Contemporary Authors®

Cumulative Index

Contemporary Authors Volumes 1-138
Contemporary Authors New Revision Series Volumes 1-39

Citations to entries in *Contemporary Authors* are identified as follows:

R after number • *Contemporary Authors* First Revision Volumes 1-44
Volume number only • *Contemporary Authors* Original Volumes 45-138
CANR • *Contemporary Authors New Revision Series,* Volumes 1-39
CAP • *Contemporary Authors Permanent Series,* Volumes 1-2
CAAS • *Contemporary Authors Autobiography Series,* Volumes 1-16
CABS • *Contemporary Authors Bibliographical Series,* Volumes 1-3

Citations to entries in other reference works are identified as follows:

AAYA • *Authors and Artists for Young Adults,* Volumes 1-9
AITN • *Authors in the News,* Volumes 1-2
BEST • *Bestsellers* (quarterly; citations appear as Year: Issue number)
BLC • *Black Literature Criticism,* Volumes 1-3
BW • *Black Writers*
CDALB • *Concise Dictionary of American Literary Biography,* 1640-1865, 1865-1917, 1917-1929, 1929-1941, 1941-1968, 1968-1988
CDBLB • *Concise Dictionary of British Literary Biography,* Before 1660, 1660-1789, 1789-1832, 1832-1890, 1890-1914, 1914-1945, 1945-1960, 1960 to Present
CLC • *Contemporary Literary Criticism,* Volumes 1-72
CLR • *Children's Literature Review,* Volumes 1-27
DC • *Drama Criticism,* Volumes 1-2
DLB • *Dictionary of Literary Biography,* Volumes 1-121
DLBD • *Dictionary of Literary Biography Documentary Series,* Volumes 1-9
DLBY • *Dictionary of Literary Biography Yearbook,* 1980-1991
HW • *Hispanic Writers*
MAICYA • *Major Authors and Illustrators for Children and Young Adults*
MTCW • *Major 20th-Century Writers*
PC • *Poetry Criticism,* Volumes 1-4
SAAS • *Something about the Author Autobiography Series,* Volumes 1-14
SATA • *Something about the Author,* Volumes 1-71
SSC • *Short Story Criticism,* Volumes 1-10
TCLC • *Twentieth-Century Literary Criticism,* Volumes 1-45
WLC • *World Literature Criticism*
YABC • *Yesterday's Authors of Books for Children,* Volumes 1-2

Note: This cumulative index supercedes all lower-numbered *CA* indexes and is not bound in any *CA* volume.

OUTSTANDING
ALA
RASD
REFERENCE SOURCE

Contemporary Authors *was named an* ***"Outstanding Reference Source"*** *by the American Library Association Reference and Adult Services Division after its 1962 inception. In 1985 it was listed by the same organization as one of the twenty-five most distinguished reference titles published in the past twenty-five years.*

Staff

Thomas Wiloch, *Index Coordinator*

Michelle M. Motowski, Susan M. Reicha, Kenneth R. Shepherd, Deborah A. Stanley, and Polly A. Vedder
Index Associates

835 Penobscot Building
Detroit, MI 48226-4094
ISBN 0-8103-8022-6

Printed in the United States of America

Published simultaneously in the United Kingdom
by Gale Research International Limited
(An affiliated company of Gale Research Inc.)

Cumulative Index

Contemporary Authors Volumes 1-138

Contemporary Authors New Revision Series Volumes 1-39

This Index Includes References to All Entries in the *Contemporary Authors* Series

Contemporary Authors--Volume 138 brings the total coverage to over 100,000 writers, both living and deceased, a large portion of whom cannot be found in other reference works. Writers in fiction, general nonfiction, poetry, journalism, drama, motion pictures, television, and other fields are all included in *CA*. Each new volume contains sketches on authors not previously listed in the series. Cumulative index published separately and distributed with even-numbered original volumes. All volumes in the series are in print.

Contemporary Authors New Revision Series--Provides completely updated information on authors listed in previous volumes of *CA*. Sketches from a number of volumes are assessed, and only entries requiring significant change are revised and published in the *CA New Revision Series*. Volumes 1-39 are in print.

(All volumes published under the former revision system, 1-4 through 41-44 First Revision, will remain in print.)

Contemporary Authors Permanent Series--Consists of updated listings for deceased and inactive authors removed from original volumes 9-36 when these volumes were revised. Two volumes only; both are in print.

Contemporary Authors Autobiography Series--Presents specially commissioned autobiographies by leading writers. Volumes 1-16 are in print.

Contemporary Authors Bibliographical Series--Contains primary and secondary bibliographies as well as analytical bibliographical essays. Volumes 1-2 are in print.

A Sample Index Entry:

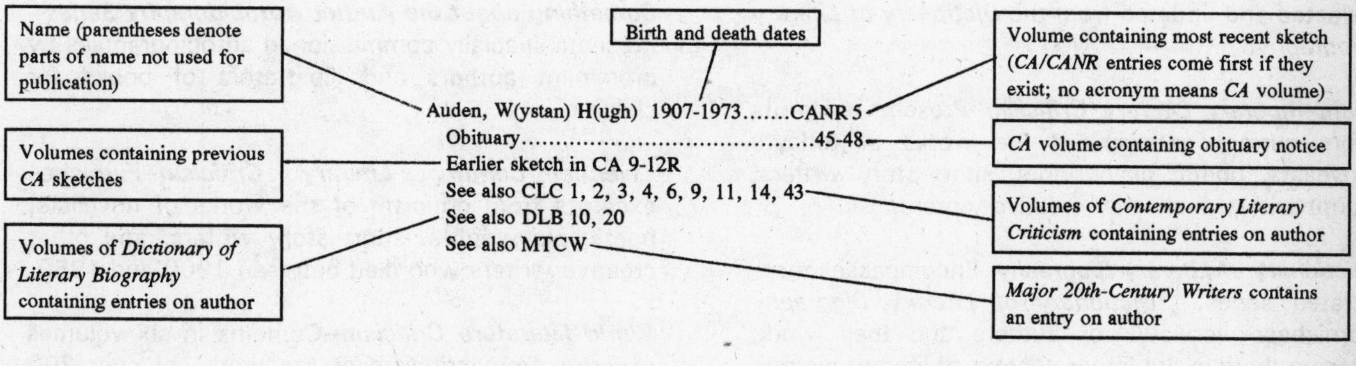

The *CA* Index Also Includes References to All Entries in These Gale Reference Works

Authors and Artists for Young Adults--Provides heavily illustrated sketches on young adult authors and creative artists of all nationalities.

Authors in the News--Reprints articles from American periodicals covering authors and members of the communications media. Two volumes, 1976-77.

Bestsellers--Furnishes information about best-selling books and their authors for the years 1989-90.

Black Literature Criticism--Contains excerpts from criticism of the most significant works of major black writers from the past two hundred years.

Black Writers--Compiles selected *CA* sketches on more than four hundred prominent twentieth-century black writers.

Children's Literature Review--Includes excerpts from reviews, criticism, and commentary on works of children's authors and illustrators.

Concise Dictionary of American Literary Biography--Contains illustrated entries on major American authors selected and updated from the *Dictionary of Literary Biography.*

Concise Dictionary of British Literary Biography--Provides illustrated entries on major British authors selected and updated from the *Dictionary of Literary Biography.*

Contemporary Literary Criticism--Presents excerpts from current criticism of the works of today's novelists, poets, playwrights, short story writers, scriptwriters, and other creative writers.

Dictionary of Literary Biography--Encompasses three related series. *Dictionary of Literary Biography* furnishes overviews of authors and their work, placing them in the larger context of literary history. *Dictionary of Literary Biography Documentary Series* illuminates the careers of major figures through a selection of literary documents. *Dictionary of Literary Biography Yearbook* summarizes the past year's literary activity and includes updated and new author entries.

Drama Criticism--Furnishes excerpts from criticism of the works of major dramatists of all eras and nationalities.

Hispanic Writers--Contains selected *CA* sketches on more than four hundred prominent twentieth-century Hispanic writers.

Major Authors and Illustrators for Children and Young Adults--Contains in six volumes both newly written and completely updated *SATA* sketches on nearly eight hundred authors and illustrators for young people.

Major 20th-Century Writers--Presents in four volumes selected *CA* sketches on over one thousand of the most influential novelists, poets, playwrights, and other creative writers of our time.

Poetry Criticism--Furnishes excerpts from criticism of the works of major poets of all eras and nationalities.

Short Story Criticism--Provides excerpts from criticism of the works of major short story writers of all eras and nationalities.

Something about the Author--Contains heavily illustrated sketches on juvenile and young adult authors and illustrators from all eras and nationalities.

Something about the Author Autobiography Series--Presents specially commissioned autobiographies by prominent authors and illustrators of books for children.

Twentieth-Century Literary Criticism--Furnishes excerpts from criticism of the works of novelists, poets, playwrights, short story writers, and other creative writers who died between 1900 and 1960.

World Literature Criticism--Contains in six volumes excerpts from criticism of the works of over 200 major writers of all eras and nationalities in world literary history.

Yesterday's Authors of Books for Children--Consists of heavily illustrated sketches on children's authors who died before 1961. Two volumes only.

Contemporary Authors®

Cumulative Index

20/1631
See Upward, Allen
A. A.
See Willis, (George) Anthony Armstrong
A. E.
See Russell, George William
See also DLB 19
See also TCLC 3, 10
A. M.
See Megged, Aharon
Aach, Herb(ert) 1923-1985 Obituary 118
Aaker, David A(llen) 1938- CANR-31
Earlier sketch in CA 49-52
Aalben, Patrick
See Jones, Noel
Aallyn, Alysse
See Clark, Melissa
Aalto, (Hugo) Alvar (Henrik)
1898-1976 Obituary 65-68
Aardema, Verna
See Vugteveen, Verna Aardema
See also CLR 17
See also MAICYA
See also SAAS 8
See also SATA 4, 68
Aaron, Benjamin 1915- 21-24R
Aaron, Chester 1923- CANR-38
Earlier sketches in CA 21-24R, CANR-8
See also MAICYA
See also SAAS 12
See also SATA 9
Aaron, Daniel 1912- CANR-7
Earlier sketch in CA 13-16R
Aaron, David (Laurence) 1938- 126
Aaron, Hank
See Aaron, Henry Louis
Aaron, Henry (Jacob) 1936- 129
Aaron, Henry Louis 1934- Brief entry 104
Aaron, James Ethridge 1927- 21-24R
Aaron, R. I.
See Aaron, Richard Ithamar
Aaron, Richard Ithamar
1901-1987 Obituary 122
Aaron, Shirley L. 1941- 123
Aaron, Sidney
See Chayefsky, Sidney
Aaron, Stephen 1936- 124
Aaronovitch, Sam 1919- 13-16R
Aarons, Edward S(idney) 1916-1975 93-96
Obituary 57-60
Aarons, Slim 1916- Brief entry 106
Aaronson, Bernard S(eymour) 1924- 29-32R
Aarsleff, Hans 1925- 21-24R
Aaseng, Nate
See Aaseng, Nathan
Aaseng, Nathan 1953- CANR-36
Earlier sketch in CA 106
See also MAICYA
See also SAAS 12
See also SATA 38, 51
Aaseng, Rolf E(dward) 1923- CANR-27
Earlier sketch in CA 49-52
Aasheim, Ashley 1942- 115
Abadinsky, Howard 1941- 110
Abagnale, Frank W. Jr. 1948- 112
Abajian, James De Tar 1914- 65-68
Abarbanel, Karin 1950- 65-68
Abarbanel, Sam X. 1914- Brief entry 106
Abasiyanik, Sait Faik 1906-1954 Brief entry 123
See also Sait Faik
Abata, Russell M(ary) 1930- 113
Abate, Frank R(obert) 1951- 118
Abayakoon, Cyrus D. F. 1912- Brief entry 115
Abbaanano, Nicola 1901- 33-36R
Abbas, Khwaja Ahmad 1914- 57-60
Abbazia, Patrick 1937- 57-60
Abbe, Elfriede (Martha) 1919- 13-16R
Abbe, George (Bancroft) 1911- CANR-10
Earlier sketch in CA 25-28R
Abbensetts, Michael 1938- CANR-37
Earlier sketch in CA 104
Abberley, Aldwyn
See Cowie, Donald
Abbey, Edward 1927-1989 ....CANR-2
Obituary 128
Earlier sketch in CA 45-48
See also CLC 36, 59
Abbey, Lloyd (Robert) 1943- 125
Brief entry 104
Abbey, Lynn
See Abbey, Marilyn Lorraine
Abbey, Margaret
See York, Margaret Elizabeth
Abbey, Marilyn Lorraine 1948- 119
Abbey, Merrill R. 1905- CANR-3
Earlier sketch in CA 1-4R
Abbington, John
See Gibson, Walter B(rown)
Abbot, Anthony
See Oursler, (Charles) Fulton
Abbot, Charles G(reeley) 1872-1973 77-80
Obituary 45-48
Abbot, Rick
See Sharkey, John Michael
Abbot, W(illiam) W(right) 1922- Brief entry 110
Abbot, Willis J(ohn) 1863-1934 Brief entry 119
See also DLB 29
Abbott, Alice
See Borland, Kathryn Kilby
and Speicher, Helen Ross S(mith)
Abbott, Anthony S. 1935- 17-20R
Abbott, Berenice 1898-1991 106
Obituary 136
Abbott, Carl (John) 1944- CANR-11
Earlier sketch in CA 65-68
Abbott, Claude Colleer 1889-1971 ....5-8R
Obituary 89-92
Abbott, Eric Symes 1906-1983 Obituary 110
Abbott, Freeland K(night) 1919-1971 ....CAP-2
Earlier sketch in CA 25-28
Abbott, George 1887- 93-96
Abbott, H(orace) Porter 1940- 45-48
Abbott, Jack Henry
See Abbott, Rufus Henry
Abbott, Jacob 1803-1879 ....DLB 1, 42
See also SATA 22
Abbott, James H(amilton) 1924- 77-80
Abbott, Jerry (Lynn) 1938- 45-48
Abbott, John J(amison) 1930- 17-20R
Abbott, John Janisen 17-20R
Abbott, Keith 1944- 121
Abbott, L(enwood) B(allard)
1908-1985 Obituary 117
Abbott, Lee K(ittredge) 1947- 124
See also CLC 48
Abbott, Lyman 1835-1922 ....DLB 79
Abbott, Manager Henry
See Stratemeyer, Edward L.
Abbott, Margaret Evans
1896-1976 Obituary 110
Abbott, Martin 1922-1977 ....33-36R
Abbott, May L(aura) 1916- 9-12R
Abbott, Pamela 1947- 135
Abbott, Philip (R.) 1944- 126
Brief entry 106
Abbott, R(obert) Tucker 1919- CANR-37
Earlier sketches in CA 9-12R, CANR-4
See also SATA 61
Abbott, Raymond H(erbert) 1942- 57-60
Abbott, Richard H(enry) 1936- 33-36R
Abbott, Robert S. 1868-1940 ....DLB 29, 91
Abbott, Rowland A(ubrey) S(amuel)
1909- 53-56
Abbott, Rufus Henry 1944- 107
Abbott, Sarah
See Zolotow, Charlotte S(hapiro)
Abbott, Scott 1949- 138
Abbott, Shirley 1934- 113
Abbott, Sidney 1937- 41-44R
Abbott, Walter M(atthew) 1923- 9-12R
Abbotts, John 1947- 73-76
Abboushi, W(asif) F(ahmi) 1931- 29-32R
Abbs, Peter 1942- 93-96
ABC
See Caddick, Arthur
Abcarian, Richard 1929- 33-36R
'Abd Al-Khaliq, Jabir
See Herbert, Nick
Abdallah, Omar
See Humbaraci, D(emir) Arslan
Abdel-Malek, Anouar 1924- 29-32R
Abdel-Quoddous, Ihsan (Mohammad)
1920(?)-1990 Obituary 130
Abdelsamad, Moustafa H(assan) 1941- 53-56
Abdul, Raoul 1929- 29-32R
See also SATA 12
Abdullah, Achmed 1881-1945 Brief entry 115
Abdullahi, Guda 1946- 93-96
Abdul-Rauf, Muhammad 1917- 101
Abeel, Erica (Hennefeld) 1937- 113
Brief entry 109
Abe Kobo 1924- CANR-24
Earlier sketch in CA 65-68
See also CLC 8, 22, 53
See also MTCW
Abel, Alan (Irwin) 1928- CANR-12
Earlier sketch in CA 17-20R
Abel, Bob
See Abel, Robert
Abel, Christopher (Graham) 1946- 127
Abel, Elie 1920- CANR-36
Earlier sketches in CA 61-64, CANR-8
Abel, Ernest L(awrence) 1943- CANR-14
Earlier sketch in CA 41-44R
Abel, I(orwith) W(ilbur) 1908-1987 Obituary 123
Brief entry 105
Abel, Jeanne 1937- 17-20R
Abel, Lionel 1910- 61-64
Abel, Raymond 1911- ....SATA 12
Abel, Reuben 1911- 37-40R
Abel, Richard L. 1941- 131
Abel, Richard (Owen) 1941- 129
Abel, Robert H(alsall) 1941- CANR-37
Earlier sketch in CA 102
Abel, Robert 1913(?)-1987 Obituary 122
Abel, Robert 1931-1981 ....CANR-11
Obituary 105
Earlier sketch in CA 65-68
Abel, Theodora M(ead) 1899- 57-60
Abel, Theodore 1896- 21-24R
Abel, Wilhelm 1904- Brief entry 119
Abelard, Peter 1079(?)-1142 ....DLB 115
Abeles, Elvin 1907- 104
Abell, Arunah S. 1806-1888 ....DLB 43
Abell, George O(gden) 1927-1983 ....CANR-3
Obituary 111
Earlier sketch in CA 9-12R
Abell, Kathleen 1938- 49-52
See also SATA 9
Abell, Kjeld 1901-1961 Obituary 111
See also CLC 15
Abell, Ron(ald F.) 1932- 119
Abella, Alex 1950- 93-96
Abella, Irving (Martin) 1940- CANR-28
Earlier sketch in CA 49-52
Abels, Harriette S(heffer) 1926- 121
See also SATA 50
Abels, Jules 1913- 61-64
Abel-Smith, Brian 1926- CANR-9
Earlier sketch in CA 21-24R
Abelson, Alan 1925- 136
Abelson, Philip Hauge 1913- Brief entry 107
Abelson, Raziel A(lter) 1921- CANR-6
Earlier sketch in CA 9-12R
Abelson, Robert P(aul) 1928- 41-44R
Abend, Norman A(nchel) 1931- 33-36R
Aber, William M(cKee) 1929- 57-60
Aberbach, David 1953- 135
Aberbach, Joel D(avid) 1940- CANR-20
Earlier sketch in CA 45-48
Abercrombie, Barbara (Mattes) 1939- 81-84
See also SATA 16
Abercrombie, Lascelles
1881-1938 Brief entry 112
See also DLB 19
Abercrombie, M(innie) L(ouie) J(ohnson)
1909(?)-1984 Obituary 115
Abercrombie, M. L. Johnson
See Abercrombie, M(innie) L(ouie) J(ohnson)
Abercrombie, Michael 1912-1979 Obituary 115
Abercrombie, Nicholas 1944- 128
Abercrombie, Nigel J(ames) 1908-1986 101
Obituary 118
Abercrombie, Stanley 1935- 117
Aberg, Sherrill E. 1924- 21-24R
Aberle, David F(riend) 1918- 21-24R
Aberle, John Wayne 1919- 1-4R
Aberle, Kathleen Gough 1925- CANR-5
Earlier sketch in CA 13-16R
Abernathy, David M(yles) 1933- CANR-37
Earlier sketch in CA 53-56
Abernathy, (M.) Elton 1913- 17-20R
Abernathy, M(abra) Glenn 1921-1990 ....13-16R
Obituary 131
Abernathy, Ralph David 1926-1990 133
Obituary 131
Abernathy, William J(ackson)
1933-1983 ....CANR-37
Obituary 111
Earlier sketch in CA 93-96
Abernethy, Francis Edward 1925- CANR-8
Earlier sketch in CA 21-24R
Abernethy, George Lawrence 1910- 1-4R
Abernethy, Peter L(ink) 1935- 69-72
Abernethy, Robert G(ordon) 1927- 21-24R
See also SATA 5
Abernethy, Thomas Perkins 1890-1975 ......CAP-1
Obituary 111
Earlier sketch in CA 19-20
Abernethy, Virginia 1934- 93-96
Abert, Donald B. 1907-1965 Obituary 116
Abisch, Roslyn Kroop 1927- CANR-10
Earlier sketch in CA 21-24R
See also SATA 9
Abisch, Roz
See Abisch, Roslyn Kroop
Abish, Walter 1931- CANR-37
Earlier sketch in CA 101
See also CLC 22
Able, James A(ugustus) Jr. 1928- 93-96
Ableman, Paul 1927- CANR-12
Earlier sketch in CA 61-64
Abler, Ronald F. 1939- CANR-4
Earlier sketch in CA 53-56
Abler, Thomas S(truthers) 1941- 101
Abley, Mark 1955- 120
Abodaher, David J. (Naiph) 1919- CANR-10
Earlier sketch in CA 17-20R
See also SATA 17
Abolafia, Yossi 1944- ....SATA 46
Abourezk, James G(eorge) 1931- 135
Abrahall, Clare Hoskyns
See Hoskyns-Abrahall, Clare (Constance Drury)
Abraham, Claude K(urt) 1931- CANR-36
Earlier sketch in CA 21-24R
Abraham, David 1946- 129
Abraham, George 1915- 110
Abraham, Gerald Ernest Heal 1904-1988 89-92
Obituary 125
Abraham, Henry Julian 1921- CANR-18
Earlier sketches in CA 5-8R, CANR-2
Abraham, Katherine 1922- 110
Abraham, Katy
See Abraham, Katherine
Abraham, Louis Arnold 1893-1983 Obituary 108
Abraham, M(annamplakkal) Francis 1939- 110
Abraham, Willard 1916- CANR-5
Earlier sketch in CA 13-16R
Abraham, William E. 1934- 13-16R
Abraham, William I(srael) 1919- 25-28R
Abrahami, Izzy 1930- Brief entry 110
Abrahamian, Ervand 1940- 110
Abrahams, Doris Caroline 1901(?)-1982(?) 129
Obituary 108
Abrahams, Edward 1949- 122
Abrahams, Gerald 1907-1980 102
Obituary 97-100
Abrahams, Hilary (Ruth) 1938- ....SATA 29
Abrahams, Howard Phineas 1904- 57-60
Abrahams, Jim 1944- 138
Abrahams, Peter (Henry) 1919- CANR-26
Earlier sketch in CA 57-60
See also BW
See also CLC 4
See also DLB 117
See also MTCW
Abrahams, R(aphael) G(arvin) 1934- 25-28R
Abrahams, Robert David 1905- CAP-2
Earlier sketch in CA 33-36
See also SATA 4
Abrahams, Roger D(avid) 1933- CANR-24
Earlier sketches in CA 9-12R, CANR-5
Abrahams, William Miller 1919- 61-64
Abrahamsen, Christine Elizabeth 1916- 101
Abrahamsen, David 1903- 65-68
Abrahamson, Irving 1925- 129
Abrahamson, Mark J. 1939- 101
Abrahamsson, Bengt 1937- 97-100
Abrahms, Sally (Ellen) 1953- 113
Abram, H(arry) S(hore) 1931-1977 ....29-32R
Abram, Morris Berthold 1918- 108
Abramov, Emil
See Draitser, Emil
Abramov, Fyodor Aleksandrovich
1920-1983 133
Obituary 109
Abramov, S(hene'ur) Zalman 1908- 134
Brief entry 108
Abramovitz, Anita (Zeltner Brooks)
1914- 97-100
See also Brooks, Anita
Abramowitz, Jack 1918- CANR-6
Earlier sketch in CA 5-8R
Abramowitz, Shalom Jacob
1835(?)-1917 Brief entry 118
Abrams, Alan E(dwin) 1941- 89-92
Abrams, Charles 1901-1970 ....CAP-2
Earlier sketch in CA 23-24
Abrams, George J(oseph) 1918-1978 ....CANR-12
Earlier sketch in CA 61-64
Abrams, Harry N(athan)
1904-1979 Obituary 93-96
Abrams, Joy 1941- 77-80
See also SATA 16
Abrams, Lawrence F. 124
See also SATA 47, 58
Abrams, Linsey 1951- CANR-18
Earlier sketch in CA 102
Abrams, M(eyer) H(oward) 1912- CANR-33
Earlier sketches in CA 57-60, CANR-13
See also CLC 24
See also DLB 67
Abrams, Mark 1906- 124
Abrams, Peter D(avid) 1936- 33-36R
Abrams, Philip 1933(?)-1981 129
Obituary 105
Abrams, Richard M. 1932- 13-16R
Abrams, Sam(uel) 1935- 21-24R
Abramsky, Chimen 1916- Brief entry 109
Abramson, Doris E. 1925- 25-28R
Abramson, Harold Alexander
1889-1980 Obituary 102
Abramson, Harold J(ulian) 1934- 45-48
Abramson, Jesse P. 1904-1979 Obituary 89-92
Abramson, Joan 1932- CANR-37
Earlier sketch in CA 25-28R
Abramson, Martin 1921- 49-52
Abramson, Michael 1944- 69-72
Abramson, Paul R(obert) 1937- CANR-37
Earlier sketches in CA 61-64, CANR-8
Abrash, Merritt 1930- 21-24R
Abrashkin, Raymond 1911-1960 115
See also SATA 50
Abravanel, Elizabeth 1944- 112
Abravanel, Elliot D(on) 1942- 112
Abrecht, Mary Ellen (Benson) 1945- 69-72
Abreu, Maria Isabel 1919- 45-48

Abruzzo, Ben(jamine Lawrence)
1930-1985 Obituary ... 115
Absalom, Roger Neil Lewis 1929- ... CANR-31
Earlier sketch in CA 111
Abse, Dannie 1923- ... CANR-4
Earlier sketch in CA 53-56
See also CAAS 1
See also CLC 7, 29
See also DLB 27
Abse, David Wilfred 1915- ... 49-52
Abse, Joan 1926- ... 108
Abse, Leo 1917- ... 137
Abshire, David M. 1926- ... CANR-37
Earlier sketches in CA 21-24R, CANR-8
Abt, Clark C(laus) 1929- ... CANR-21
Earlier sketch in CA 69-72
Abt, Lawrence Edwin 1915- ... CANR-13
Earlier sketch in CA 33-36R
Abt, Vicki 1942- ... 120
Abuba, Ernest Hawkins 1947- ... 133
Abu Jaber, Kamel S(aleh) 1932- ... CANR-14
Earlier sketch in CA 21-24R
Abu-Lughod, Ibrahim Ali 1929- ... CANR-10
Earlier sketch in CA 5-8R
Abu-Lughod, Janet L(ouise) 1928- ... CANR-10
Earlier sketch in CA 65-68
Abun-Nasr, Jamil Miri 1932- ... 69-72
Aby, Stephen H. 1949- ... 123
Abzug, Bella S(avitzky) 1920- ... 137
Brief entry ... 104
Abzug, Martin 1916-1986 Obituary ... 119
Abzug, Robert H(enry) 1945- ... CANR-21
Earlier sketch in CA 104
Academicas Mentor
See Montagu, Ashley
Academic Investor
See Reddaway, W(illiam) Brian
Accola, Louis W(ayne) 1937- ... CANR-12
Earlier sketch in CA 29-32R
Ace, Goodman 1899-1982 ... 61-64
Obituary ... 106
Aceto, Vincent J(ohn) 1932- ... 106
Achard, George
See Torres-Levin, Tereska (Szwarc)
Achard, Marcel
See Ferreol, Marcel Auguste
Achebe, (Albert) Chinua(lumogu)
1930- ... CANR-26
Earlier sketches in CA 1-4R, CANR-6
See also BLC 1
See also BW
See also CLC 1, 3, 5, 7, 11, 26, 51
See also CLR 20
See also DLB 117
See also MAICYA
See also MTCW
See also SATA 38, 40
See also WLC
Achenbaum, W(ilbert) Andrew 1947- ... CANR-34
Earlier sketches in CA 89-92, CANR-15
Acheson, David C(ampion) 1921- ... 132
Acheson, Dean (Gooderham)
1893-1971 ... CAP-2
Obituary ... 33-36R
Earlier sketch in CA 25-28
Acheson, Patricia Castles 1924- ... 1-4R
Achilles
See Lamb, Charles Bentall
Achinstein, Peter Jacob 1935- ... 111
Achtemeier, Elizabeth (Rice) 1926- ... CANR-8
Earlier sketch in CA 17-20R
Achtemeier, Paul J(ohn) 1927- ... CANR-8
Earlier sketch in CA 17-20R
Achyut
See Birla, Lakshminiwas N.
Ackart, Robert 1921- ... 109
Acker, Alison 1928- ... 125
Acker, Duane Calvin 1931- ... 33-36R
Acker, Helen ... 73-76
Acker, Kathy 1948- ... 122
Brief entry ... 117
See also CLC 45
Acker, Robert Flint 1920- ... 89-92
Acker, William R. B.
1910(?)-1974 Obituary ... 49-52
Ackerley, Chris(topher John) 1947- ... 129
Ackerley, J(oe) R(andolph) 1896-1967 ... 102
Obituary ... 89-92
Ackerman, Bruce A. 1943- ... CANR-4
Earlier sketch in CA 53-56
Ackerman, Carl W(illiam) 1890-1970 ... 73-76
Obituary ... 29-32R
Ackerman, Diane 1948- ... CANR-31
Earlier sketch in CA 57-60
See also DLB 120
Ackerman, Edward A.
1911-1973 Obituary ... 41-44R
Ackerman, Eugene (Francis)
1888-1974 ... SATA 10
Ackerman, Forrest J(ames) 1916- ... 102
Ackerman, Gerald M(artin) 1928- ... CANR-1
Earlier sketch in CA 45-48
Ackerman, J. Mark 1939- ... 53-56
Ackerman, James S(loss) 1919- ... 9-12R
Ackerman, Nathan W(ard) 1908-1971 ... CAP-2
Earlier sketch in CA 29-32
Ackerman, Robert E(dwin) 1928- ... CANR-20
Earlier sketch in CA 45-48
Ackerman, Robert K. 1933- ... 123
Ackerman, Robert W(illiam) 1910-1980 ... 103
Ackerman, Susan Rose
See Rose-Ackerman, Susan
Ackermann, Paul Kurt 1919- Brief entry ... 104
Ackermann, Robert John 1933- Brief entry ... 108
Ackerson, Duane (Wright) Jr. 1942- ... 33-36R
Ackland, Rodney 1908- ... 57-60
Ackley, Charles Walton 1913-1975 ... 41-44R
Ackley, Hugh Gardner 1915- ... 61-64
Ackley, Peggy Jo 1955- ... SATA 58
Ackley, Randall William 1931- ... CANR-6
Earlier sketch in CA 53-56
Ackoff, Russell L(incoln) 1919- ... CANR-32
Earlier sketches in CA 41-44R, CANR-15
Ackroyd, Joyce Irene ... 103
Ackroyd, Peter R(unham) 1917- ... CANR-31
Earlier sketch in CA 25-28R
Ackroyd, Peter 1949- ... 127
Brief entry ... 123
See also CLC 34, 52
Ackworth, Robert Charles 1923- ... 5-8R
Acland, Alice
See Wignall, Anne
Acland, James H. 1917-1976 ... 41-44R
Acomb, Evelyn Martha
See Acomb-Walker, Evelyn
Acomb, Frances (Dorothy)
1907- Brief entry ... 109
Acomb-Walker, Evelyn 1910- ... 85-88
Acorn, Milton 1923- ... 103
See also CLC 15
See also DLB 53
Acosta, Oscar Zeta 1935(?)- ... 131
See also DLB 82
See also HW
Acquaviva, Sabino Samele 1927- ... 101
Acquaye, Alfred Allotey 1939- ... 25-28R
Acre, Stephen
See Gruber, Frank
Acred, Arthur 1926- ... 25-28R
Acs, Laszlo (Bela) 1931- ... SATA 32, 42
Acton, Edward J. 1949- ... CANR-2
Earlier sketch in CA 45-48
Acton, Harold Mario Mitchell 1904- ... CANR-3
Earlier sketch in CA 1-4R
Acton, Jay
See Acton, Edward J.
Acton, Thomas (Alan) 1948- ... 57-60
Acuff, Frederick Gene 1931- Brief entry ... 110
Acuff, Selma Boyd 1924- ... 111
See also SATA 45
Acuna, Rodolfo
See Acuna, Rodolfo F(rancis)
Acuna, Rodolfo F(rancis) 1932- ... 131
Brief entry ... 108
See also HW
Acuna, Rudy
See Acuna, Rodolfo F(rancis)
Aczel, Tamas 1921- ... CANR-29
Earlier sketch in CA 49-52
Ada, Alma Flor 1938- ... 123
See also SATA 43
Adachi, Barbara (Curtis) 1924- ... CANR-27
Earlier sketch in CA 49-52
Adachi, Ken 1929(?)-1989 Obituary ... 128
Adair, Cecil
See Everett-Green, Evelyn
Adair, Dennis 1945- ... 107
Adair, Ian 1942- ... CANR-11
Earlier sketch in CA 69-72
See also SATA 53
Adair, Jack
See Pavey, Don
Adair, James R. 1923- ... 17-20R
Adair, James 1709(?)-1783(?) ... DLB 30
Adair, John G(lenn) 1933- ... 49-52
Adair, Margaret Weeks ... CAP-1
Earlier sketch in CA 13-14
See also SATA 10
Adair, Robert Kemp 1924- ... 136
Adam, Ben
See Drachman, Julian M(oses)
Adam, Cornel
See Lengyel, Cornel Adam
Adam, Graeme Mercer 1839-1912 ... DLB 99
Adam, Hans Christian 1948- ... 131
Adam, Helen 1909- ... CANR-7
Earlier sketch in CA 17-20R
Adam, Heribert 1936- ... 105
Adam, Jan 1920- ... CANR-38
Earlier sketch in CA 115
Adam, Michael 1919- ... CANR-37
Earlier sketches in CA 53-56
Adam, Peter 1929- ... 127
Adam, Ruth (Augusta) 1907- ... 21-24R
Adam, Thomas R(itchie) 1900- ... CAP-1
Earlier sketch in CA 19-20
Adamczewski, Zygmunt 1921- ... 13-16R
Adame, Leonard 1947- ... 131
See also DLB 82
See also HW
Adamec, Ludwig W(arren) 1924- ... CANR-24
Earlier sketches in CA 21-24R, CANR-9
Adamic, Alojzij 1899(?)-1951 Brief entry ... 109
See also Adamic, Louis
Adamic, Louis
See Adamic, Alojzij
See also DLB 9
Adamov, Arthur 1908-1970 ... CAP-2
Obituary ... 25-28R
Earlier sketch in CA 17-18
See also CLC 4, 25
See also MTCW
Adams, A. Don
See Cleveland, Philip Jerome
Adams, A. John 1931- ... 33-36R
Adams, Adrienne 1906- ... CANR-35
Earlier sketches in CA 49-52, CANR-1
See also SATA 8
Adams, Alexander B.
1917(?)-1984 Obituary ... 112
Adams, Alice (Boyd) 1926- ... CANR-26
Earlier sketch in CA 81-84
See also CLC 6, 13, 46
See also DLBY 86
See also MTCW
Adams, Andy
See Gibson, Walter B(rown)
Adams, Andy 1859-1935 ... YABC 1
Adams, Anne H(utchinson)
1935-1980 ... CANR-27
Earlier sketch in CA 41-44R
Adams, Annette
See Rowland, D(onald) S(ydney)
Adams, Ansel (Easton) 1902-1984 ... CANR-10
Obituary ... 112
Earlier sketch in CA 21-24R
See also AITN 1
Adams, Arthur E(ugene) 1917- ... CANR-4
Earlier sketch in CA 5-8R
Adams, Arthur Gray (Jr.) 1935- ... CANR-23
Earlier sketch in CA 107
Adams, Arthur Merrihew 1908- ... 53-56
Adams, Arthur Stanton 1896-1980 Obituary ... 102
Adams, Barbara
See Gardner, Virginia (Marberry)
Adams, Barbara Johnston 1943- ... SATA 60
Adams, Bart
See Bingley, David Ernest
Adams, Bernard (Paul Fornaro) 1915- ... 128
Adams, Betsy
See Pitcher, Gladys
Adams, Brooks 1848-1927 Brief entry ... 123
See also DLB 47
Adams, Bruin
See Ellis, Edward S(ylvester)
Adams, Captain Bruin
See Ellis, Edward S(ylvester)
Adams, Captain J. F. C.
See Ellis, Edward S(ylvester)
Adams, Caren 1946- ... 135
Adams, Carol J. 1951- ... 134
Adams, Cedric M. 1902-1961 Obituary ... 89-92
Adams, Charles Francis Jr.
1835-1915 Brief entry ... 113
See also DLB 47
Adams, Charles J(oseph) 1924- ... CANR-24
Earlier sketches in CA 17-20R, CANR-8
Adams, Charles Lynford 1929- ... 113
Adams, Charlotte 1899- Brief entry ... 107
Adams, Chuck
See Tubb, E(dwin) C(harles)
Adams, Cindy ... CANR-17
Earlier sketch in CA 21-24R
Adams, Cleve F(ranklin)
1895-1949 Brief entry ... 112
Adams, Clifton 1919- ... CANR-21
Earlier sketch in CA 13-16R
Adams, Clinton 1918- ... 33-36R
Adams, Dale
See Quinn, Elisabeth
Adams, Don(ald Kendrick) 1925- ... 33-36R
Adams, Donald K(napp)
1924-1987 Obituary ... 123
Brief entry ... 111
Adams, Donald R. Jr. 1940- Brief entry ... 113
Adams, Douglas (Noel) 1952- ... CANR-34
Earlier sketch in CA 106
See also AAYA 4
See also BEST 89:3
See also CLC 27, 60
See also DLBY 83
Adams, E(lie) M(aynard) 1919- ... 1-4R
Adams, Edith
See Shine, Deborah
Adams, Elsie B(onita) 1932- ... 69-72
Adams, Eugenia
See Owens, Virginia Stem
Adams, Evangeline (Smith)
1872(?)-1932 Brief entry ... 121
Adams, F(rank) Ramsay 1883-1963 ... 5-8R
Adams, Faith 1960- ... 121
Adams, Florence 1932- ... 49-52
See also SATA 61
Adams, Francis A(lexandre)
1874-1975 Obituary ... 61-64
Adams, Frank C(lyde) 1916- ... 69-72
Adams, Franklin P(ierce)
1881-1960 Obituary ... 93-96
See also DLB 29
Adams, Frederick C(harles)
1941- Brief entry ... 105
Adams, Gail Galloway 1943- ... 128
Adams, George Matthew
1878-1962 Obituary ... 93-96
Adams, George Worthington 1905- ... 41-44R
Adams, Georgia Sachs 1913- ... 37-40R
Adams, Glenda 1939- ... 104
Adams, Graham Jr. 1928- ... 17-20R
Adams, Harlen M(artin) 1904- ... CAP-1
Earlier sketch in CA 13-14
Adams, Harold 1923- ... 126
Adams, Harriet S(tratemeyer)
1892(?)-1982 ... CANR-27
Obituary ... 106
Earlier sketch in CA 17-20R
See also AITN 2
See also MAICYA
See also SATA 1, 29
Adams, Harrison ... CANR-26
Earlier sketches in CAP-2, CA 19-20
Adams, Harry Baker 1924- Brief entry ... 106
Adams, Hazard 1926- ... 9-12R
See also SATA 6
Adams, Henry (Brooks) 1838-1918 ... 133
Brief entry ... 104
See also DLB 12, 47
See also TCLC 4
Adams, Henry H(itch) 1917- ... CANR-13
Earlier sketch in CA 21-24R
Adams, Henry Mason 1907- ... CAP-1
Earlier sketch in CA 17-18
Adams, Henry T.
See Ransom, Jay Ellis
Adams, Henry 1949- ... 132
Adams, Herbert Baxter 1850-1901 ... DLB 47
Adams, Herbert Mayow 1893-1985 ... CAP-2
Obituary ... 115
Earlier sketch in CA 25-28
Adams, Howard (Joseph) 1928- ... 89-92
Adams, J(ames) Donald 1891-1968 ... CANR-1
Earlier sketch in CA 1-4R
Adams, J(ames) Mack 1933- ... 85-88
Adams, James E(dward) 1941- ... 73-76
Adams, James F(rederick) 1927- ... 17-20R
Adams, James Luther 1901- ... 41-44R
Adams, James (Macgregor David) 1951- ... 138
Adams, James R(owe) 1934- ... 41-44R
Adams, James Truslow
1878-1949 Brief entry ... 115
See also DLB 17
Adams, Jane (Ellen) 1940- ... 116
Adams, Jay Edward 1929- ... 126
Brief entry ... 108
Adams, Joanna Z.
See Koch, Joanne
Adams, Joey 1911- ... CANR-1
Earlier sketch in CA 49-52
Adams, John Anthony 1944- ... 134
See also SATA 67
Adams, John Clarke 1910- ... 1-4R
Adams, John Coldwell 1927- ... 121
Adams, John Cranford 1903-1986 Obituary ... 121
Adams, John D(avid) 1942- ... 115
Adams, John F(estus) 1930- ... 33-36R
Adams, John M(ilton) 1905-1981 ... 107
Adams, John P. 1923(?)-1983 ... 122
Obituary ... 111
Adams, John Paul
See Kinnaird, Clark
Adams, John Quincy 1767-1848 ... DLB 37
Adams, John R. 1900- ... 25-28R
Adams, John 1734-1826 ... DLB 31
Adams, John 1938- ... 111
Adams, Julian 1919- ... CANR-11
Earlier sketch in CA 25-28R
Adams, Julius J. 1901(?)-1989 Obituary ... 130
Adams, Justin
See Cameron, Lou
Adams, Kenneth Menzies 1922- ... 103
Adams, Kramer A. 1920- ... 9-12R
Adams, L(ouis) Jerold 1939- ... 49-52
Adams, Laura 1943- ... 53-56
Adams, Laurie 1941- ... 53-56
See also SATA 33
Adams, Lee (Richard) 1924- Brief entry ... 111
Adams, Leon D(avid) 1905- ... 45-48
Adams, Leonie (Fuller) 1899-1988 ... CAP-1
Obituary ... 125
Earlier sketch in CA 9-10
See also DLB 48
Adams, Les 1934- ... 97-100
Adams, Levi 1802(?)-1832 ... DLB 99
Adams, Lowell
See Joseph, James (Herz)
Adams, Marilyn Jager 1948- ... 136
Adams, Marion 1932- ... 41-44R
Adams, Mary (Grace Agnes)
1898-1984 Obituary ... 113
Adams, Maurice 1915(?)-1985 Obituary ... 116
Adams, Michael C(harles) C(orringham)
1945- ... 89-92
Adams, Michael (Evelyn) 1920- ... 33-36R
Adams, Mildred
See Kenyon, Mildred Adams
Adams, Nancy 1943(?)-1987 Obituary ... 123
Adams, Nathan Miller 1934- ... 45-48
Adams, Nicholas 1947- ... 127
Adams, Norman (Edward Albert) 1927- ... 114
Adams, Paul L(ieber) 1924- ... 61-64
Adams, Percy G(uy) 1914- ... CANR-4
Earlier sketch in CA 1-4R
Adams, Perseus 1933- ... 107
Adams, Philip R. 1908- ... 85-88
Adams, Phoebe-Lou 1918- ... 125
Brief entry ... 121
Adams, R(alph) J(ames) Q(uincy) 1943- ... 128
Adams, Rachel Leona White
1905(?)-1979 Obituary ... 93-96
Adams, Ramon Frederick
1889-1976 Obituary ... 65-68
Adams, Ramona Shepherd 1921- ... 106
Adams, Richard E(dward) W(ood) 1931- ... 106
Adams, Richard (George) 1920- ... CANR-35
Earlier sketches in CA 49-52, CANR-3
See also AITN 1, 2
See also CLC 4, 5, 18
See also CLR 20
See also MAICYA
See also MTCW
See also SATA 7, 69
Adams, Richard N(ewbold) 1924- ... CANR-12
Earlier sketch in CA 29-32R
Adams, Richard P(errill) 1917-1977 ... CAP-2
Obituary ... 69-72
Earlier sketch in CA 33-36
Adams, Robert (Franklin) 1932- ... 69-72
Adams, Robert H(ickman) 1937- ... CANR-22
Earlier sketch in CA 105
Adams, Robert Martin 1915- ... CANR-4
Earlier sketch in CA 5-8R
Adams, Robert McCormick 1926- ... CANR-39
Earlier sketches in CA 61-64, CANR-12
Adams, Robert Merrihew 1937- ... 135
Adams, Robert P. 1910- ... 13-16R

Adams, Rolland Leroy
1905(?)-1979 Obituary 89-92
Adams, Russell B(aird) Jr. 1937- 69-72
Adams, Russell L. 1930- 53-56
Adams, Ruth Joyce ....SATA 14
Adams, Sally Pepper 41-44R
Adams, Sam 1934- 57-60
Adams, Samuel A. 1933(?)-1988 Obituary 126
Adams, Samuel 1722-1803 ....DLB 31, 43
Adams, Sexton 1936- CANR-37
Earlier sketch in CA 25-28R
Adams, (Llewellyn) Sherman
1899-1986 Obituary 120
Adams, Stanley 1927- 135
Adams, Stephen J(on) 1945- 111
Adams, T(homas) W(illiam) 1933- 25-28R
Adams, Terrence Dean 1935- 33-36R
Adams, Theodore Floyd 1898-1980 ....CAP-1
Obituary 97-100
Earlier sketch in CA 11-12
Adams, Thomas Boylston 1910- 114
Adams, Thomas F. 1927- 13-16R
Adams, Thomas Randolph 1921- 107
Adams, Timothy Dow 1943- 133
Adams, Tricia
See Kite, Pat
Adams, Val 1917(?)-1983 Obituary 109
Adams, Walter 1922- CANR-37
Earlier sketches in CA 1-4R, CANR-3
Adams, Willi Paul 1940- 105
Adams, William Howard 129
Brief entry 105
Adams, William Taylor 1822-1897 ....DLB 42
See also SATA 28
Adams, William Yewdale 1927- Brief entry 104
Adamski, George 1891-1965 Obituary 112
Adam Smith, Janet (Buchanan)
1905- CANR-35
Earlier sketch in CA 113
See also SATA 63
Adam-Smith, Patricia Jean 1926- 105
Adam-Smith, Patsy
See Adam-Smith, Patricia Jean
Adamson, Alan (Herbert) 1919- 81-84
Adamson, David Grant 1927- 13-16R
Adamson, Donald 1939- CANR-39
Earlier sketch in CA 53-56
Adamson, Ed(ward Joseph)
1915(?)-1972 Obituary 37-40R
Adamson, Frank
See Adams, Robert (Franklin)
Adamson, Gareth 1925-1982(?) CANR-11
Obituary 106
Earlier sketch in CA 13-16R
See also SATA 30, 46
Adamson, George Worsley 1913- 107
See also SATA 30
Adamson, George 1906-1989 129
See also SATA 63
Adamson, Graham
See Groom, Arthur William
Adamson, Hans Christian 1890-1968 ....5-8R
Adamson, Joe
See Adamson, Joseph III
Adamson, Joseph III 1945- CANR-21
Earlier sketches in CA 45-48, CANR-1
Adamson, Joy(-Friederike Victoria)
1910-1980 ....CANR-22
Obituary 93-96
Earlier sketch in CA 69-72
See also CLC 17
See also MTCW
See also SATA 11, 22
Adamson, Lesley
See Grant-Adamson, Lesley
Adamson, M. J.
See Adamson, Mary Jo
Adamson, Mary Jo 1935- 134
Adamson, Sir John 1867-1950 ....DLB 98
Adamson, Walter L(uiz) 1946- 107
Adamson, Wendy Writson 1942- 53-56
See also SATA 22
Adamson, William Robert 1927- 21-24R
Adas, Michael 1943- 53-56
Adastra
See Mirepoix, Camille
Adburgham, Alison Haig 1912- CAP-1
Earlier sketch in CA 9-10
Adcock, Almey St. John 1894- 65-68
Adcock, Betty
See Adcock, Elizabeth S(harp)
See also DLB 105
Adcock, C(yril) John 1904- CAP-1
Earlier sketch in CA 19-20
Adcock, Elizabeth S(harp) 1938- 57-60
See also Adcock, Betty
Adcock, Fleur 1934- CANR-34
Earlier sketches in CA 25-28R, CANR-11
See also CLC 41
See also DLB 40
Adcock, Frank Ezra 1886-1968 Obituary 106
Adcock, Thomas 1947- 138
Addams, Charles (Samuel)
1912-1988 ....CANR-12
Obituary 126
Earlier sketch in CA 61-64
See also CLC 30
Addanki, Sam 1932- 109
Adde, Leo 1927(?)-1975 Obituary 57-60
Addeo, Jovita A. 1939- 103
Addie, Bob 1911(?)-1982 Obituary 105
Addie, Pauline Betz 1919(?)- Brief entry 105
Addington, Arthur Charles 1939- 105
Addington, Larry H(olbrook) 1932- 33-36R
Addison, Gwen
See Harris, Alf(red)
Addison, Herbert 1889-1982 Obituary 108
Addison, Joseph 1672-1719 ....CDBLB 1660-1789
See also DLB 101
Addison, Lloyd 1937- 45-48
Addison, William Wilkinson 1905- CANR-5
Earlier sketch in CA 13-16R
Addiss, Stephen 1935- 120
Addleshaw, George William Outram
1907(?)-1982 Obituary 107
Addona, Angelo F. 1925- 25-28R
See also SATA 14
Addy, George M(ilton) 1927- 21-24R
Addy, John 1915- 69-72
Addy, Ted
See Winterbotham, R(ussell) R(obert)
Ade, George 1866-1944 Brief entry 110
See also DLB 11, 25
Ade, Walter Frank Charles 1910- 53-56
Adelberg, Doris
See Orgel, Doris
Adelberg, Roy P. 1928- 17-20R
Adeler, Max
See Clark, Charles Heber
Adelman, Bob 1930- 69-72
Adelman, Clifford 1942- 41-44R
Adelman, Gary 1935- 33-36R
Adelman, Howard 1938- 25-28R
Adelman, Irma Glicman CANR-3
Earlier sketch in CA 5-8R
Adelman, Irving 1926- 21-24R
Adelman, Janet (Ann) 1941- 61-64
Adelman, M(orris) A(lbert) 1917- 126
Brief entry 104
Adelman, Saul J(oseph) 1944- 104
Adelmann, Frederick J(oseph) 1915- CANR-27
Earlier sketch in CA 49-52
Adelsberger, Lucie 1895-1971 Obituary 33-36R
Adelson, Daniel 1918- 69-72
Adelson, Joseph (Bernard) 1925- 17-20R
Adelson, Leone 1908- 61-64
See also SATA 11
Adelson, Sandra 1934- 105
Adelstein, Michael E. 1922- CANR-15
Earlier sketch in CA 33-36R
Aden, John M(ichael) 1918- 97-100
Adenauer, Konrad 1876-1967 Obituary 112
Adeney, David Howard 1911- 53-56
Adeney, Martin 1942- 128
Ader, Paul (Fassett) 1919- 65-68
Aderman, Ralph M(erl) 1919- 5-8R
Ades, Dawn 1943- 103
Adey, Lionel 1925- 132
Adiseshiah, Malcolm S(athianathan)
1910- 81-84
Adizes, Ichak 1937- 33-36R
Adkins, Arthur W(illiam) H(ope) 1929- 111
Brief entry 104
Adkins, Cecil (Dale) 1932- 115
Adkins, Dorothy C.
See Wood, Dorothy Adkins
Adkins, Jan 1944- 33-36R
See also CLR 7
See also MAICYA
See also SATA 8, 69
Adkins, Nelson F(rederick) 1897-1976 73-76
Obituary 65-68
Adkins, Patrick H. 1948- 126
Adlard, John 1929- CANR-21
Earlier sketches in CA 57-60, CANR-6
Adlard, (P.) Mark 1932- 65-68
Adleman, Robert H. 1919- 25-28R
Adler, Alfred (F.) 1870-1937 Brief entry 119
Adler, B.
See Adler, William
Adler, Betty 1918-1973 ....CAP-1
Earlier sketch in CA 13-14
Adler, Bill
See Adler, William
Adler, C(arole) S(chwerdtfeger) 1932- CANR-19
Earlier sketch in CA 89-92
See also AAYA 4
See also CLC 35
See also MAICYA
See also SATA 26, 63
Adler, Carol 1938- 61-64
Adler, Christopher Edward
1954(?)-1984 Obituary 114
Adler, Cyrus 1863-1940 Brief entry 122
Adler, David A. 1947- CANR-23
Earlier sketches in CA 57-60, CANR-7
See also MAICYA
See also SATA 14, 70
Adler, Denise Rinker 1908- 102
Adler, Elmer 1884-1962 Obituary 89-92
Adler, France-Michele 1942- 105
Adler, Freda 1934- CANR-27
Earlier sketches in CA 69-72, CANR-11
Adler, Gerhard 1904-1989(?) Obituary 128
Adler, H. G. 1910- CANR-10
Earlier sketch in CA 25-28R
Adler, Hans A(rnold) 1921- 49-52
Adler, Helmut E(rnest) 1920- 33-36R
Adler, Irene
See Penzler, Otto
Adler, Irving 1913- CANR-2
Earlier sketch in CA 5-8R
See also CLR 27
See also MAICYA
See also SATA 1, 29
Adler, Isidore 1925(?)-1990 Obituary 131
Adler, Jack 73-76
Adler, Jacob H(enry) 1919- 13-16R
Adler, Jacob 1873(?)-1974 Obituary 53-56
Adler, Jacob 1913- 17-20R
Adler, John Hans 1912-1980 Obituary 97-100
Adler, Joyce
See Adler, Joyce Sparer
Adler, Joyce Sparer 1915- 128
Adler, Kathleen
See Jones, Kathleen Eve
Adler, Larry 1939- 105
See also SATA 36
Adler, Lucile 1922- 105
Adler, Lulla
See Rosenfeld, Lulla
Adler, Manfred 1936- 49-52
Adler, Margot 1946- 107
Adler, Max K(urt) 1905- CANR-3
Earlier sketch in CA 9-12R
Adler, Mortimer J(erome) 1902- CANR-33
Earlier sketches in CA 65-68, CANR-7
See also MTCW
Adler, Norman Tenner 1941- CANR-20
Earlier sketch in CA 69-72
Adler, Peggy ....SATA 22
Adler, Renata 1938- CANR-22
Earlier sketches in CA 49-52, CANR-5
See also CLC 8, 31
See also MTCW
Adler, Ruth 1915-1968 ....CANR-4
Obituary 25-28R
Earlier sketch in CA 5-8R
See also SATA 1
Adler, Selig 1909-1984 ....5-8R
Obituary 114
Adler, Sol 1925- CANR-22
Earlier sketches in CA 17-20R, CANR-7
Adler, Warren 1927- CANR-11
Earlier sketch in CA 69-72
Adler, William 1929- CANR-7
Earlier sketch in CA 9-12R
Adler, William 1951- 124
Adlerblum, Nina H. 1882-1974 Obituary 49-52
Adloff, Virginia Thompson
1903-1990 Obituary 130
Adoff, Arnold 1935- CANR-37
Earlier sketches in CA 41-44R, CANR-20
See also AAYA 3
See also AITN 1
See also CLR 7
See also MAICYA
See also SATA 5, 57
Adolph, E. F.
See Adolph, Edward F(rederick)
Adolph, Edward F(rederick)
1895-1986 Obituary 121
Adomeit, Ruth E(lizabeth) 1910- 111
Adon, Aaron Bar
See Bar-Adon, Aaron
Adony, Raoul
See Launay, Andre (Joseph)
Adorjan, Carol (Madden) 1934- CANR-31
Earlier sketches in CA 41-44R, CANR-14
See also SATA 10, 71
Adorno, Theodor W(iesengrund)
1903-1969 89-92
Obituary 25-28R
Adoum, Jorge Enrique 1926- ....HW
Adrian, Arthur A(llen) 1906- CAP-2
Earlier sketch in CA 19-20
Adrian, Charles R. 1922- CANR-3
Earlier sketch in CA 1-4R
Adrian, Edgar Douglas
1889-1977 Obituary 73-76
Adrian, Frances
See Polland, Madeleine A(ngela Cahill)
Adrian, Mary
See Jorgensen, Mary Venn
Adrian, Rhys Brief entry 106
Adshead, Gladys L(ucy) 1896- 29-32R
See also SATA 3
Advani, Rukun 1955- 119
Ady, Endre 1877-1919 Brief entry 107
See also TCLC 11
Ady, Ronald W(illiam) 1934- 117
Adytum
See Curl, James Stevens
Adzigian, Denise Allard 1952- 97-100
Aebi, Ormond 1916- 89-92
Aeby, Jacquelyn CANR-24
Earlier sketch in CA 29-32R
Aero, Rita 112
Aers, David 1946- CANR-8
Earlier sketch in CA 61-64
Aeschliman, Michael D(avid) 1948- 113
Aesop, Abraham
See Newbery, John
Aesop 620 (?)-564 (?) ....CLR 14
See also MAICYA
See also SATA 64
Affabee, Eric
See Stine, R(obert) L(awrence)
Affron, Charles 1935- 21-24R
Afnan, Ruhi Muhsen 1899-1971 ....CAP-2
Earlier sketch in CA 29-32
Africa, Thomas Wilson 1927- 17-20R
Africano, Lillian 1935- CANR-29
Earlier sketches in CA 69-72, CANR-11
Aftel, Mandy 1948- 108
Afterman, Allen 1941- 103
Afton, Effie
See Harper, Frances Ellen Watkins
Agan, Patrick 1943- CANR-10
Earlier sketch in CA 65-68
Agan, Raymond J(ohn) 1919- 33-36R
Agan, (Anna) Tessie 1897- CAP-1
Earlier sketch in CA 17-18
Agapida, Fray Antonio
See Irving, Washington
Agar, Brian
See Ballard, (Willis) Todhunter
Agar, Herbert (Sebastian) 1897-1980 65-68
Obituary 102
Agar, Michael H(enry) 1945- CANR-2
Earlier sketch in CA 45-48
Agar, William (Macdonough)
1894-1972 Obituary 37-40R
Agard, H. E.
See Evans, Hilary
Agard, Nadema 1948- ....SATA 18
Agarossi, Elena 1940- CANR-20
Earlier sketch in CA 97-100
Agarwala, Amar N. 1917- CANR-13
Earlier sketch in CA 21-24R
Agassi, Joseph 1927- CANR-15
Earlier sketch in CA 41-44R
Agassiz, Jean Louis Rodolphe
1807-1873 ....DLB 1
Agawa, Hiroyuki 1920- 134
Agay, Denes 1911- 69-72
Agbodeka, Francis 1931- CANR-4
Earlier sketch in CA 53-56
Agee, James (Rufus)
1909-1955 Brief entry 108
See also AITN 1
See also CDALB 1941-1968
See also DLB 2, 26
See also TCLC 1, 19
Agee, Joel 1940- Brief entry 105
Agee, Philip 1935- 135
Brief entry 104
Agee, Warren Kendall 1916- 17-20R
Ager, Cecelia 1902-1981 Obituary 103
Ager, Derek Victor 1923- 107
Ageton, Arthur Ainsley 1900-1971 ....CANR-1
Obituary 29-32R
Earlier sketch in CA 1-4R
Aggeler, Geoffrey D(onovan) 1939- 97-100
Aggertt, Otis J. 1916-1973 ....33-36R
Aghill, Gordon
See Garrett, (Gordon) Randall (Phillip)
and Silverberg, Robert
Aginsky, Bernard W(illard) 1905- 85-88
Aginsky, Burt W.
See Aginsky, Bernard W(illard)
Aginsky, Ethel G(oldberg) 1910- 41-44R
Agle, Nan Hayden 1905- CANR-3
Earlier sketch in CA 1-4R
See also SAAS 10
See also SATA 3
Agnelli, Susanna 1922- CANR-28
Earlier sketch in CA 109
Agnew, Edith J(osephine) 1897- CAP-1
Earlier sketch in CA 17-18
See also SATA 11
Agnew, James Barron 1930- 89-92
Agnew, Patience McCormick-Goodhart
1913(?)-1976 Obituary 69-72
Agnew, Peter L(awrence) 1901-1969 ....CAP-2
Earlier sketch in CA 21-22
Agnew, Spiro T(heodore) 1918- 135
Brief entry 110
Agniel, Lucien D. 1919- 29-32R
Agnon, S(hmuel) Y(osef Halevi)
1888-1970 ....CAP-2
Obituary 25-28R
Earlier sketch in CA 17-18
See also CLC 4, 8, 14
See also MTCW
Agonito, Rosemary (Giambattista) 1937- 122
Brief entry 112
Agoos, Julie 1956- 127
Agor, Weston H(arris) 1939- CANR-29
Earlier sketch in CA 49-52
Agosin, Marjorie 1955- 131
See also HW
Agostinelli, Maria Enrica 1929- 33-36R
Agranoff, Robert 1936- CANR-14
Earlier sketch in CA 37-40R
Agree, Rose H. 1913- 21-24R
Agress, Hyman 1931- 89-92
Agress, Lynne 1941- 112
Agresto, John 1946- 115
Agronsky, Martin (Zama) 1915- 109
See also AITN 2
Aguero, Kathleen 1949- 73-76
Aguila, Pancho 1945- 105
See also HW
Aguilar, Luis E. 1926- 21-24R
Aguilar, Ricardo
See Aguilar Melantzon, Ricardo
Aguilar, Rodolfo J(esus) 1936- 53-56
Aguilar Melantzon, Ricardo 1947- ....HW
Aguilera, Donna Conant 37-40R
Aguilera, Jaime Roldos
See Roldos Aguilera, Jaime
Aguilera Malta, Demetrio 1909-1981 124
Brief entry 111
See also HW
Aguolu, Christian Chukwunedu 1940- CANR-19
Earlier sketch in CA 101
Agus, Irving A(braham) 1910-1984 ....CAP-2
Obituary 113
Earlier sketch in CA 33-36
Agus, Jacob Bernard 1911-1986 ....CANR-2
Obituary 120
Earlier sketch in CA 5-8R
Agustini, Delmira 1886-1914 ....HW
Agutter, Jennifer Ann 1952- 133
Agutter, Jenny
See Agutter, Jennifer Ann
Aguzzi-Barbagli, Danilo 1924- 49-52
Agwani, Mohammed Shafi 1928- CANR-7
Earlier sketch in CA 17-20R
Aharoni, Yohanan 1919-1976 ....CANR-15
Earlier sketch in CA 25-28R
Ahearn, Barry 1950- 110
Ahearn, Catherine 1949- 114
Ahern, Barnabas M. 1915- CANR-3
Earlier sketch in CA 5-8R
Ahern, Emily M.
See Martin, Emily

Ahern, Emily M(artin)
See Martin, Emily
Ahern, James F(rancis) 1932-1986 ....41-44R
Obituary 118
Ahern, John F(rancis) 1936- 61-64
Ahern, Margaret McCrohan 1921- 13-16R
See also SATA 10
Ahern, Thomas Francis 1947- CANR-21
Earlier sketches in CA 45-48, CANR-1
Ahern, Tim(othy James) 1952- 115
Ahern, Tom
See Ahern, Thomas Francis
Aherne, Brian (de Lacy) 1902-1986 135
Obituary 118
Brief entry 117
Aherne, Owen
See Cassill, R(onald) V(erlin)
Ahern Emily M(artin)
See Martin, Emily
Ahituv, Niv 1943- 117
Ahl, Anna Maria 1926- ....SATA 32
Ahl, Frederick Michael 1941- CANR-30
Earlier sketch in CA 111
Ahlberg, Allan 1938- CANR-38
Brief entry 111
Earlier sketch in CA 114
See also CLR 18
See also MAICYA
See also SATA 35, 68
Ahlberg, Janet 1944- 114
Brief entry 111
See also CLR 18
See also MAICYA
See also SATA 32, 68
Ahlberg, William A. 1922(?)-1985 Obituary 116
Ahlborn, Richard Eighme 1933- 108
Ahlers, John C(larke) 1927-1983 Obituary 110
Ahlert, Richard 1921-1985 Obituary 117
Ahlin, Janne 1942- 136
Ahlstroem, G(oesta) W(erner)
1918-1992 ....CANR-21
Obituary 136
Earlier sketch in CA 45-48
Ahlstrom, G(osta) W(erner)
See Ahlstroem, G(oesta) W(erner)
Ahlstrom, Sydney E(ckman) 1919-1984 .....21-24R
Obituary 113
Ahmad, Ishtiaq 1937- 53-56
Ahmad, Nafis 1913- 17-20R
Ahmad, Suleiman M(uhammad) 1943- 110
Ahmann, Mathew H(all) 1931- 9-12R
Ahnebrink, Lars 1915- 5-8R
Ahnstrom, D(oris) N. 1915- 5-8R
Aho, James (Alfred) 1942- 107
Ahokas, Jaakko (Alfred) 1923- 65-68
Ahrari, Mohammed E. 1945- 120
Ahsen, Akhter 1931- CANR-25
Earlier sketches in CA 61-64, CANR-10
Ahuja, Savitri 1924- 112
Ai 1947- 85-88
See also CAAS 13
See also CLC 4, 14, 69
See also DLB 120
Aichinger, Helga 1937- CANR-19
Earlier sketch in CA 25-28R
See also SATA 4
Aichinger, Ilse 1921- 85-88
See also DLB 85
Aichinger, Peter 1933- CANR-11
Earlier sketch in CA 61-64
Aickman, Robert (Fordyce) 1914-1981 .....CANR-3
Earlier sketch in CA 5-8R
See also CLC 57
Aidala, Thomas R(ichard) 1933- Brief entry 112
Aidells, Bruce 1944- 138
Aidenoff, Abraham 1913-1976 ....37-40R
Obituary 61-64
Aidoo, (Christina) Ama Ata 1942- 101
See also BW
See also DLB 117
Aiguillette
See Hargreaves, Reginald (Charles)
Aiken, Clarissa Lorenz 1899- CAP-2
Earlier sketch in CA 21-22
See also SATA 12
Aiken, Conrad (Potter) 1889-1973 ....CANR-4
Obituary 45-48
Earlier sketch in CA 5-8R
See also CDALB 1929-1941
See also CLC 1, 3, 5, 10, 52
See also DLB 9, 45, 102
See also MTCW
See also SATA 3, 30
See also SSC 9
Aiken, George D(avid) 1892-1984 Obituary 114
Brief entry 111
Aiken, Henry David 1912-1982 ....CANR-1
Obituary 106
Earlier sketch in CA 1-4R
Aiken, Irene (Nixon) 93-96
Aiken, Joan (Delano) 1924- CANR-34
Earlier sketches in CA 9-12R, CANR-4, 23
See also AAYA 1
See also CLC 35
See also CLR 1, 19
See also MAICYA
See also MTCW
See also SAAS 1
See also SATA 2, 30
Aiken, John (Kempton) 1913- 101
Aiken, John R(obert) 1927- 33-36R
Aiken, Lewis R(oscoe) Jr. 1931- CANR-10
Earlier sketch in CA 25-28R
Aiken, Maurice C. 1909(?)-1983 Obituary 109
Aiken, Michael Thomas 1932- CANR-9
Earlier sketch in CA 21-24R
Aikens, Tom Pitt
See Pitt-Aikens, Tom
Aikin, Charles 1901- 5-8R
Aikman, Ann
See McQuade, Ann Aikman
Aikman, David (B. T.) 1944- 65-68
Aikman, Lonnelle (Davison)
1901(?)-1986 Obituary 121
Aimes, Angelica 1943- CANR-14
Earlier sketch in CA 81-84
Ainsbury, Ray
See Paine, Lauran (Bosworth)
Ainsbury, Roy
See Paine, Lauran (Bosworth)
Ainsley, Alix
See Steiner, Barbara A(nnette)
Ainslie, Rosalynde 1932- 25-28R
Ainslie, Tom
See Carter, Richard
Ainsworth, Catherine Harris 1910- ....SATA 56
Ainsworth, Charles H(arold) 1935- 49-52
Ainsworth, Dorothy Sears
1894-1976 Obituary 69-72
Ainsworth, Ed(ward Maddin)
1902-1968 ....CANR-4
Earlier sketch in CA 5-8R
Ainsworth, G(eoffrey) C(lough) 1905- 73-76
Ainsworth, Harriet
See Cadell, (Violet) Elizabeth
Ainsworth, Katherine 1908- 29-32R
Ainsworth, Mary D(insmore) Salter
1913- CANR-8
Earlier sketch in CA 21-24R
Ainsworth, Norma CANR-5
Earlier sketch in CA 13-16R
See also SATA 9
Ainsworth, Patricia
See Bigg, Patricia Nina
Ainsworth, Ray
See Paine, Lauran (Bosworth)
Ainsworth, Roy
See Paine, Lauran (Bosworth)
Ainsworth, Ruth (Gallard) 1908- CANR-37
See also MAICYA
See also SATA 7
Ainsworth, Thomas Hargraves Jr. 1920- 123
Ainsworth, William Harrison 1805-1882 .... DLB 21
See also SATA 24
Ainsworthy, Roy
See Paine, Lauran (Bosworth)
Ainsztein, Reuben 1917-1981 110
Obituary 108
Air Chief Marshal Lord Dowding
See Dowding, Hugh Caswell Tremenheere
Aird, Catherine
See McIntosh, Kinn Hamilton
Aird, Eileen M(argaret) 1945- 49-52
Airlie, Catherine
See MacLeod, Jean Sutherland
Airola, Paavo (Olavi) 1915- 81-84
Aisenberg, Nadya 1928- 135
Aislin
See Mosher, (Christopher) Terry
Aistis, Jonas 1908(?)-1973 Obituary 41-44R
Aistrop, Jack 1916- CANR-3
Earlier sketch in CA 1-4R
See also SATA 14
Aitchison, James 1938- 137
Aitchison, Janet 1962- 57-60
Aitken, A(dam) J(ack) 1921- CANR-7
Earlier sketch in CA 13-16R
Aitken, Amy 1952- 108
See also SATA 40, 54
Aitken, Dorothy 1916- CANR-2
Earlier sketch in CA 49-52
See also SATA 10
Aitken, Douglas 1933- 115
Aitken, Hugh G(eorge) J(effrey) 1922- CANR-3
Earlier sketch in CA 1-4R
Aitken, Jonathan (William Patrick)
1942- 21-24R
Aitken, (John William) Max(well)
1910-1985 Obituary 116
Aitken, Robert (Baker) 1917- 130
Aitken, Thomas Jr. 1910- 1-4R
Aitken, W(illiam) R(ussell) 1913- 41-44R
Aitken, William Maxwell
See Beaverbrook, William Maxwell Aitken
Aitkin, Don(ald Alexander) 1937- CANR-15
Earlier sketch in CA 93-96
Aitmatov, Chingiz (Torekulovich)
1928- CANR-38
Earlier sketch in CA 103
See also CLC 71
See also MTCW
See also SATA 56
Ajami, Alfred M(ichel) 1948- Brief entry 110
Ajar, Emile
See Kacew, Romain
Ajay, Betty 1918- 69-72
Ajayi, J(acob) F(estus) Ade(niyi)
1929- CANR-18
Earlier sketch in CA 61-64
Ajegbo, Keith 1946- 122
Ajilvsgi, Geyata 1933- 124
Akaba, Suekichi 1910- ....SATA 46
Akaha, Tsuneo 1949- 120
Akalaitis, JoAnne 1937- 138
Akanji, Sangodare
See Beier, Ulli
Akare, Thomas 1950- 109
Akashi, Yoji 1928- 33-36R
Akass, John Ewart 1933-1990 Obituary 131
Akass, Jon
See Akass, John Ewart
Ake, Claude 1939- CANR-10
Earlier sketch in CA 21-24R
Akehurst, M(ichael) B(arton) 1940- 25-28R
Akens, David S. 1921- CANR-12
Earlier sketch in CA 25-28R
Akenside, Mark 1721-1770 ....DLB 109
Akenson, Donald Harman 1941- CANR-22
Earlier sketches in CA 57-60, CANR-7
Aker, George F(rederick) 1927- CANR-15
Earlier sketch in CA 41-44R
Akeret, Robert U(lrich) 1928- 45-48
Akerman, Chantal (Anne) 1950- 127
Akers, Alan Burt
See Bulmer, (Henry) Kenneth
Akers, Charles W(esley) 1920- 13-16R
Akers, Floyd
See Baum, L(yman) Frank
Akers, Keith 1949- 112
Akers, Ronald L(ouis) 1939- CANR-1
Earlier sketch in CA 45-48
Akers, Susan Grey 1889-1984 Obituary 112
Akhmadulina, Bella Akhatovna 1937- 65-68
See also CLC 53
Akhmatova, Anna 1888-1966 ....CANR-35
Obituary 25-28R
Earlier sketches in CAP-1, CA 19-20
See also CLC 11, 25, 64
See also MTCW
See also PC 2
Akhnaton, Askia
See Eckels, Jon
Akhurst, Bertram A. 1928- 45-48
Akin, Wallace E(lmus) 1923- 25-28R
Akin, William E(rnest) 1936- CANR-39
Earlier sketch in CA 116
Akinjogbin, I(saac) A(deagbo) 1930- CANR-29
Earlier sketches in CA 21-24R, CANR-12
Akins, Ellen 135
Akins, Zoe 1886-1958 Brief entry 115
See also DLB 26
Akita, George 1926- 17-20R
Akmakjian, Hiag 1926- 57-60
Akpabot, Samuel Ekpe 1932- 101
Akrigg, G(eorge) P(hillip) V(ernon)
1913- 25-28R
Aks, Patricia 1926- 136
See also SATA 68
Aksenov, Vassily
See Aksyonov, Vassily (Pavlovich)
See also CLC 22
Aksyonov, Vassily (Pavlovich) 1932- CANR-12
Earlier sketch in CA 53-56
See also Aksenov, Vassily
See also CLC 37
Akurgal, Ekrem 1911- 130
Akutagawa Ryunosuke
1892-1927 Brief entry 117
See also TCLC 16
Aladjem, Henrietta H. 1917- 105
Alailima, Fay C. 1921- 33-36R
Alain
See Brustlein, Daniel
Alain 1868-1951 ....TCLC 41
Alain-Fournier
See Fournier, Henri Alban
See also DLB 65
See also TCLC 6
Alajalov, Constantin 1900-1987 Obituary 123
See also SATA 53
Al-Amin, Jamil Abdullah 1943- 125
Brief entry 112
See also BLC 1
See also BW
Alan, Jack
See Green, Alan (Baer)
Alan, Sandy
See Ullman, Allan
Aland, Kurt 1915- CANR-12
Earlier sketch in CA 25-28R
Alas (y Urena), Leopoldo (Enrique Garcia)
1852-1901 131
Brief entry 113
See also HW
See also TCLC 29
Alaya, Flavia (M.) 1935- 33-36R
al-Azm, Sadik J. 1934- CANR-9
Earlier sketch in CA 21-24R
Alazraki, Jaime 1934- CANR-21
Earlier sketch in CA 33-36R
Alba, Nanina 1915-1968 ....DLB 41
Alba, Richard D(enis) 1942- 109
Alba, Victor 1916- CANR-25
Earlier sketches in CA 21-24R, CANR-10
Alba de Gamez, Cielo Cayetana 1920- 93-96
Albanese, Catherine L(ouise) 1940- CANR-24
Earlier sketches in CA 65-68, CANR-9
Albany, James
See Rae, Hugh C(rauford)
Albaret, Celeste (Gineste) 1891-1984 73-76
Obituary 112
Albarn, Keith 1939- 135
Albaugh, Edwin (Doll Jr.) 1935- 89-92
Albaugh, Ralph M. 1909- CAP-1
Earlier sketch in CA 13-14
Albaum, Gerald (Sherwin) 1933- CANR-38
Earlier sketches in CA 37-40R, CANR-14
Albaum, Melvin 1936- 53-56
Albee, Edward (Franklin III) 1928- CANR-8
Earlier sketch in CA 5-8R
See also CABS 3
See also AITN 1
See also CDALB 1941-1968
See also CLC 1, 2, 3, 5, 9, 11, 13, 25, 53
See also DLB 7
See also MTCW
See also WLC
Albee, George Sumner 1905-1964 ....1-4R
Alber, Mike 1938- 25-28R
Alberoni, Francesco (Saverio) 1929- 130
Albers, Anni 1899- CANR-2
Earlier sketch in CA 1-4R
Albers, Henry H. 1919- CANR-6
Earlier sketch in CA 1-4R
Albers, Josef 1888-1976 ....CANR-3
Obituary 65-68
Earlier sketch in CA 1-4R
Albert, A(braham) Adrian
1905-1972 Obituary 37-40R
Albert, Allan (Praigrod) 1945- Brief entry 116
Albert, Burton Jr. 1936- CANR-23
Earlier sketches in CA 61-64, CANR-8
See also SATA 22
Albert, Carl (Bert) 1908- 132
Albert, Ethel M(ary) 1918- 21-24R
Albert, Gail 1942- 108
Albert, Harold A. 29-32R
Albert, Linda 1939- CANR-27
Earlier sketch in CA 110
Albert, Louise 1928- 69-72
Albert, Marv 1943- 101
Albert, Marvin H(ubert) 1924- CANR-30
Earlier sketch in CA 73-76
Albert, Mimi (Abriel) 1940- 73-76
Albert, Peter J(oseph) 1946- 114
Albert, Walter E. 1930- 21-24R
Albertazzie, Ralph 1923- 101
Alberti, Johanna 1940- 136
Alberti, Rafael 1902- 85-88
See also CLC 7
See also DLB 108
Alberti, Robert E(dward) 1938- CANR-7
Earlier sketch in CA 61-64
Alberts, David Stephen 1942- 29-32R
Alberts, Frances Jacobs 1907- 5-8R
See also SATA 14
Alberts, Robert C(arman) 1907- 33-36R
Alberts, William W. 1925- 21-24R
Albertson, Chris 1931- 57-60
Albertson, Dean 1920-1989 ....CANR-3
Obituary 128
Earlier sketch in CA 1-4R
Albert the Great 1200(?)-1280 ....DLB 115
Albertyn, Dorothy
See Black, Dorothy
Albery, Nobuko 81-84
Albin, Peter S(teigman) 1934- 85-88
Albini, Joseph L(ouis) 1930- 61-64
Albinski, Henry Stephen 1931- CANR-23
Earlier sketches in CA 21-24R, CANR-8
Albinson, Jack
See Albinson, James P.
Albinson, James P. 1932- 57-60
Albion, Lee Smith ....SATA 29
Albion, Robert Greenhalgh 1896-1983 .....CANR-3
Obituary 110
Earlier sketch in CA 1-4R
Albornoz, Claudio Sanchez
See Sanchez Albornoz (y Mediuna), Claudio
Alborough, Jez 1959- 131
Albran, Kehlog
See Shacket, Sheldon R(ubin)
Albrand, Martha (a pseudonym)
1914-1981 ....CANR-11
Obituary 108
Earlier sketch in CA 13-16R
Albrecht, Lillie (Vanderveer) 1894- 5-8R
See also SATA 12
Albrecht, Milton C(harles) 1904- CANR-13
Earlier sketch in CA 33-36R
Albrecht, Robert C(harles) 1933- 21-24R
Albrecht, Ruth E. 1910- 17-20R
Albrecht, William P(rice) 1907- 73-76
Albrecht-Carrie, Rene 1904-1978 ....CANR-1
Earlier sketch in CA 1-4R
Albright, Bets Parker
See Albright, Elizabeth A.
Albright, Bliss (James F.) 1903- 33-36R
Albright, Daniel 1945- 125
Albright, Elizabeth A. 1920- 108
Albright, Horace M(arden) 1890-1987 124
Obituary 122
Albright, John Brannon 1930- 65-68
Albright, Joseph (Medill Patterson)
1937- 97-100
Albright, Peter 1926- 108
Albright, Raymond W(olf) 1901-1965 ....CAP-1
Earlier sketch in CA 9-10
Albright, Roger (Lynch) 1922- 106
Albright, Thomas 1935-1984 Obituary 112
Albright, William F(oxwell)
1891-1971 Obituary 33-36R
Albrow, Martin 1937- 33-36R
Albus, James Sacra 1935- 124
Alcala-Galiano, Juan Valera y
See Valera y Alcala-Galiano, Juan
Alcalde, E. L.
See Chaij, Fernando
Alcalde, Miguel
See Burgess, M(ichael) R(oy)
Alcantara, Ruben R(eyes) 1940- 105
Alcayaga, Lucila Godoy
See Godoy Alcayaga, Lucila
Alchemy, Jack
See Gershator, David
Alchian, Armen A(lbert) 1914- 127
Brief entry 110
Alcibiade
See Praz, Mario
Alcock, Gudrun 1908- ....SATA 33, 56
Alcock, John 1942- 125
Alcock, Vivien 1924- 110
See also AAYA 8
See also CLR 26
See also MAICYA
See also SATA 38, 45
Alcorn, Alfred 1941- 122

Alcorn, John 1935- ... SATA 30, 31
Alcorn, Marvin D. 1902- ... 13-16R
Alcorn, Pat B(arker) 1948- ... 107
Alcorn, Robert Hayden 1909- ... 5-8R
Alcosser, Sandra (B.) 1944- Brief entry ... 124
Alcott, Amos Bronson 1799-1888 ... DLB 1
Alcott, Julia
See Cudlipp, Edythe
Alcott, Louisa May
1832-1888 ... CDALB 1865-1917
See also CLR 1
See also DLB 1, 42, 79
See also MAICYA
See also WLC
See also YABC 1
Alcott, William Andrus 1789-1859 ... DLB 1
Alcyone
See Krishnamurti, Jiddu
Ald, Roy A(llison) ... CANR-24
Earlier sketch in CA 73-76
Alda, Alan 1936- ... 103
Alda, Arlene 1933- ... 114
See also SATA 36, 44
Aldan, Daisy 1923- ... CANR-25
Earlier sketches in CA 13-16R, CANR-8
Aldanov, M. A.
See Aldanov, Mark (Alexandrovich)
Aldanov, Mark (Alexandrovich)
1886(?)-1957 Brief entry ... 118
See also TCLC 23
Aldcroft, Derek H. 1936- ... CANR-29
Earlier sketches in CA 25-28R, CANR-12
Alden, Carella
See Remington, Ella-Carrie
Alden, Dauril 1926- ... 105
Alden, Douglas William 1912- ... 69-72
Alden, Henry Mills 1836-1919 ... DLB 79
Alden, Isabella (Macdonald)
1841(?)-1930 Brief entry ... 120
See also DLB 42
See also YABC 2
Alden, Jack
See Barrows, (Ruth) Marjorie
Alden, John D. 1921- ... 17-20R
Alden, John R(ichard) 1908-1991 ... CANR-11
Obituary ... 135
Earlier sketch in CA 61-64
Alden, Michele
See Avallone, Michael (Angelo, Jr)
Alden, Robert L(eslie) 1937- ... 65-68
Alden, Sue
See Francis, Dorothy Brenner
Alder, Francis A(nthony) 1937- ... 61-64
Alder, Henry (Ludwig) 1922- ... 49-52
Alderfer, Clayton P. 1940- ... 37-40R
Alderfer, E. G.
See Alderfer, E. Gordon
Alderfer, E. Gordon 1915- ... 121
Alderfer, Harold F(reed) 1903- ... 9-12R
Alderman, Clifford Lindsey 1902- ... CANR-3
Earlier sketch in CA 1-4R
See also SATA 3
Alderman, Geoffrey 1944- ... CANR-29
Earlier sketch in CA 93-96
Alderman, (Barbara) Joy 1931- ... 61-64
Aldersey-Williams, Hugh 1959- ... 138
Alderson, Jo(anne) Bartels 1930- ... 65-68
Alderson, Michael (Rowland)
1931-1988 Obituary ... 126
Alderson, (Arthur) Stanley 1927- ... 5-8R
Alderson, Sue Ann 1940- ... SATA 48, 59
Alderson, William T(homas) Jr. 1926- ... 9-12R
Alding, Peter
See Jeffries, Roderic (Graeme)
Aldington, Richard 1892-1962 ... 85-88
See also CLC 49
See also DLB 20, 36, 100
Aldis, Dorothy (Keeley) 1896-1966 ... CANR-34
Earlier sketch in CA 1-4R
See also DLB 22
See also SATA 2
Aldiss, Brian W(ilson) 1925- ... CANR-28
Earlier sketches in CA 5-8R, CANR-5
See also CAAS 2
See also CLC 5, 14, 40
See also DLB 14
See also MTCW
See also SATA 34
Aldon, Adair
See Meigs, Cornelia Lynde
Aldon, Howard
See Wilson, (Alan) Doric
Aldouby, Zwy H(erbert) 1931- ... 33-36R
Aldous, Allan (Charles) 1911- ... SATA 27
Aldous, Anthony Michael 1935- ... CANR-25
Earlier sketch in CA 69-72
Aldous, Tony
See Aldous, Anthony Michael
Aldred, Cyril 1914-1991 ... CANR-6
Obituary ... 134
Earlier sketch in CA 57-60
Aldrich, Ann
See Meaker, Marijane (Agnes)
Aldrich, C(larence) Knight 1914- ... 25-28R
Aldrich, Frederic DeLong 1899- ... CAP-1
Earlier sketch in CA 11-12
Aldrich, Jonathan 1936- Brief entry ... 112
Aldrich, Joseph C(offin) 1940- ... CANR-37
Earlier sketch in CA 114
Aldrich, Nelson Wilmarth Jr.
1935- Brief entry ... 110
Aldrich, Richard (Stoddard)
1902-1986 Obituary ... 119
Aldrich, Ruth I(sabelle) ... 105
Aldrich, Sandra Picklesimer 1945- ... 111
Aldrich, Thomas Bailey
1836-1907 Brief entry ... 111
See also DLB 42, 71, 74, 79
See also SATA 17
Aldridge, A(lfred) Owen 1915- ... 17-20R
Aldridge, Adele 1934- ... CANR-28
Earlier sketch in CA 49-52
Aldridge, Alan 1943- ... 125
See also SATA 33
Aldridge, (Harold Edward) James
1918- ... CANR-13
Earlier sketch in CA 61-64
Aldridge, Jeffrey 1938- ... 25-28R
Aldridge, John W(atson) 1922- ... CANR-3
Earlier sketch in CA 1-4R
Aldridge, Josephine Haskell ... 73-76
See also SATA 14
Aldridge, Richard Boughton 1930- ... CANR-3
Earlier sketch in CA 9-12R
Aldridge, Sarah
See Marchant, Anyda
Aldrin, Edwin E(ugene) Jr. 1930- ... 89-92
Aldwinckle, Russell (Foster) 1911- ... 69-72
Aldyne, Nathan
See McDowell, Michael
Alegria, Ciro 1909-1967 ... 131
See also DLB 113
Alegria, Claribel 1924- ... 131
See also CAAS 15
See also HW
Alegria, Fernando 1918- ... CANR-32
Earlier sketches in CA 9-12R, CANR-5
See also CLC 57
See also HW
Alegria, Ricardo E(nrique) 1921- ... CANR-32
Earlier sketches in CA 25-28R, CANR-15
See also HW
See also SATA 6
Aleichem, Sholom
See Rabinovitch, Sholem
See also TCLC 1, 35
Aleixandre, Vicente 1898-1984 ... CANR-26
Obituary ... 114
Earlier sketch in CA 85-88
See also CLC 9, 36
See also DLB 108
See also HW
See also MTCW
Alejandro, Carlos F(ederico) Diaz
See Diaz-Alejandro, Carlos F(ederico)
Aleksin, Anatolii Georgievich 1924- ... CANR-29
Earlier sketch in CA 109
See also SATA 36
Aleman, Miguel 1903(?)-1983 Obituary ... 110
Alenov, Lydia 1948- ... SATA 61
Alent, Rose Marie Bachem
See Bachem Alent, Rose M(arie Baake)
Alepoudelis, Odysseus
See Elytis, Odysseus
Aleramo, Sibilla 1876-1960 ... DLB 114
Aleshkovsky, Joseph 1929- ... 128
Brief entry ... 121
See also Aleshkovsky, Yuz
Aleshkovsky, Yuz
See Aleshkovsky, Joseph
See also CLC 44
Alessandra, Anthony J(oseph) 1947- ... 103
Alessandrini, Federico
1906(?)-1983 Obituary ... 109
Alex, Ben (a pseudonym) 1946- ... 114
See also SATA 45
Alex, Marlee (a pseudonym) 1948- ... 114
See also SATA 45
Alexander, Albert 1914- ... 25-28R
Alexander, Alfred 1908-1983 Obituary ... 110
Alexander, Anna B(arbara Cooke) 1913- ... 57-60
See also SATA 1
Alexander, Anne
See Alexander, Anna B(arbara Cooke)
Alexander, Anthony Francis 1920- ... 1-4R
Alexander, Arthur (Wilson) 1927- ... 5-8R
Alexander, Bevin (Ray) 1928- ... 122
Alexander, Bill 1910- ... 130
Alexander, Boyd 1913-1980 ... 53-56
Obituary ... 97-100
Alexander, Caroline 1956- ... 132
Alexander, Charles
See Hadfield, (Ellis) Charles (Raymond)
Alexander, Charles C(omer) 1935- ... 13-16R
Alexander, Charles Stevenson 1916- ... CANR-2
Earlier sketch in CA 5-8R
Alexander, Charles 1868-1923 ... DLB 91
Alexander, Christine (Anne) 1949- ... 117
Alexander, Christine 1893-1975 Obituary ... 61-64
Alexander, Colin James 1920- ... 13-16R
Alexander, Conel Hugh O'Donel
1909-1974 ... 73-76
Alexander, David M(ichael) 1945- ... 81-84
Alexander, David 1907-1973 ... 1-4R
Obituary ... 41-44R
Alexander, Denis 1945- ... 45-48
Alexander, Donna
See Vitek, Donna Kimel
Alexander, Edward P(orter) 1907- ... 33-36R
Alexander, Edward 1936- ... 13-16R
Alexander, Edwin P. 1905- ... 29-32R
Alexander, Elizabeth 1962- ... 135
Alexander, Eric 1910(?)-1982 Obituary ... 106
Alexander, Ernest R(obert) 1933- ... 103
Alexander, Faith
See Bentley, Margaret
Alexander, Floyce 1938- ... CANR-13
Earlier sketch in CA 33-36R
Alexander, Frances (Laura) 1888- ... CANR-35
Earlier sketch in CA 25-28R
See also SATA 4
Alexander, Frank 1943- ... 65-68
Alexander, Franklin Osborne 1897- ... CAP-2
Earlier sketch in CA 25-28
Alexander, Franz (Gabriel) 1891-1964 ... 5-8R
Alexander, Gary 1941- ... 135
Alexander, George Jonathan 1931- ... 73-76
Alexander, George M(oyer) 1914- ... 5-8R
Alexander, Gil
See Ralston, Gilbert A(lexander)
Alexander, H. G. ... 129
See also Alexander, Horace G(undry)
Alexander, Harold Lee 1934- ... 69-72
Alexander, Henry
See McAllister, Alister
Alexander, Herbert E(phraim) 1927- ... 41-44R
Alexander, Herbert (Mortimer)
1910-1988 Obituary ... 127
Alexander, Holmes (Moss)
1906-1985 ... CANR-36
Obituary ... 118
Earlier sketch in CA 61-64
Alexander, Horace G(undry)
1889-1989 Obituary ... 129
See also Alexander, H. G.
Alexander, Hubert G(riggs) 1909- ... 21-24R
Alexander, I. J. 1905(?)-1974 Obituary ... 53-56
Alexander, Ian W(elsh) 1911- ... 13-16R
Alexander, J(onathan) J(ames) G(raham)
1935- ... CANR-13
Earlier sketch in CA 21-24R
Alexander, James E(ckert) 1913- ... 73-76
Alexander, James 1691-1756 ... DLB 24
Alexander, Jan
See Banis, Victor J(erome)
Alexander, Janet 1907- ... CANR-4
Earlier sketch in CA 9-12R
See also McNeill, Janet
Alexander, Jean 1926- ... CANR-27
Earlier sketch in CA 49-52
Alexander, Joan
See Wetherell-Pepper, Joan Alexander
Alexander, Jocelyn Anne Arundel
1930- ... CANR-4
Earlier sketch in CA 1-4R
See also SATA 22
Alexander, John A(leck) 1912- ... 9-12R
Alexander, John Kurt 1941- ... 102
Alexander, John N. 1941- ... 69-72
Alexander, John T(horndike) 1940- ... 33-36R
Alexander, John W(esley) 1918- ... CANR-3
Earlier sketch in CA 5-8R
Alexander, Jon 1940- ... 33-36R
Alexander, Josephine 1909- ... 104
Alexander, (Charles) K(halil)
1923-1980 Obituary ... 103
Alexander, Karl 1944- ... 134
Alexander, Kate
See Armstrong, Tilly
Alexander, Kathryn
See Caldwell, Kathryn (Smoot)
Alexander, Ken
See Alexander, Kenneth John Wilson
Alexander, Kenneth John Wilson 1922- ... 61-64
Alexander, L(ouis) G(eorge) 1932- ... CANR-19
Earlier sketch in CA 102
Alexander, Lawrence 1939- Brief entry ... 122
Alexander, Leo 1905-1985 Obituary ... 116
Alexander, Lewis M(cElwain) 1921- ... 21-24R
Alexander, Linda 1935- ... 21-24R
See also SATA 2
Alexander, Liza
See Campbell, Louisa D.
Alexander, Lloyd (Chudley) 1924- ... CANR-38
Earlier sketches in CA 1-4R, CANR-1, 24
See also AAYA 1
See also CLC 35
See also CLR 1, 5
See also DLB 52
See also MAICYA
See also MTCW
See also SATA 3, 49
Alexander, Louis 1917- ... 121
Alexander, Marc 1929- ... CANR-34
Earlier sketches in CA 5-8R, CANR-14
Alexander, Marge
See Edwards, Roselyn
Alexander, Martha 1920- ... 85-88
See also MAICYA
See also SATA 11, 70
Alexander, Marthann 1907- ... 53-56
Alexander, Martin 1930- ... CANR-27
Earlier sketch in CA 49-52
Alexander, Mary Jean McCutcheon ... 9-12R
Alexander, Meena 1951- ... CANR-38
Earlier sketch in CA 115
Alexander, Michael (Joseph) 1941- ... CANR-22
Earlier sketch in CA 45-48
Alexander, Michael Van Cleave 1937- ... 102
Alexander, Milton 1917- ... 17-20R
Alexander, Pamela 1948- ... 122
Alexander, Pat(ricia June) 1937- ... 113
Alexander, Peter F. 1949- ... 138
Alexander, R(obert) McNeill 1934- ... 124
Alexander, R(obert) P(ercival)
1905(?)-1985 Obituary ... 117
Alexander, Rae Pace
See Alexander, Raymond Pace
Alexander, Ralph (Holland) 1936- ... 115
Alexander, Raymond Pace 1898-1974 ... 97-100
See also SATA 22
Alexander, Ric
See Long, Richard A(lexander)
Alexander, Richard Dale 1929- ... 110
Alexander, Robert
See Legat, Michael (Ronald)
Alexander, Robert
See Gross, Michael (Robert)
Alexander, Robert J. 1918- ... CANR-39
Earlier sketches in CA 1-4R, CANR-3, 18
Alexander, Robert Lester 1920- ... 108
Alexander, Robert William
1906(?)-1980 Obituary ... 97-100
Alexander, (Eben) Roy 1899(?)-1978 ... 85-88
Obituary ... 81-84
Alexander, Roy 1928- ... 118
Alexander, Shana 1925- ... CANR-26
Earlier sketch in CA 61-64
Alexander, Sidney 1912- ... CANR-6
Earlier sketch in CA 9-12R
Alexander, Stanley Walter
1895-1980 Obituary ... 97-100
Alexander, Stella Tucker 1912- ... 105
Alexander, Sue 1933- ... CANR-19
Earlier sketches in CA 53-56, CANR-4
See also SATA 12
Alexander, Taylor Richard 1915- ... 107
Alexander, Theron 1913- ... CANR-3
Earlier sketch in CA 5-8R
Alexander, Thomas G(len) 1935- ... 65-68
Alexander, Thomas W(illiamson) Jr.
1930- ... 9-12R
Alexander, Vincent Arthur
1925-1980 Obituary ... 101
See also SATA 23
Alexander, W(illiam) M(ortimer) 1928- ... 69-72
Alexander, SirWilliam 1557(?)-1640 ... DLB 121
Alexander, William M(arvin) 1912- ... 33-36R
Alexander, Yonah 1931- ... 61-64
Alexander, Zane
See Alexander, Harold Lee
Alexanderson, Gerald L(ee) 1933- ... 118
Alexandersson, Gunnar V(ilhelm) 1922- ... 17-20R
Alexandre, Philippe 1932- ... 41-44R
Alexandrowicz, Charles Henry
1902-1975 ... CANR-1
Earlier sketch in CA 1-4R
Alexeev, Wassilij 1906- ... 89-92
Alexeieff, Alexandre A. 1901- ... SATA 14
Alexeyev, Constantin (Sergeivich)
See Stanislavsky, Constantin (Sergeivich)
Alexie, Sherman (Joseph Jr.) 1966- ... 138
Alexiou, Margaret 1939- ... 69-72
Alexis, Katina
See Strauch, Katina (Parthemos)
Aley, Albert 1919-1986 Obituary ... 118
Alfandary-Alexander, Mark 1923- ... 5-8R
al-Farabi 870 (?)-950 ... DLB 115
al-Faruqi, Isma'il Raji 1921- ... CANR-13
Earlier sketch in CA 69-72
Alfau, Felipe 1902- ... 137
See also CLC 66
Alford, Bernard William Ernest 1937- ... 101
Alford, C(harles) Fred(erick) 1947- ... 131
Alford, Norman (William) 1929- ... 37-40R
Alford, Robert R(oss) 1928- ... 41-44R
Alford, Terry (L.) 1945- Brief entry ... 110
Alfred, Richard
See Haverstock, Nathan Alfred
Alfred, William 1922- ... 13-16R
Alfven, Hannes O(lof) G(oesta) 1908- ... 29-32R
Algarin, Miguel 1941- ... CANR-20
Earlier sketch in CA 69-72
Algeo, John (Thomas) 1930- ... CANR-7
Earlier sketch in CA 17-20R
Alger, Horatio Jr.
See Stratemeyer, Edward L.
Alger, Horatio Jr. 1832-1899 ... DLB 42
See also SATA 16
Alger, Leclaire (Gowans) 1898-1969 ... 73-76
See also MAICYA
See also SATA 15
Alger, Philip Langdon 1894-1979 Obituary ... 109
Algery, Andre
See Coulet du Gard, Rene
al-Ghazali 1058-1111 ... DLB 115
Algren, Nelson 1909-1981 ... CANR-20
Obituary ... 103
Earlier sketch in CA 13-16R
See also CDALB 1941-1968
See also CLC 4, 10, 33
See also DLB 9
See also DLBY 81, 82
See also MTCW
Alhaique, Claudio 1913- ... 29-32R
Ali, Ahmed 1910- ... CANR-34
Earlier sketches in CA 25-28R, CANR-15
See also CLC 69
Ali, Chaudhri Mohamad
1905-1980 Obituary ... 105
Ali, Muhammad 1942- Brief entry ... 116
Ali, Salim (A.) 1896-1987 ... 132
Obituary ... 123
Ali, Schavi M(ali) 1948- ... CANR-26
Earlier sketches in CA 61-64, CANR-11
Ali, Tariq 1943- ... CANR-10
Earlier sketch in CA 25-28R
Aliano, Richard Anthony 1946- ... CANR-10
Earlier sketch in CA 65-68
Aliav, Ruth
See Kluger, Ruth
Aliber, Robert Z. 1930- ... CANR-25
Earlier sketches in CA 21-24R, CANR-8
Alibrandi, Tom 1941- ... CANR-12
Earlier sketch in CA 65-68
Alice (Mary Victoria Augusta Pauline), Princess
1883-1981 Obituary ... 103
Aliesan, Jody 1943- ... CANR-7
Earlier sketch in CA 57-60
Alihan, Milla ... CAP-2
Earlier sketch in CA 29-32
Ali Khan, Shirley 1951- ... 118
Aliki
See Brandenberg, Aliki Liacouras
See also CLR 9

Alilunas, Leo John 1912- 17-20R
Alimayo, Chikuyo
See Franklin, Harold L(eroy)
Alinder, Martha Wheelock
See Wheelock, Martha E.
Alinsky, Saul (David) 1909-1972 133
Obituary 37-40R
Alioto, Robert F(ranklyn) 1933- 45-48
Alisky, Marvin (Howard) 1923- CANR-20
Earlier sketches in CA 13-16R, CANR-5
Alisov, Boris P. 1892-1972 Obituary 37-40R
Al-Issa, Ihsan 1931- 109
Alitto, Guy S(alvatore) 1942- 93-96
Alix, Ernest Kahlar 1939- Brief entry 112
Alkalay-Gut, Karen 1945- 129
Alkema, Chester Jay 1932- 53-56
See also SATA 12
Alker, Hayward R(ose) Jr. 1937- 17-20R
al-Khadim, Sa'd
See Elkhadem, Saad (Eldin Amin)
al-Kharrat, Edwar 1926- 136
Alkire, Leland George (Jr.) 1937- 101
Alkire, William Henry 1935- 107
Allaback, Steven Lee 1939- 97-100
Allaby, (John) Michael 1933- CANR-20
Earlier sketches in CA 45-48, CANR-1
Allaire, Joseph L(eo) 1929- 41-44R
Allamand, Pascale 1942- CANR-12
Earlier sketch in CA 69-72
See also SATA 12
Allan, Alfred K. 1930- 17-20R
Allan, Andrew 1907-1974 DLB 88
Allan, D(avid) G(uy) C(harles) 1925- CANR-15
Earlier sketch in CA 25-28R
Allan, Elkan 1922- 101
Allan, Harry T. 1928- 25-28R
Allan, J(ohn) David 1945- 41-44R
Allan, John B.
See Westlake, Donald E(dwin)
Allan, Lewis
See Meeropol, Abel
Allan, Mabel Esther 1915- CANR-18
Earlier sketches in CA 5-8R, CANR-2
See also MAICYA
See also SAAS 11
See also SATA 5, 32
Allan, Mea 1909-1982 CANR-2
Obituary 107
Earlier sketch in CA 5-8R
Allan, Norman B. 1921- Brief entry 105
Allan, Robert Alexander
1914-1979 Obituary 106
Allan, Robin 1934- 107
Allan, Ted 1916- 77-80
See also DLB 68
Allana, Ghulam Ali 1906-1985 Obituary 115
Allana, Ghulamali
See Allana, Ghulam Ali
Allanbrook, Wye J(amison) 1943- 110
Alland, Alexander Jr. 1931- 21-24R
Alland, Guy 1944- 69-72
Allard, Bessie Butler Newsom Obituary 122
Allard, Dean C(onrad) 1933- CANR-1
Earlier sketch in CA 45-48
Allard, Harry
See Allard, Harry G(rover) Jr.
Allard, Harry G(rover) Jr. 1928- CANR-38
Earlier sketch in CA 113
See also MAICYA
See also SATA 42
Allard, Michel (Adrien)
1924-1976 Obituary 65-68
Allard, Sven 1896-1975 CAP-2
Earlier sketch in CA 29-32
Allard, William Albert 1937- 115
Allardt, Erik 1925- CANR-30
Earlier sketches in CA 73-76, CANR-13
Allardt, Linda 1926- 126
Brief entry 104
Allardyce, Gilbert Daniel 1932- 33-36R
Allardyce, Paula
See Torday, Ursula
Allason, Rupert (W. S.) 1951- 132
Allaun, Frank (Julian) 1913- 103
Allbeck, Willard Dow 1898- 21-24R
Allbeury, Ted
See Allbeury, Theodore Edward le Bouthillier
See also DLB 87
Allbeury, Theodore Edward le Bouthillier
1917- CANR-34
Earlier sketches in CA 53-56, CANR-5
See also Allbeury, Ted
Allchin, A(rthur) M(acdonald) 1930- CANR-38
Earlier sketches in CA 25-28R, CANR-17
Allcorn, Seth 1946- 138
Alldridge, James Charles 1910- 29-32R
Alldritt, Keith 1935- 25-28R
See also DLB 14
Allee, John Gage (Jr.) 1918-1987 Obituary 121
Allee, Marjorie Hill 1890-1945 SATA 17
Alleger, Daniel E(ugene) 1903- 33-36R
Allegro, John Marco 1923-1988 CANR-20
Obituary 124
Earlier sketches in CA 9-12R, CANR-4
Allen, A(rthur) B(ruce) 1903-1975 CAP-2
Earlier sketch in CA 23-24
Allen, A(rvon) Dale Jr. 1935- 21-24R
Allen, Adam
See Epstein, Beryl (M. Williams)
and Epstein, Samuel
Allen, Agnes Rogers 1893-1986 Obituary 121
Allen, Alex B.
See Heide, Florence Parry
Allen, Allyn
See Eberle, Irmengarde
Allen, Anita
See Schenck, Anita A(llen)
Allen, Arthur A(ugustus) 1885-1964 CANR-19
Earlier sketch in CA 1-4R
Allen, Barbara
See Stuart, (Violet) Vivian (Finlay)
Allen, Betsy
See Harrison, Elizabeth Cavanna
Allen, Betty (Jeanne) 1929- 113
Allen, Bob 1948- 118
Allen, Brian 1952- 126
Allen, Captain Quincy CANR-26
Earlier sketches in CAP-2, CA 19-20
Allen, Carl 1961- 69-72
Allen, Catherine B(ryant) 1942- 129
Allen, Cecil J(ohn) 1886-1973 CAP-2
Earlier sketch in CA 25-28
Allen, Charles L(ivingstone) 1913- CANR-28
Earlier sketch in CA 111
Allen, Charlotte Hale 1928- 130
Allen, Charlotte Vale 1941- CANR-30
Earlier sketches in CA 69-72, CANR-12
Allen, Chester
See Holding, Vera Zumwalt
Allen, Chris 1929- 29-32R
Allen, Clabon Walter 1904-1987 Obituary 124
Allen, Clay
See Paine, Lauran (Bosworth)
Allen, Clifford Edward 1902- CAP-1
Earlier sketch in CA 9-10
Allen, Clifton Judson 1901- 108
Allen, Daniel 1947- 125
Allen, David Elliston 1932- 25-28R
Allen, David F(ranklyn) 1943- 103
Allen, David Grayson 1943- 115
Allen, David Rayvern 1938- 129
Allen, David W. 1922- Brief entry 113
Allen, David 1925- 33-36R
Allen, David 1939- 115
Allen, Derek Fortrose 1910-1975 Obituary 114
Allen, Dick 1939- 33-36R
See also CAAS 11
Allen, Diogenes 1932- CANR-25
Earlier sketches in CA 25-28R, CANR-10
Allen, Dizzy
See Allen, H(ubert) R(aymond)
Allen, Don Cameron 1903-1972 CANR-4
Earlier sketch in CA 5-8R
Allen, Donald Emerson 1917- 45-48
Allen, Donald M(erriam) 1912- CANR-10
Earlier sketch in CA 17-20R
Allen, Donald R. 1930- 45-48
Allen, Douglas (Malcolm) 1941- 113
Allen, Durward L(eon) 1910- 41-44R
Allen, Dwight W(illiam) 1931- 13-16R
Allen, E. C.
See Ward, Elizabeth Campbell
Allen, Edith Beavers 1920- 9-12R
Allen, Edith Marion CAP-1
Earlier sketch in CA 13-16
Allen, Edward D(avid) 1923- CANR-31
Earlier sketch in CA 49-52
Allen, Edward Heron
See Heron-Allen, Edward
Allen, Edward J(oseph) 1907- CAP-1
Earlier sketch in CA 17-18
Allen, Edward Lawrence
1913-1989 Obituary 130
Allen, Edward Switzer 1887-1985 Obituary 116
Allen, Edward 1948- CLC 59
Allen, Elisabeth Offutt 1895- 57-60
Allen, Elizabeth
See Thompson, Elizabeth Allen
Allen, Elizabeth Cooper
See Allen, Betty (Jeanne)
Allen, (Evelyn) Elizabeth 1918- 121
Allen, Elizabeth 1955- 122
Allen, Eric 1916- 133
Brief entry 111
Allen, Ethan 1738-1789 DLB 31
Allen, Everett S(locum) 1916- Brief entry 110
Allen, Francis A(lfred) 1919- 13-16R
Allen, Francis R(obbins) 1908- 77-80
Allen, Frank 1939- CANR-26
Earlier sketch in CA 109
Allen, Frederick G(arfield) 1936-1986 CANR-26
Obituary 121
Earlier sketch in CA 57-60
Allen, Frederick S(tetson) 1930- Brief entry 112
Allen, G(eorge) C(yril) 1900-1982 CANR-32
Obituary 107
Earlier sketches in CA 1-4R, CANR-3
Allen, G(eorge) Francis 1907- CAP-1
Earlier sketch in CA 9-10
Allen, Garland E(dward) 1936- 53-56
Allen, Gary
See Allen, Frederick G(arfield)
Allen, Gay Wilson 1903- CANR-3
Earlier sketch in CA 5-8R
See also DLB 103
Allen, Geoffrey Francis 1902- CAP-1
Earlier sketch in CA 13-14
Allen, George (Herbert) 1922- 111
Allen, George 1808-1876 DLB 59
Allen, Gerald 1942- CANR-16
Earlier sketch in CA 93-96
Allen, Gertrude E(lizabeth) 1888- 61-64
See also SATA 9
Allen, Gilbert (Bruce) 1951- 111
Allen, Gina 1918- 1-4R
Allen, Grant 1848-1899 DLB 70, 92
Allen, Gwenfread Elaine 1904- 61-64
Allen, H. Fredericka
See Allen, H(elena) G(ronlund)
Allen, H(elena) G(ronlund) 29-32R
Allen, H(ubert) R(aymond)
1919-1987 Obituary 122
Allen, Harold B(yron) 1902- CANR-10
Earlier sketch in CA 17-20R
Allen, Harold J(oseph) 1925- 45-48
Allen, Harry Cranbrook 1917- 5-8R
Allen, Hazel
See Hershberger, Hazel Kuhns
Allen, Henry
See Adams, Henry H(itch)
Allen, Henry Wilson 1912-1991 89-92
Obituary 135
See also DLBY 85
Allen, Herman R. 1913(?)-1979 Obituary 89-92
Allen, (William) Hervey (Jr.)
1889-1949 Brief entry 108
See also DLB 9, 45
Allen, Howard W. 1931- 33-36R
Allen, Ida (Cogswell) Bailey
1885-1973 Obituary 110
Allen, Ira R. 1948- 65-68
Allen, Irene 1903- CAP-1
Earlier sketch in CA 13-16
Allen, Irving L(ewis) Jr. 1931- 110
Allen, Ivan Jr. 1911- 109
Allen, Jack 1899- SATA 29
Allen, Jack 1914- CANR-4
Earlier sketch in CA 9-12R
Allen, James
See Ader, Paul (Fassett)
Allen, James B(eekman) 1931- 105
Allen, James B(rown) 1927- 105
Allen, James Egert 1896-1980 Obituary 97-100
Allen, James L(ovic) Jr. 1929- CANR-17
Earlier sketch in CA 33-36R
Allen, James Lane 1849-1925 DLB 71
Allen, James S. 1906(?)-1986 Obituary 120
Allen, James Smith 1949- 111
Allen, James 1739-1808 DLB 31
Allen, Jay Presson 1922- 73-76
See also DLB 26
Allen, Jeffrey G(rant) 1943- 116
Allen, Jeffrey (Yale) 1948- 112
See also SATA 42
Allen, Jerry 1911- 9-12R
Allen, Jim
See Allen, James L(ovic) Jr.
Allen, Johannes 1916-1973 CANR-14
Earlier sketch in CA 29-32R
Allen, John
See Perry, Ritchie (John Allen)
Allen, John Alexander 1922- 25-28R
Allen, John D(aniel) 1898-1972 CAP-2
Earlier sketch in CA 33-36
Allen, John Jay 1932- CANR-18
Earlier sketch in CA 33-36R
Allen, John Logan 1941- 85-88
Allen, John Stuart 1907-1982 Obituary 109
Allen, Jon L(ewis) 1931- 57-60
Allen, Jordan
See Dumke, Glenn S.
Allen, Judson B(oyce) 1932- CANR-17
Earlier sketch in CA 81-84
Allen, K. Eileen 1918- 113
Allen, Katharine Martin
1906(?)-1984 Obituary 113
Allen, Kenneth S. 1913-1981 CANR-32
Earlier sketch in CA 77-80
See also SATA 56
Allen, Kenneth (William) 1941- 69-72
Allen, L(ouis) David 1940- 130
Brief entry 117
Allen, Lafe Franklin 1914- Brief entry 111
Allen, Laura Jean 133
Brief entry 110
See also SATA 53
Allen, Lawrence A. 1926- 45-48
Allen, Layman E(dward) 1927- 5-8R
Allen, Lee 1915-1969 CANR-1
Earlier sketch in CA 1-4R
Allen, Leonard 1915(?)-1981 Obituary 102
Allen, Leroy 1912- 65-68
See also SATA 11
Allen, Leslie Christopher 1935- CANR-13
Earlier sketch in CA 73-76
Allen, Leslie H. 1887(?)-1973 Obituary 49-52
Allen, Linda 1925- 102
See also SATA 33
Allen, Loring
See Allen, Robert Loring
Allen, Louis A. 1917- 5-8R
Allen, Louis 1922-1991 41-44R
Obituary 136
Allen, M(arion) C. 1914- 9-12R
Allen, M(alcolm) D(ennis) 1951- 138
Allen, Marcus
See Donicht, Mark Allen
Allen, Marjorie 1931- 69-72
See also SATA 22
Allen, Marjory (Gill) 1897- CAP-1
Earlier sketch in CA 9-10
Allen, Mark
See Donicht, Mark Allen
Allen, Martha Mitten 1937- 125
Allen, Mary
See Cleveland, Mary
Allen, Mary (Charlotte Chocqueel) 1909- 109
Allen, Maury 1932- CANR-11
Earlier sketch in CA 17-20R
See also SATA 26
Allen, Merrill J(ames) 1918- 69-72
Allen, Merritt Parmelee 1892-1954 SATA 22
Allen, Michael (Derek) 1939- CANR-39
Earlier sketch in CA 77-80
Allen, Michael J(ohn) B(ridgman) 1941- 102
Allen, Michael Patrick 1945- 137
Allen, Minerva C(rantz) 1935- CANR-6
Earlier sketch in CA 57-60
Allen, Miriam Marx 1927- 138
Allen, Myron Sheppard 1901- CAP-1
Earlier sketch in CA 9-10
Allen, Nina (Stroemgren) 1935- SATA 22
Allen, Oliver E. 1922- 126
Allen, Pamela 1934- 126
See also SATA 50
Allen, Pat 1938- 118
Allen, Paul 1948- 81-84
Allen, Paula Gunn Brief entry 112
Allen, Peter Christopher 1905- 108
Allen, Phyllis (Greig) 65-68
Allen, Phyllis S(loan) 1908- 65-68
Allen, Polly Reynolds 1940- 110
Allen, R. Earl 1922- CANR-6
Earlier sketch in CA 9-12R
Allen, R(onald) R(oyce) 1930- 17-20R
Allen, Reginald E. 1931- CANR-13
Earlier sketch in CA 33-36R
Allen, (Alexander) Richard 1929- CANR-11
Earlier sketch in CA 65-68
Allen, Richard C.
See Taylor, John M(axwell)
Allen, Richard C. 1926- CANR-17
Earlier sketch in CA 25-28R
Allen, Richard (Hugh Sedley) 1903- 25-28R
Allen, Richard Sanders 1917- 21-24R
Allen, Richard V(incent) 1936- 21-24R
Allen, Roach Van 1917- 9-12R
Allen, Robert
See Garfinkel, Bernard Max
Allen, Robert C(lyde) 1950- 117
Allen, Robert Day 1927-1986 107
Obituary 125
Allen, Robert F(rancis) 1928-1987 CANR-36
Obituary 123
Earlier sketch in CA 33-36R
Allen, Robert J. 1930- 13-16R
Allen, Robert L(ee) 1942- 101
See also BW
Allen, Robert Livingston 1916- 17-20R
Allen, Robert Loring 1921- CANR-6
Earlier sketch in CA 1-4R
Allen, Robert M. 1909-1979 CANR-2
Earlier sketch in CA 1-4R
Allen, Robert Porter 1905-1963 5-8R
Allen, Robert S(haron) 1900-1981 CANR-6
Obituary 103
Earlier sketch in CA 57-60
Allen, Robert Thomas 1911- Brief entry 110
Allen, Robert 1946- 97-100
Allen, Rodney F. 1938- 61-64
See also SATA 27
Allen, Roger M(ichael) A(shley) 1942- CANR-28
Earlier sketch in CA 111
Allen, Roland
See Ayckbourn, Alan
Allen, Ronald B(arclay) 1941- 114
Allen, Ronald Royce 1930- CANR-32
Earlier sketch in CA 113
Allen, Ross R(oundy) 1928- 33-36R
Allen, Roy (George Douglas)
1906-1983 Obituary 110
Allen, Rupert C(lyde) 1927- 65-68
Allen, Ruth
See Peterson, Esther (Allen)
Allen, Ruth Finney 1898-1979 93-96
Obituary 85-88
Allen, Sam
See Allen, M(arion) C.
Allen, Samuel W(ashington) 1917- CANR-26
Earlier sketch in CA 49-52
See also BW
See also DLB 41
See also SATA 9
Allen, Sarah (Pearson) Sawyer 1920- 89-92
Allen, Sheila Rosalynd 1942- 135
Allen, Shirley Seifried 1921- 57-60
Allen, Shirley Walter 1883- CAP-2
Earlier sketch in CA 25-28
Allen, Stephen (Valentine Patrick William)
1921- CANR-18
Earlier sketch in CA 25-28R
Allen, Steve
See Allen, Stephen (Valentine Patrick William)
Allen, Sue P. 1913- 25-28R
Allen, Sydney (Earl) Jr. 1929- 29-32R
Allen, T. D.
See Allen, Terril Diener
Allen, Terril Diener 1908- CANR-2
Earlier sketch in CA 5-8R
See also SATA 35
Allen, Terry D.
See Allen, Terril Diener
Allen, Thomas B(enton) 1929- CANR-20
Earlier sketches in CA 13-16R, CANR-5
See also SATA 45
Allen, Tom
See Allen, Thomas B(enton)
Allen, Tony 1945- 77-80
Allen, Vernon L(esley) 1933- 29-32R
Allen, W(illiam) Sidney 1918- 49-52
Allen, Wallace (Wilbur) 1919- 118
Allen, Walter Ernest 1911- CANR-25
Earlier sketch in CA 61-64
See also CAAS 6
Allen, William A(ustin) 1916- CANR-13
Earlier sketch in CA 33-36R
Allen, William R(ichard) 1924- 17-20R
Allen, William Sheridan 1932- 13-16R
Allen, William Stannard 1913- 101
Allen, William 1940- 65-68
Allen, Woody 1935- CANR-38
Earlier sketches in CA 33-36R, CANR-27
See also CLC 16, 52
See also DLB 44
See also MTCW

Allende, Isabel 1942- 130
Brief entry 125
See also CLC 39, 57
See also HW
See also MTCW
Allendoerfer, Carl B(arnett)
1911-1974 ....CANR-11
Earlier sketches in CAP-2, CA 17-18
Allen of Hurtwood, Lady
See Allen, Marjory (Gill)
Allentuch, Harriet Ray 1933- 13-16R
Allentuck, Andrew 1943- 111
Allentuck, Marcia Epstein 1928- 33-36R
Allerton, Mary
See Govan, Christine Noble
Alletzhauser, Albert J. 1960- 136
Alley, Brian 1933- 111
Alley, Henry Melton 1945- CANR-35
Earlier sketch in CA 112
Alley, Louis Edward 1914- 17-20R
Alley, Norman William 1895-1981 Obituary 115
Alley, Rewi 1897-1987 ....CANR-36
Obituary 124
Earlier sketches in CA 73-76, CANR-13
Alley, Robert S. 1932- 33-36R
Alley, Stephen L(ewis) 1915- Brief entry 110
Alleyn, Ellen
See Rossetti, Christina (Georgina)
Alleyne, Mervyn (C.) 1933- 130
Allfrey, Anthony 1930- 137
Allgire, Mildred J. 1910- CAP-2
Earlier sketch in CA 25-28
Allgood, Myralyn F(rizzelle) 1939- 137
Allibone, T(homas) E(dward) 1903- 131
Alliluyeva, Svetlana (Iosifovna Stalina)
1926- 57-60
Allin, Clinton Harrop
See Harrop-Allin, Clinton
Allin, Craig Willard 1946- CANR-25
Earlier sketch in CA 108
Alline, Henry 1748-1784 ....DLB 99
Allingham, Margery (Louise)
1904-1966 ....CANR-4
Obituary 25-28R
Earlier sketch in CA 5-8R
See also CLC 19
See also DLB 77
See also MTCW
Allingham, Michael 1943- 97-100
Allingham, William 1824-1889 ....DLB 35
Allington, Richard L(loyd) 1947- CANR-30
Earlier sketch in CA 112
See also SATA 35, 39
Allinsmith, Wesley 1923- 85-88
Allinson, Beverley (Lynn Rouse) 1936- CANR-4
Earlier sketch in CA 49-52
Allinson, Gary D(ean) 1942- 77-80
Allis, Frederick Scouller Jr. 1913- 115
Allis, Oswald T(hompson)
1880-1973 Obituary 37-40R
Allison, A(ntony) F(rancis) 1916- 106
Allison, Alexander Ward 1919- 5-8R
Allison, Anne Marie 1931- 114
Allison, Anthony C(lifford) 1928- CANR-25
Earlier sketch in CA 29-32R
Allison, Bob ....SATA 14
Allison, C(hristopher) FitzSimons
1927- CANR-4
Earlier sketch in CA 1-4R
Allison, Clay
See Keevill, Henry J(ohn)
Allison, E. M. A.
See Allison, Eric W(illiam)
and Allison, Mary Ann
Allison, Eric W(illiam) 1947- 122
Allison, Graham T(illett) Jr. 1940- CANR-35
Earlier sketches in CA 49-52, CANR-2
Allison, Harrison C(larke) 1917- CANR-35
Earlier sketch in CA 49-52
Allison, Henry E(dward) 1937- 133
Brief entry 110
Allison, John Murray 1889- 73-76
Allison, Joseph D(avid) 1950- 111
Allison, Linda 1948- 113
See also SATA 43
Allison, Marian
See Reid, Frances P(ugh)
Allison, Mary Ann 1949- 122
Allison, Michael Frederick Lister 1936- 57-60
Allison, Mike
See Allison, Michael Frederick Lister
Allison, Oliver Claude 1908-1989 129
Allison, Penny
See Katz, Carol
Allison, R(ichard) Bruce 1949- CANR-19
Earlier sketches in CA 49-52, CANR-3
Allison, Ralph B(rewster) 1931- 101
Allison, Rand
See McCormick, Wilfred
Allison, Rosemary 1953- 93-96
Allison, Roy (Anthony) 1957- 119
Allison, Sam
See Loomis, Noel M(iller)
Allman, Eileen Jorge 1940- 128
Allman, James 1943- 112
Allman, John 1935- CANR-25
Earlier sketch in CA 85-88
See also CAAS 15
Allman, T. D. 1944- CANR-17
Earlier sketch in CA 93-96
Allmendinger, David F(rederick) Jr. 1938- 61-64
See also SATA 35
Allnutt, Gillian (Marguerite) 1949- 128
Allon, Yigal 1918-1980 ....CANR-36
Obituary 97-100
Earlier sketch in CA 73-76
Allott, Kenneth 1912-1973 129
Obituary 89-92
See also DLB 20
Allott, Miriam 1920- 112
Alloway, David N(elson) 1927- CANR-10
Earlier sketch in CA 21-24R
Alloway, Lawrence 1926- 41-44R
Allport, Gordon (Willard) 1897-1967 ....CANR-3
Obituary 25-28R
Earlier sketch in CA 1-4R
Allport, Susan 1950- 124
Allred, Donald M(ervin) 1923- 65-68
Allred, G. Hugh 1932- CANR-8
Earlier sketch in CA 61-64
Allred, Gordon T(hatcher) 1930- CANR-10
Earlier sketch in CA 17-20R
See also SATA 10
Allred, Ruel A(cord) 1929- 106
Allsen, Philip E(dmond) 1932- CANR-4
Earlier sketch in CA 53-56
Allsop, Kenneth 1920-1973 ....CANR-6
Earlier sketch in CA 1-4R
See also SATA 17
Allsopp, (Harold) Bruce 1912- CANR-18
Earlier sketches in CA 5-8R, CANR-2
Allston, Washington 1779-1843 ....DLB 1
Allswang, John M(yers) 1937- 41-44R
Allum, Nancy (Patricia Eaton) 1920- CAP-1
Earlier sketch in CA 9-10
Allvine, Fred C. 1936- 61-64
Allvine, Glendon 1893(?)-1977 Obituary 73-76
Allward, Maurice (Frank) 1923- CANR-19
Earlier sketches in CA 5-8R, CANR-3
Allwood, Martin (Samuel) 1916- CANR-29
Earlier sketch in CA 110
Allworth, Edward (Alfred) 1920- 101
Allyn, Jennifer
See Jones, Jeannette
Allyn, Paul
See Schosberg, Paul A.
Allyson, Kym
See Kimbro, John M.
Alma, Peter
See Nemeshegyi, Peter
Alman, David 1919- 9-12R
Al-Marayati, Abid A(min) 1931- 33-36R
Almaraz, Felix D(iaz) Jr. 1933- 33-36R
Almaz, Michael 1921- 81-84
Almedingen, E. M.
See Almedingen, Martha Edith von
See also CLC 12
See also SATA 3
Almedingen, Martha Edith von
1898-1971 ....CANR-1
Earlier sketch in CA 1-4R
See also Almedingen, E. M.
Almodovar, Pedro 1949(?)- 133
Almon, Bert 1943- 110
Almon, Clopper Jr. 1934- 21-24R
Almond, Gabriel Abraham 1911- CANR-18
Earlier sketch in CA 101
Almond, Linda Stevens
1881(?)-1987 Obituary 121
See also SATA 50
Almond, Paul 1931- 73-76
Almond, Richard 1938- 53-56
Almonte, Rosa
See Paine, Lauran (Bosworth)
Almquist, Don 1929- ....SATA 11
Almquist, Gregg (Andrew) 1948- 126
Almquist, L. Arden 1921- 29-32R
Almy, Millie 1915- 85-88
Aloff, Mindy 1947- 135
Aloian, David 1928- 25-28R
Aloma, Rene R(amon) 1947- 113
Alonso, Damaso 1898-1990 131
Obituary 130
Brief entry 110
See also CLC 14
See also DLB 108
See also HW
Alonso, J(uan) M(anuel) 1936- 102
Alonso, Maria Teresa Manjon
See Manjon De Read, Maria Teresa
Alonso, William 1933- CANR-6
Earlier sketch in CA 9-12R
Alotta, Robert I(gnatius) 1937- CANR-14
Earlier sketch in CA 65-68
Aloysius, Sister Mary
See Schaldenbrand, Mary
Alpaugh, Craig 1945- 117
Alper, Benedict S(olomon) 1905- CANR-27
Earlier sketch in CA 49-52
Alper, M(ax) Victor 1944- 69-72
Alpern, Andrew 1938- CANR-27
Earlier sketches in CA 69-72, CANR-11
Alpern, David M(ark) 1942- 73-76
Alpern, Gerald D(avid) 1932- 53-56
Alpern, Sara 1942- 128
Alperovitz, Gar 1936- CANR-29
Earlier sketch in CA 49-52
Alpers, Antony 1919- CANR-35
Earlier sketches in CA 1-4R, CANR-3
Alpers, Bernard J. 1900-1981 Obituary 105
Alpers, Edward Alter 1941- 109
Alpers, Paul (Joel) 1932- 85-88
Alpers, Svetlana (Leontief) 1936- 115
Alpert, Hollis 1916- CANR-23
Earlier sketches in CA 1-4R, CANR-6
Alpert, Jane (Lauren) 1947- 107
Alpert, Mark I(ra) 1942- 61-64
Alpert, Paul 1907- 41-44R
Alpert, Richard 1931- 89-92
Alphonso-Karkala, John B. 1923- CANR-14
Earlier sketch in CA 37-40R
Alplaus, N. Y.
See Rubin, Cynthia Elyce
Al-Qazzaz, Ayad (Sayyid Ali) 1941- 112
Alred, Gerald J(ames) 1943- 105
AlRoy, Gil Carl 1924-1985 ....CANR-17
Obituary 116
Earlier sketch in CA 41-44R
Alschuler, Rose Haas 1887-1979 ....CAP-2
Obituary 89-92
Earlier sketch in CA 25-28
Alsen, Eberhard 1939- 110
Al Sharouni, Youssef 1924- 131
al-Shaykh, Hanan 1945- 135
Alsop, George 1636- ....DLB 24
Alsop, Gulielma Fell 1881-1978 Obituary 77-80
Alsop, Joseph (Wright) 1910-1989 129
Earlier sketch in CA 122
Alsop, Mary O'Hara 1885-1980 ....CANR-4
Obituary 102
Earlier sketch in CA 9-12R
See also MAICYA
See also SATA 2, 24, 34
Alsop, Richard 1761-1815 ....DLB 37
Alsop, Stewart (Johonnot Oliver)
1914-1974 89-92
Obituary 49-52
Alsterlund, Betty
See Pilkington, Betty
Alstern, Fred
See Stern, Alfred
Alston, J(ames) M(axwell)
1901(?)-1990 Obituary 131
Alston, Mary Niven 1918- 33-36R
Alston, Patrick L(ionel) 1926- 25-28R
Alston, Robin (Carfrae) 1933- 131
Alston, Walter Emmons
1911-1984 Obituary 113
Alston, William P(ayne) 1921- CANR-37
Earlier sketches in CA 5-8R, CANR-7
Alswang, Betty 1920(?)-1978 Obituary 77-80
Alt, Betty Sowers 1931- 133
Alt, David D. 1933- CANR-27
Earlier sketch in CA 49-52
Alt, Herschel 1897(?)-1981 Obituary 105
Alt, (Arthur) Tilo 1931- 41-44R
Alta 1942- 57-60
See also CLC 19
Altabe, Joan B. 1935- 53-56
Altbach, Edith Hoshino 1941- 57-60
Altbach, Philip G(eoffrey) 1941- CANR-10
Earlier sketch in CA 25-28R
Altenberg, Peter 1859-1919 ....DLB 81
Altenbernd, (August) Lynn 1918- CANR-1
Earlier sketch in CA 45-48
Alter, J(ohn) Cecil 1879-1964 ....5-8R
Alter, Jean V(ictor) 1925- 45-48
Alter, Jonathan Hammmerman 1957- 129
Alter, Joseph Dinsmore 1923- 111
Alter, Judith (MacBain) 1938- CANR-31
Earlier sketches in CA 81-84, CANR-14
See also SATA 52
Alter, Judy
See Alter, Judith (MacBain)
Alter, Robert B(ernard) 1935- CANR-1
Earlier sketch in CA 49-52
See also CLC 34
Alter, Robert Edmond 1925-1965 ....CANR-1
Earlier sketch in CA 1-4R
See also SATA 9
Alter, Stephen 1956- 109
Alterman, Nathan 1910-1970 Obituary 25-28R
Altfest, Karen Caplan 105
Alth, Max O(ctavious) 1927- CANR-17
Earlier sketch in CA 41-44R
Althauser, Robert P(ierce) 1939- 57-60
Althea
See Braithwaite, Althea
Alther, Lisa 1944- CANR-30
Earlier sketches in CA 65-68, CANR-12
See also CLC 7, 41
See also MTCW
Althoff, Phillip 1941- 33-36R
Altholz, Josef L(ewis) 1933- CANR-35
Earlier sketch in CA 9-12R
Althouse, Larry
See Althouse, Lawrence Wilson
Althouse, LaVonne 1932- 17-20R
Althouse, Lawrence Wilson 1930- 101
Althusser, L.
See Althusser, Louis
Althusser, Louis 1918-1990 131
Obituary 132
Altick, Richard Daniel 1915- CANR-19
Earlier sketches in CA 1-4R, CANR-4
Altieri, Charles F(rancis) 1942- 106
Altizer, Thomas J(onathan) J(ackson)
1927- CANR-3
Earlier sketch in CA 1-4R
Altman, Dennis 1943- CANR-34
Earlier sketches in CA 33-36R, CANR-15
Altman, Edward I(ra) 1941- CANR-22
Earlier sketches in CA 57-60, CANR-7
Altman, Frances 1937- 65-68
Altman, Irwin 1928- 81-84
Altman, Irwin 1930- CANR-21
Earlier sketch in CA 69-72
Altman, Jack 1938- 21-24R
Altman, Janet Gurkin 1945- 128
Altman, Larry
See Altman, Irwin
Altman, Linda Jacobs 1943- CANR-30
Earlier sketch in CA 29-32R
See also SATA 21
Altman, Nathaniel 1948- CANR-21
Earlier sketches in CA 57-60, CANR-6
Altman, Richard Charles 1932- 41-44R
Altman, Rick 1945- 128
Altman, Robert A. 1943- 29-32R
Altman, Robert 1925- 73-76
See also CLC 16
Altman, Thomas
See Black, Campbell
Altman, Wilfred 1927- CAP-1
Earlier sketch in CA 9-10
Altmann, Alexander 1906-1987 ....CANR-35
Obituary 122
Earlier sketches in CA 61-64, CANR-8
Altmann, Berthold 1902(?)-1977 Obituary 69-72
Altolaguirre, Manuel 1905-1959 ....DLB 108
Altoma, Salih J(awad) 1929- 49-52
Alton, Thomas
See Bryant, T(homas) Alton
Altrocchi, Julia Cooley 1893-1972 ....CAP-1
Earlier sketch in CA 13-14
Altschul, Aaron Mayer 1914- 105
Altschul, b j 1948- 114
Altschul, Selig 1914- 108
Altschuler, Franz 1923- ....SATA 45
Altsheler, Joseph A(lexander)
1862-1919 ....YABC 1
Altshuler, Alan Anthony 1936- 108
Altshuler, Edward A. 1919- 17-20R
Altshuler, Harry 1913(?)-1990 Obituary 131
Aluko, Timothy Mofolorunso 1918- CANR-10
Earlier sketch in CA 65-68
See also BW
See also DLB 117
Alurista
See Urista, Alberto H.
See also DLB 82
Al-Van-Gar
See Radwanski, Pierre A(rthur)
Alvarez, A(lfred) 1929- CANR-33
Earlier sketches in CA 1-4R, CANR-3
See also CLC 5, 13
See also DLB 14, 40
Alvarez, Alejandro Rodriguez 1903-1965 131
Obituary 93-96
See also Casona, Alejandro
See also HW
Alvarez, Eugene 1932- 57-60
Alvarez, John
See del Rey, Lester
Alvarez, Joseph A. 1930- CANR-17
Earlier sketch in CA 33-36R
See also SATA 18
Alvarez, Luis W(alter) 1911-1988 Obituary 126
Alvarez, Lynne 131
See also HW
Alvarez, Max Joseph 1960- 112
Alvarez, Walter C(lement) 1884-1978 ....CANR-10
Earlier sketch in CA 61-64
Alvarez-Altman, Grace (DeJesus) 1926- 33-36R
Alvarez del Vayo, Julio
1891-1975 Obituary 61-64
Alvarez Murena, Hector Alberto 1923- ....HW
Alverson, Charles (E.) 1935- CANR-13
Earlier sketch in CA 25-28R
Alverson, Donna 1933- 65-68
Alverson, Marianne 1942- 126
Alves, Colin 1930- CANR-2
Earlier sketch in CA 5-8R
Alves, Marcio Moreira 1936- CANR-2
Earlier sketch in CA 45-48
Alves, Michael (Joseph) 1956- 118
Alvey, Edward Jr. 1902- 53-56
Alvey, R(ichard) Gerald 1935- 121
Alvin, Juliette (Louise) 77-80
Obituary 108
Alworth, E. P(aul) 1918- 25-28R
Alwyn, William 1905-1985 Obituary 117
Aly, Bower 1903- CANR-5
Earlier sketch in CA 5-8R
Aly, Lucile Folse 1913- 21-24R
Alyer, Philip A.
See Stratemeyer, Edward L.
Alyeshmerni, Mansoor 1943- 29-32R
Alyn, Marc (a pseudonym) 1937- 101
Alzado, Lyle (Martin) 1949- Brief entry 110
Alzaga, Florinda 1930- 73-76
Amabile, George 1936- 33-36R
Amacher, Richard Earl 1917- CANR-3
Earlier sketch in CA 1-4R
Amacher, Ryan C(uster) 1945- 105
Amadi, Elechi (Emmanuel) 1934- CANR-38
Earlier sketches in CA 29-32R, CANR-16
See also BW
See also DLB 117
Amado, Jorge 1912- CANR-35
Earlier sketch in CA 77-80
See also CLC 13, 40
See also DLB 113
See also MTCW
Amadon, Dean 1912- 61-64
Amalrik, Andrei Alekseyevich
1938-1980 Obituary 102
Amamoo, Joseph Godson 1931- 13-16R
Aman, Mohammed M(ohammed)
1940- CANR-16
Earlier sketches in CA 49-52, CANR-1
Amanda
See Wynne-Tyson, Esme
Amann, Peter H. 1927- 61-64
Amann, Richard 1945- 106
Amann, Ronald 1943- 112
Amann, Victor F(rancis) 1927- 41-44R
Amanuddin, Syed 1934- CANR-17
Earlier sketches in CA 49-52, CANR-1
Amaral, Anthony 1930-1982 ....CANR-11
Earlier sketch in CA 21-24R
Amare, Rothayne
See Byrne, Stuart J(ames)
Amaron, Douglas 1914-1985 Obituary 117
Amary, Issam B(ahjat) 1942- CANR-8
Earlier sketch in CA 61-64

Amato, Joseph Anthony 1938- CANR-6
Earlier sketch in CA 57-60
Amatora, Sister Mary 9-12R
Amaya, Ismael E(liseo)
1928-1986 Obituary 120
Amaya, Mario (Anthony) 1933-1986 ......CANR-36
Obituary 119
Earlier sketches in CA 61-64, CANR-9
Amazing Randi, The
See Randi, James
Ambasz, Emilio 1943- 73-76
Amberg, George H. 1901-1971 Obituary 110
Amberg, (Martin) Hans 1913- 77-80
Amberg, Richard H(iller) Jr. 1942- 77-80
Amberg, Richard Hiller 1912-1967 Obituary 114
Ambhanwong, Suthilak 1924- CANR-18
Earlier sketch in CA 73-76
Ambirajan, Srinivasa 1936- CANR-7
Earlier sketch in CA 17-20R
Ambler, C(hristopher) Gifford 1886- ...... SATA 29
Ambler, Effie 1936- 77-80
Ambler, Eric 1909- CANR-38
Earlier sketches in CA 9-12R, CANR-7
See also CLC 4, 6, 9
See also DLB 77
See also MTCW
Ambler, John S(teward) 1932- CANR-27
Earlier sketch in CA 49-52
Ambler, Marjane 1948- 135
Ambrose, Alice
See Lazerowitz, Alice Ambrose
Ambrose, David (Edwin) 1943- Brief entry 116
Ambrose, Eric (Samuel) 1908- CAP-1
Earlier sketch in CA 11-12
Ambrose, John W(illiam) Jr. 1931- 57-60
Ambrose, Stephen Edward 1936- CANR-3
Earlier sketch in CA 1-4R
See also SATA 40
Ambrose, W. Haydn 1922- 25-28R
Ambrosi, Hans Georg 1925- 103
Ambrosini, Maria Luisa 33-36R
Ambroz, Oton 1905- 41-44R
Ambrus, Gyozo Laszlo 1935- CANR-28
Earlier sketches in CA 25-28R, CANR-11
See also Ambrus, Victor G.
See also MAICYA
See also SATA 41
Ambrus, Victor G.
See Ambrus, Gyozo Laszlo
See also SAAS 4
See also SATA 1
Amburn, Ellis 1933- 138
Amdur, Neil 1939- 106
Amdur, Nikki 1950- 111
Amelio, Ralph J. 1939- 37-40R
Amen, Carol 1934(?)-1987 Obituary 123
Amend, Victor E(arl) 1916- 33-36R
Ament, Pat 1946- 85-88
Amerine, Maynard A(ndrew) 1911- 41-44R
Ameringer, Charles D. 1926- 57-60
Amerman, Lockhart 1911-1969 ....CAP-2
Earlier sketch in CA 29-32
See also SATA 3
Amery, (Harold) Julian 1919- 61-64
Ames, Charles Edgar 1895-1972 .... CAP-2
Earlier sketch in CA 25-28
Ames, Delano L. 1906- 107
Ames, Elinor
See Ranzini, Addis Durning
Ames, Evelyn 1908-1990 57-60
Obituary 130
See also SATA 13
See also SATO 64
Ames, Felicia
See Burden, Jean
Ames, Fisher 1758-1808 .... DLB 37
Ames, Francis H. 1900- 17-20R
Ames, Gerald 1906- 73-76
See also SATA 11
Ames, Jennifer
See Greig, Maysie
Ames, Jocelyn Green 5-8R
Ames, John Dawes 1904-1987 Obituary 122
Ames, John 1944- 111
Ames, Lee J(udah) 1921- CANR-18
Earlier sketches in CA 1-4R, CANR-3
See also SATA 3
Ames, Leslie
See Rigoni, Orlando (Joseph)
and Ross, W(illiam) E(dward) D(aniel)
Ames, Lois (Winslow Sisson) 1931- 101
Ames, Louise Bates 1908- CANR-39
Earlier sketches in CA 1-4R, CANR-3, 18
Ames, Mary Clemmer 1831-1884 .... DLB 23
Ames, Mildred 1919- CANR-11
Earlier sketch in CA 69-72
See also SATA 22
Ames, Noel
See Barrows, (Ruth) Marjorie
Ames, Norma 1920- CANR-12
Earlier sketch in CA 29-32R
Ames, Rachel 1922- 97-100
Ames, Ruth M(argaret) 1918- 29-32R
Ames, (Polly) Scribner 1908- 69-72
Ames, Van Meter 1898-1985 .... CAP-1
Obituary 117
Earlier sketch in CA 13-16
Ames, Walter Lansing 1946- 106
Ames, Winslow 1907- CAP-2
Earlier sketch in CA 25-28
Ames-Lewis, Francis 1943- 108
Amey, Lloyd Ronald 1922- CANR-20
Earlier sketch in CA 45-48
Amfitheatrof, Erik 1931- 89-92
Amft, M(arian) J(anet) 1920-1985 Obituary 117
Amichai, Yehuda 1924- 85-88
See also CLC 9, 22, 57
See also MTCW
Amick, Robert Gene 1933- 33-36R
Amidon, Bill (Vincent) 1935-1979 45-48
Obituary 103
Amidon, Stephen 1959- 132
Amiel, Barbara 1940- 101
Amiel, Joseph 1937- 101
Amies, (Edwin) Hardy 1909- 129
Amin, Ali 1913(?)-1976 Obituary 65-68
Amin, Samir 1931- CANR-35
Earlier sketches in CA 89-92, CANR-15
Amini, Johari M.
See Kunjufu, Johari M. Amini
See also DLB 41
Amir, Menachem 1930- 45-48
Amis, Breton
See Best, Rayleigh Breton Amis
Amis, Kingsley (William) 1922- CANR-28
Earlier sketches in CA 9-12R, CANR-8
See also AITN 2
See also CDBLB 1945-1960
See also CLC 1, 2, 3, 5, 8, 13, 40, 44
See also DLB 15, 27, 100
See also MTCW
Amis, Martin (Louis) 1949- CANR-27
Earlier sketches in CA 65-68, CANR-8
See also BEST 90:3
See also CLC 4, 9, 38, 62
See also DLB 14
Amishai-Maisels, Ziva
See Maisels, Maxine S.
Amling, Frederick 1926- 133
Brief entry 112
Amlund, Curtis Arthur 1927- 21-24R
Ammar, Abbas 1907(?)-1974 Obituary 53-56
Amme, Carl H. Jr. 1913- 25-28R
Ammer, Christine (Parker) 1931- 106
Ammer, Dean S. 1926- CANR-7
Earlier sketch in CA 17-20R
Ammerman, David L(eon) 1938- 57-60
Ammerman, Gale Richard 1923- 107
Ammerman, Leila T(remaine) 1912- 33-36R
Ammerman, Robert R(ay) 1927- 13-16R
Ammon, Harry 1917- 73-76
Ammons, A(rchie) R(andolph) 1926- CANR-36
Earlier sketches in CA 9-12R, CANR-6
See also AITN 1
See also CLC 2, 3, 5, 8, 9, 25, 57
See also DLB 5
See also MTCW
Amo, Tauraatua i
See Adams, Henry (Brooks)
Amoaku, J. K. 1936- 45-48
Amon, Aline 1928- CANR-8
Earlier sketch in CA 61-64
See also SATA 9
Amor, Amos
See Harrell, Irene B(urk)
Amor, Anne Clark 1933- CANR-31
Earlier sketch in CA 112
Amore, Roy Clayton 1942- 105
Amorim, Enrique (Manuel) 1900-1960 ....HW
Amory, Anne Reinberg 1931- 17-20R
Amory, Cleveland 1917- CANR-29
Earlier sketch in CA 69-72
See also AITN 1
Amory, Mark 1941- CANR-36
Earlier sketch in CA 114
Amory, Robert Jr. 1915-1989 Obituary 128
Amos, James H. Jr. 1946- 132
Amos, William E. 1926- 17-20R
Amos, Winsom 1921- CANR-27
Earlier sketch in CA 49-52
Amosov, N.
See Amosov, N(ikolai) M(ikhailovich)
Amosov, N(ikolai) M(ikhailovich)
1913- Brief entry 112
Amoss, Berthe 1925- CANR-14
Earlier sketch in CA 21-24R
See also SATA 5
Amplegirth, Antony
See Dent, Anthony Austen
Amprimoz, Alexandre 1948- CANR-15
Earlier sketch in CA 37-40R
Amram, David (Werner III) 1930- CANR-28
Earlier sketch in CA 29-32R
Amram, Philip Werner 1900-1990 Obituary 131
Amrine, Michael 1919(?)-1974 73-76
Obituary 49-52
Amsel, Abram 1922- CANR-35
Earlier sketch in CA 114
Amstead, B(illy) H(oward) 1921- 21-24R
Amster, Linda 1938- CANR-22
Earlier sketch in CA 45-48
Amsterdam, Morey 1914- Brief entry 111
Amstutz, Arnold E. 1936- 21-24R
Amstutz, Mark R(obert) 1944- 105
Amter, Joseph A. Obituary 109
Amundsen, Kirsten 1932- 37-40R
Amundsen, Roald Engelbregt Gravning
1872-1928 Brief entry 117
Amusin, Joseph 1910-1984 Obituary 113
Amuzegar, Jahangir 1920- CANR-15
Earlier sketch in CA 41-44R
Analyticus
See Wise, James Waterman
Anand, Mulk Raj 1905- CANR-32
Earlier sketch in CA 65-68
See also CLC 23
See also MTCW
Anand, Valerie 1937- CANR-13
Earlier sketch in CA 73-76
Anania, Michael 1939- 25-28R
Anastaplo, George 1925- 37-40R
Anastas, Lila L. 1940- 122
Anastas, Peter 1937- CANR-1
Earlier sketch in CA 45-48
Anastasi, Anne 1908- CANR-17
Earlier sketches in CA 5-8R, CANR-2
Anastasio, Dina 1941- 107
See also SATA 30, 37
Anastasiou, Clifford (John) 1929- CANR-18
Earlier sketches in CA 49-52, CANR-3
Anastos, Andrea La Sonde (Melrose)
1951- 117
Anatol
See Schnitzler, Arthur
Anatol, A.
See Kuznetsov, Anatoli
Anaya, Rudolfo A(lfonso) 1937- CANR-32
Earlier sketches in CA 45-48, CANR-1
See also CAAS 4
See also CLC 23
See also DLB 82
See also HW
See also MTCW
Anber, Paul
See Baker, Pauline H(alpern)
Ancel, Marc 1902- CANR-12
Earlier sketch in CA 69-72
Ancelet, Barry Jean 1951- 131
Anchell, Melvin 1919- 25-28R
Anchor, Robert 1937- 69-72
Anckarsvard, Karin Inez Maria
1915-1969 ....9-12R
Obituary 103
See also SATA 6
Ancona, George 1929- CANR-19
Earlier sketches in CA 53-56, CANR-4
See also SATA 12
Andelin, Helen B. 1920- 89-92
Andelman, Eddie 1936- 57-60
Andelman, Samuel L(ouis)
1916- Brief entry 114
Andelson, Robert V(ernon) 1931- 33-36R
Andenaes, Johannes 1912- 129
Anderegg, Karen Klok 1940- 137
Andereich, Justus
See Steiner, Gerolf
Anders, Donna Carolyn 1938- 125
Anders, Edith (Mary) England 1899- CAP-1
Earlier sketch in CA 13-16
Anders, Evelyn 1916- 29-32R
Anders, Jeanne
See Anderson, Joan Wester
Anders, Leslie 1922- 13-16R
Anders, Sarah Frances 1927- 105
Andersch, Alfred 1914-1980 ....CANR-37
Obituary 93-96
Earlier sketch in CA 33-36R
See also DLB 69
Andersch, Elizabeth Genevieve 1913- 5-8R
Andersdatter, Karla M(argaret) 1938- CANR-21
Earlier sketch in CA 104
See also SATA 34
Andersen, Arlow W. 1906- CAP-1
Earlier sketch in CA 11-12
Andersen, Benny (Allan) 1929- 101
Andersen, Christopher P(eter) 1949- CANR-31
Earlier sketches in CA 69-72, CANR-14
Andersen, D(ennis) R(ichard) 1947- 108
Andersen, Doris 1909- CANR-11
Earlier sketch in CA 21-24R
Andersen, Francis Ian 1925- CANR-27
Earlier sketch in CA 108
Andersen, Georg 1941- 112
Andersen, Hans Christian 1805-1875 .... CLR 6
See also MAICYA
See also SSC 6
See also WLC
See also YABC 1
Andersen, Jefferson
1955(?)-1979 Obituary 85-88
Andersen, Juel 1923- CANR-22
Earlier sketch in CA 105
Andersen, Kenneth E(ldon) 1933- 37-40R
Andersen, Kurt 1954- CANR-23
Earlier sketch in CA 106
Andersen, Marianne S(inger) 1934- 65-68
Andersen, Marion Lineaweaver
1912(?)-1971 Obituary 29-32R
Andersen, R(udolph) Clifton 1933- 33-36R
Andersen, Richard 1931- CANR-24
Earlier sketches in CA 57-60, CANR-8
Andersen, Richard 1946- 102
Andersen, Ted
See Boyd, Waldo T.
Andersen, Uell Stanley 1917- 1-4R
Andersen, Wayne V. 1928- 9-12R
Andersen, Wilhelm 1911- 29-32R
Andersen, Yvonne 1932- 29-32R
See also SATA 27
Anderson, A(rthur) J(ames) 1933- 106
Anderson, Alan B(rauer) 1934- 133
Anderson, Alan H. Jr. 1943- 69-72
Anderson, Alan Ross 1925-1973 .... CAP-2
Obituary 45-48
Earlier sketch in CA 17-18
Anderson, Allan 1915- 97-100
Anderson, Alpha E. 1914-1970 .... CAP-2
Earlier sketch in CA 23-24
Anderson, Ann Kiemel 1945- 121
Anderson, Arthur J(ames) O(utram)
1907- CANR-15
Earlier sketch in CA 85-88
Anderson, B(asil) W(illiam)
1901-1984 Obituary 112
Anderson, Barbara Gallatin
1926- Brief entry 111
Anderson, Barbara 1948- 93-96
Anderson, Barry (Franklin) 1935- 17-20R
Anderson, Bern 1900-1963 ....1-4R
Anderson, Bernard Eric 1936- CANR-5
Earlier sketch in CA 53-56
Anderson, Bernhard Word 1916- CANR-8
Earlier sketch in CA 57-60
Anderson, Bernice G(oudy) 1894- 101
See also SATA 33
Anderson, Bertha Moore 1892- 5-8R
Anderson, Beverly
See Nemiro, Beverly Anderson
Anderson, Beverly M.
See Nemiro, Beverly Anderson
Anderson, Bob 1947- 69-72
Anderson, Brad(ley Jay) 1924- 106
See also SATA 31, 33
Anderson, C. Farley
See Mencken, H(enry) L(ouis)
and Nathan, George Jean
Anderson, C(arl) L(eonard) 1901- 25-28R
Anderson, Camilla M(ay) 1904- 33-36R
Anderson, Carl Dicmann 1912- 33-36R
Anderson, Carl L(ennart) 1919- 41-44R
Anderson, Carolyn 1941- 73-76
Anderson, Catherine Corley 1909- 1-4R
Anderson, Charles Burroughs 1905-1985 65-68
Obituary 115
Anderson, Charles C. 1931- 29-32R
Anderson, Charles Roberts 1902- CANR-3
Earlier sketch in CA 1-4R
Anderson, Charles W(illiam) 1934- 9-12R
Anderson, Charles 1933- CANR-27
Earlier sketch in CA 49-52
Anderson, Charlotte Maria 1923- 81-84
Anderson, Chester G(rant) 1923- 25-28R
Anderson, Chester 1932- 131
Brief entry 117
Anderson, Chuck
See Anderson, Charles
Anderson, Clarence William 1891-1971 73-76
Obituary 29-32R
See also SATA 11
Anderson, Clifford
See Gardner, Richard (M.)
Anderson, Colena M(ichael) 1891- CANR-11
Earlier sketch in CA 21-24R
Anderson, Cortland 1935-1985 Obituary 118
Anderson, Courtney 1906- CAP-1
Earlier sketch in CA 19-20
Anderson, Daphne 1919- 130
Anderson, Dave
See Anderson, David Poole
See also AITN 2
Anderson, David D(aniel) 1924- CANR-5
Earlier sketch in CA 13-16R
Anderson, David L(eonard) 1919- 5-8R
Anderson, David Poole 1929- 89-92
See also Anderson, Dave
See also SATA 60
Anderson, David 1952- 130
Anderson, Dillon 1906-1974 ....1-4R
Obituary 45-48
Anderson, Don 1939- 128
Anderson, Donald F(rancis) 1938- 53-56
Anderson, Donald K(ennedy) Jr. 1922- 37-40R
Anderson, Doris (Hilda) 1925- 89-92
Anderson, Dwight G(ale) 1938- 107
Anderson, E. Ruth 1907- 93-96
Anderson, Earl Robert 1943- 111
Anderson, Edgar 1920- CANR-30
Earlier sketches in CA 33-36R, CANR-13
Anderson, Einar 1909- 13-16R
Anderson, Elbridge Gerry 1907- 69-72
Anderson, Elliott 1944- 93-96
Anderson, Eloise Adell 1927- 53-56
See also SATA 9
Anderson, Emily 1891-1962 124
Anderson, Eric (Douglas) 1949- 106
Anderson, Erica 1914- 57-60
Anderson, Eugene N(ewton) 1900- 29-32R
Anderson, E.W. 1901-1981 Obituary 104
Anderson, (William) Ferguson 1914- 107
Anderson, Frank J(ohn) 1919- CANR-4
Earlier sketch in CA 9-12R
Anderson, Fred 1949- 117
Anderson, Frederick Irving
1877-1947 Brief entry 112
Anderson, Freeman B(urket) 1922- 41-44R
Anderson, Gary Clayton 1948- 117
Anderson, Gary Lee 1939- Brief entry 115
Anderson, George
See Weissman, Jack
Anderson, George
See Groom, Arthur William
Anderson, George B.
1908(?)-1985 Obituary 114
Anderson, George Christian 1907-1976 ..... CAP-2
Obituary 69-72
Earlier sketch in CA 29-32
Anderson, George K(umler) 1901- CAP-2
Earlier sketch in CA 23-24
Anderson, George L(aVerne)
1905-1971 ....CANR-9
Earlier sketch in CA 13-16R
Anderson, George Lee 1934- Brief entry 111
Anderson, Gerald Dwight 1944- CANR-37
Earlier sketch in CA 115
Anderson, Gerald H(arry) 1930- CANR-7
Earlier sketch in CA 17-20R
Anderson, Godfrey Tryggve 1909- 41-44R
Anderson, Grace Fox 1932- 121
See also SATA 43
Anderson, Gregory 1946- 135
Anderson, H(ugh) Allen (Jr.) 1950- 120
Anderson, H(obson) Dewey 1897-1975 65-68
Obituary 61-64
Anderson, Harold H(omer) 1897- CAP-2
Earlier sketch in CA 21-22
Anderson, Harry V(ernon)
1903-1983 Obituary 110
Anderson, Henry P. 1927- 33-36R
Anderson, Howard Jeremy
1915(?)-1983 Obituary 111

Anderson, Howard Peter 1932- ... 61-64
Anderson, Hugh 1920- ... 9-12R
Anderson, Ian Gibson 1933- ... 85-88
Anderson, Irvine H(enry) 1928- ... CANR-11
Earlier sketch in CA 69-72
Anderson, J(ohn) E(dward) 1903- ... 37-40R
Anderson, J(ohn) K(inloch) 1924- ... CANR-28
Earlier sketches in CA 17-20R, CANR-10
Anderson, J(ohn) Kerby 1951- ... 97-100
Anderson, J. N.
See Anderson, (James) Norman (Dalrymple)
Anderson, J(ohn) R(ichard) L(ane)
1911-1981 ... CANR-18
Obituary ... 104
Earlier sketch in CA 25-28R
See also SATA 15, 27
Anderson, Jack(son Northman) 1922- ... CANR-6
Earlier sketch in CA 57-60
See also AITN 1
Anderson, Jack 1935- ... CANR-24
Earlier sketch in CA 33-36R
Anderson, James C(letus) 1943- ... 111
Anderson, James D(esmond) 1933- ... CANR-27
Earlier sketch in CA 49-52
Anderson, James E(lliott) 1933- ... CANR-21
Earlier sketches in CA 9-12R, CANR-6
Anderson, James F(rancis) 1910- ... 41-44R
Anderson, James G(eorge) 1936- ... 25-28R
Anderson, James LaVerne
1940- Brief entry ... 111
Anderson, James M(axwell) 1933- ... 33-36R
Anderson, (Helen) Jean 1931- ... CANR-31
Earlier sketches in CA 41-44R, CANR-14
Anderson, Jeanne 1934(?)-1979 Obituary ... 85-88
Anderson, Jennifer 1942- ... 57-60
Anderson, Jerry M(aynard) 1933- ... 41-44R
Anderson, Jessica (Margaret) Queale ... CANR-4
Earlier sketch in CA 9-12R
See also CLC 37
Anderson, Jim 1937- ... 134
Anderson, Joan Wester 1938- ... CANR-24
Earlier sketches in CA 65-68, CANR-9
Anderson, John Bayard 1922- ... 33-36R
Anderson, John F(reeman) 1945- ... 53-56
Anderson, John K.
See Anderson, J(ohn) K(inloch)
Anderson, John L(onzo) 1905- ... CANR-35
Earlier sketch in CA 25-28R
See also Anderson, Lonzo
Anderson, John M(ueller) 1914- ... 17-20R
Anderson, John Q. 1916-1975 ... CANR-3
Earlier sketch in CA 1-4R
Anderson, Jon (Stephen) 1936- ... 133
Anderson, Jon (Victor) 1940- ... CANR-20
Earlier sketch in CA 25-28R
See also CLC 9
Anderson, Joy 1928- ... 25-28R
See also SATA 1
Anderson, Judith H(elena) 1940- ... 123
Anderson, Judith I(cke) 1939- ... 112
Anderson, Karen (Kruse) 1932- ... 136
Anderson, Ken 1917- ... 25-28R
Anderson, Kenneth Norman 1921- ... CANR-18
Earlier sketch in CA 102
Anderson, Kristin
See Du Breuil, (Elizabeth) L(or)inda
Anderson, LaVere Francis Shoenfelt 1907- ... 101
See also SATA 27
Anderson, Lee Stratton 1925- ... 101
Anderson, Lee 1896-1972 ... 1-4R
Obituary ... 37-40R
Anderson, Leone Castell 1923- ... 126
See also SATA 49, 53
Anderson, Lester William 1918-1973 ... 5-8R
Obituary ... 103
Anderson, Lindsay (Gordon) 1923- ... 128
Brief entry ... 125
See also CLC 20
Anderson, Lonzo
See Anderson, John L(onzo)
See also SATA 2
Anderson, Lucia (Lewis) 1922- ... 41-44R
See also SATA 10
Anderson, Luther A(dolph) ... 65-68
Anderson, M(ary) D(esiree) 1902- ... 9-12R
Anderson, Madeleine Paltenghi 1899- ... CAP-1
Earlier sketch in CA 19-20
Anderson, Madelyn Klein ... CANR-28
Earlier sketches in CA 69-72, CANR-11
See also SATA 28
Anderson, Maggie
See Anderson, Margaret
Anderson, Malcolm 1934- ... 33-36R
Anderson, Margaret Bartlett 1922- ... 9-12R
Anderson, Margaret C(aroline) 1886-1973 ... 108
Obituary ... 45-48
See also DLB 4, 91
Anderson, Margaret J(ean) 1931- ... CANR-26
Earlier sketches in CA 69-72, CANR-11
See also SAAS 8
See also SATA 27
Anderson, Margaret J(ohnson) 1909- ... CANR-3
Earlier sketch in CA 1-4R
Anderson, Margaret (Vance) 1917- ... 21-24R
Anderson, Margaret 1948- ... 101
Anderson, Martin 1936- ... CANR-9
Earlier sketch in CA 13-16R
Anderson, Marvin Walter 1933- ... 41-44R
Anderson, Mary M. 1919- ... 136
Anderson, Mary 1939- ... CANR-16
Earlier sketches in CA 49-52, CANR-1
See also SATA 7
Anderson, Matthew Smith 1922- ... 13-16R
Anderson, Maxie (Leroy)
1934-1983 Obituary ... 115
Anderson, Maxwell 1888-1959 Brief entry ... 105
See also DLB 7
See also TCLC 2
Anderson, Michael Falconer 1947- ... 136
Anderson, Mona 1910- ... CANR-6
Earlier sketch in CA 57-60
See also SATA 40
Anderson, Nancy Fix 1941- ... 126
Anderson, Nancy Scott 1939- ... 137
Anderson, Norman Dean 1928- ... CANR-15
Earlier sketch in CA 33-36R
See also SATA 22
Anderson, Norman G(ulden) 1913- ... 133
Brief entry ... 114
Anderson, (James) Norman (Dalrymple)
1908- ... CANR-4
Earlier sketch in CA 9-12R
Anderson, O(rvil) Roger 1937- ... 33-36R
Anderson, Odin W(aldemar) 1914- ... 25-28R
Anderson, Olive M(ary) 1915- ... CANR-14
Earlier sketch in CA 81-84
Anderson, Olive Ruth 1926- ... 107
Anderson, P(aul) Howard 1947- ... 61-64
Anderson, Patrick (John MacAllister)
1915-1979 ... 93-96
Obituary ... 85-88
See also DLB 68
Anderson, Patrick 1936- ... 33-36R
Anderson, Paul E. 1925- ... 33-36R
Anderson, Paul Seward 1913-1975 ... CANR-6
Earlier sketch in CA 1-4R
Anderson, Paul Y. 1893-1938 ... DLB 29
Anderson, Peggy 1938- ... 93-96
Anderson, Poul (William) 1926- ... CANR-34
Earlier sketches in CA 1-4R, CANR-2, 15
See also CAAS 2
See also AAYA 5
See also CLC 15
See also DLB 8
See also MTCW
See also SATA 39
Anderson, Quentin 1912- ... CANR-3
Earlier sketch in CA 1-4R
Anderson, R(oy) C(laude) 1931- ... 124
Anderson, R. C. 1883(?)-1976 Obituary ... 69-72
Anderson, Rachel 1943- ... CANR-24
Earlier sketches in CA 21-24R, CANR-9
See also SATA 34
Anderson, Randall C. 1934- ... 41-44R
Anderson, Ray Sherman 1925- ... CANR-10
Earlier sketch in CA 65-68
Anderson, Raymond L(loyd) 1927- ... 106
Anderson, Richard
See Anderson, J(ohn) R(ichard) L(ane)
Anderson, Richard Chase 1934- Brief entry ... 112
Anderson, Richard Lloyd 1926- ... 37-40R
Anderson, Robert A(ndrew) 1944- ... 109
Anderson, Robert C(harles) 1930-1990 ... 85-88
Obituary ... 130
Anderson, Robert David 1942- ... 73-76
Anderson, Robert H(enry) 1918- ... CANR-27
Earlier sketch in CA 49-52
Anderson, Robert Mapes 1929- ... 108
Anderson, Robert N(orris) 1944- ... 126
Anderson, Robert Newton 1929- ... 49-52
Anderson, Robert T(homas) 1926- ... 9-12R
Anderson, Robert W(illiam) 1926- ... 17-20R
Anderson, Robert (Woodruff) 1917- ... CANR-32
Earlier sketch in CA 21-24R
See also AITN 1
See also CLC 23
See also DLB 7
Anderson, Roberta 1942- ... 115
Brief entry ... 111
Anderson, Rodney Dean 1938- ... 108
Anderson, Ronald Kinloch
1911-1984 Obituary ... 111
Anderson, Roy
See Anderson, R(oy) C(laude)
Anderson, Roy Allan 1895- ... CANR-9
Earlier sketch in CA 13-16R
Anderson, Roy 1936- ... 13-16R
Anderson, Ruth I(rene) 1919- ... CANR-18
Earlier sketch in CA 1-4R
Anderson, Ruth Nathan 1934- ... 69-72
Anderson, Scarvia (Bateman) 1926- ... CANR-14
Earlier sketch in CA 41-44R
Anderson, Sherwood 1876-1941 ... 121
Brief entry ... 104
See also CDALB 1917-1929
See also DLB 4, 9, 86
See also DLBD 1
See also MTCW
See also SSC 1
See also TCLC 1, 10, 24
See also WLC
Anderson, Sparky
See Anderson, George Lee
Anderson, Stanford 1934- ... 25-28R
Anderson, Stanley Edwin 1900-1977 ... CANR-3
Earlier sketch in CA 1-4R
Anderson, Stanley V(ictor) 1928- ... 21-24R
Anderson, Sydney 1927- ... 106
Anderson, T(heodore) W(ilbur) 1918- ... CANR-29
Earlier sketch in CA 49-52
Anderson, Teresa 1944- ... 85-88
Anderson, Terry H(oward) 1946- ... 128
Anderson, Theodore R(obert) 1927- ... 41-44R
Anderson, Thomas D. 1929- ... 111
Anderson, Thomas 1929- ... 1-4R
Anderson, Tom 1910- ... 69-72
Anderson, Tommy (Nolan) 1918- ... 45-48
Anderson, Totton J(ames) 1909-1992 ... 1-4R
Obituary ... 136
Anderson, Verily (Bruce) 1915- ... CANR-3
Earlier sketch in CA 5-8R
Anderson, Vernon E(llsworth) 1908- ... CANR-5
Earlier sketch in CA 1-4R
Anderson, Virgil Antris 1899- ... CANR-16
Earlier sketch in CA 1-4R
Anderson, Virginia (R. Cronin) 1920- ... 21-24R
Anderson, Vivienne 1916- ... 17-20R
Anderson, W. B.
See Schultz, James Willard
Anderson, Wallace Ludwig 1917- ... 17-20R
Anderson, Walt
See Anderson, Walter Truett
Anderson, Walter Truett 1933- ... 105
Anderson, Walter 1944- ... 101
Anderson, Warren DeWitt 1920- ... 17-20R
Anderson, Wayne Jeremy 1908- ... 49-52
Anderson, Wayne 1946- ... 107
See also SATA 56
Anderson, Wendell B(ernhard) 1920- ... 105
Anderson, William A(verette)
1937- Brief entry ... 114
Anderson, William Charles 1920- ... CANR-2
Earlier sketch in CA 5-8R
Anderson, William Davis 1938- ... 33-36R
Anderson, William Eugene
1926- Brief entry ... 111
Anderson, William G(ary) 1945- ... 115
Anderson, William H(arry) 1905-1972 ... 49-52
Anderson, William L(ouis) 1941- ... 135
Anderson, William Robert 1921- ... 5-8R
Anderson, William Scovil 1927- ... 61-64
Anderson, Wilton T(homas) 1916- ... 17-20R
Anderson Imbert, Enrique 1910- ... CANR-26
Earlier sketches in CA 17-20R, CANR-10
See also HW
Andersons, Edgars
See Anderson, Edgar
Anders-Richards, Donald 1928- ... 25-28R
Andersson, Ingvar 1899(?)-1974 Obituary ... 53-56
Andersson, Theodore M(urdock) 1934- ... 25-28R
Andersson, Theodore 1903- ... CANR-29
Earlier sketch in CA 49-52
Anderton, David A(lbin) 1919- ... CANR-9
Earlier sketch in CA 65-68
Anderton, Joanne (Marie) Gast 1930- ... 61-64
Anderton, Johana Gast
See Anderton, Joanne (Marie) Gast
Andervont, Howard Bancroft
1898-1981 Obituary ... 103
Andonian, Jeanne (Beghian)
1891(?)-1976 Obituary ... 65-68
Andonov-Poljanski, Hristo 1927- ... CANR-9
Earlier sketch in CA 21-24R
Andouard
See Giraudoux, (Hippolyte) Jean
Andrade, Carlos Drummond de
See Drummond de Andrade, Carlos
See also CLC 18
Andrade, E(dward) N(eville) da C(osta)
1887-1971 ... CAP-1
Earlier sketch in CA 11-12
Andrade, Jorge Carrera
See Carrera Andrade, Jorge
Andrade, Mario de 1893-1945 ... TCLC 43
Andrade, Victor (Manuel) 1905- ... 69-72
Andrain, Charles F(ranklin) 1937- ... 69-72
Andre, Evelyn M(arie) 1924- ... CANR-11
Earlier sketch in CA 69-72
See also SATA 27
Andre, (Kenneth) Michael 1946- ... 114
See also CAAS 13
Andre, Rae 1946- ... 116
Andreach, Robert J. 1930- ... 33-36R
Andreano, Ralph L(ouis) 1929- ... CANR-6
Earlier sketch in CA 5-8R
Andreas, Burton G(ould) 1921- ... 81-84
Andreas, Thomas
See Williams, Thomas (Andrew)
Andreasen, Alan R(obert) 1934- ... 65-68
Andreasen, Nancy C(oover) 1938- ... 108
Andreas-Salome, Lou 1861-1937 ... DLB 66
Andreassen, Karl
See Boyd, Waldo T.
Andree, Louise
See Coury, Louise Andree
Andree, R(ichard) V(ernon) 1919- ... CANR-8
Earlier sketch in CA 57-60
Andree, Robert G(erald) 1912-1987 ... 29-32R
Obituary ... 124
Andreissen, David
See Poyer, David
Andreopoulos, Spyros (George) 1929- ... 77-80
Andres, Glenn M(erle) 1941- ... 73-76
Andres, Stefan 1906-1970 Obituary ... 29-32R
See also DLB 69
Andresen, Jack
See Andresen, John H(enry) Jr.
Andresen, John H(enry) Jr. 1917- ... 57-60
Andresen, Julie
See Tetel, Julie
Andreski, Iris
See Gillespie, I(ris) S(ylvia)
Andreski, Stanislav Leonard 1919- ... 61-64
Andrew, Christopher (Maurice) 1941- ... 136
Andrew, David S. 1943- ... 123
Andrew, J(ames) Dudley 1945- ... CANR-9
Earlier sketch in CA 65-68
Andrew, John (Alfred III) 1943- ... 69-72
Andrew, Malcolm (Ross) 1945- ... 105
Andrew, Prudence (Hastings) 1924- ... CANR-1
Earlier sketch in CA 1-4R
Andrew, Warren 1910- ... 21-24R
Andrewes, Christopher Howard 1896- ... 17-20R
Andrewes, Patience
See Bradford, Patience Andrewes
Andrews, A. A.
See Paine, Lauran (Bosworth)
Andrews, Allen 1913- ... CANR-1
Earlier sketch in CA 49-52
Andrews, Arthur (Douglas Jr.) 1923- ... 69-72
Andrews, Barry G(eoffrey) 1943- ... CANR-2
Earlier sketch in CA 49-52
Andrews, Bart 1945- ... CANR-24
Earlier sketches in CA 65-68, CANR-9
Andrews, Benny 1930- ... 106
See also SATA 31
Andrews, Bruce 1948- ... CANR-10
Earlier sketch in CA 49-52
Andrews, Burton (Allen) 1906- ... CAP-2
Earlier sketch in CA 33-36
Andrews, Charles M(cLean)
1863-1943 Brief entry ... 119
See also DLB 17
Andrews, Cicily Fairfield
See West, Rebecca
Andrews, Claire 1940- ... 33-36R
Andrews, Clarence A(delbert) 1912- ... CANR-20
Earlier sketch in CA 33-36R
Andrews, Colin 1946- ... 133
Andrews, Donald H(atch) 1898-197 (?) ... CAP-2
Earlier sketch in CA 23-24
Andrews, Dorothea Harris
1916-1976 Obituary ... 69-72
Andrews, E(ric) M(ontgomery) 1933- ... 93-96
Andrews, Eamonn 1922-1987 ... 120
Obituary ... 124
Andrews, Edgar Harold 1932- ... 105
Andrews, Eleanor Lattimore
See Lattimore, Eleanor Frances
Andrews, Elmer 1948- ... 132
Andrews, Elton V.
See Pohl, Frederik
Andrews, Ernest E(ugene) 1932- ... 57-60
Andrews, F(rank) Emerson 1902-1978 ... CANR-1
Obituary ... 81-84
Earlier sketch in CA 1-4R
See also SATA 22
Andrews, (Earl) Frank 1937- ... 61-64
Andrews, Frank M(eredith) 1935- ... CANR-14
Earlier sketch in CA 41-44R
Andrews, George (Clinton) 1926- ... 21-24R
Andrews, George F(redrick) 1918- ... 65-68
Andrews, Henry N(athaniel) Jr. 1910- ... 93-96
Andrews, J. Cutler 1908-1972 Obituary ... 37-40R
Andrews, J(ames) S(ydney) 1934- ... 29-32R
See also SATA 4
Andrews, James David 1924- ... 53-56
Andrews, James Frederick
1936-1980 Obituary ... 107
Andrews, James J. C.
1943(?)-1985 Obituary ... 116
Andrews, James R(obertson) 1936- ... 129
Brief entry ... 117
Andrews, Jan 1942- ... 122
See also SATA 49, 58
Andrews, John F(rank) 1942- ... 119
Andrews, John Henry 1939- ... 107
Andrews, John Malcolm 1936- ... 117
Andrews, John Williams
1898-1975 Obituary ... 57-60
Andrews, Julie 1935- ... 37-40R
See also SATA 7
Andrews, Keith 1930- ... 33-36R
Andrews, Kenneth R(ichmond) 1916- ... CANR-37
Earlier sketches in CA 1-4R, CANR-16
Andrews, Kevin 1924- ... 124
Andrews, Laura
See Coury, Louise Andree
Andrews, Lewis M. 1946- ... 65-68
Andrews, (William) Linton 1886-1972 ... 9-12R
Obituary ... 120
Andrews, Lucilla (Mathew) ... 128
Brief entry ... 116
Andrews, Lyman 1938- ... 49-52
Andrews, Lynn V. ... 129
Brief entry ... 125
Andrews, Margaret E(lizabeth) ... 33-36R
Andrews, Mark Edwin 1903- ... CAP-1
Earlier sketch in CA 19-20
Andrews, (Daniel) Marshall
1899(?)-1973 Obituary ... 45-48
Andrews, Mary Evans ... 5-8R
Andrews, Michael
See Andrews, Michael Alford
Andrews, Michael Alford 1939- ... 116
Andrews, Michael F(rank) 1916- ... CANR-27
Earlier sketch in CA 49-52
Andrews, Mike
See Andrews, Michael Alford
Andrews, Miles Peter 1814- ... DLB 89
Andrews, Paul Revere 1906-1983 Obituary ... 110
Andrews, Peter 1931- ... CANR-11
Earlier sketch in CA 17-20R
Andrews, Ralph W(arren) 1897- ... 9-12R
Andrews, Raymond 1934-1991 ... CANR-15
Obituary ... 136
Earlier sketch in CA 81-84
See also BW
Andrews, Robert D.
See Andrews, (Charles) Robert Douglas (Hardy)
Andrews, (Charles) Robert Douglas (Hardy)
1908- ... CAP-1
Earlier sketch in CA 9-10
Andrews, Roy Chapman 1884-1960 ... SATA 19
Andrews, Stanley 1894- ... CANR-22
Earlier sketch in CA 45-48
Andrews, V(irginia) C(leo) ... CANR-21
Obituary ... 121
Earlier sketch in CA 97-100
See also AAYA 4
See also MTCW
See also SATA 50

Andrews, Wayne 1913-1987 .... CANR-3
Obituary 123
Earlier sketch in CA 9-12R
Andrews, William G(eorge) 1930- CANR-7
Earlier sketch in CA 5-8R
Andrews, William L(eake) 1946- 136
Andrews, William R(obert) 1937- 53-56
Andreyev, Leonid (Nikolaevich)
1871-1919 Brief entry 104
See also TCLC 3
Andreyev, Nikolay Efremych
1908-1982 Obituary 106
Andrezel, Pierre
See Blixen, Karen (Christentze Dinesen)
Andrian, Gustave W(illiam)
1918- Brief entry 114
Andrian, Leopold von 1875-1951 .... DLB 81
Andric, Ivo 1892-1975 81-84
Obituary 57-60
See also CLC 8
See also MTCW
Andriekus, (Kazimieras) Leonardas
1914- 25-28R
Andrien, Kenneth James 1951- 120
Andriessen, Hendrik (Franciscus)
1892-1981 Obituary 108
Andriola, Alfred J. 1912-1983 Obituary 109
See also SATA 34
Andrist, Ralph K. 1914- CANR-20
Earlier sketches in CA 9-12R, CANR-5
See also SATA 45
Andropov, Yuri (Vladimirovich)
1914-1984 Obituary 111
Andros, Dee G(us) 1924- 69-72
Andros, Phil
See Steward, Samuel M(orris)
Androvar
See Prado (Calvo), Pedro
Andrus, (Vincent) Dyckman 1942- 102
Andrus, Hyrum L(eslie) 1924- 37-40R
Andrus, Paul 1931- 65-68
Andrus, Vera 1895- CAP-2
Earlier sketch in CA 21-22
Andrzejewski, Jerzy 1909-1983 .... CANR-29
Obituary 109
Earlier sketch in CA 25-28R
Andrzejewski, Julie 1945- 129
Andrzeyevski, George
See Andrzejewski, Jerzy
Anduze-Dufy, Raphael
See Coulet du Gard, Rene
Anees, Munawar Ahmad 1948- 123
An Elderly Spinster
See Wilson, Margaret (Wilhemina)
Anfousse, Ginette 1944- .... SATA 48
Ang, Ien 1954- 133
Angebert, Jean
See Bertrand, Michel
Angebert, Jean-Michel
See Bertrand, Michel
Angebert, Michel
See Bertrand, Michel
Angel, Daniel D. 1939- 33-36R
Angel, Heather 1941- CANR-25
Earlier sketch in CA 69-72
Angel, J(ohn) Lawrence 1915-1986 101
Obituary 120
Angel, Marc D(wight) 1945- 101
Angel, Marie 1923- CANR-15
Earlier sketch in CA 29-32R
See also SATA 47
Angelella, Michael 1953- 97-100
Angeles, Jose 1930- 33-36R
Angeles, Peter A. 1931- 33-36R
See also SATA 40
Angeles, Philip 1909- 5-8R
Angeli, Marguerite (Lofft) de
See de Angeli, Marguerite (Lofft)
Angelilli, Frank Joseph
See Angell, Frank Joseph
Angelin, Patricia 119
Angelino, Marie
See Garbutt, Janice (D.) Lovoos
Angelique, Pierre
See Bataille, Georges
Angell, Ernest 1889-1973 Obituary 37-40R
Angell, Frank Joseph 1919- 17-20R
Angell, George 1945- 101
Angell, James Burrill 1829-1916 .... DLB 64
Angell, James W(aterhouse)
1898-1986 Obituary 119
Angell, Judie 1937- 77-80
See also SATA 22
Angell, Madeline 1919- CANR-10
Earlier sketch in CA 65-68
See also SATA 18
Angell, (Ralph) Norman 1872(?)-1967 .... CAP-1
Earlier sketch in CA 13-14
Angell, Richard B(radshaw) 1918- 13-16R
Angell, Robert Cooley 1899- 101
Angell, Roger 1920- CANR-13
Earlier sketch in CA 57-60
See also CLC 26
Angell, Tony 1940- CANR-4
Earlier sketch in CA 53-56
Angelo, Bonnie Brief entry 113
Angelo, Frank 1914- CANR-4
Earlier sketch in CA 53-56
Angelo, Valenti 1897- 73-76
See also SATA 14
Angelocci, Angelo 1926- 21-24R
Angelou, Maya 1928- CANR-19
Earlier sketch in CA 65-68
See also AAYA 7
See also BLC 1
See also BW
See also CLC 12, 35, 64
See also DLB 38
See also MTCW
See also SATA 49
Anger, Kenneth 1930- 106
Angermann, Gerhard O(tto) 1904- 65-68
Angier, Bradford CANR-7
Earlier sketch in CA 5-8R
See also SATA 12
Angier, Carole 1943- 120
Angier, Roswell P. 1940- 101
Angiolillo, Paul F(rancis) 1917- 105
Anglade, Jean 1915- CANR-20
Earlier sketch in CA 103
Angle, Jim 1946- 133
Angle, Paul M(cClelland) 1900-1975 .... CAP-2
Obituary 57-60
Earlier sketch in CA 21-22
See also SATA 20
Anglin, Douglas G(eorge) 1923- CANR-14
Earlier sketch in CA 37-40R
Anglo, Sydney 1934- 89-92
Anglund, Joan Walsh 1926- CANR-15
Earlier sketch in CA 5-8R
See also CLR 1
See also SATA 2
Ango, Fan D.
See Longyear, Barry Brookes
Angoff, Allan 1910- CANR-20
Earlier sketch in CA 45-48
Angoff, Charles 1902-1979 .... CANR-4
Obituary 85-88
Earlier sketch in CA 5-8R
Angremy, Jean-Pierre 1937- 106
Angress, R(uth) K(lueger) 1931- 37-40R
Angress, Werner T(homas) 1920- 13-16R
Angrist, Shirley S(arah) 1933- 25-28R
Angrist, Stanley W(olff) 1933- 25-28R
See also SATA 4
Anguizola, G. A.
See Anguizola, Gustave (A.)
Anguizola, Gustave (A.) 1927- Brief entry 116
Angus, Douglas Ross 1909- CANR-3
Earlier sketch in CA 1-4R
Angus, Fay 1929- CANR-33
Earlier sketches in CA 89-92, CANR-15
Angus, Ian
See Mackay, James (Alexander)
Angus, J(ohn) Colin 1907- 107
Angus, Margaret 1908- 21-24R
Angus, Sylvia 1921-1982 .... CANR-10
Earlier sketch in CA 61-64
Angus, Tom
See Powell, Geoffrey Stewart
Angus-Butterworth, Lionel Milner
1900- CANR-4
Earlier sketch in CA 53-56
Anhalt, Edward 1914- CANR-29
Earlier sketch in CA 85-88
See also DLB 26
Anicar, Tom
See Raucina, Thomas Frank
Aniebo, I(feanyichukwu) N(dubuisi) C(hikezie)
1939- 134
Anikouchine, William A(lexander)
1929- Brief entry 117
Anita
See Daniel, Anita
Ankenbrand, Frank Jr. 1905- CAP-2
Earlier sketch in CA 19-20
Anker, Charlotte 1934- 93-96
Ankerson, Dudley (Charles) 1948- 126
Anmar, Frank
See Nolan, William F(rancis)
Anna, Timothy E. 1944- 101
Annan, Noel Gilroy 1916- 61-64
Annand, J(ames) K(ing) 1908- CANR-18
Earlier sketch in CA 101
Annandale, Barbara
See Bowden, Jean
Annas, George J. 1945- 77-80
Anne-Mariel
See Goud, Anne
Annensky, Innokenty Fyodorovich
1856-1909 Brief entry 110
See also TCLC 14
Anness, Milford E(dwin) 1918- 17-20R
Annett, Cora
See Scott, Cora Annett (Pipitone)
Annett, John 1930- 29-32R
Annigoni, Pietro 1910-1988 Obituary 127
Annis, Linda Ferrill 1943- 85-88
Annixter, Jane
See Sturtzel, Jane Levington
Annixter, Paul
See Sturtzel, Howard A(llison)
Anno, Mitsumasa 1926- CANR-4
Earlier sketch in CA 49-52
See also CLR 2, 14
See also MAICYA
See also SATA 5, 38
Anobile, Richard J(oseph) 1947- CANR-5
Earlier sketch in CA 53-56
Anobile, Ulla (Kakonen) 1945- 111
Anodos
See Coleridge, Mary E(lizabeth)
Anoff, I(sador) S(amuel) 1892- 45-48
Anon, Charles Robert
See Pessoa, Fernando (Antonio Nogueira)
Anouilh, Jean (Marie Lucien Pierre)
1910-1987 .... CANR-32
Obituary 123
Earlier sketch in CA 17-20R
See also CLC 1, 3, 8, 13, 40, 50
See also MTCW
Anquillare, John 1942- 105
Ansara, Michael
See Crowther, Bruce (Ian)
Ansbacher, Heinz L(udwig) 1904- CAP-1
Earlier sketch in CA 9-10
Ansbacher, Max G. 1935- 89-92
Ansberry, William F. 1926- 33-36R
Anschel, Eugene 1907- 53-56
Anschel, Kurt R. 1936- 41-44R
Anscombe, Elizabeth
See Anscombe, G(ertrude) E(lizabeth) M(argaret)
Anscombe, G(ertrude) E(lizabeth) M(argaret)
1919- 129
Brief entry 122
Anscombe, Isabelle (Mary) 1954- 108
Ansel, Walter (Charles) 1897-1977 45-48
Obituary 73-76
Ansell, Helen 1940- 25-28R
Ansell, Jack 1925-1976 .... 17-20R
Obituary 69-72
Anselm, Felix
See Pollak, Felix
Anselm of Canterbury 1033-1109 .... DLB 115
Ansen, Alan 1922- CANR-4
Earlier sketch in CA 1-4R
Anshen, Melvin (Leon) 1912- 124
Ansley, Gladys Piatt 1906- 5-8R
Anslinger, Harry Jacob 1892-1975 .... CAP-1
Obituary 61-64
Earlier sketch in CA 11-12
Anson, Bill 1907-1983 Obituary 110
Anson, Cyril J(oseph) 1923- 49-52
Anson, Jay 1921-1980 .... CANR-29
Obituary 97-100
Earlier sketch in CA 81-84
Anson, John
See Firth, (Frederick) Anson
Anson, Peter Frederick 1889- 9-12R
Anson, Robert Sam 1945- 125
Brief entry 115
Anspach, Donald F. 1942- 69-72
Anstey, Edgar
See Slusser, George Edgar
Anstey, Edgar 1917- CANR-3
Earlier sketch in CA 5-8R
Anstey, F.
See Guthrie, Thomas Anstey
Anstey, Roger T(homas) 1927- 13-16R
Anstey, Vera (Powell) 1889- CAP-1
Earlier sketch in CA 17-18
Anstruther, Godfrey 1903-1988 Obituary 126
Anstruther, Ian 1922- 128
Anstruther, James
See Maxtone Graham, James Anstruther
An Tai-sung 1931- 133
Brief entry 113
Antell, Gerson 1926- 53-56
Antell, Will D. 1935- 104
See also SATA 31
Anthes, Richard A(llen) 1944- 107
Anthony
See Taber, Anthony Scott
Anthony, Barbara 1932- CANR-21
Earlier sketch in CA 103
See also SATA 29
Anthony, C. L.
See Smith, Dorothy Gladys
Anthony, Catherine
See Adachi, Barbara (Curtis)
Anthony, David
See Smith, William Dale
Anthony, Diana 1951- 114
Anthony, Edward 1895-1971 73-76
Obituary 33-36R
See also SATA 21
Anthony, Evelyn
See Ward-Thomas, Evelyn Bridget Patricia Stephens
Anthony, Florence
See Ai
Anthony, Geraldine C(ecilia) 1919- CANR-28
Earlier sketches in CA 69-72, CANR-11
Anthony, Gordon
See Stannus, (James) Gordon (Dawson)
Anthony, Inid E. 1925- 104
Anthony, J(oseph) Garner 1899- 61-64
Anthony, James R(aymond) 1922- CANR-27
Earlier sketch in CA 49-52
Anthony, John
See Beckett, Ronald Brymer
and Ciardi, John (Anthony)
and Sabini, John Anthony
Anthony, Julie 1948- 106
Anthony, Katharine (Susan)
1877-1965 Obituary 25-28R
Anthony, Michael 1932- CANR-27
Earlier sketches in CA 17-20R, CANR-10
See also BW
Anthony, Peter
See Shaffer, Anthony (Joshua)
and Shaffer, Peter (Levin)
Anthony, Piers 1934- CANR-28
Earlier sketch in CA 21-24R
See also CLC 35
See also DLB 8
See also MTCW
Anthony, Rebecca (Jespersen) 1950- 118
Anthony, Robert N(ewton) 1916- CANR-5
Earlier sketch in CA 13-16R
Anthony, Susan B(rownell) 1916-1991 89-92
Obituary 134
Anthony, William G. 1934- 17-20R
Anthony, William P(hilip) 1943- CANR-29
Earlier sketches in CA 77-80, CANR-13
Anthrop, Donald F. 1935- Brief entry 111
Anticaglia, Elizabeth 1939- CANR-1
Earlier sketch in CA 45-48
See also SATA 12
Antico, John 1924- 29-32R
Antill, James Macquarie 1912- CANR-13
Earlier sketch in CA 33-36R
Antin, David 1932- 73-76
Antin, Mary 1881-1949 Brief entry 118
See also DLBY 84
Antoine, Marc
See Proust, (Valentin-Louis-George-Eugene-)Marcel
Antoine-Dariaux, Genevieve 1914- 57-60
Antokoletz, Elliott (Maxim) 1942- 129
Antolini, Margaret Fishback
1904-1985 Obituary 117
See also SATA 45
Anton, Frank Robert 1920- 41-44R
Anton, Hector R(oque) 1919- 73-76
Anton, John P(eter) 1920- CANR-9
Earlier sketch in CA 21-24R
Anton, Michael J(ames) 1940- 57-60
See also SATA 12
Anton, Rita (Kenter) 1920- 9-12R
Antonacci, Robert J(oseph) 1916- CANR-9
Earlier sketch in CA 5-8R
See also SATA 37, 45
Antoncich, Betty (Kennedy) 1913- 13-16R
Antone, Evan Haywood 1922- 126
Antoni
See Iranek-Osmecki, Kazimierz
Antoniak, Helen Elizabeth 1947- 105
Antonick, Robert J. 1939- 37-40R
Antoninus, Brother
See Everson, William (Oliver)
Antonio, Robert J(ohn) 1945- 120
Antonioni, Michelangelo 1912- 73-76
See also CLC 20
Antoniutti, Ildebrando
1898-1974 Obituary 53-56
Antonovsky, Aaron 1923- CANR-12
Earlier sketch in CA 29-32R
Antony, Jonquil 1916(?)-1980 .... 13-16R
Obituary 120
Antoun, Richard T(aft) 1932- 65-68
Antreasian, Garo Z(areh) 1922- 81-84
Antrim, Harry Thomas 1936- 33-36R
Antrim, William H. 1928- 69-72
Antrobus, John 1933- CANR-11
Earlier sketch in CA 57-60
Antschel, Paul 1920-1970 .... CANR-33
Earlier sketch in CA 85-88
See also Celan, Paul
See also CLC 10, 19
See also MTCW
Anttila, Raimo (Aulis) 1935- 33-36R
Anvic, Frank
See Sherman, Jory (Tecumseh)
Anwar, Chairil 1922-1949 Brief entry 121
See also TCLC 22
Anweiler, Oskar 1925- CANR-9
Earlier sketch in CA 65-68
Anyon, G(eorge) Jay 1909- 5-8R
Anzovin, Steven 1954- 124
Aoki, Haruo 1930- CANR-27
Earlier sketch in CA 49-52
Aoki, Hisako 1942- 115
See also SATA 45
Aoki, Michiko Y(amaguchi) 107
Apel, Karl-Otto 1922- CANR-22
Earlier sketch in CA 105
Apel, Willi 1893- CANR-2
Earlier sketch in CA 1-4R
Apelian, Albert Solomon
1893-1986 Obituary 121
Apfel, Necia H(alpern) 1930- CANR-23
Earlier sketch in CA 107
See also SATA 41, 51
Apffel, Edmund R. Jr. 1948- 107
Apgar, Virginia 1909-1974 73-76
Obituary 53-56
Aphrodite, J.
See Livingston, Carole
Apikuni
See Schultz, James Willard
Apilentz
See Apelian, Albert Solomon
Apitz, Bruno 1900-1979 Obituary 85-88
Aplon, Roger 1937- 119
Apodaca, Rudy S(amuel) 1939- 131
See also DLB 82
See also HW
Apolinar, Danny 1934- 61-64
Apollinaire, Guillaume
See Kostrowitzki, Wilhelm Apollinaris de
See also TCLC 3, 8
Aponte, Barbara (Ann) Bockus
1936- Brief entry 111
Apostle, Chris(tos) N(icholas) 1935- 21-24R
Apostolon, Billy (Michael) 1930- 97-100
Apostolos-Cappadona, Diane 1948- CANR-30
Earlier sketch in CA 112
Apostolou, John L. 1930- 127
App, Austin Joseph 1902-1984 101
Obituary 112
Appadorai, A(ngadipuram) 1902- 102
Appel, Alfred Jr. 1934- 133
Brief entry 113
Appel, Allan 1946- 77-80
Appel, Allen (R.) 1945- 138

Appel, Benjamin 1907-1977 .....CANR-6
Obituary 69-72
Earlier sketch in CA 13-16R
See also SATA 21, 39
Appel, Frederic C. 1935(?)-1984 Obituary 112
Appel, John J. 1921- 33-36R
Appel, Kenneth Ellmaker
1896-1979 Obituary 89-92
Appel, Libby E(ve Sundel) 1937- 117
Appel, Martin E(liot) 1948- CANR-15
Earlier sketch in CA 85-88
See also SATA 45
Appel, Marty
See Appel, Martin E(liot)
Appel, Willa 1946- 117
Appel, William 1939- 114
Appelbaum, Diana Karter 1953- 122
Appelbaum, Judith (Pilpel) 1939- CANR-14
Earlier sketch in CA 77-80
Appelbaum, Paul S(tuart) 1951- 108
Appelbaum, Stephen A(rthur) 1926- 101
Appelfeld, Aharon 1932- 133
Brief entry 112
See also CLC 23, 47
Appell, Don 1917(?)-1990 Obituary 131
Appelman, Hyman (Jedidiah) 1902- 5-8R
Appere, Guy 1923- 117
Appiah, Peggy 1921- 41-44R
See also SATA 15
Appignanesi, Lisa 1946- CANR-27
Earlier sketch in CA 49-52
Applbaum, Ronald L. 1943- CANR-7
Earlier sketch in CA 57-60
Apple, Jacki 1941- 127
Apple, Margot .....SATA 42, 64
Apple, Max (Isaac) 1941- CANR-19
Earlier sketch in CA 81-84
See also CLC 9, 33
Apple, Michael W(hitman) 1942- 109
Apple, R(aymond) W(alter) Jr. 1934- 89-92
Applebaum, Edmond L(ewis) 1924- 117
Applebaum, Samuel 1904- 65-68
Applebaum, Stan 1922- 85-88
See also SATA 45
Applebaum, William 1906-1979(?) CANR-6
Earlier sketch in CA 9-12R
Applebee, Arthur N(oble) 1946- CANR-31
Earlier sketches in CA 81-84, CANR-14
Appleby, Andrew Bell 1929-1980 108
Appleby, David P. 1925- 110
Appleby, John T. 1909(?)-1974 Obituary 53-56
Appleby, Jon 1948- 33-36R
Appleby, Joyce Oldham 1929- CANR-11
Earlier sketch in CA 69-72
Applegarth, Margaret Tyson
1886-1976 Obituary 69-72
Applegate, James (Earl) 1923- 33-36R
Applegate, Richard
1913(?)-1979 Obituary 85-88
Applegath, John 1935- 115
Appleman, John Alan 1912-1982 .....CANR-2
Obituary 108
Earlier sketch in CA 5-8R
Appleman, M(arjorie) H. 1928- 118
Appleman, Margie
See Appleman, M(arjorie) H.
Appleman, Mark J(erome) 1917- 29-32R
Appleman, Philip (Dean) 1926- CANR-29
Earlier sketches in CA 13-16R, CANR-6
See also CLC 51
Appleman, Roy Edgar 1904- CAP-1
Earlier sketch in CA 9-10
Appleton, Arthur 1913- 93-96
Appleton, George 1902- 126
Appleton, James Henry 1919- CANR-2
Earlier sketch in CA 5-8R
Appleton, Jane (Frances) 1934- 102
Appleton, Jay
See Appleton, James Henry
Appleton, Lawrence
See Lovecraft, H(oward) P(hillips)
Appleton, Marion Brymner 1906- 105
Appleton, Sarah 1930- 37-40R
Appleton, Sheldon Lee 1933- 1-4R
Appleton, Victor CANR-27
Earlier sketches in CAP-2, CA 19-20
See also SATA 1, 67
Appleton, Victor II CANR-27
Earlier sketch in CA 17-20R
See also SATA 1, 67
Appleton, William S. 1934- 101
Appleton, William W(orthen)
1915- Brief entry 113
Applewhite, Cynthia 89-92
Applewhite, E(dgar) J(arratt Jr.) 1919- 89-92
Applewhite, Harriet Branson 1940- 106
Applewhite, James W(illiam) 1935- CANR-25
Earlier sketch in CA 85-88
See also DLB 105
Applewhite, Philip B(oatman) 1938- 112
Appley, Lawrence A. 1904- 121
Appley, M(ortimer) H(erbert) 1921- 13-16R
Appleyard, Donald 1928- CANR-4
Earlier sketch in CA 5-8R
Appleyard, Reginald Thomas 1927- 17-20R
Applezweig, M. H.
See Appley, M(ortimer) H(erbert)
Apps, Jerold W(illard) 1934- CANR-37
Earlier sketches in CA 49-52, CANR-1, 16
Apps, Jerry
See Apps, Jerold W(illard)
apRoberts, Ruth 111
Apsler, Alfred 1907- CANR-3
Earlier sketch in CA 5-8R
See also SATA 10
Apstein, Theodore 1918- 131
Apt, (Jerome) Leon 1929- 53-56
Apte, Mahadev L(akshuman) 1931- 117
Apted, M(ichael) R. 1919- 25-28R
Aptekar, Jane 1935- 81-84
Apter, David Ernest 1924- CANR-3
Earlier sketch in CA 1-4R
Apter, Emily (S.) 1954- 137
Apter, Michael J(ohn) 1939- 29-32R
Apter, Samson 1910- 104
Apter, T(erri) E. 1949- 134
Aptheker, Bettina 1944- CANR-6
Earlier sketch in CA 29-32R
Aptheker, Herbert 1915- CANR-6
Earlier sketch in CA 5-8R
Aquarius, Qass
See Buskirk, Richard H(obart)
Aquilano, Nicholas Joseph 1930- 112
Aquin, Hubert 1929-1977 105
See also CLC 15
See also DLB 53
Aquina, Sister Mary
See Weinrich, A(nna) K(atharina) H(ildegard)
Aquinas, Thomas 1224(?)-1274 .....DLB 115
Aquino, Benigno S(imeon) Jr.
1932-1983 Obituary 110
Aquino, Luis Hernandez
See Hernandez Aquino, Luis
Aquino, Ninoy
See Aquino, Benigno S(imeon) Jr.
Arad, Yitshak 1926- 134
Arafat, Ibtihaj Said 1934- 85-88
Aragbabalu, Omidiji
See Beier, Ulli
Aragon, Louis 1897-1982 .....CANR-28
Obituary 108
Earlier sketch in CA 69-72
See also CLC 3, 22
See also DLB 72
See also MTCW
Aragon, Luis Cardoza y
See Cardoza y Aragon, Luis
Aragones, Sergio 1937- 122
See also SATA 39, 48
Araki, James T(omomasa) 1925- 13-16R
Arango, Jorge Sanin 1916- 61-64
Aranha, Ray 1939- Brief entry 112
Aranow, Edward Ross 1909- 41-44R
Araoz, Daniel Leon 1930- 108
Arapoff, Nancy 1930- 29-32R
Arasteh, A(bdol) Reza 1927- 105
Arata, Esther S(pring) 1918- 89-92
Arata, Luis O(scar) 1950- 115
Arbatov, G. A.
See Arbatov, Georgi (Arkadevich)
Arbatov, Georgi (Arkadevich) 1923- 116
Arbatov, Yuri Arkadevich
See Arbatov, Georgi (Arkadevich)
Arbeiter, Jean S(onkin) 1937- 106
Arberry, A(rthur) J(ohn) 1905-1969 .....CANR-4
Earlier sketch in CA 1-4R
Arbib, Robert
See Arbib, Robert S(imeon) Jr.
Arbib, Robert S(imeon) Jr. 1915-1987 .....33-36R
Obituary 123
Arbingast, Stanley A(lan) 1910- CANR-10
Earlier sketch in CA 17-20R
Arbogast, William F. 1908-1979 Obituary 89-92
Arbuckle, Dorothy Fry 1910-1982 Obituary 108
See also SATA 33
Arbuckle, Dugald S(inclair) 1912- 13-16R
Arbuckle, Robert D(ean) 1940- 61-64
Arbuckle, W(endell) S(herwood)
1911-1987 Obituary 122
Arbuckle, Wanda Rector 1910- 41-44R
Arbus, Amy 1954- 127
Arbuthnot, John 1667-1735 .....DLB 101
Arbuthnot, May Hill 1884-1969 .....9-12R
See also SATA 2
Arbuthnott, Hugh (James) 1936- 125
Arbuzov, Alexei Nikolaevich 1908-1986 69-72
Obituary 119
Arca, Julie Anne 1953- 111
Arcana, Judith 1943- 103
Arcand, Denys 1941- 133
Arce, Hector 1935-1980 97-100
Arce, Julio G.
See Ulica, Jorge
Arceneaux, Jean
See Ancelet, Barry Jean
Arceneaux, Thelma Hoffmann Tyler .....AITN 1
Arch, E. L.
See Payes, Rachel C(osgrove)
ar C'Halan, Reun
See Galand, Rene
Archambault, John 135
See also MAICYA
See also SATA 67
Archambault, Paul 1937- 81-84
Archdeacon, Thomas J(ohn) 1942- 65-68
Archer, A. A.
See Joscelyn, Archie L.
Archer, Chalmers Jr. 1938- 138
Archer, Dennis
See Paine, Lauran (Bosworth)
Archer, Frank
See O'Connor, Richard
Archer, Fred C. 1916(?)-1974 Obituary 53-56
Archer, Fred 1915- CANR-7
Earlier sketch in CA 57-60
Archer, Gleason Leonard Jr. 1916- 65-68
Archer, H(orace) Richard 1911-1978 .....CANR-6
Obituary 89-92
Earlier sketch in CA 13-16R
Archer, Herbert Winslow
See Mencken, H(enry) L(ouis)
Archer, Ian W. 1960- 135
Archer, Jane (a pseudonym) 113
Archer, Jeffrey (Howard) 1940- CANR-22
Earlier sketch in CA 77-80
See also BEST 89:3
See also CLC 28
Archer, John H(all) 1914- 101
Archer, Jules 1915- CANR-6
Earlier sketch in CA 9-12R
See also CLC 12
See also SAAS 5
See also SATA 4
Archer, Keith (Allan) 1955- 135
Archer, Lee
See Ellison, Harlan
Archer, Leonie (Jane) 1955- 132
Archer, Marion Fuller 1917- 5-8R
See also SATA 11
Archer, Mildred 1911- 104
Archer, Myrtle (Lilly) 1926- 102
Archer, Nuala 1955- 121
Archer, Peter Kingsley 1926- CANR-2
Earlier sketch in CA 5-8R
Archer, Ron
See White, Theodore Edwin
Archer, S. E.
See Soderberg, Percy Measday
Archer, Sellers G. 1908-1980 .....17-20R
Obituary 134
Archer, Stephen H(unt) 1928- 17-20R
Archer, Stephen M(urphy) 1934- 105
Archer, W(illiam) G(eorge) 1907-1979 57-60
Obituary 125
Archer, William 1856-1924 Brief entry 108
See also DLB 10
Archerd, Armand 115
Brief entry 110
Archerd, Army
See Archerd, Armand
Archer Houblon, Doreen (Lindsay)
1899-1977 106
Archibald, Douglas N(elson) 1933- 128
Brief entry 113
Archibald, (Rupert) Douglas 1919- 101
Archibald, James Montgomery
1920-1983 Obituary 110
Archibald, Joe
See Archibald, Joseph S(topford)
Archibald, John J. 1925- 5-8R
Archibald, Joseph S(topford)
1898-1986 .....CANR-5
Obituary 118
Earlier sketch in CA 9-12R
See also SATA 3, 47
Archibald, Sandra O(rr) 1945- 113
Archibald, William 1924-1970 Obituary 29-32R
Arciniegas, German 1900- CANR-29
Earlier sketches in CA 61-64, CANR-10
See also HW
Arcone, Sonya 1925-1978 .....21-24R
Obituary 77-80
Ard, Ben N(eal) Jr. 1922- CANR-12
Earlier sketch in CA 33-36R
Ard, William (Thomas) 1922-1962(?) 5-8R
Ardagh, John 1928- 25-28R
Ardai, Charles 1969- 136
Ardalan, Nader 1939- 69-72
Arden, Barbi
See Stoutenburg, Adrien (Pearl)
Arden, Gothard Everett 1905- CAP-1
Earlier sketch in CA 11-12
Arden, J. E. M.
See Conquest, (George) Robert (Acworth)
Arden, Jane 61-64
Arden, John 1930- CANR-31
Earlier sketch in CA 13-16R
See also CAAS 4
See also CLC 6, 13, 15
See also DLB 13
See also MTCW
Arden, Leon 1932- 107
Arden, Noele
See Dambrauskas, Joan Arden
Arden, William
See Lynds, Dennis
Ardener, Edwin (William) 1927-1987 .....5-8R
Obituary 123
Ardies, Tom 1931- 33-36R
Ardizzone, Edward (Jeffrey Irving)
1900-1979 .....CANR-8
Obituary 89-92
Earlier sketch in CA 5-8R
See also CLR 3
See also MAICYA
See also SATA 1, 21, 28
Ardizzone, Tony 1949- 85-88
Ardley, Gavin 1915- 129
Ardley, Neil (Richard) 1937- CANR-39
Earlier sketch in CA 115
See also SATA 43
Ardmore, Jane Kesner 1915- 5-8R
Ardoin, John (Louis) 1935- 57-60
Ardrey, Robert 1908-1980 .....33-36R
Obituary 93-96
Arecco, Vera Lustig
See Lustig-Arecco, Vera
Areeda, Phillip E. 1930- 21-24R
Arehart-Treichel, Joan 1942- CANR-6
Earlier sketch in CA 57-60
See also SATA 22
Arellanes, Audrey Spencer 1920- 33-36R
Arellano, Diana Ramirez de
See Ramirez de Arellano, Diana (T. Clotilde)
Arellano, Rafael W(illiam) Ramirez de
See Ramirez de Arellano, Rafael W(illiam)
Arem, Joel E(dward) 1943- 89-92
Arena, Jay M(orris) 1909- 107
Arena, John I. 1929- CANR-20
Earlier sketch in CA 45-48
Arenas, Reinaldo 1943-1990 128
Obituary 133
Brief entry 124
See also CLC 41
See also HW
Arendt, Hannah 1906-1975 .....CANR-26
Obituary 61-64
Earlier sketch in CA 17-20R
See also CLC 66
See also MTCW
Arenella, Roy 1939- .....SATA 14
Arens, Richard 1921-1984 73-76
Obituary 112
Arens, William 1940- 89-92
Arensberg, Ann 1937- 114
See also DLBY 82
Arensberg, Conrad Maynadier 1910- 61-64
Arenson, Gloria 1935- 118
Arent, Arthur 1904-1972 .....CAP-2
Obituary 33-36R
Earlier sketch in CA 23-24
Areskoug, Kaj 1933- 29-32R
Aresty, Esther B(radford) 9-12R
Areta, Mavis
See Winder, Mavis Areta
Arevalo Martinez, Rafael 1884-1975 .....HW
Arey, James A(rthur) 1936-1988 .....41-44R
Obituary 125
Arey, Leslie Brainerd 1891-1988 Obituary 125
Argan, Giulio Carlo 1909- 65-68
Argenti, John 1926- 115
Argenti, Philip 1891(?)-1974 Obituary 49-52
Argenzio, Victor 1902- 53-56
Argersinger, Peter H(ayes)
1944- Brief entry 112
Arghezi, Tudor
See Theodorescu, Ion N.
Argiro, Larry 1909- 5-8R
Argo, Ellen
See Johnson, Ellen Argo
Argow, Waldemar 1916- 21-24R
Arguedas, Jose Maria 1911-1969 89-92
See also CLC 10, 18
See also DLB 113
See also HW
Arguelles, Jose A(nthony) 1939- CANR-20
Earlier sketch in CA 45-48
Arguelles, Miriam Tarcov 1943- 45-48
Argueta, Manlio 1936- 131
See also CLC 31
See also HW
Argus
See Osusky, Stefan
and Phillips-Birt, Douglas Hextall Chedzey
Argyle, Aubrey William 1910- CAP-1
Earlier sketch in CA 17-18
Argyle, Michael 1925- CANR-25
Earlier sketches in CA 21-24R, CANR-9
Argyris, Chris 1923- CANR-20
Earlier sketches in CA 1-4R, CANR-5
Arian, Alan (Asher) 1938- CANR-1
Earlier sketch in CA 49-52
Arian, Edward 1921- 33-36R
Arias, Ron(ald Francis) 1941- 131
See also DLB 82
See also HW
Arias-Misson, Alain 1936- 77-80
Arias Sanchez, Oscar 1941- .....HW
Aridas, Chris 1947- 112
Aridjis, Homero 1940- 131
See also HW
Ariel
See Moraes, Frank Robert
Aries, Philippe 1914-1984 89-92
Obituary 112
Arieti, James Alexander 1948- 108
Arieti, Silvano 1914-1981 .....CANR-10
Obituary 104
Earlier sketch in CA 21-24R
Arimond, Carroll 1909-1979 Obituary 89-92
Aring, Charles D(air) 1904- 49-52
Arinze, Francis 1932- 138
Aris, Rutherford 1929- 117
Arismendi, Rodney 1913-1989 Obituary 130
Aristides
See Epstein, Joseph
Aristophanes 450-385 .....DC 2
Ariyoshi, Sawako 1931-1984 105
Obituary 113
Ariyoshi, Shoichiro
1939(?)-1979 Obituary 89-92
Arkadyev, N.
See Shevchenko, Arkady N(ikolaevich)
Arkell, Anthony John 1898-1980 102
Obituary 97-100
Arkhurst, Frederick S(iegfried) 1920- CANR-25
Earlier sketch in CA 29-32R
Arkhurst, Joyce Cooper 1921- 17-20R
Arkin, Alan (Wolf) 1934- 112
Brief entry 110
See also SATA 32, 59
Arkin, David 1906- 21-24R
Arkin, Frieda 1917- CANR-11
Earlier sketch in CA 65-68
Arkin, Herbert 1906- 5-8R
Arkin, Joseph 1922- 5-8R
Arkin, Marcus 1926- 53-56
Arkley, Arthur J(ames) 1919- 112
Arkow, Phil 1947- 128
Arksey, Laura L(ee) 1936- 119
Arkush, Arthur Spencer
1925-1979 Obituary 85-88
Arland, Marcel 1899-1986 .....DLB 72
Arlandson, Leone 1917- 29-32R
Arlen, Michael J. 1930- CANR-13
Earlier sketch in CA 61-64

Arlen, Michael 1895-1956 Brief entry 120
See also DLB 36, 77
Arleo, Joseph 1933- 29-32R
Arley, Catherine 1935- CANR-2
Earlier sketch in CA 45-48
Arliss, Leslie 1901-1987 Obituary 124
Arlott, (Leslie Thomas) John 1914-1991 ....9-12R
Obituary 136
Arlotto, Anthony (Thomas) 1939- 33-36R
Arlow, Jacob A. 1912- 53-56
Arlt, Roberto (Godofredo Christophersen)
1900-1942 131
Brief entry 123
See also HW
See also TCLC 29
Armacost, Michael Hayden 1937- 101
Armah, Ayi Kwei 1939- CANR-21
Earlier sketch in CA 61-64
See also BLC 1
See also BW
See also CLC 5, 33
See also DLB 117
See also MTCW
Armand, Louis 1905-1971 ....CAP-2
Obituary 33-36R
Earlier sketch in CA 29-32
Armand, Octavio Rafael 1946- 131
See also HW
Armatas, James P. 1931- 41-44R
Armatrading, Joan 1950- Brief entry 114
See also CLC 17
Armbrister, Trevor 1933- 89-92
Armbruster, Carl J. 1929- 33-36R
Armbruster, F(ranz) O(wen) 1929- 49-52
Armbruster, Francis E(dward) 1923- 29-32R
Armbruster, Frank
See Armbruster, Francis E(dward)
Armbruster, Maxim Ethan 1902- 1-4R
Armens, Sven 1921- 21-24R
Armentrout, Fred S(herman) 1946- 119
Armentrout, William W(infield) 1918- 33-36R
Armer, Alberta (Roller) 1904- 5-8R
See also SATA 9
Armer, J(ohn) Michael 1937- 106
Armer, Laura (Adams) 1874-1963 65-68
See also MAICYA
See also SATA 13
Armerding, Carl Edwin 1936- 104
Armerding, George D. 1899- 85-88
Armerding, Hudson Taylor 1918- CANR-11
Earlier sketch in CA 21-24R
Armes, Roy (Philip) 1937- CANR-13
Earlier sketch in CA 73-76
Armington, John Calvin 1923- 53-56
Armington, R(aymond) Q(uintin) 1907- 131
Armistead, Samuel (Gordon) 1927- 53-56
Armitage, A(rthur) L(lewellyn)
1916-1984 Obituary 112
Armitage, Angus 1902- CAP-1
Earlier sketch in CA 13-14
Armitage, David 1943- ....SATA 38
Armitage, E(dward) Liddall 1887- CAP-1
Earlier sketch in CA 9-10
Armitage, Frank
See Carpenter, John (Howard)
Armitage, G(ary) E(dric) 1956- 121
Armitage, Merle 1893-1975 Obituary 61-64
Armitage, Michael John 1930- 117
Armitage, Ronda (Jacqueline) 1943- 121
See also SATA 38, 47
Armitage, Shelley S(ue) 1947- 121
Armitage, Simon 1963- 134
Armory, Thomas 1691(?)-1788 ....DLB 39
Armour, John
See Paine, Lauran (Bosworth)
Armour, Leslie 1931- 110
Armour, Lloyd R. 1922- 29-32R
Armour, Peter 1940- 128
Armour, Richard (Willard) 1906-1989 ....CANR-32
Obituary 128
Earlier sketches in CA 1-4R, CANR-4
See also SATA 14, 61
Armour, Rollin Stely 1929- 33-36R
Arms, George (Warren) 1912- 5-8R
Arms, Johnson
See Halliwell, David (William)
Arms, Suzanne 1944- 57-60
Armstrong, (Walter) Alan 1936- 73-76
Armstrong, Ann Seidel 1917- 9-12R
Armstrong, Anne(tte) 1924- 13-16R
Armstrong, Anthony
See Willis, (George) Anthony Armstrong
Armstrong, Anthony C.
See Armstrong, Christopher J(ohn) R(ichard)
Armstrong, (Grace) April (Oursler) 1926- 89-92
Armstrong, Arthur Hilary 1909- 69-72
Armstrong, Benjamin Leighton 1923- 93-96
Armstrong, Brian G(ary) 1936- 69-72
Armstrong, Charles B. 1923-1985 Obituary 115
Armstrong, Charlotte 1905-1969 ....CANR-3
Obituary 25-28R
Earlier sketch in CA 1-4R
Armstrong, Christopher J(ohn) R(ichard)
1935- 69-72
Armstrong, Claude Blakely
1889-1982 Obituary 108
Armstrong, D(avid) M(alet) 1926- CANR-31
Earlier sketches in CA 25-28R, CANR-11
Armstrong, (James) David 1945- 107
Armstrong, David M(ichael) 1944- 57-60
Armstrong, Diana 1943- 107
Armstrong, Douglas Albert 1920- 9-12R
Armstrong, Edward Allworthy
1900-1978 ....CANR-4
Earlier sketch in CA 5-8R
Armstrong, (Annette) Elizabeth 1917- 25-28R
Armstrong, F. W.
See Wright, T. M.
Armstrong, Frederick H(enry) 1926- 33-36R
Armstrong, Garner Ted 1929(?)- Brief entry 113
Armstrong, George D. 1927- ....SATA 10
Armstrong, Gerry (Breen) 1929- 13-16R
See also SATA 10
Armstrong, Gregory T(imon) 1933- 9-12R
Armstrong, Hamilton Fish 1893-1973 93-96
Obituary 41-44R
Armstrong, Henry
See Jackson, Henry
Armstrong, Henry H.
See Arvay, Harry
Armstrong, Herbert W. 1892-1986 Obituary 118
Brief entry 116
Armstrong, J(on) Scott 1937- CANR-1
Earlier sketch in CA 45-48
Armstrong, (A.) James 1924- 29-32R
Armstrong, Joe C. W.
See Armstrong, Joseph Charles Woodland
Armstrong, John A(lexander Jr.) 1922- CANR-3
Earlier sketch in CA 1-4R
Armstrong, John Borden 1926- 33-36R
Armstrong, John Byron 1917-1976 ....5-8R
Obituary 65-68
Armstrong, Joseph Charles Woodland
1934- 127
Armstrong, Joseph Gravitt 1943- 101
Armstrong, Judith Mary 1935- 102
Armstrong, Keith F(rancis) W(hitfield)
1950- 29-32R
Armstrong, Leslie 1940- 124
Armstrong, (Daniel) Louis
1900-1971 Obituary 29-32R
Armstrong, Louise 117
Brief entry 111
See also SATA 33, 43
Armstrong, Marjorie Moore 1912- 89-92
Armstrong, Martin 1882-1974 Obituary 49-52
Armstrong, Mary (Elizabeth) Willems 1957- 134
Armstrong, O(rland) K(ay) 1893-1987 93-96
Obituary 122
Armstrong, Paul B(radford) 1949- 112
Armstrong, (Raymond) Paul 1912- 37-40R
Armstrong, Richard B(yron) 1956- 134
Armstrong, Richard G. 1932- 73-76
Armstrong, Richard 1903- 77-80
See also SATA 11
Armstrong, Robert H(oward) 1936- 108
Armstrong, Robert L(aurence) 1926- 29-32R
Armstrong, Robert Plant 1919-1984 ....41-44R
Obituary 113
Armstrong, Roger D. 1939- 17-20R
Armstrong, Ruth Gallup 1891- CAP-1
Earlier sketch in CA 9-10
Armstrong, (Russell) Scott 1945- 108
Armstrong, Terence Ian Fytton
1912-1970 ....CAP-2
Obituary 29-32R
Earlier sketch in CA 17-18
Armstrong, Thomas 1899-1978 ....5-8R
Obituary 103
Armstrong, Tilly 1927- CANR-23
Earlier sketch in CA 107
Armstrong, Wallace Edwin
1896-1980 Obituary 97-100
Armstrong, William A(lexander) 1912- 13-16R
Armstrong, William A(rthur) 1915- 17-20R
Armstrong, William H(oward) 1914- CANR-9
Earlier sketch in CA 17-20R
See also AITN 1
See also CLR 1
See also MAICYA
See also SAAS 7
See also SATA 4
Armstrong, William M(artin) 1919- 49-52
Armstrong-Jones, Antony (Charles Robert)
1930- 118
Armstrong Jones, Tony
See Armstrong-Jones, Antony (Charles Robert)
Armytage, Walter Harry Green 1915- 9-12R
Arnade, Charles W(olfgang) 1927- 33-36R
Arnandez, Richard 1912- CANR-6
Earlier sketch in CA 13-16R
Arnason, David 1940- 114
Arnason, H(jorvardur) H(arvard)
1909-1986 ....CANR-13
Obituary 119
Earlier sketch in CA 61-64
Arnau, Frank
See Schmitt, Heinrich
Arnaud, Georges
See Girard, Henri Georges Charles Achille
Arnaz, Desi
See Arnaz y de Acha, Desiderio Alberto III
Arnaz y de Acha, Desiderio Alberto III
1917(?)-1986 Obituary 121
Brief entry 114
Arncliffe, Andrew
See Walker, Peter N.
Arndt, Elise 1943- 116
Arndt, Ernst H(einrich) D(aniel) 1899- CAP-2
Earlier sketch in CA 23-24
Arndt, Ernst Moritz 1769-1860 ....DLB 90
Arndt, H(einz) W(olfgang) 1915- CANR-29
Earlier sketches in CA 21-24R, CANR-10
Arndt, Karl John Richard 1903- CANR-23
Earlier sketches in CA 17-20R, CANR-7
Arndt, Ursula (Martha H.) ....SATA 39, 56
Arndt, Walter W(erner) 1916- CANR-5
Earlier sketch in CA 13-16R
Arnebeck, Bob 1947- 108
Arneson, D(on) J(on) 1935- 106
See also SATA 37
Arnett, Caroline
See Cole, Lois Dwight
Arnett, Carroll 1927- CANR-11
Earlier sketch in CA 21-24R
Arnett, Harold E(dward) 1931- CANR-8
Earlier sketch in CA 21-24R
Arnett, Ross H(arold) Jr. 1919- CANR-17
Earlier sketches in CA 49-52, CANR-2
Arnette, Robert
See Silverberg, Robert
Arney, William Ray 1950- 110
Arnez, Nancy Levi 1928- 29-32R
Arnheim, Daniel D(avid) 1930- CANR-5
Earlier sketch in CA 9-12R
Arnheim, Rudolf 1904- CANR-3
Earlier sketch in CA 1-4R
Arnim, Achim von (Ludwig Joachim von Arnim)
1781-1831 ....DLB 90
Arnim, Bettina von 1785-1859 ....DLB 90
Arno, Enrico 1913-1981 ....SATA 28, 43
Arno, Peter 1904-1968 73-76
Obituary 25-28R
Arnold, A(lbert) James (Jr.) 1939- 132
Arnold, Adlai F(ranklin) 1914- 33-36R
Arnold, Alan 1922- 5-8R
Arnold, Alvin L(incoln) 1929- 93-96
Arnold, Anthony 1928- 111
Arnold, Armin H. 1931- CANR-18
Earlier sketches in CA 9-12R, CANR-3
Arnold, Arnold (Ferdinand) 1921- CANR-27
Earlier sketches in CA 17-20R, CANR-10
Arnold, Bob 1952- CANR-21
Earlier sketch in CA 105
Arnold, Bruce 1936- 93-96
Arnold, Carl
See Raknes, Ola
Arnold, Caroline 1944- CANR-24
Earlier sketch in CA 107
See also SATA 34, 36
Arnold, Carroll C(lyde) 1912- Brief entry 116
Arnold, Catharine 1959- 125
Arnold, Charles Harvey 1920- 65-68
Arnold, Charlotte E(lizabeth) Cramer 57-60
Arnold, Corliss Richard 1926- 49-52
Arnold, Denis Midgley 1926-1986 ....CANR-2
Obituary 119
Earlier sketch in CA 5-8R
Arnold, Duane W(ade-) H(ampton) 1953- 127
Arnold, Edmund C(larence) 1913- CANR-3
Earlier sketch in CA 1-4R
Arnold, Edwin L(ester Linden)
1857(?)-1935 Brief entry 109
Arnold, Edwin T. 1947- 134
Arnold, Edwin 1832-1904 ....DLB 35
Arnold, Elliott 1912-1980 ....CANR-24
Obituary 97-100
Earlier sketch in CA 17-20R
See also SATA 5, 22
Arnold, Emily 1939- 109
See also McCully, Emily Arnold
See also MAICYA
See also SATA 50
Arnold, Emmy (von Hollander)
1884-1980 ....CANR-9
Earlier sketch in CA 21-24R
Arnold, Eve 1913- CANR-31
Earlier sketch in CA 112
Arnold, Francena H(arriet Long) 1888- CAP-1
Earlier sketch in CA 17-18
Arnold, G. L.
See Lichtheim, George
Arnold, Gary Howard 1942- Brief entry 117
Arnold, Gladys (M.) 1905- 128
Arnold, Guy 1932- CANR-28
Earlier sketches in CA 25-28R, CANR-11
Arnold, H(arry) J(ohn) P(hilip) 1932- CANR-2
Earlier sketch in CA 5-8R
Arnold, Heini
See Arnold, Johann Heinrich
Arnold, Herbert 1935- 37-40R
Arnold, Janet 1932- 93-96
Arnold, Johann Heinrich 1913-1982 122
Obituary 111
Arnold, John D(avid) 1933- 111
Arnold, Joseph H.
See Hayes, Joseph
Arnold, June (Davis) 1926-1982 ....21-24R
Obituary 133
Arnold, L. J.
See Cameron, Lou
Arnold, Leslie
See Lazarus, A(rnold) L(eslie)
Arnold, Lloyd R. 1906-1970 ....CAP-2
Earlier sketch in CA 25-28
Arnold, Lois B(arber) 107
Arnold, Madelyn M. 1948- 129
Arnold, Magda B(londiau) 1903- 5-8R
Arnold, Margot
See Cook, Petronelle Marguerite Mary
Arnold, Marilyn 1935- 122
Arnold, Mary Ann 1918- 65-68
Arnold, Matthew 1822-1888 .... CDBLB 1832-1890
See also DLB 32, 57
See also PC 5
See also WLC
Arnold, Milo Lawrence 1903- 57-60
Arnold, Olga Moore 1900-1981 Obituary 102
Arnold, Oren 1900- CANR-2
Earlier sketch in CA 5-8R
See also SATA 4
Arnold, Pauline 1894-1974 ....CANR-2
Earlier sketch in CA 1-4R
Arnold, Peter 1931- 123
Arnold, Peter 1943- CANR-1
Earlier sketch in CA 49-52
Arnold, R. Douglas 1950- 101
Arnold, Ray Henry 1895- 5-8R
Arnold, Richard E(ugene) 1908- CAP-2
Earlier sketch in CA 33-36
Arnold, Richard K(lein) 1923- 69-72
Arnold, Richard 1912- CANR-3
Earlier sketch in CA 9-12R
Arnold, Robert E(vans) 1932- 49-52
Arnold, Rollo (Davis) 1926- 21-24R
Arnold, Ron 1937- CANR-25
Earlier sketch in CA 108
Arnold, Stephen H. 1942- 117
Arnold, Susan (Riser) 1951- ....SATA 58
Arnold, Tedd 1949- 137
See also SATA 69
Arnold, Terrell E. 1925- 130
Arnold, Thomas 1795-1842 ....DLB 55
Arnold, Thurman Wesley 1891-1969 ....CAP-1
Earlier sketch in CA 13-16
Arnold, William Robert 1933- 29-32R
Arnold, William Van 1941- 110
Arnold-Baker, Charles 1918- 5-8R
Arnold-Forster, Mark 1920-1981 65-68
Obituary 105
Arnoldy, Julie
See Bischoff, Julia Bristol
Arnosky, James Edward 1946- CANR-32
Earlier sketches in CA 69-72, CANR-12
See also Arnosky, Jim
See also CLR 15
See also SATA 22
Arnosky, Jim
See Arnosky, James Edward
See also MAICYA
See also SATA 70
Arnothy, Christine 1930- CANR-10
Earlier sketch in CA 65-68
Arnott, (Margaret) Anne 1916- CANR-13
Earlier sketch in CA 73-76
Arnott, J(ames) F(ullarton)
1914-1982 Obituary 108
Arnott, Kathleen 1914- 57-60
See also SATA 20
Arnott, Peter D(ouglas) 1931- CANR-3
Earlier sketch in CA 1-4R
Arnoux, Alexandre (Paul)
1884-1973 Obituary 37-40R
Arnov, Boris Jr. 1926- CANR-3
Earlier sketch in CA 1-4R
See also SATA 12
Arnove, Robert Fred 1937- 111
Arnow, Harriette (Louisa) Simpson
1908-1986 ....CANR-14
Obituary 118
Earlier sketch in CA 9-12R
See also CLC 2, 7, 18
See also DLB 6
See also MTCW
See also SATA 42, 47
Arnow, L(eslie) Earle 1909- 69-72
Arnsteen, Katy Keck 1934- 136
See also SATA 68
Arnstein, Flora Jacobi 1885- 5-8R
Arnstein, Helene S(olomon) 1915- 57-60
See also SATA 12
Arnstein, Walter L(eonard) 1930- CANR-23
Earlier sketches in CA 13-16R, CANR-5
Arntson, Herbert E(dward) 1911- 17-20R
See also SATA 12
Arny, Mary (Travis) 1909- 61-64
Arny, Thomas Travis 1940- 85-88
Aron, Jean-Paul 1925(?)-1988 Obituary 126
Aron, Raymond (Claude Ferdinand)
1905-1983 ....CANR-2
Obituary 111
Earlier sketch in CA 49-52
Aron, Robert 1898-1975 93-96
Obituary 57-60
Arond, Miriam 1955- 127
Aronfreed, Justin 1930- 25-28R
Aronin, Ben 1904-1980 Obituary 102
See also SATA 25
Aronoff, Myron J(oel) 1940- CANR-24
Earlier sketch in CA 107
Aronowitz, Stanley 1933- 131
Aronson, Alex 1912- 45-48
Aronson, Alvin 1928- 25-28R
Aronson, David 1894-1988 Obituary 126
Aronson, Elliot 1932- CANR-12
Earlier sketch in CA 33-36R
Aronson, Harvey 1929- 85-88
Aronson, I(rwin) Michael 1942- 137
Aronson, J(ay) Richard 1937- CANR-34
Earlier sketch in CA 81-84
Aronson, James (Allan) 1915-1988 ....29-32R
Obituary 126
Aronson, Joseph 1898- CAP-1
Earlier sketch in CA 19-20
Aronson, Marvin L. 1925- 41-44R
Aronson, Ronald 1938- 133
Aronson, Shlomo 1936- 73-76
Aronson, Theo 1930- CANR-25
Earlier sketches in CA 9-12R, CANR-4
Aronson, Virginia 1954- CANR-25
Earlier sketch in CA 108
Arora, Shirley (Lease) 1930- 1-4R
See also SATA 2
Aros, Andrew A(lexandre) 1944- 97-100
Arout, Gabriel 1909-1982 Obituary 106
Arozarena, Marcelino 1912- ....HW
Arp, Bill
See Smith, Charles Henry
Arp, Hans
See Arp, Jean
Arp, Jean 1887-1966 81-84
Obituary 25-28R
See also CLC 5
Arpad, Joseph J(ohn) 1937- 49-52
Arpel, Adrien
See Newman, Adrien Ann
Arps, Louisa Ward 1901-1986 Obituary 118

Arquette, Cliff(ord) 1905-1974 Obituary 53-56
Arrabal
See Arrabal, Fernando
See also CLC 2, 9, 18
Arrabal, Fernando 1932- CANR-15
Earlier sketch in CA 9-12R
See also Arrabal
See also CLC 58
Arre, Helen
See Ross, Zola Helen
Arre, John
See Holt, John (Robert)
Arreola, Juan Jose 1918- 131
Brief entry 113
See also DLB 113
See also HW
Arrick, Fran ....CLC 30
Arrighi, Mel 1933-1986 ....CANR-18
Obituary 120
Earlier sketches in CA 49-52, CANR-1
Arrington, Leonard J(ames) 1917- CANR-30
Earlier sketches in CA 17-20R, CANR-9
Arriola, Gus 1917- 129
Arrow, Kenneth J(oseph) 1921- CANR-13
Earlier sketch in CA 13-16R
Arroway, Francis M.
See Rosmond, Babette
Arrowood, (McKendrick Lee) Clinton
1939- ....SATA 19
Arrowsmith, Marvin Lawrence
1913- Brief entry 116
Arrowsmith, Pat 1930- 101
See also Barton, Pat
Arrowsmith, William Ayres 1924-1992 .....CANR-4
Obituary 136
Earlier sketch in CA 9-12R
Arroyo, Antonio M. Stevens
See Stevens-Arroyo, Antonio M.
Arroyo, Stephen J(oseph) 1946- 61-64
Arrufat, Anton B. 1935- ....HW
Art, Robert (Jeffrey) 1942- 65-68
Artaud, Antonin 1896-1948 Brief entry 104
See also TCLC 3, 36
Arteaga, Lucio 1924- 49-52
Arteaga, William De
See De Arteaga, William
Artel, Jorge 1909- ....HW
Artes, Dorothy Beecher 1919- 57-60
Arther, Richard O. 1928- 17-20R
Arthos, John 1908- 9-12R
Arthur, Alan
See Edmonds, Arthur Denis
Arthur, Anthony 1937- 119
Arthur, Art(hur) 1911-1985 Obituary 116
Arthur, Burt
See Shappiro, Herbert (Arthur)
Arthur, Don(ald) R(amsay) 1917-1984 ......29-32R
Obituary 114
Arthur, Elizabeth 1953- CANR-21
Earlier sketch in CA 105
Arthur, Eric (Ross) 1898-1982 Obituary 112
Arthur, Frank
See Ebert, Arthur Frank
Arthur, George
See Phillips, Bluebell Stewart
Arthur, Gladys
See Osborne, Dorothy (Gladys) Yeo
Arthur, Herbert
See Shappiro, Herbert (Arthur)
Arthur, Hugh
See Christie-Murray, David (Hugh Arthur)
Arthur, Kay L(ee) 1932- 118
Arthur, Lee 122
Arthur, Martin (Forest) 1951- 116
Arthur, Max 1939- 121
Arthur, Percy E. 1910- CAP-1
Earlier sketch in CA 9-10
Arthur, Robert
See Feder, Robert Arthur
Arthur, Ruth M(abel) 1905-1979 ....CANR-4
Obituary 85-88
Earlier sketch in CA 9-12R
See also CLC 12
See also SATA 7, 26
Arthur, Thomas H. 1937- 122
Arthur, Tiffany
See Pelton, Robert W(ayne)
Arthur, Timothy Shay 1809-1885 .....DLB 3, 42, 79
Arthur, Tom
See Arthur, Thomas H.
Arthur, William
See Neubauer, William Arthur
Arthurs, Peter 1933- 106
Artin, Thomas 1938- Brief entry 116
Artin, Tom
See Artin, Thomas
Artis, Vicki Kimmel 1945- 53-56
See also SATA 12
Artmann, H(ans) C(arl) 1921- 101
See also DLB 85
Artobolevsky, Ivan I. 1905-1977 Obituary 73-76
Artom, Guido 1906-1982 ....CANR-12
Earlier sketch in CA 29-32R
Arts, Herwig (W. J.) 1935- CANR-32
Earlier sketch in CA 113
Artsybashev, Mikhail (Petrovich)
1878-1927 ....TCLC 31
Artz, Frederick B(inkerd) 1894-1983 ......CANR-18
Earlier sketch in CA 1-4R
Artzybasheff, Boris (Miklailovich)
1899-1965 ....SATA 14
Aruego, Ariane
See Dewey, Ariane
Aruego, Jose 37-40R
See also CLR 5
See also MAICYA
See also SATA 6, 68
Arundale, G. S.
See Arundale, George S(ydney)
Arundale, George S(ydney)
1878-1945 Brief entry 119
Arundel, Honor (Morfydd) 1919-1973 .... CAP-2
Obituary 41-44R
Earlier sketch in CA 21-22
See also CLC 17
See also SATA 4, 24
Arundel, Jocelyn
See Alexander, Jocelyn Anne Arundel
Arundel, Russell M. 1903-1978 Obituary 77-80
Arundell, Dennis Drew 1898-1988 Obituary 127
Aruri, Naseer H. 113
Arvay, Harry 1925- CANR-8
Earlier sketch in CA 57-60
Arvay, Stephen 1937- 114
Arvill, Robert
See Boote, Robert Edward
Arvin, Kay K(rehbiel) 1922- 65-68
Arvin, (Frederic) Newton (Jr.)
1900-1963 Obituary 116
See also DLB 103
Arvio, Raymond Paavo 1930-1986 77-80
Obituary 120
Ary, Donald E(ugene) 1930- 41-44R
Ary, Sheila M(ary Littleboy) 1929- 13-16R
Arya, Usharbudh 1934- 105
Arzhak, Nikolai
See Daniel, Yuli (Markovich)
Arzoomanian, Raffi
See Arzoomanian, Ralph Sarkis
Arzoomanian, Ralph Sarkis 1937- 118
Arzt, Max 1897-1975 Obituary 61-64
Asals, Frederick (John) 1935- 124
Asamani, Joseph Owusu 1934- 49-52
Asante, Molefi K(ete) 1942- CANR-21
Earlier sketch in CA 33-36R
Asare, Bediako
See Konadu, S(amuel) A(sare)
Asare, Meshack (Yaw) 1945- CANR-11
Earlier sketch in CA 61-64
Asbell, Bernard 1923- CANR-25
Earlier sketches in CA 45-48, CANR-1
Asbjoernsen, Peter Christen
1812-1885 .... MAICYA
See also SATA 15
Asbury, Herbert 1891-1963 Obituary 116
Ascani, Sparky (Wilson) 1922- 111
Asch, Frank 1946- 41-44R
See also SATA 5, 66
Asch, Nathan 1902-1964 109
See also DLB 4, 28
Asch, Peter 1937-1990 133
Brief entry 114
Asch, Sholem 1880-1957 Brief entry 105
See also TCLC 3
Aschan, Ulf 1937- 138
Ascheim, Skip 1943- 53-56
Ascher, Abraham 1928- 81-84
Ascher, Barbara Lazear 1946(?)- 138
Brief entry 130
Ascher, Carol 1941- CANR-29
Earlier sketch in CA 105
Ascher, Kate (J.) 1958- 128
Ascher, Sheila CANR-23
Earlier sketch in CA 105
Ascher/Straus
See Ascher, Sheila
and Straus, Dennis
Ascher, William (Louis) 1947- 114
Ascherson, Neal 1932- 13-16R
Aschmann, Alberta 1921- CANR-7
Earlier sketch in CA 13-16R
Aschmann, Helen Tann 13-16R
Ascoli, Max 1898-1978 Obituary 77-80
Ash, Anthony Lee 1931- CANR-3
Earlier sketch in CA 49-52
Ash, Bernard 1910- CAP-1
Earlier sketch in CA 19-20
Ash, Brian 1936- Brief entry 114
Ash, Christopher (Edward) 1914- 1-4R
Ash, David W(ilfred) 1923- 9-12R
Ash, Douglas 1914- CANR-2
Earlier sketch in CA 5-8R
Ash, John 1948- 127
Brief entry 123
See also DLB 40
Ash, Jutta 1942- ....SATA 38
Ash, Lee (Michael) 1917- 110
Ash, Mary Kay (Wagner) 112
Ash, Maurice Anthony 1917- 101
Ash, Rene Lee 1939- 57-60
Ash, Roberta
See Garner, Roberta
Ash, Sarah Leeds 1904- CAP-1
Earlier sketch in CA 9-10
Ash, Shalom
See Asch, Sholem
Ash, William Franklin 1917- CANR-18
Earlier sketches in CA 5-8R, CANR-2
Ashabranner, Brent (Kenneth) 1921- CANR-27
Earlier sketches in CA 5-8R, CANR-10
See also AAYA 6
See also CLR 28
See also MAICYA
See also SAAS 14
See also SATA 1, 67
Ashabranner, Melissa 1950- 134
Ashbaugh, Nancy 1929- 73-76
Ashbee, Paul 1918- 93-96
Ashbery, John (Lawrence) 1927- CANR-37
Earlier sketches in CA 5-8R, CANR-9
See also CLC 2, 3, 4, 6, 9, 13, 15, 25, 41
See also DLB 5
See also DLBY 81
See also MTCW
Ashbolt, Allan Campbell 1921- 104
Ashbrook, James B(arbour) 1925- CANR-31
Earlier sketches in CA 37-40R, CANR-14
Ashbrook, Joseph 1918-1980 122
Obituary 117
Ashbrook, William (Sinclair) 1922- 29-32R
Ashburne, Jim G. 1912- 1-4R
Ashby, Carter
See Paine, Lauran (Bosworth)
Ashby, Cliff 1919- 25-28R
See also CAAS 6
Ashby, Eric 1904- 61-64
Ashby, Gwynneth 1922- 25-28R
See also SATA 44
Ashby, LaVerne 1922- 21-24R
Ashby, (Darrel) LeRoy 1938- 33-36R
Ashby, Lloyd W. 1905- 89-92
Ashby, Lynn 1938- 127
Ashby, Neal 1924- 89-92
Ashby, Nora
See Africano, Lillian
Ashby, Philip Harrison 1916- 17-20R
Ashcraft, Allan Coleman 1928- 9-12R
Ashcraft, Laura 1945- 107
Ashcraft, Laurie
See Ashcraft, Laura
Ashcraft, Morris 1922- 45-48
Ashcroft, John (David) 1942- 112
Ashdown, Clifford
See Freeman, R(ichard) Austin
Ashdown, Dulcie M(argaret) 1946- 122
Brief entry 112
Ashdown, Paul G(eorge) 1944- 119
Ashe, Arthur (R. Jr.) 1943- CANR-35
Earlier sketches in CA 65-68, CANR-18
See also SATA 65
Ashe, Douglas
See Bardin, John Franklin
Ashe, Geoffrey (Thomas) 1923- CANR-31
Earlier sketches in CA 5-8R, CANR-12
See also SATA 17
Ashe, Gerald C. 1924(?)-1984 Obituary 112
Ashe, Gordon
See Creasey, John
Ashe, Mary Ann
See Lewis, Mary (Christianna)
Ashe, Penelope
See Greene, Robert W.
and Karman, Mal
and Young, Billie
Asheim, Lester E(ugene) 1914- 17-20R
Ashenfelter, David L. 1948- 108
Ashenfelter, Orley C(lark) 1942- CANR-8
Earlier sketch in CA 61-64
Asher, Don 1926- 73-76
Asher, Harry (Maurice Felix) 1909- CANR-2
Earlier sketch in CA 5-8R
Asher, Jane 1946- 133
Asher, John A(lexander) 1921- 21-24R
Asher, Maxine 1930- 105
Asher, Miriam
See Mundis, Hester
Asher, Robert Eller 1910- 61-64
Asher, Robert 1944- 111
Asher, Sandra Fenichel 1942- CANR-22
Earlier sketch in CA 105
See also Asher, Sandy
See also MAICYA
Asher, Sandy
See Asher, Sandra Fenichel
See also DLBY 83
See also SAAS 13
See also SATA 34, 36, 71
Asheron, Sara
See Moore, Lilian
Ashey, Bella
See Breinburg, Petronella
Ashford, Daisy
See Ashford, Margaret Mary
Ashford, Douglas E(lliott) 1928- CANR-37
Earlier sketches in CA 73-76, CANR-16
Ashford, Gerald 1907- 41-44R
Ashford, Janet Isaacs 1949- 113
Ashford, Jeffrey
See Jeffries, Roderic (Graeme)
Ashford, Margaret Mary
1881-1972 Obituary 33-36R
See also SATA 10
Ashford, Nicholas 1943(?)-1990 Obituary 130
Ashford, Nigel (John Gladwell) 1952- 137
Ashford, (H.) Ray 1926- 65-68
Ashford, Theodore Askounes
1908-1987 Obituary 122
Ashihara Yoshinobu 1918- 129
Ashkenazy, Vladimir D(avidovich) 1937- 137
Ashley, A.
See Aasheim, Ashley
Ashley, Bernard 1935- CANR-25
Earlier sketch in CA 93-96
See also CLR 4
See also MAICYA
See also SATA 39, 47
Ashley, Elizabeth
See Salmon, Annie Elizabeth
Ashley, (Arthur) Ernest 1906- CAP-1
Earlier sketch in CA 13-16
Ashley, Franklin 1942- CANR-1
Earlier sketch in CA 45-48
Ashley, Graham
See Organ, John
Ashley, Jack 1922- 106
Ashley, Leonard R(aymond) N(elligan)
1928- CANR-24
Earlier sketches in CA 13-16R, CANR-9
Ashley, Maurice (Percy) 1907- 41-44R
Ashley, Michael (Raymond Donald)
1948- CANR-30
Earlier sketches in CA 69-72, CANR-13
Ashley, Nova Trimble 1911- 65-68
Ashley, Paul P(ritchard) 1896-1979 ....CANR-10
Obituary 85-88
Earlier sketch in CA 21-24R
Ashley, Perry J(onathan) 1928- 120
Ashley, Ray
See Abrashkin, Raymond
Ashley, Robert P(aul) Jr. 1915- 17-20R
Ashley, Rosalind Minor 1923- 69-72
Ashley, Sally 1935- 109
Ashley, Steven
See McCaig, Donald
Ashley-Montagu, Montague Francis
See Montagu, Ashley
Ashlin, John
See Cutforth, John Ashlin
Ashlock, Patrick (Robert) 1937- 61-64
Ashlock, Robert B. 1930- CANR-28
Earlier sketches in CA 29-32R, CANR-12
Ashman, Howard (Elliott) 1950-1991 131
Obituary 133
Brief entry 122
Ashmead, John Jr. 1917-1992 ....CANR-28
Obituary 136
Earlier sketch in CA 1-4R
Ashmole, Bernard 1894-1988 106
Obituary 124
Ashmore, Harry S(cott) 1916- 13-16R
Ashmore, Jerome 1901- CAP-2
Earlier sketch in CA 33-36
Ashmore, Lewis
See Raborg, Frederick A(shton) Jr.
Ashmore, Owen 1920- 106
Ashner, Sonie Shapiro 1938- 57-60
Ashryn, Veryl M. 1948- 119
Ashton, Ann
See Kimbro, John M.
Ashton, Dore 1928- CANR-30
Earlier sketches in CA 5-8R, CANR-2
Ashton, (Arthur) Leigh (Bolland)
1897-1983 Obituary 114
Ashton, Robert 1924- CANR-3
Earlier sketch in CA 1-4R
Ashton, Rosemary 1947- 138
Ashton, Sharon
See Van Slyke, Helen (Lenore)
Ashton, (Margery) Violet 1908- 73-76
Ashton, Warren T.
See Adams, William Taylor
Ashton, Winifred 1888-1965 Obituary 93-96
See also Dane, Clemence
Ashton-Warner, Sylvia (Constance)
1908-1984 ....CANR-29
Obituary 112
Earlier sketch in CA 69-72
See also CLC 19
See also MTCW
Ashworth, Kenneth H(ayden) 1932- 41-44R
Ashworth, Mary Wells Knight 1903- 5-8R
Ashworth, Wilfred 1912- 13-16R
Ashworth, (Lewis) William 1942- 133
Ashworth, William 1920-1991 ....5-8R
Obituary 134
Asimov, Isaac 1920- CANR-36
Obituary 137
Earlier sketches in CA 1-4R, CANR-2, 19
See also BEST 90:2
See also CLC 1, 3, 9, 19, 26
See also CLR 12
See also DLB 8
See also MAICYA
See also MTCW
See also SATA 1, 26
Asimov, Janet (Jeppson) 1926- CANR-36
Asin, Alfredo Quispez
See Moro, Cesar
Asin, Cesar Quispez
See Moro, Cesar
Asinof, Eliot 1919- CANR-7
Earlier sketch in CA 9-12R
See also SATA 6
Aska, Warabe
See Masuda, Takeshi
See also SATA 56
Askari, Hussaini Muhammad
See Pereira, Harold Bertram
Askenasy, Hans George 1930- 77-80
Askew, Jack
See Hivnor, Robert
Askew, Thomas A(delbert Jr.) 1931- 130
Askew, William C(larence) 1910- 49-52
Askham, Francis
See Greenwood, Julia Eileen Courtney
Askin, A. Bradley 1943- 73-76
Askin, Alma 1911- 57-60
Askin, I(da) Jayne 1940- 109
Askwith, Betty Ellen 1909- CANR-13
Earlier sketch in CA 61-64
Askwith, Herbert 1889-1985 Obituary 117
Brief entry 113
Aslanapa, Oktay 1914- 37-40R
Aslet, Clive (William) 1955- CANR-32
Earlier sketch in CA 113
Aslin, Elizabeth (Mary) 1923-1989 Obituary 128
Asman, David 1954- 127
Aspaturian, Vernon V. 1922- 105
Aspel, Michael (Terence) 1933- Brief entry 117
Aspell, Patrick J(oseph) 1930- 25-28R
Aspin, Les 1938- 108
Aspinall, (Honor) Ruth (Alastair) 1922- CANR-2
Earlier sketch in CA 5-8R
Aspinwall, Dorothy B(rown) 1910- 49-52
Aspiz, Harold 1921- 105

Aspler, Tony 1939- CANR-25
Earlier sketch in CA 105
Asprey, Robert B. 1923- CANR-6
Earlier sketch in CA 5-8R
Asprin, Robert Lynn 1946- 85-88
Aspy, David N(athanial) 1930- CANR-20
Earlier sketch in CA 45-48
Asquith, Cynthia Mary Evelyn (Charteris)
1887-1960 Obituary 110
Asquith, Glenn Hackney 1904- CANR-16
Earlier sketches in CA 1-4R, CANR-1
Asquith, Nan
See Pattinson, Nancy Evelyn
Asquith, Stewart 1948- 116
Assael, Henry 1935- 41-44R
Assagioli, Roberto 1893(?)-1974 Obituary 53-56
Asselbroke, Archibald Algernon 1923- 77-80
Asselin, E(dward) Donald 1903-1970 ....CAP-1
Earlier sketch in CA 11-12
Asselin, Olivar 1874-1937 ....DLB 92
Asselineau, Roger (Maurice) 1915- CANR-26
Earlier sketch in CA 97-100
Assensoh, A(kwasi) B(retuo) 1946(?)- 120
Assiac
See Fraenkel, Heinrich
Astaire, Fred 1899-1987 Obituary 122
Aster, Sidney 1942- CANR-10
Earlier sketch in CA 65-68
Astier, Pierre A(rthur) G(eorges)
1927- CANR-20
Earlier sketch in CA 45-48
Astill, Kenneth N. 1923- 53-56
Astin, Alexander W(illiam) 1932- CANR-28
Earlier sketches in CA 17-20R, CANR-7
Astin, Helen S(tavridou) 1932- CANR-28
Earlier sketch in CA 29-32R
Astin, Patty Duke
See Duke, Anna Marie
Astiz, Carlos A. 1933- 25-28R
Astley, Joan Bright 1910- 33-36R
Astley, Juliet
See Lofts, Norah (Robinson)
Astley, Neil 1953- 132
Astley, Thea (Beatrice May) 1925- CANR-11
Earlier sketch in CA 65-68
See also CLC 41
Aston, Athina (Leka) 1934- 117
Aston, James
See White, T(erence) H(anbury)
Aston, Margaret 1932- 73-76
Aston, Michael (Anthony) 1946- 61-64
Aston, Trevor Henry 1925-1985 Obituary 118
Astor, (Francis) David (Langhorne)
1912- Brief entry 113
Astor, Gavin 1918-1984 Obituary 113
Astor, Gerald (Morton) 1926- CANR-24
Earlier sketch in CA 107
Astor, Mary 1906-1987 ....CANR-3
Obituary 123
Earlier sketch in CA 5-8R
Astor, Michael Langhorne 1916-1980 61-64
Obituary 97-100
Astor, Susan 1946- 105
Astrachan, Samuel 1934- 69-72
Astro, Richard 1941- CANR-27
Earlier sketch in CA 29-32R
Asturias, Miguel Angel 1899-1974 ....CANR-32
Obituary 49-52
Earlier sketches in CAP-2, CA 25-28
See also CLC 3, 8, 13
See also DLB 113
See also HW
See also MTCW
Aswad, Betsy (Becker) 1939- CANR-25
Earlier sketch in CA 104
Aswell, Mary Louise 1902-1984 Obituary 114
Aswin
See Nandakumar, Prema
Atamian, David 1892(?)-1978 Obituary 81-84
Atares, Carlos Saura
See Saura (Atares), Carlos
Atcheson, Richard 1934- 29-32R
Atchison, Sandra Dallas 1939- CANR-10
Earlier sketch in CA 17-20R
Atchity, Kenneth John 1944- CANR-16
Earlier sketches in CA 49-52, CANR-1
Atchley, Bob
See Atchley, Robert C.
Atchley, Dana W(inslow) 1941- 61-64
Atchley, Robert C. 1939- CANR-1
Earlier sketch in CA 45-48
Atene, Ann
See Atene, (Rita) Anna
Atene, (Rita) Anna 1922- ....SATA 12
Athanassiadis, Nikos 1904- CANR-17
Earlier sketch in CA 33-36R
Athans, George (Stanley) Jr. 1952- 104
Athas, Daphne 1923- CANR-3
Earlier sketch in CA 1-4R
Athay, R(obert) E. 1925- 33-36R
Athearn, Robert G(reenleaf) 1914- CANR-3
Earlier sketch in CA 1-4R
Atheling, William
See Pound, Ezra (Weston Loomis)
Atheling, William Jr.
See Blish, James (Benjamin)
Atherton, Alexine 1930- 37-40R
Atherton, Gertrude (Franklin Horn)
1857-1948 Brief entry 104
See also DLB 9, 78
See also TCLC 2
Atherton, James C(hristian) 1915- 49-52
Atherton, James S(tephen) 1910- CAP-1
Earlier sketch in CA 13-16
Atherton, Lewis E. 1905- 1-4R
Atherton, Lucius
See Masters, Edgar Lee
Atherton, Maxine 5-8R
Atherton, Pauline
See Cochrane, Pauline A(therton)
Atherton, Sarah
See Bridgman, Sarah Atherton
Atherton, Wallace N(ewman) 1927- 49-52
Athey, Irene J(owett) 1919- 61-64
Athill, Diana 1917- CANR-2
Earlier sketch in CA 1-4R
Athlone, Countess of
See Alice (Mary Victoria Augusta Pauline), Princess
Atholl, Desmond 1956- 134
Athos
See Walkerley, Rodney Lewis (de Burgh)
Athos, Anthony G(eorge) 1934- CANR-19
Earlier sketch in CA 25-28R
Atil, Esin 1938- CANR-32
Earlier sketch in CA 113
Atiya, Aziz S. 1898- 5-8R
Atiya, Nayra 1943- 128
Atiyah, P(atrick) S(elim) 1931- 37-40R
Atiyeh, George N(icholas) 1923- 57-60
Atkeson, Roy A. 1907-1990 ....CANR-11
Obituary 131
Earlier sketch in CA 69-72
Atkey, Philip 1908-1985 Obituary 118
Brief entry 112
Atkin, Flora B(lumenthal) 1919- CANR-37
Earlier sketches in CA 93-96, CANR-16
Atkin, J. Myron 1927- 45-48
Atkin, Mary Gage 1929- 81-84
Atkin, William Wilson
1912(?)-1976 Obituary 65-68
Atkins, Burton M(ark) 1944- Brief entry 115
Atkins, Chester Burton 1924- Brief entry 113
Atkins, Chester G(reenough) 1948- 45-48
Atkins, Chet
See Atkins, Chester Burton
Atkins, E(dward) Wulstan 1904- 128
Atkins, G(eorge) Douglas 1943- 114
Atkins, G(eorge) Pope 1934- CANR-17
Earlier sketch in CA 33-36R
Atkins, Gary 1949- 126
Atkins, (Arthur) Harold 1910- 105
Atkins, Harry 1933- 25-28R
Atkins, Hedley (John Barnard)
1905-1983 Obituary 111
Atkins, Jack
See Harris, Mark
Atkins, James G. 1932- 17-20R
Atkins, Jim
See Atkins, James G.
Atkins, John (Alfred) 1916- CANR-19
Earlier sketches in CA 9-12R, CANR-3
Atkins, Josiah 1755(?)-1781 ....DLB 31
Atkins, Kenneth R(obert) 1920- 73-76
Atkins, Meg Elizabeth 102
Atkins, Oliver F. 1916-1977 73-76
Atkins, Ollie
See Atkins, Oliver F.
Atkins, P(eter) W(illiam) 1940- 117
Atkins, Paul Moody 1892-1977 Obituary 69-72
Atkins, Robert C(oleman) 1930- 128
Atkins, Russell 1926- CANR-25
Earlier sketches in CA 45-48, CANR-1
See also CAAS 16
See also BW
See also DLB 41
Atkins, Stuart (Pratt) 1914- 25-28R
Atkins, Thomas R(adcliffe) 1939- CANR-8
Earlier sketch in CA 61-64
Atkinson, Allen G.
1953(?)-1987 ....SATA 46, 55, 60
Atkinson, Anthony Barnes 1944- CANR-11
Earlier sketch in CA 69-72
Atkinson, Basil F(erris) C(ampbell) 1895- 5-8R
Atkinson, (Justin) Brooks 1894-1984 ....CANR-14
Obituary 111
Earlier sketch in CA 61-64
Atkinson, Carroll (Holloway) 1896- CAP-1
Earlier sketch in CA 13-16
Atkinson, David J(ohn) 1943- 107
Atkinson, Frank 1922- 108
Atkinson, Geoffrey 1955- 118
Atkinson, Hugh C(raig) 1933-1986 ....CANR-28
Obituary 120
Earlier sketch in CA 49-52
Atkinson, James B(lakely) 1934- 119
Atkinson, James 1914- 25-28R
Atkinson, Jennifer (Elizabeth) McCabe
1937- Brief entry 116
Atkinson, John W(illiam) 1923- CANR-11
Earlier sketch in CA 21-24R
Atkinson, Linda 1941- 135
Atkinson, M. E.
See Frankau, Mary Evelyn Atkinson
Atkinson, Margaret Fleming 73-76
See also SATA 14
Atkinson, Mary
See Hardwick, Mollie
Atkinson, Phillip S. 1921- 25-28R
Atkinson, R(ichard) C(hatham) 1929- 17-20R
Atkinson, Rick 1952- 133
See also BEST 90:2
Atkinson, Ron 1932- 57-60
Atkinson, Ronald Field 1928- 17-20R
Atkinson, W. W.
See Atkinson, William Walker
Atkinson, Walter S(ydney)
1891-1978 Obituary 73-76
Atkinson, William Christopher 1902- 109
Atkinson, William Walker
1862-1932 Brief entry 120
Atkisson, Arthur A(lbert Jr.) 1930- 61-64
Atkyns, Glenn C(hadwick) 1921- 49-52
Atlas, Helen Vincent 1931- 101
Atlas, James (Robert) 1949- 138
Atlas, Martin 1914- 5-8R
Atlas, Samuel 1899-1977 Obituary 73-76
Atmore, Anthony 1932- 25-28R
Attanasio, A(lfred) A(ngelo) 1951- 137
Attaway, Robert J(oseph) 1942- 49-52
Attaway, William 1911-1986 ....BLC 1
See also DLB 76
Attea, Mary
See Spahn, Mary Attea
Atteberry, William L(ouis) 1939- 53-56
Attenborough, Bernard George CANR-2
Earlier sketch in CA 49-52
Attenborough, David (Frederick)
1926- CANR-30
Earlier sketches in CA 1-4R, CANR-6
Attenborough, John 1908- 101
Attenborough, Richard (Samuel)
1923- Brief entry 127
Atterton, Julian (Harold) 1956- 122
Attfield, Robin 137
Atthill, Robin 1912- 69-72
Atticus
See Davies, Hunter
and Fleming, Ian (Lancaster)
and Pawle, Gerald Strachan
Attiyeh, Richard E. 1937- Brief entry 113
Attlee, C. R.
See Attlee, Clement R(ichard)
Attlee, Clement R(ichard)
1883-1967 Obituary 112
Attneave, Carolyn L(ewis) 1920- CANR-1
Earlier sketch in CA 45-48
Attridge, Derek 1945- 105
Attwell, Arthur A(lbert) 1917- 49-52
Attwood, William (Hollingsworth)
1919-1989 ....21-24R
Obituary 128
Atwater, C(onstance) Elizabeth (Sullivan)
1923- 13-16R
Atwater, Eastwood 1925- 110
Atwater, Florence (Hasseltine Carroll)
1896-1979 135
See also CLR 19
See also MAICYA
See also SATA 16, 66
Atwater, James David 1928- 101
Atwater, Lynn 1935- 111
Atwater, Montgomery Meigs 1904- 73-76
See also SATA 15
Atwater, P(hyllis) M. H. 1937- 133
Atwater, Richard (Tupper) 1892-1948 135
Brief entry 111
See also CLR 19
See also MAICYA
See also SATA 27, 54, 66
Atwood, Ann (Margaret) 1913- 41-44R
See also SATA 7
Atwood, Drucy
See Morrison, Eula Atwood
Atwood, Margaret (Eleanor) 1939- CANR-33
Earlier sketches in CA 49-52, CANR-3, 24
See also BEST 89:2
See also CLC 2, 3, 4, 8, 13, 15, 25, 44
See also DLB 53
See also MTCW
See also SATA 50
See also SSC 2
See also WLC
Atwood, Robert B. ....AITN 2
Atyeo, Don 1950- 93-96
Auberjonois, Fernand 1910- 77-80
Aubert, Alvin (Bernard) 1930- CANR-26
Earlier sketch in CA 81-84
See also BW
See also DLB 41
Aubert, Rosemary 1946- 113
Aubert de Gaspe, Philippe-Ignace-Francois
1814-1841 ....DLB 99
Aubert de Gaspe, Philippe-Joseph
1786-1871 ....DLB 99
Aubery, Pierre 1920- 37-40R
Aubey, Robert T(haddeus) 1930- 21-24R
Aubigny, Pierre d'
See Mencken, H(enry) L(ouis)
Aubin, Henry (Trocme) 1942- 77-80
Aubin, Napoleon 1812-1890 ....DLB 99
Aubin, Penelope 1685-1731(?) ....DLB 39
Aubrey, Crispin 1946- 129
Aubrey-Fletcher, Henry Lancelot
1887-1969 Obituary 111
See also Wade, Henry
Aubry, Claude B. 1914-1984 106
See also SATA 29, 40
Auburn, Mark Stuart 1945- 89-92
Auchincloss, Louis (Stanton) 1917- CANR-29
Earlier sketches in CA 1-4R, CANR-6
See also CLC 4, 6, 9, 18, 45
See also DLB 2
See also DLBY 80
See also MTCW
Auchmuty, James Johnston 1909-1981 101
Obituary 109
Auchterlonie, Dorothy
See Green, Dorothy (Auchterlonie)
Auclair, Joan 1960- ....SATA 68
Audax
See Oaksey, John
Audemars, Pierre 1909- CANR-7
Earlier sketch in CA 17-20R
Auden, Renee
See West, Uta
Auden, W(ystan) H(ugh) 1907-1973 ....CANR-5
Obituary 45-48
Earlier sketch in CA 9-12R
See also CDBLB 1914-1945
See also CLC 1, 2, 3, 4, 6, 9, 11, 14, 43
See also DLB 10, 20
See also MTCW
See also PC 1
See also WLC
Audi, Robert (N.) 1941- 123
Audiard, Michel 1920-1985 Obituary 116
Audiberti, Jacques 1900-1965 Obituary 25-28R
See also CLC 38
Auel, Jean M(arie) 1936- CANR-21
Earlier sketch in CA 103
See also AAYA 7
See also BEST 90:4
See also CLC 31
Auer, J(ohn) Jeffery 1913- CANR-6
Earlier sketch in CA 9-12R
Auer, James M(atthew) 1928- 133
Auerbach, Aline B.
See Auerbach, Aline Sophie (Buchman)
Auerbach, Aline Sophie (Buchman)
1899(?)-1985 Obituary 116
Auerbach, Arnold (Jacob) 1917- 131
Auerbach, Arnold M. 1912- 17-20R
Auerbach, Erich 1892-1957 Brief entry 118
See also TCLC 43
Auerbach, Erna Obituary 61-64
Auerbach, George
1905(?)-1973 Obituary 45-48
Auerbach, Jerold S(tephen) 1936- 21-24R
Auerbach, Jessica (Lynn) 1947- 114
Auerbach, Marjorie (Hoffberg) 9-12R
Auerbach, Nina 1943- CANR-34
Earlier sketches in CA 85-88, CANR-15
Auerbach, Red
See Auerbach, Arnold (Jacob)
Auerbach, Stevanne 1938- CANR-24
Earlier sketches in CA 57-60, CANR-8
Auerbach, Stuart C(harles) 1935- 89-92
Auerbach, Sylvia CANR-4
Earlier sketch in CA 53-56
Auernheimer, Raoul 1876-1948 ....DLB 81
Auf der Maur, Nick 1942- 129
Aufricht, Hans 1902- 45-48
Augarde, Steve 1950- CANR-21
Earlier sketch in CA 104
See also SATA 25
Augarde, Tony 1936- 118
Augarten, Stan 1952- 115
Auge, Bud
See Auge, Henry J. Jr.
Auge, Henry J. Jr. 1930(?)-1983 Obituary 109
Augelli, John P(at) 1921- 17-20R
See also SATA 46
Aughtry, Charles Edward 1925- 5-8R
Augsburger, A(aron) Don(ald) 1925- 21-24R
Augsburger, David W. 1938- CANR-13
Earlier sketch in CA 33-36R
Augsburger, Myron S. 1929- CANR-6
Earlier sketch in CA 13-16R
Augspurger, Everett F.
1904(?)-1986 Obituary 118
Augstein, Rudolf (Karl) 1923- 110
Auguet, Roland (Jacques) 1935- 105
August, Eugene R(obert) 1935- CANR-27
Earlier sketch in CA 49-52
August, John
See De Voto, Bernard (Augustine)
Augustin, Ann Sutherland 1934- 57-60
Augustin, Pius 1934- 17-20R
Augustine, Erich
See Stoil, Michael Jon
Augustine, Mildred
See Benson, Mildred (Augustine Wirt)
Augustine, Norman R(alph) 1935- 121
Augustine 354-430 ....DLB 115
Augustson, Ernest
See Ryden, Ernest Edwin
Augustus, Albert Jr.
See Nuetzel, Charles (Alexander)
Aukerman, Dale 1930- 112
Aukerman, Robert C. 1910- 33-36R
Aukofer, Frank A(lexander) 1935- 65-68
Auld, Rhoda L(andsman) 105
Auleta, Michael S. 1909- CAP-2
Earlier sketch in CA 25-28
Auletta, Ken 1942- CANR-12
Earlier sketch in CA 69-72
Auletta, Richard P(aul) 1942- 53-56
Auletta, Robert 1940- 119
Brief entry 115
Aulich, James 1952- 132
Aulicino, Armand 1920(?)-1983 Obituary 109
Aulick, June L. 1906- 25-28R
Ault, Donald D(uane) 1942- 81-84
Ault, Phil
See Ault, Phillip H(alliday)
Ault, Phillip H(alliday) 1914- CANR-18
Earlier sketch in CA 101
See also SATA 23
Ault, Rosalie Sain 1942- 107
See also SATA 38
Ault, Roz
See Ault, Rosalie Sain
Aultman, Donald S. 1930- 17-20R
Aultman, Richard E(ugene) 1933- CANR-9
Earlier sketch in CA 65-68
Aumann, Francis R(obert) 1901- 41-44R
Aumbry, Alan
See Bayley, Barrington J(ohn)
Aumont, Jean-Pierre 1913- 29-32R
Aune, Bruce (Arthur) 1933- 73-76

Aung, (Maung) Htin 1909- CANR-3
Earlier sketch in CA 5-8R
See also SATA 21
Aunger, Edmund A(lexander) 1949- 112
Auntie Deb
See Coury, Louise Andree
Auntie Louise
See Coury, Louise Andree
Aurand, Harold Wilson 1940- 41-44R
Aurand, L(eonard) W(illiam) 1920- 53-56
Aurandt, Paul (Harvey II) 1948- 129
Aurandt, Paul Harvey 1918- 102
Aurelio, John R. 1937- CANR-28
Earlier sketch in CA 111
Aurelius
See Bourne, Randolph S(illiman)
Aurell, Tage 1895-1976 Obituary 113
Aurner, Robert R(ay) 1898- 5-8R
Aurthur, Robert Alan 1922-1978 ....CANR-34
Earlier sketch in CA 81-84
Ausland, John C(ampbell) 1920- 93-96
Auslander, Audrey (May) Wurdemann
1911-1960 Obituary 116
Auslander, Joseph 1897-1965 Obituary 116
Ausmus, Harry Jack 1937- 115
Austen, Jane 1775-1817 .... CDBLB 1789-1832
See also DLB 116
See also WLC
Austen, Michael (Edward) 1951- 109
Austen, Ralph A. 1937- 25-28R
Auster, Nancy (Eileen) R(oss) 1926- 65-68
Auster, Paul 1947- CANR-23
Earlier sketch in CA 69-72
See also CLC 47
Austerlitz, Robert Paul 1923- 111
Austerman, Wayne R. 1948- 122
Austgen, Robert Joseph 1932- 21-24R
Austin, Alfred 1835-1913 ....DLB 35
Austin, Allan Edward 1929- 73-76
Austin, Allen 1922- 33-36R
Austin, Anthony 1919- 33-36R
Austin, (Mildred) Aurelia 53-56
Austin, Barbara Leslie
See Linton, Barbara Leslie
Austin, Brett
See Floren, Lee
Austin, Charles M(arshall) 1941- 69-72
Austin, David E(dwards) 1926- 29-32R
Austin, Elizabeth S. 1907- CAP-2
Earlier sketch in CA 25-28
See also SATA 5
Austin, Frank
See Faust, Frederick (Shiller)
Austin, Harry
See McInerny, Ralph
Austin, Henry Wilfred 1906- 101
Austin, James C(layton) 1923- 13-16R
Austin, James Henry 1925- 81-84
Austin, John Langshaw
1911-1960 Obituary 112
Austin, John 1922- 61-64
Austin, K(enneth) A(shurst) 1911- 102
Austin, Lettie J(ane) 1925- 65-68
Austin, Lewis 1936- 73-76
Austin, Lloyd James 1915- CAP-1
Earlier sketch in CA 13-14
Austin, M(ichel) M(ervyn) 1943- CANR-19
Earlier sketch in CA 85-88
Austin, Margot 1909(?)-1990 ....CAP-1
Obituary 132
Earlier sketch in CA 9-10
See also SATA 11
See also SATO 66
Austin, Mary C(arrington) 1915- 5-8R
Austin, Mary (Hunter)
1868-1934 Brief entry 109
See also DLB 9, 78
See also TCLC 25
Austin, Neal F(uller) 1926- 25-28R
Austin, (John) Norman 1937- 89-92
Austin, Oliver L(uther) Jr. 1903-1988 49-52
Obituary 127
See also SATA 7, 59
Austin, R. G.
See Gelman, Rita Golden
Austin, (Stewart) Reid 1931- 89-92
Austin, Richard B(uckner) Jr. 1930- 73-76
Austin, Stephen
See Stevens, Austin N(eil)
Austin, Timothy R(obert) 1952- 117
Austin, William W(eaver) 1920- 21-24R
Austin, William 1778-1841 ....DLB 74
Austwick, John
See Lee, Austin
Ausubel, Herman 1920-1977 ....1-4R
Obituary 69-72
Ausubel, Marynn H.
1913(?)-1980 Obituary 97-100
Auten, James H(udson) 1938- 41-44R
Auteur, Hillary
See Gottfried, Theodore Mark
Auth, Tony
See Auth, William Anthony Jr.
Auth, William Anthony Jr. 1942- 111
Brief entry 108
See also SATA 51
Autran Dourado, Waldomiro
See Dourado, (Waldomiro Freitas) Autran
Autrey, C. E. 1904- CANR-2
Earlier sketch in CA 1-4R
Autry, Ewart (Arthur) 1900- 13-16R
Autry, (Orvon) Gene 1907- Brief entry 112
Autry, James A(rthur) 1933- 135
Brief entry 115
Autton, Norman William James 1920- 101
Auty, Phyllis 1910- CANR-2
Earlier sketch in CA 5-8R
Auty, Robert 1914-1978 Obituary 111
Auvert, Elizabeth CANR-14
Earlier sketch in CA 37-40R
Auvil, Kenneth W(illiam) 1925- 17-20R
Avakian, Arra S(teve) 1912- 85-88
Avakumovic, Ivan 1926- 41-44R
Avalle-Arce, Juan Bautista de 1927- CANR-32
Earlier sketches in CA 33-36R, CANR-13
See also HW
Avallone, Michael (Angelo, Jr) 1924- CANR-39
Earlier sketches in CA 5-8R, CANR-4
Avalon, Arthur
See Woodroffe, John George
Avanzini, John F. 1936- 122
Avarius
See Stolk, Anthonie
Avedis, Hikmet 132
Avedis, Howard
See Avedis, Hikmet
Aveline, Claude 1901- CANR-6
Earlier sketch in CA 5-8R
Aveling, Hugh
See Aveling, J(ohn) C(edric) H(ugh)
Aveling, J(ohn) C(edric) H(ugh) 1917- 131
Avendano, Fausto 1941- 131
See also DLB 82
See also HW
Aveni, Anthony F(rancis) 1938- 81-84
Averbach, Albert 1902-1975 ....CAP-2
Earlier sketch in CA 21-22
Averill, E(dgar) W(aite) 1906-1980 53-56
Averill, Esther 1902- CANR-12
Earlier sketch in CA 29-32R
See also SATA 1, 28
Averill, James H(alsey) 1947- 129
Averill, John Hillier 1923-1984 Obituary 111
Averill, Lloyd J(ames) 1923- CANR-10
Earlier sketch in CA 21-24R
Averitt, Robert T(abor) 1931- 21-24R
Averroes 1126-1198 ....DLB 115
Avers, Charlotte J(o) 1926-1990 Obituary 131
Aversa, Elizabeth Smith 1946- 127
Avery, Al
See Montgomery, Rutherford George
Avery, Burniece 1908- 73-76
Avery, Catherine B(arber) 1909- 57-60
Avery, Edwina Austin 1896-1983 Obituary 110
Avery, George C(ostas) 1926- 25-28R
Avery, Gillian (Elise) 1926- CANR-4
Earlier sketch in CA 9-12R
See also MAICYA
See also SAAS 6
See also SATA 7
Avery, Ira 1914- 81-84
Avery, James S. 1923- 126
Avery, Jeanne 1931- 111
Avery, June
See Rees, Joan
Avery, Kay 1908- 1-4R
See also SATA 5
Avery, Laurence G(reen) 1934- 33-36R
Avery, Lynn
See Cole, Lois Dwight
Avery, Martin 1955- 113
Avery, Mary Ellen 1927- 118
Avery, Peter 1923- 13-16R
Avery, Richard
See Cooper, Edmund
Avery, Robert J. Jr. 1911(?)-1983 Obituary 110
Avery, Robert Sterling 1917- 13-16R
Avery, Valeen Tippetts 1936- 129
Avery, Valerie 1940- 111
Averyt, Anne C. 1946- 127
Avey, Albert E(dwin) 1886-1963 ....CAP-1
Earlier sketch in CA 17-18
Avey, Ruby 1927- CANR-39
Earlier sketches in CA 89-92, CANR-16
Avi
See Wortis, Avi
See also CLR 24
See also SATA 71
Aviad, Janet 1942- 115
Avice, Claude (Pierre Marie) 1925- CANR-24
Earlier sketches in CA 61-64, CANR-8
Avicenna 980-1037 ....DLB 115
Avigad, Nachman 1905-1992 129
Obituary 136
Avila, Charles 1945- 129
Avila, Lilian Estelle 45-48
Avila (Penagos), Rafael 1941- 132
Avineri, Shlomo 1933- 25-28R
Avirgan, Anthony Lance 1944- CANR-31
Earlier sketch in CA 112
Avirgan, Tony
See Avirgan, Anthony Lance
Avis, Paul (David Loup) 1947- 120
Avison, Margaret 1918- 17-20R
See also CLC 2, 4
See also DLB 53
See also MTCW
Avison, N(eville) Howard 1934- 29-32R
Avi-Yonah, M(ichael) 1904-1974 ....CANR-6
Earlier sketch in CA 5-8R
Avnery, Uri 1923- CANR-25
Earlier sketch in CA 105
Avni, Abraham Albert 1921- 33-36R
Avni, Haim 1930- 133
Avramides, Anita 1952- 133
Avramovic, Dragoslav 1919- CANR-17
Earlier sketch in CA 41-44R
Avrelin, M.
See Steinberg, Aaron Zacharovich
Avrett, Robert 1901- 1-4R
Avrett, Rosalind Case 1933- 110
Avrett, Roz
See Avrett, Rosalind Case
Avrich, Paul (Henry) 1931- CANR-5
Earlier sketch in CA 49-52
Avriel, Ehud 1917-1980 69-72
Obituary 133
Avril, Pierre 1930- 29-32R
Avruch, Kevin Andrew 1950- 123
Avrutis, Raymond 1948- 69-72
Awa, Eme Onuoha 1921- 13-16R
Awad, Elias M. 1934- CANR-11
Earlier sketch in CA 17-20R
Awdry, Christopher Vere 1940- 136
See also SATA 67
Awdry, Wilbert Vere 1911- 103
See also CLR 23
See also SATA 67
Awe, Chulho 1927- 33-36R
Awolowo, Obafemi Awo 1909-1987 ....CANR-14
Obituary 122
Earlier sketch in CA 65-68
Awoonor, Kofi 1935- CANR-15
Earlier sketch in CA 29-32R
See also CAAS 13
See also BW
See also DLB 117
Awret, Irene 1921- 131
Axell, Herbert (Ernest) 1915- CANR-14
Earlier sketch in CA 81-84
Axelrad, Jacob 1899- 61-64
Axelrad, Sidney 1913-1976 122
Obituary 110
Axelrad, Sylvia Brody 1914- 104
Axelrod, Alan 1952- 110
Axelrod, D(avid) B(ruce) 1943- CANR-1
Earlier sketch in CA 45-48
Axelrod, George 1922- 65-68
Axelrod, Herbert Richard 1927- 85-88
Axelrod, Joseph 1918- 33-36R
Axelrod, Paul (Douglas) 1949- 110
Axelrod, Robert 1943- 33-36R
Axelrod, Steven Gould 1944- 81-84
Axelson, Eric (Victor) 1913- CANR-25
Earlier sketches in CA 21-24R, CANR-9
Axford, H. William 1925- 37-40R
Axford, Joseph Mack 1879-1970 ....CAP-2
Earlier sketch in CA 25-28
Axford, Lavonne B(rady) 1928- 33-36R
Axford, Roger W(illiam) 1920- 33-36R
Axinn, Donald E(verett) 1929- 125
Brief entry 115
Axinn, June 1923- 89-92
Axline, W. Andrew 1940- 25-28R
Axtell, James Lewis 1941- CANR-25
Earlier sketch in CA 108
Axthelm, Peter M(acrae) 1943- 107
Axton, David
See Koontz, Dean R(ay)
Axton, W(illiam) F(itch) 1926- 21-24R
Ayal, Igal 1942- 37-40R
Ayala, Francisco 1934- 85-88
Ayala, Mitzi 1941- 110
Ayandele, E(mmanuel) A(yankanmi)
1936- CANR-13
Earlier sketch in CA 21-24R
Ayars, Albert L(ee) 1917- 29-32R
Ayars, James S(terling) 1898- CANR-2
Earlier sketch in CA 5-8R
See also SATA 4
Ayatey, Siegfried B. Y. 1934- 25-28R
Ayckbourn, Alan 1939- CANR-31
Earlier sketch in CA 21-24R
See also CLC 5, 8, 18, 33
See also DLB 13
See also MTCW
Aycock, Don M(ilton) 1951- 106
Aydelotte, William Osgood 1910- 57-60
Aydy, Catherine
See Tennant, Emma (Christina)
Ayearst, Morley 1899-1983 ....CAP-2
Obituary 109
Earlier sketch in CA 29-32
Ayer, A(lfred) J(ules) 1910-1989 ....CANR-34
Obituary 129
Earlier sketches in CA 5-8R, 129, CANR-5
Ayer, Frederick Jr. 1917(?)-1974 73-76
Obituary 45-48
Ayer, Jacqueline 1930- 69-72
See also SATA 13
Ayer, Margaret CANR-13
Earlier sketch in CA 65-68
See also SATA 15
Ayers, Bradley Earl 1935- 69-72
Ayers, Donald Murray 1923- 17-20R
Ayers, Edward L(ynn) 1953- 115
Ayers, M(ichael) R(ichard) 1935- 25-28R
Ayers, Robert H(yman) 1918- 45-48
Ayers, Ronald 1948- 61-64
Ayers, Rose
See Greenwood, Lillian Bethel
Ayerst, David (George Ogilvy)
1904- Brief entry 113
Aykroyd, Dan(iel Edward) 1952- 123
Aykroyd, Wallace Ruddell
1899-1979 Obituary 110
Aylen, Leo (William) 1935- CANR-19
Earlier sketch in CA 102
Aylesworth, Jim 1943- CANR-22
Earlier sketch in CA 106
See also SATA 38
Aylesworth, Thomas G(ibbons) 1927- CANR-26
Earlier sketches in CA 25-28R, CANR-10
See also CLR 6
See also SATA 4
Ayling, (Harold) Keith (Oliver) 1898-1976 73-76
Obituary 69-72
Ayling, Stanley (Edward) 1909- CANR-21
Earlier sketch in CA 45-48
Aylmer, Felix
See Jones, Felix Edward Aylmer
Aylmer, G(erald) E(dward) 1926- CANR-5
Earlier sketch in CA 13-16R
Aylward, Gladys 1902(?)-1970 Obituary 111
Aylward, Marcus
See Alexander, Marc
Aymar, Brandt 1911- CANR-37
Earlier sketches in CA 1-4R, CANR-16
See also SATA 22
Aymar, Gordon C(hristian) 1893- 5-8R
Ayme, Marcel (Andre) 1902-1967 89-92
See also CLC 11
See also CLR 25
See also DLB 72
Aymes, Sister Maria de la Cruz 21-24R
Aynes, Edith A(nnette) 1909- 45-48
Aynes, Pat Edith
See Aynes, Edith A(nnette)
Aynesworth, Hugh (G.) 1931- 120
Brief entry 115
Ayrault, Evelyn West 1922- 9-12R
Ayre, Jessica
See Appignanesi, Lisa
Ayre, Robert (Hugh) 1900- 1-4R
Ayres, Alison
See Carter, Robert A(yres)
Ayres, Carole Briggs
See Briggs, Carole S(uzanne)
Ayres, James Eyvind 1939- 103
Ayres, Patricia Miller 1923-1985 Obituary 117
See also SATA 46
Ayres, Paul
See Aarons, Edward S(idney)
Ayres, Philip 1944- 134
Ayres, Robert U(nderwood) 1932- CANR-16
Earlier sketch in CA 93-96
Ayres, Ruby M(ildred)
1883-1955 Brief entry 117
Ayrton, Elisabeth Walshe
1910(?)-1991 ....CANR-21
Obituary 136
Earlier sketches in CA 5-8R, CANR-3
Ayrton, Michael 1921-1975 ....CANR-21
Obituary 61-64
Earlier sketches in CA 5-8R, CANR-9
See also CLC 7
Aytoun, SirRobert 1570-1638 ....DLB 121
Aytoun, William Edmonstoune
1813-1865 ....DLB 32
Ayub Khan, Mohammad 1907-1974 ....CAP-2
Earlier sketch in CA 23-24
Ayvazian, L. Fred 1919- 69-72
Azaid
See Zaidenberg, Arthur
Azar, Edward E(lias) 1938-1991 ....CANR-28
Obituary 134
Earlier sketch in CA 49-52
Azarian, Mary 1940- 118
Azarya, Victor 1946- 129
Azbel, Mark Ya. 1932- 105
Azcarate y Florez, Pablo de
1890-1971 Obituary 113
Azevedo, Carlos de 1918- 136
Azevedo, Ross E(ames) 105
Aziz, Sartaj 1929- 111
Aznavour, Charles
See Aznavourian, Varenagh
Aznavourian, Varenagh 1924- Brief entry 112
Azneer, J. Leonard 1921- 33-36R
Azorin
See Martinez Ruiz, Jose
See also CLC 11
Azoy, A(nastasio) C. M. 1891- CAP-1
Earlier sketch in CA 13-14
Azoy, G. Whitney 1940- 128
Azrael, Judith Anne 1938- CANR-10
Earlier sketch in CA 65-68
Azrin, Nathan H(arold) 1930- CANR-16
Earlier sketches in CA 45-48, CANR-1
Azuela, Arturo 1938- 131
See also HW
Azuela, Mariano 1873-1952 131
Brief entry 104
See also HW
See also MTCW
See also TCLC 3
Azumi, Atsushi 1907- 102
Azumi, Koya 1930- 29-32R

B

B. V.
See Thomson, James
Baack, Lawrence James 1943- 109
Baade, (Wilhelm Heinrich) W(alter)
1893-1960 Obituary 112
Baali, Fuad (G.) 1930- Brief entry 117
Baal-Teshuva, Jacob 1929- 5-8R
Baar, James A. 1929- 102
Baars, Conrad W(alterus) 1919-1981 ....CANR-8
Earlier sketch in CA 57-60
Baars, Donald Lee 1928- 121
Baarslag, Karl Herman William
1900-1984 Obituary 111
Baastad, Babbis Friis
See Friis-Baastad, Babbis Ellinor
Baatz, Charles A(lbert) 1916- 104
Baatz, Olga K. 1921- 104
Bab
See Gilbert, W(illiam) S(chwenck)

Baba, Meher 1894-1969 109
Obituary 106
Babb, Howard S(elden) 1924-1978 ....13-16R
Obituary 120
Babb, Hugh Webster 1887-197 (?) CAP-1
Earlier sketch in CA 13-14
Babb, Janice Barbara
See Bentley, Janice Babb
Babb, Lawrence Alan 1941- Brief entry 105
Babb, Lawrence 1902- CAP-2
Earlier sketch in CA 33-36
Babb, Sanora 1907- 13-16R
Babbage, Stuart Barton 1916- CANR-8
Earlier sketch in CA 5-8R
Babbidge, Homer D(aniels) Jr.
1925-1984 ....CANR-13
Obituary 112
Earlier sketch in CA 61-64
Babbie, Earl (Robert) 1938- CANR-23
Earlier sketches in CA 61-64, CANR-8
Babbis, Eleanor
See Friis-Baastad, Babbis Ellinor
Babbitt, Bruce E(dward) 1938- 97-100
Babbitt, Irving 1865-1933 .... DLB 63
Babbitt, Natalie (Zane Moore) 1932- CANR-38
Earlier sketches in CA 49-52, CANR-2, 19
See also CLR 2
See also DLB 52
See also MAICYA
See also SAAS 5
See also SATA 6, 68
Babbitt, Robert
See Bangs, Robert B(abbitt)
Babcock, C(larence) Merton 1908- CANR-5
Earlier sketch in CA 5-8R
Babcock, Dennis Arthur 1948- 61-64
See also SATA 22
Babcock, Dorothy E(llen) 1931- 65-68
Babcock, Frederic 1896- 5-8R
Babcock, Frederick Morrison
1897(?)-1983 Obituary 110
Babcock, Havilah 1898-1964 122
Obituary 110
Babcock, Leland S. 1922- Brief entry 106
Babcock, Nicolas
See Lewis, Tom
Babcock, Robert J(oseph) 1928- 13-16R
Babe, Thomas 1941- 101
Babel, Isaac (Emanuilovich)
See Babel, Isaak (Emmanuilovich)
See also TCLC 13
Babel, Isaak (Emmanuilovich)
1894-1941(?) Brief entry 104
See also Babel, Isaac (Emanuilovich)
See also TCLC 2
Baber, Walter F(rank) 1953- 120
Babiiha, Thaddeo K(itasimbwa) 1945- 110
Babin, David E. 1925- 21-24R
Babin, Maria Teresa 1910- Brief entry 107
See also HW
Babington, Anthony Patrick 1920- 61-64
Babington Smith, Constance 1912- 131
Babits, Mihaly 1883-1941 Brief entry 114
See also TCLC 14
Babitz, Eve 1943- CANR-28
Earlier sketch in CA 81-84
Babitz, Sol 1911-1982 ....CANR-28
Earlier sketch in CA 41-44R
Babladelis, Georgia 1931- CANR-8
Earlier sketch in CA 21-24R
Babris, Peter J. 1917- CANR-10
Earlier sketch in CA 21-24R
Babson, Marian 102
Babson, Roger W(ard)
1875-1967 Obituary 89-92
Babula, William 1943- CANR-21
Earlier sketch in CA 105
Baca, Jimmy Santiago 1952- 131
See also HW
Baca, Jose Santiago
See Baca, Jimmy Santiago
Bacall, Lauren 1924- 93-96
Bacchelli, Riccardo 1891-1985 ....29-32R
Obituary 117
See also CLC 19
Bacciocco, Edward J(oseph) Jr. 1935- 45-48
Bach, Alice (Hendricks) 1942- 101
See also SATA 27, 30
Bach, Bert C(oates) 1936- 21-24R
Bach, George Leland 1915- CANR-3
Earlier sketch in CA 1-4R
Bach, George Robert 1914- 104
Bach, Ira J(ohn) 1906-1985 115
Bach, Jean
See Greif, Martin
Bach, Kent 1943- 85-88
Bach, Marcus (Louis) 1906- Brief entry 115
Bach, Orville E(uing) Jr. 1946- 115
Bach, P.D.Q.
See Schickele, Peter
Bach, Richard (David) 1936- CANR-18
Earlier sketch in CA 9-12R
See also AITN 1
See also BEST 89:2
See also CLC 14
See also MTCW
See also SATA 13
Bach, Wilfrid 1936- CANR-10
Earlier sketch in CA 61-64
Bacharach, Alfred L(ouis) 1891-1966 .... CAP-1
Earlier sketch in CA 11-12
Bacharach, Bert(ram Mark)
1898-1983 Obituary 110
Bache, Benjamin Franklin 1769-1798 ...... DLB 43
Bache, Ellyn 1942- 129
Bache, William B. 1922- 25-28R

Bachelard, Gaston 1884-1962 97-100
Obituary 89-92
Bachem Alent, Rose M(arie Baake) 49-52
Bacher, June Masters 1918- 108
Bachkatov, Nina 1946- 134
Bachman, David C(hristian) 1934- 124
Bachman, Fred 1949- 53-56
See also SATA 12
Bachman, Jerald G(raybill) 1936- 41-44R
Bachman, John Walter 1916- 5-8R
Bachman, Richard
See King, Stephen (Edwin)
Bachmann, Gideon 1927- 104
Bachmann, Ingeborg 1926-1973 93-96
Obituary 45-48
See also CLC 69
See also DLB 85
Bachmura, Frank T(homas) 1922- 45-48
Bachrach, Bernard S. 1939- 113
Bachrach, Judy 1948- 114
Bacik, James Joseph 1936- 105
Back, Joe (W.) 1899-1986 .... CAP-2
Obituary 120
Earlier sketch in CA 17-18
Back, Kurt W(olfgang) 1919- 13-16R
Backer, Dorothy 1925- 85-88
Backer, John H. 1902-1985 ....33-36R
Obituary 116
Backer, Morton 1918- 17-20R
Backes, Clarus 1935-1988 Obituary 127
Backgammon, Daisy
See Murray, John F(rancis)
Backhouse, Janet 1938- CANR-26
Earlier sketch in CA 109
Backhouse, Sally 1927- 21-24R
Backlund, Ralph T. 1918- 73-76
Backman, Carl W(ard) 1923- 17-20R
Backman, Jules 1910- CANR-3
Earlier sketch in CA 1-4R
Backman, Melvin (Abraham) 1919- 21-24R
Backman, Milton V. Jr. 1927- CANR-13
Earlier sketch in CA 33-36R
Backscheider, Paula R(ice) 1943- 138
Backstrom, Charles H(erbert) 1926- 13-16R
Backus, James Gilmore
1913-1989 Obituary 129
See also SATA 63
Backus, Jean L(ouise) 1914-1986 ....33-36R
Obituary 119
Backus, Jim
See Backus, James Gilmore
Backus, Oswald P(rentiss) III 1921-1972 .... CAP-2
Obituary 37-40R
Earlier sketch in CA 33-36
Backus, (D.) William 1926- 135
Bacmeister, Rhoda W(arner) 1893-1991 .... CAP-1
Obituary 133
Earlier sketch in CA 13-16
See also SATA 11
Bacon, Daisy Sarah 1899(?)-1986 Obituary 118
Bacon, Delia 1811-1859 .... DLB 1
Bacon, Donald C(onrad) 1935- 133
Bacon, Edmund N(orwood) 1910- 41-44R
Bacon, Edward 1906-1981 ....29-32R
Obituary 102
Bacon, Elizabeth E(maline) 1904- CAP-1
Earlier sketch in CA 19-20
Bacon, Elizabeth 1914- 29-32R
See also SATA 3
Bacon, Ernst 1898-1990 Obituary 131
Bacon, Frances Atchinson 1903- 1-4R
Bacon, Francis 1561-1626 .... CDBLB Before 1660
Bacon, Joan Chase
See Bowden, Joan Chase
Bacon, John 1940- 53-56
Bacon, Josephine Dodge (Daskam)
1876-1961 97-100
See also SATA 48
Bacon, Lenice Ingram 1895- 45-48
Bacon, Margaret 106
Bacon, Margaret Frances
See Bacon, Peggy
See also SATA 50
Bacon, Margaret Hope 1921- 25-28R
See also SATA 6
Bacon, Marion 1901(?)-1975 Obituary 57-60
Bacon, Martha Sherman 1917-1981 85-88
Obituary 104
See also CLR 3
See also SATA 18, 27
Bacon, Nancy 1940- 93-96
Bacon, Peggy 1895-1987 .... CAP-2
Obituary 121
Earlier sketch in CA 23-24
See also Bacon, Margaret Frances
See also SATA 2
Bacon, Phillip 1922- 41-44R
Bacon, R(onald) L(eonard) 1924- 104
See also SATA 26
Bacon, Roger 1214(?)-1292 .... DLB 115
Bacon, Thomas 1700(?)-1768 .... DLB 31
Bacon, Wallace A(lger) 1914- 17-20R
Bacote, Clarence A(lbert) 1906- CAP-2
Earlier sketch in CA 33-36
Bacovia, G.
See Vasiliu, Gheorghe
Bacovia, George
See Vasiliu, Gheorghe
See also TCLC 24
Bacque, James 1929- 101
Badanes, Jerome 1937- .... CLC 59
Badash, Lawrence 1934- CANR-14
Earlier sketch in CA 37-40R
Badawi, M(ohamed) M(ustafa) 1925- CANR-1
Earlier sketch in CA 49-52
Badawi, Muhammed Mustafa
See Badawi, M(ohamed) M(ustafa)

Badcock, Christopher Robert 1946- 101
Baddeley, Alan D(avid) 1934- 69-72
Baddeley, Hermione 1906(?)-1986 133
Obituary 120
Baddeley, V.C. Clinton
See Clinton-Baddeley, V.C.
Baddock, James 1950- 137
Bade, Jane (Ruth) 1932- 89-92
Bade, Patrick 1951- 89-92
Baden, Robert 1936- 138
See also SATA 70
Baden-Powell, Dorothy 1920- 103
Baden-Powell, Robert (Stephenson Smyth)
1857-1941 Brief entry 114
See also SATA 16
Bader, Douglas (Robert Steuart)
1910-1982 101
Obituary 107
Bader, Julia 1944- 69-72
Bader, Robert S(mith) 1925- 120
Badger, John d'Arcy 1917- 45-48
Badger, Ralph E(astman) 1890-1978 ...... CAP-2
Obituary 73-76
Earlier sketch in CA 21-22
Badger, Reid 1942- 97-100
Badgley, John 1930- 37-40R
Badgley, Robin F(rancis) 1931- 101
Badham, Leslie (Stephen Ronald)
1908-1975 Obituary 114
Badia, Leonard F(rancis) 1934- 113
Badian, Ernst 1925- 37-40R
Badillo, Herman 1929- 85-88
Badinter, Elisabeth 1944- 118
Badough, Rose Marie 1938- 117
Badura-Skoda, Eva 1929- CANR-14
Earlier sketch in CA 37-40R
Baechler, Jean 1937- CANR-30
Earlier sketches in CA 73-76, CANR-13
Baeck, Leo 1873-1956 Brief entry 115
Baeder, John 1938- 111
Baehr, Consuelo 1938- 103
Baehr, Harry William 1907-1987 Obituary 123
Baehr, Patricia (Goehner) 1952- CANR-35
Earlier sketch in CA 103
See also SATA 65
Baen, James P. 1943- Brief entry 112
Baensch, Willy E(dward)
1893-1972 Obituary 37-40R
Baenziger, Hans 1917- 49-52
Baer, Adela S(wenson) 1931- 101
Baer, Curtis O. 1898- 49-52
Baer, Daniel J(oseph) 1929- 33-36R
Baer, Donald Merle 1931- 81-84
Baer, Earl E. 1928- 57-60
Baer, Edith R(uth) 1920- CANR-21
Earlier sketch in CA 104
Baer, Eleanora A(gnes) 1907- 9-12R
Baer, Gabriel 1919- CANR-2
Earlier sketch in CA 5-8R
Baer, George Webster 1935- 21-24R
Baer, Hans A. 1944- 119
Baer, Jean L. CANR-9
Earlier sketch in CA 13-16R
Baer, Jill
See Gilbert, (Agnes) Joan (Sewell)
Baer, John 1886-1970 Obituary 29-32R
Baer, Judith A(bbott) 1945- 81-84
Baer, Judy 1951- .... SATA 71
Baer, Marc (Bradley) 1945- 138
Baer, Marianne 1932- 81-84
Baer, Max Frank 1912- 9-12R
Baer, Rosemary 1913- 41-44R
Baer, Walter S. III 1937- 65-68
Baer, Werner 1931- 9-12R
Baerg, Harry J(ohn) 1909- CANR-4
Earlier sketch in CA 9-12R
See also SATA 12
Baerwald, Hans H(erman) 1927- 33-36R
Baerwald, Sara 1948- 61-64
Baes, Katharine Lee 1859-1929 .... DLB 71
Baetjer, Anna M(edora)
1899-1984 Obituary 112
Baetzhold, Howard G(eorge) 1923- 29-32R
Baeuml, Franz H(einrich) 1926- 49-52
Baez, Joan (Chandos) 1941- CANR-26
Earlier sketch in CA 21-24R
See also HW
Bagarag, Shibli
See Lawlor, Patrick Anthony
Bagby, George
See Stein, Aaron Marc
Bagby, Wesley M(arvin) 1922- CANR-37
Earlier sketches in CA 1-4R, CANR-16
Bagdikian, Ben Haig 1920- CANR-6
Earlier sketch in CA 9-12R
Bage, Robert 1728-1801 .... DLB 39
Bagehot, Walter 1826-1877 .... DLB 55
Bagg, Graham (William) 1917- 57-60
Bagg, Robert Ely 1935- CANR-15
Earlier sketch in CA 65-68
Baggaley, Andrew R(obert) 1923- 13-16R
Baggett, Nancy 1943- 117
Baggley, John (Samuel) 1940- 124
Bagin, Don(ald Richard) 1938- 77-80
Baginski, Frank 1938- 93-96
Bagley, Christopher 1937- 119
Bagley, Desmond 1923-1983 ....CANR-29
Obituary 109
Earlier sketch in CA 17-20R
See also DLB 87
Bagley, Edward R(osecrans) 1926- CANR-5
Earlier sketch in CA 53-56
Bagley, J(ohn) J(oseph) 1908-1989 ....CANR-2
Obituary 127
Earlier sketch in CA 5-8R
Bagley, Michael 1947- 129
Bagnall, Nigel (Thomas) 1927- 136

Bagnel, Joan 1933- 49-52
Bagni, Gwen
See Dubov, Gwen Bagni
Bagnold, Enid 1889-1981 ....CANR-5
Obituary 103
Earlier sketch in CA 5-8R
See also CLC 25
See also DLB 13
See also MAICYA
See also SATA 1, 25
Bagnold, Ralph Alger 1896-1990 Obituary 131
Bagramian, Ivan K(ristoforovich)
1897-1982 Obituary 107
Bagrjana, Elisaveta
See Belcheva, Elisaveta
Bagryana, Elisaveta
See Belcheva, Elisaveta
Bagster, Hubert
See Trumper, Hubert Bagster
Bagwell, Philip S(idney) 1914- CANR-29
Earlier sketches in CA 33-36R, CANR-13
Bagwell, William Francis Jr. 1923- CANR-31
Earlier sketch in CA 33-36R
Bahadur, K(rishna) P(rakash) 1924- CANR-28
Earlier sketch in CA 57-60
Bahat, Dan 1938- 77-80
Bahl, Roy W. (Jr.) 1939- 21-24R
Bahlke, George W(ilbon) 1934- 29-32R
Bahlke, Valerie Worth 1933- CANR-15
Earlier sketch in CA 41-44R
See also Worth, Valerie
Bahlman, Dudley Ward Rhodes 1923- 85-88
Bahm, Archie J(ohn) 1907- CANR-3
Earlier sketch in CA 9-12R
Bahmueller, Charles F(erdinand) 1942- 112
Bahn, Eugene 1906- 21-24R
Bahn, Margaret (Elizabeth) Linton
1907-1969 .... CAP-2
Earlier sketch in CA 25-28
Bahr, Edith-Jane 1926- 65-68
Bahr, Erhard 1932- 33-36R
Bahr, Hermann 1863-1934 Brief entry 121
See also DLB 81, 118
Bahr, Howard M. 1938- CANR-12
Earlier sketch in CA 29-32R
Bahr, Jerome 1909- 33-36R
Bahr, Mary 1946- 136
Bahr, Robert 1940- CANR-9
Earlier sketch in CA 65-68
See also SATA 38
Bahti, Tom 1926-1972 .... SATA 31, 57
Baier, Kurt Erich 1917- 65-68
Baigell, Matthew 1933- 107
Bai Jieming
See Barme, Geremie
Bail, Murray 1941- 127
Bailes, Kendall E(ugene) 1940- Brief entry 112
Bailey, Alfred Goldsworthy 1905- 25-28R
See also DLB 68
Bailey, Alfred M(arshall) 1894-1978 ....41-44R
Bailey, Alice A(nne La Trobe-Bateman)
1880(?)-1949 Brief entry 116
Bailey, Alice Cooper 1890- CAP-1
Earlier sketch in CA 13-16
See also SATA 12
Bailey, Anne 1958- .... SATA 71
Bailey, Anthony 1933- CANR-3
Earlier sketch in CA 1-4R
Bailey, Barry 1926- 107
Bailey, Bernadine (Freeman) 1901- CANR-7
Earlier sketch in CA 5-8R
See also SATA 14
Bailey, Beryl Loftman
1920(?)-1977 Obituary 69-72
Bailey, Carolyn Sherwin 1875-1961 73-76
See also MAICYA
See also SATA 14
Bailey, Charles W(aldo) II 1929- CANR-1
Earlier sketch in CA 1-4R
Bailey, Chris H(arvey) 1946- 65-68
Bailey, Conrad Charles Maitland 1922- 105
Bailey, D. F. 1950- 125
Bailey, D. R. Shackleton
See Shackleton Bailey, D(avid) R(oy)
Bailey, David C(harles) 1930- 45-48
Bailey, David (Royston) 1938- 120
Bailey, Derrick Sherwin 1910-1984 ....CANR-2
Obituary 112
Earlier sketch in CA 5-8R
Bailey, Don 1942- 93-96
Bailey, Donna (Veronica Anne) 1938- 136
See also SATA 68
Bailey, Dudley 1918- 17-20R
Bailey, Eric 1933- 33-36R
Bailey, F(rancis) Lee 1933- 89-92
Bailey, Fred Arthur 1947- 129
Bailey, Frederick George 1924- CANR-9
Earlier sketch in CA 13-16R
Bailey, (John) Frederick (II) 1946- 133
Bailey, Frederick Marshman 1882-1967 ..... CAP-1
Earlier sketch in CA 13-14
Bailey, George 1919- CANR-38
Earlier sketches in CA 25-28R, CANR-17
Bailey, Gerald Earl 1929- CANR-10
Earlier sketch in CA 25-28R
Bailey, Gordon Keith 1936- 112
Bailey, H(enry) C(hristopher)
1878-1961 Obituary 108
See also DLB 77
Bailey, Harold (Walter) 1899- 109
Bailey, Harry A(ugustine) Jr. 1932- 21-24R
Bailey, Helen Miller 1909- 13-16R
Bailey, Herbert S(mith) Jr. 1921- Brief entry 112
Bailey, Hillary G(oodsell) 1894- 57-60
Bailey, Hugh C(oleman) 1929- 9-12R
Bailey, J(ames) Martin 1929- 49-52

Bailey, J(ames) O(sler) 1903-1979 ....17-20R
Obituary 126
Bailey, Jackson Holbrook 1925- CANR-21
Earlier sketch in CA 45-48
Bailey, Jacob 1731-1808 .... DLB 99
Bailey, James H(enry) 1919- 106
Bailey, James R(ichard) A(be) 1919- 53-56
Bailey, (Corinne) Jane 1943- 77-80
Bailey, Jane H(orton) 1916- CANR-4
Earlier sketch in CA 53-56
See also SATA 12
Bailey, Joan H(auser) 1922- 21-24R
Bailey, Joe A(llen) 1929- 37-40R
Bailey, John A(medee) 1929- 37-40R
Bailey, John (Robert) 1940- 121
See also SATA 52
Bailey, Kenneth K(yle) 1923- 21-24R
Bailey, Kenneth P. 1912- CANR-4
Earlier sketch in CA 53-56
Bailey, Lloyd Richard 1936- CANR-15
Earlier sketch in CA 85-88
Bailey, M(innie Elizabeth) Thomas 57-60
Bailey, Maralyn Collins (Harrison) 1941- 53-56
See also SATA 12
Bailey, Martin 1947- 134
Bailey, Matilda
See Radford, Ruby L(orraine)
Bailey, Maurice Charles 1932- 53-56
See also SATA 12
Bailey, Norman A(lishan) 1931- CANR-13
Earlier sketch in CA 21-24R
Bailey, Patrick 1925- 57-60
Bailey, Paul Dayton 1906-1987 ....CANR-6
Obituary 124
Earlier sketch in CA 5-8R
Bailey, Paul 1937- CANR-16
Earlier sketch in CA 21-24R
See also CLC 45
See also DLB 14
Bailey, Pearl (Mae) 1918-1990 ....CANR-14
Obituary 132
Earlier sketch in CA 61-64
See also BW
Bailey, Philip James 1816-1902 .... DLB 32
Bailey, Ralph Edgar 1893- CAP-1
Earlier sketch in CA 17-18
See also SATA 11
Bailey, Raymond H(amby) 1938- CANR-8
Earlier sketch in CA 61-64
Bailey, Richard W(eld) 1939- CANR-10
Earlier sketch in CA 25-28R
Bailey, Robert Jr. 1945- 49-52
Bailey, Robert W(ilson) 1943- CANR-21
Earlier sketch in CA 69-72
Bailey, Stephen Kemp 1916-1982 ....CANR-4
Obituary 106
Earlier sketch in CA 1-4R
Bailey, Sydney D(awson) 1916- CANR-31
Earlier sketches in CA 69-72, CANR-12
Bailey, Thomas A(ndrew) 1902-1983 ....CANR-18
Obituary 110
Earlier sketch in CA 17-20R
Bailey, Victor 1948- 125
Bailie, Victoria Worley 1894- CAP-1
Earlier sketch in CA 13-16
Bailkey, Nels M(artin) 1911- 33-36R
Baillargeon, Pierre 1916-1967 .... DLB 88
Baillen, Claude
See Delay(-Tubiana), Claude
Baillie, Allan 1943- 118
Baillie, Hugh 1890-1966 Obituary 89-92
See also DLB 29
Baillie, Isobel 1895-1983 Obituary 110
Baillie, Joanna 1762-1851 .... DLB 93
Baillie, Kate 1957- 124
Baillie-Hamilton, George
1894-1986 Obituary 121
Baily, Charles M(ichael) 1944- 117
Baily, Leslie 1906-1976 .... CAP-2
Earlier sketch in CA 25-28
Baily, Nathan A(riel) 1920- CANR-6
Earlier sketch in CA 9-12R
Baily, Samuel L(ongstreth) 1936- 29-32R
Bailyn, Bernard 1922- CANR-8
Earlier sketch in CA 61-64
See also DLB 17
Bain, A(ndrew) D(avid) 1936- Brief entry 111
Bain, Carl E. 1930- 85-88
Bain, Chester A(rthur) 1912- 29-32R
Bain, Chester Ward 1919- 85-88
Bain, George Sayers 1939- 132
Bain, Joe S. 1912- 33-36R
Bain, Kenneth Bruce Findlater
1921-1985 93-96
Obituary 115
Bain, Kenneth Ray 1942- 104
Bain, Kenneth (Ross) 1923- 130
Bain, Robert 1932- 77-80
Bain, Willard S. Jr. 1938- 25-28R
Bainbridge, Beryl (Margaret) 1933- CANR-24
Earlier sketch in CA 21-24R
See also CLC 4, 5, 8, 10, 14, 18, 22, 62
See also DLB 14
See also MTCW
Bainbridge, Cyril 1928- 129
Bainbridge, Geoffrey 1923- 5-8R
Bainbridge, John 1913- 13-16R
Bainbridge, William Sims 1940- 120
Baine, Rodney M(ontgomery) 1913- 69-72
Baines, Anthony C(uthbert) 1912- 5-8R
Baines, Frank 1915-1987 Obituary 124
Baines, Jocelyn 1925-1973 106
Obituary 104
Baines, John (David) 1943- .... SATA 71
Baines, John M. 1935- 41-44R
Baines, John Robert 1946- 123
Bains, Larry
See Sabin, Louis
Bainton, Roland H(erbert) 1894-1984 ....CANR-5
Obituary 113
Earlier sketch in CA 1-4R
Bair, Deirdre 1935- 81-84
See also BEST 90:4
Bair, Frank E. 1927- 102
Baird, A(lbert) Craig 1883- CAP-1
Earlier sketch in CA 13-14
Baird, Alexander (John) 1925- 9-12R
Baird, Bil
See Baird, William Britton
See also SATA 30, 52
Baird, Duncan H. 1917- 65-68
Baird, Forrest J. 1905- CAP-1
Earlier sketch in CA 19-20
Baird, Irene 1901-1981 .... DLB 68
Baird, J(oseph) Arthur 1922- CANR-3
Earlier sketch in CA 5-8R
Baird, J(oseph) L. 1933- 85-88
Baird, Jack
See Baird, John Charlton
Baird, Jay Warren 1936- 41-44R
Baird, Jesse Hays 1889- 13-16R
Baird, John Charlton 1938- 126
Baird, John D. 1941- 109
Baird, John Edward 1922- 17-20R
Baird, Joseph Armstrong (Jr.) 1922- CANR-12
Earlier sketch in CA 33-36R
Baird, Lorrayne Y. 1927- 112
Baird, Marie-Terese 1918- 57-60
Baird, Martha (Joanna) 1921-1981 ....CANR-9
Earlier sketch in CA 61-64
Baird, Nancy Disher 1935- CANR-32
Earlier sketches in CA 89-92, CANR-15
Baird, Patrick D(ouglas)
1912-1984 Obituary 112
Baird, Robert D(ahlen) 1933- 53-56
Baird, Ronald J(ames) 1929- 53-56
Baird, Russell N. 1922- 17-20R
Baird, Thomas (P.) 1923-1990 ....CANR-21
Obituary 131
Earlier sketches in CA 53-56, CANR-4
See also SATA 39, 45
See also SATO 64
Baird, W(illiam) David 1939- 41-44R
Baird, William Britton 1904-1987 106
Obituary 122
See also Baird, Bil
See also SATA 30
Baird, William (Robb) 1924- 13-16R
Baird-Smith, Robin 1946- 123
Bairstow, Jeffrey N(oel) 1939- CANR-8
Earlier sketch in CA 61-64
Baity, Elizabeth Chesley 1907- 29-32R
See also SATA 1
Baitz, Jon Robin 1961- 134
Bajema, Carl Jay 1937- CANR-12
Earlier sketch in CA 33-36R
Bakal, Carl 1918- 21-24R
Bakalar, James B. 1943- 97-100
Bakalis, Michael J. 1938- 85-88
Bakan, David 1921- 25-28R
Bakan, Paul 1928- 21-24R
Bakaric, Vladimir 1912-1983 Obituary 114
Bake, William A(lbert) 1938- 110
Bakeless, John (Edwin) 1894-1978 ....CANR-5
Obituary 118
Earlier sketch in CA 5-8R
See also SATA 9
Bakeless, Katherine Little 1895- 5-8R
See also SATA 9
Bakely, Don(ald Carlisle) 1928- 65-68
Baker, Adelaide N(ichols) 1894-1974 45-48
Obituary 134
Baker, Adolph 1917- 53-56
Baker, Al .... AITN 1
Baker, Alan 1951- CANR-38
Earlier sketches in CA 97-100, CANR-16
See also SATA 22
Baker, (Allen) Albert 1910- 104
Baker, Alfred Thornton
1915(?)-1983 Obituary 110
Baker, Allison
See Crumbaker, Alice
Baker, Alton Wesley 1912- 33-36R
Baker, Asa
See Dresser, Davis
Baker, Augusta 1911- CANR-17
Earlier sketch in CA 1-4R
See also BW
See also SATA 3
Baker, Benjamin 1915- 1-4R
Baker, Betty D(oreen Flook) 1916- CANR-6
Earlier sketch in CA 9-12R
Baker, Betty Lou 1928-1987 ....CANR-38
Earlier sketches in CA 1-4R, CANR-2
See also MAICYA
See also SATA 5, 54
Baker, Bill
See Baker, C(harles) William
Baker, Bill Russell 1933- 57-60
Baker, Bill 1936- 77-80
Baker, Bobby
See Baker, Alfred Thornton
and Baker, Robert G.
Baker, C. J.
See Baker, Christopher John
Baker, C(harles) William 1919- 57-60
Baker, Carlos (Heard) 1909-1987 ....CANR-3
Obituary 122
Earlier sketch in CA 5-8R
See also DLB 103
Baker, Charlotte 1910- 17-20R
See also SATA 2
Baker, Christopher John 1948- 135
Brief entry 117
Baker, D(onald) Philip 1937- 102
Baker, David (Anthony) 1954- 118
See also DLB 120
Baker, Dennis 1942- 107
Baker, Denys Val 1917-1984 ....CANR-6
Obituary 113
Earlier sketch in CA 9-12R
Baker, Donald G(ene) 1932- 33-36R
Baker, Donald N(oel) 1936- 21-24R
Baker, Donald W(hitelaw) 1923- CANR-12
Earlier sketch in CA 73-76
Baker, Dorothy 1907-1968 ....CANR-1
Obituary 25-28R
Earlier sketch in CA 1-4R
Baker, Eleanor Z(uckerman) 1932- CANR-8
Earlier sketch in CA 57-60
Baker, Elizabeth Faulkner 1886(?)-1973 .... CAP-1
Obituary 41-44R
Earlier sketch in CA 13-16
Baker, (Mary) Elizabeth (Gillette)
1923- CANR-3
Earlier sketch in CA 1-4R
See also SATA 7
Baker, Elliott 1922- CANR-2
Earlier sketch in CA 45-48
See also CLC 8
Baker, Elsie 1929- 65-68
Baker, Elsworth F. 1903- CAP-2
Earlier sketch in CA 25-28
Baker, Eric Wilfred 1899-1973 Obituary 45-48
Baker, Eugene H. .... SATA 50
Baker, F(rederick) Sherman
1902-1976 Obituary 65-68
Baker, Falcon (O. Jr.) 1916- 135
Baker, Frank S(heaffer) 1910- 17-20R
Baker, Frank S. 1899(?)-1983 Obituary 109
Baker, Frank 1910- 9-12R
Baker, Frank 1936- CANR-18
Earlier sketches in CA 49-52, CANR-2
Baker, G. P.
See Baker, Gordon (P.)
Baker, Gary G. 1939- 21-24R
Baker, Gayle Cunningham 1950- 105
See also SATA 39
Baker, George W(alter) 1915- 21-24R
Baker, George 1915-1975 93-96
Obituary 57-60
Baker, Gilbert
See Baker, John Gilbert Hindley
Baker, Gladys L(ucille) 1910- 41-44R
Baker, Gordon (P.) 1938- 130
Baker, Gordon Pratt 1910- 1-4R
Baker, Herbert G(eorge) 1920- 41-44R
Baker, Herschel Clay 1914- 61-64
See also DLB 111
Baker, Houston A. Jr. 1943- CANR-14
Earlier sketch in CA 41-44R
See also BW
See also DLB 67
Baker, Howard H(enry) Jr. 1925- 124
Brief entry 113
Baker, Howard Wilson 1905-1990 .... CAP-2
Obituary 132
Earlier sketch in CA 19-20
Baker, Hugh D. R. 1937- CANR-12
Earlier sketch in CA 25-28R
Baker, Ivon 1928- 73-76
Baker, J(ohn) A(lec) 1926- 25-28R
Baker, James C(alvin) 1935- 125
Brief entry 117
Baker, James Lawrence 1941- 53-56
Baker, James R(upert) 1925- 29-32R
Baker, James T. 1940- 85-88
Baker, James Volant 1903- 57-60
Baker, James W. 1924- 77-80
See also SATA 22, 65
Baker, James W. 1926- 133
Baker, Jane Howard 1950- 110
Baker, Janice E(dla) 1941- 57-60
See also SATA 22
Baker, Jean Hogarth H(arvey) 1933- 41-44R
Baker, Jeannie 1950- 97-100
See also CLR 28
See also SATA 23
Baker, Jeffrey J(ohn) W(heeler) 1931- CANR-1
Earlier sketch in CA 49-52
See also SATA 5
Baker, Jerry 105
See also AITN 2
Baker, Jill 1951- 127
Baker, Jim
See Baker, James W.
Baker, John C(hester) 1909- 106
Baker, John F(leetwood)
1901-1985 Obituary 117
Baker, John F. 1931- 85-88
Baker, John Gilbert Hindley
1910-1986 Obituary 119
Baker, John H(enry) 1936- 33-36R
Baker, John R(andal) 1900-1984 ....CANR-27
Obituary 113
Earlier sketch in CA 49-52
Baker, John W(esley) 1920- 61-64
Baker, John 1901(?)-1971 Obituary 104
Baker, Joseph E(llis) 1905- 33-36R
Baker, Josephine 1906-1975 Obituary 105
Baker, Keith Michael 1938- 57-60
Baker, Kenneth F(rank) 1908- CANR-27
Earlier sketch in CA 49-52
Baker, Laura Nelson 1911- CANR-5
Earlier sketch in CA 5-8R
See also SATA 3
Baker, Lawrence M(anning) 1907- CAP-1
Earlier sketch in CA 13-14
Baker, Leonard S(tanley) 1931-1984 ....21-24R
Obituary 114
Baker, Letha Elizabeth (Mitts) 1913- 33-36R
Baker, Lewis
See Baker, Lewis T(urner) III
Baker, Lewis T(urner) III 1953- 129
Baker, Liva 1930- 29-32R
Baker, Lucinda 1916- 65-68
Baker, Lynn S. 1948- 109
Baker, M(ary) E(llen) Penny 45-48
Baker, Margaret J(oyce) 1918- CANR-22
Earlier sketches in CA 13-16R, CANR-7
See also SAAS 8
See also SATA 12
Baker, Margaret 1890- CANR-6
Earlier sketch in CA 13-16R
See also SATA 4
Baker, Marilyn 1929- Brief entry 111
Baker, Mary Gladys Steel 1892-1974 .... CAP-1
Earlier sketch in CA 13-16
See also SATA 12
Baker, Michael H(enry) C(hadwick)
1937- CANR-23
Earlier sketches in CA 57-60, CANR-8
Baker, (Robert) Michael (Graham)
1938- 25-28R
See also SATA 4
Baker, Miriam Hawthorn
See Nye, Miriam (Maurine Hawthorn) Baker
Baker, Nancy C(arolyn Moll) 1944- 81-84
Baker, Nelson B(laisdell) 1905- 17-20R
Baker, Nicholson 1957- 135
See also CLC 61
Baker, Nikki 1962- 137
Baker, Nina (Brown) 1888-1957 .... SATA 15
Baker, Norma Jean 1926-1962 129
Obituary 113
Baker, Olaf 187 (?)- 129
Baker, Oleda 1934- 69-72
Baker, Pamela J. 1947- 127
See also SATA 66
Baker, Paul R(aymond) 1927- CANR-19
Earlier sketches in CA 9-12R, CANR-4
Baker, Paul T(hornell) 1927- 33-36R
Baker, Pauline H(alpern) 1941- 105
Baker, Pearl Biddlecome 1907- 17-20R
Baker, Peter (Gorton) 1926- CANR-10
Earlier sketch in CA 21-24R
Baker, Philip John Noel
See Noel-Baker, Philip John
Baker, R(onald) J(ames) 1924- 33-36R
Baker, R. R.
See Baker, R(eginald) Robin
Baker, R(eginald) Robin 1944- 110
Baker, Rachel 1904-1978 ....5-8R
Obituary 103
See also SATA 2, 26
Baker, Ray Stannard 1870-1946 Brief entry 118
Baker, Richard M(ason) Jr. 1924-1978 ....13-16R
Obituary 135
Baker, Richard St. Barbe 1889-1982 .... CAP-1
Obituary 110
Earlier sketch in CA 11-12
Baker, Richard Terrill 1913-1981 ....1-4R
Obituary 104
Baker, Robert Allen Jr. 1921- 108
Baker, Robert Andrew 1910- 109
Baker, Robert B(ernard) 1937- CANR-6
Earlier sketch in CA 53-56
Baker, Robert D(onald) 1927- 121
Baker, Robert G. 1928- 85-88
Baker, Robert J(unior) 1920- 116
Baker, Robert K(erry) 1948- 108
Baker, Robin
See Baker, R(eginald) Robin
Baker, Robin Campbell 1941- 17-20R
Baker, (John) Roger 1934- 25-28R
Baker, Rollin H(arold) 1916- 118
Baker, Ronald L(ee) 1937- 105
Baker, Ross K(enneth) 1938- 29-32R
Baker, Russell (Wayne) 1925- CANR-11
Earlier sketch in CA 57-60
See also BEST 89:4
See also CLC 31
See also MTCW
Baker, Samm Sinclair 1909- CANR-21
Earlier sketches in CA 5-8R, CANR-3
See also SATA 12
Baker, Scott (MacMartin) 1947- 93-96
Baker, Sharlene 1954- 136
Baker, Sharon 1938- 117
Baker, Sheridan (Warner Jr.) 1918- CANR-18
Earlier sketches in CA 5-8R, CANR-2
Baker, Stephen 1921- CANR-19
Earlier sketches in CA 1-4R, CANR-3
Baker, Susan (Catherine) 1942- 105
See also SATA 29
Baker, T(homas) F(rancis) Timothy
1935- 25-28R
Baker, T(homas) Lindsay 1947- 121
Baker, Thomas George Adames 1920- 108
Baker, Thomas Harrison 1933- 33-36R
Baker, Victor Richard 1945- 109
Baker, Wesley C. 21-24R
Baker, William Avery 1911- CANR-2
Earlier sketch in CA 5-8R
Baker, William D. 1924- 105
Baker, William E(dwin) 1935- 21-24R
Baker, William Howard
See McNeilly, Wilfred (Glassford)
Baker, William Joseph 1938- CANR-24
Earlier sketch in CA 97-100
Baker, William W(allace) 1921- 73-76
Baker-Carr, Janet 1934- 93-96
Baker White, John 1902- 101

Bakewell, K(enneth) G(raham) B(artlett)
1931- ... CANR-19
Earlier sketch in CA 102
Bakewell, Paul Jr. 1889-1972 ... CAP-1
Earlier sketch in CA 11-12
Bakewell, Peter J(ohn) 1943- ... 119
Bakhtiar, Laleh Mehree 1938- ... 69-72
Bakhtin, M.
See Bakhtin, Mikhail Mikhailovich
Bakhtin, M. M.
See Bakhtin, Mikhail Mikhailovich
Bakhtin, Mikhail
See Bakhtin, Mikhail Mikhailovich
Bakhtin, Mikhail Mikhailovich 1895-1975 ... 128
Obituary ... 113
Bakish, David (Joseph) 1937- ... 45-48
Bakjian, Andy 1915- ... 53-56
Bakke, E(dward) Wight 1903-1971 Obituary ... 110
Bakke, Mary S(terling) 1904-1987 ... 37-40R
Obituary ... 121
Bakken, Dick 1941- ... CANR-25
Earlier sketch in CA 106
Bakken, Henry Harrison 1896- ... CANR-11
Earlier sketch in CA 65-68
Bakker, Cornelius B(ernardus) 1929- ... 57-60
Bakker, Elna S(undquist) 1921- ... 69-72
Bakker, James Orsen 1940- ... 128
Bakker, Jim
See Bakker, James Orsen
Bakker, Tamara Faye ... 128
Bakker, Tammy Faye
See Bakker, Tamara Faye
Bakker-Rabdau, Marianne K(atherine)
1935- ... 73-76
Baklanoff, Eric N. 1925- ... CANR-13
Earlier sketch in CA 33-36R
Bakr el Toure, Askia Muhammad Abu
See Toure, Askia Muhammad Abu Bakr el
Bakshi, Ralph 1938(?)- ... 138
Brief entry ... 112
See also CLC 26
Bakshian, Aram 1944- ... 102
Bakula, William J(ohn) Jr. 1936- ... 49-52
Bakwin, Harry 1894-1973 ... CAP-2
Obituary ... 45-48
Earlier sketch in CA 19-20
Bakwin, Ruth Morris 1898- ... 17-20R
Balaam
See Lamb, G(eoffrey) F(rederick)
Balaam, David N(orman) 1950- ... 112
Balaban, John B. 1943- ... CANR-29
Earlier sketches in CA 65-68, CANR-12
See also DLB 120
Balaban, Nancy 1928- ... 126
Balabkins, Nicholas (W.) 1926- ... 9-12R
Balachandran, M(adhavarao) 1938- ... 102
Balachandran, Sarojini 1934- ... CANR-18
Earlier sketch in CA 102
Balagura, Saul 1943- ... 81-84
Balakian, Anna (Elizabeth) 1916- ... 129
Balakian, Nona 1919-1991 ... 85-88
Obituary ... 134
Balakian, Peter 1951- ... 102
Balanchine, George 1904-1983 ... 111
Obituary ... 109
Balancy, Pierre Guy Girald
1924-1979 Obituary ... 89-92
Balandier, Georges (Leon) 1920- ... CANR-8
Earlier sketch in CA 61-64
Balas, David L(aszlo) 1929- ... 33-36R
Balaskas, Arthur 1940- ... 103
Balaskas, Janet (Marion) 1946- ... 117
Balassa, Bela 1928-1991 ... CANR-3
Obituary ... 134
Earlier sketch in CA 1-4R
Balawyder, Aloysius 1924- ... CANR-15
Earlier sketch in CA 41-44R
Balbontin, Jose Antonio 1893- ... CAP-1
Earlier sketch in CA 11-12
Balbus
See Huxley, Julian (Sorell)
Balcarce, Alberto G. 1946- ... 128
Balch, Glenn 1902- ... CANR-3
Earlier sketch in CA 1-4R
See also SAAS 11
See also SATA 3
Balchen, Bernt 1899-1973 Obituary ... 45-48
Balchin, John Frederick 1937- ... 122
Balchin, Nigel (Marlin) 1908-1970 ... CANR-21
Obituary ... 29-32R
Earlier sketch in CA 97-100
Balchin, W(illiam) G(eorge) V(ictor)
1916- ... CANR-18
Earlier sketch in CA 101
Balcomb, Raymond E. 1923- ... 21-24R
Balcon, Michael 1896-1977 ... 77-80
Obituary ... 73-76
Bald, F(rederick) Clever 1897-1970 ... CAP-1
Earlier sketch in CA 13-14
Bald, R(obert) C(ecil) 1901-1965 ... CANR-6
Earlier sketch in CA 5-8R
Bald, Wambly 1902- ... DLB 4
Baldanza, Frank 1924- ... 1-4R
Baldelli, Giovanni 1914- ... 45-48
Balderson, Margaret ... 25-28R
Balderston, Frederick E(mery) 1923- ... 133
Brief entry ... 112
Balderston, John L.
See Balderston, John Lloyd
Balderston, John Lloyd
1889-1954 Brief entry ... 121
See also DLB 26
Balderston, Katharine Canby
1895-1979 Obituary ... 93-96
Baldick, Chris(topher Giles) 1954- ... 128
Baldick, Robert 1927-1972 Obituary ... 89-92
Baldinger, Stanley 1932- ... 29-32R
Baldinger, Wallace S(pencer) 1905- ... 1-4R
Baldree, J(asper) Martin Jr. 1927- ... 53-56
Baldrey, Keith (Donald) 1958- ... 133
Baldridge, Cyrus LeRoy 1889- ... SATA 29
Baldridge, Mary Humphrey 1937- ... 114
Baldrige, Letitia (Katherine) ... CANR-17
Earlier sketch in CA 25-28R
Baldry, Harold (Caparne) 1907- ... 17-20R
Balducci, Carolyn (Feleppa) 1946- ... 33-36R
See also SATA 5
Balducci, Ernesto 1922- ... CANR-28
Earlier sketches in CA 29-32R, CANR-12
Baldwin, Alex
See Butterworth, W(illiam) E(dmund III)
Baldwin, Anne Norris 1938- ... 29-32R
See also SATA 5
Baldwin, Anne P. 1947- ... 128
Baldwin, Arthur W.
1904(?)-1976 Obituary ... 69-72
Baldwin, Bates
See Jennings, John (Edward Jr.)
Baldwin, Billy
See Baldwin, William Jr.
Baldwin, Christina 1946- ... CANR-31
Earlier sketches in CA 77-80, CANR-13
Baldwin, Clara ... 61-64
See also SATA 11
Baldwin, David A. 1936- ... 17-20R
Baldwin, Dick
See Raborg, Frederick A(shton) Jr.
Baldwin, Ed(ward A.) 1935- ... 118
Baldwin, Edward R(obinson) 1935- ... CANR-21
Earlier sketch in CA 45-48
Baldwin, Faith 1893-1978 ... CANR-4
Obituary ... 77-80
Earlier sketch in CA 5-8R
See also AITN 1
Baldwin, Gordo
See Baldwin, Gordon C.
Baldwin, Gordon C. 1908- ... CANR-3
Earlier sketch in CA 1-4R
See also SATA 12
Baldwin, Hanson W(eightman)
1903-1991 ... 61-64
Obituary ... 136
Baldwin, James (Arthur) 1924-1987 ... CANR-24
Obituary ... 124
Earlier sketches in CA 1-4R, CANR-3
See also CABS 1
See also AAYA 4
See also BLC 1
See also BW
See also CDALB 1941-1968
See also CLC 1, 2, 3, 4, 5, 8, 13, 15, 17, 42, 50, 67
See also DC 1
See also DLB 2, 7, 33
See also DLBY 87
See also MTCW
See also SATA 9, 54
See also SSC 10
See also WLC
Baldwin, James 1841-1925 Brief entry ... 111
See also SATA 24
Baldwin, John D. 1930- ... 101
Baldwin, John W(esley) 1929- ... 105
Baldwin, Joseph B(urkette) 1918- ... 111
Baldwin, Joseph Glover 1815-1864 ... DLB 3, 11
Baldwin, Joyce G(ertrude) 1921- ... CANR-8
Earlier sketch in CA 61-64
Baldwin, Leland D(ewitt) 1897-1981 ... 41-44R
Obituary ... 103
Baldwin, Lewis V. 1949- ... 135
Baldwin, Margaret
See Weis, Margaret (Edith)
Baldwin, Marshall W(hithed) 1903-1975 ... 61-64
Obituary ... 57-60
Baldwin, Michael 1930- ... CANR-3
Earlier sketch in CA 9-12R
Baldwin, Monica 1896(?)-1975 Obituary ... 104
Baldwin, Ned
See Baldwin, Edward R(obinson)
Baldwin, Neil 1947- ... 130
Baldwin, Raymond Earl
1893-1986 Obituary ... 121
Baldwin, Rebecca
See Chappell, Helen
Baldwin, Richard S(heridan) 1910- ... 105
Baldwin, Robert E(dward) 1924- ... 41-44R
Baldwin, Roger E(dwin) 1929- ... 49-52
Baldwin, Roger (Nash) 1884-1981 Obituary ... 105
Baldwin, Stan(ley C.) 1929- ... CANR-38
Earlier sketches in CA 49-52, CANR-2, 17
See also SATA 28, 62
Baldwin, William Jr. 1903-1983 ... 129
Obituary ... 111
Baldwin, William Lee 1928- ... CANR-3
Earlier sketch in CA 1-4R
Bale, Robert Osborne 1912- ... 1-4R
Bales, Carol Ann 1940- ... 45-48
See also SATA 29, 57
Bales, Jack
See Bales, James E(dward)
Bales, James D(avid) 1915- ... 5-8R
Bales, James E(dward) 1951- ... CANR-30
Earlier sketch in CA 107
Bales, Robert F(reed) 1916- ... 93-96
Bales, William Alan 1917- ... 5-8R
Balet, Jan (Bernard) 1913- ... 85-88
See also SATA 11
Baley, James A. 1918- ... CANR-5
Earlier sketch in CA 13-16R
Balfort, Neil
See Fanthorpe, R(obert) Lionel
Balfour, A. J.
See Balfour, Arthur James
Balfour, Arthur J.
See Balfour, Arthur James
Balfour, Arthur James
1848-1930 Brief entry ... 120
Balfour, Conrad George 1928- ... 53-56
Balfour, Henry H(allowell) Jr. 1940- ... 117
Balfour, James 1925- ... 25-28R
Balfour, John
See Moore, James
Balfour, Michael (Leonard) Graham
1908- ... CANR-6
Earlier sketch in CA 9-12R
Balfour, (John) Patrick Douglas
1904-1976 ... CANR-6
Earlier sketch in CA 9-12R
Balfour, Victoria 1954- ... 129
Balfour-Kinnear, George Purvis Russell
1888- ... 5-8R
Balian, Lorna 1929- ... CANR-19
Earlier sketches in CA 53-56, CANR-4
See also SATA 9
Baligh, Helmy H. 1931- ... 21-24R
Balikci, Asen 1929- ... 29-32R
Balinky, Alexander 1919- ... 21-24R
Balint, Michael 1896-1970 ... CAP-1
Earlier sketch in CA 9-10
Balis, Andrea F. 1948- ... 108
Balizet, Carol 1933- ... 114
Baljeu, Joost 1925- ... 97-100
Balk, Alfred (W.) 1930- ... 25-28R
Balk, H(oward) Wesley 1932- Brief entry ... 111
Balka, Marie
See Balkany, Marie (Romoka Zelinger) de
Balkany, Marie (Romoka Zelinger) de
1930- ... 104
Balke, Willem 1933- ... 107
Balkey, Rita 1922- ... CANR-30
Earlier sketch in CA 111
Balkin, Richard 1938- ... 77-80
Ball, Angela 1952- ... 135
Ball, B. N.
See Ball, Brian N(eville)
Ball, Brian N(eville) 1932- ... 33-36R
Ball, (Frederick) Clive 1941- Brief entry ... 114
Ball, David 1937- ... 65-68
Ball, Desmond (John) 1947- ... CANR-24
Earlier sketch in CA 106
Ball, Donald W(inston) 1934-1976 ... 122
Obituary ... 110
Ball, Donna 1951- ... 108
Ball, Doris Bell (Collier) 1897-1987 ... CANR-18
Obituary ... 122
Earlier sketches in CA 1-4R, CANR-2
Ball, Edith L. 1905- ... 85-88
Ball, (Katherine) Eve(lyn) 1890-1984 ... 122
Obituary ... 114
Ball, F(rederick) Carlton 1911- ... 17-20R
Ball, George W(ildman) 1909- ... 73-76
Ball, Howard 1937- ... CANR-17
Earlier sketch in CA 33-36R
Ball, Jane Eklund 1921- ... 33-36R
Ball, Jennifer (M. V.) 1958- ... 136
Ball, John C. 1924- ... CANR-8
Earlier sketch in CA 5-8R
Ball, John (Dudley Jr.) 1911-1988 ... CANR-18
Obituary ... 126
Earlier sketches in CA 5-8R, CANR-3
Ball, John M(iller) 1923- ... 33-36R
Ball, Joseph H. 1905- ... CAP-2
Earlier sketch in CA 23-24
Ball, Larry Durwood Sr. 1940- ... 123
Ball, M(ary) Margaret 1909- ... 25-28R
Ball, Marion J(okl) 1940- ... CANR-15
Earlier sketch in CA 89-92
Ball, Nelson 1942- ... 134
Ball, Nicole (Janice) 1948- ... CANR-31
Earlier sketch in CA 112
Ball, Robert Edward 1911- ... 108
Ball, Robert Hamilton 1902-1988 ... 9-12R
Obituary ... 127
Ball, Robert J(erome) 1941- ... 128
Ball, Robert M(yers) 1914- ... 97-100
Ball, Stuart 1956- ... 130
Ball, Sylvia Patricia 1936- ... 57-60
Ball, Terence 1944- ... 138
Ball, Zachary
See Janas, Frankie-Lee
and Masters, Kelly R.
Ballantine, Bill
See Ballantine, William (Oliver)
Ballantine, David 1926- ... 115
Ballantine, John
See da Cruz, Daniel Jr.
Ballantine, John (Winthrop) 1920- ... 53-56
Ballantine, Joseph W.
1890(?)-1973 Obituary ... 41-44R
Ballantine, Lesley Frost
See Frost, Lesley
Ballantine, Richard 1940- ... CANR-1
Earlier sketch in CA 45-48
Ballantine, William (Oliver) 1911- ... 106
Ballantyne, David (Watt) 1924- ... CANR-10
Earlier sketch in CA 65-68
Ballantyne, Dorothy Joan (Smith) 1922- ... 5-8R
Ballantyne, R(obert) M(ichael)
1825-1894 ... SATA 24
Ballantyne, Sheila 1936- ... CANR-25
Earlier sketch in CA 101
Ballard, Allen B(utler Jr.) 1930- ... 61-64
Ballard, Charles E. 1914(?)-1987 Obituary ... 123
Ballard, Dean
See Wilkes-Hunter, R(ichard)
Ballard, Edward Goodwin 1910- ... CANR-30
Earlier sketches in CA 33-36R, CANR-13
Ballard, I. Edward 1909(?)-1985 Obituary ... 117
Ballard, J(ames) G(raham) 1930- ... CANR-39
Earlier sketches in CA 5-8R, CANR-15
See also AAYA 3
See also CLC 3, 6, 14, 36
See also DLB 14
See also MTCW
See also SSC 1
Ballard, Joan Kadey 1928- ... 5-8R
Ballard, K. G.
See Roth, Holly
Ballard, Lowell C(lyne) 1904-1986 ... CAP-1
Obituary ... 120
Earlier sketch in CA 11-12
See also SATA 12, 49
Ballard, (Charles) Martin 1929- ... 25-28R
See also SATA 1
Ballard, Mignon Franklin 1934- ... 121
See also SATA 49, 64
Ballard, P. D.
See Ballard, (Willis) Todhunter
Ballard, Robert D(uane) 1942- ... 112
Ballard, (Willis) Todhunter 1903-1980 ... CANR-29
Earlier sketch in CA 13-16R
Ballard, W. T.
See Ballard, (Willis) Todhunter
Ballard, Willis T.
See Ballard, (Willis) Todhunter
Ballem, John 1925- ... 81-84
Ballen, Roger 1950- ... 103
Ballentine, Rudolph 1941- ... 114
Baller, Warren Robert 1900- ... 69-72
Ballet, Arthur H(arold) 1924- Brief entry ... 111
Balliett, Whitney 1926- ... CANR-30
Earlier sketches in CA 17-20R, CANR-13
Ballin, Caroline ... 17-20R
Balling, Robert C. Jr. 1952- ... 138
Ballingall, James (Gordon Mackie) 1958- ... 117
Ballinger, Bill S.
See Ballinger, William Sanborn
Ballinger, Harry (Russell) 1892- ... CAP-2
Earlier sketch in CA 23-24
Ballinger, James Lawrence 1919- ... 17-20R
Ballinger, Louise Bowen 1909- ... 13-16R
Ballinger, (Violet) Margaret (Livingstone)
1894-1980 ... CANR-13
Obituary ... 105
Earlier sketch in CA 61-64
Ballinger, Raymond A. 1907- ... 5-8R
Ballinger, W. A.
See McNeilly, Wilfred (Glassford)
Ballinger, William Sanborn 1912-1980 ... CANR-1
Obituary ... 97-100
Earlier sketch in CA 1-4R
Ballon, Robert J(ean) 1919- ... CANR-21
Earlier sketch in CA 45-48
Ballonoff, Paul A(lan) 1943- ... 57-60
Ballou, Arthur W. 1915-1981 ... 25-28R
Obituary ... 134
Ballou, Ellen B(artlett) 1905- ... CAP-2
Earlier sketch in CA 29-32
Ballou, Maturin Murray 1820-1895 ... DLB 79
Ballowe, James 1933- ... CANR-12
Earlier sketch in CA 29-32R
Ballstadt, Carl A. 1931- ... 124
Balma, Michael J(ames) 1930- ... 17-20R
Balmain, Pierre (Alexandre)
1914-1982 Obituary ... 107
Balme, Maurice (George) 1925- ... 61-64
Balmer, Edwin 1883-1959 Brief entry ... 114
Balmont, Konstantin (Dmitriyevich)
1867-1943 Brief entry ... 109
See also TCLC 11
Balmuth, Miriam S. ... 124
Balodis, Janis (Maris) 1950- ... 134
Balogh, Penelope 1916-1975 ... CAP-2
Earlier sketch in CA 25-28
See also SATA 1, 34
Balogh, Thomas 1905-1985 ... 57-60
Obituary ... 115
Balota, D(avid) A. 1954- ... 135
Balow, Tom 1931- ... 45-48
See also SATA 12
Baloyra, Enrique Antonio 1942- ... 111
Balsdon, (John Percy Vyvian) Dacre
1901-1977 ... CANR-13
Obituary ... 73-76
Earlier sketch in CA 5-8R
Balsdon, J.P.V.D.
See Balsdon, (John Percy Vyvian) Dacre
Balseiro, Jose Agustin 1900- ... 81-84
See also AITN 1
See also HW
Balsiger, Dave
See Balsiger, David (Wayne)
Balsiger, David (Wayne) 1945- ... CANR-28
Earlier sketches in CA 61-64, CANR-11
Balsley, Howard L(loyd) 1913- ... CANR-4
Earlier sketch in CA 1-4R
Balsley, Irol Whitmore 1912- ... 13-16R
Balswick, Jack Orville ... 136
Balswick, Judith K. 1939- ... 136
Baltake, Joe 1945- ... 118
Baltazar, Eulalio R. 1925- ... 17-20R
Baltazzi, Evan Serge 1919- ... 65-68
Baltensperger, Peter 1938- ... 115
Balterman, Marcia Ridlon 1942- ... 25-28R
See also Ridlon, Marci
Baltes, Paul B. 1939- ... 89-92
Balthasar, Hans Urs von
See von Balthasar, Hans Urs
Balthazar, Earl E(dward) 1918- ... 53-56
Baltimore, J.
See Catherall, Arthur
Baltz, Howard B(url) 1930- ... 29-32R
Baltzell, E(dward) Digby 1915- ... 33-36R
Baltzer, Hans (Adolf) 1900- ... SATA 40
Balukas, Jean 1959- Brief entry ... 111

Balwers, Renato
 See La Barre, Weston
Baly, (Alfred) Denis 1913- ... 17-20R
Baly, Monica Eileen 1914- ... 102
Balzac, Honore de 1799-1850 ... DLB 119
 See also SSC 5
 See also WLC
Balzano, Jeanne (Koppel) 1912- ... 5-8R
 See also Bell, Gina
 and Bell-Zano, Gina
 and Iannone, Jeanne
Balzer, Richard J(ay) 1944- ... 45-48
Balzer, Robert Lawrence 1912- ... 103
Bambara, Toni Cade 1939- ... CANR-24
 Earlier sketch in CA 29-32R
 See also AAYA 5
 See also BLC 1
 See also BW
 See also CLC 19
 See also DLB 38
 See also MTCW
Bamber, Linda 1945- ... 109
Bamberger, Bernard J(acob)
 1904-1980 ... CANR-6
 Obituary ... 101
 Earlier sketch in CA 13-16R
Bamberger, Carl 1902- ... CAP-2
 Earlier sketch in CA 21-22
Bamberger, Fritz 1902-1984 Obituary ... 113
Bamberger, Michael (F.) 1960- ... 134
Bambrough, (John) Renford 1926- ... 61-64
Bamdad, A.
 See Shamlu, Ahmad
Bamford, James 1946- ... 123
Bamford, Paul W(alden) 1921- ... 41-44R
Bamfylde, Walter
 See Bevan, Tom
Bamm, Peter
 See Emmrich, Curt
Bamman, Henry A. 1918- ... CANR-7
 Earlier sketch in CA 5-8R
 See also SATA 12
Ban, (Maria) Eva 1934- ... 73-76
Ban, Joseph D(aniel) 1926- ... CANR-23
 Earlier sketches in CA 21-24R, CANR-8
Ban, Thomas A. 1929- ... CANR-10
 Earlier sketch in CA 21-24R
Banani, Amin 1926- ... 33-36R
Banat, D. R.
 See Bradbury, Ray (Douglas)
Banbury, Philip 1914- ... 102
Bance, Alan F. 1939- ... 111
Banchs, Enrique J. 1888-1968 ... HW
Bancroft, Anne 1923- ... 57-60
Bancroft, Caroline 1900- ... CAP-2
 Earlier sketch in CA 21-22
Bancroft, George 1800-1891 ... DLB 1, 30, 59
Bancroft, Griffing 1907- ... 29-32R
 See also AITN 1
 See also SATA 6
Bancroft, Hubert Howe 1832-1918 ... DLB 47
Bancroft, Iris (May Nelson) 1922- ... CANR-19
 Earlier sketch in CA 102
Bancroft, Laura
 See Baum, L(yman) Frank
Bancroft, Mary 1903- ... 118
Bancroft, Peter 1916- ... 41-44R
Bancroft, Robert
 See Kirsch, Robert R.
Bandeira (Filho), Manuel (Carneiro de Sousa)
 1886(?)-1968 Obituary ... 115
Bandel, Betty 1912- ... 106
 See also SATA 47
Bander, Edward J. 1923- ... CANR-5
 Earlier sketch in CA 13-16R
Bandera, V(ladimir) N(icholas) 1932- ... 33-36R
Bandi, Hans-Georg 1920- ... 85-88
Bandinelli, Ranuccio Bianchi
 1901(?)-1975 Obituary ... 53-56
Bandman, Bertram 1930- ... 21-24R
Bandoff, Hope
 See Guthrie, Thomas Anstey
Bandow, Doug(las) 1957- ... 127
Bandura, Albert 1925- ... 13-16R
Bandy, (Eugene) Franklin 1914-1987 ... CANR-24
 Obituary ... 122
 Earlier sketch in CA 33-36R
Bandy, Leland A. 1935- ... 77-80
Bandy, Melanie 1932- ... 114
Bandy, W(illiam) T(homas) 1903-1989 ... 37-40R
 Obituary ... 129
Bandy, Way 1941(?)-1986 ... 123
 Obituary ... 120
Bane, Mary Jo 1942- ... 126
 Brief entry ... 112
Bane, Michael 1950- ... 108
Banel, Joseph 1943- ... 45-48
Baner, Skulda Vanadis 1897-1964 ... CAP-1
 Earlier sketch in CA 13-14
 See also SATA 10
Banerjee, H(emendra) N(ath)
 1929- Brief entry ... 114
Banerji, Ranan B(ihari) 1928- ... CANR-11
 Earlier sketch in CA 29-32R
Banerji, Sara 1932- ... 126
Banet, Doris Beatrice Robinson 1925- ... 5-8R
Banfield, A(lexander) W(illiam) F(rancis)
 1918- ... 61-64
Banfield, Edward C(hristie) 1916- ... 57-60
 See also AITN 1
Bang, Betsy 1912- ... 102
 See also SATA 37, 48
Bang, Garrett
 See Bang, Molly Garrett
Bang, Molly Garrett 1943- ... 102
 See also CLR 8
 See also MAICYA
 See also SATA 24, 69
Bangert, Ethel E(lizabeth) 1912- ... CANR-1
 Earlier sketch in CA 45-48
Bangert, William V(alentine) 1911- ... 45-48
Bangerter, Lowell A(llen) 1941- ... CANR-26
 Earlier sketches in CA 69-72, CANR-11
Bangham, Mary Dickerson 1896- ... CAP-2
 Earlier sketch in CA 23-24
Banghart, Charles K(enneth)
 1910(?)-1980 Obituary ... 97-100
Banghart, Kenneth
 See Banghart, Charles K(enneth)
Bangley, Bernard K. 1935- ... CANR-28
 Earlier sketch in CA 110
Bangs, Carl (Oliver) 1922- ... CANR-7
 Earlier sketch in CA 17-20R
Bangs, Carol Jane 1949- ... 114
Bangs, John Kendrick
 1862-1922 Brief entry ... 110
 See also DLB 11, 79
Bangs, Lester 1949(?)-1982 Obituary ... 106
Bangs, Richard 1950- ... 122
Bangs, Robert B(abbitt) 1914- ... 37-40R
Banham, (Peter) Reyner 1922-1988 ... CANR-35
 Obituary ... 125
 Earlier sketch in CA 29-32R
Banim, John 1798-1842 ... DLB 116
Banis, Victor J(erome) 1937- ... 81-84
Banister, Gary L. 1948- ... 57-60
Banister, Judith 1943- ... 127
Banister, Manly (Miles) 1914- ... 41-44R
Banister, Margaret
 1894(?)-1977 Obituary ... 73-76
Bank, Dena Citron 1912- ... 123
Bank, Mirra 1945- ... 102
Bank, Stephen Paul 1941- ... 110
Bank, Ted
 See Bank, Theodore P(aul) II
Bank, Theodore P(aul) II 1923- ... 41-44R
Banker, James R. 1938- ... 132
Bank-Jensen, Thea
 See Ottesen, Thea Tauber
Bankoff, George Alexis
 See Milkomane, George Alexis Milkomanovich
Bankowsky, Richard James 1928- ... 1-4R
Banks, A. L.
 See Banks, Arthur Leslie
Banks, A. Leslie
 See Banks, Arthur Leslie
Banks, Ann 1943- ... 105
Banks, Arthur Leslie 1904-1989 Obituary ... 129
Banks, Arthur S. 1926- ... CANR-27
 Earlier sketch in CA 33-36R
Banks, Brian R. 1956- ... 138
Banks, Carolyn 1941- ... CANR-23
 Earlier sketch in CA 105
Banks, Hal N(orman) 1921- ... 102
Banks, Harlan Parker 1913- ... 89-92
Banks, Iain
 See Banks, Iain M(enzies)
Banks, Iain M(enzies) 1954- ... 128
 Brief entry ... 123
 See also CLC 34
Banks, J(ohn) Houston 1911- ... 33-36R
Banks, James A(lbert) 1941- ... CANR-32
 Earlier sketches in CA 33-36R, CANR-13
Banks, James Houston 1925- ... 89-92
Banks, Jane 1913- ... 65-68
Banks, Jimmy
 See Banks, James Houston
Banks, John 1653(?)-1706 ... DLB 80
Banks, Laura Stockton Voorhees
 1908(?)-1980 Obituary ... 101
 See also SATA 23
Banks, Lynne Reid
 See Reid Banks, Lynne
 See also AAYA 6
 See also CLC 23
Banks, Oliver 1941- ... 107
Banks, Richard L. 1920- ... 9-12R
Banks, Roger 1929- ... 107
Banks, Ronald F(illmore) 1934- ... 29-32R
Banks, Russell 1940- ... CANR-19
 Earlier sketch in CA 65-68
 See also CAAS 15
 See also CLC 37, 72
Banks, Sara (Jeanne Gordon Harrell)
 See Harrell, Sara (Jeanne) Gordon
 See also SATA 26
Banks, Taylor
 See Banks, Jane
Banks, William L(ove) 1928- ... 112
Bankson, Douglas (Henneck) 1920- ... CANR-31
 Earlier sketch in CA 45-48
Bankwitz, Philip Charles Farwell 1924- ... 33-36R
Bann, Stephen 1942- ... 137
Banner, Angela
 See Maddison, Angela Mary
 See also CLR 24
Banner, Charla Ann Leibenguth
 1942- ... CANR-24
 Earlier sketch in CA 106
Banner, Hubert Stewart 1891-1964 ... CAP-1
 Earlier sketch in CA 11-12
Banner, James M(orrill) Jr. 1935- ... 49-52
Banner, Lois W(endland) 1939- ... CANR-1
 Earlier sketch in CA 49-52
Banner, Melvin Edward 1914- ... 53-56
Banner, William Augustus 1915- ... 45-48
Bannerman, Helen (Brodie Cowan Watson)
 1862(?)-1946 ... 136
 Brief entry ... 111
 See also CLR 21
 See also MAICYA
 See also SATA 19
Bannerman, Mark
 See Lewing, Anthony Charles
Bannerman, Roland
 See Hartston, W(illiam) R(oland)
Bannerman, W. Mary 1894-1984 Obituary ... 114
Bannet, Eve Tavor ... 127
Bannick, Nancy (Meredith) 1926- ... 41-44R
Banning, Evelyn I. 1903- ... 73-76
 See also SATA 36
Banning, Lance (Gilbert) 1942- ... 89-92
Banning, Margaret Culkin 1891-1982 ... CANR-4
 Obituary ... 105
 Earlier sketch in CA 5-8R
Bannister, Don
 See Bannister, Donald
Bannister, Donald 1928- ... CANR-9
 Earlier sketch in CA 61-64
Bannister, Jo 1951- ... 119
Bannister, Pat
 See Davis, Lou Ellen
Bannister, Patricia V. 1923- Brief entry ... 115
Bannister, Robert C(orwin) Jr. 1935- ... 21-24R
Bannister, Sally
 See Pratt, James Norwood
Bannock, Graham 1932- ... 33-36R
Bannon, Barbara Anne 1928- ... 101
Bannon, John Francis 1905-1986 ... CANR-4
 Obituary ... 119
 Earlier sketch in CA 1-4R
Bannon, Laura ... 1-4R
 See also SATA 6
Bannon, Peter
 See Durst, Paul
Bansemer, Roger 1948- ... 137
Banta, Martha 1928- ... CANR-29
 Earlier sketch in CA 81-84
Banta, R(ichard) E(lwell) 1904- ... CAP-2
 Earlier sketch in CA 33-36
Bantel, Linda 1943- ... 113
Banting, Keith G. 1947- ... 129
Banting, Peter M(yles) 1936- ... 112
Bantock, G(eoffrey) H(erman) 1914- ... CANR-11
 Earlier sketch in CA 25-28R
Bantock, Gavin (Marcus August) 1939- ... 33-36R
Banton, Coy
 See Norwood, Victor G(eorge) C(harles)
Banton, Michael (Parker) 1926- ... CANR-2
 Earlier sketch in CA 5-8R
Banville, John 1945- ... 128
 Brief entry ... 117
 See also CLC 46
 See also DLB 14
Banville, Thomas G(eorge) 1924- ... 81-84
Bany, Mary A. 1913- ... 9-12R
Banz, George 1928- ... 29-32R
Banziger, Hans
 See Baenziger, Hans
Bapu
 See Khare, Narayan Bhaskar
Barabas, Gabor 1948- ... 134
Barabas, Steven 1904-1983 ... 5-8R
 Obituary ... 109
Barabas, SuzAnne 1949- ... 134
Barach, Alvan L(eroy)
 1895-1977 Obituary ... 73-76
Barach, Arnold B(auer) 1913-1987 ... 97-100
 Obituary ... 122
Barack, Nathan A. 1913- ... 13-16R
Barackman, Floyd Hays Jr. 1923- ... 115
Barackman, Paul F(reeman) 1894- ... 1-4R
Baracks, Barbara 1951- ... 106
Barada, Bill
 See Barada, William Richard
Barada, William Richard 1913- ... 45-48
Bar-Adon, Aaron 1923- Brief entry ... 114
Baraheni, Reza 1935- ... 69-72
Barak, Gregg 1948- ... CANR-35
 Earlier sketch in CA 114
Barak, Michael
 See Bar-Zohar, Michael
Baraka, Amiri 1934- ... CANR-38
 Earlier sketches in CA 21-24R, CANR-27
 See also Jones, LeRoi
 See also CABS 3
 See also BLC 1
 See also BW
 See also CDALB 1941-1968
 See also CLC 1, 2, 3, 5, 10, 14, 33
 See also DLB 5, 7, 16, 38
 See also DLBD 8
 See also MTCW
 See also PC 4
Baral, Robert 1910- ... CAP-1
 Earlier sketch in CA 9-10
Baram, Phillip J(ason) 1938- ... 85-88
Baram, Robert 1919- Brief entry ... 112
Baran, Annette 1927- Brief entry ... 114
Baranet, Nancy Neiman 1933- ... 41-44R
Baranov, Alexander A.
 1931(?)-1983 Obituary ... 109
Baranson, Jack 1924- ... 119
Barany, George 1922- ... 25-28R
Barasch, Frances K. 1928- ... 37-40R
Barasch, Marc Ian 1949- ... 113
Barasch, Moshe 1920- ... 97-100
Barash, Meyer 1916- ... 1-4R
Barash, Samuel T(heodore) 1921- ... 107
Barayon, Ramon Sender
 See Sender Barayon, Ramon
Barba, Harry 1922- ... CANR-1
 Earlier sketch in CA 1-4R
Barbach, Lonnie (Villoldo) 1946- ... CANR-25
 Earlier sketches in CA 61-64, CANR-9
Barbanell, Maurice 1902-1981 Obituary ... 113
Barbara, Dominick A. 1914- ... 37-40R
Barbare, Rholf
 See Volkoff, Vladimir
Barbarese, J. T. 1948- ... 135
Barbary, James
 See Beeching, Jack
Barbash, Jack 1910- ... CANR-16
 Earlier sketch in CA 1-4R
Barbauld, Anna Laetitia
 1743-1825 ... DLB 107, 109
Barbe, Walter Burke 1926- ... 13-16R
 See also SATA 45
Barbeau, Arthur E(dward) 1936- ... 49-52
Barbeau, Clayton C(harles) 1930- ... 73-76
Barbeau, Marius 1883-1969 Obituary ... 25-28R
 See also DLB 92
Barbee, David E(dwin) 1936- ... 57-60
Barbee, Phillips
 See Sheckley, Robert
Barbellion, W. N. P.
 See Cummings, Bruce F(rederick)
 See also TCLC 24
Barber, Antonia
 See Anthony, Barbara
Barber, Benjamin R. 1939- ... CANR-32
 Earlier sketches in CA 29-32R, CANR-12
Barber, Bernard 1918- ... CANR-14
 Earlier sketch in CA 65-68
Barber, Charles (Laurence) 1915- ... CANR-22
 Earlier sketches in CA 17-20R, CANR-7
Barber, Cyril J(ohn) 1934- ... CANR-9
 Earlier sketch in CA 65-68
Barber, D(ulan) F(riar Whilberton)
 1940- ... CANR-21
 Earlier sketch in CA 61-64
Barber, James David 1930- ... CANR-6
 Earlier sketch in CA 13-16R
Barber, James G(eoffrey) 1952- ... 110
Barber, Jesse 1893-1979 Obituary ... 85-88
Barber, John Warner 1798-1885 ... DLB 30
Barber, John 1944- ... 128
Barber, Joseph 1909-1982 Obituary ... 107
Barber, Karin ... 138
Barber, Lucie W(elles) 1922- ... 108
Barber, Lucy L(ombardi)
 1882(?)-1974 Obituary ... 49-52
Barber, Lynda
 See Graham-Barber, Lynda
Barber, Lynda Graham
 See Graham-Barber, Lynda
Barber, Lynn 1944- ... 97-100
Barber, Noel (John Lysberg)
 1909-1988 Obituary ... 126
 Brief entry ... 115
Barber, Paul (Thomas) 1941- ... 134
Barber, Philip W. 1903-1981 Obituary ... 103
Barber, Red
 See Barber, Walter Lanier
Barber, Richard J. 1932- ... 29-32R
Barber, Richard (William) 1941- ... CANR-32
 Earlier sketches in CA 33-36R, CANR-13
 See also SATA 35
Barber, Samuel 1910-1981 Obituary ... 103
Barber, Stephen Guy 1921-1980 ... 69-72
 Obituary ... 97-100
Barber, T(heodore) X(enophon) 1927- ... 41-44R
Barber, Walter Lanier 1908- Brief entry ... 113
Barber, Willard F(oster) 1909- ... CAP-2
 Earlier sketch in CA 21-22
Barber, William Henry 1918- ... 5-8R
Barber, William Joseph 1925- ... CANR-8
 Earlier sketch in CA 61-64
Barbera, Henry 1929- ... 105
Barbera, Jack 1945- ... 110
 See also CLC 44
Barbera, Joe
 See Barbera, Joseph Roland
Barbera, Joseph Roland 1911- ... SATA 51
Barberis
 See Barberis, Franco
Barberis, Franco 1905- ... 25-28R
Barberis, Juan C(arlos) 1920- ... SATA 61
Barbero, Yves Regis Francois 1943- ... 57-60
Barbet, Pierre
 See Avice, Claude (Pierre Marie)
Barbette, Jay
 See Spicer, Bart
Barbey d'Aurevilly, Jules Amedee
 1808-1889 ... DLB 119
Barbieri, Elaine 1936- ... 138
Barbotin, Edmond 1920- ... 57-60
Barbour, Alan G. 1933- Brief entry ... 117
Barbour, Arthur Joseph 1926- ... 57-60
Barbour, Brian M(ichael) 1943- ... 49-52
Barbour, Douglas (Fleming) 1940- ... CANR-27
 Earlier sketches in CA 69-72, CANR-11
Barbour, Frances Martha 1895- ... 17-20R
Barbour, George 1890-1977 Obituary ... 73-76
Barbour, Hugh (Stewart) 1921- ... 21-24R
Barbour, Ian G(raeme) 1923- ... CANR-8
 Earlier sketch in CA 21-24R
Barbour, J(ames) Murray 1897-1970 ... CAP-1
 Earlier sketch in CA 11-12
Barbour, Julian B. 1937- ... 133
Barbour, Karen 1956- ... 127
 See also SATA 63
Barbour, Kenneth Michael 1921- ... CANR-7
 Earlier sketch in CA 5-8R
Barbour, Michael G(eorge) 1942- ... CANR-2
 Earlier sketch in CA 49-52
Barbour, Nevill 1895-1972 ... 5-8R
 Obituary ... 103
Barbour, Philip L(emont) 1898- ... 9-12R

Barbour, Ralph Henry 1870-1944 .... DLB 22
See also SATA 16
Barbour, Roger W(illiam) 1919- 61-64
Barbour, Russell B. 1906- CAP-2
Earlier sketch in CA 23-24
Barbour, Ruth P(eeling) 1924- 89-92
Barbour, Thomas L.
See Lesure, Thomas B(arbour)
Barbrook, Alec
See Barbrook, Alexander Thomas
Barbrook, Alexander Thomas 1927- 45-48
Barbusse, Henri 1873-1935 Brief entry 105
See also DLB 65
See also TCLC 5
Barchek, James Robert 1935- 41-44R
Barchiesi, Robert 1955- 137
Barchilon, Jacques 1923- CANR-5
Earlier sketch in CA 13-16R
Barchus, Agnes J(osephine) 1893- 97-100
Barcia, Jose Rubia
See Rubia Barcia, Jose
Barck, Oscar Theodore Jr. 1902- 21-24R
Barclay, Andrew M(ichael) 1941- 113
Barclay, Ann
See Greig, Maysie
Barclay, Barbara 1938- 29-32R
Barclay, Bill
See Moorcock, Michael (John)
Barclay, Cyril Nelson 1896- 5-8R
Barclay, Glen St. J(ohn) 1930- 77-80
Barclay, Harold B. 1924- 9-12R
Barclay, Hartley Wade 1903-1978 85-88
Obituary 81-84
Barclay, Isabel
See Dobell, I(sabel) M(arian) B(arclay)
Barclay, Oliver R(ainsford) 1919- CANR-8
Earlier sketch in CA 57-60
Barclay, Virginia
See McDonnell, Virginia B(leecker)
Barclay, William Ewert
See Moorcock, Michael (John)
Barclay, William 1907-1978 .... CANR-29
Obituary 73-76
Earlier sketch in CA 77-80
Barcus, James E(dgar) 1938- 21-24R
Barcus, Nancy B(idwell) 1937- 117
Barcynski, Leon Roger 1949- CANR-10
Earlier sketch in CA 93-96
Barcynski, Vivian G(odfrey) 1917- CANR-10
Earlier sketch in CA 61-64
Bard, Bernard 1927- 25-28R
Bard, Harry 1906-1976 .... 33-36R
Bard, James (Alan) 1925- 102
Bard, Morton 1924- 97-100
Bard, Patti 1935- 21-24R
Bard, Rachel 1921- 117
Bardach, John E(ugene) 1915- 41-44R
Bardarson, Hjalmar R(oegnvaldur) 1918- 57-60
Barden, Leonard (William) 1929- CANR-2
Earlier sketch in CA 1-4R
Barden, Thomas E(arl) 1946- 136
Bardens, Amey E. 1894(?)-1974 Obituary 53-56
Bardens, Dennis (Conrad) 1911- 5-8R
Bardi, Pietro Maria 1900- CANR-19
Earlier sketch in CA 85-88
Bardin, John Franklin 1916-1981 81-84
Obituary 104
Bardis, Panos D(emetrios) 1924- CANR-10
Earlier sketch in CA 25-28R
Bard of Avondale
See Jacobs, Howard
Bardolph, Richard 1915- 61-64
Bardon, Edward J(ohn) 1933- 81-84
Bardon, Jack Irving 1925- 101
Bardos, Marie (Dupuis) 1935- 13-16R
Bardot, Louis 1896-1975 Obituary 61-64
Bardsley, Cuthbert K(illick) N(orman)
1907-1991 .... CAP-2
Obituary 133
Earlier sketch in CA 25-28
Bardwell, George E(ldred) 1924- 1-4R
Bardwick, Judith M(arcia) 1933- CANR-19
Earlier sketch in CA 103
Bare, Arnold Edwin 1920- .... SATA 16
Bare, Colleen Stanley 102
See also SATA 32
Barea, Arturo 1897-1957 Brief entry 111
See also TCLC 14
Bareham, Terence 1937- 109
Barell, John 1938- 111
Barendrecht, Cor W(illiam) 1934- 114
Barenholtz, Bernard 1914-1989 .... SATO 64
Baretski, Charles Allan 1918- 77-80
Barfield, (Arthur) Owen 1898- CANR-2
Earlier sketch in CA 5-8R
Barfoot, Audrey Ilma 1918-1964 .... 5-8R
Barfoot, Joan 1946- 105
See also CLC 18
Barford, Carol 1931- 89-92
Barford, Philip (Trevelyan) 1925- 93-96
Bargad, Warren 1940- 122
Bargar, B(radley) D(uffee) 1924- 17-20R
Bargar, Gary W. 1947-1985 .... SATA 63
Bargate, Verity 1941(?)-1981 Obituary 103
Bargebuhr, Frederick P(erez) 1904- CAP-2
Earlier sketch in CA 33-36
Bargellini, Piero 1897-1980(?) Obituary 97-100
Barger, Harold 1907- CAP-2
Earlier sketch in CA 19-20
Barger, James (David) 1947- 57-60
Bar-Hillel, Yehoshua 1915-1975 Obituary 115
Barille, Elisabeth 1960- 137
Baring, Arnulf Martin 1932- 41-44R
Baring, Maurice 1874-1945 Brief entry 105
See also DLB 34
See also TCLC 8
Baringer, William E(ldon) 1909- 1-4R
Baring-Gould, William Stuart
1913-1967 Obituary 25-28R
Barish, Evelyn 1935- 132
Barish, Jonas A. 1922- 21-24R
Barish, Matthew 1907- 57-60
See also SATA 12
Baritz, Loren 1928- 13-16R
Barjavel, Rene (Gustave Henri)
1911- Brief entry 107
Bark, Dennis L(aistner) 1942- 117
Bark, William (Carroll) 1908- CAP-1
Earlier sketch in CA 13-14
Barkalow, Frederick Schenck Jr. 1914- 61-64
Barkan, Elliott Robert 1940- 21-24R
Barkan, Leonard 1944- 122
Brief entry 116
Barkas, J. L.
See Yager, Jan
Barkas, Janet
See Yager, Jan
Barkdoll, Robert S. 1913(?)-1984 Obituary 112
Barkee, Asouff
See Strung, Norman
Barker, A(rthur) J(ames) 1918-1981 .... CANR-7
Obituary 104
Earlier sketch in CA 13-16R
Barker, A(udrey) L(ilian) 1918- CANR-27
Earlier sketches in CA 9-12R, CANR-3
See also DLB 14
Barker, A(nthony) W(ilhelm) 1930- CANR-32
Earlier sketch in CA 113
Barker, Albert W. 1900- CANR-14
Earlier sketch in CA 73-76
See also SATA 8
Barker, Andrew (Dennison) 1943- 130
Barker, Bill
See Barker, William J(ohn)
Barker, Carol M. 1942- 45-48
Barker, Carol (Minturn) 1938- 107
See also SATA 31
Barker, Charles Albro 1904- 93-96
Barker, Charles M. Jr. 1926- 13-16R
Barker, Cicely Mary 1895-1973 121
Obituary 117
See also SATA 39, 49
Barker, Clive 1952- 129
Brief entry 121
See also BEST 90:3
See also CLC 52
See also MTCW
Barker, D(erek) R(oland) 1930- 5-8R
Barker, Dennis (Malcolm) 1929- CANR-32
Earlier sketches in CA 25-28R, CANR-14
Barker, Dudley 1910-1980(?) CANR-1
Obituary 102
Earlier sketch in CA 1-4R
Barker, E. M.
See Barker, Elsa (McCormick)
Barker, Elisabeth 1910-1986 136
Obituary 118
Barker, Elliott S(peer) 1886-1988 89-92
Obituary 125
Barker, Elsa (McCormick) 1906- CAP-2
Earlier sketch in CA 17-18
Barker, Elspeth 1940- 138
Barker, Elver A. 1920- 25-28R
Barker, Eric 1905-1973 .... CANR-27
Obituary 41-44R
Earlier sketch in CA 1-4R
Barker, Ernest 1874-1960 103
Obituary 93-96
Barker, Esther T(emperley) 1910- CANR-2
Earlier sketch in CA 49-52
Barker, Felix 1917- 130
Barker, Frank Granville 1923- CAP-1
Earlier sketch in CA 11-12
Barker, George Granville 1913-1991 .... CANR-38
Obituary 135
Earlier sketches in CA 9-12R, CANR-7
See also CLC 8, 48
See also DLB 20
See also MTCW
Barker, Gerard A(rthur) 1930- 69-72
Barker, Graham H(arold) 1949- 106
Barker, Harley Granville
See Granville-Barker, Harley
See also DLB 10
Barker, Howard 1946- 102
See also CLC 37
See also DLB 13
Barker, Jack M. 1924(?)-1985 Obituary 117
Barker, James Nelson 1784-1858 .... DLB 37
Barker, Jane Valentine 1930- CANR-11
Earlier sketch in CA 65-68
Barker, Jane 1652-1727(?) .... DLB 39
Barker, John W(alton Jr.) 1933- 17-20R
Barker, Joseph 1929- 103
Barker, Keith 1947- 135
Barker, Kenneth S(tacey) 1932- 110
Barker, Larry L(ee) 1941- CANR-17
Earlier sketch in CA 81-84
Barker, M(uhammad) A(bd-Al-)R(ahman)
1929- 116
Barker, Margaret 1944- 128
Barker, Melvern 1907- CAP-1
Earlier sketch in CA 9-10
See also SATA 11
Barker, Myrtie Lillian 1910- 5-8R
Barker, Nancy Nichols 1925- Brief entry 114
Barker, Nicolas (John) 1932- 102
Barker, Pat 1943- 122
Brief entry 117
See also CLC 32
Barker, Philip 1929- 114
Barker, Ralph 1917- CANR-38
Earlier sketches in CA 1-4R, CANR-1, 16
Barker, Robert L(ee) 1937- 25-28R
Barker, Rodney (Steven) 1942- 45-48
Barker, Roger Garlock 1903- CANR-11
Earlier sketches in CAP-1, CA 11-12
Barker, Ronald 1921(?)-1976 Obituary 65-68
Barker, S. Omar 1894- CAP-2
Earlier sketch in CA 17-18
See also SATA 10
Barker, Sally
See McMurry, Sarah L.
Barker, Sebastian 1945- 124
Barker, Shirley Frances 1911-1965 .... 5-8R
Barker, T(heodore Cardwell) 1923- CANR-5
Earlier sketch in CA 13-16R
Barker, T(erence) S(narr) 1941- CANR-21
Earlier sketch in CA 45-48
Barker, Thomas M. 1929- 21-24R
Barker, W(illiam) Alan 1923-1988(?) CANR-1
Obituary 125
Earlier sketch in CA 1-4R
Barker, Wendy B. 1942- 125
Barker, Will 1913-1983 .... 9-12R
Obituary 110
See also SATA 8
Barker, William J(ohn) 65-68
Barker, William P(ierson) 1927- 9-12R
Barker-Benfield, G(raham) J(ohn)
1941- Brief entry 113
Barkhouse, Joyce 1913- 93-96
See also SATA 48
Barkin, Carol 1944- 135
Brief entry 118
See also SATA 42, 52
Barkin, David Peter 1942- 37-40R
Barkin, Kenneth D(avid) 1939- 41-44R
Barkin, Solomon 1907- 9-12R
Barkins, Evelyn (Warner) 1919- 29-32R
Barkley, Deanne 1931- Brief entry 114
Barkley, James Edward 1941- .... SATA 6
Barkley, T(heodore) M(itchell) 1934- 120
Barkley, Vada Lee 1919- 57-60
Barkman, Alma 1939- CANR-35
Earlier sketch in CA 114
Barkman, Paul Friesen 1921- 17-20R
Barkow, Al 1932- CANR-4
Earlier sketch in CA 53-56
Barks, Carl 1901- 115
See also SATA 37
Barks, Coleman (Bryan) 1937- CANR-12
Earlier sketch in CA 25-28R
See also DLB 5
Barksdale, E(thelbert) C(ourtland) 1944- 57-60
Barksdale, Hiram C(ollier) 1921- 9-12R
Barksdale, Richard (Kenneth) 1915- 49-52
Barkton, S. Rush
See Brav, Stanley R(osenbaum)
Barkun, Michael 1938- 135
Brief entry 114
Barkworth, Peter (Wynn) 1929- 107
Barlach, Ernst 1870-1938 .... DLB 56, 118
Barlay, Bennett
See Crossen, Kendell Foster
Barlay, Stephen 1930- CANR-12
Earlier sketch in CA 25-28R
Barlett, Donald L(eon) 1936- 115
Barley, M. W.
See Barley, Maurice Willmore
Barley, Maurice Willmore 1909-1991 122
Obituary 134
Barlin, Anne L(ief) 1916- 97-100
Barling, Charles
See Barling, Muriel Vere Mant
Barling, Muriel Vere Mant 1904- 5-8R
Barlough, J(effrey) Ernest 1953- 49-52
Barlow, Claude W(illis) 1907-1976 .... CAP-2
Earlier sketch in CA 33-36
Barlow, Frank 1911- CANR-30
Earlier sketches in CA 9-12R, CANR-3
Barlow, Genevieve 1910- 21-24R
Barlow, J(ames) Stanley (Jr.) 1924- 41-44R
Barlow, James 1921-1973 .... CAP-1
Obituary 41-44R
Earlier sketch in CA 13-14
Barlow, Jane 1857-1917 Brief entry 115
Barlow, Joel 1754-1812 .... DLB 37
Barlow, John A(lfred) 1924- 21-24R
Barlow, John D(enison) 1934- 120
Barlow, Judith E(llen) 1946- 107
Barlow, Maude 1947- 135
Barlow, (Emma) Nora 1885- CAP-2
Earlier sketch in CA 25-28
Barlow, Robert O.
See Meyer, Heinrich
Barlow, Roger
See Leckie, Robert (Hugh)
Barlow, Samuel L(atham) M(itchell)
1892-1982 Obituary 107
Barlow, Sanna Morrison
See Rossi, Sanna Morrison Barlow
Barlow, T(homas) Edward 1931- CANR-3
Earlier sketch in CA 45-48
Barlow, Tani E. 1950- 130
Barlow, Wilfred 1915- 101
Barlowe, Raleigh 1914- 17-20R
Barlowe, Wayne Douglas 1958- 134
Barltrop, Robert 1922- CANR-19
Earlier sketch in CA 73-76
Barman, Alicerose 1919- 65-68
Barman, Charles R(oy) 1945- 106
Barmann, Lawrence Francis 1932- 9-12R
Barmash, Isadore 1921- CANR-17
Earlier sketches in CA 45-48, CANR-1
Barme, Geremie 1954- 131
Barmine, Alexander (G.)
1899-1987 Obituary 125
Barna, George 1954- 114
Barna, Joel Warren 1951- 138
Barna, Yon 1927- 53-56
Barnabas
See West, Charles Converse
Barnabas
See Blandford, Brian E(rnest)
Barnaby, (Charles) Frank 1927- CANR-29
Earlier sketches in CA 33-36R, CANR-13
Barnaby, Ralph S(tanton) 1893- 61-64
See also SATA 9
Barnard, (James) Alan 1928- 9-12R
Barnard, Charles N(elson III) 1924- CANR-1
Earlier sketch in CA 49-52
Barnard, Christiaan (Neethling) 1922- CANR-14
Earlier sketch in CA 61-64
Barnard, Ellsworth 1907- CANR-26
Earlier sketches in CA 21-24R, CANR-11
Barnard, F(rederick) M(echner) 1921- 25-28R
Barnard, Harry 1906-1982 .... CANR-3
Obituary 107
Earlier sketch in CA 5-8R
Barnard, Howard Clive 1884-1985 85-88
Obituary 117
Barnard, J(ohn) Darrell 1906- 5-8R
Barnard, J(ohn) Lawrence 1912-1977 77-80
Obituary 73-76
Barnard, (Virail) John 1932- 33-36R
Barnard, John 1681-1770 .... DLB 24
Barnard, Mary (Ethel) 1909- CAP-2
Earlier sketch in CA 21-22
See also CLC 48
Barnard, Robert 1936- CANR-20
Earlier sketch in CA 77-80
Barnard, William Dean 1942- 69-72
Bar-Natan, Moshe
See Louvish, Misha
Barne, Kitty
See Barne, Marion Catherine
Barne, Marion Catherine
1883-1957 Brief entry 112
Barner, Bob 1947- 93-96
See also SATA 29
Bar Ner, R.
See Brenner, Reeve R(obert)
Barnes, Adrienne Martine
See Martine-Barnes, Adrienne
Barnes, Barry 1943- 97-100
Barnes, Burton V(erne) 1930- 130
Barnes, Chesley Virginia
See Young, Chesley Virginia
Barnes, Christopher J(ohn) 1942- 132
Barnes, Clara Ernst 1895- 5-8R
Barnes, Clive (Alexander) 1927- CANR-26
Earlier sketch in CA 77-80
See also AITN 2
Barnes, Djuna 1892-1982 .... CANR-16
Obituary 107
Earlier sketch in CA 9-12R
See also CLC 3, 4, 8, 11, 29
See also DLB 4, 9, 45
See also MTCW
See also SSC 3
Barnes, Douglas 1927- CANR-19
Earlier sketch in CA 103
Barnes, Duncan 1935- 127
Barnes, Edward F.
See Marquis, Max
Barnes, Elmer Tracey CANR-26
Earlier sketches in CAP-2, CA 19-20
Barnes, (Frank) Eric Wollencott
1907-1962 .... SATA 22
Barnes, Gregory Allen 1934- CANR-25
Earlier sketches in CA 25-28R, CANR-10
Barnes, Harry Elmer 1889-1968 89-92
Obituary 25-28R
Barnes, Hazel E(stella) 1915- CANR-3
Earlier sketch in CA 5-8R
Barnes, Henry A. 1906-1968 .... CAP-1
Earlier sketch in CA 13-16
Barnes, Irston Roberts 1904-1988 Obituary 124
Barnes, J(ohn) A(rundel) 1918- 101
Barnes, J. 1944- 85-88
Barnes, Jack 1920- 89-92
Barnes, Jack 1940- CANR-9
Earlier sketch in CA 61-64
Barnes, James A(nderson) 1898- 9-12R
Barnes, James J(ohn) 1931- CANR-4
Earlier sketch in CA 9-12R
Barnes, James N(eil) 1944- 117
Barnes, Jane
See Casey, Jane Barnes
Barnes, Jim 1933- 108
Barnes, Joanna 1934- 57-60
Barnes, John (Allen) 1957- 137
Barnes, John B(ertram) 1924- 33-36R
Barnes, (Ernest) John (Ward) 1917- 108
Barnes, John 1908- CANR-2
Earlier sketch in CA 45-48
Barnes, Joseph Fels 1907-1970 Obituary 104
Barnes, Julian 1946- CANR-19
Earlier sketch in CA 102
See also CLC 42
Barnes, Kenneth Charles 1903- 106
Barnes, Leonard (John) 1895- CAP-2
Earlier sketch in CA 29-32
Barnes, Lilly I. 1935- 126
Barnes, Linda
See Barnes, Linda J(oyce)
Barnes, Linda J(oyce) 1949- 132
Barnes, Loutricia
See Barnes-Svarney, Patricia L(ou)
Barnes, Malcolm 1909(?)-1984 Obituary 114
See also SATA 41
Barnes, Margaret Ayer
1886-1967 Obituary 25-28R
See also DLB 9
Barnes, Mary 1923- 85-88
Barnes, Melvyn (Peter Keith) 1942- 122
Barnes, Michael (Anthony) 1947- 137

Barnes, Michael 1934- .... SATA 55
Barnes, Patience P(lummer) 1932- 108
Barnes, Peter 1931- CANR-34
Earlier sketches in CA 65-68, CANR-33
See also CAAS 12
See also CLC 5, 56
See also DLB 13
See also MTCW
Barnes, Phoebe 1908- CAP-2
Earlier sketch in CA 23-24
Barnes, R(ichard) G(ordon) 1932- 33-36R
Barnes, Ralph M(osser) 1900-1984 .... CAP-2
Obituary 114
Earlier sketch in CA 17-18
Barnes, Robert J(ay) 1925- 21-24R
Barnes, Robert M(orson) 1940- CANR-25
Earlier sketch in CA 45-48
Barnes, Sam(uel) G(ill) 1913- 13-16R
Barnes, Samuel H(enry) 1931- 21-24R
Barnes, Simon 1951- 130
Barnes, Stephen Emory 1952- 105
Barnes, Steven
See Barnes, Stephen Emory
Barnes, Thomas Garden 1930- CANR-1
Earlier sketch in CA 1-4R
Barnes, Timothy David 1942- 114
Barnes, Valerie 115
Barnes, Viola Florence 1885- 1-4R
Barnes, Walter 1880-1969 Obituary 116
Barnes, William 1801-1886 .... DLB 32
Barness, Richard 1917- 65-68
Barnes-Svarney, Patricia L(ou) 1953- 135
See also SATA 67
Barnet, Richard J. 13-16R
Barnet, Sylvan 1926- CANR-4
Earlier sketch in CA 1-4R
Barnetson, William Denholm
1917-1981 Obituary 103
Barnett, A. Doak 1921- CANR-15
Earlier sketch in CA 5-8R
Barnett, Adam
See Fast, Julius
Barnett, Correlli (Douglas) 1927- CANR-15
Earlier sketch in CA 13-16R
Barnett, Franklin 1903- 69-72
Barnett, George L(eonard) 1915- 29-32R
Barnett, (Nicolas) Guy 1928- 17-20R
Barnett, H(omer) G(arner) 1906- 45-48
Barnett, Isobel (Morag)
1918-1980 Obituary 105
Barnett, Ivan 1947- .... SATA 70
Barnett, James Monroe 1925- 114
Barnett, Joe R(ichard) 1933- 106
Barnett, Joel 1923- 129
Barnett, L. David
See Laschever, Barnett D.
Barnett, Leo 1925- 29-32R
Barnett, Leonard (Palin) 1919- CANR-12
Earlier sketches in CAP-1, CA 13-14
Barnett, Lincoln (Kinnear) 1909-1979 102
Obituary 89-92
See also SATA 36
Barnett, Malcolm Joel 1941- 45-48
Barnett, Marva T(uttle) 1913- 57-60
Barnett, Maurice 1917-1980 Obituary 97-100
Barnett, Michael 1930- 57-60
Barnett, Moneta 1922-1976 .... SATA 33
Barnett, Naomi 1927- CANR-7
Earlier sketch in CA 5-8R
See also SATA 40
Barnett, Peter Herbert 1945- 124
Barnett, Richard B(aity) 1941- 105
Barnett, Richard C(hambers) 1932- 33-36R
Barnett, Robert W(arren) 1911- 126
Barnett, Rosalind C(hait) 1937- 129
Barnett, S(amuel) A(nthony) 1915- CANR-6
Earlier sketch in CA 13-16R
Barnett, Sanford 1909(?)-1988 Obituary 125
Barnett, Suzanne Wilson 1940- 120
Barnett, Ursula A(nnemarie) 1924- 123
Barnett, Vivian E(ndicott) 1944- 115
Barnette, Henlee H(ulix) 1911- CANR-31
Earlier sketch in CA 49-52
Barnette, Martha 1957- 136
Barnette, W(arren) Leslie Jr. 1910- CAP-1
Earlier sketch in CA 11-12
Barnewall, Gordon G(ouverneur) 1924- 121
Barney, Harry
See Lottman, Eileen
Barney, Kenneth D. 1921- 69-72
Barney, Laura D(reyfus)
1880(?)-1974 Obituary 53-56
Barney, LeRoy 1930- 33-36R
Barney, Maginel Wright
1881(?)-1966 Obituary 111
See also SATA 32, 39
Barney, Natalie (Clifford)
1876(?)-1972 Obituary 33-36R
See also DLB 4
Barney, Stephen A(llen) 1942- 102
Barney, William L(esko) 1943- 41-44R
Barnhart, Clarence L(ewis) 1900- 13-16R
See also SATA 48
Barnhart, Joe Edward 1931- 41-44R
Barnhart, Michael A(ndrew) 1951- 127
Barnhart, Robert K. 1933- 127
Barnhill, Myrtle Fait 1896-1986 .... CAP-1
Obituary 119
Earlier sketch in CA 13-16
Barnhouse, Donald 103
Barnhouse, Donald Grey 1895-1960 123
Obituary 113
Barnhouse, Ruth Tiffany 1923- CANR-15
Earlier sketch in CA 85-88
Barnie, John 1941- 57-60
Barnitt, Nedda Lemmon 9-12R
Barnitz, Harry W. 1920-1973 .... CAP-2
Earlier sketch in CA 25-28
Barnoon, Shlomo 1940- 41-44R
Barnouw, Adriaan Jacob
1877-1968 Obituary 104
See also SATA 27
Barnouw, Erik 1908- CANR-12
Earlier sketch in CA 13-16R
Barnouw, Victor 1915- 85-88
See also SATA 28, 43
Barn Owl
See Howells, Roscoe
Barnright, Julia
See Bancroft, Iris (May Nelson)
Barns, John W(intour) B(aldwin)
1912-1974 Obituary 49-52
Barnsley, Alan Gabriel 1916-1986 ....13-16R
Obituary 121
Barnstone, Aliki 1956- 105
Barnstone, Howard 1923-1987 Obituary 122
Barnstone, Willis 1927- 17-20R
See also CAAS 15
See also SATA 20
Barnum, Jay Hyde 1888(?)-1962 .... SATA 20
Barnum, P. T. Jr.
See Stratemeyer, Edward L.
Barnum, Richard CANR-26
Earlier sketches in CAP-2, CA 19-20
See also SATA 1, 67
Barnum, Theodore
See Stratemeyer, Edward L.
Barnum, Vance CANR-26
Earlier sketches in CAP-2, CA 19-20
Barnum, W(illiam) Paul 1933- 29-32R
Barnwell, D. Robinson 1915- 17-20R
Barnwell, John (Gibbes Jr.) 1947- 113
Barnwell, William Curtis 1943- 103
Baro, Gene 1924-1982 Obituary 112
Baroff, George Stanley 1924- 101
Baroja (y Nessi), Pio 1872-1956 Brief entry 104
See also TCLC 8
Barolini, Antonio 1910-1971 ....CANR-1
Earlier sketch in CA 1-4R
Barolini, Helen 1925- CANR-39
Earlier sketches in CA 73-76, CANR-16
Barolini, Teodolinda 1951- 124
Barolsky, Paul 1941- 81-84
Baron, (Joseph) Alexander 1917- CANR-14
Earlier sketch in CA 5-8R
Baron, Beth 1958- 138
Baron, David
See Pinter, Harold
Baron, Dennis E(mery) 1944- CANR-27
Earlier sketch in CA 110
Baron, Elizabeth Frank
See Frank-Baron, Elizabeth
Baron, Frank 1936- 119
Baron, Hans 1900- 17-20R
Baron, Herman 1941- 61-64
Baron, J. W.
See Krauzer, Steven M(ark)
Baron, Mary (Kelley) 1944- CANR-2
Earlier sketch in CA 49-52
Baron, Mikan
See Barba, Harry
Baron, Oscar 1908(?)-1976 Obituary 65-68
Baron, Othello
See Fanthorpe, R(obert) Lionel
Baron, Robert Alex 1920- 41-44R
Baron, Salo W(ittmayer) 1895-1989 69-72
Obituary 130
Baron, Samuel H(askell) 1921- CANR-3
Earlier sketch in CA 9-12R
Baron, Virginia Olsen 1931- 25-28R
See also SATA 28, 46
Baron, (Ora) Wendy 1937- 41-44R
Baron Amulree
See Mackenzie, Basil William Sholto
Baron Corvo
See
Rolfe, Frederick (William Serafino Austin Lewis Mary)
Barondess, Sue K(aufman) 1926-1977 .....CANR-1
Obituary 69-72
Earlier sketch in CA 1-4R
See also Kaufman, Sue
See also CLC 8
Baron de Teive
See Pessoa, Fernando (Antonio Nogueira)
Barone, Michael 1944- 93-96
Barone, Mike
See Albert, Marvin H(ubert)
Baron Lloyd of Hampstead
See Lloyd, Dennis
Baron of Remenham
See Thomas, (William) Miles (Webster)
Baroody, Jamil Murad
1905-1979 Obituary 85-88
Barooshian, (Dickran) Vahan 1932- 85-88
Barovsky, Sharon Daley 1939- 128
Barr, Alfred H(amilton) Jr. 1902-1981 .....CANR-29
Obituary 105
Earlier sketch in CA 49-52
Barr, (Chester) Alwyn (Jr.) 1938- 33-36R
Barr, Andrew 1961- 130
Barr, Anthony 1921- 109
Barr, Betty 1932- 97-100
Barr, Beverly 61-64
Barr, Densil Neve
See Buttrey, Douglas N(orton)
Barr, Donald Roy 1938- 69-72
Barr, Donald 1921- 9-12R
See also SATA 20
Barr, Doris W(ilson) 1923- 33-36R
Barr, George 1907- CANR-1
Earlier sketch in CA 1-4R
See also SATA 2
Barr, Gladys Hutchison 1904-1976 ....CANR-6
Earlier sketch in CA 1-4R
Barr, James 1924- CANR-20
Earlier sketches in CA 1-4R, CANR-4
Barr, Jeff 1941- 69-72
Barr, Jene
See Cohen, Jene Barr
See also SATA 16, 42
Barr, Jennifer 1945- 102
Barr, John J(ay) 1942- 61-64
Barr, Margaret Scolari 1901-1987 Obituary 124
Barr, Marleen Sandra 1953- 120
Barr, Murray L(lewellyn) 1908- 130
Barr, O(rlando) Sydney 1919- 13-16R
Barr, Pat(ricia Miriam) 1934- CANR-30
Earlier sketches in CA 21-24R, CANR-12
Barr, Robert R(ussell) 1931- 110
Barr, Robert 1850-1912 ....DLB 70, 92
Barr, Roseanne 1952- ....BEST 90:1
Barr, Stephen 1904- CAP-1
Earlier sketch in CA 13-16
Barr, Stringfellow 1897-1982 ....CANR-1
Obituary 106
Earlier sketch in CA 1-4R
Barr, Tony
See Barr, Anthony
Barr, William G. 1920(?)-1987 Obituary 121
Barraclough, Geoffrey 1908-1984 101
Obituary 114
Barraclough, June (Mary) 1930- 132
Barraclough, Solon L(ovett) 1922- 41-44R
Barraga, Natalie Carter 1915- 41-44R
Barral, Carlos 1928(?)-1989 Obituary 130
Barral, Mary-Rose 1925- 33-36R
Barranger, M(illy) S(later) 1937- CANR-28
Earlier sketches in CA 29-32R, CANR-12
Barratt, G. R.
See Barratt, Glynn (Richard V.)
Barratt, G. R. V.
See Barratt, Glynn (Richard V.)
Barratt, Glynn (Richard V.) 1944- 127
Brief entry 110
Barratt-Brown, Michael 1918- CANR-38
Earlier sketches in CA 97-100, CANR-17
Barrault, Jean-Louis 1910- 105
Barrax, Gerald William 1933- CANR-10
Earlier sketch in CA 65-68
See also BW
See also DLB 41, 120
Barre, Michael Lee 1943- 118
Barreiro, Alvaro 1936- 131
Barrell, Geoffrey Richard
1917-1983 Obituary 111
Barrell, Rex A(rthur) 1921- 129
Barrell, Sarah Webb
1946(?)-1979 Obituary 89-92
Barren, Charles (MacKinnon) 1913- CANR-4
Earlier sketch in CA 9-12R
Barreno, Maria Isabel
See Martins, Maria Isabel Barreno de Faria
See also AITN 1
Barrer, Gertrude
See Barrer-Russell, Gertrude
Barrera, Mario 1939- 97-100
Barrer-Russell, Gertrude 1921- .... SATA 27
Barres, Oliver 1921- 13-16R
Barreto, Afonso Henrique de Lima
See Lima Barreto, Afonso Henrique de
Barrett, Anne Mainwaring (Gillett) 1911- CAP-2
Earlier sketch in CA 29-32
Barrett, Anthony A(rthur) 1941- 134
Barrett, Bob 1925- 73-76
Barrett, C(harles) Kingsley 1917- CANR-25
Earlier sketches in CA 21-24R, CANR-10
Barrett, C(lifton) Waller 1901- 41-44R
Barrett, Clifford L(eslie)
1894-1971 Obituary 33-36R
Barrett, Dean 1942- 69-72
Barrett, Donald N(eil) 1920- 13-16R
Barrett, Eaton Stannard 1786-1820 .... DLB 116
Barrett, Edward L(ouis) Jr. 1917- 25-28R
Barrett, Edward W(are)
1910-1989 Obituary 130
Barrett, Ethel 134
See also SATA 44
Barrett, Eugene F(rancis) 1921- 57-60
Barrett, George W(est) 1908- 17-20R
Barrett, George W. 1913(?)-1984 Obituary 114
Barrett, Gerald Van 1936- 37-40R
Barrett, Harold 1925- 81-84
Barrett, Harry B(emister) 1922- 85-88
Barrett, Henry Charles 1923- 53-56
Barrett, Ivan J. 1910- 49-52
Barrett, J(ohn) Edward 1932- 37-40R
Barrett, James H(enry) 1906- 33-36R
Barrett, James Lee 1929- 81-84
Barrett, John Gilchrist 1921- CANR-2
Earlier sketch in CA 5-8R
Barrett, John Henry 1913- 101
Barrett, Joyce Durham 1943- 138
Barrett, Judi
See Barrett, Judith
Barrett, Judith 1941- 103
See also SATA 26
Barrett, Laurence I(rwin) 1935- 69-72
Barrett, Leonard E(manuel) 1920- 65-68
Barrett, Linton Lomas 1904-1972 ....5-8R
Obituary 134
Barrett, Lois (Yvonne) 1947- 125
Barrett, Marvin 1920- CANR-11
Earlier sketch in CA 69-72
Barrett, Mary Ellin 1927- 17-20R
Barrett, Max 81-84
Barrett, Maye
See Barrett, Max
Barrett, Michael Dennis 1947- 85-88
Barrett, N. S.
See Barrett, Norman (S.)
Barrett, Nancy Smith 1942- 37-40R
Barrett, Nathan N(oble) 1933- 17-20R
Barrett, Norman (S.) 1935- CANR-24
Earlier sketch in CA 107
Barrett, Patricia 1914-1987 ....5-8R
Obituary 121
Barrett, Paul F(rancis) 1943- 117
Barrett, Raina
See Kelly, Pauline Agnes
Barrett, Ron 1937- .... SATA 14
Barrett, Rona 1936- 103
See also AITN 1
Barrett, Russel H(unter) 1919- 17-20R
Barrett, Stanley R. 1938- 128
Barrett, Susan (Mary) 1938- 138
Brief entry 109
Barrett, (Roger) Syd 1946-
See Pink Floyd
See also CLC 35
Barrett, Sylvia 1914- 25-28R
Barrett, Ward J. 1927- 29-32R
Barrett, William (Christopher) 1913- CANR-11
Earlier sketch in CA 13-16R
See also CLC 27
Barrett, William E(dmund) 1900-1986 .....CANR-22
Obituary 120
Earlier sketch in CA 5-8R
See also SATA 49
Barrett, William R. 1922(?)-1977 Obituary 73-76
Barretto, Larry
See Barretto, Laurence Brevoort
Barretto, Laurence Brevoort
1890-1971 Obituary 33-36R
Barretton, Grandall
See Garrett, (Gordon) Randall (Phillip)
Barriault, Arthur 1915(?)-1976 Obituary 65-68
Barricelli, Jean-Pierre 1924- CANR-21
Earlier sketch in CA 105
Barrick, Mac E(ugene) 1933- 33-36R
Barrie, Alexander 1923- CANR-5
Earlier sketch in CA 1-4R
Barrie, Donald C(onway) 1905- 17-20R
Barrie, J(ames) M(atthew) 1860-1937 136
Brief entry 104
See also CDBLB 1890-1914
See also CLR 16
See also DLB 10
See also MAICYA
See also TCLC 2
See also YABC 1
Barrie, Jane
See Savage, Mildred (Spitz)
Barrie, Patricia 1946- 122
Barrier, (John) Michael 1940- 109
Barrier, Norman G(erald) 1940- CANR-4
Earlier sketch in CA 53-56
Barriger, John Walker
1899-1976 Obituary 69-72
Barrile, Jackie 1943- 117
Barrington, H. W.
See Brannon, William T.
Barrington, John
See Brownjohn, Alan
Barrington, Maurice
See Brogan, D(enis) W(illiam)
Barrington, Michael
See Moorcock, Michael (John)
Barrington, P. V.
See Barling, Muriel Vere Mant
Barrington, Pamela
See Barling, Muriel Vere Mant
Barrington, Thomas Joseph 1916- 104
Barrio, Raymond 1921- CANR-32
Earlier sketches in CA 25-28R, CANR-11
See also CAAS 15
See also DLB 82
See also HW
Barrio-Garay, Jose Luis 1932- 81-84
Barrios, Eduardo 1884-1963 ....HW
Barrios, Pilar E. 1889- ....HW
Barris, Alex 1922- 61-64
Barris, Chuck 1929- Brief entry 109
Barris, George 1925- .... SATA 47
Barritt, Denis P(hillips) 1914- 21-24R
Barro, Robert Joseph 1944- 97-100
Barrol, Grady
See Bograd, Larry
Barroll, John Leeds III 1928- 101
Barron, Ann Forman 69-72
Barron, Bruce 1960- 123
Barron, Charlie Nelms
1922-1977 Obituary 69-72
Barron, Ed
See Bernhardt, Clyde Edric Barron
Barron, Frank (Xavier) 1922- CANR-8
Earlier sketch in CA 5-8R
Barron, Fred 117
Barron, Gayle 1945- 109
Barron, Gloria Joan 1934- 81-84
Barron, Greg 1952- 110
Barron, Jerome A(ure) 1933- CANR-24
Earlier sketch in CA 45-48
Barron, Judy 1939- 137
Barron, Milton L. 1918- CANR-18
Earlier sketch in CA 1-4R
Barron, (Richard) Neil 1934- CANR-37
Earlier sketch in CA 102
Barrosse, Thomas 1926- 9-12R
Barrow, Andrew 1945- 97-100
Barrow, Geoffrey W(allis) S(teuart)
1924- CANR-30
Earlier sketches in CA 17-20R, CANR-7
Barrow, Harold M(arion) 1909- 106
Barrow, Henry 1906(?)-1985 Obituary 117
Barrow, John D(avid) 1952- 115

Barrow, Joseph Louis 1914-1981 Obituary ... 103
Barrow, Keith E. 1954-1983 Obituary ... 111
Barrow, Kenneth 1945- ... 119
Barrow, Leo (Lebron) 1925- Brief entry ... 110
Barrow, Pamela
See Howarth, Pamela
Barrow, R. H. 1894(?)-1984 Obituary ... 114
Barrow, Rhoda
See Lederer, Rhoda Catharine (Kitto)
Barrow, Robin 1944- ... CANR-10
Earlier sketch in CA 65-68
Barrow, Terence 1923- ... 41-44R
Barrow, Thomas C(hurchill) 1929- ... 21-24R
Barrow, William
See Fuller, Hoyt (William)
Barrows, Anita 1947- ... CANR-31
Earlier sketch in CA 49-52
Barrows, Chester L. 1892(?)-1975 Obituary ... 104
Barrows, (Ruth) Marjorie 1892(?)-1983 ... CAP-2
Obituary ... 109
Earlier sketch in CA 21-22
Barrows, R. M.
See Barrows, (Ruth) Marjorie
Barrows, Ruth
See Barrows, (Ruth) Marjorie
Barrows, Susanna Isabel 1944- ... 108
Barrows, Sydney (Biddle) 1952- ... 126
Barry, Anne 1940- ... 85-88
Barry, Colman J. 1921- ... 13-16R
Barry, Dave 1947- ... 134
Brief entry ... 129
See also BEST 90:4
Barry, Herbert III 1930- ... CANR-14
Earlier sketch in CA 37-40R
Barry, Iris 1895-1969 Obituary ... 104
Barry, Jack 1939- ... 69-72
Barry, Jackson G(ranville) 1926- ... 29-32R
Barry, James Donald 1926- ... 33-36R
Barry, James P(otvin) 1918- ... CANR-24
Earlier sketch in CA 37-40R
See also SATA 14
Barry, Jane (Powell) 1925- ... 5-8R
Barry, Jerome B(enedict) 1894-1975 ... 1-4R
Obituary ... 61-64
Barry, Jocelyn
See Bowden, Jean
Barry, John Vincent William 1903-1969 ... 1-4R
Obituary ... 103
Barry, Joseph (Amber) 1917- ... CANR-14
Earlier sketch in CA 57-60
Barry, June 1925- ... 13-16R
Barry, Katharina Watjen 1936- ... 9-12R
See also SATA 4
Barry, Kathleen (L.) 1941- ... 129
Barry, Kevin
See Laffan, Kevin (Barry)
Barry, Lucy (Brown) 1934- ... 17-20R
Barry, Lynda (Jean) 1956- ... 138
See also AAYA 9
Barry, Margaret Stuart 1927- ... CANR-25
Earlier sketch in CA 106
Barry, Mary J(ane) 1928- ... 49-52
Barry, Mike
See Malzberg, Barry N(athaniel)
Barry, Norman P. 1944- ... 134
Barry, Philip 1896-1949 Brief entry ... 109
See also DLB 7
See also TCLC 11
Barry, Raymond Walker 1894- ... CAP-1
Earlier sketch in CA 17-18
Barry, Robert (Everett) 1931- ... CANR-2
Earlier sketch in CA 5-8R
See also SATA 6
Barry, Roger Graham 1935- ... 102
Barry, Roxana
See Robinson, Roxana (Barry)
Barry, Scott 1952- ... 89-92
See also SATA 32
Barry, Sebastian 1955- ... 117
Barry, Sheila Anne ... 135
Barry, Spranger
See Kauffmann, Stanley
Barry, Stephen P. 1948(?)-1986 ... 123
Obituary ... 120
Barry, William A(nthony) 1930- ... CANR-38
Earlier sketch in CA 115
Barry, William David 1946- ... 114
Barsacq, Andre 1909-1973 Obituary ... 41-44R
Barsacq, Leon 1906-1969 Obituary ... 113
Barsby, John A. 1935- ... 121
Barsh, Russel Lawrence 1950- ... 105
Barsis, Max 1894(?)-1973 Obituary ... 41-44R
Barsky, Arthur 1900(?)-1982(?) Obituary ... 106
Barson, John 1936- ... 85-88
Barson, Michael 1951- ... 129
Barsotti, C(harles) 1933- ... 65-68
Barstow, Anne Llewellyn 1929- ... 111
Barstow, Phyllida 1937- ... CANR-27
Earlier sketch in CA 121
Barstow, Stan(ley) 1928- ... CANR-1
Earlier sketch in CA 1-4R
See also DLB 14
Bart, Andre Schwarz
See Schwarz-Bart, Andre
Bart, Benjamin F(ranklin) 1917- ... 25-28R
Bart, Lionel 1930- ... 65-68
Bart, Pauline B(ernice) 1930- ... 53-56
Bart, Peter 1932- ... CANR-19
Earlier sketch in CA 93-96
Bartek, E(dward) J(ohn) 1921- ... 37-40R
Bartel, Pauline C(hristine) 1952- ... 81-84
Bartel, Roland 1919- ... 17-20R
Bartell, Ernest 1932- ... 33-36R
Bartell, Linda Lang 1948- ... 125
Bartels, Robert A. 1923- ... CANR-16
Earlier sketch in CA 1-4R
Bartels, Robert 1913- ... 13-16R
Bartels, Susan Ludvigson
See Ludvigson, Susan
Barten, Harvey H(arold) 1933- ... 33-36R
Bartenbach, Jean 1918- ... 115
See also SATA 40
Bartenieff, Irmgard 1900(?)-1981 Obituary ... 105
Barter, A(lice) K(nar) 1918- ... 57-60
Barth, Alan 1906-1979 ... CANR-5
Obituary ... 104
Earlier sketch in CA 1-4R
Barth, Charles P. 1895- ... CAP-2
Earlier sketch in CA 25-28
Barth, Christoph F. 1917- ... 29-32R
Barth, Edna 1914-1980 ... CANR-27
Obituary ... 102
Earlier sketch in CA 41-44R
See also SATA 7, 24
Barth, Fredrik 1928- ... CANR-11
Earlier sketch in CA 65-68
Barth, Gunther 1925- ... 103
Barth, Ilene Joan 1944- ... 134
Barth, J(ohn) Robert 1931- ... 29-32R
Barth, John (Simmons) 1930- ... CANR-23
Earlier sketches in CA 1-4R, CANR-5
See also CABS 1
See also AITN 1, 2
See also CLC 1, 2, 3, 5, 7, 9, 10, 14, 27, 51
See also DLB 2
See also MTCW
See also SSC 10
Barth, Karl 1886-1968 ... 134
Obituary ... 25-28R
Barth, Lois
See Freihofer, Lois Diane
Barth, Markus Karl 1915- ... CANR-2
Earlier sketch in CA 5-8R
Barth, Peter S. 1937- ... CANR-25
Earlier sketch in CA 106
Barth, Richard 1943- ... 81-84
Barth, Roland S(awyer) 1937- ... CANR-1
Earlier sketch in CA 45-48
Barthel, Diane L(ee) 1949- ... 115
Barthel, Joan 1932- ... 114
Brief entry ... 111
Barthelme, Donald 1931-1989 ... CANR-20
Obituary ... 129
Earlier sketch in CA 21-24R
See also CLC 1, 2, 3, 5, 6, 8, 13, 23, 46, 59
See also DLB 2
See also DLBY 80, 89
See also MTCW
See also SATA 7, 62
See also SSC 2
Barthelme, Frederick 1943- ... 122
Brief entry ... 114
See also CLC 36
See also DLBY 85
Barthelme, Peter R. 1939- ... 127
Barthelme, Steve(n) 1947- ... 136
Barthelmes, (Albert) Wes(ley Jr.)
1922-1976 ... 69-72
Obituary ... 65-68
Barthes, Roland (Gerard) 1915-1980 ... 130
Obituary ... 97-100
See also CLC 24
See also MTCW
Bartholomay, Julia A. 1923- ... 45-48
Bartholomeusz, Dennis 1930- ... 130
Bartholomew, Barbara 1941- ... 135
Brief entry ... 118
See also SATA 42
Bartholomew, Bart
See Bartholomew, Frank H.
Bartholomew, Cecilia 1907- ... CAP-1
Earlier sketch in CA 13-14
Bartholomew, Ed(ward Ellsworth) 1914- ... 25-28R
Bartholomew, Frank H.
1898-1985 Obituary ... 115
Bartholomew, James 1950- ... 132
Bartholomew, Jean
See Beatty, Patricia Robbins
Bartholomew, John Eric
See Morecambe, Eric
Bartholomew, Paul C(harles)
1907-1975 ... CANR-10
Earlier sketch in CA 17-20R
Bartier, Pierre 1945- ... 21-24R
Bartlett, Amy 1949- ... 124
Bartlett, Basil Hardington
1905-1985 Obituary ... 115
Bartlett, Bruce R(eeves) 1951- ... CANR-19
Earlier sketch in CA 89-92
Bartlett, C(hristopher) J(ohn) 1931- ... 17-20R
Bartlett, Charles (Leffingwell) 1921- ... 29-32R
Bartlett, David
See Mason, Madeline
Bartlett, Donald L. Brief entry ... 110
Bartlett, Elizabeth (Winters) 1911- ... CANR-9
Earlier sketch in CA 17-20R
Bartlett, Elsa Jaffe 1935- ... CANR-15
Earlier sketch in CA 33-36R
Bartlett, Eric George 1920- ... CANR-19
Earlier sketches in CA 5-8R, CANR-2
Bartlett, F. C.
See Bartlett, Frederic Charles
Bartlett, Frederic Charles
1886-1969 Obituary ... 115
Bartlett, Gene E(bert) 1910-1989 Obituary ... 130
Bartlett, Gerald (Robert) 1935- ... 21-24R
Bartlett, Harriett M(oulton)
1897-1987 Obituary ... 121
Bartlett, Hubert Moyse
See Moyse-Bartlett, Hubert
Bartlett, Irving H(enry) 1923- ... CANR-9
Earlier sketch in CA 21-24R
Bartlett, Jean Anne 1927- ... 97-100
Bartlett, Jennifer Losch 1941- ... 136
Bartlett, John 1820-1905 ... DLB 1
Bartlett, Jonathan 1931- ... 93-96
Bartlett, Kathleen
See Paine, Lauran (Bosworth)
Bartlett, Kim 1941- ... 89-92
Bartlett, Lee Anthony 1950- ... 114
Bartlett, Margaret Farrington 1896- ... CANR-5
Earlier sketch in CA 5-8R
Bartlett, Marie (Swan) 1918- ... 21-24R
Bartlett, Merrill L(ewis) 1939- ... 117
Bartlett, Nancy W(hite) 1913-1972 ... CAP-2
Obituary ... 41-44R
Earlier sketch in CA 23-24
Bartlett, Paul 1909- ... CAP-2
Earlier sketch in CA 17-18
Bartlett, Philip A. ... CANR-26
Earlier sketches in CAP-2, CA 19-20
See also SATA 1
Bartlett, Phyllis 1908(?)-1973 Obituary ... 41-44R
Bartlett, Richard A(dams) 1920- ... CANR-2
Earlier sketch in CA 5-8R
Bartlett, Robert (John) 1950- ... 125
Bartlett, Robert Merrill 1899- ... CANR-2
Earlier sketch in CA 5-8R
See also SATA 12
Bartlett, Robert V(irgil) 1953- ... CANR-22
Earlier sketch in CA 104
Bartlett, Ruhl J. 1897- ... CAP-1
Earlier sketch in CA 11-12
Bartlett, Ruth ... 17-20R
Bartlett, Vernon 1894-1983 ... 61-64
Obituary ... 108
Bartley, Diana E(sther) Pelaez-Rivera
1940- ... 69-72
Bartley, Leigh
See Riker, Leigh
Bartley, Numan V(ache) 1934- ... CANR-12
Earlier sketch in CA 69-72
Bartley, Robert L(eRoy) 1937- ... 97-100
Bartley, William Warren III 1934- ... CANR-15
Earlier sketch in CA 37-40R
Bartocci, Gianni 1925- ... 21-24R
Bartol, Cyrus Augustus 1813-1900 ... DLB 1
Bartole, Genevieve 1927- ... 101
Bartolome de Roxas, Juan
See Rubia Barcia, Jose
Barton, Allen H(oisington) 1924- ... CANR-10
Earlier sketch in CA 25-28R
Barton, Bernard 1784-1849 ... DLB 96
Barton, Bruce Walter 1935- ... 89-92
Barton, Byron 1930- ... CANR-13
Earlier sketch in CA 57-60
See also SATA 9
Barton, Del 1925-1971 Obituary ... 103
Barton, Erle
See Fanthorpe, R(obert) Lionel
Barton, Eustace Robert
1854-1943 Brief entry ... 114
Barton, Fredrick (Preston) 1948- ... 119
Barton, H. Arnold 1929- ... 77-80
Barton, Harriett ... SATA 43
Barton, Humphrey (Douglas Elliott)
1900- ... CAP-2
Earlier sketch in CA 19-20
Barton, Jim Tom ... 123
Barton, John Bernard Adie 1928- ... 81-84
Barton, John H(ays) 1936- ... 111
Barton, John Mackintosh Tilney 1898- ... CAP-1
Earlier sketch in CA 17-18
Barton, John (Stuart) 1957- ... 114
Barton, John 1948- ... 137
Barton, Jon
See Harvey, John (Barton)
Barton, Lee
See Fanthorpe, R(obert) Lionel
Barton, Lew(is Randolph) 1918- ... 73-76
Barton, M. Xaveria 1910- Brief entry ... 105
Barton, Margaret D(over) 1902- ... CAP-1
Earlier sketch in CA 13-16
Barton, Mary Neill 1899- ... CAP-2
Earlier sketch in CA 19-20
Barton, May Hollis ... CANR-26
Earlier sketches in CAP-2, CA 19-20
See also SATA 1, 67
Barton, Michael (Lee) 1943- ... 110
Barton, Pat
See Arrowsmith, Pat
See also SATA 59
Barton, Pat 1928- ... SATA 59
Barton, Richard F(leming) 1924- ... 61-64
Barton, Roger A(very)
1903-1976 Obituary ... 65-68
Barton, S. W.
See Whaley, Barton Stewart
Barton, Thomas Frank 1905- ... CANR-1
Earlier sketch in CA 45-48
Barton, V(ernon) Wayne ... 1-4R
Barton, Walter Elbert 1886-1983 Obituary ... 111
Barton, Wayne 1944- ... 124
Barton, Weldon V. 1938- ... 21-24R
Barton, William (Renald III) 1950- ... CANR-1
Earlier sketch in CA 45-48
Bartos, Otomar J(an) 1927- ... 105
Bartos-Hoeppner, Barbara 1923- ... CANR-10
Earlier sketch in CA 25-28R
See also SATA 5
Bartov, Hanoch 1926- ... 129
Brief entry ... 117
Bartov, Omer 1954- ... 135
Bartram, George
See Cameron, Kenneth M.
Bartram, Graham 1946- ... 116
Bartram, John 1699-1777 ... DLB 31
Bartram, William 1739-1823 ... DLB 37
Bartran, Margaret 1913-1976 ... CAP-2
Earlier sketch in CA 29-32
Bartrum, Douglas A(lbert) 1907- ... CANR-6
Earlier sketch in CA 9-12R
Bartsch, Jochen 1906- ... SATA 39
Bartsch, William H. 1933- ... 138
Bartscht, Waltraud 1924- ... 41-44R
Bartusiak, Marcia 1950- ... 129
Bartusis, Mary Ann 1930- ... 101
Bartz, Albert E(dward) 1933- ... 21-24R
Bartz, Patricia McBride 1921- ... 102
Bartz, Wayne R(onald) 1938- ... 111
Baruch, Dorothy W(alter) 1899-1962 ... SATA 21
Baruch, Grace K. 1936(?)-1988 Obituary ... 126
Baruch, Ruth-Marion 1922- ... 29-32R
Baruk, Henri Marc 1897- ... 85-88
Barwick, Steven 1921- ... 13-16R
Barwood, Hal ... 129
Brief entry ... 125
Baryshnikov, Mikhail (Nikolayevich) 1948- ... 133
Brief entry ... 113
Barzanti, Sergio 1925- ... 17-20R
Barzilay, Isaac Eisenstein 1915- ... 113
Barzini, Luigi (Giorgio Jr.) 1908-1984 ... CANR-23
Obituary ... 112
Earlier sketch in CA 13-16R
Barzman, Ben 1912- ... 132
Bar-Zohar, Michael 1938- ... CANR-35
Earlier sketches in CA 21-24R, CANR-12
Barzun, Jacques (Martin) 1907- ... CANR-22
Earlier sketch in CA 61-64
See also CLC 51
Bas, Joe 1932- ... 53-56
Bas, Rutger
See
Rutgers van der Loeff-Basenau, An(na) Maria
Basa, Eniko Molnar 1939- ... 77-80
Basart, Ann Phillips 1931- ... CANR-1
Earlier sketch in CA 1-4R
Basch, Michael Franz ... 130
Basche, James 1926- ... 29-32R
Bascio, Patrick 1927- ... 119
Bascom, David 1912- ... 93-96
Bascom, Harold A(dolphus) 1951- ... 135
Bascom, Willard N. 1916- ... CANR-6
Earlier sketch in CA 1-4R
Bascom, William R(ussel) 1912-1981 ... 17-20R
Obituary ... 125
Basdekis, Demetrios 1930- ... 25-28R
Base, Graeme (Rowland) 1958- ... 134
See also CLR 22
See also MAICYA
See also SATA 67
Baseley, Godfrey 1904- ... 102
Basgoz, M(ehmet) Ilhan 1921- ... 113
Bash, Deborah M. Blumenthal 1940- ... 109
Bash, Frank N(ess) 1937- ... 107
Bash, Harry H(arvey) 1926- ... 89-92
Basham, Don W(ilson) 1926- ... 65-68
Basham, Richard Dalton 1945- ... 111
Basham, William Randolph
1933(?)-1986 Obituary ... 118
Bashe, Patricia Ann Romanowski 1956- ... 127
Bashe, Philip (Scott) 1954- ... 134
Bashevis, Isaac
See Singer, Isaac Bashevis
Bashevkin, Sylvia B. 1954- ... 121
Bashira, Damali 1951- ... 57-60
Basho
See Matsuo Basho
Bashshur, Rashid L. 1933- ... 89-92
Basichis, Gordon (Allen) 1947- ... 85-88
Basie, Count
See Basie, William James
Basie, William James 1904(?)-1984 ... 134
Basil, Douglas C. 1923- ... 41-44R
Basil, Otto 1901-1983 ... 49-52
Obituary ... 113
Basile, Gloria Vitanza 1929- ... CANR-12
Earlier sketch in CA 69-72
Basile, Joseph 1912- ... CANR-11
Earlier sketch in CA 25-28R
Basile, Leon 1955- ... 113
Basile, Robert M(anlius) 1916- ... 53-56
Basilius, Harold A. 1905-1977 ... CANR-2
Earlier sketch in CA 1-4R
Basinger, Jeanine (Deyling) 1936- ... CANR-18
Earlier sketch in CA 97-100
Basiuk, Victor 1932- ... 93-96
Baskerville, Barnet 1916- ... 1-4R
Baskerville, Patricia 1951- ... 108
Baskett, John 1930- ... 97-100
Baskette, Floyd K(enneth) 1910-1979 ... CANR-29
Earlier sketch in CA 33-36R
Baskin, Barbara H(olland) 1929- ... CANR-22
Earlier sketch in CA 103
Baskin, Esther Tane
1926(?)-1973 Obituary ... 37-40R
Baskin, Judith R. 1950- ... 137
Baskin, Leonard 1922- ... 106
See also SATA 27, 30
Baskin, Robert E(dward)
1917-1983 Obituary ... 110
Baskin, Samuel 1921- ... 17-20R
Baskin, Wade 1924-1974 ... CAP-2
Earlier sketch in CA 23-24
Basler, Roy P(rentice) 1906-1989 ... CANR-4
Obituary ... 130
Earlier sketch in CA 5-8R
Basler, Thomas G(ordon) 1940- ... 103
Bason, Fred
See Bason, Frederick (Thomas)
Bason, Frederick (Thomas) 1907-1973 ... 5-8R
Obituary ... 89-92
Bason, Lillian 1913- ... 69-72
See also SATA 20
Bass, Altha Leah (Bierbower) 1892-1988 ... CAP-2
Obituary ... 126
Earlier sketch in CA 23-24

Bass, Althea
 See Bass, Altha Leah (Bierbower)
Bass, Bernard M(orris) 1925- CANR-19
 Earlier sketches in CA 1-4R, CANR-4
Bass, Clarence B(eaty) 1922- 5-8R
Bass, Eben E(dward) 1924- 107
Bass, Ellen 1947- CANR-2
 Earlier sketch in CA 49-52
Bass, George F(letcher) 1932- 122
Bass, Henry B(enjamin)
 1897-1975 Obituary 57-60
Bass, Herbert Jacob 1929- CANR-1
 Earlier sketch in CA 1-4R
Bass, Howard L(arry) 1942- 69-72
Bass, Howard 1923- CANR-2
 Earlier sketch in CA 5-8R
Bass, Jack A(lexander) 1946- 97-100
Bass, Jack 1934- CANR-19
 Earlier sketch in CA 29-32R
Bass, Kingsley B. Jr.
 See Bullins, Ed
Bass, Lawrence W(ade) 1898- 49-52
Bass, Madeline Tiger 1934- 116
Bass, Milton R. 1923- 25-28R
Bass, Nelson Estupinan
 See Estupinan Bass, Nelson
Bass, Rick 1958- 126
Bass, Robert D(uncan) 1904- 61-64
Bass, T. J.
 See Bassler, Thomas J(oseph)
 See also DLBY 81
Bass, Thomas A. 1951- 124
Bass, Virginia W(auchope) 1905- 61-64
Bass, William M(arvin III) 1928- CANR-31
 Earlier sketch in CA 41-44R
Bassan, Maurice 1929- 25-28R
Bassani, Giorgio 1916- CANR-33
 Earlier sketch in CA 65-68
 See also CLC 9
 See also MTCW
Basse, Eli 1904-1979 Obituary 93-96
Basse, William 1583(?)-1653 ....DLB 121
Basseches, Michael 1950- 114
Bassermann, Lujo
 See Schreiber, Hermann (Otto Ludwig)
Basset, Bernard 1909-1988 ....CANR-6
 Obituary 125
 Earlier sketch in CA 9-12R
Bassett, Edward Eryl 1940- 33-36R
Bassett, Flora Marjorie
 1890(?)-1980 Obituary 97-100
Bassett, George William 1910- 102
Bassett, Glenn Arthur 1930- 17-20R
Bassett, (Mary) Grace 1927- 73-76
Bassett, Jack
 See Rowland, D(onald) S(ydney)
Bassett, James E(lias) 1912-1978 61-64
 Obituary 81-84
Bassett, Jeni 1960- ....SATA 43, 64
Bassett, John Earl Jr. 1942- 123
Bassett, John Keith
 See Keating, Lawrence A.
Bassett, John Spencer
 1867-1928 Brief entry 122
 See also DLB 17
Bassett, Lisa 1958- 126
 See also SATA 61
Bassett, Marnie
 See Bassett, Flora Marjorie
Bassett, Richard 1900- CAP-2
 Earlier sketch in CA 25-28
Bassett, Ronald 1924- 81-84
Bassett, T(homas) D(ay) Seymour
 1913- CANR-8
 Earlier sketch in CA 21-24R
Bassett, William B. K. 1908- CAP-1
 Earlier sketch in CA 9-10
Bassett, William Travis 1923- 9-12R
Bassett, William W. 1932- CANR-34
 Earlier sketch in CA 25-28R
Bassiouni, M. Cherif 1937- CANR-34
 Earlier sketch in CA 29-32R
Bassler, Thomas J(oseph) 1932- 115
 See also Bass, T. J.
Bassnett, Susan (Edna) 1947- 128
Bassnett-McGuire, Susan
 See Bassnett, Susan (Edna)
Basso, Aldo P(eter) 1922- 65-68
Basso, (Joseph) Hamilton 1904-1964 89-92
Basso, Keith H(amilton) 1940- 131
Bassoff, Bruce 1941- 69-72
Basten, Fred E(rnest) CANR-22
 Earlier sketches in CA 57-60, CANR-7
Bastian, F(rank) 1913- 128
Bastias, Constantine
 1901(?)-1972 Obituary 37-40R
Bastico, Ettore 1876-1972 Obituary 37-40R
Bastin, J(ohn) S(turgus) 1927- CANR-11
 Earlier sketch in CA 21-24R
Bastlund, Knud 1925- 21-24R
Bastos, Augusto (Antonio) Roa
 See Roa Bastos, Augusto (Antonio)
Basu, Arindam 1948- 61-64
Basu, Asoke (Kumar) 1940- 106
Basu, Dipak R. 1951- 112
Basu, Kaushik 1952- CANR-38
 Earlier sketch in CA 115
Basu, Romen 1923- CANR-30
 Earlier sketches in CA 77-80, CANR-13
Bataille, Georges 1897-1962 101
 Obituary 89-92
 See also CLC 29
Bataille, Gretchen M. 1944- 102
Batbedat, Jean 1926- 37-40R
Batchelder, Alan Bruce 1931- 21-24R
Batchelder, Howard T(imothy) 1909- CAP-2
 Earlier sketch in CA 19-20
Batcheller, John M. 1918- 45-48
Batchelor, C(larence) D(aniel)
 1888-1977 Obituary 73-76
Batchelor, David 1943- CANR-18
 Earlier sketch in CA 101
Batchelor, Edward Jr. 1930- 110
Batchelor, John Calvin 1948- 105
Batchelor, John (Dennis) 1947- 109
Batchelor, John 1942- 93-96
Batchelor, Joy 1914- ....SATA 29
Batchelor, Julie F(rances) E(lizabeth) 1947- 109
Batchelor, Reg
 See Paine, Lauran (Bosworth)
Batcher, Elaine Kotler 1944- 109
Bate, Jonathan 1958- 134
Bate, Lucy 1939- 69-72
 See also SATA 18
Bate, Norman (Arthur) 1916- 1-4R
 See also SATA 5
Bate, Sam 1907- 102
Bate, W(alter) Jackson 1918- 5-8R
 See also DLB 67, 103
Bateman, Barbara Dee 1933- 41-44R
Bateman, Robert (Moyes Carruthers)
 1922-1973 ....CANR-7
 Earlier sketch in CA 5-8R
Bateman, Walter L(ewis) 1916- 29-32R
Bates, Alan Lawrence 1923- 17-20R
Bates, Arthenia J. 1920- 57-60
Bates, Barbara S(nedeker) 1919- 17-20R
 See also SATA 12
Bates, Betty
 See Bates, Elizabeth
 See also SATA 19
Bates, Carol Neuls
 See Neuls-Bates, Carol
Bates, Caroline (Philbrick) 1932- 103
Bates, Charles C(arpenter) 1918- 121
Bates, Daisy Lee 1914- 127
Bates, (Julian) Darrell 1913-1989 ....CAP-1
 Obituary 129
 Earlier sketch in CA 9-10
Bates, David Vincent 1922- 110
Bates, Elizabeth 1921- CANR-32
 Earlier sketches in CA 77-80, CANR-14
 See also Bates, Betty
Bates, H(erbert) E(rnest) 1905-1974 .....CANR-34
 Obituary 45-48
 Earlier sketch in CA 93-96
 See also CLC 46
 See also MTCW
 See also SSC 10
Bates, Helen L. Z.
 See Yakobson, Helen B(ates)
Bates, J(ames) Leonard 1919- 13-16R
Bates, Jefferson D(avis) 1920- CANR-34
 Earlier sketches in CA 81-84, CANR-15
Bates, Jerome E. 1917- 17-20R
Bates, Kenneth Francis 1904- CAP-1
 Earlier sketch in CA 13-14
Bates, Lucius Christopher
 1901(?)-1980 Obituary 101
Bates, Margaret J(ane) 1918- 17-20R
Bates, Marston 1906-1974 ....CANR-7
 Obituary 49-52
 Earlier sketch in CA 5-8R
Bates, Milton J(ames) 1945- 128
Bates, Paul A(llen) 1920- 37-40R
Bates, Peter Watson 1920- 102
Bates, Ralph Samuel 1906- 1-4R
Bates, Robert H(inrichs) 1942- CANR-28
 Earlier sketches in CA 69-72, CANR-11
Bates, Robert L(atimer) 1912- 121
 Brief entry 116
Bates, Ronald (Gordon Nudell) 1924- 25-28R
Bates, Scott 1923- 49-52
Bates, Stephen 1958- 122
Bates, Steven Latimer 1940- 114
Bates, Su
 See Bates, Susannah (Vacella)
Bates, Susannah (Vacella) 1941- 112
Bates, Timothy M(ason) 1946- 53-56
Bateson, Charles (Henry) 1903- 69-72
Bateson, F(rederick) W(ilse)
 1901-1978 ....CANR-6
 Earlier sketch in CA 5-8R
Bateson, Gregory 1904-1980 ....41-44R
 Obituary 101
Bateson, Mary Catherine 1939- 137
Batey, Mavis 1921- 125
Batey, Richard (Alexander) 1933- 33-36R
Batey, Tom 1946- 107
 See also SATA 41, 52
Bath, Philip Ernest 1898- CAP-1
 Earlier sketch in CA 9-10
Batherman, Muriel
 See Sheldon, Muriel
Bathke, Edwin A(lbert) 1936- 57-60
Bathke, Nancy E(dna) 1938- 57-60
Batho, Edith C(lara) 1895- CAP-1
 Earlier sketch in CA 11-12
Bathurst, Sheila
 See Sullivan, Sheila
Batista, Fulgencio
 See Batista y Zaldivar, Fulgencio
Batista y Zaldivar, Fulgencio
 1901-1973 Obituary 111
Batiuk, Thomas M(artin) 1947- 69-72
 See also SATA 40
Batki, John 1942- 45-48
Batman, Richard (Dale) 1932- 124
Bator, Robert 1939- 115
Batra, Raveendra N(ath) 1943- CANR-31
 Earlier sketch in CA 89-92
Batra, Ravi
 See Batra, Raveendra N(ath)
Batson, C(harles) Daniel 1943- 129
Batson, George (Donald) 1918-1977 ....33-36R
 Obituary 73-76
Batson, Larry 1930- 57-60
 See also SATA 35
Batson, Wade Thomas 1912- 125
Battaglia, Anthony 1939- 108
Battaglia, Aurelius 1910- ....SATA 33, 50
Battaglia, Elio Lee 1928- CANR-1
 Earlier sketch in CA 1-4R
Battalia, O. William 1928- 45-48
Battan, Louis J(oseph) 1923- 13-16R
Battcock, Gregory 1938-1980 ....CANR-11
 Obituary 105
 Earlier sketch in CA 21-24R
Battelle, Phyllis (Marie) 1922- 77-80
Batten, Charles Linwood Jr. 1942- 85-88
Batten, H(arry) Mortimer
 1888-1958 Brief entry 112
 See also SATA 25
Batten, Jack 1932- 49-52
Batten, James Knox 1936- 102
Batten, James William 1919- 33-36R
Batten, Jean (Gardner) 1909-1982 106
 Obituary 123
Batten, Joyce Mortimer
 See Mankowska, Joyce Kells Batten
Batten, Mary 1937- 41-44R
 See also SATA 5
Batten, (Richard) Peter 1916- 97-100
Batten, Thomas Reginald 1904- 13-16R
Battenhouse, Roy W(esley) 1912- 13-16R
Batterberry, Ariane Ruskin 1935- CANR-13
 Earlier sketch in CA 69-72
 See also SATA 13
Batterberry, Michael Carver 1932- 77-80
 See also SATA 32
Battersby, Christine 1946- 132
Battersby, James L(yons) 1936- 41-44R
Battersby, Martin 1914(?)-1982 Obituary 106
Battersby, William J(ohn) 1904-1976 .....CANR-4
 Earlier sketch in CA 5-8R
Battestin, Martin C(arey) 1930- 13-16R
Battie, David 1942- 135
Battin, B(rinton) W(arner) 1941- CANR-30
 Earlier sketch in CA 112
Battin, Buck
 See Battin, B(rinton) W(arner)
Battin, R(osabell) Ray 1925- CANR-6
 Earlier sketch in CA 9-12R
Battin, Wendy 1953- 121
Battis, Emery John 1915- 1-4R
Battiscombe, E(sther) Georgina (Harwood)
 1905- CANR-14
 Earlier sketches in CAP-1, CA 9-10
Battista, Miriam 1912(?)-1980 Obituary 103
Battista, O(rlando) A(loysius) 1917- CANR-7
 Earlier sketch in CA 13-16R
Battisti, Eugenio 1924- 37-40R
Battle, Allen Overton 1927- 41-44R
Battle, Gerald N(ichols) 1914- 57-60
Battle, Jean Allen 1914- 25-28R
Battle, Lois 1942- CANR-27
 Earlier sketch in CA 106
Battle, Richard John Vulliamy
 1907-1982 Obituary 106
Battle, Sol(omon Oden) 1934- 25-28R
Battles, (Roxy) Edith 1921- 41-44R
 See also SATA 7
Battles, Ford Lewis 1915- 13-16R
Batto, Bernard Frank 1941- 57-60
Batts, Michael S. 1929- 41-44R
Batty, C(harles) D(avid) 1932- 17-20R
Batty, Joyce D(orothea) 1919- 17-20R
Batty, Linda Schmidt 1940- 61-64
Battye, Gladys Starkey 1915- Brief entry 111
Battye, Louis Neville 1923- 5-8R
Baty, Gordon B(ruce) 1938- 57-60
Baty, Roger M(endenhall) 1937- 77-80
Baty, Wayne 1925- CANR-5
 Earlier sketch in CA 13-16R
Bauby, Cathrina 1927- 49-52
Bauchart
 See Camus, Albert
Baudelaire, Charles 1821-1867 ....PC 1
 See also WLC
Baudet, Henri 1919- 134
Baudhuin, John S. 1948- 112
Baudouy, Michel-Aime 1909- CAP-2
 Earlier sketch in CA 33-36
 See also SATA 7
Baudrillard, Jean 1929- ....CLC 60
Baudry, Bernard
 See Guindey, Guillaume Louis
Bauduc, R.
 See Segre, Dan V(ittorio)
Baudy, Nicolas 1904(?)-1971 Obituary 33-36R
Bauer, Caroline Feller 1935- 77-80
 See also SATA 46, 52
Bauer, E. Charles 1916- 9-12R
Bauer, Erwin A. 1919- CANR-6
 Earlier sketch in CA 9-12R
Bauer, Florence Marvyne CAP-2
 Earlier sketch in CA 17-18
Bauer, Fred 1934- CANR-13
 Earlier sketch in CA 29-32R
 See also SATA 36
Bauer, George C. 1942- 73-76
Bauer, George Howard 1933- CANR-15
 Earlier sketch in CA 29-32R
Bauer, (Jo) Hanna R(uth Goldsmith)
 1918- 57-60
Bauer, Harry C(harles) 1902-1979 ....CAP-1
 Obituary 85-88
 Earlier sketch in CA 13-14
Bauer, Helen 1900- 5-8R
 See also SATA 2
Bauer, Josef Martin 1901- CANR-5
 Earlier sketch in CA 5-8R
Bauer, K(arl) Jack 1926-1987 ....CANR-10
 Obituary 123
 Earlier sketch in CA 25-28R
Bauer, Malcolm Clair 1914- 102
Bauer, Maria 1919- 117
Bauer, Marion Dane 1938- CANR-26
 Earlier sketches in CA 69-72, CANR-11
 See also MAICYA
 See also SAAS 9
 See also SATA 20, 69
Bauer, Nancy 1934- 113
Bauer, Peter Thomas 1915- 103
Bauer, Raymond A(ugustine)
 1916-1977 ....CANR-11
 Obituary 73-76
 Earlier sketch in CA 61-64
Bauer, Robert A(lbert) 1910- 69-72
Bauer, Roy A. 1945- 137
Bauer, Royal D(aniel) M(ichael) 1889- 33-36R
Bauer, Steven 1948- 128
Bauer, Walter 1904- 101
Bauer, William Waldo 1892-1967 ....CANR-7
 Earlier sketch in CA 5-8R
Bauer, Wolfgang L(eander) 1930- 13-16R
Bauer, Yehuda 1926- CANR-12
 Earlier sketch in CA 29-32R
Bauerle, Ruth (Ellen) H(awkins) 1924- 112
Bauernfeind, Harry B. 1904- CAP-2
 Earlier sketch in CA 19-20
Bauerschmidt, Marjorie 1926- ....SATA 15
Baugh, Albert C(roll) 1891-1981 107
 Obituary 103
Baugh, Daniel A(lbert) 1931- 69-72
Baughan, Peter E(dward) 1934- 107
Baughman, Dororthy 1940- ....SATA 61
Baughman, Dorothy 1940- 65-68
Baughman, Ernest W(arren) 1916- 33-36R
Baughman, James L(ewis) 1952- 118
Baughman, James P(orter) 1936- 25-28R
Baughman, John Lee 1913- 97-100
Baughman, M(illard) Dale 1919- 41-44R
Baughman, Ray Edward 1925- CANR-22
 Earlier sketches in CA 9-12R, CANR-4
Baughman, Ronald 1940- 122
Baughman, Urbanus E. Jr.
 1905(?)-1978 Obituary 81-84
Baughn, William Hubert 1918- CANR-17
 Earlier sketch in CA 1-4R
Baukhage, Hilmar Robert
 1889-1976 Obituary 65-68
 See also AITN 2
Bauland, Peter 1932- 25-28R
Baulch, Jerry T. 1913- 77-80
Baulch, Lawrence 1926- 25-28R
Baum, Allyn Z(elton) 1924- 17-20R
 See also SATA 20
Baum, Bernard H(elmut) 1926- 37-40R
Baum, Dale 1943- 118
Baum, Daniel (Jay) 1934- CANR-6
 Earlier sketch in CA 13-16R
Baum, David William 1940- 53-56
Baum, Gregory 1923- CANR-15
 Earlier sketch in CA 25-28R
Baum, Joan 1937- 134
Baum, L. Frank
 See Thompson, Ruth Plumly
Baum, L(yman) Frank 1856-1919 133
 Brief entry 108
 See also CLR 15
 See also DLB 22
 See also MAICYA
 See also MTCW
 See also SATA 18
 See also TCLC 7
Baum, Louis F.
 See Baum, L(yman) Frank
Baum, Louis 1948- 124
 See also SATA 52, 64
Baum, Paull F(ranklin) 1886-1964 ....5-8R
 Obituary 103
Baum, Rainer C(arl) 1934- 107
Baum, Richard (Dennis) 1940- 57-60
Baum, Richard Fitzgerald 1913- 5-8R
Baum, Robert J(ames) 1941- CANR-17
 Earlier sketch in CA 85-88
Baum, Thomas 1940- 65-68
Baum, Vicki 1888-1960 93-96
 See also DLB 85
Baum, Willi 1931- 29-32R
 See also SATA 4
Bauman, Clarence 1928- CANR-32
 Earlier sketch in CA 45-48
Bauman, Edward Walter 1927- 106
Bauman, H(erman) Carl 1913- 9-12R
Bauman, Janina (G.) 1926- 134
Bauman, Karl R. 1902(?)-1989 Obituary 130
Bauman, Zygmunt 1925- 127
Baumann, Amy (Brown) Beeching
 1922- 21-24R
 See also SATA 10
Baumann, Carol Edler 1932- 33-36R
Baumann, Charles Henry 1926- 73-76
Baumann, Charly 1928- 89-92
Baumann, Edward (Weston) 1925- 109
Baumann, Elwood D. Brief entry 111
 See also SATA 33
Baumann, Gerd 1953- 125
Baumann, Hans Felix S(iegismund)
 1893-1985 Obituary 115
Baumann, Hans 1914- CANR-3
 Earlier sketch in CA 5-8R
 See also SATA 2
Baumann, Kurt 1935- CANR-13
 Earlier sketch in CA 77-80
 See also SATA 21

Baumann, Walter 1935- 29-32R
Baumbach, Jonathan 1933- CANR-12
Earlier sketch in CA 13-16R
See also CAAS 5
See also CLC 6, 23
See also DLBY 80
See also MTCW
Baumback, Clifford M(ason) 1915- CANR-6
Earlier sketch in CA 57-60
Baumber, Michael (Leslie) 1935- 133
Baume, Michael 1930- 25-28R
Baumel, Judith 1956- 125
Baumer, Franklin L(e Van)
1913- Brief entry 110
Baumer, William H(enry) 1909-1989 .... CANR-1
Obituary 127
Earlier sketch in CA 1-4R
Baumgaertel, (Max) Walter 1902- 69-72
Baumgard, Herbert Mark 1920- 13-16R
Baumgardt, David 1890-1963 .... CANR-15
Obituary 103
Earlier sketch in CA 1-4R
Baumgartel, Walter
See Baumgaertel, (Max) Walter
Baumgarten, Sylvia 1933- 112
Baumgartner, Frederic J(oseph)
1945- CANR-27
Earlier sketch in CA 110
Baumgartner, John Stanley 1924- 9-12R
Bauml, Franz H.
See Baeuml, Franz H(einrich)
Baumol, William J(ack) 1922- CANR-24
Earlier sketches in CA 13-16R, CANR-7
Baumrin, Bernard H(erbert) 1934- 9-12R
Baumrin, Stefan
See Baumrin, Bernard H(erbert)
Baur, Francis G. 1930- 111
Baur, John E(dward) 1922- 9-12R
Baur, John I(reland) H(owe)
1909-1987 Obituary 122
Baus, Herbert M(ichael) 1914- CANR-11
Earlier sketch in CA 25-28R
Bausani, Alessandro 1921- 45-48
Bausch, Richard (Carl) 1945- 101
See also CAAS 14
See also CLC 51
Bausch, Robert (Charles) 1945- 109
See also CAAS 14
Bausch, William J. 1929- CANR-11
Earlier sketch in CA 29-32R
Bausher, Mildred Jordan
1901-1982 Obituary 133
Bavarel, Michel (Joseph) 1940- CANR-35
Earlier sketch in CA 114
Bavin, Bill 1919- 73-76
Bavinck, J(ohan) H(erman)
1895-1965 Obituary 113
Bavly, Dan (Abraham) 1929- 130
Bawden, Nina (Mary Mabey) 1925- CANR-29
Earlier sketches in CA 17-20R, CANR-8
See also Kark, Nina Mary (Mabey)
See also CLR 2
See also DLB 14
See also MAICYA
Bawly, Dan
See Bavly, Dan (Abraham)
Bawn, Mary
See Wright, Mary Pamela Godwin
Bax
See Baxter, Gordon F(rancis) Jr.
Bax, Clifford 1886-1962 Obituary 113
See also DLB 10, 100
Bax, Martin C(harles) O(wen) 1933- 65-68
Bax, Roger
See Winterton, Paul
Baxandall, Rosalyn Fraad 1939- 81-84
Baxt, George 1923- 21-24R
Baxter, Angus 1912- CANR-28
Earlier sketch in CA 111
Baxter, Anne 1923-1985 114
Obituary 118
Brief entry 111
Baxter, Annette Kar 1926- CANR-4
Earlier sketch in CA 1-4R
Baxter, Batsell Barrett 1916- 33-36R
Baxter, Charles 1947- 57-60
See also CLC 45
Baxter, Craig 1929- CANR-26
Earlier sketches in CA 25-28R, CANR-11
Baxter, Douglas Clark 1942- 85-88
Baxter, Edna May 1890- CAP-1
Earlier sketch in CA 17-18
Baxter, Eric George 1918- 17-20R
Baxter, Eric P(eter) 1913- 9-12R
Baxter, George Owen
See Faust, Frederick (Shiller)
Baxter, Glen 1944- CANR-28
Earlier sketch in CA 109
Baxter, Gordon F(rancis) Jr. 1923- CANR-1
Earlier sketch in CA 45-48
Baxter, Hazel
See Rowland, D(onald) S(ydney)
Baxter, Ian F. G. CANR-11
Earlier sketch in CA 21-24R
Baxter, James K(eir) 1926-1972 77-80
See also CLC 14
Baxter, James P(hinney) III 1893-1975 65-68
Obituary 57-60
Baxter, James Sidlow 1903- 73-76
Baxter, John
See Hunt, E(verette) Howard Jr.
Baxter, John 1939- CANR-25
Earlier sketch in CA 29-32R
Baxter, Maurice Glen 1920- 13-16R
Baxter, Michael John 1944- 103
Baxter, Mike
See Baxter, Michael John
Baxter, Patricia E. W. 107
Baxter, Phyllis
See Wallmann, Jeffrey M(iner)
Baxter, Shane V.
See Norwood, Victor G(eorge) C(harles)
Baxter, Stephen B(artow) 1929- 17-20R
Baxter, Valerie
See Meynell, Laurence Walter
Baxter, William F(rancis) 1929- 89-92
Baxter, William T(hreipland) 1906- 107
Baxter(-Wright), Keith (Stanley) 1935- 135
Bay, Austin 1951- 131
Bay, Christian 1921-1990 .... 33-36R
Obituary 131
Bay, Howard 1912-1986 81-84
Obituary 121
Bayard, Jean 1923- 114
Baybars, Taner 1936- CANR-4
Earlier sketch in CA 53-56
Bayer, Eleanor
See Perry, Eleanor (Rosenfeld Bayer)
Bayer, Harold
See Gregg, Andrew K.
Bayer, Herbert 1900-1985 Obituary 117
Bayer, Jane E. Obituary 116
See also SATA 44
Bayer, Konrad 1932-1964 .... DLB 85
Bayer, Linda 1948- CANR-26
Earlier sketch in CA 107
Bayer, Oliver Weld
See Perry, Eleanor (Rosenfeld Bayer)
Bayer, Ronald 1943- 106
Bayer, Sandra Lee 1945- 127
Bayer, Sandy
See Bayer, Sandra Lee
Bayer, Sylvia
See Glassco, John
Bayer, William 1939- 33-36R
Bayer-Berenbaum, Linda
See Bayer, Linda
Bayerle, Gustav 1931- 53-56
Bayes, Marjorie 1934- 115
Bayes, Ronald H(omer) 1932- CANR-10
Earlier sketch in CA 25-28R
Bayh, Birch E(vans) Jr. 1928- 41-44R
Bayh, Marvella (Hern) 1933-1979 93-96
Obituary 85-88
Bay Laurel, Alicia
See Laurel, Alicia Bay
Baylen, Joseph O(scar) 1920- CANR-10
Earlier sketch in CA 25-28R
Bayles, Ernest E(dward) 1897- 73-76
Bayles, Martha 1948- 134
Bayles, Michael D(ale) 1941- CANR-18
Earlier sketches in CA 49-52, CANR-1
Bayless, John 1913(?)-1983 Obituary 109
Bayless, Kenneth 1913(?)-1972 Obituary 104
Bayless, Raymond 1920- 85-88
Bayley, Barrington J(ohn) 1937- CANR-14
Earlier sketch in CA 37-40R
Bayley, Charles C(alvert) 1907- 33-36R
Bayley, David H(ume) 1933- 13-16R
Bayley, Edwin Richard 1918- 108
Bayley, John (Oliver) 1925- 85-88
Bayley, Monica Worsley 1919- 111
Bayley, Nicola 1949- 118
See also MAICYA
See also SATA 41, 69
Bayley, Peter Charles 1921- 101
Bayley, Stephen 1951- 106
Bayley, Viola (Powles) 1911- CANR-5
Earlier sketch in CA 5-8R
Baylis, John 1946- CANR-39
Earlier sketches in CA 101, CANR-18
Bayliss, John Clifford 1919- 13-16R
Bayliss, Timothy
See Baybars, Taner
Baylor, Byrd 1924- 81-84
See also CLR 3
See also MAICYA
See also SATA 16, 69
Baylor, Robert 1925- 13-16R
Bayly, Joseph T(ate) 1920- 17-20R
Baym, Max I. 1895- 41-44R
Baym, Nina 1936- CANR-32
Earlier sketch in CA 112
Bayne, David C(owan) 1918- 41-44R
Bayne, Nicholas (Peter) 1937- 130
Bayne, Stephen F(ielding) Jr.
1908-1974 Obituary 45-48
Bayne-Jardine, C(olin) C(harles) 1932- 25-28R
Baynes, Cary F. 1873(?)-1977 Obituary 104
Baynes, Dorothy Colston
See Colston-Baynes, Dorothy
Baynes, John (Christopher Malcolm)
1928- 21-24R
Baynes, Ken 1934- Brief entry 110
Baynes, Pauline (Diana) 1922- CANR-37
Earlier sketch in CA 120
See also MAICYA
See also SATA 19, 59
Baynham, Henry (W. F.) 1933- 29-32R
Bayor, Ronald H(oward) 1944- 128
Bayrd, Edwin 1944- 97-100
Bays, Gwendolyn McKee 13-16R
Bazelon, David T. 1923- 17-20R
Bazelon, Irwin 1922- 102
Bazin, Andre 1918-1958 Brief entry 113
Bazin, Germain (Rene Michel)
1901-1990 .... CANR-12
Obituary 131
Earlier sketch in CA 5-8R
Bazin, Herve
See Herve-Bazin, Jean Pierre Marie
See also DLB 83
Bazin, Nancy Topping 1934- 41-44R
Bazley, Margaret C. 1938- 106
BB
See Watkins-Pitchford, Denys James
Beach, Bert Beverly 1928- 57-60
Beach, Charles
See Reid, (Thomas) Mayne
Beach, Charles Amory CANR-26
Earlier sketches in CAP-2, CA 19-20
See also SATA 1
Beach, Dale S. 1923- 13-16R
Beach, David (Williams) 1938- 115
Beach, Earl F(rancis) 1912- 13-16R
Beach, Edward L(atimer) 1918- CANR-6
Earlier sketch in CA 5-8R
See also SATA 12
Beach, Frank Ambrose 1911-1988 110
Obituary 125
Beach, Lynn
See Lance, Kathryn
Beach, Mark B. 1937- 69-72
Beach, Stewart T(aft) 1899-1979 93-96
Obituary 85-88
See also SATA 23
Beach, Sylvia (Woodbridge) 1887-1962 108
See also DLB 4
Beach, Vincent W(oodrow) 1917- 33-36R
Beach, (William) Waldo 1916- 61-64
Beachcomber
See
Morton, John (Cameron Andrieu) Bingham (Michael)
Beachcroft, Nina 1931- CANR-19
Earlier sketch in CA 97-100
See also SATA 18
Beachcroft, T(homas) O(wen) 1902- CAP-1
Earlier sketch in CA 9-10
Beachey, Duane 1948- 112
Beachum, Larry M(ahon) 1948- 113
Beachy, Lucille 1935- 77-80
Beadell, Len 1923- 102
Beadle, G. W.
See Beadle, George W(ells)
Beadle, George
See Beadle, George W(ells)
Beadle, George W(ells)
1903-1989 Obituary 128
Beadle, Leigh P(atric) 1941- 65-68
Beadle, Muriel (McClure Barnett) 1915- 21-24R
Beadles, William T(homas) 1902- 17-20R
Beagle, Peter S(oyer) 1939- CANR-4
Earlier sketch in CA 9-12R
See also CLC 7
See also DLBY 80
See also SATA 60
Beaglehole, J(ohn) C(awte) 1901-1971 .... CAP-2
Obituary 33-36R
Earlier sketch in CA 21-22
Beakley, George Carroll Jr. 1922- CANR-16
Earlier sketches in CA 45-48, CANR-1
Beal, Anthony (Ridley) 1925- 9-12R
Beal, Bob 1949- 130
Beal, George M(elvin) 1917- CANR-13
Earlier sketch in CA 21-24R
Beal, Graham W(illiam) J(ohn) 1947- 118
Beal, Gwyneth 1943- 69-72
Beal, John Robinson
1906(?)-1985 Obituary 116
Beal, M. F. 1937- 73-76
See also DLBY 81
Beal, Merrill D. 1898- CANR-5
Earlier sketch in CA 1-4R
Beal, Richard S(mith) 1945-1984 122
Obituary 114
Beale, Betty 73-76
Beale, Calvin L(unsford) 1923- 1-4R
Beale, Christopher Griffin
See Griffin-Beale, Christopher
Beale, Howard K. 1899-1959 .... DLB 17
Beale, Howard 1898- 109
Beale, Paul (Christian) 1933- 130
Beale, Walter H(enry) 1945- Brief entry 118
Bealer, Alex W(inkler III) 1921-1980 .... CANR-2
Obituary 97-100
Earlier sketch in CA 45-48
See also SATA 8, 22
Bealer, George Persson 1944- CANR-32
Earlier sketch in CA 113
Beales, Derek (Edward Dawson)
1931- CANR-16
Earlier sketch in CA 73-76
Beales, H(ugh) L(ancelot)
1889-1988 Obituary 125
Beales, Peter 1936- 122
Bealey, (Frank) William 1922- CANR-2
Earlier sketch in CA 5-8R
Beall, James Lee 1924- CANR-11
Earlier sketch in CA 65-68
Beall, Karen F(riedmann) 1938- 106
Beall, Otho T(hompson) Jr.
1908-1977 Obituary 113
Beals, Alan R(obin) 1928- 37-40R
Beals, Carleton 1893-1979 .... CANR-3
Earlier sketch in CA 1-4R
See also SATA 12
Beals, Frank Lee 1881-1972 .... 5-8R
Obituary 103
See also SATA 26
Beals, Ralph L(eon) 1901- 21-24R
Beam, Alex 1954- 135
Beam, Alvin Wesley 1912-1982 Obituary 107
Beam, C. Richard 45-48
Beam, George D(ahl) 1934- 69-72
Beam, Philip C(onway) 1910- 97-100
Beaman, Joyce Proctor 1931- 29-32R
Beame, Rona 1934- 45-48
See also SATA 12
Beamer, (George) Charles (Jr.) 1942- 121
See also SATA 43
Beamish, Annie O'Meara de Vic 1883- 13-16R
Beamish, Anthony Hamilton Obituary 109
Beamish, Huldine V. 1904- CAP-1
Earlier sketch in CA 13-14
Beamish, Noel de Vic
See Beamish, Annie O'Meara de Vic
Beamish, Tufton Victor Hamilton
See Chelwood, Tufton Victor Hamilton
Bean, Constance A(ustin) 41-44R
Bean, George E(wart) 1903-1977 .... 25-28R
Obituary 133
Bean, Henry (Schorr) 1945- 109
Bean, Keith F(enwick) 1911- CAP-1
Earlier sketch in CA 11-12
Bean, Lowell John 1931- 41-44R
Bean, Mabel Greene
1898(?)-1977 Obituary 73-76
Bean, Normal
See Burroughs, Edgar Rice
Bean, Orson 1928- 77-80
Bean, Walton (Elbert) 1914- 25-28R
Bean, William B(ennett) 1909-1989 111
Obituary 128
Beaney, Jan
See Udall, Jan Beaney
Beaney, Jane
See Udall, Jan Beaney
Bear, Bullen
See Donnelly, Austin Stanislaus
Bear, David 1949- 106
Bear, Greg(ory Dale) 1951- CANR-35
Earlier sketch in CA 113
See also SATA 65
Bear, James A(dam) Jr. 1919- 21-24R
Bear, Joan 1918- 57-60
Bear, John (Boris) 1938- CANR-29
Earlier sketches in CA 73-76, CANR-13
Bear, Roberta Meyer 1942- 21-24R
Bearce, George D(onham) 1922- 9-12R
Bearchell, Charles 1925- 93-96
Beard, Belle Boone 1898-1984 Obituary 114
Beard, Charles A(ustin)
1874-1948 Brief entry 115
See also DLB 17
See also SATA 18
See also TCLC 15
Beard, Dan(iel Carter) 1859-1941 .... SATA 22
Beard, Estle S. 1908-1983 111
Beard, Geoffrey 1929- 130
Beard, Helen 1931- CANR-32
Earlier sketch in CA 113
Beard, James (Andrews) 1903-1985 .... CANR-15
Obituary 114
Earlier sketch in CA 81-84
Beard, James F(ranklin) 1919-1989 .... 1-4R
Obituary 130
Beard, Marna L(ouise) 1942- 112
Beard, Peter H. 1938- 13-16R
Beard, Robert Eric 1911-1983 Obituary 111
Bearden, James Hudson 1933- 21-24R
Bearden, Romare (Howard) 1914(?)-1988 102
Obituary 125
See also SATA 22, 56
Beardmore, Cedric
See Beardmore, George
Beardmore, George 1908-1979 69-72
Obituary 126
See also SATA 20
Beardslee, John W(alter) III 1914- 37-40R
Beardsley, Charles Noel 1914- CANR-2
Earlier sketch in CA 1-4R
Beardsley, (John) Douglas 1941- 113
Beardsley, Elizabeth Lane 29-32R
Beardsley, John 1952- CANR-28
Earlier sketch in CA 109
Beardsley, (Betty) Lou 1925- 118
Beardsley, Monroe C(urtis) 1915-1985 .... 17-20R
Obituary 117
Beardsley, Richard K(ing) 1918-1978 .... CANR-11
Obituary 77-80
Earlier sketch in CA 17-20R
Beardsley, Theodore S(terling) Jr.
1930- 33-36R
Beardsworth, Millicent Monica 1915- 103
Beardwood, Roger 1932- 89-92
Beardwood, Valerie Fairfield 5-8R
Beare, Francis W(right) 1902- CANR-16
Earlier sketch in CA 1-4R
Beare, (M.A.) Nikki 1928- 37-40R
Bearman, Jane (Ruth) 1917- 105
See also SATA 29
Bearne, C(olin) G(erald) 1939- 97-100
Bearss, Edwin C(ole) 1923- CANR-10
Earlier sketch in CA 25-28R
Beaser, Herbert W.
1913(?)-1979 Obituary 85-88
Beasley, Jerry C(arr) 1940- CANR-14
Earlier sketch in CA 37-40R
Beasley, M. Robert 1918- 9-12R
Beasley, Maurine 1936- CANR-20
Earlier sketch in CA 104
Beasley, Rex 1925- 9-12R
Beasley, Ruth 1942- 135
Beasley, W(illiam) Conger Jr. 1940- CANR-4
Earlier sketch in CA 53-56
Beasley, W(illiam) G(erald) 1919- 53-56
Beasley-Murray, George Raymond 1916- 65-68
Beason, Robert G(ayle) 1927- 114
Beath, Paul Robert 1905- 5-8R
Beath, Warren Newton 1951- 136
Beaton, Alan A. 1947- 123
Beaton, Anne
See
Washington, (Catherine) Marguerite Beauchamp
Beaton, Cecil (Walter Hardy) 1904-1980 81-84
Obituary 93-96
Beaton, George
See Brenan, (Edward Fitz)Gerald

Beaton, (Donald) Leonard 1929-1971 ......CANR-4
Obituary 29-32R
Earlier sketch in CA 5-8R
Beaton, M. C.
See Chesney, Marion
Beaton-Jones, Cynon 1921- 5-8R
Beattie, Ann 1947- 81-84
See also BEST 90:2
See also CLC 8, 13, 18, 40, 63
See also DLBY 82
See also MTCW
Beattie, Carol 1918- 29-32R
Beattie, Edward J(ames) Jr. 1918- 106
Beattie, James 1735-1803 .... DLB 109
Beattie, Jessie Louise 1896- CANR-17
Earlier sketches in CA 5-8R, CANR-2
Beattie, John (Hugh Marshall)
1915-1990 ....37-40R
Obituary 131
Beattie, Melody 1948- ....BEST 90:4
Beattie, Sally 1941- 122
Beattie, Susan 1938- 123
Beatts, Anne Patricia 1947- 102
Beatty, Bernard 1938- 127
Beatty, Elizabeth
See Holloway, Teresa (Bragunier)
Beatty, Hetty Burlingame 1907-1971 ....1-4R
Obituary 103
See also SATA 5
Beatty, Jerome Jr. 1918- CANR-3
Earlier sketch in CA 9-12R
See also SATA 5
Beatty, John (Louis) 1922-1975 ....CANR-4
Obituary 57-60
Earlier sketch in CA 5-8R
See also SATA 6, 25
Beatty, Morgan 1902-1975 Obituary 61-64
Beatty, Patricia Robbins 1922-1991 ....CANR-3
Obituary 134
Earlier sketch in CA 1-4R
See also MAICYA
See also SAAS 4
See also SATA 1, 30
See also SATO 68
Beatty, Rita Gray 1930- 45-48
Beatty, Robert Owen
1924-1976 Obituary 69-72
Beatty, Warren
See Beaty, Warren
Beatty, William Alfred 1912- CAP-1
Earlier sketch in CA 13-14
Beatty, William K(ave) 1926- 41-44R
Beaty, Betty CANR-18
Earlier sketch in CA 73-76
Beaty, (Arthur) David 1919- CANR-18
Earlier sketches in CA 1-4R, CANR-2
Beaty, Janice J(anowski) 1930- 13-16R
Beaty, Jerome 1924- 85-88
Beaty, Shirley MacLean
See MacLaine, Shirley
Beaty, Warren 1937(?)- 126
Brief entry 109
Beaubien, Anne K(athleen) 1947- 123
Beauchamp, Edward R(obert) 1933- 61-64
Beauchamp, Gorman 1938- 121
Beauchamp, Kathleen Mansfield
1888-1923 134
Brief entry 104
See also Mansfield, Katherine
Beauchamp, Kenneth L(loyd) 1939- 29-32R
Beauchamp, Pat
See
Washington, (Catherine) Marguerite Beauchamp
Beauchamp, Tom L. 1939- CANR-13
Earlier sketch in CA 73-76
Beauchemin, Neree 1850-1931 .... DLB 92
Beauchemin, Yves 1941- 129
See also DLB 60
Beauclerk, Helen De Vere
1892-1969 Obituary 114
Beaudoin, Kenneth Lawrence 1913- 29-32R
Beaudouin, John T(yrell) 1920- Brief entry 114
Beaufitz, William
See Critchley, Julian (Michael Gordon)
Beaufort, John (David) 1912- 104
Beaufre, Andre 1902-1975 65-68
Obituary 57-60
Beaugrand, Honore 1848-1906 .... DLB 99
Beaulac, Willard L(eon) 1899-1990 ....9-12R
Obituary 132
Beaulieu, Victor-Levy 1945- .... DLB 53
Beauman, E(ric) Bentley 1891-1989 ......CANR-30
Earlier sketch in CA 9-12R
Beauman, Katharine (Burgoyne) Bentley
1902- 102
Beauman, Sally 1944(?)- 134
Beaumont, Beverly
See von Block, Sylvia
Beaumont, Charles Allen 1926- 1-4R
Beaumont, Charles 1929-1967 ....5-8R
Obituary 103
Beaumont, Cyril William 1891-1976 ....13-16R
Obituary 65-68
Beaumont, Francis
1584(?)-1616 .... CDBLB Before 1660
See also DLB 58, 121
Beaumont, George Ernest
1888-1974 Obituary 49-52
Beaumont, SirJohn 1583(?)-1627 .... DLB 121
Beaumont, Keith (Stanley) 1944- 118
Beaumont, Roger A(lban) 1935- 65-68
Beauregard, Erving E. 1920- 111
Beaurline, L(ester) A(lbert) 1927- 21-24R
Beausang, Michael F(rancis) Jr. 1936- 57-60
Beausay, Florence E(dith) 1911- 21-24R
Beausoleil, Beau 1941- CANR-14
Earlier sketch in CA 81-84
Beauvais, Robert 1911- 104
Beauvoir, Simone (Lucie Ernestine Marie Bertrand) de
1908-1986 ....CANR-28
Obituary 118
Earlier sketch in CA 9-12R
See also CLC 1, 2, 4, 8, 14, 31, 44, 50, 71
See also DLB 72
See also DLBY 86
See also MTCW
See also WLC
Beaver, Bruce (Victor) 1928- 97-100
Beaver, Frank E(ugene) 1938- 114
Beaver, Harold (Lothar) 1929- 21-24R
Beaver, (Jack) Patrick 1923- 33-36R
Beaver, Paul (Eli) 1953- 115
Beaver, R(obert) Pierce 1906- CANR-7
Earlier sketch in CA 5-8R
Beaver, Stanley H(enry)
1907-1984 Obituary 114
Beaverbrook, William Maxwell Aitken
1879-1964 103
Obituary 89-92
Beazley, John Davidson
1885-1970 Obituary 115
Bebb, Russ(ell H.) Jr. 1930- 49-52
Bebbington, D(avid) W(illiam) 1949- 133
Bebell, Mildred Hoyt 1909- CAP-1
Earlier sketch in CA 13-16
Bebey, Francis 1929- CANR-25
Earlier sketch in CA 69-72
See also BW
Bebler, A(lex) Anton 1937- CANR-2
Earlier sketch in CA 49-52
Becerra, Rosina M. 1939- 122
Bechdel, Alison 1960- 138
Becher, Ulrich 1910- 101
See also DLB 69
Bechert, Heinz 1932- 136
Bechervaise, John Mayston 1910- CANR-5
Earlier sketch in CA 13-16R
Bechhoefer, Bernhard G. 1904- 1-4R
Bechko, Peggy Anne 1950- CANR-2
Earlier sketch in CA 49-52
Bechmann, Roland 1919- 136
Becht, J. Edwin 1918- 29-32R
Bechtel, Louise Seaman 1894-1985 .... CAP-2
Obituary 116
Earlier sketch in CA 29-32
See also SATA 4, 43
Bechtel, Paul M(oyer) 1909- 116
Bechtol, William M(ilton) 1931- CANR-34
Earlier sketch in CA 49-52
Beck, Aaron T(emkin) 1921- CANR-11
Earlier sketch in CA 21-24R
Beck, Alan M(arshall) 1942- CANR-21
Earlier sketch in CA 45-48
Beck, Barbara L. 1927- 17-20R
See also SATA 12
Beck, Calvin Thomas 1937- 97-100
Beck, Carl 1930- CANR-1
Earlier sketch in CA 1-4R
Beck, Clive 1939- CANR-27
Earlier sketch in CA 49-52
Beck, Doc
See Beck, Earl Clifton
Beck, Earl Clifton 1891-1977 Obituary 110
Beck, Earl R(ay) 1916- 33-36R
Beck, Emily M(orison) 1915- 114
Beck, Evelyn Torton 1933- CANR-13
Earlier sketch in CA 33-36R
Beck, Harry
See Paine, Lauran (Bosworth)
Beck, Helen L(ouise) 1908- 73-76
Beck, Henry G(abriel) J(ustin) 1914- 9-12R
Beck, Horace P(almer) 1920- 77-80
Beck, Hubert (F.) 1931- CANR-12
Earlier sketch in CA 29-32R
Beck, James (H.) 1930- 85-88
Beck, James Murray 1914- 101
Beck, Joan (Wagner) 1923- Brief entry 118
Beck, John Jacob Jr. 1941- 53-56
Beck, Julian 1925-1985 102
Obituary 117
Beck, Leslie 1907(?)-1978 Obituary 104
Beck, Lewis White 1913- CANR-2
Earlier sketch in CA 5-8R
Beck, M. Susan 1941- 113
Beck, Marilyn (Mohr) 1928- 65-68
Beck, Mary L. (Giraudo) 1924- 131
Beck, Pamela 1954- 120
Beck, Paul 1933(?)-1985 Obituary 116
Beck, Phineas
See Chamberlain, Samuel
Beck, Robert Edward 1941- 104
Beck, Robert H(olmes) 1918- 29-32R
Beck, Robert Nelson 1924-1980 ....CANR-4
Earlier sketch in CA 1-4R
Beck, Thomas D(avis) 1943- 57-60
Beck, Toni 1925- 57-60
Beck, Victor Emanuel 1894-1963 ....5-8R
Beck, Warren Albert 1918-1991 ....CANR-6
Obituary 135
Earlier sketch in CA 5-8R
Beck, Warren 1896-1986 ....CANR-3
Obituary 119
Earlier sketch in CA 1-4R
Beckel, Graham 1913- 1-4R
Beckelhymer, (Paul) Hunter 1919- CANR-3
Earlier sketch in CA 1-4R
Becker, A(dolph) C(arl) Jr. 1920- 65-68
Becker, Abraham S(amuel) 1927- 33-36R
Becker, Albert B. 1903-1972 .... CAP-2
Earlier sketch in CA 29-32
Becker, Arthur P(eter) 1918- 29-32R
Becker, B. Jay 1904-1987 65-68
Obituary 123
Becker, Beril 1901- CAP-1
Earlier sketch in CA 9-10
See also SATA 11
Becker, Bill
See Becker, William
Becker, Bruce 57-60
Becker, Carl 1873-1945 .... DLB 17
Becker, Carol 1947- 124
Becker, Edith C. (Stepien) 1915- 13-16R
Becker, Ernest 1925-1974 97-100
Becker, Florence
See Lennon, Florence Becker (Tanenbaum)
Becker, Gary S(tanley) 1930- CANR-11
Earlier sketch in CA 61-64
Becker, George J(oseph) 1908-1989 ......CANR-7
Obituary 130
Earlier sketch in CA 5-8R
Becker, Harold K(auffman) 1933- CANR-13
Earlier sketch in CA 29-32R
Becker, Howard S(aul) 1928- 134
Brief entry 115
Becker, Irving 1945- 122
Becker, Jillian (Ruth) 1932- CANR-25
Earlier sketch in CA 77-80
Becker, John E(dward) 1930- 49-52
Becker, John (Leonard) 1901- CAP-1
Earlier sketch in CA 11-12
See also SATA 12
Becker, Joseph M(aria) 1908- CANR-7
Earlier sketch in CA 17-20R
Becker, Joyce 1936- .... SATA 39
Becker, Juergen 1932- .... DLB 75
Becker, Jurek 1937- 85-88
See also CLC 7, 19
See also DLB 75
Becker, Klaus
See Koch, Kurt E(mil)
Becker, Lawrence C(arlyle) 1939- 85-88
Becker, Lucille F(rackman) 1929- CANR-12
Earlier sketch in CA 29-32R
Becker, Manning H. 1922- 13-16R
Becker, Marion Rombauer 1903-1976 ......37-40R
Obituary 69-72
Becker, Marvin Burton 1922- 107
Becker, May Lamberton
1873-1958 Brief entry 112
See also SATA 33
Becker, Murray 1909(?)-1986 Obituary 118
Becker, Olga
See Frank, Rudolf
Becker, Paula Lee 1941- 17-20R
Becker, Peter 1921- 53-56
Becker, Robert O(tto) 1923- 123
Becker, Robin 1951- 110
Becker, Ruby Wirt 1915- 33-36R
Becker, Russell J(ames) 1923- 37-40R
Becker, Samuel L(eo) 1923- CANR-7
Earlier sketch in CA 13-16R
Becker, Seymour 1934- 25-28R
Becker, Stephen (David) 1927- CANR-3
Earlier sketch in CA 5-8R
See also CAAS 1
Becker, Ted
See Becker, Theodore L(ewis)
Becker, Theodore L(ewis) 1932- Brief entry 116
Becker, Thomas W(illiam) 1933- 5-8R
Becker, Walter 1950- .... CLC 26
Becker, Wesley C(lemence) 1928- 33-36R
Becker, William H(enry) 1943- 125
Becker, William 1903(?)-1983 Obituary 110
Beckerman, Bernard 1921-1985 ....CANR-19
Obituary 117
Earlier sketch in CA 1-4R
Beckerman, Wilfred 1925- CANR-7
Earlier sketch in CA 17-20R
Becket, Henry S. A.
See Goulden, Joseph C. (Jr.)
Beckett, Ian F(rederick) W(illiam) 1950- 120
Beckett, J(ames) C(amlin) 1912- Brief entry 114
Beckett, John A(ngus) 1916- 33-36R
Beckett, Kenneth A(lbert) 1929- CANR-28
Earlier sketches in CA 65-68, CANR-10
Beckett, Lucy 1942- 49-52
Beckett, Mary 1926- 127
Beckett, Ralph L(awrence) 1923- 5-8R
Beckett, Ronald Brymer 1891- 5-8R
Beckett, Samuel (Barclay) 1906-1989 ....CANR-33
Obituary 130
Earlier sketch in CA 5-8R
See also CDBLB 1945-1960
See also CLC 1, 2, 3, 4, 6, 9, 10, 11, 14, 18, 29, 57, 59
See also DLB 13, 15
See also DLBY 90
See also MTCW
See also WLC
Beckett, Sheilah 1913- .... SATA 33
Beckey, Fred W(olfgang) 1923- 109
Beckford, George L(eslie Fitz-Gerald)
1934- 97-100
Beckford, William 1760-1844 .... DLB 39
Beckham, Barry (Earl) 1944- CANR-26
Earlier sketch in CA 29-32R
See also BLC 1
See also BW
See also DLB 33
Beckham, Stephen Dow 1941- CANR-28
Earlier sketches in CA 61-64, CANR-12
Beckhart, Benjamin Haggott
1897-1975 Obituary 57-60
Beckingham, Charles Fraser 1914- 61-64
Beckinsale, Monica 1914- 69-72
Beckinsale, Robert Percy 1908- CANR-2
Earlier sketch in CA 5-8R
Becklake, Sue 1943- 120
Beckler, Marion Floyd 1889- CAP-1
Earlier sketch in CA 11-12
Beckles Willson, Robina (Elizabeth)
1930- CANR-20
Earlier sketches in CA 13-16R, CANR-5
See also Willson, Robina Beckles
Beckman, Aldo Bruce 1934- 73-76
Beckman, Delores 1914- 121
See also SATA 51
Beckman, Gail McKnight 1938- 53-56
Beckman, Gunnel 1910- CANR-15
Earlier sketch in CA 33-36R
See also CLC 26
See also CLR 25
See also MAICYA
See also SAAS 9
See also SATA 6
Beckman, Kaj
See Beckman, Karin
Beckman, Karin 1913- .... SATA 45
Beckman, Patti
See Boeckman, Patti
Beckman, Per (Frithiof) 1913- .... SATA 45
Beckman, Robert C(harles) 1934- 120
Beckmann, David M(ilton) 1948- CANR-8
Earlier sketch in CA 61-64
Beckmann, George Michael 1926- 5-8R
Beckmann, Martin J(osef) 1924- 37-40R
Beckmann, Petr 1924- 69-72
Beckner, Weldon (Earnest) 1933- 33-36R
Beckovic, Matiia 1939- 33-36R
Beckson, Karl 1926- CANR-2
Earlier sketch in CA 5-8R
Beckwith, B(rainerd) K(ellogg) 1902- 73-76
Beckwith, Burnham Putnam 1904- 33-36R
Beckwith, Charles E(milio) 1917- 37-40R
Beckwith, John Gordon 1918- 9-12R
Beckwith, Lillian
See Comber, Lillian
Beckwith, Paul 1905-1975 Obituary 113
Beckwith, Yvonne 106
Bedard, Michelle
See Finnigan, Joan
Bedard, Patrick Joseph 1941- 112
Bedau, Hugo Adam 1926- CANR-19
Earlier sketches in CA 9-12R, CANR-4
Beddall, Barbara G(ould) 1919- 33-36R
Beddall-Smith, Charles John 1916- 13-16R
Beddoe, Ellaruth
See Elkins, Ella Ruth
Beddoes, Richard H(erbert) 1926- 37-40R
Beddoes, Thomas Lovell 1803-1849 .... DLB 96
Bede, Andrew
See Beha, Ernest
Bede, Jean-Albert 1903-1977 Obituary 69-72
Bedeian, Arthur G(eorge) 1946- 110
Bedell, George C(hester) 1928- 41-44R
Bedell, L. Frank 1888- CAP-1
Earlier sketch in CA 13-16
Bedell, Madelon (Jane Berns)
1922(?)-1986 136
Obituary 119
Bedells, Phyllis 1893-1985 Obituary 116
Bedford, A. N.
See Watson, Jane Werner
Bedford, Ann
See Rees, Joan
Bedford, Annie North
See Watson, Jane Werner
Bedford, Charles Harold 1929- 57-60
Bedford, Donald F.
See Fearing, Kenneth (Flexner)
Bedford, Emmett G(runer) 1922- 45-48
Bedford, Henry F(rederick) 1931- 9-12R
Bedford, Kenneth
See Paine, Lauran (Bosworth)
Bedford, Norton M(oore) 1916- 5-8R
Bedford, Sybille 1911- 9-12R
Bediako, Kwabena Asare
See Konadu, S(amuel) A(sare)
Bedikian, Antriganik A.
1886(?)-1980 Obituary 93-96
Bedinger, Margery 1891- 57-60
Bedinger, Singleton B(erry) 1907- 49-52
Bedini, Silvio A. 1917- CANR-29
Earlier sketches in CA 33-36R, CANR-13
Bednarik, Charles (Philip) 1925- 77-80
Bednarik, Chuck
See Bednarik, Charles (Philip)
Bedoukian, Kerop 1907-1981 93-96
See also SATA 53
Bedoyere, Michael De La
See De La Bedoyere, Michael
Bedrij, Orest (John) 1933- CANR-16
Earlier sketch in CA 85-88
Bedsole, Adolph 1914- 13-16R
Bee, Clair (Francis) 1900-1983 ....1-4R
Obituary 109
Bee, (John) David (Ashford) 1931- 17-20R
Bee, Helen L. 1939- CANR-16
Earlier sketch in CA 89-92
Bee, Jay
See Brainerd, John W(hiting)
Bee, Robert L(awrence) 1938- 113
Beebe, (Ida) Ann 1919- 41-44R
Beebe, B(urdetta) F(aye)
See Johnson, B(urdetta) F(aye)
See also SATA 1
Beebe, Frank L(yman) 1914- 89-92
Beebe, Frederick S(essions)
1914-1973 Obituary 41-44R
Beebe, H. Keith 1921- 29-32R
Beebe, Lucius 1902-1966 Obituary 25-28R
Beebe, Maurice (Laverne) 1926- CANR-1
Earlier sketch in CA 1-4R
Beebe, Ralph K(enneth) 1932- 33-36R
Beebe, (Charles) William 1877-1962 73-76
See also SATA 19
Beeby, Betty 1923- .... SATA 25

Beeby, C(larence) E(dward) 1902- 109
Beech, George T(homas) 1931- 9-12R
Beech, Harold Reginald 1925- 25-28R
Beech, Keyes 1913-1990 ....33-36R
Obituary 130
Beech, Robert (Paul) 1940- 33-36R
Beech, Webb
See Butterworth, W(illiam) E(dmund III)
Beecham, Justin
See Wintle, Justin (Beecham)
Beecham, Thomas 1879-1961 Obituary 112
Beechcroft, William
See Hallstead, William F(inn III)
Beecher, Catharine Esther 1800-1878 .... DLB 1
Beecher, Donald A(llen) 1942- 135
Beecher, Henry Ward 1813-1887 .... DLB 3, 43
Beecher, John 1904-1980 ....CANR-8
Obituary 105
Earlier sketch in CA 5-8R
See also AITN 1
See also CLC 6
Beecher, Jonathan French 1937- 128
Beecher, Maureen Ursenbach 1935- 137
Beecher, William (M.) 1933- 65-68
Beechert, Edward D. 1920- 124
Beechhold, Henry F(rank) 1928- 33-36R
Beechick, Ruth 1925- CANR-25
Earlier sketch in CA 108
Beeching, Jack 1922- CANR-13
Earlier sketch in CA 21-24R
See also SATA 14
Beechy, Winifred
See Beechy, Winifred Nelson
Beechy, Winifred Nelson 1915- 116
Beecroft, John William Richard
1902-1966 ....5-8R
Beedell, Suzanne (Mollie) 1921- CANR-20
Earlier sketch in CA 69-72
Beeding, Francis
See Palmer, John (Leslie)
and Saunders, Hilary Aidan St. George
Beegle, Charles William 1928- 106
Beegle, Dewey Maurice 1919- 5-8R
Beegle, J(oseph) Allan 1918- 119
Beehler, Bruce M(cPherson) 1951- 127
Beek, Martin(us) A(drianus) 1909- 13-16R
Beekman, Allan 1913- 33-36R
Beekman, E(ric) M(ontague) 1939- CANR-14
Earlier sketch in CA 33-36R
Beekman, John 1918-1980 61-64
Obituary 135
Beekman, Ross
See Dey, Frederic (Merrill) Van Rensselaer
Beeks, Graydon 1919- 65-68
Beeler, Janet
See Shaw, Janet
Beeler, Nelson F(rederick) 1910- 69-72
See also SATA 13
Beeman, Richard R(oy) 1942- 77-80
Beer, Barrett L(ynn) 1936- 49-52
Beer, Edith Lynn 1930- CANR-28
Earlier sketches in CA 61-64, CANR-11
Beer, Eloise C. S. 1903- 13-16R
Beer, Ethel S(ophia) 1897-1975 ....CAP-2
Obituary 57-60
Earlier sketch in CA 25-28
Beer, Francis Anthony 1939- CANR-10
Earlier sketch in CA 25-28R
Beer, George L. 1872-1920 ....DLB 47
Beer, Jeanette (Mary Ayres) 124
Beer, John B(ernard) 1926- CANR-23
Earlier sketches in CA 5-8R, CANR-7
Beer, Kathleen Costello 1926- 25-28R
Beer, Lawrence W(ard) 1932- 37-40R
Beer, Lisl
See Beer, Eloise C. S.
Beer, Patricia 1924- CANR-13
Earlier sketch in CA 61-64
See also CLC 58
See also DLB 40
Beer, Ralph (Robert) 1947- 120
Beer, Samuel Hutchison 1911- CANR-31
Earlier sketch in CA 61-64
Beer, Vic
See Bird, Vivian
Beer, William Reed 1943- CANR-31
Earlier sketch in CA 112
Beerbohm, Henry Maximilian
1872-1956 Brief entry 104
See also DLB 34, 100
See also TCLC 1, 24
Beer-Hofmann, Richard 1866-1945 .... DLB 81
Beers, Burton F(loyd) 1927- CANR-19
Earlier sketch in CA 1-4R
Beers, Dorothy Sands 1917- 49-52
See also SATA 9
Beers, Henry A. 1847-1926 ....DLB 71
Beers, Henry Putney 1907- 13-16R
Beers, Lorna 1897- 49-52
See also SATA 14
Beers, Paul Benjamin 1931- 102
Beers, V(ictor) Gilbert 1928- CANR-36
Earlier sketches in CA 49-52, CANR-1, 16
See also SATA 9
Beers, William 1948- 137
Beery, Mary 1907- 5-8R
Beesly, Patrick 1913-1986 ....CANR-15
Obituary 120
Earlier sketch in CA 85-88
Beeson, Trevor Randall 1926- 93-96
Beeton, Max
See Redding, Robert Hull
Beeton, (Douglas) Ridley 1929- 93-96
Beevers, John (Leonard) 1911-1975 61-64
Beevor, Antony 1946- 129
Beezley, P(aul) C. 1895- 5-8R
Beezley, William H(oward Taft) 1942- CANR-27
Earlier sketch in CA 49-52
Befu, Harumi 1930- 53-56
Beg, Toran
See McKillop, Norman
Begam, Robert G(eorge) 1928- 127
Begg, A(lexander) Charles 1912- 102
Begg, Howard Bolton 1896- 5-8R
Begg, Neil Colquhoun 1915- 102
Beggs, David W(hiteford) III 1931-1966 .... CAP-1
Earlier sketch in CA 13-16
Beggs, Donald L(ee) 1941- 33-36R
Beggs, Edward Larry 1933- 89-92
Begiebing, Robert J(ohn) 1946- 122
See also CLC 70
Begin, Menachem 1913- Brief entry 109
Begin, Menahem
See Begin, Menachem
Begleiter, Henri 1935- 119
Begley, James 1929- 25-28R
Begley, Kathleen A(nne) 1948- 77-80
See also SATA 21
Begnal, Michael H(enry) 1939- 73-76
Begner, Edith 1918-1989 ....CANR-3
Obituary 129
Earlier sketch in CA 1-4R
Begon, Elisabeth 1696-1755 .... DLB 99
Beha, Ernest 1908- CAP-1
Earlier sketch in CA 13-14
Beha, Sister Helen Marie 1926- 21-24R
Behan, Brendan 1923-1964 ....CANR-33
Earlier sketch in CA 73-76
See also CDBLB 1945-1960
See also CLC 1, 8, 11, 15
See also DLB 13
See also MTCW
Behan, Dominic 1928(?)-1989 Obituary 129
Behan, Leslie
See Gottfried, Theodore Mark
Behara, Devendra Nath 1940- 41-44R
Behee, John 1933- 112
Behle, William H(arroun) 1909- 5-8R
Behler, Ernst 1928- 41-44R
Behlmer, George K(inkel) 1948- 123
Behlmer, Rudy 1926- CANR-8
Earlier sketch in CA 57-60
Behm, Marc 1925- 101
Behm, William H(erman) Jr. 1922- 13-16R
Behme, Robert Lee 1924- 57-60
Behn, Aphra 1640(?)-1689 ....DLB 39, 80
See also WLC
Behn, Harry 1898-1973 ....CANR-5
Obituary 53-56
Earlier sketch in CA 5-8R
See also DLB 61
See also SATA 2, 34
Behn, Noel 1928- 129
Brief entry 116
Behn, Robert Dietrich 1941- 137
Behney, John Bruce 1905- 101
Behnke, Charles A(lbert) 1891- CAP-2
Earlier sketch in CA 19-20
Behnke, Frances L. 33-36R
See also SATA 8
Behnke, John 1945- 69-72
Behnke, Leo 1933- 111
Behr, Edward 1926- CANR-3
Earlier sketch in CA 1-4R
Behr, Joyce 1929- ....SATA 15
Behr, Marion 1939- 105
Behrend, Jeanne 1911- 17-20R
Behrens, Earl (Charles)
1892-1985 Obituary 116
Behrens, Helen Kindler 1922- 61-64
Behrens, Herman D(aniel) 1901- 33-36R
Behrens, John C. 1933- CANR-14
Earlier sketch in CA 37-40R
Behrens, June York 1925- CANR-24
Earlier sketches in CA 17-20R, CANR-8
See also SATA 19
Behrens, Roy R(ichard) 1946- 110
Behrman, Carol H(elen) 1925- CANR-22
Earlier sketches in CA 61-64, CANR-7
See also SATA 14
Behrman, Cynthia F(ansler) 1931- 123
Behrman, Daniel 1923-1990 65-68
Obituary 131
Behrman, Jack N(ewton) 1922- CANR-30
Earlier sketch in CA 29-32R
Behrman, Lucy Creevey
See Creevey, Lucy E.
Behrman, S(amuel) N(athaniel)
1893-1973 ....CAP-1
Obituary 45-48
Earlier sketch in CA 13-16
See also CLC 40
See also DLB 7, 44
Behrstock, Barry 1948- 106
Beichman, Arnold 1913- CANR-31
Earlier sketch in CA 49-52
Beichner, Paul E(dward) 1912- 33-36R
Beidelman, T(homas) O(wen) 1931- 129
Beiderwell, Bruce 1952- 137
Beier, Ernst G(unter) 1916- 21-24R
Beier, Ulli 1922- CANR-4
Earlier sketch in CA 9-12R
Beigel, Allan 1940- 101
Beigel, Herbert 1944- 97-100
Beigel, Hugo George 1897- 37-40R
Beik, Paul H(arold) 1915- 13-16R
Beik, William (Humphrey) 1941- 123
Beilenson, Edna 1909-1981 ....CANR-29
Obituary 103
Earlier sketch in CA 85-88
Beilenson, Laurence W. 1899-1988 ....29-32R
Obituary 125
Beiler, Edna 1923- CANR-1
Earlier sketch in CA 1-4R
See also SATA 61
Beilharz, Edwin Alanson 1907-1986 ....CANR-27
Obituary 120
Earlier sketch in CA 33-36R
Beilharz, Peter 1953- 127
Beim, Norman 1923- 85-88
Beine, George Holmes 1893- 93-96
Beineix, Jean-Jacques 1946- 124
Beiner, Ronald 1953- 117
Beinhart, Larry 1947- 138
Beinicke, Steve 1956- ....SATA 69
Beirne, Barbara 1933- ....SATA 71
Beirne, Brother Kilian 1896-1976 ....21-24R
Obituary 134
Beirne, Gerald E(dward) 1936- 118
Beirne, Joseph Anthony 1911-1974 45-48
Obituary 53-56
Beiser, Arthur 1931- 93-96
See also SATA 22
Beiser, Frederick C. 1949- 128
Beiser, Germaine 1931- ....SATA 11
Beisner, Robert L(ee) 1936- 25-28R
Beissel, Henry Eric 1929- CANR-10
Earlier sketch in CA 65-68
Beisser, Arnold R(ay) 1925- 25-28R
Beistle, Shirley
See Climo, Shirley
Beit-Hallahmi, Benjamin 1943- 105
Beitler, Ethel Jane (Heinkel) 1906- CANR-2
Earlier sketch in CA 5-8R
Beitler, Stanley (Samuel) 1924- 5-8R
Beitz, Charles R(ichard) 1949- CANR-1
Earlier sketch in CA 49-52
Beitzell, Edwin Warfield
1905(?)-1984 Obituary 114
Beitzell, Robert (E.) 1930- Brief entry 115
Beitzinger, A(lfons) J(oseph) 1918- 45-48
Beizer, Boris 1934- 105
Beja, Morris 1935- 29-32R
Bejerot, Nils 1921- 29-32R
Bekessy, Jean
See Habe, Hans
Bekker, Hugo 1925- 41-44R
Bekker-Nielsen, Hans 1933- CANR-16
Earlier sketch in CA 25-28R
Belair, Felix Jr. 1907-1978 Obituary 77-80
Belair, Richard L. 1934- 13-16R
See also SATA 45
Belaney, Archibald Stansfeld
1888-1938 Brief entry 114
See also Owl, Grey
See also SATA 24
Belanger, Jerome D(avid) 1938- 69-72
Belasco, David 1853-1931 Brief entry 104
See also DLB 7
See also TCLC 3
Belcastro, Joseph 1910- CAP-2
Earlier sketch in CA 19-20
Belch, Caroline Jean 1916- 45-48
Belchem, David
See Belchem, R(onald) F(rederick) K(ing)
Belchem, R(onald) F(rederick) K(ing)
1911-1981 122
Obituary 108
Belcher, Jerry 1930-1987 Obituary 124
Belcher, Wendy (Laura) 1962- 130
Belcheva, Elisaveta 1893- ....CLC 10
Belden, Gail
See Belden, Louise Conway
Belden, Jack 1910-1989 Obituary 128
Belden, Louise Conway 1910- 104
Belden, Wilanne Schneider 1925- CANR-23
Earlier sketch in CA 106
See also SATA 56
Belding, Robert E(dward) 1911- 33-36R
Beldone, Phil "Cheech"
See Ellison, Harlan
Belehradek, Jan 1896-1980 Obituary 97-100
Beleno
See Azuela, Mariano
Belew, M. Wendell 1922- 33-36R
Belfer, Nancy 1930- 85-88
Belfield, Eversley (Michael Gallimore)
1918- CANR-11
Earlier sketch in CA 25-28R
Belfiglio, Valentine J(ohn) 1934- CANR-28
Earlier sketches in CA 49-52, CANR-11
Belford, Barbara 1935- 136
Belford, Lee A(rcher) 1913- 17-20R
Belfrage, Cedric H. 1904-1990 ....CANR-3
Obituary 132
Earlier sketch in CA 9-12R
Belfrage, Sally 1936- 105
See also SATA 65
Bel Geddes, Joan
See Geddes, Joan Bel
Belgion, (Harold) Montgomery
1892-1973 ....CAP-1
Earlier sketch in CA 13-14
Belgum, David 1922- CANR-6
Earlier sketch in CA 13-16R
Belin, David W. 1928- 85-88
Beling, Willard A(dolf) 1919- 53-56
Belinkov, Arkady Viktorovich
1922(?)-1970 Obituary 29-32R
Belisle, Louis-Alexandre
1902-1985 Obituary 117
Belitsky, A(braham) Harvey 1929- 33-36R
Belitt, Ben 1911- CANR-7
Earlier sketch in CA 13-16R
See also CAAS 4
See also CLC 22
See also DLB 5
Belk, Fred Richard 1937- 115
Belkin, Gary S(tuart) 1945- 114
Belkin, Samuel 1911-1976 ....CANR-6
Obituary 65-68
Earlier sketch in CA 1-4R
Belkind, Allen 1927- 29-32R
Belknap, B. H.
See Ellis, Edward S(ylvester)
Belknap, Boynton
See Ellis, Edward S(ylvester)
Belknap, Boynton M.D.
See Ellis, Edward S(ylvester)
Belknap, Ivan (Carl) 1916- 5-8R
Belknap, Jeremy 1744-1798 ....DLB 30, 37
Belknap, Robert H(arlan) 1917- 45-48
Belknap, Robert L(amont) 1929- 33-36R
Belknap, S(ally) Yancey 1895- CAP-1
Earlier sketch in CA 11-12
Bell, A(rthur) Donald 1920- 25-28R
Bell, Adrian (Hanbury) 1901-1980 97-100
Obituary 102
Bell, Alan P(aul) 1932- CANR-13
Earlier sketch in CA 33-36R
Bell, Anne Olivier 1916- 112
Bell, Arthur 1939-1984 85-88
Obituary 112
Bell, Barbara Currier 1941- 115
Bell, Bernard W(illiam) 1936- Brief entry 117
Bell, Betty
See Bell, Lorna Beatrice
Bell, Carol
See Flavell, Carol Willsey Bell
Bell, Carolyn
See Rigoni, Orlando (Joseph)
Bell, Carolyn Shaw 1920- 29-32R
Bell, Charles G. 1929- 37-40R
Bell, Charles Greenleaf 1916- CANR-2
Earlier sketch in CA 1-4R
See also CAAS 12
Bell, Chip R(ay) 1944- 121
Bell, (Arthur) Clive (Howard) 1881-1964 97-100
Obituary 89-92
See also MTCW
Bell, Colin (John) 1938- CANR-32
Earlier sketch in CA 29-32R
Bell, Corydon Whitten 1894- 5-8R
See also SATA 3
Bell, Daniel 1919- CANR-4
Earlier sketch in CA 1-4R
Bell, David R(obert) 1932- 93-96
Bell, David S(heffield) 1945- 61-64
Bell, David Victor John 1944- CANR-38
Earlier sketches in CA 45-48, CANR-1, 17
Bell, Derrick Albert Jr. 1930- 104
Bell, Earl Hoyt 1903-1963 ....1-4R
Bell, Eileen 1907- 33-36R
Bell, Elizabeth Rose 1912- 106
Bell, Elizabeth S. 1946- 128
Bell, Elliot V(allance) 1902-1983 Obituary 108
Bell, Emerson
See Stratemeyer, Edward L.
Bell, Emily Mary
See Cason, Mabel Earp
Bell, Frank
See Benson, Mildred (Augustine Wirt)
Bell, Gail Winther 1936- 41-44R
Bell, Gawain (Westray) 1909- 131
Bell, Geoffrey Foxall 1896-1984 Obituary 111
Bell, Geoffrey (Lakin) 1939- Brief entry 114
Bell, Gerald D(ean) 1937- 49-52
Bell, Gertrude (Wood) 1911- 13-16R
See also SATA 12
Bell, Gina
See Balzano, Jeanne (Koppel)
See also SATA 7
Bell, Gordon Bennett 1934- 104
Bell, H(arold) Idris 1879-1967 ....CAP-1
Earlier sketch in CA 13-14
Bell, Harry McAra 1899- CAP-1
Earlier sketch in CA 13-14
Bell, Herbert C(lifford Francis)
1881-1966 Obituary 113
Bell, Herbert W. 1922- 123
Bell, Irene Wood 1944- 89-92
Bell, J. Bowyer 1931- 17-20R
Bell, Jack L. 1904-1975 ....CANR-6
Obituary 61-64
Earlier sketch in CA 1-4R
Bell, James (Adrian) 1917- 73-76
Bell, James B. 1932- 101
Bell, James Edward 1941- 33-36R
Bell, James K(enton) 1937- 25-28R
Bell, James Madison 1826-1902 124
Brief entry 122
See also BLC 1
See also BW
See also DLB 50
See also TCLC 43
Bell, Janet
See Clymer, Eleanor
Bell, John
See Johnson, Victor Hugo
Bell, John C. 1902(?)-1981 Obituary 103
Bell, John (Donnelly) 1944- 97-100
Bell, John Elderkin 1913- 81-84
Bell, John Patrick 1935- 101
Bell, Joseph N. 1921- 5-8R
Bell, Josephine
See Ball, Doris Bell (Collier)
Bell, Joyce Denebrink 1936- 17-20R
Bell, Joyce 1920- CANR-8
Earlier sketch in CA 57-60
Bell, L. Nelson 1894-1973 ....CAP-1
Obituary 45-48
Earlier sketch in CA 19-20
Bell, Leland V(irgil) 1934- 49-52
Bell, Linda R. 1949- 117
Bell, Lorna Beatrice 1902- 117

Bell, Louise Price CAP-1
Earlier sketch in CA 9-10
Bell, Madison (Smartt) 1957- CANR-28
Earlier sketch in CA 111
See also CLC 41
Bell, Malcolm (H.) 1931- 122
Bell, Margaret E(lizabeth) 1898- CANR-1
Earlier sketch in CA 1-4R
See also SATA 2
Bell, Marvin (Hartley) 1937- 21-24R
See also CAAS 14
See also CLC 8, 31
See also DLB 5
See also MTCW
Bell, Mary Hayley
See Hayley Bell, Mary
Bell, Michael Davitt 1941- CANR-15
Earlier sketch in CA 81-84
Bell, Millicent (L.) CANR-36
Earlier sketch in CA 114
See also DLB 111
Bell, Neill 1946- 118
See also SATA 50
Bell, Norman (Edward) 1899- 61-64
See also SATA 11
Bell, Norman W. 1928- CANR-1
Earlier sketch in CA 1-4R
Bell, Oliver (Sydney) 1913- 53-56
Bell, Philip W(ilkes) 1924- CANR-26
Earlier sketch in CA 29-32R
Bell, Quentin (Claudian Stephen) 1910- 57-60
Bell, R(obert) C(harles) 1917- CANR-24
Earlier sketches in CA 17-20R, CANR-7
Bell, Raymond Martin 1907- 29-32R
See also SATA 13
Bell, Robert E(ugene) 1914- 138
Earlier sketch in CA 37-40R
Bell, Robert (Ivan) 1942- 101
Bell, Robert Roy 1924- CANR-1
Earlier sketch in CA 1-4R
Bell, Robert S(tanley) W(arren)
1871-1921 Brief entry 115
See also SATA 27
Bell, Robert Vaughn 1924- 110
Bell, Robin
See Jones, John F(inbar)
Bell, Roger 1947- 122
Bell, (Caroline) Rose (Buchanan) 1939- 29-32R
Bell, Roseann P. 1945- 120
Bell, Rudolph M(ark) 1942- 45-48
Bell, Sallie Lee CANR-1
Earlier sketch in CA 1-4R
Bell, Sarah Fore 1920- 53-56
Bell, Sidney 1929- 41-44R
Bell, Stephen (Scott) 1935- 65-68
Bell, Thelma Harrington 1896- 1-4R
See also SATA 3
Bell, Thornton
See Fanthorpe, R(obert) Lionel
Bell, Vicars W(alker) 1904- CAP-1
Earlier sketch in CA 13-16
Bell, W. L. D.
See Mencken, H(enry) L(ouis)
Bell, Wendell 1924- CANR-4
Earlier sketch in CA 1-4R
Bell, Whitfield Jenks Jr. 1914- 105
Bell, William J. .... AITN 1
Bell, William Stewart 1921- 1-4R
Bell, Winifred 1914- CANR-9
Earlier sketch in CA 17-20R
Bellah, James Warner 1899-1976 .... 5-8R
Obituary 69-72
Bellah, Robert N(eelly) 1927- 21-24R
Bellairs, George
See Blundell, Harold
Bellairs, John (A.) 1938-1991 .... CANR-24
Obituary 133
Earlier sketches in CA 21-24R, CANR-8
See also MAICYA
See also SATA 2, 68
See also SATO 66
Bellak, Leopold 1916- CANR-16
Earlier sketch in CA 85-88
Bellamy, Atwood C.
See Mencken, H(enry) L(ouis)
Bellamy, David (James) 1933- Brief entry 114
Bellamy, Edward 1850-1898 .... DLB 12
Bellamy, Francis Rufus
1886-1972 Obituary 33-36R
Bellamy, Guy 1935- CANR-34
Earlier sketches in CA 65-68, CANR-9
Bellamy, Harmon
See Bloom, Herman Irving
Bellamy, James A(ndrew) 1925- 49-52
Bellamy, Joe David 1941- CANR-34
Earlier sketches in CA 41-44R, CANR-15
Bellamy, Joseph 1719-1790 .... DLB 31
Bellamy, Peter 1914- Brief entry 117
Bellamy, Ralph (Rexford) 1904-1991 101
Obituary 136
Bellan, Ruben C. 1918- 13-16R
Belle, Pamela 1952- CANR-38
Earlier sketch in CA 115
Beller, Anne Scott 77-80
Beller, Elmer Adolph
1894-1980 Obituary 97-100
Beller, Jacob 1896- CAP-2
Earlier sketch in CA 25-28
Beller, Joel 1926- 113
Beller, Miles 1951- 134
Beller, Steven (Peter) 1958- 133
Beller, William Stern 1919- 5-8R
Bellerby, (Mary Eireen) Frances Parker
1899-1975 101
Bellhouse, Alan Robert
1914-1980 Obituary 108
Belli, Angela 1935- 37-40R
Belli, Carlos German 1927- 131
See also HW
Belli, Melvin M(ouron) 1907- CANR-34
Earlier sketch in CA 104
Bellin, Edward J.
See Kuttner, Henry
Bellingham, Brenda 1931- 123
See also SATA 51
Bellingham, Helen Mary Dorothea
See Beauclerk, Helen De Vere
Bellini delle Stelle, Pier Luigi
1920(?)-1984 Obituary 111
Bellis, David James 1944- 108
Bellman, Richard (Ernest) 1920-1984 .... CANR-12
Obituary 112
Earlier sketch in CA 69-72
Bellman, Samuel Irving 1926- CANR-7
Earlier sketch in CA 17-20R
Bellman, Willard F. 1920- 113
Bell-Metereau, Rebecca 1949- 122
Bello, Francis (Cesare)
1917-1987 Obituary 121
Belloc, (Joseph) Hilaire (Pierre)
1870-1953 Brief entry 106
See also DLB 19, 100
See also TCLC 7, 18
See also YABC 1
Belloc, Joseph Peter Rene Hilaire
See Belloc, (Joseph) Hilaire (Pierre)
Belloc, Joseph Pierre Hilaire
See Belloc, (Joseph) Hilaire (Pierre)
Belloc, M. A.
See Lowndes, Marie Adelaide (Belloc)
Bellochio, Marco 1939- 110
Bellocq, Louise
See Boudat, Marie-Louise
Bellonci, Maria 1902-1986 Obituary 120
Bellone, Enrico 1938- 106
Bellony, Alice 1925- 118
Bellony-Rewald, Alice
See Bellony, Alice
Bellot, Leland J(oseph) 1936- Brief entry 115
Bellotti, Laura Golden 1947- 137
Bellow, Saul 1915- CANR-29
Earlier sketch in CA 5-8R
See also CABS 1
See also AITN 2
See also BEST 89:3
See also CDALB 1941-1968
See also
CLC 1, 2, 3, 6, 8, 10, 13, 15, 25, 33, 34, 63
See also DLB 2, 28
See also DLBD 3
See also DLBY 82
See also MTCW
See also WLC
Bellows, Fiona (Ann) 1941- 115
Bellows, James G(ilbert) 1922- 102
Bellows, Roger Marion 1905- 1-4R
Bellows, Thomas J(ohn) 1935- CANR-31
Earlier sketch in CA 45-48
Bellush, Bernard 1917- 132
Brief entry 120
Bell-Villada, Gene Harold 1941- 105
Bellville, Cheryl Walsh 1944- 109
See also SATA 49, 54
Bellville, Rod 1944- 117
Bell-Zano, Gina
See Balzano, Jeanne (Koppel)
See also SATA 7
Belmont, Eleanor Robson
1879-1979 Obituary 97-100
Belmont, Georges 1909- 29-32R
Belmont, Herman S. 1920- 41-44R
Belmonte, Thomas 1946- 93-96
Belo, Fernando 1933- 131
Beloff, Max 1913- CANR-18
Earlier sketch in CA 5-8R
Beloff, Michael 1942- 21-24R
Beloff, Nora 1919- 106
Belok, Michael V(ictor) 1923- 33-36R
Beloof, Robert 1923- 21-24R
Belote, James H(ine) 1922- 33-36R
Belote, Julianne 1929- 61-64
Belote, William Milton 1922- 49-52
Belotserkovsky, Vladimir Naumovich Bill
See Bill-Belotserkovsky, Vladimir Naumovich
Belous, Russell E. 1925- 25-28R
Belozersky, Andrei (Nicolaevich)
1905-1972 Obituary 37-40R
Belpre, Pura 1899-1982 73-76
Obituary 109
See also SATA 16, 30
Belser, Lee 1925(?)-1988 73-76
Obituary 127
Belser, Reimond Karel Maria de 1929- .... CLC 14
Belshaw, Cyril S(hirley) 1921- 9-12R
Belshaw, Michael (Horace) 1928- 21-24R
Belsky, Dick 1945- 122
Belsley, David A(lan) 1939- 29-32R
Belth, Joseph M(orton) 1929- 112
Belth, Nathan C. 1909(?)-1989 Obituary 128
Belting, Natalia Maree 1915- CANR-3
Earlier sketch in CA 1-4R
See also SATA 6
Belton, John Raynor 1931- 69-72
See also SATA 22
Beltrametti, Franco 1937- .... CAAS 13
Beltran, Alberto 1923- .... SATA 43
Beltran, Miriam 1914- 33-36R
Beltran, Pedro (Gerardo) 1897-1979 93-96
Obituary 85-88
Belushi, John 1949-1982 Obituary 106
Belveal, L(orenzo) Dee 1918- 21-24R
Belvedere, Lee
See Grayland, Valerie (Merle Spanner)
Bely, Andrey
See Bugayev, Boris Nikolayevich
See also TCLC 7
Bely, Jeanette L(obach) 1916- 33-36R
Belyi, Andrei
See Bugayev, Boris Nikolayevich
Belz, Carl 1937- CANR-26
Earlier sketches in CA 29-32R, CANR-11
Belz, Herman (Julius) 1937- 65-68
Bemelmans, Ludwig 1898-1962 73-76
See also CLR 6
See also DLB 22
See also MAICYA
See also SATA 15
Bemis, Samuel Flagg 1891-1973 .... 9-12R
Obituary 45-48
See also DLB 17
Bemis, Stephen Edward
1937-1985 Obituary 115
Bemister, Henry
See Barrett, Harry B(emister)
Bemmy, Karen (Amy) 1955- 123
Bemporad, Jules (Richard) 1937- 122
Ben, Ilke
See Harper, Carol Ely
Benagh, Jim 1937- CANR-9
Earlier sketch in CA 57-60
Ben-Ami, Shlomo 1943- 116
Ben-Ami, Yitshaq 1913- 130
Ben-Amos, Dan 1934- CANR-11
Earlier sketch in CA 69-72
Ben-Amotz, Dan 1923(?)-1989 Obituary 130
Benamou, Michel J(ean) 1929-1978 .... CANR-3
Earlier sketch in CA 5-8R
Benante, Joseph P(hilip) 1936- 33-36R
Benarde, Melvin A(lbert) 1923- 25-28R
Benardete, Jane Johnson 1930- 45-48
Benario, Herbert W. 1929- 25-28R
Benarria, Allan
See Goldenthal, Allan Benarria
Benary, Margot
See Benary-Isbert, Margot
Benary-Isbert, Margot 1889-1979 .... CANR-4
Obituary 89-92
Earlier sketch in CA 5-8R
See also CLC 12
See also CLR 12
See also MAICYA
See also SATA 2, 21
Benasutti, Marion 1908- 21-24R
See also SATA 6
Benatar, Stephen (Royce) 1937- 110
Benaud, Richard 1930- 131
Benaud, Richie
See Benaud, Richard
Benavente (y Martinez), Jacinto 1866-1954 131
Brief entry 106
See also HW
See also MTCW
See also TCLC 3
Ben-Avraham, Chofetz Chaim
See Pickering, Stephen
Benbow, Charles (Clarence) 1929- 122
Bence, Evelyn 110
Bence-Jones, Mark 1930- CANR-5
Earlier sketch in CA 13-16R
Bench, Johnny (Lee) 1947- 133
Brief entry 113
Benchley, Nathaniel (Goddard)
1915-1981 .... CANR-12
Obituary 105
Earlier sketches in CA 1-4R, CANR-2
See also SATA 3, 25, 28
Benchley, Peter (Bradford) 1940- CANR-35
Earlier sketches in CA 17-20R, CANR-12
See also AITN 2
See also CLC 4, 8
See also MTCW
See also SATA 3
Benchley, Robert (Charles)
1889-1945 Brief entry 105
See also DLB 11
See also TCLC 1
Benda, Harry J(indrich) 1919-1971 .... 9-12R
Obituary 134
Benda, Julien 1867-1956 Brief entry 120
Bendavid, Avrom 1942- 41-44R
Ben-David, Joseph 1920-1986 Obituary 118
Bender, Coleman C. 1921- 33-36R
Bender, David L(eo) 1936- 123
Bender, David R(ay) 1942- 102
Bender, Frederic L(awrence) 1943- 69-72
Bender, Henry E(dwin) Jr. 1937- 33-36R
Bender, James F(rederick) 1905- 17-20R
Bender, Jay
See Deindorfer, Robert Greene
Bender, John B(ryant) 1940- 65-68
Bender, Louis W. 1927- CANR-32
Earlier sketches in CA 33-36R, CANR-14
Bender, Lucy Ellen 1942- 25-28R
See also SATA 22
Bender, Marylin 1925- CANR-12
Earlier sketch in CA 21-24R
Bender, Norman J(ohn) 1927- 118
Bender, Richard 1930- 45-48
Bender, Robert M. 1936- 33-36R
Bender, Ross Thomas 1929- 61-64
Bender, Stephen (Joseph) 1942- 61-64
Bender, Thomas 1944- CANR-35
Earlier sketches in CA 73-76, CANR-12
Bender, Todd K. 1936- CANR-24
Earlier sketches in CA 21-24R, CANR-9
Benderly, Beryl Lieff 1943- CANR-30
Earlier sketch in CA 108
Bendick, Jeanne 1919- CANR-2
Earlier sketch in CA 5-8R
See also CLR 5
See also MAICYA
See also SAAS 4
See also SATA 2, 68
Bendick, Marc Jr. 1946- 118
Bendick, Robert L(ouis) 1917- 61-64
See also SATA 11
Bendiner, Elmer 1916- CANR-7
Earlier sketch in CA 57-60
Bendiner, Kenneth Paul 1947- 119
Bendiner, Robert 1909- 9-12R
Bendit, Gladys Williams 1885- CAP-1
Earlier sketch in CA 13-14
Bendit, Laurence John 1898-1974 .... CAP-2
Earlier sketch in CA 25-28
Bendix, Reinhard 1916-1991 .... CANR-4
Obituary 133
Earlier sketch in CA 1-4R
Bendixen, Alfred 1952- 128
Bendixson, Terence 1934- 93-96
Ben-Dov, Meir
See Bernet, Michael M.
Benecke, Gerhard Obituary 117
Benedek, Therese 1892-1977 .... 41-44R
Benedetti, Mario 1920- .... DLB 113
See also HW
Benedetti, Robert L(awrence) 1939- 29-32R
Benedetto, Antonio di
See di Benedetto, Antonio
Benedetto, Arnold J(oseph) 1916-1966 .... 5-8R
Benedict, Bertram 1892(?)-1978 Obituary 77-80
Benedict, Burton 1923- 109
Benedict, Dianne 1941- 110
Benedict, Dorothy Potter 1889-1979 .... CAP-1
Obituary 93-96
Earlier sketch in CA 13-14
See also SATA 11, 23
Benedict, Elizabeth 1954- 131
Brief entry 126
Benedict, Joseph
See Dollen, Charles Joseph
Benedict, Lois Trimble 1902-1967 .... CAP-2
Earlier sketch in CA 19-20
See also SATA 12
Benedict, Marion 1923- 109
Benedict, Michael Les 1945- 45-48
Benedict, Philip (Joseph) 1949- 130
Benedict, Rex 1920- 17-20R
See also SATA 8
Benedict, Robert P(hilip) 1924-1986 .... 41-44R
Obituary 119
Benedict, Stewart H(urd) 1924- 13-16R
See also SATA 26
Benedictus, David (Henry) 1938- CANR-24
Earlier sketch in CA 73-76
See also DLB 14
Benedikt, Michael 1935- CANR-7
Earlier sketch in CA 13-16R
See also CLC 4, 14
See also DLB 5
Benefield, June 1921- 45-48
Beneke, Walter 1923- .... HW
Benell, Florence B(elle) 1912- 33-36R
Benell, Julie 1906(?)-1982 Obituary 105
Benello, C. George 1926- 33-36R
Ben-Ephraim, Gavriel 1946- 116
Benes, Jan 1936- 29-32R
Benet, Edouard
See Edwards, William B(ennett)
Benet, James 1914- CANR-8
Earlier sketch in CA 61-64
Benet, Juan 1927- .... CLC 28
Benet, Laura 1884-1979 .... CANR-6
Obituary 85-88
Earlier sketch in CA 9-12R
See also SATA 3, 23
Benet, Mary Kathleen 1943- 57-60
Benet, Stephen Vincent
1898-1943 Brief entry 104
See also DLB 4, 48, 102
See also SSC 10
See also TCLC 7
See also YABC 1
Benet, Sula 1906-1982 89-92
Obituary 108
See also SATA 21, 33
Benet, William Rose 1886-1950 Brief entry 118
See also DLB 45
See also TCLC 28
Benetar, Judith 1941- 53-56
Benevolo, Leonardo 1923- 89-92
Ben-Ezer, Ehud 1936- CANR-24
Earlier sketches in CA 61-64, CANR-8
Benezra, Barbara (Beardsley) 1921- 13-16R
See also SATA 10
Benfield, Derek 1926- CANR-30
Earlier sketches in CA 21-24R, CANR-10
Benfield, G(raham) J(ohn) Barker
See Barker-Benfield, G(raham) J(ohn)
Benfield, Richard E. 1940- 77-80
Benford, Gregory (Albert) 1941- CANR-24
Earlier sketches in CA 69-72, CANR-12
See also CLC 52
See also DLBY 82
Benford, Harry (Bell) 1917- 89-92
Benford, Timothy B(artholomew)
1941- CANR-11
Earlier sketch in CA 69-72
Benge, Eugene J(ackson) 1896- CANR-9
Earlier sketch in CA 57-60
Bengelsdorf, Irving S. 1922- 57-60
Bengtson, Vern L. 1941- CANR-4
Earlier sketch in CA 49-52
Bengtsson, Arvid 1916- 33-36R

Ben-Gurion, David 1886-1973 ... 101
  Obituary ... 45-48
Benham, Leslie 1922- ... 9-12R
  See also SATA 48
Benham, Lois (Dakin) 1924- ... 9-12R
  See also SATA 48
Benham, Mary Lile 1914- ... 102
  See also SATA 55
Ben-Horav, Naphthali
  See Kravitz, Nathaniel
Ben-Horin, Meir 1918- ... CANR-14
  Earlier sketch in CA 29-32R
Benichou, Paul 1908- ... 57-60
Beniger, James R. 1946- ... 111
Benington, John (Elson) 1921-1969 ... 5-8R
  Obituary ... 134
Ben-Israel-Kidron, Hedva ... 33-36R
Benitez, Fernando 1911- ... HW
Benitez-Rojo, Antonio 1931- ... 137
Benjamin, Alice
  See Brooke, Avery (Rogers)
Benjamin, Anna Shaw 1925- ... 41-44R
Benjamin, Annette Francis 1928- ... 17-20R
Benjamin, Bry 1924- ... 17-20R
Benjamin, Burton Richard 1917-1988 ... 101
  Obituary ... 126
Benjamin, Claude (Max Edward Pohlman)
  1911- ... 9-12R
Benjamin, Curtis G. 1901-1983 ... 122
  Obituary ... 111
Benjamin, Edward Bernard 1897-1980 ... 69-72
  Obituary ... 133
Benjamin, Gerald 1945- ... 49-52
Benjamin, Harry 1885-1986 ... CAP-1
  Obituary ... 120
  Earlier sketch in CA 11-12
Benjamin, Herbert S(tanley) 1922- ... 5-8R
Benjamin, Joseph 1921- ... 57-60
Benjamin, Judy-Lynn
  See del Rey, Judy-Lynn
Benjamin, Lois
  See Gould, Lois
Benjamin, Nora
  See Kubie, Nora Gottheil Benjamin
Benjamin, Park 1809-1864 ... DLB 3, 59, 73
Benjamin, Philip (Robert) 1922-1966 ... 5-8R
  Obituary ... 25-28R
Benjamin, Robert (Irving) 1949- ... 109
Benjamin, Roger W. 1942- ... 37-40R
Benjamin, Ruth 1934- ... 125
Benjamin, Walter 1892-1940 ... TCLC 39
Benjamin, William E(arl) 1942- ... 25-28R
Benjaminson, Peter 1945- ... CANR-12
  Earlier sketch in CA 73-76
Ben Jelloun, Tahar 1944- ... 135
Benji, Thomas
  See Robinson, Frank M(alcolm)
ben-Jochannan, Yosef 1918- ... CANR-12
  Earlier sketch in CA 69-72
Benko, Stephen 1924- ... 9-12R
Benkovitz, Miriam J(eanette)
  1911-1986 ... CANR-4
  Obituary ... 119
  Earlier sketch in CA 9-12R
Benn, Anthony Neil Wedgwood 1925- ... 131
Benn, Gottfried 1886-1956 Brief entry ... 106
  See also DLB 56
  See also TCLC 3
Benn, John Andrews 1904-1984 Obituary ... 115
Benn, June
  See Barraclough, June (Mary)
Benn, June Wedgwood
  See Barraclough, June (Mary)
Benn, Matthew
  See Siegel, Benjamin
Benn, S. I.
  See Benn, Stanley I(ssac)
Benn, Stanley I(ssac) 1920-1986 ... 129
Benn, Tony
  See Benn, Anthony Neil Wedgwood
Bennani, B(en) M(ohammed) 1946- ... CANR-13
  Earlier sketch in CA 61-64
Benne, Kenneth D(ean) 1908- ... 33-36R
Benner, Judith Ann 1942- ... 122
Benner, Ralph Eugene (Jr.) 1932- ... 33-36R
Bennet, Glin 1927- ... 123
Bennet, Ruth
  See Straubing, Harold (Elk)
Bennett, A(bram) E(lting Hasbrouck)
  1898- ... 65-68
Bennett, Addison C(urtis) 1918- ... CANR-7
  Earlier sketch in CA 5-8R
Bennett, Adrian A(rthur) 1941- ... 53-56
Bennett, Alan 1934- ... CANR-35
  Earlier sketch in CA 103
  See also CLC 45
  See also MTCW
Bennett, Alice
  See Ziner, Florence
Bennett, Anna Elizabeth 1914- ... 17-20R
Bennett, Archibald F. 1896- ... CAP-1
  Earlier sketch in CA 13-16
Bennett, (Enoch) Arnold
  1867-1931 Brief entry ... 106
  See also CDBLB 1890-1914
  See also DLB 10, 34, 98
  See also TCLC 5, 20
Bennett, Betty T. ... 115
Bennett, Boyce McLean Jr. 1928- ... 115
Bennett, Bruce L(anyon) 1917- ... 25-28R
Bennett, Bruce (William) 1952- ... 110
Bennett, Charles E(dward) 1910- ... 9-12R
Bennett, Charles 1899- ... DLB 44
Bennett, Charles 1901- ... CAP-1
  Earlier sketch in CA 13-16
Bennett, Charles 1932- ... 25-28R
Bennett, Christine
  See Neubauer, William Arthur
Bennett, Colin J. 1955- ... 138
Bennett, Daniel
  See Gilmore, Joseph L(ee)
Bennett, Daphne Nicholson ... 41-44R
Bennett, David H. 1935- ... 25-28R
Bennett, Dennis J. 1917- ... CANR-20
  Earlier sketch in CA 49-52
Bennett, Dorothea
  See Young, Dorothea Bennett
Bennett, Dwight
  See Newton, D(wight) B(ennett)
Bennett, E(thel) M. Granger 1891- ... CAP-1
  Earlier sketch in CA 13-14
Bennett, E. N.
  See Bennett, Ernest N(athaniel)
Bennett, Edward M(oore) 1927- ... 33-36R
Bennett, Edward (Martin) 1924- ... 5-8R
Bennett, Elizabeth
  See Mitchell, Margaret (Munnerlyn)
Bennett, Elizabeth Deare
  See Merwin, Sam(uel Kimball) Jr.
Bennett, Ernest N(athaniel)
  1868-1947 Brief entry ... 119
Bennett, Frances Grant 1899- ... CAP-2
  Earlier sketch in CA 25-28
Bennett, Fredna W(illis) 1906- ... CAP-1
  Earlier sketch in CA 9-10
Bennett, G. V.
  See Bennett, Gareth Vaughan
Bennett, Gareth Vaughan
  1929-1987 Obituary ... 124
Bennett, Gary L. 1940- ... 138
Bennett, Geoffrey (Martin) 1909-1983 ... 13-16R
  Obituary ... 110
Bennett, George Harold 1930- ... 97-100
  See also Bennett, Hal
  See also BW
Bennett, George 1920-1969 ... 5-8R
  Obituary ... 134
Bennett, Gertrude Ryder ... 53-56
Bennett, Gordon A(nderson) 1940- ... 29-32R
Bennett, Gordon C. 1935- ... CANR-31
  Earlier sketches in CA 33-36R, CANR-14
Bennett, Gwendolyn B. 1902-1981 ... 125
  See also BW
  See also DLB 51
Bennett, Hal
  See Bennett, George Harold
  See also CLC 5
  See also DLB 33
Bennett, Hal 1930- ... CAAS 13
Bennett, Hall
  See Hall, Bennie Caroline (Humble)
Bennett, Harold (Zina) 1936- ... 41-44R
Bennett, Harve
  See Fischman, Harve
Bennett, Howard Franklin 1911-1974 ... 1-4R
Bennett, Isadora 1900-1980 Obituary ... 93-96
Bennett, J(ohn) G(odolphin)
  1897-1974 Obituary ... 111
Bennett, Jack Arthur Walter
  1911-1981 ... CANR-6
  Obituary ... 103
  Earlier sketch in CA 9-12R
Bennett, James D(avid) 1926- ... 61-64
Bennett, James Gordon Jr. 1841-1918 ... DLB 23
Bennett, James Gordon 1795-1872 ... DLB 43
Bennett, James R(ichard) 1932- ... 33-36R
Bennett, James Thomas 1942- ... CANR-23
  Earlier sketch in CA 106
Bennett, Jay 1912- ... CANR-11
  Earlier sketch in CA 69-72
  See also CLC 35
  See also SAAS 4
  See also SATA 27, 41
Bennett, Jean Francis
  See Dorcy, Sister Mary Jean
Bennett, Jeremy
  See Bennett, John Jerome Nelson
Bennett, Jill (Crawford) 1934- ... SATA 41
Bennett, Jill 1947- ... 106
Bennett, Joan S. 1941- ... 132
Bennett, John (Frederic) 1920- ... 29-32R
Bennett, John Jerome Nelson 1939- ... 21-24R
Bennett, John M(ichael) 1942- ... CANR-18
  Earlier sketches in CA 49-52, CANR-2
Bennett, John W. 1918- ... 69-72
Bennett, John William 1915- ... CANR-4
  Earlier sketch in CA 1-4R
Bennett, John 1865-1956 ... DLB 42
  See also YABC 1
Bennett, Jon 1955- ... 127
Bennett, Jonathan (Francis) 1930- ... CANR-1
  Earlier sketch in CA 45-48
Bennett, Joseph D. 1922-1972 ... 1-4R
  Obituary ... 33-36R
Bennett, Josephine Waters 1899-1975 ... 1-4R
  Obituary ... 103
Bennett, Judith Obituary ... 85-88
Bennett, Kathleen 1946- ... 138
Bennett, Kay Curley 1922- ... 17-20R
Bennett, Kenneth A(lan) 1935- ... 131
Bennett, Lerone Jr. 1928- ... CANR-25
  Earlier sketches in CA 45-48, CANR-2
  See also BW
Bennett, Linda L(eveque) 1946- ... 115
Bennett, Louise (Simone) 1919- ... BLC 1
  See also CLC 28
  See also DLB 117
Bennett, M. J.
  See Bennett, Marcia J(oanne)
Bennett, Marcia J(oanne) 1945- ... CANR-35
  Earlier sketch in CA 114
Bennett, Margaret E(laine) 1893- ... 5-8R
Bennett, Margot 1912-1980 Obituary ... 105
Bennett, Marion T(insley) 1914- ... 9-12R
Bennett, Melba Berry 1901-1968 ... CAP-2
  Earlier sketch in CA 19-20
Bennett, Meridan 1927- ... 25-28R
Bennett, Michael 1943-1987 ... 101
  Obituary ... 122
Bennett, Mildred R. 1909-1989 ... CAP-2
  Obituary ... 130
  Earlier sketch in CA 25-28
Bennett, Neville 1937- ... CANR-19
  Earlier sketch in CA 102
Bennett, Noel 1939- ... 45-48
Bennett, Norman Robert 1932- ... CANR-39
  Earlier sketches in CA 9-12R, CANR-3, 18
Bennett, Patrick (H.) 1931- ... 122
Bennett, Paul Lewis 1921- ... CANR-4
  Earlier sketch in CA 1-4R
Bennett, Penelope Agnes 1938- ... 13-16R
Bennett, Rachel
  See Hill, Margaret (Ohler)
Bennett, Rainey 1907- ... SATA 15
Bennett, Richard 1899- ... SATA 21
Bennett, Rita (Marie) 1934- ... CANR-20
  Earlier sketch in CA 69-72
Bennett, Robert A(ndrew) 1927- ... CANR-5
  Earlier sketch in CA 13-16R
Bennett, Robert D(onald) 1947- ... 118
Bennett, Robert L. 1931- ... 41-44R
Bennett, Robert Russell
  1894-1981 Obituary ... 105
Bennett, Russell H(oradley) 1896- ... SATA 25
Bennett, Scott (Boyce) 1939- ... 33-36R
Bennett, Shelley M. 1947- ... 131
Bennett, Thomas L(eroy) 1942- ... 85-88
Bennett, Victor 1919- ... CANR-7
  Earlier sketch in CA 5-8R
Bennett, W(illiam) R(obert) 1921- ... 13-16R
Bennett, William (Ira) 1941- ... 107
Bennett, William L. 1924- ... 17-20R
Bennett-Coverley, Louise 1919- ... 97-100
Bennett-England, Rodney Charles 1936- ... 61-64
Bennetts, Pamela 1922- ... 37-40R
Bennie, William A(ndrew) 1921- ... 69-72
Bennigsen, Alexandre (A.)
  1913-1988(?) Obituary ... 125
Benning, (Barbara) Lee Edwards 1934- ... 53-56
Bennion, Barbara Elisabeth 1930- ... 110
Bennion, Sherilyn Cox 1935- ... 137
Bennis, Warren G. 1925- ... CANR-5
  Earlier sketch in CA 53-56
Benoff, Mac 1915(?)-1972 Obituary ... 37-40R
Benoist-Mechin, Jacques 1901-1983 ... 105
  Obituary ... 109
Benoit, Emile 1910-1978 ... CANR-3
  Obituary ... 77-80
  Earlier sketch in CA 5-8R
Benoit, Jacques 1941- ... DLB 60
Benoit, Leroy James 1913- ... 33-36R
Benoit, Pierre Maurice 1906-1987 ... 41-44R
  Obituary ... 122
Benoit, Pierre 1886-1962 Obituary ... 93-96
Benoit, Richard 1899(?)-1969 Obituary ... 104
Benoliel, Jeanne Quint 1919- ... CANR-27
  Earlier sketch in CA 49-52
Bense, Walter F(rederick) 1932- ... CANR-1
  Earlier sketch in CA 45-48
Bensen, Alice R. 1911- ... 69-72
Bensen, Donald R. 1927- ... CANR-20
  Earlier sketches in CA 9-12R, CANR-5
Bensko, John 1949- ... 105
Bensley, Connie 1929- ... 135
Bensman, Joseph 1922- ... CANR-10
  Earlier sketch in CA 21-24R
Bensol, Oscar
  See Gilbert, Willie
Benson, A. C. 1862-1925 ... DLB 98
Benson, A. George 1924- ... 69-72
Benson, B. A.
  See Beyea, Basil
Benson, Ben(jamin) 1915-1959 Brief entry ... 112
Benson, C(arl) David 1942- ... 123
Benson, C. Randolph 1923- ... 29-32R
Benson, Carmen 1921- ... 57-60
Benson, Charles S(cott) 1922- ... CANR-8
  Earlier sketch in CA 17-20R
Benson, Constantine Walter
  1909-1982 Obituary ... 108
Benson, Daniel
  See Cooper, Colin Symons
Benson, Dennis C(arroll) 1936- ... 37-40R
Benson, E(dward) F(rederic)
  1867-1940 Brief entry ... 114
  See also TCLC 27
Benson, Elizabeth P(olk) 1924- ... CANR-35
  Earlier sketch in CA 93-96
  See also SATA 65
Benson, Eugene 1928- ... 89-92
Benson, Frederick R. 1934- ... 33-36R
Benson, Frederick William 1948- ... CANR-19
  Earlier sketch in CA 101
Benson, Gigi (Dian Daniels) 1941- ... 108
Benson, Ginny
  See Benson, Virginia
Benson, Harry 1929- ... 108
Benson, Herbert 1935- ... 85-88
Benson, J(ack) L(eonard) 1920- ... 105
Benson, Jackson J. 1930- ... 25-28R
  See also CLC 34
  See also DLB 111
Benson, Jeffrey 1937- ... 120
Benson, John 1945- ... 131
Benson, Kathleen 1947- ... 85-88
  See also SATA 62
Benson, Larry D(ean) 1929- ... 37-40R
Benson, Lyman (David) 1909- ... CANR-32
  Earlier sketch in CA 49-52
Benson, Margaret H. Benson 1899- ... 5-8R
Benson, Mary 1919- ... CANR-17
  Earlier sketches in CA 49-52, CANR-1
Benson, Maxine (Frances) 1939- ... 65-68
Benson, Mildred (Augustine Wirt) 1905- ... 134
  See also MAICYA
  See also SATA 65
Benson, Mildred Wirt
  See Benson, Mildred (Augustine Wirt)
Benson, Peter 1956- ... 137
Benson, Rachel
  See Jowitt, Deborah
Benson, Raymond 1955- ... 118
Benson, Richard
  See Cooper, Saul
Benson, Robert G(reen) 1930- ... 29-32R
Benson, Robert S(later) 1942- ... 33-36R
Benson, Rolf Eric 1951- ... 102
Benson, Ruth Crego 1937- ... 41-44R
Benson, Sally 1900-1972 ... CAP-1
  Obituary ... 37-40R
  Earlier sketch in CA 19-20
  See also CLC 17
  See also SATA 1, 27, 35
Benson, Stella 1892-1933 Brief entry ... 117
  See also DLB 36
  See also TCLC 17
Benson, Stephana Vere 1909- ... 13-16R
Benson, Ted
  See Benson, Frederick William
Benson, Thomas Godfrey 1899- ... CAP-1
  Earlier sketch in CA 11-12
Benson, Thomas W(alter) 1937- ... CANR-19
  Earlier sketch in CA 29-32R
Benson, Virginia 1923- ... 57-60
Benson, Warren S(ten) 1929- ... 114
Benson, William Howard 1902- ... 1-4R
Benstead, Steven 1951- ... 113
Bensted-Smith, Richard (Brian) 1929- ... 13-16R
Benstock, Bernard 1930- ... CANR-29
  Earlier sketches in CA 17-20R, CANR-7
Benstock, Shari 1944- ... CANR-29
  Earlier sketch in CA 97-100
Bent, Alan Edward 1939- ... CANR-4
  Earlier sketch in CA 49-52
Bent, Charles N. 1935- ... 21-24R
Bent, Rudyard K(ipling) 1901- ... CANR-18
  Earlier sketch in CA 1-4R
Benteen, John
  See Haas, Ben(jamin) L(eopold)
Bentel, Pearl B(ucklen) 1901- ... CAP-2
  Earlier sketch in CA 21-22
Benthall, Jonathan 1941- ... 41-44R
Bentham, Frederick 1911- ... 105
Bentham, Jay
  See Bensman, Joseph
Bentham, Jeremy 1748-1832 ... DLB 107
Benthic, Arch E.
  See Stewart, Harris B(ates) Jr.
Benthul, Herman F(orrest) 1911- ... 33-36R
Bentley, Beth (Rita) 1928- ... 101
Bentley, Colin 1936- ... 118
Bentley, E(dmund) C(lerihew)
  1875-1956 Brief entry ... 108
  See also DLB 70
  See also TCLC 12
Bentley, Eric (Russell) 1916- ... CANR-6
  Earlier sketch in CA 5-8R
  See also CLC 24
Bentley, G(erald) E(ades) Jr. 1930- ... CANR-4
  Earlier sketch in CA 1-4R
Bentley, Gerald Eades 1901- ... 41-44R
Bentley, Howard Beebe 1925- ... 9-12R
Bentley, Janice Babb 1933- ... 13-16R
Bentley, Jerry H(arrell) 1949- ... 127
Bentley, Joanne 1928- ... 130
Bentley, Judith (McBride) 1945- ... CANR-23
  Earlier sketch in CA 107
  See also SATA 40
Bentley, Margaret 1926- ... CANR-25
  Earlier sketch in CA 108
Bentley, Nicolas Clerihew 1907-1978 ... CANR-11
  Obituary ... 81-84
  Earlier sketch in CA 65-68
  See also SATA 24
Bentley, Phyllis Eleanor 1894-1977 ... CANR-3
  Earlier sketch in CA 1-4R
  See also SATA 6, 25
Bentley, Richard
  See Browning, Alice C(rolley)
Bentley, Roy 1947- ... 127
  See also SATA 46
Bentley, Sarah 1946- ... 29-32R
Bentley, Toni 1958- ... 123
Bentley, Ursula 1945- ... 125
Bentley, Virginia W(illiams) 1908- ... 57-60
Bentley-Taylor, David 1915- ... CANR-14
  Earlier sketch in CA 77-80
Benton, Dorothy Gilchrist 1919- ... 57-60
Benton, F(red) Warren 1948- ... 119
Benton, Helen Hemingway
  1902(?)-1974 Obituary ... 104
Benton, John Frederic 1931-1988 ... 69-72
  Obituary ... 124
Benton, John W. 1933- ... CANR-12
  Earlier sketch in CA 29-32R
Benton, Joseph Nelson Jr.
  1924-1988 Obituary ... 124
Benton, Josephine Moffett 1905- ... 5-8R
Benton, Karla
  See Rowland, D(onald) S(ydney)
Benton, Kenneth (Carter) 1909- ... CANR-1
  Earlier sketch in CA 49-52
Benton, Lewis R(obert) 1920- ... 17-20R
Benton, (Joseph) Nelson (Jr.) 1924- ... 112
  Brief entry ... 110
Benton, Patricia 1907- ... 5-8R

Benton, Peggie 1906- CANR-31
Earlier sketch in CA 49-52
Benton, Richard G(lasscock) 1938- 81-84
Benton, Robert
See Buse, Renee
Benton, Robert (Douglass) 1932- CANR-2
Earlier sketch in CA 1-4R
See also DLB 44
Benton, Thomas Hart 1889-1975 93-96
Obituary 53-56
Benton, Wilbourn Eugene 1917- 1-4R
Benton, Will
See Paine, Lauran (Bosworth)
Benton, William 1900-1973 .... CAP-1
Obituary 41-44R
Earlier sketch in CA 13-16
Bentov, Itzhak 1923(?)-1979 Obituary 85-88
Bentsen, Cheryl 1950- 138
Bentwich, Norman 1883-1971 Obituary 111
Bentz, Thomas 1943- 112
Bentz, William F(rederick) 1940- 53-56
ben Uzair, Salem
See Horne, Richard Henry
Benveniste, Asa 1925-1990 .... CANR-33
Obituary 131
Earlier sketch in CA 69-72
Benveniste, Emile 1902-1976 Obituary 115
Benveniste, Guy 1927- CANR-8
Earlier sketch in CA 61-64
Ben-Veniste, Richard 1943- Brief entry 114
Benvenisti, Meron (Shmuel) 1934- CANR-35
Earlier sketches in CA 65-68, CANR-12
Benward, Bruce (Charles) 1921- CANR-9
Earlier sketch in CA 9-12R
Beny, Roloff
See Beny, Wilfred Roy
Beny, Wilfred Roy 1924-1984 .... CANR-32
Obituary 112
Earlier sketch in CA 21-24R
Benyo, Richard (Stephen) 1946- CANR-29
Earlier sketches in CA 77-80, CANR-13
Ben-Yosef, Avraham C(haim)
See Matsuba, Moshe
Benz, Ernst (Wilhelm) 1907-1978 .... CANR-13
Earlier sketch in CA 13-16R
Benz, Frank L(eonard) 1930- 41-44R
Benzie, William 1930- 37-40R
Benziger, Barbara Field 1918- Brief entry 115
Benziger, James 1914- 13-16R
Ben-Zion
See Weinman, Benzion
Benzoni, Juliette (Andree Marguerite)
1920- CANR-18
Earlier sketch in CA 101
Beorse, Bryn 1896- 45-48
Bequaert, Lucia H(umes) 65-68
Beranek, Leo L(eroy) 1914- 5-8R
Beranek, William 1922- 5-8R
Berard, J(ules) Aram 1933- 17-20R
Berardo, Felix M(ario) 1934- CANR-24
Earlier sketches in CA 57-60, CANR-8
Berberova, Nina (Nikolaevna) 1901- CANR-14
Earlier sketch in CA 33-36R
Berbrich, Joan D. 1925- CANR-12
Earlier sketch in CA 29-32R
Berbusse, Edward J(oseph) 1912- 21-24R
Berch, Bettina 1950- 129
Berch, William O.
See Coyne, Joseph E.
Berchen, Ursula 1919- 65-68
Berchen, William 1920- 65-68
Berck, Martin G(ans) 1928- 65-68
Berckman, Evelyn Domenica 1900- CANR-1
Earlier sketch in CA 1-4R
Bercovici, Rion 1903(?)-1976 Obituary 69-72
Bercovitch, Reuben 1923- 104
Bercovitch, Sacvan 1933- 41-44R
Berczeller, Richard 1902- 9-12R
Berdes, George R. 1931- 29-32R
Berdie, Douglas R(alph) 1946- 53-56
Berdie, Ralph F(reimuth) 1916-1974 .... CANR-11
Earlier sketch in CA 17-20R
Berding, Andrew H(enry) 1902- 5-8R
Berdyaev, Nicolas
See Berdyaev, Nikolai (Aleksandrovich)
Berdyaev, Nikolai (Aleksandrovich)
1874-1948 Brief entry 120
Bere, Rennie Montague 1907- 65-68
Bereday, George Z(ygmunt) F(ijalkowski)
1920-1983 .... CANR-4
Obituary 111
Earlier sketch in CA 1-4R
Bereiter, Carl 1930- Brief entry 113
Berelson, Bernard R(euben)
1912-1979 .... CANR-3
Obituary 89-92
Earlier sketch in CA 5-8R
Berelson, David 1943- 25-28R
Berelson, Howard 1940- .... SATA 5
Berenbaum, Linda Bayer
See Bayer, Linda
Berends, Polly Berrien 1939- 108
See also SATA 38, 50
Berendsohn, Walter A(rthur)
1884-1984(?) CANR-34
Earlier sketch in CA 33-36R
Berendt, Joachim Ernst 1922- CANR-30
Earlier sketches in CA 69-72, CANR-12
Berendzen, Richard (Earl) 1938- 85-88
Berenson, Conrad 1930- 9-12R
Berenson, F(rances) M(aria) 1929- 125
Berenstain, Jan(ice) 1923- CANR-36
Earlier sketches in CA 25-28R, CANR-14
See also CLR 19
See also MAICYA
See also SATA 12, 64
Berenstain, Michael 1951- CANR-36
Earlier sketches in CA 97-100, CANR-14
See also SATA 45
Berenstain, Stan(ley) 1923- CANR-36
Earlier sketches in CA 25-28R, CANR-14
See also CLR 19
See also MAICYA
See also SATA 12, 64
Bereny, Gail Rubin 1942- 85-88
Berenzy, Alix 1957- 133
See also SATA 65
Beresford, Anne 1929- 97-100
See also DLB 40
Beresford, Elisabeth 102
See also SATA 25
Beresford, J(ohn) D(avys)
1873-1947 Brief entry 112
Beresford, Maurice Warwick 1920- 13-16R
Beresford-Howe, Constance 1922- 53-56
See also AITN 2
See also DLB 88
Beresiner, Yasha 1940- CANR-12
Earlier sketch in CA 69-72
Beretta, Lia 1934- 17-20R
Berg, A(ndrew) Scott 1949(?)- 81-84
See also BEST 89:3
Berg, Adriane G(ilda) 1948- 119
Berg, Alan (David) 1932- CANR-22
Earlier sketch in CA 45-48
Berg, Barbara J. 124
Berg, Bjoern 1923- .... SATA 47
Berg, Darrel E. 1920- 17-20R
Berg, Dave
See Berg, David
Berg, David 1920- CANR-10
Earlier sketch in CA 21-24R
See also SATA 27
Berg, Fred Anderson 1948- 37-40R
Berg, Frederick S(ven) 1928- 53-56
Berg, Friedrich Kantor
See Kantor-Berg, Friedrich
Berg, Goesta 1903- 69-72
Berg, Irwin August 1913- 13-16R
Berg, Ivar E(lis) Jr. 1929- CANR-13
Earlier sketch in CA 21-24R
Berg, Jean Horton 1913- CANR-4
Earlier sketch in CA 53-56
See also SATA 6
Berg, Joan
See Victor, Joan Berg
Berg, Larry L(ee) 1939- 41-44R
Berg, Lasse 1943- CANR-12
Earlier sketch in CA 73-76
Berg, Leila Rita 1917- 101
Berg, Louis 1901-1972 Obituary 37-40R
Berg, Orley M. 1918- 17-20R
Berg, Paul Conrad 1921- 33-36R
Berg, Richard F(rederick) 1936- 115
Berg, Rick 1951- 93-96
Berg, Ron 1952- .... SATA 48
Berg, Stephen 1934- CANR-8
Earlier sketch in CA 13-16R
See also DLB 5
Berg, Thomas L(eRoy) 1930- 69-72
Berg, Viola Jacobson 1918- CANR-5
Earlier sketch in CA 53-56
Berg, William 1938- 97-100
Bergamini, David H(owland)
1928-1983 .... CANR-15
Obituary 110
Earlier sketch in CA 1-4R
Bergamini, John D. 1925(?)-1982 Obituary 108
Bergaust, Erik 1925-1978 .... CANR-32
Obituary 77-80
Earlier sketch in CA 73-76
See also SATA 20
Berge, Carol 1928- CANR-7
Earlier sketch in CA 13-16R
See also CAAS 10
Bergel, Egon Ernst 1894-1969 .... CAP-2
Earlier sketch in CA 21-22
Bergen, Polly 1930- 57-60
Bergendoff, Conrad J(ohn) I(mmanuel)
1895- CANR-13
Earlier sketch in CA 33-36R
Bergengruen, Werner
1892-1964(?) Obituary 114
See also DLB 56
Berger, Andrew J(ohn) 1915- CANR-14
Earlier sketch in CA 41-44R
Berger, Arthur Asa 1933- CANR-26
Earlier sketches in CA 25-28R, CANR-10
Berger, Bennett Maurice 1926- CANR-4
Earlier sketch in CA 1-4R
Berger, Brigitte (M. L.) 1928- 131
Berger, Bruce 1938- CANR-30
Earlier sketch in CA 112
Berger, Carl 1925- 9-12R
Berger, Colonel
See Malraux, (Georges-)Andre
Berger, David G. 1941- 129
Berger, David 1943- 115
Berger, Elmer 1908- 61-64
Berger, Evelyn Miller 1896- CANR-14
Earlier sketch in CA 37-40R
Berger, Fredericka 1932- 131
Berger, Gilda 1935- 134
Brief entry 118
See also SATA 42
Berger, H. Jean 1924- 13-16R
Berger, Harry Jr. 1924- 110
Berger, Hilbert J. 1920- 57-60
Berger, Ivan (Bennett) 1939- CANR-17
Earlier sketch in CA 97-100
Berger, John J(oseph) 1945- 69-72
Berger, John (Peter) 1926- 81-84
See also CLC 2, 19
See also DLB 14
Berger, Josef 1903-1971 .... 5-8R
Obituary 33-36R
See also SATA 36
Berger, Joseph 1924- 41-44R
Berger, Karen 1944- 122
Berger, Klaus 1901- CAP-1
Earlier sketch in CA 13-14
Berger, Marilyn 1935- 101
Berger, Marjorie Sue 1916- 13-16R
Berger, Mark L(ewis) 1942- Brief entry 109
Berger, Melvin H. 1927- CANR-4
Earlier sketch in CA 5-8R
See also CLC 12
See also SAAS 2
See also SATA 5
Berger, Meyer 1898-1959(?) Brief entry 120
See also DLB 29
Berger, Michael L(ouis) 1943- CANR-32
Earlier sketches in CA 77-80, CANR-14
Berger, Morroe 1917-1981 .... CANR-4
Obituary 103
Earlier sketch in CA 1-4R
Berger, Nan 1914- 113
Berger, Peter Ludwig 1929- CANR-1
Earlier sketch in CA 1-4R
Berger, Phil 1942- CANR-12
Earlier sketch in CA 61-64
See also SATA 62
Berger, Rainer 1930- 37-40R
Berger, Raoul 1901- 93-96
Berger, Raymond M(ark) 1950- 109
Berger, Robert W(illiam) 1936- 49-52
Berger, Stuart 1953- 112
Berger, Suzanne E(lizabeth) 1944- 105
Berger, Terry 1933- 37-40R
See also SATA 8
Berger, Thomas (Louis) 1924- CANR-28
Earlier sketches in CA 1-4R, CANR-5
See also CLC 3, 5, 8, 11, 18, 38
See also DLB 2
See also DLBY 80
See also MTCW
Berger, Yves 1934- 85-88
Bergeret, Ida Treat
1889(?)-1978 Obituary 77-80
Bergeron, David M(oore) 1938- CANR-2
Earlier sketch in CA 45-48
Bergeron, Paul H. 1938- 101
Bergeron, Victor (Jules Jr.) 1902-1984 89-92
Obituary 114
Berges, Emily Trafford 1937- 132
Berges, Marshall (William)
1921(?)-1988 Obituary 126
Bergeson, John B(rian) 1935- 69-72
Bergevin, Paul (Emile) 1906- CANR-2
Earlier sketch in CA 5-8R
Bergey, Alyce (Mae) 1934- CANR-7
Earlier sketch in CA 5-8R
See also SATA 45
Berggren, W(illiam) A(lfred) 1931- 123
Berghahn, Volker R(olf) 1938- CANR-20
Earlier sketch in CA 103
Bergier, Jacques 1912-1978 .... CANR-37
Obituary 81-84
Earlier sketch in CA 85-88
Bergin, Allen E. 1934- 45-48
Bergin, Kenneth Glenny
1911-1981 Obituary 103
Bergin, Thomas Goddard 1904-1987 .... CANR-3
Obituary 124
Earlier sketch in CA 9-12R
Bergland, Martha 1945- 130
Bergman, Arlene Eisen 1942- 61-64
Bergman, Bernard A(aron) 1894-1980 102
Obituary 97-100
Bergman, Bo 1869-1967 Obituary 25-28R
Bergman, David (L.) 1950- CANR-22
Earlier sketch in CA 106
Bergman, Eugene 1930- 135
Bergman, Floyd L(awrence) 1927- CANR-17
Earlier sketches in CA 49-52, CANR-2
Bergman, Hannah E(stermann)
1925-1981 69-72
Obituary 135
Bergman, Hjalmar (Frederik Elgerus)
1883-1931 Brief entry 119
Bergman, (Shmuel) Hugo
1883-1975 Obituary 57-60
Bergman, (Ernst) Ingmar 1918- CANR-33
Earlier sketch in CA 81-84
See also CLC 16, 72
Bergman, Ingrid 1915-1982 132
Obituary 107
Bergman, Jay Asa 1948- 110
Bergman, Jules (Verne) 1929-1987 108
Obituary 121
Bergman, Lewis 1918-1988 Obituary 127
Bergman, Tamar 1939- 138
Bergmann, Ernst W.
1896(?)-1977 Obituary 69-72
Bergmann, Fred L(ouis) 1916- 61-64
Bergmann, Frithjof H. 1930- 101
Bergmann, Peter G(abriel) 1915- 21-24R
Bergonzi, Bernard 1929- CANR-8
Earlier sketch in CA 17-20R
Bergonzo, Jean Louis 1939- CAP-2
Earlier sketch in CA 25-28
Bergquist, Laura (Cecelia)
1918-1982 Obituary 108
Bergreen, Laurence R. 1950- 104
See also BEST 90:4
Bergson, Abram 1914- 13-16R
Bergson, Henri 1859-1941 .... TCLC 32
Bergson, Leo
See Stebel, S(idney) L(eo)
Bergstein, Eleanor 1938- CANR-5
Earlier sketch in CA 53-56
See also CLC 4
Bergsten, C. Fred 1941- 111
Bergsten, Staffan 1932- CANR-6
Earlier sketch in CA 57-60
Bergstrom, Louise 1914- 29-32R
Beringause, Arthur F. 1919- 33-36R
Beringer, Richard E. 1933- 81-84
Berk, Fred 1911(?)-1980 Obituary 97-100
Berke, Joel S(ommers) 1936-1981 110
Obituary 105
Berke, Joseph H(erman) 1939- 57-60
Berke, Roberta 1943- 106
Berkebile, Don(ald) H(erbert) 1926- CANR-8
Earlier sketch in CA 61-64
Berkebile, Fred D(onovan) 1900-1978 .... 5-8R
Obituary 103
See also SATA 26
Berkeley, Anthony
See Cox, A(nthony) B(erkeley)
See also DLB 77
Berkeley, David S(helley) 1917- 41-44R
Berkeley, Edmund 1912- 133
Brief entry 112
Berkeley, Ellen Perry 1931- 110
Berkeley, George 1685-1753 .... DLB 101
Berkemeyer, William C. 1908- CAP-2
Earlier sketch in CA 25-28
Berkey, Barry Robert 1935- 69-72
See also SATA 24
Berkey, Helen 1898- CAP-2
Earlier sketch in CA 23-24
Berkhofer, Robert Frederick Jr. 1931- 13-16R
Berkin, Carol Ruth 1942- CANR-11
Earlier sketch in CA 69-72
Berkley, George E(ugene) 1928- 127
Brief entry 113
Berkman, Edward O(scar) 1914- CANR-9
Earlier sketch in CA 61-64
Berkman, Harold W(illiam) 1926- CANR-21
Earlier sketches in CA 53-56, CANR-5
Berkman, Richard Lyle 1946- CANR-1
Earlier sketch in CA 45-48
Berkman, Sue 1936- 45-48
Berkman, Ted
See Berkman, Edward O(scar)
Berkoff, Steven 1937- 104
See also CLC 56
Berkove, Lawrence Ivan 1930- CANR-36
Earlier sketch in CA 106
Berkovits, Eliezer 1908- CANR-37
Earlier sketches in CA 1-4R, CANR-2
Berkovitz, Irving H(erbert) 1924- 57-60
Berkovitz, Jay R. 1951- 134
Berkow, Ira 1940- 97-100
Berkowitz, Bernard 1909- .... AITN 1
Berkowitz, David Sandler 1913- 33-36R
Berkowitz, Freda Pastor 1910- CAP-1
Earlier sketch in CA 9-10
See also SATA 12
Berkowitz, Gerald M(artin) 1942- 110
Berkowitz, Leonard 1926- 125
Berkowitz, Luci 1938- 33-36R
Berkowitz, Marvin 1938- CANR-30
Earlier sketch in CA 29-32R
Berkowitz, Monroe 1919- 130
Berkowitz, Morris Ira 1931- 53-56
Berkowitz, Pearl H(enriette) 1921- 21-24R
Berkowitz, Sol 1922- CANR-1
Earlier sketch in CA 45-48
Berkowitz, William R(obby) 1939- 112
Berkson, Bill 1939- CANR-24
Earlier sketches in CA 21-24R, CANR-9
Berkson, William Koller 1944- 102
Berlak, Harold 1932- 33-36R
Berland, Alwyn 1920- 125
Berland, Theodore 1929- CANR-18
Earlier sketches in CA 5-8R, CANR-2
Berlanstein, Lenard R(ussell) 1947- 69-72
Berlant, Anthony 1941- Brief entry 112
Berlant, Tony
See Berlant, Anthony
Berle, Adolf A(ugustus) Jr. 1895-1971 .... CAP-2
Obituary 29-32R
Earlier sketch in CA 23-24
Berle, Beatrice Bishop 1902- 114
Berle, Milton 1908- 77-80
See also AITN 1
Berleant, Arnold 1932- 29-32R
Berlin, Ellin (Mackay) 1904(?)-1988 65-68
Obituary 126
Berlin, Ira 1941- 101
Berlin, Irving N. 1917- CANR-13
Earlier sketch in CA 21-24R
Berlin, Irving 1888-1989 108
Obituary 129
Berlin, Isaiah 1909- 85-88
Berlin, Michael J(oseph) 1938- 69-72
Berlin, Normand 1931- 57-60
Berlin, Richard Emmett
1894(?)-1986 Obituary 118
Berlin, Sven 1911- CANR-15
Earlier sketch in CA 85-88
Berlind, Bruce 1926- 33-36R
Berliner, Don 1930- CANR-21
Earlier sketch in CA 105
See also SATA 33
Berliner, Franz 1930- CANR-29
Earlier sketches in CA 29-32R, CANR-12
See also SATA 13
Berliner, Herman A(lbert) 1944- 77-80
Berliner, Joseph S(cholom) 1921- 69-72

Berlitz, Charles (L. Frambach) 1914- ... CANR-9
Earlier sketch in CA 5-8R
See also SATA 32
Berl-Lee, Maria
See Lee, Maria Berl
Berloni, William 1956- ... 77-80
Berlye, Milton K. 1915- ... CANR-31
Earlier sketch in CA 49-52
Berlyne, D(aniel) E(llis) 1924- ... 13-16R
Berman, Arthur I(rwin) 1925- ... 97-100
Berman, Bennett H(erbert) 1927- ... 105
Berman, Bruce D(avid) 1944- ... 41-44R
Berman, Claire 1936- ... CANR-10
Earlier sketch in CA 25-28R
Berman, Connie 1949- ... 93-96
Berman, Daniel M(arvin) 1928-1967 ... CANR-1
Earlier sketch in CA 1-4R
Berman, David 1942- ... 135
Berman, Ed 1941- ... 106
Berman, Edgar F(rank) 1915(?)-1987 ... 97-100
Obituary ... 124
Berman, Eleanor 1934- ... 85-88
Berman, Emile Zola 1902-1981 Obituary ... 104
Berman, Harold Joseph 1918- ... CANR-15
Earlier sketch in CA 89-92
Berman, Jeffrey 1945- ... 134
Berman, Larry 1951- ... 93-96
Berman, Linda 1948- ... 113
See also SATA 38
Berman, Louise M(arguerite) 1928- ... 21-24R
Berman, Marshall 1940- ... 29-32R
Berman, Milton 1924- ... 1-4R
Berman, Mitch 1956- ... 136
Berman, Morton M(ayer)
1899-1986 Obituary ... 118
Berman, Morton 1924- ... CANR-2
Earlier sketch in CA 5-8R
Berman, Paul (Lawrence) 1949- ... 110
See also SATA 66
Berman, Ronald 1930- ... 13-16R
Berman, Sanford 1933- ... 37-40R
Berman, Simeon M(oses) 1935- ... 49-52
Berman, Susan 1945- ... CANR-17
Earlier sketch in CA 65-68
Berman, William C(arl) 1932- ... 41-44R
Bermange, Barry 1933- ... 57-60
Bermant, Chaim (Icyk) 1929- ... CANR-31
Earlier sketches in CA 57-60, CANR-6
See also CLC 40
Bermant, Gordon 1936- ... 120
Bermel, Albert (Cyril) 1927- ... CANR-11
Earlier sketch in CA 69-72
Bermeo, Nancy 1951- ... 131
Bermingham, Ann 1948- ... 128
Bermont, Hubert Ingram 1924- ... CANR-5
Earlier sketch in CA 9-12R
Bermosk, Loretta Sue 1918- ... CANR-3
Earlier sketch in CA 9-12R
Bern, Maria Rasputin Soloviev
1900(?)-1977 Obituary ... 73-76
Berna, Paul 1910- ... 73-76
See also CLR 19
See also SATA 15
Bernabei, Alfio 1941- ... CANR-14
Earlier sketch in CA 77-80
Bernadette
See Watts, (Anna) Bernadette
Bernal, J(ohn) D(esmond) 1901-1971 ... 97-100
Obituary ... 33-36R
Bernal, Judith F. 1939- ... 57-60
Bernal, Martin Gardiner 1937- ... 104
Bernal, Vicente J. 1888-1915 ... DLB 82
See also HW
Bernal (y Garcia y Pimentel), Ignacio
1910-1992 ... CANR-5
Obituary ... 136
Earlier sketch in CA 9-12R
Bernanos, (Paul Louis) Georges
1888-1948 ... 130
Brief entry ... 104
See also DLB 72
See also TCLC 3
Bernard, Andre 1956- ... 132
Bernard, April 1956- ... 131
See also CLC 59
Bernard, George I. 1949- ... SATA 39
Bernard, George 1939- ... 73-76
Bernard, Guy
See Barber, Stephen Guy
Bernard, H(arvey) Russell 1940- ... 41-44R
Bernard, Harold W. 1908- ... CANR-4
Earlier sketch in CA 1-4R
Bernard, Harry 1898-1979 ... DLB 92
Bernard, Hugh Y(ancey) Jr. 1919- ... 21-24R
Bernard, Jack F. 1930- ... 21-24R
Bernard, Jacqueline (de Sieyes)
1921-1983 ... 21-24R
Obituary ... 117
See also SATA 8, 45
Bernard, Jay
See Sawkins, Raymond H(arold)
Bernard, Jean-Jacques
1888-1972 Obituary ... 37-40R
Bernard, John 1756-1828 ... DLB 37
Bernard, Kenneth A(nderson) 1906- ... 29-32R
Bernard, Kenneth 1930- ... 41-44R
Bernard, Laureat J(oseph) 1922- ... 25-28R
Bernard, Marley
See Graves, Susan B(ernard)
Bernard, Nelson T(ed) Jr. 1925- ... 123
Bernard, Oliver 1925- ... 13-16R
Bernard, Paul Peter 1929- ... 89-92
Bernard, Richard Marion 1948- ... 105
Bernard, Robert
See Martin, Robert Bernard
Bernard, Sidney 1918- ... 29-32R
Bernard, Stefan
See Baumrin, Bernard H(erbert)
Bernard, Thelma Rene 1940- ... 57-60
Bernard, Thomas J(oseph) 1945- ... 138
Bernard, Will 1915- ... 93-96
Bernard, William Spencer
1907-1986 Obituary ... 118
Bernardini, Joe 1937- ... 136
Bernardo, Aldo S(isto) 1920- ... CANR-4
Earlier sketch in CA 1-4R
Bernardo, James V. 1913- ... 17-20R
Bernardo, Stephanie
See Johns, Stephanie Bernardo
Bernard of Chartres 1060(?)-1124(?) ... DLB 115
Bernards, Neal 1963- ... SATA 71
Bernarn, Terrave
See Burnett, David (Benjamin Foley)
Bernau, George 1945- ... 127
Bernauer, George F. 1941- ... 29-32R
Bernays, Anne
See Kaplan, Anne Bernays
Bernays, Edward L. 1891- ... 17-20R
Bernazza, Ann Marie
See Haase, Ann Marie Bernazza
Bernbach, William 1911-1982 Obituary ... 108
Bernd, Joseph Laurence 1923- ... 17-20R
Berndt, Ronald Murray 1916- ... CANR-19
Earlier sketches in CA 5-8R, CANR-3
Berndt, Walter 1900(?)-1979 Obituary ... 89-92
Berndtson, Arthur 1913- ... 108
Berne, Eric (Lennard) 1910-1970 ... CANR-4
Obituary ... 25-28R
Earlier sketch in CA 5-8R
See also MTCW
Berne, Leo
See Davies, L(eslie) P(urnell)
Berne, Patricia H(iggins) 1934- ... 110
Berne, Stanley 1923- ... CANR-1
Earlier sketch in CA 45-48
Berner, Carl Walter 1902- ... CANR-37
Earlier sketch in CA 49-52
Berner, Jeff 1940- ... 89-92
Berner, Robert B(arry) 1940- ... 41-44R
Bernert, Eleanor H.
See Sheldon, Eleanor Bernert
Bernet, Michael M. 1930- ... 25-28R
Bernhard, Sandra 1955(?)- ... 137
Bernhard, Thomas 1931-1989 ... CANR-32
Obituary ... 127
Earlier sketch in CA 85-88
See also CLC 3, 32, 61
See also DLB 85
See also MTCW
Bernhard, Virginia Purington 1937- ... 112
Bernhardsen, Bris
See Bernhardsen, (Einar) Christian (Rosenvinge)
Bernhardsen, (Einar) Christian (Rosenvinge)
1923- ... 29-32R
Bernhardt, Clyde Edric Barron
1905-1986 Obituary ... 119
Bernhardt, Frances Simonsen 1932- ... 103
Bernhardt, Karl S. 1901-1967 ... CAP-1
Earlier sketch in CA 13-14
Bernheim, Evelyne 1935- ... 21-24R
Bernheim, Kayla F. 1946- ... 108
Bernheim, Marc 1924- ... 21-24R
Bernheimer, Charles 1942- ... 134
Bernheimer, Martin 1936- ... 69-72
Bernier, Alexis 1956- ... 130
Bernier, Olivier 1941- ... CANR-30
Earlier sketch in CA 105
Bernikow, Louise 1940- ... 132
Berninghausen, David K(nipe) 1916- ... 111
Berns, Julie 1899(?)-1983 Obituary ... 111
Berns, Walter (Fred) 1919- ... CANR-24
Earlier sketch in CA 101
Bernstam, Mikhail S. 1943- ... 130
Bernstein, Alvin H(owell) 1939- ... 89-92
Bernstein, Anne C(arolyn) 1944- ... 105
Bernstein, Arnold 1920- ... 29-32R
Bernstein, Barton J(annen) 1936- ... 37-40R
Bernstein, Basil (Bernard) 1924- Brief entry ... 119
Bernstein, Blanche 1912- ... 110
Bernstein, Burton 1932- ... CANR-21
Earlier sketches in CA 1-4R, CANR-4
Bernstein, Carl 1944- ... 81-84
See also AITN 1
Bernstein, Charles 1950- ... 129
Bernstein, David 1915(?)-1974 Obituary ... 53-56
Bernstein, Douglas A. 1942- ... 45-48
Bernstein, Gail Lee 1939- ... 115
Bernstein, Gerry 1927- ... 105
Bernstein, Harry 1909- ... CANR-1
Earlier sketch in CA 1-4R
Bernstein, Hilda 1915- ... 130
Bernstein, Hillel 1892(?)-1977 Obituary ... 69-72
Bernstein, Irving 1916- Brief entry ... 114
Bernstein, J(erome) S(traus) 1936- ... 25-28R
Bernstein, Jacob 1946- ... 104
Bernstein, Jane 1949- ... 104
Bernstein, Jeremy 1929- ... CANR-27
Earlier sketch in CA 13-16R
Bernstein, Jerry Marx 1908-1969 ... CAP-2
Earlier sketch in CA 25-28
Bernstein, Joanne E(ckstein) 1943- ... CANR-29
Earlier sketches in CA 77-80, CANR-13
See also SATA 15
Bernstein, John Andrew 1944- ... 124
Bernstein, Joseph M(ilton)
1908(?)-1975 Obituary ... 57-60
Bernstein, Leonard 1918-1990 ... CANR-21
Obituary ... 132
Earlier sketches in CA 1-4R, CANR-2
Bernstein, Lewis 1915- ... 33-36R
Bernstein, Margery 1933- ... 57-60
Bernstein, Marilyn 1929- ... 21-24R
Bernstein, Marver H(illel) 1919- ... CANR-2
Earlier sketch in CA 1-4R
Bernstein, Marvin David 1923- ... 45-48
Bernstein, Merton C(lay) 1923- ... 17-20R
Bernstein, Michael Andre 1947- ... 124
Bernstein, Mordechai 1893-1983 Obituary ... 109
Bernstein, Morey 1919- ... 21-24R
Bernstein, Norman R. 1927- ... CANR-13
Earlier sketch in CA 33-36R
Bernstein, Paula 1944- ... 125
Bernstein, Philip S(idney) 1901-1985 ... CANR-28
Earlier sketch in CA 49-52
Bernstein, Richard J(acob)
1932- Brief entry ... 113
Bernstein, Richard K. 1934- ... 105
Bernstein, Seymour ... CANR-26
Earlier sketch in CA 109
Bernstein, Theodore M(enline)
1904-1979 ... CANR-3
Earlier sketch in CA 1-4R
See also SATA 12, 27
Bernstein, Thomas P(aul) 1937- ... 113
Bernstein, Walter 1919- ... 106
Bernzweig, Eli P. 1927- ... CANR-26
Earlier sketch in CA 29-32R
Berofsky, Bernard 1935- ... 89-92
Berque, Jacques Augustin 1910- ... 85-88
Berquist, Goodwin F(auntleroy) 1930- ... 21-24R
Berrellez, Robert 1920(?)-1985 Obituary ... 116
Berrett, Delwyn G(reen) 1935- ... 128
Berrett, LaMar C(ecil) 1926- ... 53-56
Berrian, Albert H. 1925- ... 37-40R
Berriault, Gina 1926- ... 129
Brief entry ... 116
Berridge, Celia 1943- ... CANR-28
Earlier sketch in CA 110
Berridge, Elizabeth 1921- ... CANR-6
Earlier sketch in CA 57-60
Berridge, P(ercy) S(tuart) A(ttwood)
1901- ... 29-32R
Berrien, Edith Heal
See Heal, Edith
Berrien, F. Kenneth 1909-1971 ... CANR-1
Obituary ... 29-32R
Earlier sketch in CA 1-4R
Berrigan, Daniel 1921- ... CANR-11
Earlier sketch in CA 33-36R
See also CAAS 1
See also CLC 4
See also DLB 5
Berrigan, Edmund Joseph Michael Jr.
1934-1983 ... CANR-14
Obituary ... 110
Earlier sketch in CA 61-64
See also Berrigan, Ted
Berrigan, Philip (Francis) 1923- ... CANR-11
Earlier sketch in CA 13-16R
Berrigan, Ted
See Berrigan, Edmund Joseph Michael Jr.
See also CLC 37
See also DLB 5
Berrill, Jacquelyn (Batsel) 1905- ... 17-20R
See also SATA 12
Berrill, N(orman) J(ohn) 1903- ... 17-20R
Berrington, Hugh B(ayard) 1928- ... 49-52
Berrington, John
See Brownjohn, Alan
Berrisford, Judith Mary
See Lewis, Judith Mary
Berry, Adrian M(ichael) 1937- ... CANR-25
Earlier sketches in CA 57-60, CANR-9
Berry, B. J.
See Berry, Barbara J.
Berry, Barbara J. 1937- ... 33-36R
See also SATA 7
Berry, Boyd M(cCulloch) 1939- ... 69-72
Berry, Brewton 1901- ... CANR-3
Earlier sketch in CA 1-4R
Berry, Brian J(oe) L(obley) 1934- ... CANR-5
Earlier sketch in CA 13-16R
Berry, Bryan 1930-1955 Brief entry ... 112
Berry, Burton Yost 1901- ... 85-88
Berry, Charles Edward Anderson 1931- ... 115
See also Berry, Chuck
Berry, Charles H. 1930- ... 69-72
Berry, Chuck
See Berry, Charles Edward Anderson
See also CLC 17
Berry, Cicely 1926- ... 93-96
Berry, D. C.
See Berry, David (Chapman)
Berry, David (Adams) 1943- ... 108
Berry, David (Chapman) 1942- ... CANR-27
Earlier sketch in CA 45-48
Berry, David (Ronald) 1942- ... 29-32R
Berry, Don (George) 1932- ... 106
Berry, Edmund G(rindlay) 1915- ... 1-4R
Berry, Edward I. 1940- ... 57-60
Berry, (Julia) Elizabeth 1920- ... 21-24R
Berry, Erick
See Best, (Evangel) Allena Champlin
Berry, Faith 1939- ... 133
Berry, Francis 1915- ... CANR-5
Earlier sketch in CA 5-8R
Berry, Frederic Aroyce Jr.
1906-1978 Obituary ... 77-80
Berry, Geoffrey 1912-1988 Obituary ... 124
Berry, Helen
See Rowland, D(onald) S(ydney)
Berry, Henry 1926- ... 85-88
Berry, Herbert 1922- ... CANR-29
Earlier sketch in CA 111
Berry, I. William 1934- ... CANR-25
Earlier sketch in CA 105
Berry, J. Bill 1945- ... 137
Berry, Jack 1918- ... 37-40R
Berry, James Gomer 1883-1968 Obituary ... 89-92
Berry, James 1925- ... 135
See also CLR 22
See also SATA 67
Berry, James 1932- ... 21-24R
Berry, Jane Cobb 1915(?)-1979 Obituary ... 85-88
See also SATA 22
Berry, Jason 1949- ... 45-48
Berry, Jim
See Berry, James
Berry, Jim 1946- ... 107
Berry, Jo(ycelyn) 1933- ... CANR-18
Earlier sketch in CA 102
Berry, John Nichols (III) 1933- Brief entry ... 113
Berry, John Stevens 1938- ... 132
Berry, Jonas
See Ashbery, John (Lawrence)
Berry, Joy
See Berry, Joy Wilt
Berry, Joy Wilt 1944- ... 134
See also SATA 46, 58
Berry, Katherine F(iske) 1877- ... CAP-2
Earlier sketch in CA 17-18
Berry, Lloyd E(ason) 1935-1977 ... 13-16R
Obituary ... 133
Berry, Lynn 1948- ... 61-64
Berry, Mary Frances 1938- ... CANR-14
Earlier sketch in CA 33-36R
See also BW
Berry, Nicholas O(rlando) 1936- ... 93-96
Berry, Paul 1919- ... 102
Berry, R(obert) J(ames) 1934- ... 121
Berry, R(alph) M(arion) 1947- ... 128
Berry, Roland (Brian) 1951- ... 93-96
Berry, Ron(ald Anthony) 1920- ... 25-28R
Berry, Scyld 1954- ... 136
Berry, Sister Mary Virginia
1908(?)-1987 Obituary ... 122
Berry, Stephen Ames 1947- ... 118
Berry, Thomas Edwin 1930- ... 102
Berry, Thomas Elliott 1917- ... 33-36R
Berry, Thomas 1914- ... 21-24R
Berry, Wallace Taft 1928- ... CANR-8
Earlier sketch in CA 17-20R
Berry, Wendell (Erdman) 1934- ... 73-76
See also AITN 1
See also CLC 4, 6, 8, 27, 46
See also DLB 5, 6
Berry, William D(avid) 1926- ... 73-76
See also SATA 14
Berry, William Turner 1888- ... CAP-2
Earlier sketch in CA 23-24
Berryman, Charles (Beecher) 1939- ... 112
Berryman, James Thomas
1902-1971 Obituary ... 93-96
Berryman, Jim
See Berryman, James Thomas
Berryman, John 1914-1972 ... CANR-35
Obituary ... 33-36R
Earlier sketches in CAP-1, CA 13-16
See also CABS 2
See also CDALB 1941-1968
See also CLC 1, 2, 3, 4, 6, 8, 10, 13, 25, 62
See also DLB 48
See also MTCW
Bersani, Leo 1931- ... CANR-5
Earlier sketch in CA 53-56
Berscheid, Ellen 1936- ... 25-28R
Bershadsky, Luba 1916- ... 131
Bersianik, Louky 1930- ... DLB 60
Berson, Harold 1926- ... 33-36R
See also SATA 4
Berson, Lenora E. 1926- ... 93-96
Berssenbrugge, Mei-mei 1947- ... 104
Berst, Charles A(shton) 1932- ... 41-44R
Berst, Jesse ... 116
Bertcher, Harvey (Joseph) 1929- ... 85-88
Bertelson, David (Earl) 1934- ... 21-24R
Berthelot, Joseph A. 1927- ... 21-24R
Berthoff, Ann (Rhys) E(vans) 1924- ... 129
Berthoff, Rowland (Tappan) 1921- ... 33-36R
Berthoff, Warner (Bement) 1925- ... CANR-2
Earlier sketch in CA 5-8R
Berthold, Dennis (Alfred) 1942- ... 117
Berthold, Margot 1922- ... 73-76
Berthold, Mary Paddock 1909- ... 53-56
Berthold, Richard M(artin) 1946- ... 131
Bertholf, Diana 1946- ... 115
Berthoud, Jacques (Alexandre) 1935- ... CANR-10
Earlier sketch in CA 17-20R
Berthoud, Roger 1934- ... 128
Berthrong, Donald J(ohn) 1922- ... 81-84
Berthrong, Evelyn Nagai
See Nagai Berthrong, Evelyn
Bertin, Charles-Francois
See Berlitz, Charles (L. Frambach)
Bertin, Jack
See Bertin, John
Bertin, John 1904-1963 Obituary ... 116
Bertin, Leonard M. 1918- ... 13-16R
Bertman, Stephen (Samuel) 1937- ... 45-48
Bertocci, Peter A(nthony) 1910- ... 17-20R
Bertolino, James 1942- ... CANR-17
Earlier sketches in CA 45-48, CANR-1
Bertolucci, Bernardo 1940- ... 106
See also CLC 16
Berton, Peter (Alexander Menquez)
1922- ... 77-80
Berton, Pierre 1920- ... CANR-2
Earlier sketch in CA 1-4R
See also DLB 68
Berton, Ralph 1910- ... 49-52
Bertonasco, Marc F(rancis) 1934- ... 89-92
Bertram, Anthony 1897-1978 Obituary ... 104
Bertram, (George) Colin (Lawder) 1911- ... 13-16R
Bertram, James Munro 1910- ... 65-68
Bertram, Jean De Sales ... CANR-12
Earlier sketch in CA 45-48

Bertram, Noel
See Fanthorpe, R(obert) Lionel
Bertram-Cox, Jean De Sales
See Bertram, Jean De Sales
Bertrand, Alvin L(ee) 1918- ... CANR-30
Earlier sketch in CA 45-48
Bertrand, Charles
See Carter, David C(harles)
Bertrand, Lewis 1897(?)-1974 Obituary ... 53-56
Bertrand, Michel 1944- ... CANR-13
Earlier sketch in CA 73-76
Bertrand, Sandra 1943- ... 130
Berwanger, Eugene H. ... 21-24R
Berwick, Jean Shepherd 1929- ... 9-12R
Berwick, Keith (Bennet) 1928- ... 33-36R
Besag, Frank P. 1935- ... 119
Besanceney, Paul H. 1924- ... 45-48
Besancon, Alain J. 1932- ... 130
Besant, Annie (Wood)
1847-1933 Brief entry ... 105
See also TCLC 9
Besas, Peter 1933- ... 77-80
Beschloss, Michael R(ichard) 1955- ... 101
Besdine, Matthew 1905(?)-1986 Obituary ... 120
Beshers, James M(onahan) 1931- ... 1-4R
Beshoar, Barron B(enedict) 1907- ... 69-72
Beskow, Bo 1906- ... CANR-11
Earlier sketch in CA 61-64
Beskow, Elsa (Maartman) 1874-1953 ... 135
See also CLR 17
See also MAICYA
See also SATA 20
Besner, Neil K. 1949- ... 137
Besoyan, Rick 1924(?)-1970 Obituary ... 25-28R
Bess, Clayton
See Locke, Robert
Bessborough, Tenth Earl of
See Ponsonby, Frederick Edward Neuflize
Bessell, Peter (Joseph)
1921-1985 Obituary ... 117
Besser, Gretchen R(ous) 1928- ... CANR-14
Earlier sketch in CA 41-44R
Besser, Joe 1907-1988 Obituary ... 124
Besser, Milton 1911-1976 ... 69-72
Obituary ... 65-68
Bessette, Gerard 1920- ... CANR-14
Earlier sketch in CA 37-40R
See also DLB 53
Bessie, Alvah 1904-1985 ... CANR-2
Obituary ... 116
Earlier sketch in CA 5-8R
See also CLC 23
See also DLB 26
Bessie, Constance Ernst
1918(?)-1985 Obituary ... 115
Bessinger, Jess B(alsor) Jr. 1921- ... 13-16R
Bessom, Malcolm E(ugene) 1940-1988 ... 57-60
Obituary ... 126
Bessy, Maurice 1910- ... CANR-26
Earlier sketches in CA 65-68, CANR-10
Best, Adam
See Carmichael, William Edward
Best, Alan C.G. 1939- ... 111
Best, (Evangel) Allena Champlin
1892-1974 ... CAP-2
Earlier sketch in CA 25-28
See also SATA 2, 25
Best, Charles H(erbert) 1899-1978 ... CANR-29
Obituary ... 103
Earlier sketch in CA 45-48
Best, Ernest E. 1919- ... 112
Best, Ernest 1917- ... CANR-35
Earlier sketch in CA 114
Best, G. F. A.
See Best, Geoffrey (Francis Andrew)
Best, Gary A(llen) 1939- ... 33-36R
Best, Gary Dean 1936- ... 117
Best, Geoffrey (Francis Andrew)
1928- Brief entry ... 114
Best, (Oswald) Herbert 1894- ... CAP-2
Earlier sketch in CA 25-28
See also SATA 2
Best, Hugh 1920- ... 115
Best, James J(oseph) 1938- ... 37-40R
Best, John Wesley 1909- ... 17-20R
Best, Judith A. 1938- ... 69-72
Best, Marc
See Lemieux, Marc
Best, Marshall A. 1901(?)-1982 Obituary ... 106
Best, Michael R. ... 37-40R
Best, Nicholas 1948- ... 138
Best, Otto F(erdinand) 1929- ... CANR-25
Earlier sketch in CA 69-72
Best, Rayleigh Breton Amis 1905- ... CAP-1
Earlier sketch in CA 13-16
Best, Robin Hewitson Obituary ... 113
Best, Thomas W(aring) 1939- ... 29-32R
Bestall, A(lfred) E(dmeades)
1892-1986 Obituary ... 119
See also SATA 48
Beste, R(aymond) Vernon 1908- ... CANR-4
Earlier sketch in CA 1-4R
Bester, Alfred 1913-1987 ... CANR-36
Obituary ... 123
Earlier sketches in CA 13-16R, CANR-12
See also DLB 8
See also MTCW
Besterman, Theodore (Deocatus Nathaniel)
1904-1976 Obituary ... 105
Bestic, Alan Kent 1922- ... 13-16R
Beston, Henry 1888-1968 Obituary ... 25-28R
Bestor, Arthur (Eugene Jr.) 1908- ... CANR-6
Earlier sketch in CA 1-4R
Bestor, Dorothy K(och) ... 118
Bestul, Thomas H(oward) 1942- ... 53-56
Betancourt, Jeanne 1941- ... CANR-31
Earlier sketch in CA 49-52
See also SATA 43, 55
Betancourt, Romulo 1908-1981 ... 104
Beteille, Andre 1934- ... 130
Betenson, Lula Parker 1884-1980 ... 61-64
Obituary ... 133
Beth
See Winship, Elizabeth
Beth, Loren Peter 1920- ... CANR-3
Earlier sketch in CA 1-4R
Beth, Mary
See Miller, Mary Beth
Bethancourt, T. Ernesto
See Paisley, Tom
See also CLR 3
See also SATA 11
Bethe, H. A.
See Bethe, Hans Albrecht
Bethe, Hans A.
See Bethe, Hans Albrecht
Bethe, Hans Albrecht 1906- Brief entry ... 115
Bethea, J. D.
See Bethea, James D.
Bethea, James D. 1933(?)-1990 Obituary ... 130
Bethel, Dell 1929- ... CANR-26
Earlier sketch in CA 29-32R
See also SATA 52
Bethel, Elizabeth Rauh 1942- ... 106
Bethel, Paul D(uane) 1919- ... 25-28R
Bethell, Jean (Frankenberry) 1922- ... CANR-3
Earlier sketch in CA 9-12R
See also SATA 8
Bethell, Nicholas William 1938- ... CANR-1
Earlier sketch in CA 45-48
Bethell, Tom 1940- ... 77-80
Bethers, Ray 1902- ... CAP-1
Earlier sketch in CA 11-12
See also SATA 6
Bethge, Eberhard 1909- ... 85-88
Bethlen, T. D.
See Silverberg, Robert
Bethmann, Erich Waldemar 1904- ... CAP-2
Earlier sketch in CA 23-24
Bethune, J. G.
See Ellis, Edward S(ylvester)
Bethune, J. H.
See Ellis, Edward S(ylvester)
Bethurum, F(rances) Dorothy 1897- ... CAP-2
Earlier sketch in CA 17-18
Beti, Mongo
See Biyidi, Alexandre
See also BLC 1
See also CLC 27
Betjeman, John 1906-1984 ... CANR-33
Obituary ... 112
Earlier sketch in CA 9-12R
See also CDBLB 1945-1960
See also CLC 2, 6, 10, 34, 43
See also DLB 20
See also DLBY 84
See also MTCW
Betjeman, Penelope Chetwode
See Chetwode, Penelope
Betocchi, Carlo 1899- ... CANR-4
Earlier sketch in CA 9-12R
Bett, Walter R(eginald) 1903- ... CAP-1
Earlier sketch in CA 13-14
Bettelheim, Bruno 1903-1990 ... CANR-23
Obituary ... 131
Earlier sketch in CA 81-84
See also MTCW
Bettelheim, Charles 1913- ... CANR-13
Earlier sketch in CA 73-76
Bettelheim, Frederick A(braham) 1923- ... 49-52
Betten, Neil B. 1939- ... 105
Bettenbender, John (I.)
1921-1988 Obituary ... 125
Bettenson, Henry (Scowcroft) 1908- ... 13-16R
Betteridge, Anne
See Potter, Margaret (Newman)
Betteridge, Don
See Newman, Bernard (Charles)
Betteridge, H(arold) T(homas) 1910- ... 5-8R
Bettersworth, John K(nox) 1909- ... CANR-2
Earlier sketch in CA 5-8R
Bettey, J(oseph) H(arold) 1932- ... 130
Betti, Liliana 1939- ... 101
Betti, Ugo 1892-1953 Brief entry ... 104
See also TCLC 5
Bettina
See Ehrlich, Bettina Bauer
Bettis, Joseph Dabney 1936- ... 33-36R
Bettmann, Otto Ludwig 1903- ... 17-20R
See also SATA 46
Betts, Charles L(ancaster) Jr. 1908- ... 101
Betts, Donni 1948- ... CANR-5
Earlier sketch in CA 53-56
Betts, Doris (Waugh) 1932- ... CANR-9
Earlier sketch in CA 13-16R
See also CLC 3, 6, 28
See also DLBY 82
Betts, Emmett Albert 1903- ... 33-36R
Betts, George 1944- ... CANR-2
Earlier sketch in CA 45-48
Betts, Glynne Robinson 1934- ... 105
Betts, James
See Haynes, Betsy
Betts, John (Edward) 1939- ... 106
Betts, Raymond F. 1925- ... CANR-3
Earlier sketch in CA 1-4R
Betts, Richard K(evin) 1947- ... CANR-16
Earlier sketch in CA 85-88
Betts, William W(ilson) Jr. 1926- ... 33-36R
Betty, L(ewis) Stafford 1942- ... 118
Betz, Betty 1920- ... 1-4R
Betz, Eva Kelly 1897-1968 ... CAP-1
Earlier sketch in CA 11-12
See also SATA 10
Betz, Hans Dieter 1931- ... CANR-19
Earlier sketches in CA 53-56, CANR-4
Beuf, Ann H(ill) 1939- ... 85-88
Beum, Robert (Lawrence) 1929- ... 9-12R
Beurdeley, Michel 1911- ... CANR-30
Earlier sketch in CA 49-52
Beutel, William Charles 1930- ... 101
Beuttler, Edward Ivan Oakley ... 73-76
Beuve-Mery, Hubert 1902-1989 Obituary ... 129
Bevan, Alistair
See Roberts, Keith (John Kingston)
Bevan, Aneurin 1897-1960 Obituary ... 106
Bevan, Bryan 1913- ... 13-16R
Bevan, E. Dean 1938- ... 33-36R
Bevan, Gloria ... 134
Brief entry ... 117
Bevan, Jack 1920- ... 13-16R
Bevan, James (Stuart) 1930- ... 106
Bevan, Tom 1868-193 (?) ... YABC 2
Bevenot, Maurice 1897-1980 Obituary ... 105
Beveridge, Albert J. 1862-1927 ... DLB 17
Beveridge, Andrew A(lan) 1945- ... 93-96
Beveridge, George David Jr. 1922-1987 ... 102
Obituary ... 121
Beveridge, Meryle Secrest 1930- ... 81-84
Beveridge, Oscar Maltman 1913- ... 9-12R
Beveridge, William (Henry)
1879-1963 Obituary ... 112
Beveridge, William (Ian Beardmore) 1908- ... 106
Beverley, Mary Frances 1925- ... 120
Beverley, Robert 1673(?)-1722 ... DLB 24, 30
BeVier, Michael J(udson) ... 97-100
Bevilacqua, Alberto 1934- ... CANR-26
Earlier sketch in CA 29-32R
Bevington, David M(artin) 1931- ... CANR-3
Earlier sketch in CA 1-4R
Bevington, Helen 1906- ... 13-16R
Bevis, Em Olivia 1932- ... CANR-1
Earlier sketch in CA 49-52
Bevis, H(erbert) U(rlin) 1902- ... CAP-2
Earlier sketch in CA 29-32
Bevis, James
See Cumberland, Marten
Bevlin, Marjorie Elliott 1917- ... 9-12R
Bewes, Richard 1934- ... CANR-20
Earlier sketch in CA 102
Bewick, Thomas 1753-1828 ... SATA 16
Bewkes, Eugene Garrett 1895- ... 5-8R
Bewley, Charles Henry 1888- ... 5-8R
Bewley, Chrisina (Mary Erskine) 1924- ... 129
Bewley, Marius 1918-1973 ... CANR-3
Obituary ... 41-44R
Earlier sketch in CA 5-8R
Bey, Isabelle
See Bosticco, (Isabel Lucy) Mary
Beye, Charles Rowan 1930- ... 93-96
Beyea, Basil 1910- ... 61-64
Beyer, (Richard) Andrew 1943- ... CANR-11
Earlier sketch in CA 69-72
Beyer, Audrey White 1916- ... 13-16R
See also SATA 9
Beyer, Edvard (Freydar) 1920- ... 121
Brief entry ... 116
Beyer, Evelyn M. 1907- ... CAP-2
Earlier sketch in CA 25-28
Beyer, Glenn H. 1913-1969 ... CANR-2
Earlier sketch in CA 1-4R
Beyer, Robert 1913(?)-1978 Obituary ... 77-80
Beyer, Steven L(arsen) 1943- ... 123
Beyer, Werner William 1911- ... 9-12R
Beyerchen, Alan 1945- ... 81-84
Beyerhaus, Peter (Paul Johannes)
1929- ... CANR-38
Earlier sketches in CA 93-96, CANR-16
Beyerlin, Walter W(ilhelm) 1929- ... 124
Beyers, Charlotte K(empner) 1931- ... 85-88
Beyfus, Drusilla 1927- ... 107
Beyle, Hank
See Buchanan, James David
Beyle, Thad L. 1934- ... 37-40R
Beynon, Huw 1942- ... 107
Beynon, John
See Harris, John (Wyndham Parkes Lucas) Beynon
Beytagh, Gonville (Aubie) ffrench
See ffrench-Beytagh, Gonville (Aubie)
Bezencon, Jacqueline (Buxcel) 1924- ... SATA 48
Bezilla, Michael 1950- ... 111
Bezio, May Rowland Obituary ... 69-72
Bezruchka, Stephen (Anthony) 1943- ... 107
Bhagat, G(oberdhan) 1928- ... 29-32R
Bhagavatula, Murty S. 1921- ... 29-32R
Bhagwati, Jagdish N. 1934- ... 17-20R
Bhajan, Yogi
See Yogiji, Harbhajan Singh Khalsa
Bhaktivedanta Swami, A. C.
See Prabhupada, A. C. Bhaktivedanta
Bhana, Surendra 1939- ... 57-60
Bharati, Agehananda 1923-1991 ... CANR-4
Obituary ... 134
Earlier sketch in CA 1-4R
Bhardwaj, Surinder Mohan 1934- ... 45-48
Bharti, Ma Satya 1942- ... 102
Bhatia, Hans Raj 1904-1979 ... 53-56
Obituary ... 133
Bhatia, Jamunadevi 1919- ... 101
See also Forrester, Helen
Bhatia, June
See Bhatia, Jamunadevi
Bhatia, Krishan 1926(?)-1974 Obituary ... 53-56
Bhatnagar, Joti 1935- ... 41-44R
Bhatt, Jagdish J(eyshanker) 1939- ... CANR-31
Earlier sketches in CA 77-80, CANR-14
Bhattacharji, Sukumari 1921- ... 33-36R
Bhattacharya, Bhabani 1906- ... CANR-9
Earlier sketch in CA 5-8R
Bhave, Vinoba 1895-1982 Obituary ... 108
Bhide, Amar 1955- ... 130
Bhutto, Benazir 1953- ... 131
Bhutto, Zulfikar Ali 1928-1979 ... CANR-11
Earlier sketch in CA 53-56
Biaggini, Adriana Ivancich
1930(?)-1983 Obituary ... 109
Biagi, Shirley 1944- ... CANR-32
Earlier sketches in CA 85-88, CANR-15
Bial, Morrison David 1917- ... 61-64
See also SATA 62
Bialik, Chaim Nachman 1873-1934 ... TCLC 25
Bialk, Elisa
See Krautter, Elisa (Bialk)
Bialostocki, Jan 1921- ... 104
Bialostosky, Don H(oward) 1947- ... 120
Bianchi, Engene C(arl) 1930- ... 25-28R
Bianchi, Hombert
1912(?)-1980 Obituary ... 97-100
Bianchi, Robert S(teven) 1943- ... 109
Bianco, Anthony 1953- ... 134
Bianco, Lucien Andre 1930- ... CANR-15
Earlier sketch in CA 85-88
Bianco, Margery (Williams)
1881-1944 Brief entry ... 109
See also CLR 19
See also MAICYA
See also SATA 15
Bianco, Pamela 1906- ... 85-88
See also SATA 28
Biancolli, Louis Leopold 1907- ... 65-68
Bianconi, Lorenzo (Gennaro) 1946- ... 134
Biasin, Gian-Paolo 1933- ... 25-28R
Bibaud, Adele 1854-1941 ... DLB 92
Bibaud, Michel 1782-1857 ... DLB 99
Bibb, (David) Porter III 1937- ... 65-68
Bibby, Cyril 1914- ... CANR-7
Earlier sketch in CA 13-16R
Bibby, John F(ranklin) 1934- ... CANR-35
Earlier sketch in CA 45-48
Bibby, T(homas) Geoffrey 1917- ... CANR-4
Earlier sketch in CA 1-4R
Bibby, Violet 1908- ... 102
See also SATA 24
Bibee, John 1954- ... 112
Biberman, Edward 1904-1986 ... 49-52
Obituary ... 118
Biberman, Herbert 1900-1971 ... CAP-1
Obituary ... 33-36R
Earlier sketch in CA 13-16
Bibesco, Marthe Lucie 1887-1973 ... 93-96
Obituary ... 49-52
Bible, Charles 1937- ... 69-72
See also SATA 13
Bibo, Bobette
See Gugliotta, Bobette
Bicanic, Rudolf 1905-1968 ... 85-88
Bicat, Tony 1945- ... 130
Bice, Clare 1909-1976 ... SATA 22
Bichakjian, Bernard H. 1937- ... 136
Bichler, Joyce 1954- ... 107
Bichsel, Peter 1935- ... 81-84
See also DLB 75
Bick, Edgar Milton 1902-1978 Obituary ... 77-80
Bickel, Alexander M(ordecai)
1924-1974 ... CANR-1
Obituary ... 53-56
Earlier sketch in CA 1-4R
Bickelhaupt, David L(ynn) 1929- ... 69-72
Bickerman, Elias J(oseph) 1897-1981 ... CANR-20
Obituary ... 104
Earlier sketch in CA 25-28R
Bickers, Richard Leslie Townshend
1917- ... CANR-1
Earlier sketch in CA 45-48
Bickerstaff, Isaac
See Swift, Jonathan
Bickersteth, Geoffrey Langdale
1884-1974 Obituary ... 49-52
Bickerton, Derek 1926- ... 61-64
Bicket, Zenas J(ohan) 1932- ... 37-40R
Bickford, David 1953- ... 133
Bickford, Elwood Dale 1927- ... 61-64
Bickham, Jack M(iles) 1930- ... CANR-23
Earlier sketches in CA 5-8R, CANR-8
Bickle, Judith Brundrett ... CAP-1
Earlier sketch in CA 13-14
Bickley, R(obert) Bruce Jr. 1942- ... CANR-9
Earlier sketch in CA 65-68
Bickman, Martin 1945- ... 104
Bida, Constantine 1916- ... CANR-13
Earlier sketch in CA 61-64
Bidart, Frank ... CLC 33
Bidault, Georges 1899-1983 Obituary ... 109
Biddiss, Michael Denis 1942- ... CANR-4
Earlier sketch in CA 53-56
Biddle, Arthur W(illiam) 1936- ... 45-48
Biddle, Bruce J(esse) 1928- ... CANR-7
Earlier sketch in CA 17-20R
Biddle, Francis (Beverley) 1886-1968 ... 5-8R
Obituary ... 103
Biddle, George 1885-1973 Obituary ... 45-48
Biddle, Katherine Garrison Chapin
1890-1977 ... CANR-5
Obituary ... 73-76
Earlier sketch in CA 5-8R
Biddle, Marcia McKenna 1931- ... 112
Biddle, Perry H(arvey) Jr. 1932- ... 57-60
Biddle, Phillips R. 1933- ... 37-40R
Biddle, Wayne 1948- ... 106
Biddle, William W(ishart) 1900- ... CAP-2
Earlier sketch in CA 17-18
Biderman, Albert D. 1923- ... CANR-23
Earlier sketches in CA 5-8R, CANR-8
Biderman, Sol 1936- ... 25-28R

Bidney, David 1908- 9-12R
Bidwell, Dafne (Mary) 1929- 97-100
Bidwell, Marjory Elizabeth Sarah 77-80
Bidwell, Percy W(ells) 1888- CAP-1
Earlier sketch in CA 9-10
Bidwell, Walter Hilliard 1798-1881 .... DLB 79
Biebel, David B. 1949- 125
Bieber, Margarete 1879-1978 .... CANR-11
Obituary 77-80
Earlier sketch in CA 17-20R
Biebuyck, Daniel P. 1925- CANR-30
Earlier sketches in CA 25-28R, CANR-11
Biederman, Marcia (Squire) 1949- 127
Biegel, John E(dward) 1925- 49-52
Biegel, Paul 1925- CANR-32
Earlier sketches in CA 77-80, CANR-14
See also CLR 27
See also SATA 16
Biehler, Robert F(rederick) 1927- 37-40R
Bielby, Cliff 1919-1984 Obituary 111
Bielenberg, Christabel 1909- 29-32R
Bieler, Ludwig 1906-1981 .... 5-8R
Obituary 103
Bielfield, Sidney 1904(?)-1984 Obituary 112
Bielski, Feliks
See Giergielewicz, Mieczyslaw F.
Bielyi, Sergei
See Hollo, Anselm
Bieman, Elizabeth 1923- 137
Biemiller, Carl L(udwig Jr.) 1912-1979 121
Obituary 106
See also SATA 21, 40
Biemiller, Ruth Cobbett 1914- 37-40R
Bien, David Duckworth 1930- 5-8R
Bien, Joseph Julius 1936- CANR-31
Earlier sketches in CA 53-56, CANR-5
Bien, Peter (Adolph) 1930- 9-12R
Bienek, Horst 1930- 73-76
See also CLC 7, 11
See also DLB 75
Bienen, Henry Samuel 1939- 81-84
Bienenfeld, Florence L(ucille) 1929- CANR-23
Earlier sketch in CA 106
See also SATA 39
Bienes, Nicholas Peter 1952- 136
Bienstock, Mike
See Bienstock, Myron Joseph
Bienstock, Myron Joseph 1922- 9-12R
Bienvenu, Bernard J(efferson) 1925- 53-56
Bienvenu, Richard (Thomas) 1936- 61-64
Bier, Jesse 1925- CANR-3
Earlier sketch in CA 5-8R
Bier, William C(hristian) 1911-1980 .... 33-36R
Obituary 97-100
Bierbaum, Margaret 1916- 33-36R
Bierbaum, Otto Julius 1865-1910 .... DLB 66
Bierbrier, M(orris) L(eonard) 1947- 128
Bierce, Ambrose (Gwinett)
1842-1914(?) Brief entry 104
See also CDALB 1865-1917
See also DLB 11, 12, 23, 71, 74
See also SSC 9
See also TCLC 1, 7, 44
See also WLC
Bierhorst, John (William) 1936- CANR-28
Earlier sketches in CA 33-36R, CANR-13
See also SAAS 10
See also SATA 6
Bieri, Arthur Peter 1931- 61-64
Bierley, Paul E(dmund) 1926- CANR-13
Earlier sketch in CA 77-80
Bierman, Arthur K(almer) 1923- 85-88
Bierman, Harold Jr. 1924- CANR-9
Earlier sketch in CA 17-20R
Bierman, Judah 1917- 114
Bierman, Mildred Thornton 1912- 5-8R
Bierman, Stanley M(elvin) 1935- 106
Biermann, Lillian
See Wehmeyer, Lillian (Mabel) Biermann
Biermann, Wolf 1936- 81-84
Biernatzki, William E(ugene) 1931- CANR-6
Earlier sketch in CA 57-60
Biers, William Richard 1938- CANR-23
Earlier sketch in CA 106
Bierstedt, Robert 1913- CANR-2
Earlier sketch in CA 1-4R
Biery, William (Richard) 1933- 57-60
Biesanz, Mavis Hiltunen 1919- 33-36R
Biesanz, Richard 1944- 112
Biesterveld, Betty Parsons 1923- CANR-1
Earlier sketch in CA 1-4R
Bietenholz, Peter G(erard) 1933- 101
Biezanek, Anne C(ampbell) 1927- 17-20R
Bigard, (Albany) Barney (Leon) 1906-1980 134
Bigart, Robert James 1947- 33-36R
Bigelow, Donald N(evius) 1918- 41-44R
Bigelow, Gordon Ellsworth 1919- 110
Bigelow, Karl Worth
1898-1980 Obituary 97-100
Bigelow, Marybelle S(chmidt) 1923- 25-28R
Bigelow, Robert P(ratt) 1927- Brief entry 118
Bigelow, Robert Sydney 1918- 102
Bigelow, William F. 1879-1966 .... DLB 91
Bigg, Patricia Nina 1932- 102
Bigge, Morris L. 1908- 9-12R
Biggers, Earl Derr 1884-1933 Brief entry 108
Biggers, John Thomas 1924- CANR-2
Earlier sketch in CA 1-4R
Biggle, Lloyd Jr. 1923- CANR-35
Earlier sketches in CA 13-16R, CANR-5, 20
See also DLB 8
See also SATA 65
Biggs, Anselm G. 1914- 33-36R
Biggs, Bradley 1920- 124
Biggs, John Jr. 1895-1979 Obituary 85-88
Biggs, John B(urville) 1934- CANR-6
Earlier sketch in CA 57-60

Biggs, Margaret Key 1933- 114
Biggs, Mary 1944- 137
Biggs, (Marvin) Mouzon Jr. 1941- 111
Biggs, Peter
See Rimel, Duane (Weldon)
Biggs-Davison, John (Alec) 1918- 13-16R
Bigiaretti, Libero 1906- CANR-12
Earlier sketch in CA 29-32R
Bigler, Vernon 1922- 21-24R
Bignell, Alan 1928- 103
Bigo, Pierre (Auguste) 1906- 136
Bigsby, C(hristopher) W(illiam) E(dgar)
1941- CANR-28
Earlier sketches in CA 25-28R, CANR-11
Bihalji-Merin, Oto 1904- CANR-34
Earlier sketches in CA 81-84, CANR-15
Bihler, Penny 1940- 77-80
Bijou, Sidney W(illiam) 1908- CANR-14
Earlier sketch in CA 37-40R
Bikel, Theodore 1924- CANR-1
Earlier sketch in CA 1-4R
Bikerstaff, Isaac John 1733-1808 .... DLB 89
Bikkie, James A(ndrew) 1929- 53-56
Biklen, Douglas Paul 1945- CANR-15
Earlier sketch in CA 85-88
Bilas, Richard A(llen) 1935- 53-56
Bilbo, Queenie Obituary 37-40R
Bilbow, Antony 1932- 25-28R
Bilderback, Dean Loy 1932- 97-100
Bilderback, Diane E(lizabeth) 1951- 110
Bileck, Marvin 1920- .... SATA 40
Bilek, Arthur J(ohn) 1929- 115
Bilibin, Ivan (Iakolevich) 1876-1942 .... SATA 61
Bilich, Marion Yellin 1949- 114
Bilinsky, Yaroslav 1932- 13-16R
Bilkey, Warren J(oseph) 1920- 29-32R
Bill, Alfred Hoyt 1879-1964 107
See also SATA 44
Bill, J(ohn) Brent 1951- 117
Bill, James A(lban) 1939- Brief entry 114
Bill, Valentine T. 13-16R
Billam, Rosemary 1952- 123
See also SATA 61
Bill-Belotserkovsky, Vladimir Naumovich
1884-1970 Obituary 104
Billcliffe, Roger (George) 1946- 132
Biller, Henry B(urt) 1940- CANR-35
Earlier sketch in CA 114
Billetdoux, Francois (Paul) 1927- 21-24R
Billett, Roy O(ren) 1891- 13-16R
Billias, George Athan 1919- CANR-6
Earlier sketch in CA 9-12R
Billig, Otto 1910- 129
Billings, Charlene W(interer) 1941- CANR-24
Earlier sketch in CA 107
See also SATA 41
Billings, Charles E(dward) 1938- 121
Billings, Evelyn L(ivingston) 1918- 112
Billings, Ezra
See Halla, (Robert) Chris(tian)
Billings, Harold (Wayne) 1931- 25-28R
Billings, John Shaw 1898-1975 Obituary 104
Billings, Josh
See Shaw, Henry Wheeler
Billings, Peggy 1928- 25-28R
Billings, Richard N. 1930- 103
Billings, Robert 1949- 113
Billings, Warren M(artin) 1940- 61-64
Billings, William Dwight 1910- 113
Billingsley, Andrew 1926- 57-60
Billingsley, Edward Baxter 1910- CAP-2
Earlier sketch in CA 25-28
Billington, David P(erkins) 1927- 134
Billington, Dora May 1890-1968 .... CAP-1
Earlier sketch in CA 13-14
Billington, Elizabeth T(hain) 101
See also SATA 43, 50
Billington, James H(adley) 1929- 132
Brief entry 117
Billington, John
See Beaver, (Jack) Patrick
Billington, Joy 1931- 77-80
Billington, Michael 1939- 102
Billington, Monroe Lee 1928- 21-24R
Billington, Rachel 1942- 33-36R
See also AITN 2
See also CLC 43
Billington, Ray Allen 1903-1981 .... CANR-5
Obituary 103
Earlier sketch in CA 1-4R
Billington, Raymond John 1930- 110
Billmeyer, Fred Wallace Jr. 1919- 85-88
Billout, Guy (Rene) 1941- CANR-26
Earlier sketch in CA 85-88
See also SATA 10
Bills, Robert E(dgar) 1916- 107
Bills, Scott L(aurence) 1948- CANR-38
Earlier sketch in CA 112
Billy, Andre 1882-1971 Obituary 29-32R
Bilow, Pat 1941- 106
Bilsland, Bilko
See Bilsland, E(rnest) C(harles)
Bilsland, E(rnest) C(harles) 1931- 69-72
Bimler, Richard William 1940- CANR-14
Earlier sketch in CA 41-44R
Binchy, Maeve 1940- 134
Brief entry 127
See also BEST 90:1
Binder, Aaron 1927- 57-60
Binder, David 1931- 65-68
Binder, Eando
See Binder, Otto O(scar)
Binder, Frederick M(elvin) 1931- 29-32R
Binder, Frederick Moore 1920- 41-44R
Binder, Leonard 1927- 61-64

Binder, Otto O(scar) 1911-1974 .... CANR-3
Obituary 53-56
Earlier sketch in CA 1-4R
Binder, Pearl
See Elwyn-Jones, Pearl Binder
Binding, Rudolf G. 1867-1938 .... DLB 66
Bindman, Arthur J(oseph) 1925- 45-48
Bindoff, Stanley Thomas 1908-1980 73-76
Obituary 102
Bindra, Dalbir 1922-1980 122
Obituary 117
Binford, Chapman H(unter)
1900-1990 Obituary 130
Binford, Lewis R(oberts) 1930- 131
Bing, Elisabeth D. 1914- CANR-11
Earlier sketch in CA 69-72
Bing, Rudolf 1902- 89-92
Bingaman, Ron 1936- 61-64
Binger, Carl A(lfred) L(anning) 1889-1976 73-76
Obituary 65-68
Binger, Norman H(enry) 1914- 33-36R
Binger, Walter 1888(?)-1979 Obituary 85-88
Bingham, (George) Barry Jr. 1933- 106
Bingham, (George) Barry
1906-1988 Obituary 126
Bingham, Caleb 1757-1817 .... DLB 42
Bingham, Caroline 1938- CANR-10
Earlier sketch in CA 57-60
Bingham, Carson
See Cassiday, Bruce (Bingham)
Bingham, Charlotte (Mary Therese)
1942- CANR-11
Earlier sketch in CA 105
Bingham, David A(ndrew) 1926- 53-56
Bingham, Edwin R(alph) 1920- CANR-2
Earlier sketch in CA 5-8R
Bingham, Evangeline M(arguerite) L(adys) (Elliot)
1899- 65-68
Bingham, Jane Marie 1941- 104
Bingham, John (Michael Ward)
1908-1988 .... CANR-11
Obituary 126
Earlier sketch in CA 21-24R
Bingham, Jonathan Brewster
1914-1986 .... 33-36R
Obituary 119
Bingham, June Rossbach 1919- 1-4R
Bingham, M(orley) P(aul) 1918- 49-52
Bingham, Madeleine (Mary Ebel)
1912-1988 .... CANR-11
Obituary 124
Earlier sketch in CA 13-16R
Bingham, Melinda 1950- 119
Bingham, Mindy
See Bingham, Melinda
Bingham, Richard D. 1937- 112
Bingham, Robert C(harles) 1927- 21-24R
Bingham, Robert E. 1925- 29-32R
Bingham, Robert Kamerer
1925(?)-1982 Obituary 107
Bingham, Sallie
See Ellsworth, Sallie Bingham
Bingham, Woodbridge 1901-1986 Obituary 119
Bingley, Clive (Hamilton) 1936- 17-20R
Bingley, D. E.
See Bingley, David Ernest
Bingley, David Ernest 1920- CANR-18
Earlier sketches in CA 45-48, CANR-2
Binham, Philip Frank 1924- 107
Binion, Rudolph 1927- CANR-4
Earlier sketch in CA 1-4R
bin Ishak, Yusof
See Ishak, Yusof bin
Binkley, Anne
See Rand, Ann (Binkley)
Binkley, Luther John 1925- 5-8R
Binkley, Olin T(rivette) 1908- 45-48
Binkley, Thomas (Eden) 1931- 135
Binkley, William Campbell 1889-1970 107
Obituary 104
Binnie, G(eoffrey) M(orse)
1908-1989 Obituary 128
Binns, Archie (Fred) 1899-1971 73-76
Obituary 133
Binns, J(ames) W(allace) 1940- 53-56
Binstock, R. C. 1958- 138
Binswanger, Ludwig 1881-1966 Obituary 107
Binyon, Claude 1905-1978 Obituary 77-80
Binyon, Helen 1904-1982(?) Obituary 114
Binyon, (Robert) Laurence
1869-1943 Brief entry 115
See also DLB 19
Binyon, T(imothy) J(ohn) 1936- CANR-28
Earlier sketch in CA 111
See also CLC 34
Binzen, Bill
See Binzen, William
See also SATA 24
Binzen, Peter (Husted) 1922- 136
Binzen, William 89-92
See also Binzen, Bill
Biossat, Bruce 1910(?)-1974 Obituary 104
Biot, Francois 1923- 13-16R
Biow, Milton H. 1882(?)-1976 Obituary 65-68
Bioy Casares, Adolfo 1914- CANR-19
Earlier sketch in CA 29-32R
See also CLC 4, 8, 13
See also DLB 113
See also HW
See also MTCW
Biram, Brenda 1930(?)-1984 Obituary 112
Birch, Alison Wyrley 1922- 85-88
Birch, Anthony H(arold) 1924- CANR-5
Earlier sketch in CA 13-16R
Birch, Bruce C(harles) 1941- CANR-25
Earlier sketches in CA 65-68, CANR-10
Birch, Carol 1951- 127

Birch, Cyril 1925- 85-88
Birch, Daniel R(ichard) 1937- 101
Birch, David L. 1937- CANR-16
Earlier sketch in CA 25-28R
Birch, Herbert G. 1918-1973 Obituary 41-44R
Birch, L(ouis) C(harles) 1918- 120
Birch, Leo Bedrich 1902- 33-36R
Birch, Lionel Obituary 106
Birch, (Evelyn) Nigel (Chetwode)
1906-1981 Obituary 108
Birch, Reginald B(athurst) 1856-1943 .... SATA 19
Birch, William G(arry) 1909- 53-56
Birchall, Ian H(arry) 1939- 97-100
Bircham, Deric Neale 1934- 89-92
Bird, Al
See Mandel, Leon
Bird, Anthony (Cole) 1917-1974 .... 13-16R
Obituary 135
Bird, Brandon
See Evans, George Bird
and Evans, Kay Harris
Bird, C.
See Ellison, Harlan
Bird, Carmel 1940- 128
Bird, Caroline 1915- CANR-11
Earlier sketch in CA 17-20R
Bird, Cordwainer
See Ellison, Harlan
Bird, David 1926(?)-1987 Obituary 121
Bird, Dennis L(eslie) 1930- 116
Bird, Dorothy Maywood 1899- CAP-1
Earlier sketch in CA 17-18
Bird, E(lzy) J(ay) 1911- .... SATA 58
Bird, Florence (Bayard) 1908- 97-100
Bird, George L(loyd) 1900- CANR-2
Earlier sketch in CA 5-8R
Bird, Harrison K. 1910- 85-88
Bird, Isabella L.
See Bishop, Isabella Lucy (Bird)
Bird, James Harold 1923- 102
Bird, John 1941- 130
Bird, Junius Bouton 1907-1982 Obituary 106
Bird, (Cyril) Kenneth 1887-1965 .... CAP-1
Earlier sketch in CA 13-14
Bird, Lewis P(enhall) 1933- CANR-17
Earlier sketch in CA 97-100
Bird, Patricia Amy 1941- CANR-22
Earlier sketches in CA 61-64, CANR-7
Bird, Richard (Miller) 1938- CANR-19
Earlier sketches in CA 9-12R, CANR-4
Bird, Sarah McCabe 1949- 111
Bird, Veronica 1932- 112
Bird, Vivian 1910- 102
Bird, W(illiam) Ernest 1890- CAP-1
Earlier sketch in CA 19-20
Bird, Wendell R(aleigh) 116
Bird, Will R. 1891- 13-16R
Bird, William 1889-1963 Obituary 112
See also DLB 4
Birdsall, Steve 1944- CANR-7
Earlier sketch in CA 53-56
Birdsell, Joseph B(enjamin) 1908- 119
Birdsell, Sandra 1942- 130
Birdseye, Clarence (Frank)
1886-1956 Brief entry 122
Birdseye, Tom 1951- 133
See also SATA 66
Birdwell, Russell (Juarez)
1903-1977 Obituary 107
Birdwhistell, Ray L. 1918- 45-48
Bireley, Robert 1933- 137
Birenbaum, Arnold 1939- 108
Birenbaum, Barbara 1941- 136
See also SATA 65
Birenbaum, Halina 1929- 45-48
Birenbaum, Harvey 1936- 109
Birenbaum, William M. 1923- 29-32R
Birimisa, George 1924- 89-92
Birkenhead, Lord
See Smith, Frederick Winston Furneaux
Birkenmayer, Sigmund Stanley 1923- 21-24R
Birkerts, Sven 1951- 133
Brief entry 128
Birket-Smith, Kaj 1893- CAP-1
Earlier sketch in CA 13-14
Birkin, Andrew (Timothy) 1945- 97-100
Birkin, Charles (Lloyd) 1907- 69-72
Birkley, Marilyn 1916- 41-44R
Birkner, Michael John 1950- 125
Birkos, Alexander S(ergei) 1936- 25-28R
Birks, Tony 1937- CANR-12
Earlier sketch in CA 69-72
Birksted-Breen, Dana 1946- 102
Birla, Ghanshyamdas 1894-1983 Obituary 110
Birla, Lakshminiwas N. 1909- CAP-1
Earlier sketch in CA 13-14
Birley, Anthony R.
See Birley, Anthony (Richard)
Birley, Anthony (Richard) 1937- 129
Birley, Julia (Davies) 1928- 13-16R
Birley, Robert 1903-1982 Obituary 110
Birmelin, Blair T. 1939- 117
Birmingham, David (Bevis) 1938- 17-20R
Birmingham, F(rederic) A(lexander)
1911-1982 .... CANR-11
Obituary 107
Earlier sketch in CA 17-20R
Birmingham, Frances A(therton) 1920- 17-20R
Birmingham, John 1951- 45-48
Birmingham, Lloyd 1924- .... SATA 12
Birmingham, Maisie 1914- 101
Birmingham, Stephen 1932- CANR-20
Earlier sketches in CA 49-52, CANR-2
See also AITN 1
Birmingham, Walter (Barr) 1913- 17-20R
Birn, Donald S. 1937- 132
Birn, Randi (Marie) 1935- 73-76

Birn, Raymond Francis 1935- ... 102
Birnbach, Martin 1929- ... 1-4R
Birnbaum, Eleazar 1929- ... 37-40R
Birnbaum, Louis 1909-1983 ... 125
Birnbaum, Milton 1919- ... 33-36R
Birnbaum, Norman 1926- ... CANR-5
Earlier sketch in CA 53-56
Birnbaum, Philip 1904-1988 ... CANR-1
Obituary ... 125
Earlier sketch in CA 49-52
Birnbaum, Phyllis 1945- ... 102
Birnbaum, Solomon Asher
1891-1989 Obituary ... 130
Birnbaum, Stephen (Norman) 1937-1991 ... 129
Obituary ... 136
Brief entry ... 125
Birnbaum, Steve
See Birnbaum, Stephen (Norman)
Birnberg, Thomas B.
See Brooks, Thomas
Birne, Henry 1921- ... 17-20R
Birney, Alice L(otvin) 1938- ... 33-36R
Birney, (Alfred) Earle 1904- ... CANR-20
Earlier sketches in CA 1-4R, CANR-5
See also CLC 1, 4, 6, 11
See also DLB 88
See also MTCW
Birnie, Whittlesey 1945- ... 97-100
Birnkrant, Arthur 1906(?)-1983 Obituary ... 108
Biro, B.
See Biro, B(alint) S(tephen)
Biro, B(alint) S(tephen) 1921- ... CANR-39
Earlier sketches in CA 25-28R, CANR-11
See also Biro, Val
See also MAICYA
See also SATA 67
Biro, Charlotte Slovak 1904- ... 57-60
Biro, Val
See Biro, B(alint) S(tephen)
See also CLR 28
See also SAAS 13
See also SATA 1
Biro, Yvette ... 111
Birrell, Anne (Margaret) ... 130
Birrell, Augustine 1850-1933 ... DLB 98
Birren, Faber 1900- ... CANR-7
Earlier sketch in CA 13-16R
Birren, James E(mmett) 1918- ... 17-20R
Birse, A(rthur) H(erbert) 1889- ... CAP-2
Earlier sketch in CA 23-24
Birstein, Ann 1927- ... CANR-28
Earlier sketch in CA 17-20R
Birt, David 1936- ... CANR-35
Earlier sketches in CA 73-76, CANR-13
Bischof, Ledford Julius 1914- ... 9-12R
Bischoff, David F(redrick) 1951- ... 81-84
Bischoff, F(rederick) A(lexander) 1928- ... 89-92
Bischoff, Julia Bristol 1909-1970 ... CAP-2
Earlier sketch in CA 21-22
See also SATA 12
Bish, Robert L(ee) 1942- ... 53-56
Bishai, Wilson B. 1923- ... 33-36R
Bi Shang-guan
See Shen Congwen
Bisher, James F(urman) 1918- ... CANR-2
Earlier sketch in CA 5-8R
Bishin, William R(obert) 1939- ... 61-64
Bishir, John (William) 1933- ... 41-44R
Bishop, Bonnie 1943- ... 103
See also SATA 37
Bishop, Claire Huchet ... CANR-36
Earlier sketch in CA 73-76
See also MAICYA
See also SATA 14
Bishop, Crawford M. 1885- ... CAP-2
Earlier sketch in CA 17-18
Bishop, Curtis (Kent) 1912-1967 ... CAP-1
Earlier sketch in CA 11-12
See also SATA 6
Bishop, Donald
See Steward, Samuel M(orris)
Bishop, Donald G. 1907- ... CANR-3
Earlier sketch in CA 1-4R
Bishop, Donald H(arold) 1920- ... 105
Bishop, E. Morchard
See Stonor, Oliver
Bishop, Elizabeth 1911-1979 ... CANR-26
Obituary ... 89-92
Earlier sketch in CA 5-8R
See also CABS 2
See also CDALB 1968-1988
See also CLC 1, 4, 9, 13, 15, 32
See also DLB 5
See also MTCW
See also PC 3
See also SATA 24
Bishop, Eugene C. 1909-1983 Obituary ... 109
Bishop, Ferman 1922- ... 21-24R
Bishop, Gavin 1946- ... 121
Bishop, George (Victor) 1924- ... CANR-2
Earlier sketch in CA 49-52
Bishop, George W(esley) Jr. 1910- ... 13-16R
Bishop, Gordon (Bruce) 1938- ... 118
Bishop, Ian Benjamin 1927- ... 106
Bishop, Isabella Bird
See Bishop, Isabella Lucy (Bird)
Bishop, Isabella L.
See Bishop, Isabella Lucy (Bird)
Bishop, Isabella Lucy (Bird)
1831-1904 Brief entry ... 123
Bishop, James Alonzo 1907-1987 ... 17-20R
Obituary ... 123
See also Bishop, Jim
Bishop, James 1929- ... 97-100
Bishop, Jim
See Bishop, James Alonzo
See also AITN 1, 2
Bishop, John L(yman) 1913-1974 ... CAP-2
Earlier sketch in CA 33-36
Bishop, John Melville 1946- ... CANR-13
Earlier sketch in CA 77-80
Bishop, John Peale 1892-1944 Brief entry ... 107
See also DLB 4, 9, 45
Bishop, John Wesley 1927- ... 128
Bishop, John 1908- ... 65-68
Bishop, John 1935- ... 105
See also CLC 10
Bishop, Joseph W(arren) Jr. 1915-1985 ... 33-36R
Obituary ... 116
Bishop, Leonard 1922- ... 13-16R
Bishop, Lloyd (Ormond) 1933- ... 114
Bishop, Louis Faugeres 1901(?)-1986 ... 122
Obituary ... 119
Bishop, Martin
See Paine, Lauran (Bosworth)
Bishop, Maurice 1944-1983 ... 123
Obituary ... 111
See also BW
Bishop, Maxine H. 1919- ... 25-28R
Bishop, Michael 1945- ... CANR-9
Earlier sketch in CA 61-64
See also AITN 2
Bishop, Morchard
See Stonor, Oliver
Bishop, Morris 1893-1973 ... CANR-6
Obituary ... 45-48
Earlier sketch in CA 1-4R
Bishop, Mrs. J. F.
See Bishop, Isabella Lucy (Bird)
Bishop, Patrick 1952- ... 132
Bishop, Pike
See Obstfeld, Raymond
Bishop, Robert Lee 1931- ... 13-16R
Bishop, Robert 1938-1991 ... CANR-35
Obituary ... 135
Earlier sketches in CA 81-84, CANR-15
Bishop, Ron 1922(?)-1988 Obituary ... 124
Bishop, Susan M. 1921(?)-1970 Obituary ... 104
Bishop, Tania Kroitor 1906- ... CAP-2
Earlier sketch in CA 29-32
Bishop, Thomas W(alter) 1929- ... CANR-18
Earlier sketches in CA 1-4R, CANR-1
Bishop, Tom
See Bishop, Thomas W(alter)
Bishop, W(illiam) Arthur 1923- ... 21-24R
Bishop, Wendy 1953- ... 137
Bishop, William W(arner) Jr. 1906- ... 17-20R
Bishop of Marsland
See Duncan, Ronald
Bishop of Truro
See Leonard, Graham Douglas
Bisignani, J(oseph) D(aniel) 1947- ... CANR-35
Earlier sketch in CA 112
Biskin, Miriam 1920- ... 21-24R
Bisnow, Mark (C.) 1952- ... 130
Bisque, Anatole
See Bosquet, Alain
Bissell, Claude T(homas) 1916- ... 101
Bissell, Elaine ... 81-84
Bissell, LeClair 1928- ... 133
Bissell, Richard (Pike) 1913-1977 ... CANR-6
Obituary ... 69-72
Earlier sketch in CA 1-4R
Bisset, Donald 1910- ... CANR-13
Earlier sketch in CA 33-36R
See also SATA 7
Bisset, Ronald 1950- ... 103
bissett, bill 1939- ... CANR-15
Earlier sketch in CA 69-72
See also CLC 18
See also DLB 53
See also MTCW
Bissett, Donald J(ohn) 1930- ... 97-100
Bisson, Terry 1942- ... 127
Bisson, Thomas N(oel) 1931- ... 119
Bissoondath, Neil (Devindra) 1955- ... 136
Bissoondoyal, Basdeo 1906- ... CANR-11
Earlier sketch in CA 25-28R
Bisztray, George 1938- ... 106
Bita, Lili
See Zaller, Angelika Bita
Bite, Ben
See Schneck, Stephen
Bitker, Marjorie M(arks) 1901-1990 ... 77-80
Obituary ... 132
Bitov, Andrei (Georgievich) 1937- ... CLC 57
Bitsios, Dimitri S. 1915-1984 Obituary ... 111
Bittel, Lester Robert 1918- ... CANR-21
Earlier sketches in CA 13-16R, CANR-6
Bitter, Francis 1902-1967 Obituary ... 113
Bitter, Gary G(len) 1940- ... CANR-31
Earlier sketches in CA 69-72, CANR-14
See also SATA 22
Bittermann, Henry J(ohn) 1904- ... 33-36R
Bittinger, Desmond W(right) 1905- ... 37-40R
Bittinger, Emmert F(oster) 1925- ... 37-40R
Bittker, Boris I(rving) 1916- Brief entry ... 109
Bittle, William E(lmer) 1926- ... 53-56
Bittlinger, Arnold (Georg) 1928- ... CANR-31
Earlier sketch in CA 49-52
Bittner, Donald F(rancis) 1941- ... 122
Bittner, Vernon (John) 1932- ... 69-72
Bittner, William (Robert) 1921- ... 5-8R
Bitton, Davis 1930- ... CANR-31
Earlier sketches in CA 33-36R, CANR-14
Bitton, Livia Elvira
See Bitton Jackson, Livia E(lvira)
Bitton-Jackson, Livia
See Bitton Jackson, Livia E(lvira)
Bitton Jackson, Livia E(lvira) 1931- ... 130
Biven, W(illiam) Carl 1925- ... 21-24R
Bivins, John 1940- ... 85-88
Bixby, Jay Lewis
See Bixby, Jerome Lewis
Bixby, Jerome Lewis 1923- ... 17-20R
Bixby, Ray Z.
See Tralins, S(andor) Robert
Bixby, William (Courtney) 1920-1986 ... CANR-6
Obituary ... 118
Earlier sketch in CA 1-4R
See also SATA 6, 47
Bixler, Julius Seelye 1894-1985 Obituary ... 115
Bixler, Norma 1905- ... 49-52
Bixler, Paul (Howard) 1899- ... 69-72
Bixler, R(oy) Russell Jr. 1927- ... 61-64
Biyidi, Alexandre 1932- ... 124
Brief entry ... 114
See also Beti, Mongo
See also BW
See also MTCW
Bizardel, Yvon 1891- ... 61-64
Bizzarro, Salvatore 1939- ... 53-56
Bjarkman, Peter C(hristian) 1941- ... 130
Bjarme, Brynjolf
See Ibsen, Henrik (Johan)
Bjerke, Robert Alan 1939- ... 41-44R
Bjerke, Ward (Ollie) 1920- Brief entry ... 108
Bjerre, Jens 1921- ... 9-12R
Bjoerk, Christina 1938- ... 135
See also CLR 22
See also SATA 67
Bjoerneboe, Jens 1920-1976 ... CANR-28
Obituary ... 65-68
Earlier sketch in CA 69-72
Bjoernson, Bjoernstjerne (Martinius)
1832-1910 Brief entry ... 104
See also Bjornson, Bjornstjerne
and Bjornson, Bjornstjerne (Martinius)
See also TCLC 7
Bjorge, Gary J(ohn) 1940- ... 130
Bjork, Christina
See Bjoerk, Christina
Bjorkelo, Anders 1947- ... 138
Bjorklund, Lorence F. 1913-1978 ... SATA 32, 35
Bjorn, Thyra Ferre 1905-1975 ... CANR-3
Obituary ... 57-60
Earlier sketch in CA 5-8R
Bjornard, Reidar B(ernhard) 1917- ... 33-36R
Bjorneboe, Jens
See Bjoerneboe, Jens
Bjornson, Bjornstjerne
See Bjoernson, Bjoernstjerne (Martinius)
See also TCLC 37
Bjornson, Bjornstjerne (Martinius)
See Bjoernson, Bjoernstjerne (Martinius)
See also TCLC 7
Bjornson, Richard 1938- ... 77-80
Bjornson, (Kristjan) Val(dimar)
1906-1987 Obituary ... 121
Bjornstad, James 1940- ... 29-32R
Bjorset, Bryniolf
See Beorse, Bryn
Blachford, George 1913- ... 9-12R
Blachly, Frederick (Frank)
1881(?)-1975 Obituary ... 57-60
Blachly, Lou 1889- ... CAP-1
Earlier sketch in CA 13-14
Black, Albert George 1928- ... 45-48
Black, Algernon David 1900- ... CANR-2
Earlier sketch in CA 1-4R
See also SATA 12
Black, Angus 1943- ... 29-32R
Black, Antony 1936- ... 121
Black, Arthur (Raymond) 1943- ... 138
Black, Betty
See Schwartz, Betty
Black, Bonnie Lee 1945- ... 107
Black, Brady Forrest 1908- ... 102
Black, Campbell 1944- ... 89-92
Black, Charles
See Black, Charles L(und) Jr.
Black, Charles L(und) Jr. 1915- ... CANR-3
Earlier sketch in CA 1-4R
Black, Charles 1928- ... 132
Black, Clinton V(ane De Brosse)
1918- ... CANR-30
Earlier sketch in CA 102
Black, Creed C(arter) 1925- ... 73-76
Black, Cyril Edwin 1915-1989 ... CANR-3
Obituary ... 129
Earlier sketch in CA 1-4R
Black, D. M.
See Black, David (Macleod)
Black, David
See Way, Robert E(dward)
Black, David (Macleod) 1941- ... 25-28R
See also DLB 40
Black, David 1945- ... 136
Black, Dianne (a pseudonym) 1940- ... 97-100
Black, Dorothy 1899-1985 Obituary ... 115
Black, Dorothy 1914- ... CANR-30
Earlier sketch in CA 111
Black, Douglas M. 1896(?)-1977 Obituary ... 104
Black, Duncan 1908- ... CAP-2
Earlier sketch in CA 19-20
Black, E(dward) L(oring) 1915- ... 9-12R
Black, Earl 1942- ... 101
Black, Elizabeth 1908(?)-1987 Obituary ... 122
Black, Eugene C(harlton) 1927- ... 9-12R
Black, Eugene R(obert) 1898- ... CAP-2
Earlier sketch in CA 25-28
Black, Floyd H. 1888-1983 Obituary ... 111
Black, Gavin
See Wynd, Oswald Morris
Black, Hallie 1943- ... 108
Black, Harry George 1933- ... 61-64
Black, Hugh C(leon) 1920- ... 37-40R
Black, Hugo Lafayette
1886-1971 Obituary ... 33-36R
Black, Ian Stuart 1915- ... CANR-6
Earlier sketch in CA 9-12R
Black, Irma Simonton 1906-1972 ... CANR-6
Obituary ... 37-40R
Earlier sketch in CA 1-4R
See also SATA 2, 25
Black, Ishi
See Gibson, Walter B(rown)
Black, Ivan 1904(?)-1979 Obituary ... 85-88
Black, James A(llen) 1937- ... 121
Black, James Menzies 1913- ... CANR-5
Earlier sketch in CA 5-8R
Black, Jeremy (Martin) 1955- ... 136
Black, John N(icholson) 1922- ... CANR-13
Earlier sketch in CA 33-36R
Black, John Wilson 1906- ... CAP-1
Earlier sketch in CA 17-18
Black, Jonathan
See von Block, Bela W(illiam)
Black, Joseph E. 1921- ... 9-12R
Black, Kenneth Jr. 1925- ... CANR-7
Earlier sketch in CA 13-16R
Black, Kitty
See Black, Dorothy
Black, Lionel
See Barker, Dudley
Black, Maggie
See Black, Margaret K(atherine)
Black, Malcolm Charles Lamont 1928- ... 85-88
Black, Mansell
See Trevor, Elleston
Black, Margaret K(atherine) 1921- ... CANR-32
Earlier sketches in CA 29-32R, CANR-14
Black, Martha E(llen) 1901- ... 33-36R
Black, Mary (Childs) 1922- ... CANR-13
Obituary ... 137
Earlier sketch in CA 21-24R
Black, Matthew W(ilson) 1895- ... CAP-2
Earlier sketch in CA 25-28
Black, Max 1909- ... 61-64
Black, Michael (Hugo) 1928- ... 131
Black, Michael L(awrence) 1940- ... 121
Black, Millard H. 1912- ... 25-28R
Black, Misha 1910-1977 ... CAP-1
Obituary ... 133
Earlier sketch in CA 11-12
Black, Nancy B(reMiller) 1941- Brief entry ... 107
Black, Percy 1922- ... 33-36R
Black, R(obert) D(enis) Collison 1922- ... 131
Black, Robert
See Holdstock, Robert P.
Black, Robert B(ruce) 1920- ... 109
Black, Robert C(lifford) III 1914- ... 41-44R
Black, Robert 1946- ... 121
Black, Roe C(oddington) 1926- ... 89-92
Black, Shirley Temple 1928- ... BEST 89:2
Black, Stanley Warren III 1939- ... CANR-31
Earlier sketch in CA 45-48
Black, Susan Adams 1953- ... 105
See also SATA 40
Black, Theodore Michael 1919- ... 109
Black, Veronica
See Peters, Maureen
Black, William Joseph
1934(?)-1977 Obituary ... 73-76
Black, Winifred 1863-1936 ... DLB 25
Blackall, Eric Albert 1914-1989 ... 65-68
Obituary ... 130
Blackamore, Arthur 1679- ... DLB 24, 39
Blackbeard, Bill 1926- ... 97-100
Blackbourn, David 1949- ... 132
Blackburn, Alexander (Lambert) 1929- ... 97-100
See also DLBY 85
Blackburn, Barbara
See Leader, (Evelyn) Barbara (Blackburn)
Blackburn, Claire
See Altman, Linda Jacobs
Blackburn, George M. III 1950- ... 123
Blackburn, Graham (John) 1940- ... CANR-22
Earlier sketch in CA 69-72
Blackburn, John(ny) Brewton 1952- ... SATA 15
Blackburn, John (Fenwick) 1923- ... CANR-22
Earlier sketches in CA 1-4R, CANR-2
Blackburn, John O. 1929- ... 127
Blackburn, Joyce Knight 1920- ... 17-20R
See also SATA 29
Blackburn, Laurence Henry 1897- ... 57-60
Blackburn, Michael 1954- ... 118
Blackburn, Norma Davis 1914- ... 69-72
Blackburn, Norman 1904(?)-1990 Obituary ... 131
Blackburn, Paul 1926-1971 ... CANR-34
Obituary ... 33-36R
Earlier sketch in CA 81-84
See also CLC 9, 43
See also DLB 16
See also DLBY 81
Blackburn, R(obert) M(artin) 1934- ... 119
Blackburn, Robert T. 1923- ... 121
Blackburn, Robin 1940- ... 128
Blackburn, Simon 1944- ... 49-52
Blackburn, Thomas C(arl) 1936- ... CANR-22
Earlier sketch in CA 69-72
Blackburn, Thomas (Eliel Fenwick)
1916-1977 ... 73-76
Obituary ... 113
See also DLB 27
Blackburne, Kenneth (William)
1907-1980 Obituary ... 105
Blackburne, Neville Alfred Edmund 1913- ... 53-56
Black Elk 1863-1950 ... TCLC 33
Blacker, C(arlos) P(aton)
1895-1975 Obituary ... 57-60
Blacker, Carmen Elizabeth 1924- ... 9-12R
Blacker, Irwin R(obert) 1919-1985 ... CANR-3
Obituary ... 115
Earlier sketch in CA 1-4R
Blackett, Patrick (Maynard Stuart)
1897-1974 Obituary ... 49-52

Blackett, Veronica Heath 1927- 53-56
See also SATA 12
Blackey, Robert 1941- CANR-4
Earlier sketch in CA 53-56
Blackford, Charles Minor III 1898- 69-72
Blackford, Staige D(avis) 1931- 103
Blackhall, David Scott 1910- 5-8R
Blackham, Garth J. 1926- 33-36R
Blackham, H(arold) J(ohn) 1903- 21-24R
Black Hobart
See Sanders, (James) Ed(ward)
Blackie, Bruce L(othian) 1936- 57-60
Blackie, John (Ernest Haldane)
1904-1985 73-76
Obituary 116
Blackie, Pamela 1917- 103
Blacking, John (Anthony Randoll)
1928- CANR-3
Earlier sketch in CA 9-12R
Blackledge, Ethel H(ale) CANR-11
Earlier sketch in CA 21-24R
Blacklin, Malcolm
See Chambers, Aidan
Blackman, Audrey (Babette) 1907-1990(?) 109
Obituary 132
Blackman, Raymond V(ictor) B(ernard)
1910-1989 Obituary 128
Blackman, Sheldon 1935- 33-36R
Blackman, Sue Anne Batey 1948- 132
Blackman, Victor 1922- 103
Blackmer, Donald L. M. 1929- 33-36R
Black-Michaud, Jacob 1938- 61-64
Blackmon, C(harles) Robert 1925- 33-36R
Blackmon, Rosemary Barnsdall
1921(?)-1983 Obituary 111
Blackmore, Charles (David) 1957- 124
Blackmore, Dorothy S. 1914- 41-44R
Blackmore, John T(homas) 1931- CANR-15
Earlier sketch in CA 41-44R
Blackmore, Peter 1909-1984 9-12R
Obituary 114
Blackmore, R(ichard) D(oddridge)
1825-1900 Brief entry 120
See also DLB 18
See also TCLC 27
Blackmore, Robert Long 1919- 113
Blackmur, R(ichard) P(almer) 1904-1965 CAP-1
Obituary 25-28R
Earlier sketch in CA 11-12
See also CLC 2, 24
See also DLB 63
Blackoff, Edward M. 1934- 9-12R
Blackshear, Helen F(riedman) 1911- CANR-10
Earlier sketch in CA 25-28R
Blacksnake, George
See Richardson, Gladwell
Blackstock, Charity
See Torday, Ursula
Blackstock, Lee
See Torday, Ursula
Blackstock, Nelson 1944- 97-100
Blackstock, Paul W(illiam) 1913- 13-16R
Blackstock, Walter 1917- CANR-9
Earlier sketch in CA 5-8R
Blackstone, Bernard 1911-1983 69-72
Obituary 111
Blackstone, Geoffrey Vaughan 1910- CAP-1
Earlier sketch in CA 9-10
Blackstone, Harry
See Blackstone, Harry (Bouton) Jr.
Blackstone, Harry (Bouton) Jr. 1934- 114
Blackstone, Tessa Ann Vosper 1942- CANR-19
Earlier sketch in CA 102
Blackstone, William T(homas) 1931- CANR-11
Earlier sketch in CA 17-20R
Black Tarantula, The
See Acker, Kathy
Blackton, Peter
See Wilson, Lionel
Blackwelder, Bernice Fowler 1902- 1-4R
Blackwelder, Boyce W(atson)
1913-1976 17-20R
Obituary 135
Blackwelder, Jerry 1950- 122
Blackwell, Basil (Henry)
1889-1984 Obituary 112
Blackwell, Betsy Talbot
1905(?)-1985 Obituary 115
Blackwell, (Samuel) Earl (Jr.) 1913- 81-84
Blackwell, James E(dward) 1926- 133
Brief entry 114
Blackwell, Leslie 1885- 9-12R
Blackwell, Lois S. 1943- 85-88
Blackwell, (Annie) Louise 1919-1977 37-40R
Blackwell, Marilyn Johns 1948- 116
Blackwell, Muriel F(ontenot) 1929- 108
Blackwell, Richard Joseph 1929- 33-36R
Blackwell, Roger D(ale) 1940- 93-96
Blackwell, William L. 1929- 21-24R
Blackwood, Alan 1932- CANR-28
Earlier sketch in CA 110
See also SATA 70
Blackwood, Algernon (Henry)
1869-1951 Brief entry 105
See also TCLC 5
Blackwood, Andrew W(atterson) Jr.
1915- CANR-5
Earlier sketch in CA 1-4R
Blackwood, Andrew W(atterson)
1882-1966 5-8R
Obituary 103
Blackwood, Caroline 1931- CANR-32
Earlier sketch in CA 85-88
See also CLC 6, 9
See also DLB 14
See also MTCW
Blackwood, Cheryl Prewitt 1957- 108
Blackwood, Easley 1903- 115
Blackwood, George D(ouglas) 1919- 13-16R
Blackwood, James R. 1918- 21-24R
Blackwood, Paul Everett 1913- 102
Blade, Alexander
See Garrett, (Gordon) Randall (Phillip)
and Hamilton, Edmond
and Silverberg, Robert
Bladel, Roderick L(eRoy) 97-100
Bladen, Ashby 1929- 106
Bladen, V(incent) W(heeler) 1900- 61-64
Blades, Ann 1947- CANR-13
Earlier sketch in CA 77-80
See also CLR 15
See also MAICYA
See also SATA 16, 69
Blades, Brian Brewer
1906-1977 Obituary 73-76
Blades, James 1901- 65-68
Blades, Ruben 1948- 131
See also HW
Bladow, Suzanne Wilson 1937- 61-64
See also SATA 14
Blaffer, Sarah C.
See Hrdy, Sarah Blaffer
Blagden, Cyprian 1906-1962 1-4R
Blagden, David 1944- 53-56
Blagowidow, George 1923- 77-80
Blaher, Damian J(oseph) 1913- 21-24R
Blaich, Theodore Paul 1902- CAP-1
Earlier sketch in CA 13-14
Blaike, Avona
See MacIntosh, Joan
Blaikie, Robert J. 1923- 33-36R
Blaiklock, Edward Musgrave 1903- CANR-7
Earlier sketch in CA 17-20R
Blaine, James
See Avallone, Michael (Angelo, Jr)
Blaine, John
See Goodwin, Harold L(eland)
Blaine, Marge
See Blaine, Margery Kay
Blaine, Margery Kay 1937- 61-64
See also SATA 11
Blaine, Thomas R(obert) 1895- 106
Blaine, Tom R.
See Blaine, Thomas R(obert)
Blaine, William L(ee) 1931- 65-68
Blainey, Ann (Warriner) 1935- 25-28R
Blainey, Geoffrey (Norman) 1930- 25-28R
Blair
See Blair-Fish, Wallace Wilfrid
Blair, Anne Denton 1914- 110
See also SATA 46
Blair, Calvin Patton 1924- 13-16R
Blair, Carvel Hall 1924- 49-52
Blair, Charles E. 1920- 25-28R
Blair, Claude 1922- CANR-11
Earlier sketch in CA 5-8R
Blair, Clay Drewry Jr. 1925- 77-80
See also AITN 2
Blair, Cynthia 1953- 118
Blair, (Robert) Dike 1919- 9-12R
Blair, Don 1933- 65-68
Blair, Dorothy L. 1890- 114
Blair, Dorothy S(ara Greene)
1913- Brief entry 113
Blair, Edward H. 1938- CANR-7
Earlier sketch in CA 17-20R
Blair, Edward P(ayson) 1910- CANR-26
Earlier sketches in CAP-1, CA 13-14, CANR-11
Blair, Eric (Arthur) 1903-1950 132
Brief entry 104
See also Orwell, George
See also MTCW
See also SATA 29
Blair, Everetta Love 1907- CAP-2
Earlier sketch in CA 25-28
Blair, Francis Preston 1791-1876 DLB 43
Blair, Frank 1915- 93-96
Blair, George S(imms) 1924- 17-20R
Blair, Glenn Myers 1908- 5-8R
Blair, Gwenda (Linda) 1943- 125
Blair, Harry Wallace 1938- 109
Blair, Helen 1910- SATA 29
Blair, J(oseph) Allen 1913- 89-92
Blair, James 1655(?)-1743 DLB 24
Blair, Jane N(emec) 1911- 57-60
Blair, Jay 1953- SATA 45
Blair, John Durburrow 1759-1823 DLB 37
Blair, John G(eorge) 1934- 13-16R
Blair, John M(alcolm) 1914-1976 73-76
Obituary 69-72
Blair, Kay Reynolds 1942- 33-36R
Blair, Leon Borden 1917- 29-32R
Blair, Lorraine Louise
1899(?)-1984 Obituary 114
Blair, Lucile
See Yeakley, Marjory Hall
Blair, Paxton 1892-1974 Obituary 53-56
Blair, Peter Hunter
See Hunter Blair, Peter
Blair, Philip M(ark) 1928-1979 41-44R
Obituary 133
Blair, Ruth Van Ness 1912- 21-24R
See also SATA 12
Blair, Sam 1932- 53-56
Blair, Shannon
See Kaye, Marilyn
Blair, Thomas (Lucien Vincent) 1926- 106
Blair, Walter 1900- CANR-18
Earlier sketches in CA 5-8R, CANR-3
See also SATA 12
Blair, Wilfrid
See Blair-Fish, Wallace Wilfrid
Blair-Fish, Wallace Wilfrid 1889-1968 CAP-2
Earlier sketch in CA 29-32
Blais, Madeleine 1947- 104
Blais, Marie-Claire 1939- CANR-38
Earlier sketch in CA 21-24R
See also CAAS 4
See also CLC 2, 4, 6, 13, 22
See also DLB 53
See also MTCW
Blaisdell, Donald C(hristy) 1899-1988 37-40R
Obituary 126
Blaisdell, Foster W(arren) 1927- 69-72
Blaisdell, Harold F. 1914- 65-68
Blaisdell, Paul H(enry) 1908- 61-64
Blaisdell, Thomas C(harles) Jr.
1895-1988 Obituary 127
Blaise, Clark 1940- CANR-5
Earlier sketch in CA 53-56
See also CAAS 3
See also AITN 2
See also CLC 29
See also DLB 53
Blake, Alfred
See Janifer, Laurence M(ark)
Blake, Andrew
See Janifer, Laurence M(ark)
Blake, Brian 1918- 109
Blake, Bud
See Blake, Julian Watson
Blake, Christina
See Chandler, Bryn
Blake, David H(aven) 1940- 41-44R
Blake, Eubie
See Blake, James Hubert
Blake, Eugene Carson 1906-1985 Obituary 116
Blake, Fay M(ontaug) 1920- 53-56
Blake, Gary 1944- CANR-15
Earlier sketch in CA 85-88
Blake, Gerald H(enry) 1936- 124
Blake, Harlan Morse 1923- 25-28R
Blake, I(srael) George 1902- 21-24R
Blake, J. W.
See Blake, John William
Blake, James Hubert 1883-1983 Obituary 109
Blake, James 1922-1979 93-96
Obituary 85-88
Blake, Jennifer
See Maxwell, Patricia
Blake, John W.
See Blake, John William
Blake, John William 1911-1987 Obituary 122
Blake, Jon 1954- 135
Blake, Jonas
See Hardy, C. Colburn
Blake, Judith (Kincade) 1926- 1-4R
Blake, Julian Watson 1918- 65-68
Blake, Justin
See Bowen, John (Griffith)
Blake, Katherine
See Walter, Dorothy Blake
Blake, Kathleen 1944- 57-60
Blake, Kay
See Walter, Dorothy Blake
Blake, Ken
See Bulmer, (Henry) Kenneth
Blake, L(eslie) J(ames) 1913- CANR-11
Earlier sketch in CA 25-28R
Blake, Margaret
See Trimble, Barbara Margaret
Blake, Minden V(aughan) 1913- 69-72
Blake, Mindy
See Blake, Minden V(aughan)
Blake, Monica
See Muir, Marie
Blake, Nelson Manfred 1908- CANR-3
Earlier sketch in CA 1-4R
Blake, Nicholas
See Day Lewis, C(ecil)
See also DLB 77
Blake, Norman (Francis) 1934- 93-96
Blake, Olive
See Supraner, Robyn
Blake, Patricia 1933- 49-52
Blake, Patrick
See Egleton, Clive (Frederick)
Blake, Paul C. 1916- 25-28R
Blake, Peter (Jost) 1920- CANR-14
Earlier sketch in CA 65-68
Blake, Quentin (Saxby) 1932- CANR-37
Earlier sketches in CA 25-28R, CANR-11
See also MAICYA
See also SATA 9, 52
Blake, Reed H(arris) 1933- 57-60
Blake, Richard A(loysius) 1939- 93-96
Blake, Robert
See Davies, L(eslie) P(urnell)
Blake, Robert (Norman William)
1916- CANR-22
Earlier sketch in CA 9-12R
Blake, Robert R(ogers) 1918- CANR-13
Earlier sketch in CA 21-24R
Blake, Robert W(illiam) 1930- CANR-31
Earlier sketch in CA 33-36R
Blake, Robert 1949- SATA 42
Blake, Robin (James) 1948- 127
Blake, Sally
See Saunders, Jean
Blake, Sally Mirliss 1925-1986 17-20R
Obituary 118
Blake, Stephanie
See Pearl, Jacques Bain
Blake, Vanessa
See Brown, May
Blake, Walker E.
See Butterworth, W(illiam) E(dmund III)
Blake, Wendon
See Holden, Donald
Blake, William J(ames) 1894-1969 5-8R
Obituary 25-28R
Blake, William 1757-1827 CDBLB 1789-1832
See also DLB 93
See also MAICYA
See also SATA 30
See also WLC
Blakeborough, Jack Fairfax
See Fairfax-Blakeborough, John Freeman
Blakeborough, John Freeman Fairfax
See Fairfax-Blakeborough, John Freeman
Blakeley, Phyllis (Ruth) 1922- 61-64
Blakeley, Thomas J(ohn) 1931- CANR-3
Earlier sketch in CA 9-12R
Blakely, Allison 1940- 125
Blakely, Mary Kay 1948- 131
Blakely, R(obert) J(ohn) 1915- 37-40R
Blakemore, Colin (Brian) 1944- 85-88
Blakeney, Jay D.
See Chester, Deborah
Blaker, Alfred A(rthur) 1928- 65-68
Blakeslee, Alton (Lauren) 1913- 105
Blakeslee, Sandra 1943- 131
Blakeslee, Thomas R(obert) 1937- 101
Blakeston, Oswell
1907(?)-1985(?) Obituary 116
Blakey, George T. Jr. 1939- 120
Blakey, Scott 1936- 85-88
Blakey, Walker Jameson 1940- 69-72
Blakiston, Georgiana 1903- 69-72
Blakiston, Noel 1905-1984 Obituary 115
Blakney, Raymond D.
1897(?)-1970 Obituary 104
Blalock, Hubert M(orse) Jr. 1926-1991 CANR-5
Obituary 133
Earlier sketch in CA 13-16R
Blalock, Jane B. 1945- Brief entry 112
Blamires, David (Malcolm) 1936- CANR-14
Earlier sketch in CA 65-68
Blamires, Harry 1916- CANR-20
Earlier sketches in CA 9-12R, CANR-5
Blanc, Esther S. 1913- 131
See also SATA 66
Blanc, Mel 1908-1989 SATO 64
Blanc, Michel H(enri) A(mbroise) 1929- 133
Blance, Ellen 1931- CANR-7
Earlier sketch in CA 57-60
Blanch, Lesley 1907- 102
Blanch, Robert J. 1938- 21-24R
Blanch, Stuart Yarworth 1918- 106
Blanchard, Allan E(dward) 1929- 69-72
Blanchard, B(irdsall) Everard 1909- 41-44R
Blanchard, Carroll Henry Jr. 1928- 13-16R
Blanchard, Fessenden Seaver 1888-1963 5-8R
Blanchard, Howard L(awrence) 1909- 5-8R
Blanchard, J. Richard 1912- 89-92
Blanchard, Kendall A(llan) 1942- CANR-11
Earlier sketch in CA 69-72
Blanchard, Kenneth H(artley) 1939- 111
Blanchard, Nina 101
Blanchard, Paula (Barber) 1936- 81-84
Blanchard, Peter 1946- 117
Blanchard, Ralph Harrub 1890-1973 CAP-1
Earlier sketch in CA 13-14
Blanchard, William H(enry) 1922- CANR-8
Earlier sketch in CA 21-24R
Blanche, Pierre 1927- 25-28R
Blanchet, Eileen 1924- 57-60
Blanchette, Oliva 1929- 53-56
Blanchot, Maurice 1907- Brief entry 117
See also DLB 72
Blanck, Gertrude 1914- 85-88
Blanck, Jacob Nathaniel 1906-1974 CAP-1
Obituary 53-56
Earlier sketch in CA 11-12
Blanck, Rubin 1914- 25-28R
Blanckenburg, Christian Friedrich von
1744-1796 DLB 94
Blanco, Luis Anado 1903(?)-1975 Obituary 104
Blanco, Richard L(idio) 1926- 57-60
See also SATA 63
Blanco Fombona, Rufino 1874-1944 HW
Blanco White, Amber 1887-1981 Obituary 105
Bland, Alexander
See Gosling, Nigel
Bland, E.
See Nesbit, E(dith)
Bland, Edith Nesbit
See Nesbit, E(dith)
Bland, Fabian
See Nesbit, E(dith)
Bland, Hester Beth 1906- 57-60
Bland, Jeffrey 1946- 106
Bland, Jennifer
See Bowden, Jean
Bland, Larry I(rvin) 1940- 109
Bland, Randall Walton 1942- CANR-5
Earlier sketch in CA 53-56
Blanda, George (Frederick)
1927- Brief entry 114
Blandenship, Edward Gary 1943- 45-48
Blandford, Brian E(rnest) 1937- 118
Blandford, Percy William 1912- 9-12R
Blanding, Forrest H(arvey) 1917- 111
Blandino, Giovanni 1923- 21-24R
Blandy, Doug(las E.) 1951- 138
Blane, Gertrude
See Blumenthal, Gertrude
Blane, Howard T(homas) 1926- CANR-28
Earlier sketches in CA 25-28R, CANR-10
Blanford, James T. 1917- 33-36R
Blank, Blanche D(avis) 41-44R
Blank, Clarissa Mabel 1915-1965 SATA 62
Blank, George (W. II) 1945- 110
Blank, Joseph P. 1919- 93-96
Blank, Leonard 1927- CANR-12
Earlier sketch in CA 33-36R
Blank, Les 1935- 131
Blank, Sheldon H(aas) 1896- 1-4R

Blankenship, A(lbert) B. 1914- CANR-7
Earlier sketch in CA 13-16R
Blankenship, Edward Gary 1943- 45-48
Blankenship, Lela (McDowell) 1886- 5-8R
Blankenship, William D(ouglas) 1934- 33-36R
Blankfort, (Seymour) Michael 1907-1982 .... CANR-2
Obituary 107
Earlier sketch in CA 1-4R
Blanksten, George I(rving) 1917- CANR-1
Earlier sketch in CA 1-4R
Blanpied, Pamela Wharton 1937- 102
Blanshard, Brand 1892-1987 .... CANR-16
Obituary 124
Earlier sketch in CA 1-4R
Blanshard, Paul (Beecher) 1892-1980 135
Obituary 93-96
Blanton, (Martha) Catherine 1907- 1-4R
Blantz, Thomas E(dward) 1934- 111
Blanzaco, Andre C. 1934- 29-32R
Blasco Ibanez, Vicente 1867-1928 131
Brief entry 110
See also HW
See also MTCW
See also TCLC 12
Blase, Melvin G(eorge) 1933- 33-36R
Blaser, Robin (Francis) 1925- CANR-8
Earlier sketch in CA 57-60
Blaser, Werner 1924- 136
Blashford-Snell, John Nicholas 1936- CANR-19
Earlier sketch in CA 102
Blasier, (Stewart) Cole 1925- 21-24R
Blasing, Mutlu Konuk 1944- CANR-35
Earlier sketch in CA 89-92
Blasing, Randy 1943- CANR-35
Earlier sketch in CA 114
Blass, Birgit A(nnelise) 1940- 29-32R
Blass, Ron(ald J.) 1922-1984 Obituary 114
Blassingame, John W(esley) 1940- CANR-25
Earlier sketch in CA 49-52
See also BW
Blassingame, Wyatt Rainey 1909-1985 .... CANR-3
Obituary 114
Earlier sketch in CA 1-4R
See also SATA 1, 34, 41
Blatchford, Christie 1951- 73-76
Blathwayt, Jean 1918- 106
Blatt, Burton 1927- CANR-14
Earlier sketch in CA 41-44R
Blatt, Sidney J(ules) 1928- 37-40R
Blatter, Dorothy (Gertrude) 1901- CAP-1
Earlier sketch in CA 11-12
Blatty, William Peter 1928- CANR-9
Earlier sketch in CA 5-8R
See also CLC 2
Blau, Abram 1907-1979 Obituary 85-88
Blau, Eric 1921- 85-88
Blau, Francine D(ee) 1946- CANR-25
Earlier sketch in CA 106
Blau, Herbert 1926- CANR-36
Earlier sketch in CA 111
Blau, Joel 1945- 137
Blau, Joseph L(eon) 1909-1986 .... 9-12R
Obituary 121
Blau, Joshua 1919- CANR-7
Earlier sketch in CA 13-16R
Blau, Judith R. 1942- 122
Blau, Milton
See Blau, Eric
Blau, Peter M(ichael) 1918- CANR-1
Earlier sketch in CA 1-4R
Blau, Sheldon Paul 1935- 57-60
Blau, Tom 1913(?)-1984 Obituary 113
Blau, Yehoshua
See Blau, Joshua
Blau, Zena Smith 1922- CANR-1
Earlier sketch in CA 45-48
Blauer, Ettagale 1940- CANR-24
Earlier sketch in CA 103
See also SATA 49
Blaufarb, Douglas S(amuel) 1918- 85-88
Blaug, Mark 1927- CANR-16
Earlier sketches in CA 1-4R, CANR-1
Blaukopf, Herta 1924- 131
Blaukopf, Kurt 1914- Brief entry 114
Blauner, Peter 1959- 136
Blauner, Robert 1929- 17-20R
Blaushild, Babette 1927- 29-32R
Blaustein, Albert Paul 1921- CANR-19
Earlier sketches in CA 1-4R, CANR-1
Blaustein, Arthur I. 1933- CANR-10
Earlier sketch in CA 25-28R
Blaustein, Elliott H(arold) 1915- 41-44R
Blaustein, Esther 1935- 45-48
Blauw, Johannes 1912- 9-12R
Blauw, Pieter Wilhelmus 1942- 137
Blauw, Wim
See Blauw, Pieter Wilhelmus
Blaxland, John 1917- 5-8R
Blaxland, W(illiam) Gregory 1918- CANR-3
Earlier sketch in CA 9-12R
Blaylock, James P(aul) 1950- CANR-27
Earlier sketch in CA 110
Blayne, Sara
See Howl, Marcia (Yvonne Hurt)
Blayney, Margaret S(tatler) 1926- 53-56
Blayre, Christopher
See Heron-Allen, Edward
Blaze, Wayne 1951- 61-64
Blazek, Douglas 1941- 25-28R
Blazek, Ron(ald David) 1936- 111
Blazer, Dan G(erman) II 1944- 110
Blazer, J. S.
See Scott, Justin
Blazier, Kenneth D(ean) 1933- CANR-11
Earlier sketch in CA 69-72
Bleakley, David (Wylie) 1925- 102
Bleamer, Burton 1906(?)-1986 Obituary 118
Blechman, Barry M. 1943- 97-100
Blechman, Burt 1932- 21-24R
Bledlow, John
See Vale, (Henry) Edmund (Theodoric)
Bledsoe, Albert Taylor 1809-1877 .... DLB 3, 79
Bledsoe, Jerry 1941- 85-88
Bledsoe, Joseph C(ullie) 1918- 33-36R
Bledsoe, Thomas (Alexander) 1914- CANR-9
Earlier sketch in CA 13-16R
Bledsoe, William Ambrose
1906-1981 Obituary 104
Bleeck, Oliver
See Thomas, Ross (Elmore)
Bleeker, Mordecia
See Morgan, Fred Troy
Bleeker, Sonia
See Zim, Sonia Bleeker
See also SATA 2, 26
Blees, Robert A(rthur) 1922- 17-20R
Blegen, Carl (William)
1887-1971 Obituary 33-36R
Blegen, Theodore C. 1891-1969 .... CANR-3
Earlier sketch in CA 5-8R
Blegvad, Erik 1923- 97-100
See also MAICYA
See also SATA 14, 66
Blegvad, Lenore 1926- CANR-31
Earlier sketches in CA 69-72, CANR-14
See also SATA 14, 66
Blehl, Vincent Ferrer 1921- 9-12R
Bleiberg, Robert Marvin 1924- 103
Bleich, Alan R. 1913- 13-16R
Bleich, Harold 1930(?)-1980 Obituary 93-96
Bleich, J(udah) David 1936- 116
Bleicher, Michael N(athaniel) 1935- 37-40R
Bleier, Robert Patrick 1946- 85-88
Bleier, Rocky
See Bleier, Robert Patrick
Blench, J(ohn) W(heatley) 1926- 13-16R
Blend, Charles D(aniels) 1918-1971 .... 21-24R
Obituary 134
Blenkinsopp, Joseph 1927- 37-40R
Blennerhassett, Margaret Agnew
1773-1842 .... DLB 99
Bleser, Carol K. 1935- 107
Blesh, Rudi
See Blesh, Rudolph Pickett
Blesh, Rudolph Pickett 1899-1985 .... 17-20R
Obituary 117
Blessing, Lee 1949- .... CLC 54
Blessing, Richard Allen 1939- 53-56
Blessington, Francis C(harles) 1942- 130
Bletter, Robert 1933(?)-1976 Obituary 61-64
Bletter, Rosemarie Haag 1939- 57-60
Blevins, James Lowell 1936- 106
Blevins, Leon W(ilford) 1937- 57-60
Blevins, William L. 1937- 33-36R
Blevins, Winfred (Ernest Jr.) 1938- CANR-1
Earlier sketch in CA 45-48
Bleything, Dennis H(ugh) 1946- 61-64
Bleznick, Donald W(illiam) 1924- 21-24R
Blezzard, Judith 1944- 134
Blicker, Seymour 1940- 77-80
Blicq, Anthony 1926- 33-36R
Bligh, Norman
See Neubauer, William Arthur
Blight, John 1913- CANR-22
Earlier sketch in CA 69-72
Blight, Rose
See Greer, Germaine
Blinder, Alan S(tuart) 1945- CANR-32
Earlier sketch in CA 113
Blinder, Elliot 1949- 106
Blinderman, Abraham 1916- 61-64
Blinderman, Charles 1930- 135
Blinn, Johna
See Dorsey, Helen
Blinn, Keith Wayne 1917-1990 Obituary 131
Blinn, Walter Craig 1930- 61-64
Blish, James (Benjamin) 1921-1975 .... CANR-3
Obituary 57-60
Earlier sketch in CA 1-4R
See also CLC 14
See also DLB 8
See also MTCW
See also SATA 66
Blishen, Bernard Russell 1919- CANR-3
Earlier sketch in CA 1-4R
Blishen, Edward 1920- CANR-27
Earlier sketches in CA 17-20R, CANR-11
See also SATA 8, 66
Bliss, A. J.
See Bliss, Alan (Joseph)
Bliss, Alan (Joseph) 1921-1985 134
Obituary 118
Bliss, Carey S(tillman) 1914- 41-44R
Bliss, Carolyn (Jane) 1947- 128
Bliss, Corinne Demas 1947- CANR-28
Earlier sketch in CA 104
See also SATA 37
Bliss, Dorothy E(lizabeth) 1916-1987 118
Obituary 124
Bliss, Edward Jr. 1912- 41-44R
Bliss, Edwin C(rosby) 1923- 131
Bliss, George William 1918-1978 85-88
Obituary 81-84
Bliss, Lee 1943- 122
Bliss, (John) Michael 1941- CANR-31
Earlier sketch in CA 103
Bliss, Patricia Lounsbury 1929- 127
Bliss, Reginald
See Wells, H(erbert) G(eorge)
Bliss, Ronald G(ene) 1942- 53-56
See also SATA 12
Blissett, Marlan 1938- 41-44R
Blistein, Elmer M(ilton) 1920- 9-12R
Blitch, Fleming Lee
See Lee, Fleming
Blitchington, Evelyn G(rant) 1947- 114
Blits, Jan H. 1943- 110
Blitzer, Wolf 1948- 136
Blitzstein, Marc 1905-1964 Obituary 110
Bliven, Bruce Jr. 1916- CANR-7
Earlier sketch in CA 17-20R
See also SATA 2
Bliven, Bruce 1889-1977 .... 37-40R
Obituary 69-72
Bliven, Naomi 1925- 33-36R
Blixen, Karen (Christentze Dinesen)
1885-1962 .... CANR-22
Earlier sketches in CAP-2, CA 25-28
See also Dinesen, Isak
See also MTCW
See also SATA 44
Blizzard, S(amuel) W(ilson Jr.)
1914(?)-1976 Obituary 65-68
Bloch, Ariel A(lfred Karl) 1933- 41-44R
Bloch, Arthur McBride 1938- 128
Bloch, Barbara 1925- CANR-24
Earlier sketch in CA 106
Bloch, Bertram 1892-1987 Obituary 122
Bloch, Blanche 1890-1980 Obituary 97-100
Bloch, Chana Florence 1940- 105
Bloch, Dorothy 1912- 93-96
Bloch, Douglas 1949- 138
Bloch, E. Maurice 25-28R
Bloch, Ernst 1885-1977 .... CANR-34
Obituary 73-76
Earlier sketch in CA 29-32R
Bloch, Herbert A(aron David) 1904-1965 .... 1-4R
Obituary 134
Bloch, Herman D(avid) 1914- 29-32R
Bloch, Jeff(rey W.) 1959- 130
Bloch, Lucienne S(chupf) 1937- 93-96
Bloch, Lucienne 1909- .... SATA 10
Bloch, Marc 1886-1944 Brief entry 118
Bloch, Marie Halun 1910- CANR-19
Earlier sketches in CA 1-4R, CANR-4
See also SAAS 9
See also SATA 6
Bloch, Robert (Albert) 1917- CANR-5
Earlier sketch in CA 5-8R
See also CLC 33
See also DLB 44
See also SATA 12
Blocher, Henri (Arthur) 1937- CANR-10
Earlier sketch in CA 65-68
Blochman, Lawrence G(oldtree)
1900-1975 .... CAP-2
Obituary 53-56
Earlier sketch in CA 19-20
See also SATA 22
Block, Allan (Forrest) 1923- CANR-31
Earlier sketch in CA 49-52
Block, Andrew 1892-1985 Obituary 118
Block, Arthur John 1916(?)-1981 Obituary 105
Block, Eugene B. 1890- CANR-2
Earlier sketch in CA 5-8R
Block, Francesca (Lia) 1962- 131
Block, Hal 1914(?)-1981 Obituary 104
Block, Herbert (Lawrence) 1909- 111
Block, Irvin 1917- 17-20R
See also SATA 12
Block, Irving (Leonard) 1930- 118
Block, Jack 1921- 33-36R
Block, Jack 1931- 53-56
Block, Jean Libman 5-8R
Block, Joel D(avid) 1943- CANR-15
Earlier sketch in CA 89-92
Block, Julian 1934- 106
Block, Lawrence 1938- CANR-6
Earlier sketch in CA 1-4R
See also CAAS 11
Block, Libbie 1910(?)-1972 .... 33-36R
Block, Marvin Avram 1903-1989 106
Obituary 128
Block, Michael 1942- 101
Block, Ned Joel 1942- 117
Block, Paul Jr. 1911-1987 Obituary 122
Block, Ralph 1889-1974 Obituary 45-48
Block, Rudolph
See Lessing, Bruno
Block, Seymour Stanton 1918- 89-92
Block, Stanley Byron 1939- 85-88
Block, Thomas H(arris) 1945- CANR-18
Earlier sketch in CA 101
Block, Walter (Edward) 1941- CANR-22
Earlier sketches in CA 57-60, CANR-6
Block, Zenas 1916- 107
Blocker, Clyde (Edward) 1918- 33-36R
Blocker, H(arry) Gene 1937- 116
Blockinger, Betty
See Blocklinger, Peggy O'More
Blocklinger, Peggy O'More 1895- 5-8R
Blocksma, Mary 1942- 130
See also SATA 44
Blodgett, Beverley 1926- 57-60
Blodgett, E(dward) D(ickinson) 1935- 112
Blodgett, Geoffrey Thomas 1931- 17-20R
Blodgett, Harold William 1900- 13-16R
Blodgett, Harriet Eleanor 1919- 33-36R
Blodgett, Richard 1940- CANR-1
Earlier sketch in CA 49-52
Bloem, Diane Brummel 1935- CANR-16
Earlier sketch in CA 85-88
Bloesch, Donald G. 1928- 13-16R
Bloesser, Robert 1930- 37-40R
Blofeld, John (Eaton Calthorpe)
1913-1987 .... CANR-19
Obituary 123
Earlier sketches in CA 53-56, CANR-4
Blois, Marsden S(cott Jr.) 1919- 132
Blok, Alexander (Alexandrovich)
1880-1921 Brief entry 104
See also TCLC 5
Blok, Anton 1935- 97-100
Blom, Gaston E(ugene) 1920- 25-28R
Blom, Jan
See Breytenbach, Breyten
Blom, Karl Arne 1946- CANR-28
Earlier sketches in CA 69-72, CANR-11
Blom, Lynne Anne 1942- 120
Blom-Cooper, Louis Jacques 1926- 5-8R
Blond, Anthony 1928- 106
Blondal, Patricia 1926-1959 .... DLB 88
Blondel, Jean Fernand Pierre 1929- 101
Blondel, Nathalie 1960- 138
Blondell, (Rose) Joan 1906(?)-1979 115
Obituary 93-96
Blood, Bob
See Blood, Robert O(scar) Jr.
Blood, Charles Lewis 1929- 73-76
See also SATA 28
Blood, Jerome W. 1926- 9-12R
Blood, Marje 41-44R
Blood, Matthew
See Dresser, Davis
Blood, Robert O(scar) Jr. 1921- CANR-3
Earlier sketch in CA 1-4R
Bloodstone, John
See Byrne, Stuart J(ames)
Bloom, Alan (Herbert Vawser) 1906- CANR-3
Earlier sketch in CA 9-12R
Bloom, Alexander 1947- 114
Bloom, Allan (David) 1930- 131
Brief entry 125
Bloom, Claire 1931- 114
Bloom, Clive 1953- 131
Bloom, Daniel Halevi 1949- 120
Bloom, Edward A(lan) 1914- CANR-2
Earlier sketch in CA 1-4R
Bloom, Erick Franklin 1944- 57-60
Bloom, Floyd E(lliott) 1936- 120
Bloom, Freddy 1914- 101
See also SATA 37
Bloom, Gordon F. 1918- 13-16R
Bloom, Harold 1930- CANR-39
Earlier sketch in CA 13-16R
See also CLC 24
See also DLB 67
Bloom, Harry 1913(?)-1981 Obituary 104
Bloom, Herman Irving 1908- 102
Bloom, John Porter 1924- 49-52
Bloom, John 1921- 5-8R
Bloom, Ken(neth) 1949- CANR-38
Earlier sketch in CA 115
Bloom, Lillian D. 1920- CANR-11
Earlier sketch in CA 17-20R
Bloom, Lloyd .... SATA 43
Bloom, Lynn (Marie) Z(immerman)
1934- CANR-21
Earlier sketches in CA 13-16R, CANR-6
Bloom, Melvyn H(arold) 1938- 45-48
Bloom, Murray Teigh 1916- 17-20R
Bloom, Patrice 1936- 128
Bloom, Pauline 41-44R
Bloom, Robert 1930- 17-20R
Bloom, Samuel William 1921- CANR-3
Earlier sketch in CA 9-12R
Bloom, Ursula 1893-1984 .... 25-28R
Obituary 114
Blooman, Percy A. 1906- CAP-1
Earlier sketch in CA 11-12
Bloomberg, Edward (Michael) 1937- 41-44R
Bloomberg, Marty
See Bloomberg, Max Arthur
Bloomberg, Max Arthur 1938- 101
Bloomberg, Morton 1936- 53-56
Bloome, Enid P. 1925- 85-88
Bloomer, Amelia 1818-1894 .... DLB 79
Bloomer, Kent C(ress) 1935- 125
Bloomfield, Anthony John Westgate
1922- 1-4R
Bloomfield, Arthur Irving 1914- 41-44R
Bloomfield, Arthur (John) 1931- 65-68
Bloomfield, Aurelius
See Bourne, Randolph S(illiman)
Bloomfield, B(arry) C(ambray) 1931- CANR-5
Earlier sketch in CA 9-12R
Bloomfield, Harold H. 1944- CANR-9
Earlier sketch in CA 57-60
Bloomfield, Lincoln Palmer 1920- CANR-5
Earlier sketch in CA 1-4R
Bloomfield, Masse 1923- CANR-8
Earlier sketch in CA 61-64
Bloomfield, Maxwell H(erron III) 1931- 122
Brief entry 118
Bloomfield, Michaela 1966- .... SATA 70
Bloomfield, Morton W(ilfred)
1913-1987 .... CANR-2
Obituary 122
Earlier sketch in CA 5-8R
Bloomfield, Robert 1766-1823 .... DLB 93
Bloomingdale, Teresa 1930- CANR-21
Earlier sketch in CA 105
Bloomquist, Edward R. 1924- 29-32R
Bloomstein, Morris J. 1928- 25-28R
Blos, Joan W(insor) 1928- CANR-21
Earlier sketch in CA 101
See also CLR 18
See also MAICYA
See also SAAS 11
See also SATA 27, 33, 69
Blos, Peter 1904- 89-92
Bloss, F(red) Donald 1920- 53-56
Bloss, Meredith 1908-1982 Obituary 107
Blossom, Frederick A.
1878(?)-1974 Obituary 49-52
Blossom, Thomas 1912- 21-24R

Blotner, Joseph (Leo) 1923- CANR-35
Earlier sketches in CA 17-20R, CANR-13
See also AITN 1
See also DLB 111
Blotnick, Elihu 1939- 106
Blotnick, Srully (D.) 1941- 136
Brief entry 123
Blouet, Brian Walter 1936- CANR-15
Earlier sketches in CA 93-96, CANR-32
Blouet, Olwyn M(ary) 1948- 130
Blough, Glenn O(rlando) 1907- CAP-1
Earlier sketch in CA 11-12
See also SATA 1
Blough, Roger M(iles) 1904-1985 Obituary 117
Blount, Charles (Harold Clavell) 1913- 17-20R
Blount, Margaret 1924- 69-72
Blount, Roy (Alton) Jr. 1941- CANR-28
Earlier sketches in CA 53-56, CANR-10
See also CLC 38
See also MTCW
Bloustein, Edward J. 1925- 41-44R
Blow, Michael 1930- 130
Blow, Suzanne (Katherine) 1932- 45-48
Bloy, Leon 1846-1917 Brief entry 121
See also TCLC 22
Blu, Karen I(sobell) 1941- 121
Blue, Betty (Anne) 1922- CANR-1
Earlier sketch in CA 45-48
Blue, Frederick Judd 1937- 53-56
Blue, Martha Ward 1942- 104
Blue, Rose 1931- CANR-14
Earlier sketch in CA 41-44R
See also SATA 5
Blue, Vida (Rochelle) 1949- Brief entry 112
Blue, Wallace
See Kraenzel, Margaret (Powell)
Blue, Zachary
See Stine, R(obert) L(awrence)
Bluebond-Langner, Myra 1948- 81-84
Blue Cloud, Peter (Aroniawenrate) 1933- 117
Bluefarb, Samuel 1919- 37-40R
Bluemle, Andrew (Waltz) 1929- 1-4R
Blues, Elwood
See Aykroyd, Dan(iel Edward)
Bluestein, Daniel Thomas 1943- 65-68
Bluestein, Gene 1928- 81-84
Bluestone, Barry A(lan) 1944- 115
Bluestone, George 1928- CANR-1
Earlier sketch in CA 1-4R
Bluestone, Irving 1917- 136
Bluestone, Max 1926- 13-16R
Bluh, Bonnie 1926- 97-100
Bluhm, Heinz 1907- CAP-1
Earlier sketch in CA 17-18
Bluhm, William T(heodore) 1923- 13-16R
Blum, Albert A(lexander) 1924- CANR-11
Earlier sketch in CA 5-8R
Blum, Carol (Kathlyn) O'Brien 1934- CANR-17
Earlier sketch in CA 101
Blum, D. Steven 1951- 118
Blum, David 1935- 107
Blum, Eleanor 1914- 1-4R
Blum, Fred 1932- 13-16R
Blum, Harold P. 1929- 103
Blum, Henrik L(eo) 1915- CANR-6
Earlier sketch in CA 9-12R
Blum, Jerome 1913- CANR-19
Earlier sketch in CA 1-4R
Blum, John Morton 1921- CANR-2
Earlier sketch in CA 5-8R
Blum, Lawrence A. 1943- 124
Blum, Leon 1872-1950 Brief entry 119
Blum, Lucille Hollander 1904- 101
Blum, Mark E. 1937- 121
Blum, Ralph ....AITN 1
Blum, Richard H(osmer Adams) 1927- 13-16R
Blum, Shirley Neilsen 1932- 33-36R
Blum, Stella 1916-1985 97-100
Obituary 116
Blum, Virgil C(larence) 1913- 13-16R
Blum, William (Henry) 1933- 125
Blumberg, Arnold 1925- 33-36R
Blumberg, Dorothy Rose 1904- CAP-2
Earlier sketch in CA 25-28
Blumberg, Gary 1938- CANR-2
Earlier sketch in CA 45-48
Blumberg, Harry 1903- 73-76
Blumberg, Leda 1956- ....SATA 59
Blumberg, Leonard U. 1920- 101
Blumberg, Morris B. 1917- 123
Blumberg, Myrna 1932- 21-24R
Blumberg, Nathan(iel) Bernard 1922- 41-44R
Blumberg, Paul (Marvin) 1935- Brief entry 113
Blumberg, Phillip I(rvin) 1919- CANR-35
Earlier sketch in CA 101
Blumberg, Rena J(oy) 1934- 109
Blumberg, Rhoda L(ois Goldstein)
1926- CANR-30
Earlier sketches in CA 57-60, CANR-6
Blumberg, Rhoda 1917- CANR-26
Earlier sketches in CA 65-68, CANR-9
See also CLR 21
See also MAICYA
See also SATA 35, 70
Blumberg, Richard E(lliot) 1944- 113
Blumberg, Robert S(tephen) 1945- 57-60
Blumberg, Stanley A. 1912- 136
Blume, Friedrich 1893-1975 73-76
Blume, Helmut 1920- 138
Blume, Judy (Sussman) 1938- CANR-37
Earlier sketches in CA 29-32R, CANR-13
See also AAYA 3
See also CLC 12, 30
See also CLR 2, 15
See also DLB 52
See also MAICYA
See also MTCW
See also SATA 2, 31
Blumenfeld, Gerry 1906- 21-24R
Blumenfeld, Hans 1892- CAP-2
Earlier sketch in CA 21-22
Blumenfeld, Harold 1905(?)-1991 97-100
Obituary 133
Blumenfeld, Meyer 1905-1980 Obituary 97-100
Blumenfeld, Samuel L(eon) 1926- 41-44R
Blumenfeld, (F.) Yorick 1932- 25-28R
Blumenson, Martin 1918- CANR-21
Earlier sketches in CA 1-4R, CANR-4
Blumenstock, David Irving
1913-1963 Obituary 116
Blumenthal, Arthur L. 1936- 29-32R
Blumenthal, David Reuben 1938- 112
Blumenthal, Eileen (Flinder) 1948- 120
Blumenthal, Fred(erick G.)
1919(?)-1986 Obituary 118
Blumenthal, Gerda Renee 1923- 1-4R
Blumenthal, Gertrude 1907-1971 Obituary 104
See also SATA 27
Blumenthal, Henry 1911-1987 ....29-32R
Obituary 121
Blumenthal, Howard J. 1952- 136
Blumenthal, John 1949- 129
Blumenthal, L. Roy 1908-1975 Obituary 61-64
Blumenthal, Lassor Agoos 1926- 25-28R
Blumenthal, Michael C. 1949- 110
Blumenthal, Monica David 1930-1981 73-76
Obituary 103
Blumenthal, Norm 97-100
Blumenthal, Shirley 1943- 108
See also SATA 46
Blumenthal, Sidney 1909- 106
Blumenthal, Susan
See Tribich, Susan
Blumenthal, Walter Hart 1883- CAP-1
Earlier sketch in CA 11-12
Blumin, Stuart M(ack) 1940- 65-68
Bluming, Mildred G. 1919- 106
Blumrich, Josef F(ranz) 1913- 93-96
Blumrosen, Alfred W(illiam) 1928- 53-56
Blunck, Hans Friedrich 1888-1961 ....DLB 66
Blundel, Anne
See Conley, Enid Mary
Blundell, (Walter) Derek (George) 1929- 135
Blundell, Harold 1902- 101
Blunden, Caroline 1948- 132
Blunden, Edmund (Charles) 1896-1974 ......CAP-2
Obituary 45-48
Earlier sketch in CA 17-18
See also CLC 2, 56
See also DLB 20, 100
See also MTCW
Blunden, Margaret (Anne) 1939- 21-24R
Blunk, Frank M. 1897(?)-1976 Obituary 69-72
Blunsden, John (Beresford) 1930- 57-60
Blunsdon, Norman (Victor Charles)
1915-1968 ....CAP-1
Earlier sketch in CA 13-14
Blunt, Anthony (Frederick) 1907-1983 113
Obituary 109
Blunt, Don
See Booth, Edwin
Blunt, Wilfrid (Jasper Walter)
1901-1987 ....CANR-21
Obituary 121
Earlier sketches in CA 13-16R, CANR-5
Blunt, Wilfrid Scawen 1840-1922 ....DLB 19
Bluphocks, Lucien
See Seldes, Gilbert (Vivian)
Bluth, B(etty) J(ean) 1934- CANR-24
Earlier sketch in CA 106
Blutig, Eduard
See Gorey, Edward (St. John)
Bly, Amy Sprecher 1955- 126
Bly, Carol(yn) 1930- CANR-26
Earlier sketch in CA 108
Bly, Janet (Chester) 1945- 116
See also SATA 43
Bly, Nellie
See Cochrane, Elizabeth
Bly, Peter A(nthony) 1944- CANR-38
Earlier sketch in CA 116
Bly, Robert (Elwood) 1926- 5-8R
See also CLC 1, 2, 5, 10, 15, 38
See also DLB 5
See also MTCW
Bly, Robert W(ayne) 1957- 117
See also SATA 48
Bly, Stephen A(rthur) 1944- 121
See also SATA 43
Bly, Thomas J. 1918(?)-1979 Obituary 85-88
Blyn, George 1919- CANR-14
Earlier sketch in CA 37-40R
Blyth, Alan 1929- CANR-1
Earlier sketch in CA 49-52
Blyth, Chay 1940- Brief entry 110
Blyth, Estelle 1882(?)-1983 Obituary 109
Blyth, Henry 1910-1983 ....21-24R
Obituary 110
Blyth, Jeffrey 1926- 65-68
Blyth, John
See Hibbs, John
Blyth, Myrna 1939- CANR-10
Earlier sketch in CA 65-68
Blythe, (William) LeGette 1900- CANR-1
Earlier sketch in CA 1-4R
Blythe, Ronald (George) 1922- 5-8R
Blyton, Carey 1932- 49-52
See also SATA 9
Blyton, Enid (Mary) 1897-1968 ....CANR-33
Obituary 25-28R
Earlier sketch in CA 77-80
See also MAICYA
See also SATA 25
Boa, Kenneth 1945- CANR-27
Earlier sketches in CA 61-64, CANR-8
Boadella, David 1931- 53-56
Boaden, James 1762-1839 ....DLB 89
Boadt, Lawrence 1942- 114
Boak, Arthur Edward Romilly 1888-1962 ....5-8R
Boak, (Charles) Denis 1932- 13-16R
Boalch, Donald (Howard) 1914- 9-12R
Boalt, (Hans) Gunnar 1910- CANR-7
Earlier sketch in CA 57-60
Board, C(hester) Stephen 1942- 57-60
Board, Joseph B(reckinridge) Jr. 1931- 29-32R
Boardman, Arthur 1927- 61-64
Boardman, Barrington 1933- 130
Boardman, Brigid M. 1931- 129
Boardman, Charles C. 1932- 29-32R
Boardman, Eunice
See Meske, Eunice Boardman
Boardman, Fon Wyman Jr. 1911- CANR-3
Earlier sketch in CA 1-4R
See also SATA 6
Boardman, Francis 1915-1976 Obituary 69-72
Boardman, Gwenn R.
See Petersen, Gwenn Boardman
See also SATA 12
Boardman, John 1927- 101
Boardman, Michael Moore 1945- 118
Boardman, Neil S(ervis) 1907- CAP-1
Earlier sketch in CA 13-14
Boardman, Peter (David) 1950-1982 97-100
Obituary 108
Boardman, Robert (B.) 1943- 138
Boardman, Thomas Leslie
1919-1990 Obituary 131
Brief entry 111
Boardwell, Robert Lee 1926- 103
Boaretto, Claire 1947- 134
Boarino, Gerald L(ouis) 1931- 21-24R
Boarman, Patrick M(adigan) 1922- CANR-28
Earlier sketches in CA 13-16R, CANR-9
Boas, Claudio Villas
See Villas Boas, Claudio
Boas, Franz 1858-1942 Brief entry 115
Boas, Guy (Herman Sidney) 1896-1966 ....CAP-1
Earlier sketch in CA 11-12
Boas, Jacob 1943- 120
Boas, Louise Schutz 1885- 5-8R
Boas, Marie
See Hall, Marie Boas
Boas, Maurits Ignatius 1892- CANR-5
Earlier sketch in CA 1-4R
Boas, Orlando Villas
See Villas Boas, Orlando
Boase, Alan Martin 1902-1982 ....CANR-10
Obituary 108
Earlier sketch in CA 5-8R
Boase, Paul H(enshaw) 1915- 37-40R
Boase, Thomas Sherrer Ross
1898-1974 ....CAP-2
Earlier sketch in CA 23-24
Boase, Wendy 1944- 106
See also SATA 28
Boast, Philip 1952- 135
Boateng, E(rnest) A(mano) 1920- CANR-28
Earlier sketches in CA 21-24R, CANR-11
Boateng, Yaw Maurice
See Brunner, Maurice Yaw
Boatman, Don Earl 1913- 1-4R
Boatner, Mark Mayo III 1921- 21-24R
See also SATA 29
Boatright, Mody Coggin 1896-1970 ....CANR-3
Obituary 89-92
Earlier sketch in CA 5-8R
Boatwright, Howard (Leake Jr.) 1918- 53-56
Boatwright, James III 1933-1988 119
Obituary 126
Boaz, Martha (Tearosse) CANR-19
Earlier sketches in CA 9-12R, CANR-3
Boba, Imre 1919- 69-72
Bobb, Bernard E(arl) 1917- 5-8R
Bobbe, Dorothie de Bear 1905-1975 ....CAP-2
Obituary 57-60
Earlier sketch in CA 25-28
See also SATA 1, 25
Bobbitt, Philip 1948- 108
Bober, Harry 1915-1988 Obituary 125
Bober, P(hyllis) P(ray) 1920- 127
Bober, Stanley 1932- CANR-11
Earlier sketch in CA 21-24R
Bobette
See Simenon, Georges (Jacques Christian)
Bobette, Bibo
See Gugliotta, Bobette
Bobinski, George S(ylvan) 1929- 29-32R
Bobker, Lee R(obert) 1925- CANR-9
Earlier sketch in CA 53-56
Bobo, Lawrence (Douglas) 1958- 124
Bobri, Vladimir V. 1898- 105
See also Bobritsky, Vladimir
Bobritsky, Vladimir
See Bobri, Vladimir V.
See also SATA 32, 47
Bobroff, Edith
See Marks, Edith Bobroff
Bobrow, Davis Bernard 1936- CANR-7
Earlier sketch in CA 57-60
Bobrow, Edwin E. 1928- CANR-24
Earlier sketches in CA 21-24R, CANR-8
Bobrowski, Johannes 1917-1965 ....CANR-33
Earlier sketch in CA 77-80
See also DLB 75
Bobst, Elmer H(olmes) 1884-1978 122
Obituary 113
Bocca, Al
See Winter, Bevis (Peter)
Bocca, Geoffrey 1923-1983 Obituary 110
Boccaccio, Giovanni 1313-1375 ....SSC 10
Bochco, Steven 1943- 138
Brief entry 124
See also CLC 35
Bochenski, Innocentius M.
See Bochenski, Joseph M.
Bochenski, Joseph M. 1902- CANR-7
Earlier sketch in CA 5-8R
Bochin, Hal W(illiam) 1942- 137
Bochner, Salomon 1899- 41-44R
Bochroch, Albert R(obert) 1909- CANR-39
Earlier sketch in CA 111
Bock, Alan W(illiam) 1943- 41-44R
Bock, Carl H(einz) 1930- CAP-2
Earlier sketch in CA 19-20
Bock, Fred 1939- CANR-10
Earlier sketch in CA 25-28R
Bock, Frederick 1916- 9-12R
Bock, Gisela 1942- 138
Bock, Hal
See Bock, Harold I.
Bock, Harold I. 1939- 29-32R
See also SATA 10
Bock, Joanne 1940- 57-60
Bock, Paul J(ohn) 1922- 53-56
Bock, Philip K. 1934- CANR-11
Earlier sketch in CA 25-28R
Bock, William Sauts Netamux'we
1939- ....SATA 14
Bockelman, Wilfred 1920- 37-40R
Bockl, George 1909- 61-64
Bockle, Franz
See Boeckle, Franz
Bockmon, Guy Alan 1926- 5-8R
Bockstoce, John R(oberts) 1944- 121
Bockus, H(erman) William 1915- 53-56
Bocock, Robert (James) 1940- CANR-28
Earlier sketches in CA 69-72, CANR-12
Boczek, Boleslaw Adam 1922- CANR-4
Earlier sketch in CA 1-4R
Bod, Peter
See Vesenyi, Paul E.
Bodansky, Oscar 1901-1977 Obituary 73-76
Bodard, Lucien (Albert) 1914- Brief entry 116
Bodart, Joni
See Bodart-Talbot, Joni
Bodart-Talbot, Joni 1947- CANR-23
Earlier sketch in CA 106
Boddewyn, J(ean) J. 1929- CANR-39
Earlier sketches in CA 25-28R, CANR-17
Boddie, Charles Emerson 1911- 65-68
Boddington, Craig Thornton 1952- CANR-28
Earlier sketch in CA 111
Boddy, David 1940- 119
Boddy, Frederick A(rthur) 1914- 61-64
Boddy, Janice 1951- 134
Boddy, William Charles 1913- 101
Bode, Carl 1911- CANR-20
Earlier sketches in CA 1-4R, CANR-3
Bode, Elroy 1931- CANR-10
Earlier sketch in CA 25-28R
Bode, Janet 1943- CANR-12
Earlier sketch in CA 69-72
See also SATA 60
Bode, Roy E. 1948- 77-80
Bodecker, N(iels) M(ogens) 1922-1988 ....CANR-4
Obituary 124
Earlier sketch in CA 49-52
See also MAICYA
See also SATA 8, 54
Bodeen, DeWitt 1908-1988 ....CANR-10
Obituary 125
Earlier sketch in CA 25-28R
Bodell, Mary
See Pecsok, Mary Bodell
Bodelsen, Anders 1937- 128
Boden, Hilda
See Bodenham, Hilda Morris
Boden, Margaret A. 1936- 93-96
Bodenham, Hilda Morris 1901- CANR-6
Earlier sketch in CA 9-12R
See also SATA 13
Bodenheim, Maxwell 1892-1954 Brief entry 110
See also DLB 9, 45
See also TCLC 44
Bodenheimer, Edgar 1908- CANR-20
Earlier sketch in CA 33-36R
Bodet, Jaime Torres
See Torres Bodet, Jaime
Bodett, Thomas Edward 1955- 123
See also Bodett, Tom
Bodett, Tom
See Bodett, Thomas Edward
See also SATA 70
Bodey, Donald 1946- 128
Bodey, Hugh (Arthur) 1939- CANR-12
Earlier sketch in CA 61-64
Bodger, Joan
See Mercer, Joan Bodger
Bodian, Nat G. 1921- CANR-20
Earlier sketch in CA 103
Bodie, Idella F(allaw) 1925- 41-44R
See also SATA 12
Bodin, Paul 1909- 65-68
Bodine, Eunice
See Lapp, Eunice Willis Bodine
Bodington, Nancy H(ermione) 1912- 53-56
Bodington, Stephen 1909- 123

Bodker, Cecil 1927- ... CANR-13
Earlier sketch in CA 73-76
See also CLC 21
See also CLR 23
See also MAICYA
See also SATA 14
Bodkin, Cora 1944- ... 69-72
Bodkin, M(atthias) M'Donnell
1850-1933 Brief entry ... 114
See also DLB 70
Bodkin, Maud 1875- ... CAP-1
Earlier sketch in CA 11-12
Bodkin, Ronald G(eorge) 1936- ... 33-36R
Bodle, Yvonne Gallegos 1939- ... 33-36R
Bodley, Hal
See Bodley, Harley Ryan Jr.
Bodley, Harley Ryan Jr. 1936- ... 126
Bodmer, Johann Jakob 1698-1783 ... DLB 97
Bodmer, Walter Fred 1936- ... 102
Bodmershof, Imma von 1895-1982 ... DLB 85
Bodnar, John Edward 1944- ... 110
Bodo, Murray 1937- ... CANR-23
Earlier sketches in CA 57-60, CANR-7
Bodo, Peter T. 1949- ... 85-88
Bodoh, John J(ames) 1931- ... 45-48
Bodsworth, (Charles) Fred(erick)
1918- ... CANR-3
Earlier sketch in CA 1-4R
See also DLB 68
See also SATA 27
Bodwell, Richard
See Spring, Gerald M(ax)
Boeckle, Franz 1921- ... 101
Boeckman, Charles 1920- ... 13-16R
See also SATA 12
Boeckman, Patti ... CANR-28
Earlier sketch in CA 109
Boege, Ulrich Gustav 1940- ... 97-100
Boegehold, Betty (Doyle) 1913-1985 ... CANR-12
Obituary ... 115
Earlier sketch in CA 69-72
See also SATA 42
Boegner, Marc 1881-1970 Obituary ... 29-32R
Boehlke, Frederick J(ohn) Jr. 1926- ... 21-24R
Boehlke, Robert R(ichard) 1925- ... 5-8R
Boehlow, Robert H(enry) 1925- ... 53-56
Boehm, Christopher 1937- ... 121
Boehm, Eric H. 1918- ... 13-16R
Boehm, Herb
See Varley, John (Herbert)
Boehm, Karl 1894-1981 Obituary ... 105
Boehm, Sydney 1908- ... DLB 44
Boehm, William D(ryden) 1946- ... 61-64
Boehme, Lillian R.
See Rodberg, Lillian
Boehning, W. R.
See Bohning, W(olf) R(uediger)
Boehringer, Robert
1885(?)-1974 Obituary ... 53-56
Boelcke, Willi A(lfred) 1929- Brief entry ... 107
Boelen, Bernard J(acques) 1916- ... 41-44R
Boell, Heinrich (Theodor) 1917-1985 ... CANR-24
Obituary ... 116
Earlier sketch in CA 21-24R
See also Boll, Heinrich (Theodor)
See also CLC 2, 3, 6, 9, 11, 15, 27, 39
See also DLB 69
See also DLBY 85
See also MTCW
Boeman, John (Sigler) 1923- ... 108
Boer, Charles 1939- ... 69-72
See also DLB 5
Boer, Harry R(einier) 1913- ... CANR-4
Earlier sketch in CA 1-4R
Boerne, Ludwig 1786-1837 ... DLB 90
Boers, Arthur Paul 1957- ... 138
Boesch, Hans Heinrich
1911-1978 Obituary ... 116
Boesch, Mark J(oseph) 1917- ... 21-24R
See also SATA 12
Boesel, David 1938- ... 41-44R
Boesen, Victor 1908- ... 37-40R
See also SATA 16
Boesiger, Willi 1904- ... 102
Boessenecker, John 1953- ... 138
Boeth, Richard 1933-1982 Obituary ... 107
Boethius 480 (?)-524 (?) ... DLB 115
Boethius of Dacia 1240(?)- ... DLB 115
Boetie, Dugmore 1920(?)-1966 Obituary ... 109
Boettcher, Henry J. 1893- ... CAP-1
Earlier sketch in CA 19-20
Boettcher, Robert B.
1941(?)-1984 Obituary ... 112
Boettcher, Thomas D. 1944- ... 129
Boettinger, Henry M(aurice) 1924- ... 73-76
Boeve, Edgar G. 1929- ... 21-24R
Boewe, Charles (Ernst) 1924- ... 9-12R
Boff, Vic 1915- ... 103
Boffey, David Barnes 1945- ... 110
Bogaduck
See Lindsay, Harold Arthur
Bogan, James 1945- ... 103
Bogan, Louise 1897-1970 ... CANR-33
Obituary ... 25-28R
Earlier sketch in CA 73-76
See also CLC 4, 39, 46
See also DLB 45
See also MTCW
Bogard, Travis (Miller) 1918- ... 69-72
Bogarde, Dirk
See
Van Den Bogarde, Derek Jules Gaspard Ulric Niven
See also CLC 19
See also DLB 14
Bogardus, Emory Stephen
1882-1973 Obituary ... 116
Bogart, Carlotta 1929- ... 61-64
Bogart, E. A.
See Bogart, Eleanor A(nne)
Bogart, Eleanor A(nne) 1928- ... 137
Bogart, Leo 1921- ... CANR-14
Earlier sketch in CA 41-44R
Bogat, Shatan
See Kacew, Romain
Bogatyryov, Konstantin
1924(?)-1976 Obituary ... 65-68
Bogdan, Robert 1941- ... 128
Bogdanor, Vernon 1943- ... CANR-35
Earlier sketches in CA 81-84, CANR-14
Bogdanov, Michael 1938- ... 129
Bogdanovich, Peter 1939- ... CANR-21
Earlier sketch in CA 5-8R
Bogen, James Benjamin 1935- ... 89-92
Bogen, Laurel Ann 1950- ... CANR-35
Earlier sketch in CA 112
Bogen, Nancy R(uth) 1932- ... 97-100
Boger, Louise Ade 1909- Brief entry ... 115
Bogert, L(otta) Jean 1888-1970 ... CAP-1
Earlier sketch in CA 11-12
Boggan, E(lton) Carrington 1943- ... 101
Boggess, Louise Bradford 1912- ... CANR-28
Earlier sketches in CA 13-16R, CANR-7
Boggs, Bill
See Boggs, William III
Boggs, James 1919- ... 77-80
Boggs, Jean Sutherland 1922- ... 108
Boggs, Marcus 1947- ... 108
Boggs, Ralph Steele 1901- ... CAP-1
Earlier sketch in CA 11-12
See also SATA 7
Boggs, W(ilmot) Arthur 1916- ... 17-20R
Boggs, Wade Hamilton Jr. 1916- ... 13-16R
Boggs, William III 1942- ... 102
Bogin, George 1920- ... 104
Bogin, Ruth 1920- ... 122
Bogle, Donald ... AITN 1
Bogner, Norman 1935- ... CANR-15
Earlier sketch in CA 5-8R
See also AITN 2
Bogomolny, Robert L(ee) 1938- ... 121
Bogosian, Eric 1953- ... 138
See also CLC 45
Bogoslovsky, Christina Stael
1888(?)-1974 Obituary ... 49-52
Bograd, Larry 1953- ... 93-96
See also CLC 35
See also SATA 33
Bogue, Allan G(eorge Britton) 1921- ... 107
Bogue, Jesse C. 1912(?)-1983 Obituary ... 111
Bogue, Lucile 1911- ... CANR-13
Earlier sketch in CA 37-40R
Bogue, Merwyn (Alton) 1908- ... 131
Boguslaw, Robert 1919- ... 132
Boguslawski, Dorothy Beers
1911(?)-1978 Obituary ... 77-80
Bohan, Peter ... 33-36R
Bohana, Aileen Stein 1951- ... 103
Bohannan, Paul (James) 1920- ... 9-12R
Bohdal, Susi 1951- ... 97-100
See also SATA 22
Bohem, Endre 1901(?)-1990 Obituary ... 131
Bohen, Halcyone H(arger) 1937- ... 108
Bohen, Sister Marian 1930- ... 5-8R
Bohi, Charles W(esley) 1940- ... 89-92
Bohi, M. Janette 1927- ... 25-28R
Bohlander, Jill 1936- ... 37-40R
Bohle, Bruce 1918- ... CANR-9
Earlier sketch in CA 21-24R
Bohle, Edgar (Henry) 1909- ... 1-4R
Bohlen, Charles Eustis 1904-1974 Obituary ... 111
Bohlen, Joe M(erl) 1919- ... 5-8R
Bohlen, Nina 1931- ... SATA 58
Bohlke, L(andall) Brent 1942-1987 ... 124
Bohlman, (Mary) Edna McCaull 1897- ... CAP-1
Earlier sketch in CA 9-10
Bohlman, Herbert W(illiam) 1896- ... CAP-1
Earlier sketch in CA 19-20
Bohn, Frank 1878-1975 Obituary ... 57-60
Bohn, Joyce Illig 1940(?)-1976 Obituary ... 69-72
Bohn, Martin J(ohn) Jr. 1938- ... 116
Bohn, Ralph C. 1930- ... CANR-11
Earlier sketch in CA 17-20R
Bohner, Charles (Henry) 1927- ... 118
See also SATA 62
Bohnet, Michael 1937- ... 102
Bohning, W(olf) R(uediger) 1942- ... 111
Bohnstedt, John W(olfgang) 1927- ... 33-36R
Bohr, Niels (Henrik David)
1885-1962 Obituary ... 112
Bohr, R(ussell) L(eRoi) 1916- ... 25-28R
Bohr, Theophilus
See Thistle, Mel(ville William)
Bohren, Craig F. 1940- ... 128
Bohrnstedt, George W(illiam) 1938- ... CANR-20
Earlier sketch in CA 33-36R
Bohrod, Aaron 1907- ... 21-24R
Boice, James Montgomery 1938- ... CANR-28
Earlier sketches in CA 29-32R, CANR-12
Boie, Heinrich Christian 1744-1806 ... DLB 94
Boiko, Claire Taylor 1925- ... 93-96
Boiles, Charles Lafayette (Jr.) 1932- ... 65-68
Boime, Albert 1933- ... 125
Bois, J(oseph) Samuel 1892- ... 33-36R
Boisgilbert, Edmund
See Donnelly, Ignatius
Boissard, Janine 1932- ... SATA 59
Boisset, Caroline 1955- ... 134
Boissevain, Jeremy 1928- ... CANR-21
Earlier sketches in CA 57-60, CANR-6
Boissiere, Robert 1914- ... 119
Boissoneau, Robert 1937- ... 105
Boissonneau, Alice ... 101
Boitani, Piero 1947- ... 137
Bok, Bart J(an) 1906-1983 ... CANR-30
Obituary ... 110
Earlier sketch in CA 49-52
Bok, Cary W(illiam) 1905-1970 Obituary ... 29-32R
Bok, Derek Curtis 1930- ... 106
Bok, Edward W. 1863-1930 ... DLB 91
Bok, Priscilla F(airfield) 1896- ... 49-52
Bok, Sissela Ann 1934- ... CANR-32
Earlier sketch in CA 112
Bokenkotter, Thomas 1924- ... CANR-17
Earlier sketch in CA 85-88
Bokser, Ben Zion 1907-1984 ... CANR-11
Obituary ... 111
Earlier sketch in CA 65-68
Bokum, Fanny Butcher 1888-1987 ... 37-40R
Obituary ... 122
Bokun, Branko 1920- ... 45-48
Boland, Bridget 1913-1988 ... 101
Obituary ... 124
Boland, Charles Michael 1917- ... 9-12R
Boland, Daniel 1891- ... CAP-1
Earlier sketch in CA 13-14
Boland, Eavan 1944- ... CLC 40, 67
See also DLB 40
Boland, (Bertram) John 1913-1976 ... CANR-10
Earlier sketch in CA 9-12R
Boland, Lillian C(anon) 1919- ... 29-32R
Bolch, Ben W(ilsman) 1938- ... 57-60
Bolcom, William E(lden) 1938- ... 93-96
Bold, Alan Norman 1943- ... CANR-30
Earlier sketch in CA 25-28R
Bolding, Amy 1910- ... 73-76
Boldizsar, Ivan 1912-1988 Obituary ... 127
Boldt, Menno 1930- ... 120
Bolen, Jean Shinoda 1936- ... 110
Boles, Donald Edward 1926- ... CANR-18
Earlier sketch in CA 1-4R
Boles, Harold W(ilson) 1915- ... 17-20R
Boles, John B. 1943- ... CANR-14
Earlier sketch in CA 37-40R
Boles, Paul Darcy 1916-1984 ... CANR-4
Obituary ... 112
Earlier sketch in CA 9-12R
See also SATA 9, 38
Bolgan, Anne C(atherine) 1923-1992(?) ... 41-44R
Obituary ... 136
Bolgar, (Caius Coriolanus) R(obert) R(alph)
1913-1985 Obituary ... 117
Bolger, Philip C(unningham) 1927- ... CANR-6
Earlier sketch in CA 57-60
Bolian, Polly 1925- ... 33-36R
See also SATA 4
Bolin, Luis (A.) 1894-1969 ... CAP-2
Earlier sketch in CA 23-24
Boling, Katharine (Singleton) 1933- ... 57-60
Bolingbroke, Viscount
See St. John, Henry
Bolinger, Dwight (L.) 1907- ... CANR-7
Obituary ... 137
Earlier sketch in CA 13-16R
Bolino, August C(onstantino) 1922- ... CANR-18
Earlier sketch in CA 1-4R
Bolitho, Archie A(rdella) 1886- ... CAP-1
Earlier sketch in CA 9-10
Bolitho, Harold 1939- ... 103
Bolitho, (Henry) Hector 1897-1974 ... CAP-1
Obituary ... 53-56
Earlier sketch in CA 9-10
Bolitho, Ray D.
See Blair, Dorothy S(ara Greene)
Bolkhovitinov, Nikolai Nikolaevich 1930- ... 97-100
Bolkosky, Sidney M(arvin) 1944- ... 65-68
Boll, Carl R. 1894- ... CAP-1
Earlier sketch in CA 17-18
Boll, David 1931- ... 21-24R
Boll, Ernest
See Boll, Theophilus E(rnest) M(artin)
Boll, Heinrich (Theodor) 1917-1985
See Boell, Heinrich (Theodor)
See also CLC 2, 3, 6, 9, 11, 15, 27, 39, 72
See also DLB 69
See also DLBY 85
See also WLC
Boll, Theo
See Boll, Theophilus E(rnest) M(artin)
Boll, Theophilus E(rnest) M(artin) 1902- ... 37-40R
Bolland, O(rlando) Nigel 1943- ... 110
Bolle, Kees W. 1927- ... CANR-17
Earlier sketch in CA 25-28R
Bollen, Roger 1942(?)- ... AITN 1
See also SATA 29
Bollens, John C(onstantinus)
1920-1983 ... CANR-3
Obituary ... 111
Earlier sketch in CA 1-4R
Boller, Paul Franklin Jr. 1916- ... CANR-19
Earlier sketches in CA 1-4R, CANR-3
Bolles, (Edmund) Blair 1911-1990 ... 9-12R
Obituary ... 130
Bolles, Donald F. 1928-1976 ... 73-76
Obituary ... 65-68
Bolles, Richard Nelson 1927- ... CANR-1
Earlier sketch in CA 45-48
Bolles, Robert C(harles) 1928- ... 21-24R
Bollettieri, Nick J(ames) 1931- ... 110
Bolliger, Max 1929- ... 25-28R
See also SATA 7
Bolling, Hal
See Schwalberg, Carol(yn Ernestine Stein)
Bolling, Richard (Walker) 1916-1991 ... 17-20R
Obituary ... 134
Bolling, Robert 1738-1775 ... DLB 31
Bollinger, Lee C. 1946- ... 138
Bolloten, Burnett 1909-1987 ... 93-96
Obituary ... 123
Bolman, Frederick deWolfe Jr.
1912-1985 Obituary ... 117
Bolner, James (Jerome) 1936- ... 61-64
Bologna, Joseph ... 77-80
Bolognese, Don
See Bolognese, Donald Alan
See also SATA 71
Bolognese, Donald Alan 1934- ... 97-100
See also Bolognese, Don
See also MAICYA
See also SATA 24, 70
Bolognese, Elaine Raphael (Chionchio)
1933- ... 97-100
See also Raphael, Elaine
Bolotowsky, Ilya 1907-1981 Obituary ... 108
Bolshakoff, Serge 1901- ... 93-96
Bolster, John 1910-1984 ... 89-92
Obituary ... 111
Bolsterli, Margaret Jones 1931- ... 111
Bolt, Bruce A(lan) 1930- ... CANR-10
Earlier sketch in CA 65-68
Bolt, Carol 1941- ... 101
See also DLB 60
Bolt, David (Michael) Langstone 1927- ... CANR-6
Earlier sketch in CA 1-4R
Bolt, Ernest C(ollier) Jr. 1936- ... 77-80
Bolt, Lee
See Faust, Frederick (Shiller)
Bolt, Martin 1944- ... 118
Bolt, Robert (Oxton) 1924- ... CANR-35
Earlier sketch in CA 17-20R
See also CLC 14
See also DLB 13
See also MTCW
Bolten, Steven E. 1941- ... 37-40R
Boltho, Andrea 1939- ... 69-72
Bolton, Carole 1926- ... CANR-1
Earlier sketch in CA 49-52
See also SATA 6
Bolton, Edmund 1575(?)-1633(?) ... DLB 121
Bolton, Elizabeth
See St. John, Nicole
Bolton, Evelyn
See Bunting, Anne Evelyn
Bolton, Guy (Reginald) 1884-1979 ... 5-8R
Obituary ... 89-92
Bolton, H(arold) Philip 1944- ... 127
Bolton, Herbert E. 1870-1953 ... DLB 17
Bolton, Isabel
See Miller, Mary Britton
Bolton, James 1917(?)-1981 Obituary ... 103
Bolton, John Robert 1948- ... 115
Bolton, Kenneth (Ewart) 1914- ... 9-12R
Bolton, Maisie Sharman 1915- ... 9-12R
Bolton, Muriel Roy 1909(?)-1983 Obituary ... 109
Bolton, Theodore 1889(?)-1973 Obituary ... 45-48
Bolton, W(hitney) F(rench) 1930- ... 17-20R
Bolton, Whitney 1900-1969 Obituary ... 25-28R
Bolus, James Michael 1943- ... 111
Bolus, Jim
See Bolus, James Michael
Bolz, Frank A. Jr. 1930- ... 127
Boman, Thorleif Gustav 1894- ... 21-24R
Bomans, Godfried J(an) A(rnold)
1913-1971 ... CAP-2
Earlier sketch in CA 29-32
Bomar, Cora Paul 1913- ... 41-44R
Bombal, Maria Luisa 1910-1980 ... 127
See also HW
Bombardieri, Merle 1949- ... 107
Bombeck, Erma (Louise) 1927- ... CANR-39
Earlier sketches in CA 21-24R, CANR-12
See also AITN 1
See also BEST 89:4
See also MTCW
Bombelles, Joseph T. 1930- ... 25-28R
Bomeli, Edwin C(larence) 1920- ... 21-24R
Bomkauf
See Kaufman, Bob (Garnell)
Bommarito, James W. 1922- ... 121
Bona, Mercy
See Ziegler, Alan
Bonachea, E(nrique) Rolando 1943- ... 41-44R
Bonacich, Edna 1940- ... 45-48
Bonanno, Margaret Wander 1950- ... 85-88
Bonansea, Bernardino M(aria) 1908- ... CANR-14
Earlier sketch in CA 41-44R
Bonaparte, Felicia 1937- ... CANR-11
Earlier sketch in CA 61-64
Bonar, Veronica
See Bailey, Donna (Veronica Anne)
Bonatti, Walter 1930- ... CANR-23
Earlier sketch in CA 106
Bonaventura ... DLB 90
Bonaventure 1217(?)-1274 ... DLB 115
Bonavia, David Michael 1940-1988 ... 106
Obituary ... 126
Bonavia-Hunt, Noel Aubrey 1882-1965 ... CAP-1
Earlier sketch in CA 9-10
Bonbright, James C(ummings) 1891-1985 ... 1-4R
Obituary ... 117
Bond, Alma H(albert) 1923- ... 130
Bond, B. J.
See Heneghan, James
Bond, Brian 1936- ... CANR-6
Earlier sketch in CA 57-60
Bond, Bruce 1939- ... SATA 61
Bond, Charles R(ankin) Jr. 1915- ... 124
Bond, Christopher Godfrey 1945- ... 101
Bond, Donald F(rederic) 1898-1987 ... 13-16R
Obituary ... 121
Bond, Douglas Danford
1911-1976 Obituary ... 69-72
Bond, E(dward) J(arvis) 1930- ... 114
Bond, Edward 1934- ... CANR-38
Earlier sketch in CA 25-28R
See also CLC 4, 6, 13, 23
See also DLB 13
See also MTCW

Bond, Elaine 1924-1984 Obituary 112
Bond, Evelyn
See Hershman, Morris
Bond, Felicia 1954- 127
See also SATA 49
Bond, Geoffrey 1924-1978 ....29-32R
Obituary 134
Bond, Gladys Baker 1912- CANR-2
Earlier sketch in CA 5-8R
See also SATA 14
Bond, Harold 1939- CANR-11
Earlier sketch in CA 65-68
Bond, Horace Mann 1904-1972 ....CANR-1
Obituary 37-40R
Earlier sketch in CA 1-4R
Bond, J. Harvey
See Winterbotham, R(ussell) R(obert)
Bond, James 1900-1989 Obituary 127
Bond, Jean Carey 106
Bond, Julian 1940- 49-52
See also BW
Bond, Lewis H.
See Paine, Lauran (Bosworth)
Bond, Marshall Jr. 1908- CAP-2
Earlier sketch in CA 25-28
Bond, Mary Fanning Wickham 1898- 21-24R
Bond, Maurice Francis 1916-1983 Obituary 111
Bond, (Thomas) Michael 1926- CANR-24
Earlier sketches in CA 5-8R, CANR-4
See also CLR 1
See also MAICYA
See also SAAS 3
See also SATA 6, 58
Bond, Mrs. James
See Bond, Mary Fanning Wickham
Bond, Nancy (Barbara) 1945- CANR-36
Earlier sketches in CA 65-68, CANR-9
See also CLR 11
See also MAICYA
See also SAAS 13
See also SATA 22
Bond, Nelson S(lade) 1908- CAP-1
Earlier sketch in CA 19-20
Bond, Otto F(erdinand) 1885- 1-4R
Bond, Ray
See Smith, Richard Rein
Bond, Raymond T. 1893(?)-1981 Obituary 104
Bond, Richmond Pugh 1899- CAP-2
Earlier sketch in CA 33-36
Bond, Ruskin 1934- CANR-31
Earlier sketches in CA 29-32R, CANR-14
See also SATA 14
Bond, Simon 1947- 104
Bond, Ted
See Bond, E(dward) J(arvis)
Bond, William Henry 1915- 124
Bond, William J(oseph) 1941- CANR-26
Earlier sketch in CA 108
Bondanella, Peter Eugene 1943- CANR-29
Earlier sketches in CA 65-68, CANR-10
Bonderoff, Jason (Dennis) 1946- 97-100
Bondi, Joseph C. 1936- CANR-28
Earlier sketches in CA 29-32R, CANR-11
Bondurant, Joan V(alerie) 1918- 41-44R
Bondy, Sebastian Salazar
See Salazar Bondy, Sebastian
Bone, Edith 1889(?)-1975 Obituary 57-60
Bone, Hugh A(lvin) 1909- CANR-3
Earlier sketch in CA 1-4R
Bone, Jesse F. 1916- 57-60
Bone, Quentin 1918- 85-88
Bone, Robert (Adamson) 1924- 69-72
Bone, Robert C(larke) 1917- 37-40R
Bonehill, Captain Ralph
See Stratemeyer, Edward L.
Bonelli, Robert Allen 1950- 112
Bonellie, Helen-Janet 1937- 41-44R
Bones, James C. Jr. 1943- 125
Bones, Jim Jr.
See Bones, James C. Jr.
Boness, A. James 1928- 37-40R
Bonestell, Chesley 1888-1986 Obituary 119
See also SATA 48
Bonett, Emery
See Coulson, Felicity Carter
Bonett, John
See Coulson, John H(ubert) A(rthur)
Bonetti, Edward 1928- 93-96
Bonewits, Isaac
See Bonewits, P(hilip) E(mmons) I(saac)
Bonewits, P(hilip) E(mmons) I(saac)
1949- 93-96
Boney, Elaine E(mesette) 1921- Brief entry 110
Boney, F(rancis) N(ash) 1929- CANR-15
Earlier sketch in CA 41-44R
Boney, Mary Lily
See Sheats, Mary Boney
Boney, William Jerry 1930- 21-24R
Bonfante, Larissa CANR-11
Earlier sketch in CA 69-72
Bongar, Emmet W(ald) 1919- 33-36R
Bongartz, Heinz
See Thorwald, Juergen
Bongartz, Roy 1924-1989 ....13-16R
Obituary 128
Bongie, Laurence L(ouis) 1929- 61-64
Bonham, Barbara Thomas 1926- CANR-7
Earlier sketch in CA 17-20R
See also SATA 7
Bonham, Frank 1914-1989 ....CANR-36
Earlier sketches in CA 9-12R, CANR-4
See also AAYA 1
See also CLC 12
See also MAICYA
See also SAAS 3
See also SATA 1, 49, 62
Bonham-Carter, Victor 1913- 9-12R
Bonham Carter, (Helen) Violet (Asquith)
1887-1969 ....CAP-2
Earlier sketch in CA 17-18
Bonheim, Helmut 1930- CANR-4
Earlier sketch in CA 1-4R
Bonhoeffer, Dietrich 1906-1945 Brief entry 122
Bonhomme, Denise 1926- 104
Boni, Albert 1892-1981 65-68
Obituary 104
Boni, Margaret Bradford
1893(?)-1974 Obituary 53-56
Bonifacio, Amelia Lapena
See Lapena-Bonifacio, Amelia
Bonime, Florence 1907- 49-52
Bonime, Walter 1909- CAP-2
Earlier sketch in CA 17-18
Bonine, Gladys Nichols 1907- CAP-1
Earlier sketch in CA 13-16
Bonington, Chris(tian John Storey)
1934- CANR-34
Earlier sketches in CA 45-48, CANR-1
Bonini, Charles P(ius) 1933- 13-16R
Bonino, Louise
See Williams, Louise Bonino
Bonjean, Charles M. 1935- 41-44R
Bonk, James 1932- 123
Bonk, Wallace J. 1923- 9-12R
Bonn, Pat
See Bonn, Patricia Carolyn
Bonn, Patricia Carolyn 1948- ....SATA 43
Bonn, Robert Lewis 1937- 125
Bonn, Thomas L. 1939- 109
Bonnamy, Francis
See Walz, Audrey Boyers
Bonnar, Alphonsus 1895-1968 ....CAP-1
Earlier sketch in CA 9-10
Bonnay, Charles (Louis)
1930-1986 Obituary 119
Bonnefoy, Yves 1923- CANR-33
Earlier sketch in CA 85-88
See also CLC 9, 15, 58
See also MTCW
Bonnell, Dorothy Haworth 1914- CANR-3
Earlier sketch in CA 1-4R
Bonnell, F(raser) C(larence) 1908-1983 118
Bonnell, F(lorence Rhodes) W(inn) 1915- 118
Bonnell, John Sutherland 1893-1992 ....5-8R
Obituary 136
Bonner, Arthur 1922- 135
Bonner, Brian 1917- CANR-21
Earlier sketch in CA 104
Bonner, Gerald 1926- CANR-5
Earlier sketch in CA 9-12R
Bonner, Jack
See Paine, Lauran (Bosworth)
Bonner, James Calvin 1904- CANR-9
Earlier sketch in CA 9-12R
Bonner, Joey 1948- 122
Bonner, John Tyler 1920- 49-52
Bonner, Mary Graham 1890-1974 73-76
Obituary 49-52
See also SATA 19
Bonner, Michael
See Glasscock, Anne Bonner
Bonner, Parker
See Ballard, (Willis) Todhunter
Bonner, Paul Hyde 1893-1968 ....1-4R
Obituary 103
Bonner, Raymond T(homas) 1942- 117
Bonner, Terry Nelsen
See Castoro, Laura A(nn)
and Krauzer, Steven M(ark)
and Raeschild, Sheila
and Yarbro, Chelsea Quinn
Bonner, Thomas Jr. 1942- 110
Bonner, Thomas N(eville) 1923- 9-12R
Bonner, William H(omer) 1924- 53-56
Bonner, William Hallam
1899-1980 Obituary 115
Bonners, Susan ....SATA 48
Bonnette, Jeanne 1907- 41-44R
Bonnette, Victor
See Roy, Ewell Paul
Bonneville, Douglas A(lan) 1931- 21-24R
Bonney, Bill
See Keevill, Henry J(ohn)
Bonney, H(anning) Orrin 1903-1979 ....9-12R
Obituary 103
Bonney, Lorraine G(agnon) 1922- CANR-1
Earlier sketch in CA 45-48
Bonney, Merl E(dwin) 1902- CAP-2
Earlier sketch in CA 33-36
Bonney, (Mabel) Therese
1897-1978 Obituary 73-76
Bonnice, Joseph G(regory) 1930- 49-52
Bonnie, Fred 1945- 127
Bonnie, Richard J(effrey) 1945- CANR-4
Earlier sketch in CA 53-56
Bonnifield, Paul 1937- 104
Bonnor, William (Bowen) 1920- 9-12R
Bonny, Helen L(indquist) 1921- CANR-19
Earlier sketches in CA 49-52, CANR-2
Bono, Philip 1921- 101
Bonoma, T(homas) V(incent) 1946- CANR-33
Earlier sketches in CA 85-88, CANR-15
Bonomi, Patricia U(pdegraff) 1928- 85-88
Bonosky, Phillip 1916- 128
Bonsal, Philip Wilson 1903- 85-88
Bonsall, Crosby Barbara (Newell) 1921- 73-76
See also SATA 23
Bontebal, Henk
See Heertje, Arnold
Bontecou, Eleanor
1890(?)-1976 Obituary 65-68
Bontempo, Charles J(oseph) 1931- 61-64
Bontemps, Arna(ud Wendell)
1902-1973 ....CANR-35
Obituary 41-44R
Earlier sketches in CA 1-4R, CANR-4
See also BLC 1
See also BW
See also CLC 1, 18
See also CLR 6
See also DLB 48, 51
See also MAICYA
See also MTCW
See also SATA 2, 24, 44
Bontly, Thomas (John) 1939- 57-60
Bontrager, G(erald) Edwin 1939- 114
Bontrager, John K(enneth) 1923- 65-68
Bonvie, Thomas L. 1940- 114
Bony, Jean (Victor) 1908- 101
Bonzon, Paul-Jacques 1908-1978 93-96
See also SATA 22
Boodman, David M(orris) 1923- 21-24R
Boody, Shirley Bright 1919- 89-92
Boog Watson, Elspeth Janet 1900- CAP-1
Earlier sketch in CA 11-12
Booher, Dianna Daniels 1948- 103
See also SATA 33
Bookbinder, David J(oel) 1951- 101
Bookbinder, Robert 1950- 110
Bookchin, Murray 1921- CANR-1
Earlier sketch in CA 1-4R
Booker, Anton S.
See Randolph, Vance
Booker, Christopher (John Penrice) 1937- 136
Booker, Malcolm (Richard) 1915- 108
Booker, Simeon Saunders 1918- 9-12R
Bookman, Charlotte
See Zolotow, Charlotte S(hapiro)
Book-Senninger, Claude 1928- 45-48
Bookspan, Martin 1926- 41-44R
Bookstein, Abraham 1940- 53-56
Boom, Alfred B. 1928- CANR-14
Earlier sketch in CA 25-28R
Boom, Corrie ten
See ten Boom, Corrie
Boon, Emilie (Laetitia) 1958- 131
Boon, Francis
See Bacon, Edward
Boon, Louis-Paul 1912-1979 ....CANR-13
Earlier sketch in CA 73-76
Boone, Bruce 1940- 112
Boone, Buford 1909(?)-1983 Obituary 109
Boone, Charles Eugene
See Boone, Pat
Boone, Daniel R. 1927- CANR-12
Earlier sketch in CA 33-36R
Boone, Debby
See Boone, Deborah Ann
Boone, Deborah Ann 1956- 110
Boone, Gene 1962- CANR-33
Earlier sketch in CA 113
Boone, Gray Davis 1938- 93-96
Boone, Louis E(ugene) 1941- CANR-15
Earlier sketch in CA 41-44R
Boone, Muriel 1893- 69-72
Boone, Pat 1934- CANR-2
Earlier sketch in CA 1-4R
See also SATA 7
Boontje
See Boon, Louis-Paul
Boore, W(alter) H(ugh) 1904- CANR-5
Earlier sketch in CA 5-8R
Boorer, Wendy 1931- CANR-6
Earlier sketch in CA 57-60
Boorman, Howard L(yon) 1920- 41-44R
Boorman, John 1933- 121
Brief entry 112
See also AAYA 3
Boorman, Linda (Kay) 1940- 121
See also SATA 46
Boorman, Scott A(rcher) 1949- 29-32R
Boorman, Stanley (Harold) 1939- 127
Boorstein, Edward 1915- 73-76
Boorstin, Daniel J(oseph) 1914- CANR-28
Earlier sketches in CA 1-4R, CANR-1
See also AITN 2
See also DLB 17
See also SATA 52
Boorstin, Jon 134
Boorstin, Paul (Terry) 1944- 103
Boorstin, Ruth F.
See Boorstin, Ruth (Carolyn) Frankel
Boorstin, Ruth (Carolyn) Frankel 1917- 134
Boos, Frank Holgate 1893-1968 ....CAP-2
Earlier sketch in CA 33-36
Boot, John C. G. 1936- 17-20R
Boote, Robert Edward 1920- 65-68
Booth, Alan R. 1934- Brief entry 107
Booth, Bradford A(llen)
1909-1968 Obituary 116
Booth, Catherine Bramwell
See Bramwell-Booth, Catherine
Booth, Charles Orrell 1918- 13-16R
Booth, Edward
See Booth, Geoffrey Thornton
Booth, Edwin CANR-7
Earlier sketch in CA 17-20R
Booth, Ernest Sheldon 1915-1984 53-56
See also SATA 43
Booth, Geoffrey
See Tann, Jennifer
Booth, Geoffrey Thornton 1928- 132
Booth, George C(live) 1901- CAP-1
Earlier sketch in CA 11-12
Booth, Graham (Charles) 1935- ....SATA 37
Booth, Helen Sutton
1890(?)-1985 Obituary 117
Booth, Irwin
See Hoch, Edward D(entinger)
Booth, James 1945- 119
Booth, John A(llan) 1946- CANR-28
Earlier sketch in CA 111
Booth, John E(rlanger) 1919- 9-12R
Booth, Ken 1943- 102
Booth, Mark Haworth
See Haworth-Booth, Mark
Booth, Mark Warren 1943- 107
Booth, Martin 1944- 93-96
See also CAAS 2
See also CLC 13
Booth, Mary L. 1831-1889 ....DLB 79
Booth, Nyla 121
Booth, Pat(rick John) 1929- CAP-1
Earlier sketch in CA 9-10
Booth, Pat 1945(?)- 130
See also BEST 90:1
Booth, Paul Henry Gore
See Gore-Booth, Paul Henry
Booth, Philip 1907-1981 106
Booth, Philip 1925- CANR-5
Earlier sketch in CA 5-8R
See also CLC 23
See also DLBY 82
Booth, Rosemary Frances 1928- 53-56
Booth, Stanley 1942- 136
Booth, Stephen 1933- 69-72
Booth, Taylor L(ockwood) 1933- 53-56
Booth, Warren Scripps 1894-1987 Obituary 121
Booth, Wayne C(layson) 1921- CANR-3
Earlier sketch in CA 1-4R
See also CAAS 5
See also CLC 24
See also DLB 67
Booth, Windsor Peyton
1912-1989 Obituary 130
Boothby, Robert
See Boothby, Robert John Graham
Boothby, Robert John Graham 1900-1986 117
Obituary 120
Boothroyd, (John) Basil 1910-1988 ....CANR-13
Obituary 124
Earlier sketch in CA 33-36R
Bootle, Stan Kelly
See Kelly-Bootle, Stan
Booton, (Catherine) Kage 1919- 61-64
Booty, John Everitt 1925- CANR-17
Earlier sketch in CA 85-88
Bopp, Karl Richard 1906-1979 Obituary 107
Bor, Jonathan (Steven) 1953- 133
Bor, Josef 1906-1979 Obituary 115
Bor, Norman 1893(?)-1973 Obituary 104
Boraas, Roger S(tuart) 1926- 33-36R
Borah, Woodrow (Wilson) 1912- CANR-3
Earlier sketch in CA 5-8R
Borch, Ted
See Lund, A. Morten
Borchard, Ruth (Berendsohn) 1910- 13-16R
Borchardt, D(ietrich) H(ans) 1916- CANR-24
Earlier sketches in CA 21-24R, CANR-9
Borchardt, Frank L(ouis) 1938- 33-36R
Borchardt, Rudolf 1877-1945 ....DLB 66
Borchers, Gladys L. 1891- CAP-1
Earlier sketch in CA 17-18
Borchert, Gerald L(eo) 1932- CANR-36
Earlier sketches in CA 37-40R, CANR-14
Borchert, James 1941- 104
Borchert, Wolfgang 1921-1947 Brief entry 104
See also DLB 69
See also TCLC 5
Borden, Bob
See Rees, Clair (Francis)
Borden, Charles A. 1912-1968 ....5-8R
Borden, Henry 1901- 41-44R
Borden, Lee
See Deal, Borden
Borden, Leigh
See Deal, Borden
Borden, Linda 1951(?)- 125
Borden, Lizzie
See Borden, Linda
Borden, Louise (Walker) 1949- 136
See also SATA 68
Borden, M.
See Saxon, Gladys Relyea
Borden, Mary 1886-1968 ....CAP-1
Obituary 25-28R
Earlier sketch in CA 13-16
Borden, Morton 1925- 9-12R
Borden, Neil Hopper 1895- CANR-6
Earlier sketch in CA 1-4R
Borden, Norman E(aston) Jr. 1907- 17-20R
Borden, Richard Carman 1900- CAP-1
Earlier sketch in CA 11-12
Borden, William (Vickers) 1938- CANR-25
Earlier sketches in CA 25-28R, CANR-10
Borderieux, Carita 1874-1953 Brief entry 113
Borders, William Alexander 1939- 134
Bordes, Francois 1919-1981 Obituary 103
Bordier, Georgette 1924- ....SATA 16
Bordin, Edward S. 1913- 57-60
Bordin, Ruth B(irgitta) 1917- CANR-27
Earlier sketches in CA 21-24R, CANR-11
Bordley, James III 1900-1979 69-72
Obituary 133
Bordman, Gerald 1931- 107
Bordow, Joan (Wiener) 1944- 85-88
Borea, Phyllis Gilbert 1924- 29-32R
Boreham, Gordon F. 1928- 41-44R
Borek, Ernest 1911-1986 106
Obituary 118
Borel, Jacques 1925- CANR-13
Earlier sketch in CA 33-36R
Borel, Raymond C. 1927- 73-76
Borell, Helene
See Hegeler, Sten

Boreman, Jean 1909- CAP-2
Earlier sketch in CA 21-22
Boren, Henry C(harles) 1921- 17-20R
Boren, James H(arlan) 1925- 41-44R
Borenstein, Audrey F(arrell) 1930- CANR-28
Earlier sketches in CA 77-80, CANR-13
Borenstein, Emily 1923- 104
Borer, Mary (Irene) Cathcart 1906- CANR-4
Earlier sketch in CA 9-12R
Boretz, Allen 1900-1986 Obituary 119
Boretz, Alvin 1919- 124
Brief entry 118
Boretz, Benjamin (Aaron) 1934- 69-72
Borg, Bjoern (Rune) 1956- 134
Brief entry 114
Borg, Bjorn
See Borg, Bjoern (Rune)
Borg, Dorothy 1902- 21-24R
Borg, Susan 1947- 131
Borg, Walter R(aymond) 1921- CANR-13
Earlier sketch in CA 33-36R
Borgen, Robert 1945- 124
Borges, Jorge Luis 1899-1986 .... CANR-33
Earlier sketches in CA 21-24R, CANR-19
See also CLC 1, 2, 3, 4, 6, 8, 9, 10, 13, 19, 44, 48
See also DLB 113
See also DLBY 86
See also HW
See also MTCW
See also SSC 4
See also WLC
Borgese, Elisabeth Mann 1918- CANR-24
Earlier sketch in CA 73-76
Borghese, Junio Valerio
1906(?)-1974 Obituary 53-56
Borglum, (James) Lincoln (De La Mothe)
1912-1986 122
Obituary 118
Borgman, James Mark 1954- 133
Borgman, Jim
See Borgman, James Mark
Borgmann, Albert 1937- 117
Borgmann, Dmitri A(lfred) 1927-1985 .... 17-20R
Obituary 118
Borgo, Ludovico 1930- 65-68
Borgos, Seth 1952- 119
Borgstrom, Georg A(rne) 1912-1990 .... 17-20R
Obituary 130
Borgzinner, Jon A. 1938-1980 108
Obituary 97-100
Borhek, Mary V(irginia) 1922- 113
Borich, Michael 1949- 105
Boring, Edwin G(arrigues) 1886-1968 .... CANR-6
Earlier sketch in CA 1-4R
Boring, M(aynard) Eugene 1935- 107
Boring, Mel 1939- 106
See also SATA 35
Boring, Phyllis Zatlin
See Zatlin, Phyllis
Boris, Edna Z(wick) 1943- 113
Boris, Martin 1930- 89-92
Borish, Elaine 132
Borja, Corinne 1929- 97-100
See also SATA 22
Borja, Robert 1923- 97-100
See also SATA 22
Bork, Alfred M. 1926- 17-20R
Bork, Robert H(eron) 1927- 130
Brief entry 111
See also BEST 90:2
Borkin, Joseph 1911-1979 97-100
Obituary 89-92
Borklund, C(arl) W(ilbur) 1930- 21-24R
Borko, Harold 1922- 13-16R
Borkovec, Thomas D. 1944- 45-48
Borland, Barbara Dodge 1904(?)-1991 .... CAP-1
Obituary 133
Earlier sketch in CA 9-10
Borland, Hal
See Borland, Harold Glen
See also SATA 5, 24
Borland, Harold Glen 1900-1978 .... CANR-6
Obituary 77-80
Earlier sketch in CA 1-4R
See also Borland, Hal
Borland, Kathryn Kilby 1916- CANR-4
Earlier sketch in CA 53-56
See also SATA 16
Borman, Kathryn M. 1941- 117
Borman, William Alan 1948- 126
Bormann, Ernest G(ordon) 1925- 17-20R
Born, Adolf 1930- .... SATA 49
Born, Ernest Alexander 1898- 102
Born, Max 1882-1970 .... 5-8R
Obituary 25-28R
Borne, Dorothy
See Rice, Dorothy Mary
Borne, Lawrence Roger 1939- 121
Borneman, Ernest 1915- CANR-19
Earlier sketches in CA 9-12R, CANR-3
Borneman, H.
See Gottshall, Franklin Henry
Bornemann, Alfred H(enry) 1908-1991 .... 13-16R
Obituary 134
Bornet, Vaughn Davis 1917- CANR-20
Earlier sketches in CA 1-4R, CANR-5
Bornheimer, Deane G(ordon) 1935- 89-92
Borning, Bernard C(arl) 1913- CANR-3
Earlier sketch in CA 1-4R
Bornkamm, Guenther 1905- Brief entry 116
Bornstein, Diane (Dorothy) 1942-1984 .... CANR-8
Obituary 112
Earlier sketch in CA 57-60
Bornstein, George (Jay) 1941- 29-32R
Bornstein, Morris 1927- CANR-2
Earlier sketch in CA 5-8R
Bornstein, Sam 1913- Brief entry 112
Bornstein-Lercher, Ruth 1927- CANR-8
Earlier sketch in CA 61-64
See also SATA 14
Bornstein-Somoza, Miriam 1950- .... HW
Borntrager, Karl A. 1892- 89-92
Borodacz, William Obituary 118
Borodin, George
See Milkomane, George Alexis Milkomanovich
Boroff, David 1917-1965 .... CAP-1
Obituary 29-32R
Earlier sketch in CA 11-12
Boroson, Warren 1935- 21-24R
Borovski, Conrad 1930- 37-40R
Borovsky, Natasha 1924- 121
Borowiec, Andrew 1928- 127
Borowitz, Albert (Ira) 1930- CANR-32
Earlier sketches in CA 85-88, CANR-15
Borowitz, Eugene B(ernard) 1924- CANR-1
Earlier sketch in CA 49-52
Borowski, Tadeusz 1922-1951 Brief entry 106
See also TCLC 9
Borras, Frank Marshall Obituary 102
Borrello, Alfred 1931- 29-32R
Borrie, John 1915- 103
Borrie, Wilfred David 1913- 109
Borroff, Edith 1925- 65-68
Borroff, Marie 1923- CANR-2
Earlier sketch in CA 5-8R
Borror, Donald J(oyce) 1907-1988 .... CANR-29
Earlier sketch in CA 1-4R
Borror, Gordon L(amar) 1936- 117
Borrow, George (Henry) 1803-1881 .... DLB 21, 55
Borsch, Frederick Houk 1935- CANR-25
Earlier sketches in CA 25-28R, CANR-10
Borski, Lucia Merecka 73-76
See also SATA 18
Borsodi, Ralph 1888-1977 Obituary 73-76
Borson, Roo
See Borson, Ruth Elizabeth
Borson, Ruth Elizabeth 1952- 112
Borst, Raymond R(ichard) 1909- 107
Borsten, Orin 1912- 85-88
Borten, Helen Jacobson 1930- CANR-3
Earlier sketch in CA 5-8R
See also SATA 5
Borth, Christian C. 1895(?)-1976 Obituary 65-68
Bortin, George 114
Bortin, V. G.
See Bortin, George
and Bortin, Virginia
Bortin, Virginia 1936- 114
Bortner, Doyle M(cClean) 1915- 33-36R
Bortner, Morton 1925- 33-36R
Bortoli, Georges 1923- 65-68
Borton, Elizabeth
See Trevino, Elizabeth B(orton) de
Borton, John C. Jr. 1938- CANR-27
Earlier sketch in CA 29-32R
Borton, Terry
See Borton, John C. Jr.
Bortstein, Larry 1942- 33-36R
See also SATA 16
Bortz, Edward L(eRoy) 1896-1970 .... CAP-1
Earlier sketch in CA 11-12
Boruch, Robert F(rancis) 1942- 69-72
Borus, Michael E(liot) 1938-1987 .... 37-40R
Obituary 122
Borza, Eugene N(icholas) 1935- 25-28R
Bosanquet, N(icholas) F(rancis) G(ustavus)
1942- 131
Bosanquet, Nick
See Bosanquet, N(icholas) F(rancis) G(ustavus)
Bosanquet, Reggie
See Bosanquet, Reginald
Bosanquet, Reginald 1932-1984 Obituary 113
Bosch, David J(acobus) 1929- 118
Bosch (Gavino), Juan 1909- .... HW
Bosch, Henry G(erard) 1914- 135
Bosch, William Joseph 1928- 29-32R
Bosco, Antoinette (Oppedisano) 1928- 13-16R
Bosco, (Fernand Joseph Marius) Henri
1888-1976 69-72
Obituary 65-68
See also DLB 72
Bosco, Jack
See Holliday, Joseph
Bosco, Monique 1927- .... DLB 53
Bose, Buddhadeva 1908- Brief entry 119
Bose, Irene Mott 1899(?)-1974 Obituary 53-56
Bose, N(irmal) K(umar) 1901-1972 .... CAP-2
Earlier sketch in CA 23-24
Bose, Tarun Chandra 1931- 45-48
Boserup, Ester 1910- 57-60
Boshell, Buris R(aye) 1923- 105
Boshell, Gordon 1908- 77-80
See also SATA 15
Boshinski, Blanche 1922- 21-24R
See also SATA 10
Boskin, Joseph 1929- 25-28R
Boskoff, Alvin 1924- 13-16R
Bosland, Chelcie Clayton 1901- 5-8R
Bosler, Raymond Thomas 1915- 112
Bosley, Harold A(ugustus) 1907-1975 49-52
Obituary 53-56
Bosley, Keith 1937- CANR-6
Earlier sketch in CA 57-60
Boslooper, Thomas 1923- 81-84
Bosmajian, Haig Aram 1928- CANR-7
Earlier sketch in CA 17-20R
Bosmajian, Hamida 1936- 107
Bosquet, Alain 1919- 13-16R
Boss, Judy 1935- 57-60
Boss, Richard W(oodruff) 1937- 103
Bosschere, Jean de
1878(?)-1953 Brief entry 115
See also TCLC 19
Bosse, Malcolm J(oseph) 1933- 106
See also SATA 35
Bosserman, (Charles) Phillip 1931- 102
Bossert, Steven T(homas) 1948- 104
Bossom, Naomi 1933- 102
See also SATA 35
Bossone, Richard M. 1924- 33-36R
Bosticco, (Isabel Lucy) Mary 102
Bostick, William A(llison) 1913- 89-92
Boston, Anne 1945- 130
Boston, Charles K.
See Gruber, Frank
Boston, Lucy Maria (Wood) 1892-1990 73-76
Obituary 131
See also CLR 3
See also MAICYA
See also SATA 19
See also SATO 64
Boston, Noel 1910-1966 .... CAP-1
Earlier sketch in CA 13-16
Boston, Ray(mond J.) 1927- 128
Boston, Robert 1940- 65-68
Bostwick, Burdette Edwards 1908- 106
Boswell
See Gordon, Giles (Alexander Esme)
Boswell, Barbara (S.) 1946- 122
Boswell, Charles (Meigs Jr.) 1909- 5-8R
Boswell, Jackson Campbell 1934- 61-64
Boswell, James 1740-1795 .... CDBLB 1660-1789
See also DLB 104
See also WLC
Boswell, Jeanetta 1922- CANR-22
Earlier sketch in CA 106
Boswell, John (Eastburn) 1947- 121
Boswell, Robert 1953- 136
Boswell, Thomas 1947- 118
Bosworth, Allan R(ucker) 1901-1986 .... 1-4R
Obituary 120
Bosworth, Clifford Edmund 1928- CANR-7
Earlier sketch in CA 13-16R
Bosworth, David 1947- 113
Bosworth, Frank
See Paine, Lauran (Bosworth)
Bosworth, J. Allan 1925- .... SATA 19
Bosworth, Patricia 1933- 77-80
Bosworth, R(ichard) J(ames) B(oon)
1943- CANR-23
Earlier sketch in CA 106
Botein, Bernard 1900-1974 Obituary 45-48
Botel, Morton 1925- 105
Botham, Noel 1940- 104
Bothmer, Dietrich Felix von
See von Bothmer, Dietrich Felix
Bothwell, Jean CANR-3
Earlier sketch in CA 1-4R
See also SATA 2
Botjer, George (Francis) 1937- 97-100
Botkin, B(enjamin) A(lbert) 1901-1975 .... CAP-1
Obituary 57-60
Earlier sketch in CA 13-16
See also SATA 40
Botkin, Daniel B. 1937- 136
Botkin, James W. 1943- 112
Botman, Selma 1950- 135
Boto, Eza
See Biyidi, Alexandre
Botsch, Robert Emil 1947- 104
Botsford, Keith 1928- 9-12R
Botsford, Ward 1927- 110
See also SATA 66
Bott, George 1920- 104
Botta, Anne Charlotte (Lynch)
1815-1891 .... DLB 3
Bottel, Helen 1914- 25-28R
Botterill, Cal(vin Bruce) 1947- 57-60
Botterill, Joyce 1939- 138
Bottigheimer, Ruth B. 1939- 125
Bottiglia, William F(ilbert) 1912- 21-24R
Botting, Douglas (Scott) 1934- CANR-37
Earlier sketches in CA 45-48, CANR-1, 16
See also SATA 43
Bottner, Barbara 1943- CANR-23
Earlier sketches in CA 61-64, CANR-8
See also SATA 14
Bottom, Raymond 1927- 33-36R
Bottome, Edgar M. 1937- 33-36R
Bottome, Phyllis
See Forbes-Dennis, Phyllis
Bottomley, Gordon 1874-1948 Brief entry 120
See also DLB 10
Bottomly, Heath 1919- 105
Bottomore, T(homas) B(urton) 1920- CANR-20
Earlier sketches in CA 9-12R, CANR-4
Bottoms, A(nthony) E(dward) 1939- 73-76
Bottoms, David 1949- CANR-22
Earlier sketch in CA 105
See also CLC 53
See also DLB 120
See also DLBY 83
Bottoms, Lawrence W(endell) 1908- 89-92
Bottrall, Margaret Florence Saumarez
1909- 104
Bottrall, (Francis James) Ronald
1906-1989 53-56
Obituary 129
See also DLB 20
Botvinnik, Mikhail Moiseyevich 1911- 112
Botwinick, Jack 1923- 41-44R
Bouce, Paul-Gabriel 1936- 73-76
Bouchard, Constance B(rittain) 1948- 128
Bouchard, Lois Kalb 1938- 25-28R
Bouchard, Robert H. 1923- 17-20R
Boucher, Alan (Estcourt) 1918- CANR-24
Earlier sketches in CA 5-8R, CANR-9
Boucher, Anthony
See White, William A(nthony) P(arker)
See also DLB 8
Boucher, David 1951- 135
Boucher, Frank 1901-1977 122
Obituary 110
Boucher, John G(regory) 1930- 37-40R
Boucher, Jonathan 1738-1804 .... DLB 31
Boucher, Paul Edward 1893- CAP-1
Earlier sketch in CA 13-14
Boucher, Sandy 1936- 110
Boucher, Wayne I(rving) 1934- 53-56
Boucherville, Georges Boucher de
1814-1894 .... DLB 99
Boucolon, Maryse 1937- CANR-30
Earlier sketch in CA 110
See also Conde, Maryse
Boudat, Marie-Louise 1909- CAP-1
Earlier sketch in CA 11-12
Boudon, Raymond 1934- CANR-30
Earlier sketch in CA 49-52
Boudreau, Eugene H(oward) 1934- 45-48
Boudreaux, Patricia Duncan 1941- 33-36R
Bough, Lee
See Huser, (La)Verne (Carl)
Boughey, Arthur S(tanley) 1913- Brief entry 113
Boughner, Daniel C(liness) 1909-1974 .... CAP-2
Obituary 49-52
Earlier sketch in CA 23-24
Boughton, James M(urray) 1940- 41-44R
Boughton, Willis A(rnold)
1885-1977 Obituary 73-76
Bouissac, Paul (Antoine Rene) 1934- 65-68
Boulanger, Nadia (Juliette) 1887-1979 127
Boularan, Jacques 1890-1972 Obituary 37-40R
Boulby, Mark 1929- 37-40R
Boulding, Elise (Biorn-Hansen) 1920- CANR-26
Earlier sketches in CA 21-24R, CANR-8
Boulding, Kenneth E(wart) 1910- CANR-26
Earlier sketches in CA 5-8R, CANR-7
Boulet, Susan Seddon 1941- .... SATA 50
Boulger, James Denis 1931-1979 109
Boulle, Pierre (Francois Marie-Louis)
1912- CANR-24
Earlier sketch in CA 9-12R
See also SATA 22
Boulogne, Jean 1942- 93-96
Boult, Adrian (Cedric) 1889-1983 114
Obituary 109
Boult, S. Kye
See Cochrane, William E.
Boulter, Eric Thomas 1917-1989 Obituary 129
Boulting, John (Edward)
1913-1985 Obituary 116
Boulton, David 1935- CANR-15
Earlier sketch in CA 25-28R
Boulton, James T(hompson) 1924- 29-32R
Boulton, Jane 1921- 65-68
Boulton, Laura Theresa Craytor
1899(?)-1980 Obituary 110
Boulton, Marjorie 1924- CANR-9
Earlier sketch in CA 65-68
Boulton, Wayne G(ranberry) 1941- 115
Boultwood, Alban 1911- 118
Boulware, Marcus H(anna) 1907- CANR-1
Earlier sketch in CA 45-48
Bouma, Donald H(erbert) 1918- 41-44R
Bouma, Mary La Grand 93-96
Bouman, Pieter M(arinus) 1938- CANR-12
Earlier sketch in CA 29-32R
Bouman, Walter Richard 1929- 29-32R
Boumelha, Penelope Ann 1950- 110
Boumelha, Penny
See Boumelha, Penelope Ann
Boumphrey, Robert Stavely
1916(?)-1987 Obituary 123
Bour, Daniele 1939- .... SATA 62
Bouraoui, H(edi) A(ndre) 1932- CANR-25
Earlier sketches in CA 65-68, CANR-9
Bourassa, Napoleon 1827-1916 .... DLB 99
Bourbon, Ken
See Bauer, Erwin A.
Bourdeaux, Michael 1934- CANR-14
Earlier sketch in CA 33-36R
Bourdier, James A(aron)
1929-1987 Obituary 124
Bourdieu, Pierre 1930- 130
Bourdon, David 1934- CANR-13
Earlier sketch in CA 37-40R
See also SATA 46
Bourdon, Sylvia Diane Eve 1949- 85-88
Bouregy, Thomas 1909(?)-1978 Obituary 104
Bouret, Jean 1914- 85-88
Bourgeois, Paulette 1951- 137
Bourget, Paul (Charles Joseph)
1852-1935 Brief entry 107
See also TCLC 12
Bourgholtzer, Frank 1919- 25-28R
Bourguignon, Erika (Eichhorn) 1924- 85-88
Bourinot, John George 1837-1902 .... DLB 99
Bourjaily, Monte Ferris 1894-1979 97-100
Obituary 85-88
Bourjaily, Vance (Nye) 1922- CANR-2
Earlier sketch in CA 1-4R
See also CAAS 1
See also CLC 8, 62
See also DLB 2
Bourke, Vernon J(oseph) 1907- CANR-3
Earlier sketch in CA 9-12R
Bourke-White, Margaret 1904-1971 .... CAP-1
Obituary 29-32R
Earlier sketch in CA 13-16
Bourliaguet, Leonce 1895-1965 102
Bourliere, Francois (Marie Gabriel)
1913- Brief entry 113
Bourne, Aleck William
1885(?)-1974 Obituary 53-56
Bourne, Charles P. 1931- 9-12R
Bourne, Dorothy D(ulles) 1893- CAP-2
Earlier sketch in CA 23-24

Bourne, Edward Gaylord 1860-1908 ... DLB 47
Bourne, Eulalia ... 97-100
Bourne, Frank Card 1914- ... 17-20R
Bourne, Geoffrey Howard 1909-1988 ... 33-36R
  Obituary ... 126
Bourne, J(ohn) M. 1949- ... 124
Bourne, James R. 1897- ... CAP-2
  Earlier sketch in CA 21-22
Bourne, Joanna Watkins 1949- ... 112
Bourne, John
  See John, Owen
Bourne, Kenneth 1930- ... CANR-11
  Earlier sketch in CA 25-28R
Bourne, L(arry) S(tuart) 1939- ... CANR-27
  Earlier sketches in CA 33-36R, CANR-12
Bourne, Lesley
  See Marshall, Evelyn
Bourne, Lyle E(ugene) Jr. 1932- ... 53-56
Bourne, Miriam Anne 1931-1989 ... CANR-10
  Earlier sketch in CA 21-24R, 129
  See also SATA 16, 63
Bourne, Peter
  See Jeffries, Graham Montague
Bourne, Peter Geoffrey 1939- ... CANR-7
  Earlier sketch in CA 57-60
Bourne, Randolph S(illiman)
  1886-1918 Brief entry ... 117
  See also DLB 63
  See also TCLC 16
Bourne, Russell 1928- ... 133
Bourne, Ruth (May) 1897-1986 ... 33-36R
  Obituary ... 120
Bourneuf, Alice E. 1912-1980 Obituary ... 102
Bourricaud, Francois 1922- ... CANR-26
  Earlier sketch in CA 29-32R
Bouscaren, Anthony Trawick 1920- ... CANR-5
  Earlier sketch in CA 1-4R
Bouscaren, T(imothy) Lincoln 1884- ... CAP-1
  Earlier sketch in CA 11-12
Bousono, Carlos 1923- ... DLB 108
Bousquet, Joe 1897-1950 ... DLB 72
Bousquet, Marie-Louis Valentin
  1887(?)-1975 Obituary ... 104
Boussard, Jacques Marie 1910- ... 29-32R
Boustead, John Edmund Hugh
  1895-1980 Obituary ... 97-100
Boutell, Clarence Burley
  1908-1981 Obituary ... 104
Boutell, Clip
  See Boutell, Clarence Burley
Boutelle, Ann Edwards 1943- ... 131
Boutelle, Sara Holmes ... 130
Boutet de Monvel, (Louis) M(aurice)
  1850(?)-1913 ... SATA 30
Boutilier, Mary A(nn) 1943- ... 105
Bouton, James Alan 1939- ... 89-92
Bouton, Jim
  See Bouton, James Alan
Bouvard, Marguerite Anne 1937- ... 37-40R
Bouvier, Emile 1906- ... 37-40R
Bouvier, Leon F(rancis) 1922- ... 105
Bova, Ben(jamin William) 1932- ... CANR-11
  Earlier sketch in CA 5-8R
  See also CLC 45
  See also CLR 3
  See also DLBY 81
  See also MAICYA
  See also MTCW
  See also SATA 6, 68
Bovard, Oliver K. 1872-1945 ... DLB 25
Bovasso, Julie 1930- ... 25-28R
Bove, Emmanuel 1898-1945 ... DLB 72
Bove, Paul A(nthony) 1949- ... 125
Bovee, Courtland L(owell) 1944- ... CANR-27
  Earlier sketch in CA 49-52
Bovee, Ruth
  See Paine, Lauran (Bosworth)
Boven, William 1887(?)-1970 Obituary ... 104
Bovet, Eric D(avid) 1900- ... 118
Bovey, John (Alden Jr.) 1913- ... 107
Bovis, H(enry) Eugene 1928- ... 29-32R
Bow, Russell 1925- ... 21-24R
Bowden, Betsy 1948- ... 107
Bowden, Edwin T(urner) Jr. 1924- ... CANR-8
  Earlier sketch in CA 13-16R
Bowden, Elbert Victor 1924- ... CANR-15
  Earlier sketch in CA 41-44R
Bowden, Gregory Houston 1948- ... 41-44R
Bowden, Henry Warner 1939- ... CANR-27
  Earlier sketch in CA 49-52
Bowden, J(ocelyn) J(ean) 1927- ... 29-32R
Bowden, Jean 1925- ... CANR-7
  Earlier sketch in CA 53-56
Bowden, Jim
  See Spence, William John Duncan
Bowden, Joan Chase 1925- ... 89-92
  See also SATA 38, 51
Bowden, Leonard (Walter) 1933-1979 ... 17-20R
  Obituary ... 134
Bowden, Mary Weatherspoon 1941- ... 110
Bowden, Roland Heywood 1916- ... CANR-24
  Earlier sketch in CA 106
Bowden, Susan White
  See White-Bowden, Susan
Bowder, Diana (Ruth) 1942- ... 109
Bowditch, James L(owell) 1939- ... 89-92
Bowdle, Donald N(elson) 1935- ... 49-52
Bowdler, Roger 1934- ... 97-100
Bowdring, Paul (Edward) 1946- ... 135
Bowe, Frank 1947- ... 104
Bowe, Gabriel P(aul) 1923- ... 21-24R
Bowe, Kate
  See Taylor, Mary Ann
Bowe, (Paul Thomas) Patrick 1945- ... 106
Bowen, Barbara C(herry) 1937- ... 37-40R
Bowen, Betty Morgan
  See West, Betty
Bowen, Catherine Drinker 1897-1973 ... CANR-15
  Obituary ... 45-48
  Earlier sketch in CA 5-8R
  See also SATA 7
Bowen, Croswell 1905-1971 Obituary ... 33-36R
Bowen, David
  See Bowen, Joshua David
Bowen, Desmond 1921- ... 33-36R
Bowen, Earl Kenneth 1918- ... 5-8R
Bowen, Edmund (John)
  1898-1980 Obituary ... 105
Bowen, Elbert Russell 1918- ... 13-16R
Bowen, Elizabeth (Dorothea Cole)
  1899-1973 ... CANR-35
  Obituary ... 41-44R
  Earlier sketches in CAP-2, CA 17-18
  See also CDBLB 1945-1960
  See also CLC 1, 3, 6, 11, 15, 22
  See also DLB 15
  See also MTCW
  See also SSC 3
Bowen, Emrys George 1900-1983 Obituary ... 111
Bowen, Ezra 1927- ... 85-88
Bowen, Francis 1811-1890 ... DLB 1, 59
Bowen, Gail 1942- ... 138
Bowen, Haskell L. 1929- ... 41-44R
Bowen, Howard R(othmann)
  1908-1989 ... CANR-8
  Obituary ... 130
  Earlier sketch in CA 21-24R
Bowen, (Ivor) Ian 1908-1984 ... 105
  Obituary ... 115
Bowen, J(ean) Donald 1922- ... CANR-8
  Earlier sketch in CA 17-20R
Bowen, James Keith 1932- ... 37-40R
Bowen, John (Griffith) 1924- ... CANR-2
  Earlier sketch in CA 1-4R
  See also DLB 13
Bowen, John 1916- ... 103
Bowen, Joshua David 1930- ... 105
  See also SATA 22
Bowen, Marjorie
  See Campbell, (Gabrielle) Margaret (Vere)
Bowen, Mary
  See Hall, Mary Bowen
Bowen, Michael 1951- ... 134
Bowen, Peter 1939- ... 57-60
Bowen, Ralph H(enry) 1919- ... 69-72
Bowen, Richard M. 1928- ... 21-24R
Bowen, Robert O. 1920- ... 9-12R
Bowen, Robert Sydney 1900-1977 ... CANR-28
  Obituary ... 69-72
  Earlier sketch in CA 73-76
  See also SATA 21, 52
Bowen, Zack (Rhollie) 1934- ... 29-32R
Bowen-Judd, Sara (Hutton) 1922-1985 ... CANR-5
  Obituary ... 117
  Earlier sketch in CA 9-12R
Bower, Barbara
  See Todd, Barbara Euphan
Bower, David A(llan) 1945- ... 37-40R
Bower, Donald E(dward) 1920- ... 77-80
Bower, Eli M(ichael) 1917- ... 89-92
Bower, Fay Louise 1929- ... 53-56
Bower, Gordon H(oward) 1932- ... 17-20R
Bower, Joseph L(yon) 1938- ... 112
Bower, Julia Wells 1903- ... 41-44R
Bower, Keith
  See Beckett, Kenneth A(lbert)
Bower, Louise 1900- ... CAP-2
  Earlier sketch in CA 21-22
Bower, Muriel 1921- ... 49-52
Bower, Robert T(urrell) 1919-1990 ... CANR-27
  Obituary ... 132
  Earlier sketch in CA 49-52
Bower, Sharon Anthony 1932- ... 65-68
Bower, Ursula Violet Graham
  1914-1988 Obituary ... 127
Bower, William Clayton 1878- ... 5-8R
Bowering, George 1935- ... CANR-10
  Earlier sketch in CA 21-24R
  See also CAAS 16
  See also CLC 15, 47
  See also DLB 53
Bowering, Marilyn R(uthe) 1949- ... 101
  See also CLC 32
Bowermaster, Jon 1954- ... 127
Bowers, C. A. 1935- ... 29-32R
Bowers, Claude G. 1878-1958 ... DLB 17
Bowers, Edgar 1924- ... CANR-24
  Earlier sketch in CA 5-8R
  See also CLC 9
  See also DLB 5
Bowers, Faubion 1917- ... 5-8R
Bowers, Fredson (Thayer) 1905-1991 ... CANR-2
  Obituary ... 134
  Earlier sketch in CA 5-8R
  See also DLBY 91
Bowers, George K. 1916- ... CANR-2
  Earlier sketch in CA 1-4R
Bowers, John M. 1949- ... 126
Bowers, John Waite 1935- ... 41-44R
Bowers, John 1928- ... 33-36R
Bowers, Kenneth S. 1937- ... 97-100
Bowers, Margaretta K(eller) 1908- ... 5-8R
Bowers, Mary Beacom 1932- ... 105
Bowers, Neal 1948- ... CANR-28
  Earlier sketch in CA 110
Bowers, Q(uentin) David 1938- ... CANR-37
  Earlier sketches in CA 41-44R, CANR-16
Bowers, Ronald (Lee) 1941- ... 41-44R
Bowers, Warner Fremont 1906- ... 61-64
Bowers, William J(oseph) 1935- ... 97-100
Bowers, William L(avalle) 1930- Brief entry ... 114
Bowers, William 1916-1987 ... 102
  Obituary ... 122
Bowersock, G(len) W(arren) 1936- ... 81-84
Bowes, Anne LaBastille
  See LaBastille, Anne
Bowett, Derek William 1927- ... CANR-6
  Earlier sketch in CA 9-12R
Bowick, Dorothy Mueller
  See Mueller, Dorothy
Bowie, Andrew (S.) 1952- ... 134
Bowie, David
  See Jones, David Robert
  See also CLC 17
Bowie, Janetta (Hamilton) 1907- ... 102
Bowie, Jim
  See Norwood, Victor G(eorge) C(harles)
    and Stratemeyer, Edward L.
Bowie, Malcolm (McNaughtan) 1943- ... 128
Bowie, Norman E. 1942- ... CANR-29
  Earlier sketches in CA 33-36R, CANR-13
Bowie, Robert R(ichardson) 1909- ... CAP-1
  Earlier sketch in CA 11-12
Bowie, Sam
  See Ballard, (Willis) Todhunter
Bowie, Walter Russell 1882-1969 ... CANR-3
  Earlier sketch in CA 5-8R
Bowker, Francis E. 1917- ... 41-44R
Bowker, John (Westerdale) 1935- ... CANR-12
  Earlier sketch in CA 25-28R
Bowker, Lee Harrington 1940- ... CANR-25
  Earlier sketch in CA 108
Bowker, Margaret 1936- ... 25-28R
Bowker, R(obin) M(arsland) 1920- ... 65-68
Bowker, Richard (J.) 1950- ... 127
Bowkett, Stephen 1953- ... 134
  See also SATA 67
Bowlby, (Edward) John (Mostyn)
  1907-1990 ... CANR-34
  Obituary ... 132
  Earlier sketch in CA 49-52
Bowlby, Rachel 1957- ... 130
Bowle, John (Edward) 1905-1985 ... CANR-1
  Obituary ... 117
  Earlier sketch in CA 1-4R
Bowler, Jan Brett
  See Brett, Jan (Churchill)
Bowler, Peter J(ohn) 1944- ... 129
Bowler, R(eginald) Arthur 1930- ... 57-60
Bowles, Chester (Bliss) 1901-1986 ... 69-72
  Obituary ... 119
Bowles, D(elbert) Richard 1910- ... 33-36R
Bowles, Edmund A(ddison) 1925- ... CANR-32
  Earlier sketch in CA 33-36R
Bowles, Ella Shannon
  1886-1975 Obituary ... 57-60
Bowles, Frank H(amilton) 1907-1975 ... 13-16R
  Obituary ... 57-60
Bowles, George A. Jr.
  1924(?)-1986 Obituary ... 118
Bowles, Gordon Townsend 1904- ... CAP-1
  Earlier sketch in CA 11-12
Bowles, Jane (Sydney) 1917-1973 ... CAP-2
  Obituary ... 41-44R
  Earlier sketch in CA 19-20
  See also CLC 3, 68
Bowles, John 1938- ... 106
Bowles, Kerwin
  See Abeles, Elvin
Bowles, Norma L(ouise) ... 77-80
Bowles, Paul (Frederick) 1910- ... CANR-19
  Earlier sketches in CA 1-4R, CANR-1
  See also CAAS 1
  See also CLC 1, 2, 19, 53
  See also DLB 5, 6
  See also MTCW
  See also SSC 3
Bowles, Samuel III 1826-1878 ... DLB 43
Bowles, William Lisle 1762-1850 ... DLB 93
Bowley, Rex Lyon 1925- ... 103
Bowling, Ann (Patricia) 1951- ... 113
Bowling, Jackson M(ichael) 1934- ... 5-8R
Bowlt, John E(llis) 1943- ... 130
Bowman, Albert Hall 1921- ... 41-44R
Bowman, Alfred C(onner) 1904-1982 ... 117
Bowman, Bob
  See Bowman, Robert T.
Bowman, Bruce 1938- ... 65-68
Bowman, Clell Edgar 1904- ... 105
Bowman, David J. 1919- ... 9-12R
Bowman, Derek 1931- ... 102
Bowman, Frank Paul 1927- ... 33-36R
Bowman, Henry A(delbert) 1903- ... CAP-1
  Earlier sketch in CA 13-14
Bowman, Herbert E(ugene) 1917- ... 65-68
Bowman, James Cloyd 1880-1961 ... 97-100
  See also SATA 23
Bowman, Jeanne
  See Blocklinger, Peggy O'More
Bowman, John S(tewart) 1931- ... CANR-19
  Earlier sketches in CA 9-12R, CANR-5
  See also SATA 16
Bowman, John Wick 1894- ... CANR-6
  Earlier sketch in CA 1-4R
Bowman, Karl M. 1888-1973 Obituary ... 41-44R
Bowman, Kathleen (Gill) 1942- ... 69-72
  See also SATA 40, 52
Bowman, Larry G(ene) 1935- Brief entry ... 115
Bowman, LeRoy 1887-1971 Obituary ... 33-36R
Bowman, Locke E. Jr. 1927- ... CANR-2
  Earlier sketch in CA 5-8R
Bowman, Louise Morey 1882-1944 ... DLB 68
Bowman, Marcelle 1914- ... 25-28R
Bowman, Mary D. 1924- ... 25-28R
Bowman, Mary Jean 1908- ... 33-36R
Bowman, Ned A(lan) 1932- ... 41-44R
Bowman, Paul Hoover 1914- ... 33-36R
Bowman, Peter 1917(?)-1985 Obituary ... 114
Bowman, Raymond Albert
  1903-1979 Obituary ... 89-92
Bowman, Robert T. 1910- ... 73-76
Bowman, Robert 1928- ... 25-28R
Bowman, Sylvia E(dmonia) 1914- ... 1-4R
Bowman, Ward S(imon) Jr. 1911- ... 49-52
Bowmer, Angus L(ivingston)
  1904-1979 Obituary ... 85-88
Bowne, (William) Alan
  1945(?)-1989 Obituary ... 130
Bowne, Ford
  See Brown, Forrest
Bowness, Alan 1928- ... 130
Bowood, Richard
  See Daniell, Albert Scott
Bowra, (Cecil) Maurice 1898-1971 ... CANR-2
  Obituary ... 29-32R
  Earlier sketch in CA 1-4R
Bowring, Richard (John) 1947- ... 114
Bowron, Edgar Peters 1943- ... 130
Bowser, Eileen 1928- ... CANR-26
  Earlier sketches in CA 69-72, CANR-11
Bowser, Frederick P(ark) 1937- ... 49-52
Bowser, Hallowell 1922(?)-1990 Obituary ... 130
Bowser, Joan
  See Bowser, Pearl
Bowser, Pearl 1931- ... CANR-13
  Earlier sketch in CA 33-36R
Bowskill, Derek 1928- ... CANR-13
  Earlier sketch in CA 77-80
Bowyer, (Raymond) Chaz 1926- ... CANR-33
  Earlier sketches in CA 93-96, CANR-15
Bowyer, John W(alter) 1921- ... 37-40R
Bowyer, Mathew J(ustice) 1926- ... CANR-13
  Earlier sketch in CA 37-40R
Box, Edgar
  See Vidal, Gore
Box, Sydney 1907-1983 Obituary ... 109
Boxer, Charles Ralph 1904- ... 102
Boxer, (Charles) Mark (Edward)
  1931-1988 Obituary ... 126
Boxerman, David Samuel 1945- ... 61-64
Boxill, Roger 1928- ... 126
Boxman
  See Chambliss, William J(oseph)
Boy, Angelo V(ictor) 1929- ... 69-72
Boyajian, Cecile
  See Starr, Cecile
Boyarsky, Bill 1936- ... 25-28R
Boyce, (Joseph) Chris(topher) 1943- ... 73-76
Boyce, David George 1942- ... 103
Boyce, George A(rthur) 1898- ... 53-56
  See also SATA 19
Boyce, Gray Cowan 1899- ... 5-8R
Boyce, Joseph Nelson 1937- ... 102
Boyce, Richard Fyfe 1896-1985 ... 69-72
  Obituary ... 116
Boyce, Ronald R(eed) 1931- ... CANR-18
  Earlier sketches in CA 9-12R, CANR-3
Boycott, Desmond (Lionel) Morse
  See Morse-Boycott, Desmond (Lionel)
Boycott, Geoff
  See Boycott, Geoffrey
Boycott, Geoffrey 1940- ... 131
Boycott, Rosie 1951- ... 132
Boyd, Alamo
  See Bosworth, Allan R(ucker)
Boyd, Andrew (Kirk Henry) 1920- ... 1-4R
Boyd, Ann S.
  See Schoonmaker, Ann
Boyd, Anne Morris 1884-1974 Obituary ... 113
Boyd, Beverly M(ary) 1925- ... 69-72
Boyd, Bob
  See Boyd, Robert T(hompson)
Boyd, Candy Dawson 1946- ... 138
Boyd, Carolyn Patricia 1944- ... 112
Boyd, Carse
  See Stacton, David (Derek)
Boyd, Dean (Wallace) ... 5-8R
Boyd, E(lizabeth) 1904(?)-1974 Obituary ... 53-56
Boyd, Edward M. 1927- ... 120
Boyd, Frank
  See Kane, Frank
Boyd, Harper W(hite) Jr. 1917- ... 13-16R
Boyd, Herb 1938- ... 110
Boyd, J(ohn) Francis 1910- ... 5-8R
Boyd, Jack 1932- ... CANR-34
  Earlier sketch in CA 49-52
Boyd, James M(oore) 1919- ... 33-36R
Boyd, James S(terling) 1917- ... 49-52
Boyd, James 1888-1944 ... DLB 9
Boyd, John
  See Upchurch, Boyd (Bradfield)
  See also DLB 8
Boyd, John D. 1916- ... 25-28R
Boyd, Julian P(arks) 1903-1980 ... 65-68
  Obituary ... 97-100
Boyd, (Charles) Malcolm 1932- ... 126
Boyd, Malcolm 1923- ... CANR-26
  Earlier sketches in CA 5-8R, CANR-4
  See also CAAS 11
Boyd, Marion M.
  See Havighurst, Marion (M.)
Boyd, Martin a Beckett 1893- ... CAP-1
  Earlier sketch in CA 13-14
Boyd, Maurice 1921- ... 9-12R
Boyd, Mildred Worthy 1921- ... 17-20R
Boyd, Myron F(enton) 1909-1978 ... 41-44R
Boyd, Nancy
  See Millay, Edna St. Vincent
Boyd, Neil
  See DeRosa, Peter (Clement)
Boyd, Neil 1951- ... 129
Boyd, Pauline
  See Schock, Pauline
Boyd, R(obert) L(ewis) F(ullarton) 1922- ... 57-60
Boyd, Robert H. 1912- ... 53-56
Boyd, Robert S. 1928- ... 13-16R
Boyd, Robert T(hompson) 1914- ... 108

Boyd, Robin (Gerard Penleigh)
1919-1971 ... 17-20R
Obituary ... 133
Boyd, Selma
See Acuff, Selma Boyd
Boyd, Shylah 1945- ... 61-64
Boyd, Sue Abbott 1921- ... CANR-14
Earlier sketch in CA 65-68
Boyd, Thomas (Alexander)
1898-1935 Brief entry ... 111
See also DLB 9
Boyd, Waldo T. 1918- ... CANR-12
Earlier sketch in CA 29-32R
See also SATA 18
Boyd, William C(louser)
1903-1983 Obituary ... 109
Boyd, William Harland 1912- ... CANR-11
Earlier sketch in CA 69-72
Boyd, William 1885-1979 ... 41-44R
Obituary ... 135
Boyd, William 1952- ... 120
Brief entry ... 114
See also CLC 28, 53, 70
Boyd-Carpenter, John (Archibald) 1908- ... 131
Boyden, David D(odge)
1910-1986 Obituary ... 120
Boyden, Donald P. 1957- ... 128
Boyden, Sarah B. Obituary ... 128
Boydston, Jo Ann 1924- ... 29-32R
Boyer, Brian D. 1939- ... 45-48
Boyer, Bruce Hatton 1946- ... 101
Boyer, Carl B(enjamin)
1906-1976 Obituary ... 65-68
Boyer, Dwight 1912- ... 65-68
Boyer, Elizabeth (Mary) 1913- ... 81-84
Boyer, Ernest LeRoy 1928- ... 110
Boyer, G. G.
See Boyer, Glenn G.
Boyer, Glenn G. 1924- ... 130
Boyer, Harold W. 1908- ... 1-4R
Boyer, John (William) 1946- ... 103
Boyer, Mildred (Vinson) 1926- ... 112
Boyer, Paul Samuel 1935- ... CANR-18
Earlier sketches in CA 49-52, CANR-1
Boyer, Richard Edwin 1932- ... 21-24R
Boyer, Richard Lewis 1943- ... CANR-27
Earlier sketches in CA 69-72, CANR-11
Boyer, Richard O. 1903-1973 Obituary ... 45-48
Boyer, Rick
See Boyer, Richard Lewis
Boyer, Robert
See Lake, Kenneth R(obert)
Boyer, Robert E(rnst) 1929- ... 41-44R
See also SATA 22
Boyer, Ruth Gasink 1913- ... 114
Boyer, Sophia Ames
1907(?)-1972 Obituary ... 37-40R
Boyer, William H(arrison) 1924- ... CANR-22
Earlier sketch in CA 106
Boyer, William W. (Jr.) 1923- ... 13-16R
Boyers, Margaret Anne ... 118
Boyers, Peggy
See Boyers, Margaret Anne
Boyers, Robert 1942- ... CANR-4
Earlier sketch in CA 53-56
Boyesen, Hjalmar Hjorth 1848-1895 ... DLB 12, 71
Boyington, (Gregory) Pappy
1912-1988 Obituary ... 124
Boykin, James H(andy) 1914- ... CANR-2
Earlier sketch in CA 5-8R
Boylan, Bernard R(obert) 1927- ... 127
Boylan, Boyd
See Whiton, James Nelson
Boylan, Brian Richard 1936- ... 81-84
Boylan, Clare 1948- ... 136
Boylan, Eleanor 1916- ... 132
Boylan, James (Richard) 1927- ... CANR-16
Earlier sketches in CA 1-4R, CANR-1
Boylan, Leona Davis 1910- ... 61-64
Boylan, Lucile 1906- ... CAP-1
Earlier sketch in CA 11-12
Boylan, Mary 1913(?)-1984 Obituary ... 112
Boyle, Andrew (Philip More) 1919-1991 ... 102
Obituary ... 134
Boyle, Andrew 1923- ... 5-8R
Boyle, Ann (Peters) 1916- ... CANR-26
Earlier sketch in CA 29-32R
See also SATA 10
Boyle, Charles 1951- ... 113
Boyle, David (Courtney) 1958- ... 133
Boyle, Deirdre 1949- ... CANR-28
Earlier sketch in CA 110
Boyle, Edward Charles Gurney
1923-1981 Obituary ... 108
Boyle, Eleanor Vere (Gordon)
1825-1916 ... SATA 28
Boyle, Freddie M. 1915(?)-1984 Obituary ... 113
Boyle, Hal
See Boyle, Harold V(incent)
Boyle, Harold V(incent) 1911-1974 ... 101
Obituary ... 89-92
Boyle, Harry Joseph 1915- ... CANR-7
Earlier sketch in CA 13-16R
Boyle, J(ohn) A(ndrew) 1916-1979 ... CANR-9
Obituary ... 85-88
Earlier sketch in CA 61-64
Boyle, Jimmy 1944- ... 130
Boyle, John Hunter 1930- ... 41-44R
Boyle, John P(hillips) 1931- Brief entry ... 114
Boyle, (Emily) Joyce 1901- ... CAP-1
Earlier sketch in CA 13-14
Boyle, Kay 1902- ... CANR-29
Earlier sketch in CA 13-16R
See also CAAS 1
See also CLC 1, 5, 19, 58
See also DLB 4, 9, 48, 86
See also MTCW
See also SSC 5
Boyle, (C.) Kevin 1943- ... 123
Boyle, Leonard E(ugene) 1923- ... 127
Boyle, Mark
See Kienzle, William X(avier)
Boyle, Mary 1882(?)-1975 Obituary ... 53-56
Boyle, Patrick 1905-1982 ... 127
See also CLC 19
Boyle, Richard J(ohn) 1932- ... 129
Boyle, Robert H. 1928- ... CANR-12
Earlier sketch in CA 17-20R
See also SATA 65
Boyle, Robert (Richard) 1915- ... 13-16R
Boyle, Roger 1621-1679 ... DLB 80
Boyle, Samuel J. III 1920-1985 Obituary ... 118
Boyle, Sarah Patton 1906- ... CAP-1
Earlier sketch in CA 13-16
Boyle, Stanley E(ugene) 1927- ... 41-44R
Boyle, T. Coraghessan 1948- ... 120
See also BEST 90:4
See also CLC 36, 55
See also DLBY 86
Boyle, Ted Eugene 1933- ... 21-24R
Boyle, Thomas 1939- ... 118
Boyle, Timm
See Boyle, Timothy R(obert)
Boyle, Timothy R(obert) 1953- ... 118
Boylen, Margaret Currier 1921-1967 ... 1-4R
Obituary ... 103
Boyles, C(larence) S(cott) Jr. 1905- ... 1-4R
Boylston, Helen Dore 1895-1984 ... CANR-21
Obituary ... 113
Earlier sketch in CA 73-76
See also MAICYA
See also SATA 23, 39
Boyne, Walter J(ames) 1929- ... 107
Boynton, Lewis Delano 1909- ... CANR-6
Earlier sketch in CA 5-8R
Boynton, Peter S. 1920(?)-1971 Obituary ... 104
Boynton, Robert W(hitney)
1921- Brief entry ... 117
Boynton, Sandra (Keith) 1953- ... 126
See also SATA 38, 57
Boynton, Searles Roland 1926- ... 77-80
Boyum, Joy Gould 1934- ... 33-36R
Boyum, Keith O(rel) 1945- ... 102
Bozarth-Campbell, Alla (Linda Renee)
1947- ... 105
Boze, Arthur Phillip 1945- ... 57-60
Bozeman, Adda B(ruemmer) 1908- ... CANR-3
Earlier sketch in CA 5-8R
Bozeman, Theodore Dwight 1942- ... 85-88
Braasch, William Frederick 1878- ... CAP-2
Earlier sketch in CA 29-32
Brabazon, James
See Seth-Smith, Leslie James
Brabb, George J(acob) 1925- ... 41-44R
Brabec, Barbara 1937- ... CANR-32
Earlier sketches in CA 93-96, CANR-15
Brabson, George Dana 1900- ... CAP-1
Earlier sketch in CA 19-20
Brace, Edward Roy 1936- ... CANR-19
Earlier sketch in CA 102
Brace, Geoffrey (Arthur) 1930- ... CANR-11
Earlier sketch in CA 69-72
Brace, Gerald Warner 1901-1978 ... 13-16R
Obituary ... 81-84
Brace, Richard Munthe 1915-1977 ... CANR-15
Obituary ... 69-72
Earlier sketch in CA 1-4R
Brace, Timothy
See Pratt, Theodore
Braceairdle, Cyril 1920- ... 45-48
Bracegirdle, Brian 1933- ... 101
Braceland, Francis J(ames)
1900-1985 Obituary ... 115
Bracewell, Michael 1958- ... 135
Bracewell, Ronald N(ewbold) 1921- ... 57-60
Bracewell-Milnes, (John) Barry 1931- ... CANR-37
Earlier sketches in CA 33-36R, CANR-13
Bracey, Howard E(dwin) 1905- ... 13-16R
Bracey, John H(enry Jr.) 1941- ... 29-32R
Brach, Gerard 1927- ... 138
Bracher, Frederick (George) 1905- ... 111
Bracher, Karl Dietrich 1922- ... CANR-17
Earlier sketches in CA 45-48, CANR-1
Bracher, Marjory (Louise) 1906- ... CAP-1
Earlier sketch in CA 13-16
Brack, Harold Arthur 1923- ... 17-20R
Brack, O M Jr. 1938- ... 41-44R
Brack, Vektris
See Humphrys, Leslie George
Brack, William Dennis 1939- ... 136
Brackbill, Yvonne 1928- ... 21-24R
Bracken, Dorothy K(endall) ... 21-24R
Bracken, Joseph Andrew 1930- ... 37-40R
Bracken, Paul 1948- ... 115
Bracken, Peg 1920- ... CANR-6
Earlier sketch in CA 1-4R
Brackenbury, Alison 1953- ... 136
See also DLB 40
Brackenridge, Hugh Henry
1748-1816 ... DLB 11, 37
Brackenridge, R(obert) Douglas 1932- ... 101
Bracker, Jon 1936- ... 17-20R
Brackett, Charles 1892-1969 Obituary ... 113
See also DLB 26
Brackett, Leigh (Douglass) 1915-1978 ... CANR-1
Obituary ... 77-80
Earlier sketch in CA 1-4R
See also DLB 8, 26
Brackman, Arnold C(harles)
1923-1983 ... CANR-2
Obituary ... 111
Earlier sketch in CA 5-8R
See also AITN 1
Brackney, William (Henry) 1948- ... 123
Bracy, William 1915- ... 61-64
Bradbrook, M(uriel) C(lara) 1909- ... CANR-23
Earlier sketches in CA 13-16R, CANR-7
Bradburn, Norman M. 1933- ... CANR-13
Earlier sketch in CA 37-40R
Bradburne, E(lizabeth) S. 1915- ... 25-28R
Bradbury, Bianca (Ryley) 1908-1982 ... CANR-37
Earlier sketches in CA 13-16R, CANR-5
See also MAICYA
See also SATA 3, 56
Bradbury, Dorothy E(dith)
1902-1984 Obituary ... 113
Bradbury, Edward P.
See Moorcock, Michael (John)
Bradbury, John M(ason) 1908-1969 ... CAP-1
Earlier sketch in CA 13-16
Bradbury, Katharine L(orraine) 1946- ... 111
Bradbury, Malcolm (Stanley) 1932- ... CANR-33
Earlier sketches in CA 1-4R, CANR-1
See also CLC 32, 61
See also DLB 14
See also MTCW
Bradbury, Parnell 1904- ... 13-16R
Bradbury, Peggy 1930- ... 65-68
Bradbury, Ray (Douglas) 1920- ... CANR-30
Earlier sketches in CA 1-4R, CANR-2
See also AITN 1, 2
See also CDALB 1968-1988
See also CLC 1, 3, 10, 15, 42
See also DLB 2, 8
See also MTCW
See also SATA 11, 64
See also WLC
Braddock, Joseph (Edward)
1902- Brief entry ... 117
Braddock, Richard R(eed) 1920-1974 ... 1-4R
Obituary ... 103
Braddon, George
See Milkomane, George Alexis Milkomanovich
Braddon, Mary Elizabeth
1837(?)-1915 Brief entry ... 108
See also DLB 18, 70
Braddon, Russell (Reading) 1921- ... CANR-2
Earlier sketch in CA 1-4R
Braddy, Haldeen 1908-1980 ... 17-20R
Obituary ... 101
Brade-Birks, S(tanley) Graham 1887- ... CAP-1
Earlier sketch in CA 13-16
Bradeis, Irma 1906(?)-1990 Obituary ... 130
Braden, Charles Samuel 1887- ... 5-8R
Braden, Donna R. 1953- ... 130
Braden, Irene A.
See Hoadley, Irene Braden
Braden, Spruille 1894-1978 Obituary ... 115
Braden, Thomas (Wardell)
1918- Brief entry ... 113
Braden, Tom
See Braden, Thomas (Wardell)
Braden, Waldo W(arder) 1911- ... CANR-5
Earlier sketch in CA 5-8R
Braden, William 1930- ... 21-24R
Bradfield, James McComb 1917- ... 5-8R
Bradfield, Jolly Roger
See Bradfield, Roger
Bradfield, Nancy 1913- ... 29-32R
Bradfield, Richard 1896- ... CAP-2
Earlier sketch in CA 23-24
Bradfield, Roger 1924- ... 17-20R
Bradford, Adam M.D.
See Wassersug, Joseph D.
Bradford, Alex 1927-1978 Obituary ... 112
Bradford, Andrew 1686-1742 ... DLB 43, 73
Bradford, Ann (Liddell) 1917- Brief entry ... 116
See also SATA 38, 56
Bradford, Barbara Taylor 1933- ... CANR-32
Earlier sketch in CA 89-92
See also BEST 89:1
See also MTCW
See also SATA 66
Bradford, Benjamin 1925- ... 85-88
Bradford, David F(rantz) 1939- ... 124
Bradford, Dennis E(arle) 1946- ... 118
Bradford, Ernle (Dusgate Selby) 1922-1986 ... 101
Obituary ... 119
Bradford, Gamaliel 1863-1932 ... DLB 17
See also TCLC 36
Bradford, James C(hapin) 1945- ... CANR-29
Earlier sketch in CA 111
Bradford, John 1749-1830 ... DLB 43
Bradford, Karleen 1936- ... 112
See also SATA 48
Bradford, Leland P(owers) 1905- ... CANR-9
Earlier sketch in CA 13-16R
Bradford, Leroy 1922- ... 105
Bradford, Lois J(ean) 1936- ... 104
See also SATA 36
Bradford, M(elvin) E(ustace) 1934- ... CANR-13
Earlier sketch in CA 77-80
Bradford, Patience Andrewes 1918- ... 33-36R
Bradford, Peter Amory 1942- ... 61-64
Bradford, Reed H(oward) 1912- ... 49-52
Bradford, Richard H(eadlee) 1938- ... 89-92
Bradford, Richard (Roark) 1932- ... CANR-2
Earlier sketch in CA 49-52
See also SATA 59
Bradford, Roark 1896-1948 ... DLB 86
Bradford, Robert W(hitmore) 1918- ... 77-80
Bradford, Roy Hamilton 1920- ... 109
Bradford, Sarah (Mary Malet) 1938- ... 128
Bradford, Sax(ton) 1907-1966 ... 1-4R
Bradford, Will
See Paine, Lauran (Bosworth)
Bradford, William III 1719-1791 ... DLB 43, 73
Bradford, William C(astle) 1910- ... 9-12R
Bradford, William 1590-1657 ... DLB 24, 30
Brading, D. A. 1936- ... 136
Bradlaugh, Charles 1833-1891 ... DLB 57
Bradlee, Benjamin C(rowninshield) 1921- ... 61-64
See also AITN 2
Bradlee, Frederic 1920- ... 21-24R
Bradley, Alfred 1925-1991 ... 105
Obituary ... 134
Bradley, Bert E(dward) 1926- ... 41-44R
Bradley, Bill
See Bradley, William Warren
Bradley, Brigitte L(ooke) 1924- ... 37-40R
Bradley, C. Paul 1918- ... 106
Bradley, Concho
See Paine, Lauran (Bosworth)
Bradley, David G. 1916- ... 13-16R
Bradley, David (Henry Jr.) 1950- ... CANR-26
Earlier sketch in CA 104
See also BLC 1
See also BW
See also CLC 23
See also DLB 33
Bradley, Duane
See Sanborn, Duane
Bradley, Ed(ward R.) 1941- ... 113
Brief entry ... 108
See also BW
Bradley, Ed 1911(?)-1983 Obituary ... 110
Bradley, Erwin S(tanley) 1906- ... CAP-2
Earlier sketch in CA 33-36
Bradley, George 1953- ... 134
Bradley, Harold Whitman 1903- ... 33-36R
Bradley, Hassell 1930- ... 65-68
Bradley, Helen G(enevieve) 1932- ... 112
Bradley, Ian Campbell 1950- ... 103
Bradley, James E. 1944- ... 136
Bradley, James V(andiver) 1924- ... 37-40R
Bradley, Jerry (Wayne) 1948- ... 137
Bradley, John Ed 1959- ... CLC 55
Bradley, John (Francis Nejez) 1930- ... CANR-10
Earlier sketch in CA 25-28R
Bradley, John Lewis 1917- ... 29-32R
Bradley, Joseph F(rancis) 1917- ... 21-24R
Bradley, Kenneth (Granville) 1904- ... CAP-1
Earlier sketch in CA 13-14
Bradley, Marion Zimmer 1930- ... CANR-31
Earlier sketches in CA 57-60, CANR-7
See also CAAS 10
See also AAYA 9
See also CLC 30
See also DLB 8
See also MTCW
Bradley, Marjorie D. 1931- ... 25-28R
Bradley, Matt 1947- ... 105
Bradley, Melanie (Rose) Choukas
See Choukas-Bradley, Melanie (Rose)
Bradley, Michael
See Blumberg, Gary
Bradley, Michael 1944- ... 129
Bradley, Omar Nelson 1893-1981 Obituary ... 103
Bradley, Preston 1888-1983 Obituary ... 110
Bradley, R. C. 1929- ... CANR-14
Earlier sketch in CA 33-36R
Bradley, Ritamary 1916- ... 49-52
Bradley, Robert A(ustin) 1917- ... 21-24R
Bradley, Sam(uel McKee) 1917- ... 21-24R
Bradley, (Edward) Sculley 1897- ... 89-92
Bradley, Van Allen 1913-1984 ... 37-40R
Obituary ... 114
Bradley, Virginia 1912- ... CANR-8
Earlier sketch in CA 61-64
See also SATA 23
Bradley, William Aspenwall
1878-1939 Brief entry ... 107
See also DLB 4
Bradley, William L(ee) 1918- ... 21-24R
Bradley, William Warren 1943- ... 101
Bradley, William 1934- ... 45-48
Bradlow, Edna Rom ... CAP-1
Earlier sketch in CA 9-10
Bradlow, Frank R(osslyn) 1913- ... CANR-13
Earlier sketches in CAP-1, CA 9-10
Bradner, Enos 1892-1984 ... 57-60
Obituary ... 111
Bradshaw, Brendan 1937- ... 73-76
Bradshaw, Buck
See Paine, Lauran (Bosworth)
Bradshaw, George
1909(?)-1973 Obituary ... 45-48
Bradshaw, Gillian (Marucha) 1956- ... 103
Bradshaw, John 1933- ... 138
Bradshaw, Jon (Wayne)
1937-1986 Obituary ... 121
Bradshaw, Terry (Paxton) 1948- ... 111
Bradshaw, Thornton F(rederick) 1917- ... 108
Bradsher, Henry S(t. Amant) 1931- ... 133
Bradstock, Andrew (William) 1955- ... 127
Bradstreet, Anne
1612(?)-1672 ... CDALB 1640-1865
See also DLB 24
Bradstreet, Vallerie
See Roby, Mary Linn
Bradt, A(cken) Gordon 1896-1983 ... 57-60
Obituary ... 110
Bradwardine, Thomas 1295(?)-1349 ... DLB 115
Bradway, John S(aeger) 1890- ... CAP-2
Earlier sketch in CA 33-36
Bradwell, James
See Kent, Arthur William Charles
Brady, Alexander 1896-1985 Obituary ... 117
Brady, Ann 1947- ... 138
Brady, Charles Andrew 1912- ... 5-8R
Brady, Darlene A(nn) 1951- ... 102

Brady, Dave 1913(?)-1988 Obituary ... 125
Brady, David W(illiam) 1940- Brief entry ... 114
Brady, Esther Wood 1905-1987 ... 93-96
Obituary ... 123
See also SATA 31, 53
Brady, Frank 1924-1986 ... 13-16R
Obituary ... 120
See also DLB 111
Brady, Frank 1934- ... CANR-9
Earlier sketch in CA 61-64
Brady, Gene P(aul) 1927- ... 107
Brady, George Stuart
1887-1977 Obituary ... 73-76
Brady, Gerald Peter 1929- ... 5-8R
Brady, Ignatius Charles 1911- ... 113
Brady, Irene 1943- ... CANR-20
Earlier sketch in CA 33-36R
See also SATA 4
Brady, James Winston 1928- ... CANR-21
Earlier sketch in CA 101
Brady, Jane 1934- Brief entry ... 113
Brady, John (Mary) 1955- ... 130
Brady, John Paul 1928- ... CANR-5
Earlier sketch in CA 13-16R
Brady, John 1942- ... CANR-10
Earlier sketch in CA 65-68
Brady, Kathleen 1947- ... 129
Brady, Kristin 1949- ... 109
Brady, Leo 1917-1984 ... 69-72
Obituary ... 114
Brady, Lillian 1902- ... 105
See also SATA 28
Brady, Mary Lou 1937- ... 106
Brady, Maureen 1943- ... 112
Brady, Maxine L. 1941- ... 69-72
Brady, Michael 1928- ... 93-96
Brady, Nicholas
See Levinson, Leonard
Brady, Patricia 1943- ... 136
Brady, Peter
See Daniels, Norman
Brady, Sally Ryder 1939- ... 103
Brady, Terence 1939- ... 106
Brady, William S.
See Harvey, John (Barton)
Braeker, Ulrich 1735-1798 ... DLB 94
Braenne, Berit 1918- ... 21-24R
Braestrup, Carl Bjorn 1897-1982 Obituary ... 107
Braestrup, Peter 1929- ... 97-100
Braff, Allan James 1930- ... 108
Braganti, Nancy (Sue) 1941- ... 117
Bragdon, Clifford R(ichardson) 1940- ... 57-60
Bragdon, Elspeth MacDuffie 1897- ... CANR-5
Earlier sketch in CA 5-8R
See also SATA 6
Bragdon, Henry Wilkinson 1906-1980 ... CANR-3
Obituary ... 97-100
Earlier sketch in CA 5-8R
Bragdon, Lillian Jacot ... 73-76
See also SATA 24
Bragg, Arthur N(orris) 1897- ... CAP-1
Earlier sketch in CA 17-18
Bragg, Bill
See Bragg, William Fredrick Jr.
Bragg, Dobby
See Sykes, Roosevelt
Bragg, Mabel Caroline 1870-1945 ... SATA 24
Bragg, Melvyn 1939- ... CANR-10
Earlier sketch in CA 57-60
See also BEST 89:3
See also CLC 10
See also DLB 14
Bragg, Michael 1948- ... 128
See also SATA 46
Bragg, Richard Geoffrey 1909- ... 121
Bragg, Sir W. H.
See Bragg, William Henry
Bragg, Sir William
See Bragg, William Henry
Bragg, Sir William Henry
See Bragg, William Henry
Bragg, William Fredrick Jr. 1922- ... 109
Bragg, William Henry 1862-1942 Brief entry ... 123
Bragg, William Lawrence
1890-1971 Obituary ... 115
Braggin, Mary Vetterling
See Vetterling-Braggin, Mary (Katherine)
Braham, Allan (John Witney) 1937- ... 105
Braham, Randolph Lewis 1922- ... CANR-19
Earlier sketches in CA 1-4R, CANR-5
Brahm, Sumishta 1954- ... SATA 58
Brahms, Caryl
See Abrahams, Doris Caroline
Brahs, Stuart J(ohn) 1940- ... 57-60
Brahtz, John F(rederick) Peel 1918- ... 73-76
Braider, Donald 1923-1976 ... CAP-2
Obituary ... 65-68
Earlier sketch in CA 33-36
Braidwood, Robert John 1907- ... 108
Brailsford, Frances
See Wosmek, Frances
Braimah, Joseph Adam 1916- ... 61-64
Braiman, Susan 1943- ... 97-100
Brain, George B(ernard) 1920- ... 41-44R
Brain, J(oy) B(lundell) 1926- ... 118
Brain, James Lewton
See Lewton-Brain, James
Brain, Joseph J. 1920- ... 13-16R
Brain, Robert 1933- ... 73-76
Brainard, Harry Gray 1907- ... 1-4R
Brainard, Joe 1942- ... CANR-12
Earlier sketch in CA 65-68
Braine, John (Gerard) 1922-1986 ... CANR-33
Obituary ... 120
Earlier sketches in CA 1-4R, CANR-1
See also CDBLB 1945-1960
See also CLC 1, 3, 41
See also DLB 15
See also DLBY 86
See also MTCW
Brainerd, Barron 1928- ... 33-36R
Brainerd, Charles Jon 1944- ... 103
Brainerd, John W(hiting) 1918- ... 57-60
See also SATA 65
Braithwaite, Althea 1940- ... CANR-18
Earlier sketch in CA 97-100
See also SATA 23
Braithwaite, (Eustace) E(dward) R(icardo)
1920- ... CANR-25
Earlier sketch in CA 106
See also BW
Braithwaite, Kenneth James
See Barrow, Kenneth
Braithwaite, Max 1911- ... 93-96
Braithwaite, Richard Bevan
1900-1990 Obituary ... 131
Braithwaite, William Stanley (Beaumont)
1878-1962 ... 125
See also BLC 1
See also BW
See also DLB 50, 54
Brake, Laurel 1941- ... 138
Brake, Mike 1936- ... 93-96
Brakel, Samuel J(ohannes) 1943- ... 33-36R
Brakhage, Stan 1933- ... CANR-15
Earlier sketch in CA 41-44R
Bralver, Eleanor 1913- ... 97-100
Braly, Malcolm 1925-1980 ... CANR-12
Obituary ... 97-100
Earlier sketch in CA 17-20R
Bram, Chris
See Bram, Christopher
Bram, Christopher 1952- ... 126
Bram, Elizabeth 1948- ... CANR-9
Earlier sketch in CA 65-68
See also SATA 30
Bram, Joseph 1904-1974 Obituary ... 110
Bramah, Ernest 1868-1942 ... DLB 70
Bramall, Eric 1927- ... 9-12R
Braman, Sandra 1951- ... 114
Bramann, Jorn K(arl) 1938- ... 119
Brambell, Wilfrid 1912- ... 113
Bramble, Forbes 1939- ... 89-92
Brameld, Theodore (Burghard Hurt)
1904-1987 ... 17-20R
Obituary ... 123
Bramer, Jennie (Perkins) 1900- ... CAP-1
Earlier sketch in CA 13-14
Bramer, John C(onrad) Jr. 1924- ... 1-4R
Bramesco, Norton J. 1924- ... 106
Bramlett, John
See Pierce, John Leonard Jr.
Brammell, P(aris) Roy 1900- ... 65-68
Brammer, Lawrence M(artin) 1922- ... 13-16R
Brammer, William 1930(?)-1978 Obituary ... 77-80
See also CLC 31
Brams, Stanley Howard 1910- ... 9-12R
Brams, Steven J(ohn) 1940- ... CANR-26
Earlier sketches in CA 61-64, CANR-10
Bramsch, Joan 1936- ... 122
Bramson, Leon 1930- ... CANR-4
Earlier sketch in CA 1-4R
Bramson, Robert M(ark) 1925- ... CANR-25
Earlier sketch in CA 108
Bramson, Susan (Jane) 1940- ... 128
Bramwell, Charlotte
See Kimbro, John M.
Bramwell, Dana G. 1948- ... 57-60
Bramwell, James Guy 1911- ... 9-12R
Bramwell-Booth, Catherine
1883-1987 Obituary ... 123
Branagan, Thomas 1774-1843 ... DLB 37
Brana-Shute, Gary 1945- ... 111
Branca, Albert A. 1916- ... 13-16R
Brancaforte, Benito 1934- ... 37-40R
Brancati, Vitaliano 1907-1954 Brief entry ... 109
See also TCLC 12
Brancato, Gilda 1949- ... 107
Brancato, Robin F(idler) 1936- ... CANR-11
Earlier sketch in CA 69-72
See also AAYA 9
See also CLC 35
See also SAAS 9
See also SATA 23
Branch, Alan E(dward) 1933- ... CANR-25
Earlier sketch in CA 105
Branch, Daniel Paulk 1931- ... 17-20R
Branch, Edgar Marquess 1913- ... 13-16R
Branch, Harold F(rancis) 1894-1966 ... 5-8R
Branch, Kip 1947- ... 108
Branch, Mary 1910- ... CANR-10
Earlier sketch in CA 25-28R
Branch, Melville C(ampbell) 1913- ... CANR-14
Earlier sketch in CA 41-44R
Branch, Taylor 1947- ... 131
See also BEST 89:2
Branch, William (Blackwell) 1927- ... CANR-16
Earlier sketch in CA 81-84
See also BW
See also DLB 76
Brand, C(larence) E(ugene) 1895- ... CAP-2
Earlier sketch in CA 23-24
Brand, Carl F(remont) 1892-1981 ... 13-16R
Obituary ... 133
Brand, Charles M(acy) 1932- ... 21-24R
Brand, Charles Peter 1923- ... 13-16R
Brand, Christianna
See Lewis, Mary (Christianna)
Brand, Clay
See Norwood, Victor G(eorge) C(harles)
Brand, Eugene L(ouis) 1931- ... CANR-8
Earlier sketch in CA 61-64
Brand, Garrison
See Brandner, Gary
Brand, Gerd 1921- Brief entry ... 113
Brand, Irene B. 1929- ... 124
Brand, Jeanne L(aurel) 1919- ... 13-16R
Brand, Max
See Faust, Frederick (Shiller)
Brand, Millen 1906-1980 ... 21-24R
Obituary ... 97-100
See also CLC 7
Brand, Myles 1942- ... 37-40R
Brand, Oscar 1920- ... CANR-4
Earlier sketch in CA 1-4R
Brand, Peter
See Larsen, Erling
Brand, Sandra 1918- ... 85-88
Brand, Stewart 1938- ... 81-84
See also AITN 1
Brand, Susan
See Roper, Susan Bonthron
Brandabur, Edward 1930- ... 41-44R
Brande, Ralph T. 1921- ... 25-28R
Brandeis, Louis Dembitz
1856-1941 Brief entry ... 118
Brandel, Arthur Meyer
1913(?)-1980 Obituary ... 102
Brandel, Marc 1919- ... CANR-25
Earlier sketch in CA 108
See also SATA 71
Brandell, (Erik) Gunnar 1916- ... CANR-20
Earlier sketch in CA 103
Branden, Barbara ... CLC 44
Branden, Nathaniel 1930- ... CANR-27
Earlier sketch in CA 33-36R
Branden, Victoria (Fremlin) ... 101
Brandenberg, Aliki Liacouras 1929- ... CANR-30
Earlier sketches in CA 1-4R, CANR-4, 12
See also Aliki
See also MAICYA
See also SATA 2, 35
Brandenberg, Franz 1932- ... CANR-30
Earlier sketches in CA 29-32R, CANR-12
See also MAICYA
See also SATA 8, 35
Brandenburg, David J(ohn)
1920-1987 Obituary ... 123
Brandenburg, Frank R(alph) 1926- ... 13-16R
Brander, Michael (William) 1924- ... CANR-7
Earlier sketch in CA 53-56
Brandes, Georg (Morris Cohen)
1842-1927 Brief entry ... 105
See also TCLC 10
Brandes, Joseph 1928- ... 5-8R
Brandes, Norman Scott 1923- ... 57-60
Brandes, Paul D(ickerson) 1920- ... CANR-2
Earlier sketch in CA 45-48
Brandewyne, (Mary) Rebecca (Wadsworth)
1955- ... CANR-23
Earlier sketch in CA 107
Brandhorst, Carl T(heodore) 1898- ... CAP-2
Earlier sketch in CA 25-28
See also SATA 23
Brandi, John 1943- ... CANR-12
Earlier sketch in CA 73-76
Brandis, Marianne 1938- ... 117
See also SATA 59
Brandner, Gary 1933- ... CANR-38
Earlier sketches in CA 45-48, CANR-1, 17
Brandon, Beatrice
See Krepps, Robert W(ilson)
Brandon, Brumsic Jr. 1927- ... 61-64
See also SATA 9
Brandon, Curt
See Bishop, Curtis (Kent)
Brandon, Dick H. 1934-1981 ... CANR-10
Earlier sketch in CA 17-20R
Brandon, Donald (Wayne) 1926- ... 69-72
Brandon, Dorothy 1899(?)-1977 Obituary ... 69-72
Brandon, Frances Sweeney 1916- ... 9-12R
Brandon, Frank
See Bulmer, (Henry) Kenneth
Brandon, (Oscar) Henry 1916- ... 49-52
Brandon, James Rodger 1927- ... CANR-11
Earlier sketch in CA 69-72
Brandon, Jay (Robert) 1953- ... 119
Brandon, Joe
See Davis, Robert P.
Brandon, John G(ordon)
1879(?)-1941 Brief entry ... 112
Brandon, Johnny ... 105
Brandon, Joyce A(lmeta) 1938- ... 118
Brandon, Robert Joseph 1918- ... 105
Brandon, Robin
See Brandon, Robert Joseph
Brandon, S(amuel) G(eorge) F(rederick)
1907-1971 ... 102
Brandon, Sheila
See Rayner, Claire (Berenice)
Brandon, William 1914- ... 77-80
Brandon-Cox, Hugh 1917- ... 93-96
Brandreth, Gyles 1948- ... 65-68
See also SATA 28
Brandreth, Henry R(enaud) T(urner)
1914-1984 Obituary ... 114
Brandstatter, A(rthur) F. 1914- ... 107
Brandt, Alvin G. 1922- ... 13-16R
Brandt, Anthony 1936- ... 69-72
Brandt, Bill 1904(?)-1983 Obituary ... 111
Brandt, Carol 1904-1984 Obituary ... 114
Brandt, Catharine 1905- ... 106
See also SATA 40
Brandt, Charles 1942- ... 128
Brandt, Deborah 1951- ... 138
Brandt, Floyd S(tanley) 1930- ... 21-24R
Brandt, George W(illiam) 1920- ... 131
Brandt, Harvey
See Edwards, William B(ennett)
Brandt, Jane Lewis 1915- ... 97-100
Brandt, Keith
See Sabin, Louis
Brandt, Leslie F. 1919- ... CANR-23
Earlier sketches in CA 21-24R, CANR-8
Brandt, Lucile (Long Strayer) 1900- ... CANR-13
Earlier sketch in CA 61-64
Brandt, Nat
See Brandt, Nathan Henry Jr.
Brandt, Nathan Henry Jr. 1929- ... CANR-18
Earlier sketch in CA 102
Brandt, Rex(ford Elson) 1914- ... CANR-5
Earlier sketch in CA 13-16R
Brandt, Richard B(ooker) 1910- Brief entry ... 114
Brandt, Richard M(artin) 1922- ... 33-36R
Brandt, Roger
See Crawford, William (Elbert)
Brandt, Sue R(eading) 1916- ... 25-28R
See also SATA 59
Brandt, Tom
See Dewey, Thomas B(lanchard)
Brandt, Vincent S. R. 1924- ... 37-40R
Brandt, William E(dward) 1920- ... 5-8R
Brandt, Willy 1913- ... 85-88
Brandt, Yanna Kroyt 1933- ... 104
Brandts, Robert (Percival) 1930- ... 69-72
Brandwein, Chaim N(aftali) 1920- ... 21-24R
Brandys, Kazimierz 1916- ... CLC 62
Brandys, Marian 1912- ... 57-60
Branegan, James Augustus III 1950- ... 124
Branfield, John (Charles) 1931- ... CANR-33
Earlier sketches in CA 41-44R, CANR-14
See also SATA 11
Branfoot, Gwynneth
See Holder, Gwynneth
Branick, Vincent P(atrick) 1941- ... 113
Branigan, Keith 1940- ... 124
Branin, M(anlif) Lelyn 1901- ... 85-88
Branley, Franklyn M(ansfield) 1915- ... CANR-39
Earlier sketches in CA 33-36R, CANR-14
See also CLC 21
See also CLR 13
See also MAICYA
See also SATA 4, 68
Brann, Eva T(oni) H(elene) 1929- ... 93-96
Brannan, Robert Louis 1927- ... 21-24R
Brannen, Julia (M.) 1944- ... 130
Brannen, Noah S(amuel) 1924- ... CANR-11
Earlier sketch in CA 25-28R
Brannen, Ted R. 1924- ... 17-20R
Branner, Hans Christian 1903-1966 ... 97-100
Obituary ... 89-92
Branner, R(obert) 1927-1973 ... CANR-3
Obituary ... 45-48
Earlier sketch in CA 5-8R
Brannigan, Bill
See Brannigan, William
Brannigan, William 1936- ... 65-68
Brannon, William T. 1906- ... CAP-1
Earlier sketch in CA 13-16
Branover, Herman 1931- ... 130
Branscomb, (Bennett) Harvie 1894- ... 106
Branscum, Robbie 1937- ... CANR-8
Earlier sketch in CA 61-64
See also MAICYA
See also SATA 23, 70
Bransford, Kent Jackson 1953- ... 97-100
Bransford, Stephen 1949- ... 134
Bransom, (John) Paul 1885-1979 ... SATA 43
Branson, David 1909- ... CANR-21
Earlier sketch in CA 41-44R
Branson, Margaret Stimmann 1922- ... CANR-1
Earlier sketch in CA 49-52
Branston, (Ronald Victor) Brian 1914- ... 53-56
Brant, Charles S(tanford) 1919- ... 25-28R
Brant, Irving (Newton) 1885-1976 ... 9-12R
Obituary ... 69-72
Brant, Lewis
See Rowland, D(onald) S(ydney)
Brantley, Cynthia Louise 1943- ... 109
Branyan, Brenda
See Branyan-Broadbent, Brenda
Branyan, Robert L(ester) 1930- ... 104
Branyan-Broadbent, Brenda 1932- ... 128
Branzburg, Paul M(arshal) 1941- ... 73-76
Braque, Georges 1882-1963 Obituary ... 112
Brasch, Charles (Orwell) 1909-1973 ... 114
Obituary ... 104
Brasch, Ila Wales 1945- ... 57-60
Brasch, James D(aniel) 1929- ... 116
Brasch, Rudolph 1912- ... CANR-27
Earlier sketches in CA 21-24R, CANR-8
Brasch, Walter Milton 1945- ... CANR-23
Earlier sketches in CA 57-60, CANR-6
Brasher, Christopher William 1928- ... 5-8R
Brasher, N(orman) H(enry) 1922- ... 25-28R
Brasher, Nell 1912- ... CANR-7
Earlier sketch in CA 61-64
Brasher, Thomas L(owber) 1912- ... 69-72
Brashers, H(oward) C(harles) 1930- ... CANR-8
Earlier sketch in CA 5-8R
Brashler, William 1947- ... CANR-2
Earlier sketch in CA 45-48
Brasier, Virginia 1910- ... 61-64
Brasier-Creagh, Patrick
See Creagh, Patrick
Brasil, Emanuel 1940- ... 130
Brasnett, Bertrand R(ippington)
1893-1988 Obituary ... 124
Brason, Gill 1942- ... 112
Brass, Paul Richard 1936- ... 17-20R
Brassai
See Halasz, Gyula

Brasselle, Keefe 1923(?)-1981 Obituary 104
Brassens, Georges 1921-1981 Obituary 105
Brasseur, Pierre
See Espinasse, Albert
Braswell, George Wilbur Jr. 1936- 112
Brater, Enoch 1944- 122
Brathwaite, Edward (Kamau) 1930- CANR-26
Earlier sketches in CA 25-28R, CANR-11
See also BW
See also CLC 11
Brathwaite, Errol (Freeman) 1924- CANR-11
Earlier sketches in CA 57-60, CANR-7
Brathwaite, Sheila R. 1914- 25-28R
Bratt, Elmer Clark 1901-1970 ....1-4R
Obituary 103
Bratt, John H(arold) 1909- CANR-9
Earlier sketch in CA 17-20R
Bratter, Herbert Max 1900-1976 Obituary 65-68
Bratter, Thomas Edward 1939- 120
Brattgarg, Helge (Axel Kristian) 1920- 5-8R
Bratton, Fred Gladstone 1896- CAP-1
Earlier sketch in CA 11-12
Bratton, Helen 1899- CAP-2
Earlier sketch in CA 23-24
See also SATA 4
Brattstrom, Bayard H(olmes) 1929- 57-60
Braude, Ann (Deborah) 1955- 132
Braude, Benjamin 1945- 111
Braude, Jacob M(orton) 1896-1970 ....CANR-5
Earlier sketch in CA 5-8R
Braude, Michael 1909-1986 Obituary 121
Braude, Michael 1936- 17-20R
See also SATA 23
Braude, William Gordon 1907- 33-36R
Braudel, Fernand (Paul) 1902-1985 ......CANR-14
Obituary 117
Earlier sketch in CA 93-96
Braudy, Leo 1941- 37-40R
Braudy, Susan (Orr) 1941- CANR-10
Earlier sketch in CA 65-68
Brauer, Carl M(alcolm) 1946- 85-88
Brauer, George C(harles) Jr.
1925- Brief entry 113
Brauer, Jerald C(arl) 1921- CANR-13
Earlier sketch in CA 33-36R
Brauer, Kinley J(ules) 1935- 21-24R
Brault, Gerard Joseph 1929- CANR-3
Earlier sketch in CA 5-8R
Brault, Jacques 1933- ....DLB 53
Braun, Armin C(harles John)
1911-1986 Obituary 120
Braun, Arthur E. 1876-1976 Obituary 69-72
Braun, Edward 1936- 134
Brief entry 115
Braun, Eric 1921- 102
Braun, Henry 1930- 25-28R
Braun, Hugh 1902- 25-28R
Braun, J(oachim) Werner
1914-1972 Obituary 37-40R
Braun, John R(ichard) 1928- 33-36R
Braun, Lev 1913- 41-44R
Braun, Richard Emil 1934- 9-12R
Braun, Sidney D(avid) 1912- CANR-10
Earlier sketch in CA 65-68
Braun, Theodore E. D. 1933- CANR-7
Earlier sketch in CA 13-16R
Braun, Thomas (Felix Rudry Gerhart) 1935- 115
Braun, Volker 1939- ....DLB 75
Braunbehrens, Volkmar 1941- 134
Braunburg, Rudolf 1924- CANR-29
Earlier sketch in CA 109
Braund, Hal
See Braund, Harold
Braund, Harold 1913-1988 61-64
Obituary 124
Braunmuller, A(lbert) R(ichard) 1945- 132
Braunrot, Bruno 1936- 114
Braunstein, Daniel N(orman) 1938- 111
Braunstein, Mark M(athew) 1951- 113
Braunthal, Alfred 1898(?)-1980 Obituary 93-96
Braunthal, Gerard 1923- 13-16R
Braunthal, Julius 1891-1972 ....CAP-2
Earlier sketch in CA 23-24
Brautigan, Richard (Gary) 1935-1984 .....CANR-34
Obituary 113
Earlier sketch in CA 53-56
See also CLC 1, 3, 5, 9, 12, 34, 42
See also DLB 2, 5
See also DLBY 80, 84
See also MTCW
See also SATA 56
Brav, Stanley R(osenbaum) 1908- 25-28R
Braverman, Harry 1920-1976 53-56
Obituary 69-72
Braverman, Kate 1950- 89-92
See also CLC 67
Bravmann, Rene A. 1939- 85-88
Brawer, Florence B(lum) 1922- 37-40R
Brawley, Benjamin (Griffith) 1882-1939 125
See also BW
Brawley, Ernest 1937- 53-56
Brawley, Paul Holm
See Brawley, Paul L(eroy)
Brawley, Paul L(eroy) 1942-1988 73-76
Obituary 126
Brawn, Dympna 1931- 25-28R
Brawne, Michael 1925- 73-76
Braxton, Joanne M. 1950- ....DLB 41
Bray, Alison
See Rowland, D(onald) S(ydney)
Bray, Allen Farris III 1926- 9-12R
Bray, Anna Eliza 1790-1883 ....DLB 116
Bray, Douglas W. 1918- 13-16R
Bray, Howard 1929- 105
Bray, J(ohn) J(efferson) 1912- 102
Bray, Nicholas 1948- 135
Bray, Thomas 1656-1730 ....DLB 24
Bray, Virginia Elizabeth Nuckolls
1895(?)-1979 Obituary 93-96
Bray, Warwick 1936- CANR-15
Earlier sketch in CA 25-28R
Braybon, (Charmian) Gail 1952- 131
Braybrooke, David 1924- CANR-18
Earlier sketches in CA 9-12R, CANR-3
Braybrooke, Neville (Patrick Bellairs)
1925- 5-8R
Brayce, William
See Rowland, D(onald) S(ydney)
Brayfield, Celia 1945- 128
Brayman, Harold 1900-1988 73-76
Obituary 124
Braymer, Marguerite
See Dodd, Marguerite
Braymer, Marjorie Elizabeth 1911- 1-4R
See also SATA 6
Braynard, Frank O. 1916- CANR-8
Earlier sketch in CA 17-20R
Braza, Jacque
See McKeag, Ernest L(ionel)
Brazeau, Peter (Alden) 1942-1986 111
Obituary 119
Brazell, Karen 1938- CANR-31
Earlier sketch in CA 45-48
Brazelton, T(homas) Berry 1918- 97-100
Brazer, Harvey E(lliott) 1922-1991 111
Obituary 134
Brazil, Angela 1869(?)-1947 Brief entry 112
Brazill, William J. Jr. 1935- 53-56
Brazos, Waco
See Jennings, Michael Glenn
Breach, Robert Walter 1927- 13-16R
Breakwell, Glynis M(arie) 1952- 122
Brealey, Richard A. 1936- 53-56
Brean, Herbert (J.) 1907-1973 93-96
Obituary 41-44R
Brearley, Denis 1940- 37-40R
Brears, Peter C(harles) D(avid) 1944- 102
Breasted, Charles 1898(?)-1980 Obituary 93-96
Breasted, James Henry Jr.
1908-1983 Obituary 109
Breasted, James Henry 1865-1935 ....DLB 47
Breathed, (Guy) Berke(ley) 1957- CANR-27
Earlier sketch in CA 110
See also AAYA 5
Breathett, George 1925- 13-16R
Breatnac, Seamus
See Walsh, James P(atrick)
Breault, William 1926- CANR-6
Earlier sketch in CA 57-60
Brecher, Charles Martin 1945- CANR-4
Earlier sketch in CA 53-56
Brecher, Edward M(oritz) 1911-1989 ......CANR-7
Obituary 128
Earlier sketch in CA 13-16R
Brecher, Jeremy 1946- CANR-12
Earlier sketch in CA 69-72
Brecher, Michael 1925- CANR-4
Earlier sketch in CA 1-4R
Brecher, Ruth E(rnestine) 1911-1966 ......CAP-1
Earlier sketch in CA 13-14
Brechner, Irv 1951- 110
Brecht, Arnold 1884-1977 77-80
Obituary 73-76
Brecht, Bertolt 1898-1956 133
Brief entry 104
See also DLB 56
See also MTCW
See also TCLC 1, 6, 13, 35
See also WLC
Brecht, Edith 1895-1975 ....CAP-2
Earlier sketch in CA 25-28
See also SATA 6, 25
Brecht, Eugen Berthold Friedrich
See Brecht, Bertolt
Brecht, George 1924- 106
Breck, Allen duPont 1914- CANR-9
Earlier sketch in CA 13-16R
Breck, Vivian
See Breckenfeld, Vivian Gurney
Breckenfeld, Vivian Gurney 1895- 5-8R
See also SATA 1
Breckenridge, Adam Carlyle 1916- 29-32R
Breckinridge, Mary 1881-1965 Obituary 114
Breckler, Rosemary 1920- 101
Breda, Tjalmar
See DeJong, David C(ornel)
Bredel, Willi 1901-1964 ....DLB 56
Bredemeier, Harry Charles 1920- CANR-8
Earlier sketch in CA 5-8R
Bredemeier, Mary E(lizabeth) 1924- 81-84
Bredes, Don(ald) 1947- 110
Bredow, Miriam
See Wolf, Miriam Bredow
Bredsdorff, Elias Lunn 1912- CAP-1
Earlier sketch in CA 9-10
Bredsdorff, Jan 1942- CANR-13
Earlier sketch in CA 21-24R
Bredvold, Louis I(gnatius) 1888-1977 ....1-4R
Obituary 103
Bree, Germaine 1907- CANR-4
Earlier sketch in CA 1-4R
See also CAAS 15
Breech, (Earl) James 1944- 114
Breed, Paul F. 1916- 33-36R
Breeden, Stanley 1938- 106
Breem, Wallace (Wilfred Swinburne)
1926- Brief entry 113
Breen, Dana
See Birksted-Breen, Dana
Breen, (Joseph) John 1942- 77-80
Breen, Jon L(inn) 1943- 129
Breen, Quirinus 1896-1975 ....CAP-2
Earlier sketch in CA 33-36
Breen, Richard L. 1919-1967 Obituary 111
Breen, Richard 1935- 110
Breen, T(imothy) H(all) 1942- 101
Breen, William J(ames) 1937- 118
Breese, Dave
See Breese, David W(illiam)
Breese, David W(illiam) 1926- 118
Breese, Gerald (William) 1912- 41-44R
Breeskin, Adelyn Dohme 1896-1986 ....33-36R
Obituary 119
Breetveld, Jim Patrick 1925- CANR-2
Earlier sketch in CA 1-4R
Breeze, Katie 1929- 111
Breffort, Alexandre 1901-1971 Obituary 29-32R
Breger, Louis 1935- 69-72
Breggin, Peter R(oger) 1936- CANR-34
Earlier sketches in CA 81-84, CANR-15
Bregman, Jacob I(srael Jack) 1923- 41-44R
Bregman, Jay 1940- 109
Brehm, Sharon S(tephens) 1945- CANR-30
Earlier sketch in CA 112
Brehm, Shirley A(lice) 1926- 69-72
Breig, Joseph A(nthony) 1905- 5-8R
Breihan, Carl W(illiam) 1916- CANR-1
Earlier sketch in CA 1-4R
Breillat, Catherine 1950- 33-36R
Breimyer, Harold F(rederick) 1914- 17-20R
Breinburg, Petronella 1927- CANR-4
Earlier sketch in CA 53-56
See also SATA 11
Breines, Paul 1941- 61-64
Breines, Simon 1906- Brief entry 114
Breines, Winifred 1942- 113
Breisach, Ernst Adolf 1923- CANR-18
Earlier sketch in CA 1-4R
Breisky, William J(ohn) 1928- 53-56
See also SATA 22
Breit, Harvey 1909-1968 ....CANR-6
Obituary 25-28R
Earlier sketch in CA 5-8R
Breit, Marquita E(laine) 1942- 57-60
Breit, William (Leo) 1933- CANR-13
Earlier sketch in CA 33-36R
Breitbart, Vicki 1942- 93-96
Breitenkamp, Edward C(arlton) 1913- CANR-25
Earlier sketches in CA 25-28R, CANR-10
Breitinger, Johann Jakob 1701-1776 ....DLB 97
Breitman, George 1916-1986 ....CANR-7
Obituary 119
Earlier sketch in CA 61-64
Breitman, Richard D(avid) 1947- CANR-21
Earlier sketch in CA 105
Breitner, I. Emery 1929- 57-60
Breland, Osmond P(hilip) 1910- 9-12R
Brelis, Dean 1924- 9-12R
Brelis, Matthew 1957- 132
Brief entry 126
Brelis, Nancy (Burns) 1929- 21-24R
Brelsford, W(illiam) V(ernon) 1907- CAP-1
Earlier sketch in CA 13-14
Breman, Paul 1931- 21-24R
Brembeck, Winston Lamont
1912- Brief entry 115
Bremer, Arthur H(erman) 1950- Brief entry 113
Bremer, Francis J(ohn) 1947- 93-96
Bremer, Lisa
See Janas, Frankie-Lee
Bremner, Geoffrey 1930- CANR-38
Earlier sketch in CA 115
Bremner, John B(urton)
1920-1987 Obituary 123
Bremner, Robert H(amlett) 1917- CANR-9
Earlier sketch in CA 21-24R
Brems, Hans 1915- CANR-10
Earlier sketch in CA 25-28R
Bremser, Bonnie 1939- ....DLB 16
Bremser, Ray 1934- 17-20R
See also DLB 16
Bremyer, Jayne Dickey 1924- 61-64
Brenan, (Edward Fitz)Gerald
1894-1987 ....CANR-3
Obituary 121
Earlier sketch in CA 1-4R
Brend, Ruth M(argaret) 1927- 105
Brendel, Otto Johannes 1901-1973 97-100
Brendon, Piers (George Rundle)
1940- CANR-31
Earlier sketch in CA 101
Brendtro, Larry K. 1940- 29-32R
Brener, Milton E. 1930- 29-32R
Brengelman, Fred(erick Henry) 1928- 134
Brief entry 115
Brengelmann, Johannes Clemens 1920- 5-8R
Brenlove, Milovan S. 1948- 126
Brennan, Anne 1936- 109
Brennan, Bernard P(atrick) 1918- 5-8R
Brennan, Christopher
See Kininmonth, Christopher
Brennan, Christopher John
1870-1932 Brief entry 117
See also TCLC 17
Brennan, Donald (George)
1926-1980 Obituary 97-100
Brennan, Gale (Patrick) 1927- 125
See also SATA 53, 64
Brennan, (Harold) Geoffrey 1944- 128
Brennan, John N(eedham) H(uggard)
1914- CANR-20
Earlier sketches in CA 1-4R, CANR-4
Brennan, Joseph Gerard 1910- CANR-3
Earlier sketch in CA 1-4R
Brennan, Joseph K(illorin) 1952- 121
Brennan, Joseph Lomas 1903- CANR-2
Earlier sketch in CA 5-8R
See also SATA 6
Brennan, Joseph Payne 1918- CANR-19
Earlier sketches in CA 1-4R, CANR-4
Brennan, Lawrence D(avid) 1915- 5-8R
Brennan, Louis A(rthur) 1911-1983 ....17-20R
Obituary 109
Brennan, Maeve 1917- 81-84
See also CLC 5
Brennan, Matthew J. 1917- 106
Brennan, Maynard J. 1921- 13-16R
Brennan, Michael Joseph Jr. 1928- 13-16R
Brennan, Neil F(rancis) 1923- 37-40R
Brennan, Niall 1918- 13-16R
Brennan, Nicholas (Stephen) 1948- 106
Brennan, Ray 1908(?)-1972 Obituary 37-40R
Brennan, Richard O(liver) 1916- 89-92
Brennan, Tim
See Conroy, John Wesley
Brennan, Will
See Paine, Lauran (Bosworth)
Brennand, Frank
See Lambert, Eric
Brennecke, John H(enry) 1934- 37-40R
Brenneman, Helen Good 1925- 21-24R
Brenner, Anita 1905-1974 49-52
Obituary 53-56
See also SATA 56
Brenner, Barbara (Johnes) 1925- CANR-31
Earlier sketches in CA 9-12R, CANR-12
See also MAICYA
See also SAAS 14
See also SATA 4, 42
Brenner, David 1945- 133
Brenner, Elizabeth 1954- 123
Brenner, Erma 1911- 69-72
Brenner, Fred 1920- ....MAICYA
See also SATA 34, 36
Brenner, Gerry 1937- 110
Brenner, Isabel
See Schuchman, Joan
Brenner, Lenni 1937- 117
Brenner, Marie 1949- 73-76
Brenner, Rebecca Summer 1945- CANR-10
Earlier sketch in CA 61-64
Brenner, Reeve R(obert) 1936- Brief entry 116
Brenner, Summer
See Brenner, Rebecca Summer
Brenner, Yehojachin Simon 1926- CANR-11
Earlier sketch in CA 21-24R
Brennert, Alan (Michael) 1954- 118
Brenni, Vito J(oseph) 1923- CANR-31
Earlier sketch in CA 49-52
Brent, Beryl
See Ince, Martin (Jeffrey)
Brent, Harold Patrick 1943- 33-36R
Brent, Harry
See Brent, Harold Patrick
Brent, Hope 1935(?)-1984 ....SATA 39
Brent, Iris
See Bancroft, Iris (May Nelson)
Brent, Jonathan 1949- 113
Brent, Peter (Ludwig) 1931-1984 ....CANR-13
Obituary 114
Earlier sketch in CA 65-68
Brent, Stuart 73-76
See also SATA 14
Brentano, Bernard von 1901-1964 ....DLB 56
Brentano, Clemens 1778-1842 ....DLB 90
Brentano, Robert 1926- 21-24R
Brent-Dyer, Elinor Mary 1895-1969 101
Brent of Bin Bin
See Franklin, (Stella Maraia Sarah) Miles
Brenton, Howard 1942- CANR-33
Earlier sketch in CA 69-72
See also CLC 31
See also DLB 13
See also MTCW
Breo, Dennis L. 1942- 124
Brereton, Geoffrey 1906-1979 ....CANR-20
Earlier sketch in CA 25-28R
Bresee, Clyde W. 1916- 122
Bresky, Dushan 53-56
Breslau, Alan Jeffry 1926- 69-72
Breslauer, George W. 1946- CANR-12
Earlier sketch in CA 29-32R
Breslauer, Samuel Daniel 1942- 102
Breslin, Catherine 1936- 93-96
Breslin, Herbert H. 1924- 53-56
Breslin, James E. 1935- 33-36R
Breslin, James 1930- CANR-31
Earlier sketch in CA 73-76
See also Breslin, Jimmy
See also MTCW
Breslin, Jimmy
See Breslin, James
See also AITN 1
See also CLC 4, 43
Breslin, John B. 1943- 132
Breslin, Mark 1952- 121
Breslin, Paul 1946- 111
Breslin, Theresa 138
See also SATA 70
Breslove, David 1891- 9-12R
Breslow, Lester 1915- 115
Breslow, Lou 1900(?)-1987 Obituary 124
Breslow, Maurice (A.) 1935- 133
Breslow, Susan 1951- 137
See also SATA 69
Bressett, Kenneth E(dward) 1928- 93-96
Bressler, Leo A(lbert) 1911- 57-60
Bressler, Marion Ann 1921- 57-60
Bresson, Robert 1907- 110
See also CLC 16
Brestin, Dee 1944- 114
Bret, David 1952- 134
Bretall, Robert Walter 1913-1980 Obituary 110
Bretecher, Claire 1940- Brief entry 113
Bretnor, Reginald 1911- CANR-25
Earlier sketches in CA 65-68, CANR-10
Breton, Albert 1929- 61-64

Breton, Andre 1896-1966 .... CAP-2
Obituary 25-28R
Earlier sketch in CA 19-20
See also CLC 2, 9, 15, 54
See also DLB 65
See also MTCW
Bretscher, Paul G(erhardt) 1921- CANR-8
Earlier sketch in CA 17-20R
Brett, Bernard 1925- CANR-17
Earlier sketch in CA 97-100
See also SATA 22
Brett, Bill 1922- 122
Brett, David
See Campbell, Will D(avis)
Brett, Donna W(hitson) 1947- 134
Brett, Dorothy 1883-1977 Obituary 73-76
Brett, Edward T(racy) 1944- 134
Brett, George P(latt) Jr.
1893-1984 Obituary 112
Brett, Grace N(eff) 1900-1975 ....9-12R
Obituary 120
See also SATA 23
Brett, Hawksley
See Bell, Robert S(tanley) W(arren)
Brett, Jan (Churchill) 1949- 116
See also CLR 27
See also MAICYA
See also SATA 42, 71
Brett, John Michael
See Tripp, Miles (Barton)
Brett, Leo
See Fanthorpe, R(obert) Lionel
Brett, Lionel (Gordon Baliol) 1913- 131
Brett, Mary Elizabeth 9-12R
Brett, Michael
See Tripp, Miles (Barton)
Brett, Molly
See Brett, Mary Elizabeth
Brett, Peter David 1943- 77-80
Brett, Philip 1937- 129
Brett, Raymond Laurence 1917- CANR-3
Earlier sketch in CA 1-4R
Brett, Simon (Anthony Lee) 1945- CANR-29
Earlier sketch in CA 69-72
Brettell, Caroline B. 1950- 127
Brettell, Richard (Robson) 1949- 124
Brett-James, (Eliot) Antony 1920-1984 .....CANR-7
Obituary 112
Earlier sketch in CA 5-8R
Bretton, Henry L. 1916- CANR-2
Earlier sketch in CA 5-8R
Brettschneider, Bertram D(onald)
1924-1986 ....33-36R
Obituary 121
Brett-Smith, Richard 1923- 21-24R
Brett-Young, Jessica (Hankinson)
1883-1970 .... CAP-1
Earlier sketch in CA 9-10
Bretuo, Akwasi
See Assensoh, A(kwasi) B(retuo)
Breuer, Bessie 1893-1975 .... CAP-2
Obituary 61-64
Earlier sketch in CA 17-18
Breuer, Ernest Henry 1902-1972 .... CAP-2
Earlier sketch in CA 19-20
Breuer, Georg 1919- 105
Breuer, Gustav J. 1915-1985 Obituary 114
Breuer, Gustl
See Breuer, Gustav J.
Breuer, Lee 1937- 110
Breuer, Marcel 1902-1981 ....CANR-5
Obituary 104
Earlier sketch in CA 5-8R
Breuer, Miles J(ohn) 1888-1947 Brief entry 112
Breuer, Reinhard 1946- CANR-38
Earlier sketch in CA 115
Breuer, William B(entley) 1924- 118
Breugelmans, Rene 1925- 103
Breunig, Jerome Edward 1917- 13-16R
Breunig, LeRoy C(linton) 1915- 61-64
Brew, Douglas James
1949(?)-1985 Obituary 117
Brew, J(ohn) O(tis) 1906- 61-64
Brewer, Annie M. 1925- 107
Brewer, D(erek) S(tanley) 1923- CANR-4
Earlier sketch in CA 1-4R
Brewer, Edward S(amuel) 1933- CANR-13
Earlier sketch in CA 33-36R
Brewer, (Lucie) Elisabeth 1923- 115
Brewer, Frances Joan 1913-1965 .... CAP-1
Earlier sketch in CA 11-12
Brewer, Fredric (Aldwyn) 1921- 17-20R
Brewer, Garry Dwight 1941- CANR-14
Earlier sketch in CA 33-36R
Brewer, J(ohn) Mason 1896-1975 .... CAP-2
Earlier sketch in CA 25-28
Brewer, Jack A. 1933- 21-24R
Brewer, James H. Fitzgerald 1916- 9-12R
Brewer, Jeutonne P. 1939- CANR-14
Earlier sketch in CA 77-80
Brewer, John D(avid) 1951- 131
Brewer, Kenneth W(ayne) 1941- 110
Brewer, Margaret L. 1929- 29-32R
Brewer, Priscilla J. 1956- 122
Brewer, Sally King 1947- .... SATA 33
Brewer, Sam Pope
1909(?)-1976 Obituary 65-68
Brewer, Thomas B. 1932- 21-24R
Brewer, William C. 1897(?)-1974 Obituary 53-56
Brewer, Wilmon 1895- 5-8R
Brewi, Janice 1933- 110
Brewington, Marion Vernon 1902-1974 ....CANR-3
Obituary 53-56
Earlier sketch in CA 5-8R
Brewster, Benjamin
See Folsom, Franklin (Brewster)
Brewster, Dorothy 1883-1979 ....CANR-3
Obituary 85-88
Earlier sketch in CA 1-4R
Brewster, Elizabeth (Winifred) 1922- CANR-25
Earlier sketches in CA 25-28R, CANR-10
See also CAAS 15
See also DLB 60
Brewster, Eva 1922- 132
Brewster, Patience 1952- 121
See also SATA 51
Brewster, Townsend 1924- CANR-29
Earlier sketch in CA 105
Brewton, John E(dmund) 1898- CANR-3
Earlier sketch in CA 5-8R
See also SATA 5
Brewton, Sara Westbrook 122
Breyer, N(orman) L(ane) 1942- CANR-31
Earlier sketch in CA 49-52
Breyer, Stephen Gerald 1938- 107
Breytenbach, Breyten 1939(?)- 129
Brief entry 113
See also CLC 23, 37
Breza, Tadeusz 1905(?)-1970 Obituary 29-32R
Brezhnev, L. I.
See Brezhnev, Leonid I(lyich)
Brezhnev, Leonid
See Brezhnev, Leonid I(lyich)
Brezhnev, Leonid I(lyich) 1906-1982 132
Obituary 108
Brian
See Powell, Brian S(harples)
Brian, Alan B.
See Parulski, George R(ichard) Jr.
Brian, Denis 1923- 25-28R
Briand, Paul L. Jr. 1920- CANR-4
Earlier sketch in CA 1-4R
Briand, Rena 1935- 29-32R
Brians, Paul 1942- 127
Briarton, Grendel
See Bretnor, Reginald
Brice, Douglas 1916- 21-24R
Brice, Marshall Moore 1898- 17-20R
Brichant, Colette Dubois 1926- 13-16R
Brick, Howard 1953- 126
Brick, John 1922-1973 .... CAP-1
Obituary 45-48
Earlier sketch in CA 13-14
See also SATA 10
Brick, Michael 1922-1974 ....CANR-9
Earlier sketch in CA 13-16R
Bricker, Victoria Reifler 1940- 53-56
Brickhill, Paul Chester Jerome
1916-1991 ....9-12R
Obituary 134
Bricklin, Mark Harris 1939- 111
Brickman, Marshall 1941- 81-84
Brickman, William Wolfgang
1913-1986 ....CANR-17
Obituary 119
Earlier sketches in CA 1-4R, CANR-1
Brickner, Richard P(ilpel) 1933- CANR-2
Earlier sketch in CA 5-8R
Bricktop
See
Smith, Ada Beatrice Queen Victoria Louisa Virginia
Bricuth, John
See Irwin, John T(homas)
Bridenbaugh, Carl 1903-1992 ....CANR-4
Obituary 136
Earlier sketch in CA 9-12R
Bridge, Ann
See O'Malley, Mary Dolling (Sanders)
Bridge, Don(ald) U(lysses)
1894-1984 Obituary 112
Bridge, Raymond 1943- CANR-32
Earlier sketch in CA 69-72
Bridgecross, Peter
See Cardinal, Roger (Thomas)
Bridgeman, Harriet 1942- 85-88
Bridgeman, Richard
See Davies, L(eslie) P(urnell)
Bridgeman, William Barton 1916- 9-12R
Bridger, Adam
See Bingley, David Ernest
Bridger, Gordon (Frederick) 1932- 65-68
Bridgers, Sue Ellen 1942- CANR-36
Earlier sketches in CA 65-68, CANR-11
See also AAYA 8
See also CLC 26
See also CLR 18
See also DLB 52
See also MAICYA
See also SAAS 1
See also SATA 22
Bridges, Emily
See Bruggen, Carol (Holmes)
Bridges, Hal 1918- 1-4R
Bridges, Herb 1929- 110
Bridges, Howard
See Staples, Reginald Thomas
Bridges, James 1936- 127
Brief entry 116
Bridges, Laurie
See Bruck, Lorraine
Bridges, Robert (Seymour)
1844-1930 Brief entry 104
See also CDBLB 1890-1914
See also DLB 19, 98
See also TCLC 1
Bridges, William (Andrew) 1901- 33-36R
See also SATA 5
Bridges, William (Emery) 1933- CANR-13
Earlier sketch in CA 33-36R
Bridges-Adams, William 1889-1965 .... CAP-1
Earlier sketch in CA 13-14
Bridgman, Elizabeth 1921- 73-76
Bridgman, Richard 1927- 129
Bridgman, Sarah Atherton
1889(?)-1975 Obituary 57-60
Bridgwater, (William) Patrick 1931- 5-8R
Bridie, James
See Mavor, Osborne Henry
See also DLB 10
See also TCLC 3
Bridson, Gavin (Douglas Ruthven) 1936- 105
Bridwell, Norman 1928- CANR-20
Earlier sketches in CA 13-16R, CANR-5
See also MAICYA
See also SATA 4, 68
Briefs, Goetz Antony 1889-1974 .... CAP-2
Obituary 49-52
Earlier sketch in CA 21-22
Briegel, Ann C(arrick) 1915- 33-36R
Brien, Mimi 1929- 111
Brien, Raley
See McCulley, Johnston
Brier, Bob 1943- 102
Brier, Howard M(axwell) 1903-1969 .... CAP-1
Earlier sketch in CA 13-14
See also SATA 8
Brier, Peter A. 1935- 105
Brier, Royce 1894-1975 Obituary 93-96
Brier, Warren Judson 1931- 25-28R
Brierley, David 1936- 107
Brierley, (Louise) 1958- .... SATA 59
Brierley, Susan S.
See Isaacs, Susan (Sutherland Fairhurst)
Briffault, Herma 1898-1981 Obituary 104
Briggs, Asa 1921- CANR-7
Earlier sketch in CA 5-8R
Briggs, Austin (Eugene) Jr. 1931- 29-32R
Briggs, B(arry B.) Bruce
See Bruce-Briggs, B(arry B.)
Briggs, Berta N. 1884(?)-1976 Obituary 69-72
Briggs, Carl 1925- 114
Briggs, Carole S(uzanne) 1950- 110
See also SATA 47
Briggs, Charles Frederick 1804-1877 .... DLB 3
Briggs, Charlie 1927- CANR-1
Earlier sketch in CA 49-52
Briggs, Clarence E. III 1960- 136
Briggs, Desmond Lawther 1931- CANR-25
Earlier sketch in CA 108
Briggs, Dorothy Corkille 1924- 29-32R
Briggs, Ellis O(rmsbee) 1899-1976 73-76
Obituary 65-68
Briggs, F(red) Allen 1916- 33-36R
Briggs, Fred 1932- 73-76
Briggs, G. A. 1891(?)-1978 Obituary 104
Briggs, George M(cSpadden) 1919- 33-36R
Briggs, Jean 1925- 93-96
Briggs, Joe Bob 1959- 131
Briggs, John 1945- 132
Briggs, Katharine Mary 1898-1980 ....CANR-12
Obituary 102
Earlier sketch in CA 9-12R
See also SATA 25
Briggs, Kenneth Arthur 1941- 101
Briggs, Kenneth R. 1934- 33-36R
Briggs, L(loyd) Cabot 1909-1975 ....CANR-3
Obituary 57-60
Earlier sketch in CA 5-8R
Briggs, Michael (David) 1951- 135
Briggs, Peter 1921-1975 .... CAP-2
Obituary 57-60
Earlier sketch in CA 25-28
See also SATA 31, 39
Briggs, R(obert) C(ook) 1915- 37-40R
Briggs, Raymond Redvers 1934- 73-76
See also CLR 10
See also MAICYA
See also SATA 23, 66
Briggs, Shirley Ann 1918- 106
Briggs, Vernon M(ason) Jr. 1937- 73-76
Briggs, Walter Ladd 1919- 69-72
Briggs, Ward W(right Jr.) 1945- 135
Brigham, Besmilr 1923- CANR-12
Earlier sketch in CA 29-32R
Brigham, John C(arl) 1942- 41-44R
Brighouse, Harold 1882-1958 Brief entry 110
See also DLB 10
Bright, Deborah (Sue Tomberg) 1949- 97-100
Bright, Freda 1929- 136
Bright, Greg 1951- 93-96
Bright, John M. 1908-1989 ....5-8R
Obituary 129
Bright, Myron H. 1919- 134
Bright, Pamela Mia 1914- 109
Bright, Richard (Eugene) 1931- 69-72
Bright, Robert (Douglas Sr.) 1902-1988 73-76
Obituary 127
See also SATA 24, 60, 63
Bright, Sarah
See Shine, Deborah
Bright, William 1928- 33-36R
Brightbill, Charles K(estner) 1910-1966 ....1-4R
Obituary 103
Brightfield, Richard 1927- CANR-35
Earlier sketch in CA 118
See also SATA 53, 65
Brightfield, Rick
See Brightfield, Richard
Brightman, Robert 1920- 105
Brighton, Catherine 1943- 130
See also SATA 65
Brighton, Howard 1925- 57-60
Brighton, Wesley Jr.
See Lovin, Roger Robert
Brightwell, L(eonard) R(obert) 1889- .... SATA 29
Brignano, Russell C(arl) 1935- 57-60
Brignetti, Raffaello 1922(?)-1978 Obituary 104
Brigola, Alfredo L(uigi) 1923- 41-44R
Brijbhushan, Jamila 1918- 130
Briles, Judith 1946- 106
Briley, John (Richard) 1925- 101
Brilhart, John K. 1929- 21-24R
Brill, Earl H(ubert) 1925- 17-20R
Brill, Leon 1915- 110
Brill, Steven 85-88
Brilliant, Ashleigh 1933- CANR-11
Earlier sketch in CA 65-68
Brilliant, Eleanor L(uria) 1930- 112
Brilliant, Richard 1929- 33-36R
Briloff, Abraham J(acob) 1917- 61-64
Brim, Orville G(ilbert) Jr. 1923- CANR-2
Earlier sketch in CA 5-8R
Brimberg, Stanlee 1947- 49-52
See also SATA 9
Brimblecombe, Peter 1949- 128
Brimelow, Peter 1947- 133
Brin, David 1950- CANR-24
Earlier sketch in CA 102
See also CLC 34
See also SATA 65
Brin, Herb(ert Henry) 1915- CANR-27
Earlier sketch in CA 49-52
Brin, Ruth Firestone 1921- CANR-8
Earlier sketch in CA 17-20R
See also SATA 22
Brinckerhoff, Sidney B(urr)
1933- Brief entry 117
Brinckloe, Julie (Lorraine) 1950- 65-68
See also SATA 13
Brindel, June (Rachuy) 1919- CANR-31
Earlier sketch in CA 49-52
See also SATA 7
Brindle, Reginald Smith
See Smith Brindle, Reginald
Brindze, Ruth 1903- 73-76
See also SATA 23
Brinegar, David F(ranklin) 1910- 77-80
Brines, Russell (Dean) 1911- 69-72
Briney, Robert E(dward) 1933- CANR-19
Earlier sketches in CA 53-56, CANR-4
Bring, Mitchell 1951- 106
Bringhurst, Robert 1946- CANR-21
Earlier sketches in CA 57-60, CANR-6
Bringuier, Jean-Claude 1925- 133
Brinitzer, Carl 1907-1974 ....CANR-3
Obituary 53-56
Earlier sketch in CA 5-8R
Brink, Andre (Philippus) 1935- CANR-39
Earlier sketch in CA 104
See also CLC 18, 36
See also MTCW
Brink, Carol Ryrie 1895-1981 ....CANR-3
Obituary 104
Earlier sketch in CA 1-4R
See also MAICYA
See also SATA 1, 27, 31
Brink, Jean R. 1942- 137
Brink, T(erry) L(ee) 1949- CANR-34
Earlier sketches in CA 89-92, CANR-15
Brink, Wellington 1895-1979 Obituary 85-88
Brinker, Nancy (Goodman) 1946- 134
Brinker, Paul A. 1919- 25-28R
Brinker, Robert Durie 1901-1983 Obituary 111
Brinkerhoff, Dericksen Morgan 1921- 85-88
Brinkley, Alan 1949- 107
Brinkley, Christie 1953- 122
Brinkley, David (McClure) 1920- 97-100
Brinkley, George A. (Jr.) 1931- 17-20R
Brinkley, Joel 1952- 102
Brinkley, Roberta Florence
1892(?)-1967 Obituary 112
Brinkley, William (Clark) 1917- CANR-11
Earlier sketch in CA 21-24R
Brinkman, George L(oris) 1942- 53-56
Brinkman, Grover 1903- 73-76
Brinks, Herbert J(ohn) 1935- CANR-12
Earlier sketch in CA 29-32R
Brinley, Bertrand R(ussell) 1917- 29-32R
Brinley, Maryann B(ucknum) 1949- 130
Brinner, William M(ichael) 1924- CANR-29
Earlier sketch in CA 111
Brinnin, John Malcolm 1916- CANR-1
Earlier sketch in CA 1-4R
See also DLB 48
Brinsmead, H(esba) F(ay) 1922- CANR-10
Earlier sketch in CA 21-24R
See also CLC 21
See also MAICYA
See also SAAS 5
See also SATA 18
Brint, Armand Ian 1952- 105
Brinton, (Clarence) Crane 1898-1968 ....5-8R
Obituary 25-28R
Brinton, Henry 1901-1977 ....CANR-4
Earlier sketch in CA 1-4R
Brinton, Howard Haines 1884-1973 ....CANR-3
Earlier sketch in CA 5-8R
Brion, Guy
See Madsen, Axel
Brion, John M. 1922- 21-24R
Brion, Marcel 1895-1984 124
Obituary 114
Briquebec, John
See Rowland-Entwistle, (Arthur) Theodore (Henry)
Brisbane, Albert 1809-1890 .... DLB 3
Brisbane, Arthur 1864-1936 .... DLB 25
Brisbane, Henry R.
See Ellis, Edward S(ylvester)
Brisbane, Holly E. 1927- 33-36R
Brisbane, Katharine 1932- CANR-23
Earlier sketch in CA 107
Brisbane, Robert Hughes 1913- 77-80
Brisco, P. A.
See Matthews, Patricia (Anne)
Brisco, Patty
See Matthews, Clayton (Hartley)
and Matthews, Patricia (Anne)

Briscoe, D(avid) Stuart 1930- ... CANR-25
Earlier sketches in CA 17-20R, CANR-9
Briscoe, Jill (Pauline) 1935- ... CANR-8
Earlier sketch in CA 61-64
See also SATA 47, 56
Briscoe, John 1938- ... 118
Briscoe, Mary Louise 1937- ... 109
Brisk, Melvin J. 1924-1981 Obituary ... 104
Briskin, Jacqueline 1927- ... CANR-13
Earlier sketch in CA 29-32R
See also BEST 89:4
Briskin, Mae 1924- ... 134
Brisley, Joyce Lankester 1896- ... 97-100
See also SATA 22
Brisman, Leslie 1944- ... 61-64
Brissenden, Alan (Theo) 1932- ... 132
Brissenden, Paul F(rederick) 1885-1974 ... CAP-2
Obituary ... 53-56
Earlier sketch in CA 17-18
Brissenden, R(obert) F(rancis) 1928- ... CANR-10
Earlier sketch in CA 21-24R
Brisson, Pat 1951- ... 134
See also SATA 67
Brister, C(ommodore) W(ebster) Jr.
1926- ... CANR-7
Earlier sketch in CA 13-16R
Brister, Richard 1915- ... 13-16R
Bristol, Goldie M(ae) 1918- ... 121
Bristol, Julius
See Abel, Alan (Irwin)
Bristol, Lee Hastings Jr. 1923-1979 ... CANR-4
Obituary ... 89-92
Earlier sketch in CA 5-8R
Bristow, Allen P. 1929- ... CANR-8
Earlier sketch in CA 21-24R
Bristow, Gwen 1903-1980 ... CANR-12
Obituary ... 102
Earlier sketch in CA 17-20R
Bristow, Robert O'Neil 1926- ... 25-28R
Bristowe, Anthony (Lynn) 1921- ... CAP-1
Earlier sketch in CA 11-12
Britain, Dan
See Pendleton, Don(ald Eugene)
Britain, Ian (Michael) 1948- ... 130
Britchky, Seymour 1930- ... 102
Britindian
See Solomon, Samuel
Brito, Aristeo 1942- ... HW
Britsch, Ralph A(dam) 1912- ... 101
Britsch, Todd A(dam) 1937- ... 101
Britt, Albert 1874-1969 ... 5-8R
Obituary ... 103
See also SATA 28
Britt, Dell 1934- ... 25-28R
See also SATA 1
Britt, George (William Hughes)
1895-1988 Obituary ... 124
Britt, Steuart Henderson 1907-1979 ... CANR-2
Obituary ... 85-88
Earlier sketch in CA 1-4R
Brittain, Bill
See Brittain, William (E.)
See also SAAS 7
Brittain, Frederick ... CANR-3
Earlier sketch in CA 5-8R
Brittain, Joan Tucker 1928- ... 37-40R
Brittain, John A(shleigh) 1923- ... 73-76
Brittain, Vera (Mary) 1893(?)-1970 ... CAP-1
Obituary ... 25-28R
Earlier sketch in CA 13-16
See also CLC 23
See also MTCW
Brittain, William (E.) 1930- ... CANR-30
Earlier sketches in CA 77-80, CANR-13
See also Brittain, Bill
See also MAICYA
See also SATA 36
Brittan, Gordon G(oodhue) Jr. 1939- ... 89-92
Brittan, Samuel 1933- ... 29-32R
Britten, Milton R(eese) 1924-1985 ... 125
Obituary ... 115
Britten Austin, Paul 1922- ... CANR-13
Earlier sketch in CA 21-24R
Britter, Eric V(alentine) B(lakeney)
1906-1977 Obituary ... 73-76
Brittin, Norman A(ylsworth) 1906- ... 17-20R
Brittin, Phil (Henry) 1953- ... 108
Britton, Bryce 1943- ... 110
Britton, Christopher (Q.) 1943- Brief entry ... 118
Britton, Dorothea S(prague) 1926- ... CANR-16
Earlier sketches in CA 45-48, CANR-1
Britton, Dorothy (Guyver) 1922- ... 107
Britton, John A(ndrew) 1943- ... 126
Britton, Karl (William) 1909-1983 ... 29-32R
Obituary ... 110
Britton, Kate
See Stegeman, Janet Allais
See also SATA 49
Britton, Louisa
See McGuire, Leslie Sarah
Britton, Mattie Lula Cooper 1914- ... 5-8R
Britton, Peter Ewart 1936- ... CANR-18
Earlier sketch in CA 97-100
Brivic, Sheldon Roy 1943- ... 122
Brkic, Jovan 1927- ... 41-44R
Bro, Bernard (Gerard Marie) 1925- ... CANR-39
Earlier sketches in CA 97-100, CANR-17
Bro, Harmon Hartzell 1919- ... 25-28R
Bro, Marguerite (Harmon) 1894-1977 ... 77-80
See also SATA 19, 27
Broad, C(harlie) D(unbar) 1887-1971 ... 101
Obituary ... 89-92
Broad, Charles Lewis 1900- ... 5-8R
Broad, Jay 1930- ... CANR-19
Earlier sketch in CA 97-100
Broadbent, Donald E(ric) 1926- ... 105
Broadbent, Edward 1936- ... 45-48
Broadbent, W. W. 1919- ... 69-72
Broaddus, J(ohn) Morgan Jr. 1929- ... 21-24R
Broadfoot, Barry 1926- ... 89-92
Broadhead, Helen Cross 1913- ... 103
See also SATA 25
Broadhurst, Allan R. 1932- ... 5-8R
Broadhurst, Kent 1940- ... 137
Broadhurst, Ronald Joseph Callender
1906- ... CAP-1
Earlier sketch in CA 11-12
Broadley, Margaret E(ricson) 1904-1985 ... 97-100
Obituary ... 117
Broadribb, Violet ... 41-44R
Broadus, Catherine 1929- ... 37-40R
Broadus, Loren Jr. 1928- ... 37-40R
Broadus, Robert N(ewton) 1922- ... 73-76
Broadwell, Martin M. 1927- ... CANR-28
Earlier sketches in CA 73-76, CANR-13
Broat, I(sidore) G(erald) 1927- ... 97-100
Brobeck, Florence 1895-1979 Obituary ... 85-88
Broby-Johansen, R(udolf) 1900- ... CANR-12
Earlier sketch in CA 25-28R
Broce, Thomas Edward 1935- ... 69-72
Broch, Harald Beyer 1944- ... 135
Broch, Hermann 1886-1951 Brief entry ... 117
See also DLB 85
See also TCLC 20
Brochmann, Elizabeth 1938- ... 112
See also SATA 41
Brochu, Andre 1942- ... DLB 53
Brock, Alice May 1941- ... 41-44R
Brock, Arthur Guy Clutton
See Clutton-Brock, Arthur Guy
Brock, Ben
See Howells, Roscoe
Brock, Betty 1923- ... 29-32R
See also SATA 4
Brock, C(harles) E(dmund)
1870-1938 ... SATA 32, 42
Brock, D(ewey) Heyward 1941- ... 53-56
Brock, Delia
See Ephron, Delia
Brock, Dewey Clifton Jr. 1930- ... 5-8R
Brock, Edwin 1927- ... 130
Brief entry ... 119
See also DLB 40
Brock, Eleanor (Hope) 1921- ... 130
Brock, Emma L(illian) 1886-1974 ... 5-8R
Obituary ... 103
See also SATA 8
Brock, Gavin
See Lindsay, (John) Maurice
Brock, Gerald Wayne 1948- ... 57-60
Brock, H(enry) M(atthew) 1875-1960 ... SATA 42
Brock, Horace Rhea 1927- ... CANR-33
Earlier sketch in CA 113
Brock, Horace 1908(?)-1981 Obituary ... 105
Brock, Lou(is Clark) 1939- Brief entry ... 113
Brock, Lynn
See McAllister, Alister
Brock, Mary Duncan Howe
1909(?)-1984 Obituary ... 112
Brock, Michael George 1920- ... 93-96
Brock, P. W.
See Brock, Patrick Willet
Brock, Patrick Willet 1902- ... 112
Brock, Peter (de Beauvoir) 1920- ... CANR-5
Earlier sketch in CA 9-12R
Brock, Rose
See Hansen, Joseph
Brock, Russell Claude 1903-1980 Obituary ... 105
Brock, Stanley E(dmunde) 1936- ... 57-60
Brock, Stuart
See Trimble, Louis P(reston)
Brock, Van(dall) K(line) 1932- ... CANR-11
Earlier sketch in CA 61-64
Brock, W(illiam) H(odson) 1936- ... 21-24R
Brock, William R(anulf) 1916- ... CANR-20
Earlier sketches in CA 1-4R, CANR-4
Brockbank, (John) Philip
1922-1989 Obituary ... 129
Brockbank, Reed 1923- ... 21-24R
Brockelman, Paul T(aylor) 1935- ... 110
Brockett, Eleanor Hall 1913-1967 ... CAP-1
Earlier sketch in CA 9-10
See also SATA 10
Brockett, Oscar Gross 1923- ... CANR-22
Earlier sketches in CA 13-16R, CANR-7
Brockley, Fenton
See Rowland, D(onald) S(ydney)
Brockman, C(hristian) Frank 1902- ... 5-8R
See also SATA 26
Brockman, David Drake
See Drake-Brockman, David
Brockman, Harold 1902-1980 Obituary ... 101
Brockman, James R(aymond) 1926- ... CANR-28
Earlier sketch in CA 110
Brockman, Norbert 1934- ... 73-76
Brockriede, Wayne Elmer 1922- ... CANR-4
Earlier sketch in CA 1-4R
Brockway, Allan R(eitz) 1932- ... 21-24R
Brockway, Edith E. 1914- ... 17-20R
Brockway, (Archibald) Fenner
1888-1988 ... CAP-1
Obituary ... 125
Earlier sketch in CA 11-12
Brockway, George P(ond) 1915- ... 123
Brockway, Thomas P(armelee) 1898- ... CAP-2
Earlier sketch in CA 17-18
Brockway, Wallace 1905-1972 Obituary ... 37-40R
Brod, Max 1884-1968 ... CANR-7
Obituary ... 25-28R
Earlier sketch in CA 5-8R
See also DLB 81
Brod, Ruth Hagy 1911-1980 Obituary ... 97-100
Brodatz, Philip 1915- ... 57-60
Brodbeck, L. Emma 1893(?)-1989 Obituary ... 130
Brode, Douglas 1943- ... 57-60
Brode, Patrick 1950- ... 132
Brode, Wallace R. 1900(?)-1974 Obituary ... 53-56
Broder, David S(alzer) 1929- ... 97-100
Broder, Patricia Janis 1935- ... CANR-6
Earlier sketch in CA 57-60
Broderick, Carlfred B(artholomew)
1932- ... CANR-10
Earlier sketch in CA 25-28R
Broderick, Damien (Francis) 1944- ... CANR-28
Earlier sketch in CA 111
Broderick, Dorothy M. 1929- ... 13-16R
See also SATA 5
Broderick, Francis L(yons) 1922- ... 101
Broderick, John C(aruthers) 1926- ... 1-4R
Broderick, John F. 1909- ... CAP-2
Earlier sketch in CA 33-36
Broderick, Richard L(awrence) 1927- ... CANR-1
Earlier sketch in CA 45-48
Broderick, Robert C(arlton) 1913- ... CANR-8
Earlier sketch in CA 21-24R
Brodeur, Paul (Adrian Jr.) 1931- ... CANR-25
Earlier sketch in CA 5-8R
Brodeur, Ruth Wallace
See Wallace-Brodeur, Ruth
Brodhead, John R. 1814-1873 ... DLB 30
Brodhead, Michael John 1935- ... 105
Brodie, Bernard 1910-1978 ... CANR-10
Obituary ... 81-84
Earlier sketch in CA 17-20R
Brodie, Fawn M(cKay) 1915-1981 ... CANR-10
Obituary ... 102
Earlier sketch in CA 17-20R
Brodie, H(arlowe) Keith H(ammond) 1939- ... 103
Brodie, John (Riley) 1935- Brief entry ... 115
Brodie, Sally
See Cavin, Ruth (Brodie)
Brodin, Pierre Eugene 1909- ... 85-88
Brodine, Karen 1947- ... 123
Brodine, Virginia Warner 1915- ... 41-44R
Brodkey, Harold 1930- ... 111
See also CLC 56
Brodribb, (Arthur) Gerald (Norcott)
1915- ... CANR-33
Earlier sketch in CA 113
Brodsky, Archie 1945- ... CANR-7
Earlier sketch in CA 61-64
Brodsky, Beverly
See McDermott, Beverly Brodsky
Brodsky, Iosif Alexandrovich 1940- ... CANR-37
Earlier sketch in CA 41-44R
See also Brodsky, Joseph
See also AITN 1
See also MTCW
Brodsky, Joseph
See Brodsky, Iosif Alexandrovich
See also CLC 4, 6, 13, 36, 50
Brodsky, Louis Daniel 1941- ... 111
Brodsky, Michael Mark 1948- ... CANR-18
Earlier sketch in CA 102
See also CLC 19
Brodsky, Stanley L. 1939- ... CANR-29
Earlier sketch in CA 29-32R
Brodsky, Vera
See Lawrence, Vera Brodsky
Brodwin, Leonora Leet 1929- ... 53-56
Brody, Baruch A(lter) 1943- ... CANR-14
Earlier sketch in CA 33-36R
Brody, David 1930- ... 33-36R
Brody, Elaine 1923-1987 ... 37-40R
Obituary ... 123
Brody, J(acob) J(erome) 1929- ... CANR-32
Earlier sketch in CA 113
Brody, Jane E(llen) 1941- ... CANR-23
Earlier sketch in CA 102
Brody, Jules 1928- ... CANR-9
Earlier sketch in CA 13-16R
Brody, Marc
See Wilkes-Hunter, R(ichard)
Brody, Nathan 1935- ... 111
Brody, Polly 1919- ... 57-60
Brody, Saul Nathaniel 1938- ... 53-56
Brody, Sylvia
See Axelrad, Sylvia Brody
Broe, Mary Lynn 1946- ... 110
Broe, Ruth Hammond
1912(?)-1983 Obituary ... 110
Broeg, Bob
See Broeg, Robert M.
Broeg, Robert M. 1918- ... CANR-5
Earlier sketch in CA 13-16R
Broeger, Achim 1944- ... 107
See also SATA 31
Broegger, Fredrik Chr(istian) 1945- ... 138
Broehl, Wayne G(ottlieb) Jr. 1922- ... 9-12R
Broek, J(an) O(tto) M(arius) 1904-1974 ... CAP-2
Earlier sketch in CA 19-20
Broekel, Rainer Lothar 1923- ... CANR-19
Earlier sketches in CA 9-12R, CANR-3
See also SATA 38
Broekel, Ray
See Broekel, Rainer Lothar
Broeker, Galen 1920-1978 ... 41-44R
Obituary ... 133
Broekman, Marcel 1922- ... 57-60
Broer, Lawrence R(ichard) 1938- ... 69-72
Broer, Marion Ruth 1910- ... 13-16R
Broerman, Bruce M(artin) 1945- ... 126
Broesamle, John J(oseph) 1941- ... 57-60
Brof, Janet 1929- ... 37-40R
Brog, Molly (Jane) 1950- ... 113
Brogan, D(enis) W(illiam) 1900-1974 ... 97-100
Obituary ... 45-48
Brogan, Elise
See Urch, Elizabeth
Brogan, Frankie Fonde 1922- ... 109
Brogan, Gerald E(dward) 1924-1981 ... 29-32R
Obituary ... 104
Brogan, Jacqueline Vaught 1952- ... 125
Brogan, James E(dmund) 1941- ... 41-44R
Brogan, Phil(ip) F(rancis) 1896- ... 9-12R
Brogan, T(erry) V. F. 1951- ... 119
Broger, Achim
See Broeger, Achim
Broglie, Marguerite de
1897-1973 Obituary ... 37-40R
Broh, C(harles) Anthony 1945- ... 61-64
Broh-Kahn, Eleanor 1924- ... 45-48
Broido, Vera
See Cohn, Vera
Brokamp, Marilyn 1920- ... 49-52
See also SATA 10
Brokaw, Thomas John 1940- ... 108
Brokaw, Tom
See Brokaw, Thomas John
Brokensha, David W(arwick) 1923- ... 25-28R
Brokhin, Yuri 1934- ... 57-60
Brokhoff, John R(udolph) 1913- ... CANR-23
Earlier sketches in CA 61-64, CANR-8
Brolin, Brent C(ruse) 1940- ... 65-68
Bromage, Mary Cogan 1906- ... CAP-1
Earlier sketch in CA 13-16
Bromberg, Walter 1900- ... 65-68
Bromberger, Merry (Marie Louis)
1906-1979 Obituary ... 110
Bromberger, Serge Paul 1912- ... 29-32R
Brombert, Victor H. 1923- ... CANR-7
Earlier sketch in CA 13-16R
Brome, Richard 1590(?)-1652 ... DLB 58
Brome, (Herbert) Vincent ... CANR-14
Earlier sketch in CA 77-80
Bromell, Henry 1947- ... CANR-9
Earlier sketch in CA 53-56
See also CLC 5
Bromfield, Louis (Brucker)
1896-1956 Brief entry ... 107
See also DLB 4, 9, 86
See also TCLC 11
Bromhall, Winifred ... SATA 26
Bromhead, Peter (Alexander) 1919- ... 61-64
Bromige, David (Mansfield) 1933- ... CANR-16
Earlier sketch in CA 25-28R
Bromiley, Geoffrey W(illiam) 1915- ... CANR-19
Earlier sketches in CA 5-8R, CANR-4
Bromke, Adam 1928- ... 13-16R
Bromley, David G(rover) 1941- ... 41-44R
Bromley, Dorothy Dunbar
1896-1986 Obituary ... 118
Bromley, Dudley 1948- ... 77-80
See also SATA 51
Bromley, Gordon 1910- ... 112
Bromley, John Carter 1937- ... 33-36R
Bromley, John Selwyn 1913-1985 Obituary ... 116
Bromley, Yulian Vladimirovich
1921-1990 Obituary ... 131
Brommer, Gerald F(rederick) 1927- ... CANR-21
Earlier sketch in CA 105
See also SATA 28
Bromwich, David (Lee) 1951- ... 127
Brief entry ... 121
Bronaugh, Robert Brett 1947- ... 106
Brondfield, Jerome 1913- ... 73-76
See also SATA 22
Brondfield, Jerry
See Brondfield, Jerome
Broner, E(sther) M(asserman) 1930- ... CANR-25
Earlier sketches in CA 17-20R, CANR-8
See also CLC 19
See also DLB 28
Bronfeld, Stewart 1929- ... 109
Bronfenbrenner, Martin 1914- ... 13-16R
Bronfenbrenner, Urie 1917- ... CANR-16
Earlier sketch in CA 97-100
Bronin, Andrew 1947- ... 45-48
Bronk, William 1918- ... CANR-23
Earlier sketch in CA 89-92
See also CLC 10
Bronner, Edwin B(laine) 1920- ... CANR-22
Earlier sketches in CA 5-8R, CANR-7
Bronner, Simon J. 1954- ... 121
Bronner, Stephen Eric 1949- ... CANR-32
Earlier sketch in CA 113
Bronowski, Jacob 1908-1974 ... CANR-3
Obituary ... 53-56
Earlier sketch in CA 1-4R
See also SATA 55
Bronsen, David 1926- ... 37-40R
Bronson, Bertrand Harris 1902-1986 ... 61-64
Obituary ... 118
Bronson, Jill (Dorothy) Ireland
1936-1990 Obituary ... 131
Bronson, Lita
See Bell, Louise Price
Bronson, Lynn
See Lampman, Evelyn Sibley
Bronson, Oliver
See Rowland, D(onald) S(ydney)
Bronson, Wilfrid Swancourt 1894-1985 ... 73-76
Obituary ... 116
See also SATA 43
Bronson, William (Knox) 1926-1976 ... 41-44R
Obituary ... 65-68
Bronson, Wolfe
See Raborg, Frederick A(shton) Jr.
Bronstein, Arthur J. 1914- ... 9-12R
Bronstein, Leo 1903(?)-1976 Obituary ... 65-68
Bronstein, Lev Davidovich
See Trotsky, Leon
Bronstein, Lynne 1950- ... 77-80
Bronstein, Yetta
See Abel, Jeanne
Bronte, Anne 1820-1849 ... DLB 21

Bronte, Charlotte
1816-1855 .... CDBLB 1832-1890
See also DLB 21
See also WLC
Bronte, D(iana) Lydia 1938- 125
Bronte, (Jane) Emily
1818-1848 .... CDBLB 1832-1890
See also DLB 21, 32
See also WLC
Bronte, Louisa
See Roberts, Janet Louise
Bronwell, Arthur B. 1909- 33-36R
Bronzino, Joseph D. 1937- 136
Brook, Barry S(helley) 1918- CANR-16
Earlier sketch in CA 25-28R
Brook, David 1932- 13-16R
Brook, G. L.
See Brook, George Leslie
Brook, George Leslie 1910-1987 ....CANR-5
Obituary 123
Earlier sketch in CA 9-12R
Brook, Judith (Penelope) 1926- 122
See also SATA 51, 59
Brook, Judy
See Brook, Judith (Penelope)
Brook, Peter (Stephen Paul) 1925- CANR-38
Earlier sketch in CA 105
See also MTCW
Brook, Victor John Knight 1887-1974 ....1-4R
Obituary 103
Brooke, A. B.
See Jennings, Leslie Nelson
Brooke, Avery (Rogers) 1923- CANR-21
Earlier sketches in CA 57-60, CANR-6
Brooke, Brian 1911- 85-88
Brooke, Bryan (Nicholas) 1915- CANR-1
Earlier sketch in CA 45-48
Brooke, Carol
See Ramskill, Valerie Patricia Roskams
Brooke, Christopher N(ugent) L(awrence)
1927- CANR-18
Earlier sketches in CA 5-8R, CANR-2
Brooke, Dinah 1936- CANR-4
Earlier sketch in CA 49-52
Brooke, Eleanor (Golden)
1905(?)-1987 Obituary 122
Brooke, Frances 1724-1789 .... DLB 39, 99
Brooke, George Mercer Jr. 1914- 122
Brooke, Harold 1910- Brief entry 113
Brooke, Henry 1703(?)-1783 .... DLB 39
Brooke, James B. 1955- 135
Brooke, (Bernard) Jocelyn 1908- 5-8R
Brooke, John 1920-1985 Obituary 118
Brooke, Joshua
See Miller, Victor (Brooke)
Brooke, L(eonard) Leslie 1862-1940 .... CLR 20
See also MAICYA
See also SATA 17
Brooke, Maxey 1913- 9-12R
Brooke, Nicholas Stanton 1924- 25-28R
Brooke, Rupert (Chawner) 1887-1915 132
Brief entry 104
See also CDBLB 1914-1945
See also DLB 19
See also MTCW
See also TCLC 2, 7
See also WLC
Brooke, (Robert) Tal(iaferro) 1945- 93-96
Brooke, William J. 1946- 134
Brooke-Haven, P.
See Wodehouse, P(elham) G(renville)
Brooke-Little, John 1927- CANR-10
Earlier sketch in CA 21-24R
Brooker, Barbara 1936- 127
Brooker, Bertram 1888-1955 .... DLB 88
Brooker, Clark
See Fowler, Kenneth A(brams)
Brooker, Jewel Spears 1940- 135
Brooke-Rose, Christine 1926- 13-16R
See also CLC 40
See also DLB 14
Brookes, Edgar Harry 1897- CANR-3
Earlier sketch in CA 1-4R
Brookes, John A. 1933- 137
Brookes, Kenneth John
1909-1984 Obituary 111
Brookes, Owen
See Barber, D(ulan) F(riar Whilberton)
Brookes, Pamela 1922- 25-28R
Brookes, Reuben Solomon 1914- CAP-1
Earlier sketch in CA 9-10
Brookhouse, (John) Christopher 1938- 29-32R
Brookhouser, Frank 1912(?)-1975 ....1-4R
Obituary 61-64
Brookins, Dana 1931- 69-72
See also SATA 28
Brookman, Denise Cass 1921- 1-4R
Brookman, Rosina Francesca 1932- 61-64
Brookner, Anita 1928- CANR-37
Brief entry 114
Earlier sketch in CA 120
See also CLC 32, 34, 51
See also DLBY 87
See also MTCW
Brookover, Wilbur B(one) 1911- 33-36R
Brooks, A(lfred) Russell 1906- CAP-2
Earlier sketch in CA 33-36
Brooks, Albert
See Einstein, Albert
Brooks, Andree (Nicole) Aelion 1937- 133
Brooks, Anita
See Abramovitz, Anita (Zeltner Brooks)
See also SATA 5
Brooks, Anne Tedlock 1905- CANR-1
Earlier sketch in CA 1-4R
Brooks, B. David 1938- 113
Brooks, Bill 1939- .... SATA 59
Brooks, Bruce 137
See also AAYA 8
See also CLR 25
See also MAICYA
See also SATA 53
Brooks, C(larence) Carlyle 1888- CAP-1
Earlier sketch in CA 13-14
Brooks, Charles B(enton) 1921- 1-4R
Brooks, Charles E(dward) 1921- 53-56
Brooks, Charles (Gordon) 1920- 115
Brooks, Charles Timothy 1813-1883 .... DLB 1
Brooks, Charles V. W. 1912- 77-80
Brooks, Charlotte K. 89-92
See also SATA 24
Brooks, Cleanth 1906- CANR-35
Earlier sketches in CA 17-20R, CANR-33
See also CLC 24
See also DLB 63
See also MTCW
Brooks, D(avid) P. 1915- CANR-11
Earlier sketch in CA 25-28R
Brooks, David H(opkinson) 1929- 61-64
Brooks, Deems M(arkham) 1934- 69-72
Brooks, Douglas
See Brooks-Davies, Douglas
Brooks, Douglas L(ee) 1916- CANR-35
Earlier sketch in CA 114
Brooks, Elston (Harwood) 1930- 125
Brooks, Emerson M.
1905(?)-1982 Obituary 108
Brooks, Gary D(onald) 1942- 41-44R
Brooks, George
See Baum, L(yman) Frank
Brooks, George E(dward) Jr. 1933- 33-36R
Brooks, Gladys Rice
1886(?)-1984 Obituary 111
Brooks, Glenn E(llis) Jr. 1931- 1-4R
Brooks, Gregory 1961- 102
Brooks, Gwendolyn 1917- CANR-27
Earlier sketches in CA 1-4R, CANR-1
See also AITN 1
See also BLC 1
See also BW
See also CDALB 1941-1968
See also CLC 1, 2, 4, 5, 15, 49
See also CLR 27
See also DLB 5, 76
See also MTCW
See also SATA 6
See also WLC
Brooks, H(arold) Allen 1925- CANR-31
Earlier sketches in CA 81-84, CANR-14, 31
Brooks, Harold F(letcher) 1907- 128
Brooks, Harvey 1915- 25-28R
Brooks, Hindi Brief entry 115
Brooks, Hugh C. 1922- 29-32R
Brooks, Hunter O(tis) 1929- 77-80
Brooks, James L. 1940- CANR-32
Earlier sketch in CA 73-76
Brooks, Janice Young 1943- CANR-39
Earlier sketches in CA 65-68, CANR-9
Brooks, Jeanne
See Brooks-Gunn, Jeanne
Brooks, Jeremy 1926- CANR-7
Earlier sketch in CA 5-8R
See also DLB 14
Brooks, Jerome E(dmund)
1895(?)-1983 Obituary 109
Brooks, Jerome 1931- CANR-2
Earlier sketch in CA 49-52
See also SATA 23
Brooks, John
See Sugar, Bert Randolph
Brooks, John (Nixon) 1920- CANR-6
Earlier sketch in CA 13-16R
Brooks, Juanita 1898- Brief entry 114
Brooks, Karen 1949- 57-60
Brooks, Keith 1923- 17-20R
Brooks, (Frank) Leonard 1911- 13-16R
Brooks, LeRoy D(avis) II 1943- Brief entry 113
Brooks, Lester 1924- CANR-13
Earlier sketch in CA 33-36R
See also SATA 7
Brooks, (Mary) Louise 1906-1985 134
Obituary 117
Brooks, Lyman Beecher 1910-1984 122
Obituary 112
Brooks, Maggie
See Brooks, Margaret Ann
Brooks, Margaret Ann 1951- 132
Brooks, Maria (Zagorska) 1933- 41-44R
Brooks, Martha 136
See also SATA 68
Brooks, Maurice (Graham) 1900- .... SATA 45
Brooks, Mel
See Kaminsky, Melvin
See also CLC 12
See also DLB 26
Brooks, Nelson Herbert
1902-1978 Obituary 77-80
Brooks, Noah 1830-1903 .... DLB 42
Brooks, Pat 1931- CANR-7
Earlier sketch in CA 57-60
Brooks, Patricia 1926- CANR-11
Earlier sketch in CA 25-28R
Brooks, Paul 1909- CANR-7
Earlier sketch in CA 13-16R
Brooks, Peter Newman 1931- 131
Brooks, Peter W(right) 1920- 9-12R
Brooks, Peter 1938- CANR-1
Earlier sketch in CA 45-48
See also CLC 34
Brooks, Philip 1899(?)-1975 Obituary 104
Brooks, Polly Schoyer 1912- CANR-17
Earlier sketch in CA 1-4R
See also SATA 12
Brooks, Richard Oliver 1934- 112
Brooks, Richard 1912- 73-76
Obituary 137
See also DLB 44
Brooks, Robert A(ngus)
1920-1976 Obituary 65-68
Brooks, Robert Emanuel 1941- 57-60
Brooks, Ron(ald George) 1948- Brief entry 111
See also SATA 33
Brooks, Seth Rogers 1901-1987 Obituary 123
Brooks, Stewart M. 1923- CANR-9
Earlier sketch in CA 17-20R
Brooks, Terry 1944- CANR-14
Earlier sketch in CA 77-80
See also SATA 60
Brooks, Thomas R(eed) 1925- CANR-34
Earlier sketch in CA 73-76
Brooks, Thomas 1941- 120
Brooks, Tim(othy Haley) 1942- CANR-19
Earlier sketch in CA 102
Brooks, Van Wyck 1886-1963 ....CANR-6
Earlier sketch in CA 1-4R
See also CLC 29
See also DLB 45, 63, 103
Brooks, W. Hal 1933- 57-60
Brooks, Walter R(ollin)
1886-1958 Brief entry 111
See also SATA 17
Brooks, William D(ean) 1929- 33-36R
Brooks-Davies, Douglas 1942- CANR-12
Earlier sketch in CA 73-76
Brooks-Gunn, Jeanne 1946- 135
Brook-Shepherd, (Frederick) Gordon
1918- CANR-3
Earlier sketch in CA 9-12R
Brookshier, Frank 93-96
Brooks-Hill, Helen (Mason) 1908- .... SATA 59
Brookter, Marie 1934(?)- .... AITN 1
Broom, Leonard 1911- CANR-5
Earlier sketch in CA 13-16R
Broomall, Robert W(alter) 1946- 119
Broome, Charles L(arue) 1925- 41-44R
Broome, Harvey 1902-1968 122
Obituary 110
Broomell, Myron H(enry) 1906-1970 .... CAP-1
Earlier sketch in CA 9-10
Broomfield, Gerald W(ebb) 1895-1976 ....5-8R
Obituary 103
Broomfield, J(ohn) H(indle) 1935- 25-28R
Broomsnodder, B(radley) MacKinley
1940- CANR-8
Earlier sketch in CA 13-16R
Brophy, Ann 1931- 106
Brophy, Brigid (Antonia) 1929- CANR-25
Earlier sketch in CA 5-8R
See also CAAS 4
See also CLC 6, 11, 29
See also DLB 14
See also MTCW
Brophy, Donald F(rancis) 1934- CANR-10
Earlier sketch in CA 21-24R
Brophy, Elizabeth Bergen 1929- 61-64
Brophy, James David Jr. 1926- CANR-3
Earlier sketch in CA 1-4R
Brophy, James J(oseph) 1912- 65-68
Brophy, Jere E(dward) 1940- CANR-2
Earlier sketch in CA 45-48
Brophy, Jim
See Brophy, James J(oseph)
Brophy, John 1899-1965 .... CAP-1
Earlier sketch in CA 11-12
Brophy, Liam 1910- 9-12R
Brophy, Robert J(oseph) 1928- CANR-5
Earlier sketch in CA 53-56
Brose, Olive J(ohnson) 1919- 41-44R
Brosman, Catharine Savage 1934- CANR-21
Earlier sketch in CA 61-64
See also CLC 9
Brosnahan, Leonard Francis 1922- 102
Brosnahan, Tom 1945- 119
Brosnan, James Patrick 1929- CANR-3
Earlier sketch in CA 1-4R
See also SATA 14
Brosnan, Jim
See Brosnan, James Patrick
Bross, Irwin D(udley) J(ackson) 1921- 37-40R
Brossard, Chandler 1922- CANR-8
Earlier sketch in CA 61-64
See also CAAS 2
See also DLB 16
Brossard, Nicole 1943- 122
See also CAAS 16
See also DLB 53
Brossier, Margaret 1918(?)-1984 Obituary 113
Brostowin, Patrick Ronald 1931- 13-16R
Broszat, Martin 1926-1989 Obituary 130
Brother Antoninus
See Everson, William (Oliver)
Brother Bob
See Buell, Robert Kingery
Brother Choleric
See van Zeller, Claud
Brothers, (M.) Jay 1931- 103
Brothers, Joyce (Diane Bauer) 1929- CANR-13
Earlier sketch in CA 21-24R
See also AITN 1
Brothers Hildebrandt, The
See Hildebrandt, Tim(othy)
Brotherston, James Gordon 1939- CANR-11
Earlier sketch in CA 25-28R
Brotherton, Manfred 1900(?)-1981 Obituary 102
Broude, Norma (Freedman) 1941- 113
Broudy, Harry S(amuel) 1905- CANR-3
Earlier sketch in CA 1-4R
Broue, Pierre 1926- CANR-12
Earlier sketch in CA 69-72
Brough, James 1918- 111
Brough, John 1917-1984 Obituary 111
Brough, R(obert) Clayton 1950- CANR-7
Earlier sketch in CA 57-60
Brougham, Henry Peter 1778-1868 .... DLB 110
Brougham, John 1810-1880 .... DLB 11
Broughton, Bradford B. 1926- 21-24R
Broughton, Diane 1943- 81-84
Broughton, Geoffrey 1927- 102
Broughton, Jack(sel Markham) 1925- 73-76
Broughton, James (Richard) 1913- CANR-30
Earlier sketches in CA 49-52, CANR-2
See also CAAS 12
See also DLB 5
Broughton, Panthea Reid 1940- CANR-7
Earlier sketch in CA 57-60
Broughton, Rhoda 1840-1920 .... DLB 18
Broughton, T(homas) Alan 1936- CANR-23
Earlier sketches in CA 45-48, CANR-2
See also CLC 19
Brouillette, Jeanne S. 1-4R
Broumas, Olga 1949- CANR-20
Earlier sketch in CA 85-88
See also CLC 10
Broun, Emily
See Sterne, Emma Gelders
Broun, Heywood Hale 1918- CANR-12
Earlier sketch in CA 17-20R
Broun, Heywood Oren
1950(?)-1987 Obituary 124
Broun, Heywood 1888-1939 .... DLB 29
Broun, Hob
See Broun, Heywood Oren
Broussard, Louis 1922- 25-28R
Broussard, Vivian L.
See Martinetz, V(ivian) L.
Brouwer, Luitzen Egbertus Jan
1881-1966 Obituary 116
Brovka, Petr (Pyatrus Ustinovich)
1905-1980 Obituary 105
Brovkin, Vladimir N. 1951- 137
Brow, Robert 1924- CANR-10
Earlier sketch in CA 21-24R
Brow, Thea 1934- .... SATA 60
Broward, Donn
See Halleran, Eugene E(dward)
Broward, Robert C. 1926- 122
Browder, Earl Russell
1891(?)-1973 Obituary 45-48
Browder, Lesley H(ughes) Jr. 1935- 45-48
Browder, Olin L(orraine) Jr. 1913- 41-44R
Browder, Robert P(aul) 1921- 122
Browder, Sue 1946- 77-80
Browder, Walter Everett 1939- 53-56
Brower, Brock (Hendrickson) 1931- 25-28R
Brower, Charles Hendrickson 1901-1984 102
Obituary 113
Brower, Charlie
See Brower, Charles Hendrickson
Brower, Daniel R(oberts) 1936- 41-44R
Brower, David R(oss) 1912- CANR-9
Earlier sketch in CA 61-64
Brower, Kenneth (David) 1944- CANR-10
Earlier sketch in CA 25-28R
Brower, Linda A. 1945- 33-36R
Brower, Millicent CANR-15
Earlier sketch in CA 41-44R
See also SATA 8
Brower, Pauline 1929- 77-80
See also SATA 22
Brower, Reuben Arthur 1908-1975 ....CANR-6
Obituary 57-60
Earlier sketch in CA 1-4R
Browin, Frances Williams 1898- CAP-1
Earlier sketch in CA 19-20
See also SATA 5
Brown, A(lfred) R(eginald) Radcliffe
See Radcliffe-Brown, A(lfred) R(eginald)
Brown, Alan A. 1929- CANR-16
Earlier sketch in CA 25-28R
Brown, Alan R. 1938- 105
Brown, Alberta L(ouise) 1894- CAP-1
Earlier sketch in CA 11-12
Brown, Alexander (Crosby) 1905- CANR-3
Earlier sketch in CA 1-4R
Brown, Alexis
See Baumann, Amy (Brown) Beeching
Brown, Alice Very
See Very, Alice (N.)
Brown, Alice 1856-1948 .... DLB 78
Brown, Allen 1926- 13-16R
Brown, Andreas Le 1933- 108
Brown, Anne Ensign 1937- 101
See also SATA 61
Brown, Anne S(eddon) K(insolving)
1906-1985 ....17-20R
Obituary 117
Brown, Annice Harris 1897- 45-48
Brown, Annora 1899-1987(?) Obituary 121
Brown, Anthony Eugene 1937- 89-92
Brown, Archibald Haworth 1938- CANR-20
Earlier sketch in CA 103
Brown, Arnold 1927- 117
Brown, Arthur A(llen) 1900- 73-76
Brown, Arthur Wayne 1917- CANR-8
Earlier sketch in CA 5-8R
Brown, Ashley 1923- CANR-20
Earlier sketches in CA 1-4R, CANR-3
Brown, B(artley) Frank 1917- CANR-4
Earlier sketch in CA 9-12R
Brown, B(essie) Katherine (Taylor)
1917- 13-16R
Brown, Barbara B(anker) 1917- 69-72
Brown, Barbara W(ood) 1928- 105
Brown, Beatrice C.
See Curtis Brown, Beatrice
Brown, Benjamin F. 1930- CANR-1
Earlier sketch in CA 45-48

Brown, Bernard E(dward) 1925- CANR-21
Earlier sketches in CA 1-4R, CANR-4
Brown, Bert R(obert) 1936- 41-44R
Brown, Beth CAP-2
Earlier sketch in CA 21-22
Brown, Betty
See Jones, Elizabeth B(rown)
Brown, Bill
See Brown, William L(ouis)
Brown, Billye Walker
See Cutchen, Billye Walker
Brown, Blanche R. (Levine) 1915- 13-16R
Brown, Bob
See Brown, Robert Carlton
and Brown, Robert Joseph
See also DLB 4, 45
Brown, Bob Burton 1925- 21-24R
Brown, Buck 1936- .... SATA 45
Brown, Calvin S(mith) 1909- 49-52
Brown, Camille 1917- 9-12R
Brown, Carl F(raser) 1910- 41-44R
Brown, Carol Williams 1941- 111
Brown, Carolyn S. 1950- 127
Brown, Carrie
See Brown, Carolyn S.
Brown, Carter
See Yates, A(lan) G(eoffrey)
Brown, Cassie 1919-1986 ....CANR-23
Earlier sketch in CA 45-48
See also SATA 55
Brown, Cecil H(ooper) 1944- 109
Brown, Cecil M(orris) 1943- CANR-27
Earlier sketch in CA 73-76
See also BW
See also DLB 33
Brown, Cecil 1907-1987 Obituary 123
Brown, Charles
See Cadet, John
Brown, Charles Brockden
1771-1810 .... CDALB 1640-1865
See also DLB 37, 59, 73
Brown, Charles H. 1910- 21-24R
Brown, Charles N(ikki) 1937- 93-96
Brown, Charles T(homas) 1912- 41-44R
Brown, Christopher P(aterson) 1939- CANR-10
Earlier sketch in CA 65-68
Brown, Christy 1932-1981 105
Obituary 104
See also CLC 63
See also DLB 14
Brown, Clarence (Fleetwood Jr.)
1929- Brief entry 112
Brown, Clark 1935- 25-28R
Brown, Claude 1937- 73-76
See also AAYA 7
See also BLC 1
See also BW
See also CLC 30
Brown, Clifford Waters Jr. 1942- 77-80
Brown, (John) Clive (Anthony) 1947- 121
Brown, Conrad 1922- .... SATA 31
Brown, Constantine 1889-1966 .... CAP-1
Earlier sketch in CA 11-12
Brown, Courtney C(onrades) 1904-1990 77-80
Obituary 131
Brown, Croswell 1905(?)-1971 Obituary 104
Brown, Curtis F(ranklin) 1925- 61-64
Brown, Cynthia 1952- 121
Brown, Dale W. 1926- 37-40R
Brown, Dale 1957(?)- 138
Brief entry 129
See also BEST 89:4
Brown, Daniel G(ilbert) 1924- 45-48
Brown, Daniel Russell
See Curzon, Daniel
Brown, Daphne Faunce
See Faunce-Brown, Daphne (Bridget)
Brown, David
See Myller, Rolf
Brown, David
See Brown, David A(lan)
Brown, David A(lan) 1922-1982 129
Obituary 110
Brown, David (Clifford) 1929- 57-60
Brown, David E(arl) 1938- CANR-32
Earlier sketch in CA 113
Brown, David Grant 1936- 13-16R
Brown, David S(pringer) 1915- 29-32R
Brown, David 1916- 13-16R
Brown, Deaver David 1943- 102
Brown, Dee (Alexander) 1908- CANR-11
Earlier sketch in CA 13-16R
See also CAAS 6
See also CLC 18, 47
See also DLBY 80
See also MTCW
See also SATA 5
Brown, Delwin (Wray) 1935- 135
Brief entry 117
Brown, Denise Scott 1931- 41-44R
Brown, Dennis A(lbert) 1926-1976 ....CANR-13
Earlier sketch in CA 61-64
Brown, Derek Ernest Denny
See Denny-Brown, Derek Ernest
Brown, Diana 1928- CANR-18
Earlier sketch in CA 101
Brown, Donald Eugene 1909- CAP-1
Earlier sketch in CA 13-16
Brown, Donald Fowler 1909- 41-44R
Brown, Donald Robert 1925- 41-44R
Brown, Doris E. 1910(?)-1975 Obituary 61-64
Brown, Dorothy
See Oxley, Dorothy (Anne)
Brown, Dorothy M. 1932- 125
Brown, Douglas
See Gibson, Walter B(rown)
Brown, Douglas (Frank Lambert) 1907- 25-28R
Brown, Drollene P. 1939- 122
See also SATA 53
Brown, Duane 1937- 33-36R
Brown, E(dward) K(illoran)
1905-1951 Brief entry 107
Brown, E(ugene) Richard 1942- CANR-18
Earlier sketch in CA 97-100
Brown, Edgar S. Jr. 1922- 9-12R
Brown, Edmund G(erald) 1905- 132
Brown, Edmund G. (Pat)
See Brown, Edmund G(erald)
Brown, Edward J(ames) 1909- 25-28R
Brown, Eleanor Frances 1908- 29-32R
See also SATA 3
Brown, Eleanor Gertrude
1887-1968 Obituary 104
Brown, Elisabeth Potts 1939- 133
Brown, Elizabeth Louise 1924- 53-56
Brown, Elizabeth M(yers) 1915- 107
See also SATA 43
Brown, Emily Clara 1911- 53-56
Brown, Erik 1923- 114
Brown, Ernest Henry Phelps 1906- 108
Brown, Evelyn M. 1911- 21-24R
Brown, F(rancis) Andrew 1915- 41-44R
Brown, F. Keith 1913(?)-1976 Obituary 69-72
Brown, F(rancis Charles Claypon) Yeats
See Yeats-Brown, F(rancis Charles Claypon)
Brown, Fern G. 1918- CANR-17
Earlier sketch in CA 97-100
See also SATA 34
Brown, (Robert) Fletch 1923- 116
See also SATA 42
Brown, Fornan 1901- .... SATA 71
Brown, Forrest 49-52
Brown, (Ernest) Francis 1903- 73-76
Brown, Francis R(obert) 1914- 41-44R
Brown, Frank A(rthur) Jr. 1908- 69-72
Brown, Frank E(dward) 1908- 101
Brown, Frank London 1927-1962 .... DLB 76
Brown, Frederick G(ramm) 1932- CANR-12
Earlier sketch in CA 29-32R
Brown, Frederick 1934- 25-28R
Brown, Fredric (William) 1906-1972 121
Obituary 33-36R
See also DLB 8
Brown, G(eorge) Neville 1932- 17-20R
Brown, Geoff 1932- 61-64
Brown, George
See Wertmueller, Lina
Brown, George Alfred George
See George-Brown, George Alfred
Brown, George Douglas 1869-1902 ...... TCLC 28
Brown, George Earl 1883-1964 ....5-8R
See also SATA 11
Brown, George Isaac 1923- 73-76
Brown, George Mackay 1921- CANR-37
Earlier sketches in CA 21-24R, CANR-12
See also CAAS 6
See also CLC 5, 48
See also DLB 14, 27
See also MTCW
See also SATA 35
Brown, George Thompson 1921- 111
Brown, Gerald Saxon 1911- 9-12R
Brown, Gerald W(illiam) 1916- 33-36R
Brown, Giles T(yler) 1916- 17-20R
Brown, Ginny
See Brown, Virginia Sharpe
Brown, Gwilym Slater 1928-1974 ....9-12R
Obituary 53-56
Brown, H. Rap
See Al-Amin, Jamil Abdullah
Brown, Hamish M. 1934- 129
Brown, Harcourt 1900- CANR-20
Earlier sketch in CA 101
Brown, Harold O(gden) J(oseph)
1933- CANR-10
Earlier sketch in CA 25-28R
Brown, Harriett M. 1897- 5-8R
Brown, Harrison Scott 1917-1986 69-72
Obituary 121
Brown, Harry G(unnison)
1880-1975 Obituary 57-60
Brown, Harry M(atthew) 1921- CANR-10
Earlier sketch in CA 25-28R
Brown, Harry (Peter McNab Jr.)
1917-1986 69-72
Obituary 120
See also DLB 26
Brown, Hazel E(lizabeth) 1893- 57-60
Brown, Helen Gurley 1922- CANR-5
Earlier sketch in CA 5-8R
Brown, Herbert Ross 1902- CAP-1
Earlier sketch in CA 13-16
Brown, Howard Mayer 1930- CANR-3
Earlier sketch in CA 1-4R
Brown, Hugh Auchincloss
1879-1975 Obituary 61-64
Brown, Huntington 1899- CAP-1
Earlier sketch in CA 19-20
Brown, Ida Mae 1908- CAP-2
Earlier sketch in CA 29-32
Brown, Ina Corinne 5-8R
Brown, Ina Ladd 1905- CAP-1
Earlier sketch in CA 13-14
Brown, Ira Vernon 1922- 5-8R
Brown, Irene Bennett 1932- CANR-12
Earlier sketch in CA 29-32R
See also SATA 3
Brown, Irving
See Adams, William Taylor
Brown, Irwin
See Murray, David Stark
Brown, Ivor (John Carnegie)
1891-1974 ....CANR-12
Obituary 49-52
Earlier sketch in CA 9-12R
See also SATA 5, 26
Brown, J(ames) Douglas
1898-1986 Obituary 118
Brown, J(oseph) P(aul) S(ummers) 1930- 61-64
Brown, James Alan Calvert
1922-1984 Obituary 114
Brown, James Bush
See Bush-Brown, James
Brown, James Cooke 1921- 29-32R
Brown, James I(saac) 1908- CANR-7
Earlier sketch in CA 17-20R
Brown, James (Montgomery) 1921- 1-4R
Brown, James Patrick 1948- 29-32R
Brown, James S(eay) Jr. 1944- 120
Brown, James (Wiley) 1909-1983 77-80
Obituary 135
Brown, James Wilson 1913- 41-44R
Brown, James 1934- CANR-27
Earlier sketches in CA 65-68, CANR-10
Brown, Jamie 1945- CANR-20
Earlier sketch in CA 101
Brown, Janet 1947- 69-72
Brown, Jay A(llen) 1935- 110
Brown, Jeff
See Brown, Sevellon III
Brown, Jennifer S. H. 1940- 130
Brown, Jerry Earl 1940- 105
Brown, Jerry Wayne 1936- 25-28R
Brown, Jim (M.) 1940- 69-72
Brown, Jo Giese 1947- 108
Brown, Joan Sayers 1925(?)-1983 Obituary 110
Brown, Joe David 1915-1976 ....13-16R
Obituary 65-68
See also SATA 44
Brown, John A. 1898- 112
Brown, John Arthur 1914- CANR-11
Earlier sketch in CA 17-20R
Brown, John Buchanan
See Buchanan-Brown, John
Brown, John (E.) 1934- 25-28R
Brown, John Gracen 1936- 104
Brown, John J. 1916- 13-16R
Brown, John L(ackey) 1914- 49-52
Brown, John Mason 1900-1969 ....9-12R
Obituary 25-28R
Brown, John Pairman 1923- 33-36R
Brown, John Russell 1923- CANR-11
Earlier sketch in CA 21-24R
Brown, John 1887- CAP-1
Earlier sketch in CA 13-14
Brown, John 1920- 5-8R
Brown, Jonathan (M.) 1939- Brief entry 112
Brown, Jonathan (Mayer) 1939- 132
Brown, Joseph E(dward) 1929- CANR-6
Earlier sketch in CA 53-56
See also SATA 51, 59
Brown, Judith C(ora) 136
Brown, Judith Gwyn 1933- CANR-21
Earlier sketch in CA 93-96
See also SATA 20
Brown, Judith K. 124
Brown, Judith M(argaret) 1944- CANR-32
Earlier sketches in CA 41-44R, CANR-15
Brown, Julia (Prewitt) 1948- 93-96
Brown, Karl 1895(?)-1970 Obituary 104
Brown, Karl 1897-1990 Obituary 131
Brown, Kenneth H. 1936- 13-16R
Brown, Kevin V. 1922- 89-92
Brown, Kitt
See Vandergriff, (Lola) Aola
Brown, L(aurence) B(inet) 1927- 65-68
Brown, L. Carl
See Brown, Leon Carl
Brown, L. J.
See Du Breuil, (Elizabeth) L(or)inda
Brown, Larry
See Brown, Lawrence Jr.
Brown, (William) Larry 1951- 134
Brief entry 130
Brown, Laurene Krasny 1945- 117
See also SATA 54
Brown, Lawrence Jr. 1947- Brief entry 114
Brown, Lawrence R. 1904(?)-1986 Obituary 119
Brown, Lee Dolph 1890-1971 Obituary 29-32R
Brown, Leigh 65-68
Brown, Leland 1914- 1-4R
Brown, Lennox (John) 1934- 93-96
Brown, Leon Carl 1928- Brief entry 117
Brown, LeRoy Chester 1908- CANR-13
Earlier sketches in CAP-1, CA 11-12
Brown, Les(ter Louis) 1928- CANR-13
Earlier sketch in CA 33-36R
Brown, Leslie H(ilton) 1917-1980 ....CANR-7
Earlier sketch in CA 9-12R
Brown, Leslie Wilfrid 1912- 17-20R
Brown, Lester
See Brown, Lester R(ussell)
Brown, Lester R(ussell) 1934- 132
Brown, Letitia Woods 1915-1976 73-76
Obituary 69-72
Brown, Lloyd Arnold 1907-1966 .... CAP-1
Earlier sketch in CA 11-12
See also SATA 36
Brown, Louis M(orris) 1909- 49-52
Brown, Lyle C(larence) 1926- CANR-15
Earlier sketch in CA 41-44R
Brown, Lynne P. 1952- 138
Brown, M(ary) L(oretta) T(herese) 13-16R
Brown, Mac Alister 1924- 89-92
Brown, Mahlon A.
See Ellis, Edward S(ylvester)
Brown, Mandy
See Brown, May
Brown, Marc (Tolon) 1946- CANR-36
Earlier sketch in CA 69-72
See also MAICYA
See also SATA 10, 53
Brown, Marcia 1918- 41-44R
See also CLR 12
See also DLB 61
See also MAICYA
See also SATA 7, 47
Brown, Marel 1899- 102
Brown, Margaret Wise 1910-1952 136
Brief entry 108
See also CLR 10
See also DLB 22
See also MAICYA
See also YABC 2
Brown, Margery (Wheeler) CANR-26
Earlier sketch in CA 25-28R
See also BW
See also SATA 5
Brown, Marian A. 1911- 73-76
Brown, Marilyn McMeen Miller 1938- CANR-6
Earlier sketch in CA 57-60
Brown, Marion Marsh 1908- CANR-3
Earlier sketch in CA 1-4R
See also SATA 6
Brown, Mark H(erbert) 1900- CAP-2
Earlier sketch in CA 21-22
Brown, Marshall L. 1924- 21-24R
Brown, Marshall 1945- 111
Brown, Marvin L. Jr. 1920- 53-56
Brown, Mary Ellen 1939- 117
Brown, Mary Ward 1917- 133
Brown, Maurice F(red) 1928-1985 ....41-44R
Obituary 116
Brown, May 1913- 118
Brown, Melissa Mather 1917- 121
Brown, Merle Elliott 1925-1978 108
Brown, Michael Barratt
See Barratt-Brown, Michael
Brown, Michael H(arold) 1952- 121
Brown, Michael John 1932- 29-32R
Brown, Michael 1931- 33-36R
Brown, Michael 1938- 127
Brown, Milton Perry Jr. 1928- 9-12R
Brown, Milton W(olf) 1911- Brief entry 113
Brown, Morna Doris 1907- CANR-5
Earlier sketch in CA 5-8R
See also Ferrars, Elizabeth
Brown, Morris Cecil 1943- 37-40R
Brown, Moses
See Barrett, William (Christopher)
Brown, Muriel W(hitbeck) 1892- CAP-2
Earlier sketch in CA 23-24
Brown, Muriel 1938- 107
Brown, Murray 1929- 37-40R
Brown, Myra Berry 1918- CANR-3
Earlier sketch in CA 1-4R
See also SATA 6
Brown, Nathaniel Hapgood 1929- 101
Brown, Ned 1882(?)-1976 Obituary 65-68
Brown, Neville (George) 1932- 9-12R
Brown, Newell 1917- 97-100
Brown, Norman D(onald) 1935- 53-56
Brown, Norman O(liver) 1913- 21-24R
Brown, Oliver Madox 1855-1874 .... DLB 21
Brown, Palmer 1919- 107
See also SATA 36
Brown, Pamela (Beatrice) 1924-1989 ....13-16R
Obituary 127
See also SATA 5, 61
Brown, Parker B(oyd) 1928- 53-56
Brown, Patricia Fortini 1936- 131
Brown, Paul B. 1954- 138
Brown, Paula 1925- 110
Brown, Peter A. 1949- 138
Brown, Peter Douglas 1925- CANR-16
Earlier sketch in CA 25-28R
Brown, Peter Lancaster
See Lancaster-Brown, Peter
Brown, Peter (Robert Lamont) 1935- CANR-13
Earlier sketch in CA 21-24R
Brown, Peter 1926(?)-1984(?) Obituary 112
Brown, R(eginald) Allen 1924-1989 ....CANR-11
Obituary 128
Earlier sketch in CA 5-8R
Brown, R(onald) G(ordon) S(clater)
1929- 29-32R
Brown, Rae
See Brown, Forrest
Brown, Ralph Adams 1908- 33-36R
Brown, Raymond Bryan 1923-1977 ....17-20R
Obituary 133
Brown, Raymond E(dward) 1928- CANR-17
Earlier sketch in CA 97-100
Brown, Raymond George 1924- 109
Brown, Raymond Kay 1936- 102
Brown, Raymond Lamont
See Lamont-Brown, Raymond
Brown, Re Mona 1917- 41-44R
Brown, Rebecca 1956- 124
Brown, Rex V(andesteene) 1933- 53-56
Brown, Richard C(arl) 1917- CANR-17
Earlier sketches in CA 5-8R, CANR-2
Brown, Richard D(avid) 1939- 53-56
Brown, Richard E(ugene) 1937- 73-76
Brown, Richard E. 1946- 130
Brown, Richard (Eric) 1946- .... SATA 61
Brown, Richard H(arvey) 1940- CANR-38
Earlier sketch in CA 109
Brown, Richard H(olbrook) 1927- 9-12R
Brown, Richard Howard 1929- 57-60
Brown, Richard Maxwell 1927- CANR-11
Earlier sketch in CA 17-20R
Brown, Richard 1935- 114

Brown, Rita Mae 1944- CANR-35
Earlier sketches in CA 45-48, CANR-2, 11
See also CLC 18, 43
See also MTCW
Brown, Robert Carlton
1886-1959 Brief entry 107
See also Brown, Bob
Brown, Robert Craig 1935- 101
Brown, Robert D. 1924- CANR-20
Earlier sketch in CA 104
Brown, Robert E(ldon) 1907- 5-8R
Brown, Robert Edward 1945- CANR-15
Earlier sketch in CA 65-68
Brown, Robert Fath 1941- 111
Brown, Robert Goodell 1923- 33-36R
Brown, Robert Hanbury 1916- 112
Brown, Robert Joseph 1907- CANR-13
Earlier sketches in CAP-1, CA 9-10
See also Brown, Bob
See also SATA 14
Brown, Robert L. 1921- 21-24R
Brown, Robert McAfee 1920- CANR-7
Earlier sketch in CA 13-16R
Brown, Robert T(homas) 1943- 113
Brown, Robin 1937- 97-100
Brown, Roderick (Langmere) Haig-
See Haig-Brown, Roderick (Langmere)
Brown, Roger Glenn 1941- 77-80
Brown, Roger H(amilton) 1931- 9-12R
Brown, Roger William 1925- 13-16R
Brown, Ronald 1900- 81-84
Brown, Rosalie
See Moore, Rosalie (Gertrude)
See also SATA 9
Brown, Rosel George 1926-1967 Obituary 102
Brown, Rosellen 1939- CANR-14
Earlier sketch in CA 77-80
See also CAAS 10
See also CLC 32
Brown, Rosemary (Eleanor)
1938- Brief entry 115
Brown, Roswell
See Webb, Jean Francis
Brown, Roy (Frederick) 1921-1982 65-68
Obituary 117
See also SATA 39, 51
Brown, Rustie 1930(?)-1988 Obituary 125
Brown, Sanborn C(onner) 1913-1981 .... CANR-11
Obituary 106
Earlier sketch in CA 17-20R
Brown, Sanford J(ay) 1946- 118
Brown, Sevellon III 1913-1983 Obituary 110
Brown, Seyom 1933- CANR-17
Earlier sketch in CA 65-68
Brown, Sheldon S. 1933- 122
Brown, Sheldon S. 1937- CANR-7
Earlier sketch in CA 53-56
Brown, Sidney DeVere 1925- 33-36R
Brown, Spencer 1909- 130
Brown, Stanley (Branson) 1914- 49-52
Brown, Stanley C(oleman) 1928- 77-80
Brown, Stanley H(arold) 1927- 45-48
Brown, Stephen W. 1940- CANR-13
Earlier sketch in CA 33-36R
Brown, Sterling Allen 1901-1989 .... CANR-26
Obituary 127
Earlier sketch in CA 85-88
See also BLC 1
See also BW
See also CLC 1, 23, 59
See also DLB 48, 51, 63
See also MTCW
Brown, Steven R(andall) 1939- 49-52
Brown, Stewart 1951- 135
Brown, Stuart C(ampbell) 1938- CANR-25
Earlier sketch in CA 29-32R
Brown, Stuart Gerry 1912-1991 .... 21-24R
Obituary 135
Brown, Susan Jenkins 1896- 85-88
Brown, T. E. 1830-1897 .... DLB 35
Brown, T(illman) Merritt 1913- 41-44R
Brown, Terence 1944- CANR-19
Earlier sketch in CA 102
Brown, Theo W(atts) 1934- CANR-8
Earlier sketch in CA 61-64
Brown, Theodore L(awrence) 1928- 33-36R
Brown, Theodore M(orey) 1925- 33-36R
Brown, Thomas H. Jr. 1950- 127
Brown, Thomas H. 1930- 57-60
Brown, Thomas McPherson
1906-1989 Obituary 128
Brown, Tina 1953- 118
Brief entry 116
Brown, Tom Jr.
See Brown, Thomas H. Jr.
Brown, Truesdell S(parhawk) 1906- 13-16R
Brown, Turner Jr.
See Hample, Stuart
Brown, Velma Darbo 1921- 97-100
Brown, Vinson 1912- CANR-1
Earlier sketch in CA 1-4R
See also SATA 19
Brown, Virginia Pounds 1916- 114
Brown, Virginia Sharpe 1916- 13-16R
Brown, Virginia (Suggs) 1924- 69-72
Brown, W. Anthony 1933- Brief entry 110
Brown, W(illiam) Norman 1892-1975 61-64
Obituary 57-60
Brown, Wallace 1933- 17-20R
Brown, Walter Lee 1924- 33-36R
Brown, Walter R(eed) 1929- CANR-2
Earlier sketch in CA 45-48
See also SATA 19
Brown, Warner
See Boroson, Warren
Brown, Warren A. 1917(?)-1985 Obituary 117
Brown, Warren (William) 1894-1978 85-88
Obituary 81-84
Brown, Wayne 1944- 101
Brown, Weldon A(mzy) 1911- 65-68
Brown, Wenzell 1912- CANR-5
Earlier sketch in CA 1-4R
Brown, Wesley 1945- 125
See also BW
Brown, Wilfred A(rthur) Gavin
See Gavin-Brown, Wilfred A(rthur)
Brown, Wilfred (Banks Duncan)
1908-1985 .... 9-12R
Obituary 116
Brown, Will
See Ainsworth, William Harrison
Brown, Will C.
See Boyles, C(larence) S(cott) Jr.
Brown, William Anthony 1933- 125
Brief entry 110
See also BW
Brown, William Campbell 1928- 57-60
Brown, William E(nglish) 1907-1975 .... CAP-2
Earlier sketch in CA 29-32
Brown, William Edward 1904- 126
Brown, William F(erdinand) 1928- 33-36R
Brown, William F(rank) 1920- 33-36R
Brown, William F. 1906(?)-1990 Obituary 131
Brown, William Hill 1765-1793 .... DLB 37
Brown, William J. 97-100
Brown, William James 1889- 5-8R
Brown, William L(ouis) 1910-1964 .... 1-4R
See also SATA 5
Brown, William Wells 1813-1884 .... BLC 1
See also DC 1
See also DLB 3, 50
Brown, Zenith Jones 1898-1983 .... 9-12R
Obituary 110
Brown-Azarowicz, Marjory F. 1922- 33-36R
Brownback, Paul 1940- 113
Browne, Anthony (Edward Tudor)
1946- CANR-36
Earlier sketch in CA 97-100
See also CLR 19
See also MAICYA
See also SATA 44, 45, 61
Browne, Barum
See Saunders, Hilary Aidan St. George
Browne, Charles Farrar 1834-1867 .... DLB 11
Browne, Colette (Victoria) 1950- 121
Browne, Courtney 1915- 21-24R
Browne, Dik
See Browne, Richard Arthur Allan
See also AITN 1
See also SATA 38
Browne, E(lliott) Martin 1900-1980 .... CAP-2
Obituary 97-100
Earlier sketch in CA 25-28
Browne, Francis Fisher 1843-1913 .... DLB 79
Browne, G(erald) P(eter) 1930- 21-24R
Browne, Gary Lawson 1939- 101
Browne, George Stephenson 1890-1970 .... CAP-2
Earlier sketch in CA 29-32
Browne, Hablot Knight 1815-1882 .... SATA 21
Browne, Harry
See Browne, Henry
Browne, Harry 1933- CANR-3
Earlier sketch in CA 49-52
Browne, Henry 1918- 102
Browne, Howard 1908- 73-76
Browne, (Clyde) Jackson 1948(?)- 120
See also CLC 21
Browne, Joseph William 1914- 105
Browne, Joy 1944- 97-100
Browne, Malcolm W(ilde) 1931- 17-20R
Browne, Matthew
See Rands, William Brighty
Browne, Michael Dennis 1940- CANR-15
Earlier sketch in CA 29-32R
See also DLB 40
Browne, Ray B(roadus) 1922- CANR-11
Earlier sketch in CA 17-20R
Browne, Raymond 1897- 73-76
Browne, Richard Arthur Allan
1917-1989 Obituary 128
See also Browne, Dik
See also SATA 38, 67
Browne, Robert
See Karlins, Marvin
Browne, Robert S(pan) 1924- CANR-14
Earlier sketch in CA 37-40R
Browne, Roland A. 1910- 65-68
Browne, Sam
See Smith, Ronald Gregor
Browne, Theodore R.
1911(?)-1979 Obituary 81-84
Browne, Walter A(nderson) 1895- 37-40R
Browne, William P(aul) 1945- CANR-25
Earlier sketch in CA 109
Browne, Wynyard (Barry)
1911-1964 Obituary 113
See also DLB 13
Brownell, Blaine Allison 1942- 65-68
Brownell, John Arnold 1924- 21-24R
Brownell, W. C. 1851-1928 .... DLB 71
Browne Miller, Angela 1952- 135
Browne of Tavistock, William
1590-1645 .... DLB 121
Browning, Alice C(rolley)
1907-1985 Obituary 117
Browning, Christopher R(obert) 1944- 112
Browning, Columban
See Browning, William
Browning, David (George) 1938- 37-40R
Browning, Dixie Burrus 1930- 110
Browning, Don S(pencer) 1934- CANR-2
Earlier sketch in CA 49-52
Browning, (Grayson) Douglas 1929- 13-16R
Browning, Elizabeth Barrett
1806-1861 .... CDBLB 1832-1890
See also DLB 32
See also WLC
Browning, Elizabeth 1924- 57-60
Browning, Frank 1946- 107
Browning, Gordon 1938- 37-40R
Browning, Iben 1918- Brief entry 113
Browning, J(ohn) D. 1942- 125
Browning, John S.
See Williams, Robert Moore
Browning, L. J.
See Du Breuil, (Elizabeth) L(or)inda
Browning, Mary 1887- CAP-1
Earlier sketch in CA 11-12
Browning, Norma Lee 1914- CANR-8
Earlier sketch in CA 61-64
Browning, Peter 1928- 104
Browning, Preston M(ercer) Jr. 1929- 57-60
Browning, Reed 1938- 57-60
Browning, Robert L(ynn) 1924- CANR-16
Earlier sketch in CA 85-88
Browning, Robert
1812-1889 .... CDBLB 1832-1890
See also DLB 32
See also PC 2
See also YABC 1
Browning, Robert 1914- CANR-13
Earlier sketch in CA 33-36R
Browning, Rufus P(utnam) 1934- 124
Browning, (Zerilda) Sinclair 1946- 112
Browning, Tod 1882-1962 Obituary 117
See also CLC 16
Browning, Wilfrid (Robert Francis) 1918- 5-8R
Browning, William 1921- 113
Brownjohn, Alan 1931- 25-28R
See also DLB 40
See also SATA 6
Brownjohn, J(ohn Nevil) Maxwell 1929- 129
Brownlee, David B(ruce) 1951- 132
Brownlee, O(swald) H(arvey) 1917- 65-68
Brownlee, W(ilson) Elliot Jr. 1941- 69-72
Brownlee, W(illiam) H(ugh) 1917- 9-12R
Brownlee, Walter 1930- 57-60
See also SATA 62
Brownlie, Ian 1932- CANR-2
Earlier sketch in CA 5-8R
Brownlow, Cecil Alexander III
1926-1988 Obituary 124
Brownlow, Kevin 1938- CANR-12
Earlier sketch in CA 25-28R
See also SATA 65
Brownmiller, Susan 1935- CANR-35
Earlier sketch in CA 103
See also MTCW
Brownrigg, Walter Grant 1940- 110
Brownson, Orestes Augustus
1803-1876 .... DLB 1, 59, 73
Brownson, William C(larence) Jr. 1928- 69-72
Brownstein, Karen (Osney) 1944-1989 124
Obituary 130
Brownstein, Michael 1943- 33-36R
Brownstein, Oscar Lee 1928- 113
Brownstein, Rachel M. 1937- 122
Brownstein, Ronald J. 1958- 106
Brownstein, Samuel C. 1909- 5-8R
Brownstone, David M. 1928- CANR-21
Earlier sketch in CA 104
Broxholme, John Franklin 1930- CANR-31
Earlier sketches in CA 65-68, CANR-12
Broxon, Mildred Downey 1944- 107
Broy, Anthony 1916- 102
Broyard, Anatole 1920-1990 105
Obituary 132
Broyles, J(ohn) Allen 1934- 9-12R
Broyles, William Dodson Jr. 1944- 73-76
Brozek, Josef (Maria) 1913- 45-48
Brozen, Yale 1917- 109
Bru, Hedin
See Jacobsen, Hans Jacob
Brubach, Holly 1953- 110
Brubacher, John Seiler 1898- CANR-1
Earlier sketch in CA 1-4R
Brubaker, Carol
See Stolk, Anthonie
Brubaker, Dale L(ee) 1937- CANR-4
Earlier sketch in CA 53-56
Brubaker, Earl R(oy) 1932- 107
Brubaker, Sterling 1924- 21-24R
Bruccoli, Matthew J(oseph) 1931- CANR-7
Earlier sketch in CA 9-12R
See also CLC 34
See also DLB 103
Bruce, Ben F. Jr. 1920- 13-16R
Bruce, Charles 1906-1971 .... DLB 68
Bruce, Curt 1946- 97-100
Bruce, David (Kirkpatrick Este)
1898-1977 Obituary 105
Bruce, Debra 1951- 118
Bruce, Dickson D. Jr. 1946- 53-56
Bruce, Donald (James) 1930- 17-20R
Bruce, Dorita Fairlie 1885-1970 Obituary 107
See also SATA 27
Bruce, F(rederick) F(yvie) 1910- CANR-19
Earlier sketches in CA 1-4R, CANR-3
Bruce, George 1909- 65-68
Bruce, Harold (R.)
1934(?)-1987 Obituary 122
Bruce, Harry J. 1931- 21-24R
Bruce, Janet
See Campbell, Janet Bruce
Bruce, Jeannette M. 1922- 5-8R
Bruce, Lennart 1919- CANR-13
Earlier sketch in CA 33-36R
Bruce, Lenny
See Schneider, Leonard Alfred
See also CLC 21
Bruce, Leo
See Croft-Cooke, Rupert
See also DLB 77
Bruce, Mary 1927- 25-28R
See also SATA 1
Bruce, Maurice 1913(?)-1988 Obituary 125
Bruce, Mildred Mary 1896(?)-1990 Obituary 131
Bruce, Monica
See Melaro, Constance L(oraine)
Bruce, Philip Alexander 1856-1933 .... DLB 47
Bruce, R(aymon) R(ene) 1934- 89-92
Bruce, Richard
See Nugent, Richard Bruce
Bruce, Robert V(ance) 1923- 53-56
Bruce, Robert 1927- CAP-1
Earlier sketch in CA 9-10
Bruce, Shelley
See Merklinghaus, Michele
Bruce, Sylvia (Valerie) 1936- 33-36R
Bruce, Violet R(ose) 29-32R
Bruce-Briggs, B(arry B.) 112
Bruce-Gardyne, Jock
See Bruce-Gardyne, John
Bruce-Gardyne, John 1930-1990 Obituary 131
Bruce Lockhart, Robin 1920- 25-28R
Bruce-Novoa
See Bruce-Novoa, Juan D.
Bruce-Novoa, John David
See Bruce-Novoa, Juan D.
Bruce-Novoa, Juan D. 1944- CANR-32
Brief entry 117
See also DLB 82
See also HW
Bruch, Hilde 53-56
See also AITN 1
Bruchac, Joseph III 1942- CANR-13
Earlier sketch in CA 33-36R
See also SATA 42
Bruchey, Stuart (Weems) 1917- 33-36R
Bruck, Lilly 1918- 109
Bruck, Lorraine 1921- .... SATA 46, 55
Brucker, Clara (Hantel)
1892(?)-1980 Obituary 97-100
Brucker, Gene (Adam) 1924- Brief entry 114
Brucker, Herbert 1898-1977 .... CANR-4
Obituary 69-72
Earlier sketch in CA 5-8R
Brucker, Roger W(arren) 1929- CANR-11
Earlier sketch in CA 65-68
Bruckman, Clyde 1894-1955 .... DLB 26
Bruckner, D. J. R. 1933- 132
Bruckner, Ferdinand 1891-1958 .... DLB 118
Bruder, Judith 97-100
Bruder, Mary Newton 1939- 127
Bruegel, Johann Wolfgang 1905-1986 77-80
Obituary 121
Bruegel, John Wolfgang
See Bruegel, Johann Wolfgang
Brueggemann, Walter (A.) 1933- Brief entry 117
Bruegmann, Robert 1948- 101
Bruehl, Anton 1900-1982 Obituary 110
Bruemmer, Fred 1929- 102
See also SATA 47
Bruening, William H(arry) 1943- 57-60
Bruess, Clint E. 1941- 33-36R
Bruff, Nancy
See Gardner, Nancy Bruff
Bruffee, Kenneth A. 1934- 37-40R
Bruford, Walter Horace
1894-1988 Obituary 126
Bruggen, Carol (Holmes) 1932- 117
Brugger, Bill
See Brugger, William
Brugger, Robert J(ohn) 1943- CANR-38
Earlier sketches in CA 85-88, CANR-16
Brugger, William 1941- CANR-12
Earlier sketch in CA 73-76
Bruggink, Donald J. 1929- CANR-7
Earlier sketch in CA 13-16R
Brugioni, Dino A. 1921- 137
Bruhn, Eric (Belton Evers)
1928-1986 Obituary 118
Bruhn, John Glyndon 1934- 89-92
Bruin, John
See Brutus, Dennis
Bruins, Elton J(ohn) 1927- 53-56
Bruland, Esther (Byle) 1956- 116
Bruller, Jean (Marcel) 1902-1991 .... CANR-12
Obituary 134
Earlier sketch in CA 65-68
Brulls, Christian
See Simenon, Georges (Jacques Christian)
Brumback, Carl V. 1917(?)-1987 Obituary 123
Brumbaugh, Robert Sherrick 1918- CANR-3
Earlier sketch in CA 5-8R
Brumbaugh, Thomas B(rendle) 1921- 49-52
Brumble, H(erbert) David III 1943- 107
Brumgardt, John R(aymond) 1946- 97-100
Brumm, Ursula 1919- 29-32R
Brummel, Mark Joseph 1933- 103
Brummet, R. Lee 1921- 21-24R
Brummitt, Wyatt B. 1897- 9-12R
Brun, Ellen 1933- 103
Brun, Henri 1939- 53-56
Bruna, Dick 1927- CANR-36
Earlier sketch in CA 112
See also CLR 7
See also MAICYA
See also SATA 30, 43
Brundage, Burr Cartwright 1912- 41-44R
Brundage, Dorothy J(une) 1930- 104
Brundage, James A(rthur) 1929- CANR-7
Earlier sketch in CA 5-8R
Brundage, John Herbert 1926- 101
See also Herbert, John
Brundage, Percival F(lack) 1892-1979 101
Obituary 89-92

Brune, Lester H(ugo) 1926- CANR-13
  Earlier sketch in CA 33-36R
Bruneau, Jean
  See Sylvestre, (Joseph Jean) Guy
Bruneau, Thomas C. 1939- 53-56
Brunelli, Jean 1934- 138
Bruner, Edward M. 1924- 121
Bruner, Herbert B. 1894(?)-1974 Obituary 53-56
Bruner, Jerome S(eymour) 1915- CANR-1
  Earlier sketch in CA 45-48
Bruner, Margaret E. (Baggerly) 1886-197 (?) CAP-1
  Earlier sketch in CA 17-18
Bruner, Phillip L. 1944- 127
Bruner, Richard W(allace) 1926- 49-52
Bruner, Wally 1931- 49-52
Brunet, Michel 1917-1985 ..... CANR-18
  Obituary 117
  Earlier sketch in CA 102
Brunette, Peter (Clark Jr.) 1943- 126
Brunetti, Cledo 1910-1971 ..... CAP-2
  Earlier sketch in CA 29-32
Brunetti, Mendor Thomas 1894-1979 Obituary 89-92
Brunhoff, Jean de 1899-1937 137
  Brief entry 118
  See also CLR 4
  See also MAICYA
  See also SATA 24
Brunhoff, Laurent de 1925- 73-76
  See also CLR 4
  See also MAICYA
  See also SATA 24, 71
Brunhouse, Robert Levere 1908- CANR-2
  Earlier sketch in CA 49-52
Bruni, (Toni) Roxanna 1952- 114
Bruning, Nancy P(auline) 1948- CANR-23
  Earlier sketch in CA 106
Brunn, Harry O(tis) Jr. 1919- 1-4R
Brunner, Edmund de S(chweinitz) 1889-1973 ..... CAP-1
  Obituary 45-48
  Earlier sketch in CA 13-16
Brunner, Edward J. 1946- 127
Brunner, Elizabeth 1920-1983 Obituary 111
Brunner, James A(lbertus) 1923- 37-40R
Brunner, John (Kilian Houston) 1934- CANR-37
  Earlier sketches in CA 1-4R, CANR-2
  See also CAAS 8
  See also CLC 8, 10
  See also MTCW
Brunner, Karl 1916-1989 Obituary 128
Brunner, Maurice Yaw 1950- 103
Brunner, Theodore F(riederich) 1934- 33-36R
Brunnings, Florence E(mery) 1916- 112
Bruno, Frank
  See St. Bruno, Albert Francis
Bruno, Frank J(oe) 1930- 107
Bruno, Harold R. Jr. 1928- 77-80
Bruno, James Edward 1940- 41-44R
Bruno, Michael 1921- 33-36R
Bruno, Vincent J. 1926- 65-68
Bruns, Frederick R. Jr. 1913(?)-1979 Obituary 85-88
Bruns, George 1914(?)-1983 Obituary 109
Bruns, J(ames) Edgar 1923- CANR-2
  Earlier sketch in CA 5-8R
Bruns, Joe
  See Altshuler, Harry
Bruns, William A(lan) 1942- 113
Bruns, William J(ohn) Jr. 1935- 37-40R
Brunskill, Ronald (William) 1929- 85-88
Brunstein, Karl (Avrum) 1933- 97-100
Brunt, P(eter) A(stbury) 1917- 101
Bruntjen, Scott 1943- 111
Brunton, David W(alter) 1929- 41-44R
Brunton, Paul 1898-1981 Obituary 115
Bruntz, George G. 1901- 5-8R
Brunvand, Jan Harold 1933- CANR-26
  Earlier sketch in CA 108
Brus, Wlodzimierz 1921- 73-76
Brush, Craig B(alcombe) 1930- 21-24R
Brush, Douglas P(eirce) 1930- CANR-7
  Earlier sketch in CA 57-60
Brush, John E(dwin) 1919- 33-36R
Brush, Judith M(arie) 1938- CANR-7
  Earlier sketch in CA 57-60
Brush, Karen A(lexandra) 1960- 127
Brush, Stephanie 1954- 138
Brush, Stephen G(eorge) 73-76
Brushwood, John S(tubbs) 1920- CANR-9
  Earlier sketch in CA 21-24R
Brusiloff, Phyllis 1935- 57-60
Bruss, Elizabeth W(issman) 1944-1981 108
Brussel, Jacob 1900(?)-1979 Obituary 104
Brussel, James Arnold 1905- CANR-3
  Earlier sketch in CA 1-4R
Brussel-Smith, Bernard 1914- ..... SATA 58
Brust, Harold
  See Cheyney, (Reginald Evelyn) Peter (Southouse)
Brust, Steven K. (Zoltan) 1955- CANR-37
  Earlier sketch in CA 115
Brustein, Robert S(anford) 1927- CANR-7
  Earlier sketch in CA 9-12R
Bruster, Bill(y) G(lenn) 1940- 111
Brustlein, Daniel 1904- ..... SATA 40
Brustlein, Janice Tworkov 9-12R
  See also SATA 40
Bruteau, Beatrice 1930- 57-60
Bruton, Eric (Moore) 1915- CANR-23
  Earlier sketches in CA 13-16R, CANR-5
Bruton, Henry J(ackson) 1921- 21-24R
Bruton, J(ack) G(ordon) 1914- 9-12R
Brutten, Gene J. 1928- 37-40R
Brutten, Milton 1922- 45-48
Brutus
  See Spooner, John D.
Brutus, Dennis 1924- CANR-27
  Earlier sketches in CA 49-52, CANR-2
  See also CAAS 14
  See also BLC 1
  See also BW
  See also CLC 43
  See also DLB 117
Bruun, Bertel 1937- 45-48
Bruun, (Arthur) Geoffrey 1898-1988 ..... 1-4R
  Obituary 126
Bruun, Ruth Dowling 1937- 108
Bruyn, Kathleen 1903- CAP-2
  Earlier sketch in CA 33-36
Bruzelius, Caroline 1949- 121
Bry, Adelaide 1920- 33-36R
Bry, Gerhard 1911- 41-44R
Bryan, Ashley F. 1923- CANR-26
  Earlier sketch in CA 107
  See also BW
  See also CLR 18
  See also MAICYA
  See also SATA 31
Bryan, C(ourtlandt) D(ixon) B(arnes) 1936- CANR-13
  Earlier sketch in CA 73-76
  See also CLC 29
Bryan, Carter R(oyston) 1911- 33-36R
Bryan, Christopher 1935- CANR-20
  Earlier sketch in CA 104
Bryan, Dorothy M. 1896(?)-1984 Obituary 114
  See also SATA 39
Bryan, Ford R. 1912- 134
Bryan, G(eorge) McLeod 1920- 1-4R
Bryan, George B(arton) 1939- 117
Bryan, J(oseph) III 1904- CANR-11
  Earlier sketch in CA 61-64
Bryan, J(ack) Y(eaman) 1907- 73-76
Bryan, John E. 1931- CANR-4
  Earlier sketch in CA 53-56
Bryan, Julien (Hequembourg) 1899-1974 Obituary 53-56
Bryan, M(erwyn) Leonard 1937- 103
Bryan, Marian K(nighton) 1900(?)-1974 Obituary 53-56
Bryan, Martin 1908- 1-4R
Bryan, Mavis
  See O'Brien, Marian P(lowman)
Bryan, Michael
  See Moore, Brian
Bryan, Mina R(uese) 1908-1985 Obituary 115
Bryan, Sharon 1943- CANR-37
  Earlier sketch in CA 115
Bryan, (William) Wright 1905-1991 77-80
  Obituary 133
Bryans, Robert Harbinson 1928- CANR-11
  Earlier sketch in CA 5-8R
Bryans, Robin
  See Bryans, Robert Harbinson
Bryant, Al
  See Bryant, T(homas) Alton
Bryant, Anita
  See Green, Anita Jane
Bryant, Arthur (Wynne Morgan) 1899-1985 105
  Obituary 114
Bryant, Bear
  See Bryant, Paul W(illiam)
Bryant, Bernice (Morgan) 1908- CAP-1
  Earlier sketch in CA 9-10
  See also SATA 11
Bryant, Beth Elaine 1936- 13-16R
Bryant, Cyril E(ric Jr.) 1917- 61-64
Bryant, Donald C(ross) 1905- 13-16R
Bryant, Dorothy 1930- CANR-19
  Earlier sketches in CA 53-56, CANR-4
Bryant, Edward (Albert) 1928- CANR-11
  Earlier sketch in CA 9-12R
Bryant, Edward (Winslow Jr.) 1945- CANR-1
  Earlier sketch in CA 45-48
Bryant, Gay 1945- CANR-13
  Earlier sketch in CA 73-76
Bryant, Henry A(llen) Jr. 1943- CANR-4
  Earlier sketch in CA 53-56
Bryant, J(oseph) A(llen) Jr. 1919- 5-8R
Bryant, James C(ecil) Jr. 1931- 49-52
Bryant, Jerry H(olt) 1928- 33-36R
Bryant, Katherine Cliffton 1912- 13-16R
Bryant, Keith L(ynn) Jr. 1937- 49-52
Bryant, Margaret M. 1900- CANR-4
  Earlier sketch in CA 1-4R
Bryant, Paul W(illiam) 1913-1983 111
  Obituary 108
Bryant, Ralph C(lement) 1938- 117
Bryant, Robert H(arry) 1925- 21-24R
Bryant, Shasta M(onroe) 1924- 41-44R
Bryant, T(homas) Alton 1926- CANR-29
  Earlier sketches in CA 25-28R, CANR-10
Bryant, Traphes L(emon) 1914- 77-80
Bryant, Verda E. 1910- CAP-2
  Earlier sketch in CA 21-22
Bryant, William Cullen 1794-1878 ..... CDALB 1640-1865
  See also DLB 3, 43, 59
Bryant, Willis Rooks 1892-1965 ..... 5-8R
  Obituary 103
Bryce, Gladysann 1934- 116
Bryce, James 1934- 112
Bryce, Murray D(avidson) 1917- 13-16R
Brychta, Alex 1956- CANR-20
  Earlier sketch in CA 103
  See also SATA 21
Bryde, John F(rancis) 1920- 33-36R
Bryden, Bill
  See Bryden, William Campbell Rough
Bryden, John (Herbert) 1943- 134
Bryden, John Marshall 1941- CANR-1
  Earlier sketch in CA 49-52
Bryden, John R(ennie) 1913- 33-36R
Bryden, William Campbell Rough 1942- 105
Brydges, Samuel Egerton 1762-1837 ..... DLB 107
Bryer, Jackson R(obert) 1937- CANR-18
  Earlier sketches in CA 9-12R, CANR-3
Bryer, (Alastair) Robin (Mornington) 1944- 111
Bryers, Paul 1945- 73-76
Bryfonski, Dedria (Anne) 1947- 101
Bryher
  See Ellerman, Annie Winifred
Bryks, Rachmil 1912-1974 97-100
Brymer, Jack 1915- 110
Brynildsen, Ken(neth) 1944- 110
Brynner, Yul
  See Khan, Taidje
Bryson, Bernarda 1905- 49-52
  See also SATA 9
Bryson, Conrey 1905- 93-96
Bryson, John 1923- 133
Bryson, Phillip J(ames) 1939- 69-72
Bryson, Reid Allen 1920- 101
Bryson, W(illiam) Hamilton 1941- CANR-36
  Earlier sketch in CA 114
Bryusov, Valery Yakovlevich 1873-1924 Brief entry 107
  See also TCLC 10
Brzezinski, Zbigniew K(azimierz) 1928- CANR-5
  Earlier sketch in CA 1-4R
  See also BEST 89:3
Buarque De Holanda (Ferreira), Aurelio 1911(?)-1989 Obituary 128
Buba, Joy Flinsch 1904- ..... SATA 44
Bubar, Margaret Weber 1920(?)-1978 Obituary 77-80
Bubb, Mel
  See Whitcomb, Ian
Bube, Richard H. 1927- CANR-8
  Earlier sketch in CA 21-24R
Bubeck, Mark I(rving) 1928- 61-64
Buber, Martin 1878-1965 125
  Obituary 25-28R
  See also MTCW
Bubner, Rudiger
  See Bubner, Ruediger
Bubner, Ruediger 1941- 121
Bucaille, Maurice 1920- 137
Buccellati, Giorgio 1937- 41-44R
Bucchieri, Theresa F. 1908- 73-76
Bucco, Martin 1929- CANR-14
  Earlier sketch in CA 29-32R
Buchan, Alastair (Francis) 1918-1976 73-76
  Obituary 65-68
Buchan, Bryan 1945- 107
  See also SATA 36
Buchan, David
  See Womack, David A(lfred)
Buchan, James 1916- 130
  Brief entry 119
Buchan, John 1875-1940 Brief entry 108
  See also DLB 34, 70
  See also TCLC 41
  See also YABC 2
Buchan, Kate
  See Erskine, Barbara
Buchan, Norman Findlay 1922-1990 109
  Obituary 132
Buchan, Perdita 1940- 21-24R
Buchan, Stuart 1942-1987 57-60
  Obituary 123
  See also SATA 54
Buchan, Thomas Buchanan 1931- CANR-16
  Earlier sketch in CA 25-28R
Buchan, Tom
  See Buchan, Thomas Buchanan
Buchan, Ursula 1953- 128
Buchanan, A(lbert) Russell 1906- 13-16R
Buchanan, Annette 1933- 118
Buchanan(-Berrigan), Dawna Lisa 1954- 137
Buchanan, Betty (Joan) 1923- 101
Buchanan, Chuck
  See Rowland, D(onald) S(ydney)
Buchanan, Colin O(gilvie) 1934- 25-28R
Buchanan, Cynthia D(ee) 1937- 5-8R
Buchanan, Cynthia 1942- CANR-1
  Earlier sketch in CA 45-48
Buchanan, Daniel C(rump) 1892- 17-20R
Buchanan, David A(lan) 1949- 118
Buchanan, (Eric) David 1933- 57-60
Buchanan, Donald W(illiam) 1908- CAP-1
  Earlier sketch in CA 11-12
Buchanan, Edna (Rydzik) 1939(?)- 132
  Brief entry 125
Buchanan, George (Henry Perrott) 1904-1989 ..... CANR-3
  Obituary 129
  Earlier sketch in CA 9-12R
Buchanan, George Wesley 1921- CANR-14
  Earlier sketch in CA 37-40R
Buchanan, James David 1929- 130
Buchanan, James J(unkin) 1925- 33-36R
Buchanan, James McGill 1919- CANR-22
  Earlier sketches in CA 5-8R, CANR-3
Buchanan, Keith 1919- CANR-10
  Earlier sketch in CA 21-24R
Buchanan, Laura
  See King, Florence
Buchanan, Marie CANR-25
  Earlier sketches in CA 65-68, CANR-10
Buchanan, Patrick
  See Corley, Edwin (Raymond)
Buchanan, Pegasus 1920- 9-12R
Buchanan, R(obert) A(ngus) 1930- CANR-7
  Earlier sketch in CA 17-20R
Buchanan, Robert 1841-1901 ..... DLB 18, 35
Buchanan, Thomas G(ittings) 1919- 1-4R
Buchanan, Wiley T(homas) Jr. 1914-1986 Obituary 118
Buchanan, William
  See Buck, William Ray
Buchanan, William J(esse) 1926- CANR-39
  Earlier sketch in CA 73-76
Buchanan-Brown, John 1929- 102
Buchard, Robert 1931- 33-36R
Buchdahl, Gerd 1914- 57-60
Bucheister, Patt 1942- 122
Buchele, William Martin 1895- 57-60
Buchen, Irving H. 1930- 25-28R
Bucher, Bradley 1932- 37-40R
Bucher, Charles A(ugustus) 1912- CANR-3
  Earlier sketch in CA 9-12R
Bucher, Francois 1927- CANR-3
  Earlier sketch in CA 5-8R
Bucher, Glenn R(ichard) 1940- 57-60
Bucher, Magnus 1927- 41-44R
Buchheim, Lothar-Guenther 1918- 85-88
  See also CLC 6
Buchheimer, Naomi Barnett
  See Barnett, Naomi
Buchheit, Lee C(harles) 1950- 81-84
Buchler, Justus 1914-1991 ..... 5-8R
  Obituary 134
Buchman, Dian Dincin CANR-8
  Earlier sketch in CA 61-64
Buchman, Frank N(athan) D(aniel) 1878-1961 Obituary 112
Buchman, Herman 1920- 41-44R
Buchman, Marion 121
Buchman, Randall L(oren) 1929- CANR-1
  Earlier sketch in CA 45-48
Buchman, Sidney 1902-1975 93-96
  Obituary 61-64
  See also DLB 26
Buchsbaum, Tony 1961- 128
Buchwald, Ann 1920- 128
Buchwald, Art(hur) 1925- CANR-21
  Earlier sketch in CA 5-8R
  See also AITN 1
  See also CLC 33
  See also MTCW
  See also SATA 10
Buchwald, Emilie 1935- CANR-2
  Earlier sketch in CA 49-52
  See also SATA 7
Buck, Ashley Obituary 97-100
Buck, Charles (Henry Jr.) 1915- 33-36R
Buck, David 1934(?)-1989 Obituary 128
Buck, Doris P(itkin) 1898(?)-1980 Obituary 102
Buck, Edith V(irginia) 1919- 117
Buck, Frederick Silas 5-8R
Buck, George C(rawford) 1918- 69-72
Buck, Harry M(erwyn Jr.) 1921- CANR-13
  Earlier sketch in CA 33-36R
Buck, James H. 1924- 104
Buck, Joan Juliet 1948- CANR-25
  Earlier sketch in CA 108
Buck, John Lossing 1890-1975 ..... CANR-2
  Obituary 61-64
  Earlier sketch in CA 45-48
Buck, John N(elson) 1906- CAP-2
  Earlier sketch in CA 29-32
Buck, Lewis 1925- 73-76
  See also SATA 18
Buck, Margaret Waring 1910- 5-8R
  See also SATA 3
Buck, Marion A(shby) 1909- CAP-1
  Earlier sketch in CA 13-14
Buck, Paul H(erman) 1899-1978 Obituary 81-84
Buck, Pearl S(ydenstricker) 1892-1973 ..... CANR-34
  Obituary 41-44R
  Earlier sketches in CA 1-4R, CANR-1
  See also AITN 1
  See also CLC 7, 11, 18
  See also DLB 9, 102
  See also MTCW
  See also SATA 1, 25
Buck, Peggy S(ullivan) 1930- 65-68
Buck, Philip W(allenstein) 1900- 65-68
Buck, Robert N. 1914- 103
Buck, Ross (Workman) 1941- 128
Buck, Stratton 1906- CAP-2
  Earlier sketch in CA 17-18
Buck, Vernon E(llis) 1934- 37-40R
Buck, William Ray 1930- 1-4R
Buckaway, C. M.
  See Buckaway, Catherine M(argaret)
Buckaway, Catherine M(argaret) 1919- 130
Bucke, Charles 1781-1846 ..... DLB 110
Bucke, Richard Maurice 1837-1902 ..... DLB 99
Buckeridge, Anthony (Malcolm) 1912- CANR-2
  Earlier sketch in CA 49-52
  See also SATA 6
Buckeye, Donald A(ndrew) 1930- 49-52
Buckholdt, David R. 1942- 101
Buckholtz, Eileen (Garber) 1949- 117
  See also SATA 47, 54
Buckhout, Robert 1935-1990 45-48
  Obituary 133
Buckingham, Burdette H. 1907(?)-1977 Obituary 73-76
Buckingham, Clyde E(dwin) 1907- CAP-1
  Earlier sketch in CA 13-16
Buckingham, Edwin 1810-1833 ..... DLB 73
Buckingham, James (William) 1932-1992 ..... 29-32R
  Obituary 136
Buckingham, Jamie
  See Buckingham, James (William)
Buckingham, Joseph Tinker 1779-1861 ..... DLB 73
Buckingham, Robert W(illiam) III 113
Buckingham, Walter S(amuel) Jr. 1924-1967 ..... 1-4R
  Obituary 103
Buckingham, Willis J(ohn) 1938- 29-32R

Buckland, Michael K(eeble) 1941- 97-100
Buckland, Raymond 1934- 73-76
Buckle, (Christopher) Richard (Sandford)
1916- 97-100
Buckler, Beatrice 1933- 127
Buckler, Ernest 1908-1984 ..... CAP-1
Obituary 114
Earlier sketch in CA 11-12
See also CLC 13
See also DLB 68
See also SATA 47
Buckler, John 1945- 121
Buckler, William Earl 1924- CANR-20
Earlier sketches in CA 1-4R, CANR-5
Buckley, Anthony D. 1945- 120
Buckley, Cornelius M(ichael) 1925- 138
Buckley, Doris Heather
See Buckley Neville, Heather
Buckley, Fergus Reid 1930- 21-24R
Buckley, Fiona
See Anand, Valerie
Buckley, Francis J(oseph) 1928- CANR-13
Earlier sketch in CA 33-36R
Buckley, Helen E(lizabeth) 1918- CANR-3
Earlier sketch in CA 5-8R
See also SATA 2
Buckley, J(ames) Taylor Jr. 1939- 127
Buckley, James Lane 1923- 61-64
Buckley, Jerome Hamilton 1917- CANR-3
Earlier sketch in CA 1-4R
Buckley, Julian Gerard 1905- 41-44R
Buckley, Mary L(orraine) 53-56
Buckley, Michael F.
1880(?)-1977 Obituary 69-72
Buckley, Michael J(oseph) 1931- 73-76
Buckley, Peter 1938-1991 112
Obituary 134
Buckley, Priscilla 1921- 81-84
Buckley, Roger N(orman) 1937- 97-100
Buckley, Shawn 1943- 93-96
Buckley, Suzanne Shelton 1946- 108
Buckley, Thomas H(ugh) 1932- 29-32R
Buckley, Vincent (Thomas) 1925-1988 101
See also CLC 57
Buckley, Walter (Frederick) 1921- 121
Buckley, William F(rank) Jr. 1925- CANR-24
Earlier sketches in CA 1-4R, CANR-1
See also AITN 1
See also CLC 7, 18, 37
See also DLBY 80
See also MTCW
Buckley Neville, Heather 1910- 103
Bucklin, Louis P(ierre) 1928- 97-100
Buckman, Peter 1941- CANR-11
Earlier sketch in CA 65-68
Buckman, Rob
See Buckman, Robert (Alexander Amiel)
Buckman, Robert (Alexander Amiel) 1948- 128
Buckmaster, Henrietta
See Stephens, Henrietta Henkle
See also SATA 6
Buckminster, Joseph Stevens
1784-1812 ..... DLB 37
Bucknall, Barbara J(ane) 1933- CANR-14
Earlier sketch in CA 33-36R
Bucknell, Howard III 1924-1986 125
Buckner, Robert (Henry) 1906- 1-4R
See also DLB 26
Buckner, Sally Beaver 1931- 61-64
Buckstead, Richard C(hris) 1929- 49-52
Buckvar, Felice (Spitz) 1938- 107
Buczkowski, Leopold 1905- 41-44R
Buday, George
See Buday, Gyorgy
Buday, Gyorgy 1907-1990(?) 107
Obituary 132
Budberg, Moura 1892(?)-1974 Obituary 53-56
Budbill, David 1940- 73-76
Budd, Carol (Pellegrini) 1951- 128
Budd, Edward C(arhart) 1920- 21-24R
Budd, Elaine 1925- 101
Budd, Kenneth George 1904-1972 ..... CAP-1
Earlier sketch in CA 13-14
Budd, Lillian (Peterson) 1897- CANR-4
Earlier sketch in CA 1-4R
See also SATA 7
Budd, Louis J(ohn) 1921- CANR-3
Earlier sketch in CA 1-4R
Budd, Mavis CANR-19
Earlier sketch in CA 102
Budd, Richard W. 1934- 21-24R
Budd, Thomas ..... DLB 24
Budd, William C(laude) 1923- 49-52
Buddee, Paul Edgar 1913- 103
Budden, Julian (Medforth) 1924- 130
Budden, Laura M(adeline) 1894- 5-8R
Buddensieg, Tilmann 1928- 138
Bude, John
See Elmore, Ernest Carpenter
Budenz, Louis F(rancis)
1891-1972 Obituary 89-92
Budge, Ian 1936- CANR-12
Earlier sketch in CA 29-32R
Budgen, Frank Spencer Curtis
1882-1971 Obituary 29-32R
Budick, Sanford 1942- 33-36R
Budimir, (Simo) Velimir 1926- 65-68
Budinger, Peyton Bailey 1939- 114
Budoff, Penny Wise 1939- 110
Budrys, Algirdas Jonas 1931- CANR-20
Earlier sketches in CA 1-4R, CANR-4
See also Budrys, Algis
See also DLB 8
Budrys, Algis
See Budrys, Algirdas Jonas
See also CAAS 14
Budurowycz, Bohdan B(asil) 1921- CANR-3
Earlier sketch in CA 5-8R
Budzik, Janet K. Sims 1942- 37-40R
Budziszewski, J(ay Dalton) 1952- 125
Buechner, (Carl) Frederick 1926- CANR-39
Earlier sketches in CA 13-16R, CANR-11
See also CLC 2, 4, 6, 9
See also DLBY 80
See also MTCW
Buechner, John C(harles) 1934- 21-24R
Buechner, Thomas S(charman) 1926- 49-52
Buehler, Curt F(erdinand) 1905-1985 ..... 1-4R
Obituary 117
Buehlmann, Walbert 1916- CANR-38
Earlier sketch in CA 115
Buehnau, Ludwig
See Schreiber, Hermann (Otto Ludwig)
Buehner, Andrew J(ohn) 1905- 17-20R
Buehr, Walter Franklin 1897-1971 ..... CANR-3
Obituary 33-36R
Earlier sketch in CA 5-8R
See also SATA 3
Buehrig, Edward H(enry) 1910- 37-40R
Buehrig, Gordon M. 1904- 101
Buel, Richard (Van Wyck) Jr. 1933- CANR-13
Earlier sketch in CA 73-76
Bueler, Lois E(aton) 1940- 57-60
Bueler, William Merwin 1934- 37-40R
Buell, Ellen Lewis
See Cash, Ellen Lewis Buell
Buell, Emmett H. Jr. 1941- 138
Buell, Frederick H(enderson) 1942- 33-36R
Buell, Janet 1945- 127
Buell, John (Edward) 1927- 1-4R
See also CLC 10
See also DLB 53
Buell, Jon A. 1939- 102
Buell, Lawrence 1939- 49-52
Buell, Robert Kingery 1908-1971 ..... CAP-2
Earlier sketch in CA 25-28
Buell, Victor P(aul) 1914- CANR-8
Earlier sketch in CA 21-24R
Buelow, George J. 1929- 21-24R
Buenaventura, Enrique 1925- ..... HW
Buendia, Manuel
See Giron, Manuel Buendia Tellez
Buenker, John D(avid) 1937- CANR-16
Earlier sketches in CA 45-48, CANR-1
Bueno, Jose de la Torre
1905(?)-1980 Obituary 93-96
Bueno de Mesquita, Bruce James 1946- 108
Buergenthal, Thomas 1934- 37-40R
Buerger, Gottfried August 1747-1794 ..... DLB 94
Buerkle, Jack Vincent 1923- 41-44R
Buero Vallejo, Antonio 1916- CANR-24
Earlier sketch in CA 106
See also CLC 15, 46
See also HW
See also MTCW
Bueschel, Richard M. 1926- CANR-26
Earlier sketches in CA 25-28R, CANR-11
Buetow, Harold A(ndrew) 1919- 53-56
Buettner-Janusch, John 1924- 49-52
Obituary 138
Bufalari, Giuseppe 1927- CANR-16
Earlier sketch in CA 25-28R
Buferd, Norma Bradley 1937- 69-72
Buff, Conrad 1886-1975 135
See also MAICYA
See also SATA 19
Buff, Mary (E. Marsh) 1890-1970 135
Obituary 116
See also MAICYA
See also SATA 19
Buffa, Dudley W. 1940- 121
Buffalo Chuck
See Barth, Charles P.
Buffaloe, Neal D(ollison) 1924- 53-56
Buffett, Jimmy 1946- ..... BEST 90:2
Buffie, Margaret 1945- ..... SATA 71
Buffington, Albert F(ranklin) 1905- 33-36R
Buffington, Robert (Ray) 1933- 21-24R
Bufkin, Ernest Claude Jr. 1929- 101
Buford, Thomas O(liver) 1932- 29-32R
Bugayev, Boris Nikolayevich
1880-1934 Brief entry 104
See also Bely, Andrey
Bugbee, Emma 1888(?)-1981 Obituary 105
See also SATA 29
Bugbee, Ruth Carson 1903- CANR-1
Earlier sketch in CA 1-4R
Bugeja, Michael J. 138
Bugental, James F(rederick) T(homas)
1915- CANR-25
Earlier sketches in CA 21-24R, CANR-10
Bugg, James L(uckin) Jr. 1920- 5-8R
Bugg, Ralph 1922- 73-76
Buggie, Frederick D(enman) 1929- 97-100
Buglass, Leslie J. 1917- 13-16R
Bugliarello, George 1927- 41-44R
Bugliosi, Vincent (T.) 1934- CANR-13
Earlier sketch in CA 73-76
Bugnet, Georges 1879-1981 ..... DLB 92
Buhite, Russell D(evere) 1938- 101
Buhle, Mari Jo 1943- 108
Buhle, Paul 1944- 127
Buhler, Charlotte B(ertha) 1893-197 (?) CAP-2
Earlier sketch in CA 17-18
Buhler, Curt F(erdinand)
See Buehler, Curt F(erdinand)
Buhlmann, Walbert
See Buehlmann, Walbert
Buies, Arthur 1840-1901 ..... DLB 99
Buisseret, David 1934- 124
Buist, Charlotte
See Patterson, Charlotte (Buist)
Buist, Vincent 1919(?)-1979 Obituary 89-92
Buitenhuis, Peter (Martinus) 1925- 25-28R
Buitrago, Ann Mari 1929- 105
Bukalski, Peter J(ulian) 1941- CANR-15
Earlier sketch in CA 41-44R
Buker, George E(dward) 1923- 53-56
Bukey, Evan Burr 1940- 131
Bukharin, Nikolai (Ivanovich)
1888-1938 Brief entry 120
Bukowczyk, John J(oseph) 1950- 125
Bukowski, Charles 1920- 17-20R
See also CLC 2, 5, 9, 41
See also DLB 5
See also MTCW
Buktenica, Norman A(ugust) 1930- 33-36R
Bulatkin, Eleanor Webster 1913- 33-36R
Bulatovic, Miodrag 1930-1991 ..... CANR-21
Obituary 133
Earlier sketch in CA 5-8R
Buley, R(oscoe) Carlyle 1893-1968 ..... CAP-2
Obituary 25-28R
Earlier sketch in CA 21-22
Bulfinch, Thomas 1796-1867 ..... SATA 35
Bulgakov, Mikhail (Afanas'evich)
1891-1940 Brief entry 105
See also TCLC 2, 16
Bulger, William T(homas) 1927- 69-72
Bulgya, Alexander Alexandrovich
1901-1956 Brief entry 117
Bulka, Reuven P(inchas) 1944- 113
Bulkeley, Christy C. ..... AITN 2
Bulkeley, William M. 1950- 135
Bulkley, Dwight H(atfield) 1919- 105
Bull, Angela (Mary) 1936- CANR-24
Earlier sketches in CA 21-24R, CANR-9
See also SATA 45
Bull, Emma 1954- 127
Bull, Geoffrey Taylor 1921- CANR-3
Earlier sketch in CA 9-12R
Bull, George (Anthony) 1929- CANR-39
Earlier sketch in CA 115
Bull, Guyon B(oys) G(arrett) 1912- CANR-5
Earlier sketch in CA 5-8R
Bull, Hedley Norman 1932-1985 ..... 5-8R
Obituary 116
Bull, John 1914- 69-72
Bull, Norman John 1916- CANR-16
Earlier sketch in CA 93-96
See also SATA 41
Bull, Odd 1907- 81-84
Bull, Peter (Cecil) 1912-1984 ..... CANR-11
Obituary 112
Earlier sketch in CA 25-28R
See also SATA 39
Bull, Robert J(ehu) 1920- 97-100
Bull, Storm 1913- 9-12R
Bull, William E(merson) 1909-1972 ..... CAP-1
Earlier sketch in CA 13-16
Bulla, Clyde Robert 1914- CANR-18
Earlier sketches in CA 5-8R, CANR-3
See also MAICYA
See also SAAS 6
See also SATA 2, 41
Bullard, E(dgar) John III 1942- 33-36R
Bullard, Fred Mason 1901- 25-28R
Bullard, Helen 1902- CANR-7
Earlier sketch in CA 17-20R
Bullard, Oral 1922- CANR-23
Earlier sketches in CA 61-64, CANR-8
Bullard, Pamela 1948- 106
Bullard, Roger A(ubrey) 1937- 33-36R
Bulle, Florence (Elizabeth) 1925- CANR-15
Earlier sketch in CA 93-96
Bulleid, H(enry) A(nthony) V(aughan)
1912- CANR-13
Earlier sketches in CAP-1, CA 9-10
Bullen, Dana R(ipley) 1931- 73-76
Bullen, Keith Edward 1906-1976 Obituary 106
Bullen, Robert 1926(?)-1976 Obituary 69-72
Buller, Herman 1923- 61-64
Bulliet, Richard W(illiams) 1940- CANR-7
Earlier sketch in CA 57-60
Bullingham, Rodney
See Sladen, Norman St. Barbe
Bullins, Ed 1935- CANR-24
Earlier sketch in CA 49-52
See also CAAS 16
See also BLC 1
See also BW
See also CLC 1, 5, 7
See also DLB 7, 38
See also MTCW
Bullis, Harry Amos 1890-1963 ..... CAP-2
Earlier sketch in CA 17-18
Bullis, Jerald 1944- CANR-1
Earlier sketch in CA 49-52
Bullitt, John M(arshall) 1921-1985 Obituary 117
Bullitt, Orville H(orwitz) 1894-1979 ..... 33-36R
Obituary 89-92
Bullitt, Stimson 1919- 112
Bullitt, William C(hristian)
1891-1967 Obituary 89-92
Bulloch, John 1928- 134
Bullock, Alan Louis Charles 1914- 1-4R
Bullock, Alice 1904- 89-92
Bullock, Barbara
See Bullock-Wilson, Barbara
Bullock, C(larence) Hassell 1939- 89-92
Bullock, Charles S(pencer) III 1942- CANR-13
Earlier sketch in CA 33-36R
Bullock, Frederick W(illiam) B(agshawe)
1903- CANR-4
Earlier sketch in CA 5-8R
Bullock, Henry 1907(?)-1973 Obituary 41-44R
Bullock, Michael 1918- CANR-38
Earlier sketches in CA 17-20R, CANR-7
Bullock, Paul 1924-1986 ..... CANR-11
Obituary 118
Earlier sketch in CA 29-32R
Bullock-Wilson, Barbara 1945- 65-68
Bullough, Bonnie 1927- CANR-11
Earlier sketch in CA 69-72
Bullough, D(onald) A(uberon) 1928- 107
Bullough, Geoffrey 1901-1982 ..... CANR-5
Obituary 106
Earlier sketch in CA 1-4R
Bullough, Robert V. Jr. 1949- 135
Bullough, Vern (LeRoy) 1928- CANR-26
Earlier sketches in CA 9-12R, CANR-4, 11
Bullough, William A(lfred) 1933- 101
Bullrich (Palenque), Silvina 1915- ..... HW
Bulman, Joan (Carroll Boone) 1904- 103
Bulman, Oliver (Meredith Boone)
1902-1974 Obituary 49-52
Bulmer, (Henry) Kenneth 1921- CANR-9
Earlier sketch in CA 13-16R
Bulmer, Martin 1943- 113
Bulmer, Ralph N(eville) H(ermon)
1928-1988 Obituary 126
Bulmer-Thomas, Ivor 1905- CAP-1
Earlier sketch in CA 11-12
Buloff, Joseph 1899(?)-1985 Obituary 115
Bulpin, T(homas) V(ictor) 1918- CANR-4
Earlier sketch in CA 9-12R
Bultmann, Rudolf Karl 1884-1976 ..... CANR-29
Obituary 65-68
Earlier sketch in CA 5-8R
See also MTCW
Bulwer-Lytton, Edward (George Earle Lytton)
1803-1873 ..... DLB 21
Bumagin, Victoria E. 1923- 89-92
Bump, Jerome 1943- 109
Bumppo, Nathaniel John Balthazar
1940- 97-100
Bumppo, Natty
See Bumppo, Nathaniel John Balthazar
Bumpus, Jerry 1937- CANR-10
Earlier sketch in CA 65-68
See also DLBY 81
Bumstead, Kathleen Mary 1918-1987 121
See also SATA 53
Bumsted, J(ohn) M(ichael) 1938- 41-44R
Bunce, Alan 1939- 77-80
Bunce, Frank David 1907- CAP-1
Earlier sketch in CA 11-12
Bunce, Linda Susan (Staines) 1956- 107
Bunch, Charlotte (Anne) 1944- 126
Bunch, Clarence 53-56
Bunch, David R(oosevelt) 29-32R
Bunche, Ralph J(ohnson) 1904-1971 125
Obituary 33-36R
See also BW
Bunch-Weeks, Charlotte
See Bunch, Charlotte (Anne)
Bundtzen, Lynda K(athryn) 1947- 127
Bundy, Clarence E(verett) 1906- 85-88
Bundy, William P(utnam) 1917- 104
Bungay, Stephen 1954- 127
Bunge, Mario A(ugusto) 1919- 9-12R
Bunge, Nancy L(iddell) 1942- 124
Bunge, Robert Pierce 1930- 124
Bunge, Walter R(ichard) 1911- 25-28R
Bung Karno
See Sukarno, (Ahmed)
Buni, Andrew 1931- 21-24R
Bunim, Amos 1929- 132
Bunim, Irving M. 1901(?)-1980 Obituary 103
Bunin, Catherine 1967- 93-96
See also SATA 30
Bunin, Ivan Alexeyevich
1870-1953 Brief entry 104
See also SSC 5
See also TCLC 6
Bunin, Sherry 1925- 93-96
See also SATA 30
Buning, Sietze
See Wiersma, Stanley M(arvin)
Bunke, H(arvey) Charles 1922- 9-12R
Bunker, Edward 1933- 41-44R
Bunker, Gerald Edward 1938- 37-40R
Bunker, Linda K. 1947- CANR-29
Earlier sketch in CA 111
Bunn, John T(homas) 1924- 37-40R
Bunn, John W. 1898- CAP-2
Earlier sketch in CA 23-24
Bunn, Ronald F(reeze) 1929- 21-24R
Bunn, Scott (Middelton) 1943- 111
Bunn, Thomas 1944- 69-72
Bunnell, Peter C(urtis) 1937- CANR-30
Earlier sketches in CA 33-36R, CANR-12
Bunnell, William S(tanley) 1925- CAP-1
Earlier sketch in CA 11-12
Bunner, H. C. 1855-1896 ..... DLB 78, 79
Bunt, Lucas N(icolaas) H(endrik) 1905- 69-72
Bunting, A. E.
See Bunting, Anne Evelyn
Bunting, Anne Evelyn 1928- CANR-19
Earlier sketches in CA 53-56, CANR-5
See also Bunting, Eve
See also AAYA 5
See also SATA 18
Bunting, Bainbridge 1913-1981 ..... CANR-8
Earlier sketch in CA 61-64
Bunting, Basil 1900-1985 ..... CANR-7
Obituary 115
Earlier sketch in CA 53-56
See also CLC 10, 39, 47
See also DLB 20
Bunting, Eve
See Bunting, Anne Evelyn
See also CLR 28
See also MAICYA
See also SATA 64

Bunting, Glenn (Davison) 1957- .... SATA 22
Bunting, Josiah 1939- 45-48
Bunuan, Josefina S(antiago) 1935- 33-36R
Bunuel, Luis 1900-1983 .... CANR-32
Obituary 110
Earlier sketch in CA 101
See also CLC 16
See also HW
Bunyan, John 1628-1688 ...... CDBLB 1660-1789
See also DLB 39
See also WLC
Bunzel, John H(arvey) 1924- 17-20R
Bunzel, Ruth L(eah) 1898-1990 Obituary 130
Buol, S(tanley) W(alter) 1934- 49-52
Burack, Abraham Saul 1908-1978 .... CANR-4
Obituary 77-80
Earlier sketch in CA 9-12R
Burack, Elmer H(oward) 1927- CANR-37
Earlier sketches in CA 37-40R, CANR-16
Burack, Sylvia K. 1916- CANR-9
Earlier sketch in CA 21-24R
See also SATA 35
Burak, Linda (Gallina) 116
Buranelli, Vincent 1919- CANR-20
Earlier sketches in CA 9-12R, CANR-5
Burbank, Addison (Buswell)
1895-1961 .... SATA 37
Burbank, Garin 1940- 69-72
Burbank, Natt B(ryant) 1903- CAP-2
Earlier sketch in CA 25-28
Burbank, Nelson L(incoln) 1898- CAP-1
Earlier sketch in CA 11-12
Burbank, Rex James 1925- CANR-18
Earlier sketch in CA 1-4R
Burbidge, Peter George
1919-1985 Obituary 116
Burbridge, Branse 1921- 97-100
Burby, Raymond J(oseph) III 1942- CANR-11
Earlier sketch in CA 69-72
Burby, William E(dward) 1893- CAP-1
Earlier sketch in CA 11-12
Burch, Claire R. 1925- 101
Burch, Francis F(loyd) 1932- 29-32R
Burch, George Bosworth 1902-1973 122
Obituary 109
Burch, Jennings Michael 1941- 118
Burch, Mark H(etzel) 1953- 122
Burch, Mary Lou 1914- 104
Burch, Monte G. 1943- 103
Burch, Pat 1944- 57-60
Burch, Philip H. 1930- 106
Burch, Preston M. 1884-1978 Obituary 77-80
Burch, Robert J(oseph) 1925- CANR-17
Earlier sketches in CA 5-8R, CANR-2
See also DLB 52
See also MAICYA
See also SATA 1
Burcham, Nancy A(nn) 1942- 89-92
Burchard, John Ely 1898-1975 .... CANR-6
Obituary 61-64
Earlier sketch in CA 1-4R
Burchard, Max N(orman) 1925- 21-24R
Burchard, Peter Duncan 1921- CANR-39
Earlier sketches in CA 5-8R, CANR-3, 18
See also MAICYA
See also SAAS 13
See also SATA 5
Burchard, Rachael C(aroline) 1921- 33-36R
Burchard, S. H.
See Burchard, Sue
Burchard, Sue 1937- CANR-19
Earlier sketches in CA 53-56, CANR-4
See also SATA 22
Burchardt, Bill
See Burchardt, William Robert
Burchardt, Nellie 1921- 21-24R
See also SATA 7
Burchardt, William Robert 1917- CANR-16
Earlier sketch in CA 89-92
Burchell, Mary
See Cook, Ida
Burchell, R(obert) A(rthur) 1941- 106
Burchett, Randall E. 1-4R
Obituary 103
Burchett, Wilfred (Graham) 1911-1983 .... CANR-2
Obituary 110
Earlier sketch in CA 49-52
Burchfield, Joe D(onald) 1937- 85-88
Burchfield, Robert William 1923- CANR-35
Earlier sketches in CA 41-44R, CANR-14
Burchill, Julie 1960- 135
Burchwood, Katharine T(yler) 57-60
Burciaga, Jose Antonio 1940- 131
See also DLB 82
See also HW
Burck, Jacob 1907-1982 Obituary 106
Burckel, Nicholas C(lare) 1943- CANR-19
Earlier sketch in CA 103
Burckhardt, C(arl) J(akob) 1891-1974 93-96
Obituary 49-52
Burd, Laurence Hull 1915-1983 Obituary 109
Burd, Van Akin 1914- 41-44R
Burda, R(obert) W(arren) 1932- 73-76
Burden, Jean 1914- CANR-3
Earlier sketch in CA 9-12R
Burden, Shirley C. 1909(?)-1989 Obituary 128
Burden, William Douglas
1898-1978 Obituary 81-84
Burder, John 1940- 110
Burdett, Winston 1913- 29-32R
Burdette, Franklin L. 1911-1975 65-68
Obituary 61-64
Burdge, Rabel J(ames) 1937- 69-72
Burdick, Carol (Ruth) 1928- 132
Burdick, Donald W(alter) 1917- 53-56
Burdick, Eric 1934- 29-32R
Burdick, Eugene (Leonard) 1918-1965 .... 5-8R
Obituary 25-28R
See also SATA 22
Burdick, Loraine 1929- 57-60
Burdon, R(andal) M(athews) 1896- CAP-1
Earlier sketch in CA 13-14
Bureau, William H(obbs) 1913- 102
Buren, Martha Margareta Elisabet 1910- CAP-1
Earlier sketch in CA 13-14
Burfield, Eva
See Ebbett, (Frances) Eva
Burford, Anne M(cGill) 1942- 127
Burford, E(phraim) J(ohn) 1905- 124
Burford, Eleanor
See Hibbert, Eleanor Burford
Burford, Lolah 41-44R
Burford, Roger L(ewis) 1930- 41-44R
Burford, William (Skelly) 1927- CANR-7
Earlier sketch in CA 5-8R
Burg, B(arry) R(ichard) 1938- 129
Burg, Dale R(onda) 1942- CANR-23
Earlier sketch in CA 106
Burg, David
See Dolberg, Alexander
Burg, David F(rederick) 1936- 116
Burge, Doris 1909- 120
Burge, Ethel 1916- 65-68
Burgeon, G. A. L.
See Barfield, (Arthur) Owen
Burger, Albert E. 1941- 37-40R
Burger, Alfred 1905- 122
Burger, Angela Sutherland (Brown) 1936- 81-84
Burger, Carl 1888-1967 .... CAP-2
Earlier sketch in CA 19-20
See also SATA 9
Burger, Chester 1921- 9-12R
Burger, Edward J(ames) Jr. 1933- 110
Burger, George V(anderkarr) 1927- 57-60
Burger, Henry G. 1923- CANR-15
Earlier sketch in CA 41-44R
Burger, Hermann 1942-1989 Obituary 128
Burger, Jack
See Burger, John R(obert)
Burger, Joanna 1941- 136
Burger, John
See Marquard, Leo(pold)
Burger, John R(obert) 1942- 81-84
Burger, Nash K(err) 1908- CAP-2
Earlier sketch in CA 23-24
Burger, Robert E(ugene) 1931- 85-88
Burger, Robert S. 1913- 29-32R
Burger, Ronna Cheryl 1947- 117
Burger, Ruth (Pazen) 1917- 17-20R
Burger, Sarah Greene 1935- 69-72
Burgess, Ann Marie
See Gerson, Noel Bertram
Burgess, Anthony
See Wilson, John (Anthony) Burgess
See also AITN 1
See also CDBLB 1960 to Present
See also CLC 1, 2, 4, 5, 8, 10, 13, 15, 22, 40, 62
See also DLB 14
Burgess, Barbara Hood 1926- 138
See also SATA 69
Burgess, C(hester) F(rancis) 1922- 21-24R
Burgess, Charles (Orville) 1932- 33-36R
Burgess, Christopher Victor 1921- 9-12R
Burgess, Em
See Burgess, Mary Wyche
Burgess, Eric (Alexander) 1912- 101
Burgess, Eric 1920- CANR-18
Earlier sketches in CA 5-8R, CANR-3
Burgess, (Frank) Gelett
1866-1951 Brief entry 113
See also DLB 11
See also SATA 30, 32
Burgess, Granville Wyche 1947- 137
Burgess, Helen S(teers)
1906-1987 Obituary 123
Burgess, Jackson (Visscher) 1927- 9-12R
Burgess, Jane K. 1928- CANR-13
Earlier sketch in CA 73-76R
Burgess, John H(enry) 1923- 33-36R
Burgess, John Lawie 1912-1987 Obituary 121
Burgess, John W. 1844-1931 .... DLB 47
Burgess, Linda Cannon 1911- 73-76
Burgess, Lorraine Marshall 1913- 106
Burgess, M(argaret) Elaine 13-16R
Burgess, M(ichael) R(oy) 1948- CANR-6
Earlier sketch in CA 57-60
Burgess, Mary Wyche 1916- 61-64
See also SATA 18
Burgess, Michael
See Gerson, Noel Bertram
Burgess, Norman 1923- 25-28R
Burgess, Philip M(ark) 1939- CANR-16
Earlier sketch in CA 25-28R
Burgess, Robert F(orrest) 1927- CANR-11
Earlier sketch in CA 25-28R
See also SATA 4
Burgess, Robert H(errmann) 1913- CANR-5
Earlier sketch in CA 9-12R
Burgess, Robert L. 1938- 29-32R
Burgess, Thornton Waldo 1874-1965 73-76
See also DLB 22
See also MAICYA
See also SATA 17
Burgess, Trevor
See Trevor, Elleston
Burgess, W(arren) Randolph 1889-1978 .... CAP-2
Obituary 81-84
Earlier sketch in CA 29-32
Burgess-Kohn, Jane
See Burgess, Jane K.
Burgett, Donald R(obert) 1925- 21-24R
Burggraaff, Winfield J. 1940- Brief entry 114
Burghard, August 1901- CANR-7
Earlier sketch in CA 17-20R
See also AITN 2
Burghardt, Andrew Frank 1924- 5-8R
Burghardt, Walter J(ohn) 1914- CANR-19
Earlier sketches in CA 1-4R, CANR-4
Burgin, C(harles) David 1939- 73-76
Burgin, (Weston) Richard 1947- 25-28R
Burgos, Joseph A(gner) Jr. 1945- 106
Burgoyne, Bruce E. 1924- 135
Burgoyne, Elizabeth
See Pickles, M(abel) Elizabeth
Burgwyn, Diana 1937- 108
Burgwyn, Mebane Holoman 1914- 49-52
See also SATA 7
Burhoe, Ralph Wendell 1911- 17-20R
Buri, Fritz 1907- CANR-8
Earlier sketch in CA 17-20R
Burian, Jarka M(arsano) 1927- 33-36R
Burian, Richard M(artin) 1941- 121
Burich, Nancy J(ane) 1943- 29-32R
Burick, Si(mon) 1909-1986 85-88
Obituary 121
Burk, Bill E(ugene) 1932- 65-68
Burk, Bruce 1917- 61-64
Burk, John Daly 1772(?)-1808 .... DLB 37
Burk, Kathleen 1946- 130
Burk, Robert F(redrick) 1955- 134
Burkard, Michael 1947- 132
Burke, Alan Dennis 1949- 106
Burke, Anna Mae Walsh 1938- 111
Burke, Avid J. 1906- 21-24R
Burke, C(letus) J(oseph) 1917-1973 45-48
Burke, Carl F(rancis) 1917- 25-28R
Burke, Carol 1950- CANR-14
Earlier sketch in CA 65-68
Burke, Colin Bradley 1936- 113
Burke, David 1927- CANR-23
Earlier sketch in CA 105
See also SATA 46
Burke, Desmond William Lardner
See Lardner-Burke, Desmond William
Burke, Edmund M. 1928- 9-12R
Burke, Edmund 1729(?)-1797 .... DLB 104
See also WLC
Burke, Fielding
See Dargan, Olive (Tilford)
Burke, Fred G(eorge) 1926- 13-16R
Burke, Gerald 1914- CANR-1
Earlier sketch in CA 45-48
Burke, J(ohn) Bruce 1933- 37-40R
Burke, J(ackson) F(rederick Augustine)
1915- CANR-12
Earlier sketch in CA 65-68
Burke, James Lee 1936- CANR-22
Earlier sketches in CA 13-16R, CANR-7
Burke, James Wakefield 1916- CANR-1
Earlier sketch in CA 45-48
Burke, James 1936- CANR-28
Earlier sketch in CA 102
Burke, John
See O'Connor, Richard
Burke, John Emmett 1908- 37-40R
Burke, John (Frederick) 1922- CANR-25
Earlier sketches in CA 5-8R, CANR-9
Burke, John Garrett 1917- 77-80
Burke, John J(oseph) Jr. 1942- 114
Burke, Jonathan
See Burke, John (Frederick)
Burke, Joseph (Terence Anthony) 1913- 103
Burke, Kenneth (Duva) 1897- CANR-39
Earlier sketch in CA 5-8R
See also CLC 2, 24
See also DLB 45, 63
See also MTCW
Burke, Leda
See Garnett, David
Burke, Maggie
See Snyder, Marilyn
Burke, (Omar) Michael 1927- 73-76
Burke, Owen
See Burke, John (Frederick)
Burke, (Ulick) Peter 1937- CANR-16
Earlier sketch in CA 25-28R
Burke, Ralph
See Garrett, (Gordon) Randall (Phillip)
and Silverberg, Robert
Burke, Richard C(ullen) 1932- 53-56
Burke, Robert E(ugene) 1921- 21-24R
Burke, Russell 1946- 33-36R
Burke, S(amuel) M(artin) 1906- 49-52
Burke, Shifty
See Benton, Peggie
Burke, Stanley 1923- 101
Burke, T(homas) Patrick 1934- 121
Burke, Ted 1934(?)-1978 Obituary 77-80
Burke, Thomas 1886-1945 Brief entry 113
Burke, Tom 73-76
Burke, Vee
See Burke, Velma Whitgrove
Burke, Velma Whitgrove 1921- CANR-4
Earlier sketch in CA 53-56
Burke, Vincent John 1919-1973 122
Obituary 111
Burke, Virginia M. 1916- 45-48
Burke, W. Warner 1935- CANR-14
Earlier sketch in CA 37-40R
Burkert, Nancy Ekholm 1933- .... MAICYA
See also SAAS 14
See also SATA 24
Burkert, Walter 1931- CANR-34
Earlier sketch in CA 103
Burket, Harriet 1908- 37-40R
Burkett, David (Young III) 1934- CANR-9
Earlier sketch in CA 65-68
Burkett, Eva M(ae) 1903- 33-36R
Burkett, Jack 1914- 101
Burkett, Molly 1932- CANR-9
Earlier sketch in CA 53-56
Burkey, Richard M(ichael) 1930- 93-96
Burkhalter, Barton R. 1938- CANR-11
Earlier sketch in CA 25-28R
Burkhardt, Richard Wellington 1918- 1-4R
Burkhart, Charles 1924- 13-16R
Burkhart, James A(ustin) 1914-1979 .... 9-12R
Burkhart, John E(rnest) 1927- 116
Burkhart, Kathryn Watterson 1942- CANR-34
Earlier sketch in CA 45-48
Burkhart, Kitsi
See Burkhart, Kathryn Watterson
Burkhart, Robert E(dward) 1937- 29-32R
Burkhead, Jesse 1916- CANR-3
Earlier sketch in CA 1-4R
Burkholder, J(ames) Peter 1954- 119
Burkholder, John Richard 1928- CANR-37
Earlier sketch in CA 115
Burkholz, Herbert 1932- CANR-11
Earlier sketch in CA 25-28R
Burkill, T(om) A(lec) 1912- 33-36R
Burkitt, Denis (Parsons) 1911- 112
Burkle, Howard R(ussell) 1925- Brief entry 107
Burkman, Katherine H. 1934- 29-32R
Burkowsky, Mitchell R(oy) 1931- 29-32R
Burks, Ardath Walter 1915- 107
Burks, Arthur W(alter) 1915- 49-52
Burks, David D. 1924- 33-36R
Burks, Edward C. 1921(?)-1983 Obituary 111
Burks, Gordon E(ngledow) 1904- 1-4R
Burks, Ned
See Burks, Edward C.
Burl, (Harry) Aubrey (Woodruff) 1926- 97-100
Burland, Brian (Berkeley) 1931- CANR-23
Earlier sketches in CA 13-16R, CANR-7
See also SATA 34
Burland, C. A.
See Burland, Cottie (Arthur)
Burland, Cottie (Arthur) 1905- CANR-5
Earlier sketch in CA 5-8R
See also SATA 5
Burleigh, Anne Husted 1941- 29-32R
Burleigh, David Robert 1907- 1-4R
Burleigh, John H. S. 1894-1985 Obituary 116
Burleigh, Michael 1955- 135
Burleigh, Robert 1936- .... SATA 55
Burley, George (Joseph) 1939- Brief entry 107
Burley, W(illiam) J(ohn) 1914- CANR-29
Earlier sketches in CA 33-36R, CANR-13
Burling, Robbins 1926- 17-20R
Burlingame, Edward Livermore
1848-1922 .... DLB 79
Burlingame, (William) Roger 1889-1967 .... 5-8R
See also SATA 2
Burlingame, Virginia (Struble) 1900- CAP-2
Earlier sketch in CA 23-24
Burlingham, Dorothy (Tiffany) 1891-1979 109
Obituary 93-96
Burma, John H(armon) 1913- CANR-5
Earlier sketch in CA 1-4R
Burman, Alice Caddy 1896(?)-1977 .... SATA 24
Burman, Ben Lucien 1896-1984 .... CANR-32
Obituary 114
Earlier sketches in CA 5-8R, CANR-8
See also SATA 6, 40
Burman, Edward 1947- 134
Burman, Jose Lionel 1917- CANR-28
Earlier sketch in CA 109
Burmeister, Edwin 1939- CANR-26
Earlier sketch in CA 29-32R
Burmeister, Eva (Elizabeth) 1899- CAP-1
Earlier sketch in CA 13-14
Burmeister, Jon 1933- 29-32R
Burmeister, Lou E(lla) 1928- CANR-26
Earlier sketch in CA 45-48
Burn, A(ndrew) R(obert) 1902- CANR-17
Earlier sketches in CA 1-4R, CANR-1
Burn, Barbara 1940- CANR-17
Earlier sketch in CA 85-88
Burn, Doris 1923- 29-32R
See also SATA 1
Burn, Duncan (Lyall) 1902-1988 Obituary 124
Burn, Gordon 1948- 123
Burn, J(oshua) Harold 1892-1982 .... CAP-1
Obituary 108
Earlier sketch in CA 11-12
Burn, Mary (Wynn) 1910- 122
Burnaby, John 1891-1978 .... CAP-1
Obituary 104
Earlier sketch in CA 13-14
Burnam, Tom 1913- 61-64
Burne, Glen
See Green, Alan (Baer)
Burne, Glenn S. 1921- 21-24R
Burne, Kevin G. 1925- 13-16R
Burner, David (B.) 1937- CANR-10
Earlier sketch in CA 25-28R
Burness, Tad
See Burness, Wallace B(inny)
Burness, Wallace B(inny) 1933- CANR-21
Earlier sketch in CA 69-72
Burnet, George Bain 1894- CAP-2
Earlier sketch in CA 23-24
Burnet, Gilbert 1643-1715 .... DLB 101
Burnet, Jean R. 1920- 130
Burnet, (Frank) Macfarlane 1899-1985 73-76
Obituary 117
Burnet, Mary E(dith) 1911- 53-56
Burnett, Alfred David 1937- CANR-19
Earlier sketch in CA 102
Burnett, Anne Pippin 1925- 113
Burnett, Avis 1937- 41-44R
Burnett, Ben G(eorge) 1924-1975 .... CANR-3
Earlier sketch in CA 1-4R
Burnett, Calvin 1921- 33-36R
Burnett, Carol 1933- 127

Burnett, Collins W. 1914- CANR-3
Earlier sketch in CA 9-12R
Burnett, Constance Buel 1893-1975 ....5-8R
See also SATA 36
Burnett, David (Alan) 1946- 121
Burnett, David (Benjamin Foley)
1931-1971 ....9-12R
Obituary 33-36R
Burnett, Dorothy Kirk 1924- 5-8R
Burnett, Frances (Eliza) Hodgson
1849-1924 136
Brief entry 108
See also CLR 24
See also DLB 42
See also MAICYA
See also YABC 2
Burnett, Hallie Southgate (Zeisel)
1909(?)-1991 ....CANR-37
Obituary 135
Earlier sketches in CA 13-16R, CANR-6
Burnett, Janet 1915- 49-52
Burnett, Joe Ray 1928- 17-20R
Burnett, John 1925- 57-60
Burnett, June 1936- 113
Burnett, Laurence 1907- 49-52
Burnett, Leo 1891-1971 Obituary 116
Burnett, Leon R. 1925(?)-1983 Obituary 109
Burnett, W(illiam) R(iley) 1899-1982 ....CANR-22
Obituary 106
Earlier sketch in CA 5-8R
See also DLB 9
Burnett, Whit(ney Ewing) 1899-1973 ....CAP-2
Obituary 41-44R
Earlier sketch in CA 13-14
Burnette, O(llen) Lawrence Jr. 1927- 33-36R
Burney, Anton
See Hopkins, (Hector) Kenneth
Burney, Elizabeth (Mary) 1934- 21-24R
Burney, Eugenia 1913- 29-32R
Burney, Fanny 1752-1840 ....DLB 39
Burnford, Sheila (Philip Cochrane Every)
1918-1984 ....CANR-1
Obituary 112
Earlier sketch in CA 1-4R
See also CLR 2
See also MAICYA
See also SATA 3, 38
Burnham, Alan 1913-1984 ....13-16R
Obituary 112
Burnham, Charles
See Paine, Lauran (Bosworth)
Burnham, David (Bright) 1933- 122
Burnham, Dorothy E(dith) 1921- 65-68
Burnham, (Linden) Forbes (Sampson)
1923-1985 Obituary 117
Burnham, J. W.
See Burnham, Jack (Wesley)
Burnham, Jack (Wesley) 1931- 115
Burnham, James 1905-1987 Obituary 123
Burnham, John
See Beckwith, Burnham Putnam
Burnham, John C(hynoweth) 1929- 33-36R
Burnham, Linda Frye 1940- 125
Burnham, Richard 1940- 118
Burnham, Robert Ward Jr. 1913- 17-20R
Burnham, Sophy 1936- CANR-38
Earlier sketch in CA 41-44R
See also AITN 1
See also SATA 65
Burnham, Walter Dean 1930- 101
Burnim, Kalman A(aron) 1928- 1-4R
Burningham, John (Mackintosh)
1936- CANR-36
Earlier sketch in CA 73-76
See also CLR 9
See also MAICYA
See also SATA 16, 59
Burnley, (John) David 1941- 117
Burnley, Judith CANR-16
Earlier sketch in CA 97-100
Burns, Aidan 1943- 121
Burns, Alan Cuthbert 1887-1980 Obituary 102
Burns, Alan 1929- CANR-34
Earlier sketches in CA 9-12R, CANR-5
See also DLB 14
Burns, Allan P. 1935- 125
Burns, Alma 1919- 81-84
Burns, Arthur F(rank) 1904-1987 ....13-16R
Obituary 122
Burns, Betty 1909- CAP-2
Earlier sketch in CA 19-20
Burns, Bobby
See Burns, Vincent Godfrey
Burns, Carol 1934- 29-32R
Burns, Chester R(ay) 1937- 103
Burns, David D. 1942- 114
Burns, Diane L. 1950- 135
Burns, E(dward) Bradford 1932- 17-20R
Burns, Edward McNall 1897-1972 ....1-4R
Obituary 103
Burns, Eedson Louis Millard
1897-1985 ....CANR-5
Obituary 117
Earlier sketch in CA 5-8R
Burns, Eveline M(abel Richardson)
1900-1985 Obituary 117
Burns, Florence M. 1905-1988 ....SATA 61
Burns, Geoff 1954- 115
Burns, George 1896- 112
See also BEST 89:2
Burns, Gerald P(hillip) 1918- 17-20R
Burns, Helen M(arie) 1922- 110
Burns, Hobert Warren 1925- 1-4R
Burns, James MacGregor 1918- CANR-19
Earlier sketch in CA 5-8R
Burns, James W(illiam) 1937- 33-36R
Burns, Jean (Ellen) 1934- 103
Burns, Jim 1936- 101
Burns, Jimmy 1953- 134
Burns, Joan Simpson 1927- 65-68
Burns, John Horne 1916-1953 Brief entry 115
See also DLBY 85
Burns, John McLauren 1932- Brief entry 109
Burns, John V. 1907- CAP-2
Earlier sketch in CA 33-36
Burns, Marilyn ....SATA 33
Burns, Michael 1947- 121
Burns, Norman T(homas) 1930- 69-72
Burns, Olive Ann 1924-1990 120
Obituary 132
See also SATA 65
Burns, Paul C. CANR-4
Earlier sketch in CA 1-4R
See also SATA 5
Burns, Ralph J. 1901- CAP-2
Earlier sketch in CA 25-28
Burns, Ray
See Burns, Raymond (Howard)
Burns, Raymond (Howard) 1924- ....SATA 9
Burns, Rex (Sehler) 1935- CANR-13
Earlier sketch in CA 77-80
Burns, Richard Dean 1929- CANR-8
Earlier sketch in CA 17-20R
Burns, Richard W(ebster) 1920- 69-72
Burns, Richard (William) 1958- 128
Burns, Robert E(lliott) 1891(?)-1955 138
Burns, Robert Edward 1919- 111
Burns, Robert Grant 1938- CANR-16
Earlier sketch in CA 25-28R
Burns, Robert I(gnatius) 1921- CANR-26
Earlier sketches in CA 17-20R, CANR-7
Burns, Robert M(ilton) C(lark) Jr. 1940- 102
Burns, Robert 1759-1796 .... CDBLB 1789-1832
See also DLB 109
See also WLC
Burns, Ruby V(ermillion) 1901- 106
Burns, Scott
See Burns, Robert M(ilton) C(lark) Jr.
Burns, Sheila
See Bloom, Ursula
Burns, Stuart L(eroy) 1932- 127
Burns, Tex
See L'Amour, Louis (Dearborn)
Burns, Thomas J. 1942- 127
Burns, Thomas (Jr.) 1928- CANR-14
Earlier sketch in CA 41-44R
Burns, Thomas Stephen 1927- 49-52
Burns, Tom 1913- CANR-22
Earlier sketches in CA 5-8R, CANR-5
Burns, Vincent Godfrey 1893-1979 ....41-44R
Obituary 85-88
See also AITN 2
Burns, Wayne 1918- CANR-1
Earlier sketch in CA 1-4R
Burns, William A. 1909- CANR-11
Earlier sketches in CAP-1, CA 13-14
See also SATA 5
Burns, Zed H(ouston) 1903- 33-36R
Burns-Bisogno, Louisa 1936- 134
Burnshaw, Stanley 1906- 9-12R
See also CLC 3, 13, 44
See also DLB 48
Burnside, Wesley M(ason) 1918- 65-68
Buros, Oscar Krisen 1905-1978 Obituary 77-80
Burow, Daniel R(obert) 1931- CANR-11
Earlier sketch in CA 29-32R
Burr, Alfred Gray 1919- 25-28R
Burr, Anne 1937- 25-28R
See also CLC 6
Burr, C. Chauncey 1815(?)-1883 ....DLB 79
Burr, Charles 1922(?)-1976 Obituary 69-72
Burr, Dan 1951- ....SATA 65
Burr, Gray 1919- 69-72
Burr, John R(oy) 1933- 45-48
Burr, Keith 1946- 115
Burr, Lonnie 1943- 103
See also SATA 47
Burr, Samuel Engle Jr. 1897-1987 Obituary 124
Burr, Wesley R(ay) 1936- 37-40R
Burrell, Berkeley G(raham) 1919-1979 ....33-36R
Obituary 89-92
Burrell, David B(akewell) 1933- 33-36R
Burrell, Evelyn Patterson 1920- CANR-7
Earlier sketch in CA 53-56
Burrell, Roy E(ric) C(harles) 1923- 33-36R
Burridge, Kenelm (Oswald Lancelot)
1922- 93-96
Burridge, Trevor David 1932- 137
Burrin, Frank K. 1920- 25-28R
Burrington, David E. 1931- 73-76
Burris, B. C(ullen) 1924- 21-24R
Burris-Meyer, Harold 1902- 41-44R
Burros, Marian (Fox) CANR-30
Earlier sketch in CA 89-92
Burrough, Bryan ....BEST 90:3
Burroughs, Ben(jamin F.) 1918-1980 65-68
Obituary 122
Burroughs, Edgar Rice 1875-1950 132
Brief entry 104
See also DLB 8
See also MTCW
See also SATA 41
See also TCLC 2, 32
Burroughs, Jean Mitchell 1908- 65-68
See also SATA 28
Burroughs, John 1837-1921 Brief entry 109
See also DLB 64
Burroughs, Margaret G.
See Burroughs, Margaret Taylor (Goss)
Burroughs, Margaret Taylor (Goss)
1917- CANR-25
Earlier sketch in CA 21-24R
See also BW
See also DLB 41
Burroughs, Polly 1925- 25-28R
See also SATA 2
Burroughs, Raleigh (Simpson) 1901- 106
Burroughs, William S(eward) 1914- CANR-20
Earlier sketch in CA 9-12R
See also AITN 2
See also CLC 1, 2, 5, 15, 22, 42
See also DLB 2, 8, 16
See also DLBY 81
See also MTCW
See also WLC
Burroughs, William (Seward) Jr.
1947-1981 73-76
Obituary 112
See also DLB 16
Burrow, James Gordon 1922- CANR-2
Earlier sketch in CA 5-8R
Burrow, John A(nthony) 1932- 97-100
Burrow, John W(yon) 1935- CANR-30
Earlier sketches in CA 21-24R, CANR-12
Burroway, Janet (Gay) 1936- CANR-12
Earlier sketch in CA 21-24R
See also CAAS 6
See also DLB 6
See also SATA 23
Burrowes, Michael Anthony Bernard 1937- 103
Burrowes, Mike
See Burrowes, Michael Anthony Bernard
Burrows, Abe
See Burrows, Abram Solman
Burrows, Abram Solman 1910-1985 110
Obituary 116
Burrows, David J(ames) 1936- 41-44R
Burrows, E(dwin) G(ladding) 1917- CANR-14
Earlier sketch in CA 77-80
Burrows, Fredrika Alexander 1908- CANR-6
Earlier sketch in CA 57-60
Burrows, James C. 1944- 29-32R
Burrows, John 1945- 101
Burrows, Miles 1936- 21-24R
Burrows, Millar 1889-1980 81-84
Obituary 97-100
Burrows, William E. 1937- 65-68
Burrows, William R(ichard) 1942- 117
Burrup, Percy E. 1910- 1-4R
Bursk, Christopher 1943- CANR-24
Earlier sketch in CA 85-88
Bursk, Edward C(ollins) 1907-1990 ....CANR-5
Obituary 130
Earlier sketch in CA 1-4R
Burstall, Aubrey F(rederic)
1902-1984 Obituary 113
Burstein, Alvin G(eorge) 1931- 85-88
Burstein, Chaya M(alamud) 1923- 126
See also SATA 64
Burstein, John 1949- CANR-21
Earlier sketch in CA 69-72
See also SATA 40, 54
Burstein, Patricia (Ann) 1945- 108
Burstein, Paul 1946- 123
Burstiner, Irving 1919- 104
Burston, W. H. 1915-1981 Obituary 103
Burstyn, Harold L(ewis) 1930- CANR-5
Earlier sketch in CA 9-12R
Burt, Al(vin Victor Jr.) 1927- 25-28R
Burt, Alfred LeRoy 1888- CAP-1
Earlier sketch in CA 9-10
Burt, Cyril (Lodowic) 1883-1971 ....CAP-1
Obituary 33-36R
Earlier sketch in CA 13-14
Burt, Donald X(avier) 1929- CANR-39
Earlier sketch in CA 116
Burt, Frances R(iemer) 1917- 69-72
Burt, Jesse Clifton 1921-1976 ....CANR-4
Earlier sketch in CA 9-12R
See also SATA 20, 46
Burt, John J. 1934- CANR-11
Earlier sketch in CA 29-32R
Burt, Larry W(ayne) 1950- 122
Burt, Leonard James 1892-1983 Obituary 114
Burt, Mala S(chuster) 1943- 112
Burt, Maxwell Struthers 1882-1954 ....DLB 86
Burt, Nathaniel 1913- 17-20R
Burt, Olive Woolley 1894- CANR-5
Earlier sketch in CA 5-8R
See also SATA 4
Burt, Robert Amsterdam 1939- 102
Burt, Roger B(ivens) 1939- 113
Burt, Samuel M(athew) 1915- 21-24R
Burt, Simon 1947- 123
Burt, William Henry 1903- 106
Burtchaell, James Tunstead 1934- CANR-27
Earlier sketches in CA 25-28R, CANR-11
Burtis, C(harles) Edward 1907- 41-44R
Burtle, James (L.) 1919- Brief entry 113
Burtness, Paul Sidney 1923- 17-20R
Burton, Anthony 1933- 61-64
Burton, Anthony 1934- 97-100
Burton, Arthur 1914-1982 ....CANR-10
Earlier sketch in CA 21-24R
Burton, Carl D. 1913- 1-4R
Burton, David H(enry) 1925- CANR-3
Earlier sketch in CA 49-52
Burton, Dolores Marie 1932- 25-28R
Burton, Dwight L(owell) 1922- 61-64
Burton, Edward J. 1917- 21-24R
Burton, (Alice) Elizabeth 1908- CANR-15
Earlier sketch in CA 65-68
Burton, Gabrielle 1939- 45-48
Burton, Genevieve 1912- 33-36R
Burton, H(arry) M(cGuire Philip)
1898(?)-1979 Obituary 93-96
Burton, Hal
See Burton, Harold Bernard
Burton, Harold Bernard 1908- 97-100
Burton, Hester (Wood-Hill) 1913- CANR-10
Earlier sketch in CA 9-12R
See also CLR 1
See also MAICYA
See also SAAS 8
See also SATA 7
Burton, Ian 1935- 17-20R
Burton, Ivor Flower 1923- 109
Burton, Jane 1933- CANR-29
Earlier sketch in CA 105
Burton, Joe Wright 1907-1976 107
Burton, John A(ndrew) 1944- CANR-14
Earlier sketch in CA 65-68
Burton, John Wear 1915- 103
Burton, Katherine (Kurz) 1890-1969 77-80
Burton, Leslie
See McGuire, Leslie Sarah
Burton, Lindy 1937- 25-28R
Burton, Lloyd E. 1922- 53-56
Burton, Marilee Robin 1950- 121
See also SATA 46
Burton, Martin A. 1911-1984 Obituary 114
Burton, Mary E(lizabeth) 1900- 106
Burton, Maurice 1898- CANR-29
Earlier sketches in CA 65-68, CANR-9
See also SATA 23
Burton, Miles
See Rhode, John
Burton, Nelson Jr. 1942- 57-60
Burton, Orville Vernon 1947- 126
Burton, Philip 1904- 25-28R
Burton, Richard F. 1821-1890 ....DLB 55
Burton, Richard 1925-1984 Obituary 113
Burton, Robert E(dward) 1927- CANR-13
Earlier sketch in CA 61-64
Burton, Robert H(enderson) 1934- 37-40R
Burton, Robert (Wellesley) 1941- CANR-29
Earlier sketches in CA 45-48, CANR-1, 17
See also SATA 22
Burton, Roger V(ernon) 1928- 45-48
Burton, S(amuel) H(olroyd) 1919- 102
Burton, Sandra 132
Burton, Thomas
See Longstreet, Stephen
Burton, Thomas G(lenn) 1935- 105
Burton, Virginia Lee 1909-1968 ....CAP-1
Obituary 25-28R
Earlier sketch in CA 13-14
See also CLR 11
See also DLB 22
See also MAICYA
See also SATA 2
Burton, William Evans 1804-1860 ....DLB 73
Burton, William H(enry) 1890-1964 ....CANR-1
Earlier sketch in CA 1-4R
See also SATA 11
Burton, William L(ester) 1928- 21-24R
Burton-Bradley, Burton Gyrth 1914- 77-80
Burtschi, Mary 1911- CANR-19
Earlier sketches in CA 9-12R, CANR-5
Burtt, Edwin Arthur 1892-1989 ....5-8R
Obituary 129
Burtt, Everett Johnson Jr. 1914- 9-12R
Burtt, George 1914- CANR-11
Earlier sketch in CA 61-64
Burtt, Harold E(rnest) 1890- CAP-2
Earlier sketch in CA 17-18
Buruma, Ian 1951- 128
Burwash, Peter 1945- 119
Burwell, Adam Hood 1790-1849 ....DLB 99
Bury, Frank
See Harris, Herbert
Bury, J(ohn) P(atrick) T(uer) 1908- 17-20R
Bury, Lady Charlotte 1775-1861 ....DLB 116
Buryn, Ed(ward Casimir) 1934- 85-88
Busbee, Shirlee (Elaine) 1941- 77-80
Busby, Edith (A. Lake) Obituary 109
See also SATA 29
Busby, F. M. 1921- CANR-24
Earlier sketches in CA 65-68, CANR-9
Busby, John 1928- CANR-39
Earlier sketch in CA 116
Busby, Mabel Janice
See Stanford, Sally
Busby, Roger (Charles) 1941- 105
Buscaglia, Leo F.
See Buscaglia, (Felice) Leo(nardo)
See also BEST 89:4
Buscaglia, (Felice) Leo(nardo) 1924- CANR-30
Brief entry 110
Earlier sketch in CA 112
See also Buscaglia, Leo F.
See also SATA 65
Busch, Briton Cooper 1936- CANR-36
Earlier sketches in CA 21-24R, CANR-8
Busch, Francis X(avier) 1879-1975 ....CAP-1
Obituary 61-64
Earlier sketch in CA 13-14
Busch, Frederick 1941- 33-36R
See also CAAS 1
See also CLC 7, 10, 18, 47
See also DLB 6
Busch, Hans (Peter) 1914- 109
Busch, Julia 1940- CANR-39
Earlier sketch in CA 57-60
Busch, Niven 1903-1991 ....CANR-7
Obituary 135
Earlier sketch in CA 13-16R
See also DLB 44
Busch, Noel F(airchild) 1906-1985 49-52
Obituary 117
Busch, Phyllis S. 1909- 107
See also SATA 30
Busch, Ronald 1928-1987 Obituary 123
Buschkuehl, Matthias 1953- 121
Buschkuhl, Matthias
See Buschkuehl, Matthias

Buse, D(ieter) K(urt) 1941- 137
Buse, R. F.
See Buse, Renee
Buse, Renee 1914(?)-1979 Obituary 85-88
Buse, Rueben C. 1932- 109
Busey, James L. 1916- 5-8R
Bush, Alan (Dudley) 1900- 110
Bush, Barbara Holstein 1935- CANR-12
Earlier sketch in CA 69-72
Bush, Barry (Michael) 1938- 110
Bush, Charlie Christmas 1888(?)-1973 107
Obituary 104
Bush, Christopher
See Bush, Charlie Christmas
Bush, Clifford L(ewis) 1915- 33-36R
Bush, Donald J(ohn) 114
Bush, (John Nash) Douglas 1896-1983 .....37-40R
Obituary 109
Bush, Eric Wheler 1899-1985 65-68
Obituary 117
Bush, Frederic W(illiam) 1929- 125
Bush, George Edward Jr. 1938- 109
Bush, George P(ollock) 1892- 17-20R
Bush, George S(idney) 1925- 110
Bush, Grace A(bhau) 1936- 104
Bush, Jim 1926- 57-60
Bush, John W(illiam) 1917-1976 .... CAP-2
Earlier sketch in CA 33-36
Bush, L(uther) Russ(ell III) 1944- 121
Bush, Larry
See Bush, Lawrence Dana
Bush, Lawrence Dana 1951- 109
Bush, Lewis William 1907- 81-84
Bush, M(ichael) L(accohee) 1938- 132
Bush, Martin H(arry) 1930- CANR-12
Earlier sketch in CA 29-32R
Bush, Patricia (Jahns) 1932- CANR-24
Earlier sketch in CA 105
Bush, Richard C(larence) 1923- Brief entry 114
Bush, Robert (Burton) 1917- 116
Bush, Robert (Ray) 1920-1972 Obituary 33-36R
Bush, Ronald 1946- 136
See also CLC 34
Bush, Sargent Jr. 1937- CANR-29
Earlier sketch in CA 65-68
Bush, Susan 1933- 127
Bush, Ted J. 1922- 17-20R
Bush, Vannevar 1890-1974 97-100
Obituary 53-56
Bush, William (Shirley Jr.) 1929- CANR-32
Earlier sketches in CA 37-40R, CANR-14
Busha, Charles Henry 1931- CANR-5
Earlier sketch in CA 53-56
Bush-Brown, Albert 1926- 128
Bush-Brown, James 1892-1985 ....5-8R
Obituary 118
Bush-Brown, Louise
1896(?)-1973 Obituary 49-52
Bushell, Agnes 1949- 135
Bushell, Don(ald Gair) Jr. 1934- Brief entry 113
Bushell, Raymond 1910- CANR-20
Earlier sketches in CA 13-16R, CANR-5
Bushey, Jerry 1941- CANR-25
Earlier sketch in CA 108
Bushinsky, Jay (Joseph Mason) 1932- 77-80
Bushman, Claudia L(auper) 1934- CANR-22
Earlier sketch in CA 106
Bushman, Richard L(yman) 1931- CANR-22
Earlier sketch in CA 21-24R
Bushmiller, Ernest Paul 1905-1982 ....29-32R
Obituary 107
See also Bushmiller, Ernie
See also AITN 1
Bushmiller, Ernie
See Bushmiller, Ernest Paul
See also SATA 31
Bushnell, David S(herman) 1927- 41-44R
Bushrui, S(uheil) B(adi) 1929- 17-20R
Bushyager, Linda E(yster) 1947- 93-96
Busia, Kofi Abrefa 1913-1978 69-72
Obituary 126
Buske, Morris Roger 1912- 13-16R
Buskin, Martin 1930-1976 Obituary 65-68
Buskirk, Richard H(obart) 1927- CANR-1
Earlier sketch in CA 1-4R
Busoni, Rafaello 1900-1962 Obituary 117
See also SATA 16
Buss, Arnold H. 1924- CANR-4
Earlier sketch in CA 1-4R
Buss, Claude Albert 1903- 109
Buss, Gerald (Vere Austen) 1936- 127
Buss, Helen M.
See Clarke, Margaret
Buss, Leo W. 1953- 121
Buss, Martin J(ohn) 1930- 33-36R
Bussard, Paul 1904-1983 Obituary 109
Bussche, Henri O(mer) A(ntoine) Van den
1920-1965 ....CANR-5
Earlier sketch in CA 5-8R
Busse, Thomas V(alentine) 1941-1986 77-80
Obituary 119
Bussell, Harold L. 1941- 125
Busselle, Rebecca 1941- 135
Bussey, Ellen M(arion) 1926- CANR-2
Earlier sketch in CA 49-52
Bussieres, Arthur de 1877-1913 .... DLB 92
Bussieres, Simone 1918- 53-56
Bustad, Leo Kenneth 1920- 106
Bustamante, A(gustin) Jorge 1938- 33-36R
Bustanoby, Andre S(teven) 1930- 101
Bustard, Robert 1938- 65-68
Busteed, Marilyn 1937- 61-64
Bustos, F(rancisco)
See Borges, Jorge Luis
Bustos Domecq, H(onorio)
See Bioy Casares, Adolfo
and Borges, Jorge Luis
Bustos Domecq, H(onrio)
See Borges, Jorge Luis
Buswell, J(ames) Oliver Jr. 1895- 5-8R
Butcher, Fanny
See Bokum, Fanny Butcher
Butcher, Geoffrey (Arthur John) 1936- 111
Butcher, Grace 1934- 25-28R
Butcher, H(arold) J(ohn) 1920- 21-24R
Butcher, Harry Cecil 1901-1985 Obituary 115
Butcher, James Neal 1933- CANR-14
Earlier sketch in CA 33-36R
Butcher, (Anne) Judith 1927- 57-60
Butcher, (Charles) Philip 1918- CANR-4
Earlier sketch in CA 1-4R
Butcher, Russell Devereux 1938- CANR-8
Earlier sketch in CA 61-64
Butcher, Thomas Kennedy 1914- CAP-1
Earlier sketch in CA 11-12
Butcher, (Charles) William 1951- 131
Butchvarov, Panayot K. 1933- 33-36R
Butck, Zulie
See Jones, Thomas W(arren)
Butel, Jane
See de Calles, Jane F. Butel
Butera, Mary C. 1925- 21-24R
Buteux, Paul E. 1939- 121
Buth, Lenore 1932- 89-92
Buthelezi, Gatsha 1928- 102
Butland, Gilbert J(ames) 1910- 21-24R
Butler, Albert 1923- CANR-5
Earlier sketch in CA 13-16R
Butler, Annie L(ouise) 1920-1979 ....CANR-28
Earlier sketch in CA 33-36R
Butler, Arthur D. 1923- 1-4R
Butler, B. C.
See Butler, Basil Christopher
Butler, Basil Christopher 1902-1986 ....CANR-2
Obituary 120
Earlier sketch in CA 1-4R
Butler, Beverly Kathleen 1932- CANR-4
Earlier sketch in CA 1-4R
See also SATA 7
Butler, Bill
See Butler, Ernest Alton
and Butler, William Huxford
and Butler, William (Arthur) Vivian
Butler, Bishop B. C.
See Butler, Basil Christopher
Butler, Charles Henry 1894- CAP-2
Earlier sketch in CA 23-24
Butler, Christina Violet 1884-1982 Obituary 106
Butler, Christopher
See Butler, Basil Christopher
Butler, Colin Gasking 1913- 109
Butler, David Edgeworth 1924- CANR-13
Earlier sketch in CA 5-8R
Butler, David Francis 1928- 41-44R
Butler, David Jonathon 1946- 69-72
Butler, Dorothy 1925- 133
Butler, E(dward) H(arry) 1913- 13-16R
Butler, Edgar W(ilbur) 1929- 77-80
Butler, Erica Bracher 1905- CAP-2
Earlier sketch in CA 17-18
Butler, Ernest Alton 1926- 33-36R
Butler, Francelia McWilliams 1913- CANR-3
Earlier sketch in CA 9-12R
Butler, G(eorge) Paul 1900- CAP-2
Earlier sketch in CA 17-18
Butler, George D. 1893- 17-20R
Butler, George Tyssen 1943- 103
Butler, Grace Kipp Pratt
See Pratt-Butler, Grace Kipp
Butler, (Frederick) Guy 1918- CANR-18
Earlier sketch in CA 101
Butler, Gwendoline Williams 1922- CANR-6
Earlier sketch in CA 9-12R
Butler, Hal 1913- 57-60
Butler, Iris 1905- 21-24R
Butler, Ivan
See Beuttler, Edward Ivan Oakley
Butler, J. Donald 1908- 1-4R
Butler, Jack 1944- 114
Butler, James H(armon) 1908- 41-44R
Butler, James R(amsay) M(ontagu)
1889-1975 .... CAP-1
Earlier sketch in CA 13-14
Butler, James 1904- CAP-1
Earlier sketch in CA 11-12
Butler, Jean Campbell (MacLaurin)
1918- 9-12R
Butler, Jean Rouverol 1916- 97-100
Butler, Jeffrey (Ernest) 1922- 65-68
Butler, Jerry P. 1944- 65-68
Butler, Joan
See Alexander, Robert William
Butler, John Alfred Valentine
1899-1977 ....CANR-5
Obituary 106
Earlier sketch in CA 5-8R
Butler, Jon 1940- 134
Butler, Joseph Thomas 1932- 13-16R
Butler, Joyce 1933- CANR-25
Earlier sketches in CA 65-68, CANR-9
Butler, Juan 1942-1981 .... DLB 53
Butler, Lionel Harry 1923-1981 110
Obituary 105
Butler, Lucius (Albert Jr.) 1928- 69-72
Butler, Margaret Gwendoline 104
Butler, Marilyn (Speers) 1937- 102
Butler, Mildred Allen 1897- CAP-2
Earlier sketch in CA 29-32
Butler, Mollie 1907- 128
Butler, Natalie Sturges 1908- 53-56
Butler, Nathan
See Sohl, Jerry
Butler, Octavia E(stelle) 1947- CANR-38
Earlier sketches in CA 73-76, CANR-12, 24
See also BW
See also CLC 38
See also DLB 33
See also MTCW
Butler, Pat(rick) (Trevor) 1929- 5-8R
Butler, Rab
See Butler, Richard Austen
Butler, Richard
See Allbeury, Theodore Edward le Bouthillier
Butler, Richard Austen 1902-1982 Obituary 106
Butler, Richard 1925- CANR-8
Earlier sketch in CA 57-60
Butler, Rick 1946- 97-100
Butler, Robert Albert 1934- CANR-11
Earlier sketch in CA 61-64
Butler, Robert Lee 1918- 57-60
Butler, Robert M. 1928(?)-1989 Obituary 129
Butler, Robert N(eil) 1927- 41-44R
Butler, Robert Olen (Jr.) 1945- 112
Butler, Rohan D'Olier 1917- 109
Butler, Ron(ald William) 1934- 69-72
Butler, Ronnie 1931- 130
Butler, Samuel 1612-1680 .... DLB 101
Butler, Samuel 1835-1902 Brief entry 104
See also CDBLB 1890-1914
See also DLB 18, 57
See also TCLC 1, 33
See also WLC
Butler, Sandra (Ada) 1938- 105
Butler, Stanley 1914- 57-60
Butler, Stefan Congrat
See Congrat-Butler, Stefan
Butler, Stuart Thomas 1926- 107
Butler, Suzanne
See Perreard, Suzanne Louise Butler
Butler, Ted
See Schweitzer, Darrell
Butler, Vivian
See Butler, William (Arthur) Vivian
Butler, Walter C.
See Faust, Frederick (Shiller)
Butler, Walter E(rnest) 1898- CANR-5
Earlier sketch in CA 5-8R
Butler, William
See Butler, William (Arthur) Vivian
Butler, William E(lliott II) 1939- CANR-38
Earlier sketches in CA 25-28R, CANR-11
Butler, William F(rank) 1917-1972 Obituary 113
Butler, William Huxford 1934-1977 57-60
Obituary 133
Butler, William (Arthur) Vivian 1927- 135
Butler, William 1929- 107
Butlin, Martin (Richard Fletcher)
1929- CANR-19
Earlier sketches in CA 5-8R, CANR-2
Butlin, Ron 1949- 136
Butor, Michel (Marie Francois) 1926- CANR-33
Earlier sketch in CA 9-12R
See also CLC 1, 3, 8, 11, 15
See also DLB 83
See also MTCW
Butow, Robert J. C. 1924- 13-16R
Butrym, Zofia Teresa 1927- 103
Butsch, Richard (J.) 1943- 135
Butscher, Edward 1943- 97-100
Butt, (Howard) Edward Jr. 1927- 57-60
Butt, (Dorcas) Susan 1938- 89-92
Buttaci, Sal(vatore) St. John 1941- CANR-9
Earlier sketch in CA 65-68
Buttel, Robert (William) 1923- 102
Buttenwieser, Ann L. 1935- 128
Buttenwieser, Paul (Arthur) 1938- CANR-35
Earlier sketch in CA 104
Butter, Peter (Herbert) 1921- 5-8R
Butterfield, Fox 1939- 119
Butterfield, Herbert 1900- 1-4R
Butterfield, Lyman H(enry)
1909-1982 Obituary 106
Butterfield, Roger (Place) 1907-1981 .... CAP-1
Obituary 103
Earlier sketch in CA 9-10
Butterfield, Stephen T(homas) 1942- 57-60
Butterick, George F. 1942-1988 ....CANR-27
Obituary 126
Earlier sketches in CA 69-72, CANR-11
Butters, Dorothy Gilman
See Gilman, Dorothy
Butterworth, Douglas Stanley 1930- 108
Butterworth, Emma Macalik 1928- 105
See also SATA 43
Butterworth, F(rank) Edward (Jr.) 1917- 29-32R
Butterworth, Hezekiah 1839-1905 .... DLB 42
Butterworth, Lionel Milner Angus
See Angus-Butterworth, Lionel Milner
Butterworth, Michael 1924-1986 ....CANR-10
Obituary 121
Earlier sketch in CA 25-28R
Butterworth, Neil 1934- 125
Butterworth, Oliver 1915-1990 ....CANR-37
Obituary 132
Earlier sketch in CA 1-4R
See also MAICYA
See also SATA 1
See also SATO 66
Butterworth, W(illiam) E(dmund III)
1929- CANR-18
Earlier sketches in CA 1-4R, CANR-2
See also SATA 5
Butti, Ken(neth Michael) 1950- 104
Buttigeig, Anton 1912-1983 Obituary 109
Buttimer, Anne 1938- 37-40R
Buttinger, Joseph 1906- 21-24R
Obituary 138
Buttinger, Muriel Gardiner 1901-1985 .....CANR-39
Obituary 115
Earlier sketch in CA 77-80
Buttitta, Anthony 1907- 81-84
Buttitta, Ignazio 1899- .... DLB 114
Buttitta, Tony
See Buttitta, Anthony
Buttlar, Lois J(acqueline) 1934- 112
Buttle, Myra
See Purcell, Victor
Button, Daniel E(van) 1917- 89-92
Button, Dick 1929- 9-12R
Button, James W(ickham) 1942- 81-84
Button, Kenneth John 1948- CANR-20
Earlier sketch in CA 103
Button, (Henry) Warren 1922- 97-100
Buttress, Frederick Arthur 1908- 33-36R
Buttrey, Douglas N(orton) CANR-18
Earlier sketch in CA 101
Buttrick, George Arthur 1892-1980 61-64
Obituary 93-96
Butts, David P. 1932- 9-12R
Butts, Edward 1951- 128
Butts, Jane Roberts 1929-1984 ....CANR-15
Earlier sketch in CA 41-44R
Butts, Porter (Freeman) 1903- 41-44R
Butts, R. Freeman 1910- 13-16R
Butwell, Richard 1929- CANR-1
Earlier sketch in CA 45-48
Butzer, Karl W(ilhelm) 1934- CANR-8
Earlier sketch in CA 21-24R
Buultjens, (Edward) Ralph 1936- CANR-4
Earlier sketch in CA 53-56
Buxbaum, Edith 1902- CAP-2
Earlier sketch in CA 25-28
Buxbaum, Martin (David) 1912-1991 ....17-20R
Obituary 134
Buxbaum, Melvin H. 1934- 53-56
Buxbaum, Robert C(ourtney) 1930- 97-100
Buxton, Anne (Arundel) Brief entry 115
Buxton, Anthony 1892(?)-1970 Obituary 104
Buxton, (Evelyn June) Bonnie 1940- 69-72
Buxton, Charles R(oberts) 1913- 65-68
Buxton, Cindy 1950- 132
Buxton, Claude E(lmo) 1912- Brief entry 114
Buxton, David Roden 1910- 104
Buxton, Edward F(ulton) 1917-1990 ....41-44R
Obituary 132
Buxton, Harold J(ocelyn)
1880-1976 Obituary 104
Buxton, (Edward) John (Mawby)
1912- CANR-31
Earlier sketches in CA 9-12R, CANR-5
Buxton, Thomas H(amilton) 1940- 57-60
Buys, Donna 1944- 102
Buzan, Barry 1946- 119
Buzo, Alexander (John) 1944- CANR-39
Earlier sketches in CA 97-100, CANR-17
See also CLC 61
Buzzard, John Huxley 1912-1984 Obituary 112
Buzzati, Dino 1906-1972 Obituary 33-36R
See also CLC 36
Buzzell, Robert (Dow) 1933- 104
Buzzle, Buck
See Rubin, Charles J.
Buzzotta, V. R(alph) 1931- 37-40R
Byard, Carole (Marie) 1941- .... SATA 57
Byars, Betsy (Cromer) 1928- CANR-36
Earlier sketches in CA 33-36R, CANR-18
See also CLC 35
See also CLR 1, 16
See also DLB 52
See also MAICYA
See also MTCW
See also SAAS 1
See also SATA 4, 46
Byatt, A(ntonia) S(usan Drabble)
1936- CANR-33
Earlier sketches in CA 13-16R, CANR-13
See also CLC 19, 65
See also DLB 14
See also MTCW
Bychowski, Gustav 1895-1972 Obituary 33-36R
Byck, Robert 1933- 109
Bye, Beryl (Joyce Rayment) 1926- CANR-11
Earlier sketch in CA 61-64
Bye, Ranulph (deBayeux) 1916- 53-56
Bye, Raymond T(aylor) 1892- 5-8R
Byerly, Greg (W.) 1949- 130
Byerly, Henry Clement 1935- 53-56
Byerly, Kenneth R(hodes) 1908- 1-4R
Byerly, Victoria 1949- 127
Byers, David (Milner) 1941- 53-56
Byers, Edward A(dams) 1939-1989 119
Obituary 129
Byers, Edward E. 1921- CANR-3
Earlier sketch in CA 1-4R
Byers, (Amy) Irene 1906- CANR-3
Earlier sketch in CA 9-12R
Byers, R(ichard) McCulloch 1913- 69-72
Byfield, Barbara Ninde 1930- CANR-4
Earlier sketch in CA 1-4R
See also SATA 8
Byham, William C(larence) 1936- CANR-17
Earlier sketch in CA 25-28R
Bykau, Vasilii Uladzimiravich
See Bykov, Vasily Vladimirovich
Bykov, Vasily Vladimirovich 1924- 102
Byles, Mather 1707-1788 .... DLB 24
Bylinsky, Gene Michae 1930- 77-80
Bynagle, Hans E(dward) 1946- 120
Byng, Douglas 1893-1987 Obituary 123
Bynner, Witter 1881-1968 ....CANR-4
Obituary 25-28R
Earlier sketch in CA 1-4R
See also DLB 54

Bynum, David E(liab) 1936- ... CANR-20
Earlier sketch in CA 37-40R
Bynum, Terrell Ward 1941- ... CANR-18
Earlier sketch in CA 101
Byock, Jesse L(ewis) 1945- ... 110
Byrd, Bobby
See Byrd, Robert James
Byrd, C. L.
See Rosenkrantz, Linda
Byrd, Cecil Kash 1913- ... 17-20R
Byrd, Eldon A(rthur) 1939- ... 45-48
Byrd, Elizabeth 1912- ... CANR-5
Earlier sketch in CA 5-8R
See also SATA 34
Byrd, Emmett
See Hinden, Michael C(harles)
Byrd, John Crowe
See Hinden, Michael C(harles)
Byrd, Martha 1930- ... 29-32R
Byrd, Richard E(dward) 1931- ... CANR-7
Earlier sketch in CA 57-60
Byrd, Robert James 1942- ... 65-68
Byrd, Robert (John) 1942- ... SATA 33
Byrd, William II 1674-1744 ... DLB 24
Byrne, Charles Raymond
1916-1983 Obituary ... 111
Byrne, David 1952- ... 127
See also CLC 26
Byrne, Donald E(dward) Jr. 1942- ... 73-76
Byrne, Donn (Erwin) 1931- ... CANR-20
Earlier sketches in CA 9-12R, CANR-5
Byrne, Edmund F(rancis) 1933- ... 29-32R
Byrne, Edward M. 1935- ... 29-32R
Byrne, Frank L(oyola) 1928- ... 21-24R
Byrne, Gary C. 1942- ... 49-52
Byrne, Herbert Winston 1917- ... 1-4R
Byrne, James E. 1945- ... 81-84
Byrne, John Keyes 1926- ... 102
See also Leonard, Hugh
See also CLC 19
Byrne, John 1940- ... 104
Byrne, Malcolm 1955- ... 127
Byrne, Muriel St. Clare 1895-1983 ... CAP-1
Obituary ... 111
Earlier sketch in CA 17-18
Byrne, Peter 1925- ... 65-68
Byrne, Ralph
See Burns, Ralph J.
Byrne, Richard Hill 1915- ... 21-24R
Byrne, Robert (Eugene) 1928- Brief entry ... 110
Byrne, Robert 1930- ... CANR-35
Earlier sketches in CA 73-76, CANR-13
Byrne, Stuart J(ames) 1913- ... 102
Byrnes, Edward T(homas) 1929- ... 53-56
Byrnes, Eugene F.
1890(?)-1974 Obituary ... 49-52
Byrnes, Garrett D(avis)
1904(?)-1985 Obituary ... 118
Byrnes, James Francis 1879-1972 Obituary ... 112
Byrnes, Joseph Francis 1939- ... 114
Byrnes, Robert F. 1917- ... CANR-10
Earlier sketch in CA 25-28R
Byrnes, Thomas Edmund 1911- ... 13-16R
Byrom, James
See Bramwell, James Guy
Byrom, (Robert) Michael 1925- ... 5-8R
Byron, Carl R(oscoe) 1948- ... 97-100
Byron, Christopher M. 1944- ... 77-80
Byron, George Gordon (Noel)
1788-1824 ... CDBLB 1789-1832
See also DLB 96, 110
See also WLC
Byron, Gilbert (Valliant) 1903-1991 ... 17-20R
Obituary ... 134
Byron, John
See Armstrong, John Byron
Byron, William J(ames) 1927- ... 81-84
Bytwerk, Randall Lee 1950- ... 109
Bywater, William G(len) Jr. 1940- ... 61-64

C

C. E. M.
See Mastrangelo, Charles E.
C.3.3.
See Wilde, Oscar (Fingal O'Flahertie Wills)
Caballero, Ann Mallory 1928- ... 17-20R
Caballero, Manuel 1931- ... 132
See also HW
Caballero Bonald, Jose Manuel 1926- ... DLB 108
Caballero Calderon, E.
See Caballero Calderon, Eduardo
Caballero Calderon, Eduardo 1910- ... HW
Cabanis, Jose 1922- Brief entry ... 111
Cabaniss, J(ames) Allen 1911- ... 1-4R
See also SATA 5
Cabarga, Leslie 1954- ... CANR-13
Earlier sketch in CA 77-80
Cabassa, Victoria 1912- ... 49-52
Cabbell, Edward J. 1946- ... 121
Cabbell, Paul 1942- ... 53-56
Cabeen, David Clark 1886- ... CAP-1
Earlier sketch in CA 13-14
Cabell, James Branch
1879-1958 Brief entry ... 105
See also DLB 9, 78
See also TCLC 6
Cabezas (Lacayo), Omar 1951(?)- ... 131
See also HW
Cabibi, John F(rank) J(oseph) 1912- ... 53-56
Cable, George Washington
1844-1925 Brief entry ... 104
See also DLB 12, 74
See also SSC 4
See also TCLC 4
Cable, James (Eric) 1920- ... CANR-33
Earlier sketches in CA 85-88, CANR-15
Cable, John L(aurence) 1934- ... CANR-21
Earlier sketch in CA 69-72
Cable, Mary 1920- ... CANR-28
Earlier sketches in CA 25-28R, CANR-11
See also SATA 9
Cable, Thomas Monroe 1942- Brief entry ... 106
Cabot, Blake 1905(?)-1974 Obituary ... 53-56
Cabot, John Moors 1901-1981 Obituary ... 103
Cabot, Robert (Moors) 1924- ... 29-32R
Cabot, Thomas Dudley 1897- ... 93-96
Cabot, Tracy 1941- ... 81-84
Cabral, Alberto
See White, Richard Alan
Cabral, Amilcar 1921-1973 Obituary ... 111
Cabral, Joao de Pina
See Pina-Cabral, Joao de
Cabral, O. M.
See Cabral, Olga
Cabral, Olga 1909- ... CANR-10
Earlier sketch in CA 25-28R
See also SATA 46
Cabrera, James C. 1935- ... 109
Cabrera, Lydia 1900- ... HW
Cabrera Infante, G(uillermo) 1929- ... CANR-29
Earlier sketch in CA 85-88
See also CLC 5, 25, 45
See also DLB 113
See also HW
See also MTCW
Caccia-Dominioni, Paolo 1896- ... 21-24R
Cacciatore, Vera (Signorelli) 1911- ... CANR-5
Earlier sketch in CA 5-8R
Cachia, Pierre J. E. 1921- ... CANR-11
Earlier sketch in CA 25-28R
Cacoyannis, Michael 1922- ... 101
Cadbury, Henry J(oel) 1883-1974 ... CAP-1
Obituary ... 53-56
Earlier sketch in CA 13-16
Cadbury, Paul Strangman
1895-1984 Obituary ... 114
Caddel, Richard (Ivo) 1949- ... 137
Cadden, Joseph E. 1911(?)-1980 Obituary ... 101
Cadden, Thomas Scott 1923- ... 131
Cadden, Tom Scott
See Cadden, Thomas Scott
Caddick, Arthur 1911-1987 Obituary ... 122
Caddy, Alice
See Burman, Alice Caddy
Caddy, (Michael) Douglas 1938- ... 136
Cade, Alexander
See Methold, Kenneth (Walter)
Cade, Toni
See Bambara, Toni Cade
Cadell, (Violet) Elizabeth 1903- ... CANR-11
Earlier sketch in CA 57-60
Cadenhead, Ivie E(dward) Jr. 1923- ... 41-44R
Cadet, John 1935- ... 77-80
Cadieux, Charles L. 1919- ... 57-60
Cadieux, (Joseph Arthur) Lorenzo
1903-1976 ... 49-52
Obituary ... 103
Cadieux, (Joseph David Romeo) Marcel
1915-1981 Obituary ... 108
Cadle, Dean 1920- ... 25-28R
Cadle, Farris W(illiam) 1952- ... 135
Cadmus
See Buchan, John
Cadogan, Alexander (George Montagu)
1884-1968 Obituary ... 106
Cadogan, Mary (Rose) 1928- ... 106
Cadwallader, Clyde T(homas) ... 5-8R
Cadwallader, Sharon 1936- ... CANR-17
Earlier sketches in CA 49-52, CANR-1
See also SATA 7
Cady, Arthur 1920-1983 Obituary ... 109
Cady, Edwin Harrison 1917- ... CANR-4
Earlier sketch in CA 1-4R
See also DLB 103
Cady, Ernest (Albert) 1899-1985 Obituary ... 117
Cady, (Walter) Harrison
1877(?)-1970 Obituary ... 116
See also SATA 19
Cady, Howard Stevenson
1914-1990 Obituary ... 132
Cady, Jack A(ndrew) 1932- ... CANR-9
Earlier sketch in CA 65-68
Cady, John Frank 1901- ... CANR-4
Earlier sketch in CA 1-4R
Cady, Steve (Noel) 1927- ... 45-48
Caedmon, Father
See Wahl, Thomas (Peter)
Caefer, Raymond J(ohn) 1926- ... 17-20R
Caeiro, Alberto
See Pessoa, Fernando (Antonio Nogueira)
Caemmerer, Richard R(udolph) 1904- ... CANR-5
Earlier sketch in CA 1-4R
Caen, Herb (Eugene) 1916- ... CANR-1
Earlier sketch in CA 1-4R
See also AITN 1
Caesar, (Eu)Gene (Lee) 1927- ... CANR-1
Earlier sketch in CA 1-4R
Cafferty, Bernard 1934- ... 41-44R
Cafferty, Pastora San Juan 1940- ... 114
Caffey, David L(uther) 1947- ... 45-48
Caffrey, John G(ordon) 1922- ... 17-20R
Caffrey, Kate ... CANR-1
Earlier sketch in CA 49-52
Caffrey, Margaret M. 1947- ... 135
Cagan, Phillip D(avid) 1927- ... 17-20R
Cage, John (Milton Jr.) 1912- ... CANR-9
Earlier sketch in CA 13-16R
See also CLC 41
Caggiano, Philip 1949- ... 114
Cagle, Malcolm W(infield) 1918- ... 108
See also SATA 32
Cagle, William R(ea) 1933- ... 65-68
Cagney, James (Francis Jr.)
1899(?)-1986 Obituary ... 118
Brief entry ... 115
Cagney, Peter
See Winter, Bevis (Peter)
Cahalan, (John) Don(ald) 1912- ... 102
Cahalane, Victor H(arrison) 1901- ... CAP-2
Earlier sketch in CA 23-24
Cahan, Abraham 1860-1951 Brief entry ... 108
See also DLB 9, 25, 28
Cahen, Alfred B. 1932- ... 17-20R
Cahill, Audrey Fawcett 1929- ... 21-24R
Cahill, Daniel J(oseph) 1929- ... 69-72
Cahill, Fred V(irgil) Jr. 1916-1984 Obituary ... 112
Cahill, Gilbert A. 1912- Brief entry ... 107
Cahill, Jack
See Cahill, John Denis
Cahill, James F(rancis) 1926- ... CANR-6
Earlier sketch in CA 1-4R
Cahill, Jane (Miller) 1901- ... CAP-2
Earlier sketch in CA 23-24
Cahill, John Denis 1926- ... 131
Cahill, Kevin Michael 1936- ... CANR-18
Earlier sketch in CA 102
Cahill, Rick 1950- ... 126
Cahill, Robert S. 1933- ... 13-16R
Cahill, Susan Neunzig 1940- ... 37-40R
Cahill, Thomas (Quinn) 1940- ... 49-52
Cahill, Tom
See Cahill, Thomas (Quinn)
Cahn, Edgar S. 1935- ... 29-32R
Cahn, Rhoda 1922- ... 81-84
See also SATA 37
Cahn, Robert 1917- ... 108
Cahn, Sammy 1913- ... 85-88
Cahn, Steven M. 1942- ... CANR-29
Earlier sketches in CA 21-24R, CANR-13
Cahn, Walter 1933- ... 129
Cahn, William 1912-1976 ... 21-24R
Obituary ... 69-72
See also SATA 37
Cahn, Zvi 1896- ... CAP-2
Earlier sketch in CA 23-24
Cahnman, Werner J(acob) 1902- ... 49-52
Caiden, Gerald E(lliot) 1936- ... CANR-14
Earlier sketch in CA 29-32R
Caidin, Martin 1927- ... CANR-2
Earlier sketch in CA 1-4R
See also AITN 2
Caiger-Smith, Alan 1930- ... 13-16R
Caillois, Roger 1913-1978 ... CANR-13
Obituary ... 85-88
Earlier sketch in CA 25-28R
Caillou, Alan
See Lyle-Smythe, Alan
Cain, Arthur H(omer) 1913- ... CANR-4
Earlier sketch in CA 1-4R
See also SATA 3
Cain, Bob
See Cain, Robert Owen
Cain, Bruce E. 1948- ... 122
Cain, G.
See Cabrera Infante, G(uillermo)
Cain, George 1943- ... DLB 33
Cain, Glen G. 1933- ... 21-24R
Cain, Guillermo
See Cabrera Infante, G(uillermo)
Cain, Jackson
See Gleason, Robert
Cain, James M(allahan) 1892-1977 ... CANR-34
Obituary ... 73-76
Earlier sketches in CA 17-20R, CANR-8
See also AITN 1
See also CLC 3, 11, 28
See also MTCW
Cain, Mary (Dawson) 1904-1984 Obituary ... 112
Cain, Maureen 1938- ... 73-76
Cain, Michael Peter 1941- ... 93-96
Cain, Robert Owen 1934- ... 65-68
Cain, T. G. S. 1944- ... 124
Cain, Thomas H(enry) 1931- ... 93-96
Caine, Geoffrey
See Walker, Robert W(ayne)
Caine, (Thomas Henry) Hall
1853(?)-1931 Brief entry ... 122
Caine, Jeffrey (Andrew) 1944- ... 85-88
Caine, Lynn 1924(?)-1987 Obituary ... 124
Caine, Mark
See Raphael, Frederic (Michael)
Caine, Mitchell
See Sparkia, Roy (Bernard)
Caine, Stanley P(aul) 1940- ... 41-44R
Caine, Sydney 1902- ... CAP-2
Earlier sketch in CA 25-28
Caines, Jeannette (Franklin) ... CLR 24
See also SATA 43
Caird, George Bradford 1917-1984 ... 61-64
Obituary ... 112
Caird, Janet 1913- ... CANR-2
Earlier sketch in CA 49-52
Cairncross, Alec
See Cairncross, Alexander Kirkland
Cairncross, Alexander Kirkland 1911- ... CANR-8
Earlier sketch in CA 61-64
Cairncross, Frances (Anne) 1944- ... 57-60
Cairney, John 1930- ... 105
Cairns, David 1904- ... CANR-11
Earlier sketch in CA 61-64
Cairns, (Thomas) Dorian
1901-1972 Obituary ... 37-40R
Cairns, Earle E(dwin) 1910- ... CANR-18
Earlier sketch in CA 1-4R
Cairns, (Samuel) Ed(mund) 1945- ... 128
Cairns, Grace Edith 1907- ... CANR-18
Earlier sketch in CA 1-4R
Cairns, Huntington 1904-1985 ... CANR-5
Obituary ... 114
Earlier sketch in CA 53-56
Cairns, J(ames) F(ord) 1914- ... 105
Cairns, John C(ampbell) 1924- ... CANR-5
Earlier sketch in CA 13-16R
Cairns, Thomas W(illiam) 1931- ... 21-24R
Cairns, Trevor 1922- ... 33-36R
See also SATA 14
Cairns-Smith, A(lexander) G(raham) 1931- ... 123
Cairo, Jon
See Romano, Deane Louis
Caitlin, Elise 1953- ... 111
Cake, Patrick
See Welch, Timothy L.
Calabrese, Alphonse F. X. 1923- ... 69-72
Calabrese, Anthony 1938- ... 89-92
Calabresi, Guido 1932- ... CANR-20
Earlier sketch in CA 41-44R
Calaferte, Louis 1928- ... CANR-17
Earlier sketches in CA 45-48, CANR-1
Calais, Jean
See Rodefer, Stephen
Calamandrei, Mauro 1925- ... 69-72
Calamari, John D(aniel) 1921- ... 37-40R
Calas, Nicholas 1907-1988 Obituary ... 127
Calasibetta, Charlotte M(ankey) 1917- ... 103
Calbom, Cherie 1947- ... 138
Calde, Mark A(ugustine) 1945- ... 69-72
Caldecott, Moyra 1927- ... CANR-30
Earlier sketches in CA 77-80, CANR-13
See also SATA 22
Caldecott, Randolph (J.) 1846-1886 ... CLR 14
See also MAICYA
See also SATA 17
Calder, Alexander 1898-1976 Obituary ... 111
Calder, Angus 1942- ... CANR-38
Earlier sketch in CA 29-32R
Calder, Bruce J. 1940- ... 132
Calder, C(larence) R(oy) Jr. 1928- ... 81-84
Calder, Daniel Gillmore 1939- ... 103
Calder, Jason
See Dunmore, John
Calder, Jenni 1941- ... CANR-38
Earlier sketches in CA 45-48, CANR-1
Calder, John (Mackenzie) 1927- ... 133
Calder, Kent E(yring) 1948- ... 107
Calder, Lyn
See Calmenson, Stephanie
Calder, Nigel (David Ritchie) 1931- ... CANR-38
Earlier sketches in CA 21-24R, CANR-11
See also MTCW
Calder, Ritchie
See Ritchie-Calder, Peter Ritchie
Calder, Robert
See Mundis, Jerrold
Calder, Robert Lorin 1941- ... 65-68
Calder-Marshall, Arthur 1908- ... 61-64
Obituary ... 137
Calderon, Eduardo Caballero
See Caballero Calderon, Eduardo
Calderon, Jose Vasconcelos
See Vasconcelos (Calderon), Jose
Calderone, Mary S(teichen) 1904- ... 104
See also AITN 1
Calderwood, Ivan E. 1899- ... 57-60
Calderwood, James D(ixon) 1917- ... CANR-3
Earlier sketch in CA 5-8R
Calderwood, James L(ee) 1930- ... 21-24R
Caldicott, Helen (Mary) 1938- ... 124
Brief entry ... 114
See also MTCW
Caldwell, Ben(jamin) 1937- ... 124
Brief entry ... 117
See also BW
See also DLB 38
Caldwell, Bettye (McDonald) 1924- ... 104
Caldwell, C(harles) Edson 1906-1974 ... CAP-2
Earlier sketch in CA 29-32
Caldwell, Dan (Edward) 1948- ... 112
Caldwell, David H(epburn) 1951- ... 132
Caldwell, Doreen (Mary) 1942- ... SATA 71
Caldwell, Edward S(abiston) 1928- ... 65-68
Caldwell, Erskine (Preston)
1903-1987 ... CANR-33
Obituary ... 121
Earlier sketches in CA 1-4R, CANR-2
See also CAAS 1
See also AITN 1
See also CLC 1, 8, 14, 50, 60
See also DLB 9, 86
See also MTCW
Caldwell, Gaylon L(oray) 1920- ... 33-36R
Caldwell, Harry B(oynton) 1935- ... 37-40R
Caldwell, Helen F. 1904- ... 77-80
Caldwell, Inga Gilson 1897- ... 61-64
Caldwell, Irene Catherine (Smith)
1908-1979 ... 9-12R
Obituary ... 103
Caldwell, James
See Lowry, Robert (James Collas)
Caldwell, John C(ope) 1913- ... CANR-13
Earlier sketch in CA 21-24R
See also SATA 7
Caldwell, John 1928- ... CANR-12
Earlier sketch in CA 73-76
Caldwell, Joseph H(erman) 1934- ... 21-24R
Caldwell, Kathryn (Smoot) 1942- ... 69-72
Caldwell, Louis O(liver) 1935- ... 69-72
Caldwell, Lynton (Keith) 1913- ... CANR-12
Earlier sketch in CA 29-32R

Caldwell, (James Alexander) Malcolm
1931-1978 ....CANR-17
Earlier sketch in CA 25-28R
Caldwell, Marge 1914- 97-100
Caldwell, Nat(han Green)
1912-1985 Obituary 115
Caldwell, Oliver Johnson 1904- 37-40R
Caldwell, Robert G(ranville)
1882-1976 Obituary 65-68
Caldwell, Robert Graham 1904- 17-20R
Caldwell, Stratton F(ranklin) 1926- 136
Caldwell, (Janet Miriam) Taylor (Holland)
1900-1985 ....CANR-5
Obituary 116
Earlier sketch in CA 5-8R
See also CLC 2, 28, 39
Caldwell, William A(nthony)
1906-1986 Obituary 119
Calef, George (Waller) 1944- 132
Calef, Wesley (Carr) 1914- 13-16R
Caley, Rod
See Rowland, D(onald) S(ydney)
Calhoon, Richard P(ercival) 1909- 57-60
Calhoon, Robert M(cCluer) 1935- CANR-4
Earlier sketch in CA 53-56
Calhoun, Calfrey C. 1928- 37-40R
Calhoun, Chad
See Goulart, Ron(ald Joseph)
Calhoun, Charles W(illiam) 1948- 125
Calhoun, Conyus 1946- 111
Calhoun, Craig (Jackson) 1952- 130
Calhoun, Daniel F(airchild) 1929- 65-68
Calhoun, Don Gilmore 1914- 85-88
Calhoun, Donald W(allace) 1917- 104
Calhoun, Eric
See Turner, Robert (Harry)
Calhoun, Jackie 1936- 138
Calhoun, James Frank 1941- 109
Calhoun, John Caldwell 1782-1850 .... DLB 3
Calhoun, Mary
See Wilkins, Mary Huiskamp
See also SATA 2
Calhoun, Richard James 1926- 33-36R
Calhoun, Robert L(owery)
1896-1983 Obituary 110
Calhoun, Thomas 1940- 89-92
Calia, Vincent F(rank) 1926- 53-56
Calian, Carnegie Samuel 1933- 25-28R
Caliban
See Reid, J(ohn) C(owie)
Calif, Ruth 1922- 134
See also SATA 67
Califano, Joseph A(nthony) Jr. 1931- CANR-2
Earlier sketch in CA 45-48
Califia, Pat 1954- 133
Calimani, Riccardo 1946- 137
Calin, William (Compaine) 1936- CANR-27
Earlier sketches in CA 21-24R, CANR-11
Calinescu, Matei (Alexe) 1934- 131
Calisch, Edith Lindeman
1898-1984 Obituary 114
Calisher, Hortense 1911- CANR-22
Earlier sketches in CA 1-4R, CANR-1
See also CLC 2, 4, 8, 38
See also DLB 2
See also MTCW
Calistro, Paddy
See Calistro McAuley, Patricia Ann
Calistro McAuley, Patricia Ann 1948- 118
Calitri, Charles J(oseph) 1916- 5-8R
Calitri, Princine 33-36R
Calkin, Homer Leonard 1912- 41-44R
Calkin, Ruth Harms 1918- 102
Calkins, Fay
See Alailima, Fay C.
Calkins, Franklin
See Stratemeyer, Edward L.
Calkins, Lucy McCormick 125
Calkins, Robert G. 1932- 130
Calkins, Rodello 1920- Brief entry 105
Call, Alice E(lizabeth) LaPlant 1914- 13-16R
Call, Hughie Florence 1890- 5-8R
See also SATA 1
Calladine, Andrew G(arfield) 1941- 102
Calladine, Carole E(lizabeth) 1942- 102
Callaghan, Barry 1937- 101
Callaghan, Catherine A. 1931- 33-36R
Callaghan, Mary Rose 1944- 118
Callaghan, Morley Edward
1903-1990 ....CANR-33
Obituary 132
Earlier sketch in CA 9-12R
See also CLC 3, 14, 41, 65
See also DLB 68
See also MTCW
Callaghan, Thomas 1924- 114
Callahan, Bob 1942- 138
Callahan, Charles C(lifford) 1910- CAP-2
Earlier sketch in CA 17-18
Callahan, Claire Wallis 1890- 5-8R
Callahan, Daniel 1930- 21-24R
Callahan, Dorothy M(onahan) 1934- 114
See also SATA 35, 39
Callahan, John
See Gallun, Raymond Z(inke)
Callahan, John F(rancis) 1912- 33-36R
Callahan, Mary
See Randazzo, Mary Callahan
Callahan, Nelson J. 1927- 33-36R
Callahan, North 1908- CANR-2
Earlier sketch in CA 1-4R
Callahan, Philip Serna 1923- 102
See also SATA 25
Callahan, Raymond (Aloysius) 1938- 69-72
Callahan, Sidney Cornelia 1933- 17-20R
Callahan, Sterling G. 1916- 21-24R
Callahan, Steven (Patrick) 1952- 120
Callan, Edward T. 1917- 17-20R
Callan, Jamie 1954- 109
See also SATA 59
Callan, John P(atrick) 1939- 111
Callan, Richard J(erome) 1932- 53-56
Callard, Maurice (Frederick Thomas)
1912- CANR-3
Earlier sketch in CA 1-4R
Callard, Thomas Henry 1912- 9-12R
Callas, Theo
See McCarthy, Shaun (Lloyd)
Callaway, Ben (Anderson) 1927- 131
Callaway, Bernice (Anne) 1923- 121
See also SATA 48
Callaway, C. Wayne 1941- 138
Callaway, Joseph A(tlee) 1920- 65-68
Callaway, Kathy 1943- 107
See also SATA 36
Callcott, George H(ardy) 1929- 29-32R
Callcott, Margaret Law 1929- 61-64
Callcott, Wilfrid H(ardy)
1895-1969 Obituary 112
Calle, Francisco Rosillo
See Rosillo-Calle, Francisco
Callen, Larry
See Callen, Lawrence Willard Jr.
Callen, Lawrence Willard Jr. 1927- CANR-12
Earlier sketch in CA 73-76
See also SATA 19
Callen, William B. 1930- 21-24R
Callenbach, Ernest 1929- CANR-21
Earlier sketches in CA 57-60, CANR-6
Callender, Charles 1928- 41-44R
Callender, George 1916- 136
Callender, Julian
See Lee, Austin
Callender, Red
See Callender, George
Callender, Wesley P(ayne) Jr. 1923- 17-20R
Calleo, David P(atrick) 1934- CANR-31
Earlier sketches in CA 17-20R, CANR-10
Callicott, J(ohn) Baird 1941- 135
Callihan, E(lmer) L(ee) 1903- CAP-2
Earlier sketch in CA 25-28
Callinan, Bernard James 1913- 110
Callis, Helmut G(unther) 1906- CANR-5
Earlier sketch in CA 53-56
Callis, Robert 1920- 37-40R
Callison, Brian (Richard) 1934- CANR-31
Earlier sketch in CA 29-32R
Callister, Frank 1916- 13-16R
Callmann, Rudolf 1892-1976 69-72
Obituary 65-68
Callow, Alexander B. Jr. 1925- 21-24R
Callow, James T(homas) 1928- 41-44R
Callow, Philip Kenneth 1924- CANR-21
Earlier sketches in CA 13-16R, CANR-6
Callow, Simon 1949- 138
Calloway, Cab(ell III) 1907- Brief entry 113
Calloway, Colin G(ordon) 1953- 135
Calloway, Doris Howes 1923- 21-24R
Callum, Myles 1934- 9-12R
Callwood, June 1924- CANR-24
Earlier sketch in CA 101
Calman, Alvin R(ose) 1895-1983 Obituary 110
Calman, Mel 1931- 126
Calmann, John 1935-1980 ....21-24R
Obituary 97-100
Calmann-Levy, Robert 1899-1982 Obituary 108
Calmenson, Stephanie 1952- CANR-24
Earlier sketch in CA 107
See also SATA 37, 51
Calmer, Edgar 1907-1986 ....CANR-20
Obituary 118
Earlier sketch in CA 69-72
See also DLB 4
Calmer, Ned
See Calmer, Edgar
Calmus, Lawrence 1943- 111
Calnan, T(homas) D(aniel) 1915- 29-32R
Calne, Roy Yorke 1930- 61-64
Calonne, David Stephen 1953- 114
Calta, Louis 1913(?)-1990 Obituary 132
Caltagirone, Carmen L(illian) 1950- 114
Calter, Paul (William) 1934- CANR-31
Earlier sketches in CA 41-44R, CANR-14
Calverley, C. S. 1831-1884 .... DLB 35
Calvert, Elinor H.
See Lasell, Elinor H.
Calvert, George Henry 1803-1889 .... DLB 1, 64
Calvert, John
See Leaf, (Wilbur) Munro
Calvert, Laura D. 1922- 37-40R
Calvert, Monte A(lan) 1938- 21-24R
Calvert, Patricia 1931- CANR-21
Earlier sketch in CA 105
See also MAICYA
See also SATA 45, 69
Calvert, Peter (Anthony Richard)
1936- CANR-11
Earlier sketch in CA 25-28R
Calvert, Robert Jr. 1922- 25-28R
Calvert, Theodora 1898-1988 Obituary 128
Calvez, Jean-Yves 1927- 57-60
Calvin, Henry
See Hanley, Clifford
Calvin, Ross 1890(?)-1970 Obituary 104
Calvin, William H(oward) 1939- 123
Calvino, Italo 1923-1985 ....CANR-23
Obituary 116
Earlier sketch in CA 85-88
See also CLC 5, 8, 11, 22, 33, 39
See also MTCW
See also SSC 3
Calvo, Lino Novas
See Novas Calvo, Lino
Calvocoressi, Peter (John Ambrose)
1912- 65-68
Cam, Helen Maud 1885-1968 .... CAP-1
Earlier sketch in CA 13-14
Camara, Helder Pessoa 1909- 61-64
Camarillo, Albert (M.) 1948- 132
Camarillo, Alberto
See Camarillo, Albert (M.)
Camazine, S(cott) 1952- 129
Camber, Andrew
See Bingley, David Ernest
Cambon, Glauco (Gianlorenzo)
1921-1988 ....CANR-7
Obituary 125
Earlier sketch in CA 17-20R
Camden, Archie 1888-1979 114
Cameja, Pedro
See Camejo, Peter (Miguel)
Camejo, Pedro
See Camejo, Peter (Miguel)
Camejo, Pedro M.
See Camejo, Peter (Miguel)
Camejo, Peter (Miguel) 1939- 125
Brief entry 105
Camerini, Mario 1895-1981 Obituary 103
Cameron, A(rchibald) J(ames) 1920- 73-76
Cameron, Alan (Douglas Edward)
1938- CANR-8
Earlier sketch in CA 61-64
Cameron, Alexander
See Gibson, Alexander Cameron
Cameron, Allan Gillies 1930- 102
Cameron, Allan W(illiams) 1938- 33-36R
Cameron, Angus de Mille 1913- 102
Cameron, Angus Fraser 1941-1983 122
Obituary 109
Cameron, Ann 1943- 101
See also SATA 27
Cameron, (Barbara) Anne 1938- 136
Cameron, Betsy 1949- 101
Cameron, (Jack) Bruce 1913-1979 ....1-4R
Obituary 133
Cameron, Carey 1952- 135
See also CLC 59
Cameron, Constance Carpenter 1937- 49-52
Cameron, D. A.
See Cameron, Donald (Allan)
Cameron, D. Y.
See Cook, Dorothy Mary
Cameron, David R(obertson) 1941- 73-76
Cameron, Deborah 1958- 126
Cameron, Donald
See Bryans, Robert Harbinson
Cameron, Donald (Allan) 1937- CANR-8
Earlier sketch in CA 21-24R
Cameron, Edna M. 1905- CAP-1
Earlier sketch in CA 9-10
See also SATA 3
Cameron, Eleanor Cranston 118
Cameron, Eleanor Elford 1910- 77-80
Cameron, Eleanor (Frances) 1912- CANR-22
Earlier sketches in CA 1-4R, CANR-2
See also CLR 1
See also DLB 52
See also MAICYA
See also MTCW
See also SAAS 10
See also SATA 1, 25
Cameron, Elizabeth
See Nowell, Elizabeth Cameron
Cameron, Elizabeth Jane 1910-1976 ....CANR-1
Obituary 69-72
Earlier sketch in CA 1-4R
See also SATA 30, 32
Cameron, Elspeth 1943- 113
Cameron, Frank T. 1909- CAP-1
Earlier sketch in CA 19-20
Cameron, George Frederick 1854-1885 .... DLB 99
Cameron, George Glenn
1905-1979 Obituary 89-92
Cameron, Harold W. 1905- 81-84
Cameron, Hope
See Morritt, Hope
Cameron, Ian
See Payne, Donald Gordon
Cameron, J(ames) M(unro) 1910- CANR-2
Earlier sketch in CA 5-8R
Cameron, (Mark) James (Walter)
1911-1985 ....21-24R
Obituary 114
Cameron, James R(eese) 1929- 33-36R
Cameron, James Sorel
See Sorel-Cameron, James (Robert)
Cameron, James 1954- 137
See also AAYA 9
Cameron, John 1914- 29-32R
Cameron, Joy 1912- 132
Cameron, Julie
See Cameron, Lou
Cameron, Kate
See Du Breuil, (Elizabeth) L(or)inda
Cameron, Kenneth M. 1931- 129
Cameron, Kenneth Neill 1908- CANR-3
Earlier sketch in CA 9-12R
Cameron, Kenneth Walter 1908- CANR-24
Earlier sketches in CA 21-24R, CANR-8
Cameron, Kenneth 1922- 103
Cameron, Kim S(terling) 1946- 109
Cameron, Lorna
See Fraser, Anthea
Cameron, Lou 1924- CANR-21
Earlier sketches in CA 1-4R, CANR-4
Cameron, M(alcolm) G(ordon) Graham
See Graham-Cameron, M(alcolm) G(ordon)
Cameron, M. Graham
See Graham-Cameron, M(alcolm) G(ordon)
Cameron, Mary Owen 1915- 13-16R
Cameron, Meribeth E(lliott) 1905- 1-4R
Cameron, Mike Graham
See Graham-Cameron, M(alcolm) G(ordon)
Cameron, Neil 1920-1985 Obituary 115
Cameron, Peter 1959- 125
See also CLC 44
Cameron, Polly 1928- 17-20R
See also SATA 2
Cameron, Roderick (William)
1913-1985 Obituary 117
Brief entry 113
Cameron, Rondo (Emmett) 1925- CANR-5
Earlier sketch in CA 1-4R
Cameron, Sharon 1947- 123
Cameron, Silver Donald
See Cameron, Donald (Allan)
Cameron, William Bleasdell 1862-1951 .... DLB 99
Cameron, William Bruce 1920- 37-40R
Cameron, William J(ames)
1926- Brief entry 116
Cameron Watt, Donald 1928- CANR-14
Earlier sketch in CA 77-80
Camille, Michael 1958- 137
Camilleri, Joseph A. 1944- 117
Caminada, Jerome (Charles)
1911-1985 Obituary 117
Caminals-Heath, Roser 1956- 137
Camm, John 1718-1778 .... DLB 31
Cammack, Floyd M(cKee) 1933- CANR-6
Earlier sketch in CA 9-12R
Cammann, Schuyler (van Rensselaer)
1912- 9-12R
Cammarata, Jerry F(rank) 1947- 81-84
Cammer, Leonard 1913- 65-68
Camner, James 1950- 108
Camoin, Francois Andre 1939- 61-64
Camp, Candace P(auline) 1949- 102
Camp, Charles L. 1893-1975 Obituary 61-64
See also SATA 31
Camp, Dalton Kingsley 1920- 61-64
Camp, Fred V(alterma) 1911- 49-52
Camp, James 1923- 33-36R
Camp, Joe
See Camp, Joseph Shelton Jr.
Camp, John (Michael Francis) 1915- 93-96
Camp, John 1944- 138
Camp, Joseph Shelton Jr. 1939- 129
Camp, Roderic (Ai) 1945- CANR-18
Earlier sketch in CA 102
Camp, T(homas) Edward 1929- 13-16R
Camp, Walter (Chauncey) 1859-1925 .... YABC 1
Camp, Wesley D(ouglass) 1915- 17-20R
Camp, William (Newton Alexander) 1926- 61-64
Campa, Arthur L(eon) 1905- 73-76
See also HW
Campaigne, Jameson Gilbert 1914-1985 ....1-4R
Obituary 114
Campana, Dino 1885-1932 Brief entry 117
See also DLB 114
See also TCLC 20
Campanella, Francis B. 1936- 53-56
Campanile, Archille
1900(?)-1977 Obituary 69-72
Campanile, Pasquale Festa
See Festa Campanile, Pasquale
Campbell, A. C.
See Campbell, Andrew C.
Campbell, Alan K. 1923- CANR-3
Earlier sketch in CA 5-8R
Campbell, Alasdair Iain
See Hamilton, Iain (Betram)
Campbell, Albert A.
See Campbell, (Albert) Angus
Campbell, Alexander 1912-1977 61-64
Obituary 69-72
Campbell, Alistair 1907-1974 .... CAP-1
Earlier sketch in CA 17-18
Campbell, Alla (Linda Renee) Bozarth
See Bozarth-Campbell, Alla (Linda Renee)
Campbell, (Elizabeth) Andrea 1963- .... SATA 50
Campbell, Andrew C. 1923- Brief entry 114
Campbell, Angus
See Chetwynd-Hayes, R(onald Henry Glynn)
Campbell, (Albert) Angus 1910-1980 129
Obituary 105
Campbell, Ann R. 1925- 21-24R
See also SATA 11
Campbell, Archibald Bruce 1881- CAP-1
Earlier sketch in CA 13-16
Campbell, Arnold Everitt
1906-1980 Obituary 108
Campbell, Arthur A(ndrews) 1924- 1-4R
Campbell, Ballard Crooker Jr. 1940- 104
Campbell, Beatrice Murphy
See Murphy, Beatrice M.
Campbell, Beatrix 1947- 138
Campbell, Bernard G(rant) 1930- 21-24R
Campbell, Blanche 1902- 5-8R
Campbell, Bruce
See Epstein, Samuel
Campbell, Camilla 1905- CAP-2
Earlier sketch in CA 25-28
See also SATA 26
Campbell, Carlos Cardozo 1937- 102
Campbell, Charles Arthur
1897-1974 Obituary 49-52
Campbell, Charles S(outter) 1911- 69-72
Campbell, Clive
See MacRae, Donald G.
Campbell, Colin Dearborn 1917- 33-36R
Campbell, Cy(ril Calvin) 1925- 97-100
Campbell, D(onald)
See Gilford, C(harles) B(ernard)
Campbell, D(onald) Ross 1939- 117
Campbell, Dan H(ampton)
1907-1974 Obituary 112

Campbell, David A(itken) 1927- CANR-11
Earlier sketch in CA 25-28R
Campbell, David (John) Graham
See Graham-Campbell, David (John)
Campbell, David P. 1934- 21-24R
Campbell, David (Watt Ian) 1915-1979 97-100
Campbell, Dennis M(arion) 1945- 73-76
Campbell, Don(ald Guy) 1922-1991 .... 17-20R
Obituary 135
Campbell, Donald E. 1943- 138
Campbell, Donald 1940- CANR-30
Earlier sketch in CA 69-72
Campbell, Duane E(ugene) 1941- 116
Campbell, E(lwood) G(ordon) 1923- 107
Campbell, E. Simms 1906-1971 Obituary 93-96
Campbell, Edward D(uncomb) C(hristian) Jr.
1946- CANR-26
Earlier sketch in CA 106
Campbell, Edward F(ay) Jr. 1932- 13-16R
Campbell, Elizabeth McClure 1891- 37-40R
Campbell, Enid (Mona) 1932- 109
Campbell, Ernest Q(ueener) 1926- 37-40R
Campbell, Eugene Edward 1915- 21-24R
Campbell, Ewing 1940- CANR-29
Earlier sketches in CA 73-76, CANR-13
Campbell, F(enton) Gregory Jr. 1939- 69-72
Campbell, Francis Stuart
See Kuehnelt-Leddihn, Erik (Maria) Ritter von
Campbell, G(aylon) S(anford) 1940- 107
Campbell, George F(rederick) 1915- CANR-14
Earlier sketch in CA 65-68
Campbell, Graeme 1931- 77-80
Campbell, Hannah 9-12R
Campbell, Herbert James 1925- 97-100
Campbell, Hope 1925- CANR-10
Earlier sketch in CA 61-64
See also SATA 20
Campbell, Howard E(rnest) 1925- CANR-7
Earlier sketch in CA 57-60
Campbell, Ian 1899-1978 53-56
Obituary 103
Campbell, Ian 1942- CANR-25
Earlier sketches in CA 65-68, CANR-9
Campbell, J(ames) Arthur 1916- 53-56
Campbell, Jack K(enagy) 1927- 21-24R
Campbell, James E(dward) 1945- 107
Campbell, James Edwin 1867-1896 .... DLB 50
Campbell, James Howard 1928- 113
Campbell, James Marshall 1895-1977 73-76
Obituary 69-72
Campbell, James 1920- 57-60
Campbell, Jane
See Edwards, Jane Campbell
Campbell, Jane 1934- 41-44R
Campbell, Janet Bruce 1955- 121
Campbell, (Mary) Jean 1943- 115
Campbell, Jeff(erson) H(olland) 1931- 41-44R
Campbell, Jeffrey
See Black, Campbell
Campbell, Jeremy 1931- CANR-29
Earlier sketch in CA 109
Campbell, Jim
See Campbell, James Howard
Campbell, Joan 1929- 109
Campbell, Joanna
See Bly, Carol(yn)
Campbell, John Coert 1911- CANR-3
Earlier sketch in CA 1-4R
Campbell, John Creighton 1941- 111
Campbell, John Franklin
1940(?)-1971 Obituary 33-36R
Campbell, John Lorne 1906- 29-32R
Campbell, John R(oy) 1933- 53-56
Campbell, John W(ood Jr.)
1910-1971 .... CANR-34
Obituary 29-32R
Earlier sketches in CAP-2, CA 21-22
See also CLC 32
See also DLB 8
See also MTCW
Campbell, John 1653-1728 .... DLB 43
Campbell, John 1947- CANR-35
Earlier sketch in CA 114
Campbell, Joseph 1904-1987 .... CANR-28
Obituary 124
Earlier sketches in CA 1-4R, CANR-3
See also AAYA 3
See also BEST 89:2
See also CLC 69
See also MTCW
Campbell, Judith
See Pares, Marion (Stapylton)
Campbell, Karen
See Beaty, Betty
Campbell, Karlyn Kohrs 1937- CANR-39
Earlier sketches in CA 53-56, CANR-4, 18
Campbell, Katie 1957- 136
Campbell, Keith Oliver 1920- 110
Campbell, Keith 1938- 106
Campbell, Ken 1941- 77-80
Campbell, Kenneth
1901(?)-1979 Obituary 85-88
Campbell, Laurence R(andolph) 1903-1987 126
Campbell, Lawrence James 1931- 106
Campbell, Litta Belle 1886-1980 .... CANR-5
Earlier sketch in CA 5-8R
Campbell, Louisa D. 1958- 121
Campbell, Louisa Dresser
1907-1989 Obituary 129
Campbell, Luke
See Madison, Thomas A(lvin)
Campbell, Malcolm J(ames) 1930- CANR-21
Earlier sketches in CA 57-60, CANR-6
Campbell, Margaret 69-72
Campbell, (Gabrielle) Margaret (Vere)
1886-1952 Brief entry 116
See also Shearing, Joseph
Campbell, Margaret 1916- 106
Campbell, Maria 1940- 102
Campbell, Marjorie Wilkins 97-100
Campbell, Mary B(aine) 1954- 136
Campbell, Michael Mussen 1924-1984 102
Obituary 113
Campbell, Oscar James Jr.
1879-1970 Obituary 29-32R
Campbell, Patricia J(ean) 1930- CANR-35
Earlier sketch in CA 103
See also SATA 45
Campbell, Patricia Piatt 1901- 25-28R
Campbell, Patrick Gordon
1913-1980 Obituary 102
Campbell, Patty
See Campbell, Patricia J(ean)
Campbell, Paul N. 1923- 21-24R
Campbell, Penelope 1935- 33-36R
Campbell, Peter Anthony 1935- 21-24R
Campbell, Peter (Walter) 1926- CANR-11
Earlier sketches in CAP-1, CA 13-14
Campbell, R. T.
See Todd, Ruthven
Campbell, R. W.
See Campbell, Rosemae Wells
Campbell, R(obert) Wright 1927- CANR-24
Earlier sketches in CA 57-60, CANR-6, 21
Campbell, (John) Ramsey 1946- CANR-7
Earlier sketch in CA 57-60
See also CLC 42
Campbell, Randolph B(luford) 1940- 41-44R
Campbell, Rex R. 1931- 41-44R
Campbell, Rita Ricardo
See Ricardo-Campbell, Rita
Campbell, Robert
See Campbell, R(obert) Wright
Campbell, Robert B(lair) 1923- 69-72
Campbell, Robert C(harles) 1924- 49-52
Campbell, Robert Dale 1914- 9-12R
Campbell, Robert Wellington 1926- CANR-3
Earlier sketch in CA 1-4R
Campbell, Robert 1922-1977 .... CANR-8
Obituary 73-76
Earlier sketch in CA 53-56
Campbell, Rod 1945- .... SATA 44, 51
Campbell, Rosemae Wells 1909- 13-16R
See also SATA 1
Campbell, (Ignatius) Roy (Dunnachie)
1901-1957 Brief entry 104
See also DLB 20
See also TCLC 5
Campbell, Sheldon 1919- 41-44R
Campbell, Sid 1944- 118
Campbell, Stanley W(allace) 1926- 49-52
Campbell, Stephen K(ent) 1935- 49-52
Campbell, Thomas F. 1924- 21-24R
Campbell, Thomas M(oody) 1936- 49-52
Campbell, Thomas 1777-1844 .... DLB 93
Campbell, Tom D. 1938- 126
Campbell, Wallace J. 1910- 135
Campbell, Wilfred
See Campbell, William
See also TCLC 9
Campbell, Will D(avis) 1924- CANR-22
Earlier sketches in CA 5-8R, CANR-7
Campbell, William Edward March
1893-1954 Brief entry 108
See also March, William
Campbell, William 1858(?)-1918 Brief entry 106
See also Campbell, Wilfred
See also DLB 92
Campbell-Johnson, Alan 1913- 65-68
Campbell-Purdie, Wendy 1925- 21-24R
Campen, Richard N(ewman) 1912- 69-72
Camper, Shirley
See Soman, Shirley Camper
Campion, Donald Richard
1921-1988 Obituary 128
Campion, Jane 138
Campion, Joan 1940- 124
Campion, Nardi Reeder 1917- CANR-6
Earlier sketch in CA 1-4R
See also SATA 22
Campion, Rosamond
See Rosmond, Babette
Campion, Sidney R(onald) 1891- CAP-1
Earlier sketch in CA 9-10
Campion, Thomas
1567-1620 .... CDBLB Before 1660
See also DLB 58
Camplin, Jamie (Robert) 1947- 97-100
Campling, Christopher R(ussell) 1925- 113
Campling, Elizabeth 1948- 123
See also SATA 53
Campobello, Nellie (Francisca Ernestina)
1912- 131
See also HW
Campolo, Anthony Jr. 1935- CANR-26
Earlier sketches in CA 69-72, CANR-11
Campos, Alvaro de
See Pessoa, Fernando (Antonio Nogueira)
Camps, Arnulf (P. H. J. M.) 1925- 131
Camps, Francis Edward 1905-1972 .... 37-40R
Camps, Luis 1928- .... SATA 66
Campton, David 1924- CANR-20
Earlier sketches in CA 5-8R, CANR-5
Camus, Albert 1913-1960 89-92
See also CLC 1, 2, 4, 9, 11, 14, 32, 63, 69
See also DC 2
See also DLB 72
See also MTCW
See also SSC 9
See also WLC
Camus, Raoul Francois 1930- 65-68
Camus, (Jean) Renaud (Gabriel) 1946- 108
Camuti, Louis J(oseph) 1893-1981 101
Obituary 103
Canada, Lena 1942- 93-96
Canaday, John E(dwin) 1907-1985 .... CANR-7
Obituary 116
Earlier sketch in CA 13-16R
Canan, James William 1929- 61-64
Canary
See Conn, Canary Denise
Canary, Robert H(ughes) 1939- CANR-11
Earlier sketch in CA 29-32R
Canavan, Francis 1917- 118
Canaway, W(illiam) H(amilton) 1925- 93-96
Canby, Courtlandt 1914- 118
Canby, Henry Seidel 1878-1961 Obituary 89-92
See also DLB 91
Canby, Vincent 1924- 81-84
See also CLC 13
Cancale
See Desnos, Robert
Cancellare, Frank 1910-1985 Obituary 116
Cancian, Francesca M(icaela) 1937- 57-60
Cancian, Francis Alexander 1934- CANR-7
Earlier sketch in CA 53-56
Cancian, Frank
See Cancian, Francis Alexander
Candelaria, Cordelia (Chavez) 1943- 131
See also DLB 82
See also HW
Candelaria, Frederick (Henry) 1929- 17-20R
Candelaria, Nash 1928- CANR-32
Earlier sketches in CA 69-72, CANR-11
See also DLB 82
See also HW
Candell, Victor 1903-1977 .... SATA 24
Candida
See Hoffman, Lisa
Candilis, Wray O. 1927- CANR-10
Earlier sketch in CA 25-28R
Candland, Douglas Keith 1934- CANR-2
Earlier sketch in CA 5-8R
Candler, Julie 1919- 65-68
Candlin, Enid Saunders 1909- CANR-1
Earlier sketch in CA 45-48
Candy, Edward
See Neville, B(arbara) Alison (Boodson)
Cane, Melville (Henry) 1879-1980 .... CANR-8
Obituary 97-100
Earlier sketches in CA 1-4R, CANR-6
Canellopoulos, Panayiotis
1902-1986 Obituary 120
Canemaker, John 1943- 81-84
Caner, Mary Paul 1893- CAP-2
Earlier sketch in CA 21-22
Canetti, Elias 1905- CANR-23
Earlier sketch in CA 21-24R
See also CLC 3, 14, 25
See also DLB 85
See also MTCW
Caney, Steven 1941- 104
Canfield, Cass 1897-1986 .... 41-44R
Obituary 118
Canfield, (Fayette) Curtis
1903-1986 Obituary 120
Canfield, D(elos) Lincoln 1903- 25-28R
Canfield, Dorothea F.
See Fisher, Dorothy (Frances) Canfield
Canfield, Dorothea Frances
See Fisher, Dorothy (Frances) Canfield
Canfield, Dorothy
See Fisher, Dorothy (Frances) Canfield
Canfield, Gae Whitney 1931- 113
Canfield, James D(avid) 1937- 117
Canfield, James K(eith) 1925- 25-28R
Canfield, James Lewis 1942- 121
Canfield, Jane White 1897-1984 109
Obituary 112
See also SATA 32, 38
Canfield, John A(lan) 1941- 37-40R
Canfield, Kenneth French 1909- CAP-1
Earlier sketch in CA 13-16
Canfield, Leon Hardy 1886- 1-4R
Canfield, Muriel 1935- 115
Cang, Joel 1899-1974 .... CAP-2
Earlier sketch in CA 29-32
Cangemi, Sister Marie Lucita 1920- 21-24R
Canham, Erwin D(ain) 1904-1982 .... CAP-1
Obituary 105
Earlier sketch in CA 13-14
Canham, Kingsley 1945- 57-60
Caniff, Milton (Arthur) 1907-1988 85-88
Obituary 125
See also AITN 1
See also SATA 58
Canin, Ethan 1960- 135
Brief entry 131
See also CLC 55
Cann, Marjorie Mitchell 1924- 89-92
Cannam, Peggie 1925- 13-16R
Cannan, Denis 1919- CANR-7
Earlier sketch in CA 57-60
Cannan, Gilbert E. 1884-1955 Brief entry 111
See also DLB 10
Cannan, Joanna
See Pullein-Thompson, Joanna Maxwell
Cannell, Kathleen Biggar (Eaton)
1891-1974 106
See also DLB 4
Cannell, Skipwith 1887-1957 .... DLB 45
Cannell, Stephen J(oseph) 1941- 138
Canning, Jeff(rey Michael) 1947- 73-76
Canning, John 1920- 89-92
Canning, Paul 1947- 126
Canning, Ray R(ussell) 1920- 41-44R
Canning, Victor 1911-1986 .... CANR-6
Obituary 118
Earlier sketch in CA 13-16R
Cannon, Alexander 1896-1963(?) Obituary 111
Cannon, Beth 1951- 69-72
Cannon, Bettie (Waddell) 1922- 126
See also SATA 59
Cannon, Bill
See Cannon, William S.
Cannon, Cornelia (James)
1876-1969 Obituary 109
See also SATA 28
Cannon, Curt
See Hunter, Evan
Cannon, Garland (Hampton) 1924- CANR-30
Earlier sketches in CA 33-36R, CANR-13
Cannon, Grant Groesbeck
1911-1969 Obituary 117
Cannon, Harold C(harles) 1930- 45-48
Cannon, Helen 1921- 101
Cannon, James Monroe III 1918- 1-4R
Cannon, James P. 1890(?)-1974 Obituary 53-56
Cannon, Jimmy 1909-1973 Obituary 104
Cannon, John
See Newton, Michael
Cannon, John (Ashton) 1918- 49-52
Cannon, Le Grand Jr.
1899-1979 Obituary 93-96
Cannon, Lou(is S.) 1933- 29-32R
Cannon, Mark W(ilcox) 1928- 13-16R
Cannon, Poppy
See White, Poppy Cannon
Cannon, Ravenna
See Mayhar, Ardath
Cannon, Sarah Ophelia Colley 1912- 129
Cannon, William Ragsdale 1916- CANR-18
Earlier sketches in CA 1-4R, CANR-4
Cannon, William S. 1918- 29-32R
Canny, Nicholas P(atrick) 1944- 69-72
Cano-Ballesta, Juan 1932- CANR-1
Earlier sketch in CA 49-52
Canon, Lance Kirkpatrick 1939- 45-48
Canovan, Margaret 1939- 81-84
Cansdale, George (Soper) 1909- 9-12R
Cant, Gilbert 1909-1982 Obituary 107
Cant, Reginald (Edward)
1914-1987 Obituary 122
Cantacuzene, Julia 1876-1975 Obituary 61-64
Cantacuzino, Sherban 1928- 118
Cantalupo, Charles 1951- 126
Cantelon, John E(dward) 1924- 9-12R
Cantelon, Philip L(ouis) 1940- 124
Canterbery, E(stes) Ray 1935- 41-44R
Cantin, Eileen 1931- 53-56
Cantin, Eugene Thorpe 1944- 45-48
Cantinat, Jean 1902- 29-32R
Cantone, Vic 1933- 138
Cantor, Arthur 1920- 29-32R
Cantor, Eli 1913- CANR-14
Earlier sketch in CA 77-80
Cantor, Geoffrey 1943- 135
Cantor, George (Nathan) 1941- 138
Cantor, Gilbert M. 1929(?)-1987 Obituary 122
Cantor, Harold 1926- 136
Cantor, Leonard M(artin) 1927- 69-72
Cantor, Louis 1934- 29-32R
Cantor, Milton 1925- Brief entry 112
Cantor, Muriel G. 1923- CANR-12
Earlier sketch in CA 33-36R
Cantor, Norman F(rank) 1929- 102
Cantor, Paul A(rthur) 1945- 89-92
Cantor, Paul David 1916-1979 Obituary 89-92
Cantori, Louis J. 1934- 29-32R
Cantrell, J(ohn) A(nthony) 1952- 123
Cantril, Albert H(adley) 1940- 111
Cantu, Robert Clark 1938- 108
Cantwell, Aston
See Platt, Charles
Cantwell, Dennis P(atrick) 1940- 57-60
Cantwell, Lois 1951- 121
Cantwell, Robert Emmett 1908-1978 .... CANR-4
Obituary 81-84
Earlier sketch in CA 5-8R
See also DLB 9
Cantzlaar, George La Fond 1906-1967 .... CAP-1
Earlier sketch in CA 13-16
Canuck, Abe
See Bingley, David Ernest
Canusi, Jose
See Barker, S. Omar
Canutt, Enos Edward
1895(?)-1986 Obituary 119
Brief entry 114
Canutt, Yakima
See Canutt, Enos Edward
Canzoneri, Robert (Wilburn) 1925- 17-20R
Capaldi, Nicholas 1939- 21-24R
Cape, Judith
See Page, P(atricia) K(athleen)
Cape, Peter (Irwin) 1929- 108
Cape, William H(enry) 1920- 9-12R
Capeci, Dominic Joseph Jr. 1940- 77-80
Capek, Karel 1890-1938 Brief entry 104
See also DC 1
See also TCLC 6, 37
See also WLC
Capek, Milic 1909- CANR-4
Earlier sketch in CA 1-4R
Capel, Roger
See Sheppard, Lancelot C(apel)
Capelle, Russell B(eckett) 1917- 5-8R
Capen, Joseph 1658-1725 .... DLB 24
Capers, Gerald Mortimer Jr. 1909- 5-8R
Capitan, William H(arry) 1933- 29-32R
Capitanchik, Maurice
1929(?)-1985 Obituary 118
Capitman, Barbara Baer
1920-1990 Obituary 131
Capitman, William G(ardiner) 1921-1975 122
Obituary 111
Capizzi, Michael 1941- 41-44R

Caplan, Arthur L(eonard) 1950- CANR-22
Earlier sketch in CA 106
Caplan, David 1947- 105
Caplan, Edwin H(arvey) 41-44R
Caplan, Frank 1911(?)-1988 110
Obituary 126
Caplan, Gerald 1917- CANR-18
Earlier sketch in CA 25-28R
Caplan, Harry 1896- CAP-2
Earlier sketch in CA 23-24
Caplan, Lincoln 1950- 138
Caplan, Lionel 33-36R
Caplan, Paula J(oan) 1947- 129
Caplan, Ralph 1925- 13-16R
Caplan, Ronald Mervyn 1937- 107
Caplan, Theresa 110
Caplan, Thomas (Mark) 1946- 107
Caples, John 1900-1990 ....21-24R
Obituary 131
Caplin, Alfred Gerald 1909-1979 57-60
Obituary 89-92
See also Capp, Al
See also SATA 21
Caplovitz, David 1928- 41-44R
Caplow, Theodore 1920- CANR-20
Earlier sketches in CA 1-4R, CANR-4
Capon, Edmund (George) 1940- 107
Capon, (Harry) Paul 1912-1969 ....5-8R
Obituary 103
Capon, Peter
See Oakley, Eric Gilbert
Capon, Robert Farrar 1925- 136
Brief entry 106
Caponigri, A(loysius) Robert 1915- 37-40R
Caporale, Rocco 1927- 37-40R
Capote, Truman 1924-1984 ....CANR-18
Obituary 113
Earlier sketch in CA 5-8R
See also CDALB 1941-1968
See also CLC 1, 3, 8, 13, 19, 34, 38, 58
See also DLB 2
See also DLBY 80, 84
See also MTCW
See also SSC 2
See also WLC
Capouya, Emile 122
Brief entry 118
Capp, Al
See Caplin, Alfred Gerald
See also SATA 61
Capp, B. S.
See Capp, Bernard (Stuart)
Capp, Bernard (Stuart) 1943- 130
Capp, Glenn Richard 1910- CANR-3
Earlier sketch in CA 1-4R
Capp, Richard 1935- 81-84
Cappadona, Diane Apostolos
See Apostolos-Cappadona, Diane
Cappel, Constance 1936- CANR-10
Earlier sketch in CA 21-24R
See also SATA 22
Cappelluti, Frank Joseph 1935-1972 ....37-40R
Capper, Douglas Parode 1898(?)-1979 ....9-12R
Obituary 103
Cappo, Joseph 1936- 77-80
Cappon, Daniel 1921- 17-20R
Cappon, Lester J(esse) 1900-1981 106
Obituary 104
Capps, Benjamin (Franklin) 1922- CANR-7
Earlier sketch in CA 5-8R
See also SATA 9
Capps, Carroll M. 1917(?)-1971 Obituary 112
Capps, Clifford Lucille Sheats
1902-1976 ....37-40R
Capps, Donald E(ric) 1939- CANR-12
Earlier sketch in CA 29-32R
Capps, Jack Lee 1926- 21-24R
Capps, Walter H(olden) 1934- CANR-12
Earlier sketch in CA 29-32R
Cappy Dick
See Cleveland, George
Capra, Frank 1897-1991 61-64
Obituary 135
See also CLC 16
Capra, Fritjof 1939- 107
Capretta, Patrick J(ohn) 1929-1982 ....21-24R
Obituary 135
Caprio, Betsy
See Caprio, Elizabeth Blair
Caprio, Elizabeth Blair 1933- CANR-30
Earlier sketch in CA 110
Caprio, Frank S(amuel) 1906- 101
Capron, Alexander Morgan 1944- 115
Capron, Jean F. 1924- 21-24R
Capron, Louis (Bishop) 1891- CAP-1
Earlier sketch in CA 9-10
Capron, Walter Clark 1904-1979 .... CAP-1
Obituary 89-92
Earlier sketch in CA 17-18
Capron, William M(osher) 1920- 29-32R
Capstick, Peter Hathaway 1940- 102
Captain Kangaroo
See Keeshan, Robert J.
Captain Wheeler
See Ellis, Edward S(ylvester)
Captain X
See Power-Waters, Brian
Caputi, Anthony (Francis) 1924- CANR-3
Earlier sketch in CA 1-4R
Caputi, Jane 1953- 129
Caputo, David A(rmand) 1943- 65-68
Caputo, Philip 1941- 73-76
See also CLC 32
Caputo, Robert 1949- 101
Caradon, Lord
See Foot, Hugh Mackintosh
Caraley, Demetrios 1932- 103
Caraman, Philip 1911- CANR-21
Earlier sketches in CA 9-12R, CANR-6
Caramello, Charles 1948- 112
Carano, Paul 1919- 17-20R
Caras, Roger A(ndrew) 1928- CANR-5
Earlier sketch in CA 1-4R
See also SATA 12
Caras, Tracy 1953- 113
Carawan, Candie
See Carawan, Carolanne M.
Carawan, Carolanne M. 1939- 17-20R
Carawan, Guy H. Jr. 1927- 17-20R
Caraway, Caren 1939- ....SATA 57
Caraway, Charless 1888-1977 125
Carballido, Emilio 1925- 33-36R
See also HW
Carbaugh, Robert J(ohn) 1946- 65-68
Carbery, Thomas F. 29-32R
Carbine, Patricia (Theresa) 1931- 107
Carbonell, Reyes 1917- 9-12R
Carbonnier, Jeanne 1894-1974 ....CAP-2
Earlier sketch in CA 33-36
See also SATA 3, 34
Carbury, A.B.
See Carr, Albert H. Z(olotkoff)
Carcopino, Jerome 1881(?)-1970 Obituary 104
Card, Orson Scott 1951- CANR-27
Earlier sketch in CA 102
See also CLC 44, 47, 50
See also MTCW
Cardarelli, Joseph 1944- 77-80
Cardarelli, Vincenzo 1887-1959 ....DLB 114
Carden, Karen W(ilson) 1946- CANR-1
Earlier sketch in CA 49-52
Carden, Maren Lockwood 53-56
Carden, Patricia J. 1935- 41-44R
Cardenal (Martinez), Ernesto 1925- CANR-32
Earlier sketches in CA 49-52, CANR-2
See also CLC 31
See also HW
See also MTCW
Cardenas, Daniel N(egrete) 1917- CANR-26
Earlier sketch in CA 45-48
Cardenas, Gilbert 1947- 97-100
Cardenas, Reyes 1948- ....HW
Cardew, Cornelius 1936-1981 130
Obituary 108
Cardew, Michael (Ambrose)
1901-1983 ....CANR-30
Obituary 109
Earlier sketch in CA 49-52
Cardiff, Gray Emerson 1949- 89-92
Cardinal, Marie 1929- ....DLB 83
Cardinal, Ora 1913- 111
Cardinal, Roger (Thomas) 1940- CANR-18
Earlier sketches in CA 45-48, CANR-1
Cardinal, Sister Mary Ora
See Cardinal, Ora
Cardona, George 1936- 119
Cardona-Hine, Alvaro 1926- CANR-5
Earlier sketch in CA 9-12R
Cardone, Samuel S(teve) 1938- 17-20R
Cardoso, Onelio Jorge 1914-1986 ....HW
Cardoza y Aragon, Luis 1904- ....HW
Cardozo, Arlene Rossen 1938- CANR-19
Earlier sketch in CA 102
Cardozo, Benjamin N(athan)
1870-1938 Brief entry 117
Cardozo, Michael H. 1910- 33-36R
Cardozo, Nancy 103
Cardozo, Peter 1916- 61-64
Cardozo-Freeman, Inez 1928- 131
See also HW
Carducci, Giosue 1835-1907 ....TCLC 32
Cardui, Van
See Wayman, Tony Russell
Cardui, Vanessa
See Wayman, Tony Russell
Cardus, Neville 1889-1975 ....CANR-11
Obituary 57-60
Earlier sketch in CA 61-64
Cardwell, D(onald) S(tephen) L(owell)
1919- 101
Cardwell, Guy A(dams) 1905- 13-16R
Care, Felicity
See Coury, Louise Andree
Care, Norman S. 1937- 25-28R
Careless, J(ames) M(aurice) S(tockford)
1919- 102
Carens, James Francis 1927- CANR-12
Earlier sketch in CA 61-64
Carerra, Kathleen
See Carr, Jess(e Crowe Jr.)
Cares, Paul B. 1911- 9-12R
Caress, James M. 1947- 122
Caress, Jay
See Caress, James M.
Carette, Louis 1913- 85-88
Carew, Dorothy 1910(?)-1973 Obituary 41-44R
Carew, Dudley Charles 1903-1981 Obituary 103
Carew, Jan (Rynveld) 1925- 77-80
See also SATA 40, 51
Carew, Jocelyn
See Aeby, Jacquelyn
Carew, John Mohun 1921-1980 ....CANR-7
Earlier sketch in CA 13-16R
Carew, Rod(ney Cline) 1945- 104
Carew, Tim
See Carew, John Mohun
Carewe, S. C.
See Du Breuil, (Elizabeth) L(or)inda
Carey, Anne
See Nevill, Barry St-John
Carey, Bonnie 1941- ....SATA 18
Carey, Diane 1954- 122
Carey, Eileen
See O'Casey, Eileen (Reynolds)
Carey, Ernestine Gilbreth 1908- 5-8R
See also CLC 17
See also SATA 2
Carey, Gary 1938- CANR-34
Earlier sketches in CA 57-60, CANR-15
Carey, Henry 1687(?)-1743 ....DLB 84
Carey, James Charles 1915- 13-16R
Carey, Jane Perry (Clark) 1898-1981 73-76
Obituary 105
Carey, John A(ndrew) 1949- 109
Carey, John 1934- CANR-35
Earlier sketches in CA 57-60, CANR-6
Carey, Joseph Kuhn 1957- 135
Carey, Kenneth Moir 1908-1979 Obituary 108
Carey, M. V.
See Carey, Mary V(irginia)
Carey, Mary V(irginia) 1925- CANR-38
Earlier sketches in CA 81-84, CANR-17
See also SATA 39, 44
Carey, Mathew 1760-1839 ....DLB 37, 73
Carey, Michael
See Burton, Edward J.
Carey, Michael L(awrence) 1948- 65-68
Carey, Michael (Sausmarez)
1913-1985 Obituary 118
Carey, Mother Marme Aimee 1931- 13-16R
Carey, Omer L. 1929- CANR-23
Earlier sketches in CA 21-24R, CANR-8
Carey, Peter 1943- 127
Brief entry 123
See also CLC 40, 55
See also MTCW
Carey, Richard John 1925- 53-56
Carey, Robert George 1926- Brief entry 108
Carey, Steven Harry 1946(?)-1989 Obituary 129
Carey, Valerie Scho 1949- 128
See also SATA 60
Carey Evans, Olwen (Elizabeth) 1892- 126
Carey-Jones, N(orman) S(tewart) 1911- 21-24R
Carfagne, Cyril
See Jennings, Leslie Nelson
Carfagno, Vincent R. 1935- 41-44R
Carfax, Catherine
See Fairburn, Eleanor
Cargas, Harry J(ames) 1932- CANR-21
Earlier sketches in CA 13-16R, CANR-6
Cargill, Jennifer S(ue) 1944- 109
Cargill, Oscar 1898-1972 ....CANR-15
Obituary 33-36R
Earlier sketch in CA 1-4R
Cargill, Robert L. 1929- 25-28R
Cargo, David N(iels) 1932- 57-60
Cargo, Robert T. 1933- 85-88
Cargoe, Richard
See Payne, (Pierre Stephen) Robert
Carhart, Arthur Hawthorne 1892- CAP-1
Earlier sketch in CA 9-10
Caridi, Ronald J. 1941- 25-28R
Carigiet, Alois 1902-1985 73-76
Obituary 119
See also SATA 24, 47
Carim, Enver 1938- 136
Carin, Arthur A. 1928- 29-32R
Carin, Michael 1951- 132
Carini, Edward 1923- 61-64
See also SATA 9
Carisella, P(asquale) J. 1922- 134
Carkeet, David 1946- CANR-38
Earlier sketch in CA 102
Carl, Beverly May 1932- CANR-4
Earlier sketch in CA 53-56
Carl, Lillian Stewart 1949- 118
Carle, Eric 1929- CANR-25
Earlier sketches in CA 25-28R, CANR-10
See also CLR 10
See also MAICYA
See also SAAS 6
See also SATA 4, 65
Carlell, Lodowick 1602-1675 ....DLB 58
Carlen, Claudia 1906- 106
Carleton, Barbee Oliver 1917- 21-24R
Carleton, Captain L. C.
See Ellis, Edward S(ylvester)
Carleton, Captain Latham C.
See Ellis, Edward S(ylvester)
Carleton, Latham C.
See Ellis, Edward S(ylvester)
Carleton, Mark T. 1935- CANR-12
Earlier sketch in CA 33-36R
Carleton, R(eginal) Milton 1899-1986 69-72
Obituary 120
Carleton, Will(iam McKendree)
1845-1912 Brief entry 115
Carleton, William G(raves) 1903- CAP-2
Earlier sketch in CA 25-28
Carley, Lionel (Kenneth) 1936- 132
Carley, V(an Ness) Royal 1906-1976 ....CAP-2
Earlier sketch in CA 29-32
See also SATA 20
Carli, Angelo 1937- 49-52
Carlile, Clancy 1930- 128
Carlile, Clark S(tites) 1912- 41-44R
Carlile, Henry 1934- 33-36R
Carlile, Richard 1790-1843 ....DLB 110
Carlin, Gabriel S. 1921- 1-4R
Carlin, Thomas W(illard) 1918- 25-28R
Carlin, Vivian F. 1919- 131
Carline, Richard (Cotton)
1896-1980 Obituary 105
Carling, Francis 1945- 25-28R
Carlino, Lewis John 1932- 77-80
Carlinsky, Dan 1944- CANR-23
Earlier sketches in CA 21-24R, CANR-8
Carlise, Carris
See Pemberton, Margaret
Carlisle, Carol Jones 1919- 29-32R
Carlisle, Clark
See Holding, James (Clark Carlisle Jr.)
Carlisle, D. M.
See Cook, Dorothy Mary
Carlisle, Douglas H(ilton) 1921- 45-48
Carlisle, E(rvin) Fred 1935- 53-56
Carlisle, Fred 1915- 73-76
Carlisle, Henry (Coffin) 1926- CANR-15
Earlier sketch in CA 13-16R
See also CLC 33
Carlisle, Howard M(yron) 1928- 69-72
Carlisle, Lilian (Matarose) Baker 1912- 53-56
Carlisle, Olga Andreyev 1930- CANR-7
Earlier sketch in CA 13-16R
See also SATA 35
Carlisle, Regis 1955- CANR-17
Earlier sketch in CA 77-80
Carlisle, Rodney P. 1936- 45-48
Carlisle, Thomas (Fiske) 1944- 53-56
Carlisle, Thomas John 1913- CANR-18
Earlier sketch in CA 101
Carlock, John R(obert) 1921- 33-36R
Carlock, Lynn
See Cunningham, Marilyn
Carlon, Patricia Bernardette 13-16R
Carlquist, Sherwin 1930- 13-16R
Carls, (John) Norman 1907- CAP-2
Earlier sketch in CA 17-18
Carlsen, Chris
See Holdstock, Robert P.
Carlsen, G(eorge) Robert 1917- CANR-24
Earlier sketches in CA 17-20R, CANR-8
See also SATA 30
Carlsen, James C(aldwell) 1927- 25-28R
Carlsen, Ruth C(hristoffer) 1918- CANR-24
Earlier sketches in CA 17-20R, CANR-8
See also SATA 2
Carlson, Andrew R(aymond) 1934- 29-32R
Carlson, Arthur E(ugene) 1923- 37-40R
Carlson, Avis D(ungan) 1896-1987 73-76
Obituary 121
Carlson, Bernice Wells 1910- CANR-2
Earlier sketch in CA 5-8R
See also SATA 8
Carlson, Betty 1919- CANR-2
Earlier sketch in CA 1-4R
Carlson, C. C.
See Carlson, Carole C.
Carlson, Carl Walter 1907- 49-52
Carlson, Carole C. 1925- 113
Carlson, Dale Bick 1935- CANR-3
Earlier sketch in CA 9-12R
See also SATA 1
Carlson, Daniel (Bick) 1960- 105
See also SATA 27
Carlson, Edgar M(agnus) 1908- 105
Carlson, Ellsworth C. 1917- Brief entry 105
Carlson, Elof Axel 1931- 45-48
Carlson, Eric W(alter) 1910- 25-28R
Carlson, Esther Elisabeth 1920- 5-8R
Carlson, Harry Gilbert 1930- CANR-29
Earlier sketch in CA 109
Carlson, John A(llyn) 1933- 29-32R
Carlson, Judith Lee 1952- 104
Carlson, Leland H(enry) 1908- 17-20R
Carlson, Lewis H(erbert) 1934- 41-44R
Carlson, Loraine 1923- CANR-14
Earlier sketch in CA 37-40R
Carlson, Marvin 1935- CANR-8
Earlier sketch in CA 21-24R
Carlson, Nancy L(ee) 1953- 110
See also SATA 45, 56
Carlson, Natalie Savage 1906- CANR-3
Earlier sketch in CA 1-4R
See also MAICYA
See also SAAS 4
See also SATA 2, 68
Carlson, P. M.
See Carlson, Patricia M(cElroy)
Carlson, Patricia M(cElroy) 1940- CANR-36
Earlier sketch in CA 114
Carlson, Paul Robins 1928- 101
Carlson, Raymond 1906-1983 Obituary 109
Carlson, Reynold Edgar 1901- CANR-4
Earlier sketch in CA 1-4R
Carlson, Richard Stocks 1942- 57-60
Carlson, Richard 1912(?)-1977 Obituary 73-76
Carlson, Rick J. 1940- 65-68
Carlson, Robert E(ugene) 1922- 41-44R
Carlson, Ron(ald F.) 1947- CANR-27
Earlier sketch in CA 105
See also CLC 54
Carlson, Ronald L. 1934- CANR-35
Earlier sketches in CA 33-36R, CANR-13
Carlson, Roy L(incoln) 1930- 41-44R
Carlson, Ruth (Elizabeth) Kearney
1911- 29-32R
Carlson, Theodore L(eonard) 1905- 45-48
Carlson, Vada F. 1897- CANR-28
Earlier sketches in CA 21-24R, CANR-10
See also SATA 16
Carlson, William H(ugh) 1898- CAP-2
Earlier sketch in CA 23-24
Carlson, William S(amuel) 1905- 1-4R
Carlston, Kenneth S. 1904- 5-8R
Carlstrom, Nancy White 1948- 121
See also SATA 48, 53
Carlton, Alva
See Delk, Robert Carlton
Carlton, Charles Merritt 1928- 45-48
Carlton, Charles 1941- 53-56
Carlton, David 1938- 103
Carlton, Henry F(isk)
1893(?)-1973 Obituary 41-44R
Carlton, Jay
See Obrecht, Jas
Carlton, Lessie 1903- 49-52

Carlton, Robert G(oodrich) 1927- 17-20R
Carlton, Roger
See Rowland, D(onald) S(ydney)
Carlton, Wendy 1949- 101
Carlut, Charles E. 1911- Brief entry 107
Carlyle, Jane Welsh 1801-1866 .... DLB 55
Carlyle, Thomas 1795-1881 .... CDBLB 1789-1832
See also DLB 55
Carlyon, Richard .... SATA 55
Carm, Mac
See Armstrong, Keith F(rancis) W(hitfield)
Carmack, Robert M. 1934- 45-48
Carman, Barry (Francis) 1922- 118
Carman, (William) Bliss
1861-1929 Brief entry 104
See also DLB 92
See also TCLC 7
Carman, Dulce
See Drummond, Edith Marie Dulce Carman
Carman, J(ustice) Neale 1897-1972 .... CAP-1
Earlier sketch in CA 9-10
Carman, Robert A(rchibald) 1931- CANR-7
Earlier sketch in CA 57-60
Carman, William Y(oung) 1909- 13-16R
Carmel, Catherine 1939- 69-72
Carmel, Hesi 1937- 103
Carmell, Aryeh 1917- 118
Carmen, Arlene 1936- 69-72
Carmen, Ira H. 1934- 128
Carmen, Sister (M.) Joann 1941- 21-24R
Carmen Sylva
See Elisabeth (Ottilie Luise), Queen (Pauline)
Carmer, Carl (Lamson) 1893-1976 ....CANR-4
Obituary 69-72
Earlier sketch in CA 5-8R
See also SATA 30, 37
Carmer, Elizabeth Black 1904- .... SATA 24
Carmi, T.
See Charny, Carmi
Carmichael, Ann
See MacAlpine, Margaret H(esketh Murray)
Carmichael, Ann G(ayton) 1947- 125
Carmichael, Calum M. 1938- 53-56
Carmichael, Carrie
See Carmichael, Harriet
See also SATA 40
Carmichael, D(ouglas) R(oy) 1941- 33-36R
Carmichael, Fred 1924- CANR-25
Earlier sketches in CA 17-20R, CANR-10
Carmichael, Harriet 115
See also Carmichael, Carrie
Carmichael, Harry
See Ognall, Leopold Horace
Carmichael, Hoagland Howard
1899-1981 Obituary 108
Carmichael, Hoagy
See Carmichael, Hoagland Howard
Carmichael, Ian (Gillett) 1920- 129
Carmichael, Joel 1915- CANR-2
Earlier sketch in CA 1-4R
Carmichael, John P(eerless)
1902-1986 Obituary 119
Carmichael, Leonard 1898-1973 ....41-44R
Obituary 45-48
Carmichael, Oliver C(romwell)
1891-1966 .... CAP-1
Earlier sketch in CA 9-10
Carmichael, Peter A(rchibald) 1897- CAP-2
Earlier sketch in CA 17-18
Carmichael, Stokely 1941- CANR-25
Earlier sketch in CA 57-60
See also BW
Carmichael, Thomas N(ichols)
1919-1972 .... CAP-2
Earlier sketch in CA 29-32
Carmichael, William Edward 1922- 37-40R
Carmilly, Moshe 1908- 41-44R
Carmines, Al(vin Allison Jr.) 1936- 103
Carmody, Denise Lardner 1935- 93-96
Carmody, Jay 1900(?)-1973 Obituary 41-44R
Carmoy, Guy de 1907- 89-92
Carnac, Carol
See Rivett, Edith Caroline
Carnac, Levin
See Griffith-Jones, George Chetwynd
Carnahan, Walter H(ervey) 1891- CAP-1
Earlier sketch in CA 9-10
Carnall, Geoffrey 1927- 13-16R
Carnap, Rudolf P. 1891-1970 .... CAP-1
Obituary 29-32R
Earlier sketch in CA 9-10
Carnarvon, The Earl of
See Herbert, Henry George Alfred Marius Victor Francis
Carnegie, Dorothy Vanderpool ....AITN 1
Carnegie, Raymond Alexander 1920- CANR-11
Earlier sketch in CA 21-24R
Carnegie, Sacha
See Carnegie, Raymond Alexander
Carnegy, Patrick 1940- 81-84
Carneiro, Maurina Pereira
See Pereira Carneiro, Maurina
Carnell, Corbin Scott 1929- CANR-10
Earlier sketch in CA 65-68
Carnell, E. J.
See Carnell, (Edward) John
Carnell, Edward John 1919-1967 .... CAP-1
Earlier sketch in CA 13-14
Carnell, (Edward) John 1912-1972 ....25-28R
Obituary 104
Carner, Mosco 1904-1985 ....CANR-38
Obituary 116
Earlier sketches in CAP-1, CA 11-12, CANR-12
Carnero, Guillermo 1947- .... DLB 108
Carnes, Conrad D(ew) 1936- 85-88
Carnes, Mark C(hristopher) 1950- CANR-30
Earlier sketch in CA 112
Carnes, Paul N(athaniel)
1921-1979 Obituary 85-88
Carnes, Ralph L(ee) 1931- 33-36R
Carnes, Valerie Folts-Bohanan 1945- 33-36R
Carnevale, Anthony P(atrick) 1946- 135
Carnevali, Doris L(orrain) CANR-21
Earlier sketch in CA 69-72
Carney, Daniel 1944- 119
Carney, Dora Sanders 1903-1986 Obituary 120
Carney, Edward John 1913-1989 Obituary 128
Carney, James (Patrick) 1914- 21-24R
Carney, John J(oseph) Jr. 1932- 69-72
Carney, John Otis 1922- CANR-3
Earlier sketch in CA 1-4R
Carney, Matthew 1922- CANR-25
Earlier sketch in CA 108
Carney, Raymond 1950- 137
Carney, Richard Edward 1929- 37-40R
Carney, T(homas) F(rancis) 1931- CANR-39
Earlier sketches in CA 49-52, CANR-1, 17
Carney, W(illiam) Alderman 1922- 25-28R
Carnicelli, D(omenick) D. 1931- 61-64
Carnochan, W(alter) B(liss) 1930- 33-36R
Carnot, Joseph B(arry) 1941- 45-48
Carnoy, Martin 1938- CANR-10
Earlier sketch in CA 65-68
Caro, Francis G(eorge) 1936- CANR-28
Earlier sketches in CA 69-72, CANR-11
Caro, Robert A. 101
See also BEST 90:2
Caroe, Olaf Kirkpatrick 1892-1981 113
Carol, Bill J.
See Knott, William C(ecil Jr.)
Carol, Jacqueline
See Cooper, Jacqueline
Caroli, Betty Boyd 1938- 118
Caroll, Nonie 1926- 103
Caron, Roger 1938- 89-92
Carona, Philip B(en) 1925- CANR-4
Earlier sketch in CA 1-4R
Caronia, Guiseppe
1884(?)-1977 Obituary 69-72
Caroselli, Remus F(rancis) 1916- 97-100
See also SATA 36
Carossa, Hans 1878-1956 .... DLB 66
Carosso, Vincent Phillip 1922- CANR-3
Earlier sketch in CA 9-12R
Carothers, J. Edward 1907- 41-44R
Carothers, Robert Lee 1942- 45-48
Carousso, Georges 1909- 89-92
Carozzi, Albert V(ictor) 1925- 53-56
Carp, Frances Merchant 1918- 21-24R
Carpelan, Bo (Gustaf Bertelsson)
1926- CANR-27
Earlier sketches in CA 49-52, CANR-2
See also SATA 8
Carpenter
See Arnold, June (Davis)
Carpenter, (John) Allan 1917- CANR-3
Earlier sketch in CA 9-12R
See also SATA 3
Carpenter, Andrew 1943- 93-96
Carpenter, Angelica Shirley 1945- .... SATA 71
Carpenter, Bogdana 1941- 135
Carpenter, Cal
See Carpenter, Clarence A(lfred)
Carpenter, Charles A. (Jr.) 1929- 33-36R
Carpenter, Charles H(ope) Jr. 1916- 111
Carpenter, Clarence A(lfred) 1921- 116
Carpenter, Clarence Ray
1905-1975 Obituary 57-60
Carpenter, D(avid) A(rscott) 1946- 134
Carpenter, David A(llen) 1949- 111
Carpenter, David C. 1941- 121
Carpenter, Delores Bird 1942- 126
Carpenter, Don(ald Richard) 1931- CANR-1
Earlier sketch in CA 45-48
See also CLC 41
Carpenter, Duffy
See Hurley, John J(erome)
Carpenter, Elizabeth Sutherland 1920- 41-44R
Carpenter, Frances 1890-1972 ....CANR-4
Obituary 37-40R
Earlier sketch in CA 5-8R
See also SATA 3, 27
Carpenter, Francis Ross 1925- 101
Carpenter, Fred
See Hand, (Andrus) Jackson
Carpenter, Frederic I.
See Carpenter, Frederic Ives (Jr.)
Carpenter, Frederic Ives (Jr.)
1903-1991 ....CANR-38
Obituary 134
Earlier sketch in CA 5-8R
Carpenter, Humphrey (William Bouverie)
1946- CANR-13
Earlier sketch in CA 89-92
Carpenter, J(ohn) D(avid) 1948- 115
Carpenter, James A. 1928- 37-40R
Carpenter, John A(lcott) 1921-1978 ....9-12R
Obituary 77-80
Carpenter, John (Howard) 1948- 134
See also AAYA 2
See also SATA 58
Carpenter, John Jo
See Reese, John (Henry)
Carpenter, John (Randell) 1936- CANR-38
Earlier sketches in CA 65-68, CANR-9
Carpenter, Joyce Frances 33-36R
Carpenter, Kenneth E(dward) 1936- 137
Carpenter, Kenneth J(ohn) 1923- 124
Carpenter, Liz
See Carpenter, Elizabeth Sutherland
Carpenter, Lucas 1947- 126
Carpenter, Lynette 1951- 138
Carpenter, Margaret Haley 5-8R
Obituary 116
Carpenter, Marjorie 1896- 45-48
Carpenter, Michael (Anthony) 1940- 119
Carpenter, Mimi Gregoire 1947- CANR-30
Earlier sketch in CA 111
Carpenter, Nan Cooke 1912- 25-28R
Carpenter, Patricia (Healy Evans) 1920- 29-32R
See also SATA 11
Carpenter, Peter 1922- 13-16R
Carpenter, Rhys 1889-1980 57-60
Obituary 93-96
Carpenter, Richard C(oles) 1916- 13-16R
Carpenter, Stephen Cullen .... DLB 73
Carpenter, William 1940- 106
Carpenter, Willow
See Browning, (Zerilda) Sinclair
Carpentier (y Valmont), Alejo
1904-1980 ....CANR-11
Obituary 97-100
Earlier sketch in CA 65-68
See also CLC 8, 11, 38
See also DLB 113
See also HW
Carper, Jean Elinor 1932- CANR-7
Earlier sketch in CA 17-20R
Carper, L. Dean 1931- 49-52
Carpozi, George Jr. 1920- CANR-11
Earlier sketch in CA 13-16R
Carr, A.H.Z.
See Carr, Albert H. Z(olotkoff)
Carr, Albert H. Z(olotkoff) 1902-1971 ....CANR-1
Obituary 33-36R
Earlier sketch in CA 1-4R
Carr, Annie Roe CANR-26
Earlier sketches in CAP-2, CA 19-20
Carr, Archie (Fairly Jr.) 1909-1987 ....13-16R
Obituary 122
Carr, Arthur C(harles) 1918- 37-40R
Carr, Arthur Japheth 1914- 57-60
Carr, Bruce (A.) 1938- 114
Carr, C(harles) T(elford)
1905-1976 Obituary 65-68
Carr, Catharine
See Wade, Rosalind Herschel
Carr, David William 1911- 37-40R
Carr, Donald Eaton 1903- 13-16R
Carr, Dorothy Stevenson Laird 1912- 9-12R
Carr, Edward Hallet 1892-1982 ....CANR-14
Obituary 108
Earlier sketch in CA 61-64
Carr, Edwin George 1937- 61-64
Carr, Emily 1871-1945 .... DLB 68
See also TCLC 32
Carr, Gerald F(rancis) 1930- 118
Carr, Glyn
See Styles, (Frank) Showell
Carr, Gwen B. 1924- 41-44R
Carr, Harriett Helen 1899- CAP-1
Earlier sketch in CA 9-10
See also SATA 3
Carr, Herbert R(eginald) C(ulling)
1896-1986 Obituary 119
Carr, Ian (Henry Randell) 1933- 110
Carr, J(ames Joseph) L(loyd) 1912- CANR-37
Earlier sketch in CA 102
Carr, Janet Baker
See Baker-Carr, Janet
Carr, Jay Phillip 1936- 89-92
Carr, Jess(e Crowe Jr.) 1930-1990 ....CANR-29
Obituary 130
Earlier sketches in CA 29-32R, CANR-12
Carr, (Bettye) Jo (Crisler) 1926- 21-24R
Carr, John C(harles) 1929- 53-56
Carr, John Dickson 1906-1977 ....CANR-33
Obituary 69-72
Earlier sketches in CA 49-52, CANR-3
See also CLC 3
See also MTCW
Carr, John Laurence 1916- 49-52
Carr, Josephine 1952- 111
Carr, Lois Green 1922- 61-64
Carr, Margaret 1935- 105
Carr, Mary Jane 1899-1988 .... CAP-1
Obituary 124
Earlier sketch in CA 9-10
See also SATA 2, 55
Carr, Michael Harold 1935- 109
Carr, Pat M(oore) 1932- CANR-31
Earlier sketches in CA 65-68, CANR-14
Carr, Philippa
See Hibbert, Eleanor Burford
Carr, Raymond 1919- CANR-8
Earlier sketch in CA 17-20R
Carr, Robert K(enneth) 1908-1979 93-96
Obituary 85-88
Carr, Roberta
See Roberts, Irene
Carr, Robyn 1951- CANR-38
Earlier sketch in CA 115
Carr, Roland T. 1908(?)-1983 122
Obituary 111
Carr, Stephen L(amoni) 57-60
Carr, Terry (Gene) 1937- 81-84
Carr, Virginia Mason
See Vaughan, Virginia M(ason)
Carr, Virginia Spencer 1929- 61-64
See also CLC 34
See also DLB 111
Carr, Warren Tyree 1917- 5-8R
Carr, William G(eorge) 1901- 53-56
Carr, William H(enry) A(lexander)
1924- CANR-7
Earlier sketch in CA 13-16R
Carr, William 1921- 73-76
Carraco, Carol Crowe
See Crowe-Carraco, Carol
Carraher, Charles E. (Jr.) 1941- 135
Carranco, Lynwood 1921- CANR-21
Earlier sketches in CA 57-60, CANR-6
Carras, Mary C(alliope) 85-88
Carrasco, David 112
Carrel, Alexis 1873-1944 Brief entry 120
Carrel, Mark
See Paine, Lauran (Bosworth)
Carrell, Norman (Gerald) 1905- CAP-2
Earlier sketch in CA 25-28
Carrera Andrade, Jorge
1903-1978 Obituary 85-88
See also HW
Carretta, Vincent (Albert) 1945- 131
Carrick, A. B.
See Lindsay, Harold Arthur
Carrick, Carol (Hatfield) 1935- CANR-37
Earlier sketches in CA 45-48, CANR-1, 17
See also MAICYA
See also SATA 7, 63
Carrick, Donald (F.) 1929-1989 ....CANR-37
Earlier sketches in CA 53-56, CANR-5, 20
See also MAICYA
See also SATA 7, 63
Carrick, Edward
See Craig, Edward Anthony
Carrick, John
See Crosbie, (Hugh) Provan
Carrick, Malcolm 1945- CANR-14
Earlier sketch in CA 77-80
See also SATA 28
Carrier, Constance 1908- 33-36R
Carrier, Esther Jane 1925- 17-20R
Carrier, Jean-Guy 1945- 101
Carrier, Lark 1947- ....SATA 50, 71
Carrier, Roch 1937- 130
See also CLC 13
See also DLB 53
Carrier, Warren (Pendleton) 1918- CANR-18
Earlier sketches in CA 9-12R, CANR-3
Carrigan, Andrew G(ardner) 1935- CANR-1
Earlier sketch in CA 45-48
Carrigan, D(avid) Owen 1933- 25-28R
Carrigan, Richard A(lfred) Jr. 1932- CANR-30
Earlier sketch in CA 112
Carrighar, Sally 93-96
See also SATA 24
Carriker, Robert C(harles) 1940- 69-72
Carrillo, Lawrence W(ilbert) 1920- 13-16R
Carringer, Robert L. 1941- CANR-17
Earlier sketch in CA 97-100
Carrington, Charles Edmund 1897-1990 ....5-8R
Obituary 132
Carrington, Frank G(amble Jr.) 1936- 57-60
Carrington, George C(abell) Jr. 1928-1990 122
Obituary 132
Brief entry 118
Carrington, Grant 1938- 104
Carrington, Leonora 1917- 124
Brief entry 114
Carrington, Molly
See Matthews, C(onstance) M(ary)
Carrington, Paul D(eWitt) 1931- 29-32R
Carrington, Richard (Temple Murray)
1921- 9-12R
Carrington, William Langley 1900-1970 .... CAP-1
Earlier sketch in CA 13-14
Carrion, Arturo Morales
See Morales Carrion, Arturo
Carris, Joan Davenport 1938- CANR-27
Earlier sketch in CA 106
See also SATA 42, 44
Carrison, Daniel J. 1917- 37-40R
Carrison, Muriel Paskin 1928- 127
Carrithers, David W. 1943- 110
Carrithers, Gale H(emphill) Jr. 1932- 41-44R
Carrithers, Wallace M(axwell) 1911- 25-28R
Carrol, Shana
See Newcomb, Kerry
and Schaefer, Frank
Carroll, Anne Kristin
See Gales, Barbara J.
Carroll, Archie B(enjamin III) 1943- 109
Carroll, B(illy) D(an) 1940- 53-56
Carroll, Berenice A(nita) 1932- 41-44R
Carroll, Bob 1936- 129
Carroll, C(armal) Edward 1923- 29-32R
Carroll, Carroll 1902-1991 101
Obituary 133
Carroll, Charles Francis 1936- 53-56
Carroll, Christina
See Henderson, M(arilyn) R(uth)
Carroll, Curt
See Bishop, Curtis (Kent)
Carroll, Daniel B(ernard) 1928-1977 ....41-44R
Carroll, David
See Carroll, David L.
Carroll, David L. 1942- 129
Carroll, Dennis 1940- 114
Carroll, Donald K(ingery) 1909- CAP-2
Earlier sketch in CA 17-18
Carroll, Elizabeth
See Barkin, Carol
and James, Elizabeth
Carroll, Faye 1937- 21-24R
Carroll, Ginny 1948- 130
Carroll, Gladys Hasty 1904- CANR-5
Earlier sketch in CA 1-4R
See also DLB 9
Carroll, Herbert A(llen) 1897- CAP-1
Earlier sketch in CA 11-12
Carroll, J. Larry 1946- 129
Carroll, Jackson W(alker) 1932- CANR-16
Earlier sketch in CA 85-88
Carroll, James P. 1943(?)- 81-84
See also CLC 38
Carroll, Jeffrey 1950- 85-88

Carroll, Jim 1951- 45-48
See also CLC 35
Carroll, John B(issell) 1916- CANR-3
Earlier sketch in CA 1-4R
Carroll, John J(oseph) 1924- 13-16R
Carroll, John M(elvin) 1928- 37-40R
Carroll, John Millar 1925- CANR-23
Earlier sketches in CA 5-8R, CANR-8
Carroll, John 1735-1815 .... DLB 37
Carroll, John 1809-1884 .... DLB 99
Carroll, John 1944- CANR-7
Earlier sketch in CA 57-60
Carroll, Jonathan 1949- CANR-21
Earlier sketch in CA 105
Carroll, Joseph T(homas) 1935- 102
Carroll, Joseph 1912(?)-1989 Obituary 128
Carroll, Joy 1924- 102
Carroll, Kenneth Lane 1924- 37-40R
Carroll, L(awrence) Patrick 1936- 111
Carroll, (Archer) Latrobe 1894- CANR-3
Earlier sketch in CA 1-4R
See also SATA 7
Carroll, Laura
See Parr, Lucy
Carroll, Lewis
See Dodgson, Charles Lutwidge
See also CDBLB 1832-1890
See also CLR 2, 18
See also DLB 18
See also WLC
Carroll, Loren 1904-1978 85-88
Obituary 81-84
Carroll, Martin
See Carr, Margaret
Carroll, Mary
See Sanford, Annette
Carroll, Paul Vincent 1900-1968 ....9-12R
Obituary 25-28R
See also CLC 10
See also DLB 10
Carroll, Paul 1927- 25-28R
See also DLB 16
Carroll, Peter N(eil) 1943- 102
Carroll, Phil 1895-1971 .... CAP-1
Earlier sketch in CA 13-14
Carroll, Raymond 1924- 126
See also SATA 47
Carroll, Robert
See Alpert, Hollis
Carroll, Robert P(eter) 1941- 105
Carroll, Rosalynn
See Katz, Carol
Carroll, Ruth (Robinson) 1899- CANR-1
Earlier sketch in CA 1-4R
Carroll, St. Thomas Marion
See Carroll, Tom M.
Carroll, Sheila Baker
1918(?)-1984 Obituary 113
Carroll, Sister Mary Gerald 1913- 21-24R
Carroll, Stephen J(ohn) Jr. 1930- 41-44R
Carroll, Ted
See Carroll, Thomas Theodore Jr.
Carroll, Theodus 1928- 69-72
Carroll, Thomas J. 1909-1971 ....1-4R
Obituary 103
Carroll, Thomas Theodore Jr. 1925- 9-12R
Carroll, Tom M. 1950- 53-56
Carroll, Vern 1933- 57-60
Carroll, Vinnette (Justine) 123
Brief entry 114
See also BW
Carron, Malcolm 1917- Brief entry 105
Carrott, Richard G. 1924- 85-88
Carrouges, Michel
See Couturier, Louis (Joseph)
Carrow, Milton M(ichael) 1912- CANR-16
Earlier sketch in CA 25-28R
Carr-Saunders, Alexander (Morris)
1886-1966 ....CANR-20
Obituary 103
Earlier sketch in CA 1-4R
Carruth, Estelle 1910- 9-12R
Carruth, Gorton Veeder 1925- CANR-6
Earlier sketch in CA 57-60
Carruth, Hayden 1921- CANR-38
Earlier sketches in CA 9-12R, CANR-4
See also CLC 4, 7, 10, 18
See also DLB 5
See also MTCW
See also SATA 47
Carruthers, Ben F(rederick) 1911- 114
Carruthers, Malcolm Euan 1938- 102
Carruthers, Peter 1952- 126
Carry, (Benjamin) Peter 1942- 105
Carryaway, Nick
See Murray, John F(rancis)
Carryl, Charles E. 1841-1920 .... DLB 42
Carsac, Francis
See Bordes, Francois
Carsberg, Bryan Victor 1939- CANR-12
Earlier sketch in CA 29-32R
Carse, James P(earce) 1932- 21-24R
Carse, Robert 1902-1971 ....CANR-1
Obituary 29-32R
Earlier sketch in CA 1-4R
See also SATA 5
Carskadon, Thomas R.
1901(?)-1983(?) Obituary 108
Carson, Ada Lou 1932- 110
Carson, Alan 1951- 115
Carson, Anne (Regina) 1950- 132
Carson, Captain James CANR-26
Earlier sketches in CAP-2, CA 19-20
Carson, Ciaran 1948- Brief entry 112
Carson, Clarence B. 1925- 130
Carson, Clayborne 1944- 105
Carson, F(ranklin) John 1920- 9-12R
Carson, Gerald (Hewes) 1899-1989 ......CANR-16
Obituary 130
Earlier sketches in CA 1-4R, CANR-1
Carson, Hampton L(awrence) 1914- 5-8R
Carson, Herbert L(ee) 1929- 29-32R
Carson, J(ohn) Franklin 1920- 13-16R
See also SATA 1
Carson, Jane Dennison Obituary 114
Carson, Kit
See Carson, Xanthus
Carson, Mary 1934- 41-44R
Carson, Michael (Charles) 1946- 130
Carson, Rachel Louise 1907-1964 ....CANR-35
Earlier sketch in CA 77-80
See also CLC 71
See also MTCW
See also SATA 23
Carson, Ray F(ritziof) 1939- 61-64
Carson, Robert B. 1934- CANR-6
Earlier sketch in CA 57-60
Carson, Robert C(harles) 1930- 29-32R
Carson, Robert 1909-1983 ....21-24R
Obituary 108
Carson, Ronald A(lan) 1940- 119
Carson, Rosalind
See Chittenden, Margaret
Carson, Ruth
See Bugbee, Ruth Carson
Carson, S. M.
See Gorsline, (Sally) Marie
Carson, William Glasgow Bruce 1891- 5-8R
Carson, Xanthus 1910- 57-60
Carstairs, George Morrison 1916- 69-72
Carstairs, Kathleen
See Pendower, Jacques
Carsten, Francis Ludwig 1911- 13-16R
Carstens, Grace Pearce 1-4R
Carstensen, Roger Norwood 1920- CANR-2
Earlier sketch in CA 5-8R
Carswell, Brenda 1964- 127
Carswell, Catherine 1879-1946 .... DLB 36
Carswell, Evelyn M(edicus) 1919- 57-60
Carswell, John (Patrick) 1918- CANR-21
Earlier sketch in CA 9-12R
Carswell, Leslie
See Stephens, Rosemary
Cartano, Tony 1944- 129
Carte, Gene E(dward) 1938- 61-64
Carter, Alan 1936- 33-36R
Carter, Albert Howard 1913-1970 .... CAP-2
Earlier sketch in CA 25-28
Carter, Alden R(ichardson) 1947- 135
See also CLR 22
See also SATA 67
Carter, Alfred Edward 1914- 33-36R
Carter, Amon Giles Jr. 1919-1982 Obituary 111
Carter, Angela (Olive) 1940-1991 ....CANR-36
Obituary 136
Earlier sketches in CA 53-56, CANR-12
See also CLC 5, 41
See also DLB 14
See also MTCW
See also SATA 66
See also SATO 70
Carter, Ann
See Brooks, Anne Tedlock
Carter, Anne
See Brooks, Anne Tedlock
Carter, Anne Pitts 1925- Brief entry 106
Carter, Arthur M. 1911-1988 Obituary 125
Carter, Ashley
See Whittington, Harry (Benjamin)
Carter, Ashton B. 1954- 137
Carter, Avis Murton
See Allen, Kenneth S.
Carter, Barbara (Ellen) 1925-1988 ....CANR-10
Obituary 126
Earlier sketch in CA 53-56
Carter, Boyd (George) 1908-1980 ....CANR-7
Earlier sketch in CA 13-16R
Carter, Bruce
See Hough, Richard (Alexander)
Carter, Burnham 1901(?)-1979 Obituary 89-92
Carter, Byron L. 1924- 21-24R
Carter, C(edric) O(swald)
1917-1984 Obituary 112
Carter, Carmen 1954- 128
Carter, Carolle J(ean) 1934- 81-84
Carter, Charles Frederick 1919- CANR-20
Earlier sketches in CA 1-4R, CANR-4
Carter, Charles H(oward) 1927- 9-12R
Carter, Charles W(ebb) 1905- 21-24R
Carter, Dan T. 1940- 65-68
Carter, David C(harles) 1946- 45-48
Carter, Don E(arl) 1917- 73-76
Carter, Dorothy Sharp 1921- 49-52
See also SATA 8
Carter, E. Lawrence 1910- 25-28R
Carter, Edward Julian 1902-1982 ....5-8R
Obituary 107
Carter, Elizabeth 1717-1806 .... DLB 109
Carter, Elliott Cook 1908- 89-92
Carter, Ernestine (Marie) 130
Obituary 110
Carter, Everett 1919- 13-16R
Carter, Forrest 1927(?)-1979 107
See also SATA 32
Carter, Frances Monet 1923- 37-40R
Carter, Frances Tunnell 37-40R
Carter, George F(rancis) 1912- CANR-4
Earlier sketch in CA 5-8R
Carter, Gwendolen M(argaret)
1906-1991 ....CANR-19
Obituary 133
Earlier sketches in CA 1-4R, CANR-4
Carter, Harold 1925- 33-36R
Carter, Harry Graham 1901-1982 Obituary 106
Carter, Harvey L(ewis) 1904- 21-24R
Carter, Helene 1887-1960 .... SATA 15
Carter, Henry
See Leslie, Frank
Carter, Henry Hare 1905- 41-44R
Carter, (William) Hodding 1907-1972 .... CAP-1
Obituary 33-36R
Earlier sketch in CA 13-14
See also SATA 2, 27
Carter, Hugh 1895- 37-40R
Carter, Hurricane
See Carter, Rubin
Carter, J(ohn) Anthony 1943- 61-64
Carter, James E(dward) 1935- CANR-22
Earlier sketches in CA 57-60, CANR-7
Carter, James Earl Jr. 1924- CANR-32
Earlier sketch in CA 69-72
See also MTCW
Carter, James Puckette 1933- 33-36R
Carter, James Richard 1940- 33-36R
Carter, Jane Robbins
See Robbins, Jane (Borsch)
Carter, Janet 1938- 104
Carter, Jimmy
See Carter, James Earl Jr.
Carter, John Franklin
1897-1967 Obituary 25-28R
Carter, John Mack 1928- 103
Carter, John Stewart 1912-1965 .... CAP-1
Earlier sketch in CA 11-12
Carter, John T(homas) 1921- 33-36R
Carter, John (Waynflete) 1905-1975 ....5-8R
Obituary 57-60
Carter, Joseph 1912-1984 49-52
Obituary 112
Carter, K(ay) Codell 1939- 110
Carter, Katharine J(ones) 1905- 5-8R
See also SATA 2
Carter, Landon 1710-1778 .... DLB 31
Carter, Lief Hastings 1940- CANR-6
Earlier sketch in CA 57-60
Carter, (Bessie) Lillian (Gordy) 1898-1983 118
Obituary 111
Brief entry 105
Carter, Lin(wood Vrooman)
1930-1988 ....CANR-30
Earlier sketch in CA 41-44R
See also DLBY 81
Carter, Lonnie 1942- CANR-9
Earlier sketch in CA 65-68
Carter, Luther J(ordan) 1927- 57-60
Carter, M(argaret) L(ouise) 1948- 33-36R
Carter, Margaret (Mary) 1923- 107
Carter, Marilyn
See Ross, W(illiam) E(dward) D(aniel)
Carter, Martin (Wylde) 1927- 102
See also DLB 117
Carter, Mary CANR-5
Earlier sketch in CA 9-12R
Carter, Mary Ellen 1923- 25-28R
Carter, Mary Kennedy 65-68
Carter, Neil 1913- 17-20R
Carter, Nevada
See Paine, Lauran (Bosworth)
Carter, Nicholas
See Dey, Frederic (Merrill) Van Rensselaer
Carter, Nick
See Avallone, Michael (Angelo, Jr)
and Ballard, (Willis) Todhunter
and Crider, (Allen) Bill(y)
and Dey, Frederic (Merrill) Van Rensselaer
and Garside, (Clifford) Jack
and Hayes, Ralph E(ugene)
and Henderson, M(arilyn) R(uth)
and Lynds, Dennis
and Rasof, Henry
and Smith, Martin Cruz
and Stratemeyer, Edward L.
and Swain, Dwight V(reeland)
and Wallmann, Jeffrey M(iner)
Carter, Paul A(llen) 1926- CANR-13
Earlier sketch in CA 33-36R
Carter, Paul (Hugh) 1951- 129
Carter, Paul J(efferson) Jr. 1912-1975 ...... CAP-2
Earlier sketch in CA 21-22
Carter, Peter 1929- 69-72
See also SATA 57
Carter, Phyllis Ann
See Eberle, Irmengarde
Carter, Ralph
See Neubauer, William Arthur
Carter, Randolph 1914- 101
Carter, Richard D(uane) 1929- 111
Carter, Richard 1918- CANR-8
Earlier sketch in CA 61-64
Carter, Robert A(yres) 1923- 33-36R
Carter, Robert M(ack) 1925- 33-36R
Carter, Robert 1945- 128
Carter, Roger 1939- 119
Carter, (Eleanor) Rosalynn (Smith) 1927- 113
Carter, Rubin 1937- Brief entry 113
Carter, Samuel (Thomson) III 1904-1988 57-60
Obituary 127
See also SATA 37, 60
Carter, Sebastian 1941- 126
Carter, Steven 1956- 137
Carter, Thomas Earl 1947- 133
Carter, Tom
See Carter, Thomas Earl
Carter, Victor A(lbert) 1902- CAP-1
Earlier sketch in CA 9-10
Carter, William Ambrose 1899- CAP-1
Earlier sketch in CA 17-18
Carter, William Beverly Jr.
1921-1982 Obituary 110
Carter, William E. 1926-1983 ....17-20R
Obituary 110
See also SATA 1, 35
Carter, William Lee 1925- 1-4R
Carter, William 1934- 33-36R
Carter, Worrall Reed
1885(?)-1975 Obituary 57-60
Carterette, Edward C(alvin) 1921- 41-44R
Carter-Harrison, Paul
See Harrison, Paul Carter
Carter-Ruck, Peter F(rederick) 1914- 97-100
Cartey, Wilfred (George Onslow)
1931- CANR-25
Obituary 137
Earlier sketch in CA 73-76
See also BW
Carthy, Mother Mary Peter 1911- 13-16R
Cartier, Xam Wilson 1949(?)- 125
See also BW
Cartland, Barbara (Hamilton) 1901- CANR-34
Earlier sketches in CA 9-12R, CANR-6
See also CAAS 8
See also MTCW
Cartledge, Paul 1947- 124
Cartledge, Samuel Antoine 1903- 1-4R
Cartlidge, Barbara 1922- 121
Cartlidge, Michelle 1950- 93-96
See also SATA 37, 49
Cartnal, Alan 1950- 105
Cartner, William Carruthers 1910- 73-76
See also SATA 11
Carto, Willis A(llison) 1926- 114
Cartter, Allan Murray 1922-1976 ....CANR-8
Earlier sketch in CA 5-8R
Cartwright, Desmond S(pencer) 1924- 89-92
Cartwright, Gary 1934- 89-92
Cartwright, James McGregor
See Jennings, Leslie Nelson
Cartwright, Joseph H. 1939- 73-76
Cartwright, N.
See Scofield, Norma Margaret Cartwright
Cartwright, Reg(inald Ainsley) 1938- ...... SATA 64
Cartwright, Rosalind Dymond 1922- 81-84
Cartwright, Sally 1923- CANR-2
Earlier sketch in CA 49-52
See also SATA 9
Cartwright, Vanessa
See Preston, Harry
Cartwright, William H(olman) 1915- 9-12R
Carty, James William Jr. 1925- 53-56
Caruba, Alan 1937- 65-68
Caruso, Enrico 1873-1921 Brief entry 115
Caruso, John Anthony 1907- 33-36R
Carus-Wilson, Eleanora M(ary) 1897- 5-8R
Caruth, Donald L(ewis) 1935- 29-32R
Caruthers, Osgood 1915-1985 Obituary 117
Caruthers, William Alexander 1802-1846 .... DLB 3
Carvajal, Ricardo
See Meneses, Enrique
Carvalho-Neto, Paulo de 1923- CANR-4
Earlier sketch in CA 53-56
Carvell, Fred J. 1934- 29-32R
Carver, Dave
See Bingley, David Ernest
Carver, Frank G(ould) 1928- 49-52
Carver, Fred D(onald) 1936- 29-32R
Carver, Jeffrey A(llan) 1949- CANR-18
Earlier sketch in CA 101
Carver, John
See Gardner, Richard (M.)
Carver, Jonathan 1710-1780 .... DLB 31
Carver, (Richard) Michael (Power)
1915- CANR-14
Earlier sketch in CA 69-72
Carver, Norman F. Jr. 1928- 41-44R
Carver, Raymond 1938-1988 ....CANR-34
Obituary 126
Earlier sketches in CA 33-36R, CANR-17
See also CLC 22, 36, 53, 55
See also DLBY 84, 88
See also MTCW
See also SSC 8
Carver, Saxon Rowe 1905- CAP-1
Earlier sketch in CA 13-14
Carver, Terrell 1946- 133
Carvic, Heron 53-56
Obituary 103
Carwell, L'Ann
See McKissack, Patricia (L'Ann) C(arwell)
Cary
See Cary, Louis F(avreau)
Cary, Barbara Knapp
1912(?)-1975 Obituary 61-64
See also SATA 31
Cary, Bob 1921- 105
Cary, Diana Serra
See Cary, Peggy-Jean Montgomery
Cary, Falkland L. 1897-1989 Obituary 128
Cary, Harold Whiting 1903- CAP-1
Earlier sketch in CA 9-10
Cary, James Donald 1919- 5-8R
Cary, John H. 1926- 9-12R
Cary, (Arthur) Joyce (Lunel)
1888-1957 Brief entry 104
See also CDBLB 1914-1945
See also DLB 15, 100
See also TCLC 1, 29
Cary, Jud
See Tubb, E(dwin) C(harles)
Cary, Lee J(ames) 1925- 29-32R
Cary, Lorene 1956- 135
Cary, Louis F(avreau) 1915- .... SATA 9
Cary, Lucian 1886-1971 ....33-36R
Cary, Otis 1921- 61-64
Cary, Peggy-Jean Montgomery 1918- 57-60
Cary, Richard 1909- 21-24R
Cary, William L(ucius) 1910-1983 Obituary 109

Cary, Zenja Saft 1932(?)-1983 Obituary ... 110
Caryl, Jean
See Kaplan, Jean Caryl Korn
Caryl, Warren 1920- ... 21-24R
Casaccia, Gabriel
See Casaccia Bibolini, G(abriel)
Casaccia Bibolini, G(abriel) 1907- ... HW
Casada, James A(llen) 1942- ... 109
Casado, Pablo Gil 1931- ... 49-52
Casady, Cort (Boon) 1947- ... CANR-22
Earlier sketch in CA 105
Casady, Donald Rex 1926- ... 13-16R
Casalandra, Estelle
See Estelle, Sister Mary
Casale, Joan T(herese) 1935- ... 61-64
Casale, Ottavio M(ark) 1934- ... 104
Casals, Pablo
See Casals, Pau Carlos Salvador Defillo de
Casals, Pau Carlos Salvador Defillo de
1876-1973 ... 93-96
Obituary ... 45-48
Casares, Adolfo Bioy
See Bioy Casares, Adolfo
Casas, Penelope 1943- ... 114
Casberg, Bryan Victor 1939- ... CANR-29
Casberg, Melvin Augustus 1909- ... 104
Cascardi, Anthony J(oseph) 1953- ... 132
Cascio, Chuck 1946- ... 93-96
Casdorph, Herman Richard 1928- ... 101
Casdorph, Paul D(ouglas) 1932- ... 106
Case, Bill
See Case, Theodore Willard
Case, Brian (David) 1937- ... 25-28R
Case, David 1937- ... 107
Case, Elinor Rutt 1914- ... 1-4R
Case, Fred E. 1918- ... CANR-31
Earlier sketches in CA 5-8R, CANR-4
Case, Geoffrey ... 77-80
Case, Jack Gaylord 1918(?)-1970 Obituary ... 104
Case, John 1944- ... 114
Case, Josephine Young 1907-1990 ... CAP-2
Obituary ... 130
Earlier sketch in CA 25-28
Case, Justin
See Gleadow, Rupert Seeley
Case, L. L.
See Lewin, Leonard C(ase)
Case, Leland D(avidson) 1900- ... 17-20R
Case, Lynn M(arshall) 1903- ... 13-16R
Case, Marshal T(aylor) 1941- ... 57-60
See also SATA 9
Case, Maurice 1910-1968 ... CAP-2
Earlier sketch in CA 19-20
Case, Michael
See Howard, Robert West
Case, Patricia J(une) 1952- ... CANR-27
Earlier sketch in CA 110
Case, Theodore Willard 1920- ... 133
Case, Victoria 1897- ... 5-8R
Case, Walter 1909(?)-1983 Obituary ... 110
Casebier, Allan (Frank) 1934- ... 65-68
Casebier, Marjorie
See McCoy, Marjorie Casebier
Casebier, Virginia (Eleanor) 1918- ... 41-44R
Caseley, Judith 1951- ... 121
See also SATA 53
Caseleyr, Cam(ille Auguste Marie) 1909- ... CAP-1
Earlier sketch in CA 9-10
Casely-Hayford, J(oseph) E(phraim)
1866-1930 Brief entry ... 123
See also BLC 1
See also TCLC 24
Casement, Richard 1942-1982 Obituary ... 108
Casemore, Robert 1915- ... CANR-35
Earlier sketch in CA 73-76
Casewit, Curtis W(erner) 1922- ... CANR-21
Earlier sketches in CA 13-16R, CANR-6
See also SATA 4
Casey, Beatrice Vivian
1898(?)-1986 Obituary ... 120
Casey, Bill Harris 1930- ... 1-4R
Casey, Brigid 1950- ... CANR-28
Earlier sketch in CA 49-52
See also SATA 9
Casey, Daniel J(oseph) 1937- ... CANR-22
Earlier sketches in CA 57-60, CANR-6
Casey, Douglas R(obert) 1946- Brief entry ... 118
Casey, Edward Scott 1939- ... 102
Casey, Genevieve M(ary) 1916- ... CANR-39
Earlier sketch in CA 116
Casey, Gladys
See Grier, Barbara G(ene Damon)
Casey, Jack
See Casey, John
Casey, Jane Barnes 1942- ... 104
Casey, John (Dudley) 1939- ... CANR-23
Earlier sketch in CA 69-72
See also BEST 90:2
See also CLC 59
Casey, John 1950- ... 120
Casey, Juanita 1925- ... 49-52
See also DLB 14
Casey, Kevin 1940- ... 25-28R
Casey, Lawrence B. 1905-1977 ... 73-76
Obituary ... 69-72
Casey, Linda M. ... 136
Casey, Mart
See Casey, Michael T.
Casey, Michael T. 1922- ... 21-24R
Casey, Michael 1947- ... 65-68
See also CLC 2
See also DLB 5
Casey, Patrick
See Thurman, Wallace (Henry)
Casey, Richard Gardiner 1890-1976 ... 61-64
Obituary ... 65-68
Casey, Robert J(oseph)
1890-1962 Obituary ... 89-92
Casey, Rosemary Alice (Christmann)
1922- ... 5-8R
Casey, Rosemary 1904-1976 Obituary ... 65-68
Casey, Thomas Francis 1923- ... 13-16R
Casey, W. Wilson 1954- ... 107
Casey, Warren (Peter) 1935-1988 ... 101
Obituary ... 127
See also CLC 12
Casey, William J(oseph)
1913-1987 Obituary ... 122
Casey, William Van Etten 1914-1990 ... 57-60
Obituary ... 131
Casgrain, Therese F. 1896(?)-1981 ... 110
Obituary ... 108
Cash, Anthony 1933- ... 102
Cash, Arthur H(ill) 1922- Brief entry ... 110
Cash, Ellen Lewis Buell
1905-1989 Obituary ... 130
See also SATO 64
Cash, Grace (Savannah) 1915- ... 21-24R
Cash, Grady
See Cash, Grace (Savannah)
Cash, J(ames) Allan 1901- ... CANR-4
Earlier sketch in CA 5-8R
Cash, John R.
See Cash, Johnny
Cash, Johnny 1932- Brief entry ... 110
Cash, Joseph H(arper) 1927- ... 41-44R
Cash, Kevin (Richard) 1926-1985 ... 77-80
Obituary ... 115
Cash, Philip 1931- ... 106
Cash, Sebastian
See Smithells, Roger (William)
Cashdan, Linda 1942- ... 132
Cashen, Richard A(nthony) 1938- ... 112
Cashin, Edward J(oseph Jr.) 1927- ... CANR-9
Earlier sketch in CA 21-24R
Cashin, Edward L(awrence)
See Cashin, Edward J(oseph Jr.)
Cashin, James A. 1911-1982 ... CANR-10
Earlier sketch in CA 17-20R
Cashman, John
See Davis, Timothy Francis Tothill
Cashman, Paul Harrison 1924- ... 13-16R
Cashman, Sean Dennis 1943- ... 107
Cashmore, E. Ellis 1949- ... 116
Cashmore, Ernest
See Cashmore, E. Ellis
Casimir, H(endrik) B(rugt) G(erhard) 1909- ... 129
Casimir, Hendrik
See Casimir, H(endrik) B(rugt) G(erhard)
Caskey, John L. 1908- ... 13-16R
Casler, Lawrence (Ray) 1932- ... 49-52
Casmier, Adam A(nthony) 1934- ... 33-36R
Casmir, Fred L. 1928- ... 37-40R
Casner, A(ndrew) James 1907-1990 ... CANR-4
Obituary ... 132
Earlier sketch in CA 5-8R
Caso, Adolph 1934- ... CANR-7
Earlier sketch in CA 57-60
Casolaro, Daniel 1949- ... 114
Cason, Mabel Earp 1892-1965 ... CAP-1
Earlier sketch in CA 13-14
See also SATA 10
Casona, Alejandro
See Alvarez, Alejandro Rodriguez
See also CLC 49
Casotti, Fred 1923- ... 93-96
Caspari, Ernest W(olfgang) 1909- ... 41-44R
Caspary, Vera 1899-1987 ... CANR-9
Obituary ... 122
Earlier sketch in CA 13-16R
Casper, Barry M(ichael) 1939- ... 69-72
Casper, Bill Jr.
See Casper, William Earl Jr.
Casper, Billy
See Casper, William Earl Jr.
Casper, Henry W. 1909- ... 37-40R
Casper, Jonathan D(avid) 1942- ... 53-56
Casper, Joseph Andrew 1941- ... 65-68
Casper, Leonard Ralph 1923- ... 1-4R
Casper, Linda Ty
See Ty-Casper, Linda
Casper, William Earl Jr. 1931- ... 121
Casque, Sammy
See Davis, Sydney Charles Houghton
Casriel, H(arold) Daniel 1924-1983 ... 13-16R
Obituary ... 110
Cass, Carl Bartholomew 1901- ... CAP-1
Earlier sketch in CA 9-10
Cass, James (Michael) 1915- ... 101
Cass, Joan E(velyn) ... CANR-20
Earlier sketches in CA 1-4R, CANR-5
See also SATA 1
Cass, Ronald A(ndrew) 1949- ... 106
Cass, Zoe
See Low, Lois Dorothea
Cassady, Carolyn (Elizabeth Robinson)
1923- ... 133
See also DLB 16
Cassady, Claude
See Paine, Lauran (Bosworth)
Cassady, Neal 1926-1968 ... DLB 16
Cassady, Ralph Jr. 1900-1978 ... CANR-4
Obituary ... 77-80
Earlier sketch in CA 1-4R
Cassandra
See Connor, William (Neil)
Cassara, Ernest 1925- ... 41-44R
Cassata, Mary B. 1930- ... 121
Cassavant, Sharron Greer 1939- ... 125
Cassavetes, John 1929-1989 ... 85-88
Obituary ... 127
See also CLC 20
Cass-Beggs, Barbara 1904- ... SATA 62
Cassedy, James H(iggins) 1919- ... 1-4R
Cassedy, Sylvia 1930-1989 ... CANR-22
Earlier sketch in CA 105
See also CLR 26
See also SATA 27, 61
Cassel, Don 1942- ... CANR-28
Earlier sketch in CA 110
Cassel, Lili
See Wronker, Lili Cassel
Cassel, Mana-Zucca 1891-1981 Obituary ... 103
Cassel, Russell N. 1911- ... 37-40R
Cassel, Virginia Cunningham ... 105
Cassell, Anthony K. 1941- ... 120
Cassell, Eric J. 1928- ... 137
Cassell, Frank A(llan) 1941- ... 33-36R
Cassell, Frank Hyde 1916- ... 37-40R
Cassell, Joan 1929- ... 135
Cassell, Richard A(llan) 1921- ... 21-24R
Cassell, Sylvia 1924- ... 5-8R
Cassells, Cyrus (Curtis III) 1957- ... 112
Cassells, John
See Duncan, W(illiam) Murdoch
Casselman, Karen Leigh 1942- ... 107
Cassels, Alan 1929- ... CANR-13
Earlier sketch in CA 33-36R
Cassels, Louis 1922-1974 ... CANR-4
Obituary ... 45-48
Earlier sketch in CA 9-12R
Casserley, H(enry) C(yril) 1903- ... CANR-9
Earlier sketch in CA 65-68
Casserley, Julian Victor Langmead
1909-1978 ... 9-12R
Obituary ... 133
Casserly, John J(oseph) 1927- ... 120
Cassiday, Bruce (Bingham) 1920- ... CANR-19
Earlier sketches in CA 1-4R, CANR-4
Cassidy, Daniel J(ames) 1956- ... 119
Cassidy, Frederic Gomes 1907- ... 1-4R
Cassidy, George
See Vance, William E.
Cassidy, Harold G(omes) 1906- ... 25-28R
Cassidy, John A(lbert) 1908- ... 33-36R
Cassidy, John R(ufus) 1922- ... 89-92
Cassidy, John 1928- ... CANR-35
Earlier sketch in CA 114
Cassidy, Jude (Anne) 1955- ... 121
Cassidy, Michael 1936- ... 97-100
Cassidy, Richard J(oseph) 1942- ... 114
Cassidy, Vincent H. 1923- ... 21-24R
Cassidy, William L(awrence Robert) ... 103
Cassilis, Robert
See Edwardes, Michael (F. H.)
Cassill, Kay ... 89-92
Cassill, R(onald) V(erlin) 1919- ... CANR-7
Earlier sketch in CA 9-12R
See also CAAS 1
See also CLC 4, 23
See also DLB 6
Cassils, Peter
See Keele, Kenneth D(avid)
Cassin, Rene Samuel
1887-1976 Obituary ... 65-68
Cassinelli, C(harles) W(illiam Jr.) 1925- ... 1-4R
Cassini, Igor (Loiewski) 1915- ... 129
Cassity, (Allen) Turner 1929- ... CANR-11
Earlier sketch in CA 17-20R
See also CAAS 8
See also CLC 6, 42
See also DLB 105
Casso, Evans J(oseph) 1914- ... 57-60
Cassola, Albert M(aria) 1915- ... CAP-1
Earlier sketch in CA 9-10
Cassola, Carlo 1917-1987 ... 101
Obituary ... 121
Casson, Hugh Maxwell 1910- ... CANR-36
Earlier sketches in CA 103, CANR-20
See also SATA 65
Casson, Lionel 1914- ... CANR-3
Earlier sketch in CA 9-12R
Casstevens, Thomas W(illiam) 1937- ... 17-20R
Cast, David (Jesse Dale) 1942- ... 109
Castagna, Edwin 1909-1983 ... CAP-2
Obituary ... 111
Earlier sketch in CA 17-18
Castagnola, Lawrence A. 1933- ... CANR-12
Earlier sketch in CA 29-32R
Castaneda, Carlos 1931(?)- ... CANR-32
Earlier sketch in CA 25-28R
See also CLC 12
See also HW
See also MTCW
Castaneda, Hector-Neri 1924- ... CANR-19
Earlier sketches in CA 5-8R, CANR-3
Castaneda, James A(gustin) 1933- ... 41-44R
Castaneda, Omar S. 1954- ... 135
See also SATA 71
Castedo, Elena 1937- ... 132
See also CLC 65
Castedo-Ellerman, Elena
See Castedo, Elena
Castel, Albert 1928- ... CANR-5
Earlier sketch in CA 1-4R
Castel, J(ean) G(abriel) 1928- ... CANR-25
Earlier sketches in CA 21-24R, CANR-9
Castel, Robert 1933- ... 129
Casteleyn, Mary (Teresa) 1941- ... 131
Castellan, N(orman) John Jr. 1939- ... 37-40R
Castellaneta, Carlo 1930- ... CANR-11
Earlier sketch in CA 13-16R
Castellano, Giuseppe
1893-1977 Obituary ... 73-76
Castellanos, Jane Mollie Robinson 1913- ... 9-12R
See also SATA 9
Castellanos, Rosario 1925-1974 ... 131
Obituary ... 53-56
See also CLC 66
See also DLB 113
See also HW
Castellon, Federico 1914-1971 ... SATA 48
Castells, Manuel 1942- ... CANR-37
Earlier sketch in CA 115
Castells, Matilde O(livella) 1929- ... 69-72
Castelnuovo-Tedesco, P(ietro) 1925- ... 21-24R
Castetter, William Benjamin 1914- ... CANR-4
Earlier sketch in CA 1-4R
Castile, Rand 1938- ... 138
Castillo, Ana (Hernandez Del) 1953- ... 131
See also HW
Castillo, Debra A(nn Garsow) 1953- ... 136
Castillo, Edmund L. 1924- ... 29-32R
See also SATA 1
Castillo, Richard Griswold del
See Griswold del Castillo, Richard
Castillo Puche, Jose Luis 1919- Brief entry ... 110
Castle, Anthony (Percy) 1938- ... CANR-32
Earlier sketch in CA 113
Castle, Barbara (Anne) 1910- ... 130
Castle, Charles 1939- ... 33-36R
Castle, Coralie 1924- ... 57-60
Castle, Damon
See Smith, Richard Rein
Castle, Edgar Bradshaw
1897-1973 Obituary ... 104
Castle, Emery N(eal) 1923- ... 1-4R
Castle, Frances
See Leader, (Evelyn) Barbara (Blackburn)
Castle, Frederick Ted 1938- ... 137
Castle, Kate ... 123
Castle, Keith 1927(?)-1985 Obituary ... 118
Castle, Lee
See Ogan, George F.
and Ogan, Margaret E. (Nettles)
Castle, Leonard L. 1912(?)-1989 ... 129
Castle, Marian (Johnson) ... CAP-2
Earlier sketch in CA 17-18
Castle, Mort 1946- ... CANR-14
Earlier sketch in CA 81-84
Castle, Paul
See Howard, Vernon (Linwood)
Castle, Robert
See Hamilton, Edmond
Castle, Robert W. Jr. 1929- ... 25-28R
Castle, Sue G(aronzik) 1942- ... 105
Castle, Terry (Jacqueline) 1953- ... 112
Castle, Tony
See Castle, Anthony (Percy)
Castle, William 1914-1977 ... 77-80
Obituary ... 69-72
Castleden, Rodney 1945- ... 138
Castleman, Harry 1953- ... 109
Castleman, Michael 1950- ... 108
Castleman, (Esther) Riva 1930- ... 128
Brief entry ... 117
Castlemon, Harry
See Fosdick, Charles Austin
Castles, Francis G(eoffrey) 1943- ... CANR-17
Earlier sketch in CA 25-28R
Castles, Lance 1937- ... 25-28R
Castleton, Virginia 1925- ... 49-52
Castor, Grahame (Douglas) 1932- ... CANR-7
Earlier sketch in CA 13-16R
Castor, Henry 1909- ... 17-20R
Castoriadis, Cornelius 1922- ... 138
Castoro, Laura A(nn) 1948- ... 124
Castro, Americo 1885-1972 ... 37-40R
Castro, Antonio 1946- ... 53-56
Castro, Jan Garden 1945- ... 120
Castro, Michael 1945- ... 132
Castro (Ruz), Fidel 1926(?)- ... 129
Brief entry ... 110
Castro, Tony
See Castro, Antonio
Castro (y Quesada), Americo 1885-1972 ... HW
Castro-Klaren, Sara 1942- ... 61-64
Castronovo, David 1945- ... CANR-35
Earlier sketch in CA 114
Casty, Alan Howard 1929- ... CANR-4
Earlier sketch in CA 1-4R
Caswall, Edward 1814-1878 ... DLB 32
Caswell, Helen (Rayburn) 1923- ... 33-36R
See also SATA 12
Caswell, Margaret (Betsy) R(oss)
1903(?)-1982 Obituary ... 107
Catala, Rafael 1942- ... CANR-32
Earlier sketches in CA 73-76, CANR-13
See also HW
Catalano, Donald B(ernard) 1920- ... 57-60
Catalano, Joseph S(tellario) 1928- ... 102
Catalano, Stephen 1952- ... 135
Catalanotto, Peter 1959- ... 138
See also SATA 70
Cataldo, Michael F. 1947- ... 122
Catanese, Anthony James (Jr.) 1942- ... CANR-32
Earlier sketches in CA 29-32R, CANR-14
Catania, A(nthony) Charles 1936- ... 37-40R
Catanzariti, John 1942- ... 124
Cate, Benjamin W(ilson) 1931- ... 73-76
Cate, Curtis Wolsey 1884-1976 Obituary ... 61-64
Cate, Curtis 1924- ... CANR-9
Earlier sketch in CA 53-56
Cate, Dick
See Cate, Richard Edward Nelson
Cate, Richard Edward Nelson 1932- ... 73-76
See also SATA 28
Cate, Robert L(ouis) 1932- ... CANR-28
Earlier sketch in CA 111
Cate, William Burke 1924- ... 13-16R
Cateora, Philip Rene 1932- ... 5-8R
Cater, (Silas) Douglass 1923- ... CANR-1
Earlier sketch in CA 1-4R

Cates, Jo A. 1958- 134
Cates, Ray A. Jr. 1940- 29-32R
Cates, Tory
See Bird, Sarah McCabe
Cateura, Linda Brandi 1924- 135
Cathcart, Helen CANR-2
Earlier sketch in CA 5-8R
Cathcart, Noble Aydelotte
1898-1988 Obituary 126
Cathcart, Robert S(tephen) 1923- 101
Cather, Willa
See Cather, Willa Sibert
Cather, Willa Sibert 1873-1947 128
Brief entry 104
See also CDALB 1865-1917
See also CLC 1, 11, 31
See also DLB 9, 54, 78
See also DLBD 1
See also MTCW
See also SATA 30
See also SSC 2
See also TCLC 1, 11, 31
See also WLC
Catherall, Arthur 1906- CANR-38
Earlier sketch in CA 5-8R
See also MAICYA
See also SATA 3
Cathers, David M. 1941- 111
Cathers, Ken 1951- 112
Catherwood, (Henry) Frederick (Ross)
1925- 106
Catherwood, Mary Hartwell 1847-1902 .... DLB 78
Cathey, Cornelius Oliver 1908- 1-4R
Cathon, Laura E(lizabeth) 1908- 5-8R
See also SATA 27
Catledge, Turner 1901-1983 57-60
Obituary 109
See also AITN 1
Catlin, George E(dward) G(ordon)
1896-1979 ....13-16R
Obituary 85-88
Catlin, Warren Benjamin 1881-1968 ....1-4R
Obituary 103
Catlin, Wynelle 1930- 65-68
See also SATA 13
Catling, Darrel (Charles) 1909- 5-8R
Catling, Patrick Skene 1925- Brief entry 115
Catlow, Joanna
See Lowry, Joan (Catlow)
Cato
See Howard, Peter D(unsmore)
Cato, Nancy (Fotheringham) 1917- CAP-1
Earlier sketch in CA 49-52
Catoir, John T. 1931- CANR-11
Earlier sketch in CA 25-28R
Caton, Charles E(dwin) 1928- 9-12R
Caton, Hiram P. 1936- CANR-4
Earlier sketch in CA 53-56
Caton-Thompson, Gertrude 1888-1985 122
Obituary 116
Catran, Jack 1933- 128
Catron, Louis E. 1932- 45-48
Cattan, Henry 1906- 29-32R
Cattaui, Georges 1896-1974 .... CAP-2
Earlier sketch in CA 25-28
Cattell, Everett L(ewis) 1905- 1-4R
Cattell, Psyche 1893- 41-44R
Cattell, Raymond Bernard 1905- CANR-2
Earlier sketch in CA 5-8R
Catterall, Peter 1961- 134
Catto, Max(well Jeffrey) 1909(?)-1992 105
Obituary 137
Catton, (Charles) Bruce 1899-1978 ....CANR-7
Obituary 81-84
Earlier sketch in CA 5-8R
See also AITN 1
See also CLC 35
See also DLB 17
See also SATA 2, 24
Catton, William Bruce 1926- CANR-1
Earlier sketch in CA 1-4R
Catton, William R(obert) Jr. 1926- 109
Catudal, Honore M(arc Jr.) 1944- CANR-12
Earlier sketch in CA 69-72
Catz, Max
See Glaser, Milton
Caudell, Marian 1930- 121
See also SATA 52
Caudill, Harry M(onroe) 1922-1990 ....CANR-14
Obituary 133
Earlier sketch in CA 33-36R
Caudill, Rebecca 1899-1985 ....CANR-2
Obituary 117
Earlier sketch in CA 5-8R
See also MAICYA
See also SATA 1, 44
Caudill, William W(ayne)
1914-1983 Obituary 110
Caudle, Neil 1952- 132
Caudwell, Christopher
See Sprigg, C(hristopher) St. John
Cauffiel, Lowell 1951- 132
Cauffield, Margaret E(ileen) 1932- 122
Caughey, John L(yon) 1941- 115
Caughey, John Walton 1902- Brief entry 106
Caulder, Colline 1945- 113
Cauldwell, Frank
See King, Francis (Henry)
Cauley, John R(owan)
1908-1976 Obituary 65-68
Cauley, Lorinda Bryan 1951- 101
See also SATA 43, 46
Cauley, Terry
See Cauley, Troy Jesse
Cauley, Troy Jesse 1902- CANR-1
Earlier sketch in CA 1-4R
Caulfield, Malachy Francis 1915- CANR-14
Earlier sketch in CA 77-80
Caulfield, Max
See Caulfield, Malachy Francis
Caulfield, Peggy F. 1926-1987 ....5-8R
Obituary 123
See also SATA 53
Caulfield, Sean 1925- 108
Cauliflower, Sebastian
See Seldes, Gilbert (Vivian)
Cauman, Samuel 1910-1971 .... CAP-2
Earlier sketch in CA 23-24
See also SATA 48
Caunitz, William J. 1933- 130
Brief entry 125
See also BEST 89:3
See also CLC 34
Causley, Charles (Stanley) 1917- CANR-35
Earlier sketches in CA 9-12R, CANR-5
See also CLC 7
See also DLB 27
See also MTCW
See also SATA 3, 66
Caute, David 1936- CANR-33
Earlier sketches in CA 1-4R, CANR-1
See also CAAS 4
See also CLC 29
See also DLB 14
Cautela, Joseph R(ichard) 1927- 106
Cauthen, Baker James 1909-1985 Obituary 115
Cauthen, Irby Bruce Jr. 1919- 111
Cauthen, W(ilfred) Kenneth 1930- CANR-7
Earlier sketch in CA 5-8R
Cauvin, Jean-Pierre (Bernard) 1936- 116
Cauwels, Janice M(arie) 1949- 110
Cava, Esther Laden 1916- 37-40R
Cavafy, C(onstantine) P(eter)
See Kavafis, Konstantinos Petrou
See also TCLC 2, 7
Cavaiani, Mabel 1919- CANR-21
Earlier sketches in CA 57-60, CANR-6
Cavalcanti, Alberto (de Almeida)
1897-1982 Obituary 107
Cavalier, Julian 1931- CANR-2
Earlier sketch in CA 49-52
Cavaliero, Glen 1927- CANR-29
Earlier sketches in CA 73-76, CANR-13
Cavallari, Alberto 1927- CANR-10
Earlier sketch in CA 21-24R
Cavallaro, Ann (Abelson) 1918- 5-8R
See also SATA 62
Cavalletti, Sofia 1917- 130
Cavallo, Diana 1931- CANR-2
Earlier sketch in CA 1-4R
See also SATA 7
Cavallo, Evelyn
See Spark, Muriel (Sarah)
Cavallo, Robert M. 1932- CANR-10
Earlier sketch in CA 65-68
Cavan, Romilly 1914(?)-1975 Obituary 61-64
Cavan, Sherri 1938- 17-20R
Cavanagh, Gerald F(rancis) 1931- 41-44R
Cavanagh, Helen (Carol) 1939- 104
See also SATA 37, 48
Cavanagh, John B. 1908-1983 Obituary 110
Cavanagh, John Richard 1904- CAP-2
Earlier sketch in CA 19-20
Cavanagh, Richard E(dward) 1946- 121
Cavanah, Frances 1899-1982 ....13-16R
Obituary 133
See also SATA 1, 31
Cavanaugh, Arthur 1926- 17-20R
Cavani, Liliana 1936- 110
Cavanna, Betty
See Harrison, Elizabeth Cavanna
See also CLC 12
See also MAICYA
See also SAAS 4
See also SATA 1, 30
Cavanna, Elizabeth Allen
See Harrison, Elizabeth Cavanna
Cave, Alfred A. 1935- 37-40R
Cave, (John) David 1957- 138
Cave, Hugh Barnett 1910- CANR-2
Earlier sketch in CA 5-8R
Cave, Roderick (George James Munro)
1935- CANR-2
Earlier sketch in CA 5-8R
Cave, Thomas
See Steward, Samuel M(orris)
Cavell, Stanley (Louis) 1926- CANR-11
Earlier sketch in CA 61-64
Cavelti, Peter C(hristian) 1948- 116
Cavendish, J(ean) M(avis) 1932- 118
Cavendish, Richard 1930- CANR-20
Earlier sketches in CA 9-12R, CANR-5
Caveney, Philip (Richard) 1951- CANR-19
Earlier sketch in CA 102
Caverhill, Nicholas
See Kirk-Greene, Anthony (Hamilton Millard)
Caverhill, William Melville
1910-1983 Obituary 111
Cavers, David F(arquhar) 1902-1988 ....17-20R
Obituary 125
Cavert, Samuel McCrea 1888-1976 ....37-40R
Cavert, Walter Dudley 1891- 1-4R
Caves, Richard E(arl) 1931- CANR-19
Earlier sketches in CA 1-4R, CANR-4
Cavett, Dick
See Cavett, Richard A.
Cavett, Richard A. 1936- 108
Cavin, Ruth (Brodie) 1918- CANR-8
Earlier sketch in CA 61-64
See also SATA 38
Cavitch, David 1933- 29-32R
Cavnes, Max P(arvin) 1922- 9-12R
Cavoukian, Raffi 1948- 136
See also SATA 68
Cavrell, Jean 1927- 107
Cawein, Madison 1865-1914 .... DLB 54
Cawelti, John G(eorge) 1929- 21-24R
Cawley, Linda 1949- 113
Cawley, Robert Ralston 1893-1973 .... CAP-2
Obituary 41-44R
Earlier sketch in CA 21-22
Cawley, Winifred 1915- 69-72
See also SATA 13
Cawood, John W. 1931- 33-36R
Caws, Ian 1945- 118
Caws, Mary Ann 1933- CANR-31
Earlier sketches in CA 25-28R, CANR-10
Caws, Peter (James) 1931- CANR-8
Earlier sketch in CA 17-20R
Cawthorne, Graham
1906(?)-1980 Obituary 97-100
Cawthorne, Nigel 1951- 136
Caxton, Pisistratus
See Lytton, Edward G(eorge) E(arle) L(ytton)
Bulwer-Lytton Baron
Cayce, Edgar E(vans) 1918- 21-24R
Cayce, Hugh Lynn 1907-1982 ....CANR-34
Obituary 107
Earlier sketch in CA 25-28R
Cayley, Michael (Forde) 1950- 53-56
Cayrol, Jean 1911- 89-92
See also CLC 11
See also DLB 83
Cayton, Andrew R(obert) L(ee) 1954- 126
Cayton, Horace R(oscoe) 1903-1970 .... CAP-1
Obituary 29-32R
Earlier sketch in CA 13-14
Cayton, Mary Kupiec 1954- 137
Cazalet-Keir, Thelma 1900(?)-1989 ....25-28R
Obituary 127
Cazamian, Louis Francois
1877-1965 Obituary 93-96
Cazden, Elizabeth 1950- 65-68
Cazden, Norman 1914- 37-40R
Cazden, Robert E. 1930- 33-36R
Cazeau, Charles J(ay) 1931- 104
See also SATA 65
Cazeaux, Isabelle 1926- 53-56
Cazel, Fred A(ugustus) Jr. 1921- 9-12R
Cazelles, Brigitte Jacqueline 1944- 102
Cazemajou, Jean 1924- 73-76
Cazet, Denys 1938- 108
See also SATA 41, 52
Cazzola, Gus 1934- 108
Ceadel, Martin (Eric) 1948- 128
Cebula, Richard J(ohn) 1944- 111
Cebulash, Mel 1937- CANR-30
Earlier sketches in CA 29-32R, CANR-12
See also SATA 10
Cecchetti, Giovanni 1922- Brief entry 107
Cecelski, Elizabeth 1953- 119
Cech, John O(tto) 1944- 120
Cecil, (Edward Christian) David (Gascoyne)
1902-1986 ....CANR-34
Obituary 118
Earlier sketches in CA 61-64, CANR-13
Cecil, Henry
See Leon, Henry Cecil
Cecil, Hugh Mortimer
See Roberts, William
Cecil, Lamar (John Ryan Jr.) 1932- 21-24R
Cecil, Lord David
See Cecil, (Edward Christian) David (Gascoyne)
Cecil, R. H.
See Hewitt, Cecil Rolph
Cecil, Robert 1913- 53-56
Ceder, Georgiana Dorcas 1-4R
See also SATA 10
Cefkin, J. Leo 1916- 25-28R
Cegielka, Francis A(nthony) 1908- 37-40R
Ceitho, Dewi
See Jones, Evan David
Cejka, Jaroslav 1943- 132
Cela, Camilo Jose 1916- CANR-32
Earlier sketches in CA 21-24R, CANR-21
See also CAAS 10
See also BEST 90:2
See also CLC 4, 13, 59
See also DLBY 89
See also HW
See also MTCW
Celaeno
See Harper, George W(illiam)
Celan, Paul
See Antschel, Paul
See also CLC 53
See also DLB 69
Celaya, Gabriel 1911-1991 .... DLB 108
Celeste, Sister Marie CANR-30
Earlier sketch in CA 49-52
Celestino, Martha Laing 1951- 107
See also SATA 39
Celine, Louis-Ferdinand
See Destouches, Louis-Ferdinand
See also CLC 1, 3, 4, 7, 9, 15, 47
See also DLB 72
Celizic, Mike 1948- 135
Cell, Edward (Charles) 1928- 21-24R
Cell, John W(hitson) 1935- 41-44R
Cellario, Alberto R. 1910(?)-1984 Obituary 112
Celler, Emanuel 1888-1981 Obituary 108
Celnik, Max 1933- 17-20R
Celoria, Francis (S. C.) 1926- 102
Cemach, Harry P(aul) 1917- 57-60
Cenci, Louis 1918- 17-20R
Cendrars, Blaise
See Sauser-Hall, Frederic
Censer, Jane T(urner) 1951- 123
Cente, H. F.
See Rocklin, Ross Louis
Center, Allen Harry 1912- CANR-4
Earlier sketch in CA 5-8R
Centlivre, Susanna 1669(?)-1723 .... DLB 84
Cento
See Cobbing, Bob
Centore, F. F. 1938- 25-28R
Ceram, C. W.
See Marek, Kurt W(illi)
Ceravolo, Joseph 1934-1988 102
Obituary 126
Cerf, Bennett (Alfred) 1898-1971 .... CAP-2
Obituary 29-32R
Earlier sketch in CA 19-20
See also SATA 7
Cerf, Christopher (Bennett) 1941- 25-28R
See also SATA 2
Cerf, Jay H(enry) 1923-1974 .... CAP-2
Obituary 53-56
Earlier sketch in CA 19-20
Cerling, Charles (Edward) Jr. 1943- 111
Cermak, Laird S(cott) 1942- CANR-4
Earlier sketch in CA 53-56
Cermak, Martin
See Duchacek, Ivo D(uka)
Cerminara, Gina 17-20R
Cerney, James Vincent 1914- 21-24R
Cernuda (y Bidon), Luis 1902-1963 131
Obituary 89-92
See also CLC 54
See also HW
Cerra, Frances 1946- 97-100
Cerri, Lawrence J. 1923- CANR-17
Earlier sketch in CA 89-92
Cerruti, James Smith 1918- 103
Certner, Simon 1909(?)-1979 Obituary 89-92
Cerutti, Maria Antonietta 1932- 25-28R
Cerutti, Toni
See Cerutti, Maria Antonietta
Cerutty, Percy Wells 1895-1975 .... CAP-2
Obituary 61-64
Earlier sketch in CA 25-28
Cervantes, Alfonso J(uan)
1920-1983 Obituary 110
Cervantes, Lorna Dee 1954- 131
See also DLB 82
See also HW
Cervantes, Lucius F. 1914- 13-16R
Cervantes (Saavedra), Miguel de
1547-1616 ....WLC
Cerveri, Doris 1914- 101
Cervon, Jacqueline
See Moussard, Jacqueline
Cerwinske, Laura 1948- 111
Cerych, Ladislav 1925- CANR-7
Earlier sketch in CA 13-16R
Cesaire, Aime (Fernand) 1913- CANR-24
Earlier sketch in CA 65-68
See also BLC 1
See also BW
See also CLC 19, 32
See also MTCW
Cesara, Manda
See Poewe, Karla
Cetin, Frank Stanley 1921- 1-4R
See also SATA 2
Cetron, Marvin Jerome 1930- 107
Cetta, Lewis T(homas) 1933- 53-56
Cevasco, George A(nthony) 1924- CANR-2
Earlier sketch in CA 5-8R
Chabe, Alexander M(ichael) 1923- 53-56
Chaber, M. E.
See Crossen, Kendell Foster
Chabod, Federico 1901-1960 Obituary 116
Chabon, Michael 1965(?)- .... CLC 55
Chabrol, Claude 1930- 110
See also CLC 16
Chace, Isobel
See de Guise, Elizabeth (Mary Teresa)
Chace, James (Clarke) 1931- CANR-30
Earlier sketches in CA 1-4R, CANR-1
Chace, William M(urdough) 1938- 69-72
Chacholiades, Miltiades 1937- CANR-1
Earlier sketch in CA 45-48
Chacko, David 1942- CANR-31
Earlier sketch in CA 49-52
Chacko, George K(uttickal) 1930- CANR-13
Earlier sketch in CA 73-76
Chacon, Eusebio 1869-1948 131
See also DLB 82
See also HW
Chacon, Felipe Maximiliano 1873- .... DLB 82
Chaconas, D(oris) J. 1938- 21-24R
Chadbourne, Richard M(cClain) 1922- 21-24R
Chadeayne, Lee 1933- 53-56
Chadourne, Marc 1896(?)-1975 Obituary 53-56
Chadwick, Bruce A(lbert) 1940- 97-100
Chadwick, Henry 1920- CANR-25
Earlier sketches in CA 21-24R, CANR-9
Chadwick, James 1891-1974 Obituary 49-52
Chadwick, Janet (Bachand) 1933- 97-100
Chadwick, (Gerald William St.) John
1915- 25-28R
Chadwick, John 1920- 1-4R
Chadwick, Lee 1909- 69-72
Chadwick, Lester CANR-27
Earlier sketches in CAP-2, CA 19-20
See also SATA 1, 67
Chadwick, Margaret Lee (Gill)
1893-1984 Obituary 112
Chadwick, Nora Kershaw 1891-1972 .... CAP-1
Earlier sketch in CA 13-16
Chadwick, (William) Owen 1916- CANR-19
Earlier sketches in CA 1-4R, CANR-1
Chadwick, Ronald P(aul) 1935- 116
Chadwick, Whitney 1943- 132
Chadwin, Mark Lincoln 1939- CANR-17
Earlier sketch in CA 25-28R
Chaet, Bernard 1924- 69-72
Chafe, Wallace L. 1927- 29-32R

Chafe, William H(enry) 1942- CANR-12
Earlier sketch in CA 49-52
Chafets, Ze'ev 1947(?)- 137
Chafets, Zev
See Chafets, Ze'ev
Chafetz, Henry 1916-1978 ....CANR-3
Obituary 73-76
Earlier sketch in CA 1-4R
Chafetz, Janet Saltzman 1942- 69-72
Chafetz, Morris E(dward) 1924- CANR-5
Earlier sketch in CA 13-16R
Chaffee, Allen CAP-1
Earlier sketch in CA 9-10
See also SATA 3
Chaffee, John 1946- 85-88
Chaffee, Steven Henry 1935- 106
Chaffin, Lillie D(orton) 1925- CANR-13
Earlier sketch in CA 33-36R
See also SATA 4
Chaffin, Yule M. 1914- 21-24R
Chafin, Andrew 1937- 53-56
Chagall, David 1930- CANR-3
Earlier sketch in CA 9-12R
Chagall, Marc 1887-1985 122
Obituary 114
Chagla, M(ohamedali) C(urrim)
1900-1981 Obituary 108
Chagnon, Napoleon A. 1938- 130
Chai, Chen kang 1916- 21-24R
Chai, Ch'u 1906- 9-12R
Chai, Hon-chan 1931- 21-24R
Chai, Winberg 1932- CANR-9
Earlier sketch in CA 5-8R
Chaij, Fernando 1909- CANR-8
Earlier sketch in CA 21-24R
Chaikin, Miriam 1928- CANR-14
Earlier sketch in CA 81-84
See also SATA 24
Chais, Pamela (Herbert) 1930- 73-76
Chaisson, Eric (Joseph) 1946- CANR-25
Earlier sketch in CA 108
Chajkowsky, William E(ugene) 1938- 116
Chakerian, Charles (Garabed) 1904- 45-48
Chakour, Charles M. 1929- 33-36R
Chakravarty, Amiya (Chandra) 1901- CANR-1
Earlier sketch in CA 1-4R
Chakravarty, Birendra Narayan
1904-1980(?) 102
Chalfant, Edward Allan 1921- 111
Chalfont, Alun
See Jones, (Alun) Arthur Gwynne
Chalhoub, Michael 1932- 89-92
Chalidze, Valery Nikolaevich 1938- 103
Chalk, John Allen 1937- 57-60
Chalk, Ocania 1927- CANR-1
Earlier sketch in CA 45-48
Chalker, Jack L(aurence) 1944- 73-76
Chall, Jeanne S(ternlicht) 1921- CANR-10
Earlier sketch in CA 25-28R
Challand, Helen J(ean) 1921- 121
Brief entry 118
See also SATA 64
Challans, Mary 1905-1983 81-84
Obituary 111
See also Renault, Mary
See also SATA 23, 36
Challice, Kenneth
See Hutchin, Kenneth Charles
Challinor, John 1894- 73-76
Challis, Chris 131
Challis, George
See Faust, Frederick (Shiller)
Challoner, H. K.
See Mills, J(anet) M(elanie) A(ilsa)
Challoner, Robert
See Butterworth, Michael
Chalmers, David Mark 1927- 25-28R
Chalmers, Eric Brownlie 1929- 102
Chalmers, Floyd S(herman) 1898- CAP-2
Earlier sketch in CA 25-28
Chalmers, George 1742-1825 ....DLB 30
Chalmers, Harvey II
1890-1971 Obituary 33-36R
Chalmers, John W. 1910- 93-96
Chalmers, Malcolm 1956- 120
Chalmers, Mary (Eileen) 1927- 5-8R
See also SAAS 14
See also SATA 6
Chalmers, Penny
See Kemp, Penny
Chalon, Jean 1935- CANR-16
Earlier sketch in CA 97-100
Chalon, Jon
See Chaloner, John Seymour
Chaloner, John Seymour 1924- 93-96
Chaloner, W. H.
See Chaloner, William Henry
Chaloner, William Henry
1914-1987 Obituary 122
Chamberlain, Anne 1917- 77-80
Chamberlain, Betty 1908-1983 ....33-36R
Obituary 109
Chamberlain, Elinor 1901- CAP-1
Earlier sketch in CA 13-16
Chamberlain, Elwyn M. 1928- 131
Chamberlain, Ena
See Cooper, Penny
Chamberlain, Houston Stewart
1855-1927(?) Brief entry 120
Chamberlain, John (Rensselaer) 1903- 57-60
Chamberlain, Jonathan Mack 1928- 101
Chamberlain, Joseph Miles 1923- 107
Chamberlain, Lesley 1951- 137
Chamberlain, Margaret 1954- ....SATA 46
Chamberlain, Mary (Christina) 1947- 115
Chamberlain, Muriel Evelyn 1932- CANR-16
Earlier sketch in CA 93-96
Chamberlain, Narcisse 1924- 13-16R
Chamberlain, Neil Wolverton 1915- CANR-6
Earlier sketch in CA 13-16R
Chamberlain, (Arthur) Neville
1869-1940 Brief entry 113
Chamberlain, Robert Lyall 1923- 13-16R
Chamberlain, Samuel S. 1851-1916 ....DLB 25
Chamberlain, Samuel 1895-1975 ....CAP-2
Obituary 53-56
Earlier sketch in CA 23-24
Chamberlain, Wilson
See Crandall, Norma
Chamberlain, Wilt(on Norman) 1936- 103
Chamberland, Paul 1939- ....DLB 60
Chamberlin, E(ric) R(ussell) 1926- CANR-19
Earlier sketch in CA 97-100
Chamberlin, Enid C. S.
1900(?)-1982(?) Obituary 106
Chamberlin, J. E(ward) 1943- 85-88
Chamberlin, J(ohn) Gordon 1914- CANR-4
Earlier sketch in CA 1-4R
Chamberlin, Judi 1944- 81-84
Chamberlin, Lee
See La Pallo, A. Elise
Chamberlin, Leslie J(oseph) 1926- 53-56
Chamberlin, M. Hope 1920-1974 45-48
Obituary 49-52
Chamberlin, Mary 1914- 45-48
Chamberlin, Waldo 1905- 65-68
Chamberlin, William Henry 1897-1969 ....5-8R
See also DLB 29
Chambers, Aidan 1934- CANR-31
Earlier sketches in CA 25-28R, CANR-12
See also CLC 35
See also MAICYA
See also SAAS 12
See also SATA 1, 69
Chambers, Anne 1949- 126
Chambers, Anthony H(ood) 1943- 108
Chambers, Bradford 1922-1984 Obituary 113
See also SATA 39
Chambers, Catherine E.
See St. John, Nicole
Chambers, Charles Haddon
1860-1921 Brief entry 110
See also DLB 10
Chambers, Clarke A(lexander) 1921- 41-44R
Chambers, Colin 1950- 134
Chambers, Dewey W. 1929- CANR-12
Earlier sketch in CA 29-32R
Chambers, Edward J(ames) 1925- 17-20R
Chambers, Frances 1940- CANR-29
Earlier sketch in CA 111
Chambers, Frank P(entland) 1900- CAP-1
Earlier sketch in CA 9-10
Chambers, Howard V.
See Lowenkopf, Shelly A(lan)
Chambers, Iain 1949- 126
Chambers, James 1948- Brief entry 124
See also Cliff, Jimmy
Chambers, Jane 1937-1983 85-88
Obituary 109
Chambers, Jessie
See Lawrence, D(avid) H(erbert Richards)
Chambers, John W. 1933- 124
See also SATA 46, 57
Chambers, John Whiteclay II 1936- 137
Chambers, Jonathan David 1898-1970 ......CANR-3
Earlier sketch in CA 1-4R
Chambers, Kate
See St. John, Nicole
Chambers, Lenoir 1891-1970 111
Obituary 104
Chambers, Lucille Arcola
1909(?)-1988 Obituary 125
Chambers, M(erritt) M(adison) 1899- CANR-5
Earlier sketch in CA 9-12R
Chambers, Margaret Ada Eastwood
1911- 9-12R
See also SATA 2
Chambers, Mortimer Hardin Jr. 1927- CANR-6
Earlier sketch in CA 9-12R
Chambers, Peggy
See Chambers, Margaret Ada Eastwood
Chambers, Peter
See Phillips, D(ennis) J(ohn Andrew)
Chambers, R(aymond) J(ohn) 1917- 17-20R
Chambers, Robert W. 1865-1933 ....TCLC 41
Chambers, Robin Bernard 1942- 103
Chambers, W(illiam) Walker 1913- 29-32R
Chambers, (David) Whittaker
1901-1961 Obituary 89-92
Chambers, William E. 1943- 73-76
Chambers, William Nisbet 1916- CANR-8
Earlier sketch in CA 5-8R
Chambers, William Trout 1896- CAP-1
Earlier sketch in CA 13-14
Chambers-Schiller, Lee Virginia 1948- 120
Chambertin, Ilya
See von Block, Bela W(illiam)
and von Block, Sylvia
Chambliss, Bill
See Chambliss, William J(oseph)
Chambliss, William C.
1908(?)-1975 Obituary 57-60
Chambliss, William J(ones) 1923- 13-16R
Chambliss, William J(oseph) 1933- CANR-14
Earlier sketch in CA 77-80
Chamelin, Neil Charles 1942- 69-72
Chametzky, Jules 1928- 33-36R
Chamisso, Adelbert von 1781-1838 ....DLB 90
Chamlee, Ruth Miller
1893(?)-1983 Obituary 110
Champagne, Marian 1915- 5-8R
Champe, Flavia Waters 1902- 115
Champernowne, David (Gawen) 1912- 104
Champigny, Robert J(ean) 1922- 33-36R
Champion, Dick
See Champion, Richard Gordon
Champion, John C(arr) 1923- CANR-8
Earlier sketch in CA 17-20R
Champion, John E(lmer) 1922- 13-16R
Champion, Larry S(tephen) 1932- CANR-9
Earlier sketch in CA 21-24R
Champion, R(ichard) A(nnells) 1925- 29-32R
Champion, Richard Gordon 1931- 77-80
Champkin, Peter 1918- 5-8R
Champlin, Charles (Davenport) 1926- 69-72
Champlin, James R(aymond) 1928- 21-24R
Champlin, John Michael 1937- CANR-27
Earlier sketch in CA 110
Champlin, Joseph M(asson) 1930- CANR-20
Earlier sketches in CA 49-52, CANR-1
Champlin, Tim
See Champlin, John Michael
Champney, Freeman 1911- 25-28R
Chamson, Andre J(ules) L(ouis)
1900-1983 ....CANR-2
Obituary 111
Earlier sketch in CA 5-8R
Ch'An, Chu
See Blofeld, John (Eaton Calthorpe)
Ch'an, Chu
See Blofeld, John (Eaton Calthorpe)
Chan, Loren Briggs 1943- CANR-8
Earlier sketch in CA 57-60
Chanaidh, Fear
See Campbell, John Lorne
Chanakya
See Panikkar, K(avalam) Madhava
Chanan, Ben
See Yaffe, Richard
Chanan, Gabriel 1942- CANR-7
Earlier sketch in CA 57-60
Chanan, Michael 1946- 106
Chance, John Newton 1911-1983 102
Obituary 110
Chance, John T.
See Carpenter, John (Howard)
Chance, Jonathan
See Chance, John Newton
Chance, Michael R(obin) A(lexander)
1915- 85-88
Chance, Roger (James Ferguson)
1893-1987 Obituary 122
Chance, Stephen
See Turner, Philip (William)
Chancellor, John (William) 1927- 109
See also AITN 1
See also BEST 90:4
Chancellor, John 1900-1971 ....CAP-2
Earlier sketch in CA 23-24
Chancellor, Paul 1900-1975 Obituary 57-60
Chand, Meira (Angela) 1942- 106
Chand, Munshi Prem
See Srivastava, Dhanpat Rai
Chand, Prem
See Srivastava, Dhanpat Rai
Chanda, Asok Kumar 1902- 17-20R
Chandler, A(rthur) Bertram
1912-1984 ....CANR-13
Earlier sketch in CA 21-24R
Chandler, Alfred D(upont) Jr. 1918- CANR-4
Earlier sketch in CA 9-12R
Chandler, Alice 1931- 53-56
Chandler, Allison 1906- CAP-1
Earlier sketch in CA 9-10
Chandler, B. J. 1921- 1-4R
Chandler, Billy Jaynes 1932- 122
Chandler, Bryn 1945- 118
Chandler, Caroline A(ugusta)
1906-1979 ....17-20R
Obituary 93-96
See also SATA 22, 24
Chandler, David (Geoffrey) 1934- CANR-28
Earlier sketches in CA 25-28R, CANR-11
Chandler, David Leon CANR-38
Earlier sketches in CA 49-52, CANR-1, 16
Chandler, David Porter 1933- CANR-29
Earlier sketch in CA 45-48
See also SATA 28
Chandler, E(dwin) Russell Jr. 1932- 77-80
Chandler, Edna Walker 1908-1982 ....CANR-4
Obituary 108
Earlier sketch in CA 1-4R
See also SATA 11, 31
Chandler, Frank
See Harknett, Terry
Chandler, George 1915- CANR-5
Earlier sketch in CA 9-12R
Chandler, Harry 1864-1944 ....DLB 29
Chandler, Howard 1915(?)-1981 Obituary 104
Chandler, Jennifer
See Westwood, Jennifer
Chandler, Lester Vernon
1905-1988 Obituary 126
Chandler, Linda S(mith) 1929- CANR-23
Earlier sketch in CA 106
See also SATA 39
Chandler, Margaret Kueffner 1922- 17-20R
Chandler, Norman 1899-1973 Obituary 89-92
Chandler, Otis 1927- 111
Chandler, Raymond (Thornton) 1888-1959 129
Brief entry 104
See also CDALB 1929-1941
See also DLBD 6
See also MTCW
See also TCLC 1, 7
Chandler, Richard Eugene 1916- 5-8R
Chandler, Robert Wilbur 1921- 102
Chandler, Robert 1953- 112
See also SATA 40
Chandler, Ruth Forbes 1894-1978 ....1-4R
Obituary 103
See also SATA 2, 26
Chandler, S(tanley) Bernard 1921- 21-24R
Chandler, T(ony) J(ohn) 1928- 107
Chandler, Tertius 1915- CANR-19
Earlier sketch in CA 102
Chandola, Anoop C. 1937- CANR-14
Earlier sketch in CA 37-40R
Chandonnet, Ann F. 1943- CANR-23
Earlier sketches in CA 61-64, CANR-8
Chandor, (Peter John) Anthony 1932- CANR-26
Earlier sketch in CA 29-32R
Chandos, Fay
See Swatridge, Irene Maude (Mossop)
Chandos, John
See McConnell, John Lithgow Chandos
Chandra, Pramod 1930- 77-80
Chandra, Smita 1960- 138
Chandrasekhar, Sripati 1918- 89-92
Chaneles, Sol 1926- 41-44R
Chaney, Edward (Paul de Gruyter) 1951- 131
Chaney, Jill 1932- CANR-11
Earlier sketch in CA 25-28R
Chaney, Norman 1935- 110
Chaney, Otto Preston Jr. 1931- 33-36R
Chaney, William A(lbert) 1922- 33-36R
Chang, Chen-chi 1920- Brief entry 115
Chang, Ch'eng-chi
See Chang, Chen-chi
Chang, Chung-yuan 1900- 117
Chang, Constance D(an) 1917- 61-64
Chang, Dae H(ong) 1928- CANR-6
Earlier sketch in CA 57-60
Chang, David Wen-wei 1929- 130
Chang, Garma C. C.
See Chang, Chen-chi
Chang, Hsin-hai 1898(?)-1972 ....5-8R
Chang, Isabelle C(hin) 1924- 21-24R
Chang, Jen-chi 1903- CAP-1
Earlier sketch in CA 11-12
Chang, Jung 1952- ....CLC 71
Chang, Kia-Ngau 1889- 5-8R
Chang, Kwang-chih 1931- CANR-15
Earlier sketch in CA 41-44R
Chang, Lee
See Levinson, Leonard
Chang, Margaret (Scrogin) 1941- ....SATA 71
Chang, Parris (Hsu-Cheng) 1936- CANR-6
Earlier sketch in CA 57-60
Chang, Raymond 1939- 121
See also SATA 71
Chang, Richard T(aiwon) 1933- 61-64
Chang Chieh
See Zhang Jie
Chang Chien
See Zhang Jie
Changeux, Jean-Pierre 1936- 134
Chang-Rodriguez, Eugenio 1926- CANR-21
Earlier sketches in CA 9-12R, CANR-6
Chanin, Abraham (Solomon) 1921- 89-92
Chankin, Donald O(liver) 1934- 57-60
Channel, A. R.
See Catherall, Arthur
Channels, Vera G(race) 1915- 69-72
Channing, Edward (Perkins)
1856-1931 Brief entry 122
See also DLB 17
Channing, Edward Tyrrell 1790-1856 ....DLB 1, 59
Channing, Steven A. 1940- CANR-29
Earlier sketches in CA 33-36R, CANR-13
Channing, William Ellery II 1817-1901 .....DLB 1
Channing, William Ellery 1780-1842 .....DLB 1, 59
Channing, William Henry 1810-1884 .....DLB 1, 59
Channon, Henry 1897-1958 Brief entry 121
Chanoff, David 1943- 138
Chanover, E(dmond) Pierre 1932- 29-32R
Chanover, Hyman 1920- CANR-2
Earlier sketch in CA 49-52
Chansky, Norman M(orton) 1929- 21-24R
Chant, Barry (Mostyn) 1938- CANR-29
Earlier sketches in CA 65-68, CANR-11
Chant, Donald (Alfred) 1928- CANR-18
Earlier sketch in CA 101
Chant, Joy
See Rutter, Eileen Joyce
Chant, Ken(neth David) 1933- 89-92
Chantiles, Vilma Liacouras 1925- CANR-6
Earlier sketch in CA 57-60
Chantler, David T(homas) 1925- 93-96
Chao, Buwei Yang 1889-1981 61-64
Obituary 120
Chao, Evelina 1949- 120
Chao, Kang 1929- 33-36R
Chao, Paul 1919- 114
Chao, Yuen Ren 1892-1982 ....CAP-2
Obituary 106
Earlier sketch in CA 21-22
Chapel, Paul 1926- 25-28R
Chapelle, Howard I(rving) 1901-1975 ......CAP-2
Obituary 57-60
Earlier sketch in CA 25-28
Chapian, Marie 1938- CANR-22
Earlier sketch in CA 106
See also SATA 29
Chapin, Alene Olsen Dalton
1915(?)-1986 Obituary 119
See also SATA 47
Chapin, Dwight Allan 1938- 41-44R
Chapin, F(rancis) Stuart Jr. 1916- CANR-2
Earlier sketch in CA 5-8R
Chapin, Harry (Forster) 1942-1981 105
Obituary 104
Chapin, Henry 1893-1983 93-96
Obituary 110
Chapin, June Roediger 1931- CANR-13
Earlier sketch in CA 37-40R

Chapin, Katherine Garrison
See Biddle, Katherine Garrison Chapin
Chapin, Kim 1942- CANR-9
Earlier sketch in CA 53-56
Chapin, Louis Le Bourgeois Jr. 1918-1981 103
Chapin, Ned 1927- 13-16R
Chapin, Schuyler G(arrison) 1923- 77-80
Chapin, Victor 1919(?)-1983 Obituary 109
Chapin, William 1918- 37-40R
Chaplin, Bill
See Chaplin, W. W.
Chaplin, Charles Spencer 1889-1977 81-84
Obituary 73-76
See also Chaplin, Charlie
See also CLC 16
Chaplin, Charlie
See Chaplin, Charles Spencer
See also DLB 44
Chaplin, Dora P. 1906(?)-1990 Obituary 132
Chaplin, George 1914- 69-72
See also AITN 2
Chaplin, James P(atrick) 1919- CANR-1
Earlier sketch in CA 1-4R
Chaplin, L(inda) Tarin 1941- 116
Chaplin, Sid(ney) 1916-1986 ....CANR-39
Obituary 118
Earlier sketches in CAP-1, CA 9-10, CANR-16
Chaplin, W. W. 1895(?)-1978 Obituary 81-84
Chapman, A(rthur) H(arry) 1924- CANR-19
Earlier sketch in CA 25-28R
Chapman, Abraham 1915- 45-48
Chapman, Allen CANR-27
Earlier sketches in CAP-2, CA 19-20
See also SATA 1, 67
Chapman, Alvah H. Jr. ....AITN 2
Chapman, Brian 1923- 9-12R
Chapman, Carl H(aley) 1915-1987 133
Chapman, Carleton B(urke) 1915- 69-72
Chapman, Charles F(rederic)
1881-1976 Obituary 65-68
Chapman, Christine 1933- CANR-12
Earlier sketch in CA 73-76
Chapman, Clark Russell 1945- CANR-28
Earlier sketch in CA 110
Chapman, Colin 1937- CANR-26
Earlier sketch in CA 29-32R
Chapman, (William) Donald 1923- 109
Chapman, Dorothy Hilton 1934- 57-60
Chapman, Edmund H(aupt) 1906- CAP-1
Earlier sketch in CA 13-16
Chapman, (Constance) Elizabeth (Mann)
1919- CAP-1
Earlier sketch in CA 9-10
See also SATA 10
Chapman, Elwood N. 1916- 37-40R
Chapman, Frances
See Chapman, Frank M(onroe)
Chapman, Frank
See Chapman, Frank M(onroe)
Chapman, Frank M(onroe) 1930- 113
Chapman, G(eorge) W(arren) Vernon
1925- CANR-26
Earlier sketch in CA 29-32R
Chapman, Gaynor 1935- .... SATA 32
Chapman, George 1559(?)-1634 ...... DLB 62, 121
Chapman, Graham 1941-1989 ....CANR-35
Obituary 129
Earlier sketch in CA 116
See also Monty Python
See also CLC 21
Chapman, Guy (Patterson) 1889-1972 101
Obituary 89-92
Chapman, Hester W(olferstan)
1899-1976 ....CANR-9
Obituary 65-68
Earlier sketch in CA 9-12R
Chapman, J. Dudley 1928- CANR-8
Earlier sketch in CA 21-24R
Chapman, James (Keith) 1919- CANR-33
Earlier sketches in CA 41-44R, CANR-15
Chapman, Jean 97-100
See also SATA 34
Chapman, Jennifer 1950- 118
Chapman, John Jay 1862-1933 Brief entry 104
See also TCLC 7
Chapman, John L(eslie) 1920- 1-4R
Chapman, John Roy 1927- CANR-15
Earlier sketch in CA 77-80
Chapman, John Stanton Higham
1891-1972 Obituary 107
See also SATA 27
Chapman, John 1900-1972 Obituary 33-36R
Chapman, Joseph Irvine 1912- 61-64
Chapman, June R(amey) 1918- 5-8R
Chapman, Karen C. 1942- 65-68
Chapman, Kenneth F(rancis) 1910- CAP-1
Earlier sketch in CA 13-16
Chapman, Kenneth G. 1927- 13-16R
Chapman, Laura 1935- 105
Chapman, Loren J(ames) 1927- 53-56
Chapman, M(ary) Winslow 1903- 93-96
Chapman, Marie M(anire) 1917- CANR-11
Earlier sketch in CA 61-64
Chapman, Maristan
See Chapman, John Stanton Higham
Chapman, Nancy W(hisnant) Collins
See Collins-Chapman, Nancy W(hisnant)
Chapman, Phil 1944- 121
Chapman, Raymond 1924- CANR-2
Earlier sketch in CA 5-8R
Chapman, Richard A(rnold) 1937- 133
Brief entry 105
Chapman, Rick M. 1943- 49-52
Chapman, Robert (DeWitt) 1937- 107
Chapman, Robert L(undquist) 1920- 122
Chapman, Roger E(ddington) 1916- 21-24R
Chapman, Ronald (George) 1917- 5-8R
Chapman, Ruth 1912(?)-1979 Obituary 104
Chapman, Samuel Greeley 1929- CANR-9
Earlier sketch in CA 17-20R
Chapman, Stanley D(avid) 1935- CANR-9
Earlier sketch in CA 21-24R
Chapman, Stepan 41-44R
Chapman, Steven
See Chapman, Stepan
Chapman, Sydney 1888-1970 106
Chapman, Vera 1898- 81-84
See also SATA 33
Chapman, Victoria L(ynn) 1944- 57-60
Chapman, Walker
See Silverberg, Robert
Chapman, William 1850-1917 .... DLB 99
Chapman-Mortimer, William Charles
1907- 13-16R
Chapnick, Howard 1922- 65-68
Chappel, Bernice M(arie) 1910- CANR-37
Earlier sketches in CA 89-92, CANR-16
Chappell, Clovis G(illham) 1882-1972 65-68
Chappell, Fred (Davis) 1936- CANR-33
Earlier sketches in CA 5-8R, CANR-8
See also CAAS 4
See also CLC 40
See also DLB 6, 105
Chappell, Gordon (Stelling) 1939- 57-60
Chappell, Helen 1947- 104
Chappell, Jeannette
See Kalt, Jeannette Chappell
Chappell, Mollie 102
Chappell, Vere Claiborne 1930- 5-8R
Chappell, Warren 1904-1991 ....CANR-8
Obituary 134
Earlier sketch in CA 17-20R
See also MAICYA
See also SAAS 10
See also SATA 6, 68
See also SATO 67
Chappell, William (Evelyn) 1908- 106
Chapple, Christopher 1954- 126
Chapple, Eliot D(ismore) 1909- 41-44R
Chapple, (Clement) Gerald 1937- 111
Chapple, J(ohn) A(lfred) V(ictor) 1928- 21-24R
Chapple, Richard L(ynn) 1944- 112
Chapple, Steve 1949- 77-80
Chaput, Donald (Charles) 1933- 122
Brief entry 117
Char, K. T. Narasimha
See Narasimha Char, K. T.
Char, Rene(-Emile) 1907-1988 ....CANR-32
Obituary 124
Earlier sketch in CA 13-16R
See also CLC 9, 11, 14, 55
See also MTCW
Char, Tin-Yuke 1905- 57-60
Char, Wai Jane Chun 1912- 118
Char, Yum
See Barrett, Dean
Charanis, Peter 1908-1985 ....37-40R
Obituary 115
Charbonneau, Jean 1875-1960 .... DLB 92
Charbonneau, Louis (Henry) 1924- 85-88
Charbonneau, Robert 1911-1967 .... DLB 68
Charby, Jay
See Ellison, Harlan
Charchat, Isaac 1904(?)-1985 Obituary 116
Chard, (Maire) Brigid 1934- 105
Chard, Judy 1916- CANR-31
Earlier sketches in CA 77-80, CANR-14
Chard, Leslie F. II 1934- 33-36R
Chardiet, Bernice (Kroll) 1927(?)- 103
See also SATA 27
Chardin, Pierre Teilhard de
See Teilhard de Chardin, (Marie Joseph) Pierre
Chargaff, Erwin 1905- CANR-39
Earlier sketches in CA 101, CANR-18
Charhadi, Driss ben Hamed 13-16R
Chari, V. Krishna 1924- 17-20R
Charland, William (Alfred) Jr. 1937- 97-100
Charles, Amy M(arie) 1922- 116
Charles, C(arol) M(organ) 1931- CANR-1
Earlier sketch in CA 49-52
Charles, David
See Mondey, David (Charles)
and Taylor, Charles D(oonan)
Charles, Don C(laude) 1918- 9-12R
Charles, Donald
See Meighan, Donald Charles
Charles, Franklin
See Adams, Cleve F(ranklin)
Charles, Gerda CANR-1
Earlier sketch in CA 1-4R
See also DLB 14
Charles, Gordon H(ull) 1920- 104
Charles, Henry
See Harris, Marion Rose (Young)
Charles, Louis
See Stratemeyer, Edward L.
Charles, Maggi
See Koehler, Margaret (Hudson)
Charles, Mark
See Bickers, Richard Leslie Townshend
Charles, Nathanael
See Franklin, Benjamin V
Charles, Nicholas J.
See Kuskin, Karla (Seidman)
Charles, Ray
See Robinson, Ray Charles
Charles, Robert
See Smith, Robert Charles
Charles, Sara C(onnor) 1934- 132
Charles, Sascha 1896(?)-1972 Obituary 37-40R
Charles, Searle F(ranklin) 1923- 9-12R
Charles, Theresa
See Swatridge, Charles (John)
Charles, Will
See Willeford, Charles (Ray III)
Charles-Roux, Edmonde 1920- 85-88
Charles the Clown
See Kraus, Charles E.
Charleston, Robert E.
See Robinson, Charles M. III
Charleston, Robert Jesse 1916- 102
Charlesworth, Arthur Riggs 1911- 53-56
Charlesworth, Edward A(llison) 1949- 125
Charlesworth, James Clyde 1900-1974 ......9-12R
Obituary 45-48
Charlesworth, James H(amilton) 1940- 130
Charlesworth, John Kaye 1889- CAP-1
Earlier sketch in CA 9-10
Charlesworth, Maxwell John 1925- CANR-18
Earlier sketches in CA 1-4R, CANR-2
Charlier, Patricia (Mary) Simonet 1923- 37-40R
Charlier, Roger H(enri) 1921- CANR-31
Earlier sketches in CA 37-40R, CANR-13
Charlip, Remy 1929- 33-36R
See also CLR 8
See also MAICYA
See also SATA 4, 68
Charlot, Jean 1898-1979 ....CANR-4
Earlier sketch in CA 5-8R
See also SATA 8, 31
Charlot, John (Pierre) 1941- 120
Charlot, Martin (Day) 1944- CANR-35
Earlier sketch in CA 114
See also SATA 64
Charlotte, Susan 1954- 109
Charlson, David
See Holmes, David Charles
Charlton, David 1946- 127
Charlton, Donald Geoffrey 1925- CANR-17
Earlier sketches in CA 1-4R, CANR-1
Charlton, Evan 1912-1983 Obituary 110
Charlton, Jack
See Charlton, John
Charlton, James (Mervyn) 1939- 81-84
Charlton, John
See Woodhouse, Martin (Charlton)
Charlton, John 1935- 109
Charlton, Linda
See Murray, Linda Charlton
Charlton, Michael (Alan) 1923- .... SATA 34
Charlwood, D(onald) E(rnest) 1915- CANR-9
Earlier sketch in CA 21-24R
Charlwood, Don
See Charlwood, D(onald) E(rnest)
Charmatz, Bill 1925- 29-32R
See also SATA 7
Charme, Stuart Zane 1951- 137
Charnance, L. P.
See Hannaway, Patricia H(inman)
Charnas, Suzy McKee 1939- CANR-39
Earlier sketches in CA 93-96, CANR-18
See also SATA 61
Charney, Ann 102
Charney, David H. 1923- CANR-15
Earlier sketch in CA 81-84
Charney, George 1905(?)-1975 Obituary 61-64
Charney, Hanna (Kurtz) 1931- CANR-29
Earlier sketch in CA 49-52
Charney, Maurice (Myron) 1929- CANR-18
Earlier sketches in CA 9-12R, CANR-3
Charnin, Martin (Jay) 1934- 103
Charnley, John 1911-1982 Obituary 107
Charnley, Mitchell V(aughn) 1898- 69-72
Charnock, Joan 1903- CAP-2
Earlier sketch in CA 33-36
Charny, Carmi 1925- CANR-7
Earlier sketch in CA 13-16R
Charny, Israel W(olf) 1931- 57-60
Charosh, Mannis 1906- 29-32R
See also SATA 5
Charques, Dorothy (Taylor) 1899-1976 73-76
Obituary 65-68
Charren, Peggy 1928- 129
Charriere, Henri 1906-1973 101
Charron, Shirley 1935- 69-72
Charry, Elias 1906- 69-72
Charter, S(teve) P. R.
1915(?)-1984 Obituary 114
Charteris, Hugo (Francis Guy) 1922-1970 105
Obituary 89-92
Charteris, James Donald 1948- 117
Charteris, Leslie 1907- CANR-10
Earlier sketch in CA 5-8R
See also DLB 77
Charters, Alexander N(athaniel) 1916- 120
Charters, Ann (Danberg) 1936- CANR-34
Earlier sketches in CA 17-20R, CANR-9
Charters, Samuel (Barclay) 1929- CANR-34
Earlier sketches in CA 9-12R, CANR-9
Chartham, Robert
See Seth, Ronald (Sydney)
Chartier, Emilio
See Estenssoro, Hugo
Chartier, Normand L. 1945- .... SATA 66
Chartier, Roger 1945- 137
Chartkoff, Joseph L(ouis) 1942- 119
Chartkoff, Kerry K(ona) 1943- 119
Charvat, Frank John 1918- 1-4R
Charvet, John 1938- CANR-15
Earlier sketch in CA 85-88
Chary, Frederick B(arry) 1939- 49-52
Charyn, Jerome 1937- CANR-7
Earlier sketch in CA 5-8R
See also CAAS 1
See also CLC 5, 8, 18
See also DLBY 83
See also MTCW
Chasan, Daniel Jack 1943- 29-32R
Chase, A(lice) Elizabeth 1906- CAP-1
Earlier sketch in CA 11-12
Chase, Adam
See Fairman, Paul W.
and Marlowe, Stephen
and Thomson, James C(utting)
Chase, Alan (Louis) 1929- 1-4R
Chase, Alice
See McHargue, Georgess
Chase, Alston Hurd 1906- 5-8R
Chase, Borden
See Fowler, Frank
See also DLB 26
Chase, Chris ....AITN 1
Chase, Cleveland B(ruce)
1904(?)-1975 Obituary 53-56
Chase, Clinton I(rvin) 1927- 106
Chase, Cora G(ingrich) 1898- CANR-7
Earlier sketch in CA 61-64
Chase, Donald 1943- 53-56
Chase, Edna Woolman 1877-1957 .... DLB 91
Chase, Elaine R(aco) 1949- CANR-36
Earlier sketch in CA 114
Chase, Emily
See Aks, Patricia
and Sachs, Judith
and White, Carol
Chase, Gilbert 1906- 17-20R
Obituary 137
Chase, Glen
See Levinson, Leonard
Chase, Harold W(illiam) 1922- CANR-4
Earlier sketch in CA 9-12R
Chase, Ilka 1905-1978 ....CANR-9
Obituary 77-80
Earlier sketch in CA 61-64
Chase, James Hadley
See Raymond, Rene (Brabazon)
Chase, James S(taton) 1932- 85-88
Chase, Joan 134
Brief entry 129
Chase, Judith Wragg 1907- 41-44R
Chase, Larry
See Chase, Lawrence
Chase, Lawrence 1943- 97-100
Chase, Loriene Eck 102
Chase, Loring D. 1916- 25-28R
Chase, Lyndon
See Chard, Judy
Chase, Mary (Coyle) 1907-1981 77-80
Obituary 105
See also DC 1
See also SATA 17, 29
Chase, Mary Ellen 1887-1973 .... CAP-1
Obituary 41-44R
Earlier sketch in CA 13-16
See also CLC 2
See also SATA 10
Chase, Mildred Portney 1921- 106
Chase, Naomi Feigelson 1932- 104
Chase, Nicholas
See Hyde, Anthony
Chase, Otta Louise 1909-1987 ....CANR-32
Earlier sketch in CA 49-52
Chase, Philander D(ean) 1943- 124
Chase, Richard 1904-1988 61-64
Obituary 125
See also SATA 56, 64
Chase, Samuel B(rown) Jr. 1932- 5-8R
Chase, Stuart 1888-1985 65-68
Obituary 117
Chase, Sylvia (Belle) 1938- 115
Brief entry 110
Chase, Virginia Lowell
See Perkins, Virginia Chase
Chase, W. Linwood 1897(?)-1983 Obituary 110
Chasen, Nancy H. 1945- 130
Chase-Riboud, Barbara (Dewayne Tosi)
1939- 113
See also BW
See also DLB 33
Chasin, Barbara 1940- 69-72
Chasins, Abram 1903-1987 ....CANR-14
Obituary 122
Earlier sketch in CA 37-40R
Chasman, Herbert 1938- 121
Chastain, Madye Lee 1908- 5-8R
See also SATA 4
Chasteen, Edgar R(ay) 1935- 33-36R
Chastel, Andre (Adrien)
1912-1990 Obituary 132
Chastenet de Castaing, Jacques
1893-1978 Obituary 77-80
Chaston, Gloria Duncan 1929- 69-72
Chatalbash, Ron 1959- 111
Chateaubriand, Francois Rene de
1768-1848 .... DLB 119
Chatelain, Nicolas 1913-1976 Obituary 65-68
Chatelet, Albert 1928- CANR-6
Earlier sketch in CA 13-16R
Chater, Elizabeth (Eileen) 1910- 111
Chatfield, (Earl) Charles (Jr.) 1934- 37-40R
Chatfield, Hale 1936- CANR-13
Earlier sketch in CA 33-36R
Chatfield, Michael 1934- CANR-10
Earlier sketch in CA 25-28R
Chatham, Doug(las) M. 1938- CANR-8
Earlier sketch in CA 61-64
Chatham, James R(ay) 1931- 33-36R
Chatham, Josiah G(eorge) 1914- 49-52
Chatham, Larry
See Bingley, David Ernest
Chatham, Russell 1939- 69-72
Chatman, Seymour B(enjamin) 1928- 37-40R
Chatov, Robert 1927- 105
Chatt, Orville K(eith) 1924- 53-56
Chatterje, Sarat Chandra
1876-1936(?) Brief entry 109
See also Chatterji, Saratchandra

Chatterjee, Margaret (Gantzer) 1925- CANR-20
Earlier sketches in CA 5-8R, CANR-3
Chatterji, Saratchandra
See Chatterje, Sarat Chandra
See also TCLC 13
Chatterji, Suniti Kumar 1890- 81-84
Chatterton, Thomas 1752-1770 ..... DLB 109
Chatterton, Wayne 1921- 37-40R
Chatwin, (Charles) Bruce 1940-1989 85-88
Obituary 127
See also AAYA 4
See also BEST 90:1
See also CLC 28, 57, 59
Chaucer, Daniel
See Ford, Ford Madox
Chaucer, Geoffrey
1340(?)-1400 ..... CDBLB Before 1660
Chaudhuri, Haridas 1913- CANR-4
Earlier sketch in CA 5-8R
Chaudhuri, Nirad C(handra) 1897- 128
Chaudhuri, Sukanta 1950- 57-60
Chauffard, Rene-Jacques
1920(?)-1972 Obituary 37-40R
Chauncy, Charles 1705-1787 ..... DLB 24
Chauncy, Nan(cen Beryl Masterman)
1900-1970 ..... CANR-4
Earlier sketch in CA 1-4R
See also CLR 6
See also MAICYA
See also SATA 6
Chaundler, Christine 1887-1972 ..... CAP-2
Earlier sketch in CA 29-32
See also SATA 1, 25
Chauveau, Pierre-Joseph-Olivier
1820-1890 ..... DLB 99
Chauvin, Remy 1913- 108
Chavasse, Michael Louis Maude
1923-1983 Obituary 110
Chavchavadze, Paul 1899-1971 ..... CAP-2
Obituary 29-32R
Earlier sketch in CA 25-28
Chavel, Charles Ber 1906- CANR-4
Earlier sketch in CA 49-52
Chaves, Jonathan 1943- CANR-9
Earlier sketch in CA 65-68
Chavez, Angelico
See Chavez, Manuel
Chavez, Denise (Elia) 1948- 131
See also HW
Chavez, Fray Angelico
See Chavez, Manuel
See also DLB 82
Chavez, Fray Angelico 1910- ..... DLB 82
Chavez, John R(ichard) 1949- 118
See also HW
Chavez, Manuel 1910- CANR-32
Earlier sketch in CA 93-96
See also Chavez, Fray Angelico
See also HW
Chavez, Patricia 1934- 103
Chaviaras, Strates 1935- 105
See also Haviaras, Stratis
Chayefsky, Paddy
See Chayefsky, Sidney
See also CLC 23
See also DLB 7, 44
See also DLBY 81
Chayefsky, Sidney 1923-1981 ..... CANR-18
Obituary 104
Earlier sketch in CA 9-12R
See also Chayefsky, Paddy
Chayes, Abram 1922- CANR-14
Earlier sketch in CA 65-68
Chaytor, Lee
See Chater, Elizabeth (Eileen)
Chazanof, William 1915- 33-36R
Chaze, (Lewis) Elliott 1915- 113
Cheape, Charles Windsor 1945- CANR-28
Earlier sketch in CA 105
Cheatham, K(aryn) Follis 1943- 81-84
Cheavens, (Sam) Frank 1905- 33-36R
Cheavens, Martha Louise (Schuck)
1898-1975 Obituary 57-60
Check, Otto Premier
See Berman, Ed
Check, William A. 1943- 118
Checkland, S(ydney) G(eorge)
1916-1986 ..... 17-20R
Obituary 118
Chedid, Andree 1920- ..... CLC 47
Cheech
See Marin, Richard Anthony
Cheek, Frances Edith 1923- 41-44R
Cheek, Mavis 1948- 128
Cheeks, James E. 1930- 124
Cheesman, Paul R. 1921- CANR-1
Earlier sketch in CA 49-52
Cheetham, Erika 1939- CANR-30
Earlier sketch in CA 109
Cheetham, Hal
See Cheetham, J(ames) H(arold)
Cheetham, J(ames) H(arold) 1921- 108
Cheetham, Nicholas (John Alexander)
1910- CANR-15
Earlier sketch in CA 81-84
Cheever, Ezekiel 1615-1708 ..... DLB 24
Cheever, George Barrell 1807-1890 ..... DLB 59
Cheever, John 1912-1982 ..... CANR-27
Obituary 106
Earlier sketches in CA 5-8R, CANR-5
See also CABS 1
See also CDALB 1941-1968
See also CLC 3, 7, 8, 11, 15, 25, 64
See also DLB 2, 102
See also DLBY 80, 82
See also MTCW
See also SSC 1
See also WLC
Cheever, Susan 1943- CANR-27
Earlier sketch in CA 103
See also CLC 18, 48
See also DLBY 82
Cheffins, Ronald I. 1930- 45-48
Chehak, Susan Taylor 1951- 130
Cheifetz, Dan 1926- 69-72
Cheifetz, Philip M(orris) 1944- 53-56
Cheim, John 1953- 138
Chein, Isidor 1912- Brief entry 105
Chejne, Anwar G(eorge) 1923-1983 ..... CANR-18
Earlier sketch in CA 25-28R
Chekenian, Aram Haigaz
1900-1986 Obituary 119
Chekenian, Jane
See Gerard, Jane
Chekhonte, Antosha
See Chekhov, Anton (Pavlovich)
Chekhov, Anton (Pavlovich) 1860-1904 124
Brief entry 104
See also SSC 2
See also TCLC 3, 10, 31
See also WLC
Chekhova, Olga 1897-1980 Obituary 97-100
Chekki, Dan(esh) A(yyappa) 1935- CANR-23
Earlier sketches in CA 61-64, CANR-7
Cheldelin, Larry V(ernon) 1945- 116
Cheles, Luciano 1948- 127
Chelf, Carl P. 1937- 37-40R
Chelius, James R(obert) 1943- 115
Chellis, Marcia 1940- 121
Chelminski, Rudolph 1934- 93-96
Chelton, John
See Durst, Paul
Chelwood, Tufton Victor Hamilton
1917-1989 65-68
Obituary 128
Chen, Anthony 1929- CANR-14
Earlier sketch in CA 37-40R
See also SATA 6
Chen, Ching-chih 1937- CANR-22
Earlier sketch in CA 106
Ch'En, Chi-yun 1933- 108
Chen, Chung-Hwan 1906- 45-48
Chen, Edwin (Hung-teh) 1934- Brief entry 116
Chen, Jack 1908- CANR-15
Earlier sketch in CA 41-44R
Chen, Janey 1922- 73-76
Ch'en, Jerome 1921- CANR-9
Earlier sketch in CA 13-16R
Chen, Joseph Tao 1925- 37-40R
Chen, Kan 1928- 49-52
Chen, Kenneth K(uan-) S(heng) 1907- 17-20R
Chen, King C(hing) 1926- CANR-4
Earlier sketch in CA 53-56
Chen, Kuan I. 1926- 41-44R
Chen, Lincoln C(hih-ho) 1942- 49-52
Chen, Nai-Ruenn 1927- CANR-9
Earlier sketch in CA 21-24R
Chen, Philip S(tanley) 1903-1978 ..... CANR-5
Earlier sketch in CA 9-12R
Chen, Samuel Shih-Tsai 1915- 41-44R
Chen, Theodore Hsi-En 1902- CANR-17
Earlier sketches in CA 1-4R, CANR-1
Chen, Tony
See Chen, Anthony
Chen, Vincent 1917- 37-40R
Chen, Yuan-tsung 1932- 106
See also SATA 65
Chenault, Lawrence R(oyce) 1897- CAP-2
Earlier sketch in CA 17-18
Chenault, Nell
See Smith, Linell Nash
Chenery, Hollis Burnley 1918- 111
Chenery, Janet (Dai) 1923- 103
See also SATA 25
Chenery, William Ludlow 1884-1974 97-100
Obituary 53-56
Chenevix Trench, Charles Pocklington
1914- 9-12R
Cheney, Anne 1944- 61-64
Cheney, Brainard (Bartwell) 1900-1990 ..... CAP-2
Obituary 130
Earlier sketch in CA 25-28
Cheney, C. R.
See Cheney, Christopher Robert
Cheney, Christopher Robert
1906-1987 Obituary 123
Cheney, Cora 1916- CANR-4
Earlier sketch in CA 1-4R
See also SATA 3
Cheney, Ednah Dow (Littlehale)
1824-1904 ..... DLB 1
Cheney, Frances Neel 1906- 33-36R
Cheney, Glenn Alan 1951- 109
Cheney, Harriet Vaughan 1796-1889 ..... DLB 99
Cheney, Jean E. 1921- 118
Cheney, Lois A. 1931- 29-32R
Cheney, Lynne 1941- 89-92
Cheney, Margaret 1921- 101
Cheney, Richard B(ruce) 1941- 113
Cheney, Robert S(impson) 1922- 118
Cheney, Roberta Carkeek 1912- 73-76
Cheney, Ruth G(ordon) 1908- 113
Cheney, Sheldon Warren
1886-1980 Obituary 102
Cheney, Ted
See Cheney, Theodore Albert
Cheney, Theodore A. Rees
See Cheney, Theodore Albert
Cheney, Theodore Albert 1928- CANR-23
Earlier sketches in CA 61-64, CANR-8
See also SATA 11
Cheney, Thomas E. 1901- 41-44R
Cheney-Coker, Syl 1945- 101
Cheng, Chu-yuan 1927- CANR-20
Earlier sketches in CA 13-16R, CANR-5
Cheng, F.T.
See Cheng, Tien-hsi
Cheng, Hang-Sheng 1927- 69-72
Cheng, Hou-Tien 1944- 69-72
Cheng, J(ames) Chester 1926- 9-12R
Cheng, James K(uo) C(hiang) 1936- 25-28R
Cheng, Judith 1955- ..... SATA 36
Cheng, Ronald Ye-lin 1933- 41-44R
Cheng, Tien-hsi 1884-1970 Obituary 104
Cheng, Yi
See Cheng, James K(uo) C(hiang)
Cheng, Ying-wan 41-44R
Chen Hwei
See Stevenson, William
Chen Jia
See Shen Congwen
Chen Jo-hsi
See Tuann, Lucy H(siu-mei) C(hen)
Chennault, Anna (Chan) 1925- 61-64
Chennells, Roy D. 1912(?)-1981 Obituary 105
Chenneviere, Daniel
See Rudhyar, Dane
Chenoweth, Vida S. 1928- CANR-11
Earlier sketch in CA 25-28R
Cheraskin, Emanuel 1916- 53-56
Cherim, Stanley M(arshall) 1929- 53-56
Cherington, Paul Whiton 1918-1974 ..... CANR-6
Obituary 53-56
Earlier sketch in CA 1-4R
Chermayeff, Ivan 1932- 97-100
See also SATA 47
Chermayeff, Serge 1900- 21-24R
Chernaik, Judith 1934- CANR-39
Earlier sketches in CA 61-64, CANR-11
Chernenko, K. U.
See Chernenko, Konstantin U(stinovich)
Chernenko, Konstantin U(stinovich)
1911-1985 132
Obituary 115
Cherner, Anne 1954- 109
Chernev, Irving 1900-1981 Obituary 105
Cherniavsky, Michael
1923(?)-1973 Obituary 41-44R
Chernik, Barbara E(ileen) 1938- 117
Chernin, Kim 1940- 107
Cherniss, Harold
See Cherniss, Harold Fredrik
Cherniss, Harold Fredrik 1904-1987 93-96
Obituary 123
Cherniss, Michael D(avid) 1940- 37-40R
Cherniss, Norman A(rnold) 1926-1984 122
Obituary 114
Chernoff, Dorothy A.
See Ernst, (Lyman) John
Chernoff, Goldie Taub 1909- 33-36R
See also SATA 10
Chernoff, John Miller 1947- 105
Chernoff, Maxine 1952- 136
Chernofsky, Jacob L. 1928- 73-76
Chernow, Burt 1933- 110
Chernow, Carol 1934- 57-60
Chernow, Fred B. 1932- 57-60
Chernowitz, Maurice E.
1909-1977 Obituary 73-76
Cherns, Albert
See Cherns, Albert B(ernard)
Cherns, Albert B(ernard)
1921-1987 Obituary 122
Cherny, Robert W(allace) 1943- 131
Cherrington, Ernest H(urst) Jr. 1909- 33-36R
Cherrington, John 1909- 116
Cherrington, Leon G. 1926- 33-36R
Cherry, C. Conrad 1937- CANR-11
Earlier sketch in CA 21-24R
Cherry, Caroline L(ockett) 1942- 57-60
Cherry, Carolyn Janice 1942- CANR-10
Earlier sketch in CA 65-68
See also Cherryh, C. J.
Cherry, Charles L(ester) 1942- 57-60
Cherry, (Edward) Colin 1914-1979 ..... CANR-12
Obituary 93-96
Earlier sketch in CA 69-72
Cherry, George Loy 1905- 5-8R
Cherry, Gordon E(manuel) 1931- 125
Cherry, Kelly CANR-3
Earlier sketch in CA 49-52
See also AITN 1
See also DLBY 83
Cherry, Lynne 1952- ..... SATA 34
Cherry, Sheldon H(arold) 1934- CANR-27
Earlier sketch in CA 49-52
Cherryh, C. J.
See Cherry, Carolyn Janice
See also CLC 35
See also DLBY 80
Cherryholmes, Anne
See Price, Olive
Chertok, Haim
See Chertok, Harvey
Chertok, Harvey 1938- 127
Chervin, Ronda 1937- CANR-21
Earlier sketches in CA 57-60, CANR-6
Chervokas, John V(incent) 1936- 129
Cherwinski, Joseph 1915- CANR-5
Earlier sketch in CA 13-16R
Chesbro, George C(lark) 1940- 77-80
Chesebro, James William 1944- 108
Chesen, Eli S. 1944- 37-40R
Chesham, Henry
See Bingley, David Ernest
Chesham, Sallie CANR-26
Earlier sketch in CA 29-32R
Chesher, Kim 1955- CANR-19
Earlier sketch in CA 102
Chesher, Richard (Harvey) 1940- 106
Cheshire, David 1944- 97-100
Cheshire, Geoffrey Leonard 1917- CAP-1
Earlier sketch in CA 13-14
Cheshire, Herbert 1925(?)-1985 Obituary 118
Cheshire, Maxine 1930- 108
Cheskin, Louis 1909-1981 ..... CANR-5
Obituary 105
Earlier sketch in CA 5-8R
Chesler, Bernice 1932- CANR-16
Earlier sketch in CA 25-28R
See also SATA 59
Chesler, Phyllis 1940- CANR-4
Earlier sketch in CA 49-52
Cheslock, Louis 1898- CAP-1
Earlier sketch in CA 11-12
Chesman, Andrea 1952- 135
Chesney, Ann
See Dummett, (Agnes Margaret) Ann
Chesney, Inga L. 1928- 45-48
Chesney, Kellow (Robert) 1914- 29-32R
Chesney, Marion 1936- 115
Brief entry 111
Chesney, Weatherby
See Hyne, C(harles) J(ohn) Cutcliffe (Wright)
Chesnoff, Richard Z(eltner) 1937- CANR-10
Earlier sketch in CA 25-28R
Chesnut, J(ames) Stanley 1926- 21-24R
Chesnutt, Charles W(addell) 1858-1932 125
Brief entry 106
See also BLC 1
See also BW
See also DLB 12, 50, 78
See also MTCW
See also SSC 7
See also TCLC 5, 39
Chesnutt, David R(ogers) 1940- 122
Chess, Stella 1914- 85-88
Chess, Victoria 1939- 107
See also SATA 33
Chessare, Michele ..... SATA 42
Chesser, Eustace 1902-1973 ..... CANR-4
Obituary 45-48
Earlier sketch in CA 9-12R
Chessex, Jacques 1934- 65-68
Chesshyre, Robert (Coxhead) 1941- 128
Chessman, Caryl (Whittier) 1921-1960 73-76
Chessman, G(eorge) Wallace 1919- 13-16R
Chessman, Ruth (Green) 1910- CAP-2
Earlier sketch in CA 17-18
Chester, Alfred 1929(?)-1971 Obituary 33-36R
See also CLC 49
Chester, Allan Griffith 1900-1976 Obituary 111
Chester, Deborah 1957- CANR-18
Earlier sketch in CA 102
Chester, Edward W(illiam) 1935- CANR-13
Earlier sketch in CA 21-24R
Chester, George Randolph 1869-1924 ..... DLB 78
Chester, Laura 1949- CANR-9
Earlier sketch in CA 65-68
Chester, Michael (Arthur) 1928- CANR-1
Earlier sketch in CA 1-4R
Chester, (Daniel) Norman 1907-1986 109
Obituary 120
Chester, Peter
See Phillips, D(ennis) J(ohn Andrew)
Chester, Tessa Rose 1950- 130
Chesterman, Charles W(esley) 1913- 107
Chesterman, Clement (Clapton)
1894-1983 Obituary 110
Chesterson, Denise
See Robins, Denise (Naomi)
Chesterton, A(rthur) K(enneth) 1899- CAP-1
Earlier sketch in CA 11-12
Chesterton, G(ilbert) K(eith) 1874-1936 132
Brief entry 104
See also CDBLB 1914-1945
See also DLB 10, 19, 34, 70, 98
See also MTCW
See also SATA 27
See also SSC 1
See also TCLC 1, 6
Chestor, Rui
See Courtier, S(idney) H(obson)
Chetham-Strode, Warren 1896- CAP-1
Earlier sketch in CA 13-14
Chethimattam, John B(ritto) 1922- 25-28R
Chetin, Helen 1922- CANR-12
Earlier sketch in CA 29-32R
See also SATA 6
Chetwin, Grace 123
See also SATA 50
Chetwode, Penelope 1910-1986 102
Obituary 119
Chetwynd, Berry
See Rayner, Claire (Berenice)
Chetwynd, Lionel 1940- 137
Chetwynd, Tom 1938- 45-48
Chetwynd-Hayes, R(onald Henry Glynn)
1919- CANR-30
Earlier sketches in CA 61-64, CANR-12
Chetwynd-Talbot, Edward Hugh Frederick
1909- 116
Cheung, Steven N(g-) S(heong) 1935- 25-28R
Cheuse, Alan 1940- CANR-27
Earlier sketch in CA 49-52
Chevalier, Christa 1937- CANR-24
Earlier sketch in CA 107
See also SATA 35

Chevalier, Elizabeth (Pickett)
1896-1984 Obituary 111
Chevalier, Haakon (Maurice) 1901-1985 61-64
Obituary 116
Chevalier, Louis 1911- CANR-35
Earlier sketch in CA 85-88
Chevalier, Maurice 1888-1972 Obituary 33-36R
Chevalier, Paul Eugene George 1925- 106
Chevallier, Gabriel 1895-1969 Obituary 113
Chevallier, Raymond 1929- 103
Chevigny, Bell Gale 1936- 57-60
Chevigny, Paul G. 1935- 97-100
Cheville, Roy A(rthur) 1897- 97-100
Chevremont, Evaristo Ribera
See Ribera Chevremont, Evaristo
Chew, Allen F. 1924- 33-36R
Chew, Peter 1924- 57-60
Chew, Ruth 1920- CANR-14
Earlier sketches in CA 41-44R, CANR-31
See also SATA 7
Cheyette, Irving 1904- CANR-22
Earlier sketch in CA 69-72
Cheyney, Arnold B. 1926- CANR-23
Earlier sketches in CA 21-24R, CANR-8
Cheyney, Edward P. 1861-1947 .... DLB 47
Cheyney, (Reginald Evelyn) Peter (Southouse)
1896-1951 Brief entry 113
Chi, Madeleine 1930- CANR-11
Earlier sketch in CA 69-72
Chi, Richard Hu See-Yee 1918- 37-40R
Chi, Wen-shun 1910- 13-16R
Chiang Kai-shek 1886(?)-1975 Obituary 112
Chiang Pin-chin 1904-1986 Obituary 118
See also Ding Ling
Chiang Yee 1903-1977 .... CANR-15
Obituary 73-76
Earlier sketch in CA 65-68
Ch'iao, Sung
See Chou, Eric
Chiappelli, Fredi 1921-1990 Obituary 131
Chiara, Piero 1913-1986 .... CANR-8
Obituary 121
Earlier sketch in CA 53-56
Chiarenza, Carl 1935- CANR-29
Earlier sketch in CA 109
Chiari, Joseph 1911- CANR-29
Earlier sketches in CA 5-8R, CANR-4
Chiaromonte, Nicola Obituary 104
Chiba, Atsuko 1941(?)-1987 Obituary 123
Chibnall, Marjorie (McCallum) 1915- 29-32R
Chicago, Judy 1939- CANR-21
Earlier sketch in CA 85-88
Chichester, Francis (Charles) 1901-1972 .... CAP-1
Obituary 37-40R
Earlier sketch in CA 13-14
Chichester, Jane
See Longrigg, Jane Chichester
Chichester Clark, Emma 1955- 132
See also Clark, Emma Chichester
Chick, Edson M(arland) 1924- 21-24R
Chickering, Arthur W. 1927- 29-32R
Chickering, Roger (Philip) 1942- 73-76
Chickos, James Speros 1941- 49-52
Chicorel, Marietta 85-88
Chidsey, Donald Barr 1902-1981 .... CANR-2
Obituary 103
Earlier sketch in CA 5-8R
See also SATA 3, 27
Chidzero, Bernard Thomas Gibson 1927- 1-4R
Chiefari, Janet D. 1942- .... SATA 58
Chief Standing Bear
See Standing Bear, Luther
Chieger, Bob 1945- 114
Chielens, Edward E(rnest) 1943- 53-56
Ch'ien, Ts'un-hsun
See Tsien, Tsuen-hsuin
Ch'ien Chung-shu 1910- 130
See also CLC 22
See also MTCW
Chiesa, Francesco 1871(?)-1973 Obituary 104
Chignon, Niles
See Lingeman, Richard R(oberts)
Chigounis, Evans 1931- 45-48
Chilcote, Ronald H. 1935- CANR-24
Earlier sketches in CA 21-24R, CANR-8
Chilcott, John H(enry) 1924- 41-44R
Child, Alan
See Langner, Lawrence
Child, Francis James 1825-1896 .... DLB 1, 64
Child, Heather 1912- 9-12R
Child, Irvin L(ong) 1915- 41-44R
Child, John 1922- 93-96
Child, Julia 1912- CANR-19
Earlier sketch in CA 41-44R
Child, Kenneth 1916-1983 Obituary 111
Child, L. Maria
See Child, Lydia Maria
Child, Lydia Maria 1802-1880 .... DLB 1, 74
See also SATA 67
Child, Mrs.
See Child, Lydia Maria
Child, Philip 1898-1978 .... CAP-1
Earlier sketch in CA 13-14
See also CLC 19, 68
See also SATA 47
Child, Roderick 1949- 25-28R
Childers, (Robert) Erskine
1870-1922 Brief entry 113
See also DLB 70
Childers, Thomas (Allen) 1940- 37-40R
Children's Shepherd, The
See Westphal, Arnold Carl
Childress, Alice 1920- CANR-27
Earlier sketches in CA 45-48, CANR-3
See also AAYA 8
See also BLC 1
See also BW
See also CLC 12, 15
See also CLR 14
See also DLB 7, 38
See also MAICYA
See also MTCW
See also SATA 7, 48
Childress, James Franklin 1940- CANR-11
Earlier sketch in CA 65-68
Childress, Mark 1957- 134
Childress, William 1933- CANR-34
Earlier sketch in CA 41-44R
Childs, Barney 1926- 21-24R
Childs, Brevard S(prings) 1923- 128
Brief entry 117
Childs, C. Sand
See Childs, Maryanna
Childs, David (Haslam) 1933- CANR-31
Earlier sketches in CA 37-40R, CANR-14
Childs, Elizabeth C(atharine) 1954- 138
Childs, George W. 1829-1894 .... DLB 23
Childs, H(alla) Fay (Cochrane)
1890-1971 .... CAP-1
Earlier sketch in CA 13-16
See also SATA 1, 25
Childs, Harwood Lawrence 1898-1972 .... CAP-2
Obituary 37-40R
Earlier sketch in CA 25-28
Childs, J(ames) Rives 1893-1987 Obituary 123
Childs, James Bennett
1896-1977 Obituary 73-76
Childs, John Steven 1947- 128
Childs, Marilyn Grace Carlson 1923- 9-12R
Childs, Marquis W(illiam) 1903-1990 .... CANR-12
Obituary 132
Earlier sketch in CA 61-64
Childs, Maryanna 1910- 9-12R
Childs, Timothy 1941- 97-100
Childs, W(illiam) H(arold) J(oseph)
1905(?)-1983 Obituary 109
Chiles, Robert E(ugene) 1923- 17-20R
Chiles, Webb 1941- 108
Chill, Dan S(amuel) 1945- 69-72
Chilman, Catherine (Earles) S(treet) 1914- 121
Chilson, Richard William 1943- CANR-6
Earlier sketch in CA 57-60
Chilson, Robert 1945- 69-72
Chilton, Irma 1930- CANR-19
Earlier sketch in CA 103
Chilton, John (James) 1932- CANR-8
Earlier sketch in CA 61-64
Chilton, Lance 1944- 123
Chilton, Shirley R(ay) 1923- 77-80
Chilver, Guy (Edward Farquhar) 1910-1982 109
Obituary 107
Chilver, Peter 1933- CANR-38
Earlier sketches in CA 25-28R, CANR-17
Chimaera
See Farjeon, Eleanor
Chin, Chuan
See Chi, Richard Hu See-Yee
Chin, Frank (Chew Jr.) 1940- 33-36R
Chin, Marilyn (Mei Ling) 1955- 129
Chin, Richard (M.) 1946- 121
See also SATA 52
Chin, Robert 1918- 61-64
Chinard, Gilbert 1882(?)-1972 Obituary 104
Chinas, Beverly N(ewbold) 1924- 89-92
Chinery, Michael 1938- CANR-20
Earlier sketch in CA 103
See also SATA 26
Ching, Frank 1940- 129
Ching, James C(hristopher) 1926- 37-40R
Ching, Julia (Chia-yi) 1934- CANR-37
Earlier sketch in CA 101
Chinitz, Benjamin 1924- 9-12R
Chinmoy, Sri 1931- CANR-2
Earlier sketch in CA 49-52
Chinn, Laurene Chambers 1902-1978 .... 1-4R
Obituary 103
Chinn, Robert (Edward) 1928- 69-72
Chinn, William G. 1919- 33-36R
Chinoy, Ely 1921-1975 .... CANR-1
Obituary 57-60
Earlier sketch in CA 1-4R
Chinoy, Helen Krich 1922- 17-20R
Chinweizu 1943- 103
Chipasula, Frank (Mkalawile) 1949- 121
Chipman, Bruce L(ewis) 1946- 37-40R
Chipman, Donald E(ugene) 1928- 29-32R
Chipman, John S(omerset) 1926- 104
Chipp, D(onald) L(eslie) 1925- 108
Chipp, Herschel B(rowning) 1913- 25-28R
Chipperfield, Joseph Eugene
1912-1980(?) CANR-6
Earlier sketch in CA 9-12R
See also SATA 2
Chipperfield, Richard 1904-1988 Obituary 125
Chirenje, J. Mutero 1935- 65-68
Chirot, Daniel 1942- 132
Chirovsky, Nicholas L. 1919- CANR-4
Earlier sketch in CA 53-56
Chisholm, A(rthur) M(urray)
1872-1960 Obituary 114
Chisholm, A(lan) R(owland) 1888- 5-8R
Chisholm, Anne 109
Chisholm, Dianne 1953- 137
Chisholm, Hugh J. Jr.
1913-1972 Obituary 37-40R
Chisholm, K. Lomneth 1919- 61-64
Chisholm, Mary K(athleen) 1924- 37-40R
Chisholm, Matt
See Watts, Peter Christopher
Chisholm, Michael (Donald Inglis)
1931- 37-40R
Chisholm, R(obert) F(erguson) 1904- CAP-2
Earlier sketch in CA 29-32
Chisholm, Roderick Milton 1916- 102
Chisholm, Roger K. 1937- 33-36R
Chisholm, Sam(uel) Whitten 1919- 5-8R
Chisholm, Shirley (Anita St. Hill)
1924- CANR-27
Earlier sketch in CA 29-32R
See also BW
Chisholm, William S(herman) Jr.
1931- CANR-27
Earlier sketch in CA 49-52
Chishti, Hakim M.
See Thomson, Robert
Chislett, (Margaret) Anne 1943- .... CLC 34
Chislett, Gail (Elaine) 1948- .... SATA 58
Chisolm, Lawrence W(ashington) 1929- 9-12R
Chissell, Joan Olive 61-64
Chitham, Edward (Harry Gordon)
1932- CANR-19
Earlier sketch in CA 103
Chitnis, Anand C. 1942- 123
Chitrabhanu, Gurudev Shree 1922- 89-92
Chittenden, Elizabeth F. 1903- 61-64
See also SATA 9
Chittenden, Hiram Martin 1858-1917 .... DLB 47
Chittenden, Margaret 1935- CANR-19
Earlier sketches in CA 53-56, CANR-4
See also SATA 28
Chittick, Donald Ernest 1932- 115
Chittick, William O(liver) 1937- 41-44R
Chittum, Ida 1918- CANR-14
Earlier sketch in CA 37-40R
See also SATA 7
Chitty, Arthur Benjamin 1914- CANR-20
Earlier sketches in CA 53-56, CANR-4
Chitty, Letitia 1897-1982 Obituary 108
Chitty, Susan Elspeth 1929- CAP-1
Earlier sketch in CA 9-10
Chitty, Thomas Willes 1926- 5-8R
See also Hinde, Thomas
See also CLC 11
Chitwood, B(illy) J(ames) 1931- 97-100
Chitwood, Marie Downs 1918- 9-12R
Chitwood, Oliver Perry 1874-1971 .... CAP-1
Earlier sketch in CA 13-14
Chiu, Hong-Yee 1932- 53-56
Chiu, Hungdah 1936- CANR-31
Earlier sketches in CA 37-40R, CANR-14
Chivers, Thomas Holley 1809-1858 .... DLB 3
Chi-wei
See Shu, Austin Chi-wei
Chlamyda, Jehudil
See Peshkov, Alexei Maximovich
Chloros, A(lexander) G(eorge)
1926-1982 Obituary 108
Chloros, Aleck George
See Chloros, A(lexander) G(eorge)
Chmaj, Betty E. 1930- 97-100
Chmielarz, Sharon 1940- 121
Chmielewski, Edward 1928- 13-16R
Ch'o, Chou
See Shu-Jen, Chou
Cho, Yong Hyo 1934- Brief entry 105
Cho, Yong Sam 1925- 5-8R
Choate, Ernest A(lfred) 1900- 49-52
Choate, Gwen Peterson 1922- 1-4R
Choate, J(ulian) E(rnest Jr.) 1916- 33-36R
Choate, Judith (Newkirk) 1940- 105
See also SATA 30
Choate, R. G.
See Choate, Gwen Peterson
Chobanian, Aram V(an) 1929- 108
Chocano, Jose Santos 1875-1934 131
See also HW
Chochlik
See Radwanski, Pierre A(rthur)
Chodes, John 1939- CANR-25
Earlier sketches in CA 61-64, CANR-9
Chodorov, Edward 1904-1988 102
Obituary 126
Chodorov, Jerome 1911- CANR-15
Earlier sketch in CA 65-68
Chodorov, Stephan 1934- 17-20R
Chodorow, Nancy (Julia) 1944- 105
Chogyam Trungpa 1939-1987 .... CANR-12
Obituary 122
Earlier sketch in CA 25-28R
Choi Sunu 1916-1984 Obituary 115
Choldin, Marianna Tax 1942- CANR-26
Earlier sketch in CA 109
Choleric, Brother
See van Zeller, Claud
Chomette, Rene Lucien
1898-1981 Obituary 103
See also Clair, Rene
See also CLC 20
Chommie, John C(ampbell) 1914-1974 .... CAP-2
Earlier sketch in CA 29-32
Chomsky, (Avram) Noam 1928- CANR-28
Earlier sketch in CA 17-20R
See also MTCW
Chomsky, William 1896-1977 77-80
Obituary 73-76
Chong
See Chong, Thomas
Chong, Kyona-Jo
See Chung, Kyung Cho
Chong, Peng-Khuan 25-28R
Chong, Thomas 1938- Brief entry 112
Chong, Tommy
See Chong, Thomas
Choper, Jesse H(erbert) 1935- CANR-5
Earlier sketch in CA 13-16R
Chopin, Kate
See Chopin, Katherine
See also CDALB 1865-1917
See also DLB 12, 78
See also SSC 8
See also TCLC 5, 14
Chopin, Katherine 1851-1904 122
Brief entry 104
See also Chopin, Kate
Chopin, Rene 1885-1953 .... DLB 92
Choquette, Adrienne 1915-1973 .... DLB 68
Choquette, Robert 1905- .... DLB 68
Chorafas, Dimitris N. 1926- CANR-20
Earlier sketches in CA 5-8R, CANR-4
Chorao, (Ann Mc)Kay (Sproat) 1936- CANR-19
Earlier sketches in CA 49-52, CANR-1
See also MAICYA
See also SATA 8, 69
Chorell, Walentin 1912-1984(?) Obituary 111
Chorley, Katharine Campbell (Hopkinson)
1897-1986 Obituary 120
Chorley, R. J.
See Chorley, Richard J(ohn)
Chorley, Richard J(ohn) 1927- 121
Brief entry 116
Chorny, Merron 1922- 41-44R
Choron, Jacques 1904-1972 .... CAP-1
Obituary 33-36R
Earlier sketch in CA 9-10
Chorpenning, Charlotte (Lee Barrows)
1872-1955 Brief entry 114
See also SATA 37
Chothia, Jean 1944- 105
Chotjewitz, Peter O(tto) 1934- 129
Chotzinoff, Samuel 1889-1964 Obituary 93-96
Chou, Eric 1915- 132
Chou, Mark 1910-1988 Obituary 128
Chou, Ya-luu 1924- 41-44R
Chou, Yu-jui
See Chou, Eric
Choucri, Nazli 1943- CANR-14
Earlier sketch in CA 81-84
Choudhury, G(olam) W(ahed) 1926- CANR-17
Earlier sketch in CA 25-28R
Choudhury, Malay Roy 1939- .... CAAS 14
Choueiri, Youssef M. 1948- 136
Chou En-lai 1898-1976 Obituary 112
Choukas, Michael (Eugene) 1901-1989 .... CAP-2
Obituary 129
Earlier sketch in CA 17-18
Choukas-Bradley, Melanie (Rose) 1952- 124
Choukri, Mohamed 1935- 136
Chouraqui, Andre (Nathanael) 1917- CANR-10
Earlier sketch in CA 65-68
Chow, Gregory C. 1929- 13-16R
Chow, Yung-Teh 1916- 37-40R
Chowder, Ken 1950- 102
Chowdhary, Savitri Devi (Dumra) 1907- CAP-1
Earlier sketch in CA 11-12
Chowning, Larry S(hepherd) 1949- 111
Choy, Bong-youn 1914- 69-72
Choyce, Lesley 1951- 130
Chrimes, Stanley Bertram 1907-1984 .... 5-8R
Obituary 113
Chrislock, Carl H(endrick) 1917- 45-48
Chrisman, Arthur Bowie 1889-1953 .... YABC 1
Chrisman, Harry E. 1906- 1-4R
Chrisman, Katherine (G.)
1940(?)-1987 Obituary 122
Chrisman, Miriam Usher 1920- 131
Chriss, Nicholas C. 1928(?)-1990 Obituary 131
Christ, Carl F(inley) 1923- 21-24R
Christ, Carol T(ecla) 1944- 93-96
Christ, Henry I(rvine) 1915- CANR-2
Earlier sketch in CA 5-8R
Christ, John M(ichael) 1934- 106
Christ, Karl 1923- 120
Christ, Ronald 1936- CANR-10
Earlier sketch in CA 25-28R
Christaller, Walter 1893-1969 Obituary 115
Christelow, Eileen 1943- 111
See also SATA 35, 38
Christen, Robert J. 1928-1981 Obituary 108
Brief entry 107
Christensen, Ann 1946- 108
Christensen, Anna
See Mayer, Deborah Anne
Christensen, Clyde M. 1905- 53-56
Christensen, David E(mun) 1921- 13-16R
Christensen, Edward L. 1913- 25-28R
Christensen, Eleanor Ingalls 1913- 53-56
Christensen, Erwin O(ttomar) 1890- CAP-1
Earlier sketch in CA 13-14
Christensen, Francis 1902- CAP-2
Earlier sketch in CA 23-24
Christensen, Gardell Dano 1907- 9-12R
See also SATA 1
Christensen, Harold T(aylor) 1909- 45-48
Christensen, J(ack) A(rden) 1927- 53-56
Christensen, James L(ee) 1922- 97-100
Christensen, Jerome 1948- 110
Christensen, Jo Ippolito
See Christensen, Yolanda Maria Ippolito
Christensen, Otto H(enry) 1898- 33-36R
Christensen, Paul 1943- CANR-15
Earlier sketch in CA 77-80
Christensen, Sandra 1944- 110
Christensen, Terry 1944- 127
Christensen, Yolanda Maria Ippolito
1943- CANR-7
Earlier sketch in CA 57-60
Christenson, Cornelia V(os) 1903- CAP-2
Earlier sketch in CA 33-36
Christenson, Evelyn (Carol) 1922- 117
Christenson, Larry 1928- CANR-8
Earlier sketch in CA 57-60
Christenson, Nordis 1929- 108

Christenson, Reo M. 1918- ... 37-40R
Christesen, Barbara 1940- ... 107
See also SATA 40
Christesen, Clement Byrne 1911- ... 102
Christgau, Alice Erickson 1902- ... CAP-2
Earlier sketch in CA 17-18
See also SATA 13
Christgau, John (Frederick) 1934- ... 103
Christgau, Robert (Thomas) 1942- ... 65-68
Christian, A. B.
See Yabes, Leopoldo Y(abes)
Christian, Barbara T. 1943- ... 110
See also BW
Christian, C(urtis) W(allace) 1927- ... 21-24R
Christian, Carol (Cathay) 1923- ... 53-56
Christian, Frederick
See Gehman, Richard (Boyd)
Christian, Garth Hood 1921-1967 ... CAP-1
Earlier sketch in CA 9-10
Christian, George (Eastland) 1927- ... 65-68
Christian, Glynn 1942- ... 115
Christian, Henry A(rthur) 1931- ... CANR-14
Earlier sketch in CA 33-36R
Christian, James L(ee) 1927- ... 57-60
Christian, Jill
See Dilcock, Noreen
Christian, John
See Dixon, Roger
Christian, Louise
See Grill, Nannette L.
Christian, Marcus Bruce 1900- ... 73-76
Christian, Mary Blount 1933- ... CANR-17
Earlier sketches in CA 45-48, CANR-1
See also SATA 9
Christian, Nick
See Pollitz, Edward A(lan) Jr.
Christian, Peter
See Steinbrunner, (Peter) Chris(tian)
Christian, Portia 1908- ... 103
Christian, Rebecca 1952- ... 107
Christian, Reginald Frank 1924- ... CANR-3
Earlier sketch in CA 5-8R
Christian, Roy Cloberry 1914- ... 93-96
Christian, Shirley (Ann) 1938- ... 125
Brief entry ... 119
Christian, William A(rmistead) Jr. 1944- ... 107
Christiani, Dounia Bunis 1913- ... 13-16R
Christians, Clifford Glenn 1939- ... 104
Christiansen, Arthur 1904-1963 ... 1-4R
Christiansen, Eugene Martin 1944- ... 121
Christiansen, Harley Duane 1930- ... CANR-4
Earlier sketch in CA 53-56
Christiansen, Keith 1947- ... 112
Christiansen, Michael Robin
1927-1984 Obituary ... 113
Christiansen, Richard (Dean) 1931- ... 121
Christiansen, Rupert 1954- ... 135
Christianson, Elin B(allantyne) 1936- ... 111
Christianson, Gale E. 1942- ... 81-84
Christianson, John Robert 1934- ... 21-24R
Christie
See Ichikawa, Kon
Christie, Agatha (Mary Clarissa)
1890-1976 ... CANR-37
Obituary ... 61-64
Earlier sketches in CA 17-20R, CANR-10
See also AAYA 9
See also AITN 1, 2
See also CDBLB 1914-1945
See also CLC 1, 6, 8, 12, 39, 48
See also DLB 13, 77
See also MTCW
See also SATA 36
Christie, George C(ustis) 1934- ... 37-40R
Christie, Hugh
See Christie-Murray, David (Hugh Arthur)
Christie, Ian R(alph) 1919- ... CANR-20
Earlier sketches in CA 5-8R, CANR-2
Christie, James R(ichard) 1952- ... 129
Christie, Jean 1912- ... 101
Christie, John Aldrich 1920- ... 65-68
Christie, Keith
See Haynes, Alfred H(enry)
Christie, Lindsay H.
1906(?)-1976 Obituary ... 61-64
Christie, Milton 1921- ... 17-20R
Christie, (Ann) Philippa ... CANR-4
Earlier sketch in CA 5-8R
See also Pearce, Philippa
Christie, Trevor L. 1905-1969 ... CAP-2
Earlier sketch in CA 21-22
Christie-Murray, David (Hugh Arthur)
1913- ... CANR-4
Earlier sketch in CA 53-56
Christine, Charles T(hornton) 1936- ... 33-36R
Christine, Dorothy Weaver 1934- ... 33-36R
Christ-Janer, Albert W. 1910-1973 ... CANR-4
Obituary ... 45-48
Earlier sketch in CA 1-4R
Christman, Don(ald) R. 1919- ... 17-20R
Christman, Elizabeth 1914- ... 89-92
Christman, Henry Max 1932- ... 65-68
Christman, Henry 1906-1980 Obituary ... 103
Christman, Luther (Parmalee) 1915- ... 124
Christman, Paul J. 1952- ... 132
Christman, R(aymond) J(ohn) 1919- ... 89-92
Christmas, Joyce 1939- ... 123
Christodoulou, Anastasios 1932- ... 120
Christodoulou, Demetrios 1919- ... 136
Christoff, Peter K. 1911- ... 121
Christol, Carl Quimby 1914- ... CANR-4
Earlier sketch in CA 5-8R
Christoph, Florence A(nna) 1937- ... 137
Christoph, James B(ernard) 1928- ... CANR-4
Earlier sketch in CA 5-8R
Christoph, Peter R(ichard) 1938- ... 137
Christopher, Beth
See Steinke, Ann E(lizabeth)
Christopher, Georgia B. 1932- ... 111
Christopher, Joe R(andell) 1935- ... CANR-4
Earlier sketch in CA 53-56
Christopher, John
See Youd, (Christopher) Samuel
See also CLR 2
Christopher, John B. 1914- ... 13-16R
Christopher, Kenneth
See Brophy, Donald F(rancis)
Christopher, Louise
See Hale, Arlene
Christopher, Matt(hew F.) 1917- ... CANR-36
Earlier sketches in CA 1-4R, CANR-5
See also MAICYA
See also SAAS 9
See also SATA 2, 47
Christopher, Maurine (Brooks) ... 65-68
Christopher, Milbourne 1914(?)-1984 ... 105
Obituary ... 113
See also SATA 46
Christopher, Nicholas 1951- ... 108
Christopher, Robert Collins 1924- ... 102
Obituary ... 138
Christophersen, Paul (Hans) 1911- ... 57-60
Christowe, Stoyan 1898- ... 65-68
Christy, Betty 1924- ... 57-60
Christy, George ... 9-12R
Christy, Howard Chandler 1873-1952 ... SATA 21
Christy, Jim 1945- ... 138
Christy, Joe
See Christy, Joseph M.
Christy, Joseph M. 1919- ... CANR-14
Earlier sketch in CA 29-32R
Christy, Marian 1932- ... 65-68
Christy, Teresa E(lizabeth) 1927- ... 73-76
Chroman, Eleanor 1937- ... 45-48
Chroman, Nathan 1929- ... 77-80
Chronic, Halka (Pattison) 1923- ... 118
Chroust, Anton-Hermann 1907- ... CAP-1
Earlier sketch in CA 9-10
Chruden, Herbert J(efferson) 1918- ... 5-8R
Chrystie, Frances N(icholson)
1904-1986 ... SATA 60
Chu, Arthur (T. S.) 1916-1979 ... 81-84
Obituary ... 133
Chu, Daniel 1933- ... 13-16R
See also SATA 11
Chu, Godwin C(hien) 1927- ... 114
Chu, Grace (Goodyear) 1916- ... 81-84
Chu, Grace Zia 1899- ... CANR-4
Earlier sketch in CA 5-8R
Chu, Kong 1926- ... 49-52
Chu, Louis H. 1915- ... 13-16R
Chu, Petra ten-Doesschate 1942- ... 138
Chu, Samuel C. 1929- ... 69-72
Ch'u, Tung-tsu 1910- ... CANR-2
Earlier sketch in CA 1-4R
Chu, Valentin (Yuan-ling) 1919- ... 9-12R
Chu, W. R.
See Chu, Arthur (T. S.)
Chubb, Elmer
See Masters, Edgar Lee
Chubb, Judith (Ann) 1947- ... 113
Chubb, Thomas Caldecot 1899-1972 ... CANR-6
Obituary ... 33-36R
Earlier sketch in CA 1-4R
Chubin, Barry 1943- ... 124
Chudacoff, Howard P(eter) 1943- ... 45-48
Chudley, Ron(ald Alexander) 1937- ... 110
Chuikov, Vasili Ivanovich
1900-1982 Obituary ... 106
Chukovskaya, Lydia (Korneeva) 1907- ... 128
Brief entry ... 117
Chukovsky, Kornei (Ivanovich)
1882-1969 ... CANR-4
Obituary ... 25-28R
Earlier sketch in CA 5-8R
See also MAICYA
See also SATA 5, 34
Chulak, Armando Obituary ... 109
Chumacero, Ali 1918- ... HW
Chuman, Frank Fujio 1917- ... 69-72
Chun, Jinsie K(yung) S(hien) 1902- ... 49-52
Chun, Richard 1935- ... 65-68
Chung, Connie
See Chung, Constance Yu-Hwa
Chung, Constance Yu-Hwa 1946- ... 132
Brief entry ... 119
Chung, Edward K(oo-Young) 1931- ... 107
Chung, Hyung C(han) 1931- ... 57-60
Chung, Joseph Sang-hoon 1929- ... 49-52
Chung, Kyung Cho 1921- ... 33-36R
Chung-yu, Chu
See Hsu, Benedict (Pei-Hsiung)
Chunn, Jay Carrington II 1938- ... 116
Chupack, Henry 1915- ... 49-52
Church, Albert M(arion) 1940- ... 111
Church, Benjamin 1734-1778 ... DLB 31
Church, F(rank) Forrester (IV) 1948- ... 133
Church, Francis Pharcellus 1839-1906 ... DLB 79
Church, Jeffrey
See Kirk, Richard (Edmund)
Church, Joseph 1918- ... 1-4R
Church, Margaret 1920- ... 13-16R
Church, Peter
See Nuttall, Jeff
Church, Ralph (Bruce) 1927- ... 37-40R
Church, Richard 1893-1972 ... CANR-3
Obituary ... 33-36R
Earlier sketch in CA 1-4R
See also SATA 3
Church, Robert L(eValley) 1938- ... 61-64
Church, Ronald James Harrison
See Harrison Church, Ronald James
Church, Roy A. 1935- ... 124
Church, Ruth Ellen (Lovrien)
1910(?)-1991 ... CANR-7
Obituary ... 135
Earlier sketch in CA 5-8R
Church, Suzanne
See Bates, Susannah (Vacella)
Church, William Conant 1836-1917 ... DLB 79
Church, William Farr 1912- Brief entry ... 105
Churchill, Allen 1911-1988 ... 97-100
Obituary ... 124
Churchill, Bill
See Churchill, Gail Winston
Churchill, Caryl 1938- ... CANR-22
Earlier sketch in CA 102
See also CLC 31, 55
See also DLB 13
See also MTCW
Churchill, Charles 1731-1764 ... DLB 109
Churchill, Creighton 1912-1984 ... 69-72
Obituary ... 114
Churchill, David 1935- ... 106
Churchill, E(lmer) Richard 1937- ... CANR-30
Earlier sketches in CA 17-20R, CANR-11
See also SATA 11
Churchill, Edward Delos
1895-1972 Obituary ... 37-40R
Churchill, Elizabeth
See Hough, Richard (Alexander)
Churchill, Gail Winston
1903(?)-1984 Obituary ... 112
Churchill, Guy E. 1926- ... 29-32R
Churchill, J(ohn) H(oward)
1920-1990 Obituary ... 131
Churchill, Joyce
See Harrison, M(ichael) John
Churchill, Linda R. 1938- ... CANR-11
Earlier sketch in CA 21-24R
Churchill, R(eginald) C(harles) 1916- ... 9-12R
Churchill, Randolph (Frederick Edward Spencer)
1911-1968 Obituary ... 89-92
Churchill, Reba 1932(?)-1985 Obituary ... 116
Churchill, Rhona Adelaide 1913- ... 5-8R
Churchill, Rogers Platt 1902-1989 Obituary ... 129
Churchill, Samuel 1911- ... 17-20R
Churchill, Sarah (Millicent Hermione)
1914-1982 ... 129
Obituary ... 107
Churchill, Thomas Bell Lindsay
1907-1990 Obituary ... 131
Churchill, Ward 1947- ... 135
Churchill, Winston (Leonard Spencer)
1874-1965 ... 97-100
See also CDBLB 1890-1914
See also DLB 100
See also MTCW
Churchill, Winston S(pencer) 1940- ... 131
Churchland, Patricia Smith 1943- ... 123
Churchman, C(harles) West 1913- ... CANR-9
Earlier sketch in CA 21-24R
Churchman, Michael 1929- ... 37-40R
Chute, B(eatrice) J(oy) 1913-1987 ... 1-4R
Obituary ... 123
See also SATA 2, 53
Chute, Carolyn 1947- ... 123
See also CLC 39
Chute, Marchette (Gaylord) 1909- ... CANR-5
Earlier sketch in CA 1-4R
See also DLB 103
See also SATA 1
Chute, Robert M. 1926- ... 109
Chute, Rupert
See Cleveland, Philip Jerome
Chute, William J(oseph) 1914- ... 9-12R
Chwalek, Henryka C. 1918- ... 17-20R
Chwast, Jacqueline 1932- ... CANR-5
Earlier sketch in CA 49-52
See also SATA 6
Chwast, Seymour 1931- ... SATA 18
Chyet, Stanley F. 1931- ... 33-36R
Cialente, Fausta
See Terni-Cialente, Fausta
Cianciolo, Patricia Jean 1929- ... CANR-13
Earlier sketch in CA 37-40R
Ciaramitaro, Andrew James 1955- ... 110
Ciaramitaro, Barbara 1946- ... 107
Ciarcia, Steve 1947- ... 110
Ciardi, John (Anthony) 1916-1986 ... CANR-33
Obituary ... 118
Earlier sketches in CA 5-8R, CANR-5
See also CAAS 2
See also CLC 10, 40, 44
See also CLR 19
See also DLB 5
See also DLBY 86
See also MAICYA
See also MTCW
See also SATA 1, 46, 65
Ciavolella, Massimo 1942- ... 135
Cibber, Colley 1671-1757 ... DLB 84
Ciccorella, Aubra Dair ... 65-68
Cicellis, Kay 1926- ... CANR-3
Earlier sketch in CA 1-4R
Cicognani, Amleto Giovanni Cardinal
1883-1973 Obituary ... 45-48
Cicourel, Aaron V. 1928- ... 53-56
Cid Perez, Jose (Diego) 1906- ... CANR-4
Earlier sketch in CA 53-56
Ciechanowski, Jan
1888(?)-1973 Obituary ... 41-44R
Cienciala, Anna M(aria) 1929- ... 89-92
Cieplak, Tadeusz N(owak) 1918- ... CANR-11
Earlier sketch in CA 69-72
Cigler, Allan J(ames) 1943- ... CANR-29
Earlier sketch in CA 111
Cikovsky, Nicolai Jr. 1933- ... 113
Cilffriw, Gwynfor
See Griffith, Thomas Gwynfor
Cimbollek, Robert (Carl) 1937- ... 57-60
Ciment, Michel 1938- ... 97-100
Cimino, Michael 1943- ... 105
See also CLC 16
Cinberg, Bernard L. 1905-1979 Obituary ... 85-88
Cincinnatus
See Currey, Cecil B(arr)
Cinel, Dino 1941- ... 111
Cinquin, Emmanuelle 1908- ... 131
Cinquin, Sister Emmanuelle
See Cinquin, Emmanuelle
Cioffari, Vincenzo 1905- ... 17-20R
Cioffi, Lou(is James) 1926- ... 120
Brief entry ... 109
Cioran, E(mil) M. 1911- ... 25-28R
See also CLC 64
Cipes, Robert M. 1930- ... 21-24R
Ciplijauskaite, Birute 1929- ... CANR-14
Earlier sketches in CA 37-40R, CANR-31
Cipolla, Carlo M(anlio) 1922- ... CANR-39
Earlier sketches in CA 5-8R, CANR-2, 18
Cipolla, Joan Bagnel
See Bagnel, Joan
Cipriano, Anthony (John) 1941- ... 102
Circus, Anthony
See Hoch, Edward D(entinger)
Circus, Jim
See Roseyear, John
Cire
See Hayden, Eric W(illiam)
Cirese, Eugenio 1884-1955 ... DLB 114
Ciria, Alberto 1934- ... 73-76
Cirino, Linda D(avis) 1941- ... 65-68
Cirino, Robert 1937- ... 61-64
Cismaru, Alfred 1933- ... 61-64
Cisneros, Antonio 1942- ... 131
See also HW
Cisneros, Sandra 1954- ... 131
See also AAYA 9
See also CLC 69
See also HW
Ciszek, Walter 1904- ... CAP-1
Earlier sketch in CA 13-14
Citati, Pietro 1930- ... CANR-4
Earlier sketch in CA 53-56
Citino, David 1947- ... 104
Citrine, Walter McLennan
1887-1983 Obituary ... 109
Cittafino, Ricardo
See Bickers, Richard Leslie Townshend
Ciuba, Edward J(oseph) 1935- ... 61-64
Civille, John R(aphael) 1940- ... CANR-11
Earlier sketch in CA 69-72
Cixous, Helene 1937- ... 126
See also DLB 83
See also MTCW
Cizmar, Paula 1949- ... 122
Claassen, Harold 1905- ... CAP-2
Earlier sketch in CA 19-20
Clabaugh, Gary K(enneth) 1940- ... 69-72
Clabby, John 1911- ... 104
Clack, Robert Wood 1886-1964 ... 122
Obituary ... 110
Claerbaut, David 1946- ... CANR-1
Earlier sketch in CA 45-48
Claeyssens, Astere E(varist)
1924-1990 Obituary ... 132
Claffey, William J. 1925- ... 21-24R
Claflin, Edward 1949- ... 97-100
Clagett, John (Henry) 1916- ... CANR-6
Earlier sketch in CA 5-8R
Clagett, Marshall 1916- ... CANR-5
Earlier sketch in CA 1-4R
Claghorn, Charles Eugene 1911- ... 57-60
Clague, Ewan 1896-1987 ... 29-32R
Obituary ... 122
Clague, Maryhelen 1930- ... 81-84
Claiborne, Craig 1920- ... CANR-5
Earlier sketch in CA 1-4R
Claiborne, Robert (Watson Jr.)
1919-1990 ... CANR-31
Obituary ... 130
Earlier sketches in CA 29-32R, CANR-12
Claiborne, Sybil 1923- ... 128
Clain-Stefanelli, Vladimir 1914-1982 ... 111
Obituary ... 108
Clair, Andree ... 29-32R
See also SATA 19
Clair, Bernard (Eddy) 1951- ... 102
Clair, Rene
See Chomette, Rene Lucien
See also CLC 20
Claire, Keith
See Andrews, Claire
Claire, Keith
See Andrews, Keith
Claire, William Francis 1935- ... CANR-7
Earlier sketch in CA 57-60
Clairmont, Elva 1937- ... 117
Clammer, David 1943- ... 69-72
Clampett, Bob 1914(?)-1984 Obituary ... 112
See also Clampett, Robert
See also AITN 1
See also SATA 38
Clampett, Robert
See Clampett, Bob
See also SATA 44
Clampitt, Amy 1920- ... CANR-29
Earlier sketch in CA 110
See also CLC 32
See also DLB 105
Clance, Pauline Rose 1938- ... 126
Clancy, Francis Michael
1903-1986 Obituary ... 121
Clancy, John Gregory 1922- ... 13-16R
Clancy, Joseph P(atrick) 1928- ... CANR-18
Earlier sketch in CA 101

Clancy, King
 See Clancy, Francis Michael
Clancy, Laurence James 1942- 108
Clancy, Laurie
 See Clancy, Laurence James
Clancy, Thomas H(anley) 1923- CANR-7
 Earlier sketch in CA 13-16R
Clancy, Thomas L. Jr. 1947- 131
 Brief entry 125
 See also Clancy, Tom
 See also MTCW
Clancy, Tom
 See Clancy, Thomas L. Jr.
 See also AAYA 9
 See also BEST 89:1, 90:1
 See also CLC 45
Clancy, William 1922-1982 Obituary 106
Clanton, (Orval) Gene 1934- 41-44R
Clanton, Gordon 1942- 57-60
Clapham, Arthur Roy 1904-1990 109
 Obituary 133
Clapham, Christopher (S.) 1941- 128
Clapham, John 1908- CANR-10
 Earlier sketch in CA 25-28R
Clapp, James Gordon 1909-1970 .... CAP-1
 Earlier sketch in CA 9-10
Clapp, Margaret (Antoinette)
 1910-1974 Obituary 49-52
Clapp, Patricia 1912- CANR-37
 Earlier sketches in CA 25-28R, CANR-10
 See also MAICYA
 See also SAAS 4
 See also SATA 4
Clapp, Verner W(arren)
 1901-1972 Obituary 37-40R
Clapper, Raymond 1892-1944 .... DLB 29
Clapperton, Richard 1934- 25-28R
Clar, C(harles) Raymond 1903- 37-40R
Clardy, Andrea Fleck 1943- CANR-17
 Earlier sketch in CA 97-100
Clardy, J(esse) V. 1929- 33-36R
Clare, Elizabeth
 See Cook, Dorothy Mary
Clare, Ellen
 See Sinclair, Olga
Clare, Francis D.
 See Aschmann, Alberta
Clare, George P. 1920- 111
Clare, Helen
 See Hunter Blair, Pauline (Clarke)
Clare, John 1793-1864 .... DLB 55, 96
Clare, Josephine 1933- 73-76
Clare, Margaret
 See Maison, Margaret M(ary Bowles)
Clare, Samantha
 See Dawson, Janis
Clarens, Carlos (Figueredo y)
 1936(?)-1987 ....21-24R
 Obituary 121
Clareson, Thomas D(ean) 1926- CANR-39
 Earlier sketches in CA 1-4R, CANR-2, 18
Clarfield, Gerard Howard 1936- 103
Claridge, Gordon S. 1932- 21-24R
Clarie, Thomas C(ashin) 1943- 93-96
Clarin
 See Alas (y Urena), Leopoldo (Enrique Garcia)
Clarizio, Harvey F(rank) 1934- 33-36R
Clark, Admont Gulick 1919- 53-56
Clark, Al C.
 See Goines, Donald
Clark, Alan 1928- 13-16R
Clark, Alfred Alexander Gordon
 1900-1958 Brief entry 112
 See also Hare, Cyril
Clark, Alice S(andell) 1922- 41-44R
Clark, Andrew Hill 1911-1975 .... CAP-2
 Earlier sketch in CA 25-28
Clark, Ann L(ivezey) 1913- CANR-7
 Earlier sketch in CA 17-20R
Clark, Ann Nolan 1896- CANR-2
 Earlier sketch in CA 5-8R
 See also CLR 16
 See also DLB 52
 See also MAICYA
 See also SATA 4
Clark, Anne
 See Amor, Anne Clark
Clark, Anne 1909- 29-32R
Clark, Badger
 See Paine, Lauran (Bosworth)
Clark, Ben T. 1928- 53-56
Clark, Bill
 See Clark, William A(rthur)
Clark, Billy C(urtis) 1928- CANR-22
 Earlier sketch in CA 1-4R
Clark, (Robert) Brian 1932- 41-44R
 See also CLC 29
Clark, Bruce B(udge) 1918- 69-72
Clark, Burton R(obert) 1921- CANR-28
 Earlier sketch in CA 110
Clark, C. E. Frazer Jr. 1925- 33-36R
Clark, C. H. Douglas 1890- CAP-2
 Earlier sketch in CA 23-24
Clark, C(harles) M(anning) H(ope) 1915- 97-100
Clark, Carol (Lois) 1948- 57-60
Clark, Catherine Anthony (Smith)
 1892-1977 .... CAP-1
 Earlier sketch in CA 11-12
 See also DLB 68
Clark, Champ 1923- 108
 See also SATA 47
Clark, Charles E(dwin) 1929- 29-32R
Clark, Charles Heber 1841-1915 Brief entry 111
 See also DLB 11
Clark, Charles Tallifero 1917- 13-16R
Clark, China (Debra) 1950- 45-48
Clark, Christopher (Anthony) Stuart
 See Stuart-Clark, Christopher (Anthony)
Clark, Clifford E(dward) Jr. 1941- 81-84
Clark, Colin (Grant) 1905-1989 ....CANR-8
 Obituary 129
 Earlier sketch in CA 61-64
Clark, David
 See Hardcastle, Michael
Clark, David Allen
 See Ernst, (Lyman) John
Clark, David (George) 1939- 130
Clark, David Gillis 1933- 53-56
Clark, David Ridgley 1920- CANR-9
 Earlier sketch in CA 17-20R
Clark, Davis Wasgatt 1812-1871 .... DLB 79
Clark, Dennis E. 1916- 29-32R
Clark, Dennis J. 1927- CANR-1
 Earlier sketch in CA 1-4R
Clark, Diana Cooper
 See Cooper-Clark, Diana
Clark, Dick
 See Clark, Richard Wagstaff
Clark, D.M.J.
 See Clark, Douglas
Clark, Don(ald Henry) 1930- 29-32R
Clark, Don(ald Rowlee) 1925- 57-60
Clark, Donald E. 1933- CANR-8
 Earlier sketch in CA 21-24R
Clark, Dora Mae 1893- 41-44R
Clark, Dorothy Park 1899- 5-8R
Clark, Douglas 1919- 114
Clark, E. Ritchie 1912- 122
Clark, Edward W(illiam) 1943- 123
Clark, Eleanor 1913- 9-12R
 See also CLC 5, 19
 See also DLB 6
Clark, Electa 1910- 69-72
Clark, Eliot (Candee)
 1883-1980 Obituary 97-100
Clark, Ella E(lizabeth) 1896- 105
Clark, Ellery Harding Jr. 1909- CANR-10
 Earlier sketch in CA 65-68
Clark, Elmer Talmage 1886-1966 ....5-8R
Clark, Emma Chichester
 See Chichester Clark, Emma
 See also SATA 69
Clark, Eric 1911- CANR-9
 Earlier sketch in CA 13-16R
Clark, Eric 1937- 102
Clark, Eugenie 1922- 49-52
Clark, Evans 1888-1970 Obituary 104
Clark, Evert 1926(?)-1988 Obituary 126
Clark, F(rederick) Stephen
 1908-1977 ....CANR-14
 Earlier sketch in CA 21-24R
Clark, Francis 1919- 17-20R
Clark, Frank J(ames) 1922- CANR-17
 Earlier sketch in CA 13-16R
 See also SATA 18
Clark, Fred George 1890-1972 Obituary 37-40R
Clark, Gail 1944- CANR-16
 Earlier sketch in CA 97-100
Clark, Garel
 See Garelick, May
Clark, Garth (Reginald) 1947- 115
Clark, George Norman 1890-1979 65-68
 Obituary 85-88
Clark, George Sidney Roberts Kitson
 See Kitson Clark, George Sydney Roberts
Clark, George 1932- 136
Clark, Gerald 1918- 13-16R
Clark, Gordon H(addon) 1902-1985 ......CANR-17
 Earlier sketches in CA 1-4R, CANR-1
Clark, (John) Grahame (Douglas)
 1907- CANR-10
 Earlier sketch in CA 65-68
Clark, Gregory 1892-1977 Obituary 89-92
Clark, Harry Hayden 1901-1971 .... CAP-2
 Earlier sketch in CA 29-32
Clark, Harry 1917- 61-64
Clark, Henry B(alsley) II 1930- CANR-8
 Earlier sketch in CA 5-8R
Clark, Howard
 See Haskin, Dorothy C(lark)
Clark, Ira G(ranville Jr.) 1909- 127
Clark, J(onathan) C(harles) D(ouglas)
 1951- 121
Clark, J(ohn) H(oward) 1929- 106
Clark, J(ustus) Kent 1917- 128
Clark, J. P.
 See Clark, John Pepper
 See also DLB 117
Clark, J. R.
 See Clark, John R(ussell)
Clark, J(eff) R(ay) 1947- CANR-22
 Earlier sketch in CA 106
Clark, James Anthony 1907- 65-68
Clark, James C. 1947- 122
Clark, James M(ilford) 1930- 21-24R
Clark, James V(aughan) 1927- 13-16R
Clark, Janie 1956- 138
Clark, Jean C(ashman) 1920- 93-96
Clark, Jere Walton 1922- 21-24R
Clark, Jerome L. 1928- 37-40R
Clark, Jerry E(ugene) 1942- 73-76
Clark, Joan
 See Benson, Mildred (Augustine Wirt)
Clark, Joan 1934- 93-96
 See also SATA 59
Clark, John Desmond 1916- 61-64
Clark, John Drury 1907- 37-40R
Clark, John G(arretson) 1932- 17-20R
Clark, John Maurice 1884-1963 ....5-8R
Clark, John Pepper 1935- CANR-16
 Earlier sketch in CA 65-68
 See also Clark, J. P.
 See also BLC 1
 See also BW
 See also CLC 38
Clark, John R(ichard) 1930- 37-40R
Clark, John R(alph) K(ukeakalani) 1946- 101
Clark, John R(ussell) 1927- 120
Clark, John W(illiams) 1907- 13-16R
Clark, Joseph D(eadrick) 1893- CAP-2
 Earlier sketch in CA 33-36
Clark, Joseph James 1893-1971 .... CAP-2
 Obituary 29-32R
 Earlier sketch in CA 19-20
Clark, Joseph L(ynn) 1881- CAP-2
 Earlier sketch in CA 17-18
Clark, Joseph S(ill Jr.) 1901-1990 Obituary 130
Clark, Katerina 1941- 110
Clark, Katharine (Jarman)
 1911(?)-1986 Obituary 118
Clark, Keith 1939- 124
Clark, Kenneth B(ancroft) 1914- 33-36R
 See also BW
Clark, Kenneth (Mackenzie)
 1903-1983 ....CANR-36
 Obituary 109
 Earlier sketch in CA 93-96
 See also MTCW
Clark, L. D. 1922- CANR-1
 Earlier sketch in CA 1-4R
Clark, Laurence (Walter) 1914- 13-16R
Clark, LaVerne Harrell 1929- CANR-11
 Earlier sketch in CA 13-16R
Clark, Leonard H(ill) 1915- CANR-4
 Earlier sketch in CA 53-56
Clark, Leonard 1905-1981 ....CANR-7
 Obituary 105
 Earlier sketch in CA 13-16R
 See also SATA 29, 30
Clark, Leroy D. CANR-11
 Earlier sketch in CA 61-64
Clark, Lewis Gaylord 1808-1873 ..... DLB 3, 64, 73
Clark, Lindley H(oag) Jr. 1920- 65-68
Clark, Lydia Benson
 See Meaker, Eloise
Clark, M. R.
 See Clark, Mavis Thorpe
Clark, Mabel Margaret (Cowie) 1903-1975 101
Clark, Malcolm (Hamilton) Jr. 1917- 106
Clark, (Charles) Manning (Hope)
 1915-1991 ....9-12R
 Obituary 134
Clark, Marden J. 1916- 61-64
Clark, Margaret Goff 1913- CANR-20
 Earlier sketches in CA 1-4R, CANR-5
 See also SATA 8
Clark, Marguerite Sheridan
 1892(?)-1982 Obituary 107
Clark, Maria Louisa Guidish 1926- 5-8R
Clark, Marion L. 1943-1977 77-80
 Obituary 73-76
Clark, Marjorie A. 1911- 33-36R
Clark, Mark (Wayne) 1896-1984 Obituary 112
Clark, (Bennett) Marsh 1928-1985 122
 Obituary 117
Clark, Marv T. 37-40R
Clark, Mary Higgins 1929- CANR-36
 Earlier sketches in CA 81-84, CANR-16
 See also BEST 89:4
 See also MTCW
 See also SATA 46
Clark, Mary Jane 1915- 57-60
Clark, Mary Lou
 See Clark, Maria Louisa Guidish
Clark, Mary Margaret 1929- 113
Clark, Mary T(wibill) 102
Clark, Mavis Thorpe 1909- CANR-37
 Earlier sketches in CA 57-60, CANR-8
 See also CLC 12
 See also MAICYA
 See also SAAS 5
 See also SATA 8
Clark, Melissa 1949- CANR-22
 Earlier sketch in CA 104
Clark, Merle
 See Gessner, Lynne
Clark, Michael D(orsey) 1937- 111
Clark, Miles (Morton) 1920- 21-24R
Clark, Naomi 1932- 77-80
Clark, Neal 1950- 113
Clark, Neil M(cCullough) 1890- 5-8R
Clark, Nicholas (Alexander) 1959-1984 132
Clark, Norman H(arold) 1925- 69-72
Clark (of Herriotshall), Arthur Melville
 1895- 9-12R
Clark, Parlin
 See Trigg, Harry Davis
Clark, Patricia Finrow 1929- 17-20R
 See also SATA 11
Clark, Paul F. 1954- 138
Clark, R. Milton
 See Clark, Reginald M.
Clark, (William) Ramsey 1927- 29-32R
Clark, Randall 1957- 120
Clark, Reginald M. 1949- 128
Clark, Richard Charles 1935- 133
 Brief entry 114
Clark, Richard Wagstaff 1929- 130
 Brief entry 113
Clark, Robert Alfred 1908- 101
Clark, Robert E(dward) D(avid) 1906- CANR-21
 Earlier sketch in CA 5-8R
Clark, Robert E(ugene) 1912- 41-44R
Clark, Robert L(loyd) Jr. 1945- 103
Clark, Robert P(hillips) 1921- 126
Clark, Rolf 1937- 114
Clark, Romane Lewis 1925- 17-20R
Clark, Ronald Harry 1904- 110
Clark, Ronald William 1916-1987 ....25-28R
 Obituary 122
 See also SATA 2, 52
Clark, Ruth C(ampbell) 1920- 69-72
Clark, Samuel Delbert 1910- CANR-11
 Earlier sketches in CAP-1, CA 13-14
Clark, Samuel 1945- 89-92
Clark, Septima Poinsette 1898-1987 ....5-8R
 Obituary 124
Clark, Stephen R(ichard) L(yster)
 1945- CANR-32
 Earlier sketches in CA 77-80, CANR-13
Clark, Sue C(assidy) 1935- 41-44R
Clark, Sydney A(ylmer) 1890-1975 ....CANR-4
 Obituary 57-60
 Earlier sketch in CA 5-8R
Clark, Terry N(ichols) 1940- 25-28R
Clark, Thomas D(ionysious) 1903- CANR-4
 Earlier sketch in CA 5-8R
Clark, Thomas Willard 1941- 81-84
Clark, Tom
 See Clark, Thomas Willard
Clark, Truman R(oss) 1935- 61-64
Clark, Van D(eusen) 1909- CAP-1
 Earlier sketch in CA 13-14
 See also SATA 2
Clark, Virginia
 See Gray, Patricia (Clark)
Clark, Walter Houston 1902- 37-40R
Clark, Walter Van Tilburg 1909-1971 ....9-12R
 Obituary 33-36R
 See also CLC 28
 See also DLB 9
 See also SATA 8
Clark, Wesley James 1950- CANR-31
 Earlier sketch in CA 112
Clark, William A(rthur) 1931- 33-36R
Clark, William Bedford 1947- CANR-27
 Earlier sketch in CA 109
Clark, William (Donaldson) 1916-1985 ......29-32R
 Obituary 116
Clark, William Smith II 1900-1969 .... CAP-2
 Earlier sketch in CA 25-28
Clarke, A. F. N. 1948- 128
Clarke, Anna 1919- CANR-39
 Earlier sketches in CA 102, CANR-18
Clarke, Arthur C(harles) 1917- CANR-28
 Earlier sketches in CA 1-4R, CANR-2
 See also AAYA 4
 See also CLC 1, 4, 13, 18, 35
 See also MAICYA
 See also MTCW
 See also SATA 13, 70
 See also SSC 3
Clarke, Arthur G(ladstone) 1887- CAP-2
 Earlier sketch in CA 17-18
Clarke, Austin C(hesterfield) 1934- CANR-32
 Earlier sketches in CA 25-28R, CANR-14
 See also CAAS 16
 See also BLC 1
 See also BW
 See also CLC 8, 53
 See also DLB 53
Clarke, Austin 1896-1974 .... CAP-2
 Obituary 49-52
 Earlier sketch in CA 29-32
 See also CLC 6, 9
 See also DLB 10, 20
Clarke, Basil F(ulford) L(owther)
 1908-1978 ....CANR-4
 Obituary 89-92
 Earlier sketch in CA 5-8R
Clarke, Boden
 See Burgess, M(ichael) R(oy)
Clarke, Brenda (Margaret Lilian)
 1926- CANR-24
 Earlier sketches in CA 65-68, CANR-9
Clarke, Captain Jafar
 See Nesmith, Robert I.
Clarke, Charles Galloway
 1899-1983 Obituary 110
Clarke, Charles (Richard Astley) 1944- 118
Clarke, Clorinda 1917- 25-28R
 See also SATA 7
Clarke, D(erek) A(shdown) 1921- 125
Clarke, D(avid) Waldo 1907- 9-12R
Clarke, David E(gerton) 1920- 17-20R
Clarke, David Leonard 1937-1976 Obituary 111
Clarke, Derrick Harry 1919- 103
Clarke, Dorothy Clotelle
 See Shadi, Dorothy Clotelle Clarke
Clarke, Dudley (Wrangel) 1899-1974 .... CAP-1
 Earlier sketch in CA 13-16
Clarke, Duncan L(ynn) 1941- CANR-16
 Earlier sketch in CA 97-100
Clarke, Dwight Lancelot 1885-1971 ....1-4R
 Obituary 103
Clarke, Ernest George 1927- 102
Clarke, Garry E(vans) 1943- 77-80
Clarke, George Timothy CANR-1
 Earlier sketch in CA 1-4R
Clarke, George Wallace
 See Wallace-Clarke, George
Clarke, Gillian 1937- 106
 See also CLC 61
 See also DLB 40
Clarke, H. Harrison 1902- CANR-5
 Earlier sketch in CA 1-4R
Clarke, Hans Thacher
 1887-1972 Obituary 37-40R
Clarke, Harry Eugene Jr. 1921- 5-8R
Clarke, Henry Charles 1899- 102
Clarke, Hockley
 See Clarke, Henry Charles
Clarke, Howard William 1929- 37-40R

Clarke, Hugh Vincent 1919- CANR-19
Earlier sketch in CA 102
Clarke, I. F.
See Clarke, Ignatius (Ian) Frederick
Clarke, Ian
See Clarke, Ignatius (Ian) Frederick
Clarke, Ignatius (Ian) Frederick 1918- 116
Clarke, J(ohn) F(rederick) Gates
1905-1990 ..... CAP-1
Obituary 132
Earlier sketch in CA 13-14
Clarke, Jack Alden 1924- 29-32R
Clarke, James F(ranklin) 1906- 69-72
Clarke, James Freeman 1810-1888 ..... DLB 1, 59
Clarke, James Hall
See Rowland-Entwistle, (Arthur) Theodore (Henry)
Clarke, James W(eston) 1937- 110
Clarke, James 1934- 127
Clarke, Joan B. 1921- .....SATA 27, 42
Clarke, Joan Dorn 1924- 9-12R
Clarke, Joan (Lorraine) 1920- 104
Clarke, John
See Laklan, Carli
and Sontup, Dan(iel)
Clarke, John (Campbell) 1913- CAP-1
Earlier sketch in CA 13-16
Clarke, John Henrik 1915- CANR-24
Earlier sketch in CA 53-56
See also AITN 1
See also BW
Clarke, John Joseph 1879- CANR-5
Earlier sketch in CA 5-8R
Clarke, Kenneth W(endell) 1917- 17-20R
Clarke, Lea
See Rowland-Entwistle, (Arthur) Theodore (Henry)
Clarke, Lige 1942- 41-44R
Clarke, (Victor) Lindsay 1939- 127
Clarke, Margaret 1941- 130
Clarke, Martin Lowther 1909- CANR-2
Earlier sketch in CA 5-8R
Clarke, Mary Stetson 1911- CANR-8
Earlier sketch in CA 21-24R
See also SATA 5
Clarke, Mary Washington 1913- CANR-11
Earlier sketch in CA 25-28R
Clarke, Mary Whatley 1899- CANR-2
Earlier sketch in CA 5-8R
Clarke, Mary 1923- 104
Clarke, Michael
See Newlon, (Frank) Clarke
Clarke, Nicholas Goodrick
See Goodrick-Clarke, Nicholas
Clarke, P(eter) F(rederick) 1942- 73-76
Clarke, Pauline
See Hunter Blair, Pauline (Clarke)
See also CLR 28
See also MAICYA
Clarke, Peter 1936- 104
Clarke, Rebecca Sophia
1833-1906 Brief entry 119
See also DLB 42
Clarke, Richard
See Paine, Lauran (Bosworth)
Clarke, Richard (William Barnes)
1910-1975 Obituary 115
Clarke, Robert
See Paine, Lauran (Bosworth)
and Platt, Charles
Clarke, Robin Harwood 1937- CANR-9
Earlier sketch in CA 13-16R
Clarke, Ron 1937- 107
Clarke, Ronald Francis 1933- 21-24R
Clarke, Shirley 1925- ..... CLC 16
Clarke, Simon 1946- 122
Clarke, Stephan P(aul) 1945- 69-72
Clarke, Thomas E(mmet) 1918- 53-56
Clarke, Thomas Ernest Bennett
1907-1989 .....CANR-19
Obituary 127
Earlier sketch in CA 103
Clarke, Thurston 1946- CANR-13
Earlier sketch in CA 77-80
Clarke, Tom E(ugene) 1915- 5-8R
Clarke, William Dixon 1927- 5-8R
Clarke, William Kendall
1911(?)-1981 Obituary 104
Clarke, William M(alpas) 1922- CANR-34
Earlier sketches in CA 41-44R, CANR-15
Clarke, William Thomas 1932- 57-60
Clarke-Stewart, K(athleen) Alison
1943- CANR-32
Earlier sketch in CA 113
Clark-Kennedy, A. E.
See Clark-Kennedy, Archibald Edmund
Clark-Kennedy, Archibald Edmund
1893-1985 134
Obituary 117
Clark-Pendarvis, China 1950- 129
Clarkson, Adrienne 1939- 49-52
Clarkson, E(dith) Margaret 1915- CANR-20
Earlier sketches in CA 1-4R, CANR-5
See also SATA 37
Clarkson, Ewan 1929- CANR-17
Earlier sketch in CA 25-28R
See also SATA 9
Clarkson, Geoffrey P. E. 1934- CANR-2
Earlier sketch in CA 5-8R
Clarkson, Helen
See McCloy, Helen (Worrell Clarkson)
Clarkson, J. F.
See Tubb, E(dwin) C(harles)
Clarkson, Jan Nagel 1943- 93-96
Clarkson, Jesse Dunsmore 1897-1973 .....5-8R
Obituary 45-48
Clarkson, L(eslie) A(lbert) 1933- 73-76
Clarkson, Orman
See Richardson, Gladwell
Clarkson, Paul S(tephen) 1905- 29-32R
Clarkson, Stephen 1937- 41-44R
Clarkson, Tom 1913- 103
Clary, Jack 1932- 57-60
Clasen, Claus-Peter 1931- 41-44R
The Clash
See Headon, (Nicky) Topper
and Jones, Mick
and Simonon, Paul
and Strummer, Joe
See also CLC 30
Clasper, Paul D(udley) 1923- 1-4R
Claspy, Everett M.
1907(?)-1973 Obituary 41-44R
Claster, Daniel S(tuart) 1932- 21-24R
Clatworthy, Nancy M(oore) K. 1924- 124
Claude, Richard (P.) 1934- 29-32R
Claudel, Alice Moser CANR-2
Earlier sketch in CA 49-52
Claudel, Paul (Louis Charles Marie)
1868-1955 Brief entry 104
See also TCLC 2, 10
Claudia, Sister Mary 1906- CAP-1
Earlier sketch in CA 9-10
Claudia, Susan
See Johnston, William
Claudius, Matthias 1740-1815 ..... DLB 97
Claus, Hugo (Maurice Julius)
1929- Brief entry 116
Claus, Marshall R. 1936-1970 ..... CAP-2
Earlier sketch in CA 29-32
Clausen, Aage R. 1932- 49-52
Clausen, Andy 1943- Brief entry 117
See also DLB 16
Clausen, Christopher (John) 1942- 130
Clausen, Connie 1923- 1-4R
Clausen, Dennis M(onroe) 1943- 106
Clausen, W. V.
See Clausen, Wendell (Vernon)
Clausen, Wendell (Vernon) 1923- 121
Clauser, Suzanne (P.) 1929- 37-40R
Clavel, Bernard (Charles Henri) 1923- CANR-2
Earlier sketch in CA 45-48
Clavel, Maurice 1920-1979 Obituary 85-88
Clavell, James (duMaresq) 1925- CANR-26
Earlier sketch in CA 25-28R
See also CLC 6, 25
See also MTCW
Claverie, Jean 1946- ..... SATA 38
Clawson, Marion 1905- CANR-10
Earlier sketch in CA 65-68
Clawson, Robert W(ayne) 1939- CANR-25
Earlier sketch in CA 108
Clay, Bertha M.
See Dey, Frederic (Merrill) Van Rensselaer
Clay, Cassius
See Ali, Muhammad
Clay, Cassius Marcellus
1810-1903 Brief entry 120
See also DLB 43
Clay, Charles Travis 1885-1978 Obituary 77-80
Clay, Christopher (G. A.) 1940- 128
Clay, Comer 1910- 45-48
Clay, Diskin 1938- 115
Clay, Edith 1910- 125
Clay, Floyd M(artin) 1927- 45-48
Clay, Grady E. 1916- 93-96
Clay, James 1924- 17-20R
Clay, Jenny Strauss 125
Clay, Jim
See Clay, James
Clay, Lucius D(uBignon) 1897-1978 81-84
Obituary 77-80
Clay, Marie M(ildred) 1926- CANR-22
Earlier sketches in CA 61-64, CANR-8
Clay, Patrice 1947- 106
See also SATA 47
Clay, Roberta 1900- CAP-2
Earlier sketch in CA 29-32
Claybaugh, Amos L(incoln) 1917- 69-72
Claydon, Leslie Francis 1923- 53-56
Clayes, Stanley A(rnold) 1922- 29-32R
Claypool, Jane
See Miner, Jane Claypool
Clayre, Alasdair 1935-1984 102
Obituary 111
Clayton, Aileen Bowen 1918-1981 113
Clayton, Barbara
See Pluff, Barbara Littlefield
Clayton, Bruce 1939- 69-72
Clayton, C. Guy 1936- 122
Clayton, Charles C(urtis) 1902- 73-76
Clayton, Donald D(elbert) 1935- 65-68
Clayton, (Francis) Howard 1918- CANR-12
Earlier sketch in CA 29-32R
Clayton, Howard 1929- 65-68
Clayton, James E(dwin) 1929- 9-12R
Clayton, James L. 1931- CANR-12
Earlier sketch in CA 29-32R
Clayton, Jo 1939- 81-84
Clayton, John
See Beevers, John (Leonard)
Clayton, John J(acob) 1935- CANR-11
Earlier sketch in CA 25-28R
Clayton, John 1892-1979 .....33-36R
Obituary 89-92
Clayton, Keith (M.) 1928- CANR-11
Earlier sketch in CA 21-24R
Clayton, Lawrence (Ray) 1938- 137
Clayton, Mary 1954- 136
Clayton, Paul C(lark) 1932- 61-64
Clayton, Peter A(rthur) 1937- 130
Clayton, Richard Henry Michael
1907- CANR-29
Earlier sketches in CA 5-8R, CANR-4
Clayton, Susan
See Bailey, Alfred Goldsworthy
Clayton, Sylvia 103
Clayton, Thomas (Swoverland) 1932- 41-44R
Clayton, Thompson B(owker) 1904- 57-60
Claytor, Gertrude Boatwright
1890(?)-1973 Obituary 45-48
Cleage, Albert B. Jr. 1911- 65-68
Cleage, Pearl (Michelle) 1948- CANR-27
Earlier sketch in CA 41-44R
Cleall, Charles 1927- 5-8R
Clear, Todd R. 1949- 117
Cleare, John 1936- 65-68
Clearman, Brian (Patrick Joseph)
1941- CANR-38
Earlier sketch in CA 115
Cleary, Beverly (Atlee Bunn) 1916- CANR-36
Earlier sketches in CA 1-4R, CANR-2, 19
See also AAYA 6
See also CLR 2, 8
See also DLB 52
See also MAICYA
See also MTCW
See also SATA 2, 43
Cleary, David Powers 1915- 106
Cleary, Florence Damon 1896-1982 81-84
Obituary 133
Cleary, James W(illiam) 1927- 17-20R
Cleary, Johanna L. 1961- 122
Cleary, Jon 1917- CANR-26
Earlier sketches in CA 1-4R, CANR-3
Cleary, Robert E(dward) 1932- 41-44R
Cleator, P(hilip) E(llaby) 1908- 102
Cleaver, Anastasia N. CANR-18
Earlier sketch in CA 97-100
Cleaver, Bill ..... CLR 6
See also DLB 52
See also SATA 22, 27
Cleaver, Carole 1934- 49-52
See also SATA 6
Cleaver, Dale G. 1928- 17-20R
Cleaver, (Leroy) Eldridge 1935- CANR-16
Earlier sketch in CA 21-24R
See also BLC 1
See also BW
See also CLC 30
Cleaver, Elizabeth (Mrazik) 1939-1985 97-100
Obituary 117
See also CLR 13
See also SATA 23, 43
Cleaver, Hylton Reginald 1891-1961 73-76
See also SATA 49
Cleaver, Nancy
See Mathews, Evelyn Craw
Cleaver, Vera 1919- CANR-38
Earlier sketch in CA 73-76
See also CLR 6
See also DLB 52
See also MAICYA
See also SATA 22
Cleaver, William J(oseph) 1920-1981 .....CANR-38
Obituary 104
See also MAICYA
Cleaves, Emery N(udd) 1902- 33-36R
Cleaves, Freeman 1904- 1-4R
Cleaves, Peter S(hurtleff) 1943- 69-72
Clebsch, William Anthony 1923-1984 .....13-16R
Obituary 113
Clecak, Peter (E.) 1938- 41-44R
Cleckley, Hervey Milton 1903-1984 122
Obituary 111
Cleese, John (Marwood) 1939- CANR-35
Brief entry 112
Earlier sketch in CA 116
See also Monty Python
See also CLC 21
See also MTCW
Cleeve, Brian (Talbot) 1921- CANR-16
Earlier sketches in CA 49-52, CANR-1
Clegg, Alec
See Clegg, Alexander Bradshaw
Clegg, Alexander Bradshaw 1909- 85-88
Clegg, Charles (Myron Jr.) 1916- CANR-17
Earlier sketch in CA 25-28R
Clegg, Jerry S(tephen) 1933- 77-80
Clegg, John 1909- 118
Clegg, Reed K. 1907- CAP-1
Earlier sketch in CA 13-14
Clegg, Stewart (Roger) 1947- CANR-27
Earlier sketches in CA 69-72, CANR-11
Cleghorn, Reese 1930- 25-28R
Cleishbotham, Jebediah
See Scott, Walter
Cleland, Charles C(arr) 1924- CANR-14
Earlier sketch in CA 41-44R
Cleland, Charles E(dward) 1936- 111
Cleland, David I. 1926- CANR-10
Earlier sketch in CA 25-28R
Cleland, Hugh
See Clarke, John (Campbell)
Cleland, John 1710-1789 ..... DLB 39
Cleland, Mabel
See Widdemer, Mabel Cleland
Cleland, (Joseph) Max(well) 1942- 129
Brief entry 113
Cleland, Morton
See Rennie, James Alan
Cleland, W(illiam) Wendell
1888-1972 Obituary 37-40R
Clelland, Catherine
See Townsend, Doris McFerran
Clelland, Richard C(ook) 1921- 17-20R
Clem, Alan L(eland) 1929- CANR-3
Earlier sketch in CA 9-12R
Clemeau, Carol
See Esler, Carol Clemeau
Clemen, Wolfgang Hermann 1909- CANR-2
Earlier sketch in CA 1-4R
Clemence, Richard V(ernon) 1910- 1-4R
Clemenceau, Georges (Eugene Benjamin)
1841-1929 Brief entry 114
Clemenko, Harold B. 1905-1984 Obituary 113
Clemens, Alphonse H.
1905-1977 Obituary 73-76
Clemens, Bryan T. 1934- 97-100
Clemens, Cyril .....AITN 2
Clemens, Diane S(haver) 1936- 29-32R
Clemens, Rodgers
See Lovin, Roger Robert
Clemens, Samuel Langhorne 1835-1910 135
Brief entry 104
See also Twain, Mark
See also CDALB 1865-1917
See also DLB 11, 12, 23, 64, 74
See also MAICYA
See also YABC 2
Clemens, Virginia Phelps 1941- CANR-15
Earlier sketch in CA 85-88
See also SATA 35
Clemens, Walter C. Jr. 1933- CANR-7
Earlier sketch in CA 17-20R
Clement, A(lfred) J(ohn) 1915- 25-28R
Clement, Aeron 1936(?)-1989 Obituary 127
Clement, Charles Baxter 1940- 105
Clement, Evelyn Geer 1926- 53-56
Clement, George H. 1909- 29-32R
Clement, Hal
See Stubbs, Harry C(lement)
See also CAAS 16
See also DLB 8
Clement, Herbert F(lint) 1927- 81-84
Clement, Jane Tyson 1917- 25-28R
Clement, Roland C(harles) 1912- 49-52
Clement, Wallace 1949- CANR-28
Earlier sketch in CA 111
Clemente, Vince(nt L.) 1932- 127
Clements, A(rthur) L(eo) 1932- 29-32R
Clements, Barbara Evans 1945- 89-92
Clements, Bruce 1931- CANR-5
Earlier sketch in CA 53-56
See also SATA 27
Clements, Colleen D(ianne) 1936- 110
Clements, E(llen) Catherine (Scott)
1920- 13-16R
Clements, E(ileen) H(elen) 1905- CAP-1
Earlier sketch in CA 9-10
Clements, Frank A. 1942- 93-96
Clements, Harold M. Sr. 1907- 69-72
Clements, John 1916- CANR-11
Earlier sketch in CA 69-72
Clements, Julia 1906- CAP-1
Earlier sketch in CA 13-14
Clements, Kendrick Alling 1939- 110
Clements, Marcelle 1948- 121
Clements, Mark A. 1955- 136
Clements, Robert John 1912- CANR-5
Earlier sketch in CA 1-4R
Clements, Robert W(illiam) 1939- 110
Clements, Ronald Ernest 1929- 13-16R
Clements, Tad S. 1922- 25-28R
Clements, Traverse
1900(?)-1977 Obituary 69-72
Clements, William M(orris) 1943- 106
Clements, William 1933(?)-1983 Obituary 110
Clemhout, Simone 1934- 73-76
Cleminshaw, Clarence Higbee 1902-1985 134
Obituary 116
Brief entry 106
Clemmons, Francois 1945- 41-44R
Clemmons, Larry 1906(?)-1988 Obituary 127
Clemmons, Robert S(tarr) 1910- CAP-2
Earlier sketch in CA 21-22
Clemmons, William (Preston) 1932- 57-60
Clemo, Jack
See Clemo, Reginald John
See also DLB 27
Clemo, Reginald John 1916- CANR-6
Earlier sketch in CA 13-16R
See also Clemo, Jack
Clemo, Richard F(rederick)
1920-1976 Obituary 65-68
Clemoes, Peter Alan Martin 1920- 102
Clemons, Elizabeth
See Nowell, Elizabeth Cameron
Clemons, Harry 1879- CAP-1
Earlier sketch in CA 13-14
Clemons, Lulamae 1917- 73-76
Clemons, Walter Jr. 1929- CANR-6
Earlier sketch in CA 1-4R
Clendenen, Clarence Clemens 1899- 1-4R
Clendenin, John C(ameron) 1903- 17-20R
Clendenin, William R(itchie) 1917-1979 .....13-16R
Obituary 120
Clendenning, John 1934- 123
Clendenning, Sheila T. 1939- 25-28R
Clendinnen, Inga 1934- 138
Cleobury, Frank Harold 1892- CAP-1
Earlier sketch in CA 13-14
Clephane, Irene (Amy) 13-16R
Clepper, Henry (Edward) 1901-1987 .....CANR-1
Obituary 122
Earlier sketch in CA 45-48
Clepper, Irene E(lizabeth) 53-56
Clerc, Charles 1926- CANR-14
Earlier sketch in CA 37-40R
Clerici, Gianni 1930- 65-68
Clerihew, E.
See Bentley, E(dmund) C(lerihew)
Clerk, N. W.
See Lewis, C(live) S(taples)
Clery, (Reginald) Val(entine) 1924- CANR-3
Earlier sketch in CA 49-52
Cleugh, Mary F(rances) 1913- CANR-4
Earlier sketch in CA 1-4R
Cleve, Janita
See Rowland, D(onald) S(ydney)

Cleve, John
See Offutt, Andrew J(efferson V) and Swain, Dwight V(reeland)
Cleveland, Bob
See Cleveland, George
Cleveland, Carles 1952- 85-88
Cleveland, Clifford S.
See Goldsmith, David H(irsh)
Cleveland, George 1903(?)-1985 Obituary 116
See also SATA 43
Cleveland, (James) Harlan 1918- CANR-4
Earlier sketch in CA 1-4R
Cleveland, Harold van B(uren) 1916- CANR-13
Earlier sketch in CA 21-24R
Cleveland, John
See McElfresh, (Elizabeth) Adeline
Cleveland, Leslie 1921- 102
Cleveland, Mary 1917- 104
Cleveland, Philip Jerome 1903- 9-12R
Cleveland, Ray L(eRoy) 1929- 21-24R
Cleveland, Sidney E(arl) 1919- 9-12R
Cleven, Cathrine
See Cleven, Kathryn Seward
Cleven, Kathryn Seward 1-4R
See also SATA 2
Clevenger, Ernest Allen Jr. 1929- CANR-8
Earlier sketch in CA 57-60
Clevenger, Theodore Jr. 1929- 41-44R
Clever, (Warren) Glenn 1918- 57-60
Cleverdon, (Thomas) Douglas (James) 1903-1987 ....29-32R
Obituary 123
Cleverley Ford, D(ouglas) W(illiam) 1914- CANR-28
Earlier sketches in CA 25-28R, CANR-11
Cleves, Bernard
See Moore, Bernard
Clevin, Joergen 1920- 29-32R
See also SATA 7
Clevin, Jorgen
See Clevin, Joergen
Clew, Jeffrey Robert 1928- CANR-21
Earlier sketches in CA 57-60, CANR-6
Clew, William J(oseph) 1904- 77-80
Clewes, Dorothy (Mary) 1907- CANR-3
Earlier sketch in CA 5-8R
See also SATA 1
Clewes, Howard (Charles Vivian) 1912(?)-1988 Obituary 125
Clews, Roy 1937- 65-68
Click, J(ohn) W(illiam) 1936- 57-60
Cliff, Jimmy
See Chambers, James
See also CLC 21
Cliff, Michelle 1946- CANR-39
Earlier sketch in CA 116
See also BW
Clifford, Craig Edward 1951- 125
Clifford, Deborah Pickman 1933- 138
Clifford, Derek Plint 1915- CANR-4
Earlier sketch in CA 5-8R
Clifford, Eth
See Rosenberg, Ethel (Clifford)
Clifford, Francis
See Thompson, A(rthur) L(eonard) B(ell)
Clifford, George 1934(?)-1985 Obituary 118
Clifford, Geraldine Joncich 1931- 25-28R
Clifford, H(enry) Dalton 1911- 9-12R
Clifford, Harold B(urton) 1893- CAP-1
Earlier sketch in CA 11-12
See also SATA 10
Clifford, James L(owry) 1901-1978 ....CANR-6
Obituary 77-80
Earlier sketch in CA 1-4R
See also DLB 103
Clifford, John
See Bayliss, John Clifford
Clifford, John E(dward) 1935- 37-40R
Clifford, John Garry 1942- 53-56
Clifford, John McLean 1904-1979 85-88
Clifford, John W(illiam) 1918- 17-20R
Clifford, Laurie B(erry) 1948- 112
Clifford, Margaret Cort 1929- CANR-23
Earlier sketch in CA 25-28R
See also SATA 1
Clifford, Martin
See Hamilton, Charles (Harold St. John)
Clifford, Martin 1910- CANR-11
Earlier sketch in CA 25-28R
Clifford, Mary Louise Beneway 1926- CANR-3
Earlier sketch in CA 5-8R
See also SATA 23
Clifford, Nicholas R(owland) 1930- 21-24R
Clifford, Peggy
See Clifford, Margaret Cort
Clifford, Richard J(ohn) 1934- 112
Clifford, Sarah 1916-1976 ....CANR-11
Earlier sketch in CA 25-28R
Clifford, Theodore
See von Block, Sylvia
Cliffton, Katherine Potter
See Bryant, Katherine Cliffton
Clift, Virgil Alfred 1912- 9-12R
Clift, Wallace Bruce 1926- 110
Clifton, Bernice Marie 1901(?)-1985 ....5-8R
Obituary 116
Clifton, Bud
See Stacton, David (Derek)
Clifton, Fred J. 1935(?)-1984 Obituary 114
Clifton, Harry
See Hamilton, Charles (Harold St. John)
Clifton, Jack (Whitney) 1912- 106
Clifton, James A(lfonso) 1927- CANR-25
Earlier sketches in CA 25-28R, CANR-10
Clifton, James M(alcolm) 1930- 112
Clifton, Lewis
See Linedecker, Clifford L.
Clifton, (Thelma) Lucille 1936- CANR-24
Earlier sketches in CA 49-52, CANR-2
See also BLC 1
See also BW
See also CLC 19, 66
See also CLR 5
See also DLB 5, 41
See also MAICYA
See also MTCW
See also SATA 20, 69
Clifton, Marguerite Ann 1925- 13-16R
Clifton, Mark (Irvin) 1906-1963 136
Obituary 117
Clifton-Taylor, Alec 1907-1985 125
Clignet, Remi Pierre 1931- 104
Climo, Shirley 1928- CANR-24
Earlier sketch in CA 107
See also SATA 35, 39
Clinard, Dorothy Long 1909- 5-8R
Clinard, Helen Hall 1931- 124
Clinard, Marshall B(arron) 1911- CANR-4
Earlier sketch in CA 5-8R
Clinard, Turner N(orman) 1917-1981 ....37-40R
Obituary 135
Clinch, Nicholas (Bayard) 1930- 111
Clinchy, Everett R(oss) 1896-1986 Obituary 118
Cline, Bev
See Fink Cline, Beverly
Cline, Beverly
See Fink Cline, Beverly
Cline, Beverly Fink
See Fink Cline, Beverly
Cline, C(harles) Terry Jr. 1935- CANR-25
Earlier sketches in CA 61-64, CANR-8
Cline, Catherine Ann 1927- 17-20R
Cline, Charles (William) 1937- CANR-7
Earlier sketch in CA 61-64
Cline, Denzel C(ecil) 1903- CAP-2
Earlier sketch in CA 21-22
Cline, Edward 1946- 101
Cline, Gloria Griffen 1929-1973 ....5-8R
Obituary 125
Cline, Joan
See Hamilton, Joan Lesley
Cline, Linda 1941- 65-68
Cline, Ray S(teiner) 1918- Brief entry 106
Cline, Rodney 1903- 61-64
Cline, S(arah) L(ouise) 1948- 129
Cline, Victor (Bailey) 1925- 65-68
Clinebell, Howard J. Jr. 1922- CANR-13
Earlier sketch in CA 33-36R
Clinton, Catherine 1952- 130
Clinton, (Lloyd) D(eWitt) 1946- CANR-38
Earlier sketch in CA 116
Clinton, Dirk
See Silverberg, Robert
Clinton, F. G.
See Campbell, R(obert) Wright
Clinton, Iris A. (Corbin) 1901- CAP-1
Earlier sketch in CA 11-12
Clinton, Jeff
See Bickham, Jack M(iles)
Clinton, Jon
See Prince, J(ack) H(arvey)
Clinton, Richard Lee 1938- CANR-23
Earlier sketches in CA 61-64, CANR-8
Clinton, Rupert
See Bulmer, (Henry) Kenneth
Clinton-Baddeley, V.C. 1911(?)-1970 Obituary 104
Clipman, William 1954- 106
Clipper, Lawrence Jon 1930- 49-52
Clish, (Lee) Marian 1946- ....SATA 43
Clissmann, Anne
See Clune, Anne
Clissold, (John) Stephen (Hallet) 1913-1982 110
Obituary 107
Clistier, Adeline
See Denny, Alma
Clithero, Myrtle E(ly) 1906- CAP-2
Earlier sketch in CA 25-28
Clithero, Sally
See Clithero, Myrtle E(ly)
Clive, Clifford
See Hamilton, Charles (Harold St. John)
Clive, Geoffrey 1927-1976 ....33-36R
Clive, John
See Clive, John Leonard
Clive, John Leonard 1924-1990 85-88
Obituary 130
Clive, John 1933- 103
Clive, Mary 1907- 21-24R
Clive, William
See Bassett, Ronald
Cloake, John (Cecil) 1924- 133
Clodfelter, (William) Frank(lin) 1911- 103
Clodfelter, Micheal D. 1946- CANR-31
Earlier sketch in CA 69-72
Cloeren, Hermann J(osef) 1934- 41-44R
Cloete, Stuart 1897-1976 ....CANR-3
Obituary 65-68
Earlier sketch in CA 1-4R
Clogan, Paul M(aurice) 1934- 33-36R
Clogg, Clifford C(ollier) 1949- 112
Cloke, Richard 1916- CANR-11
Earlier sketch in CA 69-72
Clokey, Art 1921- ....SATA 59
Clokey, Richard M(ontgomery) 1936- 127
Brief entry 107
Clones, N(icholas) J. 97-100
Clopton, Beverly Virginia B(eck) 106
Clor, Harry M(ortimer) 1929- 53-56
Clore, Gerald L(ewis Jr.) 1939- 37-40R
Close, A. Kathryn 1908(?)-1973 Obituary 41-44R
Close, Frank (E.) 1945- 126
Close, Henry T(hompson) 1928- 1-4R
Close, Reginald Arthur 1909- 17-20R
Close, Upton
See Hall, Josef Washington
Closen, Michael L. 1949- 121
Closs, August 1898-1990 ....CANR-2
Obituary 132
Earlier sketch in CA 5-8R
Closs, Elizabeth
See Traugott, Elizabeth Closs
Clotfelter, Beryl E(dward) 1926- 53-56
Clotfelter, Cecil F. 1929- 53-56
Clotfelter, Charles T. 1947- 131
Clotfelter, Mary (Eunice) L(ong) 103
Clothier, Peter (Dean) 1936- 65-68
Cloud, (Joseph) Fred (Jr.) 1925- 13-16R
Cloud, Patricia
See Strother, Pat Wallace
Cloud, Preston (Ercelle) 1912-1991 93-96
Obituary 133
Cloud, Yvonne
See Kapp, Yvonne (Mayer)
Cloudsley-Thompson, J(ohn) L(eonard) 1921- CANR-23
Earlier sketches in CA 17-20R, CANR-8
See also SATA 19
Clough, Arthur Hugh 1819-1861 ....DLB 32
Clough, B(renda) W(ang) 1955- 116
Clough, Francis F(rederick) 1912- CAP-1
Earlier sketch in CA 9-10
Clough, Neil 1950- 112
Clough, Ralph Nelson 1916- Brief entry 105
Clough, Rosa Trillo 1906- 13-16R
Clough, Shepard B(ancroft) 1901-1990 ....CANR-4
Obituary 131
Earlier sketch in CA 1-4R
Clough, William A. 1899- CAP-2
Earlier sketch in CA 21-22
Clough, William 1911(?)-1976 Obituary 69-72
Clough, Wilson O(ber) 1894- 17-20R
Clouse, Robert Gordon 1931- CANR-12
Earlier sketch in CA 29-32R
Clouser, John William 1932- 61-64
Clout, Hugh Donald 1944- CANR-34
Earlier sketches in CA 41-44R, CANR-15
Cloutier, Cecile
See Cloutier-Wojciechowska, Cecile
See also DLB 60
Cloutier, David 1951- CANR-7
Earlier sketch in CA 57-60
Cloutier-Wojciechowska, Cecile 1930- CANR-12
Earlier sketch in CA 65-68
See also Cloutier, Cecile
Clover, Frank Metlar III 1940- 101
Clow, Barbara Hand 1943- 133
Clow, Martha de Mev 1932- 29-32R
Cloward, Richard Andrew 1926- 41-44R
Clower, Robert W(ayne) 1926- 89-92
Clowney, Edmund P(rosper) 1917- CANR-8
Earlier sketch in CA 5-8R
Clowse, Converse Dilworth 1929- 127
Brief entry 108
Clubb, Louise George 1930- 69-72
Clubb, O(liver) Edmund 1901-1989 ....37-40R
Obituary 128
Clubb, Oliver E. Jr. 1929- 5-8R
Clubbe, John 1938- CANR-11
Earlier sketch in CA 25-28R
Clube, (Stace) Victor (Murray) 1934- 130
Cluff, Charles E. 1937- 65-68
Clugston, Richard 1938- 41-44R
Clum, John M(acKenzie) 1941- 69-72
Clun, Arthur
See Polsby, Nelson W(oolf)
Clune, Anne 1945- 103
Clune, Francis Patrick 1893-1971 ....CAP-2
Obituary 29-32R
Earlier sketch in CA 23-24
Clune, Frank
See Clune, Francis Patrick
Clune, Henry W. 1890- CANR-5
Earlier sketch in CA 1-4R
Clunies Ross, Anthony (Ian) 1932- 53-56
Clurman, Harold 1901-1980 ....CANR-2
Obituary 101
Earlier sketch in CA 1-4R
Cluster, Dick 1947- 97-100
Clute, Morrel J. 1912- 13-16R
Clute, Robert E(ugene) 1924- 41-44R
Clutha, Janet Paterson Frame 1924- CANR-36
Earlier sketches in CA 1-4R, CANR-2
See also Frame, Janet
See also MTCW
Clutterbuck, David Ashley 1947- 113
Clutterbuck, Richard 1917- CANR-25
Earlier sketches in CA 21-24R, CANR-9
Clutton-Brock, Arthur Guy 1906- 110
Clutton-Brock, Arthur 1868-1924 ....DLB 98
Cluver, Eustace Henry 1894- CAP-1
Earlier sketch in CA 9-10
Cluysenaar, Anne (Alice Andree Jackson) 1936- 102
Clyde, Leslie
See Kipps, Harriet C(lyde)
Clyde, Norman Asa 1885-1972 ....41-44R
Clyde Cool
See Frazier, Walt(er)
Clymer, Eleanor 1906- CANR-9
Earlier sketch in CA 61-64
See also SATA 9
Clymer, (Joseph) Floyd 1895-1970 Obituary 104
Clymer, Kenton James 1943- 127
Brief entry 109
Clymer, Reuben Swinburne 1878- CAP-1
Earlier sketch in CA 11-12
Clynder, Monica
See Muir, Marie
Clyne, James F. 1898(?)-1977 Obituary 69-72
Clyne, Patricia (Edwards) 101
See also SATA 31
Clyne, Terence
See Blatty, William Peter
Clytus, John 1929- 29-32R
Cnudde, Charles F(rancis) 1938- CANR-26
Earlier sketch in CA 29-32R
Coad, F(rederick) Roy 1925- 103
Coad, Oral Sumner 1887- 45-48
Coade, Jessie 1911- 120
Coakley, Lakme 1912- 69-72
Coakley, Mary Lewis CAP-1
Earlier sketch in CA 13-16
Coakley, Michael 1947(?)-1988 Obituary 126
Coale, Samuel Chase 1943- CANR-27
Earlier sketches in CA 65-68, CANR-11
Coalson, Glo 1946- 103
See also SATA 26
Coan, Eugene V(ictor) 1943- 110
Coan, Otis W(elton) 1895- CAP-2
Earlier sketch in CA 33-36
Coan, Richard Welton 1928- CANR-12
Earlier sketch in CA 69-72
Coates, Austin 1922- 102
Coates, Belle 1896- 5-8R
See also SATA 2
Coates, Charles R(obert) 1915- 106
Coates, David 1946- 125
Coates, Donald R(obert) 1922- CANR-2
Earlier sketch in CA 49-52
Coates, Doreen (Frances) 1912- 107
Coates, Gary J(oseph) 1947- 110
Coates, Geoffrey Edward 1917- 37-40R
Coates, J(ohn) F(rancis) 1922- 123
Coates, K. S.
See Coates, Kenneth (Stephen)
Coates, Ken
See Coates, Kenneth (Stephen)
Coates, Ken S.
See Coates, Kenneth (Stephen)
Coates, Ken 1930- 123
Coates, Kenneth (Stephen) 1956- 130
Coates, Robert C(rawford) 1937- 134
Coates, Robert M(yron) 1897-1973 ....5-8R
Obituary 41-44R
See also DLB 4, 9, 102
Coates, Ruth Allison 1915- 57-60
See also SATA 11
Coates, W. Paul 1945- 136
Coates, William Ames 1916-1973 ....37-40R
Coates, Willson H(avelock) 1899-1976 ....CANR-33
Obituary 69-72
Earlier sketch in CA 37-40R
Coats, Alice M(argaret) 1905- 53-56
See also SATA 11
Coats, George W. 1936- 21-24R
Coats, Peter 1910-1990 ....CANR-1
Obituary 132
Earlier sketch in CA 49-52
Coatsworth, Elizabeth (Jane) 1893-1986 ....CANR-4
Obituary 120
Earlier sketch in CA 5-8R
See also CLR 2
See also DLB 22
See also MAICYA
See also SATA 2, 49, 56
Cobalt, Martin
See Mayne, William (James Carter)
Cobb, Alice 1909- 5-8R
Cobb, Carl W(esley) 1926- 21-24R
Cobb, Charles E. Jr. 1943- ....DLB 41
Cobb, David 1934- 112
Cobb, Faye Davis 1932- 9-12R
Cobb, Frank I. 1869-1923 ....DLB 25
Cobb, Geoffrey Belton 1892(?)-1971 Obituary 104
Cobb, Irvin S. 1876-1944 ....DLB 11, 25, 86
Cobb, James Charles 1947- CANR-31
Earlier sketch in CA 112
Cobb, Jane
See Berry, Jane Cobb
Cobb, John B(oswell) Jr. 1925- CANR-2
Earlier sketch in CA 1-4R
Cobb, Jonathan 1946- 93-96
Cobb, Nancy (Howard) 1949- 137
Cobb, Nathan 1943- 105
Cobb, R. C.
See Cobb, Richard (Charles)
Cobb, Richard (Charles) 1917- 128
Brief entry 116
Cobb, Robert A. 1941- 69-72
Cobb, Roger W(illiam) 1941- 104
Cobb, Thomas 1947- 136
Cobb, Vicki 1938- CANR-14
Earlier sketch in CA 33-36R
See also CLR 2
See also MAICYA
See also SAAS 6
See also SATA 8, 69
Cobban, Alfred 1901-1968 Obituary 111
Cobbett
See Ludovici, Anthony M(ario)
Cobbett, Richard
See Pluckrose, Henry (Arthur)
Cobbett, William 1763-1835 ....DLB 43, 107
Cobbing, Bob 1920- 101
Cobbledick, James R. 1935- 97-100
Cobbs, John L(ewis) 1917- Brief entry 115
Cobbs, Price M(ashaw) 1928- 21-24R
Coben, Lawrence A(llan) 1926- 111

Coben, Stanley 1929- 122
Cober, Alan E(dwin) 1935- ....SATA 7
Cobham, Sir Alan
See Hamilton, Charles (Harold St. John)
Coble, John (Lawrence) 1924- 9-12R
Cobleigh, Ira U(nderwood) 1903- 81-84
Coblentz, Stanton A(rthur) 1896- CANR-21
Earlier sketch in CA 5-8R
Cobley, John 1914- 13-16R
Cobos, Ruben 1911- 135
Cobrin, Harry Aaron 1902- CAP-2
Earlier sketch in CA 29-32
Coburn, Andrew 1932- CANR-36
Earlier sketches in CA 53-56, CANR-4
Coburn, Broughton 1951- 111
Coburn, D(onald) L(ee) 1938- 89-92
See also CLC 10
Coburn, John Bowen 1914- CANR-2
Earlier sketch in CA 1-4R
Coburn, Karen Levin 1941- 65-68
Coburn, Kathleen 1905-1991 93-96
Obituary 135
Coburn, L. J.
See Harvey, John (Barton)
Coburn, Louis 1915- 104
Coburn, Thomas B(owen) 1944- 110
Coburn, Walt 1889- CAP-1
Earlier sketch in CA 9-10
Cocagnac, Augustin Maurice(-Jean)
1924- CANR-17
Earlier sketch in CA 25-28R
See also SATA 7
Coccioli, Carlo 1920- CANR-9
Earlier sketches in CA 13-16R, CANR-31
Cochard, Thomas S(ylvester) 1893- 57-60
Cochet, Gabriel 1888-1973 Obituary 45-48
Cochran, Bert 1917-1984 45-48
Obituary 113
Cochran, Bobbye A. 1949- ....SATA 11
Cochran, Charles L(eo) 1940- 57-60
Cochran, Clarke E(dward) 1945- 107
Cochran, Elizabeth
See Cochrane, Elizabeth
Cochran, Hamilton 1898-1977 ....CANR-6
Obituary 73-76
Earlier sketch in CA 1-4R
Cochran, Jacqueline
1910(?)-1980 Obituary 101
Cochran, Jeff
See Durst, Paul
Cochran, John A(rthur) 1921- 122
Cochran, John R(obert) 1937- 41-44R
Cochran, Leslie H(ershel) 1939- CANR-2
Earlier sketch in CA 49-52
Cochran, Rice E.
See Monroe, Keith
Cochran, Thomas C(hilds) 1902- CANR-8
Earlier sketch in CA 61-64
See also DLB 17
Cochrane, A(rchibald) L(eman)
1909(?)-1988 Obituary 125
Cochrane, Arthur C(aspersz) 1909- CANR-4
Earlier sketch in CA 5-8R
Cochrane, Elizabeth 1867-1922 Brief entry 118
See also DLB 25
Cochrane, Eric W. 1928-1985 ....CANR-28
Obituary 118
Earlier sketch in CA 49-52
Cochrane, Glynn 1940- 53-56
Cochrane, Hugh (Ferrier) 1923- 103
Cochrane, James D(avid) 1938- 29-32R
Cochrane, James L. 1941- CANR-13
Earlier sketch in CA 33-36R
Cochrane, Jennifer (Ann Frances) 1936- 102
Cochrane, Louise Morley 1918- 9-12R
Cochrane, Pauline A(therton) 1929- 110
Cochrane, Willard W(esley) 1914- CANR-11
Earlier sketch in CA 21-24R
Cochrane, William E. 1926- 97-100
Cochrane de Alencar, Gertrude E. L.
1906- 5-8R
Cochran-Smith, Marilyn 1951- 115
Coch-y-Bonddhu
See Arnold, Richard
Cockburn, Alexander 1941- Brief entry 123
Cockburn, (Francis) Claud 1904-1981 102
Obituary 105
Cockburn, Thomas Aiden 1912- 9-12R
Cockcroft, George Powers 1932- 116
Cockcroft, James D(onald) 1935- CANR-25
Earlier sketches in CA 25-28R, CANR-10
Cockcroft, John (Douglas) 1897-1967 ....CAP-2
Earlier sketch in CA 21-22
Cockerell, H(ugh) A(nthony) L(ewis)
1909- CAP-1
Earlier sketch in CA 13-14
Cockerell, Sydney M(orris)
1906-1987 Obituary 124
Cockerill, A(rthur) W(illiam) 1929- 131
Cockerill, John A. 1845-1896 ....DLB 23
Cockett, Mary CANR-19
Earlier sketches in CA 9-12R, CANR-4
See also SATA 3
Cockfield, Jamie (Hartwell) 1945- 115
Cocking, Clive 1938- 105
Cocking, J(ohn) M(artin) 1914- 53-56
Cockrell, Amanda
See Crowe, Amanda Cockrell
Cockrell, Marian (Brown) 1909- CAP-2
Earlier sketch in CA 17-18
Cocks, Geoffrey (Campbell) 1948- 121
Cockshut, A(nthony) O(liver) J(ohn)
1927- CANR-10
Earlier sketch in CA 17-20R
Coco, James (Emil) 1930(?)-1987 Obituary 121
Cocozzella, Peter 1937- 37-40R
Cocozzoli, Gary R(ichard) 1951- 119
Cocteau, Jean (Maurice Eugene Clement)
1889-1963 ....CAP-2
Earlier sketch in CA 25-28
See also CLC 1, 8, 15, 16, 43
See also DLB 65
See also MTCW
See also WLC
Codding, George A(rthur) Jr. 1923- CANR-13
Earlier sketch in CA 33-36R
Code, Grant Hyde 1896-1974 49-52
Codel, Martin 1903(?)-1973 Obituary 41-44R
Codel, Michael R(ichard) 1939- 73-76
Coder, S(amuel) Maxwell 1902- CANR-14
Earlier sketch in CA 37-40R
Codere, Helen (Frances) 1917- 69-72
Codevilla, (Maria) Angelo 1943- 61-64
Codrescu, Andrei 1946- CANR-34
Earlier sketches in CA 33-36R, CANR-13
See also CLC 46
Codrington, Kenneth de Burgh
1899-1986 Obituary 118
Cody, Al
See Joscelyn, Archie L.
Cody, C. S.
See Waller, Leslie
Cody, D(ouglas) Thane R(omney) 1932- 57-60
Cody, Fred 1916- 107
Cody, James P.
See Rohrbach, Peter Thomas
Cody, John J. 1930- 29-32R
Cody, John 1925- 101
Cody, Liza 129
Brief entry 125
Cody, Martin L(eonard) 1941- 53-56
Cody, Morrill 1901- 125
Cody, Walt
See Norwood, Victor G(eorge) C(harles)
Coe, Charles Norton 1915- 1-4R
Coe, Christine Sadler
See Sadler, Christine
Coe, Douglas
See Epstein, Beryl (M. Williams)
and Epstein, Samuel
Coe, Fred(erick) 1914-1979 Obituary 85-88
Coe, Jonathan 1961- 133
Coe, Lloyd 1899(?)-1976 Obituary 69-72
See also SATA 30
Coe, Malcolm (James) 1930- 123
Coe, Max
See Bourne, Randolph S(illiman)
Coe, Michael Douglas 1929- CANR-19
Earlier sketches in CA 1-4R, CANR-4
Coe, Michelle E(ileen) 1917- 106
Coe, Peter 1929-1987 Obituary 122
Coe, Ralph T(racy) 1929- CANR-1
Earlier sketch in CA 1-4R
Coe, Richard L(ivingston) 1916- 65-68
Coe, Richard N(elson) 1923- CANR-12
Earlier sketch in CA 25-28R
Coe, Rodney Michael 1933- 41-44R
Coe, Tucker
See Westlake, Donald E(dwin)
Coe, William C(harles) 1930- 37-40R
Coel, Margaret 1937- CANR-39
Earlier sketch in CA 106
Coelho, George Victor 1918- CANR-1
Earlier sketch in CA 45-48
Coello, Dennis (L.) 129
Coen, Ethan 1958- 126
Coen, Joel 1955- 126
Coen, Rena Neumann 1925- 13-16R
See also SATA 20
Coens, Sister Mary Xavier 1918- 21-24R
Coerr, Eleanor (Beatrice) 1922- CANR-11
Earlier sketch in CA 25-28R
See also MAICYA
See also SATA 1, 67
Coetzee, J(ohn) M(ichael) 1940- 77-80
See also CLC 23, 33, 66
See also MTCW
Cofacci, Gino P. 1914(?)-1989 Obituary 128
Cofer, Charles N(orval) 1916- 37-40R
Cofer, Judith Ortiz 1952- CANR-32
Earlier sketch in CA 115
See also HW
Coffee, Lenore J. 1897(?)-1984 Obituary 113
See also DLB 44
Coffey, Alan R. 1931- 33-36R
Coffey, Brian
See Koontz, Dean R(ay)
Coffey, (Helen) Dairine 1933- 21-24R
Coffey, Daniel 1950- 131
Coffey, Frank 136
Coffey, J(oseph) I(rving) 1916- 41-44R
Coffey, John W(ill) Jr. 1925- 45-48
Coffey, Marilyn 1937- CANR-2
Earlier sketch in CA 45-48
Coffey, Robert E(dward) 1931- 65-68
Coffey, Thomas Patrick 1928- 120
Coffin, Arthur B. 1929- 29-32R
Coffin, Berton 1910- CANR-5
Earlier sketch in CA 9-12R
Coffin, David R(obbins) 1918- 5-8R
Coffin, Dean 1911- 33-36R
Coffin, Frank M(orey) 1919- 9-12R
Coffin, Geoffrey
See Mason, F(rancis) van Wyck
Coffin, George S(turgis) 1903- 5-8R
Coffin, Harold Glen 1926- 115
Coffin, Harold 1905(?)-1981 Obituary 104
Coffin, Joseph (John) 1899- 57-60
Coffin, Lewis A(ugustus) III 1932- 61-64
Coffin, Lyn 1943- 110
Coffin, Patricia 1912-1974 ....CAP-2
Obituary 49-52
Earlier sketch in CA 33-36
Coffin, Robert P(eter) Tristram
1892-1955 Brief entry 123
See also DLB 45
Coffin, Tristram Potter 1922- CANR-2
Earlier sketch in CA 5-8R
Coffin, Tristram 1912- 21-24R
Coffin, William Sloane Jr. 1924- 103
Coffinet, Julien 1907- 61-64
Coffman, Barbara Frances 1907- CAP-1
Earlier sketch in CA 13-16
Coffman, Charles DeWitt 1909- 102
Coffman, Edward M. 1929- 33-36R
Coffman, Paul B(rown) 1900- CAP-2
Earlier sketch in CA 21-22
Coffman, Ramon Peyton 1896- CAP-2
Earlier sketch in CA 17-18
See also SATA 4
Coffman, Virginia (Edith) 1914- CANR-2
Earlier sketch in CA 49-52
Cofyn, Cornelius
See Saunders, Hilary Aidan St. George
Cogan, Mike
See Lottman, Eileen
Cogane, Gerald
See Fonarow, Jerry
Coger, Leslie Irene 1912- 21-24R
Coggan, (Frederick) Donald 1909- 17-20R
Coggin, Philip A(nnett) 1917- 117
Coggins, Jack (Banham) 1914- CANR-2
Earlier sketch in CA 5-8R
See also SATA 2
Coggins, Paul E. 1951- 126
Coggins, Ross 1927- 13-16R
Coghill, Nevill (Henry Kendall Aylmer)
1899-1980 ....CANR-11
Obituary 102
Earlier sketch in CA 13-16R
Coghlan, Brian (Laurence Dillon) 1926- 17-20R
Coghlan, Margaret M. 1920- 106
Cogley, John 1916-1976 ....CANR-2
Obituary 65-68
Earlier sketch in CA 45-48
Cogswell, Coralie (Norris) 1930- 13-16R
Cogswell, Fred(erick William) 1917- CANR-18
Earlier sketches in CA 5-8R, CANR-3
See also DLB 60
Cogswell, James A(rthur) 1922- 33-36R
Cogswell, Mason Fitch 1761-1830 ....DLB 37
Cogswell, Theodore R. 1918- CANR-4
Earlier sketch in CA 1-4R
Cohan, Avery B(erlow) 1914-1977 61-64
Obituary 69-72
Cohan, Tony 1939- 108
Cohane, John Philip 1911- 101
Cohane, Tim(othy) 1912- 9-12R
Cohart, Mary 1911- 57-60
Cohen, Aaron (Samuel) 1935- 110
Cohen, Aharon 1910- 69-72
Cohen, Albert J. 1903(?)-1984 Obituary 114
Cohen, Albert Kircidel 1918- 13-16R
Cohen, Albert 1895(?)-1981 Obituary 105
Cohen, Allan Y. 1939- 33-36R
Cohen, Amnon 1936- 85-88
Cohen, Andrew (Z.) 1955- 135
Cohen, Anne Billings 1937- 57-60
Cohen, Anthea 1913- CANR-18
Earlier sketch in CA 97-100
Cohen, Arthur A(llen) 1928-1986 ....CANR-17
Obituary 120
Earlier sketches in CA 1-4R, CANR-1
See also CLC 7, 31
See also DLB 28
Cohen, Arthur M. 1927- 33-36R
Cohen, B(enjamin) Bernard 1922- 9-12R
Cohen, Barbara 1932- CANR-19
Earlier sketches in CA 53-56, CANR-4
See also SAAS 7
See also SATA 10
Cohen, Bella
See Spewack, Bella
Cohen, Benjamin J(erry) 1937- CANR-18
Earlier sketch in CA 101
Cohen, Benjamin Victor 1894-1983 ....CAP-1
Obituary 110
Earlier sketch in CA 11-12
Cohen, Bernard Lande 1902- 29-32R
Cohen, Bernard P. 1930- 45-48
Cohen, Bernard 1937- 103
Cohen, Bruce J. 1938- 89-92
Cohen, Carl 1931- CANR-5
Earlier sketch in CA 1-4R
Cohen, Charles 1943- 111
Cohen, Daniel (E.) 1936- CANR-20
Earlier sketches in CA 45-48, CANR-1
See also AAYA 7
See also CLR 3
See also MAICYA
See also SAAS 4
See also SATA 8, 70
Cohen, David Steven 1943- 53-56
Cohen, David 1946- 129
Cohen, David 1952- 108
Cohen, Donna 1947- 122
Cohen, Dorothy H. 1915- Brief entry 105
Cohen, Edgar H. 1913- 29-32R
Cohen, Edmund D(avid) 1943- 57-60
Cohen, Edward H. 1941- Brief entry 115
Cohen, Edward M(artin) 1936- 21-24R
Cohen, Elaine (Marsha Perlman) 1938- 110
Cohen, Elie Aron 1909- 53-56
Cohen, Eliot A(shey) 1956- 113
Cohen, Elliot D. 1951- 138
Cohen, Florence Chanock 1927- 5-8R
Cohen, Gary B(ennett) 1948- 107
Cohen, Gary G. 1934- CANR-7
Earlier sketch in CA 57-60
Cohen, George Michael 1931- 81-84
Cohen, Harry 1936- 106
Cohen, (Henry) Hennig 1919- CANR-5
Earlier sketch in CA 1-4R
Cohen, Henry 1933- 33-36R
Cohen, Howard Martin 1926- Brief entry 107
Cohen, I. Bernard 1914- 69-72
Cohen, Ira Sheldon 1924- CANR-10
Earlier sketch in CA 5-8R
Cohen, J. M.
See Cohen, John Michael
Cohen, Jack S(idney) 1938- 130
Cohen, Jacob 1918- 123
Cohen, James (E.) 1956- 137
Cohen, Jane R(abb) 1938- 130
Cohen, Janet 1940- 126
Cohen, Jean Louise 1946- 111
Cohen, Jene Barr 1900-1985 ....CANR-3
Obituary 115
Earlier sketch in CA 5-8R
See also Barr, Jene
Cohen, Jeremy 1953- 130
Cohen, Jerome Alan 1930- CANR-30
Earlier sketches in CA 49-52, CANR-13
Cohen, Jerome B(ernard) 1915-1986 ....9-12R
Obituary 121
Cohen, Joan Lebold 1932- CANR-30
Earlier sketches in CA 25-28R, CANR-13
See also SATA 4
Cohen, John Michael 1903-1989 ....CANR-4
Obituary 129
Earlier sketch in CA 5-8R
Cohen, John 1911- CANR-6
Earlier sketch in CA 13-16R
Cohen, Joseph 1926- CANR-10
Earlier sketch in CA 65-68
Cohen, Jozef 1921- 29-32R
Cohen, Judith Beth 1943- 118
Cohen, Kalman J(oseph) 1931- 13-16R
Cohen, Kathleen Rogers 1933- 53-56
Cohen, Keith 1945- 101
Cohen, Lawrence Jonathan 1923- 65-68
Cohen, Leonard (Norman) 1934- CANR-14
Earlier sketch in CA 21-24R
See also CLC 3, 38
See also DLB 53
See also MTCW
Cohen, Margie K(anter) 1912- 109
Cohen, Mark Nathan 1943- 135
Cohen, (Stephen) Marshall 1929- CANR-23
Earlier sketches in CA 45-48, CANR-2
Cohen, Martin A(aron) 1928- Brief entry 113
Cohen, Marvin 1931- CANR-17
Earlier sketch in CA 25-28R
Cohen, Matt 1942- 61-64
See also CLC 19
See also DLB 53
Cohen, Michael J. 1940- 129
Cohen, Michael P. 1944- 121
Cohen, Mike
See Cohen, Morris
Cohen, Miriam 1926- 106
See also SAAS 11
See also SATA 29
Cohen, Morris L(eo) 1927- CANR-29
Earlier sketch in CA 49-52
Cohen, Morris 1912- 17-20R
Cohen, Mortimer J. 1894-1972 Obituary 104
Cohen, Morton N(orton) 1921- CANR-28
Earlier sketches in CA 1-4R, CANR-5
Cohen, Myron 1903(?)-1986 Obituary 118
Cohen, Nancy Wainer 1947- 111
Cohen, Naomi W(iener) 1927- Brief entry 114
Cohen, Norm(an) 1936- 109
Cohen, Octavus Roy 1891-1959 Brief entry 112
Cohen, Paul Andrew 1934- 115
Cohen, Paul S. 1945- 123
See also SATA 58
Cohen, Peter Zachary 1931- CANR-12
Earlier sketch in CA 33-36R
See also SATA 4
Cohen, Philip G(ary) 1954- 136
Cohen, Ralph 1917- 138
Cohen, Richard Murry 1938- CANR-19
Earlier sketch in CA 103
Cohen, Robert Carl 1930- 57-60
See also SATA 8
Cohen, Robert 1938- CANR-34
Earlier sketches in CA 29-32R, CANR-12
Cohen, Robert 1957- 131
Cohen, Roberta G. 1937- 49-52
Cohen, Robin 1944- 134
Cohen, Ronald Dennis 1940- 105
Cohen, Ronald Jay 1949- 97-100
Cohen, Ronald 1930- CANR-29
Earlier sketches in CA 33-36R, CANR-13
Cohen, Rosalyn
See Higgins, Rosalyn (Cohen)
Cohen, S. Alan 1933- 29-32R
Cohen, S. Ralph 1917-1983 Obituary 110
Cohen, Sanford 1920- 1-4R
Cohen, Sara Kay Sherman 1943- 102
Cohen, Sarah Blacher 1936- 81-84
Cohen, Saul Bernard 1925- 130
Cohen, Scott 1946- 116
Cohen, Selma Jeanne 1920- 25-28R
Cohen, Seymour Jay 1922- 25-28R
Cohen, Sharleen Cooper CANR-19
Earlier sketch in CA 97-100
Cohen, Sheldon S. 1931- 25-28R
Cohen, Sherry Suib 1934- 102
Cohen, Sidney 1910-1987 ....13-16R
Obituary 122
Cohen, Stanley 1928- CANR-34
Earlier sketches in CA 29-32R, CANR-15
Cohen, Stephen D(avid) 1942- 111
Cohen, Stephen F(rand) 1938- CANR-35
Earlier sketch in CA 49-52

Cohen, Stephen S. 1941- 33-36R
Cohen, Stephen Z(olman) 1931- 121
Cohen, Stephen 1941- 118
Cohen, Steve (Michael) 1951- 114
Cohen, Stewart 1940- 65-68
Cohen, Susan 1938- CANR-20
Earlier sketches in CA 53-56, CANR-5
Cohen, Warren I. 1934- CANR-9
Earlier sketch in CA 21-24R
Cohen, Wilbur J(oseph) 1913-1987 CANR-17
Obituary 122
Earlier sketch in CA 25-28R
Cohen, William A(lan) 1937- CANR-19
Earlier sketch in CA 103
Cohen, William B(enjamin) 1941- 37-40R
Cohen, William Howard 1927- 17-20R
Cohen, William S(ebastian) 1940- CANR-27
Earlier sketch in CA 108
Cohen, Yehudi A(ryeh) 1928- 113
Cohen-Solal, Annie CLC 50
Cohen-Stratyner, Barbara Naomi 1951- 113
Cohler, Anne M(eyers) 1940(?)-1989 Obituary 130
Cohler, Bertram J(oseph) 1938- 109
Cohler, David Keith 1940- 104
Cohn, Adrian A. 1922- 25-28R
Cohn, Alan M(artin) 1926-1989 110
Obituary 129
Cohn, Angelo 1914- CANR-4
Earlier sketch in CA 5-8R
See also SATA 19
Cohn, Arthur 1910- 110
Cohn, Dorrit 1924- 93-96
Cohn, Elchanan 1941- 73-76
Cohn, Haim H(erman) 1911- 45-48
Cohn, Helen Desfosses
See Desfosses, Helen
Cohn, Jan Kadetsky 1933- 102
Cohn, Jules 1930- 33-36R
Cohn, Keith E(van) 1935- 107
Cohn, Lester
See Cole, Lester
Cohn, Marguerite A. 1898(?)-1984 Obituary 113
Cohn, Marvin L(ester) 1924-1990 105
Obituary 131
Cohn, Nik 1946- 102
Cohn, Norman 1915- 57-60
Cohn, Robert Greer 1921- 9-12R
Cohn, Roy M(arcus) 1927-1986 CANR-29
Obituary 119
Earlier sketch in CA 108
Cohn, Rubin (Goodman) 1911-1986 57-60
Obituary 119
Cohn, Ruby 1922- CANR-32
Earlier sketch in CA 93-96
Cohn, Samuel Kline Jr. 1949- 125
Cohn, Stanley H(arold) 1922- 29-32R
Cohn, Theodore 1923- 89-92
Cohn, Vera 1907- 97-100
Cohn, Victor (Edward) 1919- 65-68
Cohn-Sherbok, Dan 1945- 137
Cohon, Barry
See Cohon, Baruch J(oseph)
Cohon, Baruch J(oseph) 1926- 29-32R
Cohon, Beryl David 1898- CANR-6
Earlier sketch in CA 1-4R
Coigney, Virginia 1917- 103
Coit, John Hamilton 1947(?)-1986 Obituary 118
Coit, Lew Garrison 1897(?)-1985 Obituary 116
Coit, Margaret Louise 1919- CANR-5
Earlier sketch in CA 1-4R
See also SATA 2
Cojeen, Robert H. 1920- 37-40R
Coke, Tom S(tephen) 1943- 115
Coke, Van Deren 1921- CANR-22
Earlier sketches in CA 13-16R, CANR-7
Coker, C(harles) F(rederick) W(illiams) 1932-1983 Obituary 110
Coker, Carolyn 125
Coker, Elizabeth Boatwright 1909- 45-48
Coker, Gylbert 1944- 93-96
Coker, Jerry 1932- CANR-6
Earlier sketch in CA 9-12R
Coker, Syl Cheney
See Cheney-Coker, Syl
Colacci, Mario 1910-1968 5-8R
Obituary 135
Colacello, Bob 1947- 138
Coladarci, Arthur Paul 1917- 5-8R
Colaiaco, James A(lfred) 1945- 115
Colander, Pat(ricia) 1952- 110
Colaneri, John Nunzio 1930- 103
Colaw, Emerson S. 1921- 13-16R
Colbach, Edward M(ichael) 1939- 69-72
Colbeck, Maurice 1925- CANR-34
Earlier sketches in CA 13-16R, CANR-5
Colberg, Marshall R(udolph) 1913- CANR-1
Earlier sketch in CA 1-4R
Colbert, Anthony 1934- 89-92
See also SATA 15
Colbert, Douglas A(lbert) 1933- 57-60
Colbert, Edwin Harris 1905- CANR-8
Earlier sketch in CA 61-64
Colbert, Evelyn S(peyer) 1918- 102
Colbert, James 1951- 122
Colbert, Roman 1921- 53-56
Colborn, Nigel 1944- 128
Colbourn, H(arold) Trevor 1927- 33-36R
Colburn, C(lyde) William 1939- 37-40R
Colburn, David Richard 1942- 110
Colburn, George A(bbott) 1938- 41-44R
Colby, Averil 1900-1983(?) Obituary 108
Colby, Benjamin N(ick) 1931- 61-64
Colby, C(arroll) B(urleigh) 1904-1977 CANR-6
Earlier sketch in CA 1-4R
See also SATA 3, 35
Colby, Douglas (Steven) 1954- 116
Colby, Elbridge 1891-1982 CAP-1
Obituary 108
Earlier sketch in CA 13-16
Colby, Jean Poindexter 1909- CANR-5
Earlier sketch in CA 1-4R
See also SATA 23
Colby, Joan 1939- CANR-13
Earlier sketch in CA 77-80
Colby, Robert A(lan) 1920- 53-56
Colby, Roy (Edward) 1910- 25-28R
Colby, Vineta (Blumoff) 1922- 9-12R
Colby, William Egan 1920- 81-84
Colchie, Elizabeth Schneider
See Schneider, Elizabeth (Susan)
Colden, Cadwallader 1688-1776 DLB 24, 30
Coldham, James D(esmond Bowden) 1924-1987 113
Obituary 121
Coldrey, Jennifer (M.) 1940- 121
Coldsmith, Don(ald Charles) 1926- CANR-21
Earlier sketch in CA 105
Coldwell, David F(rederick) C(larke) 1923-1973 17-20R
Obituary 134
Coldwell, Joan 1936- 106
Coldwell, M(ichael) J. 1888-1974 Obituary 53-56
Cole, Adrian 1949- 121
Cole, Allison
See Coker, Carolyn
Cole, Andrew Thomas Jr. 1933- 102
Cole, Ann Kilborn
See Callahan, Claire Wallis
Cole, Ann 1937- 65-68
Cole, Annette
See Steiner, Barbara A(nnette)
Cole, Arthur C(harles) 1886-1976 Obituary 65-68
Cole, Babette 1949- SATA 61
Cole, Barry 1936- CANR-16
Earlier sketch in CA 25-28R
See also DLB 14
Cole, Bill
See Cole, William Shadrack
Cole, Brock 1938- 136
See also CLR 18
See also MAICYA
Cole, Bruce 1938- CANR-15
Earlier sketch in CA 65-68
Cole, Burt 1930- 73-76
Cole, C. Donald 1923- 125
Cole, C(harles) Robert 1939- 65-68
Cole, Cannon
See Cook, Arlene Ethel
Cole, Charles C(hester) Jr. 1922- 118
Cole, Charles L(eland) 1927- 69-72
Cole, Charles Woolsey 1906-1978 CANR-22
Obituary 77-80
Earlier sketch in CA 69-72
Cole, Clifford A. 1915- 13-16R
Cole, Cozy
See Cole, William R.
Cole, Dandridge MacFarlan 1921- 13-16R
Cole, David C(hamberlin) 1928- 127
Brief entry 106
Cole, Davis
See Elting, Mary
Cole, Diane 1952- 138
Cole, Donald Barnard 1922- 5-8R
Cole, Doris 1938- 89-92
Cole, Douglas 1934- CANR-2
Earlier sketch in CA 5-8R
Cole, E(ugene) R(oger) 1930- CANR-31
Earlier sketches in CA 53-56, CANR-4, 19
Cole, Eddie-Lou 1909- 65-68
Cole, Edward B(ender) 1923- 107
Cole, Edward C(yrus) 1904- 13-16R
Cole, Frank R(aymond) 1892- 69-72
Cole, G(eorge) D(ouglas) H(oward) 1889-1959 Brief entry 108
Cole, George F(raser) 1935- 65-68
Cole, Gordon
See Cole, Gordon H(enry)
Cole, Gordon H(enry) 1912-1988 Obituary 125
Cole, H. S. D.
See Cole, (Hugh) Sam(uel David)
Cole, (Roger) Henri 1956- 121
Cole, Howard C(handler) 1934- 49-52
Cole, Hubert (Archibald Noel) 1908- CANR-5
Earlier sketch in CA 5-8R
Cole, J(ohn) A(lfred) 1905- CAP-1
Earlier sketch in CA 13-16
Cole, J. P.
See Cole, John P(eter)
Cole, Jack
See Stewart, John (William)
Cole, Jackson
See Germano, Peter B. and Schisgall, Oscar
Cole, Janet
See Hunter, Kim
Cole, Jennifer
See Zach, Cheryl (Byrd)
Cole, Joan 1957- 113
Cole, Joanna 1944- CANR-36
Earlier sketch in CA 115
See also CLR 5
See also MAICYA
See also SATA 37, 49
Cole, John N(elson) 1923- 93-96
Cole, John P(eter) 1928- CANR-19
Earlier sketches in CA 5-8R, CANR-3
Cole, John Y(oung) Jr. 1940- CANR-19
Earlier sketch in CA 103
Cole, Jonathan R(ichard) 1942- 53-56
Cole, Juan R(icardo) I(rfan) 1952- 121
Cole, K. C. 1946- 105
Cole, Kay
See Colominas, Kathleen Adele
Cole, (Edmund) Keith 1919- CANR-19
Earlier sketch in CA 102
Cole, Larry 1936- 45-48
Cole, Leonard A(aron) 1933- 81-84
Cole, Leonard Leslie 1909-1980 103
Cole, Lester 1904(?)-1985 Obituary 117
Cole, Lewis 1946- 109
Cole, Lois Dwight 1903-1979 CANR-4
Obituary 104
Earlier sketch in CA 1-4R
See also SATA 10, 26
Cole, Luella (Winifred) 1893- CAP-1
Earlier sketch in CA 19-20
Cole, Margaret Alice CANR-6
Earlier sketch in CA 9-12R
Cole, Margaret Isabel 1893-1980 CANR-4
Obituary 97-100
Earlier sketch in CA 5-8R
Cole, Martha 1916(?)-1986 Obituary 118
Cole, Mary
See Hanna, Mary T.
Cole, Michael 1938- 97-100
Cole, Michael 1947- SATA 59
Cole, Michelle 1940- 29-32R
Cole, Monica M(ary) 1922- 1-4R
Cole, Richard Cargill 1926- 124
Cole, Robert E(van) 1937- 69-72
Cole, Robert H. 1918- 33-36R
Cole, Robert J(ason) 1925- 133
Cole, Roger L. 1933- 25-28R
Cole, (Hugh) Sam(uel David) 1943- 130
Cole, Sandi Gelles
See Gelles-Cole, Sandi
Cole, Sheila R(otenberg) 1939- CANR-4
Earlier sketch in CA 53-56
See also SATA 24
Cole, Sonia (Mary) 1918-1982 93-96
Obituary 106
Cole, Stephen
See Webbe, Gale D(udley)
Cole, Stephen 1941- 29-32R
Cole, Sylvan Jr. 1918- 69-72
Cole, Terrence (Michael) 1953- 135
Cole, (Andrew) Thomas (Jr.) 1933- 33-36R
Cole, W(illiam) Owen 1931- 118
Cole, Wayne S. 1922- 21-24R
Cole, Wendell 1914- 21-24R
Cole, William Earle 1904-1979 17-20R
Obituary 126
Cole, William Graham 1917- 17-20R
Cole, William R. 1909-1981 Obituary 108
Cole, William (Rossa) 1919- CANR-7
Earlier sketch in CA 9-12R
See also MAICYA
See also SAAS 9
See also SATA 9, 71
Cole, William Shadrack 1937- 101
Colean, Miles Lanier 1898- CAP-2
Earlier sketch in CA 21-22
Coleburt, J(ames) Russell 1920- 13-16R
Colecchia, Francesca Maria 89-92
Colegate, Isabel 1931- CANR-22
Earlier sketches in CA 17-20R, CANR-8
See also CLC 36
See also DLB 14
See also MTCW
Colegrove, Kenneth 1886-1975 CANR-4
Obituary 53-56
Earlier sketch in CA 5-8R
Coleman, A(llan) D(ouglass) 1943- CANR-15
Earlier sketch in CA 73-76
Coleman, Almand R(ouse) 1905- CAP-2
Earlier sketch in CA 29-32
Coleman, Arthur 1924- 81-84
Coleman, Bernard D(avid) 1919- 25-28R
Coleman, Bill
See Coleman, William V(incent)
Coleman, Bob
See Coleman, Robert David
Coleman, Bruce P(umphrey) 1931- 37-40R
Coleman, Buck
See Richardson, Gladwell
Coleman, Clayton W(ebster) 1901- 29-32R
Coleman, D(onald) C(uthbert) 1920- 13-16R
Coleman, Dorothy Gabe 1935- 93-96
Coleman, Elliott 1906-1980 17-20R
Obituary 97-100
Coleman, Emily Holmes 1899-1974 105
See also DLB 4
Coleman, Emily R. 1947- 135
Coleman, Emmett
See Reed, Ishmael
Coleman, Evelyn Scherabon
See Firchow, Evelyn Scherabon
Coleman, Felicia Slatkin 1916(?)-1981 Obituary 102
Coleman, Francis Xavier Jerome 1939- 108
Coleman, J(ohn) Winston Jr. 1898-1983 CANR-27
Earlier sketch in CA 49-52
Coleman, James A(ndrew) 1921- 5-8R
Coleman, James C(ovington) 1914- CANR-1
Earlier sketch in CA 1-4R
Coleman, James S(amuel) 1926- 13-16R
Coleman, James Smoot 1919- 1-4R
Coleman, Jane Candia 1939- 136
Coleman, John R(oyston) 1921- CANR-1
Earlier sketch in CA 1-4R
See also AITN 1
Coleman, Jonathan (Mark) 1951- 138
Coleman, Jonathan 1951(?)- Brief entry 129
Coleman, Kenneth 1916- CANR-33
Earlier sketches in CA 21-24R, CANR-8
Coleman, Lee
See Lapidus, Elaine
Coleman, Lonnie
See Coleman, William Laurence
Coleman, Loren (Elwood Jr.) 1947- 133
Coleman, Lucile 73-76
Coleman, Marion (Reeves) Moore 1900- CANR-11
Earlier sketch in CA 17-20R
Coleman, Michael C(hristopher) 1946- 119
Coleman, Patricia R(egister) 1936- CANR-25
Earlier sketch in CA 109
Coleman, Patty R.
See Coleman, Patricia R(egister)
Coleman, Peter J(arrett) 1926- 5-8R
Coleman, Ray 1937- 137
Coleman, Raymond James 1923- CANR-36
Earlier sketch in CA 49-52
Coleman, Richard J(ames) 1941- 41-44R
Coleman, Richard M(ark) 1951- 121
Coleman, Richard Patrick 1927- 33-36R
Coleman, Robert David 1951- 121
Coleman, Robert E(merson) 1928- CANR-35
Earlier sketches in CA 13-16R, CANR-7
Coleman, Robert William Alfred 1916- 9-12R
Coleman, Roy V. 1885-1971 Obituary 104
Coleman, Terry 1931- CANR-27
Earlier sketches in CA 13-16R, CANR-10
Coleman, Thomas R. 1942- 57-60
Coleman, Verna (Scott) 134
Coleman, Vernon 1946- 81-84
Coleman, Wanda 1946- 119
See also BW
Coleman, William L(eRoy) 1938- CANR-21
Earlier sketch in CA 69-72
See also SATA 34, 49
Coleman, William Laurence 1920-1982 CANR-39
Coleman, William V(incent) 1932- CANR-25
Earlier sketches in CA 57-60, CANR-9
Coleman-Norton, P(aul) R(obinson) 1898-1971 Obituary 29-32R
Colen, B. D. 1946- CANR-23
Earlier sketch in CA 65-68
Colenbrander, Joanna 1908- 121
Coleridge, Hartley 1796-1849 DLB 96
Coleridge, John
See Binder, Otto O(scar)
Coleridge, M. E.
See Coleridge, Mary E(lizabeth)
Coleridge, Mary E(lizabeth) 1861-1907 Brief entry 116
See also DLB 19, 98
Coleridge, Samuel Taylor 1772-1834 CDBLB 1789-1832
See also DLB 93, 107
See also WLC
Coles, Alan 1927- 124
Coles, Cyril Henry 1899-1965 CAP-1
Earlier sketch in CA 9-10
Coles, Don 1928- CANR-38
Earlier sketch in CA 115
See also CLC 46
Coles, Flournoy (Arthur) Jr. 1915- 57-60
Coles, Harry L(ewis) 1920- 9-12R
Coles, Janis
See Dawson, Janis
Coles, Joan M(yers) 1947- 133
Coles, John M(orton) 1930- CANR-34
Earlier sketches in CA 29-32R, CANR-12
Coles, Kaines Adlard 1901-1985 CAP-1
Obituary 117
Earlier sketch in CA 13-14
Coles, Manning
See Coles, Cyril Henry
Coles, Robert (Martin) 1929- CANR-32
Earlier sketches in CA 45-48, CANR-3
See also SATA 23
Coles, Robert R(eed) 1908(?)-1985 Obituary 116
Coles, S(ydney) F(rederick) Arthur 1896- 5-8R
Coles, Susan Vaughan Ebershoff
See Ebershoff-Coles, Susan Vaughan
Coles, William Allan 1930- 33-36R
Coles, William E. Jr. 1932- CANR-10
Earlier sketch in CA 61-64
Coletta, Paolo Enrico 1916- CANR-31
Earlier sketches in CA 41-44R, CANR-14
Colette, Jacques 1929- 89-92
Colette, (Sidonie-Gabrielle) 1873-1954 131
Brief entry 104
See also DLB 65
See also MTCW
See also SSC 10
See also TCLC 1, 5, 16
Colford, Paul D(ennis) 1953- 110
Colford, William E(dward) 1908-1971 5-8R
Obituary 33-36R
Colgin, Russell W(eymount) 1925- 121
Colgrave, Bertram 1888-1968 CAP-2
Earlier sketch in CA 25-28
Colie, Rosalie L(ittell) 1924-1972 Obituary 106
Colimore, Vincent J(erome) 1914- 37-40R
Colin, Ann
See Ure, Jean
Colin, Jean
See Bell, Joyce
Colina, Tessa Patterson 1915- CANR-7
Earlier sketch in CA 17-20R
Colinvaux, Paul (Alfred) 1930- CANR-14
Earlier sketch in CA 41-44R
Colish, Marcia L. 1937- CANR-10
Earlier sketch in CA 25-28R
Coll, Regina A(udrey) 1929- 112
Coll, Steve 1958- 137
Collard, Edgar Andrew 1911- 102
Collas, J. P. 1911-1984 Obituary 114

Colledge, Malcolm A(ndrew) R(ichard) 1939- ... CANR-10
Earlier sketch in CA 25-28R
Collen, Neil
See Lee, Lincoln
Coller, Richard Walter 1925- ... 119
Collery, Arnold (Peter) 1927-1989 Obituary ... 128
Collett, Barry 1934- ... 128
Collett, Rosemary K(ing) 1931- ... 69-72
Colletta, Nat J(oseph) 1944- ... 104
Collette, Christine 1947- ... 132
Colley, Ann C(heetham) 1940- ... CANR-30
Earlier sketch in CA 112
Colley, Iain 1940- ... 97-100
Colley, Linda 1949- ... 130
Collias, Joe G. 1928- ... CANR-14
Earlier sketch in CA 41-44R
Collias, Nicholas E(lias) 1914- ... 131
Collie, Michael (John) 1929- ... CANR-39
Earlier sketches in CA 49-52, CANR-3, 18
Collier, (John) Basil 1908- ... CANR-2
Earlier sketch in CA 5-8R
Collier, Boyd D(ean) 1938- ... 57-60
Collier, Calhoun C(rofford) 1916- ... 25-28R
Collier, Christopher 1930- ... CANR-33
Earlier sketches in CA 33-36R, CANR-13
See also CLC 30
See also MAICYA
See also SATA 16, 70
Collier, David S(wanson) 1923-1983 ... 21-24R
Obituary ... 111
Collier, David 1942- ... 69-72
Collier, Douglas
See Fellowes-Gordon, Ian (Douglas)
Collier, Ethel 1903- ... 65-68
See also SATA 22
Collier, Eugenia W(illiams) 1928- ... 49-52
Collier, Gary 1947- ... 138
Collier, Gaydell M(aier) 1935- ... 93-96
Collier, Gaylan Jane 1924- ... 37-40R
Collier, (Alan) Graham 1923- ... 17-20R
Collier, (James) Graham 1937- ... 105
Collier, Herbert L(eon) 1933- ... 103
Collier, James L(incoln) 1928- ... CANR-33
Earlier sketches in CA 9-12R, CANR-4
See also CLC 30
See also MAICYA
See also SATA 8, 70
Collier, Jane
See Hampson, Zena
Collier, John 1901-1980 ... CANR-10
Obituary ... 97-100
Earlier sketch in CA 65-68
See also DLB 77
Collier, Johnnie Lucille
See Collier, Lucille Ann
Collier, Joy
See Millar, (Minna Henrietta) Joy
Collier, Kenneth Gerald 1910- ... CANR-18
Earlier sketch in CA 85-88
Collier, Leo(nard) D(awson) 1908- ... 5-8R
Collier, Louise Wilbourn 1925- ... 109
Collier, Lucille Ann 1919(?)- Brief entry ... 109
Collier, Lucy Ann
See Collier, Lucille Ann
Collier, Margaret
See Taylor, Margaret Stewart
Collier, Mary 1690- ... DLB 95
Collier, Michael 1953- ... 137
Collier, Peter 1939- ... 65-68
Collier, Phyllis K(ay) 1939- ... 110
Collier, Richard 1924- ... CANR-25
Earlier sketches in CA 1-4R, CANR-5
Collier, Robert J. 1876-1918 ... DLB 91
Collier, Simon 1938- ... 21-24R
Collier, Steven 1942- ... SATA 61
Collier, Zena
See Hampson, Zena
See also SATA 23
Colligan, Francis J(ames) 1908- ... CAP-2
Earlier sketch in CA 19-20
Collignon, Jean Henri 1918- ... 1-4R
Collignon, Jeff 1953- ... 137
Collignon, Joseph 1930- ... 89-92
Collin, Marion (Cripps) 1928- ... CANR-5
Earlier sketch in CA 9-12R
Collin, Richard H(arvey) 1932- ... 122
Collin, Richard Oliver 1940- ... 105
Collings, Ellsworth 1887- ... 73-76
Collings, I. J(illie) ... CANR-38
Earlier sketch in CA 115
Collings, Michael R(obert) 1947- ... CANR-30
Earlier sketch in CA 111
Collington, Peter 1948- ... 127
See also SATA 59
Collingwood, Charles (Cummings) 1917-1985 ... 29-32R
Obituary ... 117
Collingwood, R(obin) G(eorge) 1889(?)-1943 Brief entry ... 117
Collins, Alan 1928- ... 132
Collins, Alice H(esslein) 1907- ... 65-68
Collins, Arnold Quint 1935- ... 73-76
Collins, Arthur Worth Jr. 1929- ... 131
Collins, Barbara J(ane) 1929- ... CANR-6
Earlier sketch in CA 57-60
Collins, Barry E(merson) 1937- ... CANR-7
Earlier sketch in CA 13-16R
Collins, Barry 1941- ... 102
Collins, Beulah Stowe 1923-1983 ... 122
Obituary ... 110
Collins, Bud
See Collins, Arthur Worth Jr.
Collins, Carvel 1912-1990 ... CANR-8
Obituary ... 131
Earlier sketch in CA 17-20R
Collins, Cecil (James Henry) 1908-1989 Obituary ... 128
Collins, Charles C. 1919- ... 25-28R
Collins, Charles William 1880-1964 Obituary ... 89-92
Collins, Christopher 1936- ... 49-52
Collins, Cindy
See Smith, Richard Rein
Collins, Clark
See Reynolds, Dallas McCord
Collins, Colette
See Knaack, Twila
Collins, D.
See Bulleid, H(enry) A(nthony) V(aughan)
Collins, David A(lmon) 1931- ... 21-24R
Collins, David R(aymond) 1940- ... CANR-26
Earlier sketches in CA 29-32R, CANR-11
See also SATA 7
Collins, Desmond 1940- ... CANR-14
Earlier sketch in CA 73-76
Collins, Donald E(dward) 1934- ... 122
Collins, Douglas 1912-1972 Obituary ... 33-36R
Collins, Eliza G. C. 1938- ... 129
Collins, F(rederick) Herbert 1890- ... CAP-1
Earlier sketch in CA 11-12
Collins, Fletcher Jr. 1906- ... 53-56
Collins, Freda
See Collins, Frederica Joan Hale
Collins, Frederica Joan Hale 1904- ... CAP-1
Earlier sketch in CA 13-14
Collins, Gary (Ross) 1934- ... CANR-22
Earlier sketches in CA 57-60, CANR-7
Collins, George R(oseborough) 1917- ... CANR-1
Earlier sketch in CA 1-4R
Collins, Harold R(eeves) 1915- ... 25-28R
Collins, Henry B(ascom) Jr. 1899-1987 Obituary ... 123
Collins, Henry 1917- ... 17-20R
Collins, Herbert Ridgeway 1932- ... 118
Collins, Hunt
See Hunter, Evan
Collins, Jackie ... CANR-22
Earlier sketch in CA 102
See also BEST 90:4
Collins, James Daniel 1917- ... CANR-5
Earlier sketch in CA 1-4R
Collins, Jean E(lizabeth) 1948- ... 110
Collins, Joan 1933- ... 116
Collins, Jodie 1941- ... 121
Collins, John H. 1893- ... 1-4R
Collins, John J(oseph) 1946- ... 112
Collins, John Lawrence Jr. 1929- ... CANR-19
Earlier sketch in CA 65-68
Collins, John M(artin) 1921- ... CANR-31
Earlier sketch in CA 49-52
Collins, Joseph B. 1898(?)-1975 Obituary ... 53-56
Collins, Joseph T. 1939- ... 120
Collins, Judith Graham 1942- ... 115
Collins, Judy (Marjorie) 1939- ... 103
Collins, Julie (Hubbard) 1959- ... 131
Collins, June Irene 1935- ... 37-40R
Collins, Kathleen 1931- ... 119
Collins, L(ewis) John 1905-1982 ... CAP-1
Obituary ... 108
Earlier sketch in CA 13-14
Collins, Larry
See Collins, John Lawrence Jr.
Collins, Linda 1931- ... 125
See also CLC 44
Collins, Lorraine (Hill) 1931- ... 57-60
Collins, Mabel
See Cook, Mabel Collins
Collins, Margaret (Brandon James) 1909- ... 89-92
Collins, Marie (Margaret) 1935- ... 53-56
Collins, Marjorie A(nn) 1930- ... CANR-11
Earlier sketch in CA 65-68
Collins, Marva (Deloise Nettles) 1936- ... 111
Collins, Max
See Collins, Max Allan (Jr.)
Collins, Max Allan (Jr.) 1948- ... CANR-27
Earlier sketch in CA 103
Collins, Meghan 1926- ... 101
Collins, Michael
See Lynds, Dennis
Collins, Michael 1930- ... CANR-5
Earlier sketch in CA 53-56
See also SATA 58
Collins, Miki (Dickey) 1959- ... 131
Collins, Mortimer 1827-1876 ... DLB 21, 35
Collins, Myron D(ean) 1901- ... CAP-1
Earlier sketch in CA 13-16
Collins, Myrtle T(elleen) 1915- ... 101
Collins, Nancy W.
See Collins-Chapman, Nancy W(hisnant)
Collins, Norman Richard 1907-1982 ... 105
Obituary ... 107
Collins, Orvis F(loyd) 1918- ... 69-72
Collins, Pat(ricia) Lowery 1932- ... CANR-24
Earlier sketch in CA 107
See also SATA 31
Collins, Peter (Sheridan) 1942- ... 77-80
Collins, Philip (Arthur William) 1923- ... CANR-22
Earlier sketches in CA 5-8R, CANR-8
Collins, R(obert) G(eorge) 1926- ... 112
Collins, Raymond F(rancis) 1935- ... 112
Collins, Robert E(mmet) 1927- ... 69-72
Collins, Robert M. 1943- ... 110
Collins, Robert O(akley) 1933- ... CANR-22
Earlier sketches in CA 1-4R, CANR-4
Collins, Robert 1924- ... CANR-15
Earlier sketch in CA 89-92
Collins, Rowland Lee 1934-1985 ... 9-12R
Obituary ... 116
Collins, Ruth Philpott 1890-1975 ... CANR-4
Obituary ... 53-56
Earlier sketch in CA 1-4R
See also SATA 30
Collins, Thomas Hightower 1910- ... 102
Collins, Trish 1927- ... 106
Collins, (William) Wilkie 1824-1889 ... CDBLB 1832-1890
See also DLB 18, 70
Collins, Will
See Corley, Edwin (Raymond)
Collins, William Alexander Roy 1900-1976 Obituary ... 69-72
Collins, William Bernard 1913- ... 5-8R
Collins, William 1721-1759 ... DLB 109
Collins-Chapman, Nancy W(hisnant) 1933- ... 112
Collinson, Laurence (Henry) 1925- ... 103
Collinson, Roger (Alfred) 1936- ... 110
Collis, John Stewart 1900-1984 ... 61-64
Obituary ... 112
Collis, Kevin F(rancis) 1930- ... 107
Collis, Louise 1925- ... 21-24R
Collis, Maurice 1889-1973 ... CANR-4
Obituary ... 89-92
Earlier sketch in CA 5-8R
Collis, William Robert Fitzgerald 1900- ... CAP-1
Earlier sketch in CA 9-10
Collison, David (John) 1937- ... 105
Collison, Koder M(acklin) 1910- ... 53-56
Collison, Robert Lewis Wright 1914- ... CANR-2
Earlier sketch in CA 5-8R
Colliss, Gertrude Florence Mary (Jones) 1908- ... 5-8R
Collodi, Carlo
See Lorenzini, Carlo
See also CLR 5
Collom, Jack 1931- ... 77-80
Colloms, Brenda 1919- ... CANR-7
Earlier sketch in CA 61-64
See also SATA 40
Collyer, Mary 1716(?)-1763(?) ... DLB 39
Collyns, Robin 1940- ... 69-72
Colm, Gerhard 1897-1968 ... 5-8R
Obituary ... 103
Colman, Arthur D. 1937- ... 33-36R
Colman, Benjamin 1673-1747 ... DLB 24
Colman, E(rnest) A(drian) M(ackenzie) 1930- ... 57-60
Colman, George
See Glassco, John
Colman, Hila ... CANR-7
Earlier sketch in CA 13-16R
See also AAYA 1
See also MAICYA
See also SAAS 14
See also SATA 1, 53
Colman, John E. 1923- ... 21-24R
Colman, Juliet Benita 1944- ... 61-64
Colman, Libby Lee 1940- ... 33-36R
Colman, Morris 1899(?)-1981 ... SATA 25
Colman, Warren (David) 1944- ... 136
See also SATA 67
Colmer, John (Anthony) 1921- ... CANR-34
Earlier sketches in CA 85-88, CANR-15
Colmer, Michael (J.) 1942- ... CANR-21
Earlier sketch in CA 69-72
Colodny, Robert G. 1915- ... CANR-14
Earlier sketch in CA 37-40R
Colombo, Dale
See Monroe, Keith
Colombo, Furio 1931- ... CANR-30
Earlier sketch in CA 111
Colombo, John Robert 1936- ... CANR-11
Earlier sketch in CA 25-28R
See also DLB 53
See also SATA 50
Colominas, Kathleen Adele 1948- ... 134
Colon, Jesus 1901- ... 131
See also HW
Colonel Sanders
See Sanders, Harland
Colonius, Lillian 1911- ... 21-24R
See also SATA 3
Colony, Horatio 1900-1977 ... 37-40R
Colorado, Antonio J.
See Colorado (Capella), Antonio J(ulio)
Colorado (Capella), Antonio J(ulio) 1903- ... CANR-32
Earlier sketch in CA 17-20R
See also HW
See also SATA 23
Colp, Ralph Jr. 1924- ... 126
Colquhoun, Archibald 1912-1964 ... 129
Obituary ... 89-92
Colquhoun, Frank 1909- ... 106
Colquhoun, Ithell 1906-1988 ... 13-16R
Obituary ... 125
Colquhoun, Keith 1927- ... 102
Colquitt, Betsy Feagan 1926- ... 53-56
Colson, Charles W(endell) 1931- ... CANR-29
Earlier sketch in CA 102
Colson, Elizabeth 1917- ... 53-56
Colson, Frederick
See Geis, Richard E(rwin)
Colson, Greta (Scotchmur) 1913- ... CAP-1
Earlier sketch in CA 9-10
Colson, Howard P(aul) 1910- ... 29-32R
Colson, Laramie
See Richardson, Gladwell
Colston, Lowell G(wen) 1919-1985 ... 53-56
Obituary ... 118
Colston-Baynes, Dorothy 1881(?)-1973 Obituary ... 104
Colt, Clem
See Nye, Nelson C(oral)
Colt, John W. 1900(?)-1983 Obituary ... 111
Colt, Martin
See Epstein, Beryl (M. Williams) and Epstein, Samuel
Colt, Winchester Remington
See Hubbard, L(afayette) Ron(ald)
Colt, Zandra
See Stevenson, Florence
Coltart, James M(ilne) 1903-1986 Obituary ... 120
Colter, Cyrus 1910- ... CANR-10
Earlier sketch in CA 65-68
See also BW
See also CLC 58
See also DLB 33
Colter, Shayne
See Norwood, Victor G(eorge) C(harles)
Coltharp, Lurline H(ughes) 1913- ... 17-20R
Coltman, Ernest Vivian
See Dudley, Ernest
Coltman, Will
See Bingley, David Ernest
Colton, C(larence) E(ugene) 1914- ... CANR-2
Earlier sketch in CA 5-8R
Colton, Harold S(ellers) 1881-1970 ... CANR-3
Earlier sketch in CA 1-4R
Colton, Helen 1918- ... 57-60
Colton, James
See Hansen, Joseph
Colton, James B(yers) II 1908- ... 37-40R
Colton, Joel 1918- ... CANR-2
Earlier sketch in CA 1-4R
Colton, Timothy J. 1947- ... 124
Coltrane, James
See Wohl, James P(aul)
Colum, Padraic 1881-1972 ... CANR-35
Obituary ... 33-36R
Earlier sketch in CA 73-76
See also CLC 28
See also MAICYA
See also MTCW
See also SATA 15
Columbu, Franco 1941- ... 125
Columella
See Moore, Clement Clarke
Colver, A(nthony) Wayne 1923- ... 93-96
Colver, Alice Mary (Ross) 1892- ... 69-72
Colver, Anne 1908- ... CANR-2
Earlier sketch in CA 45-48
See also SATA 7
Colvert, James B(rumley) 1921- ... 116
Colvett, Latayne
See Scott, Latayne Colvett
Colville, Derek Kent 1923- Brief entry ... 105
Colville, John Rupert 1915-1987 ... CANR-10
Obituary ... 124
Earlier sketch in CA 61-64
Colvin, Brenda 1897-1981 Obituary ... 108
Colvin, Clare 1943- ... 123
Colvin, Elaine Wright 1942- ... 106
Colvin, Howard Montagu 1919- ... 61-64
Colvin, Ian G(oodhope) 1912-1975 ... CAP-2
Obituary ... 57-60
Earlier sketch in CA 19-20
Colvin, James
See Moorcock, Michael (John)
Colvin, Ralph W(hitmore) 1920-1981 ... 107
Obituary ... 104
Colwell, C(harles) Carter 1932- ... 41-44R
Colwell, Eileen (Hilda) 1904- ... CANR-12
Earlier sketch in CA 29-32R
See also SATA 2
Colwell, Ernest Cadman 1901-1974 ... CANR-4
Obituary ... 53-56
Earlier sketch in CA 5-8R
Colwell, Richard J(ames) 1930- ... 69-72
Colwell, Robert 1931- ... 33-36R
Colwin, Laurie 1944- ... CANR-20
Earlier sketch in CA 89-92
See also CLC 5, 13, 23
See also DLBY 80
See also MTCW
Colwyn, Stewart
See Pepper, Frank S.
Colyer, Penrose 1940- ... CANR-20
Earlier sketches in CA 65-68, CANR-14
Coman, Dale Rex 1906- ... 81-84
Coman, Edwin Truman Jr. 1903- ... 9-12R
Comaroff, John L(ionel) 1945- ... 125
Comaromi, John P(hillip) 1937- ... 111
Comarow, Avery 1945- ... 127
Comay, Joan ... 103
Comber, Lillian 1916- ... CANR-3
Earlier sketch in CA 9-12R
Combs, A(rthur) W(right) 1912- ... CANR-10
Earlier sketch in CA 17-20R
Combs, Ann 1935- ... 117
Combs, David 1934- ... 108
Combs, Eugene 1934- ... 118
Combs, Harry (Benjamin) 1913- ... 129
Combs, James E(verett) 1941- ... CANR-19
Earlier sketch in CA 101
Combs, Jerald A(rthur) 1937- ... 110
Combs, Richard Earl 1934- ... 33-36R
Combs, Robert
See Murray, John
Combs, (Elisha) Tram(mell Jr.) 1924- ... 13-16R
Combuchen, Sigrid
See Combuechen, Sigrid
Combuechen, Sigrid 1942- ... 136
Comden, Betty 1919- ... CANR-2
Earlier sketch in CA 49-52
See also DLB 44
Comeau, Arthur M. 1938- ... 61-64
Comer, James P(ierpont) 1934- ... 61-64
Comey, Dennis J. 1896-1987 Obituary ... 123
Comey, James Hugh 1947- ... 65-68
Comfort, Alex(ander) 1920- ... CANR-1
Earlier sketch in CA 1-4R
See also CLC 7
Comfort, Howard 1904- ... 37-40R
Comfort, Iris Tracy ... CANR-6
Earlier sketch in CA 13-16R

Comfort, Jane Levington
See Sturtzel, Jane Levington
Comfort, Mildred Houghton 1886- ...9-12R
See also SATA 3
Comfort, Montgomery
See Campbell, (John) Ramsey
Comfort, Richard A(llen) 1933- ...21-24R
Comi, Girolamo 1890-1968 ... DLB 114
Comidas, Chinas
See Genser, Cynthia
Comini, Alessandra 1934- ...93-96
Comins, Ethel M(ae) ...CANR-8
Earlier sketch in CA 61-64
See also SATA 11
Comins, Jeremy 1933- ...CANR-14
Earlier sketch in CA 65-68
See also SATA 28
Comitas, Lambros 1927- Brief entry ...113
Comito, Terry (Allen) 1935- ...CANR-29
Earlier sketch in CA 109
Commager, Henry Steele 1902- ...CANR-26
Earlier sketch in CA 21-24R
See also DLB 17
See also MTCW
See also SATA 23
Commager, (Henry) Steele (Jr.)
1932-1984 Obituary ...112
Commins, William Dollard Sr.
1899-1983 Obituary ...109
Commire, Anne ...CANR-21
Earlier sketch in CA 69-72
Committe, Thomas C. 1922- ...65-68
Commoner, Barry 1917- ...CANR-33
Earlier sketch in CA 65-68
See also MTCW
Commons, Dorman L(eland) 1918- ...129
Como, (Michael) William 1925-1989 ...69-72
Obituary ...127
Comparetti, Alice 1907- ...37-40R
Compere, Mickie
See Davidson, Margaret
Compitello, Malcolm Alan 1946- ...136
Complo, Sister Jannita Marie 1935- ...57-60
Compo, Susan 1955- ...134
Comprone, Joseph J(ohn) 1943- ...CANR-35
Earlier sketches in CA 53-56, CANR-5
Compton, Ann
See Prebble, Marjorie Mary Curtis
Compton, Arthur Holly 1892-1962 Obituary ...116
Compton, D(avid) G(uy) 1930- ...CANR-17
Earlier sketch in CA 25-28R
Compton, Guy
See Compton, D(avid) G(uy)
Compton, Henry (Pasfield) 1909- ...9-12R
Compton, James V(incent) 1928- ...29-32R
Compton, Piers 1903- ...122
Compton-Burnett, I(vy) 1884(?)-1969 ...CANR-4
Obituary ...25-28R
Earlier sketch in CA 1-4R
See also CLC 1, 3, 10, 15, 34
See also DLB 36
See also MTCW
Compton-Hall, (Patrick) Richard
1929- ...CANR-24
Earlier sketch in CA 107
Comrey, Andrew Laurence
1923- Brief entry ...106
Comroe, Julius H(iram) Jr. 1911-1984 ...122
Obituary ...113
Comstock, Anthony 1844-1915 Brief entry ...110
See also TCLC 13
Comstock, Christine 1942- ...CANR-20
Earlier sketch in CA 104
Comstock, Gary 1954- ...127
Comstock, George Adolphe 1932- ...124
Comstock, Helen 1893-1970 ...CANR-4
Obituary ...89-92
Earlier sketch in CA 5-8R
Comstock, Henry B. 1908- ...CAP-2
Earlier sketch in CA 33-36
Comstock, Mary Bryce 1934- ...105
Comstock, W(illiam) Richard 1928- ...73-76
Comte, The Great
See Hawkesworth, Eric
Comus
See Ballantyne, R(obert) M(ichael)
Comyns, Barbara
See Comyns-Carr, Barbara Irene Veronica
Comyns-Carr, Barbara Irene Veronica
1912- ...5-8R
Conacher, D(esmond) J(ohn) 1918- ...25-28R
Conacher, J(ames) B(lennerhasset)
1916- ...25-28R
Conan, Laure 1845-1924 ...DLB 99
Conan Doyle, Adrian Malcolm 1910-1970 ...5-8R
Obituary ...29-32R
Conan Doyle, Arthur
See Doyle, Arthur Conan
Conant, Eaton H. 1930- ...53-56
Conant, Howard (Somers) 1921- ...CANR-8
Earlier sketch in CA 17-20R
Conant, James Bryant 1893-1978 ...13-16R
Obituary ...77-80
Conant, Kenneth John 1894- ...1-4R
Conant, Michael 1924- ...138
Conant, Ralph W(endell) 1926- ...CANR-31
Earlier sketches in CA 29-32R, CANR-14
Conant, Roger 1909- Brief entry ...107
Conard, Alfred Fletcher 1911- ...13-16R
Conard, Joseph W. 1911- ...13-16R
Conarroe, Joel (Osborne) 1934- ...29-32R
Conarroe, Richard R(iley) 1928- ...69-72
Conaway, James (Alley) 1941- ...33-36R
Conchon, Georges 1925-1990 Obituary ...132
Conconi, Charles N. 1938- ...77-80
Conde, Carmen 1901- ...DLB 108
Conde, Jesse C(lay) 1912- ...57-60
Conde, Maryse
See Boucolon, Maryse
See also CLC 52
Condee, Ralph Waterbury 1916- ...17-20R
Condit, Carl Wilbur 1914- ...CANR-4
Earlier sketch in CA 1-4R
Condit, Martha Olson 1913- ...73-76
See also SATA 28
Condliffe, John B(ell) 1891-1981 ...CAP-1
Obituary ...106
Earlier sketch in CA 13-16
Condon, David Rensing 1924- ...114
Condon, E(dward) U(hler)
1902-1974 Obituary ...112
Condon, Eddie 1905-1973 Obituary ...45-48
Condon, George Edward 1916- ...CANR-1
Earlier sketch in CA 45-48
Condon, Jack
See Condon, John C(arl) Jr.
Condon, Jane 1951- ...128
Condon, John C(arl) Jr. 1938- ...CANR-10
Earlier sketch in CA 21-24R
Condon, Richard (Thomas) 1915- ...CANR-23
Earlier sketches in CA 1-4R, CANR-2
See also CAAS 1
See also BEST 90:3
See also CLC 4, 6, 8, 10, 45
See also MTCW
Condon, Robert 1921(?)-1972 Obituary ...37-40R
Condor, Gladyn
See Davison, Gladys Patton
Condray, Bruno
See Humphrys, Leslie George
Condry, William Moreton 1918- ...103
Cone, Carl B. 1916- ...9-12R
Cone, Edward Toner 1917- ...110
Cone, Fairfax Mastick 1903-1977 ...73-76
Obituary ...69-72
Cone, Ferne Geller 1921- ...107
See also SATA 39
Cone, James H. 1938- ...33-36R
Cone, John F(rederick) 1926- ...17-20R
Cone, Molly Lamken 1918- ...CANR-37
Earlier sketches in CA 1-4R, CANR-1, 16
See also SAAS 11
See also SATA 1, 28
Cone, William F. 1919- ...57-60
Conerly, Perian Collier 1926- ...5-8R
Coney, Michael G(reatrex) 1932- ...97-100
See also SATA 61
Confer, Vincent 1913- ...21-24R
Conford, Ellen 1942- ...CANR-29
Earlier sketches in CA 33-36R, CANR-13
See also CLR 10
See also MAICYA
See also SATA 6, 68
Confucius
See Lund, Philip R(eginald)
Congar, Marie Joseph
See Congar, (Georges) Yves Marie-Joseph
Congar, Y. M.
See Congar, (Georges) Yves Marie-Joseph
Congar, Yves
See Congar, (Georges) Yves Marie-Joseph
Congar, Yves M.-J.
See Congar, (Georges) Yves Marie-Joseph
Congar, Yves M. J.
See Congar, (Georges) Yves Marie-Joseph
Congar, (Georges) Yves Marie-Joseph
1904- ...130
Congdon, Constance S. 1944- ...123
Congdon, Herbert Wheaton 1876-1965 ...5-8R
Congdon, Kirby 1924- ...CANR-7
Earlier sketch in CA 13-16R
Congdon, Kristin G. 1948- ...138
Congdon, Lee (Walter) 1939- ...130
Congdon, William Grosvenor 1912- ...CANR-24
Earlier sketches in CA 17-20R, CANR-7
Conger, (Seymour) Beach III
1912-1969 Obituary ...115
Conger, Jay A. 1952- ...132
Conger, John (Janeway) 1921- ...CANR-6
Earlier sketch in CA 13-16R
Conger, Lesley
See Suttles, Shirley (Smith)
Conger, Marion (C.) 1915-1990 Obituary ...130
Congrat-Butler, Stefan 1914(?)-1979 ...103
Obituary ...89-92
Congreve, Willard J(ohn) 1921-1979 ...57-60
Obituary ...134
Congreve, William
1670-1729 ...CDBLB 1660-1789
See also DC 2
See also DLB 39, 84
See also WLC
Conil, Jean 1917- ...CANR-29
Earlier sketches in CA 13-16R, CANR-13
Conine, (Odie) Ernest 1925- ...69-72
Coniston, Ed
See Bingley, David Ernest
Conkin, Paul K(eith) 1929- ...33-36R
Conkle, E(llsworth) P(routy) 1899- ...65-68
Conklin, Barbara P. 1927- ...109
Conklin, Gladys Plemon 1903- ...CANR-4
Earlier sketch in CA 1-4R
See also SATA 2
Conklin, Groff 1904-1968 ...CANR-3
Earlier sketch in CA 1-4R
Conklin, Harold C(olyer) 1926- ...118
Conklin, John E(van) 1943- ...CANR-14
Earlier sketch in CA 37-40R
Conklin, Mike 1944- ...120
Conklin, Paul ...115
Brief entry ...111
See also SATA 33, 43
Conkling, Hilda 1910- ...SATA 23
Conlay, Iris 1910- ...CAP-1
Earlier sketch in CA 11-12
Conley, Ellen Alexander 1938- ...CANR-20
Earlier sketch in CA 103
Conley, Enid Mary 1917- ...CANR-10
Earlier sketch in CA 65-68
Conley, John (Allan) 1912- ...61-64
Conley, Phillip Mallory 1887- ...69-72
Conley, Robert J(ackson) 1940- ...CANR-34
Earlier sketches in CA 41-44R, CANR-15
Conley, Verena Andermatt 1943- ...117
Conlin, David A. 1897- ...17-20R
Conlin, Joseph R. 1940- ...49-52
Conlon, Denis J. 1932- ...37-40R
Conlon, Kathleen (Annie) 1943- ...130
Brief entry ...114
Conlon-McKenna, Marita 1956- ...SATA 71
Conly, Robert Leslie 1918(?)-1973 ...73-76
Obituary ...41-44R
See also O'Brien, Robert C.
See also MAICYA
See also SATA 23
Conn, Canary Denise 1949- ...57-60
Conn, Charles Paul 1945- ...CANR-6
Earlier sketch in CA 57-60
Conn, Charles William 1920- ...CANR-10
Earlier sketch in CA 21-24R
Conn, Frances G. 1925- ...33-36R
Conn, Jan E(velyn) 1952- ...CANR-31
Earlier sketch in CA 110
Conn, Martha Orr 1935- ...93-96
Conn, Peter J. 1942- ...33-36R
Conn, Stetson 1908- ...CAP-1
Earlier sketch in CA 9-10
Conn, Stewart 1936- Brief entry ...117
Conn, Walter E(ugene) 1940- ...110
Connable, Alfred 1931- ...81-84
Connally, Eugenia (Maye) Horstman 1931- ...103
Connell, Brian (Reginald) 1916- ...CANR-4
Earlier sketch in CA 1-4R
Connell, Evan S(helby) Jr. 1924- ...CANR-39
Earlier sketches in CA 1-4R, CANR-2
See also CAAS 2
See also AAYA 7
See also CLC 4, 6, 45
See also DLB 2
See also DLBY 81
See also MTCW
Connell, Francis J. 1888- ...CAP-1
Earlier sketch in CA 13-14
Connell, Jon 1952- ...97-100
Connell, K(enneth) H(ugh) 1917-1973 ...CAP-2
Earlier sketch in CA 25-28
Connell, Kirk
See Chapman, John Stanton Higham
Connell, Maureen 1931- ...104
Connell, William Fraser 1916- ...104
Connellan, Leo 1928- ...81-84
Connelly, Bridget 1941- ...127
Connelly, Douglas 1949- ...121
Connelly, Marc(us Cook) 1890-1980 ...CANR-30
Obituary ...102
Earlier sketch in CA 85-88
See also CLC 7
See also DLB 7
See also DLBY 80
See also SATA 25
Connelly, Owen (Sergeson Jr.) 1924- ...17-20R
Connelly, Philip M(arshal)
1904(?)-1981 Obituary ...104
Connelly, Thomas L(awrence) 1938- ...CANR-11
Earlier sketch in CA 17-20R
Connely, Willard 1888-1967 ...CAP-2
Earlier sketch in CA 17-18
Conner, Berenice Gillete 1908- ...65-68
Conner, Floyd D(avis) 1951- ...119
Conner, K. Patrick 1952- ...127
Conner, Patrick Reardon 1907- ...5-8R
Conner, Patrick (Roy Mountifort) 1947- ...106
Conner, Paul Willard 1937-1984 ...17-20R
Obituary ...114
Conner, Rearden
See Conner, Patrick Reardon
Conner, Valerie Jean 1945- ...114
Conners, Bernard F. 1926- ...41-44R
Conners, Kenneth Wray 1909- ...29-32R
Connery, Donald S(tuart) 1926- Brief entry ...114
Connery, George Edward
1907(?)-1985 Obituary ...116
Connery, John (R.) 1913-1987 Obituary ...124
Connery, Robert H(owe) 1907- ...41-44R
Connett, Eugene Virginius III 1891-1969 ...CAP-1
Earlier sketch in CA 13-14
Connette, Earle 1910- ...CAP-1
Earlier sketch in CA 13-16
Connick, C(harles) Milo 1917- ...1-4R
Conniff, Frank 1914-1971 Obituary ...93-96
Conniff, James C(lifford) G(regory) ...21-24R
Conniff, Michael L(ee) 1942- ...118
Conniff, Richard 1951- ...124
Connolly, Cyril (Vernon) 1903-1974 ...CAP-2
Obituary ...53-56
Earlier sketch in CA 21-22
See also DLB 98
See also MTCW
Connolly, Francis X(avier) 1909-1965 ...CAP-1
Earlier sketch in CA 13-14
Connolly, James B. 1868-1957 ...DLB 78
Connolly, Jerome P(atrick) 1931- ...SATA 8
Connolly, Joseph 1950- ...130
Connolly, Paul
See Wicker, Thomas Grey
Connolly, Peter 1935- ...103
See also SATA 47
Connolly, Ray 1940- ...101
Connolly, Robert D(uggan Jr.) 1917- ...69-72
Connolly, S(ean) J. 1951- ...138
Connolly, Thomas Edmund 1918- ...CANR-4
Earlier sketch in CA 1-4R
Connolly, Vivian 1925- ...CANR-1
Earlier sketch in CA 49-52
Connon, Bryan (James Milne) 1927- ...137
Connor, J. Robert 1927- ...123
Connor, Jim 1935- ...107
Connor, John Anthony 1930- ...13-16R
See also Connor, Tony
Connor, Joyce Mary 1929- ...CANR-10
Earlier sketch in CA 65-68
Connor, Kevin
See O'Rourke, Frank
Connor, Lawrence S(tanton) 1925- ...89-92
Connor, Patricia 1943- ...25-28R
Connor, Ralph
See Gordon, Charles William
See also DLB 92
See also TCLC 31
Connor, Seymour V(aughan) 1923- ...53-56
Connor, Susanna Pflaum
See Pflaum, Susanna Whitney
Connor, Tony
See Connor, John Anthony
See also DLB 40
Connor, W(alter) Robert 1934- ...41-44R
Connor, Walter Downing 1942- ...106
Connor, William (Neil)
1909(?)-1967 Obituary ...25-28R
Connors, Bruton
See Rohen, Edward
Connors, Dorsey ...45-48
Connors, John Stanley 1925-1984 Obituary ...112
Connors, Joseph 1945- ...106
Conolly, L(eonard) W(illiam) 1941- ...106
Conolly, Violet 1901(?)-1988(?) Obituary ...124
Conor, Glen
See Cooney, Michael
Conot, Robert E. 1929- ...CANR-2
Earlier sketch in CA 45-48
Conover, C(harles) Eugene 1903- ...5-8R
Conover, Carole 1941- ...89-92
Conover, Chris 1950- ...128
See also SATA 31
Conover, David (Beals) 1919-1983 ...115
Conover, Hobart H. 1914- ...13-16R
Conover, Jessica Arline Wilcox
See Jones, Candy
Conover, Roger L(loyd) 1950- ...130
Conover, Ted 1958- ...129
Conquest, Edwin Parker Jr. 1931- ...29-32R
Conquest, Ned
See Conquest, Edwin Parker Jr.
Conquest, Owen
See Hamilton, Charles (Harold St. John)
Conquest, (George) Robert (Acworth)
1917- ...CANR-25
Earlier sketches in CA 13-16R, CANR-9
See also DLB 27
Conrad, Alfred Borys
1899(?)-1979 Obituary ...104
Conrad, Andree 1945- ...29-32R
Conrad, Barnaby (Jr.) 1922- ...CANR-6
Earlier sketch in CA 9-12R
Conrad, Brenda
See Brown, Zenith Jones
Conrad, David Eugene 1928- ...17-20R
Conrad, Earl 1912-1986 ...CANR-10
Obituary ...118
Earlier sketch in CA 1-4R
Conrad, Edna (G.) 1893- ...CAP-2
Earlier sketch in CA 33-36
Conrad, Hal
See Conrad, Harold
Conrad, Harold 1911-1991 ...112
Obituary ...134
Conrad, Jack (Randolph) 1923- ...9-12R
Conrad, John W(ilfred) 1935- ...CANR-4
Earlier sketch in CA 53-56
Conrad, Jon(athan) J(ames) 1920- ...114
Conrad, Joseph 1857-1924 ...131
Brief entry ...104
See also CDBLB 1890-1914
See also DLB 10, 34, 98
See also MTCW
See also SATA 27
See also SSC 9
See also TCLC 1, 6, 13, 25, 43
See also WLC
Conrad, Kenneth
See Lottich, Kenneth V(erne)
Conrad, L. K.
See Conrad, Andree
Conrad, Pam 1947- ...CANR-36
Earlier sketch in CA 121
See also CLR 18
See also MAICYA
See also SATA 49, 52
Conrad, Paul (Francis) 1924- ...CANR-38
Earlier sketch in CA 113
Conrad, Robert Arnold
See Hart, Moss
Conrad, Robert C. 1933- ...126
Conrad, Robert 1928- ...41-44R
Conrad, Susan P(hinney) 1941- Brief entry ...113
Conrad, Sybil 1921- ...21-24R
Conrad, Tod
See Wilkes-Hunter, R(ichard)
Conrad, Will C. 1882- ...CAP-1
Earlier sketch in CA 13-14
Conradi, Peter J(ohn) 1945- ...133
Conradis, Heinz 1907- ...CAP-1
Earlier sketch in CA 13-14
Conrads, Ulrich 1923- ...9-12R
Conran, Anthony 1931- ...CANR-14
Earlier sketch in CA 65-68

Conran, Shirley (Ida) 1932- CANR-22
  Earlier sketch in CA 103
  See also MTCW
Conran, Terence Orby 1931- 85-88
Conron, (Alfred) Brandon 1919- 17-20R
Conrow, Robert 1942- 57-60
Conroy, Al
  See Albert, Marvin H(ubert)
Conroy, Albert
  See Albert, Marvin H(ubert)
Conroy, Barbara 1934- 111
Conroy, Charles W. 1922- 13-16R
Conroy, Frank 1936- 77-80
Conroy, (Francis) Hilary 1919- CANR-39
  Earlier sketch in CA 115
Conroy, Jack
  See Conroy, John Wesley
  See also DLBY 81
  See also SATA 19
Conroy, John Wesley 1899-1990 .... CANR-3
  Obituary 131
  Earlier sketch in CA 5-8R
  See also Conroy, Jack
  See also SATO 65
Conroy, John 1951- 136
Conroy, Mary 1941- 110
Conroy, Michael R(alph) 1945- CANR-9
  Earlier sketch in CA 53-56
Conroy, Pat 1945- CANR-24
  Earlier sketch in CA 85-88
  See also AAYA 8
  See also AITN 1
  See also CLC 30
  See also DLB 6
  See also MTCW
Conroy, Patricia 1941- 93-96
Conroy, Peter V(incent) Jr. 1944- 53-56
Conroy, Robert
  See Goldston, Robert (Conroy)
Considine, Bob
  See Considine, Robert (Bernard)
  See also AITN 2
Considine, Douglas M(axwell) 1915- CANR-11
  Earlier sketch in CA 69-72
Considine, John J(oseph) 1897- 1-4R
Considine, Robert (Bernard) 1906-1975 93-96
  Obituary 61-64
  See also Considine, Bob
Considine, Shaun 1940- 137
Consilvio, Thomas 1947- 57-60
Consolo, Dominick P(eter) 1923- 33-36R
Constable, John W. 1922- 81-84
Constable, Trevor James 1925- 89-92
Constable, W(illiam) G(eorge) 1887-1976 .... 5-8R
  Obituary 65-68
Constant, Alberta Wilson 1908-1981 .... CANR-4
  Obituary 109
  Earlier sketch in CA 1-4R
  See also SATA 22, 28
Constant (de Rebecque), (Henri) Benjamin
  1767-1830 .... DLB 119
Constant, Jan
  See Dawson, Janis
Constantelos, Demetrios J. 1927- CANR-24
  Earlier sketches in CA 21-24R, CANR-8
Constantin, James A. 1922- 13-16R
Constantin, Robert W(ilfrid) 1937- 25-28R
Constantine, David 1944- .... DLB 40
Constantine, Greg(ory John) 1938- 117
Constantine, K. C. (a pseudonym)
  1935(?)- Brief entry 114
Constantine, K. C. 1934- 138
Constantine, Larry L(eRoy) 1943- CANR-14
  Earlier sketch in CA 81-84
Constantine, Mildred 1914- 112
  Brief entry 105
Constantine, Stephen 1947- 120
Constantino, Renato 1919- 118
Constantin-Weyer, Maurice 1881-1964 .... DLB 92
Conte, Gian Biagio 1941- 136
Contini, Gianfranco 1912-1990 Obituary 130
Conton, William (Farquhar) 1925- 1-4R
Contoski, Victor 1936- CANR-17
  Earlier sketch in CA 25-28R
Contosta, David R(ichard) 1945- 104
Contreras, Heles 1933- CANR-14
  Earlier sketch in CA 37-40R
Converse, John Marquis
  1909-1980 Obituary 102
Converse, Paul D(ulaney) 1889-1968 .... CAP-2
  Earlier sketch in CA 17-18
Converse, Philip E. 1928- CANR-6
  Earlier sketch in CA 13-16R
Convict Writer, The
  See Torok, Lou
Conway, Alan (Arthur) 1920- CANR-2
  Earlier sketch in CA 1-4R
Conway, Arlington B.
  See Burns, Eedson Louis Millard
Conway, David 1939- 106
Conway, Denise
  See Prebble, Marjorie Mary Curtis
Conway, Freda 1911- 25-28R
Conway, Gordon
  See Hamilton, Charles (Harold St. John)
Conway, J(ohn) D(onald) 1905-1967 .... CANR-2
  Earlier sketch in CA 1-4R
Conway, Jill K(er) 1934- 130
Conway, Jim 1932- CANR-39
  Earlier sketch in CA 116
Conway, Joan Ditzel 1933- 97-100
Conway, John Seymour 1929- 25-28R
Conway, (Mary) Margaret 1935- 37-40R
Conway, Moncure Daniel 1832-1907 .... DLB 1
Conway, Peter
  See Milkomane, George Alexis Milkomanovich
Conway, Sally 1934- CANR-39
  Earlier sketch in CA 116
Conway, Theresa (Ann) 1951- CANR-19
  Earlier sketch in CA 103
Conway, Thomas D(aniel) 1934- 21-24R
Conway, Thomas Daniel 1933- 112
Conway, Tim
  See Conway, Thomas Daniel
Conway, Tom
  See Yates, A(lan) G(eoffrey)
Conway, Troy
  See Avallone, Michael (Angelo, Jr)
Conway, Ward
  See Westmoreland, Reg(inald Conway)
Conway, William J. 1904-1983 Obituary 110
Conybeare, Charles Augustus
  See Eliot, T(homas) S(tearns)
Conyers, James E(rnest) 1932- 41-44R
Conyngham, William Joseph 1924- 53-56
Conyus
  See Calhoun, Conyus
Conze, Edward J. D. 1904- 13-16R
Conzelman, James Gleason
  1898-1970 Obituary 104
Conzelman, Jimmy
  See Conzelman, James Gleason
Coogan, Daniel (Francis Jr.) 1915-1980 .... 21-24R
  Obituary 134
Coogan, John W(illiam) 1947- 107
Coogan, Joseph Patrick 1925- CANR-4
  Earlier sketch in CA 1-4R
Coogan, Michael David 1942- Brief entry 112
Cook, Adrian 1940- 49-52
Cook, Alan Hugh 1922- 106
Cook, Albert S(paulding) 1925- CANR-37
  Earlier sketches in CA 1-4R, CANR-1, 16
Cook, Alice H(anson) 1903- 115
Cook, Alice Rice 1899-1973 Obituary 41-44R
Cook, Ann Jennalie 1934- 105
Cook, Arlene Ethel 1936- 65-68
Cook, Bernadine 1924- .... SATA 11
Cook, Beverly Blair 1926- 37-40R
Cook, Blanche Wiesen 1941- CANR-4
  Earlier sketch in CA 53-56
Cook, Bob 1961- 134
Cook, Bruce 1932- 33-36R
Cook, Chris(topher) 1945- CANR-23
  Earlier sketches in CA 57-60, CANR-6
Cook, Daniel J(oseph) 1938- 53-56
Cook, Daniel 1914- 33-36R
Cook, David A. 1945- 107
Cook, David C(harles) III 1912- 57-60
Cook, David (John) 1929- 107
Cook, David T. 1946- 65-68
Cook, David 1940- CANR-22
  Earlier sketch in CA 103
Cook, Don(ald Paul) 1920- CANR-14
  Earlier sketch in CA 13-16R
Cook, Don Lewis 1928- 69-72
Cook, Dorothy Mary 1907- CANR-20
  Earlier sketch in CA 103
Cook, Ebenezer 1667(?)-1732(?) .... DLB 24
Cook, Edward M(arks) Jr. 1944- 123
  Brief entry 118
Cook, Elsa E(stelle) 1932- 125
Cook, Eugene 1917(?)-1986 Obituary 120
Cook, F(rederick) P. 1937- 93-96
Cook, Fred J(ames) 1911- CANR-23
  Earlier sketches in CA 9-12R, CANR-3
  See also SATA 2
Cook, Geoffrey 1946- 77-80
Cook, George Allan 1916- 21-24R
Cook, George S. 1920- 49-52
Cook, Gervis Frere
  See Frere-Cook, Gervis
Cook, Gladys Emerson 5-8R
Cook, Gladys Moon 1907- 33-36R
Cook, Glen (Charles) 1944- 122
Cook, Glenn J. 1913- 25-28R
Cook, Gregory M(orton) 1942- 117
Cook, Harold Reed 1902- 13-16R
Cook, Hugh C(hristopher) B(ult) 1910- 57-60
Cook, Hugh (Walter Gilbert) 1956- 132
Cook, Ida Obituary 121
Cook, J(ames) Gordon 1916- 9-12R
Cook, (Harold) J. 1952- 120
Cook, J(ohn) M(anuel) 1910- 130
Cook, Jack
  See Cook, John Augustine
Cook, James Graham 1925-1966 .... 1-4R
  Obituary 103
Cook, (Harold) James 1926- 73-76
Cook, James W(yatt) 1932- 69-72
Cook, Jeffrey 1934- 97-100
Cook, Joan Marble 1920- 57-60
Cook, John Augustine 1940- 45-48
Cook, John Lennox 1923- 106
Cook, Joseph Jay 1924- CANR-2
  Earlier sketch in CA 1-4R
  See also SATA 8
Cook, Judith (Anne) 1933- 132
Cook, Kenneth (Bernard) 1929- 130
Cook, Lennox
  See Cook, John Lennox
Cook, Lila
  See Africano, Lillian
Cook, Louise (Celia) 1942-1984 Obituary 112
Cook, Luther T(ownsend) 1901- 89-92
Cook, Lyn
  See Waddell, Evelyn Margaret
Cook, Mabel Collins
  1851-1927(?) Brief entry 121
Cook, Margaret G(erry) 1903- 5-8R
Cook, Marjorie 1920- 81-84
Cook, Mark 1942- CANR-14
  Earlier sketch in CA 37-40R
Cook, Mary Jane 1929- 93-96
Cook, Melva Janice 1919- CANR-9
  Earlier sketch in CA 21-24R
Cook, Melvin A(lonzo) 1911- CANR-2
  Earlier sketch in CA 49-52
Cook, (Will) Mercer 1903-1987 .... CANR-25
  Obituary 124
  Earlier sketch in CA 77-80
  See also BW
Cook, Michael Lewis 1929- 112
Cook, Michael 1931- 123
Cook, Michael 1933- 93-96
  See also CLC 58
  See also DLB 53
Cook, Myra B. 1933- 21-24R
Cook, Nicholas (John) 1950- 128
Cook, Nilla Cram 1908-1982 Obituary 108
Cook, Olive Rambo 1892- 13-16R
Cook, Olive 1916- CANR-19
  Earlier sketches in CA 5-8R, CANR-3
Cook, P(auline) Lesley 1922- 13-16R
Cook, Paul H(arlin) 1950- 106
Cook, Peter D(onald) 1939- 112
Cook, Petronelle Marguerite Mary
  1925- CANR-15
  Earlier sketch in CA 81-84
Cook, Philip J. 1946- 133
Cook, Ramona Graham 5-8R
Cook, Ramsay 1931- CANR-25
  Earlier sketch in CA 102
Cook, Raymond Allen 1919- 45-48
Cook, Reginald L. 1903- 65-68
Cook, Richard I(rving) 1927- 21-24R
Cook, Robert Andrew 1912-1991 117
  Obituary 133
Cook, Robert I. 1920- 33-36R
Cook, Robert William Arthur 1931- 25-28R
Cook, Robin
  See Cook, Robert William Arthur
Cook, Robin 1940- 111
  Brief entry 108
  See also BEST 90:2
  See also CLC 14
Cook, Roderick 1932- 9-12R
Cook, Roy
  See Silverberg, Robert
Cook, Stanley 1922- 93-96
Cook, Stephani 1944- CANR-23
  Earlier sketch in CA 106
Cook, Stephen 1949- 118
Cook, Stuart W(ellford) 1913- CANR-1
  Earlier sketch in CA 1-4R
Cook, Sylvia (Carol) 1938- 49-52
Cook, T(homas) S(tephen) 1947- 128
Cook, Terry 1942- CANR-12
  Earlier sketch in CA 73-76
Cook, Thomas H. 1947- CANR-32
  Earlier sketch in CA 111
Cook, Thomas Ira 1907-1976 Obituary 111
Cook, W(illiam) Robert 1928- 115
Cook, Warren L. 1925- 37-40R
Cook, (George) Whitfield 1909- 107
Cook, William H(arleston) 1931- 104
Cook, William J(esse) Jr. 1938- 29-32R
Cook, William Wallace
  1867-1933 Brief entry 116
Cooke, (Alfred) Alistair 1908- CANR-34
  Earlier sketches in CA 57-60, CANR-9
  See also AITN 1
Cooke, Ann
  See Cole, Joanna
Cooke, Arthur
  See Lowndes, Robert A(ugustine) W(ard)
Cooke, Barbara
  See Alexander, Anna B(arbara Cooke)
Cooke, Barclay 1912-1981 97-100
  Obituary 105
Cooke, Bernard J. 1922- CANR-34
  Earlier sketches in CA 13-16R, CANR-9
Cooke, Charles Harris
  1904(?)-1977 Obituary 73-76
Cooke, David Coxe 1917- CANR-2
  Earlier sketch in CA 1-4R
  See also SATA 2
Cooke, Deryck (Victor) 1919-1976 Obituary 115
Cooke, Donald Ewin 1916-1985 .... CANR-4
  Obituary 117
  Earlier sketch in CA 1-4R
  See also SATA 2, 45
Cooke, Edward F(rancis) 1923- 41-44R
Cooke, Elizabeth 1948- 129
  See also CLC 55
Cooke, George Willis 1848-1923 .... DLB 71
Cooke, Gerald 1925- 13-16R
Cooke, Gilbert William 1899- CAP-1
  Earlier sketch in CA 11-12
Cooke, Greville (Vaughan Turner)
  1894- 13-16R
Cooke, Hereward Lester 1916-1973 .... CANR-1
  Obituary 45-48
  Earlier sketch in CA 1-4R
Cooke, Hope 1940- 108
Cooke, Jacob E(rnest) 1924- CANR-34
  Earlier sketch in CA 1-4R
Cooke, James Francis 1875-1960 Obituary 115
Cooke, John Byrne 1940- 119
Cooke, John D(aniel) 1892-1972 Obituary 106
Cooke, John Esten 1830-1886 .... DLB 3
Cooke, John Estes
  See Baum, L(yman) Frank
Cooke, John Fletcher
  See Fletcher-Cooke, John
Cooke, Joseph R(obinson) 1926- 65-68
Cooke, M. E.
  See Creasey, John
Cooke, Margaret
  See Creasey, John
Cooke, Michael F.R.C.
  See Cook, Michael Lewis
Cooke, Michael G(eorge) 1934-1990 110
  Obituary 132
Cooke, Philip Pendleton 1816-1850 .... DLB 3, 59
Cooke, Robert (Gordon) 1930-1987 101
  Obituary 121
Cooke, Robert William 1935- 123
Cooke, Rose Terry 1827-1892 .... DLB 12, 74
Cooke, Terence James
  1921-1983 Obituary 110
Cooke, Thomas D(arlington) 1933- 115
Cooke, William 1942- CANR-14
  Earlier sketch in CA 33-36R
Cook-Lynn, Elizabeth 1930- 133
Cookridge, E. H.
  See Spiro, Edward
Cookson, Catherine (McMullen)
  1906- CANR-28
  Earlier sketches in CA 13-16R, CANR-9
  See also MTCW
  See also SATA 9
Cookson, Frank Barton
  1912-1977 Obituary 69-72
Cookson, Peter W. Jr. 1942- 121
Cookson, Peter (W.) 1913-1990 49-52
  Obituary 130
Cookson, William 1939- CANR-30
  Earlier sketch in CA 49-52
Cool, Joyce 1938- 111
Cool, Ola C. 1890(?)-1977 Obituary 69-72
Coolbrith, Ina 1841-1928 .... DLB 54
Coole, W. W.
  See Kulski, Wladyslaw W(szebor)
Cooley, Denton A(rthur) 1920- 126
Cooley, John Kent 1927- 13-16R
Cooley, Lee Morrison 1919- CANR-3
  Earlier sketch in CA 9-12R
Cooley, Leland Frederick 1909- CANR-4
  Earlier sketch in CA 5-8R
Cooley, Margaret L. 1906(?)-1985 Obituary 117
Cooley, Peter (John) 1940- CANR-21
  Earlier sketch in CA 69-72
  See also DLB 105
Cooley, Richard A(llen) 1925- 21-24R
Coolidge, Archibald C(ary) Jr. 1928- 37-40R
Coolidge, Clark 1939- 33-36R
Coolidge, Harold Jefferson
  1904-1985 Obituary 115
Coolidge, Olivia E(nsor) 1908- CANR-2
  Earlier sketch in CA 5-8R
  See also MAICYA
  See also SATA 1, 26
Coolidge, Susan
  See Woolsey, Sarah Chauncy
Cooling, Benjamin Franklin 1938- 53-56
Coolwater, John
  See Conniff, James C(lifford) G(regory)
Coomaraswamy, A. K.
  See Coomaraswamy, Ananda K(entish)
Coomaraswamy, Ananda K(entish)
  1877-1947 Brief entry 115
Coombes, B. L. 1894(?)-1974 Obituary 53-56
Coombs, Ann
  See Pykare, Nina
Coombs, Charles Anthony 1918-1981 109
  Obituary 105
Coombs, Charles I(ra) 1914- CANR-36
  Earlier sketches in CA 5-8R, CANR-4, 19
  See also MAICYA
  See also SATA 3, 43
Coombs, Chick
  See Coombs, Charles I(ra)
Coombs, Douglas (Stafford) 1924- 13-16R
Coombs, H. Samm 1928- 93-96
Coombs, Herbert Cole 1906- 93-96
Coombs, Murdo
  See Davis, Frederick C(lyde)
Coombs, Nina
  See Pykare, Nina
Coombs, Orde M. 1939(?)-1984 .... CANR-25
  Obituary 113
  Earlier sketch in CA 73-76
  See also BW
Coombs, Patricia 1926- CANR-1
  Earlier sketch in CA 1-4R
  See also MAICYA
  See also SATA 3, 51
Coombs, (Robert) Peter 1913- 116
Coombs, Philip H(all) 1915- CANR-23
  Earlier sketches in CA 17-20R, CANR-8
Coombs, Robert H(olman) 1934- 41-44R
Coomer, Joe 1958- 125
Coon, Carleton Stevens 1904-1981 .... CANR-2
  Obituary 104
  Earlier sketch in CA 5-8R
Coon, Gene L(ee) 1924-1973 .... CANR-15
  Obituary 103
  Earlier sketch in CA 1-4R
Coon, Martha Sutherland 1884- CAP-2
  Earlier sketch in CA 25-28
Coon, Nelson 1895- 69-72
Coon, Stephen 1948- 57-60
Cooney, Barbara 1917- CANR-37
  Earlier sketches in CA 5-8R, CANR-3
  See also CLR 23
  See also MAICYA
  See also SATA 6, 59
Cooney, Caroline B. 1947- CANR-37
  Earlier sketch in CA 97-100
  See also AAYA 5
  See also MAICYA
  See also SATA 41, 48
Cooney, David M(artin) 1930- 17-20R
Cooney, Eugene J(erome) 1931- 45-48
Cooney, John 1942- 115
Cooney, Michael 1921- 25-28R

Cooney, Nancy Evans 1932- ... 105
See also SATA 42
Cooney, Ray ... CLC 62
Cooney, Seamus (Anthony) 1933- ... 53-56
Cooney, Timothy J. 1929- ... 107
Coons, Frederica Bertha (Safley) 1910- ... 17-20R
Coons, William R(ichard) 1934- ... 41-44R
Coonts, Stephen (Paul) 1946- ... 133
Brief entry ... 127
See also BEST 89:2
Coontz, Otto 1946- ... 105
See also SATA 33
Coontz, Stephanie ... 132
Coop, Howard 1928- ... 25-28R
Coope, Rosalys 1921- ... 45-48
Cooper, Alfred Morton 1890- ... CAP-1
Earlier sketch in CA 11-12
Cooper, Alice 1948- ... 106
Cooper, Allan D. 1952- ... 121
Cooper, Allan 1954- ... 118
Cooper, Anthony Ashley 1671-1713 ... DLB 101
Cooper, Arnold Cook 1933- ... 17-20R
Cooper, Artemis 1953- ... 127
Cooper, B(rian) Lee 1942- ... 117
Cooper, Barbara (Ann) 1929- ... 9-12R
Cooper, (Fraser) Barry 1943- ... 126
Cooper, Bernard 1951- ... 134
Cooper, Bernarr 1912- ... 41-44R
Cooper, Bev 1936- ... 119
Cooper, Brian (Newman) 1919- ... CANR-22
Earlier sketch in CA 1-4R
Cooper, Bruce M(ichael) 1925- ... CANR-9
Earlier sketch in CA 13-16R
Cooper, Bryan (Robert Wright) 1932- ... 25-28R
Cooper, C(hristopher) D(onald) H(untington) 1942- ... 29-32R
Cooper, Carl
See Cooper, Kenneth C(arlton)
Cooper, Charles M(uhlenberg) 1909- ... 41-44R
Cooper, Charles W(illiam) 1904- ... CAP-2
Earlier sketch in CA 21-22
Cooper, Chester L. 1917- ... 29-32R
Cooper, Christopher (John) 1941- ... 107
Cooper, (Brenda) Clare 1935- ... 118
Cooper, Colin Symons 1926- ... 102
Cooper, Darien B(irla) 1937- ... CANR-16
Earlier sketches in CA 49-52, CANR-1
Cooper, Darien B(rown) 1934- ... 116
Cooper, David D. 1948- ... 137
Cooper, David E(dward) 1942- ... CANR-31
Earlier sketch in CA 49-52
Cooper, David (Graham) 1931-1986 ... 97-100
Obituary ... 119
Cooper, Dennis 1953- ... 133
Cooper, Derek Macdonald 1925- ... 102
Cooper, Diana (Olivia Winifred Maud Manners) 1892(?)-1986 Obituary ... 119
Cooper, Dominic (Xavier) 1944- ... 65-68
Cooper, Douglas 1911-1984 ... 130
Obituary ... 112
Cooper, Edmund 1926-1982 ... CANR-31
Earlier sketch in CA 33-36R
Cooper, Elizabeth Ann 1927- ... 1-4R
Cooper, Elizabeth Keyser ... CANR-1
Earlier sketch in CA 1-4R
See also SATA 47
Cooper, Emmanuel 1938- ... CANR-3
Earlier sketch in CA 49-52
Cooper, Esther
See Kellner, Esther
Cooper, (C.) Everett
See Burgess, M(ichael) R(oy)
Cooper, Frank E(dward) 1910-1968 ... CAP-2
Earlier sketch in CA 21-22
Cooper, Giles (Stannus) 1918-1966 Obituary ... 113
See also DLB 13
Cooper, Gladys 1888-1971 Obituary ... 33-36R
Cooper, Gordon 1932- ... 61-64
See also SATA 23
Cooper, Grace Rogers 1924- ... 41-44R
Cooper, Hannah
See Spence, William John Duncan
Cooper, Harold E(ugene) 1928- ... 45-48
Cooper, Harold H. 1911(?)-1976 Obituary ... 69-72
Cooper, Harold R. 1911(?)-1978 Obituary ... 77-80
Cooper, Helen 1947- ... 129
Cooper, Henry S(potswood) F(enimore) Jr. 1933- ... CANR-13
Earlier sketch in CA 69-72
See also SATA 65
Cooper, Henry St. John
See Creasey, John
Cooper, I(rving) S(pencer) 1922-1985 ... CANR-26
Obituary ... 117
Earlier sketch in CA 69-72
Cooper, Ilene ... SATA 66
Cooper, J. C. 1905- ... 127
Cooper, J. California ... 125
See also BW
See also CLC 56
Cooper, Jackie 1922- ... 133
Cooper, Jacqueline 1924- ... 107
Cooper, James A. ... CANR-26
Earlier sketches in CAP-2, CA 19-20
Cooper, James Fenimore 1789-1851 ... CDALB 1640-1865
See also DLB 3
See also SATA 19
Cooper, James L(ouis) 1934- ... 53-56
Cooper, James M. 1939- ... 45-48
Cooper, Jamie Lee ... 9-12R
Cooper, Jane (Marvel) 1924- ... CANR-17
Earlier sketch in CA 25-28R
Cooper, Jeff 1920- ... 41-44R
Cooper, Jefferson
See Fox, G(ardner) F(rancis)
Cooper, Jeremy (Francis Peter) 1946- ... 93-96
Cooper, Jilly 1937- ... CANR-30
Earlier sketch in CA 105
Cooper, John C(harles) 1933- ... CANR-30
Earlier sketches in CA 21-24R, CANR-9
Cooper, John Cobb 1887- ... 5-8R
Cooper, John Dean
See Cooper, Jeff
Cooper, John E(llsworth) 1922- ... 25-28R
Cooper, John Irwin 1905- ... 41-44R
Cooper, John L. 1936- ... CANR-13
Earlier sketch in CA 21-24R
Cooper, John M(iller) 1912- ... 21-24R
Cooper, John Milton Jr. 1940- ... 128
Brief entry ... 105
Cooper, John O(wen) 1938- ... 89-92
Cooper, John R. ... CANR-27
Earlier sketches in CAP-2, CA 19-20
See also SATA 1
Cooper, John 1934-1984 Obituary ... 113
Cooper, Joseph Bonar 1912- ... 17-20R
Cooper, Joseph D(avid) 1917-1975 ... CANR-4
Obituary ... 57-60
Earlier sketch in CA 5-8R
Cooper, Julian M. 1945- ... 130
Cooper, Kay 1941- ... CANR-37
Earlier sketches in CA 45-48, CANR-1, 16
See also SATA 11
Cooper, Kenneth C(arlton) 1948- ... 110
Cooper, Kenneth H(ardy) 1931- ... 134
Brief entry ... 126
Cooper, Kenneth Schaaf 1918- ... 9-12R
Cooper, Kent 1880-1965 Obituary ... 89-92
See also DLB 29
Cooper, Lee Pelham 1926- ... CANR-4
Earlier sketch in CA 5-8R
See also SATA 5
Cooper, Leslie M(uir) 1930- ... 41-44R
Cooper, Lester (Irving) 1919-1985 ... 108
Obituary ... 116
See also SATA 32, 43
Cooper, Lettice (Ulpha) 1897- ... CANR-5
Earlier sketch in CA 9-12R
See also SATA 35
Cooper, Louise Field 1905- ... CANR-4
Earlier sketch in CA 1-4R
Cooper, Louise 1952- ... 107
Cooper, Lynna
See Fox, G(ardner) F(rancis)
Cooper, Mae (Klein) ... 17-20R
Cooper, Mario 1905- ... 21-24R
Cooper, Martin Du Pre 1910-1986 ... 103
Obituary ... 118
Cooper, Matthew (Heald) 1952- ... 85-88
Cooper, Mattie Lula
See Britton, Mattie Lula Cooper
Cooper, Michael (John) 1930- ... 13-16R
Cooper, Michele F(reda) 1941- ... 85-88
Cooper, Morley
See Cooper, Alfred Morton
Cooper, Neil (Louis) 1930- ... 119
Cooper, Parley J(oseph) 1937- ... CANR-26
Earlier sketches in CA 65-68, CANR-10
Cooper, Patricia J(ean) 1936- ... 97-100
Cooper, Paul F(enimore) 1900(?)-1970 Obituary ... 104
Cooper, Paul 1926- ... CANR-34
Earlier sketch in CA 49-52
Cooper, Paulette 1944- ... 37-40R
Cooper, Penny 1918- ... 137
Cooper, Peter Lee 1949- ... 111
Cooper, Philip (Jr.) 1926- ... 33-36R
Cooper, Phyllis 1939- ... 53-56
Cooper, Richard N(ewell) 1934- ... CANR-10
Earlier sketch in CA 25-28R
Cooper, Robert G(ravlin) 1943- ... 110
Cooper, Robert St. John 1905(?)-1984 Obituary ... 111
Cooper, Rosaleen 1894-1989 Obituary ... 129
Cooper, Sandi E. 1936- ... CANR-29
Earlier sketch in CA 49-52
Cooper, Saul 1934- ... 1-4R
Cooper, Signe Skott 1921- ... CANR-4
Earlier sketch in CA 53-56
Cooper, Sister Mary Ursula 1925- ... 5-8R
Cooper, Sophie
See Amory, Mark
Cooper, Susan (Mary) 1935- ... CANR-37
Earlier sketches in CA 29-32R, CANR-15
See also CLR 4
See also MAICYA
See also SAAS 6
See also SATA 4, 64
Cooper, Susan Rogers 1947- ... 136
Cooper, Sylvia 1903- ... CAP-2
Earlier sketch in CA 17-18
Cooper, Wayne 1938- ... 93-96
Cooper, Wendy (Lowe) 1919- ... CANR-6
Earlier sketch in CA 13-16R
Cooper, Wilhelmina (Behmenburg) 1939(?)-1980 Obituary ... 97-100
Cooper, Will 1929- ... 69-72
Cooper, William
See Hoff, Harry S(ummerfield)
Cooper, William F(razier) 1932- ... 69-72
Cooper, William Hurlbert 1924- ... 49-52
Cooper, William J(ames) Jr. 1940- ... 69-72
Cooper, William W(ager) 1914- ... 13-16R
Cooper, Wyatt (Emory) 1927-1978 ... 73-76
Obituary ... 77-80
See also AITN 2
Cooper-Clark, Diana 1945- ... 109
Cooper-Klein, Nina
See Cooper, Mae (Klein)
Cooperman, Hasye 1909- ... 37-40R
Cooperman, Stanley 1929-1976 ... CAP-2
Earlier sketch in CA 33-36
Coopersmith, Harry 1903- ... CAP-2
Earlier sketch in CA 21-22
Coopersmith, Jerome 1925- ... 73-76
Coopersmith, Stanley 1926-1979 ... 21-24R
Obituary ... 133
Cooter, Roger James 1948- ... 123
Cootner, Paul H(arold) 1930- ... 9-12R
Coover, James B(urrell) 1925- ... CANR-23
Earlier sketches in CA 57-60, CANR-6
Coover, Robert (Lowell) 1932- ... CANR-37
Earlier sketches in CA 45-48, CANR-3
See also CLC 3, 7, 15, 32, 46
See also DLB 2
See also DLBY 81
See also MTCW
Coox, Alvin D(avid) 1924- ... 29-32R
Copani, Peter 1942- ... 89-92
Cope, David 1941- ... 33-36R
Cope, Edward A(llen) 1948- ... 121
Cope, Jack
See Cope, Robert Knox
Cope, Jackson I(rving) 1925- ... CANR-34
Earlier sketch in CA 103
Cope, Lewis 1934- ... 125
Cope, Myron 1929- ... 57-60
Cope, Oliver 1902- Brief entry ... 109
Cope, Robert Knox 1913- ... 9-12R
Cope, (Vincent) Zachary 1881-1974 ... CAP-1
Earlier sketch in CA 9-10
Copel, Sidney L(eroy) 1930- ... 21-24R
Copelan, Rachel 1934- ... 114
Copeland, Ann
See Furtwangler, Virginia W(alsh)
Copeland, Bill
See Copeland, Paul William
Copeland, Bonnie Chapman 1919- ... 101
Copeland, Carolyn Faunce 1930- ... 65-68
Copeland, E(dwin) Luther 1916- ... CANR-3
Earlier sketch in CA 9-12R
Copeland, Gary A. 1952- ... 138
Copeland, Helen 1920- ... 25-28R
See also SATA 4
Copeland, James E(verett) 1937- ... 125
Copeland, James Isaac 1910- ... 106
Copeland, Lennie 1946- ... 120
Copeland, Melvin T. 1884-1975 ... CAP-2
Obituary ... 57-60
Earlier sketch in CA 21-22
Copeland, Miles 1916(?)-1991 ... 29-32R
Obituary ... 133
Copeland, Morris A(lbert) 1895-1989 ... CAP-1
Obituary ... 128
Earlier sketch in CA 17-18
Copeland, Paul W. ... 105
See also SATA 23
Copeland, Paul William 1917- ... 25-28R
Copeland, Ray (M.) 1926-1984 Obituary ... 112
Copeland, Ross H(ugh) 1930-1980 ... 25-28R
Obituary ... 133
Copeland, Stewart (Armstrong) 1952-
See The Police
See also CLC 26
Copeland, Thomas Wellsted 1907-1979 ... 5-8R
Copeman, George H(enry) 1922- ... CANR-8
Earlier sketch in CA 5-8R
Copenhaver, Charles L(eonard) 1915-1982 Obituary ... 107
Coper, Rudolf 1904- ... CAP-1
Earlier sketch in CA 13-14
Copetas, A. Craig 1951- ... 121
Copi, Irving M(armer) 1917- ... CANR-5
Earlier sketch in CA 1-4R
Coplan, Kate M(ildred) 1901- ... 5-8R
Copland, Aaron 1900-1990 ... 5-8R
Obituary ... 133
Coplans, John (Rivers) 1920- Brief entry ... 112
Copleston, Frederick Charles (John Paul) 1907- ... CANR-7
Earlier sketch in CA 13-16R
Copley, Frederick S.
See Greif, Martin
Copley, Gerald L. C.
See Cole, Lester
Copley (Diana) Heather Pickering 1918- ... SATA 45
Coplin, William D(avid) 1939- ... CANR-32
Earlier sketches in CA 21-24R, CANR-12
Copman, Louis 1934- ... 57-60
Copp, Andrew James (III) 1916- ... 25-28R
Copp, E. Anthony 1945- ... 102
Copp, Jim
See Copp, Andrew James (III)
Copp, (John) Terry 1938- ... 134
Coppa, Frank John 1937- ... CANR-29
Earlier sketches in CA 33-36R, CANR-13
Coppard, A(lfred) E(dgar) 1878-1957 Brief entry ... 114
See also TCLC 5
See also YABC 1
Coppard, Audrey 1931- ... CANR-27
Earlier sketch in CA 29-32R
Coppe, Abiezer
See Taylor, John (Alfred)
Coppee, Francois 1842-1908 ... TCLC 25
Coppel, Alec 1909(?)-1972 Obituary ... 33-36R
Coppel, Alfred 1921- ... CANR-10
Earlier sketch in CA 17-20R
See also CAAS 9
See also DLBY 83
Copper, (Robert) Arnold (de Vignier) 1934- ... 97-100
Copper, Basil 1924- ... 133
Copper, John Franklin 1940- ... CANR-11
Earlier sketch in CA 69-72
Copper, Marcia S(nyder) 1934- ... 53-56
Copperman, Paul 1947- ... 101
Copperud, Roy H(erman) 1915-1991 ... 9-12R
Obituary ... 136
Coppock, John (Oates) 1914- ... 13-16R
Coppock, John Terence 1921- ... 102
Coppock, Joseph D(avid) 1909- ... 49-52
Coppola, Francis Ford 1939- ... 77-80
See also CLC 16
See also DLB 44
Coppola, Raymond T(homas) 1947- ... 102
Coram, Christopher
See Walker, Peter N.
Corazzini, Sergio 1886-1907 ... DLB 114
Corbalis, Judy 1941- ... 125
Corballis, Michael C(harles) 1936- ... 115
Corbally, John Edward Jr. 1924- ... 5-8R
Corbett, Chan
See Schachner, Nat(han)
Corbett, Christopher 1951- ... 123
Corbett, Edward P(atrick) J(oseph) 1919- ... CANR-9
Earlier sketch in CA 17-20R
Corbett, Elizabeth (Frances) 1887-1981 ... CANR-2
Obituary ... 102
Earlier sketch in CA 5-8R
Corbett, Grahame ... 116
See also SATA 36, 43
Corbett, J(ack) Elliott 1920- ... 29-32R
Corbett, James A(rthur) 1908- ... 65-68
Corbett, Janice M. 1935- ... 37-40R
Corbett, (John) Patrick 1916- ... 17-20R
Corbett, Pearson H(arris) 1900- ... CAP-1
Earlier sketch in CA 9-10
Corbett, Richard 1582-1635 ... DLB 121
Corbett, Richmond McLain 1902- ... CAP-1
Earlier sketch in CA 13-16
Corbett, Ruth 1912- ... 29-32R
Corbett, Scott 1913- ... CANR-23
Earlier sketches in CA 1-4R, CANR-1
See also CLR 1
See also MAICYA
See also SAAS 2
See also SATA 2, 42
Corbett, Thomas H(enry) 1938- ... 77-80
Corbett, W(illiam) J(esse) 1938- ... 137
See also CLR 19
See also MAICYA
See also SATA 44, 50
Corbin, Arnold 1911- ... 9-12R
Corbin, Charles B. 1940- ... CANR-14
Earlier sketches in CA 29-32R, CANR-31
Corbin, Claire 1913- ... 41-44R
Corbin, Donald A(lvin) 1920- ... 33-36R
Corbin, H(ayman) Dan 1912- ... 41-44R
Corbin, Iris
See Clinton, Iris A. (Corbin)
Corbin, John B(oyd) 1935- ... CANR-22
Earlier sketch in CA 105
Corbin, Richard 1911-1988 ... CANR-3
Obituary ... 125
Earlier sketch in CA 5-8R
Corbin, Sabra Lee
See Malvern, Gladys
Corbin, Steven 1953- ... 131
Corbin, William
See McGraw, William Corbin
Corbishley, Thomas 1903-1976 ... CANR-7
Obituary ... 65-68
Earlier sketch in CA 13-16R
Corbitt, Helen Lucy 1906-1978 ... CANR-4
Obituary ... 89-92
Earlier sketch in CA 5-8R
Corby, Dan
See Catherall, Arthur
Corcoran, Barbara 1911- ... CANR-28
Earlier sketches in CA 21-24R, CANR-11
See also CAAS 2
See also CLC 17
See also DLB 52
See also SATA 3
Corcoran, Gertrude B(eatty) 1922- ... 29-32R
Corcoran, Jean (Kennedy) 1926- ... 1-4R
Corcoran, Neil (Cornelius) 1948- ... 135
Corcos, Lucille 1908-1973 ... 21-24R
Obituary ... 134
See also SATA 10
Cord, Barry
See Germano, Peter B.
Cord, Robert L. 1935- ... 33-36R
Cord, Steven Benson 1928- ... 21-24R
Cord, William O. 1921- ... 37-40R
Cordasco, Francesco 1920- ... CANR-21
Earlier sketches in CA 13-16R, CANR-6
Cordelier, Maurice
See Giraudoux, (Hippolyte) Jean
Cordell, Alexander
See Graber, Alexander
Cordell, Richard Albert 1896- ... 1-4R
Corden, W(arner) M(ax) 1927- ... 33-36R
Corder, Brice W(ood) 1936- ... 53-56
Corder, Eric
See Mundis, Jerrold
Corder, George Edward 1904- ... 110
Corder, Jim(my Wayne) 1929- ... 17-20R
Cordier, Andrew W(ellington) 1901-1975 Obituary ... 106
Cordier, Gilbert
See Scherer, Jean-Marie Maurice
Cordier, Ralph Waldo 1902- ... 37-40R
Cordingley, Patrick 1944- ... 114
Cordingly, David 1938- ... 93-96
Cordis, Lonny
See Donson, Cyril
Cords, Nicholas J. 1929- ... 105
Cordtz, Dan 1927- ... 73-76
Cordwell, Miriam 1908-1986 ... 89-92
Obituary ... 120

Corea, Gena
  See Corea, Genoveffa
Corea, Genoveffa 1946- 81-84
Corelli, Marie
  See Mackay, Mary
  See also DLB 34
Coren, Alan 1938- CANR-29
  Earlier sketch in CA 69-72
  See also SATA 32
Coren, Stanley 1942- 137
Coren, Victoria 1972- 131
Corey, Dorothy CANR-26
  Earlier sketches in CA 69-72, CANR-11
  See also SATA 23
Corey, Gerald F(rancis) 1937- 114
Corey, Paul (Frederick) 1903- CANR-2
  Earlier sketch in CA 5-8R
Corey, Stephen 1948- 124
Corfe, Thomas Howell 1928- 103
  See also SATA 27
Corfe, Tom
  See Corfe, Thomas Howell
Corfield, Conrad Laurence
  1893-1980 Obituary 105
Corfman, Eunice (Luccock)
  1928-1980 Obituary 97-100
Corina, Maurice 1936- 57-60
Cork, Patrick
  See Cockburn, (Francis) Claud
Cork, Richard (Graham) 1947- CANR-24
  Earlier sketch in CA 107
Corke, Helen 1882- CAP-1
  Earlier sketch in CA 9-10
Corke, Hilary 1921- 97-100
Corkey, R(obert) 1881-1966 .... CAP-1
  Earlier sketch in CA 13-16
Corkran, David Hudson Jr. 1902- 5-8R
Corkran, Herbert Jr. 1924- 29-32R
Corle, Edwin 1906-1956 .... DLBY 85
Corless, Roger (Jonathan) 1938- 108
Corlett, William 1938- 103
  See also SATA 39, 46
Corlew, Robert Ewing 1922- 110
Corley, (Thomas) Anthony (Buchanan)
  1923- CANR-34
  Earlier sketch in CA 1-4R
Corley, Edwin (Raymond) 1931-1981 .... CANR-12
  Obituary 105
  Earlier sketch in CA 25-28R
Corley, Ernest
  See Bulmer, (Henry) Kenneth
Corley, Nora T(eresa) 118
Corley, Ray
  See Corley, Edwin (Raymond)
Corley, Robert N(eil) 1930- CANR-19
  Earlier sketches in CA 9-12R, CANR-3
Corliss, Charlotte N(uzum) 1932- 53-56
Corliss, William R(oger) 1926- CANR-37
  Earlier sketches in CA 45-48, CANR-1, 16
Cormack, Alexander James Ross 1942- 65-68
Cormack, James Maxwell Ross
  1909-1975 .... CAP-1
  Earlier sketch in CA 9-10
Cormack, M(argaret) Grant 1913- 1-4R
  See also SATA 11
Cormack, Margaret Lawson 1912- CANR-35
  Earlier sketch in CA 1-4R
Cormack, Maribelle B. 1902-1984 .... SATA 39
Cormack, Sandy
  See Cormack, Alexander James Ross
Corman, Avery 1935- 85-88
Corman, Cid
  See Corman, Sidney
  See also CAAS 2
  See also CLC 9
  See also DLB 5
Corman, Sidney 1924- 85-88
  See also Corman, Cid
Cormany, Michael 1951- 135
Cormier, Bruno M. 1919- Brief entry 114
Cormier, Frank 1927- 21-24R
Cormier, Ramona 1923- 49-52
Cormier, Raymond J(oseph) 1938- CANR-19
  Earlier sketches in CA 53-56, CANR-4
Cormier, Robert (Edmund) 1925- CANR-23
  Earlier sketches in CA 1-4R, CANR-5
  See also AAYA 3
  See also CDALB 1968-1988
  See also CLC 12, 30
  See also CLR 12
  See also DLB 52
  See also MAICYA
  See also MTCW
  See also SATA 10, 45
Cormillot, Albert E. J. 1938- 69-72
Corn, Alfred 1943- 104
  See also CLC 33
  See also DLB 120
  See also DLBY 80
Corn, Ira George Jr. 1921-1982 .... CANR-35
  Obituary 106
  Earlier sketch in CA 85-88
Cornea, Carol
  See Koch, Kurt E(mil)
Cornebise, Alfred E(mile) 1929- CANR-38
  Earlier sketch in CA 115
Cornehls, James V(ernon) 1936- 93-96
Cornelisen, Ann 1926- CANR-17
  Earlier sketch in CA 25-28R
corneliszavandenheuvel
  See van den Heuvel, Cornelisz A.
Cornelius, Carol 1942- 115
  See also SATA 40
Cornelius, Temple H. 1891-1964 .... CAP-1
  Earlier sketch in CA 11-12
Cornelius, Wanda Pyle 1936- 105
Cornell, Douglas B. 1906(?)-1982 Obituary 106
Cornell, Felix M. 1896(?)-1970 Obituary 104
Cornell, Francis Griffith
  1906-1979 Obituary 89-92
Cornell, George W. 1920- 9-12R
Cornell, J.
  See Cornell, Jeffrey
Cornell, James (Clayton Jr.) 1938- CANR-11
  Earlier sketch in CA 69-72
  See also SATA 27
Cornell, Jean Gay 1920- CANR-1
  Earlier sketch in CA 45-48
  See also SATA 23
Cornell, Jeffrey 1945- .... SATA 11
Cornell, Katherine 1898(?)-1974 Obituary 49-52
Cornell, Tim 1946- 115
Corner, E. J. H.
  See Corner, Edred John Henry
Corner, Edred John Henry
  1906- Brief entry 116
Corner, George W(ashington) 1889-1981 102
  Obituary 104
Corner, Philip 1933- 21-24R
Cornett, Joe D(elayne) 1935- 53-56
Corney, Estelle 1911- 115
Cornfeld, Betty S. 1944(?)-1988 Obituary 128
Cornfeld, Gaalyah 1902- CANR-12
  Earlier sketch in CA 73-76
Cornford, A(ndrew) J(ohn) 1942- 112
Cornforth, Maurice 1909-1980 .... CANR-4
  Obituary 102
  Earlier sketch in CA 5-8R
Corngold, Stanley Alan 1934- CANR-32
  Earlier sketches in CA 37-40R, CANR-14
Cornillon, John Raymond Koppleman
  1941- 17-20R
Cornish, Dudley T(aylor) 1915- 17-20R
Cornish, Edward (Seymour) 1927- CANR-25
  Earlier sketch in CA 108
Cornish, Geoffrey (St. John) 1914- 125
Cornish, John (Buckley) 1914- 25-28R
Cornish, Sam(uel James) 1935- CANR-24
  Earlier sketch in CA 41-44R
  See also BW
  See also DLB 41
  See also SATA 23
Cornish, W(illiam) R(odolph) 1937- 29-32R
Cornman, James W(elton) 1929-1978 .... CANR-11
  Earlier sketch in CA 69-72
Cornock, (John) Stroud 1938- 25-28R
Cornuelle, Richard C. 1927- 17-20R
Cornwall, E(spie) Judson 1924- CANR-6
  Earlier sketch in CA 57-60
Cornwall, I(an) W(olfran) 1909- 9-12R
Cornwall, J. Spencer
  1888(?)-1983 Obituary 109
Cornwall, James (Handyside) Marshall
  See Marshall-Cornwall, James (Handyside)
Cornwall, Jim
  See Rikhoff, James C.
Cornwall, John 1928- CANR-37
  Earlier sketch in CA 115
Cornwall, Martin
  See Cavendish, Richard
Cornwall, Nellie
  See Sloggett, Nellie
Cornwell, Bernard 1944- 104
Cornwell, David (John Moore) 1931- CANR-33
  Earlier sketches in CA 5-8R, CANR-13
  See also le Carre, John
  See also CLC 9, 15
  See also MTCW
Cornwell, Elmer E(ckert) Jr.
  1924- Brief entry 118
Cornwell, Patricia Daniels 1956- 134
Cornwell, Smith
  See Smith, David (Jeddie)
Coronel, Jorge Icaza
  See Icaza Coronel, Jorge
Corpi, Lucha 1945- 131
  See also DLB 82
  See also HW
Corporal Trim
  See Bolger, Philip C(unningham)
Corradi, Gemma 1939- 21-24R
Corradi, Juan E. 1943- 113
Corrall, Alice Enid 1916- 5-8R
Corre, Alan D. 1931- 37-40R
Correa
  See Galbraith, Jean
Correa, Gustavo 1914- 49-52
Correia-Afonso, John 1924- CANR-13
  Earlier sketch in CA 33-36R
Corren, Grace
  See Hoskins, Robert
Correnti, Mario
  See Togliatti, Palmiro
Correu, Larry M. 1931- 114
Correy, Lee
  See Stine, G(eorge) Harry
Corrie, Elva
  See Clairmont, Elva
Corrigan, (Helen) Adeline 1909- 69-72
  See also SATA 23
Corrigan, Barbara 1922- 57-60
  See also SATA 8
Corrigan, Francis Joseph 1919- 5-8R
Corrigan, John D(avitt) 1900- 41-44R
Corrigan, John Thomas 1936- CANR-10
  Earlier sketch in CA 65-68
Corrigan, Kevin .... CLC 55
Corrigan, Ralph L(awrence) Jr. 1937- 33-36R
Corrigan, Robert A(nthony) 1935- 9-12R
Corrigan, Robert W(illoughby) 1927- CANR-6
  Earlier sketch in CA 5-8R
Corrigan, Timothy (J.) 1951- 129
Corrin, Jay P(atrick) 1943- 125
Corrin, Sara 1918- 120
  See also SATA 48
Corrin, Stephen 121
  See also SATA 48
Corrington, John William 1932-1988 .... CANR-8
  Earlier sketch in CA 13-16R, 127
  See also DLB 6
Corris, Peter 1942- 135
Corriveau, Monique (Chouinard)
  1927-1976 .... CANR-12
  Obituary 122
  Earlier sketch in CA 61-64
Corrothers, James D. 1869-1917 .... DLB 50
Corry, Emmett 1934- 111
Corry, J(ames) A(lexander)
  1899-1985 Obituary 120
Corsa, Helen Storm 1915- 17-20R
Corsaro, Francesco Andrea 1924- 85-88
Corsaro, Frank
  See Corsaro, Francesco Andrea
Corsaro, Maria C(ecelia) 1949- 107
Corsel, Ralph 1920- 25-28R
Corsi, Jerome R(obert) 1946- 89-92
Corsini, Raymond J. 1914- CANR-21
  Earlier sketches in CA 1-4R, CANR-3
Corso, (Nunzio) Gregory 1930- 5-8R
  See also CLC 1, 11
  See also DLB 5,16
  See also MTCW
Corson, Fred Pierce 1896-1985 .... CAP-2
  Obituary 115
  Earlier sketch in CA 23-24
Corson, Hazel W. 1906- CANR-2
  Earlier sketch in CA 1-4R
Corson, John J(ay III) 1905-1990 .... CANR-5
  Obituary 132
  Earlier sketch in CA 1-4R
Corson, Richard 41-44R
Corson-Finnerty, Adam Daniel 1944- CANR-14
  Earlier sketch in CA 81-84
Corstanje, Auspicius van
  See van Corstanje, Charles
Corstanje, Charles van
  See van Corstanje, Charles
Cort, David 1904-1983 .... 9-12R
  Obituary 111
Cort, M. C.
  See Clifford, Margaret Cort
Cort, Margaret
  See Clifford, Margaret Cort
Cort, Ned
  See Jagninski, Tom
Cortada, James W(illiam) 1946- 133
  Brief entry 114
Cortazar, Julio 1914-1984 .... CANR-32
  Earlier sketches in CA 21-24R, CANR-12
  See also CLC 2, 3, 5, 10, 13, 15, 33, 34
  See also DLB 113
  See also HW
  See also MTCW
  See also SSC 7
Cortazzi, (Henry Arthur) Hugh 1924- CANR-39
  Earlier sketch in CA 115
Cortazzo, Carman 1936- 109
Corteen, Wes
  See Norwood, Victor G(eorge) C(harles)
Corten, Irina H. 1941- 137
Cortes, Carlos E(liseo) 1934- CANR-8
  Earlier sketch in CA 61-64
Cortes, Juan B(autista) 1925- 37-40R
Cortese, A(nthony) James 1917- 65-68
Cortesi, Lawrence
  See Cerri, Lawrence J.
Cortez, Jayne 1936- CANR-31
  Earlier sketches in CA 73-76, CANR-13
  See also BW
  See also DLB 41
Cortez-Villon, Juan
  See Herzinger, Kim A(llen)
Cortinez, Carlos 1934- 123
Cortner, Richard C(arroll) 1935- 104
Cortright, Barbara 1927- 112
Cortright, David 1946- 57-60
Corty, Floyd L(ouis) 1916- 13-16R
Corwen, Leonard 1921- CANR-15
  Earlier sketch in CA 93-96
Corwin, Adele Beatrice Lewis 1922-1990 123
  Obituary 131
Corwin, Cecil
  See Kornbluth, C(yril) M.
Corwin, Edward S(amuel) 1878-1963 122
  Obituary 113
Corwin, Judith H(offman) 1946- CANR-32
  Earlier sketch in CA 113
  See also SATA 10
Corwin, Norman 1910- CANR-24
  Earlier sketches in CA 1-4R, CANR-1
  See also AITN 2
Corwin, Ronald G(ary) 1932- CANR-23
  Earlier sketches in CA 17-20R, CANR-8
Cory, Caroline
  See Freeman, Kathleen
Cory, Charlotte 1956- 137
Cory, Corrine
  See Cory, Irene E.
Cory, Daniel 1904-1972 Obituary 37-40R
Cory, David 1872-1966 Obituary 25-28R
Cory, Desmond
  See McCarthy, Shaun (Lloyd)
Cory, Howard L.
  See Jardine, Jack
Cory, Irene E. 1910- 49-52
Cory, Jean-Jacques 1947- 57-60
Cory, Ray
  See Marshall, Mel(vin D.)
Cory, William Johnson 1823-1892 .... DLB 35
Corya, I. E.
  See Cory, Irene E.
Coryell, Janet L(ee) 1955- 135
Cosby, Bill
  See Cosby, William Henry Jr.
  See also BEST 89:4
Cosby, William Henry Jr. 1937- CANR-27
  Earlier sketch in CA 81-84
  See also Cosby, Bill
  See also BW
  See also SATA 66
Cosby, Yvonne Shepard
  1886(?)-1980 Obituary 97-100
Cose, Ellis Jonathan 1951- 119
Cosell, Howard 1920- 108
Cosentino, Andrew J(oseph) 1931- 120
Cosentino, Donald J(ohn) 1941- 108
Cosentino, Frank 1937- 132
Coser, Lewis A. 1913- CANR-4
  Earlier sketch in CA 1-4R
Coser, Rose Laub 1916- 13-16R
Cosgrave, John O'Hara II 1908-1968 .... CANR-1
  Earlier sketch in CA 1-4R
  See also SATA 21
Cosgrave, Patrick 1941- 33-36R
Cosgrove, Carol Ann
  See Twitchett, Carol Cosgrove
Cosgrove, Margaret (Leota) 1926- CANR-6
  Earlier sketch in CA 9-12R
  See also SATA 47
Cosgrove, Mark P. 1947- 85-88
Cosgrove, Maynard G(iles) 1895- 57-60
Cosgrove, Rachel
  See Payes, Rachel C(osgrove)
Cosgrove, Richard A(lfred) 1941- 104
Cosgrove, Stephen E(dward) 1945- CANR-22
  Earlier sketch in CA 69-72
  See also AITN 1
  See also SATA 40, 53
Cosh, (Ethel Eleanor) Mary 5-8R
Cosic, Dobrica 1921- 138
  Brief entry 122
  See also CLC 14
Coskey, Evelyn 1932- 41-44R
  See also SATA 7
Coslow, Sam(son) 1905-1982 .... CANR-29
  Obituary 106
  Earlier sketch in CA 77-80
Cosman, Carol 104
Cosman, Madeleine Pelner 1937- 127
  Brief entry 105
Cosneck, Bernard Joseph 1912- 49-52
Cosner, Shaaron 1940- CANR-38
  Earlier sketch in CA 116
  See also SATA 43
Coss, Thurman L. 1926- 13-16R
Cossart, Theophilus
  See Glass, Montague (Marsden)
Cosseboom, Kathy Groehn
  See El-Messidi, Kathy Groehn
Cossi, Olga 1921- 81-84
  See also SATA 67
Cosslett, Tess 1947- 115
Cossman, E(li) Joseph 1918- 17-20R
Cost, March
  See Morrison, Margaret Mackie
Costa, Albert Bernard 1929- 13-16R
Costa, Gustavo 1930- 37-40R
Costa, Horacio (L.) de la
  1916-1977 Obituary 112
Costa, Richard Hauer 1921- 21-24R
Costabel, Eva Deutsch 1924- 125
  See also SATA 45
Costabel-Deutsch, Eva
  See Costabel, Eva Deutsch
Costain, Thomas B(ertram) 1885-1965 .... 5-8R
  Obituary 25-28R
  See also CLC 30
  See also DLB 9
Costantin, M(ary) M(cCaffrey) 1935- 45-48
Costantini, Humberto 1924(?)-1987 131
  Obituary 122
  See also CLC 49
  See also HW
Costas, Orlando E(nrique) 1942-1987 101
  Obituary 122
Costas, Procope 1900(?)-1974 Obituary 53-56
Coste, Donat 1912-1957 .... DLB 88
Costello, Anne 1937- 102
Costello, Bonnie 1950- 129
Costello, Chris 1947- 107
Costello, David F(rancis) 1904- 33-36R
  See also SATA 23
Costello, Donald P(aul) 1931- 17-20R
Costello, Elvis 1955- .... CLC 21
Costello, Gerald M. 1931- 127
Costello, Grace Seymour
  1883-1983 Obituary 110
Costello, John E(dward) 1943- 85-88
Costello, Joseph P(atrick) 1924- 115
Costello, Michael
  See Detzer, Karl
Costello, Peter 1946- 93-96
Costello, William Aloysious 1904-1969 .... 1-4R
  Obituary 103
Costelloe, M(artin) Joseph 1914- 41-44R
Coster, Robert
  See Barltrop, Robert
Costigan, Daniel M. 1929- CANR-31
  Earlier sketches in CA 33-36R, CANR-14
Costigan, Giovanni 1905- CAP-1
  Earlier sketch in CA 13-16
Costigan, James 1928- 73-76
Costikyan, Edward N. 1924- 17-20R
Costinescu, Tristan
  See Gross, Terence
Costis, Harry George 1928- 45-48

Costley, Bill
See Costley, William K(irkwood) Jr.
Costley, William K(irkwood) Jr. 1942- CANR-35
Earlier sketch in CA 81-84
Costonis, John J(oseph) 1937- CANR-4
Earlier sketch in CA 49-52
Cote, Richard G(eorge) 1934- 69-72
Cotes, Peter 1912- CANR-26
Earlier sketches in CA 5-8R, CANR-4
Cothem, Fayly H(ardcastle) 1926- 1-4R
Cothen, Joe H(erbert) 1926- 113
Cothran, J(oseph) Guy 1897- CAP-2
Earlier sketch in CA 29-32
Cothran, Jean 1910- 93-96
Cotich, Felicia 1926- 115
Cotler, Gordon 1923- 1-4R
Cotler, Sherwin B(arry) 1941- 65-68
Cotlow, Lewis N(athaniel) 1898-1987 65-68
Obituary 122
Cotner, Robert Crawford 1906- 37-40R
Cotner, Thomas E. 1916- 37-40R
Cott, Hugh B(amford) 1900-1987 Obituary 122
Cott, Jonathan 1942- 53-56
See also SATA 23
Cott, Nancy F. 1945- 81-84
Cottam, Clarence 1899-1974 97-100
See also SATA 25
Cottam, Keith M. 1941- 81-84
Cottam, Walter P(ace) 1894- CAP-1
Earlier sketch in CA 13-16
Cotten, Lee 1942- 127
Cotten, Nell(ie) Wyllie 1908- 1-4R
Cotter, Charles H(enry) 1919- 13-16R
Cotter, Cornelius Philip 1924- CANR-1
Earlier sketch in CA 1-4R
Cotter, Edward F(rancis) 1917- CANR-6
Earlier sketch in CA 5-8R
Cotter, James Finn 1929- 33-36R
Cotter, Janet M(errill) 1914- 61-64
Cotter, Joseph S. Sr.
See Cotter, Joseph Seamon Sr.
Cotter, Joseph Seamon Sr. 1861-1949 124
See also BLC 1
See also BW
See also DLB 50
See also TCLC 28
Cotter, Joseph Seamon Jr. 1895-1919 ..... DLB 50
Cotter, Richard V(ern) 1930- CANR-14
Earlier sketch in CA 41-44R
Cotterell, Geoffrey 1919- 5-8R
Cotterell, (Francis) Peter 1930- CANR-1
Earlier sketch in CA 49-52
Cotterill, Rodney M(ichael) J(ohn) 1933- 118
Cottingham, John (Graham) 1943- 133
Cottle, Charles
See Anderson, Robert C(harles)
Cottle, Thomas J. 1937- CANR-17
Earlier sketch in CA 33-36R
Cottle, William C(ullen) 1913- 41-44R
Cottler, Joseph 1899- CAP-2
Earlier sketch in CA 25-28
See also SATA 22
Cotton, (Thomas) Henry
1907-1987 Obituary 124
Cotton, John W(healdon) 1925- 33-36R
Cotton, John 1584-1652 ....DLB 24
Cotton, John 1925- CANR-27
Earlier sketches in CA 65-68, CANR-11
Cotton, Norris 1900- 103
Cottrell, Alan (Howard) 1919- CANR-10
Earlier sketch in CA 65-68
Cottrell, Alan P. 1935-1984 120
Cottrell, Alvin J. 1925(?)-1984 Obituary 112
Cottrell, (William) Fred(erick) 1903- 1-4R
Cottrell, Jack (Warren) 1938- CANR-23
Earlier sketch in CA 107
Cottrell, Leonard S(later) Jr. 1899-1985 107
Obituary 115
Cottrell, Leonard 1913-1974 ....CANR-4
Earlier sketch in CA 5-8R
See also SATA 24
Cottrell, Richard 1936- 130
Cottrell, Robert D(uane) 1930- 53-56
Couch, Arthur Thomas Quiller
See Quiller-Couch, Arthur Thomas
Couch, Helen F(ox) 1907- CAP-2
Earlier sketch in CA 17-18
Couch, Osma Palmer
See Tod, Osma Gallinger
Couch, William T(erry) 1901-1988 Obituary 127
Coudenhove-Kalergi, Richard N(icolas)
1894-1972 Obituary 37-40R
Coudert, Allison P(ierce) 1941- 110
Coudert, Jo 1923- 17-20R
Couffer, Jack 1924- CANR-1
Earlier sketch in CA 1-4R
Couger, J(ames) Daniel 1929- CANR-8
Earlier sketch in CA 53-56
Coughlan, John W. 1927- 21-24R
Coughlan, Margaret N(ourse) 1925- 107
Coughlan, (John) Robert 1914- 65-68
Coughlan, William C(arlisle) Jr. 1946- 115
Coughlin, Bernard J. 1922- 13-16R
Coughlin, Charles E(dward)
1891-1979 Obituary 97-100
Coughlin, George G(ordon) 1900- 107
Coughlin, Joseph Welter 1919- 1-4R
Coughlin, T(homas) Glen 1958- 136
Coughlin, Violet L(ouise) 73-76
Coughran, Larry C. 1925- 21-24R
Coughtry, Jay 1945- 111
Couldery, Fred(erick) A(lan) J(ames)
1928- 9-12R
Coulet du Gard, Rene 1919- CANR-4
Earlier sketch in CA 53-56
Coulette, Henri Anthony 1927-1988 ......CANR-14
Obituary 125
Earlier sketch in CA 65-68
Coulling, Sidney Baxter 1924- 102
Coulmas, Florian 1949- 132
Couloumbis, Theodore A. 1935- CANR-7
Earlier sketch in CA 17-20R
Coulson, C(harles) A(lfred) 1910-1974 .....CANR-4
Earlier sketch in CA 5-8R
Coulson, Felicity Carter 1906- 9-12R
Coulson, John H(ubert) A(rthur) 1906- 9-12R
Coulson, Juanita (Ruth) 1933- CANR-26
Earlier sketches in CA 25-28R, CANR-9
Coulson, N. J.
See Coulson, Noel J(ames)
Coulson, Noel J(ames) 1928-1986 124
Obituary 120
Coulson, Robert S(tratton) 1928- CANR-24
Earlier sketches in CA 21-24R, CANR-9
Coulson, Robert 1924- CANR-36
Earlier sketch in CA 49-52
Coulson, William D(onald) E(dward)
1942- 89-92
Coulter, E(llis) Merton 1890-1981 ....CANR-3
Obituary 104
Earlier sketch in CA 9-12R
Coulter, Edwin M(artin) 1937- 104
Coulter, Harris L. 1932- 136
Coulter, Hope Norman 1961- 129
Coulter, John (William) 1888-1980 ....CANR-3
Earlier sketch in CA 5-8R
See also DLB 68
Coulter, N(orman) Arthur Jr. 1920- 65-68
Coulter, Olivia W. 1915(?)-1989 Obituary 129
Coulter, Stephen 1914- Brief entry 109
Coulton, James
See Hansen, Joseph
Coultrap-McQuin, Susan (M.) 1947- 137
Council, Norman Briggs 1936- 102
Cound, John J(ames) 1928- 37-40R
Counsel, June 1926- 138
See also SATA 70
Counsell, John William 1905-1987 57-60
Obituary 121
Counselman, Mary Elizabeth 1911- 106
Counsilman, James E(dward) 1920- 126
Count, Earl W(endel) 1899- 37-40R
Counter, Kenneth (Norman Samuel)
1930- 25-28R
Countess of Romanones
See
Quintanilla, Maria Aline Griffith y Dexter Condes
Countryman, The
See Whitlock, Ralph
Countryman, Vern 1917- 13-16R
Counts, Charles Richard 1934- 49-52
Counts, George S(ylvester) 1889-1974 ....5-8R
Obituary 53-56
Couper, Heather 1949- 124
Couper, J(ohn) M(ill) 1914- 45-48
Couperus, Louis (Marie Anne)
1863-1923 Brief entry 115
See also TCLC 15
Coupey, Philippe 1937- 104
Coupling, J. J.
See Pierce, John Robinson
Courage, James Francis 1903-1963 77-80
Courant, Richard 1888-1972 Obituary 33-36R
Couratin, Arthur Hubert
1902-1988 Obituary 126
Courlander, Harold 1908- CANR-18
Earlier sketches in CA 9-12R, CANR-3
See also SATA 6
Cournos, John 1881-1966 .... CAP-2
Earlier sketch in CA 13-14
See also DLB 54
Courouci, Jennifer 1922- 29-32R
Course, Alfred George 1895- 9-12R
Course, Edwin 1922- 77-80
Coursen, Herbert R(andolph) Jr.
1932- CANR-19
Earlier sketches in CA 53-56, CANR-4
Court, Harold
See Swycaffer, Jefferson P(utnam)
Court, Margaret Smith 1942- Brief entry 106
Court, Sharon
See Rowland, D(onald) S(ydney)
Court, W(illiam) H(enry) B(assano)
1905(?)-1971 Obituary 104
Court, Wesli
See Turco, Lewis (Putnam)
Court, Wesli 1940- CANR-11
Earlier sketch in CA 69-72
Courtenay, Ashley (Reginald)
1888-1986 Obituary 121
Courtenay, Bryce 1933- 138
See also CLC 59
Courtenay, William J(ames) 1935- 9-12R
Courter, Gay 1944- CANR-26
Earlier sketches in CA 57-60, CANR-7
Courthion, Pierre (Barthelemy) 1902- CANR-14
Earlier sketch in CA 81-84
Courtice, Katie 1942- 121
Courtier, S(idney) H(obson) 1904-197 (?) CAP-2
Earlier sketch in CA 25-28
Courtine, Robert 1910- CANR-14
Earlier sketch in CA 81-84
Courtis, Stuart Appleton
1874-1969 Obituary 105
See also SATA 29
Courtland, Roberta
See Dern, Erolie Pearl Gaddis
Courtneidge, Cicely 1893-1980 Obituary 105
Courtney, Dayle
See Goldsmith, Howard
Courtney, E(dward) 1932- 129
Courtney, Gwendoline CAP-1
Earlier sketch in CA 9-10
Courtney, John
See Judd, Frederick Charles
Courtney, Nicholas (Piers) 1944- CANR-32
Earlier sketch in CA 113
Courtney, Ragan 1941- 97-100
Courtney, (John) Richard 1927- CANR-23
Earlier sketch in CA 105
Courtney, Robert
See Ellison, Harlan
Courtney, William J(ohn) 1921- 102
Courtney, Winifred F(isk) 1918- 109
Courtwright, David T(odd) 1952- CANR-28
Earlier sketch in CA 110
Courville, Donovan A(mos) 1901- 45-48
Coury, Louise Andree
1895(?)-1983 Obituary 109
See also SATA 34
Couse, Harold C. 1925- 17-20R
Cousens, Frances Reissman
1913-1985 Obituary 115
Couser, G(riffith) Thomas 1946- 89-92
Cousins, Albert Newton 1919- 41-44R
Cousins, Geoffrey (Esmond) 1900- 25-28R
Cousins, Margaret 1905- CANR-1
Earlier sketch in CA 1-4R
See also SATA 2
Cousins, Norman 1915-1990 ....CANR-33
Earlier sketches in CA 17-20R, CANR-13
See also BEST 90:2
See also MTCW
Cousins, Peter Edward 1928- 104
Cousse, Raymond 1942- 101
Cousteau, Jacques-Yves 1910- CANR-15
Earlier sketch in CA 65-68
See also CLC 30
See also MTCW
See also SATA 38
Cousteau, Philippe Pierre 1940-1979 ....33-36R
Obituary 89-92
Coustillas, Pierre 1930- 73-76
Coutard, Wanda Lundy Hale
1902(?)-1982 Obituary 106
Coutinho, Joaquim
1886(?)-1978 Obituary 77-80
Couto, Nancy Vieira 1942- 136
Couto, Richard A. 1941- CANR-15
Earlier sketch in CA 89-92
Coutts, Frederick Lee 1899-1986 ....CANR-36
Earlier sketch in CA 109
Couture, Andrea 1943- 85-88
Couturier, Louis (Joseph) 1910- 101
Couzyn, Jeni 1942- 85-88
Covarrubias, Barbara Faith 1932- 113
Covatta, Anthony Gallo 1944- 53-56
Covell, Alan C(arter) 1952- 118
Covell, Jon Carter 1910- CANR-17
Earlier sketch in CA 97-100
Coven, Brenda 110
Coveney, James 1920- 41-44R
Coventry, Francis 1725-1754 ....DLB 39
Coventry, John 1915- 93-96
Cover, Arthur Byron 1950- 107
Cover, Robert M. 1943-1986 57-60
Obituary 119
Coverdale, John F(oy) 1940- 73-76
Coverley, Louise Bennett
See Bennett-Coverley, Louise
Covert, James Thayne 1932- 37-40R
Covert, Paul 1941- CANR-20
Earlier sketch in CA 103
Covey, Cyclone 1922- 21-24R
Covey, Stephen R. 1932- CANR-12
Earlier sketch in CA 33-36R
Covici, Pascal Jr. 1930- 1-4R
Coville, Bruce 1950- CANR-22
Earlier sketch in CA 97-100
See also SATA 32
Coville, Walter J(oseph) 1914- CANR-5
Earlier sketch in CA 5-8R
Covin, Theron Michael 1947- 57-60
Covina, Gina 1952- 101
Covington, James W. 1917- 33-36R
Covington, Martin Vaden 1936- 37-40R
Covington, Vicki 1952- 133
Covino, Frank 1931- 57-60
Covino, Joseph Jr. 1954- 113
Covino, Michael 1950- 132
Covvey, H(arry) Dominic J(oseph)
1944- CANR-28
Earlier sketch in CA 110
Cowan, Alan
See Gilchrist, Alan W.
Cowan, Charles Donald 1923- 102
Cowan, Edward James 1944- 103
Cowan, G(eorge) H(amilton) 1917- 17-20R
Cowan, G(ordon) 1933- 25-28R
Cowan, Geoffrey 1942- 97-100
Cowan, George McKillop 1916- 102
Cowan, Gregory M(ac) 1935-1979 ....CANR-9
Earlier sketch in CA 65-68
Cowan, Henry J(acob) 1919- CANR-19
Earlier sketches in CA 53-56, CANR-4
Cowan, Ian Borthwick 1932-1990 ....CANR-24
Obituary 133
Earlier sketches in CA 61-64, CANR-8
Cowan, J(oseph) L(loyd) 1929- 25-28R
Cowan, James C(ostello) 1927- CANR-29
Earlier sketch in CA 29-32R
Cowan, Janice 1941- 97-100
Cowan, Louise (Shillingburg) 1916- 1-4R
Cowan, Lyn 1942- 116
Cowan, Michael H(eath) 1937- 21-24R
Cowan, Paul 1940-1990 Obituary 126
Cowan, Peter (Walkinshaw) 1914- CANR-25
Earlier sketches in CA 21-24R, CANR-9
Cowan, Richard O(lsen) 1934- 53-56
Cowan, Robert Granniss 1895- CAP-1
Earlier sketch in CA 11-12
Cowan, Ruth Schwartz 1941- 115
Cowan, Stuart DuBois 1917- 104
Cowan, Walter G(reaves) 1912- 120
Cowan, Wood (Messick) 1896-1977 69-72
Coward, Barry 1941- 131
Coward, Noel (Peirce) 1899-1973 ....CANR-35
Obituary 41-44R
Earlier sketches in CAP-2, CA 17-18
See also AITN 1
See also CDBLB 1914-1945
See also CLC 1, 9, 29, 51
See also DLB 10
See also MTCW
Cowart, David (Guyland) 1947- CANR-30
Earlier sketch in CA 104
Cowasjee, Saros 1931- CANR-20
Earlier sketches in CA 9-12R, CANR-5
Cowden, Dudley J(ohnstone) 1899- 41-44R
Cowden, Jeanne 1918- 85-88
Cowden, Joanna Dunlap 1933- 53-56
Cowdrey, A(lbert) E(dward) 1933- 17-20R
Cowdrey, (Michael) Colin 1932- 105
Cowdrey, H(erbert) E(dward) J(ohn) 1926- 129
Cowell, (John) Adrian 1934- 103
Cowell, Cyril 1888- CAP-2
Earlier sketch in CA 21-22
Cowell, Frank A. 135
Cowell, Frank Richard 1897- CANR-8
Earlier sketch in CA 53-56
Cowell, Henry Dixon 1897-1965 Obituary 116
Cowen, David L(aurence) 1909- 13-16R
Cowen, Emory L(eland) 1926- 69-72
Cowen, Eve
See Werner, Herma
Cowen, Frances
See Munthe, Frances
Cowen, Ida 1898- 45-48
See also SATA 64
Cowen, Robert Churchill 1927- 13-16R
Cowen, Ron(ald) 1944- 85-88
Cowen, Roy C(hadwell) 1930- CANR-12
Earlier sketch in CA 33-36R
Cowen, Zelman 1919- CANR-1
Earlier sketch in CA 1-4R
Cowgill, Donald O(len) 1911- 37-40R
Cowherd, Raymond Gibson 1909- 124
Cowie, Alexander 1896- 33-36R
Cowie, Donald 1911- 116
Cowie, Evelyn E(lizabeth) 1924- CANR-9
Earlier sketch in CA 13-16R
Cowie, Hamilton Russell 1931- 102
Cowie, Leonard W(allace) 1919- CANR-9
Earlier sketch in CA 13-16R
See also SATA 4
Cowie, Mervyn (Hugh) 1909- CAP-1
Earlier sketch in CA 9-10
Cowie, Peter 1939- CANR-18
Earlier sketches in CA 49-52, CANR-1
Cowle, Jerome Milton 1917- 93-96
Cowle, Jerry
See Cowle, Jerome Milton
Cowler, Rosemary (Elizabeth) 1925- 25-28R
Cowles, Fleur CANR-24
Earlier sketches in CA 9-12R, CANR-4
See also AITN 1
Cowles, Frank Jr. 1918- 57-60
Cowles, Gardner A. Jr. 1903-1985 Obituary 116
Cowles, Gardner 1861-1946 ....DLB 29
Cowles, Ginny 1924- 57-60
Cowles, John Sr. 1898-1983 Obituary 109
Cowles, Kathleen
See Krull, Kathleen
Cowles, Lois Thornburg
1909-1980 Obituary 101
Cowles, Mike
See Cowles, Gardner A. Jr.
Cowles, Raymond B(ridgeman)
1896-1975 Obituary 61-64
Cowles, S(amuel) Macon Jr. 1916- 21-24R
Cowles, Virginia (Spencer)
1912-1983 ....CANR-12
Obituary 110
Earlier sketch in CA 65-68
Cowley, Hannah 1743-1809 ....DLB 89
Cowley, Joseph (Gilbert) 1923- 106
Cowley, (Cassia) Joy 1936- CANR-11
Earlier sketch in CA 25-28R
See also SATA 4
Cowley, Malcolm 1898-1989 ....CANR-3
Obituary 128
Earlier sketch in CA 5-8R
See also CLC 39
See also DLB 4, 48
See also DLBY 81, 89
See also MTCW
Cowlin, Dorothy
See Whalley, Dorothy
Cowling, Elizabeth 1910- Brief entry 110
Cowling, Ellis 1905- CAP-1
Earlier sketch in CA 13-16
Cowling, Maurice John 1926- CANR-3
Earlier sketch in CA 5-8R
Cowlishaw, Ranson 1894- 5-8R
Cowper, Richard
See Middleton-Murry, John (Jr.)
Cowper, William 1731-1800 ....DLB 104, 109
Cox, A(nthony) B(erkeley) 1893-1970 97-100
See also Berkeley, Anthony
Cox, Albert W(esley) 1921- 53-56
Cox, Allan 1937- 93-96
Cox, Alva Irwin Jr. 1925- 17-20R
Cox, Archibald 1912- 73-76
Cox, (Christopher) Barry 1931- 103
See also SATA 62

Cox, Bertha Mae (Hill) 1901- ... 17-20R
Cox, Bill 1910- ... 9-12R
Cox, C. Benjamin 1925- ... 97-100
Cox, Carol 1946- ... 117
Cox, Charles B(rian) 1928- ... 25-28R
Cox, Claire 1919- ... CANR-2
Earlier sketch in CA 5-8R
Cox, Constance 1915- ... CANR-24
Earlier sketches in CA 21-24R, CANR-9
Cox, David (Dundas) 1933- ... 119
See also SATA 56
Cox, Donald William 1921- ... CANR-4
Earlier sketch in CA 1-4R
See also SATA 23
Cox, Edith Muriel ... 102
Cox, Edward Finch 1946- ... 29-32R
Cox, Edward Franklin 1925- ... 33-36R
Cox, Edward Locksley 1943- ... 121
Cox, Edwin B(urk) 1930- ... 37-40R
Cox, Elizabeth 1942- ... 130
Cox, Elizabeth 1953- ... 136
Cox, Erle (Harold) 1873-1950 Brief entry ... 112
Cox, Eugene L. 1931- ... 21-24R
Cox, Frank D. 1933- ... 29-32R
Cox, Fred(erick) M(oreland) 1928- ... CANR-1
Earlier sketch in CA 45-48
Cox, G. William 1949(?)-1988 Obituary ... 125
Cox, Gary D(uane) 1947- ... 113
Cox, Geoffrey Sandford 1910- ... 103
Cox, George W(yatt) 1935- ... 115
Cox, Harvey (Gallagher Jr.) 1929- ... 77-80
See also AITN 1
Cox, (William) Harvey 1939- ... 45-48
Cox, Hebe 1909- ... CAP-1
Earlier sketch in CA 13-14
Cox, Hugh Brandon
See Brandon-Cox, Hugh
Cox, Hugh S(towell) 1874-1969 ... CAP-2
Earlier sketch in CA 21-22
Cox, J(ohn) Gray 1952- ... 123
Cox, J. Halley 1910-1974 Obituary ... 112
Cox, Jack
See Cox, John Roberts
Cox, James Anthony 1926- ... 104
Cox, James M(elville) 1925- ... 13-16R
Cox, James Middleton Jr.
1903-1974 Obituary ... 89-92
Cox, James W(illiam) 1923- ... 33-36R
Cox, Jeri
See Kimes, Beverly Rae
Cox, Joan (Irene) 1942- ... 101
Cox, John H(enry) 1907-1975 Obituary ... 115
Cox, John Roberts 1915-1981 ... CANR-14
Earlier sketch in CA 29-32R
See also SATA 9
Cox, John Stuart 1931- ... 117
Cox, Joseph A. 1896(?)-1980 Obituary ... 97-100
Cox, Joseph Mason Andrew 1930- ... CANR-2
Earlier sketch in CA 49-52
See also BW
Cox, Joseph W(illiam) 1937- ... 81-84
Cox, Keith (Kohn) 1931- ... CANR-12
Earlier sketch in CA 69-72
Cox, Kevin R. 1939- ... 37-40R
Cox, LaWanda Fenlason 1909- ... 9-12R
Cox, Lee Sheridan 1916- ... 25-28R
Cox, Marie-Therese Henriette 1925-1991 ... 105
Obituary ... 136
Cox, Marion Monroe 1898-1983 Obituary ... 110
See also Monroe, Marion
Cox, Mark 1956- ... 128
Cox, Martha Heasley 1919- ... 13-16R
Cox, Mary Elizabeth
See Headapohl, Betty R.
Cox, Maxwell E. 1922- ... 25-28R
Cox, Miriam Stewart ... 9-12R
Cox, Molly
See Cox, Marie-Therese Henriette
Cox, Oliver Cromwell 1901-1974 ... 1-4R
Obituary ... 103
Cox, P(atrick) Brian ... 45-48
See also Stuart, Kenneth
Cox, Palmer 1840-1924 Brief entry ... 111
See also CLR 24
See also DLB 42
See also SATA 24
Cox, R(obert) David 1937- ... CANR-13
Earlier sketch in CA 29-32R
Cox, R(alph) Merritt 1939- ... 33-36R
Cox, Rachel Dunaway 1904- ... 33-36R
Cox, Reavis 1900- ... CAP-1
Earlier sketch in CA 13-16
Cox, Richard Howard 1925- ... CANR-8
Earlier sketch in CA 13-16R
Cox, Richard 1931- ... CANR-30
Earlier sketches in CA 21-24R, CANR-11
Cox, Roger L. 1931- ... 135
Cox, Stephen (LeRoy) 1966- ... 130
Cox, Thomas R(ichard) 1933- ... 53-56
Cox, Victoria
See Garretson, Victoria Diane
Cox, Wallace (Maynard) 1924-1973 ... 97-100
Obituary ... 41-44R
See also Cox, Wally
Cox, Wally
See Cox, Wallace (Maynard)
See also SATA 25
Cox, Warren E(arle) 1895-1977 ... CAP-2
Obituary ... 69-72
Earlier sketch in CA 33-36
Cox, William E(dwin) Jr. 1930- ... 106
Cox, William R(obert) 1901-1988 ... CANR-24
Obituary ... 126
Earlier sketches in CA 9-12R, CANR-6
See also SATA 31, 46, 57
Cox, William Trevor 1928- ... CANR-37
Earlier sketches in CA 9-12R, CANR-4
See also Trevor, William
See also CLC 9, 14, 71
See also DLB 14
See also MTCW
Coxe, Antony D(acres) Hippisley
See Hippisley Coxe, Antony D(acres)
Coxe, George Harmon 1901- ... 57-60
Coxe, Louis (Osborne) 1918- ... 13-16R
See also DLB 5
Coxe, Molly 1959- ... 137
See also SATA 69
Coxe, Tench 1755-1824 ... DLB 37
Cox-George, Noah Arthur William
1915- ... CANR-6
Earlier sketch in CA 13-16R
Coxhead, Elizabeth
1909(?)-1979 Obituary ... 89-92
Cox-Johnson, Ann
See Saunders, Ann Loreille
Coy, Harold 1902- ... CANR-4
Earlier sketch in CA 5-8R
See also SATA 3
Coyle, Beverly (Jones) 1946- ... 133
Coyle, David Cushman 1887-1969 ... CANR-15
Obituary ... 103
Earlier sketch in CA 1-4R
Coyle, J(ohn) J(ames) 1928- ... 129
Coyle, L(eslie) Patrick 1934- ... 110
Coyle, Lee
See Coyle, Leo (Perry)
Coyle, Leo (Perry) 1925- ... 41-44R
Coyle, Neva 1943- ... 138
Coyle, William 1917- ... CANR-2
Earlier sketch in CA 1-4R
Coyne, John (P.) 1940- ... CANR-12
Earlier sketch in CA 93-96
Coyne, John R(ichard) Jr. 1935- ... 37-40R
Coyne, Joseph E. 1918-1978 ... 13-16R
Obituary ... 134
Coysh, A(rthur) W(ilfred) 1905- ... CANR-13
Earlier sketch in CA 73-76
Coysh, Victor 1906- ... CANR-8
Earlier sketch in CA 61-64
Coze, Paul 1903(?)-1974 Obituary ... 53-56
Cozzens, James Gould 1903-1978 ... CANR-19
Obituary ... 81-84
Earlier sketch in CA 9-12R
See also CDALB 1941-1968
See also CLC 1, 4, 11
See also DLB 9
See also DLBD 2
See also DLBY 84
See also MTCW
Crabb, Alfred Leland 1884- ... CAP-1
Earlier sketch in CA 13-14
Crabb, Cecil V. Jr. 1924- ... 13-16R
Crabb, E(dmund) W(illiam) 1912- ... CAP-1
Earlier sketch in CA 11-12
Crabb, Lawrence J(ames) Jr. 1944- ... CANR-14
Earlier sketches in CA 65-68, CANR-31
Crabb, Richard 1914- ... 21-24R
Crabbe, Buster
See Crabbe, Clarence Linden
Crabbe, Clarence Linden 1908-1983 ... CANR-11
Obituary ... 109
Earlier sketch in CA 69-72
Crabbe, George 1754-1832 ... DLB 93
Crabbe, Katharyn W. 1945- ... 130
Crabtree, Arthur B(amford) 1910- ... CAP-2
Earlier sketch in CA 17-18
Crabtree, Judith 1928- ... 118
See also SATA 63
Crabtree, T(homas) T(avron) 1924- ... 21-24R
Crace, Jim 1946- ... 135
Brief entry ... 128
Crackel, Theodore J(oseph) 1938- ... 33-36R
Crackers, Fritz
See Frank, Philip Norman
Cracknell, Basil Edward 1925- ... 103
Cracraft, James (Edward) 1939- ... 53-56
Cracroft, Richard Holton 1936- ... 53-56
Craddock, Charles Egbert
See Murfree, Mary Noailles
Craddock, Fred B(renning) 1928- ... 132
Craddock, Patricia (Bland) 1938- ... CANR-4
Earlier sketch in CA 53-56
Craddock, William J(ames) 1946- ... 85-88
Cradock, Thomas 1718-1770 ... DLB 31
Craft, K. Y.
See Craft, Kinuko Y(amabe)
Craft, Kinuko
See Craft, Kinuko Y(amabe)
Craft, Kinuko Y(amabe) 1940- ... SATA 65
Craft, Maurice 1932- ... CANR-28
Earlier sketches in CA 65-68, CANR-11
Craft, Michael 1928- ... 25-28R
Craft, Robert 1923- ... CANR-7
Earlier sketch in CA 9-12R
Craft, Ruth 1935- ... 133
Brief entry ... 110
See also SATA 31
Crafton, Donald (Clayton) 1947- ... 138
Crafts, Glenn Alty 1918- ... 9-12R
Crafts, Kathy 1952- ... 109
Crafts, Roger Conant 1911- ... 106
Cragg, D. J.
See Cragg, Dan
Cragg, Dan 1939- ... 115
Cragg, Gerald R(obertson) 1906- ... 61-64
Cragg, (Albert) Kenneth 1913- ... CANR-22
Earlier sketches in CA 17-20R, CANR-7
Craghan, John Francis 1936- ... 53-56
Crago, Hugh 1946- ... 116
Crago, Maureen 1939- ... 116
Crago, T(homas) Howard 1907- ... CAP-1
Earlier sketch in CA 13-16
Crahan, Margaret E(llen) 1939- ... 114
Craib, Ian 1945- ... 69-72
Craib, Ralph G(rant) 1925- ... 136
Craig, A. A.
See Anderson, Poul (William)
Craig, Albert M(orton) 1927- ... 37-40R
Craig, Alec
See Craig, Alexander George
Craig, Alexander George 1897- ... CAP-1
Earlier sketch in CA 9-10
Craig, Alisa
See MacLeod, Charlotte (Matilda Hughes)
Craig, Amanda 1959- ... 137
Craig, Archibald Campbell
1888-1985 Obituary ... 117
Craig, Barbara Hinkson 1942- ... 135
Craig, Barbara M(ary St. George) 1914- ... 37-40R
Craig, Bill 1930- ... 33-36R
Craig, Brian
See Stableford, Brian (Michael)
Craig, (Robert) Cairns 1949- ... 131
Craig, Charlotte M(arie) 1929- ... 73-76
Craig, Christine (Angela) 1943- ... 120
Craig, Daniel H. 1811-1895 ... DLB 43
Craig, David
See Tucker, James
Craig, David 1932- ... CANR-37
Earlier sketches in CA 41-44R, CANR-14
Craig, Denys
See Stoll, Dennis G(ray)
Craig, Don(ald) Laurence 1946- ... 73-76
Craig, E(velyn) Quita 1917- ... 103
Craig, Edward Anthony 1905- ... 13-16R
Craig, Edward (Henry) Gordon
1872-1966 Obituary ... 25-28R
Craig, Eleanor 1929- ... 93-96
Craig, Elizabeth (Josephine)
1883-1980 ... CANR-11
Obituary ... 101
Earlier sketch in CA 9-12R
Craig, Georgia
See Dern, Erolie Pearl Gaddis
Craig, Gerald M(arquis) 1916- ... 9-12R
Craig, Gordon A(lexander) 1913- ... CANR-17
Earlier sketch in CA 25-28R
Craig, H(enry) A(rmitage) L(lewellyn)
1921-1978 ... 85-88
Obituary ... 81-84
Craig, Hazel Thompson 1904- ... 1-4R
Craig, Helen 1934- ... 117
See also SATA 46, 49
Craig, James 1930- ... 73-76
Craig, Jasmine
See Cresswell, Jasmine (Rosemary)
Craig, Jean T. 1936- ... 5-8R
Craig, John David 1903- ... CAP-2
Earlier sketch in CA 17-18
Craig, John Eland
See Chipperfield, Joseph Eugene
Craig, John Ernest 1921- ... 101
See also SATA 23
Craig, John H(erbert) 1885- ... CAP-1
Earlier sketch in CA 9-10
Craig, Jonathan
See Smith, Frank E.
Craig, Larry
See Coughran, Larry C.
Craig, Lee
See Sands, Leo G(eorge)
Craig, M. F.
See Craig, Mary (Francis) Shura
Craig, M. Jean ... 73-76
See also SATA 17
Craig, M. S.
See Craig, Mary (Francis) Shura
Craig, Margaret (Maze) 1911-1964 ... 1-4R
See also SATA 9
Craig, Mary
See Craig, Mary (Francis) Shura
Craig, Mary S.
See Craig, Mary (Francis) Shura
Craig, Mary (Francis) Shura
1923-1991 ... CANR-26
Obituary ... 133
Earlier sketches in CA 1-4R, CANR-4
See also SAAS 7
See also SATA 6
See also SATO 65
Craig, (Elizabeth) May 1889(?)-1975 ... 101
Obituary ... 89-92
Craig, Nancy
See Maslin, Alice
Craig, Pamela Tudor
See Tudor-Craig, Pamela
Craig, Patricia 1949- ... 128
Craig, Peggy
See Kreig, Margaret B. (Baltzell)
Craig, Philip R. 1933- ... 25-28R
Craig, Raymond C. 1928- ... 124
Craig, Richard B(lythe) 1935- ... 53-56
Craig, Robert B(ruce) 1944- ... 49-52
Craig, Robert C(harles) 1921- ... 17-20R
Craig, Robert D(ean) 1934- ... CANR-14
Earlier sketch in CA 81-84
Craig, Vera
See Rowland, D(onald) S(ydney)
Craig, Webster
See Russell, Eric Frank
Craig, William Lane 1949- ... 116
Craige, Betty Jean 1946- ... 117
Craighead, Frank C(ooper) Jr. 1916- ... 97-100
Craighead, W(ade) Edward
1942- Brief entry ... 118
Craigie, E(dward) Horne 1894- ... CAP-2
Earlier sketch in CA 25-28
Craik, Arthur
See Craig, Alexander George
Craik, Dinah Maria (Mulock) 1826-1887 ... DLB 35
See also MAICYA
See also SATA 34
Craik, Elizabeth M(ary) 1939- ... 131
Craik, Kenneth H(enry) 1936- ... CANR-1
Earlier sketch in CA 45-48
Craik, Thomas Wallace 1927- ... 106
Craik, W(endy) A(nn) 1934- ... 25-28R
Craille, Wesley
See Rowland, D(onald) S(ydney)
Crain, Jeff
See Meneses, Enrique
Crain, John 1926(?)-1979 Obituary ... 89-92
Crain, Robert L(ee) 1934- ... CANR-13
Earlier sketch in CA 21-24R
Crain, Sharie 1942- ... 77-80
Craine, Eugene R(ichard) 1917-1977 ... 33-36R
Craker, Lyle E(ugene) 1941- ... 116
Cram, Mildred 1889- ... 49-52
Cram, Ralph Adams 1863-1942 ... TCLC 45
Cramer, Clarence H(enley) 1905-1982 ... CANR-9
Earlier sketch in CA 13-16R
Cramer, George H. 1913- ... 21-24R
Cramer, Harold 1927- ... 29-32R
Cramer, J(an) S(olomon) 1928- ... 29-32R
Cramer, James 1915- ... 21-24R
Cramer, John F. 1913(?)-1989 Obituary ... 128
Cramer, John Francis 1899-1967 ... CAP-1
Earlier sketch in CA 17-18
Cramer, Kathryn 1943- ... 25-28R
Cramer, Richard L(ouis) 1947- ... 102
Cramer, Richard S(eldon) 1928- ... 29-32R
Cramer, Stanley H. 1933- ... 29-32R
Cramp, H(arold) St. G(eorge) 1912- ... 130
Cramp, Rosemary (Jean) 1929- ... 121
Crampton, C(harles) Gregory 1911- ... 21-24R
Crampton, Georgia Ronan 1925- ... 57-60
Crampton, Helen
See Chesney, Marion
Crampton, Roger C. 1929- ... 33-36R
Cranbrook, James L.
See Edwards, William B(ennett)
Cranch, Christopher Pearse
1813-1892 ... DLB 1, 42
Crandall, James E(dward) 1930- ... 41-44R
Crandall, Joy
See Martin, Joy
Crandall, Norma 1907- ... 69-72
Crandall, Robert Warren 1940- ... 124
Crandell, Anne (Elizabeth) Shaver
See Shaver-Crandell, Anne (Elizabeth)
Crandell, Richard F. 1901-1974 Obituary ... 53-56
Crane, Alex
See Wilkes-Hunter, R(ichard)
Crane, Barbara (Joyce) 1934- ... CANR-29
Earlier sketch in CA 107
See also SATA 31
Crane, Bill
See Crane, William B.
Crane, Caroline 1930- ... CANR-19
Earlier sketches in CA 9-12R, CANR-3
See also SATA 11
Crane, Catherine C(owle) 1940- ... 101
Crane, Diana 1933- ... 89-92
Crane, Donald P(aul) 1933- ... 61-64
Crane, (Lauren) Edgar 1917- ... 17-20R
Crane, Edna Temple
See Eicher, (Ethel) Elizabeth
Crane, Elaine Forman 1939- ... 122
Crane, Frank H. 1912- ... 89-92
Crane, (Harold) Hart 1899-1932 ... 127
Brief entry ... 104
See also CDALB 1917-1929
See also DLB 4, 48
See also MTCW
See also PC 3
See also TCLC 2, 5
See also WLC
Crane, Hewitt D(avid) 1927- ... 116
Crane, Jacob L(eslie) 1892-1988 Obituary ... 125
Crane, James G(ordon) 1927- ... 13-16R
Crane, Jim
See Crane, James G(ordon)
Crane, Joan St. C(lair) 1927- ... 73-76
Crane, Julia G(orham) 1925- ... 41-44R
Crane, M. A.
See Wartski, Maureen (Ann Crane)
Crane, Milton 1917-1985 Obituary ... 117
Crane, Morley Benjamin
1890-1983 Obituary ... 110
Crane, Philip Miller 1930- ... 9-12R
Crane, R(onald) S(almon) 1886-1967 ... 85-88
See also CLC 27
See also DLB 63
Crane, Richard (Arthur) 1944- ... 77-80
Crane, Robert
See Glemser, Bernard
and Robertson, Frank C(hester)
and Sellers, Con(nie Leslie Jr.)
Crane, Robert Dickson 1929- ... 81-84
Crane, Royston Campbell
1901-1977 Obituary ... 89-92
See also SATA 22
Crane, Stephen (Townley)
1871-1900 Brief entry ... 109
See also CDALB 1865-1917
See also DLB 12, 54, 78
See also SSC 7
See also TCLC 11, 17, 32
See also WLC
See also YABC 2
Crane, Sylvia E(ngel) 1918- ... 33-36R
Crane, Theodore Rawson 1929- ... 97-100
Crane, Verner W(inslow)
1889-1974 Obituary ... 113

Crane, Walter 1845-1915 .... MAICYA
See also SATA 18
Crane, Wilder (Willard) 1928- 45-48
Crane, William B. 1904-1981 107
Crane, William D(wight) 1892- 5-8R
See also SATA 1
Crane, William Earl 1899- 103
Cranfield, Charles E(rnest) B(urland)
1915- CANR-18
Earlier sketches in CA 5-8R, CANR-2
Cranfield, Geoffrey Alan 1920- 5-8R
Cranford, Clarence William 1906- 1-4R
Cranford, Robert J(oshua) 1908- CAP-2
Earlier sketch in CA 17-18
Cranin, A(braham) Norman 1927- 73-76
Cranko, John 1927-1973 Obituary 45-48
Crankshaw, Edward 1909-1984 ....CANR-23
Obituary 114
Earlier sketch in CA 25-28R
Cranny, Titus (Francis) 1921-1981 ....CANR-27
Earlier sketch in CA 25-28R
Cranor, Phoebe 1923- 112
Cranshaw, Stanley
See Fisher, Dorothy (Frances) Canfield
Cranston, Edward
See Fairchild, William
Cranston, Maurice (William) 1920- CANR-3
Earlier sketch in CA 5-8R
Cranston, Mechthild 53-56
Cranstone, B(ryan) A(llan) L(efevre)
1918-1989 Obituary 129
Cranton, Elmer M(itchell) 1932- 118
Cranwell, John Philips 1904- 61-64
Crapanzano, Vincent 1939- CANR-5
Earlier sketch in CA 53-56
Crapol, Edward P(aul) 1936- 45-48
Crapps, Robert W. 1925- 53-56
Crapsey, Adelaide 1878-1914 .... DLB 54
Crary, Catherine S. 1909- CAP-1
Earlier sketch in CA 13-16
Crary, Elizabeth (Ann) 1942- .... SATA 43
Crary, Margaret (Coleman) 1906- 5-8R
See also SATA 9
Crary, Ryland W(esley)
1913-1984 Obituary 113
Crase, Douglas 1944- 106
See also CLC 58
Crasweller, Robert D. 1915- 21-24R
Craster, John Montagu 1901-1975 Obituary 108
Crathern, Alice Tarbell 1894-1973 Obituary 110
Craton, Michael (John) 1931- 41-44R
Cratty, Bryant J. 1929- CANR-11
Earlier sketch in CA 25-28R
Craven, Avery (Odelle)
1885(?)-1980 Obituary 113
See also DLB 17
Craven, George M(ilton) 1929- 61-64
Craven, Margaret 1901-1980 103
See also CLC 17
Craven, Roy C. Jr. 1924- 69-72
Craven, Thomas 1889-1969 97-100
See also SATA 22
Craven, Wayne 1930- 127
Craven, Wes(ley Earl) 1939- 137
See also AAYA 6
Craven, Wesley Frank (Jr.) 1905-1981 61-64
Obituary 103
Cravens, Gwyneth 85-88
Cravens, Hamilton 1938- 103
Craveri, Marcello 1914- 21-24R
Crawells, Carl
See Herm, Gerhard
Crawford, Alan 1953- 101
Crawford, Ann Fears 1932- CANR-9
Earlier sketch in CA 21-24R
Crawford, Bill
See Crawford, William Hulfish
Crawford, C(harles) Merle 1924- 45-48
Crawford, Char 1935- 57-60
Crawford, Charles F. Obituary 109
Crawford, Charles O(len) 1934- 37-40R
Crawford, Charles P. 1945- CANR-24
Earlier sketch in CA 45-48
See also SATA 28
Crawford, Charles W(ann) 1931- CANR-8
Earlier sketch in CA 61-64
Crawford, Charles 1752-1815(?) .... DLB 31
Crawford, Cheryl 1902-1986 Obituary 120
Brief entry 112
Crawford, Christina 1939- 85-88
Crawford, Clan Jr. 1927- 57-60
Crawford, Daniel J. 1942- 136
Crawford, David
See Kettelhack, Guy
Crawford, David L.
1890(?)-1974 Obituary 45-48
Crawford, Dean (Adams) 1949- 127
Crawford, Deborah 1922- 49-52
See also SATA 6
Crawford, Donald W(esley) 1938- 45-48
Crawford, F(rancis) Marion
1854-1909 Brief entry 107
See also DLB 71
See also TCLC 10
Crawford, Fred D. 1947- 117
Crawford, Fred Roberts 1924- CANR-2
Earlier sketch in CA 45-48
Crawford, Hank
See Rummel, (Louis) Jack(son)
Crawford, Iain (Padruig) 1922- CANR-23
Earlier sketch in CA 1-4R
Crawford, Isabella Valancy 1850-1887 ..... DLB 92
Crawford, James M. 1925- 89-92
Crawford, Jean 1907(?)-1976 Obituary 104
Crawford, Jerry L(eroy) 1934- 106
Crawford, Joan
See Le Sueur, Lucille
Crawford, Joanna 1941- 9-12R
Crawford, John E(dmund) 1904-1971 .... CAP-2
Earlier sketch in CA 17-18
See also SATA 3
Crawford, John R. 1915(?)-1976 Obituary 65-68
Crawford, John Richard 1932- 106
Crawford, John S(herman) 1928- 106
Crawford, John W(illiam) 1914- CANR-30
Earlier sketch in CA 1-4R
Crawford, John W(illiam) 1936- CANR-4
Earlier sketch in CA 53-56
Crawford, Joyce 1931- 25-28R
Crawford, Kenneth G(ale) 1902-1983 81-84
Obituary 108
Crawford, Linda 1938- CANR-23
Earlier sketch in CA 65-68
Crawford, Marion (Kirk)
1910(?)-1988 Obituary 124
Crawford, Matsu W(offord) 1902- CAP-2
Earlier sketch in CA 17-18
Crawford, Max 1938- 77-80
Crawford, Mel 1925- ....SATA 33, 44
Crawford, Oliver 1917- 85-88
Crawford, Patricia 103
Crawford, Phyllis 1899- .... SATA 3
Crawford, Richard (Arthur) 1935- CANR-9
Earlier sketch in CA 57-60
Crawford, Robert
See Rae, Hugh C(rauford)
Crawford, Robert Platt 1893- CAP-2
Earlier sketch in CA 17-18
Crawford, Stanley (Gottlieb) 1937- 69-72
Crawford, T(erence Gordon) S(harman)
1945- 29-32R
Crawford, Tad 1946- 133
Brief entry 114
Crawford, Terrence Michael 1945-
See Crawford, Terry
Crawford, Terry 129
See also Crawford, Terrence Michael
Crawford, Thelmar Wyche 1905- 1-4R
Crawford, Theresa 1956- 110
Crawford, Thomas 1920- 128
Crawford, Vaughn Emerson
1917(?)-1981 Obituary 104
Crawford, Vernon (E.) 1946- 136
Crawford, Walter B(yron) 1919- 116
Crawford, William (Elbert) 1929- CANR-4
Earlier sketch in CA 1-4R
Crawford, William H.
1907(?)-1973 Obituary 104
Crawford, William Hulfish
1913-1982 Obituary 105
Crawford, William P(atrick) 1922- 106
Crawley, Aidan Merivale 1908- 61-64
Crawley, Alan 1887-1975 .... DLB 68
Crawley, C(harles) W(illiam) 1899- 109
Crawley, Gerard M(arcus) 1938- 106
Crawley, Harriet 1948- 134
Crawley, Thomas Edward 1920- 111
Crawley, Tony 1938- 129
Cray, Ed(ward) 1933- CANR-37
Earlier sketches in CA 81-84, CANR-16
Crayder, Dorothy 33-36R
See also SATA 7
Crayder, Teresa
See Colman, Hila
Crayon, Geoffrey
See Irving, Washington
Crayon, Porte
See Strother, David Hunter
Craz, Albert G. 1926- CANR-8
Earlier sketch in CA 17-20R
See also SATA 24
Creager, Alfred L(eon) 1910- 17-20R
Creagh, Patrick 1930- CANR-18
Earlier sketch in CA 25-28R
Creagh-Osborne, Richard 1928- CANR-7
Earlier sketch in CA 9-12R
Creamer, J. Shane 1929- Brief entry 116
Creamer, Robert W. 1922- 21-24R
Crean, John Edward Jr. 1939- 41-44R
Crean, Patrick (G.) 1949- 123
Creasey, John 1908-1973 ....CANR-8
Obituary 41-44R
Earlier sketch in CA 5-8R
See also CLC 11
See also DLB 77
See also MTCW
Creasy, Robert K(enwood) 1934- 118
Creasy, Rosalind R. CANR-28
Earlier sketch in CA 110
Creaturo, Barbara 1943-1990 129
Obituary 132
Crechales, Anthony George 1926- 29-32R
Crechales, Tony
See Crechales, Anthony George
Crecine, John Patrick 1939- CANR-7
Earlier sketch in CA 57-60
Crecy, Jeanne
See Williams, Jeanne
Credland, Peter (Francis) 1946- 69-72
Credle, Ellis 1902- CANR-9
Earlier sketch in CA 13-16R
See also SATA 1
Credo
See Creasey, John
Credo, Alvaro J. de
See Prado (Calvo), Pedro
Creed, David
See Guthrie, James Shields
Creekmore, Betsey B(eeler) 1915- 69-72
Creekmore, Mildred C.
1905(?)-1987 Obituary 123
Creel, George 1876-1953 Brief entry 115
See also DLB 25
Creel, Herrlee G(lessner) 1905- 85-88
Creel, Stephen Melville 1938- 69-72
Creeley, Robert (White) 1926- CANR-23
Earlier sketch in CA 1-4R
See also CAAS 10
See also CLC 1, 2, 4, 8, 11, 15, 36
See also DLB 5, 16
See also MTCW
Creelman, James 1859-1915 .... DLB 23
Creelman, Marjorie B(roer) 1908- CAP-2
Earlier sketch in CA 21-22
Creer, Thomas L(aselle) 1934- CANR-22
Earlier sketch in CA 69-72
Creese, Bethea CANR-5
Earlier sketch in CA 9-12R
Creese, Walter L(ittlefield) 1919- 125
Creeth, Edmund Homer 1928- 102
Creevey, Lucy E. 1940- 29-32R
Crefeld, Donna Carolyn Anders
See Anders, Donna Carolyn
Cregan, David (Appleton Quartus)
1931- CANR-1
Earlier sketch in CA 45-48
See also DLB 13
Creger, Ralph (Clinton) 1914- 13-16R
Cregier, Don M(esick) 1930- 69-72
Crehan, Stewart 1942- 118
Crehan, Thomas 1919- CANR-2
Earlier sketch in CA 5-8R
Creigh, Dorothy (Weyer) 1921- 105
Creighton, Basil 1885-1969 Obituary 128
Creighton, Don
See Drury, Maxine Cole
Creighton, Donald Grant 1902-1979 101
Obituary 93-96
See also DLB 88
Creighton, Helen (Evelyn) 1914- 33-36R
Creighton, (Mary) Helen 1899-1989 ....41-44R
Obituary 130
See also SATO 64
Creighton, Joanne V(anish) 1942- 69-72
Creighton, Luella Bruce 1901- CAP-1
Earlier sketch in CA 17-18
Creighton, Thomas H(awk) 1904-1984 .....CANR-6
Obituary 114
Earlier sketch in CA 5-8R
Creighton, Thomas 1915(?)-1987 Obituary 123
Crellin, John 1916- 69-72
Cremazie, Octave 1827-1879 .... DLB 99
Cremeans, Charles D(avis) 1915- 5-8R
Cremer, Jan 1940- 13-16R
Cremer, Robert Roger 1947- 61-64
Cremer, Robert Wyndham Ketton
See Ketton-Cremer, Robert Wyndham
Cremer, Victoriano 1909(?)- .... DLB 108
Cremin, Lawrence A(rthur)
1925-1990 ....CANR-29
Obituary 132
Earlier sketch in CA 33-36R
Crena de Iongh, Mary (Dows Herter Norton)
1894(?)-1985 Obituary 116
Crena de Iongh, Daniel 1888-1970 .... CAP-2
Obituary 29-32R
Earlier sketch in CA 25-28
Crenna, C. David 1944- 128
Crennen, Robert Earl 1929-1984 Obituary 112
Crenner, James 1938- 13-16R
Crenshaw, James L. 1934- CANR-34
Earlier sketches in CA 37-40R, CANR-14
Crenshaw, Mary Ann CANR-8
Earlier sketch in CA 57-60
Crepeau, Richard C(harles) 1941- 105
Crescas, Hasdai 1340(?)-1412(?) .... DLB 115
Cressey, Donald R(ay) 1919-1987 ....CANR-6
Obituary 123
Earlier sketch in CA 13-16R
Cressey, William W. 1939- 33-36R
Cresson, Bruce Collins 1930- 45-48
Cresswell, Helen 1934- CANR-37
Earlier sketches in CA 17-20R, CANR-8
See also CLR 18
See also MAICYA
See also SATA 1, 48
Cresswell, Jasmine (Rosemary)
1941- CANR-29
Earlier sketch in CA 110
Cressy, David 1946- 130
Creston, Dormer
See Colston-Baynes, Dorothy
Creswell, K(eppel) A(rchibald) C(ameron)
1879- CAP-1
Earlier sketch in CA 9-10
Cretan, Gladys (Yessayan) 1921- 29-32R
See also SATA 2
Cretcher, Dorothy 1934- 112
Cretzmeyer, F(rancis) X(avier) Jr. 1913- 13-16R
Crevecoeur, Michel Guillaume Jean de
1735-1813 .... DLB 37
Crew, Francis Albert Eley 1888-1973 .... CAP-2
Earlier sketch in CA 17-18
Crew, Helen (Cecilia) Coale
1866-1941 Brief entry 121
See also YABC 2
Crew, Linda 1951- 130
See also SATA 71
Crew, Louie 1936- 81-84
Crewdson, John (Mark) 1945- 132
Brief entry 128
Crewe, Candida 1964- 135
Crewe, Jonathan V(ere) 1941- 116
Crews, Clyde F. 1944- CANR-38
Earlier sketch in CA 116
Crews, Donald 108
See also CLR 7
See also MAICYA
See also SATA 30, 32
Crews, Frederick C(ampbell) 1933- CANR-1
Earlier sketch in CA 1-4R
Crews, Harry (Eugene) 1935- CANR-20
Earlier sketch in CA 25-28R
See also AITN 1
See also CLC 6, 23, 49
See also DLB 6
See also MTCW
Crews, Judson (Campbell) 1917- CANR-24
Earlier sketches in CA 13-16R, CANR-7
See also CAAS 14
Crews, William J. 1931- 25-28R
Cribb, Larry 1934- 109
Cribb, Robert (Bridson) 1957- 137
Cribbet, John E(dward) 1918- 17-20R
Cribbin, James J(oseph) 1915- 121
Crichton, James Dunlop 1907- CANR-5
Earlier sketch in CA 13-16R
Crichton, Jennifer 1957- 123
Crichton, John 1916- 17-20R
Crichton, Kyle Samuel
1896-1960 Obituary 89-92
Crichton, (John) Michael 1942- CANR-13
Earlier sketch in CA 25-28R
See also AITN 2
See also CLC 2, 6, 54
See also DLBY 81
See also MTCW
See also SATA 9
Crichton, Robert 1925- 17-20R
See also AITN 1
Crichton, Ronald 1913- 128
Crick, Bernard (Rowland) 1929- CANR-5
Earlier sketch in CA 1-4R
Crick, Donald Herbert 1916- 102
Crick, Francis (Harry Compton) 1916- 121
Brief entry 113
Crick, Michael (Lawrence) 1958- 118
Criddle, Joan D(ewey) 1935- 126
Criden, Joseph 1916- 77-80
Criden, Yosef
See Criden, Joseph
Crider, (Allen) Bill(y) 1941- CANR-30
Earlier sketch in CA 112
Cridland, Nancy C. 1932- 111
Crighton, John C(lark) 1903- 33-36R
Crighton, Richard E. 1921- 109
Crile, Barney
See Crile, George Jr.
Crile, George Jr. 1907- 89-92
Crim, Keith R(enn) 1924- 29-32R
Crim, Mort 1935- 41-44R
Crimmins, James Custis 1935- CANR-11
Earlier sketch in CA 5-8R
Crinkley, Richmond (Dillard) 1940-1989 .....29-32R
Obituary 127
Cripe, Helen 1932- CANR-8
Earlier sketch in CA 61-64
Cripps, (Matthew) Anthony (Leonard)
1913- 13-16R
Cripps, L(ouise) L(ilian) 1914- 97-100
Cripps, Thomas (Robert) 1932- 97-100
Crisler, Fritz
See Crisler, Herbert Orin
Crisler, Herbert Orin 1899-1982 Obituary 107
Crisler, Lois (Brown) Obituary 104
Crisp, Anthony Thomas 1937- 101
Crisp, C(olin) G(odfrey) 1936- 37-40R
Crisp, Frank R(obson) 1915- 9-12R
Crisp, Norman James 1923- 93-96
Crisp, Quentin 1908- 116
Brief entry 109
Crisp, Robert (James) 1-4R
Crisp, Tony
See Crisp, Anthony Thomas
Crispin, A(nn) C(arol) 1950- CANR-32
Earlier sketch in CA 113
Crispin, Edmund
See Montgomery, (Robert) Bruce
See also CLC 22
See also DLB 87
Crispin, John 1936- 53-56
Crispin, Ruth Helen Katz 1940- 93-96
Crispo, John 1933- 37-40R
Crissey, Elwell 1899- CAP-2
Earlier sketch in CA 23-24
Crist, Judith (Klein) 1922- CANR-17
Earlier sketch in CA 81-84
See also AITN 1
Crist, Lyle M(artin) 1924- 53-56
Crist, Raymond E. 1904- 73-76
Crist, Steven G(ordon) 1956- 101
Cristabel
See Abrahamsen, Christine Elizabeth
Cristina, Frank
See Laughlin, Tom
Cristina, Teresa
See Laughlin, Tom
Cristofer, Michael 1945(?)- Brief entry 110
See also CLC 28
See also DLB 7
Cristol, Vivian 17-20R
Cristy, Ann
See Mittermeyer, Helen (Hayton Monteith)
Cristy, R. J.
See De Cristoforo, R(omeo) J(ohn)
Criswell, Cloyd M. 1908- CAP-1
Earlier sketch in CA 17-18
Criswell, W(allie) A(mos) 1909- 17-20R
Critchfield, Howard J(ohn) 1920- 53-56
Critchfield, Richard (Patrick) 1931- CANR-16
Earlier sketch in CA 41-44R
Critchley, Edmund M(ichael) R(hys)
1931- 21-24R
Critchley, Julian (Michael Gordon) 1930- 85-88
Critchley, Lynne
See Radford, Richard F(rancis) Jr.
Critchley, T(homas) A(lan) 1919-1991 ....29-32R
Obituary 134

Crites, Ronald W(ayne) 1945- CANR-18
Earlier sketch in CA 102
Crites, Stephen D(ecatur) 1931- 41-44R
Critic
See Martin, (Basil) Kingsley
Criticus
See Harcourt, Melville
and Roe, F(rederic) Gordon
Crittenden, Mabel (Buss) 1917- 103
Crnjanski, Milos 1893- CAP-1
Earlier sketch in CA 9-10
Croall, Jonathan 1941- 130
Crobaugh, Emma ....AITN 2
Croce, Arlene 1934- 104
Croce, Benedetto 1866-1952 Brief entry 120
See also TCLC 37
Crocetti, Guido M. 1920-1979 85-88
Crock, Stan 1950- 134
Crocker, Helen Bartter 1929- 69-72
Crocker, Lester G(ilbert) 1912- CANR-5
Earlier sketch in CA 5-8R
Crocker, Lionel (George) 1897- CAP-2
Earlier sketch in CA 25-28
Crocker, Mary Wallace 1941- 93-96
Crocker, Thomas Dunstan
1936- Brief entry 108
Crocker, Walter Russell 1902- 17-20R
Crockett, Albert Stevens
1873-1969 Obituary 89-92
Crockett, Christina
See Gray, Linda Crockett
Crockett, David 1786-1836 .... DLB 3, 11
Crockett, Davy
See Crockett, David
Crockett, G(eorge) Ronald 1906- CAP-1
Earlier sketch in CA 11-12
Crockett, H(arold) Dale 1933- 111
Crockett, James Underwood
1915-1979 ....CANR-13
Obituary 89-92
Earlier sketch in CA 33-36R
Crockett, S(amuel) R(utherford)
1860-1914 Brief entry 116
Crocombe, Ronald G(ordon) 1929- 13-16R
Crofford, Emily (Ardell) 1927- 107
See also SATA 61
Crofford, Lena H(enrichson) 1908- CAP-1
Earlier sketch in CA 9-10
Croft, Julian (Charles Basset) 1941- 124
Croft, Michael (John) 1922-1986 Obituary 121
Croft, Peter John 1929-1984 122
Obituary 114
Croft, Sutton
See Lunn, Arnold
Croft-Cooke, Rupert 1903-1979 ....CANR-4
Obituary 89-92
Earlier sketch in CA 9-12R
See also Bruce, Leo
Croft-Murray, Edward 1907-1980 Obituary 102
Crofton, Denis Hayes 1908- 109
Crofts, Freeman Wills
1879-1957 Brief entry 115
See also DLB 77
Crofts, John E(rnest) V(ictor) 1887-1972 .... CAP-2
Earlier sketch in CA 25-28
Crofts, William 137
Crofut, William E. III 1934- 25-28R
See also SATA 23
Crohn, Burrill B(ernard)
1884-1983 Obituary 110
Croise, Jacques
See Schakovskoy, Zinaida
Croizier, Ralph 1935- 61-64
Croker, John Wilson 1780-1857 .... DLB 110
Croll, Carolyn 1945- 123
See also SATA 52, 56
Croly, Herbert 1869-1930 .... DLB 91
Croly, Jane Cunningham
1829(?)-1901 Brief entry 118
See also DLB 23
Croman, Dorothy Young
See Rosenberg, Dorothy
Cromie, Alice Hamilton 1914- CANR-3
Earlier sketch in CA 9-12R
See also SATA 24
Cromie, Robert (Allen) 1909- CANR-16
Earlier sketches in CA 1-4R, CANR-1
Cromie, William J(oseph) 1930- 13-16R
See also SATA 4
Crommelynck, Fernand
1885-1970 Obituary 89-92
Crompton, Anne Eliot 1930- CANR-13
Earlier sketch in CA 33-36R
See also SATA 23
Crompton, John
See Lamburn, John Battersby Crompton
Crompton, Louis (William) 1925- 33-36R
Crompton, Margaret (Norah Mair) 1901- CAP-1
Earlier sketch in CA 13-14
Crompton, Richmal
See Lamburn, Richmal Crompton
Cromwell, Chester R. 1925- 89-92
Cromwell, Elsie
See Lee, Elsie
Cromwell, Harvey 1907-1977 ....17-20R
Obituary 134
Cromwell, James H(enry) R(oberts)
1897(?)-1990 Obituary 131
Cromwell, John 1887-1979 Obituary 89-92
Cromwell, John 1914(?)-1979 Obituary 89-92
Cromwell, Link
See Kaye, Lenny
Cromwell, Richard Sidney 1925- 53-56
Cronbach, Abraham 1882-1965 ....1-4R
See also SATA 11
Crone, Alla 1923- 113
Crone, G(erald) R(oe) 1899-1982 121
Crone, Moira 1952- 125
Crone, (Hans-) Rainer 1942- CANR-14
Earlier sketch in CA 33-36R
Crone, Ruth 1919- 9-12R
See also SATA 4
Cronenberg, David 1943- 138
Croner, Helga 1914- 107
Croner, John A(lton) 1916- 121
Cronin, A(rchibald) J(oseph)
1896-1981 ....CANR-5
Obituary 102
Earlier sketch in CA 1-4R
See also CLC 32
See also SATA 25, 47
Cronin, Anthony 1926- 137
Cronin, Audrey Kurth 1958- 125
Cronin, George 1933- 101
Cronin, James E(mmet) 1908- CANR-24
Earlier sketch in CA 45-48
Cronin, John F(rancis) 1908- 37-40R
Cronin, Joseph M(arr) 1935- CANR-31
Earlier sketch in CA 49-52
Cronin, Sylvia 1929- 89-92
Cronin, Thomas E(dward) 1940- CANR-20
Earlier sketch in CA 85-88
Cronin, Vincent (Archibald Patrick)
1924- CANR-5
Earlier sketch in CA 9-12R
Cronkhite, Bernice Brown
1893-1983 Obituary 110
Cronkite, Walter (Leland Jr.) 1916- CANR-37
Earlier sketch in CA 69-72
See also AITN 1, 2
Cronley, Jay 1943- 81-84
Cronne, H(enry) A(lfred) 1904- 65-68
Cronon, E(dmund) David 1924- CANR-1
Earlier sketch in CA 1-4R
Cronon, William (John) 1954- 111
Cronus, Diodorus
See Taylor, Richard
Cronyn, Hume 1911- 123
Crook, Bette (Jean) 1921- 73-76
Crook, Beverly Courtney 115
See also SATA 35, 38
Crook, Compton Newby 1908- 121
Crook, D(avid) P(aul) 1937- 128
Crook, David 1910- 97-100
Crook, Howard (Hawthorne) 1937- 107
Crook, Isabel 1915- 97-100
Crook, J(ohn) A(nthony) 1921- 21-24R
Crook, J(oseph) Mordaunt 1937- 41-44R
Crook, Margaret Brackenbury 1886- CAP-1
Earlier sketch in CA 13-16
Crook, Roger H(awley) 1921- CANR-4
Earlier sketch in CA 1-4R
Crook, W. Melvin 1912(?)-1984 Obituary 112
Crook, William G. 1917- 129
Crook, William 1933- 102
Crookall, Robert 1890-1981 ....CANR-30
Earlier sketch in CA 33-36R
Crookenden, Napier 1915- CANR-11
Earlier sketch in CA 69-72
Crooks, James B(enedict) 1933- 25-28R
Cropp, Ben(jamin) 1936- 33-36R
Cropper, Margaret 1886-1980 Obituary 102
Crosbie, John S(haver) 1920- CANR-12
Earlier sketch in CA 73-76
Crosbie, (Hugh) Provan 1912- 9-12R
Crosbie, Sylvia Kowitt 1938- 73-76
Crosby, Alexander L. 1906-1980 ....29-32R
Obituary 93-96
See also SATA 2, 23
Crosby, Alfred W. Jr. 1931- 17-20R
Crosby, Bing
See Crosby, Harry Lillis
Crosby, (Mary Jacob) Caresse
1892-1970 Obituary 25-28R
See also DLB 4, 48
Crosby, Donald A(llen) 1932- 53-56
Crosby, Donald F(rancis) 1933- 77-80
Crosby, Faye J. 1947- CANR-36
Earlier sketch in CA 114
Crosby, Harry H(erbert) 1919- CANR-5
Earlier sketch in CA 13-16R
Crosby, Harry Lillis 1904-1977 Obituary 73-76
Crosby, Harry 1898-1929 Brief entry 107
See also DLB 4, 48
Crosby, Henry Grew
See Crosby, Harry
Crosby, Henry Sturgis
See Crosby, Harry
Crosby, Jackie
See Crosby, Jacqueline Garton
Crosby, Jacqueline Garton 1961- 133
Crosby, James O('Hea) 1924- 89-92
Crosby, Jeremiah
See Crosby, Michael (Hugh)
Crosby, John (Campbell) 1912-1991 ....CANR-4
Obituary 135
Earlier sketch in CA 1-4R
Crosby, John F. 1931- CANR-7
Earlier sketch in CA 17-20R
Crosby, Michael (Hugh) 1940- CANR-11
Earlier sketch in CA 17-20R
Crosby, Muriel (Estelle) 1908- 17-20R
Crosby, Philip B(ayard) 1926- 73-76
Crosby, Ruth 1897- 49-52
Crosby, Sumner McK(night) 1909-1982 ....13-16R
Obituary 108
Crosby, Theo 1925- 133
Crosher, G. R. 69-72
See also SATA 14
Crosland, Andrew T(ate) 1944- 53-56
Crosland, (Charles) Anthony (Raven)
1918-1977 73-76
Obituary 69-72
Crosland, Margaret 1920- CANR-21
Earlier sketches in CA 49-52, CANR-1
Cross, Aleene (Ann) 1922- CANR-26
Earlier sketch in CA 29-32R
Cross, Amanda
See Heilbrun, Carolyn G(old)
Cross, Anthony (Glenn) 1936- CANR-17
Earlier sketch in CA 37-40R
Cross, (Alan) Beverley 1931- 102
Cross, Claire 1932- 21-24R
Cross, Colin (John) 1928-1985 ....CANR-7
Obituary 118
Earlier sketch in CA 9-12R
Cross, Donna Woolfolk 1947- 97-100
Cross, Frank Moore Jr. 1921- 65-68
Cross, Gary Scott 1946- 115
Cross, George Lynn 1905- 125
Cross, Gilbert B. 1939- CANR-23
Earlier sketch in CA 105
See also SATA 51, 60
Cross, Gillian (Clare) 1945- CANR-38
Earlier sketch in CA 111
See also CLR 28
See also MAICYA
See also SATA 38, 70, 71
Cross, Helen Reeder
See Broadhead, Helen Cross
Cross, Herbert James 1934- 45-48
Cross, Ira Brown 1880-1977 Obituary 106
Cross, James
See Parry, Hugh J(ones)
Cross, Jennifer 1932- 29-32R
Cross, John Keir 1914-1967 73-76
Cross, John R(ay) 1939- 120
Cross, K(enneth) G(ustav) W(alter)
1927-1967 .... CAP-1
Earlier sketch in CA 13-16
Cross, K(athryn) Patricia 1926- CANR-13
Earlier sketch in CA 33-36R
Cross, Leslie (Frank) 1909-1977 65-68
Obituary 89-92
Cross, M. Claire
See Cross, Claire
Cross, Milton (John) 1897-1975 Obituary 53-56
Cross, Nigel 1942- CANR-38
Earlier sketch in CA 116
Cross, Ralph D(onald) 1931- CANR-17
Earlier sketch in CA 93-96
Cross, Richard K(eith) 1940- CANR-12
Earlier sketch in CA 33-36R
Cross, Richard 1950(?)-1983 Obituary 110
Cross, Robert Brandt 1914- 37-40R
Cross, Robert Dougherty 1924- 1-4R
Cross, Robert Singlehurst 1925- 5-8R
Cross, (Alfred) Rupert (Neal)
1912-1980 Obituary 102
Cross, (Alfred) Rupert (Neale) 1912-1980 105
Cross, Samuel S(tephen) 1919- 45-48
Cross, Sister Mary Francilda
1902(?)-1984 Obituary 114
Cross, Stewart
See Drago, Harry Sinclair
Cross, T. T.
See da Cruz, Daniel Jr.
Cross, Theodore L(amont) 1924- CANR-27
Earlier sketch in CA 45-48
Cross, Thomas B. 1949- 123
Cross, Victor
See Coffman, Virginia (Edith)
Cross, Wilbur Lucius III 1918- CANR-2
Earlier sketch in CA 1-4R
See also SATA 2
Crossan, Darryl
See Smith, Richard Rein
Crosscountry
See Campbell, Thomas F.
Crossen, Ken
See Crossen, Kendell Foster
Crossen, Kendell Foster 1910- CANR-4
Earlier sketch in CA 1-4R
See also Foster, Richard
Crosser, Paul K. 1902-1976 ....CANR-3
Earlier sketch in CA 1-4R
Crossette, George 1910-1984 Obituary 114
Crosskill, W. E. 1904- 129
Crossley, Archibald M(addock)
1896-1985 Obituary 116
Crossley, Robert 1945- 127
Crossley-Holland, Kevin 1941- 41-44R
See also DLB 40
See also MAICYA
See also SATA 5
Crossman, Richard (Howard Stafford)
1907-1974 61-64
Obituary 49-52
Croteau, John T(ougas) 1910- 9-12R
Crothers, George D. 1909- CAP-1
Earlier sketch in CA 13-16
Crothers, J(essie) Frances 1913- 33-36R
Crothers, Jessie F.
See Crothers, J(essie) Frances
Crothers, Rachel 1878(?)-1958 Brief entry 113
See also DLB 7
See also TCLC 19
Crotty, William J(oseph) 1936- CANR-13
Earlier sketch in CA 21-24R
Crouch, Bill Jr.
See Crouch, William Maxwell Jr.
Crouch, David 1948- 129
Crouch, Harold (Arthur) 1940- CANR-15
Earlier sketch in CA 89-92
Crouch, Marcus 1913- CANR-23
Earlier sketches in CA 9-12R, CANR-5
See also SATA 4
Crouch, Steve 1915-1983 ....CANR-9
Obituary 109
Earlier sketch in CA 53-56
Crouch, Thomas W(illiam) 1932- 73-76
Crouch, Tom D. 1944- 106
Crouch, W(illiam) George (Alfred)
1903-1970 ....5-8R
Obituary 89-92
Crouch, William Maxwell Jr. 1945- 126
Crouch, Winston Winford 1907- Brief entry 106
Croucher, Michael 1930- 128
Croudace, Glynn 1917- 29-32R
Crouse, Russell M. 1893-1966 77-80
Obituary 25-28R
Crouse, Timothy 1947- 77-80
Crouse, William H(arry) 1907- CANR-6
Earlier sketch in CA 5-8R
Crout, George C(lement) 1917- CANR-11
Earlier sketch in CA 29-32R
See also SATA 11
Crout, Robert Rhodes 1946- 116
Crouzet, Francois Marie-Joseph
1922- CANR-19
Earlier sketches in CA 9-12R, CANR-3
Croves, Hal
See Traven, B.
Crovitz, Herbert F(loyd) 1932- 29-32R
Crow, Alice (von Bauer) 1894-1966 .... CAP-1
Earlier sketch in CA 13-16
Crow, C(harles) P(atrick) 1938- 102
Crow, Charles L(loyd) 1940- 112
Crow, Donna Fletcher 1941- CANR-25
Earlier sketch in CA 108
See also SATA 40
Crow, Duncan 1920- 85-88
Crow, Elizabeth Smith 1946- 103
Crow, Francis Luther
See Luther, Frank
Crow, Jeffrey J(ay) 1947- CANR-19
Earlier sketch in CA 85-88
Crow, John A(rmstrong) 1906- 13-16R
Crow, Lester D(onald) 1897-1983 .... CAP-1
Obituary 110
Earlier sketch in CA 13-16
Crow, Mark (Alan) 1948- 57-60
Crow, Martin M(ichael) 1901- CAP-2
Earlier sketch in CA 19-20
Crow, Mary 1933- 138
Crow, William Bernard 1895-1976 .... CAP-1
Obituary 65-68
Earlier sketch in CA 13-14
Crowbate, Ophelia Mae
See Smith, C. U.
Crowcroft, Andrew 1923- 21-24R
Crowcroft, Jane
See Crowcroft, Peter
Crowcroft, Peter 1923- 101
Crowder, Christopher M. D. 1922- 103
Crowder, Herbert 1925- 127
Crowder, Michael 1934-1988 ....CANR-1
Obituary 126
Earlier sketch in CA 1-4R
Crowder, Richard (Henry) 1909- CAP-1
Earlier sketch in CA 17-18
Crowder, Robert G. 1939- 138
Crowe, Amanda Cockrell 1948- 101
Crowe, Bettina Lum 1911- 9-12R
See also SATA 6
Crowe, C. B.
See Gibson, Walter B(rown)
Crowe, Cecily (Teague) Brief entry 115
Crowe, Charles Monroe 1902-1978 ....1-4R
Obituary 103
Crowe, Charles 1928- 17-20R
Crowe, E. Odell 1925(?)-1983 Obituary 110
Crowe, F. J.
See Johnston, Jill
Crowe, Frederick Ernest 1915- CANR-29
Earlier sketch in CA 111
Crowe, Gregory D(ennis) 1963- 116
Crowe, John
See Lynds, Dennis
Crowe, Kenneth C(harles) 1934- 103
Crowe, Philip Kingsland 1908-1976 65-68
Obituary 69-72
Crowe, Robert L(ee) 1937- 69-72
Crowe, Sylvia 1901- CAP-1
Earlier sketch in CA 9-10
Crowe-Carraco, Carol 1943- 93-96
Crowell, George H. 1931- 25-28R
Crowell, Grace Noll 1877-1969 107
See also SATA 34
Crowell, Joan 1921- 57-60
Crowell, Muriel Beyea 1916- 57-60
Crowell, Norton B. 1914- 9-12R
Crowell, Pers 1910- 29-32R
See also SATA 2
Crowell, Robert Leland 1909- 109
See also SATA 63
Crowfield, Christopher
See Stowe, Harriet (Elizabeth) Beecher
Crowl, Philip A(xtell) 1914-1991 110
Obituary 134
Crowley, Aleister
See Crowley, Edward Alexander
See also TCLC 7
Crowley, Arthur McBlair 1945- 107
See also SATA 38
Crowley, Daniel J(ohn) 1921- CANR-9
Earlier sketch in CA 21-24R
Crowley, Diane 1939- 135
Crowley, Edward Alexander
1875-1947 Brief entry 104
See also Crowley, Aleister
Crowley, Ellen T(eresa) 1943- CANR-17
Earlier sketch in CA 97-100
Crowley, Frances G(eyer) 1921- 105
Crowley, George (David)
1913-1987 Obituary 123
Crowley, J(oseph) Donald 1932- 122

Crowley, James B. 1929- 21-24R
Crowley, John Edward 1943- 53-56
Crowley, John W(illiam) 1945- 69-72
Crowley, John 1942- 61-64
See also CLC 57
See also DLBY 82
See also SATA 65
Crowley, Mart 1935- 73-76
See also DLB 7
Crowley, Mary C. 1915- 97-100
Crowley, Raymond 1895-1982 Obituary 106
Crown, David A. 1928- CANR-10
Earlier sketch in CA 25-28R
Crown, Paul 1928- 17-20R
Crowne, John 1641-1712 .....DLB 80
Crownfield, Gertrude 1867-1945 .....YABC 1
Crowninshield, Frank 1872-1947 .....DLB 91
Crowson, P(aul) S(piller) 1913- 53-56
Crowther, Betty 1939- 61-64
Crowther, (Francis) Bosley
1905-1981 .....CANR-38
Obituary 103
Earlier sketch in CA 65-68
Crowther, Bruce (Ian) 1933- 128
Crowther, Duane S(wofford) 1934- CANR-17
Earlier sketch in CA 25-28R
Crowther, Geoffrey 1907-1972 Obituary 33-36R
Crowther, James Gerald 1899- 73-76
See also SATA 14
Crowther, Jean D(ecker) 1937- 120
Crowther, Wilma (Beryl) 1918-1989 .....5-8R
Obituary 128
Crowther-Hunt, Norman Crowther
1920-1987 133
Obituary 121
Croxford, Leslie 1944- 81-84
Croxton, Anthony H(ugh) 1902- 61-64
Croxton, Frederick E(mory) 1899-1991 .....CAP-2
Obituary 133
Earlier sketch in CA 23-24
Croy, Homer 1883-1965 110
Obituary 89-92
See also DLB 4
Crozet, Charlotte 1926- 25-28R
Crozetti, R(uth G.) Warner
See Warner-Crozetti, R(uth G.)
Crozier, Brian (Rossiter) 1918- CANR-3
Earlier sketch in CA 9-12R
Crozier, Lorna 1948- CANR-32
Earlier sketch in CA 113
Crozier, Michel J. 1922- 130
Crud
See Crumb, R(obert)
Cruden, Robert 1910- 33-36R
Cruger, Melvin J. 1925(?)-1983 Obituary 111
Cruickshank, Allan D(udley)
1907-1974 Obituary 53-56
Cruickshank, C. G.
See Cruickshank, Charles (Greig)
Cruickshank, Charles (Greig)
1914-1989 .....CANR-25
Obituary 128
Earlier sketches in CA 21-24R, CANR-9
Cruickshank, Helen Gere 1907- CAP-1
Earlier sketch in CA 13-14
Cruickshank, John 1924- CANR-20
Earlier sketches in CA 1-4R, CANR-4
Cruickshank, Marjorie 1920-1983 122
Obituary 111
Cruickshank, William M(ellon) 1915- 89-92
Cruikshank, George 1792-1878 .....SATA 22
Cruise, David 1950- 128
Crumarums
See Crumb, R(obert)
Crumb, R(obert) 1943- 106
See also CLC 17
Crumbaker, Alice 1911- 81-84
Crumbaugh, James C(harles) 1912- 37-40R
Crumbley, D. Larry 1941- CANR-12
Earlier sketch in CA 29-32R
Crumbum
See Crumb, R(obert)
Crumley, James 1939- CANR-21
Earlier sketch in CA 69-72
See also DLBY 84
Crumm, Lloyd C(arlton) Jr. 1927- CANR-10
Earlier sketch in CA 65-68
Crummey, Robert O(wen) 1936- CANR-17
Earlier sketch in CA 25-28R
Crump, Barry (John) 1935- CANR-8
Earlier sketch in CA 13-16R
Crump, Fred H. Jr. 1931- CANR-19
Earlier sketches in CA 9-12R, CANR-3
See also SATA 11
Crump, Galbraith Miller 1929- 57-60
Crump, Geoffrey (Herbert) 1891- CAP-1
Earlier sketch in CA 13-14
Crump, J(ames) Irving 1887-1979 73-76
Obituary 89-92
See also SATA 21, 57
Crump, Kenneth G(ordon) Jr. 1931- 21-24R
Crump, Spencer (M. Jr.) 1933- CANR-9
Earlier sketch in CA 21-24R
Crump, (Stephen) Thomas 1929- 49-52
Crumpacker, Laurie 1941- 118
Crumpet, Peter
See Buckley, Fergus Reid
Crumpler, Frank H(unter) 1935- 77-80
Crumpler, Gus H(unt) 1911- 69-72
Crumrine, N(orman) Ross II 1934- CANR-8
Earlier sketch in CA 13-16R
Crumski
See Crumb, R(obert)
Crum the Bum
See Crumb, R(obert)
Crunden, Reginald
See Cleaver, Hylton Reginald
Crunden, Robert M. 1940- CANR-15
Earlier sketch in CA 29-32R
Crunk
See Crumb, R(obert)
Cruse, Harold 77-80
Cruso, Thalassa 1909- 65-68
Crussi, F(rank) Gonzalez
See Gonzalez-Crussi, F(rank)
Crustt
See Crumb, R(obert)
Crutcher, Anne Neilson
1919-1983 Obituary 111
Crutcher, Chris(topher C.) 1946- CANR-36
Earlier sketch in CA 113
See also AAYA 9
See also CLR 28
See also MAICYA
See also SATA 52
Cruz, Arturo Jr. 1954(?)- 131
See also HW
Cruz, Gilbert R(alph) 1929- 131
See also HW
Cruz, Gilberto Rafael
See Cruz, Gilbert R(alph)
Cruz, Joan Carroll 1931- 73-76
Cruz, Nicomedes Santa
See Santa Cruz (Gamarra), Nicomedes
Cruz, Ray(mond) 1933- .....SATA 6
Cruz, Victor Hernandez 1949- CANR-32
Earlier sketches in CA 65-68, CANR-14
See also BW
See also DLB 41
See also HW
Cruz Monclova, Lidio 1899- .....HW
Cryer, Gretchen (Kiger) 1935- 123
Brief entry 114
See also CLC 21
Crying Wind
See Stafford, Linda (Crying Wind)
Crystal, David 1941- CANR-23
Earlier sketches in CA 17-20R, CANR-7
Crystal, John C(urry) 1920- 102
Csath, Geza 1887-1919 Brief entry 111
See also TCLC 13
Csicsery-Ronay, Istvan 1917- 21-24R
Csikos-Nagy, Bela 1915- 73-76
Csikszentmihalyi, Mihaly 1934- 125
Csokor, Franz Theodor 1885-1969 .....DLB 81
Ctvrtek, Vaclav 1911-1976 Obituary 107
See also SATA 27
Cua, Antonio S. 1932- CANR-7
Earlier sketch in CA 17-20R
Cuadra, Pablo Antonio 1912- 131
See also HW
Cuadrado, Carlos Mellizo
See Mellizo (Cuadrado), Carlos
Cuban, Larry 1934- CANR-12
Earlier sketch in CA 29-32R
Cubas, Braz
See Dawes, Robyn M(ason)
Cuber, John F(rank) 1911- 9-12R
Cubeta, Paul Marsden 1925- 5-8R
Cuciti, Peggy L. 1949- 123
Cudahy, Brian J(ames) 1936- 41-44R
Cuddihy, John Murray 1922- 85-88
Cuddon, John Anthony 1928- CANR-19
Earlier sketches in CA 5-8R, CANR-3
Cuddy, Don 1925- 69-72
Cudjoe, Selwyn Reginald 1943- 118
Cudlip, David 1933- .....CLC 34
Cudlipp, Edythe 1929- CANR-12
Earlier sketch in CA 33-36R
Cudlipp, Hugh 1913- Brief entry 116
Cudmore, Dana (D.) 1954- 134
Cuelho, Art 1943- 61-64
Cuevas, Clara 1933- 57-60
Cuff, Barry
See Koste, Robert Francis
Cuff, Robert Dennis 1941- Brief entry 109
Cuffari, Richard 1925-1978 .....MAICYA
See also SATA 6, 25, 66
Cugat, Xavier 1900-1990 Obituary 132
Cuisenaire, Emile-Georges
1891(?)-1976 Obituary 61-64
Cuisenier, Jean 1927- CANR-20
Earlier sketch in CA 73-76
Culbert, David H(olbrook) 1943- CANR-31
Earlier sketch in CA 112
Culbert, Samuel Alan 1938- 69-72
Culbert, T(homas) Patrick 1930- Brief entry 107
Culbertson, Don S(tuart) 1927- 9-12R
Culbertson, Hugh M. 77-80
Culbertson, J(ohn) M(athew) 1921- 9-12R
Culbertson, James T(homas) 1911- 118
Culbertson, Judi 1941- CANR-31
Earlier sketch in CA 85-88
Culbertson, Manie 1927- 49-52
Culbertson, Paul T(homas) 1905- 37-40R
Culex
See Stanier, Maida Euphemia Kerr
Culhane, Claire 1918- 118
Culhane, Shamus 1908- 121
Culican, William 1929(?)-1984 Obituary 113
Culkin, Ann Marie 1918- 9-12R
Cull, John G(uinn Jr.) 1934- 41-44R
Cullen, Charles T(homas) 1940- 53-56
Cullen, Countee 1903-1946 124
Brief entry 108
See also BLC 1
See also BW
See also CDALB 1917-1929
See also DLB 4, 48, 51
See also MTCW
See also SATA 18
See also TCLC 4, 37
Cullen, George Francis
1901-1980 Obituary 102
Cullen, Joseph P(atrick) 1920- 49-52
Cullen, Lee Stowell 1922- 103
Cullen, Maurice R(aymond) Jr. 1927- 73-76
Cullen, Patrick (Colborn) 1940- 29-32R
Cullen, Peta
See Pyle, Hilary
Cullen, Robert (B.) 1949- 134
Cullen Brown, Joanna 1930- 128
Culler, A(rthur) Dwight 1917- 17-20R
Culler, Annette Lorena
See Penney, Annette Culler
Culler, Jonathan 1944- 104
See also DLB 67
Cullerne Bown, Matthew 1956- 132
Culleton, Beatrice 1949- 120
Culley, Thomas R(obert) 1931- 33-36R
Culliford, Pierre 1928- 124
See also SATA 40
Culliford, Stanley George 1920- 65-68
Culligan, Joe
See Culligan, Matthew J(oseph)
Culligan, Matthew J(oseph) 1918- CANR-20
Earlier sketch in CA 81-84
Cullinan, Bernice Ellinger 1926- 104
Cullinan, Elizabeth 1933- CANR-11
Earlier sketch in CA 25-28R
Cullinan, Gerald 1916- 21-24R
Cullinane, Leo Patrick
1907(?)-1978 Obituary 77-80
Culliney, John L. 1942- 65-68
Cullingford, Cecil H(oward) D(unstan)
1904-1990 .....CANR-7
Obituary 132
Earlier sketch in CA 5-8R
Cullingford, Guy
See Taylor, Constance Lindsay
Cullingworth, J(ohn) Barry 1929- CANR-1
Earlier sketch in CA 1-4R
Cullman, Marguerite Wagner 1908- 1-4R
Cullman, W(illiam) Arthur 1914- 113
Cullman, W. Arthur 1914- Brief entry 111
Cullmann, Oscar 1902- 106
Cullop, Charles P. 1927- 25-28R
Cully, Iris V(irginia Arnold) 1914- CANR-17
Earlier sketches in CA 1-4R, CANR-1
Cully, Kendig Brubaker 1913- CANR-17
Earlier sketches in CA 1-4R, CANR-1
Culme, John 1946- 128
Culotta, Nino
See O'Grady, John (Patrick)
Culp, Delos Poe 1911- 17-20R
Culp, John H(ewett Jr.) 1907- 29-32R
Culp, Louanna McNary 1901-1965 .....CAP-1
Earlier sketch in CA 13-16
See also SATA 2
Culp, Paula 1941- 57-60
Culp, Stephanie (Anne) 1947- 136
Culpepper, R(ichard) Alan 1946- 115
Culpepper, Robert H(arrell) 1924- 77-80
Culross, Michael (Gerard) 1942- 33-36R
Culshaw, John (Royds) 1924-1980 .....CANR-11
Obituary 97-100
Earlier sketch in CA 21-24R
Culver, Dwight W(endell) 1921- 9-12R
Culver, Elsie Thomas 1898- CAP-2
Earlier sketch in CA 21-22
Culver, Kathryn
See Dresser, Davis
Culver, Kenneth Leon 1903- 103
Culver, Robert Duncan 1916- 120
Culver, Roger B(ruce) 1940- 104
Cum, R.
See Crumb, R(obert)
Cumberland, Charles C(urtis)
1914-1970 .....CANR-2
Earlier sketch in CA 1-4R
Cumberland, John H(ammett) 1924- 127
Brief entry 106
Cumberland, Kenneth Brailey 1913- 53-56
Cumberland, Marten 1892-1972 .....CAP-1
Earlier sketch in CA 11-12
Cumberland, Richard 1732-1811 .....DLB 89
Cumberland, William Henry 1929- 17-20R
Cumberlege, Marcus (Crossley)
1938- CANR-17
Earlier sketch in CA 97-100
Cumberlege, Vera 1908- 81-84
Cumbler, John T(aylor) 1946- 89-92
Cumes, J(ames) W(illiam) C(rawford)
1922- 73-76
Cuming, Geoffrey John 1917-1988 .....CANR-18
Obituary 125
Earlier sketches in CA 5-8R, CANR-3
Cuming, Pamela 1944- 107
Cumings, Bruce Glenn 1943- 107
Cumming, Elizabeth (Skeoch) 1948- 137
Cumming, Patricia (Arens) 1932- CANR-11
Earlier sketch in CA 61-64
Cumming, Peter 1951- 129
Cumming, Primrose Amy 1915- 33-36R
See also SATA 24
Cumming, Robert Denoon
1916- Brief entry 107
Cumming, Robert 1945- 106
See also SATA 65
Cumming, William P(atterson) 1900- 33-36R
Cummings, Ann
See Rudolph, Lee (Norman)
Cummings, Arthur J.
1920(?)-1979 Obituary 89-92
Cummings, Betty Sue 1918- CANR-14
Earlier sketch in CA 73-76
See also SAAS 9
See also SATA 15
Cummings, Bruce F(rederick)
1889-1919 Brief entry 123
See also Barbellion, W. N. P.
Cummings, Charles 1940- 107
Cummings, D(onald) W(ayne) 1935- 101
Cummings, E(dward) E(stlin)
1894-1962 .....CANR-31
Earlier sketch in CA 73-76
See also CDALB 1929-1941
See also CLC 1, 3, 8, 12, 15, 68
See also DLB 4, 48
See also MTCW
See also PC 5
See also WLC 2
Cummings, Florence
See Bonime, Florence
Cummings, Gary 1941(?)-1987 Obituary 125
Cummings, Jack
See Cummings, John W(illiam) Jr.
Cummings, Jean 1930- 33-36R
Cummings, Joe 1952- 137
Cummings, John W(illiam) Jr. 1940- 117
Cummings, Larry L(ee) 1937- 53-56
Cummings, Milton C(urtis) Jr. 1933- 13-16R
Cummings, Monette 1914- 116
Cummings, Parke 1902-1987 .....CAP-1
Obituary 123
Earlier sketch in CA 13-14
See also SATA 2, 53
Cummings, Pat 1950- 122
See also MAICYA
See also SAAS 13
See also SATA 42, 71
Cummings, Paul 1933- CANR-8
Earlier sketch in CA 21-24R
Cummings, Ray(mond King)
1887-1957 .....CANR-31
Brief entry 113
See also DLB 8
Cummings, Richard
See Gardner, Richard (M.)
Cummings, Richard LeRoy 1933- 45-48
Cummings, Richard (Marshall) 1938- 113
Cummings, Scott 112
Cummings, Thomas G(erald) 1944- CANR-16
Earlier sketch in CA 97-100
Cummings, Violet M(ay) 1905- 57-60
Cummings, W(alter) T(hies) 1933- 1-4R
Cummins, D. Duane 1935- CANR-14
Earlier sketch in CA 37-40R
Cummins, Geraldine Dorothy 1890-1969 .....CAP-1
Earlier sketch in CA 9-10
Cummins, James 1948- 122
Cummins, Maria Susanna 1827-1866 .....DLB 42
See also YABC 1
Cummins, Paul F. 1937- 33-36R
Cummins, Walter (Merrill) 1936- CANR-15
Earlier sketch in CA 41-44R
Cundiff, Edward William 1919- CANR-4
Earlier sketch in CA 1-4R
Cundiff, Margaret Joan 1932- CANR-30
Earlier sketch in CA 112
Cundy, Henry Martyn 1913- 5-8R
Cuneo, Ernest (L.) 1905-1988 Obituary 125
Cuneo, Gilbert Anthony
1913-1978 Obituary 77-80
Cuneo, John R(obert) 1911- 53-56
Cuney, Waring
See Cuney, William Waring
Cuney, William Waring 1906-1976 125
See also BW
See also DLB 51
Cunha, Euclides (Rodrigues Pimenta) da
1866-1909 Brief entry 123
See also TCLC 24
Cunha, George Martin 1911- 25-28R
Cuninggim, Merrimon 1911- 41-44R
Cuniliffe, Barrington Windsor 1939- CANR-24
Earlier sketches in CA 53-56, CANR-9
Cunliffe, Barry
See Cunliffe, Barrington Windsor
Cunliffe, Elaine 33-36R
Cunliffe, John Arthur 1933- CANR-11
Earlier sketch in CA 61-64
See also SATA 11
Cunliffe, Marcus (Falkner) 1922-1990 .....CANR-10
Obituary 132
Earlier sketch in CA 21-24R
See also SATA 37
See also SATO 66
Cunliffe, William Gordon 1929- 25-28R
Cunningham, Aline CANR-9
Earlier sketch in CA 57-60
Cunningham, Allan 1784-1842 .....DLB 116
Cunningham, Barry 1940- 73-76
Cunningham, Bob
See May, Julian
Cunningham, Captain Frank
See Glick, Carl (Cannon)
Cunningham, Cathy
See Cunningham, Chet
Cunningham, Chet 1928- CANR-19
Earlier sketches in CA 49-52, CANR-4
See also SATA 23
Cunningham, Dale S(peers) 1932- CANR-8
Earlier sketch in CA 13-16R
See also SATA 11
Cunningham, Donald H(ayward)
1935- CANR-20
Earlier sketch in CA 103
Cunningham, E. V.
See Fast, Howard (Melvin)
Cunningham, Floyd F(ranklin) 1899- CAP-1
Earlier sketch in CA 13-16
Cunningham, Frank R. 1937- 137
Cunningham, H(orace) H(erndon)
1913-1969 .....CAP-1
Earlier sketch in CA 11-12
Cunningham, Imogen
1883-1976 Obituary 65-68

Cunningham, J(ames) V(incent)
1911-1985 ... CANR-1
Obituary ... 115
Earlier sketch in CA 1-4R
See also CLC 3, 31
See also DLB 5
Cunningham, James F. 1901- ... CAP-2
Earlier sketch in CA 19-20
Cunningham, James V. 1923- ... 135
Cunningham, Jim
See Cunningham, James V.
Cunningham, John D(onovan) 1933- ... 111
Cunningham, Joseph F. X. 1925- ... 69-72
Cunningham, Joseph Sandy 1928- ... 61-64
Cunningham, Julia (Woolfolk) 1916- ... CANR-36
Earlier sketches in CA 9-12R, CANR-4, 19
See also CLC 12
See also MAICYA
See also SAAS 2
See also SATA 1, 26
Cunningham, Laura 1947- ... CANR-23
Earlier sketch in CA 85-88
Cunningham, Lawrence 1935- ... CANR-15
Earlier sketch in CA 85-88
Cunningham, Lyda Sue Martin 1938- ... 17-20R
Cunningham, Marilyn 1927- ... 125
Cunningham, Mary (Elizabeth) 1951- ... 114
Cunningham, Michael A(lan) 1945- ... 41-44R
Cunningham, Michael 1952- ... 136
See also CLC 34
Cunningham, Noble E. Jr. 1926- ... 81-84
Cunningham, Paul James Jr. 1917- ... 73-76
Cunningham, R(onnie) Walter 1932- ... 103
Cunningham, Richard 1939- ... 101
Cunningham, Robert Louis 1926- ... 41-44R
Cunningham, Robert M(aris) Jr. 1909- ... CANR-1
Obituary ... 137
Earlier sketch in CA 49-52
Cunningham, Robert Stanley 1907- ... 53-56
Cunningham, Rosemary 1916- ... 9-12R
Cunningham, Virginia
See Holmgren, Virginia C(unningham)
Cunningham, W(infield) Scott
1899(?)-1986 Obituary ... 118
Cunninghame Graham, R(obert) B(ontine)
1852-1936 Brief entry ... 119
See also Graham, R(obert) B(ontine) Cunninghame
See also DLB 98
See also TCLC 19
Cunnington, Phillis 1887-1974 Obituary ... 53-56
Cunz, Dieter 1910-1969 ... CAP-2
Earlier sketch in CA 19-20
Cuomo, George (Michael) 1929- ... CANR-7
Earlier sketch in CA 5-8R
See also DLBY 80
Cuomo, Mario Matthew 1932- ... 103
Cupitt, Don 1934- ... CANR-14
Earlier sketch in CA 41-44R
Cuppleditch, David 1946- ... CANR-38
Earlier sketch in CA 116
Cuppy, Will(iam Jacob)
1884-1949 Brief entry ... 108
See also DLB 11
Cure, Karen 1949- ... CANR-9
Earlier sketch in CA 65-68
Curiae, Amicus
See Fuller, Edmund (Maybank)
Curie, Eve 1904- ... CAP-1
Earlier sketch in CA 9-10
See also SATA 1
Curie, Marie (Sklodowska)
1867-1934 Brief entry ... 118
Curl, David H. 1932- ... 93-96
Curl, Donald Walter 1935- ... 33-36R
Curl, James Stevens 1937- ... CANR-14
Earlier sketch in CA 37-40R
Curle, Adam
See Curle, Charles T. W.
Curle, Charles T. W. 1916- ... 33-36R
Curler, (Mary) Bernice 1915- ... 85-88
Curley, Arthur 1938- ... CANR-9
Earlier sketch in CA 21-24R
Curley, Charles 1949- ... 57-60
Curley, Daniel 1918-1988 ... CANR-18
Obituary ... 127
Earlier sketches in CA 9-12R, CANR-3
See also SATA 23, 61
Curley, Dorothy Nyren
See Nyren, Dorothy Elizabeth
Curley, Michael J. 1900-1972 Obituary ... 37-40R
Curley, Walter J(oseph) P(atrick) 1922- ... 53-56
Curling, Audrey ... 61-64
Curling, Bill
See Curling, Bryan William Richard
Curling, Bryan William Richard 1911- ... 102
Curnow, (Thomas) Allen (Monro) 1911- ... 69-72
Curnow, Frank
See Atkinson, Frank
Curnow, Ray(mond) 1928- ... 117
Curran, Bob
See Curran, Robert
Curran, Charles A(rthur) 1913-1978 ... CANR-29
Earlier sketch in CA 33-36R
Curran, Charles E. 1934- ... CANR-14
Earlier sketch in CA 21-24R
Curran, Charles (John) 1921-1980 ... 130
Obituary ... 105
Curran, Dolores 1932- ... CANR-6
Earlier sketch in CA 57-60
Curran, Donald J. 1926- ... 45-48
Curran, Francis X. 1914- ... 17-20R
Curran, Jan Goldberg 1937- ... 101
Curran, Joseph M(aroney) 1932- ... 103
Curran, Mona (Elisa) ... 5-8R
Curran, Peter Malcolm 1922- ... 103
Curran, Phil(ip) R(ead) 1911- ... 73-76
Curran, Robert 1923- ... 89-92
Curran, Samuel (Crowe) 1912- ... 109
Curran, Stuart (Alan) 1940- ... 29-32R
Curran, Susan 1952- ... 113
Curran, Terrie 1942- ... 127
Curran, Thomas J(oseph) 1929- ... 45-48
Curran, Ward S(chenk) 1935- ... 41-44R
Curran, William John 1925- ... 108
Curren, Polly 1917- ... CANR-4
Earlier sketch in CA 1-4R
Current, Richard N(elson) 1912- ... CANR-5
Earlier sketch in CA 1-4R
Current-Garcia, Eugene 1908- ... 17-20R
Currer-Briggs, Noel 1919- ... CANR-13
Earlier sketch in CA 73-76
Currey, Cecil B(arr) 1932- ... CANR-25
Earlier sketch in CA 25-28R
Currey, R(onald) F(airbridge) 1894-1983 ... CAP-1
Obituary ... 109
Earlier sketch in CA 9-10
Currey, R(alph) N(ixon) 1907- ... 93-96
Currey, Richard 1949- ... 117
Currie, Ann (Brooke Peterson)
1922(?)-1980 Obituary ... 102
Currie, Barton Wood 1878-1962 Obituary ... 116
Currie, David
See Allen, Sydney (Earl) Jr.
Currie, David P(ark) 1936- ... 134
Brief entry ... 106
Currie, Donald Glenne 1926-1984 Obituary ... 111
Currie, Ellen ... CLC 44
Currie, Lauchlin (Bernard) 1902- ... CANR-15
Earlier sketch in CA 73-76
Currie, Mary Montgomerie Lamb Singleton
See Fane, Violet
Currie, Robert 1937- ... 112
Currier, Alvin C. 1932- ... 21-24R
Currier, Chester S. 1945- ... 129
Currier, Frederick P(lumer) 1923- ... 85-88
Currier, Richard L(eon) 1940- ... 57-60
Curro, Evelyn Malone 1907- ... 5-8R
Curry, Andrew 1931- ... 57-60
Curry, Avon
See Bowden, Jean
Curry, David 1942- ... 69-72
Curry, Dean C(onrad) 1952- ... 118
Curry, Estell H. 1907- ... CAP-2
Earlier sketch in CA 23-24
Curry, F. Hayden 1940- ... 108
Curry, G(len) David 1948- ... 136
Curry, George E(dward) 1947- ... 69-72
Curry, Gladys J.
See Washington, Gladys J(oseph)
Curry, Jane L(ouise) 1932- ... CANR-24
Earlier sketches in CA 17-20R, CANR-7
See also MAICYA
See also SAAS 6
See also SATA 1, 52
Curry, Jennifer 1934- ... 77-80
Curry, Kenneth 1910- ... CANR-8
Earlier sketch in CA 17-20R
Curry, Leonard Preston 1929- ... 29-32R
Curry, Lerond (Loving) 1938- ... 33-36R
Curry, Martha Mulroy 1926- ... 61-64
Curry, Paul (J.) 1917-1986 ... 49-52
Obituary ... 118
Curry, Peggy Simson 1911-1987 ... CANR-12
Obituary ... 121
Earlier sketch in CA 33-36R
See also SATA 8, 50
Curry, Richard Orr 1931- ... 13-16R
Curry, Thomas A. 1901(?)-1976 Obituary ... 69-72
Curry, Windell
See Sujata, Anagarika
Curry-Lindahl, Kai 1917- ... CANR-19
Earlier sketches in CA 49-52, CANR-2
Curtayne, Alice 1898- ... 53-56
Curteis, Ian Bayley 1935- ... CANR-36
Earlier sketch in CA 103
Curti, Merle Eugene 1897- ... CANR-4
Earlier sketch in CA 5-8R
See also DLB 17
Curtin, Dave 1955- ... 132
Curtin, Deane 1951- ... 138
Curtin, James R(udd) 1922- ... 17-20R
Curtin, Mary Ellen 1922- ... 57-60
Curtin, Patricia Romero
See Romero, Patricia W.
Curtin, Philip
See Lowndes, Marie Adelaide (Belloc)
Curtin, Phillip D. 1922- ... CANR-7
Earlier sketch in CA 13-16R
Curtin, Valerie ... 130
Curtin, William M(artin) 1927- ... 53-56
Curtis, Alan R(obert) 1936- ... 105
Curtis, Anthony 1926- ... CANR-18
Earlier sketch in CA 101
Curtis, (Hubert) Arnold 1917- ... CANR-29
Earlier sketches in CA 29-32R, CANR-12
Curtis, Bruce (Richard) 1944- ... SATA 30
Curtis, C(hristopher) Michael 1934- ... 136
Curtis, Carol Edwards 1943- ... 77-80
Curtis, Charles J(ohn) 1921- ... 21-24R
Curtis, Charles Ralph 1899- ... 5-8R
Curtis, Charlotte (Murray) 1928-1987 ... 9-12R
Obituary ... 122
See also AITN 2
Curtis, Cyrus H. K. 1850-1933 ... DLB 91
Curtis, David Paul 1942- ... CANR-13
Earlier sketch in CA 21-24R
Curtis, Donald 1915- ... CANR-20
Earlier sketch in CA 103
Curtis, Edith Roelker 1893-1977 ... 1-4R
Obituary ... 103
Curtis, George William 1824-1892 ... DLB 1, 43
Curtis, Gerald 1904-1983 Obituary ... 109
Curtis, Howard J(ames)
1906-1972 Obituary ... 37-40R
Curtis, J(osiah) Montgomery
1905-1982 Obituary ... 108
Curtis, Jack 1922- ... 103
Curtis, Jackie
See Holder, John Jr.
Curtis, James C. 1938- Brief entry ... 105
Curtis, James Malcolm 1940- ... 119
Curtis, James (Richard) 1953- ... 108
Curtis, Jared Ralph 1936- ... 101
Curtis, John
See Prebble, John Edward Curtis
Curtis, Lewis Perry 1900-1976 ... CAP-2
Obituary ... 65-68
Earlier sketch in CA 23-24
Curtis, Lindsay R(aine) 1916- ... 41-44R
Curtis, Lynn A(lan) 1943- ... 61-64
Curtis, Margaret James 1897- ... 1-4R
Curtis, Marjorie
See Prebble, Marjorie Mary Curtis
Curtis, Mark H(ubert) 1920- ... 5-8R
Curtis, Michael K. 1942- ... 128
Curtis, Michael Raymond 1923- ... CANR-22
Earlier sketch in CA 103
Curtis, Norman 1914- ... 45-48
Curtis, Patricia 1924- ... CANR-18
Earlier sketch in CA 69-72
See also SATA 23
Curtis, Paul
See Czura, R(oman) P(eter)
Curtis, Peter
See Lofts, Norah (Robinson)
Curtis, Philip (Delacourt) 1920- ... 109
See also SATA 62
Curtis, Price
See Ellison, Harlan
Curtis, Richard (Alan) 1937- ... CANR-25
Earlier sketch in CA 106
See also SATA 29
Curtis, Richard Hale
See Levinson, Leonard
and Rothweiler, Paul Roger
Curtis, Richard Kenneth 1924- ... 1-4R
Curtis, Rosemary Ann (Stevens) 1935- ... 9-12R
Curtis, Sharon 1951- ... 126
Brief entry ... 116
Curtis, Thomas Bradford 1911- ... 61-64
Curtis, Thomas Dale 1952- ... 126
Brief entry ... 116
Curtis, Tom
See Curtis, Thomas Dale
and Pendower, Jacques
Curtis, Tony 1925- ... 73-76
Curtis, Tony 1946- ... CANR-22
Earlier sketch in CA 106
Curtis, Wade
See Pournelle, Jerry (Eugene)
Curtis, Will
See Nunn, William Curtis
Curtis, William J(oseph) R. 1948- ... 110
Curtis Brown, Beatrice 1901-1974 ... CAP-2
Earlier sketch in CA 25-28
Curtiss, John S(helton) 1899- ... CAP-2
Earlier sketch in CA 19-20
Curtiss, Mina (Stein Kirstein) 1896-1985 ... 133
Obituary ... 118
Curtiss, Ursula Reilly 1923-1984 ... CANR-5
Obituary ... 114
Earlier sketch in CA 1-4R
Curtler, Hugh Mercer 1937- ... CANR-15
Earlier sketch in CA 89-92
Curto, Josephine J. 1927- ... 17-20R
Curwin, Richard L(eonard) 1944- ... 77-80
Curzon, Clare
See Buchanan, Marie
Curzon, Daniel ... 73-76
Curzon, David 1941- ... 137
Curzon, Lucia
See Stevenson, Florence
Curzon, Sam
See Krasney, Samuel A.
Curzon, Sarah Anne 1833-1898 ... DLB 99
Curzon, Virginia
See Hawton, Hector
Cusac, Marian H(ollingsworth) 1932- ... 33-36R
Cusack, (Ellen) Dymphna
1902-198 (?) ... CANR-11
Earlier sketch in CA 9-12R
Cusack, Lawrence X(avier) 1919- ... 5-8R
Cusack, Margaret 1945- ... SATA 58
Cusack, Michael J(oseph) 1928- ... 69-72
Cush, Carol Gregor
See Gregor, Carol
Cushing, Barry E(dwin) 1945- ... CANR-4
Earlier sketch in CA 53-56
Cushing, Eliza Lanesford 1794-1886 ... DLB 99
Cushing, Jane 1922- ... 29-32R
Cushing, Mary W(atkins)
189 (?)-1974 Obituary ... 53-56
Cushing, Peter (Wilton) 1913- ... 133
Cushing, Richard Cardinal
See Cushing, Richard James
Cushing, Richard James
1895-1970 Obituary ... 112
Cushing, Winifred 1907-1990 Obituary ... 132
Cushion, John P(atrick) 1915- ... 93-96
Cushman, Clarissa Fairchild
1889-1980 Obituary ... 93-96
Cushman, Dan 1909- ... CANR-18
Earlier sketches in CA 5-8R, CANR-3
Cushman, Doug 1953- ... 117
See also SATA 65
Cushman, Jerome ... 1-4R
See also SATA 2
Cushman, Joseph David Jr. 1925- ... 111
Cushman, Keith (Maxwell) 1942- ... 124
Cushman, Robert F(airchild) 1918- ... 77-80
Cushman, Stephen B. 1956- ... 123
Cusick, Philip A. 1937- ... 69-72
Cusick, Richie Tankersley 1952- ... 134
See also SATA 67
Cuskelly, Eugene James 1924- ... 5-8R
Cuskey, (Raymond) Walter 1934- ... 41-44R
Cuss, (Theodore Patrick) Camerer
1909(?)-1970 Obituary ... 104
Cussler, Clive (Eric) 1931- ... CANR-21
Earlier sketches in CA 45-48, CANR-1
See also BEST 90:4
Custer, Chester Eugene 1920- ... 41-44R
Custer, Clint
See Paine, Lauran (Bosworth)
Custer, Robert (Laverne)
1927-1990 Obituary ... 132
Cusumano, Michael A. 1954- ... 125
Cutchen, Billye Walker 1930- ... CANR-13
Earlier sketch in CA 77-80
See also SATA 15
Cutchins, Judy 1947- ... 127
See also SATA 59
Cutcliffe, Stephen H(osmer) 1947- ... 116
Cutforth, John Ashlin 1911- ... 9-12R
Cutforth, Rene 1909(?)-1984 ... 123
Obituary ... 112
Cuthbert, Diana Daphne Holman-Hunt
1913- ... 1-4R
Cuthbert, Eleonora Isabel (McKenzie)
1902- ... CAP-1
Earlier sketch in CA 11-12
Cuthbert, Mary
See Hellwig, Monika Konrad
Cuthbertson, Gilbert Morris 1937- ... 57-60
Cuthbertson, Tom 1945- ... CANR-1
Earlier sketch in CA 45-48
Cutler, Bruce 1930- ... CANR-18
Earlier sketches in CA 1-4R, CANR-2
Cutler, Carl C(uster) 1878-1966 ... 1-4R
Obituary ... 103
Cutler, Carol 1926- ... CANR-19
Earlier sketch in CA 103
Cutler, Charles L(ocke Jr.) 1930- ... 65-68
Cutler, Daniel S(olomon) 1951- ... 120
Cutler, David 1956- ... 137
Cutler, Donald R. 1930- ... 21-24R
Cutler, (May) Ebbitt 1923- ... CANR-4
Earlier sketch in CA 49-52
See also SATA 9
Cutler, Irving H. 1923- ... CANR-9
Earlier sketch in CA 21-24R
Cutler, Ivor 1923- ... CANR-9
Earlier sketch in CA 5-8R
See also SATA 24
Cutler, Katherine Noble 1905- ... CANR-4
Earlier sketch in CA 5-8R
Cutler, Roland 1938- ... CANR-25
Earlier sketch in CA 102
Cutler, Samuel
See Folsom, Franklin (Brewster)
Cutler, Stan 1925- ... 137
Cutler, William Worcester III 1941- ... 103
Cutler, Winnifred B(erg) 1944- ... 117
Cutlip, Scott M. 1915- ... 5-8R
Cutrate, Joe
See Spiegelman, Art
Cutrer, Thomas W(illiam) 1947- ... 123
Cutright, Paul Russell 1897- ... 65-68
Cutright, Phillips 1930- ... 5-8R
Cutshall, Alden 1911- ... CANR-3
Earlier sketch in CA 9-12R
Cutsumbis, Michael N(icholas) 1935- ... 45-48
Cutt, W(illiam) Towrie 1898-1981 ... 81-84
Obituary ... 115
See also SATA 16
Cutten, M. J.
See Cutten, Mervyn (James)
Cutten, Mervyn (James) 1916- ... 120
Cutter, Charles R. 1950- ... 127
Cutter, Donald C(olgett) 1922- ... CANR-13
Earlier sketch in CA 33-36R
Cutter, Fred 1924- ... 57-60
Cutter, Robert Arthur 1930- ... CANR-8
Earlier sketch in CA 57-60
Cutter, Tom
See Randisi, Robert J(oseph)
and Wallmann, Jeffrey M(iner)
Cutting, Edith E(lsie) 1918- ... 106
Cutting, Pauline 1952- ... 128
Cuttino, G(eorge) P(eddy) 1914- ... 21-24R
Cuttle, Evelyn Roeding ... 57-60
Cuttler, Charles D(avid) 1913- ... 29-32R
Cutts, John P. 1927-1986 ... 45-48
Obituary ... 121
Cutts, Richard 1923- ... 33-36R
Cutul, Ann-Marie 1945- ... 103
Cuyler, Louise E. 1908- ... 21-24R
Cuyler, Margery S(tuyvesant) 1948- ... 117
See also SATA 39
Cuyler, Stephen
See Bates, Barbara S(nedeker)
Cuyler, Susanna (Stevens) 1946- ... 61-64
Cuza Male, Belkis 1942- ... 131
See also HW
Cykler, Edmund A(lbert) 1903- ... 9-12R
Cylwicki, Albert 1932- ... CANR-38
Earlier sketch in CA 116
Cynan
See Evans-Jones, Albert
Cynthia
See King, Florence
Cyr, Arthur 1945- ... 125
Cyr, Don(ald Joseph) 1935- ... 103
Cyr, John Edwin 1915- ... 103
Czaczkes, Shmuel Yosef
See Agnon, S(hmuel) Y(osef Halevi)
Czaja, Michael 1911- ... 57-60
Czaplinski, Suzanne 1943- ... 61-64

Czerniawski, Adam 1934- ... CANR-14
Earlier sketch in CA 37-40R
Czerny, Peter G(erd) 1941- ... 65-68
Czestochowski, Joseph S(tephen) 1950- ... 113
Czigany, Lorant (Gyorgy) 1935- ... 130
Czobor, Agnes 1920- ... 37-40R
Czura, R(oman) P(eter) 1913- ... 89-92

D

D. P.
See Wells, H(erbert) G(eorge)
Daalder, Hans 1928- ... 133
Daane, Calvin J(ohn) 1925- ... 41-44R
Daane, James 1914- ... 21-24R
Dabberdt, Walter F. 1942- ... CANR-23
Earlier sketch in CA 107
Dabbs, Jack Autrey 1914- ... 17-20R
Dabbs, James McBride 1896-1970 ... CAP-1
Earlier sketch in CA 13-16
Dabcovich, Lydia ... 124
See also SATA 47, 58
Dabit, Eugene 1898-1936 ... DLB 65
Dabkin, Edwin Franden
1898(?)-1976 Obituary ... 65-68
Dabney, Dick 1933-1981 ... 69-72
Obituary ... 105
Dabney, Joseph Earl 1929- ... 49-52
Dabney, Ross H. 1934- ... 21-24R
Dabney, Virginius 1901- ... CANR-29
Earlier sketches in CA 45-48, CANR-1
Dabney, William M(inor) 1919- ... 9-12R
Daborne, Robert 1580(?)-1628 ... DLB 58
D'Abreu, Gerald Joseph 1916- ... CAP-2
Earlier sketch in CA 19-20
Dabringhaus, Erhard 1917- ... 115
Dabrowska, Maria (Szumska) 1889-1965 ... 106
See also CLC 15
Dabydeen, Cyril 1945- ... 133
Brief entry ... 122
Dabydeen, David 1955- ... 125
See also BW
See also CLC 34
DaCal, Ernesto Guerra 1911- ... CANR-19
Earlier sketches in CA 5-8R, CANR-4
Dace, Letitia (Skinner) 1941- ... 106
Dace, Tish
See Dace, Letitia (Skinner)
Dace, (Edwin) Wallace 1920- ... CANR-34
Earlier sketch in CA 61-64
Dacey, Norman F(ranklyn) 1908- ... CANR-2
Earlier sketch in CA 5-8R
Dacey, Philip 1939- ... CANR-32
Earlier sketches in CA 37-40R, CANR-14
See also CLC 51
See also DLB 105
Dachman, Ken 1958- ... 110
Dachs, David 1922-1980 ... CANR-11
Earlier sketch in CA 69-72
Dack, Gail Monroe 1901-1976 Obituary ... 111
da Cruz, Daniel Jr. 1921- ... CANR-19
Earlier sketches in CA 5-8R, CANR-3
Dacy, Douglas Calvin 1927- Brief entry ... 104
Dadie, Bernard B(inlin) 1916- ... CANR-17
Earlier sketch in CA 25-28R
See also BW
Daedalus
See Bramesco, Norton J.
Daehlin, Reidar A. 1910- ... CAP-1
Earlier sketch in CA 17-18
Daem, Thelma (Mary) Bannerman 1914- ... 5-8R
Daemer, Will
See Miller, (H.) Bill(y)
and Wade, Robert (Allison)
Daemmrich, Horst S. 1930- ... CANR-1
Earlier sketch in CA 45-48
Daenzer, Bernard John 1916- ... 53-56
Daftary, Farhad 1938- ... 136
Dagan, Avigdor 1912- ... CANR-30
Earlier sketches in CA 33-36R, CANR-13
Dagenais, James J(oseph) 1928- ... 41-44R
Dager, Edward Z(icca) 1921- ... 61-64
Dagerman, Stig (Halvard)
1923-1954 Brief entry ... 117
See also TCLC 17
Dagg, Anne Innis 1933- ... CANR-28
Earlier sketches in CA 69-72, CANR-11
Daggett, Rollin M. 1831-1901 ... DLB 79
Daglish, Eric Fitch 1892-1966 ... 102
D'Agostino, Angelo 1926- ... 17-20R
D'Agostino, Anthony 1937- ... 128
D'Agostino, Dennis John 1957- ... 106
D'Agostino, Giovanna P. 1914- ... 57-60
D'Agostino, Joseph David 1929- ... 69-72
Dagover, Lil 1897-1980 Obituary ... 105
Daheim, Mary 1937- ... 110
Dahinden, Justus 1925- ... 81-84
Dahl, Arlene 1928- Brief entry ... 105
Dahl, Borghild (Margarethe)
1890-1984 ... CANR-2
Obituary ... 112
Earlier sketch in CA 1-4R
See also SATA 7, 37
Dahl, Curtis 1920- ... CANR-2
Earlier sketch in CA 1-4R
Dahl, Georg 1905- ... 85-88
Dahl, Gordon J. 1932- ... 49-52
Dahl, Linda 1949- ... 122
Dahl, Murdoch Edgcumbe 1914- ... CAP-1
Earlier sketch in CA 9-10
Dahl, Nils A(lstrup) 1911- ... 65-68
Dahl, Roald 1916-1990 ... CANR-37
Obituary ... 133
Earlier sketches in CA 1-4R, CANR-6, 32
See also CLC 1, 6, 18
See also CLR 1, 7
See also MAICYA
See also MTCW
See also SATA 1, 26
See also SATO 65
Dahl, Robert A(lan) 1915- ... CANR-30
Earlier sketch in CA 65-68
Dahlberg, Arthur O. 1898(?)-1989 ... 124
Obituary ... 129
Dahlberg, Edward 1900-1977 ... CANR-31
Obituary ... 69-72
Earlier sketch in CA 9-12R
See also CLC 1, 7, 14
See also DLB 48
See also MTCW
Dahlberg, Edwin T(heodore) 1892-1986 ... CAP-2
Obituary ... 120
Earlier sketch in CA 17-18
Dahlberg, Jane S. 1923- ... 21-24R
Dahlhaus, Carl 1928-1989 Obituary ... 128
Dahlie, Hallvard 1925- ... 128
Dahlinger, John Cote 1923-1984 Obituary ... 114
Dahlstedt, Marden 1921- ... CANR-1
Earlier sketch in CA 45-48
See also SATA 8
Dahlsten, Donald L. 1933- ... 132
Dahlstrand, Frederick Charles 1945- ... 111
Dahlstrom, Earl C(arl) 1914- ... 17-20R
Dahl-Worlfe, Louise (Emma Augusta)
1895-1989 Obituary ... 130
Dahm, Charles W(illiam) 1937- ... 107
Dahms, Alan M(artin) 1937- ... 49-52
Dahmus, Joseph Henry 1909- ... 21-24R
Dahood, Mitchell (Joseph)
1922-1982 ... CANR-20
Obituary ... 106
Earlier sketch in CA 25-28R
Dahrendorf, Ralf 1929- ... CANR-28
Earlier sketches in CA 1-4R, CANR-3
Daiches, David 1912- ... CANR-29
Earlier sketches in CA 5-8R, CANR-7
Daigh, Ralph (Foster) 1907-1986 Obituary ... 121
Daigon, Arthur 1928- ... 33-36R
Daiken, Leslie Herbert 1912- ... 1-4R
Dailey, Charles A(lvin) 1923- ... 89-92
Dailey, Janet (Ann) 1944- ... CANR-39
Earlier sketches in CA 89-92, CANR-17
See also BEST 89:3
See also MTCW
Daily, Jay E(lwood) 1923- ... 33-36R
Daims, Diva 1925- ... 113
Dain, Martin J. 1924- ... 13-16R
See also SATA 35
Dain, Norman 1925- ... 9-12R
Dain, Phyllis 1929- ... 69-72
Dainton, (William) Courtney 1920- ... 9-12R
Daintrey, Adrian (Maurice)
1902-1988 Obituary ... 127
Daiute, Robert James 1926- ... 13-16R
Dajani, M(unther) S(uleiman) 1951- ... 132
Dakers, Elaine Kidner 1905-1978 ... CANR-30
Earlier sketch in CA 85-88
Dakin, Arthur Hazard 1905- Brief entry ... 106
Dakin, D(avid) Martin 1908- ... 73-76
Dakin, Edwin Franden 1898-1976 Obituary ... 104
Dakin, (David) Julian 1939-1971 ... CAP-2
Earlier sketch in CA 25-28
Dalal, Nergis 1920- Brief entry ... 116
Daland, Robert T(heodore) 1919- ... 21-24R
Dalbor, John B(ronislaw) 1929- ... 17-20R
Dal Co, Francesco 1945- ... 133
Dalcourt, Gerard J. 1927- ... 33-36R
Dale, (Mary) Alzina Stone 1931- ... CANR-38
Earlier sketch in CA 114
Dale, Antony 1912- ... 107
Dale, Arbie Myron Jr. 1924- ... 122
Dale, Celia (Marjorie) ... CANR-3
Earlier sketch in CA 5-8R
Dale, Colin
See Lawrence, T(homas) E(dward)
See also TCLC 18
Dale, D(ion) M(urray) C(rosbie) 1930- ... 21-24R
Dale, DeArmond 1914- ... SATA 70
Dale, Doris Cruger 1927- ... 116
Dale, Edgar 1900-1985 Obituary ... 117
Dale, Edward Everett 1879-1972 ... CANR-4
Earlier sketch in CA 5-8R
Dale, Edwin L. Jr. 1923- ... 69-72
Dale, Ernest 1917- ... 13-16R
Dale, George E.
See Asimov, Isaac
Dale, Jack
See Holliday, Joseph
Dale, James 1886-1985 ... CAP-2
Obituary ... 116
Earlier sketch in CA 33-36
Dale, John B. 1905- ... 13-16R
Dale, Kathleen 1895-1984 Obituary ... 112
Dale, Laura A(bbott) 1919-1983 Obituary ... 113
Dale, Magdalene L(arsen) 1904- ... 13-16R
Dale, Margaret J(essy) Miller 1911- ... CANR-19
Earlier sketches in CA 5-8R, CANR-3
See also SATA 39
Dale, Norman
See Denny, Norman (George)
Dale, Paul W(orthen) 1923- ... 25-28R
Dale, Penny 1954- ... 138
See also SATA 70
Dale, Peter (John) 1938- ... CANR-39
Earlier sketches in CA 45-48, CANR-1, 16
See also DLB 40
Dale, Peter N(icholas) 1950- ... 126
Dale, Reginald R. 1907- ... 21-24R
Dale, Richard 1932- ... 33-36R
Dale, Robert D(ennis) 1940- ... CANR-33
Earlier sketch in CA 113
Dale, Roman
See Czura, R(oman) P(eter)
d'Alelio, Ellen F. 1938- ... 17-20R
Dales, Douglas S. 1907(?)-1985 Obituary ... 114
Dales, Richard C(lark) 1926- ... CANR-24
Earlier sketch in CA 45-48
Daleski, H(illel) M(atthew) 1926- ... 33-36R
D'Alessandro, Robert (Philip) 1942- ... 61-64
Dalet, Roger (Charles) 1927- ... 107
Daley, Adeline 1922(?)-1984 Obituary ... 112
Daley, Arthur (John) 1904-1974 ... CAP-2
Obituary ... 45-48
Earlier sketch in CA 23-24
Daley, Bill
See Appleman, John Alan
Daley, Brian 1947- ... 126
Daley, Eliot A. 1936- ... 97-100
Daley, Harry 1901-1971 ... 134
Daley, Janet 1944- ... 125
Daley, Joseph A(ndrew) 1927- ... 53-56
Daley, Robert 1930- ... CANR-24
Earlier sketches in CA 1-4R, CANR-2
Daley, Sharon
See Barovsky, Sharon Daley
Daley, Stephen Dennis 1948- ... 133
Dalfiume, Richard Myron 1936- ... 25-28R
D'Alfonso, Antonio 1953- ... 129
D'Alfonso, John 1918- ... 29-32R
Dalgleish, Oakley Hedley
1910-1963 Obituary ... 115
Dalgliesh, Alice 1893-1979 ... 73-76
Obituary ... 89-92
See also MAICYA
See also SATA 17, 21
Dalglish, Edward R(ussell) 1913- ... 37-40R
Dali, Salvador (Domenech Felipe Jacinto)
1904-1989 ... 104
Obituary ... 127
Dall, Caroline Wells (Healey) 1822-1912 ... DLB 1
D'Allard, Hunter
See Ballard, (Willis) Todhunter
Dallas, Athena Gianakas
See Dallas-Damis, Athena G(ianakas)
Dallas, E. S. 1828-1879 ... DLB 55
Dallas, John
See Duncan, W(illiam) Murdoch
Dallas, Philip 1921- ... 61-64
Dallas, Ruth 1919- ... CANR-10
Earlier sketch in CA 65-68
Dallas, Sandra
See Atchison, Sandra Dallas
Dallas-Damis, Athena G(ianakas) 1925- ... 81-84
Dallek, Robert 1934- ... CANR-17
Earlier sketch in CA 25-28R
D'Allenger, Hugh
See Kershaw, John (Hugh D'Allenger)
Dallimore, Arnold A(rthur) 1911- ... 112
Dallin, Alexander 1924- ... CANR-19
Earlier sketches in CA 1-4R, CANR-5
Dallin, Leon 1918- ... CANR-1
Earlier sketch in CA 1-4R
Dallmann, Martha (Elsie) 1904- ... 1-4R
Dallmayr, Fred R(einhard) 1928- ... CANR-1
Earlier sketch in CA 49-52
Dally, Ann Mullins 1926- ... CANR-21
Earlier sketches in CA 5-8R, CANR-3
Dalmas, John
See Jones, John R(obert)
D'Alonzo, C(onstance) Anthony
1912-1972 Obituary ... 37-40R
Dalpadado, J(ames) Kingsley (Evold) 1922- ... 112
Dalphin, John R(obert) 1942- ... 118
Dal Poggetto, Newton Francis 1922- ... 61-64
d'Alpuget, Blanche 1944- ... 114
Dalrymple, Byron W(illiam) 1910- ... CANR-6
Earlier sketch in CA 57-60
Dalrymple, Douglas J(esse) 1934- ... 73-76
Dalrymple, Gertrude Bradley
1901(?)-1984 Obituary ... 113
Dalrymple, Ian (Murray) 1903-1989 ... 115
Obituary ... 128
Dalrymple, Jean 1910- ... CANR-5
Earlier sketch in CA 5-8R
Dalrymple, Willard 1921- ... 21-24R
Dalsass, Diana 1947- ... 106
Dalton, Alene
See Chapin, Alene Olsen Dalton
Dalton, Anne 1948- ... SATA 40
Dalton, Claire
See Burns, Alma
Dalton, Clive
See Clark, F(rederick) Stephen
Dalton, (John) David 1944- ... 97-100
Dalton, Dennis (Gilmore) 1938- ... 115
Dalton, Dorothy 1915- ... 21-24R
Dalton, Elizabeth 1936- ... 85-88
Dalton, Gene W(ray) 1928- ... 25-28R
Dalton, George 1926-1991 ... 127
Obituary ... 135
Brief entry ... 106
D'Alton, Louis (Lynch)
1900-1951 Brief entry ... 110
See also DLB 10
Dalton, Priscilla
See Avallone, Michael (Angelo, Jr)
Dalton, Richard 1930- ... 57-60
Dalton, Stephen 1937- ... 85-88
Dalven, Rae 1904- ... 33-36R
Daly, Anne 1896- ... CAP-2
Earlier sketch in CA 29-32
Daly, Cahal Brendan 1917- ... CANR-28
Earlier sketch in CA 104
Daly, Carroll John 1889-1958 Brief entry ... 112
Daly, Christopher B. 1954- ... 126
Daly, Donald F(remont) ... 69-72
Daly, Edith Iglauer ... CANR-14
Earlier sketch in CA 77-80
Daly, Elizabeth 1878-1967 ... CAP-2
Obituary ... 25-28R
Earlier sketch in CA 23-24
See also CLC 52
Daly, Emily Joseph 1913- ... 9-12R
Daly, Faye Kennedy 1936- ... 97-100
Daly, Gay 1951- ... 131
Daly, Herman E. 1938- ... 89-92
Daly, Ita 1945- ... 136
Daly, Jim
See Stratemeyer, Edward L.
Daly, John Jay 1888(?)-1976 Obituary ... 69-72
Daly, Kathleen N(orah) Brief entry ... 115
See also SATA 37
Daly, (Arthur) Leo 1920- ... CANR-25
Earlier sketch in CA 105
Daly, Lowrie John 1914- ... 13-16R
Daly, Mary Tinley 1904(?)-1979 ... 85-88
Daly, Mary 1928- ... CANR-30
Earlier sketch in CA 25-28R
See also MTCW
Daly, Maureen 1921- ... CANR-37
See also AAYA 5
See also CLC 17
See also MAICYA
See also SAAS 1
See also SATA 2
Daly, Nicholas 1946- ... CANR-36
Earlier sketch in CA 111
See also MAICYA
See also SATA 37
Daly, Niki
See Daly, Nicholas
Daly, Robert Welter 1916-1975 ... 9-12R
Obituary ... 103
Daly, Robert 1943- ... 104
Daly, Saralyn R(uth) 1924- ... 57-60
Daly, Sister Mary Virginia 1925- ... 17-20R
Daly, T(homas) A(ugustine)
1871-1948 Brief entry ... 111
See also DLB 11
Dalzel, Peter
See Dalzel Job, P(atrick)
Dalzel Job, P(atrick) 1913- ... 13-16R
Dalzell, Robert F(enton) Jr. 1937- ... 81-84
Dam, Hari N(arayan) 1921- ... 57-60
Dam, Kenneth W. 1932- ... CANR-12
Earlier sketch in CA 69-72
Damachi, (Godwin) Ukandi 1942- ... CANR-2
Earlier sketch in CA 45-48
Damas, David (John) 1926- ... 132
Damas, Leon-Gontran 1912-1978 ... 125
Obituary ... 73-76
See also BW
Damata, Ted 1909(?)-1988 Obituary ... 125
D'Amato, Alex 1919- ... CANR-18
Earlier sketch in CA 81-84
See also SATA 20
D'Amato, Anthony A. 1937- ... 29-32R
D'Amato, Barbara 1938- ... 69-72
D'Amato, Janet (Potter) 1925- ... CANR-18
Earlier sketches in CA 49-52, CANR-1
See also SATA 9
Damaz, Paul F. 1917- ... 5-8R
d'Amboise, Christopher 1960- ... 115
Dambrauskas, Joan Arden 1933- ... 104
D'Ambrosio, Charles A. 1932- ... 21-24R
D'Ambrosio, Richard A(nthony) 1927- ... 102
D'Ambrosio, Vinnie-Marie 1928- ... 45-48
Dame, Lawrence 1898- ... CAP-1
Earlier sketch in CA 11-12
D'Amelio, Dan 1927- ... 33-36R
Dameron, J(ohn) Lasley 1925- ... 53-56
Damerst, William A. 1923- ... 17-20R
Dames, Rob(ert L.) 1944- ... 133
Damiani, Bruno Mario 1942- ... 57-60
D'Amico, John Francis
1947(?)-1987 Obituary ... 124
Damis, John 1940- ... 118
Damm, John S. 1926- ... 37-40R
Damocles
See Benedetti, Mario
Damon, Gene
See Grier, Barbara G(ene Damon)
Damon, S(amuel) Foster 1893-1971 ... 101
See also DLB 45
Damon, Virgil Green 1895-1972 ... CAP-1
Obituary ... 37-40R
Earlier sketch in CA 9-10
Damor, Hakji
See Lesser, R(oger) H(arold)
D'Amore, Arcangelo R. T.
1920-1986 Obituary ... 118
Damore, Leo 1929- ... CANR-35
Earlier sketch in CA 81-84
See also BEST 89:2
Damrosch, Helen
See Tee-Van, Helen Damrosch
Damrosch, Leopold Jr. 1941- ... 45-48
Damsker, Matt(hew Harry) 1951- ... 108
Damtoft, Walter A(tkinson) 1922- ... 57-60
Dana, Amber
See Paine, Lauran (Bosworth)
Dana, Barbara 1940- ... CANR-8
Earlier sketch in CA 17-20R
See also SATA 22
Dana, Charles Anderson 1819-1897 ... DLB 3, 23
Dana, E. H.
See Hamel Peifer, Kathleen
Dana, Richard
See Paine, Lauran (Bosworth)
Dana, Richard H(enry) 1927- ... CANR-15
Earlier sketch in CA 85-88

Dana, Richard Henry Jr. 1815-1882 .... DLB 1
See also SATA 26
Dana, Robert (Patrick) 1929- 33-36R
Dana, Rose
See Ross, W(illiam) E(dward) D(aniel)
Danachair, Caoimhin O
See Danaher, Kevin
Danagher, Edward F. 1919- 9-12R
Danaher, Kevin 1913- 33-36R
See also SATA 22
Danan, Alexis 1889(?)-1979 Obituary 89-92
Danby, Hope (Smedley) 1899- CAP-1
Earlier sketch in CA 13-14
Danby, John B(lench) 1905-1983 Obituary 109
Danby, Mary (Heather) 1941- CANR-39
Danby, Miles William 1925- 13-16R
Dance, Daryl Cumber 1938- 131
Dance, E(dward) H(erbert) 1894- 37-40R
Dance, F(rancis) E(sburn) X(avier)
1929- CANR-16
Earlier sketches in CA 1-4R, CANR-1
Dance, Frank E. X.
See Dance, F(rancis) E(sburn) X(avier)
Dance, Jim 1924(?)-1983 Obituary 110
Dance, S(tanley) Peter 1932- CANR-13
Earlier sketch in CA 69-72
Dance, Stanley (Frank) 1910- CANR-8
Earlier sketch in CA 17-20R
Dancer, J. B.
See Harvey, John (Barton)
Danco, Katharine L(eck) 1929- 112
Danco, Katy
See Danco, Katharine L(eck)
Danco, Leon A(ntoine) 1923- 112
Dancocks, Daniel G. 1950- 120
D'Ancona, Mirella Levi 1919- CANR-6
Earlier sketch in CA 53-56
Dancy, John Christopher 1920- 107
Dandrea, Don(ald E.) 1936- 120
D'Andrea, Kate
See Steiner, Barbara A(nnette)
D'Andrea, Paul 1939- 120
Dandridge, Ray G.
See Dandridge, Raymond Garfield
Dandridge, Raymond Garfield 1882-1930 125
See also BW
See also DLB 51
Dandy, James Edgar 1903-1976 Obituary 104
Dane, Carl
See Adams, F(rank) Ramsay
Dane, Clemence
See Ashton, Winifred
See also DLB 10
Dane, Les(lie A.) 1925- 89-92
Dane, Mark
See Avallone, Michael (Angelo, Jr)
Dane, Mary
See Morland, Nigel
Dane, Nathan II 1916-1980 108
Obituary 97-100
Dane, Zel
See Timms, E(dward) V(ivian)
Daneff, Stephen Constantine 1931- 106
Daneke, Gregory A(llen) 1950- 112
Danelski, David J. 1930- 13-16R
Danenberg, Leigh 1893-1976 Obituary 69-72
Danford, Howard G(orby) 1904- CAP-1
Earlier sketch in CA 11-12
Danforth, Art(hur Louis)
1913(?)-1987 Obituary 122
Danforth, John 1660-1730 ....DLB 24
Danforth, Loring M(andell) 1949- 111
Danforth, Samuel I 1626-1674 ....DLB 24
Danforth, Samuel II 1666-1727 ....DLB 24
Dangaard, Colin (Edward) 1942- 85-88
D'angelo, Edward 1932- 37-40R
D'Angelo, Frank J(oseph) 1928- 120
D'Angelo, Lou
See D'Angelo, Luciano
D'Angelo, Luciano 1932- 33-36R
Dangerfield, Balfour
See McCloskey, (John) Robert
Dangerfield, Clint
See Norwood, Victor G(eorge) C(harles)
Dangerfield, George (Bubb) 1904-1986 ......9-12R
Obituary 121
Dangerfield, Harlan
See Padgett, Ron
Dangerfield, Rodney 1922(?)- 102
Danhof, Clarence H(enry) 1911- 37-40R
Dani, Ahmad Hasan 1920- 13-16R
Daniel, Alan 1939- ....SATA 53
Daniel, Anita 1893(?)-1978 Obituary 77-80
See also SATA 23, 24
Daniel, Anne
See Steiner, Barbara A(nnette)
Daniel, Becky 1947- ....SATA 56
Daniel, Charles 1933- 114
Daniel, Cletus E(dward) 1943- 107
Daniel, (Elbert) Clifton Jr. 1912- Brief entry 113
Daniel, Colin
See Windsor, Patricia (Frances)
Daniel, Daniel 1890(?)-1981 Obituary 104
Daniel, Elna Worrell
See Stone, Elna
Daniel, Emmett Randolph 1935- 102
Daniel, Errol Valentine 111
Daniel, George Bernard Jr. 1927- 13-16R
Daniel, Glenda 1943- 111
Daniel, Glyn (Edmund) 1914-1986 ....CANR-30
Obituary 121
Earlier sketches in CA 57-60, CANR-13
Daniel, Hawthorne 1890- 5-8R
See also SATA 8
Daniel, James 1916- 69-72
Daniel, Jerry C(layton) 1937- 33-36R
Daniel, John M. 1825-1865 ....DLB 43

Daniel, Julie Goldsmith 1949- CANR-14
Earlier sketch in CA 77-80
Daniel, Lee
See Reid, Daniel P. (Jr.)
Daniel, Lorne (MacLeod Lyons) 1953- 118
Daniel, Mark 1954- 133
Daniel, Norman (Alexander) 1919- CANR-6
Earlier sketch in CA 57-60
Daniel, Pete 1938- CANR-14
Earlier sketch in CA 37-40R
Daniel, Price Jr. 1941-1981 Obituary 103
Daniel, Ralph T(homas) 1921- 53-56
Daniel, Rebecca
See Daniel, Becky
Daniel, Robert L(eslie) 1923- 33-36R
Daniel, Robert W(oodham) 1915- 25-28R
Daniel, Samuel 1562(?)-1619 ....DLB 62
Daniel, Stephen H(artley) 1950- 119
Daniel, Urcel 1908(?)-1984 Obituary 113
Daniel, Walter C(larence) 1922- 110
Daniel, Wayne W. 1929- 135
Daniel, Yuli (Markovich) 1925-1988 116
Obituary 127
Daniele, Joseph William 1927- 89-92
Daniell, Albert Scott 1906-1965 ....CANR-3
Earlier sketch in CA 5-8R
Daniell, David Scott
See Daniell, Albert Scott
Daniell, Jere Rogers 1932- CANR-11
Earlier sketch in CA 29-32R
Daniell, Rosemary 1935- 118
Danielle, Maria 1945- 114
Danielli, James Frederic
1911-1984 Obituary 113
Daniells, Lorna M(cLean) 1918- CANR-18
Earlier sketch in CA 89-92
Daniells, Roy 1902-1979 57-60
See also DLB 68
Danielou, Alain 1907- CANR-31
Earlier sketches in CA 73-76, CANR-14
Danielou, Jean 1905-1974 ....CAP-2
Obituary 49-52
Earlier sketch in CA 23-24
Daniel-Rops, Henri
See Petiot, Henri Jules Charles
Daniels, Anna Kleegman
1893-1970 Obituary 29-32R
Daniels, Arlene Kaplan 1930- CANR-27
Earlier sketches in CA 29-32R, CANR-12
Daniels, Brett
See Adler, Renata
Daniels, Bruce C(olin) 1943- 122
Daniels, Charlie 1936- 138
Daniels, David 1933- 53-56
Daniels, Derick January 1926- Brief entry 112
Daniels, Dewey
See McKimmey, James
Daniels, Doris Groshen 1931- 131
Daniels, Dorothy 1915- CANR-15
Earlier sketch in CA 89-92
Daniels, Douglas Henry 1943- 125
Daniels, Draper 1913-1983 53-56
Obituary 109
Daniels, Elizabeth Adams 1920- 37-40R
Daniels, Farrington 1889-1972 ....5-8R
Obituary 37-40R
Daniels, Frank Arthur 1904-1986 Obituary 121
Daniels, Frank James
1900(?)-1983 Obituary 110
Daniels, George H. 1935- CANR-10
Earlier sketch in CA 25-28R
Daniels, George M(orris) 1927- 29-32R
Daniels, Guy 1919-1989 ....21-24R
Obituary 128
See also SATA 7, 11, 62
Daniels, Harold R(obert) 1919- 17-20R
Daniels, James R(aymond) 1956- 121
See also Daniels, Jim
Daniels, Jim
See Daniels, James R(aymond)
See also DLB 120
Daniels, John Clifford 1915- 13-16R
Daniels, John S.
See Overholser, Wayne D.
Daniels, Jonathan (Worth) 1902-1981 ....CANR-29
Obituary 105
Earlier sketch in CA 49-52
Daniels, Josephus 1862-1948 Brief entry 122
See also DLB 29
Daniels, Kate 1953- 124
Daniels, Les(lie Noel III) 1943- CANR-24
Earlier sketches in CA 65-68, CANR-9
Daniels, Mary 1937- 93-96
Daniels, Max
See Gellis, Roberta L(eah Jacobs)
Daniels, Norman CANR-15
Earlier sketch in CA 89-92
Daniels, Norman 1942- CANR-22
Earlier sketch in CA 106
Daniels, Olga
See Sinclair, Olga
Daniels, Pamela 1937- 101
Daniels, R(obertson) Balfour 1900- 49-52
Daniels, Randy (Allan) 1949- 81-84
Daniels, Robert V(incent) 1926- CANR-2
Earlier sketch in CA 1-4R
Daniels, Roger 1927- CANR-23
Earlier sketches in CA 5-8R, CANR-8
Daniels, Sally 1931- 1-4R
Daniels, Sarah 1956- 133
Daniels, Shouri
See Ramanujan, Molly
Daniels, Steven Lloyd 1945-1973 ....33-36R
Daniels, Velma Seawell 1931- 108
Danielson, Elena S(chafer) 1947- 116
Danielson, J. D.
See James, M. R.

Danielson, Michael N(ils) 1934- 33-36R
Danielson, Wayne Allen 1929- 77-80
Danielsson, Bengt (Emmerik) 1921- CANR-23
Earlier sketch in CA 107
Daniere, Andre L(ucien) 1926- 9-12R
Daniloff, Nicholas 1934- 85-88
Danilov, Victor J(oseph) 1924- CANR-21
Earlier sketches in CA 13-16R, CANR-6
Daninos, Pierre 1913- CANR-15
Earlier sketch in CA 77-80
Danish, Barbara 1948- 57-60
Dank, Gloria Rand 1955- 114
See also SATA 46, 56
Dank, Leonard D(ewey) 1929- ....SATA 44
Dank, Milton 1920- CANR-28
Earlier sketches in CA 69-72, CANR-11
See also SATA 31
Danker, Frederick William 1920- CANR-5
Earlier sketch in CA 13-16R
Danker, W(illiam) John 1914- 13-16R
Dankleff, Richard E(lden) 1925- 114
Danky, James Philip 1947- CANR-12
Earlier sketch in CA 69-72
Danly, Robert Lyons 1947- 108
Dann, Colin (Michael) 1943- 108
Dann, Jack 1945- CANR-30
Earlier sketches in CA 49-52, CANR-2
Dann, John C(hristie) 1944- 126
Dann, Max 1955- 118
See also SATA 62
Dann, Uriel 1922- 25-28R
Dannay, Frederic 1905-1982 ....CANR-39
Obituary 107
Earlier sketches in CA 1-4R, CANR-1
See also Queen, Ellery
See also CLC 11
See also MTCW
Dannelley, Paul (Edward Jr.) 1919- 122
Dannemiller, Lawrence 1925- 1-4R
Dannenfeldt, Karl H(enry) 1916- 25-28R
Danner, Margaret (Essie) 1915- 29-32R
See also BW
See also DLB 41
Dannett, Sylvia G. L. 1909- CANR-4
Earlier sketch in CA 1-4R
D'Annunzio, Gabriele
1863-1938 Brief entry 104
See also TCLC 6, 40
Danoff, I. Michael 1940- 97-100
Danowski, T(haddeus) S(tanley)
1914-1987 ....9-12R
Obituary 123
Danska, Herbert 1928- 29-32R
Danson, Lawrence Neil 1942- 85-88
d'Antibes, Germain
See Simenon, Georges (Jacques Christian)
Dantin, Louis 1865-1945 ....DLB 92
Danto, Arthur C(oleman) 1924- 17-20R
Danto, Bruce L. 1927- CANR-7
Earlier sketch in CA 53-56
Danton, J(oseph) Periam 1908- 9-12R
Danton, Rebecca
See Roberts, Janet Louise
Dantzic, Cynthia Maris 1933- 101
Dantzig, George Bernard 1914- Brief entry 106
Danvers, Dennis 1947- ....CLC 70
Danvers, Jack
See Caseleyr, Cam(ille Auguste Marie)
Danzig, Allan (Peter) 1931- 45-48
Danzig, Allison 1898-1987 ....37-40R
Obituary 121
Danzig, Fred P(aul) 1925- 65-68
Danziger, Edmund J(efferson) Jr. 1938- 102
Danziger, Kurt 1926- 41-44R
Danziger, Marlies K(allmann) 1926- CANR-16
Earlier sketch in CA 25-28R
Danziger, Nick 1958- 129
Danziger, Paula 1944- CANR-37
Brief entry 112
Earlier sketch in CA 115
See also AAYA 4
See also CLC 21
See also CLR 20
See also MAICYA
See also SATA 30, 36, 63
Danziger, Sheldon H. 1948- 119
Daoud, Hazim S. 1930-1976 122
Daoudi, M(ohammed) S(uleiman) 1946- 132
Dapper, Gloria 1922- 17-20R
Dapping, William Osborne
1880-1969 Obituary 115
D'Aprix, Roger M. 1932- 33-36R
Darack, Arthur J. 1918- CANR-37
Earlier sketch in CA 115
Darbelnet, Jean (Louis) 1904- CANR-10
Earlier sketch in CA 25-28R
Darby, Catherine
See Peters, Maureen
Darby, Edwin Wheeler 1922- 125
Darby, Gene Kegley
See Darby, Jean (Kegley)
Darby, Henry Clifford 1909- 5-8R
Darby, J. N.
See Govan, Christine Noble
Darby, Jean (Kegley) 1921- CANR-39
See also SATA 68
Darby, John 1940- 105
Darby, Michael 1944- CANR-38
Earlier sketch in CA 116
Darby, Patricia (Paulsen) 73-76
See also SATA 14
Darby, Ray(mond) 1912- 17-20R
See also SATA 7
d'Arch Smith, Timothy 1936- 13-16R
Darcy, Clare 102
D'Arcy, G(eorge) Minot 1930- 9-12R

Darcy, Jean
See Lepley, Jean Elizabeth
D'Arcy, Jean (Marie) 1913-1983 Obituary 109
D'Arcy, Margaretta (Ruth) 1934- CANR-31
Earlier sketch in CA 104
D'Arcy, Martin C(yril) 1888-1976 ....CANR-3
Obituary 69-72
Earlier sketch in CA 5-8R
D'Arcy, Pamela
See Roby, Mary Linn
D'Arcy, Paul F(rancis) 1921- 17-20R
d'Arcy, Willard
See Cox, William R(obert)
Darden, Lloyd (Nestor) 1931- Brief entry 113
Darden, Norma Jean 114
Darden, William R(aymond) 1936- 77-80
Dardess, John W(olfe) 1937- 45-48
Dardig, Jill C(arolyn) 1948- 69-72
Dardis, Tom 1926- CANR-9
Earlier sketch in CA 65-68
Dare, Evelyn
See Everett-Green, Evelyn
Dareff, Hal 1920- 65-68
Darga, Bert 1931- 110
Dargan, Olive (Tilford) 1869-1968 Obituary 111
Dargo, George 1935- 115
d'Argyre, Gilles
See Klein, Gerard
Dariaux, Genevieve Antoine
See Antoine-Dariaux, Genevieve
Darien, Peter
See Bassett, William B. K.
Daringer, Helen Fern 1892- CAP-2
Earlier sketch in CA 17-18
See also SATA 1
Dario, Ruben
See Sarmiento, Felix Ruben Garcia
See also TCLC 4
Dario, Ruben 1867-1916 131
See also HW
See also MTCW
Darion, Joe
See Darion, Joseph
Darion, Joseph 1917- Brief entry 113
Dark, Alvin Ralph 1922- 105
Dark, Harris Edward 1922- 57-60
Dark, Johnny
See Norwood, Victor G(eorge) C(harles)
Dark, Larry 1959- 136
Dark, Philip J(ohn) C(rosskey) 1918- CANR-18
Earlier sketches in CA 49-52, CANR-2
Darke, Marjorie 1929- CANR-34
Earlier sketches in CA 81-84, CANR-15
See also SATA 16
Darley, F(elix) O(ctavius) C(arr)
1822-1888 ....SATA 35
Darley, George 1795-1846 ....DLB 96
Darley, John M(cConnon) 1938- 93-96
Darling, Arthur Burr 1892-1971 ....5-8R
Obituary 33-36R
Darling, David J. 1953- 138
See also SATA 44
Darling, Edward 1907-1974 ....CANR-3
Obituary 53-56
Earlier sketch in CA 49-52
Darling, Frank Clayton 1925- 17-20R
Darling, Frank Fraser
See Fraser Darling, Frank
Darling, Jay Norwood
1876-1962 Obituary 93-96
Darling, John R(othburn) 1937- 93-96
Darling, Kathy
See Darling, Mary Kathleen
Darling, Lois MacIntyre 1917-1989 ....CANR-38
Obituary 130
Earlier sketches in CA 5-8R, CANR-3
See also MAICYA
See also SATA 3
See also SATO 64
Darling, Louis Jr. 1916-1970 ....CANR-38
Obituary 89-92
Earlier sketches in CA 5-8R, CANR-3
See also MAICYA
See also SATA 3, 23
Darling, Mary Kathleen 1943- CANR-4
Earlier sketch in CA 53-56
See also SATA 9
Darling, Richard L(ewis) 1925- 21-24R
Darling, Sandra
See Day, Alexandra
Darling, Sharon (Sandling) 1943- 128
Darlington, Alice B(enning) 1906-1973 ......CAP-2
Obituary 41-44R
Earlier sketch in CA 25-28
Darlington, C(yril) D(ean) 1903-1981 ......CANR-10
Obituary 108
Earlier sketch in CA 9-12R
Darlington, Charles F. 1904-1986 ....CAP-2
Obituary 119
Earlier sketch in CA 25-28
Darlington, David 1951- 127
Darlington, Joy 1947- 89-92
Darlington, William Aubrey (Cecil) 1890- CAP-1
Earlier sketch in CA 13-16
Darlow, Michael (George) 1934- 104
Darlton, Clark
See Ernsting, Walter
Darmstadter, Joel 1928- 121
Darnay, Arsen (Julius) 1936- 111
Darnton, John (Townsend) 1941- 126
Brief entry 119
Darnton, Robert (Choate) 1939- 116
Brief entry 113
Darr, Ann 1920- CANR-7
Earlier sketch in CA 57-60
Darracott, Joseph C(orbould) 1934- 106
Darrah, William C(ulp) 1909- 57-60

Darrell, R(obert) D(onaldson)
1903-1988 Obituary 125
Darroch, Maurice A. 1903- CAP-2
Earlier sketch in CA 19-20
Darroch, Sandra Jobson 1942- 89-92
Darrow, Ralph C(arroll) 1918- 61-64
Darrow, Richard W(illiam) 1915-1976 .... 21-24R
Obituary 120
Darrow, Whitney (Jr.) 1909- CANR-14
Earlier sketch in CA 61-64
See also SATA 13
Dart, John 1936- 65-68
Dart, Raymond A(rthur) 1893-1988 .... CAP-1
Obituary 127
Earlier sketch in CA 13-14
Darton, G(erald) C(hristopher)
1913(?)-1987 Obituary 122
Darvas, Nicolas 1920- 61-64
Darveaux, Terry A(lan) 1943- 65-68
Darvi, Andrea
See Plate, Andrea
Darvill, Fred T(homas) Jr. 1927- CANR-6
Earlier sketch in CA 57-60
Darvill, Timothy (C.) 1957- 127
Darwall, Stephen L(eicester) 1946- 113
Darwin, Charles 1809-1882 .... DLB 57
Darwin, Erasmus 1731-1802 .... DLB 93
Darwin, Len
See Darwin, Leonard
Darwin, Leonard 1916- .... SATA 24
Darwin, M. B.
See McDavid, Raven I(oor) Jr.
Darwish, Adel 1945- 135
Dary, David A. 1934- CANR-29
Earlier sketches in CA 29-32R, CANR-13
Daryush, Elizabeth 1887-1977 .... CANR-3
Earlier sketch in CA 49-52
See also CLC 6, 19
See also DLB 20
Das, Deb Kumar 1935- 102
Das, Durga 1900-1974 .... CAP-2
Obituary 49-52
Earlier sketch in CA 29-32
Das, G. K. 1934- 128
Das, Gurcharan 1943- 33-36R
Das, Jagannath Prasad 1931- CANR-6
Earlier sketch in CA 57-60
Das, Kamala 1934- CANR-27
Earlier sketch in CA 101
Das, Manmath Nath 1926- CANR-8
Earlier sketch in CA 13-16R
Dasenbrock, Reed Way 1953- 125
Dasent, Sir George Webbe
1817-1896 .... SATA 29, 62
Das Gupta, Jyotirindra 1933- 53-56
Dash, Irene G(olden) 125
Dash, Jack Brien 1907-1989 Obituary 128
Dash, Joan 1925- CANR-31
Earlier sketch in CA 49-52
Dash, Samuel 1925- Brief entry 105
Dash, Tony 1945- 33-36R
Dashiell, Alfred Sheppard
1901-1970 Obituary 89-92
Dashti, Ali 1894- 85-88
Dashwood, Edmee Elizabeth Monica de la Pasture
1890-1943 Brief entry 119
See also Delafield, E. M.
Dashwood, Robert Julian 1899- CAP-1
Earlier sketch in CA 13-14
da Silva, Howard 1909-1986 Obituary 118
DaSilva, Leon
See Wallmann, Jeffrey M(iner)
DaSilva, Zenia Sacks 1925- 121
Daskam, Josephine Dodge
See Bacon, Josephine Dodge (Daskam)
Dasmann, Raymond (Fredric) 1919- CANR-2
Earlier sketch in CA 5-8R
Dass, Ram
See Alpert, Richard
Dassault, Marcel (Bloch)
1892-1986 Obituary 119
Brief entry 115
Dassin, Jules 1911- 132
Dassonville, Michel A(uguste) 1927- 73-76
Daston, Lorraine 1951- 128
Dater, Henry M. 1909(?)-1974 Obituary 49-52
Datesh, John Nicholas 1950- 97-100
Dathorne, O(scar) R(onald) 1934- CANR-26
Earlier sketch in CA 57-60
See also BW
Daube, David 1909- CANR-1
Earlier sketch in CA 1-4R
Daubeny, Peter (Lauderdale) 1921-1975 61-64
Dauber, Kenneth Marc 1945- CANR-37
Earlier sketch in CA 114
Daudet, Leon 1867-1942 Brief entry 121
Dauenhauer, Richard L(eonard)
1942- CANR-11
Earlier sketch in CA 61-64
Dauer, Dorothea W. 1917- 37-40R
Dauer, Manning J(ulian) 1909- 89-92
Dauer, Rosamond 1934- CANR-10
Earlier sketch in CA 65-68
See also SATA 23
Dauer, Victor Paul 1909- 17-20R
Daugert, Stanley M(atthew) 1918- 17-20R
Daughdrill, James H(arold) Jr. 1934- 41-44R
Daughen, Joseph R(obert) 1935- 33-36R
Daugherty, Carroll R(oop)
1900-1988 Obituary 125
Daugherty, Charles Michael 1914- 73-76
See also SATA 16
Daugherty, James (Henry) 1889-1974 73-76
Obituary 49-52
See also MAICYA
See also SATA 13
Daugherty, Richard D(eo) 1922- 108
See also SATA 35
Daugherty, Sarah Bowyer 1949- 106
Daugherty, Sonia Medwedeff Obituary 104
See also SATA 27
Daugherty, Tracy 1955- 127
Daughtrey, Anne Scott 1920- 17-20R
d'Aulaire, Edgar Parin 1898-1986 .... CANR-29
Obituary 119
Earlier sketch in CA 49-52
See also CLR 21
See also DLB 22
See also MAICYA
See also SATA 5, 47, 66
d'Aulaire, Ingri (Mortenson Parin)
1904-1980 .... CANR-29
Obituary 102
Earlier sketch in CA 49-52
See also CLR 21
See also DLB 22
See also MAICYA
See also SATA 5, 24, 66
Daumal, Rene 1908-1944 Brief entry 114
See also TCLC 14
Daunton, M(artin) J(ames) 1949- 125
Dauster, Frank (Nicholas) 1925- 53-56
Dauten, Carl Anton 1913-1976 .... CANR-3
Earlier sketch in CA 5-8R
Dauw, Dean C(harles) 1933- CANR-6
Earlier sketch in CA 53-56
D'Avanzo, Mario Louis 1931- 41-44R
Davar, Ashok 69-72
Dave, Shyam
See Gantzer, Hugh
Daveluy, Paule Cloutier 1919- 9-12R
See also SATA 11
Davenant, William 1606-1668 .... DLB 58
Davenport, Elaine 1946- 102
Davenport, Francine
See Tate, Velma
Davenport, Francis Garvin
1905-1975 Obituary 111
Davenport, Gene L(ooney) 1935- 33-36R
Davenport, Guy (Mattison Jr.) 1927- CANR-23
Earlier sketch in CA 33-36R
See also CLC 6, 14, 38
Davenport, Gwen 1910- 9-12R
Davenport, John 1905-1987 Obituary 122
Davenport, Marcia 1903- 9-12R
Davenport, Paul 1946- 132
Davenport, Robert .... DLB 58
Davenport, Roger (Hamilton) 1946- 131
Davenport, Spencer CANR-26
Earlier sketches in CAP-2, CA 19-20
Davenport, T(homas) R(odney) H(ope)
1926- 77-80
Davenport, Walter 1889-1971 Obituary 104
Davenport, William H. 1908- CANR-4
Earlier sketch in CA 1-4R
Davenport-Hines, Richard (Peter Treadwell)
1953- 134
Daventry, Leonard John 1915- 17-20R
Daves, Delmer Lawrence
1904(?)-1977 Obituary 73-76
See also DLB 26
Daves, Francis Marion 1903- 45-48
Daves, Jessica 1898(?)-1974 Obituary 53-56
Daves, Michael 1938- 9-12R
See also SATA 40
Davey, Cyril J(ames) 1911- CANR-18
Earlier sketches in CA 5-8R, CANR-2
Davey, Frank(land Wilmot) 1940- CANR-32
Earlier sketches in CA 65-68, CANR-13
Davey, Frank 1907(?)-1983 Obituary 109
Davey, Gilbert (Walter) 1913- CANR-12
Earlier sketches in CAP-1, CA 9-10
Davey, Harold W(illiam) 1915-1986 120
Davey, Jocelyn
See Raphael, Chaim
Davey, John
See Richey, David
Davey, Peter (John) 1940- 135
Davey, Thomas A. 1954- 126
Daviau, Donald G(eorge) 1927- CANR-32
Earlier sketches in CA 81-84, CANR-14
David, A. R.
See David, A(nn) Rosalie
David, A(nn) Rosalie 1946- CANR-37
Earlier sketch in CA 114
David, Alfred 1929- 85-88
David, Andrew
See Whittingham, Richard
David, Anne 1924-1987 .... CANR-12
Obituary 122
Earlier sketch in CA 29-32R
David, Carl 1949- 108
David, Ed
See Wohlmuth, Ed
David, Emily
See Alman, David
David, Gerald 1941- 114
David, Heather M(acKinnon) 1937- 37-40R
David, Henry P. 1923- CANR-6
Earlier sketch in CA 13-16R
David, Henry 1907-1984 Obituary 111
David, Hugh (Housdon) 1954- 129
David, Irene 1921- 110
David, Jack 1946- CANR-30
Earlier sketch in CA 110
David, Jay
See Adler, William
David, Jonathan
See Ames, Lee J(udah)
David, Joseph Ben
See Ben-David, Joseph
David, Lester 1914- CANR-14
Earlier sketch in CA 37-40R
David, Marjorie 1950- 112
David, Martin H(eidenhain) 1935- 37-40R
David, Michael Robert 1932- 53-56
David, Nicholas
See Morgan, Thomas Bruce
David, Paul A(llan) 1935- 97-100
David, Paul T(heodore) 1906- CANR-2
Earlier sketch in CA 5-8R
David, R. W.
See David, Richard (W.)
David, Richard (W.) 1912- 129
David, Rosalie
See David, A(nn) Rosalie
David, Saul 1921- 124
Brief entry 114
David, Stephen M(ark) 1934-1985 .... 33-36R
Obituary 115
David, William
See Sandman, Peter M(ark)
David-Neel, Alexandra
1868-1969 Obituary 25-28R
Davidow, Mike 1913- 57-60
Davidow-Goodman, Ann
See Goodman, Ann (Davidow)
Davids, Anthony 1923- 41-44R
Davids, Bob
See Davids, L(eonard) Robert
Davids, L(eonard) Robert 1926- 115
Davids, Lewis Edmund 1917- 37-40R
Davids, Richard Carlyle 1913- 97-100
Davidson, Abraham A. 1935- 53-56
Davidson, Alan Eaton 1924- 103
Davidson, Alastair 1939- 29-32R
Davidson, Alice Joyce 1932- 115
See also SATA 45, 54
Davidson, Angus (Henry Gordon)
1898-1980 .... 25-28R
Obituary 97-100
Davidson, Arnold E(dward) 1936- 111
Davidson, Avram 1923- CANR-26
Earlier sketch in CA 101
See also Queen, Ellery
See also DLB 8
Davidson, Basil 1914- CANR-17
Earlier sketches in CA 1-4R, CANR-1
See also SATA 13
Davidson, Bill
See Davidson, William
Davidson, Bill R.
See Davidson, William R.
Davidson, Caroline 1953- 122
Davidson, Cathy Notari 1949- CANR-23
Earlier sketch in CA 106
Davidson, Chalmers Gaston 1907- 29-32R
Davidson, Chandler 1936- 45-48
Davidson, Clarissa Start
See Lippert, Clarissa Start
Davidson, Clifford 1932- 45-48
Davidson, David 1908-1985 49-52
Obituary 117
Davidson, Diane 1924- 29-32R
Davidson, Donald (Grady) 1893-1968 .... CANR-4
Obituary 25-28R
Earlier sketch in CA 5-8R
See also CLC 2, 13, 19
See also DLB 45
Davidson, Donald 1917- CANR-2
Earlier sketch in CA 45-48
Davidson, E(phraim) E(dward) 1923- 33-36R
Davidson, Ellen Prescott 49-52
Davidson, Eugene (Arthur) 1902- CANR-3
Earlier sketch in CA 1-4R
Davidson, Eva Rucker
1894(?)-1974 Obituary 53-56
Davidson, F(rank) G(eoffrey) 1920- 29-32R
Davidson, Frank P(aul) 1918- 116
Davidson, Glen W(illiam) 1936- CANR-9
Earlier sketch in CA 61-64
Davidson, Greg (Stuart) 1961- 129
Davidson, Gustav 1895-1971 Obituary 29-32R
Davidson, H(ilda) R(oderick) Ellis
1914- CANR-11
Earlier sketch in CA 17-20R
Davidson, Harold G(ordon) 1912- 65-68
Davidson, Henry A(lexander)
1905-1973 Obituary 45-48
Davidson, Herbert A(lan) 1932- 17-20R
Davidson, Hugh
See Hamilton, Edmond
Davidson, Hugh M(acCullough) 1918- 102
Davidson, Irwin Delmore
1906-1981 Obituary 105
Davidson, James Dale 1947- 107
Davidson, James West 1946- CANR-15
Earlier sketch in CA 85-88
Davidson, Jeffrey P(hilip) 1951- 122
Davidson, Jessica 1915- CANR-14
Earlier sketch in CA 41-44R
See also SATA 5
Davidson, John
See Reid, Charles (Stuart)
Davidson, John Wells 1903-1986 Obituary 120
Davidson, John 1857-1909 Brief entry 118
See also DLB 19
See also TCLC 24
Davidson, Judith 1953- 116
See also SATA 40
Davidson, Julian M. 1931- 102
Davidson, Lionel 1922- CANR-1
Earlier sketch in CA 1-4R
See also DLB 14
Davidson, Margaret 1936- CANR-17
Earlier sketch in CA 25-28R
See also SATA 5
Davidson, Marion
See Garis, Howard R(oger)
Davidson, Mark 1940- 138
Davidson, Marshall B(owman)
1907-1989 .... 33-36R
Obituary 129
Davidson, Mary R. 1885-1973 .... 5-8R
See also SATA 9
Davidson, Mary S. 1940- 107
See also SATA 61
Davidson, Max D. 1899(?)-1977 Obituary 73-76
Davidson, Melanie
See Arnold, Madelyn M.
Davidson, Michael
See Rorvik, David M(ichael)
Davidson, Michael
See Rorvik, David M(ichael)
Davidson, Michael Childers 1897- 29-32R
Davidson, Michael 1944- 106
Davidson, Mickie
See Davidson, Margaret
Davidson, Mildred 1935- 93-96
Davidson, Miriam 1960- 128
Davidson, Morris 1898-1979 85-88
Davidson, Muriel 1924(?)-1983 Obituary 110
Davidson, Norman 1933- 119
Davidson, Pamela 1954- 133
Davidson, Paul 1930- CANR-28
Earlier sketches in CA 13-16R, CANR-6
Davidson, Philip (Grant) 1902- 73-76
Davidson, Phillip B. 1915- 130
Davidson, R.
See Davidson, Raymond
Davidson, Raymond 1926- .... SATA 32
Davidson, Robert F(ranklin) 1902- 49-52
Davidson, Roger H(arry) 1936- CANR-24
Earlier sketches in CA 21-24R, CANR-9
Davidson, Rosalie 1921- 69-72
See also SATA 23
Davidson, Sandra Calder 1935- 41-44R
Davidson, Sara 1943- 81-84
See also CLC 9
Davidson, Sol M. 1924- 17-20R
Davidson, William H. 1951- 128
Davidson, William R.
1929(?)-1987 Obituary 122
Davidson, William Robert 1919- 17-20R
Davidson, William 1918- 93-96
Davidson-Houston, J(ames) Vivian
1901-1965 .... 5-8R
Davie, Donald (Alfred) 1922- CANR-1
Earlier sketch in CA 1-4R
See also CAAS 3
See also CLC 5, 8, 10, 31
See also DLB 27
See also MTCW
Davie, Elspeth 1919- 126
Brief entry 120
Davie, Ian 1924- 102
Davie, Maurice R(ea) 1893-1964 .... 5-8R
Davie, Michael 1924- 57-60
Davie, Peter (Edward Sidney) 1936- 114
Davied, Camille
See Rose, Camille Davied
Davie-Martin, Hugh
See McCutcheon, Hugh Davie-Martin
Davies, A(lfred) Mervyn 1899-1976 .... 17-20R
Obituary 69-72
Davies, Ada Hilton 1893- CAP-2
Earlier sketch in CA 17-18
Davies, Alan T(rewartha) 1933- 33-36R
Davies, Alfred T(homas) 1930- 13-16R
Davies, Andrew (Wynford) 1936- 105
See also SATA 27
Davies, Bettilu D(onna) 1942- CANR-18
Earlier sketch in CA 101
See also SATA 33
Davies, Charles (Michael) 1946- 128
Davies, Christie
See Davies, John Christopher Hughes
Davies, Colin
See Elliot, Ian
Davies, (George) Colliss (Boardman)
1912- CAP-1
Earlier sketch in CA 11-12
Davies, D(avid) Jacob 1916-1974 .... 5-8R
Obituary 103
Davies, Daniel R. 1911- 37-40R
Davies, David Margerison 1923- 5-8R
Davies, David Michael 1929- Brief entry 109
Davies, David W(illiam) 1908- CANR-3
Earlier sketch in CA 9-12R
Davies, Duncan (Sheppey) 1921-1987 124
Obituary 122
Davies, Ebenezer Thomas 1903- CAP-1
Earlier sketch in CA 13-14
Davies, Eileen Winifred 1910- CAP-1
Earlier sketch in CA 13-14
Davies, Evelyn A(dele) 1915- 61-64
Davies, Evelyn 1924- CANR-8
Earlier sketch in CA 61-64
Davies, Harriet Vaughn
1879(?)-1978 Obituary 77-80
Davies, Horton (Marlais) 1916- CANR-7
Earlier sketch in CA 5-8R
Davies, Hugh Sykes 1909-1984(?) Obituary 113
Davies, Hunter 1936- CANR-12
Earlier sketch in CA 57-60
See also SATA 45, 55
Davies, (David) Ioan 1936- 21-24R
Davies, Ivor K(evin) 1930- 53-56
Davies, J. Clarence III 1937- 29-32R
Davies, J. Kenneth 1925- 57-60
Davies, James A. 1939- 129
Davies, James Chowning 1918- 45-48
Davies, Joan 1934- 124
See also SATA 47, 50
Davies, John Christopher Hughes 1941- 93-96
Davies, John Evan Weston 1914- 113
Brief entry 111

Davies, John Gordon 1919- 69-72
Davies, John K(enyon) 1937- 120
Davies, John Paton Jr. 1908- 9-12R
Davies, L(eslie) P(urnell) 1914- CANR-9
Earlier sketch in CA 21-24R
Davies, Laurence 1926- 57-60
Davies, Loma G. 1934- 137
Davies, Mansel Morris 1913- 9-12R
Davies, Margaret C(onstance Brown)
1923- 9-12R
Davies, Margaret Lloyd 1935- 106
Davies, Marion
See Douras, Marion Cecilia
Davies, Martin Brett 1936- 102
Davies, Merton E(dward) 1917- 85-88
Davies, Morton Rees 1939- 37-40R
Davies, Nick 1953- 136
Davies, (Claude) Nigel (Byam) 1920- CANR-19
Earlier sketch in CA 102
Davies, Norman 1939- 41-44R
Davies, Oliver 1905- CAP-2
Earlier sketch in CA 25-28
Davies, P. C. W.
See Davies, Paul (Charles William)
Davies, Paul (Charles William) 1946- CANR-31
Earlier sketch in CA 106
Davies, P.C.W.
See Davies, Paul (Charles William)
Davies, (William Thomas) Pennar 1911- 13-16R
Davies, Peter J. 1937- 135
See also SATA 52
Davies, Piers (Anthony David) 1941- 103
Davies, R(onald) E. G. 1921- 17-20R
Davies, R(obert) R(ees) 1938- 135
Davies, R(eginald) T(horne) 1923- 9-12R
Davies, R(obert) W(illiam) 1925- CANR-29
Earlier sketches in CA 33-36R, CANR-13
Davies, Ray(mond Douglas)
1944- Brief entry 116
See also CLC 21
Davies, Rhys 1903-1978 ....CANR-4
Obituary 81-84
Earlier sketch in CA 9-12R
See also CLC 23
Davies, Richard Llewelyn
See Llewelyn-Davies, Richard
Davies, Richard O. 1937- 17-20R
Davies, (William) Robertson 1913- CANR-17
Earlier sketch in CA 33-36R
See also BEST 89:2
See also CLC 2, 7, 13, 25, 42
See also DLB 68
See also MTCW
See also WLC
Davies, Rod 1941- 61-64
Davies, Rosemary Reeves 1925- 49-52
Davies, Rupert Eric 1909- CANR-39
Earlier sketches in CA 5-8R, CANR-3, 18
Davies, Ruth A(nn) 1915- CANR-26
Earlier sketch in CA 29-32R
Davies, Samuel 1723-1761 .... DLB 31
Davies, Stan Gebler 1943- 65-68
Davies, Stanley Powell 1892-1985 Obituary 115
Davies, Stevan L(awrence) 1948- 107
Davies, Sumiko 1942- 126
See also SATA 46
Davies, T(refor) Rendall 1913- CAP-1
Earlier sketch in CA 9-10
Davies, Thomas M(ockett) Jr. 1940- CANR-6
Earlier sketch in CA 57-60
Davies, Thomas 1941- 115
Davies, Tom
See Davies, Thomas
Davies, W(illiam) H(enry)
1871-1940 Brief entry 104
See also DLB 19
See also TCLC 5
Davies, Walter C.
See Kornbluth, C(yril) M.
Davies, William David 1911- CANR-1
Earlier sketch in CA 1-4R
Davies, Wyndham (Roy) 1926- 25-28R
Davies of Hereford, John
1565(?)-1618 .... DLB 121
Davila, Virgilio 1869-1943 131
See also HW
Davin, D(aniel) M(arcus) 1913- CANR-30
Earlier sketches in CA 9-12R, CANR-3
Davin, Dan
See Davin, D(aniel) M(arcus)
Davin, Nicholas Flood 1840(?)-1901 .... DLB 99
Davinson, Donald E(dward) 1932- CANR-3
Earlier sketch in CA 5-8R
Daviot, Gordon
See Mackintosh, Elizabeth
See also DLB 10
Davis, Adelle 1904-1974 ....CANR-30
Obituary 49-52
Earlier sketch in CA 37-40R
Davis, Albert Belisle 1947- 138
Davis, Alice Taylor 1903-1989 Obituary 129
Davis, Allen III 1929- 108
Davis, Allen F(reeman) 1931- CANR-25
Earlier sketches in CA 21-24R, CANR-10
Davis, (William) Allison 1902-1983 125
Obituary 111
Brief entry 106
See also BW
Davis, Andrew Jackson
1826-1910 Brief entry 120
Davis, Angela (Yvonne) 1944- CANR-10
Earlier sketch in CA 57-60
See also BW
Davis, Ann E(lizabeth) 1932- 69-72
Davis, Ann 1946- 137
Davis, Archie K. 1911- 124
Davis, Arthur G. 1915- 13-16R
Davis, Arthur Hoey 1868-1935 Brief entry 121
Davis, Arthur Kennard 1910- CAP-1
Earlier sketch in CA 13-14
Davis, Arthur Kyle Jr. 1897- CAP-2
Earlier sketch in CA 17-18
Davis, Arthur P(aul) 1904- 61-64
See also BW
Davis, Audrey
See Paine, Lauran (Bosworth)
Davis, B. Lynch
See Bioy Casares, Adolfo
and Borges, Jorge Luis
Davis, Barbara Kerr 1946- 104
Davis, Barbara 1955- 108
Davis, Ben Reeves 1927- 77-80
Davis, Benjamin O(liver) Jr. 1912- 134
Davis, (Mary) Bernice
See Curler, (Mary) Bernice
Davis, Berrie 1922- 101
Davis, Bertram H(ylton) 1918- CANR-1
Earlier sketch in CA 1-4R
Davis, Bette
See Davis, Ruth Elizabeth
Davis, Bette J. 1923- 93-96
See also SATA 15
Davis, Bill C. 1951- 110
Davis, Brian 1925-1988 Obituary 126
Davis, Burke 1913- CANR-25
Earlier sketches in CA 1-4R, CANR-4
See also SATA 4
Davis, Calvin DeArmond 1927- 5-8R
Davis, Charles A. 1795-1867 .... DLB 11
Davis, Charles T(ill) 1929- 37-40R
Davis, Charles T(witchell) 1918-1981 125
See also BW
Davis, Charles 1923- CANR-21
Earlier sketch in CA 5-8R
Davis, Christopher 1928- CANR-3
Earlier sketch in CA 9-12R
See also SATA 6
Davis, Cliff
See Smith, Richard Rein
Davis, Clive E(dward) 1914- 17-20R
Davis, Clyde Brion 1894-1962 ....5-8R
See also DLB 9
Davis, Creath 1939- CANR-21
Earlier sketches in CA 57-60, CANR-6
Davis, Curtis Carroll 1916- CANR-6
Earlier sketch in CA 9-12R
Davis, Curtis Wheeler 1928-1986 136
Obituary 119
Davis, D(elbert) Dwight
1908-1965 Obituary 111
See also SATA 33
Davis, D(onald) Evan 1923-1979 ....17-20R
Obituary 122
Davis, Daniel S(heldon) 1936- 45-48
See also SATA 12
Davis, Daphne 65-68
Davis, David Brion 1927- CANR-26
Earlier sketches in CA 17-20R, CANR-9
Davis, David C(harles) L. 1928- 33-36R
Davis, David Howard 1941- 53-56
Davis, Deane C(handler) 1900- 108
Davis, Deborah 1949- 129
Davis, Dick 1945- .... DLB 40
Davis, Don
See Dresser, Davis
Davis, Donald Gordon Jr. 1939- CANR-6
Earlier sketch in CA 53-56
Davis, Dorothy Salisbury 1916- CANR-32
Earlier sketches in CA 37-40R, CANR-14
Davis, Douglas F(redell) 1935- 105
Davis, Douglas (Matthew) 1933- 111
Davis, E. Adams
See Davis, Edwin Adams
Davis, Earl C(linton) 1938- 111
Davis, Earle (Rosco) 1905- 65-68
Davis, Edwin Adams 1904- CAP-2
Earlier sketch in CA 25-28
Davis, Eleanor Harmon 1909- 106
Davis, Elise Miller 1915- 69-72
Davis, Elizabeth
See Davis, Lou Ellen
Davis, Elizabeth G.
1910(?)-1974 Obituary 53-56
Davis, Elwood Craig 1896- CANR-3
Earlier sketch in CA 1-4R
Davis, F(loyd) James 1920- CANR-4
Earlier sketch in CA 1-4R
Davis, Fitzroy 1912-1980 ....CANR-31
Obituary 102
Earlier sketch in CA 49-52
Davis, Flora 1934- CANR-10
Earlier sketch in CA 65-68
Davis, Forest K(endall) 1918- 41-44R
Davis, Francis 1946- 123
Davis, Frank (Cecil) 1892-1990 Obituary 131
Davis, Frank G(reene) 1915- 85-88
Davis, Frank Marshall 1905-1987 125
Obituary 123
See also BLC 1
See also BW
See also DLB 51
Davis, Franklin M(ilton) Jr. 1918-1981 .....CANR-4
Earlier sketch in CA 1-4R
Davis, Fred 1925- 13-16R
Davis, Frederick Barton 1909-1975 ....CANR-17
Obituary 116
Earlier sketch in CA 1-4R
Davis, Frederick C(lyde)
1902-1977 Obituary 115
Davis, Garold N(eil) 1932- 41-44R
Davis, Gary A(lan) 1938- 106
Davis, Genevieve 1928- 65-68
Davis, Genny Wright 1948- 105
Davis, George L(ittleton) Sr. 1921- 57-60
Davis, George 1939- CANR-9
Earlier sketch in CA 65-68
See also BW
Davis, Gerry 1930- Brief entry 117
Davis, Gibbs 1953- 111
See also SATA 41, 46
Davis, Gil
See Gilmore, Don
Davis, Gilbert 1899-1983 Obituary 109
Davis, Gordon
See Hunt, E(verette) Howard Jr.
and Levinson, Leonard
Davis, Gordon
See Levinson, Leonard
Davis, Gordon B(itter) 1930- CANR-4
Earlier sketch in CA 53-56
Davis, Grania 1943- CANR-39
Earlier sketches in CA 85-88, CANR-16
See also SATA 50
Davis, Grant Miller 1937- CANR-11
Earlier sketch in CA 29-32R
Davis, Gwen 1936- CANR-2
Earlier sketch in CA 1-4R
See also AITN 1
Davis, H(enry) Grady 1890- CAP-2
Earlier sketch in CA 21-22
Davis, Harley
See Green, Kay
Davis, Harold Eugene 1902-1988 ....CANR-1
Obituary 126
Earlier sketch in CA 1-4R
Davis, Harold Lenoir 1896-1960 Obituary 89-92
See also CLC 49
See also DLB 9
Davis, Harold S(eaton) 1919- 57-60
Davis, Harriet Eager
1892(?)-1974 Obituary 49-52
Davis, Harry Rex 1921- 1-4R
Davis, Henry P. 1894(?)-1970 Obituary 104
Davis, Herbert (John) 1893-1967 ....CANR-1
Earlier sketch in CA 1-4R
Davis, Hope Hale 25-28R
Davis, Hope Harding
1915(?)-1976 Obituary 69-72
Davis, Horace B(ancroft) 1898- 21-24R
Davis, Horance G(ibbs) Jr. 1924- 65-68
Davis, Howard V(aughn) 1915- 25-28R
Davis, Hubert J(ackson) 1904- 107
See also SATA 31
Davis, I(rene) M(ary) 1926- 61-64
Davis, J(ames) C(olin) 1940- 127
Davis, J(ohn) Cary 1905- 41-44R
Davis, J(ames) Madison (Jr.) 1951- 134
Davis, J. Morton 1929- 124
Davis, J(ames) William 1908- 102
Davis, Jack Leonard 1917- 106
Davis, James Allan 1929- CANR-1
Earlier sketch in CA 1-4R
Davis, James C(urran) 1895-1981 Obituary 108
Davis, James C(ushman) 1931- Brief entry 117
Davis, James H. 1932- 89-92
Davis, James Kirkpatrick 1939- 127
Davis, James Kotsilibas
See Kotsilibas-Davis, James
Davis, James Richard 1936- 65-68
Davis, James Robert 1945- CANR-16
Earlier sketch in CA 85-88
See also Davis, Jim
See also SATA 32
Davis, James W(arren Jr.) 1935- 29-32R
Davis, Jan Haddle 1950- 93-96
Davis, Jean Reynolds 1927- 61-64
Davis, Jean Walton 1909- 1-4R
Davis, Jed H(orace Jr.) 1921- 17-20R
Davis, Jenny 1953- 128
Davis, Jerome 1891-1979 ....CANR-3
Obituary 89-92
Earlier sketch in CA 5-8R
Davis, Jim
See Davis, James Robert
and Smith, Richard Rein
See also AAYA 8
Davis, Jimmie Dan 1940- 127
Davis, Jinnie Y(eh) 1945- 107
Davis, Joe Lee 1906-1974 ....5-8R
Obituary 103
Davis, Joe 1901-1978 Obituary 112
Davis, Johanna 1937-1974 ....41-44R
Obituary 53-56
Davis, John D(avid) 1937- 29-32R
Davis, John H(erbert) 1904- 29-32R
Davis, John H. 1929- CANR-18
Earlier sketch in CA 25-28R
Davis, John J(ames) 1936- 33-36R
Davis, John King 1884-1967 .... CAP-1
Earlier sketch in CA 9-10
Davis, John 1774-1854 .... DLB 37
Davis, Joseph C(ole) 1908- 97-100
Davis, Joseph S(tancliffe) 1885-1975 101
Obituary 57-60
Davis, Judith 1925- 106
Davis, Julia 1900- CANR-1
Earlier sketch in CA 1-4R
See also SATA 6
Davis, Julian 1902(?)-1974 Obituary 53-56
Davis, K(eith) 1918- CANR-20
Earlier sketches in CA 1-4R, CANR-5
Davis, Karen Padgett 1942- 112
Davis, Keith F. 1952- 123
Davis, Ken(neth Pickett) 1906-1982 49-52
Obituary 135
Davis, Kenneth Culp 1908- Brief entry 115
Davis, Kenneth R(exton) 1921- 17-20R
Davis, Kenneth S(idney) 1912- CANR-30
Earlier sketch in CA 13-16R
Davis, Kingsley 1908- CANR-8
Earlier sketch in CA 13-16R
Davis, L(awrence) J(ames) 1940- CANR-11
Earlier sketch in CA 25-28R
Davis, Lance E(dwin) 1928- 53-56
Davis, Lanny J(esse) 1945- 57-60
Davis, Lawrence B(ennion) 1939- 45-48
Davis, Lennard J. 1949- CANR-39
Earlier sketch in CA 116
Davis, Lenwood G. 1939- CANR-35
Earlier sketch in CA 25-28R
Davis, Lew A(rter) 1930- 21-24R
Davis, Linda H(onor) 1953- 127
Davis, Lloyd (Moore) 1931- 69-72
Davis, Lou Ellen 1936- 81-84
Davis, Louis E(lkin) 1918- 53-56
Davis, Louise Littleton 1921- 103
See also SATA 25
Davis, Loyal Edward 1896-1982 Obituary 107
Davis, Luther 1921- 105
Davis, M(orris) Edward 1899- 5-8R
Davis, Maggie (Hill) CANR-9
Earlier sketch in CA 13-16R
Davis, Maggie S. 1943- .... SATA 57
Davis, Maralee G.
See Gibson, Maralee G.
Davis, Marc 1934- 29-32R
Davis, Margaret Banfield 1903- CAP-1
Earlier sketch in CA 11-12
Davis, Margaret Thomson 1926- 102
See also DLB 14
Davis, Marguerite 1889- .... SATA 34
Davis, Marilyn K(ornreich) 1928- 5-8R
Davis, Martha 1942- CANR-4
Earlier sketch in CA 49-52
Davis, Mary L(ee) 1935- CANR-4
Earlier sketch in CA 49-52
See also SATA 9
Davis, Mary Octavia 1901- CAP-2
Earlier sketch in CA 25-28
See also SATA 6
Davis, Maxine
See McHugh, Maxine Davis
Davis, Mel
See Arnold, Madelyn M.
Davis, Melodie M(iller) 1951- CANR-33
Earlier sketch in CA 113
Davis, Melton S(amillow) 1910- 41-44R
Davis, (John) Michael 1940- 33-36R
Davis, Michael Justin 1925- 102
Davis, Mildred 77-80
Davis, Mildred Ann (Campbell) 1916- 5-8R
Davis, Millard C. 1930- 69-72
Davis, Monte 1949- 103
Davis, Morris 1933- CANR-11
Earlier sketch in CA 61-64
Davis, Morton D(avid) 1930- 65-68
Davis, Moshe 1916- CANR-20
Earlier sketches in CA 9-12R, CANR-4
Davis, Murray S(tuart) 1940- 53-56
Davis, Myrna (Mushkin) 1936- 69-72
Davis, Natalie Zemon 1928- 53-56
Davis, Nathaniel 1925- 128
Davis, Neil
See Davis, T(homas) Neil
Davis, Neil 1934(?)-1985 Obituary 117
Davis, Nicholas 1965- 136
Davis, Nick
See Davis, Nicholas
Davis, Nolan 1942- CANR-25
Earlier sketch in CA 49-52
See also BW
Davis, Norah Deakin 1941- 111
Davis, Norman Maurice 1936- 69-72
Davis, Norman 1913- Brief entry 106
Davis, Nuel Pharr 1915- 29-32R
Davis, Olivia 1922- 81-84
Davis, Ossie 1917- CANR-26
Earlier sketch in CA 112
See also BW
See also DLB 7, 38
Davis, Patrick (David Channer) 1925- 93-96
Davis, Patti 1952- 134
Davis, Paul (Benjamin) 1934- 135
Davis, Paxton 1925- CANR-3
Earlier sketch in CA 9-12R
See also SATA 16
Davis, Peter (Frank) 1937- CANR-29
Earlier sketch in CA 107
Davis, Philip E(dward) 1927- 49-52
Davis, Philip J. 1923- 124
Davis, Polly Ann 1931- 102
Davis, R. G. 1933- 57-60
Davis, R(alph) H(enry) C(arless)
1918-1991 ....CANR-6
Obituary 134
Earlier sketch in CA 5-8R
Davis, Ralph C(urrier) 1894- 33-36R
Davis, Rebecca (Blaine) Harding
1831-1910 Brief entry 104
See also DLB 74
See also TCLC 6
Davis, Rex D. 1924- 9-12R
Davis, Richard CANR-26
Earlier sketches in CA 53-56, CANR-7
Davis, Richard Beale 1907- CANR-2
Earlier sketch in CA 5-8R
Davis, Richard Harding
1864-1916 Brief entry 114
See also DLB 12, 23, 78, 79
See also TCLC 24
Davis, Richard W. 1935- 33-36R
Davis, Robert Con 1948- CANR-23
Earlier sketch in CA 104
Davis, Robert Murray 1934- CANR-28
Earlier sketches in CA 33-36R, CANR-12
Davis, Robert P. 1929- CANR-3
Earlier sketch in CA 5-8R
Davis, Robert Ralph Jr. 1941- 37-40R

Davis, Robert 1881-1949 ... YABC 1
Davis, Rocky 1927- ... 61-64
Davis, Ronald L(eroy) 1936- ... 37-40R
Davis, Rosemary ... 5-8R
Davis, Rosemary L.
  See Davis, Rosemary
Davis, Roy Eugene 1931- ... CANR-6
  Earlier sketch in CA 9-12R
Davis, Rupert (Charles) Hart
  See Hart-Davis, Rupert (Charles)
Davis, Russell Gerard 1922- ... 5-8R
  See also SATA 3
Davis, Ruth Elizabeth 1908-1989 ... CANR-21
  Obituary ... 129
  Earlier sketch in CA 61-64
Davis, Sammy Jr. 1925-1990 ... 108
  Obituary ... 131
Davis, Samuel Cole 1764-1809 ... DLB 37
Davis, Samuel 1930- ... 29-32R
Davis, Sandra T. W. 1937- ... 124
Davis, Sara deSaussure 1943- ... 125
Davis, Simon J. M. 1950- ... 128
Davis, Stanley Nelson 1924- ... 108
Davis, Stephen M. 1955- ... 127
Davis, Stephen 1947- ... 128
Davis, Steven Andrew 1947- ... 112
Davis, Stratford
  See Bolton, Maisie Sharman
Davis, Suzanne
  See Sugar, Bert Randolph
Davis, Sydney Charles Houghton 1887- ... 5-8R
Davis, Sylvan 1927(?)-1984 Obituary ... 112
Davis, T. N.
  See Davis, T(homas) Neil
Davis, T(homas) Neil 1932- ... 123
Davis, Terence 1924- ... 21-24R
Davis, Thomas J(oseph) 1946- ... CANR-4
  Earlier sketch in CA 53-56
Davis, Timothy Francis Tothill 1941- ... 81-84
Davis, Tom Edward 1929- ... 85-88
Davis, Verne Theodore 1889-1973 ... 1-4R
  See also SATA 6
Davis, (Benton) Vincent (Jr.) 1930- ... CANR-23
  Earlier sketches in CA 17-20R, CANR-7
Davis, W(illiam) Jackson 1942- ... 107
Davis, W(arren) Jefferson 1885-1973 ... CAP-2
  Earlier sketch in CA 29-32
Davis, W(illiam) N(ewell) Jr. 1915- ... 81-84
Davis, (Edmund) Wade 1953- ... 131
Davis, Walter A(lbert III) 1942- ... 114
Davis, Walter Richardson 1928- ... 102
Davis, Wayne H(arry) 1930- ... 33-36R
Davis, Wiley H. 1913- ... 25-28R
Davis, William C(harles) 1946- ... CANR-23
  Earlier sketches in CA 61-64, CANR-8
Davis, William H(atcher) 1939- ... 33-36R
Davis, William S(terling) 1943- ... CANR-28
  Earlier sketch in CA 111
Davis, William Virgil 1940- ... CANR-23
  Earlier sketch in CA 106
Davis, William 1933- ... CANR-28
  Earlier sketches in CA 65-68, CANR-10
Davis, Winston (Bradley) 1939- ... 104
Davis-Friedmann, Deborah 1945- ... 118
Davis-Gardner, Angela 1942- ... 110
Davis-Goff, Annabel 1942- ... 85-88
Davison, Edward 1898-1970 Obituary ... 29-32R
Davison, Frank Dalby 1893-1970 Obituary ... 116
  See also CLC 15
Davison, Geoffrey 1927- ... 110
Davison, Gladys Patton 1905- ... CAP-1
  Earlier sketch in CA 13-16
Davison, Jane 1932(?)-1981 Obituary ... 104
Davison, Jean 1937- ... CANR-10
  Earlier sketch in CA 65-68
Davison, Kenneth E(dwin) 1924- ... 9-12R
Davison, Lawrence H.
  See Lawrence, D(avid) H(erbert Richards)
Davison, Ned J. 1926- ... 45-48
Davison, Peter 1928- ... CANR-3
  Earlier sketch in CA 9-12R
  See also CAAS 4
  See also CLC 28
  See also DLB 5
Davison, Roderic H(ollett) 1916- ... 37-40R
Davison, Verne E(lbert) 1904- ... 69-72
Davisson, Charles Nelson 1917- ... 25-28R
Davisson, William I. 1929- ... CANR-11
  Earlier sketch in CA 17-20R
Davis-Weyer, Caecilia 1929- ... 41-44R
Davitt, Thomas E(dward) 1904-1980 ... 25-28R
  Obituary ... 117
Davitz, J. R.
  See Davitz, Joel R(obert)
Davitz, Joel R(obert) 1926- ... 134
  Brief entry ... 114
d'Avray, David L. ... 129
Davy, Francis X(avier) 1916- ... 29-32R
Davy, George Mark Oswald
  1898-1983 Obituary ... 110
Davy, John Charles 1927-1984 Obituary ... 114
Davys, Mary 1674-1732 ... DLB 39
Davys, Sarah
  See Manning, Rosemary (Joy)
Dawdy, Doris Ostrander ... 53-56
Dawe, (Donald) Bruce 1930- ... CANR-27
  Earlier sketches in CA 69-72, CANR-11
Dawe, Donald G. 1926- ... 33-36R
Dawe, Frederick
  See Gettings, Fred
Dawe, (Chartres) Gerald 1952- ... CANR-36
  Earlier sketch in CA 114
Dawe, Roger David 1934- ... CANR-3
  Earlier sketch in CA 9-12R
Dawes, Dorothy
  See Cooper, Parley J(oseph)
Dawes, Frank 1933- ... 69-72
Dawes, Nathaniel Thomas Jr. 1937- ... 49-52
Dawes, Neville 1926- ... 13-16R
Dawes, Robyn M(ason) 1936- ... 37-40R
Dawidowicz, Lucy S(childkret)
  1915-1990 ... CANR-18
  Obituary ... 133
  Earlier sketch in CA 25-28R
Dawis, Rene V(illaneuva) 1928- ... 45-48
Dawisha, Adeed Isam 1944- ... CANR-18
  Earlier sketch in CA 102
Dawisha, Karen (Lea) 1949- ... 120
Dawkins, Cecil 1927- ... CANR-36
  Earlier sketch in CA 5-8R
Dawkins, Louisa (a pseudonym) 1940- ... 128
Dawkins, Richard 1941- ... CANR-26
  Earlier sketch in CA 69-72
Dawley, David 1941- ... 45-48
Dawley, Powel Mills 1907- ... 57-60
Dawlish, Peter
  See Kerr, James Lennox
Dawn, C(larence) Ernest 1918- ... 61-64
Dawood, N(essim) J(oseph) 1927- ... CANR-28
  Earlier sketch in CA 49-52
Dawson, Alan David 1942- ... 77-80
Dawson, Carl 1938- ... CANR-1
  Earlier sketch in CA 45-48
Dawson, Christopher (Henry)
  1889-1970 ... CANR-6
  Obituary ... 29-32R
  Earlier sketch in CA 1-4R
Dawson, Clay
  See Levinson, Leonard
Dawson, Elizabeth
  See Geach, Christine
Dawson, Elmer A. ... CANR-27
  Earlier sketches in CAP-2, CA 19-20
  See also SATA 1, 67
Dawson, Fielding 1930- ... 85-88
  See also CLC 6
Dawson, Frank G(ates Jr.) 1925- ... 69-72
Dawson, George G(lenn) 1925- ... 37-40R
Dawson, Giles E(dwin) 1903- ... CAP-2
  Earlier sketch in CA 19-20
Dawson, Grace S(trickler) 1891- ... 17-20R
Dawson, Howard A.
  1895(?)-1979 Obituary ... 89-92
Dawson, James Lee 1949- ... 127
Dawson, Jan 1939(?)-1980 Obituary ... 101
Dawson, Janis 1936- ... 135
Dawson, Jennifer ... CANR-10
  Earlier sketch in CA 57-60
Dawson, Jerry F. 1933- ... 33-36R
Dawson, Jim
  See Dawson, James Lee
Dawson, Joseph G(reen) III 1945- ... 110
Dawson, Mary 1919- ... 21-24R
  See also SATA 11
Dawson, Mildred A(gnes) 1897- ... CANR-12
  Earlier sketch in CA 17-20R
Dawson, Minnie E. 1906-1978 ... 85-88
Dawson, Peter
  See Faust, Frederick (Shiller)
Dawson, (John) Philip 1928- ... 21-24R
Dawson, Richard E(vans) 1939- ... 73-76
Dawson, Robert L(ewis) 1943- ... 105
Dawson, Robert (Merril) 1941- ... 21-24R
Dawson, William 1704-1752 ... DLB 31
Dawson-Scott, C(atharine) A(my)
  1865-1934 Brief entry ... 113
Day, A(rthur) Grove 1904- ... CANR-23
  Earlier sketches in CA 21-24R, CANR-8
  See also SATA 59
Day, Aidan 1952- ... 132
Day, Alan Charles Lynn 1924- ... 1-4R
Day, Alan J(ohn) 1942- ... 105
Day, Albert Edward 1884-1973 ... CAP-2
  Obituary ... 45-48
  Earlier sketch in CA 23-24
Day, Albert M. 1897-1979 ... 93-96
  Obituary ... 85-88
Day, Alexandra ... 136
  See also CLR 22
  See also SATA 67
Day, Alice Taylor 1928- ... 17-20R
Day, (Stacey) B(iswas) 1927- ... CANR-29
Day, Benjamin Henry 1810-1889 ... DLB 43
Day, Beth (Feagles) 1924- ... CANR-18
  Earlier sketches in CA 9-12R, CANR-3
  See also SATA 33
Day, Bradford M(arshall) 1916- ... 104
Day, Clarence Burton 1889-1987 Obituary ... 121
Day, Clarence (Shepard Jr.)
  1874-1935 Brief entry ... 108
  See also DLB 11
  See also TCLC 25
Day, David 1944- ... 93-96
Day, (Stephen) Deforest 1941- ... 134
Day, Dianne 1938- ... 127
Day, Donald
  See Harding, Donald Edward
Day, Dorothy 1897-1980 ... 65-68
  Obituary ... 102
  See also DLB 29
Day, Douglas (Turner III) 1932- ... CANR-8
  Earlier sketch in CA 9-12R
Day, Edward C. 1932- ... 133
Day, Frank Parker 1881-1950 ... DLB 92
Day, Gardiner Mumford
  1900-1981 Obituary ... 104
Day, George Harold 1900- ... CAP-1
  Earlier sketch in CA 13-14
Day, George 1950- ... 117
Day, Gwynn McLendon 1908- ... CAP-1
  Earlier sketch in CA 11-12
Day, Holliday T. 1936- ... 137
Day, Houston
  See Day, Sam Houston
Day, J(ames) Edward 1914- ... 17-20R
Day, J(ohn) Laurence 1934- ... 65-68
Day, James F(rancis) 1917- ... 33-36R
Day, James Wentworth 1899-1983(?) ... CANR-10
  Obituary ... 108
  Earlier sketch in CA 13-16R
Day, John A(rthur) 1913- ... 17-20R
Day, John Patrick 1919- ... 5-8R
Day, John R(obert) 1917- ... CANR-9
  Earlier sketch in CA 5-8R
Day, John 1574(?)-1640(?) ... DLB 62
Day, Kenneth 1912- ... 9-12R
Day, LeRoy Judson 1917- ... 21-24R
Day, Lincoln H(ubert) 1928- ... 17-20R
Day, Lucille 1947- ... 110
Day, M(ichael) H(erbert) 1927- ... 102
Day, Martin Steele 1917- ... CANR-7
  Earlier sketch in CA 5-8R
Day, Maurice 1892- ... SATA 30
Day, Max
  See Cassiday, Bruce (Bingham)
Day, Melvin Norman 1923- ... 109
Day, Michael
  See Dempewolff, Richard F(rederic)
Day, Nancy Raines 1951- ... 111
Day, (Truman) Owen 1890- ... 69-72
Day, Paul Woodford 1916- ... 25-28R
Day, Peter (Morton) 1914- ... 1-4R
Day, Price 1907-1978 ... 85-88
  Obituary ... 81-84
Day, R(oss) H(enry) 1927- ... 29-32R
Day, Ralph L(ewis) 1926- ... CANR-7
  Earlier sketch in CA 5-8R
Day, Richard B(ruce) 1942- ... CANR-27
  Earlier sketch in CA 49-52
Day, Richard E. 1929- ... 33-36R
Day, Richard Hollis 1933- ... 114
Day, Robert Adams 1924- ... 53-56
Day, Sam Houston 1896-1984 Obituary ... 113
Day, Stacey B(iswas) 1927- ... 33-36R
Day, Thomas 1748-1789 ... DLB 39
  See also YABC 1
Dayal, Rajeshwar 1909- ... 130
Dayan, Moshe 1915-1981 ... CANR-22
  Obituary ... 105
  Earlier sketch in CA 21-24R
Dayan, Yael 1939- ... 89-92
  See also AITN 1
Dayananda, James Yesupriya 1934- ... 81-84
Daydi-Tolson, Santiago 1943- ... 127
Day Lewis, C(ecil) 1904-1972 ... CANR-34
  Obituary ... 33-36R
  Earlier sketches in CAP-1, CA 13-16
  See also Blake, Nicholas
  See also CLC 1, 6, 10
  See also DLB 15, 20
  See also MTCW
Day-Lewis, Sean (Francis) 1931- ... 132
Daynes, Byron W(ilford) 1937- ... 110
Daysh, G(eorge) H(enry) J(ohn)
  1901-1987 Obituary ... 122
Dayton, Donald W(ilber) 1942- ... CANR-24
  Earlier sketch in CA 69-72
Dayton, Edward R(isedorph) 1924- ... CANR-16
  Earlier sketch in CA 85-88
Dayton, Eldorous L. 1906-1987 Obituary ... 122
Dayton, Irene 1922- ... CANR-6
  Earlier sketch in CA 57-60
Dazai, Osamu
  See Tsushima, Shuji
  See also TCLC 11
d'Azevedo, Warren L. 1920- ... 93-96
Dazey, Agnes J(ohnston) ... CAP-2
  Earlier sketch in CA 23-24
  See also SATA 2
Dazey, Frank M. ... CAP-2
  Earlier sketch in CA 23-24
  See also SATA 2
Deacon, Eileen
  See Geipel, Eileen
Deacon, George Edward Raven
  1906-1984 Obituary ... 114
Deacon, Joseph John 1920- ... 69-72
Deacon, Richard
  See McCormick, (George) Donald (King)
Deacon, Richard 1922-1984 Obituary ... 113
Deacon, Ruth E. 1923- ... 102
Deadman, Ronald 1919-1988(?) Obituary ... 125
  See also SATA 56
Deagon, Ann (Fleming) 1930- ... 57-60
Deak, Edward Joseph Jr. 1943- ... 53-56
Deak, Francis 1899-1972 Obituary ... 33-36R
Deak, Istvan 1926- ... CANR-28
  Earlier sketches in CA 25-28R, CANR-11
Deakin, Frederick William 1913- ... CANR-5
  Earlier sketch in CA 5-8R
Deakin, James 1929- ... CANR-24
  Earlier sketches in CA 21-24R, CANR-8
Deakin, Motley F. 1920- ... 120
Deakin, Rose 1937- ... 109
Deakins, Roger Lee 1933- ... 61-64
Deal, Babs H(odges) 1929- ... CANR-1
  Earlier sketch in CA 1-4R
Deal, Borden 1922-1985 ... CANR-2
  Obituary ... 114
  Earlier sketch in CA 1-4R
  See also DLB 6
Deal, Ernest L(afayette Jr.) 1918-1984 ... 132
Deal, Terrance E. 1939- ... 130
Deal, William S(anford) 1910- ... CANR-3
  Earlier sketch in CA 5-8R
Deale, Kenneth Edwin Lee 1907- ... CANR-4
  Earlier sketch in CA 5-8R
Dealey, E(dward) M(usgrove) 1892-1969 ... CAP-2
  Earlier sketch in CA 23-24
Dealey, Ted
  See Dealey, E(dward) M(usgrove)
deAlmeida, Hermione (Beatrice) 1950- ... 118
Dean, Abner 1910-1982 Obituary ... 107
Dean, Amber 1902-1985 ... CANR-2
  Obituary ... 116
  Earlier sketch in CA 5-8R
Dean, Anabel 1915- ... CANR-14
  Earlier sketch in CA 37-40R
  See also SATA 12
Dean, Barbara 1946- ... 113
Dean, Basil (Herbert) 1888-1978 ... 69-72
  Obituary ... 134
Dean, Beryl 1911- ... 9-12R
Dean, Burton V(ictor) 1924- ... CANR-20
  Earlier sketches in CA 45-48, CANR-1
Dean, Christopher G(eorge) 1940- ... 111
Dean, Dennis R(ichard) 1938- ... 137
Dean, Dorothy 1932(?)-1987 Obituary ... 121
Dean, Dwight G(antz) 1918- ... 17-20R
Dean, E. Douglas 1916- ... 97-100
Dean, Edith M(ae) 1915- ... 111
Dean, Edwin R(obinson) 1933- ... 17-20R
Dean, Frances Mary 1905(?)-1983 Obituary ... 110
Dean, Herbert Morris 1938- ... 105
Dean, Howard E(dward) 1916- ... 41-44R
Dean, Ida
  See Grae, Ida
Dean, Jeffrey S. 1939- ... 37-40R
Dean, (Alfreda) Joan 1925- ... 101
Dean, Joan FitzPatrick 1949- ... 118
Dean, Joel 1906- ... 33-36R
Dean, John
  See Bumppo, Nathaniel John Balthazar
Dean, John A(urie) 1921- ... 53-56
Dean, John Wesley III 1938- ... 105
Dean, Karen Strickler 1923- ... CANR-26
  Earlier sketch in CA 109
  See also SATA 49
Dean, Leonard Fellows 1909- Brief entry ... 105
Dean, Luella Jo 1908(?)-1977 Obituary ... 69-72
Dean, Malcolm 1948- ... CANR-31
  Earlier sketch in CA 105
Dean, Morton 1935- ... 69-72
Dean, Nancy 1930- ... 65-68
Dean, Nell Marr 1910- ... 21-24R
Dean, Robert George
  1904(?)-1989 Obituary ... 130
Dean, Roger 1944- Brief entry ... 114
Dean, Roy 1925- ... CANR-6
  Earlier sketch in CA 57-60
Dean, Stanley (Rochelle) 1908- ... 73-76
Dean, Vera Micheles
  1903-1972 Obituary ... 37-40R
Dean, Warren 1932- ... 29-32R
Dean, William D(enard) 1937- ... 37-40R
Dean, William F(rishe) 1899-1981 Obituary ... 105
Dean, Winton Basil 1916- ... CANR-10
  Earlier sketch in CA 65-68
Dean, Yetive H(ornor) 1909- ... CAP-1
  Earlier sketch in CA 9-10
de Andrade, Carlos Drummond
  See Drummond de Andrade, Carlos
DeAndrea, William L(ouis) 1952- ... CANR-20
  Earlier sketch in CA 81-84
Deane, Dee Shirley 1928- ... 81-84
Deane, Elisabeth
  See Beilenson, Edna
Deane, Herbert Andrew 1921- ... 1-4R
Deane, James G(arner) 1923- ... 89-92
Deane, Lorna
  See Wilkinson, Lorna Hilda Kathleen
Deane, Nancy H(ilts) 1939- ... 29-32R
Deane, Norman
  See Creasey, John
Deane, Seamus (Francis) 1940- ... 118
Deane, Shirley Joan 1920- ... CANR-2
  Earlier sketch in CA 1-4R
de Angeli, Marguerite (Lofft)
  1889-1987 ... CANR-3
  Obituary ... 122
  Earlier sketch in CA 5-8R
  See also AITN 2
  See also CLR 1
  See also DLB 22
  See also MAICYA
  See also SATA 1, 27, 51
De Angelis, Barbara ... BEST 90:3
DeAngelis, William 1943- ... 113
de Antonio, Emile 1922-1989 ... 117
  Obituary ... 130
  Brief entry ... 113
Dear, William (C.) 1937- ... 125
de Aragon, Ray John 1946- ... 115
De Araugo, Tess (S.) 1930- ... 135
De Araugo-O'Mullane, Tess
  See De Araugo, Tess (S.)
Dearden, Harold 1882(?)-1962 Obituary ... 116
Dearden, James A(rthur) 1924-1976 ... 33-36R
Dearden, James S(hackley) 1931- ... CANR-12
  Earlier sketch in CA 25-28R
Dearden, James 1949- ... 136
Dearden, John 1919- ... 33-36R
Deardorff, Robert 1912- ... 61-64
Deardorff, Tom 1940- ... 89-92
Dearing, James (William) 1959- ... 114
Dearing, Vinton Adams 1920- ... 110
Dearlove, John 1944- ... 97-100
DeArmand, Frances Ullmann
  1904(?)-1984 ... 5-8R
  Obituary ... 112
  See also SATA 10, 38
de Armas, Frederick A(lfred) 1945- ... 37-40R
de Armas, Jose R(afael) 1924- ... 113
DeArment, Robert K(endall) 1925- ... 93-96
Dearmer, Geoffrey 1893- ... CAP-2
  Earlier sketch in CA 23-24
Dearmin, Jeannie Tarascou 1924- ... 5-8R

DeArmond, Dale Burlison
See Dale, DeArmond
DeArmond, Dale 1914- 138
Dearstyne, Howard (Best) 1903-1979 121
Obituary 85-88
De Arteaga, William 1943- 111
Deary, Terry 1946- 110
See also SATA 41, 51
Deason, Hilary J(ohn) 1903- 73-76
d'Easum, Cedric (Godfrey) 1907- CANR-12
Earlier sketch in CA 73-76
d'Easum, Dick
See d'Easum, Cedric (Godfrey)
Deasy, C(ornelius) M(ichael) 1918- 93-96
Deasy, Mary (Margaret) 1914- 5-8R
Deathridge, John (William) 1944- 133
Deaton, Charles W. 1942- 93-96
Deaton, John (Graydon) 1939- CANR-11
Earlier sketch in CA 61-64
Deats, Paul (Kindred) Jr. 1918- 13-16R
Deats, Randy 1954- 93-96
Deats, Richard L(ouis) 1932- 21-24R
D'Eau, Jean
See Gould, Allan (Mendel)
Deaux, George 1931- 5-8R
Deaux, Kay 1941- 114
Deaver, Julie Reece 1953- CANR-37
Earlier sketch in CA 129
See also SATA 68
DeBakey, Michael E(llis) 1908- 73-76
de Banke, Cecile 1889-1965 ....CAP-1
Earlier sketch in CA 13-14
See also SATA 11
de Bary, Brett
See Nee, Brett de Bary
deBary, William Theodore 1919- CANR-37
Earlier sketch in CA 57-60
DeBeaubien, Philip Francis
1913-1979 Obituary 85-88
de Beausobre, Iulia
See Namier, Julia
de Beauvoir, Simone (Lucie Ernestine Marie Bertrand)
See Beauvoir, Simone (Lucie Ernestine Marie Bertrand) de
de Bedts, Ralph F(ortes) 1914- 9-12R
De Beer, E(smond) S(amuel) 1895-1990 ....CAP-1
Obituary 132
Earlier sketch in CA 13-14
de Beer, Gavin R(ylands) 1899-1972 ....CAP-1
Earlier sketch in CA 13-16
DeBenedetti, Charles Louis 1943-1987 102
Obituary 121
DeBerard, Ella 1900- 73-76
Deberdt-Malaquais, Elisabeth 1937- 57-60
de Bernieres, Louis 1954- 133
de Betancourt, Cressy
See Dobkin De Rios, Marlene
DeBetz, Barbara Holstein 123
de Beus, Jacobus Gysbertus 1909- 102
Debevec Henning, Sylvie Marie 1948- 109
Debicki, Andrew P(eter) 1934- CANR-37
Earlier sketch in CA 37-40R
Debicki, Roman 1896- 1-4R
de Blank, Joost 1908-1968 ....CAP-1
Earlier sketch in CA 13-14
De Blasis, Celeste (N.) 1946- CANR-4
Earlier sketch in CA 53-56
de Blij, Harm J(an) 1935- CANR-23
Earlier sketches in CA 13-16R, CANR-8
Debo, Angie 1890-1988 69-72
Obituary 124
De Boe, David C. 1942- 127
DeBoer, John C(harles) 1923- CANR-26
Earlier sketch in CA 29-32R
DeBoer, John James 1903-1969 ....CANR-3
Earlier sketch in CA 1-4R
de Bois, Helma
See de Bois, Wilhelmina J. E.
de Bois, Wilhelmina J. E. 1923- 17-20R
de Boissiere, Ralph (Anthony) 1907- 106
DeBold, Richard C. 1927- 21-24R
DeBolt, Margaret Wayt 1930- 115
De Bona, Maurice Jr. 1926- 65-68
de Bono, Edward 1933- CANR-10
Earlier sketch in CA 21-24R
See also MTCW
See also SATA 66
De Bonville, Bob 1926- 69-72
De Borchgrave, Arnaud 1926- 73-76
De Borhegyi, Suzanne Sims 1926- 5-8R
de Born, Edith 25-28R
De Bow, James Dunwoody Brownson
1820-1867 ....DLB 3, 79
DeBoy, James J(oseph) Jr. 1942- 113
Debray, (Jules) Regis 1942- 21-24R
Debreczeny, Paul 1932- CANR-12
Earlier sketch in CA 33-36R
De Breffny, Brian (O'Rorke)
1931(?)-1989 77-80
Obituary 127
Debrett, Hal
See Dresser, Davis
Debreu, Gerard 1921- CANR-23
Earlier sketch in CA 37-40R
de Brissac, Malcolm
See Dickinson, Peter (Malcolm)
de Broca, Philippe (Claude Alex) 1933- 126
de Broglie, L.
See de Broglie, Louis (Victor Pierre Raymond)
de Broglie, Louis (Victor Pierre Raymond)
1892-1987 Obituary 122
de Brunhoff, Jean
See Brunhoff, Jean de
De Brunhoff, Laurent
See Brunhoff, Laurent de
de Bruyn, Guenter 1926- ....DLB 75
de Bruyn, Monica (Jean) G(rembowicz)
1952- 65-68
See also SATA 13
Debus, Allen G(eorge) 1926- CANR-31
Earlier sketches in CA 37-40R, CANR-14
Debussy, (Achille) Claude
1862-1918 Brief entry 118
DeBuys, William (Eno Jr.) 1949- 136
de Calles, Jane F. Butel 1938- 126
Decalo, Samuel 1937- 121
de Camp, Catherine Crook 1907- CANR-20
Earlier sketches in CA 21-24R, CANR-9
See also SATA 12
DeCamp, Graydon 1934- 97-100
de Camp, L(yon) Sprague 1907- CANR-20
Earlier sketches in CA 1-4R, CANR-1, 9
See also DLB 8
See also SATA 9
de Campi, John Webb 1939- 69-72
De Campos, L.
See Dahl, Linda
De Canio, Stephen J(ohn) 1942- 57-60
De Capite, Raymond Anthony 1924- 1-4R
Decarie, Therese Gouin 1923- 41-44R
DeCarl, Lennard 1940- 81-84
De Carlo, Andrea 1952- 132
de Castro, Fernando J(ose) 1937- 53-56
De Castro, Josue 1908-1973 ....33-36R
De Caux, Len
See De Caux, Leonard Howard
De Caux, Leonard Howard 1899- 29-32R
Decaux, Lucile
See Bibesco, Marthe Lucie
DeCecco, John Paul 1925- 17-20R
de Cervera, Alejo 1919- 21-24R
de Chair, Somerset (Struben) 1911- CANR-1
Earlier sketch in CA 45-48
DeChancie, John 1946- 118
Dechant, Emerald V(ictor) 1926- 9-12R
DeChant, John A(loysius) 1917-1974 ....CAP-2
Obituary 53-56
Earlier sketch in CA 23-24
de Chardin, Pierre Teilhard
See Teilhard de Chardin, (Marie Joseph) Pierre
deCharms, Richard IV 1927- 41-44R
de Chasca, Edmund V(illela)
1903- Brief entry 117
de Chatellerault, Victor
See Beaudoin, Kenneth Lawrence
Dechert, Charles R(ichard) 1927- CANR-10
Earlier sketch in CA 21-24R
de Chirico, Giorgio 1888-1978 89-92
Obituary 81-84
De Christoforo, Ron(ald) 1951- 81-84
Deci, Edward L(ewis) 1942- CANR-39
Earlier sketch in CA 53-56
Decker, Albert 1895-1988 Obituary 127
Decker, Beatrice 1919- 61-64
Decker, Donald M(ilton) 1923- 37-40R
Decker, Duane 1910-1964 ....5-8R
See also SATA 5
Decker, Hannah S(hulman) 1937- 85-88
Decker, Leslie E(dward) 1930- 9-12R
Decker, Robert Owen 1927- 65-68
Decker, William 1926- Brief entry 115
Deckers, Jeanine 1933(?)-1985 Obituary 115
Deckert, Alice Mae 13-16R
DeClements, Barthe 1920- CANR-22
Earlier sketch in CA 105
See also CLR 23
See also SATA 35, 71
De Cock, Liliane 1939- CANR-2
Earlier sketch in CA 45-48
Decolta, Ramon
See Whitfield, Raoul
DeConde, Alexander 1920- CANR-6
Earlier sketch in CA 5-8R
de Conte, Sieur Louis
See Clemens, Samuel Langhorne
de Costa, (George) Rene 1939- 102
deCoste, Fredrik 1910- CAP-2
Earlier sketch in CA 21-22
DeCoster, Cyrus C(ole) 1914- CANR-29
Earlier sketch in CA 49-52
deCourcy Hinds, Michael 1947- 114
DeCoursey, Virginia 1924- 114
deCoy, Robert H(arold) Jr. 1920- 25-28R
DeCredico, Mary A. 1959- 135
De Crescenzo, Luciano 1928- 133
de Crespigny, (Richard) Rafe (Champion)
1936- 57-60
De Cristoforo, R(omeo) J(ohn) 1917- CANR-3
Earlier sketch in CA 9-12R
DeCrow, Karen 1937- CANR-37
Earlier sketch in CA 33-36R
Decter, Midge (Rosenthal) 1927- CANR-2
Earlier sketch in CA 45-48
Dedek, John F. 1929- 33-36R
Dederer, John Morgan 1951- 136
Dederick, Robert 1919- Brief entry 116
de Dienes, Andre 1913- 41-44R
Dedijer, Vladimir 1914-1990 ....CANR-4
Obituary 133
Earlier sketch in CA 1-4R
Dedina, Michel 1933- 33-36R
Dedini, Eldon 1921- 65-68
Dedmon, Emmett 1918-1983 ....CANR-5
Obituary 110
Earlier sketch in CA 9-12R
Dee, Henry
See Torbett, Harvey Douglas Louis
Dee, Ruby
See Wallace, Ruby Ann
Deeb, Gary (James) 1945- 138
Deedy, John 1923- 33-36R
See also SATA 24
Deegan, Paul Joseph 1937- 102
See also SATA 38, 48
Deeken, Alfons 1932- 77-80
Deeley, Roger 1944- 53-56
Deelman, Christian Felling 1937-1964 ....CAP-1
Earlier sketch in CA 11-12
Deemer, Bill 1945- 17-20R
Deemer, Charles (Robert Jr.) 1939- 73-76
Deen, Edith Alderman 1905- CANR-2
Earlier sketch in CA 5-8R
Deener, David R(ussell) 1920-1976 ....17-20R
Obituary 134
Deep Chin
See Gould, Allan (Mendel)
Deeping, (George) Warwick
1877-1950 Brief entry 114
Deeps, Frederick
See Speed, F(rederick) Maurice
Deer, Irving 1924- 17-20R
Deer, Sandra 1940- ....CLC 45
Deese, Helen 1925- 126
Deese, James (Earle) 1921- CANR-5
Earlier sketch in CA 1-4R
Deeter, Allen C. 1931- 45-48
de Extramuros, Quixote
See Espino, Federico (Licsi Jr.)
DeFalco, Joseph Michael 1931- 13-16R
DeFanti, Charles 1942- 89-92
DeFelice, James (V.) 1940- 128
DeFelice, Louise P(aula) 1945- 61-64
De Felitta, Frank (Paul) 1921- CANR-28
Earlier sketch in CA 61-64
De Ferrari, Gabriella ....CLC 65
Deferrari, Roy J(oseph) 1890-1969 ....CAP-1
Earlier sketch in CA 13-14
DeFerrari, Sister Teresa Mary 1930- 9-12R
Deffner, Donald L(ouis) 1924- CANR-11
Earlier sketch in CA 17-20R
de Filippo, Eduardo 1900-1984 132
Obituary 114
See also MTCW
de Fletin, P.
See Fielden, T(homas) P(erceval)
Defoe, Daniel 1660(?)-1731 ....CDBLB 1660-1789
See also DLB 39, 95, 101
See also MAICYA
See also SATA 22
See also WLC
de Fontaine, Felix Gregory 1834-1896 ....DLB 43
deFontaine, Wade Hampton 1893-1969 ....5-8R
Obituary 103
De Forbes
See Forbes, DeLoris (Florine) Stanton
Deford, Frank 1938- 33-36R
deFord, Miriam Allen 1888-1975 ....CANR-4
Earlier sketch in CA 1-4R
deFord, Sara (Whitcraft) 1916- 25-28R
DeForest, Charlotte B. 1879-1971 ....CAP-2
Earlier sketch in CA 25-28
De Forest, John William
1826-1906 Brief entry 119
See also DLB 12
De Forest, Lee 1873-1961 Obituary 112
DeForest, Orrin L. 1923- 134
de Forrest, Julie
See DeWitt, Edith Openshaw
de Fossard, R(onald) A(lfred) 1929- 41-44R
de Fox, Lucia Ungaro
See Lockert, Lucia (Alicia Ungaro Fox)
deFrance, Anthony
See DiFranco, Anthony (Mario)
DeFrancis, John 1911- Brief entry 106
DeFrees, Madeline 1919- CANR-4
Earlier sketch in CA 9-12R
See also DLB 105
deFreres, Sebastian J(ean) 1936- 121
de Funiak, William Q(uinby) 1901- 33-36R
de Gamez, Cielo Cayetana Alba
See Alba de Gamez, Cielo Cayetana
de Gamez, Tana
See Alba de Gamez, Cielo Cayetana
Degani, Meir H(ershtenkorn) 1909- 102
DeGarmo, Kenneth Scott 1943- 81-84
de Gaulle, Charles (Andre Joseph Marie)
1890-1970 130
Obituary 111
de Gaury, Gerald 1897-1984 ....13-16R
Obituary 112
Degen, Bruce 1945- 124
See also SATA 47, 57
Degenhardt, Henry W(illiam) 1910- CANR-23
Earlier sketch in CA 106
De Gennaro, Angelo Anthony 1919- 13-16R
Degenshein, George A.
1918(?)-1979 Obituary 93-96
De George, Richard T(homas) 1933- CANR-39
Earlier sketches in CA 5-8R, CANR-2, 17
DeGering, Etta Fowler 1898- CAP-1
Earlier sketch in CA 9-10
See also SATA 7
Degh, Linda 1920- 85-88
Deghy, Guy (Stephen) 1912- CAP-1
Obituary 137
Earlier sketch in CA 9-10
DeGidio, Sandra 1943- 112
Degler, Carl N(eumann) 1921- CANR-3
Earlier sketch in CA 5-8R
Degler, Stanley E. 1929- 25-28R
Degnan, James Philip 1933- 41-44R
de Gourmont, Remy
See Gourmont, Remy de
De Graeff, Allen
See Blaustein, Albert Paul
de Graff, Robert F(air) 1895-1981 Obituary 105
See also DLBY 81
de Graffe, Richard
See St. Clair, Leonard
de Graft, Joe 1924-1978 ....DLB 117
DeGraft, Joseph Coleman 1932- 73-76
de Graft-Johnson, John Coleman 1919- 21-24R
de Gramont, Sanche
See Morgan, Ted
DeGrave, Philip
See DeAndrea, William L(ouis)
de Grazia, Alfred 1919- CANR-5
Earlier sketch in CA 13-16R
de Grazia, Edward 1927- 129
De Grazia, Ettore 1909-1982 ....CANR-13
Earlier sketch in CA 61-64
See also De Grazia, Ted
De Grazia, Sebastian 1917- 65-68
De Grazia, Ted
See De Grazia, Ettore
See also SATA 39
DeGre, Muriel (Harris) 1914-1971 ....CAP-1
Earlier sketch in CA 17-18
De Greene, Kenyon B(renton) CANR-14
Earlier sketch in CA 37-40R
De Gregori, Thomas R(oger) 1935- CANR-12
Earlier sketch in CA 29-32R
DeGregorio, William A(lfred) 1946- 117
DeGregory, Jerry L(ouis) 1945- 119
de Groat, Diane 1947- 107
See also SATA 31
DeGrood, David H. 1937- 33-36R
DeGroot, Alfred Thomas 1903- CANR-5
Earlier sketch in CA 5-8R
de Groot, Roy Andries 1910-1983 Obituary 110
deGros, J. H.
See Villiard, Paul
de Gruchy, John W(esley) 1939- 131
de Grummond, Lena Young CANR-1
Earlier sketch in CA 1-4R
See also SATA 6, 62
de Grunwald, Constantine 9-12R
de Guadaloupe, Brother Jose
See Mojica, Jose
Deguine, Jean-Claude 1943- 81-84
de Guingand, Francis Wilfred
1900-1979 Obituary 89-92
de Guise, Elizabeth (Mary Teresa) 1934- 126
de Gunzburg, Nicholas
See Gunzburg, Nicholas de
deGuzman, Daniel 1911- 93-96
De Haan, Margaret
See Freed, Margaret De Haan
De Haan, Richard W. 1923- 21-24R
De Haas, Elsa 1901- 45-48
de Hamel, Christopher 1950- 120
de Hamel, Joan Littledale 1924- 103
de Hart, Allen 1926- 119
de Hartmann, Olga
1883(?)-1979 Obituary 89-92
de Hartog, Jan 1914- CANR-1
Earlier sketch in CA 1-4R
See also CLC 19
De Haven, Tom 1949- 133
Dehejia, Vidya 1942- 136
de Hevesy, Paul 1883-1988 Obituary 125
Dehn, Olive 1914- 117
Dehn, Paul (Edward) 1912-1976 89-92
Dehoney, W(illiam) Wayne 1918- 17-20R
de Hostos, E. M.
See Hostos (y Bonilla), Eugenio Maria de
de Hostos, Eugenio M.
See Hostos (y Bonilla), Eugenio Maria de
de Hoyos, Angela
See Hoyos, Angela de
Dehqani-Tafti, H. B. 1920- 106
Dehr, Dorothy 1915- 29-32R
Dei-Anang, Michael 1909- 53-56
Deibler, William E. 1932- 89-92
Deighton, Lee C(ecil) 1906-1987 124
Obituary 122
Deighton, Len
See Deighton, Leonard Cyril
See also AAYA 6
See also BEST 89:2
See also CDBLB 1960 to Present
See also CLC 4, 7, 22, 46
See also DLB 87
Deighton, Leonard Cyril 1929- CANR-33
Earlier sketches in CA 9-12R, CANR-19
See also Deighton, Len
See also MTCW
Deikman, Arthur J(oseph) 1929- 65-68
Deindorfer, Robert Greene 1922-1983 ....CANR-3
Obituary 109
Earlier sketch in CA 9-12R
Deindorfer, Scott 1967- 81-84
Deinzer, Harvey T. 1908- 17-20R
de Iongh, Mary (Dows Herter Norton) Crena
See Crena de Iongh, Mary (Dows Herter Norton)
Deiss, Joseph Jay 1915- CANR-14
Earlier sketch in CA 33-36R
See also SATA 12
Deist, Wilhelm 1931- 136
Deitrick, Frances I. 1962- 137
Deitz, Susan 1934- 110
De Jaegher, Raymond-Joseph
1905-1980 ....CAP-2
Obituary 93-96
Earlier sketch in CA 21-22
DeJean, Joan (Elizabeth) 1948- 134
De Jong, Arthur J(ay) 1934- 69-72
DeJong, David C(ornel) 1905-1967 ....5-8R
See also SATA 10
deJong, Dola 5-8R
See also SATA 7
de Jong, Eveline D(orothea) 1948- 130
De Jong, Gerald Francis 1921- 61-64
de Jong, Gerrit Jr. 1892- 37-40R
De Jong, Gordon F(rederick) 1935- 25-28R

DeJong, Meindert 1906-1991 ....CANR-36
Obituary 134
Earlier sketch in CA 13-16R
See also CLR 1
See also DLB 52
See also MAICYA
See also SATA 2
See also SATO 68
De Jong, Peter 1945- 69-72
De Jong, Russell N(elson)
1907-1990 Obituary 132
de Jonge, Alex 1938- CANR-5
Earlier sketch in CA 53-56
DeJonge, Joanne E. 1943- ....SATA 56
De Jonge, Marinus 1925- 123
de Jongh, James 1942- 85-88
de Journlet, Marie
See Little, Paul H(ugo)
de Jouvenel, Bertrand
See de Jouvenel des Ursins, Edouard Bertrand
de Jouvenel, Hugues Alain 1946- 130
de Jouvenel des Ursins, Edouard Bertrand
1903-1987 Obituary 121
De Jovine, F(elix) Anthony 1927-1976 ...... CAP-2
Earlier sketch in CA 29-32
Deju, Raul A(ntonio) 1946- 53-56
DeKalb, Lorimer
See Knorr, Marian L(ockwood)
de Kay, James T(ertius) 1930- CANR-10
Earlier sketch in CA 25-28R
de Kay, Ormonde (Jr.) 1923- 49-52
See also SATA 7
de Kerpely, Theresa 1898- 119
deKieffer, Donald (Eulette) 1945- 112
de Kiewiet, Cornelis W(illem)
1902-1986 Obituary 118
de Kiewiet, Cornelius W(illiam)
See de Kiewiet, Cornelis W(illem)
de Kiewit, Cornelis W(illem)
See de Kiewiet, Cornelis W(illem)
de Kiriline, Louise
See Lawrence, Louise de Kiriline
Dekker, Carl
See Laffin, John (Alfred Charles)
and Lynds, Dennis
Dekker, George 1934- 104
Dekker, Rudolf M(ichel) 1951- 132
Dekker, Thomas
1572(?)-1632 ....CDBLB Before 1660
See also DLB 62
Dekle, Bernard 1905- 17-20R
Dekmejian, Richard Hrair 1933- 37-40R
Deknatel, F(rederick) B(rockway)
1905-1973 Obituary 45-48
Dekobra, Maurice
See Tessier, (Ernst) M(aurice)
De Koenigswerther, Edwin Raymond
1930- 49-52
DeKok, David (Paul) 1953- 124
DeKosky, Robert K. 1945- 93-96
DeKoster, Lester Ronald 1915- 13-16R
De Koven, Bernard 1941- 85-88
De Koven, Bernie
See De Koven, Bernard
Dekovic, Gene 1922- CANR-26
Earlier sketch in CA 108
deKruif, Paul (Henry) 1890-1971 ....9-12R
Obituary 29-32R
See also SATA 5, 50
de Kun, Nicolas 1923- 17-20R
De La Bedoyere, Michael
1900-1973 Obituary 104
Delacato, Carl H(enry) 1923- 41-44R
Delacorta
See Odier, Daniel
Delacorte, George T. Jr. 1894- .... DLB 91
Delacorte, Peter 1943- 105
de la Costa, Horacio (L.)
See Costa, Horacio (L.) de la
Delacour, Jean
See Delacour, Jean Theodore
Delacour, Jean Theodore
1890-1985 Obituary 117
Delacre, Lulu 1957- ....SATA 36
DeLacy, Margaret (Eisenstein) 1951- 122
DeLaet, Sigfried J(an) 1914- CANR-18
Earlier sketches in CA 5-8R, CANR-3
Delafield, E. M.
See
Dashwood, Edmee Elizabeth Monica de la Pasture
See also DLB 34
de la Garza, Rodolfo O(ropea) 1942- 77-80
De Lage, Ida 1918- CANR-14
Earlier sketch in CA 41-44R
See also SATA 11
de La Glannege, Roger-Maxe
See Legman, G(ershon)
De La Grange, Henry Louis 1924- 69-72
de la Guardia, Ernesto Jr.
1904-1983 Obituary 109
de Laguna, Frederica (Annis) 1906- 37-40R
de Laguna, Grace Mead A(ndrus)
1878-1978 .... CAP-1
Obituary 77-80
Earlier sketch in CA 11-12
Delahanty, Randolph
See Delehanty, Randolph
Delahay, E(ileen) A(vril) 1915-1982 ....25-28R
Obituary 117
Delahaye, Guy 1888-1969 .... DLB 92
De La Iglesia, Maria Elena 1936- 29-32R
de la Mare, Albinia Catherine 1932- 33-36R
de la Mare, Richard (Herbert Ingpen)
1901-1986 Obituary 118
de la Mare, Walter (John) 1873-1956 137
Brief entry 110
See also CDBLB 1914-1945
See also CLR 23
See also DLB 19
See also MAICYA
See also SATA 16
See also TCLC 4
See also WLC
DeLamarter, Jeanne
See Bonnette, Jeanne
DeLamotte, Roy Carroll 1917- CANR-15
Earlier sketch in CA 41-44R
DeLancey, Mark W(akeman) 1939- 93-96
Deland, Margaret(ta Wade Campbell)
1857-1945 Brief entry 122
See also DLB 78
Delaney, Bud
See Delaney, Francis Jr.
Delaney, C(ornelius) F. 1938- CANR-16
Earlier sketch in CA 25-28R
Delaney, Daniel J(oseph) 1938- 41-44R
Delaney, Denis
See Green, Peter (Morris)
Delaney, Edmund T. 1914- 13-16R
Delaney, Francis Jr. 1931- 57-60
Delaney, Franey
See O'Hara, John (Henry)
Delaney, Frank 1942- 126
Delaney, Harry 1932- 25-28R
See also SATA 3
Delaney, Jack J(ames) 1921- 21-24R
Delaney, John Joseph 1910-1985 ....CANR-5
Obituary 115
Earlier sketch in CA 1-4R
DeLaney, Joseph Lawrence 1917- 102
Delaney, Lolo M(ae) 1937- 57-60
Delaney, Marshall
See Fulford, Robert
Delaney, Mary Murray 1913- 53-56
Delaney, Ned
See Delaney, Thomas Nicholas III
See also SATA 28
Delaney, Norman Conrad 1932- 37-40R
Delaney, Robert Finley 1925- CANR-6
Earlier sketch in CA 1-4R
Delaney, Shelagh 1939- CANR-30
Earlier sketch in CA 17-20R
See also CDBLB 1960 to Present
See also CLC 29
See also DLB 13
See also MTCW
Delaney, Steve 1938- 121
Brief entry 110
Delaney, Thomas Nicholas III 1951- CANR-10
Earlier sketch in CA 65-68
See also Delaney, Ned
Delaney, William A(nthony) 1926- 106
de Lange, Nicholas (Robert Michael)
1944- CANR-15
Earlier sketch in CA 89-92
Delano, Anthony 1930- 102
Delano, Hugh 1933- 65-68
See also SATA 20
Delano, Isaac O. 1904- 25-28R
Delano, Kenneth J(oseph) 1934- 57-60
de Lantagne, Cecile
See Cloutier-Wojciechowska, Cecile
Delany, George (Battle) 1946- 114
Delany, Kevin F(rancis) X(avier) 1927- 73-76
Delany, Martin Robinson 1812-1885 .... DLB 50
Delany, Paul 1937- CANR-19
Earlier sketch in CA 29-32R
Delany, Samuel R(ay Jr.) 1942- CANR-27
Earlier sketch in CA 81-84
See also BLC 1
See also BW
See also CLC 8, 14, 38
See also DLB 8, 33
See also MTCW
Delany, Sheila 1940- 112
de la Pena, Augustin (Mateo) 1942- 115
Delaplane, Stanton Hill 1907-1988 ....25-28R
Obituary 125
Delaporte, Ernest P(ierre) 1924- 97-100
Delaporte, Francois Louis 1941- 137
Delaporte, Theophile
See Green, Julian (Hartridge)
de la Portilla, Marta (Rosa) 1927- 61-64
De Lapp, Ardyce Lucile 1903- 97-100
DeLapp, George Leslie 1895- 102
De La Ramee, (Marie) Louise 1839-1908
See Ouida
See also SATA 20
de la Renta, Francoise de Langlade
1921(?)-1983 Obituary 110
de la Roche, Mazo 1879-1961 ....CANR-30
Earlier sketch in CA 85-88
See also CLC 14
See also DLB 68
See also SATA 64
Delarue, Jean
See Dreze, Jean
Delasanta, Rodney 1932- 33-36R
de las Cuevas, Raymon
See Harrington, Mark Raymond
de la Torre, Jose 1943- 112
De La Torre, Lillian
See McCue, Lillian Bueno
de la Torre, Victor Raul Haya
See Haya de la Torre, Victor Raul
DeLatte, Carolyn E(lizabeth) 1943- 112
Delattre, Pierre 1930- 105
Delatush, Edith G. 1921- 124
de Laubenfels, David J(ohn) 1925- 53-56
Delaunay, Charles 1911-1988 Obituary 125
de Launay, Jacques F(orment) 1924- CANR-3
Earlier sketch in CA 9-12R
Delaunay(-Terk), Sonia 1885-1979 128
Delaune, (Jewel) Lynn (de Grummond)
...........CANR-21
Earlier sketch in CA 1-4R
See also SATA 7
DeLaura, David J(oseph) 1930- 21-24R
DeLaurentis, Louise Budde 1920- 5-8R
See also SATA 12
de la Warr, George Walter 1904-1969 ...... CAP-1
Earlier sketch in CA 13-16
Delay(-Tubiana), Claude 1944- CANR-33
Earlier sketches in CA 53-56, CANR-4
Delbanco, Nicholas (Franklin) 1942- CANR-29
Earlier sketch in CA 17-20R
See also CAAS 2
See also CLC 6, 13
See also DLB 6
del Barco, Lucy Salamanca
1900(?)-1989 ....17-20R
Obituary 130
See also SATA 64
Del Boca, Angelo 1925- 25-28R
Delbridge, Rosemary
1949(?)-1981 Obituary 105
Del Caro, Adrian 1952- 137
del Castillo, Michel 1933- 109
See also CLC 38
del Castillo, Richard Griswold
See Griswold del Castillo, Richard
Delcroix, Carlo 1896-1977 Obituary 73-76
Delderfield, Eric R(aymond) 1909- CANR-4
Earlier sketch in CA 53-56
See also SATA 14
Delderfield, Ronald Frederick 1912-1972 73-76
Obituary 37-40R
See also SATA 20
Delear, Frank J. 1914- CANR-9
Earlier sketch in CA 21-24R
Deledda, Grazia (Cosima)
1875(?)-1936 Brief entry 123
See also TCLC 23
DeLeeuw, Adele (Louise) 1899-1988 ....CANR-1
Obituary 125
Earlier sketch in CA 1-4R
See also SATA 1, 30, 56
DeLeeuw, Cateau 1903-1975 ....CANR-3
Earlier sketch in CA 1-4R
de Leeuw, Hendrik 1891-1977 Obituary 73-76
Delehanty, Randolph 1944- 123
de Leiris, Alain 1922- 73-76
DeLeon, David (Henry) 1947- Brief entry 114
De Leon, Nephtali 1945- .... DLB 82
See also HW
de Lerma, Dominique-Rene 1928- CANR-1
Earlier sketch in CA 45-48
Delessert, Etienne 1941- CANR-37
Earlier sketches in CA 21-24R, CANR-13
See also MAICYA
See also SATA 27, 46
DeLey, Herbert (Clemone Jr.) 1936- 21-24R
Delfano, M. M.
See Flammonde, Paris
Delfgaauw, Bernard(us Maria Ignatius)
1912- 21-24R
Delgado, Abelardo B(arrientos) 1931- 131
See also CAAS 15
See also DLB 82
See also HW
Delgado, Alan (George) 1909- CANR-5
Earlier sketch in CA 9-12R
Delgado, James P. 1958- 136
Delgado, Jose Manuel R(odriguez)
1915- 29-32R
Delgado, Ramon (Louis) 1937- CANR-15
Earlier sketch in CA 85-88
D'Elia, Donald John 1933- 57-60
D'Elia, Maria
See Goudiss, Maria Agnes D'Elia
De Libero, Libero 1906-1981 .... DLB 114
Delibes, Miguel
See Delibes Setien, Miguel
See also CLC 8, 18
Delibes Setien, Miguel 1920- CANR-32
Earlier sketches in CA 45-48, CANR-1
See also Delibes, Miguel
See also HW
See also MTCW
Deligiorgis, Stavros (George) 1933- 61-64
DeLillo, Don 1936- CANR-21
Earlier sketch in CA 81-84
See also BEST 89:1
See also CLC 8, 10, 13, 27, 39, 54
See also DLB 6
See also MTCW
de Lima, Agnes 1887(?)-1974 Obituary 53-56
De Lima, Clara Rosa 1922- CANR-6
Earlier sketch in CA 57-60
de Lima, Sigrid 1921- 25-28R
Delinsky, Barbara (Ruth Greenberg)
1945- CANR-30
Earlier sketch in CA 111
de Lint, Charles (Henri Diederick Hoefsmit)
1951- 126
Delisle, Francoise 1886(?)-1974 Obituary 53-56
de Lisser, H. G.
See De Lisser, Herbert George
See also DLB 117
De Lisser, Herbert George
1878-1944 Brief entry 109
See also de Lisser, H. G.
See also TCLC 12
Delius, Anthony (Ronald St. Martin)
1916- CANR-12
Earlier sketch in CA 17-20R
Delk, Robert Carlton 1920- 45-48
Dell, Belinda
See Bowden, Jean
Dell, Christopher 1927- 65-68
Dell, E(dward) T(homas) Jr. 1923- 13-16R
Dell, Edmund 1921- 103
Dell, Floyd 1887-1969 Obituary 89-92
See also DLB 9
Dell, Jeffrey 1899-1985(?) Obituary 116
Dell, Roberta E(lizabeth) 1946- 81-84
Dell, Sidney 1918- CANR-17
Earlier sketches in CA 5-8R, CANR-2
Della Femina, Jerry 1936- Brief entry 111
Della-Piana, Gabriel M. 1926- 73-76
delle Grazie, Marie Eugenie 1864-1931 .... DLB 81
Deller, John J. 1931- 134
delle Stelle, Pier Luigi Bellini
See Bellini delle Stelle, Pier Luigi
Dellheim, Charles (Jay) 1952- 128
Dellin, Lubomir A. D. 1920- 45-48
Dellinger, David (T.) 1915- 65-68
Delloff, Irving Arthur 1920- 13-16R
Delman, David 1924- Brief entry 115
Delmar, Ken 1941- 121
Del Mar, Marcia 1950- 105
Delmar, Roy
See Wexler, Jerome (LeRoy)
Delmar, Vina (Croter) 1905-1990 65-68
Obituary 130
Delmer, Denis Sefton 1904- 5-8R
Delmonico, Andrea
See Morrison, Eula Atwood
De Loach, Allen (Wayne) 1939- CANR-16
Earlier sketch in CA 85-88
DeLoach, Charles F. 1927- 37-40R
DeLoach, Clarence Jr. 1936- 57-60
Delon, Floyd G(urney) 1929- CANR-21
Earlier sketch in CA 69-72
de Lone, Richard H. 1940- 101
DeLone, Ruth
See Rankin, Ruth (DeLone) I(rvine)
De Long, Julie
See Hay, Millicent V.
DeLong, Lea Rosson 1947- 119
DeLong, Thomas A(nderton) 1935- CANR-25
Earlier sketch in CA 106
de Longchamps, Joanne (Cutten)
1923- CANR-3
Earlier sketch in CA 9-12R
De Lora, Joann S.
See Sandlin, Joann S(chepers) De Lora
DeLorean, John Z(achary) 1925- 122
DeLorenzo, Lorisa Mernette 1951- 117
DeLorenzo, Robert John 1947- 117
Deloria, Vine (Victor) Jr. 1933- CANR-20
Earlier sketches in CA 53-56, CANR-5
See also CLC 21
See also MTCW
See also SATA 21
Delorme, Andre
See Julien, Charles-Andre
Delorme, Michele
See Cranston, Mechthild
Delort, Robert 1932- 102
de los Reyes, Gabriel 45-48
de los Rios, Francisco Giner
See Giner de los Rios, Francisco
Deloughery, Grace L. 1933- 33-36R
de Loune, Henry
See Popham, Peter (Nicholas Home)
Delp, Michael W(illiam) 1948- 77-80
Delpar, Helen 1936- 53-56
Delphos, Omar
See Ald, Roy A(llison)
del Rey, Judy-Lynn 1943-1986 124
Obituary 118
del Rey, Lester 1915- CANR-17
Earlier sketch in CA 65-68
See also DLB 8
See also MTCW
See also SATA 22
Delta
See Dennett, Herbert Victor
Delton, Jina 1961- 106
Delton, Judy 1931- CANR-25
Earlier sketches in CA 57-60, CANR-8
See also AAYA 6
See also SAAS 9
See also SATA 14
Delton, Julie 1959- 108
DeLuca, A(ngelo) Michael 1912-1976 ....21-24R
Obituary 120
De Luca, Charles J. 1927- 73-76
De Lucca, John 1920- 41-44R
Delulio, John 1938- ....SATA 15
Delumeau, Jean 1923- 97-100
De Luna, Frederick Adolph 1928- 65-68
Delupis, Ingrid 1939- 103
Del Vecchio, John M(ichael) 1947- 110
See also CLC 29
See also DLBD 9
Delving, Michael
See Williams, Jay
DeLynn, Jane 1946- 77-80
DeLyser, Femmy 1935- 110
Delzell, Charles F(loyd) 1920- CANR-2
Earlier sketch in CA 1-4R
Demac, Donna A. 1952- 121
de Madariaga, Isabel 1919- 107
Demaine, Don
See Drinkall, Gordon (Don)
de Man, Paul (Adolph Michel) 1919-1983 128
Obituary 111
See also CLC 55
See also DLB 67
See also MTCW
de Mandiargues, Andre Pieyre
See Pieyre de Mandiargues, Andre

de Manio, Jack 1914-1988 61-64
Obituary 127
Demant, Vigo Auguste 1893-1983 Obituary 109
de Mar, Esmeralda
See Mellen, Ida M(ay)
Demaray, Donald E(ugene) 1926- CANR-37
Earlier sketches in CA 1-4R, CANR-1, 16
De Marco, Angelus A. 1916- 9-12R
De Marco, Arlene ....AITN 1
DeMarco, Donald 1937- CANR-24
Earlier sketches in CA 61-64, CANR-7
de Mare, Eric S. 1910- CANR-6
Earlier sketch in CA 9-12R
deMare, George 1912- 21-24R
Demarest, Bruce A(lvin) 1935- 118
Demarest, Chris(topher) L(ynn) 1951- 109
See also SATA 44, 45
Demarest, Doug
See Barker, Will
Demarest, Michael 1924(?)-1984 Obituary 112
Demarest, Phyllis Gordon
1911-1969 Obituary 104
Demarest, Rosemary Regina 1914- 116
Demarest, Victoria Booth(-Clibborn)
1890-1982 124
Obituary 112
Demaret, James Newton
1910-1983 Obituary 111
Demaret, Jimmy
See Demaret, James Newton
Demaret, Pierre 1943- CANR-12
Earlier sketch in CA 61-64
De Maria, Robert 1928- CANR-5
Earlier sketch in CA 1-4R
De Marinis, Rick 1934- CANR-25
Earlier sketches in CA 57-60, CANR-9
See also CLC 54
Demaris, Ovid
See Desmarais, Ovid E.
De Marly, Diana 1939- 125
DeMartini, Rodney J(ames) 1947- 113
De Martino, Manfred F(rank)
1924- Brief entry 117
Demas, Vida 1927- 49-52
See also SATA 9
deMatteo, Donna 1941- 25-28R
de Mauny, Erik 1920- CANR-13
Earlier sketch in CA 33-36R
deMause, Lloyd 1931- 65-68
Demb, Ada 1948- 138
Dembart, Lee 1946- 133
Dembner, Red
See Dembner, S. Arthur
Dembner, S. Arthur 1920-1990 Obituary 131
Dembo, L(awrence) S(anford) 1929- CANR-2
Earlier sketch in CA 1-4R
Dembry, R. Emmet
See Murfree, Mary Noailles
Dembski, Stephen (Michael) 1949- 128
Demby, William 1922- 81-84
See also BLC 1
See also BW
See also CLC 53
See also DLB 33
de Medici, Marino 1933- 89-92
De Mejo, Oscar 1911- 111
See also SATA 40
Dement, William Charles 1928- Brief entry 105
De Mente, Boye 1928- CANR-8
Earlier sketch in CA 21-24R
de Menton, Francisco
See Chin, Frank (Chew Jr.)
Demeny, Janos 1915- 118
Demers, James 1942- 97-100
de Mesne, Eugene (Frederick Peter Cheshire)
....CANR-25
Earlier sketch in CA 41-44R
de Mesquita, Bruce James Bueno
See Bueno de Mesquita, Bruce James
de Messieres, Nicole 1930- 107
See also SATA 39
Demetillo, Ricaredo 1920- 102
Demetrakopoulos, Stephanie Anne 1937- 111
Demetrius, James Kleon 1924- CANR-13
Earlier sketch in CA 21-24R
Demetz, Peter 1922- CANR-14
Earlier sketch in CA 65-68
Demi
See Hitz, Demi
De Michael, Don(ald Anthony)
1928-1982 Obituary 106
Demijohn, Thom
See Disch, Thomas M(ichael)
and Sladek, John
de Milan, Sister Jean
See Jean, Gabrielle (Lucille)
D'Emilio, A. Edward 1919(?)-1987 Obituary 122
D'Emilio, John 1948- 135
de Mille, Agnes
See Prude, Agnes George de Mille
DeMille, Alexandria
See Du Breuil, (Elizabeth) L(or)inda
De Mille, Cecil B(lount)
1881-1959 Brief entry 115
De Mille, James 1833-1880 ....DLB 99
De Mille, Nelson
See Levinson, Leonard
DeMille, Nelson 1943- CANR-25
Earlier sketches in CA 57-60, CANR-6
See also BEST 90:3
de Mille, Richard 1922- CANR-13
Earlier sketch in CA 21-24R
Deming, Barbara 1917-1984 ....CANR-15
Earlier sketch in CA 85-88
Deming, Kirk
See Drago, Harry Sinclair
Deming, Louise Macpherson
1916-1976 Obituary 61-64
Deming, Philander 1829-1915 ....DLB 74
Deming, Richard 1915- CANR-3
Earlier sketch in CA 9-12R
See also SATA 24
Deming, Robert H. 1937- 21-24R
DeMirjian, Arto Jr. 1931- 57-60
De Molen, Richard Lee 1938- 45-48
Demone, Harold W(ellington) Jr. 1924- CANR-9
Earlier sketch in CA 5-8R
De Monfried, Henri
1879(?)-1974 Obituary 53-56
Demong, Phyllis 1920- 106
de Montalvo, Luis Galvez
See Avalle-Arce, Juan Bautista de
DeMonte, Claudia 1947- 114
de Montebello, Guy-Philippe Lannes
1936- 45-48
de Montfort, Guy
See Johnson, Donald McI(ntosh)
de Montherlant, Henry (Milon)
See Montherlant, Henry (Milon) de
DeMontreville Polak, Doris
1904(?)-1974 Obituary 49-52
De Mordaunt, Walter J(ulius) 1925- 33-36R
Demorest, Jean-Jacques 1920- 5-8R
Demorest, Stephen 1949- CANR-20
Earlier sketch in CA 101
Demorest, William Jennings 1822-1895 ....DLB 79
De Morny, Peter
See Wynne-Tyson, Esme
Demos, John Putnam 1937- 137
Demos, Paul 1888-1983 Obituary 109
Demotes, Michael
See Burgess, M(ichael) R(oy)
DeMott, Benjamin 1924- 5-8R
De Mott, Donald W(arren) 1928- 61-64
de Mourgues, Odette (Marie Helene Louise)
1914-1988 ....5-8R
Obituary 126
Dempewolff, Richard F(rederic) 1914- CANR-1
Earlier sketch in CA 1-4R
Dempsey, David Knapp 1914- CANR-2
Earlier sketch in CA 5-8R
Dempsey, Hugh Aylmer 1929- CANR-26
Earlier sketches in CA 69-72, CANR-11
Dempsey, Jack
See Dempsey, William Harrison
Dempsey, Lotta 101
Dempsey, Paul K(enneth) 1935- CANR-19
Earlier sketch in CA 25-28R
Dempsey, Richard A(llen) 1932- 61-64
Dempsey, William Harrison 1895-1983 89-92
Obituary 109
Dempster, Barry 1952- CANR-32
Earlier sketch in CA 113
Dempster, Chris 1943- 106
Dempster, Derek David 1924- 13-16R
Dempster, Stuart 1936- 104
Demske, James Michael 1922- 29-32R
Demski, Eva 1944- 135
Demura, Fumio 1940- CANR-12
Earlier sketch in CA 61-64
Demuth, Norman (Frank) 1898-1968 ....CAP-1
Earlier sketch in CA 13-14
Demuth, Patricia Brennan 1948- 118
See also SATA 51
Den, Petr
See Radimsky, Ladislaw
Denali, Peter
See Holm, Don(ald Raymond)
de Natale, Francine
See Malzberg, Barry N(athaniel)
Denbeaux, Fred J. 1914- 5-8R
Denbie, Roger
See Green, Alan (Baer)
Denbigh, Kenneth George 1911- 106
Den Boer, James (Drew) 1937- CANR-10
Earlier sketch in CA 21-24R
Denby, Edwin (Orr) 1903-1983 138
Obituary 110
See also CLC 48
Dendel, Esther (Sietmann Warner) 1910- 102
Dender, Jay
See Deindorfer, Robert Greene
Dendle, Brian J(ohn) 1936- 116
Dendy, Marshall C(oleman) 1902- CAP-2
Earlier sketch in CA 17-18
DeNeef, Arthur Leigh 1942- 102
Deneen, James R. 1928- 45-48
Denenberg, Herbert S(idney) 1929- 37-40R
de Neufville, Richard 1939- 53-56
Denevan, William M(axfield) 1931- 41-44R
de Nevers, Noel (Howard) 1932- 37-40R
DeNevi, Donald P. 1937- 37-40R
Denevi, Marco 1922- ....HW
Denfeld, Duane (Henry) 1939- 41-44R
Deng, William 1929- 13-16R
Dengler, Dieter 1938- 102
Dengler, Marianna (Herron) 1935- 102
Dengler, Sandy 1939- CANR-30
Earlier sketch in CA 112
See also SATA 40, 54
Denham, Alice 1933- 21-24R
Denham, Avery Strakosch Obituary 104
Denham, Bertie 1927- 93-96
Denham, H(enry) M(angles) 1897- 61-64
Denham, John 1615-1669 ....DLB 58
Denham, Mary Orr 1918- CANR-2
Earlier sketch in CA 1-4R
Denham, Reginald 1894-1983 ....CAP-1
Obituary 109
Earlier sketch in CA 13-16
Denham, Robert D(ayton) 1938- 53-56
Denham, Sully
See Budd, Mavis
Denhardt, Robert Moorman 1912- 101
den Hollander, A(rie) Nicolaas Jan
1906-1976 ....CAP-2
Earlier sketch in CA 29-32
Denholm, Therese Mary Zita White
1933- 9-12R
Denholtz, Elaine (Grudin) CANR-13
Earlier sketch in CA 73-76
Dening, Greg 1931- 107
Denis, Armand 1896(?)-1971 Obituary 104
Denis, Charlotte
See Plimmer, Charlotte
and Plimmer, Denis
Denis, Julio
See Cortazar, Julio
Denis, Manuel Maldonado
See Maldonado-Denis, Manuel
Denis, Michaela Holdsworth 13-16R
Denis, Paul 1909- 21-24R
Denisoff, R. Serge 1939- 33-36R
Denison, Barbara 1926- 13-16R
Denison, Corrie
See Partridge, Eric (Honeywood)
Denison, Edward F(ulton) 1915- 21-24R
Denison, Merrill 1893-1975 ....DLB 92
Denison, (John) Michael (Terence Wellesley)
1915- 109
Denison, Norman 1925- 65-68
Denker, Henry 1912- CANR-31
Earlier sketch in CA 33-36R
See also AITN 1
Denkler, Horst 1935- CANR-19
Earlier sketches in CA 53-56, CANR-4
Denkstein, Vladimir 1906- 103
Denlinger, A(nna) Martha 1931- 113
Denman, D(onald) R(obert) 1911- CANR-8
Earlier sketch in CA 61-64
Denmark, Florence L. 1932- 85-88
Denmark, Harrison
See Zelazny, Roger (Joseph)
Dennehy, Raymond L(eo) 1934- 109
Dennes, William Ray 1898- 73-76
Dennett, Daniel C(lement) 1942- CANR-35
Earlier sketch in CA 97-100
Dennett, Herbert Victor 1893- CANR-5
Earlier sketch in CA 5-8R
Denney, Diana 1910- 104
See also SATA 25
Denney, Myron Keith 1930- 102
Denney, Reuel (Nicholas) 1913- CANR-2
Earlier sketch in CA 1-4R
Dennie, Joseph 1768-1812 ....DLB 37, 43, 59, 73
Denning, A. T.
See Denning, Alfred Thompson
Denning, Alfred Thompson
1899- Brief entry 115
Denning, Basil W. 1928- 33-36R
Denning, Candace 1946- 125
Denning, Melita
See Barcynski, Vivian G(odfrey)
Denning, Patricia
See Willis, Corinne Denneny
Dennis, Arthur
See Edmonds, Arthur Denis
Dennis, Benjamin G. 1929- 45-48
Dennis, Carl 1939- 77-80
Dennis, Charles 1946- CANR-17
Earlier sketch in CA 65-68
Dennis, Deborah Ellis 1950- 116
Dennis, Everette E. 1942- 41-44R
Dennis, Henry C(harles) 1918- 41-44R
Dennis, Ian 1952- 125
Dennis, James M(unn) 1932- 102
Dennis, John V(alue) 1916- 107
Dennis, John 1658-1734 ....DLB 101
Dennis, Landt 1937- 65-68
Dennis, Lane T(imothy) 1943- 93-96
Dennis, Lawrence 1893-1977 Obituary 73-76
Dennis, Morgan 1891(?)-1960 ....SATA 18
Dennis, Nigel (Forbes) 1912-1989 ....25-28R
Obituary 129
See also CLC 8
See also DLB 13, 15
See also MTCW
Dennis, Patrick
See Tanner, Edward Everett III
Dennis, Peggy 1909- 77-80
Dennis, Peter (John) 1945- 41-44R
Dennis, Ralph ....AITN 1
Dennis, Richard (John) 1949- 118
Dennis, Robert C. 1920-1983 101
Obituary 110
Dennis, Rutledge M(elvin) 1939- 115
Dennis, Suzanne Easton 1922- 25-28R
Dennis, Wayne 1905-1976 ....17-20R
Obituary 69-72
Dennis, Wesley 1903-1966 135
See also MAICYA
See also SATA 18
Dennis-Jones, H(arold) 1915- CANR-8
Earlier sketch in CA 57-60
Dennison, A(lfred) Dudley Jr. 1914- CANR-9
Earlier sketch in CA 57-60
Dennison, George (Harris) 1925-1987 101
Obituary 123
See also CAAS 6
Dennison, George M(arshel) 1935- 53-56
Dennison, Milo
See Cantwell, Lois
Dennison, Peter (John) 1942- 124
Dennison, Sam 1926- CANR-28
Earlier sketch in CA 109
Dennison, Shane 1933- 73-76
Denniston, Denise 1946- 69-72
Denniston, Elinore 1900-1978 Obituary 81-84
See also SATA 24
Denniston, Lyle (William) 1931- 65-68
Denny, Alma 1912- 89-92
Denny, Brian
See Doughty, Bradford
Denny, Carol
See Brandt, Carol
Denny, John Howard 1920- CAP-1
Earlier sketch in CA 9-10
Denny, Ludwell 1894-1970 Obituary 29-32R
Denny, M(aurice) Ray 1918- CANR-14
Earlier sketch in CA 41-44R
Denny, Norman (George) 1901-1982 107
See also SATA 43
Denny, Robert 1920- 135
Denny-Brown, Derek Ernest
1901-1981 Obituary 103
Dennys, Joyce (a pseudonym) 1895- 121
Dennys, Rodney Onslow 1911- 85-88
Denoeu, Francois 1898-1975 53-56
Denomme, Robert T. 1930- 25-28R
Denoon, Donald (John Noble) 1940- CANR-14
Earlier sketch in CA 73-76
DeNovo, John A(ugust) 1916- 9-12R
Densen-Gerber, Judianne 1934- 37-40R
Denslow, Sharon Phillips 1947- 136
See also SATA 68
Denslow, W(illiam) W(allace)
1856-1915 ....CLR 15
See also SATA 16
Densmore, John 1944- 136
Denson, John Lee 1903-1982 Obituary 108
Dent, Alan (Holmes) 1905-1978 ....CANR-5
Earlier sketch in CA 9-12R
Dent, Anthony Austen 1915- CANR-15
Earlier sketch in CA 25-28R
Dent, Colin 1921- 13-16R
Dent, Harold (Collett) 1894- CANR-5
Earlier sketch in CA 5-8R
Dent, Harry (Shuler) 1930- 81-84
Dent, Lester 1904(?)-1959 Brief entry 112
Dent, Robert William 1917- 105
Dent, Thomas C(ovington) 1932- 125
Brief entry 122
See also Dent, Tom
See also BW
Dent, Tom
See Dent, Thomas C(ovington)
See also DLB 38
Dentan, Robert C(laude) 1907- CANR-2
Earlier sketch in CA 1-4R
Dentinger, Jane 1951- 123
Dentinger, Stephen
See Hoch, Edward D(entinger)
Dentler, Robert A(rnold) 1928- CANR-17
Earlier sketches in CA 1-4R, CANR-1
Denton, Charles F(rederick) 1942- 37-40R
Denton, D. Keith 1948- 112
Denton, Daniel 1626(?)-1703 ....DLB 24
Denton, H(arry) M. 1882- CAP-1
Earlier sketch in CA 11-12
Denton, Herbert H(oward) Jr.
1943-1989 Obituary 128
Denton, J(effrey) H(oward) 1939- CANR-15
Earlier sketch in CA 41-44R
Denton, Jeremiah A(ndrew) Jr. 1924- CANR-31
Earlier sketch in CA 69-72
Denton, Kady MacDonald 134
See also SATA 66
Denton, Wallace 1928- 1-4R
d'Entreves, Alexander (Passerin)
1902-1985 Obituary 118
Dentry, Robert
See White, Osmar (Egmont Dorkin)
Denues, Celia 1915- 41-44R
Den Uyl, Douglas J(ohn) 1950- 117
Denver, Boone
See Rennie, James Alan
Denver, Drake C.
See Nye, Nelson C(oral)
Denver, Rod
See Edson, J(ohn) T(homas)
Denver, Walt
See Redding, Robert Hull
and Sherman, Jory (Tecumseh)
Denvir, Bernard 1917- 115
Denyer, Nicholas (Charles) 1955- 136
Denys, Teresa (a pseudonym) 1947- 105
Denzel, Justin F(rancis) 1917- CANR-4
Earlier sketch in CA 53-56
See also SATA 38, 46
Denzer, Ann Wiseman
See Wiseman, Ann (Sayre)
Denzer, Peter W(orthington) 1921- 5-8R
Denzin, Norman K(ent) 1941- CANR-30
Earlier sketches in CA 29-32R, CANR-12
de Obaldia, Rene
See Obaldia, Rene de
de Oca, Marco Antonio Montes
See Montes de Oca, Marco Antonio
de Oliveira, Paulo C(arlos) 1953- 114
Deon, Michel 1919- CANR-37
Earlier sketches in CA 37-40R, CANR-16
De Palma, Brian (Russell) 1940- 109
See also CLC 20
dePaola, Thomas Anthony 1934- CANR-37
Earlier sketches in CA 49-52, CANR-2
See also dePaola, Tomie
See also MAICYA
See also SATA 11, 59
dePaola, Tomie
See dePaola, Thomas Anthony
See also CLR 4, 24
See also DLB 61
de Paor, Risteard
See Power, Richard
Depas, Spencer 1925- 69-72
DePaul, Edith
See Delatush, Edith G.

DePauw, Linda Grant 1940- ... CANR-9
Earlier sketch in CA 21-24R
See also SATA 24
Depel, Jim 1936- ... 73-76
de Pereda, Prudencio 1912- ... CANR-4
Earlier sketch in CA 1-4R
Depestre, Rene 1926- Brief entry ... 113
Depew, Arthur M(c Kinley) 1896-1976 ... 41-44R
Depew, Wally
See Depew, Walter Westerfield
Depew, Walter Westerfield 1924- ... 5-8R
De Pietro, Albert 1913- ... 69-72
de Polman, Willem
See Nichols, Dale (William)
De Polnay, Peter 1906-1984 ... 73-76
Obituary ... 114
DePorte, Anton W. 1928- ... 124
DePorte, Michael V(ital) 1939- ... 49-52
Depp, Roberta J. 1947- ... 101
de Pre, Jean-Anne
See Avallone, Michael (Angelo, Jr)
DePree, Gladis (Lenore) 1933- ... 101
DePree, Gordon 1930- ... 101
Depta, Victor M(arshall) 1939- ... 49-52
De Puy, Norman R(obert) 1929- ... 97-100
Dequasie, Andrew 1929- ... CANR-35
Earlier sketch in CA 114
De Quincey, Thomas
1785-1859 ... CDBLB 1789-1832
See also DLB 110
D'Erasmo, Martha 1939- ... 81-84
Derber, Milton 1915- Brief entry ... 106
Derby, George Horatio 1823-1861 ... DLB 11
Derby, Pat 1942- ... 69-72
Derderian, Yeghishe
1910(?)-1990 Obituary ... 130
de Regniers, Beatrice Schenk (Freedman)
1914- ... CANR-26
Earlier sketches in CA 13-16R, CANR-6
See also MAICYA
See also SAAS 6
See also SATA 2, 68
Dereksen, David
See Stacton, David (Derek)
Deren, Eleanora 1908(?)-1961 Obituary ... 111
See also Deren, Maya
Deren, Maya
See Deren, Eleanora
See also CLC 16
Derenberg, Walter J(ulius)
1903-1975 Obituary ... 61-64
De Reneville, Mary Margaret Motley Sheridan
1912- ... 5-8R
de Reyna, Rudy 1914- ... CANR-10
Earlier sketch in CA 57-60
Derfler, (Arnold) Leslie 1933- ... CANR-9
Earlier sketch in CA 5-8R
deRham, Edith 1933- ... 13-16R
Derham, (Arthur) Morgan 1915- ... 13-16R
Der Hovanessian, Diana ... 124
Deriabin, Peter 1921- ... 134
Deric, Arthur J. 1926- ... 21-24R
Dering, Joan (Rosalind Cordelia) 1917- ... 9-12R
De Risi, William J(oseph) 1938- ... 53-56
de Rivera, Joseph H(osmer) 1932- ... 41-44R
Derleth, August (William) 1909-1971 ... CANR-4
Obituary ... 29-32R
Earlier sketch in CA 1-4R
See also CLC 31
See also DLB 9
See also SATA 5
Derman, Lou 1914(?)-1976 Obituary ... 65-68
Derman, Sarah Audrey 1915- ... CANR-17
Earlier sketch in CA 1-4R
See also SATA 11
Dermid, Jack 1923- ... 49-52
Dermout, Maria
See
Dermout-Ingermann, Helena Antonia Maria Elisabeth
Dermout-Ingermann, Helena Antonia Maria Elisabeth
1888-1962 Obituary ... 114
Dern, Erolie Pearl Gaddis 1895-1966 ... CANR-6
Obituary ... 25-28R
Earlier sketch in CA 1-4R
Dern, Karl L(udwig) 1894- ... 57-60
Dern, Peggy
See Dern, Erolie Pearl Gaddis
Dernburg, Thomas F(rederick) 1930- ... CANR-2
Earlier sketch in CA 1-4R
Der Nersessian, Sirarpie 1896- ... 102
de Robeck, Nesta 1886- ... CAP-2
Earlier sketch in CA 25-28
De Rochemont, Richard (Guertis)
1903-1982 Obituary ... 108
de Rocher, Gregory (David) 1943- ... 114
DeRoin, Nancy 1934- ... 65-68
de Romaszkan, Gregor 1894- ... 13-16R
de Roo, Anne Louise 1931- ... 103
See also SATA 25
de Roos, Robert (William) 1912- ... 9-12R
de Ropp, Robert S(ylvester) 1913- ... 17-20R
Deror, Yehezkel
See Dror, Yehezkel
deRosa, Dee ... SATA 70
DeRosa, Peter (Clement) 1932- ... CANR-9
Earlier sketch in CA 21-24R
DeRosier, Arthur H(enry) Jr. 1931- ... 29-32R
De Rosis, Helen A. 1918- ... 122
Brief entry ... 107
De Rossi, Claude J(oseph) 1942- ... 53-56
Derossi, Flavia 1926- ... 112
de Rothschild, Guy (Edward Alphonse Paul)
1909- ... 129
de Rothschild, Pauline (Fairfax-Potter)
1908(?)-1976 Obituary ... 65-68
de Rougemont, Denis 1906-1985 Obituary ... 118
de Roussan, Jacques 1929- ... 123
Brief entry ... 110
See also SATA 31
de Routisie, Albert
See Aragon, Louis
Derr, Mark (Burgess) 1950- ... 135
Derr, Richard L(uther) 1930- ... 53-56
Derr, Thomas Sieger 1931- ... 53-56
Derrett, J(ohn) Duncan M(artin)
1922- ... CANR-21
Earlier sketches in CA 13-16R, CANR-6
Derrick, Graham
See Raby, Derek Graham
Derrick, Lionel
See Cunningham, Chet
Derrick, Paul 1916- ... CAP-1
Earlier sketch in CA 9-10
Derricotte, Toi 1941- ... CANR-32
Earlier sketch in CA 113
Derrida, Jacques 1930- ... 127
Brief entry ... 124
See also CLC 24
Derriman, James Parkyns 1922- ... 106
Derry, John W(esley) 1933- ... CANR-3
Earlier sketch in CA 5-8R
Derry, (Thomas) Ramsay 1939- ... 110
Derry, Thomas Kingston 1905- ... CANR-4
Earlier sketch in CA 1-4R
Derry Down Derry
See Lear, Edward
Dershowitz, Alan M. 1938- ... CANR-11
Earlier sketch in CA 25-28R
Dersonnes, Jacques
See Simenon, Georges (Jacques Christian)
Dertouzos, Michael L. 1936- ... 21-24R
Derum, James Patrick 1893- ... CAP-1
Earlier sketch in CA 13-14
De Ruth, Jan 1922- ... 33-36R
Dervin, Brenda 1938- ... 29-32R
Dervin, Daniel A(rthur) 1935- ... 57-60
Derwent, Lavinia ... CANR-27
Earlier sketch in CA 69-72
See also SATA 14
Derwin, Jordan 1931- ... 13-16R
Dery, Tibor 1894-1977 Obituary ... 73-76
de Rycke, Laurence Joseph
1907-1989 Obituary ... 129
Desai, Anita 1937- ... CANR-33
Earlier sketch in CA 81-84
See also CLC 19, 37
See also MTCW
See also SATA 63
Desai, Boman 1950- ... 134
Desai, Meghnad 1940- ... 126
Desai, P(rasannavadan) B(hagwanji)
1924- ... 29-32R
Desai, Ram 1926- ... 5-8R
Desai, Rashmi H(arilal) 1928- ... 13-16R
Desai, Rupin W(alter) 1934- ... 45-48
de Ste. Croix, G(eoffrey) E(rnest) M(aurice)
1910- ... 73-76
de Saint-Gall, Auguste Amedee
See Strich, Christian
de St. Jorre, John 1936- ... 102
de Saint-Luc, Jean
See Glassco, John
de Saint Phalle, Therese 1930- ... CANR-21
Earlier sketch in CA 29-32R
de Saint Phalle, Thibaut 1918- ... 108
de Saint Roman, Arnaud
See Aragon, Louis
DeSalvo, Joseph S(alvatore) 1938- ... 45-48
DeSalvo, Louise A(nita) 1942- ... CANR-23
Earlier sketch in CA 102
Desan, Wilfrid 1908- ... 61-64
Desani, G(ovindas) V(ishnoodas) 1909- ... 45-48
de Santa Ana, Julio 1934- ... 132
de Santillana, Giorgio Diaz 1902- ... CAP-1
Earlier sketch in CA 13-14
DeSantis, Mary Allen (Carpe) 1930- ... 9-12R
De Santis, Vincent P. 1918- ... CANR-4
Earlier sketch in CA 9-12R
De Santo, Charles P(asquale) 1923- ... 116
De Satge, John (Cosmo) 1928-1984 ... 124
Obituary ... 113
Desatnick, Robert L(awrence) 1931- ... 41-44R
Desaulniers, Gonzalve 1863-1934 ... DLB 92
de Sausmarez, (Lionel) Maurice
1915-1969 ... CAP-1
Earlier sketch in CA 11-12
de Saussure, Eric 1925- ... 105
Desbarats, Peter 1933- ... CANR-10
Earlier sketch in CA 17-20R
See also SATA 39
Des Barres, Pamela (Ann) 1948- ... 128
Desbiens, Jean-Paul 1927- ... DLB 53
Desborough, Vincent Robin d'Arba
1914-1978 Obituary ... 111
Descargues, Pierre 1925- ... CANR-14
Earlier sketch in CA 37-40R
Deschampsneufs, Henry Pierre Bernard
1911- ... CANR-6
Earlier sketch in CA 5-8R
de Schanschieff, Juliet Dymoke 1919- ... 106
Descharnes, Robert (Pierre) 1926- ... 69-72
Deschenaux, Jacques 1945- ... 61-64
Deschin, Celia Spalter 1903- ... 104
Deschin, Jacob 1900(?)-1983 Obituary ... 110
Deschler, Lewis 1905-1976 Obituary ... 65-68
Deschner, Donald (Anthony) 1933- ... 21-24R
Deschner, (Hans) Guenther 1941- ... 41-44R
Deschner, (Hans) Gunther
See Deschner, (Hans) Guenther
Deschner, John 1923- ... 81-84
de Schweinitz, Karl 1887-1975 ... 61-64
Descombes, Vincent 1943- ... 136
de Selincourt, Aubrey 1894-1962 ... 73-76
See also SATA 14
de Sena, Jorge 1919-1978 Obituary ... 77-80
De Seversky, Alexander P(rocofieff)
1894-1974 Obituary ... 53-56
DeSeyn, Donna E. 1933- ... 21-24R
des Forets, Louis-Rene 1918- ... DLB 83
Desfosses, Helen 1945- ... 41-44R
Des Gagniers, Jean 1929- ... CANR-9
Earlier sketch in CA 65-68
DeShazo, Edith K(ind) 1920- ... 61-64
DeShazo, Elmer Anthony 1924- ... 37-40R
Deshen, Shlomo 1935- ... 57-60
Deshler, G(eorge) Byron 1903- ... 53-56
Deshpande, Chris 1950- ... 137
See also SATA 69
Deshpande, Shashi 1938- ... 128
DeSiano, Francis P(atrick) 1945- ... CANR-31
Earlier sketch in CA 112
De Sica, Vittorio 1901(?)-1974 Obituary ... 117
See also CLC 20
Desiderato, Otello 1926- ... 37-40R
de Silva, Alvaro 1949- ... 138
De Simone, Daniel V. 1930- ... 25-28R
Desjarlais, John 1953- ... 135
See also SATA 71
Desmarais, Barbara G.
See Taylor, Barbara G.
Des Marais, Louise M(ercier) 1923- ... 110
Desmarais, Ovid E. 1919- ... CANR-23
Earlier sketches in CA 1-4R, CANR-4
Desmond, Adrian J(ohn) 1947- ... CANR-8
Earlier sketch in CA 61-64
See also SATA 51
Desmond, Alice Curtis 1897- ... CANR-2
Earlier sketch in CA 1-4R
See also SATA 8
Desmond, (Clarice) J(oanne) Patrick (Scholes)
1910- ... 9-12R
Desmond, John F(rancis) 1939- ... 112
Desmond, John 1909(?)-1977 Obituary ... 73-76
Desmond, Ray 1925- ... 120
Desmond, Robert W(illiam) 1900- ... CANR-12
Earlier sketch in CA 73-76
Desmond, Shaw 1877-1960 Obituary ... 89-92
Desmonde, William H(erbert) 1921- ... 1-4R
Desnos, Robert 1900-1945 Brief entry ... 121
See also TCLC 22
De Sola, John
See Morland, Nigel
De Sola, Ralph 1908- ... 53-56
de Sousa, Ronald 1940- ... 127
Desowitz, Robert S. 1926- ... 126
Despalatovic, Elinor Murray 1933- ... 105
Despert, J(uliette) Louise 1892- ... 69-72
Desplaines, Baroness Julie
See Jennings, Leslie Nelson
Despland, Michel 1936- ... CANR-29
Earlier sketch in CA 49-52
Despres, Leo A(rthur) 1932- ... 25-28R
Des Pres, Terrence 1939-1987 ... 73-76
Obituary ... 124
DesRochers, Alfred 1901-1978 ... DLB 68
Desrosiers, Leo-Paul 1892-1967 ... DLB 68
Dess, G. D. ... 135
Dessau, Joanna 1921- ... CANR-24
Earlier sketch in CA 106
Dessauer, John H(ans) 1905- ... 104
Dessauer, John P(aul) 1924- ... 53-56
Dessaulles, Louis-Antoine 1819-1895 ... DLB 99
Dessel, Norman F(rank) 1932- ... 61-64
Dessen, Alan C(harles) 1935- ... 69-72
Dessent, Michael H(arold) 1942- ... 110
Dessi, Giuseppe 1909-1977 ... 65-68
Obituary ... 126
d'Estaing, Valery Giscard
See Giscard d'Estaing, Valery
De Steuch, Harriet Henry
1897(?)-1974 Obituary ... 49-52
Destler, Chester McArthur 1904-1984 ... CANR-16
Obituary ... 114
Earlier sketch in CA 5-8R
Destler, I. M. 1939- ... CANR-15
Earlier sketch in CA 89-92
Destouches, Louis-Ferdinand
1894-1961 ... CANR-28
Earlier sketch in CA 85-88
See also Celine, Louis-Ferdinand
See also CLC 9, 15
See also MTCW
Destry, Vince
See Norwood, Victor G(eorge) C(harles)
De Sua, William Joseph 1930- ... 13-16R
de Swaan, Abram 1942- ... CANR-13
Earlier sketch in CA 69-72
de Sylva, Donald Perrin 1928- ... 53-56
De Tabley, Lord 1835-1895 ... DLB 35
De Tarr, Francis 1926- ... 17-20R
Deter, Dean (Allen) 1945- ... 53-56
de Teran, Lisa St. Aubin
See St. Aubin de Teran, Lisa
Deterline, William A(lexander) 1927- ... CANR-8
Earlier sketch in CA 5-8R
de Terra, Helmut 1900-1981 Obituary ... 104
de Terra, Rhoda Hoff 1901- ... 1-4R
Detherage, May 1908- ... CAP-2
Earlier sketch in CA 23-24
Dethier, Vincent Gaston 1915- ... CANR-9
Earlier sketch in CA 65-68
Dethlefsen, Merle 1934- ... 119
Dethloff, Henry C(lay) 1934- ... 21-24R
De Thomasis, Louis 1940- ... 123
Detine, Padre
See Olsen, Ib Spang
de Tirtoff, Romain 1892-1990 ... 69-72
Obituary ... 131
Detjen, Ervin W(infred) 1909- ... CAP-2
Earlier sketch in CA 19-20
Detjen, Mary (Elizabeth) Ford 1904- ... CAP-1
Earlier sketch in CA 13-14
de Todany, James
See Beaudoin, Kenneth Lawrence
de Toledano, Ralph
See Toledano, Ralph de
de Tolignac, Gaston
See Griffith, D(avid Lewelyn) W(ark)
De Tolnay, Charles Erich 1899- ... 73-76
de Tonquedec, Joseph
See Tonquedec, Joseph de
de Trevino, Elizabeth B.
See Trevino, Elizabeth B(orton) de
Detrez, Conrad (Jean) 1937-1985 ... 132
Detro, Gene 1935- ... CANR-12
Earlier sketch in CA 61-64
Detter, Ingrid
See Delupis, Ingrid
Detweiler, Robert 1932- ... 33-36R
Detwiler, Donald S(caife) 1933- ... 37-40R
Detwiler, Susan Dill 1956- ... SATA 58
Detz, Joan (Marie) 1951- ... 118
Detz, Phyllis 1911- ... CAP-2
Earlier sketch in CA 33-36
Detzer, David William 1937- ... 93-96
Detzer, Karl 1891- ... CAP-1
Earlier sketch in CA 9-10
Detzler, Jack J. 1922- ... 33-36R
Detzler, Wayne Alan 1936- ... 105
Deuchar, Margaret 1952- ... 113
Deuel, Thorne 1890-1984 Obituary ... 112
Deutrich, Mabel E. 1915- ... 5-8R
Deutsch, Alfred H(enry) 1914- ... 116
Deutsch, Arnold R. 1919- ... 101
Deutsch, Babette 1895-1982 ... CANR-4
Obituary ... 108
Earlier sketch in CA 1-4R
See also CLC 18
See also DLB 45
See also SATA 1, 33
Deutsch, Bernard Francis 1925- ... 13-16R
Deutsch, Eberhard Paul
1897-1980 Obituary ... 93-96
Deutsch, Eliot (Sandler) 1931- ... CANR-10
Earlier sketch in CA 65-68
Deutsch, Eva Costabel
See Costabel, Eva Deutsch
Deutsch, Harold C(harles) 1904- ... 21-24R
Deutsch, Helen 1906- ... 112
Obituary ... 137
Brief entry ... 108
Deutsch, Helene (Rosenbach) 1884-1982 ... 128
Obituary ... 106
Deutsch, Herbert A(rnold) 1932- ... 89-92
Deutsch, Hermann Bacher
1889-1970 Obituary ... 93-96
Deutsch, John James 1911-1976 Obituary ... 111
Deutsch, Karl W(olfgang) 1912- ... 41-44R
Deutsch, Marilyn Weisberg 1950- ... 102
Deutsch, Morton 1920- ... 1-4R
Deutsch, Ronald M(artin) 1928- ... CANR-4
Earlier sketch in CA 1-4R
Deutscher, Irwin 1923- ... 25-28R
Deutscher, Isaac 1907-1967 ... CANR-4
Obituary ... 25-28R
Earlier sketch in CA 5-8R
Deutscher, Max 1916(?)-1979 Obituary ... 93-96
Deutscher, Tamara (Lebenhaft)
1913(?)-1990 Obituary ... 132
Deutscher, Thomas (Brian) 1949- ... 124
Deutschkron, Inge 1922- ... 29-32R
Deutschman, Alan (Barry) 1965- ... 116
Devadutt, Vinjamuri E(verett) 1908- ... CAP-2
Earlier sketch in CA 23-24
De Vaere, Ulric Josef 1932- ... 1-4R
Devahuti, D. 1929- ... 45-48
Devajee, Ved
See Gool, Reshard
Deval, Gord 1930- ... 124
Deval, Jacques
See Boularan, Jacques
De Valera, Eamon 1882-1975 Obituary ... 89-92
De Valera, Sinead 1879(?)-1975 Obituary ... 53-56
See also SATA 30
de Valois, Ninette 1898- Brief entry ... 115
Devaney, John 1926- ... CANR-23
Earlier sketches in CA 17-20R, CANR-7
See also SATA 12
Devaraja, N(and) K(ishore) 1917- ... 104
Devas, Nicolette (Macnamara)
1911-1987(?) ... 13-16R
Obituary ... 122
DeVault, M(arion) Vere 1922- ... CANR-20
Earlier sketches in CA 1-4R, CANR-4
De Vaux, Roland 1903-1971 Obituary ... 33-36R
De Veaux, Alexis 1948- ... CANR-26
Earlier sketch in CA 65-68
See also BW
See also DLB 38
D'Evelyn, Katherine E(dith) 1899- ... 17-20R
Dever, Joseph 1919-1970 ... CAP-2
Obituary ... 29-32R
Earlier sketch in CA 19-20
Dever, William Gwinn 1933- Brief entry ... 109
Deveraux, Jude
See White, Jude Gilliam
See also BEST 90:1
de Vere, Aubrey 1814-1902 ... DLB 35
de Vere, Jane
See Watson, Julia
Deverell, Rex (Johnson) 1941- ... 132
Deverell, William H(erbert) 1937- ... 115

Devereux, Frederick L(eonard) Jr. 1914- ... CANR-1
Earlier sketch in CA 49-52
See also SATA 9
Devereux, George 1908- ... 69-72
Devereux, Hilary 1919- ... 13-16R
Devereux, Robert (Essex) 1922- ... 5-8R
Deverson, Harry 1909(?)-1972 Obituary ... 104
De Vet, Charles V(incent) 1911- ... 102
Devi, Indra 1899- ... CAP-1
Earlier sketch in CA 13-14
Devi, Nila
See Woody, Regina Jones
Devi, Ragini 1894(?)-1982 Obituary ... 110
Deview, Lucille 1920- ... 73-76
De Vilbiss, Philip
See Mebane, John (Harrison)
Deville, Rene
See Kacew, Romain
de Villiers, Gerard 1929- ... 61-64
de Vilmorin, Louise Leveque
See Vilmorin, Louise Leveque de
de Vinck, Antoine 1924- ... 53-56
de Vinck, Catherine 1922- ... CANR-6
Earlier sketch in CA 57-60
de Vinck, (Baron) Jose M. G. A. 1912- ... 17-20R
Devine, D(avid) M(cDonald) 1920- ... CANR-1
Earlier sketch in CA 1-4R
Devine, Dominic
See Devine, D(avid) M(cDonald)
Devine, Donald J. 1937- ... 81-84
Devine, (Mary) Elizabeth 1938- ... CANR-38
Earlier sketch in CA 116
Devine, George 1941- ... CANR-1
Earlier sketch in CA 45-48
Devine, Janice 1909(?)-1973 Obituary ... 41-44R
Devine, (Joseph) Lawrence 1935- ... 73-76
Devine, T(homas) M(artin) 1945- ... 136
Devine, Thomas G. 1928- ... 17-20R
DeVinney, Richard 1936- ... 45-48
Devins, Joseph H(erbert) Jr. 1930- ... 21-24R
DeVitis, Angelo A(nthony) 1925- ... 107
De Vito, Joseph Anthony 1938- ... 37-40R
Devkota, Laxmiprasad 1909-1959 Brief entry ... 123
See also TCLC 23
Devletoglou, Nicos E. 1936- ... 41-44R
Devlin, Bernadette (Josephine) 1947- ... 105
Devlin, Diana (Mary) 1941- ... CANR-37
Earlier sketch in CA 114
Devlin, Gerard M(ichael) 1933- ... 105
Devlin, Harry 1918- ... CANR-37
Earlier sketches in CA 65-68, CANR-8
See also MAICYA
See also SATA 11
Devlin, John C. 1911(?)-1984 Obituary ... 113
Devlin, John J(oseph) Jr. 1920- ... 37-40R
Devlin, L. Patrick 1939- ... 61-64
Devlin, Otis 1916- ... 117
Devlin, Patrick (Arthur) 1905- ... 69-72
Obituary ... 138
Devlin, (Dorothy) Wende 1918- ... CANR-37
Earlier sketches in CA 61-64, CANR-8
See also MAICYA
See also SATA 11
Devney, Darcy C(ampion) 1960- ... 138
DeVoe, Shirley Spaulding 1899- ... 77-80
Devol, Kenneth S(towe) 1929- ... 49-52
Devon, D. G.
See Demorest, Stephen
and Gross, Michael (Robert)
Devon, John Anthony
See Payne, (Pierre Stephen) Robert
Devor, John W(esley) 1901- ... CAP-1
Earlier sketch in CA 11-12
Devore, Irven 1934- ... 21-24R
DeVorkin, David H(yam) 1944- ... CANR-26
Earlier sketch in CA 108
De Vorsey, Louis Jr. 1929- ... 21-24R
DeVos, George A(lphonse) 1922- ... CANR-11
Earlier sketch in CA 21-24R
De Vos, Karen Helder 1939- ... 102
de Vosjoli, Philippe L. Thyraud 1920- ... 29-32R
De Voto, Bernard (Augustine) 1897-1955 Brief entry ... 113
See also DLB 9
See also TCLC 29
de Vries, Anne 1904-1964 Obituary ... 116
De Vries, Carrow 1906- ... 53-56
deVries, Egbert 1901- ... 61-64
de Vries, Herbert A. 1917- ... CANR-13
Earlier sketch in CA 33-36R
de Vries, Jan 1943- ... CANR-26
Earlier sketch in CA 69-72
de Vries, Leonard
See Vries, Leonard de
de Vries, Manfred F. R. Kets
See Kets de Vries, Manfred F. R.
De Vries, Peter 1910- ... 17-20R
See also CLC 1, 2, 3, 7, 10, 28, 46
See also DLB 6
See also DLBY 82
See also MTCW
de Vries, Rachel (Guido) 1947- ... 123
de Vries, Simon J(ohn) 1921- ... 57-60
De Vries, Walter (Dale) 1929- ... 69-72
Dew, Charles B(urgess) 1937- ... CANR-29
Earlier sketch in CA 21-24R
Dew, Donald 1928- ... 106
Dew, Edward MacMillan 1935- ... 81-84
Dew, Joan King 1932- ... 104
Dew, Robb (Reavill) Forman 1946- ... CANR-29
Earlier sketch in CA 104
de Waal, Frans 1948- ... 110
De Waal, Ronald Burt 1932- ... CANR-14
Earlier sketch in CA 37-40R
de Waal, Victor (Alexander) 1929- ... 29-32R
de Waal Malefijt, Annemarie 1914-1982 ... 61-64
Obituary ... 109
De Waard, E(lliott) John 1935- ... CANR-2
Earlier sketch in CA 49-52
See also SATA 7
Dewald, Paul A. 1920- ... 17-20R
Dewar, David R(oss) 1913-1990 Obituary ... 131
Dewar, Deborah 1946(?)-1986 Obituary ... 118
Dewar, Diana III 1928(?)-1984 Obituary ... 112
Dewar, Margaret E(lizabeth) 1948- ... 114
Dewar, Mary (Williamson) 1921- ... 13-16R
Dewart, Edward Hartley 1828-1903 ... DLB 99
Dewart, Gilbert 1932- ... 135
Dewart, Leslie 1922- ... 9-12R
de Water, Frederic F(ranklyn) Van
See Van de Water, Frederic F(ranklyn)
Dewdney, Christopher 1951- ... 125
See also DLB 60
Dewdney, John Christopher 1928- ... 103
Dewdney, Selwyn (Hanington) 1909-1979 ... CANR-27
Earlier sketch in CA 69-72
See also DLB 68
See also SATA 64
DeWeerd, Harvey A. 1902- ... 73-76
DeWeese, Gene
See DeWeese, Thomas Eugene
DeWeese, Jean
See DeWeese, Thomas Eugene
DeWeese, Thomas Eugene 1934- ... CANR-24
Earlier sketches in CA 65-68, CANR-9
See also SATA 45, 46
De Welt, Don Finch 1919- ... CANR-1
Earlier sketch in CA 1-4R
de Wet, Hugh Oloff 1912(?)-1976(?) Obituary ... 104
Dewey, Ariane 1937- ... CANR-3
Earlier sketch in CA 49-52
See also SATA 7
Dewey, Bradley R. 1934- ... 29-32R
Dewey, Donald O(dell) 1930- ... 37-40R
Dewey, Edward R(ussell) 1895-1978 ... 41-44R
Dewey, Frank L. 1906- ... 122
Dewey, Godfrey 1887-1977 ... CAP-2
Obituary ... 73-76
Earlier sketch in CA 29-32
Dewey, Irene Sargent 1896- ... CAP-2
Earlier sketch in CA 17-18
Dewey, Jennifer (Owings) 1941- ... 126
See also SATA 48, 58
Dewey, John 1859-1952 Brief entry ... 114
Dewey, Kenneth Francis 1940- ... 112
See also SATA 39
Dewey, Melvil 1851-1931 Brief entry ... 118
Dewey, Melville Louis Kossuth
See Dewey, Melvil
Dewey, Robert D(yckman) 1923- ... 9-12R
Dewey, Robert E(ugene) 1923- ... 13-16R
Dewey, Thomas B(lanchard) 1915- ... CANR-1
Earlier sketch in CA 1-4R
Dewhirst, Ian 1936- ... 102
Dewhurst, Eileen (Mary) 1929- ... CANR-27
Earlier sketch in CA 109
Dewhurst, J(ames) Frederic 1895-1967 ... CAP-2
Earlier sketch in CA 17-18
Dewhurst, Keith 1931- ... CANR-18
Earlier sketch in CA 61-64
Dewhurst, Kenneth 1919- ... CANR-2
Earlier sketch in CA 5-8R
deWit, Dorothy (May Knowles) 1916-1980 ... 113
Obituary ... 109
See also SATA 28, 39
de Wit, Wim 1948- ... 128
DeWitt, Addison
See Newman, Kim (James)
DeWitt, Calvin B. 1935- ... 136
DeWitt, Edith Openshaw 1920- ... 111
DeWitt, James
See Lewis, Mildred D.
DeWitt, John 1910(?)-1984 Obituary ... 113
Dewlen, Al 1921- ... CANR-2
Earlier sketch in CA 1-4R
de Wohl, Louis 1903-1961 Obituary ... 111
De Wolf, L. Harold 1905- ... CANR-2
Earlier sketch in CA 1-4R
DeWolf, Rose (Doris) 1934- ... CANR-11
Earlier sketch in CA 29-32R
de Wolfe, Ivor
See Hastings, Hubert de Cronin
de Wolfe, Ivy
See Hastings, Hubert de Cronin
Dewsbury, Donald A(llen) 1939- ... CANR-15
Earlier sketch in CA 89-92
Dexter, Al
See Poindexter, Clarence Albert
Dexter, Beverly L(iebherr) 1943- ... 114
Dexter, Byron (Vinson) 1900-1973 Obituary ... 113
Dexter, (Norman) Colin 1930- ... CANR-25
Earlier sketches in CA 65-68, CANR-10
See also DLB 87
Dexter, John
See Zachary, Hugh
Dexter, Lewis Anthony 1915- ... CANR-4
Earlier sketch in CA 9-12R
Dexter, Martin
See Faust, Frederick (Shiller)
Dexter, (Ellen) Pat(ricia) Egan ... 81-84
Dexter, Pete 1943- ... 131
Brief entry ... 127
See also BEST 89:2
See also CLC 34, 55
See also MTCW
Dexter, Susan (Elizabeth) 1955- ... CANR-25
Earlier sketch in CA 108
Dey, Frederic (Merrill) Van Rensselaer 1865-1922 Brief entry ... 113
Dey, Joseph C(harles) Jr. 1907-1991 ... CAP-1
Obituary ... 133
Earlier sketch in CA 11-12
Dey, Marmaduke
See Dey, Frederic (Merrill) Van Rensselaer
Deyermond, Alan D(avid) 1932- ... CANR-6
Earlier sketch in CA 13-16R
Deyneka, Anita 1943- ... CANR-26
Earlier sketches in CA 61-64, CANR-11
See also SATA 24
Deyneka, Peter (N. Sr.) 1898-1987 Obituary ... 123
de Young, M. H. 1849-1925 ... DLB 25
DeYoung, Mary 1949- ... 112
Deyrup, Astrith Johnson 1923- ... 65-68
See also SATA 24
Deza, Ernest C. 1923- ... 53-56
Dhalla, Nariman K. 1925- ... 25-28R
Dharmi, Santana 1914- ... CANR-20
Earlier sketch in CA 101
d'Harnoncourt, Anne (Julie) 1943- ... 120
Dhavamony, Mariasusai 1925- ... 33-36R
Dhiegh, Khigh (Alx) 1910- ... 93-96
Dhokalia, (Ramaa) Prasad 1925- ... 41-44R
Dhondy, Farrukh 1944- ... 132
See also MAICYA
See also SATA 65
Dhrymes, Phoebus J(ames) 1932- ... CANR-12
Earlier sketch in CA 29-32R
Diack, Hunter 1908-1974 ... CAP-2
Earlier sketch in CA 21-22
Dial, Joan 1937- ... CANR-24
Earlier sketch in CA 81-84
Diallo, Nafissatou (Niang) 1941- ... 116
Diamano, Silmang
See Senghor, Leopold Sedar
Diamant, Lincoln 1923- ... 33-36R
Diamond, Ann
See McLean, Anne (Julia)
Diamond, Arthur Sigismund 1897- ... CAP-1
Earlier sketch in CA 9-10
Diamond, Cora A(nn) 1937- ... 121
Diamond, Donna 1950- ... 115
See also MAICYA
See also SATA 30, 35, 69
Diamond, Edwin 1925- ... CANR-9
Earlier sketch in CA 13-16R
Diamond, Ellen 1938- ... 133
Diamond, Graham 1945- ... 85-88
Diamond, Harold J(ames) 1934- ... 110
Diamond, I(sidore) A. L. 1920-1988 ... 81-84
Obituary ... 125
See also DLB 26
Diamond, Jacqueline
See Hyman, Jackie (Diamond)
Diamond, Jay 1934- ... CANR-33
Earlier sketches in CA 65-68, CANR-14
Diamond, John 1907- ... 109
Diamond, John 1934- ... 85-88
Diamond, Malcolm L(uria) 1924- ... 25-28R
Diamond, Marc 1944- ... 119
Diamond, Martin 1919-1977 ... 77-80
Obituary ... 73-76
Diamond, Milton 1934- ... 89-92
Diamond, Neil 1941- ... 108
See also CLC 30
Diamond, Norma Joyce 1933- Brief entry ... 108
Diamond, Petra
See Sachs, Judith
Diamond, Rebecca
See Sachs, Judith
Diamond, Robert Mach 1930- ... CANR-7
Earlier sketch in CA 9-12R
Diamond, Sander A. 1942- ... 49-52
Diamond, Selma 1920-1985 Obituary ... 116
Diamond, Sigmund 1920- ... 1-4R
Diamond, Solomon 1906- ... 102
Diamond, Stanley 1922-1991 ... 102
Obituary ... 134
Diamond, Stephen A(rthur) 1946- ... 89-92
Diamond, William 1917- ... 65-68
Diamonstein, Barbaralee D. ... CANR-35
Earlier sketches in CA 85-88, CANR-15
Diar, Prakash 1956- ... 137
Diara, Agadem Lumumba 1947- ... 65-68
Diara, Schavi M.
See Ali, Schavi M(ali)
Dias, Earl Joseph 1916- ... 21-24R
See also SATA 41
Dias, Ron 1937- ... SATA 71
Diaz, Janet W(inecoff) 1935- ... 53-56
Diaz, Jorge 1930- ... HW
Diaz-Alejandro, Carlos F(ederico) 1937-1985 ... 131
Obituary ... 116
See also HW
Diaz-Guerrero, Rogelio 1918- ... 101
Diaz Miron, Salvador 1858-1928 ... HW
Diaz Plaja, Guillermo 1909-1984 ... 131
Obituary ... 113
See also HW
Diaz Valcarcel, Emilio 1929- ... 135
Diaz Valcarcel, Emilo 1929- ... HW
di Bassetto, Corno
See Shaw, George Bernard
DiBattista, Maria 1947- ... 113
Dibb, Paul 1939- ... CANR-1
Earlier sketch in CA 45-48
Dibba, Ebou 1943- ... 124
Dibble, J(ames) Birney 1925- ... 17-20R
Dibble, Nancy Ann 1942- ... 103
Dibble, Vadna Davis 1902(?)-1983 Obituary ... 110
Dibdin, Michael 1947- ... 77-80
Dibelius, Otto (Friedrich Karl) 1880-1967 Obituary ... 114
Dibell, Ansen
See Dibble, Nancy Ann
Di Bella, Anna 1933- Brief entry ... 110
di Benedetto, Antonio 1922- ... HW
Di Berardino, Angelo 1936- ... 135
Dible, Donald M(eredith) 1936- ... 110
Dibner, Andrew Sherman 1926- Brief entry ... 110
Dibner, Bern 1897- ... 107
Dibner, Martin 1911-1992 ... CANR-4
Obituary ... 136
Earlier sketch in CA 1-4R
DiBona, Joseph E. 1927- Brief entry ... 109
Di Cavalcanti, Emiliano 1898(?)-1976 Obituary ... 69-72
Dice, Lee R. 1889(?)-1976 Obituary ... 69-72
Di Certo, J(oseph) J(ohn) 1933- ... CANR-13
Earlier sketch in CA 21-24R
See also SATA 60
Di Cesare, Mario A(nthony) 1928- ... CANR-3
Earlier sketch in CA 5-8R
Dichter, Ernest 1907- ... 17-20R
Dichter, Harry 1900(?)-1978(?) Obituary ... 104
Di Cicco, Pier Giorgio 1949- ... CANR-17
Earlier sketch in CA 97-100
See also DLB 60
Dick, Bernard F(rancis) 1935- ... CANR-9
Earlier sketch in CA 21-24R
Dick, Daniel T. 1946- ... 61-64
Dick, Everett 1898- ... 25-28R
Dick, Ignace 1926- ... CANR-12
Earlier sketch in CA 25-28R
Dick, Kay 1915- ... CANR-15
Earlier sketch in CA 13-16R
Dick, Philip K(indred) 1928-1982 ... CANR-16
Obituary ... 106
Earlier sketches in CA 49-52, CANR-2
See also CLC 10, 30, 72
See also DLB 8
See also MTCW
Dick, R. A.
See Leslie, Josephine Aimee Campbell
Dick, Robert C. 1938- ... 37-40R
Dick, Susan 1940- ... 120
Dick, Trella Lamson 1889-1974 ... 5-8R
See also SATA 9
Dick, Trevor J.O. 1934- Brief entry ... 106
Dick, William M(ilner) 1933- ... 41-44R
Dickason, David Howard 1907-1974 ... CAP-2
Earlier sketch in CA 33-36
Dickason, Olive Patricia 1920- ... 132
Dicke, Robert H(enry) 1916- ... 53-56
Dicken, E(ric) W(illiam) Trueman 1919- ... 9-12R
Dickens, A(rthus) G(eoffrey) 1910- ... 53-56
Dickens, Charles (John Huffam) 1812-1870 ... CDBLB 1832-1890
See also DLB 21, 55, 70
See also MAICYA
See also SATA 15
Dickens, Floyd Jr. 1940- ... 111
Dickens, Frank
See Huline-Dickens, Frank William
Dickens, Jacqueline B(ass) 1941- ... 112
Dickens, Milton 1908- ... 1-4R
Dickens, Monica (Enid) 1915- ... CANR-2
Earlier sketch in CA 5-8R
See also SATA 4
Dickens, Norman
See Eisenberg, Lawrence B(enjamin)
Dickens, Peter (Gerald Charles) 1917-1987 ... 124
Obituary ... 122
Dickens, Roy S(elman) Jr. 1938- ... CANR-9
Earlier sketch in CA 65-68
Dickenson, Fred 1909-1986 Obituary ... 119
Dickenson, James R. 1931- ... 65-68
Dickenson, Mollie 1935- ... 129
Dicker, Eva Barash 1936- ... 107
Dicker, Ralph Leslie 1914- ... 65-68
Dickerman, Edmund H. 1935- Brief entry ... 110
Dickerson, F(rederick) Reed 1909- ... 17-20R
Dickerson, Grace Leslie 1911- ... 5-8R
Dickerson, John 1939- ... 57-60
Dickerson, Martha Ufford 1922- ... 81-84
Dickerson, Nancy H(anschman) 1930- ... 69-72
Dickerson, Oliver M(orton) 1875-1966 Obituary ... 106
Dickerson, Robert B(radford) Jr. 1955- ... 106
Dickerson, Roy Ernest 1886-1965 ... 5-8R
Obituary ... 103
See also SATA 26
Dickerson, William E(ugene) 1897-1971 ... CAP-2
Earlier sketch in CA 21-22
Dickey, Charley 1920- ... 69-72
Dickey, Franklin M(iller) 1921- ... 21-24R
Dickey, Glenn (Ernest Jr.) 1936- ... CANR-4
Earlier sketch in CA 53-56
Dickey, James (Lafayette) 1923- ... CANR-10
Earlier sketch in CA 9-12R
See also CABS 2
See also AITN 1, 2
See also CDALB 1968-1988
See also CLC 1, 2, 4, 7, 10, 15, 47
See also DLB 5
See also DLBD 7
See also DLBY 82
See also MTCW
Dickey, Lee
See Bremyer, Jayne Dickey
Dickey, R(obert) P(reston) 1936- ... CANR-25
Earlier sketch in CA 29-32R
Dickey, William 1928- ... CANR-24
Earlier sketch in CA 9-12R
See also CLC 3, 28
See also DLB 5
Dickie, Edgar P(rimrose) 1897- ... CAP-1
Earlier sketch in CA 11-12
Dickie, George (Thomas) 1926- ... 33-36R
Dickie, James 1934- ... 97-100
Dickie, John 1923- ... 13-16R
Dickie, Margaret (McKenzie) 1935- ... 123

Dickie-Clark, H(amish) F(indlay) 1922- 21-24R
Dickins, A. S. M.
See Dickins, Anthony (Stewart Mackay)
Dickins, Anthony (Stewart Mackay)
1914-1987 Obituary 124
Dickinson, A(lan) E(dgar) F(rederic)
1899- 73-76
Dickinson, A(rthur) T(aylor) Jr. 1925- 5-8R
Dickinson, Charles 1951- 128
See also CLC 49
Dickinson, Don(ald Percy) 1947- 137
Dickinson, Donald C. 1927- 21-24R
Dickinson, Edward C(live) 1938- 61-64
Dickinson, Eleanor 1931- 65-68
Dickinson, Emily (Elizabeth)
1830-1886 ...... CDALB 1865-1917
See also DLB 1
See also PC 1
See also SATA 29
See also WLC
Dickinson, H(arry) T(homas) 1939- 33-36R
Dickinson, John K(ellogg) 1918- 25-28R
Dickinson, John 1732-1808 ...... DLB 31
Dickinson, Jonathan 1688-1747 ...... DLB 24
Dickinson, Leon T. 1912- 13-16R
Dickinson, Lois Stice
1898(?)-1970 Obituary 104
Dickinson, Margaret
See Muggeson, Margaret Elizabeth
Dickinson, Mary 1949- 110
See also SATA 41, 48
Dickinson, Patric Thomas 1914- CANR-3
Earlier sketch in CA 9-12R
See also DLB 27
Dickinson, Peter A(llen) 1926- 102
Dickinson, Peter (Malcolm) 1927- CANR-31
Earlier sketch in CA 41-44R
See also AAYA 9
See also CLC 12, 35
See also DLB 87
See also MAICYA
See also SATA 5, 62
Dickinson, Richard D(onald) N(ye Jr.)
1929- Brief entry 109
Dickinson, Robert Eric 1905- CANR-3
Earlier sketch in CA 5-8R
Dickinson, Ruth F(rankenstein) 1933- 37-40R
Dickinson, (William) Stirling 1909- CAP-2
Earlier sketch in CA 33-36
Dickinson, Susan 1931- 57-60
See also SATA 8
Dickinson, Thorold (Barron) 1903-1984 45-48
Obituary 112
Dickinson, W(illiam) Croft 1897-1963 ......CANR-6
Earlier sketch in CA 1-4R
See also SATA 13
Dickinson, William Boyd 1908-1978 85-88
Obituary 81-84
Dick-Lauder, George (Andrew) 1917- 102
Dickler, Gerald 1912- 9-12R
Dickman, James B(ruce) 1949- 138
Dickmeyer, Lowell A. 1939- 109
See also SATA 51
Dicks, Henry V(ictor) 1900- 102
Dicks, Russell Leslie 1906-1965 ...... CAP-1
Earlier sketch in CA 13-16
Dicks, Shirley 1940- 138
Dickson, Carr
See Carr, John Dickson
Dickson, Carter
See Carr, John Dickson
Dickson, Charles W. Jr. 1926- 25-28R
Dickson, Donald R(ichard) 1951- 126
Dickson, Franklyn 1941- 53-56
Dickson, George E(dmond) 1918- 49-52
Dickson, Gordon R(upert) 1923- CANR-6
Earlier sketch in CA 9-12R
See also DLB 8
Dickson, Helen
See Reynolds, Helen Mary Greenwood Campbell
Dickson, K. A.
See Dickson, Kwesi A(botsia)
Dickson, Kwesi A(botsia) 1929- 134
Brief entry 109
Dickson, (Horatio Henry) Lovat
1902-1987 ......13-16R
Obituary 121
Dickson, Margaret (Smith) 1947- 114
Dickson, Mora (Hope-Robertson)
1918- CANR-5
Earlier sketch in CA 13-16R
Dickson, Naida 1916- 37-40R
See also SATA 8
Dickson, Paul (Andrew) 1939- CANR-27
Earlier sketch in CA 33-36R
Dickson, Peter George Muir 1929- 13-16R
Dickson, Robert J(ames) 1919- 21-24R
Dickson, Stanley 1927- 53-56
Dickstein, Morris 1940- 85-88
Di Cyan, Erwin 1918- 37-40R
Didato, Salvatore V. 1926- 122
Brief entry 107
Didinger, Ray 1946- 93-96
Didion, Joan 1934- CANR-14
Earlier sketch in CA 5-8R
See also AITN 1
See also CDALB 1968-1988
See also CLC 1, 3, 8, 14, 32
See also DLB 2
See also DLBY 81, 86
See also MTCW
di Donato, Georgia 1932- 103
di Donato, Pietro 1911-1992 101
Obituary 136
See also DLB 9
Didsbury, Howard F(rancis) Jr. 1924- 111
Didsbury, Peter 1946- 112
Diebold, Janet
See Sylvester, Janet Hart
Diebold, Janet Oline
See Sylvester, Janet Hart
Diebold, John (Theurer) 1926- 53-56
Diebold, William Jr. 1918- CANR-6
Earlier sketch in CA 13-16R
Dieckmann, Ed(ward Adolph) Jr.
1920- CANR-21
Earlier sketch in CA 102
Dieckmann, Liselotte 1902- 97-100
Diederich, Bernard 1926- 77-80
Diefendorf, Barbara B(oonstoppel) 1946- 124
Diefendorf, Jeffry M(indlin) 1945- 104
Diefenthaler, Jon 1943- 124
Diego, Gerardo
See Diego Cendoya, Gerardo
Diego Cendoya, Gerardo
1896-1987 Obituary 123
See also HW
Diehl, (Robert) Digby 1940- CANR-7
Earlier sketch in CA 53-56
Diehl, Jackson 1956- 135
Diehl, James M(ichael) 1938- 85-88
Diehl, Katharine Smith 1906- CAP-1
Earlier sketch in CA 11-12
Diehl, Kemper 1918- 118
Diehl, Lorraine B(uscaglia) 1940- 119
Diehl, W(illiam) W(ells) 1916-1974 ......17-20R
Obituary 134
Diehl, William (Francis Jr.) 1924- CANR-13
Earlier sketch in CA 101
Diehm, Floyd L(ee) 1925- Brief entry 110
Diekhoff, John S(iemon) 1905-1976 ...... CAP-2
Obituary 69-72
Earlier sketch in CA 29-32
Diekman, John R(aymond) 1946- 110
Diekmann, Godfrey 1908- CANR-2
Earlier sketch in CA 1-4R
Diel, Paul 1893- 103
Diener, Royce 1918- Brief entry 110
Dienes, C(harles) Thomas 1940- CANR-11
Earlier sketch in CA 69-72
Dienstag, Eleanor 1938- 65-68
Dienstein, William 1909- CAP-1
Earlier sketch in CA 17-18
Dierenfield, Richard B(ruce) 1922- 17-20R
Dierickx, C(harles) W(allace) 1921- 61-64
Dierks, Jack Cameron 1930- 29-32R
Diers, Carol Jean 1933- 33-36R
Diescho, Joseph 1955- 135
Diesing, Paul R. 1922- CANR-2
Earlier sketch in CA 1-4R
Dieska, L. Joseph 1913- 37-40R
Dieskau, Dietrich Fischer
See Fischer-Dieskau, Dietrich
Dieter, William 1929- 114
Dietl, (Kirsten) Ulla 1940- 33-36R
Dietrich, John E(rb) 1913- 17-20R
Dietrich, Noah 1889-1982 45-48
Obituary 106
Dietrich, R(ichard) F(arr) 1936- 21-24R
Dietrich, Richard V(incent) 1924- CANR-19
Earlier sketches in CA 53-56, CANR-4
Dietrich, Robert
See Hunt, E(verette) Howard Jr.
Dietrich, Wilson G. 1916- 25-28R
Dietz, Betty Warner
See Dietz, Elisabeth H.
Dietz, David H(enry) 1897-1984 ......CANR-2
Obituary 114
Earlier sketch in CA 1-4R
See also SATA 10, 41
Dietz, Elisabeth H. 1908- 29-32R
Dietz, Howard 1896-1983 53-56
Obituary 110
Dietz, Lew 1907- CANR-3
Earlier sketch in CA 5-8R
See also SATA 11
Dietz, Marjorie (Priscilla) J(ohnson)
1918- CANR-14
Earlier sketch in CA 65-68
Dietz, Norman D. 1930- CANR-10
Earlier sketch in CA 21-24R
Dietz, Peter (John) 1924- 135
Dietz, Peter O(wen) 1935- 33-36R
Dietze, Charles Edgar 1919- 69-72
Dietze, Gottfried 1922- 21-24R
Dietzel, Paul F(ranklin) 1924- 21-24R
Diez Del Corral, Luis 1911- 13-16R
Diez de Medina, Raul
1909(?)-1985 Obituary 117
DiFederico, Frank R.
1933(?)-1987 Obituary 125
DiFranco, Anthony (Mario) 1945- 118
See also SATA 42
Di Franco, Fiorenza 1932- CANR-17
Earlier sketches in CA 45-48, CANR-1
Difusa, Pati
See Almodovar, Pedro
DiGaetani, John Louis 1943- CANR-35
Earlier sketch in CA 114
Digby, George (Frederick) Wingfield
See Wingfield Digby, George (Frederick)
Digby, Joan (Hildreth) 1942- 126
Digby, John (Michael) 1938- 126
Digennaro, Joseph 1939- 53-56
Diggert, Charles (P.) 1927- 128
Digges, Jeremiah
See Berger, Josef
Digges, Sister Mary Laurentia 1910- CAP-2
Earlier sketch in CA 21-22
Diggins, John P(atrick) 1935- 37-40R
Diggle, James 1944- CANR-13
Earlier sketch in CA 61-64
Diggory, James C(lark) 1920- CANR-9
Earlier sketch in CA 21-24R
Diggory, Terence (Elliott) 1951- 112
Diggs, Bernard James 1916- Brief entry 106
Diggs, Elizabeth 1939- 109
Diggs, Ellen Irene 114
Diggs, Irene
See Diggs, Ellen Irene
DiGiacomo, James J(oseph) 1924- CANR-30
Earlier sketch in CA 112
Di Girolamo, Vittorio 1928- 45-48
D'Ignazio, Fred(erick) 1949- 110
See also SATA 35, 39
Di Grazia, Thomas ...... SATA 32
Di Gregorio, Mario A(urelio Umberto) 1950- 131
di Guisa, Giano
See Praz, Mario
Dihoff, Gretchen 1942- 41-44R
Dijkstra, Bram (Abraham Jan) 1938- 37-40R
Dike, Kenneth Onwuka
1917-1983 Obituary 111
Dikshit, R(amesh) D(utta) 1939- CANR-10
Earlier sketch in CA 65-68
Dikty, Julian May
See May, Julian
Dil, Zakhmi
See Hilton, Richard
DiLauro, Stephen 1950- 112
Dilcock, Noreen 1907- 103
Di Lella, Alexander A. 1929- 21-24R
DiLello, Richard 1945- 41-44R
Di Leo, Joseph H. 1902- 33-36R
Diles, Dave 1931- CANR-8
Earlier sketch in CA 57-60
Diliberto, Gioia 1950- 128
Dilke, Annabel (Mary) 1942- CAP-1
Earlier sketch in CA 11-12
Dilke, Caroline (Sophia) 1940- 102
Dilke, Christopher Wentworth
1913(?)-1987 Obituary 125
Dilke, O(swald) A(shton) W(entworth)
1915- 69-72
Dilks, David (Neville) 1938- CANR-35
Earlier sketches in CA 61-64, CANR-8
Dill, Alonzo T(homas Jr.) 1914- 37-40R
Dill, Clarence C(leveland)
1884-1978 Obituary 115
Dill, (George) Marshall Jr. 1916- 1-4R
Dillard, Annie 1945- CANR-3
Earlier sketch in CA 49-52
See also AAYA 6
See also CLC 9, 60
See also DLBY 80
See also MTCW
See also SATA 10
Dillard, Dudley 1913-1991 ......25-28R
Obituary 135
Dillard, Emil L(ee) 1921- 57-60
Dillard, Heath (Portmann) 1933- 119
Dillard, J(oey) L(ee) 1924- CANR-31
Earlier sketches in CA 41-44R, CANR-14
Dillard, J. M. 1954- 128
Dillard, Polly Hargis 1916- CANR-5
Earlier sketch in CA 9-12R
See also SATA 24
Dillard, R(ichard) H(enry) W(ilde)
1937- CANR-10
Earlier sketch in CA 21-24R
See also CAAS 7
See also CLC 5
See also DLB 5
Dille, John M. 1921(?)-1971 Obituary 33-36R
Dille, Robert Crabtree
1924(?)-1983 Obituary 109
Dillehay, Ronald C(lifford) 1935- 21-24R
Dillenbeck, Marsden V. CAP-2
Earlier sketch in CA 25-28
Dillenberger, Jane 1916- CANR-23
Earlier sketches in CA 17-20R, CANR-7
Dillenberger, John 1918- CANR-38
Earlier sketches in CA 1-4R, CANR-2, 17
Diller, Edward 1925- 85-88
Diller, Phyllis (Ada) 1917- CANR-22
Earlier sketch in CA 81-84
Dilles, James 1923- 1-4R
Dilley, Clyde H(obson) 1939- 113
Dilley, Frank B(rown) 1931- 13-16R
Dilliard, Irving (Lee) 1904- 21-24R
Dilligan, Robert J(ames) 1940- 127
Brief entry 108
Dilling, Judith
See Rhoades, Judith G(rubman)
Dilling, Yvonne 1955- 118
Dillingham, Beth 1927- 53-56
Dillingham, William B(yron) 1930- 13-16R
Dillistone, Frederick W(illiam) 1903- CANR-5
Earlier sketch in CA 1-4R
Dillman, Audrey 1922(?)-1984 Obituary 113
Dillman, David D. 1900(?)-1983 Obituary 110
Dillon, Barbara 1927- CANR-28
Earlier sketch in CA 110
See also SATA 39, 44
Dillon, Bert 1937- 77-80
Dillon, Conley Hall 1906-1987 ......CANR-17
Obituary 123
Earlier sketch in CA 1-4R
Dillon, David 1941- 69-72
Dillon, Diane 1933- ...... MAICYA
See also SATA 15, 51
Dillon, Eilis 1920- CANR-38
Earlier sketches in CA 9-12R, CANR-4
See also CAAS 3
See also CLC 17
See also CLR 26
See also MAICYA
See also SATA 2
Dillon, George Lewis 1944- 102
Dillon, George 1906-1968 Obituary 89-92
Dillon, J(ames) T(homas) 1940- 33-36R
Dillon, John M(yles) 1939- 77-80
Dillon, Lawrence S(amuel) 1910- CANR-25
Earlier sketch in CA 45-48
Dillon, Leo 1933- ...... MAICYA
See also SATA 15, 51
Dillon, Martin 1949- 61-64
Dillon, Merton L. 1924- 13-16R
Dillon, Millicent (Gerson) 1925- CANR-12
Earlier sketch in CA 65-68
Dillon, Richard H(ugh) 1924- CANR-8
Earlier sketch in CA 17-20R
Dillon, Sharon Saseen
See Saseen, Sharon (Dillon)
Dillon, Wallace Neil 1922- 1-4R
Dillon, Wilton S(terling) 1923- 37-40R
Dillow, Harry C. 1922- 123
Dilorenzo, Ronald Eugene
1931- Brief entry 110
Dilson, Jesse 1914- 25-28R
See also SATA 24
Diltz, Bert Case 1894- CANR-9
Earlier sketch in CA 65-68
Dilworth, David A. 1934- 136
Dilworth, Sharon 1958- 135
Dimancescu, Dan 1943- 113
di Marco, Gino
See Weiss, Irving J.
Di Marco, Luis Eugenio 1937- CANR-2
Earlier sketch in CA 45-48
Dimberg, Ronald G(ilbert) 1938- 61-64
Dimbleby, Jonathan 1944- 119
Brief entry 108
Di Meglio, Clara 1933- 97-100
DiMeglio, John E(dward) 1934- 77-80
Dimen, Muriel 1942- 127
Dimen-Schein, Muriel
See Dimen, Muriel
DiMento, Joseph F(rank) 1947- 69-72
di Michele, Mary 1949- CANR-17
Earlier sketch in CA 97-100
Dimick, John M. 1898(?)-1983 Obituary 111
Dimick, Kenneth M. 1937- 29-32R
Dimitroff, Pashanko 1924- 129
Dimmette, Celia (Puhr) 1896- CAP-2
Earlier sketch in CA 29-32
Dimmitt, Richard Bertrand 1925- 17-20R
Dimock, Edward Cameron Jr. 1929- 102
Dimock, George E(dward) 1917- 133
Dimock, Gladys Ogden 1908- 5-8R
Dimock, Hedley G(ardiner) 1928- 5-8R
Dimock, Marshall E(dward) 1903-1991 ......CANR-2
Obituary 136
Earlier sketch in CA 1-4R
DiMona, Joseph 104
Dimond, E(dmunds) Grey 1918- 85-88
Dimond, Mary Clark 93-96
Dimond, Stanley E(llwood) 1905-1989 ......13-16R
Obituary 128
Dimond, Stuart J. 1938-1981 ......CANR-27
Earlier sketch in CA 33-36R
Dimondstein, Geraldine 1926- 33-36R
Dimont, Madelon 1938- 41-44R
Dimont, Max I. 1912- 17-20R
Dimont, Penelope
See Mortimer, Penelope (Ruth)
Dimrecken, B. Grayer
See de Mille, Richard
Dimson, Wendy
See Baron, (Ora) Wendy
Din, Gilbert C. 1932- 118
Dinan, Carolyn 126
See also SATA 47, 59
Dineley, David Lawrence 1927- 101
Diner, Hasia R(ena) 1946- CANR-9
Earlier sketch in CA 61-64
Diner, Steven J(ay) 1944- CANR-29
Earlier sketch in CA 110
Dinerman, Beatrice 1933- 13-16R
Dinerman, Helen Schneider
1921(?)-1974 Obituary 53-56
Dinerstein, Herbert S(amuel)
1919- Brief entry 108
Dines, (Harry) Glen 1925- 9-12R
See also SATA 7
Dines, Michael 1916- 103
Dinesen, Isak
See Blixen, Karen (Christentze Dinesen)
See also CLC 10, 29
See also SSC 7
Ding, J. N.
See Darling, Jay Norwood
Dinges, John (Charles) 1941- 101
Dingle, Graeme 1945- 123
Dingle, Herbert 1890-1978 ......13-16R
Obituary 122
Ding Ling
See Chiang Pin-chin
See also CLC 68
Dingman, Roger 1938- 93-96
Dings, John (Garetson) 1939- 41-44R
Dingwall, E(ric) J(ohn) 1890-1986 89-92
Obituary 120
Dingwall, W(illiam) Orr 1934- CANR-13
Earlier sketch in CA 21-24R
Dinhofer, A(lfred) 1929- 25-28R
Dinitz, Simon 1926- CANR-14
Earlier sketch in CA 37-40R
Dinkin, Robert J. 1940- Brief entry 107
Dinkmeyer, Don C. 1924- CANR-15
Earlier sketch in CA 41-44R
Dinman, Bertram David 1925- Brief entry 109
Dinnan, James A. 1929- 69-72
Dinneen, Betty 1929- CANR-8
Earlier sketch in CA 57-60
See also SATA 61
Dinnerstein, Harvey 1928- 112
See also SATA 42

Dinnerstein, Leonard 1934- CANR-24
Earlier sketches in CA 21-24R, CANR-9
Dino
See Dinhofer, A(lfred)
Dinsdale, Tim(othy Kay) 1924-1987 .... CANR-2
Obituary 124
Earlier sketch in CA 1-4R
See also SATA 11
Dinsky, Lazar 1891(?)-1976 Obituary 69-72
Dinsmore, Herman H.
1900(?)-1980 Obituary 97-100
Dintenfass, Mark 1941- CANR-11
Earlier sketch in CA 25-28R
See also DLBY 84
Dintiman, George B(lough) 1936- CANR-20
Earlier sketches in CA 53-56, CANR-5
Dinwiddie, Elza Teresa 110
Dinwiddy, J(ohn) R(owland)
1939-1990 Obituary 131
Dinwiddy, John
See Dinwiddy, J(ohn) R(owland)
Diole, Philippe V. 1908- 53-56
Diomede, John K.
See Effinger, George Alec
Dion, Gerard 1912- 41-44R
Dion, Peter
See Chetwynd, Lionel
Dion, Sister Anita 1918- CANR-2
Earlier sketch in CA 5-8R
Dione, Robert L(ester) 1922- 57-60
Dionisopoulos, P(anagiotes) Allan
1921- 29-32R
Diop, Birago (Ismael) 1906-1989 125
Obituary 130
See also BW
See also MTCW
See also SATO 64
Diop, Cheikh Anta 1923-1986 125
Obituary 118
Brief entry 110
See also BW
Dior, Christian 1905-1957 Brief entry 115
DiOrio, Al(bert John) 1950- CANR-9
Earlier sketch in CA 57-60
Diotima
See Wynne-Tyson, Esme
DiPalma, Ray(mond) 1943- CANR-24
Earlier sketch in CA 29-32R
DiPasquale, Dominic 1932- 57-60
DiPego, Gerald F(rancis) 1941- 85-88
DiPerna, Paula 1949- 112
DiPersio, Michael S(alvatore) 1934- 110
Di Peso, Charles C(orradino) 1920- 57-60
Di Piero, W(illiam) S. 1945- 138
Di Pietro, Robert Joseph 1932-1991 .... CANR-7
Obituary 136
Earlier sketch in CA 17-20R
Diplomaticus
See Guerra y Sanchez, Ramiro
Dipper, Alan 1922- 49-52
Dippie, Brian William 1943- CANR-25
Earlier sketch in CA 108
Dipple, Elizabeth 1937- 33-36R
di Prima, Diane 1934- CANR-13
Earlier sketch in CA 17-20R
See also DLB 5, 16
Dirac, P. A. M.
See Dirac, Paul A(drien) M(aurice)
Dirac, Paul A(drien) M(aurice) 1902-1984 133
Obituary 113
Dire, Eloise (Evangeline) Hodge 1907- 118
DiRenzo, Gordon J(ames) 1934- CANR-4
Earlier sketch in CA 53-56
Diringer, David 1900-1975 .... CANR-6
Obituary 57-60
Earlier sketch in CA 1-4R
Dirk
See Gringhuis, Richard H.
Dirk, R.
See Dietrich, Richard V(incent)
Dirks, Raymond L(ouis) 1934- 106
Dirks, Rudolph 1877-1968 Obituary 106
See also SATA 31
Dirks, Wilhelmina 1916- .... SATA 59
Dirks, Willy
See Dirks, Wilhelmina
Dirksen, Alvin Joseph 1915- 110
Dirksen, Charles J(oseph) 1912- 5-8R
Dirksen, Louella Carver 1899-1979 103
Obituary 89-92
Dirlik, Arif 1940- 97-100
di Roccaferrera Ferrero, Giuseppe M.
1912- CANR-7
Earlier sketch in CA 13-16R
Dirrim, Allen Wendell 1929- 21-24R
Dirscherl, Denis 1934- 21-24R
Dirvin, Joseph I. 1917- CANR-2
Earlier sketch in CA 5-8R
DiSalvo-Ryan, DyAnne 1954- .... SATA 59
Di Scala, Spencer M(ichael) 1941- 102
Disch, Thomas M(ichael) 1940- CANR-36
Earlier sketches in CA 21-24R, CANR-17
See also CAAS 4
See also CLC 7, 36
See also CLR 18
See also DLB 8
See also MAICYA
See also MTCW
See also SATA 54
Disch, Tom
See Disch, Thomas M(ichael)
Dischell, Judy
See Lalli, Judy
Disher, Garry 1949- 127
Disher, Maurice Willson 1893-1969 .... CAP-1
Earlier sketch in CA 9-10
Dishman, Pat(ricia L.) 1939- 17-20R

Diski, Jenny 1947- 138
d'Isly, Georges
See Simenon, Georges (Jacques Christian)
Disney, Doris Miles 1907-1976 .... CANR-3
Obituary 65-68
Earlier sketch in CA 5-8R
Disney, Walt(er Elias) 1901-1966 Obituary 107
See also DLB 22
See also SATA 27, 28
Dison, Norma 1928- 53-56
Dispenza, Joseph Ernest 1942- 81-84
Disraeli, Benjamin 1804-1881 .... DLB 21, 55
D'Israeli, Isaac 1766-1848 .... DLB 107
Disraeli, Robert 1903- CAP-1
Earlier sketch in CA 11-12
Disston, Harry 1899- 41-44R
Distel, Peter
See Koch, Kurt E(mil)
Distler, Paul Francis 1911- 5-8R
Ditchburn, R(obert) W(illiam) 1903-1987 69-72
Obituary 122
Ditcum, Steve
See Crumb, R(obert)
Dito Und Idem
See Elisabeth (Ottilie Luise), Queen (Pauline)
Ditsky, John (Michael) 1938- CANR-9
Earlier sketch in CA 65-68
Dittes, James E(dward) 1926- 61-64
Dittmer, Lowell 1941- 89-92
Ditton, James
See Clark, Douglas
Dittrich, John E(dward) 1931- 112
Ditzel, Paul C(alvin) 1926- 41-44R
Ditzen, Lowell Russell 1913-1987 .... 17-20R
Obituary 122
Ditzen, Rudolf 1893-1947 Brief entry 123
See also Fallada, Hans
Ditzion, Sidney 1908-1975 .... 41-44R
Obituary 57-60
Ditzler, James (R.) 1933- 135
Divale, William T(ulio) 1942- 33-36R
Di Valentin, Maria Messuri 1911- CANR-5
Earlier sketch in CA 5-8R
See also SATA 7
Divendal, Joost 1955- 132
Diverres, Armel Hugh 1914- 9-12R
Divine, Arthur Durham 1904-1987 103
Obituary 122
See also SATA 52
Divine, David
See Divine, Arthur Durham
Divine, Floy (Sherman) 1881-1986 113
Obituary 118
Divine, Robert A(lexander) 1929- CANR-20
Earlier sketches in CA 5-8R, CANR-3
Divine, Thomas F(rancis) 1900- 37-40R
Divinsky, N. J.
See Divinsky, Nathan (Joseph)
Divinsky, Nathan (Joseph) 1925- 132
DiVitto, Barbara A(nn) 1947- 118
Divoky, Diane 1939- 33-36R
Dix, Albert V. 1901(?)-1983 Obituary 109
Dix, Dorothea Lynde 1802-1887 .... DLB 1
Dix, Dorothy
See Gilmer, Elizabeth Meriwether
Dix, Robert H. 1930- 21-24R
Dix, William (Shepherd)
1910-1978 Obituary 77-80
Dixon, Bernard 1938- CANR-26
Earlier sketches in CA 65-68, CANR-10
Dixon, Christa Klingbeil 1935- 102
Dixon, Colin J. 1933- 105
Dixon, Dougal 1947- CANR-25
Earlier sketch in CA 107
See also SATA 45
Dixon, Franklin W. CANR-27
Earlier sketch in CA 17-20R
See also MAICYA
See also SATA 1, 67
Dixon, George
See Willis, Ted
Dixon, Graham (Peter) 1956- 121
Dixon, H(arry) Vernor 1908- CAP-1
Earlier sketch in CA 9-10
Dixon, Janice T(horne) 1932- 107
Dixon, Jeane 1918- CANR-21
Earlier sketch in CA 65-68
Dixon, Jeanne 1936- 105
See also SATA 31
Dixon, John W(esley) Jr. 1919- CANR-3
Earlier sketch in CA 9-12R
Dixon, Joseph L(awrence) 1896- 61-64
Dixon, Kenneth L. 1915(?)-1986 Obituary 119
Dixon, Laurinda S. 1948- 126
Dixon, Marjorie (Mack) 1887- CAP-2
Earlier sketch in CA 23-24
Dixon, Melvin 1950- 132
Dixon, Norman F(rank) 1922- 130
Dixon, Paige
See Corcoran, Barbara
Dixon, Penelope A(nn) 1948- 113
Dixon, Peter L(ee) 1931- CANR-2
Earlier sketch in CA 45-48
See also SATA 6
Dixon, Pierson (John) 1904-1965 .... CAP-1
Earlier sketch in CA 13-16
Dixon, Richard Watson
1833-1900 Brief entry 122
See also DLB 19
Dixon, Robert G(alloway)
1920-1980 Obituary 97-100
Dixon, Roger Edmund 1935-1983 Obituary 109
Dixon, Roger 1930- 53-56
Dixon, Rosie
See Wood, Christopher (Hovelle)
Dixon, Ruth
See Barrows, (Ruth) Marjorie

Dixon, S(ydney) L(awrence) 1930- 69-72
Dixon, Stephen 1936- CANR-17
Earlier sketch in CA 89-92
See also CLC 52
Dixon, Wheeler Winston 1950- 121
Dizard, Wilson P(aul) 1922- 17-20R
Dizenzo, Charles (John) 1938- 25-28R
Dizney, Henry (Franklin) 1926- 33-36R
Djassi, Abel
See Cabral, Amilcar
Djeddah, Eli 1911- 37-40R
Djerassi, Carl 1923- 131
Brief entry 111
Djilas, Milovan 1911- 127
Djonovich, Dusan J. 1920- 69-72
Djwa, Sandra (Ann) 1939- 131
Dluhosch, Eric 1927- 25-28R
Dluznowsky, Moshe 1906-1977 Obituary 73-76
Dmytryshyn, Basil 1925- CANR-26
Earlier sketches in CA 21-24R, CANR-11
Doak, (Dearle) Donn(ell) 1930- 65-68
Doak, Wade Thomas 1940- CANR-6
Earlier sketch in CA 57-60
Doan, Daniel 1914- 103
Doan, Eleanor Lloyd CANR-1
Earlier sketch in CA 1-4R
Doan, Richard K. 1911(?)-1989 Obituary 128
Doane, Donald P(aul) 1911- 77-80
Doane, Gilbert H(arry) 1897- CAP-1
Earlier sketch in CA 11-12
Doane, Marion S.
See Woodward, Grace Steele
Doane, (R.) Michael 1952- 135
Doane, Pelagie 1906-1966 .... CANR-6
Earlier sketch in CA 1-4R
See also SATA 7
Dobb, Maurice (Herbert) 1900-1976 .... CANR-4
Obituary 69-72
Earlier sketch in CA 9-12R
Dobbie, Elliott Van Kirk
1907-1970 Obituary 111
Dobbin, John E. 1914-1979 .... 9-12R
Obituary 103
Dobbin, Muriel 1935- 118
Dobbins, Austin C(harles) 1919- 57-60
Dobbins, Charles G(ordon) 1908-1988 .... CAP-1
Obituary 127
Earlier sketch in CA 13-16
Dobbins, Dorothy Wyeth 1929- 69-72
Dobbins, Gaines Stanley 1886-1978 .... CANR-2
Earlier sketch in CA 1-4R
Dobbins, Marybelle King 1900- 41-44R
Dobbs, Betty Jo Teeter 1930- 69-72
Dobbs, Farrell 1907-1983 .... CANR-14
Obituary 111
Earlier sketch in CA 49-52
Dobbs, Greg 1946- 65-68
Dobbs, Kildare (Robert Eric) 1923- CANR-19
Earlier sketch in CA 102
Dobbyn, John F(rancis) 1937- 53-56
Dobelis, M(iervaldis) C(hristian) 1929- 116
Dobell, Byron (Maxwell) 1927- Brief entry 112
Dobell, I(sabel) M(arian) B(arclay) 1909- CAP-1
Earlier sketch in CA 17-18
See also SATA 11
Dobell, Sydney 1824-1874 .... DLB 32
Dober, Richard P. 9-12R
Dobie, Ann B(rewster) 1935- 106
Dobie, Bertha McKee
1890(?)-1974 Obituary 53-56
Dobie, Edith 1894-1975 .... CAP-2
Obituary 57-60
Earlier sketch in CA 23-24
Dobie, J(ames) Frank 1888-1964 .... CANR-6
Earlier sketch in CA 1-4R
See also SATA 43
Dobin, Abraham 1907- 53-56
Dobinson, Charles Henry
1903-1980 Obituary 102
Dobkin, Alexander 1908-1975 Obituary 57-60
See also SATA 30
Dobkin, Bruce H. 1947- 122
Dobkin, Kathy
See Hamel Peifer, Kathleen
Dobkin, Kaye
See Hamel Peifer, Kathleen
Dobkin, Marjorie Housepian 1923- CANR-13
Earlier sketch in CA 33-36R
Dobkin De Rios, Marlene 1939- CANR-12
Earlier sketch in CA 61-64
Dobkins, J(ames) Dwight 1943- 49-52
Dobler, Bruce 1939- CANR-7
Earlier sketch in CA 53-56
Dobler, Lavinia G. 1910- CANR-2
Earlier sketch in CA 1-4R
See also SATA 6
Dobles, Fabian 1918- .... HW
Doblin, Alfred
See Doeblin, Alfred
See also TCLC 13
Dobner, Maeva Park 1918- 29-32R
Dobney, Frederick J(ohn) 1943- 53-56
Dobraczynski, Jan 1910- CAP-1
Earlier sketch in CA 11-12
Dobree, Bonamy 1891-1974 .... CANR-4
Obituary 53-56
Earlier sketch in CA 5-8R
Dobriansky, Lev E. 1918- CANR-2
Earlier sketch in CA 1-4R
Dobrin, Arnold 1928- CANR-11
Earlier sketch in CA 25-28R
See also SATA 4
Dobrin, Arthur 1943- CANR-8
Earlier sketch in CA 61-64
Dobrin, Lyn 1942- 135
Dobrin, Ronald L. 1938- 120
Dobriner, William M(ann) 1922- 65-68

Dobrovolsky, Sergei P(avlovich) 1908- CAP-2
Earlier sketch in CA 33-36
Dobrow, Larry 1925- 123
Dobrowolski, Tomasz B.
1914(?)-1976 Obituary 65-68
Dobschiner, Johanna-Ruth 1925- 97-100
Dobson, Andrew (Nicholas Howard) 1957- 132
Dobson, Austin 1840-1921 .... DLB 35
Dobson, (Richard) Barrie 1931- 33-36R
Dobson, Christopher (Joseph Edward)
1927- CANR-31
Earlier sketch in CA 97-100
Dobson, Dennis 1919(?)-1979(?) Obituary 104
Dobson, E. Philip 1910- CAP-1
Earlier sketch in CA 13-14
Dobson, Elinore (Lucille) 1934- 114
Dobson, Eric John 1913-1984 .... CANR-5
Obituary 112
Earlier sketch in CA 13-16R
Dobson, Eugene 1936- Brief entry 113
Dobson, James (Clayton Jr.) 1936- CANR-27
Earlier sketch in CA 29-32R
Dobson, Jessie Obituary 113
Dobson, John M(cCullough) 1940- 37-40R
Dobson, Julia M(argaret) 1937- 73-76
Dobson, Julia 1941- 106
See also SATA 48
Dobson, Margaret J(une) 1931- 53-56
Dobson, Rosemary 1920- 77-80
Dobson, Terry 1937- 81-84
Dobson, Theodore E(lliott) 1946- CANR-28
Earlier sketch in CA 109
Dobson, William A(rthur) C(harles) H(arvey)
1913- 13-16R
Doby, John T(homas) 1920- Brief entry 114
Doby, Tibor 1914- 5-8R
Dobyns, Henry F(armer) 1925- CANR-32
Earlier sketches in CA 37-40R, CANR-15
Dobyns, Lloyd (Allen Jr.) 1936- 119
Brief entry 110
Dobyns, Stephen 1941- CANR-18
Earlier sketches in CA 45-48, CANR-2
See also CLC 37
Dobzhansky, Theodosius 1900-1975 .... CAP-1
Obituary 61-64
Earlier sketch in CA 13-14
Doc Abraham
See Abraham, George
Docherty, James L.
See Raymond, Rene (Brabazon)
Docherty, Thomas 1955- 120
Dockeray, J(ames) C(arlton) 1907-1984 45-48
Obituary 114
Dockery, Wallene T. 1941- CANR-22
Earlier sketch in CA 105
See also SATA 27
Dockrell, William Bryan 1929- CANR-32
Earlier sketches in CA 37-40R, CANR-14
Dockstader, Frederick J. 1919- 13-16R
Doc Lochard
See Lochard, Metz T(ullus) P(aul)
Doctor Baseball
See Bjarkman, Peter C(hristian)
Doctorow, E(dgar) L(aurence) 1931- CANR-33
Earlier sketches in CA 45-48, CANR-2
See also AITN 2
See also BEST 89:3
See also CDALB 1968-1988
See also CLC 6, 11, 15, 18, 37, 44, 65
See also DLB 2, 28
See also DLBY 80
See also MTCW
Doctors, Samuel I(saac) 1936- CANR-5
Earlier sketch in CA 53-56
Doctor X
See Nourse, Alan E(dward)
Doczi, George Frederic 1909- 113
Dodd, A(rthur) E(dward) 1913- 9-12R
Dodd, Anne W(escott) 1940- 93-96
Dodd, Arthur Herbert
1893(?)-1975 Obituary 57-60
Dodd, Bella V.
See Dodd, Maria Assunta Isabella Visono
Dodd, Charles (Harold)
1884-1973 Obituary 45-48
Dodd, David L(e Fevre)
1895-1988 Obituary 126
Dodd, Donald B(radford) 1940- CANR-6
Earlier sketch in CA 57-60
Dodd, Ed(ward Benton) 1902-1991 73-76
Obituary 134
See also SATA 4
See also SATO 68
Dodd, Edward
See Dodd, Edward Howard Jr.
Dodd, Edward Howard Jr. 1905-1988 .... CANR-31
Obituary 127
Earlier sketch in CA 49-52
Dodd, James Harvey 1892-1969 .... 1-4R
Obituary 103
Dodd, Lynley (Stuart) 1941- CANR-25
Earlier sketch in CA 107
See also SATA 35
Dodd, Marguerite 1911- 5-8R
Dodd, Maria Assunta Isabella Visono
1904-1969 Obituary 111
Dodd, Martha
See Stern, Martha Eccles Dodd
Dodd, Philip W. 1904(?)-1983 Obituary 110
Dodd, Stuart C(arter) 1900-1975 .... 41-44R
Dodd, Susan M. 1946- 116
Dodd, Thomas J. 1907-1971 Obituary 29-32R
Dodd, Valerie A. 1944- 134
Dodd, Wayne (Donald) 1930- 33-36R
Dodd, William E. 1869-1940 .... DLB 17
Dodderidge, Esme 1916- 97-100
Dodds, E(ric) R(obertson) 1893-1979 101

Dodds, Edward Charles
1899-1973 Obituary 115
Dodds, Gordon Barlow 1932- 5-8R
Dodds, John W(endell) 1902- 5-8R
Dodds, Robert Clyde 1918- 5-8R
Dodds, Robert H(ungerford) 1914-1976 .... CAP-2
Earlier sketch in CA 29-32
Dodds, Tracy 1952- 85-88
Dodek, Miriam (Joyce) Selker
1909-1986 Obituary 118
Doder, Dusko 1937- 102
Doderer, Heimito von
See von Doderer, Heimito
See also DLB 85
Dodge, Bayard 1888-1972 Obituary 111
Dodge, Bertha S(anford) 1902- CANR-2
Earlier sketch in CA 5-8R
See also SATA 8
Dodge, Calvert R(enaul) 1931- 61-64
Dodge, Daniel
See Du Breuil, (Elizabeth) L(or)inda
Dodge, David (Francis) 1910- 65-68
Dodge, David L(aurence) 1931- Brief entry 112
Dodge, Dick 1918(?)-1974 Obituary 49-52
Dodge, Dorothy R(ae) 1927- 45-48
Dodge, Ernest Stanley 1913-1980 ....CANR-2
Obituary 97-100
Earlier sketch in CA 1-4R
Dodge, Fremont
See Grimes, Lee
Dodge, Gil
See Hano, Arnold
Dodge, H(arry) Robert 1929- CANR-27
Earlier sketch in CA 29-32R
Dodge, Langdon
See Wolfson, Victor
Dodge, Lowell 1940- 33-36R
Dodge, Marshall 1935- 89-92
Dodge, Mary (Elizabeth) Mapes
1831(?)-1905 137
Brief entry 109
See also DLB 42, 79
See also MAICYA
See also SATA 21
Dodge, Nicholas A. 1933- 65-68
Dodge, Norton T(ownshend) 1927- CANR-16
Earlier sketch in CA 25-28R
Dodge, Peter 1926- 37-40R
Dodge, Richard Holmes 1926- CANR-8
Earlier sketch in CA 13-16R
Dodge, Steve
See Becker, Stephen (David)
Dodge, Wendell P(hillips)
1883-1976 Obituary 65-68
Dodgshon, Robert A(ndrew) 1941- 125
Dodgson, Charles Lutwidge 1832-1898
See Carroll, Lewis
See also CLR 2
See also MAICYA
See also YABC 2
Dodsley, Robert 1703-1764 .... DLB 95
Dodson, Daniel B(oone) 1918-1991 ....CANR-3
Obituary 133
Earlier sketch in CA 9-12R
Dodson, Fitzhugh (James) 1923- CANR-24
Earlier sketch in CA 29-32R
Dodson, James L. 1910- 53-56
Dodson, Kenneth MacKenzie 1907- 1-4R
See also SATA 11
Dodson, Leonidas 1900-1977 Obituary 111
Dodson, Oscar H(enry) 1905- 5-8R
Dodson, Owen (Vincent) 1914-1983 ....CANR-24
Obituary 110
Earlier sketch in CA 65-68
See also BLC 1
See also BW
See also DLB 76
Dodson, Richard S(licer) Jr. 1896- CAP-1
Earlier sketch in CA 11-12
Dodson, Susan 1941- 97-100
See also SATA 40, 50
Dodson, Tom 1914- 29-32R
Dodwell, C(harles) R(eginald) 1922- 129
Dodwell, Peter C(arpenter) 1930- 29-32R
Dody, Sandford 1918- 129
Doebler, Charles H. 1925- 21-24R
Doebler, John (Willard) 1932- 89-92
Doeblin, Alfred 1878-1957 Brief entry 110
See also Doblin, Alfred
See also DLB 66
See also TCLC 13
Doehring, Donald G(ene) 1927- 29-32R
Doell, Charles E(dward) 1894- CAP-1
Earlier sketch in CA 13-16
Doely, Sarah Bentley
See Bentley, Sarah
Doenecke, Justus Drew 1938- CANR-20
Earlier sketch in CA 104
Doenim, Susan
See Effinger, George Alec
Doenitz, Karl 1891-1980 Obituary 103
Doerffler, Alfred 1884- 1-4R
Doering, Jeanne
See Zornes, Jeanne Doering
Doeringer, Peter B(rantley) 1941- CANR-12
Earlier sketch in CA 61-64
Doerksen, Nan 1934- 123
See also SATA 50
Doerkson, Margaret 1921- 105
Doermann, Humphrey 1930- 25-28R
Doernberg, Myrna 1939- 120
Doerr, Arthur H(arry) 1924- 41-44R
Doerr, Harriet 1910- 122
Brief entry 117
See also CLC 34
Doerrie, Doris 1955- 130
Doerschuk, Anna Beatrice
1880(?)-1974 Obituary 49-52
Doeser, Linda (Ann) 1950- 81-84
Doesticks, Q. K. Philander P. B.
See Thomson, Mortimer
Doezema, Linda Pegman 1948- 102
Dogan, Mattei 1920- CANR-30
Earlier sketches in CA 25-28R, CANR-12
Dogg, Professor R. L.
See Berman, Ed
Doggett, Frank 1906- CANR-12
Earlier sketches in CAP-2, CA 21-22
Doggett, Rachel H. 1943- 124
Dogyear, Drew
See Gorey, Edward (St. John)
Dohan, Mary Helen 1914- 85-88
Dohaney, Jean 129
Dohaney, M. T.
See Dohaney, Jean
Dohen, Dorothy M. 1923-1984 Obituary 111
Doherty, Barbara 1931- 116
Doherty, Berlie 1943- 131
See also CLR 21
See also MAICYA
Doherty, Catherine de Hueck 1900- CANR-12
Earlier sketch in CA 65-68
Doherty, Charles Hugh 1913- 9-12R
See also SATA 6
Doherty, Dennis J. 1932- 102
Doherty, Eddie
See Doherty, Edward J(oseph)
Doherty, Edward J(oseph) 1890-1975 65-68
Obituary 57-60
Doherty, Herbert J(oseph) Jr. 1926- 1-4R
Doherty, Ivy Duffy
See Doherty, Ivy R. Duffy
Doherty, Ivy R. Duffy 1922- CANR-5
Earlier sketch in CA 9-12R
Doherty, Robert W. 1935- 21-24R
Doherty, William Thomas Jr. 1923- 53-56
Doherty, William 1911(?)-1984 Obituary 113
Dohme, Alvin R(obert) L(ouis) 1910- 110
Dohrenwend, Barbara Snell
1927-1982 ....CANR-11
Earlier sketch in CA 25-28R
Doig, Desmond 1921-1983 69-72
Obituary 111
Doig, Ivan 1939- CANR-24
Earlier sketch in CA 81-84
Doig, Jameson W. 1933- CANR-32
Earlier sketches in CA 37-40R, CANR-15
Doimi di Delupis, Ingrid
See Delupis, Ingrid
Dolan, Anthony R(ossi) 1948- 73-76
Dolan, Edward F(rancis) Jr. 1924- 33-36R
See also SATA 31, 45
Dolan, Edwin G(eorge) 1943- 123
Dolan, Jay P(atrick) 1936- 81-84
Dolan, John Patrick 1923-1982(?) CANR-2
Obituary 106
Earlier sketch in CA 5-8R
Dolan, John Richard 1893- 9-12R
Dolan, Josephine A(loyse) 1913- 49-52
Dolan, Paul 1910- 9-12R
Dolan, Winthrop W(iggin) 1909- 57-60
Dolbeare, Kenneth M(arsh)
1930- Brief entry 113
Dolberg, Alexander 1933- 33-36R
Dolbier, Maurice (Wyman) 1912- 65-68
Dolby, James L(ouis) 1926- 45-48
Dolce, Philip C(harles) 1941- 57-60
Dolch, Edward William 1889-1961 .... SATA 50
Dolch, Marguerite Pierce 1891-1978 .... SATA 50
Dolci, Danilo (Bruno Pietro) 1924- 127
Brief entry 116
Dolden, A(lfred) Stuart 1893- 105
Dole, Gertrude E(velyn) 1915- 41-44R
Dole, Jeremy H(askell) 1932- 17-20R
Dolezel, Lubomir 1922- 45-48
Dolgoff, Ralph L. 1932- 33-36R
Dolgoff, Sam 1902-1990 102
Obituary 132
Dolgun, Alexander (Michael) 1926-1986 104
Obituary 120
Doliber, Earl L(awrence) 1947- 49-52
Dolim, Mary N(uzum) 1925- 17-20R
Dolin, Anton
See
Healey-Kay, (Sydney Francis) Patrick (Chippendall)
Dolin, Edwin 1928- 45-48
Doliner, Roy 1932- CANR-16
Earlier sketches in CA 1-4R, CANR-1
Dolinger, Jane ....AITN 2
Dolinsky, Meyer 1923- 57-60
Dolinsky, Mike
See Dolinsky, Meyer
Dolit, Alan 1934- 61-64
Doll, Mary A(swell) 1940- 130
Doll, (William) Richard (Shaboe) 1912- 108
Doll, Ronald C. 1913- CANR-8
Earlier sketch in CA 13-16R
Doll, Susan Marie 1954- 118
Dollar, Diane (Hills) 1933- .... SATA 57
Dollar, Jim
See Shaginyan, Marietta (Sergeyevna)
Dollar, Truman E. 1937- 97-100
Dollard, John 1900(?)-1980 Obituary 102
Dollar Investor
See D'Ambrosio, Charles A.
Dolle, Raymond F. 1952- 136
Dollen, Charles Joseph 1926- CANR-21
Earlier sketches in CA 5-8R, CANR-6
Dolley, Michael 1925-1983 123
Obituary 109
Dollimore, Jonathan 1948- 132
Dolliver, Barbara Babcock 1927- 5-8R
Dolloff, Eugene Dinsmore 1890-1972 ....1-4R
Obituary 103
Dolmatch, Theodore B(ieley) 1924- 41-44R
Dolmetsch, Carl R(ichard Jr.) 1924- 21-24R
Dolmetsch, Christopher L(ee) 1950- 111
Dolphin, Harry A. 1924- 128
Dolphin, Robert Jr. 1935- 29-32R
Dols, Michael W(alters) 1942- 69-72
Dolson, Frank(lin Robert) 1933- 112
Dolson, Hildegarde
See Lockridge, Hildegarde (Dolson)
See also SATA 5
Doman, Glenn J(oseph) 1919- 61-64
Doman, June
See Beveridge, Meryle Secrest
Domanska, Janina CANR-11
Earlier sketch in CA 17-20R
See also AITN 1
See also MAICYA
See also SATA 6, 68
Domaradzki, Theodore F(elix) 1910- CANR-1
Earlier sketch in CA 45-48
Domb, Cyril 1920- 109
Dombrowski, James A.
1897-1983 Obituary 109
Domecq, H(onorio) Bustos
See Bioy Casares, Adolfo
and Borges, Jorge Luis
Domencich, Thomas A. 29-32R
Domergue, Maurice 1907- 25-28R
Domes, Juergen (Otto) 1932- 129
Dom Helder
See Camara, Helder Pessoa
Domhoff, G(eorge) William 1936- 45-48
Dominguez, Jorge Ignacio 1945- 102
Dominguez, Richard H(enry) 1941- 102
Dominguez, Sergio D(anilo) Elizondo
See Elizondo (Dominguez), Sergio D(anilo)
Domini, Jon
See LaRusso, Dominic A(nthony)
Domini, Rey
See Lorde, Audre (Geraldine)
Dominian, Jack 1929- 104
Dominic, R. B.
See Hennissart, Martha
and Latsis, Mary J(ane)
Dominic, Sister Mary
See Gallagher, Sister Mary Dominic
Dominick, Raymond Hunter III 1945- 110
Dominique
See
Proust, (Valentin-Louis-George-Eugene-)Marcel
Dominique, Meg
See Sanford, Annette
Domino, John
See Averill, Esther
Dominowski, Roger L. 1939- CANR-1
Earlier sketch in CA 45-48
Dominy, Eric (Norman) 1918- 9-12R
Domjan, Joseph (Spiri) 1907- CANR-24
Earlier sketches in CA 9-12R, CANR-3
See also SATA 25
Domke, Helmut Georg 1914-1974 .... CAP-1
Earlier sketch in CA 13-14
Domke, Martin 1892- CAP-1
Earlier sketch in CA 13-16
Dommen, Arthur J(ohn) 1934- 9-12R
Dommermuth, William P. 1925- 17-20R
Dommeyer, Frederick Charles 1909- 37-40R
Domotor, Tekla 1914- 132
Domville, Eric 1929- 41-44R
Don, A
See Stephen, Leslie
Donabedian, Avedis 1919- CANR-12
Earlier sketch in CA 73-76
Donagan, Alan (Harry) 1925- 5-8R
Donagan, Barbara (Galley) 1927- 17-20R
Donaghy, Henry J. 1930- 53-56
Donaghy, William A.
1910(?)-1975 Obituary 53-56
Donahoe, Bernard (Frances) 1932- 17-20R
Donahue, Don 1942- 69-72
Donahue, Francis J. 1917- 17-20R
Donahue, George T. 1911- 17-20R
Donahue, Jack (Clifford) 1917-1991 ....CANR-17
Obituary 135
Earlier sketch in CA 97-100
Donahue, June (Geserick)
1918(?)-1984 Obituary 111
Donahue, Kenneth 1915- 102
Donahue, Phil(lip John) 1935- 107
Donahue, Roy L(uther) 1908- CANR-34
Earlier sketches in CA 89-92, CANR-15
Donahue, Thomas John 1943- 112
Donald, Aida DiPace 1930- 21-24R
Donald, Anabel 1944- 122
Donald, Bruce H(arry) 1935- 111
Donald, David Herbert 1920- CANR-4
Earlier sketch in CA 9-12R
See also DLB 17
Donald, Larry W(atson) 1945- 93-96
Donald, Maxwell 1897-1978 Obituary 89-92
Donald, Merlin 1939- 137
Donald, Peter (Harry) 1962- 137
Donald, R. V.
See Floren, Lee
Donald, Vivian
See Mackinnon, Charles Roy
Donalds, Gordon
See Shirreffs, Gordon D(onald)
Donaldson, Betty 1923- 103
Donaldson, Bryna
See Stevens, Bryna
Donaldson, E(thelbert) Talbot
1910-1987 ....CANR-2
Obituary 122
Earlier sketch in CA 49-52
Donaldson, Elvin F. 1903-1972 ....1-4R
Obituary 103
Donaldson, Frances (Annesley)
1907- CANR-12
Earlier sketch in CA 61-64
Donaldson, Frances (Gertrude) F(laacke)
1892(?)-1987 Obituary 122
Donaldson, Gordon 1913- CANR-22
Earlier sketches in CA 13-16R, CANR-5
See also SATA 64
Donaldson, (Charles) Ian (Edward)
1935- CANR-35
Earlier sketches in CA 69-72, CANR-12
Donaldson, Islay (Eila) Murray 1921- 135
Donaldson, John W.
1893(?)-1979 Obituary 85-88
Donaldson, Kenneth 1908- 73-76
Donaldson, Malcolm 1884-1973 .... CAP-1
Earlier sketch in CA 9-10
Donaldson, Margaret 1926- CANR-20
Earlier sketch in CA 103
Donaldson, Norman 1922- 33-36R
Donaldson, Robert Herschel 1943- CANR-15
Earlier sketch in CA 85-88
Donaldson, Sam(uel Andrew) 1934- 111
Brief entry 109
Donaldson, Scott 1928- CANR-27
Earlier sketches in CA 25-28R, CANR-11
See also DLB 111
Donaldson, Stephen R. 1947- CANR-13
Earlier sketch in CA 89-92
See also CLC 46
Donaldson, (Charles) William 1935- 77-80
Donart, Arthur C(harles) 1936- 37-40R
Donat, Anton
See Donart, Arthur C(harles)
Donat, John (Annesley) 1933- 13-16R
Donato, Anthony 1909- CAP-1
Earlier sketch in CA 13-16
Donavan, John
See Morland, Nigel
Donawerth, Jane (Lynn) 1947- 118
Donceel, Joseph F. 1906- CANR-1
Earlier sketch in CA 1-4R
Donchess, Barbara (Briggs) 1922- 57-60
Donders, Jozef G(erardus) 129
Dondis, Donis A(snin) 1924- 85-88
Donelson, Irene W(itmer) 1913- 17-20R
Donelson, Kenneth L(avern) 1927- 69-72
Donelson, Kenneth W(ilber) 1910- 17-20R
Donem, Sue
See Ross, Stanley Ralph
Doner, Mary Frances 1893- 13-16R
Donetta
See Chester, Tessa Rose
Doney, Willis (Frederick Jr.) 1925- 21-24R
Donfried, Karl Paul 1940- 108
Donheiser, Alan D. 1936- 37-40R
Donicht, Mark Allen 1946- 93-96
Donigan, Robert L. 1903(?)-1989 Obituary 128
Doniger, Lester (Laurence)
1909-1971 Obituary 104
Donin, Hayim Halevy 1928- 77-80
Donington, Robert 1907-1990(?) 33-36R
Obituary 130
Donis, Miles 1937-1979 ....29-32R
Obituary 93-96
Donkin, Nance (Clare) 1915- CANR-20
Earlier sketch in CA 103
Donleavy, J(ames) P(atrick) 1926- CANR-24
Earlier sketch in CA 9-12R
See also AITN 2
See also CLC 1, 4, 6, 10, 45
See also DLB 6
See also MTCW
Donley, Carol C(ram) 1937- 122
Donley, Marshall O(wen) Jr. 1932- CANR-14
Earlier sketch in CA 65-68
Donna, Natalie 1934-1979 ....CANR-6
Earlier sketch in CA 9-12R
See also SATA 9
Donnachie, Ian Lowe 1944- 105
Donnan, Marcia Jeanne 1932- 104
Donne, John 1572-1631 .... CDBLB Before 1660
See also DLB 121
See also PC 1
See also WLC
Donne, Maxim
See Duke, Madelaine (Elizabeth)
Donnell, David 1939(?)- .... CLC 34
Donnell, John C(orwin) 1919- 41-44R
Donnell, John D(ouglas) 1920- CANR-5
Earlier sketch in CA 53-56
Donnell, Susan 137
Donnellan, Michael T(homas) 1931- 37-40R
Donnelley, Dixon 1915-1982 Obituary 105
Donnell-Kotrozo, Carol 1947- 113
Donnelly, Alton S(tewart) 1920- 21-24R
Donnelly, Austin Stanislaus 1923- 112
Donnelly, Desmond L(ouis) 1920- 13-16R
Donnelly, Doris (Krimper) 1940- 123
Donnelly, Dorothy (Boillotat) 1903- CANR-3
Earlier sketch in CA 5-8R
Donnelly, Esmond
See Oberdorf, Charles (Donnell)
Donnelly, Gabrielle (Mary Teresa) 1952- 127
Donnelly, Ignatius 1831-1901 Brief entry 110
See also DLB 12
Donnelly, James A. III
1929(?)-1984 Obituary 112
Donnelly, James H(oward) Jr. 1941- 29-32R
Donnelly, James S(tephen) Jr. 1943- 102
Donnelly, John Patrick 1934- 81-84
Donnelly, John 1941- 93-96
Donnelly, Joseph P(eter) 1905-1982 81-84
Obituary 108
Donnelly, Sister Gertrude Joseph 1920- 13-16R

Donner, Fred McGraw 1945- ... 106
Donner, Joern 1933- ... CANR-9
  Earlier sketch in CA 13-16R
Donner, Stanley T(emple) 1910- ... 61-64
Donnison, David Vernon 1926- ... 106
Donnison, F(rank) S(iegfried) V(ernon) 1898- ... 1-4R
Donnison, Jean 1925- ... 77-80
Donnithorne, Audrey 1922- ... 17-20R
Donno, Elizabeth Story 1921- ... CANR-5
  Earlier sketch in CA 1-4R
Donoghue, Denis 1928- ... CANR-16
  Earlier sketch in CA 17-20R
Donoghue, Mildred R(ansdorf) ... CANR-10
  Earlier sketch in CA 25-28R
Donoghue, Quentin 1937- ... 122
Donoghue, William E(lliott) 1941- ... CANR-39
  Earlier sketch in CA 116
Donohoe, Thomas 1917- ... 53-56
Donohoe, Tom 1957- ... 123
Donohue, Agnes McNeill 1917- ... 127
Donohue, James F(itzgerald) 1934- ... 73-76
Donohue, John J. 1926- ... 122
Donohue, John K. 1909- ... CAP-1
  Earlier sketch in CA 11-12
Donohue, John W(aldron) 1917- ... CANR-3
  Earlier sketch in CA 5-8R
Donohue, Joseph (Walter Jr.) 1935- ... 69-72
Donohue, Mark 1937-1975 ... 57-60
  Obituary ... 89-92
Donohue, Martin
  See Gibson, Walter B(rown)
Donoso (Yanez), Jose 1924- ... CANR-32
  Earlier sketch in CA 81-84
  See also CLC 4, 8, 11, 32
  See also DLB 113
  See also HW
  See also MTCW
Donoughue, Bernard 1934- ... 17-20R
Donovan, Bonita R. 1947- ... 73-76
Donovan, Bonnie
  See Donovan, Bonita R.
Donovan, Edward J(oseph) 1904- ... 5-8R
Donovan, Frank (Robert) 1906-1975 ... CANR-6
  Obituary ... 61-64
  Earlier sketch in CA 1-4R
  See also SATA 30
Donovan, Hedley (Williams) 1914-1990 ... 115
  Obituary ... 132
  Brief entry ... 110
Donovan, James A. Jr. 1917- ... 21-24R
Donovan, James Britt 1916-1970 ... 9-12R
  Obituary ... 89-92
Donovan, John C(hauncey) 1920-1984 ... 37-40R
  Obituary ... 114
Donovan, John 1919- ... CANR-2
  Earlier sketch in CA 1-4R
Donovan, John 1928-1992 ... 97-100
  Obituary ... 137
  See also CLC 35
  See also CLR 3
  See also MAICYA
  See also SATA 29
Donovan, Josephine (Campbell) 1941- ... CANR-24
  Earlier sketch in CA 106
Donovan, Robert Alan 1921- ... 17-20R
Donovan, Robert J(ohn) 1912- ... CANR-18
  Earlier sketches in CA 1-4R, CANR-2
Donovan, Timothy Paul 1927- ... 53-56
Donovan, William
  See Berkebile, Fred D(onovan)
Donow, Herbert S(tanton) 1936- ... 112
Don Roberto
  See Cunninghame Graham, R(obert) B(ontine)
Donskoi, Mark Semyonovich 1901-1981 Obituary ... 103
Donson, Cyril 1919-1986 ... CANR-28
  Earlier sketches in CA 21-24R, CANR-11
Don-Yehiya, Eliezer 1938- ... 111
Donze, Mary Terese 1911- ... CANR-25
  Earlier sketch in CA 108
Doob, Anthony N(ewcomb) 1943- ... 33-36R
Doob, Leonard W(illiam) 1909- ... CANR-2
  Earlier sketch in CA 5-8R
  See also SATA 8
Doob, Penelope Billings Reed 1943- ... 53-56
Doody, Francis Stephen 1917- ... 13-16R
Doody, Margaret (Anne) 1939- ... CANR-27
  Earlier sketches in CA 69-72, CANR-11
Doog, K. Caj
  See Good, I(rving) John
Doohan, Leonard 1941- ... 118
Dooley, Allan C(harles) 1943- ... 138
Dooley, Arch R(ichard) 1925- ... 13-16R
Dooley, D(avid) J(oseph) 1921- ... CANR-16
  Earlier sketch in CA 25-28R
Dooley, Ebon
  See Ebon
Dooley, Howard J(ohn) 1944- ... 53-56
Dooley, John 1929(?)-1985 Obituary ... 119
Dooley, Patrick K(iaran) 1942- ... 53-56
Dooley, Paul 1928- ... 133
Dooley, Peter C(hamberlain) 1937- ... 49-52
Dooley, Roger B(urke) 1920- ... CANR-22
  Earlier sketch in CA 1-4R
Dooley, Thomas A(nthony) 1927-1961 Obituary ... 93-96
Dooley, William G(ermain) 1905(?)-1975 Obituary ... 57-60
Doolin, Dennis James 1933- ... 13-16R
Dooling, Dave
  See Dooling, David Jr.
Dooling, David Jr. 1950- ... 125
Doolittle, Hilda 1886-1961 ... CANR-35
  Earlier sketch in CA 97-100
  See also H. D.
  See also CLC 3, 8, 14, 31, 34
  See also DLB 4, 45
  See also MTCW
  See also PC 5
  See also WLC
Doolittle, Jerome (Hill) 1933- ... 53-56
Doone, Jice
  See Marshall, James Vance
Dooren, Ingrid van
  See van Dooren, Ingrid
Doorly, Ruth K. 1919- ... 25-28R
Doornkamp, John Charles 1938- ... CANR-7
  Earlier sketch in CA 57-60
Dopuch, Nicholas 1929- ... 61-64
Dor, Ana
  See Ceder, Georgiana Dorcas
Dor, Milo 1923- ... DLB 85
Doran, Adelaide L(eMert) 1908- ... 116
Doran, Charles F(rancis) 1943- ... 73-76
Doran, Madeleine 1905- ... 121
Dorant, Gene
  See Lent, D(ora) Geneva
Dorati, Antal 1906-1988 Obituary ... 127
Doray, Maya 1922- ... 45-48
Dorcy, Sister Mary Jean 1914- ... 9-12R
Dordick, Herbert S(halom) 1925- ... 116
Dore, Anita Wilkes 1914- ... 29-32R
Dore, Claire (Morin) 1934- ... 9-12R
Dore, (Louis Christophe Paul) Gustave 1832-1883 ... SATA 19
Dore, Ronald Philip 1925- ... CANR-34
  Earlier sketches in CA 89-92, CANR-15
Doreian, Patrick 1942- ... 45-48
Doremus, Robert 1913- ... SATA 30
Doremus, Thomas Edmund 1922-1962 ... 1-4R
Doren, Marion (Walker) 1928- ... 125
  See also SATA 57
Doreski, William 1946- ... CANR-17
  Earlier sketches in CA 45-48, CANR-1
Dorey, T(homas) A(lan) 1921- ... 17-20R
Dorf, Fran 1953- ... 138
Dorf, Michael C. 1964- ... 135
Dorf, Richard C. 1933- ... CANR-28
  Earlier sketch in CA 110
Dorfer, Ingemar (Nils Hans) 1939- ... 130
Dorff, Elliot N. 1943- ... 124
Dorfman, Ariel 1942- ... 130
  Brief entry ... 124
  See also CLC 48
  See also HW
Dorfman, Dan 1932- ... 116
  Brief entry ... 110
Dorfman, Eugene 1917- ... 29-32R
Dorfman, Gerald Allen 1939- ... 118
Dorfman, John 1947- ... CANR-12
  Earlier sketch in CA 69-72
Dorfman, Joseph 1904-1991 ... 45-48
  Obituary ... 135
Dorfman, Nancy S(chelling) 1922- ... 53-56
Dorfman, Nat N. 1895-1977 Obituary ... 73-76
Dorfman, Robert 1916- ... 17-20R
Dorgan, Charity Anne 1959- ... 134
Dorge, Jeanne Emilie Marie
  See Marie-Andre du Sacre-Coeur, Sister
Dorgeles, Roland 1886-1973 ... DLB 65
Doria, Charles 1938- ... 73-76
Doria, Vincent Mark 1947- ... 138
Dorian, Edith M(cEwen) 1900- ... CAP-1
  Earlier sketch in CA 9-10
  See also SATA 5
Dorian, Frederick 1902- ... CAP-1
  Earlier sketch in CA 11-12
Dorian, Harry
  See Hamilton, Charles (Harold St. John)
Dorian, Marguerite ... 17-20R
  See also SATA 7
Dorian, Nancy C(urrier) 1936- ... 104
Dorin, Patrick C(arberry) 1939- ... CANR-34
  Earlier sketches in CA 93-96, CANR-15
  See also SATA 52, 59
Doris, John Lawrence 1923- ... 102
Doris, Lillian 1899- ... 5-8R
Dorland, Henry
  See Ash, Brian
Dorland, Michael 1948- ... 102
Dorliae, Peter Gondro 1935- ... 29-32R
Dorliae, Saint
  See Dorliae, Peter Gondro
Dorman, Luke
  See Bingley, David Ernest
Dorman, Michael 1932- ... CANR-5
  Earlier sketch in CA 13-16R
  See also SATA 7
Dorman, N. B. 1927- ... 106
  See also SATA 39
Dorman, Sonya 1924- ... 73-76
Dormandy, Clara 1905- ... CAP-1
  Earlier sketch in CA 9-10
d'Ormesson, Jean (Bruno Waldemar Francois-de-Paule 1925- Brief entry ... 111
Dormon, James H(unter) Jr. 1936- ... 21-24R
Dorn, Edward (Merton) 1929- ... 93-96
  See also CLC 10, 18
  See also DLB 5
Dorn, Frank 1901-1981 ... CANR-24
  Obituary ... 104
  Earlier sketch in CA 29-32R
Dorn, Jacob H(enry) 1939- ... 21-24R
Dorn, Phyllis Moore 1910(?)-1978 Obituary ... 77-80
Dorn, Sylvia O'Neill 1918- ... 69-72
Dorn, William S. 1928- ... 65-68
Dornan, James E. Jr. 1938(?)-1979 Obituary ... 85-88
Dornberg, John Robert 1931- ... CANR-1
  Earlier sketch in CA 1-4R
Dornbusch, C(harles) E(mil) 1907- ... CAP-1
  Earlier sketch in CA 9-10
Dorner, Marjorie 1942- ... 133
Dorner, Peter Paul 1925- ... CANR-14
  Earlier sketch in CA 37-40R
Doro, Edward 1910- ... 21-24R
Doro, Marion Elizabeth 1928- ... 89-92
Doroch, Efim Yakovlevitch 1908(?)-1972 Obituary ... 37-40R
Doronzo, Emmanuel 1903- ... 21-24R
Doroshkin, Milton 1914- ... 33-36R
Dorothy, R. D.
  See Charques, Dorothy (Taylor)
Dorpalen, Andreas 1911-1982 ... 17-20R
  Obituary ... 109
Dorr, Donal 1935- ... 118
Dorr, Rheta (Louise) Childe 1866-1948 Brief entry ... 116
  See also DLB 25
Dorrie, Doris
  See Doerrie, Doris
Dorrien, Gary J. 1952- ... 135
Dorries, William (Lyle) 1923- ... 37-40R
Dorris, Michael Anthony 1945- ... CANR-19
  Earlier sketch in CA 102
  See also BEST 90:1
Dorris, R(obert) T. 1913- ... 29-32R
Dors, Diana
  See Fluck, Diana
Dorsan, Luc
  See Simenon, Georges (Jacques Christian)
Dorsange, Jean
  See Simenon, Georges (Jacques Christian)
Dorsen, Norman 1930- ... 37-40R
Dorset, Gerald (Harris) 1920- ... 112
Dorset, Phyllis (Flanders) 1924- ... 25-28R
Dorset, Ruth
  See Ross, W(illiam) E(dward) D(aniel)
Dorsett, Danielle
  See Daniels, Dorothy
Dorsett, Lyle W(esley) 1938- ... CANR-9
  Earlier sketch in CA 21-24R
Dorsey, David Frederick Jr. 1934- ... 115
Dorsey, Hebe 1925-1987 Obituary ... 124
Dorsey, Helen 1928- ... 110
Dorsey, John M(orris) 1900- ... CANR-4
  Earlier sketch in CA 5-8R
Dorsey, John R(ussell) 1938- ... 118
Dorsey, John Thornton Jr. 1924- ... 111
Dorson, Richard M(ercer) 1916-1981 ... 106
  Obituary ... 105
  See also SATA 30
Dorsonville, Max 1943- ... 65-68
Dorst, Jean (Pierre) 1924- ... CANR-19
  Earlier sketches in CA 5-8R, CANR-3
Dorst, Tankred 1925- ... CANR-30
  Earlier sketch in CA 41-44R
  See also DLB 75
Dorwart, J(effrey) M(ichael) 1944- ... 97-100
Dorwart, Reinhold August 1911- ... 65-68
Dorworth, Alice Grey 1907- ... 5-8R
Dosa, Marta Leszlei ... 45-48
Doskocilova, Hana 1936- ... CANR-23
  Earlier sketches in CA 61-64, CANR-8
Doskow, Minna 1937- ... 118
Dos Passos, John (Roderigo) 1896-1970 ... CANR-3
  Obituary ... 29-32R
  Earlier sketch in CA 1-4R
  See also CDALB 1929-1941
  See also CLC 1, 4, 8, 11, 15, 25, 34
  See also DLB 4, 9
  See also DLBD 1
  See also MTCW
  See also WLC
Doss, Helen (Grigsby) 1918- ... CANR-6
  Earlier sketch in CA 9-12R
  See also SATA 20
Doss, Margot Patterson ... CANR-12
  Earlier sketch in CA 29-32R
  See also SATA 6
Doss, Richard W(eller) 1933- Brief entry ... 112
Dossage, Jean
  See Simenon, Georges (Jacques Christian)
dos Santos, Joyce Audy 1949- ... 136
  Brief entry ... 118
  See also Zarins, Joyce Audy
  See also SATA 42
Dossick, Philip 1941- ... 81-84
Doster, William C(lark) 1921- ... 13-16R
Dostoevsky, Fedor Mikhailovich 1821-1881 ... SSC 2
  See also WLC
Dothard, Robert Loos 1909(?)-1979 Obituary ... 85-88
Doti, Lynne Pierson 1948- ... 137
Dotsenko, Paul 1894- ... 117
Dotson, Bob
  See Dotson, Robert Charles
Dotson, Floyd 1917- ... 25-28R
Dotson, John L(ouis) Jr. 1937- ... 105
Dotson, Lillian O. 1921- ... 25-28R
Dotson, Robert Charles 1946- ... 134
  Brief entry ... 119
Dott, R(obert) H(enry) Jr. 1929- ... 53-56
Dottig
  See Grider, Dorothy
Dotto, Lydia 1949- ... 125
Dotts, M. Franklin 1929- ... 57-60
Dotts, Maryann J. 1933- ... CANR-30
  Earlier sketches in CA 33-36R, CANR-12
  See also SATA 35
Doty, Brant Lee 1921- ... 17-20R
Doty, C(harles) Stewart 1928- ... 65-68
Doty, Carolyn 1941- ... CANR-23
  Earlier sketch in CA 105
Doty, Gladys 1908- ... 53-56
Doty, Gresdna Ann 1931- ... 41-44R
Doty, James Edward 1922- ... 37-40R
Doty, Jean Slaughter 1929- ... CANR-2
  Earlier sketch in CA 45-48
  See also SATA 28
Doty, Richard (George) 1942- ... 109
Doty, Robert McIntyre 1933- ... 102
Doty, Roy 1922- ... CANR-8
  Earlier sketch in CA 53-56
  See also SATA 28
Doty, William G(uy) 1939- ... CANR-20
  Earlier sketches in CA 53-56, CANR-5
Doty, William Lodewick 1919-1979 ... CANR-1
  Earlier sketch in CA 1-4R
Doubiago, Sharon 1946- ... 112
Doubleday, Neal Frank 1905-1976 ... 41-44R
Doubleday, Veronica 1948- ... 129
Doubrovsky, Serge 1928- ... 136
  Brief entry ... 110
Doubtfire, Dianne (Abrams) 1918- ... CANR-39
  Earlier sketches in CA 1-4R, CANR-1, 17
  See also SATA 29
Doucet, Clive 1946- ... 118
Doucette, Leonard E(ugene) 1936- ... 33-36R
Douds, Charles Tucker 1898-1982 Obituary ... 106
Dougall, Herbert E(dward) 1902- ... CAP-1
  Earlier sketch in CA 19-20
Dougall, Lily 1858-1923 ... DLB 92
Dougan, Michael B(ruce) 1944- ... 69-72
Dougherty, Betty 1922- ... 61-64
Dougherty, Charles 1922- ... SATA 18
Dougherty, Ching-yi (Hsu) 1915- ... 5-8R
Dougherty, David Mitchell 1903- ... 113
Dougherty, Flavian 1913(?)-1990 Obituary ... 130
Dougherty, James E(dward) 1923- ... 134
  Brief entry ... 111
Dougherty, James (Patrick) 1937- ... 106
Dougherty, Joanna Foster
  See Foster, Joanna
Dougherty, John J(oseph) 1907-1986 Obituary ... 118
Dougherty, Jude P(atrick) 1930- ... 45-48
Dougherty, Philip H(ugh) 1923-1988 Obituary ... 126
Dougherty, Richard M. 1935- ... 33-36R
Dougherty, Richard 1921-1986 ... CANR-2
  Obituary ... 121
  Earlier sketch in CA 1-4R
Doughtie, Edward (Orth) 1935- ... 45-48
Doughty, Bradford 1921- ... 65-68
Doughty, Charles M(ontagu) 1843-1926 Brief entry ... 115
  See also DLB 19, 57
  See also TCLC 27
Doughty, Nina Beckett 1911- ... 53-56
Doughty, Oswald 1889- ... CAP-1
  Earlier sketch in CA 9-10
Doughty, Paul L(arrabee) 1930- ... 85-88
Doughty, Robin W. 1941- ... 122
Douglas, Albert
  See Armstrong, Douglas Albert
Douglas, Althea (Cleveland McCoy) 1926- ... 124
Douglas, Ann C.
  See Welch, Ann Courtenay (Edmonds)
Douglas, Barbara
  See Ovstedal, Barbara
Douglas, Carole Nelson 1944- ... CANR-26
  Earlier sketch in CA 107
Douglas, Charles H(erbert) 1926- Brief entry ... 109
Douglas, Christopher
  See Neill, Christopher Harry Douglas
Douglas, David C(harles) 1898-1982 ... CANR-28
  Obituary ... 107
  Earlier sketch in CA 73-76
Douglas, Ellen
  See Haxton, Josephine Ayres and Williamson, Ellen Douglas
Douglas, Emily (Taft) 1899- ... 107
Douglas, Garry
  See Kilworth, Garry
Douglas, George H(alsey) 1934- ... CANR-14
  Earlier sketch in CA 81-84
Douglas, Glenn
  See Duckett, Alfred A.
Douglas, Gregory A.
  See Cantor, Eli
Douglas, Helen Bee
  See Bee, Helen L.
Douglas, Helen Gahagan 1900-1980 Obituary ... 101
Douglas, J(ames) D(ixon) 1922- ... CANR-21
  Earlier sketches in CA 13-16R, CANR-6
Douglas, Jack 1909(?)-1989 Obituary ... 128
Douglas, James McM.
  See Butterworth, W(illiam) E(dmund III)
Douglas, Jeff
  See Offutt, Andrew J(efferson V)
Douglas, John (Frederick James) 1929- ... 116
Douglas, Kate
  See Douglas, Kathleen
Douglas, Kathleen 1949- ... 117
Douglas, Kathryn
  See Ewing, Kathryn
Douglas, Keith 1920-1944 ... DLB 27
  See also TCLC 40
Douglas, Kirk 1916- ... 138
  See also BEST 90:4
Douglas, Lauren Wright 1947- ... 129
Douglas, Leonard
  See Bradbury, Ray (Douglas)
Douglas, Leonard M(arvin) 1910- ... CAP-2
  Earlier sketch in CA 23-24

Douglas, Lloyd C.
See Douglas, Lloyd Cassel
Douglas, Lloyd Cassel
1877-1951 Brief entry ... 120
Douglas, Louis H(artwell) 1907-1979 ... 21-24R
Obituary ... 133
Douglas, Mack R. 1922- ... 21-24R
Douglas, Marjory Stoneman 1890- ... CANR-2
Earlier sketch in CA 1-4R
See also AITN 2
See also SATA 10
Douglas, Mary (Tew) 1921- ... 97-100
Douglas, Melvyn 1901-1981 ... 135
Douglas, Michael
See Crichton, (John) Michael
Douglas, Michael
See Bright, Robert (Douglas Sr.)
Douglas, Mike 1925- ... 89-92
Douglas, (George) Norman
1868-1952 Brief entry ... 119
See also DLB 34
Douglas, Paul Howard 1892-1976 ... 69-72
Douglas, R. M.
See Mason, Douglas R(ankine)
Douglas, Robert
See Andrews, (Charles) Robert Douglas (Hardy)
Douglas, Roy (Ian) 1924- ... CANR-13
Earlier sketch in CA 73-76
Douglas, Scott
See Smith, William Scott
Douglas, Shane
See Wilkes-Hunter, R(ichard)
Douglas, Thorne
See Haas, Ben(jamin) L(eopold)
Douglas, William A(llison) 1934- ... 45-48
Douglas, William O(rville) 1898-1980 ... CANR-21
Obituary ... 93-96
Earlier sketch in CA 9-12R
Douglas-Hamilton, James 1942- ... CANR-13
Earlier sketch in CA 33-36R
Douglas-Home, Alec
See Home, Alexander Frederick
Douglas-Home, Charles (Cospatrick)
1937-1985 Obituary ... 117
Douglas-Home, Henry 1907-1980 ... 103
Obituary ... 101
Douglas-Home, Robin 1932-1968 ... CAP-2
Earlier sketch in CA 25-28
Douglas Home, William
See Home, William Douglas
Douglass, Amanda Hart
See Wallmann, Jeffrey M(iner)
Douglass, Barbara 1930- ... 114
See also SATA 40
Douglass, Billie
See Delinsky, Barbara (Ruth Greenberg)
Douglass, Donald McNutt 1899-1975 ... 1-4R
Obituary ... 103
Douglass, Elisha Peairs 1915- ... 81-84
Douglass, Frederick 1817(?)-1895 ... BLC 1
See also CDALB 1640-1865
See also DLB 1, 43, 50, 79
See also SATA 29
See also WLC
Douglass, Harl R(oy) 1892- ... 5-8R
Douglass, Herbert Edgar 1927- ... CANR-13
Earlier sketch in CA 73-76
Douglass, James W. 1937- ... CANR-10
Earlier sketch in CA 25-28R
Douglass, Malcolm P(aul) 1923- ... CANR-13
Earlier sketch in CA 73-76
Douglass, Marcia Kent
See Doty, Gladys
Douglass, Paul F(ranklin) 1904- ... CANR-3
Earlier sketch in CA 5-8R
Douglass, Robert W. 1934- ... 57-60
Douglass, Roy (Ian) 1924- ... CANR-30
Douglass, William A(nthony) 1939- ... 69-72
Douglass, William 1691(?)-1752 ... DLB 24
Douglas-Scott-Montagu, Edward
See Montagu of Beaulieu, Edward John Barrington
Doulis, Thomas 1931- ... CANR-11
Earlier sketch in CA 5-8R
Doulos, Jay
See Joyce, Jon L(oyd)
Doumato, Lamia 1947- ... 103
Dourado, (Waldomiro Freitas) Autran
1926- ... CANR-34
Earlier sketch in CA 25-28R
See also CLC 23, 60
Dourado, Waldomiro Autran
See Dourado, (Waldomiro Freitas) Autran
Douras, Marion Cecilia 1897-1961 Obituary ... 111
Douskey, Franz 1941- ... 129
Douty, Esther M(orris) 1909-1978 ... CANR-3
Obituary ... 85-88
Earlier sketch in CA 5-8R
See also SATA 8, 23
Douty, Norman F(ranklin) 1899- ... CANR-31
Earlier sketch in CA 49-52
Douvan, Elizabeth (Ann Malcolm) 1926- ... 106
Dove, Rita (Frances) 1952- ... CANR-27
Earlier sketch in CA 109
See also BW
See also CLC 50
See also DLB 120
Doveglion
See Villa, Jose Garcia
Dover, C(larence) J(oseph) 1919- ... 13-16R
Dover, K(enneth) J(ames) 1920- ... CANR-29
Earlier sketches in CA 25-28R, CANR-12
Dover Wilson, John
1881-1969 Obituary ... 25-28R
Dovey, Ken 1947- ... 120
Dovlatov, Sergei 1941-1990 ... 115
Obituary ... 132
Dow, Blanche H(innan)
1893-1973 Obituary ... 41-44R
Dow, Dorothy
See Fitzgerald, Dorothy Dow (Minerva)
Dow, Emily R. 1904- ... CAP-1
Earlier sketch in CA 11-12
See also SATA 10
Dow, George Francis
1868-1936 Brief entry ... 122
Dow, J(ose) Kamal 1936- ... 29-32R
Dow, Marguerite R(uth) 1926- ... 116
Dow, Neal 1906- ... 17-20R
Dow, Sterling 1903- ... CAP-2
Earlier sketch in CA 21-22
Dowd, Douglas F(itzgerald) 1919- ... 5-8R
Dowd, Laurence P(hillips) 1914-1980 ... 17-20R
Obituary ... 133
Dowd, Maxine
See Jensen, Maxine Dowd
Dowd, Merle E(dward) 1918- ... 85-88
Dowdell, Dorothy (Florence) Karns
1910- ... CANR-20
Earlier sketches in CA 9-12R, CANR-5
See also SATA 12
Dowden, Anne Ophelia 1907- ... CANR-18
Earlier sketches in CA 9-12R, CANR-3
See also SAAS 10
See also SATA 7
Dowden, Edward 1843-1913 ... DLB 35
Dowden, George 1932- ... CANR-22
Earlier sketches in CA 53-56, CANR-4
Dowden, Wilfred S(ellers) 1917- ... 125
Dowdey, Clifford (Shirley Jr.) 1904- ... 9-12R
Dowdey, Landon Gerald 1923- ... 89-92
See also SATA 11
Dowding, Hugh Caswell Tremenheere
1882-1970 Obituary ... 112
Dowdy, Andrew 1936- ... 49-52
Dowdy, Homer E(arl) 1922- ... 5-8R
Dowdy, Mrs. Regera
See Gorey, Edward (St. John)
Dowell, Coleman 1925-1985 ... CANR-10
Obituary ... 117
Earlier sketch in CA 25-28R
See also CLC 60
Dowell, Jack (Larder) 1908- ... 57-60
Dowell, Richard W(alker) 1931- ... 116
Dower, J. W.
See Dower, John W(illiam)
Dower, John W(illiam) 1938- ... 137
Brief entry ... 128
Dower, Penn
See Pendower, Jacques
Dowie, James Iverne 1911- ... 41-44R
Dowie, Mark 1939- ... 85-88
Dowler, James Ross 1925- ... 29-32R
Dowley, D. M.
See Marrison, L(eslie) W(illiam)
Dowley, Timothy Edward 1946- ... CANR-18
Earlier sketch in CA 101
Dowling, Allan D. 1903-1983 Obituary ... 117
Dowling, Allen 1900- ... 29-32R
Dowling, Basil (Cairns) 1910- ... 97-100
Dowling, David (Hurst) 1950- ... 118
Dowling, Eddie 1894-1976 Obituary ... 65-68
Dowling, Harry Filmore 1904- ... 102
Dowling, Joseph A(lbert) 1926- ... 37-40R
Dowling, Maria 1955- ... 123
Dowling, Thomas Jr. 1921- ... 85-88
Dowling, Tom
See Dowling, Thomas Jr.
Down, Goldie (Malvern) 1918- ... CANR-26
Earlier sketches in CA 25-28R, CANR-11
Down, Michael (Graham) 1951- ... 118
Downard, William L. 1940- ... 49-52
Downer, Alan S(eymour) 1912-1970 ... CAP-1
Obituary ... 33-36R
Earlier sketch in CA 11-12
Downer, Lesley 1949- ... 131
Downer, Marion 1892(?)-1971 Obituary ... 33-36R
See also SATA 25
Downes, Bryan Trevor 1939- ... 33-36R
Downes, David A(nthony) 1927- ... 33-36R
Downes, Edward (Olin Davenport) 1911- ... 105
Downes, Gwladys 1915- ... DLB 88
Downes, Kerry 1930- ... 119
Downes, Mollie Patricia Panter
See Panter-Downes, Mollie Patricia
Downes, Quentin
See Harrison, Michael
Downes, Randolph C(handler)
1901-1975 ... 49-52
Obituary ... 61-64
Downey, Bill
See Downey, William L(eslie)
Downey, Fairfax D(avis) 1893-1990 ... CANR-1
Obituary ... 131
Earlier sketch in CA 1-4R
See also SATA 3
See also SATO 66
Downey, Glanville 1908- ... CANR-1
Earlier sketch in CA 1-4R
Downey, Harris ... 13-16R
Downey, James 1939- ... 101
Downey, Lawrence William (Lorne)
1921- ... 17-20R
Downey, Murray William 1910- ... CANR-1
Earlier sketch in CA 1-4R
Downey, William L(eslie) 1922- ... 110
Downie, Freda (Christina) 1929- ... 106
Downie, Jill 1938- ... CANR-25
Earlier sketch in CA 108
Downie, John 1931- ... CANR-26
Earlier sketch in CA 108
Downie, Leonard Jr. 1942- ... CANR-1
Earlier sketch in CA 49-52
Downie, Mary Alice (Dawe) 1934- ... CANR-26
Earlier sketches in CA 25-28R, CANR-10
See also SATA 13
Downie, N(orville) M(organ) 1910- ... 17-20R
Downing, A(rthur) B(enjamin) 1915- ... 29-32R
Downing, Chris(tine) 1931- ... 57-60
Downing, Douglas 1957- ... 114
Downing, Graham 1954- ... 136
Downing, J. Major
See Davis, Charles A.
Downing, John (Allen) 1922- ... CANR-20
Earlier sketches in CA 53-56, CANR-5
Downing, Lester N. 1914- ... CANR-25
Earlier sketches in CA 25-28R, CANR-10
Downing, Major Jack
See Smith, Seba
Downing, Paul B(utler) 1938- ... 104
Downing, Paula E. 1951- ... 136
Downing, Warwick 1931- ... 53-56
Downs, Anthony 1930- ... CANR-28
Earlier sketch in CA 49-52
Downs, Brian W(esterdale)
1893-1984 Obituary ... 112
Downs, Cal W. 1936- ... 103
Downs, Donald (Alexander) 1948- ... 119
Downs, Hugh (Malcolm) 1921- ... CANR-2
Earlier sketch in CA 45-48
Downs, Hunton (Leache) 1918- ... 1-4R
Downs, Jacques M. 1926- ... 37-40R
Downs, James Francis 1926- ... 81-84
Downs, Lenthiel H(owell) 1915- ... 25-28R
Downs, Norton 1918-1985 ... 1-4R
Obituary ... 114
Downs, Robert B.
See Downs, Robert Bingham
Downs, Robert Bingham 1903-1991 ... CANR-17
Obituary ... 133
Earlier sketches in CA 1-4R, CANR-2
Downs, Robert C. S. 1937- ... CANR-1
Earlier sketch in CA 45-48
Downs, William Randall Jr. 1914-1978 ... 81-84
Obituary ... 77-80
Dowse, Robert E. 1933- ... 21-24R
Dowse, (Dale) Sara 1938- ... 119
Dowsey-Magog, Paul 1950- ... 105
Dowson, Ernest Christopher
1867-1900 Brief entry ... 105
See also DLB 19
See also TCLC 4
Dowst, Somerby R(ohrer) 1926-1990 ... 33-36R
Obituary ... 133
Dowty, Alan K. 1940- ... 122
Doxey, Roy W(atkins) 1908- ... 41-44R
Doxey, William S(anford Jr.) 1935- ... CANR-25
Earlier sketches in CA 65-68, CANR-9
Doxiadis, Constantinos Apostolos
1913-1975 ... 41-44R
Obituary ... 57-60
Doyle, A. Conan
See Doyle, Arthur Conan
Doyle, Adrian M. C.
See Conan Doyle, Adrian Malcolm
Doyle, Arthur Conan 1859-1930 ... 122
Brief entry ... 104
See also CDBLB 1890-1914
See also DLB 18, 70
See also MTCW
See also SATA 24
See also TCLC 7
See also WLC
Doyle, Brian 1930- ... 53-56
Doyle, Brian 1935- ... 135
See also CLR 22
See also MAICYA
See also SATA 67
Doyle, Charles (Desmond) 1928- ... CANR-26
Earlier sketches in CA 25-28R, CANR-11
Doyle, Charlotte Lackner 1937- ... 81-84
Doyle, Conan
See Doyle, Arthur Conan
Doyle, David
See Carter, David C(harles)
Doyle, Denis P. 1940- ... CANR-26
Earlier sketch in CA 109
Doyle, Don H(arrison) 1946- ... CANR-14
Earlier sketch in CA 81-84
Doyle, Donovan
See Boegehold, Betty (Doyle)
Doyle, Edward (Gerard) 1949- ... 118
Doyle, Edward Park 1907-1985 Obituary ... 115
Doyle, Esther M. 1910- ... 45-48
Doyle, Frank D. 1909(?)-1983 Obituary ... 109
Doyle, Gerald A. 1898(?)-1986 Obituary ... 119
Doyle, Harold Edmund
See Stearns, Harold Edmund
Doyle, James (Stephen) 1935- ... 73-76
Doyle, Jerry
See Doyle, Gerald A.
Doyle, John
See Graves, Robert (von Ranke)
Doyle, John Robert Jr. 1910- ... 25-28R
Doyle, Kirby 1932- ... DLB 16
Doyle, Mary Ellen 1932- ... 114
Doyle, Michael W. 1948- ... 120
Doyle, Mike
See Doyle, Charles (Desmond)
Doyle, Paul A. 1925- ... CANR-22
Earlier sketches in CA 13-16R, CANR-7
Doyle, Richard Edward 1929- ... 113
Doyle, Richard J(ames) 1923- ... 65-68
Doyle, Richard 1824-1883 ... SATA 21
Doyle, Richard 1948- ... 85-88
Doyle, Robert V(aughn) 1916- ... CANR-9
Earlier sketch in CA 65-68
Doyle, Sir A. Conan
See Doyle, Arthur Conan
Doyle, Sir Arthur Conan
See Doyle, Arthur Conan
Doyle, William 1942- ... 130
Doyno, Victor A(nthony) 1937- ... 37-40R
Dozer, Donald Marquand 1905- ... CANR-1
Earlier sketch in CA 1-4R
Dozier, Craig Lanier 1920- ... 41-44R
Dozier, Edward P. 1916-1971 Obituary ... 29-32R
Dozier, Robert R. 1932- ... 120
Dozier, Zoe
See Browning, Dixie Burrus
Dozois, Gardner R(aymond) 1947- ... CANR-27
Earlier sketch in CA 108
Dr. A
See Asimov, Isaac
and Silverstein, Alvin
Dr. Alphabet
See Morice, Dave
Dr. Hip
See Schoenfeld, Eugene
Dr. Hippocrates
See Schoenfeld, Eugene
Dr. Judy
See Kuriansky, Judith (Anne Brodsky)
Dr. NO
See Many, Seth E(dward)
Dr. Science
See Coffey, Daniel
Dr. Seuss
See Geisel, Theodor Seuss
See also CLR 9
Dr. Spektor
See Glut, Donald F(rank)
Dr. Zed
See Penrose, Gordon
Drabble, Margaret 1939- ... CANR-35
Earlier sketches in CA 13-16R, CANR-18
See also CDBLB 1960 to Present
See also CLC 2, 3, 5, 8, 10, 22, 53
See also DLB 14
See also MTCW
See also SATA 48
Drabble, Phil 1914- ... 102
Drabeck, Bernard A. 1932- ... 129
Drabek, Jan 1935- ... 93-96
Drabek, Thomas E(dward) 1940- ... CANR-37
Earlier sketches in CA 45-48, CANR-1, 16
Drach, Albert 1902- ... DLB 85
Drache, Sharon 1943- ... 118
Drachkovitch, Milorad M. 1921- ... 17-20R
Drachler, Jacob 1909- ... 61-64
Drachler, Rose 1911- ... CANR-4
Earlier sketch in CA 53-56
Drachman, Edward Ralph 1940- ... 29-32R
Drachman, Julian M(oses) 1894- ... 61-64
Drachman, Theodore S(olomon) 1904- ... 81-84
Drackett, Phil(ip Arthur) 1922- ... CANR-3
Earlier sketch in CA 9-12R
See also SATA 53
Draco, F.
See Davis, Julia
Drage, Charles H(ardinge) 1897- ... CANR-2
Earlier sketch in CA 5-8R
Drager, Marvin 1920- ... 81-84
Dragland, Stan L(ouis) 1942- ... 125
Dragnich, Alex N. 1912- ... CANR-15
Earlier sketch in CA 89-92
Drago, Edmund Leon 1942- ... 109
Drago, Harry Sinclair 1888-1979 ... 113
Obituary ... 89-92
Drago, Sinclair
See Drago, Harry Sinclair
Dragon, Caroline
See Du Breuil, (Elizabeth) L(or)inda
Dragonette, Jessica Obituary ... 97-100
Dragonwagon, Crescent 1952- ... CANR-36
Earlier sketches in CA 65-68, CANR-12
See also MAICYA
See also SAAS 14
See also SATA 11, 41
Dragun, Osvaldo 1929- ... HW
Drahos, Mary 1927- ... 116
Drainie, Bronwyn 1945- ... 129
Draitser, Emil 1937- ... CANR-18
Earlier sketch in CA 89-92
Drakakis, John 1944- ... 120
Drake, Albert (Dee) 1935- ... CANR-13
Earlier sketch in CA 33-36R
Drake, Alice Hutchins
1889(?)-1975 Obituary ... 61-64
Drake, Asa (a pseudonym) ... 113
Drake, Barbara (Ann) 1939- ... CANR-13
Earlier sketch in CA 33-36R
Drake, Bonnie
See Delinsky, Barbara (Ruth Greenberg)
Drake, Charles D(ominic) 1924- ... 116
Drake, David (Allen) 1945- ... CANR-38
Earlier sketches in CA 93-96, CANR-17
Drake, Donald C(harles) 1935- ... 85-88
Drake, Elizabeth 1948- ... 109
Drake, Francis Vivian 1894-1971 Obituary ... 104
Drake, Frank
See Hamilton, Charles (Harold St. John)
Drake, Frank D(onald) 1930- ... 17-20R
Drake, Frederick Charles 1937- ... 119
Drake, George Randolph 1938- ... CANR-11
Earlier sketch in CA 69-72
Drake, Harold Allen 1942- ... 97-100
Drake, James A. 1944- ... 130
Drake, Joan H(oward) ... CANR-24
Earlier sketch in CA 13-16R
Drake, Kimbal
See Gallagher, Rachel
Drake, Lisl
See Beer, Eloise C. S.
Drake, Michael 1935- ... CANR-16
Earlier sketch in CA 25-28R

Drake, Paul Winter 1944- ... 106
Drake, Richard Bryant 1925- ... 37-40R
Drake, Robert (Young Jr.) 1930- ... 17-20R
Drake, (John Gibbs) St. Clair (Jr.)
1911-1990 ... 65-68
Obituary ... 131
Drake, (Bryant) Stillman 1910- ... CANR-18
Earlier sketch in CA 41-44R
Drake, W. Anders
See Eshbach, Lloyd Arthur
Drake, W(inbourne) Magruder 1914- ... 41-44R
Drake, W(alter) Raymond 1913- ... CANR-5
Earlier sketch in CA 53-56
Drake, William D(onovan) 1922- ... 21-24R
Drake, William Daniel 1941- ... 69-72
Drake, William E(arle) 1903- ... CAP-1
Earlier sketch in CA 17-18
Drake-Brockman, David 1933- ... 114
Drakeford, John W. 1914- ... CANR-5
Earlier sketch in CA 1-4R
Dralle, Elizabeth (Mary) 1910- ... 1-4R
Drane, James F. 1930- ... CANR-7
Earlier sketch in CA 13-16R
Drane, John (William) 1946- ... CANR-15
Earlier sketch in CA 93-96
Drange, Theodore M. 1934- ... 37-40R
Dranoff, Linda Silver 1939- ... 129
Dransfield, Michael (John Pender)
1948-1973 ... CANR-30
Earlier sketch in CA 37-40R
Draper, Alfred 1924- ... CANR-29
Earlier sketches in CA 33-36R, CANR-13
Draper, Cena C(hristopher) 1907- ... CANR-10
Earlier sketch in CA 17-20R
Draper, Edgar 1926- ... 13-16R
Draper, (Ellinor) Elizabeth (Nancy)
1915- ... 17-20R
Draper, Hal 1914-1990 ... CANR-24
Obituary ... 130
Earlier sketches in CA 17-20R, CANR-7
Draper, Hastings
See Jeffries, Roderic (Graeme)
Draper, James T(homas) Jr. 1935- ... 89-92
Draper, Jo 1949- ... 119
Draper, John W. 1811-1882 ... DLB 30
Draper, John William 1893-1976 ... CANR-16
Obituary ... 69-72
Earlier sketches in CAP-1, CA 9-10
Draper, Lyman C. 1815-1891 ... DLB 30
Draper, Norman R(ichard) 1931- ... 53-56
Draper, Ronald Philip 1928- ... 69-72
Draper, Theodore 1912- ... 13-16R
Draper, Thomas 1928- ... 108
Drapier, M. B.
See Swift, Jonathan
Drapkin, Herbert 1916- ... 33-36R
Drapkin, Israel 1906- ... 57-60
Draskovich, Slobodan M. 1910-1982 ... 93-96
Obituary ... 108
Drath, Viola Herms 1926- ... CANR-14
Earlier sketch in CA 65-68
Drawbell, James Wedgwood 1899- ... 65-68
Drawson, Blair 1943- ... 85-88
See also SATA 17
Dray, William H(erbert) 1921- ... CANR-13
Earlier sketch in CA 33-36R
Drayer, Adam Matthew 1913- ... 9-12R
Drayham, James
See Mencken, H(enry) L(ouis)
Drayne, George
See McCulley, Johnston
Drayton, Michael 1563-1631 ... DLB 121
Drazan, Joseph Gerald 1943- ... 110
Dreadstone, Carl
See Campbell, (John) Ramsey
Drebinger, John 1891(?)-1979 Obituary ... 89-92
Drefus, Jean-Paul Etienne
1909-1985 Obituary ... 117
Dreger, Georgia 1918- ... 115
Dreger, Ralph Mason 1913- ... 73-76
Dreher, Carl 1896-1976 ... 73-76
Dreher, Diane Elizabeth 1946- ... 119
Dreher, Melanie (Creagan) 1943- ... 114
Dreifort, John E. 1943- ... 45-48
Dreifus, Claudia 1944- ... CANR-1
Earlier sketch in CA 45-48
Dreifuss, Kurt 1897- ... CANR-16
Earlier sketches in CA 1-4R, CANR-1
Dreikurs, Rudolf 1897-1972 ... CANR-6
Obituary ... 33-36R
Earlier sketch in CA 1-4R
Dreiser, Theodore (Herman Albert)
1871-1945 ... 132
Brief entry ... 106
See also CDALB 1865-1917
See also DLB 9, 12, 102
See also DLBD 1
See also MTCW
See also TCLC 10, 18, 35
See also WLC
Dreiser, Vera ... 69-72
Dreiss, Joseph G. 1949- ... 125
Dreiss-Tarasovic, Marcia M(argaret)
1943- ... 65-68
Dreitzel, Hans Peter 1935- ... 41-44R
Drekmeier, Charles 1927- ... 1-4R
Drennen, D(onald) A(rthur) 1925- ... CANR-17
Earlier sketches in CA 1-4R, CANR-2
Dresang, Eliza (Carolyn Timberlake)
1941- ... 69-72
See also SATA 19
Dresbach, Glen Ward 1889-1968 ... 5-8R
Drescher, Henrik 1955- ... 135
See also CLR 20
See also MAICYA
See also SATA 67
Drescher, Joan E(lizabeth) 1939- ... 106
See also SATA 30
Drescher, John M(ummau) 1928- ... CANR-16
Earlier sketches in CA 49-52, CANR-1
Drescher, Sandra 1957- ... CANR-16
Earlier sketch in CA 85-88
Drescher, Seymour 1934- ... CANR-4
Earlier sketch in CA 9-12R
Drescher-Lehman, Sandra
See Drescher, Sandra
Dresner, Hal 1937- ... 13-16R
Dresner, Samuel H(ayim) 1923- ... CANR-9
Earlier sketch in CA 5-8R
Dressel, Paul L(eroy) 1910- ... CANR-3
Earlier sketch in CA 9-12R
Dresser, Davis 1904-1977 ... 77-80
Obituary ... 69-72
Dresser, Helen
See McCloy, Helen (Worrell Clarkson)
Dresser, Norine 1931- ... 132
Dressman, Dennis L(ee) 1945- ... 106
Dressman, Denny
See Dressman, Dennis L(ee)
Dressman, John 1947- ... 122
Dretske, Frederick I(rwin) 1932- ... CANR-10
Earlier sketch in CA 25-28R
Dreux, William B(ehan) 1911- ... 89-92
Dreves, Veronica R. 1927-1986 Obituary ... 121
See also SATA 50
Drew, Bernard 1926(?)-1984 Obituary ... 111
Drew, Donald J. 1920- ... 57-60
Drew, Elizabeth 1887-1965 ... 5-8R
Drew, Elizabeth 1935- ... 104
Drew, Fraser Bragg Robert 1913- ... 13-16R
Drew, George A(lexander)
1894-1973 Obituary ... 113
Drew, Katherine Fischer 1923- ... 9-12R
Drew, Kenneth
See Cockburn, (Francis) Claud
Drew, Mary Anne
See Cassiday, Bruce (Bingham)
Drew, Morgan
See Price, Robert
Drew, Patricia (Mary) 1938- ... 77-80
See also SATA 15
Drew, Philip 1943- ... 107
Drew-Bear, Robert 1901- ... CAP-2
Earlier sketch in CA 33-36
Drewe, Robert (Duncan) 1943- ... 138
Drewery, Mary 1918- ... 25-28R
See also SATA 6
Drewitz, Ingeborg 1923-1986 ... DLB 75
Drewnowski, Jan 1908- ... 129
Drewry, Guy Carleton 1901-1991 ... 5-8R
Obituary ... 135
Drewry, Henry N. 1924- ... 97-100
Drewry, John E(ldridge)
1902-1983 Obituary ... 109
Drexel, Jay B.
See Bixby, Jerome Lewis
Drexler, Arthur 1925-1987 ... 97-100
Obituary ... 121
Drexler, J. F.
See Paine, Lauran (Bosworth)
Drexler, K(im) Eric 1955- ... 121
Drexler, Rosalyn 1926- ... 81-84
See also CLC 2, 6
Dreyer, Carl Theodor 1889-1968 Obituary ... 116
See also CLC 16
Dreyer, Edward C. 1937- ... 21-24R
Dreyer, Frederick 1932- ... 111
Dreyer, Peter (Richard) 1939- ... 81-84
Dreyfack, Raymond ... CANR-24
Earlier sketches in CA 65-68, CANR-9
Dreyfus, Edward A(lbert) 1937- ... 37-40R
Dreyfus, Fred
See Rosenblatt, Fred
Dreyfus, Hubert L(ederer) 1929- ... CANR-28
Earlier sketch in CA 33-36R
Dreyfus, Kay 1942- ... 124
Dreyfuss, Henry 1904-1972 ... 45-48
Obituary ... 37-40R
Dreyfuss, Joel 1945- ... 97-100
Dreyfuss, Larry 1928- ... 65-68
Dreyfuss, Randolph (Lowell) 1956- ... 97-100
Dreze, Jean 1959- ... 133
Drial, J. E.
See Laird, Jean E(louise)
Dribben, Judith Strick 1923- ... 37-40R
Driberg, Thomas Edward Neil 1905-1976 ... 65-68
Obituary ... 104
Driberg, Tom
See Driberg, Thomas Edward Neil
Drieu la Rochelle, Pierre(-Eugene)
1893-1945 Brief entry ... 117
See also DLB 72
See also TCLC 21
Driftwood, Penelope
See De Lima, Clara Rosa
Drimmer, Frederick 1916- ... CANR-23
Earlier sketches in CA 61-64, CANR-7
See also SATA 60
Drinan, Adam
See Macleod, Joseph (Todd Gordon)
Drinan, Robert F(rederick) 1920- ... CANR-3
Earlier sketch in CA 9-12R
Dring, Nathaniel
See McBroom, R. Curtis
Drinkall, Gordon (Don) 1927- ... 9-12R
Drinkle, Ruth Wolfley 1903- ... 93-96
Drinkrow, John
See Hardwick, (John) Michael (Drinkrow)
Drinkwater, Francis Harold 1886- ... CANR-1
Earlier sketch in CA 1-4R
Drinkwater, John 1882-1937 Brief entry ... 109
See also DLB 10, 19
Drinkwater, Terry 1936-1989 ... 69-72
Obituary ... 128
Drinnon, Richard 1925- ... CANR-6
Earlier sketch in CA 13-16R
Driscoll, Gertrude 1898(?)-1975 Obituary ... 61-64
Driscoll, Peter (John) 1942- ... CANR-2
Earlier sketch in CA 49-52
Driscoll, R(obert) E(ugene) 1949- ... 85-88
Driskell, David Clyde 1931- ... 102
Driskill, Frank A. 1912- ... 130
Driver, C(harles) J(onathan) 1939- ... CANR-30
Earlier sketch in CA 29-32R
Driver, Christopher (Prout) 1932- ... 57-60
Driver, Cynthia C.
See Lovin, Roger Robert
Driver, Donald 1922-1988 Obituary ... 125
Driver, Edwin D(ouglas) 1925- ... 114
Driver, Godfrey Rolles 1892-1975 ... CAP-2
Obituary ... 57-60
Earlier sketch in CA 21-22
Driver, Harold Edson 1907- ... CANR-6
Earlier sketch in CA 1-4R
Driver, Tom F(aw) 1925- ... CANR-1
Earlier sketch in CA 1-4R
Driving Hawk, Virginia
See Sneve, Virginia Driving Hawk
Drobot, Eve 1951- ... 131
Droege, Thomas Arthur 1931- ... 113
Droescher, Vitus B(ernward) 1925- ... 33-36R
Drogheda, Earl of
See Moore, Charles Garrett Ponsonby
Droit, Michel (Arnould Arthur) 1923- ... CANR-32
Earlier sketches in CA 5-8R, CANR-11
Droppers, Carl Hyink 1918- ... 5-8R
Drop Shot
See Cable, George Washington
Dror, Yehezkel 1928- ... CANR-13
Earlier sketch in CA 21-24R
Drossaart Lulofs, H(endrik) J(oan)
1906- ... 13-16R
Drotar, David Lee 1952- ... 112
Drotning, Phillip T(homas) 1920- ... CANR-10
Earlier sketch in CA 25-28R
Drought, James (William) 1931-1983 ... CANR-20
Obituary ... 110
Earlier sketch in CA 5-8R
Drouin, Francis M. 1901- ... 37-40R
Drouin, Marie-Josee 1949- ... 116
Drowatzky, John N(elson) 1936- ... 89-92
Drower, E(thel) S(tefana May)
1879-1972 ... CAP-1
Earlier sketch in CA 11-12
Drower, G(eorge) M(atthew) F(rederick)
1954- ... 131
Drown, Harold J(ames) 1904- ... 49-52
Drown, Merle 1943- ... 109
Drowne, Tatiana B(alkoff) 1913- ... 17-20R
Droz, Eugenie 1893(?)-1976 Obituary ... 104
Droze, Wilmon H(enry) 1924- ... CANR-10
Earlier sketch in CA 17-20R
Drubert, John H. 1925- ... 45-48
Druce, Christopher
See Pulling, Christopher Robert Druce
Drucker, H. M.
See Drucker, Henry M(atthew)
Drucker, Henry M(atthew) 1942- ... CANR-29
Earlier sketch in CA 106
Drucker, Malka 1945- ... CANR-31
Earlier sketches in CA 81-84, CANR-14
See also SATA 29, 39
Drucker, Mark L(ewis) 1947- ... 107
Drucker, Mort 1929- ... 133
Drucker, Peter F(erdinand) 1909- ... 61-64
Drukker, J.
See Presser, (Gerrit) Jacob
Druks, Herbert 1937- ... CANR-9
Earlier sketch in CA 21-24R
Drum, Bob
See Drum, Robert F.
Drum, Robert F. 1918- ... 5-8R
Drumheller, Sidney J(ohn) 1923- ... 53-56
Drummond, Alison 1903- ... 112
Drummond, Donald F(rasier) 1914- ... CANR-4
Earlier sketch in CA 1-4R
Drummond, Dorothy W(eitz) 1928- ... 41-44R
Drummond, Edith Marie Dulce Carman
1883-1970 ... CAP-1
Earlier sketch in CA 9-10
Drummond, Ellen Lane 1897- ... 1-4R
Drummond, Harold D. 1916- ... CANR-12
Earlier sketch in CA 33-36R
Drummond, Ian (Macdonald) 1933- ... 37-40R
Drummond, J.
See Chance, John Newton
Drummond, Jack 1923(?)-1978 Obituary ... 81-84
Drummond, John Dodds 1944- ... 102
Drummond, John 1900-1982 Obituary ... 106
Drummond, June 1923- ... CANR-7
Earlier sketch in CA 13-16R
Drummond, Kenneth H(erbert) 1922- ... 17-20R
Drummond, Maldwin Andrew Cyril
1932- ... CANR-14
Earlier sketch in CA 73-76
Drummond, Richard H(enry) 1916- ... 41-44R
Drummond, (James) Roscoe 1902-1983 ... 104
Obituary ... 110
Drummond, V(iolet) H(ilda) 1911- ... 13-16R
See also SATA 6
Drummond, Walter
See Silverberg, Robert
Drummond, William Henry 1854-1907 ... DLB 92
See also TCLC 25
Drummond, William Joe 1944- ... 77-80
See also BW
Drummond de Andrade, Carlos 1902-1987 ... 132
Obituary ... 123
See also Andrade, Carlos Drummond de
See also CLC 18
Drummond of Hawthornden, William
1585-1649 ... DLB 121
Druon, Maurice (Samuel Roger Charles)
1918- ... CANR-12
Earlier sketch in CA 13-16R
Drury, Alan 1949- ... 106
Drury, Allen (Stuart) 1918- ... CANR-18
Earlier sketch in CA 57-60
See also CLC 37
Drury, Clare Marie
See Hoskyns-Abrahall, Clare (Constance Drury)
Drury, Clifford Merrill 1897- ... CANR-3
Earlier sketch in CA 9-12R
Drury, George H(erbert) 1940- ... 121
Drury, James Westbrook 1919- ... 5-8R
Drury, John 1898-1972 ... 5-8R
Obituary ... 33-36R
Drury, John 1936- ... 133
Drury, Margaret Josephine 1937- ... 53-56
Drury, Maxine Cole 1914- ... 5-8R
Drury, Michael ... CANR-27
Earlier sketch in CA 49-52
Drury, Roger W(olcott) 1914- ... 65-68
See also SATA 15
Drury, S(hadia) B(asilious) 1950- ... 116
Drury, Treesa Way 1937- ... 53-56
Drury, William 1918- ... 125
Drutman, Irving 1910-1978 ... 85-88
Obituary ... 81-84
Druxman, Michael Barnett 1941- ... CANR-37
Earlier sketches in CA 49-52, CANR-1, 16
Drvota, Mojmir 1923- ... 57-60
Dryansky, G. Y. ... 49-52
Dryden, Cecil P(earl) 1887- ... 25-28R
Dryden, Edgar A. 1937- ... 89-92
Dryden, John
See Rowland, D(onald) S(ydney)
Dryden, John 1631-1700 ... CDBLB 1660-1789
See also DLB 80, 101
See also WLC
Dryden, Ken(neth Wayne) 1947- ... 105
Dryden, Lennox
See Steen, Marguerite
Dryden, Pamela
See St. John, Nicole
Dryhurst, Edward
See Roberts, Edward Dryhurst
Drysdale, Frank R(eiff) 1943- ... 89-92
Drysdale, George Russell
1912-1981 Obituary ... 108
Drysdale, Helena 1960- ... 125
Drysdale, Vera Louise 1923- ... 115
Drzazga, John 1907- ... CAP-1
Earlier sketch in CA 11-12
Drzemczewski, Andrew (Zbigniew) 1951- ... 116
D'Souza, Dinesh 1961- ... 118
Dua, R(am) P(arkash) 1930- ... 25-28R
Duan, Le
See Le Duan
Duane, Diane (Elizabeth) 1952- ... SATA 46, 58
Duane, Jim
See Hurley, Vic
Duane, William 1760-1835 ... DLB 43
Duarte (Fuentes), Jose Napoleon
1925-1990 ... 137
Obituary ... 131
Duarte, Joseph S(imon) 1913- ... 57-60
Dubal, David 1944- ... 118
Duball, Michael
See Ald, Roy A(llison)
Duban, James 1951- ... 125
Dubanevich, Arlene 1950- ... 116
See also SATA 56
Dubay, Robert W. 1943- ... 65-68
DuBay, Sandra 1954- ... CANR-23
Earlier sketch in CA 107
Dubay, Thomas Edward 1921- ... CANR-6
Earlier sketch in CA 1-4R
DuBay, William H. 1934- ... 17-20R
Dube, Marcel 1930- ... 129
Brief entry ... 117
See also DLB 53
Dube, Pierre Herbert 1943- ... CANR-10
Earlier sketch in CA 65-68
Dube, Rodolphe
See Hertel, Francois
Dubelaar, Thea 1947- ... SATA 60
Duberman, Lucile 1926- ... 69-72
Duberman, Martin 1930- ... CANR-2
Earlier sketch in CA 1-4R
See also CLC 8
Duberstein, Helen 1926- ... CANR-1
Earlier sketch in CA 45-48
Duberstein, Larry 1944- ... 135
Dubh, Cathal O
See Duff, Charles (St. Lawrence)
Dubie, Norman (Evans) 1945- ... CANR-12
Earlier sketch in CA 69-72
See also CLC 36
See also DLB 120
Dubin, Michael J. 1938- ... 137
Dubin, Robert 1916- ... CANR-1
Earlier sketch in CA 45-48
Dubin, Samuel Sanford 1914- ... 37-40R
Dubinsky, David 1892-1982 Obituary ... 107
Dubinsky, Rostislav (D.) 1923- ... 133
Dubitsky, Cora Marie 1933- ... 124
Dubkin, Lois Knudson 1911- ... 5-8R
du Blane, Daphne
See Groom, Arthur William
Dublin, Jack 1915- ... 21-24R
Dublin, Thomas Louis 1946- ... 101

Dubnick, Mel(vin Jay) 1946- CANR-30
Earlier sketch in CA 112
Dubnick, Randa Kay 1948- 112
Dubofsky, Melvyn 1934- CANR-37
Earlier sketches in CA 49-52, CANR-1, 16
Dubois, Charles
See Counselman, Mary Elizabeth
Du Bois, David G(raham) 1925- 65-68
See also BW
Dubois, Elfrieda T(heresia Pichler) 1916- 9-12R
DuBois, Ellen Carol 1947- 136
Brief entry 113
DuBois, Josiah Ellis Jr. 1912-1983 Obituary 114
Dubois, M.
See Kent, Arthur William Charles
DuBois, Paul M(artin) 1945- 102
DuBois, Paul Z(inkhan) 1936- 111
DuBois, Rochelle (Lynn) Holt 1946- CANR-7
Earlier sketch in CA 57-60
See also Holt, Rochelle L.
DuBois, Rosemary
See Durrant, Rita D(elores)
Du Bois, Shirley Graham 1907(?)-1977 77-80
Obituary 69-72
See also Graham, Shirley
See also BW
See also SATA 24
Du Bois, W(illiam) E(dward) B(urghardt) 1868-1963 ....CANR-34
Earlier sketch in CA 85-88
See also BLC 1
See also BW
See also CDALB 1865-1917
See also CLC 1, 2, 13, 64
See also DLB 47, 50, 91
See also MTCW
See also SATA 42
See also WLC
du Bois, William (Sherman) Pene 1916- CANR-17
Earlier sketch in CA 5-8R
See also CLR 1
See also DLB 61
See also MAICYA
See also SATA 4, 68
Dubos, Jean (Porter) 1918(?)-1988 Obituary 126
Dubos, Rene (Jules) 1901-1982 ....5-8R
Obituary 106
DuBose, Fred 1945- 118
DuBose, LaRocque (Russ) 1926- 21-24R
See also SATA 2
DuBose, Louise Jones 1901- CAP-1
Earlier sketch in CA 13-14
Du Boulay, F(rancis) R(obin) H(oussemayne) 1920- 131
du Boulay, Shirley 1933- 129
Dubout, C(harles) A(lbert) 1905-1976 Obituary 65-68
Dubov, Gwen Bagni 97-100
Dubov, Paul 97-100
Obituary 89-92
DuBow, Fredric L(ee) 1944- 25-28R
Du Breuil, (Elizabeth) L(or)inda 1924-1980 104
DuBrin, Andrew J(ohn) 1935- CANR-33
Earlier sketches in CA 41-44R, CANR-15
Dubro, Alec 1944- 133
Dubro, James (Richard) 1946- 129
Du Broff, Nedra 1931- 110
Du Broff, Sidney 1929- CANR-9
Earlier sketch in CA 21-24R
Dubrovin, Vivian 1931- CANR-9
Earlier sketch in CA 57-60
See also SATA 65
DuBruck, Alfred J(oseph) 1922- 37-40R
DuBruck, Edelgard (Conradt) 1925- 17-20R
Du Brul, Paul 1938(?)-1987 Obituary 125
Dubs, Homer H(asenpflug) 1892-1969 ....CAP-1
Earlier sketch in CA 13-16
Dubus, Andre III 1959- 132
Dubus, Andre 1936- CANR-17
Earlier sketch in CA 21-24R
See also CLC 13, 36
Dubus, Elizabeth Nell 1933- 110
Duby, Georges (Michel Claude) 1919- CANR-22
Earlier sketch in CA 104
Duca Minimo
See D'Annunzio, Gabriele
Du Cane, Peter 1901-1984 Obituary 114
du Cann, Charles Garfield Lott 1889(?)-1983 Obituary 109
Ducas, Dorothy 1905-1987 ....CANR-27
Earlier sketch in CA 5-8R
Ducasse, C(urt) J(ohn) 1881-1969 ....CANR-6
Earlier sketch in CA 1-4R
Duce, Robert 1908- 5-8R
Duchacek, Ivo D(uka) 1913-1988 ....CANR-1
Obituary 124
Earlier sketch in CA 1-4R
See also SATA 55
Du Chaillu, Paul (Belloni) 1835(?)-1903 Brief entry 112
See also SATA 26
Duchamp, (Henri-Robert) Marcel 1887-1968 116
Obituary 110
Ducharme, Rejean 1941- ....DLB 60
Duche, Jean 1915- CANR-9
Earlier sketch in CA 9-12R
Duchein, Michel 1926- 135
Duchene, Louis-Francois 1927- 105
Duchesne, Antoinette
See Paine, Lauran (Bosworth)
Duchesne, Jacques
See Saint-Denis, Michel Jacques
Duchesne, Janet 1930- Brief entry 111
See also SATA 32
Duchess Of Marlborough
See Spencer-Churchill, Laura
Duchess of Windsor
See Windsor, (Bessie) Wallis Warfield (Spencer) Simpson
Duchin, Faye 1944- 125
Duck, Stephen 1705(?)-1756 ....DLB 95
Duckat, Walter Benjamin 1911- 29-32R
Ducker, Bruce 1938- 65-68
Ducker, James H. 1950- 130
Duckert, Mary 1929- 53-56
Duckett, Alfred A. 1917(?)-1984 45-48
Obituary 114
Duckett, Eleanor Shipley 1880(?)-1976 Obituary 69-72
Duckham, A(lec) N(arraway) 1903-1988 73-76
Obituary 126
Duckham, Baron Frederick 1933- 103
Duckworth, Alistair M(cKay) 1936- 41-44R
Duckworth, F(rancis) R(obinson) G(ladstone) 1881-1964 Obituary 113
Duckworth, George E(ckel) 1903-1972 ....CANR-1
Obituary 33-36R
Earlier sketch in CA 1-4R
Duckworth, Leslie Blakey 1904- 105
Ducornet, Erica 1943- CANR-34
Earlier sketches in CA 37-40R, CANR-14
See also SATA 7
Ducornet, Rikki
See Ducornet, Erica
Duda, Margaret B(arbalich) 1941- 65-68
Dudarew-Ossetynski, Leonidas 1911(?)-1989 Obituary 128
Dudden, Arthur P(ower) 1921- CANR-3
Earlier sketch in CA 5-8R
Dudek, Louis 1918- CANR-1
Earlier sketch in CA 45-48
See also CAAS 14
See also CLC 11, 19
See also DLB 88
Dudley, B(illy) J(oseph) 1931- 25-28R
Dudley, Barbara Hudson 1921- 65-68
Dudley, Carl Safford 1932- 116
Dudley, Donald Reynolds 1910-1972 ....CANR-4
Earlier sketch in CA 5-8R
Dudley, Edward 1926- 45-48
Dudley, Ernest 1908- 13-16R
Dudley, Geoffrey A(rthur) 1917- CANR-6
Earlier sketch in CA 13-16R
Dudley, Guilford Jr. 1907- CAP-2
Earlier sketch in CA 19-20
Dudley, Guilford A(llerton) 1921-1972 ....41-44R
Dudley, Helen
See Hope Simpson, Jacynth
Dudley, James F. 1942- 130
Dudley, Jay
See Chapman, J. Dudley
Dudley, Lavinia P(ratt) 1891(?)-1984 Obituary 113
Dudley, Louise 1884- 73-76
Dudley, Martha Ward 1909(?)-1985 Obituary 117
See also SATA 45
Dudley, Nancy
See Cole, Lois Dwight
Dudley, Robert
See Baldwin, James
Dudley, Ruth H(ubbell) 1905- 61-64
See also SATA 11
Dudley Edwards, Ruth 1944- 107
Dudley-Smith, Timothy 1926- 103
Dudman, Richard (Beebe) 1918- 45-48
Due, Linnea A. 1948- 105
See also SATA 64
Dueker, Christopher W(ayne) 1939- 57-60
Dueker, Joyce S(utherlin) 1942- 57-60
Dueland, Joy V(ivian) 106
See also SATA 27
Duell, Charles Halliwell 1905-1970 Obituary 104
Duerig, Alfred W. 1926- 129
Duerr, Edwin 1904- 73-76
Duerrenmatt, Friedrich 1921-1990 ....CANR-33
Earlier sketch in CA 17-20R
See also Durrenmatt, Friedrich
See also CLC 1, 4, 8, 11, 15, 43
See also DLB 69
See also MTCW
Dufallo, Richard 1933- 133
Dufault, Peter Kane 1923- 33-36R
Dufault, Roseanna Lewis 1954- 138
Duff, Annis (James) 1904(?)-1986 Obituary 120
See also SATA 49
Duff, Charles (St. Lawrence) 1894-1966 ....CANR-2
Earlier sketch in CA 1-4R
Duff, David Skene 1912- 128
Brief entry 118
Duff, Ernest A(rthur) 1929- 25-28R
Duff, Gerald 1938- 45-48
Duff, John B. 1931- CANR-1
Earlier sketch in CA 45-48
Duff, Maggie
See Duff, Margaret K.
Duff, Margaret K. CANR-14
Earlier sketch in CA 37-40R
See also SATA 37
Duff, Raymond S(tanley) 1923- 21-24R
Duffee, David E(ugene) 1946- 104
Duffey, Bernard I. 1917- 114
Duffey, Margery 1926- 73-76
Duffield, Anne (Tate) 1893- CAP-1
Earlier sketch in CA 13-16
Duffin, Henry Charles 1884- CAP-1
Earlier sketch in CA 9-10
Duffus, R(obert) L(uther) 1888-1972 101
Obituary 37-40R
Duffy, Ben
See Duffy, Bernard C.
Duffy, Bernard C. 1902-1972 Obituary 37-40R
Duffy, Bruce ....CLC 50
Duffy, Carol Ann 1955- 119
Duffy, Charles 1940- 104
Duffy, Clinton T(ruman) 1898-1982 Obituary 108
Duffy, Dennis 1938- 113
Duffy, Edmund 1899-1962 Obituary 93-96
Duffy, Elizabeth 1904- CAP-2
Earlier sketch in CA 19-20
Duffy, Francis R(amon) 1915- CANR-30
Earlier sketch in CA 49-52
Duffy, Helene (Krainovich) 1926- 17-20R
Duffy, James (Edward) 1923- 129
Duffy, James H(enry) 1934- 131
Duffy, John J(oseph) 1934- 57-60
Duffy, John 1915- CANR-8
Earlier sketch in CA 17-20R
Duffy, Maureen 1933- CANR-33
Earlier sketch in CA 25-28R
See also CLC 37
See also DLB 14
See also MTCW
Duffy, Regis Anthony 1934- 110
Dufrechou, Carole
See Monroe, Carole
Dufresne, Isabelle 1935- 136
Dufty, William 1916- 65-68
Dugan, Alan 1923- 81-84
See also CLC 2, 6
See also DLB 5
Dugan, George 1909-1982 Obituary 107
Dugan, J(ohn) Raymond 1935- 121
Dugan, Jack
See Butterworth, W(illiam) E(dmund III)
Dugan, James (Thomas) 1912-1967 ....CANR-4
Earlier sketch in CA 5-8R
Dugan, Michael (Gray) 1947- CANR-32
Earlier sketches in CA 77-80, CANR-14
See also SATA 15
Dugard, C. J(ohn) R. 1936- 85-88
du Gard, Roger Martin
See Martin du Gard, Roger
Dugas, Marcel 1883-1947 ....DLB 92
Dugdale, Robert
See Hardy, Henry
Duggan, Alfred Leo 1903-1964 73-76
See also SATA 25
Duggan, George Henry 1912- 17-20R
Duggan, Joseph J(ohn) 1938- 29-32R
Duggan, Mary M. 1921- 25-28R
Duggan, Maurice (Noel) 1922-1974 ....CANR-17
Obituary 53-56
Earlier sketch in CA 73-76
See also SATA 30, 40
Duggan, William Redman 1915- 69-72
Duggan, William 1952- 122
Duggans, Pat
See Connolly, Robert D(uggan Jr.)
Dugger, Ronnie 1930- CANR-12
Earlier sketch in CA 21-24R
Duggins, James (Harry) Jr. 1933- 37-40R
Dughi, Nancy 1-4R
Dugmore, Clifford W(illiam) 1909-1990 ....13-16R
Obituary 132
Duguid, Charles 1884- 109
Duguid, John Bright 1895-1980 Obituary 102
Duguid, Robert
See Pring-Mill, Robert D(uguid) F(orrest)
Duhamel, Georges 1884-1966 ....CANR-35
Obituary 25-28R
Earlier sketch in CA 81-84
See also CLC 8
See also DLB 65
See also MTCW
Duhamel, Marcel 1900(?)-1977 Obituary 104
Duhamel, P(ierre) Albert 1920- 5-8R
du Hault, Jean
See Grindel, Eugene
Duhl, Leonard J. 1926- 13-16R
Duignan, Peter 1926- CANR-11
Earlier sketch in CA 13-16R
Duiker, William J(ohn) 1932- CANR-16
Earlier sketch in CA 85-88
Duis, Perry R. 1943- 124
Dujardin, Edouard (Emile Louis) 1861-1949 Brief entry 109
See also TCLC 13
du Jardin, Rosamond Neal 1902-1963 ....1-4R
Obituary 103
See also SATA 2
Duka, Ivo
See Duchacek, Ivo D(uka)
Duka, John 1949-1989 Obituary 127
Dukakis, Katharine 1937(?)- 135
Dukakis, Kitty
See Dukakis, Katharine
Duke, Alvah (Carter) 1908- 45-48
Duke, Anna Marie 1946- 130
Duke, Benjamin 1931- 49-52
Duke, Charles (Richard) 1940- CANR-28
Earlier sketches in CA 69-72, CANR-11
Duke, David C. 1940- 112
Duke, Donald Norman 1929- CANR-7
Earlier sketch in CA 17-20R
Duke, Forrest R(eagan) 1918- 77-80
Duke, James A. 1929- 135
Duke, James T(aylor) 1933- 65-68
Duke, Jim
See Duke, James A.
Duke, John
See Chalmers, Floyd S(herman)
Duke, Judith S(ilverman) 1934- 118
Duke, Madelaine (Elizabeth) 1925- CANR-9
Earlier sketch in CA 57-60
Duke, Martin 1930- 138
Duke, Maurice 1934- 112
Duke, Michael Geoffrey Hare
See Hare Duke, Michael Geoffrey
Duke, Michael S. 1940- 136
Duke, Patty
See Duke, Anna Marie
Duke, Richard DeLaBarre 1930- 57-60
Duke, Robin (Antony Hare) 1916-1984 Obituary 115
Duke, Simon (William) 1959- 127
Duke, Vernon 1903-1969 ....CAP-2
Earlier sketch in CA 29-32
Duke, Will
See Gault, William Campbell
Duke-Elder, Stewart 1896-1978 Obituary 77-80
Dukelsky, Vladimir
See Duke, Vernon
Duke of Beaufort
See Somerset, Henry Hugh Arthur FitzRoy
Duker, Abraham G(ordon) 1907- 53-56
Duker, Sam 1905-1978 ....13-16R
Obituary 77-80
Dukert, Joseph M(ichael) 1929- CANR-3
Earlier sketch in CA 5-8R
Dukes, Ashley 1885-1959 Brief entry 110
See also DLB 10
Dukes, Paul 1889-1967 Obituary 112
Dukes, Paul 1934- CANR-9
Earlier sketch in CA 21-24R
Dukes, Philip
See Bickers, Richard Leslie Townshend
Dukes, Tyrone 1946(?)-1983 Obituary 110
Dukore, Bernard F. 1931- CANR-29
Earlier sketches in CA 25-28R, CANR-12
Dukore, Margaret Mitchell 1950- CANR-23
Earlier sketch in CA 106
Dulac, Edmund 1882-1953 ....SATA 19
Dulack, Thomas 1935- 25-28R
Dulany, Don E. Jr. 1928- 69-72
Dulany, Harris 1940- 33-36R
Dulieu, Jean
See van Oort, Jan
Dull, Jonathan R(omer) 1942- 69-72
Dulles, Allen W(elsh) 1893-1969 ....CAP-2
Earlier sketch in CA 23-24
Dulles, Avery (Robert) 1918- CANR-21
Earlier sketches in CA 9-12R, CANR-3
Dulles, Eleanor Lansing 1895- 9-12R
Dulles, Foster Rhea 1900-1970 ....CAP-1
Obituary 29-32R
Earlier sketch in CA 13-14
Dulles, John Foster 1888-1959 Brief entry 115
Dulles, John W(atson) F(oster) 1913- CANR-1
Earlier sketch in CA 1-4R
Duloup, Victor
See Volkoff, Vladimir
Dulsey, Bernard M. 1914- 9-12R
Duman, Daniel 1948- 129
Dumarchais, Pierre 1882-1970 Obituary 29-32R
Dumarchey, Pierre
See Dumarchais, Pierre
Dumas, Alexandre (Davy de la Pailleterie) 1802-1870 ....DLB 119
See also SATA 18
See also WLC
Dumas, Alexandre 1824-1895 ....DC 1
Dumas, Andre 1918- CANR-29
Earlier sketches in CA 73-76, CANR-13
Dumas, Claire
See Van Weddingen, Marthe
Dumas, Claudine
See Malzberg, Barry N(athaniel)
du Mas, Frank (Maurice) 1918- 106
Dumas, Frederic 1913- 69-72
Dumas, Gerald J. 1930- 25-28R
Dumas, Henry L. 1934-1968 85-88
See also BW
See also CLC 6, 62
See also DLB 41
Dumas, Jacqueline 1946- 123
See also SATA 55
Dumas, Philippe 1940- 107
See also SATA 52
du Maurier, Daphne 1907-1989 ....CANR-6
Obituary 128
Earlier sketch in CA 5-8R
See also CLC 6, 11, 59
See also MTCW
See also SATA 27, 60
Dumbauld, Edward 1905- 129
Dumbleton, William A(lbert) 1927- 37-40R
Dumenil, Lynn 1950- 125
Dumery, Henry 1920- 101
Dumezil, Georges (Edmond Raoul) 1898-1986 Obituary 120
Dumitriu, Petru 1924- Brief entry 116
Dumke, Edward J. 1946- 124
Dumke, Glenn S. 1917-1989 ....CANR-31
Obituary 129
Earlier sketch in CA 112
Dummett, (Agnes Margaret) Ann 1930- 135
Dummett, Michael Anthony Eardley 1925- 102
Dumond, Dwight Lowell 1895-1976 69-72
Obituary 65-68
Dumont, Jean-Paul 1940- CANR-12
Earlier sketch in CA 73-76
Dumoulin, Heinrich 1905- CANR-4
Earlier sketch in CA 5-8R
Dumpleton, John Le F(evre) 1924- 13-16R
Dumpty, Humpty S.
See Denenberg, Herbert S(idney)
Dun, Angus 1892-1971 Obituary 33-36R
Dun, Mao
See Yen-Ping, Shen

Dunant, Sarah 1950- 131
Dunas, Joseph C. 1900- 17-20R
Dunathan, Arni T(homas) 1936- 53-56
Dunaway, David King 1948- 107
Dunaway, John M(arson) 1945- 89-92
Dunayevskaya, Raya 1910-1987 130
Obituary 122
Dunbabin, J(ohn) P(aul) D(elacour) 1938- 69-72
Dunbabin, Jean 1939- 119
Dunbar, Alice
See Nelson, Alice Ruth Moore Dunbar
Dunbar, Alice Moore
See Nelson, Alice Ruth Moore Dunbar
Dunbar, Charles Stuart 1900- 107
Dunbar, David
See Baxter, Craig
Dunbar, Dorothy 1923- 9-12R
Dunbar, Edward
See Smith, David MacLeod
Dunbar, Ernest 1927- 25-28R
Dunbar, Janet 1901-1989(?) CANR-6
Obituary 129
Earlier sketch in CA 9-12R
Dunbar, John Greenwell 1930- 21-24R
Dunbar, Leslie W(allace) 1921- 125
Dunbar, Maxwell John 1914- 103
Dunbar, Paul Laurence 1872-1906 124
Brief entry 104
See also BLC 1
See also BW
See also CDALB 1865-1917
See also DLB 50, 54, 78
See also PC 5
See also SATA 34
See also SSC 8
See also TCLC 2, 12
See also WLC
Dunbar, Robert E(verett) 1926- CANR-34
Earlier sketches in CA 85-88, CANR-15
See also SATA 32
Dunbar, Robert George 1907- 114
Dunbar, Tony 1949- 33-36R
Dunbar, Willis F(rederick) 1902-1970 .... CANR-4
Earlier sketch in CA 5-8R
Dunbar-Nelson, Alice
See Nelson, Alice Ruth Moore Dunbar
Dunbar-Nelson, Alice Moore
See Nelson, Alice Ruth Moore Dunbar
Dunbaugh, Frank Montgomery 1895- 45-48
Duncan, A(nthony) D(ouglas) 1930- 33-36R
Duncan, Alastair 1942- 117
Duncan, Alex
See Duke, Madelaine (Elizabeth)
Duncan, Alistair (Charteris) 1927- 61-64
Duncan, Archibald A(lexander) M(cBeth) 1926- 81-84
Duncan, Ardinelle Bean 1913- 1-4R
Duncan, (Reid) Bingham 1911- 85-88
Duncan, Bowie 1941- 33-36R
Duncan, C(yril) J(ohn) 1916- 25-28R
Duncan, Carl P(orter) 1921- Brief entry 115
Duncan, Charles T(homas) 1914- 17-20R
Duncan, Chester 1913- 93-96
Duncan, Clyde H. 1903- 17-20R
Duncan, David Douglas 1916- Brief entry 112
See also AITN 1
Duncan, David 1913- 5-8R
Duncan, Dayton 1949- 127
Duncan, Delbert J(ames) 1895- 41-44R
Duncan, Denis (Macdonald) 1920- CANR-23
Earlier sketch in CA 107
Duncan, Dora Angela
See Duncan, Isadora
Duncan, Dougal 1921- 102
Duncan, Elmer H(ubert) 1933- 69-72
Duncan, Florence Belle 1917(?)-1980 Obituary 97-100
Duncan, (Sandy) Frances (Mary) 1942- CANR-37
Earlier sketches in CA 97-100, CANR-17
See also SATA 48
Duncan, George
See Davison, Geoffrey
Duncan, Gregory
See McClintock, Marshall
Duncan, Helen (Harger Bodwell) 1902- 125
Duncan, Hugh Dalziel 1909-1970 .... CAP-2
Earlier sketch in CA 23-24
Duncan, Irma 1897-1977 49-52
Obituary 73-76
Duncan, Isadora 1878(?)-1927 Brief entry 118
Duncan, Jane
See Cameron, Elizabeth Jane
Duncan, Jennifer Ann 1940-1989 Obituary 128
Duncan, Joseph E(llis) 1921- 5-8R
Duncan, Julia Coley
See Sather, Julia Coley Duncan
Duncan, Julia K. CANR-27
Earlier sketches in CAP-2, CA 19-20
See also SATA 1
Duncan, Kenneth S(andilands) 1912- 9-12R
Duncan, Kunigunde 1886- 5-8R
Duncan, Lois 1934- CANR-36
Earlier sketches in CA 1-4R, CANR-2, 23
See also AAYA 4
See also CLC 26
See also MAICYA
See also SAAS 2
See also SATA 1, 36
Duncan, Marion Moncure 1913-1978 Obituary 77-80
Duncan, Mark (Winchester) 1952- 130
Duncan, Norman 1871-1916 Brief entry 117
See also DLB 92
See also YABC 1
Duncan, Otis Dudley 1921- CANR-22
Earlier sketches in CA 13-16R, CANR-6
Duncan, Pam 1938- 37-40R
Duncan, Pope A(lexander) 1920- 13-16R
Duncan, Quince 1940- .... HW
Duncan, Robert (Edward) 1919-1988 .... CANR-28
Obituary 124
Earlier sketch in CA 9-12R
See also CLC 1, 2, 4, 7, 15, 41, 55
See also DLB 5, 16
See also MTCW
See also PC 2
Duncan, Robert F. 1890(?)-1974 Obituary 53-56
Duncan, Robert L(ipscomb) 1927- 106
See also CAAS 2
Duncan, Ronald 1914-1982 .... CANR-4
Obituary 107
Earlier sketch in CA 5-8R
See also DLB 13
Duncan, Sara Jeannette 1861-1922 .... DLB 92
Duncan, T. Bentley 1929- 77-80
Duncan, Theodore G(arfield) 1928- 128
Duncan, Thomas (William) 1905- CANR-1
Earlier sketch in CA 1-4R
Duncan, W(illiam) Murdoch 1909-1976 .... CANR-6
Earlier sketch in CA 13-16R
Duncan, W. R.
See Duncan, Robert L(ipscomb)
Duncan, W. Raymond 1936- 41-44R
Duncan, Wilbur H(oward) 1910- 116
Duncan, William (Robert) 1944- 115
Duncanson, Michael E(dward) 1948- 57-60
Duncombe, David C(ameron) 1928- 29-32R
Duncombe, Frances (Riker) 1900- 25-28R
See also SATA 25
Dundee, Robert
See Kirsch, Robert R.
Dundes, Alan 1934- CANR-26
Earlier sketches in CA 21-24R, CANR-9
Dundy, Elaine 1937- 97-100
Dunford, Judith 1933- 107
Dungan, David L(aird) 1936- 123
Dunham, Arthur 1893- 33-36R
Dunham, Barrows 1905- 5-8R
Dunham, Bob
See Dunham, Robert
Dunham, Donald Carl 1908- CANR-17
Earlier sketch in CA 1-4R
Dunham, H(enry) Warren 1906-1985 .... CANR-8
Obituary 118
Earlier sketch in CA 13-16R
Dunham, John L. 1939- 29-32R
Dunham, Katherine 1910- CANR-17
Earlier sketch in CA 65-68
See also BW
Dunham, Lowell 1910- 37-40R
Dunham, (Bertha) Mabel 1881-1957 Brief entry 114
Dunham, Mikel 1948- 138
Dunham, Montrew Goetz 1919- 17-20R
Dunham, Robert 1931- 69-72
Dunham, William Huse Jr. 1901- 49-52
Dunham, William 1947- 133
Dunhill, Alfred H(enry) 1896(?)-1971 Obituary 104
Dunhill, Mary 1907(?)-1988 Obituary 124
Dunkel, Harold Baker 1912- 5-8R
Dunkel, Richard H(adley) 1933- 73-76
Dunkell, Samuel (V.) 1919- Brief entry 115
Dunkelman, Ben(jamin) 1913- Brief entry 111
Dunkerley, Elsie Jeanette Obituary 116
Dunkerley, James 1953- 131
Dunkerley, Roderic 1884- CAP-1
Earlier sketch in CA 13-14
Dunkin, Paul S(haner) 1905-1975 .... CAP-2
Earlier sketch in CA 33-36
Dunkle, William F(rederick) Jr. 1911- 53-56
Dunkley, Christopher 1944- 121
Dunkling, Leslie Alan 1935- CANR-14
Earlier sketch in CA 81-84
Dunkman, William E(dward) 1903- CAP-2
Earlier sketch in CA 25-28
Dunlap, Aurie N(ichols) 1907-1977 .... 37-40R
Dunlap, G(eorge) D(ale) 1923- 49-52
Dunlap, Jan 65-68
Dunlap, Jane
See Davis, Adelle
Dunlap, John 1747-1812 .... DLB 43
Dunlap, Joseph R(iggs) 1913- 85-88
Dunlap, Leslie W(hittaker) 1911- 37-40R
Dunlap, Lon
See McCormick, Wilfred
Dunlap, Orrin E(lmer) Jr. 1896-1970 .... CAP-1
Earlier sketch in CA 11-12
Dunlap, Thomas R(ichard) 1943- 126
Dunlap, William 1766-1839 .... DLB 30, 37, 59
Dunlay, Thomas W. 1944- 112
Dunleavy, Gareth W(inthrop) 1923- 33-36R
Dunleavy, Janet Egleson 1928- CANR-21
Earlier sketches in CA 57-60, CANR-6
Dunleavy, Patrick 1952- 123
Dunlop, Agnes M. R. CANR-9
Earlier sketch in CA 13-16R
Dunlop, Derrick Melville 1902-1980 Obituary 101
Dunlop, Douglas Morton 1909-1987 Obituary 123
Dunlop, Eileen (Rhona) 1938- CANR-32
Earlier sketches in CA 73-76, CANR-14
See also MAICYA
See also SAAS 12
See also SATA 24
Dunlop, Ian G(eoffrey) D(avid) 1925- CANR-24
Earlier sketches in CA 9-12R, CANR-5
Dunlop, John B. 1942- 57-60
Dunlop, John Thomas 1914- CANR-5
Earlier sketch in CA 13-16R
Dunlop, Richard (B.) 1921- CANR-25
Earlier sketches in CA 17-20R, CANR-7
Dunlop, Robert 1953- 116
Dunlop, William Tiger 1792-1848 .... DLB 99
Dunmore, John 1923- CANR-23
Earlier sketch in CA 106
Dunmore, Spencer (Sambrook) 1928- CANR-13
Earlier sketch in CA 33-36R
Dunmore, Timothy 1948- 129
Dunn, Alan (Cantwell) 1900-1974 .... CAP-2
Obituary 49-52
Earlier sketch in CA 33-36
Dunn, Carola 1946- 118
Dunn, Catherine M(ary) 1930- 37-40R
Dunn, Charles W(illiam) 1915- 49-52
Dunn, Delmer D(elano) 1941- 25-28R
Dunn, Dennis J(ohn) 1942- 129
Dunn, Donald H(arley) 1929- 33-36R
Dunn, Douglas (Eaglesham) 1942- CANR-33
Earlier sketches in CA 45-48, CANR-2
See also CLC 6, 40
See also DLB 40
See also MTCW
Dunn, Edgar S(treeter) Jr. 1921- 9-12R
Dunn, Edward D. 1883(?)-1978 Obituary 77-80
Dunn, Esther Cloudman 1891-1977 Obituary 73-76
Dunn, Ethel (Deikman) 1932- 21-24R
Dunn, Frederick Sherwood 1893-1962 Obituary 113
Dunn, Halbert Louis 1896-1975 Obituary 61-64
Dunn, (Henry) Hampton 1916- 57-60
Dunn, Harold 1929- 9-12R
Dunn, Harris
See Doerffler, Alfred
Dunn, Harvey T(homas) 1884-1952 .... SATA 34
Dunn, Hugh Patrick 1916- 122
Dunn, James
See Wilkes-Hunter, R(ichard)
Dunn, James D(ouglas Grant) 1939- 73-76
Dunn, James Taylor 1912- CANR-20
Earlier sketches in CA 5-8R, CANR-4
Dunn, Jean 1921- 109
Dunn, Jerry G. 1916- CANR-11
Earlier sketch in CA 21-24R
Dunn, John (Montfort) 1940- CANR-11
Earlier sketch in CA 69-72
Dunn, Joseph (Willcox Jr.) 1937- 122
Dunn, Judith F.
See Bernal, Judith F.
Dunn, Judy
See Spangenberg, Judith Dunn
Dunn, Katherine (Karen) 1945- 33-36R
See also CLC 71
Dunn, Kaye
See Dunham, Katherine
Dunn, Lloyd W. 1906-1991 57-60
Obituary 134
Dunn, Marion Herndon 1920- 29-32R
Dunn, Mary Lois 1930- CANR-12
Earlier sketch in CA 61-64
See also SATA 6
Dunn, Mary Maples 1931- 114
Dunn, Nell
See Sandford, Nell Mary
Dunn, Patience (Louise Ralli) 1922- 5-8R
Dunn, Peter N(orman) 1926- 122
Dunn, Richard S(lator) 1928- 134
Brief entry 112
Dunn, Ronald (Louis) 1936- Brief entry 120
Dunn, S. P.
See Dunn, Stephen P(orter)
Dunn, Samuel Watson 1918- CANR-5
Earlier sketch in CA 1-4R
Dunn, Si 1944- 77-80
Dunn, Stephen P(orter) 1928- 124
Dunn, Stephen 1939- CANR-12
Earlier sketch in CA 33-36R
See also CLC 36
See also DLB 105
Dunn, Stuart 1900- 57-60
Dunn, Thomas G(eorge) 1950- 119
Dunn, Thomas Tinsley 1901- 107
Dunn, Waldo H(ilary) 1882-1969 .... CAP-2
Earlier sketch in CA 21-22
Dunn, Walter Scott Jr. 1928- 101
Dunn, William J. 1906- 33-36R
Dunn, William L(awrence Jr.) 1924- 37-40R
Dunn, William Robert 1916- 113
Dunnahoo, Terry 1927- CANR-31
Earlier sketches in CA 41-44R, CANR-14
See also SATA 7
Dunnam, Maxie D(enton) 1934- 73-76
Dunnan, Nancy 1941- 112
Dunne, Colin 1937- 123
Dunne, Dominick 1925- 121
See also BEST 89:1, 90:4
Dunne, Finley Peter 1867-1936 Brief entry 108
See also DLB 11, 23
See also TCLC 28
Dunne, George H(arold) 1905- CANR-5
Earlier sketch in CA 1-4R
Dunne, Gerald T. 1919- CANR-1
Earlier sketch in CA 45-48
Dunne, John Gregory 1932- CANR-14
Earlier sketch in CA 25-28R
See also CLC 28
See also DLBY 80
Dunne, John S(cribner) 1929- 13-16R
Dunne, (Christopher) Lee 1934- 120
Dunne, Mary Collins 1914- CANR-14
Earlier sketch in CA 41-44R
See also SATA 11
Dunne, Mary Jo
See Dunne, Mary Collins
Dunne, Philip 1908- CANR-11
Earlier sketches in CAP-1, CA 9-10
See also DLB 26
Dunne, Phillip 1908-1992 Obituary 137
Dunne, Robert Williams 1895-1977 Obituary 69-72
Dunnell, Robert C(hester) 1942- 89-92
Dunner, Joseph 1908-1978 .... CANR-14
Earlier sketch in CA 21-24R
Dunnett, Alastair M(acTavish) 1908- 65-68
Dunnett, Dorothy 1923- CANR-3
Earlier sketch in CA 1-4R
Dunnett, Margaret (Rosalind) 1909-1977 108
See also SATA 42
Dunnigan, Alice Allison 1906-1983 125
Obituary 109
See also BW
Dunning, Brad 1957- 102
Dunning, Bruce 1940- 77-80
Dunning, Chester S(idney) L(arson) 1949- 116
Dunning, Edward
See Gilbert, R(obert) A(ndrew)
Dunning, Eric (Geoffrey) 1936- 116
Dunning, John H(arry) 1927- CANR-21
Earlier sketch in CA 104
Dunning, John 1942- CANR-16
Earlier sketch in CA 93-96
Dunning, Lawrence 1931- 77-80
Dunning, Ralph Cheever 1878-1930 Brief entry 107
See also DLB 4
Dunning, Robert William 1938- CANR-20
Earlier sketches in CA 53-56, CANR-5
Dunning, (Arthur) Stephen (Jr.) 1924- CANR-12
Earlier sketch in CA 25-28R
Dunning, William A. 1857-1922 .... DLB 17
Dunnington, Hazel Brain 1912- 21-24R
du Nouey, Pierre (-Andre-Leon) Lecomte
See Lecomte du Nouey, Pierre (-Andre-Leon)
Dunoyer, Maurice
See Domergue, Maurice
Dunoyer De Segonzac, Andre 1884-1974 Obituary 53-56
Dunphy, Jack 1914- 25-28R
Obituary 137
Dunrea, Olivier Jean-Paul Dominique 1953- 124
See also SATA 46, 59
Dunsany, Edward John Moreton Drax Plunkett 1878-1957 Brief entry 104
See also Dunsany, Lord
and Lord Dunsany
See also DLB 10
Dunsany, Lord
See Dunsany, Edward John Moreton Drax Plunkett
See also DLB 77
See also TCLC 2
Dunsheath, Joyce (Houchen) 1902- 5-8R
Dunsheath, Percy 1886- 107
Dunsmore, Roger 1938- 110
Dunson, Josh 1941- 25-28R
Duns Scotus, John 1266(?)-1308 .... DLB 115
Dunstan, Andrew
See Chandler, A(rthur) Bertram
Dunstan, Don(ald Allan) 1926- 110
Dunstan, G(ordon) R(eginald) 1917- 130
Dunstan, Reginald (Ernest) 1914- 21-24R
Dunster, Mark 1927- 85-88
Dunsterville, G(alfrid) C. K. 1905-1988 .... CAP-1
Obituary 127
Earlier sketch in CA 9-10
Dunston, Arthur John 1922- 109
Dunton, (Arnold) Davidson 1912-1987 Obituary 121
Dunton, Samuel Cady 1910(?)-1975 Obituary 61-64
Dupasquier, Philippe 1955- 130
Dupea, Bobby
See Crawley, Tony
Dupee, F(rederick) W(ilcox) 1904-1979 .... CAP-1
Obituary 85-88
Earlier sketch in CA 13-14
du Perry, Jean
See Simenon, Georges (Jacques Christian)
Dupin, August Dupont
See Taylor, John (Alfred)
Dupin, Jacques 1927- Brief entry 119
Duplessis, Yves
See Duplessis, Yvonne
Duplessis, Yvonne 1912- CANR-3
Earlier sketch in CA 9-12R
Dupont, Jacques 1915- 130
Dupont, Judith (Eva Maria) 1925- 136
Dupont, Paul
See Frewin, Leslie Ronald
DuPont, Robert L(ouis) Jr. 1936- 125
Dupre, Catherine CANR-16
Earlier sketch in CA 25-28R
Dupre, J(osef) Stefan 1936- 102
Dupre, Louis CANR-39
Earlier sketches in CA 9-12R, CANR-3, 18
Dupree, A(nderson) Hunter 1921- 9-12R
Dupree, Louis 1925- CANR-28
Earlier sketch in CA 41-44R
Dupree, Robert S(cott) 1940- 125
Dupres, Henri
See Fawcett, F(rank) Dubrez
Duprey, Richard A(llen) 1929- CANR-6
Earlier sketch in CA 5-8R
Dupuis, Adrian M(aurice) 1919- 9-12R
Dupuy, Arnold C. 1962- 135
Dupuy, R(ichard) Ernest 1887-1975 .... CANR-6
Obituary 57-60
Earlier sketch in CA 1-4R
Dupuy, T(revor) N(evitt) 1916- CANR-18
Earlier sketches in CA 1-4R, CANR-2
See also SATA 4

Durac, Jack
See Rachman, Stanley Jack
Durack, Mary 1913- CANR-17
Earlier sketch in CA 97-100
Duram, James C(arl) 1939- CANR-4
Earlier sketch in CA 53-56
Duran, Gloria Diana Bradley 1924- 107
Duran, Manuel E. 1925- CANR-11
Earlier sketch in CA 25-28R
Duran, Richard (Paul) 1943- 114
Duran, Roberto (Tinoco) 1953- 131
See also HW
Durand, G. Forbes
See Burgess, M(ichael) R(oy)
Durand, John Dana 1913-1981 ....CANR-9
Earlier sketch in CA 61-64
Durand, Loup 1933- 124
Durand, Loyal Jr. 1902-1970 ....CAP-2
Earlier sketch in CA 21-22
Durand, Lucile
See Bersianik, Louky
Durand, Robert 1944- 57-60
Durandeaux, Jacques 1926- 25-28R
Durang, Christopher (Ferdinand) 1949- 105
See also CLC 27, 38
Durant, Ariel K(aufman) 1898-1981 ....CANR-4
Obituary 105
Earlier sketch in CA 9-12R
Durant, David N(orton) 1925- 77-80
Durant, Frederick C(lark) III 1916- 113
Durant, Henry 1902-1982 Obituary 107
Durant, John 1902- CANR-5
Earlier sketch in CA 9-12R
See also SATA 27
Durant, Stuart 1932- 104
Durant, Will(iam James) 1885-1981 ....CANR-4
Obituary 105
Earlier sketch in CA 9-12R
See also MTCW
Durante, James Francis
1893-1980 Obituary 93-96
Durante, Jimmy
See Durante, James Francis
Duranti (Rossi), (Maria) Francesca 1935- 133
Duranty, Walter 1884-1957 ....DLB 29
Duras, Marguerite 1914- 25-28R
See also CLC 3, 6, 11, 20, 34, 40, 68
See also DLB 83
See also MTCW
Duratschek, (Mary) Claudia 1894- 37-40R
Duratschek, Sister Mary Claudia
See Duratschek, (Mary) Claudia
Durbahn, Walter E. 1895(?)-1981 Obituary 102
Durban, (Rosa) Pam 1947- 123
See also CLC 39
Durband, Alan 1927- CANR-20
Earlier sketches in CA 5-8R, CANR-2
Durbin, Brice 1899(?)-1983 Obituary 111
Durbin, Mary Lou 1927- 21-24R
Durbin, Richard Louis 1928- CANR-7
Earlier sketch in CA 53-56
Durbridge, Francis (Henry) 1912- CANR-24
Earlier sketches in CA 77-80, CANR-6
Durcan, Paul 1944- 134
See also CLC 43, 70
Durden, Robert Franklin 1925- 9-12R
Durell, Ann 1930- 136
See also SATA 66
Durey, Michael (John) 1947- 107
Durfee, David A(rthur) 1929- 29-32R
Durfey, Thomas 1653-1723 ....DLB 80
Durgnat, Raymond (Eric) 1932- 17-20R
Durham, David
See Vickers, Roy
Durham, Frank (Edington) 1935- 114
Durham, John
See Paine, Lauran (Bosworth)
Durham, John I 1933- CANR-13
Earlier sketch in CA 29-32R
Durham, John 1925- 107
Durham, Mae
See Roger, Mae Durham
Durham, Marilyn 1930- 49-52
Durham, Philip 1912-1977 ....CANR-7
Earlier sketch in CA 9-12R
Durka, Gloria 1939- CANR-14
Earlier sketch in CA 65-68
Durkee, Mary C. 1921- 13-16R
Durkin, Barbara W(ernecke) 1944- 123
Durkin, Henry P(aul) 1940- 53-56
Durkin, Joseph Thomas 1903- CAP-1
Earlier sketch in CA 11-12
Durland, Frances Caldwell 1892- 113
Durland, William R(eginald) 1931- CANR-7
Earlier sketch in CA 57-60
Durnbaugh, Donald F. 1927- CANR-8
Earlier sketch in CA 21-24R
Durnin, Richard G(erry) 1920- 110
Durning, Addis
See Ranzini, Addis Durning
Duroche, Leonard L(eRoy) 1933- 37-40R
DuRocher, Richard J(ames) 1955- 118
Duroselle, Jean-Baptiste (Marie Lucien Charles)
1917- CANR-18
Earlier sketches in CA 9-12R, CANR-3
Durr, Fred
See Durr, Frederick R(oland) E(ugene)
Durr, Frederick R(oland) E(ugene)
1921-1978 ....37-40R
Durr, William Kirtley 1924- 13-16R
Durrani, Mahmood Khan 1914- CAP-1
Earlier sketch in CA 13-14
Durrant, Digby 1926- CANR-13
Earlier sketch in CA 21-24R
Durrant, Rita D(elores) 108
Durrant, Theo
See Offord, Lenore Glen
Durrell, Donald D(e Witt) 1903- CANR-8
Earlier sketch in CA 17-20R
Durrell, Gerald (Malcolm) 1925- CANR-25
Earlier sketches in CA 5-8R, CANR-4
See also MTCW
See also SATA 8
Durrell, Jacqueline Sonia Rasen 1929- 21-24R
Durrell, Jacquie
See Durrell, Jacqueline Sonia Rasen
Durrell, Lawrence (George) 1912-1990 ....9-12R
Obituary 132
See also CDBLB 1945-1960
See also CLC 1, 4, 6, 8, 13, 27, 41
See also DLB 15, 27
See also DLBY 90
See also MTCW
Durrell, Zoe C(ompton) 1910- 89-92
Durrenberger, Robert Warren 1918- CANR-10
Earlier sketch in CA 21-24R
Durrenmatt, Friedrich
See Duerrenmatt, Friedrich
See also CLC 1, 4, 8, 11, 15, 43
See also DLB 69
Durslag, Melvin 1921- 101
Durst, Paul 1921- 21-24R
d'Urstelle, Pierre
See Dorst, Jean (Pierre)
Durville, Hector 1849-1923 Brief entry 117
Dury, George H(arry) 1916- 113
Duryee, Mary Ballard 1896-1988 Obituary 125
Durzak, Manfred 1938- CANR-1
Earlier sketch in CA 49-52
du Sautoy, Peter (Francis De Courcy)
1921- 5-8R
Dusay, Katherine M(ulholland) 1943- 118
Duscha, Julius (Carl) 1924- 73-76
Dusenberry, William Howard 1908- CAP-1
Earlier sketch in CA 19-20
Dusenbury, Winifred L.
See Frazer, Winifred L(oesch)
Dushkin, Alexander M(ordecai)
1890-1976 Obituary 65-68
Dushnitzky-Shner, Sara 1913- 29-32R
Duska, Ronald 1937- 97-100
Duskin, Ruthie
See Feldman, Ruth Duskin
Dusky, Lorraine 1942- 85-88
Du Soe, Robert C. 1892-1958 ....YABC 2
d'Usseau, Arnaud 1916-1990 Obituary 130
Dussel, Enrique D. 1934- 89-92
Dussere, Carol
See Dussere, Carolyn T(homas)
Dussere, Carolyn T(homas) 1942- 103
Dussinger, John A(ndrew) 1935- 113
Duster, Alfreda Barnett
1904-1983 Obituary 109
Duster, Troy 1936- 29-32R
Dustin, Charles
See Giesy, J(ohn) U(lrich)
Duthie, Charles S. 1911- CAP-2
Earlier sketch in CA 29-32
Dutile, Fernand N(eville) 1940- 107
Dutourd, Jean (Hubert) 1920- CANR-31
Earlier sketch in CA 65-68
Dutt, R(ajani) Palme 1896-1974 ....CAP-1
Obituary 53-56
Earlier sketch in CA 11-12
Dutta, Reginald 1914- 61-64
Dutta, Rex
See Dutta, Reginald
Dutton, Bertha P(auline) 1903- 122
Brief entry 117
Dutton, Diana B. 1943- 129
Dutton, Frederick G(ary) 1923- Brief entry 111
Dutton, Geoffrey (Piers Henry) 1922- CANR-17
Earlier sketches in CA 45-48, CANR-1
Dutton, H(arold) I. Obituary 116
Dutton, Joan Parry 1908- 9-12R
Dutton, John M(ason) 1926- 41-44R
Dutton, Mary 1922- 33-36R
Dutton, Paul 1943- CANR-31
Earlier sketch in CA 112
Dutton, Ralph (Stawell) 1898-1985 ....13-16R
Obituary 116
Dutton, Richard Edward 1929- Brief entry 106
Dutz
See Davis, Mary Octavia
Duun, Olav 1876-1939 Brief entry 121
Duus, Masayo 1938- 89-92
Duus, Peter 1933- 25-28R
DuVal, F(rancis) Alan 1916- 33-36R
Duval, Jean-Jacques 1930- 69-72
DuVal, John 1940- 120
Duval, Katherine
See James, Elizabeth
Duval, Margaret
See Robinson, Patricia Colbert
DuVal, Miles P(ercy) Jr.
1896-1989 Obituary 130
Duvall, Evelyn Millis 1906- CANR-1
Earlier sketch in CA 1-4R
See also SATA 9
Duvall, Richard M. 1934- 45-48
Duvall, Robert (Selden) 1931- Brief entry 116
Duvall, W(illiam) Clyde (Jr.) 1917- 17-20R
DuVaul, Virginia C.
See Coffman, Virginia (Edith)
Duveen, Geoffrey 1883-1975 Obituary 61-64
Duveneck, Josephine Whitney 1891-1978 114
Duverger, Maurice 1917- CANR-27
Earlier sketch in CA 65-68
Duvoisin, Roger Antoine 1904-1980 ....CANR-11
Obituary 101
Earlier sketch in CA 13-16R
See also CLR 23
See also DLB 61
See also MAICYA
See also SATA 2, 23, 30
Duvoisin, Roger C(lair) 1927- 132
DuWors, Richard E(dward) 1914- 45-48
Duy, Pham 1927- 61-64
Duyckinck, Evert Augustus
1816-1878 ....DLB 3, 64
Duyckinck, George Long 1823-1863 ....DLB 3
Dvoretsky, Edward 1930- CANR-31
Earlier sketches in CA 37-40R, CANR-14
Dvorkin, David 1943- 118
Dvornik, Francis 1893-1975 ....CANR-6
Obituary 61-64
Earlier sketch in CA 1-4R
Dwaraki, Leela 1942- 106
Dweck, Susan 1943- 33-36R
Dwiggins, Don(ald J.) 1913-1988 ....CANR-23
Obituary 127
Earlier sketches in CA 17-20R, CANR-8
See also SATA 4, 60
Dwight, Allan
See Cole, Lois Dwight
Dwight, John Sullivan 1813-1893 ....DLB 1
Dwight, Olivia
See Hazzard, Mary
Dwight, Timothy 1752-1817 ....DLB 37
Dworkin, Andrea 1946- CANR-39
Earlier sketches in CA 77-80, CANR-16
See also CLC 43
See also MTCW
Dworkin, Gerald 1937- 53-56
Dworkin, James B(arnet) 1948- 112
Dworkin, R. M.
See Dworkin, Ronald M(yles)
Dworkin, Rita 1928- 21-24R
Dworkin, Ronald
See Dworkin, Ronald M(yles)
Dworkin, Ronald M(yles) 1931- 127
Brief entry 123
Dwoskin, Charles 1922(?)-1980 Obituary 102
Dwoskin, Stephen 1939- 89-92
Dwyer, Augusta (Maria) 1956- 133
Dwyer, Deanna
See Koontz, Dean R(ay)
Dwyer, John C. 1930- CANR-32
Earlier sketch in CA 113
Dwyer, Judith A(nne) 1948- 117
Dwyer, K. R.
See Koontz, Dean R(ay)
Dwyer, Richard A. 1934- 135
Dwyer, T. Ryle 1944- 105
Dwyer, Thomas A. 1923- 115
Dwyer, Vincent Michael
1912-1987 Obituary 123
Dwyer-Joyce, Alice 1913- CANR-4
Earlier sketch in CA 53-56
Dyal, James A. 1928- CANR-10
Earlier sketch in CA 5-8R
Dyal, William M. Jr. 1928- 21-24R
Dyall, Valentine 1908-1985 Obituary 117
Dybek, Stuart 1942- CANR-39
Earlier sketch in CA 97-100
Dyck, Anni 1931- 25-28R
Dyck, Cornelius J(ohn) 1921- 89-92
Dyck, Harvey L(eonard) 1934- 69-72
Dyck, J. William 1918- 57-60
Dyck, Martin 1927- 41-44R
Dyckman, John William 1922-1987 ....CANR-2
Obituary 123
Earlier sketch in CA 1-4R
Dyckman, Thomas Richard 1932- CANR-13
Earlier sketch in CA 33-36R
Dye, Anne G.
See Phillips, Anne G(arvey)
Dye, Charles
See MacLean, Katherine
Dye, David L. 1925- 21-24R
Dye, Dwight L(atimer) 1931- 118
Dye, Frank Charles 1930- 103
Dye, H(ershel) Allan 1931- 93-96
Dye, Harold E(ldon) 1907- CANR-24
Earlier sketch in CA 29-32R
Dye, James W(ayne) 1934- 21-24R
Dye, Margaret 1932- 81-84
Dye, Thomas R(oy) 1935- CANR-28
Earlier sketches in CA 33-36R, CANR-12
Dyen, Isidore 1913- 53-56
Dyer, Beverly 1921- 61-64
Dyer, Braven 1900(?)-1983 Obituary 110
Dyer, Brian
See Petrocelli, Orlando R(alph)
and Rothery, Brian
Dyer, C. Raymond
See Dyer, Charles (Raymond)
Dyer, Charles (Raymond) 1928- 21-24R
See also DLB 13
Dyer, Elinor Mary Brent
See Brent-Dyer, Elinor Mary
Dyer, Esther R(uth) 1950- 102
Dyer, Frederick C. 1918- 17-20R
Dyer, Geoff 1958- 125
Dyer, George Bell 1903-1978 85-88
Obituary 81-84
Dyer, George E(dward) 1928-1974 ....37-40R
Dyer, George J(ohn) 1927- 13-16R
Dyer, George 1755-1841 ....DLB 93
Dyer, James (Frederick) 1934- 102
See also SATA 37
Dyer, John M. 1920- 13-16R
Dyer, John Percy 1902-1975 ....1-4R
Obituary 103
Dyer, John 1699-1757 ....DLB 95
Dyer, Judith Clements 1947- 112
Dyer, K(enneth) F(rank) 1939- 114
Dyer, Lucinda 1947- 105
Dyer, Raymond
See Dyer, Charles (Raymond)
Dyer, T(homas) A(llan) 1947- 101
Dyer, Thomas G(eorge) 1943- CANR-25
Earlier sketch in CA 107
Dyer, Wayne W(alter) 1940- CANR-25
Earlier sketch in CA 69-72
Dyer, William G(ibb) 1925- CANR-14
Earlier sketch in CA 41-44R
Dygard, Thomas J. 1931- CANR-15
Earlier sketch in CA 85-88
See also AAYA 7
See also SATA 24
Dygat, Stanislaw 1914-1978 Obituary 111
Dygert, James H(erbert) 1934- CANR-10
Earlier sketch in CA 65-68
Dyk, Walter 1899-1972 Obituary 37-40R
Dyke, John 1935- CANR-12
Earlier sketch in CA 25-28R
See also SATA 35
Dykema, Karl W(ashburn) 1906-1970 ....CAP-2
Earlier sketch in CA 25-28
Dykeman, Richard M(ills) 1943- 93-96
Dykeman, Wilma CANR-1
Earlier sketch in CA 1-4R
Dykes, Archie R(eece) 1931- CANR-7
Earlier sketch in CA 17-20R
Dykes, Jack
See Owen, Jack
Dykes, Jeff(erson) C(henowth) 1900- CANR-17
Earlier sketches in CA 5-8R, CANR-2
Dykhuizen, George 1899- 49-52
Dykstra, Craig Richard 1947- 112
Dykstra, Gerald 1922- 45-48
Dykstra, Robert R. 1930- 25-28R
Dylan, Bob 1941- 41-44R
See also CLC 3, 4, 6, 12
See also DLB 16
Dymally, Mervyn M(alcolm) 1926- 41-44R
Dyment, Clifford (Henry) 1914-1971 ....CAP-1
Obituary 33-36R
Earlier sketch in CA 9-10
Dymoke, Juliet
See de Schanschieff, Juliet Dymoke
Dymond, Dorothy 1891-1985 Obituary 117
Dymond, Rosalind
See Cartwright, Rosalind Dymond
Dymsza, William A(lexander) 1920- CANR-2
Earlier sketch in CA 49-52
Dyne, Michael Bradley 1918-1989 Obituary 128
Dynes, Russell R(owe) 1923- CANR-23
Earlier sketches in CA 9-12R, CANR-6
Dyott, George (Miller)
1883-1972 Obituary 37-40R
Dyrness, William A(rthur) 1943- CANR-35
Earlier sketches in CA 33-36R, CANR-13
Dyroff, Jan Michael 1942- 61-64
Dyson, A(nthony) E(dward) 1928- 57-60
Dyson, Anne Jane 1912- 21-24R
Dyson, Freeman J(ohn) 1923- CANR-17
Earlier sketch in CA 89-92
Dyson, Geoffrey Harry George
1914-1981 Obituary 114
Dyson, George (Bernard) 1953- 126
Dyson, Lowell Keith 1929- 107
Dyson, R(obert) W(illiam) 1949- 123
Dywasuk, Colette Taube 1941- 45-48
Dziech, Billie Wright 1941- 113
Dziewanowski, M(arian) Kamil 1913- 29-32R
Dzuback, Mary Ann 1950- 138
Dzwonkoski, Peter 1940- 123

E

E. V. B.
See Boyle, Eleanor Vere (Gordon)
Eade, Alfred Thompson
1891-1988 Obituary 125
Eadie, Donald 1919- 33-36R
Eadie, John W(illiam) 1935- 104
Eagan, Andrea Boroff 1943- 73-76
Eagan, Barbara Tiritilli
1935(?)-1986 Obituary 118
Eagar, Frances (Elisabeth Stuart)
1940-1978 61-64
Obituary 120
See also SATA 11, 55
Eager, Edward McMaken 1911-1964 73-76
See also DLB 22
See also MAICYA
See also SATA 17
Eager, George B. 1921- ....SATA 56
Eager, Mary Ann 1905(?)-1984 Obituary 111
Eager, Molly
See Eager, Mary Ann
Eagle, Chester (Arthur) 1933- 57-60
Eagle, Dorothy 1912- CANR-9
Earlier sketch in CA 21-24R
Eagle, Ellen 1953- ....SATA 61
Eagle, Joanna 1934- 25-28R
Eagle, Mike 1942- ....SATA 11
Eagle, Robert H(arold) 1921-1969 ....CAP-2
Earlier sketch in CA 21-22
Eagles, Charles W. 1946- 138
Eagles, Douglas Alan 1943- 110
Eaglesfield, Francis
See Guirdham, Arthur
Eagleson, John 1941- 53-56

Eagleton, Terence (Francis) 1943- CANR-23
Earlier sketches in CA 57-60, CANR-7
See also Eagleton, Terry
See also MTCW
Eagleton, Terry
See Eagleton, Terence (Francis)
See also CLC 63
Eagleton, Thomas Francis
1929- Brief entry 105
Eagly, Robert V(ictor) 1933- 49-52
Eaker, Ira
See Eaker, Ira C(larence)
Eaker, Ira C(larence) 1896-1987 Obituary 123
Eakin, Frank Edwin Jr. 1936- 53-56
Eakin, Mary K(atherine) 1917- CANR-1
Earlier sketch in CA 1-4R
Eakin, Mary Mulford 1914-1980 126
Brief entry 106
Eakin, Paul John 1938- 120
Eakin, Richard M(arshall) 1910- 61-64
Eakin, Sue 1918- 69-72
Eakins, David W(alter) 1923- 49-52
Eakins, Pamela 1953- 117
Eales, John R(ay) 1910- 9-12R
Ealy, Lawrence O(rr) 1915- 33-36R
Eames, Alexandra 1942- 105
Eames, Andrew (John) 1958- 124
Eames, David 1934- 77-80
Eames, Edwin 1930- CANR-14
Earlier sketch in CA 41-44R
Eames, Elizabeth Ramsden 1921- 125
Eames, Hugh 1917- 45-48
Eames, John Douglas 1915- 69-72
Eames, S(amuel) Morris 1916- 57-60
Ear, The
See McLellan, Diana
Eardley, George C(harles) 1926- 57-60
Earhart, H(arry) Byron 1935- CANR-14
Earlier sketch in CA 37-40R
Earl, David M(agarey) 1911- 13-16R
Earl, Donald (Charles) 1931- 57-60
Earl, Johnrae 1919(?)-1978 Obituary 77-80
Earl, Lawrence 1915- 9-12R
Earl, Maureen 1944- 137
Earl, Paul Hunter 1945- CANR-2
Earlier sketch in CA 49-52
Earle, (Mary) Alice Morse
1853(?)-1911 Brief entry 117
Earle, Jean
See Burge, Doris
Earle, Marilee
See Zdenek, Marilee
Earle, Olive L(ydia) 1888- 21-24R
See also SATA 7
Earle, Peter G. 1923- 17-20R
Earle, Ralph 1907- CANR-4
Earlier sketch in CA 1-4R
Earle, Timothy K. 1946- 125
Earle, William
See Johns, W(illiam) E(arle)
Earle, William (Alexander) 1919-1988 85-88
Obituary 127
Earley, Charity (Edna) Adams 1918- 132
Earley, Martha
See Westwater, Sister Agnes Martha
Earley, Tom 1911- CAP-2
Earlier sketch in CA 33-36
Earll, Tony
See Buckland, Raymond
Earl Mountbatten of Burma
See
Mountbatten, Louis (Francis Albert Victor Nicholas)
Earl of Arran
See
Gore, Arthur Kattendyke S(trange) D(avid) A(rchibald)
Earl of Carnarvon
See
Herbert, Henry George Alfred Marius Victor Francis
Earl of Longford
See Pakenham, Edward Arthur Henry
Earl of Orrey
See Boyle, Roger
Earlson, Ian Malcolm
See Dorn, William S.
Early, Gerald 1952- 133
Early, James 1923- 45-48
Early, Jon
See Johns, W(illiam) E(arle)
Early, Richard E(lliott) 1908- 102
Early, Robert 1940- 49-52
Earnest, Ernest (Penney) 1901- 33-36R
Earney, Fillmore C(hristy) F(idelis) 1931- 57-60
Earnshaw, Anthony 1924- 53-56
Earnshaw, Brian 1929- CANR-27
Earlier sketches in CA 25-28R, CANR-11
See also SATA 17
Earp, Virgil
See Keevill, Henry J(ohn)
Eason, Ruth P. 1898(?)-1978 Obituary 81-84
Easson, James 1895-1979 ....5-8R
Obituary 103
Easson, Roger R(alph) 1945- 112
Easson, William M(cAlpine) 1931- 65-68
East, Ben 1898- CANR-27
Earlier sketch in CA 33-36R
East, Bob 1920(?)-1985 Obituary 115
East, Charles 1924- 17-20R
East, John Marlborough 1936- 21-24R
East, John Porter 1931-1986 ....17-20R
Obituary 119
East, Michael
See West, Morris L(anglo)
East, P. D. 1921-1971 ....1-4R
Obituary 103
East, W(illiam) Gordon 1902- 69-72
Eastaugh, Kenneth 1929- 106
Eastaway, Edward
See Thomas, (Philip) Edward
Easterbrook, Frank H. 1948- 138
Easterlin, Richard A(inley) 1926- 109
Easterman, Alexander Levvey
1890-1983 Obituary 110
Eastham, Thomas 1923- 77-80
Easthope, Antony 1939- 130
Easthope, Gary 1945- 69-72
Eastin, Roy B(randon) 1917- 41-44R
Eastlake, William (Derry) 1917- CANR-5
Earlier sketch in CA 5-8R
See also CAAS 1
See also CLC 8
See also DLB 6
Eastland, Terry 1950- 97-100
Eastlick, John Taylor 1912- 106
Eastman, Addison J. 1918- 85-88
Eastman, Ann Heidbreder 1933- CANR-14
Earlier sketch in CA 37-40R
Eastman, Arthur M(orse) 1918- 21-24R
Eastman, Carol 116
See also DLB 44
Eastman, Charles 116
Eastman, Charles A(lexander)
1858-1939 ....YABC 1
Eastman, Edward Roe 1885- CAP-1
Earlier sketch in CA 13-14
Eastman, Frances W(hittier) 1915- CANR-28
Earlier sketch in CA 1-4R
Eastman, G. Don
See Oosterman, Gordon
Eastman, Harry Claude MacColl
1923- Brief entry 105
Eastman, Joel Webb 1939- 13-16R
Eastman, John 1935- 117
Eastman, Lloyd E. 1929- 126
Brief entry 112
Eastman, Max (Forrester) 1883-1969 ....9-12R
Obituary 25-28R
See also DLB 91
Eastman, P(hilip) D(ey) 1909-1986 107
Obituary 118
See also SATA 33, 46
Eastman, Richard M(orse) 1916- 17-20R
Eastman, Robert E. 1913- 93-96
Eastman, Roger (Herbert) 1931- 53-56
Easton, Allan 1916- CANR-20
Earlier sketches in CA 49-52, CANR-2
Easton, Anthony Terrence 1947- 127
Easton, Carol 1932- CANR-39
Earlier sketch in CA 65-68
Easton, David 1917- 33-36R
Easton, Edward
See Malerich, Edward P.
Easton, Elizabeth Wynne 1956- 134
Easton, Jane 1918- 138
Easton, Loyd D(avid) 1915- 21-24R
Easton, Robert (Olney) 1915- CANR-27
Earlier sketches in CA 13-16R, CANR-7
See also CAAS 14
Easton, Stewart Copinger 1907- CANR-18
Earlier sketches in CA 1-4R, CANR-2
Easton, Thomas A(twood) 1944- 114
Eastwick, Ivy (Ethel) O(live) CANR-2
Earlier sketch in CA 5-8R
See also SATA 3
Eastwood, C(harles) Cyril 1916- 5-8R
Eastwood, Cyril
See Eastwood, C(harles) Cyril
Eatock, Marjorie 1927- 89-92
Eaton, Anne T(haxter) 1881-1971 Obituary 111
See also SATA 32
Eaton, Charles Edward 1916- CANR-20
Earlier sketches in CA 5-8R, CANR-2
Eaton, Clement 1898-1980 ....CANR-4
Obituary 118
Earlier sketch in CA 1-4R
Eaton, Evelyn (Sybil Mary) 1902- 53-56
Eaton, Faith (Sybil) 1927- 103
Eaton, George L.
See Verral, Charles Spain
Eaton, J(ohn) H(erbert) 1927- CANR-19
Earlier sketches in CA 1-4R, CANR-4
Eaton, Janet
See Givens, Janet E(aton)
Eaton, Jeanette 1886-1968 73-76
See also MAICYA
See also SATA 24
Eaton, John
See Bodington, Stephen
Eaton, John P. 126
Eaton, Joseph W. 1919- CANR-4
Earlier sketch in CA 1-4R
Eaton, Leonard K. 1922- 21-24R
Eaton, Marcia M(uelder) 1938- 113
Eaton, Theodore H(ildreth) Jr. 1907- 53-56
Eaton, Tom 1940- CANR-15
Earlier sketch in CA 41-44R
See also SATA 22
Eaton, Trevor 1934- 21-24R
Eaton, William Edward 1943- 69-72
Eauclaire, Sally 1950- 118
Eaves, James Clifton 1912- 13-16R
Eaves, Morris (Emery) 1944- 120
Eaves, T(homas) C(ary) Duncan 1918- 77-80
Eavey, Charles B(enton) 1889- 5-8R
Eavey, Louise Bone 1900- 5-8R
Eayrs, James George 1926- Brief entry 106
Eban, Abba (Solomon) 1915- CANR-26
Earlier sketch in CA 57-60
Eban, Aubrey
See Eban, Abba (Solomon)
Ebb, Fred 1935- CANR-24
Earlier sketch in CA 69-72
Ebbesen, Ebbe B(ruce) 1944- CANR-2
Earlier sketch in CA 49-52
Ebbett, (Frances) Eva 1925- 103
Ebbett, Eve
See Ebbett, (Frances) Eva
Ebejer, Francis 1925- CANR-16
Earlier sketch in CA 29-32R
Ebel, Alex 1927- ....SATA 11
Ebel, Henry 1938- 53-56
Ebel, Robert L(ouis) 1910- 89-92
Ebel, Suzanne
See Goodwin, Suzanne
Ebeling, Gerhard 1912- CANR-5
Earlier sketch in CA 9-12R
Ebeling, Walter 1907- 119
Ebenstein, Ronnie Sue 1946- 103
Ebenstein, William 1910-1976 ....CANR-6
Obituary 65-68
Earlier sketch in CA 1-4R
Eber, Dorothy (Margaret) Harley 1930- 41-44R
See also SATA 27
Eber, Irene 1929- 102
Eberhard, Wolfram 1909- CANR-2
Earlier sketch in CA 49-52
Eberhardt, Newman Charles 1912- 1-4R
Eberhardt, Peter
See Adams, Robert (Franklin)
Eberhart, Dikkon 1946- 93-96
Eberhart, George M(artin) 1950- 105
Eberhart, Mignon G(ood) 1899- 73-76
See also AITN 2
Eberhart, (Wilfred) Perry 1924- 17-20R
Eberhart, Richard (Ghormley) 1904- CANR-2
Earlier sketch in CA 1-4R
See also CDALB 1941-1968
See also CLC 3, 11, 19, 56
See also DLB 48
See also MTCW
Eberle, Irmengarde 1898-1979 ....CANR-2
Obituary 85-88
Earlier sketch in CA 1-4R
See also SATA 2, 23
Eberle, Nancy (Oates)
1935(?)-1988 Obituary 125
Eberle, Paul 1928- 101
Eberman, (Gilbert) Willis 1917- 9-12R
Ebershoff-Coles, Susan Vaughan 1941- 102
Ebersohn, Wessel (Schalk) 1940- 97-100
Ebersole, A(lva) V(ernon) Jr. 1919- CANR-31
Earlier sketches in CA 37-40R, CANR-14
Eberstadt, Charles F.
1914(?)-1974 Obituary 53-56
Eberstadt, Fernanda 1960- 136
See also CLC 39
Eberstadt, Isabel 1933- 126
Eberstadt, Lindley E.
1910(?)-1985 Obituary 115
Ebert, Alan 1935- CANR-16
Earlier sketch in CA 85-88
Ebert, Arthur Frank 1902-1984 ....5-8R
Obituary 114
Ebert, John E(dward) 1922- 106
Ebert, Katherine 1921- 107
Ebert, Roger (Joseph) 1942- CANR-22
Earlier sketch in CA 69-72
Eberwein, Jane Donahue 1943- 111
Eberwein, Robert Thomas 1940- 111
Eblana, Sister 1907- CAP-1
Earlier sketch in CA 11-12
Eble, Kenneth Eugene 1923- CANR-19
Earlier sketches in CA 1-4R, CANR-4
Eblen, Jack Ericson 1936- 33-36R
Eblis, J. Philip
See Phillips, James W.
Ebner, Jeannie 1918- ....DLB 85
Ebner-Eschenbach, Marie von
1830-1916 ....DLB 81
Ebon, Martin 1917- CANR-29
Earlier sketches in CA 21-24R, CANR-10
Ebon 1942- ....DLB 41
Ebsen, Buddy
See Ebsen, Christian
Ebsen, Christian 1908- 103
Ebsworth, (George Arthur) Raymond
1911- 1-4R
Eby, Cecil D(eGrotte) 1927- CANR-4
Earlier sketch in CA 1-4R
Eby, Richard E(ngle) 1912- 112
Eccles, David (McAdam) 1904- 53-56
Eccles, Frank 1923- 103
Eccles, Henry E. 1898- CAP-1
Earlier sketch in CA 13-16
Eccles, John Carew 1903- CANR-9
Earlier sketch in CA 65-68
Eccles, W(illiam) J(ohn) 1917- 9-12R
Ecclestone, Giles 1936-1990 Obituary 132
Eccles Williams, Ferelith 1920- CANR-21
Earlier sketch in CA 105
See also Williams, Ferelith Eccles
Eccli, Sandra Fulton 1936- 102
Echegaray (y Eizaguirre), Jose (Maria Waldo)
1832-1916 ....CANR-32
Brief entry 104
See also HW
See also MTCW
See also TCLC 4
Echeruo, Michael J(oseph) C(hukwudalu)
1937- CANR-8
Earlier sketch in CA 57-60
Echevarria, Roberto Gonzalez
See Gonzalez-Echevarria, Roberto
Echeverria, Durand 1913- 9-12R
Echewa, T(homas) Obinkaram 1940- 73-76
Echikson, William 1959- 134
Echlin, Edward P. 1930- 21-24R
Echo
See
Proust, (Valentin-Louis-George-Eugene-)Marcel
Echols, Barbara E(llen) 1934- 106
Echols, John M(inor) 1913-1982 ....CANR-2
Obituary 107
Earlier sketch in CA 5-8R
Echols, Margit 1944- 97-100
Eck, Diana L. 1945- 107
Eckardt, A(rthur) Roy 1918- CANR-31
Earlier sketches in CA 37-40R, CANR-14
Eckardt, Alice L(yons) 1923- CANR-14
Earlier sketch in CA 37-40R
Eckaus, Richard S(amuel) 1926- 45-48
Eckblad, Edith Berven 1923- 17-20R
See also SATA 23
Eckbo, Garrett 1910- 25-28R
Ecke, Betty Tseng Yu-ho 1924- CANR-6
Earlier sketch in CA 5-8R
Ecke, Wolfgang 1927-1983 Obituary 111
See also SATA 37
Eckel, Malcolm W(illiam) 1912- 61-64
Eckel, Paul E(dward) 1908-1986 Obituary 119
Eckelberry, Grace Kathryn 1902- CAP-2
Earlier sketch in CA 33-36
Eckels, Jon CANR-3
Earlier sketch in CA 49-52
Ecker, Beverly A. 1938- 116
Ecker, H(erman) Paul 1922-1976 ....CAP-2
Earlier sketch in CA 29-32
Ecker-Racz, L. Laszlo 1906- 49-52
Eckerson, Olive Taylor 1901- 1-4R
Eckert, Allan W. 1931- CANR-14
Earlier sketch in CA 13-16R
See also CLC 17
See also SATA 27, 29
Eckert, Edward K(yle) 1943- 77-80
Eckert, Horst 1931- CANR-38
Earlier sketch in CA 37-40R
See also Janosch
See also MAICYA
See also SATA 8
Eckert, Ruth E(lizabeth) 1905- 13-16R
Eckes, Alfred Edward Jr. 1942- CANR-9
Earlier sketch in CA 61-64
Eckhardt, Bob
See Eckhardt, Robert Christian
Eckhardt, Robert Christian 1913- 85-88
Eckhardt, Tibor 1888-1972 Obituary 37-40R
Eckhart, Meister 1260(?)-1328(?) ....DLB 115
Eckholm, Erik P(eter) 1949- CANR-6
Earlier sketch in CA 57-60
Eckley, Grace 1932- CANR-28
Earlier sketch in CA 45-48
Eckley, Mary M. 102
Eckley, Wilton Earl Jr. 1929- CANR-28
Earlier sketch in CA 49-52
Eckman, Frederick (Willis) 1924- 33-36R
Eckman, Lester S(amuel) 1937- CANR-2
Earlier sketch in CA 49-52
Eckmar, F. R.
See de Hartog, Jan
Eckstein, Alexander 1915-1976 ....CANR-6
Obituary 69-72
Earlier sketch in CA 1-4R
Eckstein, Gustav 1890-1981 57-60
Obituary 104
Eckstein, Harry 1924- CANR-1
Earlier sketch in CA 1-4R
Eckstein, Jerome 1925- CANR-36
Eckstein, Jerome 1928- 114
Eckstein, Otto 1927-1984 ....CANR-14
Obituary 112
Earlier sketch in CA 13-16R
Eclov, Shirley
See Pfoutz, Shirley Eclov
Eco, Umberto 1932- CANR-33
Earlier sketches in CA 77-80, CANR-12
See also BEST 90:1
See also CLC 28, 60
See also MTCW
Economou, George 1934- CANR-38
Earlier sketch in CA 25-28R
Ecroyd, Donald H(owarth) 1923- CANR-4
Earlier sketch in CA 1-4R
Edari, Ronald S(amuel) 1943- 65-68
Edberg, Rolf 1912- CANR-26
Earlier sketches in CA 69-72, CANR-11
Eddenden, A(rthur) E(dward) 1928- 127
Eddings, David 1931- CANR-35
Earlier sketch in CA 110
See also BEST 90:2
Eddins, Dwight L. 1939- 33-36R
Eddison, E(ric) R(ucker)
1882-1945 Brief entry 109
See also TCLC 15
Eddison, John 1916- CANR-23
Earlier sketches in CA 61-64, CANR-8
Eddison, Roger (Tatham) 1916- CAP-1
Earlier sketch in CA 11-12
Eddleman, H(enry) Leo 1911- CANR-9
Earlier sketch in CA 13-16R
Eddy, Clifford Martin Jr.
1896-1967 Obituary 113
Eddy, C.M. Jr.
See Eddy, Clifford Martin Jr.
Eddy, Edward D(anforth Jr.) 1921- 73-76
Eddy, Elizabeth M. 1926- 21-24R
Eddy, John J(ude) 1933- 73-76
Eddy, John P(aul) 1932- CANR-9
Earlier sketch in CA 61-64
Eddy, John Percy 1881-1975 Obituary 61-64
Eddy, Mary (Morse) Baker
1821-1910 Brief entry 113
Eddy, Paul 1944- CANR-15
Earlier sketch in CA 73-76
Eddy, Roger (Whittlesey) 1920- 17-20R
Eddy, Samuel K(ennedy) 1926- CANR-17
Earlier sketch in CA 1-4R
Ede, H(arold) S(tanley) 1895-1990 131
Ede, Janina 1937- ....SATA 33

Ede, Jim
See Ede, H(arold) S(tanley)
Ede, Lisa S. 1947- ... 123
Edel, Abraham 1908- ... 1-4R
Edel, (Joseph) Leon 1907- ... CANR-22
Earlier sketches in CA 1-4R, CANR-1
See also CLC 29, 34
See also DLB 103
Edel, Marjorie
See Sinclair, Marjorie (Jane)
Edel, Matthew (David) 1941-1990 ... 29-32R
Obituary ... 133
Edel, Wilbur 1915- ... 138
Edelberg, Cynthia Dubin 1940- ... 89-92
Edelen, Georges 1924- ... 93-96
Edelhart, Michael 1951- ... 129
Edelhart, Mike
See Edelhart, Michael
Edelheit, Abraham J. 1958- ... 134
Edelheit, Hershel 1926- ... 134
Edell, Celeste ... 1-4R
See also SATA 12
Edelman, Alice Fisher 1940- ... 112
Edelman, Bernard 1946- ... 126
Edelman, Elaine ... 113
See also SATA 50
Edelman, Gerald Maurice 1929- ... 112
Edelman, John W(alter)
1893-1971 Obituary ... 113
Edelman, Lily (Judith) 1915-1981 ... 61-64
Obituary ... 102
See also SATA 22
Edelman, Marian Wright 1939- ... 124
See also BW
Edelman, Maurice 1911-1975 ... 65-68
Obituary ... 61-64
Edelman, Murray 1919- ... 33-36R
Edelman, Nathan 1911-1971 Obituary ... 113
Edelman, Paul S. 1926- ... 9-12R
Edelsberg, Herman 1909-1986 Obituary ... 120
Edelson, Edward 1932- ... CANR-13
Earlier sketch in CA 17-20R
See also SATA 51
Edelson, Julie 1949- ... 122
Edelson, Marshall 1928- Brief entry ... 111
Edelstein, Alex S. 1920(?)- ... 133
Edelstein, Arthur ... CANR-9
Earlier sketch in CA 65-68
Edelstein, David S(imeon) 1913- ... 61-64
Edelstein, J. M. 1924- ... 53-56
Edelstein, Morton A. 1925- ... 69-72
Edelstein, Scott 1954- ... 122
Edelstein, Stuart J. 1941- ... 122
Edelstein, Terese 1950- ... 135
Eden, Alvin N(oam) 1926- ... CANR-9
Earlier sketch in CA 61-64
Eden, (Robert) Anthony 1897-1977 ... 77-80
Obituary ... 69-72
Eden, Dorothy (Enid) 1912-1982 ... 81-84
Obituary ... 106
Eden, Laura
See Harrison, Claire (E.)
Eden, Robert 1942- ... 113
Edens, Cooper 1945- ... SATA 49
Edens, (Bishop) David 1926- ... 108
See also SATA 39
Eder, George Jackson 1900- ... 85-88
Eder, Richard (Gray) 1932- ... 130
Brief entry ... 123
Edes, Benjamin 1732-1803 ... DLB 43
Edey, Maitland A(rmstrong) 1910- ... CANR-6
Obituary ... 137
Earlier sketch in CA 57-60
See also SATA 25, 71
Edgar, David 1948- ... CANR-12
Earlier sketch in CA 57-60
See also CLC 42
See also DLB 13
See also MTCW
Edgar, Donald 1916- ... 121
Edgar, Frank Terrell Rhoades 1932- ... 69-72
Edgar, Josephine
See Mussi, Mary
Edgar, Ken(neth Frank) 1925- ... CANR-27
Earlier sketch in CA 49-52
Edgar, Neal Lowndes 1927-1983 ... CANR-27
Obituary ... 110
Earlier sketch in CA 69-72
Edge, David O(wen) 1932- ... 73-76
Edge, Findley B(artow) 1916- ... 5-8R
Edgell, Zee 1940- ... 135
Edgerton, Clyde (Carlyle) 1944- ... 134
Brief entry ... 118
See also CLC 39
Edgerton, David 1959- ... 138
Edgerton, Franklin 1885-1963 Obituary ... 110
Edgerton, Gary Richard 1952- ... 111
Edgerton, Harold E(ugene) 1903-1990 ... CANR-5
Obituary ... 130
Earlier sketch in CA 53-56
Edgerton, Joseph S.
1900(?)-1983 Obituary ... 109
Edgerton, Lucile Selk 1896-1987 Obituary ... 122
Edgerton, Robert B(reckenridge) 1931- ... 53-56
Edgerton, William B(enbow) 1914- ... 29-32R
Edgeworth, Maria 1767-1849 ... DLB 116
See also SATA 21
Edgington, Eugene S(inclair) 1924- ... 25-28R
Edgley, Charles K(enneth) 1943- ... 57-60
Edgley, Roy 1925- ... 29-32R
Edgren, Harry D(aniel) 1899- ... CAP-2
Earlier sketch in CA 33-36
Edgy, Wardore
See Gorey, Edward (St. John)
Edholm, O(tto) G(ustav)
1909-1985 Obituary ... 115
Edie, James M. 1927- ... 9-12R
Ediger, Peter J. 1926- ... 33-36R
Edinborough, Arnold 1922- ... 73-76
Edinger, Edward F(erdinand) 1922- ... 69-72
Edington, Andrew 1914- ... 73-76
Edison, Judith
See Paul, Judith Edison
Edison, Michael (G.) 1937- Brief entry ... 110
Edison, Theodore
See Stratemeyer, Edward L.
Edkins, Anthony 1927- ... 97-100
Edkins, Diana M(aria) 1947- ... 41-44R
Edler, Peter 1934- ... 107
Edler, Tim(othy) 1948- ... SATA 56
Edlin, Herbert Leeson 1913-1976 ... CANR-9
Obituary ... 69-72
Earlier sketch in CA 61-64
Edlin, Rosabelle Alpern 1914- ... 9-12R
Edman, David 1930- ... 37-40R
Edman, Marion (Louise) 1901- ... CAP-1
Earlier sketch in CA 17-18
Edman, Victor Raymond 1900-1967 ... CANR-6
Earlier sketch in CA 1-4R
Edmands, Allan 1942- ... 117
Edmands, Dodie 1947- ... 116
Edmisten, Patricia Taylor 1939- ... 132
Edmiston, (Helen) Jean (Mary) 1913- ... 13-16R
Edmiston, Susan 1940- ... 65-68
Edmond, Jay
See Jones, Jack
Edmond, Mary 1916- ... 121
Edmonds, Alan
See Edmonds, Arthur Denis
Edmonds, Ann C.
See Welch, Ann Courtenay (Edmonds)
Edmonds, Arthur Denis 1932- ... 73-76
Edmonds, C(ecil) J(ohn) 1889- ... CAP-1
Earlier sketch in CA 13-14
Edmonds, Charles
See Carrington, Charles Edmund
Edmonds, Helen G(rey) 1911- ... 65-68
Edmonds, I(vy) G(ordon) 1917- ... CANR-30
Earlier sketches in CA 33-36R, CANR-13
See also SATA 8
Edmonds, Jae
See Edmonds, James A.
Edmonds, James A. 1947- ... 118
Edmonds, Margaret Hammett ... 101
Edmonds, Margot
See Edmonds, Margaret Hammett
Edmonds, Paul
See Kuttner, Henry
Edmonds, R(obert) H(umphrey) G(ordon)
1920- ... 69-72
Edmonds, (Sheppard) Randolph
1900-1983 ... 125
See also BW
See also DLB 51
Edmonds, Robert 1913-1990 ... 112
Obituary ... 132
Edmonds, Robin
See Edmonds, R(obert) H(umphrey) G(ordon)
Edmonds, Ronald R. 1935-1983 Obituary ... 110
Edmonds, Vernon H. 1927- ... 37-40R
Edmonds, Walter D(umaux) 1903- ... CANR-2
Earlier sketch in CA 5-8R
See also CLC 35
See also DLB 9
See also MAICYA
See also SAAS 4
See also SATA 1, 27
Edmondson, Clifton Earl 1937- ... 102
Edmondson, G. C. 1922- ... CANR-26
Earlier sketches in CA 57-60, CANR-11
Edmondson, Garry C.
See Edmondson, G. C.
Edmondson, Wallace
See Ellison, Harlan
Edmonson, Harold A(rthur) 1937- ... 41-44R
Edmonson, Munro Sterling 1924- ... CANR-28
Earlier sketch in CA 33-36R
Edmund, Sean
See Pringle, Laurence P.
Edmunds, H(enry) Tudor 1897- ... 106
Edmunds, Malcolm 1938- ... 73-76
Edmunds, (Thomas) Murrell 1898- ... CANR-4
Earlier sketch in CA 1-4R
Edmunds, Simeon 1917- ... 17-20R
Edmunds, Stahrl W(illiam) 1917- ... 69-72
Edmundson, Bruce 1952- ... 126
Edom, Clifton C. 1907- ... 105
Edric, Robert
See Armitage, G(ary) E(dric)
Edrich, William J(ohn) 1916-1986 Obituary ... 120
Edsall, Florence S(mall)
1898(?)-1986 Obituary ... 119
Edsall, Marian (Stickney) 1920- ... CANR-27
Earlier sketch in CA 49-52
See also SATA 8
Edsall, Thomas Byrne 1941- ... 126
Edschmid, Kasimir
See Schmid, Eduard
See also DLB 56
Edson, Harold
See Hall, Asa Zadel
Edson, J(ohn) T(homas) 1928- ... CANR-30
Earlier sketches in CA 29-32R, CANR-12
Edson, Peter 1896-1977 Obituary ... 73-76
Edson, Russell ... 33-36R
See also CLC 13
Eduardi, Guillermo
See Edwards, William B(ennett)
Edwa
See Edwards, Bill
Edwardes, Allen
See Kinsley, D(aniel) A(llan)
Edwardes, Michael (F. H.) 1923- ... CANR-10
Earlier sketch in CA 57-60
Edwards, A. W. F. 1935- ... 73-76
Edwards, Al
See Nourse, Alan E(dward)
Edwards, Alexander
See Fleischer, Leonore
Edwards, Allen J(ack) 1926- ... 33-36R
Edwards, Allen L. 1914- ... CANR-10
Earlier sketch in CA 25-28R
Edwards, Anne 1927- ... CANR-33
Earlier sketches in CA 61-64, CANR-13
See also SATA 35
Edwards, Anne-Marie 1932- ... CANR-38
Earlier sketches in CA 85-88, CANR-16
Edwards, Anthony David 1936- ... 13-16R
Edwards, Audrey 1947- ... 81-84
See also SATA 31, 52
Edwards, Bertram
See Edwards, Herbert Charles
Edwards, Betty 1926- ... 105
Edwards, Bill 1929(?)-1987 Obituary ... 121
Edwards, Blake 1922- ... CANR-32
Earlier sketch in CA 81-84
Edwards, Bob
See Edwards, Robert Alan
Edwards, Bronwen Elizabeth
See Rose, Wendy
Edwards, Carl N(ormand) 1943- ... 57-60
Edwards, Cecile Pepin 1916- ... 5-8R
See also SATA 25
Edwards, Charles Edward 1930- ... 17-20R
Edwards, Charles Mundy Jr. 1903-1985 ... 45-48
Obituary ... 117
Edwards, Charlotte 1907-1987 ... CANR-35
Earlier sketch in CA 29-32R
Edwards, Christine 1902- ... CAP-1
Earlier sketch in CA 19-20
Edwards, Clifford D(uane) 1934- ... 61-64
Edwards, Corwin D. 1901-1979 ... CANR-10
Obituary ... 85-88
Earlier sketch in CA 17-20R
Edwards, David C(harles) 1937- ... 41-44R
Edwards, David L(awrence) 1929- ... CANR-29
Earlier sketches in CA 5-8R, CANR-12
Edwards, David V(andeusen) 1941- ... 126
Brief entry ... 105
Edwards, Donald Earl
See Harding, Donald Edward
Edwards, Donald (Isaac) 1904- ... 65-68
Edwards, Dorothy 1903(?)-1934 Brief entry ... 122
Edwards, Dorothy 1914-1982 ... CANR-12
Obituary ... 107
Earlier sketch in CA 25-28R
See also SATA 4, 31
Edwards, Douglas 1917-1990 ... 118
Obituary ... 132
Brief entry ... 110
Edwards, Edgar O(wen) 1919- ... CANR-6
Earlier sketch in CA 1-4R
Edwards, Eli
See McKay, Festus Claudius
Edwards, Elizabeth
See Inderlied, Mary Elizabeth
Edwards, Elwyn Hartley 1927- ... CANR-8
Earlier sketch in CA 61-64
Edwards, F. E.
See Nolan, William F(rancis)
Edwards, Francis
See Brandon, Johnny
Edwards, Frank Allyn 1908-1967 ... CANR-1
Earlier sketch in CA 1-4R
Edwards, G(erald) B(asil)
1899-1976 Obituary ... 110
See also CLC 25
Edwards, Gawain
See Pendray, George Edward
Edwards, George Charles III 1947- ... CANR-24
Earlier sketch in CA 107
Edwards, George 1914- ... 53-56
Edwards, Gerald (Kenneth Savery) Hamilton
See Hamilton-Edwards, Gerald (Kenneth Savery)
Edwards, Gillian (Mary) 1918- ... 25-28R
Edwards, Gunvor ... 107
See also SATA 32
Edwards, Gus 1939- ... 108
See also CLC 43
Edwards, Harry
See Edwards, Henry James
Edwards, Harry (Jr.) 1942- ... 111
Brief entry ... 109
Edwards, Harvey 1929- ... 25-28R
See also SATA 5
Edwards, Hazel (Eileen) 1945- ... 124
Edwards, Henry James 1893-1976 ... 13-16R
Obituary ... 122
Edwards, Herbert Charles 1912- ... 9-12R
See also SATA 12
Edwards, Hilton 1903- ... 65-68
Edwards, I(orwerth) E(iddon) S(tephen)
1909- ... CANR-7
Earlier sketch in CA 13-16R
Edwards, India 1896(?)-1990 Obituary ... 130
Edwards, James Don(ald) 1926- ... CANR-4
Earlier sketch in CA 9-12R
Edwards, James Keith O'Neill
1920-1988 Obituary ... 126
Edwards, Jane Campbell 1932- ... 13-16R
See also SATA 10
Edwards, Jaroldeen 1932- ... 102
Edwards, Jerome E(arl) 1937- ... 37-40R
Edwards, Jimmy
See Edwards, James Keith O'Neill
Edwards, John Milton
See Cook, William Wallace
Edwards, John 1943- ... 118
Edwards, Jonathan Jr. 1745-1801 ... DLB 37
Edwards, Jonathan 1703-1758 ... DLB 24
Edwards, Josephine Cunnington 1904- ... 13-16R
Edwards, Josh
See Levinson, Leonard
Edwards, Julia
See Stratemeyer, Edward L.
Edwards, Julia Spalding 1920- ... 37-40R
Edwards, Julie
See Andrews, Julie
Edwards, June
See Bhatia, Jamunadevi
Edwards, Junius 1929- ... DLB 33
Edwards, K(enneth) Morgan 1912- ... 5-8R
Edwards, Kate F(lournoy) 1877-1980 ... 107
Edwards, Lee R. 1942- ... 124
Edwards, Lee 1932- ... CANR-10
Earlier sketch in CA 25-28R
Edwards, Leo
See Lee, Edward Edson
Edwards, Linda Strauss 1948- ... 126
See also SATA 42, 49
Edwards, Lyford Paterson
1882-1984 Obituary ... 113
Edwards, Lynne 1943- ... 73-76
Edwards, Margaret (Alexander)
1902-1988 ... CAP-2
Obituary ... 125
Earlier sketch in CA 29-32
See also SATA 56
Edwards, Marie Babare ... 57-60
Edwards, Mark U(lin) Jr. 1946- ... CANR-10
Earlier sketch in CA 65-68
Edwards, (Kenneth) Martin 1955- ... 137
Edwards, Marvin L(ouis) 1915- ... 13-16R
Edwards, Max
See Benjamin, Claude (Max Edward Pohlman)
Edwards, Michael 1932- ... 85-88
Edwards, Michael 1938- ... CANR-22
Earlier sketch in CA 106
Edwards, Michelle 1955- ... 138
See also SATA 70
Edwards, Monica le Doux Newton 1912- ... 9-12R
See also SATA 12
Edwards, Nicky 1958- ... 122
Edwards, Norman
See Carr, Terry (Gene)
and White, Theodore Edwin
Edwards, O(tis) C(arl) Jr. 1928- ... 53-56
Edwards, Oliver
See Haley, William (John)
Edwards, Olwen
See Gater, Dilys
Edwards, Owen Dudley 1938- ... CANR-7
Earlier sketch in CA 57-60
Edwards, P(rior) Max(imilian) H(emsley)
1914- ... 37-40R
Edwards, Page (Lawrence Jr.) 1941- ... CANR-27
Earlier sketches in CA 45-48, CANR-1
See also SATA 59
Edwards, Paul Geoffrey 1926- ... 57-60
Obituary ... 137
Edwards, Paul M(adison) 1933- ... 41-44R
Edwards, Paul 1923- ... 85-88
Edwards, Paul 1940- ... 123
Edwards, Peter (William) 1934- ... 109
Edwards, Philip 1923- ... CANR-29
Earlier sketches in CA 25-28R, CANR-12
Edwards, Phoebe
See Bloch, Barbara
Edwards, Phyllis Irene 1916-1984 Obituary ... 114
Edwards, R. M.
See Edwards, Roselyn
Edwards, (H. C.) Ralph 1894- ... CAP-1
Earlier sketch in CA 13-16
Edwards, Raoul D(urant)
1928-1987 Obituary ... 125
Edwards, Rem B(lanchard Jr.) 1934- ... 37-40R
Edwards, Richard Alan 1934- ... 69-72
Edwards, Richard C. 1944- ... CANR-2
Earlier sketch in CA 45-48
Edwards, Richard 1524-1566 ... DLB 62
Edwards, Robert Alan 1947- ... 121
Edwards, Robert (John) 1925- ... 129
Edwards, Ron(ald George) 1930- ... 105
Edwards, Roselyn 1929- ... 25-28R
Edwards, Ruth Dudley
See Dudley Edwards, Ruth
Edwards, S. W.
See Sublette, Walter (Edwards)
Edwards, Sally (Cary) 1929- ... 25-28R
See also SATA 7
Edwards, Samuel
See Gerson, Noel Bertram
Edwards, Stephen
See Palestrant, Simon S.
Edwards, T(homas) Bentley 1906- ... CAP-2
Earlier sketch in CA 23-24
Edwards, Thomas R(obert) Jr. 1928- ... 5-8R
Edwards, Tilden Hampton Jr. 1935- ... CANR-18
Earlier sketch in CA 102
Edwards, Verne E(rvie) Jr. 1924- ... 33-36R
Edwards, Ward 1927- ... 21-24R
Edwards, William B(ennett) 1927- ... 5-8R
Edwards, William 1896- ... CAP-1
Earlier sketch in CA 13-14
Edward VIII 1894-1972 Obituary ... 33-36R
Edwin, Brother B.
See Arnandez, Richard
Eekelaar, John M(ichael) 1942- ... 116
Eekman, Thomas 1923- ... 81-84
Eells, George 1922- ... CANR-14
Earlier sketch in CA 21-24R
Eells, Richard S(edric) F(ox) 1917- ... 132
Eells, Robert J(ames) 1944- ... 102
Efemey, Raymond (Frederick) 1928- ... 21-24R
Effinger, George Alec 1947- ... CANR-23
Earlier sketch in CA 37-40R
See also DLB 8

Efird, James M(ichael) 1932- CANR-31
Earlier sketches in CA 37-40R, CANR-14
Efron, Alexander 1897- CAP-2
Earlier sketch in CA 29-32
Efron, Arthur 1931- CANR-21
Earlier sketch in CA 69-72
Efron, Benjamin 1908- CANR-5
Earlier sketch in CA 5-8R
Efron, Edith Carol 1922- 102
Efron, Marina Ivanovna Tsvetaeva
See Tsvetaeva (Efron), Marina (Ivanovna)
Efron, Marshall 1938(?)- 126
Brief entry 112
Efros, Israel (Isaac) 1891-1981 ....21-24R
Obituary 102
Efros, Susan Elyse 1947- 104
Efrot
See Efros, Israel (Isaac)
Egami, Tomi 1899- 61-64
Egan, Beresford Patrick
1905-1984 Obituary 111
Egan, David R(onald) 1943- 102
Egan, E(dward) W(elstead) 1922- CANR-9
Earlier sketch in CA 21-24R
See also SATA 35
Egan, Ferol 1923- 29-32R
Egan, Fred(erick Julian)
1905(?)-1986 Obituary 118
Egan, Gerard 1930- CANR-28
Earlier sketches in CA 29-32R, CANR-12
Egan, Harvey Daniel 1937- 113
Egan, John P. 1934- 110
Egan, Lesley
See Linington, (Barbara) Elizabeth
Egan, Lesley
See Linington, (Barbara) Elizabeth
Egan, Melinda A(nne) 1950- 102
Egan, Michael 1941- 45-48
Egan, Philip S(idney) 1920- 1-4R
Egan, Robert 1945- 77-80
Egbert, Donald Drew 1902-1973 ....CAP-2
Obituary 37-40R
Earlier sketch in CA 23-24
Egbert, Virginia Wylie
See Kilborne, Virginia Wylie
Egbuna, Obi B(enue Joseph) 1938- 102
Ege, Arvia MacKaye 1903(?)-1989 Obituary 128
Egejuru, Phanuel Akubueze 106
Egelhof, Joseph (Baird)
1919(?)-1980 Obituary 97-100
Eger, Jeffrey 1946- 125
Egermeier, Elsie E(milie) 1890-1986 ....5-8R
See also SATA 65
Egerton, Frank N(icholas) III 1936- 110
Egerton, George W(illiam) 1942- 85-88
Egerton, John (Walden) 1935- 85-88
Egerton, Lucy
See Malleson, Lucy Beatrice
Egg, Maria 1910- 29-32R
Egg-Benes, Maria
See Egg, Maria
Eggeling, Hans Friedrich 1878-1977 ....1-4R
Obituary 73-76
Eggenberger, David 1918- 9-12R
See also SATA 6
Eggenschwiler, David 1936- 37-40R
Egger, M(aurice) David 1936- 57-60
Egger, Rowland (Andrews) 1908-1979 ....CANR-4
Earlier sketch in CA 5-8R
Eggers, J(ohn) Philip 1940- 33-36R
Eggers, Kerry 1953- 137
Eggers, William T. 1912- 29-32R
Eggert, Gerald G(ordon) 1926- 21-24R
Eggert, James Edward 1943- CANR-23
Earlier sketch in CA 107
Eggert, Jim
See Eggert, James Edward
Eggleston, Edward 1837-1902 Brief entry 111
See also DLB 12
See also SATA 27
Eggleston, George T(eeple)
1906-1990 Obituary 132
Eggleston, Wilfrid 1901-1986 ....CANR-8
Obituary 119
Earlier sketch in CA 21-24R
See also DLB 92
Eggum, Arne 1936- 134
Egielski, Richard 1952- ....MAICYA
See also SATA 11, 49
Egler, Frank E(dwin) 1911- 29-32R
Egleson, Janet F.
See Dunleavy, Janet Egleson
Egleton, Clive (Frederick) 1927- CANR-22
Earlier sketch in CA 103
Egli, Ida Rae 1946- 137
Egoff, Sheila A. 1918- 132
Brief entry 116
Egremont, Max 1948- CANR-35
Earlier sketch in CA 93-96
Eguchi, Shinichi 1914-1979 Obituary 85-88
Egypt, Ophelia Settle 1903-1984 81-84
Obituary 112
See also SATA 16, 38
Ehle, John (Marsden Jr.) 1925- 9-12R
See also CLC 27
Ehler, R(ichard) L. 1930- 137
Ehlers, Henry James 1907- 13-16R
Ehlert, Lois (Jane) 1934- 137
See also CLR 28
See also MAICYA
See also SATA 35, 69
Ehmann, James 1948- 109
Ehninger, Douglas W(agner)
1913-1979 ....CANR-4
Earlier sketch in CA 5-8R
Ehre, Edward 1905- 9-12R
Ehre, Milton 1933- 53-56
Ehrenberg, Miriam 124
Ehrenberg, Otto 1926- 124
Ehrenberg, Victor (Leopold)
1891-1976 ....CANR-4
Obituary 65-68
Earlier sketch in CA 5-8R
Ehrenbourg, Ilya (Grigoryevich)
See Ehrenburg, Ilya (Grigoryevich)
Ehrenburg, Ilya (Grigoryevich) 1891-1967 102
Obituary 25-28R
See also CLC 18, 34, 62
Ehrenburg, Ilyo (Grigoryevich)
See Ehrenburg, Ilya (Grigoryevich)
Ehrenfeld, David W(illiam) 1938- 81-84
Ehrenhalt, Alan 1947- 112
Ehrenpreis, Anne Henry 1927- 53-56
Ehrenpreis, Irvin 1920-1985 121
Obituary 116
Brief entry 110
Ehrenreich, Barbara 1941- CANR-37
Earlier sketches in CA 73-76, CANR-16
See also BEST 90:4
See also MTCW
Ehrenreich, Herman 1900(?)-1970 Obituary 104
Ehrenreich, John H. 1943- 125
Ehrenstein, Albert 1886-1950 ....DLB 81
Ehrensvaerd, Goesta (Carl Henrik)
1910- CANR-2
Earlier sketch in CA 49-52
Ehrenwald, Jan 1900-1988 ....CANR-2
Obituary 125
Earlier sketch in CA 49-52
Ehrenzweig, Albert A(rmin) 1906-1974 ....CAP-2
Earlier sketch in CA 29-32
Ehresmann, Donald L(ouis) 1937- 69-72
Ehresmann, Julia M. 1939- 33-36R
Ehret, Christopher 1941- 37-40R
Ehrhardt, Reinhold 1900- 29-32R
Ehrhart, W(illiam) D(aniel) 1948- CANR-7
Earlier sketch in CA 61-64
See also DLBD 9
Ehricke, Krafft A(rnold) 1917-1984 Obituary 114
Ehrlich, Amy 1942- CANR-32
Earlier sketches in CA 37-40R, CANR-14
See also SATA 25, 65
Ehrlich, Anne (Fitzhugh) Howland
1933- CANR-8
Earlier sketch in CA 61-64
Ehrlich, Arnold 1923-1989 ....33-36R
Obituary 129
Ehrlich, Bettina Bauer 1903- CAP-1
Earlier sketch in CA 13-14
See also SATA 1
Ehrlich, Cyril 1925- 103
Ehrlich, David 1941- 127
Ehrlich, Eugene H. 1922- CANR-5
Earlier sketch in CA 1-4R
Ehrlich, Everett M. 1950- 112
Ehrlich, Howard J. 1932- 17-20R
Ehrlich, Isaac 1938- 118
Ehrlich, Jack
See Ehrlich, John Gunther
Ehrlich, Jacob Wilburn
1900-1971 Obituary 33-36R
Ehrlich, Jake
See Ehrlich, Jacob Wilburn
Ehrlich, John Gunther 1930- CANR-4
Earlier sketch in CA 1-4R
Ehrlich, Leonard Harry 1924- 102
Ehrlich, Max 1909-1983 ....CANR-1
Obituary 115
Earlier sketch in CA 1-4R
Ehrlich, Nathaniel J(oseph) 1940- 53-56
Ehrlich, Otto Hild 1892-1979 Obituary 85-88
Ehrlich, Paul R(alph) 1932- CANR-28
Earlier sketches in CA 65-68, CANR-8
Ehrlich, Robert S. 1935- 21-24R
Ehrlich, Thomas 1934- 113
Ehrlich, Walter 1921- 53-56
Ehrlichman, John Daniel 1925- 65-68
Ehrman, John (Patrick William) 1920- CANR-26
Earlier sketches in CA 5-8R, CANR-4
Ehrman, Lee 1935- 69-72
Ehrmann, Herbert B(rutus) 1891-1970 ....CAP-2
Earlier sketch in CA 25-28
Ehrsam, Theodore George 1909- 45-48
Eibl-Eibesfeldt, Irenaeus 1928- CANR-3
Earlier sketch in CA 9-12R
Eibling, Harold Henry 1905-1976 ....CANR-29
Earlier sketch in CA 37-40R
Eiby, George 1918- 53-56
Eich, Guenter 1907-1972 111
Obituary 93-96
See also CLC 15
See also DLB 69
Eichelbaum, Stanley 1926- 73-76
Eichelberger, Clark M(ell)
1896-1980 Obituary 93-96
Eichelberger, Clayton L. 1925- 41-44R
Eichelberger, Ethyl 1945-1990 Obituary 132
Eichelberger, Rosa Kohler 1896- 102
Eichenbaum, Luise 1952- 126
Eichenberg, Fritz 1901-1990 ....CANR-6
Obituary 133
Earlier sketch in CA 57-60
See also MAICYA
See also SATA 9, 50
Eichendorff, Joseph Freiherr von
1788-1857 ....DLB 90
Eichenlaub, John Ellis 1922- CANR-4
Earlier sketch in CA 1-4R
Eicher, David J(ohn) 1961- 113
Eicher, (Ethel) Elizabeth 17-20R
Eicher, Joanne B(ubolz) 1930- CANR-28
Earlier sketch in CA 49-52
Eichhorn, David Max 1906- CAP-1
Earlier sketch in CA 11-12
Eichhorn, Werner 1899- 29-32R
Eichler, Margrit 1942- 107
See also SATA 35
Eichler, Ned 1930- 132
Eichman, Mark 1949- 109
Eichner, Alfred S. 1937-1988 ....CANR-5
Obituary 124
Earlier sketch in CA 13-16R
Eichner, Hans 1921- CANR-19
Earlier sketches in CA 5-8R, CANR-4
Eichner, James A. 1927- 13-16R
See also SATA 4
Eichner, Maura 1915- CANR-14
Earlier sketch in CA 37-40R
Eichorn, Dorothy H(ansen) 1924- CANR-27
Earlier sketch in CA 49-52
Eickhoff, Andrew R(obert) 1924- 21-24R
Eicoff, Alvin Maurey 1921- 112
Eid, Leif 1908(?)-1976 Obituary 65-68
Eidelberg, Ludwig 1898-1970 ....CAP-1
Obituary 29-32R
Earlier sketch in CA 19-20
Eidelberg, Paul 1928- CANR-27
Earlier sketch in CA 21-24R
Eidenberg, Eugene 1939- 81-84
Eidesheim, Julie 1884-1972 Obituary 104
Eidsmoe, John 1945- 114
Eidsvik, Charles Vernon 1943- 101
Eidt, Robert C. 1923- 33-36R
Eiduson, Bernice T(abackman)
1921-1985 ....CANR-27
Earlier sketch in CA 1-4R
Eifert, Virginia (Louise) S(nider)
1911-1966 ....CANR-15
Earlier sketch in CA 1-4R
See also SATA 2
Eige, (Elizabeth) Lillian 1915- 136
See also SATA 65
Eigen, Manfred 1927- 108
Eigen, Michael 1936- CANR-39
Earlier sketch in CA 115
Eigner, Edwin M(oss) 1931- 21-24R
Eigner, Larry
See Eigner, Laurence (Joel)
See also CLC 9
See also DLB 5
Eigner, Laurence (Joel) 1927- CANR-6
Earlier sketch in CA 9-12R
See also Eigner, Larry
Eiland, Howard 1948- 111
Eiland, Murray L(ee) 1936- 85-88
Eilert, Richard E. 1947- 129
Eilert, Rick
See Eilert, Richard E.
Eilon, Samuel 1923- CANR-4
Earlier sketch in CA 5-8R
Eimer, D(ean) Robert 1927- 13-16R
Eimerl, Sarel (Henry) 1925- 21-24R
Einbond, Bernard Lionel 1937- 37-40R
Einhorn, Virginia Hilu
See Hilu, Virginia
Einsel, Mary E. 1929- 29-32R
Einsel, Naiad ....SATA 10
Einsel, Walter 1926- ....SATA 10
Einstein, Albert 1879-1955 133
Brief entry 121
See also MTCW
Einstein, Albert 1947- CANR-37
Brief entry 109
Earlier sketch in CA 113
Einstein, Charles 1926- CANR-29
Earlier sketch in CA 65-68
Einstein, Elizabeth (Ann) 1939- CANR-27
Earlier sketch in CA 109
Einstein, Stanley 1934- CANR-4
Earlier sketch in CA 53-56
Einstoss, Ron 1930(?)-1977 Obituary 69-72
Einzig, Paul 1897-1973 ....CANR-5
Obituary 89-92
Earlier sketch in CA 9-12R
Einzig, Susan 1922- ....SATA 43
Eire, Carlos M(arlo) N(ieto) 1950- 127
Eirelin, Glenn
See Evans, Glen
Eisdorfer, Carl 1930- 41-44R
Eisele, Albert A(lois) 1936- 41-44R
Eisele, Robert H. 1948- CANR-25
Earlier sketch in CA 108
Eiseley, Loren Corey 1907-1977 ....CANR-6
Obituary 73-76
Earlier sketch in CA 1-4R
See also AAYA 5
See also CLC 7
Eiseman, Alberta 1925- 77-80
See also SATA 15
Eiseman, Alvord L. 1916- 112
Eisen, Carol G.
See Rinzler, Carol Eisen (Gene)
Eisen, Jack 1925- 73-76
Eisen, Sydney 1929- 135
Eisenach, Eldon J(ohn) 1938- 106
Eisenberg, Azriel (Louis) 1903- CANR-10
Earlier sketch in CA 49-52
See also SATA 12
Eisenberg, Benjamin 1916-1984 Obituary 112
Eisenberg, Daniel Bruce 1946- CANR-6
Earlier sketch in CA 57-60
Eisenberg, Dennis (Harold) 1929- CANR-28
Earlier sketch in CA 25-28R
Eisenberg, Gerson G. 1909- 81-84
Eisenberg, Hershey H. 1927- 104
Eisenberg, Howard 1946- 101
Eisenberg, Larry 1919- 33-36R
Eisenberg, Lawrence B(enjamin) 77-80
Eisenberg, Lee 1946- CANR-9
Earlier sketch in CA 61-64
Eisenberg, Lisa 1949- 110
See also SATA 50, 57
Eisenberg, Maurice 1902-1972 Obituary 37-40R
Eisenberg, Phyllis Rose 1924- 111
See also SATA 41
Eisenberg, Ralph 1930-1973 ....CANR-3
Obituary 45-48
Earlier sketch in CA 5-8R
Eisenberg, Ronald L(ee) 1945- CANR-28
Earlier sketches in CA 73-76, CANR-13
Eisenberger, Kenneth 1948- 81-84
Eisenbud, Jule 1908- CANR-27
Earlier sketch in CA 49-52
Eisendrath, Craig R. 1936- 49-52
Eisenhower, Dwight D(avid)
1890-1969 ....CANR-24
Earlier sketch in CA 65-68
Eisenhower, John S(heldon) D(oud)
1922- CANR-32
Earlier sketches in CA 33-36R, CANR-14
Eisenhower, Julie Nixon 1948- 114
Eisenhower, Milton S(tover) 1899-1985 73-76
Obituary 116
Eisenman, Peter D(avid) 1932- 108
Eisenmenger, Robert Waltz 1926- 37-40R
Eisenreich, Herbert 1925-1986 ....DLB 85
Eisenschiml, Otto 1880-1963 ....1-4R
Eisenson, Jon 1907- 17-20R
Eisenstadt, A(braham) S(eldin) 1920- CANR-4
Earlier sketch in CA 9-12R
Eisenstadt, Jill 1963- ....CLC 50
Eisenstadt, Shmuel N(oah) 1923- 25-28R
Eisenstaedt, Alfred 1898- 108
Eisenstat, Jane Sperry 1920- 1-4R
Eisenstein, Elizabeth L(ewisohn) 1923- 89-92
Eisenstein, Hester 1940- 137
Eisenstein, Ira 1906- 21-24R
Eisenstein, James 1940- Brief entry 111
Eisenstein, Phyllis 1946- CANR-36
Earlier sketches in CA 85-88, CANR-16
Eisenstein, Sam(uel Abraham) 1932- CANR-16
Earlier sketch in CA 61-64
Eisenstein, Sergei (Mikhailovich)
1898-1948 Brief entry 114
Eiserer, Leonard Arnold 1948- 73-76
Eisinger, Chester E(manuel) 1915- 21-24R
Eisinger, Peter K(endall) 1942- 69-72
Eisler, Benita 1937- 136
Eisler, Colin (Tobias) 1931- 85-88
Eisler, Frieda Goldman
See Goldman-Eisler, Frieda
Eisler, Georg 1928- Brief entry 106
Eisler, George B. 1892(?)-1983 Obituary 111
Eisler, Hanns 1898-1962 Obituary 116
Eisler, Lawrence 1920- 122
Eisler, Paul (Erich) 1922-1978 61-64
Obituary 125
Eisler, Riane Tennenhaus 1931- 73-76
Eisman, Hy 1927- 65-68
Eisman, Mark 1948- 108
Eismann, Bernard N(orman) 1933- 1-4R
Eisner, Betty Grover 1915- 29-32R
Eisner, Elliot W(ayne) 1933- 123
Brief entry 118
Eisner, Gisela (Spanglet) 1925- CAP-1
Earlier sketch in CA 9-10
Eisner, Kurt 1867-1919 ....DLB 66
Eisner, Lotte (Henriette) 1896-1983 ....CANR-14
Obituary 111
Earlier sketch in CA 45-48
Eisner, Robert 1922- 107
Eisner, Sigmund 1920- 124
Eisner, Simon
See Kornbluth, C(yril) M.
Eisner, Victor 1921- 53-56
Eisner, Vivienne
See Margolis, Vivienne
Eisner, Will(iam Erwin) 1917- 108
See also SATA 31
Eiss, Harry Edwin 1950- 124
Eissenstat, Bernard W. 1927- 45-48
Eister, Allan W(ardell) 1915-1979 ....CANR-2
Earlier sketch in CA 45-48
Eiteman, David (Kurt) 1930- 45-48
Eiteman, Wilford J(ohn) 1902- CANR-4
Earlier sketch in CA 1-4R
Eitinger, Leo S(hua) 1912- CANR-16
Earlier sketch in CA 89-92
Eitington, Julius E. 1918- 120
Eitner, Lorenz E.A. 1919- CANR-5
Earlier sketch in CA 1-4R
Eitzen, Allan 1928- ....SATA 9
Eitzen, D(avid) Stanley 1934- CANR-19
Earlier sketches in CA 53-56, CANR-4
Eitzen, Ruth (Carper) 1924- 41-44R
See also SATA 9
Ekblaw, Sidney E(verette) 1903- 37-40R
Ekdahl, Janis (Kay) 1946- Brief entry 112
Ekeblad, Frederick A(lfred) 1917- 5-8R
Ekeh, Peter P(almer) 1937- 102
Ekeloef, (Bengt) Gunnar 1907-1968 123
Obituary 25-28R
See also Ekelof, (Bengt) Gunnar
See also CLC 27
Ekelof, (Bengt) Gunnar
See Ekeloef, (Bengt) Gunnar
See also CLC 27
Ekert-Rotholz, Alice Maria (Augusta) 1900- 129
Ekins, Paul (Whitfield) 1950- 123
Ekirch, A(rthur) Roger 1950- 109
Ekirch, Arthur A. Jr. 1915- CANR-2
Earlier sketch in CA 5-8R
Ekker, Charles 1930- 37-40R
Eklund, Gordon (Stewart) 1945- CANR-24
Earlier sketch in CA 33-36R
See also DLBY 83

Eklund, Jane Mary
  See Ball, Jane Eklund
Ekman, Paul 1934- ... CANR-14
  Earlier sketch in CA 37-40R
Ekman, Rosalind 1933- ... 33-36R
Ekola, Giles C(hester) 1927- ... 17-20R
Ekstein, Rudolf 1912- ... CANR-4
  Earlier sketch in CA 5-8R
Eksteins, Modris 1943- ... CANR-34
  Earlier sketch in CA 77-80
Ekstroem, (Sigrid) Margareta 1930- ... 135
Ekstrom, Margareta
  See Ekstroem, (Sigrid) Margareta
Ekstrom, Parmenia Migel
  1908-1989 Obituary ... 130
Ekvall, Robert B(rainerd) 1898- ... CANR-5
  Earlier sketch in CA 1-4R
Ekwall, Eldon E(dward) 1933- ... CANR-12
  Earlier sketch in CA 29-32R
Ekwensi, C. O. D.
  See Ekwensi, Cyprian (Odiatu Duaka)
Ekwensi, Cyprian (Odiatu Duaka)
  1921- ... CANR-18
  Earlier sketch in CA 29-32R
  See also BLC 1
  See also BW
  See also CLC 4
  See also DLB 117
  See also MTCW
  See also SATA 66
Ela, Jonathan P(ell) 1945- ... 81-84
Elaine
  See Leverson, Ada
  See also TCLC 18
Elam, Richard M(ace Jr.) 1920- ... 61-64
  See also SATA 9
El-Aref, Aref Obituary ... 41-44R
Elashoff, Janet Dixon 1942- ... 61-64
Elath, Eliahu 1903-1990 ... 13-16R
  Obituary ... 132
El-Ayouty, Yassin 1928- ... CANR-14
  Earlier sketch in CA 29-32R
Elazar, Daniel J(udah) 1934- ... CANR-13
  Earlier sketch in CA 21-24R
El-Baz, Farouk 1938- ... CANR-26
  Earlier sketches in CA 25-28R, CANR-10
Elbert, Edmund J(oseph) 1923- ... 37-40R
Elbert, George A. 1911- ... CANR-35
  Earlier sketch in CA 61-64
Elbert, Samuel H(oyt) 1907- ... CANR-5
  Earlier sketch in CA 1-4R
Elbert, Sarah 1937- ... 135
Elbert, Virginie Fowler 1912- ... CANR-35
  Earlier sketches in CA 61-64, CANR-8
Elbin, Paul Nowell 1905- ... CANR-35
  Earlier sketch in CA 69-72
Elbing, Alvar O(liver) Jr. 1928- ... 21-24R
Elbing, Carol J(eppson) 1930- ... 21-24R
Elbogen, Paul 1894- ... 5-8R
Elborn, Geoffrey 1950- ... 109
Elbow, Peter (Henry) 1935- ... CANR-28
  Earlier sketches in CA 65-68, CANR-12
Elbrecht, Paul G. 1921- ... 17-20R
El Bundukhari
  See Dent, Anthony Austen
Elchamo, Jason
  See Caballero, Manuel
Elchamo, Sebastian
  See Caballero, Manuel
Elcock, Howard J(ames) 1942- ... CANR-29
  Earlier sketches in CA 29-32R, CANR-12
El Crummo
  See Crumb, R(obert)
Eldefonso, Edward 1933- ... CANR-14
  Earlier sketch in CA 21-24R
Elder, Betty Doak 1938- ... 112
Elder, Ellen Rozanne 1940- ... 111
Elder, Gary 1939- ... 73-76
Elder, George Colman the 1732-1794 ... DLB 89
Elder, Glen(nard) H(oll) Jr. 1934- ... CANR-3
  Earlier sketch in CA 49-52
Elder, John William 1933- ... 111
Elder, John 1947- ... 133
Elder, Karl 1948- ... 77-80
Elder, Leon
  See Young, Noel
Elder, Lonne III 1931- ... CANR-25
  Earlier sketch in CA 81-84
  See also BLC 1
  See also BW
  See also DLB 7, 38, 44
Elder, Mark 1935- ... CANR-2
  Earlier sketch in CA 49-52
Elder, Michael (Aiken) 1931- ... 33-36R
Elder, Rob(ert Laurie) 1938- ... 125
Elder, Robert E(llsworth) 1915- ... 1-4R
Elder, Shirley (A.) 1931- ... 132
  Brief entry ... 118
Elderfield, John 1943- ... 132
Eldersveld, Samuel James 1917- ... 111
Eldin, Raymond
  See Morton, James (Severs)
Eldjarn, Kristjan (Thorarinsson)
  1916-1982 Obituary ... 110
Eldred, Vince 1924- ... 69-72
Eldredge, H(anford) Wentworth
  1909-1991 ... 41-44R
  Obituary ... 133
Eldredge, Laurence H(oward) 1902- ... CAP-2
  Earlier sketch in CA 25-28
Eldridge, Colin Clifford 1942- ... 107
Eldridge, Frank R. 1889(?)-1976 Obituary ... 69-72
Eldridge, J(ohn) E. T. 1936- ... CANR-11
  Earlier sketch in CA 25-28R
Eldridge, Marian (Favel Clair) 1936- ... 118
Eldridge, Paul 1888- ... 9-12R
Eldridge, Retha Hazel (Giles) 1910- ... CAP-1
  Earlier sketch in CA 13-14
Eleanor, Sister Joseph ... 25-28R
Elegant, Robert (Sampson) 1928- ... CANR-30
  Earlier sketches in CA 1-4R, CANR-1
Elek, Paul 1906(?)-1976 Obituary ... 69-72
el-Erian, Abdullah Ali 1920-1981 Obituary ... 108
Elethea, Abba
  See Thompson, James W.
Elevitch, M(orton) D. 1925- ... CANR-2
  Earlier sketch in CA 49-52
Eley, Geoff(rey Howard) 1949- ... 129
Eley, Lynn W. 1925- ... CANR-16
  Earlier sketch in CA 25-28R
Elfenbein, Julien 1897-1983 ... CANR-5
  Obituary ... 109
  Earlier sketch in CA 1-4R
Elfman, Blossom 1925- ... CANR-39
  Earlier sketches in CA 45-48, CANR-2, 17
  See also SATA 8
Elford, Homer J. R. 1912- ... CANR-9
  Earlier sketch in CA 21-24R
Elgar, Edward (William)
  1857-1934 Brief entry ... 116
Elgar, Frank 1899- ... 102
Elgin, Kathleen 1923- ... 25-28R
  See also SATA 39
Elgin, Mary
  See Stewart, Dorothy Mary
Elgin, (Patricia Anne) Suzette Haden
  1936- ... CANR-8
  Earlier sketch in CA 61-64
Elgood, Robert (Francis Willard) 1948- ... 125
el Hajjam, Mohammed ben Chaib
  1940- ... CANR-38
  Earlier sketches in CA 97-100, CANR-17
El Huitlacoche
  See Keller, Gary D.
Elia
  See Lamb, Charles
Eliach, Yaffa 1935- ... 110
Eliade, Mircea 1907-1986 ... CANR-30
  Obituary ... 119
  Earlier sketch in CA 65-68
  See also CLC 19
  See also MTCW
Elias, Albert J. 1920- ... 81-84
Elias, C(laude) E(dward) Jr. 1924- ... 13-16R
Elias, Christopher 1925- ... 33-36R
Elias, Eileen
  See Davies, Eileen Winifred
Elias, Horace J(ay) 1910- ... CANR-16
  Earlier sketch in CA 89-92
Elias, John L(awrence) 1933- ... CANR-25
  Earlier sketch in CA 69-72
Elias, Norbert 1897-1990 Obituary ... 132
Elias, Robert H(enry) 1914- ... 61-64
Elias, Taslim Olawale 1914- ... CANR-21
  Earlier sketches in CA 13-16R, CANR-6
Elias, Thomas S. 1942- ... CANR-35
  Earlier sketch in CA 114
Eliason, Joyce 1934- ... 77-80
Eliav, Arie L(ova) 1921- ... CANR-28
  Earlier sketches in CA 69-72, CANR-11
Elicker, Charles W. 1951-1978 Obituary ... 115
Elie, Robert 1915-1973 ... DLB 88
Elieff, Deanne D(esmond) 1926- ... 113
Elinson, Jack 1917- ... CANR-20
  Earlier sketches in CA 45-48, CANR-2
Elioseff, Lee Andrew 1933- ... 17-20R
Eliot, A. D.
  See Jewett, (Theodora) Sarah Orne
Eliot, Alexander 1919- ... CANR-1
  Earlier sketch in CA 49-52
Eliot, Alice
  See Jewett, (Theodora) Sarah Orne
Eliot, Anne
  See Cole, Lois Dwight
Eliot, Dan
  See Silverberg, Robert
Eliot, George Fielding
  1894-1971 Obituary ... 29-32R
Eliot, George 1819-1880 ... CDBLB 1832-1890
  See also DLB 21, 35, 55
  See also WLC
Eliot, John 1604-1690 ... DLB 24
Eliot, Sonny 1926- ... 81-84
Eliot, T(homas) S(tearns) 1888-1965 ... 5-8R
  Obituary ... 25-28R
  See also CDALB 1929-1941
  See also CLC 1, 2, 3, 6, 9, 10, 13, 15, 24, 34, 41, 55, 57
  See also DLB 7, 10, 45, 63
  See also MTCW
  See also PC 5
  See also WLC 2
Eliot, Thomas H(opkinson) 1907-1991 ... 89-92
  Obituary ... 135
Eliot Hurst, M(ichael) E(liot) 1938- ... 57-60
Eliovson, Sima (Benveniste) 1919- ... CANR-20
  Earlier sketches in CA 13-16R, CANR-5
Elis, Islwyn Ffowc 1924- ... 93-96
Elisabeth (Ottilie Luise), Queen (Pauline)
  1843-1916 Brief entry ... 123
Eliscu, Frank 1912- ... 57-60
Elish, Dan 1960- ... 136
  See also SATA 68
Elisofon, Eliot 1911-1973 Obituary ... 41-44R
  See also SATA 21
Elison, George 1937- ... 53-56
Elium, Jeanne (Ann) 1947- ... 138
Elizabeth 1866-1941 ... TCLC 41
Elizabeth Marie, Sister 1914- ... 9-12R
Elizondo (Dominguez), Sergio D(anilo)
  1930- ... 131
  See also DLB 82
  See also HW
Elizondo, Sergio
  See Elizondo (Dominguez), Sergio D(anilo)
Elizur, Joel 1952- ... 135
Elkann, Alain 1950- ... 127
Elkhadem, Saad (Eldin Amin) 1932- ... 131
Elkholy, Abdo A. 1925- ... 21-24R
Elkin, Benjamin 1911- ... CANR-4
  Earlier sketch in CA 1-4R
  See also SATA 3
Elkin, Frederick 1918- ... 41-44R
Elkin, H. V.
  See Hinkle, Vernon
Elkin, Judith Laikin 1928- ... CANR-19
  Earlier sketches in CA 53-56, CANR-4
Elkin, Stanley L(awrence) 1930- ... CANR-8
  Earlier sketch in CA 9-12R
  See also CLC 4, 6, 9, 14, 27, 51
  See also DLB 2, 28
  See also DLBY 80
  See also MTCW
Elkin, Stephen L(loyd) 1941- ... 93-96
Elkind, David 1931- ... CANR-1
  Earlier sketch in CA 45-48
Elkins, Aaron J. 1935- ... 126
  See also BEST 89:1
Elkins, Dov Peretz 1937- ... CANR-30
  Earlier sketches in CA 29-32R, CANR-12
  See also SATA 5
Elkins, Ella Ruth 1929- ... 25-28R
Elkins, Stanley Maurice 1925- ... 102
Elkins, T(homas) H(enry) 1926- Brief entry ... 111
Elkins, William R. 1926- ... 33-36R
Elkon, Jon 1949- ... 134
Elkon, Juliette
  See Elkon-Hamelecourt, Juliette
Elkon-Hamelecourt, Juliette 1912- ... 57-60
Elkouri, Frank 1921- ... 69-72
Elkus, Jonathan Britton 1931- ... 111
Ellacott, S(amuel) E(rnest) 1911- ... CANR-3
  Earlier sketch in CA 5-8R
  See also SATA 19
Elledge, Jim 1950- ... CANR-39
  Earlier sketches in CA 102, CANR-19
Elledge, Scott ... CLC 34
Elledge, W(aymon) Paul 1938- ... 25-28R
Ellen, Barbara 1938- ... 5-8R
Ellen, Jaye
  See Nixon, Joan Lowery
Ellenberger, Henri F(rederic) 1905- ... CAP-2
  Earlier sketch in CA 29-32
Ellenbogen, Eileen 1917- ... 104
Ellender, Raphael 1906-1972 Obituary ... 37-40R
Ellens, J(ay) Harold 1932- ... CANR-31
  Earlier sketches in CA 57-60, CANR-7
Ellenson, Gene 1921- ... 57-60
Eller, John 1935- ... 105
Eller, Ronald D 1948- ... 110
Eller, Scott
  See Holinger, William (Jacques)
Eller, Vernard (Marion) 1927- ... CANR-24
  Earlier sketches in CA 21-24R, CANR-9
Eller, William 1921- ... 77-80
Ellerbeck, Rosemary (Anne L'Estrange)
  ... CANR-24
  Earlier sketch in CA 106
Ellerbee, Linda 1944- ... 115
  Brief entry ... 110
Ellerman, Annie Winifred 1894-1983 ... 104
  Obituary ... 108
Ellery, John Blaise 1920- ... 9-12R
Elles, Dora Amy
  See Wentworth, Patricia
Ellet, Elizabeth F. 1818(?)-1877 ... DLB 30
Ellett, Marcella H. 1931- ... 21-24R
Ellfeldt, Lois 1910- ... 33-36R
Ellicott, V. L.
  See Ellicott, Valcoulon MeMoyne
Ellicott, Valcoulon MeMoyne
  1893-1983 Obituary ... 109
Ellin, E(lizabeth) M(uriel) 1905- ... CAP-2
  Earlier sketch in CA 29-32
Ellin, Stanley (Bernard) 1916-1986 ... CANR-28
  Obituary ... 119
  Earlier sketches in CA 1-4R, CANR-4
  See also MTCW
Elling, Karl A(lwin) 1935- ... 25-28R
Elling, Ray H. 1929- ... 33-36R
Ellingsworth, Huber W. 1928- ... CANR-10
  Earlier sketch in CA 21-24R
Ellington, Duke
  See Ellington, Edward Kennedy
Ellington, Edward Kennedy 1899-1974 ... 97-100
  Obituary ... 49-52
Ellington, James W(esley) 1927- ... 37-40R
Ellington, Mercer (Kennedy)
  1919- Brief entry ... 113
Ellington, Richard 1915(?)-1980 Obituary ... 102
Ellinwood, Leonard Webster 1905- ... 1-4R
Elliot, Alistair 1932- ... 129
Elliot, Asa
  See Blinder, Elliot
Elliot, Daniel
  See Feldman, Leonard
Elliot, Edith M(arie Farmer) 1912- ... 21-24R
Elliot, Elisabeth (Howard) 1926- ... CANR-6
  Earlier sketch in CA 5-8R
Elliot, Geraldine
  See
  Bingham, Evangeline M(arguerite) L(adys) (Elliot)
Elliot, Ian 1925- ... 69-72
Elliot, Jeffrey M. 1947- ... CANR-24
  Earlier sketch in CA 106
Elliot, John 1898-1988 Obituary ... 126
Elliott, Alan C(urtis) 1952- ... CANR-18
  Earlier sketch in CA 102
Elliott, Allan
  See Elliott, K(enneth) A(llan) C(aldwell)
Elliott, Aubrey (George) 1917- ... 93-96
Elliott, Bob
  See Elliott, Robert B.
Elliott, Brian (Robinson) 1910- ... 25-28R
Elliott, Bruce (Walter Gardner Lively Stacy)
  1915(?)-1973 Obituary ... 41-44R
Elliott, C(larence) Orville 1913- ... 33-36R
Elliott, Charles 1951- ... 138
Elliott, Chip
  See Elliott, E(scalus) E(mmert) III
Elliott, Clark A. 1941- ... 137
Elliott, David W. 1939- ... 45-48
Elliott, Don
  See Silverberg, Robert
Elliott, Donald 1928- ... 69-72
Elliott, Douglas B(yron) 1947- ... 113
Elliott, E(scalus) E(mmert) III 1945- ... 29-32R
Elliott, Ebenezer 1781-1849 ... DLB 96
Elliott, Emory 1942- ... CANR-23
  Earlier sketch in CA 69-72
Elliott, Errol T(homas) 1894- ... 69-72
Elliott, George P(aul) 1918-1980 ... CANR-2
  Obituary ... 97-100
  Earlier sketch in CA 1-4R
  See also CLC 2
Elliott, George 1923- ... DLB 68
Elliott, Harley 1940- ... CANR-4
  Earlier sketch in CA 49-52
Elliott, Hugh (Francis Ivo) 1913- Brief entry ... 112
Elliott, Inger McCabe 1933- ... 127
Elliott, James Francis 1914-1981 Obituary ... 110
Elliott, Jan Walter 1939- ... 37-40R
Elliott, Janice 1931- ... CANR-29
  Earlier sketches in CA 13-16R, CANR-8
  See also CLC 47
  See also DLB 14
Elliott, John E(d) 1931- ... CANR-5
  Earlier sketch in CA 1-4R
Elliott, John H(all) 1935- ... 126
  Brief entry ... 113
Elliott, John H(uxtable) 1930- ... CANR-3
  Earlier sketch in CA 5-8R
Elliott, John R. Jr. 1937- ... 25-28R
Elliott, John 1938- ... 25-28R
Elliott, Jumbo
  See Elliott, James Francis
Elliott, K(enneth) A(llan) C(aldwell)
  1903-1986 ... 108
  Obituary ... 119
Elliott, Kit 1936- ... 29-32R
Elliott, Lawrence 1924- ... CANR-21
  Earlier sketches in CA 5-8R, CANR-3
Elliott, Leonard M. 1902- ... CAP-1
  Earlier sketch in CA 13-14
Elliott, Lesley 1905- ... CANR-14
  Earlier sketch in CA 77-80
Elliott, Malissa Childs 1929(?)-1979 ... 101
  Obituary ... 85-88
Elliott, Marianne 1948- ... 132
Elliott, Mark Rowe 1947- ... CANR-24
  Earlier sketch in CA 107
Elliott, Neil 1939- ... 25-28R
Elliott, Osborn 1924- ... CANR-12
  Earlier sketch in CA 69-72
Elliott, P(hilip) R(oss) C(ourtney)
  1943(?)-1983 Obituary ... 110
Elliott, Ralph H. 1925- ... CANR-2
  Earlier sketch in CA 1-4R
Elliott, Ralph W(arren) V(ictor) 1921- ... 127
Elliott, Raymond Pruitt 1904- ... 17-20R
Elliott, Richard V. 1934- ... 33-36R
Elliott, Robert
  See Garfinkel, Bernard Max
Elliott, Robert B. 1923- ... 134
  Brief entry ... 109
Elliott, Robert C(arl) 1914-1981 ... CANR-21
  Earlier sketch in CA 1-4R
Elliott, Roberta ... 97-100
Elliott, Russell Richard 1912- ... 69-72
Elliott, Sarah M(cCarn) 1930- ... 41-44R
  See also SATA 14
Elliott, Sheldon D(ouglass)
  1906-1972 Obituary ... 33-36R
Elliott, Spencer H(ayward) 1883-1967 ... CAP-1
  Earlier sketch in CA 11-12
Elliott, Sumner Locke 1917-1991 ... CANR-21
  Obituary ... 134
  Earlier sketches in CA 5-8R, CANR-2
  See also CLC 38
Elliott, Susan (Anthony) 1947- ... 104
Elliott, Thomas Joseph 1941- ... 49-52
Elliott, Ward E(dward) Y(andell) 1937- ... 85-88
Elliott, William
  See Bradbury, Ray (Douglas)
Elliott, William III 1788-1863 ... DLB 3
Elliott, William Douglas 1938- ... CANR-9
  Earlier sketch in CA 65-68
Elliott, William M(arion) Jr. 1903- ... CAP-1
  Earlier sketch in CA 9-10
Elliott, William Yandell
  1896-1979 Obituary ... 85-88
Ellis, A. E. ... CLC 7
Ellis, Albert 1913- ... CANR-17
  Earlier sketches in CA 1-4R, CANR-2
Ellis, Alec (Charles Owen) 1932- ... CANR-1
  Earlier sketch in CA 45-48
Ellis, Alice Thomas
  See Haycraft, Anna
  See also CLC 40
Ellis, (Mary) Amabel (Nassau Strachey) Williams
  See
  Williams-Ellis, (Mary) Amabel (Nassau Strachey)
Ellis, Amanda M. 1898-1969 ... CAP-2
  Earlier sketch in CA 23-24
Ellis, Anyon
  See Rowland-Entwistle, (Arthur) Theodore (Henry)

Ellis, Audrey ... CANR-10
Earlier sketch in CA 65-68
Ellis, B(yron) Robert 1940- ... 53-56
Ellis, Bret Easton 1964- ... 123
Brief entry ... 118
See also AAYA 2
See also CLC 39, 71
Ellis, Brooks (Fleming)
1897-1976 Obituary ... 65-68
Ellis, C(uthbert) Hamilton 1909- ... 13-16R
Ellis, Carl F. Jr. 1946- ... 121
Ellis, Carolyn Sue 1950- ... 122
Ellis, Charles D(aniel) 1937- Brief entry ... 115
Ellis, Charles Drummond
1895-1980 Obituary ... 105
Ellis, Charles Howard 1895- ... CAP-1
Earlier sketch in CA 13-14
Ellis, Clyde T(aylor) 1908- ... CAP-2
Earlier sketch in CA 23-24
Ellis, Dan C. 1949- ... 125
Ellis, David Maldwyn 1914- ... 9-12R
Ellis, Dock (Phillip Jr.) 1945- Brief entry ... 111
Ellis, E. S.
See Ellis, Edward S(ylvester)
Ellis, Edward Robb 1911- ... 25-28R
Ellis, Edward S(ylvester)
1840-1916 Brief entry ... 122
See also DLB 42
See also YABC 1
Ellis, Ella Thorp 1928- ... CANR-2
Earlier sketch in CA 49-52
See also SAAS 9
See also SATA 7
Ellis, Elma I(srael) 1918- ... 33-36R
Ellis, Evelyn 1948- ... 138
Ellis, Florence Hawley 1906- ... 61-64
Ellis, Frank Hale 1916- ... 73-76
Ellis, (J.) Frank(lyn)
1904(?)-1976 Obituary ... 65-68
Ellis, Frank K. 1933- ... 25-28R
Ellis, Harry Bearse 1921- ... CANR-2
Earlier sketch in CA 1-4R
See also SATA 9
Ellis, (Henry) Havelock
1859-1939 Brief entry ... 109
See also TCLC 14
Ellis, Helen E. (Oickle) 1926- ... 120
Ellis, Henry C(arlton) 1927- ... CANR-17
Earlier sketch in CA 97-100
Ellis, Herbert
See Wilson, Lionel
Ellis, Hilda Roderick
See Davidson, H(ilda) R(oderick) Ellis
Ellis, Howard S(ylvester) 1898- ... CANR-28
Obituary ... 137
Earlier sketch in CA 49-52
Ellis, Howard W(oodrow) 1914- ... CANR-38
Earlier sketches in CA 1-4R, CANR-17
Ellis, Humphry F(rancis) 1907- ... 5-8R
Ellis, J(ames) H(ervey) S(tewart) 1893- ... CAP-2
Earlier sketch in CA 23-24
Ellis, J(ohn) R(ichard) 1938- ... 85-88
Ellis, Jack C(lare) 1922- ... 89-92
Ellis, Jack D. 1941- ... 121
Ellis, James 1935- ... 37-40R
Ellis, Jody 1925- ... 57-60
Ellis, John H. 1931- ... 125
Ellis, John M(artin) 1936- ... CANR-3
Earlier sketch in CA 49-52
Ellis, John Marion 1917- ... 49-52
Ellis, John O(liver) 1917- ... 85-88
Ellis, John Tracy 1905- ... CANR-5
Earlier sketch in CA 1-4R
Ellis, Joseph J(ohn) 1943- ... 53-56
Ellis, Joyce K. (Eileen) 1950- ... 116
Ellis, Julie 1933- Brief entry ... 111
Ellis, Kail C. 1940- ... 127
Ellis, Kathy
See Bentley, Margaret
Ellis, Keith Stanley 1927- ... 102
Ellis, L(ewis) Ethan 1898-1977 ... CANR-4
Earlier sketch in CA 5-8R
Ellis, Landon
See Ellison, Harlan
Ellis, Leigh 1959- ... 105
Ellis, Leo R(oy) 1909- ... 9-12R
Ellis, M(adeleine) B(lanche) 1915- ... 69-72
Ellis, M(arion) LeRoy 1928- ... 37-40R
Ellis, Marc H. 1952- ... CANR-24
Earlier sketch in CA 107
Ellis, Mark Karl 1945- ... 103
Ellis, Mary Jackson 1916- ... CANR-17
Earlier sketch in CA 1-4R
Ellis, Mary Leith 1921- ... 21-24R
Ellis, Mel(vin Richard) 1912-1984 ... 13-16R
Obituary ... 113
See also SATA 7, 39
Ellis, Norman R. 1924- ... 13-16R
Ellis, Olivia
See Wintle, Anne
Ellis, Peter Berresford 1943- ... CANR-21
Earlier sketch in CA 81-84
Ellis, Peter F(rancis) 1921- ... 115
Ellis, Ray C. 1898- ... CAP-2
Earlier sketch in CA 21-22
Ellis, Richard E(manuel) 1937- ... 61-64
Ellis, Richard (J.) 1960- ... 135
Ellis, Richard N(athaniel) 1939- ... 33-36R
Ellis, Richard White Bernard 1902- ... CAP-1
Earlier sketch in CA 13-16
Ellis, Richard 1938- ... 104
Ellis, Roger (Melville) 1943- ... 126
Ellis, Ron(ald Walter) 1941- ... 77-80
Ellis, (Christopher) Royston (George)
1941- ... 5-8R
Ellis, Sarah 1952- ... 123
See also SATA 68
Ellis, Scott
See Schorr, Mark
Ellis, Trey 1962- ... CLC 55
Ellis, Ulrich Ruegg 1904-1981 Obituary ... 108
Ellis, Walter M. 1943- ... 137
Ellis, Wesley
See Wallmann, Jeffrey M(iner)
Ellis, William Donahue 1918- ... CANR-29
Earlier sketch in CA 49-52
Ellisen, Stanley A(rthur) 1922- ... 133
Ellison, Alfred 1916- ... 1-4R
Ellison, Craig W(illiam) 1944- ... CANR-6
Earlier sketch in CA 57-60
Ellison, Fred P(ittman) 1922- Brief entry ... 113
Ellison, George R. 1907(?)-1983 Obituary ... 110
Ellison, Gerald Alexander 1910- ... CAP-1
Earlier sketch in CA 13-14
Ellison, Glenn "Tiger"
See Ellison, Glenn
Ellison, Glenn 1911- ... 89-92
Ellison, H(enry) L(eopold) 1903- ... CANR-6
Earlier sketch in CA 5-8R
Ellison, Harlan 1934- ... CANR-5
Earlier sketch in CA 5-8R
See also CLC 1, 13, 42
See also DLB 8
See also MTCW
Ellison, Henry 1931-1965 ... 5-8R
Ellison, Herbert J(ay) 1929- ... 13-16R
Ellison, James E. 1927- ... 13-16R
Ellison, James Whitfield 1929- ... CANR-1
Earlier sketch in CA 1-4R
Ellison, Jerome 1907-1981 ... 29-32R
Obituary ... 104
Ellison, John Malcus 1889-1979 ... CANR-25
Earlier sketch in CA 1-4R
Ellison, Katherine (White) 1941- ... 101
Ellison, Katherine 1957- ... 127
Ellison, Lucile Watkins 1907(?)-1979 ... 109
Obituary ... 93-96
See also SATA 22, 50
Ellison, Max 1914-1985 ... 57-60
Obituary ... 116
See also AITN 1
Ellison, Ralph (Waldo) 1914- ... CANR-24
Earlier sketch in CA 9-12R
See also BLC 1
See also BW
See also CDALB 1941-1968
See also CLC 1, 3, 11, 54
See also DLB 2, 76
See also MTCW
See also WLC
Ellison, Randall Erskine
1904-1984 Obituary ... 113
Ellison, Reuben Young 1907- ... 13-16R
Ellison, Virginia H(owell) 1910- ... 33-36R
See also SATA 4
Ellison, William McLaren
1919(?)-1978 Obituary ... 81-84
Elliston, Frederick Allen 1944- ... 105
Elliston, Thomas R(alph)
1919-1977 Obituary ... 73-76
Elliston, Valerie Mae (Watkinson) 1929- ... 9-12R
Ellithorpe, Harold (Earle) 1925- ... 77-80
Ellman, Michael 1942- ... 45-48
Ellmann, Lucy (Elizabeth) 1956- ... 128
See also CLC 61
Ellmann, Richard (David) 1918-1987 ... CANR-28
Obituary ... 122
Earlier sketches in CA 1-4R, CANR-2
See also BEST 89:2
See also CLC 50
See also DLB 103
See also DLBY 87
See also MTCW
Ellroy, James 1948- ... 138
See also BEST 90:4
Ellsberg, Daniel 1931- ... 69-72
Ellsberg, Edward 1891- ... 5-8R
See also SATA 7
Ellsworth, L(ida) E(lizabeth) 1948- ... 118
Ellsworth, P(aul) T(heodore) 1897- ... 17-20R
Ellsworth, Ralph Eugene 1907- ... CANR-2
Earlier sketch in CA 1-4R
Ellsworth, S(amuel) George 1916- ... 45-48
Ellsworth, Sallie Bingham 1937- ... CANR-18
Earlier sketch in CA 1-4R
Ellsworth, Scott 1954- ... 109
Ellul, Jacques 1912- ... 81-84
Ellvinger, Barbara Anne Price
See Price, Barbara Anne Ellvinger
Ellwood, Edith E(lizabeth)
See Muesing-Ellwood, Edith E(lizabeth)
Ellwood, Gracia-Fay 1938- ... 29-32R
Ellwood, Robert S(cott) Jr. 1933- ... CANR-14
Earlier sketch in CA 41-44R
El Mallakh, Ragaei (William) 1925- ... 112
Elman, Richard 1934- ... 17-20R
See also CAAS 3
See also CLC 19
Elman, Robert 1930- ... CANR-3
Earlier sketch in CA 45-48
Elmandjra, Mahdi 1933- ... 89-92
Elmblad, Mary (B.) 1927- ... 108
El-Meligi, A(bdel) Moneim 1923- ... 17-20R
Elmen, Paul H. 1913- ... 89-92
Elmendorf, Mary Lindsay 1917- ... 57-60
Elmer, Carlos Hall 1920- ... 102
Elmer, Gary W. 1941- ... 122
Elmer, Irene (Elizabeth) 1937- ... 1-4R
El-Messidi, Kathy Groehn 1946- ... 57-60
Elmhirst, Leonard Knight
1893-1974 Obituary ... 115
Elmore, Ernest Carpenter
1901-1957 Brief entry ... 114
Elmore, (Carolyn) Patricia 1933- ... 114
See also SATA 35, 38
Elms, Alan C(linton) 1938- ... 69-72
Elmslie, Kenward 1929- ... CANR-25
Earlier sketches in CA 21-24R, CANR-9
Elmslie, William Alexander Leslie
1885-1965 ... CAP-1
Earlier sketch in CA 13-14
Elmstrom, George P. 1925- ... 5-8R
El Muhajir 1944- ... CANR-26
Earlier sketch in CA 49-52
See also Marvin X
See also BW
Elon, Amos 1926- ... 128
Brief entry ... 121
Elovitz, Mark H(arvey) 1938- ... 69-72
Elphick, Richard Hall 1943- ... 112
Elphinstone, Francis
See Powell-Smith, Vincent (Walter Francis)
Elphinstone, Murgatroyd
See Kahler, Hugh (Torbert) MacNair
Elrick, George S(eefurth) 1921- ... 112
Elron
See Hubbard, L(afayette) Ron(ald)
el Ropo, Smokestack
See Perry, Charles
El Saadawi, Nawal 1931- ... 118
See also CAAS 11
El Saffar, Ruth (Ann) 1941- ... 69-72
Elsasser, Albert B(ertrand) 1918- ... CANR-22
Earlier sketch in CA 69-72
Elsasser, Glen Robert 1935- ... 65-68
Elsberry, Terence 1943- ... 45-48
Elsbree, Langdon 1929- ... 33-36R
Else, Gerald Frank 1908-1982 ... 61-64
Obituary ... 107
Elsea, Janet G(ayle) 1942- ... 119
Elsen, Albert E(dward) 1927- ... CANR-26
Earlier sketches in CA 5-8R, CANR-11
El-Shabazz, El-Hajj Malik
See Little, Malcolm
Elshtain, Jean Bethke 1941- ... 106
Elsmere, Jane Shaffer 1932- ... 37-40R
Elsner, Gisela 1937- ... 9-12R
Elsner, Henry Jr. 1930- ... 21-24R
Elsom, John Edward 1934- ... 65-68
Elson, Edward L(ee) R(oy) 1906- ... CANR-3
Earlier sketch in CA 5-8R
Elson, Lawrence M(cClellan) 1935- ... 53-56
Elson, R. N.
See Nelson, R(adell) Faraday
Elson, Robert T(ruscott) 1906-1987 ... 77-80
Obituary ... 121
Elson, Ruth Miller 1917- ... 13-16R
Elspeth
See Bragdon, Elspeth MacDuffie
Elstar, Dow
See Gallun, Raymond Z(inke)
Elstob, Peter 1915- ... CANR-1
Earlier sketch in CA 1-4R
Elston, Allan Vaughan 1887-1976 ... CANR-3
Earlier sketch in CA 1-4R
Elston, Gene 1922- ... 33-36R
Elston, Robert 1934-1987 Obituary ... 124
Elston, Wilbur E(vans) 1913- Brief entry ... 112
Elstun, Esther N(ies) 1935- ... 117
Elsy, (Winifred) Mary ... 93-96
Elting, John R(obert) 1911- ... CANR-31
Earlier sketch in CA 112
Elting, Mary 1906- ... CANR-19
Earlier sketches in CA 9-12R, CANR-4
See also SATA 2
Eltis, David 1940- ... 127
Eltis, Walter (Alfred) 1933- ... 131
Elton, Edwin J(oel) 1939- ... 53-56
Elton, G(eoffrey) R(udolph) 1921- ... CANR-30
Earlier sketches in CA 9-12R, CANR-3
Elton, John
See Marsh, John
Elton, W(illiam) R. 1921- Brief entry ... 111
el-Toure, Askia Muhammad Abu Bakr
See Toure, Askia Muhammad Abu Bakr el
Eltringham, S(tewart) K(eith) 1929- ... 110
Eluard, Paul
See Grindel, Eugene
See also TCLC 7, 41
El Uqsor
See Borgmann, Dmitri A(lfred)
Elvenstar, Diane C.
See Medved, Diane
Elvin, Drake
See Beha, Ernest
Elvin, Harold 1909-1985 ... CANR-4
Obituary ... 115
Earlier sketch in CA 5-8R
Elvin, (Herbert) Lionel 1905- ... CAP-1
Earlier sketch in CA 13-14
Elvin, Mark 1938- ... 73-76
Elward, James (Joseph) 1928- ... CANR-12
Earlier sketch in CA 29-32R
Elwart, Joan Potter 1927- ... 25-28R
See also SATA 2
Elwell, Fayette Herbert 1885- ... 5-8R
Elwell, Jerry MacElroy 1922- ... 57-60
Elwell, Stillman J. 1894-1977 Obituary ... 110
Elwell, Walter A(lexander) 1937- ... 119
Elwell-Sutton, L(aurence) P(aul)
1912-1984 ... 5-8R
Obituary ... 114
Elwin, Malcolm 1903-1973 Obituary ... 89-92
Elwin, William
See Ebenstein, William
Elwood, Ann 1931- ... 125
See also SATA 52, 55
Elwood, Catharyn 1903(?)-1975 Obituary ... 61-64
Elwood, Douglas J(ames) 1924- ... 116
Elwood, Muriel 1902- ... CAP-1
Earlier sketch in CA 9-10
Elwood, Roger 1943- ... CANR-10
Earlier sketch in CA 57-60
See also SATA 58
Elwyn-Jones, Pearl Binder 1904- ... 107
Ely, David 1927- ... 53-56
Ely, Donald P(aul) 1930- ... 29-32R
Ely, James W(allace) Jr. 1938- ... 73-76
Ely, John Hart 1938- ... 103
Ely, John Wilton
See Wilton-Ely, John
Ely, Paul (Henri) 1897-1975 Obituary ... 53-56
Ely, Scott 1944- ... 127
Ely, Virginia (Shackelford) 1899- ... CANR-24
Earlier sketch in CA 1-4R
Elytis, Odysseus 1911- ... 102
See also CLC 15, 49
See also MTCW
Elzinga, Kenneth G(erald) 1941- ... CANR-13
Earlier sketches in CA 49-52, CANR-1
Emans, Robert 1934- ... 53-56
Emanuel, James A. 1921- ... CANR-12
Earlier sketch in CA 29-32R
See also BW
See also DLB 41
Ember, Carol R(uchlis) 1943- ... 77-80
Emberley, Barbara A(nne) 1932- ... CANR-5
Earlier sketch in CA 5-8R
See also CLR 5
See also MAICYA
See also SATA 8, 70
Emberley, Ed(ward Randolph) 1931- ... CANR-36
Earlier sketches in CA 5-8R, CANR-5
See also CLR 5
See also MAICYA
See also SATA 8, 70
Emberley, Michael 1960- ... 104
See also SATA 34
Embey, Philip
See Philipp, Elliot Elias
Emblen, D(onald) L(ewis) 1918- ... 33-36R
Embling, John 1952- ... 111
Emboden, William A(llen) Jr. 1935- ... CANR-34
Earlier sketches in CA 41-44R, CANR-14
Embree, Ainslie Thomas 1921- ... CANR-2
Earlier sketch in CA 1-4R
Embry, Margaret Jacob 1919-1975 ... CANR-3
Earlier sketch in CA 1-4R
See also SATA 5
Emecheta, (Florence Onye) Buchi
1944- ... CANR-27
Earlier sketch in CA 81-84
See also BLC 2
See also BW
See also CLC 14, 48
See also DLB 117
See also MTCW
See also SATA 66
Emeneau, Murray Barnson 1904- ... CANR-5
Earlier sketch in CA 1-4R
Emenegger, Bob
See Emenegger, Robert
Emenegger, Robert 1933- ... 102
Emenhiser, JeDon A(llen) 1933- ... 37-40R
Emerick, Kenneth F(red) 1925- ... 53-56
Emerson, Alice B. ... CANR-27
Earlier sketches in CAP-2, CA 19-20
See also SATA 1, 67
Emerson, Caroline D. 1891-1973 ... CAP-1
Obituary ... 45-48
Earlier sketch in CA 17-18
Emerson, Caryl (Geppert) 1944- ... 123
Emerson, Connie 1930- ... 109
Emerson, (Alan) David 1900- ... CANR-2
Earlier sketch in CA 5-8R
Emerson, Donald (Conger) 1913- ... 21-24R
Emerson, Earl W. 1948- ... 123
Emerson, Everett Harvey 1925- ... CANR-22
Earlier sketches in CA 13-16R, CANR-5
Emerson, Frank C(reighton) 1936- ... 53-56
Emerson, H(enry) O(liver) 1893- ... CAP-2
Earlier sketch in CA 23-24
Emerson, James G(ordon) Jr. 1926- ... 17-20R
Emerson, Kathy Lynn 1947- ... 127
See also SATA 63
Emerson, Laura S(alome) 1907- ... CAP-1
Earlier sketch in CA 13-16
Emerson, Mary Lee
See Kennedy, Mary
Emerson, O. B. 1922- ... CANR-16
Earlier sketch in CA 25-28R
Emerson, Ralph Waldo
1803-1882 ... CDALB 1640-1865
See also DLB 1, 59, 73
See also WLC
Emerson, Ronald
See Scotland, James
Emerson, Ru 1944- ... 121
See also SATA 70
Emerson, Rupert 1899-1979 ... CANR-2
Obituary ... 85-88
Earlier sketch in CA 1-4R
Emerson, Thomas I(rwin) 1907-1991 ... 21-24R
Obituary ... 134
Emerson, William K(eith) 1925- ... 41-44R
See also SATA 25
Emerson, William 1769-1811 ... DLB 37
Emery, Alan E(glin) H(eathcote) 1928- ... 69-72
Emery, Allan C(omstock) Jr. 1919- ... 104
Emery, Anne (McGuigan) 1907- ... CANR-2
Earlier sketch in CA 1-4R
See also SATA 1, 33
Emery, David A(mos) 1920- ... 29-32R
Emery, Edwin 1914- ... CANR-11
Earlier sketch in CA 69-72
Emery, Fred 1933- ... 65-68

Emery, Gary 1942- ... CANR-29
Earlier sketch in CA 110
Emery, Glenn D. 1954- ... 135
Emery, Kenneth Orris 1914- ... 107
Emery, Marc 1932- ... 132
Emery, Michael 1940- ... 73-76
Emery, Pierre-Yves 1929- ... 101
Emery, Robert F(irestone) 1927- ... 37-40R
Emery, Walter Byron 1907-1973 ... CANR-22
Earlier sketch in CA 1-4R
Emett, Rowland 1906-1990 ... 102
Obituary ... 133
Emig, Janet Ann ... 73-76
Emlen, Robert P. 1946- ... 135
Emma, Ronald David 1920- ... 25-28R
Emmanuel, Philip D. 1909- ... CAP-1
Earlier sketch in CA 13-16
Emmanuel, Pierre
See Mathieu, Noel Jean
Emme, Eugene M(orlock) 1919-1985 ... CANR-8
Obituary ... 116
Earlier sketch in CA 13-16R
Emmel, Thomas C. 1941- Brief entry ... 111
Emmens, Carol Ann 1944- ... 106
See also SATA 39
Emmerich, Andre 1924- ... 9-12R
Emmerick, R(onald) E(ric) 1937- ... CANR-11
Earlier sketch in CA 25-28R
Emmerson, Donald K(enneth) 1940- ... CANR-32
Earlier sketches in CA 65-68, CANR-14
Emmerson, Henry Russell 1899- ... 5-8R
Emmerson, John K(enneth)
1908-1984 ... CANR-14
Obituary ... 112
Earlier sketch in CA 57-60
Emmerson, Richard Kenneth 1948- ... 106
Emmet, Dorothy Mary 1904- ... 9-12R
Emmet, E(ric) R(evell) 1909- ... 107
Emmett, Bruce 1949- ... 57-60
Emmitt, Robert (P.) 1925- ... 29-32R
Emmons, Charles F(rank) 1942- ... 110
Emmons, Della (Florence) Gould
1890-1983 Obituary ... 111
See also SATA 39
Emmons, Michael 1938- ... 107
Emmons, Nuel 1927- ... 125
Emmott, Bill
See Emmott, William John
Emmott, William John 1956- ... 136
Emmrich, Curt 1897-1975 ... CAP-2
Earlier sketch in CA 29-32
Emmrich, Kurt
See Emmrich, Curt
Emorey, N.
See Ellison, Jerome
Emory, Alan (Steuer) 1922- ... CANR-12
Earlier sketch in CA 69-72
Empey, Arthur Guy 1883-1963 Obituary ... 107
Empey, LaMar T(aylor) 1923- ... CANR-30
Earlier sketch in CA 29-32R
Employee X
See Fautsko, Timothy F(rank)
Empringham, Antoinette F(leur) 1939- ... 124
Empringham, Toni
See Empringham, Antoinette F(leur)
Empson, William 1906-1984 ... CANR-31
Obituary ... 112
Earlier sketch in CA 17-20R
See also CLC 3, 8, 19, 33, 34
See also DLB 20
See also MTCW
Emrich, Duncan (Black Macdonald)
1908-197 (?) ... CANR-9
Earlier sketch in CA 61-64
See also SATA 11
Emshwiller, Carol ... 53-56
Emsley, Clare
See Plummer, Clare (Emsley)
Emsley, Michael Gordon 1930- ... 97-100
Emslie, M. L.
See Simpson, Myrtle L(illias)
Emswiler, Sharon Neufer 1944- ... 119
Emy, Hugh (Vincent) 1944- ... 77-80
Enamurado Cuesta, Jose 1892- ... HW
Encausse, Gerard (Anaclet Vincent)
1865-1916 Brief entry ... 113
Encel, Sol
See Encel, Solomon
Encel, Solomon 1925- ... CANR-37
Earlier sketch in CA 115
Enchi Fumiko (Ueda) 1905-1986 ... 129
Obituary ... 121
See also CLC 31
Endacott, G(eorge) B(eer) 1901- ... 5-8R
Endacott, M(arie) Violet 1915- ... 9-12R
Ende, Jean 1947- ... 53-56
Ende, Michael (Andreas Helmuth)
1929- ... CANR-36
Brief entry ... 118
Earlier sketch in CA 124
See also CLC 31
See also CLR 14
See also DLB 75
See also MAICYA
See also SATA 42, 61
Ende, Richard Chaffey von
See von Ende, Richard Chaffey
Endelman, Todd M(ichael) 1946- ... 125
Enderle, Judith (Ann) Ross 1941- ... CANR-22
Earlier sketch in CA 106
See also SATA 38
Enders, Richard
See Fenster, Robert
Endersby, Clive 1944- ... 133
Endfield, Mercedes
See von Block, Bela W(illiam)
Endicott, Frank S(impson)
1904-1990 Obituary ... 131
Endicott, Ruth Belmore ... CANR-26
Earlier sketches in CAP-2, CA 19-20
Endicott, Stephen Lyon 1928- ... 107
Endler, Norman S(olomon) 1931- ... CANR-9
Earlier sketch in CA 21-24R
Endo, Mitsuko 1942- ... 65-68
Endo, Shusaku 1923- ... CANR-21
Earlier sketch in CA 29-32R
See also CLC 7, 14, 19, 54
See also MTCW
Endore, (Samuel) Guy 1900-1970 ... CANR-6
Obituary ... 25-28R
Earlier sketch in CA 1-4R
Endres, Clifford 1941- ... 108
Endy, Melvin B(ecker) Jr. 1938- ... 81-84
Enelow, Allen J(ay) 1922- ... CANR-7
Earlier sketch in CA 17-20R
Enfield, Carrie
See Smith, Susan Vernon
Eng--, Tom
See Engelhardt, Thomas Alexander
Engberg, Edward 1928- ... 21-24R
Engberg, Holger L(aessoe) 1930- ... 37-40R
Engberg, (Johanna) Susan 1940- ... 117
Engdahl, Sylvia Louise 1933- ... CANR-14
Earlier sketch in CA 29-32R
See also CLR 2
See also MAICYA
See also SAAS 5
See also SATA 4
Engebrecht, P(atricia) A(nn) 1935- ... 57-60
Engel, A. J.
See Engel, Arthur (Jason)
Engel, Alan
See Engelberg, Alan (D.)
Engel, Alan S(tuart) 1932- ... 37-40R
Engel, Arthur (Jason) 1944- ... 129
Engel, Bernard F. 1921- ... 13-16R
Engel, Diana 1947- ... 138
See also SATA 70
Engel, Herbert M. 1918- ... 120
Engel, Howard 1931- ... 112
Engel, J. Ronald 1936- ... 124
Engel, James F. 1934- ... CANR-13
Earlier sketch in CA 21-24R
Engel, (Aaron) Lehman 1910-1982 ... CANR-31
Obituary ... 107
Earlier sketch in CA 41-44R
Engel, Louis (Henry Jr.) 1909-1982 ... 21-24R
Obituary ... 108
Engel, Lyle Kenyon 1915-1986 ... 85-88
Obituary ... 120
Engel, Madeline H(elena) 1941- ... 85-88
Engel, Marian 1933-1985 ... CANR-12
Earlier sketch in CA 25-28R
See also CLC 36
See also DLB 53
Engel, Mary June Montgomery
1920(?)-1985 Obituary ... 117
Engel, Monroe 1921- ... 5-8R
Engel, Pauline Newton 1918- ... 17-20R
Engel, Peter H. 1935- ... CANR-15
Earlier sketch in CA 81-84
Engel, S(rul) Morris (von) 1931- ... CANR-14
Earlier sketch in CA 37-40R
Engel, Salo 1908-1972 ... CAP-2
Earlier sketch in CA 33-36
Engel, Samuel G. 1904-1984 Obituary ... 112
Engelbach, David (Charles) 1946- ... 133
Engelberg, Alan (D.) 1941- ... 132
Engelberg, Edward 1929- ... 37-40R
Engelhard, Jack 1940- ... 132
Engelhardt, Frederick
See Hubbard, L(afayette) Ron(ald)
Engelhardt, Thomas Alexander 1930- ... 133
Engelhardt, Tom
See Engelhardt, Thomas Alexander
Engelhart, Margaret S. 1924- ... 122
See also SATA 59
Engelking, L. L. 1903(?)-1980 Obituary ... 102
Engell, James 1951- ... 135
Engelman, Rose C.
1919(?)-1979 Obituary ... 89-92
Engelmann, Hugo O(tto) 1917- ... 41-44R
Engelmann, Larry 1941- ... 101
Engelmann, Ruth 1919- ... 106
Engelmann, Siegfried E. 1931- ... CANR-13
Earlier sketch in CA 21-24R
Engelmayer, Sheldon David 1945- ... 114
Engels, Donald (W.) 1946- ... 102
Engels, John David 1931- ... CANR-6
Earlier sketch in CA 13-16R
Engels, Norbert (Anthony) 1903- ... CAP-2
Earlier sketch in CA 17-18
Engeman, Thomas S(ledge) 1944- ... 109
Engen, Rodney K(ent) 1948- ... CANR-15
Earlier sketch in CA 65-68
Enger, Norman L. 1937- ... CANR-10
Earlier sketch in CA 25-28R
Engerman, Stanley L(ewis) 1936- ... 53-56
Enggass, Robert 1921- ... CANR-9
Earlier sketch in CA 13-16R
Engh, M(ary) J(ane) 1933- ... 69-72
Engh, Rohn 1938- ... 69-72
Engholm, Eva 1909- ... 93-96
Engl, Lieselotte 1918- ... 49-52
Engl, Theodor 1925- ... 49-52
England, Anthony Bertram 1939- ... 85-88
England, Barry 1932- ... 25-28R
England, Colin
See Jeans, Michael
England, E. M.
See Anders, Edith (Mary) England
England, E Squires
See Ball, Sylvia Patricia
England, George Allan
1877-1936 Brief entry ... 112
England, George W(illiam) 1927- ... 104
England, John C(arol) 1930- ... 116
England, Martha Winburn 1909- ... CAP-1
Earlier sketch in CA 11-12
England, Maurice Derrick 1908-1980 ... 104
England, Rodney Charles Bennett
See Bennett-England, Rodney Charles
England, Wilbur Birch 1903- ... 1-4R
Engle, Eloise
See Paananen, Eloise (Katherine)
See also SATA 9
Engle, Jeff(rey) 1947- ... 103
Engle, John D(avid) Jr. 1922- ... CANR-25
Earlier sketches in CA 57-60, CANR-7
Engle, Louise Boardman Proctor
1897(?)-1987 Obituary ... 121
Engle, Parke F. 1900(?)-1984 Obituary ... 111
Engle, Paul (Hamilton) 1908-1991 ... CANR-5
Obituary ... 134
Earlier sketch in CA 1-4R
See also DLB 48
Engle, T(helburn) L(aRoy) 1901- ... 13-16R
Englebert, Victor 1933- ... 57-60
See also SATA 8
Englefield, Ronald 1891-1975 Obituary ... 105
Englehart, Bob
See Englehart, Robert (Wayne) Jr.
Englehart, Robert (Wayne) Jr. 1945- ... 133
Englekirk, John E(ugene)
1905-1983 Obituary ... 112
Engleman, Finis E(wing) 1895-1978 ... 9-12R
Obituary ... 134
Engleman, Paul 1953- ... 131
Engler, Larry 1949- ... 53-56
Engler, Richard E(mil) Jr. 1925- ... 37-40R
Engler, Robert 1922- ... CANR-2
Earlier sketch in CA 1-4R
Englert, Clement Cyril 1910- ... CANR-5
Earlier sketch in CA 1-4R
English, Adrian J(oseph) 1939- ... 118
English, Arnold
See Hershman, Morris
English, Barbara (Anne) 1933- ... CANR-13
Earlier sketch in CA 33-36R
English, Charles
See Nuetzel, Charles (Alexander)
English, David 1931- ... 69-72
English, Deirdre (Elena) 1948- ... 85-88
English, E(ugene) Schuyler 1899-1981 ... 107
Obituary ... 103
English, Earl (Franklin) 1905- ... 37-40R
English, Edward (H.) Obituary ... 41-44R
English, Fenwick Walter 1939- ... CANR-1
Earlier sketch in CA 45-48
English, Isobel 1925- ... 53-56
English, James W(ilson) 1915- ... 21-24R
See also SATA 37
English, (Emma) Jean M(artin) 1937- ... 29-32R
English, John W(esley) 1940- ... 69-72
English, Maurice 1909-1983 ... CANR-12
Obituary ... 111
Earlier sketch in CA 9-12R
English, O(liver) Spurgeon 1901- ... CAP-2
Earlier sketch in CA 33-36
English, Ronald (Frederick) 1913- ... CAP-1
Earlier sketch in CA 9-10
English, Thomas H(opkins) 1895- ... CANR-2
Earlier sketch in CA 5-8R
English, Thomas Saunders
1928- Brief entry ... 105
Englizian, H. Crosby 1923- ... 21-24R
Engquist, Richard 1933- ... 29-32R
Engren, Edith
See McCaig, Robert Jesse
Engs, Robert Francis 1943- ... 101
Engstrand, Iris (H.) Wilson 1935- ... 107
Engstrom, Ted W.
See Engstrom, Theodore W(ilhelm)
Engstrom, Theodore W(ilhelm) 1916- ... CANR-25
Earlier sketches in CA 65-68, CANR-9
Engstrom, W(infred) A(ndrew) 1925- ... 57-60
Enis, Ben M(elvin) 1942- ... CANR-22
Earlier sketches in CA 57-60, CANR-7
Enke, Stephen 1916-1974 ... 65-68
Obituary ... 53-56
Enloe, Cynthia H(olden) 1938- ... CANR-39
Earlier sketches in CA 37-40R, CANR-17
Enlow, David R(oland) 1916- ... CANR-10
Earlier sketch in CA 5-8R
Ennes, James M(arquis) Jr. 1933- ... CANR-34
Earlier sketch in CA 102
Ennis, Bruce J. 1940- Brief entry ... 110
Ennis, Robert H(ugh) 1927- ... CANR-10
Earlier sketch in CA 25-28R
Eno, Susan ... 101
Enoch, Kurt 1895-1982 Obituary ... 106
Enockson, Paul G(eorge) 1938- ... 110
Enomiya-Lassalle, Hugo M(akibi) 1898- ... 21-24R
Enquist, Per Olov 1934- Brief entry ... 109
Enrick, Norbert Lloyd 1920- ... CANR-6
Earlier sketch in CA 13-16R
Enright, D(ennis) J(oseph) 1920- ... CANR-1
Earlier sketch in CA 1-4R
See also CLC 4, 8, 31
See also DLB 27
See also SATA 25
Enright, Elizabeth 1909-1968 ... 61-64
Obituary ... 25-28R
See also CLR 4
See also DLB 22
See also MAICYA
See also SATA 9
Enright, Maureen Patricia Ford
1908(?)-1983 Obituary ... 111
Enroth, Clyde A(dolph) 1926- ... 37-40R
Enscoe, Gerald (Eugene) 1926- ... CANR-10
Earlier sketch in CA 5-8R
Ense, Wolfgang
See Frank, Rudolf
Ensign, Thomas 1940- ... 101
Ensign, Tod
See Ensign, Thomas
Ensley, Evangeline 1907- ... 122
Brief entry ... 114
Ensley, Francis Gerald 1907- ... CAP-1
Earlier sketch in CA 13-16
Enslin, Morton S(cott) 1897-1980 ... 17-20R
Obituary ... 134
Enslin, Theodore (Vernon) 1925- ... CANR-19
Earlier sketches in CA 53-56, CANR-4
See also CAAS 3
Enslow, Sam 1946- ... 136
Ensminger, Marion Eugene 1908- ... CANR-16
Earlier sketches in CA 49-52, CANR-1
Ensor, Allison (Rash) 1935- ... 25-28R
Ensor, (Alick Charles) David(son)
1906-1987 Obituary ... 121
Enstrom, Robert (William) 1946- ... 104
Enteman, Willard F(inley) 1936- ... 33-36R
Entenza, John Dymock
1905-1984 Obituary ... 112
Enterline, James Robert 1932- ... 41-44R
Enters, Angna 1907-1989 Obituary ... 128
Enthoven, Alain C(harles) 1930- ... CANR-27
Earlier sketch in CA 49-52
Entine, Alan D(avid) 1936- ... 21-24R
Entman, Robert M. 1949- ... 130
Entwisle, Doris R(oberts) 1924- ... 5-8R
Entwistle, Florence Vivienne
1889(?)-1982 Obituary ... 105
Entwistle, Harold 1923- ... 29-32R
Entwistle, Noel (James) 1936- ... CANR-39
Earlier sketches in CA 93-96, CANR-16
Entwistle, (Arthur) Theodore (Henry) Rowland
See Rowland-Entwistle, (Arthur) Theodore (Henry)
Enyeart, James L(yle) 1943- ... 113
Enys, Sarah L.
See Sloggett, Nellie
Enz, Jacob J(ohn) 1919- ... 41-44R
Enzensberger, Hans Magnus 1929- ... 119
Brief entry ... 116
See also CLC 43
Enzler, Clarence J.
1910(?)-1976 Obituary ... 69-72
Epafrodito
See Wagner, C(harles) Peter
Epand, Len 1950- ... 85-88
Epernay, Mark
See Galbraith, John Kenneth
Ephraim, Gavriel Ben
See Ben-Ephraim, Gavriel
Ephron, Amy 1955- ... 138
Ephron, Delia 1944- ... CANR-12
Earlier sketch in CA 97-100
See also SATA 50, 65
Ephron, Henry 1911- ... 73-76
Ephron, Nora 1941- ... CANR-39
Earlier sketches in CA 65-68, CANR-12
See also AITN 2
See also CLC 17, 31
Ephron, Phoebe (Wolkind)
1916-1971 Obituary ... 33-36R
Epler, Percy H. 1872-1975 Obituary ... 57-60
Epp, Eldon Jay 1930- ... CANR-7
Earlier sketch in CA 17-20R
Epp, Frank H(enry) 1929-1986 ... CANR-29
Earlier sketch in CA 29-32R
Epp, Margaret A(gnes) 1913- ... CANR-3
Earlier sketch in CA 9-12R
See also SATA 20
Eppard, Philip B(lair) 1945- ... 112
Eppenbach, Sarah 1947- ... 114
Eppenstein, Louise (Kohn)
1892-1987 Obituary ... 123
See also SATA 54
Epperly, Elizabeth Rollins 1951- ... 106
Epperson, Gordon 1921- ... 25-28R
Eppie
See Naismith, Helen
Eppinga, Jacob D. 1917- ... 33-36R
Eppinger, Josh 1940- ... 89-92
Eppink, Norman R(oland) 1906- ... 53-56
Epple, Anne Orth 1927- ... 33-36R
See also SATA 20
Epps, Bernard 1936- ... DLB 53
Epps, Edgar G(ustavas) 1929- ... 49-52
Epps, Garrett 1950- ... 69-72
Epps, Jack Jr. 1949- ... 133
Epps, Preston H(erschel) 1888-1982 ... 37-40R
Obituary ... 133
Epps, Robert L(ee) 1932- ... 17-20R
Epsilon, John 1895-1988 Obituary ... 125
Epsilon
See Betjeman, John
Epstein, Ann Wharton
See Wharton, Annabel Jane
Epstein, Anne Merrick 1931- ... 69-72
See also SATA 20
Epstein, Barbara 1928- Brief entry ... 110
Epstein, Benjamin Robert 1912-1983 ... 45-48
Obituary ... 109
Epstein, Beryl (M. Williams) 1910- ... CANR-39
Earlier sketches in CA 5-8R, CANR-2, 18
See also CLR 26
See also SATA 1, 31
Epstein, Charlotte 1921- ... CANR-8
Earlier sketch in CA 61-64
Epstein, Cy(ril Robert) 1942- Brief entry ... 108
Epstein, Cynthia Fuchs 1933- ... CANR-14
Earlier sketch in CA 29-32R

Epstein, Daniel Mark 1948- CANR-2
Earlier sketch in CA 49-52
See also CLC 7
Epstein, David G(eorge) 1943- 69-72
Epstein, Dena J. 1916- 41-44R
Epstein, Edmund L(loyd) 1931- 118
Epstein, Edward Jay 1935- CANR-13
Earlier sketch in CA 17-20R
Epstein, Edwin M(ichael) 1937- 25-28R
Epstein, Ellen Robinson 1947- 115
Epstein, Erwin H(oward) 1939- 29-32R
Epstein, Eugene 1944- 69-72
Epstein, Fritz T(heodor) 1898-1979 .... CANR-22
Earlier sketch in CA 69-72
Epstein, Helen 1947- 89-92
Epstein, Howard M(ichael) 1927- 21-24R
Epstein, Jacob 1880-1959 Brief entry 120
Epstein, Jacob 1956- 114
See also CLC 19
Epstein, Jason 1928- 57-60
Epstein, Joseph 1937- 119
Brief entry 112
See also CLC 39
Epstein, Judith Sue 1947- 69-72
Epstein, Julius J. 1909- 124
Brief entry 113
See also DLB 26
Epstein, Julius 1901-1975 Obituary 57-60
Epstein, June CANR-30
Earlier sketches in CA 73-76, CANR-13
Epstein, Lawrence J(effrey) 1946- 132
Epstein, Lee 1958- 119
Epstein, Leon D. 1919- 13-16R
Epstein, Leslie 1938- CANR-23
Earlier sketch in CA 73-76
See also CAAS 12
See also CLC 27
Epstein, Melech (Michael)
1889(?)-1979 Obituary 89-92
Epstein, Morris 1921-1973 .... CAP-1
Obituary 45-48
Earlier sketch in CA 13-16
Epstein, Perle S(herry) 1938- CANR-9
Earlier sketch in CA 65-68
See also SATA 27
Epstein, Philip G. 1909-1952 Brief entry 117
See also DLB 26
Epstein, Samuel S(tanley) 1926- 115
Epstein, Samuel 1909- CANR-39
Earlier sketches in CA 9-12R, CANR-4, 18
See also CLR 26
See also SATA 1, 31
Epstein, Seymour 1917- CANR-25
Earlier sketches in CA 1-4R, CANR-5
Epstein, William H(enry) 1944- 61-64
Epstein, William 1912- CANR-11
Earlier sketch in CA 69-72
Epton, Nina C(onsuelo) CANR-11
Earlier sketch in CA 5-8R
Equiano, Olaudah 1745(?)-1797 .... BLC 2
See also DLB 37, 50
Eramus, M. Nott
See Stuber, Stanley I(rving)
Erasmus, Charles J(ohn) 1921- 1-4R
Erasmus, M. Nott
See Stuber, Stanley I(rving)
Erazmus, Edward T. 1920- Brief entry 106
Erb, Alta Mae 1891- CAP-1
Earlier sketch in CA 9-10
Erb, Paul 1894- 9-12R
Erb, Peter C. 1943- CANR-32
Earlier sketch in CA 113
Erbsen, Claude E. 1938- 89-92
Ercoli, Ercole
See Togliatti, Palmiro
Erdahl, Carol Syvertsen 1932- 108
Erdahl, Lowell O. 1931- 109
Erdman, David V(orse) 1911- CANR-17
Earlier sketches in CA 1-4R, CANR-1
Erdman, Howard Loyd 1935- 21-24R
Erdman, Loula Grace CANR-10
Earlier sketch in CA 5-8R
See also SATA 1
Erdman, Nikolai R.
1902(?)-1970 Obituary 29-32R
Erdman, Paul E(mil) 1932- CANR-13
Earlier sketch in CA 61-64
See also AITN 1
See also CLC 25
Erdoes, Richard 1912- 77-80
See also SATA 28, 33
Erdos, Paul L(ouis) 1914- 29-32R
Erdrich, Louise 1954- 114
See also BEST 89:1
See also CLC 39, 54
See also MTCW
Erdt, Terrence 1942- 106
Ereira, Alan 1943- 137
Erenberg, Arthur 1909(?)-1980 Obituary 114
Erenberg, Lewis A. 1944- 125
Erenburg, Ilya (Grigoryevich)
See Ehrenburg, Ilya (Grigoryevich)
Erens, Patricia 1938- 93-96
Erhard, Ludwig 1897-1977 Obituary 112
Erhard, Thomas A. 1923- CANR-29
Earlier sketches in CA 33-36R, CANR-13
Erhard, Walter 1920- .... SATA 30
Erhart, Margaret 1953- 127
Eribon, Didier 1953- 138
Eric, Kenneth
See Henley, Arthur
Erichsen, Heino R(ichard) 1924- 110
Erichsen-Nelson, Jean 1934- 109
Ericksen, Ephraim Gordon 1917- 5-8R
Ericksen, Gerald L(awrence) 1931- 29-32R
Ericksen, Kenneth J(errold) 1939- 37-40R
Ericksen, Stanford Clark 1911- Brief entry 108
Erickson, Arthur (Charles) 1924- 89-92
Erickson, Arvel Benjamin 1905-1974 .... CAP-2
Earlier sketch in CA 21-22
Erickson, Bonnie H(eather) 1944- 112
Erickson, Carolly 1943- CANR-11
Earlier sketch in CA 69-72
Erickson, Don 1932- 110
Erickson, Donald A(rthur) 1925- 29-32R
Erickson, E(rnst) Walfred 1911- CANR-5
Earlier sketch in CA 5-8R
Erickson, Edsel L(ee) 1928- 53-56
Erickson, Erling Arthur 1934- 33-36R
Erickson, John R. 1943- 138
See also SATA 70
Erickson, John 1929- 101
Erickson, Keith V. 1943- 29-32R
Erickson, M(elvin) E(ddy) 1918- 9-12R
Erickson, Marilyn T. 1936- 73-76
Erickson, Marion J. 1913- 17-20R
Erickson, Millard J. 1932- 93-96
Erickson, Milton H(yland) 1901-1980 106
Obituary 97-100
Erickson, Peter (Brown) 1945- 126
Erickson, Phoebe CANR-3
Earlier sketch in CA 1-4R
See also SATA 59
Erickson, Robert 1917- Brief entry 109
Erickson, Russell E(verett) 1932- 93-96
See also SATA 27
Erickson, Sabra Rollins 1912- CANR-5
Earlier sketch in CA 5-8R
See also SATA 35
Erickson, Stephen A(nthony) 1940- 85-88
Erickson, Stephen Michael 1950- 129
See also Erickson, Steve
Erickson, Steve
See Erickson, Stephen Michael
See also CLC 64
Erickson, W(alter) Bruce 1938- 49-52
Ericson, Edward E(inar) 1939- 69-72
Ericson, Joe Ellis 1925- 41-44R
Ericson, Julia
See Leisy, James (Franklin)
Ericson, Walter
See Fast, Howard (Melvin)
Ericson, Walter
See Fast, Howard (Melvin)
Ericsson, Emily (Alice)
1904-1976 Obituary 65-68
Ericsson, Mary Kentra 1910- CANR-20
Earlier sketches in CA 1-4R, CANR-5
Ericsson, Ronald James 1935- 110
Erikson, Erik H(omburger) 1902- CANR-33
Earlier sketch in CA 25-28R
See also MTCW
Erikson, Kai T(heodor) 1931- Brief entry 107
Erikson, Mel 1937- .... SATA 31
Erikson, Roy L. 1939(?)-1985 Obituary 116
Erikson, Stanley 1906- 37-40R
Eriksson, Buntel
See Bergman, (Ernst) Ingmar
Eriksson, Edward 1941- 77-80
Eriksson, Marguerite A. 1911- 13-16R
Erim, Kenan Tevfik 1929-1990 Obituary 132
Eringer, Robert 1954- 114
Erisman, Fred (Raymond) 1937- CANR-29
Earlier sketch in CA 110
Eriugena, John Scottus
810 (?)-877 (?) .... DLB 115
Erlander, Tage Fritiof 1901-1985 Obituary 116
Erlanger, Baba
See Trahey, Jane
Erlanger, Ellen (Louise) 1950- CANR-32
Earlier sketches in CA 85-88, CANR-15
See also SATA 52
Erlanger, Philippe 1903- CANR-20
Earlier sketches in CA 5-8R, CANR-5
Erlanger, Steven Jay 1952- 133
Erlich, Alexander 1912-1985 Obituary 114
Erlich, Gloria C. 125
Erlich, Lillian (Feldman) 1910- CANR-5
Earlier sketch in CA 1-4R
See also SATA 10
Erlich, Victor 1914- CANR-3
Earlier sketch in CA 9-12R
Erline, N. T.
See Ragen, Naomi
Ermarth, Elizabeth 1939- 117
Ermine, Will
See Drago, Harry Sinclair
Ermolaev, Herman Sergei 1924- 107
Ernest, Victor (Hugo) 1911- CAP-2
Earlier sketch in CA 33-36
Ernest, William
See Berkebile, Fred D(onovan)
Ernharth, Ronald Louis 1936- 45-48
Erno, Richard B. 1923- 13-16R
Ernst, Barbara 1945- 65-68
Ernst, Carl Henry 1938- 45-48
Ernst, Clara
See Barnes, Clara Ernst
Ernst, Earle 1911- 5-8R
Ernst, Eldon G(ilbert) 1939- 85-88
Ernst, Jimmy 1920-1984 Obituary 112
Ernst, (Lyman) John 1940- 45-48
See also SATA 39
Ernst, Joseph Albert 1931- Brief entry 109
Ernst, Kathryn (Fitzgerald) 1942- CANR-12
Earlier sketch in CA 61-64
See also SATA 25
Ernst, Lisa Campbell 1957- 114
See also SATA 44, 55
Ernst, Margaret Samuels 1894- CAP-1
Earlier sketch in CA 13-14
Ernst, Margot Klebe 1939- 21-24R
Ernst, Max 1891-1976 Obituary 65-68
Ernst, Morris L(eopold) 1888-1976 .... CANR-7
Obituary 65-68
Earlier sketch in CA 5-8R
Ernst, Paul 1866-1933 .... DLB 66, 118
Ernst, Robert 1915- 21-24R
Ernst, Sheila 1941- 109
Ernsting, Walter 1920- 37-40R
Erny, Pierre Jean Paul 1933- CANR-13
Earlier sketch in CA 73-76
Eron, Carol (Lehman) 1945- 112
Eron, Leonard D(avid) 1920- Brief entry 110
Errington, Frederick (Karl) 1940- 104
Errington, Jane 1951- 128
Erskine, Barbara 1944- 123
Erskine, Chester 1904(?)-1986 Obituary 121
Erskine, Jim 1956- 107
Erskine, John 1879-1951 Brief entry 112
See also DLB 9, 102
Erskine, Laurie York
1894(?)-1976 Obituary 69-72
Erskine, Margaret
See Williams, (Margaret) Wetherby
Erskine, Noel Leo 116
Erskine, Rosalind
See Longrigg, Roger (Erskine)
Erskine, Thomas L(eonard) 1939- 65-68
Erskine, Wilson Fiske 1911-1972(?) 1-4R
Obituary 134
Erskine-Lindop, Audrey (Beatrice Noel)
1920-1986 69-72
Obituary 121
Erte
See de Tirtoff, Romain
Ertel, (Richard) James 1922-1985 .... 9-12R
Obituary 117
Ertz, Susan 1894-1985 .... 5-8R
Obituary 116
Ervin, Janet Halliday 1923- 29-32R
See also SATA 4
Ervin, Sam(uel) J(ames) Jr. 1896-1985 119
Obituary 115
Brief entry 113
Ervin, Susan
See Ervin-Tripp, Susan Moore
Ervin, Theodore Robert 1928- 13-16R
Ervine, St. John Greer
1883-1971 Obituary 29-32R
See also DLB 10
Ervin-Tripp, Susan Moore 1927- 53-56
Erwin, Annabel
See Barron, Ann Forman
Erwin, Edward (James) 1937- 29-32R
Erwin, John D(raper) 1883-1983 Obituary 109
Erwin, John Seymour 1911- 105
Erwin, Will
See Eisner, Will(iam Erwin)
Esau, Helmut 1941- 57-60
Esbensen, Barbara Juster 1925- 134
See also SATA 53, 62
Escandon, Ralph 1928- CANR-33
Earlier sketches in CA 37-40R, CANR-14
Escarpenter, Claudio 1922-1977 .... 17-20R
Obituary 120
Escarraz, Donald Ray 1932- 21-24R
Eschelbach, Claire John 1929- 1-4R
Eschenbach, Wolfram von
See Wolfram von Eschenbach
Eschenburg, Johann Joachim
1743-1820 .... DLB 97
Escher, Franklin (Jr.) 1915- 9-12R
Escherich, Elsa Falk 1888- 5-8R
Eschholz, Paul A(nderson) 1942- CANR-14
Earlier sketch in CA 37-40R
Eschmeyer, R(einhart) E(rnst) 1898- 105
See also Eshmeyer, R. E.
Eschmeyer, William N(eil) 1939- 112
Escott, Colin 1949- 107
Escott, Jonathan 1922- CANR-20
Earlier sketch in CA 65-68
Escott, Paul David 1947- 93-96
Escriva, Josemaria
See Escriva de Balaguer, Josemaria
Escriva de Balaguer, Josemaria
1902-1975 Obituary 57-60
Eseki, Bruno
See Mphahlele, Ezekiel
Esenin, Sergei (Alexandrovich)
1895-1925 Brief entry 104
See also TCLC 4
Esfandiary, F M
See Fm-2030
Eshbach, Lloyd Arthur 1910- 118
Eshelman, Byron E(lias) 1915- 1-4R
Esherick, Joseph W(harton) 1942- 65-68
Eshleman, Clayton 1935- 33-36R
See also CAAS 6
See also CLC 7
See also DLB 5
Eshleman, Edwin D(uing)
1920-1985 Obituary 114
Eshleman, J. Ross 1936- 101
Eshmeyer, R. E.
See Eschmeyer, R(einhart) E(rnst)
See also SATA 29
Eskelin, Neil J(oyner) 1938- 33-36R
Eskelund, Karl 1918-1972 .... CAP-2
Earlier sketch in CA 23-24
Eskenazi, Gerald 1936- CANR-7
Earlier sketch in CA 61-64
Eskey, Kenneth 1930- 77-80
Eskin, Frada 1936- 37-40R
Eskow, John 1949- 105
Eskow, Seymour 1924- 9-12R
Esler, Anthony (James) 1934- CANR-26
Earlier sketches in CA 21-24R, CANR-8
Esler, Carol Clemeau 1935- 108
Esler, William K. 1930- CANR-5
Earlier sketch in CA 53-56
Esman, Aaron H(irsh) 1924- CANR-11
Earlier sketch in CA 61-64
Esman, Milton J. 1918- 81-84
Esmein, Jean 1923- CANR-31
Earlier sketch in CA 49-52
Esmond, Harriet
See Burke, John (Frederick)
Esohg, Lama
See Ghose, Amal
Eson, Morris E. 1921- 13-16R
Espeland, Pamela (Lee) 1951- 107
See also SATA 38, 52
Espenshade, Edward B(owman) Jr. 1910- 1-4R
Esper, Erwin A(llen) 1895- CAP-1
Earlier sketch in CA 13-16
Espey, John (Jenkins) 1913- CANR-25
Earlier sketches in CA 5-8R, CANR-4
Espinasse, Albert 1905-1972 Obituary 37-40R
'Espinasse, Margaret
1903(?)-1980 Obituary 114
Espino, Federico (Licsi Jr.) 1939- 93-96
Espinosa, Aurelio M(acedonio) Jr. 1907- 131
See also HW
Espinosa, Aurelio M(acedonio) 1880-1958 131
See also HW
Espinosa, Jose E(dmundo) 1900-1967 .... CAP-2
Earlier sketch in CA 25-28
Espinosa, Rudy
See Espinoza, Rudolph Louis
Espinoza, Guillermo
See Robinson, William I.
Espinoza, Rudolph Louis 1933- 73-76
Esposito, John C(abrino) 1940- 33-36R
Esposito, John L(ouis) 1940- 116
Esposito, Joseph L(ouis) 1941- CANR-35
Earlier sketch in CA 114
Esposito, Phil(ip Anthony) 1942- Brief entry 108
Espriella, Don Manuel Alvarez
See Southey, Robert
Espriu, Salvador 1913-1985 Obituary 115
See also CLC 9
Espy, Richard 1952- 105
Espy, Willard R(ichardson) 1910- CANR-2
Earlier sketch in CA 49-52
See also SATA 38
Esquenazi-Mayo, Roberto 1920- 45-48
Essame, Hubert 1896-1976 .... CANR-28
Obituary 65-68
Earlier sketch in CA 49-52
Esse, James
See Stephens, James
Esser, Robin 1933- 29-32R
Esses, Michael (Isaiah) 1923- Brief entry 110
Essex, Harry J. 33-36R
Essex, Mary
See Bloom, Ursula
Essex, Rosamund (Sibyl) 1900-1985 107
Obituary 116
Essick, Robert N(ewman) 1942- CANR-19
Earlier sketches in CA 53-56, CANR-5
Esslin, Martin (Julius) 1918- CANR-27
Earlier sketch in CA 85-88
See also MTCW
Esslinger, Dean R(obert) 1942- 61-64
Esslinger, Pat M.
See Carr, Pat M(oore)
Essoe, Gabe (Attila) 1944- 25-28R
Essop, Ahmed 1931- 123
Essrig, Harry 1912- 108
See also SATA 66
Estabrook, Robert Harley 1918- 69-72
Estabrooks, George H.
1896(?)-1973 Obituary 45-48
Estang, Luc 1911- 61-64
Estarellas, Juan 1918- CANR-2
Earlier sketch in CA 45-48
Estaver, Marguerite M. 1893- 97-100
Estelle, Sister Mary 1907- CAP-1
Earlier sketch in CA 11-12
Estenssoro, Hugo 1946- 69-72
Estep, Irene Compton 1-4R
See also SATA 5
Estep, W(illiam) R(oscoe) Jr. 1920- CANR-25
Earlier sketches in CA 13-16R, CANR-9
Esterbrook, Tom
See Hubbard, L(afayette) Ron(ald)
Estergreen, M. Morgan
See Estergreen, Marian Morgan
Estergreen, Marian Morgan 1910- 17-20R
Esterly, Glenn 1942- 33-36R
Estermann, Carlos Obituary 105
Esterow, Milton 1928- 17-20R
Estes, Bill 1941- 107
Estes, Eleanor 1906-1988 .... CANR-20
Obituary 126
Earlier sketches in CA 1-4R, CANR-5
See also CLR 2
See also DLB 22
See also MAICYA
See also SATA 7, 56
Estes, J(oseph) Worth 1934- 104
Estes, John E(dward) 1939- 57-60
Estes, Rice 1907- CAP-1
Earlier sketch in CA 11-12
Estes, Richard J. 1942- 118
Estes, Steve(n Douglas) 1952- 97-100
Estes, Winston M(arvin) 1917-1982 .... 29-32R
Obituary 126
Estess, Sybil P. 1942- 129
Estess, Ted L(ynn) 1942- 114
Estey, George F. 1924- 33-36R
Esthus, Raymond Arthur 1925- 13-16R

Estleman, Loren D. 1952- CANR-27
Earlier sketch in CA 85-88
See also CLC 48
See also MTCW
Estner, Lois J(ane) 1947- 114
Estock, Anne (Martin) 1923- 1-4R
Estoril, Jean
See Allan, Mabel Esther
Estrada, Doris (Perkins) 1923- 17-20R
Estrada, Jacquelyn (Ann) 1946- 29-32R
Estragon, Vladimir
See Stokes, Geoffrey
Estrin, Herman A. 1915- CANR-7
Earlier sketch in CA 17-20R
Estroff, Sue E. 1950- 105
Estupinan Bass, Nelson 1915- ....HW
Esty, John Cushing Jr. 1928- Brief entry 106
Eszterhas, Joe
See Eszterhas, Joseph A.
Eszterhas, Joseph A. 130
Brief entry 124
Etchebaster, Pierre 1894-1980 102
Obituary 97-100
Etchemendy, Nancy 1952- 106
See also SATA 38
Etcheson, Craig Carlyle 1955- 117
Etcheson, Warren W(ade) 1920- 41-44R
Etchison, Birdie L(ee) 1937- 106
See also SATA 38
Etchison, Dennis (William) 1943- 118
Brief entry 115
Eterovich, Adam S(lav) 1930- CANR-27
Earlier sketch in CA 49-52
Eterovich, Francis Hyacinth
1913-1980 ....CANR-28
Earlier sketch in CA 37-40R
Ethell, Jeffrey L(ance) 1947- CANR-39
Earlier sketches in CA 101, CANR-18
Etherege, George 1636-1692 .... DLB 80
Etheridge, Eugene Wesley 1925- 5-8R
Etherington, Charles Leslie 1903- 5-8R
Etherington, Frank 1945- .... SATA 58
Etherton, Michael (James) 1939- 121
Ethridge, James M(erritt) 1921- 114
Ethridge, Mark Foster Jr.
1924-1985 Obituary 115
Ethridge, Mark Foster 1896-1981 Obituary 103
Ethridge, Willie Snow 1900-1983(?) 17-20R
Obituary 108
See also AITN 1
Etienne
See King-Hall, (William) Stephen (Richard)
Etkin, Anne (Dunwody Little) 1923- 73-76
Etmekjian, James 1915- CANR-3
Earlier sketch in CA 5-8R
Eton, Robert
See Meynell, Laurence Walter
Etra, Jonathan 1952-1991 102
Obituary 133
Ets, Marie Hall 1893- CANR-4
Earlier sketch in CA 1-4R
See also DLB 22
See also MAICYA
See also SATA 2
Ets-Hokin, Judith Diane 1938- 61-64
Etteldorf, Raymond P. 1911- 9-12R
Etter, Dave 1928- CANR-24
Earlier sketches in CA 17-20R, CANR-8
See also DLB 105
Etter, Les(ter Frederick) 1904- 25-28R
Etter, Patricia A. 1932- 120
Ettin, Andrew V(ogel) 1943- 124
Ettinger, Elzbieta 1925- 29-32R
Ettinger, Richard Prentice
1893-1971 Obituary 29-32R
Ettinger, Robert C(hester) W(ilson)
1918- 13-16R
Ettinghausen, Maurice Leon
1883-1974 Obituary 116
Ettinghausen, Richard 1906-1979 ....CANR-9
Obituary 85-88
Earlier sketch in CA 65-68
Ettleson, Abraham 1897- CAP-2
Earlier sketch in CA 23-24
Ettling, John 1944- 125
Ettlinger, Gerard H(erman) 1935- 61-64
Ettlinger, L. D.
See Ettlinger, Leopold David
Ettlinger, Leopold D.
See Ettlinger, Leopold David
Ettlinger, Leopold David
1913-1989 Obituary 129
Brief entry 111
Etulain, Richard W(ayne) 1938- CANR-16
Earlier sketches in CA 45-48, CANR-1
Etzioni, Amitai (Werner) 1929- CANR-22
Earlier sketches in CA 1-4R, CANR-5
Etzioni, Minerva M(orales)
1938(?)-1985 Obituary 118
Etzioni-Halevy, Eva 1934- 127
Etzkorn, K(laus) Peter 1932- 49-52
Etzkowitz, Henry 1940- 25-28R
Etzold, Thomas H(erman) 1945- CANR-14
Earlier sketch in CA 81-84
Eubank, (Weaver) Keith (Jr.) 1920- CANR-2
Earlier sketch in CA 5-8R
Eubank, Nancy 1934- 41-44R
Eubanks, Ralph T(ravis) 1920- 17-20R
Eucken, Rudolf (Christof)
1846-1926 Brief entry 119
Eulau, Heinz 1915- Brief entry 107
Eulenspiegel, Alexander
See Shea, Robert (Joseph)
Eulert, Don(ald Dean) 1935- CANR-18
Earlier sketches in CA 49-52, CANR-2
Euller, John E(lmer) 1926- 9-12R
Eulo, Ken 1939- 126
Brief entry 109
Eunson, (John) Dale 1904- 41-44R
See also SATA 5
Eunson, Robert C(harles) 1912-1975 ....13-16R
Obituary 61-64
Euphan
See Todd, Barbara Euphan
Euphemides, Aristos
See von Koerber, Hans Nordewin
Eurich, Alvin C(hristian) 1902-1987 ....17-20R
Obituary 123
Eurich, Nell 1919- CANR-12
Earlier sketch in CA 73-76
European
See Mosley, Oswald (Ernald)
Eusden, John (Dykstra) 1922- 45-48
Eustace, Cecil John 1903- 49-52
Eustace, May (Corcoran) 1904- 5-8R
Eustace, Robert
See Barton, Eustace Robert
Eustis, Alvin Allen Jr. 1917- 102
Eustis, Laurette
See Murdock, Laurette P.
Eustis, O. B.
See Eustis, Orville B.
Eustis, Orville B. 1913-1986 124
Euwe, Machgielis 1901-1981 Obituary 105
Euwe, Max
See Euwe, Machgielis
Evain, Elaine 1931- 57-60
Evan, Carol
See Goldsmith, Carol Evan
Evan, Evin
See Faust, Frederick (Shiller)
Evan, William (Martin) 1922- CANR-2
Earlier sketch in CA 1-4R
Evang, Karl 1902- 65-68
Evanier, David Brief entry 108
Evanoff, Vlad 1916- CANR-6
Earlier sketch in CA 5-8R
See also SATA 59
Evans, A(lfred) Alexander 1905- CAP-1
Earlier sketch in CA 9-10
Evans, Abbie Huston 1881- 57-60
Evans, Alan
See Stoker, Alan
Evans, Albert 1917- 85-88
Evans, Alice Frazer 1939- CANR-30
Earlier sketch in CA 112
Evans, Arthur Bruce 1948- 61-64
Evans, Barbara Lloyd
See Lloyd Evans, Barbara
Evans, Benjamin Ifor 1899-1982 Obituary 107
Evans, Bennett
See Berger, Ivan (Bennett)
Evans, Bergen (Baldwin) 1904-1978 ....CANR-4
Obituary 77-80
Earlier sketch in CA 5-8R
Evans, Bruce A. 1946- 134
Evans, C(harles) Stephen 1948- CANR-29
Earlier sketches in CA 33-36R, CANR-13
Evans, Chad (Arthur) 1951- 131
Evans, (Jean) Cherry (Drummond) 1928- CAP-1
Earlier sketch in CA 9-10
Evans, Christopher (Riche) 1931-1979 102
Evans, Clifford 1916(?)-1983 Obituary 110
Evans, Constance May 1890- 9-12R
Evans, Craig A. 1952- 129
Evans, D(avid) Ellis 1930- CANR-16
Earlier sketch in CA 25-28R
Evans, Dale
See Rogers, Dale Evans
Evans, David Allan 1940- CANR-31
Earlier sketch in CA 49-52
Evans, David Beecher 1928- Brief entry 105
Evans, David Huhn Jr. 1944- 110
Evans, David R(ichard) 1940- CANR-39
Earlier sketch in CA 116
Evans, David R(ussell) 1937- CANR-17
Earlier sketch in CA 33-36R
Evans, David S(tanley) 1916- 41-44R
Evans, Debra 1953- 122
Evans, Don 1938- 111
Evans, Donald (Dwight) 1927- 41-44R
Evans, Donald P(aul) 1930- CANR-7
Earlier sketch in CA 57-60
Evans, Donald 1884-1921 Brief entry 123
See also DLB 54
Evans, Dorinda 1944- 121
Evans, E(myr) Estyn 1905-1989 ....CANR-5
Obituary 129
Earlier sketch in CA 5-8R
Evans, E(dward) Everett
1893-1958 Brief entry 113
Evans, Edward G(ordon) Jr. 1916- 45-48
Evans, Eli N. 1936- 45-48
See also AITN 1
Evans, Elizabeth 1932- 53-56
Evans, Ellen
See Du Breuil, (Elizabeth) L(or)inda
Evans, Emerald
See Du Breuil, (Elizabeth) L(or)inda
Evans, Eric J(ohn) 1945- 108
Evans, Eva (Knox) 1905- 73-76
See also SATA 27
Evans, Evan
See Faust, Frederick (Shiller)
Evans, (Francis) Fallon 1925- 1-4R
Evans, Fanny-Maude 1914- 117
Evans, F.M.G.
See Higham, Florence May Grier
Evans, Frances Monet Carter
See Carter, Frances Monet
Evans, Frank Bernard 1927- CANR-36
Earlier sketch in CA 114
Evans, G. B.
See Evans, Gwynne Blakemore
Evans, G. Blakemore
See Evans, Gwynne Blakemore
Evans, G(ayle) Edward 1937- 33-36R
Evans, G(eraint) N(antglyn) D(avies)
1935-1971 ....CAP-2
Earlier sketch in CA 33-36
Evans, G. R.
See Evans, Gillian (Rosemary)
Evans, Gareth Lloyd
See Lloyd Evans, Gareth
Evans, Geoffrey (Charles) 1901-1987 ....17-20R
Obituary 121
Evans, George Bird 1906- CANR-2
Earlier sketch in CA 1-4R
Evans, George Ewart 1909-1988(?) 61-64
Obituary 124
Evans, George Henry 1805-1856 .... DLB 43
Evans, George W(illiam) II 1920- 21-24R
Evans, Gillian (Rosemary) 1944- 126
Evans, Glen 1921- 85-88
Evans, Gordon H(eyd) 1930- 13-16R
Evans, Gwynfor 1912- 61-64
Evans, Gwynne B.
See Evans, Gwynne Blakemore
Evans, Gwynne Blakemore 1912- 125
Evans, Harold Matthew 1928- 41-44R
Evans, Harold 1911-1983 129
Obituary 109
Evans, Harris
See Evans, George Bird
and Evans, Kay Harris
Evans, Harry 1896(?)-1988 Obituary 126
Evans, Herndon J. 1895-1976 69-72
Evans, Hilary 1929- CANR-20
Earlier sketches in CA 1-4R, CANR-5
Evans, Howard Ensign 1919- CANR-27
Earlier sketches in CA 5-8R, CANR-6
Evans, Hubert John Filmer
1904-1989 Obituary 129
Evans, Hubert Reginald 1892-1986 103
Obituary 119
See also DLB 92
See also SATA 48
Evans, Humphrey (Marshall Jr.) 1914- 29-32R
Evans, I(drisyn) O(liver) 1894-1977 ....CANR-15
Earlier sketch in CA 13-16R
Evans, Idella M(arie Crowe) 1924- 29-32R
Evans, Ilona 1918(?)-1980 Obituary 102
Evans, J(ames) A(llan) S(tewart) 1931- 37-40R
Evans, J(ohn) D(avid) G(emmill) 1942- 127
Evans, J. Martin 1935- 85-88
Evans, J(ack) N(aunton) 1920- 25-28R
Evans, J(ohn) Robert 1942- CANR-7
Earlier sketch in CA 57-60
Evans, Jacob A. 1920- 25-28R
Evans, James Allen 1926(?)-1983 Obituary 110
Evans, Jay 1925- 61-64
Evans, Jean 1939- 102
Evans, Jessica
See Lottman, Eileen
Evans, Joan 1893-1977 ....13-16R
Obituary 73-76
Evans, John
See Browne, Howard
Evans, John Davies 1925- 127
Evans, John Lewis 1930- 85-88
Evans, John W(alker) 1904- 33-36R
Evans, John X(avier) 1933- 37-40R
Evans, Jonathan
See Freemantle, Brian Harry
Evans, Joseph S. Jr. 1909(?)-1978 85-88
Obituary 81-84
Evans, Joseph W(illiam) 1921- 21-24R
Evans, Julia (Rendel) 1913- 13-16R
Evans, K(athleen) M(arianne) 1911- 9-12R
Evans, Katherine (Floyd) 1901-1964 ....5-8R
See also SATA 5
Evans, Kay Harris 1906- CANR-2
Earlier sketch in CA 1-4R
Evans, (Cyril) Kenneth 1917- 53-56
Evans, Kenneth R. 1938- 134
Brief entry 110
Evans, Larry (Melvyn) 1932- 129
Evans, Laurence 1923- 37-40R
Evans, Lawrence Watt 1954- CANR-32
Earlier sketch in CA 102
Evans, Lee
See Forrest, Richard (Stockton)
Evans, Lloyd (Lloyd Thomas) 1927- 69-72
Evans, Louis Hadley Sr. 1897-1981 116
Evans, Luther Harris 1902-1981 ....CANR-9
Obituary 106
Earlier sketch in CA 17-20R
Evans, M(edford) Stanton 1934- 65-68
Evans, Mari 1923- CANR-27
Earlier sketches in CA 49-52, CANR-2
See also BW
See also DLB 41
See also SATA 10
Evans, Mark 65-68
See also SATA 19
Evans, Marvin R(ussell) 1915- 49-52
Evans, Mary Ann
See Eliot, George
Evans, Mary 1946- 122
Evans, Max 1925- CANR-1
Earlier sketch in CA 1-4R
Evans, Medford (Bryon) 1907- 25-28R
Evans, Mel 1912(?)-1984 Obituary 112
Evans, Melbourne G(riffith) 1912- CAP-2
Earlier sketch in CA 33-36
Evans, Michael K(aye) 1938- 132
Evans, Morgan
See Davies, L(eslie) P(urnell)
Evans, N(orman) Dean 1925- CANR-13
Earlier sketch in CA 21-24R
Evans, Nancy 1950- CANR-34
Earlier sketch in CA 77-80
See also SATA 65
Evans, Nathaniel 1742-1767 .... DLB 31
Evans, Oliver 1915- 17-20R
Evans, Olwen (Elizabeth) Carey
See Carey Evans, Olwen (Elizabeth)
Evans, Patricia Healy
See Carpenter, Patricia (Healy Evans)
Evans, Paul Richer 1925- Brief entry 106
Evans, Peter (Andrew) 131
Evans, Philip 1944- Brief entry 110
Evans, Rand B(oyd) 1942- Brief entry 107
Evans, Richard Evan 1898-1983 Obituary 109
Evans, Richard I(sadore) 1922- 131
Brief entry 108
Evans, Richard J. 1947- 138
Evans, Richard L(ouis) 1906-1971 ....9-12R
Obituary 103
Evans, Richard 1939- 106
Evans, Robert Jr. 1932- 17-20R
Evans, Robert Allen 1937- 112
Evans, Robert F(ranklin) 1930-1974 .... CAP-2
Earlier sketch in CA 23-24
Evans, Robert Henry 1937- 21-24R
Evans, Robert L(eonard) 1917- CANR-32
Earlier sketch in CA 49-52
Evans, Robert Owen 1919- 13-16R
Evans, Robert P. 1918- 13-16R
Evans, Rodney E(arl) 1939- 49-52
Evans, Rowland Jr. 1921- CANR-15
Earlier sketch in CA 21-24R
Evans, Rupert N. 1921- 37-40R
Evans, Sara 1943- 93-96
Evans, Sebastian 1830-1909 .... DLB 35
Evans, Shirlee 1931- 61-64
See also SATA 58
Evans, Stanley G(eorge) 1912-1965 .... CAP-1
Earlier sketch in CA 9-10
Evans, Stuart 1934- 124
Brief entry 118
Evans, Susan H(ope) 1951- 115
Evans, Tabor
See Cameron, Lou
and Knott, William C(ecil Jr.)
and Wallmann, Jeffrey M(iner)
Evans, Thomas W(illiam) 1930- 45-48
Evans, Travers Moncure 1938- 57-60
Evans, Virginia Moran 1909- CANR-5
Earlier sketch in CA 5-8R
Evans, W(illiam) Glyn 1918- 89-92
Evans, W(illiam) McKee 1923- 21-24R
Evans, Walker 1903-1975 Obituary 89-92
Evans, (William Edis) Webster
1908-1982 ....41-44R
Obituary 133
Evans, Wilbur 1913- 97-100
Evans, William David 1912-1985 Obituary 117
Evans, William Howard 1924- 21-24R
Evans, William R. 1938- 105
Evans, William 1895-1988 81-84
Obituary 126
Evans Davies, Gloria 1932- 5-8R
Evansen, Virginia Besaw 1921- 13-16R
Evans-Jones, Albert 1895- 5-8R
Evans-Pritchard, Edward Evan
1902-1973 65-68
Evarts, Esther
See Benson, Sally
Evarts, Hal G(eorge) 1887-1934 Brief entry 121
Evarts, Hal G. (Jr.) 1915- CANR-2
Earlier sketch in CA 49-52
See also SATA 6
Eve, Barbara
See Reiss, Barbara Eve
Eveland, Bill
See Eveland, Wilbur Crane
Eveland, Wilbur Crane 1918- 101
Eveling, (Harry) Stanley 1925- 61-64
Evely, Louis 1910- 85-88
Evelyn, Anthony
See
Ward-Thomas, Evelyn Bridget Patricia Stephens
Evelyn, (John) Michael 1916- CANR-22
Earlier sketches in CA 5-8R, CANR-6
Evenhuis, Gertie 1932- 107
Everage, Dame Edna
See Humphries, Barry
Evered, James F(letcher) 1928- 107
Everest, Allan S(eymour) 1913- CANR-26
Earlier sketches in CA 29-32R, CANR-11
Everett, Alexander Hill 1790-1847 .... DLB 59
Everett, Arthur (W. Jr.) 1914- 103
Everett, Donald E(dward) 1920- 9-12R
Everett, Edward 1794-1865 .... DLB 1, 59
Everett, Gail
See Hale, Arlene
Everett, Glenn D. 1921- 69-72
Everett, Percival
See Everett, Percival L.
Everett, Percival L. 1956- 129
See also CLC 57
Everett, Peter W(illiam) 1924- 13-16R
Everett, Peter 1931- CANR-31
Earlier sketch in CA 69-72
Everett, T(homas) H(enry) 1903(?)-1986 133
Obituary 120
Everett, Walter 1936- 93-96
Everett-Green, Evelyn
1856-1932 Brief entry 114
Evergood, Philip 1901-1973 Obituary 41-44R
Everhart, James W(illiam) Jr. 1924- 89-92
Everhart, Jim
See Everhart, James W(illiam) Jr.

Everitt, Alan (Milner) 1926- CANR-11
Earlier sketch in CA 21-24R
Everitt, Arva Graham Johnson
1916(?)-1982 Obituary 107
Everitt, Bridget Mary 1924- 45-48
Everitt, C(harles) W(illiam) F(rancis)
1934- 65-68
Everitt, David Samuel 1952- 110
Everman, Welch D(uane) 1946- 57-60
Evernden, Margery 1916- 5-8R
See also SATA 5
Evers, (James) Charles 1923(?)- Brief entry 111
Evers, Christopher 1940- 122
Evers, Larry 1946- 135
Eversley, D(avid) E(dward) C(harles)
1921- CANR-1
Earlier sketch in CA 1-4R
Eversole, Finley T. 1933- 9-12R
Everson, Dale Millar 1928- 17-20R
Everson, David H. 1941- 124
Everson, Ida Gertrude 1898- 37-40R
Everson, R(onald) G(ilmour) 1903- 17-20R
See also CLC 27
See also DLB 88
Everson, William Keith 1929- CANR-2
Earlier sketch in CA 1-4R
Everson, William (Oliver) 1912- CANR-20
Earlier sketch in CA 9-12R
See also CLC 1, 5, 14
See also DLB 5, 16
See also MTCW
Eversz, Robert McLeod 1954- 127
Everton, Macduff 1947- 104
Evertts, Eldonna L(ouise) 1917- 21-24R
Everwine, Peter Paul 1930- 73-76
Every, George 1909- CANR-6
Earlier sketch in CA 13-16R
Eves, Douglas 1922- 119
Evetts, Julia 1944- 69-72
Evins, Joseph Landon 1910- 61-64
Evitts, William J(oseph) 1942- 121
Brief entry 112
EVOE
See Knox, Edmund George Valpy
Evold, Bent 1936- 129
Evoy, John J(oseph) 1911- 5-8R
Evslin, Bernard 1922- CANR-9
Earlier sketch in CA 21-24R
See also SATA 28, 45
Evslin, Dorothy 1923- 57-60
Evtushenko, Evgenii Aleksandrovich
See Yevtushenko, Yevgeny (Alexandrovich)
Ewald, Wendy Taylor 1951- 120
Ewald, William Bragg Jr. 1925- CANR-27
Earlier sketch in CA 107
Ewans, Michael (Christopher) 1946- 129
Ewart, Andrew 1911- 17-20R
Ewart, Charles
See Lyte, Charles
Ewart, Gavin (Buchanan) 1916- CANR-17
Earlier sketch in CA 89-92
See also CLC 13, 46
See also DLB 40
See also MTCW
Ewart, Simon
See Herd, Michael
Ewbank, Henry L(ee) Jr. 1924- 73-76
Ewbank, Walter F(rederick) 1918- CANR-38
Earlier sketches in CA 25-28R, CANR-17
Ewell, Barbara C(laire) 1947- CANR-35
Earlier sketch in CA 114
Ewell, Judith 1943- 107
Ewen, David 1907-1985 .... CANR-2
Obituary 118
Earlier sketch in CA 1-4R
See also SATA 4, 47
Ewen, Elizabeth 1943- 124
Ewen, Frederic 1899-1988 73-76
Obituary 126
Ewen, Robert B. 1940- CANR-15
Earlier sketch in CA 37-40R
Ewen, Stuart 1945- CANR-12
Earlier sketch in CA 69-72
Ewens, James 1939- 116
Ewers, Hanns Heinz 1871-1943 Brief entry 109
See also TCLC 12
Ewers, John C(anfield) 1909- CANR-22
Earlier sketches in CA 17-20R, CANR-7
Ewert, David 1922- 105
Ewing, Alfred Cyril 1899-1973 .... CANR-4
Earlier sketch in CA 5-8R
Ewing, David Walkley 1923- CANR-5
Earlier sketch in CA 1-4R
Ewing, Donald M. 1895(?)-1978 Obituary 81-84
Ewing, Elizabeth 1904- 41-44R
Ewing, Frederick R.
See Sturgeon, Theodore (Hamilton)
Ewing, George W(ilmeth) 1923- 45-48
Ewing, John A(lexander) 1923- 125
Brief entry 105
Ewing, John Melvin 1925- 53-56
Ewing, John S(inclair) 1916- 13-16R
Ewing, Juliana (Horatia Gatty)
1841-1885 .... DLB 21
See also SATA 16
Ewing, Kathryn 1921- CANR-7
Earlier sketch in CA 61-64
See also SATA 20
Ewing, Sherman 1901-1975 Obituary 57-60
Ewton, Ralph W(aldo) Jr. 1938- 81-84
Ewy, Donna 1934- CANR-14
Earlier sketch in CA 33-36R
Ewy, Rodger 1931- CANR-14
Earlier sketch in CA 33-36R
Exall, Barry
See Nugent, John Peer
Excellent, Matilda
See Farson, Daniel (Negley)
Exell, Frank Kingsley 1902- 5-8R
Exetastes
See Harakas, Stanley Samuel
Exley, Frederick (Earl) 1929- 81-84
Obituary 138
See also AITN 2
See also CLC 6, 11
See also DLBY 81
Exley, Jo Ella Powell 1940- 122
Exman, Eugene 1900-1975 .... CAP-1
Obituary 61-64
Earlier sketch in CA 17-18
Ex - R. S. M.
See Lindsay, Harold Arthur
Exton, Clive (Jack Montague) 1930- 61-64
Exton, William Jr. 1907-1988 45-48
Obituary 127
Eyck, Frank 1921- CANR-11
Earlier sketch in CA 25-28R
Eye, Glen G(ordon) 1904- CANR-2
Earlier sketch in CA 49-52
Eyen, Jerome
See Eyen, Tom
Eyen, Tom 1941-1991 .... CANR-22
Obituary 134
Earlier sketch in CA 25-28R
Eyerly, Jeannette Hyde 1908- CANR-19
Earlier sketches in CA 1-4R, CANR-4
See also SAAS 10
See also SATA 4
Eyestone, Robert 1942- 41-44R
Eykman, Christoph 1937- 41-44R
Eyles, Wilfred Charles 1891- CAP-2
Earlier sketch in CA 17-18
Eynhardt, Guillermo
See Quiroga, Horacio (Sylvestre)
Eyre, Annette
See Worboys, Anne(tte Isobel) Eyre
Eyre, Dorothy
See McGuire, Leslie Sarah
Eyre, Frank 1910-1988 .... SATA 62
Eyre, Katherine Wigmore
1901-1970 Obituary 104
See also SATA 26
Eyre, Richard M(elvin) 1944- CANR-13
Earlier sketch in CA 61-64
Eyre, Ronald 1929- 104
Eyre, S(amuel) R(obert) 1922- 21-24R
Eysenck, Hans J(urgen) 1916- CANR-25
Earlier sketches in CA 9-12R, CANR-4
Eysenck, Michael (William) 1944- 131
Eysman, Harvey (Allen) 1939- 106
Eyster, C(harles) William 1917- 29-32R
Eyvindson, Peter (Knowles) 1946- 124
See also SATA 52
Ezekiel, Mordecai J(oseph) B(rill)
1899-1974 65-68
Obituary 53-56
Ezekiel, Nissim 1924- 61-64
See also CLC 61
Ezekiel, Raphael S. 1931- 53-56
Ezekiel, Tish O'Dowd 1943- 129
See also CLC 34
Ezell, Edward C(linton) 1939- 128
Ezell, Harry E(ugene) 1918-1974 .... 1-4R
Obituary 103
Ezell, John Samuel 1917- 1-4R
Ezell, Macel D. 1934- 77-80
Ezera, Kalu 1925- 13-16R
Ezergailis, Andrew 1930- 89-92
Ezorsky, Gertrude 89-92
Ezzell, Marilyn 1937- 109
See also SATA 38, 42

F

Faas, (K.) Ekbert 1938- 130
Faas, Larry A(ndrew) 1936- 29-32R
Fabbri, Diego 1911-1980 Obituary 105
Fabe, Maxene 1943- 77-80
See also SATA 15
Faber, Adele 1928- CANR-37
Earlier sketch in CA 77-80
Faber, Charles F(ranklin) 1926- CANR-12
Earlier sketch in CA 29-32R
Faber, Doris (Greenberg) 1924- CANR-30
Earlier sketches in CA 17-20R, CANR-8
See also SATA 3
Faber, Frederick William 1814-1863 .... DLB 32
Faber, Harold 1919- CANR-29
Earlier sketches in CA 13-16R, CANR-8
See also SATA 5
Faber, John Henry 1918- 13-16R
Faber, Nancy W(eingarten) 1909-1976 .... 5-8R
Obituary 65-68
Faber, Richard Stanley 1924- 61-64
Faber-Kaiser, Andreas 1944- 73-76
Fabian, Donald L(eroy) 1919- 21-24R
Fabian, Josephine C(unningham)
1903-1984 .... CAP-1
Obituary 114
Earlier sketch in CA 9-10
Fabian, Robert (Honey) 1901-1978 81-84
Obituary 77-80
Fabian, Ruth
See Quigley, Aileen
Fabinyi, Andrew 1908-1978 Obituary 108
Fabio, Sarah Webster 1928-1979 .... CANR-22
Earlier sketch in CA 69-72
See also BW
Fabisch, Judith Patricia 1938- CANR-19
Earlier sketch in CA 103
Fabos, Julius Gy(ula) 1932- 97-100
Fabre, Genevieve E. 1936- 109
Fabre, Jean Henri (Casimir)
1823-1915 .... SATA 22
Fabre, Michel J(acques) 1933- CANR-37
Earlier sketches in CA 45-48, CANR-1, 16
Fabrega, Horacio Jr. 1934- 73-76
Fabri, Ralph 1894-1975 .... CAP-2
Obituary 57-60
Earlier sketch in CA 19-20
Fabricand, Burton Paul 1923- 93-96
Fabricant, Carole 1944- 113
Fabricant, Solomon 1906-1989 Obituary 129
Fabricius, Johan (Johannes) 1899- CANR-5
Earlier sketch in CA 53-56
Fabrizio, Ray 1930- 33-36R
Fabrizius, Peter
See Fabry, Joseph B(enedikt)
and Knight, Max
Fabry, Joseph B(enedikt) 1909- 25-28R
Fabrycky, Wolter Joseph 1932- 21-24R
Fabun, Don 1920- 45-48
Fackenheim, Emil L(udwig) 1916- 21-24R
Facklam, Margery (Metz) 1927- CANR-21
Earlier sketches in CA 5-8R, CANR-6
See also SATA 20
Fackler, Eli
See Fackler, Elizabeth
Fackler, Elizabeth 1947- 118
Fackre, Gabriel Joseph 1926- CANR-7
Earlier sketch in CA 17-20R
Facos, James F(rancis) 1924- 41-44R
Factor, Regis A(nthony) 1937- 118
Fader, Daniel 1930- 33-36R
Fader, Shirley Sloan 1931- CANR-14
Earlier sketch in CA 77-80
Faderman, Lillian 1940- CANR-37
Earlier sketches in CA 33-36R, CANR-16
Fadeyev, A.
See Bulgya, Alexander Alexandrovich
Fadeyev, Alexander
See Bulgya, Alexander Alexandrovich
Fadiman, Clifton (Paul) 1904- CANR-9
Earlier sketch in CA 61-64
See also SATA 11
Fadiman, Edwin Jr. 1925- 29-32R
Fadiman, James 1939- 33-36R
Fadiman, Jeffrey A(ndrew) 1936- 116
Fadner, Frank (Leslie) 1910-1987 .... 9-12R
Obituary 123
Faegre, Torvald 1941- 89-92
Faelten, Sharon 1950- CANR-23
Earlier sketch in CA 106
Faessler, Shirley 1921(?)- 106
Fagan, Brian M(urray) 1936- CANR-31
Earlier sketches in CA 41-44R, CANR-14
Fagan, Cary 1957- 136
Fagan, Edward R(ichard) 1924- CANR-20
Earlier sketches in CA 9-12R, CANR-5
Fage, John Donnelly 1921- CANR-7
Earlier sketch in CA 5-8R
Fagen, Donald 1948- .... CLC 26
Fagen, Richard R. 1933- CANR-22
Earlier sketches in CA 17-20R, CANR-7
Fagen, Stanley Alan 1936- 102
Fager, Charles E(ugene) 1942- 21-24R
Fagerstrom, Stan 1923- 57-60
Fagg, Elizabeth
See Olds, Elizabeth Fagg
Fagg, John (Edwin) 1916- 81-84
Fagg, William Buller 1914- 102
Fagles, Robert 1933- Brief entry 104
Fagley, Richard M(artin) 1910- 1-4R
Fagon, Alfred 1937-1986 Obituary 120
Fagothey, Austin 1901- CAP-1
Earlier sketch in CA 11-12
Fague, William Robert 1927- 109
Fagundo, Ana Maria 1938- 37-40R
Fagunwa, D(aniel) O(lorunfemi)
1910(?)-1963 Obituary 116
Fagyas, Maria 33-36R
Faherty, William B(arnaby) 1914- CANR-5
Earlier sketch in CA 5-8R
Fahey, David (Allen) 1948- 131
Fahey, Frank M(ichael) 1917- 101
Fahey, James C(harles)
1903-1974 Obituary 53-56
Fahlstrom, Oyvind (Axel Christian)
1928-1976 Obituary 69-72
Fahmy, Ismail 1922- 133
Fahnestock, Beatrice Beck
1899(?)-1980 Obituary 97-100
Fahs, Ivan J. 1932- 45-48
Fahs, Sophia Blanche Lyon
1876-1978 Obituary 77-80
Fahy, Christopher 1937- CANR-29
Earlier sketches in CA 69-72, CANR-11
Fain, Haskell 1926- 33-36R
Fain, Tyrus Gerard 1933- 104
Fainlight, Ruth (Esther) 1931- CANR-26
Earlier sketches in CA 17-20R, CANR-8
Fainsod, Merle 1907-1972 .... CAP-1
Obituary 33-36R
Earlier sketch in CA 13-16
Fainstein, Norman Ira 1944- 102
Fainstein, Susan S. 1938- 93-96
Fainzilberg, Ilya Arnoldovich
1897-1937 Brief entry 120
See also Ilf, Ilya
Fair, A. A.
See Gardner, Erle Stanley
Fair, Charles M. 1916- CANR-10
Earlier sketch in CA 13-16R
Fair, Harold L(loyd) 1924- 89-92
Fair, James R(utherford) Jr. 1920- CANR-34
Earlier sketch in CA 29-32R
Fair, James 1898(?)-1984 Obituary 112
Fair, Marvin L(uke) 1897(?)-1983 Obituary 110
Fair, Ray C(larence) 1942- 29-32R
Fair, Ronald L. 1932- CANR-25
Earlier sketch in CA 69-72
See also BW
See also CLC 18
See also DLB 33
Fair, Sylvia 1933- 69-72
See also SATA 13
Fairbairn, Ann
See Tait, Dorothy
Fairbairn, Douglas 1926- 33-36R
Fairbairn, Garry L. 1947- 77-80
Fairbairn, Helen
See Southard, Helen Fairbairn
Fairbairn, Ian J(ohn) 1933- 53-56
Fairbairns, Zoe (Ann) 1948- CANR-21
Earlier sketch in CA 103
See also CLC 32
Fairbank, Alfred John 1895-1982 .... CANR-6
Obituary 106
Earlier sketch in CA 5-8R
Fairbank, John K(ing) 1907-1991 .... CANR-3
Obituary 135
Earlier sketch in CA 1-4R
Fairbanks, Carol 1935- 69-72
Fairbanks, Henry G(eorge)
1914- Brief entry 112
Fairbrother, Nan 1913-1971 .... CANR-3
Obituary 33-36R
Earlier sketch in CA 5-8R
Fairburn, Eleanor 1928- CANR-8
Earlier sketch in CA 61-64
Fairchild, Hoxie Neale 1894-1973 .... 5-8R
Obituary 45-48
Fairchild, John B(urr) 1927- Brief entry 117
Fairchild, Louis W. 1901-1981 Obituary 105
Fairchild, William 73-76
Fairclough, Adam 1952- 127
Fairclough, Chris 1951- 112
Faire, Zabrina
See Stevenson, Florence
Fairfax, Ann
See Chesney, Marion
Fairfax, Beatrice
See Scarberry, Alma Sioux
Fairfax, Beatrice
See Manning, Marie
and McCarroll, Marion C(lyde)
Fairfax, Felix
See Gibson, Walter B(rown)
Fairfax, John 1930- 97-100
Fairfax, John 1937- 49-52
Fairfax, Warwick (Oswald)
1901-1987 Obituary 121
Fairfax-Blakeborough, Jack
See Fairfax-Blakeborough, John Freeman
Fairfax-Blakeborough, John Freeman
1883-1978(?) 102
Fairfax-Lucy, Brian (Fulke Cameron-Ramsay)
1898-1974 .... CAP-2
Earlier sketch in CA 29-32
See also SATA 6, 26
Fairfield, Darrell
See Larkin, Rochelle
Fairfield, James G(lencairn) T(homson)
1926- 126
Fairfield, John
See Livingstone, Harrison Edward
Fairfield, Lesley 1949- 130
Fairfield, Leslie P(arke) 1941- Brief entry 107
Fairfield, Richard 1937- 41-44R
Fairfield, Roy P(hillip) 1918- 33-36R
Fairhall, David Keir 1934- 103
Fairholme, Elizabeth 1910- 97-100
Fairless, Caroline S. 1947- 105
Fairley, Barker 1887-1986 .... 1-4R
Obituary 121
Fairley, Irene R. 1940- 73-76
Fairley, James Stewart 1940- 102
Fairley, John (Alexander) 1939- 131
Fairley, M(ichael) C(harles) 1937- CANR-14
Earlier sketch in CA 37-40R
Fairley, Peter 1930- CANR-24
Earlier sketch in CA 29-32R
Fairlie, Gerard 1899-1983 Obituary 109
See also DLB 77
See also SATA 34
Fairlie, Henry (Jones) 1924-1990 104
Obituary 131
Fairman, Charles 1897- 45-48
Fairman, Herbert Walter 1907-1982 111
Obituary 108
Fairman, Honora C.
1927(?)-1978 Obituary 81-84
Fairman, Joan A(lexandra) 1935- 33-36R
See also SATA 10
Fairman, Paul W. 1916-1977 Obituary 114
Fairn, (Richard) Duncan
1906-1986 Obituary 119
Fairweather, Digby 1946- 127
Fairweather, Eileen 1954- 125
Fairweather, Eugene Rathbone
1920- Brief entry 108
Fairweather, George W. 1921- 13-16R
Fairweather, Janet (Anne) 1945- 124
Fairweather, Sally (Hallberg) 1917- 112
Fairweather, Virginia 1922- 29-32R
Faison, S(amson) Lane Jr. 1907- 89-92
Faissler, Margareta 1902- 5-8R

Fait, Hollis F. 1918- CANR-5
Earlier sketch in CA 1-4R
Faith, Barbara
See Covarrubias, Barbara Faith
Faith, (Richard) Mack 1944- 125
Faith, William Robert
See Fague, William Robert
Faithfull, Gail 1936- 57-60
See also SATA 8
Faiz, Faiz Ahmad 1912(?)-1984 Obituary 115
Fakhry, Majid 1923- 29-32R
Fakinos, Aris 1935- 81-84
Falassi, Alessandro 1945- 105
Falb, Lewis W(illiam) 1935- 102
Falck, (Adrian) Colin 1934- 65-68
Falco, Edward 1948- 134
Falco, Gian
See Papini, Giovanni
Falco, Maria J(osephine) 1932- CANR-12
Earlier sketch in CA 61-64
Falcoff, Mark 1941- 65-68
Falcon
See Nestle, John Francis
Falcon, Richard
See Shapiro, Samuel
Falcon, Walter P(hillip) 1936- 126
Brief entry 109
Falcon, William D(yche) 1932- 17-20R
Falcon-Barker, Ted 1923- 25-28R
Falconer, A. F.
See Falconer, Alexander Frederick
Falconer, Alexander Frederick
1908-1987 Obituary 122
Falconer, Alun Obituary 104
Falconer, James
See Kirkup, James
Falconer, Kenneth
See Kornbluth, C(yril) M.
Falconer, Lee N.
See May, Julian
Falconieri, John V(incent) 1920- 130
Falero, Frank Jr. 1937- 37-40R
Fales, Dean Abner Jr. 1925- Brief entry 110
Fales, Edward (Daniel Jr.) 1906- 97-100
Falk, Candace 1947- 136
Falk, Charles J(ohn) 1899-1971 ....CAP-2
Earlier sketch in CA 23-24
Falk, Doris Virginia 1919- Brief entry 111
Falk, Elsa
See Escherich, Elsa Falk
Falk, Eugene H(annes) 1913- 116
Falk, Gerhard 1931- CANR-39
Earlier sketch in CA 117
Falk, Harvey 1932- 127
Brief entry 112
Falk, I(sidore) S(ydney)
1899-1984 Obituary 114
Falk, Irving A. 1921- 21-24R
Falk, Kathryn 1940- CANR-20
Earlier sketch in CA 97-100
Falk, Lee
See Copper, Basil
Falk, Lee Harrison 1915- 97-100
Falk, Leslie A. 1915- 9-12R
Falk, Louis A. 1896(?)-1979 Obituary 85-88
Falk, Marvin W. 1943- 122
Falk, Minna Regina 1900-1983 Obituary 109
Falk, Pamela S. 1953- 122
Falk, Quentin 1948- 122
Falk, Richard A(nderson) 1930- CANR-12
Earlier sketch in CA 5-8R
Falk, Robert 1914- 89-92
Falk, Roger (Salis) 1910- 65-68
Falk, S(tephen) J(ohn) 1942- 124
Falk, Signi Lenea 1906- 5-8R
Falk, Stanley L(awrence) 1927- CANR-2
Earlier sketch in CA 1-4R
Falk, Susan Meyers 1942- 117
Falk, Toby
See Falk, S(tephen) J(ohn)
Falk, Ursula Adler 114
Falk, Ze'ev W(ilhelm) 1923- CANR-15
Earlier sketch in CA 21-24R
Falkender, Baroness Marcia
See Williams, Marcia
Falkirk, Richard
See Lambert, Derek
Falkland, Samuel
See Heijermans, Herman
Falkner, Leonard 1900- 21-24R
See also SATA 12
Falkner, Murry (Charles) 1899- CAP-2
Earlier sketch in CA 23-24
Falk-Roenne, Arne 1920- CANR-14
Earlier sketch in CA 21-24R
Falkus, Hugh Edward Lance 1917- 111
Fall, Bernard B. 1926-1967 ....CANR-6
Obituary 25-28R
Earlier sketch in CA 1-4R
Fall, Frieda Kay 1913- 41-44R
Fall, Thomas
See Snow, Donald Clifford
Fallaci, Oriana 1930- CANR-15
Earlier sketch in CA 77-80
See also CLC 11
See also MTCW
Fallada, Hans
See Ditzen, Rudolf
See also DLB 56
Fallaw, Wesner 1907- 1-4R
Faller, Kevin 1920- CANR-4
Earlier sketch in CA 53-56
Fallere, Felicia
See Knist, F(rances) Emma
Fallers, Lloyd A(shton Jr.) 1925-1974 ....CANR-4
Obituary 49-52
Earlier sketch in CA 9-12R
Falley, Margaret Dickson
1898-1983 Obituary 110
Fallon, Carlos 1909- 41-44R
Fallon, Eileen Brydon 1954- 118
Fallon, Frederic (Michael) 1944-1970 ....41-44R
Fallon, George
See Bingley, David Ernest
Fallon, Ivan (Gregory) 1944- 137
Fallon, Jack
See Fallon, John W(illiam)
Fallon, John W(illiam) 1924- 77-80
Fallon, Martin
See Patterson, Harry
Fallon, Padraic 1905-1974 103
Obituary 89-92
Fallon, Peter 1951- 133
Brief entry 106
Fallon, Robert T(homas) 1927- 121
Fallowell, Duncan (Richard) 1948- 137
Fallows, James M(ackenzie) 1949- CANR-2
Earlier sketch in CA 45-48
Falls, C(harles) B(uckles)
1874-1960 Obituary 116
See also SATA 27, 38
Falls, Cyril Bentham 1888- CAP-1
Earlier sketch in CA 13-14
Falls, Joe 1928- 77-80
Falwell, Marshall Leigh Jr. 1943- 69-72
Falorp, Nelson P.
See Jones, Stephen (Phillip)
Falstein, Louis 1909- 97-100
See also SATA 37
Faltas Youssef, Edwar Kolta
See al-Kharrat, Edwar
Faludi, Susan 1959- 138
Faludy, George 1913- 21-24R
See also CLC 42
Faludy, Gyoergy
See Faludy, George
Falvey, Jack 1938- 122
Falwell, Jerry 1933- 102
Fama, Eugene F. 1939- Brief entry 113
Famiglietti, Eugene Paul
1931(?)-1980 Obituary 97-100
Famularo, Joseph John 1922- CANR-4
Earlier sketch in CA 1-4R
Fan, Kuang Huan 1932- 21-24R
Fanburg, Walter H. 1936- Brief entry 114
Fancher, Betsy 1928- ....DLBY 83
Fancher, Ewilda 1928- 61-64
Fancher, Raymond E(lwood) Jr. 1940- 69-72
Fancher, Robert T. 1954- 135
Fanchon, Lisa
See Floren, Lee
Fancutt, Walter 1911- CANR-12
Earlier sketches in CAP-1, CA 9-10
Fandel, John 1925- CANR-23
Earlier sketch in CA 69-72
Fane, Bron
See Fanthorpe, R(obert) Lionel
Fane, Julian Charles 1927- CANR-6
Earlier sketch in CA 13-16R
Fane, Violet 1843-1905 ....DLB 35
Fang, Chaoying 1908(?)-1985 Obituary 116
Fang, Irving E. 1929- CANR-31
Earlier sketch in CA 49-52
Fang, Josephine (Maria) Riss 1922- 69-72
Fang, L. Z.
See Fang Lizhi
Fanger, Donald (Lee) 1929- 13-16R
Fang Lizhi 1936- 135
Fann, K(uang) T(ih) 1937- 61-64
Fann, William E(dwin) 1930- CANR-2
Earlier sketch in CA 49-52
Fannin, Allen 1939- 69-72
Fanning, Buckner 1926- 69-72
Fanning, Charles (Frederick Jr.) 1942- 81-84
Fanning, Leonard M(ulliken) 1888-1967 ....5-8R
See also SATA 5
Fanning, Louis A(lbert) 1927- 69-72
Fanning, Michael 1942- 89-92
Fanning, Odom 1920- 53-56
Fanning, Robbie 1947- CANR-31
Earlier sketches in CA 77-80, CANR-14
Fanon, Frantz 1925-1961 116
Obituary 89-92
See also BLC 2
See also BW
Fanshawe, David 1942- 97-100
Fant, Joseph Lewis III 1928- 13-16R
Fant, Louis J(udson) Jr. 1931- 37-40R
Fanta, J. Julius 1907- 33-36R
Fante, John (Thomas) 1911-1983 ....CANR-23
Obituary 109
Earlier sketch in CA 69-72
See also CLC 60
See also DLBY 83
Fantel, Hans 1922- CANR-31
Earlier sketch in CA 49-52
Fanthorpe, Patricia Alice 1938- CANR-14
Earlier sketch in CA 89-92
Fanthorpe, R(obert) Lionel 1935- CANR-32
Earlier sketches in CA 73-76, CANR-14
Fantini, Mario D. 1927(?)-1989 77-80
Obituary 129
Fantoni, Barry (Ernest) 1940- 129
Farabee, Barbara 1944- 57-60
Faraday, Ann 1935- 77-80
Faraday, M. M.
See Rorvik, David M(ichael)
Faragher, John Mack 1945- Brief entry 111
Farago, Ladislas 1906-1980 ....CANR-10
Obituary 102
Earlier sketch in CA 65-68
Farah, Caesar Elie 1929- 41-44R
Farah, Madelain 1934- 73-76
Farah, Nuruddin 1945- 106
See also BLC 2
See also CLC 53
Fàralla, Dana 1909- 49-52
See also SATA 9
Faralla, Dorothy W.
See Faralla, Dana
Faramelli, Norman Joseph
1932- Brief entry 109
Farau, Alfred 1904-1972 Obituary 37-40R
Farb, Peter 1929-1980 ....CANR-12
Obituary 97-100
Earlier sketch in CA 13-16R
See also SATA 12, 22
Farber, Bernard 1922- 21-24R
Farber, Donald C. CANR-30
Earlier sketches in CA 29-32R, CANR-13
Farber, Edward (Rolke)
1914-1982 Obituary 110
Farber, Joseph C. 1903- 33-36R
Farber, Leslie Hillel 1912-1981 110
Obituary 103
Farber, Marvin 1901- 49-52
Farber, Norma 1909-1984 102
Obituary 112
See also DLB 61
See also MAICYA
See also SATA 25, 38
Farber, Paul Lawrence 1944- 112
Farber, Seymour M(organ) 1912- 57-60
Farber, Stephen E. 1943- CANR-19
Earlier sketch in CA 103
Farber, Susan L. 1945- 106
Farber, Thomas (David) 1944- 103
Farberman, Harvey A(lan) 1939- CANR-35
Earlier sketch in CA 45-48
Farberow, Norman L(ouis) 1918- CANR-7
Earlier sketch in CA 17-20R
Farca, Marie C. 1935- 37-40R
Farcau, Bruce 1951- 138
Farel, Conrad
See Bardens, Dennis (Conrad)
Farely, Alison
See Poland, Dorothy (Elizabeth Hayward)
Farer, Tom J. 1935- CANR-8
Earlier sketch in CA 17-20R
Farewell, Nina
See Cooper, Mae (Klein)
Fargis, Paul (McKenna) 1939- CANR-13
Earlier sketch in CA 21-24R
Fargo, Doone
See Norwood, Victor G(eorge) C(harles)
Fargo, Joe
See Rikhoff, James C.
Fargue, Leon-Paul
1876(?)-1947 Brief entry 109
See also TCLC 11
Farhi, Moris 1935- CANR-13
Earlier sketch in CA 77-80
Faria, A(nthony) J(ohn) 1944- CANR-19
Earlier sketch in CA 102
Farias, Victor 1940- 135
Faricy, Robert L(eo) 1926- CANR-34
Earlier sketches in CA 37-40R, CANR-15
Faridi, S. N.
See Faridi, Shah Nasiruddin Mohammad
Faridi, Shah Nasiruddin Mohammad
1929- 29-32R
Faries, Clyde J. 1928- 37-40R
Faries, David A(llan) 1938- 112
Farigoule, Louis
See Romains, Jules
Farina, John 1950- 114
Farina, Richard 1936(?)-1966 81-84
Obituary 25-28R
See also CLC 9
Faris, (Earl) Barry 1889-1966 Obituary 114
Faris, Robert E. L(ee) 1907- 17-20R
Faris, Wendy B(ush) 1945- 115
Farisani, Tshenuwani Simon 1947- 134
Farish, Donald J(ames) 1942- 106
Farish, Margaret Kennedy 1918- 5-8R
Farish, Terry 1947- 137
Farjeon, (Eve) Annabel 1919- 53-56
See also SATA 11
Farjeon, Eleanor 1881-1965 ....CAP-1
Earlier sketch in CA 11-12
See also MAICYA
See also SATA 2
Farkas, Emil 1946- CANR-32
Earlier sketch in CA 69-72
Farkas, Philip (Francis) 1914- CANR-31
Earlier sketch in CA 49-52
Farley, Carol 1936- CANR-25
Earlier sketches in CA 21-24R, CANR-10
See also SATA 4
Farley, (William) Edward 1929- 61-64
Farley, Eugene J. 1916- CANR-12
Earlier sketch in CA 33-36R
Farley, James A(loysius)
1888-1976 Obituary 65-68
Farley, Jean 1928- 21-24R
Farley, Jennie (Tiffany Towle) 1932- 132
Farley, Miriam Southwell
1907(?)-1975 Obituary 57-60
Farley, Rawle 1922- 45-48
Farley, Walter (Lorimer) 1915-1989 ....CANR-29
Earlier sketches in CA 17-20R, CANR-8
See also CLC 17
See also DLB 22
See also MAICYA
See also SATA 2, 43
Farley-Hills, David 1931- 73-76
Farlie, Barbara L(eitzow) 1936- 65-68
Farlow, John King
See King-Farlow, John
Farmacevten
See Holm, Sven (Aage)
Farmar, Hugh William 1908-1987 Obituary 123
Farmer, Albert J(ohn) 1894-1976 ....21-24R
Obituary 120
Farmer, Bernard James 1902- 5-8R
Farmer, Bertram Hughes 1916- 104
Farmer, Charles J(oseph) 1943- CANR-10
Earlier sketch in CA 57-60
Farmer, David Hugh 1923- 125
Farmer, Don 1938- 65-68
Farmer, Gary R(ay) 1923- 57-60
Farmer, Gene 1919-1972 Obituary 37-40R
Farmer, Herbert Henry
1892-1981(?) Obituary 102
Farmer, Kathleen 1946- CANR-10
Earlier sketch in CA 65-68
Farmer, Laurence 1895(?)-1976 Obituary 65-68
Farmer, Martha L(ouise) 1912- 21-24R
Farmer, Norman K(ittrell Jr.) 1934- 123
Farmer, Penelope (Jane) 1939- CANR-37
Earlier sketches in CA 13-16R, CANR-9
See also CLR 8
See also MAICYA
See also SATA 39, 40
Farmer, Peter 1950- ....SATA 38
Farmer, Philip Jose 1918- CANR-35
Earlier sketches in CA 1-4R, CANR-4
See also CLC 1, 19
See also DLB 8
See also MTCW
Farmer, R. L.
See Lamont, Rosette C(lementine)
Farmer, Richard Neil 1928- CANR-8
Earlier sketch in CA 17-20R
Farmer, Robert Allen 1938- 21-24R
Farmer, William R(euben) 1921- 123
Brief entry 109
Farmer Jones
See Jones, Bryan L.
Farmiloe, Dorothy Alicia 1920- CANR-8
Earlier sketch in CA 61-64
Farnan, D(orothy) J(eanne-Therese) 1919- 130
Farnash, Hugh
See Luff, S(tanley) G(eorge) A(nthony)
Farndale, W(illiam) A(rthur) J(ames)
1916- CANR-11
Earlier sketch in CA 25-28R
Farner, Donald S(ankey) 1915- 53-56
Farnham, Burt
See Clifford, Harold B(urton)
Farnham, Emily 1912- 69-72
Farnham, Marynia F.
1900(?)-1979 Obituary 85-88
Farnham, Thomas J(avery) 1938- CANR-4
Earlier sketch in CA 53-56
Farnie, D(ouglas) A(ntony) 1926- CANR-12
Earlier sketch in CA 73-76
Farnsworth, Clyde A.
1908(?)-1984 Obituary 112
Farnsworth, Dana (Lyda) 1905-1986 61-64
Obituary 119
Farnsworth, E(dward) Allan 1928- 13-16R
Farnsworth, James
See Pohle, Robert W(arren) Jr.
Farnsworth, Jerry 1895- CAP-1
Earlier sketch in CA 13-16
Farnsworth, Lee W(infield) 1932- 33-36R
Farnsworth, Paul Randolph 1899- CAP-2
Earlier sketch in CA 29-32
Farnsworth, Robert M. 1929- 53-56
Farnum, K. T.
See Rips, Ervine M(ilton)
Farnworth, Warren 1935- 93-96
Farny, Michael H(olt) 1934- 65-68
Faron, Louis C. 1923- 9-12R
Farquhar, Aardvark Z. 1929- 113
Farquhar, Francis P(eloubet) 1887-1975 ....CAP-1
Obituary 57-60
Earlier sketch in CA 19-20
Farquhar, George 1677-1707 ....DLB 84
Farquhar, Margaret C(utting) 1905- 69-72
See also SATA 13
Farquharson, Alexander 1944- ....SATA 46
Farquharson, Charlie
See Harron, Don(ald)
Farquharson, Martha
See Finley, Martha
Farr, Bill
See Farr, William T.
Farr, David M. L. 1922- 37-40R
Farr, Diana (Pullein-Thompson) CANR-20
Earlier sketches in CA 13-16R, CANR-7
See also Pullein-Thompson, Diana
Farr, Dorothy M(ary) 1905- 77-80
Farr, Douglas
See Gilford, C(harles) B(ernard)
Farr, Finis (King) 1904-1982 ....CANR-1
Obituary 105
Earlier sketch in CA 1-4R
See also SATA 10
Farr, John
See Webb, Jack (Randolph)
Farr, Judith 1937- CANR-12
Earlier sketch in CA 29-32R
Farr, Kenneth R(aymond) 1942- 73-76
Farr, Michael 1924- 29-32R
Farr, Roger C. 33-36R
Farr, Sidney Saylor 1932- 114
Farr, Walter Greene Jr. 1925- Brief entry 106
Farr, William T. 1934-1987 Obituary 121
Farra, Madame E.
See Fawcett, F(rank) Dubrez
Farrant, Leda 1927- 21-24R
Farrar, John C(hipman) 1896-1974 65-68
Obituary 53-56

Farrar, Lancelot Leighton Jr. 1932- CANR-4
Earlier sketch in CA 53-56
Farrar, Larston Dawn 1915-1970 ....1-4R
Obituary 29-32R
Farrar, Margaret Petherbridge
1897-1984 Obituary 113
Farrar, Richard B(artlett) Jr. 1939- 65-68
Farrar, Ronald T(ruman) 1935- 33-36R
Farrar, Rowena Rutherford 1903- 108
Farrar, Susan Clement 1917- 101
See also SATA 33
Farrar-Hockley, Anthony Heritage 1924- 69-72
Farrell, Alan 1920- 13-16R
Farrell, Anne A. 1916- 25-28R
Farrell, B. A.
See Farrell, Brian Anthony
Farrell, Barry 1935(?)-1984 Obituary 114
Farrell, Ben
See Cebulash, Mel
Farrell, Brian
See Farrell, Brian Anthony
Farrell, Brian Anthony 1912- 130
Farrell, Brian 1929- 135
Farrell, Bryan (Henry) 1923- CANR-2
Earlier sketch in CA 49-52
Farrell, C(larence) Frederick Jr. 1934- 122
Farrell, Catharine
See O'Connor, Sister Mary Catharine
Farrell, Cliff 1899-1977 65-68
Obituary 125
Farrell, David
See Smith, Frederick E(screet)
Farrell, Desmond
See Organ, John
Farrell, Edith R(odgers) 1933- 122
Farrell, Edmund J(ames) 1927- 120
Farrell, Francis (Thomas)
1912-1983 Obituary 109
Farrell, Frank
See Farrell, Francis (Thomas)
Farrell, J(ames) G(ordon) 1935-1979 ....CANR-36
Obituary 89-92
Earlier sketch in CA 73-76
See also CLC 6
See also DLB 14
See also MTCW
Farrell, James T(homas) 1904-1979 ....CANR-9
Obituary 89-92
Earlier sketch in CA 5-8R
See also CLC 1, 4, 8, 11, 66
See also DLB 4, 9, 86
See also DLBD 2
See also MTCW
Farrell, John J(oseph) 1934- Brief entry 110
Farrell, John Philip 1939- 102
Farrell, Kathleen (Amy) 1912- 5-8R
Farrell, Kirby 1942- 33-36R
Farrell, M. J.
See Keane, Mary Nesta (Skrine)
Farrell, Matthew Charles 1921- 49-52
Farrell, Melvin L(loyd) 1930- CANR-5
Earlier sketch in CA 13-16R
Farrell, Michael 1944- CANR-23
Earlier sketch in CA 69-72
Farrell, Patricia
See Zelver, Patricia (Farrell)
Farrell, Robert T(homas) 1938- 93-96
Farrell, Susan Caust 1944- 112
Farrell, William E. 1936(?)-1985 Obituary 115
Farrelly, M(ark) John 1927- 13-16R
Farrelly, Peter (John) 1956- 127
Farren, David
See McFerran, Douglass David
Farren, Richard J.
See Betjeman, John
Farren, Richard M.
See Betjeman, John
Farrer, Claire R(afferty) 1936- CANR-26
Earlier sketches in CA 65-68, CANR-10
Farrer, (Bryan) David 1906-1983 ....25-28R
Obituary 109
Farrer, Katharine Dorothy (Newton) 1911- 5-8R
Farrer, Keith Thomas Henry 1916- 110
Farrimond, John 1913- 102
Farrington, Benjamin 1891-1974 65-68
Obituary 53-56
See also SATA 20
Farrington, D. P.
See Farrington, David P.
Farrington, David P. 1944- 130
Farrington, (Mary) Elizabeth Pruett
1898-1984 Obituary 113
Farrington, (Roland) Gene 1931- 130
Farrington, S(elwyn) Kip Jr. 1904-1983 73-76
Obituary 109
See also SATA 20
Farris, Jack 1921- 129
Farris, John 101
Farris, Martin T(heodore) 1925- CANR-11
Earlier sketch in CA 21-24R
Farris, Paul L(eonard) 1919- 9-12R
Farrison, William Edward 1902- 29-32R
Farriss, N(ancy) M(arguerite) 1938- 25-28R
Farrow, J.
See Fonarow, Jerry
Farrow, James S.
See Tubb, E(dwin) C(harles)
Farson, Daniel (Negley) 1927- CANR-37
Earlier sketches in CA 93-96, CANR-16
Farson, (James Scott) Negley
1890-1960 Obituary 93-96
Farstad, Arthur L(eonard) 1935- 109
Farthing, Alison 1936- 117
See also SATA 36, 45
Farwell, Byron E. 1921- CANR-9
Earlier sketch in CA 13-16R
Farwell, George Michell 1911-1976 ....21-24R
Obituary 69-72
Farwell, Loring C(hapman)
1915- Brief entry 111
Farzan, Massud 1936- 53-56
Fasana, Paul James 1933- CANR-14
Earlier sketch in CA 37-40R
Fasel, George W(illiam) 1938- 21-24R
Fasick, Adele M(ongan) 1930- 125
Fasold, Ralph W(illiam August) 1940- 29-32R
Fass, Paula S. 1947- 129
Brief entry 112
Fassbinder, Rainer Werner
1946-1982 ....CANR-31
Obituary 106
Earlier sketch in CA 93-96
See also CLC 20
Fassett, James 1904-1986 49-52
Obituary 121
Fassler, Joan (Grace) 1931- 61-64
See also SATA 11
Fast, Barbara 1924- 104
Fast, Howard (Melvin) 1914- CANR-33
Earlier sketches in CA 1-4R, CANR-1
See also CLC 23
See also DLB 9
See also SATA 7
Fast, Jonathan (David) 1948- CANR-34
Earlier sketch in CA 77-80
Fast, Julius 1919- CANR-27
Earlier sketches in CA 25-28R, CANR-11
Fastlife
See Grogan, Emmett
Fatchen, Max 1920- CANR-28
Earlier sketches in CA 25-28R, CANR-11
See also SATA 20
Fate, Terry 1949- 116
Fatemi, Nasrollah S(aifpour) 1910-1990 77-80
Obituary 131
Father Xavier
See Hurwood, Bernhardt J.
Fathy, Hassan 1900-1989 Obituary 130
Fatigati, (Frances) Evelyn 1948- 77-80
See also SATA 24
Fatio, Louise 1904- 37-40R
See also SATA 6
Fatjo, Thomas Joseph Jr. 1940- 107
Fatouros, A(rghyrios) A. 1932- 13-16R
Fatout, Paul 1897- 21-24R
Fatt, Amelia 1943- 118
Faucher, Real 1940- 101
Faucher, W. Thomas 1945- 57-60
Faulcon, Robert
See Holdstock, Robert P.
Faulhaber, Charles Bailey 1941- 53-56
Faulhaber, Martha 1926- 33-36R
See also SATA 7
Faulk, Charles Johnson Jr.
1916(?)-1990 Obituary 131
Faulk, John Henry 1913-1990 102
Obituary 131
Faulk, Odie B. 1933- CANR-14
Earlier sketch in CA 25-28R
Faulkes, Anthony 1937- 138
Faulkner, Alex 1905(?)-1983 Obituary 109
Faulkner, Anne Irvin 1906- CANR-2
Earlier sketch in CA 1-4R
See also SATA 23
Faulkner, Charles H. 1937- 25-28R
Faulkner, Christopher G(raham) 1942- 125
Faulkner, Edwin J. 1900(?)-1987 Obituary 121
Faulkner, Elsie 1905- 65-68
Faulkner, Frank
See Ellis, Edward S(ylvester)
Faulkner, Harold Underwood 1890-1968 ....1-4R
Obituary 103
Faulkner, Howard J. 1945- 135
Faulkner, John 1901-1963 ....CANR-1
Earlier sketch in CA 1-4R
Faulkner, Joseph E. 1928- 45-48
Faulkner, Nancy
See Faulkner, Anne Irvin
Faulkner, Peter 1933- CANR-20
Earlier sketches in CA 5-8R, CANR-3
Faulkner, Ray (Nelson) 1906- 5-8R
Faulkner, Trader 1930- 102
Faulkner, Virginia (Louise) 1913-1980 ....CANR-11
Earlier sketch in CA 65-68
Faulkner, (Herbert Winthrop) Waldron
1898-1979 93-96
Obituary 85-88
Faulkner, William (Cuthbert)
1897-1962 ....CANR-33
Earlier sketch in CA 81-84
See also AAYA 7
See also CDALB 1929-1941
See also CLC 1, 3, 6, 8, 9, 11, 14, 18, 28, 52, 68
See also DLB 9, 11, 44, 102
See also DLBD 2
See also DLBY 86
See also MTCW
See also SSC 1
See also WLC
Faulknor, Cliff(ord Vernon) 1913- CANR-8
Earlier sketch in CA 17-20R
Faulks, Neville 1908-1985 Obituary 118
Faulks, Sebastian 1953- 131
Faunce, Roland Cleo 1905- 1-4R
Faunce, William A(lden) 1928- 25-28R
Faunce-Brown, Daphne (Bridget) 1938- 115
Faupel, John F(rancis) 1906- 5-8R
Faure, Lucie 1908-1977 Obituary 73-76
Faure, William C(aldwell) Jr. 1949- 109
Faurot, Albert 1914- 77-80
Faurot, Jean H(iatt) 1911- 29-32R
Faurot, Jeannette 1943- 106
Faurot, Ruth Marie 1916- 85-88
Fauset, Arthur Huff 25-28R
Fauset, Jessie Redmon 1884(?)-1961 109
See also BLC 2
See also BW
See also CLC 19, 54
See also DLB 51
Fausold, Martin L. 1921- 21-24R
Fausset, Hugh I'Anson
1895-1965 Obituary 93-96
Faust, Clarence H(enry)
1901-1975 Obituary 57-60
Faust, Drew Gilpin 1947- 110
Faust, Frederick (Shiller)
1892-1944(?) Brief entry 108
Faust, Irvin 1924- CANR-28
Earlier sketch in CA 33-36R
See also CLC 8
See also DLB 2, 28
See also DLBY 80
Faust, Naomi F(lowe) 61-64
Fausti, Remo P(hilip) 1917- 41-44R
Fausto-Sterling, Anne 1944- 137
Fauth, Robert T. 1916- 1-4R
Fautsko, Timothy F(rank) 1945- 85-88
Faux, Marian 1945- CANR-14
Earlier sketch in CA 81-84
Fava, Sylvia Fleis 1927- 115
Faverty, Frederic Everett 1902-1981 45-48
Obituary 104
Faville, David Ernest 1899-1970 ....1-4R
Obituary 103
Favret, Andrew G. 1925- 17-20R
Favretti, Rudy J(ohn) 1932- CANR-4
Earlier sketch in CA 53-56
Fawcett, Brian 1906- 102
Fawcett, Chris 1950- 107
Fawcett, Clara Hallard 1887- CAP-1
Earlier sketch in CA 13-16
Fawcett, Claude W(eldon) 1911- 49-52
Fawcett, F(rank) Dubrez 1891-1968 ....CAP-1
Earlier sketch in CA 9-10
Fawcett, J(ames) E(dmund) S(anford)
1913- 97-100
Fawcett, Ken(neth Richard) 1944- 104
Fawcett, Marion
See Sanderson, Sabina W(arren)
Fawcett, Robin P(owell) 1937- 119
Fawcett, Roger Knowlton
1909-1979 Obituary 89-92
Fawdry, Marguerite 1912- 135
Fawkes, Guy
See Benchley, Robert (Charles)
Fawkes, Richard (Brian) 1944- CANR-20
Earlier sketch in CA 103
Fax, Elton Clay 1909- CANR-15
Earlier sketch in CA 13-16R
See also SATA 25
Faxon, Alicia Craig 1931- CANR-29
Earlier sketch in CA 69-72
Faxon, Arba D. 1895(?)-1975 Obituary 61-64
Faxon, Lavinia
See Russ, Lavinia (Faxon)
Fay, Allen 1934- 123
Brief entry 118
Fay, Erica
See Stopes, Marie (Charlotte) Carmichael
Fay, Frederic L(eighton) 1890- CAP-2
Earlier sketch in CA 21-22
Fay, Gerard (Francis Arthur) 1913-1968 ....CAP-1
Earlier sketch in CA 13-16
Fay, Gordon S(haw) 1912- 53-56
Fay, John 1921- 57-60
Fay, Leo (Charles) 1920- 13-16R
Fay, Mary Helen
See Fagyas, Maria
Fay, Peter Ward 1924- 57-60
Fay, S(amuel) P(rescott) Jr. 1926- 89-92
Fay, Stanley
See Shulman, Fay Grissom Stanley
Fay, Stephen (Francis John) 1938- CANR-31
Earlier sketch in CA 25-28R
Fay, Thomas A(rthur) 1927- 102
Faye, Jean Pierre 1925- 102
Fayer, Mischa Harry 1902-1977 ....CANR-6
Earlier sketch in CA 1-4R
Fayer, Steve 1935- 132
Fayerweather, John 1922- CANR-1
Earlier sketch in CA 1-4R
Fazakas, Ray 1932- 101
Fazakerley, George Raymond 1921- 13-16R
Fazal, M(uhammad) A(bul) 1939- 29-32R
Fazzano, Joseph E. 1929- 5-8R
Feagans, Lynne 1945- 117
Feagans, Raymond (John) 1953- 57-60
Feagin, Joe R(ichard) 1938- CANR-13
Earlier sketch in CA 37-40R
Feagles, Anita M(acRae) 1927- CANR-4
Earlier sketch in CA 1-4R
See also SATA 9
Feagles, Elizabeth
See Day, Beth (Feagles)
Feague, Mildred H. 1915- 29-32R
See also SATA 14
Feal-Deibe, Carlos 1935- 37-40R
Fear, David E. 1941- 53-56
Fear, Richard Arthur 1909- 125
Fear Chanaidh
See Campbell, John Lorne
Fearing, Kenneth (Flexner) 1902-1961 93-96
See also CLC 51
See also DLB 9
Fearon, George Edward 1901- CAP-1
Earlier sketch in CA 9-10
Fearon, John D(aniel) 1920- 37-40R
Fearon, Peter (Shaun) 1942- 29-32R
Fears, Gerald 81-84
Feather, John 1947- 122
Feather, Leonard G(eoffrey) 1914- 61-64
Feather, Norman T(homas) 1930- 73-76
Feather, Norman 1904-1978 Obituary 111
Featherstone, D.
See Warren, David
Featherstone, Helen 1944- 102
Featherstone, Joseph (Luke) 1940- 33-36R
Featherstonehaugh, Francis
See MacGregor, Alasdair Alpin (Douglas)
Feaver, George (Arthur) 1937- 29-32R
Feaver, J(ohn) Clayton 1911- CAP-2
Earlier sketch in CA 25-28
Feaver, Vicki 1943- 129
Feaver, William Andrew 1942- 103
February, Vernie A.
See February, Vernon Alexander
February, Vernon Alexander 1938- 129
Fecamps, Elise
See Creasey, John
Fecher, Charles A(dam) 1917- 81-84
Fecher, Constance
See Heaven, Constance
Fechter, Alyce Shinn 1909- CAP-1
Earlier sketch in CA 13-16
Feck, Luke 1935- 69-72
Fedde, Norman A(ndreas) 1914- 5-8R
Fedden, Henry (Romilly) 1908- 9-12R
Fedden, Robin
See Fedden, Henry (Romilly)
Fedder, Edwin H(ersh) 1929- 37-40R
Fedder, Norman J(oseph) 1934- CANR-25
Earlier sketches in CA 21-24R, CANR-9
Fedder, Ruth 1907- CANR-2
Earlier sketch in CA 5-8R
Feder, Bernard 1924- CANR-15
Earlier sketch in CA 33-36R
Feder, Ernest 1913- 37-40R
Feder, Jane 1940- 93-96
Feder, Jose 1917- 105
Feder, Karah (Tal) 1920- 17-20R
Feder, Lillian 41-44R
Feder, Paula (Kurzband) 1935- 105
See also SATA 26
Feder, Robert Arthur 1909-1969 Obituary 110
See also SATA 35
Federbusch, Simon
See Federbush, Simon
Federbush, Arnold 1935- 104
Federbush, Simon 1892(?)-1969 Obituary 115
Federico, Ronald Charles 1941- 89-92
Federman, Raymond 1928- CANR-10
Earlier sketch in CA 17-20R
See also CAAS 8
See also CLC 6, 47
See also DLBY 80
Federoff, Alexander
1927(?)-1979 Obituary 89-92
Federspiel, J(uerg) F. 1931- ....CLC 42
Fedin, Konstantin A(lexandrovich)
1892-1977 ....CANR-28
Obituary 73-76
Earlier sketch in CA 81-84
Fedler, Fred 1940- 97-100
Fedoroff, Alexander 1927-1979 ....CANR-5
Earlier sketch in CA 1-4R
Fedorov, Yevgeny Konstantinovich
1910-1981 Obituary 106
Fedorowicz, J(an) K(rzysztof) 1949- 130
Feduccia, (John) Alan 1943- 124
Fedyshyn, Oleh S(ylvester) 1928- 49-52
Fee, Elizabeth 1946- 126
Fee, Gordon D(onald) 1934- 117
Feegel, John R(ichard) 1932- CANR-9
Earlier sketch in CA 57-60
Feeley, Gregory 1955- 135
Feeley, Kathleen 1929- 33-36R
Feeley, Malcolm McCollum
1942- Brief entry 105
Feeley, Pat(ricia Falk) 1941- 81-84
Feelings, Muriel (Grey) 1938- 93-96
See also BW
See also CLR 5
See also MAICYA
See also SAAS 8
See also SATA 16
Feelings, Thomas 1933- CANR-25
Earlier sketch in CA 49-52
See also Feelings, Tom
See also BW
See also MAICYA
See also SATA 8
Feelings, Tom
See Feelings, Thomas
See also CLR 5
See also SATA 69
Feely, Terence John 1928- CANR-25
Earlier sketch in CA 106
Feenberg, Eugene 1906-1977 Obituary 73-76
Feeney, Leonard 1897-1978 81-84
Obituary 77-80
Feeney, Stephanie S(inger) 1939- 118
Feenstra, Henry John 1936- 37-40R
Feerick, John D(avid) 1936- 69-72
Fegan, Camilla 1939- 21-24R
Fegan, Patrick W. 1947- 111
Fegely, Thomas D(avid) 1941- 97-100
Fehl, Philipp P(inhas) 1920- 33-36R
Fehr, Howard Franklin 1901-1982 Obituary 106
Fehren, Henry 1920- CANR-9
Earlier sketch in CA 21-24R
Fehrenbach, T(heodore) R(eed Jr.)
1925- CANR-1
Earlier sketch in CA 1-4R
See also SATA 33
Fehrenbacher, Don E. 1920- CANR-2
Earlier sketch in CA 1-4R

Fehrman, Carl (Abraham Daniel) 1915- 133
Brief entry 113
Feibes, Walter 1928- 53-56
Feibleman, James K(ern) 1904- CANR-22
Earlier sketches in CA 5-8R, CANR-7
See also AITN 2
Feibleman, Peter S(teinam) 1930- 110
Brief entry 108
Feider, Paul 1951- CANR-35
Earlier sketch in CA 114
Feied, Frederick (James) 1925- 13-16R
Feierman, Steven 1940- 53-56
Feifel, Herman 1915- 101
Feiffer, Jules (Ralph) 1929- CANR-30
Earlier sketch in CA 17-20R
See also AAYA 3
See also CLC 2, 8, 64
See also DLB 7, 44
See also MTCW
See also SATA 8, 61
Feig, Barbara Krane 1937- 104
See also SATA 34
Feig, Douglas 1946- 114
Feige, Hermann Albert Otto Maximilian
See Traven, B.
Feigelson, Naomi
See Chase, Naomi Feigelson
Feigenbaum, Edward A(lbert) 1936- 134
Feigenbaum, Lawrence H. 1918- 25-28R
Feigert, Frank B(rook) 1937- CANR-19
Earlier sketches in CA 53-56, CANR-4
Feigl, Herbert 1902- CAP-1
Earlier sketch in CA 13-14
Feigon, Lee (Nathan) 1945- 117
Fei-Kan, Li
See Li Fei-kan
Feikema, Feike
See Manfred, Frederick (Feikema)
Feil, Hila 1942- 37-40R
See also SATA 12
Feild, Reshad 1934- CANR-25
Earlier sketch in CA 69-72
Feilding, Charles (Rudolph) 1902- CAP-2
Earlier sketch in CA 25-28
Feilen, John
See May, Julian
Feiler, Seymour 1919- 41-44R
Fein, Albert 1930-1989 115
Obituary 128
Fein, Helen 1934- 110
Fein, Irving A(shley) 1911- 69-72
Fein, John M(orton) 1922- 120
Fein, Judith 1941- 107
Fein, Leah Gold 49-52
Fein, Leonard J. 1934- 13-16R
Fein, Rashi 1926- 122
Fein, Richard J(acob) 1929- 45-48
Feinberg, Abraham L. 1899-1986 ....9-12R
Obituary 120
Feinberg, Barbara Jane 1938- CANR-22
Earlier sketch in CA 106
See also SATA 58
Feinberg, Barry (Vincent) 1938- 29-32R
Feinberg, Beatrice Cynthia Freeman
1915(?)-1988 ....CANR-29
Obituary 126
Earlier sketch in CA 81-84
Feinberg, Charles E. 1899-1988 ....DLBY 88
Feinberg, David B. 1956- 135
See also CLC 59
Feinberg, Gerald 1933- CANR-12
Earlier sketch in CA 25-28R
Feinberg, Gloria (Granditer)
1923- Brief entry 109
Feinberg, Hilda 49-52
Feinberg, Joel 1926- CANR-22
Earlier sketch in CA 17-20R
Feinberg, Lawrence B(ernard) 1940- 73-76
Feinberg, Leonard 1914- CANR-2
Earlier sketch in CA 5-8R
Feinberg, Mortimer R(obert) 1922- 102
Feinberg, Renee 1940- 112
Feinberg, Walter 1937- 57-60
Feinbloom, Deborah Heller 1940- 65-68
Feinbloom, Richard I. 1935- 135
Feingold, Ben(jamin) F(ranklin)
1900-1982 97-100
Obituary 106
Feingold, Eugene (Neil) 1931- CANR-22
Earlier sketch in CA 17-20R
Feingold, Henry L(eo) 1931- CANR-31
Earlier sketch in CA 29-32R
Feingold, Jessica 1910- CAP-2
Earlier sketch in CA 25-28
Feingold, Michael 1945- 89-92
Feingold, S. Norman 1914- CANR-30
Earlier sketches in CA 13-16R, CANR-13
Feininger, Andreas (Bernhard Lyonel)
1906- CANR-20
Earlier sketch in CA 85-88
Feinman, Jeffrey 1943- CANR-10
Earlier sketch in CA 65-68
Feinsilver, Alexander 1910- 13-16R
Feinsilver, Lillian Mermin 1917- 29-32R
Feinsinger, Nathan Paul
1902-1983 Obituary 111
Feinstein, Alan (Shawn) 1931- 25-28R
Feinstein, David 1946- 135
Feinstein, Elaine 1930- CANR-31
Earlier sketch in CA 69-72
See also CAAS 1
See also CLC 36
See also DLB 14, 40
See also MTCW
Feinstein, George W(illiamson) 1913- 73-76
Feinstein, John 1956- 133
Feinstein, Lloyd L(eonard) 1941- 113
Feinstein, Moshe 1895-1986 Obituary 118
Feinstein, Otto 1930- 104
Feinstein, Roni 1954- 134
Feinstein, Sherman C. 1923- CANR-7
Earlier sketch in CA 57-60
Feintuch, Burt H. 1949- 124
Feirstein, Bruce 1953- 108
Feirstein, Frederick 1940- CANR-1
Earlier sketch in CA 45-48
See also CAAS 11
Feis, Herbert 1893-1972 ....CAP-1
Obituary 33-36R
Earlier sketch in CA 9-10
Feis, Ruth (Stanley-Brown) 1892- CAP-2
Earlier sketch in CA 19-20
Feise, Ernst 1884-1966 ....CAP-2
Earlier sketch in CA 17-18
Feist, Aubrey (Noel Lydston) 1903- 41-44R
Feist, Gene 1930- 129
Feit, E(wald) Edward 1924- CANR-10
Earlier sketch in CA 5-8R
Feitel, Donald G. 1925(?)-1976 Obituary 65-68
Feith, Herbert 1930- 1-4R
Feiwel, George R(ichard) 1929- CANR-23
Earlier sketches in CA 17-20R, CANR-8
Feiwel, Raphael Joseph 1907-1985 129
Obituary 117
Fejes, Claire 1920- CANR-13
Earlier sketch in CA 21-24R
Fejes, Endre 1923- 25-28R
Fejto, Francois (Philippe) 1909- 29-32R
Fekete, John 1946- 129
Fekrat, M. Ali 1937- 45-48
Felber, Stanley B. 1932- 77-80
Feld, Bernard (David III) 1947- 125
Feld, Bernard T(aub) 1919- 104
Feld, Michael 1938- 33-36R
Feld, Rose Caroline 1895-1981 Obituary 105
Feld, Ross 1947- CANR-16
Earlier sketch in CA 33-36R
Feld, Werner (Joachim) 1910- CANR-24
Earlier sketches in CA 21-24R, CANR-8
Feldbaum, Eleanor G. 1935- 117
Feldberg, Michael 1943- 113
Feldenkrais, Moshe (Pinchas) 1904- 73-76
Felder, David W. 1945- 136
Felder, Paul
See Wellen, Edward (Paul)
Felder, Raoul Lionel 1934- 33-36R
Felderman, Eric 1944- 69-72
Feldkamp, Fred 1915(?)-1981 Obituary 105
Feldkamp, Phyllis 102
Feldman, Abraham J(ehiel) 1893-1977 81-84
Obituary 73-76
Feldman, Alan 1945- CANR-13
Earlier sketch in CA 73-76
Feldman, Anne (Rodgers) 1939- 73-76
See also SATA 19
Feldman, Annette (Gerber)
1913-198 (?) CANR-34
Earlier sketch in CA 69-72
Feldman, Burton 1926- 33-36R
Feldman, Daniel L(ee) 1949- 131
Feldman, Edmund Burke 1924- 33-36R
Feldman, Edwin B(arry) 1925- CANR-2
Earlier sketch in CA 5-8R
Feldman, Egal 1925- 125
Feldman, Ellen (Bette) 1941- CANR-39
Earlier sketches in CA 97-100, CANR-18
Feldman, George J(ay) 1904- CAP-1
Earlier sketch in CA 13-14
Feldman, Gerald D(onald) 1937- CANR-27
Earlier sketches in CA 21-24R, CANR-9
Feldman, Herbert (H. S.) 1910- 29-32R
Feldman, Irving (Mordecai) 1928- CANR-1
Earlier sketch in CA 1-4R
See also CLC 7
Feldman, Kenneth A. 1937- 29-32R
Feldman, Leon A(ryeh) 1921- CANR-16
Earlier sketch in CA 97-100
Feldman, Leonard 1927- 69-72
Feldman, Leslie ....AITN 1
Feldman, Louis H(arry) 1926- 53-56
Feldman, Lynne B. 1956- 138
Feldman, M(aurice) P(hilip) 1933- 41-44R
Feldman, Marty 1934(?)-1982 110
Obituary 108
Feldman, Paula R. 1948- 128
Feldman, Richard 1949- 128
Feldman, Robert A.
See Feldman, Robert Alan
Feldman, Robert Alan 1953- 123
Feldman, Ruth Duskin 1934- 119
Feldman, Ruth 1911- CANR-31
Earlier sketch in CA 106
Feldman, Samuel Nathan 1931- 25-28R
Feldman, Sandor S.
1891(?)-1973 Obituary 41-44R
Feldman, Saul D(aniel) 1943- 41-44R
Feldman, Sidney 1902(?)-1986 Obituary 121
Feldman, Silvia (Dash) 1928- 97-100
Feldman, Sol(omon) E. 1933- 25-28R
Feldman, Sophie 1930-1978 Obituary 108
Feldman, Stephen L. 1946-1990 Obituary 132
Feldmann, Susan Judith
1928-1969 Obituary 104
Feldmeir, Daryle M(atthew) 1923-1987 73-76
Obituary 122
Feldon, Leah 1944- 97-100
Feldstein, Martin S(tuart) 1939- 73-76
Feldstein, Paul J(oseph) 1933- 89-92
Feldstein, Stuart A(lan) 1948- 113
Feldt, Allan Gunnar 1932- 41-44R
Feldzamen, A(lvin) N(orman) 1931- 25-28R
Felheim, Marvin 1914- 1-4R
Felice, Cynthia 1942- 107
Felipe, Leon 1884-1968 ....DLB 108
Felix
See Vincent, Felix
Felix, Christopher
See McCargar, James (Goodrich)
Felix, David 1921- 45-48
Felix-Tchicaya, Gerald
See Tchicaya, Gerald Felix
Felkenes, George T(heodore) 1930- CANR-8
Earlier sketch in CA 57-60
Felker, Clay S(chuette) 1925- 73-76
Felker, Evelyn H. 1933- 57-60
Felker, Jere L. 1934- 21-24R
Felknor, Bruce L(ester) 1921- 21-24R
Fell, Barry
See Fell, H(oward) Barraclough
Fell, Derek (John) 1939- CANR-25
Earlier sketch in CA 108
Fell, H(oward) Barraclough 1917- 33-36R
Fell, James E(dward) Jr. 1944- 107
Fell, John L(ouis) 1927- 53-56
Fell, Joseph P(hineas) III 1931- CANR-6
Earlier sketch in CA 13-16R
Fellini, Federico 1920- CANR-33
Earlier sketch in CA 65-68
See also CLC 16
Fellman, Gordon 1934- 53-56
Fellman, Michael (Dinion) 1943- 45-48
Fellmeth, Robert C(harles) 1945- CANR-2
Earlier sketch in CA 49-52
Fellner, William John 1905-1983 ....CANR-2
Obituary 110
Earlier sketch in CA 1-4R
Fellowes, Anne
See Mantle, Winifred (Langford)
Fellowes-Gordon, Ian (Douglas)
1921- CANR-10
Earlier sketch in CA 5-8R
Fellows, Brian John 1936- 25-28R
Fellows, Donald Keith 1920- 41-44R
Fellows, Hugh P. 1915- 37-40R
Fellows, Jay 1940- CANR-11
Earlier sketch in CA 61-64
Fellows, Lawrence (Perry) 1924- 49-52
Fellows, Malcolm Stuart 1924- 9-12R
Fellows, Muriel H. 53-56
See also SATA 10
Fellows, Otis (Edward) 1908- CANR-1
Earlier sketch in CA 1-4R
Fellows, Richard A(stley) 1947- 121
Felmly, Lloyd McPherson
1894-1984 Obituary 112
Felperin, Howard (Michael) 1941- 136
Fels, Ludwig 1946- ....DLB 75
Fels, Rendigs 1917- 37-40R
Felsen, Henry Gregor 1916- CANR-1
Earlier sketch in CA 1-4R
See also CLC 17
See also SAAS 2
See also SATA 1
Felsenstein, Walter 1901-1975 Obituary 111
Felsenthal, Carol 1949- 108
Felsher, Howard D. 1927- 17-20R
Felstein, Ivor 1933- 41-44R
Felstiner, L. John Jr. 1936- 45-48
Felt, Jeremy P(ollard) 1930- 21-24R
Felt, Margaret Elley 1917- 9-12R
Felter, Emma K. (Schroeder) 1896- CAP-1
Earlier sketch in CA 13-16
Felton, Bruce 1946- 65-68
Felton, Cornelius Conway 1807-1862 ....DLB 1
Felton, Harold William 1902- CANR-1
Earlier sketch in CA 1-4R
See also SATA 1
Felton, John Richard 1917- 89-92
Felton, Ronald Oliver 1909- CANR-3
Earlier sketch in CA 9-12R
See also SATA 3
Felton, Sandra 1935- 120
Felts, Shirley 1934- ....SATA 33
Feltskog, E(lmer) N. 1935- 37-40R
Felver, Charles S(tanley) 1916- 33-36R
Femiano, Samuel D. 1932- 21-24R
Femina, Jerry Della
See Della Femina, Jerry
Fen, Elisaveta
See Jackson, Lydia
Fenady, Andrew J. 1928- CANR-13
Earlier sketch in CA 77-80
Fenander, Elliot W(atkins) 1938- 21-24R
Fenberg, Matilda 1888(?)-1977 Obituary 73-76
Fenby, Eric (William) 1906- 25-28R
Fendell, Bob 1925- 57-60
Fendelman, Helaine Woll 1942- 69-72
Fenderson, Lewis H. Jr. 1907-1983 106
Obituary 111
See also SATA 37, 47
Fenelon, Fania 1918-1983 77-80
Obituary 111
Fenelon, Kevin G(erard) 1898-1983 73-76
Obituary 109
Feng, Chin
See Liu, Sydney (Chieh)
Fenger, Henning Johannes Hauch 1921- 73-76
Fenical, Marlin Edward 1907-1983 Obituary 110
Fenichel, Carol Hansen 1935- 119
Fenichell, Stephen 1956- 108
Fenick, Barbara 1951- 118
Fenik, Bernard Carl 1934- 122
Fenin, George N(icolaievich) 1916- 9-12R
Fenlon, Dick 1930- 89-92
Fenlon, Paul Edward 1921- 13-16R
Fenn, Charles (Henry) 1907- 9-12R
Fenn, Dan H(untington) Jr. 1923- CANR-1
Earlier sketch in CA 1-4R
Fenn, Elizabeth A. 1959- 115
Fenn, Henry Courtenay
1894-1978 Obituary 81-84
Fennario, David 1947- ....DLB 60
Fennell, Francis L(e Roy) Jr. 1942- CANR-39
Earlier sketch in CA 116
Fennell, John L(ister) I(llingworth)
1918- CANR-19
Earlier sketches in CA 1-4R, CANR-1
Fennell, William Oscar 1916- 101
Fennelly, Catherine 1918- 37-40R
Fennelly, John F(auntleroy)
1899-1974 Obituary 53-56
Fennelly, Parker W. 1891-1988 Obituary 125
Fennelly, Tony 1945- 119
Fennema, Owen Richard 1929- CANR-3
Earlier sketch in CA 49-52
Fenner, Carol Elizabeth 1929- CANR-3
Earlier sketch in CA 5-8R
See also SATA 7
Fenner, H(arry) Wolcott 1911-1972 ....CAP-2
Obituary 37-40R
Earlier sketch in CA 33-36
Fenner, James R.
See Tubb, E(dwin) C(harles)
Fenner, James 1923- 37-40R
Fenner, Kay Toy CAP-1
Earlier sketch in CA 9-10
Fenner, Mildred Sandison 1910- 33-36R
Fenner, Phyllis R(eid) 1899-1982 ....CANR-2
Obituary 106
Earlier sketch in CA 5-8R
See also SATA 1, 29
Fenner, Theodore (Lincoln) 1919- 37-40R
Fennimore, Keith John 1917- 57-60
Fenno, John 1751-1798 ....DLB 43
Fenno, R(ichard) Francis Jr. 1926- 5-8R
Fensch, Edwin A. 1903- CAP-1
Earlier sketch in CA 13-16
Fensch, Thomas 1943- CANR-29
Earlier sketches in CA 25-28R, CANR-11
Fenster, Robert 1946- CANR-32
Earlier sketch in CA 113
Fenster, Valmai (Ruth) Kirkham 1939-1984 110
Obituary 114
Fensterheim, Herbert 1921- 112
Fenstermaker, J(oseph) Van 1933- 29-32R
Fenten, Barbara D(oris) 1935- CANR-5
Earlier sketch in CA 53-56
See also SATA 26
Fenten, D(onald) X. 1932- CANR-5
Earlier sketch in CA 33-36R
See also SATA 4
Fenton, Alexander 1929- 131
Fenton, Carroll Lane 1900-1969 ....CANR-6
Obituary 29-32R
Earlier sketch in CA 1-4R
See also SATA 5
Fenton, Clyde 1901-1982 Obituary 106
Fenton, Edward 1917- CANR-34
Earlier sketches in CA 9-12R, CANR-13
See also SATA 7
Fenton, Frank 1903-1971 Obituary 33-36R
Fenton, Freda
See Rowland, D(onald) S(ydney)
Fenton, James Martin 1949- 102
See also CLC 32
See also DLB 40
Fenton, John C(harles) 1921- CAP-1
Earlier sketch in CA 9-10
Fenton, John H(arold) 1921- 37-40R
Fenton, John Y(oung) 1933- 53-56
Fenton, Joseph Clifford 1906- 5-8R
Fenton, Julia
See Fenton, Robert L.
Fenton, Mildred Adams 1899- 77-80
See also SATA 21
Fenton, Robert L. 1929- 135
Fenton, Shane
See Stardust, Alvin
Fenton, Sophia Harvati 1914- 33-36R
Fenton, Thomas Patrick 1943- 89-92
Fenton, Thomas Trail 1930- 102
Fenton, William N(elson) 1908- 93-96
Fentress, John Simmons
1925(?)-1981 Obituary 104
Fenvessy, Stanley J(ohn) 1918- 106
Fenwick, Charles G(hequiere)
1880-1973 Obituary 41-44R
Fenwick, Kay
See Bean, Keith F(enwick)
Fenwick, (Ian Graham) Keith 1941- 102
Fenwick, Millicent Hammond 1910- 112
Fenwick, Patti
See Grider, Dorothy
Fenwick, Sheridan 1942- 69-72
Fenwick-Owen, Roderic (Franklin Rawnsley)
1921- 129
Brief entry 111
Fenyvesi, Charles 1937- 102
Feola, Jose (Maria) 1926- 69-72
Feravolo, Rocco Vincent 1922- CANR-1
Earlier sketch in CA 1-4R
See also SATA 10
Ferazani, Larry 1938- 61-64
Ferber, Andrew 1935- 53-56
Ferber, Edna 1887-1968 ....5-8R
Obituary 25-28R
See also AITN 1
See also CLC 18
See also DLB 9, 28, 86
See also MTCW
See also SATA 7
Ferber, Ellen 1939- 102
Ferber, Robert 1922- 37-40R
Ferdinand, Theodore N(ichols) 1929- 21-24R
Ferdinand, Vallery III
See Salaam, Kalamu ya
Ferdon, Edwin N(elson) Jr. 1913- 21-24R
Ferejohn, John A(rthur) 1944- 53-56

Ferencz, Benjamin B(erell) 1920- CANR-19
Earlier sketch in CA 97-100
Fergus, Jan 1943- 125
Fergus, Patricia M(arguerita) 1918- 53-56
Ferguson, Alfred R(iggs) 1915-1974 ....CANR-6
Obituary 49-52
Earlier sketch in CA 1-4R
Ferguson, Annabelle Evelyn 1923- 102
Ferguson, Arthur B(owles) 1913- 5-8R
Ferguson, Bob
See Ferguson, Robert Bruce
Ferguson, C(harles) E(lmo) 1928-1972 ......17-20R
Obituary 134
Ferguson, Cecil 1931- ....SATA 45
Ferguson, Charles Albert 1921- 69-72
Ferguson, Charles Austin 1937- 121
Ferguson, Charles W. 1901-1987 ....13-16R
Obituary 124
Ferguson, Chris(topher Wilson) 1944- 57-60
Ferguson, Clarence Clyde Jr.
1924-1983 ....CANR-6
Obituary 111
Earlier sketch in CA 5-8R
Ferguson, David L. 1930- 73-76
Ferguson, Donald N(ivison) 1882-1985 ....5-8R
Obituary 116
Ferguson, E(lmer) James 1917- 61-64
Ferguson, Everett 1933- 33-36R
Ferguson, Franklin C(ole) 1934- 69-72
Ferguson, Harry 1903-1980 Obituary 97-100
Ferguson, Helen
See Kavan, Anna
Ferguson, Howard 1908- CAP-1
Earlier sketch in CA 11-12
Ferguson, J(ohn) Halcro 1920-1968 ....1-4R
Obituary 103
Ferguson, James M(ilton) 1936- 21-24R
Ferguson, John Henry 1907- 13-16R
Ferguson, John 1921- CANR-25
Earlier sketches in CA 5-8R, CANR-8
Ferguson, M(ilton) Carr Jr. 1931- CANR-30
Earlier sketch in CA 49-52
Ferguson, Margaret W(illiams) 1948- 112
Ferguson, Marilyn 1938- 114
Brief entry 110
Ferguson, Mary Anne 1918- 77-80
Ferguson, Oliver W(atkins) 1924- 5-8R
Ferguson, Pamela 1943- 101
Ferguson, Peter R(oderick) I(nnes)
1933- CANR-3
Earlier sketch in CA 5-8R
Ferguson, Robert A. 1942- 131
Ferguson, Robert Bruce 1927- 69-72
See also SATA 13
Ferguson, Robert D(ouglas) 1921- 17-20R
Ferguson, Robert (Thomas) 1948- 135
Ferguson, Robert W(illiam) 1940- CANR-12
Earlier sketch in CA 61-64
Ferguson, Ronald 1939- 134
Ferguson, Rowena 1904- 85-88
Ferguson, Samuel 1810-1886 ....DLB 32
Ferguson, Sarah (Margaret) 1959- 135
See also SATA 66
Ferguson, Suzanne 1939- 57-60
Ferguson, Sybil (Rae) 1934- 129
Ferguson, Ted 1936- 65-68
Ferguson, Tom 1943- 107
Ferguson, Trevor 1947- 116
Ferguson, Walter (W.) 1930- 107
See also SATA 34
Ferguson, William M(cDonald) 1917- 117
Ferguson, William (Rotch) 1943- CANR-33
Earlier sketch in CA 49-52
Ferguson, William Scott 1875-1954 ....DLB 47
Fergusson, Adam 1932- Brief entry 112
Fergusson, Bernard Edward
1911-1980 ....CANR-7
Obituary 102
Earlier sketch in CA 9-12R
Fergusson, Erna 1888-1964 ....CAP-1
Earlier sketch in CA 13-14
See also SATA 5
Fergusson, Francis (De Liesseline)
1904-1986 ....CANR-3
Obituary 121
Earlier sketch in CA 9-12R
Fergusson, Harvey 1890-1971 Obituary 33-36R
Fergusson, James 1904-1973 Obituary 104
Fergusson, Robert 1750-1774 ....DLB 109
Fergusson, Rosalind (Joyce) 1953- 117
Fergusson Hannay, Doris
1902(?)-1982 ....CANR-6
Obituary 107
Earlier sketch in CA 9-12R
Fericano, Paul 1951- CANR-29
Earlier sketches in CA 69-72, CANR-12
Ferkiss, Victor C(hristopher) 1925- 21-24R
Ferland, Albert 1872-1943 ....DLB 92
Ferland, Carol 1936- 102
Ferling, Lawrence
See Ferlinghetti, Lawrence (Monsanto)
Ferlinghetti, Lawrence (Monsanto)
1919(?)- CANR-3
Earlier sketch in CA 5-8R
See also CDALB 1941-1968
See also CLC 2, 6, 10, 27
See also DLB 5, 16
See also MTCW
See also PC 1
Ferlita, Ernest (Charles) 1927- CANR-26
Earlier sketches in CA 29-32R, CANR-11
Ferm, Betty 1926- 21-24R
Ferm, Deane William 1927- CANR-13
Earlier sketch in CA 33-36R
Ferm, Max A(rnold) 1929- 116
Ferm, Robert Livingston 1931- 13-16R
Ferm, Vergilius (Ture Anselm)
1896-1974 ....9-12R
Obituary 49-52
Ferman, Edward L(ewis) 1937- 106
Ferman, Joseph W(olfe)
1906-1975 Obituary 104
Fermi, Enrico 1901-1954 Brief entry 115
Fermi, Laura 1907-1977 ....CANR-6
Earlier sketch in CA 1-4R
See also SATA 6, 28
Fermor, Patrick Leigh
See Leigh Fermor, Patrick (Michael)
Fern, Alan M(axwell) 1930- CANR-12
Earlier sketch in CA 33-36R
Fern, Eugene A. 1919-1987 ....CANR-16
Obituary 123
Earlier sketch in CA 1-4R
See also SATA 10, 54
Fern, Fanny
See Parton, Sara Payson Willis
Fernald, John (Bailey) 1905-1985 ....CAP-2
Obituary 115
Earlier sketch in CA 23-24
Fernandez, Benedict J. (III) 1936- 85-88
Fernandez, Gladys Craven 1939- 106
Fernandez, Happy Craven
See Fernandez, Gladys Craven
Fernandez, James William 1930- CANR-23
Earlier sketch in CA 107
Fernandez, John P(eter) 1941- CANR-10
Earlier sketch in CA 65-68
Fernandez, Jose S(alvador)
1893-1967 Obituary 113
Fernandez, Joseph A. 1921- 37-40R
Fernandez, Julio A. 1936- 33-36R
Fernandez, Roberto G. 1951- 131
See also HW
Fernandez, Vicente Garcia Huidobro
See Huidobro Fernandez, Vicente Garcia
Fernandez de la Reguera, Ricardo
1914- CANR-3
Earlier sketch in CA 5-8R
Fernandez-Marina, R(amon) 1909- 41-44R
Fernandez Mendez, E.
See Fernandez Mendez, Eugenio
Fernandez Mendez, Eugenio 1924- ....HW
Fernandez Moreno, Baldomero 1886-1950 .....HW
Fernandez Moreno, Cesar 1919- 131
See also HW
Fernandez Retamar, Roberto 1930- 131
See also HW
Fernando, Ajith 1948- 122
Fernando, Lloyd 1926- 77-80
Fernea, Elizabeth Warnock 1927- CANR-29
Earlier sketches in CA 13-16R, CANR-12
Fernea, Robert Alan 1932- CANR-29
Earlier sketch in CA 33-36R
Fernett, Gene 1924- 49-52
Fernie, Eric (Campbell) 1939- 119
Ferns, H(enry) S(tanley) 1913- CANR-19
Obituary 137
Earlier sketches in CA 5-8R, CANR-4
Fernsworth, Lawrence
1893(?)-1977(?) Obituary 89-92
Ferracuti, Franco 1927- CANR-30
Earlier sketches in CA 25-28R, CANR-11
Ferrante, Don
See Gerbi, Antonello
Ferrante, Joan M(arguerite Aida) 1936- 85-88
Ferrar, Harold 1935- Brief entry 116
Ferrara, V(ernon) Peter
1912-1988 Obituary 127
Ferrari, Enzo 1898-1988 Obituary 126
Ferrari, R(onald) L(eslie) 1930- 135
Ferrarini, Elizabeth M. 1948- 124
Ferraro, Gary P(aul) 1940- 89-92
Ferrars, E. X.
See Brown, Morna Doris
Ferrars, Elizabeth
See Brown, Morna Doris
See also DLB 87
Ferrat, Jacques Jean
See Merwin, Sam(uel Kimball) Jr.
Ferrater-Mora, Jose 1912- CANR-29
Earlier sketch in CA 1-4R
See also HW
Ferre, Frederick 1933- 13-16R
Ferre, Gustave A. 1918- 1-4R
Ferre, Nels F(redrik) S(olomon)
1908-1971 ....CAP-2
Earlier sketch in CA 29-32
Ferre, Rosario 1942- 131
See also HW
Ferreira de Castro, Jose Maria 1898-1974 102
Obituary 49-52
Ferrell, Frank 1940- 136
Ferrell, Mallory Hope 1935- CANR-30
Earlier sketches in CA 33-36R, CANR-13
Ferrell, Nancy Warren 1932- 138
See also SATA 70
Ferrell, Robert H(ugh) 1921- CANR-22
Earlier sketches in CA 5-8R, CANR-6
Ferrell, Robert W(illingham) 1913- 13-16R
Ferreol, Marcel Auguste 1899-1974 97-100
Obituary 53-56
Ferrer, Aldo 1927- CANR-28
Earlier sketches in CA 25-28R, CANR-11
Ferrer, Gabriel (Francisco Victor) Miro
See Miro (Ferrer), Gabriel (Francisco Victor)
Ferrer, Gloria M. Pagan
See Pagan Ferrer, Gloria M.
Ferrer, Sister Vincent
See Doherty, Barbara
Ferreri, Marco 1928- 126
Ferres, John H(oward) 1932- 41-44R
Ferridge, Philippa 1933- CANR-18
Earlier sketch in CA 102
Ferrier, Janet Mackay 1919- 9-12R
Ferrier, Lucy
See Penzler, Otto
Ferrier, Susan (Edmonstone)
1782-1854 ....DLB 116
Ferrigno, Robert ....CLC 65
Ferril, Thomas Hornsby 1896-1988 65-68
Obituary 127
Ferrill, Arther 1938- 129
Ferrini, Vincent 1913- ....DLB 48
Ferris, Helen Josephine 1890-1969 77-80
See also SATA 21
Ferris, James Cody CANR-27
Earlier sketches in CAP-2, CA 19-20
See also SATA 1
Ferris, James Cody
See McFarlane, Leslie (Charles)
Ferris, Jean 1939- CANR-38
Earlier sketch in CA 116
See also SATA 50, 56
Ferris, Norman (Bernard) 1931- 81-84
Ferris, Paul (Frederick) 1929- CANR-22
Earlier sketches in CA 5-8R, CANR-3
Ferris, Theodore P(arker)
1908-1972 Obituary 37-40R
Ferris, Timothy 1944- CANR-30
Earlier sketches in CA 69-72, CANR-11
Ferris, Tom
See Walker, Peter N.
Ferris, William (R.) 1942- 136
Ferriss, Abbott Lamoyne 1915- 29-32R
Ferritor, Daniel Edward 1939- CANR-35
Earlier sketch in CA 49-52
Ferro, Marc 1924- 77-80
Ferro, Robert (Michael) 1941-1988 ....29-32R
Obituary 126
Ferron, Jacques 1921-1985 129
Brief entry 117
See also DLB 60
Ferron, Madeleine 1922- ....DLB 53
Ferruolo, Stephen C(arl) 1949- 120
Ferry, Anne Davidson 1930- 17-20R
Ferry, Charles 1927- CANR-16
Earlier sketch in CA 97-100
See also SATA 43
Ferry, David (Russell) 1924- 13-16R
Ferry, W(illiam) Hawkins 1914(?)-1988 61-64
Obituary 124
Fersh, Seymour H. 1926- CANR-14
Earlier sketch in CA 37-40R
Ferster, C(harles) B(ohris) 1922-1981 97-100
Obituary 102
Ferster, Dorothy C(oben) 1922- 111
Ferster, Marilyn B(ender)
See Gilbert, Marilyn B(ender)
Ferullo, Dan 1948- 106
Feshbach, Norma Deitch 1926- CANR-8
Earlier sketch in CA 61-64
Feshbach, Seymour 1925- CANR-8
Earlier sketch in CA 37-40R
Fesler, James W(illiam) 1911- 21-24R
Fesperman, John (Thomas Jr.) 1925- CANR-2
Earlier sketch in CA 5-8R
Fess, Philip E. 1931- 33-36R
Fessel, Murray 1927- 21-24R
Fessenden, Katherine
1896(?)-1974 Obituary 53-56
Fessenden, Seth A(rthur) 1903-1976 .....CANR-10
Earlier sketch in CA 17-20R
Fessenko, Tatiana (Sviatenko) 1915- 13-16R
Fessier, Michael 1905(?)-1988 Obituary 126
Fessler, Loren W. 1923- 9-12R
Fest, Joachim C. 1926- 49-52
Fest, Thorrel B(rooks) 1910- CAP-1
Earlier sketch in CA 13-16
Festa Campanile, Pasquale
1927-1986 Obituary 118
Festa-McCormick, Diana 117
Festinger, Leon 1919-1989 ....CANR-31
Obituary 127
Earlier sketch in CA 1-4R
Fetherling, Dale 1941- 77-80
Fetler, Andrew 1925- 13-16R
Fetridge, William Harrison 1906-1989 73-76
Obituary 129
Fetros, John G. 1932- 57-60
Fetscher, Iring 1922- CANR-12
Earlier sketch in CA 69-72
Fettamen, Ann
See Hoffman, Anita
Fetter, Elizabeth Head 1904-1973 ....5-8R
Obituary 41-44R
Fetter, Frank Whitson 1899-1991 106
Obituary 135
Fetter, Richard (Leland) 1943- CANR-15
Earlier sketch in CA 89-92
Fetterley, Judith 1938- Brief entry 113
Fetterman, Elsie 1927- 97-100
Fetterman, John (Davis) 1920-1975 93-96
Obituary 61-64
Fettig, Art(hur John) 1929- CANR-29
Earlier sketches in CA 73-76, CANR-13
Fetz, Ingrid 1915- ....SATA 30
Fetzer, John F(rancis) 1931- 61-64
Feucht, Oscar E(mil) 1895- 103
Feuchtwanger, E(dgar) J(oseph)
1924- CANR-11
Earlier sketch in CA 69-72
Feuchtwanger, Lion 1884-1958 Brief entry 104
See also DLB 66
See also TCLC 3
Feuer, Avrohom Chaim 1946- CANR-32
Earlier sketch in CA 113
Feuer, Kathryn Beliveau 1926- 102
Obituary 137
Feuer, Lewis S(amuel) 1912- CANR-3
Earlier sketch in CA 5-8R
Feuerlicht, Ignace CAP-2
Earlier sketch in CA 33-36
Feuerlicht, Roberta Strauss 1931-1991 .....17-20R
Obituary 135
Feuerstein, Georg 1947- 123
Feuerstein, Phyllis A. 1930- 105
Feuerwerger, Marvin C(harles) 1950- 104
Feuerwerker, Albert 1927- CANR-8
Earlier sketch in CA 21-24R
Feulner, Edwin J(ohn) Jr. 1941- 115
Feulner, Patricia N(ancy) 1946- 105
Feur, D. C.
See Stahl, Fred Alan
Feurey, Benita S. 1940(?)-1989 Obituary 129
Fewster, Kevin (John) 1953- 125
Fey, Harold E(dward) 1898-1990 ....17-20R
Obituary 130
Feydeau, Georges (Leon Jules Marie)
1862-1921 Brief entry 113
See also TCLC 22
Feydy, Anne Lindbergh
See Sapieyevski, Anne Lindbergh
See also SATA 32
Feynman, R. P.
See Feynman, Richard Phillips
Feynman, Richard
See Feynman, Richard Phillips
Feynman, Richard P.
See Feynman, Richard Phillips
See also BEST 89:3
Feynman, Richard Phillips 1918-1988 129
Obituary 125
Brief entry 119
See also Feynman, Richard P.
See also MTCW
Fezler, William 1945- 122
Ffinch, Michael 1934- 137
ffolkes
See Davis, Brian
Ffolkes, Michael
See Davis, Brian
ffolliott, Rosemary 1934- 97-100
ffrench-Beytagh, Gonville (Aubie) 1912- 103
ffrench Blake, Neil (St. John) 1940- 69-72
ffrench Blake, Robert L(ifford) V(alentine)
1913- 61-64
Fiacc, Padraic
See O'Connor, Patrick Joseph
Fialkowski, Barbara 1946- 77-80
Fiammenghi, Gioia 1929- ....SATA 9, 66
Fiandt, Mary K. 1914- 89-92
Fiarotta, Noel
See Ficarotta, Noel
See also SATA 15
Fiarotta, Phyllis
See Ficarotta, Phyllis
See also SATA 15
Fiber, Alan 102
Ficarotta, Noel 1944- CANR-11
Earlier sketch in CA 69-72
See also Fiarotta, Noel
Ficarotta, Phyllis 1942- CANR-11
Earlier sketch in CA 69-72
See also Fiarotta, Phyllis
Fichte, Johann Gottlieb 1762-1814 ....DLB 90
Fichtelius, Karl-Erik 1924- 53-56
Fichter, Andrew J(ohn) 1945- 117
Fichter, George S. 1922- CANR-23
Earlier sketches in CA 17-20R, CANR-7
See also SATA 7
Fichter, Joseph 1908- CANR-19
Earlier sketches in CA 1-4R, CANR-4
Ficke, Arthur Davison 1883-1945 ....DLB 54
Ficken, Frederick A(rthur)
1910-1978 Obituary 81-84
Ficker, Victor B. 1937- CANR-13
Earlier sketch in CA 33-36R
Fickert, Kurt J(on) 1920- CANR-31
Earlier sketches in CA 37-40R, CANR-14
Fickett, Harold L. Jr. 1918- 13-16R
Fickett, Lewis P. Jr. 1926- 21-24R
Fickle, James Edward 1939- 106
Fickling, G. G.
See Fickling, Skip Forrest
Fickling, Skip Forrest 1925- 5-8R
Fidelio
See Hunt, Edgar H(ubert)
Fidler, James M. 1900-1988 Obituary 126
Fidler, Jimmie
See Fidler, James M.
Fidler, Kathleen (Annie) 1899-1980 ......CANR-20
Obituary 117
Earlier sketch in CA 25-28R
See also SATA 3, 45
Fidrych, Mark 1954- Brief entry 112
Fie, Jacquelyn Joyce 1937- 57-60
Fiedel, Stuart J(ay) 1952- 128
Fiedler, Fred E(dward) 1922- 21-24R
Fiedler, Jean(nette Feldman) CANR-11
Earlier sketch in CA 29-32R
See also SATA 4
Fiedler, Leslie A(aron) 1917- CANR-7
Earlier sketch in CA 9-12R
See also CLC 4, 13, 24
See also DLB 28, 67
See also MTCW
Fiedler, Lois (Wagner) 1928- 17-20R
Fieg, Victor P. 1924- 106
Field, Adelaide (Anderson) 1916- 106
Field, Andrew 1938- CANR-25
Earlier sketch in CA 97-100
See also CLC 44
Field, Arthur J(ordan) 1927-1975 ....33-36R
Field, Barbara 1935- 110
Field, Carol 1940- 113
Field, Charles
See Rowland, D(onald) S(ydney)

Field, Daniel 1938- ... 65-68
Field, David D(udley) 1918- ... 73-76
Field, David (McLucas) 1944- ... 133
Field, Dawn Stewart 1940- ... 57-60
Field, Dick 1912- ... 57-60
Field, Edward 1924- ... CANR-10
Earlier sketch in CA 13-16R
See also DLB 105
See also SATA 8
Field, Eleanor S. 1932- ... 122
Field, Elinor Whitney 1889-1980 Obituary ... 109
See also SATA 28
Field, Ernest R. 1925- ... 5-8R
Field, Eugene 1850-1895 ... DLB 23, 42
See also MAICYA
See also SATA 16
Field, Frances Fox
1913(?)-1977 Obituary ... 69-72
Field, Frank Chester
See Robertson, Frank C(hester)
Field, Frank McCoy 1887-1978 ... 45-48
Obituary ... 103
Field, Frank 1936- ... 21-24R
Field, Frederick V.
See Field, Frederick Vanderbilt
Field, Frederick Vanderbilt 1905- ... 130
Field, G(eorge) W(allis) 1914- ... 37-40R
Field, Gans T.
See Wellman, Manly Wade
Field, George B(rooks) 1929- ... 101
Field, Gordon Lawrence 1939- ... 17-20R
Field, Harry
See Field, Henry
Field, Hartry H(amlin) 1946- ... 124
Field, Hazel E(lizabeth) 1891- ... CAP-1
Earlier sketch in CA 19-20
Field, Henry 1902-1986 ... 69-72
Obituary ... 118
Field, Hermann Haviland 1910- ... 135
Field, Irving M(edcraft) 1934- ... 25-28R
Field, James A(lfred) Jr. 1916- ... 25-28R
Field, Joanna
See Milner, Marion (Blackett)
Field, John (Leslie) 1910- ... 33-36R
Field, John P(aul) 1936- ... 37-40R
Field, Joyce W(olf) 1932- ... 29-32R
Field, Leslie A. 1926- ... 29-32R
Field, Mark G(eorge) 1923- ... 37-40R
Field, Michael ... TCLC 43
Field, Michael 1915-1971 Obituary ... 29-32R
Field, Minna (Kagan) ... 25-28R
Field, Nathan 1587-1620(?) ... DLB 58
Field, Penelope
See Giberson, Dorothy (Dodds)
Field, Peter
See Hobson, Laura Z(ametkin)
Field, Phyllis Frances 1946- ... 107
Field, Rachel (Lyman) 1894-1942 ... 137
Brief entry ... 109
See also CLR 21
See also DLB 9, 22
See also MAICYA
See also SATA 15
Field, Stanley 1911- ... CANR-9
Earlier sketch in CA 21-24R
Field, Thomas P(arry) 1914- ... 9-12R
Field, Walter S(herman) 1899- ... 49-52
Fielden, Charlotte ... 93-96
Fielden, T(homas) P(erceval) 1882- ... 5-8R
Fielder, Mildred (Craig) 1913- ... CANR-10
Earlier sketch in CA 13-16R
Fielding, A. W.
See Wallace, Alexander Fielding
Fielding, Daphne Winifred Louise 1904- ... 9-12R
Fielding, G(ordon) J. 1934- ... 97-100
Fielding, Gabriel
See Barnsley, Alan Gabriel
Fielding, Henry 1707-1754 ... CDBLB 1660-1789
See also DLB 39, 84, 101
See also WLC
Fielding, Joy 1945- ... CANR-2
Earlier sketch in CA 49-52
Fielding, Nancy (Parker)
1913-1983 Obituary ... 111
Brief entry ... 108
Fielding, Nigel G(oodwin) 1950- ... 131
Fielding, Raymond E. 1931- ... CANR-8
Earlier sketch in CA 17-20R
Fielding, Sarah 1710-1768 ... DLB 39
Fielding, Temple (Hornaday)
1913-1983 ... CANR-14
Obituary ... 109
Earlier sketch in CA 21-24R
Fielding, Waldo L. 1921- ... 45-48
Fielding, William J(ohn) 1886-1973 ... 13-16R
Obituary ... 134
Fielding, Xan
See Wallace, Alexander Fielding
Fields, Alan
See Duprey, Richard A(llen)
Fields, Arthur C. 1926(?)-1974 Obituary ... 49-52
Fields, Beverly 1917- ... 49-52
Fields, Dorothy 1905-1974 ... 93-96
Obituary ... 49-52
Fields, Gracie 1898-1979 Obituary ... 112
Fields, Howard K(enneth) 1938- ... 81-84
Fields, James Thomas 1817-1881 ... DLB 1
Fields, Jeff ... AITN 2
Fields, Joseph 1895-1966 Obituary ... 25-28R
Fields, Julia 1938- ... CANR-26
Earlier sketch in CA 73-76
See also BW
See also DLB 41
Fields, Kenneth (Wayne) 1939- Brief entry ... 110
Fields, Morgan
See Morgan, J(ill) M(eredith)
Fields, Nora ... 49-52
Fields, Rick 1942- ... CANR-27
Earlier sketches in CA 65-68, CANR-9
Fields, Rona M(arcia) 1934- ... 69-72
Fields, Scott (Gary) 1956- ... 134
Fields, Suzanne 1936- ... 129
Fields, Totie
See Feldman, Sophie
Fields, Victor A(lexander) 1901- ... 5-8R
Fields, W. C. 1880-1946 ... DLB 44
Fields, Wayne 1942- ... 134
Fields, Wilbert J. 1917- ... 13-16R
Fields, Wilmer Clemont 1922- Brief entry ... 106
Fieler, Frank B(ernard) 1933- ... 41-44R
Fiene, Donald M(ark) 1930- ... 69-72
Fiene, Ernest 1894-1965 ... CAP-1
Earlier sketch in CA 13-14
Fiennes, Ranulph (Twisleton-Wykeham)
1944- ... CANR-20
Earlier sketches in CA 45-48, CANR-3
Fiennes, Richard
See
Twisleton-Wykeham-Fiennes, Richard Nathaniel
Fiering, Norman Sanford 1935- ... 105
Fierro, Robert Daniel 1945- ... 109
Fierstein, Harvey (Forbes) 1954- ... 129
Brief entry ... 123
See also CLC 33
Fieser, Louis F(rederick)
1899-1977 Obituary ... 73-76
Fieser, Max E(ugene) 1930- ... 13-16R
Fiester, Mark (Lafayette) 1907- ... 65-68
Fieve, Ronald R(obert) 1930- Brief entry ... 107
Fife, Austin E(dwin) 1909- ... 53-56
Fife, Dale (Odile Hollerbach) 1901- ... CANR-19
Earlier sketch in CA 85-88
See also SATA 18
Fife, Robert Oldham 1918- ... 37-40R
Fifer, Ken 1947- ... 104
Fifield, Christopher G(eorge) 1945- ... 130
Fifield, William 1916-1987 ... CANR-9
Obituary ... 124
Earlier sketch in CA 13-16R
Fifo, Ray
See Glazar, Bob
Fifoot, Cecil Herbert Stuart
1899-1975 Obituary ... 107
Figes, Eva 1932- ... CANR-4
Earlier sketch in CA 53-56
See also CLC 31
See also DLB 14
Figgins, Ross 1936- ... CANR-11
Earlier sketch in CA 69-72
Figh, Margaret Gillis 1896- ... CAP-2
Earlier sketch in CA 29-32
Fighter Pilot, A
See Johnston, H(ugh) A(nthony) S(tephen)
Figler, Howard Elliot 1939- ... 127
Brief entry ... 109
Figler, Stephen K(enneth) 1942- ... 117
Figuera, Angela 1902-1984 ... DLB 108
Figueroa, John
See Figueroa, John J(oseph Maria)
Figueroa, John J(oseph Maria) 1920- ... 125
Brief entry ... 108
See also BW
Figueroa, John L(ewis) 1936- ... 65-68
Figueroa, Loida
See Figueroa-Mercado, Loida
See also HW
Figueroa, Pablo 1938- ... 61-64
See also HW
See also SATA 9
Figueroa-Chapel, Ramon 1935- ... 45-48
Figueroa-Mercado, Loida 1917- ... CANR-9
Earlier sketches in CAP-28, CA 57-60
See also Figueroa, Loida
Figurito, Joseph 1922- ... 29-32R
Fijan, Carol 1918- ... 53-56
See also SATA 12
Fikso, Eunice Cleland 1927- ... 5-8R
Filas, Francis L(ad) 1915-1985 ... CANR-2
Obituary ... 115
Earlier sketch in CA 5-8R
Filby, P(ercy) William 1911- ... CANR-27
Earlier sketches in CA 9-12R, CANR-3
Filene, Peter G. 1940- ... 21-24R
Filep, Robert Thomas 1931- ... CANR-19
Earlier sketches in CA 45-48, CANR-1
Filicchia, Ralph 1935- ... 103
Filip, Raymond 1950- ... 113
Filipovitch, Anthony J(oseph) 1947- ... 102
Filippo, Eduardo de
See de Filippo, Eduardo
Fill, Joseph Herbert 1924- Brief entry ... 112
Filler, Louis 1912- ... CANR-2
Earlier sketch in CA 1-4R
Fillmer, Henry Thompson 1932- ... 21-24R
Fillmore, Lowell 1882- ... CAP-1
Earlier sketch in CA 9-10
Fillmore, Parker H(oysted) 1878-1944 ... YABC 1
Fillmore, Roscoe Alfred 1887- ... 5-8R
Filmer, Henry
See Childs, J(ames) Rives
Filosa, Gary Fairmont Randolph de Marco II
1931- ... 65-68
Filreis, Alan 1956- ... 125
Filson, Floyd V(ivian) 1896- ... 61-64
Filson, John 1753(?)-1788 ... DLB 37
Filstrup, Chris
See Filstrup, E(dward) Christian
Filstrup, E(dward) Christian 1942- ... 113
See also SATA 43
Filstrup, Jane (Merrill) 1946- ... 110
Filstrup, Janie
See Filstrup, Jane (Merrill)
Filtzer, Donald 1948- ... 126
Finan, John J(oseph) 1925- ... 117
Finberg, H(erbert) P(atrick) R(eginald)
1900-1974 ... CAP-1
Obituary ... 53-56
Earlier sketch in CA 13-16
Finch, Anne 1661-1720 ... DLB 95
Finch, Christopher 1939- ... 138
Brief entry ... 112
Finch, Donald George 1937- ... 53-56
Finch, Henry LeRoy 1918- ... 41-44R
Finch, Matthew
See Fink, Merton
Finch(-Rayner), Sheila 1935- ... 121
Finch, Robert (Charles) 1943- ... 137
Finch, Robert (Duer Claydon) 1900- ... CANR-24
Earlier sketches in CA 57-60, CANR-9
See also CLC 18
See also DLB 88
Fincham, A(nthony) A(rthur) 1943- ... 117
Fincher, Cameron Lane 1926- ... 41-44R
Fincher, Ernest B(arksdale) 1910-1985 ... CANR-9
Obituary ... 115
Earlier sketch in CA 53-56
Finck, Furman J(oseph) 1900- ... CAP-2
Earlier sketch in CA 33-36
Fincke, Gary (William) 1945- ... 57-60
Finckenauer, James O(liver) 1939- ... 108
Finder, Joseph 1958- ... 113
Finder, Martin
See Salzmann, Siegmund
Findlater, Richard
See Bain, Kenneth Bruce Findlater
Findlay, Bruce Allyn 1895-1972 ... CAP-1
Earlier sketch in CA 13-14
Findlay, Campbell K(irkman) 1909- ... 5-8R
Findlay, David K. 1901- ... CAP-1
Earlier sketch in CA 13-14
Findlay, James Arthur 1883-1964 Obituary ... 111
Findlay, James F(ranklin) Jr. 1930- ... 49-52
Findlay, John N(iemeyer) 1903-1987 ... CANR-5
Obituary ... 123
Earlier sketch in CA 5-8R
Findlay, Robert R. 1932- ... 45-48
Findley, Carter Vaughn 1941- ... 102
Findley, Paul 1921- ... 29-32R
Findley, Timothy 1930- ... CANR-12
Earlier sketch in CA 25-28R
See also CLC 27
See also DLB 53
Findling, John Ellis 1941- ... 102
Fine, Anne 1947- ... CANR-38
Earlier sketch in CA 105
See also CLR 25
See also MAICYA
See also SATA 29
Fine, Benjamin 1905-1975 ... CANR-4
Obituary ... 57-60
Earlier sketch in CA 5-8R
Fine, Carla 1946- ... 112
Fine, Elsa Honig 1930- ... CANR-28
Earlier sketch in CA 49-52
Fine, Estelle
See Jelinek, Estelle C.
Fine, Gary Alan 1950- ... 111
Fine, I(sadore) V. 1918- ... 17-20R
Fine, John (Van Antwerp) Jr. 1939- ... 117
Fine, Judylaine 1948- ... 117
Fine, Marshall 1950- ... 137
Fine, Nathan 1893(?)-1979 Obituary ... 89-92
Fine, Ralph Adam 1941- ... 29-32R
Fine, Reuben 1914- ... CANR-12
Earlier sketch in CA 17-20R
Fine, S(eymour) Morton 1930- ... 104
Fine, Seymour H(oward) 1925- ... CANR-30
Earlier sketch in CA 111
Fine, Sidney 1920- ... CANR-1
Earlier sketch in CA 1-4R
Fine, Warren 1943- ... 21-24R
Fine, William Michael 1924- ... 13-16R
Fineberg, Robert Gene 1940- ... 107
Finegan, Jack 1908- ... CANR-1
Earlier sketch in CA 1-4R
Finegan, T(homas) Aldrich
1929- Brief entry ... 108
Fineman, Howard (David) 1948- ... 133
Fineman, Irving 1893- ... 5-8R
Fineman, Joel 1947-1989 ... 127
Obituary ... 128
Finer, Leslie 1921- ... 13-16R
Finer, Samuel Edward 1915- ... 41-44R
Finestone, Harold 1920- Brief entry ... 110
Finestone, Harry 1920- ... 45-48
Fingarette, Herbert 1921- ... 77-80
Finger, Charles J(oseph)
1869(?)-1941 Brief entry ... 119
See also SATA 42
Finger, Seymour Maxwell 1915- ... 104
Finger, William R(atliff) 1947- ... 111
Fingerhut, Eugene R. 1932- ... 111
Fingesten, Peter 1916-1987 ... 13-16R
Obituary ... 123
Finifter, Ada W(eintraub) 1938- ... CANR-21
Earlier sketch in CA 104
Fink, Arthur Emil 1903- ... 1-4R
Fink, Augusta 1916- ... CANR-13
Earlier sketch in CA 33-36R
Fink, Carole 1940- ... 135
Fink, Edith 1918- ... 61-64
Fink, Eli E. 1908(?)-1979 Obituary ... 85-88
Fink, Gary M. 1936- ... 53-56
Fink, Ida 1921- ... 136
Fink, Joanne 1954- ... 123
Fink, Joseph 1915- ... 57-60
Fink, Karl J. 1942- ... 138
Fink, Lawrence Alfred 1930- ... 97-100
Fink, Leon 1948- ... 135
Fink, Merton 1921- ... 9-12R
Fink, Paul Jay 1933- ... 53-56
Fink, Stevanne Auerbach
See Auerbach, Stevanne
Fink, William
See Mencken, H(enry) L(ouis)
Fink, William B(ertrand) 1916- ... 41-44R
See also SATA 22
Fink, Z(era) S(ilver) 1902- ... CAP-1
Earlier sketch in CA 9-10
Fink Cline, Beverly 1951- ... 113
Finke, Blythe Foote 1922- ... 65-68
See also SATA 26
Finke, Jack A. 1918(?)-1979 Obituary ... 89-92
Finkel, Alvin 1949- ... 131
Finkel, Donald 1929- ... CANR-29
Earlier sketches in CA 21-24R, CANR-9
Finkel, George (Irvine) 1909-1975 ... CAP-2
Earlier sketch in CA 17-18
See also SATA 8
Finkel, Lawrence S. 1925- ... 13-16R
Finkel, LeRoy 1939- ... 105
Finkelhor, David 1947- ... 118
Finkelhor, Dorothy Cimberg 1902- ... 110
Finkell, Max
See Catto, Max(well Jeffrey)
Finkelman, Paul 1949- ... CANR-22
Earlier sketch in CA 105
Finkelstein, Bonnie B(lumenthal) 1946- ... 85-88
Finkelstein, Jacob Joel
1922-1974 Obituary ... 53-56
Finkelstein, Leonid Vladimirovitch
1924- ... 21-24R
Finkelstein, Louis 1895-1991 ... 13-16R
Obituary ... 136
Finkelstein, Marina S.
1921(?)-1972 Obituary ... 33-36R
Finkelstein, Milton 1920- ... 89-92
Finkelstein, Miriam 1928- ... 108
Finkelstein, Sidney
1910(?)-1974 Obituary ... 45-48
Finkle, Jason L(eonard) 1926- ... 21-24R
Finklehoffe, Fred F. 1910-1977 Obituary ... 73-76
Finkler, Kaja 1935- ... 114
Finlator, John Haywood 1911- ... 102
Finlay, Campbell K(irkman) 1909- ... 5-8R
Finlay, David J(ames) 1934- ... CANR-16
Earlier sketch in CA 25-28R
Finlay, Fiona
See Stuart, (Violet) Vivian (Finlay)
Finlay, Ian Hamilton 1925- ... 81-84
See also DLB 40
Finlay, Matthew Henderson 1916- ... 13-16R
Finlay, Roger (Anthony Peter) 1952- ... 132
Finlay, William
See Mackay, James (Alexander)
Finlay, Winifred Lindsay Crawford (McKissack)
1910- ... 9-12R
See also SATA 23
Finlayson, Ann 1925- ... 29-32R
See also SATA 8
Finlayson, Geoffrey B(eauchamp) A(listair) M(oubray)
1934- ... 131
Finlayson, Michael G(eorge) 1938- ... 128
Finlayson, Roderick (David) 1904- ... 81-84
Finler, Joel W(aldo) 1938- ... CANR-32
Earlier sketch in CA 77-80
Finletter, Thomas K(night)
1893-1980 Obituary ... 101
Finley, Gerald Eric 1931- ... 105
Finley, Glenna
See Witte, Glenna Finley
Finley, Harold M(arshall) 1916- ... 17-20R
Finley, James 1943- ... 97-100
Finley, Joseph E(dwin) 1919- ... 69-72
Finley, Lewis M(erren) 1929- ... 61-64
Finley, M(oses) I. 1912-1986 ... CANR-10
Obituary ... 119
Earlier sketch in CA 5-8R
Finley, Martha 1828-1909 Brief entry ... 118
See also DLB 42
See also SATA 43
Finman, Ted 1931- Brief entry ... 110
Finn, David 1921- ... 73-76
Finn, Doug(las Arthur) 1946- ... 115
Finn, Edward E(rnest) 1908- ... 115
Finn, Geraldine 1947- ... 118
Finn, James 1924- Brief entry ... 108
Finn, Jonathan 1884(?)-1971 Obituary ... 29-32R
Finn, R. Welldon
See Finn, Reginald Patrick Arthur Welldon
Finn, Ralph L(eslie) 1912- ... CANR-9
Earlier sketch in CA 5-8R
Finn, Reginald Patrick Arthur Welldon
1900-1971 ... CANR-10
Earlier sketch in CA 13-16R
Finn, Rex Welldon
See Finn, Reginald Patrick Arthur Welldon
Finn, (Patrick) Timothy 1938- ... 129
Finnegan, Mary Jeremy 1907- ... 135
Finnegan, Robert
See Ryan, Paul William
Finnegan, Ruth H(ilary) 1933- ... CANR-12
Earlier sketch in CA 25-28R
Finnegan, William (Patrick) 1952- ... 136
Finneran, Richard J(ohn) 1943- ... CANR-29
Earlier sketches in CA 29-32R, CANR-12
Finnerty, Adam Daniel
See Corson-Finnerty, Adam Daniel
Finnerty, Daniel John
See Corson-Finnerty, Adam Daniel
Finney, Ben R(udolph) 1933- ... CANR-1
Earlier sketch in CA 45-48
Finney, Charles G(randison) 1905-1984 ... CAP-2
Obituary ... 112
Earlier sketch in CA 29-32
Finney, Ernest J. ... 134

Finney, Gertrude Elva (Bridgeman)
1892- CAP-1
Earlier sketch in CA 13-16
Finney, Gretchen Ludke 1901- 9-12R
Finney, Humphrey S. 1902- 97-100
Finney, Jack
See Finney, Walter Braden
See also DLB 8
Finney, Mark
See Muir, Kenneth (Arthur)
Finney, Nathaniel Solon
1903-1982 Obituary 108
Finney, Patricia 1958- 97-100
Finney, Paul B(urnham) 1929- 73-76
Finney, Shan 1944- 111
See also SATA 65
Finney, Theodore M(itchell) 1902- 61-64
Finney, Walter Braden 1921- 133
Brief entry 110
See also Finney, Jack
Finnigan, Joan 1925- CANR-29
Earlier sketches in CA 17-20R, CANR-13
Finnin, (Olive) Mary 106
Finnis, John M(itchell) 1940- 136
Finocchiaro, Mary (Bonomo) 1913- CANR-27
Earlier sketch in CA 29-32R
Fins, Alice 1944- 110
Finson, Jon W(illiam) 1950- 125
Finstad, Suzanne 1955- 131
Finucane, Ronald C(harles) 135
Fiore, Edith 1930- 85-88
Fiore, Michael V. 1934- 45-48
Fiore, Peter Amadeus 1927- 33-36R
Fiore, Robert Louis 1935- 73-76
Fiore, Silvestro 1921- 17-20R
Fiorenza, Elisabeth Schuessler 1938- CANR-39
Earlier sketch in CA 106
Fiorenza, Francis S(chuessler) 1941- CANR-39
Earlier sketch in CA 115
Fiori, Pamela A. 1944- 89-92
Fiorina, Morris Paul Jr. 1946- 85-88
Fiorino, A(ngelo) John 1926- 29-32R
Fiorio, Franco Emilio 1912-1975 Obituary 61-64
Firbank, Louis 1942- Brief entry 117
See also Reed, Lou
Firbank, (Arthur Annesley) Ronald
1886-1926 Brief entry 104
See also DLB 36
See also TCLC 1
Firchow, Evelyn Scherabon 1932- CANR-11
Earlier sketch in CA 21-24R
Firchow, Peter (Edgerly) 1937- 37-40R
Firebrace, Aylmer (Newton George) 1886- 5-8R
Firer, Ben Zion
See Firer, Benzion
Firer, Benzion 1914- 131
See also SATA 64
Fires, Alicia
See Oglesby, Joseph
Fireside, Harvey 1929- 29-32R
Firestone, Harvey S(amuel) Jr.
1898-1973 Obituary 41-44R
Firestone, O(tto) J(ohn) 1913- 41-44R
Firestone, Robert W. 1930- 130
Firestone, Tom
See Newcomb, Duane G(raham)
Firey, Walter Irving (Jr.) 1916- 1-4R
Firkins, Peter (Charles) 1926- 107
Firmage, George J(ames) 1928- 9-12R
Firmat, Gustavo (Francisco) Perez
See Perez-Firmat, Gustavo (Francisco)
Firmin, Charlotte 1954- CANR-23
Earlier sketch in CA 106
See also SATA 29
Firmin, Giles 1615-1697 .... DLB 24
Firmin, Peter 1928- CANR-17
Earlier sketch in CA 81-84
See also SATA 15, 58
Firor, John (W.) 1927- 136
Firsoff, V(aldemar) Axel 1910- 93-96
First, Ruth 1925-1982 .... CANR-10
Obituary 107
Earlier sketch in CA 53-56
Firth, (Frederick) Anson 1902- 117
Firth, Grace (Ushler) 1922- 73-76
Firth, J. R.
See Firth, John Rupert
Firth, John Rupert 1890-1960 Obituary 116
Firth, Raymond (William) 1901- 65-68
Firth, Robert E. 1921- 77-80
Firth, Tony 1937(?)-1980 Obituary 97-100
Fisch, Edith L. 1923- 77-80
Fisch, Gerald G(rant) 1922- 13-16R
Fisch, Harold 1923- 37-40R
Fisch, Martin L. 1924- 109
Fisch, Max H(arold) 1900- 33-36R
Fisch, Richard 1926- Brief entry 106
Fischbach, Julius 1894- CANR-2
Earlier sketch in CA 5-8R
See also SATA 10
Fischel, Walter J(oseph) 1902-1973 .... CAP-2
Obituary 41-44R
Earlier sketch in CA 23-24
Fischer, Alfred (George) 1920- 73-76
Fischer, Ann 1919-1971 .... CAP-2
Earlier sketch in CA 25-28
Fischer, Arlene 1934- 111
Fischer, Bobby
See Fischer, Robert James
Fischer, Bruno 1908- 77-80
Fischer, Carl H(ahn) 1903- 17-20R
Fischer, Claude S(erge) 1948- 107
Fischer, David Hackett 1935- 17-20R
Fischer, Dietrich 1941- 117
Fischer, Donald E(dward) 1935- 41-44R
Fischer, Edward (Adam) 1914- CANR-37
Earlier sketches in CA 1-4R, CANR-1, 16
Fischer, Ernst 1899-1972 Obituary 37-40R
Fischer, Fritz 1908- CANR-9
Earlier sketch in CA 65-68
Fischer, George 1923- CANR-9
Earlier sketch in CA 53-56
Fischer, George 1932- 25-28R
Fischer, Gerald C(harles) 1928- CANR-9
Earlier sketch in CA 21-24R
Fischer, J(ohn) L(yle) 1923- 17-20R
Fischer, Joel 1939- CANR-19
Earlier sketches in CA 53-56, CANR-4
Fischer, John Irwin 1940- 129
Fischer, John Martin 1952- 124
Fischer, John 1910-1978 .... CANR-4
Obituary 81-84
Earlier sketch in CA 9-12R
Fischer, Karoline Auguste Fernandine
1764-1842 .... DLB 94
Fischer, LeRoy H(enry) 1917- CANR-8
Earlier sketch in CA 17-20R
Fischer, Louis 1896-1970 .... CAP-1
Obituary 25-28R
Earlier sketch in CA 11-12
Fischer, Lucy Rose 1944- 138
Fischer, Michael R(obert) 1949- 118
Fischer, Robert H. 1918- 37-40R
Fischer, Robert James 1943- 103
Fischer, Roger Adrian 1939- Brief entry 109
Fischer, Vera Kistiakowsky
See Kistiakowsky, Vera
Fischer, Victor 1924- Brief entry 110
Fischer, William F(rank) 1934- Brief entry 111
Fischer, Wolfgang Georg 1933- 33-36R
Fischer-Dieskau, Dietrich 1925- 97-100
Fischer-Fabian, Siegfried 1922- 130
Fischer-Galati, Stephen A(lexander) 1924- 127
Brief entry 117
Fischer-Nagel, Andreas 1951- 123
See also SATA 56
Fischer-Nagel, Heiderose 1956- 123
See also SATA 56
Fischetti, John 1916-1980 Obituary 102
Fischl, Viktor
See Dagan, Avigdor
Fischler, Alan 1952- 137
Fischler, Shirley (Walton) 136
See also SATA 66
Fischler, Stan(ley I.) 128
Brief entry 116
See also SATA 36, 66
Fischman, Harve 1930- Brief entry 113
Fischman, Leonard L(ipman) 1919- CANR-10
Earlier sketch in CA 13-16R
Fischtrom, Harvey 1933-1974 .... CAP-2
Obituary 53-56
Earlier sketch in CA 25-28
See also Zemach, Harve
Fish, Byron 1908- 45-48
Fish, Julian
See Campbell, Blanche
Fish, Kenneth L(loyd) 1926- 29-32R
Fish, Margery (Townshend) 1892-1969 .... CANR-4
Earlier sketch in CA 5-8R
Fish, Peter Graham 1937- 69-72
Fish, Robert L. 1912-1981 .... CANR-13
Obituary 103
Earlier sketch in CA 13-16R
Fish, Roy J(ason) 1930- 123
Brief entry 118
Fish, Stanley
See Fish, Stanley Eugene
Fish, Stanley E.
See Fish, Stanley Eugene
Fish, Stanley Eugene 1938- 132
Brief entry 112
See also DLB 67
Fishacre, Richard 1205(?)-1248 .... DLB 115
Fishback, Margaret
See Antolini, Margaret Fishback
Fishback, Price V(anmeter) 1955- 138
Fishbane, Michael A(lton) 1943- 113
Fishbein, Harold D(ennis) 1938- 126
Brief entry 105
Fishbein, Meyer H(arry) 1916- 41-44R
Fishbein, Morris 1889-1976 .... CANR-4
Obituary 69-72
Earlier sketch in CA 5-8R
Fishburn, Hummel 1901- CAP-1
Earlier sketch in CA 19-20
Fishburn, Janet Forsythe 1937- 108
Fishburn, Peter C(lingerman) 1936- 45-48
Fishel, Elizabeth 1950- 103
Fishel, Leslie H(enry) Jr. 1921- 21-24R
Fishel, Wesley R(obert) 1919-1977 73-76
Obituary 69-72
Fisher, A(rnold) Garth 1933- 104
Fisher, A(rthur) Stanley T(heodore) 1906- 93-96
Fisher, Aileen (Lucia) 1906- CANR-37
Earlier sketches in CA 5-8R, CANR-2, 17
See also MAICYA
See also SATA 1, 25
Fisher, Alan W(ashburn) 1939- 53-56
Fisher, Alan 1929- 121
Fisher, Alden L(owell) 1928-1970 .... CAP-2
Earlier sketch in CA 25-28
Fisher, Allan C(arroll) Jr. 1919- 112
Fisher, Allan G(eorge) B(arnard)
1895-1976 .... 33-36R
Fisher, Allen J. 1907(?)-1980 Obituary 102
Fisher, Ameel J(oseph) 1909- 104
Fisher, Anne B. 1957- 135
Fisher, Arthur 1931- 110
Fisher, Barbara 1940- CANR-30
Earlier sketch in CA 104
See also SATA 34, 44
Fisher, Bart (Steven) 1943- 45-48
Fisher, Benjamin Franklin IV 1940- CANR-30
Earlier sketch in CA 112
Fisher, Bob
See Fisher, Robert Percival
Fisher, Bruce 1931- 118
Fisher, C(harles) William 1916- CANR-6
Earlier sketch in CA 5-8R
Fisher, Carrie (Frances) 1956- 135
See also BEST 90:4
Fisher, Charles Alfred
1916-1982(?) Obituary 105
Fisher, Clavin C(argill) 1912- 65-68
See also SATA 24
Fisher, Clay
See Allen, Henry Wilson
Fisher, David E(limelech) 1932- CANR-22
Earlier sketches in CA 53-56, CANR-4
Fisher, Dominic (Mayne Maitland) 1953- 124
Fisher, Don 1933(?)-1983 Obituary 111
Fisher, Dorothy (Frances) Canfield
1879-1958 136
Brief entry 114
See also DLB 9, 102
See also MAICYA
See also YABC 1
Fisher, Douglas Mason 1919- 89-92
Fisher, Douglas 1934- 102
Fisher, Douglas 1954- 118
Fisher, Edward 1902- 1-4R
Fisher, Elizabeth 1941- 117
Fisher, Ernest Arthur 1887- 13-16R
Fisher, Esther Oshiver 1910- 85-88
Fisher, Eugene J(oseph) 1943- CANR-22
Earlier sketch in CA 105
Fisher, Florence (Anna) 1928- Brief entry 112
Fisher, Franklin M(arvin) 1934- 17-20R
Fisher, Fred L(ewis) 1911- CANR-5
Earlier sketch in CA 1-4R
Fisher, (Donald) Gary 1938- 103
Fisher, Gene H. 1922- 41-44R
Fisher, Gene L(ouis) 1947- 81-84
Fisher, George E(dward) 1923- 127
Fisher, George W. 1910(?)-1987 Obituary 124
Fisher, Glen H(arry) 1922- Brief entry 111
Fisher, Glenn W(illiam) 1924- 53-56
Fisher, Gordon N(eil) 1928-1985 Obituary 117
Fisher, Harold H. 1890-1975 Obituary 61-64
Fisher, Harvey Irvin 1916- 69-72
Fisher, Helen E(lizabeth) 1945- 108
Fisher, Humphrey J(ohn) 1933- 33-36R
Fisher, J(ohn) R(obert) 1943- CANR-1
Earlier sketch in CA 45-48
Fisher, J(oseph) Thomas 1936- 33-36R
Fisher, James (Maxwell McConnell)
1912-1970 126
Obituary 89-92
Fisher, James R(aymond) Jr. 1937- 81-84
Fisher, Joe 1947- 103
Fisher, Johanna 1922- 93-96
Fisher, John C(harles) 1927- 41-44R
Fisher, John H(urt) 1919- CANR-11
Earlier sketch in CA 21-24R
Fisher, John J(acob) III
1951(?)-1990 Obituary 131
Fisher, John (Oswald Hamilton) 1909- 81-84
See also SATA 15
Fisher, Kenneth L(awrence) 1950- 118
Fisher, Kim N. 1948- 121
Fisher, Laine
See Howard, James A(rch)
Fisher, Laura Harrison 1934- 13-16R
See also SATA 5
Fisher, Lawrence V. 1923- 17-20R
Fisher, Lee 1908- 33-36R
Fisher, Leonard Everett 1924- CANR-37
Earlier sketches in CA 1-4R, CANR-2
See also CLR 18
See also DLB 61
See also MAICYA
See also SAAS 1
See also SATA 4, 34
Fisher, Lillian Estelle 1891- CAP-1
Earlier sketch in CA 13-16
Fisher, Lois H(amilton) 1936- 113
Fisher, Lois I. 1948- 113
See also SATA 35, 38
Fisher, Lois Jeannette 1909- 5-8R
Fisher, Louis 1934- 37-40R
Fisher, M(ary) F(rances) K(ennedy)
1908- 77-80
Obituary 138
Fisher, Malcolm R(obertson)
1923- Brief entry 110
Fisher, Margaret B(arrow) 1918- 17-20R
Fisher, Margery (Turner) 1913- 73-76
See also SATA 20
Fisher, Margot
See Paine, Lauran (Bosworth)
Fisher, Marvin 1927- 21-24R
Fisher, Mary L. 1928- 33-36R
Fisher, Michael John 1933- CANR-3
Earlier sketch in CA 1-4R
Fisher, Miles Mark 1899-1970 .... CAP-1
Earlier sketch in CA 13-16
Fisher, Miriam Louise (Scharfe) 1939- 13-16R
Fisher, Morris 1922- 21-24R
Fisher, Neal F(loyd) 1936- 106
Fisher, Nigel 1913- 102
Fisher, Norman George
1910-1972 Obituary 107
Fisher, Peter Jack 1930- 69-72
Fisher, Philip A(rthur) 1907- 61-64
Fisher, Philip 1941- CANR-33
Earlier sketch in CA 113
Fisher, R. A.
See Fisher, Ronald A(ylmer)
Fisher, Ralph Talcott Jr. 1920- 41-44R
Fisher, Rhoda Lee 1924- 65-68
Fisher, Richard B(ernard) 1919- 77-80
Fisher, Richard 1936- 17-20R
Fisher, Robert C(harles) 1930- 53-56
Fisher, Robert J(ay) 1924- 61-64
Fisher, Robert Percival 1935- 93-96
Fisher, Robert (Tempest) 1943- CANR-26
Earlier sketch in CA 109
See also SATA 47
Fisher, Roger (Dummer) 1922- 37-40R
Fisher, Ronald A(ylmer)
1890-1962 Obituary 112
Fisher, Roy 1930- CANR-16
Earlier sketch in CA 81-84
See also CAAS 10
See also CLC 25
See also DLB 40
Fisher, Rudolph 1897-1934 124
Brief entry 107
See also BLC 2
See also BW
See also DLB 51, 102
See also TCLC 11
Fisher, Seymour 1922- CANR-12
Earlier sketch in CA 33-36R
Fisher, Shelton 1911-1985 Obituary 115
Fisher, Sidney Thomson 1908- 124
Fisher, Sterling Wesley 1899(?)-1978 85-88
Obituary 81-84
Fisher, Susan M(ichal) 1937- 119
Fisher, Suzanne
See Staples, Suzanne Fisher
Fisher, Sydney G.
See Fisher, Sydney George
Fisher, Sydney George
1856-1927 Brief entry 122
See also DLB 47
Fisher, Vardis (Alvero) 1895-1968 .... 5-8R
Obituary 25-28R
See also CLC 7
See also DLB 9
Fisher, Wade
See Norwood, Victor G(eorge) C(harles)
Fisher, Wallace E. 1918- CANR-10
Earlier sketch in CA 21-24R
Fisher, Walter R. 1931- 13-16R
Fisher, Welthy Honsinger 1879-1980 .... CANR-2
Obituary 102
Earlier sketch in CA 1-4R
Fisher, Wesley Andrew 1944- 104
Fisher, William Bayne 1916-1984 65-68
Obituary 113
Fishler, Mary Shiverick 1920- 5-8R
Fishlock, David (Jocelyn) 1932- 130
Fishman, Betty G(oldstein) 1918- 5-8R
Fishman, Burton J(ohn) 1942- 45-48
Fishman, Charles 1942- CANR-7
Earlier sketch in CA 57-60
Fishman, George Samuel 1937- 25-28R
Fishman, Jack 1920- CANR-7
Earlier sketch in CA 9-12R
Fishman, Joshua A(aron) 1926- CANR-34
Earlier sketches in CA 41-44R, CANR-15
Fishman, Katherine Davis 1937- 130
Fishman, Ken 1950- 105
Fishman, Leo 1914-1975 .... 17-20R
Obituary 120
Fishman, Lew 1939- CANR-11
Earlier sketch in CA 61-64
Fishman, Robert (Lawrence) 1946- 112
Fishman, Sterling 1932- 45-48
Fishof, David 1956- 115
Fishwick, Marshall William 1923- CANR-6
Earlier sketch in CA 5-8R
Fisk, E(rnest) K(elvin) 1917- 17-20R
Fisk, Erma J(onnie) 1905(?)-1990 Obituary 130
Fisk, McKee 1900- CAP-2
Earlier sketch in CA 21-22
Fisk, Nicholas 1923- CANR-28
Earlier sketches in CA 65-68, CANR-11
See also SATA 25
Fisk, Pauline 1948- 136
See also SATA 66
Fisk, Samuel 1907- 57-60
Fiske, Edward B. 1937- CANR-16
Earlier sketch in CA 85-88
Fiske, John 1608-1677 .... DLB 24
Fiske, John 1842-1901 .... DLB 47, 64
Fiske, Marjorie CANR-1
Earlier sketch in CA 45-48
Fiske, Roger E(lwyn) 1910- 13-16R
Fiske, Sharon
See Hill, Pamela
Fiske, Tarleton
See Bloch, Robert (Albert)
Fisketjon, Gary 1954- 129
Brief entry 123
Fiskin, A(bram) M. I. 1916-1975 .... CAP-2
Earlier sketch in CA 23-24
Fison, Joseph Edward 1906-1972 Obituary 114
Fiss, Owen M(itchell) 1938- 112
Fiszel, Henryk 1910- 29-32R
Fiszman, Joseph R. 1921- 41-44R
Fitch, Alger Morton Jr. 1919- 53-56
Fitch, Bob
See Fitch, Robert Beck
Fitch, Clarke
See Sinclair, Upton (Beall)
Fitch, (William) Clyde
1865-1909 Brief entry 110
See also DLB 7
Fitch, Donald S(heldon) 1949- 106
Fitch, Edwin M(edbery) 1902- CAP-2
Earlier sketch in CA 25-28
Fitch, George Ashmore
1883-1979 Obituary 85-88

Fitch, Geraldine T(ownsend)
1892(?)-1976 Obituary 69-72
Fitch, James Marston 1909- 89-92
Fitch, John IV
See Cormier, Robert (Edmund)
Fitch, Kenneth (Leonard) 1929- 49-52
Fitch, Lyle C(raig) 1913- 13-16R
Fitch, Raymond E(dward) 1930- 110
Fitch, Robert Beck 1938- 21-24R
Fitch, Stanley K. 1920- 29-32R
Fitch, Thomas 1700(?)-1774 .... DLB 31
Fitch, William Clyde 1865-1909 .... DLB 7
Fitch, Willis Stetson
1896(?)-1978 Obituary 81-84
Fite, Gilbert C(ourtland) 1918- 33-36R
Fite, James David 1933- 107
Fite, Mack
See Schneck, Stephen
Fitgerald, Penelope 1916- .... CLC 61
Fitler, Mary Biddle
1878(?)-1966 Obituary 25-28R
Fitschen, Dale 1937- 77-80
See also SATA 20
Fitt, Mary
See Freeman, Kathleen
Fitter, Richard Sidney Richmond
1913- CANR-11
Earlier sketch in CA 65-68
Fitting, Greer A. 1943- 81-84
Fitting, James E. 1939- 45-48
Fitting, Melvin (Chris) 1942- CANR-11
Earlier sketch in CA 29-32R
Fitton, James 1899-1982 Obituary 106
Fitts, Dudley 1903-1968 93-96
Obituary 25-28R
Fitts, Henry (King) 1914- 113
Fitts, William Howard 1918- 21-24R
Fitz, Jean DeWitt 1912- 29-32R
Fitzalan, Roger
See Trevor, Elleston
Fitzell, John 1922- 13-16R
Fitzgeffrey, Charles 1575(?)-1638 .... DLB 121
Fitzgerald, Arlene J. CANR-8
Earlier sketch in CA 21-24R
Fitzgerald, Barbara
See Value, Barbara Ann
Fitzgerald, Barbara
See Newman, Mona Alice Jean
Fitzgerald, Barry Charles 1939- 37-40R
FitzGerald, Brian Seymour Vesey
See Vesey-FitzGerald, Brian Seymour
FitzGerald, C(harles) P(atrick) 1902- CANR-11
Obituary 137
Earlier sketch in CA 17-20R
Fitzgerald, Captain Hugh
See Baum, L(yman) Frank
Fitz-Gerald, Carolyn 1932- 41-44R
FitzGerald, Cathleen 1932-1987 .... 33-36R
Obituary 121
See also SATA 50
Fitzgerald, Dorothy Dow (Minerva)
1903(?)-1989 Obituary 128
Fitzgerald, E(dmund) V(alpy) K(nox)
1947- 73-76
Fitzgerald, Edward Earl 1919- 73-76
See also SATA 20
FitzGerald, Edward 1809-1883 .... DLB 32
Fitzgerald, Edward 1898(?)-1982 Obituary 108
Fitzgerald, Ellen
See Stevenson, Florence
Fitzgerald, Ernest A. 1925- CANR-12
Earlier sketch in CA 29-32R
Fitzgerald, F(rancis) A(nthony) 1940- .... SATA 15
Fitzgerald, F(rancis) Scott (Key) 1896-1940 123
Brief entry 110
See also AITN 1
See also CDALB 1917-1929
See also DLB 4, 9, 86
See also DLBD 1
See also DLBY 81
See also MTCW
See also SSC 6
See also TCLC 1, 6, 14, 28
See also WLC
FitzGerald, Frances 1940- CANR-32
Earlier sketch in CA 41-44R
FitzGerald, Garret 1926- 109
Fitzgerald, George R. 1932- CANR-17
Earlier sketch in CA 97-100
Fitzgerald, Gerald E(dward) 1920- 25-28R
Fitzgerald, Gerald (Norman)
1932-1990 Obituary 131
Fitzgerald, Gerald (Pierce) 1930- 37-40R
Fitz Gerald, Gregory 1923- CANR-1
Earlier sketch in CA 49-52
Fitzgerald, Hal
See Johnson, Joseph E(arl)
Fitzgerald, Harold Alvin
1896-1984 Obituary 114
Fitzgerald, Hiram E(arl) 1940- CANR-16
Earlier sketch in CA 77-80
Fitzgerald, Jack
See Shea, John Gerald
Fitzgerald, James A(ugustine) 1892- CANR-1
Earlier sketch in CA 1-4R
Fitzgerald, James V.
1889(?)-1976 Obituary 69-72
Fitzgerald, John
See Fazzano, Joseph E.
Fitzgerald, John D(ennis) 1907(?)-1988 93-96
Obituary 126
See also CLR 1
See also MAICYA
See also SATA 20, 56
Fitzgerald, John Joseph 1928- 37-40R
Fitzgerald, Judith 1952- CANR-32
Earlier sketch in CA 113
Fitzgerald, Julia
See Watson, Julia
FitzGerald, Kathleen Whalen 1938- 109
Fitzgerald, Kitty 1946- 129
Fitzgerald, Laurine Elisabeth 1930- 37-40R
Fitzgerald, Lawrence P(ennybaker)
1906-1976 .... CANR-2
Earlier sketch in CA 1-4R
Fitzgerald, Maury 1906(?)-1986 Obituary 121
Fitzgerald, Merni Ingrassia 1955- 124
See also SATA 53
Fitzgerald, Michael G(arrett) 1950- 77-80
Fitzgerald, Nancy 1951- 85-88
Fitzgerald, Patrick (John) 1928- 9-12R
Fitzgerald, Penelope 1916- 85-88
See also CAAS 10
See also CLC 19, 51
See also DLB 14
Fitzgerald, Randall 1950- 118
Fitzgerald, Richard (Ambrose) 1938- 45-48
FitzGerald, Robert D(avid) 1902-1987 .... 17-20R
See also CLC 19
Fitzgerald, Robert (Stuart) 1910-1985 .... CANR-1
Obituary 114
Earlier sketch in CA 1-4R
See also CLC 39
See also DLBY 80
FitzGerald, Stephen (Arthur) 1938- 97-100
FitzGerald, Tamsin 1950- 97-100
Fitzgerald, Thomas 1819-1891 .... DLB 23
Fitzgerald, Zelda (Sayre) 1900-1948 126
Brief entry 117
See also DLBY 84
FitzGibbon, (Robert Louis) Constantine (Lee-Dillon)
1919-1983 .... CANR-2
Obituary 109
Earlier sketch in CA 1-4R
Fitzgibbon, Russell H(umke)
1902-1979 .... CANR-14
Earlier sketch in CA 65-68
FitzGibbon, Theodora (Joanne Eileen Winifred)
Rosling 1916- CANR-3
Earlier sketch in CA 5-8R
Fitzgibbons, James P.
1912(?)-1983 Obituary 110
Fitzhardinge, Joan Margaret 1912- CANR-36
Earlier sketches in CA 13-16R, CANR-6, 23
See also Phipson, Joan
See also MAICYA
See also SATA 2
Fitzhenry, Robert Irvine 1918- 110
FitzHerbert, Margaret 1942-1986 130
Fitzhugh, Louise 1928-1974 .... CANR-34
Obituary 53-56
Earlier sketches in CAP-2, CA 29-32
See also CLR 1
See also DLB 52
See also MAICYA
See also SATA 1, 24, 45
Fitzhugh, Percy Keese 1876-1950 133
See also SATA 65
Fitzhugh, Robert Tyson
1906-1981 Obituary 104
Fitzhugh, William 1651(?)-1701 .... DLB 24
Fitzlyon, (Cecily) April (Mead) 1920- 5-8R
Fitzlyon, Kyril 1910- 93-96
Fitzmaurice, Gabriel 1952- 137
Fitzmaurice, George 1877-1963 Obituary 93-96
Fitzmyer, Joseph A(ugustine) 1920- CANR-5
Earlier sketch in CA 9-12R
Fitzpatrick, Daniel Robert
1891-1969 Obituary 89-92
Fitzpatrick, James K(evin) 1942- 65-68
Fitzpatrick, Joseph P(atrick) 1913- 17-20R
Fitzpatrick, Kathryn 1934- 113
FitzPatrick, Paul Joseph
1894-1984 Obituary 111
Fitzpatrick, Tom 1927- Brief entry 111
Fitzpatrick, Vincent (dePaul III) 1950- 131
FitzRalph, Matthew
See McInerny, Ralph
Fitz-Randolph, Jane (Currens) 1915- 103
See also SATA 51
FitzRoy, Charles (Patrick Hugh) 1957- 136
Fitzroy, Rosamond
See Briggs, Desmond Lawther
Fitzsimmons, Cleo 1900- 1-4R
Fitzsimmons, Michael P. 1949- 129
Fitzsimmons, Thomas 1926- CANR-15
Earlier sketch in CA 33-36R
Fitz-Simon, Christopher 1934- 113
Fitzsimons, Louise 1932- 61-64
Fitzsimons, M(athew) A(nthony) 1912- 13-16R
Fitzsimons, Neal 1928- 33-36R
FitzSimons, Raymund CANR-15
Earlier sketch in CA 33-36R
FitzSimons, Ruth M(arie Mangan) 53-56
Fitzwilliam, Michael
See Lyons, J. B.
Five, Billy
See Obrecht, Jas
Fivelson, Scott 1954- 117
Fix, Paul
See Morrison, Paul Fix
Fix, William R. 1941- CANR-15
Earlier sketch in CA 85-88
Fixel, Lawrence 1917- 137
Fixler, Michael 1927- 13-16R
Fixx, James F(uller) 1932-1984 .... CANR-13
Earlier sketch in CA 73-76
Fixx, Jim
See Fixx, James F(uller)
Fizer, John 1925- 53-56
Fjelde, Rolf (Gerhard) 1926- 17-20R
Flach, Frederic F(rancis) 1927- 81-84
Flachmann, Michael 1942- 117
Flack, Audrey L. 1931- CANR-26
Earlier sketch in CA 106
Flack, Dora D(utson) 1919- CANR-21
Earlier sketches in CA 57-60, CANR-6
Flack, Elmer Ellsworth 1894- 17-20R
Flack, Jerry D(avid) 1943- 131
Flack, Marjorie 1897-1958 136
Brief entry 112
See also CLR 28
See also MAICYA
See also YABC 2
Flack, Naomi John White CANR-1
Earlier sketch in CA 1-4R
See also SATA 35, 40
Flacks, Niki 1943- 110
Flacks, Richard 1938- 49-52
Fladeland, Betty 1919- 45-48
Flader, Susan L. 1941- 81-84
Flagg, Fannie 1941- 111
Flagg, Kenneth
See Ayvazian, L. Fred
Flagstad, Kirsten 1895-1962 Obituary 112
Flaherty, Daniel Leo 1929- 89-92
Flaherty, David H(arris) 1940- 25-28R
Flaherty, Doug(las Ernest) 1939- 33-36R
Flaherty, Gloria 1938- 85-88
Flaherty, Joe 1936(?)-1983 Obituary 111
Flaherty, Mary Pat 1955- 132
Brief entry 127
Flaherty, Robert J(oseph)
1884-1951 Brief entry 115
Flaherty, Robert Joseph 1933- 73-76
Flaherty, Vincent X.
1908(?)-1977 Obituary 73-76
Flaiano, Ennio 1910-1972 Obituary 37-40R
Flake, Chad J(ohn) 1929- 29-32R
Flambeau, Blossom
See Stocking, Kathleen
Flamholtz, Eric 1943- 57-60
Flamm, Dudley 1931- 25-28R
Flamm, Gerald R(obert) 1916- 77-80
Flamm, Jerry
See Flamm, Gerald R(obert)
Flammarion, (Nicolas) Camille
1842-1925 Brief entry 120
Flammarion, Henri (Claude)
1910-1985 Obituary 117
Flammer, Philip M(eynard) 1928- 45-48
Flammonde, Paris 17-20R
Flanagan, Dennis 1919- 128
Flanagan, Dorothy Belle
See Hughes, Dorothy B(elle)
Flanagan, John C(lemans) 1906- CANR-1
Earlier sketch in CA 1-4R
Flanagan, John T(heodore) 1906- 17-20R
Flanagan, Joseph David Stanislaus
1903- 13-16R
Flanagan, Mary 1943- 125
Flanagan, Mike 1950- 133
Flanagan, Neal M. 1920-1985 .... 17-20R
Obituary 117
Flanagan, Owen J. 1949- 125
Flanagan, Robert (James) 1941- 33-36R
Flanagan, Thomas (James Bonner) 1923- 108
See also CLC 25, 52
See also DLBY 80
See also MTCW
Flanagan, William G(eorge) 1940- CANR-15
Earlier sketch in CA 93-96
Flanagan, William G(eorge) 1942- 119
Flanagan, William I. 1916(?)-1986 Obituary 118
Flanders, Helen Hartness 1890-1972 .... CAP-1
Obituary 33-36R
Earlier sketch in CA 13-16
Flanders, Henry Jackson Jr. 1921- 33-36R
Flanders, James P(rescott) 1942- 69-72
Flanders, Jane (Hess) 1940- 110
Flanders, Michael (Henry) 1922-1975 .... CANR-4
Obituary 57-60
Earlier sketch in CA 5-8R
Flanders, Ned A. 1918- 37-40R
Flanders, Ralph Edward 1880-1970 .... CAP-1
Earlier sketch in CA 11-12
Flanders, Rebecca
See Ball, Donna
Flanders, Robert Bruce 1930- 17-20R
Flanery, E(dward) B(oyd) 1932- 61-64
Flanigan, James 1936- 134
Flanigan, Lloyd A(llen) 1933- 33-36R
Flanner, Hildegarde
See Monhoff, June Hildegarde Flanner
See also DLB 48
Flanner, Janet 1892-1978 .... CANR-13
Obituary 81-84
Earlier sketch in CA 65-68
See also DLB 4
Flannery, Edward H(ugh) 1912- 13-16R
Flannery, Harry W. 1900-1975 .... CAP-1
Obituary 57-60
Earlier sketch in CA 9-10
Flannery, James W(illiam) 1936- Brief entry 110
Flannery, Peter 1951- 104
Flannery, Sean
See Hagberg, David J(ames)
Flasch, Joy 1932- 37-40R
Flaster, Donald J(ohn) 1932- 115
Flath, Arnold W(illiam) J. 1929- 65-68
Flato, Charles 1908(?)-1984 Obituary 111
Flattau, Edward 1937- 65-68
Flaubert, Gustave 1821-1880 .... DLB 119
See also WLC
Flavell, Carol Willsey Bell 1939- 73-76
Flavell, John H(urley) 1928- CANR-11
Earlier sketch in CA 17-20R
Flavin, Martin 1883-1967 .... 5-8R
Obituary 25-28R
See also DLB 9
Flavius, Brother
See Ellison, James E.
Flaxman, Traudl 1942- 25-28R
Flayderman, Phillip C(harles) 1930-1969 .... CAP-2
Earlier sketch in CA 23-24
Fleck, Betty
See Paine, Lauran (Bosworth)
Fleck, Henrietta 1903- 77-80
Fleck, Richard Francis 1937- CANR-18
Earlier sketch in CA 102
Flecker, (Herman) James Elroy
1884-1915 Brief entry 109
See also DLB 10, 19
See also TCLC 43
Fleece, Jeffrey (Atkinson) 1920- 17-20R
Fleege, Urban H(erman) 1908- CANR-1
Earlier sketch in CA 45-48
Fleer, Jack D(avid) 1937- 25-28R
Fleeson, Doris 1901-1970 Obituary 93-96
See also DLB 29
Fleet, Michael 1941- 131
Fleetwood, Frances 1902- CANR-17
Earlier sketches in CA 45-48, CANR-1
Fleetwood, Frank
See Fleetwood, Frances
Fleetwood, Hugh (Nigel) 1944- Brief entry 112
Fleetwood-Hesketh, (Charles) Peter (Fleetwood)
1905-1985 Obituary 115
Flegg, (Henry) Graham 1924- 114
Fleischbein, Sister M. Catherine Frederic
1902- 5-8R
Fleischer, Cornell H(ugh) 1950- 128
Fleischer, Jane
See Oppenheim, Joanne
Fleischer, Leonore Brief entry 109
See also SATA 47
Fleischer, Manfred P(aul) 1928- 29-32R
Fleischer, Max 1889-1972 Obituary 109
See also SATA 30
Fleischer, Nathaniel S.
1888(?)-1972 Obituary 37-40R
Fleischhauer-Hardt, Helga 1936- 102
See also SATA 30
Fleischman, Harry 1914- CANR-3
Earlier sketch in CA 5-8R
Fleischman, Paul 1952- CANR-37
Earlier sketch in CA 113
See also CLR 20
See also MAICYA
See also SATA 32, 39
Fleischman, (Albert) Sid(ney) 1920- CANR-37
Earlier sketches in CA 1-4R, CANR-5
See also CLR 1, 15
See also MAICYA
See also SATA 8, 59
Fleischmann, Glen H(arvey) 1909- 33-36R
Fleischmann, Harriet 1904- CAP-2
Earlier sketch in CA 21-22
Fleischmann, Raoul H(erbert)
1885-1969 Obituary 115
Fleischmann, Wolfgang Bernard 1928- 116
Fleisher, Belton Mendel 1935- 69-72
Fleisher, Frederic 1933- 21-24R
Fleisher, Martin 1925- 45-48
Fleisher, Michael (Lawrence) 1942- 25-28R
Fleisher, Paul 1948- 137
Fleisher, Robbin 1951-1977 .... SATA 49, 52
Fleisher, Wilfried 1897(?)-1976 Obituary 65-68
Fleishman, Avrom (Hirsch) 1933- 21-24R
Fleishman, Edwin A(lan) 1927- CANR-11
Earlier sketch in CA 21-24R
Fleishman, Lazar 1944- 133
Fleishman, Seymour 1918- 133
Brief entry 111
See also SATA 32, 66
Fleisser, Marieluise
See Haindl, Marieluise
See also DLB 56
Flemer, William III 1922- 61-64
Fleming, Alice Mulcahey 1928- CANR-2
Earlier sketch in CA 1-4R
See also SATA 9
Fleming, Amalia 1912-1986 Obituary 118
Fleming, Berry 1899-1989 .... CANR-18
Obituary 129
Earlier sketches in CA 1-4R, CANR-2
Fleming, C(harlotte) M(ary) 1894- 5-8R
Fleming, D(enna) F(rank) 1893- CANR-1
Earlier sketch in CA 1-4R
Fleming, David A(rnold) 1939- 93-96
Fleming, Donald M(ethuen) 1905-1986 130
Obituary 121
Fleming, Elizabeth P. 1888-1985 Obituary 119
See also SATA 48
Fleming, George J(oseph) 1917- 37-40R
Fleming, George James
1904(?)-1990 Obituary 132
Fleming, Gerald 1921- 53-56
Fleming, Guy
See Masur, Harold Q.
Fleming, H(orace) K(ingston) 1901- 33-36R
Fleming, Harold (Lee) 1927- 17-20R
Fleming, Harold M(anchester) 1900- CAP-2
Earlier sketch in CA 21-22
Fleming, Ian (Lancaster) 1908-1964 .... 5-8R
See also CDBLB 1945-1960
See also CLC 3, 30
See also DLB 87
See also MTCW
See also SATA 9
Fleming, Irene 1923(?)-1979 Obituary 89-92
Fleming, Jennifer Baker 1943- 77-80
Fleming, Joan Margaret 1908-1980 81-84
Obituary 102
Fleming, John 1919- 129
Fleming, June 1935- 110
Fleming, Kate 1946- 137

Fleming, Lady Amalia
See Fleming, Amalia
Fleming, Laurence (William Howie) 1929- 107
Fleming, Macklin 1911- 77-80
Fleming, May Agnes 1840-1880 ...... DLB 99
Fleming, Miles 1919-1978 ......29-32R
Obituary 134
Fleming, Oliver
See MacDonald, Philip
Fleming, (Robert) Peter
1907-1971 Obituary 33-36R
Fleming, Ray(mond) 1945- 115
See also BW
Fleming, Reid
See Obrecht, Jas
Fleming, Robert H(enry)
1912-1984 Obituary 114
Fleming, Ronald Lee 1941- 108
See also SATA 56
Fleming, Sandford 1888- CAP-1
Earlier sketch in CA 9-10
Fleming, Stuart
See Knight, Damon (Francis)
Fleming, Susan 1932- CANR-14
Earlier sketch in CA 81-84
See also SATA 32
Fleming, Theodore B(owman) Jr. 1917- 45-48
Fleming, Thomas (James) 1927- CANR-10
Earlier sketch in CA 5-8R
See also CLC 37
See also SATA 8
Fleming, William (Coleman) 1909- 17-20R
Flemming, Nicholas Coit 1936- 97-100
Flemmons, Jerry 1936- 124
Flender, Harold 1924-1975 49-52
Obituary 135
Flesch, Janos Laszlo
1933(?)-1983 Obituary 111
Flesch, Rudolf (Franz) 1911-1986 ......CANR-3
Obituary 120
Earlier sketch in CA 9-12R
Flesch, Y.
See Flesch, Yolande (Catarina)
Flesch, Yolande (Catarina) 1950- 122
See also SATA 55
Flescher, Irwin 1926- 37-40R
Flescher, Joachim 1906(?)-1976 Obituary 65-68
Fletcher, Adele (Whitely) 1898- CAP-1
Earlier sketch in CA 17-18
Fletcher, Alan Mark 1928- 73-76
Fletcher, Angus (John Stewart) 1930- 104
Fletcher, Anthony John 1941- 73-76
Fletcher, Arnold Charles 1917- 17-20R
Fletcher, Banister F.
See Fletcher, Banister Flight
Fletcher, Banister Flight
1866-1953 Brief entry 123
Fletcher, Barbara (Helen) 1935- 110
Fletcher, Basil Alais 1900-1983 65-68
Obituary 109
Fletcher, Bramwell 1904(?)-1988 Obituary 125
Fletcher, Charlie May Hogue 1897- 9-12R
See also SATA 3
Fletcher, Colin 1922- CANR-11
Earlier sketch in CA 13-16R
See also AITN 1
See also SATA 28
Fletcher, David
See Barber, D(ulan) F(riar Whilberton)
Fletcher, Dirk
See Cunningham, Chet
Fletcher, Geoffrey Scowcroft 1923- 103
Fletcher, George U.
See Pratt, (Murray) Fletcher
Fletcher, Gordon A(lan) 1942- 127
Fletcher, Grace Nies 1895- 5-8R
Fletcher, H(arry) L(utf) V(erne)
1902-197 (?) CANR-4
Earlier sketch in CA 9-12R
Fletcher, Harold Roy 1907-1978 Obituary 111
Fletcher, Harris Francis 1892-1979 ......1-4R
Obituary 103
Fletcher, Harvey 1884-1981 Obituary 108
Fletcher, Helen Jill 1911- 9-12R
See also SATA 13
Fletcher, Henry Lancelot Aubrey
See Aubrey-Fletcher, Henry Lancelot
Fletcher, Ian 1920-1988 Obituary 127
Brief entry 124
Fletcher, (Minna) Inglis 5-8R
See also AITN 1
Fletcher, J(oseph) S(mith)
1863-1935 Brief entry 109
See also DLB 70
Fletcher, Jesse C. 1931- CANR-4
Earlier sketch in CA 9-12R
Fletcher, John C(aldwell) 1931- 124
Fletcher, John Gould
1886-1950 Brief entry 107
See also DLB 4, 45
See also TCLC 35
Fletcher, John (Walter James) 1937- CANR-15
Earlier sketch in CA 81-84
Fletcher, John 1579-1625 ...... CDBLB Before 1660
See also DLB 58
Fletcher, Joseph (Francis III)
1905-1991 ......CANR-11
Obituary 135
Earlier sketch in CA 21-24R
Fletcher, Leon 1921- CANR-33
Earlier sketch in CA 49-52
Fletcher, Lucille
See Wallop, Lucille Fletcher
Fletcher, Marilyn P(endleton) 1940- 106
Fletcher, Marjorie 1941- Brief entry 113
Fletcher, Mary ......AITN 1
Fletcher, (William) Miles (III) 1946- 114
Fletcher, Phineas 1582-1650 ...... DLB 121
Fletcher, Richard E. 1917(?)-1983 Obituary 109
See also SATA 34
Fletcher, Rick
See Fletcher, Richard E.
Fletcher, Robert H.
1885(?)-1972 Obituary 37-40R
Fletcher, Roger A(nthony) 1942- 121
Fletcher, Ronald 1921- CANR-13
Earlier sketch in CA 33-36R
Fletcher, Sir Banister
See Fletcher, Banister Flight
Fletcher, Susan (Clemens) 1951- 138
See also SATA 70
Fletcher, William C(atherwood) 1932- 21-24R
Fletcher, William W(higham) 1918- CANR-15
Earlier sketch in CA 81-84
Fletcher, Winston 1937- 118
Fletcher-Cooke, John 1911- 102
Fletcher the Younger, Giles
1585(?)-1623 ...... DLB 121
Flett, Una (Leonie) 1932- 137
Fleur, Anne 1901- ...... SATA 31
Fleur, Paul
See Pohl, Frederik
Fleure, H. J.
See Fleure, Herbert John
Fleure, Herbert John 1877-1969 Obituary 115
Fleuridas, Ellie Rae
See Sherman, Eleanor Rae
Fleury, Delphine
See Amatora, Sister Mary
Flew, Antony G(arrard) N(ewton)
1923- CANR-18
Earlier sketches in CA 5-8R, CANR-3
Flexner, Eleanor 1908- 45-48
Flexner, James Thomas 1908- CANR-37
Earlier sketches in CA 1-4R, CANR-2
See also SATA 9
Flexner, Stuart Berg 1928-1990 ......CANR-11
Obituary 133
Earlier sketch in CA 13-16R
Flick, Carlos Thomas 1927- 89-92
Fliegel, Frederick C(hristian) 1925- 49-52
Flieger, Wilhelm 1931- 25-28R
Flier, Michael S(tephen) 1941- CANR-32
Earlier sketches in CA 37-40R, CANR-14
Fliess, Peter J(oachim) 1915- 21-24R
Fligstein, Neil 1951- 135
Flinders, Neil J. 1934- 21-24R
Flink, James J(ohn) 1932- Brief entry 112
Flink, Salomon J. 1906-1983 ......CANR-17
Earlier sketch in CA 1-4R
Flinn, M(ichael) W(alter) 1917-1983 ......CANR-13
Obituary 110
Earlier sketch in CA 17-20R
Flint, Betty M. 1920- 21-24R
Flint, Cort R(ay) 1915- 49-52
Flint, E. de P.
See Fielden, T(homas) P(erceval)
Flint, F(rank) S(tuart) 1885-1960 Obituary 113
See also DLB 19
Flint, Helen 1952- 128
Flint, Homer Eon 1892-1924 Brief entry 114
Flint, Jeremy 1928(?)-1989 Obituary 130
Flint, Jerry 1931- 127
Flint, John E(dgar) 1930- 37-40R
Flint, Lucy
See Flint-Gohlke, Lucy
Flint, Timothy 1780-1840 ...... DLB 73
Flint-Gohlke, Lucy 1954- CANR-37
Flippo, Chet 1943- 89-92
Flippo, Edwin B(ly) 1925- CANR-13
Earlier sketch in CA 33-36R
Flitner, David P(erkins) Jr. 1949- CANR-1
Earlier sketch in CA 45-48
See also SATA 7
Floan, Howard R(ussell) 1918- 17-20R
Floethe, Louise Lee 1913- CANR-2
Earlier sketch in CA 1-4R
See also SATA 4
Floethe, Richard 1901- 33-36R
See also SATA 4
Floherty, John Joseph 1882-1964 ...... SATA 25
Flood, Charles Bracelen 1929- 41-44R
Flood, Curt(is Charles) 1938- Brief entry 115
Flood, E(dward) Thadeus 1932-1977 49-52
Obituary 133
Flood, John A(nthony) 1949- 129
Flood, John M(ichael) 1947- 127
Flood, Kenneth Urban 1925- 9-12R
Flood, Norman 1935- 134
Flood, Robert G. 1935- CANR-22
Earlier sketch in CA 106
Flooglebuckle, Al
See Spiegelman, Art
Flook, Maria 1952- 110
Flora, Fletcher 1914-1969 ......CANR-3
Earlier sketch in CA 1-4R
Flora, James (Royer) 1914- CANR-3
Earlier sketch in CA 5-8R
See also SAAS 6
See also SATA 1, 30
Flora, Joseph M(artin) 1934- CANR-21
Earlier sketches in CA 13-16R, CANR-5
Flora, Paul 1922- Brief entry 113
Floren, Lee 1910- CANR-18
Earlier sketches in CA 5-8R, CANR-3
Floren, Myron (Howard) 1919- 129
Florence, Philip Sargant
1890-1982 Obituary 106
Florence, Ronald 1942- CANR-15
Earlier sketch in CA 33-36R
Florentin, Eddy 1923- 49-52
Flores, Angel 1900- CANR-32
Earlier sketches in CA 103, CANR-19
See also HW
Flores, Dan Louie 1948- 121
Flores, Ivan 1923- CANR-22
Earlier sketches in CA 17-20R, CANR-7
Flores, Janis 1946- CANR-26
Earlier sketches in CA 65-68, CANR-10
Flores, John 1943- 77-80
Florescu, Radu R. 1925- 41-44R
Florez, Pablo de Azcarate y
See Azcarate y Florez, Pablo de
Florian, Douglas 1950- 123
See also SATA 19
Florian, Tibor 1908- 73-76
Florin, Lambert F. 1905- CANR-7
Earlier sketch in CA 17-20R
Florinsky, Michael T(imothy)
1894-1981 ......CANR-15
Obituary 105
Earlier sketch in CA 1-4R
Floriot, Rene 1902-1975 Obituary 61-64
Florit, Eugenio 1903- 104
Florit (y Sanchez de Fuentes), Eugenio
1903- CANR-32
See also HW
Florman, Samuel C(harles) 1925- 102
Florovsky, Georges (Vasilievich)
1893-1979 Obituary 111
Flory, Charles D(avid) 1902- 41-44R
Flory, Harry R. 1899-1976 Obituary 69-72
Flory, Jane Trescott 1917- CANR-3
Earlier sketch in CA 9-12R
See also SATA 22
Flory, Julia McCune 1882-1971 ...... CAP-2
Obituary 29-32R
Earlier sketch in CA 21-22
Flory, Paul J(ohn) 1910-1985 Obituary 117
Flory, Wendy Stallard 1943- 132
Floud, Roderick 1942- CANR-1
Earlier sketch in CA 45-48
Flournoy, Don Michael 1937- 126
Flower, Dean S. 1938- 21-24R
Flower, Desmond (John Newman) 1907- 9-12R
Flower, Elizabeth Farquhar 1914- 103
Flower, Harry A(lfred) 1901- CAP-1
Earlier sketch in CA 11-12
Flower, Joe
See Flower, Joseph Edward
Flower, (Harry) John 1936- 37-40R
Flower, Joseph Edward 1950- 130
Flower, Margaret Cameron Coss 61-64
Flower, Milton E(mbick) 1910- 129
Flower, (Walter) Newman
1879-1964 Obituary 109
Flower, Raymond (Charles) 1921- 108
Flowerdew, Phyllis 103
See also SATA 33
Flowers, Ann Moore 1923- 9-12R
Flowers, Betty S(ue) 1947- 65-68
Flowers, Charles E(ly Jr.) 1920- 93-96
Flowers, Charles V. Jr.
1926(?)-1990 Obituary 130
Flowers, Charles 1942- 29-32R
Flowers, John V(ictor) 1938- 106
Flowers, Paul Abbott 1905-1984 Obituary 112
Floyd, Barry Neil 1925- 33-36R
Floyd, Gareth 1940- ......SATA 31, 62
Floyd, Harriet 1925- 69-72
Floyd, Lois Gray 1910(?)-1978 85-88
Obituary 81-84
Floyd, Samuel A(lexander) Jr. 1937- CANR-39
Earlier sketch in CA 115
Floyd, Troy S(mith) 1920- 37-40R
Floyd, W(illiam) E(dward) G(regory)
1939- 33-36R
Floyd, William Anderson 1928- 29-32R
Fluchere, Henri (Auguste)
1898-1987 Obituary 123
Fluchere, Henri 1914- 77-80
See also SATA 40
Fluck, Diana 1931-1984 Obituary 113
Fluck, Reginald Alan Paul 1928- 9-12R
Flume, Violet S(igoloff) 116
Flumiani, Carlo M(aria) 1911- CANR-9
Earlier sketch in CA 13-16R
Fluno, Robert Y(ounger) 1916- 33-36R
Flusser, Martin 1947- 73-76
Flute, Molly
See Lottman, Eileen
Fly, Claude L(ee) 1905- 97-100
Flyat, Sten G(unnar) 1911- 9-12R
Flying Officer X
See Bates, H(erbert) E(rnest)
Flynn, Barbara 1928- ...... SATA 9
Flynn, Bernice (Lydia Carlson) 1922- 114
Flynn, Carol Houlihan 1945- 112
Flynn, Charles F(rederick) 1949- 57-60
Flynn, David H(oughton) 1953- 115
Flynn, Don
See Flynn, Donald R(obert)
Flynn, Donald R(obert) 1928- CANR-30
Earlier sketches in CA 29-32R, CANR-12
Flynn, Elizabeth Gurley
1890-1964 Obituary 111
Flynn, Fahey 1916-1983 Obituary 110
Flynn, George
See Paine, Lauran (Bosworth)
Flynn, George L. 1931- CANR-24
Earlier sketches in CA 65-68, CANR-9
Flynn, George Q(uitman) 1937- 25-28R
Flynn, Gerard (Cox) 1924- 41-44R
Flynn, Jackson
See Bensen, Donald R.
and Shirreffs, Gordon D(onald)
Flynn, James Joseph 1911- 21-24R
Flynn, James R. 1934- 21-24R
Flynn, John Joseph 1936- 17-20R
Flynn, John Thomas 1882-1964 Obituary 89-92
Flynn, Leslie Bruce 1918- CANR-37
Earlier sketches in CA 1-4R, CANR-2, 17
Flynn, Paul P(atrick) 1942- 37-40R
Flynn, Robert (Lopez) 1932- 29-32R
Flynt, Candace 1947- 102
Flynt, Larry ......AITN 2
Flynt, Wayne 1940- CANR-13
Earlier sketch in CA 37-40R
Flythe, Starkey S(harp) Jr. 1935- 69-72
Fm-2030 ......CANR-31
Fo, Dario 1926- 128
Brief entry 116
See also CLC 32
See also MTCW
Foat Tugay, Emine 1897- CAP-1
Earlier sketch in CA 13-14
Fobel, James M. 1946- 129
Fobel, Jim
See Fobel, James M.
Foda, Aun
See Foxe, Arthur N(orman)
Fodaski-Black, Martha 1929- 73-76
Fodden, Simon R. 1944- 131
Fodor, Eugene 1905-1991 ......CANR-14
Obituary 133
Earlier sketch in CA 21-24R
Fodor, M. W. 1890(?)-1977 Obituary 69-72
Fodor, Nandor 1895-1964 Obituary 112
Fodor, R(onald) V(ictor) 1944- CANR-15
Earlier sketch in CA 65-68
See also SATA 25
Foell, Earl W(illiam) 1929- 69-72
Foerster, Eberhard
See Weisenborn, Guenther
Foerster, Leona M(itchell) 1930- 89-92
Foerster, Lotte B(rand) 1910-1986 77-80
Obituary 119
Foerster, Norman 1887- 5-8R
Foff, Arthur R(aymond) 1925-1973 ...... CAP-2
Earlier sketch in CA 33-36
Fogarty, John J. 1931- 128
Fogarty, Jonathan Titulescu Esq.
See Farrell, James T(homas)
Fogarty, Michael P(atrick) 1916- CANR-9
Earlier sketch in CA 21-24R
Fogarty, Robert S(tephen) 1938- CANR-9
Earlier sketch in CA 65-68
Fogel, Daniel
See Kahn-Fogel, Daniel (Mark)
Fogel, Daniel (Mark) Kahn
See Kahn-Fogel, Daniel (Mark)
Fogel, Ephim G(regory) 1920- 120
Fogel, Robert W(illiam) 1926- CANR-13
Earlier sketch in CA 77-80
Fogel, Ruby 17-20R
Fogelquist, Donald Frederick 1906- 69-72
Fogelson, Robert M(ichael) 1937- 81-84
Fogg, Sam R. 1917(?)-1987 Obituary 123
Fogle, Bruce 1944- 106
Fogle, French R(owe) 1912- 37-40R
Fogle, James 1936- 134
Fogle, Richard Harter 1911- CANR-5
Earlier sketch in CA 5-8R
Foglio, Frank 1921- 57-60
Foiles, Keith Andrew 1926-1983 Obituary 109
Foin, Theodore C(hin) 1940- 93-96
Foisie, Jack 1919- 104
Fokkema, D(ouwe) W(essel) 1931- CANR-23
Earlier sketches in CA 17-20R, CANR-7
Fol, Alexander 1933- Brief entry 111
Foladare, Joseph 1909- 102
Folb, Edith A(rlene) 1938- 102
Folch-Ribas, Jacques 1928- 69-72
Folda, Jaroslav (Thayer III) 1940- 127
Foldessy, Edward P(atrick) 1941- 126
Folds, Thomas M. 93-96
Folejewski, Zbigniew 1910- CANR-7
Earlier sketch in CA 17-20R
Foley, Allen Richard 1898-1978 45-48
Obituary 77-80
Foley, (Anna) Bernice Williams 1902- CANR-12
Earlier sketch in CA 29-32R
See also SATA 28
Foley, Charles 1908- CAP-1
Earlier sketch in CA 13-16
Foley, Daniel J(oseph) 1913- CANR-5
Earlier sketch in CA 5-8R
Foley, Doug 1942- 57-60
Foley, Duncan K(arl) 1942- 93-96
Foley, Gerald (Patrick) 1936- CANR-11
Earlier sketch in CA 69-72
Foley, Helen
See Fowler, Helen Rosa Huxley
Foley, (Cedric) John 1917-1974 ......CANR-4
Obituary 53-56
Earlier sketch in CA 9-12R
Foley, John Miles 1947- 111
Foley, June 1944- 109
See also SATA 44
Foley, Leonard 1913- 89-92
Foley, (Mary) Louise Munro 1933- 37-40R
See also SATA 40, 54
Foley, Martha 1897(?)-1977 117
Obituary 73-76
Foley, Mary Mix 1918- 102
Foley, Michael F(rancis)
1940-1984 Obituary 113
Foley, Paul 1914-1983 Obituary 111
Foley, Rae
See Denniston, Elinore
Foley, Richard N. 1910(?)-1980 Obituary 102
Foley, Richard 1947- 126
Foley, Scott
See Dareff, Hal
Foley, Vincent D. 1933- 57-60
Foley, William E. 1938- 33-36R
Foley, Winifred 1914- 102

Folk, Jerry 114
Folkard, Charles James
1878-1963 Obituary 109
See also SATA 28
Folke, Will
See Bloch, Robert (Albert)
Folkenflik, Robert 1939- Brief entry 111
Folkers, George Fulton 1929- 49-52
Folkerts, George W(illiam) 1938- 53-56
Folkman, Jerome (Daniel) 1907- CAP-2
Earlier sketch in CA 29-32
Follain, Jean (Rene) 1903-1971 130
Folland, H(arold) F(reeze) 1906- 49-52
Follen, Eliza Lee (Cabot) 1787-1860 .... DLB 1
Follett, Helen Thomas
1884(?)-1970 Obituary 107
See also SATA 27
Follett, James 1939- 134
Brief entry 112
Follett, Ken(neth Martin) 1949- CANR-33
Earlier sketches in CA 81-84, CANR-13
See also AAYA 6
See also BEST 89:4
See also CLC 18
See also DLB 87
See also DLBY 81
See also MTCW
Follett, Robert J(ohn) R(ichard) 1928- CANR-23
Earlier sketches in CA 21-24R, CANR-8
Folley, Terence T. 1931- 21-24R
Folley, Vern L(eRoy) 1936- 49-52
Folliard, Edward T(homas)
1899-1976 Obituary 69-72
Follis, Anne Bowen 1947- 106
Follmann, J(oseph) F(rancis) Jr.
1908-1989 ....CANR-7
Obituary 128
Earlier sketch in CA 17-20R
Folmar, J. Kent
See Folmar, John Kent
Folmar, John Kent 1932- 116
Folmsbee, Stanley J(ohn) 1899-1974 .... CAP-2
Earlier sketch in CA 29-32
Folsom, Anne (Ferril) 1922- Brief entry 114
Folsom, Burton W(hitmore) Jr. 1947- 118
Folsom, Franklin (Brewster) 1907- CANR-2
Earlier sketch in CA 1-4R
See also SATA 5
Folsom, Jack
See Folsom, John B(entley)
Folsom, John B(entley) 1931- 45-48
Folsom, Kenneth E(verett) 1921- 21-24R
Folsom, Marion Bayard 1893- CAP-2
Earlier sketch in CA 17-18
Folsom, Marvin Hugh 1929- 57-60
Folsom, Michael (Brewster) 1938- 112
See also SATA 40
Folsom, Robert S(lade) 1915- 77-80
Folster, David 1937- 134
Folta, Jeannette R. 1934- 25-28R
Foltin, Lore Barbara 1913- CAP-2
Earlier sketch in CA 25-28
Foltz, William J(ay) 1936- 9-12R
Fombona, Rufino Blanco
See Blanco Fombona, Rufino
Fomin
See Golomstock, Igor (Naumovitch)
Fomon, Samuel J(oseph) 1923- 53-56
Fonarow, Jerry 1935- CANR-4
Earlier sketch in CA 53-56
Fonda, Henry (Jaynes) 1905-1982 Obituary 107
Fonda, Jane (Seymour) 1937- 138
Fonda, Peter 1939(?)- Brief entry 112
Fon Eisen, Anthony T. 1917- 13-16R
Foner, Eric 1943- CANR-12
Earlier sketch in CA 29-32R
Foner, Jack D(onald) 1910- 77-80
Foner, Nancy 1945- 53-56
Foner, Philip (Sheldon) 1910- CANR-3
Earlier sketch in CA 9-12R
Fong, Leo 1928- 127
Fong, Wen Chih 1930- 103
Fong-Torres, Ben 1945- 93-96
Fonseca, Aloysius Joseph 1915- CANR-9
Earlier sketch in CA 13-16R
Fonseca, John R. 1925- CANR-8
Earlier sketch in CA 17-20R
Fonstad, Karen Wynn 1945- 104
Fontaine, Andre (Lucien Georges)
1921- CANR-12
Earlier sketch in CA 25-28R
Fontaine, Andre 1910- 65-68
Fontaine, Joan 1917- 81-84
Fontana, Bernard L(ee) 1931- CANR-7
Earlier sketch in CA 17-20R
Fontana, Biancamaria 1952- 124
Fontana, Thomas M(ichael) 1951- 130
Brief entry 113
Fontana, Vincent James 1923- 13-16R
Fontanet, Joseph 1921-1980 Obituary 105
Fontcreuse, Marquis de
See Jaeger, Cyril Karel Stuart
Fontenay, Charles L(ouis) 1917- 25-28R
Fontenelle, Don H(arris) 1946- 106
Fontenot, Chester J. 1950- 112
Fontenot, Mary Alice 1910- CANR-31
Earlier sketches in CA 37-40R, CANR-14
See also SATA 34
Fontenrose, Joseph 1903- 5-8R
Fontes, Montserrat 1940- 136
Fonteyn, Margot
See Fonteyn de Arias, Margot
Fonteyn de Arias, Margot 1919-1991 117
Obituary 133
Brief entry 110
Fonzi, Bruno 1913(?)-1976 Obituary 65-68
Foon, Dennis 1951- CANR-28
Earlier sketch in CA 111
Fooner, Michael 81-84
See also SATA 22
Foord, Archibald Smith 1914-1969 .... CAP-1
Earlier sketch in CA 11-12
Foosaner, Samuel J.
1907(?)-1988 Obituary 125
Foot, David 1929- 136
Foot, Hugh Mackintosh 1907- 9-12R
Foot, M(ichael) R(ichard) D(aniell)
1919- CANR-3
Earlier sketch in CA 5-8R
Foot, Michael 1913- 108
Foot, Paul Mackintosh 1937- 17-20R
Foot, Philippa Ruth 1920- 101
Foote, A(von) Edward 1937- CANR-13
Earlier sketch in CA 73-76
Foote, Arthur 1911- 114
Foote, Darby Mozelle 1942- 61-64
Foote, Dorothy Norris (McBride) 1908- CAP-2
Earlier sketch in CA 21-22
Foote, Geoffrey 1950- 123
Foote, Horton 1916- CANR-34
Earlier sketch in CA 73-76
See also CLC 51
See also DLB 26
Foote, Samuel 1721-1777 .... DLB 89
Foote, Shelby 1916- CANR-3
Earlier sketch in CA 5-8R
See also DLB 2, 17
Foote, Timothy (Gilson) 1926- 93-96
See also SATA 52
Foote, Victoria 1954- 118
Foote, Wilder 1905-1975 Obituary 57-60
Foote-Smith, Elizabeth 1913- 69-72
Footitt, Hilary 1948- 132
Footman, David (John) 1895-1983 97-100
Obituary 111
Footman, Robert 1916- 126
Footner, (William) Hulbert
1879-1944 Brief entry 114
Foran, Donald J. 1943- 33-36R
Forberg, Ati
See Forberg, Beate Gropius
See also SATA 22
Forberg, Beate Gropius 1925- 105
See also Forberg, Ati
Forbes, Bryan 1926- 69-72
See also SATA 37
Forbes, Cabot L.
See Hoyt, Edwin P(almer) Jr.
Forbes, Calvin 1945- CANR-26
Earlier sketch in CA 49-52
See also CAAS 16
See also BW
See also DLB 41
Forbes, Clarence A(llen) 1901- 77-80
Forbes, Colin
See Sawkins, Raymond H(arold)
Forbes, Daniel
See Kenyon, Michael
Forbes, DeLoris (Florine) Stanton
1923- CANR-5
Earlier sketch in CA 9-12R
Forbes, Donald (Galen)
1918-1987 Obituary 122
Forbes, Elliot 1917- 9-12R
Forbes, Eric Gray 1933-1984 ....CANR-10
Obituary 114
Earlier sketch in CA 65-68
Forbes, Esther 1891-1967 .... CAP-1
Obituary 25-28R
Earlier sketch in CA 13-14
See also CLC 12
See also CLR 27
See also DLB 22
See also MAICYA
See also SATA 2
Forbes, Graham B. CANR-27
Earlier sketches in CAP-2, CA 19-20
See also SATA 1
Forbes, Henry W(illiam) 1918- 1-4R
Forbes, J(ohn) V(an) G(elder) 1916- 9-12R
Forbes, Jack D. 1934- CANR-4
Earlier sketch in CA 1-4R
Forbes, Joanne R. (Triebel) 1930- 37-40R
Forbes, John Douglas 1910- 53-56
Forbes, Kathryn
See McLean, Kathryn (Anderson)
Forbes, Malcolm S(tevenson)
1919-1990 ....CANR-28
Obituary 131
Earlier sketch in CA 69-72
Forbes, Murray (M.) 1906-1987 Obituary 121
Forbes, (Christopher) Patrick 1925- 25-28R
Forbes, Rosita
See McGrath, Joan Rosita (Torr)
Forbes, Stanton
See Forbes, DeLoris (Florine) Stanton
Forbes, Thomas Rogers 1911- 41-44R
Forbes-Boyd, Eric 1897-1979 ....13-16R
Obituary 125
Forbes-Dennis, Phyllis
1884-1963 Obituary 93-96
Forbes-Robertson, Diana
See Sheean, Diana
Forbis, Judith 1934- 101
Forbis, William H. 1918- CANR-15
Earlier sketch in CA 37-40R
Forbus, Ina B(ell) 1935- 1-4R
Forcade, Robert J. 1935- 125
Force, Peter 1790-1868 .... DLB 30
Force, Roland W(ynfield) 1924- 41-44R
Force, William M. 1916- 21-24R
Forcey, Charles B(udd) 1925- CANR-1
Earlier sketch in CA 1-4R
Forche, Carolyn (Louise) 1950- 117
Brief entry 109
See also CLC 25
See also DLB 5
Forchheimer, Paul 1913- 53-56
Forcione, Alban Keith 1938- CANR-13
Earlier sketch in CA 33-36R
Ford, A(lec) G(eorge) 1926- 5-8R
Ford, Adam 1940- 111
Ford, Agnes Gibbs 1902- CAP-2
Earlier sketch in CA 21-22
Ford, Albert Lee
See Stratemeyer, Edward L.
Ford, Alice 1906- CAP-1
Earlier sketch in CA 19-20
Ford, Amasa B. 1922- 21-24R
Ford, Arthur A. 1897-1971 Obituary 112
Ford, Arthur L(ewis) 1937- 57-60
Ford, Barbara 134
Brief entry 112
See also SATA 34, 56
Ford, Betty
See Ford, Elizabeth Anne Bloomer
Ford, Boris 1917- 112
Ford, Brian J(ohn) 1939- CANR-34
Earlier sketches in CA 41-44R, CANR-15
See also SATA 49
Ford, Cathy Diane 1952- 105
Ford, Charles Henri 1913- CANR-13
Earlier sketch in CA 25-28R
See also DLB 4, 48
Ford, Colin John 1934- 85-88
Ford, Collier
See Ford, James L(awrence) C(ollier)
Ford, Corey 1902-1969 Obituary 25-28R
See also DLB 11
Ford, D(ouglas) W(illiam) Cleverley
See Cleverley Ford, D(ouglas) W(illiam)
Ford, Daniel (Francis) 1931- CANR-11
Earlier sketch in CA 17-20R
Ford, David
See Harknett, Terry
Ford, Donald (Frank William) 1924- 5-8R
Ford, Donald H(erbert) 1926- 41-44R
Ford, Edmund Brisco 1901-1988 85-88
Obituary 124
Ford, Edsel 1928-1970 .... CAP-1
Obituary 29-32R
Earlier sketch in CA 13-16
Ford, Edward (Charles) 1928- 89-92
Ford, Eileen (Otte) 1922- 120
Ford, Elaine 1938- CANR-19
Earlier sketch in CA 102
Ford, Elbur
See Hibbert, Eleanor Burford
Ford, Elizabeth
See Bidwell, Marjory Elizabeth Sarah
Ford, Elizabeth Anne Bloomer 1918- CANR-23
Earlier sketch in CA 105
Ford, Florence
See Novelli, Florence
Ford, Ford Madox 1873-1939 132
Brief entry 104
See also CDBLB 1914-1945
See also DLB 34, 98
See also MTCW
See also TCLC 1, 15, 39
Ford, Frank B(ernard) 1932- 85-88
Ford, Franklin L(ewis) 1920- 17-20R
Ford, Fred
See Doerffler, Alfred
Ford, George Barry 1885-1978 Obituary 81-84
Ford, George D. 1880(?)-1974 Obituary 53-56
Ford, George H(arry) 1914- CANR-2
Earlier sketch in CA 1-4R
Ford, George (Jr.) 107
See also SATA 31
Ford, George L(onnie) 1914- 5-8R
Ford, Gerald R(udolph Jr.) 1913- 114
Brief entry 110
Ford, Gordon B(uell) Jr. 1937- CANR-13
Earlier sketch in CA 21-24R
Ford, Guy B(arrett) 1922- 5-8R
Ford, Harvey Seabury
1905(?)-1978 Obituary 73-76
Ford, Henry II 1917-1987 Obituary 123
Brief entry 111
Ford, Henry 1863-1947 Brief entry 115
Ford, Herbert Paul 1927- 17-20R
Ford, Hilary
See Youd, (Christopher) Samuel
Ford, Hilary
See Youd, (Christopher) Samuel
Ford, Hildegarde
See Morrison, Velma Ford
Ford, Hugh D. 1925- Brief entry 114
Ford, J. Massingberd
See Ford, Josephine Massyngbaerde
Ford, James Allan 1920- CAP-1
Earlier sketch in CA 9-10
Ford, James L(awrence) C(ollier) 1907- 29-32R
Ford, Jesse Hill (Jr.) 1928- CANR-1
Earlier sketch in CA 1-4R
See also DLB 6
Ford, John 1586- .... CDBLB Before 1660
See also DLB 58
Ford, John 1895-1973 Obituary 45-48
See also CLC 16
Ford, Josephine Massyngbaerde 41-44R
Ford, Kathleen 1932- 25-28R
Ford, Kirk
See Spence, William John Duncan
Ford, Lee 1936- 25-28R
Ford, Leighton F. S. 1931- 17-20R
Ford, LeRoy 1922- 9-12R
Ford, Leslie
See Brown, Zenith Jones
Ford, Lewis
See Patten, Lewis B(yford)
Ford, Lewis S. 1933- 137
Ford, Marcia
See Radford, Ruby L(orraine)
Ford, Marcus Peter 1950- 108
Ford, Margaret Patricia 1925- 9-12R
Ford, Mary Forker 1905- 9-12R
Ford, Murray J(ohn) S(tanley) 1923- 93-96
Ford, Nancy K(effer) 1906-1961 Obituary 109
See also SATA 29
Ford, Nick Aaron 1904-1982 ....CANR-11
Earlier sketch in CA 25-28R
See also BW
Ford, Norman D(ennis) 1921- CANR-10
Earlier sketch in CA 21-24R
Ford, Norrey
See Dilcock, Noreen
Ford, Patrick 1914- 21-24R
Ford, Paul F(rancis X.) 1947- CANR-22
Earlier sketch in CA 105
Ford, Percy 1894-1983 Obituary 110
Ford, Peter 1936- 126
See also SATA 59
Ford, Philip J(ohn) 1949- 115
Ford, Phyllis M(arjorie) 1928- CANR-30
Earlier sketches in CA 33-36R, CANR-13
Ford, R(obert) A(rthur) D(ouglass)
1915- CANR-19
Earlier sketch in CA 97-100
See also DLB 88
Ford, R(ichard) Clyde
1870-1951 Brief entry 121
Ford, Richard Brice 1935- 37-40R
Ford, Richard 1944- CANR-11
Earlier sketch in CA 69-72
See also CLC 46
Ford, Robert E. 1913-1975 .... CAP-2
Earlier sketch in CA 29-32
Ford, Robert N(icholas) 1909- 33-36R
Ford, Stephen 1949- 77-80
Ford, Thomas R(obert) 1923- 49-52
Ford, Thomas W(ellborn) 1924- 21-24R
Ford, W(illiam) Clay(ton Jr.) 1946- 93-96
Ford, W(illiam) Herschel 1900- CANR-5
Earlier sketch in CA 9-12R
Ford, Webster
See Masters, Edgar Lee
Ford, Whitey
See Ford, Edward (Charles)
Ford, Worthington C. 1858-1941 .... DLB 47
Forde, Gerhard O(laf) 1927- 89-92
Forde-Johnston, James (Leo) 1927- CANR-3
Earlier sketch in CA 9-12R
Fordham, Frieda 1903-1988 Obituary 124
Fordham, Peta 1905- 106
Fordin, Hugh 1935- 57-60
Fordyce, Rachel (Poole) 1942- 121
Brief entry 118
Fore, William Frank 1928- 5-8R
Forell, George W(olfgang) 1919- CANR-16
Earlier sketches in CA 1-4R, CANR-1
Foreman, Carl 1914-1984 ....41-44R
Obituary 113
See also DLB 26
Foreman, Clark H(owell)
1902-1977 Obituary 69-72
Foreman, Gene 1934- 77-80
Foreman, Harry 1915- 33-36R
Foreman, Kenneth Joseph 1891- CAP-2
Earlier sketch in CA 33-36
Foreman, L(eonard) L(ondon) 1901- CANR-5
Earlier sketch in CA 5-8R
Foreman, Lawton Durant 1913- 9-12R
Foreman, Michael 1938- CANR-38
Earlier sketches in CA 21-24R, CANR-10
See also MAICYA
See also SATA 2
Foreman, Richard 1937- CANR-32
Earlier sketch in CA 65-68
See also CLC 50
Foreman, Russell 1921- 77-80
Forer, Lois G(oldstein) 1914- 29-32R
Forer, Lucille K(remith) 37-40R
Forer, Mort 1922- 97-100
Fores, John 1914- 25-28R
Forest, Antonia 103
See also SATA 29
Forest, Dial
See Gault, William Campbell
Forest, Ilse 1896- CAP-2
Earlier sketch in CA 19-20
Forest, James H. 1941- 136
Forest, Jim
See Forest, James H.
Forest, Lee
See Woods, Clee
Forester, Bruce (Michael) 1939- CANR-25
Earlier sketch in CA 107
Forester, C(ecil) S(cott) 1899-1966 73-76
Obituary 25-28R
See also CLC 35
See also SATA 13
Forester, Frank
See Herbert, Henry William
Forester, Tom 1949- 127
Foreyt, John P(aul) 1943- 118
Forez
See Mauriac, Francois (Charles)
Forgie, George B(arnard) 1941- 89-92
Forgus, Ronald (Henry) 1928- 41-44R
Forio, Robert
See Weiss, Irving J.
Forisha, Barbara L.
See Forisha-Kovach, Barbara L(usk)
Forisha-Kovach, Barbara L(usk) 1941- 107
Forker, Charles R(ush) 1927- 136

Forkosch, Morris D(avid) 1908- ... 41-44R
Form, William H. 1917- ... 65-68
Forma, Warren 1923- ... 45-48
Forman, Brenda 1936- ... CANR-6
Earlier sketch in CA 9-12R
See also SATA 4
Forman, Celia Adler
1890(?)-1979 Obituary ... 85-88
Forman, Charles William 1916- ... 13-16R
Forman, Harrison 1904-1978 ... 5-8R
Obituary ... 77-80
Forman, Henry James 1879-1966 ... 5-8R
Forman, James Douglas 1932- ... CANR-19
Earlier sketches in CA 9-12R, CANR-4
See also CLC 21
See also MAICYA
See also SATA 8, 70
Forman, Joan ... 102
Forman, Jonathan 1887-1974 ... CAP-2
Earlier sketch in CA 23-24
Forman, Leona S. 1940- ... 25-28R
Forman, Marc A(llan) 1935- ... 57-60
Forman, Max Leon 1909- ... 112
Forman, Milos 1932- ... 109
Forman, Robert E(dgar) 1924- ... 9-12R
Forman, Shepard (Lewis) 1938- Brief entry ... 112
Forman, (James Adam) Sholto 1915- ... 25-28R
Formby, William A(rthur) 1943- ... 109
Formento, Dan 1954- ... 112
Formhals, Robert W(illard) Y(ates) S(arguszko)
1919- ... 53-56
Formisano, Ronald P. 1939- Brief entry ... 115
Formwalt, Lee W(illiam) 1949- ... 119
Fornara, Charles William 1935- ... 130
Fornari, Franco 1921- ... CANR-12
Earlier sketch in CA 29-32R
Fornari, Harry D(avid) 1919- ... 69-72
Fornell, Earl Wesley 1915-1969 ... 1-4R
Obituary ... 103
Fornes, Maria Irene 1930- ... CANR-28
Earlier sketch in CA 25-28R
See also CLC 39, 61
See also DLB 7
See also HW
See also MTCW
Forno, Lawrence J(oseph) 1943- ... 37-40R
Forrest, A(lfred) C(linton) 1916-1978 ... CANR-27
Obituary ... 103
Earlier sketch in CA 49-52
Forrest, Anthony
See MacKenzie, Norman (Ian)
Forrest, Caleb
See Telfer, Dariel (Doris)
Forrest, David
See Forrest-Webb, Robert
Forrest, Derek W(illiam) 1926- ... 77-80
Forrest, Earle Robert 1883-1969 ... 1-4R
Obituary ... 103
Forrest, Felix C.
See Linebarger, Paul M(yron) A(nthony)
Forrest, Gary Gran 1943- ... CANR-32
Earlier sketch in CA 113
Forrest, James Taylor 1921- ... 115
Forrest, John Galbraith
1898-1982 Obituary ... 107
Forrest, Julian
See Wagenknecht, Edward (Charles)
Forrest, Julie de
See DeWitt, Edith Openshaw
Forrest, Katherine V(irginia) 1939- ... 131
Forrest, Leon 1937- ... CANR-25
Earlier sketch in CA 89-92
See also CAAS 7
See also BW
See also CLC 4
See also DLB 33
Forrest, Norman
See Morland, Nigel
Forrest, Richard (Stockton) 1932- ... CANR-25
Earlier sketches in CA 57-60, CANR-9
Forrest, Sybil
See Markun, Patricia Maloney
Forrest, W(illiam) G(eorge) 1925- ... 25-28R
Forrest, Wilbur S. 1887-1977 Obituary ... 69-72
Forrestal, Dan J(oseph) Jr. 1912- ... 77-80
Forrester, Duncan B(aillie) 1933- ... 131
Forrester, Frank H. 1919(?)-1986 Obituary ... 119
See also SATA 52
Forrester, Helen
See Bhatia, Jamunadevi
See also SATA 48
Forrester, Jay W(right) 1918- ... CANR-1
Earlier sketch in CA 45-48
Forrester, Larry 1924- ... 25-28R
Forrester, Leland S.
1905(?)-1978 Obituary ... 81-84
Forrester, Leo
See Lee, Edward Edson
Forrester, Marian
See Schachtel, Roger (Bernard)
Forrester, Martyn (John) 1952- ... 129
Forrester, Mary
See Humphries, Mary
Forrester, (William) Ray 1911- ... 21-24R
Forrester, Rex Desmond 1928- ... 103
Forrester, Victoria 1940- ... CANR-25
Earlier sketch in CA 108
See also SATA 35, 40
Forrest-Webb, Robert 1929- ... CANR-4
Earlier sketch in CA 49-52
Forsberg, (Charles) Gerald 1912- ... 102
Forsberg, Malcolm I. 1908- ... 21-24R
Forsberg, Roberta Jean 1914- Brief entry ... 105
Forsee, (Frances) Aylesa ... CANR-1
Earlier sketch in CA 1-4R
See also SATA 1
Forsey, Chris 1950- ... SATA 59
Forshay-Lunsford, Cin 1965- ... 119
See also SATA 60
Forssmann, Werner Theodor Otto
1904-1979 Obituary ... 111
Forster, Arnold 1912- ... 13-16R
Forster, E(dward) M(organ) 1879-1970 ... CAP-1
Obituary ... 25-28R
Earlier sketch in CA 13-14
See also AAYA 2
See also CDBLB 1914-1945
See also CLC 1, 2, 3, 4, 9, 10, 13, 15, 22, 45
See also DLB 34, 98
See also MTCW
See also SATA 57
See also WLC
Forster, Georg 1754-1794 ... DLB 94
Forster, Kent 1916-1981 ... 21-24R
Obituary ... 125
Forster, Klaus 1945- ... 131
Forster, Marc R. 1959- ... 138
Forster, Margaret 1938- ... 133
Forster, Mark Arnold
See Arnold-Forster, Mark
Forster, Merlin H(enry) 1928- ... 41-44R
Forster, Peter 1926(?)-1982 Obituary ... 107
Forster, Robert 1926- ... 41-44R
Forstman, H(enry) Jackson 1929- ... 13-16R
Forsyth, Bill 1948- ... 122
Forsyth, David J(ames) C(ameron)
1940- ... 41-44R
Forsyth, David P(ond) 1930- ... 9-12R
Forsyth, Frederick 1938- ... CANR-38
Earlier sketch in CA 85-88
See also BEST 89:4
See also CLC 2, 5, 36
See also DLB 87
See also MTCW
Forsyth, George H(oward) Jr.
1901-1991 ... 37-40R
Obituary ... 133
Forsyth, Ilene (Haering) 1928- ... 37-40R
Forsyth, James (Law) 1913- ... 73-76
Forsyth, Michael (de Jong) 1951- ... 133
Forsyth (Outram), Anne 1933- ... CANR-29
Earlier sketches in CA 29-32R, CANR-12
Forsyth, Richard S(andes) 1948- ... 116
Forsythe, Elizabeth 1927- ... 93-96
Forsythe, Irene
See Hanson, Irene (Forsythe)
Forsythe, Robert
See Crichton, Kyle Samuel
Forsythe, Sidney A. 1920- ... 41-44R
Fort, John 1942- ... 77-80
Fort, Paul
See Stockton, Francis Richard
Fort, Paul 1872-1960 Obituary ... 114
Fort, Williams Edwards Jr. 1905- ... 37-40R
Fortas, Abe 1910-1982 Obituary ... 106
Forte, Allen 1926- ... 41-44R
Forte, Dan 1935- ... 65-68
Forte, David F. 1941- ... 53-56
Fortebraccia, Donato
See Forte, Dan
Forten, Charlotte
See Grimke, Charlotte L(ottie) Forten
Forten, Charlotte L.
See Grimke, Charlotte L(ottie) Forten
See also BLC 2
See also DLB 50
See also TCLC 16
Fortes, Meyer 1906-1983 ... 129
Obituary ... 109
Fortescue, William (Archer Irvine) 1945- ... 122
Fortman, Edmund J. 1901-1990 ... CANR-28
Obituary ... 130
Earlier sketches in CA 21-24R, CANR-11
Fortnum, Peggy
See Nuttall-Smith, Margaret Emily Noel
See also SATA 26
Fortune, T(imothy) Thomas
1856-1928 Brief entry ... 112
See also DLB 23
Forty, Adrian 1948- ... 123
Forty, George 1927- ... CANR-34
Earlier sketches in CA 89-92, CANR-15
Forward, Luke
See Patrick, Johnstone G(illespie)
Forward, Robert L(ull) 1932- ... CANR-20
Earlier sketch in CA 103
Forward, Susan ... 130
See also BEST 90:1
Forzano, Giovacchino 1884-1970 Obituary ... 104
Fosburgh, Hugh (Whitney)
1916-1976 Obituary ... 69-72
Fosburgh, Lacey 1942- ... CANR-22
Earlier sketch in CA 85-88
Fosburgh, Liza 1930- ... CANR-30
Earlier sketch in CA 112
Fosburgh, Pieter Whitney
1914(?)-1978 Obituary ... 77-80
Foscue, Edwin Jay 1899-1972 ... 1-4R
Obituary ... 103
Fosdick, Charles Austin
1842-1915 Brief entry ... 119
See also DLB 42
Fosdick, Harry Emerson
1878-1969 Obituary ... 25-28R
Fosdick, Raymond B(laine)
1883-1972 Obituary ... 37-40R
Foshay, Toby (Avard) 1950- ... 119
Foshee, John (Hugh) 1931- ... 69-72
Foskett, D(ouglas) J(ohn) 1918- ... CANR-5
Earlier sketch in CA 1-4R
Foskett, Daphne 1911- ... 102
Foskett, Reginald 1909-1973 ... CAP-2
Earlier sketch in CA 21-22
Foss, Christopher F(rank) 1946- ... 93-96
Foss, Clive (Frank Wilson) 1939- ... 132
Foss, Dennis C(arleton) 1947- ... 104
Foss, Phillip Oliver ... 13-16R
Foss, William O(tto) 1918- ... 17-20R
Fosse, Alfred
See Jelly, George Oliver
Fosse, Bob
See Fosse, Robert Louis
See also CLC 20
Fosse, Robert Louis 1927-1987 Obituary ... 123
Brief entry ... 110
See also Fosse, Bob
Fossedal, Gregory
See Fossedal, Gregory A.
Fossedal, Gregory A. 1959- ... 125
Fossey, Dian 1932-1985 ... CANR-34
Obituary ... 118
Earlier sketch in CA 113
See also MTCW
Fossum, Robert H. 1923- ... 25-28R
Foster, Alan Dean 1946- ... CANR-22
Earlier sketches in CA 53-56, CANR-5
See also SATA 70
Foster, Brad W. 1955- ... SATA 34
Foster, Brian 1920- Brief entry ... 112
Foster, Carno A(ugustus) 1916- ... 41-44R
Foster, Catharine Osgood 1907- ... 65-68
Foster, Cedric 1900-1975 Obituary ... 89-92
Foster, Charles Howell 1913- ... 17-20R
Foster, Charles I(rving) 1898-197 (?) ... 1-4R
Obituary ... 134
Foster, Charles R(obert) 1927- ... 110
Foster, Charles William 1939- ... 57-60
Foster, Daniel W(illet) 1930- ... 108
Foster, David Manning 1944- ... CANR-39
Earlier sketches in CA 97-100, CANR-18
Foster, David William (Anthony)
1940- ... CANR-22
Earlier sketches in CA 21-24R, CANR-8
Foster, David 1908- ... 97-100
Foster, Don(ald) 1948- ... 33-36R
Foster, Donald (LeRoy) 1928- ... 53-56
Foster, Donald W. 1950- ... 132
Foster, Doris Van Liew 1899- ... 102
See also SATA 10
Foster, Dorothy 1936- ... 93-96
Foster, E(lizabeth) C(onnell) 1902- ... 53-56
See also SATA 9
Foster, Earl M(asters) 1940- ... 57-60
Foster, Edward Halsey 1942- ... CANR-18
Earlier sketches in CA 49-52, CANR-2
Foster, Elizabeth Read 1912- ... 106
Foster, Elizabeth 1902- ... 85-88
See also SATA 12
Foster, Elizabeth 1905-1963 ... 1-4R
See also SATA 10
Foster, F. Blanche 1919- ... 61-64
See also SATA 11
Foster, Frances Smith 1944- ... 135
Foster, (Reginald) Francis 1896-1975 ... 109
Obituary ... 107
Foster, Frederick
See Godwin, John (Frederick)
Foster, G(eorge) Allen 1907-1969 ... 9-12R
See also SATA 26
Foster, Genevieve Stump 1893-1979 ... CANR-4
Obituary ... 89-92
Earlier sketch in CA 5-8R
See also CLR 7
See also DLB 61
See also MAICYA
See also SATA 2, 23
Foster, Genevieve W(akeman) 1902- ... 69-72
Foster, George
See Haswell, Chetwynd John Drake
Foster, George M(cClelland Jr.)
1913- Brief entry ... 113
Foster, H. Lincoln 1906-1989 ... CAP-1
Obituary ... 128
Earlier sketch in CA 19-20
Foster, Hal
See Foster, Harold (Rudolf)
See also AITN 2
Foster, Hannah Webster 1758-1840 ... DLB 37
Foster, Harold D(ouglas) 1943- ... 111
Foster, Harold (Rudolf)
1892-1982 Obituary ... 107
See also Foster, Hal
See also SATA 31
Foster, Harry
See Paine, Lauran (Bosworth)
Foster, Henry H(ubbard) Jr. 1911-1988 ... CANR-2
Obituary ... 125
Earlier sketch in CA 1-4R
Foster, Herbert L(awrence) 1928- ... 57-60
Foster, Herbert W.
1920(?)-1979 Obituary ... 89-92
Foster, Idris Llywelyn 1911-1984 Obituary ... 113
Foster, Iris
See Posner, Richard
Foster, J(ames) A(nthony) 1932- ... 130
Foster, Jack Donald 1930- ... 29-32R
Foster, James C(aldwell) 1943- ... CANR-7
Earlier sketch in CA 57-60
Foster, Jeanne Robert (Ollivier)
1884-1970 Obituary ... 104
Foster, Joanna 1928- ... CANR-8
Earlier sketch in CA 5-8R
Foster, John (Andrew) 1941- ... 126
Foster, John Burt Jr. 1945- ... 106
Foster, John L(awrence) 1930- ... 53-56
Foster, John (Thomas) 1925- ... 33-36R
See also SATA 8
Foster, John 1648-1681 ... DLB 24
Foster, John 1915- ... 5-8R
Foster, Joseph O'Kane 1898- ... 49-52
Foster, Julian F(rancis) S(herwood)
1926- ... 29-32R
Foster, K(enneth) Neill 1935- ... CANR-4
Earlier sketch in CA 53-56
Foster, Laura Louise (James) 1918- ... 17-20R
See also SATA 6
Foster, (William) Lawrence 1947- ... 131
Foster, Lee Edwin 1943- ... 33-36R
Foster, Lee 1923(?)-1977 Obituary ... 69-72
Foster, Lynn 1952- ... CANR-32
Earlier sketch in CA 113
Foster, M(ichael) A(nthony) 1939- ... CANR-25
Earlier sketches in CA 57-60, CANR-9
Foster, Malcolm (Burton) 1931- ... 109
Foster, Margaret Lesser
1899(?)-1979 Obituary ... 89-92
See also SATA 21
Foster, Margery S(omers) 1914- ... 5-8R
Foster, Marguerite H. 1909- ... CAP-2
Earlier sketch in CA 21-22
Foster, Marian Curtis 1909-1978 ... 73-76
Obituary ... 85-88
See also SATA 23
Foster, Marion
See Shea, Shirley
Foster, Mark Stewart 1939- ... 106
Foster, Martha S(tanding) ... 5-8R
Foster, Michael S(immler) 1942- ... 117
Foster, Michael 1904-1956 Brief entry ... 110
See also DLB 9
Foster, Nancy Haston ... 122
Foster, O'Kane
See Foster, Joseph O'Kane
Foster, Paul 1931- ... CANR-26
Earlier sketches in CA 21-24R, CANR-9
Foster, Peter 1947- ... CANR-25
Earlier sketch in CA 108
Foster, Philip (John) 1927- ... 69-72
Foster, Richard ... 137
See also Crossen, Kendell Foster
Foster, Richard J(ames) 1942- ... CANR-34
Earlier sketches in CA 85-88, CANR-15
Foster, Robert A(lfred) 1949- ... 81-84
Foster, Ruel Elton 1916- ... 33-36R
Foster, Sally ... SATA 58
Foster, Shirley 1943- ... 122
Foster, Steven 1957- ... 135
Foster, Timothy R(ichard) V(ernon) 1938- ... 112
Foster, Tony
See Foster, J(ames) A(nthony)
Foster, Virginia Ramos ... 29-32R
Foster, Walter Roland 1925- Brief entry ... 116
Foster-Harris, William
1903(?)-1978 Obituary ... 104
Fothergill, (Arthur) Brian 1921-1990 ... 17-20R
Obituary ... 132
Fothergill, Philip G(ilbert) 1908- ... 5-8R
Fotheringham, Nick 1943- ... 121
Fotiler, Myron David 1941- ... CANR-14
Earlier sketch in CA 37-40R
Foucault, Michel 1926-1984 ... CANR-34
Obituary ... 113
Earlier sketch in CA 105
See also CLC 31, 34, 69
See also MTCW
Fougasse
See Bird, (Cyril) Kenneth
Fought, John G(uy) 1938- Brief entry ... 113
Fouhy, Ed(ward Michael) 1934- ... 69-72
Foulds, Elfrida Vipont 1902- ... CANR-38
Earlier sketches in CA 53-56, CANR-4
See also MAICYA
See also SATA 52
Foulke, Adrienne 1915- ... 65-68
Foulke, Robert (Dana) 1930- ... 45-48
Foulke, Roy Anderson 1896- ... CANR-1
Earlier sketch in CA 1-4R
Foulkes, A(lbert) Peter 1936- ... 37-40R
Foulkes, (William) David 1935- Brief entry ... 107
Foulkes, Fred K. 1941- ... CANR-12
Earlier sketch in CA 33-36R
Fountain, Charles (Francis) 1950- ... 118
Fountain, Leatrice 1924- ... 21-24R
Fouque, Caroline de la Motte
1774-1831 ... DLB 90
Fouque, Friedrich Heinrich Karl de la Motte
1777-1843 ... DLB 90
Fouraker, Lawrence Edward 1923- ... 1-4R
Fourastie, Jean Joseph Hubert
1907-1990 Obituary ... 132
Fourcade, Marie-Madeleine
1909-1989 Obituary ... 129
Four Corners, George
See Viereck, George Sylvester
Fourest, Henry-Pierre 1911- ... 136
Brief entry ... 109
Fourest, Michel
See Wynne-Tyson, (Timothy) Jon (Lyden)
Fournet, Jean-Claude 1932- ... 124
Fournier, Frank
See Chapman, Frank M(onroe)
Fournier, Henri Alban
1886-1914 Brief entry ... 104
See also Alain-Fournier
Fournier, Pierre 1916- ... CANR-16
Earlier sketch in CA 89-92
See also Gascar, Pierre
See also CLC 11
Fourth, Clifton
See Morse, H(enry) Clifton IV
Fourth Brother, The
See Aung, (Maung) Htin
Fourth Earl of Chesterfield
See Stanhope, Philip Dormer
Foust, Paul J(ohn) 1920- ... 49-52
Fouste, E(thel) Bonita Rutledge 1926- ... 13-16R
Fout, John C(alvin) 1937- ... 57-60

Fowke, Edith (Margaret) 1913- 37-40R
See also SATA 14
Fowkes, Robert Allen 1913- Brief entry 106
Fowle, Eleanor Cranston
See Cameron, Eleanor Cranston
Fowler, Alastair (David Shaw) 1930- CANR-39
Earlier sketch in CA 13-16R
Fowler, Austin 1928- 21-24R
Fowler, Carolyn 117
Fowler, Charles B(runer) 1931- CANR-24
Earlier sketches in CA 57-60, CANR-8
Fowler, Christopher 1953- 137
Fowler, David Covington 1921- CANR-28
Earlier sketch in CA 1-4R
Fowler, David Henry 1924- Brief entry 112
Fowler, Don D. 1936- CANR-15
Earlier sketch in CA 33-36R
Fowler, Doreen (Angela) 1948- 119
Fowler, Douglas 1940- 57-60
Fowler, Elaine W(ootten) 1914- 93-96
Fowler, Elizabeth Millspaugh 1921- 102
Fowler, Eugene Devlan 1890-1960 97-100
Obituary 89-92
Fowler, Frank 1900-1971 Obituary 113
See also Chase, Borden
Fowler, Gene
See Fowler, Eugene Devlan
Fowler, Gene 1931- CANR-20
Earlier sketches in CA 53-56, CANR-5
Fowler, George P(almer) 1909- 41-44R
Fowler, Guy 1893(?)-1966 Obituary 25-28R
Fowler, Harry (Jr.) 1934- CANR-1
Earlier sketch in CA 45-48
Fowler, Heather T.
See Remoff, Heather T(rexler)
Fowler, Helen Rosa Huxley 1917- CAP-1
Earlier sketch in CA 9-10
Fowler, James W(iley) III 1940- 104
Fowler, Jim
See Fowler, James W(iley) III
Fowler, John M(ajor) 1926- 103
Fowler, Kenneth A(brams) 1900-1987 ....5-8R
Obituary 122
Fowler, Marian (Elizabeth) 1929- 114
Fowler, Mark 1949- 65-68
Fowler, Mary Elizabeth 1911- CAP-2
Earlier sketch in CA 29-32
Fowler, Mary Jane
See Wheeler, Mary Jane
Fowler, (Edward) Michael (Coulson) 1929- 109
Fowler, Raymond Dalton Jr.
1930- Brief entry 110
Fowler, Raymond E(veleth) 1933- 85-88
Fowler, Richard A(lan) 1948- CANR-36
Earlier sketch in CA 113
Fowler, Richard Hindle 1910- 130
Fowler, Robert H(oward) 1926- 73-76
Fowler, Roger 1938- 65-68
Fowler, Sandra (Lynn) 1937- 106
Fowler, Virginie
See Elbert, Virginie Fowler
Fowler, Wilfred 1907- CAP-1
Earlier sketch in CA 13-14
Fowler, Will 1922- 5-8R
Fowler, William Morgan Jr. 1944- CANR-31
Earlier sketches in CA 45-48, CANR-1
Fowler, Wilton B(onham) 1936- 53-56
Fowles, Jib 1940- 69-72
Fowles, John 1926- CANR-25
Earlier sketch in CA 5-8R
See also CDBLB 1960 to Present
See also CLC 1, 2, 3, 4, 6, 9, 10, 15, 33
See also DLB 14
See also MTCW
See also SATA 22
Fowlie, Wallace 1908- CANR-5
Earlier sketch in CA 5-8R
Fox, Adam 1883-1977 ....CANR-10
Earlier sketches in CAP-1, CA 13-14
Fox, Aileen 1907- CANR-5
Earlier sketch in CA 5-8R
See also SATA 58
Fox, Alan John 13-16R
Fox, Alistair 1948- CANR-39
Earlier sketch in CA 116
Fox, Allan M(ark) 1948- 41-44R
Fox, Annette Baker 1912- Brief entry 109
Fox, Anthony
See Fullerton, Alexander (Fergus)
Fox, Bill
See Fox, William
Fox, Brian
See Ballard, (Willis) Todhunter
Fox, C(arol) Lynn 1948- CANR-29
Earlier sketch in CA 110
Fox, Charles Elliot 1878- CAP-1
Earlier sketch in CA 9-10
Fox, Charles Philip 1913- CANR-1
Earlier sketch in CA 1-4R
See also SATA 12
Fox, Col. Victor J.
See Winston, R(obert) A(lexander)
Fox, Connie
See Fox, Hugh (Bernard Jr.)
Fox, Daniel Michael 1938- 112
Fox, David J(oseph) 1927- 13-16R
Fox, Dorothea Warren 1914- 61-64
Fox, Douglas A(llan) 1927- CANR-17
Earlier sketch in CA 41-44R
Fox, Douglas McMurray 1940- CANR-15
Earlier sketch in CA 33-36R
Fox, E(dward) Inman 1933- 17-20R
Fox, Edward J(ackson) 1913- 1-4R
Fox, Edward L. 1938-1983 134
Brief entry 110
Fox, Edward Whiting 1911- Brief entry 106
Fox, Eleanor
See St. John, Wylly Folk
Fox, Fontaine Talbot Jr.
1884-1964 Obituary 89-92
See also SATA 23
Fox, Frances Margaret
See Field, Frances Fox
Fox, Frank W(ayne) 1940- 109
Fox, Fred 1903(?)-1981 Obituary 104
See also SATA 27
Fox, Frederic Ewing 1917-1981 ....1-4R
Obituary 103
Fox, Freeman
See Hamilton, Charles (Harold St. John)
Fox, G(ardner) F(rancis) 1911- CANR-5
Earlier sketch in CA 5-8R
Fox, G(eoffrey) P. 1938- CANR-11
Earlier sketch in CA 21-24R
Fox, Gail 1942- CANR-19
Earlier sketch in CA 103
Fox, George (Richard) 1934- 37-40R
Fox, Gilbert T(heodore) 1915- 69-72
Fox, Gill
See Fox, Gilbert T(heodore)
Fox, Grace
See Anderson, Grace Fox
Fox, Grace (Estelle) 1899-1984 ....37-40R
Obituary 111
Fox, Grace Imogene 1907- 1-4R
Fox, H(enry) B(enjamin) 1910- 57-60
Fox, Harrison W(illiam) Jr. 1944- 126
Fox, Helen Morgenthau
1885(?)-1974 Obituary 45-48
Fox, Hugh (Bernard Jr.) 1932- CANR-29
Earlier sketches in CA 25-28R, CANR-11
Fox, Jack C(urtis) 1925-1987 ....21-24R
Obituary 122
Fox, Jack Vernon 1918-1982 Obituary 106
Fox, James (Lyttleton) 1945- 120
Fox, James M. 1908(?)-1989 102
Obituary 128
Fox, John
See Todd, John M(urray)
Fox, John H(oward) 1925- CANR-8
Earlier sketch in CA 5-8R
Fox, John Roger 1896-1987 Obituary 125
Fox, John (William) Jr.
1862(?)-1919 Brief entry 108
See also DLB 9
Fox, John 1906-1984 Obituary 114
Fox, John 1952-1990 Obituary 132
Fox, Joseph M(ichael) 1934- 106
Fox, Karl A(ugust) 1917- CANR-7
Earlier sketch in CA 17-20R
Fox, Kenneth 1944- 125
Fox, Larry 106
See also SATA 30
Fox, Levi 1914- CANR-31
Earlier sketches in CA 77-80, CANR-14
Fox, Logan J(ordan) 1922- 53-56
Fox, Lorraine 1922-1976 ....SATA 11, 27
Fox, Lucia
See Lockert, Lucia (Alicia Ungaro Fox)
Fox, Marcia R(ose) 1942- 105
Fox, Mary Virginia 1919- CANR-12
Earlier sketch in CA 29-32R
See also SATA 39, 44
Fox, Matthew (Timothy) 1940- 126
Brief entry 109
Fox, Mem
See Fox, Merrion Frances
See also CLR 23
See also MAICYA
Fox, Merrion Frances 1946- 127
See also Fox, Mem
See also SATA 51
Fox, Michael A(llen) 1940- CANR-19
Earlier sketch in CA 103
Fox, Michael W(ilson) 1937- CANR-14
Earlier sketch in CA 73-76
See also SATA 15
Fox, Milton S. 1904-1971 Obituary 33-36R
Fox, Nancy L. 1917- 122
Fox, Norman A(rnold) 1911-1960 Obituary 114
Fox, Owen
See Farmer, Bernard James
Fox, Paula 1923- CANR-36
Earlier sketches in CA 73-76, CANR-20
See also AAYA 3
See also CLC 2, 8
See also CLR 1
See also DLB 52
See also MAICYA
See also MTCW
See also SATA 17, 60
Fox, Ralph H(artzler) 1913-1973 Obituary 49-52
Fox, Ray Errol 1941- 85-88
Fox, Renee C(laire) 1928- 49-52
Fox, Richard G(abriel) 1939- 41-44R
Fox, Richard Kyle 1846-1922 .... DLB 79
Fox, Richard Wightman 1945- CANR-27
Earlier sketch in CA 93-96
Fox, Robert Barlow 1930- 13-16R
Fox, Robert J. 1927- CANR-17
Earlier sketches in CA 45-48, CANR-1
See also SATA 33
Fox, Robert 1943- 77-80
Fox, Robin 1934- 135
Fox, Ruth 1895-1989 73-76
Obituary 128
Fox, Samuel J. 1919- 53-56
Fox, Samuel 1905- CAP-2
Earlier sketch in CA 21-22
Fox, Sharon E(lizabeth) 1938- 45-48
Fox, Siv Cedering 1939- 41-44R
Fox, Sonny 1925- 41-44R
Fox, Stephen
See Furthmann, Julius Grinnell
Fox, Stephen R. 1945- CANR-12
Earlier sketch in CA 29-32R
Fox, Ted
See Fox, Theodore J.
Fox, Ted
See Fox, Gilbert T(heodore)
Fox, Terry Curtis 1948- 117
Fox, Theodore J. 1954- 123
Fox, Uffa 1898-1972 Obituary 37-40R
Fox, V. Helen
See Couch, Helen F(ox)
Fox, Vernon (Brittain) 1916- CANR-35
Earlier sketch in CA 37-40R
Fox, Willard 1919- 21-24R
Fox, William Lloyd 1921- 17-20R
Fox, William McNair 1924- 5-8R
Fox, William Price (Jr.) 1926- CANR-11
Earlier sketch in CA 17-20R
See also CLC 22
See also DLB 2
See also DLBY 81
Fox, William Thornton Rickert
1912- Brief entry 108
Fox, William W(ellington) 1909- 1-4R
Fox, William 1919(?)-1985 Obituary 116
Foxall, Raymond (Jehoiada Campbell)
1916- CANR-5
Earlier sketch in CA 9-12R
Foxe, Arthur N(orman) 1902-1982 ....CANR-4
Obituary 108
Earlier sketch in CA 9-12R
Foxell, Nigel 1931- 97-100
Fox-Genovese, Elizabeth 1941- CANR-26
Earlier sketches in CA 65-68, CANR-10
Foxley, William M(cLachlan) 1926-1978 77-80
Foxley-Norris, Christopher Neil 1917- 109
Fox-Lockert, Lucia
See Lockert, Lucia (Alicia Ungaro Fox)
Foxman, Sherri 1950- 112
Fox-Martin, Milton 1914(?)-1977 Obituary 69-72
Foxon, A(ndrew David) 1956- 121
Foxon, David Fairweather 1923- 102
Fox-Sheinwold, Patricia 102
Foxworth, Thomas G(ordon) 1937- 114
Foxx, Jack
See Pronzini, Bill
Foxx, Redd 1922-1991 89-92
Obituary 135
Foxx, Richard M(ichael) 1944- CANR-17
Earlier sketches in CA 45-48, CANR-1
Foxx, Rosalind
See Haydon, June
and Simpson, Judith H(olroyd)
Foxx, Teralene S. 1939- 122
Foy, George 1952- 116
Foy, Kenneth R(ussell) 1922- 25-28R
Foy, Nancy 1934- CANR-2
Earlier sketch in CA 45-48
Fozdar, Jamshed K(hodadad) 1926- 49-52
F.P.A.
See Adams, Franklin P(ierce)
Fraber, Daniel A. 1950- 128
Fracchia, Charles A(nthony) 1937- 89-92
Frackenpohl, Arthur R(oland) 1924- 17-20R
Frackman, Nathaline
1903(?)-1977 Obituary 69-72
Fraddle, Farragut
See Mearns, David Chambers
Fradin, Dennis Brindell 1945- 69-72
See also SATA 29
Fradkin, Elvira (Thekla) Kush
1890(?)-1972 Obituary 37-40R
Fradkin, Philip L(awrence) 1935- 107
Fraelich, Richard O(ddly) 1924- 5-8R
Fraenkel, Gerd 1919-1970 .... CAP-1
Earlier sketch in CA 11-12
Fraenkel, Gottfried S(amuel)
1901-1984 Obituary 114
Fraenkel, Heinrich 1897- 13-16R
Fraenkel, Jack R(unnels) 1932- 29-32R
Fraenkel, Michael 1896-1957 Brief entry 107
See also DLB 4
Fraenkel, Osmond K. 1888-1983 .... CAP-2
Obituary 109
Earlier sketch in CA 23-24
Frager, Robert 1940- 81-84
Frahm, Anne B. Schwerdt 1927- 9-12R
Fraiberg, Louis Benjamin 1913- 1-4R
Fraiberg, Selma 1918-1981 97-100
Obituary 105
Fraine, Harold G(eorge) 1900- 1-4R
Frair, Wayne Franklin 1926- 113
Fraistat, Neil (Richard) 1952- 122
Fraistat, Rose Ann C. 1952- 123
Frake, Warner
See Musciano, Walter A.
Frakes, George Edward 1932- 29-32R
Fraley, Oscar (B.) 1914- Brief entry 109
Fram, Eugene Harry 1929- 17-20R
Frame, Donald M(urdoch) 1911-1991 ....17-20R
Obituary 133
Frame, Janet
See Clutha, Janet Paterson Frame
See also CLC 2, 3, 6, 22, 66
Frame, Paul 1914- Brief entry 111
See also SATA 33
Framo, James L(awrence) 1922- CANR-15
Earlier sketch in CA 41-44R
Frampton, Hollis 1936-1984 Obituary 112
Frampton, Kenneth Brian 1930- 105
Frampton, Merle E(lbert) 1903- CAP-2
Earlier sketch in CA 25-28
Frampton, Peter (Kenneth)
1950- Brief entry 117
Franc, Helen M. 1908- 103
Franca, Celia 1921- 89-92
Franca, Jose-Augusto 1922- CANR-19
Earlier sketch in CA 102
France, Anatole
See Thibault, Jacques Anatole Francois
See also TCLC 9
France, Anna Kay 1940- 103
France, Beulah Sanford
1891-1971 Obituary 33-36R
France, Claire
See Dore, Claire (Morin)
France, Evangeline
See France-Hayhurst, Evangeline (Chaworth-Musters)
France, Harold L(eroy) 1930- 49-52
France, Malcolm 1928- 21-24R
France, Pierre Mendes
See Mendes-France, Pierre
France, Richard 1938- 93-96
See also DLB 7
France-Hayhurst, Evangeline (Chaworth-Musters)
1904- CAP-1
Earlier sketch in CA 9-10
Francesca, Rosina
See Brookman, Rosina Francesca
Franchere, Ruth 73-76
See also SATA 18
Franchi, Eda
See Vickers, Antoinette L.
Francis, Anne
See Bird, Florence (Bayard)
and Wintle, Anne
Francis, Arlene 1912- 89-92
Francis, Arthur
See Gershwin, Ira
Francis, Basil (Hoskins) 1906- CAP-1
Earlier sketch in CA 13-14
Francis, Cat
See Francis, Emile (Percy)
Francis, C.D.E.
See Howarth, Patrick (John Fielding)
Francis, Charles
See Holme, Bryan
Francis, Clare 1946- CANR-34
Earlier sketches in CA 77-80, CANR-15
Francis, Claude ....CLC 50
Francis, Convers 1795-1863 ....DLB 1
Francis, Daniel
See Cranny, Titus (Francis)
Francis, Daniel 1947- 111
Francis, (Alan) David 1900- 21-24R
Francis, David Noel 1904- 5-8R
Francis, David R(ichard) 1933- 133
Francis, Dee
See Haas, Dorothy F.
Francis, Dennis S. 1943(?)-1980 Obituary 102
Francis, Devon (Earl) 1901-1986 61-64
Obituary 118
Francis, Dick 1920- CANR-9
Earlier sketch in CA 5-8R
See also AAYA 5
See also BEST 89:3
See also CDBLB 1960 to Present
See also CLC 2, 22, 42
See also DLB 87
See also MTCW
Francis, Dorothy Brenner 1926- CANR-24
Earlier sketches in CA 21-24R, CANR-9
See also SATA 10
Francis, Emile (Percy) 1926- Brief entry 112
Francis, Frank Chalton 1901-1988 65-68
Obituary 126
Francis, Gloria A(ileen)
1930-1988 Obituary 125
Brief entry 113
Francis, H(erbert) E(dward Jr.) 1924- CANR-10
Earlier sketch in CA 25-28R
Francis, Helen Dannefer 1915- 13-16R
Francis, John M(ichael) 1939- 118
Francis, Marilyn 1920- CANR-3
Earlier sketch in CA 5-8R
Francis, Matthew (Charles) 1956- 132
Francis, Michael J(ackson) 1938- 89-92
Francis, Michel
See Cattaui, Georges
Francis, Mother Mary
See Aschmann, Alberta
Francis, Nelle (Trew) 1914- 37-40R
Francis, Pamela (Mary) 1926- 29-32R
See also SATA 11
Francis, Paul
See Engleman, Paul
Francis, Philip
See Lockyer, Roger
Francis, Philip S(heridan) 1918- 17-20R
Francis, R. Mabel 1880- CAP-2
Earlier sketch in CA 25-28
Francis, Richard (H.) 1945- CANR-24
Earlier sketch in CA 102
Francis, Robert (Churchill) 1901-1987 .....CANR-1
Obituary 123
Earlier sketch in CA 1-4R
See also CLC 15
Francis, Roy G. 1919- 1-4R
Francis, Wayne L(ouis) 1935- 41-44R
Francisco, Charles 1930- 109
Francisco, Clyde Taylor 1916- Brief entry 106
Francis-Williams, Lord
See Williams, Edward Francis
Franck, Frederick 1909- CANR-5
Earlier sketch in CA 1-4R
Franck, Harry Alverson
1881-1962 Obituary 110
Franck, Irene M(ary) 1941- CANR-21
Earlier sketch in CA 104
Franck, Phyllis 1928- 53-56

Franck, Sebastian
See Jacoby, Henry
Franck, Thomas M. 1931- 33-36R
Francke, Donald Eugene
1910-1978 Obituary 81-84
Francke, Kuno 1855-1930 .....DLB 71
Francke, Linda Bird 1939- CANR-15
Earlier sketch in CA 85-88
Franco, Eloise (Bauder) 1910- .....SATA 62
Franco, Jean 1914-1971 .....CAP-2
Earlier sketch in CA 25-28
Franco, Jean 1924- CANR-9
Earlier sketch in CA 21-24R
Franco, Johan (Henri Gustave) 1908- 97-100
See also SATA 62
Franco, Marjorie 114
See also SATA 38
Francoeur, Anna K(otlarchyk) 1940- 53-56
Francoeur, Robert T(homas) 1931- CANR-31
Earlier sketches in CA 37-40R, CANR-14
Francois, Andre 1915- 93-96
See also SATA 25
Francois, Pierre 1932- 17-20R
Francois, William E. 1924- CANR-5
Earlier sketch in CA 13-16R
Francoise
See Seignobosc, Francoise
Francoise 1863-1910 .....DLB 92
Francois-Poncet, Andre
1887-1978 Obituary 73-76
Franda, Marcus F. 1937- CANR-9
Earlier sketch in CA 21-24R
Frandsen, Arden N. 1902- 1-4R
Frandsen, Julius 1907-1976 Obituary 69-72
Franey, Pierre 1921- CANR-15
Earlier sketch in CA 89-92
Frangsmyr, Tore (Lennart) 1938- 129
Frank, Adolph F(rederick) 1918- 106
Frank, Andre Gunder 1929- CANR-28
Earlier sketch in CA 21-24R
Frank, Anne(lies Marie) 1929-1945 133
Brief entry 113
See also MTCW
See also SATA 42
See also TCLC 17
See also WLC
Frank, Benis M. 1925- 37-40R
Frank, Benjamin 1902-1984 Obituary 113
Frank, Bernhard 1931- 105
Frank, Bruno 1887-1945 .....DLB 118
Frank, Charles E(dward) 1911- 21-24R
Frank, Charles Paul 1935- Brief entry 112
Frank, Charles Raphael (Jr.) 1937- 37-40R
Frank, Daniel B. 1956- 117
See also SATA 55
Frank, Elizabeth 1945- 126
Brief entry 121
See also CLC 39
Frank, Florence Kiper
1885(?)-1976 Obituary 65-68
Frank, Frederick S. 1935- 138
Frank, Gerold 1907- Brief entry 109
Frank, Goldalie 1908- CAP-1
Earlier sketch in CA 17-18
Frank, H(ans) Eric 1921- 49-52
Frank, Harry Thomas 1933-1980 53-56
Obituary 103
Frank, Helene
See Vautier, Ghislaine
Frank, Helmut J(ack) 1922- CANR-7
Earlier sketch in CA 17-20R
Frank, Irving 1910- CAP-2
Earlier sketch in CA 21-22
Frank, Isaiah 1917- CANR-1
Earlier sketch in CA 1-4R
Frank, Jacqueline Obituary 114
Frank, Janet
See Dunleavy, Janet Egleson
Frank, Jeffrey 1942- 21-24R
Frank, Jerome D(avid) 1909- CANR-3
Earlier sketch in CA 5-8R
Frank, Jerome (New)
1889-1957 Brief entry 121
Frank, John G. 1896(?)-1978 Obituary 81-84
Frank, Joseph (Nathaniel) 1918- CANR-32
Earlier sketch in CA 77-80
Frank, Joseph 1916- CANR-1
Earlier sketch in CA 1-4R
Frank, Josette 1893-1989 .....CAP-1
Obituary 129
Earlier sketch in CA 19-20
See also SATA 10, 63
Frank, Judith M. 127
Frank, Katherine 124
Frank, Lawrence K(elso) 1890-1968 .....1-4R
Obituary 103
Frank, Lee
See Griffin, Arthur J.
Frank, Leonhard 1882-1961 Obituary 116
See also DLB 56, 118
Frank, Mary 1933- .....SATA 34
Frank, Melvin 1913(?)-1988 Obituary 126
See also DLB 26
Frank, Morton 1912- 102
Frank, Murray 1908-1977 .....37-40R
Obituary 73-76
Frank, Nathalie D. 1918- 9-12R
Frank, Pat (Harry Hart) 1907-1964 .....5-8R
Frank, Peter (Solomon) 1950- CANR-15
Earlier sketch in CA 81-84
Frank, Philip Norman 1943- 113
Frank, Philipp (G.) 1884-1966 Obituary 25-28R
Frank, R. Jr.
See Ross, Frank (Xavier) Jr.
Frank, Reuven 1920- 81-84
Frank, Robert G(regg) Jr. 1943- 134
Brief entry 113
Frank, Robert J(oseph) 1939- 65-68
Frank, Robert Worth Jr. 1914- 13-16R
Frank, Roberta 1941- 115
Frank, Ronald E(dward) 1933- CANR-18
Earlier sketches in CA 5-8R, CANR-3
Frank, Rudolf 1886-1979 121
Frank, Sheldon 1943- 77-80
Frank, Stanley B. 1908-1979 .....5-8R
Obituary 85-88
Frank, T. C.
See Laughlin, Tom
Frank, Thaisa 1943- 117
Frank, Waldo (David) 1889-1967 93-96
Obituary 25-28R
See also DLB 9, 63
Frank, William G.
See Frank, Rudolf
Frank, William L(uke) 1929- 106
Frankau, Mary Evelyn Atkinson 1899- CAP-1
Earlier sketch in CA 9-10
See also SATA 4
Frankau, Pamela 1908-1967 Obituary 25-28R
Frank-Baron, Elizabeth
1911(?)-1982 Obituary 108
Franke, C(arl) W(ilfred) 1928- 21-24R
Franke, Christopher 1941- 77-80
Franke, David 1938- 49-52
Franke, Herbert W. 1927- Brief entry 110
Franke, Holly L(ambro) 1943- 49-52
Frankel, A(rthur) Steven 1942- 53-56
Frankel, Alona 1937- 135
See also SATA 66
Frankel, Bernice 61-64
See also SATA 9
Frankel, Charles 1917-1979 .....CANR-4
Obituary 89-92
Earlier sketch in CA 5-8R
Frankel, Edward 1910- 85-88
See also SATA 44
Frankel, Eliot 1922-1990 77-80
Obituary 130
Frankel, Ellen 1951- 135
Frankel, Flo 1923- 105
Frankel, Hans H(ermann) 1916- 61-64
Frankel, Haskel 1926- 89-92
Frankel, Hermann F.
1899(?)-1977 Obituary 69-72
Frankel, J(oseph) 1913- CANR-3
Earlier sketch in CA 5-8R
Frankel, Julie 1947- CANR-36
Earlier sketch in CA 113
See also SATA 34, 40
Frankel, Max 1930- 65-68
Frankel, Otto (Herzberg) 1900- 108
Frankel, Sandor 1943- 33-36R
Frankel, Tobia (Brown)
1935(?)-1987 Obituary 122
Frankel, Valerie 1965- 138
Frankel, William 1917- 106
Frankel, Zygmunt 1929- 41-44R
Franken, Rose (Dorothy)
1895(?)-1988 Obituary 125
See also DLBY 84
Frankena, William K(laas) 1908- CANR-10
Earlier sketch in CA 17-20R
Frankenberg, Celestine Gilligan 9-12R
Frankenberg, Lloyd 1907-1975 .....CANR-6
Obituary 57-60
Earlier sketch in CA 1-4R
Frankenberg, Robert 1911- .....SATA 22
Frankenstein, Alfred Victor 1906-1981 .....CANR-2
Obituary 104
Earlier sketch in CA 1-4R
Frankenstein, Carl 1905- 9-12R
Frankenthal, Kate 1889-1976 Obituary 65-68
Frankfort, Ellen 1936-1987 .....29-32R
Obituary 122
Frankforter, A(lbertus) Daniel (III) 1939- 81-84
Frankfurt, Harry Gordon 1929- 41-44R
Frankfurter, Felix 1882-1965 Brief entry 124
Frankl, Razelle 1932- 133
Frankl, Viktor E(mil) 1905- 65-68
Frankland, Mark 1934- 69-72
Frankland, (Anthony) Noble 1922- CANR-14
Earlier sketch in CA 65-68
Franklin, A.
See Arnold, Adlai F(ranklin)
Franklin, Ada C(rogman) Obituary 111
Franklin, Adele 1887(?)-1977 Obituary 69-72
Franklin, Alexander (John) 1921- 13-16R
Franklin, Alfred White 1905- CANR-7
Earlier sketch in CA 57-60
Franklin, Ben(jamin) A. 1927- 89-92
Franklin, Benjamin
See Hasek, Jaroslav (Matej Frantisek)
Franklin, Benjamin V 1939- CANR-39
Earlier sketch in CA 115
Franklin, Benjamin
1706-1790 .....CDALB 1640-1865
See also DLB 24, 43, 73
Franklin, Billy J(oe) 1940- 33-36R
Franklin, Bob 1949- 124
Franklin, Burt 1903-1972 .....CAP-1
Earlier sketch in CA 13-16
Franklin, Charles
See Usher, Frank (Hugh)
Franklin, Cheryl J. 1955- 138
See also SATA 70
Franklin, Colin 1923- 77-80
Franklin, Denson Nauls 1914- 1-4R
Franklin, Edward Herbert 1930- 13-16R
Franklin, Elizabeth
See Campbell, Hannah
Franklin, Eugene
See Bandy, (Eugene) Franklin
Franklin, George E. 1890-1971 .....CAP-1
Earlier sketch in CA 19-20
Franklin, H. Bruce 1934- CANR-9
Earlier sketch in CA 5-8R
Franklin, Harold L(eroy) 1934- 57-60
Franklin, Harold 1926- 29-32R
See also SATA 13
Franklin, Harry 1906- CANR-12
Earlier sketches in CAP-1, CA 13-14
Franklin, J(ennie) E(lizabeth) 1937- 61-64
See also BW
Franklin, James 1697-1735 .....DLB 43
Franklin, Jay
See Carter, John Franklin
Franklin, Jerome L(ee) 1943- 102
Franklin, Jill (Leslie) 1928-1988 Obituary 125
Franklin, Jimmie Lewis 1939- 126
Brief entry 106
Franklin, Joe 1926- 134
Brief entry 108
Franklin, John Hope 1915- CANR-26
Earlier sketches in CA 5-8R, CANR-3
See also BW
Franklin, John 1786-1847 .....DLB 99
Franklin, Jon (Daniel) 1942- CANR-27
Earlier sketch in CA 104
Franklin, Kay 1933- 118
Franklin, Keith
See Foy, Kenneth R(ussell)
Franklin, Kerry
See Caldwell, Stratton F(ranklin)
Franklin, Linda Campbell 1941- CANR-26
Earlier sketch in CA 105
Franklin, Marc A. 1932- 29-32R
Franklin, Marshall 1929- 53-56
Franklin, Max
See Deming, Richard
Franklin, (Stella Maraia Sarah) Miles
1879-1954 Brief entry 104
See also TCLC 7
Franklin, Nat
See Bauer, Erwin A.
Franklin, Olga 1912-1985 102
Obituary 115
Franklin, Penelope (Florence) 1948- 125
Franklin, R(alph) W(illiam) 1937- CANR-9
Earlier sketch in CA 21-24R
Franklin, Richard 1918- 21-24R
Franklin, Robert M(ichael) 1954- 135
Franklin, S(amuel) Harvey 1928- CANR-26
Earlier sketch in CA 105
Franklin, Sidney 1903-1976 Obituary 65-68
Franklin, Steve
See Stevens, Franklin
Franklin, Ursula 1929- 112
Franklin, Wayne S(teven) 1945- 125
Franklyn, Charles Aubrey Hamilton
1896- 9-12R
Franklyn, Julian 1899-1970 Obituary 112
Franklyn, Robert Alan 1918- 89-92
Franko, Lawrence G. 1942- 37-40R
Frankowski, Leo 1943- 120
Franks, C(harles) E(dward) S(elwyn)
1936- 77-80
Franks, Claudia Stillman 1947- 117
Franks, Cyril Maurice 1923- 13-16R
Franks, Ed
See Brandon, Johnny
Franks, Felix 1926- 125
Franks, Helen 1934- 133
Franks, Kenny Arthur 1945- 123
Franks, Lucinda 1946- 53-56
Franks, Marlene Strong 1955- 125
Franks, Maurice R(udolph) 1942- 112
Franks, Robert S(leightholme) 1871-1963 .....5-8R
Fransella, Fay CANR-13
Earlier sketch in CA 25-28R
Frantz, Charles 1925- CANR-3
Earlier sketch in CA 5-8R
Frantz, Douglas 1949- 126
Frantz, Harry Warner 1891-1982 Obituary 106
Frantz, Joe B. 1917- CANR-1
Earlier sketch in CA 1-4R
Frantz, Ralph Jules 1902-1979 77-80
Obituary 89-92
See also DLB 4
Frantzen, Allen J. 1947- 121
Franz, Barbara E(van) 1946- 110
Franz, Carl 1944- 107
Franz, William S(trasser) 1945- 110
Franzblau, Abraham N(orman)
1901-1982 .....29-32R
Obituary 108
Franzblau, Rose N(adler) 1905-1979 .....29-32R
Obituary 89-92
Franzen, Gosta Knut 1906- 41-44R
Franzen, Jonathan 1959- 129
Franzen, Lavern G(erhardt) 1926- CANR-7
Earlier sketch in CA 61-64
Franzen, Nils-Olof 1916- CANR-25
Earlier sketch in CA 29-32R
See also SATA 10
Franzen, William Edward 1952- 129
Franzero, Carlo Maria 1892-1986 .....CANR-5
Obituary 120
Earlier sketch in CA 1-4R
Franzero, Charles Marie
See Franzero, Carlo Maria
Franzius, Enno 1901- 25-28R
Franzke, Andreas 1938- 129
Franzmann, Martin H. 1907-1976 .....CANR-3
Earlier sketch in CA 1-4R
Franzwa, Gregory M. 1926- CANR-9
Earlier sketch in CA 21-24R
Frary, Michael 1918- 77-80
Frasca, John (Anthony) 1916-1979 .....CANR-3
Obituary 93-96
Earlier sketch in CA 49-52
Frascatoro, Gerald
See Hornback, Bert G(erald)
Frascino, Edward CANR-37
Brief entry 111
Earlier sketch in CA 114
See also MAICYA
See also SAAS 9
See also SATA 33, 48
Frascona, Joseph Lohengrin 1910- 17-20R
Frasconi, Antonio 1919- CANR-1
Earlier sketch in CA 1-4R
See also MAICYA
See also SAAS 11
See also SATA 6, 53
Frase, Larry E. 1945- 41-44R
Frase, Robert W(illiam) 1912- 33-36R
Fraser, Alex
See Brinton, Henry
Fraser, Allan 1900- 57-60
Fraser, Amy Stewart 1892- CANR-9
Earlier sketch in CA 49-52
Fraser, Anthea CANR-25
Earlier sketches in CA 65-68, CANR-10
Fraser, Antonia (Pakenham) 1932- 85-88
See also CLC 32
See also MTCW
See also SATA 32
Fraser, Arthur Ronald
1888-1974 Obituary 53-56
Fraser, Arvonne S. 1925- 33-36R
Fraser, B. Kay 1941- 69-72
Fraser, Betty
See Fraser, Elizabeth Marr
Fraser, Blair 1909-1968 .....CAP-2
Earlier sketch in CA 23-24
Fraser, Bruce (Donald) 1910- 109
Fraser, Colin 1935- 21-24R
Fraser, Conon 1930- CAP-1
Earlier sketch in CA 9-10
Fraser, D(onald) M(urray) 1946-1985 117
Fraser, David (William) 1920- 129
Fraser, (William) Dean 1916- 45-48
Fraser, Diane Lynch
See Lynch-Fraser, Diane
Fraser, Dorothy May
1903(?)-1980 Obituary 102
Fraser, Douglas Ferrar 1929- CANR-4
Earlier sketch in CA 1-4R
Fraser, Douglas 1910- 102
Fraser, Edith Emily Rose Oram 1903- CAP-1
Earlier sketch in CA 11-12
Fraser, Elise Parker 1903- 1-4R
Fraser, Elizabeth Marr 1928- .....SATA 31
Fraser, Eric (George) 1902-1983 .....SATA 38
Fraser, Flora 1958- 124
Fraser, G(eorge) S(utherland) 1915-1980 85-88
Obituary 105
See also DLB 27
Fraser, George MacDonald 1925- CANR-2
Earlier sketch in CA 45-48
See also CLC 7
Fraser, Gordon Holmes 1898- CAP-1
Earlier sketch in CA 13-16
Fraser, Hamish 1913-1986 Obituary 120
Fraser, (William Jocelyn) Ian
1897-1974 Obituary 53-56
Fraser, J(ulius) T(homas) 1923- CANR-27
Earlier sketches in CA 61-64, CANR-8
Fraser, James
See White, Alan
Fraser, Jane
See Pilcher, Rosamunde
Fraser, Janet Hobhouse
See Hobhouse, Janet
Fraser, John 1931- 29-32R
Fraser, Kathleen 1937- 106
Fraser, Keath 1944- 125
Fraser, Margot 1936- 135
Fraser, Maxwell
See Fraser, Dorothy May
Fraser, Morris 1941- 102
Fraser, Neil McCormick 1902- 5-8R
Fraser, Peter (Malcolm) 1928-1987 107
Obituary 121
Fraser, Peter (Shaw) 1932- 33-36R
Fraser, Ray
See Fraser, Raymond (Joseph)
Fraser, Raymond (Joseph) 1941- 130
Brief entry 107
Fraser, Robert (H.) 1947- 134
Fraser, Ronald
See Tiltman, Ronald Frank
Fraser, Ronald
See Fraser, Arthur Ronald
Fraser, Ronald (Angus) 1930- 131
Fraser, Russell A(lfred) 1927- 37-40R
Fraser, Stewart Erskine 1929- CANR-32
Earlier sketches in CA 13-16R, CANR-10
Fraser, Stuart
See Wood, James (Alexander Fraser)
Fraser, Sylvia 1935- CANR-16
Earlier sketches in CA 45-48, CANR-1
See also CLC 64
Fraser, W(aller) B(rown) 1905- CAP-2
Earlier sketch in CA 25-28
Fraser, W(illiam) Hamish 1941- 103
Fraser, W(illiam) Lionel CAP-1
Earlier sketch in CA 9-10
Fraser Darling, Frank 1903-1979 61-64
Obituary 89-92
Fraser Harrison, Brian 1918- CAP-1
Earlier sketch in CA 9-10
Fraser Roberts, J(ohn) A(lexander)
See Roberts, J(ohn) A(lexander) Fraser
Frasier, Debra 1953- 137
See also SATA 69
Frasier, James E(dwin) 1923- 17-20R

Frassanito, William A(llen) 1946- ... CANR-9
Earlier sketch in CA 57-60
Frasure, David W(illiam) 1942- ... 113
Fratcher, William F(ranklin) 1913- ... CANR-3
Earlier sketch in CA 5-8R
Frater Perdurabo
See Crowley, Edward Alexander
Fraticelli, Marco 1945- ... 118
Fratti, Mario 1927- ... 77-80
Frautschi, R(ichard) L(ane) 1926- ... 17-20R
Frawley, Ernest D(avid)
1920-1984 Obituary ... 114
Frawley, William John 1953- ... 114
Fraydas, Stan 1918- ... 57-60
Frayling, Christopher 1946- ... 110
Frayn, Michael 1933- ... CANR-30
Earlier sketch in CA 5-8R
See also CLC 3, 7, 31, 47
See also DLB 13, 14
See also MTCW
Frayser, Suzanne G. 1943- ... 127
Fraze, Candida (Merrill) 1945- ... 126
See also CLC 50
Frazee, Charles A(aron) 1929- ... 37-40R
Frazee, Steve 1909- ... CANR-5
Earlier sketch in CA 5-8R
Frazen, Bill
See Franzen, William Edward
Frazer, Andrew
See Marlowe, Stephen
Frazer, Fred
See Avallone, Michael (Angelo, Jr)
Frazer, J(ames) G(eorge)
1854-1941 Brief entry ... 118
See also TCLC 32
Frazer, Mark Petrovich
See Maclean, Donald Duart
Frazer, Robert Caine
See Creasey, John
Frazer, Robert W(alter) 1911- ... 17-20R
Frazer, Sir James George
See Frazer, J(ames) G(eorge)
Frazer, William J(ohnson) Jr. 1924- ... 17-20R
Frazer, Winifred Dusenbury
See Frazer, Winifred L(oesch)
Frazer, Winifred L(oesch) ... 25-28R
Frazer-Hurst, Douglas 1883- ... CAP-1
Earlier sketch in CA 9-10
Frazetta, Frank 1928- ... 104
See also SATA 58
Frazier, Allie M. 1932- Brief entry ... 110
Frazier, Anitra 1937- ... 113
Frazier, Arthur
See Bulmer, (Henry) Kenneth
Frazier, Claude A(lbee) 1920- ... CANR-32
Earlier sketch in CA 29-32R
Frazier, Cliff(ord) 1934- Brief entry ... 109
Frazier, Edward Franklin
1894-1962 Obituary ... 108
Frazier, George 1911-1974 ... CAP-2
Obituary ... 49-52
Earlier sketch in CA 25-28
Frazier, Ian 1951- ... 130
See also CLC 46
Frazier, Kendrick (Crosby) 1942- ... CANR-39
Earlier sketches in CA 101, CANR-17
Frazier, Neta (Osborn) Lohnes
1890-1990 ... CANR-1
Obituary ... 131
Earlier sketch in CA 1-4R
See also SATA 7
Frazier, Sarah
See Wirt, Winola Wells
Frazier, Shervert Hughes 1921- ... 85-88
Frazier, Thomas R(ichard) 1931- ... 33-36R
Frazier, Walt(er) 1945- ... 103
Frears, J(ohn) R(ussell) 1936- ... 107
Freas, Frank Kelly 1922- ... CANR-21
Earlier sketch in CA 102
Freburger, William J. 1940- ... 115
Frech, Frances 1923- ... 97-100
Frechette, Louis-Honore 1839-1908 ... DLB 99
Freddi, Cris 1955- ... 106
Freddland, Michael 1934- ... CANR-29
Frede, Richard 1934- ... CANR-32
Earlier sketch in CA 69-72
Fredeman, William E(van) 1928- ... 33-36R
Fredenburgh, Franz A(lvah) 1906- ... 33-36R
Frederic, Harold 1856-1898 ... DLB 12, 23
Frederic, Mike
See Cox, William R(obert)
Frederic, Sister M. Catherine
See Fleischbein, Sister M. Catherine Frederic
Frederick, Carl Louis 1942- ... 65-68
Frederick, Dick
See Dempewolff, Richard F(rederic)
Frederick, John
See Faust, Frederick (Shiller)
Frederick, John H(utchinson) 1896- ... 1-4R
Frederick, John Towner
1893-1975 Obituary ... 111
Frederick, Lee
See Nussbaum, Al(bert F.)
Frederick, Oswald
See Snelling, O(swald) F(rederick)
Frederick, Pauline 1908-1990 ... 102
Obituary ... 131
Frederick, Robert Allen 1928- ... CANR-3
Earlier sketch in CA 45-48
Fredericks, Carlton 1910-1987 ... CANR-7
Obituary ... 123
Earlier sketch in CA 53-56
See also AITN 1
Fredericks, Frank
See Franck, Frederick
Fredericks, Frohm
See Kerner, Fred
Fredericks, Pierce Griffin 1920-1985 ... 13-16R
Obituary ... 117
Fredericks, Vic
See Majeski, William
Frederics, Jocko
See Frede, Richard
Frederics, Macdowell
See Frede, Richard
Frederika (Louise), Queen
1917-1981 Obituary ... 108
Frederiksen, Alan Ryle 1935- ... 113
Frederiksen, Martin W. 1930-1980 Obituary ... 101
Frederikson, Edna 1904- ... 49-52
Fredge, Frederique 1906- ... CAP-2
Earlier sketch in CA 21-22
Fredman, Alice G(reen) 1924- ... 102
Fredman, Henry John 1927- ... 29-32R
Fredman, John
See Fredman, Henry John
Fredman, Ruth Gruber 1934- ... 106
Fredricks, Edgar J(ohn) 1942- ... 25-28R
Fredrickson, George M(arsh) 1934- ... CANR-24
Earlier sketches in CA 17-20R, CANR-8
Fredrickson, Olive A(lta) 1901- ... 49-52
Fredriksson, Don 1926- ... 110
Fredriksson, Kristine 1940- ... 122
Free
See Hoffman, Abbie
Free, Ann Cottrell ... 9-12R
Free, James S(tillman) 1908- ... 77-80
Free, Lloyd A. 1908- ... 13-16R
Free, William Joseph 1933- ... 9-12R
Free, William Norris 1933- ... 25-28R
Freeborn, Brian (James) 1939- ... 65-68
Freeborn, Richard H. 1926- ... CANR-1
Earlier sketch in CA 1-4R
Freed, Alvyn M. 1913- ... CANR-8
Earlier sketch in CA 61-64
See also SATA 22
Freed, Arthur 1894-1973 Obituary ... 41-44R
Freed, Barry
See Hoffman, Abbie
Freed, Donald 1932- ... 85-88
Freed, Louis Franklin 1903- ... 5-8R
Freed, Lynn (R.) 1945- ... CANR-27
Earlier sketch in CA 108
Freed, Margaret De Haan 1917- ... 73-76
Freed, Ray 1939- ... 117
Freedberg, S(ydney) J(oseph) 1914- ... CANR-17
Earlier sketches in CA 1-4R, CANR-1
Freedeman, Charles E(ldon) 1926- ... 102
Freeden, Michael S(tephen) 1944- ... 127
Freedgood, Lillian (Fischel) 1911- ... 13-16R
Freedgood, Morton 1912- ... 128
Brief entry ... 108
See also AITN 1
Freedland, Michael 1934- ... CANR-11
Earlier sketch in CA 65-68
Freedland, Nat(haniel) 1936- ... 65-68
Freedley, George (Reynolds)
1904-1967 ... CANR-4
Earlier sketch in CA 5-8R
Freedman, Alfred M(ordecai) 1917- ... CANR-4
Earlier sketch in CA 49-52
Freedman, Arthur M(erton) 1916- ... 41-44R
Freedman, Benedict 1919- ... 69-72
See also SATA 27
Freedman, Dan 1952- ... 126
Freedman, Daniel X. 1921- ... 41-44R
Freedman, David M(ichael) 1949- ... 112
Freedman, David Noel 1922- ... CANR-1
Earlier sketch in CA 1-4R
Freedman, Hy 1914- ... 85-88
Freedman, Leonard 1924- ... CANR-1
Earlier sketch in CA 1-4R
Freedman, M(orris) David 1938- ... CANR-16
Earlier sketch in CA 41-44R
Freedman, Marcia K(ohl) 1922- ... CANR-10
Earlier sketch in CA 25-28R
Freedman, Maurice 1920-1975 ... CAP-2
Obituary ... 61-64
Earlier sketch in CA 25-28
Freedman, Mervin B. 1920- ... 29-32R
Freedman, Monroe H(enry)
1928- Brief entry ... 107
Freedman, Morris 1920- ... CANR-3
Earlier sketch in CA 5-8R
Freedman, Nancy 1920- ... CANR-19
Earlier sketches in CA 45-48, CANR-1
See also SATA 27
Freedman, Paul H(arris) 1949- ... 122
Freedman, Ralph (William Bernard) 1920- ... 128
Brief entry ... 112
Freedman, Richard 1932-1991 ... 77-80
Obituary ... 134
Freedman, Robert Owen 1941- ... CANR-13
Earlier sketch in CA 33-36R
Freedman, Ronald 1917- ... CANR-6
Earlier sketch in CA 9-12R
Freedman, Russell (Bruce) 1929- ... CANR-23
Earlier sketches in CA 17-20R, CANR-7
See also AAYA 4
See also CLR 20
See also MAICYA
See also SATA 16
Freedman, Russell 1929- ... SATA 71
Freedman, Samuel Sumner 1927- ... 112
Freedman, Warren 1921- ... 17-20R
Freehill, Maurice F(rancis) 1915- ... 5-8R
Freehling, Alison Goodyear 1941- ... 112
Freehof, Solomon B(ennett) 1892-1990 ... 93-96
Obituary ... 131
Freeland, Jay
See McLeod, John F(reeland)
Freeland, John Maxwell 1920- ... 13-16R
Freeland, Richard M. 1941- ... 81-84
Freeland, Stephen L.
1911(?)-1977 Obituary ... 69-72
Freeley, Austin J. 1922- ... 5-8R
Freeling, Nicolas 1927- ... CANR-17
Earlier sketches in CA 49-52, CANR-1
See also CAAS 12
See also CLC 38
See also DLB 87
Freely, Maureen 1952- ... 97-100
Freeman, A. Myrick III 1936- ... 85-88
Freeman, Anne Frances 1936- ... 1-4R
Freeman, Arthur 1938- ... CANR-1
Earlier sketch in CA 1-4R
Freeman, Barbara C(onstance) 1906- ... 73-76
See also SATA 28
Freeman, Barbara M. 1947- ... 132
Freeman, Bill
See Freeman, William Bradford
Freeman, Bjorn
See Pratney, William Alfred
Freeman, C(lifford) Wade 1906- ... 5-8R
Freeman, Charles K.
1900-1980 Obituary ... 97-100
Freeman, Cynthia
See Feinberg, Beatrice Cynthia Freeman
Freeman, Darlene 1934- ... 29-32R
Freeman, Dave
See Freeman, David
Freeman, David E(dgar) 1945- ... 131
Brief entry ... 108
Freeman, David Hugh 1924- ... CANR-17
Earlier sketch in CA 1-4R
Freeman, David 1922- ... 102
Freeman, Davis
See Friedman, David F.
Freeman, Don 1908-1978 ... 77-80
See also MAICYA
See also SATA 17
Freeman, Donald Cary 1938- ... 53-56
Freeman, Donald McKinley 1931- ... CANR-15
Earlier sketch in CA 37-40R
Freeman, Douglas Southall
1886-1953 Brief entry ... 109
See also DLB 17
See also TCLC 11
Freeman, Eugene 1906- ... CANR-26
Earlier sketch in CA 41-44R
Freeman, G(raydon) L(a Verne)
1904- ... CANR-13
Earlier sketch in CA 13-16R
Freeman, Gary 1945- ... 93-96
Freeman, Gillian 1929- ... CANR-3
Earlier sketch in CA 5-8R
Freeman, Harrop A(rthur) 1907- ... 13-16R
Freeman, Harry 1906-1978 ... 77-80
Freeman, Howard E(dgar) 1929- ... CANR-23
Earlier sketches in CA 5-8R, CANR-6
Freeman, Ira Henry 1906- ... CAP-1
Earlier sketch in CA 13-16
Freeman, Ira Maximilian 1905- ... 73-76
See also SATA 21
Freeman, James Dillet 1912- ... 17-20R
Freeman, James Montague 1936- ... 102
Freeman, Jean Kenny 1929- ... 115
Freeman, Jean Todd 1929- ... 25-28R
Freeman, Jo 1945- ... CANR-8
Earlier sketch in CA 61-64
Freeman, John Crosby 1941- ... 13-16R
Freeman, Joseph 1897-1965 Obituary ... 89-92
Freeman, Judith 1946- ... CLC 55
Freeman, Kathleen 1897-1959 Brief entry ... 112
Freeman, Larry
See Freeman, G(raydon) L(a Verne)
Freeman, Lea David
1887(?)-1976 Obituary ... 69-72
Freeman, Legh Richmond 1842-1915 ... DLB 23
Freeman, Leslie J(ane) 1944- ... 106
Freeman, Linton C(larke) 1927- ... 69-72
Freeman, Lucy (Greenbaum) 1916- ... CANR-3
Earlier sketch in CA 5-8R
See also SATA 24
Freeman, Mae (Blacker) 1907- ... 73-76
See also SATA 25
Freeman, Margaret B. 1899-1980 ... 109
Obituary ... 97-100
Freeman, Margaret C(ooper) 1913- ... 57-60
Freeman, Margaret N(adgwick) 1915- ... 9-12R
Freeman, Mary Eleanor Wilkins
1852-1930 Brief entry ... 106
See also DLB 12, 78
See also SSC 1
See also TCLC 9
Freeman, Max Herbert 1907- Brief entry ... 109
Freeman, Morton S(igmund) 1912- ... 118
Freeman, Nancy 1932- ... SATA 61
Freeman, Paul 1929(?)-1980 Obituary ... 101
Freeman, Peter J.
See Calvert, Patricia
Freeman, R(ichard) Austin
1862-1943 Brief entry ... 113
See also DLB 70
See also TCLC 21
Freeman, R(ichard) B(roke) 1915-1986 ... 133
Obituary ... 120
Freeman, Richard B(arry) 1944- ... CANR-15
Earlier sketch in CA 85-88
Freeman, Richard Borden 1908- ... CANR-17
Earlier sketch in CA 1-4R
Freeman, Roger A(dolph) 1904-1991 ... 25-28R
Obituary ... 136
Freeman, Roger A(nthony Wilson)
1928- ... CANR-26
Earlier sketches in CA 65-68, CANR-10
Freeman, Roger K. 1935- ... 127
Freeman, Roger L(ouis) 1928- ... CANR-12
Earlier sketch in CA 69-72
Freeman, Ruth B(enson) 1906- ... 41-44R
Freeman, Ruth (Lazear) S(underlin)
1907- ... CANR-13
Earlier sketches in CAP-1, CA 13-16
Freeman, Sarah (Caroline) 1940- ... 133
See also SATA 66
Freeman, Simon (David) 1952- ... 133
Freeman, Susan Tax 1938- ... 85-88
Freeman, T(homas) W(alter) 1908-1988 ... 5-8R
Obituary ... 125
Freeman, Thomas 1919- ... 93-96
Freeman, Tony ... 134
See also SATA 44
Freeman, Walter (Jackson Jr.)
1895-1972 ... CAP-1
Obituary ... 33-36R
Earlier sketch in CA 17-18
Freeman, Warren S(amuel) 1911- ... 5-8R
Freeman, William Bradford 1938- ... SATA 48, 58
Freeman, William M. 1913-1990 Obituary ... 130
Freeman-Grenville, Greville Stewart Parker
1918- ... CANR-3
Earlier sketch in CA 5-8R
Freeman-Ishill, Rose 1895- ... CAP-1
Earlier sketch in CA 9-10
Freemantle, Brian Harry 1936- ... CANR-16
Earlier sketch in CA 65-68
Freemon, Frank R(eed) 1938- ... 45-58
Freer, Coburn 1939- ... 125
Brief entry ... 105
Freer, Harold Wiley 1906- ... CAP-2
Earlier sketch in CA 21-22
Freese, Arthur S. 1917- ... 77-80
Freestrom, Hubert J. 1928- ... 37-40R
Freeth, Zahra 1925- ... 121
Fregault, Guy 1918-1977 ... 101
Frege, (Friedrich Ludwig) Gottlob
1848-1925 Brief entry ... 120
Fregly, Bert 1922- ... CANR-8
Earlier sketch in CA 57-60
Fregosi, Claudia (Anne Marie) 1946- ... 69-72
See also SATA 24
Frei, Eduardo
See Frei Montalva, Eduardo
Frei, Hans W(ilhelm) 1922-1988 Obituary ... 126
Brief entry ... 111
Freiberg, Stanley K(enneth) 1923- ... CANR-31
Earlier sketch in CA 112
Freiberger, Steven Z. 1950- ... 138
Freid, Jacob L. 1913- ... CANR-17
Earlier sketch in CA 1-4R
Freidel, Frank (Burt Jr.) 1916- ... CANR-5
Earlier sketch in CA 1-4R
Freidenreich, Harriet Pass 1947- ... 114
Freides, Thelma K(atz) 1930- ... 49-52
Freidin, Seymour K(enneth)
1917-1991 ... CANR-2
Obituary ... 134
Earlier sketch in CA 1-4R
Freidson, Eliot 1923- ... CANR-8
Earlier sketch in CA 5-8R
Freihofer, Lois Diane 1933- ... 13-16R
Freilich, Joan S(herman) 1941- ... 57-60
Freilich, Morris 1928- ... 37-40R
Frei Montalva, Eduardo
1911-1982 Obituary ... 110
Freire, P.
See Freire, Paulo
Freire, Paulo 1921- ... 132
Brief entry ... 116
Freire-Maia, Newton 1918- ... 29-32R
Freitas, Margarete Elisabeth 1927- ... 45-48
Freivalds, John 1944- ... 69-72
Freixedo, Salvador 1923- ... 29-32R
Frelinghuysen, Joseph S. 1912- ... 134
Fremantle, Anne 1910- ... 13-16R
Fremgen, James Morgan 1933- ... 17-20R
Fremlin, Celia
See Goller, Celia (Fremlin)
Fremont, W. B.
See Bowers, Warner Fremont
Fremont-Smith, Eliot 1929- ... 105
Frenay, Henri 1905-1988 Obituary ... 126
French, Alfred 1916- ... 102
French, Alice 1850-1934 ... DLB 74
French, Allen 1870-1946 Brief entry ... 122
See also YABC 1
French, Ashley
See Robins, Denise (Naomi)
French, Bevan M(eredith) 1937- ... 97-100
French, Brandon 1944- ... 89-92
French, Calvin L(eonard) 1934- ... 53-56
French, Charles E(zra) 1923- ... CANR-1
Earlier sketch in CA 45-48
French, Christopher W.
1940(?)-1989 Obituary ... 129
French, David 1939- ... 101
See also DLB 53
French, Doris
See Shackleton, Doris (Cavell)
French, Dorothy Kayser 1926- ... CANR-3
Earlier sketch in CA 9-12R
See also SATA 5
French, Edward L(ivingstone)
1916-1969 ... CAP-2
Earlier sketch in CA 21-22
French, Fiona 1944- ... 29-32R
See also MAICYA
See also SATA 6
French, Herbert E(liot) 1912- ... 45-48
French, Kathryn
See Mosesson, Gloria R(ubin)
French, Marilyn 1929- ... CANR-31
Earlier sketches in CA 69-72, CANR-3
See also CLC 10, 18, 60
See also MTCW
French, Michael 1944- ... 89-92
See also SATA 38, 49

French, Paul
See Asimov, Isaac
French, Peter A(ndrew) 1942- CANR-38
Earlier sketches in CA 45-48, CANR-1, 17
French, Peter 1918- 1-4R
French, Philip (Neville) 1933- 103
French, R(obert) B(utler) D(igby)
1904-1981 .... CAP-2
Obituary 104
Earlier sketch in CA 25-28
French, R(oger) K(enneth) 1938- 118
French, Richard (De Land) 1947- CANR-11
Earlier sketch in CA 69-72
French, Ruth M. 1921(?)-1987 Obituary 122
French, Scott Robert 1948- 57-60
French, Simon 1957- CANR-22
Earlier sketch in CA 105
French, Warren G(raham) 1922- CANR-16
Earlier sketches in CA 1-4R, CANR-1
French, Wendell L(owell) 1923- 116
French, Will 1890(?)-1979 Obituary 89-92
French, William (Harold) 1926- 69-72
French, William Marshall 1907- CAP-1
Earlier sketch in CA 13-16
Frend, A.
See Cleveland, Philip Jerome
Frend, W(illiam) H(ugh) C(lifford) 1916- CANR-9
Earlier sketch in CA 21-24R
Freneau, Philip Morin 1752-1832 ....DLB 37, 43
Frenkel, Jacob A(haron) 1943- 89-92
Frenkel, Richard E(ugene) 1924- 21-24R
Frentzen, Jeffrey 1956- 109
Frenz, Horst 1912- 29-32R
Frenzel, Louis (Earl) Jr. 1938- 112
Frere, A. S.
See Frere-Reeves, Alexander Stuart
Frere, Emile (George) 1917-1974 ....41-44R
Frere, James Arnold 1920- 5-8R
Frere, Paul 1917- CANR-14
Earlier sketch in CA 5-8R
Frere, Sheppard (Sunderland) 1916- 21-24R
Frere-Cook, Gervis 1928- Brief entry 111
Frere-Reeves, Alexander Stuart
1892-1984 Obituary 114
Frerichs, A(lbert) C(hristian) 1910- CAP-2
Earlier sketch in CA 25-28
Freschet, Berniece (Louise Speck)
1927- CANR-11
Earlier sketch in CA 17-20R
Frese, Dolores Warwick 1936- CANR-9
Earlier sketch in CA 5-8R
Fretheim, Terence E(rling) 1936- CANR-11
Earlier sketch in CA 25-28R
Fretter, T. W.
See Andre, (Kenneth) Michael
Fretter, William Bache 1916- 113
Fretwell, Stephen DeWitt 1942- 53-56
Freuchen, (Lorence) Peter (Elfred)
1886-1957 Brief entry 114
Freud, Anna 1895-1982 ....CANR-34
Obituary 108
Earlier sketch in CA 112
See also MTCW
Freud, Clement (Raphael) 1924- 102
Freud, Sigmund 1856-1939 133
Brief entry 115
See also MTCW
Freud, Sophie 1924- 134
Freudberg, Frank 1953- 118
Freudenberger, C(arlton) Dean 1930- 135
Freudenberger, Herman 1922- 13-16R
Freudenheim, Leslie Ann Mandelson
1941- 69-72
Freudenheim, Yehoshua (Oskar)
1894-1975 .... CAP-2
Earlier sketch in CA 21-22
Freudenthal, Hans 1905- CANR-27
Earlier sketches in CA 25-28R, CANR-11
Freund, E(rnest) Hans 1905- 1-4R
Freund, Edith 1931- 118
Freund, Gerald 1930- CANR-1
Earlier sketch in CA 1-4R
Freund, Gisele 1912- 49-52
Freund, John E(rnst) 1921- 13-16R
Freund, Otto Kahn
See Kahn-Freund, Otto
Freund, Paul A(braham) 1908-1992 ....1-4R
Obituary 136
Freund, Philip (Herbert) 1909- CANR-12
Earlier sketch in CA 13-16R
Freund, Rudolf 1915-1969 .... SATA 28
Freundlich, August L. 1924- 49-52
Frevert, Peter 1938- 81-84
Frew, David R(ichard) 1943- 77-80
Frewer, Glyn (M.) 1931- CANR-10
Earlier sketch in CA 13-16R
See also SATA 11
Frewin, Leslie Ronald 1917- CANR-11
Earlier sketch in CA 5-8R
Frey, Andrew 1905(?)-1983 Obituary 109
Frey, Erich A. 1931- 45-48
Frey, Frederick Ward 1929- 53-56
Frey, Henry A. 1923- 33-36R
Frey, John Andrew 1929- 89-92
Frey, Leonard H(amilton) 1927- 29-32R
Frey, Marlys
See Mayfield, Marlys
Frey, Richard L(incoln) 1905-1988 89-92
Obituary 126
Frey, Robert Seitz 1955- 128
Freyberg, Paul 1923- 135
Freyer, Frederic
See Ballinger, William Sanborn
Freyre, Gilberto (de Mello) 1900-1987 126
Brief entry 117
Freyre, Ricardo Jaimes
See Jaimes Freyre, Ricardo
Freytag, Joseph
See Cooper, Parley J(oseph)
Freytag, Josephine
See Cooper, Parley J(oseph)
Friar, Kimon 1911- 85-88
Friar Tuck
See Tucker, Irwin St. John
Fribourg, Marjorie G. 1920- CANR-4
Earlier sketch in CA 1-4R
Frick, C. H.
See Irwin, Constance Frick
Frick, Constance
See Irwin, Constance Frick
Frick, Ford Christopher
1894-1978 Obituary 89-92
Frick, George F(rederick) 1925- 13-16R
Fricke, Cedric V. 1928- 13-16R
Fricker, E(dward) G(eorge) 1910- 125
Fricker, Mary 1940- 134
Friday, Nancy 1937- CANR-28
Earlier sketch in CA 77-80
See also MTCW
Friday, Peter
See Harris, Herbert
Fridenson, Patrick 1944- 129
Frideres, James S(tephen) 1943- 113
Fridy, (William) Wallace 1910- CANR-17
Earlier sketch in CA 1-4R
Friebert, Stuart (Alyn) 1931- 65-68
Fried, Barbara 1924- 45-48
Fried, Charles 1935- CANR-12
Earlier sketch in CA 29-32R
Fried, Eleanor L.
See Furman, Eleanor L.
Fried, Emanuel 1913- 73-76
Fried, Erich 1921-1988 126
Obituary 127
Brief entry 114
See also DLB 85
Fried, Eunice 124
Fried, Frederick 1908- 77-80
Fried, John J(ames) 1940- CANR-12
Earlier sketch in CA 33-36R
Fried, Jonathan L(ester) 1955- 113
Fried, Joseph P. 1939- 37-40R
Fried, Lawrence 1926-1983 Obituary 110
Fried, Marc (Allen) 1922- 77-80
Fried, Marc B(ernard) 1944- 77-80
Fried, Mary McKenzie Hill 1914- 93-96
Fried, Morton H(erbert) 1923-1986 ....21-24R
Obituary 121
Fried, Peter A(lexander) 1943- 108
Fried, Richard M(ayer) 1941- 73-76
Fried, William 1945- 57-60
Friedan, Betty (Naomi) 1921- CANR-18
Earlier sketch in CA 65-68
See also MTCW
Friedberg, Ardy 1935- 108
Friedberg, Gertrude (Tonkonogy)
1908(?)-1989 ....21-24R
Obituary 129
Friedberg, Joan Brest 1927- 124
Friedberg, Maurice 1929- CANR-5
Earlier sketch in CA 1-4R
Friede, Eleanor Kask 1920- 101
Friedeberg-Seeley, Frank (J. B.) 1912- 138
Friedelbaum, Stanley H(erman) 1927- 37-40R
Friedell, Aaron 1890(?)-1985 Obituary 116
Frieden, Bernard J. 1930- CANR-10
Earlier sketch in CA 13-16R
Frieden, Ken(neth) 1955- 118
Friedenberg, Edgar Zodiag 1921- CANR-29
Earlier sketch in CA 65-68
Friedenberg, Walter Drew 1928- 89-92
Friedenreich, Harriet Pass
See Freidenreich, Harriet Pass
Friedenthal, Richard 1896-1979 103
Obituary 89-92
Frieder, Emma 1891- CAP-2
Earlier sketch in CA 33-36
Friederich, Werner P(aul) 1905- 13-16R
Friederichsen, Kathleen (Hockman)
1910- 17-20R
Friedgut, Theodore H. 1931- 89-92
Friedheim, Robert L(yle) 1934- CANR-12
Earlier sketch in CA 21-24R
Friedkin, William 1939- 107
Friedl, Ernestine 1920- 37-40R
Friedl, John 1945- CANR-4
Earlier sketch in CA 53-56
Friedlaender, Walter (Ferdinand)
1873-1966 Obituary 115
Friedland, Ronald Lloyd 1937-1975 .... CAP-2
Obituary 57-60
Earlier sketch in CA 33-36
Friedland, Ronnie 1945- 106
Friedland, Seymour 1928- CANR-17
Earlier sketch in CA 25-28R
Friedland, William H. 1923- 13-16R
Friedlander, Albert H(oschander)
1927- CANR-25
Earlier sketches in CA 21-24R, CANR-9
Friedlander, Howard 1941- 105
Friedlander, Joanne K(ohn) 1930- 61-64
See also SATA 9
Friedlander, Saul 1932- 130
Brief entry 117
Friedlander, Stanley Lawrence 1938- 17-20R
Friedlander, Walter A(ndreas) 1891- 37-40R
Friedman, Alan
See Horowitz, Shel Alan
Friedman, Alan J(acob) 1942- 125
Friedman, Alan Warren 1939- 25-28R
Friedman, Albert B(arron) 1920- CANR-17
Earlier sketch in CA 1-4R
Friedman, Alice R. 1900- 41-44R
Friedman, Amy 1952- 133
Friedman, Arnold D'Arcy
1900-1981 Obituary 109
Friedman, Arnold P(hineas) 1909- CANR-1
Earlier sketch in CA 45-48
Friedman, Avner 1932- 53-56
Friedman, B(ernard) H(arper) 1926- CANR-3
Earlier sketch in CA 1-4R
See also CLC 7
Friedman, Bernard 1896-1983 Obituary 110
Friedman, Bruce Jay 1930- CANR-25
Earlier sketch in CA 9-12R
See also CLC 3, 5, 56
See also DLB 2, 28
Friedman, Charles 1902-1984 Obituary 113
Friedman, David F. 1923- 134
Friedman, David 1945- 89-92
Friedman, Edward H. 1948- 127
Friedman, Edward Ludwig 1903- 1-4R
Friedman, Elizabeth 1893(?)-1980 Obituary 102
Friedman, Estelle (Ehrenwald) 1920- 5-8R
See also SATA 7
Friedman, Frieda 1905- .... SATA 43
Friedman, Hal
See Friedman, Harold
Friedman, Harold 1942- 89-92
Friedman, Herbert 1916- Brief entry 112
Friedman, Ina R(osen) 1926- 53-56
See also SATA 41, 49
Friedman, Irving S(igmund) 1915-1989 ....CANR-3
Obituary 130
Earlier sketch in CA 45-48
Friedman, Isaiah 1921- 53-56
Friedman, Jerrold David
See Gerrold, David
Friedman, John Block 1934- 125
Friedman, John S(aul) 1942- 118
Friedman, Josephine Troth 1928- 77-80
Friedman, Josh Alan 1956- 122
Friedman, Josh(ua M.) 1941- Brief entry 126
Friedman, Joy Troth
See Friedman, Josephine Troth
Friedman, Judi 1935- 65-68
See also AITN 2
See also SATA 59
Friedman, Julian R. 1920(?)-1983 Obituary 111
Friedman, Kathy V(allone) 1943- CANR-38
Earlier sketch in CA 114
Friedman, Ken(neth Scott) 65-68
Friedman, Kenneth 1939- 25-28R
Friedman, Lawrence J. 1940- 53-56
Friedman, Lawrence Meir 1930- CANR-5
Earlier sketch in CA 13-16R
Friedman, Lenemaja 1924- 61-64
Friedman, Leon 1933- 81-84
Friedman, Lester David 1945- 108
Friedman, Marcia 1925- 57-60
Friedman, Marvin 1930- .... SATA 33, 42
Friedman, Maurice S(tanley) 1921- 13-16R
Friedman, Max Motel
1899(?)-1988 Obituary 125
Friedman, Melvin J(ack) 1928- 21-24R
Friedman, Meyer 1910- 127
Brief entry 113
Friedman, Michael H(enry) 1945- 101
Friedman, Michael J(an) 1955- 119
Friedman, Michaele Thompson 1944- 111
Friedman, Mickey
See Friedman, Michaele Thompson
Friedman, Milton 1912- CANR-22
Earlier sketches in CA 1-4R, CANR-1
See also MTCW
Friedman, Murray 1926- 57-60
Friedman, Myles I(van) 1924- CANR-6
Earlier sketch in CA 57-60
Friedman, Nancy 1950- 107
Friedman, Norman 1925- CANR-1
Earlier sketch in CA 1-4R
Friedman, Paul Belais 1953- 110
Friedman, Paul 1899-1972 Obituary 37-40R
Friedman, Paul 1937- 122
Friedman, Ralph 1916- 69-72
Friedman, Rochelle (Rame) 1942- 112
Friedman, Rose D(irector) CANR-22
Earlier sketch in CA 101
Friedman, (Eve) Rosemary (Tibber)
1929- CANR-21
Earlier sketches in CA 5-8R, CANR-3
Friedman, Roslyn Berger 1924- 17-20R
Friedman, Roy 1934- 25-28R
Friedman, Sanford 1928- 73-76
Friedman, Sara Ann 1935- 77-80
Friedman, Saul S. 1937- 57-60
Friedman, Stuart 1913- 1-4R
Friedman, Susan Stanford 1943- 109
Friedman, Thomas L(oren) 1953- CANR-38
Earlier sketch in CA 109
See also BEST 90:1
Friedman, Warner G(eorge) 1934- 97-100
Friedman, Winifred
1923(?)-1975 Obituary 61-64
Friedman, Yona 1923- 130
Friedmann, Arnold 1925- 41-44R
Friedmann, Deborah Davis
See Davis-Friedmann, Deborah
Friedmann, Georges
1902(?)-1977 Obituary 104
Friedmann, Herbert 1900-1987 106
Obituary 122
Friedmann, John 1926- CANR-15
Earlier sketch in CA 85-88
Friedmann, Thomas 1947- 118
Friedmann, Wolfgang (Gaston)
1907-1972 ....CANR-6
Earlier sketch in CA 1-4R
Friedmann, Yohanan 1936- 33-36R
Friedrich, Anton
See Strich, Christian
Friedrich, Carl Joachim 1901-1984 ....CANR-30
Obituary 113
Earlier sketch in CA 69-72
Friedrich, Dick
See Friedrich, Richard
Friedrich, Gustav W(illiam)
1941- Brief entry 111
Friedrich, Otto (Alva) 1929- CANR-3
Earlier sketch in CA 5-8R
See also SATA 33
Friedrich, Paul 1927- CANR-12
Earlier sketch in CA 29-32R
Friedrich, Priscilla 1927- 113
See also SATA 39
Friedrich, Richard 1936- 103
Friedrichs, Christopher R(ichard) 1947- 89-92
Friedrichs, Robert W(inslow) 1923- 49-52
Friedson, Anthony M(artin) 1924- 108
Friel, Brian 1929- CANR-33
Earlier sketch in CA 21-24R
See also CLC 5, 42, 59
See also DLB 13
See also MTCW
Frielink, A(braham) Barend 1917- 21-24R
Friend, Joseph H(arold) 1909-1972 .... CAP-2
Earlier sketch in CA 25-28
Friend, Krebs 1895(?)-1967(?) .... DLB 4
Friend, Robert 1913- CANR-7
Earlier sketch in CA 13-16R
Friend, Theodore (Wood III) 1931- 138
Friendlich, Dick
See Friendlich, Richard J.
Friendlich, Richard J. 1909- CAP-1
Earlier sketch in CA 13-16
See also SATA 11
Friendly, Alfred 1911-1983 101
Obituary 111
Friendly, Fred W. 1915- CANR-14
Earlier sketch in CA 21-24R
Friendly, Henry Jacob 1903-1986 103
Obituary 118
Frier, Bruce W(oodward) 1943- 125
Friermood, Elisabeth Hamilton 1903- CANR-1
Earlier sketch in CA 1-4R
See also SATA 5
Fries, Albert Charles 1908- CANR-4
Earlier sketch in CA 1-4R
Fries, Fritz Rudolf 1935- CANR-11
Earlier sketch in CA 25-28R
See also DLB 75
Fries, James Franklin 1938- 89-92
Fries, Robert Francis 1911- 106
Friesel, Evyatar 1930- 135
Friesen, Garry 1947- 114
Friesen, Gerald 1943- 120
Friesen, Patrick 1945- CANR-32
Earlier sketch in CA 113
Friesner, Esther M.
See Friesner-Stutzman, Esther M.
See also SATA 71
Friesner-Stutzman, Esther M. 1951- 125
See also Friesner, Esther M.
Friess, Horace L(eland) 1900-1975 65-68
Obituary 61-64
Friggens, Arthur (Henry) 1920- 103
Friis, Erik J(ohan) 1913- 69-72
Friis, Harald T(rap) 1893-1976 Obituary 65-68
Friis-Baastad, Babbis Ellinor 1921-1970 ....17-20R
Obituary 134
See also CLC 12
See also SATA 7
Frijling-Schreuder, E(lisabeth) C. M.
1908- 61-64
Frillmann, Paul W. 1911-1972 .... CAP-2
Obituary 37-40R
Earlier sketch in CA 25-28
Friman, Alice 1933- 129
Frimbo, E. M.
See Whitaker, Rogers E(rnest) M(alcolm)
Friml, Rudolf 1879-1972 Obituary 37-40R
Frimmer, Steven 1928- 33-36R
See also SATA 31
Frimoth, Lenore B(eck) 1927- 5-8R
Frindall, Bill
See Frindall, William Howard
Frindall, William Howard 1939- 135
Frings, Ketti 1915-1981 101
Obituary 103
Frings, Manfred S. 1925- CANR-26
Earlier sketches in CA 17-20R, CANR-8
Frink, Maurice 1895-1972 .... CAP-2
Earlier sketch in CA 25-28
Frinta, Mojmir S(vatopluk) 1922- 25-28R
Fripp, Patricia 1945- 93-96
Frisbie, Louise K(elley) 1913- 61-64
Frisbie, Margery (Rowbottom) 1923- 5-8R
Frisbie, Richard P(atrick) 1926- CANR-38
Earlier sketches in CA 5-8R, CANR-2, 17
Frisby, Terence (Peter Michael) 1932- 65-68
Frisch, Karl (Ritter) von 1886-1982 85-88
Obituary 115
Frisch, Max (Rudolf) 1911-1991 ....CANR-32
Obituary 134
Earlier sketch in CA 85-88
See also CLC 3, 9, 14, 18, 32, 44
See also DLB 69
See also MTCW
Frisch, Michael H(erbert) 1942- 126
Frisch, Morton J. 1923- 33-36R
Frisch, O(tto) R(obert) 1904- 9-12R
Frisch, Paul Z. 1926(?)-1977 Obituary 73-76
Frisch, Ragnar Anton Kittil
1895-1973 Obituary 115
Frischauer, Willi 1906- CANR-7
Earlier sketch in CA 5-8R
Frischer, Bernard D(avid) 1949- 113
Frischmuth, Barbara 1941- .... DLB 85

Frischwasser-Ra'Anan, H. F.
  See Ra'Anan, Uri
Friskey, Margaret (Richards) 1901- CANR-2
  Earlier sketch in CA 5-8R
  See also SATA 5
Frison, George C(arr) 1924- 93-96
Frist, William H. 1952- 136
Fritchman, Stephen Hole 1902- Brief entry 105
Frith, David (Edward John) 1937- 138
Frith, H(arold) J(ames) 1921- 102
Frith, Nigel (Andrew Silver) 1941- 69-72
Fritsch, Albert Joseph 1933- 102
Fritsch, Bruno 1926- CANR-11
  Earlier sketch in CA 69-72
Fritsch, Charles Theodore 1912- 112
Fritschler, A. Lee 1937- 33-36R
Fritts, Mary Bahr
  See Bahr, Mary
Fritz
  See Whitehall, Harold
Fritz, Henry E(ugene) 1927- 17-20R
Fritz, Jean (Guttery) 1915- CANR-37
  Earlier sketches in CA 1-4R, CANR-5, 16
  See also CLR 2, 14
  See also DLB 52
  See also MAICYA
  See also SAAS 2
  See also SATA 1, 29
Fritz, Leah 1931- 93-96
Fritze, Julius Arnold 1918- 103
Fritzell, Peter A(lgren) 1940- 133
Fritzsch, Harald 1943- 113
Frobish, Nestle J(ohn) 1930- 101
Froboess, Harry (August) 1899- CAP-2
  Earlier sketch in CA 17-18
Froehlich, Gustav 1902-1987 Obituary 124
Froehlich, Margaret W(alden) 1930- 115
  See also SATA 56
Froelich, Robert E. 1929- CANR-3
  Earlier sketch in CA 45-48
Frohlich, Gustav
  See Froehlich, Gustav
Frohlich, Norman 1941- 77-80
Frohman, Charles E(ugene) 1901-1976 ....CAP-2
  Earlier sketch in CA 29-32
Frohock, W(ilbur) M(errill) 1908-1984 73-76
  Obituary 113
Froissard, Lily Powell CANR-25
  Earlier sketch in CA 45-48
Froissart, Jean 1338(?)-1410(?) ....SATA 28
Froman, Elizabeth Hull 1920-1975 ....CAP-1
  Obituary 53-56
  Earlier sketch in CA 13-16
  See also SATA 10
Froman, Lewis A(crelius) Jr. 1935- 5-8R
Froman, Robert (Winslow) 1917- CANR-1
  Earlier sketch in CA 1-4R
  See also SATA 8
Frome, David
  See Brown, Zenith Jones
Frome, Frieda
  See Krieger, Frieda Frome
Frome, Michael 1920- CANR-16
  Earlier sketches in CA 1-4R, CANR-1
Fromer, Margot J(oan) 1939- 110
Fromkin, David 1932- 109
Fromkin, Howard L(arry) 1939- 121
  Brief entry 118
Fromkin, Victoria A(lexandria) 1923- 89-92
Fromm, Erich 1900-1980 ....CANR-29
  Obituary 97-100
  Earlier sketch in CA 73-76
  See also MTCW
Fromm, Erika 1910- 9-12R
Fromm, Gary 1933- CANR-7
  Earlier sketch in CA 17-20R
Fromm, Gloria G(likin) 1931- Brief entry 112
Fromm, Harold 1933- 21-24R
Fromm, Herbert 1905- CANR-1
  Earlier sketch in CA 49-52
Fromm, Lilo 1928- 81-84
  See also SATA 29
Fromme, Babbette Brandt 1925- 106
Frommer, Harvey 1937- CANR-26
  Earlier sketch in CA 103
  See also SATA 41
Frommer, Myrna 1941- 111
Froncek, Thomas (Walter) 1942- 81-84
Frondizi, Risieri 1910- 41-44R
Frontier, Tex
  See Miller, J(ames) P.
Frooks, Dorothy 1899- 57-60
Froomkin, Joseph 1927- CANR-13
  Earlier sketch in CA 21-24R
Frosch, Thomas Richard 1943- 69-72
Froscher, Wingate 1918- 1-4R
Frost, A(rthur) B(urdett) 1851-1928 136
  See also MAICYA
  See also SATA 19
Frost, Carol 1948- CANR-11
  Earlier sketch in CA 69-72
Frost, David (Paradine) 1939- CANR-31
  Earlier sketch in CA 69-72
Frost, Erica
  See Supraner, Robyn
Frost, Ernest 1918- 9-12R
Frost, Everett L(loyd) 1942- 65-68
Frost, Frank (Jasper) 1929- 89-92
Frost, Frederick
  See Faust, Frederick (Shiller)
Frost, Gavin 1930- CANR-1
  Earlier sketch in CA 45-48
Frost, Gerhard Emanuel 1909- CAP-1
  Earlier sketch in CA 9-10
Frost, Gregory 1951- 118
Frost, Helen 1898- CAP-1
  Earlier sketch in CA 13-14
Frost, James A(rthur) 1918- 37-40R
Frost, Jason
  See Obstfeld, Raymond
Frost, Joe L. 1933- 25-28R
Frost, Joni
  See Paine, Lauran (Bosworth)
Frost, Lawrence A(ugust) 1907-1990 ....CANR-26
  Obituary 132
  Earlier sketches in CA 69-72, CANR-11
Frost, Lesley 1899-1983 ....21-24R
  Obituary 110
  See also SATA 14, 34
Frost, Leslie Miscampbell
  1895-1973 Obituary 41-44R
Frost, M(ax) Gilbert 1908- CAP-1
  Earlier sketch in CA 13-14
Frost, Marjorie 1914- 25-28R
Frost, O(rcutt) W(illiam) 1926- 136
Frost, Paul
  See Castle, Anthony (Percy)
Frost, Peter Kip 1936- 33-36R
Frost, Richard H(indman) 1930- 25-28R
Frost, Richard T. 1926-1972 ....CAP-1
  Obituary 37-40R
  Earlier sketch in CA 13-16
Frost, Richard 1929- 33-36R
Frost, Robert Carlton 1926- 53-56
Frost, Robert (Lee) 1874-1963 ....CANR-33
  Earlier sketch in CA 89-92
  See also CDALB 1917-1929
  See also CLC 1, 3, 4, 9, 10, 13, 15, 26, 34, 44
  See also DLB 54
  See also DLBD 7
  See also MTCW
  See also PC 1
  See also SATA 14
  See also WLC
Frost, Roon 1943- 126
Frost, S. E. Jr. 1899- CAP-2
  Earlier sketch in CA 19-20
Frost, Stanley Brice 1913- 61-64
Frost, William 1917- 41-44R
Frostic, Gwen 1906- 17-20R
Frostick, Michael 1917- 9-12R
Frothingham, Octavius Brooks
  1822-1895 ....DLB 1
Froude, James Anthony 1818-1894 ....DLB 18, 57
Frow, John 1948- 120
Froy, Herald
  See Deghy, Guy (Stephen)
  and Waterhouse, Keith (Spencer)
Frucht, Abby 1957- 127
Frucht, Phyllis 1936- 57-60
Fruchtenbaum, Arnold G(enekovich)
  1943- CANR-11
  Earlier sketch in CA 61-64
Fruchter, Benjamin 1914- 1-4R
Fruchter, Norman D. 81-84
Frude, Neil 1946- 114
Fruehling, Rosemary T(herese) 1933- CANR-35
  Earlier sketches in CA 33-36R, CANR-13
Frugoni, Cesare 1881-1978 Obituary 73-76
Fruhan, William E(dward) Jr. 1943- 41-44R
Frum, Barbara 1937- 101
  Obituary 137
Fruman, Norman 1923- 37-40R
Frumkes, Lewis Burke 1939- CANR-36
  Earlier sketch in CA 114
Frumkin, Gene 1928- CANR-4
  Earlier sketch in CA 9-12R
Frumkin, Robert M. 1928- CANR-9
  Earlier sketch in CA 21-24R
Fruton, Joseph S(tewart) 1912- CANR-34
  Earlier sketch in CA 49-52
Fruzzetti, Lina M(aria) 1942- 113
Fry, Alan 1931- CANR-1
  Earlier sketch in CA 45-48
Fry, Barbara 1932- 25-28R
Fry, C(harles) George 1936- CANR-31
  Earlier sketches in CA 37-40R, CANR-14
Fry, Christine 1943- 107
Fry, Christopher 1907- CANR-30
  Earlier sketches in CA 17-20R, CANR-9
  See also CLC 2, 10, 14
  See also DLB 13
  See also MTCW
  See also SATA 66
Fry, David
  See Roper, William L(eon)
Fry, Dennis Butler 1907-1983 109
  Obituary 110
Fry, Donald K(lein Jr.) 1937- 25-28R
Fry, E(dwin) Maxwell 1899-1987 65-68
  Obituary 123
Fry, Earl H(oward) 1947- 102
Fry, Edward Bernard 1925- CANR-5
  Earlier sketch in CA 9-12R
  See also SATA 35
Fry, Hilary G. 1922- 17-20R
Fry, Howard T(yrrell) 1919- 37-40R
Fry, John 1930- 93-96
Fry, Maggie Culver 1900- ....AITN 1
Fry, Maxwell
  See Fry, E(dwin) Maxwell
Fry, Michael G(raham) 1934- CANR-23
  Earlier sketch in CA 69-72
Fry, P(atricia) Eileen 1947- 104
Fry, Paul H. 1944- 129
Fry, Plantagenet Somerset
  See
  Somerset Fry, (Peter George Robin) Plantagenet
Fry, Roger (Eliot) 1866-1934 Brief entry 115
Fry, Ronald W(illiam) 1949- 57-60
Fry, Rosalie Kingsmill 1911- 9-12R
  See also SAAS 11
  See also SATA 3
Fry, Thomas Frederick 1919- 118
Fry, Tom
  See Fry, Thomas Frederick
Fry, William F(inley Jr.) 1924- 5-8R
Fryatt, Norma R. 57-60
Fryburger, Vernon R(ay) Jr. 1918- 1-4R
Fryd, Norbert 1913-1976 Obituary 65-68
Frydman, Szajko 1911- 25-28R
Frye, (Charles) Alton 1936- 21-24R
Frye, Ellen 1940- 49-52
Frye, John 1910- CANR-28
  Earlier sketch in CA 49-52
Frye, Keith 1935- 53-56
Frye, (Herman) Northrop 1912-1991 ....CANR-37
  Obituary 133
  Earlier sketches in CA 5-8R, CANR-8
  See also CLC 24, 70
  See also DLB 67, 68
  See also MTCW
Frye, Richard N(elson) 1920- CANR-3
  Earlier sketch in CA 5-8R
Frye, Roland Mushat 1921- 9-12R
Frye, William R(uggles) 1918- 73-76
Fryer, Donald S.
  See Sidney-Fryer, Donald
Fryer, Holly C(laire) 1908- CAP-1
  Earlier sketch in CA 19-20
Fryer, Jonathan 1950- 85-88
Fryer, Judith 1939- 69-72
Fryer, Mary Beacock 1929- 97-100
Fryer, William T. 1900(?)-1980 Obituary 93-96
Frykenberg, Robert Eric 1930- 25-28R
Fryklund, Verne C(harles) 1896-1980 ....13-16R
  Obituary 126
Frykman, John H(arvey) 1932- 33-36R
Frym, Gloria 1947- 105
Frymier, Jack R(immel) 1925- 17-20R
Fryscak, Milan 1932- 53-56
Fuchida, Mitsuo 1902(?)-1976 Obituary 65-68
Fuchs, Daniel 1909- 81-84
  See also CAAS 5
  See also CLC 8, 22
  See also DLB 9, 26, 28
Fuchs, Daniel 1934- CANR-14
  Earlier sketch in CA 37-40R
  See also CLC 34
Fuchs, Elinor 1933- 105
Fuchs, Erich 1916- 29-32R
  See also SATA 6
Fuchs, Estelle 57-60
Fuchs, Guenter Bruno 1928-1977 Obituary 114
Fuchs, Jacob 1939- 21-24R
Fuchs, Jerome H(erbert) 1922- 69-72
Fuchs, Josef 1912- 21-24R
Fuchs, Lawrence H. 1927- CANR-5
  Earlier sketch in CA 1-4R
Fuchs, Lucy 1935- CANR-30
  Earlier sketches in CA 73-76, CANR-12
  See also SATA 52
Fuchs, Roland J(ohn) 1933- CANR-14
  Earlier sketch in CA 81-84
Fuchs, Victor R(obert) 1924- CANR-18
  Earlier sketches in CA 1-4R, CANR-2
Fuchs, Vivian (Ernest) 1908- CANR-21
  Earlier sketch in CA 104
Fuchshuber, Annegert 1940- 112
  See also SATA 43
Fucilla, Joseph G(uerin) 1897- 89-92
Fucini, Joseph J(ames) 1951- 120
Fucini, Suzy 1951- 120
Fudge, William Kingston
  1904-1985 Obituary 116
Fuegi, John 1936- 37-40R
Fueloep-Miller, Rene 1891-1963 Obituary 110
Fuentes, Carlos 1928- CANR-32
  Earlier sketches in CA 69-72, CANR-10
  See also AAYA 4
  See also AITN 2
  See also CLC 3, 8, 10, 13, 22, 41, 60
  See also DLB 113
  See also HW
  See also MTCW
  See also WLC
Fuentes, Gregorio Lopez y
  See Lopez y Fuentes, Gregorio
Fuentes, Martha Ayers 1923- 73-76
Fuentes, Roberto 1934- 57-60
Fuentes Mohr, Alberto
  1928(?)-1979 Obituary 85-88
Fuerer-Haimendorf, Christoph von
  1909- CANR-13
  Earlier sketch in CA 13-16R
Fuermann, George Melvin 1918- 103
Fuertes, Gloria 1918- ....DLB 108
Fufuka, Karama
  See Morgan, Sharon A(ntonia)
Fugard, (Harold) Athol 1932- CANR-32
  Earlier sketch in CA 85-88
  See also CLC 5, 9, 14, 25, 40
  See also MTCW
Fugard, Sheila 1932- 125
  See also CLC 48
Fugate, Bryan I(rven) 1943- 120
Fugate, Francis L(yle) 1915- 25-28R
Fugate, Joe K. 1931- 21-24R
Fugate, Roberta B(auslin) 1917- 111
Fugate, Terence (McCuddy) 1930- 5-8R
Fugitt, Eva D(raper) 1929- 110
Fuhrman, Ellsworth R(aymond) 1946- 112
Fuhrman, Lee 1903(?)-1977 Obituary 73-76
Fuhrmann, Joseph T(heodore) 1940- 73-76
Fuhro, Wilbur J. 1914- 9-12R
Fujikawa, Gyo 1908- 113
  See also CLR 25
  See also MAICYA
  See also SATA 30, 39
Fujita, Tamao 1905- 37-40R
  See also SATA 7
Fujiwara, Iwaichi 1908- 132
Fujiwara, Michiko 1946- 77-80
  See also SATA 15
Fujiwara, Yoichi 1909- CANR-22
  Earlier sketch in CA 105
Fuka, Vladimir 1926-1977 Obituary 104
  See also SATA 27
Fukei, Gladys Arlene (Harper) 1920- 13-16R
Fuks, Ladislav 1923- 118
Fukuda, Haruko 1946- 109
Fukuda, Tsutomu 1905- 103
Fukui, Haruhiro 1935- 29-32R
Fukutake, Tadashi 1917- CANR-5
  Earlier sketch in CA 13-16R
Fukuyama, Yoshio 1921- 41-44R
Fulbright, J(ames) William 1905- 9-12R
Fulbrook, Mary (Jean Alexandra) 1951- 121
Fulco, William J(ames) 1936- 49-52
Fuld, James J. 1916- 21-24R
Fuld, Leonard M. 1953- 120
Fulda, Carl H. 1909-1975 ....CAP-2
  Earlier sketch in CA 33-36
Fuldauer, Ivan 1927- 69-72
Fuldheim, Dorothy (Violet Snell)
  1893-1989 ....CANR-29
  Obituary 130
  Earlier sketch in CA 49-52
Fulford, Robert 1932- 89-92
Fulford, Roger (Thomas Baldwin)
  1902-1983 65-68
  Obituary 109
Fulghum, Robert 1937- ....BEST 89:2
Fulks, Bryan 1897- 97-100
Full, Harold 1919- 17-20R
Fuller, Alfred C(arl) 1885-1973 Obituary 45-48
Fuller, Beverley 1927- 69-72
Fuller, Blair 1927- 9-12R
Fuller, Buckminster
  See Fuller, R(ichard) Buckminster (Jr.)
Fuller, Catherine Leuthold 1916- 29-32R
  See also SATA 9
Fuller, Charles (H. Jr.) 1939- 112
  Brief entry 108
  See also BLC 2
  See also BW
  See also CLC 25
  See also DC 1
  See also DLB 38
  See also MTCW
Fuller, Curtis G. 1912- Brief entry 120
Fuller, Daniel P(ayton) 1925- 127
  Brief entry 112
Fuller, David O(tis) 1903- 53-56
Fuller, Dorothy Mason 1898- 101
Fuller, Edgar 1904-1973 Obituary 45-48
Fuller, Edmund (Maybank) 1914- 77-80
  See also SATA 21
Fuller, Edward C. 1907- 53-56
Fuller, Elizabeth 1946- CANR-33
  Earlier sketch in CA 113
Fuller, Harold 1940- 65-68
Fuller, Helen 1914(?)-1972 Obituary 37-40R
Fuller, Henry Blake 1857-1929 Brief entry 108
  See also DLB 12
Fuller, Hoyt (William) 1927-1981 53-56
  Obituary 103
  See also BW
Fuller, Iola
  See McCoy, Iola Fuller
Fuller, Jack (William) 1946- 130
  Brief entry 125
Fuller, Jean (Violet) Overton 1915- CANR-19
  Earlier sketches in CA 5-8R, CANR-4
Fuller, John Frederick Charles
  1878-1966 ....CAP-1
  Earlier sketch in CA 13-16
Fuller, John G(rant Jr.) 1913-1990 ....CANR-2
  Obituary 133
  Earlier sketch in CA 1-4R
  See also SATA 65
Fuller, John (Harold) CAP-1
  Earlier sketch in CA 9-10
Fuller, John (Leopold) 1937- CANR-9
  Earlier sketch in CA 21-24R
  See also CLC 62
  See also DLB 40
Fuller, Ken 1946- 125
Fuller, Lois Hamilton 1915- CANR-29
  Earlier sketch in CA 1-4R
  See also SATA 11
Fuller, Lon (Luvois) 1902-1978 ....CAP-2
  Obituary 77-80
  Earlier sketch in CA 33-36
Fuller, Margaret
  See Ossoli, Sarah Margaret (Fuller marchesa d')
Fuller, Maud
  See Petersham, Maud (Sylvia Fuller)
Fuller, Miriam Morris 1933- 37-40R
Fuller, Paul E(ugene) 1932- 73-76
Fuller, Peter (Michael) 1947- 97-100
Fuller, R(ichard) Buckminster (Jr.)
  1895-1983 ....CANR-12
  Obituary 109
  Earlier sketch in CA 9-12R
  See also MTCW
Fuller, Reginald H(orace) 1915- CANR-39
  Earlier sketches in CA 5-8R, CANR-3, 18
Fuller, Robert C(harles) 1952- CANR-38
  Earlier sketch in CA 116
Fuller, Roger
  See Tracy, Don(ald Fiske)
Fuller, Roy (Broadbent) 1912-1991 ....5-8R
  Obituary 135
  See also CAAS 10
  See also CLC 4, 28
  See also DLB 15, 20

Fuller, Ruth
See Perry, Ruth (Fuller)
Fuller, Sam
See Fuller, Samuel (Michael)
Fuller, Samuel (Michael) 1912- ... 129
Brief entry ... 112
See also DLB 26
Fuller, Sarah Margaret
1810-1850 ... CDALB 1640-1865
See also DLB 1, 59, 73
Fuller, Steve William 1959- ... 137
Fuller, Thomas C(harles) 1918- ... 126
Fuller, Wayne E(dison) 1919- ... 13-16R
Fuller, William A(lbert) 1924- ... 41-44R
Fullerton, Alexander (Fergus) 1924- ... CANR-23
Earlier sketches in CA 17-20R, CANR-7
Fullerton, Gail Jackson 1927- ... 37-40R
Fullerton, Gail Putney
See Fullerton, Gail Jackson
Fullinwider, Robert King 1942- ... 108
Fullinwider, S. P(endleton) 1933- ... 127
Brief entry ... 109
Fullmer, Daniel W(arren) 1922- ... CANR-29
Earlier sketches in CA 33-36R, CANR-13
Fullmer, June Z(immerman) 1920- ... 25-28R
Fulmer, Robert M(arion) 1939- ... CANR-10
Earlier sketch in CA 57-60
Fulop-Miller, Rene
See Fueloep-Miller, Rene
Fulton, A(lbert) R(ondthaler) 1902- ... 1-4R
Fulton, Alice 1952- ... 116
See also CLC 52
Fulton, Gere (Burke) 1939- ... 53-56
Fulton, Len 1934- ... 57-60
See also DLBY 86
Fulton, Norman 1927- ... 37-40R
Fulton, Paul C(edric) 1901-1985 ... CAP-1
Obituary ... 118
Earlier sketch in CA 13-16
Fulton, Robert Lester 1926- Brief entry ... 105
Fulton, Robin 1937- ... CANR-38
Earlier sketches in CA 33-36R, CANR-16
See also DLB 40
Fults, John Lee 1932- ... 53-56
See also SATA 33
Fultz, Walter J. 1924(?)-1971 Obituary ... 104
Fulweiler, Howard Wells 1932- ... 77-80
Fumento, Rocco 1923- ... 1-4R
Funabashi, Seiichi 1904(?)-1976 Obituary ... 65-68
Funai, Mamoru (Rolland) 1932- ... SATA 46
Fundaburk, Emma Lila 1922- ... 41-44R
Funderburk, Guy B(ernard) 1902- ... 45-48
Funderburk, Thomas R(ay) 1928- ... 17-20R
Fung, Gong
See Goon, Fook Mun
Fung, Raymond (Wai Man) 1940- ... 123
Funigiello, Philip J. 1939- ... 65-68
Funk, Arthur Layton 1914- ... 21-24R
Funk, Charles Earle Jr. 1913- ... 122
Funk, Peter V(an) K(euren) 1921- ... CANR-13
Earlier sketch in CA 21-24R
Funk, Rainer 1943- ... 109
Funk, Robert W(alter) 1926- ... 33-36R
Funk, Thompson 1911- ... CANR-2
Earlier sketch in CA 49-52
See also SATA 7
Funk, Tom
See Funk, Thompson
Funk, Wilfred (John) 1883-1965 Obituary ... 89-92
Funke, Lewis 1912- ... 49-52
See also SATA 11
Funkhouser, Erica 1949- ... 135
Funston, Richard Y(ork) 1943- ... 123
Brief entry ... 118
Funt, Julian 1907(?)-1980 Obituary ... 97-100
Funt, Marilyn 1937- ... 102
Fuoss, Robert Martin
1912-1980 Obituary ... 93-96
Furbank, P(hilip) N(icholas) 1920- ... CANR-18
Earlier sketch in CA 21-24R
Furbee, Leonard J.
1896(?)-1975 Obituary ... 61-64
Furchgott, Terry 1948- ... 105
See also SATA 29
Furcolo, Foster 1917- ... 117
Furer, Howard B(ernard) 1934- ... 33-36R
Furer-Haimendorf, Christoph von
See Fuerer-Haimendorf, Christoph von
Furey, Michael
See Ward, Arthur Henry Sarsfield
Furfey, Paul Hanly 1896- ... CAP-2
Earlier sketch in CA 23-24
Furgurson, Ernest B(aker Jr.) 1929- ... 73-76
Furgurson, Pat
See Furgurson, Ernest B(aker Jr.)
Furia, Philip (G.) 1943- ... 136
Furley, David John 1922- ... 108
Furlong, Monica (Mavis) 1930- Brief entry ... 117
Furlonge, Geoffrey (Warren)
1903-1984 Obituary ... 114
Furman, Bess 1894-1969 Obituary ... 115
Furman, Eleanor L. 1913- ... CANR-12
Earlier sketch in CA 29-32R
Furman, Gertrude Lerner Kerman
1909- ... CANR-31
Furman, Laura (J.) 1945- ... CANR-30
Earlier sketch in CA 104
See also DLBY 86
Furman, Roger 1924(?)-1983 Obituary ... 111
Furnas, J(oseph) C(hamberlain) 1905- ... 77-80
Furneaux, Robin
See Smith, Frederick William Robin
Furneaux, Rupert 1908- ... CANR-1
Earlier sketch in CA 1-4R
Furness, Edna L(ue) 1906- ... 37-40R
Furness, Horace Howard 1833-1912 ... DLB 64
Furness, William Henry 1802-1896 ... DLB 1

Furnier, Vincent Damon
See Cooper, Alice
Furnish, Dorothy Jean 1921- ... 106
Furnish, Victor Paul 1931- ... CANR-25
Earlier sketches in CA 21-24R, CANR-10
Furniss, Edgar S(tephenson)
1890-1972 Obituary ... 37-40R
Furniss, Norman Francis 1922- ... 1-4R
Furniss, Tim 1948- ... CANR-29
Earlier sketch in CA 109
See also SATA 49
Furniss, W(arren) Todd 1921- ... 57-60
Furphy, Joseph 1843-1912 ... TCLC 25
Furrer, Juerg 1939- ... 69-72
Furry, Elda 1890-1966 ... 113
Obituary ... 89-92
Furse, John 1932- ... 109
Furst, Alan 1941- ... CANR-34
Earlier sketches in CA 69-72, CANR-12
Furst, Lilian Renee 1931- ... CANR-18
Earlier sketch in CA 102
Furtado, Celso 1920- ... CANR-25
Earlier sketches in CA 17-20R, CANR-9
Furth, Alex
See Sasuly, Richard
Furth, George 1932- ... 73-76
Furth, Hans G. 1920- ... 45-48
Furthman, Jules
See Furthmann, Julius Grinnell
See also DLB 26
Furthmann, Julius Grinnell
1888-1966 Obituary ... 113
See also Furthman, Jules
Furtwangler, Albert (J.) 1942- ... 118
Furtwangler, Virginia W(alsh) 1932- ... 118
Furubotn, Eirik G. 1923- ... 137
Furukawa, Toshi 1924- ... CANR-2
Earlier sketch in CA 45-48
See also SATA 24
Fusco, Margie 1949- ... 85-88
Fusero, Clemente 1913-1975 ... 81-84
Fusfeld, Daniel R(oland) 1922- ... 45-48
Fusi (Aizpurua), Juan Pablo 1945- ... 131
See also HW
Fuson, Benjamin Willis 1911- ... 37-40R
Fuson, Robert H(enderson) 1927- ... 89-92
Fuss, Peter 1932- ... CANR-9
Earlier sketch in CA 21-24R
Fussell, Betty
See Fussell, Betty Harper
Fussell, Betty Harper 1927- ... 121
Fussell, Edwin 1922- ... 53-56
Fussell, G(eorge) E(dwin) 1889- ... CANR-3
Earlier sketch in CA 5-8R
Fussell, Paul 1924- ... CANR-35
Earlier sketches in CA 17-20R, CANR-8, 21
See also BEST 90:1
See also MTCW
Fussner, F(rank) Smith 1920- ... CANR-5
Earlier sketch in CA 1-4R
Futabatei, Shimei 1864-1909 ... TCLC 44
Futrell, Allan W. 1952- ... 123
Futrell, Gene Allen 1928- ... 107
Futrelle, Jacques 1875-1912 Brief entry ... 113
See also TCLC 19
Futuyma, Douglas Joel 1942- ... 108
Fye, W(allace) Bruce (III) 1946- ... 126
Fyffe, Don(ald Lewis) 1925- ... 25-28R
Fyfield, Frances
See Hegarty, Frances
Fyleman, Rose (Amy)
1877-1957 Brief entry ... 111
See also SATA 21
Fyler, John (Morgan) 1943- ... 89-92
Fyodorov, Yevgeny Konstantinovich
See Fedorov, Yevgeny Konstantinovich
Fysh, Wilmot Hudson 1895-1974 ... 17-20R
Obituary ... 134
Fyson, J(enny) G(race) 1904- ... CAP-2
Earlier sketch in CA 21-22
See also SATA 42
Fyvel, T. R.
See Feiwel, Raphael Joseph
Fyvel, Tosco Raphael
See Feiwel, Raphael Joseph

G

G. B.
See Boas, Guy (Herman Sidney)
G. B. S.
See Shaw, George Bernard
Gaa, Charles J(ohn) 1911- ... 17-20R
Gaan, Margaret 1914- ... 81-84
See also SATA 65
Gaard, David 1945- ... 25-28R
Gaastra, F(emme) S(imon) 1945- ... 132
Gaathon, A(ryeh) L(udwig) 1898- ... 49-52
Gabbard, Glen O(wens) 1949- ... 126
Gabbard, Krin 1948- ... 126
Gabbard, Lucina P(aquet) 1922- ... 110
Gabbett, Harry 1910(?)-1985 Obituary ... 116
Gabel, (W.) Creighton 1931- Brief entry ... 106
Gabel, Joseph 1912- ... 101
Gabel, Margaret 1938- ... 33-36R
Gabel, Medard 1946- ... CANR-11
Earlier sketch in CA 65-68
Gabin, Sanford B(yron) 1936- ... 114
Gable, Tom 1944- ... 93-96
Gablehouse, Charles 1928- ... 21-24R
Gabler-Hover, Janet A. 1953- ... 135

Gablik, Suzi 1934- ... 33-36R
Gabo, Naum 1890-1977 ... CAP-2
Obituary ... 73-76
Earlier sketch in CA 33-36
Gabor, Dennis 1900-1979 ... 17-20R
Obituary ... 120
Gabor, Georgia M. 1930- ... 108
Gabor, Mark 1939- ... 81-84
Gaboury, Antonio 1919- ... CANR-2
Earlier sketch in CA 45-48
Gabre-Medhin, Tsegaye (Kawessa) 1936- ... 101
Gabre-Tsadick, Marta 1932- ... 115
Gabriel, A(strik) L. 1907- ... CANR-6
Earlier sketch in CA 5-8R
Gabriel, H(enry) 1922- ... 77-80
Gabriel, Joyce 1949- ... 97-100
Gabriel, Jueri (Evald) 1940- ... 93-96
Gabriel, Mabel McAfee
1884(?)-1976 Obituary ... 65-68
Gabriel, Philip L(ouis) 1918- ... 93-96
Gabriel, Ralph Henry 1890-1987 ... 13-16R
Obituary ... 122
Gabriel, Richard Alan 1942- Brief entry ... 104
Gabriel, Roman 1940- Brief entry ... 107
Gabriel-Robinet, Louis
1909-1975 Obituary ... 61-64
Gabrielson, Frank 1911(?)-1980 Obituary ... 93-96
Gabrielson, Ira N(oel) 1889-1977 ... CAP-1
Obituary ... 73-76
Earlier sketch in CA 9-10
Gabrielson, James B. 1917- ... 29-32R
Gabrys, Ingrid Schubert
See Schubert-Gabrys, Ingrid
Gach, Gary 1947- ... 77-80
Gach, Michael Reed 1952- ... CANR-29
Earlier sketch in CA 110
Gackenbach, Dick 1927- ... CANR-38
Earlier sketch in CA 115
See also MAICYA
See also SATA 30, 48
Gadamer, Hans-Georg 1900- ... 85-88
Gadd, David 1912- ... 57-60
Gadd, Maxine 1940- ... 116
Gadda, Carlo Emilio 1893-1973 ... 89-92
See also CLC 11
Gaddes, Peter
See Sheldon, Peter
Gaddis, J. Wilson 1910(?)-1975 Obituary ... 57-60
Gaddis, John Lewis 1941- ... CANR-30
Earlier sketch in CA 45-48
Gaddis, Peggy
See Dern, Erolie Pearl Gaddis
Gaddis, Thomas E(ugene)
1908-1984 ... CANR-16
Obituary ... 114
Earlier sketch in CA 29-32R
Gaddis, Vincent H. 1913- ... 13-16R
See also SATA 35
Gaddis, William 1922- ... CANR-21
Earlier sketch in CA 17-20R
See also CLC 1, 3, 6, 8, 10, 19, 43
See also DLB 2
See also MTCW
Gaddy, C(urtis) Welton 1941- ... 61-64
Gaddy, David Winfred 1932- ... 129
Gadler, Steve J. 1905- ... 97-100
See also SATA 36
Gadney, Reg 1941- ... CANR-18
Earlier sketches in CA 49-52, CANR-3
Gado, Frank 1936- ... CANR-31
Earlier sketch in CA 49-52
Gadol, Peter 1964- ... 134
Gadpaille, Warren J(oseph) 1924- ... 61-64
Gaebelein, Frank Ely 1899- ... CANR-2
Earlier sketch in CA 13-16R
Gaeddert, Lou Ann (Bigge) 1931- ... CANR-29
Earlier sketches in CA 73-76, CANR-13
See also SATA 20
Gaedeke, Ralph M(ortimer) 1941- ... CANR-24
Earlier sketches in CA 65-68, CANR-9
Gaeng, Paul A. 1924- ... 37-40R
Gaenzl, Kurt (Friedrich) 1946- ... 134
Gaer, Joseph 1897-1969 ... 9-12R
Obituary ... 122
Gaer, Yossef
See Gaer, Joseph
Gaess, Roger 1943- ... 104
Gaff, Jerry G(ene) 1936- ... 85-88
Gaffen, Fred 1944- ... 127
Gaffney, Edward McGlynn Jr. 1941- ... 114
Gaffney, James 1931- ... CANR-6
Earlier sketch in CA 57-60
Gaffney, (Merrill) Mason 1923- ... CANR-3
Earlier sketch in CA 49-52
Gaffney, Timothy R. 1951- ... 137
See also SATA 69
Gag, Flavia 1907-1979 ... 5-8R
Obituary ... 104
See also SATA 24
Gag, Wanda (Hazel) 1893-1946 ... 137
Brief entry ... 113
See also CLR 4
See also DLB 22
See also MAICYA
See also YABC 1
Gagan, Bernard 1915-1984 Obituary ... 112
Gagarin, Michael 1942- ... 89-92
Gagarin, Yuri (Alekseevich)
1934-1968 Obituary ... 112
Gage, Diane 1954- ... 116
Gage, Edwin 1943- ... 85-88
Gage, Joy P. 1930- ... CANR-35
Earlier sketch in CA 114
Gage, Nathaniel Lees 1917- ... 69-72
Gage, Nicholas
See Ngagoyeanes, Nicholas
Gage, S. R. 1945- ... 134

Gage, William W(hitney) 1925- ... 13-16R
Gage, William 1915-1973 ... CAP-2
Earlier sketch in CA 25-28
Gage, Wilson
See Steele, Mary Q(uintard Govan)
Gager, John Goodrich Jr. 1937- Brief entry ... 104
Gager, Nancy Land
1932(?)-1980 Obituary ... 93-96
Gagliano, Frank 1931- ... CANR-1
Earlier sketch in CA 45-48
Gagliardo, John G(arver) 1933- ... 21-24R
Gagliardo, Ruth Garver
1895(?)-1980 Obituary ... 104
See also SATA 22
Gagne, Cole 1954- ... 112
Gagne, Robert M(ills) 1916- ... 121
Brief entry ... 116
Gagnier, Ed 1936- ... 65-68
Gagnier, Regenia (A.) 1953- ... 126
Gagnon, Cecile 1936- ... SATA 58
Gagnon, Jean-Louis 1913- ... 21-24R
Gagnon, John H(enry) 1931- ... 33-36R
Gagnon, Madeleine 1938- ... DLB 60
Gagnon, Paul Adelard 1925- Brief entry ... 104
Gahagan, Helen
See Douglas, Helen Gahagan
Gahagan, Jayne D. 1929(?)-1983 Obituary ... 110
Gaherty, Sherry 1951- ... 57-60
Gail, Marzieh ... CANR-11
Earlier sketch in CA 69-72
Gailey, Harry A(lfred) 1926- ... CANR-16
Earlier sketches in CA 45-48, CANR-1
Gailey, James H(erbert) Jr. 1916- ... 5-8R
Gailmor, William S. 1910(?)-1970 Obituary ... 104
Gaiman, Neil (Richard) 1960- ... 133
Gaine, Hugh 1726-1807 ... DLB 43
Gainer, Bernard 1944- Brief entry ... 109
Gaines, Bill
See Gaines, William Maxwell
Gaines, Charles (Latham Jr.) 1942- ... 119
Gaines, Diana 1912- ... 1-4R
Gaines, Donna 1951- ... 136
Gaines, Ernest J(ames) 1933- ... CANR-24
Earlier sketches in CA 9-12R, CANR-6
See also AITN 1
See also BLC 2
See also BW
See also CDALB 1968-1988
See also CLC 3, 11, 18
See also DLB 2, 33
See also DLBY 80
See also MTCW
Gaines, Jack
See Gaines, Jacob
Gaines, Jacob 1918- ... 101
Gaines, Pierce Welch 1905- ... 13-16R
Gaines, Richard L. 1925- ... 49-52
Gaines, William Maxwell 1922- Brief entry ... 108
Gainham, Sarah
See Ames, Rachel
Gains, Larry 1900-1983 Obituary ... 110
Gainsbrugh, Glen M. 1949- ... 25-28R
Gainsbrugh, Martin R(euben)
1907-1977 Obituary ... 69-72
Gainsburg, Joseph (Charles) 1894- ... 5-8R
Gainza Paz, Alberto 1899-1977 ... 77-80
Obituary ... 73-76
Gaiser, Gerd 1908-1976 ... DLB 69
Gaite, Francis
See Coles, Cyril Henry
Gaither, Gant 1917- ... 9-12R
Gaither, Norman 1937- ... 112
Gaitskell, Charles D(udley) 1908- ... 29-32R
Gaitskell, H.T.N.
See Gaitskell, Hugh (Todd Naylor)
Gaitskell, Hugh (Todd Naylor)
1906-1963 Obituary ... 112
Gaitskill, Mary 1954- ... 128
See also CLC 69
Gajdusek, Robert Elemer 1925- ... 102
Gajdusek, Robin
See Gajdusek, Robert Elemer
Gakwandi, Shatto Arthur 1943- ... 131
Gal, Allon 1934- ... CANR-1
Earlier sketch in CA 45-48
Gal, Hans 1890- ... 5-8R
Gal, Istvan 1912-1982 Obituary ... 107
Gal, Laszlo 1933- ... SATA 32, 52
Galai, Shmuel 1933- ... 107
Galambos, Louis (Paul) 1931- ... 81-84
Galamian, Ivan (Alexandrovitch)
1903-1981 Obituary ... 108
Galand, Rene 1923- ... CANR-24
Earlier sketch in CA 45-48
Galanoy, Terry 1927- ... CANR-4
Earlier sketch in CA 45-48
Galanskov, Yuri 1939(?)-1972 Obituary ... 37-40R
Galantay, Ervin Yvan 1930- ... 101
Galante, Jane Hohfeld 1924- ... 132
Galante, Pierre 1909- ... 13-16R
Galanter, Eugene 1924- ... 1-4R
Galanter, Marc 1931- ... 122
Galarza, Ernest
See Galarza, Ernesto
Galarza, Ernesto 1905-1984 ... 131
Obituary ... 113
See also HW
Galassi, Jonathan (White) 1949- ... 101
Galati, Stephen A(lexander) Fischer
See Fischer-Galati, Stephen A(lexander)
Galatopoulos, Stelios 1932- Brief entry ... 110
Galay, Ted 1941- ... 122
Galbraith, Clare K(earney) 1919- ... 33-36R
Galbraith, Georgie Starbuck 1909-1980 ... CAP-1
Obituary ... 97-100
Earlier sketch in CA 9-10
Galbraith, James K. 1952- ... 130

Galbraith, Jean 1906- ... 37-40R
Galbraith, John Kenneth 1908- ... CANR-34
Earlier sketch in CA 21-24R
See also MTCW
Galbraith, John S. 1916- ... CANR-6
Earlier sketch in CA 5-8R
Galbraith, Madelyn 1897-1976 ... CAP-2
Earlier sketch in CA 33-36
Galbraith, Vivian Hunter 1889-1976 ... CANR-29
Obituary ... 69-72
Earlier sketch in CA 73-76
Galbreath, Robert (Carroll) 1938- ... 41-44R
Galdone, Paul 1907(?)-1986 ... CANR-13
Obituary ... 121
Earlier sketch in CA 73-76
See also CLR 16
See also MAICYA
See also SATA 17, 49, 66
Galdos, Benito Perez
See Perez Galdos, Benito
Gale, Barry 1935- ... 110
Gale, Bill
See Gale, William
Gale, Bob
See Gale, Michael Robert
Gale, Elliot N(yman) 1938- Brief entry ... 110
Gale, Herbert M(orrison) 1907- ... CAP-1
Earlier sketch in CA 13-16
Gale, John
See Gaze, Richard
Gale, Linda A(nn) 1939- ... 112
Gale, Michael Robert 1951- ... 133
Gale, Patrick (Evelyn Hugh Sadler) 1962- ... 124
Gale, Raymond F(loyd) 1918- ... 25-28R
Gale, Richard M. 1932- ... 25-28R
Gale, Richard Nelson 1896-1982 Obituary ... 107
Gale, Robert L(ee) 1919- ... CANR-18
Earlier sketches in CA 9-12R, CANR-3
Gale, Vi ... 33-36R
Gale, William C.
See Giles, Carl H(oward)
Gale, William Daniel 1906- ... 107
Gale, William 1925- ... 97-100
Gale, Zona 1874-1938 Brief entry ... 105
See also DLB 9, 78
See also TCLC 7
Galeano, Eduardo (Hughes) 1940- ... CANR-32
Earlier sketches in CA 29-32R, CANR-13
See also CLC 72
See also HW
Galella, Ron 1931- ... CANR-14
Earlier sketch in CA 53-56
See also AITN 1
Galenson, Walter 1914- ... CANR-27
Earlier sketches in CA 25-28R, CANR-11
Gales, Barbara J. 1940- ... CANR-14
Earlier sketch in CA 81-84
Galewitz, Herb 1928- ... CANR-14
Earlier sketch in CA 41-44R
Galfo, Armand J. 1924- ... 17-20R
Galiano, Juan Valera y Alcala
See Valera y Alcala-Galiano, Juan
Galich, Alexander 1918(?)-1977 Obituary ... 73-76
Galilea, Segundo 1928- ... 105
Galindo, P.
See Hinojosa(-Smith), Rolando (R.)
Galinsky, Ellen 1942- ... CANR-9
Earlier sketch in CA 65-68
See also SATA 23
Galinsky, G(otthard) Karl 1942- ... 33-36R
Galkin, Elliott W(ashington)
1921-1990 Obituary ... 131
Gall, Auguste Amedee de Saint
See Strich, Christian
Gall, Elizabeth Cornelia 1898- ... 37-40R
Gall, Meredith D(amien) 1942- ... CANR-21
Earlier sketches in CA 53-56, CANR-6
Gall, Morris 1907- ... 45-48
Gall, Sally M(oore) 1941- ... 110
Gall, Sandy 1927- ... 130
Gallager, Gale
See Oursler, Will(iam Charles)
Gallagher, Buell Gordon 1904-1978 ... 65-68
Obituary ... 133
Gallagher, Charles A(ugustus) 1927- ... CANR-9
Earlier sketch in CA 61-64
Gallagher, David P. 1944- ... 45-48
Gallagher, Dorothy 1935- ... 65-68
Gallagher, Edward J.
1892(?)-1978 Obituary ... 81-84
Gallagher, Gary W(illiam) 1950- ... 136
Gallagher, Idella J(ane Smith)
1917- Brief entry ... 108
Gallagher, J(ames) Roswell 1903- ... 57-60
Gallagher, James J(ohn) 1926- ... 114
Gallagher, Jock 1938- ... 129
Gallagher, John (Andrew) 1919-1980 ... 133
Gallagher, John F(redrick) 1936- ... 17-20R
Gallagher, (John) Joseph 1929- ... 122
Gallagher, Kent G(rey) 1933- ... 33-36R
Gallagher, Louis J(oseph)
1885-1972 Obituary ... 37-40R
Gallagher, (Joseph) Mark 1953- ... 123
Gallagher, Marsha V. 1943- ... 117
Gallagher, Mary 1947- ... 97-100
Gallagher, Matthew P(hilip) 1919- ... 5-8R
Gallagher, Maureen 1938- ... 118
Gallagher, Neil 1941- ... 114
Gallagher, Patricia ... CANR-27
Earlier sketches in CA 65-68, CANR-11
Gallagher, Patricia C. 1957- ... 138
Gallagher, Patrick (Francis) 1930- ... 45-48
Gallagher, Rachel ... 89-92
Gallagher, Richard
See Levinson, Leonard
Gallagher, Richard (Farrington) 1926- ... CANR-6
Earlier sketch in CA 1-4R
Gallagher, Robert E(mmett) 1922- ... 13-16R
Gallagher, Sister Mary Dominic 1917- ... 17-20R
Gallagher, Stephen 1954- ... 138
Gallagher, Susan VanZanten 1955- ... 137
Gallagher, Tess 1943- ... 106
See also CLC 18, 63
See also DLB 120
Gallagher, Thomas (Michael) ... CANR-5
Earlier sketch in CA 1-4R
Gallagher, Vera 1917- ... CANR-38
Earlier sketch in CA 115
Gallagher, William Davis 1808-1894 ... DLB 73
Gallagher, William M.
1923-1975 Obituary ... 89-92
Gallaher, Art Jr. 1925- ... CANR-3
Earlier sketch in CA 1-4R
Gallaher, John G(erard) 1928- ... 126
Brief entry ... 112
Gallaher, (William) Rhea Jr. 1945- ... 136
Gallahue, David L(ee) 1943- ... CANR-30
Earlier sketches in CA 77-80, CANR-13
Gallahue, John (Jeremiah)
1930- Brief entry ... 110
Gallant, Christine C. 1940- Brief entry ... 106
Gallant, Mavis 1922- ... CANR-29
Earlier sketch in CA 69-72
See also CLC 7, 18, 38
See also DLB 53
See also MTCW
See also SSC 5
Gallant, Roy A(rthur) 1924- ... CANR-29
Earlier sketches in CA 5-8R, CANR-4
See also CLC 17
See also MAICYA
See also SATA 4, 68
Gallant, T(homas) Grady 1920- ... 5-8R
Gallardo, Edward ... 131
See also HW
Gallati, Mary Ernestine ... 5-8R
Gallati, Robert R. J. 1913- ... CANR-1
Earlier sketch in CA 1-4R
Galle, F(rederick) C(harles) 1919- ... 61-64
Galle, William 1938- ... 93-96
Gallegly, J(oseph) S(tephen) 1898- ... 5-8R
Gallego, Laura (Matilde) 1924- ... HW
Gallegos (Freire), Romulo 1884-1969 ... 131
See also HW
See also MTCW
Gallen, John (J.) 1932- Brief entry ... 113
Gallenkamp, Charles (Benton) 1930- ... 131
Galler, David 1929- ... 25-28R
Galler, Meyer 1914- ... 89-92
Gallerite, The
See Bason, Frederick (Thomas)
Gallery, Dan
See Gallery, Daniel V.
Gallery, Daniel V. 1901-1977 ... 13-16R
Obituary ... 69-72
Gallico, Paul (William) 1897-1976 ... CANR-23
Obituary ... 69-72
Earlier sketch in CA 5-8R
See also AITN 1
See also CLC 2
See also DLB 9
See also MAICYA
See also SATA 13
Gallie, Duncan (Ian Dunbar) 1946- ... 123
Gallie, Menna (Patricia Humphreys)
1920- ... CANR-1
Earlier sketch in CA 1-4R
Gallie, W(alter) B(ryce) 1912- ... 85-88
Galligan, Edward L(awrence) 1926- ... 126
Gallimard, Gaston 1881-1975 Obituary ... 61-64
Gallimore, Ronald 1938- ... 65-68
Gallin, Sister Mary Alice 1921- ... 13-16R
Gallinger, Osma Couch
See Tod, Osma Gallinger
Gallison, Kate
See Gallison, Kathleen
Gallison, Kathleen 1939- ... 120
Gallistel, C(harles) R(ansom) 1941- ... 119
Gallix, Francois 1939- ... CANR-26
Earlier sketch in CA 109
Gallman, Waldemar J(ohn) 1899-1980 ... CAP-1
Obituary ... 101
Earlier sketch in CA 11-12
Gallner, Sheldon M(ark) 1949- ... 53-56
Gallo, Max 1932- ... 85-88
Gallo, Rose Adrienne 1938- Brief entry ... 107
Gallois, Claire 1938- ... CANR-18
Earlier sketch in CA 85-88
Gallon, Arthur J(ames) 1915- ... 57-60
Gallop, David 1928- ... 65-68
Gallop, Jane 1952- ... 107
Galloping Gourmet
See Kerr, Graham
Galloway, A(llan) D(ouglas) 1920- ... 25-28R
Galloway, David D(arryl) 1937- ... CANR-37
Earlier sketches in CA 21-24R, CANR-16
Galloway, George Barnes 1898-1967 ... 1-4R
Obituary ... 103
Galloway, Janice 1956- ... 137
Galloway, John C. 1915-1970 ... CAP-2
Earlier sketch in CA 25-28
Galloway, Jonathan F(uller) 1939- ... 77-80
Galloway, Joseph L(ee) 1941- ... CANR-12
Earlier sketch in CA 73-76
Galloway, Margaret C(ecilia) 1915- ... 13-16R
Galloway, Patricia Kay 1945- ... CANR-30
Earlier sketch in CA 112
Galloway, Priscilla 1930- ... 112
See also SATA 66
Gallu, Samuel ... 85-88
See also AITN 2
Gallucci, Robert L(ovis) 1946- ... 61-64
Gallun, Raymond Z(inke) 1911- ... CANR-9
Earlier sketch in CA 65-68
Gallup, Dick 1941- ... 33-36R
Gallup, Donald (Clifford) 1913- ... CANR-27
Earlier sketches in CA 25-28R, CANR-11
Gallup, George (Horace) 1901-1984 ... CANR-13
Earlier sketch in CA 13-16R
Gallup, Ralph
See Whitemore, Hugh (John)
Gallwey, W. Timothy 1938- ... CANR-4
Earlier sketch in CA 53-56
Gallwitz, Klaus 1930- ... 131
Brief entry ... 109
Galouye, Daniel Francis 1920-1976 ... 9-12R
Obituary ... 134
Galper, Harvey 1937- ... 119
Galster, George C(harles) 1948- ... 126
Galston, Arthur William 1920- ... 102
Galsworthy, John 1867-1933 Brief entry ... 104
See also CDBLB 1890-1914
See also DLB 10, 34, 98
See also TCLC 1, 45
See also WLC 2
Galt, Alfreda Sill ... 114
Galt, Anthony H(oward) 1944- ... 137
Galt, John 1779-1839 ... DLB 99, 116
Galt, Serena
See Donald, Anabel
Galt, Thomas Franklin Jr. 1908- ... 5-8R
See also SATA 5
Galt, Tom
See Galt, Thomas Franklin Jr.
Galton, Francis 1822-1911 Brief entry ... 121
Galton, Lawrence 1913- ... CANR-6
Earlier sketch in CA 57-60
Galub, Jack 1915- ... 85-88
Galus, Henry S(tanley) 1923- ... 5-8R
Galvez (Baluzera), Manuel 1882-1962 ... HW
Galvez de Montalvo, Luis
See Avalle-Arce, Juan Bautista de
Galvin, Brendan 1938- ... CANR-24
Earlier sketches in CA 45-48, CANR-1
See also CAAS 13
See also DLB 5
Galvin, James 1951- ... CANR-26
Earlier sketch in CA 108
See also CLC 38
Galvin, John R(ogers) 1929- ... CANR-13
Earlier sketch in CA 21-24R
Galvin, Patrick Joseph 1927- ... CANR-18
Earlier sketch in CA 102
Galvin, Thomas J(ohn) 1932- ... CANR-10
Earlier sketch in CA 13-16R
Galway, James 1939- Brief entry ... 105
Gam, Rita (Elenore) 1927- ... 45-48
Gamarra, Eduardo (A.) 1957- ... 131
See also HW
Gambaccini, Peter 1950- ... 105
Gambaro, Griselda 1928- ... 131
See also HW
Gamba-Stonehouse, Virginia (Silvia Isabel)
1954- ... 134
Gambill, Edward Lee 1936- ... 112
Gambino, Thomas D(ominic) 1942- ... 101
Gamble, Andrew (Michael) 1947- ... CANR-12
Earlier sketch in CA 69-72
Gamble, Ed 1943- ... 133
Gamble, Frederick (John) 1904- ... CAP-1
Earlier sketch in CA 9-10
Gamble, Mary
See Murry, Mary Middleton
Gamble, Michael (Wesley) 1943- ... 110
Gamble, Sidney David 1890-1968 ... CAP-1
Earlier sketch in CA 11-12
Gamble, Teri (Susan) Kwal 1947- ... 110
Gamboa, Federico 1864-1939 ... TCLC 36
Gamboa, Harry Jr. ... HW
Gambrell, Herbert (Pickens) 1898- ... 1-4R
Gambrill, Eileen 1934- ... CANR-34
Earlier sketches in CA 89-92, CANR-15
Gambs, John S(ake) 1899- ... 13-16R
Gamer, Robert E(manuel) 1938- ... 65-68
Gamerman, Martha 1941- ... 77-80
See also SATA 15
Gamm, David B(ernard) 1948- ... 69-72
Gammage, Allen Z. 1917- ... CANR-11
Earlier sketch in CA 5-8R
Gammage, Bill
See Gammage, William Leonard
Gammage, William Leonard 1942- ... CANR-10
Earlier sketch in CA 57-60
Gammell, Stephen 1943- ... 135
See also MAICYA
See also SATA 53
Gammell, Susanna Valentine Mitchell
1897(?)-1979 Obituary ... 85-88
Gammie, John G(lenn) 1929- ... 121
Gammon, Roland I. 1920-1981 ... 49-52
Obituary ... 103
Gammon, Samuel Rhea (III)
1924- Brief entry ... 112
Gammond, Peter 1925- ... CANR-31
Earlier sketches in CA 81-84, CANR-14
Gamoran, Mamie (Goldsmith) 1900- ... CANR-3
Earlier sketch in CA 5-8R
Gamow, George 1904-1968 ... 102
Obituary ... 93-96
Gamson, William A. 1934- ... CANR-13
Earlier sketch in CA 33-36R
Gamst, Frederick C(harles) 1936- ... CANR-11
Earlier sketch in CA 29-32R
Gance, Abel 1889-1981 Obituary ... 108
Ganci, Dave 1937- ... 115
Gandalac, Lennard
See Berne, Eric (Lennard)
Gandee, Lee R(auss) 1917- ... 33-36R
Gandevia, Bryan Harle 1925- ... CANR-22
Earlier sketch in CA 106
Gandhi, Indira (Priyadarshini Nehru)
1917-1984 ... 128
Obituary ... 113
Gandhi, M. K.
See Gandhi, Mohandas Karamchand
Gandhi, Mahatma
See Gandhi, Mohandas Karamchand
Gandhi, Mohandas Karamchand
1869-1948 ... 132
Brief entry ... 121
See also MTCW
Gandley, Kenneth Royce 1920- ... CANR-12
Earlier sketch in CA 69-72
Gandolfo, Joe M. 1936- ... 105
Gandossy, Robert P. 1951- ... 120
Gangel, Kenneth O(tto) 1935- ... CANR-39
Earlier sketches in CA 25-28R, CANR-17
Gangemi, Kenneth 1937- ... 29-32R
Gangewere, Robert J(ay) 1936- ... 89-92
Gangloff, Deborah 1952- ... 130
Ganley, Albert Charles 1918- ... 13-16R
Ganley, Gladys Dickens 1929- ... 113
Ganley, Oswald Harold 1929- ... 112
Ganly, Helen (Mary) 1940- ... 125
See also SATA 56
Gann, Ernest Kellogg 1910-1991 ... CANR-1
Obituary ... 136
Earlier sketch in CA 1-4R
See also AITN 1
See also CLC 23
Gann, L(ewis) H(enry) 1924- ... CANR-31
Earlier sketches in CA 5-8R, CANR-3
Gannett, Frank E(rnest)
1876-1957 Brief entry ... 117
See also DLB 29
Gannett, Lewis Stiles
1891-1966 Obituary ... 89-92
Gannett, Ruth Chrisman (Arens)
1896-1979 ... SATA 33
Gannett, Ruth Stiles 1923- ... 21-24R
See also SATA 3
Gannon, Frank 1952- ... 126
Gannon, Robert Haines 1931- ... CANR-4
Earlier sketch in CA 9-12R
See also SATA 8
Gannon, Robert I(gnatius) 1893-1978 ... CAP-1
Obituary ... 77-80
Earlier sketch in CA 13-16
Gannon, Thomas M(ichael) 1936- ... CANR-26
Earlier sketch in CA 109
Gans, Bruce Michael 1951- ... 81-84
Gans, Eric L. 1941- ... 33-36R
Gans, Herbert J. 1927- ... CANR-6
Earlier sketch in CA 1-4R
Gans, Roma 1894- ... CANR-32
Earlier sketch in CA 77-80
See also SATA 45
Gansberg, Judith M. 1947- ... 85-88
Ganshof, Francois-Louis 1895- ... CAP-2
Earlier sketch in CA 19-20
Gansler, Jacques Singleton 1934- ... 135
Gans-Ruedin, E(rwin) 1915- ... 65-68
Ganss, George Edward 1905- ... CANR-31
Earlier sketch in CA 49-52
Gant, Chuck
See Galub, Jack
Gant, Jonathan
See Adams, Clifton
Gant, Matthew
See Hano, Arnold
Gant, Phyllis 1922- ... 57-60
Gant, Richard
See Freemantle, Brian Harry
Gantner, Neilma 1922- ... 104
Gantner, Susan (Verble) 1939- ... SATA 63
Gantos, Jack
See Gantos, John (Bryan) Jr.
See also CLR 18
Gantos, John (Bryan) Jr. 1951- ... CANR-15
Earlier sketch in CA 65-68
See also Gantos, Jack
See also SATA 20
Gantry, Susan Nadler 1947- ... 61-64
Gantt, Fred Jr. 1922-197 (?) ... CANR-3
Earlier sketch in CA 9-12R
Gantt, William Andrew Horsley 1893-1980 ... 102
Obituary ... 97-100
Gantz, Charlotte Orr 1909- ... 49-52
Gantzer, Hugh 1931- ... 61-64
Ganz, Arthur (Frederick) 1928- ... 49-52
Ganz, David L(awrence) 1951- ... 105
Ganz, Margaret 1927- ... 45-48
Ganz, Yaffa 1938- ... 115
See also SATA 52, 61
Ganzalass, Martin Richard 1941- ... 33-36R
Ganzel, Dewey Alvin Jr. 1927- ... 25-28R
Ganzl, Kurt
See Gaenzl, Kurt (Friedrich)
Gapanov, Boris 1934(?)-1972 Obituary ... 37-40R
Gar, The
See Garfinkel, Charles H.
Gara, Larry 1922- ... 53-56
Garab, Arra M. 1930- ... 81-84
Garafola, Lynn 1946- ... 135
Garagiola, Joe
See Garagiola, Joseph Henry
Garagiola, Joseph Henry 1926- ... 126
Garard, Ira D(ufresne) 1888- ... 73-76
Garavaglia, Louis A(ubrey) 1940- ... 119
Garb, Solomon 1920- ... CANR-9
Earlier sketch in CA 13-16R
Garbarino, Joseph W. 1919- ... 53-56
Garbarino, Merwyn S(tephens) ... 77-80
Garbe, Ruth Moore
See Moore, Ruth (Ellen)
Garber, Anne (Theresa) 1946- ... 138
Garber, Emil 1901(?)-1985 Obituary ... 115

Garber, Eugene K. 1932- ... CANR-6
Earlier sketch in CA 57-60
Garber, Frederick 1929- ... 53-56
Garber, Joseph R(ene) 1943- ... 132
Garber, Lawrence (Arnold) 1937- ... 122
Garber, Lee O(rville) 1900- ... 37-40R
Garber, Steven D(aniel) 1954- ... 128
Garbett, Colin (Campbell) 1881- ... CAP-1
Earlier sketch in CA 9-10
Garbini, Giovanni 1931- ... CANR-25
Earlier sketches in CA 21-24R, CANR-9
Garbo, Norman 1919- ... CANR-9
Earlier sketch in CA 17-20R
Garbus, Martin 1934- ... 133
Garbutt, Bernard 1900- Brief entry ... 110
See also SATA 31
Garbutt, Janice (D.) Lovoos ... 124
Garceau, Oliver 1911- ... CAP-2
Earlier sketch in CA 29-32
Garchik, Leah (Lieberman) 1945- ... 133
Garchik, Morton (Lloyd) 1929- ... 119
Garcia, Ann O'Neal 1939- ... 108
Garcia, C(elso-) R(amon) 1921- ... 118
Garcia, F(laviano) Chris 1940- ... CANR-4
Earlier sketch in CA 53-56
Garcia, George Haddad
See Haddad-Garcia, George
Garcia, Lionel G. 1935- ... 131
See also DLB 82
See also HW
Garcia, Mario R(amon) 1947- ... 77-80
Garcia, Nasario 1936- ... 134
Garcia, Richard A. 1941- ... HW
Garcia, Sam 1957- ... HW
Garcia Castaneda, Salvador 1932- ... 61-64
Garcia Lorca, Federico 1898-1936 ... 131
Brief entry ... 104
See also DC 2
See also DLB 108
See also HW
See also MTCW
See also PC 3
See also TCLC 1, 7
See also WLC
Garcia Marquez, Gabriel (Jose) 1928- ... CANR-28
Earlier sketches in CA 33-36R, CANR-10
See also Marquez, Gabriel (Jose) Garcia
See also AAYA 3
See also BEST 89:1, 90:4
See also CLC 2, 3, 8, 10, 15, 27, 47, 55
See also DLB 113
See also HW
See also MTCW
See also SSC 8
See also WLC
Garcia-Marquez, Vicente 1953- ... 134
Garcia Ponce, Juan 1932- ... 131
See also HW
Garcia Rocha, Rina 1954- ... HW
Garcia Sanchez, Javier 1955- ... 136
Gard, Janice
See Latham, Jean Lee
Gard, Joyce
See Reeves, Joyce
Gard, Richard A(bbott) 1914- ... CANR-1
Earlier sketch in CA 1-4R
Gard, Robert Edward 1910- ... 85-88
See also SATA 18
Gard, Roger Martin du
See Martin du Gard, Roger
Gard, (Sanford) Wayne 1899-1986 ... 1-4R
Obituary ... 120
See also SATA 49
Gardam, Jane 1928- ... CANR-33
Earlier sketches in CA 49-52, CANR-2, 18
See also CLC 43
See also CLR 12
See also DLB 14
See also MAICYA
See also MTCW
See also SAAS 9
See also SATA 28, 39
Gardaphe, Fred L(ouis) 1952- ... 136
Garden, Alexander 1685(?)-1756 ... DLB 31
Garden, Bruce
See Mackay, James (Alexander)
Garden, Edward J(ames) C(larke)
1930- ... 25-28R
Garden, Graeme 1943- ... 107
Garden, John
See Fletcher, H(arry) L(utf) V(erne)
Garden, Nancy 1938- ... CANR-30
Earlier sketches in CA 33-36R, CANR-13
See also SAAS 8
See also SATA 12
Garden, Robert Hal 1937- ... 69-72
Gardiner, C(linton) Harvey 1913- ... CANR-16
Earlier sketches in CA 1-4R, CANR-1
Gardiner, Charles Wrey
1901-1981 Obituary ... 103
Gardiner, Dorothy 1894-1979 Obituary ... 93-96
Gardiner, Glenn Lion 1896-1962 ... 1-4R
Gardiner, John Reynolds 1944- ... 127
See also SATA 64
Gardiner, Judith Kegan 1941- ... 138
Gardiner, Judy 1922- ... CANR-9
Earlier sketch in CA 21-24R
Gardiner, Mary Summerfield
1896-1982 Obituary ... 106
Gardiner, Muriel
See Buttinger, Muriel Gardiner
Gardiner, Patrick (Lancaster) 1922- ... CANR-5
Earlier sketch in CA 1-4R
Gardiner, Robert K. A. 1914- ... 21-24R
Gardiner, Robert W(orthington) 1932- ... 53-56
Gardiner, Stephen 1925- ... 97-100
Gardinier, David E(lmer) 1932- ... 112
Gardiol, Rita M(azzetti) ... 81-84
Gardner, Alan (Harold) 1925- ... 21-24R
Gardner, Angela Davis
See Davis-Gardner, Angela
Gardner, Anne
See Shultz, Gladys Denny
Gardner, Beau ... SATA 50
Gardner, (Robert) Brian 1931- ... 13-16R
Gardner, Carl 1931- ... 107
Gardner, D(avid) Bruce 1924- ... 49-52
Gardner, David P(ierpont) 1933- ... 21-24R
Gardner, Dic
See Gardner, Richard (M.)
Gardner, Dorothy E. M. 1900-1972 ... CAP-2
Earlier sketch in CA 23-24
Gardner, E(dward) Clinton 1920- ... 13-16R
Gardner, Eldon J(ohn) 1909- ... 41-44R
Gardner, Erle Stanley 1889-1970 ... CANR-13
Obituary ... 25-28R
Earlier sketch in CA 5-8R
See also MTCW
Gardner, Frank Matthias
1908-1980 Obituary ... 109
Gardner, G(erald) B(rosseau)
1884-1964 Obituary ... 112
Gardner, Gerald 1929- ... CANR-5
Earlier sketch in CA 1-4R
Gardner, Helen (Louise) 1908- ... 97-100
Gardner, Herb ... CLC 44
Gardner, Howard 1943- ... CANR-9
Earlier sketch in CA 65-68
Gardner, Hugh 1910-1986 Obituary ... 120
See also SATA 49
Gardner, Hy 1908-1989 ... 101
Obituary ... 128
Gardner, Isabella (Stewart) 1915-1981 ... 97-100
Obituary ... 104
Gardner, Jack Irving 1934- ... 102
Gardner, Jani 1943- ... 25-28R
Gardner, Jeanne LeMonnier 1925- ... 17-20R
See also SATA 5
Gardner, Jeffrey
See Fox, G(ardner) F(rancis)
Gardner, John (Champlin) Jr.
1933-1982 ... CANR-33
Obituary ... 107
Earlier sketch in CA 65-68
See also AITN 1
See also CLC 2, 3, 5, 7, 8, 10, 18, 28, 34
See also DLB 2
See also DLBY 82
See also MTCW
See also SATA 31, 40
See also SSC 7
Gardner, John E(dward) 1917- ... 17-20R
Gardner, John (Edmund) 1926- ... CANR-15
Earlier sketch in CA 103
See also CLC 30
See also MTCW
Gardner, John W(illiam) 1912- ... CANR-4
Earlier sketch in CA 1-4R
Gardner, Joseph L(awrence) 1933- ... CANR-30
Earlier sketch in CA 29-32R
Gardner, Lawrence
See Brannon, William T.
Gardner, Leonard 1934- Brief entry ... 111
Gardner, Lewis 1943- ... 65-68
Gardner, Lloyd C(alvin) 1934- ... CANR-3
Earlier sketch in CA 9-12R
Gardner, (Alice) Lucille 1913- ... 69-72
Gardner, Marilyn ... 101
Gardner, Martin 1914- ... 73-76
See also SATA 16
Gardner, Mary A(delaide) 1920- ... 21-24R
Gardner, Mary 1936- ... 124
Gardner, Nancy Bruff 1915- ... 13-16R
Gardner, Noel
See Kuttner, Henry
Gardner, Paul ... 69-72
Gardner, R(ufus) H(allette III) 1918- ... 33-36R
Gardner, Ralph D(avid) 1923- ... CANR-6
Earlier sketch in CA 13-16R
Gardner, Richard A. 1931- ... CANR-34
Earlier sketch in CA 33-36R
See also SATA 13
Gardner, Richard Kent 1928- ... CANR-27
Earlier sketch in CA 69-72
Gardner, Richard (M.) 1931- ... CANR-10
Earlier sketch in CA 21-24R
See also SATA 24
Gardner, Richard N(ewton) 1927- ... 89-92
Gardner, Riley W(etherell) 1921- ... 13-16R
Gardner, Robert 1911- ... 61-64
Gardner, Robert 1929- ... SATA 43
Gardner, Sandra 1940- ... 138
See also SATA 70
Gardner, Sheldon 1934- ... 104
See also SATA 33
Gardner, Virginia (Marberry) 1904-1992 ... 112
Obituary ... 136
Gardner, Wanda Kirby 1914- ... 73-76
Gardner, Wayland Downing 1928- ... 73-76
Gardner, William Earl 1928- ... CANR-18
Earlier sketches in CA 5-8R, CANR-3
Gardner, William Henry 1902-1969 ... CAP-1
Earlier sketch in CA 13-16
Gardner, Wynelle B. 1918- ... 65-68
Gardner-Smith, Percival 1888-1985 ... CAP-2
Obituary ... 116
Earlier sketch in CA 17-18
Gardons, S. S.
See Snodgrass, William D(e Witt)
Garduk, Harry David 1910(?)-1985 Obituary ... 116
Gare, Fran
See Mandell, Fran Gare
Gareau, Etienne 1915- ... 45-48
Gareau, Frederick H(enry) 1923- ... 5-8R
Garebian, Keith 1943- ... 129
Gareffa, Peter M(ichael) 1952- ... 118
Garelick, May 1910-1989 ... 73-76
Obituary ... 130
See also SATA 19
Garetz, Mark 1953- ... 112
Garfield, Brian (Wynne) 1939- ... CANR-6
Earlier sketch in CA 1-4R
Garfield, Eugene 1925- ... 114
Garfield, Evelyn Picon 1940- ... CANR-25
Earlier sketches in CA 57-60, CANR-9
Garfield, James B. 1881-1984 Obituary ... 112
See also SATA 6, 38
Garfield, Leon 1921- ... CANR-38
Earlier sketch in CA 17-20R
See also AAYA 8
See also CLC 12
See also CLR 21
See also MAICYA
See also SATA 1, 32
Garfield, Patricia L(ee) 1934- ... 85-88
Garfield, Sol L(ouis) 1918- ... CANR-12
Earlier sketch in CA 29-32R
Garfield, Sydney 1916(?)-1988 Obituary ... 124
Garfinkel, Alan 1941- ... CANR-21
Earlier sketch in CA 105
Garfinkel, Bernard Max 1929- ... CANR-17
Earlier sketch in CA 25-28R
Garfinkel, Charles H. 1939- ... 112
Garfinkel, Charlie
See Garfinkel, Charles H.
Garfinkel, Herbert 1920- ... 1-4R
Garfinkel, Perry 1948- ... 121
Garfinkle, Adam M. 1951- ... 112
Garfinkle, Louis (Alan) 1928- Brief entry ... 112
Garfitt, Roger 1944- ... CANR-13
Earlier sketch in CA 33-36R
Garforth, Francis William 1917- ... 9-12R
Garfunkel, Louis X.
1897(?)-1972 Obituary ... 37-40R
Gargan, Edward T(homas)
1922- Brief entry ... 111
Gargan, William Dennis
1905-1979 Obituary ... 106
Gargan, William (Michael) 1950- ... 111
Garibaldi, Gerald 1951- ... 108
Gariepy, Henry 1930- ... CANR-2
Earlier sketch in CA 49-52
Garioch, Robert Sutherland 1909-1981 ... 103
Garis, Howard R(oger) 1873-1962 ... CANR-27
Earlier sketch in CA 73-76
See also DLB 22
See also SATA 13
Garis, Robert (Erwin) 1925- ... 17-20R
Garitano, Rita 1939- ... 118
Garlan, Patricia Wallace 1926- ... 120
Garland, Bennett
See Garfield, Brian (Wynne)
Garland, Charles T(albot)
1910(?)-1976 Obituary ... 69-72
Garland, George
See Roark, Garland
Garland, (Hannibal) Hamlin
1860-1940 Brief entry ... 104
See also DLB 12, 71, 78
See also TCLC 3
Garland, Hazel (Barbara)
1913-1988 Obituary ... 125
Garland, Madge 1900(?)-1990 ... 25-28R
Obituary ... 132
Garland, Mary 1922- ... 89-92
Garland, Phyl(lis T.) 1935- ... 69-72
Garland, Robert (Sandford John) 1947- ... 120
Garland, Sarah 1944- ... SATA 62
Garlick, Peter C(yril) 1923- ... 41-44R
Garlick, Raymond 1926- ... CANR-4
Earlier sketch in CA 53-56
Garlington, Phil 1943- ... 81-84
Garlington, Warren K(ing) 1923- ... 9-12R
Garlinski, Jozef 1914- ... 108
Garmaise, Freda 1928- ... 134
Garment, Grace R. 1927(?)-1976 Obituary ... 104
Garmey, Jane 1942- ... 114
Garmon, William S. 1926- ... 21-24R
Garms, Walter I(rving Jr.) 1925- ... 120
Garn, Edwin Jacob 1932- ... 107
Garn, Jake
See Garn, Edwin Jacob
Garneau, Francois-Xavier 1809-1866 ... DLB 99
Garneau, Michel 1939- ... DLB 53
Garneau, (Hector de) Saint-Denys
1912-1943 Brief entry ... 111
See also DLB 88
See also TCLC 13
Garner, Alan (Francis) 1950- ... 132
Garner, Alan 1934- ... CANR-15
Earlier sketch in CA 73-76
See also CLC 17
See also CLR 20
See also MAICYA
See also MTCW
See also SATA 18, 69
Garner, Claud Wilton 1891- ... 9-12R
Garner, Dwight L. 1913- ... 25-28R
Garner, Graham
See Rowland, D(onald) S(ydney)
Garner, H(essle) F(ilmore) 1926- ... 73-76
Garner, Harry Hyman 1910-1973 ... 17-20R
Obituary ... 134
Garner, Helen 1942- ... 127
Brief entry ... 124
Garner, Hugh 1913-1979 ... CANR-31
Earlier sketch in CA 69-72
See also CLC 13
See also DLB 68
Garner, Joseph John Saville
1908-1983 Obituary ... 111
Garner, (Samuel) Paul 1910- ... 37-40R
Garner, Roberta 1943- ... 85-88
Garner, Rolf
See Berry, Bryan
Garner, (Lafayette) Ross 1914- ... 33-36R
Garner, Wendell R(ichard) 1921- ... CANR-11
Earlier sketch in CA 5-8R
Garner, William R(obin) 1936- ... 21-24R
Garner, William 1920- ... CANR-12
Earlier sketch in CA 29-32R
Garnet, Eldon 1946- ... CANR-9
Earlier sketch in CA 61-64
Garnett, A(rthur) Campbell 1894-1970 ... CANR-2
Earlier sketch in CA 1-4R
Garnett, Angelica 1918- ... 136
Garnett, Bill
See Garnett, William John
Garnett, Christopher Browne
1906-1975 Obituary ... 61-64
Garnett, David 1892-1981 ... CANR-17
Obituary ... 103
Earlier sketch in CA 5-8R
See also CLC 3
See also DLB 34
Garnett, Eve C. R. 1900-1991 ... CANR-2
Obituary ... 134
Earlier sketch in CA 1-4R
See also SATA 3
See also SATO 70
Garnett, Henrietta (Catherine Vanessa)
1945- ... 125
Garnett, Lynne 1942- ... 138
Garnett, Richard (Duncan Carey) 1923- ... 5-8R
Garnett, Roger
See Morland, Nigel
Garnett, Tay 1894(?)-1977 Obituary ... 73-76
Garnett, William John 1941- ... 102
Garnham, Nicholas 1937- ... 33-36R
Garofalo, Reebee
See Garofalo, Robert L.
Garofalo, Robert L. 1944- ... 77-80
Garoogian, Andrew 1928- Brief entry ... 113
Garoogian, Rhoda 1933- ... CANR-19
Earlier sketch in CA 102
Garos, Stephanie
See Katz, Steve
Garou, Louis P.
See Bowkett, Stephen
Garoyan, Leon 1925- ... CANR-5
Earlier sketch in CA 1-4R
Garrad, Larch S(ylvia) 1936- ... 61-64
Garrard, Gene
See Garrard, Jeanne Sue
Garrard, J(ohn) G(ordon) 1934- Brief entry ... 114
Garrard, Jeanne Sue ... 81-84
Garrard, L(ancelot) A(ustin) 1904- ... CAP-1
Earlier sketch in CA 9-10
Garrard, Mary D(ubose) 1937- ... 125
Garrard, Timothy F(rancis) 1943- ... 131
Garraty, John A(rthur) 1920- ... CANR-36
Earlier sketches in CA 1-4R, CANR-2
See also DLB 17
See also SATA 23
Garreau, Joel 1948- ... 101
Garret, Maxwell R. 1917- ... 106
See also SATA 39
Garretson, Lucy Reed 1936- ... 97-100
Garretson, Robert L. 1920- ... 17-20R
Garretson, Victoria Diane 1945- ... 108
See also SATA 44
Garrett, Albert Charles 1915-1983 Obituary ... 109
Garrett, Alfred B. 1906- ... 5-8R
Garrett, Charles 1925-1977 Obituary ... 73-76
Garrett, Clarke 1935- ... 73-76
Garrett, Eileen J(eanette) 1893-1970 ... CAP-2
Earlier sketch in CA 25-28
Garrett, Franklin M(iller) 1906- ... 57-60
Garrett, Garet 1878-1954 Brief entry ... 122
Garrett, George (Palmer) 1929- ... CANR-1
Earlier sketch in CA 1-4R
See also CAAS 5
See also CLC 3, 11, 51
See also DLB 2, 5
See also DLBY 83
Garrett, Gerald R. 1940- ... CANR-28
Earlier sketches in CA 73-76, CANR-12
Garrett, Gerard 1928- ... 73-76
Garrett, Gordon
See Garrett, (Gordon) Randall (Phillip)
Garrett, Helen 1895- ... SATA 21
Garrett, Howard 1931- ... 61-64
Garrett, James Leo Jr. 1925- ... CANR-13
Earlier sketch in CA 33-36R
Garrett, (Ruth) Jane 1914- ... 105
Garrett, Jennifer 1960- ... 122
Garrett, John (Allen) 1920- ... CANR-16
Earlier sketch in CA 33-36R
Garrett, Leonard J(oseph) 1926- ... 17-20R
Garrett, Leslie 1931- ... 17-20R
Garrett, Lillian ... 29-32R
Garrett, Peter K. 1940- ... 25-28R
Garrett, (Gordon) Randall (Phillip)
1927-1987 ... 130
Garrett, Richard 1920- ... CANR-37
Earlier sketches in CA 81-84, CANR-16
Garrett, Romeo Benjamin 1910- ... 37-40R
Garrett, Stephen A(rmour) 1939- ... 111
Garrett, Thomas M(ichael) 1924- ... CANR-5
Earlier sketch in CA 1-4R
Garrett, Thomas S(amuel) 1913-1980 ... CANR-3
Earlier sketch in CA 1-4R
Garrett, Tom
See Garrett, Thomas S(amuel)
Garrett, Truman
See Judd, Margaret Haddican
Garrett, Wendell D(ouglas) 1929- ... 9-12R

Garrett, William 1890-1967 ... CAP-1
Earlier sketch in CA 11-12
Garrick, David 1717-1779 ... DLB 84
Garrigan, Owen (Walter) 1928- ... 21-24R
Garrigue, Jean 1914-1972 ... CANR-20
Obituary ... 37-40R
Earlier sketch in CA 5-8R
See also CLC 2, 8
Garrigue, Sheila 1931- ... 69-72
See also SATA 21
Garrigus, Charles B(yford) 1914- ... 136
Garrison, Barbara 1931- ... SATA 19
Garrison, Christian (Bascom) 1942- ... 65-68
Garrison, Daniel H. 1937- ... 136
Garrison, Dee 1934- ... 125
Garrison, Frederick
See Sinclair, Upton (Beall)
Garrison, J. Ritchie 1951- ... 137
Garrison, James (Dale) 1943- ... 61-64
Garrison, Jim (C.) 1921- ... 132
Brief entry ... 111
Garrison, Joan
See Neubauer, William Arthur
Garrison, Karl C(laudius) 1900-1980 ... CANR-31
Earlier sketch in CA 37-40R
Garrison, Omar V. 1913- ... 33-36R
Garrison, Paul 1918- ... 122
Garrison, Phil
See Brandner, Gary
Garrison, R. Benjamin 1926- ... CANR-5
Earlier sketch in CA 13-16R
Garrison, Webb B(lack) 1919- ... CANR-18
Earlier sketches in CA 1-4R, CANR-2
See also SATA 25
Garrison, William Lloyd
1805-1879 ... CDALB 1640-1865
See also DLB 1, 43
Garrison, Winfred Ernest 1874-1969 ... CANR-6
Earlier sketch in CA 1-4R
Garrity
See Gerrity, David James
Garrity, Dave
See Gerrity, David James
Garrity, Devin Adair 1905-1981 ... 107
Obituary ... 103
Garrity, Joan Terry 1940- ... 69-72
See also AITN 1
Garrity, Richard (George) 1903- ... 77-80
Garrity, Terry
See Garrity, Joan Terry
Garro, Elena 1920(?)- ... 131
See also HW
Garrod, Rene J(eannette) 1954- ... 120
Garrow, David J(effries) 1953- ... 93-96
Garroway, Dave
See Garroway, David Cunningham
Garroway, David Cunningham
1913-1982 Obituary ... 107
Garry, Charles R. 1909- ... 73-76
Garside, Charles Jr. 1927-1987 Obituary ... 122
Garside, (Clifford) Jack 1924- ... 127
Garside, Roger R(amsay) 1938- ... 107
Garskof, Michele Hoffnung
See Hoffnung, Michele
Garson, Barbara ... 33-36R
Garson, Clee
See Fairman, Paul W.
Garson, G(eorge) David 1943- ... CANR-4
Earlier sketch in CA 53-56
Garson, Helen Sylvia 1925- ... 107
Garson, Noel George 1931- ... 29-32R
Garson, Paul 1946- ... 49-52
Garst, Doris Shannon 1894- ... 1-4R
See also SATA 1
Garst, John Fredric 1932- ... 45-48
Garst, Robert E(dward) 1900-1980 ... 108
Obituary ... 97-100
Garst, Shannon
See Garst, Doris Shannon
Garstang, Jack
See Garstang, James Gordon
Garstang, James Gordon 1927- ... 13-16R
Garstein, Oskar Bernhard 1924- ... 13-16R
Gart, Murray Joseph 1924- ... 103
Garten, Hugh F(rederick) 1904-1975 ... CANR-3
Earlier sketch in CA 5-8R
Gartenberg, Egon 1911- ... 57-60
Gartenberg, Leo 1906- ... 9-12R
Garth, Samuel 1661-1719 ... DLB 95
Garth, Will
See Hamilton, Edmond
and Kuttner, Henry
Garthoff, Raymond L(eonard) 1929- ... 5-8R
Garthwaite, Malaby
See Dent, Anthony Austen
Garthwaite, Marion H(ook) 1893- ... 5-8R
See also SATA 7
Gartland, Robert Aldrich 1927- ... 17-20R
Gartman, Louise 1920- ... 17-20R
Gartner, Alan 1935- ... CANR-34
Earlier sketches in CA 33-36R, CANR-15
Gartner, Carol B(licker) 1935- ... 114
Gartner, Chloe (Maria) 1916- ... CANR-20
Earlier sketches in CA 1-4R, CANR-5
Gartner, Lloyd P. 1927- ... CANR-2
Earlier sketch in CA 1-4R
Gartner, Michael G(ay) 1938- ... 77-80
Garton, Charles 1926- ... CANR-21
Earlier sketch in CA 45-48
Garton, Janet 1944- ... CANR-36
Earlier sketch in CA 114
Garton, Jean Staker 1929- ... 114
Garton, Malinda D(ean) ... 1-4R
Obituary ... 103
See also SATA 26
Garton, Nancy Wells 1908- ... 5-8R
Garton, Nina R. 1905- ... CAP-2
Earlier sketch in CA 21-22
Garve, Andrew
See Winterton, Paul
See also DLB 87
Garver, Richard B(ennett) 1934- ... 33-36R
Garvey, Amy Jacques
1896(?)-1973 Obituary ... 45-48
Garvey, Edward B. 1914- ... 41-44R
Garvey, Gerald (Thomas) 1935- Brief entry ... 112
Garvey, John 1944- ... CANR-14
Earlier sketch in CA 65-68
Garvey, Marcus (Moziah Jr.) 1887-1940 ... 124
Brief entry ... 120
See also BLC 2
See also BW
See also TCLC 41
Garvey, Mona C. 1934- ... CANR-34
Earlier sketch in CA 29-32R
Garvey, Robert 1908-1983 ... 107
Obituary ... 109
Garvey, Steve(n Patrick) 1948- ... 133
Garvey, Terence Willcocks 1915- ... 103
Garvie, A(lexander) F(emister) 1934- ... 73-76
Garvin, Charles D. 1929- ... CANR-6
Earlier sketch in CA 57-60
Garvin, Glenn 1954- ... 136
Garvin, (Hilda) Katharine 1904- ... 5-8R
Garvin, Lawrence 1945- ... 53-56
Garvin, Paul L(ucian) 1919- ... CANR-5
Earlier sketch in CA 13-16R
Garvin, Philip 1947- ... 73-76
Garvin, Richard M. 1934- ... 49-52
Garvin, Thomas Christopher 1943- ... 113
Garvin, Tom
See Garvin, Thomas Christopher
Garvin, William 1922- ... 25-28R
Garwood, Darrell (Nelson) 1909- ... 29-32R
Garwood, Julie 1946- ... 138
Gary, Romain
See Kacew, Romain
See also CLC 25
See also DLB 83
Garza, Roberto J(esus) 1934- ... 104
See also HW
Garzilli, Enrico 1937- ... 41-44R
Gasca, Philip D. Ortego
See Ortego y Gasca, Philip D.
Gascar, Pierre
See Fournier, Pierre
See also CLC 11
Gasche, Rodolphe 1938- ... 135
Gascoigne, Bamber 1935- ... CANR-28
Earlier sketches in CA 25-28R, CANR-10
See also SATA 62
Gascoigne, John 1951- ... 133
Gascoigne, Marguerite
See Lazarus, Marguerite
Gascon, The
See Miller, F(rederick) W(alter) G(ascoyne)
Gascoyne, David (Emery) 1916- ... CANR-28
Earlier sketches in CA 65-68, CANR-10
See also CLC 45
See also DLB 20
See also MTCW
Gash, Joe
See Granger, Bill
Gash, Jonathan
See Grant, John
Gash, Norman 1912- ... CANR-1
Earlier sketch in CA 1-4R
Gaskell, Elizabeth Cleghorn
1810-1865 ... CDBLB 1832-1890
See also DLB 21
Gaskell, Jane 1941- ... CANR-11
Earlier sketch in CA 5-8R
Gaskell, (John) Philip (Wellesley)
1926- ... CANR-3
Earlier sketch in CA 5-8R
Gaskell, Thomas F. 1916- ... 17-20R
Gaskill, Harold V. 1905-1975 Obituary ... 57-60
Gaskin, Catherine 1929- ... CANR-10
Earlier sketch in CA 65-68
Gaskin, David Edward 1939- ... 69-72
Gaskin, Ina May 1940- ... 129
Gaskin, J(ohn) C(harles) A(ddison) 1936- ... 131
Gaskin, Stephen (F.) 1935- ... 129
Gasnick, Roy M(ichael) 1933- ... 117
Gasparini, Graziano 1926- ... 41-44R
Gasparotti, Elizabeth Seifert
1897-1983 ... CANR-2
Obituary ... 110
Earlier sketch in CA 1-4R
Gasper, Louis 1911- ... 13-16R
Gasperini, Jim 1952- ... 122
See also SATA 49, 54
Gaspey, Thomas 1788-1871 ... DLB 116
Gasque, W(oodrow) Ward 1939- ... CANR-15
Earlier sketch in CA 65-68
Gass, William H(oward) 1924- ... CANR-30
Earlier sketch in CA 17-20R
See also CLC 1, 2, 8, 11, 15, 39
See also DLB 2
See also MTCW
Gassan, Arnold 1930- ... 73-76
Gassenheimer, Linda 1942- ... 137
Gassert, Robert G(eorge) 1921- ... 17-20R
Gasset, Jose Ortega y
See Ortega y Gasset, Jose
Gassier, Pierre 1915- ... CANR-34
Earlier sketch in CA 49-52
Gassner, John Waldhorn 1903-1967 ... CANR-3
Obituary ... 25-28R
Earlier sketch in CA 1-4R
Gassner, Julius S(tephen) 1915- ... 37-40R
Gast, Kelly P.
See Edmondson, G. C.
Gaster, T(heodor) Herzl 1906-1992 ... 73-76
Obituary ... 136
Gastil, Raymond D(uncan) 1931- ... 29-32R
Gastmann, Albert (Lodewijk) 1921- ... 97-100
Gaston, Edwin W(illmer) Jr. 1925- ... CANR-2
Earlier sketch in CA 1-4R
Gaston, Georg M(eri-) A(kri) 1938- ... 109
Gaston, Jerry (Collins) 1940- ... CANR-1
Earlier sketch in CA 45-48
Gaston, Wilber
See Gibson, Walter B(rown)
Gat, Dimitri V(sevolod) 1936- ... CANR-31
Earlier sketch in CA 29-32R
Gatch, Jean 1924- ... 127
Gatch, Milton McC(ormick Jr.) 1932- ... CANR-27
Earlier sketch in CA 29-32R
Gatell, Frank Otto 1931- ... 9-12R
Gatenby, Greg 1950- ... 97-100
Gatenby, Rosemary 1918- ... CANR-9
Earlier sketch in CA 21-24R
Gater, Dilys 1944- ... 112
See also SATA 41
Gater, Hubert 1913(?)-1980 Obituary ... 101
Gates, Albert
See Glotzer, Albert
Gates, Arthur Irving
1890-1972 Obituary ... 37-40R
Gates, David Murray 1921- ... 81-84
Gates, Doris 1901-1987 ... CANR-1
Obituary ... 124
Earlier sketch in CA 1-4R
See also DLB 22
See also MAICYA
See also SAAS 1
See also SATA 1, 34, 54
Gates, Frieda 1933- ... 93-96
See also SATA 26
Gates, Henry Louis Jr. 1950- ... CANR-25
Earlier sketch in CA 109
See also BW
See also DLB 67
Gates, J(eannette) M(cPherson) 1924- ... CANR-7
Earlier sketch in CA 57-60
Gates, Jean Key 1911- ... 33-36R
Gates, John A(lexander) 1898- ... 5-8R
Gates, John D. 1939- ... 89-92
Gates, John Floyd 1915- ... 1-4R
Gates, Lewis E. 1860-1924 ... DLB 71
Gates, Lillian Francis 1901- ... CAP-2
Earlier sketch in CA 25-28
Gates, Natalie ... 21-24R
Gates, Norman T(immins) 1914- ... 77-80
Gates, Paul W(allace) 1901- ... CANR-2
Earlier sketch in CA 1-4R
Gates, Philomene (A.) 1918- ... 134
Gates, Robbins L(adew) 1922- ... 13-16R
Gates, William Byram
1917-1975 Obituary ... 61-64
Gatewood, Willard B. Jr. 1931- ... 17-20R
Gathercole, Adrienne Lois
See Kaeppler, Adrienne Lois
Gatheridge, R. Edward
See Wilson, Robert (Edward)
Gathorne-Hardy, Jonathan G. 1933- ... CANR-39
Earlier sketch in CA 104
See also SATA 26
Gatley, Jimmy 1931(?)-1985 Obituary ... 115
Gatley, Richard Harry 1936- ... 101
Gatlin, Douglas S. 1928- ... 21-24R
Gatlin, Lila L(ee) 1928- ... 101
Gatner, Elliott S(herman) M(ozian)
1914- ... CANR-3
Earlier sketch in CA 9-12R
Gato, J. A.
See Keller, John E(sten)
Gattegno, Caleb 1911-1988 Obituary ... 126
Gattey, Charles Neilson 1921- ... CANR-20
Earlier sketches in CA 13-16R, CANR-5
Gatti, Arthur Gerard 1942- ... 65-68
Gatti, Daniel Jon 1946- ... 45-48
Gatti, Enzo
See Gatti, Vincenzo
Gatti, Richard DeY 1947- ... 45-48
Gatti, Vincenzo 1942- ... CANR-8
Earlier sketch in CA 61-64
Gattmann, Eric 1925- ... 49-52
Gatto, Alfonso 1909-1976 ... DLB 114
Gatty, Juliana Horatia
See Ewing, Juliana (Horatia Gatty)
Gatty, Margaret Scott 1809-1873 ... SATA 27
Gatty, Ronald 1929- ... 85-88
Gatzke, Hans W(ilhelm) 1915-1987 ... CANR-5
Obituary ... 123
Earlier sketch in CA 1-4R
Gauch, Patricia Lee 1934- ... CANR-9
Earlier sketch in CA 57-60
See also SATA 26
Gauchat, Dorothy 1921- ... 97-100
Gaudet, Frederick J(oseph) 1902-1977 ... 5-8R
Obituary ... 73-76
Gaudiose, Dorothy M(arie) 1920- ... 89-92
Gauer, Harold 1914- ... 13-16R
Gaugh, Harry F. ... 116
Gaul, Randy 1959- ... SATA 63
Gauld, Charles A(nderson) 1911- ... 13-16R
Gaulden, Ray 1914- ... CANR-8
Earlier sketch in CA 17-20R
Gauldie, Enid 1928- ... CANR-14
Earlier sketch in CA 77-80
Gauldie, (William) Sinclair 1918- ... 33-36R
Gaulle, Charles (Andre Joseph Marie) de
See de Gaulle, Charles (Andre Joseph Marie)
Gault, Clare 1925- ... 97-100
See also SATA 36
Gault, Frank 1926-1982 ... CANR-11
Earlier sketch in CA 69-72
See also SATA 30, 36
Gault, Henri (Andre Paul Victor) 1929- ... 130
Gault, Mark
See Cournos, John
Gault, Peter 1958- ... 138
Gault, William Campbell 1910- ... CANR-37
Earlier sketches in CA 49-52, CANR-1, 16
See also SATA 8
Gaumnitz, Jack E(rwin) 1935- ... 120
Gaumnitz, Walter Herbert
1891-1979 Obituary ... 89-92
Gaunt, Leonard 1921- ... CANR-3
Earlier sketch in CA 5-8R
Gaunt, Michael
See Robertshaw, (James) Denis
Gaunt, Peter
See Eshbach, Lloyd Arthur
Gaunt, William 1900-1980 ... CANR-6
Obituary ... 97-100
Earlier sketch in CA 9-12R
Gauquelin, Michel (Roland) 1928- ... CANR-31
Earlier sketch in CA 57-60
Gaur, Albertine 1932- ... 121
Gaus, Gerald F. 1952- ... 112
Gaustad, Edwin Scott 1923- ... CANR-1
Earlier sketch in CA 1-4R
Gautier, Theophile 1811-1872 ... DLB 119
Gauvreau, Claude 1925-1971 ... DLB 88
Gavaskar, Sunil 1949- ... 131
Gaver, Becky
See Gaver, Rebecca
Gaver, Jack 1906-1974 ... 97-100
Obituary ... 53-56
Gaver, Jessyca (Russell) 1915- ... CANR-9
Earlier sketch in CA 53-56
Gaver, Mary Virginia 1906-1991 ... CANR-34
Obituary ... 136
Earlier sketch in CA 1-4R
Gaver, Rebecca 1952- ... SATA 20
Gavett, J(oseph) William 1921- ... 25-28R
Gavett, Thomas W(illiam) 1932- ... 13-16R
Gavin
See Frost, Gavin
Gavin, Amanda
See Gibson-Jarvie, Clodagh
Gavin, Bill
See Gavin, William S.
Gavin, Catherine ... CANR-1
Earlier sketch in CA 1-4R
Gavin, Eileen A. 1931- ... 45-48
Gavin, James M(aurice) 1907-1990 ... CAP-1
Obituary ... 131
Earlier sketch in CA 13-16
Gavin, Jamila 1941- ... 110
Gavin, Thomas F. 1910- ... 108
Gavin, Thomas 1941- ... 85-88
Gavin, William
See Houston, Douglas (Norman)
Gavin, William S. 1907(?)-1985 Obituary ... 114
Gavin-Brown, Wilfred A(rthur) 1904- ... CAP-1
Earlier sketch in CA 9-10
Gavron, Daniel 1935- ... CANR-12
Earlier sketch in CA 29-32R
Gavronsky, Serge 1932- ... CANR-9
Earlier sketch in CA 65-68
Gavshon, Arthur L(eslie) 1916- ... 5-8R
Gaw, Walter A. 1904- ... 1-4R
Gawain, Shakti 1948- ... 93-96
Gawaine, John
See Hamilton-Hill, Donald
Gawron, Jean Mark 1953- ... 103
Gawsworth, John
See Armstrong, Terence Ian Fytton
and Bates, H(erbert) E(rnest)
Gawthrop, Louis C. 1930- ... 81-84
Gaxotte, Pierre 1895-1982 ... 111
Obituary ... 108
Gay, A. Nolder
See Koelsch, William Alvin
Gay, Amelia
See Hogarth, Grace (Weston Allen)
Gay, Carlo T(eofilo) E(berhard) 1913- ... CANR-27
Earlier sketch in CA 49-52
Gay, Ebenezer 1696-1787 ... DLB 24
Gay, Francis
See Gee, H(erbert) L(eslie)
Gay, John E(dward) 1942- ... 81-84
Gay, John 1685-1732 ... DLB 84, 95
Gay, Kathlyn 1930- ... CANR-25
Earlier sketches in CA 21-24R, CANR-8
See also SATA 9
Gay, Marie-Louise 1952- ... 135
See also CLR 27
See also SATA 68
Gay, Peter (Jack) 1923- ... CANR-18
Earlier sketch in CA 13-16R
Gay, Volney P(atrick) 1948- ... 117
Gay, Zhenya 1906-1978 ... 73-76
See also SATA 19
Gaya-Nuno, Juan Antonio 1913-1975 ... CANR-31
Earlier sketch in CA 81-84
Gayarre, Charles E. A. 1805-1895 ... DLB 30
Gay-Crosier, Raymond 1937- ... CANR-15
Earlier sketch in CA 41-44R
Gaydos, Michael J. 1940- ... 53-56
Gaye, Carol
See Shann, Renee
Gaye, Marvin (Penze) 1939-1984 Obituary ... 112
See also CLC 26
Gay-Kelly, Doreen 1952- ... 61-64
Gayle, Addison Jr. 1932-1991 ... CANR-13
Obituary ... 135
Earlier sketch in CA 25-28R
See also BW
Gayle, Emma
See Fairburn, Eleanor
Gayle, Marilyn
See Hoff, Marilyn

Gayle, Stephen H. 1948(?)-1982 Obituary 107
Gayles, Anne Richardson 1923- 53-56
Gaylin, Willard (M.) 1925- CANR-13
Earlier sketch in CA 21-24R
Gaylord, Billy
See Gaylord, William (Gilbert)
Gaylord, Edward King
1873-1974 Obituary 89-92
Gaylord, Sherwood Boyd 1914- Brief entry 105
Gaylord, William (Gilbert) 1945-1985 69-72
Obituary 118
Gayn, Mark J. 1909-1981 Obituary 105
Gaynor, Harry J. 134
Gayre, G(eorge) R(obert) 1907- CANR-4
Earlier sketch in CA 5-8R
Gayre of Gayre, R.
See Gayre, G(eorge) R(obert)
Gayre of Gayre and Nigg, Robert
See Gayre, G(eorge) R(obert)
Gazaway, Rena 1910- CAP-2
Earlier sketch in CA 29-32
Gazda, George M(ichael) 1931- CANR-29
Earlier sketches in CA 61-64, CANR-13
Gazdanov, Gaito 1903-1971 Obituary 104
Gazdanov, Georgii
See Gazdanov, Gaito
Gaze, Richard 1917- 1-4R
Gazell, James A(lbert) 1942- 49-52
Gazi, Stephen 1914-1978 45-48
Obituary 103
Gazis, Denos C(onstantinos) 1930- 57-60
Gazley, John G(erow) 1895- 61-64
Gazzaniga, Michael S(aunders) 1939- 121
Gdanski, Marek
See Thee, Marek
Geach, Christine 1930- CANR-10
Earlier sketch in CA 25-28R
Geach, Patricia Sullivan 1916- 29-32R
Geach, Peter Thomas 1916- 103
Gealt, Adelheid (Medicus) 1946- CANR-36
Earlier sketch in CA 114
Geanakoplos, Deno John 1916- CANR-2
Earlier sketch in CA 1-4R
Geaney, Dennis J(oseph) 1914- CANR-20
Earlier sketches in CA 5-8R, CANR-5
Gear, C. William 1935- 53-56
Gear, Kathleen O'Neal 1954- ....SATA 71
Gear, Sheila 1942- 114
Gear, W. Michael 1955- ....SATA 71
Geare, Michael 1919- 117
Geare, Mildred Mahler
1888(?)-1977 Obituary 73-76
Gearey, John 1926- CANR-23
Earlier sketch in CA 45-48
Gearhart, Sally Miller 1931- 57-60
Gearheart, B(ill) R. 1928- CANR-9
Earlier sketch in CA 21-24R
Gearing, Catherine 1916- 103
Gearing, Fred(erick) O(smond) 1922- 29-32R
Gearing-Thomas, G.
See Norwood, Victor G(eorge) C(harles)
Geary, Douglas 1931- 13-16R
Geary, Frederick Charles
1886(?)-1975(?) Obituary 104
Geary, Herbert Valentine (Rupert)
1894-1965 ....CAP-1
Earlier sketch in CA 9-10
Geary, Patricia (Carol) 1951- 134
Geary, Patrick J(oseph) 1948- 104
Geary, Roger 1950- 123
Geasland, Jack
See Geasland, John Buchanan Jr.
Geasland, John Buchanan Jr. 1944- 81-84
Gebhard, Anna Laura Munro 1914- 5-8R
Gebhard, Bruno (Frederic) 1901- 73-76
Gebhard, Paul H(enry) 1917- 5-8R
Gebhart, Benjamin 1923- 53-56
Gebler, Carlo (Ernest) 1954- 133
Brief entry 119
See also CLC 39
Gebler, Ernest 1915- CANR-3
Earlier sketch in CA 5-8R
Geck, Francis J(oseph) 1900- 73-76
Geckle, George L. 1939- 77-80
Gecys, Casimir C. 1904- CAP-2
Earlier sketch in CA 19-20
Gedda, George 1941- 77-80
Geddes, Charles L(ynn) 1928- CANR-2
Earlier sketch in CA 49-52
Geddes, Gary 1940- ....DLB 60
Geddes, Joan Bel 1916- 57-60
Geddes, Paul 1922- 136
Geddes, Virgil 1897- ....DLB 4
Geddie, John 1937- 69-72
Gedo, John E. 1927- 121
Gedo, Mary M(athews) 1925- 104
Geduld, Harry M(aurice) 1931- CANR-20
Earlier sketches in CA 9-12R, CANR-5
Gedye, George Eric Rowe
1890-1970 Obituary 93-96
Gee, H(erbert) L(eslie) 1901-1977 ....9-12R
Obituary 103
See also SATA 26
Gee, Maggie (Mary) 1948- 130
See also CLC 57
Gee, Maurice (Gough) 1931- 97-100
See also CLC 29
See also SATA 46
Geehr, Richard S. 1938- 136
Geemis, Joseph (Stephen) 1935- 69-72
Geen, Russell Glenn 1932- CANR-22
Earlier sketch in CA 104
Geer, Charles 1922- 108
See also SATA 32, 42
Geer, Stephen (DuBois) 1930- 69-72
Geer, William D. 1906(?)-1976 Obituary 104
Geering, R(onald) G(eorge) 1918- 133
Geertz, Clifford (James) 1926- CANR-36
Earlier sketch in CA 33-36R
Geertz, Hildred 1927- 77-80
Geeslin, Campbell 1925- 102
Geffen, Maxwell Myles 1896-1980 Obituary 102
Geffen, Roger 1919- 17-20R
Gefvert, Constance J(oanna) 1941- 53-56
Gega, Peter C(hristopher) 1924- 73-76
Geggus, David Patrick 1949- CANR-37
Earlier sketch in CA 114
Geha, Joseph (A.) 1944- 134
Geherin, David J(ohn) 1943- CANR-39
Earlier sketches in CA 101, CANR-17
Gehlbach, Frederick Renner 1935- 106
Gehlen, Reinhard 1902-1979 Obituary 89-92
Gehman, Betsy Holland 1932- 17-20R
Gehman, Christian 1948- 119
Gehman, Henry Snyder 1888- 13-16R
Gehman, Richard (Boyd) 1921-1972 ....CANR-16
Obituary 33-36R
Earlier sketch in CA 1-4R
Gehr, Mary ....SATA 32
Gehrels, Franz 1922- 101
Gehri, Alfred 1896(?)-1972 Obituary 33-36R
Gehrig, Klaus 1946- 137
Gehring, Wes D(avid) 1950- 137
Gehris, Paul 1934- 45-48
Geier, Arnold 1926- 1-4R
Geier, Woodrow A. 1914- 21-24R
Geigel Polanco, Vicente
1904-1979 Obituary 85-88
See also HW
Geiger, Don(ald) Jesse 1923- 5-8R
Geiger, H(omer) Kent 1922- CANR-5
Earlier sketch in CA 1-4R
Geiger, John (Grigsby) 1960- 129
Geiger, Louis G. 1913- 13-16R
Geiger, Ray(mond Aloysius) 1910- 118
See also AITN 1
Geiger, Theodore 1915- Brief entry 114
Geipel, Eileen 1932- 107
See also SATA 30
Geipel, John 1937- CANR-13
Earlier sketch in CA 73-76
Geiringer, Irene (Steckel)
1899-1983 Obituary 111
Geiringer, Karl (Johannes) 1899-1989 ....13-16R
Obituary 127
Geis, Darlene Stern CANR-5
Earlier sketch in CA 1-4R
See also SATA 7
Geis, Florence L(indauer) 1933- CANR-8
Earlier sketch in CA 57-60
Geis, Gilbert 1925- CANR-6
Earlier sketch in CA 9-12R
Geis, Richard E(rwin) 1927- 101
Geisel, Helen 1898-1967 Obituary 107
See also SATA 26
Geisel, Theodor Seuss 1904-1991 ....CANR-32
Obituary 135
Earlier sketches in CA 13-16R, CANR-13
See also Dr. Seuss
and Seuss, Dr.
See also CLR 1
See also DLB 61
See also DLBY 91
See also MAICYA
See also MTCW
See also SATA 1, 28
See also SATO 67
Geiser, Robert L(ee) 1931- 97-100
Geisert, Arthur 1941- 120
See also SATA 52, 56
Geisinger, David L. 1938- 110
Geisler, Norman L(eo) 1932- CANR-27
Earlier sketches in CA 25-28R, CANR-10
Geismar, L(udwig) L(eo) 1921- CANR-11
Earlier sketch in CA 25-28R
Geismar, Maxwell (David) 1909-1979 ....CANR-33
Obituary 104
Earlier sketch in CA 1-4R
Geismer, L(udwig) L(eo) 1921- CANR-29
Geissman, Erwin William
1920-1980 Obituary 101
Geist, Harold 1916- CANR-22
Earlier sketches in CA 17-20R, CANR-7
Geist, Kenneth L(ee) 1936- 81-84
Geist, Robert John 1912- 41-44R
Geist, Roland C. 1896- 89-92
Geist, Sidney 1914- Brief entry 112
Geist, Valerius 1938- CANR-8
Earlier sketch in CA 61-64
Geitgey, Doris A. 1920- 53-56
Geiwitz, P(eter) James 1938- CANR-11
Earlier sketch in CA 29-32R
Gelatt, Roland 1920-1986 ....13-16R
Obituary 121
Gelb, Alan
See Gelb, Alan Lloyd
Gelb, Alan Lloyd 1950- 126
Gelb, Arthur 1924- CANR-21
Earlier sketch in CA 1-4R
See also DLB 103
Gelb, Barbara (Stone) 1926- CANR-21
Earlier sketch in CA 1-4R
See also DLB 103
Gelb, Ignace J(ay) 1907-1985 ....9-12R
Obituary 118
Gelb, Joyce 1940- 61-64
Gelb, Leslie H(oward) 1937- CANR-19
Earlier sketch in CA 103
Gelb, Norman 1929- CANR-30
Earlier sketch in CA 108
Gelbart, Larry (Simon) 1923- 73-76
See also CLC 21, 61
Gelber, Harry G. 1926- 25-28R
Gelber, Jack 1932- CANR-2
Earlier sketch in CA 1-4R
See also CLC 1, 6, 14
See also DLB 7
Gelber, Lionel (Morris) 1907-1989 ....13-16R
Obituary 129
Gelber, Steven M(ichael) 1943- 53-56
Geld, Ellen Bromfield 1932- 37-40R
Geldard, Frank A(rthur) 1904-1984 ....41-44R
Obituary 114
Geldart, William 1936- ....SATA 15
Gelderman, Carol Wettlaufer 1935- 105
Gelernt, Jules 1928- 21-24R
Gelfand, Elissa D(eborah) 1949- 114
Gelfand, Lawrence Emerson 1926- CANR-3
Earlier sketch in CA 5-8R
Gelfand, Morris Arthur 1908- 49-52
Gelfman, Dick 1947- 122
Gelfman, Judith S(chlein) 1937- 65-68
Gelfond, Rhoda 1946- CANR-12
Earlier sketch in CA 49-52
Gelinas, Gratien 1909- ....DLB 88
Gelinas, Paul J. 1911- 41-44R
See also SATA 10
Gell, Frank
See Kowet, Don
Gell, Paul (Frederick William) 1928- 116
Gellatly, Peter 1923- Brief entry 111
Geller, Allen 1941- 25-28R
Geller, Bruce 1930-1978 Obituary 77-80
Geller, Evelyn
See Gottesfeld, Evelyn
Geller, Uri 1946- 69-72
Gellerman, Saul W(illiam) 1929- CANR-8
Earlier sketch in CA 5-8R
Gellert, Christian Furchtegott
1715-1769 ....DLB 97
Gellert, Judith 1925- 33-36R
Gellert, Lew
See Wellen, Edward (Paul)
Gelles, Richard J. 1946- CANR-22
Earlier sketches in CA 61-64, CANR-8
Gelles, Sandi
See Gelles-Cole, Sandi
Gelles-Cole, Sandi 1949- 121
Gelley, Alexander 1933- 127
Brief entry 108
Gellhorn, Ernst 1893-1973 ....CAP-2
Earlier sketch in CA 21-22
Gellhorn, Martha Ellis 1908- 77-80
See also CLC 14, 60
See also DLBY 82
Gellhorn, Walter 1906- 13-16R
Gellinek, Christian 1930- CANR-9
Earlier sketch in CA 21-24R
Gellinek, Janis Little
See Solomon, Janis Little
Gellis, Roberta L(eah Jacobs) 1927- CANR-22
Earlier sketches in CA 5-8R, CANR-3
Gellman, Estelle Sheila 1941- 53-56
Gellman, Irwin F(rederick) 1942- CANR-1
Earlier sketch in CA 45-48
Gellner, Ernest (Andre) 1925- CANR-22
Earlier sketches in CA 5-8R, CANR-4
Gellner, John 1907- 29-32R
Gellrich, Jesse M. 1942- 118
Gelman, David Graham 1926- 103
Gelman, Jan 1963- ....SATA 58
Gelman, Juan 1930- ....HW
Gelman, Milton S. 1920(?)-1990 Obituary 131
Gelman, Mitch(ell Barry) 1962- 124
Gelman, Rita Golden 1937- CANR-16
Earlier sketch in CA 81-84
See also SATA 51
Gelman, Steve 1934- CANR-16
Earlier sketch in CA 25-28R
See also SATA 3
Gelman, Woodrow 1915(?)-1978 Obituary 104
Gelman, Woody
See Gelman, Woodrow
Gelmis, Joseph S(tephan) 1935- 45-48
Gelperin, L.
See Halpern, Leivick
Gelpi, Albert 1931- 33-36R
Gelpi, Barbara Charlesworth 1933- 112
Gelpi, Donald L. 1934- CANR-7
Earlier sketch in CA 17-20R
Geltman, Max 1906(?)-1984 Obituary 112
Gelula, Abner Joseph 1906-1985 Obituary 116
Gelven, (Charles) Michael 1937- 29-32R
Gelzer, Matthias 1886-1974 ....CAP-2
Earlier sketch in CA 25-28
Gemme, Francis Robert 1934- 21-24R
Gemme, Leila Boyle 1942- 81-84
Gemmell, Alan Robertson 1913- 114
Gemmett, Robert J(ames) 1936- 33-36R
Gemmill, Jane Brown 1898- 1-4R
Gemmill, Paul F. 1890(?)-1976 Obituary 69-72
Gemming, Elizabeth 1932- CANR-9
Earlier sketch in CA 65-68
See also SATA 11
Gems, (Iris) Pam(ela) 1925- 107
See also DLB 13
Genauer, Emily 1911- 106
Gendel, Evelyn W. 1916(?)-1977 Obituary 104
See also SATA 27
Gendell, Murray 1924- CANR-5
Earlier sketch in CA 9-12R
Gendlin, Eugene T. 1926- 1-4R
Gendron, George M. 1949- 93-96
Gendzier, Irene Lefel 1936- 21-24R
Gendzier, Stephen J(ules) 1930- 33-36R
General, Lloyd 1924(?)-1986 Obituary 119
Genet
See Flanner, Janet
Genet, Jean 1910-1986 ....CANR-18
Earlier sketch in CA 13-16R
See also CLC 1, 2, 5, 10, 14, 44, 46
See also DLB 72
See also DLBY 86
See also MTCW
Genevoix, Maurice Charles Louis
1890-1980 Obituary 102
See also DLB 65
Geng, Veronica 1941- 124
Brief entry 119
Genn, Calder
See Gillie, Christopher
Gennaro, Joseph F(rancis) Jr. 1924- 101
See also SATA 53
Genne, Elizabeth Steel 1911- Brief entry 108
Genne, William H. 1910- 17-20R
Genovese, Eugene D(ominick) 1930- CANR-10
Earlier sketch in CA 69-72
See also DLB 17
Genoves Tarazaga, Santiago 1923- 127
Brief entry 107
Gensemer, Robert Eugene
1936- Brief entry 110
Genser, Cynthia 1950- 69-72
Gensler, Kinereth 1922- 116
Genszler, G(eorge) William II 1915- CANR-9
Earlier sketch in CA 65-68
Gent, Peter 1942- 89-92
See also AITN 1
See also CLC 29
See also DLBY 82
Genthe, Charles V(incent) 1937- 29-32R
Gentil, Richard 1917- 102
Gentile, Gennaro L. 1946- 115
Gentile, Giovanni 1875-1944 Brief entry 119
Gentile, John S(amuel) 1956- 132
Gentle, Mary 1956- 106
See also SATA 48
Gentleman, David (William) 1930- CANR-15
Earlier sketch in CA 25-28R
See also SATA 7
Gentles, Frederick (Ray) 1912- 29-32R
Gentry, Byron B. 1913- 13-16R
Gentry, Curt 1931- CANR-5
Earlier sketch in CA 9-12R
Gentry, Diane Koos 1943- 128
Gentry, Dwight L. 1919- 1-4R
Gentry, Marshall Bruce 1953- 121
Gentry, Peter
See Newcomb, Kerry
and Schaefer, Frank
Gentz, William Howard 1918- 107
Gentzler, J(ennings) Mason 1930- 93-96
Geoff
See Dyson, Geoffrey Harry George
Geoffrey, Theodate
See Wayman, Dorothy G.
Geoghegan, Sister Barbara 1902- CAP-1
Earlier sketch in CA 11-12
Geoghegan, Thomas Dolan
1917(?)-1987 Obituary 121
Georgakas, Dan 1938- CANR-22
Earlier sketches in CA 45-48, CANR-1
George, Alexander Lawrence 1920- 13-16R
George, Alfred Raymond 1912- 108
George, Barbara
See Katz, Bobbi
George, Charles H(illes) 1922- 9-12R
George, Chief Dan 1899-1981 110
Obituary 108
George, Claude Swanson Jr. 1920- 13-16R
George, Collins Crusor 1909-1980 77-80
Obituary 133
George, Dan
See George, Chief Dan
George, David
See Vogenitz, David George
George, E(dgar) Madison 1907-1975 ....1-4R
Obituary 103
George, Elizabeth 1949- 137
George, Emery E(dward) 1933- CANR-36
Earlier sketches in CA 41-44R, CANR-16
George, Emily
See Katz, Bobbi
George, Eugene
See Chevalier, Paul Eugene George
George, Gail
See Katz, Bobbi
George, Henry 1839-1897 ....DLB 23
George, Hermon Jr. 1945- 126
George, Jay
See Strachan, J(ohn) George
George, Jean Craighead 1919- CANR-25
Earlier sketch in CA 5-8R
See also AAYA 8
See also CLC 35
See also CLR 1
See also DLB 52
See also MAICYA
See also SATA 2, 68
George, John E(dwin) 1936- 53-56
George, John L(othar) 1916- 5-8R
See also SATA 2
George, John 1936- 132
George, Jonathan
See Burke, John (Frederick)
and Theiner, George (Fredric)
George, M(ary) Dorothy CAP-1
Earlier sketch in CA 13-16
George, Malcom F(arris) 1930- 57-60
George, Marion
See Benjamin, Claude (Max Edward Pohlman)
George, Mary Carolyn Hollers Jutson
1930- CANR-12
Earlier sketch in CA 73-76
George, Mary Yanaga 1940- 29-32R

George, N(orvil) L(ester) 1902- ... CAP-2
Earlier sketch in CA 29-32
George, Nelson 1957- ... 119
George, Peter 1924-1966 Obituary ... 25-28R
George, Richard R(obert) 1943- ... 104
George, Robert Esmonde Gordon
1890-1969 ... CAP-1
Earlier sketch in CA 11-12
George, Rolf 1930- ... 110
George, Roy E(dwin) 1923- ... CANR-14
Earlier sketch in CA 37-40R
George, S(idney) C(harles) 1898- ... 53-56
See also SATA 11
George, Sally 1945- ... 105
George, Sara 1947- ... 65-68
George, Stefan (Anton)
1868-1933 Brief entry ... 104
See also TCLC 2, 14
George, Susan Akers 1934- ... 77-80
George, W(illiam) Lloyd
1900(?)-1975 Obituary ... 53-56
See also SATA 30
George, W(illiam) R(ichard) P(hilip) 1912- ... 69-72
George, Wilfred R(aymond) 1928- ... 111
George, Wilma
See Crowther, Wilma (Beryl)
George-Brown, George Alfred
1914-1985 Obituary ... 116
Brief entry ... 110
Georges, Georges Martin
See Simenon, Georges (Jacques Christian)
Georges, Robert A(ugustus) 1933- ... 111
Georgescu, Vlad 1937(?)-1988 Obituary ... 127
Georgescu-Roegen, Nicholas 1906- ... CANR-9
Earlier sketch in CA 21-24R
Georges-Michel, Michel
1883-1985 Obituary ... 116
Georgi, Charlotte ... CANR-17
Earlier sketches in CA 1-4R, CANR-2
Georgiana, Sister
See Terstegge, Mabel Alice
Georgiou, Constantine 1927- ... 13-16R
See also SATA 7
Georgiou, Steven Demetre 1948- ... 101
Georgopoulos, Basil S(pyros) 1926- ... 73-76
Gephart, William J(ay) 1928- ... 69-72
Geraci, Philip C. 1929- ... 77-80
Gerald, J(ames) Edward 1906- ... 5-8R
Gerald, John Bart 1940- ... CANR-22
Earlier sketches in CA 5-8R, CANR-7
Gerald, Ziggy
See Zeigerman, Gerald
Gerard, Albert S(tanislas) 1920- ... CANR-13
Earlier sketch in CA 29-32R
Gerard, Andrew
See Gatti, Arthur Gerard
Gerard, Charles (Franklin) 1914- ... 29-32R
Gerard, Dave 1909- ... 53-56
Gerard, David 1923- ... 77-80
Gerard, Elaine
See Ryder, Eileen
Gerard, H(arold) B(enjamin)
1923- Brief entry ... 110
Gerard, Jane 1930- ... 1-4R
Gerard, Jean Ignace Isidore
1803-1847 ... SATA 45
Gerard, Jules B(ernard) 1929- ... 110
Gerard, Karen (Nina) 1932- ... 120
Gerard, Louise 1878(?)-1970 Obituary ... 104
Gerard, Ralph W(aldo)
1900-1974 Obituary ... 49-52
Gerard-Libois, Jules C. 1923- ... 33-36R
Geras, Adele (Daphne) 1944- ... CANR-19
Earlier sketch in CA 97-100
See also SATA 23
Geras, Norman (Myron) 1943- ... CANR-19
Earlier sketch in CA 102
Gerasimov, Gennadi (Ivanovitch)
1930- ... CANR-32
Earlier sketch in CA 69-72
Gerasimov, Innokentii Petrovich
1905-1985 Obituary ... 115
Gerasimov, Mikhail Mikhaylovich
1907-1970 Obituary ... 107
Gerassi, John 1931- ... CANR-8
Earlier sketch in CA 5-8R
Geraud, (Charles Joseph) Andre
1882-1974 ... 69-72
Obituary ... 53-56
Gerber, Albert B(enjamin) 1913- ... 17-20R
Gerber, Barbara (Lin) 1942- ... 117
Gerber, Bobbie
See Gerber, Barbara (Lin)
Gerber, Dan 1940- ... 33-36R
Gerber, David A(llison) 1944- ... 77-80
Gerber, Douglas E(arl) 1933- ... CANR-15
Earlier sketch in CA 29-32R
Gerber, Ellen W. 1936- Brief entry ... 107
Gerber, Helmut E. 1920-1981 ... CANR-10
Earlier sketch in CA 21-24R
Gerber, Israel J(oshua) 1918- ... 77-80
Gerber, John C(hristian) 1908- ... 102
Gerber, John 1907(?)-1981 Obituary ... 103
Gerber, Merrill Joan 1938- ... CANR-26
Earlier sketches in CA 13-16R, CANR-10
See also SATA 64
Gerber, Philip Leslie 1923- Brief entry ... 108
Gerber, Rudolph Joseph 1938- ... 105
Gerber, Sanford E(dwin) 1933- ... CANR-1
Earlier sketch in CA 49-52
Gerber, William 1908- ... 37-40R
Gerberding, Richard A. 1945- ... 128
Gerberg, Mort 1931- ... SATA 64
Gerbers, Teresa 1933- ... 53-56
Gerbi, Antonello 1904-1976 ... 77-80
Gerbner, George 1919- ... CANR-1
Earlier sketch in CA 45-48
Gerboth, Walter W(illiam) 1925-1984 ... 13-16R
Obituary ... 112
Gerchunoff, Alberto 1883-1950 ... HW
Gerden, Friedrich Carl
See Greve, Felix Paul (Berthold Friedrich)
Gerdes, Florence Marie 1919- ... 25-28R
Gerdts, William H. 1929- ... CANR-10
Earlier sketch in CA 13-16R
Gergely, Tibor 1900-1978 ... 107
Obituary ... 106
See also SATA 20, 54
Gergen, Kenneth J(ay) 1934- ... 33-36R
Gerhard, Happy 1920- ... 57-60
Gerhardi, William Alexander
See Gerhardie, William Alexander
Gerhardie, William Alexander
1895-1977 ... CANR-18
Obituary ... 73-76
Earlier sketch in CA 25-28R
See also CLC 5
See also DLB 36
Gerhardt, Lydia A(nn) 1934- ... CANR-10
Earlier sketch in CA 61-64
Gerhart, Gail M. 1943- ... 85-88
Gerhart, Genevra 1930- ... 57-60
Gerig, Reginald R(oth) 1919- ... 57-60
Gerin, Winifred 1901(?)-1981 ... CANR-20
Obituary ... 104
Earlier sketch in CA 25-28R
Geringer, Laura 1948- ... 107
See also SATA 29
Gerlach, Barbara A(nn) 1946- ... 114
Gerlach, Don R(alph) 1932- ... 9-12R
Gerlach, John 1941- ... 101
Gerlach, Larry R(euben) 1941- ... 133
Brief entry ... 109
Gerlach, Luther P(aul) 1930- ... 41-44R
Gerlach, Russel L(ee) 1939- ... 89-92
Gerlach, Vernon S(amuel) 1922- ... 61-64
Gerler, William R(obert) 1917- ... 65-68
See also SATA 47
Germain, Edward B. 1937- ... 89-92
Germain, Walter 1889-1962 Obituary ... 112
German, Donald R(obert) 1931-1986 ... CANR-22
Obituary ... 119
Earlier sketches in CA 57-60, CANR-7
German, Gene Arlin 1933- ... 45-48
German, Joan W(olfe) 1933- ... CANR-22
Earlier sketches in CA 57-60, CANR-7
German, Tony 1924- ... 97-100
Germane, Gayton E. 1920- ... CANR-18
Earlier sketches in CA 1-4R, CANR-2
Germani, Gino 1911-1979 ... CANR-7
Earlier sketch in CA 53-56
Germanicus
See Dunner, Joseph
Germann, A(lbert) C(arl) 1921- ... 1-4R
Germann, Richard Wolf 1930- ... 104
Germano, Peter B. 1913- Brief entry ... 116
Germany, (Vera) Jo(sephine) ... CANR-9
Earlier sketch in CA 65-68
Germar, Herb
See Germar, William H(erbert)
Germar, William H(erbert) 1911- ... 21-24R
Germeshausen, Anna Louise
1906-1968 Obituary ... 108
Germino, Dante (Lee) 1931- ... 53-56
Germond, Jack W. 1928- ... 112
Brief entry ... 108
Gernert, Eleanor Towles 1928- ... 37-40R
Gernes, Sonia 1942- ... 107
Gernsback, Hugo 1884-1967 Obituary ... 93-96
See also DLB 8
Gernsheim, Helmut 1913- ... CANR-22
Earlier sketches in CA 5-8R, CANR-5
Gernstein, Mordicai Brief entry ... 117
See also SATA 36
Geroely, Kalman
See Gabel, Joseph
Gerold, Karl 1906-1973 Obituary ... 41-44R
Gerold, William 1932- ... 17-20R
Geroly, Kalman
See Gabel, Joseph
Gerome
See Thibault, Jacques Anatole Francois
Gerosa, Guido 1933- ... 73-76
Gerould, Daniel C(harles) 1928- ... CANR-33
Gerould, Daniel C. 1928- ... 29-32R
Gerould, Katharine Fullerton
1879-1944 ... DLB 78
Gerow, Edwin 1931- ... 53-56
Gerow, Josh(ua R.) 1941- ... 103
Gerrard, A. J.
See Gerrard, John
Gerrard, Jean 1933- ... 115
See also SATA 51
Gerrard, John 1944- ... 135
Gerrard, Roy 1935- ... 110
See also CLR 23
See also SATA 45, 47
Gerrietts, John 1912-1992 ... 77-80
Obituary ... 136
Gerring, Ray H. 1926- ... 13-16R
Gerrish, B(rian) A(lbert) 1931- ... CANR-4
Earlier sketch in CA 5-8R
Gerrity, David James 1923- ... CANR-4
Earlier sketch in CA 1-4R
Gerrold, David 1944- ... 93-96
See also DLB 8
See also SATA 66
Gerschenkron, Alexander (Pavlovich)
1904-1978 ... CANR-1
Earlier sketch in CA 45-48
Gersh, Harry 1912- ... CANR-1
Earlier sketch in CA 1-4R
Gershator, David 1937- ... 115
Gershator, Phillis 1942- ... 102
Gershen, Martin 1924-1985 ... 33-36R
Obituary ... 114
Gershenson, Daniel E(noch) 1935- ... 5-8R
Gershman, Herbert S. 1926-1971 ... CAP-2
Obituary ... 33-36R
Earlier sketch in CA 25-28
Gershon, Karen
See Tripp, Karen
Gershoy, Leo 1897-1975 ... CAP-1
Obituary ... 57-60
Earlier sketch in CA 13-14
Gershwin, Ira 1896-1983 Obituary ... 110
Brief entry ... 108
Gerson, Corinne 1927- ... CANR-25
Earlier sketch in CA 93-96
See also SATA 37
Gerson, Louis Leib 1921- ... 17-20R
Gerson, Noel Bertram 1914-1988 ... 81-84
Obituary ... 127
See also SATA 22, 60
Gerson, Walter (Max) 1935- ... 41-44R
Gerson, Wolfgang 1916- ... 33-36R
Gersoni, Diane 1947- ... 53-56
Gersonides 1288-1344 ... DLB 115
Gersoni-Stavn, Diane
See Gersoni, Diane
Gerstad, John (Leif) 1924-1981 ... 103
Obituary ... 105
Gerstein, Arnold A. 1940- ... 124
Gerstein, Linda (Groves) 1938- Brief entry ... 110
Gerstein, Mordicai 1935- ... CANR-36
Earlier sketch in CA 127
See also MAICYA
See also SATA 47
Gerstenberg, Heinrich Wilhelm von
1737-1823 ... DLB 97
Gerstenberger, Donna Lorine 1929- ... CANR-4
Earlier sketch in CA 5-8R
Gerster, Georg (Anton) 1928- ... 37-40R
Gerster, Patrick G(eorge) 1942- ... 57-60
Gerstine, Jack
See Gerstine, John
Gerstine, John 1915- ... 5-8R
Gerstl, Joel E. 1932- ... 21-24R
Gerstle, Kurt H(erman) 1923- ... 53-56
Gerstler, Amy 1956- ... CLC 70
Gerstner, Edna Suckau 1914- ... 1-4R
Gerstner, John H(enry) 1914- ... CANR-2
Earlier sketch in CA 1-4R
Gert, Bernard 1934- ... 29-32R
Gerteiny, Alfred G(eorges) 1930- ... 21-24R
Gerteis, Louis S(axton) 1942- ... 45-48
Gerth, Donald Rogers 1928- ... 45-48
Gerth, Hans Heinrich
1908-1978 Obituary ... 81-84
Gertler, Menard M. 1919- ... 9-12R
Gertler, T. ... 121
Brief entry ... 116
See also CLC 34
Gertman, Samuel 1915- ... 1-4R
Gertz, Elmer 1906- ... CANR-11
Earlier sketch in CA 13-16R
Gertz, Theodore G(erson) 1936- ... 115
Gertzog, Irwin N(orman) 1933- ... 29-32R
Gerulaitis, Leonardas Vytautas 1928- ... 77-80
Gervais, C(harles) H(enry) 1946- ... 97-100
Gervais, Marty
See Gervais, C(harles) H(enry)
Gervasi, Eugene Michael
1937-1989 Obituary ... 127
Gervasi, Frank H(enry) 1908-1990 ... CAP-1
Obituary ... 130
Earlier sketch in CA 13-16
Gervasi, Tom
See Gervasi, Eugene Michael
Gerwig, Anna Mary (Gerwig) 1907- ... CAP-2
Earlier sketch in CA 17-18
Gerwin, Donald 1937- ... 25-28R
Gerzon, Mark ... 81-84
Gesch, Dorothy K(atherine) 1923- ... 29-32R
Gesch, Roy G(eorge) 1920- ... 21-24R
Geschickter, Charles F(reeborn)
1901-1987 Obituary ... 123
Geschwender, James A(rthur) 1933- ... 41-44R
Gesell, Arnold Lucius 1880-1961 Obituary ... 116
Geserick, June
See Donahue, June (Geserick)
Gesler, Wilbert M. 1941- ... 138
Gesner, Carol 1922- ... 29-32R
Gesner, Clark 1938- ... 109
See also SATA 40
Gesner, Elsie Miller 1919- ... 17-20R
Gess, Denise 1952- ... 135
Gessert, Kate Rogers 1948- ... 113
Gessner, Lynne 1919- ... CANR-10
Earlier sketch in CA 25-28R
See also SATA 16
Gessner, Salomon 1730-1788 ... DLB 97
Geston, Mark S(ymington) 1946- ... 102
See also DLB 8
Gethers, Peter 1953- ... CANR-31
Earlier sketch in CA 103
Gethers, Steven 1922(?)-1989 Obituary ... 130
Gething, Thomas W(ilson) 1939- ... 41-44R
Getlein, Dorothy Woolen 1921- ... 9-12R
Getlein, Frank 1921- ... CANR-6
Earlier sketch in CA 9-12R
Getman, Gerald Nathan
1914(?)-1990 Obituary ... 131
Gettel, Ronald 1931- ... 112
Gettens, Rutherford John
1900(?)-1974 Obituary ... 49-52
Gettings, Eunice J.
1901(?)-1978 Obituary ... 81-84
Gettings, Fred 1937- ... 123
Gettleman, Marvin E. 1933- ... 37-40R
Gettleman, Susan
See Braiman, Susan
Getty, Gerald W(inkler) 1913- ... 57-60
Getty, Hilda F. 1938- ... 61-64
Getty, J(ean) Paul 1892-1976 ... 69-72
Obituary ... 65-68
Getty, Mary Ann 1943- ... 114
Getz, Gene A(rnold) 1932- ... CANR-29
Earlier sketches in CA 29-32R, CANR-12
Getz, Malcolm 1945- ... CANR-18
Earlier sketch in CA 101
Getz, Oscar 1897-1983 Obituary ... 110
Getzels, Jacob Warren 1912- ... CANR-30
Earlier sketch in CA 45-48
Getzoff, Carole 1943- ... 61-64
Geubtner, Virginia Reidel
See Reidel-Geubtner, Virginia
Geve, Thomas 1929- ... 127
Gevirtz, Don L(ee) 1928- ... 121
Gevirtz, Eliezer 1950- ... 121
See also SATA 49
Gevirtz, Stanley 1929-1988 Obituary ... 126
Brief entry ... 109
Gewe, Raddory
See Gorey, Edward (St. John)
Gewecke, Clifford George Jr. 1932- ... 21-24R
Gewehr, Wolf M(ax) 1939- ... CANR-1
Earlier sketch in CA 45-48
Gewirth, Alan 1912- Brief entry ... 107
Gewirtz, Jacob L(eon) 1924- ... 45-48
Gewirtz, Leonard Benjamin 1918- ... 1-4R
Geyer, Alan (Francis) 1931- ... 9-12R
Geyer, Georgie Anne 1935- ... CANR-17
Earlier sketch in CA 29-32R
Geyl, Pieter (Catharinus Arie) 1887-1966 ... 103
Obituary ... 89-92
Geyman, John P. 1931- ... CANR-14
Earlier sketch in CA 37-40R
Gezi, Kal
See Gezi, Kalil I(smail)
Gezi, Kalil I(smail) 1930- ... CANR-17
Earlier sketch in CA 25-28R
Ghadimi, Hossein 1922- ... 61-64
Ghai, Dharam P. 1936- ... CANR-34
Earlier sketches in CA 21-24R, CANR-15
Gheddo, Piero 1929- ... CANR-15
Earlier sketch in CA 73-76
Ghelardi, Robert (Anthony) 1939- ... 69-72
Ghelderode, Michel de 1898-1962 ... 85-88
See also CLC 6, 11
Gheorghiu, (Constantin) Virgil 1916- ... CANR-30
Obituary ... 138
Earlier sketch in CA 33-36R
Gherity, James Arthur 1929- ... 17-20R
Gherman, Beverly 1934- ... 136
See also SATA 68
Ghezzi, Bert (Bentil W.) 1941- ... 133
Ghigna, Charles 1946- ... 77-80
Ghine, Wunnakyawhtin U Ohn
See Maurice, David (John Kerr)
Ghiotto, Renato 1923- ... 49-52
Ghiradella, Robert 1934- ... 114
Ghiselin, Brewster 1903- ... CANR-13
Earlier sketch in CA 13-16R
See also CAAS 10
See also CLC 23
Ghiselin, Michael T(enant) 1939- ... 49-52
Ghiselli, Edwin E(rnest) 1907- ... 37-40R
Ghnassia, Maurice (Jean-Henri)
1920- ... CANR-34
Earlier sketch in CA 49-52
Ghose, Amal 1929- ... CANR-28
Earlier sketch in CA 106
Ghose, Sri Chinmoy Kumar
See Chinmoy, Sri
Ghose, Sudhin(dra) N(ath) 1899- ... 5-8R
Ghose, Zulfikar 1935- ... 65-68
See also CLC 42
Ghosh, Amitav 1956- ... CLC 44
Ghosh, Arun Kumar 1930- ... CANR-26
Earlier sketches in CA 21-24R, CANR-10
Ghosh, Dipali 1945- ... 124
Ghosh, Jyotis Chandra
1904(?)-1975 Obituary ... 57-60
Ghosh, Tapan 1928- ... 53-56
Ghougassian, Joseph P(eter) 1944- ... 49-52
Ghurye, G(ovind) S(adashiv) 1893- ... CANR-3
Earlier sketch in CA 5-8R
Giacosa, Giuseppe 1847-1906 Brief entry ... 104
See also TCLC 7
Giacumakis, George Jr. 1937- ... 41-44R
Giallombardo, Rose (Mary) 1925- ... 61-64
Giamatti, A(ngelo) Bartlett 1938-1989 ... 97-100
Obituary ... 129
Giamatti, Valentine 1911-1982 Obituary ... 106
Gianakaris, C(onstantine) J(ohn) 1934- ... 25-28R
Giannaris, George (B.) 1936- ... CANR-22
Earlier sketches in CA 45-48, CANR-2
Giannestras, Nicholas James
1909-1978 Obituary ... 105
Giannetti, Louis D. 1937- ... 33-36R
Giannini, Enzo 1946- ... SATA 68
Giannone, Richard 1934- ... 21-24R
Giannoni, Carlo Borromeo 1939- ... 41-44R
Giap Vo Nguyen
See Vo Nguyen Giap
Giardina, Anthony 1950- ... 118
Giardina, Denise 1951- ... 119
Giauque, William Francis
1895-1982 Obituary ... 106
Gibaldi, Joseph 1942- ... CANR-15
Earlier sketch in CA 89-92
Gibans, Nina Freedlander 1932- ... 116
Gibb, Hamilton (Alexander Rosskeen)
1895-1971 ... CANR-6
Obituary ... 33-36R
Earlier sketch in CA 1-4R

Gibb, Jack (Rex) 1914- ... 17-20R
Gibb, Lee
See Deghy, Guy (Stephen)
and Waterhouse, Keith (Spencer)
Gibbard, Allan (Fletcher) 1942- ... 136
Gibbard, Graham S(tewart) 1942- ... 53-56
Gibbens, T(revor) C(harles) N(oel)
1912-1983 Obituary ... 111
Gibberd, Frederick 1908-1984 Obituary ... 111
Gibbins, Peter 1947- ... 127
Gibble, Kenneth L(ee) 1941- ... 130
Gibbon, Edward 1737-1794 ... DLB 104
Gibbon, John Murray 1875-1952 ... DLB 92
Gibbon, Lewis Grassic
See Mitchell, James Leslie
See also TCLC 4
Gibbon, (William) Monk 1896-1987 ... 69-72
Obituary ... 124
Gibbon, Vivian 1917- ... 103
Gibbons, Barbara (Halloran) 1934- ... CANR-10
Earlier sketch in CA 61-64
Gibbons, Bob
See Gibbons, Robert
Gibbons, Brian 1938- ... CANR-11
Earlier sketch in CA 25-28R
Gibbons, Don C(ary) 1926- Brief entry ... 110
Gibbons, Euell (Theophilus) 1911-1975 ... CAP-2
Obituary ... 61-64
Earlier sketch in CA 23-24
See also AITN 1
Gibbons, Faye 1938- ... 109
See also SATA 65
Gibbons, Felton L(ewis) 1929-1990 ... 124
Obituary ... 131
Gibbons, (Raphael) Floyd (Phillips)
1887-1939 Brief entry ... 113
See also DLB 25
Gibbons, Gail 1944- ... CANR-12
Earlier sketch in CA 69-72
See also CLR 8
See also MAICYA
See also SAAS 12
See also SATA 23
Gibbons, Helen Bay 1921- ... 17-20R
Gibbons, J. Whitfield 1939- ... CANR-35
Earlier sketch in CA 114
Gibbons, John H(oward) 1929- ... 127
Gibbons, John William 1907-1983 Obituary ... 109
Gibbons, Kaye 1960- ... CLC 50
Gibbons, Maurice 1931- ... 89-92
Gibbons, Reginald 1947- ... CANR-18
Earlier sketch in CA 97-100
See also DLB 120
Gibbons, Robert 1949- ... CANR-39
Earlier sketch in CA 116
Gibbons, Stella (Dorothea) 1902-1989 ... 13-16R
Obituary ... 130
Gibbons, Whit
See Gibbons, J. Whitfield
Gibbons, William ... DLB 73
Gibbs, A(twood) James 1922- ... 17-20R
Gibbs, A(nthony) M(atthews) 1933- ... 33-36R
Gibbs, Alonzo (Lawrence) 1915- ... CANR-5
Earlier sketch in CA 5-8R
See also SATA 5
Gibbs, Anthony 1902-1975 ... CAP-2
Earlier sketch in CA 29-32
Gibbs, Barbara 1912- ... 25-28R
Gibbs, C. Earl 1935- ... 69-72
Gibbs, Esther 1904- ... 57-60
Gibbs, George 1870-1942 Brief entry ... 120
Gibbs, Henry
See Rumbold-Gibbs, Henry St. John Clair
Gibbs, Jack P(orter) 1927- ... 122
Brief entry ... 118
Gibbs, James A.
See Gibbs, James Atwood
Gibbs, James Atwood 1922- ... CANR-29
Earlier sketches in CA 69-72, CANR-11
Gibbs, Jim
See Gibbs, James Atwood
Gibbs, Joanifer 1947- ... 57-60
Gibbs, John G(amble) 1930- ... 41-44R
Gibbs, Mark 1920- ... 5-8R
Gibbs, Mary Ann
See Bidwell, Marjory Elizabeth Sarah
Gibbs, (Cecilia) May 1877-1969 Obituary ... 104
See also SATA 27
Gibbs, Norman Henry 1910-1990 Obituary ... 131
Gibbs, Paul T(homas) 1897- ... 9-12R
Gibbs, Peter Bawtree 1903- ... 1-4R
Gibbs, Philip (Hamilton)
1877-1962 Obituary ... 89-92
Gibbs, Rafe
See Gibbs, Raphael Sanford
Gibbs, Raphael Sanford 1912- ... 5-8R
Gibbs, Tony
See Gibbs, Wolcott Jr.
Gibbs, William E. 1936- ... CAP-2
Earlier sketch in CA 21-22
Gibbs, Wolcott Jr. 1935- ... 85-88
See also SATA 40
Gibbs-Smith, Charles Harvard
1909-1981 ... CANR-4
Obituary ... 108
Earlier sketch in CA 9-12R
Gibbs-Wilson, Kathryn (Beatrice)
1930- ... CANR-10
Earlier sketch in CA 65-68
Gibby, Robert Gwyn 1916- ... 13-16R
Giberson, Dorothy (Dodds) ... CANR-2
Earlier sketch in CA 1-4R
Gibian, George 1924- ... CANR-19
Earlier sketches in CA 1-4R, CANR-5
Giblin, Charles Homer 1928- ... 41-44R
Giblin, James Cross 1933- ... CANR-24
Earlier sketch in CA 106
See also MAICYA
See also SAAS 12
See also SATA 33
Giblon, Shirley T(enhouse) 1935- ... 131
Gibney, Frank (Bray) 1924- ... CANR-11
Earlier sketch in CA 69-72
Gibney, Harriet
See Harvey, Harriet
Gibney, Sheridan 1904(?)-1988 Obituary ... 125
Giboire, Clive (John) 1945- ... 118
Gibran, Jean 1933- ... 69-72
Gibran, Kahlil 1883-1931 Brief entry ... 104
See also TCLC 1, 9
Gibson, Alexander Cameron 1926- ... 134
Gibson, Alexander Dunnett
1901-1978 Obituary ... 77-80
Gibson, Anne (E.) 1954- ... 125
Gibson, Arrell Morgan 1921- ... 41-44R
Gibson, Arthur 1943- ... 130
Gibson, Charles (Edmund) 1916- ... 5-8R
Gibson, Charles 1920- ... 21-24R
Gibson, Charline 1937- ... 69-72
Gibson, D. Parke 1930-1979 ... 93-96
Obituary ... 85-88
Gibson, Derlyne 1936- ... 21-24R
Gibson, Donald B. 1933- ... 25-28R
See also BW
Gibson, E(rnest) Dana 1906- ... 29-32R
Gibson, E(dward) Lawrence 1935- ... 93-96
Gibson, Elizabeth 1949- ... 118
Gibson, Elsie (Edith) 1907- ... 61-64
Gibson, Eva 1939- ... CANR-35
Earlier sketch in CA 114
Gibson, Evan K(eith) 1909- ... 105
Gibson, Frank K. 1924- ... 37-40R
Gibson, George H(orner) 1932- Brief entry ... 114
Gibson, Gerald Don 1938- ... 104
Gibson, Gertrude Hevener 1906- ... 5-8R
Gibson, Gifford Guy 1943- ... 77-80
Gibson, Graeme 1934- ... 130
See also DLB 53
Gibson, H(amilton) B(ertie) 1914- ... 102
Gibson, Harry Clark
See Hubler, Richard Gibson
Gibson, James C.
See Gibson, James (Charles)
Gibson, James (Charles) 1919- ... 117
Gibson, James J(erome) 1904- ... 85-88
Gibson, James L(awrence) 1935- ... CANR-8
Earlier sketch in CA 5-8R
Gibson, James W(illiam) 1932- ... 41-44R
Gibson, Janice T(horne) 1934- ... 41-44R
Gibson, John M(endinghall) 1899- ... 1-4R
Obituary ... 134
Gibson, John 1907- ... 33-36R
Gibson, Josephine
See Hine, Al(fred Blakelee)
and Hine, Sesyle Joslin
Gibson, Karon Rose (White) 1946- ... 105
Gibson, Maralee G. 1924- ... 17-20R
Gibson, Margaret 1944- ... 77-80
See also DLB 120
Gibson, Margaret 1948- ... 103
Gibson, Miles 1947- ... CANR-18
Earlier sketch in CA 102
Gibson, Morgan 1929- ... CANR-14
Earlier sketch in CA 25-28R
Gibson, (William) Morris(on) 1916- ... 117
Gibson, Nevin H(erman) 1915- ... 49-52
Gibson, Raymond E(ugene) 1924- ... 21-24R
Gibson, Reginald Walter 1901- ... CAP-1
Earlier sketch in CA 13-14
Gibson, Richard (Thomas) 1931- ... 41-44R
Gibson, Robert (Donald Davidson) 1927- ... 65-68
Gibson, Robert L(eone) 1927- ... 121
Gibson, Robert William Jr. 1923- ... 107
Gibson, Ronald George 1909- ... 109
Gibson, Rosemary
See Newell, Rosemary
Gibson, Shirley 1927- ... 103
Gibson, (William) Walker 1919- ... CANR-1
Earlier sketch in CA 1-4R
Gibson, Walter B(rown) 1897-1985 ... 110
Obituary ... 118
Brief entry ... 108
Gibson, Walter Samuel 1932- ... 102
Gibson, Wilfrid Wilson 1878-1962 Obituary ... 113
See also DLB 19
Gibson, William Carleton 1913- ... 17-20R
Gibson, William E(dward) 1944- ... 33-36R
Gibson, William (Ford) 1948- ... 133
Brief entry ... 126
See also CLC 39, 63
Gibson, William M(erriam) 1912- ... 121
Gibson, William 1914- ... CANR-9
Earlier sketch in CA 9-12R
See also CLC 23
See also DLB 7
See also SATA 66
Gibson-Jarvie, Clodagh 1923- ... 105
Gichon, Mordechai 1922- ... 89-92
Gicovate, Bernard 1922- ... 37-40R
Gidal, Nachum
See Gidal, Tim N(achum)
Gidal, Peter 1946- ... 103
Gidal, Sonia (Epstein) 1922- ... CANR-14
Earlier sketch in CA 5-8R
See also SATA 2
Gidal, Tim N(achum) 1909- ... CANR-20
Earlier sketches in CA 5-8R, CANR-14
See also SATA 2
Gidalewitsch, Nachum
See Gidal, Tim N(achum)
Giddings, James Louis 1909-1964 ... CAP-1
Earlier sketch in CA 11-12
Giddings, John Calvin 1930- ... 109
Giddings, Paula 1948- ... 125
See also BW
Giddings, Robert (Lindsay) 1935- ... CANR-9
Earlier sketch in CA 21-24R
Giddins, Gary 1948- ... CANR-32
Earlier sketches in CA 77-80, CANR-13
Giddy, Ian H. 1948- ... 114
Gide, Andre (Paul Guillaume) 1869-1951 ... 124
Brief entry ... 104
See also DLB 65
See also MTCW
See also TCLC 5, 12, 36
See also WLC
Gideonse, Harry David 1901-1985 Obituary ... 115
Gidley, Charles
See Wheeler, (Charles) Gidley
Gidley, (Gustavus) M(ick) 1941- ... 102
Gidlow, Elsa 1898-1986 ... 77-80
Obituary ... 119
Gidney, James B. 1914- ... 45-48
Giedion, Sigfried 1888(?)-1968 Obituary ... 116
Giegling, John A(llan) 1935- ... 29-32R
See also SATA 17
Giele, Janet Z(ollinger) 1934- ... CANR-36
Earlier sketch in CA 114
Gielgud, Gwen Bagni
See Dubov, Gwen Bagni
Gielgud, (Arthur) John 1904- Brief entry ... 111
Gielgud, Val (Henry) 1900- ... CANR-5
Earlier sketch in CA 9-12R
Giere, Ronald N(elson) 1938- ... CANR-4
Earlier sketch in CA 49-52
Giergielewicz, Mieczyslaw F. 1901-1983 ... CAP-2
Obituary ... 113
Earlier sketch in CA 25-28
Gierow, Karl Ragnar (Knut)
1904-1982 Obituary ... 108
Giersch, Julius
See Arnade, Charles W(olfgang)
Giertz, Bo H(arald) 1905- ... CANR-9
Earlier sketch in CA 21-24R
Gies, Frances 1915- ... CANR-9
Earlier sketch in CA 25-28R
Gies, Joseph (Cornelius) 1916- ... CANR-9
Earlier sketch in CA 5-8R
Gies, Thomas G(eorge) 1921- ... 33-36R
Giesbrecht, Martin Gerhard 1933- ... CANR-4
Earlier sketch in CA 53-56
Gieseking, Hal E. 1932- ... 131
Giesey, Ralph E(dwin) 1923- ... 25-28R
Giessler, Phillip Bruce 1938- ... CANR-8
Earlier sketch in CA 61-64
Giesy, J(ohn) U(lrich)
1877-1947 Brief entry ... 112
Giff, Patricia Reilly 1935- ... CANR-18
Earlier sketch in CA 101
See also MAICYA
See also SATA 33, 70
Giffen, Daniel H. 1938- ... 107
Giffin, Frederick Charles 1938- ... 41-44R
Giffin, James Manning 1935- ... 105
Giffin, Mary (Elizabeth) 1919- ... 130
Giffin, Sidney F. 1907-1977 Obituary ... 73-76
Gifford, Barry (Colby) 1946- ... CANR-30
Earlier sketches in CA 65-68, CANR-9
See also CLC 34
Gifford, Denis 1927- ... CANR-18
Earlier sketch in CA 101
Gifford, Don (Creighton) 1919- ... 53-56
Gifford, Edward S(tewart) Jr. 1907- ... CAP-2
Earlier sketch in CA 19-20
Gifford, Francis Newton
See Gifford, Frank
Gifford, Frank 1930- Brief entry ... 109
Gifford, Griselda 1931- ... CANR-24
Earlier sketch in CA 107
See also SATA 42
Gifford, (Charles) Henry 1913- ... 17-20R
Gifford, James Fergus Jr. 1940- ... 57-60
Gifford, Prosser 1929- ... CANR-39
Earlier sketches in CA 101, CANR-18
Gifford, Terry 1946- ... CANR-24
Earlier sketch in CA 106
Gifford, Thomas (Eugene) 1937- ... 77-80
Gifford-Jones, W.
See Walker, Kenneth Francis
Gigerenzer, Gerd 1947- ... 135
Giggal, Kenneth 1927- ... CANR-20
Earlier sketch in CA 104
Giglio, Ernest D(avid) 1931- ... 33-36R
Giglio, James N. 1939- ... 138
Giguere, Diane 1937- ... 25-28R
See also DLB 53
Giguere, Roland 1929- ... DLB 60
Gih, Andrew 1901- ... 21-24R
Gil, David G(eorg) 1924- ... CANR-12
Earlier sketch in CA 29-32R
Gil, Federico Guillermo 1915- ... CANR-2
Earlier sketch in CA 1-4R
Gilb, Corinne Lathrop 1925- ... 17-20R
Gilbar, Steven 1941- ... 106
Gilbert, Alan Graham 1944- ... 112
Gilbert, Allan H. 1888- ... 9-12R
Gilbert, Amy M(argaret) 1895-1980 ... 49-52
Obituary ... 133
Gilbert, Ann
See Taylor, Ann
Gilbert, Anna
See Lazarus, Marguerite
Gilbert, Anne 1927- ... CANR-7
Earlier sketch in CA 57-60
Gilbert, Anthony
See Malleson, Lucy Beatrice
See also DLB 77
Gilbert, Arlene E(lsie) 1934- ... 49-52
Gilbert, Arthur 1926-1976 ... CANR-9
Earlier sketch in CA 17-20R
Gilbert, Ben W(illiam) 1918- ... 45-48
Gilbert, Benjamin Franklin 1918- ... CANR-22
Earlier sketches in CA 17-20R, CANR-7
Gilbert, Bentley B(rinkerhoff) 1924- ... 25-28R
Gilbert, Bil 1927- ... 134
Brief entry ... 129
Gilbert, Bill 1931- ... 105
Gilbert, Celia 1932- ... 115
Gilbert, Charles 1913- ... 41-44R
Gilbert, Christine B(ell) 1909- ... 103
Gilbert, Christopher 1949- ... 120
See also BW
Gilbert, Creighton (Eddy) 1924- ... CANR-15
Earlier sketch in CA 33-36R
Gilbert, David T(hompson) 1953- ... 106
Gilbert, David 1913- ... 137
Gilbert, Doris Wilcox ... 17-20R
Gilbert, Doug 1938-1979 Obituary ... 104
Gilbert, Douglas L. 1925- ... 13-16R
Gilbert, Douglas 1942- ... 53-56
Gilbert, Edmund W(illiam) 1900-1973 ... 65-68
Gilbert, Edwin 1907-1976 ... 77-80
Obituary ... 69-72
Gilbert, Felix 1905- ... 132
Brief entry ... 106
Gilbert, George 1922- ... 69-72
Gilbert, Glenn Gordon 1936- ... CANR-13
Earlier sketch in CA 33-36R
Gilbert, Gordon Allan 1942- ... 103
Gilbert, Gorman 1943- ... 114
Gilbert, Gustave M. 1911-1977 Obituary ... 69-72
Gilbert, Harriett 1948- ... CANR-9
Earlier sketch in CA 57-60
See also SATA 30
Gilbert, Harry 1946- ... 106
Gilbert, Herman Cromwell 1923- ... CANR-12
Earlier sketch in CA 29-32R
Gilbert, Jack G(lenn) 1934- ... 25-28R
Gilbert, Jack 1925- ... 123
Brief entry ... 116
Gilbert, James B(urkhart) 1939- ... 129
Gilbert, James 1935- ... 29-32R
Gilbert, Jarvey 1917- ... 33-36R
Gilbert, (Agnes) Joan (Sewell) 1931- ... 21-24R
See also SATA 10
Gilbert, John (Raphael) 1926- ... 107
See also SATA 36
Gilbert, Julie Goldsmith
See Daniel, Julie Goldsmith
Gilbert, Manu
See West, Joyce (Tarlton)
Gilbert, Marilyn B(ender) 1926- ... CANR-1
Earlier sketch in CA 1-4R
Gilbert, Martin (John) 1936- ... CANR-31
Earlier sketch in CA 9-12R
Gilbert, Michael (Francis) 1912- ... CANR-28
Earlier sketches in CA 1-4R, CANR-1
See also CAAS 15
See also DLB 87
Gilbert, Milton 1909(?)-1979 Obituary ... 93-96
Gilbert, Miriam
See Presberg, Miriam Goldstein
Gilbert, Nan
See Gilbertson, Mildred Geiger
Gilbert, Neil 1940- ... 77-80
Gilbert, R(obert) A(ndrew) 1942- ... 124
Gilbert, Robert E(mile) 1939- ... 53-56
Gilbert, Rod(rigue Gabriel)
1941- Brief entry ... 109
Gilbert, Russell Wieder 1905-1985 ... CANR-27
Obituary ... 115
Earlier sketch in CA 45-48
Gilbert, Ruth Gallard Ainsworth
See Ainsworth, Ruth (Gallard)
Gilbert, S(tuart) R(eid) 1948- ... 101
Gilbert, Sandra M(ortola) 1936- ... CANR-33
Earlier sketches in CA 41-44R, CANR-14
See also DLB 120
See also MTCW
Gilbert, Sara (Dulaney) 1943- ... CANR-6
Earlier sketch in CA 57-60
See also SATA 11
Gilbert, Stephen 1912- ... 25-28R
Gilbert, W(illiam) S(chwenck)
1836-1911 Brief entry ... 104
See also SATA 36
See also TCLC 3
Gilbert, Willie 1916-1980 ... CANR-37
Earlier sketch in CA 45-48
Gilbert, (Lerman) Zack 1925- ... 65-68
Gilberts, Helen 1909- ... 29-32R
Gilbertson, Merrill Thomas 1911- ... 9-12R
Gilbertson, Mildred Geiger 1908- ... CANR-2
Earlier sketch in CA 5-8R
See also SATA 2
Gilbo, Patrick F(rancis) 1937- ... 107
Gilboa, Amir 1917-1984 Obituary ... 114
Gilboa, Yehoshua A. 1918-1981 ... CANR-35
Earlier sketch in CA 29-32R
Gilborn, Alice 1936- ... 69-72
Gilbreath, Alice 1921- ... CANR-25
Earlier sketches in CA 25-28R, CANR-10
See also SATA 12
Gilbreath, (Larry) Kent 1945- ... 45-48
Gilbreth, Frank B. Jr. 1911- ... 9-12R
See also CLC 17
See also SATA 2
Gilbreth, Lillian Moller
1878-1972 Obituary ... 33-36R
Gilcher, Edwin L. 1909- ... 29-32R
Gilchrist, Agnes A(ddison)
1907-1976 Obituary ... 65-68
Gilchrist, Alan W. 1913- ... 21-24R
Gilchrist, Andrew (Graham) 1910- ... CANR-26
Earlier sketch in CA 109

Gilchrist, Ellen 1935- 116
Brief entry 113
See also CLC 34, 48
See also MTCW
Gilchrist, J(ohn Thomas) 1927- 25-28R
Gilday, Robert M. 1925(?)-1980 Obituary 101
Gil de Biedma, Jaime 1929-1990 ....DLB 108
Gilden, Bert 1915(?)-1971 ....CAP-1
Obituary 29-32R
Earlier sketch in CA 11-12
Gilden, K. B.
See Gilden, Bert
and Gilden, Katya Alpert
Gilden, Katya Alpert 1919(?)-1991 ....9-12R
Obituary 134
Gilder, Eric 1911- CANR-15
Earlier sketch in CA 89-92
Gilder, George F. 1939- CANR-26
Earlier sketches in CA 17-20R, CANR-9
See also AITN 1
Gilder, Jeannette L. 1849-1916 ....DLB 79
Gilder, Richard Watson 1844-1909 ....DLB 64, 79
Gilder, Rosamond de Kay 1891-1986 ....1-4R
Obituary 120
Gildersleeve, Basil 1831-1924 ....DLB 71
Gildersleeve, Thomas R(obert) 1927- 29-32R
Gildner, Gary 1938- CANR-12
Earlier sketch in CA 33-36R
Gildner, Judith 1943- 89-92
Gildrie, Richard P(eter) 1945- 73-76
Gildzen, Alex 1943- 41-44R
Gilead, Zerubavel 1912- 123
Giles, C(harles) W(ilfred) Scott
See Scott-Giles, C(harles) W(ilfred)
Giles, Carl H(oward) 1935- CANR-39
Earlier sketch in CA 29-32R
Giles, Elizabeth
See Holt, John (Robert)
Giles, Frank (Thomas Robertson) 1919- 133
Giles, Frederick John 1928- 93-96
Giles, Geoffrey J(ohn) 1947- 122
Giles, Gordon A.
See Binder, Otto O(scar)
Giles, Henry 1809-1882 ....DLB 64
Giles, James R(ichard) 1937- 73-76
Giles, Janice Holt 1909-1979 ....CANR-3
Earlier sketch in CA 1-4R
Giles, Jeff 1965- 137
Giles, John 1921- 104
Giles, Kris
See Nielsen, Helen Berniece
Giles, Mary E(lizabeth) 1934- 108
Giles, Molly 1942- 126
See also CLC 39
Giles, Raymond
See Holt, John (Robert)
Giles, Robert H(artmann) 1933- Brief entry 122
Giles of Rome 1243(?)-1316 ....DLB 115
Gilfillan, Edward S(mith) Jr. 1906- 57-60
Gilfillan, Merrill (C.) 1945- 138
Gilfond, Henry CANR-24
Earlier sketches in CA 21-24R, CANR-9
See also SATA 2
Gilford, C(harles) B(ernard) 1920- 17-20R
Gilford, Madeline Lee 1923- 85-88
Gilge, Jeanette 1924- 61-64
See also SATA 22
Gilgen, Albert R(udolph) 1930- 37-40R
Gilgoff, Alice 1946- 85-88
Gilgun, John F(rancis) 1935- 117
Gilhooley, Jack
See Gilhooley, John
Gilhooley, John 1940- CANR-31
Earlier sketch in CA 85-88
Gilhooley, Leonard 1921- 37-40R
Gili, Phillida 1944- ....SATA 70
Gilien, Sasha 1925(?)-1971 Obituary 33-36R
Giliomee, Hermann (Buhr) 1938- 102
Gilison, Jerome Martin 1935- 103
Gilkerson, William 1936- 127
Gilkes, A(ntony) N(ewcombe) 1900- 5-8R
Gilkey, Langdon (Brown) 1919- CANR-7
Earlier sketch in CA 17-20R
Gilkyson, Bernice Kenyon
1898(?)-1982 Obituary 106
Gill, Alan
See Gillespie, Alfred
Gill, Anton 1948- 130
Gill, B. M.
See Trimble, Barbara Margaret
Gill, Bartholomew
See McGarrity, Mark
Gill, Bob 1931- 1-4R
Gill, Brendan 1914- CANR-37
Earlier sketch in CA 73-76
See also MTCW
Gill, (Ronald) Crispin 1916- CANR-12
Earlier sketch in CA 21-24R
Gill, David (Lawrence William) 1934- CANR-12
Earlier sketch in CA 29-32R
Gill, Derek (Lewis Theodore) 1919- CANR-19
Earlier sketches in CA 49-52, CANR-4
See also SATA 9
Gill, Dominic 1941- 106
Gill, (Arthur) Eric (Rowton Peter Joseph)
1882-1940 Brief entry 120
See also DLB 98
Gill, Evan Robertson 1892- 9-12R
Gill, Frederick (Cyril) 1898- 5-8R
Gill, Gillian
See Gill, Gillian C(atherine)
Gill, Gillian C(atherine) 1942- 134
Gill, I(nayat) K(hera) 1924- 61-64
Gill, Jerry H. 1933- CANR-28
Earlier sketches in CA 33-36R, CANR-12
Gill, John Edward 1938- 106
Gill, Joseph 1901- CANR-3
Earlier sketch in CA 9-12R
Gill, Kay 1944- 111
Gill, Margery Jean 1925- ....SATA 22
Gill, Merton M(ax) 1914- 122
Gill, Patrick
See Creasey, John
Gill, Peter 1939- CANR-22
Earlier sketch in CA 103
Gill, Richard T(homas) 1927- CANR-13
Earlier sketch in CA 21-24R
Gill, Richard 1922-1989 ....41-44R
Obituary 128
Gill, Sam D. 1943- 130
Gill, Stephen 1932- ....SATA 63
Gill, Suzanne L(utz) 1941- 136
Gill, Traviss 1891- CAP-1
Earlier sketch in CA 13-14
Gillan, Garth J. 1939- 102
Gillan, Patricia Wagstaff 1936- 102
Gillchrest, Muriel Noyes 1905- 25-28R
Gillelan, G(eorge) Howard 1917- CANR-6
Earlier sketch in CA 1-4R
Gillen, Lucy
See Stratton, Rebecca
Gillen, Mollie 1908- 41-44R
Gillen, Robert L(eonard) 1946- 114
Gillenson, Lewis William 1918- 5-8R
Giller, Robert M(aynard) 1942- 124
Gilles, Albert S(imeon) Sr. 1888- 57-60
Gilles, Anthony E(ugene) 1945- 114
Gilles, Daniel 1917- 103
Gillese, John Patrick 1920- 13-16R
Gillespie, A(braham) Lincoln Jr.
1895-1950 Brief entry 115
See also DLB 4
Gillespie, Alfred 1924- 77-80
Gillespie, Angus Kress 1942- 132
Gillespie, Cynthia K. 1941- 133
Gillespie, Diane Filby 1943- 130
Gillespie, Dizzy
See Gillespie, John Birks
Gillespie, Gerald 1933- CANR-10
Earlier sketch in CA 25-28R
Gillespie, I(ris) S(ylvia) 1923- 65-68
Gillespie, James E(rnest) Jr. 1940- 53-56
Gillespie, Janet Wicks 1913- 5-8R
Gillespie, John Birks 1917- 104
Gillespie, John E. 1921- 17-20R
Gillespie, John T(homas) 1928- CANR-31
Earlier sketches in CA 73-76, CANR-13
Gillespie, Kingsley 1895-1984 Obituary 112
Gillespie, Link
See Gillespie, A(braham) Lincoln Jr.
Gillespie, Marcia Ann 1944- 134
See also AITN 2
Gillespie, Michael Patrick 1946- 127
Gillespie, Neal C(ephas) 1933- 33-36R
Gillespie, Robert B(yrne) 1917- CANR-29
Earlier sketch in CA 110
Gillespie, Robert W. 1922(?)-1983 Obituary 110
Gillespie, Susan
See Turton-Jones, Edith Constance (Bradshaw)
Gillet, Lev 1892(?)-1980 Obituary 97-100
Gillett, Charlie 1942- 33-36R
Gillett, Edward 1915- 131
Gillett, Eric (Walkey) 1893-1978 ....CANR-3
Earlier sketch in CA 5-8R
Gillett, J(ohn) D(avid) 1913- 49-52
Gillett, Margaret 1930- CANR-39
Earlier sketches in CA 1-4R, CANR-2, 17
Gillett, Mary (Bledsoe) CAP-2
Earlier sketch in CA 25-28
See also SATA 7
Gillette, Arnold S(impson) 1904- CANR-2
Earlier sketch in CA 1-4R
Gillette, Henry Sampson 1915- 5-8R
See also SATA 14
Gillette, J(ay) Michael 1939- 113
Gillette, Michael
See Gillette, J(ay) Michael
Gillette, Paul 1938- 53-56
Gillette, Virginia M(ary) 1920- 57-60
Gillette, William 1933- 108
Gilley, Sheridan (Wayne) 1945- 133
Gillham, Bill
See Gillham, W(illiam) E(dwin) C(harles)
Gillham, D. G. 1921- 21-24R
Gillham, W(illiam) E(dwin) C(harles) 1936- 113
See also SATA 42
Gilliam, Dorothy B(utler) 1936- 97-100
Gilliam, Florence ....DLB 4
Gilliam, Stan 1946- ....SATA 35, 39
Gilliam, Terry (Vance) 1940- CANR-35
Brief entry 108
Earlier sketch in CA 113
See also Monty Python
See also CLC 21
Gillian, Jerry
See Gilliam, Terry (Vance)
Gillian, Kay
See Smith, Kay Nolte
Gilliatt, Penelope (Ann Douglass) 1932- 13-16R
See also AITN 2
See also CLC 2, 10, 13, 53
See also DLB 14
Gillie, Christopher 1914- 102
Gillie, Oliver (John) 1937- CANR-12
Earlier sketch in CA 65-68
Gillies, Archibald L. 127
Gillies, John 1925- CANR-28
Earlier sketches in CA 73-76, CANR-12
Gillies, Malcolm 1954- 137
Gillies, Mary Davis 1900- CAP-2
Earlier sketch in CA 25-28
Gilligan, Edmund 1898-1973 Obituary 45-48
Gilligan, Sonja Carl 1936- 57-60
Gilliland, Alexis A(rnaldus) 1931- CANR-25
Earlier sketch in CA 108
Gilliland, Charles
See Muller, Charles G(eorge Geoffrey)
Gilliland, Charles Edward Jr.
1916-1975 Obituary 110
Gilliland, (Cleburne) Hap 1918- CANR-5
Earlier sketch in CA 53-56
Gillin, Caroline J(ulia) 1932- 45-48
Gillin, Donald George 1930- 33-36R
Gillin, John P(hilip) 1907-1973 ....41-44R
Obituary 45-48
Gillingham, John (Bennett) 1940- CANR-18
Earlier sketch in CA 97-100
Gillings, Richard John 1902- 77-80
Gillion, Kenneth Lowell (Oliver) 1929- 93-96
Gillis, Chester 1951- 136
Gillis, Daniel 1935- 106
Gillis, Everett A(lden) 1914- CANR-15
Earlier sketch in CA 41-44R
Gillis, John R. 1939- 33-36R
Gillis, Patricia Ingle 1932- Brief entry 108
Gillis, Phyllis 1945- 116
Gillispie, Charles C(oulston) 1918- 13-16R
Gillman, Olga Marjorie 1894- 5-8R
Gillman, Peter (Charles) 1942- 131
Gillman, Richard 1929- 17-20R
Gillmer, Thomas C(harles) 1911- CANR-6
Earlier sketch in CA 57-60
Gillmer, Tom
See Gillmer, Thomas C(harles)
Gillmor, C(harles) Stewart 1938- 45-48
Gillmor, Daniel S. 1917(?)-1975 Obituary 61-64
Gillmor, Donald M(iles) 1926- 41-44R
Gillmor, Frances 1903- CAP-2
Earlier sketch in CA 17-18
Gillmore, David 1934- 21-24R
Gillmore, Margalo 1897-1986 Obituary 119
Gillon, Adam 1921- CANR-8
Earlier sketch in CA 5-8R
Gillon, Diana (Pleasance Case) 1915- 13-16R
Gillon, Meir Selig 1907- 13-16R
Gillon, Werner 1905- 126
Gillott, Jacky 1939-1980 102
See also DLB 14
Gillquist, Peter E. 1938- CANR-12
Earlier sketch in CA 29-32R
Gilluly, James 1896-1980 Obituary 102
Gillum, Helen L(ouise) 1909- 69-72
Gilman, Andrew D. 1951- 137
Gilman, C(harles) Malcolm B(rookfield)
1898-1981 107
Gilman, Caroline (Howard)
1794-1888 ....DLB 3, 73
Gilman, Charlotte (Anna) Perkins (Stetson)
1860-1935 Brief entry 106
See also TCLC 9, 37
Gilman, Dorothy 1923- CANR-30
Gilman, Esther 1925- ....SATA 15
Gilman, George G.
See Harknett, Terry
Gilman, J. D.
See Fishman, Jack
and Orgill, Douglas
Gilman, James
See Gilmore, Joseph L(ee)
Gilman, Phoebe 1940- ....SATA 58
Gilman, Richard 1925- CANR-5
Earlier sketch in CA 53-56
Gilman, Robert Cham
See Coppel, Alfred
Gilman, Sander L(awrence) 1944- CANR-5
Earlier sketch in CA 53-56
Gilman, Stephen 1917- 107
Gilman, William H(enry) 1911-1976 ....17-20R
Obituary 65-68
Gilman, William 1909-1978 ....1-4R
Gilmer, Ann
See Ross, W(illiam) E(dward) D(aniel)
Gilmer, B(everley) von Haller 1909- CANR-5
Earlier sketch in CA 5-8R
Gilmer, Elizabeth Meriwether
1861(?)-1951 Brief entry 114
See also DLB 29
Gilmer, Francis Walker 1790-1826 ....DLB 37
Gilmer, (Frank) Walker 1935- 33-36R
Gilmer, Wesley Jr. 1928- 115
Gil-Montero, Martha 1940- ....HW
Gilmore, Alec 1928- 93-96
Gilmore, Al-Tony 1946- CANR-7
Earlier sketch in CA 57-60
Gilmore, Cecile
See MacMillan, Cecile
Gilmore, Charles L(ee) 33-36R
Gilmore, Christopher Cook 1940- CANR-17
Earlier sketch in CA 101
Gilmore, Daniel F(rancis) 1922-1988 65-68
Obituary 126
Gilmore, David D. 1943- 133
Gilmore, Don 1930- 29-32R
Gilmore, Eddy (Lanier King) 1907- 5-8R
Gilmore, Edith Spacil 1920- 1-4R
Gilmore, Gene 1920- 33-36R
Gilmore, Grant 1910-1982 Obituary 111
Gilmore, Harold L(awrence) 1931- 53-56
Gilmore, Haydn 1928- 85-88
Gilmore, Iris 1900- 97-100
See also SATA 22
Gilmore, J. Herbert Jr. 1925- 33-36R
Gilmore, Jene Carlton 1933- 33-36R
Gilmore, John (Norman) 1951- 133
Gilmore, John 1935- 25-28R
Gilmore, Joseph L(ee) 1929- 81-84
Gilmore, Maeve 102
Obituary 110
Gilmore, Mary (Jean Cameron) 1865-1962 114
See also SATA 49
Gilmore, Richard 1943- 107
Gilmore, Susan 1954- ....SATA 59
Gilmore, Thomas B(arry Jr.) 1932- 73-76
Gilmore, William J(ames) 1945- 120
Gilmour, Barbara
See Trimble, Barbara Margaret
Gilmour, David 1944- 138
See also Pink Floyd
See also CLC 35
Gilmour, Garth (Hamilton) 1925- CAP-1
Earlier sketch in CA 9-10
Gilmour, H. B. 1939- 81-84
Gilmour, John C. 1939- 136
Gilmour, Robert S(cott) 1940- 69-72
Gilmour, Robin 1943- 124
Gilner, Elias 1888(?)-1976 Obituary 65-68
Gilot, Francoise 1921- 108
Gilpatrick, Eleanor G(ottesfocht) 1930- CANR-9
Earlier sketch in CA 21-24R
Gilpin, Alan 1924- CANR-28
Earlier sketches in CA 25-28R, CANR-11
Gilpin, Alec Richard 1920- 45-48
Gilpin, John 1930-1983 Obituary 114
Gilpin, Laura 1891-1979 Obituary 111
Gilpin, Robert G. Jr. 1930- 5-8R
Gilray, J. D.
See Mencken, H(enry) L(ouis)
Gilray, James
See Madsen, (Mark) Hunter
Gilroy, Beryl 1924- 135
Gilroy, Frank D(aniel) 1925- CANR-32
Earlier sketch in CA 81-84
See also CLC 2
See also DLB 7
Gilroy, Harry 1908(?)-1981 Obituary 104
Gilroy, Thomas Laurence 1951- 103
Gilroy, Tom
See Gilroy, Thomas Laurence
Gilson, Barbara
See Gilson, Charles James Louis
Gilson, Charles James Louis
1878-1943 ....YABC 2
Gilson, Etienne Henry 1884-1978 102
Obituary 81-84
Gilson, Goodwin Woodrow 1918- 17-20R
Gilson, Jamie 1933- 111
See also SATA 34, 37
Gilson, Thomas Q(uinleven) 1916- 5-8R
Gilstrap, Robert L(awrence) 1933- 9-12R
Gilzean, Elizabeth Houghton Blanchet
1913- 9-12R
Gimbel, John 1922- CANR-2
Earlier sketch in CA 1-4R
Gimbutas, Marija (Alseika) 1921- 13-16R
Gimmestad, Victor E(dward) 1912-1982 57-60
Obituary 109
Gimpel, Herbert J. 1915- 17-20R
Gimpel, Jean 1918- 69-72
Gimson, Alfred Charles 1917-1985 ....5-8R
Obituary 116
Ginandes, Shepard 1928- 41-44R
Ginder, Richard 1914- 65-68
Gindin, James 1926- CANR-2
Earlier sketch in CA 5-8R
Giner de los Rios, Francisco
1839-1915 Brief entry 105
Gingell, Benjamin Broughton 1924- 104
Ginger, Ann Fagan 1925- CANR-19
Earlier sketches in CA 53-56, CANR-4
Ginger, Helen 1916- 17-20R
Ginger, John 1933- 25-28R
Gingerich, Martin E(llsworth) 1933- 118
Gingerich, Melvin 1902-1975 ....CAP-2
Earlier sketch in CA 25-28
Gingerich, Owen (Jay) 1930- CANR-22
Earlier sketches in CA 53-56, CANR-5
Gingher, Marianne 1947- 138
Gingland, David R. 1913- 17-20R
Gingold, Hermione (Ferdinanda)
1897-1987 ....5-8R
Obituary 122
Gingrich, Arnold 1903-1976 ....13-16R
Obituary 69-72
Gingrich, F(elix) Wilbur 1901- CAP-2
Earlier sketch in CA 17-18
Gingrich, Newt(on Leroy) 1943- 131
Giniger, Carol Virginia Wilkins
1929(?)-1985 Obituary 117
Giniger, Kenneth Seeman 1919- CANR-3
Earlier sketch in CA 5-8R
Ginn, Robert Jay Jr. 1946- 107
Ginnings, Harriett W.
See Harriett
Ginns, Patsy (Lee) M(oore) 1937- 69-72
Ginns, Ronald 1896- CAP-1
Earlier sketch in CA 11-12
Ginori Lisci, Leonardo 1908-1987 Obituary 122
Ginott, Haim G. 1922-1973 Obituary 45-48
Ginsberg, Allen 1926- CANR-2
Earlier sketch in CA 1-4R
See also AITN 1
See also CDALB 1941-1968
See also CLC 1, 2, 3, 4, 6, 13, 36, 69
See also DLB 5, 16
See also MTCW
See also PC 4
See also WLC 3
Ginsberg, Benjamin 1947- 121
Ginsberg, Harold Louis
1903-1990 Obituary 132
Ginsberg, Joanne
See Summerfield, Joanne
Ginsberg, Leon H(erman) 1936- 105
Ginsberg, Louis 1895-1976 ....13-16R
Obituary 65-68
Ginsberg, Morris 1889-1970 Obituary 116
Ginsberg, Robert 1937- 25-28R

Ginsburg, Faye D(iana) 1952- 133
Ginsburg, Herbert (Paul) 1939- CANR-12
Earlier sketch in CA 73-76
Ginsburg, Mirra CANR-28
Earlier sketches in CA 17-20R, CANR-11
See also SATA 6
Ginsburg, Ruth Bader 1933- 53-56
Ginsburg, Seymour 1927- CANR-13
Earlier sketch in CA 21-24R
Ginsburgh, Robert N(eville) 1923- 13-16R
Ginsburgs, George 1932- CANR-4
Earlier sketch in CA 53-56
Ginsbury, Norman 1902- 5-8R
Ginter, Maria 1922- 105
Ginther, John R(obert) 1922- Brief entry 107
Gintis, Herbert 1940- 57-60
Ginzberg, Eli 1911- CANR-27
Earlier sketches in CA 5-8R, CANR-8
Ginzberg, Yevgeniya
1906(?)-1977 Obituary 69-72
Ginzburg, Natalia 1916-1991 ....CANR-33
Obituary 135
Earlier sketch in CA 85-88
See also CLC 5, 11, 54, 70
See also MTCW
Ginzburg, Ralph 1929- 21-24R
Ginzkey, Franz Karl 1871-1963 ....DLB 81
Gioia, (Michael) Dana 1950- 130
See also DLB 120
Gioia, Ted 1957- 127
Giono, Jean 1895-1970 ....CANR-35
Obituary 29-32R
Earlier sketches in CA 45-48, CANR-2
See also CLC 4, 11
See also DLB 72
See also MTCW
Giordan, Alma Roberts 1917- 57-60
Giordan, Marion Obituary 110
Giordanetti, Elmo 1925-1984 Obituary 113
Giorno, John 1936- 33-36R
Gioseffi, Daniela 1941- CANR-3
Earlier sketch in CA 45-48
Giotti, Virgilio 1885-1957 ....DLB 114
Giovacchini, Peter L(ouis) 1922- 101
Giovannetti, Alberto 1913- 9-12R
Giovanni, Nikki 1943- CANR-18
Earlier sketch in CA 29-32R
See also CAAS 6
See also AITN 1
See also BLC 2
See also BW
See also CLC 2, 4, 19, 64
See also CLR 6
See also DLB 5, 41
See also MAICYA
See also MTCW
See also SATA 24
Giovannitti, Len 1920- 13-16R
Obituary 137
Giovanopoulos, Paul (Arthur) 1939- ....SATA 7
Giovene, Andrea 1904- 85-88
See also CLC 7
Gipe, George 1933-1986 77-80
Obituary 120
Gippius, Zinaida (Nikolayevna)
1869-1945 Brief entry 106
See also Hippius, Zinaida
Gipson, Fred(erick Benjamin)
1908-1973 ....CANR-3
Obituary 45-48
Earlier sketch in CA 1-4R
See also MAICYA
See also SATA 2, 24
Gipson, John (Durwood) 1932- 61-64
Gipson, Lawrence Henry 1880-1971 ....CANR-3
Obituary 33-36R
Earlier sketch in CA 5-8R
See also DLB 17
Giragosian, Newman H. 1922- 93-96
Girard, Hazel Batten 1901- 112
Girard, Henri Georges Charles Achille
1917-1987 Obituary 121
Girard, James P(reston) 1944- 69-72
Girard, Joe 1928- CANR-9
Earlier sketch in CA 77-80
Girard, Linda (Walvoord) 1942- 114
See also SATA 41
Girard, Marvin Eugene 1924- 112
Girard, Mustang Marve
See Girard, Marvin Eugene
Girard, Rene N(oel) 1923- CANR-28
Earlier sketches in CA 9-12R, CANR-4
Girard, Robert C(olby) 1932- 101
Girard, Rodolphe 1879-1956 ....DLB 92
Girardi, Joe
See Girard, Joe
Girardot, Norman J(ohn) 1943- 110
Giraud, Marcel 1900- 77-80
Giraudoux, (Hippolyte) Jean
1882-1944 Brief entry 104
See also DLB 65
See also TCLC 2, 7
Girdlestone, Cuthbert Morton
1895-1975 ....CANR-3
Obituary 65-68
Earlier sketch in CA 5-8R
Girgus, Sam B. 1941- 127
Girion, Barbara 1937- CANR-15
Earlier sketch in CA 85-88
See also SAAS 14
See also SATA 26
Girling, John L(awrence) S(cott) 1926- 106
Girling, Richard 1945- 108
Girod, Gerald R(alph) 1939- 53-56
Girod, Gordon H. 1920- 1-4R
Girodias, Maurice 1919-1990 129
Obituary 132
Brief entry 112
Girodo, Michel 1945- 81-84
Giron, Manuel Buendia Tellez
1926(?)-1984 Obituary 112
See also HW
Girondo, Oliverio 1891-1967 ....HW
Gironella, Jose Maria 1917- 101
See also CLC 11
Giroud, Francoise 1916- CANR-39
Earlier sketches in CA 81-84, CANR-17
See also AITN 1
Giroux, E. X.
See Shannon, Doris
Giroux, Henry A(rmand) 1943- CANR-30
Earlier sketch in CA 112
Giroux, Joan 1922- 93-96
Giroux, Robert 1914- CANR-28
Earlier sketch in CA 107
Girri, A.
See Girri, Alberto
Girri, Alberto 1919- ....HW
Girson, Rochelle 21-24R
Girtin, Thomas 1913- 9-12R
Girtin, Tom
See Girtin, Thomas
Girvan, Helen (Masterman) 1891- 73-76
Girvetz, Harry K(enneth)
1910-1974 Obituary 111
Girzaitis, Loretta 1920- CANR-2
Earlier sketch in CA 49-52
Girzone, Joseph F(rancis) 1930- 130
See also BEST 90:1
Giscard, Valery
See Giscard d'Estaing, Valery
Giscard d'Estaing, Valery 1926- Brief entry 111
Giscombe, C. S. 1950- 127
Gish, Arthur G. 1939- 29-32R
Gish, Lillian (Diana) 1896(?)- 128
Gish, Nancy K. 1942- 132
Gish, Robert F. 1940- 133
Gishford, Anthony (Joseph)
1908-1975 Obituary 53-56
Gisolfi, Anthony M. 1909- CAP-2
Earlier sketch in CA 17-18
Gisselquist, David 1947- 112
Gissen, Max 1909(?)-1984 Obituary 114
Gissing, George (Robert)
1857-1903 Brief entry 105
See also DLB 18
See also TCLC 3, 24
Gissler, Sig(vard Gunnar Jr.) 1935- 134
Gist, Noel P(itts) 1899- CANR-1
Earlier sketch in CA 1-4R
Gist, Ronald R. 1932- 21-24R
Gitchoff, G(eorge) Thomas 1938- 53-56
Gitchoff, Tom
See Gitchoff, G(eorge) Thomas
Gitelman, Zvi Y(echiel) 1940- 128
Brief entry 112
Gitin, David (Daniel) 1941- CANR-2
Earlier sketch in CA 49-52
Gitin, Maria (Brians) 1946- CANR-8
Earlier sketch in CA 61-64
Gitisetan, Dariush 118
Gitisetan, Darrin Dariush
See Gitisetan, Dariush
Gitlin, Murray 1903- 1-4R
Gitlin, Todd 1943- CANR-25
Earlier sketch in CA 29-32R
Gitlow, A(braham) Leo 1918- 1-4R
Gitlow, Benjamin 1891-1965 Obituary 89-92
Gittell, Marilyn 1931- CANR-29
Earlier sketches in CA 21-24R, CANR-9
Gittelsohn, Roland B(ertram) 1910- CANR-2
Earlier sketch in CA 5-8R
Gittelson, Celia 105
Gitter, A. George 1926- 102
Gittinger, J(ames) Price 41-44R
Gittings, Clare (St. Quentin) 1954- 130
Gittings, Jo (Grenville) Manton 1919- CANR-3
Earlier sketch in CA 5-8R
See also SATA 3
Gittings, John 1938- CANR-9
Earlier sketch in CA 21-24R
Gittings, Robert (William Victor)
1911-1992 ....25-28R
Obituary 136
See also SATA 6
See also SATO 70
Gittins, Diana 1946- 113
Gittleman, Edwin 1929- 21-24R
Gittleman, Sol 1934- 65-68
Gittler, Joseph B(ertram) 1912- 37-40R
Giudici, Ann Couper 1929- 73-76
Giuliani, George A. 1938- 120
Giunti, Renato 1905-1983 Obituary 109
Giurlani, Aldo
See Palazzeschi, Aldo
Giuseppi, John (Anthony) 1900- CAP-2
Earlier sketch in CA 23-24
Giuttari, Theodore Richard 1931- 29-32R
Givens, Charles J. 1942(?)- ....BEST 90:3
Givens, David B(radley) 1944- 119
Givens, Janet E(aton) 1932- 111
See also SATA 60
Givens, John 1943- 77-80
Givner, Abraham 1944- 89-92
Givner, Joan Mary 1936- CANR-25
Earlier sketch in CA 108
Gizycka, Eleanor M.
See Patterson, Eleanor Medill
Gizzi, Michael 1949- 117
Gjertsen, Derek 1933- 125
Glaab, Charles N(elson) 1927- CANR-8
Earlier sketch in CA 5-8R
Glad, Betty 1929- 21-24R
Glad, Donald 1915- 13-16R
Glad, John 1941- 133
Glad, Paul W(ilbur) 1926- 73-76
Gladden, E(dgar) Norman 1897- 21-24R
Gladden, Vivianne Cervantes 1927- 102
Glade, William P(atton) Jr. 1929- 41-44R
Gladilin, Anatoly (Tikhonovich) 1935- CANR-18
Earlier sketch in CA 101
Gladish, David F(rancis) 1928- 41-44R
Gladkov, Fyodor (Vasilyevich)
1883-1958 ....TCLC 27
Gladney, Heather 1957- 127
Gladney Glasserow, Marion 1925- 118
Gladstone, Arthur M. 1921- 97-100
Gladstone, Eve
See Werner, Herma
Gladstone, Gary 1935- 29-32R
See also SATA 12
Gladstone, Josephine 1938- 21-24R
Gladstone, M(yron) J. 1923- 53-56
See also SATA 37
Gladstone, Maggie
See Gladstone, Arthur M.
Gladstone, Meredith 1939- 69-72
Gladstone, William Ewart 1809-1898 ....DLB 57
Gladwin, William Zachary
See Zollinger, Gulielma
Gladych, B. Michael 1910- 5-8R
Glaeser, Ernst 1902-1963 ....DLB 69
Glaettli, Walter E(ric) 1920- 21-24R
Glahe, Fred R(ufus) 1934- CANR-14
Earlier sketch in CA 37-40R
Glaister, John 1892-1971 Obituary 104
Glaister, Lesley (G.) 1956- 134
Glamis, Walter
See Schachner, Nat(han)
Glancy, Diane 1941- 136
Glantz, David M. 1942- 135
Glantz, Kalman 1937- 132
Glanville, Brian (Lester) 1931- CANR-3
Earlier sketch in CA 5-8R
See also CAAS 9
See also CLC 6
See also DLB 15
See also SATA 42
Glanville, Maxwell 1918- 85-88
Glanville, Ranulph 1946- 114
Glanz, Edward C(oleman) 1924- 1-4R
Glanz, Karen 1953- 135
Glanz, Rudolf 1892-1978 ....CANR-3
Earlier sketch in CA 49-52
Glanzman, Louis S. 1922- ....SATA 36
Glapthorne, Henry 1610-1643(?) ....DLB 58
Glaser, Daniel 1918- 61-64
Glaser, Dianne E(lizabeth) 1937- 77-80
See also SATA 31, 50
Glaser, E(ric) M(ichael) 1913- 21-24R
Glaser, Edward 1918-1972 Obituary 37-40R
Glaser, Eleanor Dorothy
See Zonik, Eleanor Dorothy
Glaser, Elizabeth 1947- 138
Glaser, Elton 1945- 111
Glaser, Eva Schocken 1918-1982 Obituary 105
Glaser, Isabel Joshlin 1929- 77-80
Glaser, Kurt 1914- CANR-5
Earlier sketch in CA 1-4R
Glaser, Lynn 1943- 21-24R
Glaser, Milton 1929- CANR-11
Earlier sketch in CA 17-20R
See also SATA 11
Glaser, Robert 1921- CANR-7
Earlier sketch in CA 17-20R
Glaser, Rollin Oliver 1932- CANR-10
Earlier sketch in CA 25-28R
Glaser, William A(rnold) 1925- CANR-21
Earlier sketches in CA 1-4R, CANR-6
Glasgow, Douglas G. 108
Glasgow, Ellen (Anderson Gholson)
1873(?)-1945 Brief entry 104
See also DLB 9, 12
See also TCLC 2, 7
Glasgow, Eric 1924- 69-72
Glasgow, Gordon H(enry) H(arper)
1926- 29-32R
Glasgow, Jack
See Larson, Doran
Glasgow, Mary Cecilia 1905-1983 Obituary 111
Glasheen, Adaline 1920- 101
Glasheen, Patrick 1897- CAP-1
Earlier sketch in CA 13-14
Glaskin, G(erald) M(arcus) 1923- CANR-5
Earlier sketch in CA 53-56
Glaskowsky, Nicholas A(lexander) Jr.
1928- CANR-3
Earlier sketch in CA 5-8R
Glaspell, Susan (Keating)
1882(?)-1948 Brief entry 110
See also DLB 7, 9, 78
See also YABC 2
Glasrud, Bruce (Alden) 1940- 41-44R
Glass, Albert J(ulius) 1908-1983 Obituary 109
Glass, Andrew 134
See also SATA 46
Glass, Andrew J(ames) 1935- 65-68
Glass, Bill 1935- CANR-13
Earlier sketch in CA 73-76
Glass, David Victor 1911-1978 85-88
Obituary 81-84
Glass, Ian Cameron 1926- 77-80
Glass, Joanna (McClelland) 1936- 81-84
Glass, John F(ranklin) 1936- 53-56
Glass, Justine C.
See Corrall, Alice Enid
Glass, Malcolm (Sanford) 1936- CANR-20
Earlier sketch in CA 104
Glass, Montague (Marsden)
1877-1934 Brief entry 117
See also DLB 11
Glass, Ruth 1912-1990 Obituary 131
Glass, Sandra
See Shea, Robert (Joseph)
Glass, Stanley T(homas) 1932- 21-24R
Glassberg, B(ertrand) Y(ounker) 1902- CAP-1
Earlier sketch in CA 13-16
Glassburner, Bruce 1920- 33-36R
Glassco, John 1909-1981 ....CANR-15
Obituary 102
Earlier sketch in CA 13-16R
See also CLC 9
See also DLB 68
Glasscock, Amnesia
See Steinbeck, John (Ernst)
Glasscock, Anne Bonner 1924- 1-4R
Glasscock, Sarah (Jean) 1952- 130
Glasse, Robert Marshall 1929- 29-32R
Glasser, Allen 1918- 9-12R
Glasser, Ira 1938- 137
Glasser, Paul H(arold) 1929- CANR-15
Earlier sketch in CA 29-32R
Glasser, Perry 1948- 127
Glasser, Ronald J. 1940(?)- ....CLC 37
Glasser, Selma 110
Glasser, Stephen A(ndrew) 1943- 53-56
Glasser, William 1925- 73-76
Glasserow, Mario N.
See Gladney Glasserow, Marion
Glasserow, Marion Gladney
See Gladney Glasserow, Marion
Glassford, Wilfred
See McNeilly, Wilfred (Glassford)
Glassgold, Peter 1939- 103
Glassie, Henry H(aywood)
1914-1987 Obituary 124
Glassman, Bernard Tetsugen 1939- 112
Glassman, James K(enneth) 1947- 127
Glassman, Jon David 1944- 69-72
Glassman, Joyce
See Johnson, Joyce
Glassman, Michael 1899- 13-16R
Glassman, Peter Joel 1945- 113
Glassman, Ronald M. 1937- 134
Brief entry 111
Glassner, Barry 1952- 135
Glassner, Lester 1939- 107
Glassner, Martin Ira 1932- CANR-34
Earlier sketches in CA 41-44R, CANR-15
Glasson, Thomas Francis 1906- CAP-1
Earlier sketch in CA 9-10
Glassop, (Jack) Lawson 1913-1966 ....CAP-1
Earlier sketch in CA 9-10
Glasstone, Victor 1924- CANR-10
Earlier sketch in CA 65-68
Glatstein, Jacob 1896-1971 Obituary 33-36R
Glatthorn, Allan A. 1924- 13-16R
Glattstein, Judy 1942- 137
Glatzer, Hal 1946- 57-60
Glatzer, Nahum Norbert 1903-1990 ....CANR-7
Obituary 131
Earlier sketch in CA 13-16R
Glauber, Uta (Heil) 1936- 29-32R
See also SATA 17
Glaus, Marlene 1933- 21-24R
Glauser, Friedrich 1896-1938 ....DLB 56
Glavin, John P(atrick) 1933- 57-60
Glazar, Bob 1954- 115
Glaze, Andrew (Louis III) 1920- CANR-24
Earlier sketches in CA 17-20R, CANR-8
Glaze, Eleanor 1930- 49-52
Glaze, Thomas E(dward) 1914- 1-4R
Glazebrook, G(eorge) P(arkin) de T(wenebrokes)
1899- 102
Glazebrook, Philip 1937- 29-32R
Glazener, Mary U(nderwood) 1921- 17-20R
Glazer, Daphne (Fae) 1938- 119
Glazer, Nathan 1923- 5-8R
Glazer, Nona Y.
See Glazer-Malbin, Nona
Glazer, Sidney 1905-1983 ....1-4R
Obituary 111
Glazer, Tom 1914- CANR-8
Earlier sketch in CA 61-64
See also SATA 9
Glazer-Malbin, Nona 1932- 33-36R
Glazier, Kenneth MacLean 1912- 9-12R
Glazier, Lyle (Edward) 1911- 37-40R
Glazier, Stephen 1947- 108
Glazner, Joseph Mark 1945- 104
Gleadow, Rupert Seeley 1909-1974 ....9-12R
Obituary 103
Gleasner, Diana (Cottle) 1936- CANR-33
Earlier sketches in CA 65-68, CANR-15
See also SATA 29
Gleason, Abbott 1938- CANR-21
Earlier sketch in CA 104
Gleason, Eugene Franklin 1914- 1-4R
Gleason, Gene
See Gleason, Eugene Franklin
Gleason, Harold 1892- CAP-1
Earlier sketch in CA 9-10
Gleason, John J(ames) Jr. 1934- 120
Gleason, John (Marquis) 1942- 107
Gleason, Judith 1929- CANR-9
Earlier sketch in CA 61-64
See also SATA 24
Gleason, Ralph J(oseph) 1917-1975 65-68
Obituary 61-64
Gleason, Robert J(ames) 1906- 73-76
Gleason, Robert Walter 1917- CANR-4
Earlier sketch in CA 1-4R
Gleason, Robert 1945- 118
Gleason, S(arel) Everett
1905-1974 Obituary 53-56

Gleave, T(om) P. 1908- ... 127
Gleaves, Robert M(ilnor) 1938- ... 53-56
Gleaves, Suzanne 1904- ... 9-12R
Gleckner, Robert Francis 1925- ... CANR-17
Earlier sketches in CA 1-4R, CANR-2
Gledhill, Alan 1895-1983 ... CAP-1
Obituary ... 110
Earlier sketch in CA 9-10
Glees, Anthony 1948- ... 134
Gleeson, Ruth (Ryall) 1925- ... 9-12R
Gleick, James (W.) 1954- ... 137
Brief entry ... 131
Gleim, Johann Wilhelm Ludwig
1719-1803 ... DLB 97
Gleiman, Lubomir 1923- ... 41-44R
Gleisser, Marcus D(avid) 1923- ... 17-20R
Gleitman, Lila R. 1929- ... 114
Gleitzman, Morris 1953- ... 131
Glemser, Bernard 1908-1990 Obituary ... 131
Glen, Duncan (Munro) 1933- ... CANR-12
Earlier sketch in CA 21-24R
Glen, Eugene
See Fawcett, F(rank) Dubrez
Glen, Frank Grenfell 1933- ... 106
Glen, J(ohn) Stanley 1907-1986 ... CAP-1
Obituary ... 118
Earlier sketch in CA 9-10
Glen, Robert S. 1925- ... 29-32R
Glenday, Alice 1920- ... 57-60
Glendenning, Donn
See Paine, Lauran (Bosworth)
Glendenning, Raymond Carl
1907-1974 Obituary ... 114
Glendinning, Richard 1917- ... 21-24R
See also SATA 24
Glendinning, Sally
See Glendinning, Sara W(ilson)
Glendinning, Sara W(ilson) 1913- ... CANR-2
Earlier sketch in CA 49-52
See also SATA 24
Glendinning, Victoria 1937- ... 127
Brief entry ... 120
See also CLC 50
Glendon, Mary Ann 1938- ... 41-44R
Glenn, Armon 1912- ... 107
Glenn, Christine Genevieve 1947- ... 115
Glenn, Constance W(hite) 1933- ... 128
Glenn, Edmund S(tanislas) 1915- ... 113
Glenn, Frank 1901-1982 Obituary ... 106
Glenn, Harold T(heodore) 1910- ... CANR-5
Earlier sketch in CA 5-8R
Glenn, Jacob B. 1905-1974 ... CANR-4
Obituary ... 49-52
Earlier sketch in CA 9-12R
Glenn, James
See Paine, Lauran (Bosworth)
Glenn, Jerry (Hesmer Jr.) 1938- ... 45-48
Glenn, Lois (Ruth) 1941- ... 61-64
Glenn, Mel 1943- ... 123
See also SATA 45, 51
Glenn, Morton B(ernard) 1922- ... 61-64
Glenn, Norval Dwight 1933- ... 17-20R
Glennon, James 1900- ... 25-28R
Glennon, Maurade 1926- ... 25-28R
Glenny, Lyman A. 1918- ... CANR-7
Earlier sketch in CA 17-20R
Glenny, Michael Valentine 1927-1990 ... 102
Obituary ... 132
Gles, Margaret Breitmaier 1940- ... 57-60
See also SATA 22
Gleser, Goldine C(ohnberg) 1915- ... 17-20R
Gless, Darryl James 1945- ... 102
Glessing, Robert J(ohn) 1930- ... 29-32R
Gliauda, Jurgis 1906- ... CANR-3
Earlier sketch in CA 5-8R
Glick, Carl (Cannon) 1890-1971 ... 5-8R
Obituary ... 103
See also SATA 14
Glick, Edward Bernard 1929- ... CANR-8
Earlier sketch in CA 21-24R
Glick, G(arland) Wayne 1921- ... 25-28R
Glick, Paul C(harles) 1910- ... 5-8R
Glick, Paula Brown
See Brown, Paula
Glick, Ruth (Burtnick) 1942- ... CANR-16
Earlier sketch in CA 89-92
Glick, Thomas F(rederick) 1939- ... CANR-34
Earlier sketches in CA 29-32R, CANR-15
Glick, Virginia Kirkus 1893-1980 ... CAP-2
Obituary ... 101
Earlier sketch in CA 21-22
See also SATA 23
Glick, Wendell 1916- ... 111
Glickman, Albert S(eymour) 1923- ... 53-56
Glickman, Arthur P. 1940- ... 61-64
Glickman, Beatrice Marden 1919- ... 102
Glickman, Gary 1959- ... 128
Glickman, Norman J. 1942- ... 135
Glickman, S(teven) Craig 1947- ... 116
Glickman, Susan 1953- ... CANR-38
Earlier sketch in CA 116
Glicksberg, Charles Irving 1900- ... CANR-2
Earlier sketch in CA 1-4R
Glicksman, Abraham M(orton) 1911- ... 5-8R
Glidden, Frederick D(illey) 1908-1975 ... CAP-2
Obituary ... 61-64
Earlier sketch in CA 21-22
Glidden, Horace Knight 1901- ... CAP-1
Earlier sketch in CA 13-16
Glidewell, John Calvin 1919- ... CANR-23
Earlier sketches in CA 13-16R, CANR-7
Glieberman, Herbert A(llen) 1930- ... 112
Gliewe, Unada (Grace) 1927- ... CANR-12
Earlier sketch in CA 29-32R
See also SATA 3
Glikes, Erwin 1937- ... 13-16R
Glimcher, Arnold B. 1938- ... 81-84
Glimm, James Y(ork) 1942- ... 132
Glimmerveen, Ulco 1958- ... 132
Glines, Carroll V(ane) Jr. 1920- ... CANR-2
Earlier sketch in CA 1-4R
See also SATA 19
Gliozzo, Charles 1932- ... 45-48
Glissant, Edouard 1928- ... CLC 10, 68
Glisson, Jerry (Lee) 1923- ... 113
Gloag, John (Edwards) 1896-1981 ... CANR-10
Obituary ... 104
Earlier sketch in CA 65-68
Gloag, Julian 1930- ... CANR-10
Earlier sketch in CA 65-68
See also AITN 1
See also CLC 40
Glob, Peter Vilhelm 1911-1985 ... 97-100
Obituary ... 117
Globe, Leah Ain 1900- ... 107
See also SATA 41
Glock, Charles Y(oung) 1919- ... CANR-5
Earlier sketch in CA 53-56
Glock, Marvin D(avid) 1912- ... 21-24R
Gloer, (William) Hulitt 1950- ... 126
Glogau, Art(hur H.) 1922- ... 53-56
Glogau, Lillian Flatow Fleischer 1925- ... 85-88
Glogowski, Maryruth F(rancine) P(helps)
1950- ... 120
Glorfeld, Louis E(arl) 1916- ... 53-56
Glos, Raymond E(ugene) 1903- ... 21-24R
Gloss, Molly 1944- ... 132
Glotzer, Albert 1908- ... 133
Glovach, Linda 1947- ... CANR-31
Earlier sketches in CA 37-40R, CANR-14
See also SATA 7
Glover, Albert Gould 1942- ... 89-92
Glover, Bob
See Glover, Robert H.
Glover, Denis (James Matthews)
1912-1980 ... CANR-30
Obituary ... 101
Earlier sketch in CA 77-80
See also SATA 7
Glover, Donald E(llsworth) 1933- ... 116
Glover, Douglas 1948- ... 137
Glover, Harry 1912- ... 77-80
Glover, Janice 1919- ... 17-20R
Glover, John D(esmond) 1915- ... CANR-2
Earlier sketch in CA 5-8R
Glover, Jon 1943- ... 133
Glover, Judith 1943- ... CANR-22
Earlier sketch in CA 106
Glover, Leland E(llis) 1917- ... 9-12R
Glover, Michael 1922- ... CANR-23
Earlier sketches in CA 17-20R, CANR-8
Glover, Richard 1712-1785 ... DLB 95
Glover, Robert H. 1946- ... 116
Glover, (David) Tony "Harp Dog" 1939- ... 13-16R
Gloversmith, Frank 1936- ... 127
Glowacki, Janusz 1938- ... 116
Glubb, John Bagot 1897-1986 ... CANR-5
Obituary ... 118
Earlier sketch in CA 9-12R
Glubb Pasha
See Glubb, John Bagot
Glubok, Shirley (Astor) 1933- ... CANR-4
Earlier sketch in CA 5-8R
See also CLR 1
See also MAICYA
See also SAAS 7
See also SATA 6, 68
Gluck, Carol 1941- ... 126
Gluck, Felix 1923-1981 Obituary ... 103
See also SATA 25
Gluck, Herb 1925- ... CANR-31
Earlier sketches in CA 45-48, CANR-2
Gluck, Jay 1927- ... CANR-12
Earlier sketch in CA 21-24R
Gluck, Louise 1943- ... 33-36R
See also Glueck, Louise
See also CLC 7, 22, 44
See also DLB 5
Gluck, Mary 1947- ... 127
Gluck, Robert 1947- ... CANR-32
Earlier sketch in CA 113
Gluckin, Doreen Sandra 1949- ... 108
Gluckman, Max 1911-1975 ... 9-12R
Obituary ... 57-60
Glucksberg, Harold 1939- ... 105
Glueck, Eleanor T(ouroff) 1898-1972 ... CANR-9
Obituary ... 37-40R
Earlier sketches in CAP-2, CA 17-18
Glueck, Louise
See Gluck, Louise
See also CLC 7, 22
See also DLB 5
Glueck, Nelson 1900-1971 ... CAP-2
Earlier sketch in CA 17-18
Glueck, Sheldon 1896-1980 ... CANR-9
Obituary ... 97-100
Earlier sketch in CA 5-8R
Glueck, William F(rank) 1934-1980 ... CANR-27
Earlier sketch in CA 33-36R
Glueckauf, Eugen 1906-1981 Obituary ... 108
Gluss, Brian 1930- ... 104
Glustrom, Simon W. 1924- ... 21-24R
Glut, Donald F(rank) 1944- ... CANR-13
Earlier sketch in CA 33-36R
Gluyas, Constance 1920- ... 136
Brief entry ... 115
Gluzman, Brian
See Gluss, Brian
Glyn, Anthony 1922- ... 53-56
Glyn, Caroline 1947- ... CANR-5
Earlier sketch in CA 9-12R
Glyn, Richard Hamilton 1907-1980 ... 105
Obituary ... 102
Glynn, James A. 1941- ... 57-60
Glynn, Jeanne Davis 1932- ... 29-32R
Glynn, Jenifer 1929- ... 128
Glynn, Leonard M. 1948- ... 130
Glynn, Prudence (Loveday) 1935-1986 ... 129
Obituary ... 120
Glynn, Thomas P(eter) 1935- ... 93-96
Glynne-Jones, M(arjorie) L(ilian)
1936- Brief entry ... 111
Glynne-Jones, William 1907- ... 5-8R
See also SATA 11
Gmelch, George 1944- ... 103
Gmelch, Sharon Bohn 1947- ... 103
Gmelch, Walter H(oward) 1947- ... 112
Gnaegy, Charles 1938- ... 89-92
Gnagey, Thomas D(avid) 1938- ... 49-52
Gnagy, Jon
See Gnagy, Michael Jacques
Gnagy, Michael Jacques
1907(?)-1981 Obituary ... 103
Gnarowski, Michael 1934- ... 41-44R
Gniffke, Rudolf
See Hartmann, Rudolf A.
Gnosticus
See Weschcke, Carl L(ouis)
Gnuse, Robert K(arl) 1947- ... 121
Go, Puan Seng 1904- ... CAP-2
Earlier sketch in CA 29-32
Goacher, Denis 1925- ... 104
Goaman, Muriel
See Cox, Edith Muriel
Gobar, Ash 1930- ... 41-44R
Gobbato, Imero 1923- ... SATA 39
Gobbi, Tito 1915-1984 ... 129
Obituary ... 112
Brief entry ... 105
Goble, Danney 1946- ... 136
Goble, Dorothy ... 93-96
See also SATA 26
Goble, Frank G. 1917- ... 112
Goble, (Lloyd) Neil 1933- ... 29-32R
Goble, Paul 1933- ... CANR-16
Earlier sketch in CA 93-96
See also CLR 21
See also MAICYA
See also SATA 25, 69
Goble, Warwick ... SATA 46
Gocek, Matilda A(rkenbout) 1923- ... CANR-1
Earlier sketch in CA 49-52
Gochfeld, Michael 1940- ... 137
Gockel, Herman W. 1906- ... CANR-1
Earlier sketch in CA 1-4R
Godard, Jean-Luc 1930- ... 93-96
See also CLC 20
Godbold, E(dward) Stanly Jr. 1942- ... 37-40R
Godbolt, Jim 1922- ... 129
Godbout, Jacques 1933- Brief entry ... 125
See also DLB 53
Goddard, Alfred
See Harper, Carol Ely
Goddard, Burton L(eslie) 1910- ... 21-24R
Goddard, Donald 1934- ... CANR-28
Earlier sketches in CA 17-20R, CANR-11
Goddard, Gladys Benjamin
1881(?)-1976 Obituary ... 61-64
Goddard, J(ack) R. 1930- ... 29-32R
Goddard, Kenneth (William) 1946- ... 110
Goddard, Morrill 1865-1937 ... DLB 25
Goddard, Robert Hutchings
1882-1945 Brief entry ... 118
Goddard, Robert (William) 1954- ... 134
Goddard, William 1740-1817 ... DLB 43
Godden, Geoffrey 1929- ... 102
Godden, Jon 1906-1984 ... CANR-27
Obituary ... 112
Earlier sketch in CA 77-80
Godden, (Margaret) Rumer 1907- ... CANR-36
Earlier sketches in CA 5-8R, CANR-4, 27
See also AAYA 6
See also CLC 53
See also CLR 20
See also MAICYA
See also SAAS 12
See also SATA 3, 36
Gode, Alexander
See
Gode von Aesch, Alexander (Gottfried Friedrich)
Godechot, Jacques Leon 1907- ... CANR-25
Earlier sketches in CA 65-68, CANR-9
Godefroy, Vincent 1912- ... 69-72
Godel, Kurt
See Goedel, Kurt
Gode von Aesch, Alexander (Gottfried Friedrich)
1906-1970 ... CAP-1
Earlier sketch in CA 9-10
See also SATA 14
Godey, John
See Freedgood, Morton
Godey, Louis A. 1804-1878 ... DLB 73
Godfrey, Cuthbert John ... 5-8R
Godfrey, (William) Dave 1938- ... CANR-11
Earlier sketch in CA 69-72
See also DLB 60
Godfrey, Eleanor S(mith) 1914- ... 69-72
Godfrey, Ellen 1942- ... 113
Godfrey, Frederick M. 1901-1974 ... CAP-1
Earlier sketch in CA 13-14
Godfrey, Henry F. 1906-1975 ... CAP-2
Earlier sketch in CA 25-28
Godfrey, Jane
See Bowden, Joan Chase
Godfrey, Laurie R(ohde) 1945- ... 113
Godfrey, Lionel (Robert Holcombe)
1932- ... 81-84
Godfrey, Martyn N. 1949- ... 126
Godfrey, Michael A. 1940- ... CANR-14
Earlier sketch in CA 81-84
Godfrey, Peter 1917- ... 124
Godfrey, Thomas 1736-1763 ... DLB 31
Godfrey, Vincent H.
1895(?)-1975 Obituary ... 57-60
Godfrey, William
See Youd, (Christopher) Samuel
Godin, Gabriel 1929- ... 73-76
Godine, David R(ichard) 1944- ... 101
Godkin, Celia (Marilyn) 1948- ... 133
See also SATA 66
Godkin, E. L. 1831-1902 ... DLB 79
Godley, John
See Kilbracken, John (Raymond Godley)
Godly, J. P.
See Plawin, Paul
Godman, Arthur 1916- ... CANR-24
Earlier sketch in CA 106
Godolphin, Francis R(ichard) B(orroum)
1903-1974 ... 65-68
Obituary ... 53-56
Godown, Marian Bailey ... 103
Godoy Alcayaga, Lucila 1889-1957 ... 131
Brief entry ... 104
See also Mistral, Gabriela
See also HW
See also MTCW
Godsey, John Drew 1922- ... 13-16R
Godshalk, William Leigh 1937- ... 41-44R
Godson, John 1937- ... 77-80
Godson, Joseph 1913-1986 Obituary ... 120
Godson, Roy (S.) 1942- Brief entry ... 111
Godwin, Anthony Richard James Wylie
1920(?)-1976 Obituary ... 104
Godwin, Gail (Kathleen) 1937- ... CANR-15
Earlier sketch in CA 29-32R
See also CLC 5, 8, 22, 31, 69
See also DLB 6
See also MTCW
Godwin, Gaylord 1906(?)-1979 Obituary ... 85-88
Godwin, George (Stanley) 1889- ... 5-8R
Godwin, Harry 1901-1985 ... 109
Obituary ... 117
Godwin, John (Frederick) 1922- ... CANR-19
Earlier sketch in CA 102
Godwin, John 1929- ... CANR-16
Earlier sketches in CA 1-4R, CANR-1
Godwin, Joscelyn 1945- ... CANR-29
Earlier sketches in CA 69-72, CANR-12
Godwin, Parke 1816-1904 Brief entry ... 119
See also DLB 3, 64
Godwin, Phillip E(arl) 1954-1989 Obituary ... 130
Godwin, Tony
See Godwin, Anthony Richard James Wylie
Godwin, William 1756-1836 ... CDBLB 1789-1832
See also DLB 39, 104
Godwin-Jones, Robert 1949- ... 137
Goebbels, Josef
See Goebbels, (Paul) Joseph
Goebbels, Joseph Paul
See Goebbels, (Paul) Joseph
Goebbels, (Paul) Joseph
1897-1945 Brief entry ... 115
Goebel, Dorothy (Burne) 1898-1976 ... 69-72
Obituary ... 65-68
Goebel, Julius Jr. 1893(?)-1973 Obituary ... 45-48
Goedecke, W(alter) Robert 1928- ... 29-32R
Goedel, Kurt 1906-1978 Obituary ... 108
Goedertier, Joseph M. 1907- ... CAP-2
Earlier sketch in CA 25-28
Goedicke, Hans 1926- ... CANR-19
Earlier sketches in CA 45-48, CANR-1
Goedicke, Patricia (McKenna) 1931- ... CANR-27
Earlier sketches in CA 25-28R, CANR-11
Goedicke, Victor (Alfred) 1912- ... 17-20R
Goel, M(adan) Lal 1936- ... 53-56
Goeldner, Charles R. 1932- ... 128
Goeller, Carl 1930- ... 21-24R
Goelz, Paul Cornelius 1914- ... 109
Goen, Clarence C(urtis) Jr. 1924-1990 ... 1-4R
Obituary ... 133
Goen, Rayburne Wyndham Jr. 1942- ... 107
Goen, Tex Jr.
See Goen, Rayburne Wyndham Jr.
Goeney, William M(orton) 1914- ... 5-8R
Goerdt, Arthur L(inus) 1912- ... 41-44R
Goergen, Donald 1943- ... 61-64
Goering, Helga
See Wallmann, Jeffrey M(iner)
Goering, Reinhard 1887-1936 ... DLB 118
Goerling, Lars 1931-1966 ... CAP-2
Obituary ... 25-28R
Earlier sketch in CA 21-22
Goerner, E(dward) A(lfred) 1929- ... 49-52
Goerres, Joseph 1776-1848 ... DLB 90
Goertz, Donald C(harles) 1939- ... 53-56
Goertzel, Ted George 1942- ... 69-72
Goes, Albrecht 1908- ... DLB 69
Goetchius, Eugene Van Ness 1921- ... 118
Goethals, George W. 1920- ... 13-16R
Goethe, Johann Wolfgang von
1749-1832 ... DLB 94
See also PC 5
See also WLC 3
Goetsch-Trevelyan, Katherine
See Trevelyan, Katharine
Goettel, Elinor 1930- ... 29-32R
See also SATA 12
Goetz, Billy E. 1904- ... CAP-1
Earlier sketch in CA 13-14
Goetz, Delia 1898- ... 73-76
See also SATA 22
Goetz, Ignacio L. 1933- ... 37-40R
Goetz, Johann Nikolaus 1721-1781 ... DLB 97
Goetz, Joseph (William) 1933- ... 118
Goetz, Lee Garrett 1932- ... 25-28R
Goetze, Albrecht E. R.
1897-1971 Obituary ... 33-36R
Goetzmann, William H. 1930- ... 21-24R

Goetz-Stankiewicz, Marketa ... 122
Goff, Charles Ray 1889-1984 Obituary ... 114
Goff, Frederick Richmond 1916-1982 ... CANR-7
Obituary ... 108
Earlier sketch in CA 17-20R
Goff, James R. Jr. 1957- ... 126
Goff, Martyn 1923- ... CANR-2
Earlier sketch in CA 5-8R
Goffart, Walter (Andre) 1934- ... CANR-38
Earlier sketches in CA 37-40R, CANR-16
Goffe, Thomas 1592(?)-1629 ... DLB 58
Goffe, Toni 1936- ... SATA 61
Goffen, Rona 1944- ... 121
Goffin, Raymond C.
1890(?)-1976 Obituary ... 65-68
Goffman, Erving 1922-1982 ... CANR-9
Obituary ... 108
Earlier sketch in CA 21-24R
Goffstein, (Marilyn) Brooke 1940- ... CANR-28
Earlier sketches in CA 21-24R, CANR-9
See also Goffstein, M. B.
See also CLR 3
See also DLB 61
See also MAICYA
See also SATA 8, 70
Goffstein, M. B.
See Goffstein, (Marilyn) Brooke
See also CLR 3
See also DLB 61
See also SATA 8
Gofman, John W(illiam) 1918- ... 65-68
Goforth, Ellen
See Francis, Dorothy Brenner
Gogarty, Oliver St. John
1878-1957 Brief entry ... 109
See also DLB 15, 19
See also TCLC 15
Goggin, Dan 1943- ... 126
Goggin, Terrence P(atrick) 1941- ... 103
Gogisgi
See Arnett, Carroll
Gogol, Nikolai (Vasilyevich) 1809-1852 ... DC 1
See also SSC 4
See also WLC
Goh, Cheng-Teik 1943- ... 41-44R
Gohdes, Clarence Louis Frank 1901- ... 13-16R
Gohman, Fred Joseph 1918- ... 5-8R
Goines, Donald 1937(?)-1974 ... 124
Obituary ... 114
See also AITN 1
See also BLC 2
See also BW
See also DLB 33
Goins, Ellen H(aynes) 1927-1979 ... CANR-26
Earlier sketch in CA 33-36R
Goist, Park Dixon 1936- ... 37-40R
Goitein, S(helomo) D(ov) 1900-1985 ... CANR-8
Obituary ... 115
Earlier sketch in CA 61-64
Goitein, Solomon Dob Fritz
See Goitein, S(helomo) D(ov)
Gokak, Vinayak Krishna 1909- ... 69-72
Gokhale, Balkrishna Govind 1919- ... CANR-4
Earlier sketch in CA 1-4R
Gokhale, Namita 1956- ... 123
Golan, Aviezer 1922- ... 104
Golan, Matti 1936- ... 101
Golann, Cecil Paige 1921- ... 33-36R
See also SATA 11
Golann, Stuart E(ugene) 1936- ... 57-60
Golant, William 1937- ... 65-68
Golay, Frank H(indman) 1915- ... CANR-1
Earlier sketch in CA 1-4R
Golbin, Andree 1923- ... SATA 15
Golburgh, Stephen J. 1935- ... 21-24R
Golby, J(ohn) M(ichael) 1935- ... 127
Gold, Aaron 1937-1983 ... 101
Obituary ... 109
Gold, Alan R(obert) 1948- ... 45-48
Gold, Alison Leslie 1945- ... 136
Gold, Arthur 1917- ... 132
Gold, Artie 1947- ... 114
Gold, Barbara K(irk) 1945- ... CANR-29
Earlier sketch in CA 110
Gold, Don 1931- ... CANR-9
Earlier sketch in CA 61-64
Gold, Doris B. 1919- ... CANR-9
Earlier sketch in CA 21-24R
Gold, Douglas 1894- ... CAP-1
Earlier sketch in CA 11-12
Gold, Herbert 1924- ... CANR-17
Earlier sketch in CA 9-12R
See also CLC 4, 7, 14, 42
See also DLB 2
See also DLBY 81
Gold, Ivan 1932- ... CANR-3
Earlier sketch in CA 5-8R
Gold, Joseph 1933- ... 21-24R
Gold, Lee 1919(?)-1985 Obituary ... 116
Gold, Martin 1931- ... 29-32R
Gold, Michael
See Granich, Irving
See also DLB 9, 28
Gold, Michael Evan 1943- ... 138
Gold, Milton J. 1917- ... 17-20R
Gold, Phyllis
See Goldberg, Phyllis
See also SATA 21
Gold, Robert S(tanley) 1924- ... 53-56
See also SATA 63
Gold, Seymour M(urray) 1933- ... CANR-21
Earlier sketch in CA 41-44R
Gold, Sharlya ... CANR-8
Earlier sketch in CA 61-64
See also SATA 9
Gold, Todd 1958- ... 136
Gold, Victor Roland 1924- ... 53-56
Gold, William E(mil) 1912- ... 69-72
Goldbarth, Albert 1948- ... CANR-6
Earlier sketch in CA 53-56
See also CLC 5, 38
See also DLB 120
Goldbeck, David M. 1942- ... CANR-30
Earlier sketch in CA 49-52
Goldbeck, Frederick E(rnest) 1902- ... 102
Goldbeck, Nikki 1947- ... CANR-30
Earlier sketch in CA 49-52
Goldbeck, Willis 1899(?)-1979 Obituary ... 89-92
Goldberg, Albert (Levi) 1898-1990 Obituary ... 130
Goldberg, Alvin Arnold 1931- ... 41-44R
Goldberg, Anatol 1910-1982 ... 131
Obituary ... 117
See also CLC 34
Goldberg, Arnold I(rving) 1929- ... CANR-19
Earlier sketch in CA 103
Goldberg, Arthur J(oseph) 1908-1990 ... 65-68
Obituary ... 130
Goldberg, Barney 1918- ... 21-24R
Goldberg, Benjamin 1915- ... 120
Goldberg, Carl 1938- ... CANR-18
Earlier sketches in CA 49-52, CANR-3
Goldberg, David J. 1939- ... 127
Goldberg, Dick 1947- ... 97-100
See also DLB 7
Goldberg, Dorothy K(urgans) 1909(?)-1988 ... 103
Obituary ... 124
Goldberg, E(lliott) Marshall 1930- ... CANR-26
Earlier sketches in CA 69-72, CANR-11
Goldberg, Edward M(orris) 1931- ... 53-56
Goldberg, Fats
See Goldberg, Larry
Goldberg, George 1935- ... 69-72
Goldberg, Gerald Jay 1929- ... 49-52
Goldberg, Harvey E(llis) 1939- ... CANR-25
Earlier sketch in CA 45-48
Goldberg, Herb 1937- ... CANR-9
Earlier sketch in CA 61-64
Goldberg, Herbert S. 1926- ... 5-8R
See also SATA 25
Goldberg, Herman Raphael 1915- ... CANR-5
Earlier sketch in CA 9-12R
Goldberg, Hillel 1946- ... 116
Goldberg, Hyman 1908(?)-1970 Obituary ... 104
Goldberg, Jacob 1948- ... 120
Goldberg, Jan
See Curran, Jan Goldberg
Goldberg, Jane G. 1946- ... 138
Goldberg, Joan Rachel 1955- ... 110
Goldberg, Jonathan 1943- ... 122
Goldberg, Joseph P(hilip) 1918- ... 37-40R
Goldberg, Kenneth P(hilip) 1945- ... 116
Goldberg, Larry 1934- ... 113
Goldberg, Leah 1911-1970 Obituary ... 25-28R
Goldberg, Lester 1924- ... 126
Goldberg, Louis
See Grant, Louis T(heodore)
Goldberg, Louis 1908- ... 13-16R
Goldberg, Lucianne Cummings 1935- ... 85-88
Goldberg, M(ilton) A(llan) 1919-1970 ... CAP-2
Earlier sketch in CA 25-28
Goldberg, M(elvyn) Hirsh 1942- ... 73-76
Goldberg, Marie Waife
See Waife-Goldberg, Marie
Goldberg, Maxwell Henry 1907- ... CANR-24
Earlier sketch in CA 103
Goldberg, Miriam Levin 1914- ... 41-44R
Goldberg, Moses H(aym) 1940- ... CANR-15
Earlier sketch in CA 93-96
Goldberg, Nathan 1903(?)-1979 Obituary ... 85-88
Goldberg, Norman L(ewis) 1906-1982 ... 81-84
Obituary ... 133
Goldberg, P(ercy) Selvin 1917- ... 5-8R
Goldberg, Paul (Boris) 1959- ... 135
Goldberg, Philip 1944- ... CANR-15
Earlier sketch in CA 85-88
Goldberg, Phyllis 1941- ... 57-60
See also Gold, Phyllis
Goldberg, Ray A(llan) 1926- ... 49-52
Goldberg, Reuben L(ucius) 1883-1970 ... CANR-9
Earlier sketch in CA 5-8R
Goldberg, Robert Alan 1949- ... 105
Goldberg, RoseLee 1947- ... 120
Goldberg, Rube
See Goldberg, Reuben L(ucius)
Goldberg, Samuel Louis 1926- ... 112
Goldberg, Sidney 1931- ... 77-80
Goldberg, Stan J. 1939- ... 49-52
See also SATA 26
Goldberg, Steven 1941- ... 53-56
Goldberg, Susan 1948- ... SATA 71
Goldberger, Arthur Stanley 1930- ... 9-12R
Goldberger, Judith M. 1948- ... 112
Goldberger, Leo 1930- ... 127
Goldberger, Nancy Rule 1937- ... 124
Goldberger, Paul (Jesse) 1950- ... 129
Brief entry ... 122
Golde, Peggy 1930- ... 37-40R
Golde, Roger A(llan) 1934- ... 69-72
Goldemberg, Isaac 1945- ... CANR-32
Earlier sketches in CA 69-72, CANR-11
See also CAAS 12
See also CLC 52
See also HW
Goldemberg, Rose Leiman ... CANR-2
Earlier sketch in CA 49-52
Golden, Arthur 1924- ... 33-36R
Golden, Eve 1957- ... 136
Golden, Harry Jr. 1928(?)-1988 Obituary ... 125
Golden, Harry (Lewis) 1902-1981 ... CANR-2
Obituary ... 104
Earlier sketch in CA 1-4R
Golden, James L. 1919- Brief entry ... 109
Golden, Jeffrey S. 1950- ... 33-36R
Golden, L(ouis) L(awrence) L(ionel)
1909(?)-1983 ... 21-24R
Obituary ... 111
Golden, Leon 1930- ... 17-20R
Golden, Marita 1950- ... 111
See also BW
Golden, Mark 1948- ... 135
Golden, Morris 1926- ... 1-4R
Golden, Richard M(artin) 1947- ... 138
Golden, Robert Edward 1945- ... 65-68
Golden, Ruth I(sbell) 1910- ... CAP-2
Earlier sketch in CA 17-18
Golden, Samuel A(dler) 1909- Brief entry ... 110
Golden, Sean V(alentine) 1948- ... 107
Golden, Sherry (Lazar) 1945- ... 123
Goldenbaum, Sally 1941- ... 124
Goldenberg, Edie N. 1945- ... 69-72
Goldenberg, Herbert 1926- ... 41-44R
Goldenberg, I(sidore) Ira 1936- ... 110
Goldenberg, Robert 1942- ... 109
Goldenberg, Susan 1944- ... 134
Golden Silver
See Storm, Hyemeyohsts
Goldensohn, Barry 1937- ... 77-80
Goldenson, Daniel R. 1944- ... 25-28R
Goldenson, Robert M(yar) 1908- ... 29-32R
Goldenthal, Allan Benarria 1920- ... 17-20R
Goldfader, Edward H. 1930- ... 29-32R
Goldfarb, Clare R(osett) 1934- ... 113
Goldfarb, Nathan 1913- ... 13-16R
Goldfarb, Ronald L. 1933- ... CANR-9
Earlier sketch in CA 21-24R
Goldfarb, Russell M. 1934- ... 37-40R
Goldfarb, Sally F(ay) 1957- ... 104
Goldfeder, Cheryl
See Pahz, (Anne) Cheryl Suzanne
Goldfeder, James
See Pahz, James Alon
Goldfeder, Jim
See Pahz, James Alon
Goldfein, Donna 1933- ... 116
Goldfrank, David M. ... 118
Goldfrank, Esther S(chiff) 1896- ... 61-64
Goldfrank, Helen Colodny 1912- ... CANR-3
Earlier sketch in CA 1-4R
See also SATA 6
Goldfrank, Lewis 1941- ... 127
Goldfried, Marvin R(obert) 1936- ... 37-40R
Goldgar, Bertrand A(lvin) 1927- ... 65-68
Goldhaber, Gerald Martin 1944- ... CANR-9
Earlier sketch in CA 57-60
Goldhamer, Herbert 1907-1977 ... CANR-2
Earlier sketch in CA 45-48
Goldhurst, Richard 1927- ... 57-60
Goldhurst, William 1929- ... 5-8R
Goldie, Frederick 1914-1980 Obituary ... 105
Goldie, Terrence William 1950- ... CANR-32
Earlier sketch in CA 113
Goldie, Terry
See Goldie, Terrence William
Goldin, Augusta 1906- ... CANR-7
Earlier sketch in CA 17-20R
See also SATA 13
Goldin, Barbara Diamond 1946- ... 132
Goldin, Grace 1916- ... 115
Goldin, Judah 1914- ... 33-36R
Goldin, Kathleen Mckinney 1943- ... 133
Brief entry ... 118
Goldin, Milton 1927- ... 61-64
Goldin, Stephen 1947- ... 77-80
Golding, Lawrence A(rthur) 1926- ... 61-64
Golding, Louis 1907- ... CAP-1
Earlier sketch in CA 9-10
Golding, Martin Philip 1930- ... 101
Golding, Morton J(ay) 1925- ... 21-24R
Golding, Peter 1947- ... 103
Golding, William (Gerald) 1911- ... CANR-33
Earlier sketches in CA 5-8R, CANR-13
See also AAYA 5
See also CDBLB 1945-1960
See also CLC 1, 2, 3, 8, 10, 17, 27, 58
See also DLB 15, 100
See also MTCW
See also WLC
Goldknopf, David 1918- ... 53-56
Goldman, A(ndrew) E. O. 1947- ... 57-60
Goldman, Alan H(arris) 1945- ... 93-96
Goldman, Albert 1927- ... CANR-9
Earlier sketch in CA 17-20R
See also BEST 89:2
Goldman, Alex J. 1917- ... 49-52
See also SATA 65
Goldman, Alvin I(ra) 1938- ... 77-80
Goldman, Alvin L. 1938- ... CANR-1
Earlier sketch in CA 45-48
Goldman, Arnold (Melvyn) 1936- ... 17-20R
Goldman, Bernard 1922- ... 53-56
Goldman, Bo 1932- ... 112
Brief entry ... 109
Goldman, Bruce (Eliot) 1942- ... 61-64
Goldman, Carl A(lexander) 1942- ... 101
Goldman, Charles R(emington) 1930- ... 53-56
Goldman, Dave 1927- ... 107
Goldman, E. S. 1913- ... 128
Goldman, Emma 1869-1940 Brief entry ... 110
See also TCLC 13
Goldman, Eric (Frederick) 1915-1989 ... 5-8R
Obituary ... 127
Goldman, Frederick 1921- ... 81-84
Goldman, George D(avid) 1923- ... 107
Goldman, Howard H(irsch) 1949- ... 112
Goldman, Irving 1911- ... 29-32R
Goldman, Jacquelin (Roberta) 1934- ... 69-72
Goldman, James A. 1927- ... CANR-1
Earlier sketch in CA 45-48
Goldman, Lee A. 1946- ... 25-28R
Goldman, Leo 1920- ... 85-88
Goldman, Lorraine 1940- ... 111
Goldman, Louis 1925- ... 125
Goldman, Marcus Selden 1894- ... 41-44R
Goldman, Marshall I(rwin) 1930- ... 9-12R
Goldman, Martin (Raymond Rubin) 1920- ... 69-72
Goldman, Martin 1950(?)-1984 Obituary ... 113
Goldman, Merle 1931- ... 33-36R
Goldman, Michael (Paul) 1936- ... CANR-8
Earlier sketch in CA 17-20R
Goldman, Norma Wynick 1922- ... 110
Goldman, Paul (Henry Joseph) 1950- ... 129
Goldman, Peter (Louis) 1933- ... CANR-24
Earlier sketches in CA 21-24R, CANR-8
Goldman, Phyllis W. 1927- ... 29-32R
Goldman, Ralph M(orris) 1920- ... 89-92
Goldman, Richard Franko 1910-1980 ... CANR-5
Obituary ... 93-96
Earlier sketch in CA 9-12R
Goldman, Ronald ... 21-24R
Goldman, Sheldon 1939- ... 21-24R
Goldman, Sherli E(vens) 1930- ... 25-28R
Goldman, Shifra M(eyerowitz) 1926- ... CANR-25
Earlier sketch in CA 106
Goldman, Susan 1939- ... 65-68
Goldman, William (W.) 1931- ... CANR-29
Earlier sketch in CA 9-12R
See also CLC 1, 48
See also DLB 44
Goldman-Eisler, Frieda
1909(?)-1982 Obituary ... 105
Goldmann, Lucien 1913-1970 ... CAP-2
Earlier sketch in CA 25-28
See also CLC 24
Goldmann, Nahum 1895-1982 Obituary ... 107
Goldmark, Peter C(arl) 1906-1977 ... 77-80
Obituary ... 73-76
Goldner, Bernard (Burton) 1919- ... 5-8R
Goldner, Jack 1900- ... CAP-2
Earlier sketch in CA 25-28
Goldner, Nancy 1943- ... 57-60
Goldner, Orville (Charles) 1906- ... 53-56
Goldovsky, Boris 1908- ... CANR-16
Earlier sketch in CA 81-84
Goldring, Douglas 1887-1960 Obituary ... 93-96
Goldring, Patrick (Thomas Zachary)
1921- ... 29-32R
Goldsberry, Steven 1949- ... 131
See also CLC 34
Goldsborough, June 1923- ... SATA 19
Goldsborough, Robert (Gerald) 1937- ... 138
Goldscheider, Calvin 1941- ... 122
Brief entry ... 108
Goldscheider, Ludwig 1896- ... 5-8R
Goldschmidt, Clara Malraux
See Malraux, Clara (Goldschmidt)
Goldschmidt, Walter Rochs 1913- ... 9-12R
Goldschmidt, Yaagov 1927- ... 29-32R
Goldsen, Rose Kohn 1918- ... CANR-33
Earlier sketch in CA 1-4R
Goldsmith
See Miller, Lynne (Ellen)
Goldsmith, Arnold L(ouis) 1928- ... 41-44R
Goldsmith, Arthur (A. Jr.) 1926- ... CANR-5
Earlier sketch in CA 13-16R
Goldsmith, Barbara 1931- ... CANR-5
Earlier sketch in CA 53-56
Goldsmith, Carol Evan 1930- ... 29-32R
Goldsmith, David H(irsh) 1933- ... 117
Goldsmith, Donald 1943- ... 77-80
Goldsmith, Edward ... 104
Goldsmith, Emanuel S(idney)
1935- Brief entry ... 109
Goldsmith, Howard 1943- ... CANR-21
Earlier sketch in CA 101
See also SATA 24
Goldsmith, Ilse Sondra (Weinberg)
1933- ... 37-40R
Goldsmith, Jack 1931- ... 57-60
Goldsmith, Joel S. 1892(?)-1964 Obituary ... 109
Goldsmith, John Herman Thorburn
1903-1987 Obituary ... 122
See also SATA 52
Goldsmith, John 1947- ... 125
Goldsmith, Oliver
1728-1774 ... CDBLB 1660-1789
See also DLB 39, 89, 104, 109
See also SATA 26
See also WLC
Goldsmith, Oliver 1794-1861 ... DLB 99
Goldsmith, Peter
See Priestley, J(ohn) B(oynton)
Goldsmith, Raymond W(illiam) 1904-1988 ... 115
Obituary ... 126
Goldsmith, Robert Hillis 1911- ... 49-52
Goldsmith, Ruth M. 1919- ... SATA 62
Goldsmith, Sharon S(weeney) 1948- ... 57-60
Goldsmith, Walter (Kenneth) 1938- ... 120
Goldson, Rae L(illian) Segalowitz 1893- ... 5-8R
Goldstein, Abraham S(amuel) 1925- ... CANR-29
Earlier sketch in CA 33-36R
Goldstein, Abraham 1903(?)-1982 Obituary ... 106
Goldstein, Alvin H. Sr.
1902-1972 Obituary ... 33-36R
Goldstein, Arthur D(avid) 1937- ... 73-76
Goldstein, Bernard R. 1938- ... 57-60
Goldstein, Carl 1938- ... 130
Goldstein, David I. 1924-1987(?) ... 130
Goldstein, David 1933- ... CANR-11
Earlier sketch in CA 17-20R
Goldstein, Donald M(aurice) 1932- ... CANR-26
Earlier sketch in CA 108
Goldstein, E. Ernest 1918- ... 9-12R
Goldstein, Edward 1923- ... 9-12R
Goldstein, Ernest A. 1933- ... 110
See also SATA 52
Goldstein, Gersham 1938- Brief entry ... 108
Goldstein, Howard 1922- ... 93-96

Goldstein, Irwin L. 1937- 41-44R
Goldstein, Israel 1896-1986 53-56
Obituary 119
Goldstein, Jack 1930- 73-76
Goldstein, Jeffrey H(askell) 1942- CANR-32
Earlier sketches in CA 81-84, CANR-14
Goldstein, Jerome 1931- 101
Goldstein, Joan 1932- CANR-35
Earlier sketch in CA 114
Goldstein, Jonathan A(mos) 1929- 25-28R
Goldstein, Joseph 1923- 17-20R
Goldstein, Kenneth M(ichael) 1940- 33-36R
Goldstein, Kenneth S. 1927- Brief entry 107
Goldstein, Laurence
1937(?)-1972 Obituary 33-36R
Goldstein, Laurence 1943- 93-96
Goldstein, Leo S. 1924- 13-16R
Goldstein, Leon J. 1927- 69-72
Goldstein, Lisa 1953- CANR-25
Earlier sketch in CA 108
Goldstein, Malcolm 1925- CANR-32
Earlier sketch in CA 49-52
Goldstein, Marc 1948- 109
Goldstein, Martin E(ugene) 1939- 41-44R
Goldstein, Melvyn C. 1938- 121
Goldstein, Michael J(oseph) 1930- 103
Goldstein, Milton 1915- CANR-24
Earlier sketch in CA 45-48
Goldstein, Nathan 1927- CANR-16
Earlier sketches in CA 45-48, CANR-1
See also SATA 47
Goldstein, Philip 1910- 53-56
See also SATA 23
Goldstein, Rhoda L.
See Blumberg, Rhoda L(ois Goldstein)
Goldstein, Richard 1944- 25-28R
Goldstein, Robert Justin 1947- 131
Goldstein, Roberta Butterfield 1917- 9-12R
Goldstein, Robin 1952- 133
Goldstein, Robin 1955(?)-1989 Obituary 129
Goldstein, Ruth M(artha) 1913- 113
Goldstein, Ruth Tessler 1924- 69-72
Goldstein, Sidney 1927- CANR-25
Earlier sketches in CA 21-24R, CANR-9
Goldstein, Stanley 1922- 103
Goldstein, Stephen R(obert) 1938- CANR-30
Earlier sketches in CA 61-64, CANR-13
Goldstein, Stewart 1941- 65-68
Goldstein, Thomas Eugene
1913- Brief entry 108
Goldstein, William Isaac 1932- 13-16R
Goldstein-Jackson, Kevin 1946- 106
Goldstine, Herman Heine 1913- 110
Goldston, Robert (Conroy) 1927- CANR-13
Earlier sketch in CA 17-20R
See also SATA 6
Goldstone, Aline L(ewis)
1878(?)-1976 Obituary 65-68
Goldstone, Harmon H(endricks) 1911- 77-80
Goldstone, Herbert 1921- 77-80
Goldstone, Lawrence A.
See Treat, Lawrence
Goldstone, Richard H. 1921- 33-36R
Goldsworthy, David 1938- 33-36R
Goldsworthy, Graeme 1934- CANR-35
Earlier sketch in CA 114
Goldsworthy, Peter 1951- 118
Goldszmit, Henryk 1878-1942 133
See also Korczak, Janusz
Goldthorpe, J(ohn) E(rnest) 1921- CANR-33
Earlier sketch in CA 49-52
Goldthorpe, Rhiannon 1934- 126
Goldthwaite, Eaton K. 1907- 25-28R
Goldthwaite, Richard A(llen) 1933- 136
Brief entry 108
Goldwasser, Thomas 1939- 135
Goldwater, Barry (Morris) 1909- 41-44R
Goldwater, Eleanor Lowenstein
1909(?)-1980 Obituary 102
Goldwater, John ....AITN 1
Goldwater, John L. 1916- 131
Goldwater, Robert 1907-1973 Obituary 41-44R
Goldwater, Walter Delmar
1907-1985 Obituary 116
Goldwin, Robert Allen 1922- 102
Goldwyn, Robert M(alcolm) 1930- 122
Gole, Victor Leslie 1903- CANR-23
Earlier sketch in CA 107
Goleman, Daniel 1946- 111
Golembiewski, Robert T(homas)
1932- CANR-21
Earlier sketches in CA 5-8R, CANR-6
Golenbock, Peter 1946- CANR-8
Earlier sketch in CA 57-60
Golenpaul, Ann 1907(?)-1986 Obituary 119
Golf, Loyal E.
See Golv, Loyal E(ugene)
Golffing, Francis (Charles) 1910- CANR-5
Earlier sketch in CA 5-8R
Goliard, Roy
See Shipley, Joseph T(wadell)
Golightly, Bonnie H(elen) 1919- 1-4R
Goll, Reinhold W(eimar) 1897- 5-8R
See also SATA 26
Gollan, Robin 1917- 13-16R
Gollancz, Victor 1893-1967 Obituary 116
Golledge, Reginald G(eorge) 1937- 41-44R
Goller, Celia (Fremlin) 1914- CANR-5
Earlier sketch in CA 13-16R
Golley, Frank Benjamin 1930- Brief entry 106
Gollin, Gillian Lindt
See Lindt, Gillian
Gollings, Franklin O. A. 1919- 21-24R
Gollmar, Robert H. 1903(?)-1987 Obituary 123
Gollwitzer, Heinz 1917- 25-28R
Gologor, Ethan 1940- 101
Golomb, Claire 1928- 103
Golomb, Louis 1943- CANR-16
Earlier sketch in CA 85-88
Golombek, Harry 1911- 103
Golomstock, Igor (Naumovitch) 1929- 134
Golon, Serge(anne)
1903-1972 Obituary 37-40R
Golovine, Michael N(icholas) 1903-1965 ....5-8R
Golson, G(eorge) Barry 1944- CANR-33
Earlier sketch in CA 69-72
Golv, Loyal E(ugene) 1926- CANR-1
Earlier sketch in CA 1-4R
Golz, R(einhardt) Lud 1936- CANR-5
Earlier sketch in CA 13-16R
Gom, Leona 1946- 116
Gombault, Charles Henri
1907-1983 Obituary 110
Gomberg, Adeline Wishengrad 1915- 17-20R
Gomberg, William 1911-1985 ....17-20R
Obituary 118
Gombossy, Zoltan
See Gabel, Joseph
Gombrich, E(rnst) H(ans Josef) 1909- CANR-32
Earlier sketches in CA 53-56, CANR-5
Gombrich, Richard Francis 1937- 138
Gombrowicz, Witold 1904-1969 ....CAP-2
Obituary 25-28R
Earlier sketch in CA 19-20
See also CLC 4, 7, 11, 49
Gomery, Douglas 1945- CANR-29
Earlier sketch in CA 110
Gomez, Alberto Perez
See Perez-Gomez, Alberto
Gomez, Carlos F. 1958- 129
Gomez, David F(ederico) 1940- 49-52
Gomez, Joseph A(nthony) 1942- 104
Gomez, Rudolph 1930- 53-56
Gomez de la Serna, Ramon
1888-1963 Obituary 116
See also CLC 9
See also HW
Gomez-Gil, Alfredo 1936- 41-44R
See also AITN 1
Gomez-Quinones, Juan (H.) 1942- 131
See also HW
Gomez Rosa, Alexis 1950-
See Rosa, Alexis Gomez
See also HW
Gomi, Taro 1945- ....SATA 64
Gomori, George 1934- CANR-9
Earlier sketch in CA 21-24R
Gompertz, Rolf 1927- CANR-11
Earlier sketch in CA 69-72
Gondosch, Linda 1944- 127
See also SATA 58
Gongora, Maria Eugenia 1948- 104
Gonick, Jean 1950- 121
Gonick, Larry 1946- 127
Gontarski, S(tanley) E. 1942- 114
Gontier, Fernande ....CLC 50
Gonzales, (Elizabeth) Anne H. 1944- 138
Gonzales, John
See Terrall, Robert
Gonzales, Manuel G(arcia) 1943- 111
Gonzales, Pancho
See Gonzales, Richard Alonzo
Gonzales, Richard Alonzo
1928- Brief entry 105
Gonzales, Sylvia Alicia 1943- 77-80
See also HW
Gonzalez, Alfonso 1927- 41-44R
Gonzalez, Angel 1925- CANR-15
Earlier sketch in CA 85-88
See also DLB 108
Gonzalez, Arturo 1928- 77-80
Gonzalez, Catherine Gunsalus 1934- 136
Gonzalez, Cesar A.
See Gonzalez T(rujillo), Cesar A.
Gonzalez, Edward 1933- Brief entry 109
Gonzalez, Gloria 1940- CANR-24
Earlier sketch in CA 65-68
See also SATA 23
Gonzalez, Jaime Jose 1925- 103
Gonzalez, Jose Luis 1926- 131
See also HW
Gonzalez, Justo L(uis) 1937- CANR-16
Earlier sketch in CA 29-32R
Gonzalez, N(estor) V(icente) M(adali)
1915- CANR-2
Earlier sketch in CA 1-4R
Gonzalez, Nancie L(oudon) 1929- 103
Gonzalez, Richard F(lorentz) 1927- 114
Gonzalez, Sergio A(ntonio) Torres
See Torres Gonzalez, Sergio A(ntonio)
Gonzalez-Aller, Faustino 1922- 81-84
Gonzalez-Crussi, F(rank) 1936- 126
Brief entry 121
See also HW
Gonzalez-Echevarria, Roberto 1943- 106
Gonzalez-Gerth, Miguel 1926- 69-72
Gonzalez Lopez, Emilio 1903- CANR-2
Earlier sketch in CA 49-52
Gonzalez Martinez, Enrique 1871-1952 ....HW
Gonzalez-Mena, Janet 1937- 111
Gonzalez-Paz, Elsie E. 1913- 45-48
Gonzalez Prada, Manuel 1844-1918 ....HW
Gonzalez-T., Cesar A. 1931- ....DLB 82
Gonzalez T(rujillo), Cesar A. 1931- ....HW
Gonzalez-Wippler, Migene 1936- 109
Gooby, Peter Taylor
See Taylor-Gooby, Peter
Gooch, Bob
See Gooch, Robert M(iletus)
Gooch, Brad 1952- 132
Gooch, Brison D(owling) 1925- 13-16R
Gooch, Bryan Niel Shirley 1937- 93-96
Gooch, George Peabody 1873-1968 ....5-8R
Gooch, John 1945- 126
Gooch, Robert M(iletus) 1919- CANR-29
Earlier sketches in CA 77-80, CANR-13
Gooch, Stan(ley Alfred) 1932- CANR-14
Earlier sketch in CA 77-80
Gooch, Steve 1945- CANR-20
Earlier sketch in CA 101
Good, Carter V(ictor) 1897- 5-8R
Good, David F(ranklin) 1943- 125
Good, Edwin M(arshall) 1928- CANR-11
Earlier sketch in CA 17-20R
Good, H(arry) G(ehman) 1880-1971 ....1-4R
Obituary 103
Good, I(rving) John 1916- CANR-3
Earlier sketch in CA 5-8R
Good, Kenneth 1942- 134
Good, Lawrence R. 1924- 13-16R
Good, Paul 1929- 85-88
Good, Robert Crocker 1924- 73-76
Good, Thomas L(indall) 1943- CANR-22
Earlier sketches in CA 57-60, CANR-8
Goodacre, Elizabeth Jane 1929- 102
Goodall, Daphne Machin
See Machin Goodall, Daphne (Edith)
Goodall, H(arold) L(loyd) Jr. 1952- 132
Goodall, Jane 1934- CANR-2
Earlier sketch in CA 45-48
See also MTCW
Goodall, John Strickland 1908- 33-36R
See also CLR 25
See also MAICYA
See also SATA 4, 66
Goodall, Leonard E. 1937- 85-88
Goodall, Marcus C(ampbell) 1914- 33-36R
Goodall, Melanie
See Drachman, Julian M(oses)
Goodall, Norman 1896-1985 Obituary 115
Goodall, Vanne Morris
See Morris-Goodall, Vanne
Goodavage, Joseph F. 1925- 25-28R
Goodbody, Slim
See Burstein, John
Goodchild, Peter 1939- 106
Goode, Barry 1938- 118
Goode, Diane 1949- ....SATA 15
Goode, Erich 1938- CANR-37
Earlier sketches in CA 49-52, CANR-1, 16
Goode, Gerald 1899(?)-1983 Obituary 111
Goode, James M. 1939- 93-96
Goode, James 1924- 123
Goode, John 1927- 103
Goode, Kenneth G. 1932- 49-52
Goode, Richard (Benjamin) 1916- 17-20R
Goode, Ruth 1905- 77-80
Goode, Stephen H(ogue) 1924- CANR-2
Earlier sketch in CA 45-48
Goode, Stephen Ray 1943- CANR-18
Earlier sketch in CA 57-60
See also SATA 40, 55
Goode, William Josiah 1917- 102
Goodell, Charles E(llsworth) 1926-1987 81-84
Obituary 121
Goodell, Donald (James) 1938- 45-48
Goodell, John S. 1939- 73-76
Goodell, Rae 1944- 77-80
Goodenough, Erwin R(amsdell)
1893-1965 ....5-8R
Goodenough, Evelyn
See Pitcher, Evelyn G(oodenough)
Goodenough, Ward Hunt 1919- CANR-2
Earlier sketch in CA 1-4R
Goodenow, Earle 1913- ....SATA 40
Gooders, John 1937- CANR-6
Earlier sketch in CA 57-60
Goodfellow, Peter 1935- 115
Goodfield, (Gwyneth) June 1927- 9-12R
Goodfriend, Arthur 1907- 5-8R
Goodgold, Edwin 1944- CANR-23
Earlier sketch in CA 21-24R
Goodhart, A. L.
See Goodhart, Arthur Lehman
Goodhart, Arthur Lehman 1891-1978 ......CANR-31
Obituary 81-84
Earlier sketch in CA 85-88
Goodhart, Robert S(tanley) 1909- 89-92
Goodheart, Barbara 1934- 33-36R
Goodheart, Eugene 1931- CANR-39
Earlier sketches in CA 5-8R, CANR-3, 18
Goodheart, Lawrence B. 1944- 135
Goodin, Gayle 1938- 33-36R
Goodin, Robert Edward 1950- CANR-22
Earlier sketch in CA 105
Gooding, Cynthia 1924- 33-36R
Gooding, John (Ervine) 1940- 21-24R
Gooding, Judson 1926- 73-76
Gooding, Kathleen (Tinney) 116
Goodis, David 1917-1967 ....1-4R
Goodkin, Sanford R(onald) 1929- 104
Goodkind, Henry M. 1904(?)-1970 Obituary 104
Goodlad, John I. 1920- CANR-19
Earlier sketches in CA 5-8R, CANR-3
Goodman, A(lvin) Harold 1924- 103
Goodman, A(dolph) W(inkler) 1915- 57-60
Goodman, Ann (Davidow) 1932- 107
Goodman, Arnold Abraham 1913- 109
Goodman, Benjamin David
1909(?)-1986 Obituary 119
Goodman, Benny
See Goodman, Benjamin David
Goodman, Celia (Mary) 1916- 123
Goodman, Charles S(chaffner) 1916- 33-36R
Goodman, Charlotte Margolis 1934- 134
Goodman, David (Allen) 1941- 119
Goodman, David Michael 1936- 17-20R
Goodman, David S. 1917- 29-32R
Goodman, Deborah Lerme 1956- 121
See also SATA 49, 50
Goodman, Edward J(ulius) 1916- 111
Goodman, Elaine 1930- 37-40R
See also SATA 9
Goodman, Elizabeth B. 1912- 25-28R
Goodman, Ellen (Holtz) 1941- 104
Goodman, Elliot R(aymond) 1923- 1-4R
Goodman, Emily Jane 1940- 65-68
Goodman, Eugene B(enedict) 1922- 113
Goodman, Felicitas D(aniels) 1914- CANR-23
Earlier sketches in CA 53-56, CANR-4
Goodman, George J(erome) W(aldo)
1930- CANR-31
Earlier sketch in CA 21-24R
Goodman, Grant K(ohn) 1924- CANR-15
Earlier sketch in CA 41-44R
Goodman, Hannah Grad
See Sverdlin, Hannah Grad
Goodman, Harriet Wilinsky 111
Goodman, Herman 1894-1971 Obituary 105
Goodman, James M(arion) 1929- 117
Goodman, Jay S. 1940- 37-40R
Goodman, Joan Elizabeth 1950- 126
See also SATA 50
Goodman, Jonathan 1931- CANR-13
Earlier sketch in CA 33-36R
Goodman, Joseph Irving 1908- 102
Goodman, Kenneth S. 1927- 25-28R
Goodman, Lenn Evan 1944- 53-56
Goodman, Leonard H(enry) 1941- 103
Goodman, Linda 1925- 89-92
Goodman, Louis Wolf 1942- 25-28R
Goodman, Mark 1939- 126
Goodman, Melvin A. 1938- 138
Goodman, Michael B(arry) 1949- 107
Goodman, Mitchell 1923- CANR-4
Earlier sketch in CA 1-4R
Goodman, (Henry) Nelson 1906- 45-48
Goodman, Norman 1934- CANR-17
Earlier sketches in CA 49-52, CANR-1
Goodman, Paul 1911-1972 ....CANR-34
Obituary 37-40R
Earlier sketches in CAP-2, CA 19-20
See also CLC 1, 2, 4, 7
See also MTCW
Goodman, Percival 1904-1989 ....1-4R
Obituary 129
Goodman, Philip 1911- 33-36R
Goodman, Randolph 1908- CANR-2
Earlier sketch in CA 5-8R
Goodman, Rebecca Gruver 1931- 77-80
Goodman, Richard Merle 1932- CANR-18
Earlier sketch in CA 102
Goodman, Richard 1945- 136
Goodman, Roger B. 1919- CANR-9
Earlier sketch in CA 21-24R
Goodman, Ronald A. 1938- 73-76
Goodman, Rubin Robert
1913-1978 Obituary 81-84
Goodman, Saul 1919- 103
Goodman, Seymour S. 1931- CANR-22
Earlier sketch in CA 45-48
Goodman, Sonya
See Arcone, Sonya
Goodman, Stanley J(oshua) 1910- 110
Goodman, Steve 1948-1984 Obituary 113
Goodman, Steven M(ichael) 1957- 126
Goodman, Walter 1927- CANR-7
Earlier sketch in CA 9-12R
See also SATA 9
Goodnough, David L. 1930- 93-96
Goodnow, Henry F(rank) 1917- 13-16R
Goodnow, Jacqueline (Jarrett) 1924- CANR-5
Earlier sketch in CA 13-16R
Goodovitch, I(srael) M(eir) 1934- 25-28R
Goodpaster, Andrew J(ackson) 1915- 109
Goodpaster, Kenneth E(dwin) 1944- CANR-17
Earlier sketch in CA 97-100
Goodpasture, H(enry) McKennie 1929- 134
Goodreau, William Joseph Jr. 1931- 1-4R
Goodrich, Chris 1956- 134
Goodrich, David L(loyd) 1930- 85-88
Goodrich, Donna Clark 1938- 117
Goodrich, Foster E(dward)
1908-1972 Obituary 37-40R
Goodrich, Frances C. 1933- 21-24R
Goodrich, Frances 1890(?)-1984 Obituary 111
See also DLB 26
Goodrich, L(uther) Carrington
1894-1986 ....CANR-2
Obituary 120
Earlier sketch in CA 5-8R
Goodrich, Leland Matthew 1899- 81-84
Goodrich, Lloyd 1897-1987 ....CANR-31
Obituary 122
Earlier sketch in CA 69-72
Goodrich, Norma Lorre 1917- 53-56
Goodrich, Robert E(dward) Jr. 1909- 33-36R
Goodrich, Samuel Griswold
1793-1860 ....DLB 1, 42, 73
See also SATA 23
Goodrich, William Lloyd
1910(?)-1975 Obituary 61-64
Goodrick, Edward W(illiam) 1913- CANR-29
Earlier sketch in CA 111
Goodrick-Clarke, Nicholas 1953- 123
Goodrum, Charles A(lvin) 1923- CANR-27
Earlier sketches in CA 25-28R, CANR-12
Goodsall, Robert Harold 1891- CANR-4
Earlier sketch in CA 5-8R
Goodsell, Charles T(rue) 1932- CANR-8
Earlier sketch in CA 61-64
Goodsell, Fred Field 1880-1976 ....1-4R
Obituary 69-72
Goodsell, Jane Neuberger
1921(?)-1988 Obituary 126
See also SATA 56
Goodson, Felix E(mmett) 1922- 49-52
Goodspeed, Donald J(ames) 1919- 5-8R

Goodspeed, Edgar Johnson
1871-1962 Obituary 93-96
Goodspeed, Peter 1944- 110
Goodstein, David B. 1932(?)-1985 Obituary 116
Goodstein, Leonard D(avid) 1927- CANR-13
Earlier sketch in CA 33-36R
Goodstein, Marvin (Elias) 1927- 125
Goodstein, R(euben) L(ouis) 1912-1985 53-56
Obituary 116
Goodwin, Albert 1906- 5-8R
Goodwin, Bennie Eugene II 1933- 112
Goodwin, Craufurd D(avid) W(ycliffe)
1934- CANR-14
Earlier sketch in CA 37-40R
Goodwin, Dave 1926- 113
Goodwin, Derek 1920- 93-96
Goodwin, Donald W(illiam) 1931- 65-68
Goodwin, Doris (Helen) Kearns 1943- CANR-23
Goodwin, Eugene D.
See Kaye, Marvin (Nathan)
Goodwin, Geoffrey (Lawrence) 1916- 106
Goodwin, H(arry) Eugene 1922- 126
Goodwin, Hal
See Goodwin, Harold L(eland)
Goodwin, Harold L(eland) 1914-1990 ....CANR-29
Obituary 131
Earlier sketches in CA 1-4R, CANR-2
See also SATA 13, 51
See also SATO 65
Goodwin, Harold 1919- 57-60
Goodwin, John Lonnen 1921- 108
Goodwin, John R(obert) 1929- 77-80
Goodwin, Ken(neth Leslie) 1934- 131
Goodwin, Leonard 1929- 41-44R
Goodwin, Mark
See Matthews, Stanley G(oodwin)
Goodwin, (Trevor) Noel 1927- 124
Goodwin, Richard M(urphey) 1913- CANR-29
Earlier sketches in CA 29-32R, CANR-12
Goodwin, Richard N(aradhof)
1931- Brief entry 111
Goodwin, Robert L. 1928(?)-1983 Obituary 109
Goodwin, Stephen 1943- CANR-8
Earlier sketch in CA 57-60
See also DLBY 82
Goodwin, Suzanne CANR-31
Earlier sketches in CA 77-80, CANR-14
Goodwyn, Floyd L(owell) 1940- 113
Goodwyn, Lawrence 1928- 21-24R
Goody, Joan Edelman 1935- 17-20R
Goodyear, Frank H. Jr. 1944- 122
Goodyear, John H(enry) III 1941- 111
Gookin, Daniel 1612-1687 ....DLB 24
Gool, Reshard 1931- 97-100
Goolagong, Evonne 1951- 89-92
Goold-Adams, Richard 1916- 13-16R
Goon, Fook Mun 1917(?)-1984 Obituary 113
Gooneratne, (Malini) Yasmine 1935- CANR-18
Earlier sketch in CA 29-32R
Goonetilleke, D(evapriya) C(hitra) R(anjan) A(lwis)
1938- 130
Goor, Nancy (Ruth Miller) 1944- CANR-32
Earlier sketch in CA 113
See also SATA 34, 39
Goor, Ron(ald Stephen) 1940- CANR-32
Earlier sketch in CA 113
See also SATA 34, 39
Goossen, Agnes
See Epp, Margaret A(gnes)
Goossen, Irvy W. 37-40R
Goot, Mary Vander
See Vander Goot, Mary
Gopal, Sarvepalli 1923- 104
Gopalakrishnan, Chennat 1936- CANR-30
Earlier sketch in CA 112
Gopen, George D(avid) 1945- 113
Gorak, Jan 1952- 126
Goralski, Robert 1928-1988 105
Obituary 125
Goran, Lester 1928- 45-48
Goran, Morris 1918- CANR-2
Earlier sketch in CA 1-4R
Gorbachev, Mikhail (Sergeyevich) 1931- 132
See also MTCW
Gorbanevskaya, Natalya 1936- 111
Gorbatov, Alexander V.
1891(?)-1973 Obituary 45-48
Gorden, Raymond L(owell) 1919- 53-56
Gordenker, Leon 1923- 21-24R
Gordett, Marea (Beth) 1949- 117
Gordh, George (Rudolph) 1912- 13-16R
Gordimer, Nadine 1923- CANR-28
Earlier sketches in CA 5-8R, CANR-3
See also CLC 3, 5, 7, 10, 18, 33, 51, 70
See also MTCW
Gordin, Richard Davis 1928- 53-56
Gordis, Robert 1908- CANR-9
Earlier sketch in CA 13-16R
Gordon, Ad
See Hano, Arnold
Gordon, Alan F. 1947- 102
Gordon, Albert I(saac) 1903-1968 ....CAP-1
Earlier sketch in CA 11-12
Gordon, Alex
See Cotler, Gordon
Gordon, Alison (Ruth) 1943- 121
Gordon, Alvin J. 1912-1989 ....33-36R
Obituary 130
Gordon, Ambrose Jr. 1920-1987 ....33-36R
Obituary 122
Gordon, Andrew (Mark) 1945- 115
Gordon, Angela
See Paine, Lauran (Bosworth)
Gordon, Anne Wolrige
See Wolrige Gordon, Anne
Gordon, Antoinette K.
1892(?)-1975 Obituary 57-60
Gordon, Archibald Victor Dudley
1913-1984 Obituary 114
Gordon, Archie
See Gordon, Archibald Victor Dudley
Gordon, Arthur 1912- 5-8R
Gordon, Barbara 1935- CANR-17
Earlier sketch in CA 89-92
Gordon, Barry (Lewis John) 1934- 102
Gordon, Bernard K. 1932- 85-88
Gordon, Bernard Ludwig 1931- 29-32R
See also SATA 27
Gordon, Bertram M(artin) 1943- 101
Gordon, Beverly 1948- 93-96
Gordon, Burton L(e Roy) 1920- 114
Gordon, Caroline 1895-1981 ....CANR-36
Obituary 103
Earlier sketches in CAP-1, CA 11-12
See also CLC 6, 13, 29
See also DLB 4, 9, 102
See also DLBY 81
See also MTCW
Gordon, Charles William
1860-1937 Brief entry 109
See also Connor, Ralph
Gordon, Colonel H. R.
See Ellis, Edward S(ylvester)
Gordon, Cyrus H(erzl) 1908- CANR-5
Earlier sketch in CA 1-4R
Gordon, Dane R. 1925- 33-36R
Gordon, David
See Garrett, (Gordon) Randall (Phillip)
Gordon, David Cole 1922- 25-28R
Gordon, David J. 1929- Brief entry 105
Gordon, David Michael 1944- 128
Gordon, Deborah Hannes 1946- 130
Gordon, Diana
See Andrews, Lucilla (Mathew)
Gordon, Diana R(ussell) 1938- CANR-28
Earlier sketch in CA 49-52
Gordon, Donald
See Payne, Donald Gordon
Gordon, Donald Craigie 1911- 17-20R
Gordon, Donald E(dward)
1931-1984 Obituary 112
Gordon, Donald Ramsay 1929- CANR-31
Earlier sketches in CA 37-40R, CANR-14
Gordon, Doreen
See Chard, Judy
Gordon, Dorothy 1893-1970 73-76
See also SATA 20
Gordon, Edmund Wyatt 1921- 37-40R
Gordon, Edwin 1927- CANR-10
Earlier sketch in CA 17-20R
Gordon, Eric A(rthur) 1945- 132
Gordon, Ernest 1916- CANR-2
Earlier sketch in CA 1-4R
Gordon, (Alexander) Esme 1910- 108
Gordon, Esther S(aranga) 1935- CANR-7
Earlier sketch in CA 53-56
See also SATA 10
Gordon, Ethel Edison 1915- 53-56
Gordon, Felice 1939- 97-100
Gordon, Frederick CANR-26
Earlier sketches in CAP-2, CA 19-20
See also SATA 1
Gordon, Fritz
See Jarvis, Fred(erick) G(ordon Jr.)
Gordon, Gary
See Edmonds, I(vy) G(ordon)
Gordon, George
See Hasford, (Jerry) Gustav
Gordon, George Byron 1911- 33-36R
Gordon, George J(acob) 1943- 111
Gordon, George N(ewton) 1926- CANR-5
Earlier sketch in CA 1-4R
Gordon, Gerald 1909- CAP-1
Earlier sketch in CA 13-14
Gordon, Giles (Alexander Esme) 1940- 41-44R
See also DLB 14
Gordon, Gordon 1912- CANR-7
Earlier sketch in CA 5-8R
Gordon, Guanetta Stewart 37-40R
Gordon, Hal
See Goodwin, Harold L(eland)
Gordon, Harold J(ackson) Jr. 1919- 33-36R
Gordon, Harry 137
See also Gordon, Henry Alfred
Gordon, (Charles) Harry (Clinton) Pirie
See Pirie-Gordon, (Charles) Harry (Clinton)
Gordon, Henry Alfred 1925- CANR-5
Earlier sketch in CA 53-56
See also Gordon, Harry
Gordon, I(an) R(obert) F(raser) 1939- 69-72
Gordon, Ian
See Fellowes-Gordon, Ian (Douglas)
Gordon, Ian A(listair) 1908- CANR-11
Earlier sketch in CA 25-28R
Gordon, Ida L. 1907- CAP-2
Earlier sketch in CA 33-36
Gordon, Ira J(ay) 1923-1978 ....CANR-26
Earlier sketch in CA 69-72
Gordon, (Gilbert) James 1918- 61-64
Gordon, Jane
See Lee, Elsie
Gordon, Jeffie Ross
See Enderle, Judith (Ann) Ross
and Tessler, Stephanie Gordon
Gordon, Joanne J(oy) 1956- 108
Gordon, John
See Gesner, Clark
Gordon, John Fraser 1916- CANR-22
Earlier sketch in CA 105
Gordon, John (Rutherford)
1890-1974 Obituary 104
Gordon, John Steele 1944- 57-60
Gordon, John (William) 1925- CANR-27
Earlier sketches in CA 103, CANR-11
Gordon, Kermit 1916-1976 Obituary 65-68
Gordon, Kurtz
See Kurtz, C(larence) Gordon
Gordon, Leland J(ames) 1897-1982 ....41-44R
Obituary 133
Gordon, Leonard A. 1938- 37-40R
Gordon, Leonard H. D. 1928- 29-32R
Gordon, Leonard 1935- 53-56
Gordon, Lesley
See Elliott, Lesley
Gordon, Lew
See Baldwin, Gordon C.
Gordon, Lillian L. 1925-1977 ....29-32R
Gordon, Lincoln 1913- 117
Gordon, (Irene) Linda 1940- CANR-25
Earlier sketches in CA 65-68, CANR-10
Gordon, Lois G. 1938- CANR-29
Earlier sketches in CA 33-36R, CANR-13
Gordon, Lou 1917(?)-1977 Obituary 69-72
Gordon, Margaret (Anna) 1939- ....SATA 9
Gordon, Margaret T(aber) 1939- 81-84
Gordon, Mark 1942- 118
Gordon, Mary (Catherine) 1949- 102
See also CLC 13, 22
See also DLB 6
See also DLBY 81
See also MTCW
Gordon, Mary Ebbitt
See Winters, Catherine (Mary)
Gordon, Mary McDougall 1929- 130
Gordon, Michael (David) 1952- 123
Gordon, Michael 1940- 41-44R
Gordon, Mildred 1912-1979 ....CANR-7
Obituary 85-88
Earlier sketch in CA 5-8R
See also SATA 24
Gordon, Mitchell 1925- 5-8R
Gordon, Myron J(ules) 1920- CANR-6
Earlier sketch in CA 5-8R
Gordon, Nancy
See Heinl, Nancy G(ordon)
Gordon, Noah 1926- 17-20R
Gordon, Oliver
See Emerson, H(enry) O(liver)
Gordon, Patricia 1909- 21-24R
Gordon, Percival Hector 1884-1975 ....41-44R
Gordon, Peter
See Wilkes-Hunter, R(ichard)
Gordon, Peter H. 1948- 130
Gordon, R(ichard) L(aurence)
1920- Brief entry 114
Gordon, Ray
See Wainwright, Gordon Ray
Gordon, Rex
See Hough, S(tanley) B(ennett)
Gordon, Richard
See Ostlere, Gordon (Stanley)
Gordon, Richard L(ewis) 1934- 29-32R
Gordon, Robert A(aron) 1908-1978 ....CANR-4
Obituary 77-80
Earlier sketch in CA 5-8R
Gordon, Robert C(oningsby) 1921- 5-8R
Gordon, Robert J. 1947- 121
Gordon, Ruth 1896-1985 ....CANR-31
Obituary 117
Earlier sketch in CA 81-84
Gordon, Samuel 1907(?)-1984 Obituary 114
Gordon, Sanford D(aniel) 1924- 33-36R
Gordon, Sarah (Ann) 1944- 132
Gordon, Selma
See Lanes, Selma Gordon
Gordon, Sheila 1927- 132
See also CLR 27
Gordon, Shirley 1921- 97-100
See also SATA 41, 48
Gordon, Sol 1923- CANR-4
Earlier sketch in CA 53-56
See also CLC 26
See also SATA 11
Gordon, Steve 1938(?)-1982 Obituary 108
Gordon, Stewart
See Shirreffs, Gordon D(onald)
Gordon, Strathearn 1902-1983 Obituary 109
Gordon, Suzanne 1945- CANR-4
Earlier sketch in CA 49-52
Gordon, Sydney 1914- 29-32R
Gordon, Theodore J. 1930- 17-20R
Gordon, Thomas 1918- 29-32R
Gordon, Tom
See Thomas, Gordon
Gordon, Walter Kelly 1930- 33-36R
Gordon, Walter L(ockhart) 1906-1987 97-100
Obituary 122
Gordon, Wendell (Chaffee) 1916- 17-20R
Gordon, William A. 1950- 135
Gordone, Charles 1925- 93-96
See also BW
See also CLC 1, 4
See also DLB 7
See also MTCW
Gordons, The
See Gordon, Gordon
and Gordon, Mildred
Gordon Walker, Patrick (Chrestien)
1907- 29-32R
Gordon-Watson, Mary 1948- CANR-37
Earlier sketch in CA 112
Gordy, Berry Sr. 1888-1978 102
Gore, Albert (Arnold) 1907- Brief entry 112
Gore, Arthur Kattendyke S(trange) D(avid) A(rchibald)
1910-1983 Obituary 109
Gore, Catherine 1800-1861 ....DLB 116
Gore, Christopher 1946(?)-1988 Obituary 125
Gore, John Francis 1885-1983 Obituary 110
Gore, Robert Hayes 1886-1972 Obituary 89-92
Gore, William Jay 1924- 9-12R
Goreau, Angeline 1951- 102
Gore-Booth, Paul Henry
1909-1984 Obituary 113
Gorecki, Jan 1926- 57-60
Gorelick, Bryna Siegel
See Siegel-Gorelick, Bryna
Gorelick, Molly C. 1920- 21-24R
See also SATA 9
Gorelik, Mordecai 1899-1990 ....CAP-2
Obituary 131
Earlier sketch in CA 23-24
Goren, Arthur A(ryeh) 1926- 127
Brief entry 111
Goren, Charles H(enry)
See Vadakin, James C(harles)
Goren, Charles H(enry) 1901- 69-72
Goren, Judith 1933- 61-64
Goren, Roberta C. 1943-1983 135
Gorenko, Anna Andreevna
See Akhmatova, Anna
Gorenstein, Paul 1934- 114
Gorenstein, Shirley 1928- 73-76
Gorer, Geoffrey (Edgar) 1905-1985 69-72
Obituary 116
Gores, Joe
See Gores, Joseph N(icholas)
Gores, Joseph N(icholas) 1931- CANR-28
Earlier sketches in CA 25-28R, CANR-10
Gorey, Edward (St. John) 1925- CANR-30
Earlier sketches in CA 5-8R, CANR-9
See also DLB 61
See also MAICYA
See also SATA 27, 29, 70
Gorey, Hays 57-60
Gorham, Charles Orson 1911-1975 ....CANR-6
Obituary 61-64
Earlier sketch in CA 1-4R
See also SATA 36
Gorham, J(eanne) U(rich) 1920- 53-56
Gorham, Maurice Anthony Coneys 1902- 9-12R
Gorham, Michael
See Folsom, Franklin (Brewster)
Gorkin, Jess 1913-1985 Obituary 115
Gorky, Maxim
See Peshkov, Alexei Maximovich
See also TCLC 8
See also WLC
Gorling, Lars
See Goerling, Lars
Gorman, Beth
See Paine, Lauran (Bosworth)
Gorman, Burton W(illiam) 1907- 29-32R
Gorman, Edward 1941- 138
Gorman, George H. 1916-1982 Obituary 106
Gorman, Ginny
See Zachary, Hugh
Gorman, John Andrew 1938- 41-44R
Gorman, Katherine CAP-2
Earlier sketch in CA 29-32
Gorman, Ralph 1897-1972 Obituary 37-40R
Gorman, T. Walter
1916(?)-1972 Obituary 37-40R
Gorman, Thomas David 1919-1986 123
Obituary 120
Gorman, Tom
See Gorman, Thomas David
Gormley, Beatrice 1942- 113
See also SATA 35, 39
Gormley, Gerard (Joseph) 1931- CANR-14
Earlier sketch in CA 81-84
Gormley, Mike 1945- 69-72
Gorn, Janice L(eonora) 1915- 53-56
Gorn, Mordechai Martin
1890-1986 Obituary 119
Gorney, Roderic 1924- 73-76
Gorney, Sondra 1918- 45-48
Gorni, Yosef
See Gorny, Yosef
Gornick, Vivian 1935- 101
Gorny, Joseph
See Gorny, Yosef
Gorny, Yosef 1933- 130
Goro, Fritz 1901-1986 Obituary 121
Gorodetsky, Gabriel 1945- 69-72
Gorog, Judith (Allen) 1938- 114
See also SATA 39
Gorostiza, Celestino ....HW
Gorostiza, Jose 1901-1973 131
See also HW
Gorrell, Robert Mark 1914- CANR-5
Earlier sketch in CA 1-4R
Gorsline, Douglas (Warner) 1913-1985 ....CANR-9
Obituary 116
Earlier sketch in CA 61-64
See also SATA 11, 43
Gorsline, (Sally) Marie 1928- 106
See also SATA 28
Gorsline, S. M.
See Gorsline, (Sally) Marie
Gorst, Elliot Marcet 1885-1973 Obituary 104
Gortner, Ross A(iken) Jr. 1912- 5-8R
Gortner, Willis Alway 1913- 108
Gorton, Kaitlyn
See Emerson, Kathy Lynn
Gorton, Richard A. 1932- CANR-7
Earlier sketch in CA 57-60
Goryan, Sirak
See Saroyan, William
Goscilo, Helena 1945- 118
Goscinny, Rene 1926-1977 117
Obituary 113
See also SATA 39, 47
Gosden, Freeman F(isher)
1899-1982 Obituary 108
Gosden, Peter Henry John Heather
1927- 93-96
Gosdin, Rex 1938(?)-1983 Obituary 109
Gose, Elliott B(ickley) Jr. 1926- 33-36R

Goshay, Robert C. 1931- 13-16R
Goshen, Charles E(rnest) 1916- CANR-13
Earlier sketch in CA 21-24R
Goshen-Gottstein, Esther 1928- 137
Goshgarian, Gary 1942- 112
Goshorn, Elizabeth 1953- 61-64
Goslin, David A. 1936- 9-12R
Gosling, J(ustin) C(yril) B(ertrand) 1930- 77-80
Gosling, John Neville 1905- 5-8R
Gosling, Nigel 1909-1982 129
Obituary 106
Gosling, Paula 1939- CANR-30
Earlier sketch in CA 111
Gosling, William Flower 1901- 5-8R
Goslovich, Marianne
See Brown, Morris Cecil
Gosnell, Betty
See Gosnell, Elizabeth Duke Tucker
Gosnell, Elizabeth Duke Tucker 1921- 29-32R
Gosnell, Harold F(oote) 1896- 41-44R
Goss, Clay 1946- 57-60
Gosse, Edmund (William)
1849-1928 Brief entry 117
See also DLB 57
See also TCLC 28
Gosselin, Chris(topher C.) 1929- 110
Gosselin, Peter G. 1951- 133
Gosset, W(illiam) P(atrick) 1946- 126
Gossett, Philip 1941- CANR-15
Earlier sketch in CA 89-92
Gossett, Thomas F. 1916- 13-16R
Gossman, Lionel 1929- CANR-7
Earlier sketch in CA 17-20R
Gossop, Michael 1948- 127
Gostelow, Mary 1943- CANR-8
Earlier sketch in CA 61-64
Goswami, Amit 1936- 129
Goswami, Maggie 1937- 117
Gotchi, Iris 1933- 132
Gotesky, Rubin 1906- 45-48
Gotfryd, Bernard 1924- 133
Gotfurt, Frederick 1902(?)-1973 Obituary 104
Gotlieb, Phyllis Fay (Bloom) 1926- CANR-7
Earlier sketch in CA 13-16R
See also CLC 18
See also DLB 88
Gotlieb, Sondra 1936- Brief entry 111
Gotoff, Harold C(harles) 1936- Brief entry 112
Gots, Ronald E(ric) 1943- 65-68
Gotshalk, D(ilman) W(alter) 1901-1973 ....CANR-6
Earlier sketch in CA 1-4R
Gott, K(enneth) D(avidson) 1923- 81-84
Gott, Richard (Willoughby) 1938- 81-84
Gottehrer, Barry H. 1935- 13-16R
Gotterer, Malcolm H(arold) 1924- 37-40R
Gottesfeld, Evelyn 1948- 104
Gottesfeld, Mary L. 1926(?)-1984 Obituary 113
Gottesman, Irving I(sadore) 1930- 37-40R
Gottesman, Ronald 1933- CANR-13
Earlier sketch in CA 33-36R
Gottesman, S. D.
See Kornbluth, C(yril) M.
and Lowndes, Robert A(ugustine) W(ard)
and Pohl, Frederik
Gottfried, Alex 1919- 1-4R
Gottfried, Manfred 1900-1985 Obituary 117
Gottfried, Martin 1933- CANR-14
Earlier sketch in CA 21-24R
Gottfried, Robert Steven 1949- 111
Gottfried, Theodore Mark 1928- CANR-18
Earlier sketch in CA 33-36R
Gottlieb, Adolph 1903-1974 Obituary 49-52
Gottlieb, Alan M(erril) 1947- 125
Gottlieb, Alex 1906-1988 Obituary 126
Gottlieb, Alma 1954- 138
Gottlieb, Annie 1946- 135
Gottlieb, Arthur 1929- 137
Gottlieb, Beatrice M.
1889(?)-1979 Obituary 89-92
Gottlieb, Bernhardt Stanley 1898- 1-4R
Gottlieb, Carla 1912- 119
Gottlieb, Darcy 1922- 77-80
Gottlieb, Elaine 61-64
Gottlieb, Freema (Peninah) 1946- 137
Gottlieb, Gerald 1923- 5-8R
See also SATA 7
Gottlieb, Gilbert 1929- 138
Gottlieb, Lois Davidson 1926- 17-28R
Gottlieb, Moshe R(aphael) 1931- 113
Gottlieb, Naomi R(uth) 1925- 57-60
Gottlieb, Paul 1936- 93-96
Gottlieb, Robert A(dams) 1931- 129
Brief entry 125
Gottlieb, Robin (Grossman) 1928- CANR-2
Earlier sketch in CA 1-4R
Gottlieb, Stephen E. 1941- 138
Gottlieb, (Anne Ruth) Vera 1945- 117
Gottlieb, William P(aul) 1917- 101
See also SATA 24
Gottman, John M(ordechai) 1942- CANR-12
Earlier sketch in CA 69-72
Gottschalk, Elin Toona
See Toona, Elin(-Kai)
Gottschalk, Laura Riding
See Jackson, Laura (Riding)
Gottschalk, Louis A(ugust) 1916- CANR-19
Earlier sketches in CA 53-56, CANR-5
Gottschalk, Louis (Reichenthal)
1899-1975 ....CANR-9
Obituary 57-60
Earlier sketch in CA 13-16R
Gottschalk, Paul A. 1939- 61-64
Gottschalk, Shimon S. 1929- 89-92
Gottschalk, Stephen 1940- 77-80
Gottschall, Edward M(aurice) 1915- 133
Gottsched, Johann Christoph
1700-1766 ....DLB 97
Gottsegen, Abby J. 1956- 105
Gottsegen, Gloria Behar 1930- 77-80
Gottshall, Franklin Henry 1902- CANR-2
Earlier sketch in CA 5-8R
Gottstein, Esther Goshen
See Goshen-Gottstein, Esther
Gottwald, Norman Karol 1926- 108
Gotwals, Vernon (Detwiler Jr.) 1924- 5-8R
Gotz, Ignacio L.
See Goetz, Ignacio L.
Gotzsche, Anne-Lise 1939- 97-100
Goubert, Pierre 1915- 136
Goud, Anne 1917- 61-64
Goudeket, Maurice 1889-1977 Obituary 69-72
Goudey, Alice E. 1898- 73-76
See also SATA 20
Goudge, Eileen 1950- 126
See also AAYA 6
Goudge, Elizabeth (de Beauchamp)
1900-1984 ....CANR-5
Obituary 112
Earlier sketch in CA 5-8R
See also MAICYA
See also SATA 2, 38
Goudie, Andrew Shaw 1945- CANR-38
Earlier sketches in CA 49-52, CANR-1, 17
Goudinoff, Peter Alexis 1941- 112
Goudiss, Maria Agnes D'Elia 1941- 114
Goudsmit, Samuel A(braham)
1902-1978 Obituary 81-84
Gouge, Orson
See Larner, Jeremy
Gougeon, Len (G.) 1947- 135
Gough, Barry Morton 1938- CANR-30
Earlier sketches in CA 61-64, CANR-11
Gough, Bill
See Gough, William (John)
Gough, Catherine
See Mulgan, Catherine
See also SATA 24
Gough, John W(iedhofft) 1900- 13-16R
Gough, Kathleen
See Aberle, Kathleen Gough
Gough, Philip 1908- ....SATA 45
Gough, Vera 25-28R
Gough, William (John) 1945- 131
Gougov, Nikola Delchev 1914- CANR-37
Earlier sketch in CA 45-48
Goulart, Frances Sheridan 1938- CANR-25
Earlier sketches in CA 57-60, CANR-7
Goulart, Ron(ald Joseph) 1933- CANR-7
Earlier sketch in CA 25-28R
See also SATA 6
Goulbourne, Harry 1948- 137
Gould, Alan
See Canning, Victor
Gould, Alfred Ernest 1909- 5-8R
Gould, Allan (Mendel) 1944- 132
Gould, Beatrice Blackmar 1898-1989 .... CAP-2
Obituary 127
Earlier sketch in CA 25-28
Gould, (Charles) Bruce 1898-1989 Obituary 129
Gould, Bruce Grant 1942- CANR-22
Earlier sketch in CA 45-48
Gould, Bryan 1939- 136
Gould, Carol C. 1946- 103
Gould, Cecil (Hilton Monk) 1918- CANR-9
Earlier sketch in CA 21-24R
Gould, Chester 1900-1985 ....CANR-30
Obituary 116
Earlier sketch in CA 77-80
See also AAYA 7
See also SATA 43, 49
Gould, Douglas Parsons 1919- 1-4R
Gould, Ed(win Orrin) 1936- CANR-16
Earlier sketch in CA 93-96
Gould, Felix CAP-1
Earlier sketch in CA 11-12
Gould, James A(dams) 1922- 33-36R
Gould, James L. 1945- 130
Gould, James Warren 1924- CANR-2
Earlier sketch in CA 5-8R
Gould, Jay R(eid) 1906- CANR-24
Earlier sketch in CA 45-48
Gould, Jean R(osalind) 1919- CANR-21
Earlier sketches in CA 5-8R, CANR-3
See also SATA 11
Gould, Joan 1927- 107
Gould, John A(llen) 1944- 57-60
Gould, John (Thomas) 1908- 65-68
Gould, Joseph E(dmund) 1912- 9-12R
Gould, Josiah B(ancroft) 1928- 45-48
Gould, Joy
See Boyum, Joy Gould
Gould, Judith
See Bienes, Nicholas Peter
Gould, Leroy C. 1937- 93-96
Gould, Leslie 1902-1977 Obituary 73-76
Gould, Lettie
See Paxson, Ethel
Gould, Lewis L(udlow) 1939- 41-44R
Gould, Lilian CANR-2
Earlier sketch in CA 49-52
See also SATA 6
Gould, Lois CANR-29
Earlier sketch in CA 77-80
See also CLC 4, 10
See also MTCW
Gould, Marilyn 1928- ....SATA 15
Gould, Mary Earle 1885- 5-8R
Gould, Maurice M. 1909- CANR-5
Earlier sketch in CA 5-8R
Gould, Milton Samuel 1909- 93-96
Gould, Peter R(obin) 1932- CANR-27
Earlier sketch in CA 1-4R
Gould, Philip 1925- 124
Gould, Randall 1898(?)-1979 Obituary 89-92
Gould, Richard A(llan) 1939- CANR-7
Earlier sketch in CA 53-56
Gould, Roger L(ouis) 1935- Brief entry 110
Gould, Ronald 1904- 102
Gould, Shirley (Goldman) 81-84
Gould, Stephen Jay 1941- CANR-27
Earlier sketches in CA 77-80, CANR-10
See also BEST 90:2
See also MTCW
Gould, Wallace 1882-1940 ....DLB 54
Gould, Warwick 1947- 110
Gould, Wesley Larson 1917- CANR-2
Earlier sketch in CA 1-4R
Gould, William B(enjamin IV) 1936- 132
Brief entry 118
Goulden, Joseph C. (Jr.) 1934- CANR-31
Earlier sketches in CA 17-20R, CANR-8
Goulden, Mark 1896(?)-1980 Obituary 101
Goulder, Grace
See Izant, Grace Goulder
Goulding, Brian 1933- 103
Goulding, Dorothy Jane 1923- 65-68
Goulding, Peter Geoffrey 1920- 106
Goulding, Ray(mond Walter)
1922-1990 ....CANR-36
Obituary 131
Earlier sketch in CA 85-88
Gouldner, Alvin W(ard) 1920-1980 ....CANR-17
Obituary 102
Earlier sketch in CA 13-16R
See also MTCW
Gouled, Vivian G(loria) 1911- 41-44R
Goulet, Denis A. 1931- CANR-15
Earlier sketch in CA 41-44R
Goulet, John 1942- 85-88
Goulet, Robert (Joseph) 1924- 1-4R
Goulet, Rosalina Morales 1930- 119
Goulett, Harlan M(ador) 1927-1969 .... CAP-2
Earlier sketch in CA 21-22
Goulianos, Joan Rodman 1939- 49-52
Gouliashki, (Stoianov) Andrei 1914- CANR-19
Earlier sketch in CA 101
Goullart, Peter 1902- CAP-1
Earlier sketch in CA 13-14
Goulson, Carlyn Floyd 1922- 113
Goulson, Cary F.
See Goulson, Carlyn Floyd
Gourdie, Thomas 1913- CANR-1
Earlier sketch in CA 1-4R
Gourevitch, Doris-Jeanne 17-20R
Gourevitch, Peter A(lexis) 1943- 112
Gourhan, Andre (Georges Leandre) Leroi
See Leroi-Gourhan, Andre (Georges Leandre)
Gouri, Haim 1923- 103
Gourlay, Elizabeth 1917- CANR-30
Earlier sketch in CA 112
Gourley, G(erald) Douglas 1911- 1-4R
Gourley, Jay 1947- 73-76
Gourlie, Norah Dundas CAP-1
Earlier sketch in CA 9-10
Gourmont, Remy de 1858-1915 Brief entry 109
See also TCLC 17
Gourse, Leslie 1939- 1-4R
Gourvish, T(erry) R. 1943- 125
Gouzenko, Igor 1919-1982 Obituary 107
Govan, Christine Noble 1898- CANR-2
Earlier sketch in CA 1-4R
See also SATA 9
Govan, Thomas P(ayne) 1907-1979 ....CANR-2
Earlier sketch in CA 45-48
Gove, Philip Babcock 1902-1972 ....CAP-1
Obituary 37-40R
Earlier sketch in CA 13-14
Gove, Samuel K(imball) 1923- 33-36R
Gove, Walter R(oberts) 1938- 118
Goveia, Elsa V(esta) 1925- 21-24R
Govenar, Alan B(ruce) 1952- 109
Gover, (John) Robert 1929- 9-12R
Govern, Elaine 1939- 53-56
See also SATA 26
Govier, Katherine 1948- CANR-18
Earlier sketch in CA 101
See also CLC 51
Govinda, Anagarika Brahmacari
1898- CANR-14
Earlier sketch in CA 21-24R
Govinda, Lama Anagarika Brahmacari
See Govinda, Anagarika Brahmacari
Govoni, Albert P(eter) 1914-1982 53-56
Obituary 108
Govoni, Corrado 1884-1965 ....DLB 114
Govoni, Laura E. 1914- 33-36R
Govorchin, Gerald Gilbert 1912- 13-16R
Gow, Donald 1920- 41-44R
Gow, Ronald 1897- CANR-13
Earlier sketches in CAP-2, CA 25-28
Gowan, Donald E(lmer) 1929- 69-72
Gowan, John Curtis 1912-1986 ....CANR-5
Obituary 121
Earlier sketch in CA 13-16R
Gowans, Alan 1923- CANR-18
Earlier sketches in CA 1-4R, CANR-2
Gowar, Antonia
See Dunford, Judith
and Margolis, Susanna
Gowar, Michael Robert 1951- 127
Gowar, Mick
See Gowar, Michael Robert
Gowen, (Samuel) Emmett 1902- CAP-1
Earlier sketch in CA 11-12
Gowen, James A(nthony) 1928-1981 ....17-20R
Obituary 134
Gower, Herschel 1919- 5-8R
Gowers, Ernest (Arthur)
1880-1966 Obituary 89-92
Gowin, D(ixie) Bob 1925- CANR-26
Earlier sketch in CA 108
Gowing, Lawrence (Burnett) 1918-1991 ......9-12R
Obituary 133
Gowing, Margaret (Margaret Mary) 1921- 81-84
Gowing, Peter Gordon 1930- 53-56
Gowland, Mariano E(zequiel) 1933- 5-8R
Goy, Richard J(ohn) 1947- 118
Goyder, George Armin 1908- 105
Goyen, (Charles) William 1915-1983 ....CANR-6
Obituary 110
Earlier sketch in CA 5-8R
See also AITN 2
See also CLC 5, 8, 14, 40
See also DLB 2
See also DLBY 83
Goyeneche, Gabriel
See Avalle-Arce, Juan Bautista de
Goyer, Robert S(tanton) 1923- CANR-16
Earlier sketch in CA 41-44R
Goytisolo, Juan 1931- CANR-32
Earlier sketch in CA 85-88
See also CLC 5, 10, 23
See also HW
See also MTCW
Gozzano, Guido 1883-1916 ....DLB 114
Gozzi, Raymond D(ante) 1920- 116
Graaf, Peter
See Youd, (Christopher) Samuel
Grabar, Andre 1896- 111
Grabar, Oleg 1929- 124
Grabbe, Crockett L(ane) 1951- 138
Grabbe, Paul 1902- 93-96
Graber, Alexander 1914- CANR-1
Earlier sketch in CA 1-4R
See also SATA 7
Graber, Doris A. 1923- CANR-13
Earlier sketch in CA 33-36R
Graber, Gerry S(amuel) 1928- 81-84
Graber, Richard (Fredrick) 1927- 85-88
See also SATA 26
Grabes, Herbert 1936- 130
Grabianski, Janusz 1928-1976 ....CANR-2
Earlier sketch in CA 45-48
See also SATA 30, 39
Grabill, Joseph L. 1931- 29-32R
Grabner-Haider, Anton 1940- 73-76
Grabo, Norman Stanley 1930- 1-4R
Graboff, Abner 1919- 107
See also SATA 35
Grabois, Aryeh 1930- 105
Grabosky, Peter Nils 1945- 85-88
Grabow, Stephen (Harris) 1943- 121
Grabowski, Z(bigniew) Anthony 1903- 5-8R
Graburn, Nelson H(ayes) H(enry)
1936- CANR-1
Earlier sketch in CA 45-48
Gracchus, Sidney J(oseph) 1930- 97-100
Grace, Deborah
See Winer, Deborah Grace
Grace, Edward
See de Grazia, Edward
Grace, F(rances Jane) 111
See also SATA 45
Grace, Gerald R(upert) 1936- CANR-22
Earlier sketch in CA 45-48
Grace, Helen K(ennedy) 1935- 53-56
Grace, J. Peter 1913- 126
Grace, Joan C(arroll) 1921- 61-64
Grace, John Patrick 1942- CANR-31
Earlier sketch in CA 112
Grace, Joseph
See Hornby, John (Wilkinson)
Grace, Patricia 1937- ....CLC 56
Grace, Sherrill E(lizabeth) 1944- 110
Grace, William J(oseph) Jr. 1948- CANR-38
Earlier sketch in CA 111
Grace, William Joseph 1910- CAP-1
Earlier sketch in CA 13-14
Gracey, Harry L(ewis) 1933- 41-44R
Gracia, Jorge J(esus) E(miliano)
1942- CANR-30
Earlier sketch in CA 109
See also HW
Gracie, Archibald 1859-1912 Brief entry 122
Gracq, Julien
See Poirier, Louis
See also CLC 11, 48
See also DLB 83
Gracy, David B(ergen) II 1941- CANR-16
Earlier sketch in CA 25-28R
Gracza, Margaret Young 1928- 13-16R
See also SATA 56
Grad, Bonnie L(ee) 1949- 117
Grad, Eli 1928- 115
Grad, Frank P. 1924- 33-36R
Grade, Arnold (Edward) 1928- 29-32R
Grade, Chaim 1910-1982 93-96
Obituary 107
See also CLC 10
Gradidge, Roderick 1929- 117
Gradon, Pamela O(live) E(lizabeth)
1915- 97-100
Graduate of Oxford, A
See Ruskin, John
Gradwohl, David M(ayer) 1934- 125
Grady, Don(ald Wyndham) 1929- 115
Grady, Henry W. 1850-1889 ....DLB 23
Grady, James (Thomas) 1949- CANR-22
Earlier sketch in CA 104
Grady, Ronan Calistus Jr. 1921- 49-52
Grady, Tex
See Webb, Jack (Randolph)
Grae, Ida 1918- 97-100
Graeber, Charlotte Towner 134
See also SATA 44, 56
Graebner, Alan 1938- 61-64
Graebner, Norman A. 1915- CANR-24
Earlier sketches in CA 13-16R, CANR-7

Graebner, Walter 1909- ... CAP-1
Earlier sketch in CA 13-16
Graebner, William Sievers 1943- ... 104
Graedon, Joe (David) 1945- ... 77-80
Graedon, Teresa 1947- ... 127
Graef, Hilda C(harlotte) 1907- ... 5-8R
Graeff, Grace M. 1918- ... 21-24R
Graeme, Bruce
See Jeffries, Graham Montague
Graeme, David
See Jeffries, Graham Montague
Graeme, Roderic
See Jeffries, Roderic (Graeme)
Graeme, Sheila 1944- ... 25-28R
Graf, Le Roy Philip 1915- ... 41-44R
Graf, Oskar Maria 1894-1967 Obituary ... 115
See also DLB 56
Graf, Rudolf F. 1926- ... 9-12R
Grafe, Felix
See Greve, Felix Paul (Berthold Friedrich)
Graff, George 1886-1973 Obituary ... 41-44R
Graff, Gerald (Edward) 1937- ... CANR-31
Earlier sketch in CA 29-32R
Graff, Harvey J. 1949- ... 127
Graff, Henry F(ranklin) 1921- ... CANR-17
Earlier sketches in CA 1-4R, CANR-1
Graff, Polly Anne Colver
See Colver, Anne
Graff, (S.) Stewart 1908- ... CANR-29
Earlier sketch in CA 49-52
See also SATA 9
Grafftey, Heward 1928- ... 127
Grafftey-Smith, Laurence Barton
1892-1989 Obituary ... 128
Grafton, Ann
See Owens, Thelma
Grafton, Carl 1942- ... 53-56
Grafton, David 1930- ... 126
Grafton, Sue 1940- ... CANR-31
Earlier sketch in CA 108
See also BEST 90:3
Gragg, Rod 1950- ... 134
Graglia, Lino A(nthony) 1930- ... 69-72
Graham, A(lexander) John 1930- ... CANR-8
Earlier sketch in CA 13-16R
Graham, A(lexander) S(teel) 1917- ... 104
Graham, Ada 1931- ... CANR-4
Earlier sketch in CA 29-32R
See also SATA 11
Graham, Aelred 1907-1984 ... CANR-5
Obituary ... 114
Earlier sketch in CA 5-8R
Graham, Alice Walworth 1905- ... CANR-5
Earlier sketch in CA 1-4R
Graham, Alistair (Dundas) 1938- ... 49-52
Graham, Andrew Guillemard
1913-1981 Obituary ... 103
Graham, Angus (Charles) 1919-1991 ... 17-20R
Obituary ... 134
Graham, Billy
See Graham, William Franklin
Graham, Bob 1942- ... SATA 63
Graham, Brenda Knight 1942- ... 103
See also SATA 32
Graham, Carlotta
See Wallmann, Jeffrey M(iner)
Graham, Caroline 1931- ... 119
Graham, Charles S.
See Tubb, E(dwin) C(harles)
Graham, Charlotte
See Bowden, Joan Chase
Graham, Clarence H.
1906-1971 Obituary ... 33-36R
Graham, Cosmo 1956- ... 138
Graham, Daniel O(rrin) 1925- ... 132
Graham, David (Duane) 1927- ... 69-72
Graham, Desmond 1940- ... 73-76
Graham, Don(ald R.) 1947- ... 133
Graham, Don B. 1940- ... CANR-39
Earlier sketches in CA 102, CANR-18
Graham, Donald W(ilkinson) 1903- ... CAP-2
Earlier sketch in CA 29-32
Graham, Eleanor 1896-1984 ... 73-76
Obituary ... 112
See also SATA 18, 38
Graham, Elizabeth
See Edmonds, Arthur Denis
Graham, Frank Jr. 1925- ... CANR-4
Earlier sketch in CA 9-12R
See also SATA 11
Graham, Fred P(atterson) 1931- ... 37-40R
Graham, Gene S(wann) 1924- ... 41-44R
Graham, George J(ackson) Jr. 1938- ... 45-48
Graham, George Rex 1813-1894 ... DLB 73
Graham, Gerald (Sandford) 1903-1988 ... 102
Obituary ... 126
Graham, Grace 1910- ... CAP-1
Earlier sketch in CA 13-14
Graham, Gwethalyn 1913-1965 ... DLB 88
Graham, Harriet 1935- ... 127
Graham, Harry Edward 1940- ... 29-32R
Graham, Henry 1930- ... 103
Graham, Howard Jay 1905- ... CAP-2
Earlier sketch in CA 33-36
Graham, Hugh
See Barrows, (Ruth) Marjorie
Graham, Hugh Davis 1936- ... CANR-13
Earlier sketch in CA 21-24R
Graham, Ian (James Alastair) 1923- ... CANR-2
Earlier sketch in CA 45-48
Graham, Ilse 1914-1988 ... CANR-8
Obituary ... 127
Earlier sketch in CA 57-60
Graham, J. W. 1925- ... 93-96
Graham, J(ames) Walter 1906- ... 1-4R
Graham, James
See Patterson, Harry
Graham, John
See Phillips, David Graham
Graham, John Alexander 1941- ... 25-28R
Graham, John Remington 1940- ... 33-36R
Graham, John Thomas 1928- ... 53-56
Graham, John 1926- ... 33-36R
See also SATA 11
Graham, Jorie 1951- ... 111
See also CLC 48
See also DLB 120
Graham, Jory 1925-1983 ... CANR-13
Obituary ... 109
Earlier sketch in CA 29-32R
Graham, Joseph M. 1911(?)-1971 Obituary ... 104
Graham, Katharine (Meyer) 1917- ... 105
See also AITN 1
Graham, (George) Kenneth 1936- ... 77-80
Graham, Kennon
See Harrison, David L(ee)
Graham, Larry
See Graham, Lawrence (Otis)
Graham, Lawrence (Otis) 1962- ... 116
See also SATA 63
Graham, Lawrence S(herman) 1936- ... 45-48
Graham, Lee E. 1913(?)-1977 Obituary ... 73-76
Graham, Lloyd M. 1889- ... 97-100
Graham, Loren R. 1933- ... CANR-13
Earlier sketch in CA 21-24R
Graham, Lorenz (Bell) 1902-1989 ... CANR-25
Obituary ... 129
Earlier sketch in CA 9-12R
See also BW
See also CLR 10
See also DLB 76
See also MAICYA
See also SAAS 5
See also SATA 2, 63
Graham, Malcolm 1923- ... 53-56
Graham, Margaret Althea 1924- ... 9-12R
Graham, Margaret Bloy 1920- ... 77-80
See also SATA 11
Graham, Martha 1894-1991 ... 129
Obituary ... 134
Graham, Matthew
See Arnold, Peter
Graham, Michael Angelo
1921-1985 Obituary ... 117
Graham, Michael 1898-1972 Obituary ... 104
Graham, Milton D(uke) 1916- ... 45-48
Graham, Neile 1958- ... 113
Graham, Neill
See Duncan, W(illiam) Murdoch
Graham, (Roger) Neill 1941- ... CANR-26
Earlier sketch in CA 109
Graham, Otis L. Jr. 1935- ... CANR-11
Earlier sketch in CA 21-24R
Graham, Patricia Albjerg 1935- ... 25-28R
Graham, Peter W(illiam) 1951- ... 121
Graham, Philip Leslie
1915-1963 Obituary ... 89-92
Graham, R(obert) B(ontine) Cunninghame
See Cunninghame Graham, R(obert) B(ontine)
See also DLB 98
Graham, Rachel (Metcalf) 1895- ... CAP-1
Earlier sketch in CA 13-16
Graham, Ramona
See Cook, Ramona Graham
Graham, Richard 1934- ... CANR-34
Earlier sketches in CA 29-32R, CANR-15
Graham, Robert
See Haldeman, Joe (William)
Graham, Robert G. 1925- ... CANR-12
Earlier sketch in CA 25-28R
Graham, Robin Lee 1949- ... 49-52
See also SATA 7
Graham, Ron 1948- ... 133
Graham, Ruth
See Evans, Jean
Graham, Sean 1920- ... 21-24R
Graham, Sheilah 1904(?)-1988 ... 108
Obituary ... 127
See also AITN 1
Graham, Shirley
See Du Bois, Shirley Graham
See also DLB 76
Graham, Sonia
See Sinclair, Sonia
Graham, Stephen 1884-1975 Obituary ... 93-96
Graham, (Maude Fitzgerald) Susan
1912- ... 17-20R
Graham, Thomas F(rancis) 1923- ... 21-24R
Graham, Tom
See Lewis, (Harry) Sinclair
Graham, Vanessa
See Fraser, Anthea
Graham, Victor E(rnest) 1920- ... 93-96
Graham, Virginia
See Guttenberg, Virginia
Graham, W(illiam) Fred 1930- ... 33-36R
Graham, W(illiam) S(ydney) 1918-1986 ... 73-76
Obituary ... 118
See also CLC 29
See also DLB 20
Graham, William Franklin 1918- ... CANR-20
Earlier sketch in CA 9-12R
Graham, Winston (Mawdsley) 1910- ... CANR-22
Earlier sketches in CA 49-52, CANR-2
See also CLC 23
See also DLB 77
Graham-Barber, Lynda 1944- ... 113
See also SATA 42
Graham-Cameron, M.
See Graham-Cameron, M(alcolm) G(ordon)
Graham-Cameron, M(alcolm) G(ordon)
1931- ... 123
See also SATA 45, 53
Graham-Cameron, Mike
See Graham-Cameron, M(alcolm) G(ordon)
Graham-Campbell, David (John) 1912- ... 113
Grahame, Kenneth 1859-1932 ... 136
Brief entry ... 108
See also CLR 5
See also DLB 34
See also MAICYA
See also YABC 1
Graham Scott, Peter 1923- ... 108
Graham-White, Anthony 1940- ... 61-64
Graham-Yooll, Andrew M(ichael)
1944- ... CANR-28
Earlier sketch in CA 108
Grahn, Judith L. 1940- ... 122
Brief entry ... 116
Grahn, Judy
See Grahn, Judith L.
Grainger, A(nthony) J(ohn) 1929- ... 33-36R
Grainger, J(ohn) H(erbert) 1917- ... 77-80
Grainger, Margaret 1936- ... 116
Grainger, Martin Allerdale 1874-1941 ... DLB 92
Gralapp, Leland Wilson 1921- ... 13-16R
Gram, Harold A(lbert) 1927- ... 25-28R
Gram, Moltke (Stefanus) 1938- ... CANR-13
Earlier sketch in CA 69-72
Gramatky, Hardie 1907-1979 ... CANR-3
Obituary ... 85-88
Earlier sketch in CA 1-4R
See also AITN 1
See also CLR 22
See also DLB 22
See also MAICYA
See also SATA 1, 23, 30
Grambling, Lois G. 1927- ... SATA 71
Grambs, Jean D(resden) 1919-1989 ... CANR-7
Obituary ... 129
Earlier sketch in CA 17-20R
Gramet, Charles ... 1-4R
Gramick, Jeannine 1942- ... 113
Grammaticus
See Blaiklock, Edward Musgrave
Grammer, June Amos 1927- ... SATA 58
Grampp, William D(yer) 1914- ... 33-36R
Grams, Armin 1924- ... 45-48
Granados, Paul
See Kent, Arthur William Charles
Granat, Robert 1925- ... CANR-2
Earlier sketch in CA 1-4R
Granatstein, J(ack) L(awrence) 1939- ... CANR-10
Earlier sketch in CA 25-28R
Granbeck, Marilyn
See Henderson, M(arilyn) R(uth)
Granberg, W(ilbur) J(ohn) 1906- ... 5-8R
Granberry, Edwin 1897- ... CAP-2
Earlier sketch in CA 21-22
Granby, Milton
See Wallmann, Jeffrey M(iner)
Grand, Samuel 1912- ... 107
See also SATA 42
Granda, Chabuca
See Larco, Isabel Granda
Grandbois, Alain 1900-1975 ... DLB 92
Grande, Luke M. 1922- ... CANR-2
Earlier sketch in CA 5-8R
Grande Vitesse
See Walkerley, Rodney Lewis (de Burgh)
Grandfield, Raymond J(oseph) 1931- ... 53-56
Grandower, Elissa
See Waugh, Hillary Baldwin
Grandville, J. J.
See Gerard, Jean Ignace Isidore
Grandville, Jean Ignace Isidore Gerard
See Gerard, Jean Ignace Isidore
Grandy, Richard (Edward) 1942- ... 77-80
Granfield, Linda 1950- ... 128
Grange, Chris
See Gnaegy, Charles
Grange, Cyril 1900- ... CAP-1
Earlier sketch in CA 13-16
Grange, Peter
See Nicole, Christopher Robin
Granger, Bill 1941- ... 131
Brief entry ... 127
Granger, Bruce Ingham 1920- ... 1-4R
Granger, Byrd Howell 1912- ... 107
Granger, Clive W(illiam) J(ohn) 1934- ... CANR-8
Earlier sketch in CA 9-12R
Granger, Darius John
See Marlowe, Stephen
Granger, Margaret Jane
1925(?)-1977 Obituary ... 104
See also SATA 27
Granger, Peggy
See Granger, Margaret Jane
Granger, Percy 1945- ... 136
Granich, Irving 1894-1967 ... 97-100
Obituary ... 45-48
See also Gold, Michael
Granick, David 1926- ... 1-4R
Granick, Harry 1898- ... 85-88
Granik, (S.) Theodore
1906-1970 Obituary ... 89-92
Granit, Arthur 1917- ... 120
Granite, Harvey R. 1927- ... CANR-15
Earlier sketch in CA 33-36R
Granite, Tony
See Politella, Dario
Grannis, Chandler B(rinkerhoff)
1912- Brief entry ... 111
Granovetter, Mark S. 1943- ... 85-88
Granovsky, Anatoli 1922-1974 Obituary ... 53-56
Granowsky, Alvin 1936- ... 21-24R
Gransden, Antonia 1928- ... CANR-30
Earlier sketch in CA 77-80
Granstaff, Bill 1925- ... SATA 10
Grant, Alan
See Kennington, (Gilbert) Alan
Grant, Alexander T(homas) K(ingdom)
1906- ... 53-56
Grant, Ambrose
See Raymond, Rene (Brabazon)
Grant, Anthony
See Pares, Marion (Stapylton)
Grant, Barbara M(oll) 1932- ... 53-56
Grant, Barry Keith 1947- ... 138
Grant, Ben
See Henderson, M(arilyn) R(uth)
Grant, Brian W. 1939- ... CANR-7
Earlier sketch in CA 57-60
Grant, Bruce Alexander 1925- ... 107
Grant, Bruce 1893-1977 ... CANR-6
Obituary ... 69-72
Earlier sketch in CA 1-4R
See also SATA 5, 25
Grant, C.B.S.
See Haga, Enoch J.
Grant, Charles L. 1942- ... 85-88
Grant, Cynthia D. 1950- ... CANR-20
Earlier sketch in CA 104
See also SATA 33
Grant, David
See Thomas, Craig (David)
Grant, Don
See Glut, Donald F(rank)
Grant, Donald J. 1939-1984 Obituary ... 113
Grant, Dorothy Fremont 1900- ... CAP-2
Earlier sketch in CA 23-24
Grant, Dorothy 1927- ... 114
Grant, Elliott Mansfield 1895-1969 ... CANR-5
Earlier sketch in CA 5-8R
Grant, Ellsworth Strong 1917- ... 57-60
Grant, Eva 1907- ... 49-52
See also SATA 7
Grant, Evva H. 1913-1977 Obituary ... 104
See also SATA 27
Grant, Frederick C(lifton) 1891-1974 ... 1-4R
Obituary ... 49-52
Grant, George Monro 1835-1902 ... DLB 99
Grant, George (Parkin) 1918-1988 Obituary ... 126
See also DLB 88
Grant, Gerald 1938- ... 81-84
Grant, Gordon 1875-1962 ... 102
See also SATA 25
Grant, Gwen(doline Ellen) 1940- ... CANR-22
Earlier sketch in CA 106
See also SATA 47
Grant, H. Roger 1943- ... 89-92
Grant, Harry J(ohnston)
1881-1963 Obituary ... 114
See also DLB 29
Grant, Hilda Kay 1910- ... 1-4R
Grant, Isabel F(rances)
1887-1983 Obituary ... 110
Grant, J(ohn) B(arnard) 1940- ... CANR-28
Earlier sketches in CA 57-60, CANR-6
Grant, Jack
See Grant, J(ohn) B(arnard)
Grant, James
See Crowther, Bruce (Ian)
Grant, James Edward 1905-1966 Obituary ... 113
See also DLB 26
Grant, James G. 1926(?)-1979 Obituary ... 89-92
Grant, James Russell 1924- ... CANR-17
Earlier sketch in CA 101
Grant, Jane
See Leader, (Evelyn) Barbara (Blackburn)
Grant, Jane (Cole) 1895-1972 ... CAP-2
Obituary ... 33-36R
Earlier sketch in CA 25-28
Grant, Joan
See Kelsey, Joan Marshall
Grant, Joanne B(enzel) 1940- ... 106
Grant, John E(rnest) 1925- ... 41-44R
Grant, John J. 1932- ... 53-56
Grant, John Webster 1919- ... CANR-6
Earlier sketch in CA 5-8R
Grant, John 1933- ... 77-80
Grant, Judith 1929- ... 21-24R
Grant, Kay ... 21-24R
Grant, Kerry S. 1945- ... 121
Grant, Landon
See Gribble, Leonard (Reginald)
Grant, (Alice) Leigh 1947- ... SATA 10
Grant, Louis T(heodore) 1943- ... 53-56
Grant, Madeleine Parker 1895- ... 73-76
Grant, Margaret
See Franken, Rose (Dorothy)
Grant, Mary A(melia) 1890- ... CAP-2
Earlier sketch in CA 25-28
Grant, Mary Kathryn 1941- ... 81-84
Grant, Matthew G.
See May, Julian
Grant, Maxwell
See Gibson, Walter B(rown)
and Lynds, Dennis
Grant, Michael 1914- ... CANR-25
Earlier sketches in CA 1-4R, CANR-4
Grant, Myrna (Lois) 1934- ... CANR-4
Earlier sketch in CA 53-56
See also SATA 21
Grant, Neil 1938- ... CANR-34
Earlier sketches in CA 33-36R, CANR-15
See also SATA 14
Grant, Nigel (Duncan Cameron) 1932- ... CANR-7
Earlier sketch in CA 17-20R
Grant, Ozro F. 1908- ... CAP-2
Earlier sketch in CA 21-22
Grant, Patrick 1941- ... 132
Grant, Richard B(abson) 1925- ... CANR-4
Earlier sketch in CA 1-4R
Grant, Robert B(ruce) 1933- ... 45-48
Grant, Robert M(cQueen) 1917- ... 65-68

Grant, Roderick 1941- Brief entry 112
Grant, Skeeter
See Spiegelman, Art
Grant, Ulysses S. III 1881-1968 Obituary 111
Grant, Verne E(dwin) 1917- 53-56
Grant, Vernon W(esley) 1904- 17-20R
Grant, W(illiam) Leonard 1914- 17-20R
Grant, Wilson Wayne 1941- 97-100
Grant, Wyn(ford) 1947- CANR-35
Earlier sketch in CA 114
Grant, Zalin (Belton) 1941- 73-76
Grant-Adamson, Lesley 1942- 121
Grantham, Alexander (William George Herder) 1899- CAP-2
Earlier sketch in CA 19-20
Grantham, Dewey Wesley 1921- CANR-1
Earlier sketch in CA 1-4R
Grantland, Keith
See Beaumont, Charles
Granton, Ester Fannie 1914(?)-1980 Obituary 101
Grant Wallace, Lewis
See Wallace, Lewis Grant
Granville, Joseph E(nsign) 1923- 65-68
Granville, W. Wilfred 1905- CAP-1
Earlier sketch in CA 9-10
Granville-Barker, Harley 1877-1946 Brief entry 104
See also Barker, Harley Granville
See also TCLC 2
Grape, Oliver
See Wood, Christopher (Hovelle)
Grapho
See Oakley, Eric Gilbert
Grass, Guenter (Wilhelm) 1927- CANR-20
Earlier sketch in CA 13-16R
See also CLC 1, 2, 4, 6, 11, 15, 22, 32, 49
See also DLB 75
See also MTCW
See also WLC
Grassi, Joseph A(ugustus) 1922- CANR-19
Earlier sketch in CA 103
Grassi, Maggi Lidchi
See Lidchi Grassi, Maggi
Grasso, Domenico 1917- 73-76
Grasty, Charles H. 1863-1924 ....DLB 25
Grater, Michael 1923- ....SATA 57
Grathwohl, Larry D(avid) 1947- 65-68
Grattan, C(linton) Hartley 1902-1980 ....CANR-1
Obituary 101
Earlier sketch in CA 1-4R
Grattan, Virginia L(ee) 1932- 115
Grattan-Guinness, I. 1941- 73-76
Gratton, Thomas
See Hulme, T(homas) E(rnest)
Gratus, Jack 1935- 93-96
Grau, Joseph A(ugust) 1921- 65-68
Grau, Shirley Ann 1929- CANR-22
Earlier sketch in CA 89-92
See also CLC 4, 9
See also DLB 2
See also MTCW
Graubard, Mark A. 1904- CANR-5
Earlier sketch in CA 1-4R
Graubard, Paul S. 1932- 103
Graubard, Stephen R(ichards) 1924- Brief entry 113
Graubart, David 1907(?)-1984 Obituary 112
Grauer, Ben(jamin Franklin) 1908-1977 Obituary 69-72
Grauer, Neil A(lbert) 1947- 122
Graulich, Melody 1951- 128
Grauman, Lawrence Jr. 1935- 33-36R
Graupe, Daniel 1934- 41-44R
Graupera, Carlos M(anuel) 1915- 49-52
Grava, Sigurd 1934- 77-80
Gravagnuolo, Benedetto 1949- 112
Grave, S(elwyn) A(lfred) 1916- 5-8R
Gravel, Fern
See Hall, James Norman
Gravel, Mike 1930- 41-44R
Gravelle, Karen 1942- 135
Gravely, William B(ernard) 1939- 49-52
Graver, Elizabeth 1964- 135
See also CLC 70
Graver, Jane (Ann) 1931- 117
Graver, Lawrence 1931- 25-28R
Graver, Suzanne 1936- 117
Graversen, Pat 1935- 109
Graves, Allen W(illis) 1915- 17-20R
Graves, Barbara Farris 1938- 41-44R
Graves, Charles Parlin 1911-1972 ....CANR-4
Obituary 37-40R
Earlier sketch in CA 5-8R
See also SATA 4
Graves, Edgar B(aldwin) 1898-1983 Obituary 109
Graves, Eleanor MacKenzie 1926- 102
Graves, John (Alexander III) 1920- CANR-9
Earlier sketch in CA 13-16R
See also DLBY 83
Graves, Leon B(erneil) 1946- 29-32R
Graves, Michael A(rthur) R(oy) 1933- 131
Graves, Nora Calhoun 1914- 73-76
Graves, Phillip E(arl) 1945- 115
Graves, Ralph (Augustus) 1924- 138
Graves, Richard L(atshaw) 1928- 57-60
Graves, Richard L(ayton) 1931- 53-56
Graves, Richard Perceval 1945- CANR-26
Earlier sketches in CA 65-68, CANR-9
See also CLC 44
Graves, Richard 1715-1804 ....DLB 39
Graves, Robert (von Ranke) 1895-1985 ....CANR-36
Obituary 117
Earlier sketches in CA 5-8R, CANR-5
See also CDBLB 1914-1945
See also CLC 1, 2, 6, 11, 39, 44, 45
See also DLB 20, 100
See also DLBY 85
See also MTCW
See also SATA 45
Graves, Susan B(ernard) 1933- 41-44R
Graves, Tricia
See Graversen, Pat
Graves, W(illiam) Brooke 1899- CAP-1
Earlier sketch in CA 9-10
Graves, Wallace 1922- 33-36R
Graves, Warren 1933- 128
Graveson, R(onald) H(arry) 1911- 122
Grawbarger, Josephine (Clara) 1908- 121
Grawoig, Sheila
See Raeschild, Sheila
Gray, A(lbert) W(illiam) 1940- 127
Gray, Alasdair (James) 1934- 126
See also CLC 41
See also MTCW
Gray, Alexander 1882-1968 ....5-8R
Gray, Alfred O(rren) 1914- CANR-7
Earlier sketch in CA 17-20R
Gray, Amlin 1946- 138
See also CLC 29
Gray, Angela
See Daniels, Dorothy
Gray, Anne 1931- CANR-9
Earlier sketch in CA 65-68
Gray, Asa 1810-1888 ....DLB 1
Gray, Barry 1916- 61-64
Gray, Basil 1904-1989 ....CAP-1
Obituary 128
Earlier sketch in CA 9-10
Gray, Betsy
See Poole, Gray Johnson
Gray, Bettyanne 1934- 81-84
Gray, Bradford H(itch) 1942- 57-60
Gray, Captain Bill
See Gray, William Bittle
Gray, Charles A(ugustus) 1938- 17-20R
Gray, Clifford F. 1930- 25-28R
Gray, Darrell 1945- 65-68
Gray, David 1838-1861 ....DLB 32
Gray, David 1927-1983 Obituary 110
Gray, Dorothea Helen Forbes Obituary 110
Gray, Dorothy (Kamer) 1936- 69-72
Gray, Dorothy Kate 1918- 102
Gray, Douglas 1930- 117
Gray, Dulcie CANR-24
Earlier sketches in CA 5-8R, CANR-3
Gray, Dwight E(lder) 1903- CAP-2
Earlier sketch in CA 23-24
Gray, Eden 1907- 93-96
Gray, Edna Redmond 1905(?)-1983 Obituary 110
Gray, Edwyn 1927- 41-44R
Gray, Elizabeth Janet
See Vining, Elizabeth Gray
Gray, Ellington
See Jacob, Naomi Ellington
Gray, Ernest
See Gray, Ernest Alfred
Gray, Ernest A.
See Gray, Ernest Alfred
Gray, Ernest Alfred 1908- 118
Gray, Farnum 1940- 49-52
Gray, Floyd (Francis) 1926- CANR-10
Earlier sketch in CA 25-28R
Gray, Francine du Plessix 1930- CANR-33
Earlier sketches in CA 61-64, CANR-11
See also CAAS 2
See also BEST 90:3
See also CLC 22
See also MTCW
Gray, Genevieve S(tuck) 1920- 33-36R
See also SATA 4
Gray, George Hugh 1922- CANR-7
Earlier sketch in CA 17-20R
Gray, Gibson 1922- 33-36R
Gray, Giles Wilkeson 1889- 5-8R
Gray, Gordon 1909-1982 Obituary 109
Gray, H(enry) Peter 1924- Brief entry 111
Gray, Harold James 1907- 107
Gray, Harold (Lincoln) 1894-1968 107
See also SATA 32, 33
Gray, Harriet
See Robins, Denise (Naomi)
Gray, J(esse) Glenn 1913-1977 ....37-40R
Obituary 73-76
Gray, J(ames) M(artin) 1930- 53-56
Gray, J(ohn) Richard 1929- CANR-5
Earlier sketch in CA 1-4R
Gray, J(ohn) Stanley 1894- CAP-2
Earlier sketch in CA 17-18
Gray, Jack 1927- 103
Gray, James H(enry) 1906- 97-100
Gray, James R(obert) 1921- 33-36R
Gray, James 1899- 13-16R
Gray, Jane
See Evans, Constance May
Gray, Jeffrey A(lan) 1934- 104
Gray, Jenny
See Gray, Genevieve S(tuck)
Gray, John E(dmund) 1922- 65-68
Gray, John (Henry) 1866-1934 Brief entry 119
See also TCLC 19
Gray, John Milner 1889-1970 Obituary 29-32R
Gray, John Morgan 1907- 103
Gray, John Rodger 1913-1984 Obituary 113
Gray, John S(tephens) 1910- 73-76
Gray, John W(ylie) 1935- 17-20R
Gray, John 1913- 9-12R
Gray, Juanita R(uth) 1918- 61-64
Gray, Lee Learner 1924- 73-76
Gray, Linda Crockett 1943- 109
Gray, Malcolm
See Stuart, Ian
Gray, Margaret K. 1949- 123
Gray, Marian
See Pierce, Edith Gray
Gray, Marianne 1947- 110
Gray, Martin 1926- CANR-14
Earlier sketch in CA 77-80
See also AITN 1
Gray, Mayo Loiseau 1938- 104
Gray, Michael H(aslam) 1946- 103
Gray, Nicholas Stuart 1922-1981 ....CANR-11
Obituary 103
Earlier sketch in CA 21-24R
See also SATA 4, 27
Gray, Nicolete (Mary) 1911- 103
Gray, Nigel 1941- 85-88
See also SATA 33
Gray, (Lucy) Noel (Clervaux) 1898-1983 65-68
See also SATA 47
Gray, Oscar S(halom) 1926- 29-32R
Gray, Parke H. 1936(?)-1987 Obituary 121
Gray, Patricia (Clark) 29-32R
See also SATA 7
Gray, Patsey
See Gray, Patricia (Clark)
Gray, Peter 1908- 41-44R
Gray, Philip
See Perlman, Jess
Gray, Ralph D(ale) 1933- CANR-24
Earlier sketches in CA 21-24R, CANR-8
Gray, Richard
See Gray, J(ohn) Richard
Gray, Richard B(utler) 1922- CANR-2
Earlier sketch in CA 1-4R
Gray, Richard G(eorge) 1932-1984 Obituary 114
Gray, Robert (Archibald Speir) 1942- 134
Gray, Robert F(red) 1912- 17-20R
Gray, Robert Keith 1923- 1-4R
Gray, Robert Mack 1922- 13-16R
Gray, Ronald (Douglas) 1919- CANR-22
Earlier sketches in CA 17-20R, CANR-7
Gray, Ronald Francis 1918- 5-8R
Gray, Russell
See Fischer, Bruno
Gray, Seymour 1911- 130
Gray, Simon (James Holliday) 1936- CANR-32
Earlier sketch in CA 21-24R
See also CAAS 3
See also AITN 1
See also CLC 9, 14, 36
See also DLB 13
See also MTCW
Gray, Spalding 1941- 128
See also CLC 49
Gray, Stephen E. 1925- 73-76
Gray, Thomas 1716-1771 ....CDBLB 1660-1789
See also DLB 109
See also PC 2
See also WLC
Gray, Tony
See Gray, George Hugh
Gray, Vanessa
See Aeby, Jacquelyn
Gray, Wellington Burbank 1919-1977 ....1-4R
Obituary 103
Gray, William Bittle 1891-1974 ....CANR-11
Earlier sketch in CA 13-16R
Gray, William R(alph) 1946- 97-100
Gray, Wood 1905(?)-1977 Obituary 69-72
Graybar, Lloyd J(oseph) 1938- 57-60
Graybeal, David M(cConnell) 1921- 17-20R
Graybill, Florence Curtis 1898- 97-100
Graybill, Ron(ald D.) 1944- 33-36R
Grayeff, Felix 1906- 77-80
Grayland, Eugene C(harles) 1916-1976 ....CANR-11
Earlier sketches in CAP-1, CA 9-10
Grayland, V. Merle
See Grayland, Valerie (Merle Spanner)
Grayland, Valerie (Merle Spanner) CANR-11
Earlier sketch in CA 9-12R
See also SATA 7
Graymont, Barbara 81-84
Graysmith, Robert 1942- 117
Grayson, A(lbert) K(irk) 1935- 41-44R
Grayson, Alice Barr
See Grossman, Jean Schick
Grayson, Benson Lee 1932- 93-96
Grayson, C(harles) Jackson Jr. 1923- 106
Grayson, Cary Travers Jr. 1919- CANR-10
Earlier sketch in CA 17-20R
Grayson, Cecil 1920- 13-16R
Grayson, Charles 1905-1973 Obituary 41-44R
Grayson, David
See Baker, Ray Stannard
Grayson, Henry (Wesley) 1910- 41-44R
Grayson, Janet 1934- 53-56
Grayson, L(inda) M(ary) 1947- 89-92
Grayson, Marion F. 1906-1976 ....CANR-4
Obituary 69-72
Earlier sketch in CA 5-8R
Grayson, Melvin J(ay) 1924- 45-48
Grayson, Richard (A.) 1951- CANR-31
Earlier sketches in CA 85-88, CANR-14
See also CLC 38
Grayson, Robert A. 1927- 33-36R
Grayson, Ruth (King) 1926- 73-76
Grayson, William John 1788-1863 ....DLB 3, 64
Graystone, Lynn
See Brennan, Joseph Lomas
Grayzel, Solomon 1896-1980 ....CANR-4
Earlier sketch in CA 1-4R
Grazhdanin, Misha
See Burgess, M(ichael) R(oy)
Graziano, Anthony M(ichael) 1932- 93-96
Grealey, Thomas Louis 1916- 81-84
Grealis, Walt(er) 1929- 77-80
Grealy, Desmond 1923(?)-1979 Obituary 85-88
Grean, Stanley 1920- 29-32R
Greanias, George C. 1948- 126
Great Merlini, The
See Rawson, Clayton
Greatorex, Wilfred 1921- 103
Greaves, H(arold) R(ichard) G(oring) 1907- 5-8R
Greaves, (Brian) John 1898- 103
Greaves, Margaret 1914- CANR-18
Earlier sketch in CA 25-28R
See also SATA 7
Greaves, Percy L(aurie) Jr. 1906- 49-52
Greaves, Richard L(ee) 1938- CANR-39
Earlier sketches in CA 33-36R, CANR-16
Greaves, William 1926- 125
See also BW
Grebanier, Bernard (David N.) 1903-1977 ....CANR-10
Earlier sketch in CA 21-24R
Grebe, Maria Ester 1928- 25-28R
Greben, Stanley E(dward) 1927- 120
Greber, Judith 1939- 116
Grebstein, Lawrence C(harles) 1937- 29-32R
Grebstein, Sheldon Norman 1928- CANR-5
Earlier sketch in CA 1-4R
Greco, Jose 1918- 85-88
Greco, Margaret
See Fry, Barbara
Gree, Alain 1936- 89-92
See also SATA 28
Greeley, Andrew M(oran) 1928- CANR-7
Earlier sketch in CA 5-8R
See also CAAS 7
See also CLC 28
See also MTCW
Greeley, Dana McLean 1908-1986 Obituary 119
Greeley, Horace 1811-1872 ....DLB 3, 43
Greeley, Valerie 1953- 118
Green, A(dwin) Wigfall 1900-1971(?) CAP-1
Earlier sketch in CA 9-10
Green, Abel 1900-1973 Obituary 41-44R
Green, Adam
See Weisgard, Leonard Joseph
Green, Adolph 1915- 130
Brief entry 110
See also DLB 44
Green, Alan (Baer) 1906-1975 53-56
Obituary 57-60
Green, Alan Singer 1907- 85-88
Green, Andrew (Malcolm) 1927- CANR-12
Earlier sketch in CA 73-76
Green, Anita Jane 1940- 85-88
Green, Anna Katharine 1846-1935 Brief entry 112
Green, Anne Canevari 1943- ....SATA 62
Green, Anne M. 1922- 1-4R
Green, Anne (Mitchell) 1947- 120
Green, Arnold W(ilfred) 1914- 5-8R
Green, Arthur S(amuel) 1927- 5-8R
Green, Ben K. 1911(?)-1974 Obituary 115
See also AITN 1
Green, Benny
See Green, Bernard
Green, Bernard 1927- 25-28R
Green, Betty Radley 1926-1978 Obituary 111
Green, Brian
See Card, Orson Scott
Green, Bryan S(tuart) W(estmacott) 1901- CAP-1
Earlier sketch in CA 13-14
Green, Celia (Elizabeth) 1935- 65-68
Green, Cliff(ord) 1934- 131
Green, Constance McLaughlin 1897-1975 ....9-12R
Obituary 61-64
Green, D.
See Casewit, Curtis W(erner)
Green, Daniel W(illiam) E(dward) 1958- 121
Green, David Bronte 1910- 13-16R
Green, David M(arvin) 1932- 41-44R
Green, David 1942- 77-80
Green, Deborah 1948- 104
Green, Dennis Howard 1922- 110
Green, Donald E(dward) 1936- CANR-1
Earlier sketch in CA 45-48
Green, Donald Ross 1924- 37-40R
Green, Dorothy (Auchterlonie) 1915- 112
Green, Duff 1791-1875 ....DLB 43
Green, Edith Pinero 1929- CANR-15
Earlier sketch in CA 77-80
Green, Edward 1920- 13-16R
Green, Edwin 1948- CANR-38
Earlier sketch in CA 116
Green, Elizabeth A(dine) H(erkimer) 1906- 21-24R
Green, Elmer Ellsworth 1917- 103
Green, Ernestene L(everne) 1939- 57-60
Green, Evelyn Everett
See Everett-Green, Evelyn
Green, F(rederick) C(harles) 1891-1964 Obituary 89-92
Green, Fitzhugh 1917-1990 77-80
Obituary 132
Green, Fletcher Melvin 1895-1978 ....CANR-6
Earlier sketch in CA 1-4R
Green, Frederick Pratt 1903- 102
Green, Galen 1949- 57-60
Green, George D(avid) 1938- Brief entry 114

Green, George MacEwan 1931- 81-84
Green, George S(herman) 1930- 97-100
Green, Georgia M. 1944- 93-96
Green, Gerald 1922- CANR-8
Earlier sketch in CA 13-16R
See also DLB 28
Green, Gil(bert) 1906- 73-76
Green, H(enry) Gordon 1912- 110
Green, Hannah
See Greenberg, Joanne (Goldenberg)
Green, Hannah 73-76
See also CLC 3
Green, Harold P(aul) 1922-...............13-16R
Green, Harvey 1946- CANR-37
Earlier sketch in CA 115
Green, Henry
See Yorke, Henry Vincent
See also CLC 2, 13
See also DLB 15
Green, Hollis Lynn 1933- 103
Green, J(ames) C. R. 1949- 104
Green, James L(eroy) 1919- 17-20R
Green, James R(obert) 1944- 130
Green, Jane Nugent 1918- 61-64
Green, Jane 1937- 61-64
See also SATA 9
Green, Janet 1939- CANR-30
Earlier sketch in CA 112
Green, Jeffrey P(hillip) 1944- 111
Green, Jerome Frederic 1928- 125
Green, Jerry
See Green, Jerome Frederic
Green, Jim 1941- 114
Green, Joann 1938- 115
Green, John Alden 1925- CANR-3
Earlier sketch in CA 5-8R
Green, John F. 1943- 126
Green, John L(afayette) Jr. 1929- CANR-22
Earlier sketch in CA 45-48
Green, Jonas 1712-1767 .... DLB 31
Green, Jonathan (William) 1939- CANR-9
Earlier sketch in CA 61-64
Green, Jonathon 1948- 134
Green, Joseph F(ranklin) Jr. 1924- 13-16R
Green, Joseph 1706-1780 .... DLB 31
Green, Joseph 1931- 29-32R
Green, Judith
See Galbraith, Jean
and Rodriguez, Judith Green
Green, Julian (Hartridge) 1900- CANR-33
Earlier sketch in CA 21-24R
See also CLC 3, 11
See also DLB 4, 72
See also MTCW
Green, Julien
See Green, Julian (Hartridge)
Green, Kay 1927- 117
See also CAAS 11
Green, Landis K(night) 1940- 57-60
Green, Lawrence W(inter) 1940- CANR-12
Earlier sketch in CA 69-72
Green, Leslie Claude 1920- 13-16R
Green, Lewis W(allace) 1932- 119
Green, Lewis 1946- 125
Green, Louis 1929- 45-48
Green, Marc Edward 1943- 117
Green, Margaret (Murphy) 1926- CANR-1
Earlier sketch in CA 1-4R
Green, Maria del Rosario
See Rosario Green (de Heller), Maria del
Green, Mark J(oseph) 1945- 41-44R
Green, Martin (Burgess) 1927- CANR-29
Earlier sketches in CA 17-20R, CANR-9
Green, Martyn 1899-1975 Obituary 57-60
Green, Mary McBurney 1896- CAP-2
Earlier sketch in CA 29-32
Green, Mary Moore 1906- CAP-1
Earlier sketch in CA 13-14
See also SATA 11
Green, Maureen Patricia 1933- 101
Green, Maurice B(erkeley) 1920- 77-80
Green, (James) Maurice (Spurgeon)
1906-1987 Obituary 123
Green, Maurice R(ichard) 1922- 13-16R
Green, Maury 1916- 29-32R
Green, Michael Frederick 1927- CANR-19
Earlier sketch in CA 102
Green, Milton D(ouglas) 1903- 41-44R
Green, Morton 1937- 57-60
See also SATA 8
Green, Norma B(erger) 1925- 41-44R
See also SATA 11
Green, O. O.
See Durgnat, Raymond (Eric)
Green, Otis H(oward) 1898- 9-12R
Green, Paul E(dgar) 1927- CANR-27
Earlier sketches in CA 69-72, CANR-11
Green, Paul (Eliot) 1894-1981 ....CANR-3
Obituary 103
Earlier sketch in CA 5-8R
See also AITN 1
See also CLC 25
See also DLB 7, 9
See also DLBY 81
Green, Peter
See Bulmer, (Henry) Kenneth
Green, Peter (Morris) 1924- CANR-4
Earlier sketch in CA 5-8R
Green, Phyllis 1932- CANR-17
Earlier sketches in CA 45-48, CANR-1
See also SATA 20
Green, R. P. H. 1943- 138
Green, Rayna (Diane) 1942- 114
Green, Reginald Herbold 1935- CANR-17
Earlier sketch in CA 25-28R
Green, Richard .... AITN 1
Green, Richard 1936- Brief entry 111
Green, Robert
See Smith, Richard Rein
Green, Robert D(avid) 1942- 77-80
Green, Robert L(ee) 1933- CANR-15
Earlier sketch in CA 65-68
Green, Roger C(urtis) 1932- CANR-24
Earlier sketch in CA 45-48
Green, Roger James 1944- 123
See also SATA 52
Green, Roger (Gilbert) Lancelyn
1918-1987 ....CANR-2
Obituary 123
Earlier sketch in CA 1-4R
See also SATA 2, 53
Green, Roland (James) 1944- 77-80
Green, Ronald Michael 1942- 85-88
Green, Rosalie B(eth) 1917- 1-4R
Green, Rose Basile 1914- CANR-39
Earlier sketches in CA 41-44R, CANR-15
Green, Samuel 1921(?)-1983 Obituary 111
Green, Samuel 1948- 77-80
Green, Scott E. 1951- 132
Green, Sharon 1942- 120
Green, Sheila Ellen 1934- CANR-39
Earlier sketches in CA 1-4R, CANR-2, 17
See also SATA 8
Green, Smith Wendell
1917(?)-1987 Obituary 124
Green, Stanley 1923-1990 ....CANR-17
Obituary 133
Earlier sketches in CA 1-4R, CANR-1
Green, Stephen J(ohn) 1940- 131
Green, Susan 1941- 81-84
Green, Thomas Andrew 1940- 125
Green, Thomas F. 1927- 57-60
Green, Thomas J(ohn) 1946- 113
Green, Timothy (Seton) 1936- CANR-22
Earlier sketches in CA 49-52, CANR-5
Green, Vivian Hubert Howard 1915- 9-12R
Green, William A. Jr. 1935- 85-88
Green, William Baillie 1927- 118
Green, William M(ark) 1929- CANR-35
Earlier sketch in CA 45-48
Green, William 1926- 53-56
Greenacre, Phyllis 1894- 5-8R
Greenall, Jack 1905-1983 Obituary 110
Greenawalt, R(obert) Kent 1936- 33-36R
Greenaway, George W(illiam) 1903- 118
Greenaway, Gladys 1901- 93-96
Greenaway, Kate 1846-1901 137
See also CLR 6
See also MAICYA
See also YABC 2
Greenaway, Peter 1942- 127
Greenbank, Anthony Hunt 1933- CANR-19
Earlier sketches in CA 49-52, CANR-4
See also SATA 39
Greenbaum, Fred 1930- 37-40R
Greenbaum, Leonard 1930- 21-24R
Greenbaum, Sidney 1929- CANR-33
Earlier sketches in CA 33-36R, CANR-15
Greenberg, Alfred Henry
1924-1990 Obituary 131
Greenberg, Alvin (David) 1932- 33-36R
Greenberg, Arthur
See Granit, Arthur
Greenberg, Barbara L(evenson) 1932- 53-56
Greenberg, Bernard L(ouis) 1917- 41-44R
Greenberg, Bernard 1922- 69-72
Greenberg, Bradley S(ander) 1934- 104
Greenberg, Carl 1908-1984 Obituary 114
Greenberg, Clement 1909- CANR-2
Earlier sketch in CA 1-4R
Greenberg, Daniel A. 1934- 5-8R
Greenberg, Daniel S. 1931- 29-32R
Greenberg, Dolores 1934- 112
Greenberg, Douglas 1947- 117
Greenberg, Edward (Seymour) 1942- 53-56
Greenberg, Eliezer
1897(?)-1977 Obituary 69-72
Greenberg, Eric Rolfe 1945- 114
Greenberg, Harvey R. 1935- 33-36R
See also SATA 5
Greenberg, Herbert 1935- 25-28R
Greenberg, Ira A(rthur) 1924- CANR-2
Earlier sketch in CA 49-52
Greenberg, Ivan 1908-1973 85-88
See also Rahv, Philip
Greenberg, Jae W. 1894(?)-1974 Obituary 104
Greenberg, James B(rian) 1945- 105
Greenberg, Jan W(eingarten) 1943- 118
Greenberg, Jan 1942- ....SATA 61
Greenberg, Jay (R.) 1942- 137
Greenberg, Joanne (Goldenberg)
1932- CANR-32
Earlier sketches in CA 5-8R, CANR-14
See also CLC 7, 30
See also SATA 25
Greenberg, Jonathan D. 1958- 133
Greenberg, Joseph Harold 1915- 102
Greenberg, Judith Anne
See Azrael, Judith Anne
Greenberg, Kenneth R(ay) 1930- 57-60
Greenberg, Kenneth S. 1947- 124
Greenberg, Louis M. 1933- Brief entry 112
Greenberg, Martin Harry 1941- 49-52
Greenberg, Martin J. 1945- 131
Greenberg, Milton 1927- 25-28R
Greenberg, Morrie
See Greenberg, Morris S.
Greenberg, Morris S. 1924- 33-36R
Greenberg, Moshe 1928- 13-16R
Greenberg, Norman 1945- Obituary 129
Greenberg, Paul 1937- 69-72
Greenberg, Pearl 1927- 93-96
Greenberg, Polly 1932- 85-88
See also SATA 43, 52
Greenberg, Richard 1959(?)- 138
See also CLC 57
Greenberg, Robert Arthur 1930-1989 ......CANR-4
Obituary 129
Earlier sketch in CA 1-4R
Greenberg, Roger P(aul) 1941- 131
Greenberg, Selig 1904- 49-52
Greenberg, Selma 1930- 29-32R
Greenberg, Sidney 1917- CANR-3
Earlier sketch in CA 9-12R
Greenberg, Simon 1901- CANR-14
Earlier sketch in CA 77-80
Greenberg, Stan 1931- 119
Greenberg, Stanley Bernard 1945- 53-56
Greenberg, Uri Zvi 1898-1981 Obituary 103
Greenberger, Allen J(ay) 1937- 41-44R
Greenberger, Evelyn Barish
See Barish, Evelyn
Greenberger, Howard 1924- 45-48
Greenberger, Martin 1931- CANR-8
Earlier sketch in CA 61-64
Greenbie, Barrie B(arstow) 1920- 107
Greenbie, Marjorie Barstow
1889(?)-1976 Obituary 61-64
Greenblat, Cathy S(tein) 1940- 133
Brief entry 118
Greenblatt, Augusta 1912- CANR-6
Earlier sketch in CA 57-60
Greenblatt, Edwin 1920- 49-52
Greenblatt, M(anuel) H(arry) 1922-1972 ..... CAP-2
Earlier sketch in CA 17-18
Greenblatt, Richard 1952- 130
Greenblatt, Robert Benjamin 1906-1987 .... CAP-1
Obituary 123
Earlier sketch in CA 11-12
Greenblatt, Stephen J(ay) 1943- 49-52
Greenblum, Joseph 1925- 21-24R
Greenburg, Dan 1936- CANR-25
Earlier sketches in CA 13-16R, CANR-9
Greenburger, Francis 1949- 85-88
Greenburger, Ingrid Elisabeth 1913- 104
Greene, A(lvin) C(arl) 1923- CANR-14
Earlier sketch in CA 37-40R
Greene, Adam
See Scott, Peter Dale
Greene, Anthony Hamilton Millard Kirk
See Kirk-Greene, Anthony (Hamilton Millard)
Greene, Asa 1789-1838 .... DLB 11
Greene, Bert 1923-1988 ....CANR-27
Obituary 125
Earlier sketches in CA 57-60, CANR-6
Greene, Bette 1934- CANR-4
Earlier sketch in CA 53-56
See also AAYA 7
See also CLC 30
See also CLR 2
See also MAICYA
See also SATA 8
Greene, Bob
See Greene, Robert Bernard Jr.
Greene, Carla 1916- CANR-1
Earlier sketch in CA 1-4R
See also SATA 1, 67
Greene, Carol 134
See also SATA 44, 66
Greene, Charles Jerome
1910-1983 Obituary 110
Greene, Constance C(larke) 1924- CANR-38
Earlier sketches in CA 61-64, CANR-8
See also AAYA 7
See also MAICYA
See also SAAS 11
See also SATA 11
Greene, David B(eckwith) 1939- 117
Greene, David H. 1913- 21-24R
Greene, David L(ouis) 1944- Brief entry 114
Greene, David M(ason) 1920- 118
Greene, Donald J(ohnson) 1916- CANR-2
Earlier sketch in CA 1-4R
Greene, Ellin 1927- 77-80
See also SATA 23
Greene, Felix 1909-1985 ....CANR-6
Obituary 116
Earlier sketch in CA 1-4R
Greene, Fred
See Cadet, John
Greene, Gael CANR-10
Earlier sketch in CA 13-16R
See also CLC 8
Greene, Gayle 1943- 137
Greene, Graham (Henry) 1904-1991 .....CANR-35
Obituary 133
Earlier sketch in CA 13-16R
See also AITN 2
See also CDBLB 1945-1960
See also CLC 1, 3, 6, 9, 14, 18, 27, 37, 70, 72
See also DLB 13, 15, 77, 100
See also DLBY 91
See also MTCW
See also SATA 20
See also WLC
Greene, Harlan 1953- 137
Greene, Harris 1921- 13-16R
Greene, Harry A. 1889- CAP-2
Earlier sketch in CA 17-18
Greene, Harry J(oseph) 1906- 57-60
Greene, Herbert 1898- CAP-1
Earlier sketch in CA 9-10
Greene, Howard R. 1937- 61-64
Greene, Hugh (Carleton) 1910-1987 102
Obituary 121
Greene, Jack P(hillip) 1931- CANR-18
Earlier sketches in CA 9-12R, CANR-3
Greene, James H. 1915- 17-20R
Greene, Janet (Churchill) 1917- 5-8R
Greene, Janice Presser
See Presser, Janice
Greene, Jay E(lihu) 1914- CANR-5
Earlier sketch in CA 5-8R
Greene, Jerry
See Greene, Charles Jerome
Greene, John C(olton) 1917- 89-92
Greene, John William Jr. 1946- 89-92
Greene, Johnny
See Greene, John William Jr.
Greene, Jonathan Edward 1943- CANR-12
Earlier sketch in CA 33-36R
Greene, Laura 1935- CANR-23
Earlier sketch in CA 107
See also SATA 38
Greene, Lawrence J. 1943- 113
Greene, Lee S(eifert) 1905- CANR-5
Earlier sketch in CA 13-16R
Greene, Leonard M(ichael) 1918- 109
Greene, Lorenzo Johnston
1899-1988 Obituary 124
Greene, Mabel
See Bean, Mabel Greene
Greene, Mark R. 1923- CANR-5
Earlier sketch in CA 1-4R
Greene, Maxine 1917- CANR-13
Earlier sketch in CA 21-24R
Greene, Melissa Fay 1952- 138
Greene, Mott T(uthill) 1945- CANR-28
Earlier sketch in CA 110
Greene, Naomi 1942- 45-48
Greene, Nathanael 1935- 25-28R
Greene, Owen (John) 1954- 124
Greene, Pamela
See Forman, Joan
Greene, Philip L(eon) 1924- Brief entry 113
Greene, Reynolds W(illiam) Jr. 1924- CANR-2
Earlier sketch in CA 5-8R
Greene, Richard C. 1941- 111
Greene, Richard Leighton 1904-1983 ......CANR-2
Obituary 111
Earlier sketch in CA 5-8R
Greene, Robert
See Deindorfer, Robert Greene
Greene, Robert Bernard Jr. 1947- CANR-27
Earlier sketch in CA 107
Greene, Robert W(illiam) 1933- Brief entry 111
Greene, Robert W. 1929- 104
Greene, Robert 1558-1592 .... DLB 62
Greene, Ruth Altman 1896- 73-76
Greene, Sara
See Strong, June
Greene, Sheldon L. 1934- 132
Greene, Shirley E(dward) 1911- 1-4R
Greene, Stephanie 1953- 61-64
Greene, Stephen 1914-1979 Obituary 89-92
Greene, Thomas M(cLernon) 1926- 9-12R
Greene, Victor R(obert) 1933- 25-28R
Greene, Vivian .... AITN 2
Greene, Wade 1933- .... SATA 11
Greene, Walter E. 1929- 25-28R
Greene, Wilda 1911- CANR-9
Earlier sketch in CA 21-24R
Greene, William C. 1933- 13-16R
Greene, Yvonne
See Flesch, Yolande (Catarina)
Greenebaum, Louise G(uggenheim)
1919- 69-72
Greener, Leslie 1900-1974 .... CAP-2
Earlier sketch in CA 21-22
Greener, Michael (John) 1931- 25-28R
Greenewalt, Crawford Hallock 1902- CANR-2
Earlier sketch in CA 1-4R
Greenfeder, Paul 1925(?)-1983 Obituary 109
Greenfeld, Howard CANR-19
Earlier sketch in CA 81-84
See also SATA 19
Greenfeld, Josh 1927(?)- Brief entry 116
See also SATA 62
Greenfeld, Liah 1954- 138
Greenfield, Darby
See Ward, Philip
Greenfield, Edward 1928- Brief entry 110
Greenfield, Eloise 1929- CANR-19
Earlier sketches in CA 49-52, CANR-1
See also BW
See also CLR 4
See also MAICYA
See also SATA 19, 61
Greenfield, Gerald Michael 1943- 114
Greenfield, Harry I. 1922- 127
Brief entry 109
Greenfield, Howard 1937(?)-1986 Obituary 118
Greenfield, Irving A. 1928- 33-36R
Greenfield, James Lloyd 1924- 73-76
Greenfield, Jeanette 134
Greenfield, Jeff 1943- CANR-24
Earlier sketch in CA 37-40R
Greenfield, Jerome 1923- 5-8R
Greenfield, Jerry
See Greenfield, Jerome
Greenfield, Jonas Carl 1926- Brief entry 110
Greenfield, Meg 1930- 128
Brief entry 123
Greenfield, Norman S(amuel) 1923- 41-44R
Greenfield, Patricia Marks 1940- CANR-24
Earlier sketches in CA 21-24R, CANR-9
Greenfield, Sidney M(artin) 1932- 21-24R
Greenfield, Stanley B(rian) 1922- 9-12R
Greenfield, Thelma N. 1922- 25-28R
Greengold, Jane
See Stevens, Jane Greengold
Greengrass, Mark 1949- 118
Greengroin, Artie
See Brown, Harry (Peter McNab Jr.)
Greenhalgh, P(eter) A(ndrew) L(ivsey)
1945- CANR-1
Earlier sketch in CA 49-52
Greenhalgh, Paul 1955- 130

Greenhaus, Thelma Nurenberg
1903-1984 69-72
Obituary 113
See also SATA 45
Greenhaw, H(arold) Wayne 1940- CANR-24
Earlier sketches in CA 21-24R, CANR-9
Greenhill, Basil (Jack) 1920- CANR-38
Earlier sketches in CA 5-8R, CANR-2, 17
Greenhood, (Clarence) David 1895-1983 .... 1-4R
Obituary 109
Greenhouse, Linda 1947- 77-80
Greenhow, Robert 1800-1854 .... DLB 30
Greenhut, Melvin L. 1921- 13-16R
Greening, Hamilton
See Hamilton, Charles (Harold St. John)
Greenland, Colin 1954- 117
Greenlaw, Jean-Pierre 1910- 69-72
Greenlaw, Paul S(tephen) 1930- CANR-5
Earlier sketch in CA 1-4R
Greenleaf, Barbara Kaye 1942- 29-32R
See also SATA 6
Greenleaf, Peter 1910- 85-88
See also SATA 33
Greenleaf, Richard Edward 1930- 25-28R
Greenleaf, Robert Kiefner 1904- 125
Greenleaf, Stephen (Howell) 1942- 102
Greenleaf, William 1917- 9-12R
Greenlee, Douglas 1935-1979 45-48
Obituary 103
Greenlee, J(acob) Harold 1918- 17-20R
Greenlee, James W(allace) 1933- CANR-11
Earlier sketch in CA 69-72
Greenlee, Sam 1930- 69-72
See also BW
Greenlick, Merwyn R(onald) 1935- 41-44R
Greenman, Robert 1939- CANR-38
Earlier sketch in CA 115
Greenman, Russell Lester
1904-1983 Obituary 111
Greenough, Horatio 1805-1852 .... DLB 1
Greenough, Malcolm W(helen) Jr. 1926- 128
Greenough, Sarah 1951- 126
Greenough, William Croan 1914-1989 .... 13-16R
Obituary 130
Greenslade, S(tanley) L(awrence)
1905-1977 Obituary 111
Greenson, Ralph R(omeo)
1911- Brief entry 114
Greenspan, Bud 1927- 103
Greenspan, Cappy Petrash
See Greenspan, Constance Anne Petrash
Greenspan, Charlotte L. 1921- 33-36R
Greenspan, Constance Anne Petrash
1932(?)-1983 Obituary 110
Greenspan, Elaine 1929- 110
Greenspan, Emily 1953- 124
Greenspan, Sophie 1906- 97-100
Greenspoon, Leonard J(ay) 1945- CANR-30
Earlier sketch in CA 111
Greenspun, H(erman) M(ilton)
1909-1989 .... CAP-2
Obituary 129
Earlier sketch in CA 21-22
See also AITN 2
Greenspun, Hank
See Greenspun, H(erman) M(ilton)
Greenspun, Roger (Austin) 1929- 102
Greenstein, Fred I(rwin) 1930- CANR-4
Earlier sketch in CA 49-52
Greenstein, George 1940- 130
Greenstein, Jack 1915- 130
Greenstock, David Lionel 1912- 9-12R
Greenstone, J. David 1937- 25-28R
Greenup, Ruth (Robinson)
1912(?)-1984 Obituary 113
Greenwald, Harold 1910- CANR-4
Earlier sketch in CA 1-4R
Greenwald, Jerry 1923- 57-60
Greenwald, Sheila
See Green, Sheila Ellen
Green-Wanstall, Kenneth 1918- 13-16R
Greenway, Hugh D(avids) S(cott) 1935- 73-76
Greenway, John 1919- 9-12R
Greenway, Roger S(elles) 1934- CANR-4
Earlier sketch in CA 53-56
Greenwell, Dora 1821-1882 .... DLB 35
Greenwood, Barbara 1940- 134
Greenwood, David Charles 1927-1984 61-64
Obituary 112
Greenwood, Duncan 1919- 21-24R
Greenwood, Edward Alister 1930- CANR-30
Earlier sketches in CA 29-32R, CANR-12
Greenwood, Frank 1924- CANR-10
Earlier sketch in CA 25-28R
Greenwood, Gordon E(dward) 1935- 37-40R
Greenwood, Gordon 1913- CANR-9
Earlier sketch in CA 21-24R
Greenwood, Grace
See Lippincott, Sara Jane Clarke
Greenwood, Julia Eileen Courtney 1910- CAP-1
Earlier sketch in CA 13-14
Greenwood, Kathryn Moore 1922- 93-96
Greenwood, Lillian Bethel 1932- 104
Greenwood, Marianne (Hederstrom)
1926- CANR-6
Earlier sketch in CA 9-12R
Greenwood, Ned H. 1932- Brief entry 110
Greenwood, Ted
See Greenwood, Edward Alister
Greenwood, Theresa 1936- 29-32R
Greenwood, Val D(avid) 1937- 73-76
Greenwood, Walter 1903-1974 93-96
Obituary 53-56
See also DLB 10
Greer, Ann Lennarson 1944- 53-56
Greer, Art(hur Ellis Jr.) 1929- 81-84
Greer, Ben 1948- 102
See also DLB 6
Greer, Carlotta C(herryholmes)
1879-1965 .... CAP-1
Earlier sketch in CA 13-16
Greer, Francesca
See Janas, Frankie-Lee
Greer, Georgeanna H(errmann) 1922- CANR-6
Earlier sketch in CA 57-60
Greer, Germaine 1939- CANR-33
Earlier sketch in CA 81-84
See also AITN 1
See also MTCW
Greer, Herb 1929- CANR-8
Earlier sketch in CA 5-8R
Greer, Louise 1899- CAP-1
Earlier sketch in CA 13-16
Greer, Philip 1930-1985 Obituary 116
Greer, Rebecca Ellen 1935- 103
Greer, Richard
See Silverberg, Robert
Greer, Richard
See Garrett, (Gordon) Randall (Phillip)
and Silverberg, Robert
Greer, Rita 1942- 97-100
Greer, Scott (Allen) 1922- 45-48
Greer, Thomas H(oag) 1914- 21-24R
Greeson, Janet 1952- 121
Greet, Brian Aubrey 1922- 105
Greet, Kenneth (Gerald) 1918- CANR-25
Earlier sketches in CA 5-8R, CANR-6
Greet, T(homas) Y(oung) 1923- 13-16R
Greet, William Cabell
1901-1972 Obituary 37-40R
Greever, William S(t. Clair) 1916- 5-8R
Greeves, Frederic 1903-1985 Obituary 115
Greevy, David U(pton) 1953- 112
Greg, W. R. 1809-1881 .... DLB 55
Greger, Debora 1949- CANR-31
Earlier sketch in CA 112
Gregersen, Edgar (Alstrup) 1937- 120
Gregg, Andrew K. 1929- CANR-15
Earlier sketch in CA 29-32R
Gregg, Charles T(hornton) 1927- CANR-14
Earlier sketch in CA 81-84
See also SATA 65
Gregg, Davis W(einert) 1918- 17-20R
Gregg, Hubert 1916- 102
Gregg, James E(rwin) 1927- 21-24R
Gregg, James R. 1914- 21-24R
Gregg, Jess 1926- 61-64
Gregg, John E(dwin) 1925- 45-48
Gregg, Larry
See Leighton, Lauren G(ray)
Gregg, Linda (Alouise) 1942- 113
Gregg, Martin
See McNeilly, Wilfred (Glassford)
Gregg, Pauline 5-8R
Gregg, Richard A(lexander) 1927- 13-16R
Gregg, Robert J(ohn) 1912- Brief entry 110
Gregg, Walter H(arold) 1919- 73-76
See also SATA 20
Gregg, William H. 1904(?)-1983 Obituary 109
Gregor, A(nthony) James 1929- 57-60
Gregor, Arthur 1923- CANR-11
Earlier sketch in CA 25-28R
See also CAAS 10
See also CLC 9
See also SATA 36
Gregor, Carol 1943- 117
Gregor, Howard F(rank) 1920- CANR-2
Earlier sketch in CA 5-8R
Gregor, Lee
See Pohl, Frederik
Gregor, Rex H. 1922- 13-16R
Gregori, Leon 1919- .... SATA 15
Gregorian, Joyce Ballou 1946- CANR-24
Earlier sketch in CA 107
See also SATA 30
Gregorian, Vartan 1935- 29-32R
Gregorich, Barbara 1943- 117
See also SATA 66
Gregorios, Paulos Mar 1922- CANR-11
Earlier sketch in CA 25-28R
Gregorowski, Christopher 1940- CANR-15
Earlier sketch in CA 89-92
See also SATA 30
Gregory, Bettina 1946- 69-72
Gregory, Chuck
See Gnaegy, Charles
Gregory, Diana (Jean) 1933- 97-100
See also SATA 42, 49
Gregory, Dick 1932- CANR-7
Earlier sketch in CA 45-48
See also BW
Gregory, Elizabeth
See Gilford, C(harles) B(ernard)
Gregory, Frederick 1942- 138
Gregory, Freida 1938- 69-72
Gregory, H(ollingsworth) F(ranklin) 1906- 69-72
Gregory, Harry
See Gottfried, Theodore Mark
Gregory, Hilton
See Ferguson, Charles W.
Gregory, Horace (Victor) 1898-1982 .... CANR-22
Obituary 106
Earlier sketches in CA 5-8R, CANR-3
See also DLB 48
Gregory, Isabella Augusta (Persse)
1852-1932 Brief entry 104
See also DLB 10
See also TCLC 1
Gregory, J. Dennis
See Williams, John A(lfred)
Gregory, J. S.
See Gregory, James S(tothert)
Gregory, James S(tothert) 1912-1983 77-80
Obituary 133
Gregory, Jean
See Ure, Jean
Gregory, K(enneth) J(ohn) 1938- 107
Gregory, Kenneth (Malcolm) 1921- 73-76
Gregory, Lisa
See Camp, Candace P(auline)
Gregory, Lydia
See Carey, Diane
Gregory, Mark
See Burch, Monte G.
Gregory, Paul Roderick 1941- 53-56
Gregory, Peter 1924- 41-44R
Gregory, Philippa 1954- 131
Gregory, R(ichard) L(angton) 1923- 57-60
Gregory, Richard Claxton
See Gregory, Dick
Gregory, Robert G(ranville) 1924- 41-44R
Gregory, Robert Lloyd 1892- 29-32R
Gregory, Ross 1933- 29-32R
Gregory, Roy 1935- 37-40R
Gregory, Ruth W(ilhelmine) 1910- 77-80
Gregory, Sean
See Hossent, Harry
Gregory, Sinda 1947- 115
Gregory, Stephan
See Pendleton, Don(ald Eugene)
Gregory, Stephen
See Penzler, Otto
Gregory, Stephen 1952- 136
Gregory, Steven
See Jones, Stephen
Gregory, Susan 1945- 108
Gregory, Thomas B(ernard) 1940- 45-48
Gregory, Timothy E(dmund) 1943- 111
Gregory, Vahan 1927- 69-72
Gregory, Violet L(efler) 1907- CANR-8
Earlier sketch in CA 57-60
Gregory, William King
1876-1970 Obituary 29-32R
Gregory, Yvonne 1919(?)-1979 Obituary 89-92
Gregory of Rimini 1300(?)-1358 .... DLB 115
Gregson, Paul
See Oakley, Eric Gilbert
Gregston, Gene 1925- 81-84
Greider, William (F.) 117
Greif, E(dwin) Charles 1915- 1-4R
Greif, Martin 1938- CANR-25
Earlier sketches in CA 65-68, CANR-10
Greiff, Barrie S(anford) 1935- 134
Brief entry 114
Greig, Cicely Obituary 116
Greig, Maysie 1902-1971 102
Obituary 104
Greimas, A. J.
See Greimas, Algirdas Julien
Greimas, Algirdas Julien 1917- 132
Greiner, Donald J(ames) 1940- CANR-37
Earlier sketches in CA 45-48, CANR-1, 16
Greinke, (Lawrence) Eric 1948- 41-44R
Greisman, Joan Ruth 1937- 103
See also SATA 31
Grele, Ronald J(ohn) 1934- 73-76
Gremillion, Joseph 1919- 102
Gremmels, Marion Louise Chapman 1924- 111
Grenander, M(ary) E(lizabeth) 1918- CANR-4
Earlier sketch in CA 53-56
Grendahl, J(ay) Spencer 1943- 29-32R
Grendler, Paul F(rederick) 1936- 41-44R
Grendon, Edward
See LeShan, Lawrence L(ee)
Grendon, Stephen
See Derleth, August (William)
Grene, Marjorie (Glicksman) 1910- CANR-25
Earlier sketches in CA 13-16R, CANR-8
Grenelle, Lisa
See Munroe, Elizabeth L(ee)
Grenfell, Joyce (Irene) 1910-1979 .... CANR-20
Obituary 89-92
Earlier sketch in CA 81-84
Grenfell, Wilfred Thomason 1865-1940 .... DLB 92
Grenier, Judson A(chille) 1930- 89-92
Grenier, Mildred 1917- CANR-12
Earlier sketch in CA 29-32R
Grennan, Eamon 1941- 133
Grennan, Margaret R(ose) 41-44R
Grenville, Bryan P(eter) 1955- 117
Grenville, J(ohn) A(shley) S(oames)
1928- CANR-5
Earlier sketch in CA 9-12R
Grenville, Kate 1950- 118
See also CLC 61
Grenville, Pelham
See Wodehouse, P(elham) G(renville)
Grenyer, Norman 1913-1983 Obituary 110
Gresham, Anthony
See Russell, Roy
Gresham, Claude Hamilton Jr. 1922- CANR-8
Earlier sketch in CA 5-8R
Gresham, Elizabeth (Fenner) 1904- 81-84
Gresham, Grits
See Gresham, Claude Hamilton Jr.
Gresham, Perry E(pler) 1907- 45-48
Gresser, Seymour 1926- 29-32R
Gresser, Sy
See Gresser, Seymour
Gressley, Gene M(aurice) 1931- CANR-10
Earlier sketch in CA 17-20R
Greteman, James 1933- 112
Greteman, Jim
See Greteman, James
Gretz, Susanna 1937- CANR-28
Earlier sketch in CA 29-32R
See also SATA 7
Gretzer, John .... SATA 18
Gretzky, Walter 1938- 120
Greulach, Victor A(ugust) 1906- 49-52
Grevatt, Wallace 1925- 129
Greve, Elsa
See Greve, Felix Paul (Berthold Friedrich)
Greve, Felix Paul (Berthold Friedrich)
1879-1948 Brief entry 104
See also Grove, Frederick Philip
Greville, Fulke 1554-1628 .... DLB 62
Grew, James Hooper 1906- 103
Grew, Raymond 1930- 13-16R
Grewdead, Roy
See Gorey, Edward (St. John)
Grewer, Eira M(ary) 1931- 21-24R
Grex, Leo
See Gribble, Leonard (Reginald)
Grey, Abby (Bartlett) Weed
1903(?)-1983 Obituary 110
Grey, Anthony 1938- CANR-29
Earlier sketch in CA 29-32R
Grey, Beryl (Elizabeth) 1927- 109
Grey, Brenda
See Mackinlay, Leila Antoinette Sterling
Grey, Carenna Jane
See Kalpakian, Laura Anne
Grey, Carol
See Lowndes, Robert A(ugustine) W(ard)
Grey, Charles
See Tubb, E(dwin) C(harles)
Grey, David Lennox 1935- 93-96
Grey, Dorothy 1913- 120
Grey, Elizabeth
See Hogg, Elizabeth (Tootill)
Grey, Georgina
See Roby, Mary Linn
Grey, Ian 1918- CANR-2
Earlier sketch in CA 5-8R
Grey, J. David 1935- 133
Grey, Jerry 1926- CANR-20
Earlier sketches in CA 53-56, CANR-5
See also SATA 11
Grey, Lindsey
See Peel, Colin D(udley)
Grey, Marian Powys 1883(?)-1972 Obituary 104
Grey, Robert Waters 1943- 49-52
Grey, Robin
See Gresham, Elizabeth (Fenner)
Grey, Vivian (Hoffman) 17-20R
Grey, Zane 1872-1939 132
Brief entry 104
See also DLB 9
See also MTCW
See also TCLC 6
Grey Owl
See Belaney, Archibald Stansfeld
Greyser, Stephen A. 1935- 33-36R
Gri
See Denney, Diana
Gribbin, John 1946- 113
Gribbin, Lenore S. 1922- 33-36R
Gribbin, William James 1943- CANR-17
Earlier sketches in CA 45-48, CANR-1
Gribble, Charles E(dward) 1936- 41-44R
Gribble, Harry Wagstaff (Graham)
1891(?)-1981 Obituary 102
Gribble, James 1938- 29-32R
Gribble, Jennifer 1937- 116
Gribble, Leonard (Reginald) 1908- CANR-7
Earlier sketch in CA 53-56
Gribbons, Warren D(avid) 1921- 29-32R
Grice, Frederick 1910- CANR-3
Earlier sketch in CA 9-12R
See also SATA 6
Grice, Grimes
See Kamp, Irene Kittle
Grice, Julia (Haughey) 1940- CANR-16
Earlier sketch in CA 77-80
Gridban, Volsted
See Tubb, E(dwin) C(harles)
Grider, Dorothy 1915- .... SATA 31
Grider, Jay
See Miller, John Grider
Gridley, Marion E(leanor) 1906-1974 45-48
Obituary 103
See also SATA 26, 35
Gridley, Roy E. 1935- 127
Brief entry 109
Gridzewski, Mieczylawski
1895(?)-1970 Obituary 104
Grieb, Kenneth J. 1939- CANR-12
Earlier sketch in CA 29-32R
Grieb, Lyndal 1940- 61-64
Grieder, Jerome B. 1932- 130
Grieder, Josephine 1939- 53-56
Grieder, Terence 1931- CANR-35
Earlier sketch in CA 114
Grieder, Theodore 1926- 45-48
Grieder, Walter 1924- 41-44R
See also SATA 9
Grieg, Michael 1922- 17-20R
Grieg, (Johan) Nordahl (Brun)
1902-1943 Brief entry 107
See also TCLC 10
Grier, B. R. 1913- 25-28R
Grier, Barbara G(ene Damon) 1933- 107
Grier, Edward F(rancis) 1917- 121
Grier, Eldon 1917- 113
See also DLB 88
Grier, Frances Belle Powner
1886(?)-1980(?) Obituary 104
Grier, Katherine C. 1953- 132
Grier, Roosevelt 1932- 113
Grier, Rosey
See Grier, Roosevelt
Grierson, Edward 1914- CANR-4
Earlier sketch in CA 1-4R
Grierson, Francis Durham
1888-1972 Obituary 104

Grierson, Herbert John Clifford
1886-1960 Obituary ... 93-96
Grierson, John 1898-1972 Obituary ... 116
Grierson, John 1909-1977 ... CAP-2
Obituary ... 69-72
Earlier sketch in CA 19-20
Grierson, (Monica) Linden 1914- ... CAP-1
Earlier sketch in CA 9-10
Grierson, Philip 1910- ... 129
Gries, Tom 1923(?)-1977 Obituary ... 69-72
Griese, Arnold A(lfred) 1921- ... CANR-1
Earlier sketch in CA 49-52
See also SATA 9
Grieson, Ronald Edward 1943- ... CANR-1
Earlier sketch in CA 49-52
Griesse, Carolyn 1941- ... 107
Griessman, Benjamin Eugene 1934- ... 41-44R
Griest, Guinevere L(indley) 1924- ... 65-68
Grieve, Andrew W. 1925- ... 9-12R
Grieve, C(hristopher) M(urray)
1892-1978 ... CANR-33
Obituary ... 85-88
Earlier sketch in CA 5-8R
See also MacDiarmid, Hugh
See also CLC 11, 19
See also MTCW
Grieves, Forest L(eslie) 1938- ... 53-56
Grifalconi, Ann 1929- ... CANR-35
Earlier sketches in CA 5-8R, CANR-9
See also MAICYA
See also SATA 2, 66
Griff
See Fawcett, F(rank) Dubrez
and McKeag, Ernest L(ionel)
Griffen, Edmund
See Du Breuil, (Elizabeth) L(or)inda
Griffen, (James) Jeff(erds) 1923- ... 13-16R
Griffin, A(rthur) H(arold) 1911- ... CANR-9
Earlier sketch in CA 21-24R
Griffin, Al 1919- ... 33-36R
Griffin, Anne J.
See Griffin, Arthur J.
Griffin, Arthur J. 1921- ... CANR-1
Earlier sketch in CA 49-52
Griffin, Barbara C(ook) 1945- ... 53-56
Griffin, Bryan F(rederick) ... 120
Brief entry ... 113
Griffin, C. F.
See Fikso, Eunice Cleland
Griffin, C. S.
See Griffin, Clifford S(tephen)
Griffin, C(harles) W(illiam) 1925- ... 53-56
Griffin, Charles C(arroll)
1902-1976 Obituary ... 65-68
Griffin, Charles Henry 1922- ... 17-20R
Griffin, Clifford S(tephen) 1929- Brief entry ... 111
Griffin, (George) Dan(iel)
1937-1984 Obituary ... 112
Griffin, David Ray 1939- ... 77-80
Griffin, Donald (Redfield) 1915- ... CANR-15
Earlier sketch in CA 37-40R
Griffin, Dustin H(adley) 1943- ... 120
Griffin, Edward M(ichael) 1937- ... 89-92
Griffin, Emilie Russell Dietrich 1936- ... CANR-21
Earlier sketch in CA 103
Griffin, Ernest G(eorge) 1916- ... 25-28R
Griffin, Gerald G(ehrig) 1933- ... CANR-9
Earlier sketch in CA 57-60
Griffin, Gillett Good 1928- ... SATA 26
Griffin, Glen C. 1934- ... CANR-17
Earlier sketch in CA 29-32R
Griffin, (Arthur) Gwyn
1922(?)-1967 Obituary ... 89-92
Griffin, Jacqueline P. 1927- ... 33-36R
Griffin, James A. 1934- ... 29-32R
Griffin, John Howard 1920-1980 ... CANR-2
Obituary ... 101
Earlier sketch in CA 1-4R
See also AITN 1
See also CLC 68
Griffin, John Q(uealy) 1948- ... 77-80
Griffin, Jonathan
See Griffin, Robert John Thurlow
Griffin, Judith Berry ... 108
See also SATA 34
Griffin, Keith B(roadwell) 1938- ... CANR-7
Earlier sketch in CA 57-60
Griffin, (Samuel) Marvin
1907-1982 Obituary ... 108
Griffin, Mary Claire 1924- ... 17-20R
Griffin, Mary 1916- ... 61-64
Griffin, Merv(yn) Edward Jr.) 1925- ... 130
Griffin, Peni R(ae) 1961- ... 134
See also SATA 67
Griffin, Peter ... CLC 39
Griffin, Peter 1942- ... 136
Griffin, Robert John Thurlow 1906- ... 129
Griffin, Robert 1936- ... 53-56
Griffin, Russell M(organ) 1943- ... 114
Griffin, Stuart 1917- ... 5-8R
Griffin, Susan 1943- ... CANR-27
Earlier sketches in CA 49-52, CANR-3
Griffin, Thomas E. Jr. 1946- ... 131
Griffin, Tom
See Griffin, Thomas E. Jr.
Griffin, W. E. B.
See Butterworth, W(illiam) E(dmund III)
Griffin, Walter 1937- ... 73-76
Griffin, William D(enis) 1936- ... 122
Griffin, (Henry) William 1935- ... 93-96
Griffin, William Lloyd 1938- ... 21-24R
Griffin-Beale, Christopher 1947- ... 118
Griffiss, James E(dward) 1928- ... 132
Brief entry ... 118
Griffith, A. Kinney 1897- ... CANR-17
Earlier sketch in CA 1-4R
Griffith, A(rthur) Leonard 1920- ... CANR-5
Earlier sketch in CA 9-12R
Griffith, Albert J(oseph Jr.) 1932- ... 37-40R
Griffith, Benjamin Woodward Jr.
1922- ... CANR-20
Earlier sketches in CA 1-4R, CANR-5
Griffith, Bill
See Granger, Bill
Griffith, Bill 1944- ... 129
Griffith, Corinne 1898(?)-1979 Obituary ... 89-92
Griffith, D(avid Lewelyn) W(ark)
1875-1948 Brief entry ... 119
Griffith, Elizabeth 1727-1793 ... DLB 89
Griffith, Elizabeth 1727(?)-1793 ... DLB 39
Griffith, Ernest S(tacey) 1896- ... 13-16R
Griffith, Francis 1906- ... 106
Griffith, G(uy) T(hompson)
1908-1985 Obituary ... 117
Griffith, George
See Griffith-Jones, George Chetwynd
Griffith, Helen V(irginia) 1934- ... CANR-22
Earlier sketch in CA 105
See also SATA 39
Griffith, Jeannette
See Eyerly, Jeannette Hyde
Griffith, Jerry 1932- ... 53-56
Griffith, Kathryn 1923- ... 73-76
Griffith, Kenneth 1921- ... CANR-21
Earlier sketch in CA 69-72
Griffith, Lawrence
See Griffith, D(avid Lewelyn) W(ark)
Griffith, Leon Odell 1921- ... CANR-2
Earlier sketch in CA 1-4R
Griffith, Lucille B(lanche) 1905- ... 17-20R
Griffith, Patricia Browning 1935- ... CANR-35
Earlier sketches in CA 77-80, CANR-13
Griffith, Paul 1921-1983 ... 21-24R
Obituary ... 109
Griffith, Richard (Edward) 1912-1969 ... CANR-6
Earlier sketch in CA 1-4R
Griffith, Robert 1940- ... 45-48
Griffith, Samuel Blair II 1906-1983 Obituary ... 109
Griffith, Thomas Gwynfor 1926- ... 103
Griffith, Thomas 1915- ... 21-24R
Griffith, William E(dgar) 1920- ... 61-64
Griffith, Winthrop 1931- ... 9-12R
Griffith-Jones, George Chetwynd
1857-1906 Brief entry ... 112
Griffith-Jones, Stephany 1947- ... 126
Griffiths, A(lan) Bede 1906- ... CANR-7
Earlier sketch in CA 13-16R
Griffiths, Alison 1953- ... 128
Griffiths, Brian 1941- ... 120
Griffiths, Bryn(lyn) David 1933- ... 101
Griffiths, Daniel E(dward) 1917- ... 25-28R
Griffiths, G. D.
See Griffiths, (Edith) Grace (Chalmers)
Griffiths, G(ordon) D(ouglas) 1910-1973 ... CAP-2
Earlier sketch in CA 21-22
See also SATA 20
Griffiths, (Edith) Grace (Chalmers)
1921- ... CANR-22
Earlier sketch in CA 106
Griffiths, Helen 1939- ... CANR-25
Earlier sketches in CA 17-20R, CANR-7
See also SAAS 5
See also SATA 5
Griffiths, John C(harles) 1934- ... 108
Griffiths, John Gwyn 1911- ... 106
Griffiths, Kitty Anna ... 105
Griffiths, Linda 1956- ... 132
Griffiths, Louise (Benckenstein) 1907- ... 1-4R
Griffiths, (Thomas) Mel(vin) 1910- ... 85-88
Griffiths, Michael C(ompton) 1928- ... CANR-31
Earlier sketches in CA 37-40R, CANR-14
Griffiths, Naomi 1934- ... 101
Griffiths, Paul (Anthony) 1947- ... 107
Griffiths, Percival Joseph 1899- ... 103
Griffiths, Ralph A(lan) 1937- ... CANR-22
Earlier sketch in CA 105
Griffiths, Richard M(athias) 1935- ... CANR-8
Earlier sketch in CA 17-20R
Griffiths, Robert David 1952- ... 118
Griffiths, Sally 1934- ... 25-28R
Griffiths, Stephen Gareth 1949- ... 131
Griffiths, Steve
See Griffiths, Stephen Gareth
Griffiths, Trevor 1935- ... 97-100
See also CLC 13, 52
See also DLB 13
Griffiths, Vincent Llewellyn
1902(?)-1984 Obituary ... 113
Griffy
See Griffith, Bill
Grigg, Charles M(eade) 1918- ... 13-16R
Grigg, John (Edward Poynder) 1924- ... 104
Griggs, Charles Irwin 1902- ... 1-4R
Griggs, Earl Leslie 1899- ... 73-76
Griggs, Gary B(ruce) 1943- ... 118
Griggs, Lee 1928- ... 69-72
Griggs, Mary
See Phillips, Bluebell Stewart
Griggs, Sutton Elbert
1872-1930(?) Brief entry ... 123
See also DLB 50
Griggs, Tamar 1941- ... 77-80
Grignon, Claude-Henri 1894-1976 ... DLB 68
Grigoli, Valorie 1955- ... 122
Grigorovich, Yuri Nikolayevich 1927- ... 126
Grigsby, Gordon 1927- ... CANR-19
Earlier sketch in CA 97-100
Grigson, Geoffrey (Edward Harvey)
1905-1985 ... CANR-33
Obituary ... 118
Earlier sketches in CA 25-28R, CANR-20
See also CLC 7, 39
See also DLB 27
See also MTCW
Grigson, Jane (McIntire) 1928-1990 ... CANR-20
Obituary ... 131
Earlier sketches in CA 49-52, CANR-1
See also SATA 63
Grill, Johnpeter Horst 1943- ... 112
Grill, Nannette L. 1935- ... 65-68
Grilli, Peter M. 1942- ... 120
Grilliot, Harold J(ohn) 1937- ... 107
Grillo, John 1942- Brief entry ... 117
Grillo, Ralph David 1940- ... 49-52
Grillo, Virgil 1938- ... 53-56
Grim, John A(llen) 1946- ... 117
Grim, Patrick 1950- ... CANR-37
Earlier sketch in CA 115
Grim, Ronald E(ugene) 1946- ... 118
Grimal, Pierre Antoine 1912- ... CANR-7
Earlier sketch in CA 13-16R
Grimaldi, J(ohn) V. 1916- ... CANR-19
Earlier sketches in CA 5-8R, CANR-3
Grimaud, Michel (Robert) 1945- ... 129
Grimault, Berthe 1940- ... 13-16R
Grimble, Ian 1921- ... CANR-39
Earlier sketches in CA 5-8R, CANR-2, 18
Grimble, Reverend Charles James
See Eliot, T(homas) S(tearns)
Grime, Harol (Riley) 1896-1984 Obituary ... 114
Grimes, Alan P. 1919- ... CANR-1
Earlier sketch in CA 1-4R
Grimes, (Lewis) Howard 1915- ... 25-28R
Grimes, Johnnie Marie ... 103
Grimes, Joseph E(vans) 1928- ... 37-40R
Grimes, Lee 1920- ... CANR-37
Earlier sketch in CA 61-64
See also SATA 68
Grimes, Martha ... 117
Brief entry ... 113
See also BEST 90:1
See also MTCW
Grimes, Nikki 1950- ... 77-80
Grimes, Orville F(rank) Jr. 1943- ... 106
Grimes, Paul 1924- ... 77-80
Grimes, Ronald L. 1943- ... CANR-17
Earlier sketches in CA 45-48, CANR-1
Grimes, W(illiam) H(enry)
1892-1972 Obituary ... 33-36R
Grimke, Angelina (Emily) Weld 1880-1958 ... 124
See also BW
See also DLB 50, 54
Grimke, Charlotte L(ottie) Forten
1837(?)-1914 ... 124
Brief entry ... 117
See also Forten, Charlotte L.
See also BW
Grimley, Mildred H(ess) 1919- ... 5-8R
Grimm, Charles John
1898(?)-1983 Obituary ... 111
Grimm, Charlie
See Grimm, Charles John
Grimm, Cherry Barbara 1930- ... 101
See also SATA 43
Grimm, Hans 1875-1959 ... DLB 66
Grimm, Harold J(ohn) 1901- ... 13-16R
Grimm, Jacob Ludwig Karl 1785-1863 ... DLB 90
See also MAICYA
See also SATA 22
Grimm, Reinhold 1931- ... CANR-23
Earlier sketches in CA 61-64, CANR-8
Grimm, Wilhelm Karl 1786-1859 ... DLB 90
See also MAICYA
See also SATA 22
Grimm, William C(arey) 1907- ... CANR-34
Earlier sketch in CA 49-52
See also SATA 14
Grimond, Joseph 1913- ... 108
Grimsditch, Herbert Borthwick
1898-1971 Obituary ... 104
Grimshaw, Allen Day 1929- ... CANR-9
Earlier sketch in CA 65-68
Grimshaw, James A(lbert) Jr. 1940- ... 109
Grimshaw, Mark
See McKeag, Ernest L(ionel)
Grimshaw, Nigel (Gilroy) 1925- ... CANR-17
Earlier sketch in CA 101
See also SATA 23
Grimsley, Gordon
See Groom, Arthur William
Grimsley, Linda 1940- ... 81-84
Grimsley, Ronald 1915- ... CANR-3
Earlier sketch in CA 5-8R
Grimsley, Will (Henry) 1914- ... 33-36R
Grimson, Todd 1952- ... 129
Grimstead, Hettie 1903- Brief entry ... 115
Grimsted, David Allen 1935- ... 25-28R
Grimsted, Patricia Kennedy 1935- ... 77-80
Grindal, Bruce T. 1940- ... 41-44R
Grindal, Gracia (Marie) 1943- ... 116
Grindea, Miron 1909- ... CANR-5
Earlier sketch in CA 5-8R
Grindel, Carl W(illiam) 1905- ... 85-88
Grindel, Eugene 1895-1952 Brief entry ... 104
See also Eluard, Paul
Grindel, John Anthony 1937- ... 65-68
Grindell, Robert M(aclean) 1933- ... 13-16R
Grinder, Michael 1942- ... 61-64
Grindle, Carleton
See Page, Gerald W(ilburn)
Grindley, John (Thomas Ellam) 1926- ... 25-28R
Grindley, (Jane) Sally 1953- ... 121
Grindrod, Muriel (Kathleen) 1902- ... 5-8R
Gringhuis, Dirk
See Gringhuis, Richard H.
Gringhuis, Richard H. 1918-1974 ... CANR-5
Earlier sketch in CA 1-4R
See also SATA 6, 25
Grinnell, David
See Wollheim, Donald A(llen)
Grinnell, George Bird 1849-1938 ... SATA 16
Grinnell, Isabel Hoopes
1899(?)-1988 Obituary ... 124
Grinsell, Leslie Valentine 1907- ... CANR-3
Earlier sketch in CA 9-12R
Grinspoon, Lester 1928- ... 81-84
Grinstead, David 1939- ... 105
Grinstein, Alexander 1918- ... CANR-5
Earlier sketch in CA 13-16R
Gripari, Pierre 1925- ... CANR-31
Earlier sketch in CA 29-32R
Gripe, Maria (Kristina) 1923- ... CANR-39
Earlier sketches in CA 29-32R, CANR-17
See also CLR 5
See also MAICYA
See also SATA 2
Grise, Jeannette
See Thomas, Jeannette Grise
Grisewood, Harman (Joseph Gerard)
1906- ... CAP-2
Earlier sketch in CA 29-32
Grisez, Germain G. 1929- ... CANR-21
Earlier sketches in CA 13-16R, CANR-6
Grisham, John 1955(?)- ... 138
Grisham, Noel 1916- ... CANR-10
Earlier sketch in CA 25-28R
Grispino, Joseph Aloysius 1922- ... 17-20R
Grissim, John 1941- ... 113
Grissom, Fay
See Shulman, Fay Grissom Stanley
Grissom, Ken 1945- ... 135
Griswold, Charles L. Jr. 1951- ... 123
Griswold, Erwin N(athaniel) 1904- ... CAP-1
Earlier sketch in CA 13-16
Griswold, George
See Dean, Robert George
Griswold, Jerome 1947- ... 130
Griswold, Lawrence T.
1904(?)-1984 Obituary ... 113
Griswold, Rufus Wilmot 1815-1857 ... DLB 3, 59
Griswold, Wesley S(outhmayd) 1909- ... 1-4R
Griswold del Castillo, Richard 1942- ... 101
Gritsch, Eric W. 1931- ... CANR-10
Earlier sketch in CA 21-24R
Grivas, Theodore 1922- ... 9-12R
Grizzard, Lewis (M. Jr.) 1946- ... 129
Brief entry ... 123
See also MTCW
Grob, Alan 1932- Brief entry ... 113
Grob, Gerald N. 1931- ... CANR-20
Earlier sketches in CA 1-4R, CANR-5
Grobel, Lawrence 1947- ... 131
Grobman, Alex 1946- ... 116
Grobstein, Clifford 1916- ... 130
Groch, Judith (Goldstein) 1929- ... 9-12R
See also SATA 25
Grode, Redway
See Gorey, Edward (St. John)
Groden, Michael (Lewis) 1947- ... 131
Grodnick, Susan 1951- ... 122
Groemping, Franz A(lbert)
1909(?)-1987 Obituary ... 123
Groenbjerg, Kirsten A(ndersen)
1946- ... CANR-15
Earlier sketch in CA 85-88
Groene, Bertram Hawthorne 1923- ... 45-48
Groene, Janet 1936- ... 37-40R
Groener, Carl
See Lowndes, Robert A(ugustine) W(ard)
Groenhoff, Edwin L. 1924- ... 57-60
Groening, Matt ... 138
See also AAYA 8
Groennings, Sven O. 1934- ... 45-48
Groenoset, Dagfinn 1920- ... 93-96
Groeschel, Benedict J(oseph) 1933- ... CANR-37
Earlier sketch in CA 115
Grof, Stanislav 1931- ... 73-76
Groff, Patrick J(ohn) 1924- ... 41-44R
Groff, Warren F(rederick) 1924- ... 53-56
Grogan, Emmett 1942-1978 ... 41-44R
Groh, Ed(win Charles) 1910- ... 49-52
Groh, George W. 1922-1984 ... 85-88
Obituary ... 114
Grohman, Joann Sills 1928- ... 107
Grohskopf, Bernice ... CANR-3
Earlier sketch in CA 5-8R
See also SATA 7
Groia, Phil(ip) 1941- ... 53-56
Grol, Lini R(icharda) 1913- ... CANR-25
Earlier sketches in CA 61-64, CANR-8
See also SATA 9
Grollman, Earl A. 1925- ... 21-24R
See also SATA 22
Grollman, Sharon Hya 1954- ... CANR-15
Earlier sketch in CA 81-84
Grollmes, Eugene E. 1931- ... 29-32R
Gromacki, Robert Glenn 1933- ... CANR-19
Earlier sketches in CA 53-56, CANR-4
Gromada, Thaddeus V(ladimir) 1929- ... 45-48
Groman, George L. 1928- ... 21-24R
Grombach, John V(alentin) 1901- ... 103
Gromyko, Andrei (Andreevich) 1909-1989 ... 134
Gronbeck, Bruce E(lliot) 1941- ... 132
Brief entry ... 118
Gronbjerg, Kirsten A(ndersen)
See Groenbjerg, Kirsten A(ndersen)
Grondona, L(eo) St. Clare 1890-1982 ... 103
Obituary ... 108
Groneman, Chris Harold 1906- ... CANR-1
Earlier sketch in CA 1-4R

Gronert, Bernard G(eorge)
1920-1985 Obituary 116
Gronewold, Sue Ellen
See Gronewold, Susan Ellen
Gronewold, Susan Ellen 1947- 115
Groninger, William C.
1928(?)-1983 Obituary 111
Gronowicz, Antoni 1913-1985 ....25-28R
Obituary 117
Groocock, J(ohn) M(ichael) 1929- 57-60
Groom, Arthur William 1898-1964 ....CANR-1
Earlier sketch in CA 1-4R
See also SATA 10
Groom, Bernard 1892- CAP-2
Earlier sketch in CA 21-22
Groom, Nigel 1924- 117
Groom, Winston 1943- CANR-34
Earlier sketch in CA 85-88
Groome, Thomas H(enry) 1945- 110
Gropius, Walter 1883-1969 Obituary 25-28R
Gropman, Donald S(heldon) 1936- 101
Gropp, Louis (Oliver) 1935- 120
Gropper, William 1897-1977 102
Obituary 89-92
Grosbard, Ulu 1929- 25-28R
Grose, B(url) Donald 1943- CANR-22
Earlier sketch in CA 45-48
Grose, Christopher (Waldo)
1939- Brief entry 114
Grose, Peter (Bolton) 1934- Brief entry 119
Groseclose, Elgin E. 1899-1983 .... CAP-2
Obituary 109
Earlier sketch in CA 21-22
Groseclose, Kel(vin) 1940- CANR-32
Earlier sketch in CA 113
Grosman, Brian A(llen) 1935- 73-76
Grosman, Ladislav 1921- 102
Grosman, Tatyana 1904-1982 Obituary 107
Grosofsky, Leslie
See Gross, Leslie
Gross, Alan 1947- CANR-24
Earlier sketch in CA 89-92
See also SATA 43, 54
Gross, Albert C. 1947- 125
Gross, Anthony 1905-1984 Obituary 114
Gross, Beatrice 1935- 77-80
Gross, Ben Samuel 1891-1979 97-100
Obituary 89-92
Gross, Bertram M(yron) 1912- CANR-9
Earlier sketch in CA 13-16R
Gross, Beverly 1938- 29-32R
Gross, Carl H. 1911- 13-16R
Gross, Daniel R(ussell) 1942- 53-56
Gross, David C(harles) 1923- 102
Gross, Ernest A(rnold) 1906- 5-8R
Gross, Ernie 1913- 136
See also SATA 67
Gross, Feliks 1906- CANR-12
Earlier sketch in CA 29-32R
Gross, Franz B(runo) 1919- 29-32R
Gross, Gerald 1932- 9-12R
Gross, Hanns 1928- 41-44R
Gross, Harvey S(eymour) 1922- CANR-8
Earlier sketch in CA 13-16R
Gross, Helen Shimota 1931- 9-12R
Gross, Irma H(annah) 1892- CAP-1
Earlier sketch in CA 13-16
Gross, James A. 1933- 57-60
Gross, Joel 1951- CANR-31
Earlier sketches in CA 29-32R, CANR-14
Gross, Johannes Heinrich 1916- 29-32R
Gross, John J. 1912-1970 .... CAP-2
Earlier sketch in CA 25-28
Gross, John (Jacob) 1935- CANR-39
Earlier sketch in CA 29-32R
Gross, John Owen 1894-1971 .... CAP-2
Earlier sketch in CA 17-18
Gross, Kenneth G. 1939- 25-28R
Gross, Kenneth 1954- 118
Gross, Leonard 1928- 118
Brief entry 112
Gross, Leslie 1927- 5-8R
Gross, Llewellyn (Zwicker) 1914- 25-28R
Gross, Martin (Arnold) 1934- CANR-11
Earlier sketch in CA 13-16R
Gross, Martin L(ouis) 1925- CANR-7
Earlier sketch in CA 9-12R
Gross, Mary Anne 1943- 49-52
Gross, Michael (Robert) 1952- CANR-20
Earlier sketch in CA 93-96
Gross, Michael 1891(?)-1979 Obituary 97-100
Gross, Milt 1895-1953 .... DLB 11
Gross, Milton ....AITN 1
Gross, Milton 1912(?)-1973 Obituary 41-44R
Gross, Neal 1920-1981 Obituary 108
Gross, Philip (John) 1952- 131
Gross, Phyllis P(ennebaker) 1915- 93-96
Gross, Polly 1952- 128
Gross, Richard Edmund 1920- CANR-1
Earlier sketch in CA 1-4R
Gross, Ronald 1935- CANR-5
Earlier sketch in CA 5-8R
Gross, Ruth Belov 1929- .... SATA 33
Gross, S(amuel Harry) 1933- CANR-27
Earlier sketch in CA 45-48
Gross, Sarah Chokla 1906-1976 61-64
Obituary 65-68
See also SATA 9, 26
Gross, Seymour L. 1926- CANR-3
Earlier sketch in CA 1-4R
Gross, Sheldon H(arvey) 1921- 81-84
Gross, Shelley 1938- 21-24R
Gross, Shelly
See Gross, Sheldon H(arvey)
Gross, Stuart D. 1914- 57-60
Gross, Suzanne 1933- 17-20R
Gross, Terence 1947- 101
Gross, Theodore L(awrence) 1930- CANR-14
Earlier sketch in CA 41-44R
Gross, Walter 1923- 21-24R
Gross, William Joseph 1894- CAP-1
Earlier sketch in CA 11-12
Grossack, Irvin Millman 1927- 97-100
Grossack, Martin Myer 1928- CANR-6
Earlier sketch in CA 9-12R
Grossbach, Robert 1941- CANR-13
Earlier sketch in CA 33-36R
Grossbart, Ted A. 1946- 126
Grossberger, Lewis 1940(?)- Brief entry 121
Grossen, Neal E. 1943- 93-96
Grosser, Alfred 1925- CANR-20
Earlier sketches in CA 45-48, CANR-2
Grosser, Arthur E(dward) 1934- 116
Grosser, Morton 1931- CANR-17
Earlier sketch in CA 97-100
Grosseteste, Robert 1160(?)-1253 .... DLB 115
Grossfeld, Stan 1951- 136
Grosshans, Henry 1921- 29-32R
Grossholtz, Jean 1929- 13-16R
Grossinger, Richard (Selig) 1944- CANR-19
Earlier sketch in CA 103
Grossinger, Tania 1937- CANR-4
Earlier sketch in CA 53-56
Grosskurth, Phyllis 1924- CANR-9
Earlier sketch in CA 13-16R
Grossman, Alfred 1927- 5-8R
Grossman, Allen (R.) 1932- CANR-38
Earlier sketches in CA 1-4R, CANR-1, 16
Grossman, David 138
See also CLC 67
Grossman, Edith Marian 1936- 108
Grossman, Ellie 110
Grossman, Frances Kaplan 1939- 57-60
Grossman, Gary H(oward) 1948- 69-72
Grossman, Herbert 1934- 17-20R
Grossman, Jean Schick
1894-1972 Obituary 37-40R
Grossman, Joan (Adess) 1940- 120
Grossman, Joan Delaney 1928- 111
Grossman, Julian 1931- 53-56
Grossman, Karl (H.) 1942- 130
Grossman, Kurt R. 1897-1972 Obituary 33-36R
Grossman, Lawrence 1945- 65-68
Grossman, Lee 1931- 69-72
Grossman, Louis Irwin 1901-1988 Obituary 125
Grossman, Manuel Lester 1939- Brief entry 106
Grossman, Martin A. 1951- 102
Grossman, Martin (Allen) 1943- CANR-13
Earlier sketch in CA 77-80
Grossman, Mary Louise 1930- 77-80
Grossman, Morton Charles 1919- CANR-2
Earlier sketch in CA 1-4R
Grossman, Nancy 1940- .... SATA 29
Grossman, Richard L(ee) 1921- 97-100
Grossman, Robert 1940- .... SATA 11
Grossman, Ronald P(hilip) 1934- 21-24R
Grossman, Samuel 1897- 53-56
Grossman, Sebastian P. 1934- 21-24R
Grossman, Shelly 1928(?)-1975 Obituary 57-60
Grossman, Vasily (Semenovich) 1905-1964 130
Brief entry 124
See also CLC 41
See also MTCW
Grossman, William L(eonard) 1906-1980 .... CAP-2
Obituary 97-100
Earlier sketch in CA 23-24
Grossmann, Reinhardt S. 1931- CANR-20
Earlier sketch in CA 33-36R
Grossmith, Robert (Anthony) 1954- 134
Grossu, Sergiu 1920- CANR-8
Earlier sketch in CA 57-60
Grossvogel, David I. 1925- CANR-4
Earlier sketch in CA 1-4R
Grosswirth, Marvin 1931-1984 ....33-36R
Obituary 112
Grosvenor, Donna K(erkam) 1938- 109
Grosvenor, Gilbert (Hovey)
1875-1966 Obituary 93-96
See also DLB 91
Grosvenor, Kali Diana 1960- 69-72
Grosvenor, Melville Bell 1901-1982 ....CANR-34
Obituary 106
Earlier sketch in CA 69-72
Grosvenor, Verta Mae 1938- 69-72
See also BW
Grote, David (G.) 1945- 130
Groten, Dallas 1951- CANR-38
Earlier sketch in CA 115
See also SATA 64
Groth, Alexander J(acob) 1932- CANR-14
Earlier sketch in CA 41-44R
Groth, Jeanette L(ue) 1947- 111
Groth, John (August) 1908-1988 101
Obituary 125
See also SATA 21, 56
Grotjahn, Martin 1904-1990 ....CANR-15
Obituary 132
Earlier sketch in CA 41-44R
Grotowski, Jerzy 1933- Brief entry 105
Groulx, Lionel 1878-1967 .... DLB 68
Grounds, Roger (Ransford Paterson)
1938- 97-100
Grounds, Vernon C(arl) 1914- 122
Groundwater, William
1906(?)-1982 Obituary 106
Groupe, Darryl R.
See Bunch, David R(oosevelt)
Groussard, Serge 1921- 108
Grout, Donald Jay 1902-1987 102
Obituary 121
Grout, Jack 1910- 69-72
Grout, Ruth E(llen) 1901- CAP-2
Earlier sketch in CA 17-18
Grove, Andrew S. 1936- 130
Grove, Fred(erick) 1913- CANR-37
Earlier sketches in CA 1-4R, CANR-2, 17
Grove, Frederick Philip
See Greve, Felix Paul (Berthold Friedrich)
See also DLB 92
See also TCLC 4
Grove, Jack William 1920- 5-8R
Grove, Lee E(dmonds) Obituary 104
Grove, Pearce S(eymour) 1930- 73-76
Grove, Will O.
See Brister, Richard
Grovelands, Sarah
See Schneider, Myra
Grover, David H(ubert) 1925- 13-16R
Grover, David S(teele) 1939- 89-92
Grover, John W(agner) 1927- 77-80
Grover, Linda 1934- 29-32R
Grover, Philip 1929- 104
Grover, Wayne 1934- 137
See also SATA 69
Groves, Colin Peter 1942- 61-64
Groves, Don(ald) George 106
Groves, Francis Richard 1889- CAP-1
Earlier sketch in CA 13-14
Groves, Georgina
See Symons, (Dorothy) Geraldine
Groves, H(arry) E(dward) 1921- 5-8R
Groves, Harold M(artin) 1897-1969 ....5-8R
Obituary 134
Groves, Naomi Jackson 1910- 117
Groves, Paul 1930- CANR-17
Earlier sketch in CA 93-96
Groves, Reg(inald) 1908- 13-16R
Groves, Ruth Clouse 1902- CAP-2
Earlier sketch in CA 17-18
Grow, Lawrence 1939- CANR-25
Earlier sketches in CA 73-76, CANR-10
Growe, Sarah Jane 1939- 134
Grozny, I. L.
See Berger, Ivan (Bennett)
Grub, Phillip D. 1932- CANR-32
Earlier sketches in CA 25-28R, CANR-14
Grubar, Francis S(tanley) 1924- 33-36R
Grubb
See Crumb, R(obert)
Grubb, Davis Alexander 1919-1980 ....CANR-4
Obituary 101
Earlier sketch in CA 1-4R
See also DLB 6
Grubb, Frederick (Crichton-Stuart) 1930- 101
Grubb, Kenneth George 1900-1980 .... CAP-1
Obituary 97-100
Earlier sketch in CA 9-10
Grubb, Norman (Percy) 1895- CANR-13
Earlier sketches in CAP-1, CA 13-16
Grubb, W. Norton 1948- 110
Grubbs, David H(arold) 1929- 117
Grubbs, Donald H. 1936- 81-84
Grubbs, Frank Leslie Jr. 1931- 29-32R
Grubbs, Robert L(owell) 1919- CANR-2
Earlier sketch in CA 1-4R
Grube, Georges M(aximilien) A(ntoine)
1899- CAP-1
Earlier sketch in CA 13-14
Grubel, Herbert G(unter) 1934- CANR-5
Earlier sketch in CA 9-12R
Gruber, Frank 1904-1969 .... CAP-1
Obituary 25-28R
Earlier sketch in CA 13-14
Gruber, Frederick C(harles) 1903- 49-52
Gruber, Gary R. 1940- CANR-24
Earlier sketches in CA 53-56, CANR-9
Gruber, Helmut 1928- 103
Gruber, Howard E(rnest) 1922- 119
Brief entry 113
Gruber, Ira D(empsey) 1934- Brief entry 110
Gruber, Jacob W(illiam) 1921- 1-4R
Gruber, Joseph John Jr. 1930- CANR-6
Earlier sketch in CA 5-8R
Gruber, Katherine 1952- 123
Gruber, Martin Jay 1937- CANR-8
Earlier sketch in CA 53-56
Gruber, Ruth CANR-12
Earlier sketch in CA 25-28R
Gruber, Terry (deRoy) 1953- 97-100
See also SATA 66
Gruberg, Martin 1935- 33-36R
Grubian, Motel 1909(?)-1972 Obituary 104
Grudin, Louis 1898- 1-4R
Gruelle, John (Barton)
1880-1938 Brief entry 115
See also Gruelle, Johnny
See also SATA 32, 35
Gruelle, Johnny
See Gruelle, John (Barton)
See also DLB 22
Gruelle, Worth ....AITN 2
Gruen, Erich S(tephen) 1935- 131
Gruen, John 1926- CANR-8
Earlier sketch in CA 17-20R
Gruen, Victor (David) 1903-1980 ....CANR-10
Obituary 97-100
Earlier sketch in CA 13-16R
Gruen, Yetta Fisher 125
Gruenbaum, Adolf 1923- CANR-20
Earlier sketches in CA 9-12R, CANR-5
Gruenbaum, Ludwig
See Gaathon, A(ryeh) L(udwig)
Gruenberg, Benj(amin) C(harles)
1875-1965 .... CAP-1
Earlier sketch in CA 13-14
Gruenberg, Sidonie Matsner 1881-1974 ..... CAP-1
Obituary 49-52
Earlier sketch in CA 13-16
See also SATA 2, 27
Gruenberger, Fred J(oseph) 1918- 118
Grueneberg, Hans 1907-1982 Obituary 108
Gruenhagen, Robert W. 1932- 29-32R
Gruening, Ernest (Henry) 1887-1974 .....CANR-34
Earlier sketch in CA 49-52
Gruenstein, Peter 1947- 77-80
Gruenther, Alfred M(aximilian)
1899-1983 Obituary 109
Gruffydd, Peter 1935- 104
Gruhn, Carrie Myers 1907- CAP-1
Earlier sketch in CA 11-12
Gruits, Patricia Beall 1923- 105
Grulow, Leo 1913- 5-8R
Grumbach, Doris (Isaac) 1918- CANR-9
Earlier sketch in CA 5-8R
See also CAAS 2
See also CLC 13, 22, 64
Grumbling Gourmet, The
See Chapman, Frank M(onroe)
Grumelli, Antonio 1928- 37-40R
Grumet, Robert Steven 1949- 102
Grumich, Charles A. 1905(?)-1981 Obituary 104
Grumley, Michael 1941-1988 ....29-32R
Obituary 125
Grumme, Marguerite (Evelyn) 5-8R
Grummer, Arnold E(dward) 1923- 106
See also SATA 49
Grun, Bernard 1901-1972 Obituary 37-40R
Grunbaum, Adolf
See Gruenbaum, Adolf
Grund, Josef Carl 1920- 73-76
Grundberg, Andy
See Grundberg, John Andrew
Grundberg, John Andrew 1947- 103
Grundlehner, Philip 1945- 115
Grundstein, Nathan D(avid) 1913- CANR-15
Earlier sketch in CA 37-40R
Grundt, Leonard 1936- 57-60
Grundy, J(ohn) B(rownsdon) C(lowes)
1902-1987 Obituary 123
Grundy, J(ohn) Owen 1911-1985 Obituary 114
Grundy, Joan 1920- 109
Grundy, Kenneth W(illiam) 1936- CANR-12
Earlier sketch in CA 73-76
Grundy, Lester H. 1914(?)-1985 Obituary 116
Gruneau, Richard S(teven) 1948- CANR-30
Earlier sketch in CA 110
Gruneberg, Hans
See Grueneberg, Hans
Grunewalt, Pine
See Kunhardt, Edith
Grunfeld, Frederic V(olker)
1929-1987 ....CANR-18
Obituary 124
Earlier sketch in CA 73-76
Grunge
See Crumb, R(obert)
Grunlan, Stephen Arthur 1942- CANR-39
Earlier sketches in CA 101, CANR-18
Grunwald, Constantine de
See de Grunwald, Constantine
Grunwald, Henry Anatole 1922- 107
Grunwald, Joseph 1920- 115
Grunwald, Lisa 1959- 120
See also CLC 44
Grunwald, Stefan 1933- 29-32R
Grupp, Stanley E(ugene) 1927- 53-56
Grusa, Jiri 1938- 117
Grusd, Edward Elihu 1904- CAP-2
Earlier sketch in CA 19-20
Grushow, Ira 1933- 128
Gruskin, Alan D(aniel) 1904-1970 .... CAP-1
Obituary 29-32R
Earlier sketch in CA 11-12
Gruson, Edward S. 1929- 45-48
Gruss, Edmond C(harles) 1933- 53-56
Grutz, Mariellen Procopio 1946- 93-96
Grutzmacher, Harold M(artin) Jr. 1930- 29-32R
Gruver, Rebecca
See Goodman, Rebecca Gruver
Gruver, William R. II 1929- 45-48
Gruzen, Lee Ferguson 1945- 128
Grylls, David (Stanway) 1947- 85-88
Grylls, (Mary) Rosalie Glynn
1905(?)-1988 65-68
Obituary 127
Grynberg, Henryk 1936- CANR-34
Earlier sketch in CA 29-32R
Gryst, Edward (George) 1911- 1-4R
Grzimek, Bernhard (Klemens Maria H. P.)
1909-1987 133
Obituary 121
Guadaloupe, Brother Jose de
See Mojica, Jose
Guado, Sergio
See Gerosa, Guido
Guandagnolo, Joseph F(rancis) 1912- 5-8R
Guandolo, John 1919- 21-24R
Guaragna, Salvatore 1893-1981 Obituary 105
Guard, Dave
See Guard, David
Guard, David 1934-1991 77-80
Obituary 134
Guardia, Ernesto de la Jr.
See de la Guardia, Ernesto Jr.
Guardo, Carol Joan 1939- 103
Guare, John 1938- CANR-21
Earlier sketch in CA 73-76
See also CLC 8, 14, 29, 67
See also DLB 7
See also MTCW
Guarendi, Raymond N(icholas) 1952- 120
Guareschi, Giovanni 1908-1968 105
Obituary 25-28R
Guarino, Dagmar
See Guarino, Deborah
Guarino, Deborah 1954- 136
See also SATA 68
Guarino, M(artin) Vincent 1939- 41-44R

Guay, Georgette (Marie Jeanne) 1952- 132
See also SATA 54
Guback, Thomas H(enry) 1937- 25-28R
Gubar, Susan (David) 1944- 108
See also MTCW
Gubern, Santiago (Garriga-Nogues)
1933- CANR-2
Earlier sketch in CA 45-48
Gubert, Betty Kaplan 1934- 112
Gubrium, Jaber F(andy) 1943- CANR-4
Earlier sketch in CA 53-56
Gubser, Nicholas J. 1938- 17-20R
Guccione, Robert Jr. ....AITN 2
Guches, Richard (Clement) 1938- 115
Guck, Dorothy 1913- 49-52
See also SATA 27
Gudde, Erwin G(ustav) 1889-1969 ....CANR-4
Earlier sketch in CA 5-8R
Gudenian, Haig (Krikor)
1918-1985(?) Obituary 115
Guder, Eileen (Likens) 1919- 17-20R
Gudiol, Jose
See Gudiol i Ricart, Josep
Gudiol i Ricart, Josep 1904- 81-84
Gudiol Ricart, Jose M.
See Gudiol i Ricart, Josep
Gudiol Ricart, Josep
See Gudiol i Ricart, Josep
Gudjonsson, Halldor Kiljan 1902- 103
See also Laxness, Halldor
Gudschinsky, Sarah C(aroline)
1919-1975 ....CAP-2
Earlier sketch in CA 33-36
Guede, Norina (Maria Esterina) Lami
1913- 9-12R
Guehenne, Jean
See Guehenno, Jean Marcel Jules Marie
Guehenno, Jean Marcel Jules Marie
1890-1978 Obituary 104
Guelich, Robert A(llison) 1939- CANR-17
Earlier sketches in CA 45-48, CANR-2
Guemple, Lee 1930- 41-44R
Guenderrode, Caroline von 1780-1806 ..... DLB 90
Guenette, Robert (Homer) 1935- 25-28R
Guenter, Erich
See Eich, Guenter
Guenther, Charles (John) 1920- 29-32R
Guenther, Herbert V. 1917- 73-76
Guenther, John (Lewis) CANR-9
Earlier sketch in CA 5-8R
Guenther, (Robert) Wallace 1929- 65-68
Guerard, Albert Joseph 1914- CANR-2
Earlier sketch in CA 1-4R
See also CAAS 2
Guerin, Wilfred L(ouis) 1929- 17-20R
Guerlac, Henry (Edward)
1910-1985 Obituary 116
Guerlac, Rita 1916- 116
Guerney, Bernard G(uilbert) Jr. 1930- 93-96
Guerney, Bernard Guilbert
1894-1979 Obituary 85-88
Guernsey, Bruce H(ubbard) 1944- 108
Guernsey, James Lee 1923- 37-40R
Guernsey, Otis L(ove) Jr. 1918- 89-92
Guerny, Gene
See Gurney, Gene
Guerra, Emilio Louis
1909-1980 Obituary 97-100
Guerrant, Edward Owings 1911- 21-24R
Guerra y Sanchez, Ramiro
1880-1970 Obituary 104
Guerrero, Rogelio Diaz
See Diaz-Guerrero, Rogelio
Guerrette, Richard H(ector) 1930- 49-52
Guerrier, Dennis 1923- 29-32R
Guers-Villate, Yvonne 1924- 41-44R
Guess, Edward Preston 1925- 73-76
Guest, A(nthony) G(ordon) 1930- CANR-1
Earlier sketch in CA 1-4R
Guest, Barbara 1920- CANR-11
Earlier sketch in CA 25-28R
See also CLC 34
See also DLB 5
Guest, Edgar A(lbert)
1881-1959 Brief entry 112
Guest, Harry
See Guest, Henry Bayly
Guest, Henry Bayly 1932- CANR-9
Earlier sketch in CA 65-68
Guest, Ivor (Forbes) 1920- CANR-20
Earlier sketches in CA 5-8R, CANR-2
Guest, Judith (Ann) 1936- CANR-15
Earlier sketch in CA 77-80
See also AAYA 7
See also CLC 8, 30
See also MTCW
Guest, Lynn 1939- 131
Guetersloh, Albert Paris 1887-1973 .... DLB 81
Guett, Dieter 1924- 65-68
Gueulette, David G(eorge) 1941- 111
Guevara, Che
See Guevara (Serna), Ernesto
Guevara (Serna), Ernesto 1928-1967 127
Obituary 111
See also HW
Guevremont, Germaine 1893-1968 .... DLB 68
Guffey, George
See Guffey, George Robert
Guffey, George R.
See Guffey, George Robert
Guffey, George Robert 1932- 132
Brief entry 118
Guffin, Gilbert L. 1906- 17-20R
Gugas, Chris 1921- 97-100
Gugelyk, M(yron) Ted 1938- 120
Guggenheim, Edward Armand
1901-1970 Obituary 104
Guggenheim, Hans Georg 1927- 125
Guggenheim, Harry Frank
1890-1971 Obituary 89-92
Guggenheim, Marguerite
1898-1979 Obituary 105
Guggenheim, Martin 1946- 129
Guggenheim, Peggy
See Guggenheim, Marguerite
Guggenheimer, Richard 1906-1977 ....41-44R
Obituary 69-72
Guggenmos, Josef 1922- 81-84
Guggisberg, C(harles) A(lbert) W(alter)
1913- 81-84
Gugliotta, Bobette 1918- CANR-31
Earlier sketches in CA 41-44R, CANR-14
See also SATA 7
Guhin, Michael A(lan) 1940- 41-44R
Guiberson, Brenda Z. 1946- ....SATA 71
Guice, John D(avid) W(ynne) 1931- 41-44R
Guicharnaud, June 1922-1989 93-96
Obituary 129
Guido, Beatriz 1924-1988 ....HW
Guido, (Cecily) Margaret 1912- 65-68
Guild, Lurelle Van Arsdale 1898- CAP-2
Earlier sketch in CA 29-32
Guild, Nicholas M. 1944- 93-96
See also CLC 33
Guild, Thelma S(croggs) 1911- 118
Guild, Vera Palmer 1906- Brief entry 106
Guilds, John C(aldwell Jr.) 1924- 77-80
Guiles, Fred Lawrence 1920- CANR-12
Earlier sketch in CA 25-28R
Guilford, J(oy) Paul 1897- CANR-4
Earlier sketch in CA 1-4R
Guilford, Joan S. 1928- 29-32R
Guillaume, Alfred 1888- CAP-1
Earlier sketch in CA 13-16
Guillaume, Jeanette G. Flierl 1899- 1-4R
See also SATA 8
Guille, Frances V(ernor) 1908-1975 45-48
Obituary 61-64
Guillemin, Henri 1903- 81-84
Guillemin, Jacques
See Sartre, Jean-Paul
Guillen, Jorge 1893-1984 89-92
Obituary 112
See also CLC 11
See also DLB 108
See also HW
Guillen, Mauro (Federico) 1964- 134
Guillen, Tomas 1949- 134
Guillen (y Batista), Nicolas (Cristobal)
1902-1989 125
Obituary 129
Brief entry 116
See also BLC 2
See also BW
See also CLC 48
See also HW
Guillet, Edwin C(larence) 1898-1975 107
Guillet, Jacques 1910- 102
Guillevic, (Eugene) 1907- 93-96
See also CLC 33
Guillois
See Desnos, Robert
Guillot, Rene 1900-1969 ....CANR-39
Earlier sketch in CA 49-52
See also CLR 22
See also SATA 7
Guilloux, Louis 1899-1980 Obituary 104
See also DLB 72
Guilmartin, John Francis Jr. 1940- 53-56
Guimaraes, Dona 1926(?)-1989 Obituary 129
Guimary, Donald L(ee) 1932- 73-76
Guimond, James K. 1936- 25-28R
Guin, Wyman (Woods) 1915- 102
Guinagh, Kevin (Joseph) 1897- 17-20R
Guinan, Michael D(amon) 1939- 117
Guindey, Guillaume Louis
1909-1989 Obituary 128
Guinee, Kathleen K. 1902(?)-1982 Obituary 109
Guiney, Louise Imogen 1861-1920 .... DLB 54
See also TCLC 41
Guiney, Mortimer 1930- 53-56
Guinn, Paul (Spencer Jr.) 1928- 13-16R
Guinness, Bryan (Walter) 1905- 102
Guinness, (Ian) Os(wald) 1941- 65-68
Guinther, John 1927- CANR-28
Earlier sketches in CA 69-72, CANR-11
Guion, Robert M(organ) 1924- CANR-7
Earlier sketch in CA 17-20R
Guiraldes, Ricardo (Guillermo) 1886-1927 131
See also HW
See also MTCW
See also TCLC 39
Guirdham, Arthur 1905- 103
Guisewite, Cathy (Lee) 1950- 113
Brief entry 111
See also AAYA 2
See also SATA 57
Guisinger, Stephen Edward 1941- 103
Guitar, Mary Anne 1922- Brief entry 113
Guiterman, Arthur 1871-1943 Brief entry 120
See also DLB 11
Guither, Harold D. 1927- 29-32R
Gula, Richard M(ichael) 1947- 109
Gula, Robert J(ohn) 1941- 97-100
Gulick, Bill
See Gulick, Grover C.
Gulick, Edward Vose 1915- 113
Gulick, Grover C. 1916- CANR-39
Earlier sketches in CA 33-36R, CANR-17
Gulick, Robert Lee Jr. 1912-1987 Obituary 122
Gulik, Robert H(ans) van
See van Gulik, Robert Hans
Gulker, Virgil G. 1947- 65-68
Gullace, Gino 1925- CANR-17
Earlier sketch in CA 69-72
Gullans, Charles (Bennett) 1929- CANR-39
Earlier sketches in CA 1-4R, CANR-4, 18
Gullason, Thomas A(rthur) 1924- CANR-8
Earlier sketch in CA 21-24R
Gulley, Halbert E(dison) 1919- CANR-6
Earlier sketch in CA 5-8R
Gulley, Judie 1942- ....SATA 58
Gulley, Norman 1920- 33-36R
Gullick, Charles Francis William Rowley
1907- 5-8R
Gullick, Etta 1916- 89-92
Gullick, John M(ichael) 1916- 13-16R
Gulliford, Andrew 1953- 120
Gulliford, Ronald 1920- 13-16R
Gulliver, Harold S. 1935- 97-100
Gulliver, Lemuel
See Hastings, Macdonald
Gulston, Charles 1913-1981 122
Gummere, Richard M(ott) Jr. 1912- 45-48
Gump, Richard (Benjamin) 1906- CAP-1
Earlier sketch in CA 9-10
Gump, Sally
See Stanford, Sally
Gumpertz, Robert 1925- 69-72
Gumperz, John J(oseph) 1922- 132
Gunders, Henry 1924- 29-32R
Gundersheimer, Karen 1939- 133
See also SATA 44
Gundersheimer, Werner L. 1937- 53-56
Gunderson, Doris V. 29-32R
Gunderson, Frank L(ester)
1902-1983 Obituary 110
Gunderson, Keith (Robert) 1935- 33-36R
Gunderson, Robert Gray 1915- 1-4R
Gundrey, Elizabeth 1924- CANR-6
Earlier sketch in CA 13-16R
See also SATA 23
Gundry, Robert H(orton) 1932- 29-32R
Gundry, Stanley Norman 1937- 114
Gundy, Elizabeth 112
Gundy, H(enry) Pearson) 1905- 45-48
Guney, Yilmaz 1937(?)-1984 Obituary 113
Gunji, Masakatsu 1913- 29-32R
Gunlicks, Arthur B. 1936- 126
Gunn, Bill
See Gunn, William Harrison
See also CLC 5
See also DLB 38
Gunn, Brooke
See Brooks-Gunn, Jeanne
Gunn, Christopher Eaton 1944- 117
Gunn, Diana Maureen 1926- CANR-18
Earlier sketch in CA 97-100
Gunn, Drewey Wayne 1939- 57-60
Gunn, Elizabeth
See Gunn, Diana Maureen
Gunn, Giles B(uckingham) 1938- 57-60
Gunn, Helen Montgomery
1900(?)-1987 Obituary 122
Gunn, J(ohn) A(lexander) W(ilson)
1937- CANR-20
Earlier sketch in CA 25-28R
Gunn, James E(dwin) 1923- CANR-22
Earlier sketches in CA 9-12R, CANR-5
See also CAAS 2
See also DLB 8
See also SATA 35
Gunn, John (Charles) 1937- CANR-29
Earlier sketch in CA 49-52
Gunn, Mrs. Aneas 1870-1961 Obituary 115
Gunn, Neil M(iller) 1891-1973 Obituary 37-40R
See also DLB 15
Gunn, Peter (Nicholson) 1914- CANR-18
Earlier sketches in CA 25-28R, CANR-10
Gunn, S(teven) J(ohn) 1960- 128
Gunn, Sister Agnes Marie 1928- 17-20R
Gunn, Thom(son William) 1929- CANR-33
Earlier sketches in CA 17-20R, CANR-9
See also CDBLB 1960 to Present
See also CLC 3, 6, 18, 32
See also DLB 27
See also MTCW
Gunn, William Harrison 1934(?)-1989 .....CANR-25
Obituary 128
Earlier sketches in CA 13-16R, CANR-12
See also Gunn, Bill
See also AITN 1
See also BW
Gunnars, Kristjana 1948- 113
See also CLC 69
See also DLB 60
Gunnarsson, Gunnar 1889-1975 Obituary 61-64
Gunnell, Bryn 1933- 103
Gunnell, John G. 1933- 25-28R
Gunneweg, Antonius H. J. 1922- CANR-16
Earlier sketch in CA 89-92
Gunning, Monica Olwen 1930- 65-68
Gunning, Robert 1908-1980 ....CAP-2
Obituary 97-100
Earlier sketch in CA 25-28
Gunsalus Gonzalez, Catherine
See Gonzalez, Catherine Gunsalus
Gunston, Bill
See Gunston, William Tudor
Gunston, William Tudor 1927- CANR-19
Earlier sketches in CA 49-52, CANR-3
See also SATA 9
Gunstone, A(ntony) J. H.
1937(?)-1984 Obituary 112
Gunter, (J.) Bradley (Hunt) 1940- 29-32R
Gunter, Pete A(ddison) Y(ancey)
1936- CANR-34
Earlier sketches in CA 33-36R, CANR-15
Gunterman, Bertha Lisette
1886(?)-1975 Obituary 104
See also SATA 27
Gunther, A(lbert) E(verard) 1903- 29-32R
Gunther, Bernard 1929- CANR-2
Earlier sketch in CA 45-48
Gunther, Gerald 1927- CANR-13
Earlier sketch in CA 33-36R
Gunther, John 1901-1970 ....9-12R
Obituary 25-28R
See also SATA 2
Gunther, Marc 1951- 129
Gunther, Max 1927- 13-16R
Gunther, Peter F. 1920- 9-12R
Gunther, Richard (Paul) 1946- 103
Gunton, Sharon R(ose) 1952- 102
Guntrip, Harry
See Guntrip, Henry James Samuel
Guntrip, Henry James Samuel
1901-1975 ....CANR-5
Earlier sketch in CA 5-8R
Gunzburg, Nicholas de 1904-1981 Obituary 103
Guppy, Nicholas (Gareth Lechmere)
1925- CANR-6
Earlier sketch in CA 5-8R
Guppy, Shusha 1938- 128
Gupta, Brijen K(ishore) 1929- CANR-16
Earlier sketches in CA 45-48, CANR-1
Gupta, Marie (Jacqueline) 1946- 57-60
Gupta, Pranati Sen
See Sen Gupta, Pranati
Gupta, Ram Chandra 1927- CANR-13
Earlier sketch in CA 21-24R
Gupta, S(ushil) (Kumar) 1927- 57-60
Gupta, Shiv K(umar) 1930- 57-60
Gupta, Sulekh Chandra 1928- 13-16R
Gupta, Sunetra 1965- 137
Guptara, Prabhu S(iddhartha) 1949- 81-84
Guptill, Nathanael M(ann) 1917- 45-48
Gura, Philip F(rancis) 1950- 111
Gurdus, Luba Krugman 1914- 120
Gurganus, Allan 1947- 135
See also BEST 90:1
See also CLC 70
Gurik, Robert 1932- 129
See also DLB 60
Gurin, Joel 1953- 108
Gurko, Leo 1914- CANR-5
Earlier sketch in CA 5-8R
See also SATA 9
Gurko, Miriam 1910(?)-1988 ....1-4R
Obituary 126
See also SATA 9, 58
Gurman, Alan S(tephen) 1945- CANR-5
Earlier sketch in CA 53-56
Gurnee, Jeanne 1926- 93-96
Gurnee, Russell H(ampton) 1922- 107
Gurney, A(lbert) R(amsdell) Jr. 1930- CANR-32
Earlier sketch in CA 77-80
See also CLC 32, 50, 54
Gurney, Gene 1924- CANR-9
Earlier sketch in CA 5-8R
See also SATA 65
Gurney, George 1939- 119
Gurney, Ivor (Bertie) 1890-1937 ....TCLC 33
Gurney, J. Eric CANR-2
Earlier sketch in CA 1-4R
Gurney, Nancy Jack
1915(?)-1973 Obituary 45-48
Gurney, Peter
See Gurney, A(lbert) R(amsdell) Jr.
Gurr, Andrew (John) 1936- 33-36R
Gurr, David 1936- 132
Brief entry 125
Gurr, Ted Robert 1936- CANR-16
Earlier sketch in CA 41-44R
Gurrey, Percival 1890-1980 Obituary 97-100
Gurtov, Melvin 1941- Brief entry 112
Gurwitsch, Aron 1901-1973 ....CAP-1
Obituary 41-44R
Earlier sketch in CA 13-16
Gusfield, Joseph R. 1923- 53-56
Gusikoff, Lynne
See Hawes, Lynne Gusikoff Salop
Guss, Donald L(eroy) 1929- 17-20R
Guss, Leonard M. 1926- 21-24R
Gussman, Boris (William) 1914- 5-8R
Gussow, Alan 1931- Brief entry 111
Gussow, Don 1907-1992 132
Obituary 136
Gussow, Joan Dye 1928- 29-32R
Gussow, Mel 1933- 107
Gustaf, King of Sweden
1882-1973 Obituary 45-48
Gustafson, Alrik 1903-1970 ....1-4R
Obituary 103
Gustafson, Anita 1942- 112
See also SATA 45
Gustafson, Donald F. 1934- CANR-36
Earlier sketch in CA 9-12R
Gustafson, James M(oody) 1925- CANR-37
Earlier sketch in CA 25-28R
Gustafson, James 1949- 125
Gustafson, Jim
See Gustafson, James
Gustafson, Paula Catherine 1941- 106
Gustafson, Ralph (Barker) 1909- CANR-8
Earlier sketch in CA 21-24R
See also CLC 36
See also DLB 88
Gustafson, Richard C(larence)
1933-1977 Obituary 111
Gustafson, Richard F(olke) 1934- 17-20R
Gustafson, Sarah R.
See Riedman, Sarah R(egal)
Gustafson, Scott 1956- ....SATA 34
Gustafson, W(illiam) Eric 1933- 57-60

Gustafsson, Lars 1936- 85-88
Gustaitis, Rasa 1934- 25-28R
Gustavson, Carl G(ustav) 1915- 17-20R
Gustin, Lawrence Robert 1937- CANR-37
Earlier sketch in CA 57-60
Gustkey, Earl 1940- 57-60
Gut, Gom
See Simenon, Georges (Jacques Christian)
Gutch, John 1905-1988 Obituary 124
Gutcheon, Beth R(ichardson) 1945- CANR-2
Earlier sketch in CA 49-52
Gutek, Gerald L(ee) 1935- CANR-17
Earlier sketch in CA 81-84
Gutenberg, Arthur W(illiam) 1920- 37-40R
Guterman, Norbert 1900-1984 Obituary 113
Guterman, Simeon L(eonard) 1907- 41-44R
Guterman, Stanley S(anford) 1934- 29-32R
Guterson, David 1956- 132
Guth, DeLloyd J. 1938- 129
Gutheim, Frederick 1908- CANR-9
Earlier sketch in CA 21-24R
Guthke, Karl S(iegfried) 1933- CANR-37
Earlier sketches in CA 41-44R, CANR-15
Guthman, Edwin 1919- 33-36R
Guthman, William H(arold) 1924- CANR-37
Earlier sketch in CA 57-60
Guthmann, Harry G. 1896- 1-4R
Guthrie, A(lfred) B(ertram) Jr.
1901-1991 ....CANR-24
Obituary 134
Earlier sketch in CA 57-60
See also CLC 23
See also DLB 6
See also SATA 62
See also SATO 67
Guthrie, Anne 1890-1979 ....5-8R
Obituary 134
See also SATA 28
Guthrie, Arlo (Davy) 1947- 113
Guthrie, David
See Allen, H(ubert) R(aymond)
Guthrie, Donald 1916- CANR-23
Earlier sketches in CA 13-16R, CANR-7
Guthrie, Donna W. 1946- ....SATA 63
Guthrie, Harvey Henry Jr. 1924- 13-16R
Guthrie, Hugh
See Freeman, John Crosby
Guthrie, Hunter 1901-1974 65-68
Obituary 53-56
Guthrie, Isobel
See Grieve, C(hristopher) M(urray)
Guthrie, James Shields 1931- CANR-15
Earlier sketch in CA 33-36R
Guthrie, James W. 1936- 41-44R
Guthrie, John A(lexander) 1907- 1-4R
Guthrie, John 1908- 106
Guthrie, Judith Bretherton
1905(?)-1972 Obituary 37-40R
Guthrie, Marjorie (Greenblatt Mazia)
1917-1983 Obituary 117
Guthrie, Ramon 1896-1973 ....5-8R
Obituary 45-48
See also DLB 4
Guthrie, Robert V(al) 1930- 53-56
Guthrie, Russell Dale 1936- Brief entry 106
Guthrie, T.
See Guthrie, (William) Tyrone
Guthrie, Thomas Anstey
1856-1934 Brief entry 113
Guthrie, (William) Tyrone 1900-1971 123
Obituary 29-32R
Guthrie, William Keith Chambers
1906-1981 ....CANR-11
Obituary 103
Earlier sketch in CA 65-68
Guthrie, Woodrow Wilson 1912-1967 113
Obituary 93-96
See also Guthrie, Woody
Guthrie, Woody
See Guthrie, Woodrow Wilson
See also CLC 35
Gutierrez, Donald 1932- CANR-36
Earlier sketch in CA 109
Gutierrez, Gustavo
See Gutierrez Merino, Gustavo
Gutierrez M., Gustavo
See Gutierrez Merino, Gustavo
Gutierrez Merino, Gustavo 1928- 130
See also HW
Gutierrez-Vega, Zenaida 1924- CANR-19
Earlier sketch in CA 41-44R
Gutin, Bernard 1934- 112
Gutkin, Harry 1915- 101
Gutkind, Erwin A(nton) 1886-1968 ....CANR-8
Earlier sketch in CA 5-8R
Gutkind, Lee 1943- CANR-20
Earlier sketches in CA 53-56, CANR-5
Gutkind, Peter C(laus) W(olfgang) 1925- 116
Gutman, Bill 135
See also SATA 43, 67
Gutman, Dan 1955- 133
Gutman, David 1957- 127
Gutman, Herbert G(eorge)
1928-1985 ....CANR-36
Obituary 116
Earlier sketch in CA 65-68
Gutman, Judith Mara 1928- 21-24R
Gutman, Kellie O. 1952- 124
Gutman, Naham 1899(?)-1981 Obituary 102
See also SATA 25
Gutman, Richard J(ay) S(tephen) 1949- 101
Gutman, Robert W. 1925- 25-28R
Gutman, Robert 1926- 45-48
Gutman, Roy (W.) 1944- 131
Gutman, Stanley T. 1943- 127
Gutman, Walter
See Gutman, Walter Knowlton
Gutman, Walter Knowlton
1903-1986 Obituary 119
Gutmann, Amy 1949- 128
Gutmann, David L(eo) 1925- 135
Gutmann, James 1897-1988 ....CAP-2
Obituary 127
Earlier sketch in CA 21-22
Gutmann, Joseph 1923- CANR-37
Earlier sketches in CA 49-52, CANR-1, 17
Gutmann, Myron P. 1949- 127
Brief entry 105
Gutnik, Martin J(erome) 1942- CANR-3
Earlier sketch in CA 49-52
Gutowski, Armin (Ferdinand) 1930-1987 136
Gutsche, Thelma 1915- 21-24R
Gutstein, Morris A(aron)
1905-1987 Obituary 122
Gutt, Dieter
See Guett, Dieter
Guttenberg, Barnett 89-92
Guttenberg, Virginia 1914- 81-84
Guttentag, Marcia 1932-1977 ....CANR-8
Earlier sketch in CA 57-60
Gutteridge, Anne C(hristine) 1943- 108
Gutteridge, Bernard 1916-1985 Obituary 117
Gutteridge, Don(ald George) 1937- CANR-36
Earlier sketches in CA 65-68, CANR-9
Gutteridge, Lindsay 1923- 49-52
Gutteridge, Richard (Joseph Cooke) 1911- 122
Gutteridge, William F(rank) 1919- 13-16R
Gutterson, Herbert (Lindsley Jr.) 1915- 9-12R
Gutting, Gary (Michael) 1942- CANR-37
Earlier sketch in CA 103
Guttmacher, Alan F(rank) 1898-1974 ......CANR-6
Obituary 49-52
Earlier sketch in CA 1-4R
Guttmacher, Manfred S(chanfarber)
1898-1966 ....CAP-1
Earlier sketch in CA 11-12
Guttmann, Alexander 29-32R
Guttmann, Allen 1932- CANR-39
Earlier sketches in CA 1-4R, CANR-1, 16
Guttridge, Leonard F(rancis) 1918- 85-88
Guttsman, Wilhelm Leo 1920- 9-12R
Gutwirth, Samuel William
1903-1983 Obituary 111
Gutzke, Manford G(eorge) 1896- 17-20R
Guy, Anne W(elsh) 5-8R
Guy, David 1948- 105
Guy, Harold A. 1904- 17-20R
Guy, Mary E. 1947- 138
Guy, Ray 1939- ....DLB 60
Guy, Rosa (Cuthbert) 1928- CANR-34
Earlier sketches in CA 17-20R, CANR-14
See also AAYA 4
See also BW
See also CLC 26
See also CLR 13
See also DLB 33
See also MAICYA
See also SATA 14, 62
Guyer, Paul 1948- CANR-24
Earlier sketch in CA 105
Guymer, (Wilhelmina) Mary 1909- ....SATA 50
Guyot, James F(ranklin) 1932- 53-56
Guyton, Arthur C(lifton) 1919- CANR-7
Earlier sketch in CA 17-20R
Guzie, Tad W(alter) 1934- CANR-5
Earlier sketch in CA 13-16R
Guzman (Franco), Martin Luis 1887-1976 ......HW
Guzman, Ralph C. 1924-1985 Obituary 117
Guzzetti, Alfred F. 1942- 136
Guzzo, Lou(is Richard) 1919- 135
Guzzo, Sandra E(lizabeth) 1941- 120
Guzzwell, John 1930- 13-16R
Gwaltney, Francis Irby 1921- CANR-2
Earlier sketch in CA 1-4R
Gwaltney, John Langston 1928- 77-80
Gwendolyn
See Bennett, (Enoch) Arnold
Gwilliam, Kenneth M(ason) 1937- 17-20R
Gwin, Lucy 1943- 109
Gwinup, Thomas 1932- 73-76
Gwirtzman, Milton S. 1933- 29-32R
Gwyn, Julian 1937- 57-60
Gwyn, Richard J. 1934- CANR-17
Earlier sketch in CA 25-28R
Gwyn, W(illiam) B(rent) 1927- CANR-36
Earlier sketches in CA 13-16R, CANR-5
Gwynn, Denis (Rolleston) 1893- CAP-1
Earlier sketch in CA 13-14
Gwynn, Mary 1952- 111
Gwynn, Robin D(avid) 1942- 121
Gwynne, Erskine 1898-1948 Brief entry 107
See also DLB 4
Gwynne, Fred(erick Hubbard) 1926- 113
See also SATA 27, 41
Gwynne, Oscar A.
See Ellis, Edward S(ylvester)
Gwynne, Oswald A.
See Ellis, Edward S(ylvester)
Gwynne, Peter 1941- 89-92
Gwynne-Jones, Allan 1892-1982 Obituary 107
Gwynne-Thomas, E(ric) H(ubert) 1917- 120
Gyftopolous, Elias Panayiotis 1927- CANR-36
Earlier sketch in CA 104
Gyldenvand, Lily M. 1917- CANR-6
Earlier sketch in CA 13-16R
Gyles, John 1680-1755 ....DLB 99
Gyllenhammar, Pehr G(ustaf) 1935- CANR-13
Earlier sketch in CA 73-76
Gyoergyi, Albert (von Nagyrapolt) Szent
See Szent-Gyoergyi, Albert (von Nagyrapolt)
Gyorgy, Andrew 1917- 122
Gyorgyey, Clara 1936- 77-80
Gyorgyi, Albert (von Nagyrapolt) Szent
See Szent-Gyoergyi, Albert (von Nagyrapolt)
Gysbers, Norman C(harles) 1932- 61-64
Gysin, Brion 1916-1986 117
Obituary 120
Brief entry 113
See also DLB 16
Gzowski, Peter 1934- 106

H

H. D.
See Doolittle, Hilda
See also CLC 3, 8, 14, 31, 34
See also PC 5
H. F. E.
See Everett-Green, Evelyn
H. M. S.
See Kirk-Greene, Anthony (Hamilton Millard)
H. M. W.
See Wang, Hui-Ming
Haaby, Lawrence O. 1915- 33-36R
Haac, Oscar A(lfred) 1918- 33-36R
Haack, Susan 1945- 61-64
Haaf, Beverly T(erhune) 1936- 97-100
Haaften, Julia Van
See Van Haaften, Julia
Haag, Jessie Helen 1917- CANR-5
Earlier sketch in CA 13-16R
Haagensen, Cushman D(avis)
1900-1990 Obituary 132
Haaker, Ann M. 25-28R
Haakonssen, Knud 1947- 124
Haan, Aubrey Edwin 1908- 1-4R
Haar, Charles M(onroe) 1920- 33-36R
Haar, Francis 1908- 53-56
Haar, Franklin B. 1906- CAP-1
Earlier sketch in CA 11-12
Haar, Jaap ter
See ter Haar, Jaap
See also CLR 15
Haar, James 1929- 21-24R
Haarer, Alec Ernest 1894-1970 ....CANR-4
Earlier sketch in CA 5-8R
Haarhoff, Theodore Johannes
1892-1971 ....CAP-1
Earlier sketch in CA 13-14
Haas, Albert E. 1917- 21-24R
Haas, Antonio 1923- 131
Haas, Ben(jamin) L(eopold) 1926-1977 ....CANR-8
Obituary 73-76
Earlier sketch in CA 9-12R
Haas, Carolyn Buhai 1926- CANR-9
Earlier sketch in CA 65-68
See also SATA 43
Haas, Charles A. 1947- 125
Haas, Charlie 1952- 73-76
Haas, Dorothy F. CANR-20
Earlier sketches in CA 5-8R, CANR-3
See also SAAS 43
See also SATA 43, 46
Haas, Ernst B(ernard) 1924- 81-84
Haas, Ernst 1921-1986 Obituary 120
Haas, Gerda (Schild) 1922- 110
Haas, Harold I(rwin) 1925- 29-32R
Haas, Irene 1929- 97-100
See also SATA 17
Haas, Irvin 1916- 41-44R
Haas, J(ohn) Eugene 1926- 41-44R
Haas, James E(dward) 1943- CANR-7
Earlier sketch in CA 61-64
See also SATA 40
Haas, Jessie 1959- 114
Haas, Kenneth B(rooks) Sr. 1898- CANR-6
Earlier sketch in CA 57-60
Haas, Kurt 53-56
Haas, LaVerne 1942- 49-52
Haas, Lynne 1939- 65-68
Haas, Marilyn L(oomis) 1931- 117
Haas, Mary Odin 1910- CAP-1
Earlier sketch in CA 13-14
Haas, Mary R(osamond) 1910- 9-12R
Haas, Merle S. 1896(?)-1985 Obituary 114
See also SATA 41
Haas, Michael 1938- 53-56
Haas, Raymond Michael 1935- 37-40R
Haas, Robert Bartlett 1916- Brief entry 108
Haas, Robert Lewis 1936- 101
Haase, Ann Marie Bernazza 1942- 33-36R
Haase, John 1923- CANR-14
Earlier sketch in CA 5-8R
Haavikko, Paavo Juhani 1931- 106
See also CLC 18, 34
Habbema, Koos
See Heijermans, Herman
Habe, Hans 1911-1977 ....CANR-2
Obituary 73-76
Earlier sketch in CA 45-48
Habegger, Alfred (Carl) 1941- 131
Habel, Norman C. 1932- 17-20R
Habenstreit, Barbara 1937- 29-32R
See also SATA 5
Haber, Audrey 1940- CANR-13
Earlier sketch in CA 33-36R
Haber, Carole R. 1951- 124
Haber, Eitan 1940- 104
Haber, Francis Colin 1920-1990 Obituary 131
Haber, Heinz 1913- 73-76
Haber, Jack 1939-1984 69-72
Obituary 114
Haber, Joyce 1932- 65-68
Haber, Louis 1910- 29-32R
See also SATA 12
Haber, Ralph Norman 1932- 33-36R
Haber, Samuel 1928- 9-12R
Haber, Tom Burns 1900- CAP-2
Earlier sketch in CA 17-18
Haber, William 1899- CAP-2
Earlier sketch in CA 21-22
Haberer, Joseph 1929- 65-68
Haberler, Gottfried 1900- 103
Haberly, David T(ristram) 1942- 106
Haberly, Loyd 1896-1981 105
Obituary 103
Haberman, Daniel 1933-1991 110
Obituary 135
Haberman, David A. 1928- 126
Haberman, Donald (Charles) 1933- 21-24R
Haberman, Martin 1932- 57-60
Haberman, Shelby J(oel) 1947- 103
Habermann, Helen M(argaret) 1927- 53-56
Habermas, Juergen 1929- 109
Habermas, Jurgen
See Habermas, Juergen
Haberstroh, Chadwick John 1927- 41-44R
Habgood, John Stapylton 1927- CANR-22
Earlier sketches in CA 13-16R, CANR-5
Habig, Marion A(lphonse) 1901-1984 .....CANR-20
Obituary 114
Earlier sketches in CA 5-8R, CANR-5
Hablutzel, Philip 1935- 37-40R
Habsburg-Lothringen, Geza Louis Eusebius Gebhard
See
von Habsburg-Lothringen, Geza Louis Eusebius
Hach, Clarence Woodrow 1917- 13-16R
Hachey, Thomas E(ugene) 1938- 37-40R
Hachten, Harva 108
Hachten, William Andrews 1924- 107
Hacikyan, A(gop) J. 1931- 33-36R
Hack, Walter G. 1925- 29-32R
Hackady, Hal Brief entry 105
Hacker, Andrew 1929- CANR-1
Earlier sketch in CA 1-4R
Hacker, Carlotta 1931- 118
Hacker, Frederick J. 1914-1989 Obituary 129
Brief entry 104
Hacker, Jeffrey H. 1954- 125
Hacker, Leonard
See Hackett, Buddy
Hacker, Louis M(orton) 1899-1987 ....17-20R
Obituary 122
Hacker, Marilyn 1942- 77-80
See also CLC 5, 9, 23, 72
See also DLB 120
Hacker, Mary Louise 1908- CAP-2
Earlier sketch in CA 17-18
Hacker, Rose (Goldbloom) 1906- 13-16R
Hacker, Shyrle 1910- 101
Hackes, Peter Sidney 1924- 102
Hackett, Albert 1900- ....DLB 26
Hackett, Blanche Ann 1924- 73-76
Hackett, Buddy 1924- Brief entry 108
Hackett, Cecil Arthur 1908- 13-16R
Hackett, Charles J(oseph) 1915- 73-76
Hackett, Donald F. 1918- 29-32R
Hackett, Francis 1883-1962 108
Obituary 89-92
Hackett, Herbert L(ewis) 1917-1964 ....1-4R
Hackett, Jan Michele 1952- 105
See also Kerouac, Jan
Hackett, John W. 1924- 17-20R
Hackett, John Winthrop 1910- 89-92
See also SATA 65
Hackett, Laura Lyman 1916- 17-20R
Hackett, Lee
See Arkley, Arthur J(ames)
Hackett, Marie G. 1923- 37-40R
Hackett, Pat 105
Hackett, Paul 1920- 29-32R
Hackett, Peter 1940- Brief entry 108
Hackett, Philip 1941- 77-80
Hackett, Roger F(leming) 1922- 77-80
Hackett, William H. Y. Jr.
1921(?)-1986 Obituary 118
Hackford, Robert 1921(?)-1983 Obituary 111
Hackforth-Jones, (Frank) Gilbert 1900- 13-16R
Hacking, Ian 1936- 69-72
Hackl, Erich 1954- 137
Hackleman, Michael A(lan) 1946- 106
Hackler, James C(ourtland) 1930- 112
Hackman, J(ohn) Richard 1940- CANR-1
Earlier sketch in CA 49-52
Hackman, Martha L. 1912- 29-32R
Hackney, Alan 1924- 5-8R
Hackney, Rod(erick Peter) 1942- 135
Hackney, Sheldon 1933- 41-44R
Hackney, Vivian 1914- 21-24R
Hackwell, W. John 1942- 126
Hackworth, David H. 1931- 130
See also BEST 89:4
Hadas, Moses 1900-1966 ....CANR-6
Obituary 25-28R
Earlier sketch in CA 1-4R
Hadas, Pamela White 1946- CANR-16
Earlier sketch in CA 93-96
Hadas, Rachel 1948- CANR-29
Earlier sketch in CA 111
See also DLB 120
Hadawi, Sami 1904- CANR-13
Earlier sketch in CA 21-24R
Hadda, Janet (Ruth) 1945- 128
Haddad, George M. 1910- 17-20R
Haddad, Gladys 1930- 138
Haddad, Robert M(itchell) 1930- 69-72
Haddad, William Frederick
1928- Brief entry 108
Haddad, Yvonne Y(azbeck) 1935- CANR-25
Earlier sketch in CA 108
Haddad-Garcia, George 1954- 107
Haddan, Eugene E. 1918- Brief entry 108

Hadden, Briton 1898-1929 .... DLB 91
Hadden, Jeffrey K(eith) 1936- 106
Hadden, Maude Miner 1880-1967 .... CAP-2
Earlier sketch in CA 17-18
Haddix, Cecille
See Haddix-Kontos, Cecille P.
Haddix-Kontos, Cecille P. 1937- 69-72
Haddo, Oliver
See Puechner, Ray
Haddock, Sally 1954- 121
Haddon, Celia 1944- 130
Haddon, Christopher
See Palmer, John (Leslie)
Haddox, John H(erbert) 1929- 45-48
Hader, Berta (Hoerner) 1890(?)-1976 73-76
Obituary 65-68
See also MAICYA
See also SATA 16
Hader, Elmer Stanley 1889-1973 73-76
See also MAICYA
See also SATA 16
Hadfield, Alice M(ary) 1908- CANR-26
Earlier sketch in CA 108
Hadfield, (Ellis) Charles (Raymond)
1909- CANR-26
Earlier sketches in CA 13-16R, CANR-7
Hadfield, E. C. R.
See Hadfield, (Ellis) Charles (Raymond)
Hadfield, John (Charles Heywood) 1907- 128
Hadfield, Miles H(eywood) 1903-1982 ...... CAP-1
Obituary 106
Earlier sketch in CA 13-16
Hadfield, Vic(tor Edward) 1940- Brief entry 106
Hadham, John
See Parkes, James William
Hadik, Laszlo 1932(?)-1973 Obituary 45-48
Hadingham, Evan 1951- 102
Hadithi, Mwenye
See Hobson, Bruce
Hadley, Arthur T. 1924- 89-92
Hadley, Charles D(avid) Jr. 1942- CANR-31
Earlier sketch in CA 110
Hadley, Eleanor M(artha) 1916- 29-32R
Hadley, Franklin
See Winterbotham, R(ussell) R(obert)
Hadley, Hamilton 1896-.................... CAP-1
Earlier sketch in CA 9-10
Hadley, Jay 1947- 114
Hadley, Joan
See Hess, Joan
Hadley, Lee 1934- CANR-36
Earlier sketches in CA 101, CANR-19
See also Irwin, Hadley
See also MAICYA
See also SATA 38, 47
Hadley, Leila 1925- CANR-14
Earlier sketch in CA 41-44R
Hadley, Michael L(lewellyn) 1936- 118
Hadley, Morris 1894-1979 Obituary 85-88
Hadley, Rollin van N. 1927- 127
Hadley Chase, James
See Raymond, Rene (Brabazon)
Hadlich, Roger L(ee) 1930- Brief entry 108
Hadlow, Leonard Harold 1908- CAP-1
Earlier sketch in CA 13-14
Hadrill, Andrew (Frederic) Wallace
See Wallace-Hadrill, Andrew (Frederic)
Hadrill, John Michael Wallace
See Wallace-Hadrill, John Michael
Hadwiger, Don F. 1930- 21-24R
Haeberle, Erwin J(akob) 1936- CANR-29
Earlier sketch in CA 29-32R
Haebich, Kathryn A. 1899- 5-8R
Haedrich, Marcel (pseudonym) 1913- 85-88
Haefele, John W(illiam) 1913- 1-4R
Haefner, Richard 1929- 108
Haeger, John Denis 1942- 137
Haegerstrand, (Stig) Torsten (Erik)
1916- Brief entry 116
Haegg, Tomas 1938- 111
Haegglund, Bengt 1920- CANR-10
Earlier sketch in CA 25-28R
Haekkerup, Per 1915-1979 Obituary 85-88
Haenicke, Diether H. 1935- 33-36R
Haentzschel, Adolph T(heodore)
1881-1971 ....1-4R
Obituary 103
Haering, Bernhard 1912- CANR-9
Earlier sketch in CA 5-8R
Haertling, Peter 1933- CANR-22
Earlier sketch in CA 101
See also Hartling, Peter
See also DLB 75
See also MAICYA
See also SATA 66
Haessler, Herbert A(lfred) 1926- 125
Haessly, Jacqueline 1937- 120
Hafemeister, David W(alter) 1934- 124
Hafen, Ann Woodbury 1893-1970 Obituary 111
Hafen, Brent Q(ue) 1940- 112
Hafen, LeRoy R(euben) 1893- 65-68
Hafer, W(illiam) Keith 108
Hafertepe, Kenneth 1955- 137
Haffenden, Philip Spencer 1926- 61-64
Haffner, J. Lilliwhite
See Speed, F(rederick) Maurice
Hafley, James 1928- 17-20R
Hafner, Lawrence E. 1924- CANR-10
Earlier sketch in CA 25-28R
Hafner, Marylin 1925- .... SATA 7
Haga, Enoch J. 1931- 25-28R
Hagan, Arthur Peter 1912- 107
Hagan, Charles B(anner) 1905- 37-40R
Hagan, Chet 1922- CANR-25
Earlier sketch in CA 107
Hagan, John T(homas) 1926- 25-28R
Hagan, Kenneth J(ames) 1936- 41-44R

Hagan, Patricia
See Howell, Patricia Hagan
Hagan, William T(homas) 1918- CANR-8
Earlier sketch in CA 5-8R
Hagar, George
See Maria Del Rey, Sister
Hagarty, Britt 1949- 110
Hagberg, David J(ames) 1942- 106
Hagbrink, Bodil 1936- 104
Hage, Jerald 1932- 37-40R
Hagedorn, Hermann 1882-1964 Obituary 116
Hagedorn, Robert (Bruce) 1925- CANR-28
Earlier sketch in CA 49-52
Hagee, John C(harles) 1940- CANR-3
Earlier sketch in CA 45-48
Hagelman, Charles W(illiam) Jr. 1920- 21-24R
Hagelstange, Rudolf 1912-1984 81-84
See also DLB 69
Hageman, Howard G(arberich) 1921- CANR-5
Earlier sketch in CA 1-4R
Hagen, Clifford (Warren Jr.) 1943- 29-32R
Hagen, Elizabeth Pauline 1915- 13-16R
Hagen, Everett E(inar) 1906- CANR-1
Earlier sketch in CA 1-4R
Hagen, John Milton 1902- 57-60
Hagen, John William 1940- 61-64
Hagen, Lorinda
See Du Breuil, (Elizabeth) L(or)inda
Hagen, Richard L(ionel) 1935- 93-96
Hagen, Uta 1919- 77-80
Hager, Alice Rogers 1894-1969 ....5-8R
Obituary 103
See also SATA 26
Hager, Henry B. 1926- 17-20R
Hager, Jean 1932- 101
Hager, Judith
See Polley, Judith (Anne)
Hager, Robert M. 1938- 65-68
Hager, Thomas Arthur 1953- 126
Hagerman, Edward 1939- 130
Hagerman, Paul Stirling 1949- 106
Hagerstrand, (Stig) Torsten (Erik)
See Haegerstrand, (Stig) Torsten (Erik)
Hagerty, James C(ampbell) 1909-1981 129
Obituary 103
Hagerty, Nancy K. 1935- 33-36R
Hagerty, Sheward 1930-1983 Obituary 109
Hagg, G. Eric 1908(?)-1979 Obituary 85-88
Hagg, Tomas
See Haegg, Tomas
Haggai, Thomas Stephens 1931- 93-96
Haggar, R. G.
See Haggar, Reginald George
Haggar, Reginald G.
See Haggar, Reginald George
Haggar, Reginald George
1905-1988 Obituary 128
Haggard, H(enry) Rider
1856-1925 Brief entry 108
See also DLB 70
See also SATA 16
See also TCLC 11
Haggard, Howard W. 1902- 121
Haggard, Merle 1937- Brief entry 112
Haggard, Paul
See Longstreet, Stephen
Haggard, Raymond (Gordon Rider)
1921- Brief entry 109
Haggard, Virginia 1915- 122
Haggard, William
See Clayton, Richard Henry Michael
Haggerson, Nelson L. 1927- 41-44R
Haggerty, Brian A(rthur) 1943- CANR-32
Earlier sketch in CA 113
Haggerty, James J(oseph) 1920- 41-44R
See also SATA 5
Haggerty, P(atrick) E(ugene)
1914-1980 Obituary 105
Haggett, Peter 1933- 73-76
Haggie, Paul 1949- 124
Haggin, B(ernard) H. 1900-1987 ....CANR-18
Obituary 122
Earlier sketch in CA 102
Hagiwara, Michio Peter 1932- CANR-13
Earlier sketch in CA 73-76
Hagler, Erwin Harrison 1947- 120
Hagler, Skeeter
See Hagler, Erwin Harrison
Haglund, Elaine J(ean) 1937- 109
Hagman, Bette 1922- 53-56
Hagman, Donald Gerald
1932-1982 Obituary 114
Hagner, Donald Alfred 1936- 110
Hagon, Priscilla
See Allan, Mabel Esther
Hagopian, John V. 1923- 41-44R
Hagopian, Mark N. 1940- CANR-28
Earlier sketch in CA 49-52
Hagstrom, Jerry 1947- CANR-34
Earlier sketch in CA 111
Hagstrom, Julie 1950- 111
Hagstrom, Warren Olaf 1930- 21-24R
Hagstrum, Jean (Howard) 1913- 17-20R
Hague, Douglas Chalmers 1926- CANR-20
Earlier sketch in CA 69-72
Hague, Harlan 1932- 116
Hague, (Susan) Kathleen 1949- 125
See also SATA 45, 49
Hague, Michael R. 1948- CANR-36
Brief entry 111
Earlier sketch in CA 123
See also MAICYA
See also SATA 32, 48
Hague, Richard 1947- 126
Hague, William Edward Jr. 1919- 85-88
Hagy, Alyson 1960- 137

Hagy, Ruth Geri
See Brod, Ruth Hagy
Hahn, Emily 1905- CANR-27
Earlier sketches in CA 1-4R, CANR-1
See also CAAS 11
See also SATA 3
Hahn, F. E.
See Hahn, Friedrich Ernest
Hahn, Fred E.
See Hahn, Friedrich Ernest
Hahn, Fred Ernest
See Hahn, Friedrich Ernest
Hahn, Fred 1906- 45-48
Hahn, Friedrich Ernest 1916-1989 Obituary 129
Hahn (Garces), Oscar (Arturo) 1938- 131
See also HW
Hahn, Gloria 1926-1987 Obituary 123
Hahn, H. George 1942- 107
Hahn, Hannelore CANR-3
Earlier sketch in CA 5-8R
See also SATA 8
Hahn, Harlan 1939- 33-36R
Hahn, James (Sage) 1947- CANR-17
Earlier sketches in CA 49-52, CANR-2
See also SATA 9
Hahn, (Mona) Lynn 1949- CANR-17
Earlier sketches in CA 49-52, CANR-2
See also SATA 9
Hahn, Mary Downing 1937- 122
See also MAICYA
See also SAAS 12
See also SATA 44, 50
Hahn, Otto 1879-1968 Obituary 112
Hahn, Paul H. 1932- 117
Hahn, Robert H. 1920- 123
Hahn, Robert O(scar) 1916- 69-72
Hahn, Roger 1932- 33-36R
Hahn, Steven 1951- 123
Hahner, June E(dith) 1940- CANR-11
Earlier sketch in CA 25-28R
Hahon, James
See Swift, Patrick
Haiblum, Isidore 1935- CANR-19
Earlier sketches in CA 53-56, CANR-4
Haidu, Peter 1931- 37-40R
Haig, Alexander M(eigs) Jr. 1924- 138
Brief entry 124
Haig, Fenil
See Ford, Ford Madox
Haig, (Irvine Reid) Stirling 1936- 33-36R
Haigaz, Aram
See Chekenian, Aram Haigaz
Haig-Brown, Roderick (Langmere)
1908-1976 ....CANR-38
Obituary 69-72
Earlier sketches in CA 5-8R, CANR-4
See also CLC 21
See also DLB 88
See also MAICYA
See also SATA 12
Haigerty, Leo James 1924- 1-4R
Haigh, Christopher 1944- 126
Haight, Amanda 1939- 77-80
Haight, Anne Lyon 1895-1977 .... CAP-2
Obituary 73-76
Earlier sketch in CA 33-36
See also SATA 30
Haight, Gordon S(herman) 1901-1985 ...... CAP-2
Obituary 118
Earlier sketch in CA 25-28
See also DLB 103
Haight, John McVickar Jr. 1917- 29-32R
Haight, M. R. 1938- 124
Haight, Mabel V. Jackson
See Jackson-Haight, Mabel V.
Haight, Mary Ellen Jordan
See Jordan Haight, Mary Ellen
Hail, Marshall 1905- 5-8R
Haile, H(arry) G(erald) 1931- 65-68
Hailes, Julia 1961- 130
Hailey, Arthur 1920- CANR-36
Earlier sketches in CA 1-4R, CANR-2
See also AITN 2
See also BEST 90:3
See also CLC 5
See also DLB 88
See also DLBY 82
See also MTCW
Hailey, Elizabeth Forsythe 1938- CANR-15
Earlier sketch in CA 93-96
See also CAAS 1
See also CLC 40
Hailey, Johanna
See Howl, Marcia (Yvonne Hurt)
Hailey, Johanna
See Jarvis, Sharon
Hailey, (Elizabeth) Kendall 1966- 136
Hailey, Oliver 1932- CANR-15
Earlier sketch in CA 41-44R
Hailey, Sheila 1927- 85-88
Hailperin, Herman 1899-1973 ....5-8R
Obituary 103
Hailstones, Thomas J(ohn) 1919- 41-44R
Hailwood, Mike
See Hailwood, Stanley Michael Bailey
Hailwood, Stanley Michael Bailey
1940-1981 Obituary 108
Haiman, Franklyn S(aul) 1921- 37-40R
Haiman, Robert James 1936- 133
Haimann, Theo 1911- CANR-2
Earlier sketch in CA 5-8R
Haime, Agnes Irvine Constance (Adams)
1884- CAP-1
Earlier sketch in CA 9-10
Haimes, Norma 53-56
Haimo, Ethan 1950- 128
Haimowitz, Morris (Loeb) 1918- 37-40R

Haimowitz, Natalie Reader 1923- 53-56
Haimson, Leopold Henri 1917- 126
Brief entry 109
Hain, Peter 1950- 131
Hainaux, Rene 1918- 73-76
Haindl, Marieluise 1901-1974 Obituary 49-52
See also Fleisser, Marieluise
Haine, Edgar A. 1908- 97-100
Haines, Charles G(rove)
1906-1976 Obituary 65-68
Haines, Charles 1928- 41-44R
Haines, Edward Burdette
1910-1984 Obituary 112
Haines, Francis D. Jr. 1923- 53-56
Haines, Francis 1899- 5-8R
Haines, Gail Kay 1943- CANR-31
Earlier sketches in CA 37-40R, CANR-14
See also SATA 11
Haines, George H(enry) Jr. 1937- 33-36R
Haines, Harry B. 1949(?)-1984 Obituary 112
Haines, John
See Richardson, Gladwell
Haines, John (Meade) 1924- CANR-34
Earlier sketches in CA 17-20R, CANR-13
See also CLC 58
See also DLB 5
Haines, Max 1931- CANR-15
Earlier sketch in CA 85-88
Haines, Pamela Mary 1929- CANR-24
Earlier sketch in CA 106
Haines, Perry Franklin 1889- 5-8R
Haines, Walter W(ells) 1918- 1-4R
Haines, William Wister 1908-1989 .... CAP-1
Obituary 130
Earlier sketch in CA 9-10
Haining, Peter 1940- CANR-1
Earlier sketch in CA 45-48
See also SATA 14
Hainworth, Henry Charles 1914- 109
Hair, Donald S(herman) 1937- 69-72
Hair, P(aul) E(dward) H(edley) 1926- 25-28R
Hair, William Ivy 1930- 29-32R
Haire, Wilson John 1932- 101
Haislip, Harvey (Shadle) 1889-1978 ....1-4R
Obituary 103
Haislip, John 1925- 33-36R
Haislip, Martha Pratt
1889(?)-1984 Obituary 112
Haithcox, John Patrick 1933- 29-32R
Haj, Fareed 1935- 29-32R
Hake, Thomas Gordon 1809-1895 .... DLB 32
Hakeda, Yoshito S. 1924(?)-1983 Obituary 110
Hakes, Joseph Edward 1916- 9-12R
Hakim, Seymour 1933- 65-68
Hakutani, Yoshinobu 1935- 101
Halabi, Rafik 1946- 127
Halaby, Najeeb E(lias) 1915- Brief entry 107
Halacy, D(aniel) S(tephen) Jr. 1919- CANR-9
Earlier sketch in CA 5-8R
See also Halacy, Dan
See also SATA 36
Halacy, Dan
See Halacy, D(aniel) S(tephen) Jr.
See also SAAS 8
Halal, William E. 1933- 123
Halam, Ann
See Jones, Gwyneth A.
Halas, Celia (Mary) 1922- 103
Halas, George Stanley 1895-1983 Obituary 111
Halas, John 1912- 108
Halasz, Gyula 1899-1984 126
Obituary 113
Halasz, Nicholas 1895-1985 ....17-20R
Obituary 116
Halbach, Edward C(hristian) Jr. 1931- 93-96
Halbe, Max 1865-1944 .... DLB 118
Halberg, Arvo Kusta
See Hall, Gus
Halberstadt, John 1941- 49-52
Halberstadt, William Harold 1930- 1-4R
Halberstam, David 1934- CANR-10
Earlier sketch in CA 69-72
See also BEST 89:4
Halberstam, Michael J(oseph)
1932-1980 ....CANR-10
Obituary 102
Earlier sketch in CA 65-68
Halbert, Frederic (Leslie) 1945- 122
Brief entry 118
Halbert, Sandra (Edith) 1943- 123
Halbrook, Stephen P. 121
Halcomb, Ruth 1936- 97-100
Halcrow, Harold Graham 1911- 17-20R
Haldane, A(rchibald) R(ichard) B(urdon)
1900-1982 120
Obituary 108
Haldane, J(ohn) B(urdon) S(anderson)
1892-1964 101
Haldane, R(obert) A(ylmer) 1907- 69-72
Haldane, Roger John 1945- .... SATA 13
Haldane-Stevenson, James Patrick
1910- CANR-14
Earlier sketch in CA 45-48
Haldeman, Charles (Heuss) 1931- 5-8R
Haldeman, H(arry) R(obbins) 1926- 81-84
Haldeman, Jack C(arroll II)
1941- Brief entry 119
Haldeman, Joe (William) 1943- CANR-6
Earlier sketch in CA 53-56
See also CLC 61
See also DLB 8
Haldeman, Linda (Wilson) 1935- 85-88
Halder, Ras Mohun 1905(?)-1990 Obituary 131
Hale, Agnes Burke 1890-1981 Obituary 103
Hale, Allean Lemmon 1914- CANR-30
Earlier sketch in CA 33-36R

Hale, Arlene 1924-1982 ....CANR-1
Earlier sketch in CA 1-4R
See also SATA 49
Hale, Bob
See Hale, Robert D(avid)
Hale, Charles A(dams) 1930- 25-28R
Hale, Charlotte
See Allen, Charlotte Hale
Hale, Clarence B(enjamin) 1905- 69-72
Hale, David G(eorge) 1938- 45-48
Hale, Dennis 1944- 25-28R
Hale, Edward Everett
1822-1909 Brief entry 119
See also DLB 1, 42, 74
See also SATA 16
Hale, Francesca
See Halpern, Frances J(oy)
Hale, Francis Joseph 1922- 53-56
Hale, Frank (Wilbur) Jr. 1927- 65-68
Hale, Glenn
See Walker, Robert W(ayne)
Hale, Helen
See Mulcahy, Lucille Burnett
Hale, Irina 1932- 105
See also SATA 26
Hale, J. Russell 1918- 101
Hale, Jade
See Hyatt, Betty H(ale)
Hale, Janet Campbell 1947- 49-52
Hale, John (Barry) 1926- 102
Hale, John Rigby 1923- CANR-19
Earlier sketch in CA 102
Hale, Judson (Drake) 1933- 69-72
Hale, Julian A(nthony) S(tuart) 1940- 41-44R
Hale, Kathleen 1898- 73-76
See also SATA 17, 66
Hale, Keith 1955- 126
Hale, Leo Thomas
See Ebon
Hale, Leon 1921- CANR-10
Earlier sketch in CA 17-20R
Hale, (Charles) Leslie 1902-1985 .... CAP-1
Obituary 116
Earlier sketch in CA 13-16
Hale, Linda (Howe) 1929- 5-8R
See also SATA 6
Hale, Lionel Ramsay 1909-1977 Obituary 107
Hale, Lucretia P.
See Hale, Lucretia Peabody
Hale, Lucretia Peabody 1820-1900 136
Brief entry 122
See also DLB 42
See also MAICYA
See also SATA 26
Hale, Margaret
See Higonnet, Margaret Randolph
Hale, Mason E(llsworth Jr.)
1928-1990 Obituary 131
Hale, Michael
See Bullock, Michael
Hale, Nancy 1908-1988 ....5-8R
Obituary 126
See also DLB 86
See also DLBY 80, 88
See also SATA 31, 57
Hale, Nathan Cabot 1925- 53-56
Hale, Oron James 1902-1991 ....13-16R
Obituary 135
Hale, Patricia Whitaker 1922- 53-56
Hale, Philip
See Eastwood, C(harles) Cyril
Hale, Richard W(alden)
1909-1976 Obituary 65-68
Hale, Robert Beverly 1901-1985 Obituary 117
Hale, Robert D(avid) 1928- 134
Hale, Robert William 1937- 114
Hale, Sarah Josepha (Buell)
1788-1879 ....DLB 1, 42, 73
Hale, Wanda
See Coutard, Wanda Lundy Hale
Hale, William Harlan 1910-1974 93-96
Obituary 49-52
Hale, William 1940- 125
Hales, Ann
See Hales-Tooke, Ann (Mary Margaret)
Hales, E(dward) E(lton) Y(oung) 1908- 85-88
Hales, Edward John 1927- 106
Hales, Loyde (Wesley) 1933- 89-92
Hales, Norman
See Young, Vernon
Hales, Peter Bacon 1950- 132
Hales-Tooke, Ann (Mary Margaret) 1926- 123
Brief entry 116
Halevi, Z'ev ben Shimon
See Kenton, Warren
Halevy, Eva Etzioni
See Etzioni-Halevy, Eva
Haley, Alex(ander Murray Palmer)
1921-1992 77-80
Obituary 136
See also BLC 2
See also BW
See also CLC 8, 12
See also DLB 38
See also MTCW
Haley, Andrew G(allagher) 1904- CAP-1
Earlier sketch in CA 13-16
Haley, Bruce Everts 1933- Brief entry 108
Haley, Earl. J. 1898(?)-1987 Obituary 122
Haley, Gail E(inhart) 1939- CANR-35
Earlier sketches in CA 21-24R, CANR-14
See also CLR 21
See also MAICYA
See also SAAS 13
See also SATA 28, 43
Haley, Jack Jr.
See Haley, John J. Jr.
Haley, James L(ewis) 1951- 77-80
Haley, Jay 1923- CANR-9
Earlier sketch in CA 21-24R
Haley, John J. Jr. 1933- 135
Haley, Joseph E. 1915- 13-16R
Haley, K(enneth) H(arold) D(obson)
1920- 25-28R
Haley, Margaret Angela
1861-1939 Brief entry 112
Haley, Michael 1952- 109
Haley, Neale 41-44R
See also SATA 52
Haley, P. Edward 130
Haley, (Harry) Russell 1934- 118
Haley, William (John) 1901-1987 Obituary 123
Half, Robert 1918- 107
Haliburton, Thomas Chandler
1796-1865 ....DLB 11, 99
Halifax, Joan (Squire) 1942- 85-88
Halio, Jay L(eon) 1928- CANR-10
Earlier sketch in CA 25-28R
Halivni, David
See Weiss, David
Halivni, David Weiss
See Weiss, David
Halkett, John G(eorge) 1933- 57-60
Halkin, Abraham S. 1903-1990 Obituary 131
Halkin, Shimon 1899- 53-56
Halkin, Simon
See Halkin, Shimon
Hall, Adam
See Trevor, Elleston
Hall, Adele 1910- 1-4R
See also SATA 7
Hall, Adrian 1927- CANR-22
Earlier sketch in CA 106
Hall, Al(fred) Rupert 1920- 9-12R
Hall, Alice Clay 1900- 73-76
Hall, Andrew 1935- 21-24R
Hall, Angus 1932- CANR-13
Earlier sketch in CA 21-24R
Hall, Ann
See Duckert, Mary
Hall, Anna Gertrude 1882-1967 .... CAP-1
Earlier sketch in CA 11-12
See also SATA 8
Hall, Anthony Stewart 1945- 102
Hall, Ariel Perry 1906- 69-72
Hall, Arlene Stevens 1923- 17-20R
Hall, Asa Zadel 1875-1965 ....CANR-4
Earlier sketch in CA 1-4R
Hall, Austin 1882(?)-1933 Brief entry 114
Hall, Aylmer
See Hall, Norah E. L.
Hall, B(axter) C(larence) 1936- CANR-9
Earlier sketch in CA 57-60
Hall, B. K. 1932- 106
Hall, Barbara 1960- 135
See also SATA 68
Hall, Bennie Caroline (Humble) 1-4R
Hall, Borden
See Yates, Raymond F(rancis)
Hall, Brian (Jonathan) 1959- 137
Hall, Brian P(atrick) 1935- CANR-9
Earlier sketch in CA 61-64
See also SATA 31
Hall, C(onstance) Margaret 1937- CANR-12
Earlier sketch in CA 73-76
Hall, Calvin (Springer) 1909- 13-16R
Hall, Cameron
See del Rey, Lester
Hall, Cameron P(arker) 1898- 49-52
Hall, Carl W. 1924- 135
Hall, Carolyn Vosburg 1927- 61-64
Hall, Caryl
See Hansen, Caryl (Hall)
Hall, Challis A(lva) Jr. 1917-1968 ....1-4R
Obituary 103
Hall, Charles A(rthur) M(ann)
1924- Brief entry 107
Hall, Clarence W(ilbur) 1902-1985 Obituary 114
Hall, Claudia
See Floren, Lee
Hall, Clifton L. 1898- CAP-1
Earlier sketch in CA 11-12
Hall, D(onald) J(ohn) 1903- 13-16R
Hall, Daniel George Edward 1891-1979 103
Hall, David D(risko) 1936- 125
Brief entry 108
Hall, Don Alan 1938- 108
Hall, Don 1929- 110
Hall, Donald (Andrew Jr.) 1928- CANR-2
Earlier sketch in CA 5-8R
See also CAAS 7
See also CLC 1, 13, 37, 59
See also DLB 5
See also SATA 23
Hall, Donald Ray 1933- 33-36R
Hall, Dorothy Judd 1928- 122
Hall, Douglas John 1928- CANR-14
Earlier sketch in CA 69-72
Hall, Douglas Kent 1938- 33-36R
Hall, Douglas 1931- ....SATA 43
Hall, Edward Twitchell (Jr.) 1914- 65-68
Hall, Elizabeth Cornelia 1898- 37-40R
Hall, Elizabeth 1929- CANR-31
Earlier sketches in CA 65-68, CANR-14
Hall, Elvajean 1910- CANR-8
Earlier sketch in CA 13-16R
See also SATA 6
Hall, Eric J(ohn) 1933- 97-100
Hall, Evan
See Halleran, Eugene E(dward)
Hall, F. H. 1926- 77-80
Hall, Fernau 102
Hall, Frederic Sauser
See Sauser-Hall, Frederic
Hall, Gene E(rwin) 1941- 93-96
Hall, Geoffrey Fowler 1888-1970 .... CAP-1
Earlier sketch in CA 13-14
Hall, George F(ridolph) 1908- CANR-22
Earlier sketch in CA 45-48
Hall, George R. 1930- 123
Hall, George 1941- CANR-15
Earlier sketch in CA 85-88
Hall, Georgette Brockman 1915- 57-60
Hall, Geraldine M(arion) 1935- 33-36R
Hall, Gimone 1940- CANR-33
Earlier sketches in CA 29-32R, CANR-15
Hall, Gladys 1891(?)-1977 Obituary 73-76
Hall, Gordon Langley
See Simmons, Dawn Langley
Hall, Gus 1910- 137
Brief entry 108
Hall, Gwendolyn Midlo 1929- 41-44R
Hall, H(essel) Duncan 1891-1976 .... CAP-2
Obituary 65-68
Earlier sketch in CA 29-32
Hall, H(ugh) Gaston 1931- 131
Hall, Halbert Weldon 1941- 53-56
Hall, Haywood 1898- 77-80
Hall, Helen 1892- 104
Hall, Henry M(arion) 1877- 5-8R
Hall, J(ohn) C(live) 1920- 101
Hall, J(ames) Curtis 1926- 53-56
Hall, J. De P.
See McKelway, St. Clair
Hall, J. Tillman 1916- CANR-6
Earlier sketch in CA 1-4R
Hall, Jacquelyn (Dowd) 1943- 97-100
Hall, James
See Kuttner, Henry
Hall, James Andrew 1935- 118
Hall, James B(yron) 1918- CANR-1
Earlier sketch in CA 1-4R
See also CAAS 12
Hall, James Baker 1935- 116
Hall, James (Herrick Jr.) 1933- 53-56
Hall, James Norman 1887-1951 Brief entry 123
See also SATA 21
See also TCLC 23
Hall, James W(illiam) 1937- CANR-22
Earlier sketch in CA 45-48
Hall, James 1793-1868 ....DLB 73, 74
Hall, James 1918- 102
Hall, Jay C.
See Hall, John C.
Hall, Jay 1932- 127
Hall, Jean R(ogers) 1941- 105
Hall, Jerome 1901- CAP-1
Obituary 137
Earlier sketch in CA 11-12
Hall, Jesse
See Boesen, Victor
Hall, John C. 1915- 57-60
Hall, John F. 1919- CANR-17
Earlier sketch in CA 1-4R
Hall, John O. P. 1911- 9-12R
Hall, John Whitney 1916- 25-28R
Hall, John 1937- 93-96
Hall, Josef Washington
1894-1960 Obituary 89-92
Hall, Joseph (Sargent) 1906- 41-44R
Hall, Joseph 1574-1656 ....DLB 121
Hall, Julie (Ann) 1943- Brief entry 110
Hall, Kathleen M(ary) 1924- CANR-3
Earlier sketch in CA 5-8R
Hall, Katy
See McMullan, Kate Hall
Hall, Kendall
See Heath, Harry E(ugene) Jr.
Hall, Kenneth F(ranklin) 1926- 17-20R
Hall, Kermit L(ance) 1944- 101
Hall, Kirsten Marie 1974- 135
See also SATA 67
Hall, Laurence James 1940- 97-100
Hall, Lawrence Sargent 1915- 1-4R
Hall, (Frederick) Leonard 1899- CANR-27
Earlier sketch in CA 65-68
Hall, Leslie 1948- 126
Hall, Linda B(iesele) 1939- CANR-23
Earlier sketch in CA 106
Hall, Livingston 1903- CAP-2
Earlier sketch in CA 21-22
Hall, Louis Brewer 1920- 110
Hall, Luella J(emima) 1890-1973 45-48
Obituary 103
Hall, Lynn 1937- CANR-25
Earlier sketches in CA 21-24R, CANR-37, 9
See also AAYA 4
See also MAICYA
See also SAAS 4
See also SATA 2, 47
Hall, Malcolm 1945- CANR-4
Earlier sketch in CA 49-52
See also SATA 7
Hall, Manly Palmer 1901-1990 93-96
Obituary 132
Hall, Marie Boas 1919- 9-12R
Hall, Marjory
See Yeakley, Marjory Hall
Hall, Mark W. 1943- 33-36R
Hall, Martin Hardwick 1925-1979(?) CANR-35
Earlier sketch in CA 33-36R
Hall, Mary Ann 1942- 116
Hall, Mary Bowen 1932- 21-24R
Hall, MaryAnne 1934- CANR-25
Earlier sketch in CA 29-32R
Hall, Michael Garibaldi 1926- 13-16R
Hall, Monty 1924- Brief entry 108
Hall, N(orman) John 1933- CANR-31
Earlier sketches in CA 61-64, CANR-12
Hall, Nancy Lee 1923- 57-60
Hall, Natalie Watson 1923- 5-8R
Hall, Neal (Gordon) 1952- 134
Hall, Noel (Frederick) 1902-1983 Obituary 109
Hall, Norah E. L. 1914- 97-100
Hall, O. M.
See Hall, Oakley (Maxwell)
Hall, Oakley (Maxwell) 1920- CANR-3
Earlier sketch in CA 9-12R
Hall, Patrick 1932- 21-24R
Hall, Penelope C(oker) 1933- 17-20R
Hall, Peter (Geoffrey) 1932- CANR-24
Earlier sketches in CA 17-20R, CANR-8
Hall, Peter (Reginald Frederick) 1930- 133
Hall, Phil 1953- 102
Hall, R(obert) Cargill 1937- CANR-1
Earlier sketch in CA 49-52
Hall, (Marguerite) Radclyffe
1886(?)-1943 Brief entry 110
See also TCLC 12
Hall, (Patrick) Richard Compton
See Compton-Hall, (Patrick) Richard
Hall, Richard H(ammond) 1934- CANR-13
Earlier sketch in CA 77-80
Hall, Richard (Seymour) 1925- CANR-9
Earlier sketch in CA 17-20R
Hall, Robert A(nderson) Jr. 1911- CANR-5
Earlier sketch in CA 13-16R
Hall, Robert Benjamin 1918- 57-60
Hall, Robert Burnett Jr. 1923- Brief entry 109
Hall, Robert E(lliott) 1924- CANR-13
Earlier sketch in CA 17-20R
Hall, Robert E(rnest) 1943- 114
Hall, Robert Lee 1941- 73-76
Hall, Robert T(om) 1938- Brief entry 110
Hall, Rodney 1935- 109
See also CLC 51
Hall, Roger (Leighton) 1939- 134
Hall, Roger (Wolcott) 1919- 29-32R
Hall, Roger 1945- 112
Hall, Rosalys Haskell 1914- 9-12R
See also SATA 7
Hall, Ross H(ume) 1926- 61-64
Hall, Rubylea (Ray) 1910- CAP-2
Earlier sketch in CA 17-18
Hall, Ruth 1933(?)-1981 Obituary 104
Hall, Sam 1936- 137
Hall, Steven (Leonard) 1960- 93-96
Hall, Susan 1940- 57-60
Hall, T(homas) William 1921- 118
Hall, Ted Byron 1902- CAP-2
Earlier sketch in CA 33-36
Hall, Thor 1927- 37-40R
Hall, Tom T. 1936- 102
Hall, Tony
See Hall, Anthony Stewart
Hall, Tord (Erik Martin) 1910- 29-32R
Hall, Trevor H(enry) 1910-1991 ....CANR-16
Obituary 134
Earlier sketch in CA 29-32R
Hall, Van Beck 1934- 45-48
Hall, Vernon Jr. 1913- CANR-3
Earlier sketch in CA 5-8R
Hall, Wade H. 1934- CANR-6
Earlier sketch in CA 5-8R
Hall, Walter (Earl Jr.) 1940- CANR-13
Earlier sketch in CA 21-24R
Hall, Wayne E(dward) 1947- 105
Hall, William N(orman)
1915-1974 Obituary 53-56
Hall, Willis 1929- CANR-36
Earlier sketch in CA 101
See also MTCW
See also SATA 66
Hall, Wilson (Dudley) 1922-1991 69-72
Obituary 133
Halla, (Robert) Chris(tian) 1949- CANR-18
Earlier sketch in CA 77-80
Hallahan, William H(enry) Brief entry 109
Hallahmi, Benjamin Beit
See Beit-Hallahmi, Benjamin
Hallam, Arthur Henry 1811-1833 ....DLB 32
Hallam, (Samuel Benoni) Atlantis 1915- 5-8R
Hallam, Elizabeth M. 1950- 123
Hallam, H(erbert) E(noch) 1923- 21-24R
Hallam, J(ohn) Harvey 1917- 13-16R
Hallard, Peter
See Catherall, Arthur
Hallas, Richard
See Knight, Eric (Mowbray)
Hallberg, Charles William 1899- CAP-1
Earlier sketch in CA 17-18
Hallberg, Edmond C. 1931- Brief entry 111
Hallberg, Peter 1916- CANR-4
Earlier sketch in CA 53-56
Hall-Clarke, James
See Rowland-Entwistle, (Arthur) Theodore (Henry)
Halle, Jean-Claude 1939- CANR-17
Earlier sketch in CA 93-96
Halle, Katherine Murphy 41-44R
Halle, Kay
See Halle, Katherine Murphy
Halle, Louis J(oseph) 1910- CANR-2
Earlier sketch in CA 1-4R
Halleck, Fitz-Greene 1790-1867 ....DLB 3
Halleck, Seymour L(eon) 1929- CANR-13
Earlier sketch in CA 21-24R
Haller, Archibald O(rben) Jr. 1926- 45-48
Haller, Bill
See Bechko, Peggy Anne
Haller, Dorcas Woodbury 1946- 117
See also SATA 46
Haller, Ellis M(etcalf) 1915-1981 Obituary 103
Haller, John Samuel Jr. 1940- 61-64
Haller, Mark H(ughlin) 1928- CANR-5
Earlier sketch in CA 9-12R
Haller, Mike 1945- 110
Haller, Robert S(pencer) 1933- CANR-2
Earlier sketch in CA 1-4R

Haller, Robin Meredith 1944- ...65-68
Haller, William 1885-1974 Obituary ...49-52
Halleran, Eugene E(dward) 1905- ...1-4R
Hallet, Jean-Pierre 1927- ...17-20R
Hallett, Ellen Kathleen 1899- ...CAP-1
Earlier sketch in CA 13-16
Hallett, Garth L(ie) 1927- ...CANR-13
Earlier sketch in CA 69-72
Hallett, George H(ervey) Jr.
1895-1985 Obituary ...116
Hallett, Graham 1929- ...CANR-16
Earlier sketch in CA 25-28R
Hallett, Judith Peller 1944- ...124
Hallett, Kathryn J(osephine) 1937- ...57-60
Hallett, Robin 1926- ...103
Halley, Anne 1928- ...121
Halley, Laurence
See O'Keeffe, Laurence
Hallgarten, George W(olfgang) F(elix)
1901-1975 ...65-68
Obituary ...57-60
Hallgarten, Peter A(lexander) 1931- ...97-100
Hallgarten, Siegfried Fritz 1902- ...CANR-18
Earlier sketches in CA 5-8R, CANR-3
Hallgren, Chris 1947- ...115
Halliburton, David (Garland)
1933- Brief entry ...116
Halliburton, Richard 1900-1939(?) ...135
Brief entry ...114
Halliburton, Rudia Jr. 1929- ...81-84
Halliburton, Warren J. 1924- ...CANR-24
Earlier sketch in CA 33-36R
See also BW
See also SATA 19
Halliday, Brett
See Dresser, Davis
and Terrall, Robert
Halliday, David 1948- ...113
Halliday, Dorothy
See Dunnett, Dorothy
Halliday, E(rnest) M(ilton) 1913- ...1-4R
Halliday, Ena
See Baumgarten, Sylvia
Halliday, F(rank) E(rnest) 1903-1982 ...CANR-2
Obituary ...106
Earlier sketch in CA 1-4R
Halliday, Fred 1937- ...53-56
Halliday, James
See Symington, David
Halliday, Jerry 1949- ...69-72
Halliday, Jon 1939- ...97-100
Halliday, M(ichael) A(lexander) K(irkwood)
1925- ...126
Brief entry ...112
Halliday, Michael
See Creasey, John
Halliday, Richard 1905-1973 Obituary ...41-44R
Halliday, Tim (Richard) 1945- ...112
Halliday, William R(oss) 1926- ...49-52
See also SATA 52
Hallie, Philip P. 1922- ...CANR-9
Earlier sketch in CA 13-16R
Hallier, Amedee 1913- ...73-76
Halligan, Nicholas 1917- ...CANR-5
Earlier sketch in CA 13-16R
Hallin, Emily Watson ...CANR-26
Earlier sketches in CA 25-28R, CANR-10
See also SATA 6
Hallinan, Hazel Hunkins
1891(?)-1982 Obituary ...106
Hallinan, Nancy 1921- ...CANR-3
Earlier sketch in CA 9-12R
Hallinan, P(atrick) K(enneth) 1944- ...CANR-11
Earlier sketch in CA 69-72
See also SATA 37, 39
Hallinan, Vincent 1896- ...1-4R
Hallion, Richard P(aul Jr.) 1948- ...41-44R
Halliwell, David (William) 1936- ...CANR-31
Earlier sketches in CA 65-68, CANR-11
Halliwell, Leslie 1929-1989 ...CANR-16
Obituary ...127
Earlier sketches in CA 49-52, CANR-1
Hall-Jones, Frederick George
1891-1982 Obituary ...108
Hallman, Frank Curtis
1943(?)-1975 Obituary ...104
Hallman, G(eorge) Victor III 1930- ...101
Hallman, Howard W(esley) 1928- ...116
Hallman, Ralph J(efferson) 1911- ...13-16R
Hallman, Ruth 1929- ...CANR-15
Earlier sketch in CA 85-88
See also SATA 28, 43
Hallo, William W. 1928- ...CANR-15
Earlier sketch in CA 37-40R
Hallock, G. B. F.
See Hallock, Gerard B(enjamin) F(leet)
Hallock, Gerard B(enjamin) F(leet)
1856-1953 Brief entry ...122
Hallock, Robert Lay 1898(?)-1986 Obituary ...120
Halloran, Richard (Colby) 1930- ...29-32R
Halloway, Vance 1916- ...53-56
Hallowell, A(lfred) Irving 1892-1974 ...5-8R
Obituary ...53-56
Hallowell, Christopher L. 1945- ...93-96
Hallowell, John H(amilton) 1913- ...CANR-5
Earlier sketch in CA 13-16R
Hallowell, Tommy
See Hill, Thomas
Hallpike, C. R. 1938- ...41-44R
Hall-Quest, (Edna) Olga W(ilbourne)
1899-1986 ...5-8R
Obituary ...118
See also SATA 11, 47
Halls, Geraldine (Mary) 1919- ...103
Halls, W(ilfred) D(ouglas) 1918- ...CANR-5
Earlier sketch in CA 1-4R
Hallstead, William F(inn III) 1924- ...CANR-21
Earlier sketches in CA 5-8R, CANR-6
See also SATA 11
Hallstein, Walter 1901-1982 Obituary ...106
Hallstroem, Per (August Leonard)
1866-1960 Obituary ...116
Hallstrom, Per (August Leonard)
See Hallstroem, Per (August Leonard)
Hallus, Tak
See Robinett, Stephen (Allen)
Hallward, Michael 1889- ...49-52
See also SATA 12
Halm, George N(ikolaus) 1901- ...21-24R
Halman, Talat Sait 1931- ...CANR-4
Earlier sketch in CA 53-56
Halmos, Paul 1911-1977 ...CANR-8
Earlier sketch in CA 17-20R
Halper
See Halpern, Leivick
Halper, Albert 1904-1984 ...CANR-3
Obituary ...111
Earlier sketch in CA 5-8R
See also DLB 9
Halper, Nathan 1908(?)-1983 Obituary ...110
Halper, Sam 1916-1989 Obituary ...128
Halper, Thomas 1942- ...41-44R
Halperin, David M(artin) 1952- ...117
Halperin, Don A(kiba) 1925- ...57-60
Halperin, Edwin G. 1935(?)-1987 Obituary ...123
Halperin, Irving 1922- ...29-32R
Halperin, Joan Ungersma 1932- ...137
Halperin, John 1941- ...CANR-6
Earlier sketch in CA 53-56
See also DLB 111
Halperin, Jonathan L. 1949- ...132
Halperin, Mark (Warren) 1940- ...CANR-9
Earlier sketch in CA 65-68
Halperin, Maurice 1906- ...73-76
Halperin, Morton H. 1938- ...CANR-3
Earlier sketch in CA 9-12R
Halperin, S(amuel) William 1905-1979 ...97-100
Obituary ...85-88
Halperin, Samuel 1930- ...CANR-1
Earlier sketch in CA 1-4R
Halpern, A(braham) M(eyer) 1914- ...17-20R
Halpern, Barbara Kerewsky
See Kerewsky-Halpern, Barbara
Halpern, Barbara Strachey 1912- ...106
Halpern, Ben(jamin) 1912-1990 Obituary ...131
Brief entry ...115
Halpern, Daniel 1945- ...33-36R
See also CLC 14
Halpern, Frances J(oy) ...114
Halpern, Howard Marvin 1929- ...93-96
Halpern, Joel M. 1929- ...CANR-3
Earlier sketch in CA 5-8R
Halpern, L.
See Halpern, Leivick
Halpern, Leivick 1888-1962 Obituary ...114
Halpern, Manfred 1924- ...9-12R
Halpern, Martin 1929- ...CANR-7
Earlier sketch in CA 5-8R
Halpern, Oscar Saul 1912- ...97-100
Halpern, Paul G. 1937- ...45-48
Halpern, Paul J(oseph) 1942- ...CANR-7
Earlier sketch in CA 57-60
Halpern, Stephen Mark 1940- ...57-60
Halpert, Inge D. 1926- ...21-24R
Halpert, Stephen 1941- ...37-40R
Halpin, Andrew W(illiams) 1911- ...17-20R
Halprin, Anna Schuman 1920- ...85-88
Halprin, Lawrence 1916- ...41-44R
Hals, Ronald M. 1926- ...33-36R
Halsall, Elizabeth 1916- ...33-36R
Halsall, Eric 1920- ...107
Halsband, Robert 1914-1989 ...CANR-8
Obituary ...130
Earlier sketch in CA 17-20R
Halsell, Grace (Eleanor) 1923- ...CANR-13
Earlier sketch in CA 21-24R
See also AITN 1
See also SATA 13
Halsey, A(lbert) H(enry) 1923- ...CANR-7
Earlier sketch in CA 17-20R
Halsey, Elizabeth Tower
1903(?)-1976 Obituary ...65-68
Halsey, Elizabeth 1890- ...CAP-2
Earlier sketch in CA 17-18
Halsey, George Dawson 1889-1970 ...1-4R
Obituary ...103
Halsey, Margaret (Frances) 1910- ...81-84
Halsey, Martha T. 1932- ...CANR-14
Earlier sketch in CA 37-40R
Halsey, William D(arrach) 1918- Brief entry ...117
Halsman, Philippe 1906-1979 ...CANR-10
Obituary ...89-92
Earlier sketch in CA 21-24R
Halstead, Dirck S. 1936- ...133
Halstead, Murat 1829-1908 ...DLB 23
Halstead, William Perdue
1906-1982 Obituary ...109
Halsted, Anna Roosevelt
1906-1975 Obituary ...61-64
See also SATA 30
Halstock, Max
See Caulfield, Malachy Francis
Halter, Carl 1915- ...17-20R
Halter, Jon C(harles) 1941- ...CANR-13
Earlier sketch in CA 61-64
See also SATA 22
Halton, David 1940- ...73-76
Halton, Eugene Rochberg
See Rochberg-Halton, Eugene
Haltrecht, Montague 1932- ...29-32R
Halverson, Alton C. O. 1922- ...61-64
Halverson, Richard C. 1916- ...CANR-3
Earlier sketch in CA 1-4R
Halverson, Richard P(aul) 1941- ...109
Halverson, William H(agen) 1930- ...37-40R
Halvorson, Arndt L(eroy) 1915- ...CANR-3
Earlier sketch in CA 5-8R
Halvorson, Marilyn 1948- ...132
Halward, Leslie G. 1904(?)-1976 Obituary ...65-68
Ham, Wayne 1938- ...CANR-11
Earlier sketch in CA 21-24R
Hamachek, Don E. 1933- ...17-20R
Hamada, Hirosuke 1893- ...45-48
Hamady, Walter ...AITN 1
Hamalainen, Pekka Kalevi 1938- ...97-100
Hamalainen, Pertti (Olavi) 1952- ...138
Hamalian, Leo 1920- ...CANR-2
Earlier sketch in CA 5-8R
See also SATA 41
Hamann, Johann Georg 1730-1788 ...DLB 97
Hamberg, Daniel 1924- ...1-4R
Hamberger, Conrad P. 1900- ...13-16R
Hamberger, John 1934- ...69-72
See also SATA 14
Hambletonian
See Fairfax-Blakeborough, John Freeman
Hamblett, Theora 1895(?)-1977 Obituary ...69-72
Hamblin, C(harles) L(eonard) 1922- ...25-28R
Hamblin, Dora Jane 1920- ...37-40R
See also SATA 36
Hamblin, Douglas H. 1923- ...115
Hamblin, Robert L(ee) 1927- ...97-100
Hamblin, Robert W(ayne) 1938- ...131
Hamblin, W. K. 1928- ...53-56
Hambourg, Maria Morris 1949- ...130
Hambrick-Stowe, Charles E(dwin) 1948- ...125
Hamburg, Carl H(einz) 1915- ...37-40R
Hamburg, David A(llen) 1925- Brief entry ...109
Hamburg, Morris 1922- Brief entry ...114
Hamburger, Ernest
1891(?)-1980 Obituary ...97-100
Hamburger, Estelle 1898(?)-1983 Obituary ...110
Hamburger, Kaete 1896- ...CANR-14
Earlier sketch in CA 29-32R
Hamburger, Max 1897-1970 ...CAP-2
Earlier sketch in CA 17-18
Hamburger, Michael J(ay) 1938- ...CANR-3
Earlier sketch in CA 45-48
Hamburger, Michael (Peter Leopold)
1924- ...CANR-2
Earlier sketch in CA 5-8R
See also CAAS 4
See also CLC 5, 14
See also DLB 27
Hamburger, Philip 1914- ...5-8R
Hamburger, Robert (A. Jr.) 1943- ...CANR-8
Earlier sketch in CA 61-64
Hamburgh, Max 1922- ...61-64
Hamby, Alonzo L. 1940- ...CANR-15
Earlier sketch in CA 37-40R
Hamel, Peter Michael 1947- ...97-100
Hamel Dobkin, Kathleen
See Hamel Peifer, Kathleen
Hamelin, Louis-Edmond 1923- ...110
Hamell, Patrick Joseph 1910- ...CAP-1
Earlier sketch in CA 13-16
Hamelman, Paul W(illiam) 1930-1976 ...41-44R
Hamel Peifer, Kathleen 1945- ...CANR-28
Earlier sketch in CA 110
Hamer, David Allan 1938- ...CANR-35
Earlier sketch in CA 45-48
Hamer, Frank 1929- ...105
Hamer, Mick 1946- ...109
Hamer, Philip (May) 1891-1971 Obituary ...104
Hamermesh, Daniel S(elim)
1943- Brief entry ...110
Hamermesh, Morton 1915- ...5-8R
Hamerow, Theodore S(tephen) 1920- ...CANR-28
Earlier sketch in CA 49-52
Hamerstrom, Frances 1907- ...69-72
See also SATA 24
Hames, (Alice) Inez 1892- ...29-32R
Hamey, J(ohn) A(nthony) 1956- ...109
Hamey, L(eonard) A(rnold) 1918- ...109
Hamil, Sharon Hide 1939- ...122
Hamil, Thomas Arthur 1928- ...73-76
See also SATA 14
Hamill, Denis 1951- ...110
Hamill, Ethel
See Webb, Jean Francis
Hamill, Pete 1935- ...CANR-18
Earlier sketch in CA 25-28R
See also CLC 10
Hamill, Robert H(offman) 1912-1975 ...CAP-2
Earlier sketch in CA 33-36
Hamill, Sam ...CAAS 15
Hamilton, A(lbert) C(harles) 1921- ...133
Hamilton, Adam
See Henderson, M(arilyn) R(uth)
Hamilton, (John) Alan 1943- ...CANR-36
Earlier sketch in CA 115
See also SATA 66
Hamilton, Alex John 1939- ...103
Hamilton, Alexander 1712-1756 ...DLB 31
Hamilton, Alexander 1755(?)-1804 ...DLB 37
Hamilton, Alfred Starr 1914- ...53-56
Hamilton, Alice
See Cromie, Alice Hamilton
Hamilton, B(ertram) L(awson) St. John
1914- ...13-16R
Hamilton, Beth Alleman 1927- ...110
Hamilton, (Arthur Douglas) Bruce
1900-1974 Obituary ...109
Hamilton, Buzz
See Hemming, Roy
Hamilton, Carl 1914- ...53-56
Hamilton, Carlos D. 1908- ...69-72
Hamilton, Charles D(aniel)
1940- Brief entry ...112
Hamilton, Charles F(ranklin) 1915- ...89-92
Hamilton, Charles Granville
1905-1984 ...CANR-15
Earlier sketch in CA 41-44R
Hamilton, Charles (Harold St. John)
1876-1961 ...CANR-29
Earlier sketch in CA 73-76
See also SATA 13
Hamilton, Charles Vernon 1929- ...77-80
Hamilton, Charles W(alter) 1890- ...5-8R
Hamilton, Charles 1913- ...CANR-20
Earlier sketches in CA 5-8R, CANR-3
See also SATA 65
Hamilton, Cicely (Mary)
1872-1952 Brief entry ...113
See also DLB 10
Hamilton, Clare
See Lawless, Bettyclare Hamilton
Hamilton, Clive
See Lewis, C(live) S(taples)
Hamilton, Dave
See Troyer, Byron L(eRoy)
Hamilton, David (Boyce Jr.) 1918- ...29-32R
Hamilton, David (Peter) 1935- ...119
Hamilton, David 1939- ...126
Hamilton, (Charles) Denis 1918-1988 ...109
Obituary ...125
Hamilton, Donald (Bengtsson) 1916- ...CANR-39
Earlier sketches in CA 1-4R, CANR-2, 18
Hamilton, Dorothy (Drumm) 1906-1983 ...33-36R
Obituary ...110
See also SATA 12, 35
Hamilton, Earl J(efferson) 1899-1989 ...CAP-1
Obituary ...128
Earlier sketch in CA 9-10
Hamilton, Edith 1867-1963 ...77-80
See also SATA 20
Hamilton, Edmond 1904-1977 ...CANR-3
Earlier sketch in CA 1-4R
See also CLC 1
See also DLB 8
Hamilton, Edward G. 1897- ...CAP-1
Earlier sketch in CA 11-12
Hamilton, Eleanor Poorman 1909- ...CANR-2
Earlier sketch in CA 1-4R
Hamilton, (Muriel) Elizabeth (Mollie)
1906- ...CAP-1
Earlier sketch in CA 9-10
See also SATA 23
Hamilton, Elizabeth 1758-1816 ...DLB 116
Hamilton, Elizabeth 1928- ...97-100
Hamilton, Ernest
See Merril, Judith
Hamilton, Eugene (Jacob) Lee
See Lee-Hamilton, Eugene (Jacob)
Hamilton, Floyd (Garland)
1908(?)-1984 Obituary ...113
Hamilton, Franklin
See Silverberg, Robert
Hamilton, Franklin Willard 1923- ...33-36R
Hamilton, Gail
See Corcoran, Barbara
Hamilton, Gene 1943- ...120
Hamilton, George Baillie
See Baillie-Hamilton, George
Hamilton, George Rostrevor
1888-1967 Obituary ...93-96
Hamilton, Hamish 1900-1988 Obituary ...125
Hamilton, Henry W. 1898- ...33-36R
Hamilton, Hervey
See Robins, Denise (Naomi)
Hamilton, Holman 1910-1980 ...CANR-10
Obituary ...97-100
Earlier sketch in CA 13-16R
Hamilton, Horace E(rnst) 1911- ...21-24R
Hamilton, Howard Devon 1920- ...13-16R
Hamilton, Hugo 1953- ...138
Hamilton, Iain (Betram) 1920-1986 ...130
Hamilton, (Robert) Ian 1938- ...106
See also DLB 40
Hamilton, J(ames) A(lan) B(ousfield)
1899-1971 Obituary ...116
Hamilton, J(ames) Wallace 1900-1968 ...CAP-1
Earlier sketch in CA 13-14
Hamilton, Jack
See Brannon, William T.
Hamilton, James Robertson 1921- ...103
Hamilton, Janet 1951- ...114
Hamilton, Jean Tyree 1909- ...33-36R
Hamilton, Joan Lesley 1942- ...102
Hamilton, John
See Hayden, Sterling
Hamilton, John Maxwell 1947- ...121
Hamilton, Julia
See Watson, Julia
Hamilton, Katie 1945- ...118
Hamilton, Kay
See DeLeeuw, Cateau
Hamilton, Kenneth (Morrison) 1917- ...17-20R
Hamilton, Marshall Lee 1937- ...37-40R
Hamilton, Mary (E.) 1927- ...123
See also SATA 55
Hamilton, Michael (Pollock) 1927- ...CANR-30
Earlier sketch in CA 29-32R
Hamilton, Milton W(heaton) 1901-1989 ...CAP-1
Obituary ...128
Earlier sketch in CA 13-16
Hamilton, Mollie
See Kaye, M(ary) M(argaret)
Hamilton, Morse 1943- ...108
See also SATA 35
Hamilton, Nancy 1908-1985 Obituary ...115
Hamilton, Neill Q. 1925- ...61-64
Hamilton, (Charles) Nigel 1944- ...101
Hamilton, (Anthony Walter) Patrick
1904-1962 Obituary ...113
See also CLC 51
See also DLB 10

Hamilton, Patrick Macfarlan
1892-1977 Obituary 108
Hamilton, Paul
See Dennis-Jones, H(arold)
Hamilton, Peter (Edward) 1947- 73-76
Hamilton, Peter N(apier)
1925(?)-1989 Obituary 128
Hamilton, Ralph
See Stratemeyer, Edward L.
Hamilton, Raphael N(oteware) 1892- CAP-2
Earlier sketch in CA 29-32
Hamilton, Richard F(rederick) 1930- CANR-26
Earlier sketch in CA 108
Hamilton, Richard 1922- Brief entry 116
Hamilton, Robert W. CANR-26
Earlier sketches in CAP-2, CA 19-20
Hamilton, Ronald 1909- 13-16R
Hamilton, Russell G(eorge) 1934- 61-64
Hamilton, Seena M. 1926- 17-20R
Hamilton, Virginia 1936- CANR-37
Earlier sketches in CA 25-28R, CANR-20
See also AAYA 2
See also BW
See also CLC 26
See also CLR 1, 11
See also DLB 33, 52
See also MAICYA
See also MTCW
See also SATA 4, 56
Hamilton, W(illiam) B(askerville)
1908-1972 .... CAP-1
Obituary 37-40R
Earlier sketch in CA 17-18
Hamilton, W(illis) D(avid) 1936- 105
Hamilton, Wade
See Floren, Lee
Hamilton, Wallace 1919-1983 ....CANR-15
Obituary 110
Earlier sketch in CA 85-88
Hamilton, Walter 1908-1988 109
Obituary 124
Hamilton, William Jr. 1924- 53-56
Hamilton, William B(aillie) 1930- 102
Hamilton, William 1939- CANR-15
Earlier sketch in CA 69-72
Hamilton-Edwards, Gerald (Kenneth Savery)
1906- CANR-14
Earlier sketch in CA 21-24R
Hamilton-Hill, Donald 1915-1985 Obituary 117
Hamilton-Paterson, James 1941- 137
Hamizrachi, Yoram 1942- 107
Hamlet, Ova
See Lupoff, Richard A(llen)
Hamlet, Sybil E. 1913(?)-1989 Obituary 129
Hamley, Dennis 1935- CANR-26
Earlier sketches in CA 57-60, CANR-11
See also SATA 39, 69
Hamlin, Charles Hughes 1907- 69-72
Hamlin, Gladys E(va) 37-40R
Hamlin, Griffith Askew 1919- 37-40R
Hamlin, Marjorie (Day) 1921- 105
Hamlin, Wilfrid G(ardiner) 1918- 93-96
Hamlyn, D(avid) W(alter) 1924- 132
Hamm, Charles Edward 1925- 103
Hamm, Cleve 1927(?)-1984 Obituary 112
Hamm, Edward Frederick Jr.
1908-1985 Obituary 115
Hamm, Glenn B(ruce) 1936-1980 53-56
Obituary 125
Hamm, Jack 1916- CANR-9
Earlier sketch in CA 5-8R
Hamm, Marie Roberson 1917- 65-68
Hamm, Michael Franklin 1943- 89-92
Hamm, Robert M(acGowan) 1950- 116
Hamm, Russell Leroy 1926- CANR-2
Earlier sketch in CA 5-8R
Hamm, Thomas D. 1957- 137
Hammack, David C(onrad) 1941- 115
Hammack, James W. Jr. 1937- 81-84
Hamman, Henry (Longley) 1946- 119
Hamman, Ray T(racy) 1945- 69-72
Hammar, Russell A(lfred) 1920- 104
Hammarskjoeld, Dag (Hjalmar Agne Carl)
1905-1961 77-80
Hammarskjold, Dag
See Hammarskjoeld, Dag (Hjalmar Agne Carl)
Hammel, Eric M(axwell) 1946- CANR-35
Earlier sketch in CA 107
Hammel, Faye 1929- CANR-5
Earlier sketch in CA 1-4R
Hammen, Carl Schlee 1923- 53-56
Hammen, Oscar J(ohn) 1907- CAP-2
Earlier sketch in CA 25-28
Hammer, Armand 1898-1990 Obituary 134
Hammer, Carl Jr. 1910- 53-56
Hammer, Charles 1934- ....SATA 58
Hammer, David Harry
1893(?)-1978 Obituary 81-84
Hammer, Emanuel F(rederick) 1926- 29-32R
Hammer, Jacob
See Oppenheimer, Joel (Lester)
Hammer, Jeanne-Ruth 1912- 9-12R
Hammer, Jefferson J(oseph) 1933- 41-44R
Hammer, Kenneth M. 1918- 85-88
Hammer, Reuven 1933- 127
Hammer, Richard 1928- CANR-11
Earlier sketch in CA 25-28R
See also SATA 6
Hammer, Signe 102
Hammerman, Donald R. 1925- 13-16R
Hammerman, Gay M(orenus) 1926- 33-36R
See also SATA 9
Hammerschlag, Carl A(llen) 1939- 128
Hammerstein, Oscar (Greeley Glendenning) II
1895-1960 101
Hammes, John A(nthony) 1924- 13-16R
Hammes, Tobi Gillian Sanders
1948(?)-1987 Obituary 122
Hammett, (Samuel) Dashiell 1894-1961 81-84
See also AITN 1
See also CDALB 1929-1941
See also CLC 3, 5, 10, 19, 47
See also DLBD 6
See also MTCW
Hammick, Georgina 1939- 126
Hammil, Joel 1909- 114
Hamming, Richard W. 1915- 57-60
Hammon, Jupiter 1711(?)-1800(?) ....BLC 2
See also DLB 31, 50
Hammond, Albert L(anphier) 1892-1970 ....1-4R
Obituary 103
Hammond, Antony Derek 1938- 114
Hammond, Brean S(imon) 1951- 119
Hammond, Charles Montgomery Jr. 1922- 106
Hammond, Dorothy 1924- 69-72
Hammond, Edwin Hughes 1919- 13-16R
Hammond, Gerald (Arthur Douglas) 1926- 107
Hammond, Guyton B(owers) 1930- 17-20R
Hammond, J(ames) D(illard) 1933- CANR-22
Earlier sketch in CA 45-48
Hammond, J(ohn) R. 1933- 130
Hammond, Jane
See Poland, Dorothy (Elizabeth Hayward)
Hammond, John .... DLB 24
Hammond, John (Henry Jr.) 1910-1987 106
Obituary 123
Hammond, Keith
See Kuttner, Henry
Hammond, Laurence 104
Hammond, Lawrence 1925- 81-84
Hammond, Mac (Sawyer) 1926- 17-20R
Hammond, Mason 1903- 65-68
Hammond, N(icholas) G(eoffrey) L(empriere)
1907- CANR-21
Earlier sketches in CA 13-16R, CANR-5
Hammond, Norman 1944- CANR-19
Earlier sketches in CA 49-52, CANR-3
Hammond, Paul Y(oung) 1929- CANR-2
Earlier sketch in CA 1-4R
Hammond, Paul 1947- 57-60
Hammond, Peter B(oyd) 1928- 69-72
Hammond, Philip C. 1924- 5-8R
Hammond, Phillip E(verett) 1931- CANR-7
Earlier sketch in CA 17-20R
Hammond, Ralph
See Hammond Innes, Ralph
Hammond, Richard J(ames) 1911-1982 61-64
Obituary 122
Hammond, Ross W(illiam) 1918- 33-36R
Hammond, Thomas T(aylor) 1920- 9-12R
Hammond, W(illiam) Rogers 1920- 45-48
Hammond, Winifred G(raham) 1899- 107
See also SATA 29
Hammond Innes, Ralph 1913- CANR-26
Earlier sketches in CA 5-8R, CANR-4
Hammonds, Michael (Galen) 1942- 45-48
Hammontree, Marie (Gertrude) 1913- 5-8R
See also SATA 13
Hamner, Earl (Henry) Jr. 1923- 73-76
See also AITN 2
See also CLC 12
See also DLB 6
Hamner, Robert Daniel 1941- 106
Hamod, (Hamode) Sam(uel) 1936- CANR-22
Earlier sketch in CA 45-48
Hamori, Laszlo Dezso 1911- 9-12R
Hamovitch, Mitzi Berger 1924- 112
Hamp, Eric P(ratt) 1920- 17-20R
Hampden, John 1898- 109
Hampden-Turner, Charles M. 1934- 33-36R
Hamper, Ben 1956(?)- 138
Hampl, Patricia 1946- CANR-21
Earlier sketch in CA 104
Hample, Stuart 1926- 108
Hampsch, George H(arold) 1927- 13-16R
Hampshire, Joyce Gregorian
See Gregorian, Joyce Ballou
Hampshire, Stuart (Newton)
1914- Brief entry 116
Hampshire, Susan 1942- 129
Brief entry 112
Hampson, Anne 117
Brief entry 111
Hampson, (Richard) Denman 1929- .... SATA 15
Hampson, Frank 1918(?)-1985 Obituary 117
See also SATA 46
Hampson, Norman 1922- 25-28R
Hampson, Robert (Gavin) 1948- 135
Hampson, Zena 1926- CANR-19
Earlier sketches in CA 1-4R, CANR-3
See also Collier, Zena
Hampton, Angeline A.
See Kelly, A(ngeline) A(gnes)
Hampton, Christopher (James) 1946- 25-28R
See also CLC 4
See also DLB 13
See also MTCW
Hampton, Christopher 1929- CANR-4
Earlier sketch in CA 53-56
Hampton, David
See Fairclough, Chris
Hampton, David R(ichard) 1933- 81-84
Hampton, H(arold) Duane 1932- 33-36R
Hampton, Jim
See Hampton, John Lewis
Hampton, John Lewis 1935- 133
Hampton, Kathleen 1923- 1-4R
Hampton, Mark
See Norwood, Victor G(eorge) C(harles)
Hampton, Robert E. 1924- 33-36R
Hampton, William (Albert) 1929- CANR-13
Earlier sketch in CA 33-36R
Hamre, Leif 1914- CANR-4
Earlier sketch in CA 5-8R
See also SATA 5
Hamrick, Samuel J. Jr. 1929- 120
Brief entry 115
Hams, Thomas M. Jr. 1928- 9-12R
Hamsa, Bobbie 1944- 106
See also SATA 38, 52
Hamscher, Albert N(elson) 1946- 73-76
Hamsher, J. Herbert 1938- 57-60
Hamshere, Cyril (Eric) 1912- 41-44R
Hamson, C. J.
See Hamson, Charles John
Hamson, Charles John 1905-1987 Obituary 124
Hamsun, Knut
See Pedersen, Knut
See also TCLC 2, 14
Hamsund, Knut Pedersen
See Pedersen, Knut
Han, Henry H. 1932- 125
Han, Seung Soo 1936- CANR-2
Earlier sketch in CA 45-48
Han, Sungjoo 1940- 53-56
Han, Suyin 1917- 17-20R
Hanagan, Eva (Helen) 1923- 101
Hanagan, Michael Patrick 1947- 109
Hanaghan, Jonathan 1887-1967 65-68
Hanami, Tadashi (Akamatsu) 1930- 89-92
Hanan, Patrick Dewes 1927- 106
Hanau, Laia 1916- 89-92
Hanawalt, Barbara A(nn) 1941- 101
Hanbury, Victor
See Losey, Joseph (Walton)
Hanbury-Tenison, Marika 1938-1982 104
Obituary 108
Hanbury-Tenison, (Airling) Robin 1936- 57-60
Hance, Kenneth G(ordon) 1903- 85-88
Hance, William A(dams) 1916- 9-12R
Hanchett, William 1922- 33-36R
Hancock, Alice Van Fossen 1890- 1-4R
Hancock, Carla 89-92
Hancock, Carol Helen Brooks
See Hancock, Morgan
Hancock, Edward L(eslie) 1930- CANR-1
Earlier sketch in CA 45-48
Hancock, Geoffrey 1946- CANR-19
Earlier sketch in CA 101
Hancock, Harold B(ell) 1913- 53-56
Hancock, Joy Bright 1898-1986 Obituary 120
Hancock, Keith
See Hancock, W(illiam) K(eith)
Hancock, Leslie 1941- 21-24R
Hancock, Lyn 1938- 77-80
Hancock, M. Donald 1939- 33-36R
Hancock, Malcolm 1936- 25-28R
Hancock, Mary A. 1923- 37-40R
See also SATA 31
Hancock, Maxine 1942- CANR-8
Earlier sketch in CA 61-64
Hancock, Morgan 1941- 103
Hancock, Niel Anderson 1941- CANR-21
Earlier sketch in CA 97-100
Hancock, Ralph Lowell 1903- CAP-1
Earlier sketch in CA 9-10
Hancock, Roger Nelson 1929- 97-100
Hancock, Sheila 1942- 49-52
Hancock, Sibyl 1940- CANR-16
Earlier sketches in CA 49-52, CANR-1
See also SATA 9
Hancock, Taylor 1920- 97-100
Hancock, W(illiam) K(eith) 1898-1988 ......CANR-5
Obituary 126
Earlier sketch in CA 5-8R
Hand, Elizabeth 1957- 136
Hand, G(eoffrey) J(oseph Philip Macaulay)
1931- 25-28R
Hand, J(oan) C(arole) 1943- 57-60
Hand, (Andrus) Jackson 1913- CANR-10
Earlier sketch in CA 61-64
Hand, John
See Pierson, John H(erman) G(roesbeck)
Hand, Thomas A(lypius) 1915- 13-16R
Hand, Wayland D(ebs) 1907-1986 ....41-44R
Obituary 120
Handel, Gerald 1924- CANR-11
Earlier sketch in CA 21-24R
Handel, Michael I. 1942- 131
Handelman, Howard 1943- 57-60
Handelman, John R(obert) 1948- 77-80
Handelman, Susan A. 1949- 137
Handel-Mazzetti, Enrica von 1871-1955 .... DLB 81
Handelsman, Judith Florence 1948- 61-64
Handford, Martin (John) 1956- 137
See also CLR 22
See also MAICYA
See also SATA 64
Handforth, Thomas (Schofield)
1897-1948 Brief entry 120
See also SATA 42
Handke, Peter 1942- CANR-33
Earlier sketch in CA 77-80
See also CLC 5, 8, 10, 15, 38
See also DLB 85
See also MTCW
Handl, Irene 1902(?)-1987 103
Obituary 124
Handler, Jerome S(idney) 1933- 53-56
Handler, Joel F. 1932- Brief entry 113
Handler, Julian Harris 1922- 21-24R
Handler, Meyer Srednick
1905-1978 Obituary 77-80
Handler, Milton 1903- 61-64
Handler, Philip 1917-1981 ....33-36R
Obituary 105
Handley, Graham Roderick 1926- CANR-24
Earlier sketch in CA 105
Handley-Taylor, Geoffrey 1920- CANR-7
Earlier sketch in CA 5-8R
Handlin, Mary (Flug) 1913-1976 ....CAP-2
Obituary 65-68
Earlier sketch in CA 33-36
Handlin, Oscar 1915- CANR-23
Earlier sketches in CA 1-4R, CANR-5
See also DLB 17
Handman, Herbert Ira 1932- 89-92
Handover, P(hyllis) M(argaret)
1923(?)-1974 ....9-12R
Obituary 53-56
Handscombe, Richard 1935- 37-40R
Handville, Robert (Tompkins) 1924- .... SATA 45
Handy, Edward Smith Craighill
1893(?)-1980 Obituary 102
Handy, Robert T(heodore) 1918- CANR-2
Earlier sketch in CA 5-8R
Handy, Rollo 1927- 9-12R
Handy, Toni 1930- 97-100
Handy, W(illiam) C(hristopher)
1873-1958 Brief entry 121
Handy, William J. 1918- 45-48
Hane, Mikiso 1922- CANR-15
Earlier sketch in CA 81-84
Hane, Roger 1940-1974 .... SATA 20
Hanenkrat, Frank (Thomas) 1939- 93-96
Haner, F(rederick) T(heodore) 1929- 53-56
Hanes, Bailey C(ass) 1915- 77-80
Hanes, Elizabeth Sill 1-4R
Hanes, Frank Borden 1920- CANR-28
Earlier sketch in CA 1-4R
Hanes, Mary (a pseudonym)
1940(?)- Brief entry 117
Haney, David P. 1938- CANR-21
Earlier sketches in CA 57-60, CANR-6
Haney, Eleanor H(umes) 1931- Brief entry 114
Haney, John B. 1931- 29-32R
Haney, Lynn 1941- CANR-1
Earlier sketch in CA 49-52
See also SATA 23
Haney, Thomas K. 1936- 13-16R
Haney, Thomas R. 45-48
Haney, William V. 1925- 17-20R
Hanff, Helene CANR-3
Earlier sketch in CA 5-8R
See also SATA 11
Hanfmann, George M(axim) A(nossov)
1911-1986 Obituary 118
Brief entry 117
Hanford, Lloyd D(avid) 1901-1979 ....CANR-11
Earlier sketch in CA 13-16R
Hanford, S. A. 1898-1978 Obituary 81-84
Hang, T(ing-)Y(ung) 1908(?)-1987 Obituary 122
Hangen, (Putnam) Welles 1930- 9-12R
Hanifi, M(ohammed) Jamil 1935- 61-64
Hanigan, James Patrick 1938- 125
Haning, Bob
See Haning, James R(obert)
Haning, James R(obert) 1928- CANR-2
Earlier sketch in CA 45-48
Hanke, Howard August 1911- 1-4R
Hanke, Lewis (Ulysses) 1905- 65-68
Hankey, Cyril Patrick 1886-1973 ....1-4R
Obituary 103
Hankey, Rosalie A.
See Wax, Rosalie (Amelia) H.
Hankey, Roy 1932- 108
Hankin, C(herry) A(nne) 1937- 131
Hankin, (Edward Charles) St. John (Emile Clavering)
1869-1909 Brief entry 110
See also DLB 10
Hankins, Clabe
See McDonald, Erwin L(awrence)
Hankins, Frank Hamilton
1877-1970 Obituary 104
Hankins, John Erskine 1905- 49-52
Hankins, Norman E(lijah) 1935- CANR-11
Earlier sketch in CA 61-64
Hankins, Thomas Leroy 1933- 108
Hankinson, Alan 1926- 130
Hankinson, Cyril (Francis James) 1895- CAP-1
Earlier sketch in CA 9-10
Hankla, Cathryn 1958- CANR-39
Earlier sketch in CA 116
Hanks, Lucien M(ason) 1910- 37-40R
Hanks, Stedman Shumway
1889-1979 Obituary 85-88
Hanle, Dorothea Zack 1917- 13-16R
Hanley, Boniface Francis 1924- 9-12R
See also SATA 65
Hanley, Clifford 1922- CANR-23
Earlier sketches in CA 9-12R, CANR-3
See also DLB 14
Hanley, Elizabeth
See Du Breuil, (Elizabeth) L(or)inda
Hanley, Evelyn A(lice) 1916-1980 ....41-44R
Obituary 97-100
Hanley, Gerald (Anthony) 1916- CANR-6
Earlier sketch in CA 1-4R
Hanley, Hope Anthony 1926- CANR-5
Earlier sketch in CA 9-12R
Hanley, James 1901-1985 ....CANR-36
Obituary 117
Earlier sketch in CA 73-76
See also CLC 3, 5, 8, 13
See also MTCW
Hanley, Katharine Rose 1932- 37-40R
Hanley, Michael F. IV 1941- 65-68
Hanley, Mike
See Hanley, Michael F. IV
Hanley, Theodore Dean 1917- 5-8R
Hanley, Thomas O'Brien 1918- CANR-1
Earlier sketch in CA 1-4R
Hanley, William 1931- 41-44R
Hanlon, Emily 1945- 77-80
See also SATA 15

Hanlon, John J(oseph) 1912- ... 57-60
Hanmer, Davina
  See Courtney, Nicholas (Piers)
Hann, C. M. 1953- ... 121
Hann, Jacquie 1951- ... CANR-13
  Earlier sketch in CA 73-76
  See also SATA 19
Hanna, Alfred Jackson 1893-1978 ... CANR-2
  Earlier sketch in CA 45-48
Hanna, Bill
  See Hanna, William
Hanna, David 1917- ... CANR-6
  Earlier sketch in CA 57-60
Hanna, Frank A(llan) 1907-1978 Obituary ... 111
Hanna, J. Marshall 1907- ... CANR-24
  Earlier sketch in CA 1-4R
Hanna, John Paul 1932- ... CANR-1
  Earlier sketch in CA 45-48
Hanna, Lavone Agnes 1896- ... 13-16R
Hanna, Mary Carr 1905- ... 45-48
Hanna, Mary T. 1935- ... 97-100
Hanna, Nell(ie L.) 1908- ... SATA 55
Hanna, Paul R(obert) 1902- ... 45-48
  See also SATA 9
Hanna, S(uhail) S(alim) 1943- ... 126
Hanna, Thomas 1928- ... CANR-1
  Earlier sketch in CA 1-4R
Hanna, Warren L(eonard) 1898- ... 130
Hanna, William John 1931- ... CANR-8
  Earlier sketch in CA 61-64
Hanna, William 1910- ... SATA 51
Hannaford, John 1918- ... 45-48
Hannaford, Peter (Dor) 1932- ... 130
Hannah, (Juliel) Barbara 1891- ... 97-100
Hannah, Barry 1942- ... 110
  Brief entry ... 108
  See also CLC 23, 38
  See also DLB 6
  See also MTCW
Hannah, Norman B(ritton) 1919- ... 127
Hannak, Johann Jacques 1892- ... CAP-1
  Earlier sketch in CA 9-10
Hannam, Charles 1925- ... CANR-11
  Earlier sketch in CA 61-64
  See also SATA 50
Hannan, Joseph F(rancis) 1923- ... CANR-3
  Earlier sketch in CA 9-12R
Hannas, Linda 1913- ... 113
Hannau, Hans W(alter) 1904- ... CANR-10
  Earlier sketch in CA 21-24R
Hannavy, John Michael 1946- ... CANR-11
  Earlier sketch in CA 69-72
Hannaway, Patricia H(inman) 1929- ... 61-64
Hannaway, Patti
  See Hannaway, Patricia H(inman)
Hannay, Alastair 1932- ... 130
Hannay, Allen 1946- ... 109
Hannay, Doris Fergusson
  See Fergusson Hannay, Doris
Hannay, James 1827-1873 ... DLB 21
Hannay, Margaret Patterson 1944- ... CANR-21
  Earlier sketch in CA 104
Hanneman, Audre (Louise) 1926- ... 21-24R
Hanney, Peter 1930-1976 Obituary ... 105
Hannibal
  See Alexander, Stanley Walter
Hannibal, Edward 1936- ... CANR-28
  Earlier sketch in CA 29-32R
Hannifin, Jerry (Bernard) 1917- ... 77-80
Hanning, Hugh 1925- ... 25-28R
Hanning, Robert William 1938- ... 93-96
Hannon, Ezra
  See Hunter, Evan
Hannula, Reino 1918- ... 105
Hannum, Alberta Pierson 1906-1985 ... 65-68
  Obituary ... 115
Hano, Arnold 1922- ... CANR-5
  Earlier sketch in CA 9-12R
  See also SATA 12
Hanover, Terri
  See Huff, Tanya (Sue)
Hanrahan, Barbara 1939- ... 127
  Brief entry ... 121
Hanrahan, John D(avid) 1938- ... CANR-15
  Earlier sketch in CA 77-80
Hanrieder, Wolfram F. 1931- ... CANR-23
  Earlier sketches in CA 21-24R, CANR-8
Hans, Valerie P(atricia) 1951- ... 126
Hansberry, Lorraine (Vivian) 1930-1965 ... 109
  Obituary ... 25-28R
  See also CABS 3
  See also BLC 2
  See also BW
  See also CDALB 1941-1968
  See also CLC 17, 62
  See also DC 2
  See also DLB 7, 38
  See also MTCW
Hanscom, Leslie Rutherford 1924- ... 135
Hansel, C(harles) E(dward) M(ark)
  1917- Brief entry ... 115
Hansel, Robert R(aymond)
  1936- Brief entry ... 110
Hansell, Antonina
  See Looker, Antonina (Hansell)
Hansen, Al(fred Earl) 1927- ... 17-20R
Hansen, Alvin H(arvey) 1887-1975 ... CAP-1
  Obituary ... 57-60
  Earlier sketch in CA 13-16
Hansen, Arlen J. 1936- ... 133
Hansen, Bertrand Lyle 1922- ... 9-12R
Hansen, Brooks 1965- ... 132
Hansen, Carl (Francis) 1906-1983 ... CANR-2
  Obituary ... 110
  Earlier sketch in CA 5-8R
Hansen, Carol
  See Fenichel, Carol Hansen
Hansen, Caryl (Hall) 1929- ... 108
  See also SATA 39
Hansen, Cecil
  See Huffaker, Clair
Hansen, Cecil Dan
  See Huffaker, Clair
Hansen, Chadwick (Clarke) 1926- ... 29-32R
Hansen, Donald A(ndrew) 1933- ... 73-76
Hansen, Donald Charles 1935- ... 33-36R
Hansen, Emmanuel 1937- ... 104
Hansen, Flemming 1938- ... 93-96
Hansen, Forest Warnyr 1931- ... 45-48
Hansen, Gary B(arker) 1935- ... CANR-21
  Earlier sketches in CA 9-12R, CANR-3
Hansen, Harry 1884-1977 ... 73-76
  Obituary ... 69-72
Hansen, Joseph 1923- ... CANR-16
  Earlier sketch in CA 29-32R
  See also CLC 38
Hansen, Joyce 1942- ... 105
  See also CLR 21
  See also MAICYA
  See also SATA 39, 46
Hansen, Kenneth H(arvey) 1917- ... 13-16R
Hansen, Klaus J(uergen) 1931- ... 21-24R
Hansen, Leroy John 1922-1990 Obituary ... 132
Hansen, Martin A. 1909-1955 ... TCLC 32
Hansen, Mary Lewis (Patterson) 1933- ... 17-20R
Hansen, Niles M(aurice) 1937- ... CANR-30
  Earlier sketches in CA 25-28R, CANR-13
Hansen, Norman J. 1918- ... 29-32R
Hansen, Richard H(erbert) 1929- ... 1-4R
Hansen, Rodney Thor 1940- ... 53-56
Hansen, Roger D(ennis) 1935-1991 ... 105
  Obituary ... 133
Hansen, Ron 1947- ... CANR-17
  Earlier sketch in CA 89-92
  See also SATA 56
Hansen, Rosanna 1947- ... 105
Hansen, Terrence Leslie 1920-1974 ... 37-40R
Hansen, W(illiam) Lee 1928- ... 29-32R
Hansen, William F(reeman) 1941- ... CANR-30
  Earlier sketch in CA 49-52
Hanser, Richard (Frederick)
  1909-1981 ... CANR-8
  Earlier sketch in CA 5-8R
  See also SATA 13
Hanshew, Thomas W.
  1857-1914 Brief entry ... 113
Hansi
  See Hirschmann, Maria Anne
Hanson, A(lbert) H(enry) 1913-1971 ... CANR-4
  Obituary ... 89-92
  Earlier sketch in CA 5-8R
Hanson, Agnes O(lin) 1905- ... 107
Hanson, Anne Coffin 1921- ... 21-24R
Hanson, Anthony Tyrrell 1916-1991 ... CANR-24
  Obituary ... 134
  Earlier sketches in CA 21-24R, CANR-9
Hanson, Charles G(oring) 1934- ... 138
Hanson, Dirk 1950- ... 111
Hanson, E(ugene) Kenneth 1930- ... 13-16R
Hanson, Earl D(orchester) 1927- ... CANR-12
  Earlier sketch in CA 73-76
Hanson, Earl Parker 1899-1978 ... 41-44R
Hanson, Eric O. 1942- ... 125
Hanson, F(ridolf) Allan 1939- ... 41-44R
Hanson, Harvey 1941- ... 65-68
Hanson, Howard Gordon 1931- ... 21-24R
Hanson, Howard (Harold)
  1896-1981 Obituary ... 103
Hanson, Irene (Forsythe) 1898- ... 49-52
Hanson, Isabel 1929- ... 106
Hanson, James Arthur 1940- ... CANR-30
  Earlier sketch in CA 49-52
Hanson, Jim 1953- ... 97-100
Hanson, Joan 1938- ... CANR-15
  Earlier sketch in CA 33-36R
  See also SATA 8
Hanson, Joseph E. 1894(?)-1971 Obituary ... 104
  See also SATA 27
Hanson, June Andrea 1941- ... 97-100
Hanson, Kenneth O(stlin) 1922- ... CANR-7
  Earlier sketch in CA 53-56
  See also CLC 13
Hanson, Kristine 1958- ... 123
Hanson, Michael James 1942- ... 61-64
Hanson, Norwood Russell 1924-1967 ... CANR-8
  Earlier sketch in CA 5-8R
Hanson, Paul D(avid) 1939- ... 61-64
Hanson, Paul R. 1952- ... 134
Hanson, Pauline ... 45-48
Hanson, Peggy 1934- ... CANR-12
  Earlier sketch in CA 29-32R
Hanson, Philip 1936- ... 103
Hanson, R(ichard) P(atrick) C(rosland)
  1916-1988 ... CANR-9
  Obituary ... 127
  Earlier sketch in CA 21-24R
Hanson, Richard S(imon) 1931- ... 37-40R
Hanson, Robert Carl 1926- ... 37-40R
Hanson, Robert P(aul) 1918- ... 9-12R
Hanson, Roy (Francis) 1934-1989 Obituary ... 128
Hanson, Ruth Katie 1900- ... 5-8R
Hanson, Simon
  See Hanson, Richard S(imon)
Hanson, William S(tewart) 1950- ... 123
Hansson, Gunilla 1939- ... SATA 64
Hansten, Philip D. 1943- ... 33-36R
Hanushek, Eric Alan 1943- ... 41-44R
Hanzlicek, C(harles) G(eorge) 1942- ... CANR-12
  Earlier sketch in CA 73-76
Hao, Qian
  See Qian Hao
Hao, Yen-ping 1934- ... 53-56
Hapgood, Charles Hutchins 1904- ... 17-20R
Hapgood, David 1926- ... 13-16R
Hapgood, Fred 1942- ... 93-96
Hapgood, Norman 1868-1937 ... DLB 91
Hapgood, Ruth K(nott) 1920- ... 49-52
Hapke, Laura 1946- ... 138
Happe, Peter 1932- ... CANR-28
  Earlier sketch in CA 45-48
Happel, Robert A. 1916- ... 1-4R
Happel, Stephen 1944- ... 114
Happold, F(rederick) C(rossfield) 1893- ... 101
Haq, Mahbub ul 1934- ... 13-16R
Harakas, Stanley Samuel 1932- ... 134
Harald, Eric
  See Boesen, Victor
Haraldsson, Erlendur 1931- ... 101
Haran, Maeve 1950- ... 136
Harap, Henry 1893-1981 Obituary ... 104
Harap, Louis 1904- ... 57-60
Harari, Ehud 1935- ... 65-68
Harary, Keith 1953- ... 120
Harary, Stuart Blue
  See Harary, Keith
Harasymiw, Bohdan 1936- ... 124
Haraway, Donna Jeanne 1944- ... 73-76
Harbach, Otto (Abels) 1873-1963 Obituary ... 112
Harbage, Alfred (Bennett) 1901-1976 ... CANR-5
  Obituary ... 65-68
  Earlier sketch in CA 5-8R
Harbaugh, John W(arvelle) 1926- ... CANR-30
  Earlier sketch in CA 49-52
Harbaugh, William Henry 1920- ... 1-4R
Harberger, Arnold C. 1924- ... CANR-6
  Earlier sketch in CA 13-16R
Harbert, Earl N(orman) 1934- ... CANR-29
  Earlier sketches in CA 33-36R, CANR-13
Harbert, Mary Ann 1945- ... 61-64
Harbeson, Georgiana Brown
  1894(?)-1980 Obituary ... 101
Harbeson, Gladys Evans ... 21-24R
Harbeson, John Willis 1938- ... 57-60
Harbin, Calvin E(dward) 1916- ... 21-24R
Harbin, Robert
  See Williams, Ned
Harbinson, Robert
  See Bryans, Robert Harbinson
Harbinson, W(illiam) A(llen) 1941- ... CANR-25
  Earlier sketches in CA 61-64, CANR-9
Harbison, Frederick Harris
  1912-1976 Obituary ... 65-68
Harbison, Peter 1939- ... 65-68
Harbison, Robert 1940- ... 102
Harbottle, Michael (Neale) 1917- ... 29-32R
Harbron, John D(avison) 1924- ... 9-12R
Harburg, E(dgar) Y(ipsel) 1896-1981 ... 85-88
  Obituary ... 103
Harburg, Yip
  See Harburg, E(dgar) Y(ipsel)
Harbury, Colin (Desmond) 1922- ... 102
Harcave, Sidney S(amuel) 1916- ... 17-20R
Harcleroad, Fred F(arley) 1918- ... CANR-23
  Earlier sketches in CA 17-20R, CANR-8
Harcourt, Ellen Knowles
  1890(?)-1984 Obituary ... 111
  See also SATA 36
Harcourt, G(eoffrey) C(olin) 1931- ... CANR-16
  Earlier sketch in CA 25-28R
Harcourt, Melville 1909- ... 5-8R
Harcourt, Palma ... CANR-31
  Earlier sketches in CA 77-80, CANR-14
Harcourt, Peter 1931- ... 81-84
Hard, Edward W(ilhelm) Jr. 1939- ... 85-88
Hard, Frederick 1897- ... CAP-2
  Earlier sketch in CA 25-28
Hard, Margaret (Steel)
  1888(?)-1974 Obituary ... 49-52
Hard, T. W.
  See Hard, Edward W(ilhelm) Jr.
Hard, Walter (Rice) 1882-1966 Obituary ... 116
Hardach, Gerd 1941- ... 105
Hardach, Karl 1936- ... 130
Hardaway, Francine 1941- ... 81-84
Hardcastle, Michael 1933- ... CANR-12
  Earlier sketch in CA 25-28R
  See also SATA 38, 47
Harden, Blaine 1952- ... 135
Harden, Donald B(enjamin) 1901- ... 5-8R
Harden, Edgar F(rederick) 1932- ... 123
Harden, Ian (John) 1954- ... 126
Harden, Oleta Elizabeth (McWhorter)
  1935- ... 37-40R
Harden, (John) William 1903- ... 93-96
Harder, Eleanor (Loraine) 1925- ... 37-40R
Harder, Geraldine Gross 1926- ... 53-56
Harder, Raymond Wymbs Jr. 1920- ... 85-88
Hardesty, Nancy A(nn) 1941- ... CANR-23
  Earlier sketches in CA 57-60, CANR-8
Hardesty, Sarah 1951- ... 126
Hardesty, Von 1939- ... 112
Hardgrave, Robert L(ewis) Jr. 1939- ... CANR-11
  Earlier sketch in CA 25-28R
Hardie, Frank 1911-1989 ... 33-36R
  Obituary ... 127
Hardie, Sean 1947- ... 135
Hardie, William Francis Ross
  1902-1990 Obituary ... 132
Hardiman, James W. 1919- ... 33-36R
Hardin, Charles M(eyer) 1908- ... CANR-30
  Earlier sketch in CA 49-52
Hardin, Clement
  See Newton, D(wight) B(ennett)
Hardin, Garrett James 1915- ... CANR-9
  Earlier sketch in CA 17-20R
Hardin, J. D.
  See Riefe, Alan
  and Sheldon, Walter J.
Hardin, James N(eal) 1939- ... CANR-35
  Earlier sketch in CA 114
Hardin, Paul III 1931- ... 25-28R
Hardin, Peter
  See Vaczek, Louis
Hardin, Richard F(rancis) 1937- ... 45-48
Hardin, Robert 1934- ... 77-80
Hardin, Tim 1941(?)-1981 Obituary ... 102
Hardin, Tom
  See Bauer, Erwin A.
Hardin, Wes
  See Keevill, Henry J(ohn)
Harding, A(nthony) F(ilmer) 1946- ... 77-80
Harding, Barbara 1926- ... 41-44R
Harding, Bertita (Leonarz de) 1902- ... 5-8R
Harding, Carl B.
  See Barker, Elver A.
Harding, D(ouglas) E(dison)
  1909- Brief entry ... 116
Harding, D(ennis) W(illiam) 1940- ... 41-44R
Harding, D(enys Clement) W(yatt)
  1906- ... CANR-16
  Earlier sketches in CAP-1, CA 13-16
Harding, Davis P. 1915(?)-1970 Obituary ... 104
Harding, Donald Edward 1916- ... CANR-4
  Earlier sketch in CA 53-56
Harding, Georgina 1955- ... 133
Harding, Harold F(riend) 1903- ... 37-40R
Harding, Harry (Jr.) 1946- ... CANR-28
  Earlier sketch in CA 109
Harding, Jack 1914- ... 29-32R
Harding, James 1929- ... CANR-32
  Earlier sketches in CA 33-36R, CANR-14
Harding, John 1948- ... 97-100
Harding, Kenneth
  See Little, Paul H(ugo)
Harding, Lee 1937- ... 106
  See also SATA 31, 32
Harding, Maria
  See Goudiss, Maria Agnes D'Elia
Harding, Matt
  See Floren, Lee
Harding, Matthew Whitman
  See Floren, Lee
Harding, Neil 1942- ... 125
Harding, Peter
  See Burgess, M(ichael) R(oy)
Harding, Sandra G. 1935- ... 120
Harding, Susan Friend 1946- ... 126
Harding, T(imothy) D. 1948- ... 85-88
Harding, Thomas G(rayson) 1937- ... 21-24R
Harding, Virginia Hamlet 1909- ... 45-48
Harding, Walter Roy 1917- ... CANR-17
  Earlier sketches in CA 1-4R, CANR-1
  See also DLB 111
Harding, Wes
  See Keevill, Henry J(ohn)
Harding, William Harry 1945- ... 93-96
Hardinge, Helen (Mary Cecil) 1901- ... CAP-2
  Earlier sketch in CA 29-32
Hardingham, John (Frederick Watson)
  1916- ... CAP-1
  Earlier sketch in CA 11-12
Hardison, O(sborne) B(ennett Jr.)
  1928-1990 ... CANR-6
  Obituary ... 132
  Earlier sketch in CA 5-8R
  See also BEST 90:2
Hardman, John (David) 1944- ... 45-48
Hardman, Keith (Jordan) 1931- ... 116
Hardman, Richards Lynden 1924- ... 13-16R
Hardon, John A(nthony) 1914- ... CANR-2
  Earlier sketch in CA 1-4R
Hardoy, Jorge Enrique 1926- ... 33-36R
Hardt, Helga Fleischhauer
  See Fleischhauer-Hardt, Helga
Hardt, J(ohn) Pearce 1922- ... CANR-3
  Earlier sketch in CA 5-8R
Hardwick, Adam
  See Connor, John Anthony
Hardwick, Clyde T(homas) 1915- ... 5-8R
Hardwick, Elizabeth 1916- ... CANR-32
  Earlier sketches in CA 5-8R, CANR-3
  See also CLC 13
  See also DLB 6
  See also MTCW
Hardwick, Homer
  See Rogers, Paul (Patrick)
Hardwick, Joan 1940- ... 135
Hardwick, (John) Michael (Drinkrow)
  1924-1991 ... CANR-2
  Obituary ... 134
  Earlier sketch in CA 49-52
Hardwick, Mollie ... CANR-2
  Earlier sketch in CA 49-52
Hardwick, Richard Holmes Jr. 1923- ... CANR-9
  Earlier sketch in CA 5-8R
  See also SATA 12
Hardwick, Sylvia
  See Doherty, Ivy R. Duffy
Hardy, Adam
  See Bulmer, (Henry) Kenneth
Hardy, Alan 1932- ... 73-76
Hardy, Alexander G(eorge)
  1920-1973 Obituary ... 45-48
Hardy, Alice Dale ... CANR-26
  Earlier sketches in CAP-2, CA 19-20
  See also SATA 1, 67
Hardy, Alister C(lavering) 1896-1985 ... 85-88
  Obituary ... 116
Hardy, Barbara (Gladys) ... 85-88
Hardy, C. Colburn 1910- ... CANR-21
  Earlier sketches in CA 53-56, CANR-6
Hardy, David A(ndrews) 1936- ... CANR-8
  Earlier sketch in CA 61-64
  See also SATA 9
Hardy, Dennis 1941- ... 124
Hardy, Douglas
  See Andrews, (Charles) Robert Douglas (Hardy)

Hardy, Edward R(ochie) 1908- CAP-1
Earlier sketch in CA 13-16
Hardy, Eric 61-64
Hardy, Evelyn 1902- 21-24R
Hardy, Henry 1949- 113
Hardy, J(ohn) P(hillips) 1933- 25-28R
Hardy, Jason
See Oxley, William
Hardy, John Edward 1922- 13-16R
Hardy, Jon 1958- 123
See also SATA 53
Hardy, Jonathan G. Gathorne
See Gathorne-Hardy, Jonathan G.
Hardy, Laura
See Holland, Sheila
Hardy, Leroy C(lyde) 1927- 29-32R
Hardy, Melissa Arnold 1952- 102
Hardy, Michael (James Langley) 1933- 25-28R
Hardy, Peter 1931- 65-68
Hardy, Richard E(arl) 1938- 37-40R
Hardy, Richard P(eter) 1940- 117
Hardy, Ronald Harold 1919- 5-8R
Hardy, Stuart
See Schisgall, Oscar
Hardy, Thomas 1840-1928 123
Brief entry 104
See also CDBLB 1890-1914
See also DLB 18, 19
See also MTCW
See also SSC 2
See also TCLC 4, 10, 18, 32
See also WLC
Hardy, Tom 1943- 116
Hardy, W(illiam) G(eorge) 1895-1979 .... CANR-5
Earlier sketch in CA 5-8R
Hardy, Willene S(chaefer) 1937- 112
Hardy, William M(arion) 1922- CANR-2
Earlier sketch in CA 1-4R
Hardyck, Curtis D(ale) 1929- 29-32R
Hare, A(lexander) Paul 1923- CANR-2
Earlier sketch in CA 1-4R
Hare, Bill
See Hare, William Moorman
Hare, Cyril
See Clark, Alfred Alexander Gordon
See also DLB 77
Hare, David 1947- CANR-39
Earlier sketch in CA 97-100
See also CLC 29, 58
See also DLB 13
See also MTCW
Hare, Douglas Robert Adams 1929- 45-48
Hare, Eric B. 1894- CAP-1
Earlier sketch in CA 13-16
Hare, F(rederick) Kenneth 1919- CANR-14
Earlier sketch in CA 37-40R
Hare, John 1935- 21-24R
Hare, Nathan 1934- CANR-24
Earlier sketch in CA 41-44R
See also BW
Hare, Norma Q(uarles) 1924- 101
See also SATA 41, 46
Hare, Peter H. 1935- 33-36R
Hare, R(ichard) M(ervyn) 1919- CANR-31
Earlier sketches in CA 5-8R, CANR-2
Hare, Richard (Gilbert) 1907-1966 .... CAP-1
Earlier sketch in CA 13-14
Hare, Ronald 1899- 77-80
Hare, Thomas Blenman
See Hare, Thomas William
Hare, Thomas William 1952- 122
Hare, Van Court Jr. 1929- 25-28R
Hare, William Moorman 1934- 101
Hare, William 1944- CANR-28
Earlier sketch in CA 111
Hare Duke, Michael Geoffrey 1925- 111
Harel, Isser 1912- CANR-10
Earlier sketch in CA 65-68
Hareven, Shulamith 1931- Brief entry 117
Hareven, Tamara K. 1937- CANR-30
Earlier sketches in CA 25-28R, CANR-13
Harewood, George Henry Hubert Lascelles
1923- 125
Harford, David K(ennedy) 1947- 49-52
Harford, Henry
See Hudson, W(illiam) H(enry)
Harger, Rolla N(eil) 1890-1983 Obituary 114
Harger, William Henderson 1936- 57-60
Hargrave, John Gordon
1894-1982 Obituary 110
Hargrave, Leonie
See Disch, Thomas M(ichael)
Hargrave, O. T. 1936- 33-36R
Hargrave, Rowena 1906- 33-36R
Hargraves, Thomas
See Ainsworth, Thomas Hargraves Jr.
Hargreaves, Alec G(ordon) 1948- 131
Hargreaves, Harry 1922- 5-8R
Hargreaves, John D(esmond) 1924- 9-12R
Hargreaves, Mary W(ilma) M(assey)
1914- CANR-14
Earlier sketch in CA 37-40R
Hargreaves, Reginald (Charles) 1888- CAP-1
Earlier sketch in CA 9-10
Hargreaves, (Charles) Roger
1935-1988 Obituary 126
See also SATA 56
Hargreaves-Mawdsley, W(illiam) Norman
1921-1980 .... CANR-7
Earlier sketch in CA 9-12R
Hargroder, Charles M(erlin) 1926- 73-76
Hargrove, Barbara Watts 1924- 33-36R
Hargrove, Erwin C. 1930- Brief entry 111
Hargrove, James 1947- 120
See also SATA 50, 57
Hargrove, Jim
See Hargrove, James
Hargrove, Katharine T. 33-36R
Hargrove, Marion 1919- .... DLB 11
Hargrove, Merwin Matthew 1910- 9-12R
Hargrove, Nancy Duvall 1941- 97-100
Hargrove, Richard J(ohn) Jr. 1941- 116
Harik, Iliya F. 1934- CANR-16
Earlier sketch in CA 25-28R
Haring, Bernard
See Haering, Bernhard
Haring, Firth 1937- 25-28R
Haring, Jo 1934- 116
Haring, Joseph E(merick) 1931- 33-36R
Haring, Norris G. 1923- CANR-2
Earlier sketch in CA 1-4R
Haring, Philip S(myth) 1915- 37-40R
Harington, Donald 1935- CANR-7
Earlier sketch in CA 13-16R
Harjo, Joy 1951- CANR-35
Earlier sketch in CA 114
See also DLB 120
Hark, Mildred
See McQueen, Mildred Hark
Harkabi, Yehoshafat 1921- CANR-27
Earlier sketch in CA 73-76
Harkavy, Robert E(dward) 1936- CANR-30
Earlier sketch in CA 111
Harkaway, Hal
See Stratemeyer, Edward L.
Harker, Kenneth 1927- 97-100
Harker, Ronald 1909- 77-80
Harkey, Ira B(rown) Jr. 1918- 57-60
Harkey, William G. 1914- 25-28R
Harkins, Arthur M(artin) 1936- 97-100
Harkins, Paul W(illiam) 1911- 116
Harkins, Philip 1912- 29-32R
See also SATA 6
Harkins, William E(dward) 1921- 33-36R
Harkness, Bruce 1923- 13-16R
Harkness, D(avid) W(illiam) 1937- CANR-15
Earlier sketch in CA 29-32R
Harkness, David J(ames) 1913- CANR-3
Earlier sketch in CA 9-12R
Harkness, Edward 1947- 77-80
Harkness, Georgia (Elma) 1891-1974 .... CANR-6
Obituary 53-56
Earlier sketch in CA 1-4R
Harkness, Gladys Estelle Suiter
1908(?)-1973 Obituary 41-44R
Harkness, Jack
See Harkness, John Leigh
Harkness, John Leigh 1918- 120
Harkness, Marjory Gane 1880- CAP-2
Earlier sketch in CA 23-24
Harknett, Terry 1936- CANR-21
Earlier sketches in CA 57-60, CANR-6
Harlan
See Shaw, William Harlan
Harlan, Elizabeth 1945- 111
See also SATA 35, 41
Harlan, Glen
See Cebulash, Mel
Harlan, John Marshall
1899-1971 Obituary 33-36R
Harlan, Louis R(udolph) 1922- CANR-25
Earlier sketch in CA 21-24R
See also CLC 34
Harlan, William K(eith) 1938- 45-48
Harle, Elizabeth
See Roberts, Irene
Harlequin
See Reed, A(lexander) W(yclif)
Harley, John
See Marsh, John
Harling, Robert 1951(?)- .... CLC 53
Harling, Thomas
See Eastham, Thomas
Harlow, Enid 1939- 102
Harlow, Francis H(arvey) 1928- 57-60
Harlow, Harry F(rederick) 1905- 97-100
Harlow, Joan Hiatt 1932- 89-92
Harlow, LeRoy F(rancis) 1913- 85-88
Harlow, Lewis A(ugustus) 1901- CAP-1
Earlier sketch in CA 13-14
Harlow, Neal 1908- 109
Harlow, Robert 1923- 128
See also DLB 60
Harlow, Samuel Ralph 1885-1972 .... 1-4R
Obituary 37-40R
Harlow, W(illiam) M(orehouse)
1900-1986 .... 13-16R
Obituary 119
Harman, Alec
See Harman, Richard Alexander
Harman, Barbara Leah 1946- 126
Harman, Claire
See Schmidt, Claire Harman
Harman, David 1944- 105
Harman, Fred 1902(?)-1982 Obituary 106
See also SATA 30
Harman, Gilbert H(elms) 1938- 73-76
Harman, Harry E. III 1917- CANR-39
Earlier sketch in CA 116
Harman, Hugh 1903-1982 Obituary 108
See also SATA 33
Harman, Jane
See Harknett, Terry
Harman, Jeanne Perkins 1919- CANR-39
Earlier sketches in CA 69-72, CANR-11
Harman, Mark 1951- 118
Harman, Nicholas 1933- 101
Harman, P(eter) M(ichael) 1943- 110
Harman, R. Alec
See Harman, Richard Alexander
Harman, Richard Alexander 1917- CANR-5
Earlier sketch in CA 9-12R
Harman, Willis W(alter) 1918- 5-8R
Harmel, Robert 1950- 110
Harmelink, Barbara (Mary) 61-64
See also SATA 9
Harmer, Mabel 1894- 9-12R
See also SATA 45
Harmer, Ruth Mulvey 1919- 9-12R
Harmin, Merrill 1928- 89-92
Harmon, A(llen) J(ackson) 1926- 21-24R
Harmon, Frederick G(ardner) 1932- 119
Harmon, Gary L. 1935- 37-40R
Harmon, Glynn 1933- 45-48
Harmon, H. H.
See Williams, Robert Moore
Harmon, James Judson 1933- 21-24R
Harmon, Jim
See Harmon, James Judson
Harmon, Lily 1912- 105
Harmon, Lyn S. 1930- 21-24R
Harmon, Margaret 1906- 69-72
See also SATA 20
Harmon, Maurice 1930- CANR-9
Earlier sketch in CA 21-24R
Harmon, Nolan B(ailey) 1892- 89-92
Harmon, (Norman) Paul 1942- 122
Harmon, Robert Bartlett 1932- CANR-23
Earlier sketches in CA 17-20R, CANR-8
Harmon, Susanna M(arie) 1940- 57-60
Harmon, William (Ruth) 1938- CANR-35
Earlier sketches in CA 33-36R, CANR-14, 32
See also CLC 38
See also SATA 65
Harms, Ernest 1895-1974 .... CAP-1
Obituary 49-52
Earlier sketch in CA 13-14
Harms, John 1900- 17-20R
Harms, Leroy Stanley 1928- CANR-8
Earlier sketch in CA 53-56
Harms, Robert T(homas) 1932- 37-40R
Harms, Valerie 1940- CANR-2
Earlier sketch in CA 49-52
Harmsel, Henrietta Ten
See Ten Harmsel, Henrietta
Harmsen, Dorothy B. Bahneman 103
Harmsen, Frieda 1931- 107
Harmston, Olivia
See Weber, Nancy
Harmsworth, Esmond Cecil
1898-1978 Obituary 89-92
Harnack, Curtis (Arthur) 1927- CANR-22
Earlier sketches in CA 1-4R, CANR-2
Harnack, R(obert) Victor 1927- 13-16R
Harnack, William J. 1953- 125
Harnan, Terry 1920- 45-48
See also SATA 12
Harnden, Ruth Peabody 73-76
Harned, David Baily 1932- 135
Brief entry 112
Harner, James L(owell) 1946- 110
Harner, Michael J(ames) 1929- 134
Brief entry 114
Harness, Charles L(eonard)
1915- Brief entry 113
See also DLB 8
Harnett, Bertram 1923- 119
Harnett, Cynthia (Mary) 1893-1981 .... CAP-1
Obituary 111
Earlier sketch in CA 9-10
See also SATA 5, 32
Harnetty, Peter 1927- 37-40R
Harnik, Bernard 1910- 93-96
Harnsberger, Caroline Thomas
1902-1991 61-64
Obituary 134
Harnwell, Gaylord Probasco
1903-1982 Obituary 106
Haro, Robert P(eter) 1936- 33-36R
Harodoy, Jorge Enrique 1926- 33-36R
Harold, Fred(erick) G(ordon) 1937- 118
Haroldson, William
See King, Harold
Haroutunian, Joseph 1904-1968 Obituary 111
Harper, Anita 1943- 114
See also SATA 41
Harper, Bill
See Harper, William A(rthur)
Harper, Carol Ely 61-64
Harper, Daniel
See Brossard, Chandler
Harper, David
See Corley, Edwin (Raymond)
Harper, Douglas A(lbert) 1948- 117
Harper, Elaine
See Hallin, Emily Watson
Harper, F. E. W.
See Harper, Frances Ellen Watkins
Harper, Fletcher 1806-1877 .... DLB 79
Harper, Floyd H(enry)
1899-1978 Obituary 77-80
Harper, Frances E. W.
See Harper, Frances Ellen Watkins
Harper, Frances E. Watkins
See Harper, Frances Ellen Watkins
Harper, Frances Ellen
See Harper, Frances Ellen Watkins
Harper, Frances Ellen Watkins 1825-1911 125
Brief entry 111
See also BLC 2
See also BW
See also DLB 50
See also TCLC 14
Harper, George Mills 1914- 136
Brief entry 114
Harper, George W(illiam) 1927- 113
Harper, Harold W. 89-92
Harper, Harry H(alsted) Jr.
1910-1983 Obituary 110
Harper, Howard M(orrall) Jr. 1930- CANR-22
Earlier sketch in CA 21-24R
Harper, Howard (V.) 1904-1978 .... 17-20R
Obituary 133
Harper, J(ohn) Russell 1914-1983 .... CANR-13
Earlier sketch in CA 33-36R
Harper, James E(dwin) 1927- 41-44R
Harper, Joan (Marie) 1932- 101
Harper, John C(arsten) 1924- 103
Harper, John Dickson 1910- 103
Harper, Karen 1945- 114
Harper, Kate
See Harper, Katherine E(rna)
Harper, Katherine E(rna) 1946- 103
Harper, M(ichael) J(ohn) K(ennedy) 1935- 116
Harper, Marjory(-Ann Denoon) 1956- 129
Harper, Marvin Henry 1901- 49-52
Harper, Mary Wood
See Dixon, Jeanne
Harper, Michael S(teven) 1938- CANR-24
Earlier sketch in CA 33-36R
See also BW
See also CLC 7, 22
See also DLB 41
Harper, Michael 1931- CANR-15
Earlier sketch in CA 65-68
Harper, Mrs. F. E. W.
See Harper, Frances Ellen Watkins
Harper, Paula (Hays) 1938- 105
Harper, Robert A(lexander) 1924- 17-20R
Harper, Robert J(ohnston) C(raig)
1927- 13-16R
Harper, Stephen (Dennis) 1924- 97-100
Harper, Tom 1923(?)-1983 Obituary 110
Harper, Wilhelmina 1884-1973 .... CAP-1
Earlier sketch in CA 17-18
See also SATA 4, 26
Harper, William A(rthur) 1944- 77-80
Harpham, Geoffrey Galt 1946- 111
Harpole, Charles H(enry) 1943- 111
Harpole, Patricia Chayne 1933- 37-40R
Harpur, Patrick 1950- 114
Harpur, Thomas William 1929- 137
Harpur, Tom
See Harpur, Thomas William
Harr, Wilber C. 1908-1971 .... 1-4R
Obituary 103
Harragan, Betty Lehan 1921- CANR-17
Earlier sketch in CA 77-80
Harrah, Barbara K. 1938- 107
Harrah, David Fletcher 1949- 65-68
Harrah, David 1926- 5-8R
Harrah, Michael 1940- 115
See also SATA 41
Harral, Stewart 1906-1964 .... 5-8R
Harrar, E(llwood) S(cott) 1905- CAP-1
Earlier sketch in CA 11-12
Harrar, J(acob) George
1906-1982 Obituary 110
Harre, John 1931- 21-24R
Harre, (Horace) Rom(ano) 1927- CANR-21
Earlier sketches in CA 5-8R, CANR-2
Harrell, Allen W(aylan) 1922- 29-32R
Harrell, Anne
See Neggers, Carla A(malia)
Harrell, Costen J(ordan) 1885- 5-8R
Harrell, David Edwin Jr. 1930- CANR-34
Earlier sketches in CA 37-40R, CANR-15
Harrell, Irene B(urk) 1927- CANR-25
Earlier sketches in CA 21-24R, CANR-9
Harrell, Janice 1945- 138
See also SATA 70
Harrell, John G(rinnell) 1922- CANR-18
Earlier sketches in CA 9-12R, CANR-3
Harrell, Sara (Jeanne) Gordon 1940- 105
See also Banks, Sara (Jeanne Gordon Harrell)
Harrell, (Clyde) Stevan 1947- 106
Harrell, Thomas Willard 1911- 1-4R
Harrelson, Walter (Joseph) 1919- 9-12R
Harrer, Heinrich 1912- CANR-31
Earlier sketches in CA 17-20R, CANR-7
Harrier, Richard C(harles) 1923- 122
Brief entry 117
Harries, Joan 1922- 107
See also SATA 39
Harries, Karsten 1937- 25-28R
Harries, Owen 1930- 127
Harries, Richard (Douglas) 1936- 116
Harriett 1905- 77-80
Harrigan, Anthony (Hart) 1925- 21-24R
Harrigan, Kathryn Rudie 1951- CANR-26
Earlier sketch in CA 109
Harrigan, Stephen 1948- 122
Harriman, Ann 1932- 111
Harriman, Averell
See Harriman, W(illiam) Averell
Harriman, Edward 1922- 114
Harriman, Margaret 1928- 21-24R
Harriman, Richard L(evet) 1944- 33-36R
Harriman, Sarah 1942- 57-60
Harriman, W(illiam) Averell
1891-1986 Obituary 119
Brief entry 111
Harrington, Alan 1919- 73-76
Harrington, Charles (Christopher)
1942- CANR-9
Earlier sketch in CA 65-68
Harrington, Curtis 1928- 103
Harrington, Denis J(ames) 1932- 69-72
Harrington, Donald Szantho 1914- 21-24R
Harrington, Elbert W(ellington) 1901- 37-40R
Harrington, Evelyn Davis 1911- CANR-4
Earlier sketch in CA 5-8R
See also Harrington, Lyn
Harrington, Gary 1953- 135
Harrington, Geri CANR-21
Earlier sketches in CA 57-60, CANR-6
Harrington, Harold David 1903-1981 .... CANR-11
Earlier sketch in CA 25-28R

Harrington, Jack 1918- 57-60
Harrington, Jeremy 1932- 41-44R
Harrington, John P. 1952- 138
Harrington, John W(ilbur) 1918-1986 132
Harrington, Joseph Daniel 1923- 89-92
Harrington, K.
See Bean, Keith F(enwick)
Harrington, Lyn
See Harrington, Evelyn Davis
See also SATA 5
Harrington, Mark Raymond 1882-1971 .... CAP-2
Earlier sketch in CA 17-18
Harrington, (Edward) Michael
1928-1989 ....CANR-19
Obituary 129
Earlier sketch in CA 17-20R
Harrington, Norman W.
1922(?)-1987 Obituary 123
Harrington, (Peter) Ty(rus) 1951- 102
Harrington, William 1931- CANR-19
Earlier sketches in CA 9-12R, CANR-4
Harriott, Edwin Thomas 1933- 117
Harriott, Ted
See Harriott, Edwin Thomas
Harris, Alan 1928- 5-8R
See also SATA 71
Harris, Albert J(osiah) 1908-1990 ....CANR-5
Obituary 132
Earlier sketch in CA 1-4R
Harris, Alex(ander Eisemann) 1949- 124
Harris, Alf(red) 1928- 53-56
Harris, Alice Kessler 1941- CANR-14
Earlier sketch in CA 37-40R
Harris, Andrea
See Connolly, Vivian
and Walker, Irma Ruth (Roden)
Harris, Andrew
See Poole, Frederick King
Harris, Ann Sutherland 1937- 126
Harris, Aurand 1915- CANR-36
Earlier sketches in CA 93-96, CANR-16
See also SATA 37
Harris, Barbara J. 1942- 115
Harris, Barbara S(eger) 1927- 49-52
Harris, Ben(jamin) Charles 1907-1978 57-60
Obituary 89-92
Harris, Ben(jamin) M(axwell) 1923- CANR-2
Earlier sketch in CA 5-8R
Harris, Benjamin ....DLB 42, 43
Harris, Bernice K(elly) 1892-1973 ....5-8R
Obituary 45-48
Harris, Bertha 1937- 29-32R
Harris, Beulah Obituary 104
Harris, Bill
See Harris, William F. Jr.
Harris, Brian
See King, Harold
Harris, Brownie 1949- 107
Harris, Carl V(ernon) 1937- 97-100
Harris, Catherine
See Ainsworth, Catherine Harris
Harris, Charlaine 1951- 105
Harris, Charles B(urt) 1940- 53-56
Harris, Charles H(ouston) III 1937- 13-16R
Harris, Charles 1923- 102
Harris, Chauncy D(ennison) 1914- 29-32R
Harris, Chester W(illiam) 1910- CAP-1
Earlier sketch in CA 11-12
Harris, Christie (Lucy) Irwin 1907- CANR-6
Earlier sketch in CA 5-8R
See also CLC 12
See also DLB 88
See also MAICYA
See also SAAS 10
See also SATA 6
Harris, Clyde E. Jr. 21-24R
Harris, Colver
See Colver, Anne
Harris, Curtis C(lark) Jr. 1930- 53-56
Harris, Cyril 1891- CAP-1
Earlier sketch in CA 11-12
Harris, Dale B(enner) 1914- 13-16R
Harris, Daniel A(rthur) 1942- 89-92
Harris, David (Victor) 1946- 69-72
Harris, David W. 1948- Brief entry 107
Harris, Deborah Turner 1951- 135
Harris, Del(mer William) 1937- CANR-8
Earlier sketch in CA 61-64
Harris, Donald 1931- 126
Harris, Dorothy Joan 1931- CANR-1
Earlier sketch in CA 45-48
See also SATA 13
Harris, Douglas H(ershel Jr.) 1930- 25-28R
Harris, Edward Arnold
1910-1976 Obituary 65-68
Harris, Elizabeth 1944- 136
Harris, Elliot 1932- 25-28R
Harris, Ernest E(dward) 1914- 33-36R
Harris, Errol E(ustace) 1908- CANR-18
Earlier sketches in CA 49-52, CANR-2
Harris, F(rank) Brayton 1932- 21-24R
Harris, Francis 1957- 130
Harris, Frank 1856(?)-1931 Brief entry 109
See also TCLC 24
Harris, Fred (Roy) 1930- CANR-26
Earlier sketch in CA 77-80
Harris, Frederick John 1943- 57-60
Harris, Gene Gray 1929- 17-20R
Harris, George A. 1950- 130
Harris, George Washington
1814-1869 ....DLB 3, 11
Harris, Geraldine (Rachel) 1951- 116
See also SATA 54
Harris, Gertrude (Margaret) 1916- 57-60
Harris, H(arold) A(rthur) 1902-1974 ....CANR-30
Earlier sketch in CA 49-52
Harris, H(enry) S(ilton) 1926- 130
Harris, Harold (Morris) 1915- 132
Harris, Helen(a Barbara Mary) 1927- 61-64
Harris, Herbert 1911- 102
Harris, Herbert 1914(?)-1974 Obituary 49-52
Harris, Hyde
See Harris, Timothy Hyde
Harris, Ian (Anthony) 1937- 107
Harris, Irving David 1914- 13-16R
Harris, Jacqueline L. 1929- 126
See also SATA 62
Harris, James E(dward) 1928- 126
Brief entry 110
Harris, Jana 1947- 105
Harris, Jane Allen 1918- 1-4R
Harris, Jane Gary 111
Harris, Janet 1932-1979 ....CANR-28
Obituary 93-96
Earlier sketch in CA 33-36R
See also SATA 4, 23
Harris, Janice Hubbard 1943- 118
Harris, Jay S(tephen) 1938- 85-88
Harris, Jean (S.) 1923- 137
Harris, Jed
See Horowitz, Jacob
Harris, Jessica L.
See Milstead, Jessica L(ee)
Harris, Jocelyn 1939- 128
Harris, Joel Chandler 1848-1908 137
Brief entry 104
See also DLB 11, 23, 42, 78, 91
See also MAICYA
See also TCLC 2
See also YABC 1
Harris, John (Wyndham Parkes Lucas) Beynon
1903-1969 102
Obituary 89-92
See also CLC 19
Harris, John (Roy) 1915- CANR-2
Earlier sketch in CA 5-8R
Harris, John S(harp) 1917- 29-32R
Harris, John S(terling) 1929- 65-68
Harris, John 1916-1991 93-96
Obituary 134
Harris, Jonathan 1921- 121
See also SATA 52
Harris, Joseph E(arl) 1929- 122
Brief entry 117
Harris, Joseph Pratt 1896-1985 ....1-4R
Obituary 115
Harris, Julian (Earle) 1896-1988 ....CANR-31
Earlier sketch in CA 1-4R
Harris, Julie 1925- 103
Harris, Karen H(arriman) 1934- CANR-22
Earlier sketch in CA 103
Harris, Kathleen
See Humphries, Adelaide M.
Harris, Kathryn Gibbs
See Gibbs-Wilson, Kathryn (Beatrice)
Harris, Kenn 1947- 116
Harris, Kenneth 1904-1983 Obituary 109
Harris, Kenneth 1919- 129
Harris, Larry M.
See Janifer, Laurence M(ark)
Harris, Larry Vincent 1939- ....SATA 59
Harris, Lavinia
See St. John, Nicole
Harris, Leon A. Jr. 1926- CANR-3
Earlier sketch in CA 9-12R
See also SATA 4
Harris, Leonard 1929- CANR-9
Earlier sketch in CA 65-68
Harris, Lloyd J(ohn) 1947- 61-64
Harris, Lorle K(empe) 1912- 97-100
See also SATA 22
Harris, Louis 1921- 13-16R
Harris, Louise 1903- CANR-7
Earlier sketch in CA 17-20R
Harris, M(iddleton) A. 1908-1977 Obituary 111
Harris, MacDonald
See Heiney, Donald (William)
Harris, Madalene 1925- 105
Harris, Marcia Lee 1951- 109
Harris, Marie 1943- CANR-20
Earlier sketch in CA 104
Harris, Marilyn
See Springer, Marilyn Harris
Harris, Marion Rose (Young) 1925- CANR-30
Earlier sketches in CAP-1, CA 9-10, CANR-12
Harris, Marjorie Silliman 1890- CAP-1
Earlier sketch in CA 13-14
Harris, Mark C(harles) 1955- 113
Harris, Mark Jonathan 1941- CANR-21
Earlier sketch in CA 104
See also SATA 32
Harris, Mark 1922- CANR-2
Earlier sketch in CA 5-8R
See also CAAS 3
See also CLC 19
See also DLB 2
See also DLBY 80
Harris, Marshall (Dees) 1903- CANR-1
Earlier sketch in CA 1-4R
Harris, Martyn 1952- 132
Harris, Marvin 1927- 124
Brief entry 110
Harris, Mary B(ierman) 1943- 53-56
Harris, Mary (Emma) 1943- 135
Harris, Mary Imogene 49-52
Harris, Mary K. 1905-1966 ....CAP-1
Earlier sketch in CA 13-16
Harris, Mary Law 1892(?)-1980 Obituary 102
Harris, Maynard L(awrence)
1902-1974 Obituary 49-52
Harris, Michael H(ope) 1941- 57-60
Harris, Michael R(ichard) 1936- 29-32R
Harris, Michael (Terry) 1948- 125
Harris, Miles F(itzgerald) 1913- CANR-6
Earlier sketch in CA 5-8R
Harris, P(eter) B(ernard) 1929- 104
Harris, Patricia 57-60
Harris, Philip R(obert) 1926- CANR-25
Earlier sketches in CA 17-20R, CANR-8
Harris, R(ansom) Baine 1927- 73-76
Harris, R(obert) J(ohn) C(ecil)
1922-1980 ....CANR-15
Earlier sketch in CA 65-68
Harris, R(obert) Laird 1911- CANR-1
Earlier sketch in CA 1-4R
Harris, Radie 65-68
Harris, Raymond 1919-1989 Obituary 129
Harris, Rex 1904-1985 Obituary 118
Harris, Richard Colebrook 1936- 97-100
Harris, Richard H. 1942- 103
Harris, Richard J(ohn) 1948- 115
Harris, Richard N(elson) 1942- 77-80
Harris, Richard (S.) 1928(?)-1987 129
Obituary 123
Harris, Richard 1934- 107
Harris, Richard 1955- 126
Harris, Ricky 1922- 103
Harris, Robert Dalton 1921- 93-96
Harris, Robert Harry 1941- 108
Harris, Robert (Jennings) 1907- 5-8R
Harris, Robert Samuel 1904-1983 Obituary 111
Harris, Robert T(aylor) 1912- 5-8R
Harris, Robie H. ....SATA 53
Harris, Robin
See Shine, Deborah
Harris, Robin S(utton) 1919- 21-24R
Harris, Roger
See Wilson, R(oger) H(arris) L(ebus)
Harris, Ronald W(alter) 1916- 5-8R
Harris, Rosemary (Jeanne) CANR-30
Earlier sketches in CA 33-36R, CANR-13
See also SAAS 7
See also SATA 4
Harris, Roy J. 1903(?)-1980 Obituary 93-96
Harris, S(eymour) E(dwin) 1897-1974 65-68
Obituary 53-56
Harris, Sara Lee
See Stadelman, S(ara) L(ee)
Harris, Sheldon H(oward) 1928- 37-40R
Harris, Sherwood 1932- 97-100
See also SATA 25
Harris, Stephen E. 1943- Brief entry 111
Harris, Stephen L(eRoy) 1937- 29-32R
Harris, Steven Michael 1957- 121
See also SATA 55
Harris, (William) Stewart 1922- 104
Harris, Stuart
See Fantoni, Barry (Ernest)
Harris, Styron 1936- 112
Harris, Sydney J(ustin) 1917-1986 ....CANR-11
Obituary 120
Earlier sketch in CA 61-64
Harris, T George 1924- 69-72
Harris, Thistle Y.
See Stead, Thistle Yolette
Harris, Thomas A(nthony) 1913(?)- 93-96
Harris, Thomas Cunningham
1908-1985 Obituary 114
Harris, Thomas Harold 1933- 125
Harris, Thomas J. 1892(?)-1983 Obituary 109
Harris, Thomas O(rville) 1935- 73-76
Harris, Thomas 1940(?)- CANR-35
Earlier sketch in CA 113
Harris, Timothy Hyde 1946- 101
Harris, (Jonathan) Toby 1953- 118
Harris, Tom
See Harris, Thomas Cunningham
Harris, Trudier 1948- 115
Harris, Valentina 1957- 128
Harris, Walter A. 1929- 29-32R
Harris, Warren G(ene) 1936- CANR-26
Earlier sketch in CA 77-80
Harris, Wendell V. 1932- 111
Harris, William Bliss 1901(?)-1981 Obituary 104
Harris, William C. 1933- 21-24R
Harris, William F. Jr. 1933- CANR-30
Earlier sketch in CA 109
Harris, William Foster
See Foster-Harris, William
Harris, William Hamilton 1944- 111
Harris, William J(oseph) 1942- CANR-19
Earlier sketches in CA 53-56, CANR-5
Harris, William McKinley Sr. 1941- 126
Harris, (Theodore) Wilson 1921- CANR-27
Earlier sketches in CA 65-68, CANR-11
See also CAAS 16
See also BW
See also CLC 25
See also DLB 117
See also MTCW
Harris, Yvonne L. 138
Harrison, Allan E(ugene) 1925- CANR-6
Earlier sketch in CA 57-60
Harrison, Antony H. 1948- 132
Harrison, Barbara Grizzuti 1934- CANR-15
Earlier sketch in CA 77-80
Harrison, Barbara 1941- CANR-28
Earlier sketches in CA 29-32R, CANR-12
Harrison, Barry (Joseph Douglas) 1935- 129
Harrison, Bennett 1942- 53-56
Harrison, Bernard 1933- 93-96
Harrison, Beverly Wildung 1932- 111
Harrison, Bill
See Harrison, William C.
Harrison, Billy R. 1937- 121
Harrison, Brian Fraser
See Fraser Harrison, Brian
Harrison, C. William 1913- 107
See also SATA 35
Harrison, Carey 1944- 61-64
Harrison, Charles Yale 1898-1954 ....DLB 68
Harrison, Chip 1952- 29-32R
Harrison, Claire (E.) 1946- CANR-28
Earlier sketch in CA 111
Harrison, Colin 1960- 138
Harrison, Cynthia Ellen 1946- 57-60
Harrison, David L(akin) 1926- 117
Harrison, David L(ee) 1937- 93-96
See also SATA 26
Harrison, Deloris 1938- 61-64
See also SATA 9
Harrison, Don(ald Dean) 1941- 112
Harrison, Edward Hardy 1926- CANR-39
Earlier sketch in CA 116
See also SATA 56
Harrison, Elizabeth Cavanna 1909- CANR-27
Earlier sketches in CA 9-12R, CANR-6
See also Cavanna, Betty
Harrison, Eric George William Warde
1893-1987 Obituary 124
Harrison, Everett F(alconer) 1902- CAP-1
Earlier sketch in CA 11-12
Harrison, Francis Llewelyn
1905-1987 Obituary 124
Harrison, Frank Llewelyn
See Harrison, Francis Llewelyn
Harrison, Frank R(ussell) III 1935- 53-56
Harrison, Fred
See Paine, Lauran (Bosworth)
Harrison, Fred 1917- 29-32R
Harrison, Frederic 1831-1923 ....DLB 57
Harrison, G(eorge) B(agshawe)
1894-1991 ....CANR-3
Obituary 136
Earlier sketch in CA 1-4R
Harrison, George Russell 1898-1979 ....CANR-27
Earlier sketches in CAP-2, CA 19-20
Harrison, Hank 1940- 41-44R
Harrison, Harry (Max) 1925- CANR-21
Earlier sketches in CA 1-4R, CANR-5
See also CLC 42
See also DLB 8
See also SATA 4
Harrison, Helen Amy 1943- 114
Harrison, Helen P(atricia) 1935- 102
Harrison, Howard 1930- 5-8R
Harrison, J(ohn) F(letcher) C(lews)
1921- CANR-10
Earlier sketch in CA 25-28R
Harrison, J(ames) P. 77-80
Harrison, James (Thomas) 1937- CANR-8
Earlier sketch in CA 13-16R
See also Harrison, Jim
Harrison, Jay S(molens)
1927-1974 Obituary 53-56
Harrison, Jeffrey (Woods) 1957- 127
Harrison, Jim
See Harrison, James (Thomas)
See also CLC 6, 14, 33, 66
See also DLBY 82
Harrison, Joan (Mary) 1909- 104
Harrison, John A(rmstrong)
1915- Brief entry 111
Harrison, John Baugham 1907- 1-4R
Harrison, John M(arshall) 1914- 25-28R
Harrison, John R(aymond) 1933- 101
See also AITN 2
Harrison, John 1924- 129
Harrison, K(enneth) C(ecil) 1915- CANR-3
Earlier sketch in CA 9-12R
Harrison, Kathryn 1961- ....CLC 70
Harrison, Keith Edward 1932- 73-76
Harrison, Lawrence E. 1932- 127
Harrison, Louise C(ollbran) 1908- CAP-1
Earlier sketch in CA 11-12
Harrison, Lowell H(ayes) 1922- 37-40R
Harrison, M(ichael) John 1945- 53-56
Harrison, Marcus 1924- 102
Harrison, Marshall 1933- 138
Harrison, Martin 1930- 49-52
Harrison, Mary
See Rash, Nancy
Harrison, Max 69-72
Harrison, Michael A. 1936- 126
Harrison, Michael 1907- 97-100
Harrison, Michelle Jessica 1942- 109
Harrison, Molly 1909- 108
See also SATA 41
Harrison, Nicolas 1937(?)-1984 Obituary 114
Harrison, Paul Carter 1936- 125
Brief entry 117
See also BW
See also DLB 38
Harrison, Paul M. 1923- 53-56
Harrison, Randall P(aul) 1929- CANR-11
Earlier sketch in CA 69-72
Harrison, Ray(mond Vincent) 1928- 126
Harrison, Raymond H. 1911- 17-20R
Harrison, Reginald Carey
1908-1990 Obituary 131
Harrison, Rex
See Harrison, Reginald Carey
Harrison, Richard A(rnold) 1945- 107
Harrison, Richard John 1920- 109
Harrison, Robert (Ligon) 1932- 25-28R
Harrison, Robert Pogue 1954- 138
Harrison, Roland Kenneth 1920- 49-52
Harrison, Rosina 1899- 102
Harrison, (Thomas) Ross 1943- CANR-9
Earlier sketch in CA 61-64
Harrison, Royden John 1927- 17-20R
Harrison, S(ydney) Gerald 1924- 13-16R
Harrison, Sarah 1946- 102
See also SATA 63
Harrison, Saul I. 1925- CANR-10
Earlier sketch in CA 21-24R
Harrison, Selig S(eidenman) 1927- 85-88

Harrison, Stanley R. 1927- 41-44R
Harrison, Sue 1950- 135
Harrison, Susan Frances 1859-1935 .... DLB 99
Harrison, Ted
See Harrison, Edward Hardy
Harrison, Tony 1937- 65-68
See also CLC 43
See also DLB 40
See also MTCW
Harrison, Wallace (Kirkman)
1895-1981 Obituary 108
Harrison, Whit
See Whittington, Harry (Benjamin)
Harrison, Wilfrid 1909- CAP-1
Earlier sketch in CA 11-12
Harrison, William C. 1919- 25-28R
Harrison, William 1933- CANR-9
Earlier sketch in CA 17-20R
Harrison Church, Ronald James 1915- 13-16R
Harriss, C(lement) Lowell 1912- CANR-2
Earlier sketch in CA 1-4R
Harriss, Joseph 1936- 57-60
Harriss, R(obert) P(reston) 1902-1989 73-76
Obituary 129
Harriss, Will(ard Irvin) 1922- 111
See also CLC 34
Harrisse, Henry 1829-1910 .... DLB 47
Harrity, Richard 1907-1973 Obituary 41-44R
Harrod, Leonard Montague 1905- 13-16R
Harrod, Roy Forbes 1900-1978 ....9-12R
Obituary 103
Harrold, Stanley 1946- 128
Harrold, William E(ugene) 1936- 41-44R
Harron, Don(ald) 1924- 104
Harrop-Allin, Clinton 1936- 107
Harroun, Catherine 1907- 109
Harrow, Benjamin 1888-1970 Obituary 104
Harrowe, Fiona
See Hurd, Florence
Harrower, Elizabeth 1928- 101
Harrower, Molly 1906- 5-8R
Harry, Deborah Ann 1945- 129
Harry, M.
See Lewis, Sasha Gregory
Harsany, Peter 1913- 111
Harsch, Ernest 1951- 69-72
Harsch, Hilya
See Jelly, George Oliver
Harsch, Joseph C(lose) 1905- 102
Harsent, David 1942- 93-96
See also DLB 40
Harsh, George 1908(?)-1980 Obituary 93-96
Harsh, Wayne C. 1924- CANR-15
Earlier sketch in CA 29-32R
Harshaw, Ruth H(etzel)
1890-1968 Obituary 107
See also SATA 27
Harshbarger, David Dwight 1938- 53-56
Harshman, Marc 1950- .... SATA 71
Harson, Sley
See Ellison, Harlan
Harss, Luis 1936- 17-20R
Harstad, Peter Tjernagel 1935- 37-40R
Harston, Ruth 1944- 41-44R
Hart, A(rthur) Tindal 1908- 9-12R
Hart, Albert Bushnell 1854-1943 Brief entry 116
See also DLB 17
Hart, Albert Gailord 1909- CAP-2
Earlier sketch in CA 23-24
Hart, Alexandra 1939- CANR-6
Earlier sketch in CA 57-60
See also Jacopetti, Alexandra
Hart, Allan H(untley) 1935- 106
Hart, Archibald D(aniel) 1932- CANR-15
Earlier sketch in CA 93-96
Hart, Barry
See Bloom, Herman Irving
Hart, Basil Henry Liddell
See Liddell Hart, Basil Henry
Hart, Benjamin 1958- 126
Brief entry 118
Hart, Bruce 1938- 107
See also SATA 39, 57
Hart, Carol 1944- 65-68
Hart, Carole 1943- 107
See also SATA 39, 57
Hart, Carolyn G(impel) 1936- CANR-25
Earlier sketch in CA 13-16R
Hart, Charles (A.) 1940- 133
Hart, David K(irkwood) 1933- 123
Brief entry 117
Hart, David M(ontgomery) 1927- 136
Hart, David 1944- 128
Hart, Donald J(ohn) 1917- 9-12R
Hart, Douglas C. 1950- 101
Hart, Edward J(ack) 1941- 53-56
Hart, Edward L. 1916- CANR-14
Earlier sketch in CA 37-40R
Hart, Ellis
See Ellison, Harlan
Hart, Ernest H(untley) 1910- 102
Hart, Frances (Newbold) Noyes
1890-1943 Brief entry 112
Hart, Francis
See Paine, Lauran (Bosworth)
Hart, Francis Dudley 1909- CANR-25
Earlier sketch in CA 108
Hart, Gary (Warren) 1936(?)- 124
Brief entry 114
Hart, Gavin 1939- 106
Hart, George L. III 1942- 93-96
Hart, H(erbert) L(ionel) A(dolphus)
1907- CANR-2
Earlier sketch in CA 1-4R
Hart, Henry C(owles) 1916- 1-4R
Hart, Henry Hersch 1886-1968 .... CAP-1
Earlier sketch in CA 9-10
Hart, Henry (W.) 1954- 128
Hart, Herbert Michael 1928- 9-12R
Hart, Hornell (Norris) 1888-1967 Obituary 111
Hart, James D(avid) 1911-1990 ....CANR-1
Obituary 132
Earlier sketch in CA 1-4R
Hart, Jane (Meyers) 1922- 107
Hart, Jeanne
See Schrager, Jeanne Hart
Hart, Jeffrey Allen 1947- 109
Hart, Jenifer 1914- 138
Hart, Jim Allee 1914- 13-16R
Hart, John E(dward) 1917- 33-36R
Hart, John Fraser 1924- 37-40R
Hart, John Lewis 1931- CANR-4
Earlier sketch in CA 49-52
See also Hart, Johnny
Hart, John Mason 1935- 132
Hart, John 1942- 109
Hart, John 1948- CANR-11
Earlier sketch in CA 65-68
Hart, Johnny
See Hart, John Lewis
See also AITN 1
Hart, Jon
See Harvey, John (Barton)
Hart, Joseph 1945- 85-88
Hart, Josephine 1942(?)- 138
See also CLC 70
Hart, Judith 1924- 109
Hart, Julia Catherine 1796-1867 .... DLB 99
Hart, Kate
See Kramer, Roberta
Hart, Kevin 1954- 135
Hart, Kitty 1926- 117
Hart, Larry 1920- 33-36R
Hart, Lois B(orland) 1941- 117
Hart, Marie 1932- 41-44R
Hart, Marilyn M(cGuire) 1926- 45-48
Hart, Marion Rice 1892(?)-1990 Obituary 132
Hart, Martin
See 't Hart, Maarten
Hart, Matthew 1945- 125
Hart, Milton R. 1896(?)-1983 Obituary 109
Hart, Moss 1904-1961 109
Obituary 89-92
See also CLC 66
See also DLB 7
Hart, Oliver 1723-1795 .... DLB 31
Hart, Patricia Susan 1950- 118
Hart, Patrick 1925- 53-56
Hart, Ray L(ee) 1929- 29-32R
Hart, Richard (Harry) 1908- CAP-1
Earlier sketch in CA 9-10
Hart, Robert A(llan) 1929- Brief entry 117
Hart, Roderick P(atrick) 1945- 106
Hart, Sandra Lynn Housby 1948- CANR-25
Earlier sketch in CA 108
Hart, Stan 1929- 118
Hart, Stephanie 1949- 97-100
Hart, Sue
See Hart, Susanne
Hart, Susanne 1927- CANR-20
Earlier sketch in CA 102
Hart, V(orhis) Donn 1918- 13-16R
Hart, Walter 1906(?)-1973 Obituary 45-48
Hart, Winston Scott
1903(?)-1979 Obituary 89-92
Hartcup, Adeline 1918- 116
Hartcup, Guy 1919- 29-32R
Hart-Davis, Duff 1936- CANR-27
Earlier sketch in CA 29-32R
Hart-Davis, Phyllida
See Barstow, Phyllida
Hart-Davis, Rupert (Charles) 1907- 134
Brief entry 115
Hartdegen, Stephen J. 1907-1989 Obituary 130
Harte, (Francis) Bret(t)
1836(?)-1902 Brief entry 104
See also CDALB 1865-1917
See also DLB 12, 64, 74, 79
See also SATA 26
See also SSC 8
See also TCLC 1, 25
See also WLC
Harte, Marjorie
See McEvoy, Marjorie Harte
Harte, Samantha
See Hart, Sandra Lynn Housby
Harte, Thomas Joseph
1914-1974 Obituary 53-56
Hartel, Klaus Dieter
See Vandenberg, Philipp
Hartendorp, A(bram) V(an) H(eyningen)
1893- CAP-1
Earlier sketch in CA 13-16
Harter, Eugene C(laudius) 1926- 119
Harter, Helen (O'Connor) 1905- 5-8R
Harter, Hugh A(nthony) 1922- 110
Harter, Kenneth W. 1912(?)-1984 Obituary 112
Harter, Lafayette George Jr. 1918- 9-12R
Hartfeld, Hermann 1942- 136
Hartford, Claire 1913- 29-32R
Hartford, Ellis F(ord) 1905- CAP-1
Earlier sketch in CA 13-14
Hartford, (George) Huntington II 1911- 17-20R
Hartford, Margaret E(lizabeth) 1917- 41-44R
Hartford, Via
See Donson, Cyril
Harth, Erica 116
Harth, Erich 1919- 107
Harth, (John) Phillip 1926- Brief entry 116
Harth, Robert 1940- 33-36R
Harthan, John Plant 1916- 102
Harthoorn, A(ntonie) M(arinus) 1923- 53-56
Hartich, Alice 1888- CAP-2
Earlier sketch in CA 17-18
Hartill, Rosemary (Jane) 1949- 127
Harting, Emilie Clothier 1942- 73-76
Hartje, Robert G(eorge) 1922- 25-28R
Hartjen, Clayton A(lfred) 1943- 69-72
Hartke, Vance 1919- 25-28R
Hartland, Michael 1941- 110
Hartlaub, Felix 1913(?)-1945 .... DLB 56
Hartlaub, G(ustav) F(riedrich)
1884-1963 Obituary 112
Hartle, Anthony E. 1942- 137
Hartleben, Otto Erich 1864-1905 .... DLB 118
Hartley, Dorothy 1893-1985 105
Obituary 118
Hartley, Ellen (Raphael) 1915-1980 ....CANR-4
Earlier sketch in CA 5-8R
See also SATA 23
Hartley, Fred Allan III 1953- 106
See also SATA 41
Hartley, Jean 1933- 135
Hartley, John I(rvin) 1921- 5-8R
Hartley, Keith 1940- CANR-37
Earlier sketch in CA 115
Hartley, L(eslie) P(oles) 1895-1972 ....CANR-33
Obituary 37-40R
Earlier sketch in CA 45-48
See also CLC 2, 22
See also DLB 15
See also MTCW
Hartley, Livingston 1900- 61-64
Hartley, Lodwick (Charles) 1906-1979 ....CANR-1
Earlier sketch in CA 1-4R
Hartley, Margaret L(ohlker) 1909-1983 97-100
Obituary 110
Hartley, Marie 1905- 9-12R
Hartley, Marsden 1877-1943 Brief entry 123
See also DLB 54
Hartley, Peter (Roy) 1933- 103
Hartley, Rachel M. 1895- 5-8R
Hartley, Robert E. 1936- 130
Hartley, Robert F(rank) 1927- CANR-28
Earlier sketches in CA 69-72, CANR-11
Hartley, Shirley Foster 1928- CANR-13
Earlier sketch in CA 73-76
Hartley, Travis
See Paine, Lauran (Bosworth)
Hartley, William B(rown) 1913-1980 ....CANR-4
Earlier sketch in CA 5-8R
See also SATA 23
Hartling, Peter
See Haertling, Peter
See also DLB 75
Hartman, Berl
See Hartman, Berl Mendelson
Hartman, Berl Mendelson 1938- 122
Hartman, (Howard) Carl 1917- 122
Hartman, Carl 1928- 104
Hartman, Charles O(ssian) 1949- 108
Hartman, Chester W(arren) 1936- 57-60
Hartman, David N. 1921- 13-16R
Hartman, Evert 1937- 113
See also SATA 35, 38
Hartman, Geoffrey H. 1929- 125
Brief entry 117
See also CLC 27
See also DLB 67
Hartman, George E(dward) 1926- 41-44R
Hartman, Hermene D(emaris) 1948- 122
Hartman, Jan 1938- 65-68
Hartman, Jane E(vangeline) 1928- CANR-22
Earlier sketch in CA 105
See also SATA 47
Hartman, John J(acob) 1942- 49-52
Hartman, Louis F(rancis) 1901-1970 .... CAP-2
Earlier sketch in CA 23-24
See also SATA 22
Hartman, Mary S(usan) 1941- 81-84
Hartman, Nancy Carol 1942- 53-56
Hartman, Olov 1906-1982 ....CANR-14
Earlier sketch in CA 29-32R
Hartman, Patience
See Zawadsky, Patience
Hartman, Rachel (Frieda) 1920-1972 ....5-8R
Obituary 33-36R
Hartman, Rhondda Evans 1934- 61-64
Hartman, Robert K(intz) 1940- 41-44R
Hartman, Robert S. 1910-1973 .... CAP-2
Obituary 45-48
Earlier sketch in CA 17-18
Hartman, Roger
See Mehta, Rustam Jehangir
Hartman, Shirley 1929- 57-60
Hartman, William E(llis) 1919- 69-72
Hartman, William T(aylor) 1942- 117
Hartmann, Betsy
See Hartmann, Elizabeth
Hartmann, Edward George 1912- 41-44R
Hartmann, Elizabeth 1951- 126
Hartmann, Ernest 1934- 21-24R
Hartmann, Franz 1838-1912 Brief entry 115
Hartmann, Frederick Howard 1922- CANR-38
Earlier sketches in CA 1-4R, CANR-1, 16
Hartmann, Heinz 1894-1970 Obituary 104
Hartmann, Helmut Henry 1931- 105
Hartmann, Klaus 1925- 21-24R
Hartmann, Michael 1944- 97-100
Hartmann, Rudolf A. 1937- Brief entry 111
Hartmann, Sadakichi 1867-1944 .... DLB 54
Hartmann, Susan M(arie) 1940- 41-44R
Hartmann, William K(enneth) 1939- 69-72
Hartnack, Justus 1912- 41-44R
Hartnett, D(avid) W(illiam) 1952- 122
Hartnett, Ken(neth Owen) 1934- 118
Hartnett, Michael 1941- 130
Hartnoll, Phyllis 1906- 81-84
Hartocollis, Peter 1922- CANR-1
Earlier sketch in CA 45-48
Hartog, Diana 1942- 123
Hartog, Joseph 1933- 102
Hartshorn, Ruth M. 1928- .... SATA 11
Hartshorne, Charles 1897- CANR-29
Earlier sketches in CA 9-12R, CANR-4
Hartshorne, Richard 1899- 5-8R
Hartshorne, Thomas L(lewellyn) 1935- 37-40R
Hart-Smith, William 1911- CANR-11
Earlier sketch in CA 21-24R
Hartsoe, Colleen Ivey 1925- 109
Hartston, W(illiam) R(oland) 1947- 116
Hartsuch, Paul Jackson 1902- 57-60
Hartt, Julian N(orris) 1911- 132
Hartt, Julian 1916(?)-1984 Obituary 113
Hartung, Albert Edward 1923- 103
Hartung, Hans (Heinrich Ernst)
1904-1989 Obituary 130
Hartup, Willard W(ert) 1927- 25-28R
Hartwell, Dickson Jay 1906-1981 .... CAP-1
Obituary 103
Earlier sketch in CA 11-12
Hartwell, Nancy
See Callahan, Claire Wallis
Hartwell, Ronald Max 1921- 25-28R
Hartwick, Sylvia
See Doherty, Ivy R. Duffy
Hartwig, Marie (Dorothy) 1906- 1-4R
Hartwig, Richard E(ric) 1942- 118
Harty, (Fredric) Russell
1934-1988 Obituary 125
Hartz, Fred R. 1933- 122
Hartz, Jim .... AITN 2
Hartz, Louis 1919-1986 Obituary 118
Hartzler, Daniel David 1941- 61-64
Haruf, Kent .... CLC 34
Haruki Murakami 1949- 136
Harvard, Andrew Carson 1949- 69-72
Harvard, Charles
See Gibbs-Smith, Charles Harvard
Harvard, Stephen 1948- 57-60
Harvester, Simon
See Rumbold-Gibbs, Henry St. John Clair
Harvey, Andrew 1952- 132
Brief entry 126
Harvey, Anne 1933- 121
Harvey, Anthony Peter 1940- 106
Harvey, Barbara (Fitzgerald) 1928- 116
Harvey, Brett 1936- 126
See also SATA 61
Harvey, C(harles) J(ohn) D(errick) 1922- 9-12R
Harvey, David Dow 1931- 65-68
Harvey, David (W.) 1935- Brief entry 117
Harvey, David 1935- 123
Harvey, Donald J(oseph) 1922- 41-44R
Harvey, Earle (Sherburn) 1906- CANR-29
Earlier sketch in CA 109
Harvey, Edith 1908(?)-1972 Obituary 104
See also SATA 27
Harvey, Edward Burns 1939- 41-44R
Harvey, Frank (Laird) 1913- 5-8R
Harvey, Frank 1912-1981 Obituary 105
Harvey, Geoffrey 1943- 126
Harvey, Gina Cantoni 1922- CANR-33
Earlier sketch in CA 45-48
Harvey, Harriet 1924- 109
Harvey, Ian Douglas 1914-1987 .... CAP-1
Obituary 121
Earlier sketch in CA 9-10
Harvey, James C(ardwell) 1925- 45-48
Harvey, James O. 1926- 17-20R
Harvey, James 1929- 135
Harvey, Jean-Charles 1891-1967 .... DLB 88
Harvey, Joan C. 1948- 132
Harvey, Joan M(argaret) 1918- 102
Harvey, John B.
See Harvey, John (Barton)
Harvey, John (Barton) 1938- 125
Harvey, John F(rederick) 1921- CANR-23
Earlier sketches in CA 13-16R, CANR-8
Harvey, John Hooper 1911- CANR-21
Earlier sketches in CA 5-8R, CANR-6
Harvey, John Robert 1942- 93-96
Harvey, Jonathan 1939- 61-64
Harvey, Karen (E.) G(iddens) 1944- 117
Harvey, Kenneth 1919(?)-1979 Obituary 89-92
Harvey, Lashley Grey 1900- 37-40R
Harvey, Maria Luisa Alvarez 1938- 53-56
Harvey, Marian 1927- 89-92
Harvey, Michael G. 1944- 110
Harvey, Mose Lofley 1910-1985 Obituary 115
Harvey, Nancy Lenz 1935- 65-68
Harvey, Nigel 1916- CANR-30
Earlier sketches in CA 73-76, CANR-13
Harvey, O. J. 1927- 37-40R
Harvey, P(aul) D(ean) A(dshead) 1930- 112
Harvey, Paul
See Aurandt, Paul Harvey
Harvey, Paulett
See Tumay, Paulett
Harvey, (Brian) Peter 1951- 135
Harvey, Rachel
See Bloom, Ursula
Harvey, Richard B(lake) 1930- 49-52
Harvey, Robert 1884- 5-8R
Harvey, Roland 1945- .... SATA 71
Harvey, Ruth C(harlotte) 1918-1980 ....1-4R
Obituary 102
Harvey, Stephen 1949- 134
Harvey, Van A(ustin) 1926- 33-36R
Harvey, Virginia I(sham) 1917- 57-60
Harvey, William Burnett 1922- 41-44R
Harvey Wood, (Elizabeth) Harriet 1934- 123
Harvie-Watt, George Steven 1903- 109
Harvor, Beth
See Harvor, (Erica) Elisabeth (Arendt Deichmann)
Harvor, (Erica) Elisabeth (Arendt Deichmann)
1936- 134
Harward, Donald W. 1939- 93-96

Harward, Timothy Blake 1932- ... 25-28R
Harwell, Ann (Manning) J. 1936- ... 57-60
Harwell, Ernie
See Harwell, William Earnest
Harwell, Richard Barksdale 1915- ... CANR-17
Earlier sketches in CA 1-4R, CANR-2
Harwell, William Earnest 1918- ... 128
Brief entry ... 116
Harwick, B. L.
See Keller, Beverly
Harwin, Brian
See Henderson, LeGrand
Harwit, Martin Otto 1931- ... 105
Harwood, Alan 1935- ... 113
Harwood, Alice (Mary) ... 5-8R
Harwood, (Henry) David 1938- ... 104
Harwood, Edwin 1939- ... 29-32R
Harwood, Gina
See Battiscombe, E(sther) Georgina (Harwood)
Harwood, Gwen(doline Nessie) 1920- ... 97-100
Harwood, Jonathan 1943- ... 103
Harwood, Lee 1939- ... CANR-9
Earlier sketch in CA 21-24R
See also DLB 40
Harwood, Michael 1934(?)-1989 Obituary ... 130
Harwood, Pearl Augusta (Bragdon)
1903- ... 13-16R
See also SATA 9
Harwood, Raymond C(harles)
1906-1987 Obituary ... 122
Harwood, Ronald 1934- ... CANR-4
Earlier sketch in CA 1-4R
See also CLC 32
See also DLB 13
Harzfeld, Lois 1932- ... 107
Hasan, Saiyid Zafar 1930- ... 73-76
Hasan, Sana ... 128
Hasbrouck, Kenneth E(dward) Sr.
1916- ... CANR-31
Earlier sketch in CA 49-52
Hasegawa, Nyozekan 1875-1969 Obituary ... 111
Hasegawa, Tsuyoshi 1941- ... 109
Hasek, Jaroslav (Matej Frantisek)
1883-1923 ... 129
Brief entry ... 104
See also MTCW
See also TCLC 4
Hasel, Gerhard F(ranz) 1935- ... CANR-15
Earlier sketch in CA 41-44R
Haselden, John
See Forrester, Martyn (John)
Haselden, Kyle (Emerson) 1913-1968 ... 5-8R
Haseler, Stephen Michael Alan 1942- ... 85-88
Haseley, Dennis ... SATA 44, 57
Hasenclever, Herbert Frederick
1924-1978 Obituary ... 81-84
Hasford, (Jerry) Gustav 1947- ... 85-88
Hashmi, Aurangzeb Alamgir 1951- ... CANR-16
Earlier sketch in CA 77-80
Haskell, Arnold L(ionel) 1903-1981(?) ... CANR-7
Obituary ... 102
Earlier sketch in CA 5-8R
See also SATA 6
Haskell, Douglas 1899-1979 Obituary ... 89-92
Haskell, Edward Froehlich
1906- Brief entry ... 105
Haskell, Francis (James Herbert)
1928- ... CANR-6
Earlier sketch in CA 9-12R
Haskell, Harry 1954- ... 129
Haskell, John Duncan Jr. 1941- ... CANR-25
Earlier sketch in CA 107
Haskell, Martin R(oy) 1912- ... 41-44R
Haskell, Molly 1939- ... 135
Haskett, Edythe Rance 1915- ... 21-24R
Haskin, Dorothy C(lark) 1905- ... 5-8R
Haskin, Gretchen 1936- ... 103
Haskins, Barbara
See Stone, Barbara Haskins
Haskins, Charles Homer 1870-1937 ... DLB 47
Haskins, George Lee 1915-1991 ... CANR-1
Obituary ... 135
Earlier sketch in CA 1-4R
Haskins, Ilma 1919- ... 45-48
Haskins, James S. 1941- ... CANR-25
Earlier sketch in CA 33-36R
See also Haskins, Jim
See also BW
See also CLR 3
See also MAICYA
See also SATA 9, 69
Haskins, Jim
See Haskins, James S.
See also SAAS 4
Haskins, Sam(uel Joseph) 1926- ... 103
Haslam, Gerald W. 1937- ... CANR-27
Earlier sketches in CA 29-32R, CANR-11
Hasler, Eveline 1937- ... 106
Hasler, Joan 1931- ... 29-32R
See also SATA 28
Haslerud, George M(artin) 1906- ... 45-48
Hasley, Louis (Leonard) 1906- ... 37-40R
Hasley, Lucile (Charlotte Hardman)
1909- ... CAP-1
Earlier sketch in CA 11-12
Hasling, John 1928- ... 33-36R
Haslip, Joan 1912- ... 107
Hasluck, Nicholas 1942- ... 137
Hasluck, Paul (Meernaa Caedwalla) 1905- ... 109
Haspel, Eleanor C. 1944- ... 69-72
Hass, C(harles) Glen 1915- ... 17-20R
Hass, Eric 1905(?)-1980 Obituary ... 102
Hass, Hans 1919- ... 108
Hass, Michael 1938- ... 37-40R
Hass, Robert 1941- ... CANR-30
Earlier sketch in CA 111
See also CLC 18, 39
See also DLB 105
Hassall, Anthony J. 1939- ... 126
Hassall, Christopher (Vernon)
1912-1963 Obituary ... 89-92
Hassall, Joan 1906-1988 ... SATA 43, 56
Hassall, Mark (William Cory) 1940- ... CANR-13
Earlier sketch in CA 73-76
Hassall, William Owen 1912- ... 13-16R
Hassan, Ihab Habib 1925- ... CANR-19
Earlier sketches in CA 5-8R, CANR-3
See also CAAS 12
Hassan, William Ephraim Jr. 1923- ... 33-36R
Hasse, John Edward 1948- ... 119
Hassel, David John 1923- ... CANR-32
Earlier sketch in CA 113
Hassel, Odd 1897-1981 Obituary ... 108
Hassel, R. Chris Jr. 1939- ... 129
Hassel, Sven 1917- ... 93-96
Hassenger, Robert (Leo) 1937- ... 21-24R
Hassing, Per 1916- ... 37-40R
Hassinger, Edward W(esley) 1925- ... 125
Hassler, Donald M. (II) 1937- ... CANR-31
Earlier sketches in CA 41-44R, CANR-14
Hassler, Jon (Francis) 1933- ... CANR-21
Earlier sketch in CA 73-76
See also SATA 19
Hassler, Warren W. Jr. 1926- ... 9-12R
Hassler, William T(homas) 1954- ... 104
Hassrick, Peter H(eyl) 1941- ... CANR-16
Earlier sketches in CA 49-52, CANR-1
Hast, Adele 1931- ... 119
Hastings, Adrian 1929- ... CANR-23
Earlier sketches in CA 17-20R, CANR-7
Hastings, Alan
See Williamson, Geoffrey
Hastings, Arthur Claude 1935- ... 37-40R
Hastings, Beverly
See Barkin, Carol
and James, Elizabeth
Hastings, Brooke
See Gordon, Deborah Hannes
Hastings, Cecily Mary Eleanor 1924- ... 5-8R
Hastings, Graham
See Jeffries, Roderic (Graeme)
Hastings, Harrington
See Marsh, John
Hastings, Hubert de Cronin 1902-1986 ... 109
Obituary ... 121
Hastings, Hudson
See Kuttner, Henry
Hastings, Ian 1912- ... 45-48
See also SATA 62
Hastings, Macdonald 1909- ... CANR-9
Earlier sketch in CA 53-56
Hastings, March
See Levinson, Leonard
Hastings, Margaret 1910- ... 41-44R
Hastings, (Macdonald) Max 1945- ... 81-84
Hastings, Michael
See Bar-Zohar, Michael
Hastings, Michael (Gerald) 1938- ... 97-100
Hastings, Paul G(uiler) 1914- ... CANR-24
Earlier sketch in CA 1-4R
Hastings, Philip Kay 1922- ... 102
Hastings, Phyllis (Dora Hodge) ... CANR-8
Earlier sketch in CA 9-12R
Hastings, Robert J. 1924- ... 122
Hastings, Robert Paul 1933- ... 73-76
Hastings, Robin Hood William Stewart
1917-1990 Obituary ... 131
Hastings, Roderic
See Jeffries, Graham Montague
Hastings, Selina ... CLC 44
Hastings, Susan 1942- ... 128
Hastings, William T(homson) 1881- ... 5-8R
Haston, Dougal 1940-1977 Obituary ... 105
Hastorf, Albert H(erman) 1920- ... 97-100
Hasty, Olga Peters 1951- ... 128
Hasty, Ronald W. 1941- ... CANR-4
Earlier sketch in CA 53-56
Haswell, Chetwynd John Drake 1919- ... 41-44R
Haswell, Harold Alanson Jr. 1912- ... 45-48
Haswell, Jock
See Haswell, Chetwynd John Drake
Haszard, Patricia Moyes 1923- ... CANR-29
Earlier sketches in CA 17-20R, CANR-13
See also Moyes, Patricia
Hatch, Alden 1898-1975 ... 65-68
Obituary ... 57-60
Hatch, (Alden) Denison 1935- ... 33-36R
Hatch, Elvin (James) 1937- ... 45-48
Hatch, Eric S(towe)
1902(?)-1973 Obituary ... 41-44R
Hatch, James V(ernon) 1928- ... 41-44R
Hatch, John (Charles) 1917- ... 9-12R
Hatch, Mary Cottam 1912-1970 Obituary ... 109
See also SATA 28
Hatch, Nathan O(rr) 1946- ... 129
Brief entry ... 109
Hatch, Preble D(elloss) K(ellogg) 1898- ... CAP-2
Earlier sketch in CA 23-24
Hatch, Raymond N(orris) 1911- ... 21-24R
Hatch, Richard A(llen) 1940- ... CANR-9
Earlier sketch in CA 21-24R
Hatch, Robert McConnell 1910- ... 93-96
Hatch, William H(enry) P(aine)
1875-1972 Obituary ... 37-40R
Hatcher, George W. 1906(?)-1983 Obituary ... 110
Hatcher, Harlan (Henthorne) 1898- ... CAP-2
Earlier sketch in CA 19-20
Hatcher, John S(outhall) 1940- ... 97-100
Hatcher, John 1942- ... 33-36R
Hatcher, Nat(han) B(razzell) 1897- ... 1-4R
Hatcher, Robert Anthony 1937- ... 93-96
Hatcher, William S(pottswood) 1935- ... 123
Hatem, Mohamed Abdel-Kader
See Hatim, Muhammad 'Abd al-Qadir
Hatfield, Antoinette Kuzmanich 1929- ... 85-88
Hatfield, Dorothy B(lackmon) 1921- ... 53-56
Hatfield, Elaine (Catherine) 1937- ... CANR-38
Earlier sketches in CA 25-28R, CANR-10, 17
Hatfield, Henry Caraway 1912- ... 65-68
Hatfield, Julie (Stockwell) 1940- ... 126
Hatfield, Mark O(dom) 1922- ... 77-80
Hatfield, Michael (Vernon) 1935- ... 119
Hathaway, Baxter L. 1909- ... CANR-5
Earlier sketch in CA 1-4R
Hathaway, Bo 1942- ... 106
Hathaway, Dale E(rnest) 1925- ... 9-12R
Hathaway, Jan
See Neubauer, William Arthur
Hathaway, Lulu (Bailey) 1903- ... 13-16R
Hathaway, Mavis
See Avery, Ira
Hathaway, Nancy 1946- ... 108
Hathaway, Richard Dean 1927- ... 125
Hathaway, Sibyl Collings 1884-1974 ... 1-4R
Obituary ... 103
Hathaway, Starke R(osecrans) 1903-1984 ... 5-8R
Obituary ... 113
Hathaway, William 1944- ... 73-76
See also DLB 120
Hathcock, Louise ... 1-4R
Hathorn, Richmond Y(ancey) 1917- ... CANR-1
Earlier sketch in CA 1-4R
Hatim, Muhammad 'Abd al-Qadir 1918- ... 89-92
Hatlen, Burton (Norval) 1936- ... 109
Hatley, George B(erton) 1924- ... 106
Hatlo, Jimmy 1898-1963 Obituary ... 93-96
See also SATA 23
Hatmon, Paul W. 1921- ... 106
Hatt, Harold E(rnest) 1932- ... 21-24R
Hatta, Mohammed 1902-1980 Obituary ... 97-100
Hattaway, Herman (Morell) 1938- ... 65-68
Hattaway, Michael 1941- ... CANR-39
Earlier sketch in CA 116
Hattendorf, John B(rewster) 1941- ... 135
Hatteras, Amelia
See Mencken, H(enry) L(ouis)
Hatteras, Owen
See Mencken, H(enry) L(ouis)
Hatteras, Owen
See Nathan, George Jean
See also TCLC 18
Hatteras, Owen III
See McDavid, Raven I(oor) Jr.
Hatterer, Lawrence J(ohn)
1925- Brief entry ... 118
Hattersley, Ralph (Marshall Jr.) 1921- ... 103
Hattersley, Roy (Sydney George) 1932- ... 103
Hattersley-Smith, Geoffrey (Francis) 1923- ... 118
Hattery, Lowell H(arold) 1916- ... 17-20R
Hatton, Ragnhild Marie 1913- ... CANR-12
Earlier sketch in CA 25-28R
Hatton, Robert Wayland 1934- ... 37-40R
Hatton, Thomas J(enison) 1935- ... 114
Hattwick, Richard E(arl) 1938- ... 73-76
Hatvary, George Egon ... 53-56
Hatzenbuehler, Ronald L(ee) 1945- ... 117
Hatzfeld, Helmut A(nthony) 1892-1979 ... 97-100
Obituary ... 85-88
Hauberg, Clifford A(lvin) 1906- ... 37-40R
Hauck, Allan 1925- ... 1-4R
Hauck, Paul A(nthony) 1924- ... CANR-14
Earlier sketch in CA 41-44R
Hauck, Richard Boyd 1936- ... 53-56
Haueisen, Kathryn M. 1946- ... 128
Haueisen, Kathy
See Haueisen, Kathryn M.
Hauerwas, Stanley Martin 1940- ... 57-60
Hauff, Wilhelm 1802-1827 ... DLB 90
Haug, C(harles) James 1946- ... CANR-38
Earlier sketch in CA 116
Haugaard, Erik Christian 1923- ... CANR-38
Earlier sketches in CA 5-8R, CANR-3
See also CLR 11
See also MAICYA
See also SAAS 12
See also SATA 4, 68
Haugaard, William Paul 1929- ... 25-28R
Hauge, Sharon K(aye) 1943- ... 116
Haugeland, John (Christian) 1945- ... 133
Haugen, Edmund Bennett 1913- ... 17-20R
Haugen, Einar (Ingvald) 1906- ... CANR-25
Earlier sketches in CA 21-24R, CANR-9
Haugen, Tormod 1945- ... 135
See also SATA 66
Haugh, Richard (Stanley) 1942- ... CANR-9
Earlier sketch in CA 57-60
Haugh, Robert F(ulton) 1910- ... 61-64
Haughey, John C. 1930- ... 77-80
Haughey, Thomas Brace 1943- ... 113
Haught, James A(lbert Jr.)
1932- Brief entry ... 122
Haught, John F(rancis) 1942- ... 85-88
Haughton, Claire Shaver 1901- ... 85-88
Haughton, Rosemary (Luling) 1927- ... CANR-35
Earlier sketch in CA 5-8R
Haughton, Sidney Henry
1888-1982 Obituary ... 107
Haughton-James, Jean Rosemary
1924-1981 Obituary ... 105
Haugland, Vern(on Arnold) 1908-1984 ... 93-96
Obituary ... 113
Hauk, Maung
See Hobbs, Cecil (Carlton)
Haule, James M(ark) 1945- ... CANR-27
Earlier sketch in CA 109
Hauman, Doris 1898- ... SATA 32
Hauman, George 1890-1961 ... SATA 32
Haun, Paul 1906-1969 ... CAP-2
Earlier sketch in CA 17-18
Hau'Ofa, Epeli 1939- ... 124
Haupt, Christopher (Charles Herbert) Lehmann
See Lehmann-Haupt, Christopher (Charles Herbert)
Haupt, Zygmunt 1907(?)-1975 Obituary ... 61-64
Hauptly, Denis J(ames) 1945- ... 118
See also SATA 57
Hauptman, Don 1947- ... 138
Hauptman, Terry 1947- ... 111
Hauptman, William 1942- ... 128
Hauptmann, Carl 1858-1921 ... DLB 66, 118
Hauptmann, Gerhart (Johann Robert)
1862-1946 Brief entry ... 104
See also DLB 66, 118
See also TCLC 4
Haury, Emil W(alter) 1904- ... 65-68
Hausdorff, Don 1927- ... 45-48
Hause, Steven C. 1942- ... 127
Hauser, Bengamin Gayelord
1895-1984 Obituary ... 114
Brief entry ... 111
Hauser, Carl Maria 1895-1985 Obituary ... 117
Hauser, Charles McCorkle 1929- ... 69-72
Hauser, Gayelord
See Hauser, Bengamin Gayelord
Hauser, Hillary 1944- ... CANR-30
Earlier sketches in CA 69-72, CANR-11
Hauser, Margaret L(ouise) 1909- ... CAP-1
Earlier sketch in CA 11-12
See also SATA 10
Hauser, Marianne 1910- ... CANR-13
Earlier sketches in CAP-1, CA 11-12
See also CAAS 11
See also DLBY 83
Hauser, Phillip M(orris) 1909- ... 17-20R
Hauser, Robert Mason 1942- ... 109
Hauser, Thomas 1946- ... 85-88
Hauser, William B(arry) 1939- ... 69-72
Hausknecht, Murray 1925- ... 37-40R
Hausknecht, Richard 1929- ... 121
Hausman, Gerald 1945- ... CANR-38
Earlier sketches in CA 45-48, CANR-2, 17
See also SATA 13
Hausman, Gerry
See Hausman, Gerald
Hausman, Patricia 1953- ... CANR-26
Earlier sketch in CA 107
Hausman, Warren H. 1939- ... 17-20R
Hausmann, Bernard A(ndrew) 1899- ... CAP-2
Earlier sketch in CA 23-24
Hausmann, Manfred 1898-1986 Obituary ... 120
Hausmann, Winifred 1922- ... CANR-26
Earlier sketches in CA 21-24R, CANR-11
Hausrath, Alfred Hartmann 1901- ... 41-44R
Haussig, Hans Wilhelm 1916- ... 29-32R
Hausvater, Alexander 1948- ... 130
Hauther, Brenda 1951- ... 113
Hautzig, Deborah 1956- ... 89-92
See also SATA 31
Hautzig, Esther Rudomin 1930- ... CANR-20
Earlier sketches in CA 1-4R, CANR-5
See also CLR 22
See also MAICYA
See also SATA 4, 68
Havard, William C(lyde) Jr. 1923- ... CANR-5
Earlier sketch in CA 1-4R
Havel, J(ean) E(ugene Martial) 1928- ... 41-44R
Havel, Vaclav 1936- ... CANR-36
Earlier sketch in CA 104
See also CLC 25, 58, 65
See also MTCW
Havelock, Christine Mitchell 1924- ... 85-88
Havelock, Eric A(lfred) 1903-1988 ... CAP-1
Obituary ... 125
Earlier sketch in CA 13-16
Havelock, Ronald G(eoffrey) 1935- ... 85-88
Haveman, Robert H. 1936- ... 17-20R
Havemann, Ernest (Carl) 1912- ... 1-4R
Havemann, Ernst 1918- ... 135
Havemann, Joel 1943- ... 85-88
Havemann, Robert (Hans Gunther)
1910-1982 Obituary ... 110
Havemeyer, Loomis
1886-1971 Obituary ... 33-36R
Haven, Richard 1924- ... 25-28R
Havens, Daniel F(rederick) 1931- ... 69-72
Havens, George R(emington)
1890-1977 ... CANR-4
Obituary ... 73-76
Earlier sketch in CA 5-8R
Havens, Gordon 1903-1983 Obituary ... 111
Havens, Leston Laycock 1924- ... 119
Havens, Murray Clark 1932- ... 41-44R
Havens, Shirley E(lise) 1925- ... 89-92
Havens, Thomas R. H. 1939- ... CANR-34
Earlier sketches in CA 41-44R, CANR-15
Haver, Ronald D. 1939- ... 109
Haverkamp-Begemann, Egbert 1923- ... CANR-11
Earlier sketch in CA 17-20R
Haverstick, John (Mitchell) 1919- ... 25-28R
Haverstock, Mary Sayre 1932- ... 81-84
Haverstock, Nathan Alfred 1931- ... 53-56
Havet, Jose (L.) 1937- ... 137
Haviaras, Stratis
See Chaviaras, Strates
See also CLC 33
Havighurst, Alfred F(reeman)
1904-1991 ... 33-36R
Obituary ... 133
Havighurst, Marion (M.) 1894-1974 ... CAP-1
Obituary ... 49-52
Earlier sketch in CA 13-14
Havighurst, Robert J(ames) 1900-1991 ... 21-24R
Obituary ... 133

Havighurst, Walter (Edwin) 1901- CANR-29
Earlier sketches in CA 1-4R, CANR-1
See also SATA 1
Haviland, Virginia 1911-1988 ....CANR-12
Obituary 124
Earlier sketch in CA 17-20R
See also SATA 6, 54
Havill, Steven 1945- CANR-25
Earlier sketch in CA 108
Havis, Allan 1951- CANR-28
Earlier sketch in CA 108
Havlice, Patricia Pate 1943- CANR-12
Earlier sketch in CA 29-32R
Havlik, John F(ranklin) 1917-1984 ....CANR-24
Earlier sketch in CA 45-48
Havoc, June 1916- 107
Havran, Martin J. 1929- CANR-1
Earlier sketch in CA 1-4R
Havrevold, Finn 1905- 109
Havrilesky, Thomas M(ichael) 1939- CANR-19
Earlier sketches in CA 53-56, CANR-4
Haw, Richard Claude 1913- CAP-1
Earlier sketch in CA 9-10
Hawes, Evelyn (Johnson) 13-16R
See also AITN 1
Hawes, Frances Cooper (Richmond)
1897- CAP-1
Earlier sketch in CA 9-10
Hawes, Gene R(obert) 1922- CANR-39
Earlier sketches in CA 5-8R, CANR-3, 18
Hawes, Grace M. 1926- 69-72
Hawes, Hampton 1929(?)-1977 Obituary 69-72
Hawes, John T. 1906(?)-1983 Obituary 109
Hawes, Joseph M(ilton) 1938- 53-56
Hawes, Judy 1913- 33-36R
See also SATA 4
Hawes, Louis 1931- 114
Hawes, Louise 1943- ....SATA 60
Hawes, Lynne Gusikoff Salop 1931- CANR-22
Earlier sketch in CA 106
Hawes, William (Kenneth) 1931- 77-80
Hawgood, John Arkas 1905-1971 Obituary 104
Hawk, Alex
See Garfield, Brian (Wynne)
Hawk, Grace E. 1905-1983 Obituary 110
Hawk, Philip B(ovier) 1874-1966 Obituary 116
Hawke, David Freeman 1923- CANR-18
Earlier sketch in CA 102
Hawke, Gary Richard 1942- 102
Hawke, Nancy
See Nugent, Nancy
Hawke, Simon
See Yermakov, Nicholas
Hawken, William R. 1917- CANR-5
Earlier sketch in CA 9-12R
Hawker, Robert Stephen 1803-1875 .... DLB 32
Hawkes, (Charles Francis) Christopher
1905- Brief entry 105
Hawkes, G(ary) W(arren) 1953- 138
Hawkes, Glenn R(ogers) 1919- 17-20R
Hawkes, J(ohn) G(regory) 1915- 135
Hawkes, (Jessie) Jacquetta (Hopkins)
1910- CANR-15
Earlier sketch in CA 69-72
Hawkes, John (Clendennin Burne Jr.)
1925- CANR-2
Earlier sketch in CA 1-4R
See also CLC 1, 2, 3, 4, 7, 9, 14, 15, 27, 49
See also DLB 2, 7
See also DLBY 80
See also MTCW
Hawkes, Judith 1949- 132
Hawkes, Kevin 1959- 135
Hawkes, Robert E(rnest) 1930- 113
Hawkes, Terence 1932- 17-20R
Hawkesworth, (Elizabeth) Celia 1942- 121
Hawkesworth, Eric 1921- 29-32R
See also SATA 13
Hawking, S. W.
See Hawking, Stephen W(illiam)
Hawking, Stephen W(illiam) 1942- 129
Brief entry 126
See also BEST 89:1
See also CLC 63
Hawkins, A. Desmond
See Hawkins, (Alec) Desmond
Hawkins, Angus 1953- 126
Hawkins, Arthur 1903- CANR-8
Earlier sketch in CA 21-24R
See also SATA 19
Hawkins, Brett W(illiam) 1937- CANR-11
Earlier sketch in CA 21-24R
Hawkins, (Alec) Desmond 1908- CANR-9
Earlier sketch in CA 65-68
Hawkins, Edward H. 1934- 85-88
Hawkins, Frances P(ockman) 1913- 105
Hawkins, Gary J(ames) 1937- 115
Hawkins, Gerald S(tanley) 1928- 17-20R
Hawkins, Gordon 1919- 41-44R
Hawkins, Harriett B(loker) 1934- Brief entry 112
Hawkins, Hugh (Dodge) 1929- CANR-31
Earlier sketch in CA 1-4R
Hawkins, Jack
See Hawkins, John Edward
Hawkins, Jim 1944- 73-76
Hawkins, John C(harles) 1948- 106
Hawkins, John Edward 1910-1973 120
Obituary 111
Hawkins, John Noel 1944- CANR-8
Earlier sketch in CA 61-64
Hawkins, John P. 1946- 120
Hawkins, John 1719-1789 ....DLB 104
Hawkins, Joyce M(ary) 1928- 128
Hawkins, Odie 1937- 57-60
Hawkins, Peter S(tephen) 1945- 110
Hawkins, (Helena Ann) Quail 1905- 17-20R
See also SATA 6
Hawkins, Richard (Anthony James) 1938- 129
Hawkins, Robert O(usley) Jr. 1938- 117
Hawkins, Robert 1923- CANR-14
Earlier sketch in CA 21-24R
Hawkins, Walter Everette 1883(?)- .... DLB 50
Hawkins, William (Waller) 1912- 1-4R
Hawkinson, John (Samuel) 1912- 21-24R
See also SATA 4
Hawkinson, Lucy (Ozone) 1924-1971 103
See also SATA 21
Hawks. Howard (Winchester)
1896-1977 Obituary 73-76
Hawksworth, Henry D. 1933- 73-76
Hawley, Amos H(enry) 1910- 37-40R
Hawley, Beatrice
See Jagel, Beatrice Hawley
Hawley, Cameron 1905-1969 ....1-4R
Obituary 25-28R
Hawley, Donald Frederick 1921- 108
Hawley, Donald Thomas 1923- CANR-11
Earlier sketch in CA 65-68
Hawley, Ellis W. 1929- CANR-7
Earlier sketch in CA 17-20R
Hawley, Florence M.
See Ellis, Florence Hawley
Hawley, Gessner G. 1906(?)-1983 Obituary 110
Hawley, Henrietta Ripperger
1890(?)-1974 Obituary 49-52
Hawley, Isabel (Allen) L(ockwood)
1935- CANR-7
Earlier sketch in CA 57-60
Hawley, Jane Stouder 1936- 21-24R
Hawley, John Stratton 1941- 110
Hawley, Mabel C. CANR-26
Earlier sketches in CAP-2, CA 19-20
See also SATA 1, 67
Hawley, Richard A. 1945- 123
Hawley, Robert C(oit) 1933- CANR-22
Earlier sketches in CA 57-60, CANR-7
Hawley, Willis D(avid) 1938- 114
Haworth, Don 1924- 128
Haworth, Lawrence 1926- 5-8R
Haworth, Mary
See Young, Mary Elizabeth Reardon
Haworth-Booth, Mark 1944- 124
Haworth-Booth, Michael 1896- 116
Haws, Duncan 1921- 97-100
Hawthorn, Jeremy 1942- 97-100
Hawthorne, Captain R. M.
See Ellis, Edward S(ylvester)
Hawthorne, (Ivy Ellen) Jennie Crawley
1916- CAP-1
Earlier sketch in CA 9-10
Hawthorne, Julian 1846-1934 .... TCLC 25
Hawthorne, Nathaniel
1804-1864 .... CDALB 1640-1865
See also DLB 1, 74
See also SSC 3
See also WLC
See also YABC 2
Hawton, Hector 1901- 13-16R
Haxton, Josephine Ayres 1921- 115
Hay, David M(cKechnie) 1935- 53-56
Hay, Dennis 1952- 105
Hay, Denys 1915- 13-16R
Hay, Elizabeth (Jean) 1936- 131
Hay, Eloise K(napp) 1926- 9-12R
Hay, Jacob 1920- 25-28R
Hay, James G(ordon) 1936- CANR-4
Earlier sketch in CA 53-56
Hay, John (Milton) 1838-1905 Brief entry 108
See also DLB 12, 47
Hay, John 1915- CANR-9
Earlier sketch in CA 65-68
See also SATA 13
Hay, Leon Edwards 25-28R
Hay, Melba Porter 1949- 133
Hay, Millicent V. 1945- 128
Hay, Peter 1935- 21-24R
Hay, Robert D(ean) 1921- CANR-8
Earlier sketch in CA 61-64
Hay, Sara Henderson 1906-1987 .... CAP-1
Obituary 123
Earlier sketch in CA 13-16
Hay, Stephen N(orthup) 1925- 5-8R
Hay, Thomas Robson
1888-1974 Obituary 49-52
Hay, Timothy
See Brown, Margaret Wise
Hay, Vicky
See Hay, Millicent V.
Haya de la Torre, Victor Raul
1895-1979 Obituary 89-92
Hayakawa, S(amuel) I(chiye) 1906- CANR-20
Obituary 137
Earlier sketch in CA 13-16R
Hayami, Yujiro 1932- 77-80
Hayano, David M(amoru) 1942- 115
Hayaseca y Eizaguirre, Jorge
See Echegaray (y Eizaguirre), Jose (Maria Waldo)
Hayashi, Tetsumaro 1929- CANR-14
Earlier sketch in CA 37-40R
Hayashi Fumiko 1904-1951 .... TCLC 27
Haycock, Ken(neth) Roy 1948- 104
Haycock, Ronald G. 1942- 123
Haycraft, Anna 122
See also Ellis, Alice Thomas
Haycraft, Howard 1905-1991 ....21-24R
Obituary 136
See also SATA 6
See also SATO 70
Haycraft, John (Stacpoole) 1926- 133
Haycraft, Molly Costain 1911- 13-16R
See also SATA 6
Hayden, Albert A(rthur) 1923- 33-36R
Hayden, C. Gervin
See Wicker, Randolfe Hayden
Hayden, Carl T(rumbull)
1877-1972 Obituary 33-36R
Hayden, Dolores 1945- CANR-9
Earlier sketch in CA 65-68
Hayden, Donald E(ugene) 1915- CANR-10
Earlier sketch in CA 25-28R
Hayden, Eric W(illiam) 1919- CANR-2
Earlier sketch in CA 5-8R
Hayden, Gwendolen Lampshire 1904- .... SATA 35
Hayden, Howard K. 1930- 17-20R
Hayden, Jay
See Paine, Lauran (Bosworth)
Hayden, Jay G. 1884-1971 Obituary 89-92
Hayden, John O(lin) 1932- CANR-10
Earlier sketch in CA 25-28R
Hayden, Julia Elizabeth
1939(?)-1981 Obituary 104
Hayden, Julie
See Hayden, Julia Elizabeth
Hayden, Martin S(choll) 1912- 69-72
Hayden, (Holden) Mike 1920-1984 120
Hayden, Naura 1942- CANR-12
Earlier sketch in CA 73-76
Hayden, Robert C(arter) Jr. 1937- CANR-24
Earlier sketch in CA 69-72
See also BW
See also SATA 28, 47
Hayden, Robert E(arl) 1913-1980 ....CANR-24
Obituary 97-100
Earlier sketch in CA 69-72
See also CABS 2
See also BLC 2
See also BW
See also CDALB 1941-1968
See also CLC 5, 9, 14, 37
See also DLB 5, 76
See also MTCW
See also SATA 19, 26
Hayden, Sterling 1916-1986 111
Obituary 119
Hayden, Stirling
See Hayden, Sterling
Hayden, Thomas E(mmet) 1939- 107
Hayden, Tom
See Hayden, Thomas E(mmet)
Hayden, Torey L(ynn) 1951- CANR-35
Earlier sketch in CA 103
See also SATA 65
Haydn, Hiram 1907-1973 .... CAP-1
Obituary 45-48
Earlier sketch in CA 9-10
Haydn, Richard 1905-1985 Obituary 115
Haydon, A(lbert) Eustace
1880-1975 Obituary 61-64
Haydon, Benjamin Robert 1786-1846 ..... DLB 110
Haydon, Glen 1896-1966 .... CAP-1
Earlier sketch in CA 9-10
Haydon, June 1932- 109
Haydon, Roger (Malcolm) 1950- 118
Hayek, F(riedrich) A(ugust von) 1899- CANR-20
Obituary 137
Earlier sketch in CA 93-96
See also MTCW
Hayes, Alden C(ary) 1916- 57-60
Hayes, Alfred 1911-1985 106
Obituary 117
Hayes, Ann L(ouise) 1924- 25-28R
Hayes, Anna Hansen 1886- 1-4R
Hayes, Bartlett (Harding Jr.) 1904-1988 77-80
Obituary 124
Hayes, Billy 97-100
Hayes, Carlton J(oseph) H(untley)
1882-1964 ....CANR-3
Earlier sketch in CA 1-4R
See also SATA 11
Hayes, Denis A(llen) 1944- 132
Hayes, (Robert) Dennis 1952- 130
Hayes, Dorsha 1897(?)-1990 77-80
Obituary 133
Hayes, Douglas A(nderson) 1918- CANR-18
Earlier sketch in CA 1-4R
Hayes, E(ugene) Nelson 1920- 29-32R
Hayes, Edward C(ary) 1937- CANR-35
Earlier sketch in CA 45-48
Hayes, Edward L(ee) 1931- 29-32R
Hayes, Elvin 1945- Brief entry 111
Hayes, Francis Clement 1904- CAP-2
Earlier sketch in CA 21-22
Hayes, Geoffrey 1947- CANR-25
Earlier sketches in CA 65-68, CANR-9
See also SATA 26
Hayes, Grace Person 1919- 33-36R
Hayes, Harold T(homas) P(ace)
1926-1989 ....CANR-22
Obituary 128
Earlier sketch in CA 69-72
Hayes, Helen 1900- 138
Hayes, James T(homas) 1923- 29-32R
Hayes, John F. 1904- CAP-1
Earlier sketch in CA 13-14
See also SATA 11
Hayes, John H(aralson) 1934- CANR-21
Earlier sketch in CA 69-72
Hayes, John Michael 1919- 108
See also DLB 26
Hayes, John P(hillip) 1949- CANR-15
Earlier sketch in CA 93-96
Hayes, John R(ichard) 1929- 108
Hayes, John S. 1910-1981 Obituary 108
Hayes, Joseph 1918- CANR-30
Earlier sketches in CA 17-20R, CANR-7
Hayes, Louis D. 1940- 29-32R
Hayes, Margaret 1925- 21-24R
Hayes, Mary Anne 1956- 105
Hayes, Mary-Rose 1939- 102
Hayes, Nelson (Taylor) 1903-1971 ....1-4R
Obituary 33-36R
Hayes, Paul J(ames) 1922- 57-60
Hayes, Paul Martin 1942- 77-80
Hayes, Penny (a pseudonym) 1940- 121
Hayes, Ralph E(ugene) 1927- CANR-15
Earlier sketch in CA 21-24R
Hayes, Robert M(ayo) 1926- 9-12R
Hayes, Samuel P(erkins) 1910- CANR-3
Earlier sketch in CA 5-8R
Hayes, Sheila 1937- CANR-22
Earlier sketch in CA 106
See also SATA 50, 51
Hayes, Steven C(harles) 1948- CANR-31
Earlier sketch in CA 112
Hayes, W. Woodrow
See Hayes, Wayne Woodrow
Hayes, Wayland J(ackson) 1893-1972 ...... CAP-1
Earlier sketch in CA 13-14
Hayes, Wayne Woodrow
1913-1987 Obituary 121
Hayes, Will 5-8R
See also SATA 7
Hayes, William D(imitt) 1913- 5-8R
See also SATA 8
Hayes, Wilson
See Gibbs-Wilson, Kathryn (Beatrice)
Hayes, Woody
See Hayes, Wayne Woodrow
Hayes, Zachary (Jerome) 1932- CANR-39
Earlier sketch in CA 115
Hayford, Charles W. 1941- 136
Hayford, Fred Kwesi 1937- 45-48
Hayford, Harrison (Mosher) 1916- 118
Hayford, J(oseph) E(phraim) Casely
See Casely-Hayford, J(oseph) E(phraim)
Hayford, Taria
See Haydon, June
Hayley, Barbara 1938- 131
Hayley, William 1745-1820 .... DLB 93
Hayley Bell, Mary 25-28R
Haylock, John (Mervyn) 1918- 133
Hayman
See Peel, H(azel) M(ary)
Hayman, Carol Bessent 1927- 53-56
Hayman, David 1927- CANR-7
Earlier sketch in CA 17-20R
Hayman, John L(uther) Jr. 1929- 25-28R
Hayman, LeRoy 1916- 85-88
Hayman, Max 1908- 17-20R
Hayman, Robert 1575-1629 .... DLB 99
Hayman, Ronald 1932- CANR-18
Earlier sketch in CA 25-28R
See also CLC 44
Haymes, Robert C. 1931- 33-36R
Haymon, S. T.
See Haymon, Sylvia (Theresa)
Haymon, Sylvia (Theresa) 1918(?)- 131
Brief entry 127
Hayn, Annette 1922- 65-68
Haynal, Andre (Emeric) 1930- 120
Hayne, Paul Hamilton 1830-1886 .... DLB 3, 64, 79
Haynes, Alfred H(enry) 1910- 5-8R
Haynes, Anne
See Madlee, Dorothy (Haynes)
Haynes, Betsy 1937- CANR-8
Earlier sketch in CA 57-60
See also SATA 37, 48
Haynes, Brian 1939- 111
Haynes, Glynn W(alker) 1936- 65-68
Haynes, James Almand 1933- 131
Haynes, James 1932- 110
Haynes, Jim
See Haynes, James Almand
Haynes, Lincoln 1924- 116
Haynes, Linda
See Swinford, Betty (June Wells)
Haynes, Maria S(chnee) 1912- 25-28R
Haynes, Mary 1938- CANR-35
Earlier sketch in CA 111
See also SATA 65
Haynes, Pat
See McKeag, Ernest L(ionel)
Haynes, Renee (Oriana Tickell)
1906- CANR-34
Earlier sketch in CA 49-52
Haynes, Richard F(rederick) 1935- 49-52
Haynes, Robert Talmadge Jr. 1926- 1-4R
Haynes, Robert Vaughn 1929- 41-44R
Haynes, Sybille 1926- 57-60
Haynes, William Warren 1921- CANR-8
Earlier sketch in CA 5-8R
Haynie, Hugh 1927- 121
Haynie, Sandra (B.) 1943- Brief entry 121
Hays, (Lawrence) Brooks 1898-1981 .... CAP-1
Obituary 105
Earlier sketch in CA 11-12
Hays, David G(lenn) 1928- CANR-14
Earlier sketch in CA 21-24R
Hays, Donald 1947- 132
Hays, Elinor Rice 1-4R
Hays, H(offmann) R(eynolds)
1904-1980 ....CANR-31
Obituary 105
Earlier sketch in CA 81-84
See also SATA 26
Hays, Helen Ireland 1903- 61-64
Hays, Paul R. 1903-1980 .... CAP-2
Obituary 93-96
Earlier sketch in CA 19-20
Hays, Peter L. 1938- 33-36R
Hays, R. Vernon 1902- 89-92
Hays, Richard D. 1942- 37-40R
Hays, Robert Glenn 1935- 53-56
Hays, Samuel Pfrimmer 1921- 103
Hays, Terence E(ugene) 1942- 69-72

Hays, Wilma Pitchford 1909- ... CANR-5
Earlier sketch in CA 1-4R
See also MAICYA
See also SAAS 3
See also SATA 1, 28
Haystead, Wes
See Haystead, Wesley
Haystead, Wesley 1942- ... CANR-22
Earlier sketches in CA 57-60, CANR-6
Hayter, Adrian (Goodenough)
1914-1990 Obituary ... 131
Hayter, Alethea 1911- ... 29-32R
Hayter, Earl W(iley) 1901- ... 41-44R
Hayter, Stanley William
1901-1988 Obituary ... 125
Hayter, William Goodenough 1906- ... CANR-9
Earlier sketch in CA 21-24R
Haythornthwaite, Philip John 1951- ... CANR-19
Earlier sketch in CA 103
Hayton, Richard Neil 1916- ... 57-60
Hayward, Brooke 1937- ... 81-84
Hayward, Charles H(arold) 1898- ... CANR-7
Earlier sketch in CA 9-12R
Hayward, Jack 1931- ... CANR-21
Earlier sketches in CA 57-60, CANR-6
Hayward, John F(orrest) 1916-1983 ... 9-12R
Obituary ... 109
Hayward, John F(rank) 1918- ... 5-8R
Hayward, Linda 1943- ... 112
See also SATA 39
Hayward, Max 1925(?)-1979 ... 93-96
Obituary ... 85-88
Hayward, Richard
See Kendrick, Baynard H(ardwick)
Hayward, Richard 1893- ... CAP-1
Earlier sketch in CA 9-10
Hayward, Stephen 1954- ... 133
Haywood, C. Robert 1921- ... 137
Haywood, Carolyn 1898-1990 ... CANR-20
Obituary ... 130
Earlier sketches in CA 5-8R, CANR-5
See also CLR 22
See also MAICYA
See also SATA 1, 29, 64
Haywood, Charles 1904- ... CANR-22
Earlier sketch in CA 1-4R
Haywood, Dixie 1933- ... 105
Haywood, Eliza 1693(?)-1756 ... DLB 39
Haywood, H(erbert) Carl(ton) 1931- ... CANR-3
Earlier sketch in CA 49-52
Haywood, Harry
See Hall, Haywood
Haywood, John Alfred 1913- ... 17-20R
Haywood, Richard Mansfield 1905-1977 ... CAP-2
Obituary ... 69-72
Earlier sketch in CA 33-36
Haywood, Richard Mowbray 1933- ... 25-28R
Haywood, Stephen Patrick 1949- ... 138
Hazam, Louis J. 1911-1983 Obituary ... 110
Hazan, Marcella (Maddalena) 1924- ... 128
Brief entry ... 116
Hazan, Victor 1928- ... 114
Hazard, David 1955- ... 116
Hazard, Harry W(illiams) 1918- ... 122
Hazard, Jack
See Booth, Edwin
Hazard, John N(ewbold) 1909- ... CANR-31
Earlier sketch in CA 1-4R
Hazard, Leland 1893-1980 ... 17-20R
Obituary ... 133
Hazard, Patrick D. 1927- ... 13-16R
Hazel, Paul 1944- ... 114
Hazelgrove, William E(lliot III) 1959- ... 138
Hazelrigg, Meredith K(ent) 1942- ... 33-36R
Hazelton, Alexander
See Armstrong, William A(lexander)
Hazelton, Roger 1909- ... CANR-16
Earlier sketches in CA 1-4R, CANR-1
Hazen, Allen T(racy) 1904- ... CAP-1
Earlier sketch in CA 13-14
Hazen, Barbara Shook 1930- ... CANR-22
Earlier sketch in CA 105
See also SATA 27
Hazen, Helen 1943- ... 116
Hazen, Margaret Hindle 1948- ... 126
Hazen, Robert M(iller) 1948- ... 112
Hazlehurst, Cameron 1941- ... 103
Hazleton, Lesley 1945- ... 128
Brief entry ... 126
Hazlett, Bill
See Hazlett, William Scott
Hazlett, William Scott 1931-1983 Obituary ... 110
Hazlitt, Henry 1894- ... CANR-3
Earlier sketch in CA 5-8R
Hazlitt, Joseph
See Strage, Mark
Hazlitt, William 1778-1830 ... DLB 110
Hazo, Robert G. 1931- ... 21-24R
Hazo, Samuel (John) 1928- ... CANR-31
Earlier sketches in CA 5-8R, CANR-8
See also CAAS 11
Hazzard, Lowell B(restel)
1898-1978 Obituary ... 77-80
Hazzard, Mary 1928- ... 105
Hazzard, Shirley 1931- ... CANR-4
Earlier sketch in CA 9-12R
See also CLC 18
See also DLBY 82
See also MTCW
Heacox, Cecil E. 1903- ... 101
Heacox, Kim 1951- ... 137
Head, Alice Maud 1886-1981 Obituary ... 116
Head, Ann
See Morse, Anne Christensen
Head, Bessie 1937-1986 ... CANR-25
Obituary ... 119
Earlier sketch in CA 29-32R
See also BLC 2
See also BW
See also CLC 25, 67
See also DLB 117
See also MTCW
Head, Constance 1939- ... 37-40R
Head, Edith 1898(?)-1981 Obituary ... 105
Head, Gay
See Hauser, Margaret L(ouise)
Head, Gwen 1940- ... 89-92
Head, K(enneth) Maynard 1938- ... 110
Head, (Joanne) Lee 1931-1983 ... 65-68
Obituary ... 110
Head, Matthew
See Canaday, John E(dwin)
Head, Raymond (Victor) 1948- ... 136
Head, Richard G(lenn) 1938- ... CANR-35
Earlier sketch in CA 53-56
Head, Robert V. 1929- ... CANR-15
Earlier sketch in CA 41-44R
Head, Sydney W(arren) 1913- ... CANR-9
Earlier sketch in CA 65-68
Head, Timothy E. 1934- ... 13-16R
Headapohl, B. R.
See Headapohl, Betty R.
Headapohl, Betty R. 1940- ... 122
Headings, Mildred J. 1908- ... 37-40R
Headington, Bonnie Jay 1940- ... 114
Headington, Christopher John Magenis
1930- Brief entry ... 106
Headley, Elizabeth
See Harrison, Elizabeth Cavanna
Headley, Gwyn 1946- ... 125
Headley, Joel T. 1813-1897 ... DLB 30
Headley, John M. 1929- ... 130
Headon, (Nicky) Topper 1956(?)-
See The Clash
See also CLC 30
Headstrom, (Birger) Richard 1902- ... CANR-13
Earlier sketches in CA 1-4R, CANR-2
See also SATA 8
Heady, Earl O(rel) 1916- ... CANR-8
Earlier sketch in CA 17-20R
Heady, Eleanor B(utler) 1917-1979 ... CANR-31
Earlier sketch in CA 41-44R
See also SATA 8
Heady, Harold F(ranklin) 1916- ... CANR-31
Earlier sketch in CA 53-56
Heagney, Anne 1901- ... 5-8R
Heal, Edith 1903- ... CANR-2
Earlier sketch in CA 1-4R
See also SATA 7
Heal, Jane 1946- ... 132
Heal, Jeanne (Bennett) 1917- ... CAP-1
Earlier sketch in CA 9-10
Heald, Charles Brehmer
1882-1974 Obituary ... 49-52
Heald, Edward Thornton 1885- ... 17-20R
Heald, Gordon 1941- ... 128
Heald, Morrell 1922- Brief entry ... 111
Heald, Suzette 1943- ... 132
Heald, Tim(othy Villiers) 1944- ... CANR-30
Earlier sketches in CA 49-52, CANR-2
Healey, B. J.
See Healey, Ben (James)
Healey, Ben (James) 1908- ... CANR-17
Earlier sketch in CA 77-80
Healey, Brooks
See Albert, Burton Jr.
Healey, Denis Winston 1917- ... 110
Healey, Dorothy (Ray) 1914- ... 138
Healey, F(rancis) G(eorge) 1903- ... CAP-2
Earlier sketch in CA 21-22
Healey, James Stewart 1931- ... 57-60
Healey, James 1936- ... 53-56
Healey, Joseph G(raham) 1938- ... 116
Healey, Larry 1927- ... 101
See also SATA 42, 44
Healey, Robert (Mathieu) 1921- ... 61-64
Healey-Kay, (Sydney Francis) Patrick (Chippendall)
1904-1983 Obituary ... 111
Healy, David F(rank) 1926- ... 17-20R
Healy, Dermot 1947- ... 114
Healy, Fleming 1911- ... 5-8R
Healy, George Robert 1923- ... 17-20R
Healy, George W(illiam) Jr. 1905-1980 ... 69-72
Obituary ... 125
Healy, Jeremiah (F. III) 1948- ... 137
Healy, John D(elaware) 1921- ... 93-96
Healy, Kent T(enney) 1902-1985 Obituary ... 114
Healy, Patrick III 1910- Brief entry ... 110
Healy, Paul F(rancis) 1915-1984 ... 17-20R
Obituary ... 114
Healy, Richard J. 1916- ... 25-28R
Healy, Sean D(esmond) 1927- ... CANR-11
Earlier sketch in CA 25-28R
Healy, Sister Kathleen ... 61-64
Healy, Sophia (Warner) 1938- ... 136
Healy, Timothy S. 1923- ... 41-44R
Heaney, John J. 1925- ... CANR-5
Earlier sketch in CA 9-12R
Heaney, Seamus (Justin) 1939- ... CANR-25
Earlier sketch in CA 85-88
See also CDBLB 1960 to Present
See also CLC 5, 7, 14, 25, 37
See also DLB 40
See also MTCW
Heany, Donald Francis 1918-1990 Obituary ... 132
Heap, Desmond 1907- ... CANR-15
Earlier sketches in CAP-1, CA 9-10
Heaps, Willard A(llison) 1908- ... 85-88
See also SATA 26
Heard, (George) Alexander 1917- ... 17-20R
Heard, Anthony Hazlitt 1937- ... 134
Heard, (Henry Fitz) Gerald 1889-1971 ... CAP-2
Obituary ... 29-32R
Earlier sketch in CA 21-22
Heard, H. F.
See Heard, (Henry Fitz) Gerald
Heard, J(oseph) Norman 1922- ... 9-12R
Heard, Nathan C(liff) 1936- ... CANR-25
Earlier sketch in CA 53-56
See also BW
See also DLB 33
Hearden, Patrick J. 1942- ... 138
Hearder, Harry 1924- ... 5-8R
Hearn, Charles R(alph) 1937- ... 77-80
Hearn, Emily
See Valleau, Emily
Hearn, Janice W. 1938- ... 65-68
Hearn, John 1920- ... 97-100
Hearn, (Patricio) Lafcadio (Tessima Carlos)
1850-1904 Brief entry ... 105
See also DLB 12, 78
See also TCLC 9
Hearn, M(illard) F(illmore Jr.) 1938- ... 115
Hearn, Sneed
See Gregg, Andrew K.
Hearnden, Arthur (George) 1931- ... 65-68
Hearne, Betsy Gould 1942- ... CANR-35
Earlier sketch in CA 114
See also SATA 38
Hearne, John (Edgar Caulwell) 1926- ... 125
Brief entry ... 116
See also BW
See also DLB 117
See also MTCW
Hearne, Samuel 1745-1792 ... DLB 99
Hearne, Vicki 1946- ... CLC 56
Hearnshaw, Leslie Spencer 1907- ... 89-92
Hearon, Shelby 1931- ... CANR-18
Earlier sketch in CA 25-28R
See also AITN 2
See also CLC 63
Hearsey, John E(dward) N(icholl)
1928- ... CANR-8
Earlier sketch in CA 5-8R
Hearst, David Whitmire
1915-1986 Obituary ... 119
Hearst, George Randolph
1904-1972 Obituary ... 89-92
Hearst, James 1900-1983 ... CANR-15
Earlier sketch in CA 85-88
Hearst, Patricia Campbell 1954- ... 136
Hearst, Patty
See Hearst, Patricia Campbell
Hearst, William Randolph
1863-1951 Brief entry ... 118
See also DLB 25
Heartman, Harold
See Mebane, John (Harrison)
Heasman, Kathleen Joan 1913- ... CAP-1
Earlier sketch in CA 9-10
Heater, Derek (Benjamin) 1931- ... CANR-6
Earlier sketch in CA 57-60
Heath, Catherine 1924-1991 ... CANR-30
Obituary ... 136
Earlier sketch in CA 93-96
See also DLB 14
Heath, Charles C(hastain) 1921- ... 69-72
Heath, Charles D(ickinson) 1941- ... 121
See also SATA 46
Heath, Douglas H(amilton) 1925- ... 17-20R
Heath, Dwight B(raley) 1930- ... CANR-7
Earlier sketch in CA 17-20R
Heath, Edward Richard George 1916- ... 33-36R
Heath, G. Louis 1944- ... 37-40R
Heath, Harry E(ugene) Jr. 1919- ... CANR-28
Earlier sketch in CA 85-88
Heath, (Ernest) James 1920- ... 17-20R
Heath, Jim F(rank) 1931- ... 29-32R
Heath, Malcolm (Frederick) 1957- ... 130
Heath, Mary Ellen 1928- ... 115
Heath, Monica
See Fitzgerald, Arlene J.
Heath, (Charles) Monro 1899-1966 ... CAP-1
Earlier sketch in CA 9-10
Heath, Peter (Lauchlan) 1922- ... 41-44R
Heath, Robert L. 1941- ... 126
Heath, Robert W. 1931- ... 13-16R
Heath, Roy A(ubrey) K(elvin) 1926- ... CANR-33
Earlier sketch in CA 106
See also DLB 117
See also MTCW
Heath, Roy 1917- ... 9-12R
Heath, Royton E(dward) 1907- ... 9-12R
Heath, Sandra
See Wilson, Sandra
Heath, Terrence (George) 1936- ... CANR-36
Earlier sketch in CA 97-100
Heath, Veronica
See Blackett, Veronica Heath
Heath, William (Webster) 1929- ... CANR-31
Earlier sketch in CA 1-4R
Heathcott, Mary
See Keegan, Mary Heathcott
Heath-Stubbs, John (Francis Alexander)
1918- ... 13-16R
See also DLB 27
Heat-Moon, William Least
See Trogdon, William (Lewis)
See also AAYA 9
See also CLC 29
Heaton, Charles Huddleston 1928- ... CANR-20
Earlier sketch in CA 1-4R
Heaton, Eric William 1920- ... 61-64
Heaton, Herbert 1890-1973 ... 5-8R
Obituary ... 41-44R
Heaton, Peter 1919- ... 104
Heaton, Rose Henniker
1884-1975 Obituary ... 61-64
Heaton, Thomas Peter Starke 1928- ... 134
Heaton, Tom
See Heaton, Thomas Peter Starke
Heaton-Ward, William Alan 1919- ... 102
Heatter, Gabriel 1890-1972 Obituary ... 89-92
Heaven, Constance 1911- ... CANR-18
Earlier sketches in CA 49-52, CANR-2
See also SATA 7
Heavysege, Charles 1816-1876 ... DLB 99
Hebard, Edna L(aura Henriksen) 1913- ... 9-12R
Hebb, D(onald) O(lding) 1904-1985 ... CANR-2
Obituary ... 118
Earlier sketch in CA 1-4R
Hebblethwaite, Brian Leslie 1939- ... CANR-27
Earlier sketch in CA 109
Hebblethwaite, Margaret 1951- ... 129
Hebblethwaite, Peter 1930- ... 69-72
Hebden, Mark
See Harris, John
Hebel, Johann Peter 1760-1826 ... DLB 90
Heberer, Thomas 1947- ... 135
Hebert, Anne 1916- ... 85-88
See also CLC 4, 13, 29
See also DLB 68
See also MTCW
Hebert, Ernest 1941- ... 102
Hebert, F(elix) Edward 1901-1979 ... 110
Obituary ... 106
Hebert, (Arthur) Gabriel 1886-1963 ... 1-4R
Hebert, Jacques 1923- ... CANR-27
Earlier sketches in CA 25-28R, CANR-11
See also DLB 53
Hebert, Tom 1938- ... 69-72
Hebson, Ann (Hellebusch) 1925- ... 17-20R
Hechinger, Fred M(ichael) 1920- ... 77-80
Hechler, David (S.) 1950- ... 127
Hechler, Ken 1914- ... 109
Hecht, Anthony (Evan) 1923- ... CANR-6
Earlier sketch in CA 9-12R
See also CLC 8, 13, 19
See also DLB 5
Hecht, Ben 1894-1964 ... 85-88
See also CLC 8
See also DLB 7, 9, 25, 26, 28, 86
Hecht, George J(oseph)
1895-1980 Obituary ... 97-100
See also SATA 22
Hecht, Henri Joseph 1922- ... 29-32R
See also SATA 9
Hecht, James L(ee) 1926- ... 33-36R
Hecht, Jeff(rey Charles) 1947- ... 131
Hecht, Joseph C. 1924- ... 29-32R
Hecht, Marie B(ergenfeld) 1918- ... 21-24R
Hecht, Robert A(nthony) 1929- ... 114
Hecht, Roger 1926- ... 17-20R
Hecht, Warren Jay 1946- ... 103
Hechter, Michael 1943- ... 69-72
Hechtkopf, Henryk 1910- ... SATA 17
Hechtlinger, Adelaide 1914- ... 29-32R
Heck, Alfons 1928- ... 131
Heck, Bessie Holland 1911- ... 5-8R
See also SATA 26
Heck, Frank H(opkins) 1904-1983 ... 69-72
Obituary ... 126
Heck, Harold J(oseph) 1906- ... 41-44R
Heck, Peter M. 1937- ... 53-56
Heck, Suzanne Wright 1939- ... 53-56
Heckart, Barbara Hooper 1937- ... 118
Heckart, Beverly Anne 1938- ... 103
Heckel, Robert V. 1925- ... 9-12R
Heckelmann, Charles N(ewman)
1913- ... CANR-30
Earlier sketch in CA 49-52
Hecker, Isaac Thomas 1819-1888 ... DLB 1
Heckert, J(osiah) Brooks 1893- ... 5-8R
Heckler, Jonellen (Beth) 1943- ... 109
Heckman, Hazel 1904- ... 21-24R
Heckman, William O(scar) 1921- ... 21-24R
Heckmann, Wolf 1929- ... 114
Heckscher, August 1913- ... CANR-35
Earlier sketch in CA 1-4R
Hedayat, Sadeq 1903-1951 Brief entry ... 120
See also TCLC 21
Hedberg, Nancy 1944- ... 122
Hedde, Wilhelmina G(enevava) 1895- ... 5-8R
Hedden, Walter Page
1898(?)-1976 Obituary ... 65-68
Hedden, Worth Tuttle 1896-1985 ... CAP-2
Obituary ... 117
Earlier sketch in CA 21-22
Hedderwick, Mairi 1939- ... 137
See also MAICYA
See also SATA 30
Hederman, Thomas M(artin) Jr.
1911-1985 Obituary ... 114
Hedge, Frederic Henry 1805-1890 ... DLB 1, 59
Hedge, Leslie (Joseph) 1922- ... 9-12R
Hedgeman, Anna Arnold 1899-1990 ... CAP-1
Obituary ... 130
Earlier sketch in CA 13-16
Hedges, Bob A(tkinson) 1919- ... 45-48
Hedges, David (Paget) 1930- ... 45-48
Hedges, Elaine R(yan) 1927- ... CANR-7
Earlier sketch in CA 57-60
Hedges, Inez (Kathleen) 1947- ... 116
Hedges, Joseph
See Harknett, Terry
Hedges, Sid(ney) G(eorge) 1897-1974 ... CANR-4
Earlier sketch in CA 9-12R
See also SATA 28
Hedges, Trimble R(aymond) 1906- ... CAP-2
Earlier sketch in CA 21-22
Hedges, Ursula M. 1940- ... 29-32R
Hedges, William L(eonard) 1923- ... 37-40R
Hedin, Mary ... 103
Hedley, George (Percy) 1899- ... CAP-2
Earlier sketch in CA 19-20

Hedley, (Gladys) Olwen 1912- CANR-9
Earlier sketch in CA 61-64
Hedlund, Ronald D(avid) 1941- 33-36R
Hedren, Paul L(eslie) 1949- CANR-37
Earlier sketch in CA 114
Hedrick, Addie M. 1903- CAP-2
Earlier sketch in CA 25-28
Hedrick, Basil C(alvin) 1932- CANR-21
Earlier sketch in CA 33-36R
Hedrick, Floyd D(udley) 1927- 33-36R
Hedrick, Joan Doran 1944- 107
Hedrick, Travis K. 1904(?)-1977 Obituary 69-72
Heeney, Brian 1933- 89-92
Heer, David MacAlpine 1930- 13-16R
Heer, John E(dward) Jr. 1921- Obituary 113
Heer, Nancy Whittier 33-36R
Heeresma, Heere 1932- 25-28R
Heeresma Inc.
See Heeresma, Heere
Heermance, J. Noel 1939- 25-28R
Heertje, Arnold 1934- 131
Heerwagen, Paul K. 1895- 29-32R
Heesterman, J(ohannes) C(ornelis) 1925- 128
Heezen, Bruce C(harles) 1924-1977 ....CANR-29
Obituary 69-72
Earlier sketch in CA 49-52
Heffer, Eric S(amuel) 1922- 123
Heffern, Richard 1950- 61-64
Heffernan, James A(nthony) W(alsh)
1939- 25-28R
Heffernan, Michael 1942- CANR-18
Earlier sketch in CA 77-80
Heffernan, Patrick
See O'Heffernan, Patrick
Heffernan, Paul 1905(?)-1983 Obituary 110
Heffernan, Thomas Farel 1933- 107
Heffernan, Thomas J(ohn Andrew) 1944- 125
Heffernan, Thomas (Patrick Carroll)
1939- 81-84
Heffernan, William A. 1937- 25-28R
Heffley, Wayne 1927- 9-12R
Heffner, Richard D(ouglas) 1925- 69-72
Heffron, Dorris 1944- CANR-36
Earlier sketch in CA 49-52
See also SATA 68
Heffron, Mary J. 1935- 135
Hefley, James C(arl) 1930- CANR-7
Earlier sketch in CA 13-16R
Heflin, Donald
See Wallmann, Jeffrey M(iner)
Hefner, Hugh (Marston) 1926- Brief entry 110
See also AITN 1
Hefner, Paul
See Tabori, Paul
Hefner, Robert W(illiam) 1952- 119
Hefter, Richard 1942- CANR-23
Earlier sketch in CA 107
See also SATA 31
Hegarty, Edward J. 1891- CANR-5
Earlier sketch in CA 1-4R
Hegarty, Ellen 1918- 37-40R
Hegarty, Frances 1948- 135
Hegarty, Reginald Beaton 1906-1973 ....CAP-1
Obituary 41-44R
Earlier sketch in CA 13-16
See also SATA 10
Hegarty, Sister M(ary) Loyola
See Hegarty, Ellen
Hegarty, Walter 1922- 65-68
Hegel, Georg Wilhelm Friedrich
1770-1831 ....DLB 90
Hegel, Richard 1927- CANR-6
Earlier sketch in CA 57-60
Hegel, Robert Earl 1943- 108
Hegeler, Sten 1923- 107
Hegeman, Elizabeth Blair 1942- 61-64
Hegenberger, John 1947- 135
Hegener, Mark Paul 1919-1988 Obituary 125
Heger, Theodore Ernest 1907- 33-36R
Hegesippus
See Schonfield, Hugh J(oseph)
Heggoy, Alf Andrew 1938- CANR-14
Earlier sketch in CA 37-40R
Hegi, Ursula 1946- 104
Heginbotham, Stanley J. 1938- Brief entry 106
Heglar, Mary Schnall 1934- 49-52
Hegner, William 1928- 93-96
Hegre, Theodore A. 1908-1984 Obituary 115
Hegstad, Roland R(ex) 1926- 57-60
Heiber, Helmut 1924- 49-52
Heiby, Walter A(lbert) 1918- 21-24R
Heichberger, Robert Lee 1930- 53-56
Heichelheim, Fritz M(oritz)
1901-1968 Obituary 116
Heicher, Merlo K. W. 1882-1967 ....CAP-1
Earlier sketch in CA 13-14
Heidbreder, Margaret Ann
See Eastman, Ann Heidbreder
Heide, Florence Parry 1919- CANR-19
Earlier sketch in CA 93-96
See also MAICYA
See also SAAS 6
See also SATA 32, 69
Heide, Robert 1939- CANR-20
Earlier sketch in CA 103
Heidegger, Martin 1889-1976 ....CANR-34
Obituary 65-68
Earlier sketch in CA 81-84
See also CLC 24
See also MTCW
Heidelberger, Michael (Johannes) 1947- 130
Heideman, Eugene P. 1929- 69-72
Heiden, Carol A. 1939- 57-60
Heiden, Konrad 1901-1966 Obituary 116
Heidenreich, Charles A(lbert) 1917- 25-28R
Heidenstam, (Carl Gustaf) Verner von
1859-1940 Brief entry 104
See also TCLC 5
Heider, Karl G(ustav) 1935- 132
Heiderstadt, Dorothy 1907- CANR-1
Earlier sketch in CA 1-4R
See also SATA 6
Heidi, Gloria 69-72
Heidingsfield, Myron S(amuel)
1914-1969 ....CANR-31
Obituary 103
Earlier sketch in CA 1-4R
Heidish, Marcy Moran 1947- 101
See also DLBY 82
Heidmann, Jean 1923- 130
Heiferman, Ronald Ian 1941- 61-64
Heifetz, Harold 1919- CANR-10
Earlier sketch in CA 25-28R
Heifetz, Milton D. 1921- 57-60
Heifner, Jack 1946- 105
See also CLC 11
Heiges, P. Myers 1887-1968 ....CAP-1
Earlier sketch in CA 13-16
Heijermans, Herman 1864-1924 Brief entry 123
See also TCLC 24
Heijke, John 1927- 21-24R
Heikal, M. Hassanein
See Heikal, Mohamed Hassanein
Heikal, Mohamed
See Heikal, Mohamed Hassanein
Heikal, Mohamed H.
See Heikal, Mohamed Hassanein
Heikal, Mohamed Hassanein 1923- 127
Brief entry 112
Heil, John 112
Heil, Ruth 1947- 112
Heilbron, J(ohn) L(ewis) 1934- CANR-19
Earlier sketches in CA 53-56, CANR-4
Heilbroner, Joan Knapp 1922- 1-4R
See also SATA 63
Heilbroner, Robert L(ouis) 1919- CANR-21
Earlier sketches in CA 1-4R, CANR-4
Heilbronner, Walter L(eo) 1924- 25-28R
Heilbrun, Carolyn G(old) 1926- CANR-28
Earlier sketches in CA 45-48, CANR-1
See also CLC 25
Heilbrun, Lois Hussey
1922(?)-1987 Obituary 123
See also SATA 54
Heilbrunn, Otto 1906-1969 ....CAP-1
Earlier sketch in CA 13-16
Heilig, Matthias R. 1881- CAP-2
Earlier sketch in CA 23-24
Heiliger, Edward Martin 1909- 13-16R
Heilman, Arthur (William) 1914- CANR-5
Earlier sketch in CA 5-8R
Heilman, Grant 1919- 53-56
Heilman, Joan Rattner CANR-21
Earlier sketches in CA 57-60, CANR-6
See also SATA 50
Heilman, Robert Bechtold 1906- CANR-27
Earlier sketches in CA 13-16R, CANR-9
Heilman, Samuel C(hiel) 1946- 69-72
Heilner, Van Campen
1899-1970 Obituary 29-32R
Heim, Alice (Winifred) 1913- CANR-14
Earlier sketch in CA 33-36R
Heim, Bruno Bernard 1911- 89-92
Heim, Kathleen M(cEntee) 1948- 111
Heim, Ralph D(aniel) 1895-1983 73-76
Obituary 133
Heiman, Ernest J(ean) 1930- CANR-4
Earlier sketch in CA 53-56
Heiman, Grover G(eorge Jr.) 1920- CANR-6
Earlier sketch in CA 5-8R
Heiman, Judith 1935- 1-4R
Heimann, Marcel 1909-1976 Obituary 65-68
Heimann, Robert Karl 1918-1990 Obituary 130
Heimann, Susan 1940- 33-36R
Heimarck, Theodore 1906- 5-8R
Heimbeck, Raeburne S(eeley) 1930- 29-32R
Heimberg, Marilyn Markham
See Ross, Marilyn (Ann) Heimberg
Heimdahl, Ralph 1909- 69-72
Heimer, Mel(vin Lytton) 1915-1971 ....CANR-4
Obituary 29-32R
Earlier sketch in CA 1-4R
Heimert, Alan (Edward) 1928- 5-8R
Heimler, Eugene 1922- CANR-8
Earlier sketch in CA 13-16R
Heimlich, Henry Jay 1920- 102
Heims, Steve J(oshua) 1926- 131
Heims, Steve Paul
See Heims, Steve J(oshua)
Heimsath, Charles H. 1928- 17-20R
Hein, Eleanor C(harlotte) 1933- 61-64
Hein, John 1921- CANR-16
Earlier sketches in CA 45-48, CANR-1
Hein, Leonard William 1916- 53-56
Hein, Lucille Eleanor 1915- CANR-2
Earlier sketch in CA 5-8R
See also SATA 20
Hein, Marvin Lester 1925- 125
Hein, Norvin 1914- 61-64
Hein, Piet 1905- CANR-4
Earlier sketch in CA 49-52
Hein, Rolland Neal 1932- 112
Heinberg, Paul (Julius) 1924- CANR-23
Earlier sketch in CA 45-48
Heindel, Richard Heathcote
1912-1979 Obituary 89-92
Heine, Arthur J. 1940- 138
Heine, Carl 1936- 57-60
Heine, Heinrich 1797-1856 ....DLB 90
Heine, Helme 1941- 135
See also CLR 18
See also MAICYA
See also SATA 67
Heine, Lala Koehn
See Koehn-Heine, Lala
Heine, Ralph W(illiam) 1914- 41-44R
Heine, William C(olbourne) 1919- 97-100
Heineman, Benjamin Walter Jr. 1944- CANR-28
Earlier sketch in CA 105
Heineman, Helen 1936- 125
Heinemann, George Alfred 1918- ....SATA 31
Heinemann, Katherine 1918- 77-80
Heinemann, Larry (Curtiss) 1944- CANR-31
Earlier sketch in CA 110
See also CLC 50
See also DLBD 9
Heinemann, Ronald L(ynton) 1939- 112
Heinen, Hubert (Plummer) 1937- 41-44R
Heinerman, John 1946- 128
Heiney, Donald (William) 1921- CANR-3
Earlier sketch in CA 1-4R
See also CLC 9
Heinke, Clarence H. 1912- 53-56
Heinl, Nancy G(ordon) 1916- 81-84
Heinl, Robert Debs Jr. 1916-1979 ....CANR-4
Obituary 85-88
Earlier sketch in CA 5-8R
Heinlein, Robert A(nson) 1907-1988 ....CANR-20
Obituary 125
Earlier sketches in CA 1-4R, CANR-1
See also CLC 1, 3, 8, 14, 26, 55
See also DLB 8
See also MAICYA
See also MTCW
See also SATA 9, 56, 69
Heinrich, Bernd 1940- 109
Heinrich, Willi 1920- CANR-15
Earlier sketch in CA 93-96
See also DLB 75
Heinrichs, Waldo H(untley) Jr. 1925- 122
Heins, A(rthur) James 1931- 5-8R
Heins, Ethel L(eah) 1918- 102
Heins, Marjorie 1946- 69-72
Heins, Paul 1909- 69-72
See also SATA 13
Heinse, Wilhelm 1746-1803 ....DLB 94
Heinsohn, A(ugereau) G(ray) Jr. 1896- CAP-1
Earlier sketch in CA 11-12
Heinsohn, Thomas William
1934- Brief entry 118
Heinsohn, Tommy
See Heinsohn, Thomas William
Heintz, Ann Christine 1930-1989 ....CANR-8
Obituary 127
Earlier sketch in CA 61-64
Heintz, Bonnie L(ee) 1924- 69-72
Heintz, John 1936- 45-48
Heintze, Carl 1922- 57-60
See also SATA 26
Heintzelman, Donald S(haffer) 1938- CANR-16
Earlier sketch in CA 93-96
Heinz, G.
See Gerard-Libois, Jules C.
Heinz, W(ilfred) C(harles) 1915- CANR-4
Earlier sketch in CA 5-8R
See also SATA 26
Heinz, William Frederick 1899-1976 ....CANR-12
Earlier sketch in CA 61-64
Heinze, Robert H(arold)
1920-1984 Obituary 113
Heinzelman, Kurt 1947- 101
Heinzen, Mildred
See Masters, Mildred
Heinzerling, Larry E(dward) 1945- 73-76
Heinzerling, Lynn Louis
1906-1983 Obituary 111
Heinzman(n), George (Melville) 1916- 1-4R
Heirich, Max 1931- 29-32R
Heise, David R(euben) 1937- 89-92
Heise, Edward Tyler 1912- 1-4R
Heise, Kenan 1933- 57-60
Heisenberg, Werner 1901-1976 Obituary 65-68
Heiser, Charles B(ixler) Jr. 1920- 45-48
Heiser, Victor George
1893-1972 Obituary 33-36R
Heiserman, Arthur Ray 1929-1975 ....CANR-15
Obituary 103
Earlier sketch in CA 1-4R
Heiserman, David L(ee) 1940- CANR-8
Earlier sketch in CA 61-64
Heisey, Alan Milliken 1928- 57-60
Heiskell, John Netherland
1872-1972 Obituary 89-92
Heisler, Martin O. 1938- CANR-23
Earlier sketch in CA 45-48
Heisler, Philip Samuel 1915-1988 Obituary 127
Heiss, Jerold (Sheldon) 1930- 126
Brief entry 111
Heissenbuettel, Helmut 1921- 81-84
See also Heissenbuttel, Helmut
See also DLB 75
Heissenbuttel, Helmut
See Heissenbuettel, Helmut
See also DLB 75
Heisserer, Andrew Jackson 1935- 111
Heitler, Walter (Heinrich) 1904-1981 ....CANR-8
Earlier sketch in CA 13-16R
Heitman, Sidney 1924- 9-12R
Heitner, Robert R. 1920- 5-8R
Heitzmann, William Ray 1948- CANR-17
Earlier sketch in CA 97-100
Heizer, Robert Fleming 1915-1979 102
Hekker, Terry 1932- 97-100
Hekman, Susan J(ean) 1949- 114
Helbig, Althea K. 1928- CANR-37
Earlier sketches in CA 97-100, CANR-17
Helbing, Terry 1951- 89-92
Helbling, Robert E(ugene) 1923- 49-52
Helck, C. Peter 1893- CANR-1
Earlier sketch in CA 1-4R
Held, David 1951- 110
Held, Jack Preston 1926- 33-36R
Held, Jacqueline 1936- CANR-14
Earlier sketch in CA 73-76
Held, Joseph 1930- 45-48
Held, Julius Samuel 1905- 103
Held, Peter
See Vance, John Holbrook
Held, R(over) Burnell 1921- 33-36R
Held, Ray E(ldred) 1918- 45-48
Held, Richard 1922- 41-44R
Held, Virginia (Potter) 1929- CANR-16
Earlier sketches in CA 1-4R, CANR-1
Helder, Dom
See Camara, Helder Pessoa
Heldman, Dan C(hristopher) 1943- 110
Heldman, Gladys M(edalie)
1922- Brief entry 111
Heleniak, Kathryn Moore 110
Helfen, Otto J. Maenchen
See Maenchen, Otto John
Helfert, Erich A(nton) 1931- 9-12R
Helfgott, Daniel (Andrew) 1952- CANR-22
Earlier sketch in CA 106
Helfgott, Roy B. 1925- 81-84
Helfman, Elizabeth S(eaver) 1911- CANR-5
Earlier sketch in CA 5-8R
See also SATA 3
Helfman, Harry 1910- 25-28R
See also SATA 3
Helforth, John
See Doolittle, Hilda
Helfritz, Hans 1902- 41-44R
Helgerson, Richard 1940- 116
Helgesen, Sally 1948- 115
Helion, Jean 1904-1987 Obituary 124
Helitzer, Florence (Saperstein) 1928- 17-20R
Hellberg, Hans-Eric 1927- CANR-18
Earlier sketch in CA 101
See also SATA 38
Helldorfer, M.C. 1954- 129
Hellegers, Andre E. 1926-1979 Obituary 85-88
Hellen, J(ohn) A(nthony) 1935- 61-64
Hellenhofferu, Vojtech Kapristian z
See Hasek, Jaroslav (Matej Frantisek)
Heller
See Iranek-Osmecki, Kazimierz
Heller, Abraham M. 1898-1975 Obituary 57-60
Heller, Bernard 1896-1976 Obituary 65-68
Heller, Celia S(topnicka) 37-40R
Heller, David (A.) 1922-1968 ....CAP-1
Earlier sketch in CA 9-10
Heller, David 1957- 124
Heller, Dawn Hansen 1932- 125
Heller, Deane Fons 1924- 9-12R
Heller, Erich 1911-1990 ....CANR-8
Obituary 132
Earlier sketch in CA 13-16R
Heller, Francis H(oward) 1917- CANR-31
Earlier sketch in CA 1-4R
Heller, H(einz) Robert 1940- CANR-22
Earlier sketch in CA 69-72
Heller, Herbert L. 1908- 21-24R
Heller, Jean 1942- 73-76
Heller, John H(erbert) 1921- 114
Heller, John 1896(?)-1987 Obituary 124
Heller, Joseph 1923- CANR-8
Earlier sketch in CA 5-8R
See also CABS 1
See also AITN 1
See also CLC 1, 3, 5, 8, 11, 36, 63
See also DLB 2, 28
See also DLBY 80
See also MTCW
See also WLC
Heller, Keith 1949- 119
Heller, Linda 1944- 108
See also SATA 40, 46
Heller, Mark (Francis) 1914- CANR-10
Earlier sketch in CA 61-64
Heller, Michael (David) 1937- CANR-26
Earlier sketch in CA 45-48
Heller, Mike
See Hano, Arnold
Heller, Peter 1920- CANR-32
Earlier sketches in CA 41-44R, CANR-14
Heller, Rachelle S(ara) 1943- 111
Heller, Reinhold (August Friedrich) 1940- 77-80
Heller, Robert (Gordon Barry) 1932- 132
Heller, Robert W(illiam) 1933- 25-28R
Heller, Robert 1899(?)-1973 Obituary 41-44R
Heller, Ruth M. 1924- 130
See also SATA 66
Heller, Shelly
See Heller, Rachelle S(ara)
Heller, Sipa 1897(?)-1980 Obituary 97-100
Heller, Trudy (Marie) 1944- 115
Heller, Walter W(olfgang) 1915-1987 ....21-24R
Obituary 122
Heller, Wilson Battin 1893-1983 Obituary 110
Hellerman, Herbert 1927- 53-56
Hellerstein, David (Joel) 1953- 120
Hellerstein, Jerome R. 1907- CAP-1
Earlier sketch in CA 13-14
Hellerstein, Kathryn (Ann) 1952- 114
Hellie, Ann 1925- CANR-15
Earlier sketch in CA 77-80
Hellie, Richard 1937- CANR-36
Earlier sketches in CA 33-36R, CANR-14
Hellinga, Lotte 1932- 129
Hellinga, Wytze (Gs) 1908-1985 Obituary 116
Hellinger, Douglas A(llan) 1948- CANR-21
Earlier sketch in CA 69-72

Hellinger, Stephen H(enry) 1948- CANR-21
Earlier sketch in CA 69-72
Hellison, Donald R(aymond) 1938- 53-56
Hellman, Anna 1902(?)-1972 Obituary 33-36R
Hellman, Arthur D(avid) 1942- 69-72
Hellman, C(larisse) Doris
1910-1973 Obituary 41-44R
Hellman, Geoffrey T(heodore)
1907-1977 ....CANR-30
Obituary 73-76
Earlier sketch in CA 69-72
Hellman, Hal
See Hellman, Harold
Hellman, Harold 1927- CANR-10
Earlier sketch in CA 25-28R
See also SATA 4
Hellman, Hugo E. 1908- CAP-2
Earlier sketch in CA 19-20
Hellman, John 1940- 129
Hellman, Judith Adler 1945- 113
Hellman, Lillian (Florence) 1906-1984 ....CANR-33
Obituary 112
Earlier sketch in CA 13-16R
See also AITN 1, 2
See also CLC 2, 4, 8, 14, 18, 34, 44, 52
See also DC 1
See also DLB 7
See also DLBY 84
See also MTCW
Hellman, Peter 1943- 107
Hellman, Robert 1919-1984 ....17-20R
Obituary 113
Hellmann, Donald C(harles) 1933- CANR-28
Earlier sketch in CA 45-48
Hellmann, Ellen 1908- 106
Hellmann, John 1948- CANR-24
Earlier sketch in CA 105
Hellmuth, Jerome 1911- 13-16R
Hellmuth, William Frederick Jr. 1920- CANR-4
Earlier sketch in CA 1-4R
Hellstrom, Ward 1930- 33-36R
Hellwig, Monika Konrad 1929- 37-40R
Helly, Dorothy O. 1931- 122
Hellyer, A(rthur) G(eorge) L(ee)
1902- CANR-19
Earlier sketches in CA 9-12R, CANR-4
Hellyer, Arthur
See Hellyer, A(rthur) G(eorge) L(ee)
Hellyer, Clement David 1914- 118
Hellyer, David Tirrell 1913- 17-20R
Hellyer, Jill 1925- 118
Hellyer, Paul (Theodore) 1923- CANR-14
Earlier sketch in CA 69-72
Helm, Bertrand P. 1929- 37-40R
Helm, Ernest Eugene 1928- CANR-2
Earlier sketch in CA 1-4R
Helm, Everett 1913- 49-52
Helm, P(eter) J(ames) 1916- CANR-3
Earlier sketch in CA 9-12R
Helm, Robert Meredith 1917- 17-20R
Helm, Thomas (William) 1919- 5-8R
Helmer, John 1946- 41-44R
Helmer, William F. 1926- 33-36R
Helmer, William J(oseph) 1936- 73-76
Helmericks, Bud
See Helmericks, Harmon R.
Helmericks, Constance (Chittenden)
1918-1987 ....9-12R
Obituary 122
Helmericks, Harmon R. 1917- 29-32R
Helmering, Doris Wild 1942- 65-68
Helmers, George Dow 1906- 61-64
Helmholz, R(ichard) H(enry) 1940- CANR-29
Earlier sketch in CA 61-64
Helmi, Jack
See Sands, Leo G(eorge)
Helming, Ann 1924- CANR-2
Earlier sketch in CA 1-4R
Helminiak, Daniel A. 1942- 126
Helmker, Judith Anne 1940- 33-36R
Helmlinger, (Benita) Trudy 1943- 69-72
Helmore, G(eoffrey) A(nthony) 1922- 29-32R
Helm-Pirgo, Marian 1897- 77-80
Helmreich, Ernst Christian 1902- 1-4R
Helmreich, Jonathan Ernst
1936- Brief entry 105
Helmreich, Paul C(hristian) 1933- 53-56
Helmreich, Robert Louis 1937- 65-68
Helmreich, William B. 1945- 105
Helms, Christine Moss 129
Helms, Jesse (Alexander Jr.)
1921- Brief entry 124
Helms, Randel 1942- 49-52
Helms, Roland Thomas Jr. 1940- 102
Helms, Tom
See Helms, Roland Thomas Jr.
Helmstadter, Gerald C. 1925- 13-16R
Heloise
See Reese, Heloise (Bowles)
Helper, Rose 77-80
Helpern, Milton 1902-1977 73-76
Obituary 69-72
Helprin, Mark 1947- 81-84
See also CLC 7, 10, 22, 32
See also DLBY 85
See also MTCW
Helps, Racey 1913-1971 ....CAP-2
Obituary 29-32R
Earlier sketch in CA 23-24
See also SATA 2, 25
Helson, Harry 1898- CAP-1
Earlier sketch in CA 11-12
Helterman, Jeffrey A. 1942- 103
Helton, David (Kirby) 1940- 25-28R
Helton, Tinsley 1915- 1-4R
Helvick, James
See Cockburn, (Francis) Claud
Helweg, Hans H. 1917- 126
See also SATA 33, 50
Helwig, David (Gordon) 1938- 33-36R
See also DLB 60
Helwig, Maggie
See Helwig, Sarah Magdalen
Helwig, Sarah Magdalen 1961- 130
Helyar, Jane Penelope Josephine
1933- CANR-26
Earlier sketches in CA 21-24R, CANR-10
See also Poole, Josephine
Helyar, John ....BEST 90:3
Hemans, Felicia 1793-1835 .... DLB 96
Hembree, Charles R. 1938- 33-36R
Hembry, Phyllis (May) 1916- 136
Hemdahl, Reuel Gustaf 1903-1977 ....37-40R
Hemel Dobkin, Kathleen
See Hamel Peifer, Kathleen
Hemenway, Robert 1921- 33-36R
Hemenway, Ruby 1884(?)-1987 Obituary 123
Hemery, Eric 1914- 111
Hemesath, Caroline 1899- 61-64
Hemeze
See Caballero, Manuel
Hemeze, Sebastian
See Caballero, Manuel
Hemington, Judith 1949- 129
Hemingway, Ernest (Miller)
1899-1961 ....CANR-34
Earlier sketch in CA 77-80
See also CDALB 1917-1929
See also CLC 1, 3, 6, 8, 10, 13, 19, 30, 34, 39, 41, 44, 50, 61
See also DLB 4, 9, 102
See also DLBD 1
See also DLBY 81, 87
See also MTCW
See also SSC 1
See also WLC
Hemingway, Gregory H.
1931(?)- Brief entry 112
Hemingway, Leicester C.
1915-1982 Obituary 107
Hemingway, Maggie 1946- 125
Hemingway, Mary Welsh 1908-1986 73-76
Obituary 121
Hemingway, Patricia Drake 1926-1978 69-72
Obituary 73-76
Hemingway, Taylor
See Rywell, Martin
Heminway, John (H. Jr.) 1944- 25-28R
Hemleben, Sylvester John 1902- CAP-2
Earlier sketch in CA 25-28
Hemley, Cecil Herbert 1914-1966 ....CANR-1
Obituary 25-28R
Earlier sketch in CA 1-4R
Hemley, Elaine Gottlieb
See Gottlieb, Elaine
Hemley, Robin 1958- 130
Hemlow, Joyce 1906- 5-8R
Hemmant, Lynette 1938- ....SATA 69
Hemmerechts, Kristien 1955- 133
Hemming, (Laurence) Charles 1950- 132
Hemming, John (Henry) 1935- CANR-12
Earlier sketch in CA 29-32R
Hemming, Roy 1928- 61-64
See also SATA 11
Hemmings, F(rederic) W(illiam) J(ohn)
1920- CANR-27
Earlier sketch in CA 97-100
Hemmings, Susan 1941- 118
Hemon, Louis 1880-1913 ....DLB 92
Hempel, Amy 1951- 137
Brief entry 118
See also CLC 39
Hempel, Carl G.
See Hempel, Carl Gustav
Hempel, Carl Gustav 1905- Brief entry 116
Hemphill, A. Marcus 1930(?)-1986 Obituary 120
Hemphill, Betty
See Hemphill, Elizabeth Anne
Hemphill, Charles F. Jr. 1917- 101
Hemphill, Christopher (Glenn)
1950-1987 Obituary 122
Hemphill, Elizabeth Anne 1920- 115
Hemphill, George 1922- 13-16R
Hemphill, Herbert Waide Jr. 1929- 116
Hemphill, John K(nox) 1919- 53-56
Hemphill, Kenneth S. 1948- 134
Hemphill, Martha Locke 1904-1973 ....37-40R
See also SATA 37
Hemphill, Paul 1936- CANR-29
Earlier sketches in CA 49-52, CANR-12
See also AITN 2
See also DLBY 87
Hemphill, W(illiam) Edwin 1912- 21-24R
Hempstone, Smith 1929- CANR-1
Earlier sketch in CA 1-4R
Hempton, David 1952- 125
Hemschemeyer, Judith 1935- 49-52
Henaghan, Jim 1919- 102
Henahan, Donal 1921- Brief entry 111
Henault, Gilles 1920- ....DLB 88
Henault, Marie (Josephine) 1921- 33-36R
Henbest, Nigel 1951- 124
See also SATA 52, 55
Henbos
See Bosch, Henry G(erard)
Hench, John B(ixler) 1943- 131
Henchman, Daniel 1689-1761 ....DLB 24
Hencken, Hugh O'Neill 1902-1981 Obituary 104
Hendee, John C(lare) 1938- 93-96
Hendel, Charles William 1890-1982 ......CANR-13
Obituary 108
Earlier sketches in CAP-1, CA 13-16
Hendel, Samuel 1909-1984 ....CANR-1
Obituary 113
Earlier sketch in CA 1-4R
Hendelson, William H. 1904-1975 Obituary 104
Henderley, Brooks CANR-26
Earlier sketches in CAP-2, CA 19-20
See also SATA 1
Henderlite, Rachel 1905- 1-4R
Hendershot, Ralph
1896(?)-1979 Obituary 89-92
Henderson, Alexander (John) 1910- CAP-1
Earlier sketch in CA 13-16
Henderson, Algo D(onmyer)
1897-1988 ....CANR-1
Obituary 126
Earlier sketch in CA 1-4R
Henderson, Alice Corbin 1881-1949 .... DLB 54
Henderson, Archibald
1877-1963 Obituary 93-96
See also DLB 103
Henderson, Archibald 1916- 53-56
Henderson, Bert C. 1904- CAP-1
Earlier sketch in CA 9-10
Henderson, Bill 1941- 33-36R
Henderson, Brian 1941- 112
Henderson, C(rispin) A(listair) P(oland)
1955- 119
Henderson, C(elia) Nell 1959- 135
Henderson, C(harles) William 1925- 65-68
Henderson, Charles Jr. 1923- 45-48
Henderson, Charles P(ackard) Jr. 1941- 41-44R
Henderson, Charles W(illiam) 1948- 135
Henderson, Dan Fenno 1921- 17-20R
Henderson, David 1942- CANR-10
Earlier sketch in CA 25-28R
See also BW
See also DLB 41
Henderson, Dion (Winslow) 1921-1984 ....CANR-5
Obituary 114
Earlier sketch in CA 9-12R
Henderson, Donald
See Laughlin, Tom
Henderson, Dwight F. 1937- 41-44R
Henderson, Edwin Bancroft
1883-1977 Obituary 116
Henderson, Eva Pendleton 1890- 115
Henderson, F. C.
See Mencken, H(enry) L(ouis)
Henderson, G. D. S.
See Henderson, George (David Smith)
Henderson, G(eorge) P(atrick) 1915- 29-32R
Henderson, G(eorge) P(oland) 1920- 37-40R
Henderson, George (David Smith)
1931- CANR-27
Earlier sketch in CA 25-28R
Henderson, George L(eslie) 1925- 69-72
Henderson, George Wylie 1904- 125
See also BW
See also DLB 51
Henderson, Gordon 1950- .... SATA 53
Henderson, Harold G(ould)
1889-1974 Obituary 53-56
Henderson, Harold H(ale) 1928- 114
Henderson, Harry B(rinton) Jr.
1914- Brief entry 109
Henderson, Hazel 1933- 129
Henderson, Ian 1910-1969 ....CAP-2
Earlier sketch in CA 17-18
Henderson, Isabel 1933- 25-28R
Henderson, James Youngblood 1944- 110
Henderson, James 1934- CANR-13
Earlier sketch in CA 33-36R
Henderson, Jean Carolyn Glidden 1916- 102
Henderson, Jennifer 1929- 107
Henderson, John S(teele) 1919- 5-8R
Henderson, John W(illiam) 1910- 25-28R
Henderson, John 1906(?)-1982 Obituary 108
Henderson, John 1915- 5-8R
Henderson, K(enneth) D(avid) D(ruitt)
1903- CAP-1
Earlier sketch in CA 13-16
Henderson, Katherine Usher 1937- 126
Henderson, Kathy 1949- 123
See also SATA 53, 55
Henderson, (Alan) Keith 1883-1982 107
Obituary 106
Henderson, Keith M. 1934- 21-24R
Henderson, Laurance G.
1924(?)-1977 Obituary 73-76
Henderson, Laurence 1928- 53-56
Henderson, Lawrence W. 1921- 103
Henderson, LeGrand 1901-1965 ....5-8R
See also SATA 9
Henderson, Linda Dalrymple 1948- 124
Henderson, Lois T(hompson) 1918- 81-84
Henderson, M(arilyn) R(uth) 1927- CANR-27
Henderson, Mary
See Mavor, Osborne Henry
Henderson, Mary C. 1928- 77-80
Henderson, (Andrew) Maxwell 1908- 132
Henderson, Michael (Douglas) 1932- CANR-27
Earlier sketch in CA 110
Henderson, Monika 1954- 129
Henderson, Nancy Wallace 1916- 97-100
See also SATA 22
Henderson, Nancy 1943- 41-44R
Henderson, (John) Nicholas 1919- 132
Henderson, Paul (III) 1939- Brief entry 122
Henderson, Peter 1904-1983 108
Obituary 111
Henderson, Philip (Prichard)
1906-1977 ....CANR-14
Obituary 104
Earlier sketches in CAP-1, CA 9-10
Henderson, Randall 1888- CAP-1
Earlier sketch in CA 13-14
Henderson, Richard B(eveir) 1921- 77-80
Henderson, Richard I(van) 1926- CANR-11
Earlier sketch in CA 69-72
Henderson, Richard 1924- CANR-20
Earlier sketches in CA 13-16R, CANR-5
Henderson, Robert M. 1926- 33-36R
Henderson, Robert W(augh) 1920- 1-4R
Henderson, Robert William
1888-1985 Obituary 117
Henderson, Robert 1906- 106
Henderson, S(hirley) P(rudence) A(nn)
1929- 37-40R
Henderson, Stephen E. 1925- 29-32R
See also BW
Henderson, Sylvia
See Ashton-Warner, Sylvia (Constance)
Henderson, Thomas W(alter) 1949- 73-76
Henderson, Vivian (Wilson) 1923-1976 65-68
Obituary 61-64
Henderson, W(illiam) O(tto) 1904- CANR-4
Earlier sketch in CA 1-4R
Henderson, William III 1922- 17-20R
Henderson, William L(eroy) 1927- 33-36R
Henderson, Zenna (Chlarson)
1917-1983 ....CANR-1
Obituary 133
Earlier sketch in CA 1-4R
See also DLB 8
See also SATA 5
Henderson-Howat, Gerald
See Howat, Gerald Malcolm David
Hendin, David (Bruce) 1945- 41-44R
Hendin, Herbert (Martin) 1926- 129
Brief entry 117
Hendin, Josephine 1946- 102
Hendley, Coit (Taylor) Jr.
1920-1985 Obituary 116
Hendon, William S(cott) 1933- CANR-35
Earlier sketch in CA 45-48
Hendra, Tony 102
Hendren, Ron 1945- 77-80
Hendrich, Paula Griffith 1928- CANR-1
Earlier sketch in CA 1-4R
Hendrick, George 1929- CANR-23
Earlier sketches in CA 13-16R, CANR-8
Hendrick, Irving G(uilford) 1936- 81-84
Hendrick, Ives 1898-1972 ....CAP-1
Obituary 33-36R
Earlier sketch in CA 11-12
Hendrick, T(homas) W(illiam) 1909- 108
Hendricks, Faye N(eidhold) 1913- 69-72
Hendricks, Frances Wade Kellam
1900- 37-40R
Hendricks, Gay 1945- 73-76
Hendricks, George D. 1913- 5-8R
Hendricks, J(ames) Edwin 1935- CANR-34
Earlier sketches in CA 41-44R, CANR-15
Hendricks, Robert J(oseph) 1944- 45-48
Hendricks, Walter 1892-1979 Obituary 103
Hendricks, William Lawrence 1929- CANR-17
Earlier sketches in CA 49-52, CANR-2
Hendrickson, David C. 1953- 126
Hendrickson, Donald E(ugene) 1941- 93-96
Hendrickson, James E. 1932- 21-24R
Hendrickson, Paul 1944- 108
Hendrickson, Robert A(ugustus)
1923- CANR-12
Earlier sketch in CA 29-32R
Hendrickson, Robert 1933- CANR-1
Earlier sketch in CA 49-52
Hendrickson, Walter Brookfield Jr.
1936- CANR-1
Earlier sketch in CA 1-4R
See also SATA 9
Hendrie, Don(ald Franz) Jr. 1942- CANR-18
Earlier sketches in CA 49-52, CANR-3
Hendriks, A(rthur) L(emiere) 1922- 97-100
Hendriksen, Eldon Sende 1917- 13-16R
Hendrix, Harville 1935- 130
Hendry, Allan 1950- 106
Hendry, Diana 1941- 136
See also SATA 68
Hendry, J(ames) F(indlay) 1912- 29-32R
Hendry, John (Lovat) 1952- 136
Hendry, Joy (McLaggan) 1953- 133
Hendry, Thomas 1929- 69-72
Hendry, Tom
See Hendry, Thomas
Hendy, M(ichael) F(rank) 1942- 137
Hendy, Philip (Anstiss) 1900-1980 Obituary 102
Henegan, Lucius Herbert Jr.
1902(?)-1979 Obituary 85-88
Heneghan, James 1930- 129
See also SATA 53
Heneman, Herbert Gerhard Jr. 1916- CANR-1
Earlier sketch in CA 1-4R
Henfil
See Souza Filho, Henrique de
Henfrey, Colin (Vere Fleetwood) 1941- 13-16R
Henfrey, Norman 1929- 25-28R
Henig, Gerald S(heldon) 1942- 57-60
Henig, Martin (Edward) 1942- 114
Henig, Robin Marantz 1953- 108
Henig, Ruth B(eatrice) 1943- 49-52
Henig, Suzanne 1936- CANR-2
Earlier sketch in CA 45-48
Henige, David 1938- CANR-39
Earlier sketch in CA 103
Heninger, S(imeon) K(ahn) Jr. 1922- CANR-1
Earlier sketch in CA 1-4R
Henisch, Bridget Ann 1932- 127
Henisch, Heinz K. 1922- 73-76
Henisch, Peter 1943- ....DLB 85
Henissart, Paul 1923- 29-32R
Henke, Dan (Ferdinand) 1924- 53-56
Henke, Emerson O(verbeck) 1916- CANR-12
Earlier sketch in CA 17-20R
Henkel, Barbara Osborn 1921- 9-12R

Henkel, Stephen C. 1933- ... 37-40R
Henkels, Robert M(acAllister) Jr. 1936- ... 57-60
Henkes, Kevin 1960- ... CANR-38
Earlier sketch in CA 114
See also CLR 23
See also MAICYA
See also SATA 43
Henkes, Robert 1922- ... CANR-29
Earlier sketches in CA 33-36R, CANR-13
Henkin, Harmon 1940(?)-1980 Obituary ... 101
Henkin, Louis 1917- ... CANR-13
Earlier sketch in CA 33-36R
Henkle, Roger B. 1935- ... 129
Henle, Faye Obituary ... 37-40R
Henle, Fritz 1909- ... 73-76
Henle, James 1891(?)-1973 Obituary ... 37-40R
Henle, Jane 1913- ... 77-80
Henle, Mary 1913- ... 33-36R
Henle, Robert John 1909- ... 110
Henle, Theda O. 1918- ... 33-36R
Henley, Arthur 1921- ... 21-24R
Henley, Beth
See Henley, Elizabeth Becker
See also CABS 3
See also CLC 23
See also DLBY 86
Henley, Elizabeth Becker 1952- ... CANR-32
Earlier sketch in CA 107
See also Henley, Beth
See also MTCW
Henley, Gail 1952- ... CANR-21
Earlier sketch in CA 89-92
Henley, Karyn 1952- ... 102
Henley, Nancy Eloise Main
1934- Brief entry ... 106
Henley, Norman 1915- ... 17-20R
Henley, Virginia 1935- ... 109
Henley, W(illiam) Ballentine 1905- ... 61-64
Henley, Wallace (Boynton) 1941- ... CANR-14
Earlier sketch in CA 65-68
Henley, William Ernest
1849-1903 Brief entry ... 105
See also DLB 19
See also TCLC 8
Henn, Harry George 1919- ... CANR-36
Earlier sketch in CA 45-48
Henn, Thomas Rice 1901-1974 ... CANR-4
Earlier sketch in CA 5-8R
Hennacy, Ammon 1893-1970 Obituary ... 104
Henne, Frances E. 1906-1985 Obituary ... 118
Hennedy, Hugh L(ouis) 1929- ... 41-44R
Henneman, John Bell Jr. 1935- ... CANR-31
Earlier sketch in CA 45-48
Hennesey, James J. 1926- ... 33-36R
Hennessey, Caroline
See von Block, Bela W(illiam)
and von Block, Sylvia
Hennessey, R(oger) A(nthony) S(ean)
1937- ... 29-32R
Hennessy, Bernard C. 1924- ... 13-16R
Hennessy, David James George
1932- ... CANR-22
Earlier sketch in CA 106
Hennessy, James Pope
See Pope-Hennessy, James
Hennessy, Jossleyn (Michael Stephen Philip)
1903- ... 9-12R
Hennessy, Mary L. 1927- ... 21-24R
Hennessy, Max
See Harris, John
Hennessy, Peter 1947- ... 123
Hennessy, Thomas C(hristopher) 1916- ... 115
Hennig, Margaret (Marie) 1940- ... 81-84
Henning, Basil Duke 1910-1990 Obituary ... 130
Henning, Charles N(athaniel) 1915- ... 1-4R
Henning, Daniel H(oward) 1931- ... CANR-2
Earlier sketch in CA 45-48
Henning, Edward B. 1922- ... 17-20R
Henning, Standish 1932- Brief entry ... 107
Henning, Sylvie Marie Debevec
See Debevec Henning, Sylvie Marie
Henninger, G. Ross 1898-1984 Obituary ... 112
Hennings, Dorothy Grant 1935- ... CANR-4
Earlier sketch in CA 53-56
Hennings, Josephine Silva
1899(?)-1985 Obituary ... 117
Hennissart, Martha ... 85-88
See also Lathen, Emma
Henrey, Madeleine 1906- ... CANR-6
Earlier sketch in CA 13-16R
Henrey, Mrs. Robert
See Henrey, Madeleine
Henrey, Robert
See Henrey, Madeleine
Henri, Adrian (Maurice) 1932- ... CANR-34
Earlier sketches in CA 25-28R, CANR-15
See also MTCW
Henri, Florette 1908-1985 ... 73-76
Obituary ... 117
Henri, G.
See Clement, George H.
Henrichsen, Walt(er Arlie) Jr. 1934- ... 89-92
Henricks, Kaw
See Wolfe, Charles Keith
Henries, A. Doris Banks 1913(?)-1981 ... 125
Obituary ... 103
See also BW
Henries, Doris
See Henries, A. Doris Banks
Henriksen, Louise Levitas 1917- ... 128
Henriksen, Thomas H(ollinger) 1939- ... 112
Henrikson, Arthur A. 1921- ... 130
Henriod, Lorraine 1925- ... 45-48
See also SATA 26
Henriques, Veronica 1931- ... 102
Henry, Alexander 1739-1824 ... DLB 99
Henry, Avril (Kay) 1935- ... 123
Henry, Bessie Walker 1921- ... 9-12R
Henry, Bill
See Henry, William Mellors
Henry, Buck 1930- ... 77-80
See also DLB 26
Henry, Carl F(erdinand) H(oward)
1913- ... CANR-21
Earlier sketches in CA 13-16R, CANR-6
Henry, (William) Claud 1914- ... 45-48
Henry, Daniel
See Kahnweiler, Daniel-Henry
Henry, David Dodds 1905- ... 106
Henry, David Lee
See Hill, R. Lance
Henry, Desmond Paul 1921- ... 132
Henry, DeWitt (Pawling II) 1941- ... 131
Henry, Eric P(utnam) 1943- ... 108
Henry, Fran Worden 1948- ... 111
Henry, Frances 1931- ... 77-80
Henry, Francoise 1902-1982 Obituary ... 106
Henry, Harold Wilkinson 1926- ... 37-40R
Henry, Harriet
See De Steuch, Harriet Henry
Henry, James P(aget) 1914- ... 104
Henry, James S(helburne) 1950- ... 49-52
Henry, Janet Cope 1925(?)-1986 Obituary ... 118
Henry, Jeanne Heffernan 1940- ... 105
Henry, Joanne Landers 1927- ... 17-20R
See also SATA 6
Henry, John Case 1905-1990 Obituary ... 132
Henry, Joseph B. 1901- ... CAP-2
Earlier sketch in CA 17-18
Henry, Jules 1904-1969 Obituary ... 109
Henry, Kenneth 1920- ... 57-60
Henry, Laurin L(uther) 1921- ... 1-4R
Henry, Marguerite 1902- ... CANR-9
Earlier sketch in CA 17-20R
See also CLR 4
See also DLB 22
See also MAICYA
See also SAAS 7
See also SATA 11, 69
Henry, Marie H. 1935- ... SATA 65
Henry, Marion
See del Rey, Lester
Henry, O.
See Porter, William Sydney
See also SSC 5
See also TCLC 1, 19
See also WLC
Henry, Oliver
See Porter, William Sydney
Henry, Peter 1926- ... 109
Henry, Robert Selph 1889-1970 ... CANR-17
Obituary ... 103
Earlier sketch in CA 1-4R
See also DLB 17
Henry, Shirley 1925(?)-1972 Obituary ... 33-36R
Henry, Sondra 1930- ... 119
Henry, T. E.
See Rowland-Entwistle, (Arthur) Theodore (Henry)
Henry, Vera 1909(?)-1987 ... CAP-2
Obituary ... 123
Earlier sketch in CA 21-22
Henry, W. P. 1929- ... 17-20R
Henry, Will
See Allen, Henry Wilson
Henry, William A(lfred) III 1950- ... 130
Brief entry ... 116
Henry, William Earl 1917- Brief entry ... 108
Henry, William Mellors
1890-1970 Obituary ... 89-92
Henry of Ghent 1217(?)-1293 ... DLB 115
Henschel, Elizabeth Georgie ... 107
See also SATA 56
Henschke, Alfred
See Klabund
Hensey, Frederick G(erald) 1931- ... 89-92
Hensey, Fritz
See Hensey, Frederick G(erald)
Henshall, A(udrey) S(hore) 1927- ... 9-12R
Henshaw, James Ene 1924- ... 101
Henshaw, Richard 1945- ... 101
Henshaw, Tom 1924- ... 103
Henshel, Richard L(ee) 1939- ... 57-60
Hensley, Charles S(tanley) 1919- ... 41-44R
Hensley, Jeff (Lane) 1947- ... 117
Hensley, Joe L. 1926- ... CANR-31
Earlier sketches in CA 33-36R, CANR-14
Hensley, Sophie Almon 1866-1946 ... DLB 99
Hensley, (Malcolm) Stewart
1914(?)-1976 Obituary ... 65-68
Henslin, James M(arvin) 1937- ... CANR-34
Earlier sketches in CA 41-44R, CANR-15
Henson, Clyde E(ugene) 1914- ... 5-8R
Henson, James Maury 1936-1990 ... 124
Obituary ... 131
Brief entry ... 106
See also SATA 43
See also SATO 65
Henson, Jim
See Henson, James Maury
Henson, Margaret Swett 1924- ... 122
Henstell, Bruce 1945- ... 131
Henstell, Diana
See Silber, Diana
Henstra, Friso 1928- ... SAAS 14
See also SATA 8
Henthorn, William E(llsworth) 1928- ... 41-44R
Hentoff, Nat(han Irving) 1925- ... CANR-25
Earlier sketches in CA 1-4R, CANR-5
See also CAAS 6
See also AAYA 4
See also CLC 26
See also CLR 1
See also MAICYA
See also SATA 27, 42, 69
Henty, G(eorge) A(lfred)
1832-1902 Brief entry ... 112
See also DLB 18
See also SATA 64
Hentz, Caroline Lee (Whiting) 1800-1856 ... DLB 3
Henwood, James N. J. 1932- ... 29-32R
Henze, Donald F(rank) 1928- ... 21-24R
Hepburn, Andrew H.
1899(?)-1975 Obituary ... 57-60
Hepburn, James Gordon 1922- ... CANR-29
Earlier sketch in CA 85-88
Hepburn, Ronald W(illiam) 1927- ... 13-16R
Hepner, Harry W(alker) 1893-1984 ... 29-32R
Obituary ... 114
Hepner, James O(rville) 1933- ... 57-60
Heppenheimer, T(homas) A(dolph)
1947- ... CANR-16
Earlier sketch in CA 93-96
Heppenstall, Margit Strom 1913- ... 21-24R
Heppenstall, (John) Rayner
1911-1981 ... CANR-29
Obituary ... 103
Earlier sketch in CA 1-4R
See also CLC 10
Hepple, Alex 1904(?)-1983 Obituary ... 111
Hepple, Bob (Alexander) 1934- ... CANR-12
Earlier sketch in CA 29-32R
Hepple, Peter 1927- ... 81-84
Heppner, Sam(uel) 1913-1983 ... 25-28R
Obituary ... 109
Hepworth, James B. 1910- ... 1-4R
Hepworth, James Michael 1938- ... CANR-13
Earlier sketch in CA 73-76
Hepworth, Mike
See Hepworth, James Michael
Hepworth, (Charles) Philip 1912- ... 17-20R
Her
See Deal, Borden
Herail, Rene James 1939- ... 118
Herald, Earl Stannard 1914-1973 Obituary ... 112
Herald, George William 1911- ... 73-76
Herald, Kathleen
See Peyton, Kathleen Wendy
Heraud, Brian J(eremy) 1934- ... 73-76
Heraud, Javier 1942-1963 ... 131
See also HW
Heravi, Mehdi 1940- ... 29-32R
Herber, Bernard P. 1929- ... 21-24R
Herber, Harold L. 1929- ... 108
Herber, Lewis
See Bookchin, Murray
Herberg, Will 1909-1977 ... 73-76
Obituary ... 69-72
Herberger, Charles F. 1920- ... 41-44R
Herbers, John N. 1923- ... 33-36R
Herbert, A(lan) P(atrick) 1890-1971 ... 97-100
Obituary ... 33-36R
See also DLB 10
Herbert, Anthony B(ernard) 1930- ... 77-80
Herbert, Arthur
See Shappiro, Herbert (Arthur)
Herbert, Brian 1947- ... 133
Herbert, Cecil
See Hamilton, Charles (Harold St. John)
Herbert, Cynthia Ridgeway 1943- ... 118
Herbert, David T(homas) 1935- ... CANR-18
Earlier sketches in CA 49-52, CANR-2
Herbert, Don(ald Jeffrey) 1917- ... CANR-30
Earlier sketch in CA 29-32R
See also SATA 2
Herbert, Edward 1583-1648 ... DLB 121
Herbert, Eugenia W(arren) 1929- ... CANR-35
Earlier sketch in CA 93-96
Herbert, Frank (Patrick) 1920-1986 ... CANR-5
Obituary ... 118
Earlier sketch in CA 53-56
See also CLC 12, 23, 35, 44
See also DLB 8
See also MTCW
See also SATA 9, 37, 47
Herbert, George
1593-1633 ... CDBLB Before 1660
See also PC 4
Herbert, Gilbert 1924- ... CANR-23
Earlier sketch in CA 107
Herbert, Helen (Jean) 1947- ... SATA 57
Herbert, Henry George Alfred Marius Victor Francis
1898-1987 Obituary ... 123
Herbert, Henry William 1807-1858 ... DLB 3, 73
Herbert, Ian 1939- ... 111
Herbert, (Edward) Ivor (Montgomery)
1925- ... CANR-19
Earlier sketches in CA 53-56, CANR-4
Herbert, James 1943- ... 81-84
Herbert, Jean (Daniel Fernand)
1897-1980 ... CANR-9
Earlier sketch in CA 17-20R
Herbert, John
See Brundage, John Herbert
See also DLB 53
Herbert, John (David) 1924- ... CANR-13
Earlier sketch in CA 21-24R
Herbert, Kevin (Barry John) 1921- ... 17-20R
Herbert, Marie 1941- ... 69-72
Herbert, Martin 1933- ... 103
Herbert, Miranda C(arleton) 1950- ... 97-100
Herbert, Nick 1936- ... 128
Herbert, Robert L(ouis) 1929- ... CANR-36
Earlier sketches in CA 9-12R, CANR-5
Herbert, Sandra (Swanson) 1942- ... 130
Herbert, Theodore T(erence) 1942- ... CANR-15
Earlier sketch in CA 65-68
Herbert, Thomas Walter Jr. 1938- ... 104
Herbert, Victor 1927- ... 112
Herbert, Wally
See Herbert, Walter William
Herbert, Walter William 1934- ... CANR-15
Earlier sketch in CA 69-72
See also SATA 23
Herbert, William 1580-1630 ... DLB 121
Herbert, (Alfred Francis) Xavier
1901-1984 ... 69-72
Obituary ... 114
Herbert, Zbigniew 1924- ... CANR-36
Earlier sketch in CA 89-92
See also CLC 9, 43
See also MTCW
Herbertson, Gary J. 1938- ... 25-28R
Herblock
See Block, Herbert (Lawrence)
Herbrand, Jan(ice M.) 1931- ... 49-52
Herbruck, Christine Comstock
See Comstock, Christine
Herbst, Anthony F(rancis) 1941- ... CANR-35
Earlier sketch in CA 114
Herbst, Josephine (Frey) 1897-1969 ... 5-8R
Obituary ... 25-28R
See also CLC 34
See also DLB 9
Herbst, Jurgen (F. H.) 1928- ... 37-40R
Herbst, Robert L(eroy) 1935- ... 61-64
Herburger, Guenter 1932- ... DLB 75
Hercules, Frank (E. M.) ... CANR-2
Earlier sketch in CA 1-4R
See also BW
See also DLB 33
Herd, Dale 1940- ... 61-64
Herd, Michael 1937- ... 128
Herdan, Gustav 1897- ... 1-4R
Herdeck, Donald E. 1924- ... 53-56
Herdeg, Klaus 1937- ... 130
Herder, Johann Gottfried von
1744-1803 ... DLB 97
Herdt, Gilbert H(enry) 1949- ... 105
Herdt, Sheryll (Enette) Patterson 1941- ... 57-60
Hereford, John
See Fletcher, H(arry) L(utf) V(erne)
Heren, Louis (P.) 1919- ... CANR-12
Earlier sketch in CA 25-28R
Herfindahl, Orris C(lemens) 1918-1972 ... 41-44R
Obituary ... 37-40R
Herge
See Remi, Georges
See also CLR 6
Hergenhahn, B(aldwin) R(oss) 1934- ... 123
Brief entry ... 118
Hergenhan, L(aurence) T(homas) 1931- ... 127
Hergenhan, Laurie
See Hergenhan, L(aurence) T(homas)
Hergesheimer, Joseph
1880-1954 Brief entry ... 109
See also DLB 102, 9
See also TCLC 11
Herget, Paul 1908(?)-1981 Obituary ... 105
Herian, V.
See Gregorian, Vartan
Heriat, Philippe
See Payelle, Raymond-Gerard
Hering, Doris (Minnie) 1920- ... 128
Herington, C. J(ohn) 1924- ... CANR-15
Earlier sketch in CA 29-32R
Heriot, Angus 1927- ... 5-8R
Heriteau, Jacqueline 1925- ... CANR-37
Earlier sketches in CA 45-48, CANR-1, 16
Herity, Michael 1929- ... 49-52
Herken, Gregg (Franklin) 1947- ... CANR-20
Earlier sketch in CA 104
Herkimer, L(awrence) R(ussell) 1925(?)- ... 110
See also SATA 42
Herlihy, David (Joseph) 1930-1991 ... 41-44R
Obituary ... 133
Herlihy, James Leo 1927- ... CANR-2
Earlier sketch in CA 1-4R
See also CLC 6
Herlin, Hans 1925- ... 77-80
Herling, John 1907- Brief entry ... 112
Herm, Gerhard 1931- ... CANR-22
Earlier sketch in CA 104
Hermalyn, Gary 1952- ... 123
Herman, A(rthur) L(udwig) 1930- ... 65-68
Herman, Ben 1927- ... 104
Herman, Charlotte 1937- ... CANR-34
Earlier sketches in CA 41-44R, CANR-15
See also SATA 20
Herman, Donald L. 1928- ... CANR-29
Earlier sketches in CA 53-56, CANR-4
Herman, Esther 1935- ... 102
Herman, George E(dward) 1920- ... 69-72
Herman, George R(ichard) 1925- ... 5-8R
Herman, Jan (Jacob) 1942- ... 45-48
Herman, John R(ufus) 1928- ... 119
Herman, Judith 1943- ... 49-52
Herman, Justin B. 1907(?)-1983 Obituary ... 111
Herman, Kenneth Neil 1954- ... 77-80
Herman, Louis Jay 1925- ... 53-56
Herman, Marguerite Shalett 1914-1977 ... 41-44R
Herman, Masako ... 103
Herman, Melvin (Jerome) 1922- Brief entry ... 111
Herman, Melvin 1922(?)-1983 Obituary ... 109
Herman, Michelle 1955- ... 136
Herman, Richard Jr. 1939- ... 137
Herman, Roger E. 1943- ... 128
Herman, Simon N(athan) 1912- ... 29-32R
Herman, Sondra R(enee) 1932- ... 25-28R
Herman, Stanley M. 1928- ... 25-28R
Herman, Vic(tor J.) 1919- ... 107
Herman, Victor 1916(?)-1985 Obituary ... 115
Herman, Walter
See Wager, Walter H(erman)
Herman, William 1926- ... 126
Hermand, Jost 1930- ... CANR-31
Earlier sketches in CA 41-44R, CANR-14

Hermann, Donald H(arold) J(ames) 1943- CANR-17
Earlier sketches in CA 45-48, CANR-2
Hermann, Edward J(ulius) 1919- 17-20R
Hermann, John 1917- 49-52
Hermann, Philip J. 1916- 117
Hermann, (Theodore) Placid 1909- CAP-1
Earlier sketch in CA 13-16
Hermanns, Peter
See Brannon, William T.
Hermanns, William 1895- CANR-15
Earlier sketch in CA 37-40R
Hermans, Willem Frederik 1921- CAP-1
Earlier sketch in CA 9-10
Hermansen, Gustav 1909- 117
Hermansen, John 1918- 45-48
Hermanson, Dennis (Everett) 1947- .... SATA 10
Hermeren, Goeran A. 1938- CANR-15
Earlier sketch in CA 89-92
Hermes
See Flammarion, (Nicolas) Camille
Hermes, Johann Timotheus 1738-1821 .... DLB 97
Hermes, Patricia 1936- CANR-22
Earlier sketch in CA 104
See also SATA 31
Hermlin, Stephen 1915- .... DLB 69
Hern, (George) Anthony 1916- 21-24R
Hern, Nicholas 1944- 115
Hernadi, Paul 1936- CANR-15
Earlier sketch in CA 41-44R
Hernandez, Al 1909- CAP-2
Earlier sketch in CA 21-22
Hernandez, Amado V. 1903-1970 Obituary 112
Hernandez, Frances 1926- 37-40R
Hernandez, Juana Amelia 45-48
Hernandez, Luis F. 1923- 61-64
Hernandez, Pedro F(elix) 1925- 45-48
Hernandez Aquino, Luis 1907- ....HW
Herndl, George C. 1927- 33-36R
Herndon, Booton 1915- CANR-4
Earlier sketch in CA 9-12R
Herndon, James 1926- 89-92
Herndon, Terry (Eugene) 1939- 130
Herndon, Venable 1927- CANR-32
Earlier sketch in CA 109
Herner, Charles H. 1930- 29-32R
Hernes, Helga Maria 1938- CANR-20
Earlier sketch in CA 103
Hernon, Peter 1944- CANR-8
Earlier sketch in CA 61-64
Hernton, Calvin C(oolidge) 1934- CANR-26
Earlier sketches in CA 9-12R, CANR-3
See also BW
See also DLB 38
Hero, Alfred O(livier) Jr. 1924- 21-24R
Herold, Brenda 1948- 33-36R
Herold, J(ean) Christopher 1919-1964 .... CAP-1
Earlier sketch in CA 9-10
Heron, Alasdair I(ain) C(ampbell) 1942- 115
Heron, David Winston 1920- 112
Heron, Laurence Tunstall 1902- 49-52
Heron, Patrick 1920- 109
Heron-Allen, Edward 1861-1943 Brief entry 113
Herpel, George L(loyd) 1921- CANR-15
Earlier sketch in CA 41-44R
Herr, Dan(iel J.) 1917-1990 ....1-4R
Obituary 132
Herr, Edwin L. 1933- 37-40R
Herr, Ethel 1936- 112
Herr, Michael 1940(?)- 89-92
See also MTCW
Herr, Pamela (Staley) 1939- 126
Herr, Richard 1922- 1-4R
Herrera, Juan Felipe 1948- 131
See also HW
Herrera-Sobek, Maria 131
See also HW
Herrera y Reissig, Julio 1875-1910 ....HW
Herrero, Stephen M(atthew) 1939- 118
Herreshoff, David 1921- 21-24R
Herreshoff, L. Francis 1890-1972 .... CAP-1
Obituary 37-40R
Earlier sketch in CA 13-14
Herrick, Bruce Hale 1936- CANR-7
Earlier sketch in CA 17-20R
Herrick, Joy Field 1930- 101
Herrick, Marvin Theodore 1899-1966 ....CANR-1
Earlier sketch in CA 1-4R
Herrick, Neal Q(uentin) 1927- 49-52
Herrick, Robert L(ee) 1930- 61-64
Herrick, Robert (Welch) 1868-1938 Brief entry 119
See also DLB 9, 12, 78
Herrick, Tracy Grant 1933- 112
Herrick, Walter R(ussell) Jr. 1918- 21-24R
Herrick, William 1915- CANR-9
Earlier sketch in CA 21-24R
See also DLBY 83
Herridge, Robert 1914(?)-1981 Obituary 104
Herring, George C. Jr. 1936- CANR-14
Earlier sketch in CA 41-44R
Herring, Hubert Clinton 1889-1967 Obituary 105
Herring, Jack W(illiam) 1925- 115
Herring, Ralph A(lderman) 1901- CAP-2
Earlier sketch in CA 21-22
Herring, Reuben 1922- CANR-7
Earlier sketch in CA 17-20R
Herring, Robert H(erschel) 1938- CANR-21
Earlier sketch in CA 105
Herrington, James L(awrence) 1928- 73-76
Herrington, Pat
See Herrington, Patricia (Murphy)
Herrington, Patricia (Murphy) 1927- 114
Herrington, Stuart A. 1941- 109
Herriot, James
See Wight, James Alfred
See also AAYA 1
See also CLC 12
Herriot, Peter 1939- CANR-25
Earlier sketch in CA 29-32R
Herriott, Robert E. 1929- CANR-7
Earlier sketch in CA 17-20R
Herrmann, Dorothy 1941- 107
See also CLC 44
Herrmann, Frank 1927- CANR-10
Earlier sketch in CA 21-24R
Herrmann, John 1900-1959 Brief entry 107
See also DLB 4
Herrmann, Klaus J(acob) 1929- 37-40R
Herrmann, Luke John 1932- 103
Herrmann, Nina 1943- 77-80
Herrmann, R(obert) L(awrence) 1928- 109
Herrmann, Richard K. 1952- 124
Herrmann, Robert O(mer) 1932- 41-44R
Herrmann, Taffy
See Herrmann, Dorothy
Herrmanns, Ralph 1933- CANR-18
Earlier sketches in CA 9-12R, CANR-3
See also SATA 11
Herrnstadt, Richard L. 1926- 33-36R
Herrnstein, Barbara
See Smith, Barbara Herrnstein
Herrnstein, Richard J(ulius) 1930- Brief entry 107
Herron, Don 1952- CANR-29
Earlier sketch in CA 111
Herron, Edward A(lbert) 1912- 5-8R
See also SATA 4
Herron, Ima Honaker 1899- CAP-2
Earlier sketch in CA 25-28
Herron, Lowell William 1916- 1-4R
Herron, Orley R. Jr. 1933- CANR-12
Earlier sketch in CA 25-28R
Herron, Shaun 1912- 29-32R
Herron, William George 1933- 37-40R
Herschberger, Ruth (Margaret) 1917- 33-36R
Herschensohn, Bruce 1932- 69-72
Herscher, Uri David 1941- 107
Herscovici, Alan 1948- 138
Hersey, George Leonard 1927- 41-44R
Hersey, Jean 1902- CANR-3
Earlier sketch in CA 9-12R
Hersey, John (Richard) 1914- CANR-33
Earlier sketch in CA 17-20R
See also CLC 1, 2, 7, 9, 40
See also DLB 6
See also MTCW
See also SATA 25
Hersey, William Dearborn 1910- CAP-1
Earlier sketch in CA 11-12
Hersh, Burton 1933- 73-76
Hersh, Jacques 1935- 103
Hersh, Reuben 1927- 125
Hersh, Seymour M. 1937- CANR-15
Earlier sketch in CA 73-76
See also AITN 1
Hershan, Stella K. 1915- 33-36R
Hershatter, Richard Lawrence 1923- 81-84
Hershberg, David 1935- 45-48
Hershberger, Hazel Kuhns 5-8R
Hershenson, David Bert 1933- 41-44R
Hershenson, Maurice (Eugene) 1933- 41-44R
Hersher, Leonard 1925- 41-44R
Hershey, Burnet 1896-1971 .... CAP-2
Obituary 33-36R
Earlier sketch in CA 25-28
Hershey, Daniel 1931- CANR-16
Earlier sketch in CA 89-92
Hershey, Ed
See Hershey, Edward (Norman)
Hershey, Edward (Norman) 1944- Brief entry 118
Hershey, Gerald L. 1931- 53-56
Hershey, Lenore 104
Hershey, Nathan 1930- 117
Hershey, Olive 130
Hershey, Robert Delp 1909- 69-72
Hershfield, Harry 1885-1974 Obituary 53-56
Hershhorn, Bernard S(eymour) 1928- 119
Hershkowitz, Leo 1924- 25-28R
Hershman, Morris 1926- CANR-5
Earlier sketch in CA 53-56
Hershon, Robert 1936- CANR-13
Earlier sketch in CA 33-36R
Herskovits, Frances Shapiro 1897-1972 Obituary 33-36R
Herskowitz, Herbert Bennett 1925- 17-20R
Herskowitz, Mickey 81-84
Herst, Herman Jr. 1909- CANR-2
Earlier sketch in CA 1-4R
Herstein, I(srael) N(athan) 1923-1988 Obituary 125
Herstein, Sheila R. 1942- 119
Hertel, Francois 1905-1985 .... DLB 68
Herter, Christian A(rchibald) 1895-1966 Obituary 116
Hertling, G(unter) H. 1930- 41-44R
Hertling, James E. 1935- 93-96
Hertsens, Marcel 1918- 9-12R
Hertweck, Alma Louise 1937- 122
Hertz, Aleksander 1895-1983 Obituary 109
Hertz, David Michael 1954- 125
Hertz, Grete Janus 1915- 101
See also SATA 23
Hertz, Jackoline G. 1920- 69-72
Hertz, Jacky
See Hertz, Jackoline G.
Hertz, Karl H(erbert) 1917- 73-76
Hertz, Leah 1937-1988 Obituary 126
Hertz, Peter Donald 1933- 37-40R
Hertz, Richard C(ornell) 1916- 21-24R
Hertz, Solange (Strong) 1920- 5-8R
Hertzberg, Arthur 1921- 17-20R
Hertzberg, Hazel W(hitman) 1918-1988 73-76
Obituary 126
Hertzberg, Hendrik 1943- 126
Hertzberg, Sidney 1910-1984 Obituary 114
Hertzler, Daniel 1925- 115
Hertzler, Joyce O(ramel) 1895-1975 ....1-4R
Obituary 103
Hertzler, Lois Shank 1927- 57-60
Hertzman, Lewis 1927- 9-12R
Herum, John (Maurice) 1931- 61-64
Herve, Jean-Luc
See Humbaraci, D(emir) Arslan
Herve-Bazin, Jean Pierre Marie 1911- 81-84
See also Bazin, Herve
Hervent, Maurice
See Grindel, Eugene
Hervey, Evelyn
See Keating, H(enry) R(eymond) F(itzwalter)
Hervey, Jane
See McGaw, Naomi Blanche Thoburn
Hervey, John 1696-1743 .... DLB 101
Hervey, Michael 1920- 9-12R
Herwig, Holger H(einrich) 1941- CANR-7
Earlier sketch in CA 61-64
Herz, Irene 1948- 93-96
Herz, Jerome Spencer 45-48
Herz, Jerry
See Herz, Jerome Spencer
Herz, John H(ermann) 1908- 41-44R
Herz, Martin F(lorian) 1917-1983 ....CANR-9
Obituary 111
Earlier sketch in CA 21-24R
Herz, Peggy 1936- 37-40R
Herz, Stephanie M(argarette) 1900- 101
Herzberg, Donald Gabriel 1925-1980 Obituary 101
Herzberg, Joseph Gabriel 1907-1976 Obituary 65-68
Herzberger, Maximillian Jacob 1899-1982 Obituary 106
Herzel, Catherine (Williams) 1908- 5-8R
Herzfeld, Thomas J. 1945- 107
Herzinger, Kim A(llen) 1946- 114
Herzka, Heinz (Stefan) 1935- 37-40R
Herzl, Theodor 1860-1904 .... TCLC 36
Herzog, Arthur (III) 1927- CANR-30
Earlier sketches in CA 17-20R, CANR-9
Herzog, Chaim 1918- 103
Herzog, E.
See Maurois, Andre
Herzog, Frederick 1925- 116
Herzog, Gerard 1920- 104
Herzog, John P(hillip) 1931- 29-32R
Herzog, Kristin (K. H.) 1929- 114
Herzog, Peter Emilius 1925- 125
Herzog, Stephen J(oel) 1938- 33-36R
Herzog, Werner 1942- 89-92
See also CLC 16
Herzstein, Robert Edwin 1940- CANR-7
Earlier sketch in CA 57-60
Hesburgh, Theodore M(artin) 1917- 13-16R
Heschel, Abraham Joshua 1907-1972 ....CANR-4
Obituary 37-40R
Earlier sketch in CA 5-8R
Heseltine, George Coulehan 1895-1980 Obituary 97-100
Heseltine, Nigel 1916- 9-12R
Heskes, Irene 1928- 93-96
Hesketh, (Charles) Peter (Fleetwood) Fleetwood
See Fleetwood-Hesketh, (Charles) Peter (Fleetwood)
Hesketh, Phoebe Rayner 1909- CANR-14
Earlier sketches in CAP-1, CA 9-10
Heskett, J(ames) L(ee) 1933- CANR-8
Earlier sketch in CA 13-16R
Hesky, Olga CAP-2
Obituary 53-56
Earlier sketch in CA 25-28
Hesla, David H(eimarck) 1929- 33-36R
Heslep, Robert D(urham) 1930- 37-40R
Heslin, Jo-Ann 1946- CANR-16
Earlier sketch in CA 93-96
Heslin, Richard 1936- 37-40R
Heslop, J. Malan 1923- 37-40R
Hespro, Herbert
See Robinson, Herbert Spencer
Hess, Albert G(unter) 1909- CAP-1
Earlier sketch in CA 19-20
Hess, Alexander 1898(?)-1981 Obituary 105
Hess, Bartlett L(eonard) 1910- CANR-21
Earlier sketch in CA 61-64
Hess, Beth B(owman) CANR-24
Earlier sketches in CA 65-68, CANR-9
Hess, Earl J(ohn) 1955- 118
Hess, Eckhard H(einrich) 1916-1986 57-60
Obituary 118
Hess, Gary R(ay) 1937- 21-24R
Hess, Hannah S(pier) 1934- 45-48
Hess, Hans 1908-1975 Obituary 53-56
Hess, J(ohn) Daniel 1937- 116
Hess, Joan 1949- 134
Hess, John L(oft) 1917- 102
Hess, John M(ilton) 1929- 21-24R
Hess, Karen 1918- 105
Hess, Karl 1923- 81-84
Hess, Lilo 1916- CANR-12
Earlier sketch in CA 33-36R
See also SATA 4
Hess, Margaret Johnston 1915- CANR-21
Earlier sketches in CA 57-60, CANR-6
Hess, Robert D(aniel) 1920- CANR-13
Earlier sketch in CA 21-24R
Hess, Robert L(ee) 1932-1992 ....29-32R
Obituary 136
Hess, (Walther Richard) Rudolf 1894-1987 Obituary 123
Hess, Stephen 1933- CANR-30
Earlier sketches in CA 17-20R, CANR-10
Hess, Thomas B(aer) 1920-1978 81-84
Obituary 77-80
Hess, William N. 1925- 29-32R
Hesse, Hermann 1877-1962 .... CAP-2
Earlier sketch in CA 17-18
See also CLC 1, 2, 3, 6, 11, 17, 25, 69
See also DLB 66
See also MTCW
See also SATA 50
See also SSC 9
See also WLC
Hesse, Mary (Brenda) 1924- CANR-12
Earlier sketch in CA 17-20R
Hesselgesser, Debra 1939- 69-72
Hesselgrave, David J(ohn) 1924- 81-84
Hesseltine, William Best 1902-1963 ....1-4R
Hessert, Paul 1925- 33-36R
Hessing, Dennis
See Dennis-Jones, H(arold)
Hession, Charles H(enry) 1911- 33-36R
Hession, Roy 1908- 81-84
Hessler, Gene 1928- 73-76
Hesslink, George K. 1940-1980 ....21-24R
Obituary 120
Hest, Amy 1950- 115
See also SATA 55
Hester, Hubert Inman 1895- CANR-5
Earlier sketch in CA 5-8R
Hester, Hugh Bryan 1895-1983 Obituary 111
Hester, James J. 1931- 37-40R
Hester, Kathleen B. 1905- CAP-2
Earlier sketch in CA 19-20
Hester, M(arvin) Thomas 1941- 131
Hester, Marcus B. 1937- 33-36R
Hester, Randolph Thompson Jr. 1944- CANR-34
Earlier sketch in CA 113
Hester, Thomas R(oy) 1946- CANR-32
Earlier sketch in CA 113
Hester, William
See Hester, William C.
Hester, William C. 1934- 129
Hesterman, Vicki 1951- 112
Heston, Alan (Wiley) 1934- 97-100
Heston, Charlton 1924- 110
Brief entry 108
Heston, Edward 1908(?)-1973 Obituary 45-48
Heston, Leonard L(ancaster) 1930- 101
Heth, Meir 1932- 21-24R
Hetherington, (Hector) Alastair 1919- 109
Hetherington, Eileen Mavis (Plenderleith) 1926- 115
Hetherington, Hugh W(illiam) 1903- 5-8R
Hetherington, John (Aikman) 1907-1974 93-96
Obituary 53-56
Hetherington, Norriss Swigart 1942- 126
Hethmon, Robert H(enry) 1925- 13-16R
Hettinger, Herman Strecker 1902-1972 Obituary 37-40R
Hettlinger, Richard F(rederick) 1920- CANR-7
Earlier sketch in CA 17-20R
Hetzell, Margaret Carol 1917-1978 85-88
Obituary 81-84
Hetzler, Florence M(ary) 1926- CANR-25
Earlier sketch in CA 107
Hetzler, Stanley Arthur 1919- 37-40R
Hetzron, Robert 1937- 33-36R
Heuer, John (Michael) 1941- CANR-14
Earlier sketch in CA 69-72
Heuer, Kenneth John 1927- CANR-30
Earlier sketch in CA 110
See also SATA 44
Heuman, William 1912-1971 ....CANR-7
Earlier sketch in CA 5-8R
See also SATA 21
Heumann, Milton 1947- 110
Heuscher, Julius E(rnst) 1918- 9-12R
Heuser, Beatrice 1961- 138
Heuss, John 1908-1966 .... CAP-1
Earlier sketch in CA 9-10
Heussler, Robert 1924- CANR-8
Earlier sketch in CA 5-8R
Heussner, Ralph C(lyde) Jr. 1949- 119
Heuterman, Thomas H(enry) 1934- 101
Heuvelmans, Bernard (Joseph Pierre) 1916- 97-100
Heuvelmans, Martin 1903- 49-52
Heuving, Jeanne 1951- 138
Heuyer, Georges 1884-1977 Obituary 73-76
Hevener, John W(atts) 1933- 103
Heward, Edmund (Rawlings) 1912- 93-96
Heward, William L(ee) 1949- CANR-4
Earlier sketch in CA 53-56
Hewat, Alexander 1743(?)-1824 .... DLB 30
Hewens, Frank Edgar 1912- 45-48
Hewer, Humphrey Robert 1903-1974 Obituary 105
Hewes, Agnes Danforth 1874-1963 Obituary 113
See also SATA 35
Hewes, Cady
See De Voto, Bernard (Augustine)
Hewes, Dorothy W. 1922- 37-40R
Hewes, Hayden 1943- 85-88
Hewes, Henry 1917- 13-16R
Hewes, Jeremy Joan 1944- 77-80
Hewes, Laurence (Ilsley) 1902- 105
Hewes, Leslie 1906- 41-44R
Hewett, Anita 1918- 21-24R
See also SATA 13
Hewett, Dorothy Coade 1923- 97-100
Hewett, John H(arris) 1952- 115
Hewett, William S. 1924- 21-24R

Hewins, Geoffrey Shaw 1889- CAP-1
Earlier sketch in CA 9-10
Hewins, Ralph Anthony 1909-1984(?) CAP-1
Obituary 112
Earlier sketch in CA 9-10
Hewison, Robert 1943- 81-84
Hewitson, John Nelson 1917- 29-32R
Hewitt, Arthur Wentworth 1883- 69-72
Hewitt, Bernard (Wolcott) 1906- 13-16R
Hewitt, Cecil Rolph 1901- CANR-18
Earlier sketch in CA 102
Hewitt, David (Sword) 1942- 118
Hewitt, Don (S.) 1922- Brief entry 119
Hewitt, Emily Clark 1944- CANR-2
Earlier sketch in CA 45-48
Hewitt, Foster (William)
1903(?)-1985 Obituary 115
Hewitt, Garnet (William) 1939- 110
Hewitt, Geof (George F.) 1943- 33-36R
Hewitt, H(erbert) J(ames) 1890- 13-16R
Hewitt, James 1928- CANR-21
Earlier sketches in CA 57-60, CANR-6
Hewitt, Jean D(aphne) 1925- 77-80
Hewitt, John (Harold) 1907-1987 ....CANR-16
Obituary 123
Earlier sketch in CA 97-100
See also DLB 27
Hewitt, John P(aul) 1941- 53-56
Hewitt, Nicholas 1945- 132
Hewitt, Philip Nigel 1945- 81-84
Hewitt, Robert L. 1917(?)-1983 Obituary 111
Hewitt, Sue Whitsett
1919(?)-1984 Obituary 111
Hewitt, William Henry 1936- 17-20R
Hewlett, Dorothy Obituary 85-88
Hewlett, Frank West
1909(?)-1983 Obituary 110
Hewlett, Maurice (Henry)
1861-1923 Brief entry 121
See also DLB 34
Hewlett, Richard Greening 1923- 9-12R
Hewlett, Roger S. 1911(?)-1977 Obituary 73-76
Hewlett, Sylvia Ann 1946- 123
Brief entry 118
Hewlett, Virginia B.
1912(?)-1979 Obituary 85-88
Hewson, John 1930- 37-40R
Hewton, Eric 1934- 126
Hexham, Irving 1943- 125
Hexner, Ervin Paul 1893-1968 ....5-8R
Obituary 103
Hext, Harrington
See Phillpotts, Eden
Hextall, David
See Phillips-Birt, Douglas Hextall Chedzey
Hexter, J(ack) H. 1910- 13-16R
Hey, John D(enis) 1944- 106
Hey, Nigel S(tewart) 1936- 33-36R
See also SATA 20
Hey, Robert P(ierpont) 1935- 133
Heyd, David 1945- 118
Heydenburg, Harry E.
1891(?)-1979 Obituary 89-92
Heydenreich, Ludwig Heinrich
1903- Brief entry 105
Heydon, Peter Richard 1913-1971 .... CAP-1
Earlier sketch in CA 19-20
Heydron, Vicki Ann 1945- 131
Heyduck-Huth, Hilde 1929- 57-60
See also SATA 8
Heyel, Carl 1908- CANR-22
Earlier sketches in CA 17-20R, CANR-7
Heyen, William 1940- 33-36R
See also CAAS 9
See also CLC 13, 18
See also DLB 5
Heyer, Carol 1950- 130
Heyer, Georgette 1902-1974 93-96
Obituary 49-52
See also DLB 77
See also MTCW
Heyer, Marilee 1942- 125
See also SATA 64
Heyerdahl, Thor 1914- CANR-22
Earlier sketches in CA 5-8R, CANR-5
See also CLC 26
See also MTCW
See also SATA 2, 52
Heyler, David B. Sr. 1905(?)-1983 Obituary 110
Heyliger, William 1884-1955 .... YABC 1
Heylin, Clinton (M.) 1960- 135
Heym, Georg (Theodor Franz Arthur)
1887-1912 Brief entry 106
See also TCLC 9
Heym, Stefan 1913- CANR-4
Earlier sketch in CA 9-12R
See also CLC 41
See also DLB 69
Heyman, Abigail 1942- 57-60
Heyman, Ken(neth Louis) 1930- 112
See also SATA 34
Heyman, Neil Michael 1937- 113
Heymann, C. David
See Heymann, Clemens Claude
See also BEST 89:4
Heymann, Clemens Claude 1945- 129
See also Heymann, C. David
Heymann, Frederick Gotthold
1900-1983 Obituary 111
Heymann, Thomas N. 1958- 135
Heymann, Tom
See Heymann, Thomas N.
Heymanns, Betty 1932- 85-88
Heymanson, Randal 1903-1984 Obituary 113
Heyn, Ernest V(ictor) 1904- 134
Brief entry 111
Heyne, Paul 1931- 89-92
Heynen, Jim 1940- 77-80
Heyns, Barbara 1943- 85-88
Heyrman, Christine Leigh 1950- 115
Heyse, Paul (Johann Ludwig von)
1830-1914 Brief entry 104
See also TCLC 8
Heyst, Axel
See Grabowski, Z(bigniew) Anthony
Heytesbury, William 1310(?)-1372(?) ..... DLB 115
Heyward, Carter 1945- 65-68
Heyward, Dorothy (Hartzell Kuhns)
1890-1961 Obituary 112
See also DLB 7
Heyward, (Edwin) DuBose
1885-1940 Brief entry 108
See also DLB 7, 9, 45
See also SATA 21
Heywood, Christopher 1928- 41-44R
Heywood, Colin 1947- 130
Heywood, Hugh Christopher Lempriere
1896-1987 Obituary 122
Heywood, Joe T.
See Heywood, Joseph (T.)
Heywood, Joseph (T.) 1943- 134
Brief entry 128
Heywood, Karen 1946- .... SATA 48
Heywood, Lorimer D.
1899(?)-1977 Obituary 73-76
Heywood, Philip 1938- 69-72
Heywood, Rosalind 1895- 89-92
Heywood, Terence CAP-1
Earlier sketch in CA 9-10
Heywood, Thomas 1573(?)-1641 .... DLB 62
Heyworth, Laurence 1955- 134
Heyworth, Peter (Lawrence Frederick)
1921-1991 65-68
Obituary 135
Heyworth-Dunne, James Obituary 53-56
Hezel, Francis X(avier) 1939- 118
Hiaasen, Carl 1953- CANR-22
Earlier sketch in CA 105
Hian
See Higginson, William J(ohn)
Hiat, Elchik
See Katz, Menke
Hiatt, Howard H(aym) 1925- 133
Hibbard, George Richard 1915- 85-88
Hibbard, Howard 1928-1984 ....CANR-9
Obituary 114
Earlier sketch in CA 53-56
Hibben, Frank Cummings 1910- CANR-2
Earlier sketch in CA 1-4R
Hibberd, Andrew Stuart
1893-1983(?) Obituary 111
Hibberd, Jack 1940- 103
Hibbert, Alun 1949- 130
Hibbert, Christopher 1924- CANR-2
Earlier sketch in CA 1-4R
See also SATA 4
Hibbert, Eleanor Burford 1906- CANR-28
Earlier sketches in CA 17-20R, CANR-9
See also BEST 90:4
See also CLC 7
See also SATA 2
Hibbett, Howard (Scott) 1920- 106
Hibbs, Ben 1901-1975 65-68
Obituary 104
Hibbs, Douglas A(lbert) Jr. 1944- CANR-3
Earlier sketch in CA 49-52
Hibbs, John 1925- CANR-19
Earlier sketch in CA 103
Hibbs, Paul 1906- CAP-1
Earlier sketch in CA 13-16
Hibdon, James E(dward) 1924- 25-28R
Hick, John (Harwood) 1922- CANR-22
Earlier sketches in CA 9-12R, CANR-6
Hickel, Walter J(oseph) 1919- 41-44R
Hicken, Mandy
See Hicken, Marilyn E.
Hicken, Marilyn E. 1937- 135
Hicken, Victor 1921- 21-24R
Hickerson, J(ohn) Mel(ancthon) 1897- 25-28R
Hickey, Edward Shelby 1928(?)-1978 85-88
Obituary 81-84
Hickey, Joseph J(ames) 1907- 41-44R
Hickey, Michael 1929- 102
Hickey, Neil 1931- 1-4R
Hickey, Raymond 1936- CANR-37
Earlier sketch in CA 114
Hickey, William
See Driberg, Thomas Edward Neil
Hickford, Jessie 1911- 53-56
Hickin, Norman E(rnest) 1910- CANR-15
Earlier sketch in CA 85-88
Hickinbotham, Tom 1903-1983 Obituary 111
Hickler, Holly 1923- 117
Hickling, C(harles) F(rederick)
1902-1977 Obituary 117
Hickman, Bert G(eorge) Jr. 1924- 108
Hickman, C(harles) Addison 1916- 103
Hickman, Charles 1905-1983 Obituary 109
Hickman, (Gertrud) Hannah 1928- 123
Hickman, Hoyt L(eon) 1927- 121
Hickman, Janet 1940- CANR-10
Earlier sketch in CA 65-68
See also SATA 12
Hickman, Katie 1960- 128
Hickman, Martha Whitmore 1925- CANR-26
Earlier sketches in CA 25-28R, CANR-10
See also SATA 26
Hickman, Martin B(erkeley) 1925- 65-68
Hickman, Peggy 1906- 73-76
Hickman, Tracy Raye 1955- 126
Hickman, William Albert 1877-1957 .... DLB 92
Hickok, Dorothy Jane 1912- 73-76
Hickok, Lorena A. 1892(?)-1968 73-76
See also SATA 20
Hickok, Robert (Blair) 1927- 61-64
Hickok, Will
See Harrison, C. William
Hicks, Charles B(alch) 1916- 5-8R
Hicks, Clifford B. 1920- CANR-24
Earlier sketches in CA 5-8R, CANR-9
See also SATA 50
Hicks, Darryl E(dwin) 1948- 120
Hicks, David E. 1931- CANR-7
Earlier sketch in CA 9-12R
Hicks, Donald A(lbert) 1947- 111
Hicks, Eleanor B.
See Coerr, Eleanor (Beatrice)
Hicks, George L(eon) 1935- 65-68
Hicks, Granville 1901-1982 ....CANR-13
Obituary 107
Earlier sketch in CA 9-12R
Hicks, Harvey
See Stratemeyer, Edward L.
Hicks, J. L.
See Hicks, Jim(my Lyn)
Hicks, Jack 1942- 97-100
Hicks, James L. 1915(?)-1986 Obituary 118
Hicks, Jim(my Lyn) 1937- 107
Hicks, John D(onald) 1890-1972 ....CANR-2
Earlier sketch in CA 1-4R
Hicks, John Edward 1890(?)-1971 Obituary 104
Hicks, John H(arland) 1919- 45-48
Hicks, John (Kenneth) 1918- 25-28R
Hicks, John (Richard) 1904-1989 ....CANR-13
Obituary 128
Earlier sketch in CA 65-68
Hicks, John V(ictor) 1907- CANR-30
Earlier sketch in CA 110
Hicks, Raymond L. 1926- 61-64
Hicks, Robert E(lden) 1920- Brief entry 109
Hicks, Roger W(illiam) 1950- 124
Hicks, Ronald G(raydon) 1934- 73-76
Hicks, Thomas 1936- 129
Hicks, Tyler Gregory 1921- 103
Hicks, Ursula Kathleen (Webb) 1896-1985 103
Obituary 117
Hicks, Warren B(raukman) 1921- 33-36R
Hicks, Wilson 1897-1970 Obituary 29-32R
Hicky, Daniel Whitehead 1902- .... AITN 1
Hicyilmaz, Gay 1947- 133
Hidalgo, Jose Luis 1919-1947 .... DLB 108
Hidden, (Frederick) Norman 1913- 77-80
Hidore, John J. 1932- CANR-21
Earlier sketches in CA 57-60, CANR-6
Hidy, Muriel E(mmie) 1906- 97-100
Hidy, Ralph W(illard) 1905- 5-8R
Hieatt, A(llen) Kent 1921- 21-24R
Hieatt, Constance B(artlett) 1928- CANR-23
Earlier sketches in CA 5-8R, CANR-8
See also SATA 4
Hiebel, Friedrich 1903- CANR-11
Earlier sketch in CA 65-68
Hiebert, Clarence 1927- 61-64
Hiebert, D(avid) Edmond 1910- 17-20R
Hiebert, Paul (Gerhardt) 1892-1987 ......CANR-17
Earlier sketches in CAP-2, CA 23-24
See also DLB 68
Hiebert, Ray Eldon 1932- CANR-7
Earlier sketch in CA 17-20R
See also SATA 13
Hiernaux, Jean 1921- 57-60
Hieronymus, Clara (Booth) 1913- 73-76
Hierro, Jose 1922- .... DLB 108
Hiers, John Turner 1945- 102
Hiers, Richard H(yde) 1932- 53-56
Hiesberger, Jean Marie 1941- 41-44R
Hiesinger, Kathryn B(loom) 1943- 119
Hiestand, Dale L(eroy) 1925- 41-44R
Hiestand, Emily (L.) 1947- 134
Hifler, Joyce (Sequichie) 1925- 21-24R
Higashiuchi, Yoshio 1915(?)-1987 Obituary 122
Higbe, (Walter) Kirby 1915-1985 Obituary 116
Higbee, Edward (Counselman) 1910- 13-16R
Higbee, Kenneth Leo 1941- 101
Higby, Mary Jane 25-28R
Higdon, David Leon 1939- 77-80
Higdon, Hal 1931- CANR-3
Earlier sketch in CA 9-12R
See also SATA 4
Higenbottam, Frank 1910-1982 ....25-28R
Obituary 117
Higgie, Lincoln William 1938- 5-8R
Higginbotham, A(loysius) Leon Jr. 1928- 110
Higginbotham, (Prieur) Jay 1937- CANR-37
Earlier sketches in CA 93-96, CANR-17
Higginbotham, John E. 1933- 29-32R
Higginbotham, R(obert) Don 1931- 17-20R
Higginbotham, Sanford Wilson
1913- Brief entry 105
Higginbotham, Virginia 1935- 115
Brief entry 110
Higginbottom, J(effrey) Winslow
1945- .... SATA 29
Higgins, A(lbert) C(orbin) 1930- 37-40R
Higgins, A(ngus) J(ohn) B(rockhurst)
1911- 13-16R
Higgins, Aidan 1927- 9-12R
See also DLB 14
Higgins, Alice 1924(?)-1974 Obituary 53-56
Higgins, Chester (Archer Jr.) 1946- 73-76
Higgins, Colin 1941-1988 ....CANR-30
Obituary 126
Earlier sketch in CA 33-36R
See also DLB 26
Higgins, D. S(ydney) 1938- 132
Higgins, Dick
See Higgins, Richard C(arter)
See also CAAS 8
Higgins, Don 1928- CANR-14
Earlier sketch in CA 25-28R
Higgins, George V(incent) 1939- CANR-17
Earlier sketch in CA 77-80
See also CAAS 5
See also CLC 4, 7, 10, 18
See also DLB 2
See also DLBY 81
See also MTCW
Higgins, Ink
See Weiss, Morris S(amuel)
Higgins, Jack
See Patterson, Harry
See also BEST 89:3
Higgins, James E(dward) 1926- 73-76
Higgins, Jean C. 1932- 29-32R
Higgins, Joan 1948- 125
Higgins, John A(loysius) 1931- CANR-13
Earlier sketch in CA 77-80
Higgins, John C(layborn) 1934- 132
Higgins, John J(oseph) 1935- 45-48
Higgins, John 1934- 138
Higgins, Judith Holden 1930- 102
Higgins, Kathleen M(arie) 1954- 138
Higgins, Lionel G(eorge) 1891-1985 123
Higgins, Marguerite 1920-1966 ....5-8R
Obituary 25-28R
Higgins, Paul C. 1950- 106
Higgins, Paul Lambourne 1916- CANR-17
Earlier sketches in CA 1-4R, CANR-2
Higgins, Reynold Alleyne 1916- 25-28R
Higgins, Richard C(arter) 1938- CANR-29
Earlier sketches in CA 13-16R, CANR-8
See also Higgins, Dick
Higgins, Ronald 1929- 81-84
Higgins, Rosalyn (Cohen) 1937- CANR-3
Earlier sketch in CA 9-12R
Higgins, Thomas J(oseph) 1899- CANR-5
Earlier sketch in CA 1-4R
Higgins, Trumbull 1919-1990 ....17-20R
Obituary 131
Higgins, W(illiam) Robert 1938- 37-40R
Higgins, William R(eynolds) 1935- 128
Higginson, Fred H(all) 1921- 1-4R
Higginson, Margaret V(alliant) 1923- 105
Higginson, Thomas Wentworth
1823-1911 .... DLB 1, 64
See also TCLC 36
Higginson, William J(ohn) 1938- 123
Higgs, David (Clive) 1939- 61-64
Higgs, E(ric) S(idney) 1908-1976 ....9-12R
Obituary 69-72
Higgs, Gerald B. 1921- 106
Higgs, Gertrude Monro
See Monro-Higgs, Gertrude
Higgs, Robert J(ackson) 1932- 115
High, Dallas M. 1931- 21-24R
High, Monique Raphel 1949- CANR-21
Earlier sketch in CA 102
High, Philip E(mpson) 1914- 97-100
High, Stanley (Hoflund)
1895-1961 Obituary 89-92
Higham, Charles 1931- CANR-17
Earlier sketch in CA 33-36R
See also BEST 89:1
Higham, David (Michael) 1949- 126
See also SATA 50
Higham, David 1895-1978 ....CANR-2
Earlier sketch in CA 1-4R
Higham, Florence May Grier
1896-1980 Obituary 97-100
Higham, John 1920- CANR-6
Earlier sketch in CA 1-4R
Higham, Jon Atlas
See Higham, Jonathan Huw
Higham, Jonathan Huw 1960- 127
See also SATA 59
Higham, Robin (David Stewart) 1925- CANR-31
Earlier sketches in CA 1-4R, CANR-1
Higham, Roger 1935- 33-36R
Higham, T. F.
See Higham, Thomas Farrant
Higham, Thomas Farrant
1890-1975 Obituary 116
Highberger, Ruth 1917- 65-68
Highet, Gilbert (Arthur) 1906-1978 ....CANR-6
Obituary 73-76
Earlier sketch in CA 1-4R
Highet, Helen
See MacInnes, Helen (Clark)
Highfield, (John) Roger (Loxdale) 1922- 130
Highland, Dora
See Avallone, Michael (Angelo, Jr)
Highland, Monica
See Kendall, Lisa See
Highland, Monica
See Espey, John (Jenkins)
and Kendall, Lisa See
and See, Carolyn (Penelope)
Highsmith, (Mary) Patricia 1921- CANR-20
Earlier sketches in CA 1-4R, CANR-1
See also CLC 2, 4, 14, 42
See also MTCW
Highsmith, Richard M(organ) Jr. 1920- 37-40R
Hightower, Florence Cole 1916-1981 .....CANR-35
Obituary 103
Earlier sketch in CA 1-4R
See also SATA 4, 27
Hightower, John M(urmann)
1909-1987 Obituary 121
Hightower, Paul
See Collins, Thomas Hightower

Highwater, Jamake (Mamake)
1942(?)- ... CANR-34
Earlier sketches in CA 65-68, CANR-10
See also CAAS 7
See also AAYA 7
See also CLC 12
See also CLR 17
See also DLB 52
See also DLBY 85
See also MAICYA
See also SATA 30, 32, 69
Higley, John (Clark) 1938- Brief entry ... 116
Higman, B(arry) W(illiam) 1943- ... 81-84
Higman, Francis M(ontgomery) 1935- ... CANR-12
Earlier sketch in CA 25-28R
Hignett, Sean 1934- ... 49-52
Higonnet, Margaret Randolph 1941- ... 61-64
Higonnet, Patrice Louis-Rene 1938- ... 65-68
Higson, James D(oran) 1925- ... 49-52
Hijirida, Kyoko 1937- ... 126
Hijuelos, Oscar 1951- ... 123
See also BEST 90:1
See also CLC 65
See also HW
Hikmet, Nazim 1902-1963 Obituary ... 93-96
See also CLC 40
Hilary, Christopher
1927(?)-1979 Obituary ... 89-92
Hilberg, Raul 1926- ... 33-36R
Hilberry, Conrad (Arthur) 1928- ... CANR-10
Earlier sketch in CA 25-28R
See also DLB 120
Hilborn, Ann 1942- ... 109
Hilborn, Harry (Warren) 1900- ... CAP-2
Earlier sketch in CA 33-36
Hild, Jack
See Garside, (Clifford) Jack
Hild, Jack
See Preston, John
Hildebidle, John 1946- ... 114
Hildebrand, George H(erbert) 1913- ... CANR-8
Earlier sketch in CA 17-20R
Hildebrand, Grant 1934- ... 57-60
Hildebrand, Joel H(enry) 1881-1983 ... CAP-1
Obituary ... 109
Earlier sketch in CA 11-12
Hildebrand, John 1949- ... 131
Hildebrand, Verna 1924- ... CANR-28
Earlier sketches in CA 33-36R, CANR-13
Hildebrandt, Franz 1909-1985 ... 118
Hildebrandt, Greg 1939- ... 104
See also SATA 33, 55
Hildebrandt, Tim(othy) 1939- ... 122
Brief entry ... 111
See also SATA 33, 55
Hildebrandts, The
See Hildebrandt, Tim(othy)
Hilder, Rowland 1905- ... SATA 36
Hilderbrand, Robert Clinton 1947- ... 105
Hildesheimer, Wolfgang 1916-1991 ... 101
Obituary ... 135
See also CLC 49
See also DLB 69
Hildick, E. W.
See Hildick, (Edmund) Wallace
See also SAAS 6
Hildick, (Edmund) Wallace 1925- ... 25-28R
See also Hildick, E. W.
See also MAICYA
See also SATA 2, 68
Hildreth, Gertrude Howell
1898-1984 Obituary ... 112
Hildreth, Margaret Holbrook 1927- ... 89-92
Hildreth, Richard 1807-1865 ... DLB 1, 30, 59
Hildum, Donald C(layton) 1930- ... 21-24R
Hildyard, Nicholas 1955- ... 122
Hilfer, Anthony Channell 1936- ... 73-76
Hilfiker, David 1945- ... 123
Hilgard, Ernest R(opiequet) 1904- ... CANR-32
Earlier sketch in CA 113
Hilgartner, Beth 1957- ... SATA 58
Hilgartner, Stephen 1956- ... 111
Hilger, Sister Mary Inez 1891-1977 ... 73-76
Hilken, Glen A. 1936-1976 ... 61-64
Obituary ... 134
Hill, Aaron 1685-1750 ... DLB 84
Hill, Ab
See Hill, Abram (Barrington)
Hill, Abram (Barrington)
1910(?)-1986 Obituary ... 120
Hill, Adrian Keith Graham 1895-1977 ... CANR-29
Earlier sketch in CA 77-80
Hill, Alexis
See Craig, Mary (Francis) Shura
and Glick, Ruth (Burtnick)
Hill, Alfred T(uxbury) 1908- ... 21-24R
Hill, Archibald A(nderson) 1902- ... 49-52
Hill, Arthur Norman 1920(?)-1988 Obituary ... 125
Hill, Barrington Julian Warren 1915- ... 5-8R
Hill, Bennett D(avid) 1934- ... 111
Hill, Bob
See Hill, Robert C(ecil)
Hill, Brian (Merrikin) 1896- ... CAP-1
Earlier sketch in CA 9-10
Hill, Carol (Dechellis) 1942- ... 77-80
Hill, Charles William Jr. 1940- ... 125
Hill, Charles 1904-1989 Obituary ... 129
Hill, (John Edward) Christopher 1912- ... CANR-22
Earlier sketches in CA 9-12R, CANR-4
Hill, Christopher R. 1935- ... 128
Hill, Claude 1911-1991 ... 21-24R
Obituary ... 136
Hill, Clifford S. 1927- ... CANR-27
Earlier sketches in CA 13-16R, CANR-7
Hill, Daniel G. Jr. 1896(?)-1979 Obituary ... 89-92
Hill, Dave
See Hill, David John
Hill, Dave
See Hill, David Charles
Hill, David Charles 1936- ... CANR-11
Earlier sketch in CA 17-20R
Hill, David John 1958- ... 132
Hill, Deborah 1936- ... 108
Hill, Dee
See Zucker, Dolores Mae Bolton
Hill, Denise 1919- ... CANR-23
Earlier sketch in CA 106
Hill, (Richard) Desmond 1920-1984 ... 5-8R
Obituary ... 114
Hill, Devra Z.
See Zucker, Dolores Mae Bolton
Hill, Dilys M(ary) 1935- ... 61-64
Hill, Donald Hamilton
See Hamilton-Hill, Donald
Hill, Donald (Routledge) 1922- ... 122
Hill, Donna (Marie) ... CANR-25
Earlier sketches in CA 13-16R, CANR-7
See also SATA 24
Hill, Douglas (Arthur) 1935- ... CANR-4
Earlier sketch in CA 53-56
See also SATA 39
Hill, Draper
See Hill, L(eroy) Draper Jr.
Hill, Earle 1941- ... 33-36R
Hill, Eileen
See Stack, Nicolete Meredith
Hill, Elizabeth Starr 1925- ... CANR-31
Earlier sketch in CA 17-20R
See also SATA 24
Hill, Ellen Wise 1942- ... 77-80
Hill, Eric 1927- ... 134
See also CLR 13
See also MAICYA
See also SATA 53, 66
Hill, Ernest 1915- ... 53-56
Hill, Errol Gaston 1921- ... CANR-26
Earlier sketch in CA 45-48
See also BW
Hill, Evan 1919- ... CANR-5
Earlier sketch in CA 9-12R
Hill, Fiona
See Pall, Ellen Jane
Hill, (Charles) Fowler
1901(?)-1973 Obituary ... 37-40R
Hill, (James William) Francis
1899-1980 Obituary ... 108
Hill, Frank Ernest 1888-1969 ... 73-76
Hill, Gene 1928- ... 97-100
Hill, Geoffrey (William) 1932- ... CANR-21
Earlier sketch in CA 81-84
See also CDBLB 1960 to Present
See also CLC 5, 8, 18, 45
See also DLB 40
See also MTCW
Hill, George E(dward) 1907- ... CAP-1
Earlier sketch in CA 17-18
Hill, George Roy 1921- ... 122
Brief entry ... 110
See also CLC 26
Hill, Gladwin 1914- ... 25-28R
Hill, Grace Brooks ... CANR-26
Earlier sketches in CAP-2, CA 19-20
See also SATA 1, 67
Hill, Grace Livingston 1865-1947 ... YABC 2
Hill, (Norman) Graham 1929-1975 Obituary ... 108
Hill, H. D. N.
See Disston, Harry
Hill, Hamlin (Lewis) 1931- ... CANR-18
Earlier sketches in CA 9-12R, CANR-3
Hill, Harold E(verett) 1905- ... CANR-11
Earlier sketch in CA 69-72
Hill, Helen
See Miller, Helen Hill
Hill, Helen M(orey) 1915- ... 57-60
See also SATA 27
Hill, Henry Bertram 1907- ... 1-4R
Hill, Herbert 1924- ... 65-68
Hill, Hyacinthe
See Anderson, Virginia (R. Cronin)
Hill, I(saac) William 1908- ... 65-68
Hill, J(ohn) C(ampbell) 1888- ... 37-40R
Hill, James
See Jameson, (Margaret) Storm
Hill, James N(ewlin) 1934- ... 33-36R
Hill, Jane Bowers 1950- ... 126
Hill, Jim Dan 1897- ... CAP-1
Earlier sketch in CA 11-12
Hill, John
See Koontz, Dean R(ay)
Hill, John Hugh 1905- ... CANR-5
Earlier sketch in CA 1-4R
Hill, John L. 1960- ... 124
Hill, John P(aul) 1936- ... 29-32R
Hill, John S(tanley) 1929- ... 37-40R
Hill, John Wiley 1890-1977 Obituary ... 69-72
Hill, Johnson
See Kunhardt, Edith
Hill, Kathleen Louise 1917- ... CANR-3
Earlier sketch in CA 9-12R
See also SATA 4
Hill, Kay
See Hill, Kathleen Louise
Hill, Ken(neth) 1937- ... 108
Hill, King
See Robertson, Frank C(hester)
Hill, Knox C(alvin) 1910- ... CAP-1
Earlier sketch in CA 19-20
Hill, L(eslie) A(lexander) 1918- ... 21-24R
Hill, L(eroy) Draper Jr. 1935- ... CANR-12
Earlier sketch in CA 17-20R
Hill, Larry D(ean) 1935- ... 73-76
Hill, Lawrence 1912-1988 Obituary ... 125
Hill, Lawson (Traphagen) 1927- ... 118
Hill, Lee H(alsey) 1899-1974 ... 37-40R
Obituary ... 45-48
Hill, Leslie Pinckney 1880-1960 ... 125
See also BW
See also DLB 51
Hill, Lew
See Skene-Melvin, (Lewis) David (St. Columb)
Hill, Lorna 1902- ... CANR-14
Earlier sketches in CAP-1, CA 9-10
See also SATA 12
Hill, Lowell Dean 1930- ... 114
Hill, M(elba) Anne 1953- ... 123
Hill, Malcolm R(onald) 1942- ... 130
Hill, Margaret (Ohler) 1915- ... CANR-16
Earlier sketches in CA 1-4R, CANR-1
See also SATA 36
Hill, Marnesba D. 1913- ... 101
Hill, Marvin S(idney) 1928- ... 61-64
Hill, Mary A. 1939- ... 102
Hill, Mary Raymond 1923- ... CANR-6
Earlier sketch in CA 57-60
Hill, Mary V. 1941- ... 102
Hill, Meg
See Hill, Margaret (Ohler)
Hill, Meredith
See Craig, Mary (Francis) Shura
Hill, Mike 1944- ... 122
Hill, Monica
See Watson, Jane Werner
Hill, Nancy Klenk 1936- ... 108
Hill, Napoleon 1883(?)-1970 Obituary ... 104
Hill, Nellie
See Hill, Ellen Wise
Hill, Norman Llewellyn 1895- ... 5-8R
Hill, Pamela 1920- ... CANR-37
Earlier sketches in CA 49-52, CANR-1, 16
Hill, Pati ... 69-72
Hill, Peter Proal 1926- ... 33-36R
Hill, Philip G(eorge) 1934- ... 33-36R
Hill, Polly
See Humphreys, Mary Eglantyne Hill
Hill, R(ufus) Carter 1945- ... 110
Hill, R. Lance 1943- ... CANR-11
Earlier sketch in CA 65-68
Hill, Ralph Nading 1917-1987 ... CANR-1
Obituary ... 124
Earlier sketch in CA 1-4R
See also SATA 65
Hill, Rebecca 1944- ... 111
Hill, Reginald (Charles) 1936- ... CANR-32
Earlier sketch in CA 73-76
Hill, Reuben (Lorenzo Jr.) 1912-1985 ... 131
Obituary ... 117
Hill, Richard E. 1920- ... 33-36R
Hill, Richard (Fontaine) 1941- ... 33-36R
Hill, Richard Johnson 1925- ... CANR-4
Earlier sketch in CA 9-12R
Hill, Richard 1901- ... CANR-1
Earlier sketch in CA 1-4R
Hill, Robert A. 1943- ... 132
Hill, Robert C(ecil) 1929- ... 118
Hill, Robert W(hite) 1919-1982 ... 9-12R
Obituary ... 107
See also SATA 12, 31
Hill, Roger
See Paine, Lauran (Bosworth)
Hill, Rosalind M(ary) T(heodosia) 1908- ... CAP-1
Earlier sketch in CA 11-12
Hill, Roscoe E(arl) 1936- ... 37-40R
Hill, Rowland
See Wallace-Clarke, George
Hill, Roy Gerald 1926- ... 111
Hill, Ruth A.
See Viguers, Ruth Hill
Hill, Ruth Beebe 1913- ... 89-92
Hill, Ruth Livingston
See Munce, Ruth Hill
Hill, Samuel E(rvin) 1913- ... 17-20R
Hill, Samuel S(mythe) Jr. 1927- ... CANR-5
Earlier sketch in CA 9-12R
Hill, Selima 1945- ... 117
Hill, "Sir" John 1714(?)-1775 ... DLB 39
Hill, Stephen 1946- ... 111
Hill, Susan (Elizabeth) 1942- ... CANR-29
Earlier sketch in CA 33-36R
See also CLC 4
See also DLB 14
See also MTCW
Hill, Thomas E(nglish) Jr. 1937- ... 137
Hill, Thomas English 1909- ... 13-16R
Hill, Thomas 1960- ... 135
Hill, W. M.
See Dodd, Edward Howard Jr.
Hill, W(illiam) Speed 1935- ... 41-44R
Hill, Walter 1942- Brief entry ... 109
See also DLB 44
Hill, Weldon
See Scott, William R(alph)
Hill, West T(hompson) Jr. 1915- ... 37-40R
Hill, Wilhelmina 1902- ... 57-60
Hill, William Joseph 1924- ... 37-40R
Hill, Winfred F(arrington) 1929- ... 29-32R
Hillaby, John (D.) 1917- Brief entry ... 109
Hillam, Ray C. 1928- Brief entry ... 107
Hillard, Darla 1946- ... 135
Hillard, James M(ilton) 1920- ... 73-76
Hillary, Edmund (Percival) 1919- ... 112
Hillary, Peter 1954- ... 123
Hillas, Julian
See Dashwood, Robert Julian
Hillbruner, Anthony 1914- ... 41-44R
Hillcourt, William 1900- ... 93-96
See also SATA 27
Hillegas, Mark R(obert) 1926- ... 33-36R
Hillel, Yehoshua Bar
See Bar-Hillel, Yehoshua
Hillenbrand, Barry R. 1941- ... 73-76
Hillenbrand, Martin Joseph 1915- ... 108
Hiller, Catherine 1946- ... 106
Hiller, Doris
See Nussbaum, Al(bert F.)
Hiller, Flora
See Hurd, Florence
Hiller, Herbert L. 1931- ... 125
Hiller, Ilo (Ann) 1938- ... 121
See also SATA 59
Hiller, Lejaren A(rthur) Jr. 1924- ... 1-4R
Hillerbrand, Hans J(oachim) 1931- ... 134
Brief entry ... 111
Hillerich, Robert L(ee) 1927- ... 112
Hillerman, Anne 1949- ... 118
Hillerman, Tony 1925- ... CANR-21
Earlier sketch in CA 29-32R
See also AAYA 6
See also BEST 89:1
See also CLC 62
See also SATA 6
Hillers, Delbert R(oy) 1932- ... 77-80
Hillers, H(erman) W(illiam) 1925- ... 73-76
Hillert, Margaret 1920- ... CANR-17
Earlier sketches in CA 49-52, CANR-1
See also AITN 1
See also SATA 8
Hillery, George A(nthony) Jr. 1927- ... 25-28R
Hilles, Frederick W(hiley) 1900-1975 ... 5-8R
Obituary ... 61-64
Hillesum, Etty 1914-1943 ... 137
Hillgarth, J(ocelyn) N(igel) 1929- ... 37-40R
Hillgruber, Andreas (Fritz) 1925-1989 ... 106
Obituary ... 128
Hilliard, Jan
See Grant, Kay
Hilliard, Noel (Harvey) 1929- ... CANR-7
Earlier sketch in CA 9-12R
See also CLC 15
Hilliard, Robert L. 1925- ... 107
Hilliard, Sam B(owers) 1930- ... 61-64
Hillier, Bevis 1940- ... 29-32R
Hillier, Jack R(onald) 1912- ... CANR-3
Earlier sketch in CA 5-8R
Hillier, James Martin 1941- ... 113
Hillier, Jim
See Hillier, James Martin
Hillier, Tristram (Paul) 1905-1983 Obituary ... 114
Hilliker, Grant 1921- ... 33-36R
Hilling, David 1935- ... CANR-12
Earlier sketch in CA 29-32R
Hillinger, Brad 1952- ... 73-76
Hillis, Charles Richard 1913- ... 13-16R
Hillis, Dave 1945- ... 57-60
Hillis, Dick
See Hillis, Charles Richard
Hillis, Rick 1956- ... 134
See also CLC 66
Hillix, W(illiam) A(llen) 1927- ... 89-92
Hillman, Arthur 1909-1985 Obituary ... 115
Hillman, Barry L(eslie) 1942- ... 102
Hillman, Brenda 1951- ... 129
Hillman, Howard 1934- ... CANR-20
Earlier sketch in CA 41-44R
Hillman, James 1926- ... 89-92
Hillman, Martin
See Hill, Douglas (Arthur)
Hillman, Priscilla 1940- ... 108
See also SATA 39, 48
Hillman, Ruth Estelyn 1925- ... 53-56
Hillocks, George Jr. 1934- ... 53-56
Hill-Reid, William Scott 1890- ... 5-8R
Hills, Argentina Schifano 1921- ... 136
Hills, C(harles) A(lbert) R(eis) 1955- ... CANR-23
Earlier sketch in CA 106
See also SATA 39
Hills, Christopher B. 1926- ... 114
Hills, Denis (Cecil) 1913- ... CANR-10
Earlier sketch in CA 65-68
Hills, George 1918- ... 25-28R
Hills, L(awrence) Rust 1924- ... 25-28R
Hills, Lawrence Donegan
1911-1990 Obituary ... 132
Hills, Lee 1906- ... 101
See also AITN 2
Hills, P. J.
See Hills, Philip J(ames)
Hills, Patricia Gorton Schulze 1936- ... 103
Hills, Philip
See Hills, Philip J(ames)
Hills, Philip J(ames) 1933- ... 129
Brief entry ... 117
Hills, Stuart Lee 1932- ... 33-36R
Hills, Theo(dore) L(ewis) 1925- ... 5-8R
Hills, Tina ... AITN 2
Hills, Tina
See Hills, Argentina Schifano
Hillson, Maurie 1925- ... 17-20R
Hillstrom, Tom 1943- ... 102
Hillus, Wilhelm
See Hillers, H(erman) W(illiam)
Hillway, Tyrus 1912- ... CANR-4
Earlier sketch in CA 1-4R
Hillyard, Brian P. 1949- ... 111
Hillyer, Robert (Silliman)
1895-1961 Obituary ... 89-92
See also DLB 54
Hilmes, Michele 1953- ... 136
Hilscher, Herb(ert H.) 1902-1987 Obituary ... 122
Hilsdale, (Eric) Paul 1922- ... 9-12R
Hilsenrath, Edgar 1926- ... 49-52
Hilsman, Roger 1919- ... 5-8R
Hilt, Douglas Richard 1932- ... 65-68
Hiltebeitel, Alf 1942- ... 103
Hiltner, Seward 1909-1984 ... CANR-1
Obituary ... 114
Earlier sketch in CA 1-4R

Hilton, Alec
See Chesser, Eustace
and Fullerton, Alexander (Fergus)
Hilton, Alice Mary 1924- ... 29-32R
Hilton, Bruce 1930- ... CANR-8
Earlier sketch in CA 5-8R
Hilton, Conrad N(icholson)
1887-1979 Obituary ... 81-84
Hilton, Della (Marion) 1934- ... 69-72
Hilton, Earl (Raymond) 1914- ... 21-24R
Hilton, George W(oodman) 1925- ... CANR-4
Earlier sketch in CA 1-4R
Hilton, Howard H(oyt Jr.) 1926- ... 105
Hilton, Irene Pothus ... 1-4R
See also SATA 7
Hilton, James 1900-1954 Brief entry ... 108
See also DLB 34, 77
See also SATA 34
See also TCLC 21
Hilton, John Buxton 1921- ... CANR-5
Earlier sketch in CA 53-56
Hilton, Lewis B. 1920- ... CANR-8
Earlier sketch in CA 57-60
Hilton, Margaret Lynette 1946- ... 136
See also SATA 68
Hilton, (Howard) Nelson 1950- ... 110
Hilton, Nette
See Hilton, Margaret Lynette
Hilton, Peter 1913- ... 69-72
Hilton, R. H.
See Hilton, Rodney (Howard)
Hilton, Ralph 1907- ... 29-32R
See also SATA 8
Hilton, Richard 1894- ... CAP-1
Earlier sketch in CA 9-10
Hilton, Rodney (Howard) 1916- ... 134
Brief entry ... 112
Hilton, Ronald 1911- ... 29-32R
Hilton, Suzanne 1922- ... CANR-30
Earlier sketches in CA 29-32R, CANR-12
See also SATA 4
Hilton, Thomas Leonard 1924- ... 13-16R
Hilton Smith, Robert D(ennis) Obituary ... 53-56
Hilts, Philip J(ames) 1947- ... 110
Hilu, Virginia 1929(?)-1976 Obituary ... 104
Hilvert, John (Peter Paul) 1945- ... 124
Him
See Deal, Borden
Him, George 1900-1982 Obituary ... 106
See also SATA 30
Himber, Jacob 1907- ... 105
Himelick, (James) Raymond 1910- ... 33-36R
Himelstein, Morgan Y(ale) 1926- ... 5-8R
Himes, Chester (Bomar) 1909-1984 ... CANR-22
Obituary ... 114
Earlier sketch in CA 25-28R
See also BLC 2
See also BW
See also CLC 2, 4, 7, 18, 58
See also DLB 2, 76
See also MTCW
Himes, Joseph S(andy) 1908- ... 25-28R
Himler, Ann 1946- ... 53-56
See also SATA 8
Himler, Ronald (Norbert) 1937- ... CANR-5
Earlier sketch in CA 53-56
See also SATA 6
Himmelfarb, Gertrude 1922- ... CANR-28
Earlier sketch in CA 49-52
Himmelfarb, Milton 1918- ... 101
Himmelheber, Diana Martin 1938- ... 17-20R
Himmelman, John (Carl) 1959- ... 114
See also SATA 47
Himmelstein, Jerome L(ionel) 1948- ... 113
Himstreet, William Charles 1923- ... CANR-16
Earlier sketches in CA 1-4R, CANR-1
Hinchliff, Peter Bingham 1929- ... 102
Hinchliffe, Arnold P. 1930- ... CANR-14
Earlier sketch in CA 77-80
Hinckle, Warren James III 1938- ... 89-92
Hinckley, Barbara 1937- ... 57-60
Hinckley, Helen
See Jones, Helen Hinckley
Hinckley, Ted C(harles) 1925- ... 57-60
Hind, Dolores (Ellen) 1931- ... 129
See also SATA 49, 53
Hind, Robert James 1931- ... 45-48
Hinde, Richard Standish Elphinstone
1912- ... CAP-1
Earlier sketch in CA 9-10
Hinde, Robert A(ubrey) 1923- ... CANR-30
Earlier sketch in CA 109
Hinde, Thomas
See Chitty, Thomas Willes
See also CLC 6, 11
Hinde, Wendy 1919- ... 103
Hindemith, Paul 1895-1963 Obituary ... 112
Hinden, Michael C(harles) 1941- ... 109
Hinderer, Walter (Hermann) 1934- ... CANR-1
Earlier sketch in CA 45-48
Hindin, Nathan
See Bloch, Robert (Albert)
Hinding, Andrea 1942- ... 126
Hindle, Brooke 1918- ... CANR-23
Earlier sketches in CA 13-16R, CANR-7
Hindle, Lee J(ohn) 1965- ... 117
Hindle, W(ilfred) H(ope) 1903-1967 ... CAP-2
Earlier sketch in CA 23-24
Hindley, Geoffrey 1935- ... 109
Hindman, Jane F(erguson) 1905- ... CANR-10
Earlier sketch in CA 25-28R
Hindman, Jo(sephine Long) 1910- ... 97-100
Hindmarch, Gladys 1940- ... 128
Hinds, Dudley S. 1926- ... 115
Hinds, E. M.
See Hinds, (Evelyn) Margery
Hinds, (Evelyn) Margery ... 9-12R
Hinds, Michael deCourcy
See deCourcy Hinds, Michael
Hindus, Maurice (Gerschon)
1891-1969 Obituary ... 25-28R
Hindus, Michael S(tephen) 1946- ... 105
Hindus, Milton Henry 1916- ... CANR-7
Earlier sketch in CA 17-20R
Hine, Al(fred Blakelee) 1915- ... CANR-2
Earlier sketch in CA 1-4R
Hine, (William) Daryl 1936- ... CANR-20
Earlier sketches in CA 1-4R, CANR-1
See also CAAS 15
See also CLC 15
See also DLB 60
Hine, Frederick R. 1925- ... 37-40R
Hine, James R. 1909- ... CANR-17
Earlier sketches in CA 45-48, CANR-2
Hine, Robert Van Norden Jr. 1921- ... CANR-1
Earlier sketch in CA 1-4R
Hine, Sesyle Joslin 1929- ... 13-16R
See also Joslin, Sesyle
Hine, Thomas 1947- ... 123
Hine, Virginia H(aglin) 1920- ... 97-100
Hiner, Louis C(hase) 1919- ... 73-76
Hiner, N. Ray Jr. 1937- ... 127
Hines, Anna G(rossnickle) 1946- ... CANR-36
Earlier sketch in CA 114
See also SATA 45, 51
Hines, Barry (Melvin) 1939- ... 102
Hines, Bede F(rancis) 1918- ... 45-48
Hines, Donald M. 1931- ... 136
Hines, Earl Kenneth 1905-1983 Obituary ... 109
Hines, Fatha
See Hines, Earl Kenneth
Hines, Jerome 1921- ... 130
Hines, Neal O(ldfield) 1908- ... CANR-2
Earlier sketch in CA 5-8R
Hines, Paul (David) 1934- ... 29-32R
Hines, Robert Stephan 1926- ... CANR-3
Earlier sketch in CA 9-12R
Hines, Terence (Michael) 1951- ... 128
Hines, Thomas S(pight) 1936- ... CANR-5
Earlier sketch in CA 53-56
Hines, William H. 1909(?)-1976 Obituary ... 65-68
Hinger, Charlotte 1940- ... 123
Hingley, Ronald F(rancis) 1920- ... 5-8R
Hingorani, R(up) C. 1925- ... CANR-26
Earlier sketch in CA 29-32R
Hinkel, John V.
See Hinkel, John Vincent
Hinkel, John Vincent 1906-1986 Obituary ... 121
Hinkemeyer, Michael T(homas) 1940- ... CANR-34
Earlier sketches in CA 69-72, CANR-11
Hinkle, Douglas P(addock) 1923- ... 69-72
Hinkle, Gerald H(ahn) 1931- ... 89-92
Hinkle, Olin Ethmer 1902- ... 1-4R
Hinkle, Vernon 1935- ... CANR-30
Earlier sketch in CA 109
Hinkson, James 1943- ... 69-72
Hinkson, Katharine Tynan
See Tynan, Katharine
Hinkson, Pamela 1900(?)-1982 Obituary ... 107
Hinman, Charlton (Joseph Kadio)
1911-1977 ... CANR-3
Obituary ... 89-92
Earlier sketch in CA 5-8R
Hinman, George W. Jr.
1891-1977 Obituary ... 73-76
Hinman, Robert B(enedict) 1920- ... 5-8R
Hinnebusch, Paul (Gerard) 1917- ... CANR-35
Earlier sketch in CA 114
Hinnebusch, Raymond A. 1946- ... 136
Hinnebusch, William A(quinas) 1908- ... 37-40R
Hinnells, John R(ussell) 1941- ... 49-52
Hinojosa(-Smith), Rolando (R.) 1929- ... 131
See also Hinojosa-Smith, Rolando
See also DLB 82
See also HW
Hinojosa-S., Rolando R.
See Hinojosa(-Smith), Rolando (R.)
Hinojosa-Smith, Rolando
See Hinojosa(-Smith), Rolando (R.)
See also CAAS 16
Hinrichsen, Max (Henry) 1901-1965 ... CAP-1
Earlier sketch in CA 13-14
Hinshaw, Cecil E(ugene) 1911- ... 13-16R
Hinshaw, H(orton) Corwin 1902- ... 104
Hinshaw, Randall (Weston) 1915- ... CANR-15
Earlier sketch in CA 41-44R
Hinshaw, Robert E(ugene) 1933- ... 57-60
Hinshaw, Seth B(ennett) 1908- ... 112
Hinshelwood, Cyril (Norman)
1897-1967 Obituary ... 116
Hinsley, F(rancis) H(arry) 1918- ... 17-20R
Hinson, E(dward) Glenn 1931- ... CANR-8
Earlier sketch in CA 21-24R
Hinson, (Grady) Maurice 1930- ... CANR-38
Earlier sketches in CA 45-48, CANR-2, 17
Hinterhoff, Eugene 1895- ... CAP-1
Earlier sketch in CA 9-10
Hintikka, (Kaarlo) Jaakko (Juhani)
1929- ... CANR-2
Earlier sketch in CA 1-4R
Hinton, Ann Pearlman 1941- ... 108
Hinton, Bernard L. 1937- ... 33-36R
Hinton, Harold C(lendenin) 1924- ... 17-20R
Hinton, John 1926- ... 49-52
Hinton, Milt
See Hinton, Milton John
Hinton, Milton John 1910- ... 134
Hinton, Nigel 1941- ... 85-88
Hinton, Richard W.
See Angoff, Charles
Hinton, S(usan) E(loise) 1950- ... CANR-32
Earlier sketch in CA 81-84
See also AAYA 2
See also CLC 30
See also CLR 3, 23
See also MAICYA
See also MTCW
See also SATA 19, 58
Hinton, Sam 1917- ... 73-76
See also SATA 43
Hinton, Ted C. 1904(?)-1977 Obituary ... 73-76
Hinton, William H. 1919- ... CANR-18
Earlier sketch in CA 25-28R
Hintz, (Loren) Martin 1945- ... CANR-30
Earlier sketches in CA 65-68, CANR-12
See also SATA 39, 47
Hintze, Guenther 1906- ... CAP-2
Earlier sketch in CA 21-22
Hintze, Naomi A. 1909- ... CANR-1
Earlier sketch in CA 45-48
Hinxman, Margaret 1924- ... 124
Hinz, Evelyn J. 1938- ... CANR-10
Earlier sketch in CA 65-68
Hipp, George
See Abrams, George J(oseph)
Hippel, Theodor Gottlieb von
1741-1796 ... DLB 97
Hippisley Coxe, Antony D(acres)
1912-1988 ... 103
Obituary ... 124
Hippius, Zinaida
See Gippius, Zinaida (Nikolayevna)
See also TCLC 9
Hipple, Theodore W(allace) 1935- ... CANR-10
Earlier sketch in CA 65-68
Hipple, Walter J(ohn) Jr. 1921- ... 41-44R
Hippler, Arthur E(dwin) 1935- ... 57-60
Hippopotamus, Eugene H.
See Kraus, Robert
Hipps, Juanita Redmond
1913(?)-1979 Obituary ... 85-88
Hipskind, Judith 1945- ... 97-100
Hipskind, Verne K(enneth) 1925-1975 ... CAP-2
Earlier sketch in CA 21-22
Hirano, Cathy 1957- ... SATA 68
Hirano, Marsha
See Hirano-Nakanishi, Marsha J(oyce)
Hirano-Nakanishi, Marsha J(oyce) 1949- ... 119
Hiraoka, Kimitake 1925-1970 ... 97-100
Obituary ... 29-32R
See also Mishima, Yukio
See also MTCW
Hiro, Dilip ... CANR-32
Earlier sketches in CA 77-80, CANR-14
Hirsch, Abby 1946- ... 45-48
Hirsch, Barbara B. 1938- ... 73-76
Hirsch, Charles S. 1942- ... 105
Hirsch, David H. 1930- ... 97-100
Hirsch, E(ric) D(onald) Jr. 1928- ... CANR-27
Earlier sketch in CA 25-28R
See also DLB 67
See also MTCW
Hirsch, Edward 1950- ... CANR-20
Earlier sketch in CA 104
See also CLC 31, 50
See also DLB 120
Hirsch, Ernest A(lbert) 1924-1977 ... CANR-11
Earlier sketch in CA 25-28R
Hirsch, Foster (Lance) 1943- ... CANR-39
Earlier sketches in CA 45-48, CANR-2, 17
Hirsch, Fred 1931-1978 ... CANR-28
Obituary ... 77-80
Earlier sketch in CA 25-28R
Hirsch, Herbert 1941- ... CANR-15
Earlier sketch in CA 41-44R
Hirsch, Karen 1941- ... 105
See also SATA 61
Hirsch, Lester M. 1925- ... 17-20R
Hirsch, Linda 1949- ... 105
Hirsch, Marianne 1949- ... 113
Hirsch, Mark David 1910-1989 ... 89-92
Obituary ... 128
Hirsch, Miriam F. 1927- ... 106
Hirsch, Monroe J(erome) 1917- ... 41-44R
Hirsch, Morris Isaac 1915- ... 103
Hirsch, Phil 1926- ... 102
See also SATA 35
Hirsch, S. Carl 1913- ... CANR-2
Earlier sketch in CA 5-8R
See also SAAS 7
See also SATA 2
Hirsch, Seev 1931- ... 33-36R
Hirsch, Steven R(ichard) 1937- ... CANR-32
Earlier sketch in CA 113
Hirsch, Thomas L. 1931- ... 49-52
Hirsch, Walter 1919- ... 13-16R
Hirsch, Werner Z. 1920- ... CANR-7
Earlier sketch in CA 17-20R
Hirsch, William Randolph
See Kitman, Marvin
and Lingeman, Richard R(oberts)
Hirschberg, Cornelius 1901- ... CAP-2
Earlier sketch in CA 17-18
Hirschfeld, Albert 1903- ... CANR-2
Earlier sketch in CA 1-4R
Hirschfeld, Burt 1923- ... 134
Brief entry ... 111
Hirschfeld, Charles 1913- ... 127
Brief entry ... 105
Hirschfeld, Herman 1905- ... CAP-1
Earlier sketch in CA 13-16
Hirschfelder, Joseph Oakland
1911-1990 Obituary ... 131
Hirschfield, Robert S(idney) 1928- ... 45-48
Hirschhorn, Clive 1940- ... CANR-9
Earlier sketch in CA 57-60
Hirschhorn, Howard H(arvey) 1931- ... CANR-16
Earlier sketch in CA 93-96
Hirschhorn, Richard Clark 1933- ... 69-72
Hirschi, Ron 1948- ... 120
See also SATA 56
Hirschi, Travis 1935- ... CANR-13
Earlier sketch in CA 77-80
Hirschman, A. O.
See Hirschman, Albert O.
Hirschman, Albert O. 1915- ... CANR-37
Earlier sketches in CA 1-4R, CANR-1, 16
Hirschman, Jack 1933- ... CANR-22
Earlier sketch in CA 105
Hirschmann, Linda (Ann) 1941- ... 106
See also SATA 40
Hirschmann, Maria Anne ... 85-88
Hirschmeier, Johannes 1921- ... CANR-5
Earlier sketch in CA 13-16R
Hirsh, James E(ric) 1946- ... 109
Hirsh, M(ary) E(lizabeth) 1947- ... 125
Hirsh, Marilyn 1944-1988 ... CANR-16
Obituary ... 126
Earlier sketches in CA 49-52, CANR-1
See also SATA 7, 58
Hirshberg, Al(bert Simon) 1909-1973 ... CANR-4
Obituary ... 41-44R
Earlier sketch in CA 1-4R
See also SATA 38
Hirshfield, Daniel S. 1942- ... 29-32R
Hirshson, Stanley Philip 1928- ... 1-4R
Hirst, David W(ayne) 1920- ... 37-40R
Hirst, Paul H(eywood) 1927- ... 65-68
Hirst, Paul Quentin 1946- ... 104
Hirst, Rodney Julian 1920- ... 9-12R
Hirst, Stephen M(ichael) 1939- ... 53-56
Hirst, Wilma E(llis) 1914- ... 13-16R
Hirt, Howard (Franklin) 1924-1987 ... 131
Hirt, Michael L(eonard) 1934- ... 9-12R
Hisamatsu, (Hoseki) Shin'ichi 1889- ... 81-84
Hiscock, Bruce 1940- ... 122
See also SATA 57
Hiscock, Eric C(harles) 1908-1986 ... 107
Obituary ... 120
Hiscock, Eric 1899-1989(?) ... 109
Obituary ... 127
Hiscocks, C(harles) Richard 1907- ... 53-56
Hiscoe, Helen B. 1919- ... 137
Hiser, Constance 1950- ... SATA 71
Hiser, Iona Seibert ... CANR-2
Earlier sketch in CA 1-4R
See also SATA 4
Hiskett, Mervyn 1920- ... 61-64
Hislop, Codman 1906- ... CAP-2
Earlier sketch in CA 33-36
Hisrich, Robert D(ale) 1944- ... 112
Hiss, Alger 1904- ... 33-36R
Hiss, Tony 1941- ... 77-80
Hissey, Jane (Elizabeth) 1952- ... 124
See also SATA 58
Hitchcock, Alfred (Joseph)
1899-1980 Obituary ... 97-100
See also CLC 16
See also SATA 24, 27
Hitchcock, Alma Reville
1899-1982 Obituary ... 107
Hitchcock, George 1914- ... CANR-13
Earlier sketch in CA 33-36R
See also CAAS 12
Hitchcock, H(ugh) Wiley 1923- ... CANR-17
Earlier sketches in CA 45-48, CANR-1
Hitchcock, Henry-Russell 1903-1987 ... 125
Obituary ... 122
Hitchcock, James 1938- ... 33-36R
Hitchcock, Raymond (John) 1922- ... 85-88
Hitchcock, Susan Tyler 1950- ... CANR-18
Earlier sketch in CA 102
Hitchens, Dolores 1908(?)-1973 Obituary ... 45-48
Hitchin, Martin Mewburn 1917- ... 13-16R
Hitching, (John) Francis 1933- ... 103
Hitchman, James H. 1932- ... 37-40R
Hitchman, Janet 1916-1980 ... 21-24R
Obituary ... 97-100
Hite, James (Cleveland) 1941- ... 53-56
Hite, Molly 1947- ... 124
Hite, Shere 1942- ... CANR-31
Earlier sketch in CA 81-84
See also MTCW
Hitiris, Theodore 1938- ... 41-44R
Hitler, Adolf 1889-1945 Brief entry ... 117
Hitrec, Joseph George 1912-1972 ... CAP-2
Earlier sketch in CA 17-18
Hitsman, J(ohn) Mackay 1917-1970 ... CAP-1
Earlier sketch in CA 17-18
Hitt, Russell T(rovillo) 1905- ... 1-4R
Hitt, William D(ee) 1929- ... 49-52
Hitte, Kathryn 1919- ... 21-24R
See also SATA 16
Hitti, Philip K(huri) 1886-1978 ... CANR-6
Obituary ... 81-84
Earlier sketch in CA 1-4R
Hitz, Demi 1942- ... CANR-35
Earlier sketches in CA 61-64, CANR-8
See also MAICYA
See also SATA 11, 66
Hitz-Holman, Betsy
See Holman, Betsy Hitz
Hively, Pete (Chester) 1934- ... 69-72
Hivnor, Robert 1916- ... CANR-28
Earlier sketch in CA 65-68
Hix, Charles (Arthur) 1942- ... CANR-21
Earlier sketch in CA 102
Hixon, Don L(ee) 1942- ... 73-76
Hixson, Joseph R(andolph) 1927- ... 65-68
Hixson, Richard F. 1932- ... 21-24R
Hixson, William B(utler) Jr. 1940- ... 37-40R
Hjelte, George 1893-1979 ... CANR-23
Earlier sketch in CA 29-32R

Hjortsberg, William (Reinhold) 1941- 33-36R
Hlasko, Marek 1933(?)-1969 Obituary 25-28R
Hlybinny, Vladimir
See Seduro, Vladimir
Hnizdovsky, Jacques 1915- ....SATA 32
Ho, Alfred K(uo-liang) 1919- CANR-35
Earlier sketch in CA 25-28R
Ho, Minfong 1951- 77-80
See also CLR 28
See also SATA 15
Ho, Ping-ti 1917- CANR-11
Earlier sketch in CA 5-8R
Hoa, Nguyen-Dinh
See Nguyen, Dinh Hoa
Hoadley, Irene Braden 1938- 29-32R
Hoadley, Walter E(vans) 1916- 102
Hoag, Edwin 1926- 13-16R
Hoag, Tami 1959- 138
Hoagland, Edward 1932- CANR-31
Earlier sketches in CA 1-4R, CANR-2
See also CLC 28
See also DLB 6
See also SATA 51
Hoagland, Everett (III) 1942- CANR-25
Earlier sketch in CA 33-36R
See also BW
See also DLB 41
Hoagland, Jimmie Lee 1940- 101
Hoagland, John 1947(?)-1984 Obituary 112
Hoagland, Kathleen M(ary) Dooher
1909(?)-1984 ....5-8R
Obituary 112
Hoagland, Mahlon B(ush) 1921- 85-88
Hoang Van Chi 1915- CANR-7
Earlier sketch in CA 13-16R
Hoare, Merval Hannah 1914- 103
Hoare, Philip 1958- 134
Hoare, Robert J(ohn) 1921-1975 ....CANR-6
Earlier sketch in CA 9-12R
See also SATA 38
Hoare, Wilber W. Jr. 1921-1976 Obituary 65-68
Hoban, Lillian 1925- CANR-23
Earlier sketch in CA 69-72
See also MAICYA
See also SATA 22, 69
Hoban, Russell (Conwell) 1925- CANR-37
Earlier sketches in CA 5-8R, CANR-23
See also CLC 7, 25
See also CLR 3
See also DLB 52
See also MAICYA
See also MTCW
See also SATA 1, 40
Hoban, Tana CANR-23
Earlier sketch in CA 93-96
See also CLR 13
See also MAICYA
See also SAAS 12
See also SATA 22, 70
Hobart, Alice Nourse 1882-1967 ....5-8R
Obituary 25-28R
Hobart, Alice Tisdale
See Hobart, Alice Nourse
Hobart, Billie 1935- 49-52
Hobart, Lois (Elaine) 5-8R
See also SATA 7
Hobbing, Enno 1920- 89-92
Hobbs, Albert Hoyt 1940- 125
Hobbs, Anne
See Purdy, Anne S.
Hobbs, Anne Stevenson 1942- 133
Hobbs, Cecil (Carlton) 1907- 21-24R
Hobbs, Charles R(ene) 1931- 13-16R
Hobbs, (Carl) Fredric 1931- 81-84
Hobbs, Herschel Harold 1907- CANR-2
Earlier sketch in CA 5-8R
Hobbs, J. Kline 1928- 108
Hobbs, John Leslie 1916-1964 ....5-8R
Hobbs, Michael 1934- 111
Hobbs, Perry
See Blackmur, R(ichard) P(almer)
Hobbs, Peter V(ictor) 1936- 53-56
Hobbs, Richard (Wright) 1931- 123
Brief entry 118
Hobbs, Robert C(arleton) 1946- CANR-24
Earlier sketch in CA 106
Hobbs, William (Beresford) 1939- 21-24R
Hobbs, Williston C.
1925(?)-1978 Obituary 81-84
Hobby, Bertram Maurice
1905-1983 Obituary 110
Hobby, Elaine (Ann) 1956- 130
Hobby, Gladys L(ounsbury) 1910- 119
Hobby, Oveta Culp 1905- 81-84
Hobby, William P. 1932- 85-88
Hobday, Charles (Henry) 1917- 132
Hobday, Victor C(arr) 1914- 97-100
Hobel, Phil
See Fanthorpe, R(obert) Lionel
Hoben, John B. 1908- 37-40R
Hoberecht, Earnest 1918- 21-24R
Hoberman, Gerald 1943- 111
Hoberman, Mary Ann 1930- 41-44R
See also CLR 22
See also MAICYA
See also SATA 5
Hobfoll, Stevan E(arl) 1951- 123
Hobgood, Burnet M. 1922- 101
Hobhouse, Christina 1941- 25-28R
Hobhouse, Hermione 1934- CANR-15
Earlier sketch in CA 41-44R
Hobhouse, Janet 1948-1991 57-60
Obituary 133
Hobhouse, Penelope
See Malins, Penelope
Hobkirk, Michael D(algliesh) 1924- 119
Hobley, Leonard Frank 1903- CANR-5
Earlier sketch in CA 13-16R
Hobsbaum, Philip (Dennis) 1932- CANR-29
Earlier sketches in CA 9-12R, CANR-3
See also DLB 40
Hobsbawm, Eric J(ohn Ernest) 1917- CANR-3
Earlier sketch in CA 5-8R
Hobson, Anthony (Robert Alwyn) 1921- 33-36R
Hobson, Bruce 1950- 127
See also SATA 62
Hobson, Burton (Harold) 1933- CANR-2
Earlier sketch in CA 5-8R
See also SATA 28
Hobson, Edmund (Schofield) 1931- 45-48
Hobson, Fred Colby Jr. 1943- CANR-5
Earlier sketch in CA 53-56
Hobson, Geary 1941- 122
Hobson, Hank
See Hobson, Harry
Hobson, Harold 1904- 81-84
Obituary 137
Hobson, Harry 1908- CAP-1
Earlier sketch in CA 9-10
Hobson, Julius W(ilson) 1922(?)-1977 102
See also BW
Hobson, Laura Z(ametkin) 1900-1986 ....17-20R
Obituary 118
See also CLC 7, 25
See also DLB 28
See also SATA 52
Hobson, Mary 1926- 106
Hobson, Polly
See Evans, Julia (Rendel)
Hobson, William 1911- 103
Hobzek, Mildred J(ane) 1919- 101
Hoch, Edward D(entinger) 1930- CANR-27
Earlier sketches in CA 29-32R, CANR-11
Hoch, Paul L(awrence) 1942- CANR-27
Earlier sketch in CA 65-68
Hochbaum, H(ans) Albert 1911- 103
Hochfield, George 1926- 1-4R
Hochhuth, Rolf 1931- CANR-33
Earlier sketch in CA 5-8R
See also CLC 4, 11, 18
See also MTCW
Ho Chi Minh 1890(?)-1969 Obituary 112
Hochman, Baruch 1930- 128
Hochman, Harold M(arvin) 1936- 108
Hochman, Sandra 1936- 5-8R
See also CLC 3, 8
See also DLB 5
Hochman, Shel 1944- 69-72
Hochman, Shirley D(ean) 1917- 61-64
Hochman, Stanley Richard 1928- 103
Hochschild, Adam 1942- 125
Brief entry 121
Hochschild, Arlie Russell 1940- 57-60
See also BEST 89:4
See also SATA 11
Hochschild, Harold K. 1892-1981 Obituary 103
Hochstein, Rolaine CANR-23
Earlier sketch in CA 45-48
Hochstetter, Leo D. 1911(?)-1987 Obituary 122
Hochwaelder, Fritz 1911-1986 ....29-32R
Obituary 120
See also Hochwalder, Fritz
See also CLC 36
See also MTCW
Hochwald, Werner 1910- 17-20R
Hochwalder, Fritz
See Hochwaelder, Fritz
See also CLC 36
Hockaby, Stephen
See Mitchell, Gladys (Maude Winifred)
Hockenberry, Hope
See Newell, Hope Hockenberry
Hocker, Karla
See Hoecker, Karla
Hockett, Charles F(rancis) 1916- 17-20R
Hocking, Anthony 1938- 102
Hocking, Brian 1914-1974 ....CAP-2
Earlier sketch in CA 17-18
Hocking, Mary (Eunice) 1921- CANR-18
Earlier sketch in CA 101
See also CLC 13
Hocking, William Ernest 1873-1966 ....CAP-1
Earlier sketch in CA 13-14
Hockley, G(raham) C(harles) 1931- 29-32R
Hockney, David 1937- Brief entry 116
Hocks, Richard A(llen) 1936- 81-84
Hodder-Williams, Christopher 1926- CANR-1
Earlier sketch in CA 1-4R
Hoddinott, Ralph Field 1913- 127
Hode, W(illiam) Stanley 1903- 17-20R
Hodeir, Andre 1921- CANR-34
Earlier sketches in CA 85-88, CANR-15
Hodes, Aubrey 1927- 33-36R
Hodes, Scott 1937- 49-52
Hodgart, Matthew (John Caldwell)
1916- CANR-9
Earlier sketch in CA 5-8R
Hodge, Alan 1915-1979 Obituary 89-92
Hodge, David W(ayne) 1935- 61-64
Hodge, Francis (Richard) 1915- CANR-12
Earlier sketch in CA 33-36R
Hodge, Gene (Meany) 1898- 45-48
Hodge, James L(ee) 1935- 41-44R
Hodge, Jane Aiken 1917- CANR-3
Earlier sketch in CA 5-8R
Hodge, Marshall Bryant 1925- CAP-2
Earlier sketch in CA 23-24
Hodge, P(aul) W(illiam) 1934- CANR-14
Earlier sketch in CA 33-36R
See also SATA 12
Hodge, Robert 1940- 128
Hodge, William H(oward) 1932- CANR-15
Earlier sketch in CA 65-68
Hodgell, P(atricia) C(hristine) 1951- 109
See also SATA 42
Hodges, C(yril) Walter 1909- CANR-5
Earlier sketch in CA 13-16R
See also SATA 2
Hodges, Carl G. 1902-1964 ....5-8R
See also SATA 10
Hodges, Devon Leigh 1950- 125
Hodges, Donald Clark 1923- CANR-24
Earlier sketches in CA 53-56, CANR-6
Hodges, Doris M(arjorie) 1915- CANR-11
Earlier sketch in CA 25-28R
Hodges, Elizabeth Jamison 9-12R
See also SATA 1
Hodges, Gil(bert Ray) 1924-1972 Obituary 109
Hodges, Graham R(ushing) 1915- 5-8R
Hodges, Harold Mellor 1922- 17-20R
Hodges, Henry G. 1888- 5-8R
Hodges, Henry (Woolmington MacKenzie)
1920- 37-40R
Hodges, Herbert Arthur 1905-1976 73-76
Obituary 69-72
Hodges, John C(unyus) 1892-1967 ....5-8R
Obituary 103
Hodges, Louis W. 1933- 81-84
Hodges, Luther (Hartwell)
1898-1974 Obituary 53-56
Hodges, Margaret Moore 1911- CANR-30
Earlier sketches in CA 1-4R, CANR-2
See also MAICYA
See also SAAS 9
See also SATA 1, 33
Hodges, Michael P. 1941- 136
Hodges, Richard E(dwin) 1928- CANR-15
Earlier sketch in CA 41-44R
Hodges, Turner
See Morehead, Albert H(odges)
Hodges, Zane Clark 1932- CANR-15
Earlier sketch in CA 41-44R
Hodgetts, A(lfred) Birnie 1911- 101
Hodgetts, Blake Christopher 1967- 114
See also SATA 43
Hodgetts, J(ohn) E(dwin) 1917- 13-16R
Hodgetts, Richard M(ichael) 1942- CANR-23
Earlier sketches in CA 57-60, CANR-8
Hodgins, Bruce W(illard) 1931- 37-40R
Hodgins, Eric 1899-1971 104
Obituary 29-32R
Hodgins, Jack 1938- 93-96
See also CLC 23
See also DLB 60
Hodgkin, Robert Allason 1916- 102
Hodgkin, Robin A.
See Hodgkin, Robert Allason
Hodgkin, Thomas Lionel
1910-1982 Obituary 115
Hodgkinson, Anthony 1916-1983 126
Hodgkinson, Christopher 1928- 115
Hodgkinson, Edith 1959- 117
Hodgkinson, Liz 1943- 124
Hodgkinson, Marie Elisabeth
1921(?)-1983 Obituary 110
Hodgkiss, A(lan) G(eoffrey) 1921- 124
Hodgman, Helen 1945- 131
Brief entry 117
See also DLB 14
Hodgson, D(avid) H(argraves) 1939- 25-28R
Hodgson, David
See Lewis, David
Hodgson, Derek 1929- 118
Hodgson, Godfrey (Michael Talbot)
1934- 25-28R
Hodgson, John A(lfred) 1945- 125
Hodgson, Leonard 1889-1969 ....CAP-1
Earlier sketch in CA 9-10
Hodgson, Margaret
See Ballinger, (Violet) Margaret (Livingstone)
Hodgson, Marshall G. S. 1922-1968 ....CAP-2
Earlier sketch in CA 21-22
Hodgson, Martha (Keeling) 1906- 57-60
Hodgson, Norma
See Russell, Norma Hull Lewis
Hodgson, Pat 1928- CANR-7
Earlier sketch in CA 57-60
Hodgson, Peter Crafts 1934- CANR-15
Earlier sketch in CA 29-32R
Hodgson, Peter E(dward) 1928- 9-12R
Hodgson, Phyllis 1909- CAP-1
Earlier sketch in CA 13-14
Hodgson, Ralph 1871-1962 102
See also DLB 19
Hodgson, Richard Sargeant 1924- CANR-7
Earlier sketch in CA 13-16R
Hodgson, Robert D(avid) 1923- 5-8R
Hodgson, William Hope
1877(?)-1918 Brief entry 111
See also DLB 70
See also TCLC 13
Hodin, J(osef) P(aul) 1905- 41-44R
Hodnett, Edward 1901-1984 ....CANR-5
Obituary 114
Earlier sketch in CA 13-16R
Hodsdon, Nicholas E(dward) 1941- 49-52
Hodsdon, Nick
See Hodsdon, Nicholas E(dward)
Hodson, Henry V(incent) 1906- CANR-3
Earlier sketch in CA 5-8R
Hodson, Peregrine 128
Hoebel, Edward Adamson 1906- CANR-1
Earlier sketch in CA 1-4R
Hoecker, Karla 1901- CANR-2
Earlier sketch in CA 49-52
Hoehling, A(dolph) A. 1915- CANR-1
Earlier sketch in CA 1-4R
Hoehling, Mary 1914- 93-96
Hoehn, Richard A(lbert) 1936- 116
Hoehner, Harold W. 1935- 37-40R
Hoekema, Anthony A(ndrew) 1913- 9-12R
Hoeksema, Gertrude 1921- 106
Hoel, Robert F(loyd) 1942- 53-56
Hoelderlin, Friedrich 1770-1843 ....DLB 90
Hoelldobler, Bert(hold Karl) 1936- 134
Hoelterhoff, Manuela (Vali) 1949- 120
Brief entry 114
Hoelty, Ludwig Christoph Heinrich
1748-1776 ....DLB 94
Hoelzel, Alfred 1934- 41-44R
Hoenig, J(ulius) 1916- 29-32R
Hoenig, Sidney B(enjamin) 1907-1979 .....CANR-2
Earlier sketch in CA 45-48
Hoeniger, F(rederick) David 1921- 41-44R
Hoenigswald, Henry M(ax) 1915- CANR-39
Earlier sketch in CA 13-16R
Hoepfl, Harro (Maximilian) 1943- 129
Hoequist, Charles Ernest Jr. 1954- 108
Hoerr, John P. (III) 1930- 135
Hoest, Bill
See Hoest, William P.
Hoest, William P. 1926-1988 ....CANR-23
Obituary 127
Earlier sketch in CA 69-72
Hoetink, H(armannus) 1931- 21-24R
Hoeveler, Diane Long 1949- 102
Hoeveler, J. David Jr. 1943- 129
Hoexter, Corinne K. 1927- CANR-27
Earlier sketch in CA 49-52
See also SATA 6
Hoey, Joanne Nobes 1936- 106
Hofer, Peter
See Kortner, Peter
Hofer, Philip 1898-1984 Obituary 114
Hoff, Carol 1900- CAP-2
Earlier sketch in CA 21-22
See also SATA 11
Hoff, Ebbe Curtis 1906- 57-60
Hoff, Harry S(ummerfield) 1910- CANR-20
Earlier sketches in CA 1-4R, CANR-2
Hoff, Joan
See Wilson, Joan Hoff
Hoff, Marilyn 1942- CANR-7
Earlier sketch in CA 17-20R
Hoff, Syd(ney) 1912- CANR-38
Earlier sketches in CA 5-8R, CANR-4
See also MAICYA
See also SAAS 4
See also SATA 9
Hoffa, James R(iddle)
1913-1975(?) Obituary 109
Hoffecker, Carol E(leanor) 1938- 85-88
Hoffecker, (John) Savin 1908- 5-8R
Hoffeld, Donald R(aymond) 1933- 29-32R
Hoffeld, Laura 1946(?)-1982 Obituary 106
Hoffenberg, Jack 1906-1977 81-84
Hoffenberg, Mason 1922(?)-1986 Obituary 119
Hoffenstein, Samuel Goodman
1890-1947 Brief entry 111
See also DLB 11
Hoffer, Charles R(ussell) 1929- CANR-22
Earlier sketches in CA 13-16R, CANR-7
Hoffer, Eric 1902-1983 ....CANR-18
Obituary 109
Earlier sketch in CA 13-16R
Hoffer, Thomas William 1938- 118
Hoffer, William 1943- CANR-27
Earlier sketch in CA 65-68
Hofferbert, Richard I(ra) 1937- 29-32R
Hoffine, Lyla 1897- 1-4R
Hoffman, Abbie 1936-1989 ....CANR-35
Obituary 128
Earlier sketches in CA 21-24R, CANR-8
See also MTCW
Hoffman, Abraham 1938- 106
Hoffman, Adeline M(ildred)
1908-1979 ....CANR-23
Earlier sketch in CA 29-32R
Hoffman, Alice 1952- CANR-34
Earlier sketch in CA 77-80
See also CLC 51
See also MTCW
Hoffman, Andrew Jay 1956- 138
Hoffman, Anita 1942- 69-72
Hoffman, Arthur S. 1926- CANR-10
Earlier sketch in CA 25-28R
Hoffman, Arthur W(olf) 1921- 5-8R
Hoffman, Bengt R(uno) 1913- 69-72
Hoffman, Bernard G(ilbert) 1925- 41-44R
Hoffman, Betty Hannah 1918- 9-12R
Hoffman, Calvin 1908(?)-1986 Obituary 118
Hoffman, Charles Fenno 1806-1884 ....DLB 3
Hoffman, Daniel (Gerard) 1923- CANR-4
Earlier sketch in CA 1-4R
See also CLC 6, 13, 23
See also DLB 5
Hoffman, David Herbert
1932(?)-1985 Obituary 115
Hoffman, Dominic M. 1913- 116
Hoffman, Donald S(tone) 1936- 57-60
Hoffman, Edward 106
Hoffman, Edwin D. 101
See also SATA 49
Hoffman, Elizabeth P(arkinson) 1921- 77-80
Hoffman, Eva 1945- 132
Hoffman, Frederick J(ohn) 1909-1967 .....CANR-6
Earlier sketch in CA 1-4R
Hoffman, Gail 1896- 5-8R
Hoffman, George W(alter) 1914- 13-16R
Hoffman, Harry G. 1911(?)-1977 Obituary 69-72
Hoffman, Helmut 1912- CANR-17
Earlier sketch in CA 1-4R
Hoffman, Herbert H(einz) 1928- 117
Hoffman, Hester R(osalyn) 1895- CAP-1
Earlier sketch in CA 9-10
Hoffman, Jo Ann S. 1942- 81-84

Hoffman, Joseph G(ilbert) 1909-1974 65-68
Obituary 53-56
Hoffman, Joy 1954- 108
Hoffman, Julius Jennings
1895-1983 Obituary 110
Hoffman, L. Richard 1930- 13-16R
Hoffman, Lee 1932- CANR-18
Earlier sketch in CA 25-28R
See also CAAS 10
Hoffman, Lisa 1919- 29-32R
Hoffman, Lois Wladis 1929- 13-16R
Hoffman, Mark S. 1952- 125
Hoffman, Marshall 1942- 106
Hoffman, Mary (Margaret) 1945- 131
See also Lassiter, Mary
See also SATA 59
Hoffman, Michael Allen 1944-1990 106
Obituary 131
Hoffman, Michael J(erome) 1939- 29-32R
Hoffman, Nancy Jo 1942- 107
Hoffman, Paul 1934-1984 .... CANR-28
Obituary 112
Earlier sketches in CA 45-48, CANR-1
Hoffman, Philip T(homas) 1947- 119
Hoffman, Phyllis M(iriam) 1944- CANR-28
Earlier sketches in CA 29-32R, CANR-12
See also SATA 4
Hoffman, Richard L(ester) 1937-1981 .... CANR-23
Earlier sketch in CA 29-32R
Hoffman, Robert C. 1899(?)-1985 Obituary 116
Hoffman, Robert L. 1937- 37-40R
Hoffman, Ronald 1941- 133
Brief entry 112
Hoffman, Rosekrans 1926- CANR-15
Earlier sketch in CA 89-92
See also SATA 15
Hoffman, Ross John Swartz 1902- 65-68
Hoffman, Stanley 1944- 77-80
See also CLC 5
Hoffman, Willa M(athews) 1914- 61-64
Hoffman, William M(oses) 1939- CANR-11
Earlier sketch in CA 57-60
See also CLC 40
Hoffman, William 1925- CANR-9
Earlier sketch in CA 21-24R
Hoffmann, Ann (Marie) 1930- 37-40R
Hoffmann, Banesh 1906-1986 .... CANR-3
Obituary 119
Earlier sketch in CA 5-8R
Hoffmann, Charles G. 1921- 13-16R
Hoffmann, Charles 1921- 106
Hoffmann, Donald 1933- 25-28R
Hoffmann, E(rnst) T(heodor) A(madeus)
1776-1822 .... DLB 90
See also SATA 27
Hoffmann, Eleanor 1895- CAP-1
Earlier sketch in CA 13-16
Hoffmann, Erik P(eter) 1939- CANR-29
Earlier sketches in CA 33-36R, CANR-13
Hoffmann, Felix 1911-1975 .... CAP-2
Obituary 57-60
Earlier sketch in CA 29-32
See also SATA 9
Hoffmann, Frank W(illiam) 1949- 106
Hoffmann, Hilde 1927- 25-28R
Hoffmann, Leon-Francois 1932- 49-52
Hoffmann, Malcolm A(rthur) 1912- 65-68
Hoffmann, Margaret Jones 1910- CANR-2
Earlier sketch in CA 5-8R
See also SATA 48
Hoffmann, Peggy
See Hoffmann, Margaret Jones
Hoffmann, Peter (Conrad Werner)
1930- CANR-14
Earlier sketch in CA 81-84
Hoffmann, Peter R. 1935- 108
Hoffmann, Stanley (H.) 1928- CANR-14
Earlier sketches in CA 81-84, CANR-1
Hoffmann, Yoel 1937- 97-100
Hoffmeister, Adolf 1903-1973 Obituary 41-44R
Hoffmeister, Donald F(rederick) 1916- 53-56
Hoffmeister, Gerhart 1936- 130
Hoffnung, Michele 1944- 81-84
Hoff-Wilson, Joan
See Wilson, Joan Hoff
Hofheinz, Roy Mark Jr. 1935- 110
Hofinger, Johannes 1905- CAP-1
Earlier sketch in CA 19-20
Hofling, Charles K(reimer) 1920-1980 .... CANR-34
Earlier sketch in CA 41-44R
Hofman, Anton
See Hollo, Anselm
Hofmann, Adele Dellenbaugh 1926- 97-100
Hofmann, Gert 1931- 128
See also CLC 54
Hofmann, Hans 1923- CANR-4
Earlier sketch in CA 1-4R
Hofmann, Melita C(ecelia) 5-8R
Obituary 69-72
Hofmann, Michael 1957- .... DLB 40
Hofmann, Paul Leopold 1912- 107
Hofmann, William J(ohn) 1931- 114
Hofmannsthal, Hugo von
1874-1929 Brief entry 106
See also DLB 81, 118
See also TCLC 11
Hofsinde, Robert 1902-1973 73-76
Obituary 45-48
See also SATA 21
Hofsommer, Don(ovan) L(owell)
1938- CANR-24
Earlier sketches in CA 65-68, CANR-9
Hofstadter, Albert 1910- 33-36R
Hofstadter, Douglas R(ichard) 1945- 105
See also MTCW
Hofstadter, Richard 1916-1970 .... CANR-4
Obituary 29-32R
Earlier sketch in CA 1-4R
See also DLB 17
Hofstede, Geert
See Hofstede, Gerard H(endrik)
Hofstede, Geert H.
See Hofstede, Gerard H(endrik)
Hofstede, Gerard H(endrik) 1928- CANR-35
Earlier sketches in CA 41-44R, CANR-15
Hofstetter, Richard R(yan) 1956- 117
Hofvendahl, Russ(ell Lloyd) 1921- 116
Hogan, Bernice Harris 1929- CANR-7
Earlier sketch in CA 13-16R
See also SATA 12
Hogan, Dennis P. 1950- 110
Hogan, Desmond 1950- 102
See also DLB 14
Hogan, Inez 1895- CANR-1
Earlier sketch in CA 1-4R
See also SATA 2
Hogan, James P(atrick) 1941- CANR-15
Earlier sketch in CA 81-84
Hogan, John Charles 1919- 17-20R
Hogan, John D. 1927- 45-48
Hogan, Judy 1937- CANR-39
Earlier sketches in CA 77-80, CANR-16
Hogan, Lawrence D(aniel) 1944- 124
Hogan, Linda 1947- 120
Hogan, Michael 1943- CANR-34
Earlier sketches in CA 77-80, CANR-14
Hogan, Patrick Colm 1957- 134
Hogan, Paul 1927- 61-64
Hogan, (Eugene) Pendleton 1907- 127
Hogan, (Robert) Ray 1908- CANR-4
Earlier sketch in CA 9-12R
Hogan, Robert F(rancis) 1927- 41-44R
Hogan, Robert (Goode) 1930- CANR-19
Earlier sketches in CA 1-4R, CANR-1
Hogan, Thom(as Eugene Jr.) 1952- 103
Hogan, Ursula 1899- 5-8R
Hogan, Willard N(ewton) 1909- CAP-2
Earlier sketch in CA 21-22
Hogan, William Francis 1930- 25-28R
Hogan, William T. 1919- 97-100
Hogarth, Burne 1911- 93-96
See also SATA 63
Hogarth, Charles
See Bowen, (Ivor) Ian
and Creasey, John
Hogarth, Douglas
See Phillips-Birt, Douglas Hextall Chedzey
Hogarth, Emmett
See Polonsky, Abraham (Lincoln)
Hogarth, Grace (Weston Allen) 1905- 89-92
Hogarth, John
See Finnin, (Olive) Mary
Hogarth, Jr.
See Kent, Rockwell
Hogarth, (Arthur) Paul 1917- CANR-27
Earlier sketch in CA 49-52
See also SATA 41
Hogben, Lancelot T. 1895-1975 73-76
Obituary 61-64
Hogbin, H(erbert) Ian 1904- 9-12R
Hogbotel, Sebastian
See Gott, K(enneth) D(avidson)
Hoge, Cecil C(unningham) Sr. 1913- 116
Hoge, Dean R(ichard) 1937- CANR-27
Earlier sketch in CA 53-56
Hoge, James O(tey) 1944- 89-92
Hoge, Phyllis
See Thompson, Phyllis Hoge
Hoge, Warren McClamroch 1941- 102
Hogendorn, Jan S(tafford) 1937- CANR-14
Earlier sketch in CA 37-40R
Hogg, Beth
See Hogg, Elizabeth (Tootill)
Hogg, Clayton L(eRoy) 1924- 104
Hogg, Elizabeth (Tootill) 1917- CANR-10
Earlier sketch in CA 5-8R
Hogg, Enderby
See Meades, Jonathan (Turner)
Hogg, Garry 1902-1976 .... CANR-10
Earlier sketch in CA 21-24R
See also SATA 2
Hogg, Helen (Battles) Sawyer 1905- 69-72
Hogg, Ian V(ernon) 1926- CANR-12
Earlier sketch in CA 29-32R
Hogg, James (Dalby) 1937- 137
Hogg, James 1770-1835 .... DLB 93, 116
Hogg, Oliver Frederick Gillilan 1887-1979 93-96
Obituary 85-88
Hogg, Quintin McGarel 1907- CANR-14
Earlier sketches in CAP-1, CA 11-12
Hogg, Robert (Lawrence) 1942- 53-56
Hogg, W(illiam) Richey 1921- 1-4R
Hoggart, Richard 1918- 9-12R
Hogins, James Burl 1936- 53-56
Hogner, Dorothy Childs 33-36R
See also SATA 4
Hogner, Nils 1893-1970 77-80
See also SATA 25
Hogrefe, Pearl CAP-1
Earlier sketch in CA 13-16
Hogrogian, Nonny 1932- CANR-2
Earlier sketch in CA 45-48
See also CLR 2
See also MAICYA
See also SAAS 1
See also SATA 7
Hogue, Arthur R(eed) 1906-1986 .... 37-40R
Obituary 118
Hogue, C(harles) B(illy) 1928- 69-72
Hogue, Charles Leonard 1935- 105
Hogue, Richard 1946- 49-52
Hogue, W. Lawrence 1951- 126
Hoguet, Susan Ramsay 1945- 119
Hogwood, Brian W(alter) 1950- 128
Hogwood, Christopher (Jarvis Haley) 1941- 127
Brief entry 120
Hoh, Diane 1937- 120
See also SATA 48, 52
Hohenberg, Dorothy Lannuier
1905(?)-1977 Obituary 73-76
Hohenberg, John 1906- CANR-6
Earlier sketch in CA 13-16R
Hohenberg, Paul M(arcel) 1933- 25-28R
Hohendahl, Peter Uwe 1936- CANR-17
Earlier sketches in CA 45-48, CANR-2
Hohenstein, C(harles) Louis 1930- 116
Hohenstein, Henry J(ohn) 1931- 53-56
Hohenzollern, Friedrich Wilhelm (Victor Albert)
1859-1941 Brief entry 120
Hohimer, Frank 1928- 57-60
Hohl, Ludwig 1904-1980 .... DLB 56
Hohler, Robert T(illman) 1951- 123
Hohlfelder, Robert Lane 1938- 45-48
Hohlwein, Kathryn Joyce 1930- 125
Hohn, Hazel (Stamper) 5-8R
Hohnen, David 1925- 21-24R
Hohoff, Tay
See Torrey, Therese von Hohoff
Hoig, Stan(ley Warlick) 1924- CANR-1
Earlier sketch in CA 1-4R
Hoijer, Harry 1904-1976 73-76
Obituary 65-68
Hoisington, Harland
1896(?)-1973 Obituary 45-48
Hoke, Helen
See Watts, Helen L. Hoke
See also SATO 65
Hoke, Helen L.
See Watts, Helen L. Hoke
Hoke, John (Lindsay) 1925- 41-44R
See also SATA 7
Holabird, Katharine 1948- 121
See also SATA 62
Holaday, Allan Gibson 1916- 37-40R
Holan, Vladimir 1905-1980 Obituary 114
Holbeach, Henry
See Rands, William Brighty
Holbeche, Philippa Jack 1919- CAP-1
Earlier sketch in CA 9-10
Holberg, Ruth L(angland) 1889- 5-8R
See also SATA 1
Holbik, Karel 1920- 37-40R
Holbo, Paul Sothe 1929- 25-28R
Holborn, Hajo 1902-1969 .... CAP-2
Earlier sketch in CA 25-28
Holborn, Louise W. 1898- CAP-2
Earlier sketch in CA 25-28
Holborn, Mark 1949- 104
Holbrook, Bill 1921- 61-64
Holbrook, Clyde A(mos)
1911-1989 Obituary 130
Holbrook, David (Kenneth) 1923- CANR-3
Earlier sketch in CA 5-8R
See also DLB 14, 40
Holbrook, Jennifer Kearns 1931- 102
Holbrook, John
See Vance, John Holbrook
Holbrook, Peter
See Glick, Carl (Cannon)
Holbrook, Sabra
See Erickson, Sabra Rollins
Holbrook, Stewart Hall 1893-1964 .... CAP-1
Earlier sketch in CA 9-10
See also SATA 2
Holbrooke, Richard 1941- 135
Holburn, James 1900-1988 Obituary 124
Holck, Manfred Jr. 1930- 17-20R
Holcomb, Adele M(ansfield) 1930- 113
Holcomb, Donald F(rank) 1925- 97-100
Holcomb, George L. 1911- 45-48
Holcomb, Jerry (Leona) 1927- 25-28R
Holcombe, Arthur N(orman) 1884-1977 .... CAP-2
Obituary 73-76
Earlier sketch in CA 29-32
Holcombe, Randall G(regory) 1950- CANR-29
Earlier sketch in CA 111
Holcroft, Thomas 1745-1809 .... DLB 39, 89
Holden, Anthony (Ivan) 1947- 101
Holden, Anton 1934- 108
Holden, Curry
See Holden, William Curry
Holden, David (Shipley) 1924-1977 .... 41-44R
Holden, Donald 1931- CANR-18
Earlier sketches in CA 45-48, CANR-2
Holden, Edith 1871-1920 Brief entry 113
Holden, Genevieve
See Pou, Genevieve Long
Holden, George S(cott) 1926- 106
Holden, Inez 1906-1974 Obituary 53-56
Holden, Jonathan 1941- CANR-37
Earlier sketches in CA 45-48, CANR-1, 16
See also DLB 105
Holden, Matthew
See Parkinson, Roger
Holden, Matthew Jr. 1931- 57-60
Holden, Molly 1927-1981 .... 25-28R
Obituary 133
See also DLB 40
Holden, Paul E. 1894(?)-1976 Obituary 65-68
Holden, Raymond (Peckham)
1894-1972 .... CANR-4
Obituary 37-40R
Earlier sketch in CA 5-8R
Holden, Ursula 1921- CANR-22
Earlier sketch in CA 101
See also CAAS 8
See also CLC 18
Holden, Vincent F. 1911-1972 Obituary 37-40R
Holden, W. C.
See Holden, William Curry
Holden, W(illis) Sprague 1909-1973 .... 1-4R
Obituary 45-48
Holden, William Curry 1898(?)- Brief entry 117
Holder, Bob N.
See Mullarky, Taylor
Holder, Glenn 1906- 41-44R
Holder, Gwynneth 1943- 119
Holder, John Jr. 1947-1985 103
Obituary 116
Holder, Ray 1913- 102
Holder, William G. 1937- CANR-10
Earlier sketch in CA 25-28R
Holderlin, (Johann Christian) Friedrich
1770-1843 .... PC 4
Holdgate, Martin Wyatt 1931- 109
Holdheim, William Wolfgang 1926- CANR-2
Earlier sketch in CA 1-4R
Holding, Charles H. 1897- CAP-1
Earlier sketch in CA 11-12
Holding, Elizabeth Sanxay
1889-1955 Brief entry 111
Holding, James (Clark Carlisle Jr.)
1907- 25-28R
See also SATA 3
Holding, Vera Zumwalt 1894-1984 Obituary 114
Holditch, W(illiam) Kenneth 1933- 119
Holdren, Bob R. 1922- 37-40R
Holdren, John P(aul) 1944- 33-36R
Holdstock, Robert
See Holdstock, Robert P.
Holdstock, Robert P. 1948- 131
See also CLC 39
Holdsworth, Christopher (John) 1931- 124
Holdsworth, Irene CAP-1
Earlier sketch in CA 9-10
Holdsworth, Mary (Zvegintzov) 1908- CAP-1
Earlier sketch in CA 13-16
Hole, Christina 1896-1985 Obituary 118
Hole, Dorothy (Henrietta Field) 135
Hole, Tahu Ronald Charles Pearce
1908-1985 Obituary 118
Holenstein, Elmar 1937- CANR-28
Earlier sketches in CA 65-68, CANR-11
Holford, Ingrid 1920- 102
Holford, William Graham
1907-1975 Obituary 108
Holiday, F(rederick) W(illiam) 1921- 25-28R
Holiday, Homer
See DeBeaubien, Philip Francis
Holinger, William (Jacques) 1944- 123
Holisher, Desider 1901-1972 .... CAP-2
Obituary 37-40R
Earlier sketch in CA 19-20
See also SATA 6
Holl, Adelaide Hinkle 1910- CANR-2
Earlier sketch in CA 1-4R
See also SATA 8
Holl, Adolf 1930- 101
Holl, Jack M. 1937- 57-60
Holl, Kristi D(iane) 1951- 114
See also SATA 51
Holladay, Sylvia A(gnes) 1936- 57-60
Holladay, William L(ee) 1926- 53-56
Holland, Ada Morehead 1911- 122
Holland, Alma Boice 29-32R
Holland, Barbara A(dams) 1925- 57-60
Holland, Brud
See Holland, Jerome H(eartwell)
Holland, Cecelia (Anastasia) 1943- CANR-9
Earlier sketch in CA 17-20R
Holland, Cecil Fletcher
1907-1978 Obituary 77-80
Holland, Deborah K(atherine) 1947- 57-60
Holland, DeWitte T(almage) 1923- 45-48
Holland, Elizabeth (Anne) 1928- 124
Holland, Francis Ross Jr. 1927- 33-36R
Holland, Gail Bernice 1940- 126
Holland, Glen A. 1920- 37-40R
Holland, Harrison M(elsher) 1921- 117
Holland, Hilda 1901(?)-1975 Obituary 57-60
Holland, Isabelle 1920- CANR-25
Earlier sketches in CA 21-24R, CANR-10
See also CLC 21
See also MAICYA
See also SATA 8, 70
Holland, Jack H. 1922- 81-84
Holland, Jack 1947- 105
Holland, James C(larence) 1935- 112
Holland, James Gordon 1927- 1-4R
Holland, James R. 1944- 37-40R
Holland, Janice 1913-1962 73-76
See also SATA 18
Holland, Jerome H(eartwell)
1916-1985 Obituary 114
Holland, John L(ewis) 1919- CANR-17
Earlier sketch in CA 25-28R
See also SATA 20
Holland, Joyce
See Morice, Dave
Holland, Joyce (Flint) 1921- 5-8R
Holland, Kel
See Whittington, Harry (Benjamin)
Holland, Kenneth J(ohn) 1918- 33-36R
Holland, Kenneth 1948- 118
Holland, Laurence B(edwell) 1920-1980 .... 17-20R
Obituary 102
Holland, Louise Adams 1893- 89-92
Holland, Lynwood M. 1905- 41-44R
Holland, Lys
See Gater, Dilys
Holland, Marcus
See Caldwell, (Janet Miriam) Taylor (Holland)
Holland, Marion 1908-1989 61-64
Obituary 128
See also SATA 6, 61

Holland, Max (Mendel) 1950-.................135
Holland, Norman N(orwood) 1927-.........17-20R
See also DLB 67
Holland, Patricia G. 1940-....................115
Holland, Philip Welsby 1917-..................109
Holland, Robert 1940-.......................33-36R
Holland, Sheila 1937-....................CANR-15
Earlier sketch in CA 85-88
Holland, Thomas E(dward) 1934-...........53-56
Holland, Tim 1931-..........................57-60
Holland, Tom 1947-..........................126
Holland, Vyvyan (Beresford) 1886-1967.....97-100
Obituary.....................................25-28R
Holland, William E. 1940-....................124
Hollander, A(rie) Nicolaas Jan den
See den Hollander, A(rie) Nicolaas Jan
Hollander, Anne 1930-........................131
Hollander, Hans 1899-1986...................103
Obituary...120
Hollander, Herbert S.
1904(?)-1976 Obituary.....................69-72
Hollander, John 1929-....................CANR-1
Earlier sketch in CA 1-4R
See also CLC 2, 5, 8, 14
See also DLB 5
See also SATA 13
Hollander, Lee M(ilton) 1880-..................1-4R
Hollander, Paul
See Silverberg, Robert
Hollander, Paul 1932-...................CANR-13
Earlier sketch in CA 37-40R
Hollander, Phyllis 1928-.................CANR-18
Earlier sketch in CA 97-100
See also SATA 39
Hollander, Richard Isaac
1912-1985 Obituary..........................117
Hollander, Robert 1933-..................CANR-5
Earlier sketch in CA 13-16R
Hollander, Sophie Smith 1911-............13-16R
Hollander, Stanley C(harles) 1919-........37-40R
Hollander, Zander 1923-.................CANR-18
Earlier sketch in CA 65-68
See also SATA 63
Hollands, Roy (Derrick) 1924-...........CANR-37
Earlier sketch in CA 114
Hollandsworth, James G. Jr. 1944-............135
Hollaway, Otto 1903-..........................69-72
Hollberg, John
See Hall, Gus
Holldobler, Bert
See Hoelldobler, Bert(hold Karl)
Holldobler, Turid 1939-...................SATA 26
Holleb, Arthur Irving 1921-...................103
Hollender, Edward A. 1899-...................105
Hollenweger, Walter J(acob) 1927-.......CANR-19
Earlier sketches in CA 53-56, CANR-4
Holler, Frederick L. 1921-...................97-100
Holler, Ronald F. 1938-........................53-56
Holleran, Andrew 1943(?)-.................CLC 38
Holles, Everett R. 1904(?)-1978 Obituary.....77-80
Holles, Robert Owen 1926-.................CANR-18
Earlier sketches in CA 5-8R, CANR-3
Holley, Bobbie Lee 1927-...................33-36R
Holley, Edward Gailon 1927-..............CANR-6
Earlier sketch in CA 5-8R
Holley, Frederick S. 1924-......................109
Holley, I(rving) B(rinton) Jr. 1919-.....CANR-14
Earlier sketch in CA 37-40R
Holley, Marietta 1836(?)-1926 Brief entry.......118
See also DLB 11
Holli, Melvin G(eorge) 1933-.............CANR-26
Earlier sketches in CA 25-28R, CANR-11
Hollick, Ann L(orraine) 1941-..................57-60
Holliday, Barbara Gregg 1917-................73-76
Holliday, Joe
See Holliday, Joseph
Holliday, Joseph 1910-......................CAP-2
Earlier sketch in CA 29-32
See also SATA 11
Hollindale, Peter 1936-.........................103
Holling, Holling C(lancy)
1900-1973 Obituary..........................106
See also MAICYA
See also SATA 15, 26
Hollingdale, R(eginald) J(ohn) 1930-...........102
Hollinghurst, Alan 1954-.......................114
See also CLC 55
Hollings, Michael 1921-.........................81-84
Hollingshead, August deBelmont
1907-1980.....................................13-16R
Obituary..120
Hollingshead, (Ronald) Kyle 1941-.......CANR-11
Earlier sketch in CA 21-24R
Hollingsworth, Alvin C(arl) 1930-........SATA 39
Hollingsworth, Brian 1923-......................130
Hollingsworth, Dorothy Frances 1916-.......85-88
Hollingsworth, Harold M(arvin) 1932-.......53-56
Hollingsworth, J(oseph) Rogers
1932-...CANR-22
Earlier sketches in CA 13-16R, CANR-7
Hollingsworth, Kent 1929-......................81-84
Hollingsworth, Lyman B(urgess) 1919-.......45-48
Hollingsworth, Margaret 1942-..................123
See also DLB 60
Hollingsworth, Mary H(ead) 1910-...........69-72
Hollingsworth, Paul M. 1932-.................29-32R
Hollingworth, Clare 1911-........................121
Hollinrake, Roger (Barker) 1929-..............115
Hollis, C(harles) Carroll 1911-.................125
Hollis, (Maurice) Christopher 1902-1977.......73-76
Obituary...69-72
Hollis, Daniel W(alker) 1922-....................5-8R
Hollis, Daniel W(ebster) III 1942-...............118
Hollis, Florence 1907-1987 Obituary...........123
Hollis, Harry Newcombe Jr. 1938-...............57-60
Hollis, Helen Rice 1908-.........................61-64
Hollis, James R(ussell) 1940-..................41-44R
Hollis, Jim
See Summers, Hollis (Spurgeon Jr.)
Hollis, Joseph W(illiam) 1922-...............25-28R
Hollis, Lucile U(ssery) 1921-.................25-28R
Hollis, Marcia 1937-..............................114
Hollister, Bernard C(laiborne) 1938-.......CANR-3
Earlier sketch in CA 49-52
Hollister, C(harles) Warren 1930-.........CANR-25
Earlier sketches in CA 1-4R, CANR-1
Hollister, Charles A(mmon) 1918-............17-20R
Hollister, George E(rwin) 1905-.............CAP-2
Earlier sketch in CA 17-18
Hollister, Herbert A(llen) 1933-................104
Hollister, Leo E. 1920-......................CANR-14
Earlier sketch in CA 21-24R
Hollister, William G(ray) 1915-.................122
Hollmann, Clide John 1896-1966.................5-8R
Hollo, Anselm 1934-..........................CANR-9
Earlier sketch in CA 21-24R
See also DLB 40
Hollom, Philip Arthur Dominic 1912-.........13-16R
Hollon, W. Eugene 1913-.....................CANR-2
Earlier sketch in CA 1-4R
See also AITN 1
Hollow, John Walter 1939-......................111
Holloway, Brenda W(ilmar) 1908-.............CAP-1
Earlier sketch in CA 9-10
Holloway, David 1924-..........................107
Holloway, (Rufus) Emory 1885-1977..........49-52
Obituary..73-76
See also DLB 103
Holloway, (Percival) Geoffrey 1918-.......CANR-27
Earlier sketch in CA 49-52
Holloway, George (Edward Talbot)
1921-..25-28R
Holloway, Harry (Albert) 1925-..................9-12R
Holloway, James Y(oung) 1927-..................53-56
Holloway, Jean
See Tobin, Jean Holloway
Holloway, John 1920-...........................CANR-3
Earlier sketch in CA 5-8R
See also DLB 27
Holloway, Joseph E(dward) 1948-...............111
Holloway, Marcella M(arie) 1913-..............89-92
Holloway, Mark 1917-...........................21-24R
Holloway, Maurice 1920-..........................9-12R
Holloway, Nigel 1953-.............................135
Holloway, Robert J. 1921-......................13-16R
Holloway, Stanley 1890-1982 Obituary.........106
Holloway, Teresa (Bragunier) 1906-..........17-20R
See also SATA 26
Holloway, Thomas H(alsey) 1944-...............106
Holloway, W(illiam) V(ernon) 1903-..........CANR-2
Earlier sketch in CA 1-4R
Hollowell, John 1945-.............................102
Hollowood, Albert Bernard 1910-1981..........9-12R
Obituary...103
Holly, J(ohn) Fred 1915-.......................CANR-6
Earlier sketch in CA 5-8R
Holly, Joan C(arol) 1932-......................CANR-1
Earlier sketch in CA 1-4R
Holly, Joan Hunter
See Holly, Joan C(arol)
Holly, Michael Ann 1944-.........................121
Hollyday, Frederic B(lackmar) M(umford)
1928-...45-48
Holm, (Else) Anne (Lise) 1922-................17-20R
See also MAICYA
See also SAAS 7
See also SATA 1
Holm, Bill
See Holm, Oscar William
Holm, Don(ald Raymond) 1918-...............33-36R
Holm, Jeanne M(arjorie) 1921-..................130
Holm, John Cecil 1904-1981 Obituary..........116
Holm, Marilyn D. (Franzen) 1944-.............17-20R
Holm, Oscar William 1925- Brief entry..........117
Holm, Sven (Aage) 1902-........................CAP-1
Earlier sketch in CA 11-12
Holman, Betsy Hitz 1951-.........................119
Holman, Bob
See Holman, Robert
Holman, C(larence) Hugh 1914-1981.....CANR-21
Earlier sketch in CA 5-8R
Holman, Dennis (Idris) 1915-....................9-12R
Holman, Felice 1919-..........................CANR-18
Earlier sketches in CA 5-8R, CANR-3
See also SATA 7
Holman, Harriet R. 1912-.......................37-40R
Holman, John (William) 1951-....................133
Holman, L(loyd) Bruce 1939-....................61-64
Holman, Mary A(lida) 1933-.....................93-96
Holman, Portia Grenfell
1903-1983 Obituary.............................109
Holman, Robert 1936-.............................116
Holman, William R(oger) 1926-.................49-52
Holmans, Alan Edward 1934-.....................1-4R
Holme, Bryan 1913-1990..........................103
Obituary...132
See also SATA 26
See also SATO 66
Holme, (Edith) Constance
1880(?)-1955 Brief entry........................118
See also DLB 34
Holme, K. E.
See Hill, (John Edward) Christopher
Holme, Thea 1903-..............................41-44R
Holmelund, Paul 1890-............................5-8R
Holmer, Paul L(eroy) 1916-....................37-40R
Holmes, Abraham S. 1821(?)-1908.........DLB 99
Holmes, Ann 1936(?)-1985 Obituary.............114
Holmes, Arthur F. 1924-........................33-36R
Holmes, Arthur 1890-1965 Obituary.............116
Holmes, Barbara Ware 1945-.....................120
See also SATA 65
Holmes, Burnham 1942-........................97-100
Holmes, C. Raymond 1929-.....................57-60
Holmes, Charles M(ason) 1923-...............29-32R
Holmes, Charles S(hiveley) 1916-1976.......41-44R
Obituary...61-64
Holmes, Charles Warfield
1931-1984 Obituary..............................112
Holmes, Colin 1938-...........................CANR-11
Earlier sketch in CA 25-28R
Holmes, David Charles 1919-...................9-12R
Holmes, David M(orton) 1929-.................33-36R
Holmes, Douglas 1933-.........................41-44R
Holmes, Edward M(orris) 1910-..............CANR-14
Earlier sketch in CA 37-40R
Holmes, Efner Tudor 1949-.......................65-68
Holmes, Eric M(ills) 1943-.........................121
Holmes, Frank Wakefield 1924-...................109
Holmes, Frederic L(awrence) 1932-..............93-96
Holmes, Geoffrey (Shorter) 1928-.............25-28R
Holmes, George (Arthur) 1927-....................128
Holmes, Grant
See Fox, James M.
Holmes, H. H.
See White, William A(nthony) P(arker)
Holmes, Jack D(avid) L(azarus)
1930-..CANR-24
Earlier sketch in CA 41-44R
Holmes, Jay
See Holmes, Joseph Everett
Holmes, Jeffrey 1934-..............................120
Holmes, John
See Souster, (Holmes) Raymond
Holmes, John (Albert) 1904-1962 Obituary.....115
Holmes, John Clellon 1926-1988...............CANR-4
Obituary...125
Earlier sketch in CA 9-12R
See also CLC 56
See also DLB 16
Holmes, John Haynes
1879-1964 Obituary...............................89-92
Holmes, John L. 1925-..............................115
Holmes, John W(endell) 1910-1989..............134
Brief entry...109
Holmes, John 1913-..................................104
Holmes, Jon 1948-...................................114
Holmes, Joseph Everett 1922-..................CANR-1
Earlier sketch in CA 1-4R
Holmes, Joseph R. 1928(?)-1983 Obituary.....109
Holmes, Kenneth L(loyd) 1915-..............CANR-27
Earlier sketch in CA 37-40R
Holmes, Kim R(ene) 1952-.........................111
Holmes, Lowell D(on) 1925-....................33-36R
Holmes, Marjorie (Rose) 1910-..............CANR-23
Earlier sketches in CA 1-4R, CANR-5
See also AITN 1
See also SATA 43
Holmes, Martin (Rivington) 1905-............CANR-1
Earlier sketch in CA 49-52
Holmes, (John) Michael (Aleister) 1931-....25-28R
Holmes, Michael Stephan 1942-.................77-80
Holmes, Nancy 1921-...............................69-72
Holmes, Olive 1911-.................................115
Holmes, Oliver Wendell Jr.
1841-1935 Brief entry.............................114
Holmes, Oliver Wendell
1809-1894.......................CDALB 1640-1865
See also DLB 1
See also SATA 34
Holmes, Parker Manfred 1895-...................CAP-1
Earlier sketch in CA 13-14
Holmes, Paul Allen 1901-1985...................CAP-2
Obituary...114
Earlier sketch in CA 19-20
Holmes, Paul Carter 1926-....................CANR-11
Earlier sketch in CA 21-24R
Holmes, Peggy 1898-................................121
See also SATA 60
Holmes, Raymond
See Souster, (Holmes) Raymond
Holmes, (Edward) Richard 1946-.............CANR-25
Earlier sketch in CA 106
Holmes, Richard 1945-..............................133
Brief entry..126
Holmes, Rick
See Hardwick, Richard Holmes Jr.
Holmes, Robert A(lexander) 1943-..............57-60
Holmes, Robert L(awrence) 1935-.............41-44R
Holmes, Robert Merrill 1925-....................89-92
Holmes, Thomas K.............................CANR-26
Earlier sketches in CAP-2, CA 19-20
Holmes, Tiffany 1944-..............................97-100
Holmes, Tommy 1903-1975 Obituary............57-60
Holmes, Urban T(igner) 1900-1972..............CAP-2
Earlier sketch in CA 21-22
Holmes, W(ilfred) J(ay) 1900-..................29-32R
Holmes, William Kersley 1882-...................CAP-1
Earlier sketch in CA 9-10
Holmgren, Helen Jean 1930-....................97-100
See also SATA 45
Holmgren, Norah 1939-...............................102
Holmgren, Sister George Ellen
See Holmgren, Helen Jean
Holmgren, Virginia C(unningham) 1909-.........107
See also SATA 26
Holmquist, Anders 1933-..........................29-32R
Holmquist, Eve 1921-...............................53-56
See also SATA 11
Holmstrand, Marie Juline (Gunderson)
1908-...5-8R
Holmstrom, (John) Edwin 1898-.................CAP-1
Earlier sketch in CA 11-12
Holmstrom, Lynda Lytle 1939-...................33-36R
Holmvik, Oyvind 1914-.............................17-20R
Holod, Renata O. 1942-...............................119
Holoien, Martin O. 1928-..............................112
Holquist, (James) Michael 1935-...............CANR-17
Earlier sketches in CA 45-48, CANR-2
Holroyd, Michael (de Courcy Fraser)
1935-...CANR-35
Earlier sketches in CA 53-56, CANR-4, 18
See also MTCW
Holroyd, Sam
See Burton, S(amuel) H(olroyd)
Holroyd, Stuart 1933-...............................93-96
Holsaert, Eunice Obituary.........................53-56
Holsinger, Jane Lumley............................17-20R
Holske, Katherine Obituary..........................104
Holsopple, Barbara 1943-...........................73-76
Holst, Hermann E. von 1841-1904..............DLB 47
Holst, Imogen (Clare) 1907-1984 Obituary......112
Holst, Johan J(oergen) 1937-...................CANR-11
Earlier sketch in CA 25-28R
Holst, Lawrence E(berhardt) 1929-..............61-64
Holsti, Kalevi J(acque) 1935-...................21-24R
Holsti, Ole R(udolf) 1933-......................CANR-28
Earlier sketches in CA 25-28R, CANR-11
Holt, Andrew
See Anhalt, Edward
Holt, Edgar Crawshaw 1900-1975..............CANR-6
Obituary...61-64
Earlier sketch in CA 1-4R
Holt, Elizabeth B(asye) G(ilmore)
1906(?)-1987...124
Holt, Gavin
See Rodda, Charles
Holt, Georgia 1927-.....................................129
Holt, (Wilma) Geraldene..............................137
Holt, Helen
See Paine, Lauran (Bosworth)
Holt, (Laurence) James 1939-....................25-28R
Holt, John Agee 1920-.................................1-4R
Holt, John (Caldwell) 1923-1985...............CANR-32
Obituary...117
Earlier sketch in CA 69-72
Holt, John (Robert) 1926-........................CANR-11
Earlier sketch in CA 25-28R
Holt, John 1721-1784...............................DLB 43
Holt, Kaare 1917- Brief entry.......................111
Holt, Kare
See Holt, Kaare
Holt, L. Emmett Jr. 1895-1974 Obituary........53-56
Holt, Lee E(lbert) 1912-............................13-16R
Holt, Margaret Van Vechten (Saunders)
1899-1963 Obituary.....................................111
See also SATA 32
Holt, Margaret 1937-..............................17-20R
See also SATA 4
Holt, Michael F(itzgibbon) 1940-.................81-84
Holt, Michael (Paul) 1929-.........................CANR-5
Earlier sketch in CA 53-56
See also SATA 13
Holt, Pat Mayo 1920-...................................111
Holt, Rackham
See Holt, Margaret Van Vechten (Saunders)
Holt, Robert R(utherford) 1917-...............CANR-35
Earlier sketches in CA 41-44R, CANR-15
Holt, Robert T. 1928-..............................37-40R
Holt, Rochelle L.
See DuBois, Rochelle (Lynn) Holt
See also SATA 41
Holt, Stephen
See Thompson, Harlan (Howard)
Holt, Tex
See Joscelyn, Archie L.
Holt, Thelma Jewett 1913-........................29-32R
Holt, Thomas Charles Louis 1961-..................135
Holt, Thomas J(ung) 1928-............................102
Holt, Tom
See Holt, Thomas Charles Louis
Holt, Victoria
See Hibbert, Eleanor Burford
Holt, Will 1929-...105
Holt, William 1897-1977.............................CAP-1
Obituary..69-72
Earlier sketch in CA 17-18
Holtan, Orley I. 1933-..............................33-36R
Holtby, Robert Tinsley 1921-........................108
Holter, Don W. 1905-.................................37-40R
Holthusen, Hans Egon 1913-........................45-48
See also DLB 69
Holtje, Herbert F(ranklin) 1931-.................CANR-8
Earlier sketch in CA 61-64
Holton, Felicia Antonelli 1921-.....................69-72
Holton, Gerald (James) 1922-.....................13-16R
Holton, Leonard
See Wibberley, Leonard (Patrick O'Connor)
Holton, (William) Milne 1931-....................41-44R
Holton, Richard H(enry) 1926- Brief entry.......107
Holtrop, William Frans 1908-........................57-60
Holtz, Avraham 1934-...............................29-32R
Holtz, Barry W(illiam) 1947-..........................109
Holtz, Herman R(alph) 1919-.........................105
Holtze, Sally Holmes 1952-...........................123
See also SATA 64
Holtzman, Abraham 1921-..........................CANR-2
Earlier sketch in CA 1-4R
Holtzman, Harry 1912-1987 Obituary..............123
Holtzman, Jerome 1926-............................CANR-4
Earlier sketch in CA 53-56
See also SATA 57
Holtzman, Paul D(ouglas) 1918-...................33-36R
Holtzman, Wayne H(arold) 1923-...............CANR-34
Earlier sketches in CA 37-40R, CANR-15
Holtzman, Will 1951-.....................................102
Holub, Miroslav 1923-..............................CANR-10
Earlier sketch in CA 21-24R
See also CLC 4
Holub, Robert C(harles) 1949-...................CANR-35
Earlier sketch in CA 114
Holum, Dianne 1951-...................................123
Holway, John 1929-....................................57-60
Holyer, Erna Maria 1925-..........................CANR-12
Earlier sketch in CA 29-32R
See also SATA 22

Holyer, Ernie
See Holyer, Erna Maria
Holz, Arno 1863-1929 .... DLB 118
Holz, Loretta (Marie) 1943- CANR-10
Earlier sketch in CA 65-68
See also SATA 17
Holz, Robert K(enneth) 1930- 53-56
Holzapfel, Rudolf Patrick 1938- CAP-1
Earlier sketch in CA 11-12
Holzberger, William George 1932- 53-56
Holzel, Thomas Martin 1940- 126
Holzel, Tom
See Holzel, Thomas Martin
Holzer, Hans 1920- CANR-22
Earlier sketches in CA 13-16R, CANR-7
Holzer, Harold 1949- CANR-39
Earlier sketch in CA 116
Holzman, Franklyn Dunn 1918- 61-64
Holzman, Philip Seidman 1922- 37-40R
Holzman, Red
See Holzman, William
Holzman, Robert S(tuart) 1907- CANR-2
Earlier sketch in CA 1-4R
Holzman, William 1920- 101
Holzner, Burkart 1931- 93-96
Hom, Ken 1949- CANR-26
Earlier sketch in CA 109
Hom, Marlon Kau 1947- 131
Homan, Robert Anthony 1929- 5-8R
Homans, Abigail Adams
1879-1974 Obituary 104
Homans, George Caspar 1910-1989 107
Obituary 128
Homans, Peter 1930- CANR-28
Earlier sketches in CA 21-24R, CANR-11
Homberger, Eric (Ross) 1942- CANR-23
Earlier sketch in CA 106
Homburger, Erik
See Erikson, Erik H(omburger)
Home, Alexander Frederick 1903- 102
Home, Charles (Cospatrick) Douglas
See Douglas-Home, Charles (Cospatrick)
Home, Henry Douglas
See Douglas-Home, Henry
Home, Henry 1696-1782 .... DLB 104
Home, John 1722-1808 .... DLB 84
Home, Michael
See Bush, Charlie Christmas
Home, William Douglas 1912- 102
See also DLB 13
Homel, Michael W. 1944- 126
Homer, Frank X. J. 1941- 127
Homer, Frederic D(onald) 1939- 65-68
Homer, Sidney 1902-1983 Obituary 110
Homer, Williams Innes 1929- 13-16R
Homes, A(my) M. 136
Homes, Geoffrey
See Mainwaring, Daniel
Homewood, Charles H.
1914(?)-1984 Obituary 112
Homewood, Harry
See Homewood, Charles H.
Homola, Priscilla 1947- 116
Homola, Samuel 1929- 97-100
Homolya, Istvan 1940- 131
Homosap
See Nuttall, Jeff
Homrighausen, Elmer George 1900- 45-48
Homsher, Lola Mae 1913- 1-4R
Homze, Alma C. 1932- 29-32R
See also SATA 17
Homze, Edward L. 1930- 33-36R
Honan, Park 1928- CANR-14
Earlier sketch in CA 77-80
See also DLB 111
Honan, William H(olmes) 1930- 123
Honce, Charles E. 1895-1975 Obituary 61-64
Honderich, John A. 1946- 128
Honderich, Ted 1933- CANR-35
Earlier sketches in CA 33-36R, CANR-14
Hone, Joseph 1937- CANR-35
Earlier sketches in CA 65-68, CANR-14
Hone, Ralph E(merson) 1913- CANR-9
Earlier sketch in CA 21-24R
Hone, William 1780-1842 .... DLB 110
Honerkamp, Nicholas 1950- 138
Honey, Martha S(pencer) 1945- CANR-31
Earlier sketch in CA 112
Honey, P(atrick) J(ames) 1922- 13-16R
Honey, William (Houghton) 1910- 33-36R
Honeycombe, Gordon 1936- CANR-34
Earlier sketches in CA 77-80, CANR-15
Honeycutt, Ann 1902(?)-1989 Obituary 129
Honeycutt, Benjamin L(awrence) 1938- 57-60
Honeycutt, Roy L(ee) Jr. 1926- 41-44R
Honeyman, Brenda
See Clarke, Brenda (Margaret Lilian)
Hong, Edna H. 1913- CANR-9
Earlier sketch in CA 21-24R
Hong, Howard V(incent) 1912- CANR-9
Earlier sketch in CA 21-24R
Hong, Jane Fay 1954- 93-96
Hong, Yong Ki 1929(?)-1979 Obituary 85-88
Hongo, Garrett Kaoru 1951- 133
See also DLB 120
Honhart, Frederick L(ewis III) 1943- 112
Honig, Donald 1931- CANR-24
Earlier sketches in CA 17-20R, CANR-9
See also SATA 18
Honig, Edwin 1919- CANR-4
Earlier sketch in CA 5-8R
See also CAAS 8
See also CLC 33
See also DLB 5
Honig, Louis 1911-1977 77-80
Obituary 73-76
Honigfeld, Gilbert
See Howard, Gilbert
Honigmann, E(rnst) A(nselm) J(oachim)
1927- CANR-9
Earlier sketch in CA 21-24R
Honigmann, John J(oseph) 1914-1977 .....CANR-2
Earlier sketch in CA 1-4R
Honnalgere, Gopal 1944- 73-76
Honness, Elizabeth H. 1904- 25-28R
See also SATA 2
Honnold, John Otis Jr. 1915- CANR-8
Earlier sketch in CA 13-16R
Honore, Antony Maurice 1921- CANR-1
Earlier sketch in CA 1-4R
Honour, Hugh 1927- 103
Honourable Member for X
See de Chair, Somerset (Struben)
Honri, Peter 1929- 103
Hoobler, Dorothy CANR-27
Earlier sketches in CA 69-72, CANR-11
See also SATA 28
Hoobler, Thomas CANR-27
Earlier sketches in CA 69-72, CANR-11
See also SATA 28
Hood, Ann 1956- 136
Hood, Bruce 1936- 130
Hood, Buck 1907(?)-1983 Obituary 110
Hood, David Crockett 1937- 37-40R
Hood, Donald W(ilbur) 1918- 37-40R
Hood, Dora (Ridout) 1885- CAP-2
Earlier sketch in CA 17-18
Hood, F(rancis) C(ampbell) 1895-1971 ...... CAP-1
Earlier sketch in CA 13-14
Hood, Flora M(ae) 1898- 5-8R
Hood, Graham 1936- 77-80
Hood, Hugh (John Blagdon) 1928- CANR-33
Earlier sketches in CA 49-52, CANR-1
See also CLC 15, 28
See also DLB 53
Hood, Joseph F. 1925- 33-36R
See also SATA 4
Hood, Lynley (Jane) 1942- 135
Hood, Margaret Page 1892- 1-4R
Hood, Mary 1946- 128
Hood, Robert E. 1926- 21-24R
See also SATA 21
Hood, Roger (Grahame) 1936- 128
Hood, Sarah
See Killough, (Karen) Lee
Hood, (Martin) Sinclair (Frankland)
1917- CANR-9
Earlier sketch in CA 21-24R
Hood, Thomas 1799-1845 .... DLB 96
Hood, William (Joseph) 1920- CANR-26
Earlier sketch in CA 109
Hoofnagle, Keith Lundy 1941- 13-16R
Hoogasian-Villa, Susie 1921-1978 ....17-20R
Obituary 114
Hoogenboom, Ari (Arthur) 1927- CANR-25
Earlier sketch in CA 45-48
Hoogenboom, Olive 1927- 21-24R
Hoogestraat, Wayne E. 5-8R
Hook, Andrew 1932- 53-56
Hook, Diana ffarington 1918- 61-64
Hook, Donald D(wight) 1928- CANR-4
Earlier sketch in CA 53-56
Hook, Frances 1912- 105
See also SATA 27
Hook, Frank S(cott) 1922- 21-24R
Hook, Hilary 1917-1990 Obituary 132
Hook, J(ulius) N(icholas) 1913- CANR-38
Earlier sketches in CA 5-8R, CANR-2, 17
Hook, Judith 1941(?)-1984 Obituary 113
Hook, Martha 1936- 105
See also SATA 27
Hook, Sidney 1902-1989 ....CANR-7
Obituary 129
Earlier sketch in CA 9-12R
Hook, Theodore 1788-1841 .... DLB 116
Hooke, Nina Warner 1907- 73-76
Hooker, C(lifford) A(lan) 1942- CANR-19
Earlier sketches in CA 49-52, CANR-4
Hooker, Craig Michael 1951- 57-60
Hooker, Frances
See Horovitz, Frances Margaret
Hooker, James Ralph 1929- 21-24R
Hooker, (Peter) Jeremy 1941- CANR-22
Earlier sketch in CA 77-80
See also CLC 43
See also DLB 40
Hooker, Richard
See Hornberger, H. Richard
Hooker, Richard J(ames) 1912- 122
Hooker, Ruth 1920- 69-72
See also SATA 21
Hooker, Stanley (George)
1907-1984 Obituary 112
Hooker, Thomas 1586-1647 .... DLB 24
Hookham, Hilda Henriette (Kuttner)
1915- 9-12R
Hooks, G(aylor) Eugene 1927- 1-4R
Hooks, Gene
See Hooks, G(aylor) Eugene
Hooks, William H(arris) 1921- CANR-19
Earlier sketch in CA 81-84
See also SATA 16
Hoole, Daryl Van Dam 1934- 21-24R
Hoole, W(illiam) Stanley 1903- CANR-7
Earlier sketch in CA 17-20R
Hooper, Biff
See Obrecht, Jas
Hooper, Byrd
See St. Clair, Byrd Hooper
Hooper, David (Vincent) 1915- 85-88
Hooper, Douglas 1927- CANR-18
Earlier sketch in CA 25-28R
Hooper, Finley (Allison) 1922- 123
Hooper, Hedley Colwill 1919- 124
Hooper, John W(illiam) 1926- 29-32R
Hooper, Johnson Jones 1815-1862 ......DLB 3,11
Hooper, Judith 1949- 136
Hooper, Kay 1957- 122
Hooper, Meredith (Jean) 1939- CANR-22
Earlier sketch in CA 106
See also SATA 28
Hooper, Patricia 1941- 127
Hooper, Paul F(ranklin) 1938- CANR-18
Earlier sketch in CA 101
Hooper, Peter
See Hooper, Hedley Colwill
Hooper, Walter (McGehee) 1931- CANR-22
Earlier sketches in CA 17-20R, CANR-7
Hooper, William Loyd 1931- CANR-19
Earlier sketches in CA 5-8R, CANR-3
Hoopes, Clement R. 1906-1979 73-76
Obituary 89-92
Hoopes, David S. 1928- 118
Hoopes, Donelson F(arquhar) 1932- 33-36R
Hoopes, James 1944- CANR-10
Earlier sketch in CA 65-68
Hoopes, Lyn Littlefield 1953- 120
See also SATA 44, 49
Hoopes, Ned E(dward) 1932- 17-20R
See also SATA 21
Hoopes, Robert (Griffith) 1920- CANR-1
Earlier sketch in CA 1-4R
Hoopes, Roy 1922- CANR-15
Earlier sketch in CA 21-24R
See also SATA 11
Hoopes, Townsend Walter 1922- 97-100
Hoople, Cheryl G. Brief entry 111
See also SATA 32
Hoops, Richard A(llen) 1933- 41-44R
Hoor, Elvie (Marie Mortensen) Ten
See Ten Hoor, Elvie (Marie Mortensen)
Hoornik, Ed(uard Jozef Antonie Marie)
1910-1970 Obituary 104
Hoos, Ida Russakoff 1912- 17-20R
Hooson, David J. M. 1926- 17-20R
Hooten, William J(arvis) 1900- 61-64
Hooton, Charles
See Rowe, Vivian C(laud)
Hooton, Joy 1935- 127
Hoover, Calvin Bryce 1897-1974 .... CAP-1
Obituary 49-52
Earlier sketch in CA 13-14
Hoover, Dorothy Estheryne 1918- 49-52
Hoover, Dwight W(esley) 1926- 33-36R
Hoover, Edgar M. 1907- 13-16R
Hoover, F(rancis) Louis 1913- 41-44R
Hoover, H(elen) M(ary) 1935- CANR-36
Earlier sketches in CA 105, CANR-22
See also MAICYA
See also SAAS 8
See also SATA 33, 44
Hoover, Hardy 1902- 29-32R
Hoover, Helen (Drusilla Blackburn)
1910-1984 ....21-24R
Obituary 113
See also SATA 12, 39
Hoover, Herbert (Clark) 1874-1964 108
Obituary 89-92
Hoover, Herbert Theodore 1930- 106
Hoover, J(ohn) Edgar 1895-1972 ....CANR-2
Obituary 33-36R
Earlier sketch in CA 1-4R
Hoover, John P. 1910- 53-56
Hoover, Kenneth H(arding) 1920- CANR-7
Earlier sketch in CA 57-60
Hoover, Kenneth R(ay) 1940- 132
Hoover, Marjorie L(awson) 1910- 41-44R
Hoover, Mary B(idgood) 1917- 93-96
Hoover, Thomas 1941- 102
Hopcraft, Arthur 1932- CANR-35
Earlier sketches in CA 25-28R, CANR-14
Hope, A(lec) D(erwent) 1907- CANR-33
Earlier sketch in CA 21-24R
See also CLC 3, 51
See also MTCW
Hope, A(shley) Guy 1914-1982 ....25-28R
Obituary 133
Hope, Amanda
See Lewis, Judith Mary
Hope, Andrew
See Hern, (George) Anthony
Hope, Bob 1903- 101
See also BEST 90:4
Hope, Brian
See Creasey, John
Hope, C(harles) E(velyn) G(raham)
1900-1971 .... CAP-1
Earlier sketch in CA 13-16
Hope, Christopher (David Tully) 1944- 106
See also CLC 52
See also SATA 62
Hope, David
See Fraser, Douglas
Hope, Felix
See Williamson, Claude C(harles) H.
Hope, Jack 1940- 81-84
Hope, Jane 1938- 110
Hope, Karol 93-96
Hope, Laura Lee CANR-27
Earlier sketch in CA 17-20R
See also SATA 1, 67
Hope, Margaret
See Knight, Alanna
Hope, Marjorie (Cecelia) 1923- 29-32R
Hope, Norman Victor 1908-1983 Obituary 110
Hope, Quentin M(anning) 1923- 13-16R
Hope, Ronald (Sidney) 1921- CANR-3
Earlier sketch in CA 9-12R
Hope, Welborn 1903- 29-32R
Hope-Jones, Arthur 1911-1984 Obituary 112
Hopes, David Brendan 1953- CANR-26
Earlier sketch in CA 109
Hope Simpson, Jacynth 1930- CANR-7
Earlier sketch in CA 13-16R
See also SATA 12
Hope-Wallace, Philip (Adrian)
1911-1979 Obituary 93-96
Hopewell, S(ydney) 1924- 25-28R
Hopf, Alice (Martha) L(ightner)
1904-1988 ....CANR-9
Obituary 124
Earlier sketch in CA 17-20R
See also SATA 5, 55
Hopke, William E. 1918- 21-24R
Hopkin, Alannah 1949- CANR-27
Earlier sketch in CA 109
Hopkins, A. T.
See Turngren, Annette
Hopkins, Antony 1921- CANR-17
Earlier sketch in CA 101
Hopkins, Bill 1928- 9-12R
Hopkins, C(harles) Howard 1905- 123
Hopkins, Clark 1895-1976 129
Obituary 109
See also SATA 34
Hopkins, David 1948- 122
Hopkins, Donald R(oswell) 1941- 123
Hopkins, Fred W(right) Jr. 1935- 69-72
Hopkins, George E(mil) 1937- 33-36R
Hopkins, Gerard Manley
1844-1889 .... CDBLB 1890-1914
See also DLB 35, 57
See also WLC
Hopkins, Harry 1913- 29-32R
Hopkins, J(ohn) F(eely) 1922- 102
Hopkins, J. L. 1938- 77-80
Hopkins, Jack W(alker) 1930- 25-28R
Hopkins, James Franklin 1909- 1-4R
Hopkins, Jasper (Stephen Jr.) 1936- CANR-31
Earlier sketches in CA 37-40R, CANR-14
Hopkins, Jerry 1935- CANR-18
Earlier sketch in CA 25-28R
Hopkins, John (Richard) 1931- 85-88
See also CLC 4
Hopkins, Joseph G(erard) E(dward)
1909- CANR-5
Earlier sketch in CA 1-4R
See also SATA 11
Hopkins, Joseph Martin 1919- 49-52
Hopkins, Keith 1934- 130
Hopkins, (Hector) Kenneth 1914-1988 .....CANR-1
Obituary 125
Earlier sketch in CA 1-4R
See also SATA 58
Hopkins, Lee Bennett 1938- CANR-29
Earlier sketch in CA 25-28R
See also MAICYA
See also SAAS 4
See also SATA 3, 68
Hopkins, Lee (Wallace) 57-60
Hopkins, Lemuel 1750-1801 .... DLB 37
Hopkins, Lightnin'
See Hopkins, Sam
Hopkins, Lyman
See Folsom, Franklin (Brewster)
Hopkins, Marjorie 1911- 21-24R
See also SATA 9
Hopkins, Mark W(yatt) 1931- 29-32R
Hopkins, Milton 1906-1983 Obituary 109
Hopkins, Nicholas S(nowden) 1939- 77-80
Hopkins, Pauline Elizabeth 1859-1930 .... BLC 2
See also DLB 50
See also TCLC 28
Hopkins, Prynce (C.) 1885-1970 .... CAP-2
Earlier sketch in CA 21-22
Hopkins, Pryns
See Hopkins, Prynce (C.)
Hopkins, Raymond F(rederick) 1939- CANR-28
Earlier sketch in CA 49-52
Hopkins, Robert A. 1923- 89-92
Hopkins, Robert S(ydney) 1930- CANR-38
Earlier sketch in CA 115
Hopkins, Sam 1912-1982 Obituary 106
Hopkins, Samuel 1721-1803 .... DLB 31
Hopkins, Terence K(ilbourne) 1928- 9-12R
Hopkins, Thomas H(ollis) 1945- 116
Hopkins, Thomas J(ohns) 1930- 37-40R
Hopkins, Viola
See Winner, Viola Hopkins
Hopkins, Vivian C. 1909- CAP-2
Earlier sketch in CA 33-36
Hopkinson, Diana 1912- 29-32R
Hopkinson, Francis 1737-1791 .... DLB 31
Hopkinson, Henry Thomas 1905-1990 ......17-20R
Obituary 132
Hopkinson, Tom
See Hopkinson, Henry Thomas
Hopkirk, Peter 1930- 107
Hopley, George
See Hopley-Woolrich, Cornell George
Hopley-Woolrich, Cornell George
1903-1968 .... CAP-1
Earlier sketch in CA 13-14
Hoppe, Art(hur Watterson) 1925- CANR-3
Earlier sketch in CA 5-8R
Hoppe, Eleanor Sellers 1933- 73-76
Hoppe, Emil Otho 1878- 9-12R
Hoppe, Joanne 1932- 81-84
See also SATA 42
Hoppe, Ronald A. 1931- 45-48
Hoppen, K(arl) Theodore 1941- 119
Hoppenstedt, Elbert M. 1917- 1-4R
Hopper, Columbus B(urwell) 1931- 33-36R
Hopper, David H. 1927- 21-24R
Hopper, Dennis 1936- 114
Hopper, Hedda
See Furry, Elda

Hopper, John 1934- ... 17-20R
Hopper, Nancy J. 1937- ... CANR-38
Earlier sketch in CA 115
See also SATA 35, 38
Hopper, R(obert) J(ohn) 1910-1987 ... 123
Hopper, Robert 1945- ... CANR-9
Earlier sketch in CA 65-68
Hopper, Vincent Foster 1906-1976 ... CANR-6
Obituary ... 61-64
Earlier sketch in CA 1-4R
Hoppin, Richard H(allowell) 1913- ... 41-44R
Hoppock, Robert 1901- ... 1-4R
Hopson, Dan Jr. 1930- ... 21-24R
Hopson, Janet L(ouise) 1950- ... 89-92
Hopwood, Robert R. 1910- ... CAP-1
Earlier sketch in CA 13-14
Hora, F. Bayard 1909(?)-1984 Obituary ... 112
Horak, M. Stephan 1920- ... 9-12R
Horan, Francis Harding
1900-1978 Obituary ... 81-84
Horan, James David 1914-1981 ... CANR-9
Obituary ... 105
Earlier sketch in CA 13-16R
Horan, (Harold) Joseph Taaffe
1898(?)-1985 Obituary ... 117
Horan, William D. 1933- ... 25-28R
Horatio
See
Proust, (Valentin-Louis-George-Eugene-)Marcel
Horatio, Algernon ... 89-92
Horatio, Jane
See Cudlipp, Edythe
Horbach, Michael 1924-1986 ... CANR-25
Obituary ... 120
Earlier sketch in CA 29-32R
Horchler, Richard (Thomas) 1925- ... 5-8R
Horchow, (Samuel) Roger 1928- ... 106
Horder, Mervyn 1910- ... 104
Hordern, William (Edward) 1920- ... 13-16R
Hordon, Harris E(ugene) 1942- ... 53-56
Horecky, Paul Louis 1913- ... CANR-2
Earlier sketch in CA 5-8R
Horelick, Arnold L(awrence) 1928- ... CANR-8
Earlier sketch in CA 17-20R
Horgan, Denis E. 1941- ... 101
Horgan, Edward R. 1934- ... 109
Horgan, John J(oseph) 1910- ... 61-64
Horgan, John Joseph 1881-1967 Obituary ... 116
Horgan, Paul 1903- ... CANR-35
Earlier sketches in CA 13-16R, CANR-9
See also CLC 9, 53
See also DLB 102
See also DLBY 85
See also MTCW
See also SATA 13
Hori, Ichiro 1910-1974 ... CAP-2
Earlier sketch in CA 25-28
Horie, Shigeo 1903- ... CAP-1
Earlier sketch in CA 13-14
Horikoshi, Jiro 1904(?)-1982 Obituary ... 110
Horka-Follick, Lorayne Ann 1940- ... 29-32R
Horkheimer, Max 1895-1973 Obituary ... 41-44R
Horlak, E. E.
See Tepper, Sheri S.
Horman, Richard E. 1945- ... 29-32R
Horn, D(avid) B(ayne) 1901-1969 ... CANR-6
Earlier sketch in CA 1-4R
Horn, Daniel 1934-1991 ... 21-24R
Obituary ... 134
Horn, Edward Newman
1903(?)-1976 Obituary ... 65-68
Horn, Francis H(enry) 1908- ... 53-56
Horn, George F(rancis) 1917- ... CANR-8
Earlier sketch in CA 5-8R
Horn, Henry Eyster 1913- ... 21-24R
Horn, Jeanne P. 1925- ... 5-8R
Horn, John L(eonard) 1928- ... CANR-14
Earlier sketch in CA 37-40R
Horn, Linda L(ouise) 1947- ... 101
Horn, Maurice 1931- ... CANR-22
Earlier sketch in CA 89-92
Horn, Pamela (Lucy Ray) 1936- ... CANR-30
Earlier sketch in CA 69-72
Horn, Peter
See Kuttner, Henry
Horn, Peter (Rudolf Gisela) 1934- ... 103
Horn, Pierre L(aurence) 1942- ... 119
Horn, Richard 1954-1989 ... 105
Obituary ... 128
Horn, Robert M. 1933- ... 29-32R
Horn, Siegfried H(erbert) 1908- ... 37-40R
Horn, Stefan F. 1900- ... CAP-1
Earlier sketch in CA 13-16
Horn, (John) Stephen 1931- ... 13-16R
Horn, Stephen (McCaffrey Moore) 1931- ... 45-48
Horn, Thomas D. 1918- ... 13-16R
Horn, Vivi 1878(?)-1971 Obituary ... 104
Horn, Walter (William) 1908- ... 21-24R
Hornback, Bert G(erald) 1935- ... CANR-22
Earlier sketch in CA 29-32R
Hornbaker, Alice 1927- ... 77-80
Hornbein, Thomas Frederic 1930- ... 53-56
Hornberger, H. Richard ... 105
Hornberger, Theodore 1906-1975 ... CANR-3
Earlier sketch in CA 5-8R
Hornblow, Arthur Jr. 1893-1976 ... 89-92
Obituary ... 65-68
See also SATA 15
Hornblow, Leonora (Schinasi) 1920- ... 73-76
See also SATA 18
Hornblower, Harry C.
See Shriver, Harry C(lair)
Hornbruch, Frederick William Jr. 1913- ... 109
Hornby, John (Wilkinson) 1913- ... 9-12R
Hornby, Leslie 1949- ... 103
Hornby, Richard 1938- ... 89-92
Hornby, William H(arry) 1923- ... 106
Horne, A(lexander) D(ouglas) 1932- ... 109
Horne, Aaron 1940- ... 138
Horne, Alistair (Allan) 1925- ... CANR-9
Earlier sketch in CA 5-8R
Horne, Bernard Shea 1905-1970 Obituary ... 104
Horne, Chevis Ferber 1914- ... CANR-16
Earlier sketch in CA 97-100
Horne, Cynthia Miriam 1939- ... 5-8R
Horne, Donald (Richmond) 1921- ... CANR-20
Earlier sketch in CA 103
Horne, Elliott 1922(?)-1989 Obituary ... 129
Horne, Frank (Smith) 1899-1974 ... 125
Obituary ... 53-56
See also BW
See also DLB 51
Horne, Geoffrey 1916- ... 9-12R
Horne, Howard
See Payne, (Pierre Stephen) Robert
Horne, Hugh Robert 1915- ... 5-8R
Horne, Kenneth 1900-1975 Obituary ... 115
Horne, Lewis 1932- ... 110
Horne, Marilyn 1934- ... 133
Horne, Peter 1947- ... 69-72
Horne, R(alph) A(lbert) 1929- ... 106
Horne, Richard Henry 1803-1884 ... DLB 32
See also SATA 29
Horne, Roman L(emuel)
1901-1987 Obituary ... 121
Horne, Shirley (Faith) 1919- ... 49-52
Horner, Althea (Jane) 1926- ... 81-84
See also SATA 36
Horner, Dave 1934- ... 17-20R
See also SATA 12
Horner, David Stuart
1900(?)-1983(?) Obituary ... 111
Horner, George F(rederick) 1899-1974 ... CAP-2
Earlier sketch in CA 33-36
Horner, J. C.
See Horner, John Curwen
Horner, John Curwen 1922- ... 103
Horner, Joyce Mary 1903-1980 Obituary ... 112
Horner, Kenric Lancaster
1902-1973 Obituary ... 111
Horner, Lance
See Horner, Kenric Lancaster
Horner, Thomas Marland 1927- ... 37-40R
Horner, Tom (Julian) 1913- ... 121
Horner, Winifred Bryan 1922- ... 118
Horney, Karen (Clementine Theodore Danielsen)
1885-1952 Brief entry ... 114
Horngren, Charles T(homas) 1926- ... 57-60
Hornig, Doug 1943- ... 117
Hornik, Edith Lynn
See Beer, Edith Lynn
Hornik-Beer, Edith Lynn
See Beer, Edith Lynn
Horning, Alice S. 1950- ... 137
Hornman, Wim 1920- Brief entry ... 106
Hornos, Axel 1907- ... CAP-2
Earlier sketch in CA 29-32
See also SATA 20
Hornsby, Albert Sidney
1898(?)-1978 Obituary ... 104
Hornsby, Alton Jr. 1940- ... 37-40R
Hornsby, Ken 1934- ... 105
Hornsby, Roger A. 1926- ... 21-24R
Hornsby-Smith, Michael P(eter) 1932- ... 126
Hornstein, Harvey A. 1938- ... 53-56
Hornstein, Lillian Herlands 1909- ... 45-48
Hornstein, Reuben Aaron 1912- ... 106
See also SATA 64
Hornung, Clarence Pearson 1899- ... CANR-9
Earlier sketch in CA 17-20R
Hornung, E(rnest) W(illiam)
1866-1921 Brief entry ... 108
See also DLB 70
Hornung, Erik 1933- ... 117
Hornung, Maximilian 1942- ... 107
Horobin, Ian M. 1899-1976 Obituary ... 69-72
Horovitz, Frances Margaret
1938-1983 Obituary ... 111
Horovitz, Israel 1939- ... 33-36R
See also CLC 56
See also DLB 7
Horovitz, Michael 1935- ... 81-84
Horowitz, Al
See Horowitz, I(srael) A.
Horowitz, David A. 1941- ... 89-92
Horowitz, David Charles 1937- ... 89-92
Horowitz, David (Joel) 1939- ... 13-16R
Horowitz, David 1903- ... 69-72
Horowitz, Donald L(eonard) 1939- ... 126
Horowitz, Edward 1904- ... CANR-4
Earlier sketch in CA 1-4R
Horowitz, Esther 1920- ... 49-52
Horowitz, Gene 1930- ... 77-80
Horowitz, Helen Lefkowitz 1942- ... 125
Horowitz, I(srael) A.
1907-1973 Obituary ... 41-44R
Horowitz, Ira 1934- ... 41-44R
Horowitz, Irving Louis 1929- ... 41-44R
Horowitz, Jacob 1900-1979 Obituary ... 89-92
Horowitz, Joseph 1948- ... CANR-27
Earlier sketch in CA 109
Horowitz, Laura (Godofsky)
1943-1983 Obituary ... 110
Horowitz, Leonard M(artin) 1937- ... 37-40R
Horowitz, Lois 1940- ... 119
Horowitz, Mardi J(on) 1934- ... 33-36R
Horowitz, Michael M. 1933- ... CANR-15
Earlier sketch in CA 41-44R
Horowitz, Morris A(aron) 1919- ... CANR-9
Earlier sketch in CA 65-68
Horowitz, Robert S. 1924- ... 9-12R
Horowitz, Shel Alan 1956- ... 120
Horrell, C. William 1918- ... CANR-13
Earlier sketch in CA 61-64
Horricks, Raymond 1933- ... 129
Horrock, Berta Crone
1896(?)-1983 Obituary ... 110
Horrock, Nicholas (Morton) 1936- ... 49-52
Horrocks, Brian (Gwynne)
1895-1985 Obituary ... 114
Horrocks, Edna M. 1908- ... CAP-2
Earlier sketch in CA 17-18
Horrocks, John E(dwin) 1913- ... 5-8R
Horsbrugh, Ian 1941- ... 111
Horsburgh, David Michael
1923-1984 Obituary ... 114
Horsburgh, H(oward) J(ohn) N(eate)
1918- ... 25-28R
Horsfield, J(ohn) Keith 1901- ... 5-8R
Horsely, Ramsbottom
See Berne, Eric (Lennard)
Horseman, Elaine Hall 1925- ... 13-16R
Horsford, Howard C(larke) 1921- ... 136
Horsley, David
See Bingley, David Ernest
Horsley, James (Allen) 1938- ... 45-48
Horsman, Reginald 1931- ... CANR-17
Earlier sketches in CA 1-4R, CANR-2
Horst, Irvin B(uckwalter) 1915- ... 41-44R
Horst, Samuel (Levi) 1919- ... 21-24R
Horstman, Allen (Henry) 1943- ... 122
Horton, Arthur MacNeill Jr. 1947- ... CANR-35
Earlier sketch in CA 114
Horton, Felix Lee
See Floren, Lee
Horton, Frank E. 1939- ... 29-32R
Horton, George Moses 1797(?)-1883(?) ... DLB 50
Horton, J(ames) Wright (Jr.) 1950- ... 138
Horton, James O(liver) 1943- ... CANR-35
Earlier sketch in CA 114
Horton, John (William) 1905- ... CANR-18
Earlier sketches in CA 9-12R, CANR-3
Horton, Louise 1916- ... CANR-2
Earlier sketch in CA 49-52
Horton, Lowell 1936- ... 53-56
Horton, Michael Scott 1964- ... 135
Horton, Patricia Campbell 1943- ... 89-92
Horton, Paul Burleigh 1916- ... CANR-20
Earlier sketch in CA 1-4R
Horton, Paul Chester 1942- ... 106
Horton, Philip C. 1911(?)-1989 Obituary ... 129
Horton, Rod W(illiam) 1910- ... 49-52
Horton, Russell M. 1946- ... 97-100
Horton, Stanley M(onroe) 1916- ... CANR-6
Earlier sketch in CA 57-60
Horton, Susan R. 1941- ... 109
Horvat, Branko 1928- ... 53-56
Horvath, Betty 1927- ... 17-20R
See also SATA 4
Horvath, Janos 1921- ... 41-44R
Horvath, Joan 1944- ... 81-84
Horvath, Odon von
See Horvath, Oedoen von
See also DLB 85
Horvath, Oedoen von
1901-1938 Brief entry ... 118
See also Horvath, Odon von
See also TCLC 45
Horvath, Polly 1957- ... 132
Horvath, Violet M. 1924- ... 29-32R
Horwich, Frances R(appaport) 1908- ... CAP-1
Earlier sketch in CA 13-16
See also SATA 11
Horwitz, Elinor Lander ... CANR-13
Earlier sketch in CA 77-80
See also SATA 33, 45
Horwitz, Julius 1920-1986 ... CANR-12
Obituary ... 119
Earlier sketch in CA 9-12R
See also CLC 14
Horwitz, Richard P(aul) 1949- ... 122
Horwitz, Simi L(ouise) 1949- ... 103
Horwitz, Sylvia L(aibman) 1911- ... 61-64
Horwood, Harold (Andrew) 1923- ... CANR-25
Earlier sketches in CA 21-24R, CANR-9
See also CAAS 15
See also DLB 60
Hosek, Chaviva (Milada) 1946- ... 127
Hoselitz, Bert(hold) F(rank) 1913- ... CANR-1
Earlier sketch in CA 1-4R
Hosford, Bowen I. 1916- ... CANR-24
Earlier sketch in CA 107
Hosford, Dorothy (Grant) 1900-1952 ... SATA 22
Hosford, Jessie 1892- ... 41-44R
See also SATA 5
Hosford, Philip L(ewis) 1926- ... 57-60
Hosford, Ray E. 1933- ... 85-88
Hosie, Stanley W(illiam) 1922- ... 25-28R
Hosier, Helen Kooiman 1928- ... CANR-8
Earlier sketch in CA 61-64
Hosier, Peter
See Clark, Douglas
Hosken, Fran(ziska) P(orges) 1919- ... CANR-6
Earlier sketch in CA 57-60
Hoskin, Cyril Henry 1911(?)-1981 Obituary ... 102
Hosking, Eric (John) 1909- ... CANR-17
Earlier sketch in CA 101
Hosking, Geoffrey A(lan) 1942- ... CANR-19
Earlier sketch in CA 85-88
Hoskins, Katharine Bail 1924- ... 65-68
Hoskins, Katherine (de Montalant) 1909- ... CAP-2
Earlier sketch in CA 25-28
Hoskins, Percy 1904-1989 Obituary ... 127
Hoskins, Robert 1933- ... 29-32R
Hoskins, William George 1908-1992 ... 13-16R
Obituary ... 136
Hoskyns, John 1566-1638 ... DLB 121
Hoskyns-Abrahall, Clare (Constance Drury)
... 29-32R
See also SATA 13
Hosley, Richard 1921- ... CANR-8
Earlier sketch in CA 5-8R
Hosmer, Charles B(ridgham) Jr. 1932- ... 13-16R
Hosmon, Robert Stahr 1943- ... 45-48
Hosokawa, Bill
See Hosokawa, William K.
Hosokawa, William K. 1915- ... CANR-11
Earlier sketch in CA 29-32R
Hospers, John Jr. 1918- ... CANR-2
Earlier sketch in CA 1-4R
Hospital, Janette Turner 1942- ... 108
See also CLC 42
Hoss, Marvin Allen 1929- ... 29-32R
Hoss, Norman 1923(?)-1983 Obituary ... 111
Hossent, Harry 1916- ... CAP-1
Earlier sketch in CA 9-10
Hostetler, Beulah Stauffer 1926- ... 126
Hostetler, Marian 1932- ... CANR-24
Earlier sketches in CA 65-68, CANR-9
Hostetter, B(enjamin) Charles 1916- ... CANR-1
Earlier sketch in CA 1-4R
Hostler, Charles W(arren) 1919- ... 21-24R
Hostos, Adolfo de 1887- ... 131
See also HW
Hostos, E. M. de
See Hostos (y Bonilla), Eugenio Maria de
Hostos, Eugenio M. de
See Hostos (y Bonilla), Eugenio Maria de
Hostos, Eugenio Maria
See Hostos (y Bonilla), Eugenio Maria de
Hostos (y Bonilla), Eugenio Maria de
1839-1903 ... 131
Brief entry ... 123
See also HW
See also TCLC 24
Hostovsky, Egon 1908-1973 Obituary ... 89-92
Hostrop, Richard Winfred 1925- ... 25-28R
Hotaling, Edward 1937- ... 77-80
Hotchkiss, Bill 1936- ... 104
Hotchkiss, Jeanette 1901- ... 21-24R
Hotchkiss, Ralf D. 1947- ... 33-36R
Hotchner, A(aron) E(dward) 1920- ... CANR-27
Earlier sketch in CA 69-72
Hotchner, Tracy 1950- ... 102
Hothem, Lar(ry Lee) 1938- ... 106
Hothersall, David 1940- ... 111
Hotson, John H(argrove) 1930- ... 25-28R
Hotspur
See Curling, Bryan William Richard
Hottois, James W. 1943- ... 77-80
Hotz, Robert B(ergmann) 1914- ... 101
Hou, Chi-ming 1924- ... 21-24R
Hou, Fu-Wu
See Houn, Franklin W.
Houblon, Doreen (Lindsay) Archer
See Archer Houblon, Doreen (Lindsay)
Houchin, Thomas D(ouglas) 1925- ... 77-80
Houck, Carter 1924- ... CANR-14
Earlier sketch in CA 77-80
See also SATA 22
Houck, John W(illiam) 1931- ... CANR-11
Earlier sketch in CA 29-32R
Houdini
See Lovecraft, H(oward) P(hillips)
Houdini, Merlin X.
See Borgmann, Dmitri A(lfred)
Houedard, Pierre-Sylvester 1924- ... 103
Houfe, Simon (Richard) 1942- ... CANR-19
Earlier sketch in CA 103
Hougan, Carolyn ... CLC 34
Hougan, James Richard 1942- ... 77-80
Hougan, Jim
See Hougan, James Richard
Hough, (Helen) Charlotte 1924- ... CANR-5
Earlier sketch in CA 9-12R
See also SATA 9
Hough, Denny C. 1925(?)-1983 Obituary ... 111
Hough, Emerson 1857-1923 Brief entry ... 120
See also DLB 9
Hough, George A(nthony) III 1920- ... 121
Brief entry ... 117
Hough, Graham (Goulder) 1908-1990 ... CANR-25
Obituary ... 132
Earlier sketch in CA 69-72
Hough, Henry Beetle 1896-1985 ... CANR-2
Obituary ... 116
Earlier sketch in CA 1-4R
Hough, Henry W(ade) 1906-197 (?) ... 25-28R
Obituary ... 122
Hough, Hugh 1924-1986 ... 73-76
Obituary ... 119
Hough, Jerry F(incher) 1935- ... 137
Brief entry ... 114
Hough, John T. Jr. 1946- ... 33-36R
Hough, Joseph C(arl) Jr. 1933- ... 21-24R
Hough, Judy Taylor 1932- ... 124
See also SATA 51, 56, 63
Hough, Lindy Downer 1944- ... CANR-8
Earlier sketch in CA 61-64
Hough, Louis 1914- ... 37-40R
Hough, Michael 1928- ... 133
Hough, Richard (Alexander) 1922- ... CANR-18
Earlier sketches in CA 5-8R, CANR-3
See also SATA 17
Hough, S(tanley) B(ennett) 1917- ... CANR-3
Earlier sketch in CA 5-8R
Houghteling, James L(awrence) Jr. 1920- ... 5-8R
Houghton, Bernard 1935- ... 77-80
Houghton, Diane 1940- ... 123
Houghton, Elizabeth
See Gilzean, Elizabeth Houghton Blanchet
Houghton, Eric 1930- ... CANR-2
Earlier sketch in CA 1-4R
See also SATA 7
Houghton, George William 1905- ... 13-16R
Houghton, Katharine 1945- ... 130

Houghton, Neal D(oyle) 1895- CAP-2
Earlier sketch in CA 25-28
Houghton, (Charles) Norris 1909- 21-24R
Houghton, Peter 1938- 119
Houghton, R(alph) E(dward) C(unliffe)
1896-1990 Obituary 132
Houghton, Samuel G(ilbert) 1902-1975 65-68
Houghton, (William) Stanley
1881-1913 Brief entry 110
See also DLB 10
Houghton, Walter Edwards 1904-1983 ...... CAP-1
Obituary 109
Earlier sketch in CA 9-10
Houlbrooke, Ralph (A.) 1944- 132
Houlden, J(ames) L(eslie) 1929- 77-80
Houle, Cyril O(rvin) 1913- CANR-3
Earlier sketch in CA 5-8R
Houlehen, Robert J. 1918- 49-52
See also SATA 18
Houlgate, Deke 1930- 61-64
Houlgate, Stephen (Glynn) 1954- 127
Hoult, Norah 1898-1984 Obituary 112
Hoult, Thomas Ford 1920- Brief entry 116
Houlton, Peggy Mann 1925(?)-1990 ......CANR-35
See also Mann, Peggy
Houn, Franklin W. 1920- 21-24R
Hounshell, David A. 1950- 129
Hounsome, Terry 1944- 109
Houpt, Katherine Albro 1939- 105
Hourani, Cecil 1917- 129
Hourani, George F(adlo) 1913-1984 ......CANR-23
Earlier sketch in CA 45-48
Hours, Madeleine 1915- CANR-28
Earlier sketch in CA 49-52
Hours-Miedan, Madeleine
See Hours, Madeleine
Hours-Miedan, Magdeleine
See Hours, Madeleine
House, Anne W.
See McCauley, Elfrieda B(abnick)
House, Charles (Albert) 1916- 25-28R
House, Ernest R(obert) 1937- CANR-23
Earlier sketch in CA 45-48
House, Gloria 1941- 117
House, H(ershel) Wayne 1948- 119
House, John William 1919-1984 106
Obituary 112
House, Karen Elliott 1947- 130
Brief entry 125
House, Kurt D(uane) 1947- 104
House, Robert Burton 1892- CAP-1
Earlier sketch in CA 11-12
House, Robert J. 1932- 101
House, Robert W(illiam) 1920- 53-56
House, Ruth Sizemore 1946- 116
House, Victor 1893-1983 Obituary 109
Household, Geoffrey (Edward West)
1900-1988 77-80
Obituary 126
See also CLC 11
See also DLB 87
See also SATA 14, 59
Houselander, (Frances) Caryll
1901-1954 Brief entry 110
See also SATA 31
Houseman, Barton L(eroy) 1933- 61-64
Houseman, Gerald L. 1935- 108
Houseman, John 1902-1988 Obituary 127
Brief entry 110
Housepian, Marjorie
See Dobkin, Marjorie Housepian
Houser, Caroline 115
Housley, Norman (James) 1952- 108
Housman, A(lfred) E(dward) 1859-1936 125
Brief entry 104
See also DLB 19
See also MTCW
See also PC 2
See also TCLC 1, 10
Housman, Laurence 1865-1959 Brief entry 106
See also DLB 10
See also SATA 25
See also TCLC 7
Houston, Beverle (Ann) 1936-1988 89-92
Obituary 124
Houston, C(larence) Stuart 1927- 119
Houston, Cecil J(ames) 1943- 135
Houston, David 1938- 118
Houston, Douglas (Norman) 1947- 123
Houston, James A(rchibald) 1921- CANR-38
Earlier sketch in CA 65-68
See also CLR 3
See also MAICYA
See also SATA 13
Houston, James D. 1933- CANR-29
Earlier sketch in CA 25-28R
See also CAAS 16
Houston, James M(ackintosh) 1922- 13-16R
Houston, Jean Brief entry 115
Houston, Jeanne (Toyo) Wakatsuki
1934- CANR-29
Earlier sketch in CA 103
See also CAAS 16
Houston, Joan 1928- 17-20R
Houston, John Porter 1933-1987 ....CANR-3
Obituary 123
Earlier sketch in CA 9-12R
Houston, Neal B. 1928- 41-44R
Houston, Peyton (H.) 1910- CANR-1
Earlier sketch in CA 49-52
Houston, R. B.
See Rae, Hugh C(rauford)
Houston, Robert 1935- 37-40R
Houston, W(illiam) Robert Jr. 1928- CANR-18
Earlier sketches in CA 5-8R, CANR-3
Houston, Will
See Paine, Lauran (Bosworth)
Houston, William Neil 1948- 123
Houtart, Francois 1925- 13-16R
Houthakker, Hendrik S(amuel) 1924- 17-20R
Houton, Kathleen
See Kilgore, Kathleen
Houts, Marshall (Wilson) 1919- CANR-13
Earlier sketch in CA 21-24R
Houts, Peter S. 1933- 49-52
Houwald, Ernst von 1778-1845 .... DLB 90
Hovannisian, Richard G. 1932- 21-24R
Hovda, Robert W(alker) 1920-1992 ....CANR-3
Obituary 136
Earlier sketch in CA 9-12R
Hovde, A(nnis) J(orgen) 1917- 112
Hovde, Christian A(rneson) 1922- 5-8R
Hovde, Howard 1928- 25-28R
Hovell, Lucille A. (Peterson) 1916- 5-8R
Hovell, Lucy A.
See Hovell, Lucille A. (Peterson)
Hoverland, H. Arthur 1928- 45-48
Hoversten, Chester E. 1922- 5-8R
Hovey, E(lwyn) Paul 1908- CANR-1
Earlier sketch in CA 1-4R
Hovey, Richard B(ennett) 1917- 25-28R
Hovey, Richard 1864-1900 .... DLB 54
Hovey, Sonya 1898-1960 Obituary 113
See also Levien, Sonya
Hoveyda, Fereydoun 1924- 101
Hovick, Rose Louise
1914(?)-1970 Obituary 113
Hoving, Thomas 1931- 101
Howald, Reed Anderson 1930- 57-60
Howar, Barbara 1934- 89-92
See also AITN 1, 2
Howard, A(rthur) E(llsworth) Dick 1933- 13-16R
Howard, Alan 1922- .... SATA 45
Howard, Alan 1934- CANR-20
Earlier sketch in CA 37-40R
Howard, Alvin Wendell 1922-1975 ....33-36R
Howard, Alyssa
See Glick, Ruth (Burtnick)
Howard, Alyssa
See Titchener, Louise
Howard, Alyssa
See Buckholtz, Eileen (Garber)
Howard, Anthony (Michell) 1934- 109
Howard, Barbara 1930- 53-56
Howard, Ben(jamin Willis) 1944- 73-76
Howard, Bill
See Shannon, Mike
Howard, Bion B. 1912- 13-16R
Howard, Blanche 1923- 101
Howard, C(hester) Jeriel 1939- CANR-31
Earlier sketches in CA 29-32R, CANR-14
Howard, Carleton
See Howe, Charles H(orace)
Howard, Cecil
See Smith, Cecil (Howard III)
Howard, Charles Frederick 1904- 17-20R
Howard, Christopher 1913- 21-24R
Howard, Clark 122
Howard, Clive Obituary 53-56
Howard, Constance (Mildred) 1910- CANR-11
Earlier sketch in CA 69-72
Howard, Coralie
See Cogswell, Coralie (Norris)
Howard, D(erek) L(ionel) 1930- CANR-8
Earlier sketch in CA 5-8R
Howard, Daniel F(rancis) 1928- 41-44R
Howard, David M(orris) 1928- CANR-10
Earlier sketch in CA 25-28R
Howard, Deborah (Janet) 1946- 124
Howard, Dick 1943- 77-80
Howard, Don (Marcel) 1940- CANR-22
Earlier sketch in CA 106
Howard, Donald R(oy) 1927-1987 ....CANR-1
Obituary 121
Earlier sketch in CA 1-4R
Howard, Donald 1927-1987 .... DLB 111
Howard, Dorothy (Arlynne) 1912- 65-68
Howard, Dorothy Gray 1902- 93-96
Howard, Edmund (Bernard Carlo) 1909- 85-88
Howard, Edward G(arfield)
1918(?)-1972 Obituary 104
Howard, Edwin J(ohnston) 1901- CAP-1
Earlier sketch in CA 11-12
Howard, Edwin 1924- 65-68
Howard, Elizabeth
See Paine, Lauran (Bosworth)
Howard, Elizabeth Fitzgerald 1927- 128
Howard, Elizabeth Jane 1923- CANR-8
Earlier sketch in CA 5-8R
See also CLC 7, 29
Howard, Ellen 1943- 130
See also SATA 67
Howard, Frances Minturn Brief entry 111
Howard, Fred D(avid) 1919- CANR-19
Earlier sketches in CA 1-4R, CANR-4
Howard, Frederick James 1904- 109
Howard, Gerald J(ohn) 1950- 108
Howard, Gilbert 1934- 49-52
Howard, Harold P. 1905- CAP-2
Earlier sketch in CA 33-36
Howard, Harry Nicholas 1902-1987 ......CANR-34
Obituary 123
Earlier sketch in CA 49-52
Howard, Hartley
See Ognall, Leopold Horace
Howard, Helen Addison 1904- CANR-3
Earlier sketch in CA 5-8R
Howard, Ian P. 1927- 21-24R
Howard, J. Grant 1929- 125
Howard, J. Woodford Jr. 1931- 33-36R
Howard, James A(rch) 1922- CANR-8
Earlier sketch in CA 13-16R
Howard, James H(enri) 1925- 41-44R
Howard, James K(enton) 1943- 85-88
Howard, James T(homas) 1934- 101
Howard, Jane (Temple) 1935- CANR-13
Earlier sketch in CA 29-32R
Howard, Jean
See MacGibbon, Jean
Howard, Jessica
See Schere, Monroe
Howard, John
See Hewitt, John (Harold)
Howard, John (Arnold) 1916- 41-44R
Howard, John R(obert) 1933- 53-56
Howard, John Tasker
1890-1964 Obituary 89-92
Howard, Joseph Leon 1917- CANR-1
Earlier sketch in CA 1-4R
Howard, Joyce 1922- 5-8R
Howard, Kenneth I(rwin) 1932- 115
Howard, Kenneth Samuel 1882-1972 ....9-12R
Obituary 103
Howard, Kez
See Houston, David
Howard, Lee M(ilton) 1922- 108
Howard, Leigh
See Lee Howard, Leon Alexander
Howard, Leon Alexander Lee
See Lee Howard, Leon Alexander
Howard, Leon 1903-1982 109
Howard, Leslie G(raham) 1947- 114
Howard, Lowell B(ennett) 1925- 13-16R
Howard, Marie
See Lena, Marie H(oward)
Howard, Mark
See Rigsby, Howard
Howard, Mary
See Mussi, Mary
Howard, Maureen 1930- CANR-31
Earlier sketch in CA 53-56
See also CLC 5, 14, 46
See also DLBY 83
See also MTCW
Howard, Michael (Eliot) 1922- CANR-2
Earlier sketch in CA 1-4R
Howard, Michael S. 1922-1974 Obituary 53-56
Howard, Moses L(eon) 1928- 109
Howard, Munroe 1913-1974 .... CAP-2
Earlier sketch in CA 23-24
Howard, Nona
See Luxton, Leonora Kathrine
Howard, Oliver Otis 1830-1909 Brief entry 109
Howard, Patricia (Lowe) 1937- CANR-7
Earlier sketch in CA 17-20R
Howard, Paul Jack 1908-1984 Obituary 113
Howard, Peter D(unsmore) 1908-1965 ...... CAP-1
Earlier sketch in CA 11-12
Howard, Philip 1933- 65-68
Howard, Prosper
See Hamilton, Charles (Harold St. John)
Howard, Richard C. 1929- 53-56
Howard, Richard 1929- CANR-25
Earlier sketch in CA 85-88
See also AITN 1
See also CLC 7, 10, 47
See also DLB 5
Howard, Robert Ervin
1906-1936 Brief entry 105
See also TCLC 8
Howard, Robert West 1908- CANR-1
Earlier sketch in CA 1-4R
See also SATA 5
Howard, Robert 1926- 41-44R
Howard, Roger 1938- CANR-39
Earlier sketches in CA 93-96, CANR-17
Howard, Ron .... AAYA 8
Howard, Ronnalie Roper
See Roper, Ronnalie J.
Howard, Ross 1946- 120
Howard, Roy Joseph 1925- 112
Howard, Roy Wilson 1883-1964 Obituary 89-92
See also DLB 29
Howard, Sidney 1891-1939 .... DLB 7, 26
Howard, Stanley E. 1888(?)-1980 Obituary 102
Howard, Ted
See Howard, Theodore Korner
Howard, Theodore Korner 1915- 103
Howard, Thomas T(rumbull) 1935- 111
Howard, Thomas 1930- 37-40R
Howard, Troy
See Paine, Lauran (Bosworth)
Howard, Vechel
See Rigsby, Howard
Howard, Vernon (Linwood) 1918- 108
See also SATA 40
Howard, Warren F.
See Pohl, Frederik
Howard, Warren Starkie 1930- 5-8R
Howard-Hill, Trevor Howard 1933- 85-88
Howard-Williams, Jeremy (Napier)
1922- CANR-22
Earlier sketch in CA 106
Howarth, David (Armine) 1912-1991 ......CANR-25
Obituary 134
Earlier sketches in CA 13-16R, CANR-9
See also SATA 6
See also SATO 68
Howarth, Donald 1931- 25-28R
Howarth, Pamela 1954- 102
Howarth, Patrick (John Fielding) 1916- 77-80
Howarth, Stephen (William Russell)
1953- CANR-25
Earlier sketch in CA 107
Howarth, T(homas) E(dward) B(rodie)
1914-1988(?) Obituary 125
Howarth, W(illiam) D(river) 1922- CANR-35
Earlier sketch in CA 45-48
Howarth, William Louis 1940- CANR-20
Earlier sketch in CA 37-40R
Howat, Gerald Malcolm David 1928- CANR-16
Earlier sketch in CA 93-96
Howat, John K(eith) 1937- 49-52
Howatch, Joseph 1935- 65-68
Howatch, Susan 1940- CANR-24
Earlier sketch in CA 45-48
See also AITN 1
Howe, Charles H(orace) 1912- 53-56
Howe, Charles L. 1932- 17-20R
Howe, Christopher (Barry) 1937- 121
Howe, Daniel Walker 1937- 29-32R
Howe, Deborah 1946-1978 105
See also SATA 29
Howe, Doris Kathleen CANR-3
Earlier sketch in CA 49-52
Howe, E. W. 1853-1937 .... DLB 12, 25
Howe, Ellic (Paul) 1910-1991 ....25-28R
Obituary 135
Howe, Fanny 1940- 117
See also CLC 47
See also SATA 52
Howe, Florence 1929- 124
Brief entry 109
Howe, G(eorge) Melvyn 1920- 101
Howe, George Frederick
1901-1988 Obituary 124
Howe, George Locke
1898(?)-1977 Obituary 69-72
Howe, Helen 1905-1975 .... CAP-2
Obituary 57-60
Earlier sketch in CA 23-24
Howe, Henry 1816-1893 .... DLB 30
Howe, Hubert S(hattuck) Jr. 1942- 57-60
Howe, Irving 1920- CANR-21
Earlier sketch in CA 9-12R
See also DLB 67
See also MTCW
Howe, James Robinson 1935- 69-72
Howe, James 1946- CANR-22
Earlier sketch in CA 105
See also CLR 9
See also MAICYA
See also SATA 29, 71
Howe, Jonathan Trumbull 1935- 29-32R
Howe, Joseph 1804-1873 .... DLB 99
Howe, Josephine (Mary) O'Connor
See O'Connor Howe, Josephine (Mary)
Howe, Julia Ward 1819-1910 Brief entry 117
See also DLB 1
See also TCLC 21
Howe, Leland W(right) 1940- 123
Brief entry 118
Howe, Louise Kapp 1934-1984 Obituary 111
Howe, Mark Anthony DeWolfe
1864-1960 Obituary 89-92
Howe, Neil 1951- 132
Howe, Nelson 1935- 33-36R
Howe, Quincy 1900-1977 49-52
Obituary 69-72
Howe, Reuel L(anphier) 1905- 21-24R
Howe, Richard J. 1937- 77-80
Howe, Russell Warren 1925- CANR-27
Earlier sketch in CA 49-52
Howe, Susan 1937- .... CLC 72
See also DLB 120
Howe, Tina 1937- 109
See also CLC 48
Howe, W(arren) Asquith 1910- 29-32R
Howe, William Hugh 1928- 65-68
Howell, Anthony 1945- 128
Howell, Barbara 1937- 49-52
Howell, Benjamin Franklin
1890-1976 Obituary 65-68
Howell, Bette 1920- 130
Howell, Clark Sr. 1863-1936 .... DLB 25
Howell, Clinton T(almage) 1913-1981 ....29-32R
Obituary 133
Howell, David Arthur Russell 1936- 109
Howell, Elsworth Seaman
1915-1987 Obituary 122
Howell, Evan P(ark) 1839-1905 Brief entry 119
See also DLB 23
Howell, Helen (Jane) 1934- 57-60
Howell, James Edwin 1928- CANR-20
Earlier sketch in CA 1-4R
Howell, John
See Hall, Gus
Howell, John C(hristian) 1924- CANR-9
Earlier sketch in CA 21-24R
Howell, John M(ichael) 1933- 33-36R
Howell, Joseph T(oy III) 1942- CANR-24
Earlier sketch in CA 45-48
Howell, Leon 1936- 25-28R
Howell, Michael J. 1932(?)-1986 Obituary 118
Howell, Pat 1947- .... SATA 15
Howell, Patricia Hagan 1939- 81-84
Howell, Paul (Philip) 1917- 135
Howell, Peter (Adrian) 1941- 128
Howell, Reet 1945- 110
Howell, Richard W(esley) 1926- 57-60
Howell, Robert Lee 1928- 25-28R
Howell, Roger (Jr.) 1936- CANR-11
Earlier sketch in CA 21-24R
Howell, S.
See Styles, (Frank) Showell
Howell, Thomas 1944- 73-76
Howell, Virginia
See Ellison, Virginia H(owell)
Howell, Wilbur Samuel 1904- 33-36R
Obituary 137
Howell, William C(arl) 1932- 93-96
Howells, J(ames) Harvey 1912- 97-100
Howells, John G(wilym) 1918- CANR-24
Earlier sketches in CA 21-24R, CANR-9
Howells, Roscoe 1919- 104
Howells, W. D.
See Howells, William Dean

Howells, William D.
See Howells, William Dean
Howells, William Dean 1837-1920 134
Brief entry 104
See also CDALB 1865-1917
See also DLB 12, 64, 74, 79
See also TCLC 41, 7, 17
Howells, William White 1908- CANR-19
Earlier sketches in CA 1-4R, CANR-2
Hower, Edward 1941- 106
Hower, Ralph M(erle) 1903-1973 ....1-4R
Obituary 45-48
Howes, Alan B(arber) 1920- Brief entry 112
Howes, Barbara 1914- 9-12R
See also CAAS 3
See also CLC 15
See also SATA 5
Howes, Connie B. 1933- 89-92
Howes, Frank Stewart 1891-1974 Obituary 115
Howes, Michael 1904- 61-64
Howes, Paul Griswold 1892-1984 ....29-32R
Obituary 113
Howes, Raymond F(loyd) 1903- CAP-1
Earlier sketch in CA 17-18
Howes, Robert Gerard 1919- CANR-4
Earlier sketch in CA 1-4R
Howes, Royce (Bucknam) 1901-1973 ....CAP-2
Obituary 41-44R
Earlier sketch in CA 19-20
Howes, Wright 1882-1978 Obituary 104
Howick, William Henry 1924- 33-36R
Howie, Carl G(ordon) 1920- 13-16R
Howith, Harry 1934- 25-28R
Howitt, Mary 1799-1888 ....DLB 110
Howitt, William 1792-1879 ....DLB 110
Howitzer, Bronson
See Hardman, Richards Lynden
Howker, Janni 1957- 137
See also AAYA 9
See also CLR 14
See also MAICYA
See also SAAS 13
See also SATA 46
Howkins, John 1945- CANR-32
Earlier sketches in CA 65-68, CANR-14
Howl, Marcia (Yvonne Hurt) 1947- 121
Howland, Bette 1937- 85-88
Howland, Harold Edward
1913-1980 Obituary 102
Howlett, D(onald) Roger 1945- 135
Howlett, Duncan 1906- 107
Howlett, John (Reginald) 1940- CANR-12
Earlier sketch in CA 69-72
Howorth, Beckett 1902- 114
Howorth, M. K.
See Black, Margaret K(atherine)
Howorth, Muriel CAP-1
Earlier sketch in CA 9-10
Howse, Ernest Marshall 1902- 49-52
Howson, Susan 1945- 113
Howton, F(rank) William 1925- 29-32R
Hoxie, Frederick E(ugene) 1947- 117
Hoxie, R(alph) Gordon 1919- 103
Hoy, Cyrus H. 1926- 21-24R
Hoy, David 1930- 17-20R
Hoy, James F(ranklin) 1939- 57-60
Hoy, John C. 1933- CANR-9
Earlier sketch in CA 21-24R
Hoy, Linda 1946- 130
See also SATA 65
Hoy, Nina
See Roth, Arthur J(oseph)
Hoye, Anna Scott 1915- 13-16R
Hoyem, Andrew 1935- 9-12R
See also DLB 5
Hoyer, George W. 1919- CANR-4
Earlier sketch in CA 1-4R
Hoyer, H(arvey) Conrad 1907- 33-36R
Hoyer, Mildred N(aeher) 57-60
Hoyland, Michael 1925- 21-24R
Hoyle, Fred 1915- CANR-29
Earlier sketches in CA 5-8R, CANR-3
See also MTCW
Hoyle, Geoffrey 1942- CANR-29
Earlier sketches in CA 53-56, CANR-6
See also SATA 18
Hoyle, Martha Byrd
See Byrd, Martha
Hoyle, Peter 1939- 124
Hoyles, J(ames) Arthur 1908- 5-8R
Hoyos, Angela de 1940(?)- 131
See also DLB 82
See also HW
Hoyt, Charles Alva 1931- 33-36R
Hoyt, Charles K(ing) 1938- 110
Hoyt, Clark 1942- 69-72
Hoyt, Edwin P(almer) Jr. 1923- CANR-1
Earlier sketch in CA 1-4R
See also SATA 28
Hoyt, Elizabeth E(llis) 1893- 37-40R
Hoyt, Erich 1950- 106
See also SATA 65
Hoyt, Herman A(rthur) 1909- 29-32R
Hoyt, Homer 1896-1984 ....CANR-1
Obituary 114
Earlier sketch in CA 1-4R
Hoyt, Jo Wasson 1927- 21-24R
Hoyt, Joseph B(ixby) 1913- 5-8R
Hoyt, Kenneth B(oyd) 1924- CANR-1
Earlier sketch in CA 45-48
Hoyt, Mary Finch 1924(?)- 107
Hoyt, Murray 1904- 9-12R
Hoyt, Olga (Gruhzit) 1922- 25-28R
See also SATA 16
Hoyt, (Edwin) Palmer
1897-1979 Obituary 89-92
Hoyt, Richard (Duane) 1941- 129
Hoyt, Robert S(tuart) 1918-1971 Obituary 111
Hoyt, Waite (Charles) 1899-1984 Obituary 113
Hozeny, Tony 1946- 61-64
Hozjusz
See Dobraczynski, Jan
Hrabal, Bohumil 1914- 106
See also CAAS 12
See also CLC 13, 67
Hrdy, Sarah Blaffer 1946- CANR-35
Earlier sketch in CA 107
Hromadka, Josef L(ukl) 1889-1971 ....CAP-1
Earlier sketch in CA 9-10
Hruska-Cortes, Elias 1943- 45-48
Hruza, Zdenek 1926- 61-64
Hsia, Adrian (Rue Chun) 1938- 77-80
Hsia, C(hih)-T(sing) 1921- CANR-17
Earlier sketches in CA 1-4R, CANR-2
Hsia, David Yi-Yung
1925-1972 Obituary 33-36R
Hsia, Hsiao
See Liu, Wu-chi
Hsia, Tsi-an 1916-1965 ....CAP-2
Earlier sketch in CA 25-28
Hsiang, Yeh
See Liu, Sydney (Chieh)
Hsiao, Katharine H(uei-Ying Huang)
1923- 77-80
Hsiao, Kung-Chuan 1897- 1-4R
Hsiao, Tso-liang 1910- 1-4R
Hsiung, James Chieh 1935- 37-40R
Hsu, Benedict (Pei-Hsiung) 1933- 69-72
Hsu, Cho-yun 1930- CANR-9
Earlier sketch in CA 17-20R
Hsu, Francis L(ang) K(wang) 1909- CANR-16
Earlier sketches in CA 1-4R, CANR-1
Hsu, Immanuel C. Y. 1923- 1-4R
Hsu, K.
See Hsu, Kenneth J(inghwa)
Hsu, K. J.
See Hsu, Kenneth J(inghwa)
Hsu, K. Jinghwa
See Hsu, Kenneth J(inghwa)
Hsu, Kai-yu 1922-1982 ....CANR-14
Earlier sketch in CA 21-24R
Hsu, Kenneth J(inghwa) 1929- 135
Hsueh, Chun-tu 1922- CANR-34
Earlier sketches in CA 41-44R, CANR-15
Hsun, Lu
See Shu-Jen, Chou
See also TCLC 3
Hsu Ying 1935- 124
Htin Aung, U.
See Aung, (Maung) Htin
Hu, Shi Ming
See Hu, Shu Ming
Hu, Shu Ming 1927- 85-88
Hu, Sze-Tsen 1914- 41-44R
Huaco, George A. 1927- 17-20R
Huang, David S(hih-Li) 1930- 9-12R
Huang, Parker (Po-fei) 1914- CANR-2
Earlier sketch in CA 45-48
Huang, Philip C(hung-Chih) 1940- 127
Huang, Philip Chung-Chih 1940- Brief entry 105
Huang, Po-fei
See Huang, Parker (Po-fei)
Huang, Ray (Jen-yu) 1918- CANR-8
Earlier sketch in CA 61-64
Huang, Stanley S(hang) C(hien) 1923- 77-80
Huan Yue
See Shen Congwen
Hubach, Robert R(ogers) 1916- 1-4R
Hubartt, Paul L(eroy) 1919- 5-8R
Hubback, David 1916- 128
Hubbard, Barbara Marx 1929- 103
Hubbard, D(onald) L(ee) 1929- 21-24R
Hubbard, David Allan 1928- CANR-16
Earlier sketch in CA 33-36R
Hubbard, David G(raham) 1920- 33-36R
Hubbard, Don 1926- 109
Hubbard, Edward (Horton) 1937-1989 124
Obituary 128
Hubbard, Elbert 1856-1915 ....DLB 91
Hubbard, Frank T. 1921(?)-1976 Obituary 65-68
Hubbard, Freeman (Henry) 1894- 5-8R
Hubbard, George (Barron)
1884-1958 Brief entry 122
Hubbard, J(ake) T(imothy) W(illiam) 1935- 124
Hubbard, (Frank Mc)Kin(ney)
1868-1930 Brief entry 113
See also DLB 11
Hubbard, L(afayette) Ron(ald)
1911-1986 ....CANR-22
Obituary 118
Earlier sketch in CA 77-80
See also CLC 43
Hubbard, Lucien 1889(?)-1971 Obituary 33-36R
Hubbard, Margaret Ann
See Priley, Margaret Hubbard
Hubbard, P(hilip) M(aitland) 1910-1980 85-88
Obituary 97-100
Hubbard, Paul H. 1900(?)-1983 Obituary 109
Hubbard, Preston John 1918- 5-8R
Hubbard, (Andrew) Ray 1924- 103
Hubbard, Robert Hamilton 1916- CANR-21
Earlier sketch in CA 1-4R
Hubbard, Ruth 1924- 116
Hubbard, Susan (S.) 1951- 138
Hubbard, Thomas K. 1956- 136
Hubbard, Thomas Leslie Wallan 1905- CAP-1
Earlier sketch in CA 13-14
Hubbard, William 1621(?)-1704 ....DLB 24
Hubbell, Harriet Weed 1909- 5-8R
Hubbell, Harry M. 1881-1971 Obituary 29-32R
Hubbell, Jay B(roadus) 1885-1979 ....CANR-17
Obituary 116
Earlier sketch in CA 1-4R
Hubbell, John G(erard) 1927- 65-68
Hubbell, Lindley Williams 1901- CAP-1
Earlier sketch in CA 13-16
Hubbell, Patricia 1928- 17-20R
See also SATA 8
Hubbell, Richard Whittaker 1914- 13-16R
Hubbell, Sue 1935- 120
Hubber, Therese 1764-1829 ....DLB 90
Hubbs, Carl Leavitt 1894-1979 Obituary 89-92
Hubbs, G(uy) Ward 1952- 114
Hubenka, Lloyd J(ohn) 1931- 49-52
Huber, Jack T(ravis) 1918- 21-24R
Huber, Joan 1925- CANR-13
Earlier sketch in CA 77-80
Huber, Leonard Victor 1903- CANR-6
Earlier sketch in CA 57-60
Huber, Morton Wesley 1923- 17-20R
Huber, Peter W. 1952- 128
Huber, Richard M(iller) 1922- 33-36R
Huber, Thomas Michael 1944- 112
Huber, Thomas 1937- 29-32R
Huberman, Edward 1910- 13-16R
Huberman, Elizabeth Duncan Lyle
1915- 13-16R
Huberman, Leo 1903-1968 ....CANR-4
Earlier sketch in CA 1-4R
Hubert, Cam
See Cameron, (Barbara) Anne
Hubert, James Lee 1947- 73-76
Hubert, Jim
See Hubert, James Lee
Hubert, Renee Riese 1916- 61-64
Hubin, Allen J. 1936- 33-36R
Hubka, Betty (Josephine Morgan)
1924- 13-16R
Hubka, Thomas C. 1946- 126
Hubler, David 1941- 110
Hubler, Edward L(orenzo) 1902-1965 ....CAP-1
Earlier sketch in CA 13-14
Hubler, Herbert Clark 1910- 85-88
Hubler, Richard Gibson 1912- CANR-2
Earlier sketch in CA 1-4R
Hubley, Faith Elliot 1924- CANR-29
Earlier sketch in CA 81-84
See also SATA 48
Hubley, John 1914-1977 ....SATA 24, 48
Huby, Pamela M(argaret Clark) 1922- 21-24R
Huch, Friedrich 1873-1913 ....DLB 66
Huch, Ricarda (Octavia)
1864-1947 Brief entry 111
See also DLB 66
See also TCLC 13
Huchel, Peter 1903- 81-84
Huck, Gabe (Donald Joseph) 1941- CANR-30
Earlier sketch in CA 112
Huckaby, Elizabeth (Paisley) 1905- 106
Huckaby, Gerald 1933- 33-36R
Hucker, Charles O(scar) 1919- 69-72
Huckins, Wesley C. 1918- 21-24R
Huckleberry, E(vermont) R(obbins)
1894- CANR-11
Earlier sketch in CA 61-64
Huckshorn, Robert J(ack) 1928- 97-100
Hudd, Roy 1936- 105
Huddle, David 1942- 57-60
See also CLC 49
Huddle, Frank Jr. 1943- 37-40R
Huddleston, Eugene L(ee) 1931- CANR-19
Earlier sketch in CA 102
Huddleston, Lee Eldridge 1935- 21-24R
Huddleston, Rodney D(esmond) 1937- 33-36R
Huddy, Delia 1934- CANR-19
Earlier sketch in CA 25-28R
Hudgens, A(lice) Gayle 1941- 37-40R
Hudgins, Andrew (Leon Jr.) 1951- 132
See also DLB 120
Hudgins, H(erbert) C(ornelius) Jr. 1932- 33-36R
Hudnut, Robert K(ilborne) 1934- CANR-38
Earlier sketches in CA 25-28R, CANR-17
Hudoba, Michael 1913-1984 Obituary 113
Hudon, Edward Gerard 1915- 5-8R
Hudson, Alec
See Holmes, W(ilfred) J(ay)
Hudson, Arthur Palmer
1894(?)-1978 Obituary 111
Hudson, Charles M(elvin Jr.) 1932- 33-36R
Hudson, Danny L. 1940- 122
Hudson, Darril 1931- 45-48
Hudson, Derek (Rommel) 1911- 9-12R
Hudson, Geoffrey Francis
1903-1974 Obituary 49-52
Hudson, Gladys W(atts) 1926- 33-36R
Hudson, Gossie Harold 1930- 93-96
Hudson, Helen
See Lane, Helen
Hudson, Henry Norman 1814-1886 ....DLB 64
Hudson, Henry T(homas) 1932- 118
Hudson, Herman 1923- 97-100
Hudson, James A(lbert) 1924- 33-36R
Hudson, James J(ackson) 1919- 25-28R
Hudson, James R. 1933- 124
Hudson, Jan 1954- 136
Hudson, Jean B(arlow) 1915- 93-96
Hudson, Jeffery
See Crichton, (John) Michael
Hudson, John A(llen) 1927- 25-28R
Hudson, Kenneth 1916- 128
Brief entry 117
Hudson, (Margaret) Kirsty 1947- 107
See also SATA 32
Hudson, Liam 1933- CANR-12
Earlier sketch in CA 29-32R
Hudson, Lois Phillips 1927- 1-4R
Hudson, Marc 1947- 116
Hudson, Mark 1957- 132
Hudson, Meg
See Koehler, Margaret (Hudson)
Hudson, Michael C(raig) 1938- 37-40R
Hudson, Michael Huckleberry 1939- CANR-13
Earlier sketch in CA 33-36R
Hudson, Miles (Matthew Lee) 1925- 132
Hudson, (Arthur) Palmer 1892- CAP-2
Earlier sketch in CA 19-20
Hudson, Peggy
See Herz, Peggy
Hudson, R(obert) Lofton 1910- 13-16R
Hudson, Randolph H(oyt) 1927- 17-20R
Hudson, Richard (McLain Jr.) 1925- 65-68
Hudson, Robert
See Oleksy, Walter
Hudson, Robert P(aul) 1926- 116
Hudson, Robert Vernon 1932- 109
Hudson, Theodore R. 45-48
Hudson, W(illiam) H(enry)
1841-1922 Brief entry 115
See also DLB 98
See also SATA 35
See also TCLC 29
Hudson, Wilma J(ones) 1916- 33-36R
Hudson, Wilson Mathis 1907- 102
Hudson, Winthrop Still 1911- CANR-2
Earlier sketch in CA 1-4R
Hudspeth, Robert N. 1936- 103
Huebel, Harry Russell 1943- 77-80
Huebener, Theodore 1895-1983 Obituary 111
Huebner, Anna (Ismelda Mathews)
1877(?)-1974 Obituary 53-56
Huebner, Fredrick D. 1955- 133
Huebner, Klaus H(ermann) 1916- 126
Huebner, Kurt 1921- 132
Hueffer, Ford Madox
See Ford, Ford Madox
Huegli, A(lbert) G(eorge) 1913- 13-16R
Huelsman, Richard J(oseph) 1921- 111
Huelsmann, Carl (M.) 1914- 130
Huelsmann, Eva 1928- ....SATA 16
Huerlimann, Bettina 1909-1983 109
Obituary 110
See also Hurlimann, Bettina
See also MAICYA
See also SATA 34, 39
Huerlimann, Ruth 1939- 107
See also Hurlimann, Ruth
See also SATA 31, 32
Huerta, Jorge
See Huerta, Jorge A(lfonso)
Huerta, Jorge A(lfonso) 1942- 131
See also HW
Huessy, Hans R. 1921- 21-24R
Hueter, John E(dwin) 1918- 114
Huether, Anne Frances
See Freeman, Anne Frances
Huey, F. B. Jr. 1925- CANR-23
Earlier sketch in CA 106
Huey, Lynda 1947- 65-68
Hufana, A(lejandrino) G. 1926- 77-80
Hufbauer, Karl (George) 1937- 109
Huff, Afton (A.) W(alker) 1928- 65-68
Huff, Barbara A. 1929- 135
See also SATA 67
Huff, Betty Tracy 25-28R
Huff, Darrell 1913- CANR-5
Earlier sketch in CA 1-4R
Huff, Robert 1924- CANR-6
Earlier sketch in CA 13-16R
Huff, T(om) E. 1938(?)- 93-96
See also AITN 2
Huff, T. S.
See Huff, Tanya (Sue)
Huff, Tanya (Sue) 1957- 128
Huff, Vaughn E(dward) 1935- 29-32R
Huff, Vivian 1948- ....SATA 59
Huffaker, Clair 1926(?)-1990 113
Obituary 131
Huffaker, Sandy 1943- ....SATA 10
Huffard, Grace Thompson 1892- CAP-1
Earlier sketch in CA 11-12
Huffert, Anton M. 1912- 13-16R
Huffington, Arianna Stassinopoulos 1950- 129
Huffman, Carolyn 1928- 69-72
Huffman, Claire (De Cesare Licari) 116
Huffman, Franklin E(ugene) 1934- CANR-12
Earlier sketch in CA 29-32R
Huffman, James Lamar 1941- 102
Huffman, Laurie 1916- 45-48
Huffman, Phyllis
See Atwater, P(hyllis) M. H.
Huffman, Tom ....SATA 24
Hufford, Susan 1940- CANR-9
Earlier sketch in CA 57-60
Hufschmidt, Maynard Michael 1912- CANR-15
Earlier sketch in CA 41-44R
Hufton, Olwen H. 1938- 21-24R
Hug, Bernal D(ean) 1896- 57-60
Huggan, Isabel 1943- 119
Huggett, Frank E(dward) 1924- CANR-19
Earlier sketches in CA 9-12R, CANR-3
Huggett, Joyce 1937- 126
Huggett, Richard 1929- 53-56
Huggett, William Turner 53-56
Huggins, Alice Margaret 1891-1971 ....CAP-1
Earlier sketch in CA 17-18
Huggins, Charles B(renton)
1901- Brief entry 115
Huggins, Nathan Irvin 1927-1989 ....CANR-25
Obituary 130
Earlier sketch in CA 29-32R
See also BW
See also SATA 63
Hughart, Barry 137
See also CLC 39
Hughes, Alan 1935- 97-100
Hughes, Alice 1899(?)-1977 Obituary 104
Hughes, Andrew 1937- 61-64
Hughes, Anthony John 1933- 9-12R

Hughes, Arthur Joseph 1928- 17-20R
Hughes, Arthur Montague D'Urban
1873-1974 Obituary 49-52
Hughes, B(asil) P(erronet) 1903- 61-64
Hughes, C(hristopher) J(ohn) 1918- 17-20R
Hughes, C. J. Pennethorne
See Hughes, (Charles James) Pennethorne
Hughes, Catharine R(achel)
1935-1987 ....CANR-27
Obituary 123
Earlier sketch in CA 41-44R
Hughes, Charles C(ampbell) 1929- 41-44R
Hughes, Charles L(loyd) 1933- CANR-11
Earlier sketch in CA 17-20R
Hughes, (John) Cledwyn 1920-1978 ....13-16R
Obituary 126
Hughes, Colin
See Creasey, John
Hughes, Colin A(nfield) 1930- CANR-25
Earlier sketches in CA 21-24R, CANR-9
Hughes, Daniel T(homas) 1930- 89-92
Hughes, Daniel 1929- 33-36R
Hughes, David (John) 1930- 129
Brief entry 116
See also CLC 48
See also DLB 14
Hughes, Dean Aubrey
1908(?)-1987 Obituary 122
Hughes, Dean 1943- CANR-22
Earlier sketch in CA 106
See also SATA 33
Hughes, Dorothy B(elle) 1904- 104
Hughes, Dorothy (Berry) 1910- CAP-2
Earlier sketch in CA 33-36
Hughes, Douglas A(llan) 1938- 29-32R
Hughes, Dusty
See Hughes, Richard Holland
Hughes, Eden
See Butterworth, W(illiam) E(dmund III)
Hughes, Elizabeth
See Zachary, Hugh
Hughes, Emmet John 1920-1982 69-72
Obituary 107
Hughes, Erica 1931- CANR-28
Earlier sketch in CA 109
Hughes, Everett Cherrington 1897-1983 103
Obituary 108
Hughes, Felicity 1938- 33-36R
Hughes, G(eorge) E(dward) 1918- 21-24R
Hughes, Gerald (Thomas) 1930- 117
Hughes, Gervase 1905- 9-12R
Hughes, Glyn 1935- CANR-35
Earlier sketches in CA 33-36R, CANR-13
Hughes, Graham 1928- 57-60
Hughes, Gwilym Fielden 1899- 97-100
Hughes, H(enry) Stuart 1916- CANR-2
Earlier sketch in CA 1-4R
Hughes, Harold K(enneth) 1911- 9-12R
Hughes, Heather 1954- 133
Hughes, Helen (Gintz) 1928- 13-16R
Hughes, Howard (Robard)
1905-1976 Obituary 112
Hughes, Irene Finger 103
Hughes, J(ohnson) Donald 1932- CANR-10
Earlier sketch in CA 65-68
Hughes, James Monroe 1890-1971 ....1-4R
Obituary 103
Hughes, James Pennethorne
See Hughes, (Charles James) Pennethorne
Hughes, James Quentin 1920- CANR-6
Earlier sketch in CA 13-16R
Hughes, James W(ilfred) 1934- 77-80
Hughes, John A(nthony) 1941- 41-44R
Hughes, John Jay 1928- 57-60
Hughes, John L(ewis) 1938- 77-80
Hughes, John Paul 1920-1974 ....1-4R
Obituary 53-56
Hughes, (Robert) John 1930- CANR-4
Earlier sketch in CA 1-4R
Hughes, John 1677-1720 ....DLB 84
Hughes, John 1950(?)- 129
Brief entry 124
See also AAYA 7
Hughes, Jonathan R(oberts) T(yson)
1928- 81-84
Obituary 137
Hughes, Judith M(arkham) 1941- 33-36R
Hughes, Judy 1943- 69-72
Hughes, Kathleen W.
1927(?)-1977 Obituary 69-72
Hughes, Ken(neth) 1922- CANR-39
Earlier sketches in CA 5-8R, CANR-16
Hughes, (James) Langston
1902-1967 ....CANR-34
Obituary 25-28R
Earlier sketches in CA 1-4R, CANR-1
See also BLC 2
See also BW
See also CDALB 1929-1941
See also CLC 1, 5, 10, 15, 35, 44
See also CLR 17
See also DLB 4, 7, 48, 51, 86
See also MAICYA
See also MTCW
See also PC 1
See also SATA 4, 33
See also SSC 6
See also WLC
Hughes, Leo 1908- 41-44R
Hughes, Libby ....SATA 71
Hughes, Margaret Kelly
1894(?)-1980 Obituary 101
Hughes, Marija Matich 97-100
Hughes, Mary Gray 1930- 61-64
Hughes, Mary Louise 1910- 29-32R
Hughes, Mary 1951- 122
Hughes, Matilda
See MacLeod, Charlotte (Matilda Hughes)
Hughes, Merrit Y(erkes) 1893-1970 ....CAP-1
Earlier sketch in CA 17-18
Hughes, Monica (Ince) 1925- CANR-23
Earlier sketch in CA 77-80
See also CLR 9
See also MAICYA
See also SAAS 11
See also SATA 15, 70
Hughes, Nathaniel Cheairs Jr. 1930- 17-20R
Hughes, Owain (Gardner Collingwood)
1943- 21-24R
Hughes, Patrick 1939- 61-64
Hughes, Paul L(ester) 1915- 9-12R
Hughes, (Charles James) Pennethorne
1907-1967 ....CAP-2
Earlier sketch in CA 21-22
Hughes, Philip Edgcumbe 1915- CANR-18
Earlier sketches in CA 9-12R, CANR-3
Hughes, Philip 1895-1967 ....CAP-2
Earlier sketch in CA 17-18
Hughes, (James) Quentin 1920- 29-32R
Hughes, R(ichard) E(dward) 1927- CANR-6
Earlier sketch in CA 5-8R
Hughes, Richard (Arthur Warren)
1900-1976 ....CANR-4
Obituary 65-68
Earlier sketch in CA 5-8R
See also CLC 1, 11
See also DLB 15
See also MTCW
See also SATA 8, 25
Hughes, Richard Holland 1947- 131
Hughes, Richard 1906-1984 Obituary 111
Hughes, Richard 1941- 107
Hughes, Riley 1914-1981 107
Obituary 103
Hughes, Robert (Studley Forrest) 1938(?)- 112
Brief entry 110
Hughes, Robert 1929(?)-1972 Obituary 37-40R
Hughes, Russell C. 1893(?)-1982 Obituary 108
Hughes, Russell Meriwether
1898(?)-1988 Obituary 124
Hughes, Sam
See Wilks, Brian
Hughes, Shirley 1927- CANR-24
Earlier sketch in CA 85-88
See also CLR 15
See also MAICYA
See also SATA 16, 70
Hughes, Stella 1916- 127
Hughes, Stephen Ormsby 1924- 61-64
Hughes, Ted 1930- CANR-33
Earlier sketches in CA 1-4R, CANR-1
See also CLC 2, 4, 9, 14, 37
See also CLR 3
See also DLB 40
See also MAICYA
See also MTCW
See also SATA 27, 49
Hughes, Terry A. 1933- 65-68
Hughes, Theodore E(rmond) 1942- 116
Hughes, Thomas M(ears) 1927- 65-68
Hughes, Thomas Parke 1923- 29-32R
Hughes, Thomas 1822-1896 ....DLB 18
See also SATA 31
Hughes, Virginia
See Campbell, Hope
Hughes, Walter (Llewellyn) 1910- CANR-1
Earlier sketch in CA 1-4R
See also SATA 26
Hughes, William J. Jr.
1897(?)-1974 Obituary 45-48
Hughes, William W(auters) 1918- 126
Hughes, Zach
See Zachary, Hugh
Hughes, Zachary
See Zachary, Hugh
Hughes-Hallett, Lucy 1951- 138
Hughey, Roberta 1942- ....SATA 61
Hughey, Ruth Willard 1899- 1-4R
Hugill, Stan(ley) James 1906- CAP-2
Earlier sketch in CA 23-24
Hugo, Grant
See Cable, James (Eric)
Hugo, Herbert W. 1930(?)-1979 Obituary 89-92
Hugo, Richard F(ranklin) 1923-1982 ....CANR-3
Obituary 108
Earlier sketch in CA 49-52
See also CLC 6, 18, 32
See also DLB 5
Hugo, Victor (Marie) 1802-1885 ....DLB 119
See also SATA 47
See also WLC
Huhne, Christopher 1954- 133
Huhta, James K(enneth) 1937- 37-40R
Huidobro, Vicente
See Huidobro Fernandez, Vicente Garcia
Huidobro Fernandez, Vicente Garcia
1893-1948 131
See also HW
See also TCLC 31
Huie, William Bradford 1910-1986 ....CANR-7
Obituary 121
Earlier sketch in CA 9-12R
See also AITN 1
Huie, William O(rr) 1911- 21-24R
Huisken, Ronald H(erman) 1946- 93-96
Hula, Harold L. 1930- 25-28R
Hulbert, Ann 1956- 138
Hulbert, Jack 1892-1978 Obituary 115
Hulet, Claude Lyle 1920- CANR-9
Earlier sketch in CA 53-56
Hulicka, Irene M(ackintosh) 1927- 37-40R
Hulicka, Karel 1913- 41-44R
Huline-Dickens, Frank William 1931- 107
See also SATA 34
Hulke, Malcolm 1924- 81-84
Hull, Cary Schuler 1946- 106
Hull, Charles
See Charles, Gordon H(ull)
Hull, David L(ee) 1935- 77-80
Hull, David Stewart 1938- 25-28R
Hull, Denison Bingham 1897- 37-40R
Hull, Eleanor (Means) 1913- CANR-19
Earlier sketches in CA 9-12R, CANR-4
See also SATA 21
Hull, Eric Traviss
See Harnan, Terry
Hull, Eugene L(eslie) 1928- 37-40R
Hull, George F. 1909(?)-1974 Obituary 53-56
Hull, Gloria T(heresa Thompson)
1944- CANR-25
Earlier sketch in CA 108
See also BW
Hull, H. Braxton
See Jacobs, Helen Hull
Hull, Helen (Rose) 1888(?)-1971 ....CAP-1
Obituary 29-32R
Earlier sketch in CA 9-10
Hull, J(ohn) H(owarth) E(ric) 1923- 25-28R
Hull, Jesse Redding
See Hull, Jessie Redding
Hull, Jessie Redding 1932- 109
See also SATA 51
Hull, John M. 1935- 137
Hull, Katharine 1921-1977 ....29-32R
See also SATA 23
Hull, Lynda 1954- 126
Hull, Marion A(da) 1911- 105
Hull, Opal
See Lehnus, Opal (Hull)
Hull, Oswald 1919- 25-28R
Hull, R(ichard) F(rancis) C(arrington)
1913(?)-1974 Obituary 53-56
Hull, Raymona E. 1907- 116
Hull, Raymond 1919-1985 ....CANR-11
Obituary 116
Earlier sketch in CA 25-28R
Hull, Richard W. 1940- CANR-25
Earlier sketch in CA 45-48
Hull, Richard 1896-1973 ....DLB 77
Hull, Roger H. 1942- 25-28R
Hull, Suzanne W(hite) 1921- 125
Hull, William (Doyle) 1918- CANR-5
Earlier sketch in CA 13-16R
Hull, William E(dward) 1930- CANR-24
Earlier sketches in CA 17-20R, CANR-7
Hulland, J(ennifer) R(osemary) 1936- 122
Hulley, Clarence C(harles) 1905- 41-44R
Hulme, Hilda Mary 1914- 77-80
Hulme, Kathryn 1900-1981 ....CAP-1
Obituary 104
Earlier sketch in CA 9-10
Hulme, Keri 1947- 125
See also CLC 39
Hulme, T(homas) E(rnest)
1883-1917 Brief entry 117
See also DLB 19
See also TCLC 21
Hulme, William E(dward) 1920- CANR-5
Earlier sketch in CA 13-16R
Hulse, Clark 1947- 106
Hulse, Erroll 1931- CANR-21
Earlier sketch in CA 104
Hulse, James Warren 1930- 9-12R
Hulse, (Herman) LaWayne 1922- 29-32R
Hulse, Michael (William) 1955- 118
Hulse, Stewart H(arding) Jr. 1931- CANR-14
Earlier sketch in CA 33-36R
Hult, Ruby El 1912- 57-60
Hulteng, John L. 1921- CANR-13
Earlier sketch in CA 33-36R
Hultgren, Thor 1902- CAP-1
Earlier sketch in CA 17-18
Hultkrantz, Aake G. B. 1920- 130
Hultkrantz, Ake G. B.
See Hultkrantz, Aake G. B.
Hultman, Charles W(illiam) 1930- CANR-1
Earlier sketch in CA 1-4R
Hults, Dorothy Niebrugge 1898- CAP-1
Earlier sketch in CA 9-10
See also SATA 6
Humbaraci, D(emir) Arslan 1923- 49-52
Humbard, (Alpha) Rex (Emmanuel)
1919- Brief entry 111
Humber, William 1949- 124
Humble, Richard 1945- CANR-17
Earlier sketches in CA 45-48, CANR-2
See also SATA 60
Humble, William F(rank) 1948- 21-24R
Humboldt, Alexander von 1769-1859 ....DLB 90
Humboldt, Wilhelm von 1767-1835 ....DLB 90
Hume, Arthur W. J. G. Ord
See Ord-Hume, Arthur W. J. G.
Hume, Basil
See Hume, George Haliburton
Hume, (Alexander) Brit(ton) 1943- 126
Brief entry 119
Hume, David 1711-1776 ....DLB 104
Hume, Fergus(on Wright)
1859-1932 Brief entry 109
See also DLB 70
Hume, George Haliburton 1923- 126
Hume, John E. N. Jr. 1915-1986 Obituary 118
Hume, John Robert 1939- 106
Hume, Kathryn 1945- 57-60
Hume, L(eonard) J(ohn) 1926- 135
Hume, Lotta Carswell CAP-1
Earlier sketch in CA 9-10
See also SATA 7
Hume, Martha 1947- 112
Hume, Paul Chandler 1915- 102
Hume, Robert D. 1944- CANR-12
Earlier sketch in CA 29-32R
Hume, Ruth Fox 1922-1980 Obituary 97-100
See also SATA 22, 26
Hume, Stephen 1947- 125
Humes, D(ollena) Joy 1921- 1-4R
Humes, H(arold) L. 1926- 5-8R
Humes, James C. 1934- CANR-1
Earlier sketch in CA 45-48
Humes, John Portner 1921-1985 Obituary 117
Humes, Samuel 1930- 5-8R
Humez, Jean McMahon 1944- 124
Humfrey, C.
See Osborne, C(harles) H(umfrey) C(aufeild)
Humfrey, (James) Michael 1936- 127
Hummel, Berta 1909-1946 ....SATA 43
Hummel, Charles E. 1923- 17-20R
Hummel, Madeline
See Moore, Madeline (Roberta)
Hummel, Monte 1946- 135
Hummel, Ray O(rvin) Jr. 1909- 33-36R
Hummel, Ruth Stevenson 1929- 5-8R
Hummel, Sister Maria Innocentia
See Hummel, Berta
Hummer, T(erry) R. 1950- 128
See also DLB 120
Humphreville, Frances Tibbetts 1909- 9-12R
Humphrey, David C(hurchill) 1937- 85-88
Humphrey, Henry (III) 1930- 77-80
See also SATA 16
Humphrey, Hubert Horatio 1911-1978 69-72
Obituary 73-76
Humphrey, J(ames) Edward 1918- 93-96
Humphrey, James (Earl) 1939- 45-48
Humphrey, James H(arry) 1911- CANR-23
Earlier sketches in CA 61-64, CANR-8
Humphrey, Mary Ann 1943- 134
Humphrey, Michael (Edward) 1926- 29-32R
Humphrey, Paul 1915- 110
Humphrey, Robert L. 1923- 57-60
Humphrey, William 1924- 77-80
See also CLC 45
See also DLB 6
Humphreys, A(rthur) R(aleigh)
1911-1988 Obituary 126
Humphreys, Alexander J(eremiah)
1913- 33-36R
Humphreys, Alice Lee 1893- 5-8R
Humphreys, (Travers) Christmas
1901-1983 77-80
Obituary 109
Humphreys, David 1752-1818 ....DLB 37
Humphreys, Emyr Owen 1919- CANR-24
Earlier sketches in CA 5-8R, CANR-3
See also CLC 47
See also DLB 15
Humphreys, George G(ary) 1949- 138
Humphreys, Graham 1945- ....SATA 32
Humphreys, J(ohn) R(ichard) Adams
1918- CANR-22
Earlier sketch in CA 1-4R
Humphreys, Josephine 1945- 127
Brief entry 121
See also CLC 34, 57
Humphreys, (Robert Allan) Laud
1930-1988 ....29-32R
Obituary 126
Humphreys, Martha 1943- ....SATA 71
Humphreys, Mary Eglantyne Hill 1914- CANR-6
Earlier sketch in CA 5-8R
Humphreys, R(obert) A(rthur) 1907- 129
Humphreys, Robin A.
See Humphreys, R(obert) A(rthur)
Humphreys, Susan L.
See Lowell, Susan
Humphreyville, Theresa R. 1918- 13-16R
Humphries, Adelaide M. 1898- CAP-1
Earlier sketch in CA 13-16
Humphries, Barry 1934- 129
Humphries, Helen Speirs Dickie 1915- CAP-1
Earlier sketch in CA 9-10
Humphries, (John) Jefferson 1955- CANR-36
Earlier sketch in CA 114
Humphries, Mary 1905- 53-56
Humphries, (George) Rolfe 1894-1969 ....CANR-3
Obituary 25-28R
Earlier sketch in CA 5-8R
Humphries, Sydney Vernon 1907- 103
Humphry, Derek 1930- 41-44R
Humphrys, Geoffrey
See Humphrys, Leslie George
Humphrys, Leslie George 1921- 107
Humpstone, Charles Cheney 1931- 49-52
Huncke, Herbert E(dwin) 1915- 130
See also DLB 16
Hundley, Joan Martin 1921- 45-48
Hundley, Norris (Cecil) Jr. 1935- CANR-8
Earlier sketch in CA 17-20R
Huneker, James Gibbons 1857-1921 ....DLB 71
Huneryager, S(herwood) G(eorge) 1933- 1-4R
Hungerford, Cy(rus Cotton)
1889(?)-1983 Obituary 109
Hungerford, Edward Buell 1900- 37-40R
Hungerford, Harold R(alph) 1928- 33-36R
Hungerford, Mary Jane 1913- 77-80
Hungerford, Pixie
See Brinsmead, H(esba) F(ay)
Hungry Wolf, Adolf 1944- CANR-38
Earlier sketch in CA 115
Hungry Wolf, Beverly 1950- CANR-38
Earlier sketch in CA 117
Hunker, Henry L. 1924- 13-16R
Hunkin, Timothy Mark Trelawney 1950- 102
See also SATA 53
Hunkins, Francis P(eter) 1938- 57-60
Hunkins, Lee(cynth) 1930- 108

Hunnex, Milton D(eVerne) 1917- 29-32R
Hunnicutt, Benjamin Kline 1943- 130
Hunnings, Neville March 1929- CANR-12
Earlier sketch in CA 25-28R
Hunnisett, Basil 1923- 119
Hunsaker, David M(alcolm) 1944- 33-36R
Hunsberger, Edith Mae 1927- 109
Hunsberger, Warren S(eabury) 1911- 41-44R
Hunsehe, Raymond W.
1891(?)-1983 Obituary 111
Hunsinger, George 1945- 65-68
Hunsinger, Paul 1919- 33-36R
Hunsinger, Walter (William) 1923- 122
Hunt, Abby Campbell 1933(?)-1985 135
Obituary 116
Hunt, Barbara
See Watters, Barbara H(unt)
Hunt, Bernice (Kohn) 1920- CANR-21
Earlier sketch in CA 9-12R
See also Kohn, Bernice
Hunt, Bruce J. 1956- 136
Hunt, Charles Butler 1906- 110
Hunt, Charlotte
See Hodges, Doris M(arjorie)
Hunt, Chester L. 1912- CANR-5
Earlier sketch in CA 13-16R
Hunt, Clarence
See Holman, C(larence) Hugh
Hunt, Dave
See Hunt, David C(harles Hadden)
Hunt, David C(harles Hadden) 1926- CANR-9
Earlier sketch in CA 57-60
Hunt, David C(urtis) 1935- CANR-38
Earlier sketches in CA 89-92, CANR-16
Hunt, David (Wathen Stather) 1913- 102
Hunt, David 1942- 33-36R
Hunt, Douglas 1918- 13-16R
Hunt, E(verette) Howard Jr. 1918- CANR-2
Earlier sketch in CA 45-48
See also AITN 1
See also CLC 3
Hunt, E. K. 1937- 77-80
Hunt, Earl B. 1933- 93-96
Hunt, Earl W(ilbur) 1926- 85-88
Hunt, Edgar H(ubert) 1909- CAP-1
Earlier sketch in CA 9-10
Hunt, Elgin F(raser) 1895-1978 ....1-4R
Hunt, Everett Lee 1890(?)-1984 Obituary 112
Hunt, F(lorence) V(ance) 132
Hunt, Florine E(lizabeth) 1928- 13-16R
Hunt, Francis CANR-26
Earlier sketches in CAP-2, CA 19-20
Hunt, Frazier 1885-1967 Obituary 93-96
Hunt, Garry Edward 1942- 115
Hunt, Geoffrey 1915(?)-1974 Obituary 104
Hunt, George Laird 1918- 49-52
Hunt, George W(illiam) 1937- 120
Hunt, Gill
See Tubb, E(dwin) C(harles)
Hunt, Gladys M. 1926- CANR-13
Earlier sketch in CA 29-32R
Hunt, (Leslie) Gordon 1906-1970 ....CAP-2
Earlier sketch in CA 29-32
Hunt, H(arry) Draper 1935- 37-40R
Hunt, Harrison
See Ballard, (Willis) Todhunter
Hunt, Herbert James 1899-1973 Obituary 89-92
Hunt, Hugh 1911- CANR-3
Earlier sketch in CA 5-8R
Hunt, Ignatius 1920- 17-20R
Hunt, Inez Whitaker 1899- CAP-1
Earlier sketch in CA 17-18
Hunt, Irene 1907- CANR-8
Earlier sketch in CA 17-20R
See also CLR 1
See also DLB 52
See also MAICYA
See also SATA 2
Hunt, J(oseph) McVicker 1906-1991 ....37-40R
Obituary 133
Hunt, J. William Jr. 1930- 53-56
Hunt, James Gerald 1932- CANR-31
Earlier sketches in CA 65-68, CANR-14
Hunt, John
See Paine, Lauran (Bosworth)
Hunt, John Dixon 1936- CANR-17
Earlier sketch in CA 85-88
Hunt, (Henry Cecil) John 1910- 109
Hunt, John J. 1929- 33-36R
Hunt, John P(aul) 1915-1988 ....33-36R
Obituary 124
Hunt, John W(esley) 1927- 21-24R
Hunt, Joyce 1927- CANR-22
Earlier sketch in CA 106
See also SATA 31
Hunt, June 1944- 103
Hunt, Kari (Eleanor B.) 1920- 41-44R
Hunt, Kellogg W(esley) 1912- 5-8R
Hunt, Kenneth E(dward)
1917(?)-1978 Obituary 104
Hunt, Kyle
See Creasey, John
Hunt, Lawrence J. 1920- 5-8R
Hunt, Leigh 1784-1859 ....DLB 96, 110
Hunt, Leon (Gibson) 1931- 65-68
Hunt, Linda 1940- 106
See also SATA 39
Hunt, Lynn (Avery) 1945- 131
Hunt, Mabel Leigh 1892-1971 ....CAP-1
Obituary 106
Earlier sketch in CA 9-10
See also SATA 1, 26
Hunt, Marsha 1946- ....CLC 70
Hunt, Maurice P. 1915- 25-28R
Hunt, Michael H. 1942- 127
Hunt, Morton M(agill) 1920- CANR-21
Earlier sketch in CA 5-8R
See also SATA 22
Hunt, Nan
See Ray, N(ancy) L(ouise)
Hunt, Nancy (Ridgely) 1927- 103
Hunt, Nigel
See Greenbank, Anthony Hunt
Hunt, Noel Aubrey Bonavia
See Bonavia-Hunt, Noel Aubrey
Hunt, Noreen 1931- 103
Hunt, Norman C.
See Crowther-Hunt, Norman Crowther
Hunt, Norman Crowther Crowther
See Crowther-Hunt, Norman Crowther
Hunt, Patricia Joan CANR-21
Earlier sketch in CA 103
Hunt, Patricia 1922(?)-1983 Obituary 120
Hunt, Penelope
See Napier, Priscilla
Hunt, Peter (Leonard) 1945- CANR-32
Earlier sketch in CA 113
Hunt, Peter 1922- 5-8R
Hunt, Ray(mond) C(hamp) Jr. 1919- 122
Hunt, Raymond G(eorge) 1928- CANR-3
Earlier sketch in CA 9-12R
Hunt, Richard N(orman) 1931- 9-12R
Hunt, Richard (Patrick) 1938- 137
Hunt, Richard (Paul) 1921- 73-76
Hunt, Robert C(ushman) 1934- CANR-9
Earlier sketch in CA 21-24R
Hunt, Sam 1946- 110
Hunt, Stoker
See Piotrowski, Andrew
Hunt, Tim(othy A.) 1949- 121
Hunt, Todd T. 1938- 13-16R
Hunt, V. Daniel 1939- 111
Hunt, Virginia Lloyd
1888(?)-1977 Obituary 73-76
Hunt, William A(lvin) 1903-1986 Obituary 118
Hunt, William Dudley Jr. 1922-1987 ....CANR-14
Obituary 122
Earlier sketch in CA 33-36R
Hunt, William Gibbes 1791-1833 ....DLB 73
Hunt, William R(aymond) 1929- 93-96
Hunt, William 1934- CANR-3
Earlier sketch in CA 49-52
Hunter, A(rchibald) M(acbride) 1906- CANR-6
Earlier sketch in CA 9-12R
Hunter, Alan (James Herbert) 1922- CANR-18
Earlier sketches in CA 9-12R, CANR-3
Hunter, Allan A(rmstrong) 1893- 5-8R
Hunter, Anson
See Orrmont, Arthur
Hunter, Beatrice Trum 1918- CANR-22
Earlier sketches in CA 17-20R, CANR-7
Hunter, Bernice Thurman 1922- 119
See also SATA 45
Hunter, Bill R. 1932(?)-1990 Obituary 131
Hunter, Bruce (William) 1952- 123
Hunter, C. Bruce 1917- 61-64
Hunter, Captain Marcy
See Ellis, Edward S(ylvester)
Hunter, Christine
See Hunter, Maud L(ily)
Hunter, Clark 124
Hunter, Clingham M.D.
See Adams, William Taylor
Hunter, Dard 1883-1966 ....CAP-1
Obituary 25-28R
Earlier sketch in CA 13-16
Hunter, Doris A. 1929- 37-40R
Hunter, E. Waldo
See Sturgeon, Theodore (Hamilton)
Hunter, Edith Fisher 1919- 107
See also SATA 31
Hunter, Edward 1902-1978 ....5-8R
Obituary 77-80
Hunter, Elizabeth
See de Guise, Elizabeth (Mary Teresa)
Hunter, Evan 1926- CANR-38
Earlier sketches in CA 5-8R, CANR-5
See also CLC 11, 31
See also DLBY 82
See also MTCW
See also SATA 25
Hunter, Frederick J(ames) 1916- 33-36R
Hunter, Geoffrey (Basil Bailey) 1925- 33-36R
Hunter, George
See Ballard, (Willis) Todhunter
Hunter, George E.
See Ellis, Edward S(ylvester)
Hunter, Gordon C. 1924- 106
Hunter, (James) Graham 136
Hunter, Hall
See Marshall, Edison
Hunter, Henry MacGregor 1929- Brief entry 109
Hunter, Hilda 1921- 49-52
See also SATA 7
Hunter, Howard Eugene 1929- 41-44R
Hunter, J(ames) A(lston) H(ope)
1902- CANR-14
Earlier sketches in CAP-1, CA 9-10
Hunter, J(ohn) F(letcher) M(acGregor)
1924- 37-40R
Hunter, J(ames) Paul 1934- CANR-24
Earlier sketches in CA 21-24R, CANR-9
Hunter, Jack D(ayton) 1921- CANR-29
Earlier sketches in CA 5-8R, CANR-6
Hunter, James H(ogg) 1890- 85-88
Hunter, Jane (Harlow) 1949- 125
Hunter, Jim 1939- CANR-7
Earlier sketch in CA 9-12R
See also DLB 14
See also SATA 65
Hunter, Joan
See Yarde, Jeanne Betty Frances
Hunter, Joe
See McNeilly, Wilfred (Glassford)
Hunter, John
See Ballard, (Willis) Todhunter
and Hunter, Maud L(ily)
Hunter, John M(erlin) 1921- 13-16R
Hunter, Kim 1922- 61-64
Hunter, Kristin (Eggleston) 1931- CANR-13
Earlier sketch in CA 13-16R
See also AITN 1
See also BW
See also CLC 35
See also CLR 3
See also DLB 33
See also MAICYA
See also SAAS 10
See also SATA 12
Hunter, Leigh
See Etchison, Birdie L(ee)
Hunter, Leona Wesley
See Greif, Martin
Hunter, Leslie S(tannard) 1890-1983 ....CAP-1
Obituary 110
Earlier sketch in CA 19-20
Hunter, Lieutenant Ned
See Ellis, Edward S(ylvester)
Hunter, Louis C. 1898(?)-1984 Obituary 112
Hunter, Louise H(arris) 41-44R
Hunter, Mac
See Hunter, Henry MacGregor
Hunter, Marjorie 1922- 69-72
Hunter, Mark 1952- 128
Hunter, Marvin H(erbert) 1930- Brief entry 111
Hunter, Mary Vann 1937- 107
Hunter, Maud L(ily) 1910- CANR-4
Earlier sketch in CA 9-12R
Hunter, Mel 1927- 93-96
See also SATA 39
Hunter, Michael (Cyril William) 1949- 104
Hunter, Milton R(eed) 1902-1975 Obituary 104
Hunter, Mollie 1922- CANR-37
See also McIlwraith, Maureen Mollie Hunter
See also CLC 21
See also CLR 25
See also MAICYA
See also SAAS 7
See also SATA 54
Hunter, Ned
See Ellis, Edward S(ylvester)
Hunter, Norman Charles
1908-1971 Obituary 29-32R
See also DLB 10
Hunter, Norman (George Lorimer)
1899- CANR-15
Earlier sketch in CA 93-96
See also SATA 26
Hunter, Richard 1923-1981 Obituary 105
Hunter, Robert E(dwards) 1940- CANR-33
Earlier sketches in CA 41-44R, CANR-15
Hunter, Robert Grams 1927- 93-96
Hunter, Rodello
See Calkins, Rodello
Hunter, Sam 1923- CANR-8
Earlier sketch in CA 13-16R
Hunter, Stephen 1946- CANR-19
Earlier sketch in CA 102
Hunter, Thomas 1932- 108
Hunter, Tim 1947- 85-88
Hunter, Valancy
See Meaker, Eloise
Hunter, Vickie
See Hunter, Victoria Alberta
Hunter, Victoria Alberta 1929- 5-8R
Hunter, William A(lbert) 1908- 13-16R
Hunter, William B(ridges) Jr. 1915- 77-80
Hunter Blair, Pauline (Clarke) 1921- 29-32R
See also Clarke, Pauline
See also SATA 3
Hunter Blair, Peter 1912-1982 Obituary 108
Brief entry 107
Hunter-Duvar, John 1821-1899 ....DLB 99
Hunting, Constance 1925- CANR-23
Earlier sketch in CA 45-48
Huntingdon, Eugenia 1910- 127
Huntington, Anna Hyatt
1876-1973 Obituary 45-48
Huntington, (E.) Gale 1902- 9-12R
Huntington, Harriet E(lizabeth) 1909- CANR-5
Earlier sketch in CA 5-8R
See also SATA 1
Huntington, Henry S. Jr.
1892-1981 Obituary 103
Huntington, John (Willard) 1940- 112
Huntington, Madge 1937- 126
Huntington, Samuel P(hillips) 1927- CANR-1
Earlier sketch in CA 1-4R
Huntington, Thomas W(aterman)
1893-1973 Obituary 45-48
Huntington, Virginia 1889- 21-24R
Huntley, Chester Robert 1911-1974 97-100
Obituary 49-52
See also AITN 1
Huntley, Chet
See Huntley, Chester Robert
Huntley, Frank Livingstone 1902- 33-36R
Huntley, H(erbert) E(dwin) 1892- CAP-1
Earlier sketch in CA 13-14
Huntley, James L(ewis) 1914- 101
Huntley, James Robert 1923- CANR-12
Earlier sketch in CA 29-32R
Huntley, Timothy Wade 1939- 102
Hunton, Mary
See Gilzean, Elizabeth Houghton Blanchet
Hunton, Richard E(dwin) 1924- 21-24R
Huntress, Keith G(ibson) 1913- 5-8R
Huntsberger, John (Paul) 1931- 5-8R
Huntsberry, William E(mery) 1916- CANR-2
Earlier sketch in CA 1-4R
See also SATA 5
Hunzicker, Beatrice Plumb 1886- 5-8R
Hupka, Robert 1919- 61-64
Huppe, Bernard F. 1911- CANR-3
Earlier sketch in CA 5-8R
Huppert, George 1934- 29-32R
Hurd, Charles (Wesley Bolick)
1903-1968 ....CAP-1
Earlier sketch in CA 11-12
Hurd, Clement (G.) 1908-1988 ....CANR-24
Obituary 124
Earlier sketches in CA 29-32R, CANR-9
See also MAICYA
See also SATA 2, 54, 64
Hurd, Douglas (Richard) 1930- CANR-10
Earlier sketch in CA 25-28R
Hurd, Edith (Thacher) 1910- CANR-24
Earlier sketches in CA 13-16R, CANR-9
See also MAICYA
See also SAAS 13
See also SATA 2, 64
Hurd, Florence 1918- CANR-19
Earlier sketch in CA 103
Hurd, John C(oolidge) Jr. 1928- 17-20R
Hurd, Michael John 1928- CANR-12
Earlier sketch in CA 65-68
Hurd, (John) Thacher 1949- CANR-36
Earlier sketches in CA 106, CANR-24
See also MAICYA
See also SATA 45, 46
Hure, Anne 1918- 9-12R
Hureau, Jean (Emile Pierre)
1915- Brief entry 110
Hurewitz, J(acob) C(oleman) 1914- CANR-2
Earlier sketch in CA 1-4R
hurkey, rooan
See Holzapfel, Rudolf Patrick
Hurkos, Peter 1911-1988 Obituary 125
Hurlbut, Allen F. 1910-1983 Obituary 110
Hurlbut, Cornelius S(earle) Jr. 1906- CANR-11
Earlier sketch in CA 25-28R
Hurlbutt, Robert H(arris) III 1924- 13-16R
Hurley, Alfred F(rancis) 1928- 97-100
Hurley, Doran 1900-1964 ....5-8R
Hurley, F(orrest) Jack 1940- CANR-25
Earlier sketch in CA 45-48
Hurley, Jane (Hezel) 1928- 13-16R
Hurley, John J(erome) 1930- 104
Hurley, John 1928- CANR-13
Earlier sketch in CA 33-36R
Hurley, Kathy 1947- 109
Hurley, Leslie J(ohn) 1911- 49-52
Hurley, Mark J(oseph Jr.) 1919- 53-56
Hurley, Neil 1925- 29-32R
Hurley, Vic 1898-1978 ....1-4R
Obituary 103
Hurley, W(illiam) Maurice 1916- 37-40R
Hurley, Wilfred G(eoffrey) 1895-1973 ....CAP-2
Obituary 45-48
Earlier sketch in CA 17-18
Hurley, William James Jr. 1924- 9-12R
Hurlimann, Bettina
See Huerlimann, Bettina
See also SATA 34, 39
Hurlimann, Ruth
See Huerlimann, Ruth
See also SATA 31, 32
Hurlock, Elizabeth B. 1898- 41-44R
Hurlow, (Wilma) Janet 1939- 118
Hurm, Ken 1934- 106
Hurmence, Belinda ....CLR 25
Hurne, Ralph 1932- 21-24R
Hurok, Sol(omon) 1888-1974 Obituary 49-52
Hursch, Carolyn J(udge) 41-44R
Hurst, A(lexander) A(nthony) 1917- 5-8R
Hurst, Charles G. Jr. 1928- 37-40R
Hurst, Fannie 1889-1968 ....CAP-1
Obituary 25-28R
Earlier sketch in CA 13-16
See also DLB 86
Hurst, G(eorge) Cameron III 1941- 85-88
Hurst, James M(arshall) 1924- 29-32R
Hurst, James Willard 1910- 130
Hurst, M(ichael) E(liot) Eliot
See Eliot Hurst, M(ichael) E(liot)
Hurst, Michael (Charles) 1931- 21-24R
Hurst, Norman 1944- 53-56
Hurst, Richard Maurice 1938- 101
Hurst, Virginia Radcliffe
1914(?)-1976 Obituary 69-72
Hurstfield, Joel 1911-1980 ....CANR-6
Obituary 102
Earlier sketch in CA 53-56
Hurston, Zora Neale 1903-1960 85-88
See also BLC 2
See also BW
See also CLC 7, 30, 61
See also DLB 51, 86
See also MTCW
See also SSC 4
Hurt, C(harlie) D(euel III) 1950- 127
Hurt, Freda M(ary) E(lizabeth) 1911- 103
Hurt, Henry 1942- 106
Hurt, James (Riggins) 1934- CANR-23
Earlier sketch in CA 45-48
Hurt, Ray Douglas 1946- 125
Hurtado, Albert L. 1946- 130
Hurtgen, Andre O(scar) 1932- 81-84
Hurtig, Mel 137
Hurvitz, Leon Nahum 1923- 106
Hurwitz, Abraham B. 1905-1981 ....29-32R
Obituary 133
Hurwitz, Edith F(arber) 1941- 108
Hurwitz, Howard L(awrence) 1916- 37-40R

Hurwitz, Johanna 1937- CANR-25
Earlier sketches in CA 65-68, CANR-10
See also MAICYA
See also SATA 20, 71
Hurwitz, Ken 1948-........................33-36R
Hurwitz, Samuel J(ustin) 1912-1972 .... CAP-2
Earlier sketch in CA 25-28
Hurwitz, Stephan 1901-1981 Obituary 103
Hurwood, Bernhardt J. 1926-1987..........25-28R
Obituary 121
See also SATA 12, 50
Husar, John 1937- 81-84
Husband, William Hollow
1899(?)-1978 Obituary 81-84
Huse, Dennis P(aul) 1944- 115
Huseman, Richard C. 1939- 127
Brief entry 109
Husen, Torsten 1916- CANR-27
Earlier sketches in CA 21-24R, CANR-9
Huser, (La)Verne (Carl) 1931- CANR-22
Earlier sketch in CA 106
Huson, Paul (Anthony) 1942- CANR-12
Earlier sketch in CA 29-32R
Huss, Roy 1927- 25-28R
Huss, Sandy 1953- 138
Hussein, Taha 1889-1973 Obituary 45-48
Husserl, E. G.
See Husserl, Edmund (Gustav Albrecht)
Husserl, Edmund (Gustav Albrecht)
1859-1938 133
Brief entry 116
Hussey, David Edward 1934- CANR-9
Earlier sketch in CA 57-60
Hussey, John A(dam) 1913- 61-64
Hussey, Mark 1956- 135
Hussey, Maurice Percival 1925- 9-12R
Hussey, (John) Walter (Atherton)
1909-1985 133
Hussman, Lawrence Eugene Jr. 1932- 115
Hustak, Alan (Joseph) 1944- 128
Huste, Annemarie 1943- 57-60
Husted, Darrell 1931- 81-84
Huston, Anne Marshall 116
Huston, Fran
See Miller, R. S.
Huston, James A(lvin) 1918- CANR-33
Earlier sketches in CA 41-44R, CANR-15
Huston, John (Marcellus) 1906-1987 .....CANR-34
Obituary 123
Earlier sketch in CA 73-76
See also CLC 20
See also DLB 26
Huston, Luther A. 1888- CAP-2
Earlier sketch in CA 21-22
Huston, Mervyn James 1912- CANR-8
Earlier sketch in CA 61-64
Hustvedt, Lloyd (Merlyn) 1922- 21-24R
Hustvedt, Siri 1955- 137
Huszar, George B(ernard) de 1919- CAP-2
Earlier sketch in CA 19-20
Hutchcroft, Vera 1923- 102
Hutchens, Eleanor Newman 1919- 13-16R
Hutchens, John Kennedy 1905- 65-68
Hutchens, Paul 1902-1977 61-64
See also SATA 31
Hutcheon, Linda (Ann) 1947- 131
Hutcheson, Richard G(ordon) Jr. 1921- 107
Hutchin, Kenneth Charles 1908- 110
Hutchings, Alan Eric 1910- 1-4R
Hutchings, Arthur (James Bramwell)
1906- CANR-6
Earlier sketch in CA 5-8R
Hutchings, Bill
See Hutchings, William Bruce
Hutchings, Edward Jr. 1912- 126
Hutchings, Margaret (Joscelyne) 1918- CANR-3
Earlier sketch in CA 9-12R
Hutchings, Monica Mary 1917- 9-12R
Hutchings, Patrick A(elfred) 1929- CANR-4
Earlier sketch in CA 53-56
Hutchings, Raymond 1924- CANR-12
Earlier sketch in CA 33-36R
Hutchings, William Bruce 1948- 111
Hutchins, Carleen Maley 1911- 17-20R
See also SATA 9
Hutchins, Charles R. 1928- 123
Hutchins, Francis Gilman 1939- 21-24R
Hutchins, Hazel J. 1952- 123
See also SATA 51
Hutchins, Maude (Phelps McVeigh) 61-64
Hutchins, Myldred Flanigan 1910- 112
Hutchins, Pat 1942- CANR-32
Earlier sketches in CA 81-84, CANR-15
See also CLR 20
See also MAICYA
See also SATA 15, 70
Hutchins, Robert Maynard 1899-1977 69-72
Hutchins, Ross Elliott 1906- CANR-5
Earlier sketch in CA 9-12R
See also SATA 4
Hutchinson, Arthur Stuart Menteth
1879-1971 Obituary 29-32R
Hutchinson, C(ecil) Alan 1914-1981 ....29-32R
Obituary 133
Hutchinson, D(ouglas) S(tanley) 1955- 128
Hutchinson, David (Christopher) 1960- 119
Hutchinson, Earl Ofari 1945- 138
Hutchinson, Eliot Dole 1900- 61-64
Hutchinson, G(eorge) Evelyn
1903-1991 ....CANR-14
Obituary 134
Earlier sketches in CAP-1, CA 13-14
Hutchinson, George
1920-1980 Obituary 97-100
Hutchinson, H(ugh) Lester 1904- 17-20R
Hutchinson, John 1921- 45-48
Hutchinson, Joseph (Burtt) 1902-1988 109
Obituary 124
Hutchinson, Margaret Massey 1904- CAP-1
Earlier sketch in CA 13-16
Hutchinson, Mary Jane 1924- 106
Hutchinson, Michael E. 1925- 17-20R
Hutchinson, (William Patrick Henry) Pearse
1927- 103
Hutchinson, Peter 1943- CANR-8
Earlier sketch in CA 61-64
Hutchinson, Ray Coryton 1907-1975 ......CANR-3
Obituary 61-64
Earlier sketch in CA 1-4R
Hutchinson, Richard Wyatt 1894-1970 ....5-8R
Obituary 89-92
Hutchinson, Robert 1924- 13-16R
Hutchinson, Thomas 1711-1780 .... DLB 30, 31
Hutchinson, Vernal 1922- 49-52
Hutchinson, Veronica S(omerville)
1895-1961 Obituary 111
Hutchinson, Warner Alton Jr. 1929- 110
Hutchinson, William K(enneth) 1945- 102
Hutchinson, William M(iller) 1916- 112
Hutchison, (William) Bruce 1901- 103
Hutchison, Chester Smith 1902- CAP-2
Earlier sketch in CA 17-18
Hutchison, (Dorothy) Dwight
1890(?)-1975 Obituary 57-60
Hutchison, E(arl) R. 1926- CANR-10
Earlier sketch in CA 25-28R
Hutchison, Emery 1919(?)-1985 Obituary 116
Hutchison, Harold Frederick 1900- CANR-4
Earlier sketch in CA 1-4R
Hutchison, Jane Campbell 1932- 37-40R
Hutchison, John Alexander 1912- 69-72
Hutchison, Sidney C(harles) 1912- 25-28R
Hutchison, T(erence) W(ilmot) 1912- 129
Hutchison, William Robert 1930- 21-24R
Huth, Angela 1938- CANR-20
Earlier sketch in CA 85-88
Huth, Marta 1898- Brief entry 106
Huth, Mary Jo(sephine) 1929- 103
Huth, Tom 1941- 97-100
Huthmacher, J. Joseph 1929- 21-24R
See also SATA 5
Hutin, Magdeleine 1898-1989 Obituary 130
Hutmacher (MacLean), Barbara Anne
1926- 112
Hutman, Norma Louise 1935- 25-28R
Hutschnecker, Arnold A. 1898- 81-84
Hutslar, Donald Andrew 1931- 127
Hutson, Anthony Brian Austen 1934- 93-96
Hutson, James H(oward) 1937- 85-88
Hutson, Jan 1932- 106
Hutson, Joan 1929- 89-92
Hutt, Maurice George 1928- 13-16R
Hutt, Max L. 1908- 57-60
Hutt, W(illiam) H(arold) 1899-1988 57-60
Obituary 125
Huttenback, Robert A. 1928- 25-28R
Hutter, Albert David 1941- 130
Huttig, Jack W(ilfred) 1919- 53-56
Huttner, Matthew 1915-1975 Obituary 104
Hutto, Nelson (Allen) 1904- CAP-1
Earlier sketch in CA 9-10
See also SATA 20
Hutton, Ann 1929- 108
Hutton, Barbara (Audrey) 1920- 132
Hutton, Clarke 1898- 107
Hutton, Geoffrey (William) 1909- 130
Hutton, Geoffrey 1928- 41-44R
Hutton, Ginger
See Hutton, Virginia Carol
Hutton, Harold 1912- 102
Hutton, J(oseph) Bernard 1911- CANR-14
Earlier sketch in CA 21-24R
Hutton, J(ohn) H(enry) 1885-1968 .... CAP-1
Earlier sketch in CA 13-14
Hutton, James 1902-1980 ....CANR-27
Earlier sketch in CA 77-80
Hutton, John (Harwood) 1928- 107
Hutton, Malcolm 1921- CANR-24
Earlier sketch in CA 107
Hutton, Paul Andrew 1949- 133
Hutton, Richard Holt 1826-1897 .... DLB 57
Hutton, Richard 1949- 109
Hutton, Ronald 1953- 131
Hutton, Virginia Carol 1940- 77-80
Hutton, Warwick 1939- CANR-9
Earlier sketch in CA 61-64
See also SATA 20
Hutton, Will(iam Nicholas) 1950- 130
Huus, Helen 1913- CANR-1
Earlier sketch in CA 1-4R
Huvos, Kornel 1913- 49-52
Huws, Daniel 1932- 81-84
Huxhold, Harry N(orman) 1922- 61-64
Huxley, Aldous (Leonard) 1894-1963 85-88
See also CDBLB 1914-1945
See also CLC 1, 3, 4, 5, 8, 11, 18, 35
See also DLB 36, 100
See also MTCW
See also SATA 63
See also WLC
Huxley, Anthony J(ulian) 1920- CANR-22
Earlier sketches in CA 9-12R, CANR-7
Huxley, Elspeth (Josceline Grant)
1907- CANR-28
Earlier sketch in CA 77-80
See also DLB 77
See also SATA 62
Huxley, George 1932- 21-24R
Huxley, Herbert H(enry) 1916- 5-8R
Huxley, Judith 1927(?)-1983 Obituary 111
Huxley, Julian (Sorell) 1887-1975 ....CANR-7
Obituary 57-60
Earlier sketch in CA 9-12R
See also MTCW
Huxley, Laura Archera 13-16R
Huxley, T. H. 1825-1895 .... DLB 57
Huxley-Blythe, Peter J(ames) 1925- 17-20R
Huxtable, Ada Louise (Landman) 1921- 120
Huxtable, (William) John (Fairchild)
1912- 13-16R
Huy, Nguyen Ngoc
See Nguyen Ngoc Huy
Huyck, Dorothy Boyle
1925(?)-1979 Obituary 89-92
Huyck, Margaret Hellie 1939- 49-52
Huyck, Peter H(azelwood) 1940- 107
Huyck, Willard 1945(?)- 128
Brief entry 111
Huygen, Wil(librord Joseph) 1922- CANR-15
Earlier sketch in CA 81-84
Huyghe, Patrick 1952- 135
Huyghe, Rene (Louis) 1906- CANR-20
Earlier sketch in CA 81-84
Huyghue, Douglas Smith 1816-1891 .... DLB 99
Huyler, Jean Wiley 1935- CANR-35
Earlier sketches in CA 69-72, CANR-13
Huynh, Quang Nhuong 1946- 107
Huysmans, Charles Marie Georges
1848-1907 Brief entry 104
See also Huysmans, Joris-Karl
Huysmans, Joris-Karl
See Huysmans, Charles Marie Georges
See also TCLC 7
Huzar, Eleanor G(oltz) 1922- 85-88
Hvidt, Kristian 1929- 130
Hwang, David Henry 1957- 132
Brief entry 127
See also CLC 55
Hy, Ronald John 1942- 115
Hyam, Ronald 1936- 97-100
Hyams, Barry 1911-1989 ....13-16R
Obituary 129
Hyams, Edward (Solomon) 1910-1975 .....CANR-8
Obituary 61-64
Earlier sketch in CA 5-8R
Hyams, Joe
See Hyams, Joseph
Hyams, Joseph 1923- CANR-22
Earlier sketches in CA 17-20R, CANR-7
Hyatt, Betty H(ale) 1927- 125
Hyatt, Carole S. 1935- 93-96
Hyatt, Daniel
See James, Daniel (Lewis)
Hyatt, I. Ralph 1927- 115
Hyatt, J(ames) Philip 1909-1972 ....9-12R
Obituary 134
Hyatt, Richard Herschel 1944- 101
Hybels, Bill 1951- 126
Hybels, Saundra 1938- 57-60
Hyde, Anthony 1946- 136
See also CLC 42
Hyde, Charles K(eith) 1945- 116
Hyde, Dayton O(gden) 25-28R
See also SATA 9
Hyde, Douglas (Arnold) 1911- Brief entry 109
Hyde, Edward 1609-1674 .... DLB 101
Hyde, Elisabeth 1953- 122
Hyde, Fillmore 1896(?)-1970 Obituary 104
Hyde, George E. 1882-1968 ....5-8R
Obituary 133
Hyde, H(arford) Montgomery 1907-1989 ....5-8R
Obituary 129
Hyde, Hawk
See Hyde, Dayton O(gden)
Hyde, Janet Shibley 1948- CANR-10
Earlier sketch in CA 65-68
Hyde, L(ouis) K(epler Jr.) 1901- CAP-1
Earlier sketch in CA 13-14
Hyde, Laurence 1914- 17-20R
Hyde, Margaret O(ldroyd) 1917- CANR-36
Earlier sketches in CA 1-4R, CANR-1
See also CLC 21
See also CLR 23
See also MAICYA
See also SAAS 8
See also SATA 1, 42
Hyde, Mary (Morley Crapo) 1912- CANR-27
Earlier sketch in CA 49-52
Hyde, Nina Solomon 1932-1990 Obituary 131
Hyde, Shelley
See Reed, Kit
Hyde, Simeon Jr. 1919- 21-24R
Hyde, Stuart W(allace) 1923- 61-64
Hyde, Tracy Elliot
See Venning, Corey
Hyde, W. Lewis 1945- 104
Hyde, Wayne Frederick 1922- 1-4R
See also SATA 7
Hyden, (Sten Gustav Vilhelm) Goeran
1938- CANR-20
Earlier sketch in CA 103
Hyder, Clyde Kenneth 1902- 33-36R
Hyder, O(liver) Quentin 1930- 127
Brief entry 105
Hyer, James Edgar 1923- 77-80
Hyer, Paul Van 1926- 104
Hyers, M. Conrad 1933- 33-36R
Hyett, Barbara Helfgott 1945- 120
Hygen, Johan B(ernitz) 1911- 21-24R
Hyink, Bernard L(ynn) 1913- 45-48
Hyland, Douglas K(irk) S(amuel) 1949- 124
Hyland, Drew A(lan) 1939- CANR-15
Earlier sketch in CA 89-92
Hyland, Jean Scammon 1926- 49-52
Hyland, Paul 1947- 121
Hyland, (Henry) Stanley 1914- 9-12R
Hylander, Clarence J(ohn) 1897-1964 ....5-8R
See also SATA 7
Hylton, Delmer P(aul) 1920- 17-20R
Hyma, Albert 1893- 17-20R
Hyman, Alan 1910- 102
Hyman, Ann 1936- 53-56
Hyman, (Robert) Anthony 1928- 132
Hyman, B(arbara) D(avis) 1947- 125
Hyman, David N(eil) 1943- CANR-22
Earlier sketches in CA 57-60, CANR-7
Hyman, Dick 1904- CANR-7
Earlier sketch in CA 17-20R
Hyman, Frieda Clark 1913- 5-8R
Hyman, Harold M(elvin) 1924- CANR-29
Earlier sketch in CA 5-8R
Hyman, Helen Kandel 1920- 105
Hyman, Herbert H(iram) 1918-1985 ....21-24R
Obituary 118
Hyman, Irwin A(braham Meltzer) 1935- 93-96
Hyman, Jackie (Diamond) 1949- CANR-28
Earlier sketch in CA 108
Hyman, Jeremy (A.) 125
Hyman, Lawrence W. 1919- 41-44R
Hyman, Miranda
See Miller, Miranda
Hyman, Paula 1946- 89-92
Hyman, Richard J(oseph) 1921- CANR-1
Earlier sketch in CA 45-48
Hyman, Robin P(hilip) 1931- CANR-15
Earlier sketch in CA 41-44R
See also SATA 12
Hyman, Ronald T. 1933- CANR-25
Earlier sketches in CA 21-24R, CANR-9
Hyman, Sidney 1917- 102
Hyman, Stanley Edgar 1919-1970 85-88
Obituary 25-28R
Hyman, Trina Schart 1939- CANR-36
Earlier sketches in CA 49-52, CANR-2
See also DLB 61
See also MAICYA
See also SATA 7, 46
Hymans, Jacques Louis 1937- 57-60
Hymes, Dell H(athaway) 1927- 13-16R
Hymes, Lucia M(anley) 1907- 5-8R
See also SATA 7
Hymoff, Edward 1924- 17-20R
Hynd, Alan 1904(?)-1974 Obituary 45-48
Hyndman, Donald W(illiam) 1936- CANR-27
Earlier sketch in CA 57-60
Hyndman, Jane Andrews Lee
1912-1978 ....CANR-5
Obituary 89-92
Earlier sketch in CA 5-8R
See also SATA 1, 23, 46
Hyndman, Robert Utley 1906-1973 97-100
See also SATA 18
Hynds, Frances Jane 1929- 77-80
Hyne, C(harles) J(ohn) Cutcliffe (Wright)
1865-1944 Brief entry 111
Hynek, J(osef) Allen 1910-1986 81-84
Obituary 119
Hyneman, Charles S(hang) 1900-1985 ...... CAP-1
Obituary 114
Earlier sketch in CA 13-14
Hynes, James 1956(?)- .... CLC 65
Hynes, Samuel (Lynn) 1924- CANR-32
Earlier sketch in CA 105
Hyslop, Beatrice F.
1900(?)-1973 Obituary 45-48
Hyslop, James H(ervey)
1854-1920 Brief entry 123
Hyslop, Lois Boe 1908- 41-44R
Hysom, John L(eland Jr.) 1934- 115
Hytier, Jean (Pierre) 1899-1983 Obituary 109
Hyun, Peter 1906- 136

I

I. W.
See Watts, Isaac
Iacocca, Lee
See Iacocca, Lido Anthony
See also BEST 89:1
Iacocca, Lido Anthony 1924- 125
See also Iacocca, Lee
Iacone, Salvatore J(oseph) 1945- CANR-15
Earlier sketch in CA 85-88
Iacuzzi, Alfred 1896-1977 Obituary 73-76
Iams, Jack
See Iams, Samuel Harvey Jr.
Iams, Samuel Harvey Jr.
1910-1990 Obituary 130
Ian, Janis 1951- Brief entry 105
See also CLC 21
Iannelli, Richard 1949- 118
Ianni, Francis A(nthony) J(ames)
1926- CANR-28
Earlier sketch in CA 45-48
Ianniello, Lynne Young 1925- 17-20R
Iannone, Jeanne
See Balzano, Jeanne (Koppel)
See also SATA 7
Iannone, Ron(ald Vincent) 1940- 53-56
Iannuzzi, John Nicholas 1935- 93-96
Iatrides, John O(restes) 1932- CANR-10
Earlier sketch in CA 25-28R
Ibanez, Carlos G. Velez
See Velez-Ibanez, Carlos G(uillermo)
Ibanez, Vicente Blasco
See Blasco Ibanez, Vicente
Ibarbourou, Juana de 1895-1979 ....HW

Ibarguengoitia, Jorge 1928-1983 124
Obituary 113
See also CLC 37
See also HW
Ibarra, Crisostomo
See Yabes, Leopoldo Y(abes)
Ibbotson, Eva 1925- CANR-15
Earlier sketch in CA 81-84
See also SATA 13
Ibbotson, M. C(hristine) 1930- 25-28R
See also SATA 5
Ibele, Oscar Herman 1917- Brief entry 106
Ibingira, G(race) S(tuart) K(atebarirwe)
1932- 103
Iblacker, Reinhold A. 1930- 130
Ibn Bajja 1077(?)-1138 ....DLB 115
Ibn Gabirol, Solomon 1021(?)-1058(?) ....DLB 115
Ibrahim, Abdel-Sattar 1939- 69-72
Ibrahim, Ibrahim Abdelkader 1923- 13-16R
Ibsen, Henrik (Johan)
1828-1906 Brief entry 104
See also DC 2
See also TCLC 2, 8, 16, 37
See also WLC
Ibuka, Masaru 1908- 102
Ibuse Masuji 1898- 127
See also CLC 22
Icaza Coronel, Jorge 1906-1978 89-92
Obituary 85-88
See also HW
Ice, Jackson Lee 1925- 25-28R
Icenhower, Joseph Bryan 1913- CANR-5
Earlier sketch in CA 5-8R
Ichikawa, Kon 1915- 121
See also CLC 20
Ichikawa, Satomi 1949- 126
Brief entry 116
See also SATA 36, 47
Ichimura, Shinichi 1925- 129
Ichioka, Yuji 1936- 128
Icks, Robert J(oseph) 1900- 41-44R
Icolari, Daniel Leonardo 1942- 17-20R
Iddon, Don 1913(?)-1979 Obituary 89-92
Ide, Richard S(myth) 1943- 120
Idelsohn, Abraham Zevi
1882-1938 Brief entry 109
Iden, William
See Green, William M(ark)
Idle, Eric 1943- CANR-35
Earlier sketch in CA 116
See also Monty Python
See also CLC 21
Idone, Christopher 1937- 122
Idriess, Ion L. 1891(?)-1979 Obituary 89-92
Iduarte (Foucher), Andres 1907- 33-36R
Idyll, C(larence) P(urvis) 1916- CANR-8
Earlier sketch in CA 9-12R
Ierardi, Francis B. 1886-1970 Obituary 104
Iffland, August Wilhelm 1759-1814 ....DLB 94
Ifft, James B(rown) 1935- 53-56
Ifkovic, Edward 1943- CANR-33
Earlier sketches in CA 61-64, CANR-8
Iggers, Georg G(erson) 1926- CANR-33
Earlier sketch in CA 25-28R
Iggers, Wilma Abeles 1921- 25-28R
Iggulden, John Manners 1917- 9-12R
Iglauer, Edith
See Daly, Edith Iglauer
Iglehart, Alfreda P(aulette) 1950- 109
Iglehart, Louis Tillman 1915-1981 Obituary 104
Iglesias, Mario 1924- CANR-25
Earlier sketch in CA 45-48
Iglitzin, Lynne 1931- 41-44R
Ignatieff, George 1913- 119
Ignatius, David 1950- 128
Ignatow, David 1914- CANR-31
Earlier sketch in CA 9-12R
See also CAAS 3
See also CLC 4, 7, 14, 40
See also DLB 5
Ignotus, Paul 1901-1978 ....CANR-8
Obituary 77-80
Earlier sketch in CA 5-8R
Igo, John N. Jr. 1927- CANR-33
Earlier sketch in CA 13-16R
Igoe, James (Thomas) 1935- 108
Igoe, (Lesly) Lynn Moody 1937- 108
Ihde, Don 1934- CANR-13
Earlier sketch in CA 33-36R
Ihimaera, Witi 1944- 77-80
See also CLC 46
Ihnat, Steve 1935(?)-1972 Obituary 33-36R
Iiams, Thomas M. Jr. 1928- CANR-35
Earlier sketch in CA 9-12R
Iino, (David) Norimoto 1918- 61-64
Ike, Nobutaka 1916- 21-24R
Ikeda, Daisaku 1928- 85-88
Ikeda, Kiyoshi 1928- Brief entry 104
Ikejiani, Okechukwu 1917- 17-20R
Ikenberry, Oliver Samuel 1908-1978 53-56
Obituary 134
Ikerman, Ruth C. (Percival) 1910- 13-16R
Ikle, Fred Charles 1924- 45-48
Iko, Momoko 1940- CANR-14
Earlier sketch in CA 77-80
Ilardi, Vincent 1925- 29-32R
Ilardo, Joseph A(nthony) 1944- 89-92
Ilchman, Warren Frederick 1934- CANR-1
Earlier sketch in CA 1-4R
Iles, Bert
See Ross, Zola Helen
Iles, Francis
See Cox, A(nthony) B(erkeley)
Iles, Jane 1954- 135
Ilf, Ilya
See Fainzilberg, Ilya Arnoldovich
See also TCLC 21
Ilg, Frances L(illian) 1902-1981 107
Obituary 104
Ilgen, Thomas
See Ilgen, Thomas L.
Ilgen, Thomas L. 1946- 120
Ilich, John 1933- 106
Ilie, Paul 1932- CANR-10
Earlier sketch in CA 25-28R
Illan, Jose M(anuel) 1924- 45-48
Illes, Robert E(noch) 1914- 103
Illiano, Antonio 1934- 41-44R
Illich, Ivan 1926- CANR-35
Earlier sketches in CA 53-56, CANR-10
See also AITN 2
See also MTCW
Illick, Joseph E. 1934- 17-20R
Illingworth, Frank (M. B.) 1908- CANR-5
Earlier sketch in CA 5-8R
Illingworth, John 1904(?)-1980 Obituary 97-100
Illingworth, Neil 1934- 13-16R
Illingworth, Ronald Stanley
1909-1990(?) CANR-3
Obituary 131
Earlier sketch in CA 9-12R
Illwitzer, Elinor G. 1934- 29-32R
Illyes, Gyula 1902-1983 114
Obituary 109
Ilma, Viola 1911(?)-1989 Obituary 129
Ilowite, Sheldon A. 1931- 106
See also SATA 27
Ilsey, Dent
See Chapman, John Stanton Higham
Ilsley, Dent
See Chapman, John Stanton Higham
Ilsley, Velma (Elizabeth) 1918- CANR-3
Earlier sketch in CA 9-12R
See also SATA 12
Ilson, Robert (Frederick) 1937- 124
Iltinger, Paula 1944- 124
Ilyin, Mikhail Andreyevich
1878-1942 Brief entry 119
Imai, Masaaki 1930- 129
Imamura, Anne E(lizabeth Sommers) 1946- 126
Imamura, Shigeo 1922- 77-80
Imber, Gerald 1941- 89-92
Imbert, Enrique Anderson
See Anderson Imbert, Enrique
Imbrie, John 1925- Brief entry 107
Imbrie, Katherine P(almer) 1952- 104
Imbs, Bravig (Wilbur Eugene)
1904-1946 Brief entry 107
See also DLB 4
Imershein, Betsy 1953- ....SATA 62
Imerti, Arthur D. 1915- 37-40R
Imfeld, Al 1935- CANR-29
Earlier sketches in CA 69-72, CANR-13
Imhoof, Maurice Lee 1930- Brief entry 108
Immaculata, Sister
See Maxwell, Sister Mary
Immel, Mary Blair 1930- CANR-6
Earlier sketch in CA 13-16R
See also SATA 28
Immerman, Leon Andrew 1952- 103
Immerman, Richard H. 1949- 129
Immerwahr, Sara Anderson
1914- Brief entry 108
Immoos, Thomas 1918- CANR-35
Earlier sketches in CA 85-88, CANR-15
Immroth, John Phillip 1936-1976 ....CAP-2
Earlier sketch in CA 33-36
Imperato, Pascal James 1937- 127
Brief entry 106
Impey, Oliver (Richard) 1936- 108
Impey, Rose 1947- 137
See also SATA 69
Imrie, Richard
See Pressburger, Emeric
Inada, Lawson Fusao 1938- 33-36R
Inalcik, Halil 1916- CANR-28
Earlier sketch in CA 49-52
Inayat-Khan, Pir Vilayat 1916- 93-96
Inbau, Fred E. 1909- CANR-1
Earlier sketch in CA 1-4R
Inber, Vera Mikhailovna
1893-1972 Obituary 37-40R
Ince, Basil A(ndre) 1933- 57-60
Ince, Martin (Jeffrey) 1952- 110
Ince, W(alter) N(ewcombe)
1927(?)-1988 Obituary 126
Inch, Morris Alton 1925- CANR-11
Earlier sketch in CA 29-32R
Inchbald, Elizabeth 1753-1821 ....DLB 39, 89
Inchbald, Peter 1919- 130
Inciardi, James A(nthony) 1939- CANR-8
Earlier sketch in CA 61-64
Inclan, Ramon (Maria) del Valle
See Valle-Inclan, Ramon (Maria) del
Incogniteau, Jean-Louis
See Kerouac, Jean-Louis Lebris de
Ind, Allison 1903-1974 ....CAP-1
Earlier sketch in CA 13-16
Indelman, Elchanan Chonon
1908(?)-1983 Obituary 109
Indelman-Yinnon, Moshe
1895(?)-1977 Obituary 73-76
Inderlied, Mary Elizabeth 1945- 49-52
Indik, Bernard P(aul) 1932- 33-36R
Inez, Colette 1931- 37-40R
See also CAAS 10
Infante, G(uillermo) Cabrera
See Cabrera Infante, G(uillermo)
Infield, Glenn (Berton) 1920-1981 ....CANR-5
Obituary 103
Earlier sketch in CA 5-8R
Ing, Dean 1931- CANR-23
Earlier sketch in CA 106
Ingalls, Daniel H(enry) H(olmes) 1916- 17-20R
Ingalls, David Sinton 1899-1985 Obituary 116
Ingalls, Jeremy 1911- CANR-27
Earlier sketch in CA 1-4R
Ingalls, Rachel (Holmes) 1940- 127
Brief entry 123
See also CLC 42
Ingalls, Robert Paul 1941- 110
Brief entry 107
Ingamells, Rex 1913-1955 ....TCLC 35
Ingard, K(arl) Uno 1921- 33-36R
Ingarden, Roman Witold
1893-1970 Obituary 113
Ingate, Mary 1912- 73-76
Ingbar, Mary Lee 1926- 41-44R
Inge, M(ilton) Thomas 1936- CANR-25
Earlier sketches in CA 17-20R, CANR-9
Inge, W. R.
See Inge, William Ralph
Inge, William Motter 1913-1973 ....9-12R
See also CDALB 1941-1968
See also CLC 1, 8, 19
See also DLB 7
See also MTCW
Inge, William Ralph 1860-1954 Brief entry 116
Ingel, Florence Courtney 1963- 130
Ingelfinger, Franz Joseph
1910-1980 Obituary 97-100
Ingelow, Jean 1820-1897 ....DLB 35
See also SATA 33
Ingermann, Helena Antonia Maria Elisabeth
Dermout
See Dermout-Ingermann, Helena Antonia Maria
Elisabeth
Ingersol, Jared
See Paine, Lauran (Bosworth)
Ingersoll, David E(dward) 1939- 41-44R
Ingersoll, John H. 1925- 73-76
Ingersoll, Ralph (McAllister) 1900-1985 ....CAP-1
Obituary 115
Earlier sketch in CA 13-14
Ingersoll, Robert Franklin 1933- 104
Ingham, Colonel Frederic
See Hale, Edward Everett
Ingham, Daniel
See Lambot, Isobel
Ingham, Jennie 1944- 108
Ingham, John N. 1939- 138
Ingham, Kenneth 1921- 110
Brief entry 108
Ingham, (Ann) Mary 1947- 120
Ingham, Richard Arnison 1935- 104
Ingham, Robert E(dward) 1934- 108
Ingilby, Joan Alicia 1911- 9-12R
Ingle, Clifford 1915-1977 ....29-32R
Obituary 134
Ingle, Dwight Joyce 1907- CAP-1
Earlier sketch in CA 9-10
Ingle, Joseph B. 1946- 136
Ingle, Stephen (James) 1940- 127
Ingleby, Terry 1901- 106
Ingles, G(lenn) Lloyd 1901- CAP-1
Earlier sketch in CA 19-20
Inglis, Brian (St. John) 1916- CANR-23
Earlier sketches in CA 17-20R, CANR-7
Inglis, David Rittenhouse 1905- CANR-5
Earlier sketch in CA 5-8R
Inglis, James 1927- 21-24R
Inglis, John K(enneth) 1933- 106
Inglis, R(obert) M(orton) G(all)
1910-1975 ....CANR-8
Earlier sketch in CA 13-16R
Inglis, Ruth Langdon 1927- CANR-1
Earlier sketch in CA 49-52
Inglis, Stuart J(ohn) 1923- 41-44R
Ingman, Nicholas 1948- 134
See also SATA 52
Ingold, Gerard (Antoine Hubert)
1922- CANR-23
Earlier sketch in CA 106
Ingold, Klara (Schmid) 1913-1980 61-64
Obituary 134
Ingraham, Barton L(ee) 1930- 119
Ingraham, Joseph Holt 1809-1860 ....DLB 3
Ingraham, Leonard W(illiam) 1913- 25-28R
See also SATA 4
Ingraham, Mark H(oyt) 1896-1982 61-64
Obituary 109
Ingraham, Vernon L. 1924- 33-36R
Ingram, Anne (Whitten) Bower 1937- 102
Ingram, (Mildred Rebecca) Bowen (Prewett)
....37-40R
Ingram, Collingwood 1880-1981 61-64
Obituary 103
Ingram, Derek (Thynne) 1925- 9-12R
Ingram, Forrest L(eo) 1938- 53-56
Ingram, Gregory Keith 1944- 77-80
Ingram, Helen Moyer 1937- CANR-22
Earlier sketch in CA 105
Ingram, James C(arlton) 1922- 5-8R
Ingram, (Archibald) Kenneth 1882-1965 ....CAP-1
Earlier sketch in CA 13-14
Ingram, R(eginald W(illiam) 1930-1989 129
Ingram, Thomas Henry 1924- CANR-2
Earlier sketch in CA 49-52
Ingram, Tom
See Ingram, Thomas Henry
Ingram, William 1930- 41-44R
Ingram, Willis J.
See Harris, Mark
Ingrams, Doreen 1906- CANR-12
Earlier sketch in CA 33-36R
See also SATA 20
Ingrams, Richard (Reid) 1937- 103
Ingrao, Charles W(illiam) 1948- 101
Ingstad, Helge Marcus 1899- 65-68
Ingwersen, Faith 1934- CANR-15
Earlier sketch in CA 69-72
Ingwersen, Niels 1935- CANR-15
Earlier sketch in CA 69-72
Ingwersen, Will (Alfred Theodore)
1905-1990 Obituary 132
Inkeles, Alex 1920- CANR-1
Earlier sketch in CA 1-4R
Inkiow, (Janakiev) Dimiter 1932- 101
Inkster, Ian 1949- 113
Inlow, Gail M(aurice) 1910- CANR-4
Earlier sketch in CA 5-8R
Inman, Arthur Crew 1895-1963 122
Inman, Billie (Jo) Andrew 1929- CANR-28
Earlier sketches in CA 29-32R, CANR-12
Inman, Jack (Ingles) 1919- 25-28R
Inman, John 1805-1850 ....DLB 73
Inman, Robert (Anthony) 1931- 17-20R
Inman, Will 1923- CANR-12
Earlier sketch in CA 25-28R
Inmerito
See Javitch, Daniel Gilbert
Inmon, W(illiam) H(arvey) 1945- 110
Innaurato, Albert (F.) 1948(?)- 122
Brief entry 115
See also CLC 21, 60
Innerhofer, Franz 1944- 101
See also DLB 85
Innes, Brian 1928- CANR-14
Earlier sketch in CA 21-24R
Innes, C(atherine) L(ynette) 1940- 123
Innes, Christopher David 1941- 107
Innes, Frank C. 1934- 45-48
Innes, Hammond
See Hammond Innes, Ralph
Innes, Jean
See Saunders, Jean
Innes, Michael
See Stewart, J(ohn) I(nnes) M(ackintosh)
Innes, Ralph Hammond
See Hammond Innes, Ralph
Innes, Rosemary E(lizabeth Jackson) 25-28R
Innes, Stephen 1946- 116
Innis, Donald Quayle 1924- 41-44R
Innis, Harold Adams 1894-1952 ....DLB 88
Innis, Mary Quayle 1899-1972 ....DLB 88
Innis, Pauline B. (Coleman) 1918- CANR-4
Earlier sketch in CA 1-4R
Innis, Robert E(dward) 1941- 130
Inoguchi, Takashi 1944- 131
Inoue, Yukitoshi 1945- 25-28R
Inouye, Daniel K(en) 1924- 25-28R
Insall, Donald W(illiam) 1926- 61-64
Insana, Tino 1948- 123
Insel, Deborah (June) 1949- 110
Insight, James
See Coleman, Robert William Alfred
Insingel, Mark 1935- 131
Brief entry 110
Insolia, Anthony Edward 1926- 120
Intriligator, Michael D(avid) 1938- 53-56
Inwood, M(ichael) J(ames) 1944- 117
Inyart, Gene
See Namovicz, Gene Inyart
See also SATA 6
Ione
See Ione, Carole
Ione, Carole 1937- 137
Ionesco, Eugene 1912- 9-12R
See also CLC 1, 4, 6, 9, 11, 15, 41
See also MTCW
See also SATA 7
See also WLC
Ionescu, Ghita G. 1913- 103
Iongh, Mary (Dows Herter Norton) Crena de
See Crena de Iongh, Mary (Dows Herter Norton)
Iorio, James 1921- 61-64
Iorio, John 1925- 49-52
Iorizzo, Luciano J(ohn) 1930- 73-76
Ipcar, Dahlov (Zorach) 1917- CANR-9
Earlier sketch in CA 17-20R
See also MAICYA
See also SAAS 8
See also SATA 1, 49
Ippolito, Donna 1945- 104
Ipsen, D(avid) C(arl) 1921- 33-36R
Iqbal, Afzal 1919- CANR-26
Earlier sketches in CA 61-64, CANR-10
Iqbal, Muhammad 1873-1938 ....TCLC 28
Iqbal, Sabiha 1950- 111
Iranek-Osmecki, Kazimierz 1897-1984 49-52
Obituary 113
Irby, Kenneth (Lee) 1936- CANR-22
Earlier sketch in CA 69-72
Ireland, Ann 1953- 127
Ireland, David 1927- CANR-29
Earlier sketch in CA 25-28R
Ireland, Earl (Crowell) 1928- 5-8R
Ireland, Jill (Dorothy) 1936-1990 135
Ireland, Joe C. 1936- 73-76
Ireland, Kevin (Mark) 1933- 73-76
Ireland, Norma Olin 1907- CANR-3
Earlier sketch in CA 9-12R
Ireland, Patrick
See O'Doherty, Brian
Ireland, Robert M(ichael) 1937- CANR-25
Earlier sketch in CA 45-48
Ireland, Sandra L(eora) Jones 1942- 137
Iremonger, Lucille (d'Oyen)
1915-1989(?) CANR-6
Obituary 127
Earlier sketch in CA 9-12R
Iremonger, Valentin 1918- 101
Ireson, Barbara (Francis) 1927- CANR-21
Earlier sketch in CA 5-8R
Ireton, Rollo
See Shirley, Ralph
Irfani, Suroosh 1947- 118
Irgang, Jacob 1930- 85-88

Iribarne, Louis 1940- 123
Irion, Mary Jean 1922- 21-24R
Irion, Paul E(rnst) 1922- 21-24R
Irion, Ruth (Hershey) 1921- 65-68
Irish, Donald P(aul) 1919- 49-52
Irish, Jerry 125
Irish, Marian D(oris) 1909- 9-12R
Irish, Richard K. 1932- 65-68
Irish, William
 See Hopley-Woolrich, Cornell George
Iriye, Akira 1934- CANR-11
 Earlier sketch in CA 25-28R
Irland, David
 See Green, Julian (Hartridge)
Iron, Ralph
 See Schreiner, Olive (Emilie Albertina)
Ironmaster, Maximus
 See Wilkinson, John (Donald)
Irons, Peter
 See Irons, Peter H(anlon)
Irons, Peter H(anlon) 128
Ironside, Henry Allan 1876-1951 Brief entry 115
Ironside, Jetske 1940- .... SATA 60
Ironside, Virginia 1944- 120
Iron Thunderhorse
 See Sekaxsu Petakwonexnajunkis
Irsfeld, John H(enry) 1937- 65-68
Irvin, Bob
 See Irvin, Robert W.
Irvin, Dona L. 1917- 138
Irvin, Fred 1914- .... SATA 15
Irvin, Rea 1881-1972 Obituary 93-96
Irvin, Robert W. 1933-1980 Obituary 103
Irvine, Betty Jo 1943- 77-80
Irvine, Demar (Buel) 1908- 33-36R
Irvine, Janice M. 1951- 135
Irvine, John Henry 1951- 119
Irvine, Keith 1924- 29-32R
Irvine, Lucy 1956- 118
Irvine, R(obert) R(alstone) 1936- CANR-15
 Earlier sketch in CA 81-84
Irvine, Reed (John) 1922- 128
Irvine, Sidney H(erbert) 1931- Brief entry 106
Irvine, William 1906-1964 Obituary 106
Irving, Alexander
 See Hume, Ruth Fox
Irving, Blanche M(cDaniel) 1904- 114
Irving, Brian William 1932- 53-56
Irving, Clifford Michael 1930- CANR-2
 Earlier sketch in CA 1-4R
 See also AITN 1
Irving, Clive 1933- CANR-22
 Earlier sketch in CA 85-88
Irving, David (John Cawdell) 1938- CANR-25
 Earlier sketch in CA 13-16R
Irving, Edward B(urroughs) Jr.
 1923- Brief entry 112
Irving, Gordon 1918- 25-28R
Irving, Henry
 See Kanter, Hal
Irving, John (Winslow) 1942- CANR-28
 Earlier sketch in CA 25-28R
 See also AAYA 8
 See also BEST 89:3
 See also CLC 13, 23, 38
 See also DLB 6
 See also DLBY 82
 See also MTCW
Irving, R(obert) L(ock) Graham
 1877-1969 .... CAP-1
 Earlier sketch in CA 13-16
Irving, Robert
 See Adler, Irving
Irving, T(homas) B(allantine) 1914- 37-40R
Irving, Washington
 1783-1859 .... CDALB 1640-1865
 See also DLB 3, 11, 30, 59, 73, 74
 See also SSC 2
 See also WLC
 See also YABC 2
Irwin, Ann(abelle Bowen) 1915- CANR-36
 Earlier sketches in CA 101, CANR-19
 See also Irwin, Hadley
 See also MAICYA
 See also SATA 38, 44
Irwin, Constance Frick 1913- CANR-5
 Earlier sketch in CA 1-4R
 See also SATA 6
Irwin, Cynthia C.
 See Irwin-Williams, Cynthia (Cora)
Irwin, David 1933- 53-56
Irwin, Francis William 1905- Brief entry 105
Irwin, G. H.
 See Palmer, Raymond A.
Irwin, George 1910-1971 .... 41-44R
Irwin, Grace (Lilian) 1907- 17-20R
 See also DLB 68
Irwin, Graham W(ilkie) 1920-1991 121
 Obituary 135
 Brief entry 118
Irwin, Hadley
 See Hadley, Lee
 and Irwin, Ann(abelle Bowen)
 See also SAAS 14
Irwin, Inez Haynes 1873-1970 102
Irwin, James W. 1891(?)-1977 Obituary 73-76
Irwin, John T(homas) 1940- 53-56
Irwin, John V(aleur) 1915- CANR-1
 Earlier sketch in CA 45-48
Irwin, Keith Gordon 1885-1964 .... 5-8R
 See also SATA 11
Irwin, Margaret 1889-1967 Obituary 93-96
Irwin, P. K.
 See Page, P(atricia) K(athleen)
Irwin, (Joseph) Paul 1940- 107
Irwin, Raymond 1902- CAP-1
 Earlier sketch in CA 9-10
Irwin, Robert (Graham) 1946- 121
Irwin, Ruth Beckey 1906- 29-32R
Irwin, Theodore 1907- 65-68
Irwin, Vera Rushforth 1913- 33-36R
Irwin, W(illiam) R(obert) 1915- 65-68
Irwin, Will(iam Henry)
 1873-1948 Brief entry 117
 See also DLB 25
Irwin-Williams, Cynthia (Cora) 1936- CANR-1
 Earlier sketch in CA 45-48
Isaac, Erich 1928- 45-48
Isaac, Glynn Llewelyn 1937-1985 Obituary 117
Isaac, Joanne 1934- 25-28R
 See also SATA 21
Isaac, Joseph Ezra 1922- 115
Isaac, Paul E(dward) 1926- 17-20R
Isaac, Rael Jean (Isaacs) 1933- 17-20R
Isaac, Rhys L(lywelyn) 1937- 113
Isaac, Stephen 1925- 33-36R
Isaacs, Alan 1925- CANR-3
 Earlier sketch in CA 9-12R
Isaacs, Bernard 1924- 107
Isaacs, E. Elizabeth 1917- 5-8R
Isaacs, Edith Somborn
 1884-1978 Obituary 77-80
Isaacs, Harold Robert 1910-1986 .... CANR-2
 Obituary 119
 Earlier sketch in CA 1-4R
Isaacs, Jacob
 See Kranzler, George G(ershon)
Isaacs, Neil D. 1931- CANR-9
 Earlier sketch in CA 5-8R
Isaacs, Norman Ellis 1908- 81-84
Isaacs, Stan 1929- 13-16R
Isaacs, Stephen D(avid) 1937- 81-84
Isaacs, Susan (Sutherland Fairhurst)
 1885-1948 Brief entry 120
Isaacs, Susan 1943- CANR-20
 Earlier sketch in CA 89-92
 See also BEST 89:1
 See also CLC 32
 See also MTCW
Isaacson, Joel 1930- Brief entry 114
Isaacson, Judith Magyar 1925- 133
Isaacson, Philip M(arshal) 1924- 128
Isaacson, Robert L. 1928- CANR-7
 Earlier sketch in CA 17-20R
Isaacson, Walter (Seff) 1952- 112
Isaak, Robert A(llen) 1945- CANR-13
 Earlier sketch in CA 61-64
Isadora, Rachel 1953(?)- 137
 Brief entry 111
 See also CLR 7
 See also MAICYA
 See also SATA 32, 54
Isais, Juan M. 1926- 29-32R
Isakovsky, Mikhail Vasilyevich
 1900-1973 Obituary 41-44R
Isaksson, Ulla (Margareta Lundberg)
 1916- Brief entry 109
Isard, Walter 1919- 114
 Brief entry 112
Isban, Samuel 1905- CANR-2
 Earlier sketch in CA 49-52
Isbister, Clair
 See Isbister, Jean Sinclair
Isbister, Jean Sinclair 1915- CANR-39
 Earlier sketches in CA 1-4R, CANR-1, 18
Ise, John 1885-196 (?) CAP-1
 Earlier sketch in CA 13-14
Isely, Flora Kunigunde Duncan
 See Duncan, Kunigunde
Isely, Helen Sue (Pearson) 1917-1978 .... 5-8R
 Obituary 120
Iseminger, Gary 1937- 37-40R
Isenberg, Irwin M. 1931-1979 .... CANR-11
 Earlier sketch in CA 17-20R
Isenberg, Seymour 1930- 33-36R
Isenhour, Thomas Lee 1939- 57-60
Iser, Wolfgang 1926- 57-60
Ishak, Fayek (Matta) 1922- 41-44R
Ishak, Yusof bin 1910(?)-1970 Obituary 104
Isham, Charlotte H(ickock) 1912- 73-76
 See also SATA 21
Isham, Linda (Rose) 1938- Brief entry 107
Ishee, John A. 1934- CANR-18
 Earlier sketch in CA 25-28R
Isherwood, Christopher (William Bradshaw)
 1904-1986 .... CANR-35
 Obituary 117
 Earlier sketch in CA 13-16R
 See also CLC 1, 9, 11, 14, 44
 See also DLB 15
 See also DLBY 86
 See also MTCW
Isherwood, Robert M. 1935- 126
Ishida, Takeshi 1923- CANR-38
 Earlier sketches in CA 97-100, CANR-16
Ishigo, Estelle 1899- 61-64
Ishiguro, Kazuo 1954- 120
 See also BEST 90:2
 See also CLC 27, 56, 59
 See also MTCW
Ishikawa Takuboku
 1886(?)-1912 Brief entry 113
 See also TCLC 15
Ishino, Iwao 1921- 17-20R
Ish-Kishor, Judith 1892-1972 .... 1-4R
 Obituary 103
 See also SATA 11
Ish-Kishor, Sulamith 1896-1977 73-76
 Obituary 69-72
 See also SATA 17
Ishlon, Deborah 1925- 1-4R
Ishmael, Woodi 1914- .... SATA 31
Ishmole, Jack 1924- 49-52
Ishwaran, K(arigoudar) 1922- 49-52
Isichei, Elizabeth 1939- CANR-5
 Earlier sketch in CA 53-56
Isis
 See Torbett, Harvey Douglas Louis
Iskander, Fazil 1929- 102
 See also CLC 47
Islam, A(bul) K(hair) M(uhammed) Aminul
 1933- 41-44R
Islam, Kazi Nazrul 1899(?)-1976 Obituary 69-72
Islas, Arturo 1938- 131
 See also HW
Isle, Walter (Whitfield) 1933- 25-28R
Isler, Betty
 See Isler, Elizabeth
Isler, Elizabeth 1915- 114
Ismach, Arnold H(arvey) 1930- 85-88
Ismael, Tareq Y. 125
Ismail, A. H. 1923- 25-28R
Isogai, Hiroshi 1940- 102
Ispahani, Mirza Abol Hassan
 1902-1981 Obituary 108
Israel, Abby 1942- 107
Israel, Charles E(dward) 1920- 1-4R
Israel, Elaine 1945- CANR-9
 Earlier sketch in CA 53-56
 See also SATA 12
Israel, Fred L. 1934- CANR-12
 Earlier sketch in CA 17-20R
Israel, Gerard 1928- 81-84
Israel, Jerry (Michael) 1941- 29-32R
Israel, John (Warren) 1935- 21-24R
Israel, Jonathan I. 1946- 109
Israel, Marion Louise 1882-1973 .... 1-4R
 Obituary 103
 See also SATA 26
Israel, Martin 1927- 109
Israel, Peter 1933- 128
Israel, Philip 1935- 133
Israel, Saul 1910-1990 .... CAP-1
 Obituary 131
 Earlier sketch in CA 13-16
Israeloff, Roberta 1952- 118
Israelowitz, Oscar 1949- CANR-32
 Earlier sketch in CA 113
Issachar
 See Stanford, J(ohn) K(eith)
Issawi, Charles Philip 1916- CANR-20
 Earlier sketches in CA 5-8R, CANR-4
Isser, Natalie 1927- 53-56
Issler, Anne Roller 1892- 49-52
Iswolsky, Helene 1896-1975 .... 5-8R
 Obituary 61-64
Italiaander, Rolf (Bruno Maximilian)
 1913- CANR-23
 Earlier sketches in CA 5-8R, CANR-6
Itani, Frances (Susan) 1942- 138
Iterson, S(iny) R(ose) Van
 See Van Iterson, S(iny) R(ose)
Itim, Talang
 See Lapena-Bonifacio, Amelia
Itse, Elizabeth M(yers) 1930- CANR-1
 Earlier sketch in CA 49-52
Itule, Bruce D. 1947- 125
Itwaru, Arnold (Harrichand) 1942- 134
Itzin, Catherine 1944- CANR-14
 Earlier sketch in CA 77-80
Itzkoff, Seymour W(illiam) 1928- 33-36R
Ivan, Martha Miller Pfaff 1909- CAP-2
 Earlier sketch in CA 19-20
Ivancevich, John M(ichael) 1939- CANR-25
 Earlier sketch in CA 29-32R
Ivanov, Miroslav 1929- 81-84
Ivanov, Vsevolod Vyacheslavovich
 1895-1963 Obituary 93-96
Ivanov, Vyacheslav Ivanovich
 1866-1949 Brief entry 122
 See also TCLC 33
Ivask, George 1910-1986 Obituary 118
Ivask, Ivar Vidrik 1927- CANR-24
 Earlier sketch in CA 37-40R
 See also CLC 14
Ivens, Georg Henri Anton
 1898(?)-1989 Obituary 129
Ivens, Joris
 See Ivens, Georg Henri Anton
Ivens, Michael 1924- 5-8R
Ivens, Virginia R(uth) 1922- 105
Ivers, Larry E(dward) 1936- 77-80
Iversen, Gudmund R(agnvaldsson)
 1934- CANR-4
 Earlier sketch in CA 53-56
Iversen, Nick 1951- 73-76
Iverson, Genie 1942- CANR-9
 Earlier sketch in CA 65-68
 See also SATA 52
Iverson, Jeffrey (James) 1934- 105
Iverson, Lucille K(arin) 1925- 61-64
Iverson, Peter James 1944- 106
Ives, Burl (Icle Ivanhoe) 1909- 103
Ives, Charles Edward
 1874-1954 Brief entry 113
Ives, Colta Feller 1943- 118
Ives, Edward D(awson) 1925- 25-28R
Ives, Lawrence
 See Woods, Frederick
Ives, Sandy
 See Ives, Edward D(awson)
Ives, Sumner 1911- 9-12R
Ivey, Allen E(ugene) 1933- CANR-2
 Earlier sketch in CA 49-52
Ivey, Donald 1918- 89-92
Ivey, James Burnett 1925- 119
Ivey, Jim
 See Ivey, James Burnett
Ivie, Robert L(ynn) 1945- 115
Ivie, Robert M. 1930- 9-12R
Ivins, Molly 1944(?)- 138
Ivnev, Riurik
 See Kovalev, Mikhail A(leksandrovich)
Ivo, Ledo 1924- 129
Ivory, James (Francis) 1928- Brief entry 109
Ivry, Alfred Lyon 1935- CANR-1
 Earlier sketch in CA 45-48
Ivy, Ralph 1938- 120
Iwamatsu, Jun Atsushi 1908- 73-76
 See also Yashima, Taro
 See also MAICYA
 See also SATA 14
Iwamura, Kazuo 1939- 129
Iwaniuk, Wactaw 1915- 130
Iwasaki (Matsumoto), Chihiro
 1918-1974 .... CLR 18
Iwaszkiewicz, Jaroslaw
 1894-1980 Obituary 97-100
Iwata, Masakazu 1917- 17-20R
Iyengar, B(ellur) K(rishnamachar) S(undararaja)
 1918- 97-100
Iyengar, K(odaganallur) R(amaswami) Srinivasa
 1908- CANR-8
 Earlier sketch in CA 5-8R
Iyengar, S. Kesava 1894- 17-20R
Iyer, Raghavan (Narasimhan) 1930- CANR-22
 Earlier sketches in CA 57-60, CANR-6
Izant, Grace Goulder 1893- CAP-1
 Earlier sketch in CA 9-10
Izard, Barbara 1926- 29-32R
Izard, Carroll E(llis) 1923- CANR-4
 Earlier sketch in CA 49-52
Izban, Samuel
 See Isban, Samuel
Izenberg, Gerald N(athan) 1939- 105
Izenour, George Charles 1912- 93-96
Izzo, Herbert J(ohn) 1928- 41-44R

J

"J"
 See Garrity, Joan Terry
J. L.-M.
 See Lees-Milne, James
Jaanus, Maire 1940- 120
Jabay, Earl 1925- 21-24R
Jabber, Fuad (Amin)
 See Jabber, Paul
Jabber, Paul 1943- CANR-27
 Earlier sketch in CA 113
Jabes, Edmond 1912-1991 127
 Obituary 133
Jabez
 See Nicol, Eric (Patrick)
Jablon, Howard 1939- 116
Jablonski, Edward 1922- CANR-18
 Earlier sketches in CA 1-4R, CANR-2
Jablonski, Ronald E. 1929- Brief entry 104
Jablonsky, David 1938- 133
Jablow, Martha M(oraghan) 1944- 112
Jabs, Carolyn 1950- 110
Jac, Lee
 See Morton, Lee Jack Jr.
Jaccottet, Philippe 1925- 129
 Brief entry 116
Jack, Daniel Thomson 1901-1984 Obituary 115
Jack, Donald Lamont 1924- CANR-3
 Earlier sketch in CA 1-4R
Jack, Homer A(lexander) 1916- CANR-14
 Earlier sketch in CA 41-44R
Jack, Ian 1923- 57-60
Jack, R. D. S.
 See Jack, Ronald D(yce) S(adler)
Jack, R(obert) Ian 1935- CANR-3
 Earlier sketch in CA 49-52
Jack, Ronald D(yce) S(adler) 1941- 120
Jackall, Robert 135
Jackendoff, Ray S. 1945- CANR-6
 Earlier sketch in CA 53-56
Jacker, Corinne L(itvin) 1933- 17-20R
Jackins, Harvey 1916- CANR-37
 Earlier sketches in CA 49-52, CANR-1, 17
Jacklin, Anthony 1944- 85-88
Jacklin, Tony
 See Jacklin, Anthony
Jackman, E(dwin) R(ussell) 1894- CAP-1
 Earlier sketch in CA 13-16
Jackman, Jarrell C(lark) 1943- 120
Jackman, Leslie (Arthur James)
 1919- CANR-29
 Earlier sketch in CA 29-32R
Jackman, Michael R. 1952- 120
Jackman, Robert W(illiam) 1946- 124
Jackman, Stuart 1922- CANR-18
 Earlier sketch in CA 101
Jackman, Sydney W(ayne) 1925- CANR-19
 Earlier sketches in CA 1-4R, CANR-1
Jackont, Amnon 1948- 130
Jackowska, Nicki 1942- 119
Jacks, L(awrence) P(earsall)
 1860-1955 Brief entry 113
Jacks, Oliver
 See Gandley, Kenneth Royce
Jackson, A(lexander) B(rooks) 1925- 104
Jackson, Alan 1938- 101
Jackson, Albert 1943- 93-96
Jackson, Albina
 See Geis, Richard E(rwin)
Jackson, Allan 1905(?)-1976 Obituary 65-68
Jackson, Angela 1951- .... DLB 41
Jackson, Anna J. 1926- 103

Jackson, Anne
See Jackson, Anna J.
Jackson, Anne 1896(?)-1984 ... SATA 37
Jackson, Anthony 1926- ... CANR-11
Earlier sketch in CA 69-72
Jackson, Archibald Stewart 1922- ... 61-64
Jackson, Arlene M(arjorie) 1938- ... 118
Jackson, Arthur 1921- Brief entry ... 104
Jackson, B(erkley) R. 1937- ... 25-28R
Jackson, Barbara Garvey Seagrave
1929- ... 21-24R
Jackson, Barbara (Ward) 1914-1981 ... CANR-6
Obituary ... 103
Earlier sketch in CA 45-48
Jackson, Basil 1920- ... CANR-8
Earlier sketch in CA 57-60
Jackson, Blyden 1910- ... 57-60
Jackson, Brian 1933(?)-1983 Obituary ... 110
Jackson, Brooks 1941- ... 97-100
Jackson, Bruce 1936- ... 89-92
Jackson, C(hester) O(scar) 1901- ... CAP-1
Earlier sketch in CA 13-16
Jackson, C(aary) Paul 1902- ... CANR-6
Earlier sketch in CA 5-8R
See also SATA 6
Jackson, Caary
See Jackson, C(aary) Paul
Jackson, Carlton (Luther) 1933- ... 21-24R
Jackson, Carole ... 104
Jackson, Charles O. 1935- ... 126
Brief entry ... 112
Jackson, Charles (Reginald) 1903-1968 ... 101
Obituary ... 25-28R
Jackson, Charlotte E. (Cobden)
1903(?)-1989 Obituary ... 128
See also SATA 62
Jackson, Christine E(lisabeth) 1936- ... 121
Jackson, Clarence J.-L.
See Bulliet, Richard W(illiams)
Jackson, Daniel
See Wingrove, David (John)
Jackson, Dave
See Jackson, J. David
Jackson, David Cooper 1931- ... 109
Jackson, Derrick 1939- ... 77-80
Jackson, Diane 1938- ... 115
Jackson, Don(ald) D(e Avila) 1920-1968 ... CAP-1
Earlier sketch in CA 11-12
Jackson, Donald Dale 1935- ... CANR-19
Earlier sketches in CA 49-52, CANR-1
Jackson, Donald (Dean) 1919-1987 ... 17-20R
Obituary ... 124
Jackson, Dorothy Virginia Steinhauer
1924- ... 13-16R
Jackson, Douglas N. 1929- ... 37-40R
Jackson, E. F.
See Tubb, E(dwin) C(harles)
Jackson, Edgar (Newman) 1910- ... CANR-29
Earlier sketches in CA 77-80, CANR-13
Jackson, Ellen B. 1943- ... 110
Jackson, Elmore 1910- ... 112
Jackson, Esther Merle 1922- ... 13-16R
Jackson, Everatt
See Muggeson, Margaret Elizabeth
Jackson, Frank 1951- ... 120
Jackson, Franklin Jefferson
See Watkins, Mel
Jackson, G. Mark 1952- ... 132
Jackson, Gabriel 1921- ... 21-24R
Jackson, Gabriele Bernhard 1934- ... 29-32R
Jackson, Geoffrey (Holt Seymour)
1915-1987 ... 61-64
Obituary ... 123
See also SATA 53
Jackson, George D. 1929- ... 81-84
Jackson, George (Lester) 1941-1971 ... 120
Obituary ... 111
See also BW
Jackson, George S(tuyvesant)
1906-1976 ... CAP-1
Obituary ... 61-64
Earlier sketch in CA 17-18
Jackson, Gordon 1934- ... 104
Jackson, Graham 1949- ... 112
Jackson, Guida M. 1930- ... CANR-37
Earlier sketches in CA 93-96, CANR-16
See also SATA 71
Jackson, Harvey H(ardaway III) 1943- ... 119
Jackson, Helen Hunt 1830-1885 ... DLB 42, 47
Jackson, Henry F. 1939-1991 ... 129
Obituary ... 135
Jackson, Henry Martin 1912-1983 Obituary ... 110
Jackson, Henry 1912-1988 Obituary ... 126
Jackson, Herbert C(ross) 1917- ... 9-12R
Jackson, Herbert G. Jr. 1928- ... 37-40R
Jackson, Holbrook 1874-1948 ... DLB 98
Jackson, J. David 1944- ... CANR-18
Earlier sketch in CA 81-84
Jackson, J. P.
See Atkins, (Arthur) Harold
Jackson, Jacqueline 1928- ... 45-48
See also SATA 65
Jackson, Jacquelyne Johnson 1932- ... 37-40R
Jackson, James Charles
1936-1979 Obituary ... 117
Jackson, James P(ierre) 1925- ... CANR-14
Earlier sketch in CA 77-80
Jackson, Jesse 1908-1983 ... CANR-27
Obituary ... 109
Earlier sketch in CA 25-28R
See also BW
See also CLC 12
See also CLR 28
See also MAICYA
See also SATA 2, 29, 48
Jackson, John A. 1943- ... 138
Jackson, John Archer 1929- ... 13-16R
Jackson, John E(dgar) 1942- ... 101
Jackson, John Howard 1932- ... 41-44R
Jackson, John N(icholas) 1925- ... CANR-31
Earlier sketches in CA 37-40R, CANR-14
Jackson, Jon A(nthony) 1938- ... 81-84
Jackson, Jonathan (Charles) 1966- ... 116
Jackson, Joseph Hollister 1912- ... 120
Jackson, Joseph 1924-1987 ... CANR-11
Obituary ... 122
Earlier sketches in CAP-1, CA 9-10
Jackson, Joy J(uanita) 1928- ... 29-32R
Jackson, Julia A(ndreasen) 1939- ... 119
Jackson, Karl (Dion) 1942- ... 102
Jackson, Katherine Gauss
1904-1975 Obituary ... 57-60
Jackson, (William) Keith 1928- ... CANR-8
Earlier sketch in CA 61-64
Jackson, Kenneth T. 1939- ... 21-24R
Jackson, Kevin Goldstein
See Goldstein-Jackson, Kevin
Jackson, Laura (Riding) 1901-1991 ... CANR-28
Obituary ... 135
Earlier sketch in CA 65-68
See also Riding, Laura
See also CLC 7
See also DLB 48
Jackson, Livia Bitton
See Bitton Jackson, Livia E(lvira)
Jackson, Louise A(llen) 1937- ... 93-96
Jackson, Lowell G(eorge) 1934- ... 118
Jackson, Lucille
See Strauss, (Mary) Lucille Jackson
Jackson, Lydia 1900(?)-1983 Obituary ... 110
Jackson, MacDonald P. 1938- ... 125
Jackson, Mae 1946- ... 81-84
Jackson, Mahalia 1901-1972 Obituary ... 33-36R
Jackson, Margaret Weymouth
1895-1974 Obituary ... 115
See also AITN 1
Jackson, Mark
See Kurz, Ron
Jackson, Martin A(lan) 1941- ... 89-92
Jackson, Mary 1924- ... 61-64
Jackson, Melvin H. 1914(?)-1983 Obituary ... 111
Jackson, Michael P. 1947- ... 125
Jackson, Miles M(errill) 1929- ... 41-44R
Jackson, Neta J. 1944- ... CANR-18
Earlier sketch in CA 89-92
Jackson, Neville
See Glaskin, G(erald) M(arcus)
Jackson, Nora
See Tennant, Nora Jackson
Jackson, Norman 1932- ... CANR-17
Earlier sketch in CA 25-28R
Jackson, O. B.
See Jackson, C(aary) Paul
Jackson, Paul R. 1905- ... CAP-1
Earlier sketch in CA 13-16
Jackson, Percival Ephrates 1891-1970 ... CANR-3
Earlier sketch in CA 1-4R
Jackson, Philip W(esley) 1928- ... 21-24R
Jackson, R. E.
See Innes, Rosemary E(lizabeth Jackson)
Jackson, R(ichard) Eugene 1941- ... CANR-28
Earlier sketch in CA 109
Jackson, R(ichard) W(illiam) 1939- ... 119
Jackson, Reggie
See Jackson, Reginald Martinez
Jackson, Reginald Martinez
1946- Brief entry ... 112
Jackson, Richard A(rlen) 1937- ... 125
Jackson, Richard 1946- ... 110
Jackson, Robert B(lake) 1926- ... CANR-6
Earlier sketch in CA 5-8R
See also SATA 8
Jackson, Robert J. 1936- ... 25-28R
Jackson, Robert L(owell) 1935- ... 73-76
Jackson, Robert Louis 1923- ... 109
Jackson, Robert S(umner) 1926- ... 29-32R
Jackson, Robert 1911- ... 9-12R
Jackson, Ruth A. ... 45-48
Jackson, Sally
See Kellogg, Jean (Defrees)
Jackson, Sam
See Trumbo, Dalton
Jackson, Sara
See Thomas, Sara (Sally)
and Wingrove, David (John)
Jackson, Scoop
See Jackson, Henry Martin
Jackson, Shirley 1919-1965 ... CANR-4
Obituary ... 25-28R
Earlier sketch in CA 1-4R
See also AAYA 9
See also CDALB 1941-1968
See also CLC 11, 60
See also DLB 6
See also SATA 2
See also SSC 9
See also WLC
Jackson, Stanley W(ebber) 1920- ... 124
Jackson, Stephanie
See Werner, Vivian
Jackson, Teague 1938- ... 93-96
Jackson, W. A. Douglas
See Jackson, William Arthur Douglas
Jackson, W(illiam) G(odfrey) F(othergill)
1917- ... 25-28R
Jackson, W(illiam) T(homas) H(obdell)
1915-1983 ... CANR-1
Obituary ... 117
Earlier sketch in CA 1-4R
Jackson, W(illiam) Turrentine 1915- ... 13-16R
Jackson, Wallace 1930- ... 114
Jackson, Wes 1936- ... CANR-22
Earlier sketches in CA 49-52, CANR-3
Jackson, William Arthur Douglas
1923- ... CANR-28
Earlier sketch in CA 45-48
Jackson, William Vernon 1926- ... CANR-13
Earlier sketch in CA 21-24R
Jackson, Wilma 1929- ... CANR-12
Earlier sketch in CA 73-76
Jackson-Haight, Mabel V. 1912- ... 25-28R
Jaco, E(gbert) Gartly 1923- ... CANR-1
Earlier sketch in CA 1-4R
Jacob, Alaric 1909- ... 5-8R
Jacob, Charles E. 1931- ... CANR-5
Earlier sketch in CA 13-16R
Jacob, Ernest Fraser 1894-1971 ... CANR-3
Earlier sketch in CA 1-4R
Jacob, Francois 1920- ... 102
Jacob, Fred E. 1899- ... 105
Jacob, Gordon (Percival Septimus)
1895-1984 Obituary ... 113
Jacob, Helen Pierce 1927- ... 69-72
See also SATA 21
Jacob, Herbert 1933- ... 77-80
Jacob, J. R.
See Jacob, James R.
Jacob, James R. 1940- ... 132
Jacob, John 1950- ... 126
Jacob, Margaret C(andee) 1943- ... CANR-37
Earlier sketches in CA 65-68, CANR-16
Jacob, (Cyprien-)Max
1876-1944 Brief entry ... 104
See also TCLC 6
Jacob, Nancy L. 1943- ... 29-32R
Jacob, Naomi Ellington
1884(?)-1964 Obituary ... 115
Jacob, Paul 1940- ... 103
Jacob, Philip E(rnest) 1914- ... CANR-4
Earlier sketch in CA 53-56
Jacobi, Carl (Richard) 1908- ... CAP-1
Earlier sketch in CA 13-14
Jacobi, Friedrich Heinrich 1743-1819 ... DLB 94
Jacobi, Johann Georg 1740-1814 ... DLB 97
Jacobi, Jolande (Szekacs) 1890- ... 9-12R
Jacobi, Kathy ... SATA 42
Jacobowitz, Ellen 1948- ... 121
Jacobs, Al(bert T.) 1903-1985 Obituary ... 115
Jacobs, Arthur (David) 1922- ... CANR-21
Earlier sketches in CA 5-8R, CANR-4
Jacobs, Barry (Douglas) 1932- ... 101
Jacobs, Bradford (McElderry) 1920- ... 121
Jacobs, Clyde E(dward) 1925- ... 37-40R
Jacobs, Dan(iel) N(orman) 1924- ... CANR-4
Earlier sketch in CA 5-8R
Jacobs, David Michael 1942- ... 57-60
Jacobs, Diane 1948- ... 73-76
Jacobs, Donald M(artin) 1937- ... 110
Jacobs, Flora Gill 1918- ... CANR-21
Earlier sketch in CA 1-4R
See also SATA 5
Jacobs, Francine 1935- ... CANR-18
Earlier sketches in CA 49-52, CANR-1
See also SATA 42, 43
Jacobs, Frank 1929- ... CANR-6
Earlier sketch in CA 13-16R
See also SATA 30
Jacobs, G(enevieve) Walker 1948- ... 49-52
Jacobs, Garry (Lawrence) 1946- ... 120
Jacobs, Glenn 1940- ... 29-32R
Jacobs, Harold 1941- ... 45-48
Jacobs, Harvey (Collins) 1915- ... 21-24R
Jacobs, Harvey 1930- ... 29-32R
Jacobs, Hayes B(enjamin) 1919- ... 9-12R
Jacobs, Helen Hull 1908- ... 9-12R
See also SATA 12
Jacobs, Herbert (Austin) 1903-1987 ... 13-16R
Obituary ... 122
Jacobs, Howard 1908- ... 65-68
Jacobs, James B. 1947- ... CANR-39
Earlier sketches in CA 101, CANR-18
Jacobs, Jane 1916- ... CANR-15
Earlier sketch in CA 21-24R
Jacobs, Jerome L. 1931- ... 89-92
Jacobs, Jerry 1932- ... CANR-11
Earlier sketch in CA 29-32R
Jacobs, Jill
See Bharti, Ma Satya
Jacobs, Jim 1942- ... 97-100
See also CLC 12
Jacobs, John (Kedzie) 1918- ... 21-24R
Jacobs, Joseph 1854-1916 ... 136
Brief entry ... 111
See also MAICYA
See also SATA 25
Jacobs, Judy 1952- ... 137
See also SATA 69
Jacobs, Laurence Wile 1939- ... 53-56
Jacobs, Leah
See Gellis, Roberta L(eah Jacobs)
Jacobs, Leland Blair 1907- ... 73-76
Obituary ... 137
See also SATA 20, 71
Jacobs, Lewis 1906- ... 77-80
Jacobs, Linda
See Altman, Linda Jacobs
Jacobs, Lou(is) Jr. 1921- ... CANR-9
Earlier sketch in CA 21-24R
See also SATA 2
Jacobs, Louis 1920- ... CANR-38
Earlier sketches in CA 1-4R, CANR-1, 17
Jacobs, Melville 1902-1971 ... 1-4R
Obituary ... 103
Jacobs, Michael (Stephen) 1955- ... 123
Jacobs, Milton 1920- ... 37-40R
Jacobs, Nehama 1951- ... 126
Jacobs, Norman (Gabriel) 1924- ... 77-80
Jacobs, Paul 1918-1978 ... 13-16R
Obituary ... 73-76
Jacobs, Pepita Jimenez 1932- ... 17-20R
Jacobs, Philip E. 1914(?)-1985 Obituary ... 116
Jacobs, Renee 1962- ... 125
Jacobs, Robert D(urene) 1918- ... 41-44R
Jacobs, Roderick A(rnold) 1934- ... 21-24R
Jacobs, Ruth Harriet 1924- ... CANR-33
Earlier sketches in CA 89-92, CANR-15
Jacobs, Sheldon 1931- ... 106
Jacobs, Sophia Yarnall 1902- ... 106
Jacobs, Sue-Ellen 1936- ... 111
Jacobs, Susan
See Quinn, Susan
See also SATA 30
Jacobs, T. C. H.
See Pendower, Jacques
Jacobs, Travis Beal 1936- Brief entry ... 113
Jacobs, Vernon K(enneth) 1936- ... 117
Jacobs, Vivian 1916(?)-1981 Obituary ... 103
Jacobs, W(illiam) W(ymark)
1863-1943 Brief entry ... 121
See also TCLC 22
Jacobs, Walter Darnell 1922- ... 17-20R
Jacobs, Wilbur R(ipley) 1918- ... 13-16R
Jacobs, William Jay 1933- ... CANR-7
Earlier sketch in CA 57-60
See also SATA 28
Jacobsen, Hans Jacob 1901-1987 Obituary ... 122
Jacobsen, Josephine 1908- ... CANR-23
Earlier sketch in CA 33-36R
See also CLC 48
Jacobsen, K(enneth) C. 1939- ... 133
Jacobsen, Lydik S.
1897(?)-1976 Obituary ... 69-72
Jacobsen, Lyle E. 1929- ... 13-16R
Jacobsen, Marion Leach 1908- ... 61-64
Jacobsen, O(le) Irving 1896- ... CAP-2
Earlier sketch in CA 25-28
Jacobsen, Phebe R(obinson) 1922- ... 73-76
Jacobsen, Thorkild 1904- Brief entry ... 105
Jacobsohn, Gary J. 1946- ... 89-92
Jacobson, Bernard Isaac 1936- ... 109
Jacobson, Beverly 1927- ... 113
Jacobson, Boyd 1942- ... 118
Jacobson, Cliff 1940- ... 85-88
Jacobson, Dan 1929- ... CANR-25
Earlier sketches in CA 1-4R, CANR-2
See also CLC 4, 14
See also DLB 14
See also MTCW
Jacobson, Daniel 1923- ... 53-56
See also SATA 12
Jacobson, David B(ernard) 1928- ... 53-56
Jacobson, Edith 1897(?)-1978 Obituary ... 85-88
Jacobson, Edmund 1888- ... 9-12R
Jacobson, Ethel ... 37-40R
Jacobson, Frederick L(awrence) 1938- ... 49-52
Jacobson, Gary Charles 1944- ... 109
Jacobson, Gerald F. 1922-1987 Obituary ... 123
Jacobson, Harold Karan 1929- ... CANR-19
Earlier sketches in CA 9-12R, CANR-3
Jacobson, Helen S(altz) 1921- ... CANR-6
Earlier sketch in CA 57-60
Jacobson, Howard Boone 1925- ... 1-4R
Jacobson, Jon 1938- ... 61-64
Jacobson, Julius 1922- ... 45-48
Jacobson, Marcia 1941- ... 115
Jacobson, Mark 1948- ... 136
Jacobson, Michael F. 1943- ... CANR-13
Earlier sketch in CA 77-80
Jacobson, Morris K(arl) 1906- ... CANR-3
Earlier sketch in CA 45-48
See also SATA 21
Jacobson, Nils Olof 1937- Brief entry ... 110
Jacobson, Nolan Pliny 1909- ... CANR-23
Earlier sketches in CA 21-24R, CANR-8
Jacobson, Robert (Marshall) 1940-1987 ... 89-92
Obituary ... 122
Jacobson, Rodolfo 1915- ... 41-44R
Jacobson, Sheldon A(lbert) 1903- ... 37-40R
Jacobson, Sibyl C(hafer) 1942- ... 65-68
Jacobson, Stephen A. 1934- ... 97-100
Jacobson, Steve
See Jacobson, Stephen A.
Jacobstein, J(oseph) Myron 1920- ... 53-56
Jacobus, Donald L(ines) 1887-1970 ... CANR-4
Earlier sketch in CA 5-8R
Jacobus, Elaine Wegener 1908- ... 33-36R
Jacobus, Lee A. 1935- ... CANR-30
Earlier sketches in CA 33-36R, CANR-13
Jacobus, Mary 1944- ... 105
Jacoby, Henry 1905- ... 77-80
Jacoby, Joseph E. 1944- ... 97-100
Jacoby, Neil H(erman) 1909-1979 ... CANR-10
Obituary ... 89-92
Earlier sketch in CA 21-24R
Jacoby, Oswald 1902-1984 ... 107
Obituary ... 113
Jacoby, Russell 1945- ... CANR-15
Earlier sketch in CA 77-80
Jacoby, Sidney B(ernard)
1908-1990 Obituary ... 130
Jacoby, Stephen M(ichael) 1940- ... 57-60
Jacoby, Susan ... 108
Jacopetti, Alexandra
See Hart, Alexandra
See also SATA 14
Jacot, B. L.
See Jacot de Boinod, Bernard Louis
Jacot, Michael 1924- ... 104
Jacot de Boinod, Bernard Louis
1898-1977 ... 9-12R
Obituary ... 77-80
Jacoway, Elizabeth 1944- ... 110
Jacqueline
See Carpentier (y Valmont), Alejo
Jacqueney, Mona G(raubart) ... 41-44R
Jacqueney, Theodore
1943(?)-1979 Obituary ... 89-92

Jacques, Brian 1939- 127
See also CLR 21
See also SATA 62
Jacques, David (Lawson) 1948- 123
Jacques, Robin 1920- .... MAICYA
See also SAAS 5
See also SATA 30, 32
Jacquet, Constant Herbert Jr. 1925- 106
Jade, Jacqueline
See Hyman, Jackie (Diamond)
Jaded Observer
See Zolf, Larry
Jados, Stanley S. 1912-1977 .... 33-36R
Jaeck, Lois Marie 1946- 137
Jaediker, Kermit 1912(?)-1986 Obituary 118
Jaeger, Cyril Karel Stuart 1912- 1-4R
Jaeger, Edmund C(arroll) 1887-1983 .... CAP-2
Obituary 110
Earlier sketch in CA 23-24
Jaeger, Harry J. Jr.
1919(?)-1979 Obituary 85-88
Jaeger, Lorenz Cardinal
1892-1975 Obituary 57-60
Jaeger, Walter H(enry) E(dward)
1902(?)-1982 Obituary 108
Jaen, Didier Tisdel 1933- 29-32R
Jaenen, Cornelius John 1927- CANR-15
Earlier sketch in CA 85-88
Jaffa, George
See Wallace-Clarke, George
Jaffa, Harry V(ictor) 1918- 33-36R
Jaffe, A(bram) J. 1912- 5-8R
Jaffe, Aniela 1903- 125
Jaffe, Bernard 1896-1986 .... 5-8R
Obituary 121
Jaffe, Betsy
See Jaffe, Elizabeth Latimer
Jaffe, Dan 1933- CANR-17
Earlier sketch in CA 25-28R
Jaffe, David 1911-1990 Obituary 131
Jaffe, Dennis T(heodore) 1946- CANR-32
Earlier sketches in CA 89-92, CANR-15
Jaffe, Elizabeth Latimer 1935- 135
Jaffe, Elsa
See Bartlett, Elsa Jaffe
Jaffe, Eugene D. 1937- 37-40R
Jaffe, Frederick S. 1925-1978 .... CANR-5
Earlier sketch in CA 9-12R
Jaffe, Gabriel Vivian 1923- 13-16R
Jaffe, Harold 1940- CANR-30
Earlier sketch in CA 29-32R
Jaffe, Hilde 1927- 105
Jaffe, Irma B(lumenthal) CANR-1
Earlier sketch in CA 45-48
Jaffe, Joseph 1924- Brief entry 113
Jaffe, Lorna S. 1941- 128
Jaffe, Louis Leventhal 1905- 21-24R
Jaffe, (Andrew) Michael 1923- 21-24R
Jaffe, Nora Crow 1944- 106
Jaffe, Rona 1932- CANR-24
Earlier sketch in CA 73-76
See also AITN 1
See also BEST 90:3
See also MTCW
Jaffe, Sam(uel Adason)
1929(?)-1985 Obituary 115
Jaffe, Sandra Sohn 1943- 101
Jaffe, Sherril 1945- CANR-19
Earlier sketch in CA 103
Jaffe, William 1898-1980 57-60
Obituary 122
Jaffee, Al(lan) 1921- 135
Brief entry 116
See also SATA 37, 66
Jaffee, Annette Williams 1945- 131
Jaffee, Dwight M. 1943- 57-60
Jaffee, Mary L.
See Lindsley, Mary F(rances)
Jaffin, David 1937- CANR-34
Earlier sketches in CA 65-68, CANR-15
Jagel, Beatrice Hawley
1944(?)-1985 Obituary 116
Jagendorf, Moritz (Adolf) 1888-1981 .... 5-8R
Obituary 102
See also SATA 2, 24
Jager, Okke 1928- CANR-23
Earlier sketches in CA 61-64, CANR-8
Jager, Ronald (Albert) 1932- 41-44R
Jaggard, Geoffrey (William) 1902-1970 .... CAP-2
Earlier sketch in CA 21-22
Jagger, John Hubert 1880- CAP-1
Earlier sketch in CA 9-10
Jagger, Mick 1944- .... CLC 17
Jagger, Peter (John) 1938- CANR-21
Earlier sketch in CA 103
Jaglom, Henry 1941- 127
Jagninski, Tom 1935- 137
Jagoda, Robert 1923- 73-76
Jahan, Rounaq 1944- CANR-29
Earlier sketch in CA 49-52
Jaher, Frederic Cople 1934- 9-12R
Jahier, Piero 1884-1966 .... DLB 114
Jahn, Ernst A(dalbert) 1929- 69-72
Jahn, Janheinz 1918-1973 Obituary 111
Jahn, Joseph C. 1914(?)-1984 Obituary 113
Jahn, Joseph Michael 1943- CANR-5
Earlier sketch in CA 49-52
See also SATA 28
Jahn, Melvin E(dward) 1938- 9-12R
Jahn, Michael
See Jahn, Joseph Michael
Jahn, Mike
See Jahn, Joseph Michael
Jahnn, Hans Henny 1894-1959 .... DLB 56
Jahoda, Gloria (Adelaide Love)
1926-1980 .... CANR-4
Obituary 104
Earlier sketch in CA 1-4R
See also AITN 1
Jahoda, Gustav 1920- 135
Brief entry 114
Jahsmann, Allan Hart 1916- 106
See also SATA 28
Jaimes, M. Annette 1946- 137
Jaimes Freyre, Ricardo 1868-1933 .... HW
Jain, Girilal 1922- 9-12R
Jain, Rajendra K. 1951- 134
Jain, Ravindra Kumar 1937- 29-32R
Jain, Sagar C. 1930- CANR-10
Earlier sketch in CA 25-28R
Jain, Sharad Chandra 1933- CANR-21
Earlier sketch in CA 25-28R
Jaini, Padmanabh S. 1923- 103
Jakes, John (William) 1932- CANR-10
Earlier sketch in CA 57-60
See also BEST 89:4
See also CLC 29
See also DLBY 83
See also MTCW
See also SATA 62
Jakle, John Allais 1939- 107
Jakobovits, Immanuel 1921- 108
Jakobovits, Leon Alex 1938- 25-28R
Jakobson, Roman 1896-1982 .... CANR-31
Obituary 107
Earlier sketch in CA 77-80
Jaksch, Wenzel 1896-1966 .... CAP-1
Earlier sketch in CA 13-14
Jakubauskas, Edward B(enedict) 1930- 57-60
Jakubowski, Patricia (Ann) 1941- 65-68
Jalland, Pat(ricia) 1941- 133
Jamba, Sousa 1966- 134
James, Alan Geoffrey 1943- 104
James, Allen
See Allen, James L(ovic) Jr.
James, Amalia
See Neggers, Carla A(malia)
James, Andrew
See Kirkup, James
James, Anne Eleanor Scott
See Scott-James, Anne Eleanor
James, Anthony
See Hanna, David
James, (Eliot) Antony Brett
See Brett-James, (Eliot) Antony
James, Bernard (Joseph) 1922- Brief entry 110
James, Bessie (Williams) Rowland
1895-1974 107
James, Bill
See James, George W(illiam)
James, Brian
See Thomas, Gordon
and Tierney, John Lawrence
James, Bruno S(cott) 1906- 5-8R
James, (David) Burnett (Stephen)
1919-1987 .... 5-8R
Obituary 122
James, C. B.
See Coover, James B(urrell)
James, C(yril) L(ionel) R(obert) 1901-1989 125
Obituary 128
Brief entry 117
See also BW
See also CLC 33
See also MTCW
James, C. W.
See Cumes, J(ames) W(illiam) C(rawford)
James, Captain Lew
See Stratemeyer, Edward L.
James, Cary A(mory) 1935- 29-32R
James, Charles J(oseph) 1944- CANR-5
Earlier sketch in CA 53-56
James, Charles L(yman) 1934- 29-32R
James, Clive (Vivian Leopold) 1939- 128
Brief entry 105
See also MTCW
James, Coy Hilton 1915- 103
James, Cy
See Watts, Peter Christopher
James, D(orris) Clayton 1931- 29-32R
James, D(avid) G(wilym) 1905-1968 .... CANR-4
Earlier sketch in CA 1-4R
James, Daniel (Lewis) 1911-1988 Obituary 125
See also Santiago, Danny
James, David
See Hagberg, David J(ames)
James, David W(illiam) 1910- 128
James, David 1955- 119
James, Denise 29-32R
James, Diana
See Gunn, Diana Maureen
James, Don(ald H.) 1905- CANR-2
Earlier sketch in CA 1-4R
James, Dorothy Buckton 1937- Brief entry 109
James, Dynely
See Mayne, William (James Carter)
James, Edgar C. 1933- CANR-5
Earlier sketch in CA 13-16R
James, Edward
See Masur, Harold Q.
James, Edward (Frank Willis)
1907-1984 Obituary 115
James, Edward T(opping) 1917- 33-36R
James, Edwin
See Gunn, James E(dwin)
James, Edwin Oliver 1889-1972 .... CAP-1
Earlier sketch in CA 13-16
James, Eleanor 1912- 41-44R
James, Elizabeth 1942- 121
See also SATA 39, 45, 52
James, Eric Arthur 1925- CAP-1
Earlier sketch in CA 9-10
James, Estelle 1935- 37-40R
James, F(rank) Cyril 1903-1973 Obituary 114
James, Fleming Jr. 1904- CAP-1
Earlier sketch in CA 17-18
James, Gene Gray 1934- 114
James, George P. R. 1801-1828 .... DLB 116
James, George W(illiam) 1949- CANR-35
Earlier sketch in CA 109
James, H(enry) Thomas 1915- 25-28R
James, Harold 1956- 127
James, Harry Clebourne 1896-1978 .... CANR-4
Earlier sketch in CA 5-8R
See also SATA 11
James, Heather 1914- CANR-31
Earlier sketch in CA 45-48
James, Henry 1843-1916 132
Brief entry 104
See also CDALB 1865-1917
See also DLB 12, 71, 74
See also MTCW
See also SSC 8
See also TCLC 2, 11, 24, 40
See also WLC
James, Howard (Anthony Jr.)
1935- Brief entry 111
James, Hunter 1932- 114
James, Jean Rosemary Haughton
See Haughton-James, Jean Rosemary
James, (David) John 45-48
James, John 1633(?)-1729 .... DLB 24
James, Josef C. 1916(?)-1973 Obituary 45-48
James, Joseph B. 1912- 17-20R
James, Josephine
See Sterne, Emma Gelders
James, Judith
See Jennings, Leslie Nelson
James, Kelvin Christopher 138
James, Kristin
See Camp, Candace P(auline)
James, Leigh Franklin
See Little, Paul H(ugo)
James, Leonard F(rank) 1904- 49-52
James, Lloyd E.
See Laughlin, Tom
James, (William) Louis (Gabriel) CANR-6
Earlier sketch in CA 13-16R
James, M. R. 1940- 57-60
James, Marlise Ann 1945- 57-60
James, Martin
See Kisner, James (Martin Jr.)
James, Mary
See Meaker, Marijane (Agnes)
James, Matthew
See Lucey, James D(ennis)
James, Michael 1922(?)-1981 Obituary 104
James, Monica
See Nonhebel, Clare
James, Montague (Rhodes)
1862-1936 Brief entry 104
See also TCLC 6
James, Muriel 85-88
James, Naomi 1949- 102
James, Noel David Glaves 1911- 107
James, Norah C(ordner) 29-32R
James, P. D.
See White, Phyllis Dorothy James
See also BEST 90:2
See also CDBLB 1960 to Present
See also CLC 18, 46
See also DLB 87
James, Paul
See Warburg, James Paul
James, Paul 1921- 125
James, Peter N. 1940- 57-60
James, Philip
See del Rey, Lester
and Moorcock, Michael (John)
James, Philip S(eaforth) 1914- CAP-1
Earlier sketch in CA 9-10
James, Preston E(verett) 1899-1986 .... CANR-29
Earlier sketch in CA 45-48
James, Rebecca
See Elward, James (Joseph)
James, Robert A. 1946-1983 Obituary 109
James, Robert C(larke) 1918- 5-8R
James, Robert (Vidal) Rhodes
See Rhodes James, Robert (Vidal)
James, Robin (Irene) 1953- 126
See also SATA 50
James, Ronald
See Preston, James
James, Russell 1942- 137
James, Simon
See Kunen, James Simon
James, Stanton
See Flemming, Nicholas Coit
James, Susan
See Griffin, Arthur J.
James, Sydney V(incent Jr.) 1929- CANR-21
Earlier sketch in CA 1-4R
James, Thelma Gray 1899-1988 .... 5-8R
Obituary 124
James, Theodore Jr. 1934- 33-36R
James, Theodore E(arle) 1913- 57-60
James, Thomas N.
See Neal, James T(homas)
James, Trevor
See Constable, Trevor James
James, Vanessa
See Beauman, Sally
James, (Arthur) Walter 1912- 5-8R
James, Walter S.
See Sheldon, Walter J.
James, Warren A. 1960- 133
James, Warren E(dward) 1922- 45-48
James, Weldon (Bernard) 1912- 1-4R
James, Will(iam Roderick) 1892-1942 137
See also MAICYA
See also SATA 19
James, William
See Craddock, William J(ames)
James, William C(losson) 1943- 126
James, William M.
See Harknett, Terry
and Harvey, John (Barton)
James, William Milbourne 1881- CAP-1
Earlier sketch in CA 11-12
James, William 1842-1910 Brief entry 109
See also TCLC 15, 32
James, Wilma Roberts 1905- 105
James, Wilmot G. 1953- 138
Jameson, Anna 1794-1860 .... DLB 99
Jameson, Eric
See Trimmer, Eric J.
Jameson, Fredric 1934- .... DLB 67
Jameson, J. Franklin 1859-1937 .... DLB 17
Jameson, Judith
See Neyland, James (Elwyn)
Jameson, Kenneth (Ambrose) 1913- 77-80
Jameson, Kenneth P(eter) 1942- 112
Jameson, Sam 1936- 136
Jameson, Samuel H(aig) 1896- 45-48
Jameson, (Margaret) Storm 1891-1986 81-84
Obituary 120
See also DLB 36
Jameson, Vic(tor Loyd) 1924- 17-20R
Jamie, Kathleen 1962- 128
Jamieson, Bob
See Jamieson, Robert John
Jamieson, Paul F(letcher) 1903- CAP-1
Earlier sketch in CA 9-10
Jamieson, Robert John 1943- 116
Brief entry 110
Jamison, A(lbert) Leland 1911- 89-92
Jamison, Andrew 1948- 29-32R
Jamme, Albert (Joseph) 1916- 5-8R
Jampolsky, Gerald G(ershan) 1925- 111
Jan
See Noble, John (Appelbe)
Jan, Emerson
See Bixby, Jerome Lewis
Jan, George P(okung) 1925- 21-24R
Janas, Frankie-Lee 1908- CANR-24
Earlier sketch in CA 106
Jancar, Barbara Wolfe 1935- Brief entry 111
Jance, J. A.
See Jance, Judith A(nn)
Jance, Judith A(nn) 1944- 118
See also SATA 50
Janda, Kenneth (Frank) 1935- 13-16R
Jandl, Ernst 1925- .... CLC 34
Jandl, H(enry) Ward 1946- 121
Jandt, Fred E(dmund) 1944- 53-56
Jandy, Edward Clarence
1899-1980 Obituary 97-100
Jane, Mary Childs 1909- CANR-4
Earlier sketch in CA 1-4R
See also SATA 6
Jane, Nancy 1946- 89-92
Janeczko, Paul B(ryan) 1945- CANR-22
Earlier sketch in CA 104
See also AAYA 9
See also SATA 53
Janello, Amy (Elizabeth) 1962- 136
Janes, Edward C. 1908- 93-96
See also SATA 25
Janes, J(oseph) Robert 1935- 123
See also SATA 50
Janes, Percy 1922- 113
Janes, Regina (Mary) 1946- 120
Janeshutz, Patricia M(arie) 1947- 121
Janeshutz, Trish
See Janeshutz, Patricia M(arie)
Janeway, Eliot 1913- 130
Brief entry 112
Janeway, Elizabeth (Hall) 1913- CANR-2
Earlier sketch in CA 45-48
See also AITN 1
See also SATA 19
Janger, Allen R(obert) 1932- CANR-12
Earlier sketch in CA 29-32R
Janger, Kathleen N. 1940- 125
See also SATA 66
Janice
See Brustlein, Janice Tworkov
Janifer, Laurence M(ark) 1933- CANR-5
Earlier sketch in CA 9-12R
Janik, Allan (Stanley Peter) 1941- 53-56
Janik, Carolyn 1940- CANR-33
Earlier sketches in CA 89-92, CANR-15
Janik, Del Ivan 1945- 117
Janik, Phyllis 1944- 111
Janis, Irving L(ester) 1918- CANR-23
Earlier sketches in CA 17-20R, CANR-8
Janis, J(ack) Harold 1910- 13-16R
Janis, Sidney 1896-1989 Obituary 130
Janjigian, Robert 1957- 127
Jankelevitch, Vladimir 1903-1985 Obituary 117
Janko, Richard 1955- CANR-30
Earlier sketch in CA 111
Jankowsky, Kurt Robert 1928- 37-40R
Janner, Greville Ewan 1928- CANR-8
Earlier sketch in CA 13-16R
Janos, Andrew C(saba) 1934- 106
Janos, Leo 1933- 127
Janosch
See Eckert, Horst
See also CLR 26
Janov, Arthur 1924- 116
Janovy, John Jr. 1937- CANR-19
Earlier sketch in CA 97-100

Janowitz, Morris 1919-1988 ....13-16R
Obituary 127
Janowitz, Phyllis 93-96
Janowitz, Tama 1957- 106
See also CLC 43
Janowski, Tadeus M(arian) 1923- 53-56
Janowsky, Oscar Isaiah 1900- CANR-5
Earlier sketch in CA 5-8R
Janrup, (Ruth) Birgit 1931- 97-100
Jans, Zephyr
See Zekowski, Arlene
Jansen, Clifford J. 1935- 33-36R
Jansen, G(odfrey) H(enry) 1919- 114
Jansen, Godfrey
See Jansen, G(odfrey) H(enry)
Jansen, Jared
See Cebulash, Mel
Jansen, John Frederick 1918- 21-24R
Jansen, Marius B(erthus) 1922- 130
Jansen, Michael (Elin) 1940- 130
Jansen, Robert B(ruce) 1922- 81-84
Janson, Anthony F(rederick) 1943- 121
Janson, Donald 1921- 5-8R
Janson, Dora Jane (Heineberg) 1916- 106
See also SATA 31
Janson, H(orst) W(oldemar)
1913-1982 ....CANR-4
Obituary 107
Earlier sketch in CA 1-4R
See also SATA 9
Janson, Hank
See Hobson, Harry
and Norwood, Victor G(eorge) C(harles)
Janson-Smith, Celina 1909-1985 Obituary 118
Janssen, Al(fred Guthrie) 1949- 121
Janssen, Lawrence H(arm) 1921- 13-16R
Janssens, Paul Mary 1914- 53-56
Jansson, Tove Marika 1914- CANR-38
Earlier sketch in CA 17-20R
See also CLR 2
See also MAICYA
See also SATA 3, 41
Janta, Alexander 1908-1974 101
Obituary 53-56
Jantsch, Erich 1929-1980 ....CANR-10
Earlier sketch in CA 65-68
Jantscher, Gerald R.
1939(?)-1987 Obituary 123
Jantzen, Hans 1881-1967 Obituary 111
Jantzen, Steven L(loyd) 1941- 77-80
Janus
See Clery, (Reginald) Val(entine)
Janus, Grete
See Hertz, Grete Janus
Janus, Sam (Shep) 1930- 134
Brief entry 111
Januz, Lauren Robert 1939- 108
Janzen, John M(arvin) 1937- 81-84
Japhson, Robert 1736-1803 ....DLB 89
Jaques, Elliott 1917- CANR-6
Earlier sketch in CA 13-16R
Jaques, Faith 1923- CANR-20
Earlier sketch in CA 103
See also MAICYA
See also SATA 21, 69
Jaques, Florence Page 1890-1972 103
Obituary 104
Jaques, Francis Lee 1887-1969 ....SATA 28
Jaquette, Jane Stallmann 1942- Brief entry 105
Jaquin, Noel 1894(?)-1974 Obituary 112
Jaquith, Priscilla 1908- 121
See also SATA 51
Jaramillo, Samuel 1925- 41-44R
Jarausch, Konrad H(ugo) 1941- 130
Jarchow, Merrill E(arl) 1910- CANR-14
Earlier sketch in CA 41-44R
Jardim, Anne 1936- 107
Jardim, Vasco S. 1900(?)-1983 Obituary 111
Jardine, Alice (Ann) 1951- 117
Jardine, Jack 1931- 21-24R
Jareed
See Faridi, Shah Nasiruddin Mohammad
Jares, Joe 1937- CANR-12
Earlier sketch in CA 33-36R
Jarmain, W. Edwin 1938- 13-16R
Jarman, A(lfred) O(wen) H(ughes) 1911- 130
Jarman, Cosette C(otterell) 1909- CAP-2
Earlier sketch in CA 21-22
Jarman, Douglas 1942- 133
Jarman, Mark Anthony 1955- 118
See also DLB 120
Jarman, Rosemary Hawley 1935- CANR-2
Earlier sketch in CA 49-52
See also SATA 7
Jarman, Thomas Leckie 1907- CANR-4
Earlier sketch in CA 5-8R
Jarman, Walton Maxey
1904-1980 Obituary 108
Jarmusch, Jim 1953(?)- 132
Jarmuth, Sylvia L. 1912- 25-28R
Jarnow, Jeannette 1909- 53-56
Jaroch, F(rancis) A(nthony) Randy 1947- 89-92
Jaroch, Randy
See Jaroch, F(rancis) A(nthony) Randy
Jaroff, Leon Morton 1927- 135
Jarolimek, John 1921- Brief entry 114
Jaron, Lou
See Spender, Lynne
Jarreau, Al(wyn Lopez) 1940- 117
Brief entry 116
Jarrell, John W. 1908(?)-1978 Obituary 81-84
Jarrell, Mary Von Schrader 1914- 77-80
See also SATA 35
Jarrell, Randall 1914-1965 ....CANR-34
Obituary 25-28R
Earlier sketches in CA 5-8R, CANR-6
See also CABS 2
See also CDALB 1941-1968
See also CLC 1, 2, 6, 9, 13, 49
See also CLR 6
See also DLB 48, 52
See also MAICYA
See also MTCW
See also SATA 7
Jarrett, (John) Derek 1928- 57-60
Jarrett, H(arold) Reginald 1916- CANR-3
Earlier sketch in CA 9-12R
Jarrett, James Louis 1917- 53-56
Jarrett, Marjorie 1923- 105
Jarrett, Philip (Martin) 1946- 127
Jarrett, Roxanne
See Werner, Herma
Jarriel, Thomas Edwin 1934- 120
Brief entry 109
Jarriel, Tom
See Jarriel, Thomas Edwin
Jarrott, Mattie L. 1881(?)-1973 Obituary 41-44R
Jarry, Alfred 1873-1907 Brief entry 104
See also TCLC 2, 14
Jarvie, Clodagh Gibson
See Gibson-Jarvie, Clodagh
Jarvie, I(an) C(harles) 1937- 53-56
Jarvik, Lissy E. 128
Jarvis, Ana C(ortesi) 1936- CANR-14
Earlier sketch in CA 65-68
Jarvis, Charles E(fthemios) 1921- 111
Jarvis, E. K.
See Bloch, Robert (Albert)
and Ellison, Harlan
and Fairman, Paul W.
and Silverberg, Robert
Jarvis, F(rank) Washington 1939- 37-40R
Jarvis, Fred(erick) G(ordon Jr.) 1930- 33-36R
Jarvis, Howard (Arnold) 1902(?)-1986 122
Obituary 120
Brief entry 111
Jarvis, Jennifer M(ary) 1935- 13-16R
Jarvis, Martin 1941- CANR-25
Earlier sketch in CA 105
Jarvis, Rupert Charles 1899- 103
Jarvis, Sharon 1943- 119
Jarvis, William Don(ald) 1913- CAP-1
Earlier sketch in CA 13-16
Jasen, David A(lan) 1937- CANR-27
Earlier sketch in CA 29-32R
Jasenas, Michael 1912- Brief entry 113
Jashemski, Wilhelmina Feemster 1910- CAP-1
Earlier sketch in CA 13-16
Jasmin, Claude 1930- 123
See also DLB 60
Jasner, W. K.
See Watson, Jane Werner
Jasny, Naum 1883- CAP-1
Earlier sketch in CA 9-10
Jason
See Munro, (Macfarlane) Hugh
and Stannus, (James) Gordon (Dawson)
Jason
See Stannus, (James) Gordon (Dawson)
Jason
See Caballero, Manuel
Jason, Johnny
See Glut, Donald F(rank)
Jason, Kathrine 1953- 126
Jason, Philip K(enneth) 1941- CANR-35
Earlier sketch in CA 114
Jason, Stuart
See Avallone, Michael (Angelo, Jr)
and Floren, Lee
Jaspan, Norman 103
Jasper, David 1951- 128
Jasper, James M(acdonald) 1957- 138
Jasper, Ronald Claud Dudley
1917-1990 Obituary 131
Jaspers, Karl (Theodor) 1883-1969 122
Obituary 25-28R
Jaspersohn, William 1947- 102
Jassal, Harjinder (Singh) 1938- 111
Jassem, Kate
See Oppenheim, Joanne
Jassy, Marie-France Perrin
See Perrin Jassy, Marie-France
Jastak, Joseph Florian 1901-1979 ....CANR-4
Obituary 85-88
Earlier sketch in CA 5-8R
Jastrow, Robert 1925- CANR-18
Earlier sketch in CA 21-24R
Jauch, Lawrence R. 1943- 112
Jauncey, James H(enry) 1916- CANR-20
Earlier sketches in CA 1-4R, CANR-5
Jauss, Anne Marie 1902(?)-1991 ....CANR-4
Obituary 135
Earlier sketch in CA 1-4R
See also SATA 10
See also SATO 69
Jauss, David 1951- 121
Jaussi, Laureen Richardson 1934- 73-76
Javitch, Daniel Gilbert 1941- 103
Javits, Benjamin A(braham)
1894-1973 Obituary 41-44R
Javits, Eric Moses 1931- 1-4R
Javits, Jacob K(oppel) 1904-1986 ....CANR-17
Obituary 118
Earlier sketches in CA 1-4R, CANR-1
Javor, Frank A. 1916- 135
Jawien, Andrzej
See John Paul II, Pope
Jaworska, Wladyslawa Jadwiga 1910- 53-56
Jaworski, Francis Anthony
See Javor, Frank A.
Jaworski, Leon 1905-1982 ....CAP-1
Obituary 108
Earlier sketch in CA 13-16
Jaworskyj, Michael 1921- 61-64
Jaxon, Milt
See Kimbro, John M.
Jay, Antony (Rupert) 1930- 25-28R
Jay, Bill 1940- Brief entry 117
Jay, Charlotte
See Halls, Geraldine (Mary)
Jay, Donald
See Meyer, Charles R(obert)
Jay, Douglas (Patrick Thomas) 1907- CANR-12
Earlier sketch in CA 65-68
Jay, Elisabeth 1947- 124
Jay, Eric George 1907- 5-8R
Jay, G. S.
See Halls, Geraldine (Mary)
Jay, Gregory S. 1952- 130
Jay, Hilda L(ease) 1921- 117
Jay, James M(onroe) 1927- 53-56
Jay, John 1745-1829 ....DLB 31
Jay, Karla 1947- 85-88
Jay, M(argaret) Ellen 1946- 118
Jay, Marion
See Spalding, Ruth
Jay, Martin (Evan) 1944- 53-56
Jay, Mel
See Fanthorpe, R(obert) Lionel
Jay, Peter A. 1940- 101
Jay, Peter (Anthony Charles) 1945- 97-100
Jay, Peter 1937- 109
Jay, Robert Ravenelle 1925- Brief entry 106
Jay, Ruth I(ngrid) 1920- 93-96
Jay, Ruth Johnson
See Jay, Ruth I(ngrid)
Jay, Simon
See Alexander, Colin James
Jayawardena, Visakha Kumari 1931- 45-48
Jayme, William North 1925- 9-12R
Jayne, Lieutenant R. H.
See Ellis, Edward S(ylvester)
Jayne, Sears 1920- 13-16R
Jaynes, Clare
See Mayer, Jane Rothschild
Jaynes, Julian 1923- 41-44R
Jaynes, Richard A(ndrus) 1935- 65-68
Jaynes, Roger W. 1946- 85-88
Jaynes, Ruth 1899- CAP-2
Earlier sketch in CA 25-28
Jazayery, M(ohammad) Ali 1924- CANR-9
Earlier sketch in CA 21-24R
Jeake, Samuel Jr.
See Aiken, Conrad (Potter)
Jeal, Tim 1945- CANR-9
Earlier sketch in CA 21-24R
Jean, Gabrielle (Lucille) 1924- CANR-14
Earlier sketch in CA 37-40R
Jean, Marcel 1900- 25-28R
Jean-Louis
See Kerouac, Jean-Louis Lebris de
Jeannerat, Pierre Gabriel 1902- 5-8R
Jeanneret, Marsh 1917-1990 132
Jeanniere, Abel 1921- CANR-28
Earlier sketch in CA 49-52
Jeans, Marylu Terral 1914- 89-92
Jeans, Michael 127
Jeansonne, Glen 1946- 122
Jeanty, Ninette Helene
See Raven, Ninette Helene Jeanty
Jebb, (Hubert Miles) Gladwyn 1900- 21-24R
Jedamus, Paul 1923- 37-40R
Jedlitzka, Maria
See Jeritza, Maria
Jedrey, Christopher M(ichael) 1949- 101
Jedrzejewicz, Waclaw 1893- 25-28R
Jeef, Kalle
See Tshiamala, Kabasele
Jeeves, Malcolm A(lexander) 1926- CANR-12
Earlier sketch in CA 29-32R
Jeffares, A(lexander) Norman 1920- CANR-39
Earlier sketches in CA 85-88, CANR-16
Jeffer, Marsha 1940- 41-44R
Jefferds, Vincent H(arris) 1916- 127
See also SATA 49, 59
Jefferies, (John) Richard 1848-1887 ....DLB 98
See also SATA 16
Jefferies, Susan Herring 1903- CAP-1
Earlier sketch in CA 13-14
Jefferis, Barbara (Tarlton) 1917- 81-84
Jeffers, H(arry) Paul 1934- 93-96
Jeffers, Jo
See Johnson, Joan Helen
Jeffers, Lance 1919-1985 ....CANR-25
Earlier sketch in CA 65-68
See also BW
See also DLB 41
Jeffers, (John) Robinson 1887-1962 ....CANR-35
Earlier sketch in CA 85-88
See also CDALB 1917-1929
See also CLC 2, 3, 11, 15, 54
See also DLB 45
See also MTCW
See also WLC
Jeffers, Susan 97-100
See also MAICYA
See also SATA 17, 70
Jefferson, Alan 1921- CANR-29
Earlier sketches in CA 33-36R, CANR-13
Jefferson, Blanche (Waugaman) 1909- 5-8R
Jefferson, Carter (Alfred) 1927- 17-20R
Jefferson, Ian
See Davies, L(eslie) P(urnell)
Jefferson, Janet
See Mencken, H(enry) L(ouis)
Jefferson, Omar Xavier
See Jefferson, Xavier T(homas)
Jefferson, Roland S. 1939- CANR-35
Earlier sketch in CA 111
See also BW
Jefferson, Sarah
See Farjeon, (Eve) Annabel
Jefferson, Thomas
1743-1826 ....CDALB 1640-1865
See also DLB 31
Jefferson, Xavier T(homas) 1952- CANR-13
Earlier sketch in CA 73-76
Jeffery, Grant 1924- 1-4R
Jeffery, Ransom 1943- 21-24R
Jefferys, Allan 93-96
Jefford, Bat
See Bingley, David Ernest
Jeffress, Philip W. 1941- Brief entry 111
Jeffrey, Adi-Kent Thomas 1916- 37-40R
Jeffrey, Christopher
See Leach, Michael
Jeffrey, David Lyle 1941- CANR-24
Earlier sketches in CA 57-60, CANR-7
Jeffrey, Francis 1773-1850 ....DLB 107
Jeffrey, Francis 1950- 135
Jeffrey, Julie Roy 1941- 93-96
Jeffrey, L(illian) H(amilton) 1915- 1-4R
Jeffrey, Lawrence 1953- 130
Jeffrey, Lloyd Nicholas 1918- 37-40R
Jeffrey, Mildred (Mesurac) 5-8R
Jeffrey, Richard Carl 1926- 103
Jeffrey, Ruth
See Bell, Louise Price
Jeffrey, Thomas E. 1947- 136
Jeffrey, William
See Wallmann, Jeffrey M(iner)
Jeffrey, William
See Pronzini, Bill
Jeffrey, William P. Jr. 1919- 57-60
Jeffreys, Harold 1891-1989 109
Obituary 128
Jeffreys, J. G.
See Healey, Ben (James)
Jeffreys, Montagu Vaughan Castelman
1900-1985 ....CANR-4
Obituary 117
Earlier sketch in CA 5-8R
Jeffreys-Jones, Rhodri 1942- CANR-13
Earlier sketch in CA 77-80
Jeffries, Charles Joseph 1896-1972 ....CANR-4
Earlier sketch in CA 5-8R
Jeffries, Derwin J(ames) 1915- 57-60
Jeffries, Don 1940- 137
Jeffries, Graham Montague
1900-1982 ....CANR-25
Earlier sketch in CA 77-80
Jeffries, John Worthington 1942- 103
Jeffries, Lewis I(ngles) 1942- 103
Jeffries, Ona (Griffin)
1893(?)-1973 Obituary 41-44R
Jeffries, Roderic (Graeme) 1926- CANR-25
Earlier sketches in CA 17-20R, CANR-9
See also SATA 4
Jeffries, Virginia M(urrill) 1911- 5-8R
Jeffs, Julian 1931- 37-40R
Jeffs, Rae 1921- 25-28R
Jefkins, Frank William 1920- CANR-9
Earlier sketch in CA 13-16R
Jehlen, Myra 1940- 101
Jekel, Pamela (L.) 1948- 135
Jelagin, Juri 1910-1987 Obituary 123
Jelakowitch, Ivan
See Heijermans, Herman
Jelavich, Barbara 1923- 53-56
Jelenski, Constantin 1922- 101
Jelinek, Elfriede 1946- ....DLB 85
Jelinek, Estelle C. 1935- 102
Jelinek, Hena Maes
See Maes-Jelinek, Hena
Jellema, Roderick 1927- 41-44R
Jellicoe, (Patricia) Ann 1927- 85-88
See also CLC 27
See also DLB 13
Jellicoe, Geoffrey Alan 1900- 13-16R
Jellicoe, Sidney 1906-1973 ....CAP-2
Earlier sketch in CA 33-36
Jellinek, George 1919- 89-92
Jellinek, J(oseph) Stephan 1930- 81-84
Jellinek, Paul 1897- 13-16R
Jellison, Charles Albert Jr. 1924- CANR-27
Earlier sketch in CA 1-4R
Jelly, George Oliver 1909- 103
Jemie, Onwuchekwa 1940- 89-92
Jemyma
See Holley, Marietta
Jen, Gish
See Jen, Lillian
See also CLC 70
Jen, Lillian 1956(?)- 135
See also Jen, Gish
Jena, Ruth Michaelis
See Ratcliff, Ruth
Jencks, Charles 1939- CANR-2
Earlier sketch in CA 49-52
Jencks, Christopher 1936- CANR-2
Earlier sketch in CA 49-52
Jencks, Harlan W(ardell) 1941- 111
Jenison, Don P. 1897- CANR-7
Earlier sketch in CA 17-20R
Jenkin, A(lfred) K(enneth) Hamilton
1900-1980 Obituary 102
Jenkins, Alan 1914- CANR-6
Earlier sketch in CA 57-60
Jenkins, Cecil 1927- 107
Jenkins, Clive 1926- CANR-5
Earlier sketch in CA 13-16R
Jenkins, Dan (Thomas B.) 1929- 126
Brief entry 111
Jenkins, Daniel T(homas) 1914- 127

Jenkins, David E(dward) 1925- Brief entry 114
Jenkins, David L. 1931- 136
Jenkins, David 1928- 97-100
Jenkins, Dorothy Helen
1907-1972 Obituary 37-40R
Jenkins, Edith A(rnstein) 1913- 137
Jenkins, (Margaret) Elizabeth (Heald)
1905- CANR-13
Earlier sketch in CA 73-76
Jenkins, Emyl 1941- 114
Jenkins, Ferrell 1936- CANR-6
Earlier sketch in CA 57-60
Jenkins, Frances Briggs 1905- CAP-2
Earlier sketch in CA 25-28
Jenkins, Geoffrey 1920- CANR-16
Earlier sketch in CA 5-8R
Jenkins, (Thomas) Gilmour
1894-1981 Obituary 108
Jenkins, Gladys Gardner 1901- CANR-4
Earlier sketch in CA 1-4R
Jenkins, Gordon (Hill) 1910-1984 Obituary 112
Jenkins, Gwyn 1919- 1-4R
Jenkins, Hal
See Jenkins, Harold L.
Jenkins, Harold L. 1909(?)-1987 Obituary 124
Jenkins, Harold 1909- 9-12R
Jenkins, Holt M. 1920- 17-20R
Jenkins, Hugh (Gater) 1908- 104
Jenkins, Iredell 1909- 106
Jenkins, James J(erome) 1923- 13-16R
Jenkins, Jerry B(ruce) 1949- CANR-20
Earlier sketches in CA 49-52, CANR-5
Jenkins, John Geraint 1929- 21-24R
Jenkins, John H(olmes III) 1940- CANR-10
Earlier sketch in CA 65-68
Jenkins, John J. 1937- 132
Jenkins, John (Robert Graham)
1928- CANR-28
Earlier sketch in CA 45-48
Jenkins, Kenneth V(incent) 1930- 53-56
Jenkins, Linda Walsh 1944- 111
Jenkins, Louis 1942- CANR-4
Earlier sketch in CA 53-56
Jenkins, Marie M(agdalen) 1909- 41-44R
See also SATA 7
Jenkins, Mark 1958- 137
Jenkins, Michael (Romilly Heald) 1936- 25-28R
Jenkins, Nancy (Harmon) 1937- 109
Jenkins, Patricia 1927-1982 106
Jenkins, Peter (George James) 1934- 135
Jenkins, Peter 1951- 89-92
Jenkins, Phyllis
See Schwalberg, Carol(yn Ernestine Stein)
Jenkins, Ray(mond Leonard) 1935- 103
Jenkins, Reese V(almer) 1938- 65-68
Jenkins, (John) Robin 1912- CANR-1
Earlier sketch in CA 1-4R
See also CLC 52
See also DLB 14
Jenkins, Romilly James Heald
1907-1969 ......CANR-5
Earlier sketch in CA 5-8R
Jenkins, Roy (Harris) 1920- CANR-30
Earlier sketches in CA 9-12R, CANR-13
Jenkins, Simon 1943- 81-84
Jenkins, Will(iam) F(itzgerald)
1896-1975 ......CANR-4
Obituary 57-60
Earlier sketch in CA 9-12R
See also Leinster, Murray
Jenkins, William A(twell) 1922- 61-64
See also SATA 9
Jenkins, William Marshall Jr.
1918- Brief entry 105
Jenkinson, Edward B(ernard) 1930- 21-24R
Jenkinson, Michael 1938- 25-28R
Jenks, Almet 1892-1966 ......CAP-1
Earlier sketch in CA 13-14
Jenks, C(larence) Wilfred 1909-1973 ......CANR-4
Earlier sketch in CA 9-12R
Jenks, George C(harles)
1850-1929 Brief entry 119
Jenks, James M. 1922- 122
Jenks, Randolph 1912- 9-12R
Jenks, Tom 1950- 137
Jenkyns, Chris 1924- ......SATA 51
Jenkyns, Richard (Henry Austen) 1949- 108
Jenner, Bruce 1949- 110
Jenner, Chrystie 1950- 77-80
Jenner, Delia 1944- 21-24R
Jenner, Heather
See James, Heather
Jenner, Philip Norman 1921- 89-92
Jenner, W(illiam) J(ohn) F(rancis)
1940- CANR-12
Earlier sketch in CA 29-32R
Jenness, Aylette 1934- 25-28R
Jennifer, Susan
See Hoskins, Robert
Jennings, Coleman A(lonzo) 1933- 124
See also SATA 64
Jennings, Dana Close 1923- 53-56
Jennings, Dean Southern
1905-1969 Obituary 89-92
Jennings, Edward M(orton III) 1936- 29-32R
Jennings, Elizabeth (Joan) 1926- CANR-39
Earlier sketches in CA 61-64, CANR-8
See also CAAS 5
See also CLC 5, 14
See also DLB 27
See also MTCW
See also SATA 66
Jennings, Gary (Gayne) 1928- CANR-29
Earlier sketches in CA 5-8R, CANR-9
See also SATA 9
Jennings, (William) Ivor 1903-1965 ......5-8R
Jennings, James M(urray) 1924- 37-40R
Jennings, Jerry (Edward) 1935- CANR-7
Earlier sketch in CA 53-56
Jennings, Jesse David 1909- CANR-13
Earlier sketch in CA 33-36R
Jennings, John (Edward Jr.) 1906-1973 ......CAP-1
Obituary 45-48
Earlier sketch in CA 13-14
Jennings, Karla (Mari) 1956- 134
Jennings, Lane (Eaton) 1944- CANR-19
Earlier sketch in CA 102
Jennings, Leslie Nelson 1890-1972 ......CAP-1
Earlier sketch in CA 9-10
Jennings, Marianne Moody 1953- 118
Jennings, Michael Glenn 1931- CANR-24
Earlier sketch in CA 69-72
Jennings, Patrick
See Mayer, S(ydney) L(ouis)
Jennings, Paul (Francis) 1918- CANR-19
Earlier sketches in CA 9-12R, CANR-4
Jennings, Peter (Charles Archibald Ewart)
1938- 134
Brief entry 114
Jennings, Phillip C. 1946- 126
Jennings, Raymond P(olson) 1924- 110
Jennings, Richard (Wormington) 1907- 17-20R
Jennings, Robert
See Hamilton, Charles (Harold St. John)
Jennings, Robert E(dward) 1931- CANR-11
Earlier sketch in CA 61-64
Jennings, S. M.
See Meyer, Jerome Sydney
Jennings, Sharon (Elizabeth) 1954- 134
Jennings, Talbot 1895(?)-1985 Obituary 116
Jennings, Ted C(harles) 1949- 81-84
Jennings, Vivien 61-64
Jennings, Waylon 1937- ......CLC 21
Jennings, William Dale 1917- 25-28R
Jennison, C. S.
See Starbird, Kaye
Jennison, Christopher 1938- 53-56
Jennison, Keith Warren 1911- 73-76
See also SATA 14
Jennison, Peter S(axe) 1922- CANR-4
Earlier sketch in CA 9-12R
Jenny, Hans H(einrich) 1922- 103
Jenoff, Marvyne 1942- 117
Jens, Walter 1923- CANR-15
Earlier sketch in CA 89-92
See also DLB 69
Jensen, Ad(olph) E. 1899-1965 ......CAP-2
Earlier sketch in CA 19-20
Jensen, Alan F(rederick) 1938- 53-56
Jensen, Albert C(hristian) 1924- 85-88
Jensen, Andrew F(rederick) Jr. 1929- 57-60
Jensen, Ann 21-24R
Jensen, Arthur R(obert) 1923- CANR-2
Earlier sketch in CA 1-4R
Jensen, Clayne R. 1930- CANR-8
Earlier sketch in CA 17-20R
Jensen, De Lamar 1925- CANR-7
Earlier sketch in CA 9-12R
Jensen, Dwight 1934- 85-88
Jensen, Ejner J. 1937- 138
Jensen, Frede 1926- 57-60
Jensen, Gordon Duff 1926- Brief entry 106
Jensen, Gwendolyn Evans 1936- 57-60
Jensen, H. James 1933- 25-28R
Jensen, Irene K(hin Khin Myint) 1925- 69-72
Jensen, Irving L. 1920- CANR-7
Earlier sketch in CA 17-20R
Jensen, J(ohn) Vernon 1922- 49-52
Jensen, Jo
See Pelton, Beverly Jo
Jensen, Joan M(aria) 1934- 127
Jensen, Johannes V. 1873-1950 ......TCLC 41
Jensen, John H(jalmar) 1929- 21-24R
Jensen, John Martin 1893- CAP-1
Earlier sketch in CA 13-16
Jensen, Julie
See McDonald, Julie
Jensen, Larry Cyril 1938- 106
Jensen, Laura (Linnea) 1948- 103
See also CLC 37
Jensen, Lawrence N(eil) 1924- 17-20R
Jensen, Lloyd 1936- 61-64
Jensen, Margaret Ann 1948- 123
Jensen, Marlene 1947- 81-84
Jensen, Mary Ten Eyck Bard 1904-1970 ......5-8R
Obituary 29-32R
Jensen, Maxine Dowd 1919- 65-68
Jensen, Merrill (Monroe) 1905-1980 77-80
Obituary 112
See also DLB 17
Jensen, Michael C(harles) 1934- 127
Jensen, Michael C(ole) 1939- CANR-32
Earlier sketch in CA 49-52
Jensen, Niels 1927- 49-52
See also SATA 25
Jensen, Ole Klindt
See Klindt-Jensen, Ole
Jensen, Oliver (Ormerod) 1914- CANR-10
Earlier sketch in CA 25-28R
Jensen, Paul K. 1916- 17-20R
Jensen, Paul M(orris) 1944- 53-56
Jensen, Pauline Marie (Long) 1900- CAP-2
Earlier sketch in CA 17-18
Jensen, Peter
See Wallmann, Jeffrey M(iner)
Jensen, Richard C(arl) 1936- 49-52
Jensen, Richard J. 1941- 33-36R
Jensen, Robert (Earl) 1938-1990 111
Obituary 132
Jensen, Rolf (Arthur) 1912- 21-24R
Jensen, Rosalie (Seymour) 1938- 57-60
Jensen, Vernon H(ortin) 1907- 106
Jensen, Virginia Allen 1927- CANR-1
Earlier sketch in CA 45-48
See also SATA 8
Jensi, Muganwa Nsiku
See Shorter, Aylward
Jenson, Robert W(illiam) 1930- CANR-9
Earlier sketch in CA 5-8R
Jenson, William R(obert) 1946- 101
Jentleson, Bruce W. 1951- 124
Jentz, Gaylord A. 1931- CANR-31
Earlier sketches in CA 25-28R, CANR-14
Jenyns, R(oger) Soame 1904-1976 73-76
Obituary 69-72
Jenyns, Soame
See Jenyns, R(oger) Soame
Jephcott, E(dmund) F(rancis) N(eville)
1938- Brief entry 115
Jeppson, J. O.
See Asimov, Janet (Jeppson)
Jepsen, Stanley M(arius) 1912- 77-80
Jepson, Selwyn 1899-1989 Obituary 128
Jeram, Anita 1965- ......SATA 71
Jerdee, Thomas H(arlan) 1927- 118
Jeremias, Joachim 1900- CANR-11
Earlier sketch in CA 5-8R
Jeremy, David J(ohn) 1939- 129
Jeremy, Sister Mary 5-8R
Jerina, Carol 1947- 126
Jeritza, Maria 1887-1982 Obituary 107
Jermain, Clive 1966(?)-1988 Obituary 124
Jerman, James (Auguste) 1920- 123
Jerman, Sylvia Paul
See Cooper, Sylvia
Jernick, Ruth 1948- 107
Jerome, Jerome K(lapka)
1859-1927 Brief entry 119
See also DLB 10, 34
See also TCLC 23
Jerome, John 1932- CANR-2
Earlier sketch in CA 45-48
Jerome, Joseph
See Sewell, Brocard
Jerome, Judson (Blair) 1927- CANR-20
Earlier sketches in CA 9-12R, CANR-4
See also CAAS 8
See also DLB 105
Jerome, Lawrence E(dmund) 1944- 77-80
Jerome, Mark
See Appleman, Mark J(erome)
Jerome, Stuart 1918(?)-1983 Obituary 111
Jerrybilt
See Shields, Gerald R.
Jersild, Arthur T(homas) 1902- CANR-21
Earlier sketch in CA 1-4R
Jersild, P. C.
See Jersild, Per Christian
Jersild, Paul T(homas) 1931- 37-40R
Jersild, Per Christian 1935- 130
Jervell, Jacob 1925- CANR-23
Earlier sketches in CA 61-64, CANR-8
Jervey, Edward D(rewry) 1929- 133
Jeschke, Marlin 1929- 45-48
Jeschke, Susan 1942- 77-80
See also SATA 27, 42
Jeske, Richard Lee 1936- 111
Jesmer, Elaine 1939- 49-52
See also AITN 1
Jespersen, James 1934- 103
Jesse, F(ryniwyd) Tennyson
1889-1958 Brief entry 112
See also DLB 77
Jesse, Michael
See Baldwin, Michael
Jessel, Camilla (Ruth) 1937- CANR-23
Earlier sketch in CA 104
See also SATA 29
Jessel, George (Albert) 1898-1981 89-92
Obituary 103
Jessel, John
See Weinbaum, Stanley Grauman
Jessen, Carl A. 1887(?)-1978 Obituary 77-80
Jessey, Cornelia
See Sussman, Cornelia Silver
Jessner, Lucie Ney 1896-1979 Obituary 93-96
Jessop, Thomas Edmund 1896- 9-12R
Jessor, Richard 1924- 41-44R
Jessup, Frances
See Van Briggle, Margaret F(rances) Jessup
Jessup, John K(nox) 1907-1979 101
Obituary 89-92
Jessup, Michael H(yle) 1937- Brief entry 109
Jessup, Paul F(rederick) 1939- 111
Jessup, Philip C(aryl) 1897-1986 77-80
Obituary 118
Jessup, Richard 1925(?)-1982 Obituary 108
Jesty, P(eter) H(ugh) 1948- 121
Jeter, Jacky
See Jeter, Jacquelyn I.
Jeter, Jacquelyn I. 1935- 25-28R
Jett, Stephen C(linton) 1938- CANR-10
Earlier sketch in CA 25-28R
Jette, Fernand 1921- 5-8R
Jeune, Paul 1950- 101
Jevons, Frederic Raphae 1929- 61-64
Jevons, Marshall
See Breit, William (Leo)
and Elzinga, Kenneth G(erald)
Jewell, Derek 1927-1985 ......CANR-20
Earlier sketches in CA 33-36R, CANR-13
Jewell, Edmund F.
1896(?)-1978 Obituary 81-84
Jewell, Malcolm E(dwin) 1928- CANR-5
Earlier sketch in CA 1-4R
Jewell, Nancy 1940- CANR-7
Earlier sketch in CA 61-64
See also SATA 41
Jewess, Kathleen
See Burk, Kathleen
Jewett, Alyce Lowrie (Williams) 1908- CAP-1
Earlier sketch in CA 13-14
Jewett, Ann E(lizabeth) 1921- 93-96
Jewett, Claudia L(owe) 1939- 112
Jewett, Eleanore Myers 1890-1967 ......5-8R
See also SATA 5
Jewett, Paul King 1919-1991 53-56
Obituary 135
Jewett, Robert 1933- CANR-2
Earlier sketch in CA 45-48
Jewett, (Theodora) Sarah Orne 1849-1909 127
Brief entry 108
See also DLB 12, 74
See also SATA 15
See also SSC 6
See also TCLC 1, 22
Jewison, Norman (Frederick)
1926- Brief entry 113
Jewitt, John Rodgers 1783-1821 ......DLB 99
Jewsbury, Geraldine (Endsor)
1812-1880 ......DLB 21
Jezard, Alison 1919- 29-32R
See also SATA 34, 57
Jezer, Marty 1940- CANR-27
Earlier sketch in CA 109
Jezewski, Bohdan O(lgierd) 1900-1980 ......5-8R
Obituary 103
Jha, Akhileshwar 1932- 107
Jha, Lakshmi Kant 1913-1988 Obituary 125
Jhabvala, Ruth Prawer 1927- CANR-29
Earlier sketches in CA 1-4R, CANR-2
See also CLC 4, 8, 29
See also MTCW
Jianou, Ionel 1905- CANR-9
Earlier sketch in CA 21-24R
Jidejian, Nina 1921- 29-32R
Jie, Zhang
See Zhang Jie
Jiler, John 1946- 114
See also SATA 35, 42
Jiles, Paulette 1943- 101
See also CLC 13, 58
Jillson, Joyce 1950- 111
Jimenez, Francisco 1943- 131
See also HW
Jimenez, Janey (Renee) 1953- 77-80
Jimenez (Mantecon), Juan Ramon
1881-1958 131
Brief entry 104
See also HW
See also MTCW
See also TCLC 4
Jimenez, Neal (Randall) 1960- 138
Jimenez, Ramon
See Jimenez (Mantecon), Juan Ramon
Jimenez Mantecon, Juan
See Jimenez (Mantecon), Juan Ramon
Jinks, William Howard Jr. 1938- 41-44R
Jipson, Wayne R(ay) 1931- 45-48
Jiskogo
See Harrington, Mark Raymond
Jo, Yung-Hwan 1932- 45-48
Joachim, Leo H. 1898-1985 Obituary 117
Joan, Polly 1933- 101
Joans, Ted 1928- CANR-25
Earlier sketches in CA 45-48, CANR-2
See also BW
See also DLB 16, 41
Jobb, Jamie 1945- 85-88
See also SATA 29
Jobe, Brock (William) 1948- 118
Jobes, Gertrude Blumenthal 1907- CAP-1
Earlier sketch in CA 11-12
Jobson, Gary Alan 1950- 93-96
Jobson, Hamilton 1914- 73-76
Jobson, Sandra
See Darroch, Sandra Jobson
Jocelyn, Richard
See Clutterbuck, Richard
Jochnowitz, George 1937- 49-52
Joedicke, Juergen 1925- 17-20R
Joel, Asher Alexander 1912- 108
Joel, Billy
See Joel, William Martin
See also CLC 26
Joel, William Martin 1949- 108
See also Joel, Billy
Joels, Merrill E. 1915- 25-28R
Joelson, Annette 1903-1971 Obituary 29-32R
Joerns, Consuelo 114
Brief entry 111
See also SATA 33, 44
Joers, Lawrence E(ugene) C(laire)
1900- 41-44R
Joesting, Edward Henry 1925- 103
Jofen, Jean 1922- 37-40R
Joffe, Josef 1944- 126
Joffe, Joyce 1940- 77-80
Johannes, John R. 1943- 111
Johannes, R.
See Moss, Rose
Johannesen, Richard L(ee) 1937- 17-20R
Johannesson, Olof
See Alfven, Hannes O(lof) G(oesta)
Johanningmeier, E(rwin) V(irgil) 1937- 104
Johannis, Theodore B(enjamin) Jr.
1914- 33-36R
Johannsen, Hano D. 1933- CANR-29
Earlier sketch in CA 29-32R
Johannsen, Robert Walter 1925- 1-4R
Johansen, Bruce Elliott 1950- 110
Johansen, Dorothy O. 1904- CAP-1
Earlier sketch in CA 13-14
Johanson, Donald C(arl) 1943- 107
Johanson, Stanley Morris 1933- 45-48

Johansson, Thomas (Hugo) B(ernard)
1943- CANR-19
Earlier sketch in CA 102
John, Angela V. 1948- 125
John, B.
See John, Elizabeth Beaman
John, Betty
See John, Elizabeth Beaman
John, Colin
See Hagan, Chet
John, Dane
See Major, Alan P(ercival)
John, DeWitt 1915-1985 Obituary 117
John, Elizabeth Beaman 1907- CANR-8
Earlier sketch in CA 5-8R
John, Errol 1924-1988 Obituary 126
John, Helen James 1930- 61-64
John, Joyce .... SATA 59
John, Owen 1918- Brief entry 117
John, Robert 29-32R
John, Sandra D(eanne Thompson) 1951- 114
John, Vera P.
See John-Steiner, Vera P(olgar)
Johnn, David
See Engle, John D(avid) Jr.
John of Dumbleton 1310(?)-1349(?) .... DLB 115
John Paul I, Pope 1912-1978 .... CANR-29
Earlier sketch in CA 81-84
John Paul II, Pope 1920- 133
Brief entry 106
Johnpoll, Bernard K(eith) 1918- CANR-24
Earlier sketches in CA 21-24R, CANR-9
Johns, Albert Cameron 1914- CANR-6
Earlier sketch in CA 49-52
Johns, Avery
See Cousins, Margaret
Johns, Claude J. Jr. 1930- 77-80
Johns, Edward Alistair 1936- 45-48
Johns, Elizabeth 1937- 121
Johns, Eric 1907-1975 Obituary 116
Johns, Foster
See Seldes, Gilbert (Vivian)
Johns, Geoffrey
See Warner, (George) Geoffrey John
Johns, Glover S. Jr.
1911(?)-1976 Obituary 65-68
Johns, Janetta
See Quin-Harkin, Janet
Johns, John E(dwin) 1921- 9-12R
Johns, June 1925- 57-60
Johns, Kenneth
See Bulmer, (Henry) Kenneth
Johns, Marston
See Fanthorpe, R(obert) Lionel
Johns, Ray E(arl) 1900- 41-44R
Johns, Richard A(lton) 1929- 17-20R
Johns, Stephanie Bernardo 1947- CANR-30
Earlier sketch in CA 112
Johns, W(illiam) E(arle) 1893-1968 .... CANR-30
Earlier sketch in CA 73-76
See also MAICYA
See also SATA 55
Johns, Warren L. 1929- 21-24R
Johns, Whitey
See White, John I(rwin)
Johnsen, Trevor Bernard Meldal
See Meldal-Johnsen, Trevor Bernard
Johnsgard, Karin L(uisa) 1964- 118
Johnsgard, Paul A(ustin) 1931- CANR-39
Earlier sketches in CA 49-52, CANR-1, 17
Johnson, A.
See Johnson, Annabell (Jones)
Johnson, A. E.
See Johnson, Annabell (Jones)
and Johnson, Edgar (Raymond)
Johnson, A(lison) Findlay 1947- 132
Johnson, Alan P(ackard) 1929- 17-20R
Johnson, Albert (Franklin) 1904- CANR-6
Earlier sketch in CA 9-12R
Johnson, Alden Porter 1914-1972 Obituary 104
Johnson, Alison
See Johnson, A(lison) Findlay
Johnson, Allen 85-88
Johnson, Allison H(eartz) 1910- 41-44R
Johnson, Alvin 1874-1971 Obituary 29-32R
Johnson, Amandus 1877-1974 Obituary 49-52
Johnson, Andrew N(isseu) 1887-1982 61-64
Obituary 120
Johnson, Angela 1961- 138
See also SATA 69
Johnson, Ann Braden 1945- 135
Johnson, Ann Cox
See Saunders, Ann Loreille
Johnson, Annabel
See Johnson, Annabell (Jones)
Johnson, Annabell (Jones) 1921- CANR-37
Earlier sketch in CA 9-12R
See also MAICYA
See also SATA 2
Johnson, Arno Hollock 1901-1985 Obituary 116
Johnson, Arnold W(aldemar) 1900- CAP-1
Earlier sketch in CA 13-14
Johnson, Arthur Menzies 1921- 21-24R
Johnson, Arthur W(illiam) 1920- 117
Johnson, Aubrey Rodway
1901-1985 Obituary 117
Johnson, Audrey P(ike) 1915- CANR-15
Earlier sketch in CA 93-96
Johnson, B(owen) C(harleston) 1945- 107
Johnson, B(urdetta) F(aye) 1920- CANR-3
Earlier sketch in CA 1-4R
See also Beebe, B(urdetta) F(aye)
Johnson, B(asil) L(eonard) C(lyde) 1919- 120
Johnson, B(ryan) S(tanley William)
1933-1973 .... CANR-9
Obituary 53-56
Earlier sketch in CA 9-12R
See also CLC 6, 9
See also DLB 14, 40
Johnson, Barbara F(erry) 1923- 73-76
Johnson, Barclay G(iddings)
1909-1985 Obituary 116
Johnson, Barry L(ee) 1943- 61-64
Johnson, Barry L(ynn) 1934- 33-36R
Johnson, Bea Obituary 65-68
Johnson, Ben E(ugene) 1940- CANR-8
Earlier sketch in CA 61-64
Johnson, Benj. F. of Boo
See Riley, James Whitcomb
Johnson, Benjamin A. 1937- CANR-9
Earlier sketch in CA 21-24R
Johnson, Benjamin F. of Boo
See Riley, James Whitcomb
Johnson, Benton 1928- 81-84
Johnson, Bernard 1933- 33-36R
Johnson, Bertha French 1906- 41-44R
Johnson, Beth 1953- 118
Johnson, Bob 1950- 130
Johnson, Bradford 1937- 57-60
Johnson, Brian (Martin) 1925- CANR-23
Earlier sketch in CA 106
Johnson, Bruce 1933- 33-36R
Johnson, Bryan 1948- 133
Johnson, Burges 1877-1963 Obituary 89-92
Johnson, Byron Lindberg 1917- 21-24R
Johnson, C. Edward
See Johnson, Carl E(dward)
Johnson, C. F.
See Goulart, Frances Sheridan
Johnson, Carl E(dward) 1937- 25-28R
Johnson, Carl G(raves) 1915- 101
Johnson, Carol Virginia 1928- CANR-6
Earlier sketch in CA 9-12R
Johnson, Carroll B(ernard) 1938- 73-76
Johnson, Cecil Edward 1927- 33-36R
Johnson, Chalmers A(shby) 1931- CANR-6
Earlier sketch in CA 5-8R
Johnson, Charlene
See Crawford, Char
Johnson, Charles Benjamin
1928-1980 .... CANR-4
Earlier sketch in CA 5-8R
Johnson, Charles Ellicott 1920-1969 .... 1-4R
Obituary 103
Johnson, Charles R. 1925- 65-68
See also SATA 11
Johnson, Charles (Richard) 1948- 116
See also BLC 2
See also BW
See also CLC 7, 51, 65
See also DLB 33
Johnson, Charles S.
See Edwards, William B(ennett)
Johnson, Charles S(purgeon) 1893-1956 125
See also BW
See also DLB 51, 91
Johnson, Charles W(illiam) 1934- 107
Johnson, Charles 1679-1748 .... DLB 84
Johnson, Charlotte Buel
See von Wodtke, Charlotte Buel Johnson
See also SATA 46
Johnson, Christine 1943- 123
Johnson, Christopher Howard
1937- Brief entry 106
Johnson, Christopher 1931- CANR-8
Earlier sketch in CA 13-16R
Johnson, Chuck
See Johnson, Charles R.
Johnson, Clair 1915(?)-1980 Obituary 97-100
Johnson, Claudia Alta (Taylor) 1912- 89-92
Johnson, Claudia D(urst) 1938- 114
Johnson, Clive (White Jr.) 1930- 29-32R
Johnson, Colin 1939- 130
Johnson, Crockett
See Leisk, David Johnson
Johnson, Curt(is Lee) 1928- 33-36R
Johnson, Curtiss Sherman 1899- 45-48
Johnson, D(onald) Barton 1933- 33-36R
Johnson, D(avid) Bruce 1942- 61-64
Johnson, D(avid) Gale 1916- 17-20R
Johnson, D(ana) William 1945- 97-100
See also SATA 23
Johnson, Dale A(rthur) 1936- 37-40R
Johnson, Dale L(eonard) 1934- 130
Johnson, Dave W(illiam) 1931- 93-96
Johnson, David G(eorge) 1906- 9-12R
Johnson, David Lawrence 1943- 114
Johnson, David Ralph 1942- 117
Johnson, David 1927- CANR-8
Earlier sketch in CA 13-16R
Johnson, Deidre A(nn) 1953- 116
Johnson, Denis 1949- 121
Brief entry 117
See also CLC 52
See also DLB 120
Johnson, Diane (Lain) 1934- CANR-17
Earlier sketch in CA 41-44R
See also CLC 5, 13, 48
See also DLBY 80
See also MTCW
Johnson, Dick
See Johnson, Richard A.
Johnson, Dolores 1949- 137
See also SATA 69
Johnson, Don 1934- 116
Johnson, Donald Bruce 1921-1981 .... CANR-25
Earlier sketch in CA 1-4R
Johnson, Donald D. 1917- 137
Johnson, Donald M(cEwen) 1909- 1-4R
Johnson, Donald McI(ntosh) 1903- CANR-8
Earlier sketch in CA 5-8R
Johnson, Donna Kay 1935- 106
Johnson, Donovan A(lbert) 1910- CANR-5
Earlier sketch in CA 5-8R
Johnson, Doris McNeely 1941- 111
Johnson, Dorothy Biddle
1887(?)-1974 Obituary 53-56
Johnson, Dorothy E(thel) 1920- 53-56
Johnson, Dorothy M(arie) 1905-1984 .... CANR-6
Obituary 114
Earlier sketch in CA 5-8R
See also SATA 6, 40
Johnson, Dorris 1914- 109
Johnson, Douglas W(ayne) 1934- CANR-21
Earlier sketches in CA 57-60, CANR-6
Johnson, E(dgar) A(ugustus) J(erome)
1900-1972 .... CAP-1
Obituary 37-40R
Earlier sketch in CA 17-18
Johnson, E(arly) Ashby 1917- 33-36R
Johnson, E(ugene) Harper .... SATA 44
Johnson, E. Ned
See Johnson, Enid
Johnson, E(mil) Richard 1937- 104
Johnson, E(dward) W(arren) 1941- 29-32R
Johnson, Earl Jr. 1933- CANR-10
Earlier sketch in CA 61-64
Johnson, Earl S.
See Johnson, Earl Shepard
Johnson, Earl Shepard 1894-1986 Obituary 119
Johnson, Edgar (Raymond)
1912-1990 .... CANR-37
Earlier sketch in CA 9-12R
See also MAICYA
See also SATA 2
Johnson, Edgar 1901- 9-12R
See also DLB 103
Johnson, Edward A(ndrew) 1915- 37-40R
Johnson, Edward 1598-1672 .... DLB 24
Johnson, Edwin Clark (Toby) 1945- CANR-25
Earlier sketch in CA 107
Johnson, Eleanor
See Seymour, Dorothy Jane Z(ander)
Johnson, Eleanor Murdock
1892-1987 Obituary 123
See also SATA 54
Johnson, Electa Search 1909- 1-4R
Johnson, Elizabeth 1911-1984 .... CANR-4
Obituary 117
Earlier sketch in CA 1-4R
See also SATA 7, 39
Johnson, Ellen Argo 1933-1983 .... CANR-13
Obituary 110
Earlier sketch in CA 73-76
Johnson, Ellen H(ulda) 1910- CANR-15
Obituary 137
Earlier sketch in CA 37-40R
Johnson, Elmer Douglas 1915- CANR-3
Earlier sketch in CA 9-12R
Johnson, Elmer Hubert 1917- 13-16R
Johnson, Enid 1892- 73-76
Johnson, Eola 1909- 49-52
Johnson, Eric W(arner) 1918- CANR-4
Earlier sketch in CA 5-8R
See also SATA 8
Johnson, Eugene J. 1937- 127
Johnson, Evelyne 1922- CANR-21
Earlier sketch in CA 69-72
See also SATA 20
Johnson, Eyvind (Olof Verner)
1900-1976 .... CANR-34
Obituary 69-72
Earlier sketch in CA 73-76
See also CLC 14
Johnson, Falk S(immons) 1913- 17-20R
Johnson, Fenton 1888-1958 124
Brief entry 118
See also BLC 2
See also BW
See also DLB 45, 50
Johnson, Ferd 1905- 69-72
Johnson, Forrest B(ryant) 1935- 106
Johnson, Franklyn A(rthur) 1921- CANR-4
Earlier sketch in CA 1-4R
Johnson, Fred .... SATA 63
Johnson, Frederick 1932- 73-76
Johnson, Fridolf (Lester) 1905-1988 103
Obituary 126
Johnson, Frosty
See Johnson, Forrest B(ryant)
Johnson, G(eorge) Orville 1915- CANR-4
Earlier sketch in CA 1-4R
Johnson, Gaylord 1884- CAP-1
Earlier sketch in CA 9-10
See also SATA 7
Johnson, Geoffrey 1893-1966 .... CAP-1
Earlier sketch in CA 13-14
Johnson, George (Laclede) 1952- 123
Johnson, George 1917- 5-8R
Johnson, George 1952- 133
Johnson, Georgia Douglas (Camp)
1886-1966 125
See also BW
See also DLB 51
Johnson, Gerald White 1890-1980 85-88
Obituary 97-100
See also DLB 29
See also SATA 19, 28
Johnson, Gertrude F(alk) 1929- 57-60
Johnson, Greer 1920(?)-1974 Obituary 53-56
Johnson, H(arold) B(enjamin) Jr. 1931- 29-32R
Johnson, H(erbert) Webster 1906- CANR-4
Earlier sketch in CA 5-8R
Johnson, Halvard 1936- 33-36R
Johnson, Harold L. 1924- 13-16R
Johnson, Harold Scholl 1929- 37-40R
Johnson, Harold V. 1897- CANR-5
Earlier sketch in CA 1-4R
Johnson, Harper
See Johnson, E(ugene) Harper
Johnson, Harriett 1908-1987 Obituary 123
See also SATA 53
Johnson, Harry Alleyn 1921- CANR-31
Earlier sketch in CA 45-48
Johnson, Harry G(ordon) 1923-1977 .... CANR-29
Obituary 69-72
Earlier sketch in CA 5-8R
Johnson, Harry L. 1929- 29-32R
Johnson, Harry Morton 1917- 9-12R
Johnson, Harvey L(eroy) 1904- 37-40R
Johnson, Haynes Bonner 1931- CANR-12
Earlier sketch in CA 5-8R
Johnson, Helen (Louise) Kendrick
1844(?)-1917 Brief entry 123
Johnson, Helene 1907- .... DLB 51
Johnson, Henry
See Hammond, John (Henry Jr.)
Johnson, Herbert A(lan) 1934- CANR-4
Earlier sketch in CA 5-8R
Johnson, Herbert J. 1933- 29-32R
Johnson, Hildegard Binder 1908- CANR-3
Earlier sketch in CA 9-12R
Johnson, Howard Albert 1915-1974 .... 1-4R
Obituary 49-52
Johnson, Hubert C. 1930- 130
Johnson, Hugh 1939- CANR-39
Earlier sketches in CA 93-96, CANR-16
Johnson, Humphrey Wynne
1925-1976 Obituary 61-64
Johnson, Irma Bolan 1903- CANR-1
Earlier sketch in CA 1-4R
Johnson, Irving McClure 1905-1991 .... 1-4R
Obituary 133
Johnson, J. R.
See James, C(yril) L(ionel) R(obert)
Johnson, J. Stewart 1925- 127
Johnson, Jack
See Johnson, John Arthur
Johnson, Jalmar Edwin 1905- 5-8R
Johnson, James A(llen) 1932- Brief entry 110
Johnson, James Craig 1944- 53-56
Johnson, James E(dgar) 1927- 77-80
Johnson, James H(enry) 1930- CANR-11
Earlier sketch in CA 25-28R
Johnson, James J(ay) 1939- 33-36R
Johnson, James L. 1927- CANR-9
Earlier sketch in CA 21-24R
Johnson, James P(earce) 1937- 81-84
Johnson, James Ralph 1922- CANR-2
Earlier sketch in CA 1-4R
See also SATA 1
Johnson, James Rosser 1916- 9-12R
Johnson, James Turner 1938- 61-64
Johnson, James Weldon 1871-1938 125
Brief entry 104
See also BLC 2
See also BW
See also CDALB 1917-1929
See also DLB 51
See also MTCW
See also SATA 31
See also TCLC 3, 19
Johnson, James William 1927- 53-56
Johnson, Jane M(axine) 1914- 49-52
Johnson, Jane 1951- CANR-28
Earlier sketch in CA 110
See also SATA 48
Johnson, Jann
See Johnson, Paula Janice
Johnson, Jay 1951(?)-1990 Obituary 131
Johnson, Jean Dye 1920- 21-24R
Johnson, (Hettie) Jean 1937- 126
Johnson, Jerry Mack 1927- CANR-4
Earlier sketch in CA 53-56
Johnson, Jim
See Johnson, James A(llen)
Johnson, Jinna
See Johnson, Virginia
Johnson, Joan D. 1929- Brief entry 106
Johnson, Joan Helen 1931- 61-64
Johnson, Joan J. 1942- 122
See also SATA 59
Johnson, Joe Donald 1943- 57-60
Johnson, John Arthur
1878-1946 Brief entry 115
Johnson, John Bockover Jr.
1912-1972 Obituary 106
Johnson, John E(mil) 1929- 110
See also SATA 34
Johnson, John H(arold) 1918- 135
Brief entry 128
Johnson, John J. 1912- 9-12R
Johnson, John M(yrton) 1941- 93-96
Johnson, Johnni 1922- 13-16R
Johnson, Jory (F.) 1950- 137
Johnson, Joseph A. Jr.
1914(?)-1979 Obituary 89-92
Johnson, Joseph E(arl) 1946- 37-40R
Johnson, Joseph M.
1883(?)-1973 Obituary 45-48
Johnson, Josephine W(inslow)
1910-1990 .... 25-28R
Obituary 131
Johnson, Joy Duvall 1932- 110
Johnson, Joyce 1935- 129
Brief entry 125
See also CLC 58
Johnson, Karen 1939- 69-72
Johnson, Kathryn 1929- 33-36R
Johnson, Keith B(arnard) 1933- 29-32R
Johnson, Kendall 1928- 69-72
Johnson, Kenneth G(ardner) 1922- 41-44R
Johnson, Kenneth M(itchell) 1903- 5-8R

Johnson, Kim "Howard"
See Johnson, Kim
Johnson, Kim 1955- 133
Johnson, Kristi Planck 1944- 57-60
Johnson, L. D. 1916-1981 ....CANR-28
Earlier sketch in CA 33-36R
Johnson, La Verne B(ravo) 1925- 65-68
See also SATA 13
Johnson, Lady Bird
See Johnson, Claudia Alta (Taylor)
Johnson, Lemuel A. 1941- 53-56
Johnson, LeRoy C. 1937- 126
Johnson, Lewis Kerr 1904- 1-4R
Johnson, Lincoln F. Jr. 1920- 81-84
Johnson, Linnea 1946- 138
Johnson, Lionel (Pigot)
1867-1902 Brief entry 117
See also DLB 19
See also TCLC 19
Johnson, Lissa H(alls) 1955- 136
See also SATA 65
Johnson, Loch K. 1942- 121
Johnson, Lois Smith 1894- CAP-1
Earlier sketch in CA 9-10
See also SATA 6
Johnson, Lois Walfrid 1936- CANR-6
Earlier sketch in CA 57-60
See also SATA 22
Johnson, LouAnne 1953- 138
Johnson, Louis 1924- CANR-18
Earlier sketch in CA 101
Johnson, Luke Timothy 1943- 127
Brief entry 107
Johnson, Lyndon Baines 1908-1973 ....CANR-23
Obituary 41-44R
Earlier sketch in CA 53-56
Johnson, Lynn Eric 1932- Brief entry 108
Johnson, M. Glen 1936- 41-44R
Johnson, M. L.
See Abercrombie, M(innie) L(ouie) J(ohnson)
Johnson, Malcolm L. 1937- 69-72
Johnson, Malcolm (Malone) 1904-1976 69-72
Obituary 65-68
Johnson, Manly 1920- 89-92
Johnson, Margaret S(weet)
1893-1964 Obituary 113
See also SATA 35
Johnson, Margaret 1926- 37-40R
Johnson, Marilue Carolyn 1931- CANR-1
Earlier sketch in CA 45-48
Johnson, Marion Georgina Wikeley
1912-1980 ....9-12R
Obituary 97-100
Johnson, Mark 1949- 115
Johnson, Marshall D. 1935- 33-36R
Johnson, Mary Anne 1943- 53-56
Johnson, Mary Ellen 1949- 120
Johnson, Mary Frances K.
1929(?)-1979 Obituary 104
See also SATA 27
Johnson, Mary Louise
See King, Mary Louise
Johnson, Mary Ritz 1904- CAP-1
Earlier sketch in CA 9-10
Johnson, Maryanna 1925- 33-36R
Johnson, Maud Battle
1918(?)-1985 Obituary 117
See also SATA 46
Johnson, Maurice (O.) 1913-1978 ....CANR-20
Earlier sketch in CA 1-4R
Johnson, Mauritz (Jr.) 1922- 41-44R
Johnson, Mel
See Malzberg, Barry N(athaniel)
Johnson, Mendal W(illiam) 1928-1976 101
Johnson, Merle Allison 1934- 37-40R
Johnson, Michael L(illard) 1943- CANR-19
Earlier sketches in CA 53-56, CANR-4
Johnson, Michael P(aul) 1941- 132
Johnson, Mike
See Sharkey, John Michael
Johnson, Mildred D. 132
Johnson, Milton 1932- ....SATA 31
Johnson, Nancy E(dith) 1941- 125
Johnson, Neil (James) 1955- 123
Johnson, Nicholas 1934- 29-32R
Johnson, Niel M(elvin) 1931- 41-44R
Johnson, Nora 1933- 106
Johnson, Nunnally 1897-1977 81-84
Obituary 69-72
See also DLB 26
Johnson, Olga Weydemeyer 1901- CAP-2
Earlier sketch in CA 29-32
Johnson, Oliver A(dolph) 1923- CANR-12
Earlier sketch in CA 29-32R
Johnson, Owen 1878-1952 ....DLBY 87
Johnson, Pamela Hansford
1912-1981 ....CANR-28
Obituary 104
Earlier sketches in CA 1-4R, CANR-2
See also CLC 1, 7, 27
See also DLB 15
See also MTCW
Johnson, Pamela 1949- ....SATA 71
Johnson, Patrick Spencer 1938- 9-12R
Johnson, Paul (Bede) 1928- CANR-34
Earlier sketch in CA 17-20R
See also BEST 89:4
Johnson, Paul C(ornelius) 1904- 81-84
Johnson, Paul E(manuel) 1898-1974 ....13-16R
Obituary 134
Johnson, Paul Victor 1920- 1-4R
Johnson, Paula Janice 1946- 106
Johnson, Pauline B. 1-4R
Johnson, Pauline 1861-1913 ....DLB 92
Johnson, Penelope D(elafield) 1938- 124
Johnson, Peter 1930- 65-68
Johnson, Philip A(rthur) 1915-1991 ....13-16R
Obituary 133
Johnson, Philip Cortelyou 1906- Brief entry 106
Johnson, Phillip E. 1940- 136
Johnson, Phyllis (Anne) 1937-1985 126
Brief entry 108
Johnson, Pierce 1921- 41-44R
Johnson, Quentin G. 1930- 9-12R
Johnson, R(obbin) S(inclair) 1946- 29-32R
Johnson, Rachel H(arris)
1887-1983 Obituary 110
Johnson, Ralph W(hitney) 1923- 77-80
Johnson, Ray DeForest 1926-1989 65-68
Obituary 130
Johnson, Ray(mond Edward) 1927- 17-20R
Johnson, Raynor C(arey) 1901- Brief entry 115
Johnson, Rebecca L. 1956- 136
See also SATA 67
Johnson, Richard
See Richey, David
Johnson, Richard A(ugust) 1937- 37-40R
Johnson, Richard A. 1955- 135
Johnson, Richard B(righam) 1914-1977 ....41-44R
Johnson, Richard C. 1919- 33-36R
Johnson, Richard D(avid) 1927- 109
Johnson, Richard N(ewhall)
1900-1971 Obituary 104
Johnson, Richard R(igby) 1942- 116
Johnson, Richard Tanner
See Pascale, Richard Tanner
Johnson, Robert A. 1921- 61-64
Johnson, Robert C(lyde) 1919- 5-8R
Johnson, Robert E. 1908(?)-1989 Obituary 128
Johnson, Robert Erwin 1923- 37-40R
Johnson, Robert I(var) 1933- 53-56
Johnson, Robert J. 1933- 21-24R
Johnson, Robert L(eon Jr.) 1930- 33-36R
Johnson, Robert L. 1919- 33-36R
Johnson, Robert Owen 1926- 33-36R
Johnson, Robert Sherlaw 1932- 61-64
Johnson, Robert W(illard) 1921- 17-20R
Johnson, Roger N(ylund) 1939- 53-56
Johnson, Ronald C. 1927- 81-84
Johnson, Ronald M(aberry) 1936- 126
Brief entry 108
Johnson, Ronald 1935- CANR-20
Earlier sketches in CA 9-12R, CANR-4
Johnson, Rossall J(ames) 1917- 21-24R
Johnson, Ruby Kelley 1928- 33-36R
Johnson, Ruth I.
See Jay, Ruth I(ngrid)
Johnson, (Walter) Ryerson 1901- CANR-2
Earlier sketch in CA 5-8R
See also SATA 10
Johnson, S(amuel) Lawrence
1909-1978 ....CANR-12
Earlier sketch in CA 29-32R
Johnson, Sabina Thorne
See Thorne, Sabina
Johnson, Sam Houston 1914(?)-1978 89-92
Obituary 81-84
Johnson, Samuel A(ugustus) 1895- 17-20R
Johnson, Samuel 1696-1772 ....DLB 24
Johnson, Samuel
1709-1784 ....CDBLB 1660-1789
See also DLB 39, 95, 104
See also WLC
Johnson, Samuel 1822-1882 ....DLB 1
Johnson, Sherman E(lbridge) 1908- 53-56
Johnson, Sherman Ellsworth
1896-1978 Obituary 77-80
Johnson, Shirley K(ing) 1927- 9-12R
See also SATA 10
Johnson, Siddie Joe 1905-1977 Obituary 106
See also SATA 20
Johnson, Sonia 1936- 118
Johnson, Spencer 1938- 110
See also SATA 38
Johnson, Stanley J. F.
1920(?)-1978 Obituary 77-80
Johnson, Stanley L(ewis) 1920- 17-20R
Johnson, Stanley (Patrick) 1940- CANR-13
Earlier sketch in CA 21-24R
Johnson, (John) Stephen 1947- 107
Johnson, (Edward) Stowers 5-8R
Johnson, Susan E. 1940- 138
Johnson, Susan (Ruth) 1956- 137
Johnson, Sylvia A. ....SATA 52
Johnson, Thomas Frank 1920- 9-12R
Johnson, Thomas Herbert 1902-1985 124
Johnson, Thomas William 1946- Brief entry 110
Johnson, Una E. 134
Brief entry 109
Johnson, Uwe 1934-1984 ....CANR-39
Obituary 112
Earlier sketches in CA 1-4R, CANR-1
See also CLC 5, 10, 15, 40
See also DLB 75
See also MTCW
Johnson, Van L(oran) 1908- 37-40R
Johnson, Vernon E(dwin) 1920- 93-96
Johnson, Victor Hugo 1912- Brief entry 110
Johnson, Virginia E. 1925- CANR-34
Earlier sketch in CA 21-24R
Johnson, Virginia W(eisel) 1910- 17-20R
Johnson, Virginia 1914-1975 ....CAP-2
Earlier sketch in CA 33-36
Johnson, W. Bolingbroke
See Bishop, Morris
Johnson, W(illiam) Branch 1893- CANR-5
Earlier sketch in CA 5-8R
Johnson, W(illiam) E(rnest)
1858-1931 Brief entry 122
Johnson, W(alter) R(alph) 1933- CANR-9
Earlier sketch in CA 65-68
Johnson, W(endell) Stacy 1927-1990 ....CANR-17
Obituary 131
Earlier sketches in CA 1-4R, CANR-2
Johnson, Walter Frank Jr. 1914- 5-8R
Johnson, Walter 1915-1985 89-92
Obituary 116
Johnson, Warren Arthur 1937- 33-36R
Johnson, Warren T(hurston) 1925- 131
Johnson, Wayne G(ustave) 1930- 113
Johnson, Wayne 1956- 135
Johnson, Wendell (Andrew Leroy)
1906-1965 ....CANR-1
Earlier sketch in CA 1-4R
Johnson, Willard R(aymond) 1935- 105
Johnson, William Alexander 1932- 5-8R
Johnson, William C(lark Jr.) 1945- CANR-8
Earlier sketch in CA 61-64
Johnson, William R. CANR-25
Earlier sketches in CA 17-20R, CANR-7
See also SATA 38
Johnson, William Weber 1909- 17-20R
See also SATA 7
Johnson, Winifred (MacNally) 1905- 5-8R
Johnson Abercrombie, M. L.
See Abercrombie, M(innie) L(ouie) J(ohnson)
Johnson-Marshall, Percy E. A. 1915- 21-24R
John-Steiner, Vera P(olgar) 121
Johnston, A(aron) Montgomery 1915- CANR-11
Earlier sketch in CA 29-32R
Johnston, Agnes Christine
See Dazey, Agnes J(ohnston)
Johnston, Alan (William) 1942- 103
Johnston, Albert H. 1914- 69-72
Johnston, Angus James II 1916- 9-12R
Johnston, Annie Fellows
1863-1931 Brief entry 116
See also DLB 42
See also SATA 37
Johnston, (William) Arnold 1942- 77-80
Johnston, Arthur 1924- 21-24R
Johnston, Arvin Harry 1906- 1-4R
Johnston, Basil H. 1929- CANR-28
Earlier sketches in CA 69-72, CANR-11
See also DLB 60
Johnston, Bernard 1934- 17-20R
Johnston, Bernice Houle 1914-1971 ....CAP-2
Earlier sketch in CA 33-36
Johnston, Brenda A(rlivia) 1944- 57-60
Johnston, Brian 1932- 65-68
Johnston, Bruce F(oster) 1919- CANR-14
Earlier sketch in CA 41-44R
Johnston, Charles (Hepburn)
1912-1986 ....CANR-5
Obituary 119
Earlier sketch in CA 13-16R
Johnston, Colin 1946- 108
Johnston, Dan 1912- 123
Johnston, David (Cay Boyle) 1948- 131
Johnston, (William) Denis 1901-1984 ....CAP-2
Obituary 113
Earlier sketch in CA 21-22
See also DLB 10
Johnston, Dorothy Grunbock
1915-1979 ....CANR-5
Earlier sketch in CA 5-8R
See also SATA 54
Johnston, Ellen Turlington 1929- 65-68
Johnston, Fran(ces Jonsson) 1925- 13-16R
Johnston, Francis E. 1931- CANR-4
Earlier sketch in CA 53-56
Johnston, George (Benson) 1913- CANR-20
Earlier sketches in CA 1-4R, CANR-5
See also CLC 51
See also DLB 88
Johnston, George Burke 1907- CAP-1
Earlier sketch in CA 17-18
Johnston, George 1913- CANR-15
Earlier sketch in CA 89-92
Johnston, Ginny 1946- ....SATA 60
Johnston, Gordon (Frederick) 1920-1983 122
Johnston, H(ugh) A(nthony) S(tephen)
1913-1967 ....CAP-2
Earlier sketch in CA 21-22
See also SATA 14
Johnston, H(ugh) J(ames) M(orton)
1939- 41-44R
Johnston, Hank
See Johnston, Henry
Johnston, Henry 1922- 25-28R
Johnston, Herbert (Leo) 1912- 5-8R
Johnston, Hugh Buckner 1913- 69-72
Johnston, Janet 1944- ....SATA 71
Johnston, Jennifer 1930- 85-88
See also CLC 7
See also DLB 14
Johnston, Jill 1929- 53-56
Johnston, Johanna 1914(?)-1982 ....CANR-7
Obituary 108
Earlier sketch in CA 57-60
See also SATA 12, 33
Johnston, John H(ubert) 1921- 9-12R
Johnston, John M.
1898(?)-1979 Obituary 89-92
Johnston, Kenneth R(ichard) 1938- 121
Johnston, Leonard 1920- CANR-11
Earlier sketch in CA 13-16R
Johnston, Lynn (Beverley) 1947- 110
Johnston, Marguerite 1917- 138
Johnston, Mary E(lizabeth)
1919-1989 Obituary 128
Johnston, Mary 1870-1936 Brief entry 109
See also DLB 9
Johnston, Minton C(oyne) 1900- 5-8R
Johnston, Mireille 1940- 49-52
Johnston, Norma
See St. John, Nicole
See also SATA 29
Johnston, Norman (Bruce) 1921- CANR-18
Earlier sketch in CA 93-96
Johnston, Norman J. 1918- 120
Johnston, Portia
See Takakjian, Portia
Johnston, R(onald) J(ohn) 1941- CANR-18
Earlier sketch in CA 101
Johnston, Randolph W(ardell) 1904- CANR-15
Earlier sketch in CA 85-88
Johnston, Richard Malcolm 1822-1898 ....DLB 74
Johnston, Richard W(yckoff)
1915-1981 Obituary 104
Johnston, Robert Kent 1945- 104
Johnston, Ronald Carlyle
1907-1990 Obituary 131
Johnston, Ronald 1926- 13-16R
Johnston, Russell G. 1933- 118
Johnston, S(amuel) Paul
1899-1985 Obituary 117
Johnston, Stanley H(oward) Jr. 1946- 137
Johnston, Susan Taylor 1942- CANR-15
Earlier sketch in CA 41-44R
See also Johnston, Tony
Johnston, Terry C(onrad) 1947- 113
Johnston, Thomas E. 1931- 13-16R
Johnston, Thomas 1945- 104
Johnston, Tony
See Johnston, Susan Taylor
See also SATA 8
Johnston, Velma B.
1912(?)-1977 Obituary 69-72
Johnston, Wayne 1958- 125
Johnston, William M(urray) 1936- 37-40R
Johnston, William 1924- 85-88
Johnston, William 1925- 33-36R
Johnstone, Charles 1719(?)-1800(?) ....DLB 39
Johnstone, D(onald) Bruce 1909- 104
Johnstone, Henry W(ebb) Jr. 1920- 1-4R
Johnstone, Iain 1943- 108
Johnstone, Kathleen Yerger 1906- 9-12R
Johnstone, Keith 129
Johnstone, Lammy Olcott 1949- CANR-14
Earlier sketch in CA 81-84
Johnstone, Parker Lochiel 1903- 69-72
Johnstone, Rex
See Chapman, Frank M(onroe)
Johnstone, Robert Morton Jr. 1939- 81-84
Johnstone, Robert 1951- 118
Johnstone, T(homas) M(uir)
1924-1983 Obituary 114
Johnstone, Ted
See McDaniel, David (Edward)
Johnstone, William D(avid) G(ordon)
1935- 77-80
Johnston-Saint, Peter
1889-1974 Obituary 53-56
John XXIII, Pope 1881-1963 134
Obituary 113
Joiner, Charles A(drian) 1932- 77-80
Joiner, Charles W(ycliffe) 1916- CANR-1
Earlier sketch in CA 1-4R
Joiner, Edward Earl 1924- 49-52
Joiner, Verna J(ones) 1896- 1-4R
Joki, Virginia (Carville)
1909(?)-1986 Obituary 120
Jolas, Eugene 1894-1952 Brief entry 107
See also DLB 4, 45
Joliat, Eugene 1910- 49-52
Joliffe, John E(dward) A(ustin) 1891-1964 ....5-8R
Jolin, Stephen Towne 1941- 45-48
Jolivet, R(egis) 1891-1966 ....CAP-1
Earlier sketch in CA 9-10
Joll, (Dowrish) Evelyn (Louis) 1925- 101
Joll, James (Bysse) 1918- CANR-7
Earlier sketch in CA 5-8R
Jolley, (Monica) Elizabeth 1923- 127
See also CAAS 13
See also CLC 46
Jolley, (Stephen) Nicholas 1948- 120
Jolliffe, H(arold) R(ichard) 1904-1978 ....1-4R
Obituary 103
Jolliffe, John (Hedworth) 1935- 133
Jolly, Alison 1937- CANR-15
Earlier sketch in CA 41-44R
Jolly, Clifford J. 1939- Brief entry 108
Jolly, Cyril Arthur 1910- CAP-1
Earlier sketch in CA 9-10
Jolly, Hugh R. 1918-1986 85-88
Obituary 118
Jolly, W(illiam) P(ercy) 1922- CANR-4
Earlier sketch in CA 53-56
Jolly Cholly
See Grimm, Charles John
Jolson, Marvin A(rnold) 1922- CANR-1
Earlier sketch in CA 49-52
Joly, Cyril Bencraft 1918- CAP-1
Earlier sketch in CA 9-10
Jonas, A(dolphe) David 1913- 107
Jonas, Ann 1919- 105
Jonas, Ann 1932- 136
Brief entry 118
See also CLR 12
See also MAICYA
See also SATA 42, 50
Jonas, Arthur 1930- 13-16R
Jonas, Carl 1913-1976 ....9-12R
Obituary 69-72
Jonas, Doris F(rances) 1916- CANR-8
Earlier sketch in CA 61-64
Jonas, George 1935- CANR-32
Earlier sketch in CA 29-32R
Jonas, Gerald 1935- 65-68
Jonas, Hans 1903- CANR-23
Earlier sketches in CA 61-64, CANR-7
Jonas, Ilsedore B. 1920- 33-36R
Jonas, Klaus W(erner) 1920- CANR-2
Earlier sketch in CA 1-4R

Jonas, Manfred 1927- CANR-8
Earlier sketch in CA 21-24R
Jonas, Norman N. 1931-1988 Obituary 125
Jonas, Paul 1922- CANR-13
Earlier sketch in CA 73-76
Jonas, Steven 1936- 89-92
Jonassen, Christen T(onnes) 1912- 41-44R
Joncich, Geraldine
See Clifford, Geraldine Joncich
Jones, A(rnold) H(ugh) M(artin)
1904-1970 Obituary 89-92
Jones, A(rthur) Morris 1899- CAP-1
Earlier sketch in CA 13-14
Jones, Adam Mars
See Mars-Jones, Adam
Jones, Adrienne 1915- CANR-28
Earlier sketch in CA 33-36R
See also SAAS 10
See also SATA 7
Jones, Alan Griffith 1943- CANR-19
Earlier sketch in CA 103
Jones, Alan Moore Jr. 1942- 53-56
Jones, Alan William 1940- 117
Jones, Alex S. 1946- 135
Jones, Alexander 1906-1970 .... CANR-2
Obituary 103
Earlier sketch in CA 1-4R
Jones, Alfred Winslow 1900-1989 Obituary 128
Jones, Alice C. 1853-1933 .... DLB 92
Jones, Allan Gwynne
See Gwynne-Jones, Allan
Jones, Andrew (Eric) 1950- 111
Jones, Andrew 1921- 93-96
Jones, Annabel
See Lewis, Mary (Christianna)
Jones, Anne Hudson 1944- 135
Jones, Antony Armstrong
See Armstrong-Jones, Antony (Charles Robert)
Jones, Archer 1926- CANR-18
Earlier sketches in CA 1-4R, CANR-4
Jones, Archie N(eff) 1900- CAP-1
Earlier sketch in CA 13-16
Jones, Arthur F(rederick) 1945- 81-84
Jones, Arthur Glyn Prys
See Prys-Jones, Arthur Glyn
Jones, (Alun) Arthur Gwynne 1919- 128
Brief entry 120
Jones, Arthur Hope
See Hope-Jones, Arthur
Jones, Arthur (Mervyn) Keppel
See Keppel-Jones, Arthur (Mervyn)
Jones, Arthur Llewellyn
1863-1947 Brief entry 104
See also Machen, Arthur
Jones, Aubrey 1911- 103
Jones, Barbara (Mildred) 1917(?)-1978 .... CANR-4
Obituary 81-84
Earlier sketch in CA 1-4R
Jones, Bessie 1902-1984 Obituary 114
Jones, Betty Millsaps 1940- 109
See also SATA 54
Jones, Bill
See Jones, William David Anthony
Jones, Billy M(ac) 1925- CANR-25
Earlier sketches in CA 21-24R, CANR-10
Jones, Bob
See Jones, Robert Reynolds Jr.
Jones, Bobby
See Jones, Robert Tyre Jr.
Jones, Brennon 1945- 136
Jones, Brian 1938- Brief entry 119
Jones, Bryan L. 1945- 110
Jones, C(lifton) Clyde 1922- 109
Jones, C. M.
See Jones, Clarence Medlycott
Jones, C(harles) Robert 1932- 129
Jones, Calico
See Richardson, Gladwell
Jones, Candy 1925-1990 107
Obituary 130
Jones, Capt. Wilbur
See Edwards, William B(ennett)
Jones, Carolyn (Sue) 1933-1983 .... 29-32R
Obituary 110
Jones, Charles Alfred 1921-1982 Obituary 107
Jones, Charles C. Jr. 1831-1893 .... DLB 30
Jones, Charles Edwin 1932- CANR-23
Earlier sketch in CA 49-52
Jones, Charles M(artin) 1912- 129
See also Jones, Chuck
See also SATA 53
Jones, Charles O(scar) 1931- CANR-7
Earlier sketch in CA 17-20R
Jones, Charles W(illiams) 1905- 13-16R
Jones, Charles 1910- CAP-1
Earlier sketch in CA 9-10
Jones, Cheslyn Peter Montague
1918-1987(?) Obituary 125
Jones, Christina Hendry 1896- 73-76
Jones, (Audrey) Christine 1937- 61-64
Jones, Christopher 1937- 21-24R
Jones, Chuck
See Jones, Charles M(artin)
See also AAYA 2
Jones, Clarence Medlycott
1913(?)-1986 Obituary 118
Jones, Clifford M(erton) 1902- 17-20R
Jones, Craig 1945- CANR-34
Earlier sketch in CA 81-84
Jones, Cranston E(dward) 1918-1991 .... CANR-26
Obituary 134
Earlier sketch in CA 1-4R
Jones, Cyril Meredith 1904- CAP-2
Earlier sketch in CA 23-24
Jones, D(ennis) F(eltham) Brief entry 111
Jones, D(ouglas) G(ordon) 1929- CANR-13
Earlier sketch in CA 29-32R
See also CLC 10
See also DLB 53
Jones, D(avid) Gareth 1940- 106
Jones, D(onald) L(ewis) 1925- 25-28R
Jones, D(avid) Mervyn 1922- 21-24R
Jones, Daisy (Marvel) 1906- 17-20R
Jones, Dan Burne 1908- 65-68
Jones, Daniel 1881-1967 .... CANR-6
Earlier sketch in CA 5-8R
Jones, Daryl (Emrys) 1946- 134
Jones, David Arthur 1946- CANR-13
Earlier sketch in CA 73-76
Jones, David (Erik) Hay 1959- 133
Jones, David (Michael) 1895-1974 .... CANR-28
Obituary 53-56
Earlier sketch in CA 9-12R
See also CDBLB 1945-1960
See also CLC 2, 4, 7, 13, 42
See also DLB 20, 100
See also MTCW
Jones, David Pryce
See Pryce-Jones, David
Jones, David Rhodes 1932- 101
Jones, David Richard 1942- 125
Jones, David Robert 1947- 103
See also Bowie, David
Jones, David W(yn) 1950- 131
Jones, Diana Wynne 1934- CANR-26
Earlier sketches in CA 49-52, CANR-4
See also CLC 26
See also CLR 23
See also MAICYA
See also SAAS 7
See also SATA 9, 70
Jones, Dolores Blythe 1947- 120
Jones, Don 1924- 125
Jones, (Gene) Donald 1931- CANR-34
Earlier sketches in CA 85-88, CANR-15
Jones, Donald (Lawrence) 1938- 17-20R
Jones, Dorothy Holder 1925(?)-1991 .... 9-12R
Obituary 134
Jones, Dorothy V. 1927- 138
Jones, Douglas C(lyde) 1924- CANR-12
Earlier sketch in CA 21-24R
See also SATA 52
Jones, DuPre Anderson 1937- 21-24R
Jones, E(li) Stanley 1884-1973 93-96
Obituary 41-44R
Jones, E(ndsley) Terrence 1941- 33-36R
Jones, E(lbert) Winston 1911- 13-16R
Jones, Ebenezer 1820-1860 .... DLB 32
Jones, Edgar A(llen) Jr. 1921- 89-92
Jones, (Hilary) Edgar 1953- 118
Jones, Edward A(llen)
See Larson, Victor E.
Jones, Edward A(llen) 1903- 25-28R
Jones, Edward E(llsworth) 1926- 17-20R
Jones, Edward H(arral) Jr. 1922- 13-16R
Jones, Eldred D(urosimi) 1925- CANR-30
Earlier sketch in CA 45-48
Jones, Elizabeth B(rown) 1907- 61-64
Jones, Elizabeth Orton 1910- 77-80
See also SATA 18
Jones, Elwyn 1923-1982 .... CANR-21
Obituary 106
Earlier sketch in CA 69-72
Jones, Emlyn (David) 1912-1975 .... CAP-2
Earlier sketch in CA 23-24
Jones, Emrys 1920- 17-20R
Jones, Enid (Mary) Huws 1911- 49-52
Jones, Eric Lionel 1936- 104
Jones, (Alfred) Ernest
1879-1958 Brief entry 121
Jones, Ernest 1819-1868 .... DLB 32
Jones, Eva (Eleonore) 1913- 131
Jones, Evan David 1903-1987 Obituary 122
Jones, Evan 1915- CANR-6
Earlier sketch in CA 9-12R
See also SATA 3
Jones, Eve (Spiro-John) 1924- 1-4R
Jones, Everett L(ee) 1915-1990 .... 13-16R
Obituary 131
Jones, Ezra Earl 1939- 57-60
Jones, F(rank) Lancaster 1937- 29-32R
Jones, Faustine Childress
See Jones-Wilson, Faustine C(hildress)
Jones, Felix Edward Aylmer 1889- CAP-1
Earlier sketch in CA 9-10
Jones, Francis P(rice) 1890- 9-12R
Jones, Frank E(dward) 1917- 13-16R
Jones, Frank Pierce 1905-1975 Obituary 110
Jones, Frank 1937- 119
Jones, Franklin Ross 1921- 53-56
Jones, Frederick George Hall
See Hall-Jones, Frederick George
Jones, G. Brian 1935- 128
Jones, G(eorge) Curtis 1911- CANR-3
Earlier sketch in CA 5-8R
Jones, G(wyn) O(wain) 1917- 25-28R
Jones, G(eorge) William 1931- CANR-11
Earlier sketch in CA 21-24R
Jones, Gareth (Elwyn) 1939- CANR-19
Earlier sketch in CA 102
Jones, Garth N(elson) 1925- 81-84
Jones, Gary M(artin) 1925- 17-20R
Jones, Gayl 1949- CANR-27
Earlier sketch in CA 77-80
See also BLC 2
See also BW
See also CLC 6, 9
See also DLB 33
See also MTCW
Jones, Gene 1928- 21-24R
Jones, Geoffrey (Gareth) 1952- 122
Jones, George Chetwynd Griffith
See Griffith-Jones, George Chetwynd
Jones, George Fenwick 1916- CANR-7
Earlier sketch in CA 13-16R
Jones, George Hilton 1924- 33-36R
Jones, George Thaddeus 1917- 53-56
Jones, Geraldine
See McCaughrean, Geraldine
Jones, Gillingham
See Hamilton, Charles (Harold St. John)
Jones, (Morgan) Glyn 1905- CANR-3
Earlier sketch in CA 9-12R
See also DLB 15
Jones, Gordon W(illis) 1915- 45-48
Jones, Goronwy J(ohn) 1915- 9-12R
Jones, Grant D(rummond) 1941- 129
Jones, Guy Salisbury
See Salisbury-Jones, Guy
Jones, Gwen 1951(?)-1988 Obituary 124
Jones, Gwendolyn 33-36R
Jones, Gwilym Peredur
1892-1975 Obituary 57-60
Jones, Gwyn 1907- 124
Brief entry 117
See also DLB 15
Jones, Gwyneth A. 1952- 107
Jones, H(ouston) G(wynne) 1924- CANR-13
Earlier sketch in CA 33-36R
Jones, H(enry) John F(ranklin) 1924- 9-12R
Jones, Hardin Blair 1914-1978 Obituary 77-80
Jones, Harold
See Page, Gerald W(ilburn)
Jones, Harold 1904- CANR-15
Earlier sketch in CA 85-88
See also SATA 14
Jones, Harriet
See Marble, Harriet Clement
Jones, Harry Lee 1921(?)-1983 Obituary 110
Jones, Helen Hinckley 1903- CANR-5
Earlier sketch in CA 5-8R
See also SATA 26
Jones, Helen L(ouise) 1903-1973 Obituary 104
See also SATA 22
Jones, Helen 1917- 105
Jones, (Max Him) Henri 1921- 41-44R
Jones, Henry Albert 1889-1981 Obituary 103
Jones, Henry Arthur 1851-1929 Brief entry 110
See also DLB 10
Jones, Hettie 1934- 81-84
See also SATA 27, 42
Jones, Hortense P. 1918- 61-64
See also SATA 9
Jones, Howard Mumford 1892-1980 85-88
Obituary 97-100
Jones, Howard P(alfry) 1899-1973 Obituary 111
Jones, Howard 1940- 85-88
Jones, Hugh 1692(?)-1760 .... DLB 24
Jones, Iris Sanderson 1932- 73-76
Jones, J. Barrie 1946- 131
Jones, J. Farragut
See Levinson, Leonard
Jones, J(ohn) Ithel 1911- CAP-2
Earlier sketch in CA 25-28
Jones, Jack
See Jones, James Larkin
Jones, Jack 1884-1970 Obituary 115
Jones, Jack 1913-1984 Obituary 113
Brief entry 109
Jones, Jack 1924- 85-88
Jones, Jacqueline 1948- 122
See also BW
Jones, James C(linton) 1922- 69-72
Jones, James Henry
1907(?)-1977 Obituary 73-76
Jones, James Larkin 1913- CANR-27
Earlier sketch in CA 109
Jones, James T. 1948- 124
Jones, James 1921-1977 .... CANR-6
Obituary 69-72
Earlier sketch in CA 1-4R
See also AITN 1, 2
See also CLC 1, 3, 10, 39
See also DLB 2
See also MTCW
Jones, Jeanie Schmit Kayser
See Kayser-Jones, Jeanie Schmit
Jones, Jeanne 1937- CANR-28
Earlier sketches in CA 61-64, CANR-12
Jones, Jeannette 1944- 110
Jones, Jenkin Lloyd 1911- 9-12R
Jones, Jessie Mae Orton
1887(?)-1983 Obituary 111
See also SATA 37
Jones, Jimmy
See Jones, Clarence Medlycott
Jones, Jo 33-36R
Jones, Joanna
See Burke, John (Frederick)
Jones, Johanna 1909- 118
Jones, John Bush 1940- 33-36R
Jones, John F(inbar) 1929- 130
Jones, John Griffin 1955- 113
Jones, John J.
See Lovecraft, H(oward) P(hillips)
Jones, John Paul Jr. 1912- CANR-11
Earlier sketch in CA 69-72
Jones, John Philip 1930- 130
Jones, John R(obert) 1926- 116
Jones, Joseph Jay 1908- CANR-16
Earlier sketches in CA 1-4R, CANR-1
Jones, Joseph L. 1897-1980 Obituary 102
Jones, Joseph Marion Jr.
1908-1990 Obituary 132
Jones, Judith Paterson 1938- 106
Jones, K. Westcott
See Westcott-Jones, K(enneth)
Jones, Karen Midkiff 1948- 104
Jones, Katharine M(acbeth) 1900- 5-8R
Jones, Kathleen Eve 1944- 102
Jones, Kathleen 1922- 81-84
Jones, Kaylie (Ann) 1960- 123
Jones, Ken D(uane) 1930- CANR-31
Earlier sketch in CA 49-52
Jones, Kenley 1935- 69-72
Jones, Kenneth E(ffner) 1920- 57-60
Jones, Kenneth Glyn 1915- 115
Jones, Kenneth LaMar 1931- 53-56
Jones, Kenneth S. 1919- 21-24R
Jones, Kenneth W. 1934- Brief entry 113
Jones, Landon Y(oung) 1943- 105
Jones, Leon 1936- 101
Obituary 137
Jones, Leonidas M(onroe) Sr. 1923- 45-48
Jones, LeRoi
See Baraka, Amiri
See also CLC 1, 2, 3, 5, 10, 14
Jones, Leroy P. 1941- 118
Jones, Lewis Pinckney 1916- 61-64
Jones, Lewis 1897-1939 .... DLB 15
Jones, Linda Phillips
See Phillips-Jones, Linda
Jones, Lisa 1961- 130
Jones, Lloyd S(cott) 1931- CANR-4
Earlier sketch in CA 1-4R
Jones, Louis B. .... CLC 65
Jones, Louis C(lark) 1908-1990 .... 5-8R
Obituary 133
Jones, Lyndon Hamer 1927- CANR-22
Earlier sketch in CA 103
Jones, M(arjorie) L(ilian) Glynne
See Glynne-Jones, M(arjorie) L(ilian)
Jones, Madeline Adams 1913- 21-24R
Jones, Madison (Percy Jr.) 1925- CANR-7
Earlier sketch in CA 13-16R
See also CAAS 11
See also CLC 4
Jones, Major J. 1919- 33-36R
Jones, Major Joseph
See Thompson, William Tappan
Jones, Malcolm V(ince) 1940- 103
Jones, Maldwyn Allen 1922- CANR-4
Earlier sketch in CA 1-4R
Jones, Marc Edmund 1888- 33-36R
Jones, Margaret Boone 25-28R
Jones, Margaret E. W. 1938- 37-40R
Jones, Marvin 1886-1976 Obituary 65-68
Jones, Mary Alice 1898(?)-1980 .... 17-20R
Obituary 118
See also SATA 6
Jones, Mary Brush 1925- 25-28R
Jones, Mary (Elizabeth) 1942- 120
Jones, Mary Voell 1933- 21-24R
Jones, Maxwell (Shaw) 1907- 25-28R
Jones, Maynard Benedict
1904-1972 Obituary 93-96
Jones, McClure 112
See also SATA 34
Jones, Mervyn 1922- CANR-1
Earlier sketch in CA 45-48
See also CAAS 5
See also CLC 10, 52
See also MTCW
Jones, Michael (Christopher Emlyn)
1940- CANR-20
Earlier sketch in CA 104
Jones, Michael Owen 1942- 101
Jones, Mick 1956(?)-
See The Clash
See also CLC 30
Jones, Miriam
See Schuchman, Joan
Jones, Morris Val 1914- 5-8R
Jones, Nard
See Jones, Maynard Benedict
Jones, Nettie (Pearl) 1941- 137
See also CLC 34
Jones, Noel 1939- 81-84
Jones, O(wen) R(ogers) 1922- 1-4R
Jones, Oakah L. Jr. 1930- CANR-8
Earlier sketch in CA 17-20R
Jones, Orlando
See Looker, Antonina (Hansell)
Jones, P(eter) M(ichael) 1949- 122
Jones, Pat
See Jones, Virgil Carrington
Jones, Paul Davis 1940- 49-52
Jones, Paul J. 1897(?)-1974 Obituary 53-56
Jones, Pearl Binder Elwyn
See Elwyn-Jones, Pearl Binder
Jones, Peggy 1947- 109
Jones, Penelope 1938- CANR-14
Earlier sketch in CA 81-84
See also SATA 31
Jones, Peter (Austin) 1929- CANR-4
Earlier sketch in CA 53-56
Jones, Peter d'Alroy 1931- CANR-20
Earlier sketches in CA 5-8R, CANR-3
Jones, Peter Gaylord 1929- 73-76
Jones, Peter 1920- 103
Jones, Peter 1921- 5-8R
Jones, Philip Howard 1937- 102
Jones, Phillip L. 1928(?)-1979 Obituary 89-92
Jones, Pirkle 1914- 29-32R
Jones, Preston 1936-1979 73-76
Obituary 89-92
See also CLC 10
See also DLB 7
Jones, R(ichard) Ben(jamin) 1933- CANR-12
Earlier sketch in CA 25-28R
Jones, R(oger) W(illiam) 1941- 128
Jones, Ray O. 1930- 89-92
Jones, Raymond F. 1915- Brief entry 106

Jones, Rebecca C(astaldi) 1947- CANR-22
Earlier sketch in CA 106
See also SATA 33
Jones, Reginald L(anier) 1931- 45-48
Jones, Reginald Victor 1911- 103
Jones, Richard Allan 1943- 103
Jones, Richard Granville 1926- 112
Jones, Richard H(utton) 1914- 49-52
Jones, Richard M(atthew) 1925- 93-96
Jones, Richard 1926- CANR-2
Earlier sketch in CA 49-52
Jones, Richard 1953- 121
Jones, Robert B(rinkley) 1942- 114
Jones, Robert Emmet 1928- CANR-2
Earlier sketch in CA 1-4R
Jones, Robert Epes 1908- CAP-1
Earlier sketch in CA 13-14
Jones, Robert F(rancis) 1934- CANR-2
Earlier sketch in CA 49-52
See also CLC 7
Jones, Robert Godwin
See Godwin-Jones, Robert
Jones, Robert H(uhn) 1927- CANR-2
Earlier sketch in CA 5-8R
Jones, Robert O(wen) 1928- 29-32R
Jones, Robert R(ussell) 1927- 69-72
Jones, Robert Reynolds Jr. 1911- CANR-11
Earlier sketch in CA 25-28R
Jones, Robert Tyre Jr. 1902-1971 Obituary 113
Jones, Robin Lloyd
See Lloyd-Jones, Robin
Jones, Rod 1953- 128
See also CLC 50
Jones, Rodney W(illiam) 1943- CANR-33
Earlier sketch in CA 113
Jones, Rodney 1950- 133
See also DLB 120
Jones, Roger Stanley 1934- 113
Jones, Roger (Winston) 1939- 101
Jones, Royston Oscar 1925-1974 85-88
Jones, Ruby Aileen Hiday 1908- CAP-1
Earlier sketch in CA 11-12
Jones, Russell Bradley 1894- 1-4R
Jones, Russell 1918-1979 106
Obituary 89-92
Jones, Ruth Ann 1928- 107
Jones, Ruth Dorval 93-96
Jones, Sally Roberts 1935- 102
Jones, Sandra L.
See Ireland, Sandra L(eora) Jones
Jones, Sandra (Redmond) 1937- 132
Jones, Sandy 1943- CANR-15
Earlier sketch in CA 85-88
Jones, Sanford W.
See Thorn, John
Jones, Scott N. 1929- 29-32R
Jones, Seaborn (Gustavus) Jr. 1942- 104
Jones, Simmons 1920- 136
Jones, Simon (C.) 1957- 128
Jones, Sonia 1938- 127
Jones, Stacy V(anderhoof) 1894-1989 ....1-4R
Obituary 127
Jones, Stanley L(lewellyn) 1918- 9-12R
Jones, Stephen D(wight) 1948- 112
Jones, Stephen (Phillip) 1935- CANR-2
Earlier sketch in CA 49-52
Jones, Stephen 1953- 134
Jones, Susan Mann
See Mann, Susan
Jones, T(homas) Anthony 1940- 110
Jones, Tad
See Jones, Thaddeus B.
Jones, Terence Graham Parry 1942- CANR-35
Brief entry 112
Earlier sketch in CA 116
See also Jones, Terry
and Monty Python
See also CLC 21
See also SATA 51
Jones, Terry
See Jones, Terence Graham Parry
See also SATA 67
Jones, Thaddeus B. 1952- 125
Jones, Theador Edward 1937- 138
Jones, Thomas B. 1929- 25-28R
Jones, Thomas M(artin) 1916- 29-32R
Jones, Thomas W(arren) 1947- 53-56
Jones, Tim(othy) Wynne
See Wynne-Jones, Tim(othy)
Jones, Tom 1928- CANR-6
Earlier sketch in CA 53-56
Jones, Tony Armstrong
See Armstrong-Jones, Antony (Charles Robert)
Jones, Trevor Arthur 1936- 105
Jones, Trevor David 1908-1984 Obituary 114
Jones, Tristan 1924- 73-76
Jones, Turkel
See McKimmey, James
Jones, Vane A. 1917- 21-24R
Jones, Vernon 1897- 53-56
Jones, (Charles) Victor 1919- 5-8R
Jones, Virgil Carrington 1906- CANR-2
Earlier sketch in CA 1-4R
Jones, Volcano
See Mitchell, Adrian
Jones, W(alton) Glyn 1928- CANR-29
Earlier sketch in CA 49-52
Jones, W(illiam) J(ohn) 1932- 129
Jones, W(alter) Paul 1891- CAP-1
Earlier sketch in CA 11-12
Jones, W(illiam) T(homas) 1910- 37-40R
Jones, Walter Benton 1893- 1-4R
Jones, Webb
See Henley, Arthur
Jones, Weyman (B.) 1928- 17-20R
See also SAAS 11
See also SATA 4
Jones, Wilbur Devereux 1916- CANR-2
Earlier sketch in CA 1-4R
Jones, William Alfred 1817-1900 ....DLB 59
Jones, William David Anthony 1946- 113
Jones, William Glynne
See Glynne-Jones, William
Jones, William H(ugh) 1939-1982 112
Obituary 108
Jones, William M(cKendrey) 1927- CANR-7
Earlier sketch in CA 61-64
Jones, William Monarch
See Guthrie, Thomas Anstey
Jones, William P(owell) 1901- 1-4R
Jones, William R(onald) 1933- 104
Jones, William 1746-1794 ....DLB 109
Jones, Willis Knapp 1895- 13-16R
Jones, Zelda
See Schuchman, Joan
Jones-Evans, Eric 1898- 21-24R
Jones-Jackson, Pat
See Jones-Jackson, Patricia
Jones-Jackson, Patricia
1946-1986 Obituary 124
Jones-Ryan, Maureen 1943- 93-96
Jones-Wilson, Faustine C(hildress)
1927- CANR-27
Earlier sketch in CA 77-80
Jong, Erica 1942- CANR-26
Earlier sketch in CA 73-76
See also AITN 1
See also BEST 90:2
See also CLC 4, 6, 8, 18
See also DLB 2, 5, 28
See also MTCW
Jongeward, Dorothy 1925- CANR-3
Earlier sketch in CA 49-52
Jonk, Clarence 1906- 5-8R
See also SATA 10
Jonke, Gert F 1946- ....DLB 85
Jonnes, Jill 1952- 121
Jonsen, Albert R(upert) 1931- CANR-28
Earlier sketches in CA 25-28R, CANR-11
Jonson, Ben(jamin)
1572(?)-1637 ....CDBLB Before 1660
See also DLB 62, 121
See also WLC
Jonsson, Snaebjorn
1888(?)-1978 Obituary 81-84
Joos, Martin (George) 1907- CAP-1
Earlier sketch in CA 13-16
Joosse, Barbara M(onnot) 1949- 109
See also SATA 52
Joost, Nicholas (Teynac) 1916-1980 ....13-16R
Obituary 97-100
Joplin, Scott 1868-1917 Brief entry 123
Jopp, Hal
See Jopp, Harold Dowling Jr.
Jopp, Harold Dowling Jr. 1946- 57-60
Joralemon, Ira B(eaman)
1884-1975 Obituary 61-64
Joravsky, David 1925- CANR-2
Earlier sketch in CA 1-4R
Jordan, Alexis Hill
See Titchener, Louise
Jordan, Alexis Hill
See Glick, Ruth (Burtnick)
Jordan, Alma Theodora 1929- 33-36R
Jordan, Amos A(zariah) 1922- 33-36R
Jordan, Anne Devereaux 1943- 135
Jordan, Barbara (Charline) 1936- 123
Brief entry 113
See also BW
Jordan, Bill
See Jordan, William
Jordan, Borimir 1933- 89-92
Jordan, Carrie
See Cudlipp, Edythe
Jordan, Clarence L(eonard) 1912-1969 ..... CAP-2
Earlier sketch in CA 23-24
Jordan, Dale R(oderick) 1931- 45-48
Jordan, Daniel P(orter) Jr. 1938- 130
Jordan, David K. 1942- 61-64
Jordan, David M(alcolm) 1935- 33-36R
Jordan, David P(aul) 1939- 57-60
Jordan, David William 1940- 93-96
Jordan, Don
See Howard, Vernon (Linwood)
Jordan, Donald A. 1936- 65-68
Jordan, E(mil) L(eopold) 1900- ....SATA 31
Jordan, Franklin Everard
1904(?)-1983 Obituary 110
Jordan, Gail
See Dern, Erolie Pearl Gaddis
Jordan, Gerald Ray 1896-1964 ....CAP-1
Earlier sketch in CA 13-14
Jordan, Gilbert John 1902- CANR-28
Earlier sketch in CA 49-52
Jordan, Gill
See Gilbert, George
Jordan, Grace Edgington CANR-2
Earlier sketch in CA 1-4R
Jordan, Hope Dahle 1905- CANR-13
Earlier sketch in CA 77-80
See also SATA 15
Jordan, Jael (Michal) 1949- ....SATA 30
Jordan, John E(mory) 1919- CANR-20
Earlier sketch in CA 1-4R
Jordan, John 1930- 103
Jordan, June 1936- CANR-25
Earlier sketch in CA 33-36R
See also AAYA 2
See also BW
See also CLC 5, 11, 23
See also CLR 10
See also DLB 38
See also MAICYA
See also MTCW
See also SATA 4
Jordan, Lee
See Scholefield, Alan
Jordan, Leonard
See Levinson, Leonard
Jordan, Lewis 1912-1983 Obituary 111
Jordan, Lois B(reedlove) 1912- 57-60
Jordan, Mildred
See Bausher, Mildred Jordan
Jordan, Mildred Arlene 1918- 110
Jordan, Monica
See Caruba, Alan
Jordan, Neil 1950(?)- 130
Brief entry 124
Jordan, Norman 1938- 33-36R
Jordan, Pascual 1902-1982(?) Obituary 112
Jordan, Pat(rick M.) 1941- 33-36R
See also CLC 37
Jordan, Philip D(ean) 1940- 110
Jordan, Philip Dillon 1903- 9-12R
Jordan, Robert Paul 1921- 29-32R
Jordan, Robert S(mith) 1929- CANR-1
Earlier sketch in CA 45-48
Jordan, Robin 1947- 65-68
Jordan, Ruth 1926- CANR-7
Earlier sketch in CA 57-60
Jordan, Sherryl 1949- ....SATA 71
Jordan, Stello 1914- 29-32R
Jordan, Terry G(ilbert) 1938- CANR-9
Earlier sketch in CA 21-24R
Jordan, Thomas E(dward) 1929- 120
Jordan, Thurston C. Jr. 1940- 25-28R
Jordan, Wayne 1903(?)-1979 Obituary 85-88
Jordan, Weymouth T(yree) 1912-1968 ......CAP-2
Earlier sketch in CA 17-18
Jordan, Wilbur K(itchener) 1902-1980 .....CANR-5
Obituary 97-100
Earlier sketch in CA 5-8R
Jordan, William A. 1928- 33-36R
Jordan, William H. Jr. 1944- 114
Jordan, William J(ohnston) 1924- CANR-39
Earlier sketch in CA 114
Jordan, William S(tone) Jr. 1917- 13-16R
Jordan, William 1941- Brief entry 118
Jordan, Winthrop D(onaldson) 1931- 25-28R
Jordan, Z(bigniew) A(ntoni) 1911-1977 ......25-28R
Obituary 89-92
Jordan Haight, Mary Ellen 1927- 136
Jordan-Smith, Paul 1885(?)-1971 Obituary 104
Jorden, Eleanor Harz CANR-8
Earlier sketch in CA 5-8R
Jordy, William H(enry) 1917- CANR-25
Earlier sketch in CA 1-4R
Jorgens, Jack J(ohnstone) 1943- 65-68
Jorgensen, Christine 1926-1989 Obituary 128
Jorgensen, Ivar
See Ellison, Harlan
and Garrett, (Gordon) Randall (Phillip)
Jorgensen, James (Aleck) 1931- CANR-19
Earlier sketch in CA 103
Jorgensen, James D(ale) 1932- 41-44R
Jorgensen, Joseph G(ilbert) 1934- CANR-7
Earlier sketch in CA 61-64
Jorgensen, Mary Venn CANR-1
Earlier sketch in CA 1-4R
See also SATA 36
Jorgensen, Neil 1934- 53-56
Jorgenson, Allen
See Stine, Henry Eugene
Jorgenson, Ivar
See Silverberg, Robert
Jorgenson, Lloyd P. 1912- 125
Jorn, Asger 1914-1973 Obituary 41-44R
Jorstad, Erling (Theodore) 1930- CANR-30
Earlier sketches in CA 29-32R, CANR-12
Joscelyn, Archie L. 1899- CANR-5
Earlier sketch in CA 1-4R
Jose, F(rancisco) Sionil
See Sionil Jose, F(rancisco)
Jose, James R(obert) 1939- 29-32R
Josefowitz, Natasha 1926- 114
Josefsberg, Milt 1911-1987 ....CANR-29
Obituary 124
Earlier sketch in CA 81-84
Joselovitz, Ernest A. 1942- 108
Joselow, Beth Baruch 1948- CANR-36
Earlier sketch in CA 114
Joseph, Alexander 1907-1976 ....13-16R
Obituary 120
Joseph, Bertram L(eon) 1915-1981 ....CANR-6
Obituary 104
Earlier sketch in CA 5-8R
Joseph, David I(glauer) 1941- 9-12R
Joseph, Dov 1899-1980 Obituary 93-96
Joseph, Franz
See Schnaubelt, Franz Joseph
Joseph, Helen (Beatrice May) 1905- 128
Joseph, James (Herz) 1924- CANR-2
Earlier sketch in CA 1-4R
See also SATA 53
Joseph, Jenny 1932- CANR-25
Earlier sketch in CA 107
See also DLB 40
Joseph, Joan 1939- CANR-17
Earlier sketch in CA 25-28R
See also SATA 34
Joseph, John 1923- 1-4R
Joseph, Jonathan
See Fineman, Irving
Joseph, Joseph M(aron) 1903-1979 ....5-8R
See also SATA 22
Joseph, M(ichael) K(ennedy)
1914-1981 ....CANR-6
Earlier sketch in CA 9-12R
Joseph, Marie 109
Joseph, Marjory L(ockwood) 1917- 77-80
Joseph, Mark (Chester) 1946- 120
Joseph, R. F.
See Joseph, Robert Farras
Joseph, Richard 1910-1976 ....CANR-6
Obituary 69-72
Earlier sketch in CA 1-4R
Joseph, Robert F.
See Joseph, Robert Farras
Joseph, Robert Farras 1935- 129
Joseph, Stephen M. 1938- 25-28R
Joseph, Stephen 1921-1967 ....9-12R
Obituary 103
Joseph, William A(llen) 1947- 118
Josephs, Arthur
See Gottlieb, Arthur
Josephs, Ray 1912- 9-12R
Josephs, Rebecca
See Talbot, Toby
See also SATA 14
Josephs, Stephen
See Dolmatch, Theodore B(ieley)
Josephson, Clifford A. 1922- 17-20R
Josephson, Elmer A. 1909- 121
Josephson, Halsey D.
1906(?)-1977 Obituary 69-72
Josephson, Hannah 1900-1976 ....CAP-2
Obituary 69-72
Earlier sketch in CA 29-32
Josephson, Harold 1942- 61-64
Josephson, Matthew 1899-1978 81-84
Obituary 77-80
See also DLB 4
Josephy, Alvin M. Jr. 1915- CANR-8
Earlier sketch in CA 17-20R
Josey, E(lonnie) J(unius) 1924- 29-32R
Josh
See Clemens, Samuel Langhorne
Joshee, O(m) K(umar) 1934- 117
Joshi, Irene M(arian) 1934- 110
Joshi, S(unand) T(ryambak) 1958- 131
Joshi, Shivkumar 1916- 77-80
Joshua, Wynfred 1930- 29-32R
Josiah Allen's Wife
See Holley, Marietta
Josipovici, Gabriel 1940- 37-40R
See also CAAS 8
See also CLC 6, 43
See also DLB 14
Joskow, Paul L. 1947- 124
Joslin, Sesyle
See Hine, Sesyle Joslin
See also SATA 2
Jospe, Alfred 1909- 106
Joss, John 1934- 101
Josselyn, John ....DLB 24
Josten, Josef 1913-1985 Obituary 118
Jotischky, Andrew 1965- 133
Joubert, Andre J. 1924- 49-52
Joubert, Ingrid 1942- 110
Joudry, Patricia 1921- 65-68
See also DLB 88
Jouhandeau, Marcel Henri
1888-1979 Obituary 85-88
Jourard, Sidney M(arshall) 1926-1974 .....CANR-6
Obituary 53-56
Earlier sketch in CA 5-8R
Jourdain, Alice M. 1923- 53-56
Jourdain, Rose (Leonora) 1932- 89-92
Journet, Charles 1891-1975 65-68
Obituary 57-60
Journlet, Marie de
See Little, Paul H(ugo)
Jouve, Pierre Jean 1887-1976 Obituary 65-68
See also CLC 47
Jouvenel, Bertrand de
See de Jouvenel des Ursins, Edouard Bertrand
Jouvet, Jean
See Strich, Christian
Jovanovich, William (Iliya) 1920- 107
Jowett, Garth Samuel 1940- CANR-10
Earlier sketch in CA 65-68
Jowett, Paul (Melville) 1959- 120
Jowitt, Deborah 1934- 103
Joy, Barbara Ellen 1898- 5-8R
Joy, David Anthony Welton 1942- CANR-20
Earlier sketch in CA 103
Joy, Donald Marvin 1928- 13-16R
Joy, Edward T(homas) 1909- 9-12R
Joy, Kenneth Ernest 1908- CAP-2
Earlier sketch in CA 23-24
Joy, Thomas Alfred 1904- 102
Joyaux, Philippe
See Sollers, Philippe
Joyce, Adrien
See Eastman, Carol
Joyce, Bill
See Joyce, William
Joyce, Brian T(homas) 1938- 106
Joyce, Bruce R(ogers) 1930- Brief entry 114
Joyce, Ernest 1899-1975 ....CAP-2
Earlier sketch in CA 33-36
Joyce, J(ames) Avery 1902-1987 ....CANR-10
Obituary 121
Earlier sketch in CA 65-68
See also SATA 11, 50

Joyce, James (Augustine Aloysius)
1882-1941 126
Brief entry 104
See also CDBLB 1914-1945
See also DLB 10, 19, 36
See also MTCW
See also SSC 3
See also TCLC 3, 8, 16, 35
See also WLC
Joyce, James Daniel 1921- 9-12R
Joyce, Jon L(oyd) 1937- CANR-10
Earlier sketch in CA 65-68
Joyce, Joyce Ann 1949- 137
Joyce, Julia
See Tetel, Julie
Joyce, Mary Rosera 1930- 29-32R
Joyce, Patrick 1945- 128
Joyce, R(oger) B(ilbrough) 1924- CANR-1
Earlier sketch in CA 45-48
Joyce, Robert E(dward) 1934- 29-32R
Joyce, William L(eonard) 1942- 111
Joyce, William W(alter) 1934- CANR-15
Earlier sketch in CA 85-88
Joyce, William 1959(?)- 124
See also CLR 26
See also SATA 46
Joyner, Charles W. 1935- 37-40R
Joyner, Jerry 1938- 107
See also SATA 34
Joyner, William T. 1934- 21-24R
Joynson, R(obert) B(illington) 1922- 57-60
Joynt, Carey Bonthron 1924- 124
Joynt, Robert R(ichard) 1915- 106
Jozsef, Attila 1905-1937 Brief entry 116
See also TCLC 22
Juarroz, Roberto 1925- 131
See also HW
Jucker, Sita 1921- CANR-12
Earlier sketch in CA 29-32R
See also SATA 5
Jucovy, Milton Edward 1918- 109
Juda, L(yon) 1923- 9-12R
Judah, Aaron 1923- 103
Judah, J(ay) Stillson 1911- 21-24R
Judd, Cyril
See Kornbluth, C(yril) M.
and Merril, Judith
and Pohl, Frederik
Judd, Deane B(rewster) 1900-1972 ....CAP-1
Earlier sketch in CA 13-14
Judd, Denis (O'Nan) 1938- CANR-13
Earlier sketch in CA 25-28R
See also SATA 33
Judd, Dennis R. 1943- CANR-16
Earlier sketch in CA 93-96
Judd, Frances K. CANR-27
Earlier sketches in CAP-2, CA 19-20
See also SATA 1
Judd, Frederick Charles 1914- CANR-6
Earlier sketch in CA 5-8R
Judd, Gerrit P(armele) 1915-1971 ....5-8R
Obituary 29-32R
Judd, H(oward) Stanley 1936- CANR-21
Earlier sketch in CA 69-72
Judd, Harrison
See Daniels, Norman
Judd, Larry R. 1937- 45-48
Judd, Margaret Haddican 1906- 5-8R
Judd, Robert 1939- CANR-38
Earlier sketch in CA 85-88
Judd, Sara (Hutton) Bowen
See Bowen-Judd, Sara (Hutton)
Judd, Sylvester 1813-1853 ....DLB 1
Judelle, Beatrice 1908- 33-36R
Judge, Harry George 1928- 124
Judovitz, Dalia 1951- 130
Judson, Clara Ingram 1879-1960 137
See also MAICYA
See also SATA 27, 38
Judson, David (Malcolm) 1941- 93-96
Judson, Horace Freeland 1931- 89-92
Judson, John 1930- CANR-12
Earlier sketch in CA 13-16R
Judson, Lewis Van Hagen
1893-1973 Obituary 41-44R
Judson, Margaret Atwood 1899-1991 102
Obituary 134
Judson, Sylvia Shaw 1897-1978 ....41-44R
Obituary 133
Judson, William
See Corley, Edwin (Raymond)
Judy, Marvin T(hornton) 1911- 33-36R
Judy, Stephen
See Tchudi, Stephen N.
Judy, Stephen N.
See Tchudi, Stephen N.
Judy, Susan J(ane) 1944- 107
Judy, Will(iam Lewis) 1891- 5-8R
Juel, Donald H. 1942- CANR-35
Earlier sketch in CA 114
Juel-Nielsen, Niels 1920- 106
Juengel, Eberhard 1934- Brief entry 118
Juenger, Ernst 1895- CANR-21
Earlier sketch in CA 101
See also Junger, Ernst
See also DLB 56
Juergens, George Ivar 1932- 109
Juergensen, Hans 1919- CANR-8
Earlier sketch in CA 21-24R
Juergensmeyer, Jane Stuart
See Stuart, (Jessica) Jane
Juergensmeyer, John Eli 1934- 41-44R
Juergensmeyer, Mark (Karl) 1940- 129
Jugenheimer, Donald W(ayne) 1943- 125
Juhasz, Anne McCreary 1922- 53-56
Juhasz, Leslie A.
See Shepard, Leslie Albert
Juhasz, Suzanne 1942- 85-88
Jukes, (James Thomas) Geoffrey 1928- 29-32R
Jukes, Mavis 1947- 127
Brief entry 121
See also MAICYA
See also SAAS 12
See also SATA 43
Jukic, Ilija 1901-1977 49-52
Obituary 103
Julesberg, Elizabeth Rider Montgomery
1902-1985 ....CANR-3
Obituary 115
Earlier sketch in CA 1-4R
See also Montgomery, Elizabeth Rider
See also SATA 3, 34
Jules-Rosette, Bennetta (Washington)
1948- 112
Julian, Jane
See Wiseman, David
Juliard, Pierre 1939- 41-44R
Julie
See Robbins, June
Julien, Charles-Andre 1891- 103
Julie of Colorado Springs
See Robbins, June
Julin, Virginia Cheatham 1918- 5-8R
Julin, Joseph R. 1926- 37-40R
Juline, Ruth Bishop
See Ritchie, Ruth
Julitte, Pierre (Gaston Louis) 1910- 37-40R
Julius
See Curling, Bryan William Richard
Jullian, Philippe 1919-1977 73-76
Julty, Sam 1927- 61-64
July, Robert W(illiam) 1918- 41-44R
Jumper, Andrew Albert 1927- 17-20R
Jumpp, Hugo
See MacPeek, Walter G.
Jumsai, Sumet 1939- 129
Jun, Jong S(up) 1936- 53-56
June, Jennie
See Croly, Jane Cunningham
Jung, C(arl) G(ustav) 1875-1961 117
See also MTCW
Jung, Franz 1888-1963 ....DLB 118
Jung, Hwa Yol 1932- 37-40R
Jung, John A. 1937- 17-20R
Jung, Leo 1892-1987 Obituary 124
Junge, Mark G(ene) 1943- 122
Jungel, Eberhard
See Juengel, Eberhard
Junger, Ernst
See Juenger, Ernst
See also DLB 56
Jungk, Robert 1913- 85-88
Jungle Doctor
See White, Paul Hamilton Hume
Jungreis, Esther 1936- 110
Jung-Stilling, Johann Heinrich
1740-1817 ....DLB 94
Juniper, D(ean) F(rancis) 1929- CANR-18
Earlier sketch in CA 97-100
Junius
See Luxemburg, Rosa
Junker, Karin Stensland 1916- CANR-3
Earlier sketch in CA 9-12R
Junkins, Donald 1931- 33-36R
Junor, John 1919- 108
Jupo, Frank J. 1904- CANR-2
Earlier sketch in CA 5-8R
See also SATA 7
Jupp, James 1932- CANR-11
Earlier sketch in CA 21-24R
Jupp, Kenneth 1939- 65-68
Juptner, Joseph Paul 1913- 5-8R
Jur, Jerzy
See Lerski, George Jan
Jurek, Martin 1942- 77-80
Jurgela, Constantine R.
1904-1988 Obituary 124
Jurgens, Curt 1912-1982 Obituary 107
Jurgens, W(illiam) A(nthony) 1928- 41-44R
Jurgensen, Barbara (Bitting) 1928- 17-20R
Juris, Hervey A(sher) 1938- CANR-5
Earlier sketch in CA 53-56
Jurjevich, Ratibor-Ray (Momchila)
1915- 37-40R
Jurji, Edward J. 1907-1990 ....13-16R
Obituary 132
Jurmain, Suzanne 1945- 133
Jurnak, Sheila
See Raeschild, Sheila
Jussim, Estelle 1927- CANR-29
Earlier sketch in CA 81-84
Just, Ward (Swift) 1935- CANR-32
Earlier sketch in CA 25-28R
See also CLC 4, 27
Juster, F. Thomas 1926- CANR-2
Earlier sketch in CA 45-48
Juster, Norton 1929- CANR-13
Earlier sketch in CA 13-16R
See also MAICYA
See also SATA 3
Justice, Blair 1927- CANR-1
Earlier sketch in CA 45-48
Justice, Donald (Rodney) 1925- CANR-26
Earlier sketch in CA 5-8R
See also CLC 6, 19
See also DLBY 83
Justice, William G(ross) Jr. 1930- CANR-20
Earlier sketches in CA 53-56, CANR-5
Justiciar
See Powell-Smith, Vincent (Walter Francis)
Justus, May 1898- 9-12R
See also SATA 1
Justus, Moeser 1720-1794 ....DLB 97
Juta, Jan 1895- 49-52
Juta, Rene
See Juta, Jan
Jute, Andre 1945- 131
Jutikkala, Eino Kaarlo Ilmari 1907- CAP-1
Earlier sketch in CA 9-10
Jutson, Mary Carolyn Hollers
See George, Mary Carolyn Hollers Jutson
Juvenilia
See Taylor, Ann
Juvenis
See Bourne, Randolph S(illiman)
Juviler, Peter H(enry) 1926- 77-80
Jwaideh, Nizar 1933(?)-1988 Obituary 124

K

K. M.
See Beauchamp, Kathleen Mansfield
Kaapu, Myrtle King 1898-1985 Obituary 119
Kaba, Lansine 1941- 61-64
Kabadi, Sunder 1898(?)-1983 Obituary 111
Kabaker, Ray 1934(?)-1990 Obituary 132
Kabaphe, Konstantinos Petrou
See Kavafis, Konstantinos Petrou
Kabaphes, Konstantinos Petrou
See Kavafis, Konstantinos Petrou
Kabasele, Joseph
See Tshiamala, Kabasele
Kabbani, Rana 1958- 125
Kabdebo, Tamas
See Kabdebo, Thomas
Kabdebo, Thomas 1934- CANR-23
Earlier sketches in CA 53-56, CANR-7
See also SATA 10
Kabibble, Ish
See Bogue, Merwyn (Alton)
Kabibble, Osh
See Jobb, Jamie
Kabotie, Fred 1900- 118
Kabraji, Fredoon 1897- CAP-1
Earlier sketch in CA 13-14
Kac, Arthur W(ayne) 1904- 117
Kac, Mark 1914-1984 Obituary 114
Kacew, Romain 1914-1980 108
Obituary 102
See also Gary, Romain
Kacew, Roman
See Kacew, Romain
Kachru, Braj B(ehari) 1932- CANR-23
Earlier sketches in CA 61-64, CANR-8
Kaczer, Illes 1887- CAP-1
Earlier sketch in CA 9-10
Kadai, Heino Olavi 1931- 21-24R
Kadans, Joseph M(ichael) 1912- 118
Kadare, Ismail 1936- ....CLC 52
Kadesch, Robert R(udstone) 1922- 57-60
See also SATA 31
Kadic, Ante 1910- Brief entry 107
Kadish, Alon 1950- 131
Kadish, Ferne 1940- 61-64
Kadish, Mortimer Raymond
1916- Brief entry 106
Kadler, Eric H(enry) 1922- 29-32R
Kadohata, Cynthia ....CLC 59
Kadushin, Alfred 1916- 25-28R
Kadushin, Charles 1932- 25-28R
Kaegi, Walter Emil Jr. 1937- CANR-10
Earlier sketch in CA 25-28R
Kael, Pauline 1919- CANR-6
Earlier sketch in CA 45-48
Kaelbling, Rudolf 1928- 17-20R
Kaelin, Eugene F(rancis) 1926- 45-48
Kaellberg, Sture 1928- CANR-25
Earlier sketch in CA 107
Kaempfert, Wade
See del Rey, Lester
Kaempffert, Waldemar (Bernhard)
1877-1956 Brief entry 113
Kaeppler, Adrienne Lois 1935- Brief entry 107
Kaese, Harold 1909(?)-1975 Obituary 57-60
Kaestle, Carl F(rederick) 1940- 85-88
Kaestner, Dorothy 1920- 61-64
Kaestner, Erich 1899-1974 73-76
Obituary 49-52
See also Kastner, Erich
See also CLR 4
See also DLB 56
See also MAICYA
See also SATA 14
Kaeuper, Richard W(illiam)
1941- Brief entry 115
Kafe, Joseph Kofi Thompson 1933- 49-52
Kafka, Barbara 1933- 136
Kafka, Franz 1883-1924 126
Brief entry 105
See also DLB 81
See also MTCW
See also SSC 5
See also TCLC 2, 6, 13, 29
See also WLC
Kafka, Sherry 1937- 21-24R
Kafka, Vincent W(infield) 1924- 61-64
Kafker, Frank A. 1931- 37-40R
Kafu
See Nagai Sokichi
Kagan, Abram S. 1889(?)-1983 Obituary 111
Kagan, Andrew 1947- 123
Kagan, Benjamin 1914- 21-24R
Kagan, Donald 1932- CANR-9
Earlier sketch in CA 21-24R
Kagan, Jerome 1929- CANR-24
Earlier sketches in CA 5-8R, CANR-2
Kagan, Richard C(lark) 1938- 53-56
Kagan, Richard (Lauren) 1943- 57-60
Kagan, Robert A. 1938- 126
Kagan-Kans, Eva 1928- 49-52
Kaganoff, Nathan M. 1926- 126
Brief entry 108
Kagarlitsky, Boris 1958- 134
Kagy, Frederick D(avid) 1917- 13-16R
Kahan, Arcadius 1920-1982 135
Kahan, Gerald 1923- 33-36R
Kahan, Stanley 1931- 5-8R
Kahan, Stuart 1936- 93-96
Kahane, Claire 1935- 126
Kahane, Howard 1928- CANR-1
Earlier sketch in CA 49-52
Kahane, Meir (David) 1932-1990 133
Brief entry 112
Kaharl, Victoria A(nn) 1952- 137
Kahin, Audrey R. 1934- 121
Kahl, Ann Hammel 1929- 17-20R
Kahl, Joseph A(lan) 1923- Brief entry 109
Kahl, M(arvin) P(hilip) 1934- 107
See also SATA 37
Kahl, Virginia 1919- CANR-2
Earlier sketch in CA 49-52
See also SATA 38, 48
Kahle, Roger (Raymond) 1943- 33-36R
Kahlenberg, Mary Hunt 1940- CANR-2
Earlier sketch in CA 45-48
Kahlenberg, Richard D(awson) 1963- 138
Kahler, Erich Gabriel 1885-1970 ....CANR-7
Obituary 29-32R
Earlier sketch in CA 5-8R
Kahler, Hugh (Torbert) MacNair 1883-1969 102
Kahler, Woodland 1895- 1-4R
Kahm, H(arold) S. 101
Kahn, Albert E(ugene) 1912-1979 118
Obituary 89-92
Kahn, Alfred E(dward) 1917- 41-44R
Kahn, Alfred J. 1919- CANR-32
Earlier sketches in CA 5-8R, CANR-15
Kahn, Alice 1943- 119
Kahn, Arnold Dexter 1939- 101
Kahn, Balthazar
See Carlisle, Thomas (Fiske)
Kahn, Charles H(enry) 1928- 132
Kahn, Coppelia 1939- 129
Kahn, Dan 1933(?)-1989 Obituary 129
Kahn, David 1930- CANR-12
Earlier sketch in CA 25-28R
Kahn, E(ly) J(acques) Jr. 1916- 65-68
Kahn, Ely Jacques 1884-1972 Obituary 37-40R
Kahn, Frank J(ules) 1938- 33-36R
Kahn, Gilbert 1912-1971 ....CANR-6
Earlier sketch in CA 1-4R
Kahn, Grace Leboy 1891-1983 Obituary 109
Kahn, Hannah 1911- CANR-14
Earlier sketch in CA 77-80
See also AITN 2
Kahn, Herman 1922-1983 65-68
Obituary 110
Kahn, Herta Hess 1919- 25-28R
Kahn, James M. 1903(?)-1978 Obituary 77-80
Kahn, James 1947- CANR-27
Earlier sketch in CA 109
Kahn, Joan 1914- 77-80
See also SATA 48
Kahn, John (Ellison) 1950- 135
Kahn, Judd 1940- 101
Kahn, Kathy 1945- 41-44R
Kahn, Lawrence E(dwin) 1937- 103
Kahn, Lothar 1922- 25-28R
Kahn, Louis I. 1901-1974 Obituary 49-52
Kahn, Ludwig W(erner) 1910- 41-44R
Kahn, Madeleine (H.) 1955- 137
Kahn, Margaret 1949- 101
Kahn, Michael A. 1952- 138
Kahn, Michael D. 1936- CANR-27
Earlier sketch in CA 109
Kahn, Michele 1940- 130
Kahn, Peggy
See Katz, Bobbi
Kahn, Richard (Ferdinand Karn)
1905-1989 97-100
Obituary 128
Kahn, Robert I(rving) 1910- 5-8R
Kahn, Robert L(ouis) 1918- CANR-10
Earlier sketch in CA 17-20R
Kahn, Roger 1927- 25-28R
See also CLC 30
See also SATA 37
Kahn, Samuel 1897-1981 Obituary 106
Kahn, Sanders A(rthur) 1919-1987 89-92
Obituary 121
Kahn, Sandra S(utker) 1942- 106
Kahn, Sholom J(acob) 1918- 102
Kahn, Si(mon) 1944- 33-36R
Kahn, Stephen 1940-1988 ....5-8R
Obituary 127
Kahn, Steve
See Kahn, Stephen
Kahn, Sy M. 1924- CANR-10
Earlier sketch in CA 25-28R
Kahn, Theodore C(harles) 1912- 33-36R
Kahn-Fogel, Daniel (Mark) 1948- 97-100
Kahn-Freund, Otto 1900-1979 Obituary 108
Kahnweiler, Daniel-Henry 1884-1979 ....29-32R
Obituary 85-88
Kahrl, George M(orrow) 1904- 105
Kahrl, Stanley J. 1931- 9-12R
Kahrl, William L. 1946- 109
Kaid, Lynda Lee 1948- CANR-16
Earlier sketch in CA 89-92
Kaikini, P(rabhakar) R(amrao) 1912- 61-64
Kaikkonen, Gus 1951- 129

Kaiko, Takeshi 1930- 104
Kaim-Caudle, Peter Robert 1916- 21-24R
Kain, John F(orrest) 1935- 29-32R
Kain, Malcolm
See Oglesby, Joseph
Kain, Philip J(oseph) 1943- 132
Kain, Richard M(organ) 1908-1990 ....CANR-2
Obituary 131
Earlier sketch in CA 5-8R
Kain, Richard Y(erkes) 1936- 37-40R
Kain, Saul
See Sassoon, Siegfried (Lorraine)
Kains, Josephine
See Goulart, Ron(ald Joseph)
Kainz, Howard Paul 1933- CANR-35
Earlier sketch in CA 114
Kairys, Anatolijus 1914- CANR-32
Earlier sketch in CA 102
Kaisari, Uri 1899(?)-1979 Obituary 85-88
Kaiser, Artur 1943- 97-100
Kaiser, Bill
See Sumner, David (W. K.)
Kaiser, Christopher B(arina) 1941- 114
Kaiser, Daniel H. 1945- 126
Kaiser, Edward J(ohn) 1935- 93-96
Kaiser, Edwin George 1893-1984 45-48
Obituary 114
Kaiser, Ernest 1915- CANR-16
Earlier sketches in CA 49-52, CANR-1
Kaiser, Frances E(lkan) 1922- 57-60
Kaiser, Georg 1878-1945 Brief entry 106
See also TCLC 9
Kaiser, Harvey H. 1936- CANR-14
Earlier sketch in CA 81-84
Kaiser, Leo M(ax) 1918- 116
Kaiser, Otto 1924- 85-88
Kaiser, Robert Blair 1930- 9-12R
Kaiser, Robert G(reeley) 1943- CANR-31
Earlier sketch in CA 65-68
Kaiser, Walter Christian Jr. 1933- 114
Kaiser, Walter (Jacob) 1931- CANR-36
Earlier sketches in CA 37-40R, CANR-15
Kaiser, Ward L(ouis) 1923- 53-56
Kaiser Wilhelm II
See Hohenzollern, Friedrich Wilhelm (Victor Albert)
Kaitz, Edward M. 1928- CANR-13
Earlier sketch in CA 29-32R
Kajencki, Francis C(asimir) 1918- CANR-38
Earlier sketch in CA 115
Kakapo, Leilani 1939- CANR-9
Earlier sketch in CA 17-20R
Kakar, Sudhir 1938- 33-36R
Kaki
See Heinemann, Katherine
Kakimoto, Kozo 1915- ....SATA 11
Kakonen, Ulla
See Anobile, Ulla (Kakonen)
Kakonis, Thomas E. 1930- 57-60
Kakonis, Tom E.
See Kakonis, Thomas E.
Kakugawa, Frances H(ideko) 1936- 77-80
Kaland, William J. 1915(?)-1983 Obituary 111
Kalashnikoff, Nicholas 1888-1961 73-76
See also SATA 16
Kalb, Bernard 1932- Brief entry 109
Kalb, Jonah 1926- CANR-4
Earlier sketch in CA 53-56
See also SATA 23
Kalb, Jonathan 1959- 135
Kalb, Marvin L. 1930- 5-8R
Kalb, S(am) William 1897- 33-36R
Kalberer, Augustine 1917- 61-64
Kalcheim, Lee 1938- 85-88
Kaldor, Mary 1946- 93-96
Kaldor, Nicholas 1908-1986 134
Kale, Arvind and Shanta
See Gantzer, Hugh
Kalechofsky, Roberta 1931- CANR-2
Earlier sketch in CA 49-52
See also DLB 28
Kaledin, Eugenia 1929- 109
Kalem, T(heodore) E(ustace)
1919-1985 Obituary 116
Kalemkerian, Zarouhi
1874(?)-1971 Obituary 104
Kalenik, Sandra 1945- 73-76
Kaler, Anne K(atherine) 1935- 138
Kaler, James Otis 1848-1912 Brief entry 120
See also DLB 42
See also SATA 15
Kales, Emily Fox 1944- 21-24R
Kaletski, Alexander 1946- Brief entry 118
See also CLC 39
Kalfus, Melvin 1931- 134
Kalia, Narendra Nath 1942- CANR-30
Earlier sketch in CA 112
Kalich, Jacob 1891-1975 Obituary 89-92
Kalich, Richard 1947- 127
Kalich, Robert 1947- 106
Kalicki, Jan H(enryk) 1948- 65-68
Kalijarvi, Thorsten V(alentine)
1897-1980 ....CAP-1
Obituary 97-100
Earlier sketch in CA 19-20
Kalin, Martin (Gregory) 1943- 53-56
Kalin, Robert 1921- CANR-8
Earlier sketch in CA 61-64
Kalin, Rudolf 1938- 45-48
Kalina, Sigmund 1911-1977 ....CANR-3
Earlier sketch in CA 49-52
Kalins, Dorothy (G.) 1942- CANR-17
Earlier sketch in CA 25-28R
Kalinsky, George 1936- CANR-2
Earlier sketch in CA 49-52
Kalish, Betty McKelvey 1913- 45-48
Kalish, Donald 1919- 9-12R
Kalish, Richard A(llan) 1930- CANR-25
Earlier sketches in CA 5-8R, CANR-10
Kalisher, Simpson 1926- 17-20R
Kallas, James (Gus) 1928- CANR-10
Earlier sketch in CA 17-20R
Kallaus, Norman F. 1924- 33-36R
Kallberg, Sture
See Kaellberg, Sture
Kallberg, Sture
See Kaellberg, Sture
Kallen, (Marc) Christian 1950- 120
Kallen, Horace M(eyer) 1882-1974 93-96
Obituary 49-52
Kallen, Laurence 1944- 41-44R
Kallen, Lucille 97-100
Kallenbach, Joseph E(rnest) 1903- 77-80
Kallenbach, W(illiam) Warren 1926- 9-12R
Kallesser, Michael 1886(?)-1975 Obituary 61-64
Kallet, Arthur 1902-1972 Obituary 33-36R
Kallet, Marilyn 1946- 104
Kallich, Martin 1918- CANR-2
Earlier sketch in CA 5-8R
Kallifatides, Theodor 1938- CANR-15
Earlier sketch in CA 85-88
Kallir, Jane K(atherine) 1954- CANR-25
Earlier sketch in CA 109
Kallir, Otto 1894-1978 49-52
Obituary 81-84
Kallman, Chester (Simon) 1921-1975 ......CANR-3
Obituary 53-56
Earlier sketch in CA 45-48
See also CLC 2
Kallmann, Helmut Max 1922- 108
Kallsen, T(heodore) J(ohn) 1915- 5-8R
Kalman, Bobbie 1947- ....SATA 63
Kalman, Harold David 1943- 103
Kalme, Egils 1909- 81-84
Kalmijn, Jo 1905- CAP-2
Earlier sketch in CA 21-22
Kalmus, Ain
See Mand, Ewald
Kalmus, Hans 1906(?)-1988 Obituary 128
Kalnay, Francis 1899- 49-52
See also SATA 7
Kalnoky, Ingeborg L(ouise) 1909- 61-64
Kalow, Gert 1921- 29-32R
Kalow, Gisela 1946- 107
See also SATA 32
Kalpakian, Laura Anne 1945- CANR-15
Earlier sketch in CA 81-84
Kals, W(illiam) S(teven) 1910- CANR-24
Earlier sketch in CA 45-48
Kalson, Albert E(ugene) 1932- 132
Kalstone, David (Michael)
1932-1986 Obituary 119
Kalstone, Shirlee A(nn) 1932- CANR-8
Earlier sketch in CA 61-64
Kalt, Bryson R. 1934- 33-36R
Kalt, Jeannette Chappell
1898(?)-1976 Obituary 69-72
Kaltenborn, Hans Von
1878-1965 Obituary 93-96
Kalter, Joanmarie 1951- 102
Kalu, Ogbu Uke 1944- 93-96
Kaluger, George 1921- 29-32R
Kaluger, Meriem Fair 1921- 81-84
Kalven, Harry Jr. 1914-1974 Obituary 53-56
Kalyanaraman, Aiyaswamy 1903- CAP-2
Earlier sketch in CA 33-36
Kamal, Aleph 1950- 134
Kamarck, Andrew M(artin) 1914- CANR-10
Earlier sketch in CA 21-24R
Kamarck, Lawrence 1927- CANR-32
Earlier sketch in CA 73-76
Kamath, M(adhav) V(ithal) 1921- CANR-21
Earlier sketch in CA 69-72
Kamboureli, Smaro 1955- 127
Kambu, Joseph
See Amamoo, Joseph Godson
Kamen, Betty 1925- 114
Kamen, Gloria 1923- CANR-35
Earlier sketch in CA 114
See also SATA 9
Kamen, Henry Arthur 1936- CANR-7
Earlier sketch in CA 5-8R
Kamen, Isai
See Stein, Jess
Kamen, Martin D(avid) 1913- 118
Kamen, Paula 1967- 137
Kamen, Si 1920- 114
Kamenetsky, Ihor 1927- CANR-4
Earlier sketch in CA 1-4R
Kamenetz, Rodger 1950- CANR-30
Earlier sketch in CA 112
Kamenka, Eugene 1928- CANR-2
Earlier sketch in CA 5-8R
Kamerman, Jack B. 1940- 115
Kamerman, Sheila B(rody) 1928- CANR-10
Earlier sketch in CA 65-68
Kamerman, Sylvia E.
See Burack, Sylvia K.
Kamerschen, David R(oy) 1937- 53-56
Kamien, Marcia 1940- CANR-22
Earlier sketch in CA 105
Kamil, Alan C(urtis) 1941- 134
Brief entry 109
Kamil, Jill 1930- CANR-7
Earlier sketch in CA 57-60
Kamin, Leon J. 1927- 103
Kamin, Nick
See Antonick, Robert J.
Kamins, Jeanette 5-8R
Kamins, Robert Martin 1918- Brief entry 105
Kaminska, Ida 1899-1980 Obituary 97-100
Kaminskaya, Dina 1920- 115
Kaminski, Margaret (Joan) 1944- CANR-8
Earlier sketch in CA 61-64
Kaminsky, Alice R. 33-36R
Kaminsky, Howard 1940- 105
Kaminsky, Jack 1922- 21-24R
Kaminsky, Marc 1943- CANR-24
Earlier sketches in CA 53-56, CANR-5
Kaminsky, Melvin 1926- CANR-16
Earlier sketch in CA 65-68
See also Brooks, Mel
Kaminsky, Peretz 1916- 33-36R
Kaminsky, Stuart M(elvin) 1934- CANR-29
Earlier sketch in CA 73-76
See also CLC 59
Kaminsky, Susan Stanwood 1937- 115
Brief entry 110
Kamisar, Yale 1929- CANR-13
Earlier sketch in CA 69-72
Kamitses, Zoe 1941- 111
Kamm, Antony 1931- 117
Kamm, (Jan) Dorinda 1952- CANR-14
Earlier sketch in CA 37-40R
Kamm, Herbert 1917- 69-72
Kamm, Jacob Oswald 1918- 5-8R
Kamm, Josephine (Hart) 1905- CANR-5
Earlier sketch in CA 9-12R
See also SATA 24
Kamm, Phyllis S. 1918- 112
Kamman, Madeleine M(arguerite Pin)
1930- 85-88
Kamman, William 1930- 25-28R
Kammen, Michael G(edaliah) 1936- CANR-34
Earlier sketches in CA 25-28R, CANR-22
See also MTCW
Kammerer, Gladys M. 1909-1970 ....CANR-16
Obituary 103
Earlier sketch in CA 1-4R
Kammeyer, Kenneth C(arl) W(illiam)
1931- 29-32R
Kamp, Irene Kittle 1910-1985 Obituary 116
Kampelman, Max M. 1920- 41-44R
Kampen, Irene Trepel 1922- CANR-1
Earlier sketch in CA 1-4R
Kampen, Michael Edwin 1939- Brief entry 110
Kampf, Abraham 1920- 21-24R
Kampf, Avram
See Kampf, Abraham
Kampf, Louis 1929- 33-36R
Kamphoefner, Walter D. 1948- 137
Kampov, Boris Nikolayevich 1908-1981 108
Obituary 104
Kampowski, Walter 1929- ....DLB 75
Kamrany, Nake M. 1934- CANR-14
Earlier sketch in CA 37-40R
Kamstra, Leslie D. 1920- 69-72
Kan, Sergei 1953- 137
Kanahele, George Sanford 1930- 102
Kanazawa, Masakata 1934- 25-28R
Kanazawa, Roger
See Kanazawa, Masakata
Kanchier, Carole 132
Kandaouroff, Berice 1912- 33-36R
Kandel, Denise Bystryn 1933- 13-16R
Kandel, I(saac) L(eon) 1881-1965 ....CANR-3
Earlier sketch in CA 1-4R
Kandel, Lenore 1932- ....DLB 16
Kandel, Thelma E. 1932- 111
Kandell, Alice S. 1938- CANR-13
Earlier sketch in CA 33-36R
See also SATA 35
Kandinsky, Nina 1896(?)-1980 101
Kandinsky, Wassily 1866-1944 Brief entry 118
Kando, Thomas M. 1941- CANR-2
Earlier sketch in CA 49-52
Kane, Aarno
See Kagan, Andrew
Kane, Basil G(odfrey) 1931- CANR-24
Earlier sketch in CA 69-72
Kane, Bob ....AAYA 8
Kane, Dennis Cornelius 1918- 41-44R
Kane, E. B. 1944- 57-60
Kane, Edward J(ames) 1935- 41-44R
Kane, Elizabeth 1942- 136
Kane, Frank R. 1925- 77-80
Kane, Frank 1912-1968 ....5-8R
Obituary 25-28R
Kane, George 1916- 103
Kane, Gerard Thomas Matthew 1946- 133
Kane, H. Victor 1906- 29-32R
Kane, Harnett T(homas)
1910-1984 Obituary 113
Kane, Henry Bugbee 1902-1971 73-76
See also SATA 14
Kane, J. Herbert 1910- 97-100
Kane, Jack
See Baker, (Allen) Albert
Kane, James
See Germano, Peter B.
Kane, Jim
See Germano, Peter B.
Kane, John Joseph 1909- CAP-2
Earlier sketch in CA 13-14
Kane, Julia
See Robins, Denise (Naomi)
Kane, L. A.
See Mannetti, Lisa
Kane, Pablo
See Zachary, Hugh
Kane, Paul
See Simon, Paul
Kane, Penelope Susan 1945- 131
Kane, Penny
See Kane, Penelope Susan
Kane, Peter E(vans) 1932- CANR-31
Earlier sketch in CA 112
Kane, Robert S. 1925- CANR-23
Earlier sketches in CA 9-12R, CANR-7
Kane, Robert W. 1910- ....SATA 18
Kane, Rod
See Kane, Gerard Thomas Matthew
Kane, Thomas S. 1925- 114
Kane, William Everett 1943- 49-52
Kane, Wilson
See Bloch, Robert (Albert)
Kanellos, Nicolas 1945- 131
See also HW
Kanet, Roger E(dward) 1936- CANR-14
Earlier sketch in CA 33-36R
Kanetzke, Howard W(illiam) 1932- 112
See also SATA 38
Kanfer, Allen 1905(?)-1983 Obituary 110
Kanfer, Frederick H. 1925- CANR-32
Earlier sketches in CA 41-44R, CANR-15
Kanfer, Stefan 1933- 103
Kang, Shin T. 1935- 33-36R
Kang, Younghill 1903-1972 Obituary 37-40R
Kanigel, Robert 1946- 132
Kanin, Garson 1912- CANR-7
Earlier sketch in CA 5-8R
See also AITN 1
See also CLC 22
See also DLB 7
Kanin, Michael 1910- 61-64
Kanin, Ruth 1920- 107
Kanitz, Walter 1910- 97-100
Kaniuk, Yoram 1930- 134
See also CLC 19
Kaniut, Larry (LeRoy) 1942- 114
Kann, Mark E. 1947- 130
Kann, Robert A(dolf) 1906-1981 129
Kann, Robert A. 1906-1981 Obituary 105
Kannappan, Subbiah 1927- 93-96
Kanner, Catherine 1954- 123
Kanner, Leo 1894-1981 ....17-20R
Obituary 103
Kanof, Abram 1903- 29-32R
Kanovsky, Eliyahu 1922- 33-36R
Kansil, Joli 1943- 81-84
Kant, Hermann 1926- ....DLB 75
Kant, Immanuel 1724-1804 ....DLB 94
Kantar, Edwin B(ruce) 1932- 41-44R
Kantaris, Sylvia 1936- 139
Kantarizis, Sylvia
See Kantaris, Sylvia
Kanter, Arnold 1945- 89-92
Kanter, Hal 1918- 81-84
Kanter, Rosabeth Moss 1943- CANR-14
Earlier sketch in CA 77-80
Kanto, Peter
See Zachary, Hugh
Kantonen, T(aito) A(lmar) 1900- 33-36R
Kantor, Hal 1924- 77-80
Kantor, Harry 1911- CANR-2
Earlier sketch in CA 1-4R
Kantor, Herman I. 1909- 57-60
Kantor, James 1927-1974 ....CAP-2
Earlier sketch in CA 21-22
Kantor, Leonard 1924(?)-1984 Obituary 112
Kantor, MacKinlay 1904-1977 61-64
Obituary 73-76
See also CLC 7
See also DLB 9, 102
Kantor, Marvin 1934- CANR-2
Earlier sketch in CA 49-52
Kantor, Seth 1926- 81-84
Kantor, Tim 1932- 128
Kantor-Berg, Friedrich 1908-1979 133
Obituary 89-92
See also Torberg, Friedrich
Kantorovich, L(eonid) V(italevich)
1912-1986 Obituary 119
Kantowicz, Edward Robert 1943- 114
Kantrowitz, Arnie 1940- 77-80
Kantrowitz, Joanne Spencer 1931- 81-84
Kantzer, Kenneth S(ealer) 1917- 106
Kanungo, R(abindra) N. 1935- 135
Kanwar, Mahfooz A. 1939- 37-40R
Kany, Charles E(mil) 1895-1968 ....CANR-3
Earlier sketch in CA 1-4R
Kanya-Forstner, A(lexander) S(ydney)
1940- CANR-17
Earlier sketch in CA 25-28R
Kanza, Thomas R. (Nsenga) 1933- CANR-5
Earlier sketch in CA 53-56
Kanzawa, Toshiko
See Furukawa, Toshi
Kanzer, Mark 1908- 37-40R
Kao, Charles C. L. 1932- 85-88
Kao, George 1912- 132
Kapel, Andrew
See Burgess, M(ichael) R(oy)
Kapel, David E(dward) 1932- 125
Kapelner, Alan 5-8R
Kapelrud, Arvid Schou 1912- 102
Kapfer, Miriam B(ierbaum) 1935- 33-36R
Kapfer, Philip G(ordon) 1936- 33-36R
Kapitsa, Pyotr L(eonidovich)
1894-1984 Obituary 112
Kaplan, Abraham 1918- 13-16R
Kaplan, Allan 1932- 33-36R
Kaplan, Andrew (Gary) 1941- 125
Kaplan, Anne Bernays 1930- CANR-5
Earlier sketch in CA 1-4R
See also SATA 32
Kaplan, Arthur 1925- 5-8R
Kaplan, Benjamin 1911- 1-4R
Kaplan, Bernard 1944- CANR-2
Earlier sketch in CA 49-52
Kaplan, Berton H(arris) 1930- 61-64
Kaplan, Bess 1927- 85-88
See also SATA 22
Kaplan, Boche 1926- CANR-10
Earlier sketch in CA 21-24R
See also SATA 24
Kaplan, Charles 1919- 9-12R

Kaplan, David Gordon 1908- ... 61-64
Kaplan, David Michael 1946- ... CLC 50
Kaplan, Doris
See Willens, Doris
Kaplan, E(lizabeth) Ann 1936- ... 127
Kaplan, Edward 1946- ... CANR-11
Earlier sketch in CA 69-72
Kaplan, Eugene H(erbert) 1932- ... 81-84
Kaplan, Flora S(tewart) ... 109
Kaplan, Fred
See Kaplan, Fred Michael
Kaplan, Fred M.
See Kaplan, Fred Michael
Kaplan, Fred Michael 1954- ... 127
Brief entry ... 121
Kaplan, Fred 1937- ... CANR-14
Earlier sketch in CA 41-44R
See also DLB 111
Kaplan, Frederick I(srael) 1920- ... 21-24R
Kaplan, H. Roy 1944- ... 89-92
Kaplan, Harold 1916- ... 17-20R
Kaplan, Helen Singer 1929- ... 102
See also AITN 1
Kaplan, Howard B(ernard) 1932- ... CANR-22
Earlier sketches in CA 61-64, CANR-8
Kaplan, Howard 1950- ... 69-72
Kaplan, Hymen R. 1910- ... 102
Kaplan, Irma 1900- ... 29-32R
See also SATA 10
Kaplan, Jack A(rnold) 1947- ... 57-60
Kaplan, Jacob J. 1920- ... CANR-10
Earlier sketch in CA 21-24R
Kaplan, James 1951- ... 135
See also CLC 59
Kaplan, Janet A(nn) 1945- ... 130
Kaplan, Janice Ellen 1955- ... 117
Kaplan, Jean Caryl Korn 1926- ... 5-8R
See also SATA 10
Kaplan, Jim 1944- ... 126
Kaplan, Joel 1956- ... 134
Kaplan, Johanna 1942- ... 77-80
See also DLB 28
Kaplan, John 1929-1989 Obituary ... 130
Kaplan, Joseph 1916(?)-1980 Obituary ... 97-100
Kaplan, Justin 1925- ... CANR-8
Earlier sketch in CA 17-20R
See also DLB 111
Kaplan, Lawrence Jay 1915- ... 21-24R
Kaplan, Lawrence S(amuel) 1924- ... 33-36R
Kaplan, Leonard 1918(?)-1977 Obituary ... 69-72
Kaplan, Martin F(rancis) 1940- ... 93-96
Kaplan, Martin (Harold) 1950- ... 65-68
Kaplan, Max 1911- ... CANR-20
Earlier sketches in CA 1-4R, CANR-5
Kaplan, Milton 1910- ... 65-68
Kaplan, Milton 1918-1988 Obituary ... 127
Kaplan, Mordecai M(enahem)
1881-1983 Obituary ... 111
Kaplan, Morton A. 1921- ... CANR-7
Earlier sketch in CA 5-8R
Kaplan, Norman Mayer 1931- ... 110
Kaplan, Philip 1916- ... 13-16R
Kaplan, Richard 1929- ... 73-76
Kaplan, Robert B. 1928- ... CANR-22
Earlier sketches in CA 13-16R, CANR-7
Kaplan, S(aul) Howard 1938- ... 25-28R
Kaplan, Samuel 1935- ... 21-24R
Kaplan, Sidney 1913- ... 85-88
Kaplan, Steven B. 1953- ... 135
Kaplan, Stuart R(onald) 1932- ... CANR-21
Earlier sketches in CA 49-52, CANR-2
Kaplan, Sydney Janet 1939- ... 110
Kaplan, William 1957- ... 126
Kapler, Aleksei (Yaklovlevich)
1904(?)-1979 Obituary ... 89-92
Kaplon, Morton F(ischel) 1921- ... 21-24R
Kaplow, Herb(ert Elias) 1927- ... 119
Brief entry ... 110
Kaplow, Jeffry 1937- ... 17-20R
Kaplow, Robert 1954- ... 138
See also SATA 70
Kapoor, Ashok 1940- ... 85-88
Kapoor, Sukhbir Singh 1937- ... CANR-29
Earlier sketch in CA 109
Kapp, Colin 1928(?)- ... 132
Kapp, K(arl) William 1910-1976 ... CANR-8
Obituary ... 65-68
Earlier sketch in CA 5-8R
Kapp, Reginald Otto 1885-1966 ... 5-8R
Kapp, Yvonne (Mayer) 1903- ... 103
Kappauf, William Emil (Jr.) 1913- ... 106
Kappel, Philip 1901- ... CAP-1
Earlier sketch in CA 13-16
Kappelman, Murray M(artin) 1931- ... 73-76
Kappel-Smith, Diana 1951- ... 121
Kappen, Charles Vaughan 1910- ... 9-12R
Kaprow, Allan 1927- ... 105
Kapsner, Oliver L(eonard) 1902- ... 116
Kapstein, I(srael) J(ames)
1904-1983 Obituary ... 110
Kaptchuk, Ted J(ack) 1947- ... CANR-27
Earlier sketch in CA 110
Kapur, Harish 1929- ... CANR-34
Earlier sketches in CA 85-88, CANR-15
Kapur, Rajiv A. 1951- ... 136
Kapuscinski, Ryszard 1932- ... 114
Kapusta, Paul
See Bickers, Richard Leslie Townshend
Karageorge, Michael
See Anderson, Poul (William)
Karageorghis, Vassos 1929- ... CANR-33
Earlier sketches in CA 81-84, CANR-15
Karamanski, Theodore J. 1953- ... 126
Karan, Pradyumna P(rasad) 1930- ... CANR-35
Earlier sketch in CA 114
Karanikas, Alexander 1916- ... 33-36R
Karapanou, Margarita 1946- ... 101
See also CLC 13
Karas, Jim 1949-1981 ... 126
Obituary ... 108
Karas, Joza 1926- ... 124
Karas, Phyllis 1944- ... 105
Karasu, Toksoz B(yram) 1935- ... 105
Karasz, Ilonka 1896-1981 ... SATA 29
Karbo, Joe 1925(?)-1980 Obituary ... 115
Kardiner, Abram 1891-1981 ... 107
Obituary ... 104
Kardish, Laurence 1945- ... CANR-30
Earlier sketch in CA 49-52
Kardouche, G(eorge) Khalil 1935- ... 17-20R
Karel, Leonard 1912- ... 49-52
Karen
See Aldrich, Sandra Picklesimer
Karen, Robert L(e Roy) 1925- ... 73-76
Karen, Ruth 1922-1987 ... CANR-11
Obituary ... 123
Earlier sketch in CA 17-20R
See also SATA 9, 54
Karg, Elissa Jane 1951- ... 21-24R
Karger, Delmar William 1913- ... CANR-8
Earlier sketch in CA 17-20R
Kargon, Robert Hugh 1938- ... CANR-28
Earlier sketch in CA 45-48
Kariel, Henry S. 1924- ... 13-16R
Karin, Sidney 1943- ... 126
Karina
See Goud, Anne
Kariuki, Josiah Mwangi 1929- ... 107
Kark, Nina Mary (Mabey)
See Bawden, Nina (Mary Mabey)
See also SATA 4
Karkala, John A.
See Alphonso-Karkala, John B.
Karkala, John B. A.
See Alphonso-Karkala, John B.
Karkhanis, Sharad 1935- ... 110
Karkoschka, Erhard 1923- ... 45-48
Karl, Barry D(ean) 1927- ... 102
Karl, Dennis (R.) 1954- ... 134
Karl, Frederick R(obert) 1927- ... CANR-3
Earlier sketch in CA 5-8R
See also CLC 34
Karl, Jean E(dna) 1927- ... CANR-12
Earlier sketch in CA 29-32R
See also SAAS 10
See also SATA 34
Karl, Roger
See Trouve, Roger
Karlan, Richard 1919- ... 17-20R
Karlen, Arno 1937- ... CANR-5
Earlier sketch in CA 1-4R
Karlen, Delmar 1912-1988 ... CANR-2
Obituary ... 127
Earlier sketch in CA 5-8R
Karlgren, (Klas) Bernhard (Johannes)
1889- ... CAP-1
Earlier sketch in CA 9-10
Karlin, Bernie 1927- ... 136
See also SATA 68
Karlin, Eugene 1918- ... SATA 10
Karlin, Jules 1899- ... CAP-2
Earlier sketch in CA 25-28
Karlin, Muriel S.
See Trachman, Muriel Karlin
Karlin, Nurit ... SATA 63
Karlin, Robert 1918- ... 9-12R
Karlin, Wayne (Stephen) 1945- ... 133
Karlins, Marvin 1941- ... CANR-17
Earlier sketch in CA 25-28R
Karlowich, Robert A. 1927- ... 125
Karlsson, Elis (Viktor) 1905- ... CAP-1
Earlier sketch in CA 13-16
Karlsson, T. Edward 1915(?)-1984 Obituary ... 113
Karman, James W. 1947- ... 126
Karman, Mal 1944- ... 103
Karmel, Alex 1931- ... 21-24R
Karmel, Roberta S(arah) 1937- ... 108
Karmel-Wolfe, Henia 1923- ... 49-52
Karmen, Roman Lazarevich
1906-1978 Obituary ... 77-80
Karmi, Abdul Karim 1907(?)-1980 Obituary ... 102
Karmi, Hasan Said 1908- ... 45-48
Karmin, Monroe William 1929- ... 101
Karnad, Girish 1938- ... 65-68
Karnes, Merle B(riggs) 1916- ... 85-88
Karnes, Thomas L(indas) 1914- ... 21-24R
Karney, Beulah Mullen ... 13-16R
Karniewski, Janusz
See Wittlin, Thaddeus (Andrew)
Karno, Bung
See Sukarno, (Ahmed)
Karnow, Stanley 1925- ... CANR-31
Earlier sketch in CA 57-60
See also MTCW
Karol, Alexander
See Kent, Arthur William Charles
Karol, K. S.
See Kewes, Karol
Karolevitz, Bob
See Karolevitz, Robert F.
Karolevitz, Robert F. 1922- ... CANR-22
Earlier sketches in CA 17-20R, CANR-7
Karolides, Nicholas J(ames) 1928- ... 21-24R
Karolyi, Catherine (Andrassy)
1898-1985 Obituary ... 116
Karon, Bertram Paul 1930- ... CANR-7
Earlier sketch in CA 61-64
Karp, Abraham J. 1921- ... CANR-18
Earlier sketches in CA 5-8R, CANR-3
Karp, Alan 1947- ... 107
Karp, David 1922- ... CANR-1
Earlier sketch in CA 1-4R
Karp, Ivan C. 1926- ... 17-20R
Karp, Laurence E(dward) 1939- ... 77-80
Karp, Lila 1933- ... 25-28R
Karp, Mark 1922- ... 1-4R
Karp, Naomi J. 1926- ... 81-84
See also SATA 16
Karp, Stephen A(rnold) 1928- ... CANR-6
Earlier sketch in CA 1-4R
Karp, Walter 1934(?)-1989 Obituary ... 129
Karpat, Kemal H(asim) 1925- ... CANR-11
Earlier sketch in CA 69-72
Karpatkin, Marvin M. 1926-1975 Obituary ... 53-56
Karpau, Uladzimir
See Karpov, Vladimir
Karpel, Bernard 1911-1986 ... 106
Obituary ... 118
Karpel, Craig S. 1944- ... 65-68
Karpeles, Maud 1885- ... 25-28R
Karpf, Holly W. 1946- ... 37-40R
Karpin, Fred L(eon) 1913-1986 ... CANR-9
Obituary ... 119
Earlier sketch in CA 13-16R
Karplus, Walter J. 1927- ... 21-24R
Karpman, Harold L(ew) 1927- ... 77-80
Karpov, Vladimir 1912(?)-1977 Obituary ... 73-76
Karr, E(arl) R(alph) 1918- ... 1-4R
Karr, Phyllis Ann 1944- ... CANR-18
Earlier sketch in CA 101
Karras, Alex(ander G.) 1935- ... 107
Karrass, Chester L. 1923- ... 101
Karren, Keith J(ohn) 1943- ... 116
Karrer, Paul 1889-1971 Obituary ... 113
Karris, Robert J(oseph) 1938- ... CANR-5
Earlier sketch in CA 53-56
Karsavina, Jean (Faterson) 1908- ... 101
Karsavina, Tamara 1885-1978 Obituary ... 77-80
Karsch, Anna Louisa 1722-1791 ... DLB 97
Karsch, Robert F(rederick) 1909- ... 77-80
Karsen, Sonja (Petra) 1919- ... 41-44R
Karsh, Bernard 1921- ... 103
Karsh, Yousuf 1908- ... 33-36R
Karshner, Roger 1928- ... 33-36R
Karst, Kenneth L(eslie) 1929- ... 132
Karsten, Peter 1938- ... CANR-13
Earlier sketch in CA 37-40R
Karta, Nat
See Norwood, Victor G(eorge) C(harles)
Kartiganer, Donald M. 1937- ... 97-100
Karttunen, Frances 1942- ... 138
Karu, Baruch 1899-1972 Obituary ... 104
Karve, Dinakar Dhondo 1899-1980 ... 5-8R
Obituary ... 103
Karve, Irawati (Karmarkar) 1905-1970 ... CAP-1
Earlier sketch in CA 19-20
Kary, Elizabeth N. (a pseudonym) 1947- ... 122
Kasack, Hermann 1896-1966 ... DLB 69
Kasarda, John Dale 1945- ... 103
Kaschnitz, Marie Luise
See von Kaschnitz-Weinberg, Marie Luise
See also DLB 69
Kasdan, Lawrence 1949- ... 109
Kasdan, Sara (Moskovitz) 1911- ... 1-4R
Kasdorf, Hans 1928- ... 116
Kase, Francis J(oseph) 1910- ... 21-24R
Kaselow, Joseph 1912-1986 Obituary ... 119
Kaser, David 1924- ... 17-20R
Kaser, Michael (Charles) 1926- ... CANR-10
Earlier sketch in CA 17-20R
Kaser, Paul 1944- ... 104
Kash, Don E(ldon) 1934- ... CANR-9
Earlier sketch in CA 21-24R
Kasha, Lawrence N(athan)
1934(?)-1990 Obituary ... 132
Kashdan, Isaac 1905-1985 Obituary ... 115
Kashima, Tetsuden 1940- ... 81-84
Kashiwagi, Isami 1925- ... SATA 10
Kashner, Rita 1942- ... CANR-27
Earlier sketch in CA 105
Kasinitz, Philip 1957- ... 137
Kaske, Robert Earl 1921-1989 Obituary ... 129
Kaslow, Florence W(hiteman) 1930- ... CANR-18
Earlier sketches in CA 45-48, CANR-1
Kasper, Shirl(ey Elaine) 1948- ... 137
Kasper, Sydney H. 1911- ... 1-4R
Kasper, Walter 1933- ... 130
Kasperson, Roger E. 1938- ... 29-32R
Kasrils, Ronald 1938- ... 29-32R
Kass, Edward H(arold) 1917- ... 129
Kass, Jerome 1923(?)-1973 Obituary ... 104
Kass, Jerome 1937- ... 57-60
Kass, Linda Stern 1953- ... 138
Kass, Norman 1934- ... 29-32R
Kass, Ray 1944- ... 118
Kassalow, Everett M(alcolm) 1918- ... CANR-25
Earlier sketch in CA 45-48
Kassebaum, Gene G(irard) 1929- ... 17-20R
Kassem, Lou 1931- ... 128
See also SATA 51, 62
Kassewitz, Jack 1914(?)-1984 Obituary ... 112
Kassis, Hanna (Emmanuel) 1932- ... 125
Kassler, J. C.
See Kassler, Jamie C(roy)
Kassler, Jamie C(roy) 1938- ... 135
Kassof, Allen 1930- ... 21-24R
Kasson, John F(ranklin) 1944- ... 81-84
Kassorla, Irene Chamie 1931- ... 110
Kast, Fremont E. 1926- ... 21-24R
Kastan, David Scott 1946- ... 109
Kastein, Shulamith 1903-1983 ... 105
Obituary ... 110
Kastel, Warren
See Silverberg, Robert
Kastenbaum, Robert (Jay) 1932- ... CANR-9
Earlier sketch in CA 13-16R
Kaster, Joseph 1912- ... CAP-1
Earlier sketch in CA 19-20
Kastl, Albert J(oseph) 1939- ... 57-60
Kastl, Lena 1942- ... 61-64
Kastle, Herbert D(avid) 1924-1987 ... CANR-1
Obituary ... 123
Earlier sketch in CA 1-4R
Kastner, Erich
See Kaestner, Erich
See also CLR 4
See also DLB 56
See also SATA 14
Kastner, Jill (Marie) 1964- ... SATA 70
Kastner, Jonathan 1937- ... 25-28R
Kastner, Joseph 1907- ... 85-88
Kastner, Marianna 1940- ... 25-28R
Kastner, Patricia Wilson
See Wilson-Kastner, Patricia
Kasulis, T(homas) P(atrick) 1948- ... 124
Kasuya, Masahiro 1937- ... CANR-29
Earlier sketch in CA 110
See also SATA 51
Kaszner, Kurt
See Serwicher, Kurt
Kaszubski, Marek 1951- ... 105
Kataev, Evgeny Petrovich
1903-1942 Brief entry ... 120
See also Petrov, Evgeny
Katahn, Martin 1928- ... 114
Katan, Norma-Jean 1936- ... 113
Kataphusin
See Ruskin, John
Katayev, Valentin (Petrovich) 1897-1986 ... 131
Obituary ... 119
Brief entry ... 117
Katcha, Vahe
See Katchadourian, Vahe
Katchadourian, Herant A(ram) 1933- ... CANR-20
Earlier sketch in CA 103
Katchadourian, Vahe 1928- ... CANR-25
Earlier sketch in CA 29-32R
Katchen, Carole 1944- ... 61-64
See also SATA 9
Katchmer, George Andrew 1916- ... 1-4R
Kateb, George (Anthony) 1931- ... 123
Brief entry ... 118
Katen, Thomas Ellis 1931- ... 53-56
Kater, Michael H(ans) 1937- ... 114
Kates, Brian 1946- ... 119
Kates, Carol A. 1943- ... 115
Kates, Gary (Richard) 1952- ... 125
Kates, Robert W. 1929- ... CANR-24
Earlier sketches in CA 17-20R, CANR-8
Kathman, Michael D(ennis) 1943- ... 109
Kathryn
See Searle, Kathryn Adrienne
Kati
See Rekai, Kati
Katicic, Radoslav 1930- ... 37-40R
Katkov, George 1903-1985 Obituary ... 115
Katkov, Norman 1918- ... 13-16R
Kato, Hidetoshi 1930- ... 115
Kato, Shuichi 1919- ... 37-40R
Kato, Tsuyoski 1943- ... 126
Katona, Edita 1913- ... 69-72
Katona, George 1901-1981 ... 128
Obituary ... 104
Katona, Robert 1949- ... SATA 21
Katope, Christopher G. 1918- ... 21-24R
Katoppo, (Henriette) Marianne 1943- ... 123
Katrovas, Richard 1953- ... 126
Katsarakis, Joan Harries
See Harries, Joan
Katsaros, Thomas 1926- ... 57-60
Katsh, Abraham I(saac) 1908- ... CANR-8
Earlier sketch in CA 5-8R
Katsh, M. Ethan 1945- ... 133
Katsh, Salem M(ichael) 1948- ... 110
Kattan, Naim 1928- ... CANR-11
Earlier sketch in CA 69-72
See also DLB 53
Katterjohn, Arthur D.
1930(?)-1980 Obituary ... 93-96
Katz, Abraham 1926- ... 49-52
Katz, Albert M(ichael) 1938- ... 93-96
Katz, Alfred
See Allan, Alfred K.
Katz, Alfred 1938- ... 77-80
Katz, Arthur M. 1942- ... 124
Katz, Basho
See Gatti, Arthur Gerard
Katz, Benjamin 1904-1985 Obituary ... 115
Katz, Bobbi 1933- ... CANR-37
Earlier sketches in CA 37-40R, CANR-16
See also SATA 12
Katz, Carol 1939- ... 115
Katz, Daniel 1903- ... 41-44R
Katz, Elias 1912- ... 29-32R
Katz, Ellis 1938- ... 29-32R
Katz, Eve 1938- ... CANR-1
Earlier sketch in CA 45-48
Katz, Fred E(mil) 1927- ... 77-80
Katz, Fred(eric Phillip) 1938- ... 49-52
See also SATA 6
Katz, Friedrich 1927- ... 134
Brief entry ... 113
Katz, Gloria 1945(?)- ... 107
Katz, Herbert Melvin 1930- ... 103
Katz, Irving I. 1907- ... 1-4R
Katz, Jack 1944- ... 111
Katz, Jacob 1904- ... CANR-4
Earlier sketch in CA 1-4R
Katz, Jane B(resler) 1934- ... 85-88
See also SATA 33
Katz, Jay 1922- ... 118
Katz, John Stuart 1938- ... CANR-14
Earlier sketch in CA 37-40R
Katz, Jonathan 1938- ... 85-88
Katz, Josef 1918- ... 53-56
Katz, Joseph 1910- ... CANR-2
Earlier sketch in CA 1-4R

Katz, Judith Milstein 1943- 106
Katz, Leon 1919- CANR-20
Earlier sketches in CA 49-52, CANR-4
Katz, Leonard 1926- 21-24R
Katz, Lewis R(obert) 1938- 116
Katz, Lilian G(onshaw) 1932- 111
Katz, Marjorie P.
See Weiser, Marjorie P(hillis) K(atz)
Katz, Martin 1929- 21-24R
Katz, Marvin C(harles) 1930- 25-28R
Katz, Menke 1906-1991 .... CANR-11
Obituary 134
Earlier sketch in CA 13-16R
See also CAAS 9
Katz, Michael B(arry) 1939- CANR-13
Earlier sketch in CA 33-36R
Katz, Michael M. 1956(?)-1988 Obituary 126
Katz, Michael Ray 1944- CANR-39
Earlier sketches in CA 102, CANR-18
Katz, Mickey
See Katz, Myron Meyer
Katz, Milton 1907- CAP-1
Earlier sketch in CA 11-12
Katz, Mort 1925- CANR-11
Earlier sketch in CA 61-64
Katz, Myron Meyer 1909-1985 81-84
Obituary 116
Katz, Robert L. 1917- 9-12R
Katz, Robert 1933- CANR-11
Earlier sketch in CA 25-28R
Katz, Samuel 1914- CANR-12
Earlier sketch in CA 25-28R
Katz, Sanford N. 1933- CANR-13
Earlier sketch in CA 33-36R
Katz, Shmuel
See Katz, Samuel
Katz, Stan
See Chapman, Frank M(onroe)
Katz, Stanley Nider 1934- 9-12R
Katz, Steve 1935- CANR-12
Earlier sketch in CA 25-28R
See also CAAS 14
See also CLC 47
See also DLBY 83
Katz, Steven T(heodore) 1944- 132
Katz, Susan 1944(?)-1982 Obituary 107
Katz, Welwyn Wilton 1948- .... SATA 62
Katz, William A(rmstrong) 1924- CANR-10
Earlier sketch in CA 25-28R
Katz, William Loren 1927- CANR-9
Earlier sketch in CA 21-24R
See also SATA 13
Katz, William 1940- 85-88
Katzander, Howard L.
1911(?)-1983 Obituary 110
Katzenbach, John 1950- 119
Katzenbach, Maria 1953- 77-80
Katzenbach, William E.
1904-1975 Obituary 61-64
Katzenstein, Mary Fainsod 1945- 93-96
Katzenstein, Peter J(oachim) 1945- CANR-17
Earlier sketch in CA 93-96
Ka-Tzetnik 135633 .... CANR-27
Earlier sketch in CA 29-32R
Katzman, Allen 1937- 29-32R
Katzman, Anita 1920- 57-60
Katzman, David Manners 1941- CANR-5
Earlier sketch in CA 53-56
Katzman, Martin T(heodore) 1941- 111
Katznelson-Shazar, Rachel
1888-1975 Obituary 61-64
Katzner, Kenneth 1930- 5-8R
Kau, Michael Y. M.
See Kau, Ying-mao
Kau, Ying-mao 1934- Brief entry 114
Kauder, Emil 1901- 17-20R
Kaufelt, David Allan 1939- CANR-38
Earlier sketches in CA 45-48, CANR-1, 16
Kauffeld, Carl F. 1911-1974 Obituary 49-52
Kauffman, Christmas Carol 1902- 1-4R
Kauffman, Christopher J. 1936- 107
Kauffman, Donald T(homas) 1920- CANR-11
Earlier sketch in CA 25-28R
Kauffman, Dorotha S(trayer) 1925- 17-20R
Kauffman, Draper L. 1946- 108
Kauffman, George B(ernard) 1930- 17-20R
Kauffman, Henry J. 1908- 13-16R
Kauffman, James M(ilton) 1940- CANR-7
Earlier sketch in CA 57-60
Kauffman, Janet 1945- 117
See also CLC 42
See also DLBY 86
Kauffman, Joseph F(rank) 1921- CANR-1
Earlier sketch in CA 45-48
Kauffman, Milo (Franklin) 1898- 89-92
Kauffmann, C. Michael 1931- 125
Kauffmann, Georg (Friedrich) 1925- 49-52
Kauffmann, (Franklin) Lane
1922(?)-1988 Obituary 125
Kauffmann, Lane 1921- 17-20R
Kauffmann, Samuel Hay
1898-1971 Obituary 89-92
Kauffmann, Stanley 1916- CANR-6
Earlier sketch in CA 5-8R
Kaufman, Alan 1952- 128
Kaufman, Arnold S. 1927- 25-28R
Kaufman, Arthur 1934- CANR-25
Earlier sketch in CA 107
Kaufman, Barry Neil 1942- CANR-17
Earlier sketch in CA 97-100
Kaufman, Bel CANR-13
Earlier sketch in CA 13-16R
See also AAYA 4
See also SATA 57
Kaufman, Bob (Garnell) 1925-1986 .... CANR-22
Obituary 118
Earlier sketch in CA 41-44R
See also BW
See also CLC 49
See also DLB 16, 41
Kaufman, Burton I. 1940- 33-36R
Kaufman, Daniel 1949- 85-88
Kaufman, Debra Renee 1941- 109
Kaufman, Donald D(avid) 1933- 29-32R
Kaufman, Edmund George 1891- 73-76
Kaufman, George S. 1889-1961 108
Obituary 93-96
See also CLC 38
See also DLB 7
Kaufman, Gerald (Bernard) 1930- 21-24R
Kaufman, Gershen 1943- 117
Kaufman, Gloria (Shapiro) 1929- 122
Kaufman, Gordon Dester 1925- CANR-7
Earlier sketch in CA 13-16R
Kaufman, H(arold) G(erson) 1939- 69-72
Kaufman, Herbert 1922- 137
Brief entry 115
Kaufman, I(sadore) 1892-1978 Obituary 77-80
Kaufman, Irving 1920- 21-24R
Kaufman, Jacob J(oseph) 1914- 41-44R
Kaufman, Joe 1911- 107
See also SATA 33
Kaufman, Lloyd 1927- 93-96
Kaufman, Martin 1940- CANR-28
Earlier sketch in CA 109
Kaufman, Menahem 1921- 138
Kaufman, Mervyn D. 1932- 5-8R
See also SATA 4
Kaufman, Paul 1886-1979 Obituary 89-92
Kaufman, Paula T. 1946- 126
Kaufman, Philip 1936- 121
Brief entry 112
Kaufman, Polly W(elts) 1929- 114
Kaufman, Robert 1931- CANR-25
Earlier sketch in CA 17-20R
Kaufman, Roger (Alexander) 1932- CANR-9
Earlier sketch in CA 53-56
Kaufman, Rosamond (Arleen) V(an) P(oznak)
1923- CANR-7
Earlier sketch in CA 9-12R
Kaufman, Sherwin A. 1920- CANR-10
Earlier sketch in CA 25-28R
Kaufman, Shirley 1923- 49-52
Kaufman, Sidney 1910-1983 Obituary 110
Kaufman, Stuart Bruce 1942- 123
Kaufman, Sue
See Barondess, Sue K(aufman)
See also CLC 3, 8
Kaufman, Wallace 1939- CANR-10
Earlier sketch in CA 25-28R
Kaufman, William I(rving) 1922- CANR-24
Earlier sketches in CA 13-16R, CANR-7
Kaufman, Wolfe 1905(?)-1970 Obituary 29-32R
Kaufmann, Angelika 1935- .... SATA 15
Kaufmann, Edgar Jr. 1910-1989 Obituary 129
Kaufmann, Harry 1927- 45-48
Kaufmann, Helen L(oeb) 1887- CANR-7
Earlier sketch in CA 5-8R
Kaufmann, Henry William 1913- 41-44R
Kaufmann, John 1931- 81-84
See also SATA 18
Kaufmann, Myron S. 1921- 25-28R
Kaufmann, R(alph) James 1924- 13-16R
Kaufmann, Thomas DaCosta
1948- Obituary 129
Kaufmann, U(rlin) Milo 1934- 41-44R
Kaufmann, Ulrich George 1920- 21-24R
Kaufmann, Walter 1921-1980 .... CANR-1
Obituary 101
Earlier sketch in CA 1-4R
Kaufmann, Walter 1933- 61-64
Kaufmann, William J(ohn) III 1942- 93-96
Kaufmann, William W. 1918- 13-16R
Kaul, Donald 1934- 65-68
Kaula, Edna Mason 1906- 5-8R
See also SATA 13
Kaumeyer, Dorothy 1914- 134
Brief entry 105
Kaunda, K. D.
See Kaunda, Kenneth David
Kaunda, Kenneth
See Kaunda, Kenneth David
Kaunda, Kenneth D.
See Kaunda, Kenneth David
Kaunda, Kenneth David 1924- 133
Kauper, Paul Gerhardt 1907-1974 .... CANR-6
Obituary 49-52
Earlier sketch in CA 1-4R
Kaur, Sardarni Premka 1943- 77-80
Kaur Khalsa, Dayal 1943(?)-1989 Obituary 129
Kausler, Donald H(arvey) 1927- 17-20R
Kauth, Benjamin 1914- 5-8R
Kautsky, Karl (Johann)
1854-1938 Brief entry 123
Kauvar, Gerald B(luestone) 1938- 45-48
Kavafis, Konstantinos Petrou
1863-1933 Brief entry 104
See also Cavafy, C(onstantine) P(eter)
Kavaler, Lucy 1930- CANR-22
Earlier sketches in CA 57-60, CANR-7
See also SATA 23
Kavaler, Rebecca 1932- CANR-16
Earlier sketch in CA 89-92
Kavan, Anna 1901-1968 .... CANR-6
Earlier sketch in CA 5-8R
See also CLC 5, 13
See also MTCW
Kavanagh, Aidan 1929- 112
Kavanagh, Dan
See Barnes, Julian
Kavanagh, Dan(iel) 1946- 125
Kavanagh, James H. 1948- 126
Kavanagh, Jennifer 1947- 119
Kavanagh, Michael 1945- 118
Kavanagh, P(atrick) J(oseph Gregory)
1931- 81-84
See also DLB 40
Kavanagh, Patrick (Joseph) 1904-1967 123
Obituary 25-28R
See also CLC 22
See also DLB 15, 20
See also MTCW
Kavanagh, Peter 1916- 132
Kavanaugh, Cynthia
See Daniels, Dorothy
Kavanaugh, Ian
See Webb, Jean Francis
Kavanaugh, James J(oseph) 1934- CANR-38
Earlier sketches in CA 13-16R, CANR-17
Kavanaugh, John F(rancis) 1941- 115
Kavanaugh, Kieran 1928- 25-28R
Kavanaugh, Robert E. 1926- 29-32R
Kavasch, E(lizabeth) Barrie 1942- 110
Kavenagh, W(illiam) Keith 1926- 37-40R
Kavesh, Robert A(llyn) 1927- 17-20R
Kavet, Robert 1924- 37-40R
Kavifis, Konstantinos Petrou
See Kavafis, Konstantinos Petrou
Kavli, Guthorm 1917- CAP-1
Earlier sketch in CA 9-10
Kavner, Richard S. 1936- 93-96
Kavolis, Vytautas 1930- 25-28R
Kawabata, Yasunari 1899-1972 93-96
Obituary 33-36R
See also CLC 2, 5, 9, 18
Kawahito, Kiyoshi 1939- 37-40R
Kawai, Kazuo 1904-1963 .... 1-4R
Kawakami, Tovo S(uvemoto) 1916- 33-36R
Kawin, Bruce F. 1945- CANR-13
Earlier sketch in CA 37-40R
Kawin, Ethel CAP-1
Earlier sketch in CA 11-12
Kay, Barbara Ann 1929- 13-16R
Kay, Brian Ross 1924- 1-4R
Kay, David A(llen) 1940- Brief entry 114
Kay, Donald 1939- 57-60
Kay, E(lizabeth) Alison 1928- 65-68
Kay, Ellen
See DeMille, Nelson
Kay, Ernest 1915- CANR-24
Earlier sketches in CA 13-16R, CANR-6
Kay, George
See Lambert, Eric
Kay, George 1936- 21-24R
Kay, Guy Gavriel 1954- 134
Kay, Harry 1919- 25-28R
Kay, Helen
See Goldfrank, Helen Colodny
Kay, J(ohn) A(nderson) 1948- 119
Kay, Jane Holtz 1938- CANR-22
Earlier sketch in CA 106
Kay, Kenneth (Edmond) 1915- CANR-6
Earlier sketch in CA 9-12R
Kay, Mara CANR-2
Earlier sketch in CA 5-8R
See also SATA 13
Kay, Mary
See Ash, Mary Kay (Wagner)
Kay, Norman (Forber) 1929- 45-48
Kay, (Sydney Francis) Patrick (Chippendall) Healey
See
Healey-Kay, (Sydney Francis) Patrick (Chippendall)
Kay, Paul 1934- 41-44R
Kay, Reed 1925- 77-80
Kay, Ronald
See Knox-Mawer, Ronald
Kay, Terence 1918- 17-20R
Kay, Teresa
See de Kerpely, Theresa
Kay, Terry
See Kay, Terence
Kay, Terry (Winter) 1938- 110
Kay, Thomas O(bed) 1932- 1-4R
Kay, (Albert) William 1930-1976 .... CAP-2
Earlier sketch in CA 29-32
Kay, Zell
See Kemp, Roy Z(ell)
Kayal, Joseph M(itchell) 1942- 57-60
Kayal, Philip M(itchell) 1943- 57-60
Kayden, Xandra 1939- 127
Kaye, Alan
See Horowitz, Shel Alan
Kaye, Barbara
See Muir, Marie
Kaye, Bruce (Norman) 1939- 93-96
Kaye, Buddy 1918- 81-84
Kaye, Danny 1913-1987 Obituary 121
See also SATA 50
Kaye, Evelyn 1937- 57-60
Kaye, Geraldine (Hughesdon) 1925- CANR-22
Earlier sketches in CA 13-16R, CANR-7
See also SATA 10
Kaye, H. R.
See Knox, Hugh (Randolph)
Kaye, Harvey E(arle) 1927- 101
Kaye, Harvey J(ordan) 1949- 121
Kaye, Hilary 1950- 116
Kaye, Howard L. 1951- 126
Kaye, Joanne
See Payes, Rachel C(osgrove)
Kaye, Julian B(ertram) 1925- 1-4R
Kaye, Kenneth Peter 1946- 111
Kaye, Lenny 1946- Brief entry 121
Kaye, M(ary) M(argaret) 1909- CANR-24
Earlier sketch in CA 89-92
See also CLC 28
See also MTCW
See also SATA 62
Kaye, Marilyn 1949- CANR-24
Earlier sketch in CA 107
See also SATA 56
Kaye, Marvin (Nathan) 1938- CANR-19
Earlier sketches in CA 53-56, CANR-5
Kaye, Mollie
See Kaye, M(ary) M(argaret)
Kaye, Myrna 1930- 57-60
Kaye, Peggy 1948- 116
Kaye, Philip A. 1920- 37-40R
Kaye, Phyllis Johnson 102
Kaye-Smith, Sheila 1887-1956 Brief entry 118
See also DLB 36
See also TCLC 20
Kayira, Legson Didimu 1942- 17-20R
See also BW
Kaymor, Patrice Maguilene
See Senghor, Leopold Sedar
Kaysen, Carl 1920- CANR-11
Earlier sketch in CA 17-20R
Kayser, Elmer Louis 1896-1985 .... 37-40R
Obituary 116
Kayser, Hugh F. 1926- 107
Kayser-Jones, Jeanie Schmit 1935- 105
Kaysing, Bill
See Kaysing, William C.
Kaysing, William C. 1922- 33-36R
Kayyali, Abdul-Wahhab (Said)
1939-1981 Obituary 108
Kazakov, Yuri Pavlovich 1927- CANR-36
Earlier sketch in CA 5-8R
See also MTCW
Kazamias, Andreas M. 1927- 17-20R
Kazan, Elia 1909- CANR-32
Earlier sketch in CA 21-24R
See also CLC 6, 16, 63
Kazan, Frances 1946- 125
Kazantzakis, Nikos 1883(?)-1957 132
Brief entry 105
See also MTCW
See also TCLC 2, 5, 33
Kazarian, Edward A(rshak) 1931- 53-56
Kazdin, Alan E(dward) 1945- 104
Kazee, Buell H(ilton) 1900-1976 Obituary 111
Kazemzadeh Firuz 1924- 21-24R
Kazhdan, Alexander P. 1922- 138
Kazickas, Jurate C(atherine) 1943- 102
Kazimiroff, Theodore L. 1941- 109
Kazin, Alfred 1915- CANR-1
Earlier sketch in CA 1-4R
See also CAAS 7
See also CLC 34, 38
See also DLB 67
Kazin, Michael 1948- 127
Kazis, Richard 1952- 112
Kazmer, Daniel (Raphael) 1947- 102
Kazmier, Leonard J(ohn) 1930- 107
Kazziha, Walid W. 1941- 65-68
Keach, Richard L(eroy) 1919- 89-92
Kealey, Edward J(oseph) 1936- CANR-14
Earlier sketch in CA 37-40R
Kealy, Sean P(atrick) 1937- 114
Kean, Benjamin Harrison 1912- 103
Kean, Charles Duell 1910-1963 .... 5-8R
Kean, Edmund (Stanley) 1915- 102
Keane, Betty Winkler 1914- 93-96
Keane, Bil 1922- CANR-13
Earlier sketch in CA 33-36R
See also SATA 4
Keane, John B. 1928- 29-32R
See also DLB 13
Keane, Mary Nesta (Skrine) 1904- 114
Brief entry 108
See also Keane, Molly
Keane, Molly
See Keane, Mary Nesta (Skrine)
See also CLC 31
Keane, Noel 1938- 133
Keane, Patrick J(oseph) 1939- CANR-1
Earlier sketch in CA 45-48
Keaney, Marian 1944- 103
Kearey, Charles 1916- 45-48
Kearley, F(loyd) Furman 1932- 57-60
Kearney, Hugh Francis 1924- 5-8R
Kearney, James R(obert III) 1929- 25-28R
Kearney, Jean Nylander 1923- 65-68
Kearney, Robert N(orman) 1930- 81-84
Kearney, Ruth Elizabeth
See Carlson, Ruth (Elizabeth) Kearney
Kearns, Doris Helen
See Goodwin, Doris (Helen) Kearns
Kearns, Francis E(dward) 1931- 29-32R
Kearns, Frank T. 1903-1984 Obituary 111
Kearns, Frank 1917(?)-1986 Obituary 119
Kearns, James A(loysius) III 1949- 29-32R
Kearns, Lionel 1937- CANR-11
Earlier sketch in CA 17-20R
Kearns, Martha 1945- 57-60
Kearns, Michael S. 1947- 126
Kearny, Edward N. III 1936- 29-32R
Kearny, Jillian
See Goulart, Ron(ald Joseph)
Keasey, Carol Tomlinson
See Tomlinson-Keasey, Carol
Keast, James D. 1930- 25-28R
Keast, William R(ea) 1914- 13-16R
Keates, Jonathan .... CLC 34
Keating, Bern
See Keating, Leo Bernard
Keating, Charlotte Matthews 1927- 33-36R
Keating, Diane 1940- CANR-18
Earlier sketch in CA 101
Keating, Edward M. 1925- 13-16R

Keating, H(enry) R(eymond) F(itzwalter)
1926- CANR-34
Earlier sketches in CA 33-36R, CANR-18
See also CAAS 8
See also DLB 87
See also MTCW
Keating, John J. 1918(?)-1975 Obituary 61-64
Keating, L(ouis) Clark 1907- 21-24R
Keating, Lawrence A. 1903-1966 .... 5-8R
See also SATA 23
Keating, Leo Bernard 1915- 29-32R
See also SATA 10
Keating, Michael (F.) 1932- 49-52
Keating, Michael (Irvine) 1943- 129
Keating, Micheline 1904(?)-1989 Obituary 127
Keating, Tom 1917-1984 Obituary 112
Keaton, Buster 1895-1966 .... CLC 20
Keats, Charles B. 1905- CAP-1
Earlier sketch in CA 13-16
Keats, Emma 1899(?)-1979(?) 135
See also SATA 68
Keats, Ezra Jack 1916-1983 77-80
Obituary 109
See also AITN 1
See also CLR 1
See also DLB 61
See also MAICYA
See also SATA 14, 34, 57
Keats, John (C.) 1920- 73-76
Keats, John 1795-1821 .... CDBLB 1789-1832
See also DLB 96, 110
See also PC 1
See also WLC
Keats, Mark 1905- 77-80
Keaveney, Arthur 1951- 124
Keaveney, Sydney Starr 1939- 53-56
Keay, Frederick 1915- 33-36R
Keay, John (Stanley Melville) 1941- 65-68
Kebbe, Charles Maynard 1913- 114
Kebin, Jodi
See Lawrence, Jodi
Keble, John 1792-1866 .... DLB 32, 55
Kebschull, Harvey G(ustav) 1932- 41-44R
Keck, Leander Earl 1928- 104
Keddell, Georgina (Murray) 1913- 25-28R
Keddie, Nikki R(agozin) 1930- CANR-13
Earlier sketch in CA 25-28R
Kedgley, Susan (Jane) 1948- 61-64
Kedourie, Elie 1926- CANR-31
Earlier sketches in CA 21-24R, CANR-10
Kedzie, Daniel Peter 1930- 17-20R
Kee, (Alexander) Alistair 1937- 89-92
Kee, Howard Clark 1920- CANR-10
Earlier sketch in CA 21-24R
Kee, Robert 1919- 130
Brief entry 113
Keeble, John 1944- CANR-14
Earlier sketch in CA 29-32R
See also DLBY 83
Keeble, Neil H(oward) 1944- 135
Keech, William J(ohn) 1904- CAP-1
Earlier sketch in CA 9-10
Keech, William R(obertson) 1939- 25-28R
Keedy, Mervin L(averne) 1920- CANR-5
Earlier sketch in CA 53-56
Keefe, Carolyn 1928- 57-60
Keefe, Donald Joseph 1924- 37-40R
Keefe, John Edwin 1942- 107
Keefe, Michael 1946- 93-96
Keefe, Robert 1938- 89-92
Keefe, Susan E. 1947- 126
Keefe, Terry 1940- 125
Keefer, Catherine
See Ogan, George F.
and Ogan, Margaret E. (Nettles)
Keefer, Janice Kulyk
See Kulyk Keefer, Janice
Keefer, T(ruman) Frederick 1930- 21-24R
Keeffe, Barrie (Colin) 1945- Brief entry 116
See also DLB 13
Keegan, Frank L. 1925- 45-48
Keegan, John (Desmond Patrick) 1934- 136
Brief entry 130
See also BEST 90:3
Keegan, Marcia 1943- CANR-32
Earlier sketch in CA 49-52
See also SATA 9
Keegan, Mary Heathcott 1914- CANR-3
Earlier sketch in CA 5-8R
Keegan, Terence J(ames) 1939- 117
Keegan, Warren J(oseph) 1936- 57-60
Keehn, Sally M. 1947- 137
Keel, Frank
See Keeler, Ronald F(ranklin)
Keel, John A.
See Kiehle, John Alva
Keele, Kenneth D(avid) 1909- 5-8R
Keele, Reba Lou 1941- Brief entry 106
Keeler, Mary Frear 1904- 77-80
Keeler, Ronald F(ranklin) 1913-1983 107
See also SATA 47
Keeley, Edmund (Leroy) 1928- CANR-22
Earlier sketches in CA 1-4R, CANR-1
Keeley, James 1867-1934 .... DLB 25
Keeley, Joseph C(harles) 1907- 25-28R
Keeley, Steve 1949- 93-96
Keeling, Clinton Harry 1932- CANR-7
Earlier sketch in CA 9-12R
Keeling, E. B.
See Curl, James Stevens
Keeling, Jill Annette (Shaw) 1923- CANR-12
Earlier sketches in CAP-1, CA 9-10
Keely, Charles C(larke) Jr.
1934-1985 Obituary 116
Keely, Harry Harris 1904- 65-68
Keely, Jane 1922- 107

Keen, Benjamin 1913- 136
Brief entry 114
Keen, (John) Ernest 1937- 33-36R
Keen, Geraldine
See Norman, Geraldine (Lucia)
Keen, M. H.
See Keen, Maurice Hugh
Keen, Martin L. 1913- 33-36R
See also SATA 4
Keen, Maurice
See Keen, Maurice Hugh
Keen, Maurice Hugh 1933- 122
Keen, Sam 137
Keen, Tommy 1923- 108
Keenan, Angela Elizabeth 1890-1983 61-64
Obituary 111
Keenan, Boyd R(aymond) 1928- 17-20R
Keenan, Deborah (Anne) 1950- CANR-30
Earlier sketches in CA 69-72, CANR-11
Keenan, Desmond (Joseph) 1933- 125
Keenan, Joseph H(enry)
1900-1977 Obituary 73-76
Keenan, Martha 1927- 77-80
Keene, Burt
See Bickers, Richard Leslie Townshend
Keene, Carolyn
See McFarlane, Leslie (Charles)
Keene, Carolyn CANR-27
Earlier sketch in CA 17-20R
See also MAICYA
See also SATA 65
Keene, Donald 1922- CANR-5
Earlier sketch in CA 1-4R
See also CLC 34
Keene, J(ames) Calvin 1908- CAP-1
Earlier sketch in CA 17-18
Keene, James A(llen) 1932- 109
Keene, R. D.
See Keene, Raymond D(ennis)
Keene, Ray
See Keene, Raymond D(ennis)
Keene, Raymond D(ennis)
1948- Brief entry 112
Keener, Frederick M(ichael) 1937- CANR-15
Earlier sketch in CA 53-56
Keeney, Charles James 1912- 5-8R
Keeney, Chuck
See Keeney, Charles James
Keeney, Ralph L(yons) 1944- CANR-16
Earlier sketch in CA 97-100
Keeney, William (Echard) 1922- CANR-15
Earlier sketch in CA 41-44R
Keenleyside, Hugh Llewellyn 1898- CAP-1
Earlier sketch in CA 17-18
Keenleyside, T(erence) A(shley) 1940- 77-80
Keeny, S. M.
See Keeny, Spurgeon Milton
Keeny, Spurgeon Milton
1893-1988 Obituary 126
Keep, Carolyn 1940- 65-68
Keep, David (John) 1936- 61-64
Keep, John (Leslie Howard) 1926- 9-12R
Keeping, Charles (William James)
1924-1988 .... CANR-11
Obituary 125
Earlier sketch in CA 21-24R
See also MAICYA
See also SATA 9, 56, 69
Keery, Sam 1929- 124
Kees, Beverly (Ann) 1941- 81-84
Keese, Parton 1926- 109
Keesecker, William Francis 1918- 33-36R
Keeshan, Robert J. 1927- CANR-5
Earlier sketch in CA 5-8R
See also SATA 32
Keesing, Nancy (Florence) 1923- CANR-27
Earlier sketches in CA 9-12R, CANR-6
Keeslar, Oreon 1907- CAP-1
Earlier sketch in CA 13-14
Keeton, Elizabeth B(aker) 1919- 29-32R
Keeton, George Williams 1902- 13-16R
Keeton, Kathy 1939- 125
See also AITN 2
Keeton, Morris Teuton 1917- CANR-4
Earlier sketch in CA 1-4R
Keeton, Robert E(rnest) 1919- CANR-2
Earlier sketch in CA 5-8R
Keeton, William T(insley) 1933-1980 124
Obituary 105
Keever, Jack 1938- 53-56
Keevill, Henry J(ohn) 1914- CAP-1
Earlier sketch in CA 9-10
Keezer, Dexter Merriam 1895- 1-4R
Kefferstan, Jean
See Pedrick, Jean
Kegan, Adrienne Koch
1912-1971 Obituary 33-36R
Kegel, Charles H. 1924- 1-4R
Kegley, Charles W(illiam) Jr. 1944- CANR-36
Earlier sketch in CA 114
Kegley, Charles William 1912- CANR-2
Earlier sketch in CA 5-8R
Kehayan, V. Alex 1944- 110
Kehl, D(elmar) G(eorge) 1936- 33-36R
Kehl, James Arthur 1922- 112
Kehle, Roberta L(unsford) 1936- 116
Kehm, Freda (Irma) S(amuels) CAP-2
Earlier sketch in CA 29-32
Kehoe, Constance (DeMuzio) 1933- 13-16R
Kehoe, Monika 1909- 21-24R
Kehoe, Patricia D. 1951- 120
Kehoe, Patrick E(mmett) 1941- 57-60
Kehoe, William F. 1933- 13-16R
Kehrer, Daniel M(ark) 1953- 120
Kehrer, James P(aul) 1951- 117
Keidel, Eudene 1921- 109
Keidel, Levi (Jr.) 1927- 115

Keifetz, Norman 1932- 89-92
Keiger, John F(rederick) V(ictor) 1952- 125
Keightley, David N(oel) 1932- 97-100
Keil, (Harold) Bill 1926- 81-84
Keil, Sally Van Wagenen 1946- 89-92
Keillor, Garrison
See Keillor, Gary (Edward)
See also AAYA 2
See also BEST 89:3
See also CLC 40
See also DLBY 87
See also SATA 58
Keillor, Gary (Edward) 1942- CANR-36
Brief entry 111
Earlier sketch in CA 117
See also Keillor, Garrison
See also MTCW
Keilstrup, Margaret 1945- 138
Keim, Charles J. 1921- CANR-13
Earlier sketch in CA 33-36R
Keimberg, Allyn
See Kimbro, John M.
Keinzley, Frances 1922- 85-88
Keir, Christine
See Popescu, Christine
Keir, David E(dwin) 1906-1969 .... CAP-1
Earlier sketch in CA 9-10
Keir, David Lindsay 1895-1973 .... CAP-2
Earlier sketch in CA 21-22
Keirstead, Burton Seely 1907- 5-8R
Keiser, Bea(trice) 1931- 97-100
Keiser, Norman F(red) 1930- 13-16R
Keislar, Evan R(ollo) 1913- 21-24R
Keisling, Bill
See Keisling, William
Keisling, William 1958- 113
Keisman, Michael E(dward) 1932- 25-28R
Keister, Elinore
See Dobson, Elinore (Lucille)
Keitges, Julie 1940- 110
Keith, Agnes Newton 1901- 17-20R
Keith, Carlton
See Robertson, Keith (Carlton)
Keith, David
See Steegmuller, Francis
Keith, Donald
See Monroe, Keith
Keith, Elmer (Merrifield) 1899- 101
Keith, Eros 1942- 114
See also SATA 52
Keith, Hal 1934- .... SATA 36
Keith, Hamish
See Chapman, James (Keith)
Keith, Harold Verne 1903- CANR-2
Earlier sketch in CA 5-8R
See also MAICYA
See also SATA 2
Keith, Herbert F. 1895- 37-40R
Keith, J. Kilmeny
See Malleson, Lucy Beatrice
Keith, Jean E. 1921-1979 Obituary 85-88
Keith, Jennie 1942- 116
Keith, Judith 1923- 49-52
Keith, K. Wymand 1924- 33-36R
Keith, Larry Ficquette 1947- 97-100
Keith, Lee
See Sunners, William
Keith, Marian 1874(?)-1961 .... DLB 92
Keith, Michael
See Hubbard, L(afayette) Ron(ald)
Keith, Michael C(urtis) 1945- 132
Keith, Nancy 1916-1990 138
Keith, Noel L(eonard) 1903-1981 57-60
Obituary 133
Keith, Robert
See Applebaum, Stan
Keith, Ronald (A.) 1914(?)-1985 Obituary 117
Keith, Sam 1921- 65-68
Keith, Stuart 1931- 126
Keith, W(illiam) J(ohn) 1934- CANR-11
Earlier sketch in CA 17-20R
Keithley, Erwin M. 1905- 73-76
Keithley, George 1935- 37-40R
Keith-Lucas, Alan 1910- CANR-20
Earlier sketches in CA 5-8R, CANR-2
Keith-Lucas, Bryan 1912- 107
Keith-Spiegel, Patricia 1939- 41-44R
Keith X
See Armstrong, Keith F(rancis) W(hitfield)
Kekes, John 1936- 65-68
Kekkonen, Sylvi 1900(?)-1974 Obituary 53-56
Kelber, Magda 1908- 5-8R
Kelch, Ray Alden 1923- 85-88
Kelder, Diane 1934- CANR-18
Earlier sketch in CA 25-28R
Keldysh, Mstislav V(sevolodovich)
1911-1978 Obituary 77-80
Kele, Max H(erschel) 1936- Brief entry 114
Keleher, Will(iam Aloysius)
1886-1972 Obituary 37-40R
Keleinikov, Andrei 1924- .... SATA 65
Keleman, Stanley 1931- CANR-14
Earlier sketch in CA 81-84
Kelemen, Pal 1894- 104
Kelen, Emery 1896-1978 .... 9-12R
Obituary 103
See also SATA 13, 26
Kelen, Stephen 1912- 107
Kelf-Cohen, Reuben 1895- 49-52
Kelikian, Hampar 1899(?)-1983 Obituary 110
Kell, Joseph
See Wilson, John (Anthony) Burgess
Kell, Richard (Alexander) 1927- CANR-8
Earlier sketch in CA 5-8R
Kellam, Sheppard (Gordon) 1931- 73-76
Kelland, Clarence Budington
1881-1964 Obituary 89-92

Kellar, Kenneth C(hambers) 1906- 45-48
Kellaway, Frank (Gerald) 1922- 9-12R
Kellaway, George P(ercival) 1909- CAP-2
Earlier sketch in CA 23-24
Kelleam, Joseph E(veridge) 1913-1975 107
See also SATA 31
Kelleher, Catherine McArdle 1939- 125
Brief entry 115
Kelleher, Patrick J(oseph)
1917-1985 Obituary 116
Kelleher, Stephen J(oseph) 1915- 69-72
Kelleher, Victor (Michael Kitchener) 1939- 126
See also SATA 52
Keller, Allan 1904-1981 .... CANR-29
Earlier sketch in CA 29-32R
Keller, Betty 1930- 121
Keller, Beverly CANR-38
Earlier sketches in CA 49-52, CANR-1, 17
See also SATA 13
Keller, Charles 1942- CANR-2
Earlier sketch in CA 49-52
See also SATA 8
Keller, Clair W(ayne) 1932- 53-56
Keller, Dean H(oward) 1933- 53-56
Keller, Dick 1923- .... SATA 36
Keller, Dolores Elaine 1926- 104
Keller, Edward A(nthony) 1942- 73-76
Keller, Evelyn Fox 1936- 125
Keller, Frances Richardson 1914- 81-84
Keller, Franklin J. 1887(?)-1976 Obituary 65-68
Keller, Fred S(immons) 1899- CANR-11
Earlier sketch in CA 69-72
Keller, Gail Faithfull
See Faithfull, Gail
Keller, Gary D. 1943- 131
See also DLB 82
See also HW
Keller, George 1928- 123
Keller, Helen (Adams) 1880-1968 101
Obituary 89-92
See also MTCW
Keller, Holly Brief entry 118
See also SATA 42
Keller, Howard H(ughes) 1941- 45-48
Keller, Irene (Barron) 1927- 116
See also SATA 36
Keller, James Gregory
1900-1977 Obituary 69-72
Keller, John E(sten) 1917- 45-48
Keller, Karl 1933- CANR-12
Earlier sketch in CA 57-60
Keller, Marti 1948- 97-100
Keller, Mitzie Stuart 111
Keller, Mollie .... SATA 50
Keller, Morton 1929- 5-8R
Keller, Suzanne 1930- 65-68
Keller, Thomas F(ranklin) 1931- CANR-3
Earlier sketch in CA 9-12R
Keller, W(alter) D(avid) 1900- 41-44R
Keller, Werner (Rudolf August Wolfgang)
1909- CANR-13
Earlier sketch in CA 21-24R
Kellerman, Barbara 1939- 110
Kellerman, Faye 1952- 120
Kellerman, Jonathan 1949- CANR-29
Earlier sketch in CA 106
See also BEST 90:1
See also CLC 44
Kellett, Arnold 1926- CANR-19
Earlier sketch in CA 103
Kelley, Alden D(rew) 1903- 1-4R
Kelley, Alice van Buren 1944- 81-84
Kelley, Allen C(harles) 1937- 104
Kelley, Arleon L(eigh) 1935- 115
Kelley, (Albert) Ben 1936- 45-48
Kelley, Brooks Mather 1929- 111
Kelley, Cecil B. Sr. 1911(?)-1987 Obituary 123
Kelley, Clarence M(arion) 1911- 127
Kelley, Dean M(aurice) 1926- 81-84
Kelley, Donald R(eed) 1931- CANR-12
Earlier sketch in CA 29-32R
Kelley, Earl Clarence 1895- 5-8R
Kelley, Edith Summers
1884-1956 Brief entry 109
See also DLB 9
Kelley, Eugene J(ohn) 1922- 13-16R
Kelley, H. N. 1911- 45-48
Kelley, Hubert (Williams) Jr. 1926- 5-8R
Kelley, J(ohn) Charles 1913- 97-100
Kelley, Jane Holden 1928- 45-48
Kelley, Joanna (Elizabeth) 1910- CAP-2
Earlier sketch in CA 23-24
Kelley, Jonathan 107
Kelley, Joseph J(ohn) Jr. 1914- CANR-8
Earlier sketch in CA 61-64
Kelley, Kevin J. 1948- 120
Kelley, Kitty 1942- CANR-27
Earlier sketch in CA 81-84
Kelley, Leo P(atrick) 1928- CANR-24
Earlier sketch in CA 107
See also SATA 31, 32
Kelley, Mary 1943- 124
Kelley, Maurice (Willyle) 1903- 119
Kelley, Page H(utto) 1924- 25-28R
Kelley, Ray
See Paine, Lauran (Bosworth)
Kelley, Robert E(mmett) 1938- 53-56
Kelley, Robert 1925- 25-28R
Kelley, Ruby M.
See Johnson, Ruby Kelley
Kelley, Stanley Jr. 1926- 13-16R
Kelley, True (Adelaide) 1946- CANR-23
Earlier sketch in CA 105
See also SATA 39, 41

Kelley, William Melvin 1937- CANR-27
Earlier sketch in CA 77-80
See also BW
See also CLC 22
See also DLB 33
Kelley, William T(homas) 1917- 37-40R
Kelley, William 1929- CANR-6
Earlier sketch in CA 5-8R
Kelley, Win 1923- 89-92
Kellin, Sally Moffet 1932- 61-64
See also SATA 9
Kelling, Furn L. 1914- 17-20R
See also SATA 37
Kelling, George W(alton) 1944- CANR-9
Earlier sketch in CA 57-60
Kelling, Hans-Wilhelm 1932- 37-40R
Kellison, Stephen G. 1942- 53-56
Kellman, Steven G. 1947- CANR-29
Earlier sketch in CA 112
Kellner, Bruce 1930- CANR-27
Earlier sketches in CA 29-32R, CANR-11
Kellner, Douglas Mackay 1943- 116
Kellner, Esther 13-16R
Kellner, L. 1904- 5-8R
Kellock, Archibald P.
See Mavor, Osborne Henry
Kellogg, Alfred Latimer 1915- 41-44R
Kellogg, Ansel Nash 1832-1886 .... DLB 23
Kellogg, Charles Edwin
1902-1980 Obituary 97-100
Kellogg, Charles Flint 1909- CAP-2
Earlier sketch in CA 23-24
Kellogg, Gene
See Kellogg, Jean (Defrees)
Kellogg, James C. III 1915-1980 Obituary 103
Kellogg, Jean (Defrees) 1916-1978 ....CANR-7
Earlier sketch in CA 9-12R
See also SATA 10
Kellogg, Marion S(chuyler) 1920- 120
Kellogg, Marjorie 1922- 81-84
See also CLC 2
Kellogg, Mary Alice 1948- 81-84
Kellogg, Steven 1941- CANR-1
Earlier sketch in CA 49-52
See also CLR 6
See also DLB 61
See also MAICYA
See also SATA 8, 57
Kellogg, Virginia 1907-1981 Obituary 108
Kellogg, Winthrop N(iles) 1898-1971 ....1-4R
Kellough, Richard Dean 1935- 53-56
Kellow, Kathleen
See Hibbert, Eleanor Burford
Kellow, Norman B. 1914- 21-24R
Kellum, D(avid) F(ranklin) 1936- 61-64
Kelly, A(ngeline) A(gnes) 1924- 128
Kelly, Alfred H. 1907-1976 ....5-8R
Obituary 65-68
Kelly, Alison 1913- 105
Kelly, Balmer H(ancock) 1914- 17-20R
Kelly, C(harles) Brian 1935- 89-92
Kelly, Carla 1947- 118
Kelly, Charles E. 1920(?)-1985 Obituary 114
Kelly, Charles M. 1932- 128
Kelly, Charles Patrick Bernard
1891(?)-1971 Obituary 29-32R
Kelly, Clarence 1941- 61-64
Kelly, C.M.O.
See Gibbs, (Cecilia) May
Kelly, Commando
See Kelly, Charles E.
Kelly, Dave
See Kelly, David M(ichael)
Kelly, David M(ichael) 1938- CANR-12
Earlier sketch in CA 29-32R
Kelly, Edward H(anford) 1930- 37-40R
Kelly, Emmett (Leo) 1898-1979 Obituary 85-88
Kelly, Eric Philbrook 1884-1960 Obituary 93-96
See also MAICYA
See also YABC 1
Kelly, Faye L(ucius) 1914- 21-24R
Kelly, Frank K. 1914- CANR-39
Earlier sketches in CA 1-4R, CANR-1, 16
Kelly, Frederic Joseph 1922- 53-56
Kelly, Gail P(aradise) 1940-1991 81-84
Obituary 133
Kelly, Gary F(rank) 1943- 89-92
Kelly, George A. 1916- CANR-11
Earlier sketch in CA 17-20R
Kelly, George Armstrong
1932-1987 Obituary 125
Kelly, George E. 1887-1974 Obituary 49-52
See also AITN 1
See also DLB 7
Kelly, George V(incent) 1919- 93-96
Kelly, George W. 1894- CANR-9
Earlier sketch in CA 65-68
Kelly, Gerald R(ay) 1930- 29-32R
Kelly, Grace (Patricia) 1929-1982 Obituary 107
Kelly, Guy
See Moore, Nicholas
Kelly, H(enry) A(nsgar) 1934- CANR-30
Earlier sketch in CA 25-28R
Kelly, Hugh 1739-1777 .... DLB 89
Kelly, Ian
See Kelly, John Spence
Kelly, J(ohn) M(aurice) 1931-1991 109
Obituary 133
Kelly, James B(urton) 1905- 49-52
Kelly, James Patrick 1951- 135
Kelly, James Plunkett 1920- 53-56
See also Plunkett, James
Kelly, Jeff
See Kelly, Jeffrey
Kelly, Jeffrey A(llen) 1948- 114
Kelly, Jeffrey 1946- 136
See also SATA 65
Kelly, Joan Berlin 1939- 107
Kelly, Joan 1928(?)-1982 Obituary 107
Kelly, John M. Jr. 1919- 13-16R
Kelly, John N(orman) D(avidson)
1909- CANR-5
Earlier sketch in CA 5-8R
Kelly, John Rivard 1939- 103
Kelly, John Spence 1934- 125
Kelly, John 1921- 73-76
Kelly, John 1943- 127
Kelly, Joyce 1933- 106
Kelly, Karen 1935- 101
Kelly, Kathleen M. 1964- .... SATA 71
Kelly, Kathleen Sheridan White 1945- 49-52
Kelly, Kevin 1934- 130
Kelly, L(ouis) G(erard) 1935- 107
Kelly, Laurence 1933- CANR-15
Earlier sketch in CA 81-84
Kelly, Lawrence C(harles) 1932- CANR-8
Earlier sketch in CA 21-24R
Kelly, Leo J. 1925- 41-44R
Kelly, (Alison) Linda 1936- 103
Kelly, M(ilton) T(erry) 1947- CANR-19
Earlier sketch in CA 97-100
See also CLC 55
Kelly, Mahlon (George) 1939- 53-56
Kelly, Marguerite (Lelong) 1932- 65-68
Kelly, Martha Rose 1914-1983 69-72
See also SATA 37
Kelly, Marty
See Kelly, Martha Rose
Kelly, Mary Coolican 1927- CANR-2
Earlier sketch in CA 1-4R
Kelly, Mary J(osephine) 1944- 117
Kelly, Maurice Anthony 1931- 53-56
Kelly, Maurice N. 1919- 21-24R
Kelly, Nora (Hickson) 1910- 101
Kelly, Patrick
See Allbeury, Theodore Edward le Bouthillier
Kelly, Paula 1949- 114
Kelly, Pauline Agnes 1936- 45-48
Kelly, Philip John 1896-1972 ....5-8R
Obituary 37-40R
Kelly, Ralph
See Geis, Darlene Stern
Kelly, Ray
See Paine, Lauran (Bosworth)
Kelly, Regina Z(immerman) 1898- CANR-2
Earlier sketch in CA 1-4R
See also SATA 5
Kelly, Richard J(ohn) 1938- 41-44R
Kelly, Richard (Michael) 1937- CANR-34
Earlier sketch in CA 107
Kelly, Rita Mae 1939- 81-84
Kelly, Robert Glynn 1920- 1-4R
Kelly, Robert 1935- 17-20R
See also DLB 5
Kelly, Rosalie (Ruth) CANR-11
Earlier sketch in CA 61-64
See also SATA 43
Kelly, Russell 1949- 123
Kelly, Stan
See Kelly-Bootle, Stan
Kelly, Stephen E(ugene) 1919-1978 110
Obituary 104
Kelly, Susan Croce 1947- 129
Kelly, Thomas 1909- CAP-1
Earlier sketch in CA 9-10
Kelly, Thomas 1929- 109
Kelly, Tim 1935- 13-16R
Kelly, Timothy Michael 1947- 133
Kelly, Walt(er Crawford) 1913-1973 73-76
Obituary 45-48
See also SATA 18
Kelly, William Leo 1924- 13-16R
Kelly, William W(atkins) 1928- 9-12R
Kelly-Bootle, Stan 1929- 110
Kelly-Gadol, Joan 61-64
Kelm, Karlton 1908(?)-1987 Obituary 121
Kelman, Charles D. 1930- 110
Kelman, Herbert C(hanoch) 1927- 13-16R
Kelman, James 1946- .... CLC 58
Kelman, Mark 1951- 93-96
Kelman, Steven 1948- CANR-12
Earlier sketch in CA 29-32R
Kelsay, Isabel Thompson 1905- 121
Kelsen, Hans 1881-1973 Obituary 115
Kelsey, Alice Geer 1896- 5-8R
See also SATA 1
Kelsey, Joan Marshall 1907- 5-8R
Kelsey, Morton T(rippe) 1917- CANR-26
Earlier sketches in CA 21-24R, CANR-10
Kelsey, Robert J(ohn) 1927- 103
Kelso, Louis O(rth) 1913-1991 ....25-28R
Obituary 133
Kelso, Ruth 1885-1986 Obituary 119
Kelson, Allen H(oward) 1940- CANR-13
Earlier sketch in CA 77-80
Keltner, John W(illiam) 1918- 29-32R
Kelton, Elmer 1926- CANR-36
Earlier sketches in CA 21-24R, CANR-12
See also AITN 1
Kelvin, Norman 1924- Brief entry 118
Kemal, Salim 1948- 125
Kemal, Yashar 1923- 89-92
See also CLC 14, 29
Kemble, Fanny 1809-1893 .... DLB 32
Kemble, James CAP-2
Earlier sketch in CA 29-32
Kemelman, Harry 1908- CANR-6
Earlier sketch in CA 9-12R
See also AITN 1
See also CLC 2
See also DLB 28
Kemeny, Jean A(lexander) 1930- 117
Kemeny, John G(eorge) 1926- 33-36R
Kemeny, Peter 1938-1975 53-56
Obituary 89-92
Kemerer, Frank R(obert) 1940- CANR-26
Earlier sketches in CA 65-68, CANR-10
Kemmerer, Donald L(orenzo) 1905- 1-4R
Kemp, Anthony 1939- CANR-25
Earlier sketch in CA 105
Kemp, Arnold 1938- Brief entry 110
Kemp, Bernard Peter 1942- 107
Kemp, Betty 1916- 9-12R
Kemp, Charles F. 1912- CANR-5
Earlier sketch in CA 9-12R
Kemp, Diana Moyle 1919- CAP-1
Earlier sketch in CA 9-10
Kemp, Edward C. 1929- 81-84
Kemp, Gene 1926- CANR-12
Earlier sketch in CA 69-72
See also MAICYA
See also SATA 25
Kemp, Jack (French) 1935- 109
Kemp, Jerrold E(dwin) 1921- 77-80
Kemp, John C(rocker) 1942- 93-96
Kemp, Lysander (Schaffer Jr.) 1920- CANR-1
Earlier sketch in CA 45-48
Kemp, Martin (John) 1942- 108
Kemp, Patrick S(amuel) 1932- 53-56
Kemp, Penny 1944- 130
Kemp, Peter (Mant Macintyre) 1915- 25-28R
Kemp, Robert 1908-1967 .... CAP-1
Earlier sketch in CA 13-16
Kemp, Roy Z(ell) 1910- 9-12R
Kemp, Tom 1921- 25-28R
Kempe, C(harles) Henry 1922-1984 122
Kempe, Frederick 1954- 138
Kemper, Donald J. 1929- 21-24R
Kemper, Inez 1906- CAP-1
Earlier sketch in CA 13-14
Kemper, Rachel H. 1931- 102
Kemper, Robert V(an) 1945- 104
Kemper, Troxey 1915- 136
Kemperman, Steve (Richard) 1955- 108
Kempfer, Lester Leroy 1932- 49-52
Kempher, Ruth Moon 1934- CANR-17
Earlier sketch in CA 25-28R
Kempner, Mary Jean 1913-1969 .... CAP-2
Earlier sketch in CA 29-32
See also SATA 10
Kempner, S. Marshall 1898- 85-88
Kempowski, Walter 1929- Brief entry 122
Kempson, Rachel 1910- 130
Kempster, Mary Yates 1911- CAP-1
Earlier sketch in CA 9-10
Kempster, Norman 1936- 77-80
Kempton, James Murray Jr.
1945(?)-1971 Obituary 33-36R
Kempton, Jean Goldschmidt
1946(?)-1971 Obituary 33-36R
Kempton, Jean Welch 1914- 49-52
See also SATA 10
Kempton, (James) Murray 1918- 97-100
Kempton, Richard 1935- 106
Kemsley, Viscount
See Berry, James Gomer
Kemsley, William George Jr. 1928- 85-88
Kenda, Margaret 1942- .... SATA 71
Kendal, Geoffrey
See Bragg, Richard Geoffrey
Kendal, Wallis 1937- 107
Kendall, Alan 1939- 131
Kendall, Aubyn 1919- 107
Kendall, Carol (Seeger) 1917- CANR-25
Earlier sketches in CA 5-8R, CANR-7
See also MAICYA
See also SAAS 7
See also SATA 11
Kendall, David Evan 1944- 29-32R
Kendall, Dorothy Steinbomer 1912- 57-60
Kendall, E(dith) Lorna 1921- 5-8R
Kendall, Edward C(alvin)
1886-1972 Obituary 111
Kendall, Elaine (Becker) 1929- 17-20R
Kendall, Elizabeth B(emis) 1947- 81-84
Kendall, Gordon
See Lewitt, Shariann (N.)
Kendall, Henry Madison 1901-1966 ....5-8R
Kendall, Jane (F.) 1952- 137
Kendall, Kenneth E(verett) 1913- 45-48
Kendall, Lace
See Stoutenburg, Adrien (Pearl)
Kendall, Laurel 1947- 121
Kendall, Lisa See 1955- CANR-25
Earlier sketch in CA 111
Kendall, Lyle H(arris) Jr. 1919- 17-20R
Kendall, Marjorie 1930- 121
Kendall, Maurice (George)
1907-1983 Obituary 109
Kendall, Patricia Louise
1921-1990 Obituary 131
Kendall, Paul Murray 1911-1973 .... CAP-1
Earlier sketch in CA 13-16
Kendall, R(obert) T(illman) 1935- 93-96
Kendall, Robert 1934- CANR-6
Earlier sketch in CA 13-16R
Kendall, T(homas) Robert 1935- 69-72
Kendall, Willmoore 1909-1967 ....CANR-6
Earlier sketch in CA 5-8R
Kendle, John Edward 1937- 61-64
Kendler, Howard H(arvard) 1919- 17-20R
Kendrake, Carleton
See Gardner, Erle Stanley
Kendrick, Baynard H(ardwick)
1894-1977 ....CANR-4
Obituary 69-72
Earlier sketch in CA 1-4R
Kendrick, David Andrew 1937- CANR-9
Earlier sketch in CA 21-24R
Kendrick, Frank J(enness) 1928- 41-44R
Kendrick, John (Stafford) 1917- 121
Kendrick, John W(hitefield) 1917- 127
Brief entry 110
Kendrick, Thomas Downing 1895- 81-84
Kendrick, Walter 1947- 112
Kendricks, James
See Fox, G(ardner) F(rancis)
Kendris, Christopher 1923- CANR-24
Earlier sketches in CA 5-8R, CANR-7
Keneally, Thomas (Michael) 1935- CANR-10
Earlier sketch in CA 85-88
See also CLC 5, 8, 10, 14, 19, 27, 43
See also MTCW
Kenealy, James P. 1927- 93-96
See also SATA 29, 52
Kenealy, Jim
See Kenealy, James P.
Keneas, Alexander 1938(?)-1984 Obituary 113
Kenelly, John W(illis Jr.) 1935- 25-28R
Kenen, Isaiah Leo 1905- 107
Kenen, Peter B(ain) 1932- CANR-22
Earlier sketches in CA 5-8R, CANR-7
Kenesson, Frank G. 1913(?)-1985 Obituary 119
Kenez, Peter 1937- 29-32R
Kenian, Paul Roger
See Clifford, Martin
Kenin, Richard (Metz) 1947-1983 Obituary 111
Kenison, Katrina 1958- 138
Keniston, Kenneth 1930- 25-28R
Kenjo, Takashi 1940- 137
Kenkel, William F(rancis) 1925- 61-64
Kenna, Peter 1930- 61-64
Kennamer, Lorrin Jr. 1924- CANR-6
Earlier sketch in CA 5-8R
Kennan, George Frost 1904- CANR-39
Earlier sketches in CA 1-4R, CANR-2
Kennan, Kent (Wheeler) 1913- 1-4R
Kennard, George (Arnold Ford) 1915- 134
Kennard-Davis, Arthur (Shelley) 1910- CAP-1
Earlier sketch in CA 9-10
Kennaway, Adrienne 1945- .... SATA 60
Kennaway, James (Pebles Ewing)
1928-1968 103
Obituary 89-92
Kenneally, Michael 1945- 133
Kennealy (Morrison), Patricia 1946- 120
Kennebeck, Edwin 1924- 41-44R
Kennebeck, Paul 1943- 53-56
Kennecott, G. J.
See Viksnins, George J(uris)
Kennedy, Adam CANR-24
Earlier sketch in CA 107
See also AITN 1
Kennedy, Adrienne (Lita) 1931- CANR-26
Earlier sketch in CA 103
See also CABS 3
See also BLC 2
See also BW
See also CLC 66
See also DLB 38
Kennedy, Andrew (Karpati) 1931- 61-64
Kennedy, Betty 1926- 121
Kennedy, Brendan 1970- 123
See also SATA 57
Kennedy, Bruce M. 1929- 57-60
Kennedy, Carol CANR-21
Earlier sketch in CA 105
Kennedy, Caroline 1944- 125
Kennedy, Charles J(oseph)
1935-1984 Obituary 114
Kennedy, Chuck
See Kennedy, Charles J(oseph)
Kennedy, D. James 1930- 61-64
Kennedy, Dane K(eith) 1951- 126
Kennedy, David M. 1941- CANR-13
Earlier sketch in CA 29-32R
Kennedy, Dennis (Edward) 1940- 120
Kennedy, Don H(enry) 1911- 61-64
Kennedy, Dorothy M(intzlaff) 1931- 116
See also SATA 53
Kennedy, Eddie C. 1910- 89-92
Kennedy, Edward Moore 1932- 110
Kennedy, Edward R(idgway)
1923(?)-1975 Obituary 104
Kennedy, Elliot
See Godfrey, Lionel (Robert Holcombe)
Kennedy, (Robert) Emmet (Jr.) 1941- 132
Kennedy, Eugene C(ullen) 1928- 25-28R
Kennedy, Gail 1900-1972 Obituary 33-36R
Kennedy, Gavin 1940- CANR-9
Earlier sketch in CA 61-64
Kennedy, George (Alexander) 1928- CANR-2
Earlier sketch in CA 5-8R
Kennedy, George 1899(?)-1977 Obituary 73-76
Kennedy, Gerald (Hamilton) 1907- CANR-6
Earlier sketch in CA 5-8R
Kennedy, Gerald Studdert
See Studdert-Kennedy, (William) Gerald
Kennedy, Harold J. 1915(?)-1988 Obituary 124
Kennedy, Hubert (Collings) 1931- 93-96
Kennedy, Hugh 1947- 127
Kennedy, J. Gerald 1947- 127
Kennedy, J(ames) Hardee 1915- 13-16R
Kennedy, James
See Monahan, James (Henry Francis)
Kennedy, James G(ettier) 1932- 81-84
Kennedy, James William 1905- CANR-1
Earlier sketch in CA 1-4R
Kennedy, James Y(oung) 1916- 77-80
Kennedy, Jimmy 1903(?)-1984 Obituary 112
Kennedy, John Fitzgerald 1917-1963 ....CANR-1
Earlier sketch in CA 1-4R
See also MTCW
See also SATA 11
Kennedy, John J(oseph) 1914- 57-60
Kennedy, John Pendleton 1795-1870 ....DLB 3

Kennedy, Joseph Charles 1929- ... CANR-30
Earlier sketches in CA 1-4R, CANR-4
See also Kennedy, X. J.
See also CLC 8
See also SATA 14
Kennedy, Judith M(ary) 1935- ... 41-44R
Kennedy, Kathleen
1947(?)-1975 Obituary ... 57-60
Kennedy, Kenneth A(drian) R(aine)
1930- ... CANR-1
Earlier sketch in CA 45-48
Kennedy, Kieran A. 1935- ... 37-40R
Kennedy, L. D. 1924- ... 45-48
Kennedy, Leigh 1951- ... 122
Kennedy, Lena
See Smith, Lena (Kennedy)
Kennedy, Leo 1907- ... DLB 88
Kennedy, Leonard Anthony 1922- ... 37-40R
Kennedy, Leonard M(ilton) 1925- ... 73-76
Kennedy, Ludovic Henry Coverley 1919- ... 65-68
Kennedy, Malcolm D(uncan) 1895- ... 9-12R
Kennedy, Margaret 1896-1967 Obituary ... 25-28R
See also DLB 36
Kennedy, Marilyn Moats 1943- ... CANR-32
Earlier sketch in CA 109
Kennedy, Mary ... 102
Kennedy, Michael 1926- ... CANR-23
Earlier sketches in CA 13-16R, CANR-5
Kennedy, Moorhead 1930- ... 123
Kennedy, P(eter) J(ohn) 1925- ... 123
Kennedy, Paul E(dward) 1929- ... SATA 33
Kennedy, Paul M.
See Kennedy, Paul (Michael)
Kennedy, Paul (Michael) 1945- ... CANR-30
Earlier sketches in CA 65-68, CANR-9
See also BEST 89:1
Kennedy, Ralph Dale 1897-1965 ... 1-4R
Kennedy, Raymond A. 1934- ... 5-8R
Kennedy, (Jerome) Richard 1932- ... CANR-26
Earlier sketches in CA 57-60, CANR-7
See also SATA 22
Kennedy, Richard (Pitt) 1910-1989 ... 102
Obituary ... 127
See also SATA 60
Kennedy, Richard S(ylvester) 1920- ... CANR-29
Earlier sketches in CA 5-8R, CANR-3
See also DLB 111
Kennedy, Robert E(mmet) Jr. 1937- ... 37-40R
Kennedy, Robert F(rancis) Jr. 1954- ... 110
Kennedy, Robert F(rancis) 1925-1968 ... CANR-1
Earlier sketch in CA 1-4R
Kennedy, Robert L(ee) 1930- ... 57-60
Kennedy, Robert Woods 1911- ... 49-52
Kennedy, Robert 1938- ... SATA 63
Kennedy, Roger G(eorge) 1926- ... 115
Kennedy, Rose (Fitzgerald) 1890- ... 53-56
Kennedy, Sighle Aileen 1919- ... 53-56
Kennedy, Stetson 1916- ... 5-8R
Kennedy, Susan Estabrook 1942- ... 45-48
Kennedy, T(eresa) A. 1953- ... 114
See also SATA 35, 42
Kennedy, T(homas) F(illans) 1921- ... 53-56
Kennedy, Ted
See Kennedy, Edward Moore
Kennedy, Teresa
See Kennedy, T(eresa) A.
Kennedy, Theodore Reginald 1936- ... 105
Kennedy, Thomas C. 1937- ... 125
Kennedy, Thomas 1920- ... 116
Kennedy, William B(ean) 1926- ... 116
Kennedy, William J(ohn) 1942- ... 117
Kennedy, William 1928- ... CANR-31
Earlier sketches in CA 85-88, CANR-14
See also AAYA 1
See also CLC 6, 28, 34, 53
See also DLBY 85
See also MTCW
See also SATA 57
Kennedy, X. J.
See Kennedy, Joseph Charles
See also CAAS 9
See also CLC 42
See also CLR 27
See also DLB 5
Kennedy-Martin, Ian 1936- ... 101
Kenneggy, Richard
See Nettell, Richard (Geoffrey)
Kennel, LeRoy E(ldon) 1930- ... 77-80
Kennell, Ruth Epperson 1893-1977 ... CAP-2
Earlier sketch in CA 29-32
See also SATA 6, 25
Kennelly, Brendan 1936- ... CANR-5
Earlier sketch in CA 9-12R
See also DLB 40
Kenner, Charles Leroy 1933- ... 25-28R
Kenner, (William) Hugh 1923- ... CANR-28
Earlier sketch in CA 21-24R
See also DLB 67
Kennerly, David Hume 1947- ... 101
See also AITN 2
Kennerly, Karen 1940- ... 33-36R
Kennett, (Houn) Jiyu 1924- ... 93-96
Kennett, Lee 1931- ... 21-24R
Kennett, Peggy Teresa Nancy
See Kennett, (Houn) Jiyu
Kenney, Alice P(atricia) 1937-1985 ... CANR-10
Obituary ... 115
Earlier sketch in CA 25-28R
Kenney, Catherine (McGehee) 1948- ... 135
Kenney, Charles 1950- ... 135
Kenney, Douglas C. 1947(?)-1980 ... 107
Obituary ... 101
Kenney, Edwin James Jr. 1942- ... 53-56
Kenney, George Churchill 1889- ... CAP-1
Earlier sketch in CA 11-12
Kenney, John Paul 1920- ... 17-20R
Kenney, Lona B(ronberg) 1921- ... 115
Kenney, Richard (L.) 1948- ... 134
Kenney, Susan (McIlvaine) 1941- ... CANR-37
Earlier sketch in CA 115
Kenney, Sylvia W. 1922- ... CAP-1
Earlier sketch in CA 19-20
Kennick, W(illiam) E(lmer) 1923- ... 13-16R
Kennington, (Gilbert) Alan
1906-1986 Obituary ... 121
Kennington, Alice Eve 1935- ... 119
Kennon, Donald R. 1948- ... 122
Kenny, Anthony
See Kenny, Anthony John Patrick
Kenny, Anthony John Patrick 1931- ... CANR-23
Earlier sketch in CA 101
Kenny, Charles J.
See Gardner, Erle Stanley
Kenny, Ellsworth Newcomb 1909-1971 ... 5-8R
Obituary ... 103
See also SATA 26
Kenny, Herbert Andrew 1912- ... 41-44R
See also SATA 13
Kenny, James Andrew 1933- ... CANR-26
Earlier sketch in CA 107
Kenny, Jean
See Freeman, Jean Kenny
Kenny, John P. 1909- ... 17-20R
Kenny, John Peter 1916- ... CANR-1
Earlier sketch in CA 45-48
Kenny, Kathryn
See Bowden, Joan Chase
and Krull, Kathleen
and Sanderlin, Owenita (Harrah)
and Stack, Nicolete Meredith
Kenny, Kevin
See Krull, Kathleen
Kenny, Mary 1936- ... 108
Kenny, Michael 1923- ... CANR-5
Earlier sketch in CA 1-4R
Kenny, Nicholas Napoleon
1895-1975 Obituary ... 89-92
Kenny, Nick
See Kenny, Nicholas Napoleon
Kenny, Shirley (Elise) Strum 1934- ... CANR-31
Earlier sketch in CA 45-48
Kenny, Vincent 1919- ... 45-48
Kenny, W. Henry 1918- ... 37-40R
Kenofer, C(harles) Louis 1923- ... 69-72
Kenoyer, Natlee Peoples 1907- ... CANR-5
Earlier sketch in CA 5-8R
Kenrick, Donald Simon 1929- ... 81-84
Kenrick, Tony 1935- ... 104
Kenshalo, Daniel R(alph) 1922- ... 41-44R
Kensinger, George
See Fichter, George S.
Kent, Alexander
See Reeman, Douglas Edward
Kent, Allegra 1938(?)- ... 126
Brief entry ... 105
Kent, Allen 1921- ... CANR-39
Earlier sketches in CA 9-12R, CANR-3, 18
Kent, Arden
See Marion, Frieda
Kent, Arthur William Charles 1925- ... 102
Kent, Bill
See Kent, Carleton Volney Jr.
Kent, Carleton Volney Jr.
1909-1985 Obituary ... 114
Kent, Christopher 1940- ... 129
Kent, Cromwell
See Sparshott, Francis (Edward)
Kent, David
See Lambert, David (Compton)
Kent, Deborah Ann 1948- ... 103
See also SATA 41, 47
Kent, Donald P(eterson) 1916-1972 ... 17-20R
Obituary ... 120
Kent, Edward Allen 1933- ... 45-48
Kent, Ernest W(illiam) 1940- ... 104
Kent, Fortune
See Toombs, John
Kent, Frank R(ichardson)
1877-1958 Brief entry ... 121
See also DLB 29
Kent, Frank (Richardson Jr.)
1907(?)-1978 Obituary ... 81-84
Kent, George O(tto) 1919- ... 37-40R
Kent, George W. 1928- ... 25-28R
Kent, Harold W(infield) 1900- ... 65-68
Kent, Helen
See Polley, Judith (Anne)
Kent, Homer A(ustin) Jr. 1926- ... CANR-3
Earlier sketch in CA 9-12R
Kent, Jack
See Kent, John Wellington
Kent, John Henry Somerset 1923- ... 9-12R
Kent, John Wellington 1920-1985 ... CANR-16
Obituary ... 117
Earlier sketch in CA 85-88
See also SATA 24, 45
Kent, Katherine
See Dial, Joan
Kent, Kelvin
See Kuttner, Henry
Kent, Leonard J. 1927- ... 77-80
Kent, Louise Andrews 1886-1969 ... CANR-4
Obituary ... 25-28R
Earlier sketch in CA 1-4R
Kent, Malcolm 1932- ... 45-48
Kent, Mallory
See Lowndes, Robert A(ugustine) W(ard)
Kent, Margaret 1894- ... CAP-2
Earlier sketch in CA 25-28
See also SATA 2
Kent, Neil (Lowell) 1951- ... 129
Kent, Noel J(ay) 1944- ... 111
Kent, Nora 1899- ... CAP-1
Earlier sketch in CA 9-10
Kent, Pete
See Richardson, Gladwell
Kent, Philip
See Bulmer, (Henry) Kenneth
Kent, Rockwell 1882-1971 ... CANR-4
Obituary ... 29-32R
Earlier sketch in CA 5-8R
See also SATA 6
Kent, Sherman 1903-1986 ... 53-56
Obituary ... 118
See also SATA 20, 47
Kent, Sherry 1955- ... 128
Kent, Simon
See Catto, Max(well Jeffrey)
Kent, Stella
See Phillips, Stella
Kent, Tony
See Crechales, Anthony George
Kent, Valerie 1947- ... 114
Kentfield, Calvin 1924- ... 5-8R
Kenton, Leslie 1941- ... 113
Kenton, Maxwell
See Hoffenberg, Mason
and Southern, Terry
Kenton, Warren 1933- ... CANR-29
Earlier sketch in CA 29-32R
Kenward, James (Macara) 1908- ... 5-8R
Kenward, Jean 1920- ... 108
See also SATA 42
Kenward, Michael 1945- ... 103
Kenworthy, Brian J(ohn) 1920- ... 103
Kenworthy, Leonard S. 1912- ... CANR-1
Earlier sketch in CA 1-4R
See also SATA 6
Kenyatta, Jomo 1891(?)-1978 ... 124
Obituary ... 113
See also BW
See also MTCW
Kenyon, Bernice
See Gilkyson, Bernice Kenyon
Kenyon, Ernest M(onroe) 1920- ... 85-88
Kenyon, F(rank) W(ilson) 1912- ... CANR-1
Earlier sketch in CA 1-4R
Kenyon, J(ohn) P(hilipps) 1927- ... CANR-3
Earlier sketch in CA 9-12R
Kenyon, James William 1910- ... CAP-1
Earlier sketch in CA 9-10
Kenyon, Jane 1947- ... 118
See also DLB 120
Kenyon, John R(obert) 1948- ... 127
Kenyon, Karen 1938- ... 106
Kenyon, Kate
See Adorjan, Carol (Madden)
and Ransom, Candice F.
Kenyon, Kathleen Mary 1906-1978 ... CANR-13
Earlier sketch in CA 21-24R
Kenyon, Ley 1913- ... 13-16R
See also SATA 6
Kenyon, Michael 1931- ... CANR-12
Earlier sketch in CA 13-16R
Kenyon, Mildred Adams 1894-1980 ... 108
Obituary ... 105
Kenyon, Paul
See Freedland, Nat(haniel)
Kenyon, Robert O.
See Kuttner, Henry
Kenyon, W. A.
See Kenyon, Walter Andrew
Kenyon, Walter
See Kenyon, Walter Andrew
Kenyon, Walter A.
See Kenyon, Walter Andrew
Kenyon, Walter Andrew
1917-1986 Obituary ... 121
Kenzer, Robert C. 1955- ... 126
Keogh, Dermot (Francis) 1945- ... 126
Keogh, James 1916- ... 45-48
Keogh, Lilian Gilmore 1927- ... 9-12R
Keohane, Nannerl O(verholser) 1940- ... 106
Keohane, Robert O(wen) 1941- ... CANR-33
Earlier sketch in CA 45-48
Kepes, Gyorgy 1906- ... 101
Kepes, Juliet A(ppleby) 1919- ... 69-72
See also SATA 13
Kephart, Horace 1862-1931 Brief entry ... 119
Kephart, Newell C. 1911-1973 ... CAP-2
Earlier sketch in CA 17-18
Kephart, William M. 1921- ... 41-44R
Kepler, Thomas Samuel 1897-1963 ... 1-4R
Keppel, Charlotte
See Torday, Ursula
Keppel, Sonia 1900-1986 ... 107
Obituary ... 120
Keppel-Jones, Arthur (Mervyn) 1909- ... 118
Kepple, Ella Huff 1902- ... CAP-2
Earlier sketch in CA 17-18
Keppler, Ann B(lystad) 1946- ... 117
Keppler, C(arl) F(rancis) 1909- ... 17-20R
Keppler, Herbert 1925- ... 85-88
Keppler, Victor 1904-1987 Obituary ... 124
Ker, Jill
See Conway, Jill K(er)
Ker, Neil Ripley 1908-1982 Obituary ... 107
Ker, William Paton 1855-1923 Brief entry ... 121
Kerber, August Frank 1917- ... 21-24R
Kerber, Linda K(aufman) 1940- Brief entry ... 115
Kerby, Bill 1937- ... 104
Kerby, Joe Kent 1933- ... 53-56
Kerby, Philip Pearce 1911- Brief entry ... 116
Kerby, Robert L(ee) 1934- ... 41-44R
Kerby, Susan Alice
See Burton, (Alice) Elizabeth
Kercheval, Jesse Lee 1956- ... 126
Kerckhoff, Alan C(hester) 1924- ... CANR-32
Earlier sketch in CA 113
Kerek, Andrew 1936- ... 102
Kerekes, Tibor 1893-1969 ... CAP-2
Earlier sketch in CA 17-18
Kerensky, Alexandr Fedorovich
1881-1970 Obituary ... 113
Kerensky, Oleg 1930- ... CANR-12
Earlier sketch in CA 29-32R
Kerensky, V(asil) M(ichael) 1930- ... 53-56
Keres, Paul (Petrovich)
1916-1975 Obituary ... 57-60
Kerestesi, Michael 1929- ... 109
Kereszty, Roch A(ndrew) 1933- ... 29-32R
Kerewsky-Halpern, Barbara 1931- ... 102
Kerferd, G(eorge) B(riscoe) 1915- ... 132
Kerigan, Florence 1896- ... 29-32R
See also SATA 12
Kerin, Roger A(nthony) 1947- ... CANR-26
Earlier sketch in CA 109
Kerina, Mburumba 1932- ... 129
Kerkvliet, Benedict J(ohn) 1943- ... 93-96
Kerlan, Irvin 1912-1963 ... 5-8R
Kerlinger, Fred N(ichols) 1910- ... CANR-2
Earlier sketch in CA 49-52
Kerman, Cynthia Earl 1923- ... 57-60
Kerman, Gertrude
See Furman, Gertrude Lerner Kerman
Kerman, Gertrude Lerner 1909- ... 5-8R
See also SATA 21
Kerman, Joseph Wilfred 1924- ... CANR-15
Earlier sketch in CA 65-68
Kerman, Judith (Berna) 1945- ... 77-80
Kerman, Sheppard 1928- ... CANR-26
Earlier sketch in CA 85-88
Kermani, Taghi Thomas 1929- ... 25-28R
Kermode, (John) Frank 1919- ... CANR-1
Earlier sketch in CA 1-4R
Kern, Alfred 1924- ... 33-36R
Kern, Canyon
See Raborg, Frederick A(shton) Jr.
Kern, E. R.
See Kerner, Fred
Kern, Edith 1912- ... 113
Kern, Gary 1938- ... 65-68
Kern, Gregory
See Tubb, E(dwin) C(harles)
Kern, Janet (Rosalie) 1924- ... 5-8R
Kern, Jean B(ordner) 1913- ... 85-88
Kern, Mary Margaret 1906- ... 101
Kern, Robert W(illiam) 1934- ... CANR-7
Earlier sketch in CA 61-64
Kern, Seymour 1913- ... 93-96
Kern, Stephen 1943- ... 69-72
Kern, Walter O(tto) 1930- ... 117
Kernaghan, Eileen 1939- ... CANR-28
Earlier sketch in CA 111
Kernan, Alvin B(ernard) 1923- ... CANR-33
Earlier sketch in CA 49-52
Kernan, Jerome B(ernard) 1932- ... 25-28R
Kernan, Julia K. 1901(?)-1988 Obituary ... 125
Kernan, Michael 1927- ... 81-84
Kerner, Fred 1921- ... CANR-22
Earlier sketches in CA 9-12R, CANR-6
Kerner, Justinus 1786-1862 ... DLB 90
Kernochan, Sarah 1947- ... 73-76
Kernodle, George R(iley) 1907- ... 65-68
Kerns, Frances Casey 1937- ... 81-84
Kerns, J(ames) Alexander
1894-1975 Obituary ... 104
Kerns, Robert Louis 1929- ... 77-80
Kerouac, Jack
See Kerouac, Jean-Louis Lebris de
See also CDALB 1941-1968
See also CLC 1, 2, 3, 5, 14, 29, 61
See also DLB 2, 16
See also DLBD 3
Kerouac, Jan
See Hackett, Jan Michele
See also DLB 16
Kerouac, Jean-Louis Lebris de
1922-1969 ... CANR-26
Obituary ... 25-28R
Earlier sketch in CA 5-8R
See also Kerouac, Jack
See also AITN 1
See also MTCW
See also WLC
Kerouac, John
See Kerouac, Jean-Louis Lebris de
Kerpelman, Larry C(yril) 1939- ... 37-40R
Kerr, Alex A. 1922- ... 125
Kerr, Alex(ander McBride) 1921- ... 61-64
Kerr, Andy
See Kerr, Alex A.
Kerr, Barbara 1913- ... 89-92
Kerr, Ben
See Ard, William (Thomas)
Kerr, Carole
See Carr, Margaret
Kerr, Catherine 1945- ... 102
Kerr, Clark 1911- ... CANR-22
Earlier sketches in CA 45-48, CANR-1
Kerr, D(onald) G(ordon) G(rady)
1913-1976 ... CANR-6
Earlier sketch in CA 1-4R
Kerr, Donna H(anneman) 1944- ... 112
Kerr, Elizabeth M. 1905- ... 37-40R
Kerr, Frederick
See Kerner, Fred
Kerr, Graham 1934- ... 108
Kerr, Harry P(rice) 1928- ... 5-8R
Kerr, Homer L(ee) 1921- ... 120
Kerr, Howard Hastings 1931- ... 103
Kerr, Hugh Thomson 1909- ... 103
Obituary ... 137
Kerr, James Lennox 1899-1963 ... 102
Kerr, James Stolee 1928- ... 17-20R

Kerr, Jean 1923- CANR-7
Earlier sketch in CA 5-8R
See also CLC 22
Kerr, Jessica 1901- CAP-2
Earlier sketch in CA 29-32
See also SATA 13
Kerr, Joan P. 1921- 81-84
Kerr, (Anne-) Judith 1923- 93-96
See also SATA 24
Kerr, K(athel) Austin 1938- 25-28R
Kerr, M. E.
See Meaker, Marijane (Agnes)
See also AAYA 2
See also CLC 12, 35
See also SAAS 1
Kerr, Malcolm (Hooper) 1931-1984 97-100
Obituary 111
Kerr, Norman D.
See Sieber, Sam Dixon
Kerr, Orpheus C.
See Newell, Robert Henry
Kerr, Phyllis Forbes 1942- 120
Kerr, Robert .... CLC 55
Kerr, Robert (a pseudonym) 1899- 69-72
Kerr, Rose Netzorg 1892-1974 .... CAP-2
Earlier sketch in CA 23-24
Kerr, Stanley E. 1894(?)-1976 Obituary 69-72
Kerr, Walter (Francis) 1913- CANR-7
Earlier sketch in CA 5-8R
Kerrigan, (Thomas) Anthony 1918- CANR-4
Earlier sketch in CA 49-52
See also CAAS 11
See also CLC 4, 6
Kerrigan, Catherine 1939- 117
Kerrigan, Kate Lowe
See Rickett, Frances
Kerrigan, William J(oseph) CANR-2
Earlier sketch in CA 49-52
Kerry, Frances
See Kerigan, Florence
Kerry, Lois
See Duncan, Lois
Kersell, John E(dgar) 1930- 45-48
Kersey, Katharine C(lark) 1935- CANR-38
Earlier sketch in CA 116
Kersey, Tanya-Monique 1961- 138
Kersh, Cyril 1925- 104
Kersh, Gerald 1911-1968 Obituary 25-28R
Kershaw, Alister (Nasmyth) 1921- CANR-19
Earlier sketches in CA 5-8R, CANR-3
Kershaw, Gordon Ernest 1928- 85-88
Kershaw, Ian 1943- 137
Kershaw, John (Hugh D'Allenger) 73-76
Kershner, Howard E(ldred) 1891- 73-76
Kershner, Richard B(randon)
1913-1982 Obituary 110
Kerslake, Susan 1943- CANR-17
Earlier sketch in CA 93-96
Kersnowski, Frank L. 1934- 41-44R
Kertesz, Andre 1894-1985 85-88
Obituary 117
Kertesz, Louise 1939- 102
Kertesz, Stephen D(enis) 1904- CAP-2
Earlier sketch in CA 21-22
Kertzer, David I(srael) 1948- 106
Kertzer, Morris Norman 1910-1983 .... CANR-1
Obituary 111
Earlier sketch in CA 1-4R
Ker Wilson, Barbara 1929- CANR-7
Earlier sketch in CA 5-8R
See also SATA 20, 70
Kerwood, John R. 1942- 53-56
Kesey, Ken (Elton) 1935- CANR-38
Earlier sketches in CA 1-4R, CANR-22
See also CDALB 1968-1988
See also CLC 1, 3, 6, 11, 46, 64
See also DLB 2, 16
See also MTCW
See also SATA 66
See also WLC
Keshet, Harry F(inkelstein) 1940- 109
Keshishian, John M. 1923- 25-28R
Kesich, Veselin 1921- Brief entry 111
Kesler, (William) Jackson (II) 1938- 102
Kesler, Jay 1935- CANR-26
Earlier sketches in CA 61-64, CANR-8
See also SATA 65
Kess, Joseph Francis 1942- 65-68
Kessel, Dmitri 1902- 120
Kessel, John H(oward) 1928- CANR-21
Earlier sketch in CA 21-24R
Kessel, John (Joseph Vincent) 1950- 120
Kessel, Joseph (Elie) 1898-1979 105
Obituary 89-92
See also DLB 72
Kessel, Joyce Karen 1937- 105
See also SATA 41
Kessel, Lipmann 1914- 13-16R
Kessel, Martin 1901- .... DLB 56
Kessell, John L(ottridge) 1936- 93-96
Kesselman, Judi R.
See Kesselman-Turkel, Judi
Kesselman, Louis Coleridge
1919-1974 Obituary 110
Kesselman, Mark J. CANR-14
Earlier sketch in CA 37-40R
Kesselman-Turkel, Judi 1934- CANR-37
Kesselring, Joseph (Otto) 1902-1967 .... CLC 45
Kessen, William 1925- CANR-1
Earlier sketch in CA 1-4R
Kessler, Diane Cooksey 1947- 57-60
Kessler, Edward 1927- 61-64
Kessler, Ethel 1922- 121
Brief entry 115
See also SATA 37, 44
Kessler, Francis P(aschal) 1944- 109
Kessler, Frank
See Kessler, Francis P(aschal)
Kessler, Gail 1937- 65-68
Kessler, Henry H(oward)
1896-1978 Obituary 73-76
Kessler, Herbert L(eon) 1941- 125
Kessler, Jascha (Frederick) 1929- CANR-8
Earlier sketch in CA 17-20R
See also CLC 4
Kessler, Kaye (Warren) 1923- 112
Kessler, Lauren J. 1950- 127
Kessler, Leonard P. 1921- 77-80
See also SATA 14
Kessler, Merle (Bruce) 1949- 128
Kessler, Milton 1930- CANR-2
Earlier sketch in CA 1-4R
Kessler, Rod 1949- 117
Kessler, Ronald (Borek) 1943- CANR-28
Earlier sketches in CA 69-72, CANR-13
Kessler, Sheila 57-60
Kessler, Walter R. 1913-1978 Obituary 81-84
Kessler-Harris, Alice 1941- CANR-32
Kessner, Lawrence 1957- 109
Kessner, Thomas 1946- CANR-11
Earlier sketch in CA 69-72
Kesteloot, Lilyan 1931- CANR-19
Earlier sketch in CA 73-76
Kesten, Hermann 1900- .... DLB 56
Kester, Dana R(ay) 1943- 116
Kesterson, David B(ert) 1938- 41-44R
Kesterton, Wilfred (Harold) 1914- 41-44R
Kesteven, G. R.
See Crosher, G. R.
Kestler, Frances Roe 1929- 135
Kestner, Joseph A(loysius) 1943- 89-92
Ketch, Jack
See Tibbetts, John C(arter)
Ketcham, Carl H(untington) 1923- 29-32R
Ketcham, Charles B(rown) 1926- 29-32R
Ketcham, Hank
See Ketcham, Henry King
Ketcham, Henry King 1920- 105
See also SATA 27, 28
Ketcham, Howard 1902-1982 Obituary 106
Ketcham, Katherine 1949- 118
Ketcham, Orman W(eston) 1918- CANR-9
Earlier sketch in CA 21-24R
Ketcham, Ralph (Louis) 1927- CANR-4
Earlier sketch in CA 9-12R
Ketcham, Rodney K(enneth) 1909- CANR-4
Earlier sketch in CA 1-4R
Ketchum, Carlton Griswold 1892- 85-88
Ketchum, Cliff
See Paine, Lauran (Bosworth)
Ketchum, Creston Donald 1922- 9-12R
Ketchum, Frank
See Paine, Lauran (Bosworth)
Ketchum, J.
See Frentzen, Jeffrey
Ketchum, Jack
See Paine, Lauran (Bosworth)
Ketchum, Marshall D(ana) 1905- CAP-1
Earlier sketch in CA 17-18
Ketchum, Richard M(alcolm) 1922- 25-28R
Ketchum, Robert Glenn 1947- CANR-23
Earlier sketch in CA 107
Ketchum, William C(larence) Jr.
1931- CANR-28
Earlier sketches in CA 33-36R, CANR-12
Keteyian, Armen 1953- 122
Kets de Vries, Manfred F. R. 1942- 111
Kett, Joseph F. 1938- 25-28R
Kettani, M. Ali 1941- 133
Kettelhack, Guy 1951- 134
Kettelkamp, Larry (Dale) 1933- CANR-16
Earlier sketch in CA 29-32R
See also CLC 12
See also SAAS 3
See also SATA 2
Ketterer, David (Anthony Theodor)
1942- CANR-21
Earlier sketches in CA 53-56, CANR-4
Ketterman, Grace H(orst) 1926- CANR-22
Earlier sketch in CA 106
Kettl, Donald F. 1952- CANR-34
Earlier sketch in CA 111
Kettle, Arnold (Charles) 1916-1986 .... CANR-6
Obituary 121
Earlier sketch in CA 9-12R
Kettle, Jocelyn Pamela 1934- 25-28R
Kettle, Pamela
See Kettle, Jocelyn Pamela
Kettle, Peter
See Glover, Denis (James Matthews)
Kettner, Elmer Arthur 1906-1964 .... 1-4R
Kettner, James H(arold) 1944- 89-92
Ketton-Cremer, Robert Wyndham
1906-1969 Obituary 106
Keucher, William F. 1918- 49-52
Keuls, Eva C(lara) 1928- 123
Keuls, Hans 1910-1985 Obituary 117
Keun, Irmgard 1905-1982 .... DLB 69
Kevan, Martin 1949- CANR-27
Earlier sketch in CA 110
Keve, Paul W(illard) 1913- CANR-6
Earlier sketch in CA 9-12R
Kevern, Barbara
See Shepherd, Donald (Lee)
Keveson, Peter 1919-1986 Obituary 118
Kevill-Davies, Sally 1945- 138
Kevin, Jodi
See Lawrence, Jodi
Kevles, Barbara (Lynne) 1940- 128
Kevles, Bettyann 1938- CANR-27
Earlier sketches in CA 69-72, CANR-11
See also SATA 23
Kevles, Daniel J(erome) 1939- CANR-27
Earlier sketch in CA 85-88
Kew, Stephen 1947- 103
Kewes, Karol 1924- 9-12R
Key, Alexander (Hill) 1904-1979 .... CANR-6
Obituary 89-92
Earlier sketch in CA 5-8R
See also SATA 8, 23
Key, Jack D(ayton) 1934- CANR-30
Earlier sketch in CA 112
Key, Mary Ritchie 1924- CANR-38
Earlier sketches in CA 45-48, CANR-1, 16
Key, Ted
See Key, Theodore
Key, Theodore 1912- 13-16R
Key, V(aldimer) O(rlando) Jr. 1908-1963 .... 1-4R
Key, William H(enry) 1919- 45-48
Key, Wilson Bryan 1925- CANR-2
Earlier sketch in CA 49-52
Keyes, Claire J. 1938- 126
Keyes, Daniel 1927- CANR-26
Earlier sketches in CA 17-20R, CANR-10
See also SATA 37
Keyes, Edward 1927- 103
Keyes, Evelyn 1919(?)- 85-88
Keyes, Fenton 1915- 107
See also SATA 34
Keyes, Frances Parkinson 1885-1970 .... CANR-7
Obituary 25-28R
Earlier sketch in CA 5-8R
Keyes, Kenneth S(cofield) Jr. 1921- CANR-24
Earlier sketches in CA 17-20R, CANR-8
Keyes, Langley Carleton Jr. 1938- 25-28R
Keyes, Margaret Frings 1929- 57-60
Keyes, Noel
See Keightley, David N(oel)
Keyes, Ralph 1945- CANR-3
Earlier sketch in CA 49-52
Keyfitz, Nathan 1913- CANR-10
Earlier sketch in CA 25-28R
Keyhoe, Donald E(dward)
1897-1988 Obituary 127
Keyishian, Harry 1932- 61-64
Keylock, Leslie R(obert) 1933- 117
Keylor, Arthur (W.) 1920(?)-1981 Obituary 104
Keylor, William R(obert) 1944- 89-92
Keynes, Edward 1940- 120
Keynes, Geoffrey Langdon 1887-1982 103
Obituary 107
Keynes, John Maynard
1883-1946 Brief entry 114
Keynes, Richard Darwin 1919- 114
Keys, Ancel 1904- 61-64
Keys, Donald (Fraser) 1924- 115
Keys, Ivor Christopher Banfield 1919- 103
Keys, John D. 1938- 9-12R
Keys, Thomas Edward 1908- CAP-1
Earlier sketch in CA 11-12
Keyser, Daniel J. 1935- 121
Keyser, (George) Gustave 1910- 77-80
Keyser, Lester Joseph 1943- 105
Keyser, Marcia 1933- 116
See also SATA 42
Keyser, Samuel Jay 1935- 106
Keyser, Sarah
See McGuire, Leslie Sarah
Keyser, William R(ussell) 1916- 69-72
Keyserling, Eduard von 1855-1918 .... DLB 66
Keyserling, Leon H. 1908-1987 61-64
Obituary 123
Keyserlingk, Robert H. 1933- 131
Keyssar, Alexander 1947- 121
Keyt, David (Alan) 1930- 1-4R
Kezdi, Paul 1914- 77-80
Kezys, Algimantas 1928- CANR-31
Earlier sketches in CA 81-84, CANR-14
Kgositsile, Keorapetse (William)
1938- CANR-25
Earlier sketch in CA 77-80
See also BW
Khadduri, Majid 1909- CANR-2
Earlier sketch in CA 1-4R
Khaketla, B. M.
See Khaketla, B(ennett) Makalo
Khaketla, B(ennett) Makalo
1913- Brief entry 113
Khalatbari, Adel-Sultan
1901(?)-1977 Obituary 69-72
Khalsa, Dayal Kaur 1943-1989 137
See also MAICYA
See also SATA 62
Khan, Hassina
See Ali Khan, Shirley
Khan, Lurey 1927- 97-100
Khan, Mohammed Masud R. 1927(?)-1989 129
Khan, (Chaudhri) Muhammad Zafrulla
1893-1985 Obituary 117
Khan, Pir Vilayat Inayat
See Inayat-Khan, Pir Vilayat
Khan, Shirley Ali
See Ali Khan, Shirley
Khan, Taidje 1920(?)-1985 Obituary 117
Khan, Zillur Rahman 1938- CANR-14
Earlier sketch in CA 41-44R
Khanna, J(aswant) L(al) 1925- 21-24R
Khanshendel, Chiron
See Rose, Wendy
Kharasch, Robert Nelson 1926- 103
Khare, Narayan Bhaskar 1882- CAP-1
Earlier sketch in CA 11-12
Kharitonov, Yevgeny
1941(?)-1981 Obituary 104
Khatchadourian, Haig 1925- 53-56
Khatena, Joe
See Khatena, Joseph
Khatena, Joseph 1925- CANR-39
Earlier sketch in CA 116
Khazzoom, J. Daniel 1932- 17-20R
Khedouri, Franklin 1944- 101
Kher, Inder Nath 1933- 93-96
Khera, S(ucha) S(ingh) 1903- 13-16R
Kherdian, David 1931- CANR-39
Earlier sketch in CA 21-24R
See also CAAS 2
See also CLC 6, 9
See also CLR 24
See also MAICYA
See also SATA 16
Khlebnikov, Velimir
See Khlebnikov, Viktor Vladimirovich
See also TCLC 20
Khlebnikov, Viktor Vladimirovich
1885-1922 Brief entry 117
See also Khlebnikov, Velimir
Khodasevich, Vladislav (Felitsianovich)
1886-1939 Brief entry 115
See also TCLC 15
Khomaini, Ayatullah Sayyed Ruholla Mousavi
See Khomeini, Ruhollah (Mussavi)
Khomeini, Ayatollah
See Khomeini, Ruhollah (Mussavi)
Khomeini, Ayatollah Ruhollah
See Khomeini, Ruhollah (Mussavi)
Khomeini, Imam
See Khomeini, Ruhollah (Mussavi)
Khomeini, Ruhollah (Mussavi)
1900(?)-1989 117
Obituary 128
Khornak, Lucille 1953- 110
Khoroche, Peter (Andrew) 1947- 136
Khosla, G(opal) D(as) 1901- 113
Khouri, Fred J(ohn) 1916- 25-28R
Khouri, Mounah A(bdallah) 1918- 114
Khrushchev, Nikita Sergeyevich 1894-1971 112
Khrushchev, Sergei (Nikitich) 1935- 136
Khubchandani, Lachman M(ulchand) 1932- 128
Khumeini, Ruhollah
See Khomeini, Ruhollah (Mussavi)
Kiang, Ying-cheng 17-20R
Kianto, Ilmari 1874-1970 Obituary 29-32R
Kibbe, Pat (Hosley) 125
See also SATA 60
Kibbee, Roland 1914-1984 Obituary 113
Kibler, James Everett Jr. 1944- CANR-22
Earlier sketch in CA 105
Kibler, Robert J(oseph) 1934- 29-32R
Kibler, William W. 1942- 37-40R
Kibre, Pearl 1902(?)-1985 Obituary 116
Kicknosway, Faye 1936- CANR-7
Earlier sketch in CA 57-60
Kicza, John E(dward) 1947- 120
Kidd, Adam 1802(?)-1831 .... DLB 99
Kidd, Aline H(alstead) 1922- 17-20R
Kidd, Charles (William) 1952- 134
Kidd, David Lundy 1926- CANR-1
Earlier sketch in CA 1-4R
Kidd, Elisabeth
See Triegel, Linda (Jeanette)
Kidd, Harry 1917- 29-32R
Kidd, I(an) G(ray) 1922- 132
Kidd, J(ames) R(obbins) 1915- CANR-3
Earlier sketch in CA 5-8R
Kidd, J. Roby
See Kidd, J(ames) R(obbins)
Kidd, Janet (Gladys) Aitken
1908(?)-1988 Obituary 127
Kidd, Ronald 1948- CANR-39
Earlier sketch in CA 116
See also SATA 42
Kidd, Russ
See Donson, Cyril
Kidd, Virginia 1921- CANR-10
Earlier sketch in CA 65-68
Kidd, Walter E. 1917- 21-24R
Kiddell, John 1922- 29-32R
See also SATA 3
Kiddell-Monroe, Joan 1908- CAP-1
Earlier sketch in CA 13-14
See also SATA 55
Kidder, Barbara (Ann) 1933- 41-44R
Kidder, J(onathan) Edward (Jr.) 1922- 107
Kidder, Rushworth M(oulton) 1944- 77-80
Kidder, Tracy 1945- 109
See also BEST 90:1
See also MTCW
Kiddle, Lawrence B(ayard) 1907- 33-36R
Kidner, (Frank) Derek 1913- 41-44R
Kidney, Dorothy Boone 1919- CANR-3
Earlier sketch in CA 9-12R
Kidney, Walter C(urtis) 1932- CANR-19
Earlier sketches in CA 53-56, CANR-4
Kido, Koichi 1890(?)-1977 Obituary 69-72
Kidwell, Carl 1910- .... SATA 43
Kidwell, Catherine (Arthelia) 1921- 109
Kieckhefer, Richard 1946- 93-96
Kiefer, Bill
See Kiefer, Tillman W.
Kiefer, Christie Weber 1937- 103
Kiefer, Frederick (Paul) 1945- 114
Kiefer, Irene 1926- CANR-11
Earlier sketch in CA 69-72
See also SATA 21
Kiefer, Louis Sr. 1936- 131
Kiefer, Tillman W. 1898- CAP-2
Earlier sketch in CA 29-32
Kiefer, Warren 1929- 77-80
Kiefer, William Joseph 1925- 1-4R
Kiehle, John Alva 1930- Brief entry 115
Kiehtreiber, Albert Conrad
See Guetersloh, Albert Paris
Kiell, Norman 1916- CANR-5
Earlier sketch in CA 13-16R
Kiell, Paul J(acob) 1930- 124
Brief entry 118

Kielland, Alexander Lange
1849-1906 Brief entry 104
See also TCLC 5
Kiely, Benedict 1919- CANR-2
Earlier sketch in CA 1-4R
See also CLC 23, 43
See also DLB 15
Kiely, Robert (James) 1931- 131
Kiemel, Ann
See Anderson, Ann Kiemel
Kieniewicz, Stefan 1907- 29-32R
Kienzle, William X(avier) 1928- CANR-31
Earlier sketches in CA 93-96, CANR-9
See also CAAS 1
See also CLC 25
See also MTCW
Kiepper, Shirley Morgan 1933- 37-40R
See also Morgan, Shirley
Kieran, John Francis 1892-1981 101
Obituary 105
Kieran, Sheila 1930- 97-100
Kierland, Joseph Scott 1937- 61-64
Kierman, Frank Algerton Jr. 1914- 125
Kiernan, Brian 1937- 107
Kiernan, Robert F(rancis) 1940- 115
Kiernan, Thomas 113
Kiernan, (E.) V(ictor) G(ordon) 1913- CANR-11
Earlier sketch in CA 25-28R
Kiernan, Walter 1902-1978 Obituary 73-76
Kies, Cosette (Nell) 1936- 124
Kiesel, Stanley 1925- 104
See also SATA 35
Kieser, Rolf 1936- 77-80
Kiesler, Charles A(dolphus) 1934- CANR-10
Earlier sketch in CA 25-28R
Kiesler, Sara B(eth) 1940- CANR-16
Earlier sketch in CA 25-28R
Kiesling, Christopher (Gerald)
1925-1986 .... CANR-12
Obituary 120
Earlier sketch in CA 29-32R
Kiesling, Herbert J. 1934- 45-48
Kiester, Edwin Jr. 1927- 110
Kieszak, Kenneth 1939- 89-92
Kiev, Ari 1933- CANR-3
Earlier sketch in CA 9-12R
Kiev, I. Edward 1905-1975 Obituary 104
Kiger, Joseph Charles 1920- 125
Kihl, Armand
See Ald, Roy A(llison)
Kihl, Young Whan 1932- 127
Kihss, Peter (Frederick)
1912(?)-1984 Obituary 114
Kijima Hajime
See Kojima Shozo
Kikel, Rudy (John) 1942- 117
Kiker, B(ill) F(razier) 1937- 61-64
Kiker, Douglas 1930-1991 65-68
Obituary 135
Kikukawa, Cecily H(arder) 1919- 113
See also SATA 35, 44
Kilander, H(olger) Frederick 1900-1969 .... CAP-2
Earlier sketch in CA 17-18
Kilborne, Virginia Wylie 1912- 21-24R
Kilbourn, Jonathan
1916(?)-1976 Obituary 65-68
Kilbourn, William (Morley) 1926- CANR-11
Earlier sketch in CA 21-24R
Kilbracken, John (Raymond Godley)
1920- 5-8R
Kilburn, Henry
See Rigg, H(enry Hemmingway) K(ilburn)
Kilburn, Robert E(dward) 1931- 17-20R
Kilby, Clyde Samuel 1902-1986 .... CANR-9
Obituary 120
Earlier sketch in CA 13-16R
Kilby, Peter 1935- CANR-17
Earlier sketch in CA 25-28R
Kildahl, John P. 1927- 89-92
Kildahl, Phillip A. 1912- 21-24R
Kildare, Maurice
See Richardson, Gladwell
Kilduff, (Mary) Dorrell 1901- 5-8R
Kiley, Dan (Edward) 1942- 132
Brief entry 125
Kiley, Frederick 1932- CANR-15
Earlier sketch in CA 37-40R
Kiley, Jed
See Kiley, John Gerald
See also DLB 4
Kiley, John Gerald 1889-1962 Obituary 112
See also Kiley, Jed
Kiley, Margaret A(nn) 53-56
Kilgallen, Dorothy (Mae)
1913-1965 Obituary 89-92
Kilgallen, James L. 1888(?)-1982 Obituary 108
Kilgo, James 1941- 127
Kilgore, James C(olumbus) 1928-1988 .... 33-36R
Obituary 127
Kilgore, John
See Paine, Lauran (Bosworth)
Kilgore, Kathleen 1946- CANR-27
Earlier sketch in CA 109
See also SATA 42
Kilgore, William J(ackson) 1917- 45-48
Kilgour, John Graham 1937- 105
Kilgour, Raymond L(incoln) 1903- CAP-1
Earlier sketch in CA 13-16
Kilian, Crawford 1941- CANR-22
Earlier sketch in CA 105
See also SATA 35
Kilina, Patricia
See Warren, Patricia Nell
Kiljunen, Kimmo (Roobert) 1951- 132
Killam, (Gordon) Douglas 1930- CANR-3
Earlier sketch in CA 49-52
Killanin, Lord
See Morris, Michael
Kille, Mary F. 1948- 33-36R
Killeen, Jacqueline 1931- 61-64
Killen, Linda 1945- 118
Killenberg, George A(ndrew) 1917- 77-80
Killens, John Oliver 1916-1987 .... CANR-26
Obituary 123
Earlier sketch in CA 77-80
See also CAAS 2
See also BW
See also CLC 10
See also DLB 33
Killian, Ida F(aith) 1910- 65-68
Killian, James R(hyne) Jr. 1904-1988 97-100
Obituary 124
Killian, Larry
See Wellen, Edward (Paul)
Killian, Lewis M(artin) 1919- 9-12R
Killian, Ray A. 1922- 21-24R
Killigrew, Thomas 1612-1683 .... DLB 58
Killilea, Marie (Lyons) 1913- 5-8R
See also SATA 2
Killingback, Julia 1944- .... SATA 63
Killinger, George G(lenn) 1908- 102
Killinger, John 1933- 81-84
Killingley, Carl A(rthur) 1918- 118
Killingsworth, Frank R.
1873(?)-1976 Obituary 65-68
Killion, Katheryn L. 1936- 17-20R
Killion, Ronald G(ene) 1931- 61-64
Killorin, Joseph I(gnatius) 1926- 111
Killough, (Karen) Lee 1942- CANR-32
Earlier sketches in CA 89-92, CANR-15
See also SATA 64
Killy, Jean-Claude 1943- Brief entry 115
Kilmann, Peter R(ichard) 1945- 118
Kilmartin, Edward J(ohn) 1923- 17-20R
Kilmer, (Alfred) Joyce
1886-1918 Brief entry 120
See also DLB 45
Kilmer, Kenton 1909- 1-4R
Kilmer, Nicholas (John) 1941- 129
Kilmister, C(live) W(illiam) 1924- 119
Kilodney, Crad 1948- CANR-37
Earlier sketch in CA 115
Kilpatrick, Carroll 1913- 69-72
Kilpatrick, F(ranklin) P(eirce) 1920- 21-24R
Kilpatrick, James Jackson 1920- CANR-1
Earlier sketch in CA 1-4R
See also AITN 1, 2
Kilpatrick, Sarah
See Underwood, Mavis Eileen
Kilpatrick, Terrence 1920- 81-84
Kilreon, Beth
See Walker, Barbara (Jeanne) K(erlin)
Kilroy, James F(rancis) 1935- 133
Kilroy, Thomas 1934- 53-56
Kilson, Marion 1936- 37-40R
Kilson, Martin Luther Jr. 1931- 103
Kilvert, B. Cory Jr. 1930- 45-48
Kilwardby, Robert 1215(?)-1279 .... DLB 115
Kilworth, Garry 1941- 128
Kim
See Simenon, Georges (Jacques Christian)
Kim, C(hong-) I(k) Eugene 1930- 37-40R
Kim, Chin W. 1936- 37-40R
Kim, Chong Lim 1937- 114
Kim, Choong Soon 1938- 116
Kim, David U(ngchon) 1932- 109
Kim, Elaine H(aikyung) 1942- 130
Kim, Hee-Jin 1927- 106
Kim, Helen 1899-1970 .... CAP-1
Earlier sketch in CA 13-16
Kim, Hyung-chan 1938- 57-60
Kim, Ilpyong J(ohn) 1931- 53-56
Kim, Jung-Gun 1933- 53-56
Kim, K(wan) H(o) 1936- 29-32R
Kim, Kwan-Bong 1936- 37-40R
Kim, Kyung-Won 1936- 29-32R
Kim, Richard C(hong) C(hin) 1923- 29-32R
Kim, Richard E. 1932- 5-8R
Kim, Samuel S(oonki) 1935- 104
Kim, Se-Jin 1933- 53-56
Kim, Seung Hee 1936- 29-32R
Kim, Sung Bok 1932- Brief entry 113
Kim, Yong Choon 1935- 57-60
Kim, Yong-ik 1920- 17-20R
Kim, Yoon Hough 1934-1976 .... 33-36R
Kim, Young Hum 1920- 21-24R
Kimball, Arthur G(ustaf) 1927- 41-44R
Kimball, Dean 1912- 69-72
Kimball, Frank
See Paine, Lauran (Bosworth)
Kimball, Gayle 1943- 107
Kimball, George 1943- 53-56
Kimball, John P. 1941- CANR-2
Earlier sketch in CA 45-48
Kimball, John W(ard) 1931- CANR-15
Earlier sketch in CA 93-96
Kimball, Michael 1949- 120
Kimball, Nancy
See Upson, Norma
Kimball, Penn T(ownsend) 1915- CANR-18
Earlier sketch in CA 102
Kimball, Philip 1941- 117
Kimball, Ralph
See Paine, Lauran (Bosworth)
Kimball, Richard Laurance 1939- CANR-7
Earlier sketch in CA 53-56
Kimball, Robert Eric 1939- Brief entry 106
Kimball, Roger 1953- 136
Kimball, Solon T(oothaker) 1909- 21-24R
Kimball, Spencer L(evan) 1918- CANR-1
Earlier sketch in CA 1-4R
Kimball, Spencer W(oolley)
1895-1985 .... CANR-39
Obituary 117
Earlier sketch in CA 45-48
Kimball, Stanley B(uchholz) 1926- CANR-26
Earlier sketches in CA 17-20R, CANR-10
Kimball, Warren F. 1935- 25-28R
Kimball, Yeffe 1914-1978 .... SATA 37
Kimberley, Hugh
See Morland, Nigel
Kimberly, Gail 81-84
Kimble, Daniel Porter 1934- 41-44R
Kimble, David 1921- 13-16R
Kimble, George H(erbert) T(inley) 1908- 108
Kimble, Gregory A(dams) 1917- 21-24R
Kimbrell, Grady 1933- 33-36R
Kimbro, Harriet
See Kofalk, Harriet
Kimbro, Jean
See Kimbro, John M.
Kimbro, John M. 1929- CANR-2
Earlier sketch in CA 45-48
Kimbrough, Emily 1899-1989 .... 17-20R
Obituary 127
See also SATA 2, 59
Kimbrough, Katheryn
See Kimbro, John M.
Kimbrough, Ralph B(radley) 1922- 73-76
Kimbrough, Richard B(enito) 1931- 41-44R
Kimbrough, Robert (Alexander III)
1929- CANR-6
Earlier sketch in CA 9-12R
Kimbrough, Sara Dodge 1901- 93-96
Kimche, David 103
Kimenye, Barbara 1940(?)- 101
Kimes, Beverly Rae 1939- 122
Brief entry 107
Kimmel, Arthur S(andor) 1930- 41-44R
Kimmel, Douglas C(harles) 1943- 53-56
Kimmel, Eric A. 1946- CANR-3
Earlier sketch in CA 49-52
See also SATA 13
Kimmel, Jo 1931- CANR-4
Earlier sketch in CA 53-56
Kimmel, Margaret Mary 1938- 124
See also SATA 43
Kimmel, Melvin 1930- 25-28R
Kimmel, Stanley (Preston)
1894(?)-1982 Obituary 109
Kimmel, William (Breyfogel)
1908-1982 Obituary 109
Kimmelman, Elaine 1925- 111
Kimmelman, Leslie (Grodinsky) 1958- 132
Kimmens, Andrew C(harles) 1942- 124
Kimmey, John Lansing 1922- Brief entry 108
Kimmich, Christoph M(artin) 1939- 69-72
Kimmich, Flora (Graham Horne) 1939- 106
Kimpel, Ben D(rew) 1915- 57-60
Kimpel, Ben F(ranklin) 1905- 1-4R
Kimrey, Grace (Evelyn) Saunders
1910- CANR-24
Earlier sketch in CA 45-48
Kim Ronyoung
See Hahn, Gloria
Kimura, Jiro 1949- 85-88
Kincaid, Alan
See Rikhoff, James C.
Kincaid, Jamaica 1949- 125
See also BLC 2
See also BW
See also CLC 43, 68
Kincaid, James R(ussell) 1937- CANR-15
Earlier sketch in CA 65-68
Kincaid, Suzanne (Moss) 1936- 9-12R
Kinch, Sam E. Jr. 1940- 45-48
Kincheloe, Raymond McFarland 1909- 61-64
Kincl, (Gladys) Kay Owens 1955- 106
Kindall, Alva Frederick 1906- 1-4R
Kindem, Gorham A(nders) 1948- 125
Kinder, Faye 1902- 5-8R
Kinder, Gary 1946- 109
Kinder, James S. 1895- 13-16R
Kinder, Kathleen
See Potter, Kathleen Jill
Kinder, Marsha 1940- CANR-15
Earlier sketch in CA 41-44R
Kinderlehrer, Jane 1913- 106
Kindleberger, Charles P(oor) II 1910- CANR-36
Earlier sketches in CA 73-76, CANR-12
Kindley, Jeffrey (Bowman) 1945- 130
Brief entry 125
Kindred, Alton R(ichard) 1922- 109
Kindred, Leslie W(ithrow) 1905- 41-44R
Kindred, Wendy (Good) 1937- 37-40R
See also SATA 7
Kindregan, Charles P(eter) 1935- CANR-10
Earlier sketch in CA 21-24R
Kineji, Maborushi
See Gibson, Walter B(rown)
Kinert, Reed (Charles) 1911(?)- 107
Kines, Pat Decker 1937- 65-68
See also SATA 12
Kines, Thomas Alvin 1922- 13-16R
Kines, Tom
See Kines, Thomas Alvin
King, Adam
See Hoare, Robert J(ohn)
King, Adele Cockshoot 1932- CANR-8
Earlier sketch in CA 13-16R
King, Alan 1927- 89-92
King, Alec Hyatt
See King, Alexander Hyatt
King, Alexander Hyatt 1911- 124
King, Alexander 1909- 110
King, Alfred M. 1933- 25-28R
King, Algin B(raddy) 1927- CANR-15
Earlier sketch in CA 41-44R
King, Alison
See Martini, Teri
King, Alvy L(eon) 1932- 33-36R
King, Annette 1941- 33-36R
King, Anthony (Stephen) 1934- 17-20R
King, Archdale Arthur 1890-1972 .... CAP-1
Earlier sketch in CA 17-18
King, Ben F(rank) 1937- 57-60
King, Bert T(homas) 1927- 45-48
King, Betty (Alice) 1919- 103
King, Betty Patterson 1925- 9-12R
King, Billi
See Caulder, Colline
King, Billie Jean 1943- CANR-10
Earlier sketch in CA 53-56
See also SATA 12
King, Bruce Obituary 61-64
King, Bruce A. 1933- CANR-19
Earlier sketches in CA 53-56, CANR-4
King, C(lyde) Richard 1924- CANR-11
Earlier sketch in CA 69-72
King, Captain Charles
See King, Charles
King, Cecil
See King, Cecil H(armsworth)
King, Cecil H(armsworth) 1901-1987 110
Obituary 122
King, Charles (Lester) 1922- 57-60
King, Charles 1844-1933 Brief entry 122
King, Clarence (Rivers)
1842-1901 Brief entry 110
See also DLB 12
King, Clarence 1884(?)-1974 Obituary 53-56
King, (David) Clive 1924- 104
See also SATA 28
King, Clyde S(tuart) 1919- 17-20R
King, Coretta Scott 1927- CANR-27
Earlier sketch in CA 29-32R
See also BW
King, Cynthia 1925- CANR-36
Earlier sketch in CA 29-32R
See also SATA 7
King, Daniel P(atrick) 1942- CANR-4
Earlier sketch in CA 53-56
King, Deborah 1950- CANR-31
Earlier sketch in CA 112
King, (William) Dennis 1941- 130
King, Donald B. 1913- 13-16R
King, Edith W(eiss) 1930- CANR-14
Earlier sketch in CA 33-36R
King, Edmund J(ames) 1914- CANR-2
Earlier sketch in CA 5-8R
King, Edmund L(udwig) 1914- CANR-13
Earlier sketch in CA 33-36R
King, Edward L. 1928- 81-84
King, Elizabeth A.
See Abravanel, Elizabeth
King, Florence 1936- CANR-7
Earlier sketch in CA 57-60
See also AITN 1
See also DLBY 85
King, Francis Edward 1931- 61-64
King, Francis (Henry) 1923- CANR-33
Earlier sketches in CA 1-4R, CANR-1
See also CLC 8, 53
See also DLB 15
See also MTCW
King, Francis P(aul) 1922- 13-16R
King, Frank A.
See King, Franklin Alexander
King, Frank H(enry) H(aviland) 1926- 119
King, Frank O. 1883-1969 Obituary 89-92
See also SATA 22
King, Franklin Alexander 1923- 45-48
King, Frederick Murl 1916- CANR-2
Earlier sketch in CA 5-8R
King, General Charles
See King, Charles
King, Glen D. 1925- 9-12R
King, Grace (Elizabeth)
1852(?)-1932 Brief entry 116
See also DLB 12, 78
King, Graham (Peter) 1930- 132
King, Harold 1898-1990 Obituary 132
King, Harold 1945- CANR-7
Earlier sketch in CA 57-60
King, Helen H(ayes) 1937- 33-36R
King, Homer W. 1907- CAP-1
Earlier sketch in CA 13-16
King, Horace Maybray
See Maybray-King, Horace
King, Irving H(enry) 1935- 89-92
King, Ivan R(obert) 1927- 89-92
King, Jack
See Dowling, Allen
King, James Cecil 1924- CANR-14
Earlier sketch in CA 41-44R
King, James G. 1898(?)-1979 Obituary 89-92
King, James T(errell) 1933- 37-40R
King, James W. 1920- 9-12R
King, James 1942- 121
King, Janet Kauffman 1935- Brief entry 110
King, Jere Clemens 1910- 5-8R
King, Jerome Babcock 1927- 103
King, (Frederick) Jerry 1941- 97-100
King, Joan (M.) 1930- 123
King, Joe 1909(?)-1979 Obituary 85-88
King, John
See McKeag, Ernest L(ionel)
King, John Edward 1947- 102
King, John L(afayette) 1917- 41-44R
King, John N. 1945- CANR-32
Earlier sketch in CA 113
King, John O(zias) 1923- Brief entry 108
King, John Q. Taylor 1921- 25-28R
King, Josie
See Germany, (Vera) Jo(sephine)

King, Joyce
See Ching, Julia (Chia-yi)
King, K. DeWayne (Dewey) 1925- 13-16R
King, Katherine Callen 1942- 127
King, Kathleen (Marie) 1948- 114
King, Kimball 1934- CANR-31
Earlier sketch in CA 110
King, Larry L. 1929- CANR-24
Earlier sketch in CA 13-16R
See also MTCW
See also SATA 66
King, Larry 1933- Brief entry 111
King, Leila Pier 1882-1981 Obituary 105
King, Leslie John 1934- Brief entry 106
King, Lester S(now) 1908- 33-36R
King, Louise W(ooster) CANR-7
Earlier sketch in CA 13-16R
King, Marcet (Alice Hines) 1922- 25-28R
King, Margaret L(eah) 1947- 123
King, Marian 1900(?)-1986 ....CANR-2
Obituary 118
Earlier sketch in CA 5-8R
See also SATA 23, 47
King, Marjorie Cameron 1909- 33-36R
King, Mark 1945- 61-64
King, Martha L. 1918- 127
Brief entry 109
King, Martin Luther Sr. 1899-1984 125
Obituary 117
See also BW
King, Martin Luther Jr. 1929-1968 ....CANR-27
Earlier sketches in CAP-2, CA 25-28
See also BLC 2
See also BW
See also MTCW
See also SATA 14
King, Mary Louise 1911- 21-24R
King, Michael
See Buse, Renee
and Kahane, Meir (David)
King, Michael J(ulius) 1941- 119
King, Morton Brandon 1913- 102
King, Noel Q(uixote) 1922- CANR-19
Earlier sketches in CA 1-4R, CANR-4
King, Norman A.
See Tralins, S(andor) Robert
King, O. H. P. 1902- 1-4R
King, Patricia 1930- 5-8R
King, Paul
See Drackett, Phil(ip Arthur)
King, Paula
See Downing, Paula E.
King, Pauline 1917- 119
King, Peggy Cameron
See King, Marjorie Cameron
King, Peter (John) 1940-1989 Obituary 127
King, Peter 1925- 125
King, Philip B(urke) 1903-1987 125
Obituary 122
King, Philip 1904- 103
King, Preston (Theodore) 1936- CANR-26
Earlier sketches in CA 21-24R, CANR-10
King, Ray A(iken) 1933- 21-24R
King, Richard A(ustin) 1929- 21-24R
King, Richard G. 1922- 37-40R
King, Richard H. 1942- 77-80
King, Richard L(ouis) 1937- CANR-1
Earlier sketch in CA 45-48
King, Robert B. 1949- 125
King, Robert Charles 1928- 17-20R
King, Robert G. 1929- 21-24R
King, Robert H(arlen) 1935- 45-48
King, Robert L. 1950- 77-80
King, Robert R(ay) 1942- CANR-8
Earlier sketch in CA 61-64
King, Robin 1919- 5-8R
King, Roma Alvah Jr. 1914- CANR-1
Earlier sketch in CA 1-4R
King, Ronald (Wilfred) 1914- 107
King, Rufus 1917- 25-28R
King, Ruth Rodney
See Manley, Ruth Rodney King
King, Spencer B(idwell) Jr. 1904- CAP-1
Earlier sketch in CA 17-18
King, Stanley H(all) 1921- Brief entry 110
King, Stella 69-72
King, Stephen (Edwin) 1947- CANR-30
Earlier sketches in CA 61-64, CANR-1
See also AAYA 1
See also BEST 90:1
See also CLC 12, 26, 37, 61
See also DLBY 80
See also MTCW
See also SATA 9, 55
King, Stephen W(illiam) 1947- 61-64
King, Steve
See King, Stephen (Edwin)
King, T(homas) J(ames) 1925- 37-40R
King, Tabitha (Jane) 1949- CANR-30
Earlier sketch in CA 105
King, Teri 1940- 89-92
King, Terry Johnson 1929-1978 ....17-20R
Obituary 77-80
King, Thomas M(ulvihill) 1929- 57-60
King, Tony 1947- 109
See also SATA 39
King, Veronica
See King, Florence
King, Vincent
See Vinson, Rex Thomas
King, Willard L. 1893-1981 ....1-4R
Obituary 103
King, William Donald Aelian 1910- 89-92
King, William R(ichard) 1938- CANR-8
Earlier sketch in CA 21-24R
King, Winston L(ee) 1907- 41-44R
King, Woodie Jr. 1937- CANR-25
Earlier sketch in CA 103
See also BW
See also DLB 38
Kingdon, Frank 1894-1972 Obituary 33-36R
Kingdon, John W(ells) 1940- 25-28R
Kingdon, Robert M(cCune) 1927- 21-24R
Kingdon, Roger 1891-1984 Obituary 113
Kingery, Robert E(rnest) 1913-1978 ....9-12R
Obituary 103
King-Farlow, John 1932- 111
King-Hall, Magdalen 1904-1971 ....CAP-1
Obituary 29-32R
Earlier sketch in CA 9-10
King-Hall, (William) Stephen (Richard)
1893-1966 ....5-8R
King-Hamilton, Alan 1904- 130
King-Hele, Desmond (George) 1927- CANR-32
Earlier sketches in CA 29-32R, CANR-14
Kinghorn, A(lexander) M(anson) 1926- 93-96
Kinghorn, Kenneth Cain 1930- CANR-31
Earlier sketches in CA 41-44R, CANR-14
Kinglake, Alexander William 1809-1891 ....DLB 55
Kingman, Dong (Moy Shu) 1911- 112
See also SATA 44
Kingman, Lee
See Natti, (Mary) Lee
See also CLC 17
See also SAAS 3
See also SATA 1, 67
Kingman, Russ 1917- CANR-17
Earlier sketch in CA 101
Kingry, Philip L. 1942- 53-56
Kingsbury, Arthur 1939- 29-32R
Kingsbury, Donald (MacDonald) 1929- 124
Kingsbury, Jack Dean 1934- 37-40R
Kingsbury, John M(erriam) 1928- CANR-6
Earlier sketch in CA 13-16R
Kingsbury, Robert C(arrick) 1924- CANR-2
Earlier sketch in CA 1-4R
Kingsbury-Smith, Joseph 1908- 133
Kingsland, Leslie William 1912- 69-72
See also SATA 13
Kingsland, Sharon E. 1951- 124
Kingsley, Charles 1819-1875 ....DLB 21, 32
See also YABC 2
Kingsley, Charlotte Mary
See Hanshew, Thomas W.
Kingsley, Daniel T(hain) 1932- 117
Kingsley, Emily Perl 1940- 107
See also SATA 33
Kingsley, Henry 1830-1876 ....DLB 21
Kingsley, Michael J.
1918(?)-1972 Obituary 37-40R
Kingsley, Sidney 1906- 85-88
See also CLC 44
See also DLB 7
Kingsley-Smith, Terence 1940- 57-60
King-Smith, Dick 1922- CANR-22
Earlier sketch in CA 105
See also MAICYA
See also SATA 38, 47
Kingsnorth, George W(illiam) 1924- 5-8R
Kingsolver, Barbara 1955- 134
Brief entry 129
See also CLC 55
Kingston, Albert J(ames) 1917- 21-24R
Kingston, Jeremy Henry Spencer 1931- 103
Kingston, Maxine (Ting Ting) Hong
1940- CANR-38
Earlier sketches in CA 69-72, CANR-13
See also AAYA 8
See also CLC 12, 19, 58
See also DLBY 80
See also MTCW
See also SATA 53
Kingston, Syd
See Bingley, David Ernest
Kingston, (Frederick) Temple 1925- CANR-12
Earlier sketch in CA 33-36R
Kingston-Mann, Esther 112
Kingston-Stoops, Joyce 1923- 81-84
Kington, Miles (Beresford) 1941- 130
Kininmonth, Christopher 1917- 53-56
Kinkade, Richard P(aisley) 1939- CANR-31
Earlier sketches in CA 37-40R, CANR-14
Kinkaid, Matt
See Adams, Clifton
Kinkaid, Wyatt E.
See Jennings, Michael Glenn
Kinkead, Eugene (Francis) 1906- CANR-1
Earlier sketch in CA 1-4R
Kinkead-Weekes, Mark 1931- 124
Kinkley, Jeffrey C(arroll) 1948- 125
Kinley, Phyllis (Elaine Gillespie) 1930- 1-4R
Kinloch, A. Murray 1923- 103
Kinmonth, Earl H. 1946- 107
Kinnaird, Clark 1901-1983 ....CANR-1
Obituary 111
Earlier sketch in CA 45-48
Kinnaird, John (William) 1924-1980 124
Obituary 97-100
Kinnaird, William M(cKee) 1928- 101
Kinnamon, Keneth 1932- 37-40R
Kinnane, John F. 1921-1987 Obituary 123
Kinnard, Douglas 1921- CANR-14
Earlier sketch in CA 77-80
Kinnear, Elizabeth K. 1902- CAP-2
Earlier sketch in CA 33-36
Kinnear, Michael 1937- 37-40R
Kinneavy, James Louis 1920- 69-72
Kinneir, (Richard) Jock 1917- 121
Kinnell, Galway 1927- CANR-34
Earlier sketches in CA 9-12R, CANR-10
See also CLC 1, 2, 3, 5, 13, 29
See also DLB 5
See also DLBY 87
See also MTCW
Kinney, Arthur F(rederick) 1933- CANR-14
Earlier sketch in CA 37-40R
Kinney, C. Cle(land) 1915- 9-12R
See also SATA 6
Kinney, Francis S(herwood) 1915- 106
Kinney, Harrison 1921- 1-4R
See also SATA 13
Kinney, James (Joseph) 1942- 120
Kinney, James R(oser)
1902(?)-1978 Obituary 81-84
Kinney, Jean Stout 1912- 9-12R
See also SATA 12
Kinney, Lucien Blair 1895-1971 ....CAP-2
Earlier sketch in CA 23-24
Kinney, Peter 1943- 73-76
Kinney, Richard 1924(?)-1979 Obituary 85-88
Kinnicutt, Susan Sibley 1926- 77-80
Kinnison, William A(ndrew) 1932- 21-24R
Kinor, Jehuda
See Rothmuller, Aron Marko
Kinoshita Junji 1914- 124
Kinross, Lord
See Balfour, (John) Patrick Douglas
Kinsbruner, Jay 1939- 25-28R
Kinsel, Paschal 1895(?)-1976 Obituary 69-72
Kinsella, James 1959- 134
Kinsella, Paul L. 1923- 21-24R
Kinsella, Thomas 1928- CANR-15
Earlier sketch in CA 17-20R
See also CLC 4, 19
See also DLB 27
See also MTCW
Kinsella, W(illiam) P(atrick) 1935- CANR-35
Earlier sketches in CA 97-100, CANR-21
See also CAAS 7
See also AAYA 7
See also CLC 27, 43
See also MTCW
Kinsey, Alfred C(harles)
1894-1956 Brief entry 115
Kinsey, Barry Allan 1931- 17-20R
Kinsey, Elizabeth
See Clymer, Eleanor
Kinsey-Jones, Brian
See Ball, Brian N(eville)
Kinsey-Warnock, Natalie 1956- ....SATA 71
Kinsley, D(aniel) A(llan) 1939- 45-48
Kinsley, James 1922-1984 ....CANR-2
Obituary 114
Earlier sketch in CA 1-4R
Kinsolving, Charles McIlvaine
1893-1984 Obituary 114
Kinstler, Everett Raymond 1926- 33-36R
Kinter, Judith 1928- 109
Kintgen, Eugene R(obert) Jr. 1942- 116
Kintner, Earl W(ilson) 1912- CANR-1
Earlier sketch in CA 45-48
Kintner, Robert Edmonds
1909-1980 Obituary 103
Kintner, William R(oscoe) 1915- CANR-6
Earlier sketch in CA 5-8R
Kinton, Jack F(ranklin) 1939- CANR-7
Earlier sketch in CA 57-60
Kintsch, Walter 1932- 29-32R
Kinyatti, Maina wa
See wa Kinyatti, Maina
Kinzel, Dorothy 1950- ....SATA 57
Kinzel, Dottie
See Kinzel, Dorothy
Kinzer, Betty 1922- 21-24R
Kinzer, Donald Louis 1914- 53-56
Kinzer, H(arless) M(ahlon)
1923(?)-1975 Obituary 57-60
Kinzer, Nora Scott 1936- 126
Brief entry 106
Kinzie, Mary 1944- 133
Kiparsky, Valentin (Julius Alexander)
1904- 17-20R
Kipfer, Barbara Ann 1954- 134
Kiple, Kenneth F(ranklin) 1939- 120
Kipling, (Joseph) Rudyard 1865-1936 ....CANR-33
Brief entry 105
Earlier sketch in CA 120
See also CDBLB 1890-1914
See also DLB 19, 34
See also MAICYA
See also MTCW
See also PC 3
See also SSC 5
See also TCLC 8, 17
See also WLC
See also YABC 2
Kiplinger, Austin H(untington) 1918- 57-60
Kiplinger, Willard Monroe
1891-1967 Obituary 89-92
Kipnis, Aaron R. 1948- 137
Kipnis, Claude 1938-1981 107
Obituary 103
Kipnis, Kenneth 1943- 129
Kippax, Janet 1926- 97-100
Kippenhahn, Rudolf 1926- 130
Kipphardt, Heinar 1922-1982 89-92
Obituary 108
Kippley, John F(rancis) 1930- 29-32R
Kippley, Sheila K. 1939- 61-64
Kipps, Harriet C(lyde) 1926- 124
Kiraly, Bela (Kalman) 1912- CANR-8
Earlier sketch in CA 61-64
Kiratli, Cemile
See Schimmel, Annemarie (Brigitte)
Kirby, (George) Blaik 1928- 77-80
Kirby, D(avid) P(eter) 1936- 25-28R
Kirby, David G. 1942- 101
Kirby, David K(irk) 1944- 53-56
Kirby, Douglas J. 1929- 25-28R
Kirby, E(dward) Stuart 1909- CANR-22
Earlier sketches in CA 13-16R, CANR-7
Kirby, Emily B(aruch) 1929- 117
Kirby, F(rank) E(ugene) 1928- 65-68
Kirby, Gilbert W(alter) 1914- 103
Kirby, Jack Temple 1938- 25-28R
Kirby, James
See Kirby, James C(ordell) Jr.
Kirby, James C(ordell) Jr.
1928-1989 Obituary 130
Kirby, Jean
See Robinson, Chaille Howard (Payne)
Kirby, Jean
See McDonnell, Virginia B(leecker)
Kirby, John B(yron) 1938- 105
Kirby, M(ary) Sheelah Flanagan 1916- 5-8R
Kirby, Mark
See Floren, Lee
Kirby, Rollin 1875-1952 Brief entry 118
Kirby, Susan E. 1949- ....SATA 62
Kirby, Thomas Austin 1904- 5-8R
Kirby, William 1817-1906 ....DLB 99
Kirchhofer, Alfred H.
1892(?)-1985 Obituary 117
Kirchhoff, Frederick (Thomas) 1942- 111
Kirchner, Audrey Burie 1937- CANR-12
Earlier sketch in CA 73-76
Kirchner, Emil J. 1942- 130
Kirchner, Glenn 1930- 29-32R
Kirchner, Walther 1905- CANR-1
Earlier sketch in CA 1-4R
Kirchwey, Freda 1893-1976 93-96
Obituary 61-64
Kirdar, Uner 1933- 21-24R
Kirgis, Frederic L(ee) Jr. 1934- 125
Kirk, Alexandra
See Woods, Sherryl
Kirk, Clara M(arburg) 1898-1976 ....CAP-1
Obituary 69-72
Earlier sketch in CA 17-18
Kirk, Cooper 1920- 116
Kirk, David 1935- 29-32R
Kirk, Donald R. 1935- 57-60
Kirk, Donald 1938- 37-40R
Kirk, Elizabeth D(oan) 1937- 53-56
Kirk, G(eoffrey) S(tephen) 1921- CANR-2
Earlier sketch in CA 5-8R
Kirk, George (Eden) 1911- 1-4R
Kirk, H(enry) David 1918- CANR-11
Earlier sketch in CA 17-20R
Kirk, Irene 1926- CANR-6
Earlier sketch in CA 5-8R
Kirk, Irina
See Kirk, Irene
Kirk, James A(lbert) 1929- 37-40R
Kirk, Jeremy
See Powell, Richard (Pitts)
Kirk, Jerome (Richard) 1937- 49-52
Kirk, John Esben 1905-1975 Obituary 57-60
Kirk, John Foster 1824-1904 ....DLB 79
Kirk, John T(homas) 1933- 49-52
Kirk, John W. 1932- 129
Kirk, Lydia (Chapin) 1896-1984 Obituary 114
Kirk, Marshall (Kenneth) 1957- 135
Kirk, Mary Wallace 1889- 57-60
Kirk, Michael
See Knox, William
Kirk, Philip
See Levinson, Leonard
Kirk, R.
See Dietrich, Richard V(incent)
Kirk, Richard (Edmund) 1931- 13-16R
Kirk, Robert Warner 9-12R
Obituary 103
Kirk, Roger E(dward) 1930- 41-44R
Kirk, Rudolf 1898-1989 Obituary 130
Kirk, Russell (Amos) 1918- CANR-20
Earlier sketches in CA 1-4R, CANR-1
See also CAAS 9
See also AITN 1
See also MTCW
Kirk, Ruth (Kratz) 1925- CANR-9
Earlier sketch in CA 13-16R
See also SATA 5
Kirk, Samuel A(lexander) 1904- CANR-1
Earlier sketch in CA 45-48
Kirk, T(homas) H(obson) 1899- CAP-2
Earlier sketch in CA 23-24
Kirk, Ted
See Bank, Theodore P(aul) II
Kirk, Wayne
See Kock, Winston E(dward)
Kirkaldy, John F(rancis)
1908-1990 Obituary 132
Kirkbride, Norma Jean
1924(?)-1983 Obituary 111
Kirkbride, Ronald (de Levington) 1912- CANR-2
Earlier sketch in CA 1-4R
Kirkconnell, Watson 1895-1977 125
Obituary 108
See also DLB 68
Kirkendall, Don(ald M.) 1923- 49-52
Kirkendall, Lester A(llen) 1903- CANR-5
Earlier sketch in CA 1-4R
Kirkendall, Richard Stewart 1928- 77-80
Kirk-Greene, Anthony H. M.
See Kirk-Greene, Anthony (Hamilton Millard)
Kirk-Greene, Anthony (Hamilton Millard)
1925- CANR-27
Earlier sketches in CA 61-64, CANR-11
Kirk-Greene, Christopher Walter Edward
1926- 13-16R
Kirkham, E. Bruce 1938- 37-40R

Kirkham, George L. 1941- ... 77-80
Kirkham, Michael 1934- ... 25-28R
Kirkland, Bryant M(ays) 1914- ... 21-24R
Kirkland, Caroline M. 1801-1864 ... DLB 3, 73, 74
Kirkland, Edward Chase 1894-1975 ... CANR-6
Obituary ... 104
Earlier sketch in CA 1-4R
Kirkland, Joseph 1830-1893 ... DLB 12
Kirkland, Sally 1912-1989 Obituary ... 129
Kirkland, Wallace W.
1891(?)-1979 Obituary ... 89-92
Kirkland, Will
See Hale, Arlene
Kirkman, James S(pedding) 1906-1989 ... 93-96
Obituary ... 128
Kirkpatrick, Diane 1933- ... 53-56
Kirkpatrick, Donald L(ee) 1924- ... 41-44R
Kirkpatrick, Doris (Upton) 1902- ... 93-96
Kirkpatrick, Dow (Napier) 1917- ... 21-24R
Kirkpatrick, Evron M(aurice) 1911- ... 57-60
Kirkpatrick, Frank 1924- ... 108
Kirkpatrick, Ivone Augustine 1897-1964 ... CAP-1
Earlier sketch in CA 9-10
Kirkpatrick, Jean 1923- ... 81-84
Kirkpatrick, Jeane D(uane) J(ordan)
1926- ... CANR-7
Earlier sketch in CA 53-56
Kirkpatrick, John 1905-1991 ... 45-48
Obituary ... 136
Kirkpatrick, Lyman B(ickford) Jr. 1916- ... 33-36R
Kirkpatrick, Oliver (Austin) 1911- ... 49-52
Kirkpatrick, Ralph 1911-1984 ... 49-52
Obituary ... 112
Kirkpatrick, Samuel A(lexander) III
1943- ... 41-44R
Kirkpatrick, Sidney D(ale) 1955- ... 136
Kirkpatrick, Smith 1922- ... 49-52
Kirkup, James 1918- ... CANR-2
Earlier sketch in CA 1-4R
See also CAAS 4
See also CLC 1
See also DLB 27
See also SATA 12
Kirkus, Virginia
See Glick, Virginia Kirkus
Kirkwood, Ellen Swan 1904- ... 25-28R
Kirkwood, G(ordon) M(acdonald) 1916- ... 93-96
Kirkwood, James 1930(?)-1989 ... CANR-6
Obituary ... 128
Earlier sketch in CA 1-4R
See also AITN 2
See also CLC 9
Kirkwood, Kenneth P. 1899-1968 ... 37-40R
Kirn, Ann Minette 1910- ... 93-96
Kirp, David L(eslie) 1944- ... 109
Kirsch, Anthony Thomas 1930- ... 103
Kirsch, Arthur C(lifford) 1932- ... 13-16R
Kirsch, Charlotte 1942- ... 109
Kirsch, Herbert 1924(?)-1978 Obituary ... 104
Kirsch, Irving 1943- ... 136
Kirsch, James Isaac 1901-1989 Obituary ... 128
Kirsch, Leonard Joel 1934-1977 ... 37-40R
Kirsch, Paul John 1914- ... 108
Kirsch, Robert R. 1922-1980 ... CANR-13
Obituary ... 102
Earlier sketch in CA 33-36R
Kirsch, Sarah 1935- ... DLB 75
Kirschen, Leonard 1908-1983 Obituary ... 109
Kirschenbaum, Aaron 1926- ... 33-36R
Kirschenbaum, Howard 1944- ... 89-92
Kirschner, Allen 1930- ... 29-32R
Kirschner, Fritz
See Bickers, Richard Leslie Townshend
Kirschner, Joseph 1930- ... 121
Kirschner, Linda Rae 1939- ... 33-36R
Kirschten, Ernest 1902-1974 ... CAP-1
Obituary ... 49-52
Earlier sketch in CA 11-12
Kirshenbaum, Jerry 1938- ... 107
Kirshenblatt-Gimblett, Barbara 1942- ... CANR-15
Earlier sketch in CA 81-84
Kirshner, Gloria Ifland ... 41-44R
Kirsner, Douglas 1947- ... 77-80
Kirsner, Robert 1921- ... 21-24R
Kirst, Hans Hellmut 1914-1989 ... 104
Obituary ... 128
See also DLB 69
Kirst, Michael W(eile) 1939- ... CANR-24
Earlier sketch in CA 45-48
Kirstein, George G(arland)
1909-1986 Obituary ... 118
Kirstein, Lincoln (Edward) 1907- ... 128
Brief entry ... 117
Kirsten, Grace 1900- ... 104
Kirtland, G. B.
See Hine, Al(fred Blakelee)
and Hine, Sesyle Joslin
Kirtland, Helen Johns
1890(?)-1979 Obituary ... 89-92
Kirtland, Kathleen 1945- ... 65-68
Kirvan, John J. 1932- ... CANR-10
Earlier sketch in CA 21-24R
Kirwan, Albert D(ennis) 1904-1971 ... CANR-4
Earlier sketch in CA 1-4R
Kirwan, Laurence Patrick 1907- ... 1-4R
Kirwan, Molly (Morrow) 1906- ... CAP-1
Earlier sketch in CA 13-14
Kirwin, Harry Wynne 1911-1963 ... 1-4R
Kirzner, Israel M(ayer) 1930- ... CANR-3
Earlier sketch in CA 1-4R
Kis, Danilo 1935-1989 ... 118
Obituary ... 129
Brief entry ... 109
See also CLC 57
See also MTCW
Kisamore, Norman D(ale) 1928- ... 5-8R
Kiser, Clyde V(ernon) 1904- ... 25-28R
Kiser, Lisa J. 1949- ... 114
Kish, G. Hobab
See Kennedy, Gerald (Hamilton)
Kish, George 1914- ... CANR-1
Earlier sketch in CA 1-4R
Kish, Kathleen Vera 1942- ... CANR-12
Earlier sketch in CA 69-72
Kish, Leslie 1910- ... CAP-1
Earlier sketch in CA 19-20
Kishel, Patricia G(unter) 1948- ... 117
Kishida, Eriko 1929- ... CANR-7
Earlier sketch in CA 53-56
See also SATA 12
Kishon, Ephraim 1924- ... CANR-2
Earlier sketch in CA 49-52
Kishtainy, Khalid 1929- ... 115
Kisiel, Marie 1929- ... 112
Kisinger, Grace Gelvin (Maze)
1913-1965 ... CAP-1
Earlier sketch in CA 13-14
See also SATA 10
Kisker, George W. 1912- ... 21-24R
Kismaric, Carole 1942- ... CANR-23
Earlier sketches in CA 33-36R, CANR-8
Kisner, James (Martin Jr.) 1947- ... CANR-35
Earlier sketch in CA 113
Kisor, Henry (Du Bois) 1940- ... 73-76
Kissam, Edward 1943- ... 61-64
Kissane, John M(ichael) 1928- ... 53-56
Kissane, Leedice McAnelly 1905- ... CAP-2
Earlier sketch in CA 25-28
Kissen, Fan(ny) 1904- ... CAP-1
Earlier sketch in CA 13-16
Kissick, Gary 1946- ... 118
Kissin, Eva H. 1923- ... 29-32R
See also SATA 10
Kissinger, Henry A(lfred) 1923- ... CANR-33
Earlier sketches in CA 1-4R, CANR-2
See also MTCW
Kissinger, Warren S(tauffer) 1922- ... 116
Kissling, Dorothy (Hight)
1904-1969 Obituary ... 105
Kissling, Fred R. Jr. 1930- ... 21-24R
Kiste, Robert Carl 1936- ... 61-64
Kister, Kenneth F. 1935- ... 25-28R
Kistiakowsky, George B(ogdan)
1900-1982 Obituary ... 108
Kistiakowsky, Vera 1928- ... 21-24R
Kistler, Mark O(liver) 1918- ... 77-80
Kistner, Robert William 1917- ... CANR-13
Earlier sketch in CA 61-64
Kitagawa, Daisuke 1910- ... CAP-2
Earlier sketch in CA 17-18
Kitagawa, Joseph M. 1915- ... CANR-2
Earlier sketch in CA 1-4R
Kitamura, Satoshi 1956- ... SATA 62
Kitano, Harry H. L. 1926- ... 29-32R
Kitao, T(imothy) Kaori 1933- ... 106
Kitchel, Denison 1908- ... 105
Kitchen, Bert
See Kitchen, Herbert Thomas
Kitchen, Helen (Angell) ... CANR-23
Earlier sketches in CA 9-12R, CANR-8
Kitchen, Herbert Thomas 1940- ... 138
See also SATA 70
Kitchen, Herminie B(roedel) 1901-1973 ... CAP-1
Earlier sketch in CA 17-18
Kitchen, Martin 1936- ... CANR-26
Earlier sketches in CA 61-64, CANR-10
Kitchen, Paddy 1934- ... CANR-21
Earlier sketch in CA 25-28R
Kitchener, Richard Frank 1941- ... 124
Kitcher, Philip 1947- ... 113
Kitchin, C. H. B. 1895-1967 ... DLB 77
Kitchin, Laurence 1913- ... 104
Kite, Larry
See Schneck, Stephen
Kite, Pat 1940- ... 119
Kiteley, Brian 1956- ... 132
Kitman, Marvin 1929- ... 101
Kitson, Jack William 1940- ... 25-28R
Kitson Clark, George Sydney Roberts
1900-1975 ... CANR-14
Earlier sketch in CA 21-24R
Kitt, Eartha (Mae) 1928- ... 77-80
Kitt, Tamara
See de Regniers, Beatrice Schenk (Freedman)
Kittelson, David James 1931- ... 119
Kittler, Glenn D. 1920(?)-1986 Obituary ... 119
Kitto, Crispin 1951- ... 119
Kitto, H(umphrey) D(avy) F(indley)
1897-1982 ... CAP-1
Obituary ... 105
Earlier sketch in CA 11-12
Kittredge, William 1932- ... 111
Kittrie, Nicholas N(orbert Nehemiah)
1928- ... 81-84
Kituomba
See Odaga, Asenath (Bole)
Kitzinger, Ernst 1912- ... 108
Kitzinger, Sheila 1929- ... 37-40R
See also SATA 57
Kitzinger, U(we) W(ebster) 1928- ... CANR-1
Earlier sketch in CA 1-4R
Kivenson, Gilbert 1920- ... 112
Kivy, Peter Nathan 1934- ... 103
Kiyota, Minoru 1923- ... CANR-32
Earlier sketch in CA 113
Kizer, Carolyn (Ashley) 1925- ... CANR-24
Earlier sketch in CA 65-68
See also CAAS 5
See also CLC 15, 39
See also DLB 5
Kjelgaard, James Arthur 1910-1959 ... 137
Brief entry ... 109
See also MAICYA
See also SATA 17
Kjelgaard, Jim
See Kjelgaard, James Arthur
Kjome, June C(reola) 1920- ... 5-8R
Klaas, Joe 1920- ... CANR-12
Earlier sketch in CA 29-32R
Klaassen, Leo(nardus) H(endrik)
1920- ... CANR-26
Earlier sketches in CA 21-24R, CANR-11
Klaassen, Walter 1926- ... 115
Klabund 1890-1928 ... DLB 66
See also TCLC 44
Kladstrup, Don(ald) 1943- ... 77-80
Klafs, Carl E. 1911- ... 13-16R
Klagsbrun, Francine (Lifton) ... 21-24R
See also SATA 36
Klaiber, Jeffrey L. 1943- ... 85-88
Klaich, Dolores 1936- ... 49-52
Klaidman, Stephen 1938- ... 125
Klainikite, Anne
See Gehman, Betsy Holland
Klaits, Barrie 1944- ... 73-76
See also SATA 52
Klaits, Joseph (Aaron) 1942- ... 126
Klamer, Arjo 1953- ... 116
Klamkin, Charles 1923- ... 61-64
Klamkin, Lynn 1950- ... 45-48
Klamkin, Marian 1926- ... CANR-1
Earlier sketch in CA 49-52
Klaniczay, Tibor 1923- ... 132
Klann, Margaret L. 1911- ... 77-80
Klaperman, Gilbert 1921- ... 49-52
See also SATA 33
Klaperman, Libby Mindlin 1921-1982 ... 9-12R
Obituary ... 107
See also SATA 31, 33
Klapp, Orrin E. 1915- ... 9-12R
Klapper, Charles F(rederick) 1905- ... CAP-1
Earlier sketch in CA 9-10
Klapper, Joseph T(homas)
1917-1984 Obituary ... 112
Klapper, M(olly) Roxana 1937- ... 53-56
Klapper, Marvin 1922- ... 17-20R
Klappert, Peter 1942- ... 33-36R
See also CLC 57
See also DLB 5
Klappholz, Kurt 1913-1975 Obituary ... 61-64
Klapthor, Margaret B(rown) 1922- ... 119
Klare, George R(oger) 1922- ... 5-8R
Klare, Hugh J(ohn) 1916- ... 103
Klare, Michael T(homas) 1942- ... 130
Klaren, Peter F(indell) 1938- ... 57-60
Klarsfeld, Beate 1939- ... 65-68
Klarsfeld, Serge 1935- ... 115
Klass, Allan Arnold 1907- ... 65-68
Klass, Morton 1927- ... CANR-5
Earlier sketch in CA 1-4R
See also SATA 11
Klass, Perri 1958- ... 126
Klass, Philip J. 1919- ... 25-28R
Klass, Sheila Solomon 1927- ... CANR-37
Earlier sketches in CA 37-40R, CANR-13
See also SATA 45
Klass, Sholom 1916- ... 21-24R
Klassen, Albert D(ale Jr.) 1931- ... 133
Klassen, Frank Roy 1910- ... 113
Klassen, Peter J(ames) 1930- ... CANR-1
Earlier sketch in CA 45-48
Klassen, Randolph Jacob 1933- ... 61-64
Klassen, Walter
See Klaassen, Walter
Klassen, William 1930- ... CANR-10
Earlier sketch in CA 25-28R
Klauber, John 1917-1981 Obituary ... 104
Klauber, Laurence M(onroe)
1883-1968 Obituary ... 105
Klauck, Daniel L. 1947- ... 69-72
Klauder, Francis John 1918- ... 53-56
Klaue, Lola Shelton 1903- ... 5-8R
Klause, John L(ouis) 1943- ... 118
Klausler, Alfred P(aul) 1910- ... 21-24R
Klausmeier, Herbert J. 1915- ... CANR-20
Earlier sketches in CA 1-4R, CANR-5
Klausner, Abraham J. 1915- ... 108
Klausner, Lawrence D(avid) 1939- ... 110
Klausner, Margot 1905-1976(?) Obituary ... 61-64
Klausner, Samuel Z(undel) 1923- ... 17-20R
Klavans, J(odie) K(ay) 1956- ... 118
Klaw, Spencer 1920- ... 25-28R
Klawans, Harold L(eo) 1937- ... 106
Klayman, Maxwell Irving 1917- ... 29-32R
Klebe, Charles Eugene 1907- ... CAP-2
Earlier sketch in CA 23-24
Klebe, Gene
See Klebe, Charles Eugene
Kleberger, Ilse 1921- ... CANR-39
Earlier sketches in CA 41-44R, CANR-15
See also SATA 5
Klee, James B(utt) 1916- ... 109
Kleeberg, Irene (Flitner) Cumming
1932- ... CANR-35
Earlier sketches in CA 61-64, CANR-12
See also SATA 65
Kleeblatt, Norman L(eslie) 1948- ... 128
Kleene, Stephen Cole 1909- ... 41-44R
Klees, Fredric (Spang) 1901- ... CAP-2
Earlier sketch in CA 19-20
Klehr, Harvey 1945- ... 111
Kleiler, Frank Munro 1914- ... 89-92
Kleiman, Ed 1932- ... 135
Kleiman, Mark A. R. 1951- ... 138
Kleiman, Robert 1918- ... 13-16R
Klein, A(braham) M(oses) 1909-1972 ... 101
Obituary ... 37-40R
See also CLC 19
See also DLB 68
Klein, Aaron E. 1930- ... CANR-19
Earlier sketch in CA 25-28R
See also SATA 28, 45
Klein, Alan F(redric) 1911- ... 57-60
Klein, Alexander 1918- ... CANR-14
Earlier sketch in CA 5-8R
Klein, Allen 1938- ... 131
Klein, Arnold William 1945- ... 37-40R
Klein, Bernard 1921- ... 17-20R
Klein, Carole (Doreen) 1934- Brief entry ... 118
Klein, Charlotte 1925- ... 101
Klein, Daniel M(artin) 1939- ... CANR-28
Earlier sketches in CA 61-64, CANR-11
Klein, Dave 1940- ... 89-92
Klein, David Ballin 1897- ... 41-44R
Klein, David 1919- ... CANR-18
Earlier sketches in CA 1-4R, CANR-1
See also SATA 59
Klein, Donald C(harles) 1923- ... 25-28R
Klein, Donald W(alker) 1929- Brief entry ... 114
Klein, Doris F.
See Jonas, Doris F(rances)
Klein, Edward 1936- ... 69-72
Klein, Elizabeth 1939- ... 110
Klein, Ernest 1899- ... CAP-2
Earlier sketch in CA 21-22
Klein, Fannie J. 1903-1984 Obituary ... 113
Klein, Fred 1932- Brief entry ... 115
Klein, Frederic Shriver 1904- ... 13-16R
Klein, Gene 1921- ... 126
Klein, Gerard 1937- ... 49-52
Klein, Gerda Weissmann 1924- ... 116
See also SATA 44
Klein, H(erbert) Arthur ... 13-16R
See also SATA 8
Klein, Herbert Sanford 1936- ... CANR-17
Earlier sketches in CA 93-96, CANR-37
Klein, Heywood 1954(?)-1984 Obituary ... 111
Klein, Holger Michael 1938- ... 65-68
Klein, Isaac 1905- ... 57-60
Klein, Jeffrey B. 1948- ... 77-80
Klein, Joe
See Klein, Joseph
Klein, John J(acob) 1929- ... 17-20R
Klein, Joseph 1946- ... 85-88
Klein, Josephine (F. H.) 1926- ... 1-4R
Klein, Julius 1901-1984 Obituary ... 112
Klein, K. K.
See Turner, Robert (Harry)
Klein, Karl
See Sala, Charles
Klein, Kathleen Gregory 1946- ... 130
Klein, Lawrence R(obert) 1920- Brief entry ... 116
Klein, Leonore (Glotzer) 1916- ... CANR-1
Earlier sketch in CA 1-4R
See also SATA 6
Klein, Marcus 1928- ... 9-12R
Klein, Martin A. 1934- ... 21-24R
Klein, Marymae E. 1917- ... 97-100
Klein, Maury 1939- ... 33-36R
Klein, Maxine 1934- ... CANR-10
Earlier sketch in CA 61-64
Klein, Melanie 1882-1960 Obituary ... 111
Klein, Milton M(artin) 1917- ... 93-96
Klein, Mina C(ooper) 1906-1979 ... 37-40R
Obituary ... 133
See also SATA 8
Klein, Muriel Walzer 1920- ... 29-32R
Klein, Norma 1938-1989 ... CANR-37
Obituary ... 128
Earlier sketches in CA 41-44R, CANR-15
See also AAYA 2
See also CLC 30
See also CLR 2, 19
See also MAICYA
See also SAAS 1
See also SATA 7, 57
Klein, Philip A(lexander) 1927- ... 17-20R
Klein, Philip Shriver 1909- ... CANR-1
Earlier sketch in CA 1-4R
Klein, Randolph Shipley 1942- ... 73-76
Klein, Richard C. 1916(?)-1983 Obituary ... 111
Klein, Richard G. 1941- ... 120
Klein, Richard M. 1923- ... CANR-25
Earlier sketch in CA 108
Klein, Robin 1936- ... 116
See also CLR 21
See also MAICYA
See also SATA 45, 55
Klein, Rose (Shweitzer) 1918- ... 21-24R
Klein, Stanley D. 1936- ... 77-80
Klein, Stanley 1930- ... 57-60
Klein, Stuart M(arc) 1932- ... 134
Brief entry ... 111
Klein, Suzanne Marie 1940- ... 57-60
Klein, T(heodore) E(ibon) D(onald) 1947- ... 119
See also CLC 34
Klein, Ted U. 1926- ... 25-28R
Klein, Thomas D(icker) 1941- ... 61-64
Klein, Walter J(ulian) 1923- ... 69-72
Klein, Woody 1929- ... 13-16R
Klein, Zachary 1948- ... 135
Kleinbauer, W(alter) Eugene 1937- ... 37-40R
Kleinbaum, Abby Wettan 1943- ... 113
Kleinberg, Seymour 1933- ... 105
Kleine, Glen 1936- ... 73-76
Kleine-Ahlbrandt, W(illiam) Laird 1932- ... 29-32R
Kleiner, Art 1954- ... 124
Kleiner, Dick
See Kleiner, Richard Arthur
Kleiner, Richard Arthur 1921- ... 129
Kleinfeld, Gerald R. 1936- ... 103
Kleinfeld, Judith S. 1944- ... CANR-15
Earlier sketch in CA 77-80
Kleinfeld, Vincent A. 1907- ... CANR-10
Earlier sketch in CA 17-20R

Kleinfield, N(athan) R(ichard) 1950- CANR-18
Earlier sketch in CA 97-100
Kleinfield, Sonny
See Kleinfield, N(athan) R(ichard)
Kleinhans, Theodore John 1924-............5-8R
Kleinke, Chris (Lynn) 1944- CANR-15
Earlier sketch in CA 89-92
Kleinman, Arthur (Michael) 1941- CANR-22
Earlier sketch in CA 105
Kleinman, Philip (Julian) 1932- 131
Kleinman, Ruth 1929- 125
Kleinmann, Jack H(enry) 1932- 21-24R
Kleinmuntz, Benjamin 1930- 33-36R
Kleinsmith, Bruce John 1942- 132
Kleinzahler, August 1949- 125
Kleist, Ewald von 1715-1759 .... DLB 97
Kleist, Heinrich von 1777-1811 .... DLB 90
Klejment, Anne M. 1950- CANR-17
Earlier sketch in CA 101
Klem, Kaye Wilson 1941- 89-92
Klement, Frank L(udwig) 1908- 9-12R
Klemer, Richard Hudson 1918-1972 ....CANR-4
Obituary 37-40R
Earlier sketch in CA 5-8R
Klemesrud, Judy 1939(?)-1985 89-92
Obituary 117
Klemin, Diana 49-52
See also SATA 65
Klemke, E(lmer) D. 1926- CANR-10
Earlier sketch in CA 25-28R
Klemm, Edward G. Jr. 1910- 57-60
See also SATA 30
Klemm, Roberta K(ohnhorst) 1884- 61-64
See also SATA 30
Klemm, W(illiam) R(obert) 1934- 93-96
Klemperer, Otto 1885-1973 Obituary 116
Klempner, Irving M(ax) 1924- 53-56
Klempner, John 1898(?)-1972 Obituary 37-40R
Klenbort, Charlotte
See Sempell, Charlotte
Klenicki, Leon 1930- 106
Klenk, Robert W(illiam) 1934- 29-32R
Klenz, William 1915- 5-8R
Klerer, Melvin 1926- 21-24R
Klerman, Lorraine V(ogel) 1929- CANR-15
Earlier sketch in CA 81-84
Klett, Guy S(oulliard) 1897- CAP-1
Earlier sketch in CA 13-14
Kleuser, Louise C(aroline)
1889(?)-1976 Obituary 65-68
Klevin, Jill Ross 1935- 111
See also SATA 38, 39
Klewin, W(illiam) Thomas 1921- 29-32R
Kleyman, Paul (Fred) 1945- 57-60
Kleypas, Lisa 1964- 127
Kliban, B(ernard) 1935-1990 106
Obituary 132
See also SATA 35
See also SATO 66
Klibansky, Raymond 1905- Brief entry 117
Kliever, Lonnie D(ean) 1931- 29-32R
Kliewer, Evelyn 1933- 101
Kliewer, Warren 1931- CANR-2
Earlier sketch in CA 45-48
Kligerman, Jack 1938- 85-88
Kligman, Ruth 1930- 101
Klima, Ivan 1931- CANR-17
Earlier sketch in CA 25-28R
See also CLC 56
Kliman, Gilbert W(allace) 1929- 117
Klimas, Antanas 1924- 41-44R
Klimas, John E(dward) 1927-1975 Obituary 111
Klimek, David E(rnest) 1941- 89-92
Klimenko, Michael 1924- 73-76
Klimentov, Andrei Platonovich
1899-1951 Brief entry 108
See also Platonov, Andrei
Klimisch, Sister Mary Jane 1920- 17-20R
Klimo, Jake
See Klimo, Vernon
Klimo, Vernon 1914- 101
Klimowicz, Barbara 1927- 21-24R
See also SATA 10
Klin, George 1931- 53-56
Klinck, Carl Frederick 1908- 17-20R
Klinck, George Alfred 1903-1973 ....9-12R
Obituary 103
Klindt-Jensen, Ole 1918-1980 ....CANR-10
Obituary 101
Earlier sketch in CA 21-24R
Kline, George L(ouis) 1921- CANR-9
Earlier sketch in CA 17-20R
Kline, Linda 1940- 126
Kline, Lloyd W. 1931- 33-36R
Kline, Morris 1908- CANR-2
Earlier sketch in CA 5-8R
Kline, Nancy Meadors 1946- 57-60
Kline, Nathan S(chellenberg)
1916-1983 ....CANR-36
Obituary 109
Earlier sketch in CA 81-84
Kline, Peter 1936- 25-28R
Kline, Stephen Edward 1945- 132
Kline, Steve
See Kline, Stephen Edward
Kline, Suzy 1943- 120
See also SATA 48, 67
Kline, Thomas J(efferson) 1942- 85-88
Klineberg, Stephen L(ouis) 1940- 77-80
Klinefelter, Walter 1899- CANR-3
Earlier sketch in CA 9-12R
Klineman, George A(lfred) 1947- 107
Kling, Robert E(dward) Jr. 1920- 29-32R
Kling, Simcha 1922- 13-16R
Kling, Woody 1926(?)-1988 Obituary 125
Klingelhofer, E(dwin) L(ewis) 1920- 124
Klinger, Eric 1933- CANR-29
Earlier sketches in CA 33-36R, CANR-13
Klinger, Friedrich Maximilian von
1752-1831 .... DLB 94
Klinger, Kurt 1914- 17-20R
Klinghoffer, Arthur Jay 1941- 65-68
Klingman, Lawrence (Lewis)
1918-1986 Obituary 120
Klingstedt, Joe Lars 1938- 53-56
Klink, Johanna L. 1918- CANR-8
Earlier sketch in CA 61-64
Klinkowitz, Jerome 1943- CANR-1
Earlier sketch in CA 45-48
See also CAAS 9
Klipper, Miriam Z(eldner) 108
Klise, Eugene Storm 1908- 5-8R
Klise, Thomas S. 1928-1978 57-60
Obituary 134
Klitzman, Robert (L.) 1958- 135
Klobuchar, James John 1928- 73-76
Klobuchar, Jim
See Klobuchar, James John
Kloepfer, Marguerite (Fonnesbeck)
1916- 97-100
Kloesel, Christian Johannes Wilhelm 1942- 113
Kloetzli, Walter (Jr.) 1921- 1-4R
Klonglan, Gerald E(dward) 1936- 41-44R
Klonis, N. I.
See Clones, N(icholas) J.
Klonsky, Milton 1921(?)-1981 Obituary 105
Kloos, Peter 1936- 93-96
Klooster, Fred H. 1922- 1-4R
Klopf, Donald W(illiam) 1923- CANR-34
Earlier sketches in CA 89-92, CANR-15
Klopfer, Donald S(imon)
1902-1986 Obituary 119
Klopfer, Peter H(ubert) 1930- 85-88
Klopfer, Walter G(eorge) 1923- 89-92
Kloppenburg, Boaventura 1919- CANR-15
Earlier sketch in CA 65-68
Klopstock, Friedrich Gottlieb
1724-1803 .... DLB 97
Klopstock, Meta 1728-1758 .... DLB 97
Klos, Frank W(illiam) Jr. 1924- 13-16R
Klose, Kevin 1940- 53-56
Klose, Norma Cline 1936- 17-20R
Klosinski, Emil 1922- 65-68
Kloss, Phillips 1902- CAP-1
Earlier sketch in CA 13-16
Kloss, Robert J(ames) 1935- 45-48
Kloss, Robert Marsh 1938- 65-68
Klosty, James (Michael) 1943- Brief entry 112
Klotman, Phyllis Rauch 93-96
Klotman, Robert Howard 1918- 53-56
Klots, Alexander Barrett 1903-1989 107
Obituary 128
See also SATA 62
Klotter, James C(hristopher) 1947- 77-80
Klotter, John C(harles) 1918- 93-96
Klotz, Lynn C(harles) 1940- 116
Klubertanz, George Peter 1912- 5-8R
Kluckhohn, Frank L. 1907-1970 ....5-8R
Obituary 29-32R
Klueger, Ruth
See Kluger, Ruth
Klug, Eugene F(rederick Adolf) 1917- CANR-1
Earlier sketch in CA 45-48
Klug, Ron(ald) 1939- CANR-24
Earlier sketch in CA 107
See also SATA 31
Kluge, Alexander 1932- 81-84
See also DLB 75
Kluge, Eike-Henner W. 1942- 61-64
Kluge, P(aul) F(rederick) 1942- CANR-37
Earlier sketches in CA 73-76, CANR-16
Kluger, James R. 1939- 29-32R
Kluger, Richard 1934- CANR-28
Earlier sketches in CA 9-12R, CANR-6
Kluger, Ruth 1914-1980 116
Obituary 108
Kluger, Steve 1952- 138
Klugh, Henry E(licker III) 1927- 53-56
Klugman, Edgar 1925- 132
Kluver, Billy
See Kluver, J. Wilhelm
Kluver, J. Wilhelm 1927- 133
Kluwe, Mary Jean 1905-1975 .... CAP-2
Earlier sketch in CA 23-24
Kmoch, Hans 1897(?)-1973 Obituary 41-44R
Knaack, Twila 1944- 119
Knaak, Richard A. 1961- 128
Knachel, Philip A(therton) 1926- 21-24R
Knack, Martha C(arol) 1948- 118
Knaplund, Paul (Alexander) 1885-1964 .... CAP-1
Earlier sketch in CA 11-12
Knapp, Bettina (Liebowitz) CANR-21
Earlier sketches in CA 13-16R, CANR-6
Knapp, David A(llan) 1938- 41-44R
Knapp, Edward
See Kunhardt, Edith
Knapp, Herbert W. 1931- 105
Knapp, J(ohn) Merrill 1914- 53-56
Knapp, James F(ranklin) 1940- 107
Knapp, John (Allen) II 1940- 116
Knapp, Joseph G(eorge) 1924- 41-44R
Knapp, Joseph G(rant) 1900-1983 ....37-40R
Obituary 110
Knapp, Joseph Palmer 1864-1951 .... DLB 91
Knapp, Lewis M(ansfield) 1894- 21-24R
Knapp, Mark L(ane) 1938- 81-84
Knapp, Mary L. 1931- 105
Knapp, Peggy A(nn) 1937- 119
Knapp, Robert Hampden 1915-1974 .... CAP-2
Obituary 53-56
Earlier sketch in CA 13-16
Knapp, Ron 1952- 103
See also SATA 34
Knapp, Ronald Gary 1940- CANR-30
Earlier sketch in CA 112
Knapp, Ronald J(ames) 1935- 119
Knapp, Samuel Lorenzo 1783-1838 .... DLB 59
Knapp, William R. 1920(?)-1990 Obituary 132
Knapper, Christopher (Kay) 1940- CANR-12
Earlier sketch in CA 29-32R
Knapton, Ernest John 1902- CANR-1
Earlier sketch in CA 1-4R
Knaub, Richard K. 1928- 41-44R
Knaus, William A. 1946- 105
Knauss, Peter R(ichard)
1937-1990 Obituary 131
Knauth, Percy 1914- 57-60
Knauth, Victor W. 1895(?)-1977 Obituary 73-76
Kneale, Matthew (Nicholas Kerr) 1960- 125
Kneale, (Thomas) Nigel 1922- 132
Knebel, Fletcher 1911- CANR-36
Earlier sketches in CA 1-4R, CANR-1
See also CAAS 3
See also AITN 1
See also CLC 14
See also SATA 36
Knecht, R(obert) J(ean) 1926- CANR-13
Earlier sketch in CA 33-36R
Knechtges, David R(ichard) 1942- 65-68
Kneebone, Geoffrey Thomas 1918- 5-8R
Kneese, Allen V(ictor) 1930- CANR-8
Earlier sketch in CA 13-16R
Knef, Hildegard 1925- CANR-4
Earlier sketch in CA 45-48
Kneller, John W(illiam) 1916- 17-20R
Knelman, Fred H. 1919- 102
Knelman, Martin 1943- 73-76
Knepler, Henry (William) 1922- 21-24R
Knevitt, Charles (Philip Paul) 1952- 132
Knezevich, Stephen J(oseph) 1920- CANR-10
Earlier sketch in CA 5-8R
Knickerbocker, Charles H(errick) 1922- 13-16R
Knickerbocker, Cholly
See Cassini, Igor (Loiewski)
Knickerbocker, Diedrich
See Irving, Washington
Knickerbocker, Kenneth L(eslie) 1905- 5-8R
Knickmeyer, Steve 1944- 85-88
Knies, Elizabeth 1941- 109
Knifesmith
See Cutler, Ivor
Kniffen, Fred B(owerman) 1900- 1-4R
Knigge, Adolph Franz Friedrich Ludwig Freiherr von
1752-1796 .... DLB 94
Knigge, Robert (R.) 1921(?)-1987 Obituary 121
See also SATA 50
Knight, Adam
See Lariar, Lawrence
Knight, Alan 1946- 125
Knight, Alanna CANR-33
Earlier sketches in CA 81-84, CANR-15
Knight, Alice Valle 1922- 81-84
Knight, Amy 1946- 128
Knight, Anne (Katherine) 1946- .... SATA 34
Knight, Arthur Winfield 1937- CANR-19
Earlier sketches in CA 53-56, CANR-4
Knight, Arthur 1916-1991 ....41-44R
Obituary 135
Knight, B(etty) Carolyn 1944- 118
Knight, Bernard 1931- CANR-2
Earlier sketch in CA 49-52
Knight, Bertram 1904- 103
Knight, Charles Landon .... AITN 2
Knight, Charles W. 1891- CAP-1
Earlier sketch in CA 9-10
Knight, Charles 1910- 109
Knight, Clayton 1891-1969 .... CAP-1
Earlier sketch in CA 9-10
Knight, Damon (Francis) 1922- CANR-36
Earlier sketches in CA 49-52, CANR-3, 17
See also CAAS 10
See also DLB 8
See also SATA 9
Knight, David
See Prather, Richard S(cott)
Knight, David C(arpenter) 1925- 73-76
See also SATA 14
Knight, David Marcus 1936- CANR-7
Earlier sketch in CA 57-60
Knight, Denis 1921- 137
Knight, Doug(las E.) 1925- 85-88
Knight, Douglas M(aitland) 1921- CANR-2
Earlier sketch in CA 49-52
Knight, Eric (Mowbray) 1897-1943 137
See also MAICYA
See also SATA 18
Knight, Etheridge 1931-1991 ....CANR-23
Obituary 133
Earlier sketch in CA 21-24R
See also BLC 2
See also BW
See also CLC 40
See also DLB 41
Knight, Everett 1919- 33-36R
Knight, Francis Edgar 1905- 73-76
See also SATA 14
Knight, Frank
See Knight, Francis Edgar
Knight, Frank H(yneman)
1885-1972 Obituary 33-36R
Knight, Franklin Willis 1942- 101
Knight, Frida 1910- CANR-2
Earlier sketch in CA 49-52
Knight, G(ilfred) Norman 1891-1978 ......CANR-17
Earlier sketch in CA 25-28R
Knight, G(eorge) Wilson 1897-1985 ......CANR-10
Obituary 115
Earlier sketch in CA 13-16R
Knight, Gareth
See Wilby, Basil Leslie
Knight, Geoffrey Egerton 1921- 122
Knight, George Angus Fulton 1909- 1-4R
Knight, Glee 1947-1975 57-60
Obituary 120
Knight, H(erbert) Ralph 1895- CAP-2
Earlier sketch in CA 25-28
Knight, Harold V(incent) 1907- 21-24R
Knight, Hattie M. 1908-1976 .... CAP-2
Earlier sketch in CA 29-32
Knight, Hilary 1926- 73-76
See also MAICYA
See also SATA 15, 69
Knight, Hugh McCown 1905- 5-8R
Knight, Ione Kemp 1922- 37-40R
Knight, Isabel F(rances) 1930- 25-28R
Knight, James
See Schneck, Stephen
Knight, James A(llen) 1918- CANR-6
Earlier sketch in CA 13-16R
Knight, Janet M(argaret) 1940- 93-96
Knight, Jesse F. 1946- 129
Knight, John S. III .... AITN 2
Knight, John Shively 1894-1981 93-96
Obituary 103
See also AITN 2
See also DLB 29
Knight, K(enneth) G(raham) 1921- 25-28R
Knight, Karl F. 1930- 17-20R
Knight, Kathryn Lasky
See Lasky, Kathryn
Knight, Mallory T.
See Hurwood, Bernhardt J.
Knight, Margaret K(ennedy) Horsey
1903- CAP-1
Earlier sketch in CA 9-10
Knight, Max 1909- 93-96
Knight, Maxwell 1900- CAP-1
Earlier sketch in CA 13-14
Knight, Michael E(mery) 1935- 105
Knight, Norman L(ouis) 1895- CAP-2
Earlier sketch in CA 23-24
Knight, Oliver (Holmes) 1919- 21-24R
Knight, Paul Emerson 1925- 13-16R
Knight, R(oy) C(lement) 1907- 13-16R
Knight, Richard S. 1936- 115
Knight, Robin 1943- 73-76
Knight, Roderic C(opley) 1942- 61-64
Knight, Ruth Adams 1898-1974 ....5-8R
Obituary 49-52
See also SATA 20
Knight, Sarah Kemble 1666-1727 .... DLB 24
Knight, Stephen 1951-1985 ....CANR-34
Obituary 117
Earlier sketch in CA 69-72
Knight, Thomas J(oseph) 1937- 102
Knight, Thomas S(tanley Jr.) 1921- 17-20R
Knight, Vick R(alph) Jr. 1928- CANR-37
Earlier sketches in CA 45-48, CANR-1, 16
Knight, Vick (Ralph) Sr.
1908-1984 Obituary 112
Knight, W(illiam) Nicholas 1939- 37-40R
Knight, Walker L(eigh) 1924- CANR-13
Earlier sketch in CA 37-40R
Knight, Wallace E(dward) 1926- CANR-11
Earlier sketch in CA 65-68
Knight, William E. 1922- 128
Knightley, Phillip 1929- 25-28R
Knight-Patterson, W. M.
See Kulski, Wladyslaw W(szebor)
Knights, John Keell 1930(?)-1981 Obituary 102
Knights, L(ionel) C(harles) 1906- CANR-3
Earlier sketch in CA 5-8R
Knights, Peter R(oger) 1938- 37-40R
Knights, Ward A(rthur) Jr. 1927- 97-100
Knigin, Michael Jay 1942- 85-88
Kniker, Charles Robert 1936- 77-80
Knipe, Humphry 1941- 37-40R
Knipe, Wayne Bishop III 1946- 53-56
Knipschield, Don(ald Harold) 1940- 5-8R
Kniskern, David Paul 1948- 112
Knist, F(rances) Emma 1948- CANR-5
Earlier sketch in CA 53-56
Knister, Raymond 1899-1932 .... DLB 68
Knittel, John (Herman Emanuel)
1891-1970 Obituary 104
Knitter, Paul F(rancis) 1939- 129
Knobel, Lance 1956- 121
Knoblauch, C(yril) H. 1945- 124
Knobler, Nathan 1926- 33-36R
Knobler, Peter (Stephen) 1946- 97-100
Knoblock, Edward 1874-1945 Brief entry 108
See also DLB 10
Knock, Warren 1932- 65-68
Knoebl, Kuno 1936- 25-28R
Knoepfle, John 1923- CANR-29
Earlier sketches in CA 13-16R, CANR-12
See also SATA 66
Knoepflmacher, U(lrich) C(amillus)
1931- CANR-10
Earlier sketch in CA 13-16R
Knoerle, Jeanne 1928- 45-48
Knoke, David (Harmon) 1947- CANR-26
Earlier sketches in CA 65-68, CANR-10
Knoles, (Michael Clive) David 1896- 5-8R
Knoles, George Harmon 1907- 5-8R
Knoll, Erwin 1931- 89-92
Knoll, Gerald M. 1942- 29-32R
Knoll, Paul W(endell) 1937- 107
Knoll, Robert Edwin 1922- CANR-5
Earlier sketch in CA 1-4R
Knollenberg, Bernhard 1892-1973 .... CAP-2
Obituary 41-44R
Earlier sketch in CA 21-22
Knoop, Faith Yingling 1896- 97-100
Knop, Werner 1912(?)-1970 Obituary 29-32R

Knopf, Alfred A. 1892-1984 106
Obituary 113
See also DLBY 84
Knopf, Edwin H. 1899-1982(?) Obituary 105
Knopf, Irwin J(ay) 1924- 119
Knopf, Kenyon A(lfred) 1921- 77-80
Knopf, Terry Ann 1940- CANR-17
Earlier sketch in CA 25-28R
Knopp, Josephine Zadovsky 1941- 103
Knorr, Albert Scofield 1929- 25-28R
Knorr, Dandi 1949- 112
Knorr, K. E.
See Knorr, Klaus E(ugene)
Knorr, Klaus
See Knorr, Klaus E(ugene)
Knorr, Klaus E(ugene) 1911-1990 134
Obituary 131
Brief entry 113
Knorr, Marian L(ockwood) 1910- 102
Knott, Bill
See Knott, William C(ecil Jr.)
Knott, John R(ay) Jr. 1937- 57-60
Knott, Kim 1955- 124
Knott, Leonard L(ewis) 1905- 107
Knott, Will C.
See Knott, William C(ecil Jr.)
Knott, William C(ecil Jr.) 1927- CANR-22
Earlier sketches in CA 5-8R, CANR-7
See also SATA 3
Knotts, Howard (Clayton Jr.) 1922- CANR-11
Earlier sketch in CA 69-72
See also SATA 25
Knowland, A(nthony) S(tephen) 1919- 116
Knowland, William Fife
1908-1974 Obituary 89-92
Knowler, John 1933(?)-1979 Obituary 85-88
Knowles, A(lbert) Sidney Jr. 1926- 101
Knowles, Alison 1933- CANR-29
Earlier sketches in CA 17-20R, CANR-8
Knowles, Anne 1933- 102
See also SATA 37
Knowles, Asa S(mallidge) 1909-1990 ....29-32R
Obituary 132
Knowles, Clayton 1908-1978 81-84
Obituary 73-76
Knowles, (Michael Clive) David
1896-1974 ....CANR-4
Obituary 53-56
Earlier sketch in CA 5-8R
Knowles, Dorothy 1906- 25-28R
Knowles, Henry P(aine) 1912- 61-64
Knowles, John H(ilton) 1926-1979 101
Obituary 85-88
Knowles, John 1926- 17-20R
See also CDALB 1968-1988
See also CLC 1, 4, 10, 26
See also DLB 6
See also MTCW
See also SATA 8
Knowles, Joseph W(illiam) 1922- 21-24R
Knowles, Louis L(eonard) 1947- 29-32R
Knowles, Mabel Winifred
1875-1949 Brief entry 122
Knowles, Malcolm Shepherd 1913- CANR-5
Earlier sketch in CA 5-8R
Knowles, Valerie (J.) 1934- 128
Knowles, Yereth K(ahn) 1920- 93-96
Knowlton, Derrick 1921- CANR-6
Earlier sketch in CA 57-60
Knowlton, Edgar C(olby) Jr. 1921- 41-44R
Knowlton, James 1943- 120
Knowlton, Robert A(lmy) 1914-1968 ....1-4R
Obituary 103
Knowlton, William H. 1927- 17-20R
Knox, Alexander 1907- 81-84
Knox, Bernard M(acGregor) W(alker) 1914- 128
Brief entry 117
Knox, Bill
See Knox, William
Knox, Calvin M.
See Silverberg, Robert
Knox, Caroline 1938- 120
Knox, Cleone
See King-Hall, Magdalen
Knox, Collie T. 1897-1977 77-80
Obituary 73-76
Knox, David H. Jr. 1943- 41-44R
Knox, Donald E(dward) 1936-1986 ....CANR-39
Obituary 119
Earlier sketch in CA 45-48
Knox, Edmund George Valpy 1881-1971 112
Obituary 29-32R
Knox, (Mary) Eleanor Jessie 1909- .... MAICYA
See also SATA 30, 59
Knox, Frank 1874-1944 .... DLB 29
Knox, George A(lbert) 1918- 121
Knox, George 1922- 138
Knox, Henry M(acdonald) 1916- 13-16R
Knox, Hugh (Randolph) 1942- 103
Knox, Israel 1906-1986 Obituary 119
Knox, James
See Brittain, William (E.)
Knox, John Armory 1850-1906 .... DLB 23
Knox, John Ballenger 1909- CAP-1
Earlier sketch in CA 9-10
Knox, John 1900-1990 ....13-16R
Obituary 132
Knox, Katharine McCook
1890(?)-1983 Obituary 110
Knox, (Thomas) Malcolm 1900-1980 103
Obituary 97-100
Knox, Robert Buick 1918- 25-28R
Knox, Ronald A(rbuthnott)
1888-1957 Brief entry 111
See also DLB 77
Knox, Sanka (Lutins) 1906-1984 Obituary 112
Knox, Vera Huntingdon 9-12R
Knox, Warren Barr 1925- 49-52
Knox, William 1928- CANR-1
Earlier sketch in CA 1-4R
Knox-Johnston, Robin 1939- CANR-15
Earlier sketch in CA 29-32R
Knox-Mawer, Ronald 1925- 123
Knox-Mawer, Ronnie
See Knox-Mawer, Ronald
Knudsen, Hans August Heinrich
1886-1971 Obituary 29-32R
Knudsen, James 1950- 111
See also SATA 42
Knudson, Danny (Alan) 1940- CANR-11
Earlier sketch in CA 61-64
Knudson, R. R.
See Knudson, Rozanne
Knudson, Richard L(ewis) 1930- CANR-20
Earlier sketch in CA 104
See also SATA 34
Knudson, Rozanne 1932- CANR-35
Earlier sketches in CA 33-36R, CANR-15
See also SATA 7
Knudtson, Peter M(ichael) 1947- 129
Knuemann, Carl H(einz) 1922- 77-80
Knusel, Jack L(eonard) 1923- 25-28R
Knuth, Helen 1912- 53-56
Knutson, Donald C. 1931(?)-1990 Obituary 131
Knutson, Harold Christian 1928- 112
Knutson, Jeanne N(ickell) 1934- 41-44R
Knutson, Kent S(iguart) 1924-1973 .... CAP-2
Obituary 41-44R
Earlier sketch in CA 33-36
Knutson, Roger M. 1933- 126
Knye, Cassandra
See Disch, Thomas M(ichael)
Ko, Kanzein
See Isogai, Hiroshi
Ko, Won 1925- 61-64
Kobal, John 1943(?)-1991 ....CANR-11
Obituary 135
Earlier sketch in CA 61-64
Kobayashi, Koji 1907- 133
Kobayashi, Masako Matsuno 1935- CANR-31
Earlier sketches in CA 5-8R, CANR-13
See also Matsuno, Masako
Kobayashi, Noritake 1932- 53-56
Kobayashi, Tetsuya 1926- 69-72
Kober, Arthur 1900-1975 .... CAP-1
Obituary 57-60
Earlier sketch in CA 13-14
See also DLB 11
Kobler, Arthur L(eon) 1920- 13-16R
Kobler, (Albert) John (Jr.) 1910- 65-68
Kobler, (Mary) Turner S. 1930- 37-40R
Kobrak, Peter 1936- 104
Kobre, Sidney 1907- 65-68
Kobrin, David 1941- 41-44R
Kobrin, Janet 1942- 57-60
Kobryn, A(llen) P(aul) 1949- 93-96
Koch, C(hristopher) J(ohn) 1932- 127
See also CLC 42
Koch, Charlotte 85-88
Koch, Christopher
See Koch, C(hristopher) J(ohn)
Koch, Claude (F.) 1918- 9-12R
Koch, Dorothy Clarke 1924- 5-8R
See also SATA 6
Koch, Edward I(rving) 1924- 113
Koch, Eric 1919- 69-72
Koch, H(annsjoachim) W(olfgang)
1933- CANR-15
Earlier sketch in CA 93-96
Koch, Hans-Gerhard 1913- 17-20R
Koch, Helen L(ois) 1895- CAP-2
Earlier sketch in CA 21-22
Koch, Howard 1902- 73-76
See also DLB 26
Koch, James Harold 1926- 106
Koch, Joanne 1940- CANR-32
Earlier sketches in CA 69-72, CANR-15
Koch, Kenneth 1925- CANR-36
Earlier sketches in CA 1-4R, CANR-6
See also CLC 5, 8, 44
See also DLB 5
See also SATA 65
Koch, Kurt E(mil) 1913-1987 107
Obituary 122
Koch, Lew(is) Z. 1935- 69-72
Koch, Michael 1916(?)-1981 Obituary 103
Koch, Raymond 85-88
Koch, Richard 1921- 29-32R
Koch, Robert 1918- 9-12R
Koch, Stephen 1941- 77-80
Koch, Thilo 1920- CANR-11
Earlier sketch in CA 25-28R
Koch, Thomas J(ohn) 1947- 61-64
Koch, Thomas Walter 1933- 17-20R
Koch, William H. Jr. 1923- 17-20R
Kochan, Lionel 1922- 105
Kochan, Miriam (Louise) 1929- 103
Kochan, Paul C(ranston) 1906- 45-48
Kochan, Thomas A(nton) 1947- 123
Kochanek, Stanley A(nthony) 1934- CANR-38
Earlier sketch in CA 116
Kochen, Manfred 1928- 21-24R
Kochenburger, Ralph J. 1919- 53-56
Kocher, Eric 1912- 57-60
Kocher, Paul H(arold) 1907- 65-68
Kochetov, Vsevolod A(nisimovich)
1912-1973 Obituary 45-48
Kochiss, John (Matthew) 1926- 97-100
Kochka, Mary Murray
1894(?)-1984 Obituary 112
Kochman, Thomas 1936- 37-40R
Kock, Winston E(dward) 1909-1982 110
Kocka, Juergen 1941- 133
Kocka, Jurgen
See Kocka, Juergen
Kockelmans, Joseph J(ohn) 1923- 117
Brief entry 113
Kocsis, J. C.
See Paul, James
Kocsis, Robert
See Kossez, Robes
Koda-Callan, Elizabeth 1944- 136
See also SATA 67
Kodaly, Zoltan 1882-1967 Obituary 112
Kodama, Sanehide 1932- 120
Kodanda Rao, Pandurangi 1889- 13-16R
Koda Rohan
See Koda Shigeyuki
Koda Shigeyuki 1867-1947 Brief entry 121
See also Rohan, Koda
Kodera, Takashi James 1945- 111
Koehler, Alan (Robert) 1928- 13-16R
Koehler, Frank
See Paine, Lauran (Bosworth)
Koehler, G(eorge) Stanley 1915- 37-40R
Koehler, George E. 1930- 25-28R
Koehler, Ludmila 1917- 53-56
Koehler, Lyle P(eter) 1944- 109
Koehler, Margaret (Hudson) CANR-30
Earlier sketch in CA 85-88
Koehler, Nikki 1951- 25-28R
Koehler, Phoebe 1955- 132
Koehler, W(illiam) R. 1914- 9-12R
Koehler, Wolfgang 1887-1967 Obituary 111
Koehn, Ilse
See Van Zwienen, Ilse Charlotte Koehn
Koehn, Lala
See Koehn-Heine, Lala
Koehn-Heine, Lala 1936- 112
Koelb, Clayton T. 1942- 132
Koelsch, William Alvin 1933- 104
Koen, Ross Y. 1918- 1-4R
Koenig, Allen Edward 1939- 21-24R
Koenig, C(lyde) Eldo 1919- 21-24R
Koenig, Duane (Walter) 1918- 37-40R
Koenig, Franz 1905- 101
Koenig, Fritz H(ans) 1940- 53-56
Koenig, John (Thomas) 1938- 102
Koenig, Laird CANR-32
Earlier sketch in CA 29-32R
Koenig, Linda Lee 1948- 113
Koenig, Louis William 1916- 1-4R
Koenig, Rene 1906- CANR-15
Earlier sketch in CA 81-84
Koenig, Samuel 1899-1972 .... CAP-2
Obituary 37-40R
Earlier sketch in CA 17-18
Koenig, Walter 1936- 104
Koenigsberg, Moses 1879-1945 .... DLB 25
Koenigsberger, H(elmut) G(eorg) 1918- 33-36R
Koenigswald, (Gustav Heinrich) Ralph von
See von Koenigswald, (Gustav Heinrich) Ralph
Koenker, Diane 1947- 112
Koenker, Ernest Benjamin
1920- Brief entry 106
Koenner, Alfred 1921- CANR-18
Earlier sketch in CA 101
Koepf, Michael 1940- 81-84
Koepke, Paul 1918- 114
Koepke, Wulf 1928- CANR-39
Earlier sketches in CA 93-96, CANR-16
Koeppel, Gary 1938- 49-52
Koeppen, Wolfgang 1906- .... DLB 69
Koering, Ursula 1921-1976 .... SATA 64
Koerner, James D. 1923- 9-12R
Koerner, Stephan 1913- 1-4R
Koerner, Theodor 1791-1813 .... DLB 90
Koerner, W(illiam) H(enry) D(avid)
1878-1938 .... SATA 21
Koerte, Mary Norbert 1934- 103
Koertge, Noretta 1935- CANR-22
Earlier sketch in CA 106
Koertge, Ronald 1940- CANR-25
Earlier sketches in CA 65-68, CANR-9
See also DLB 105
See also SATA 53
Koestenbaum, Peter 1928- CANR-13
Earlier sketch in CA 29-32R
Koestenbaum, Phyllis 1930- CANR-25
Earlier sketch in CA 107
Koestenbaum, Wayne 1958- 134
Koester, Helmut 1926- 110
Koestler, Arthur 1905-1983 ....CANR-33
Obituary 109
Earlier sketches in CA 1-4R, CANR-1
See also CDBLB 1945-1960
See also CLC 1, 3, 6, 8, 15, 33
See also DLBY 83
See also MTCW
Koestler, Cynthia 1928(?)-1983 Obituary 114
Koethe, John (Louis) 1945- 49-52
Kofalk, Harriet 1937- CANR-30
Earlier sketch in CA 112
Koff, Richard Myram 1926- CANR-15
Earlier sketch in CA 89-92
See also SATA 62
Kofoed, Jack
See Kofoed, John C.
Kofoed, John C. 1894-1979 ....5-8R
Obituary 93-96
Kofsky, Frank (Joseph) 1935- 57-60
Kogan, Bernard Robert 1920- 9-12R
Kogan, Deborah
See Kogan Ray, Deborah
See also SATA 50
Kogan, Herman 1914-1989 ....CANR-20
Obituary 128
Earlier sketches in CA 9-12R, CANR-5
Kogan, Judith 1956- 126
Kogan, Leonard S(aul)
1919-1976 Obituary 65-68
Kogan, Maurice 1930- 107
Kogan, Norman 1919- 1-4R
Kogan Ray, Deborah 1940- CANR-22
Earlier sketches in CA 57-60, CANR-7
See also Kogan, Deborah
and Ray, Deborah
Kogawa, Joy Nozomi 1935- CANR-19
Earlier sketch in CA 101
Koger, Lisa (Jan) 1953- 133
Kogiku, K(iichiro) C(hris) 1927- 33-36R
Koginos, Manny T. 1933- 21-24R
Kogos, Frederick 1907-1974 .... CAP-2
Obituary 53-56
Earlier sketch in CA 29-32
Koh, Byung Chul 1936- 17-20R
Koh, Sung Jae 1917- 17-20R
Kohak, Erazim V. 1933- CANR-31
Earlier sketches in CA 37-40R, CANR-14
Kohake, Rosanne 1951- 114
Kohan, Rhea 89-92
Kohanski, Alexander S(iskind) 1902-1987 108
Obituary 123
Kohavi, Y.
See Stern, Jay B(enjamin)
Kohen-Raz, Reuven 1921- 37-40R
Kohfeldt, Mary Lou 1939- 119
Kohl, Benjamin G. 1938- 126
Kohl, Herbert 1937- CANR-14
Earlier sketch in CA 65-68
See also SATA 47
Kohl, Irene C(aistor) 1927- 119
Kohl, James (Virgil) 1942- 57-60
Kohl, Marvin 1932- 85-88
Kohlberg, Lawrence 1927-1987 125
Obituary 122
Kohlenberg, Robert J(oseph) 1937- 111
Kohler, Foy D(avid) 1908-1990 ....29-32R
Obituary 133
Kohler, Heinz 1934- 21-24R
Kohler, Julilly H(ouse) 1908-1976 77-80
Obituary 69-72
See also SATA 20
Kohler, Mary Conway 1903-1986 135
Obituary 119
Kohler, Saul 1928- 69-72
Kohler, Sheila (May) 1941- 137
Kohler, Sister Mary Hortense 1892- 5-8R
Kohler, Wolfgang
See Koehler, Wolfgang
Kohlmeier, Louis M(artin) Jr. 1926- 49-52
Kohls, R. L.
See Kohls, Richard L(ouis)
Kohls, Richard L(ouis) 1921- 126
Brief entry 106
Kohlstedt, Sally Gregory 1943- 69-72
Kohmescher, Matthew Franklin 1921- 113
Kohn, Alexander 1919- 123
Kohn, Alfie 1957- 122
Kohn, Bernice
See Hunt, Bernice (Kohn)
See also SATA 4
Kohn, Clyde Frederick 1911-1989 Obituary 130
Brief entry 109
Kohn, Eugene 1887-1977 Obituary 69-72
Kohn, George C(hilds) 1940- CANR-19
Earlier sketch in CA 103
Kohn, Hans 1891-1971 ....CANR-4
Obituary 29-32R
Earlier sketch in CA 1-4R
Kohn, Howard 1947- 124
Kohn, Jacob 1881-1968 ....5-8R
Obituary 103
Kohn, John S. (Van E.)
1906-1976 Obituary 104
Kohn, Marek (Czeslaw Patrick) 1958- 128
Kohn, Melvin L(ester) 1928- 41-44R
Kohn, Richard H(enry) 1940- CANR-37
Earlier sketch in CA 115
Kohn, Walter S(amuel) G(erst) 1923- 107
Kohner, Frederick 1905-1986 ....CANR-1
Obituary 119
Earlier sketch in CA 1-4R
See also SATA 10, 48
Kohout, Pavel 1928- CANR-3
Earlier sketch in CA 45-48
See also CLC 13
Kohr, Louise Hannah 1903- 41-44R
Kohs, Samuel C(almin)
1890-1984 Obituary 111
Koht, Halvdan 1873-1965 85-88
Kohut, Heinz 1913-1981 ....CANR-1
Obituary 105
Earlier sketch in CA 45-48
Kohut, Les
See Kohut, Nester C(larence)
Kohut, Nester C(larence) 1925- 45-48
Koidahl, Ilona 1924- 97-100
Koide, Tan 1938-1986 132
See also SATA 50
Koi Hai
See Palmer, (Nathaniel) Humphrey
Koilpillai, (Jesudas) Charles 41-44R
Koilpillai, Das
See Koilpillai, (Jesudas) Charles
Koinange, Mbiyu (Peter)
1907-1981 Obituary 108
Koiner, Richard B. 1929- 17-20R
Koizumi, Yakumo
See Hearn, (Patricio) Lafcadio (Tessima Carlos)
Kojecky, Roger 1943- 85-88
Kojima, Naomi 1950- 109
Kojima, Takashi 1902- CAP-1
Earlier sketch in CA 9-10
Kojima Shozo 1928- 69-72

Kokoschka, Oskar 1886-1980 109
Obituary 93-96
Kokyshev, Lazor 1933(?)-1975 Obituary..........104
Kolaja, Jiri Thomas 1919- 9-12R
Kolakowski, Leszek 1927- 49-52
Kolars, Frank 1899-1973......................5-8R
Obituary 37-40R
Kolasky, John 1915- 25-28R
Kolatch, Alfred Jacob 1916- 107
Kolatch, Jonathan 1943- 41-44R
Kolb, Annette 1870-1967 .... DLB 66
Kolb, Carolyn 1942- 89-92
Kolb, David A(llen) 1939- CANR-15
Earlier sketch in CA 65-68
Kolb, Erwin J(ohn) 1924- 37-40R
Kolb, Gwin Jackson 1919- 1-4R
Kolb, Harold H(utchinson) Jr. 1933- CANR-12
Earlier sketch in CA 29-32R
Kolb, (Gwin) Jack (II) 1946- 125
Kolb, John F. 1916(?)-1974 Obituary 53-56
Kolb, Ken(neth) 1926- 21-24R
Kolb, Lawrence 1911-1972 Obituary 37-40R
Kolb, Philip 1907- CANR-4
Earlier sketch in CA 53-56
Kolba, St. Tamara 97-100
See also SATA 22
Kolbas, Grace Holden 1914- 93-96
Kolbe, Henry E(ugene) 1907- 5-8R
Kolbenheyer, Erwin Guido 1878-1962 ..... DLB 66
Kolbenschlag, Madonna (Claire)
1935- Brief entry 115
Kolbrek, Loyal 1914- 29-32R
Kolchin, Peter 1943- 41-44R
Kolde, Endel Jakob 1917- CANR-1
Earlier sketch in CA 45-48
Kolenda, Konstantin 1923- 13-16R
Kolers, Paul A. 1926- 97-100
Kolesar, Paul 1927- 105
Kolesnik, Walter B(ernard) 1923- CANR-2
Earlier sketch in CA 5-8R
Kolevzon, Edward R.
1913(?)-1976 Obituary 69-72
Kolin, Philip C(harles) 1945- 119
Kolins, William 1926(?)-1973 Obituary 104
Kolinski, Charles J(ames) 1916- 17-20R
Kolinsky, Martin 1936- CANR-8
Earlier sketch in CA 61-64
Koljevic, Svetozar 1930- CANR-7
Earlier sketch in CA 17-20R
Kolker, Robert Phillip 1940- 112
Kolko, Gabriel 1932- CANR-4
Earlier sketch in CA 5-8R
Kolko, Joyce 1933- 130
Kolkowicz, Roman 1929- Brief entry 116
Kollat, David T(ruman) 1938- 41-44R
Kollek, Teddy
See Kollek, Theodore
Kollek, Theodore 1911- CAP-2
Earlier sketch in CA 29-32
Koller, Ann Marie 128
Koller, Charles W. 1896(?)-1983 61-64
Obituary 109
Koller, James 1936- CANR-39
Earlier sketches in CA 49-52, CANR-2, 18
See also CAAS 5
Koller, John M. 1938- 33-36R
Koller, Larry
See Koller, Lawrence Robert
Koller, Lawrence Robert 1912-1967 ....CANR-6
Earlier sketch in CA 1-4R
Koller, Marvin Robert 1919- 13-16R
Kolleritsch, Alfred 1931- .... DLB 85
Kollmar, Dick
See Kollmar, Richard Tompkins
Kollmar, Richard Tompkins
1910-1971 Obituary 89-92
Kollock, Will(iam Raymond) 1940- 33-36R
Kollontai, Alexandra (Mikhailovna)
1872-1952 Brief entry 112
Kollstedt, Paula Lubke 1946- 113
Kolmar, Gertrud 1894-1943 .... TCLC 40
Kolmerten, Carol A. 1946- 135
Kolmogorov, Andrei Nikolayevich
1903-1987 Obituary 123
Kolnai, Aurel (Thomas) 1900-1973 103
Kolodin, Irving 1908-1988 93-96
Obituary 125
Kolodny, Annette 1941- CANR-8
Earlier sketch in CA 61-64
See also DLB 67
Kolodny, Ralph (Leonard) 1923- 116
Kolodziej, Edward Albert 1935- 97-100
Kolon, Aleksander 1947- CANR-30
Kolon, Nita
See Onadipe, (Nathaniel) Kola(wole)
Kolosimo, Peter 1922- CANR-7
Earlier sketch in CA 53-56
Kolsky, Thomas A. 1942- 135
Kolson, Clifford J(ohn) 1920- 9-12R
Kolstoe, Oliver P(aul) 1920- 17-20R
Koltes, Bernard-Marie 1948-1989 Obituary 128
Koltun, Frances Lang 69-72
Kolumban, Nicholas 1937- 111
Kolve, Carolee Nance 1946- 122
Kolyer, John (McNaughton) 1933- CANR-39
Earlier sketches in CA 69-72, CANR-11
Komai, Akira 1908(?)-1983 Obituary 111
Komaiko, Jean R. 1922(?)-1984 Obituary 114
Komar, Kathleen L(enore) 1949- 128
Komarnicki, Tytus 1896- CAP-1
Earlier sketch in CA 9-10
Komarovsky, Mirra CAP-1
Earlier sketch in CA 17-18
Komatsu Sakyo 1931- Brief entry 113
Kome, Penney 1948- 116
Komer, Robert W(illiam) 1922- 108
Kometani, Foumiko 1930- 135
Komisar, Lucy 1942- 33-36R
See also SATA 9
Kommers, Donald P. 1932- 116
Komoda, Beverly 1939- 85-88
See also SATA 25
Komoda, Kiyo 1937- ....SATA 9
Komroff, Manuel 1890-1974 ....CANR-4
Obituary 53-56
Earlier sketch in CA 1-4R
See also DLB 4
See also SATA 2, 20
Komunyakaa, Yusef 1947- .... DLB 120
Konadu, Asare
See Konadu, S(amuel) A(sare)
Konadu, S(amuel) A(sare) 1932- CANR-26
Earlier sketch in CA 21-24R
See also BW
Konchalovsky, Andrei
See Mikhalkov-Konchalovsky, Andrei (Sergeyevich)
Konczacki, Zbigniew Andrzej 1917- CANR-10
Earlier sketch in CA 21-24R
Kondoleon, Harry 1955- 112
Kondracke, Morton 1939- 127
Brief entry 119
Kondrashin, Kiril (Petrovich)
1914-1981 Obituary 108
Kondrashov, Stanislav (Nikolaevich)
1928- 69-72
Konecky, Edith 1922- 69-72
Konefsky, Samuel J.
1915-1970 Obituary 29-32R
Konek, Carol (Wolfe) 1934- Brief entry 114
Koner, Marvin 1921(?)-1983 Obituary 109
Koner, Pauline 1912- 132
Kong, Shiu Loon 1934- 108
Konick, Marcus 1914- 37-40R
Konig, David Thomas 1947- 97-100
Konig, Franz
See Koenig, Franz
Konig, Fritz H(ans)
See Koenig, Fritz H(ans)
Konig, Rene
See Koenig, Rene
Konigsberg, Conrad Isidore 1916-1976 .....21-24R
Obituary 134
Konigsburg, E(laine) L(obl) 1930- CANR-39
Earlier sketches in CA 21-24R, CANR-17
See also AAYA 3
See also CLR 1
See also DLB 52
See also MAICYA
See also MTCW
See also SATA 4, 48
Koning, Hans
See Koningsberger, Hans
Koningsberger, Hans 1921- CANR-2
Earlier sketch in CA 1-4R
See also SATA 5
Konkel, Wilbur Stanton 1912- 111
Konkle, Janet Everest 1917- 1-4R
See also SATA 12
Konner, Alfred
See Koenner, Alfred
Konner, Linda 1951- 102
Konner, Melvin Joel 1946- Brief entry 116
Konnyu, Leslie 1914- CANR-7
Earlier sketch in CA 13-16R
Konopka, Gisela 1910- 9-12R
Konovalov, Sergey 1899-1982 Obituary 106
Konrad, Evelyn 1930- 33-36R
Konrad, George
See Konrad, Gyoergy
Konrad, Gyoergy 1933- 85-88
See also CLC 4, 10
Konrad, James
See Maclean, Charles
Konstan, David 1940- CANR-32
Earlier sketch in CA 113
Kontos, Cecille
See Haddix-Kontos, Cecille P.
Kontos, Peter G(eorge) 1935-1977 ....CANR-17
Obituary 115
Earlier sketch in CA 25-28R
Konvitz, Jeffrey 1944- CANR-7
Earlier sketch in CA 53-56
Konvitz, Milton Ridvas 1908- CANR-4
Earlier sketch in CA 1-4R
Konwicki, Tadeusz 1926- CANR-39
Earlier sketch in CA 101
See also CAAS 9
See also CLC 8, 28, 54
See also MTCW
Koo, Anthony Y(ing) C(hang) 1918- 57-60
Koo, Samuel 1941- 77-80
Koo, V(i) K(yuin) Wellington 1888-1985 81-84
Obituary 117
Koob, C(harles) Albert 1920- 41-44R
Koob, Derry D(elos) 1933- 37-40R
Koob, Joseph E. II 1948- 121
Koob, Theodora (J. Foth) 1918- 5-8R
See also SATA 23
Kooiker, Leonie
See Kooyker-Romijn, Johanna Maria
Kooiman, Gladys 1927- 89-92
Kooiman, Helen W.
See Hosier, Helen Kooiman
Koon, George William 1942- 116
Koon, Helene Wickham 1924- 120
Koonce, Ray F. 1913- 9-12R
Koons, Carolyn 136
Koonts, Jones Calvin 1924- 49-52
Koontz, Dean R(ay) 1945- CANR-36
Earlier sketches in CA 108, CANR-19
See also AAYA 9
See also BEST 89:3, 90:2
See also MTCW
Koontz, Harold 1908-1984 ....41-44R
Obituary 112
Koontz, Robin Michal 1954- 138
See also SATA 70
Koonz, Claudia
See Koonz, Claudia Ann
Koonz, Claudia Ann 131
Brief entry 126
Koop, Katherine C. 1923- 17-20R
Koop, Theodore Frederick
1907(?)-1988 Obituary 126
Koopman, LeRoy George 1935- 101
Koopmans, Tjalling (Charles)
1910-1985 Obituary 115
Koopowitz, Harold 1940- 114
Kooser, Ted
See Kooser, Theodore
See also DLB 105
Kooser, Theodore 1939- CANR-15
Earlier sketch in CA 33-36R
See also Kooser, Ted
Kootz, Samuel Melvin 1898-1982 Obituary 107
Kooyker-Romijn, Johanna Maria
1927- CANR-34
Earlier sketch in CA 107
See also SATA 48
Kooyker-Romyn, Johanna Maria
See Kooyker-Romijn, Johanna Maria
Kopal, Zdenek 1914- 93-96
Kopelev, Lev (Zinovievich) 1912- 123
Kopelev, Raissa (Davydovna) Orlova
See Orlova-Kopelev, Raissa (Davydovna)
Kopelman, Arie 1937- 113
Koperwas, Sam 1948- CANR-22
Earlier sketch in CA 105
Kopf, David 1930- 89-92
Kopff, E(dward) Christian 1946- 117
Kopit, Arthur (Lee) 1937- 81-84
See also CABS 3
See also AITN 1
See also CLC 1, 18, 33
See also DLB 7
See also MTCW
Kopkind, Andrew D(avid) 1935- 29-32R
Koplin, H(arry) T(homas) 1923- 33-36R
Koplinka, Charlotte
See Lukas, Charlotte Koplinka
Koplitz, Eugene D(e Vere) 1928- 37-40R
Kopman, H(enri Marshall) 1918- 89-92
Kopp, Anatole 1915- CANR-12
Earlier sketch in CA 29-32R
Kopp, Harriet Green 41-44R
Kopp, O(swald) W. 1918- 33-36R
Kopp, Richard L. 1934- CANR-13
Earlier sketch in CA 33-36R
Kopp, Sheldon B(ernard) 1929- 37-40R
Kopp, William LaMarr 1930- 65-68
Koppel, Lillian 1926- 108
Koppel, Shelley R(uth) 1951- 108
Koppel, Ted 1940(?)- 103
Kopper, Edward A(nthony) Jr. 1937- CANR-33
Earlier sketches in CA 69-72, CANR-15
Kopper, Lisa (Esther) 1950- ....SATA 51
Kopper, Philip (Dana) 1937- 97-100
Kopperman, Paul Edward 1945- 69-72
Koppett, Leonard 1923- CANR-11
Earlier sketch in CA 25-28R
Koppitz, Elizabeth M(unsterberg)
1919-1983 ....CANR-14
Obituary 111
Earlier sketch in CA 13-16R
Koppman, Lionel 1920- CANR-6
Earlier sketch in CA 9-12R
Kops, Bernard 1926- 5-8R
See also CLC 4
See also DLB 13
Kopulos, Stella 1906- 49-52
Kopycinski, Joseph V(alentine) 1923- 33-36R
Korach, Mimi 1922- ....SATA 9
Koralek, Jenny 1934- ....SATA 71
Koran, Dennis 1947- 120
Korb, Lawrence J(oseph) 1939- 77-80
Korbel, John 1918- 9-12R
Korbel, Josef 1909-1977 ....37-40R
Obituary 73-76
Korbonski, Andrzej 1927- 9-12R
Korbonski, Stefan 1903-1989 ....CANR-5
Obituary 128
Earlier sketch in CA 5-8R
Korczak, Janusz
See Goldszmit, Henryk
See also SATA 65
Korda, Michael (Vincent) 1933- CANR-39
Earlier sketch in CA 107
See also BEST 89:3
Kordel, Lelord 1904- 106
Korelitz, Jean Hanff 1961- 132
Koren, Edward 1935- CANR-11
Earlier sketch in CA 25-28R
See also SATA 5
Koren, Henry J(oseph) 1912- CANR-35
Earlier sketch in CA 9-12R
Korenbaum, Myrtle 1915- 57-60
Korenblit, Joan B(ravo) 1952- 113
Korey, William 1922- Brief entry 112
Korfker, Dena 1908- CANR-17
Earlier sketch in CA 1-4R
Korg, Jacob 1922- CANR-2
Earlier sketch in CA 5-8R
Korges, James 1930-1975 .... CAP-2
Earlier sketch in CA 25-28
Korinets, Iurii Iosifovich
See Korinetz, Yuri (Iosifovich)
Korinetz, Yuri (Iosifovich) 1923- CANR-11
Earlier sketch in CA 61-64
See also CLR 4
See also SATA 9
Korman, A. Gerd 1928- CANR-35
Earlier sketch in CA 53-56
Korman, Gordon 1963- CANR-34
Earlier sketch in CA 112
See also CLR 25
See also MAICYA
See also SATA 41, 49
Korman, Justine 1958- 138
See also SATA 70
Korman, Keith 1956- 102
Kormendi, Ferenc 1900-1972 Obituary 37-40R
Kormondy, Edward J(ohn) 1926- CANR-13
Earlier sketch in CA 33-36R
Korn, Alfons L(udwig) 1906-1986 ....CANR-34
Obituary 119
Earlier sketch in CA 93-96
Korn, Bertram Wallace 1918-1979 ....CANR-1
Earlier sketch in CA 1-4R
Korn, Frank J(ames) 1935- 115
Korn, Henry James 1945- 69-72
Korn, Noel 1923- 73-76
Korn, Peggy
See Liss, Peggy K(orn)
Korn, Walter 1908- 73-76
Kornai, J(anos) 1928- CANR-35
Earlier sketch in CA 13-16R
Kornblatt, Joyce Reiser 1944- CANR-27
Earlier sketch in CA 106
Kornbluh, Marvin 1927-1987 Obituary 124
Kornblum, Allan 1949- 69-72
Kornblum, Cinda 1950- 69-72
Kornblum, Sylvan 1927- 41-44R
Kornbluth, C(yril) M. 1923-1958 Brief entry 105
See also DLB 8
See also TCLC 8
Kornbluth, Jesse 1946- CANR-17
Earlier sketch in CA 25-28R
Korneichuk, Aleksandr Y.
1905-1972 Obituary 33-36R
Korner, Stephan
See Koerner, Stephan
Kornfeld, Anita Clay 1928- 97-100
Kornfeld, Paul 1889-1942 .... DLB 118
Kornfeld, Robert J(onathan) 1919- 104
Kornhauser, David H(enry) 1918- CANR-14
Earlier sketch in CA 41-44R
Kornhauser, Jincy
See Willett, Jincy
Kornhauser, William 1925- 1-4R
Kornheiser, Tony 1948- 138
Kornrich, Milton 1933- 17-20R
Korol, Alexander G. 1900- 5-8R
Korolenko, V. G.
See Korolenko, Vladimir Galaktionovich
Korolenko, Vladimir
See Korolenko, Vladimir Galaktionovich
Korolenko, Vladimir G.
See Korolenko, Vladimir Galaktionovich
Korolenko, Vladimir Galaktionovich
1853-1921 Brief entry 121
See also TCLC 22
Korotkin, Judith 1931- 53-56
Korr, Charles Paul 1939- 112
Kors, Alan Charles 1943- 77-80
Kort, Carol 1945- 106
Kort, Wesley A(lbert) 1935- CANR-34
Earlier sketch in CA 37-40R
Korte, Mary Norbert
See Koerte, Mary Norbert
Korten, David C(raig) 1937- CANR-34
Earlier sketches in CA 41-44R, CANR-15
Kortepeter, C(arl) Max 1928- CANR-26
Earlier sketch in CA 41-44R
Korth, Francis N(icholas) 1912- 25-28R
Korth, Philip A. 1936- 137
Kortner, Peter 1924-1991 ....33-36R
Obituary 133
Korty, Carol 1937- 77-80
See also SATA 15
Korty, John Van Cleave 1936- 106
Kory, Robert B(ruce) 1950- 65-68
Korzenik, Diana 1941- 133
Korzenny, Felipe 1947- 116
Korzybski, Alfred (Habdank Skarbek)
1879-1950 Brief entry 123
Kos, Erih 1913- Brief entry 106
Kosa, John 1914-1972 ....CANR-34
Earlier sketch in CA 5-8R
Kosch, Erich
See Kos, Erih
Koschade, Alfred 1928- 21-24R
Koscielniak, Bruce 1947- 134
See also SATA 67
Kosel, Janice E. 1948- 116
Koshetz, Herbert 1907(?)-1977 Obituary 73-76
Koshi, George M. 1911- CAP-2
Earlier sketch in CA 29-32
Koshland, Ellen 1947- CANR-13
Earlier sketch in CA 33-36R
Kosinski, Jerzy (Nikodem) 1933-1991 ......CANR-9
Obituary 134
Earlier sketch in CA 17-20R
See also CLC 1, 2, 3, 6, 10, 15, 53, 70
See also DLB 2
See also DLBY 82
See also MTCW
Kosinski, Leonard V. 1923- 25-28R
Koskenmaki, Rosalie
See Maggio, Rosalie
Koskoff, David E(lihu) 1939- 49-52
Koslow, Jules 1916- CANR-6
Earlier sketch in CA 1-4R
Kosmala, Hans 1904(?)-1981 Obituary 104
Kosof, Anna 1945- CANR-35
Earlier sketch in CA 85-88
Koss, Stephen E(dward) 1940-1984 ....25-28R
Obituary 114

Kossez, Robes 1935- CANR-12
Earlier sketch in CA 29-32R
Kossin, Sandy (Sanford) 1926- .... SATA 10
Kosslyn, Stephen Michael 1948- 117
Kossmann, Rudolf R(ichard) 1934- 37-40R
Kossoff, David 1919- CANR-35
Earlier sketch in CA 61-64
Kost, Mary Lu 1924- 45-48
Kost, Robert John 1913- 1-4R
Kostash, Myrna 1944- 65-68
Koste, Robert Francis 1933- 81-84
Kostelanetz, Andre 1901-1980 Obituary 107
Kostelanetz, Richard (Cory) 1940- CANR-38
Earlier sketch in CA 13-16R
See also CAAS 8
See also CLC 28
Kosten, Andrew 1921- 1-4R
Koster, Donald N(elson) 1910- 53-56
Koster, John (Peter Jr.) 1945- CANR-5
Earlier sketch in CA 53-56
Koster, R(ichard) M(orton) 1934- 37-40R
Kostich, Dragos D. 1921- CANR-10
Earlier sketch in CA 5-8R
Kostis, Nicholas 103
Kostiuk, Hryhory 1902- 77-80
Kostka, Edmund Karl 1915- 17-20R
Kostrowitzki, Wilhelm Apollinaris de
1880-1918 Brief entry 104
See also Apollinaire, Guillaume
Kostrubala, Thaddeus 1930- 101
Kostyu, Frank A(lexander) 1919- CANR-1
Earlier sketch in CA 49-52
Kosygin, Alexei Nikolayevich
1904-1980 Obituary 102
Kot, Stanislaw 1886(?)-1976 Obituary 65-68
Kotarba, Joseph A(nthony) 1947- 111
Kotarbinski, Tadeusz (Marian)
1886-1981 Obituary 105
Kotcheff, Ted
See Kotcheff, William Theodore
Kotcheff, William Theodore 1931- 115
Kothari, Rajni 1928- CANR-35
Earlier sketch in CA 33-36R
Kotin, Armine Avakian
See Mortimer, Armine Kotin
Kotker, Norman 1931- CANR-35
Earlier sketches in CA 25-28R, CANR-10
Kotker, Zane 1934- CANR-3
Earlier sketch in CA 49-52
Kotler, Milton 1935- CANR-25
Earlier sketch in CA 29-32R
Kotler, Philip 1931- CANR-13
Earlier sketch in CA 33-36R
Kotlowitz, Alex 1955(?)- 138
Kotlowitz, Robert 1924- CANR-36
Earlier sketch in CA 33-36R
See also CLC 4
Kotowska, Monika 1942- 93-96
Kotowski, Joanne 1930- 57-60
Kotre, John N(icholas) 1940- 81-84
Kotrozo, Carol Donnell
See Donnell-Kotrozo, Carol
Kotschevar, Lendal H(enry) 1908- CANR-10
Earlier sketch in CA 17-20R
Kotschnig, Walter M(aria)
1901-1985 Obituary 117
Kotsilibas-Davis, James 1940- 106
Kotsuji, Abraham S(etsuzau) 1899-1973 .... CAP-1
Obituary 45-48
Earlier sketch in CA 13-16
Kott, Jan 1914- 13-16R
Kottler, Dorothy 1918- 97-100
Kottler, Jeffrey (A.) 1951- 136
Kottman, Richard N(orman) 1932- 25-28R
Kotz, David M(ichael) 1943- 81-84
Kotz, Mary Lynn 1936- 104
Kotz, Nick 1932- CANR-32
Earlier sketch in CA 29-32R
Kotz, Samuel 1930- CANR-34
Earlier sketches in CA 13-16R, CANR-7
Kotzebue, August (Friedrich Ferdinand) von
1761-1819 .... DLB 94
Kotzin, Michael C(harles) 1941- 37-40R
Kotzwinkle, William 1938- CANR-3
Earlier sketch in CA 45-48
See also CLC 5, 14, 35
See also CLR 6
See also MAICYA
See also SATA 24, 70
Koubourlis, Demetrius J(ohn) 1938- 57-60
Koufax, Sandy
See Koufax, Sanford
Koufax, Sanford 1935- 89-92
Kouhi, Elizabeth 1917- 126
See also SATA 49, 54
Koulack, David 1938- 102
Koumoulides, John (Thomas Anastassios)
1938- CANR-34
Earlier sketch in CA 41-44R
Koupernik, Cyrille 1917- CANR-35
Earlier sketch in CA 57-60
Kourdakov, Sergei 1951-1973 Obituary 115
Kourvetaris, George A.
See Kourvetaris, Yorgos A.
Kourvetaris, Yorgos A. 1933- 127
Kousoulas, D(imitrios) George 1923- 17-20R
Kousser, J(oseph) Morgan 1943- CANR-32
Earlier sketch in CA 57-60
Koutoukas, H. M. 1947- 69-72
See also Rivoli, Mario
Kouts, Anne 1945- 29-32R
See also SATA 8
Kouts, Hertha Pretorius 1922-1973 ....1-4R
Obituary 103
Kouwenhoven, John A(tlee) 1909-1990 ....1-4R
Obituary 132
Kouyoumdjian, Dikran
See Arlen, Michael
Kovach, Barbara L(usk) Forisha
See Forisha-Kovach, Barbara L(usk)
Kovach, Bill 1932- CANR-11
Earlier sketch in CA 69-72
Kovach, Francis J(oseph) 1918- CANR-35
Earlier sketch in CA 61-64
Kovach, Thomas A(llen) 1949- 129
Kovacs, Alexander
1930(?)-1977 Obituary 73-76
Kovacs, Imre 1913-1980 ....CANR-34
Obituary 102
Earlier sketch in CA 21-24R
Kovacs, Steven 1946- 130
Kovaleff, Theodore Philip 1943- 116
Kovalev, Mikhail A(leksandrovich)
1893-1981 Obituary 108
Kovalik, Nada 1926- 25-28R
Kovalik, Vladimir 1928- 25-28R
Kovalski, Maryann 1951- .... SATA 58
Kovarik, Bill
See Kovarik, William
Kovarik, William 1951- 113
Kovarsky, Irving 1918- 29-32R
Kovel, Joel S. 1936- CANR-32
Earlier sketches in CA 29-32R, CANR-14
Kovel, Ralph CANR-23
Earlier sketches in CA 17-20R, CANR-8
Kovel, Terry 1928- CANR-23
Earlier sketches in CA 17-20R, CANR-8
Kovic, Ron 1946- 138
Kovner, Aba 1918-1987 Obituary 123
Kovner, B.
See Adler, Jacob
Kovrig, Bennett 1940- CANR-12
Earlier sketch in CA 29-32R
Kowalewski, David 1943- 112
Kowalke, Kim H. 1948- 132
Kowalski, Frank 1907- 37-40R
Kowet, Don 1937- CANR-35
Earlier sketches in CA 57-60, CANR-10
Kowit, Steve 1938- 118
Kowitt, Sylvia
See Crosbie, Sylvia Kowitt
Kowitz, Gerald T(homas) 1928- 33-36R
Kownslar, Allan O(wen) 1935- CANR-35
Earlier sketch in CA 61-64
Koyama, Kosuke 1929- CANR-35
Earlier sketches in CA 57-60, CANR-7
Koykka, Arthur S(idney) 1937- 116
Koyre, Alexandre 1892-1964 Obituary 111
Kozak, Jan B(lahoslav)
1889(?)-1974 Obituary 45-48
Kozak, Roman 1948(?)-1988 Obituary 126
Kozar, Andrew Joseph 1930- 103
Kozelka, Paul 1909- CAP-2
Earlier sketch in CA 25-28
Kozer, Jose 1940- CANR-34
Earlier sketches in CA 49-52, CANR-2
Kozicki, Henry 1924- 103
Kozicki, Richard J(oseph) 1929- 125
Brief entry 118
Koziebrodzki, Leopold B(olesta) 1906- 41-44R
Kozintsev, Grigori (Mikhailovich)
1905-1973 53-56
Kozlenko, William 1917- 57-60
Kozloff, Max 1933- 127
Brief entry 114
Kozlow, Mark J.
See Newton, Michael
Kozlowski, Theodore T(homas) 1917- CANR-19
Earlier sketches in CA 9-12R, CANR-4
Kozol, Jonathan 1936- CANR-16
Earlier sketch in CA 61-64
See also CLC 17
Kozoll, Michael 1940(?)- .... CLC 35
Kozulin, Alex 1949- 122
Kpomassie, Tete-Michel 1941- 123
Kra, Siegfried J. 1930- 129
Kraay, Colin M(ackennal)
1918-1982 Obituary 116
Kracmar, John Z. 1916- 37-40R
Krader, Lawrence 1919- 21-24R
Kraditor, Aileen S. 1928- CANR-35
Earlier sketch in CA 13-16R
Kraehe, Enno E(dward) 1921- CANR-35
Earlier sketch in CA 9-12R
Kraemer, Kenneth L(eo) 1936- CANR-35
Earlier sketch in CA 111
Kraemer, Richard H(oward) 1920- CANR-35
Earlier sketches in CA 53-56, CANR-4
Kraenzel, Carl F(rederick) 1906- 73-76
Kraenzel, Margaret (Powell) 1899- 1-4R
Kraf, Elaine 1946- CANR-11
Earlier sketch in CA 65-68
See also DLBY 81
Krafft, C(onrad) James 1923- 119
Krafft, Jim
See Krafft, C(onrad) James
Krafft, Maurice 1946-1991 ....CANR-10
Obituary 134
Earlier sketch in CA 65-68
Krafsur, Richard Paul 1940- 103
Kraft, Barbara 1939- 97-100
Kraft, Betsy Harvey 1937- 89-92
Kraft, Charles H(oward) 1932- CANR-16
Earlier sketches in CA 45-48, CANR-1
Kraft, Charlotte 1922- 103
Kraft, Dean 1950- 114
Kraft, Eric (Lance) 1944- 108
Kraft, Hy(man Solomon) 1899-1975 ....CANR-36
Obituary 57-60
Earlier sketch in CA 41-44R
Kraft, Joseph 1924-1986 ....CANR-34
Obituary 118
Earlier sketch in CA 9-12R
Kraft, Ken(neth) 1907- CANR-1
Earlier sketch in CA 1-4R
Kraft, Kenneth H. Sr. 1896-1983 Obituary 111
Kraft, Leo 1922- 41-44R
Kraft, Leonard E(dward) 1923- 29-32R
Kraft, Robert Alan 1934- 37-40R
Kraft, Stephanie (Barlett) 1944- 105
Kraft, Virginia 1932- 21-24R
Kraft, Walter Andreas
See Friedlander, Walter A(ndreas)
Kraft, William F. 1938- 33-36R
Kragen, Jinx
See Morgan, Judith A(dams)
Krahn, Fernando 1935- CANR-11
Earlier sketch in CA 65-68
See also CLR 3
See also SATA 31, 49
Kraig, Bruce 1939- CANR-18
Earlier sketch in CA 102
Krailsheimer, Alban John 1921- CANR-2
Earlier sketch in CA 5-8R
Kraines, Oscar 1916- 97-100
Kraines, Samuel H(enry) 1906- 77-80
Krajenke, Robert William 1939- 29-32R
Krajewski, Frank R. 1938- CANR-10
Earlier sketch in CA 65-68
Krajewski, Robert J(oseph) 1940- 97-100
Krakel, Dean Fenton 1923- 45-48
Krakowski, Lili 1930- 85-88
Kramarz, Joachim 1931- 25-28R
Kramer, A(lfred) T(heodore) 1892- CAP-1
Earlier sketch in CA 11-12
Kramer, Aaron 1921- CANR-12
Earlier sketch in CA 21-24R
Kramer, Anthony .... SATA 42
Kramer, Bernard M(ordecai) 1923- 77-80
Kramer, Charles 1915-1988 Obituary 125
Kramer, Dale 1936- CANR-5
Earlier sketch in CA 53-56
Kramer, Daniel C(aleb) 1934- 53-56
Kramer, Douglas 1950- 138
Kramer, Edith 1916- 33-36R
Kramer, Edna E.
See Kramer-Lassar, Edna Ernestine
Kramer, Eugene F(rancis) 1921- 37-40R
Kramer, Frank Raymond 1908- CAP-1
Earlier sketch in CA 11-12
Kramer, Gene 1927- 69-72
Kramer, George
See Heuman, William
Kramer, Hilton 1928- 113
Brief entry 109
Kramer, Jack 1923- 41-44R
Kramer, Jane 1938- 102
Kramer, Joel (Herbert) 1937- 97-100
Kramer, John Eichholtz Jr. 1935- 108
Kramer, Jonathan D. 1942- 130
Kramer, Jonathan M. 1946- 121
Kramer, Judith Rita 1933-1970 ....1-4R
Obituary 103
Kramer, Kathryn .... CLC 34
Kramer, Larry 1935- 126
Brief entry 124
See also CLC 42
Kramer, Lawrence (Eliot) 1946- 120
Kramer, Leonie Judith 1924- CANR-39
Earlier sketches in CA 81-84, CANR-17
Kramer, Mark (William) 1944- CANR-17
Earlier sketch in CA 97-100
Kramer, Milton D. 1915-1973 Obituary 37-40R
Kramer, Nancy 1942- 101
Kramer, Nora 1896(?)-1984 107
Obituary 113
See also SATA 26, 39
Kramer, Paul J(ackson) 1904- CANR-1
Earlier sketch in CA 45-48
Kramer, (Simon) Paul 1914- 21-24R
Kramer, Rita 1929- CANR-31
Earlier sketch in CA 69-72
Kramer, Roberta 1935- 103
Kramer, Roland Laird 1898- 5-8R
Kramer, Samuel Noah 1897-1990 ....9-12R
Obituary 133
Kramer, Ted
See Steward, Samuel M(orris)
Kramer, Victor A. 1939- CANR-16
Earlier sketch in CA 85-88
Kramer-Lassar, Edna Ernestine 1902-1984 107
Obituary 113
Kramish, Arnold 1923- CANR-7
Earlier sketch in CA 5-8R
Krammer, Arnold Paul 1941- CANR-27
Earlier sketches in CA 61-64, CANR-11
Kramon, Florence 1920- 25-28R
Kramrisch, Stella 1898- CAP-2
Earlier sketch in CA 21-22
Kranidas, Kathleen
See Collins, Kathleen
Krantz, Hazel Newman 1920- CANR-16
Earlier sketches in CA 1-4R, CANR-1
See also SATA 12
Krantz, Judith 1927- CANR-33
Earlier sketches in CA 81-84, CANR-11
See also BEST 89:1
See also MTCW
Krantz, Les(lie Jay) 1945- 120
Kranz, E(dwin) Kirker 1949- 33-36R
Kranz, Stewart D(uane) 1924- 101
Kranzberg, Melvin 1917- CANR-11
Earlier sketch in CA 21-24R
Kranzler, David 1930- 93-96
Kranzler, George G(ershon) 1916- CANR-12
Earlier sketch in CA 57-60
See also SATA 28
Kranzler, Gershon
See Kranzler, George G(ershon)
Krapf, Norbert 1943- 117
Krapp, R. M.
See Adams, Robert Martin
Krar, Stephen Frank 1924- CANR-20
Earlier sketches in CA 53-56, CANR-4
Kraselchik, R.
See Dyer, Charles (Raymond)
Krashen, Stephen D. 1941- 132
Krasilovsky, M(arvin) William 1926- 61-64
Krasilovsky, Phyllis 1926- CANR-11
Earlier sketch in CA 29-32R
See also MAICYA
See also SAAS 5
See also SATA 1, 38
Kraske, Robert Brief entry 116
See also SATA 36
Kraslow, David 1926- 29-32R
Krasna, Norman 1909-1984 Obituary 114
See also DLB 26
Krasne, Betty
See Levine, Betty K(rasne)
Krasner, Jack Daniel 1921-1978 ....CANR-3
Earlier sketch in CA 49-52
Krasner, Leonard 1924- 33-36R
Krasner, Stephen D(avid) 1942- CANR-15
Earlier sketch in CA 85-88
Krasner, William 1917- CANR-35
Earlier sketches in CA 37-40R, CANR-15
Krasney, Samuel A. 1922- 1-4R
Krasnov, Vladislav Georgievich 1937- 132
Krasnow, Erwin G(ilbert) 1936- 103
Krasovskaya, Vera (Mikhailovna) 1915- 130
Brief entry 106
Krass, Alfred C(harles) 1936- 116
Krasser, Wilhelm 1925(?)-1979 Obituary 89-92
Krassner, Paul 1932- CANR-11
Earlier sketch in CA 21-24R
Krasso, Miklos 1929(?)-1986 Obituary 118
Kratcoski, Peter C(harles) 1936- 111
Kratochvil, Paul 1932- 25-28R
Kratos
See Power, Norman S(andiford)
Kratovil, Robert 1910- CANR-5
Earlier sketch in CA 5-8R
Kratzenstein, Jossef J. 1904- CAP-2
Earlier sketch in CA 17-18
Krauch, Velma 1916- 37-40R
Kraues, Judith E. 101
Kraus, Albert L(awson) 1920- 41-44R
Kraus, Barbara 1929-1977 102
Kraus, Bruce R. 1954- 97-100
Kraus, C(lyde) Norman 1924- CANR-33
Earlier sketches in CA 41-44R, CANR-15
Kraus, Charles E. 1946- 111
Kraus, Constantine Raymond 1900- 129
Kraus, George 1930- 25-28R
Kraus, H. P.
See Kraus, Hans P(eter)
Kraus, Hans P(eter) 1907-1988 ....CAP-2
Obituary 127
Earlier sketch in CA 29-32
Kraus, Joanna Halpert 1937- CANR-21
Earlier sketch in CA 104
Kraus, Joe 1939- CANR-15
Earlier sketch in CA 89-92
Kraus, Joseph 1925- CANR-4
Earlier sketch in CA 53-56
Kraus, Karl 1874-1936 Brief entry 104
See also DLB 118
See also TCLC 5
Kraus, Michael 1901-1990 ....5-8R
Obituary 132
Kraus, Richard G(ordon) 1923- CANR-11
Earlier sketch in CA 13-16R
Kraus, Robert 1925- 33-36R
See also MAICYA
See also SAAS 11
See also SATA 4, 65
Kraus, Sidney 1927- CANR-10
Earlier sketch in CA 5-8R
Kraus, W. Keith 1934- 21-24R
Krause, Frank H(arold) 1942- 104
Krause, Harry D(ieter) 1932- 33-36R
Krause, Herbert 1905-1976 49-52
Obituary 103
Krause, Lawrence Berle 1929- 113
Krause, Pat 1930- CANR-37
Earlier sketch in CA 114
Krause, Sydney J(oseph) 1925- 21-24R
Krause, Walter 1917- CANR-1
Earlier sketch in CA 1-4R
Kraushaar, John L. 1917- 45-48
Kraushaar, Otto F(rederick) 1901- 37-40R
Krauskopf, Konrad B(ates) 1910- 77-80
Krauss, Bob
See Krauss, Robert G.
Krauss, Bruno
See Bulmer, (Henry) Kenneth
Krauss, Clifford 1953- 136
Krauss, Ellis S(aunders) 1944- CANR-8
Earlier sketch in CA 61-64
Krauss, Herbert Harris 1940- 85-88
Krauss, Paul Gerhardt 1905- 1-4R
Krauss, Robert G. 1924- CANR-2
Earlier sketch in CA 1-4R
Krauss, Robert M. 1931- 17-20R
Krauss, Rosalind E(pstein) 1940- 81-84
Krauss, Ruth (Ida) 1911- CANR-13
Earlier sketches in CA 1-4R, CANR-1
See also DLB 52
See also MAICYA
See also SATA 1, 30
Krausz, Ernest 1931- 104
Krausz, Michael 1942- CANR-4
Earlier sketch in CA 53-56
Krausz, Norman G(eorge) P(hilip) 1920- 41-44R
Kraut, Benny 1947- 113
Kraut, Richard 1944- 130

Krauthammer, Charles 1950- 127
Brief entry 121
Krautheimer, Richard 1897- 103
Krautter, Elisa (Bialk) 1912(?)-1990 CANR-1
Obituary 131
Earlier sketch in CA 1-4R
See also SATA 1
See also SATO 65
Krauze, Andrzej 1947- SATA 46
Krauzer, Steven M(ark) 1948- CANR-25
Earlier sketch in CA 109
Kravetz, Nathan 1921- 9-12R
Kravis, Irving B(ernard) 1916- CANR-7
Earlier sketch in CA 17-20R
Kravitz, Nathan
See Kravitz, Nathaniel
Kravitz, Nathaniel 1905- 49-52
Krawiec, Richard 1952- 122
Krawiec, T(heophile) S(tanley) 1913- CANR-10
Earlier sketch in CA 25-28R
Krawitz, Henry 1947- 45-48
Krawitz, Herman E(verett) 1925- 61-64
Krawitz, Ruth (Lifshitz) 1929- 9-12R
Kraybill, Donald B(rubaker) 1945- 69-72
Krebs, Alfred H. 1920- 21-24R
Krebs, Hans (Adolf) 1900-1981 129
Obituary 108
Krech, David 1909-1977 Obituary 73-76
Krech, Shepard III 1944- 119
Kredel, Fritz 1900-1973 Obituary 41-44R
See also SATA 17
Kredenser, Gail 1936- 21-24R
Kreeft, Peter 1937- CANR-31
Earlier sketches in CA 81-84, CANR-14
Krefetz, Gerald 1932- CANR-15
Earlier sketch in CA 33-36R
Krefetz, Ruth 1931-1972 CAP-2
Obituary 37-40R
Earlier sketch in CA 33-36
Kregel, J(an) A(llen) 1944- 41-44R
Kreh, Bernard 1925- 57-60
Kreider, Barbara 1942- 41-44R
Kreider, Carl 1914- 37-40R
Kreider, Jan F(rederick) 1942- 111
Kreidl, John Francis 1939- 81-84
Kreig, Margaret B. (Baltzell) 1922- 13-16R
Krein, David F(rederick) 1942- 85-88
Kreindler, Lee (Stanley) 1924- 17-20R
Kreingold, Shana
1889(?)-1972 Obituary 37-40R
Kreinin, Mordechai 1930- 9-12R
Kreisel, Henry 1922- 61-64
See also DLB 88
Kreiser, B(ernard) Robert 1943- 116
Kreisler, Fritz 1875-1962 Obituary 115
Kreisman, Leonard T(heodore) 1925- 13-16R
Kreisman, Marvin 1933(?)-1979(?) Obituary 102
Kreitler, Hans 1916- 45-48
Kreitler, Shulamith 1938- 45-48
Krejci, Jaroslav 1916- CANR-31
Earlier sketches in CA 41-44R, CANR-14
Kremen, Bennett 1936- 57-60
Kremenliev, Boris A(ngeloff) 1911-1988 45-48
Obituary 125
Krementz, Jill 1940- CANR-23
Earlier sketch in CA 41-44R
See also AITN 1, 2
See also CLR 5
See also MAICYA
See also SAAS 8
See also SATA 17, 71
Kremer, Laura Evelyn 1921- 103
Kremer, William F. 1919- 69-72
Kreml, Anne Lee 1930- 21-24R
Krempel, Daniel S(partakus) 1926- 33-36R
Kren, George M. 1926- 102
Krenek, Ernst 1900-1991 57-60
Obituary 136
Krenkel, John H(enry) 1906- CAP-2
Earlier sketch in CA 33-36
Krensky, Stephen (Alan) 1953- CANR-13
Earlier sketch in CA 73-76
See also SATA 41, 47
Krentel, Mildred White 1921- 5-8R
Krents, Harold Eliot 1944-1987 37-40R
Obituary 121
Krentz, Edgar (Martin) 1928- 21-24R
Krepon, Michael 1946- 128
Krepps, Robert W(ilson) 1919-1980 CANR-1
Earlier sketch in CA 1-4R
Kreps, Juanita M(orris) 1921- 130
Kresge, George Joseph Jr.
See Kreskin
Kresh, Paul 1919- CANR-13
Earlier sketch in CA 13-16R
See also SATA 61
Kreskin 1935- 101
Kress, Nancy 1948- 126
Kress, Paul F(rederick) 1935- 29-32R
Kress, Robert (Lee) 1932- CANR-8
Earlier sketch in CA 61-64
Kress, Roy A(lfred) 1916- 107
Kress, Stephen W. 1945- 122
Kressel, Kenneth 1942- 119
Kressy, Michael 1936- CANR-8
Earlier sketch in CA 61-64
Kretsch, Robert W.
1913(?)-1979 Obituary 89-92
Kretzmann, Adalbert Raphael 1903- CAP-1
Earlier sketch in CA 13-16
Kretzmann, Norman 1928- 49-52
Kretzmer, Herbert 1925- 105
Kreuder, Ernst 1903-1972 DLB 69
Kreuger, Miles 1934- 81-84
Kreusler, Abraham A(rthur) 1897- 65-68
Kreuter, Kent 1932- 29-32R
Kreuzer, James R. 1913-1971 CAP-1
Earlier sketch in CA 11-12
Kreve (Mickevicius), Vincas
1882-1954 TCLC 27
Krevitsky, Nathan I. 1914- 9-12R
Krevitsky, Nik
See Krevitsky, Nathan I.
Krevolin, Nathan 1927- CANR-14
Earlier sketch in CA 41-44R
Krewer, Semyon E(fimovich) 1915- 105
Kreyche, Gerald F. 1927- 37-40R
Kreyche, Robert J(oseph) 1920-1974 13-16R
Obituary 133
Kreymborg, Alfred 1883-1966 Obituary 25-28R
See also DLB 4, 54
Krich, A. M.
See Krich, Aron
Krich, Aron M.
See Krich, Aron
Krich, Aron 1916- 120
Krich, John 1951- 108
Krieg, Saul 1917- 81-84
Kriegel, Gail 1942- 108
Kriegel, Harriet 104
Kriegel, Leonard 1933- CANR-12
Earlier sketch in CA 33-36R
Krieger, Frieda Frome 1925- 128
Krieger, Leonard 1918-1990 CANR-7
Obituary 132
Earlier sketch in CA 17-20R
Krieger, Martin H. 1944- 138
Krieger, Murray 1923- CANR-2
Earlier sketch in CA 1-4R
See also DLB 67
Krieghbaum, Hillier (Hiram) 1902- CANR-2
Earlier sketch in CA 5-8R
Kriegman, Oscar M(arvin) 1930- 9-12R
Kriensky, Morris (Edward) 1917- 57-60
Krier, James E(dward) 1939- 81-84
Kriesberg, Louis 1926- CANR-12
Earlier sketch in CA 29-32R
Krikorian, Yervant H(ovhannes)
1892-1977 CANR-2
Obituary 73-76
Earlier sketch in CA 45-48
Krim, Seymour 1922-1989 CANR-4
Obituary 129
Earlier sketch in CA 5-8R
See also DLB 16
Krimerman, Leonard Isaiah 1934- 17-20R
Krims, Milton Robert
1904(?)-1988 Obituary 126
Krimsky, Joseph (Hayylm)
1883(?)-1971 Obituary 104
Krimsky, Sheldon 1941- CANR-33
Earlier sketch in CA 113
Krin, Sylvie
See Fantoni, Barry (Ernest)
Kring, Hilda Adam 1921- 77-80
Kring, Walter Donald 1916- 116
Krinsky, Carol Herselle 1937- 37-40R
Kripalani, J(iwatram) B(hagwandas)
1888-1982 Obituary 110
Kripke, Dorothy Karp 17-20R
See also SATA 30
Kripke, Saul A(aron) 1940- 130
Krippendorff, Klaus 1932- 77-80
Krippner, Stanley (Curtis) 1932- CANR-32
Earlier sketches in CA 81-84, CANR-15
Krisch, Henry 1931- 134
Brief entry 111
Krise, Raymond (Owens Jr.) 1949- 109
Krisher, Bernard 1931- CANR-18
Earlier sketch in CA 77-80
Krishna, Gopi
See Shivpuri, Gopi Krishna
Krishnamurti, Jiddu 1895-1986 CANR-39
Obituary 118
Earlier sketches in CA 61-64, CANR-11
Krislov, Alexander
See Lee Howard, Leon Alexander
Krislov, Joseph 1927- 41-44R
Krislov, Samuel 1929- CANR-18
Earlier sketches in CA 9-12R, CANR-3
Krispyn, Egbert 1930- 13-16R
Kriss, Ronald P(aul) 1934- 69-72
Krist, Gary (Michael) 1957- 132
Kristein, Marvin M(ichael) 1926- 29-32R
Kristeller, Paul Oskar 1905- CANR-6
Earlier sketch in CA 9-12R
Kristensen, Thorkil 1899-1989 130
Kristian, Hans
See Neerskov, Hans Kristian
Kristof, Jane 1932- 29-32R
See also SATA 8
Kristof, Ladis K(ris) D(onabed) 1918- 61-64
Kristof, Nicholas D(onabet) 1959- 126
Kristofferson, Kris 1936- 104
See also CLC 26
Kristol, Irving 1920- CANR-28
Earlier sketch in CA 25-28R
Kritsick, Stephen M(ark) 1951- 112
Kritz, Mary M. 138
Kritzeck, James 1930- 5-8R
Kriyananda
See Walters, J. Donald
Kriyananda, S.
See Walters, J. Donald
Kriyananda, Sri
See Walters, J. Donald
Kriyananda, Swami
See Walters, J. Donald
Krizanc, John 1956- CLC 57
Krizay, John 1926- 61-64
Krleza, Miroslav 1893-1981 97-100
Obituary 105
See also CLC 8
Krmpotic, Vesna 1932- CANR-20
Earlier sketch in CA 102
Kroc, Ray(mond Albert) 1902-1984 118
Obituary 111
Kroch, Adolph A. 1882-1978 Obituary 81-84
Krochmal, Arnold 1919- CANR-14
Earlier sketch in CA 69-72
Krochmal, Connie 1949- 41-44R
Krock, Arthur 1887-1974 CAP-2
Obituary 49-52
Earlier sketch in CA 33-36
See also AITN 1
See also DLB 29
Krodel, Gerhard 1926- 61-64
Kroeber, A(lfred) L(ouis) 1876-1960 129
Obituary 110
Kroeber, Clifton B(rown) 1921- CANR-32
Earlier sketch in CA 110
Kroeber, Donald W(alter) 1934- 115
Kroeber, Karl 1926- CANR-32
Earlier sketch in CA 57-60
Kroeber, Theodora (Kracaw)
1897-1979 CANR-32
Obituary 89-92
Earlier sketches in CA 5-8R, CANR-5
See also Quinn, Theodora K.
See also SATA 1
Kroeger, Arthur 1908- 13-16R
Kroeger, Frederick P(aul) 1921- 33-36R
Kroepcke, Karol
See Krolow, Karl (Gustav Heinrich)
Kroetsch, Robert 1927- CANR-38
Earlier sketches in CA 17-20R, CANR-8
See also CLC 5, 23, 57
See also DLB 53
See also MTCW
Kroetz, Franz
See Kroetz, Franz Xaver
Kroetz, Franz Xaver 1946- 130
See also CLC 41
Kroger, William S. 1906- CAP-1
Earlier sketch in CA 13-14
Krohn, Ernst C(hristopher) 1888-1975 37-40R
See also AITN 1
Krohn, Norman Odya 1920- 116
Krohn, Robert 1937- 45-48
Krok-Paszkowski, Jan 1925- 130
Kroll, Burt
See Rowland, D(onald) S(ydney)
Kroll, Ernest 1914- 97-100
Kroll, Francis Lynde 1904-1973 CAP-1
Earlier sketch in CA 13-16
See also SATA 10
Kroll, John (Leon) 1925-1986 Obituary 119
Kroll, Judith 1943- 65-68
Kroll, Morton 1923- 49-52
Kroll, Steven 1941- CANR-35
Earlier sketches in CA 65-68, CANR-9, 25
See also SAAS 7
See also SATA 19, 66
Kroller, Eva-Marie 1949- 128
Krolow, Karl (Gustav Heinrich) 1915- 81-84
Kromer, Helen CANR-34
Earlier sketch in CA 93-96
Kromminga, John H(enry) 1918- 77-80
Kronegger, Maria Elisabeth 1932- 25-28R
Kronenberg, Henry Harold 1902- 1-4R
Kronenberg, Maria Elizabeth
1881(?)-1970 Obituary 104
Kronenberger, Louis 1904-1980 CANR-2
Obituary 97-100
Earlier sketch in CA 1-4R
Kronenwetter, Michael 1943- SATA 62
Kroner, Richard 1884- 9-12R
Kronhausen, Eberhard W(ilhelm)
1915- CANR-6
Earlier sketch in CA 9-12R
Kronhausen, Phyllis C(armen) 1929- CANR-6
Earlier sketch in CA 9-12R
Kronick, David A(braham) 1917- 9-12R
Kronick, Joseph G. 1953- 122
Kroninger, Robert H(enry) 1923- 13-16R
Kronk, Gary (Wayne) 1956- 115
Kronman, Anthony T(ownsend) 1945- 113
Kronstadt, Henry L(ippin) 1915- 73-76
Kronus, Sidney J. Jr. 1937- Brief entry 107
Krook, Dorothea 1920- 123
Krooss, Herman E. 1912-1975 CAP-2
Obituary 57-60
Earlier sketch in CA 17-18
Kropf, Linda S(toddart) 1947- 49-52
Kropf, Richard W(illiam Bartlett)
1932- CANR-10
Earlier sketch in CA 65-68
Kropotkin, Peter (Aleksieevich)
1842-1921 Brief entry 119
See also TCLC 36
Kropp, Lloyd 25-28R
Kropp, Paul (Stephan) 1948- 112
See also SATA 34, 38
Krosby, H(ans) Peter 1929- 89-92
Krosney, Mary Stewart 1939- 17-20R
Krotki, Karol J(ozef) 1922- 41-44R
Krotkov, Yuri 1917- 102
See also CLC 19
Krout, John Allen 1896-1979 97-100
Obituary 85-88
Kruchkow, Diane 1947- 69-72
Kruck, William E(vert) 1942- 114
Kruckeberg, Arthur R(ice) 1920- 137
Krueger, Anne O. 1934- CANR-32
Earlier sketches in CA 37-40R, CANR-15
Krueger, Christoph 1937- 33-36R
Krueger, Hardy 1928- 77-80
Krueger, Henrik S. 1938- 130
Krueger, John R(ichard) 1927- CANR-33
Earlier sketches in CA 21-24R, CANR-10
Krueger, Lorenz 1932- 136
Krueger, Ralph R. 1927- CANR-2
Earlier sketch in CA 49-52
Krueger, Robert B(lair) 1928- 57-60
Krueger, Thomas A. 1936- 21-24R
Kruell, Marianne 1936- 132
Kruess, James 1926- CANR-5
Earlier sketch in CA 53-56
See also Kruss, James
See also CLR 9
See also MAICYA
See also SATA 8
Krug, Edward August 1911-1980 CANR-4
Earlier sketch in CA 5-8R
Krug, Mark M. 1915- Brief entry 109
Krug, Samuel E(dward) 1943- 121
Kruger, Arthur N(ewman) 1916- CANR-1
Earlier sketch in CA 1-4R
Kruger, Daniel H(erschel) 1922- 25-28R
Kruger, Hardy
See Krueger, Hardy
Kruger, Lorenz
See Krueger, Lorenz
Kruger, Mollee (Coppel) 1929- CANR-21
Earlier sketch in CA 69-72
Kruger, Paul
See Sebenthall, R(oberta) E(lizabeth)
Kruger, (Charles) Rayne 5-8R
Kruglak, Haym 1909- 53-56
Kruh, David (S.) 1956- 138
Kruh, Louis 1923- 138
Kruise, Carol Sue 1939- 125
Krukowski, Lucian 1929- 125
Krulewitch, Melvin Levin 1895-1978 103
Krulik, Stephen 1933- CANR-8
Earlier sketch in CA 17-20R
Krull, Felix
See White, Stanley
Krull, Kathleen 1952- 106
See also SATA 39, 52
Krull, Marianne
See Kruell, Marianne
Krumb
See Crumb, R(obert)
Krumboltz, John D(wight) 1928- Brief entry 110
Krumgold, Joseph (Quincy) 1908-1980 CANR-7
Obituary 101
Earlier sketch in CA 9-12R
See also CLC 12
See also MAICYA
See also SATA 1, 23, 48
Krumm, John McGill 1913- 109
Krummel, Donald William 1929- 106
Krump, John M. 1929(?)-1990 Obituary 132
Krumpelmann, John T(heodore) 1892- 41-44R
Krumwitz
See Crumb, R(obert)
Krupat, Arnold 1941- 126
Krupat, Edward 1945- 77-80
Krupinski, Loretta 1940- SATA 67
Krupnick, Mark L. 1939- 130
Krupnik, Baruch
See Karu, Baruch
Krupp, E(dwin) C(harles) 1944- CANR-21
Earlier sketch in CA 105
See also SATA 53
Krupp, Nate 1935- CANR-10
Earlier sketch in CA 21-24R
Krupp, Robin Rector 1946- 135
See also SATA 53
Krupp, Sherman Roy 1926-1988 1-4R
Obituary 125
Krusch, Werner E. 1927- 5-8R
Kruschke, Earl R(oger) 1934- 41-44R
Kruse, Alexander Z.
1888(?)-1972 Obituary 33-36R
Kruse, Harry D(ayton)
1900-1977 Obituary 73-76
Kruse, John 1919- CANR-35
Earlier sketch in CA 114
Krush, Beth 1918- MAICYA
See also SATA 18
Krush, Joe 1918- MAICYA
See also SATA 18
Krusich, Walter S(teve) 1922- 49-52
Kruskal, William H(enry) 1919- 33-36R
Kruss, James
See Kruess, James
See also CLR 9
Kruszewski, Z. Anthony 1928- 134
Brief entry 113
Krutch, Joseph Wood 1893-1970 CANR-4
Obituary 25-28R
Earlier sketch in CA 1-4R
See also CLC 24
See also DLB 63
Krutilla, John Vasil 1922- CANR-9
Earlier sketch in CA 21-24R
Krutzch, Gus
See Eliot, T(homas) S(tearns)
Kruuk, Hans 1937- 61-64
Kruzas, Anthony T(homas) 1914- CANR-17
Earlier sketches in CA 1-4R, CANR-2
Krymow, Virginia P(auline) 1930- 69-72
Krypton
See Graham, Lloyd M.
Krysl, Marilyn 1943- 105
Krythe, Maymie Richardson 17-20R
Krzywan, Jozef
See Krotki, Karol J(ozef)
Krzyzaniak, Marian 1911- 9-12R
Krzyzanowski, Jerzy R(oman) 1922- 37-40R
Krzyzanowski, Ludwik
1907(?)-1986 Obituary 118
Kselman, Thomas A. 1948- 110
K-Turkel, Judi
See Kesselman-Turkel, Judi

Kubal, David L(awrence) 1936- ... 45-48
Kubat, Daniel 1928- Brief entry ... 114
Kubeck, James (Ernest) 1920- ... 17-20R
Kubek, Anthony 1920- ... 104
Kubelka, Susanna 1942- ... 113
Kube-McDowell, Michael P(aul) 1954- ... 119
Kubiak, T(imothy) J(ames) 1942- ... 61-64
Kubiak, William J. 1929- ... 33-36R
Kubicek, Robert V(incent) 1935- ... 29-32R
Kubie, Eleanor Gottheil
See Kubie, Nora Gottheil Benjamin
Kubie, Lawrence S.
1896(?)-1973 Obituary ... 45-48
Kubie, Nora Benjamin
See Kubie, Nora Gottheil Benjamin
Kubie, Nora Gottheil Benjamin 1899-1988 ... 5-8R
Obituary ... 126
See also SATA 39, 59
Kubin, Alfred 1877-1959 Brief entry ... 112
See also DLB 81
See also TCLC 23
Kubinyi, Laszlo 1937- ... 85-88
See also SATA 17
Kubis, Pat 1928- ... 25-28R
Kubler, George (Alexander) 1912- ... 9-12R
Kubler-Ross, Elisabeth
See Kuebler-Ross, Elisabeth
Kublin, Hyman 1919- ... 9-12R
Kubly, Herbert (Oswald Nicholas)
1915- ... CANR-4
Earlier sketch in CA 5-8R
Kubo, Sakae 1926- ... CANR-7
Earlier sketch in CA 57-60
Kubose, Gyomay M(asao) 1905- ... 49-52
Kubota, Akira 1932- ... 37-40R
Kubrick, Stanley 1928- ... CANR-33
Earlier sketch in CA 81-84
See also CLC 16
See also DLB 26
Kucera, Henry 1925- ... 21-24R
Kucharek, Casimir (Anthony) 1928- ... 57-60
Kucharski, Kasimir
See Koch, Kurt E(mil)
Kucharsky, David (Eugene) 1931- ... 65-68
Kucherov, Alexander 1927-1985 Obituary ... 117
Kucich, John (Richard) 1952- ... 112
Kuczkir, Mary 1933- ... 115
Brief entry ... 111
Kuczynski, Pedro-Pablo 1938- ... 77-80
Kudian, Mischa ... 107
Kudrle, Robert Thomas 1942- ... 112
Kuebler-Ross, Elisabeth 1926- ... 25-28R
Kuebrich, David 1943- ... 134
Kuehl, John 1928- ... 21-24R
Kuehl, Linda 1939(?)-1978 Obituary ... 104
Kuehl, Warren F(rederick) 1924- ... CANR-7
Earlier sketch in CA 17-20R
Kuehn, Dorothy Dalton
See Dalton, Dorothy
Kuehn, Heinz R(ichard) 1919- ... 130
Kuehn, Thomas James 1950- ... 116
Kuehnelt-Leddihn, Erik (Maria) Ritter von
1909- ... CANR-20
Earlier sketches in CA 9-12R, CANR-3
Kuemmerly, Walter 1903- ... 49-52
Kuen, Alfred (F.) 1921- ... CANR-25
Earlier sketch in CA 107
Kuenan, Philip Henry 1902-1976 Obituary ... 116
Kueng, Hans 1928- ... 53-56
See also MTCW
Kuenne, Robert E(ugene) 1924- ... 5-8R
Kuenstler, Morton 1927- ... SATA 10
Kuenzli, Alfred E(ugene) 1923- ... 17-20R
Kuesel, Harry N. 1892(?)-1977 Obituary ... 73-76
Kuester, David 1938- ... 53-56
Kuether, Edith Lyman 1915- ... 49-52
Kufeldt, George 1923- ... 37-40R
Kuffler, Stephen 1913-1980 Obituary ... 105
Kufner, Herbert L(eopold) 1927- ... 5-8R
Kugel, James 1945- ... 29-32R
Kugelman, Richard 1908- ... 41-44R
Kugelmass, J. Alvin 1910-1972 ... CANR-4
Obituary ... 33-36R
Earlier sketch in CA 5-8R
Kugi, Constance Todd 1939- ... 127
Kuh, Charlotte 1892(?)-1985 Obituary ... 115
See also SATA 43
Kuh, Edwin 1925-1986 ... CANR-36
Obituary ... 119
Earlier sketch in CA 21-24R
Kuh, Frederick Robert
1895-1978 Obituary ... 89-92
Kuh, Katharine W. 1904- ... 13-16R
Kuh, Richard H. 1921- ... 21-24R
Kuhatschek, Jack 1949- ... 122
Kuhfeld, Mary Pulver 1943- ... 128
Kuhl, Ernest Peter 1881-1981 ... CANR-39
Obituary ... 133
Earlier sketch in CA 41-44R
Kuhlken, Ken(neth Wayne) 1945- ... 102
Kuhlman, James A(llen) 1941- ... 85-88
Kuhlman, John M(elville) 1923- ... 17-20R
Kuhlman, Kathryn 1910(?)-1976 ... CANR-12
Obituary ... 65-68
Earlier sketch in CA 57-60
Kuhlmann, Susan
See Lohafer, Susan
Kuhn, Alfred 1914-1981 ... CANR-37
Earlier sketches in CA 9-12R, CANR-3
Kuhn, Annette 1945- ... CANR-29
Earlier sketch in CA 111
Kuhn, Bowie (Kent) 1926- ... 126
Kuhn, Delia (Wolf) 1903-1989 ... 130
Kuhn, Edward Jr. 1924(?)-1979 ... 102
Obituary ... 93-96
Kuhn, Ferdinand 1905-1978 ... CANR-36
Obituary ... 81-84
Earlier sketch in CA 5-8R
Kuhn, Harold B(arnes) 1911- ... 49-52
Kuhn, Heinz R(ichard)
See Kuehn, Heinz R(ichard)
Kuhn, Irene Corbally ... CAP-1
Earlier sketch in CA 9-10
Kuhn, Karl F(rancis) 1939- ... CANR-37
Earlier sketch in CA 65-68
Kuhn, Maggie
See Kuhn, Margaret E.
Kuhn, Margaret E. 1905- Brief entry ... 109
Kuhn, Martin A(rno) 1924- ... 9-12R
Kuhn, Reinhard (Clifford) 1930-1980 ... CANR-34
Earlier sketch in CA 45-48
Kuhn, Thomas S(amuel) 1922- ... CANR-11
Earlier sketch in CA 21-24R
Kuhn, Tillo E. 1919- ... 5-8R
Kuhn, William Ernst 1922- ... 37-40R
Kuhn, Wolfgang Erasmus 1914- ... 5-8R
Kuhne, Cecil 1952- ... 93-96
Kuhne, Marie (Ahnighito Peary)
1893-1978 Obituary ... 77-80
Kuhner, Herbert 1935- ... 25-28R
Kuhns, Dennis R(ay) 1947- ... 113
Kuhns, Dorothy
See Heyward, Dorothy (Hartzell Kuhns)
Kuhns, Grant (Wilson) 1929- ... 9-12R
Kuhns, Richard F(rancis Jr.) 1924- ... CANR-36
Earlier sketch in CA 37-40R
Kuhns, William 1943- ... 21-24R
Kuhse, Helga 1940- ... 122
Kuic, Vukan 1923- ... 37-40R
Kuiper, Gerard Peter 1905-1973 ... CAP-2
Obituary ... 45-48
Earlier sketch in CA 17-18
Kuisel, Richard F(rancis) 1935- ... 21-24R
Kuist, J(ames) M(arquis) 1935- ... 124
Kuitert, H(arminus) Martinus 1924- ... CANR-37
Earlier sketch in CA 25-28R
Kujawa, Duane 1938- ... 33-36R
Kujoth, Jean Spealman 1935-1975 ... CAP-2
Earlier sketch in CA 25-28
See also SATA 30
Kukla, Robert J(ohn) 1932- ... 49-52
Kuklick, Bruce 1941- ... 41-44R
Kuklin, Susan 1941- ... 130
See also SATA 63
Kuleshov, Arkady A. 1914-1978 Obituary ... 77-80
Kulick, John
See Pinchot, Ann (Kramer)
Kulka, Richard A. 1945- ... 130
Kulkarni, Hemant B(alvantrao) 1916- ... CANR-1
Earlier sketch in CA 45-48
Kulkarni, R(amchandra) G(anesh)
1931- ... 29-32R
Kulkarni, Venkatesh S(rinivas) 1945- ... 113
Kulkin, Mary-Ellen
See Siegel, Mary-Ellen Kulkin
Kull, Andrew 1947- ... 138
Kull, Steven 1951- ... 128
Kullman, Harry 1919-1982 ... CANR-39
Earlier sketch in CA 93-96
See also SATA 35
Kulshrestha, Chirantan 1946- ... 107
Kulski, Julian (Eugeniusz) 1929- ... CANR-14
Earlier sketch in CA 21-24R
Kulski, Wladyslaw W(szebor) 1903- ... CANR-37
Earlier sketch in CA 5-8R
Kulstein, David J. 1916-1974 ... CAP-2
Earlier sketch in CA 25-28
Kultermann, Udo 1927- ... 85-88
Kulukundis, Elias 1937- ... 21-24R
Kulyk Keefer, Janice 1952- ... 127
Kumar, (Jagdish) Krishan 1942- ... 130
Kumar, Krishna 1942- ... 109
Kumar, Satish 1933- ... 112
Kumar, Shiv K(umar) 1921- ... CANR-7
Earlier sketch in CA 9-12R
Kumbel
See Hein, Piet
Kumin, Maxine (Winokur) 1925- ... CANR-21
Earlier sketches in CA 1-4R, CANR-1
See also CAAS 8
See also AITN 2
See also CLC 5, 13, 28
See also DLB 5
See also MTCW
See also SATA 12
Kummel, Bernhard 1919- ... 33-36R
Kummerly, Walter
See Kuemmerly, Walter
Kun, Michael (Stuart) 1962- ... 132
Kunce, Joseph T(yree) 1928- ... 41-44R
Kuncewicz, Maria (Szczepanska) 1899- ... CAP-1
Earlier sketch in CA 9-10
Kuncewiczowa, Maria
See Kuncewicz, Maria (Szczepanska)
Kundera, Milan 1929- ... CANR-19
Earlier sketch in CA 85-88
See also AAYA 2
See also CLC 4, 9, 19, 32, 68
See also MTCW
Kundsin, Ruth Blumfeld 1916- ... 106
Kunen, James Simon 1948- ... 25-28R
Kunene, Mazisi (Raymond) 1930- ... 125
See also BW
See also DLB 117
Kuner, M(ildred) C(hristophe) 1922- ... 41-44R
Kunert, Guenter 1929- ... DLB 75
Kung, Hans
See Kueng, Hans
Kung, Shien Woo 1905- ... 1-4R
Kunhappa, Murkot 1905- ... 69-72
Kunhardt, Dorothy (Meserve) 1901-1979 ... 107
Obituary ... 93-96
See also SATA 22, 53
Kunhardt, Edith 1937- ... 134
See also SATA 67
Kunhardt, Philip B(radish) Jr. 1928- ... CANR-37
Earlier sketch in CA 85-88
Kunhi Krishnan, T(aramal) V(anmeri)
1919- ... 61-64
Kuniczak, W(ieslaw) S(tanislaw) 1930- ... 85-88
Kuniholm, Bruce Robellet 1942- ... CANR-27
Earlier sketch in CA 93-96
Kuniholm, Whitney 1954- ... 112
Kunin, Madeleine May 1933- ... 93-96
Kunin, Richard A(llen) 1932- ... 107
Kunitz, Joshua 1896(?)-1980 Obituary ... 97-100
Kunitz, Stanley (Jasspon) 1905- ... CANR-26
Earlier sketch in CA 41-44R
See also CLC 6, 11, 14
See also DLB 48
See also MTCW
Kunjufu, Johari M. Amini 1935- ... 41-44R
See also Amini, Johari M.
See also BW
Kunkel, Francis L(eo) 1921- ... 45-48
Kunnes, Richard 1941- ... 33-36R
Kuno, Susumu 1933- ... 41-44R
Kunreuther, Howard Charles 1938- ... CANR-37
Earlier sketch in CA 25-28R
Kunst, David W(illiam) 1939- ... 85-88
Kunstler, James Howard 1948- ... CANR-18
Earlier sketch in CA 101
Kunstler, Morton
See Kuenstler, Morton
Kunstler, William M(oses) 1919- ... CANR-5
Earlier sketch in CA 9-12R
Kuntz, J(ohn) Kenneth 1934- ... CANR-9
Earlier sketch in CA 21-24R
Kuntz, Kenneth A. 1916- ... 1-4R
Kuntz, Paul G. 1915- ... 5-8R
Kuntzleman, Charles T(homas) 1940- ... CANR-22
Earlier sketches in CA 57-60, CANR-7
Kunz, Marji 1939(?)-1979 Obituary ... 89-92
Kunz, Phillip Ray 1936- ... CANR-19
Earlier sketch in CA 37-40R
Kunz, Roxane (Brown) 1932- ... 121
See also SATA 53
Kunz, Virginia B(rainard) 1921- ... CANR-37
Earlier sketch in CA 21-24R
Kunze, Reiner 1933- ... 93-96
See also CLC 10
See also DLB 75
Kunzle, David Mark 1936- ... CANR-36
Earlier sketches in CA 53-56, CANR-5
Kunzur, Sheela
See Geis, Richard E(rwin)
Kuo, Ping-chia 1908- ... 5-8R
Kuo, Shirley W. Y. 1930- ... 115
Kuo, Ting-yee 1904(?)-1975 Obituary ... 61-64
Kuo Mo-Jo 1892-1978 Obituary ... 77-80
Kup, Alexander Peter 1924- ... CANR-9
Earlier sketch in CA 13-16R
Kup, Karl 1903-1981 Obituary ... 104
Kuper, Adam (Jonathan) 1941- ... CANR-20
Earlier sketch in CA 103
Kuper, Hilda Beemer 1911- ... CANR-2
Earlier sketch in CA 1-4R
Kuper, Jack 1932- ... 21-24R
Kuper, Leo 1908- ... CANR-35
Earlier sketches in CA 21-24R, CANR-11
Kuper, Yuri
See Kuperman, Yuri
Kuperman, Yuri 1940- ... 102
Kupfer, Fern 1946- ... CANR-36
Earlier sketch in CA 106
Kupferberg, Herbert 1918- ... 29-32R
See also SATA 19
Kupferberg, Naphtali 1923- ... CANR-13
Earlier sketch in CA 21-24R
See also Kupferberg, Tuli
Kupferberg, Tuli
See Kupferberg, Naphtali
See also DLB 16
Kupperman, Joel J. 1936- ... CANR-36
Earlier sketch in CA 33-36R
Kupperman, Karen O(rdahl) 1939- ... 111
Kuprin, Aleksandr Ivanovich
1870-1938 Brief entry ... 104
See also TCLC 5
Kuralt, Charles Bishop 1934- ... 89-92
Kurath, Gertrude Prokosch 1903- ... 13-16R
Kurath, Hans 1891- ... 9-12R
Kuratomi, Chizuko 1939- ... CANR-10
Earlier sketch in CA 21-24R
See also SATA 12
Kurdi, Abdulrahman Abdulkadir 1941- ... 133
Kurdsen, Stephen
See Noon, Brian
Kureishi, Hanif 1954- ... CLC 64
Kurelek, William 1927-1977 ... CANR-3
Earlier sketch in CA 49-52
See also CLR 2
See also MAICYA
See also SATA 8, 27
Kurian, George 1928- ... 107
See also SATA 65
Kuriansky, Judith (Anne Brodsky) 1947- ... 132
Kurien, C(hristopher) T(homas) 1931- ... CANR-13
Earlier sketch in CA 33-36R
Kurihara, Kenneth Kenkichi 1910-1972 ... CANR-6
Obituary ... 37-40R
Earlier sketch in CA 1-4R
Kurkjian, Stephen A(noosh) 1943- ... 129
Brief entry ... 116
Kurkul, Edward 1916- ... 25-28R
Kurland, Gerald 1942- ... CANR-14
Earlier sketch in CA 41-44R
See also SATA 13
Kurland, Michael (Joseph) 1938- ... CANR-11
Earlier sketch in CA 61-64
See also SATA 48
Kurland, Philip B. 1921- ... CANR-7
Earlier sketch in CA 9-12R
Kurman, George 1942- ... 53-56
Kurnitz, Harry 1909-1968 Obituary ... 25-28R
Kuroda, Yasumasa 1931- ... CANR-35
Earlier sketch in CA 45-48
Kuropas, Myron B(ohdon) 1932- ... 45-48
Kurosawa, Akira 1910- ... 101
See also CLC 16
Kurowski, Eugeniusz
See Dobraczynski, Jan
Kurrik, Maire Jaanus 1940- ... 101
Kursh, Charlotte Olmsted 1912- ... 9-12R
Kursh, Harry 1919- ... 9-12R
Kurten, Bjorn (Olof) 1924-1988 ... CANR-20
Earlier sketch in CA 25-28R
See also SATA 64
Kurth-Voigt, Lieselotte E. 1923- Brief entry ... 110
Kurtis, Arlene Harris 1927- ... 25-28R
Kurtis, Bill
See Kurtis, William Horton
Kurtis, William Horton 1940- ... 133
Brief entry ... 124
Kurtz, C(larence) Gordon 1902- ... 65-68
Kurtz, David L(ee) 1941- ... 41-44R
Kurtz, Donna Carol 1943- ... 93-96
Kurtz, Ernest 1935- ... 112
Kurtz, Harold 1913- ... 17-20R
Kurtz, Irma 1935- ... 118
Kurtz, Katherine (Irene) 1944- ... CANR-25
Earlier sketch in CA 29-32R
Kurtz, Kenneth H(assett) 1928- ... 33-36R
Kurtz, Lester R. 1949- ... 126
Kurtz, Michael L(ouis) 1941- ... CANR-36
Earlier sketch in CA 107
Kurtz, Paul 1925- ... CANR-25
Earlier sketches in CA 13-16R, CANR-5
Kurtz, Stephen G(uild) 1926- ... 9-12R
Kurtzman, Jeffrey G(ordon) 1940- ... 110
Kurtzman, Joel 1947- ... CANR-30
Earlier sketch in CA 29-32R
Kurtz-Phelan, James L(anham) 1946- ... 49-52
Kuryluk, Ewa 1946- ... 135
Kurys, Diane 1949- ... 125
Kurz, Artur R.
See Scortia, Thomas N(icholas)
Kurz, Isolde 1853-1944 ... DLB 66
Kurz, Mordecai 1934- ... CANR-12
Earlier sketch in CA 29-32R
Kurz, Otto 1908-1975 ... 107
Obituary ... 104
Kurz, Paul Konrad 1927- ... 29-32R
Kurz, Ron 1940- ... CANR-14
Earlier sketch in CA 81-84
Kurzer, Siegmund F.
1907(?)-1973 Obituary ... 104
Kurzman, Dan 1927- ... CANR-32
Earlier sketches in CA 69-72, CANR-14
Kurzman, Paul A(lfred) 1938- ... CANR-13
Earlier sketch in CA 33-36R
Kurzweg, Bernhard F. 1926- ... 17-20R
Kurzweil, Arthur 1951- ... 97-100
Kurzweil, Edith ... 110
Kurzweil, Raymond (C.) 1948- ... 134
Kurzweil, Zvi Erich 1911- ... CANR-36
Earlier sketches in CAP-1, CA 11-12
Kusan, Ivan 1933- ... CANR-6
Earlier sketch in CA 9-12R
Kusche, Larry
See Kusche, Lawrence David
Kusche, Lawrence David 1940- ... CANR-5
Earlier sketch in CA 53-56
Kusenberg, Kurt 1904-1983 ... DLB 69
Kushel, Gerald 1930- ... CANR-11
Earlier sketch in CA 25-28R
Kushner, Carol 1950- ... 133
Kushner, David Z(arkeri) 1935- ... 53-56
Kushner, Donn (J.) 1927- ... CANR-35
Earlier sketch in CA 113
See also SATA 52
Kushner, Harold S(amuel) 1935- ... CANR-36
Earlier sketch in CA 107
See also BEST 90:2
Kushner, Harvey W(olf) 1941- ... 110
Kushner, Howard Irvin 1943- ... 81-84
Kushner, Irving 1929- ... 119
Kushner, James A(lan) 1945- ... 132
Kushner, Jill Menkes 1951- ... SATA 62
Kushner, Malcolm 1952- ... 134
Kushner, Rose 1929-1990 ... 61-64
Obituary ... 130
Kushner, Sam 1915(?)-1987 Obituary ... 123
Kusin, Vladimir V(ictor) 1929- ... CANR-13
Earlier sketch in CA 33-36R
Kuske, Martin 1940- ... 97-100
Kuskin, Karla (Seidman) 1932- ... CANR-22
Earlier sketches in CA 1-4R, CANR-4
See also CLR 4
See also MAICYA
See also SAAS 3
See also SATA 2, 68
Kuslan, Louis I(saac) 1922- ... CANR-1
Earlier sketch in CA 45-48
Kusmer, Kenneth Leslie 1945- ... 102
Kusnick, Barry A. 1910- ... CANR-37
Earlier sketch in CA 53-56
Kusniewicz, Andrzej 1904- ... 107
Kuspit, Donald B(urton) 1935- ... CANR-37
Earlier sketch in CA 97-100
Kussmaul, Ann (Sturm) 1945- ... 110

Kustermeir, Rudolf
1893(?)-1977 Obituary 73-76
Kustow, Michael (David) 1939- Brief entry 106
Kutash, Samuel Benjamin 1912-1979 ......CANR-2
Earlier sketch in CA 1-4R
Kuten, Jay 1935- Brief entry 108
Kuter, Laurence S(herman)
1905-1979 Obituary 113
Kutler, Stanley I. 1934- CANR-36
Earlier sketch in CA 21-24R
Kutner, Luis 1908- 109
Kutner, Nanette 1906(?)-1962 ....1-4R
Kutsche, Paul 1927- 114
Kutscher, Charles L(awrence) 1936- 77-80
Kutsky, Roman Joseph 1922- Brief entry 110
Kuttna, Mari 1934-1983 Obituary 109
Kuttner, Henry 1915-1958 Brief entry 107
See also DLB 8
See also TCLC 10
Kuttner, Paul 1931- CANR-30
Earlier sketches in CA 77-80, CANR-13
See also SATA 18
Kutz, LeRoy M. 1922- 13-16R
Kutza, Elizabeth Ann 111
Kuwayama, George 1925- CANR-39
Earlier sketch in CA 116
Kuyk, Dirk (A. Jr.) 1934- 135
Kuykendall, Eleanor 1938- Brief entry 109
Kuykendall, Jack L(awrence) 1940- 57-60
Kuykendall, Ralph S(impson) 1885-1963 ....1-4R
Kuzma, Greg 1944- 33-36R
See also CLC 7
Kuzma, Kay 1941- CANR-23
Earlier sketch in CA 106
See also SATA 39
Kuzmich, Natalie 1932- 127
Kuzmin, Mikhail 1872(?)-1936 ....TCLC 40
Kuznets, Simon (Smith)
1901-1985 Obituary 116
Brief entry 108
Kuznetsov, Anatoli 1929-1979 Obituary 89-92
Kuznetsov, (Edward) 1939- CANR-39
Earlier sketch in CA 57-60
Kuzniewski, Anthony J(oseph) 1945- 107
Kuzwayo, Ellen (Kate) 1914- 134
Kvale, Velma R(uth) 1898- CAP-2
Earlier sketch in CA 25-28
See also SATA 8
Kvam, Wayne (Eugene) 1938- 45-48
Kvasnicka, Robert M(ichael) 1935- 97-100
Kwabena Nketia, J. H.
See Nketia, J(oseph) H(anson) Kwabena
Kwamena-Poh, M(ichael Albert) 1932- 132
Kwan, Kian M(oon) 1929- 17-20R
Kwant, R. C.
See Kwant, Remigius C(ornelis)
Kwant, Remigius C(ornelis) 1918- CANR-18
Earlier sketches in CA 9-12R, CANR-3
Kwant, Remy C.
See Kwant, Remigius C(ornelis)
Kwanten, Luc 1944- 93-96
Kwavnick, David 1940- 45-48
Kweder, Adele 1910- 5-8R
Kweder, David James 1905- 5-8R
Kweit, Robert W(illiam) 1946- CANR-37
Earlier sketch in CA 112
Kwiatkowska, Hanna Yaxa
1907(?)-1980 Obituary 97-100
Kwitny, Jonathan 1941- CANR-23
Earlier sketches in CA 49-52, CANR-1
Kwolek, Constance
See Porcari, Constance Kwolek
Kyburg, Henry (Guy) E(ly) Jr. 1928- CANR-36
Earlier sketches in CA 5-8R, CANR-8
Kyd, Thomas
See Harbage, Alfred (Bennett)
Kyd, Thomas 1558-1594 ....DLB 62
Kydd, Sam(uel) 1917-1982 109
Obituary 106
Kyemba, Henry 1939- 81-84
Kyes, Robert L(ange) 1933- CANR-37
Earlier sketch in CA 49-52
Kyger, Joanne (Elizabeth) 1934- CANR-17
Earlier sketch in CA 101
See also CAAS 16
See also DLB 16
Kyle, Duncan
See Broxholme, John Franklin
Kyle, Elisabeth
See Dunlop, Agnes M. R.
Kyle, Keith 1925- 137
Kyle, Marlaine
See Hager, Jean
Kyle, Robert
See Terrall, Robert
Kyle, Sefton
See Vickers, Roy
Kyme, Ernest Hector 1906- 103
Kynaston, SirFrancis 1587-1642 ....DLB 121
Kyne, Peter B. 1880-1957 ....DLB 78
Kynett, Harold Havelock
1889-1973 Obituary 106
Kyper, Frank 1940- 85-88
Kyprianos, Iossif
See Samarakis, Antonis
Kyre, Joan Randolph 1935- 25-28R
Kyre, Martin (Theodore Jr.) 1928- 25-28R
Kyrle, Roger (Ernie) Money
See Money-Kyrle, Roger (Ernie)
Kysar, Robert (Dean) 1934- CANR-22
Earlier sketch in CA 69-72
Kyselka, Will 1921- 106
Kyte, Kathy S. 1946- ....SATA 44, 50
Kytle, Elizabeth 112
Kytle, Ray(mond) 1941- 29-32R
Kyvig, David E(dward) 1944- CANR-36
Earlier sketch in CA 101

L

La-Anyane, Seth 1922- 9-12R
Laas, William M. 1910(?)-1975 Obituary 61-64
LaBar, Tom 1937- 25-28R
Labaree, Benjamin Woods 1927- CANR-6
Earlier sketch in CA 9-12R
Labaree, Leonard W(oods) 1897-1980 73-76
Obituary 97-100
Labarge, Margaret Wade 1916- CANR-11
Earlier sketch in CA 25-28R
LaBarge, William Howard 1948- 116
La Barr, Creighton
See von Block, Bela W(illiam)
La Barre, Weston 1911- CANR-22
Earlier sketch in CA 1-4R
LaBastille, Anne 1938- CANR-8
Earlier sketch in CA 57-60
L'Abate, Luciano 1928- 111
Labatut, Jean 1899-1986 Obituary 121
Labbe, John T. CANR-17
Earlier sketch in CA 97-100
La Beau, Dennis (George) 1941- 97-100
LaBelle, Maurice Marc 1939- 113
Laber, Jeri 1931- CANR-9
Earlier sketch in CA 65-68
Laberge, Albert 1871-1960 ....DLB 68
Laberge, Marie 1950- ....DLB 60
LaBier, Douglas 1944- 124
Labin, Suzanne (Devoyon) 1913- CANR-32
Earlier sketches in CA 29-32R, CANR-14
Labor, Earle G. 1928- 21-24R
LaBorde, Rene
See Neuffer, Irene LaBorde
Labovitz, I(srael) M(ilton) 1907- 5-8R
Labrador, James
See Hamel Peifer, Kathleen
Labrador, Judy
See Hamel Peifer, Kathleen
LaBrecque, Claude X. 85-88
La Brie, Henry George III 1946- 57-60
Labrie, Roger P(aul) 1952- 113
Labroca, Mario 1897(?)-1973 Obituary 41-44R
Labus, Marta Haake 1943- 109
Labuta, Joseph A(nthony) 1931- 57-60
Labuz, Ronald M. 1953- 123
Labys, Walter C(arl) 1937- CANR-34
Earlier sketch in CA 73-76
La Camera, Anthony
1914(?)-1984 Obituary 114
Lacan, Jacques (Marie Emile) 1901-1981 121
Obituary 104
LaCapra, Dominick 1939- CANR-28
Earlier sketch in CA 109
La Capria, Raffaele 1922- CANR-4
Earlier sketch in CA 9-12R
Lacarriere, Jacques 1925- Brief entry 125
La Casce, Steward 1935- 37-40R
Laccetti, (Silvio) Richard 1941- CANR-13
Earlier sketch in CA 37-40R
Lace, O(live) Jessie 1906- 17-20R
Lacerda, Carlos 1914-1977 Obituary 69-72
Lacey, A(lan) R(obert) 1926- 112
Lacey, Archie L(ouis) 1923- 9-12R
Lacey, Douglas R(aymond) 1913-1973 ....29-32R
Obituary 134
Lacey, Elizabeth A. 1954- 132
Lacey, Jeannette F. 77-80
Lacey, John
See Alexander, Boyd
Lacey, Louise 1940- 81-84
Lacey, Nicola 1958- 130
Lacey, Paul A. 1934- 41-44R
Lacey, Peter 1929- 21-24R
Lacey, Robert 1944- CANR-16
Earlier sketch in CA 33-36R
Lacey, W(alter) K(irkpatrick) 1921- CANR-11
Earlier sketch in CA 25-28R
Lach, Donald F(rederick) 1917- 102
La Chapelle, Mary 1955- 132
La Charite, Virginia Anding 1937- 29-32R
Lachenbruch, David 1921- 89-92
Lachenmeyer, Charles W(illiam) 1943- 105
Lachmann, Frank M(ichael) 1929- 103
Lachs, John 1934- 21-24R
Lack, David Lambert 1910-1973 ....CANR-4
Obituary 89-92
Earlier sketch in CA 5-8R
Lackey, Douglas Paul 1945- 103
Lackey, Mercedes R. 1950- 126
Lackmann, Ron(ald) 1934- CANR-13
Earlier sketch in CA 29-32R
Lackner, Stephan 1910- CANR-15
Earlier sketch in CA 29-32R
Lacks, Cecilia 1945- 69-72
Lacks, Cissy
See Lacks, Cecilia
Lacks, Roslyn 1933- 102
La Clair, Earl E. 1916- 21-24R
La Claustra, Vera Berneicia (Derrick)
1903- 53-56
LaCocque, Andre (Marie) 1927- CANR-31
Earlier sketch in CA 112
Lacocque, Pierre-Emmanuel 1952- 112
La Colere, Francois
See Aragon, Louis
Lacolere, Francois
See Aragon, Louis
La Colere, Francois
See Aragon, Louis
Lacolere, Francois
See Aragon, Louis
Lacombe, Gabriel
1905(?)-1973 Obituary 37-40R
Lacoste, Paul 1923- CANR-1
Earlier sketch in CA 45-48
Lacouture, Jean Marie Gerard 1921- 101
Lacretelle, Jacques de 1888-1985 ....DLB 65
Lacroix, Louise
See Swift, Helen C(ecilia)
LaCroix, Mary 1937- CANR-22
Earlier sketch in CA 106
Lacroix, Ramon
See McKeag, Ernest L(ionel)
LaCrosse, E. Robert 1937- 33-36R
Lacy, A(lexander) D(acre) 1894-1969 ....CAP-2
Earlier sketch in CA 25-28
Lacy, Charles
See Hippisley Coxe, Antony D(acres)
Lacy, Creighton (Boutelle) 1919- 13-16R
Lacy, Dan (Mabry) 1914- 37-40R
Lacy, Donald Charles 1933- 105
Lacy, Eric Russell 1933- 17-20R
Lacy, Gene M(elvin) 1934- 53-56
Lacy, Gerald M(orris) 1940- 77-80
Lacy, Leslie Alexander 1937- 33-36R
See also SATA 6
Lacy, Mary Lou (Pannill) 1914- 17-20R
Lacy, Norris J(oiner) 1940- CANR-23
Earlier sketches in CA 61-64, CANR-8
Ladany, L.
See Ladany, Laszlo
Ladany, Laszlo 1914-1990 Obituary 132
Ladas, Alice Kahn 129
Ladas, Gerasimos 1937- 53-56
Ladas, Stephen P(ericles) 1898-1976 102
Ladd, Brian 1957- 137
Ladd, Bruce 1936- 25-28R
Ladd, Edward T(aylor) 1918-1973 ....CANR-4
Earlier sketch in CA 5-8R
Ladd, Everett Carll Jr. 1937- CANR-11
Earlier sketch in CA 25-28R
Ladd, George E(ldon) 1911- CANR-5
Earlier sketch in CA 5-8R
Ladd, Helen F. 1945- 111
Ladd, John 1917- 81-84
Ladd, Joseph Brown 1764-1786 ....DLB 37
Ladd, Veronica
See Miner, Jane Claypool
Ladenson, Alex 1907- 17-20R
Ladenson, Robert Franklin 1943- 113
Lader, Lawrence 1919- CANR-2
Earlier sketch in CA 1-4R
See also SATA 6
Laderman, Carol (C.) 121
La Deshabilleuse
See Simenon, Georges (Jacques Christian)
Ladman, Jerry R. 1935- 128
Ladner, Joyce A(nn) 1943- 124
Brief entry 122
See also BW
Ladner, Kurt
See DeMille, Nelson
Ladner, Mildred D. 1918- 97-100
Lado, Robert 1915- CANR-7
Earlier sketch in CA 9-12R
Ladurie, Emmanuel Le Roy
See Le Roy Ladurie, Emmanuel
Lady, A
See Taylor, Ann
Lady Gregory
See Gregory, Isabella Augusta (Persse)
Ladyman, Phyllis 103
Lady Mears
See Tempest, Margaret Mary
Lady of Quality, A
See Bagnold, Enid
Lael, Richard L(ee) 1946- 111
Laemmar, Jack W. 1909- 1-4R
Laertes, Joseph
See Saltzman, Joseph
Laestadius, Lars-Levi 1909-1982 Obituary 107
Laeuchli, Samuel 1924- CANR-4
Earlier sketch in CA 5-8R
Laevastu, Taivo 1923- CANR-15
Earlier sketch in CA 41-44R
LaFantasie, Glenn W(arren) 1949- 125
La Farge, Oliver (Hazard Perry)
1901-1963 ....CANR-30
Earlier sketch in CA 81-84
See also DLB 9
See also SATA 19
La Farge, Phyllis 73-76
See also SATA 14
Lafarge, Rene 1902- CAP-2
Earlier sketch in CA 29-32
LaFauci, Horatio M(ichael) 1917- 33-36R
Lafayette, Carlos
See Boiles, Charles Lafayette (Jr.)
Lafayette, Rene
See Hubbard, L(afayette) Ron(ald)
LaFeber, Walter (Fredrick) 1933- CANR-5
Earlier sketch in CA 9-12R
Laffal, Julius 1920- 49-52
Laffan, Kevin (Barry) 1922- 37-40R
Lafferty, Perry (Francis) 1917- CANR-6
Earlier sketch in CA 9-12R
Lafferty, R(aphael) A(loysius) 1914- CANR-32
Earlier sketches in CA 57-60, CANR-12
See also DLB 8
Laffin, John (Alfred Charles) 1922- CANR-23
Earlier sketches in CA 53-56, CANR-7
See also SATA 31
Laffont, Jean-Pierre 1935- 115
Laffrado, Laura 1959- 138
LaFitte, Pat Chew 1950- 107
LaFleur, William R. 1936- 115
La Follette, Marcel (Evelyn) Chotkowski
1944- 114
La Follette, Suzanne
1894(?)-1983 Obituary 109
LaFontaine, Blanche
See Schwalberg, Carol(yn Ernestine Stein)
LaFontaine, Charles Vivian 1936- 57-60
La Fontaine, Jean de 1621-1695 ....MAICYA
See also SATA 18
Lafore, Laurence Davis 1917-1985 ....13-16R
Obituary 118
LaForte, Robert Sherman 1933- 57-60
La Fountaine, George 1934- CANR-7
Earlier sketch in CA 57-60
Lafourcade, Bernard 1934-1986 115
Obituary 118
LaFraniere, Sharon 1955- 136
La Freniere, (B. Marie) Celine 1950- 132
Lafreniere, Gyslaine F. 1948- 116
Lagace, Louise Lambert
See Lambert-Lagace, Louise
LaGattuta, Margo 1942- CANR-38
Earlier sketch in CA 115
Lagemann, Ellen Condliffe 1945- 128
Lager, Marilyn 1939- 121
See also SATA 52
Lagercrantz, Rose (Elsa) 1947- 108
See also SATA 39
Lagerkvist, Paer (Fabian) 1891-1974 85-88
Obituary 49-52
See also CLC 7, 10, 13, 54
See also MTCW
Lagerkvist, Par
See Lagerkvist, Paer (Fabian)
Lagerloef, Selma (Ottiliana Lovisa)
1858-1940 Brief entry 108
See also Lagerlof, Selma (Ottiliana Lovisa)
See also CLR 7
See also SATA 15
See also TCLC 4, 36
Lagerlof, Selma (Ottiliana Lovisa)
See Lagerloef, Selma (Ottiliana Lovisa)
See also CLR 7
See also SATA 15
Lagerwall, Edna 45-48
Lagerwerff, Ellen Best 1919- 85-88
Lagevi, Bo
See Blom, Karl Arne
Lagneau-Kesteloot, Lilyan
See Kesteloot, Lilyan
Lago, Mary M(cClelland) 1919- CANR-15
Earlier sketch in CA 85-88
LaGrand, Louis E. 1935- 33-36R
La Grange, Henry Louis De
See De La Grange, Henry Louis
LaGuardia, David M(ichael) 1943- 118
La Guardia, Fiorello Henry
1882-1947 Brief entry 120
Laguerre, Andre 1915(?)-1979 97-100
Obituary 85-88
Laguerre, Enrique A(rturo) 1906- 131
See also HW
Laguerre, Michel S(aturnin) 1945- 115
La Guma, (Justin) Alex(ander)
1925-1985 ....CANR-25
Obituary 118
Earlier sketch in CA 49-52
See also BW
See also CLC 19
See also DLB 117
See also MTCW
La Gumina, Salvatore John 1928- 77-80
LaHaye, Tim 1926- CANR-9
Earlier sketch in CA 65-68
Lahee, Frederic Henry 1884-1968 ....CAP-2
Earlier sketch in CA 19-20
Lahey, Edwin A(loysius)
1902-1969 Obituary 115
Lahontan, Louis-Armand de Lom d'Arce Baron
1666-1715(?) ....DLB 99
LaHood, Marvin J(ohn) 1933- CANR-10
Earlier sketch in CA 25-28R
Lahr, John (Henry) 1941- CANR-21
Earlier sketch in CA 25-28R
Lahr, Raymond M(errill)
1914-1973 Obituary 41-44R
Lahue, Kalton C. 1934- CANR-7
Earlier sketch in CA 13-16R
Lai, David Chuenyan 1937- 138
Lai, T'ien-Ch'ang 1921- CANR-11
Earlier sketch in CA 69-72
Lai, Violet Lau 1916- 119
Laidlaw, A. K.
See Grieve, C(hristopher) M(urray)
Laidlaw, Harry Hyde Jr. 1907- 5-8R
Laidlaw, Marc 1960- 119
Laidlaw, Ross 1931- 118
Laidlaw, W(illiam) A(llison)
1898-1983 Obituary 109
Laidler, Harry W(ellington) 1884-1970 ....CANR-5
Obituary 29-32R
Earlier sketch in CA 5-8R
Laiken, Deirdre S(usan) 1948- 104
See also SATA 40, 48
Laikin, Paul 1927- 5-8R
Laimgruber, Monika 1946- ....SATA 11
Laine, Barry 1951-1987 Obituary 123
Laine, Gloria
See Hanna, David
Lainez, Manuel Mujica
See Mujica Lainez, Manuel
See also HW
Laing, Alastair 1944- 127
Laing, Alexander (Kinnan) 1903-1976 ....CANR-4
Obituary 65-68
Earlier sketch in CA 5-8R
Laing, Anne C.
See Schachterle, Nancy (Lange)
Laing, Frederick 105
Laing, Jennifer 1948- 106

Laing, Lloyd (Robert) 1944- CANR-5
Earlier sketch in CA 53-56
Laing, Martha
See Celestino, Martha Laing
Laing, R(onald) D(avid) 1927-1989 .... CANR-34
Obituary 129
Earlier sketch in CA 107
See also MTCW
Lair, Jacqueline Carey 1930- 119
Lair, Jess K. 1926- CANR-14
Earlier sketch in CA 41-44R
Lair, Robert L(eland) 1932- 53-56
Laird, Bailey
See Goodwin, Richard N(aradhof)
Laird, Betty A(nn) 1925- CANR-33
Earlier sketches in CA 33-36R, CANR-15
Laird, Carobeth 1895-1983 .... CANR-8
Obituary 110
Earlier sketch in CA 61-64
See also DLBY 82
Laird, Charlton G(rant) 1901- 13-16R
Laird, David
See Laird, W(ilbur) David Jr.
Laird, Donald A(nderson) 1897-1969 .... 5-8R
Obituary 25-28R
Laird, Dorothy
See Carr, Dorothy Stevenson Laird
Laird, Dugan 1920- CANR-12
Earlier sketch in CA 73-76
Laird, Eleanor Childs 1908- 73-76
Laird, Elizabeth (Mary Risk) 1943- 128
Laird, Helen 1933- 122
Laird, J(ohn) T(udor) 1921- 69-72
Laird, Jean E(louise) 1930- CANR-6
Earlier sketch in CA 9-12R
See also SATA 38
Laird, Melvin R(obert) 1922- 65-68
Laird, Robbin F. 1946- 113
Laird, Roy D(ean) 1925- CANR-33
Earlier sketches in CA 33-36R, CANR-15
Laird, W(ilbur) David Jr. 1937- 113
Lait, Robert 1921- CANR-2
Earlier sketch in CA 1-4R
Laite, Gordon 1925- .... SATA 31
Laite, William Edward Jr. 1932- 37-40R
Laithwaite, Eric Roberts 1921- 103
Laitin, Joseph 1914- 136
Laitin, Ken 1963- 102
Laitin, Lindy 1968- 108
Laitin, Steve 1965- 102
Lajoie, Antoine Gerin 1824-1882 .... DLB 99
Lajolo, Davide 1913(?)-1984 Obituary 113
Lakatos, Imre 1922-1974 Obituary 116
Lake, Alice (Dannenberg)
1916-1990 Obituary 131
Lake, Carolyn 1932- 25-28R
Lake, David J. 1929- CANR-10
Earlier sketch in CA 65-68
Lake, Frank 1914-1982 .... CANR-10
Earlier sketch in CA 21-24R
Lake, Harriet
See Taylor, Paula (Wright)
Lake, Kenneth R(obert) 1931- CANR-5
Earlier sketch in CA 53-56
Lakeland, Paul 1946- 137
Lakeman, Enid 1903- 107
Laken, Bob
See Holman, Robert
Laker, Rosalind
See Ovstedal, Barbara
Lakey, George (Russell) 1937- CANR-7
Earlier sketch in CA 17-20R
Lakhu
See Khubchandani, Lachman M(ulchand)
Lakin, Martin 1925- 73-76
Laklan, Carli 1907- CANR-1
Earlier sketch in CA 1-4R
See also SATA 5
Lakoff, George 1941- CANR-27
Earlier sketch in CA 29-32R
Lakoff, Robin Tolmach 1942- CANR-27
Earlier sketch in CA 103
Lakoff, Sanford A(llan) 1931- CANR-1
Earlier sketch in CA 1-4R
Lakritz, Esther Himmelman 1928- 1-4R
Lal, Gobind Behari 1890(?)-1982 Obituary 106
Lal, Kishori Saran 1920- 21-24R
Lal, P. 1929- CANR-9
Earlier sketch in CA 13-16R
Laliberte, Norman 1925- 104
Lalicki, Barbara 119
See also SATA 61
Lalley, Joseph M. 1897(?)-1980 Obituary 102
Lalli, Judy 1949- 110
Lally, Michael (David) 1942- CANR-32
Earlier sketches in CA 77-80, CANR-14
La Londe, Bernard J. 1933- 33-36R
Lalonde, Michele 1937- .... DLB 60
Lalonde, Robert 1947- 109
Lalumia, Joseph 1916- 21-24R
Lam, Charlotte (Dawson) 1924- 37-40R
Lam, Truong Buu 1933- 25-28R
Laman, Russell 1907- CAP-1
Earlier sketch in CA 9-10
LaMancusa, Katherine C.
See Koop, Katherine C.
Lamanna, Dolores B. 1930-1980 .... 9-12R
Obituary 97-100
Lamantia, Philip 1927- 117
Brief entry 111
See also DLB 16
Lamar, Howard R(oberts) 1923- 17-20R
Lamar, Jake 1961- 137
Lamar, Lavoisier 1907- 5-8R
Lamar, Nedra Newkirk 69-72
Lamarque, Peter 1948- 120
LaMarre, Virgil E. 1910(?)-1985 Obituary 115
LaMarsh, Judy
See LaMarsh, Julia Verlyn
LaMarsh, Julia Verlyn 1924-1980 .... CANR-13
Obituary 105
Earlier sketch in CA 29-32R
Lamb, Andrew (Martin) 1942- 137
Lamb, Antonia 1943- 21-24R
Lamb, Beatrice Pitney 1904- 5-8R
See also SATA 21
Lamb, Charles Bentall 1914-1981 102
Obituary 105
Lamb, Charles M(oody) 1945- 124
Lamb, Charles 1775-1834 .... CDBLB 1789-1832
See also DLB 93, 107
See also SATA 17
See also WLC
Lamb, Charlotte
See Holland, Sheila
Lamb, Dana S(torrs) 1900-1986 134
Obituary 120
Lamb, David 1940- 110
Lamb, Edward 1902-1987 108
Obituary 122
Lamb, Eleanor 1917- 69-72
Lamb, Elizabeth Searle 1917- 33-36R
See also SATA 31
Lamb, F(rank) Bruce 1913- 33-36R
Lamb, G(eoffrey) F(rederick) CANR-19
Earlier sketches in CA 53-56, CANR-4
See also SATA 10
Lamb, H(ubert) H(orace) 1913- 21-24R
Lamb, Harold (Albert) 1892-1962 101
Obituary 89-92
See also SATA 53
Lamb, Helen B.
See Lamont, Helen Lamb
Lamb, Hugh 1946- CANR-1
Earlier sketch in CA 49-52
Lamb, James B(arrett) 1919- 133
Lamb, Karl A(llen) 1933- CANR-18
Earlier sketches in CA 5-8R, CANR-3
Lamb, Lady Caroline 1785-1828 .... DLB 116
Lamb, Lawrence E(dward) 1926- 97-100
Lamb, Lynton (Harold) 1907-1977 .... CANR-4
Earlier sketch in CA 1-4R
See also SATA 10
Lamb, Marion M(inerva) 1905- 5-8R
Lamb, Mary Ann 1764-1847 .... SATA 17
Lamb, Patricia Frazer 1931- 126
Lamb, Robert (Boyden) 1941- CANR-35
Earlier sketch in CA 29-32R
See also SATA 13
Lamb, Ruth S(tanton) CANR-21
Earlier sketch in CA 45-48
Lamb, Sydney M(acDonald) 1929- 33-36R
Lamb, William
See Jameson, (Margaret) Storm
Lamb, William Kaye 1904- 81-84
Lambasa, Frank Slavko
1921-1987 Obituary 123
Lambdin, William 1936- 102
Lambec, Zoltan
See Kimbro, John M.
Lamberg, Robert F(elix) 1929- 65-68
Lamberg-Karlovsky, Clifford Charles
1937- 85-88
Lambert, Angela Maria 1940- 138
Lambert, B. Geraldine 1922- 41-44R
Lambert, Betty
See Lambert, Elizabeth (Minnie)
See also DLB 60
Lambert, Byron Cecil 1923- 97-100
Lambert, Darwin (Seymour) 1916- CANR-2
Earlier sketch in CA 5-8R
Lambert, David (Compton) 1932- 122
See also SATA 49
Lambert, Derek 1929- CANR-17
Earlier sketch in CA 25-28R
Lambert, Eleanor 102
Lambert, Elisabeth
See Ortiz, Elisabeth Lambert
Lambert, Elizabeth (Minnie) 1933-1983 102
See also Lambert, Betty
Lambert, Eric 1918-1966 .... CAP-1
Earlier sketch in CA 13-14
Lambert, Gavin 1924- CANR-1
Earlier sketch in CA 1-4R
Lambert, Hazel Margaret 1-4R
Lambert, Herbert H. 1929- 69-72
Lambert, J(ack) W(alter) 1917-1986 108
Obituary 120
Lambert, Jacques Edward 1901- CAP-2
Earlier sketch in CA 23-24
Lambert, Janet 1895(?)-1973 Obituary 41-44R
See also SATA 25
Lambert, John (Robin) 1936- CANR-8
Earlier sketch in CA 5-8R
Lambert, Mark 1942- 73-76
Lambert, Ronald Dick 1936- 108
Lambert, Roy Eugene 1918- 37-40R
Lambert, Royston James
1932-1982 Obituary 108
Lambert, Saul 1928- 106
See also SATA 23
Lambert, Sheila 1926- 85-88
Lambert, William Wilson 1919- 9-12R
Lamberti, Marjorie 1937- 103
Lambert-Lagace, Louise 1941- CANR-29
Earlier sketch in CA 111
Lamberton, Donald McLean 1927- 103
Lamberts, J(acob) J. 1910- 37-40R
Lambeth, Edmund Barry 1932- 123
Lambi, Ivo Nikolai 1931- 132
Lambley, Peter 1946- 109
Lambo, Thomas Adeoye 1923- 29-32R
Lamborn, LeRoy L(eslie) 1937- 21-24R
Lambot, Isobel 1926- 73-76
Lambourne, John
See Lamburn, John Battersby Crompton
Lambrick, Hugh Trevor 1904- CANR-6
Earlier sketch in CA 9-12R
Lambright, William Henry 1939- 103
Lambro, Donald (Joseph) 1940- CANR-25
Earlier sketches in CA 57-60, CANR-7
Lambton, Anne (Patricia St. Clair) 1918- 85-88
Lamburn, John Battersby Crompton
1893- CAP-1
Earlier sketch in CA 9-10
Lamburn, Richmal Crompton 1890-1969 .... CAP-1
Obituary 25-28R
Earlier sketch in CA 9-10
See also SATA 5
Lame Deer 1895(?)-1976 Obituary 69-72
Lamensdorf, Leonard 1930- 29-32R
La Meri
See Hughes, Russell Meriwether
L'Ami, Charles Ernest 1896- 102
Lamirande, Emilien 1926- CANR-8
Earlier sketch in CA 17-20R
Lamis, Alexander P. 1946- 125
Lamm, Joyce 1933- 57-60
Lamm, Maurice 1930- 17-20R
Lamm, Norman 1927- CANR-28
Earlier sketch in CA 49-52
Lamme, Linda Leonard 1942- 102
Lamming, George (William) 1927- CANR-26
Earlier sketch in CA 85-88
See also BLC 2
See also BW
See also CLC 2, 4, 66
See also MTCW
Lamming, R. M. 1949- 125
Brief entry 119
Lamon, Lester C(rawford) 1942- 89-92
Lamond, Henry George
1885-1969 Obituary 25-28R
Lamont, Corliss 1902- CANR-11
Earlier sketch in CA 13-16R
Lamont, Douglas Felix 1937- 41-44R
Lamont, Helen Lamb
1906(?)-1975 Obituary 61-64
Lamont, Lansing 1930- CANR-11
Earlier sketch in CA 17-20R
Lamont, Marianne
See Rundle, Anne
Lamont, N. B.
See Barnitt, Nedda Lemmon
Lamont, Nedda
See Barnitt, Nedda Lemmon
Lamont, Rosette C(lementine) 33-36R
Lamont, William D(awson) 1901-1982 .... CAP-1
Obituary 108
Earlier sketch in CA 11-12
Lamont-Brown, Raymond 1939- CANR-32
Earlier sketches in CA 73-76, CANR-14
Lamorisse, Albert (Emmanuel) 1922-1970 101
See also SATA 23
Lamott, Kenneth (Church) 1923-1979 .... 25-28R
Obituary 89-92
Lamotte, Etienne 1904(?)-1983 Obituary 109
Lamour, Dorothy
See Kaumeyer, Dorothy
L'Amour, Louis (Dearborn)
1908-1988 .... CANR-25
Obituary 125
Earlier sketches in CA 1-4R, CANR-3
See also AITN 2
See also BEST 89:2
See also CLC 25, 55
See also DLBY 80
See also MTCW
Lamparski, Richard 21-24R
Lampe, David 1923- CANR-1
Earlier sketch in CA 1-4R
Lampedusa, Giuseppe (Tomasi) di
See Tomasi di Lampedusa, Giuseppe
See also TCLC 13
Lampell, Millard 1919- 9-12R
Lampert, Emily 1951- 121
See also SATA 49, 52
Lamphere, Louise (Anne) 1940- 89-92
Lampitt, Dinah 1937- 132
Lampkin, William R(obert) 1932- 106
Lampl, Paul 1915- Brief entry 104
Lamplugh, Lois 1921- CANR-24
Earlier sketches in CA 13-16R, CANR-9
See also SATA 17
Lampman, Archibald 1861-1899 .... DLB 92
Lampman, Ben Hur 1886-1954 Brief entry 111
Lampman, Evelyn Sibley 1907-1980 .... CANR-11
Obituary 101
Earlier sketch in CA 13-16R
See also SATA 4, 23
Lampman, Robert James 1920- 103
Lampo, Hubert 1920- Brief entry 105
Lamport, Felicia 1916- 1-4R
Lamppa, William R(ussell) 1928- 53-56
Lamprecht, Sterling P(ower) 1890-1973 .... CAP-1
Earlier sketch in CA 17-18
Lamprey, Louise 1869-1951 Brief entry 117
See also YABC 2
Lampson, Robin 1900-1978 Obituary 77-80
Lampton, Chris
See Lampton, Christopher F.
Lampton, Christopher
See Lampton, Christopher F.
Lampton, Christopher .... SATA 67
Lampton, Christopher F. CANR-37
Earlier sketch in CA 125
See also SATA 47
Lamsa, George M(amishisho)
1892-1975 .... CANR-9
Earlier sketches in CAP-2, CA 23-24
Lamson, Peggy 1912- 25-28R
La Mure, Pierre 1909-1976 Obituary 104
Lan, David 1952- CANR-24
Earlier sketch in CA 97-100
Lana, Robert E(dward) 1932- 33-36R
Lancaster, Bob 1943- 111
Lancaster, Bruce 1896-1963 .... CAP-1
Earlier sketch in CA 9-10
See also CLC 36
See also SATA 9
Lancaster, Burt(on Stephen) 1913- 122
Brief entry 116
Lancaster, Clay 1917- CANR-8
Earlier sketch in CA 5-8R
Lancaster, David
See Heald, Tim(othy Villiers)
Lancaster, Evelyn
See Sizemore, Chris(tine) Costner
Lancaster, F. Donald
See Fredriksson, Don
Lancaster, F(rederick) Wilfrid 1933- CANR-19
Earlier sketches in CA 53-56, CANR-4
Lancaster, Kelvin (John) 1924- 33-36R
Lancaster, Lydia
See Meaker, Eloise
Lancaster, Marie-Jaqueline 1922- 25-28R
Lancaster, Matthew 1973(?)-1983 Obituary 117
See also SATA 45
Lancaster, Osbert 1908-1986 105
Obituary 119
Lancaster, Otis Ewing 1909- 103
Lancaster, Richard 21-24R
Lancaster, Sheila
See Holland, Sheila
Lancaster-Brown, Peter 1927- CANR-19
Earlier sketches in CA 53-56, CANR-4
Lance, Derek (Paul) 1932- CANR-9
Earlier sketch in CA 13-16R
Lance, H(ubert) Darrell 1935- 115
Lance, James Waldo 1926- 65-68
Lance, Kathryn 1943- 122
Lance, LaBelle D(avid) 1931- 81-84
Lance, Leslie
See Swatridge, Charles (John)
Lancer, Jack CANR-27
Earlier sketch in CAP-2
Lanchester, Elsa 1902-1986 134
Obituary 121
Lanciano, Claude O(lwen) Jr. 1922- CANR-1
Earlier sketch in CA 45-48
Lancour, Gene
See Fisher, Gene L(ouis)
Lancour, (Adlore) Harold 1908-1981 .... 21-24R
Obituary 105
Lancy, David F(alcon) 1945- 110
Land
See Landry, Robert John
Land, Aubrey C(hristian) 1912- 41-44R
Land, Barbara (Neblett) 1923- 81-84
See also SATA 16
Land, (Reginald) Brian 1927- 101
Land, George T(homas) Lock 1933- 53-56
Land, Jane
See Borland, Kathryn Kilby
and Speicher, Helen Ross S(mith)
Land, Myrick (Ebben) 1922- CANR-11
Earlier sketch in CA 13-16R
See also SATA 15
Land, Ross
See Borland, Kathryn Kilby
and Speicher, Helen Ross S(mith)
Landar, Herbert (Jay) 1927- 33-36R
Landau, Elaine 1948- CANR-5
Earlier sketch in CA 53-56
See also SATA 10
Landau, Genevieve Millet 1927- 107
Landau, Jacob M. 1924- CANR-24
Earlier sketches in CA 17-20R, CANR-8
Landau, Jacob 1917- .... SATA 38
Landau, Lev Davidovich
1908-1968 Obituary 113
Landau, Mark Alexandrovich
See Aldanov, Mark (Alexandrovich)
Landau, Martin 1921- 45-48
Landau, Rom 1899-1974 .... CANR-4
Obituary 49-52
Earlier sketch in CA 1-4R
Landau, Saul (I.) 1936- 130
Landau, Sidney I(van) 1933- CANR-7
Earlier sketch in CA 57-60
Landau, Sol 1920- CANR-31
Earlier sketch in CA 49-52
Landau-Aldanov, Mark Alexandrovich
See Aldanov, Mark (Alexandrovich)
Landauer, Carl 1891-1983 .... CANR-21
Earlier sketch in CA 1-4R
Landauer, Jerry Gerd 1932-1981 109
Obituary 103
Lande, Henry F(rank) 1920- 29-32R
Lande, Lawrence (Montague) 1906- 105
Lande, Nathaniel 1939- 104
Landeck, Beatrice 1904- 73-76
See also SATA 15
Landecker, Manfred 1929- 29-32R
Landeen, William M. 1891-1982 Obituary 109
Landeira, Ricardo L(opez) 1917- 81-84
Landen, Robert Geran 1930- 21-24R
Lander, Ernest McPherson Jr. 1915- CANR-4
Earlier sketch in CA 1-4R
Lander, Jack Robert 1921- 101
Lander, Jeannette 1931- 33-36R
Lander, Louise 1938- 85-88
Lander, Mamie Stubbs
1891(?)-1975 Obituary 53-56
Landers, Ann
See Lederer, Esther Pauline
Landers, Gunnard W(illiam) 1944- 93-96

Landes, David S(aul) 1924- ...CANR-22
Earlier sketch in CA 103
Landes, Marie Gisele
See Landes-Fuss, Marie-Gisele
Landes, Ruth 1908-1991 ...CAP-2
Obituary ...133
Earlier sketch in CA 29-32
Landes, Sonia 1925- ...CANR-22
Earlier sketch in CA 104
Landes-Fuss, Marie-Gisele 1936- ...129
Landesman, Charles 1932- ...85-88
Landesman, Fran(ces) 1927- ...127
Brief entry ...120
See also DLB 16
Landesman, Jay (Irving) 1919- ...127
Brief entry ...118
See also DLB 16
Landgren, Marchal E.
1907(?)-1983 Obituary ...109
Landi, Ferruccio Rossi
See Rossi-Landi, Ferruccio
Landin, Les 1923- ...5-8R
See also SATA 2
Landis, Benson Y. 1897-1966 ...CAP-1
Earlier sketch in CA 13-14
Landis, Dennis Channing 1947- ...110
Landis, Fred S(imon) 1943- ...107
Landis, J(ames) D(avid) 1942- ...126
See also SATA 52, 60
Landis, Jessie Royce
1904-1972 Obituary ...33-36R
Landis, John 1950- ...122
Brief entry ...112
See also CLC 26
Landis, Judson R(ichard) 1935- ...33-36R
Landis, Lincoln 1922- ...45-48
Landis, Paul H(enry) 1901- ...CANR-5
Earlier sketch in CA 5-8R
Landman, David 1917- ...CANR-11
Earlier sketch in CA 69-72
Lando, Barry Mitchell 1939- ...77-80
Landolfi, Tommaso 1908-1979 ...127
Obituary ...117
See also CLC 11, 49
Landon, Donald D. 1930- ...25-28R
Landon, H(oward) C(handler) Robbins
1926- ...CANR-34
Earlier sketches in CA 77-80, CANR-13
Landon, Letitia Elizabeth 1802-1838 ... DLB 96
Landon, Lucinda 1950- ...123
See also SATA 51, 56
Landon, Margaret (Dorothea Mortenson)
1903- ... CAP-1
Earlier sketch in CA 13-14
See also SATA 50
Landon, Michael de L(aval) 1935- ...CANR-30
Earlier sketch in CA 29-32R
Landor, Walter Savage 1775-1864 ... DLB 93, 107
Landorf, Joyce 1932- ...124
See also AITN 1
Landow, George P(aul) 1940- ...CANR-19
Earlier sketches in CA 53-56, CANR-4
Landowska, Wanda (Aleksandra)
1879-1959 Brief entry ...122
Landreth, Bill 1964- ...138
Landreth, Catherine 1899- ...77-80
Landrith, Harold Fochone 1919- ...103
Landrum, Phil 1939- ...81-84
Landry, Hilton (James) 1924- ...13-16R
Landry, Napoleon-P. 1884-1956 ... DLB 92
Landry, Robert John 1903-1991 ...69-72
Obituary ...134
Landsberg, Hans H. 1913- ...CANR-10
Earlier sketch in CA 17-20R
Landsberg, Helmut Erich 1906-1985 ...107
Obituary ...118
Landsberg, Michele 1939- ...123
Landsbergis, Algirdas J. 1924- ...CANR-13
Earlier sketch in CA 33-36R
Landsburg, Alan William 1933- ...103
Landsburg, Sally (Breit) 1933- ...57-60
Landshoff, Fritz Helmut
1901-1988 Obituary ...125
Landshoff, Ursula 1908- ...29-32R
See also SATA 13
Landsman, Ned C. 1951- ...126
Landstrom, Bjorn O(lof) 1917- ...13-16R
Landsverk, O(le) G(odfred) 1901- ...61-64
Landvater, Dorothy 1927- ...103
Landwehr, Arthur J. II 1934- ...37-40R
Landwirth, Heinz 1927- ...CANR-7
Earlier sketch in CA 9-12R
See also Lind, Jakov
Landy, David 1917- ...77-80
Landy, Eugene E(llsworth) 1934- ...41-44R
Landy, John (Michael) 1930- ...128
Landynski, Jacob W. 1930- ...21-24R
Lane, Allen 1902-1970 Obituary ...29-32R
Lane, Ann J(udith) 1931- ...126
Brief entry ...110
Lane, Anthony 1916- ...13-16R
Lane, Arthur (Ernest) 1937- ...41-44R
Lane, Carl D(aniel) 1899- ...105
Lane, Carolyn 1926- ...CANR-12
Earlier sketch in CA 29-32R
See also SATA 10
Lane, Charles
See Gatti, Arthur Gerard
Lane, Charles 1800-1870 ... DLB 1
Lane, David (Stuart) ...CANR-39
Earlier sketches in CA 29-32R, CANR-17
Lane, E(ugene Numa) 1936- ...37-40R
Lane, Frank Walter 1908- ...9-12R
Lane, Frederic C(hapin) 1900-1984 ...105
Obituary ...114
Lane, Gary 1943- ...37-40R
Lane, Hana Umlauf 1946- ...118
Lane, Harlan (Lawson) 1936- ...126
Brief entry ...111
Lane, Helen R(uth) ...CANR-2
Earlier sketch in CA 45-48
Lane, Helen 1920- ...123
Lane, Irving M(ark) 1944- ...53-56
Lane, Jack C(onstant) 1932- ...CANR-4
Earlier sketch in CA 53-56
Lane, James B(uchanan) 1942- ...93-96
Lane, Jane
See Dakers, Elaine Kidner
Lane, Jan-Erik 1946- ...138
Lane, Jerry
See Martin, Patricia Miles
Lane, John (Richard) 1932- ...106
See also SATA 15
Lane, Laura Gordon 1913- ...102
Lane, Laurence W. 1890-1967 ... DLB 91
Lane, M(illicent) Travis 1934- ...112
See also DLB 60
Lane, Marc J(ay) 1946- ...CANR-21
Earlier sketch in CA 105
Lane, Margaret 1907- ...CANR-29
Earlier sketches in CA 25-28R, CANR-13
See also SATA 38, 65
Lane, Mark 1927- ...CANR-21
Earlier sketch in CA 61-64
Lane, Mary (Lois) B(eauchamp) 1911- ...CANR-9
Earlier sketch in CA 13-16R
Lane, Mary D.
See Delaney, Mary Murray
Lane, Michael (John) 1941- ...85-88
Lane, Patrick 1939- ...97-100
See also CLC 25
See also DLB 53
Lane, Pinkie Gordon 1923- ...CANR-25
Earlier sketch in CA 41-44R
See also BW
See also DLB 41
Lane, Raymond A.
1894(?)-1974 Obituary ...53-56
Lane, Richard 1926- ...CANR-10
Earlier sketch in CA 21-24R
Lane, Robert E(dwards) 1917- ...CANR-6
Earlier sketch in CA 1-4R
Lane, Roger 1934- ...105
Lane, Ronnie M(ack) 1949- ...41-44R
Lane, Rose Wilder 1887-1968 ...102
See also SATA 28, 29
Lane, Roumelia
See Green, Kay
Lane, Sherry
See Smith, Richard Rein
Lane, Sylvia 1916- ...CANR-8
Earlier sketch in CA 5-8R
Lane, Thomas A(lphonsus) 1906-1975 ...13-16R
Obituary ...125
Lane, Wheaton J. 1902-1983 Obituary ...111
Lane, William G(uerrant) 1919- ...25-28R
Lane, William L(ister) 1931- ...CANR-27
Earlier sketch in CA 29-32R
Lane, Yoti ...1-4R
Lanegran, David A(ndrew) 1941- ...CANR-37
Earlier sketches in CA 89-92, CANR-16
Lanes, Selma Gordon 1929- ...25-28R
See also SATA 3
Laney, Al 1896- ...108
See also DLB 4
Laney, J(ohn) Carl 1948- ...CANR-35
Earlier sketch in CA 114
Laney, James Thomas 1927- ...103
Lanford, H(orace) W(haley) 1919- ...41-44R
Lang, Allen Kim 1928- ...17-20R
Lang, Andrew 1844-1912 ...137
Brief entry ...114
See also DLB 98
See also MAICYA
See also SATA 16
See also TCLC 16
Lang, Barbara 1935- ...9-12R
Lang, Berel 1933- ...CANR-34
Earlier sketches in CA 41-44R, CANR-15
Lang, Daniel 1915-1981 ...CANR-4
Obituary ...105
Earlier sketch in CA 5-8R
Lang, David Marshall 1924-1991 ...CANR-17
Obituary ...134
Earlier sketches in CA 5-8R, CANR-2
Lang, David 1913- ...106
Lang, Derek 1913- ...102
Lang, Frances
See Mantle, Winifred (Langford)
Lang, Fritz 1890-1976 ...CANR-30
Obituary ...69-72
Earlier sketch in CA 77-80
See also CLC 20
Lang, George 1924- ...101
Lang, Gottfried O(tto) 1919- ...45-48
Lang, Grace
See Floren, Lee
Lang, Gregor
See Birren, Faber
Lang, H. Jack 1904- ...115
Lang, Jack (Frederick) 1921- ...5-8R
Lang, Jenifer Harvey 1951- ...138
Lang, Jovian Peter 1919- ...CANR-15
Earlier sketch in CA 41-44R
Lang, King
See Tubb, E(dwin) C(harles)
Lang, Kurt 1924- ...33-36R
Lang, Mabel L(ouise) 1917- ...126
Brief entry ...106
Lang, Martin
See Birren, Faber
Lang, Martin A(ndrew) 1930- ...115
Lang, Maud
See Williams, Claerwen
Lang, Michel (Jules Jean Marcel) 1939- ...129
Lang, Miriam (Milman) 1915- ...5-8R
Lang, Nancy M.
See Mace, Nancy L(awson)
Lang, Ned
See Sheckley, Robert
Lang, Paul Henry 1901-1991 ...103
Obituary ...135
Lang, Robert (Peregrine) 1912- ...41-44R
Lang, Ronald William 1933- ...103
Lang, Rupert
See Turner, E(rnest) S(ackville)
Lang, Susan S. 1950- ...136
See also SATA 68
Lang, T. T.
See Taylor, Theodore
Lang, William Rawson 1909- ...CANR-21
Earlier sketch in CA 103
Langacker, Ronald W(ayne) 1942- ...21-24R
Langan, Ruth Ryan 1937- ...CANR-24
Earlier sketch in CA 107
Langan, Thomas 1929- ...CANR-17
Earlier sketch in CA 1-4R
Langart, Darrell T.
See Garrett, (Gordon) Randall (Phillip)
Langbaum, Robert (Woodrow) 1924- ...CANR-1
Earlier sketch in CA 45-48
Langbein, John H(arriss) 1941- ...124
Langdale, Cecily 1939- ...126
Langdale, Eve
See Craig, E(velyn) Quita
Langdon, Charles 1934- ...77-80
Langdon, Frank C(orriston) 1919- ...21-24R
Langdon, George D(orland) Jr. 1933- ...21-24R
Langdon, Grace 1889- ...1-4R
Langdon, John 1913- ...5-8R
Langdon, Margaret Hoffmann (Storms)
1926- Brief entry ...107
Langdon, Philip 1937- ...109
Langdon, Philip 1947- ...129
Langdon, Robert Adrian 1924- ...CANR-20
Earlier sketch in CA 104
Lange, Dorothea 1895-1965 Obituary ...107
Lange, Gerald 1946- ...69-72
Lange, John
See Crichton, (John) Michael
Lange, John Frederick Jr. 1931- ...CANR-25
Earlier sketches in CA 97-100, CANR-8
Lange, (Leo) Joseph (Jr.) 1932- ...CANR-8
Earlier sketch in CA 17-20R
Lange, Kelly ...89-92
Lange, Martin 1955- ...130
Lange, Oliver (a pseudonym) 1927- ...CANR-23
Earlier sketch in CA 103
Lange, Oskar (Richard)
1904-1965 Obituary ...116
Lange, Suzanne 1945- ...29-32R
See also SATA 5
Lange, (Hermann Walter) Victor 1908- ...9-12R
Langendoen, D(onald) Terence 1939- ...33-36R
Langer, Elinor 1939- ...121
See also CLC 34
Langer, Ellen J(ane) 1947- ...CANR-30
Earlier sketch in CA 49-52
Langer, Erick D. 1955- ...137
Langer, Jonas 1936- ...33-36R
Langer, Lawrence L(ee) 1929- ...CANR-11
Earlier sketch in CA 65-68
Langer, Marshall J. 1928- ...105
Langer, Susanne (Katherina) K(nauth)
1895-1985 ...CANR-34
Obituary ...116
Earlier sketch in CA 41-44R
See also MTCW
Langer, Sydney 1914- ...109
Langer, Thomas Edward 1929- ...5-8R
Langer, Walter Charles 1899-1981 ...102
Obituary ...104
Langer, William L(eonard) 1896-1977 ...CANR-14
Obituary ...73-76
Earlier sketch in CA 29-32R
Langevin, Andre 1927- ... DLB 60
Langevin, Sister Jean Marie 1917- ...53-56
Langford, Alec J. 1926- ...97-100
Langford, David 1953- ...135
Langford, Gary R(aymond) 1947- ...CANR-20
Earlier sketch in CA 103
Langford, George 1939- ...53-56
Langford, Gerald 1911- ...CANR-32
Earlier sketch in CA 1-4R
Langford, James R(ouleau) 1937- ...53-56
Langford, Jane
See Mantle, Winifred (Langford)
Langford, Jerome J.
See Langford, James R(ouleau)
Langford, Thomas Anderson 1929- ...9-12R
Langford, Walter McCarty 1908- ...33-36R
Langgaesser, Elisabeth (Maria)
1899-1950 Brief entry ...121
See also Langgasser, Elisabeth (Maria)
See also DLB 69
Langgasser, Elisabeth (Maria)
See Langgaesser, Elisabeth (Maria)
See also DLB 69
Langguth, A(rthur) J(ohn) 1933- ...CANR-30
Earlier sketch in CA 61-64
Langhoff, Severin Peter Jr.
1910-1987 Obituary ...122
Langholm, Neil
See Bulmer, (Henry) Kenneth
Langhorne, Elizabeth ...49-52
Langhorne, John 1735-1779 ... DLB 109
Langhorne, Richard (Tristan Bailey) 1940- ...122
Langiulli, Nino 1932- ...53-56
Langland, Elizabeth 1948- ...112
Langland, Joseph (Thomas) 1917- ...CANR-8
Earlier sketch in CA 5-8R
Langley, Adria (Locke)
1899(?)-1983 Obituary ...110
Langley, Bob 1936- ...85-88
Langley, Dorothy
See Kissling, Dorothy (Hight)
Langley, Gill(ian Rose) 1952- ...133
Langley, Harold D. 1925- ...21-24R
Langley, Helen
See Rowland, D(onald) S(ydney)
Langley, James Maydon 1916-1983 ...102
Obituary ...109
Langley, Lester D(anny) 1940- ...CANR-19
Earlier sketch in CA 102
Langley, Michael (John) 1933- ...97-100
Langley, Noel 1911-1980 ...CANR-30
Obituary ...102
Earlier sketch in CA 13-16R
See also SATA 25
Langley, Raymond J. 1935- Brief entry ...108
Langley, Roger 1930- ...73-76
Langley, Stephen G(ould) 1938- ...41-44R
Langley, Tania
See Armstrong, Tilly
Langley, Wright 1935- ...57-60
Langlois, Walter G(ordon) 1925- ...CANR-9
Earlier sketch in CA 21-24R
Langman, Ida Kaplan 1904- ... CAP-1
Earlier sketch in CA 13-16
Langman, Larry 1930- ...109
Langner, Lawrence 1890-1962 Obituary ...116
Langner, Nola 1930- ...CANR-15
Earlier sketch in CA 37-40R
See also SATA 8
Langone, John (Michael) 1929- ...CANR-1
Earlier sketch in CA 49-52
See also SATA 38, 46
Langsam, Walter Consuelo 1906-1985 ...CANR-2
Obituary ...117
Earlier sketch in CA 1-4R
Lang-Sims, Lois Dorothy 1917- ...106
Langsley, Donald G(ene) 1925- ...CANR-4
Earlier sketch in CA 53-56
Langstaff, J(ohn) Brett 1889-1985 ...CANR-29
Obituary ...115
Earlier sketch in CA 1-4R
Langstaff, John Meredith 1920- ...CANR-4
Earlier sketch in CA 1-4R
See also CLR 3
See also MAICYA
See also SATA 6, 68
Langstaff, Josephine
See Herschberger, Ruth (Margaret)
Langstaff, Launcelot
See Irving, Washington
Langstaff, Nancy 1925- ...CANR-12
Earlier sketch in CA 73-76
Langton, Anne 1804-1893 ... DLB 99
Langton, Clair V(an Norman) 1895- ...5-8R
Langton, Daniel J(oseph) 1927- ...93-96
Langton, Jane (Gillson) 1922- ...CANR-18
Earlier sketches in CA 1-4R, CANR-1
See also MAICYA
See also SAAS 5
See also SATA 3, 68
Langton, Kenneth P(atrick) 1933- ...25-28R
Langwill, Lyndesay Graham 1897- ...13-16R
Langworth, Richard M(ichael) 1941- ...73-76
Langworthy, Harry W(ells III) 1939- ...57-60
Lanham, Charles Trueman
1902-1978 Obituary ...81-84
Lanham, Edwin (Moultrie) 1904-1979 ...9-12R
Obituary ...89-92
See also DLB 4
Lanham, Frank W(esley) 1914- ...CANR-6
Earlier sketch in CA 1-4R
Lanham, Richard Alan 1936- ...CANR-10
Earlier sketch in CA 25-28R
Lanham, Url(ess Norton) 1918- ...25-28R
Lanier, Alison Raymond 1917- ...CANR-12
Earlier sketch in CA 17-20R
Lanier, Sidney 1842-1881 ... DLB 64
See also MAICYA
See also SATA 18
Lanier, Sterling E(dmund) 1927- Brief entry ...118
Lanigan, Catherine 1947- ...108
Laning, Edward 1906- ...53-56
Lank, Edith H(andleman) 1926- ...109
Lanker, Brian T(imothy) 1947- ...134
Lankevich, George J(ohn) 1939- ...CANR-13
Earlier sketch in CA 77-80
Lankford, John (Errett) 1934- ...17-20R
Lankford, Nelson D. 1948- ...138
Lankford, Philip Marlin 1945- ...CANR-7
Earlier sketch in CA 57-60
Lankford, T(homas) Randall 1942- ...65-68
Lanks, Herbert C(harles)
1899-1987 Obituary ...122
Lanne, William F.
See Leopold, Nathan F.
Lanner, Ronald Martin 1930- ...107
Lanning, Edward P(utnam) 1930- ...17-20R
Lanning, George (William) Jr. 1925- ...9-12R
Lanning, John Tate 1902-1976 Obituary ...108
Lanoil, Georgia Hope Witkin
See Witkin-Lanoil, Georgia Hope
Lanoue, Fred Richard 1908-1965 ... CAP-1
Earlier sketch in CA 13-14
La Noue, George R(ichard) 1937- ...73-76
Lanouette, William (John) 1940- ...136
Lanoux, Armand 1913-1983 Obituary ...109
Lansbury, Angela 1946- ...81-84
Lansdale, Edward Geary
1908-1987 Obituary ...121
Lansdale, Joe R(ichard) 1951- ...CANR-32
Earlier sketch in CA 113
Lansdale, Robert Tucker
1900-1980 Obituary ...103

Lansdowne, J(ames) F(enwick) 1937- CANR-30
Earlier sketch in CA 49-52
Lanser, Susan Sniader 107
Lansing, Alfred 1921-1975 ....13-16R
Obituary 61-64
See also SATA 35
Lansing, Elisabeth Hubbard 1911- 5-8R
Lansing, Gerrit (Yates) 1928- 73-76
Lansing, Henry
See Rowland, D(onald) S(ydney)
Lansing, John B(elcher)
1919-1970 Obituary 108
Lansing, Karen E. 1954- ....SATA 71
Lansky, Bruce 1941- CANR-29
Earlier sketch in CA 109
Lansky, Vicki 1942- CANR-26
Earlier sketch in CA 81-84
Lanson, Lucienne (Therese)
1930- Brief entry 108
Lant, Harvey
See Rowland, D(onald) S(ydney)
Lant, Jeffrey Ladd 1947- CANR-30
Earlier sketch in CA 109
Lanterman, Ray(mond E.) 1916- 106
Lantis, David W(illiam) 1917- 13-16R
Lantis, Margaret (Lydia) 1906- CAP-2
Earlier sketch in CA 29-32
Lantry, Mike
See Tubb, E(dwin) C(harles)
Lantz, Fran
See Lantz, Francess L(in)
Lantz, Francess L(in) 1952- CANR-39
Earlier sketch in CA 115
See also SATA 63
Lantz, Herman R. 1919-1987 ....37-40R
Obituary 122
Lantz, Louise K. 1930- 45-48
Lantz, Paul 1908- ....SATA 45
Lantz, Walter 1900- Brief entry 108
See also SATA 37
Lanyer, Aemilia 1569-1645 .... DLB 121
Lanyon, Carla 1906-1971 .... CAP-1
Earlier sketch in CA 13-14
Lanzillotti, Robert F(ranklin) 1921- 77-80
Lao, Kan 1907- 41-44R
Lao She
See Shu Ch'ing-ch'un
Lapage, Geoffrey 1888- CAP-1
Earlier sketch in CA 9-10
La Pallo, A. Elise 128
La Palombara, Joseph 1925- CANR-31
Earlier sketches in CA 1-4R, CANR-6
Lapaquellerie, Yvon
See Bizardel, Yvon
Lapati, Americo D. 1924- CANR-1
Earlier sketch in CA 1-4R
La Patra, Jack W(illiam) 1927- 93-96
Lape, Esther Everett 1881-1981 Obituary 108
Lape, Fred 1900- 102
Lapedes, Daniel N.
1913(?)-1979 Obituary 93-96
Lapena-Bonifacio, Amelia 1930- 130
LaPenta, Anthony V(incent) Jr. 1943- 69-72
Lapeza, David (Henry) 1950- 73-76
Lapham, Arthur L(owell) 1922- 49-52
Lapham, Lewis H(enry) 1935- CANR-33
Earlier sketch in CA 77-80
Lapham, Maxwell E(dward)
1900(?)-1983 Obituary 110
Lapham, Samuel Jr. 1892-1972 Obituary 106
Lapide, Phinn E.
See Lapide, Pinchas E.
Lapide, Pinchas E. 1922- CANR-13
Earlier sketch in CA 21-24R
Lapidus, Elaine 1939- 21-24R
Lapidus, Jacqueline (Anita) 1941- 97-100
Lapidus, Morris 1902- 77-80
Lapierre, Dominique 1931- CANR-19
Earlier sketch in CA 69-72
LaPierre, Laurier L. 1929- Brief entry 107
La Pietra, Mary 1929- 61-64
Lapin, Howard S(idney) 1922- 17-20R
Lapin, Jackie 1951- 85-88
Lapine, James (Elliot) 1949- 130
Brief entry 123
See also CLC 39
Lapinski, Susan 1948- 115
La Place, John 1922- 103
LaPointe, Frank 1936- 93-96
Lapointe, Gatien 1931-1983(?) .... DLB 88
Lapointe, Paul-Marie 1929- Brief entry 109
See also DLB 88
Laponce, Jean Antoine 1925- 53-56
Laporte, Jean 1924- 41-44R
Laporte, Maurice 1901(?)-1987 Obituary 123
LaPorte, Robert Jr. 1940- 41-44R
Lapp, Charles (Leon) 1914- CANR-1
Earlier sketch in CA 45-48
Lapp, Chuck
See Lapp, Charles (Leon)
Lapp, Eleanor J. 1936- 69-72
Lapp, Eunice Willis Bodine 1905- 123
Lapp, John Allen 1933- 41-44R
Lapp, John Clarke 1917-1977 85-88
Lapp, Ralph Eugene 1917- 81-84
Lapp, Rudolph M(athew) 1915- 113
Lappe, Frances Moore 1944- 37-40R
Lappe, Marc 1943- 126
Lappin, Ben
See Lappin, Bernard William
Lappin, Bernard William 1916- 9-12R
Lappin, Peter 1911- CANR-25
Earlier sketches in CA 57-60, CANR-7
See also SATA 32
Lapping, Brian 1937- 25-28R
Laprade, William Thomas
1883-1975 Obituary 89-92
LaPray, (Margaret) Helen 1916- CANR-7
Earlier sketch in CA 53-56
Lapsley, James N(orvell) 1930- 25-28R
La Puma, Salvatore 1929- 136
Laqueur, Walter (Ze'ev) 1921- CANR-23
Earlier sketch in CA 5-8R
Laquian, Aprodicio A(rcilla) 1935- CANR-26
Earlier sketch in CA 29-32R
Lara
See Griffith-Jones, George Chetwynd
Lara, Agustin 1900-1970 Obituary 104
Lara, Jan
See Hinkemeyer, Michael T(homas)
Laramore, Darryl 1928- 101
Larangeira, Crispin 1940- 129
Larbaud, Valery (Nicolas)
1881-1957 Brief entry 106
See also TCLC 9
Larco, Isabel Granda
1911(?)-1983 Obituary 109
Lardas, Konstantinos 1927- 13-16R
Lardner, George Jr. 1934- 73-76
Lardner, James 1948- 118
Lardner, John (Abbott)
1912-1960 Obituary 93-96
Lardner, Ring
See Lardner, Ring(gold) W(ilmer)
Lardner, Ring(gold Wilmer) Jr. 1915- CANR-13
Earlier sketch in CA 25-28R
See also DLB 26
Lardner, Ring W. Jr.
See Lardner, Ring(gold) W(ilmer)
Lardner, Ring(gold) W(ilmer) 1885-1933 131
Brief entry 104
See also CDALB 1917-1929
See also DLB 11, 25, 86
See also MTCW
See also TCLC 2, 14
Lardner-Burke, Desmond William
1909-1984 Obituary 114
Laredo, Betty
See Codrescu, Andrei
Laredo, Johnny
See Caesar, (Eu)Gene (Lee)
La Reyniere
See Courtine, Robert
Large, Peter Somerville
See Somerville-Large, Peter
Large, R(ichard) Geddes 1901- 102
Large, Stephen S(toker) 1942- 120
Largo, Michael 1950- 73-76
Lariar, Lawrence 1908- CAP-1
Earlier sketch in CA 9-10
Larimore, Bertha B(urnham) 1915- 61-64
La Rivers, Ira II 1915-1977 ....41-44R
Larkey, Patrick Darrel 1943- 85-88
Larkin, Amy
See Burns, Olive Ann
Larkin, Emmet 1927- CANR-9
Earlier sketch in CA 13-16R
Larkin, John A(lan) 1936- 41-44R
Larkin, John Day 1897-1986 Obituary 118
Larkin, Maia
See Wojciechowska, Maia (Teresa)
Larkin, Maurice (John Milner) 1932- 102
Larkin, Miriam Therese 1930- Brief entry 108
Larkin, Oliver Waterman 1896-1970 ....1-4R
Obituary 29-32R
Larkin, Philip (Arthur) 1922-1985 ....CANR-24
Obituary 117
Earlier sketch in CA 5-8R
See also CDBLB 1960 to Present
See also CLC 3, 5, 8, 9, 13, 18, 33, 39, 64
See also DLB 27
See also MTCW
Larkin, R. T.
See Larkin, Rochelle
Larkin, Rochelle 1935- CANR-13
Earlier sketch in CA 33-36R
Larkin, Sarah
See Loening, Sarah (Elizabeth) Larkin
Larlham, Hattie 1914- 113
Larminie, Margaret Beda 1924- CANR-18
Earlier sketches in CA 5-8R, CANR-2
Larmore, Lewis 1915- 45-48
Larn, Richard (James Vincent) 1930- CANR-20
Earlier sketch in CA 103
Larnach, Rupert
See Nevill, Barry St-John
Larner, Christina (Ross) Obituary 115
Larner, Jeremy 1937- 9-12R
Larner, John (Patrick) 1930- 81-84
Larneuil, Michel
See Batbedat, Jean
Laroche, Giles 1956- ....SATA 71
Laroche, Rene
See McKeag, Ernest L(ionel)
La Roche, Sophie von 1730-1807 .... DLB 94
Larock, Bruce Edward 1940- 53-56
La Rocque, Gilbert 1943-1984 .... DLB 60
Larom, Henry V. 1903(?)-1975 Obituary 61-64
See also SATA 30
Laroque de Roquebrune, Robert
See Roquebrune, Robert
La Rosa, Paul (Frank) 1953- 113
Larose, Paul 1947- 114
LaRouche, Lyndon H(ermyle) Jr. 1922- 138
Brief entry 124
Larrabee, Carroll Burton
1896-1983 Obituary 110
Larrabee, Eric 1922-1990 ....CANR-1
Obituary 133
Earlier sketch in CA 1-4R
Larrabee, Harold A(tkins) 1894-1979 .... CAP-1
Obituary 85-88
Earlier sketch in CA 11-12
Larranaga, Robert O. 1940- 49-52
Larrea, Jean-Jacques 1960- 45-48
Larrecq, John M(aurice)
1926-1980 ....SATA 25, 44
Larrick, Nancy 1910- CANR-1
Earlier sketch in CA 1-4R
See also DLB 61
See also SATA 4
Larrie, Reginald R. 1928- 123
Brief entry 118
Larrison, Earl J(unior) 1919- CANR-9
Earlier sketch in CA 57-60
Larrowe, Charles P(atrick) 1916- 41-44R
Larry
See Parkes, Terence
Larsen, Beverly (Namen) 1929- 17-20R
Larsen, Carl 1934- CANR-27
Earlier sketch in CA 77-80
Larsen, Charles E(dward) 1923- 33-36R
Larsen, David C(harles) 1944- 73-76
Larsen, E(gner) John 1926- CANR-16
Earlier sketch in CA 25-28R
Larsen, Egon 1904- CANR-3
Earlier sketch in CA 9-12R
See also SATA 14
Larsen, Elyse 1957- 41-44R
Larsen, Eric 1941- 132
See also CLC 55
Larsen, Erik 1911- 41-44R
Larsen, Erling 1909- 13-16R
Larsen, Ernest 1946- 106
Larsen, Gaylord 1932- CANR-30
Earlier sketch in CA 112
Larsen, J(akob) A(ll) O(tteson)
1888-1974 Obituary 111
Larsen, Jack Lenor 1927- 126
Larsen, Jeanne (Louise) 1950- 134
Larsen, Jens Peter 1902-1988 Obituary 126
Larsen, Kalee 1952- 41-44R
Larsen, Knud S(onderhede) 1938- 53-56
Larsen, Lawrence H. 1931- 21-24R
Larsen, Nella 1891-1964 125
See also BLC 2
See also BW
See also CLC 37
See also DLB 51
Larsen, Otto N. 1922- CANR-2
Earlier sketch in CA 1-4R
Larsen, Paul E(manuel) 1933- 93-96
Larsen, Peter 1933- CANR-22
Earlier sketch in CA 29-32R
Larsen, Rebecca 1944- 122
See also SATA 54
Larsen, Ronald J(ames) 1948- 41-44R
Larsen, Roy E(dward)
1899-1979 Obituary 89-92
Larsen, Stephen 1941- 69-72
Larsen, Susan C(arol) 1946- 125
Larsen, Tony 1949- 107
Larsen, Wendy Wilder 1940- 120
Larsen, William E(dward) 1936- 17-20R
Larsgaard, Mary L(ynette) 1946- 122
Larson, Albert J. 1934- 112
Larson, Andrew Karl 1899- CAP-2
Earlier sketch in CA 33-36
Larson, Arthur 1910- CANR-1
Earlier sketch in CA 1-4R
Larson, Bob 1944- CANR-5
Earlier sketch in CA 53-56
Larson, Bruce L(lewellyn) 1936- 85-88
Larson, Bruce 1925- CANR-30
Earlier sketches in CA 57-60, CANR-13
Larson, Calvin J(ames) 1933- CANR-31
Earlier sketch in CA 49-52
Larson, Carl M. 1916- 41-44R
Larson, Cedric Arthur 1908- 65-68
Larson, Charles R(aymond) 1938- CANR-4
Earlier sketch in CA 53-56
See also CLC 31
Larson, Charles U(rban) 1940- 97-100
Larson, Charles 1922- 25-28R
Larson, Clinton F(oster) 1919- 57-60
Larson, Donald (Norman) 1925- 57-60
Larson, Doran 1957- 124
Larson, E. Richard 1944- 105
Larson, Esther Elisabeth 1908-1978 ....17-20R
Obituary 134
Larson, Eve
See St. John, Wylly Folk
Larson, Gary O(tto) 1949- 115
Larson, Gary 1950- 118
See also AAYA 1
See also SATA 57
Larson, George C(harles) 1942- CANR-9
Earlier sketch in CA 65-68
Larson, Gerald James 1938- 93-96
Larson, Glen A. 1937(?)- Brief entry 115
Larson, Gustive O(lof) 1897-1978 ....29-32R
Obituary 125
Larson, Harold J. 1934- 53-56
Larson, Henrietta M(elia) 1894-1983 .... CAP-2
Obituary 110
Earlier sketch in CA 23-24
Larson, James F(rederick) 1947- 115
Larson, Janet Karsten 1945- 104
Larson, Jean Russell 1930- 21-24R
Larson, Jeanne 1920- 57-60
Larson, Knute (G.) 1919- 9-12R
Larson, Kris 1953- 77-80
Larson, Magali Sarfatti 1936- 97-100
Larson, Martin Alfred 1897- CANR-2
Earlier sketch in CA 5-8R
Larson, Mel(vin Gunnard) 1916- 5-8R
Larson, Muriel 1924- CANR-24
Earlier sketches in CA 21-24R, CANR-9
Larson, Norita D(ittberner) 1944- 105
See also SATA 29
Larson, Orvin Prentiss 1910- 77-80
Larson, P(aul) Merville 1903- 41-44R
Larson, Peggy (Ann Pickering) 1931- 81-84
Larson, Reed (W.) 1950- 128
Larson, Richard Francis 1931- CANR-15
Earlier sketch in CA 41-44R
Larson, Robert H(erbert) 1942- 113
Larson, Robert W. 1927- 85-88
Larson, Simeon 1925- 61-64
Larson, T(aft) A(lfred) 1910- 33-36R
Larson, Thomas B(ryan) 1914- 25-28R
Larson, Victor E. 1898-1981 ....25-28R
Obituary 134
Larson, William H. 1938- 21-24R
See also SATA 10
Larsson, Carl (Olof) 1853-1919 Brief entry 115
See also SATA 35
Larsson, Flora (Benwell) 1904- 93-96
Lartigue, Jacques-Henri 1894-1986 ....33-36R
Obituary 120
La Rue, Daniel Wolford Jr.
1878-1969 Obituary 116
Larue, Gerald A(lexander) 1916- 21-24R
LaRue, L. H. 1938- 135
LaRusso, Dominic A(nthony) 1924- 33-36R
Lary, N(ikita) M(ichael) 1940- 61-64
Lasagna, Louis (Cesare) 1923- Brief entry 106
LaSalle, Charles A.
See Ellis, Edward S(ylvester)
LaSalle, Charles E.
See Ellis, Edward S(ylvester)
La Salle, Donald (Philip) 1933- 29-32R
La Salle, Dorothy (Marguerite) 1895-1980 .....5-8R
Obituary 126
LaSalle, Peter 1947- 103
La Salle, Victor
See Fanthorpe, R(obert) Lionel
Lasater, Alice E(lizabeth) 1936- 57-60
Lasby, Clarence G(eorge) 1933- 105
Lasch, Christopher 1932- CANR-25
Earlier sketch in CA 73-76
See also MTCW
Lasch, Robert 1907- 102
Laschever, Barnett D. 1924- CANR-6
Earlier sketch in CA 1-4R
LaScola, Ray(mond) L. 1915- 1-4R
Lasdun, James 1958- 137
Lasdun, Susan 1929- 111
Lasell, Elinor H. 1929- CANR-7
Earlier sketch in CA 5-8R
See also SATA 19
Lasell, Fen H.
See Lasell, Elinor H.
Lasenby, Jack 1931- 130
See also SATA 65
Laser, Marvin 1914- 9-12R
Lash, Jeffrey N. 1949- 136
Lash, Joseph P. 1909-1987 ....CANR-16
Obituary 123
Earlier sketch in CA 17-20R
See also SATA 43
Lasher, Albert C. 1928- 25-28R
Lasher, Faith B. 1921- 37-40R
See also SATA 12
Laska
See Laska, P(eter) J(erome)
Laska, P(eter) J(erome) 1938- CANR-15
Earlier sketch in CA 65-68
Laska, Vera
See Laska, Vera O(ravec)
Laska, Vera O(ravec) 1923- 119
Lasker, David 1950- 112
See also SATA 38
Lasker, Edward 1885-1981 ....5-8R
Obituary 103
Lasker, Gabriel Ward 1912- 1-4R
Lasker, Joe
See Lasker, Joseph Leon
Lasker, Joseph Leon 1919- CANR-38
Earlier sketches in CA 49-52, CANR-1
See also SATA 9
Lasker, Judith N. 1947- 130
Lasker-Schueler, Else 1869-1945 ....DLB 66
Laski, Marghanita 1915-1988 105
Obituary 124
See also SATA 55
Laskin, Bora 1912-1984 Obituary 112
Laskowski, Jerzy 1919- 77-80
Lasky, Betty 1927- 119
Lasky, Jesse Louis Jr. 1910- CANR-20
Earlier sketches in CA 1-4R, CANR-4
See also AITN 1
Lasky, Kathryn 1944- CANR-11
Earlier sketch in CA 69-72
See also CLR 11
See also MAICYA
See also SATA 13, 69
Lasky, Melvin J(onah) 1920- 53-56
Lasky, Victor 1918-1990 ....CANR-10
Obituary 131
Earlier sketch in CA 5-8R
See also AITN 1
Lasky, William R(aymond) 1921- 97-100
Laslett, John H(enry) M(artin) 1933- CANR-12
Earlier sketch in CA 29-32R
Laslett, Peter 1915- CANR-12
Earlier sketch in CA 73-76
Lasley, Jack
See Lasley, John Wayne III
Lasley, John Wayne III 1925- 17-20R
Lasnier, Rina 1915- ....DLB 88
LaSor, William Sanford 1911-1991 ....CANR-21
Obituary 133
Earlier sketches in CA 1-4R, CANR-2
La Sorte, A(ntonio) Michael 1931- 13-16R
La Spina, (Fanny) Greye 1880- CAP-1
Earlier sketch in CA 13-14
Lass, Abraham H(arold) 1907- 9-12R

Lass, Betty (Lipschitz)
1908(?)-1976 Obituary 69-72
Lass, Roger 1937- 132
Lass, William E(dward) 1928- CANR-2
Earlier sketch in CA 1-4R
Lass, William M. 1910(?)-1975 Obituary 104
Lassaigne, Jacques 1910(?)-1982 129
Lassalle, C. E.
See Ellis, Edward S(ylvester)
Lassam, Robert (Errington) 1914- 112
Lassen-Willems, James
See Willems, J. Rutherford
Lassers, Willard J. 1919- 17-20R
Lassimonne, Denise 25-28R
Lassiter, Adam
See Krauzer, Steven M(ark)
Lassiter, Isaac Steele 1941- 33-36R
Lassiter, Mary
See Hoffman, Mary (Margaret)
See also SATA 59
Lassiter, (Albin) Perry (Jr.) 1935- 97-100
Lassiter, Roy L(eland) Jr. 1927- 21-24R
Lassner, Jacob 1935- CANR-20
Earlier sketch in CA 29-32R
Lasson, Kenneth (Lee) 1943- CANR-13
Earlier sketch in CA 33-36R
Lasswell, Harold D. 1902-1978 Obituary 104
Lasswell, Marcia 1927- 97-100
Lasswell, Thomas Ely 1919- 17-20R
Last, Jef
See Last, Josephus Carel Franciscus
Last, Joan 1908- 107
Last, Josephus Carel Franciscus
1898-1972 .... CAP-2
Earlier sketch in CA 33-36
Laster, Ann A(ppleton) 1936- 29-32R
Laszlo, Ervin 1932- 41-44R
Laszlo, Miklos 1904(?)-1973 Obituary 41-44R
Latane, Bibb 1937- 37-40R
Latch, William 1950(?)-1985 Obituary 117
Latchaw, Marjorie Elizabeth 1914- 5-8R
Lateiner, Donald 1944- 135
Latham, Aaron 1943- 33-36R
Latham, Barbara 1896- .... SATA 16
Latham, Caroline S. 1940- 125
Latham, Donald Crawford 1932- 9-12R
Latham, Earl Ganson 1907- 103
Latham, Frank B(rown) 1910- 49-52
See also SATA 6
Latham, Harold Strong 1887-1969 .... CAP-1
Earlier sketch in CA 9-10
Latham, Ian 1956- 109
Latham, Jean Lee 1902- CANR-7
Earlier sketch in CA 5-8R
See also AITN 1
See also CLC 12
See also MAICYA
See also SATA 2, 68
Latham, John H. 1917- 5-8R
Latham, Joyce 1943- 73-76
Latham, Lenn Learner 1901-197 (?) 1-4R
Obituary 135
Latham, Lorraine 1948- 65-68
Latham, Marte Hooper 1924- 9-12R
Latham, Mavis
See Clark, Mavis Thorpe
Latham, Peter 1910- CAP-1
Earlier sketch in CA 11-12
Latham, Philip
See Richardson, Robert S(hirley)
Latham, Roger M. 1914(?)-1979 Obituary 85-88
Lathen, Emma
See Hennissart, Martha
and Latsis, Mary J(ane)
See also CLC 2
Lathrop, Dorothy P(ulis) 1891-1980 73-76
Obituary 102
See also DLB 22
See also MAICYA
See also SATA 14, 24
Lathrop, Francis
See Leiber, Fritz (Reuter Jr.)
Lathrop, George Parsons 1851-1898 ...... DLB 71
Lathrop, Irvin T(unis) 1927- CANR-22
Earlier sketch in CA 45-48
Lathrop, JoAnna 1931- 61-64
Lathrop, John Jr. 1772-1820 .... DLB 37
Latimer, Dean 1945- 129
See also AAYA 2
Latimer, H(enry) C. 1893- 29-32R
Latimer, Jonathan (Wyatt)
1906-1983 Obituary 110
Latman, Alan 1930-1984 Obituary 113
Latner, Helen (Stambler) 1918- 106
Latner, Pat Wallace
See Strother, Pat Wallace
Latorre, Dolores L(aguarta Blasco) 1903- 65-68
Latorre, Felipe A(ugusto) 1907- 65-68
La Tour du Pin, Patrice de
1911-1975 Obituary 115
Latourelle, Rene 1918- 130
La Tourette, Aileen 1946- 119
Latourette, Kenneth Scott 1884-1967 ...... CAP-2
Earlier sketch in CA 23-24
La Tourrette, Jacqueline 1926- CANR-34
Earlier sketch in CA 49-52
Latow, (Muriel) Roberta 1931- 116
Latsis, Mary J(ane) 85-88
See also Lathen, Emma
Latta, Richard 1946- CANR-19
Earlier sketches in CA 53-56, CANR-4
Latta, William (Charlton Jr.) 1929- 115
Lattimer, John Kingsley 1914- 106
Lattimore, Eleanor Frances 1904-1986 ....CANR-6
Obituary 119
Earlier sketch in CA 9-12R
See also SATA 7, 48
Lattimore, Jessie
See Dresser, Norine
and Fontes, Montserrat
Lattimore, Owen 1900-1989 97-100
Obituary 128
Lattimore, Richmond (Alexander)
1906-1984 ....CANR-1
Obituary 112
Earlier sketch in CA 1-4R
See also CLC 3
Lattin, Ann
See Cole, Lois Dwight
Lattin, Harriet Pratt 1898- 33-36R
Latukefu, Sione 1927- 73-76
Latzer, Beth Good 1911- 65-68
Lau, Charles Richard 1933-1984 Obituary 112
Lau, Charley
See Lau, Charles Richard
Lau, Joseph S(hui) M(ing) 1934- 77-80
Laub, (Martin) Julian 1929- 37-40R
Laubach, Frank Charles 1884-1970 .... CAP-1
Earlier sketch in CA 9-10
Laube, Clifford J(ames)
1891-1974 Obituary 53-56
Laubenthal, Sanders Anne 1943- 61-64
Lauber, Lynn 1952- 133
Lauber, Patricia (Grace) 1924- CANR-38
Earlier sketches in CA 9-12R, CANR-6, 24
See also CLR 16
See also MAICYA
See also SATA 1, 33
Lauber, Volkmar 1944- 132
Laubin, Gladys (Winifred) 111
Laubin, Reginald K(arl) 111
Laucanno, Christopher Sawyer
See Sawyer-Laucanno, Christopher
Lauck, Carol 1934- 93-96
Laudan, Larry L. 1941- 129
Lauder, George
See Dick-Lauder, George (Andrew)
Lauder, George (Andrew) Dick
See Dick-Lauder, George (Andrew)
Lauder, Phyllis 1898- 93-96
Lauder, Robert E(dward) 1934- 134
Lauderdale, Pat 1944- 101
Laudicina, Paul A(ndrew) 1949- 93-96
Laudin, Harvey 1922- 77-80
Laue, Max Theodor Felix von
1879-1960 Obituary 113
Lauer, Evelyn G(erda) 1938- 29-32R
Lauer, Jeanette C(arol) 1935- CANR-19
Earlier sketch in CA 104
Lauer, Jean-Philippe 1902- 85-88
Lauer, Robert H(arold) 1933- CANR-19
Earlier sketches in CA 53-56, CANR-4
Lauer, Rosemary Zita 1919- 5-8R
Lauer, Theodore E. 1931- 37-40R
Lauerman, David A(nthony) 1931- 17-20R
Lauersen, Niels H(elth) 1939- CANR-33
Earlier sketches in CA 85-88, CANR-15
Lauf, Detlef I. Charles 1936- 103
Laufe, Abe 1906- 17-20R
Laufer, Leopold 1925- 21-24R
Laufer, Robert S. 1942(?)-1989 Obituary 129
Lauffer, Armand A(lbert) 1933- CANR-19
Earlier sketches in CA 53-56, CANR-5
Laugesen, Mary E(akin) 1906- CAP-2
Earlier sketch in CA 29-32
See also SATA 5
Laughbaum, Steve 1945- .... SATA 12
Laughlin, Clarence John
1905-1985 Obituary 114
Laughlin, Florence Young 1910- 9-12R
See also SATA 3
Laughlin, Henry Prather 1916- CANR-8
Earlier sketch in CA 61-64
Laughlin, James 1914- CANR-9
Earlier sketch in CA 21-24R
See also CLC 49
See also DLB 48
Laughlin, Ledlie Irwin 1890-1977 ....37-40R
Laughlin, P. S.
See Shea, Patrick
Laughlin, Tom 1938(?)- 138
Brief entry 116
Laughton, Bruce (Kyle Blake) 1928- 133
Laughton, Tom 1904(?)-1984 Obituary 112
Laugier, Odile 1956- 108
Laugier, R.
See Cumberland, Marten
Laumann, Edward O. 1938- 33-36R
Laumer, (John) Keith 1925- CANR-7
Earlier sketch in CA 9-12R
See also DLB 8
Launay, Andre (Joseph) 1930- 25-28R
Launay, Droo
See Launay, Andre (Joseph)
Laune, Paul Sidney 1899- 17-20R
Launitz-Schurer, Leopold (Sidney) Jr.
1942- 103
Laurance, Alfred D.
See Tralins, S(andor) Robert
Laurance, Alice (a pseudonym) 1938- 101
Laure, Ettagale
See Blauer, Ettagale
Laure, Jason 1940- 104
See also SATA 44, 50
Laurel, Alicia Bay 1949- 41-44R
Lauren, Linda
See Bunce, Linda Susan (Staines)
Laurence, Dan H. 1920- CANR-32
Earlier sketches in CA 17-20R, CANR-13
Laurence, Ester Hauser 1935- 29-32R
See also SATA 7
Laurence, Gerald (Robert) 1948- 131
Laurence, John 1939- 69-72
Laurence, (Jean) Margaret (Wemyss)
1926-1987 ....CANR-33
Obituary 121
Earlier sketch in CA 5-8R
See also CLC 3, 6, 13, 50, 62
See also DLB 53
See also MTCW
See also SATA 50
See also SSC 7
Laurence, Michael M(arshall) 1940- 33-36R
Laurence, Will
See Smith, Willard L(aurence)
Laurence, William Leonard 1888-1977 77-80
Obituary 69-72
Laurent, Antoine 1952- .... CLC 50
Laurent, Lawrence (Bell) 1925- 69-72
Laurenti, Joseph L(ucian) 1931- CANR-31
Earlier sketch in CA 49-52
Laurentin, Rene 1917- 106
Laurents, Arthur 1918- CANR-8
Earlier sketch in CA 13-16R
See also DLB 26
Lauria, Frank (Jonathan) 1935- 103
Laurie, Annie
See Black, Winifred
and Scarberry, Alma Sioux
Laurie, Bruce 1943- 115
Laurie, Edward J(ames) 1925- CANR-8
Earlier sketch in CA 17-20R
Laurie, Harry C.
See Cahn, Zvi
Laurie, James 1947- 69-72
Laurie, Michael M. 1932- 126
Laurie, Rona CANR-33
Laurie, Rona 1916- CANR-15
Earlier sketch in CA 85-88
See also SATA 55
Laurin, Anne
See McLaurin, Anne
Lauritsen, John (Phillip) 1939- 57-60
Lauritzen, Elizabeth Moyes 1909- CAP-1
Earlier sketch in CA 13-16
Lauritzen, Jonreed 1902- 5-8R
See also SATA 13
Lauri-Volpi, Giacomo
1893(?)-1979 Obituary 85-88
Lauro, Shirley (Shapiro) Mezvinsky 1933- 126
Laury, Jean Ray 1928- 77-80
Lauscher, Hermann
See Hesse, Hermann
Laut, Agnes Christina 1871-1936 .... DLB 92
Lautenbach, Renee 1932- 110
Lauter
See Chamson, Andre J(ules) L(ouis)
Lauter, Geza Peter 1932- 41-44R
Lauter, Paul 1932- 13-16R
Lauterbach, Albert 1904- CANR-1
Earlier sketch in CA 1-4R
Lauterstein, Ingeborg 1935- 130
Lauwerys, Joseph (Albert) 1902-1981 ......13-16R
Obituary 104
Laux, Dorothy 1920- 61-64
See also SATA 49
Laux, James M(ichael) 1927- 33-36R
Laux, P(eter) J(ohn) 1922- 25-28R
Lavagnino, Allessandra 1927- CANR-2
Earlier sketch in CA 45-48
LaValle, Irving H(oward) 1939- 33-36R
Lavan, Spencer 1937- CANR-8
Earlier sketch in CA 57-60
Lavater, Johann Kaspar 1741-1801 .... DLB 97
Lave, Lester B(ernard) 1939- CANR-33
Earlier sketches in CA 41-44R, CANR-15
Lavelle, Mike 1933- 65-68
Lavelle, Sheila 1939- 109
Lavender, David (Sievert) 1910- CANR-18
Earlier sketches in CA 1-4R, CANR-2
See also SATA 64
Lavender, William 1921- CANR-10
Earlier sketch in CA 65-68
Lavenson, James H. 1919- 103
Lavenson, Jim
See Lavenson, James H.
Laver, James 1899-1975 ....CANR-3
Obituary 57-60
Earlier sketch in CA 1-4R
Laver, Michael 1949- CANR-23
Earlier sketch in CA 107
Laver, Rod(ney George) 1938- Brief entry 112
La Verdiere, Eugene Armand 1936- CANR-19
Earlier sketch in CA 102
Lavers, Annette 1932- 130
Lavers, Norman 1935- 104
Laverty, Carroll D(ee) 1906- 77-80
Laverty, Donald
See Blish, James (Benjamin)
and Knight, Damon (Francis)
Lavery, Emmet (Godfrey)
1902-1986 Obituary 118
Laves, Walter H(erman) C(arl)
1902-1983 Obituary 111
La Vey, Anton Szandor 1930- Brief entry 109
Lavin, David E(dwin) 1931- CANR-2
Earlier sketch in CA 1-4R
Lavin, Henry St. C. 1921-1985 Obituary 114
Lavin, J(oseph) A(nthony) 1932- 33-36R
Lavin, Marilyn Aronberg 1925- 106
Lavin, Mary 1912- CANR-33
Earlier sketch in CA 9-12R
See also CLC 4, 18
See also DLB 15
See also MTCW
See also SSC 4
Lavine, David 1928- .... SATA 31
Lavine, Harold 1915-1984 ....41-44R
Obituary 113
Lavine, Richard A. 1917- 21-24R
Lavine, Sigmund Arnold 1908- CANR-19
Earlier sketches in CA 1-4R, CANR-4
See also SATA 3
Lavington, H(arold) Dude 1907- 117
Lavinson, Joseph
See Kaye, Marvin (Nathan)
Laviolette, Emily A. 1923(?)-1975 .... SATA 49
Lavitt, Wendy (Adler) 1939- 127
Lavond, Paul Dennis
See Kornbluth, C(yril) M.
and Lowndes, Robert A(ugustine) W(ard)
and Pohl, Frederik
Lavori, Nora 1950- 93-96
Lavrentiev, Alexander (Nikolaevich) 1954- 135
Lavrin, Janko Matthew 1887-1986 ....9-12R
Obituary 120
Law, Alexander 1904- 128
Law, Carol Russell 106
Law, Howard W(illiam) 1919- 21-24R
Law, Janice
See Trecker, Janice Law
Law, Marie Hamilton 1884-1981 Obituary 106
Law, Richard 1901-1980 Obituary 105
Law, Virginia W.
See Shell, Virginia Law
Lawder, Douglas W(ard) 1934- CANR-1
Earlier sketch in CA 45-48
Lawford, J(ames) P(hilip) 1915-1977 ......CANR-28
Earlier sketch in CA 33-36R
Lawford, Paula Jane 1960- 125
See also Martyr, Paula (Jane)
See also SATA 53
Lawhead, Victor B(ernard) 1919- 41-44R
Lawhorne, Clifton O. 1927-1983 104
Obituary 110
Lawler, Donald L(ester) 1935- 105
Lawler, James R. 1929- 57-60
Lawler, Lillian B. 1898- 13-16R
Lawler, Patrick 1948- 136
Lawler, Philip F(rederick) 1950- 110
Lawler, Raymond Evenor 1922- 103
See also CLC 58
Lawler, Ronald (David) 1926- 126
Brief entry 110
Lawless, Anthony
See MacDonald, Philip
Lawless, Bettyclare Hamilton 1915- 61-64
Lawless, Dorothy (Mae) Kennedy 1906- 5-8R
Lawless, Edward W(illiam) 1931- 114
Lawless, Elaine J. 1947- 126
Lawless, Gary 1951- CANR-13
Earlier sketch in CA 73-76
Lawlor, Florine 1925- 65-68
Lawlor, John (James) 1918- 5-8R
Lawlor, Monica (Mary) 1926- 9-12R
Lawlor, Pat
See Lawlor, Patrick Anthony
Lawlor, Patrick Anthony 1893- CAP-1
Earlier sketch in CA 9-10
Lawlor, Rob(ert Thomas) 1936- 127
Lawner, Lynne 1935- 9-12R
Lawrence, A. R.
See Foff, Arthur R(aymond)
Lawrence, Alexander Atkinson 1906-1979 102
Lawrence, Ann (Margaret) 1942-1987 104
See also SATA 41, 54
Lawrence, Ariadne
See Ling, Amy
Lawrence, Berta 73-76
Lawrence, Bill 1930- 25-28R
Lawrence, C(lifford) H(ugh) 1921- 132
Lawrence, D. Baloti 1950- CANR-32
Earlier sketch in CA 113
Lawrence, D(avid) H(erbert Richards)
1885-1930 121
Brief entry 104
See also CDBLB 1914-1945
See also DLB 10, 19, 36, 98
See also MTCW
See also SSC 4
See also TCLC 2, 9, 16, 33
See also WLC
Lawrence, Daniel 1940- 57-60
Lawrence, David Jr. 1942- 73-76
Lawrence, David 1888-1973 102
Obituary 41-44R
See also DLB 29
Lawrence, E. S.
See Bradburne, E(lizabeth) S.
Lawrence, Eddie
See Eisler, Lawrence
Lawrence, Edward
See Eisler, Lawrence
Lawrence, Elizabeth L. 1904-1985 124
Lawrence, Emeric Anthony 1908- CANR-5
Earlier sketch in CA 1-4R
Lawrence, Francis L(eo) 1937- 49-52
Lawrence, Gale 1941- 126
Lawrence, George H(ill Mathewson)
1910-1978 Obituary 81-84
Lawrence, H(enry) L(ionel) 1908- CAP-1
Earlier sketch in CA 9-10
Lawrence, Helen M(ary) 1925- CANR-28
Earlier sketch in CA 111
Lawrence, Isabelle (Wentworth) .... SATA 29
Lawrence, J. D.
See Lawrence, James Duncan
Lawrence, J. T.
See Rowland-Entwistle, (Arthur) Theodore (Henry)
Lawrence, Jack
See Fitzgerald, Lawrence P(ennybaker)
Lawrence, James Duncan 1918- CANR-27
Earlier sketch in CA 17-20R
Lawrence, Jerome 1915- 41-44R
See also SATA 65
Lawrence, Jim
See Lawrence, James Duncan

Lawrence, Jock
See Lawrence, Justus Baldwin
Lawrence, Jodi 1938- ... CANR-3
Earlier sketch in CA 45-48
Lawrence, John
See Lawrence, Jodi
Lawrence, John A. 1908-1976 Obituary ... 65-68
Lawrence, John S(helton) 1938- ... 123
Brief entry ... 107
Lawrence, John (Waldemar) 1907- ... 81-84
Lawrence, John 1933- ... CANR-24
Earlier sketch in CA 107
See also SATA 30
Lawrence, Joseph D(ouglas) 1895- ... 126
Lawrence, Josephine 1890(?)-1978 ... 77-80
See also SATA 24
Lawrence, Justus Baldwin
1903-1987 Obituary ... 122
Lawrence, Karen 1949- ... 126
Lawrence, Karen 1951- ... 126
Lawrence, Karl
See Foff, Arthur R(aymond)
Lawrence, Kathleen Rockwell 1945- ... 136
Lawrence, Kenneth G.
See Ringgold, Gene
Lawrence, Lesley
See Lewis, Lesley
Lawrence, Louise ... SATA 38
Lawrence, Louise de Kiriline 1894- ... 25-28R
See also SATA 13
Lawrence, Margaret Morgan 1914- ... 33-36R
Lawrence, Margot ... 132
Lawrence, Marjorie 1907-1979 Obituary ... 85-88
Lawrence, Martin
See Greif, Martin
and Grow, Lawrence
Lawrence, Mary
See Young, Mary Lou Daves
Lawrence, Mary Margaret 1920- ... 93-96
Lawrence, Melinda
See Weinhouse, Beth
Lawrence, Merle 1915- ... 21-24R
Lawrence, Michael
See Lariar, Lawrence
Lawrence, Mildred Elwood 1907- ... CANR-5
Earlier sketch in CA 1-4R
See also SATA 3
Lawrence, Nathaniel (Morris)
1917-1986 ... CANR-22
Earlier sketch in CA 45-48
Lawrence, P.
See Tubb, E(dwin) C(harles)
Lawrence, Peter 1921-1988 Obituary ... 124
Lawrence, R(onald) D(ouglas) 1921- ... CANR-11
Earlier sketch in CA 65-68
See also SATA 55
Lawrence, Richard A.
See Leopold, Nathan F.
Lawrence, Robert
See Beum, Robert (Lawrence)
Lawrence, Robert A(llen) 1948- ... 118
Lawrence, Robert 1912(?)-1981 Obituary ... 105
Lawrence, Roy 1930- ... 45-48
Lawrence, Samuel A. 1928- ... 21-24R
Lawrence, Sharon 1945- ... 65-68
Lawrence, Steven C.
See Murphy, Lawrence A(gustus)
Lawrence, T(homas) E(dward)
1888-1935 Brief entry ... 115
See also Dale, Colin
See also TCLC 18
Lawrence, Thomas
See Roberts, Thom(as Sacra)
Lawrence, Vera Brodsky 1909- Brief entry ... 109
Lawrence, William Howard
1916-1972 Obituary ... 33-36R
Lawrence, William J(ohn) C(ooper)
1899(?)-1985 Obituary ... 118
Lawrence Of Arabia
See Lawrence, T(homas) E(dward)
Lawrenson, Helen 1907-1982 ... 117
Obituary ... 106
Lawrenson, Thomas Edward
1918-1982 Obituary ... 106
Lawry, Jon Sherman 1924- ... 5-8R
Laws, G(eorge) Malcolm Jr. 1919- ... 37-40R
Laws, Priscilla W(atson) 1940- ... 73-76
Lawshe, C(harles) H(ubert) 1908- ... CAP-2
Earlier sketch in CA 23-24
Lawson, (Richard) Alan 1934- ... 53-56
Lawson, Annetta 1939- ... 116
Lawson, Annette 1936- ... 129
Lawson, Carol (Antell) 1946- ... SATA 42
Lawson, Chet
See Tubb, E(dwin) C(harles)
Lawson, David 1927- ... 57-60
Lawson, Don(ald Elmer) 1917-1990 ... CANR-26
Earlier sketches in CA 1-4R, 130, CANR-2
See also SATA 9
Lawson, Donna Roberta 1937- ... 41-44R
Lawson, E(verett) LeRoy 1938- ... CANR-19
Earlier sketches in CA 53-56, CANR-4
Lawson, Evelyn 1917- ... 57-60
Lawson, F(loyd) Melvyn 1907- ... 53-56
Lawson, Frederick Henry
1897-1983 Obituary ... 109
Lawson, H(orace) L(owe) 1900- ... 5-8R
Lawson, H. Lowe
See Lawson, H(orace) L(owe)
Lawson, Henry (Archibald Hertzberg)
1867-1922 Brief entry ... 120
See also TCLC 27
Lawson, Jacob
See Burgess, M(ichael) R(oy)
Lawson, James 1938- ... 65-68
Lawson, Joan 1906- ... 103
See also SATA 55
Lawson, John ... DLB 24
Lawson, John Howard 1894-1977 ... CAP-1
Obituary ... 73-76
Earlier sketch in CA 13-16
Lawson, John 1909- ... CANR-3
Earlier sketch in CA 1-4R
Lawson, Kay 1933- ... 104
Lawson, Lewis A. 1931- ... 21-24R
Lawson, M. C.
See Lawson, H(orace) L(owe)
Lawson, Marion Tubbs 1896- ... CAP-1
Earlier sketch in CA 9-10
See also SATA 22
Lawson, Michael
See Ryder, M(ichael) L(awson)
Lawson, Philip J. 1908(?)-1978 Obituary ... 77-80
Lawson, (Phillippe) Reed 1929- ... 5-8R
Lawson, Richard H(enry) 1919- ... CANR-8
Earlier sketch in CA 17-20R
Lawson, Robert G. 1938- ... 118
Lawson, Robert 1892-1957 ... 137
Brief entry ... 118
See also CLR 2
See also DLB 22
See also MAICYA
See also YABC 2
Lawson, Ronald (Lynton) 1940- ... 126
Lawson, Ruth C(atherine) 1911- ... 9-12R
Lawson, S. Alexander 1912- ... 57-60
Lawson, Sarah (Anne) 1943- ... 120
Lawson, Steve
See Turner, Robert (Harry)
Lawson, Steven F(red) 1945- ... 122
Lawson, Victor F. 1850-1925 ... DLB 25
Lawson, W. B.
See Jenks, George C(harles)
Lawton, Charles
See Heckelmann, Charles N(ewman)
Lawton, Dennis
See Faust, Frederick (Shiller)
Lawton, Harry Wilson 1927- ... 33-36R
Lawton, Manny
See Lawton, Marion R(ussell)
Lawton, Marion R(ussell) 1918-1986 ... 118
Lawton, Sherman P(axton) 1908- ... CAP-2
Earlier sketch in CA 19-20
Lawyer, Annabel Glenn
1906(?)-1974 Obituary ... 53-56
Law Yone, Edward Michael
1911(?)-1980 Obituary ... 101
Lax, Eric 1944- ... 138
Lax, Robert 1915- ... CANR-27
Earlier sketches in CA 25-28R, CANR-11
Laxalt, Robert P(eter) 1923- ... CANR-38
Earlier sketch in CA 13-16R
Laxness, Halldor
See Gudjonsson, Halldor Kiljan
See also CLC 25
Lay, Bennett 1910- ... CAP-1
Earlier sketch in CA 11-12
Lay, Bierne Jr. 1909-1982 Obituary ... 107
Lay, Daniel W(ayne) 1914- ... 118
Lay, Nancy Duke S. 1938- ... CANR-21
Earlier sketch in CA 105
Lay, Norvie L(ee) 1940- ... 49-52
Lay, S(amuel) Houston 1912- ... 33-36R
Lay, Shawn 1953- ... 124
Layard, (Peter) Richard (Grenville) 1934- ... 128
Laybourne, Lawrence E.
1914(?)-1976 Obituary ... 65-68
Laycock, Ellen (Mae) 1921- ... 112
Laycock, George (Edwin) 1921- ... CANR-19
Earlier sketches in CA 5-8R, CANR-4
See also SATA 5
Laycock, Harold R. (I. O.) 1916- ... 5-8R
Laye, Camara 1928-1980 ... CANR-25
Obituary ... 97-100
Earlier sketch in CA 85-88
See also BLC 2
See also BW
See also CLC 4, 38
See also MTCW
Layman, Constance 1943- ... 111
Layman, Emma McCloy 1910- ... 81-84
Layman, Richard 1947- ... CANR-35
Earlier sketch in CA 65-68
Laymon, Charles Martin 1904- ... CANR-7
Earlier sketch in CA 9-12R
Layne, Bobby
See Layne, Robert Lawrence
Layne, Laura
See Knott, William C(ecil Jr.)
Layne, Robert Lawrence
1927-1986 Obituary ... 121
Layton, Andrea
See Bancroft, Iris (May Nelson)
Layton, Aviva 1933- ... 116
Layton, Edwin T(homas) Jr. 1928- ... 29-32R
Layton, Felix 1910- ... CAP-2
Earlier sketch in CA 23-24
Layton, Irving (Peter) 1912- ... CANR-33
Earlier sketches in CA 1-4R, CANR-2
See also CLC 2, 15
See also DLB 88
See also MTCW
Layton, Marilyn Smith 1941- ... 114
Layton, Max 1946- ... 128
Layton, Robert 1930- ... 21-24R
Layton, Thomas Arthur 1910- ... 9-12R
Layton, Wilbur L. 1922- Brief entry ... 106
Layton, William (Isaac) 1913- ... 17-20R
Lazar, Wendy 1939- ... 104
Lazare, Gerald John 1927- ... SATA 44
Lazare, Jerry
See Lazare, Gerald John
Lazareff, Pierre 1907-1972 Obituary ... 33-36R
Lazareth, William Henry 1928- ... CANR-16
Earlier sketches in CA 1-4R, CANR-1
Lazarevich, Mila 1942- ... SATA 17
Lazaron, Hilda R(othschild) 1895- ... 49-52
Lazarre, Jane D(eitz) 1943- ... 101
Lazarsfeld, Paul F(elix) 1901-1976 ... CANR-29
Obituary ... 69-72
Earlier sketch in CA 73-76
Lazarus, A(rnold) L(eslie) 1914- ... CANR-11
Earlier sketch in CA 25-28R
Lazarus, Arnold A(llan) 1932- ... CANR-14
Earlier sketch in CA 41-44R
Lazarus, Arthur 1892(?)-1978 Obituary ... 77-80
Lazarus, Edward H. 1959- ... 122
Lazarus, Felix
See Cable, George Washington
Lazarus, Harold 1927- ... 21-24R
Lazarus, John 1947- ... 132
Lazarus, Keo Felker 1913- ... 41-44R
See also SATA 21
Lazarus, Marguerite 1916- ... 106
Lazarus, Mell 1927- ... CANR-11
Earlier sketch in CA 17-20R
Lazarus, Pat 1935- ... 130
Lazarus, Paul N. 1913- ... 126
Lazarus, Richard S(tanley) 1922- ... CANR-5
Earlier sketch in CA 1-4R
Lazarus, Simon 1941- ... 57-60
Lazear, Edward P. 1948- ... 129
LaZebnik, Edith 1897- ... 85-88
Lazell, James Draper Jr. 1939- ... 65-68
Lazenby, Walter S(ylvester) Jr. 1930- ... 65-68
Lazer, William 1924- ... CANR-19
Earlier sketches in CA 1-4R, CANR-4
Lazere, Donald 1935- ... 105
Lazerowitz, Alice Ambrose 1906- ... CANR-17
Earlier sketches in CA 49-52, CANR-1
Lazerowitz, Morris 1907- ... CANR-17
Earlier sketches in CA 9-12R, CANR-3
Lazlo, Kate
See Angus, Sylvia
Lazo, Hector 1899-1965 ... CANR-3
Earlier sketch in CA 1-4R
Lazreg, Marnia 1941- ... 69-72
Lea, Alec 1907- ... 73-76
See also SATA 19
Lea, David A(lexander) M(aclure)
1934- ... CANR-10
Earlier sketch in CA 21-24R
Lea, F(rank) A(lfred) 1915-1977 ... CANR-3
Earlier sketch in CA 1-4R
Lea, Frederick (Measham)
1900-1984 Obituary ... 113
Lea, Henry Charles 1825-1909 Brief entry ... 122
See also DLB 47
Lea, James F(ranklin) 1945- ... 130
Lea, Joan
See Neufeld, John (Arthur)
Lea, John Sedgwick 1910(?)-1987 Obituary ... 124
Lea, Kathleen M(arguerite) 1903- ... 119
Lea, Sydney (L. Wright Jr.) 1942- ... CANR-22
Earlier sketch in CA 106
See also DLB 120
Lea, Timothy
See Wood, Christopher (Hovelle)
Lea, Tom 1907- Brief entry ... 115
See also DLB 6
Leab, Daniel Josef 1936- ... CANR-11
Earlier sketch in CA 29-32R
Leabo, Dick A. 1921- ... 9-12R
Leacacos, John P. 1908-1986 ... 25-28R
Obituary ... 121
Leach, Aroline Beecher 1899- ... 61-64
Leach, Barry Arthur 1930- ... 102
Leach, Bernard Howell 1887-1979 ... 97-100
Obituary ... 85-88
Leach, Douglas Edward 1920- ... 17-20R
Leach, E. R.
See Leach, Edmund Ronald
Leach, Edmund
See Leach, Edmund Ronald
Leach, Edmund R.
See Leach, Edmund Ronald
Leach, Edmund Ronald
1910-1989 Obituary ... 127
Leach, Eleanor Winsor 1937- ... 103
Leach, Gerald Adrian 1933- ... CANR-21
Earlier sketch in CA 5-8R
Leach, Graham (John) 1948- ... 122
Leach, John Robert 1922- ... 21-24R
Leach, Joseph (Lee) 1921- ... 29-32R
Leach, Maria 1892-1977 ... 53-56
Obituary ... 69-72
See also SATA 28, 39
Leach, (Richard) Max(well) 1909- ... 41-44R
Leach, Michael 1940- ... 73-76
Leach, Paul Roscoe 1890-1977 Obituary ... 73-76
Leach, Penelope (Jane) 1937- ... CANR-21
Earlier sketch in CA 97-100
Leach, Richard H(eald) 1922- ... 127
Brief entry ... 113
Leach, Robert J. 1916- ... 29-32R
Leach, (Carson) Wilford 1932(?)-1988 ... CANR-2
Obituary ... 125
Earlier sketch in CA 45-48
Leachman, Robert Briggs 1921- ... 104
Leacock, Eleanor Burke 1922-1987 ... CANR-15
Obituary ... 122
Earlier sketch in CA 37-40R
Leacock, John 1729-1802 ... DLB 31
Leacock, Ruth 1926- ... 37-40R
Leacock, Stephen (Butler)
1869-1944 Brief entry ... 104
See also DLB 92
See also TCLC 2
Leacroft, Helen (Mabel Beal) 1919- ... CANR-2
Earlier sketch in CA 5-8R
See also SATA 6
Leacroft, Richard (Vallance Becher)
1914- ... CANR-2
Earlier sketch in CA 5-8R
See also SATA 6
Leadbetter, Eric 1892(?)-1971 Obituary ... 104
Leadbitter, Mike 1942- ... 41-44R
Leader, (Evelyn) Barbara (Blackburn)
1898- ... 61-64
Leader, Charles
See Smith, Robert Charles
Leader, Mary (Bartelt) ... 85-88
Leader, Ninon 1933- ... 21-24R
Leader, Shelah Gilbert 1943- ... CANR-27
Earlier sketch in CA 110
Leader, Zachary 1946- ... 138
Leaf, David 1952- ... 117
Leaf, Margaret P. 1909(?)-1988 Obituary ... 124
See also SATA 55
Leaf, (Wilbur) Munro 1905-1976 ... CANR-29
Obituary ... 69-72
Earlier sketch in CA 73-76
See also CLR 25
See also MAICYA
See also SATA 20
Leaf, Murray J(ohn) 1939- ... CANR-1
Earlier sketch in CA 45-48
Leaf, Paul 1929- ... 132
Leaf, Russell C(harles) 1935- ... 21-24R
Leaf, VaDonna Jean 1929- ... 57-60
See also SATA 26
Leagans, John Paul 1911- ... 103
Leahy, James E. 1919- ... 138
Leahy, Syrell Rogovin 1935- ... CANR-29
Earlier sketches in CA 57-60, CANR-12
Leake, Chauncey D(epew) 1896-1978 ... CANR-3
Obituary ... 73-76
Earlier sketch in CA 49-52
Leake, Jane Acomb 1928- ... 21-24R
Leakey, Louis S(eymour) B(azett)
1903-1972 ... 97-100
Obituary ... 37-40R
See also MTCW
Leakey, Mary (Douglas Nicol) 1913- ... CANR-18
Earlier sketch in CA 97-100
Leakey, Richard E(rskine Frere)
1944- ... CANR-18
Earlier sketch in CA 93-96
See also SATA 42
Leal, Luis 1907- ... 131
See also HW
Leale, B(arry) C(avendish) 1930- ... 132
Leaman, David R(ay) 1947- ... 115
Leamer, Edward E(mery) 1944- ... 29-32R
Leamer, Laurence Allen 1941- ... CANR-35
Earlier sketches in CA 65-68, CANR-13
Leaming, Barbara ... CANR-25
Earlier sketch in CA 107
Lean, Arthur E(dward) 1909- ... 73-76
Lean, David 1908-1991 ... 134
Brief entry ... 111
Lean, E(dward) Tangye
1911-1974 Obituary ... 53-56
Lean, Garth Dickinson 1912- ... CANR-17
Earlier sketch in CA 29-32R
Leander, Ed
See Richelson, Geraldine
Leaney, Alfred Robert Clare 1909- ... CANR-2
Earlier sketch in CA 5-8R
Leaning, Jennifer 1945- ... 132
Leap, Harry P(atrick) 1908-1976 ... 1-4R
Obituary ... 103
Leapman, Michael 1938- ... 109
Leapor, Mary 1722-1746 ... DLB 109
Lear, Edward 1812-1888 ... CLR 1
See also DLB 32
See also MAICYA
See also SATA 18
Lear, Floyd Seyward 1895- ... CAP-1
Earlier sketch in CA 17-18
Lear, John 1909- ... 37-40R
Lear, Martha Weinman 1930- ... CANR-9
Earlier sketch in CA 9-12R
Lear, Melva Gwendoline Bartlett 1917- ... 5-8R
Lear, Norman (Milton) 1922- ... 73-76
See also CLC 12
Lear, Peter
See Lovesey, Peter (Harmer)
Leard, G(eorge) Earl 1918- ... 9-12R
Leard, John E. 1916- ... 73-76
Learmonth, Andrew Thomas Amos
1916- ... 13-16R
Learned, Edmund Philip 1900- ... 104
Learning, Walter J. 1938- ... 130
Leary, David E. 1945- ... 124
Leary, Edward A(ndrew) 1913- ... CANR-12
Earlier sketch in CA 29-32R
Leary, James F. 1942- ... 126
Leary, John P(atrick) 1919- ... 9-12R
Leary, Lewis (Gaston) 1906-1990 ... CANR-4
Obituary ... 131
Earlier sketch in CA 1-4R
Leary, Paris 1931- ... 17-20R
Leary, Timothy (Francis) 1920- ... 107
See also DLB 16
See also MTCW
Leary, William G(ordon) 1915- ... CANR-31
Earlier sketch in CA 49-52
Leary, William M. Jr. 1934- ... 93-96
Leas, Speed 1937- ... CANR-30
Earlier sketch in CA 49-52
Lease, Benjamin 1917- Brief entry ... 114
Lease, Gary 1940- ... CANR-38
Earlier sketch in CA 45-48
Leasher, Evelyn M(arie) 1941- ... 115

Leask, Ian Graham 1951- 138
Leaska, Mitchell A(lexander) 1934- CANR-39
Earlier sketches in CA 77-80, CANR-13
Leasor, (Thomas) James 1923- CANR-2
Earlier sketch in CA 1-4R
See also SATA 54
Least Heat Moon, William
See Trogdon, William (Lewis)
Leasure, Robert E. 1921- 112
Leather, Edwin (Hartley Cameron)
1919- 97-100
Leather, George
See Swallow, Norman
Leatherman, LeRoy 1922-1984 ....21-24R
Obituary 112
Leaton, Anne 1932- 130
Leautaud, Paul 1872-1956 .... DLB 65
Leavell, Landrum P(inson) II 1926- 89-92
Leavenworth, Carol 1940- CANR-14
Earlier sketch in CA 81-84
Leavenworth, James Lynn 1915- 21-24R
Leaver, Robin Alan 1939- CANR-9
Earlier sketch in CA 61-64
Leavey, John P(eter) Jr. 1951- 127
Leavis, F(rank) R(aymond) 1895-1978 ......21-24R
Obituary 77-80
See also CLC 24
See also MTCW
Leavis, Q(ueenie) D(orothy) 1906-1981 97-100
Obituary 108
Leavitt, David 1961- 122
Brief entry 116
See also CLC 34
Leavitt, Harold J(ack) 1922- 125
Brief entry 117
Leavitt, Hart Day 1909- 13-16R
Leavitt, Harvey R(obert) 1934- 65-68
Leavitt, Jack 1931- 97-100
Leavitt, Jerome E(dward) 1916- CANR-17
Earlier sketches in CA 1-4R, CANR-1
See also SATA 23
Leavitt, Judith A(nn) 1947- CANR-27
Earlier sketch in CA 110
Leavitt, Richard Freeman 1929- 89-92
Leavitt, Ruby R.
See Rohrlich, Ruby
Leavitt, William J. 1928-1984 Obituary 112
Leavy, Stanley A(rnold) 1915- 120
LeBar, Lois E. 1907- 21-24R
LeBar, Mary E(velyn) 1910-1982 ....CANR-25
Earlier sketch in CA 107
See also SATA 35
LeBaron, Charles W. 1943- CANR-9
Earlier sketch in CA 61-64
LeBeau, Roy
See Smith, Mitchell
Lebeaux, Richard 1946- CANR-12
Earlier sketch in CA 73-76
Lebedoff, David (Michael) 1938- 126
Leber, George L. 1917(?)-1976 Obituary 61-64
Lebergott, Stanley 1918- 103
Lebert, Randy
See Brannon, William T.
Lebeson, Anita Libman 1896-1987 ....29-32R
Obituary 121
LeBlanc, Annette M. 1965- .... SATA 68
LeBlanc, L(ee) 1913- .... SATA 54
Leblanc, Maurice (Marie Emile)
1864-1941 Brief entry 110
LeBlanc, Rena Dictor 1938- 104
Leblon, Jean (Marcel Jules) 1928- 41-44R
Lebo, Dell 1922- 57-60
LeBoeuf, Michael 1942- CANR-15
Earlier sketch in CA 93-96
Le Boutillier, Cornelia Geer
1894(?)-1973 Obituary 45-48
Lebovich, William Louis 1948- CANR-37
Earlier sketch in CA 115
Lebovitz, Harold Paul 1916- 77-80
Lebow, Eileen F. 1925- 132
Lebow, Jeanne 1951- 135
Lebow, Richard Ned 1942- 129
Lebow, Victor 1902-1980 ....37-40R
Obituary 133
Lebowitz, Alan 1934- 25-28R
Lebowitz, Albert 1922- 73-76
Lebowitz, Fran(ces Ann) 1951(?)- CANR-14
Earlier sketch in CA 81-84
See also CLC 11, 36
See also MTCW
Lebowitz, Naomi 1932- 37-40R
Leboyer, Frederick 1918- 106
Lebra, Joyce C(hapman) CANR-1
Earlier sketch in CA 45-48
Lebra, Takie Sugiyama 1930- 77-80
Lebra, William P(hilip) 1922- 33-36R
Lebrecht, Norman 1948- 117
Lebreo, Steward
See Weiner, Stewart
Lebreo, Stewart
See Weiner, Stewart
Le Breton, Auguste
See Montfort, Auguste
Le Bris, Michel 1944- 131
Le Brown, Andreas
See Brown, Andreas Le
Lebrun, Claude 1929- 136
See also SATA 66
LeBrun, Gautier
See Gibson, Walter B(rown)
LeBrun, George P. 1862-1966 ....5-8R
Lebrun, Richard Allen 1931- 41-44R
Le Cain, Errol John 1941-1989 ....CANR-13
Obituary 127
Earlier sketch in CA 33-36R
See also MAICYA
See also SATA 6, 60, 68
Lecale, Errol
See McNeilly, Wilfred (Glassford)
Lecar, Helene Lerner 1938- 25-28R
le Carre, John
See Cornwell, David (John Moore)
See also BEST 89:4
See also CDBLB 1960 to Present
See also CLC 3, 5, 9, 15, 28
See also DLB 87
Lecavele, Roland
See Dorgeles, Roland
Le Chanois, Jean-Paul
See Drefus, Jean-Paul Etienne
Lechlitner, Ruth N. 1901- 105
See also DLB 48
Lechner, Robert F(irman) 1918- 33-36R
Lecht, Charles Philip 1933- 21-24R
Lecht, Leonard A. 1920- CANR-28
Earlier sketches in CA 25-28R, CANR-11
Lechtenberg, Richard 1947- 125
Lecker, Robert 1951- CANR-28
Earlier sketch in CA 111
Leckey, Dolores (Conklin) 1933- 109
Leckie, Keith (Ross) 1952- 130
Leckie, Robert (Hugh) 1920- 13-16R
Leckie, William H. 1915- 21-24R
LeClair, Thomas 1944- 113
LeClair, Tom
See LeClair, Thomas
LeClaire, Gordon 1905- 69-72
Leclant, Jean 1920- 132
Leclerc, Felix 1914- ....DLB 60
Leclerc, Ivor 1915- 33-36R
Leclerc, Victor
See Parry, Albert
Le Clercq, Jacques Georges Clemenceau
1898-1972 Obituary 37-40R
Le Clezio, J(ean) M(arie) G(ustave) 1940- 128
Brief entry 116
See also CLC 31
See also DLB 83
Le Cocq, Rhoda P(riscilla) 1921- 73-76
Lecoin, Louis 1888(?)-1971 Obituary 33-36R
Lecomber, Brian 1945- CANR-13
Earlier sketch in CA 73-76
LeCompte, (Nancy) Jane 1948- 133
Lecompte, Janet 1923- 122
Le Comte, Edward (Semple) 1916- CANR-5
Earlier sketch in CA 1-4R
Lecomte du Nouey
See Lecomte du Nouey, Pierre (-Andre-Leon)
Lecomte du Nouey, P.
See Lecomte du Nouey, Pierre (-Andre-Leon)
Lecomte du Nouey, Pierre (-Andre-Leon)
1883-1947 Brief entry 119
Lecomte du Nouy, Pierre (-Andre-Leon)
See Lecomte du Nouey, Pierre (-Andre-Leon)
Le Coq, Monsieur
See Simenon, Georges (Jacques Christian)
LeCroy, Anne K(ingsbury) 1930- CANR-16
Earlier sketch in CA 41-44R
LeCroy, Ruth Brooks 45-48
Ledbetter, J(ack) T(racy) 1934- 73-76
Ledbetter, Jack Wallace 1930- 5-8R
Ledbetter, Joe O(verton) 1927- 45-48
Ledbetter, Ken(neth Lee) 1931- 117
Ledbetter, Les 1941(?)-1985 Obituary 116
Ledbetter, Virgil C. 1918- CAP-1
Earlier sketch in CA 13-16
Ledderose, Lothar 1942- 85-88
Leder, Jane Mersky 1945- 117
See also SATA 51, 61
Leder, Lawrence H. 1927- 25-28R
Leder, Rudolf
See Hermlin, Stephen
Lederer, Charles 1910-1976 Obituary 65-68
See also DLB 26
Lederer, Chloe 1915- 77-80
Lederer, Edith Madelon 1943- 97-100
Lederer, Esther Pauline 1918- 89-92
Lederer, Ivo J(ohn) 1929- 9-12R
Lederer, Jiri 1922-1983 Obituary 111
Lederer, Joseph 1927- 73-76
Lederer, Lajos 1904-1985 Obituary 118
Lederer, Laura 1951- 121
Lederer, Muriel 1929- 77-80
See also SATA 48
Lederer, Paul Joseph 1944- 111
Lederer, Rhoda Catharine (Kitto)
1910- CANR-22
Earlier sketches in CA 9-12R, CANR-6
Lederer, Richard 1938- 132
Lederer, William J(ulius) 1912- CANR-5
Earlier sketch in CA 1-4R
See also SATA 62
Lederman, Leonard L(awrence) 1931- 61-64
Ledermann, Erich Kurt 1908- 107
Ledermann, Walter 1911- CANR-30
Earlier sketch in CA 49-52
Ledesert, (Dorothy) Margaret 1916- CANR-28
Earlier sketch in CA 45-48
Ledesert, R(ene) P(ierre) L(ouis)
1913-1984 ....CANR-28
Obituary 114
Earlier sketch in CA 45-48
Ledoux, Paul (Martin) 1949- 131
Le Duan 1908(?)-1986 Obituary 119
Le Duc, Don R(aymond) 1933- CANR-31
Earlier sketch in CA 49-52
Leduc, Violette 1907-1972 .... CAP-1
Obituary 33-36R
Earlier sketch in CA 13-14
See also CLC 22
Ledwidge, Francis 1887(?)-1917 Brief entry 123
See also DLB 20
See also TCLC 23
Ledwidge, William (Bernard) John 1915- 103
Ledwith, Frank 1907- 103
Ledyard, Gleason H(ines) 1919- 5-8R
Lee, A. R.
See Ash, Rene Lee
Lee, A(rthur) Robert 1941- 130
Lee, Addison E(arl) 1914- 9-12R
Lee, Adrian Iselin Jr. 1920- 89-92
Lee, Al(fred Matthew) 1938- 45-48
Lee, Alfred McClung 1906- CANR-19
Obituary 137
Earlier sketches in CA 1-4R, CANR-3
Lee, Alvin A. 1930- 33-36R
Lee, Amanda
See Baggett, Nancy
and Buckholtz, Eileen (Garber)
and Glick, Ruth (Burtnick)
Lee, Amber
See Baldwin, Faith
Lee, Andrea
See Toona, Elin(-Kai)
Lee, Andrea 1953- 125
See also BLC 2
See also BW
See also CLC 36
Lee, Andrew
See Auchincloss, Louis (Stanton)
Lee, Arthur M(atthias) 1918- 41-44R
Lee, Asher 1909- 73-76
Lee, Audrey 25-28R
Lee, Austin 1904- CAP-1
Earlier sketch in CA 13-16
Lee, Barbara A(nne) 1949- 128
Lee, Barbara (Moore) 1934- CANR-9
Earlier sketch in CA 53-56
Lee, Barbara 1932- 109
Lee, Benjamin 1921- 104
See also SATA 27
Lee, Betsy 1949- 106
See also SATA 37
Lee, Betty
See Lambert, Elizabeth (Minnie)
Lee, Betty 1921- 103
Lee, Bill
See Lee, William Saul
Lee, Bob
See McGrath, Robert L(ee)
Lee, Brother Basil Leo
1909-1974 Obituary 53-56
Lee, C(live) H(oward) 1942- 126
Lee, C(harles) Nicholas 1933- 49-52
Lee, C(larence) P(endleton) 1913- 49-52
Lee, C(hin)-Y(ana) 1917- 9-12R
Lee, Calvin B. T. 1934- 33-36R
Lee, Carol
See Fletcher, Helen Jill
Lee, Carolina
See Dern, Erolie Pearl Gaddis
Lee, Carvel (Bigham) 1910- CAP-1
Earlier sketch in CA 13-14
Lee, Charles Robert Jr. 1929- 5-8R
Lee, Charles 1913- 33-36R
Lee, Charlotte I(rene) 1909- 21-24R
Lee, Chong-Sik 1931- CANR-15
Earlier sketch in CA 41-44R
Lee, Christine Eckstrom 1952- 110
Lee, Christopher Frank Carandini 1922- 73-76
Lee, David Dale 1948- 117
Lee, David 1944- CANR-29
Earlier sketch in CA 111
Lee, Deemer 1905-1979 111
Lee, Dennis (Beynon) 1939- CANR-31
Earlier sketches in CA 25-28R, CANR-11
See also CLR 3
See also DLB 53
See also MAICYA
See also SATA 14
Lee, Derek 1937- 107
Lee, (Henry) Desmond (Pritchard) 1908- 102
Lee, Devon
See Pohle, Robert W(arren) Jr.
Lee, Don L.
See Madhubuti, Haki R.
See also CLC 2
Lee, Doris Emrick 1905-1983 Obituary 110
See also SATA 35, 44
Lee, Dorris M(ay Potter) 1905- 13-16R
Lee, Douglas A(llen) 1932- 53-56
Lee, Dwight E(rwin) 1898- 5-8R
Lee, Eddie H. 1917- 69-72
Lee, Edward Edson 1884-1944 128
See also AITN 1
Lee, Edward N(icholls) 1935- 29-32R
Lee, Elizabeth Briant 1908- 37-40R
Lee, Elsie 1912- 85-88
Lee, Eric
See Lee, Fleming
and Page, Gerald W(ilburn)
Lee, Essie E. 1920- CANR-4
Earlier sketch in CA 49-52
Lee, Eugene (Huey) 1941- 49-52
Lee, Fleming 1933- CANR-7
Earlier sketch in CA 9-12R
Lee, Florence Henry 1910- CAP-1
Earlier sketch in CA 17-18
Lee, Francis Nigel 1934- CANR-8
Earlier sketch in CA 57-60
Lee, Frank F(reeman) 1920- 1-4R
Lee, Fred 1927- 109
Lee, G. Avery 1916- 104
Lee, George J. 1920(?)-1976 Obituary 65-68
Lee, George Leslie
See Lee, Brother Basil Leo
Lee, George W(ashington) 1894-1976 125
See also BLC 2
See also BW
See also CLC 52
See also DLB 51
Lee, Gerard (Majella) 1951- 93-96
Lee, Ginffa 1900(?)-1976 Obituary 69-72
Lee, Gordon C(anfield) 1916-1972 ....13-16R
Obituary 135
Lee, Gypsy Rose
See Hovick, Rose Louise
Lee, H. Alton 1942- 81-84
Lee, Hahn-Been 1921- CANR-11
Earlier sketch in CA 25-28R
Lee, Harold N(ewton) 1899- 37-40R
Lee, (Nelle) Harper 1926- 13-16R
See also CDALB 1941-1968
See also CLC 12, 60
See also DLB 6
See also MTCW
See also SATA 11
See also WLC
Lee, Harriet 1757-1851 .... DLB 39
Lee, Harry J. Jr. 1914-1985 Obituary 118
Lee, Hector (Haight) 1908- 97-100
Lee, Helen Clara 1919- 49-52
Lee, Helen Jackson 1908- 81-84
Lee, Henry F(oster) 1913- 89-92
Lee, Henry (Walsh) 1911- 5-8R
Lee, Herbert d'H.
See Kastle, Herbert D(avid)
Lee, Hermione 1948- CANR-15
Earlier sketch in CA 73-76
Lee, Howard
See Goulart, Ron(ald Joseph)
Lee, Irvin H. 1932-1980 ....21-24R
Obituary 133
Lee, J(erry) W(allace) 1932- 93-96
Lee, James A(lvin) 1922- 126
Lee, James F. 1905(?)-1975 Obituary 61-64
Lee, James Michael 1931- CANR-30
Earlier sketches in CA 17-20R, CANR-13
Lee, James W. 1931- 25-28R
Lee, Janet 1904-1988 Obituary 127
Lee, Janice (Jeanne) 1944- 33-36R
Lee, Jennie
See Lee, Janet
Lee, Joe Won 1921- 41-44R
Lee, John A(lexander) 1891- CANR-7
Earlier sketch in CA 53-56
Lee, John (Darrell) 1931- CANR-9
Earlier sketch in CA 25-28R
Lee, John Eric 1919- 33-36R
Lee, John Michael 1932- CANR-6
Earlier sketch in CA 13-16R
Lee, John R(obert) 1923-1976 57-60
Obituary 120
See also SATA 27
Lee, Jordan
See Scholefield, Alan
Lee, Judith Yaross 1949- 137
Lee, Judy
See Carlson, Judith Lee
Lee, Julian
See Latham, Jean Lee
Lee, Jung Young 1935- 33-36R
Lee, Kay
See Kelly, Karen
Lee, L(awrence) L(ynn) 1924- 73-76
Lee, Lamar Jr. 1911- 17-20R
Lee, Lance 1942- CANR-13
Earlier sketch in CA 77-80
Lee, Larry
See Lee, Lawrence
Lee, Laurel 1945(?)- 138
Brief entry 113
Lee, Laurie 1914- CANR-33
Earlier sketch in CA 77-80
See also DLB 27
See also MTCW
Lee, (Enoch) Lawrence 1912- 13-16R
Lee, Lawrence 1903- 25-28R
See also CLC 34
Lee, Lawrence 1941-1990 Obituary 131
Lee, Leo Ou-fan 1939- 102
Lee, Lincoln 1922- 9-12R
Lee, Linda 1947- CANR-13
Earlier sketch in CA 77-80
Lee, Loyd Ervin 1939- 102
Lee, Lucy
See Talbot, Charlene Joy
Lee, M(ark) Owen 1930- 33-36R
Lee, Mabel Barbee
1886(?)-1978 Obituary 85-88
Lee, Mabel 1886-1985 134
Lee, Malka 1905(?)-1976 Obituary 65-68
Lee, Manfred B(ennington) 1905-1971 ....CANR-2
Obituary 29-32R
Earlier sketch in CA 1-4R
See also Queen, Ellery
See also CLC 11
Lee, Manning de Villeneuve
1894-1980 Obituary 104
See also SATA 22, 37
Lee, Maria Berl 1924- CANR-9
Earlier sketch in CA 61-64
Lee, Marian
See Clish, (Lee) Marian
Lee, Marjorie 1921- CANR-4
Earlier sketch in CA 1-4R
Lee, Mark W. 1923- CANR-18
Earlier sketches in CA 9-12R, CANR-3
Lee, Martin A. 1954- 121
Lee, Mary Price 1934- CANR-24
Earlier sketches in CA 57-60, CANR-9
See also SATA 8
Lee, Mary 1949- 29-32R
Lee, Maryat 1923-1989 ....25-28R
Obituary 129
Lee, Matt
See Merwin, Sam(uel Kimball) Jr.

Lee, Maurice (duPont) Jr. 1925- CANR-21
Earlier sketch in CA 45-48
Lee, Meredith 1945- 93-96
Lee, Mildred
See Scudder, Mildred Lee
See also SATA 6
Lee, Mildred 1908- ....SAAS 12
Lee, Molly K(yung) S(ook) C(hang) 1934- 53-56
Lee, Muna 1895-1965 Obituary 25-28R
Lee, Nata
See Frackman, Nathaline
Lee, Nathaniel 1645(?)-1692 ....DLB 80
Lee, Norma E. 1924- 65-68
Lee, Oliver M(inseem) 1927- 41-44R
Lee, Pali Jae 1929- CANR-31
Earlier sketches in CA 29-32R, CANR-13
Lee, Parker
See Turner, Robert (Harry)
Lee, Patricia 1941- 115
Lee, Patrick C(ornelius) 1936- 65-68
Lee, Peter H(acksoo) 1929- CANR-3
Earlier sketch in CA 9-12R
Lee, Peter 1947- 127
Lee, Philip J. 1932- 124
Lee, Polly Jae
See Lee, Pali Jae
Lee, R(oy) Alton 1931- 21-24R
Lee, Raymond L(awrence) 1911- 41-44R
Lee, Raymond 1910(?)-1974 Obituary 49-52
Lee, Rebecca Smith 1894- 5-8R
Lee, Rensselaer W(right)
1898-1984 Obituary 114
Lee, Richard
See Lee, Richard B(orshay)
Lee, Richard B(orshay) 1937- CANR-20
Earlier sketch in CA 45-48
Lee, Robert
See Fairman, Paul W.
Lee, Robert C. 1931- CANR-10
Earlier sketch in CA 25-28R
See also SATA 20
Lee, Robert E. A. 1921- 9-12R
Lee, Robert E(arl) 1906- 53-56
See also AITN 1
Lee, Robert E(dwin) 1918- CANR-2
Earlier sketch in CA 45-48
See also SATA 65
Lee, Robert Edson 1921- 25-28R
Lee, Robert Edward 1912- 111
Lee, Robert Greene 1886- CANR-3
Earlier sketch in CA 1-4R
Lee, Robert J. 1921- ....SATA 10
Lee, Robert 1929- CANR-3
Earlier sketch in CA 5-8R
Lee, Roberta
See McGrath, Robert L(ee)
Lee, Ronald 1934- 37-40R
Lee, Rowena
See Bartlett, Marie (Swan)
Lee, Roy
See Hopkins, Clark
Lee, Roy Stuart 1899- CAP-1
Earlier sketch in CA 9-10
Lee, Russel V(an Arsdale)
1895-1982 Obituary 110
Lee, Ruth (Wile) 1892- CAP-2
Earlier sketch in CA 23-24
Lee, S(amuel) E(dgar) 1894- 73-76
Lee, S(idney) G(illmore) M(cKenzie)
1920-1973 ....CAP-2
Earlier sketch in CA 33-36
Lee, Sally 1943- 134
See also SATA 67
Lee, Samuel J(ames) 1906- CAP-2
Earlier sketch in CA 29-32
Lee, Shelton Jackson 1957(?)- 125
See also Lee, Spike
See also BW
Lee, Sherman Emery 1918- CANR-1
Earlier sketch in CA 1-4R
Lee, Sophia 1750-1824 ....DLB 39
Lee, Spike
See Lee, Shelton Jackson
See also AAYA 4
Lee, Stan 1922- 111
Brief entry 108
See also AAYA 5
See also CLC 17
Lee, Stewart M(unro) 1925- 57-60
Lee, Susan 135
Lee, Susan Dye 1939- 85-88
Lee, Susan 1944- 110
Lee, Tammie
See Townsend, Thomas L.
Lee, Tanith 1947- 37-40R
See also CLC 46
See also SATA 8
Lee, Terence R(ichard) 1938- 29-32R
Lee, Tom(my L.) 1950- 65-68
Lee, Vernon
See Paget, Violet
See also DLB 57
See also TCLC 5
Lee, Virginia (Yew) 1927- 9-12R
Lee, Virginia 1905(?)-1981 Obituary 105
Lee, W. Storrs
See Lee, William Storrs
Lee, Walt(er William Jr.) 1931- 61-64
Lee, Warner
See Battin, B(rinton) W(arner)
Lee, Warren M. 1908- 77-80
Lee, Wayne C. 1917- CANR-17
Earlier sketches in CA 1-4R, CANR-2
Lee, William
See Burroughs, William S(eward)
Lee, William R(owland) 1911- CANR-19
Earlier sketches in CA 9-12R, CANR-4
Lee, William Saul 1938- 104
Lee, William Storrs 1906- CANR-1
Earlier sketch in CA 1-4R
Lee, Willy
See Burroughs, William S(eward)
Lee, Yur Bok 1934- 29-32R
Leech, Alfred B. 1918(?)-1974 Obituary 49-52
Leech, Bryan Jeffery 1931- 93-96
Leech, Clifford 1909-1977 ....CANR-4
Earlier sketch in CA 1-4R
Leech, Geoffrey N(eil) 1936- CANR-29
Earlier sketches in CA 29-32R, CANR-12
Leech, Kenneth 1939- 103
Leech, Margaret (Kernochan) 1893-1974 93-96
Obituary 49-52
Leecing, Walden A. 1932- 33-36R
Leed, Eric J. 1942- 89-92
Leed, Jacob R. 1924- CANR-7
Earlier sketch in CA 17-20R
Leed, Richard L. 1929- 13-16R
Leed, Theodore W(illiam) 1927- 126
Brief entry 106
Leedham, Charles 1926- 13-16R
Leedham, John 1912- CANR-13
Earlier sketch in CA 21-24R
Leeds, Anthony 1925- 17-20R
Leeds, Barry H. 1940- 29-32R
Leeds, Morton (Harold) 1921- 13-16R
Leeds, Patricia (Miriam)
1920(?)-1985 Obituary 114
Leedy, Jack J. 1921- 21-24R
Leedy, Loreen (Janelle) 1959- 122
See also SATA 50, 54
Leedy, Paul D. 1908- CANR-1
Earlier sketch in CA 1-4R
Leefeldt, Christine 1941- 93-96
Lee-Hamilton, Eugene (Jacob)
1845-1907 Brief entry 117
See also TCLC 22
Lee-Hostetler, Jeri 1940- ....SATA 63
Lee Howard, Leon Alexander
1914-1979(?) Obituary 104
Leek, Sybil 1923-1982 102
Obituary 108
Leekley, Richard N. 1912-1976 Obituary 69-72
Leekley, Thomas B(riggs) 1910- 5-8R
See also SATA 23
Leeman, Wayne A(lvin) 1924- 13-16R
Leeming, David Adams 1937- 49-52
Leeming, Donald 1944- 114
Leeming, Glenda 1943- CANR-4
Earlier sketch in CA 53-56
Leeming, Jo Ann
See Leeming, Joseph
Leeming, John F(ishwick) 1900- CAP-1
Earlier sketch in CA 9-10
Leeming, Joseph 1897-1968 73-76
See also SATA 26
Leeming, Owen (Alfred) 1930- CANR-15
Earlier sketch in CA 65-68
Leenhouts, Keith J(ames) 1925- 61-64
Leepa, Allen 1919- 45-48
Leeper, Sarah H(ammond) 1912- 57-60
Leepson, Marc 1945- 111
Leer, Norman Robert 1937- 17-20R
Leerburger, Benedict A. Jr. 1932- 9-12R
Lees, Andrew 1940- 122
Lees, Carlton Brown 1924- 103
Lees, Charles J. 1919- 25-28R
Lees, Dan 1927- CANR-13
Earlier sketch in CA 33-36R
Lees, Francis A(nthony) 1931- CANR-9
Earlier sketch in CA 65-68
Lees, Gene 1928- CANR-24
Earlier sketches in CA 21-24R, CANR-9
Lees, Hannah
See Fetter, Elizabeth Head
Lees, Hilda Frances 1900-1983 Obituary 111
Lees, John D(avid) 1936- 53-56
Lees, John G(arfield) 1931- 57-60
Lees, Lynn Hollen 1941- 113
Lees, Ray 1931- CANR-8
Earlier sketch in CA 61-64
Lees, Richard 1948- CANR-26
Earlier sketch in CA 108
Leese, Elizabeth 1937- 85-88
Lee Six, Abigail (Etta) 1960- 132
Lees-Milne, James 1908- CANR-31
Earlier sketches in CA 9-12R, CANR-13
Leeson, C(harles) Roland 1926- 93-96
Leeson, Howard A(lfred) 1942- 118
Leeson, Muriel 1920- ....SATA 54
Leeson, R. A.
See Leeson, Robert (Arthur)
Leeson, Robert (Arthur) 1928- CANR-22
Earlier sketch in CA 105
See also MAICYA
See also SATA 42
Leet, Judith 1935- ....CLC 11
Le Fanu, Joseph Sheridan
1814-1873 ....DLB 21, 70
Lefco, Helene 1922- 53-56
Lefcoe, George 1938- 21-24R
Lefcowitz, Barbara F(reedgood) 1935- 104
Lefebure, Marcus 1933- 113
Lefebure, Molly 57-60
Lefebvre, Henri 1901- CANR-11
Earlier sketch in CA 25-28R
Lefebvre d'Argence, Rene-Yvon
1928- CANR-11
Earlier sketch in CA 21-24R
Le Feuvre, Amy Brief entry 111
Lefever, D(avid) Welty 1901- 49-52
Lefever, Ernest W(arren) 1919- CANR-1
Earlier sketch in CA 1-4R
LeFevre, Adam 1950- 81-84
Lefevre, Carl A(nthony) 1913- CANR-7
Earlier sketch in CA 9-12R
Lefevre, Gui
See Bickers, Richard Leslie Townshend
Lefevre, Helen (Elveback) 17-20R
LeFevre, Perry D(eyo) 1921- CANR-25
Earlier sketches in CA 21-24R, CANR-10
LeFevre, Robert (Thomas) 1911-1986 ....CANR-9
Obituary 119
Earlier sketch in CA 57-60
Leff, Arthur A(llen) 1935-1981 Obituary 105
Leff, Gordon 1926- CANR-3
Earlier sketch in CA 9-12R
Leff, Leonard J. 1942- 128
Leff, Nathaniel H. 1938- 25-28R
Leffelaar, Hendrik Louis 1929- 5-8R
Lefferts, George 1921- CANR-14
Earlier sketch in CA 69-72
Leffland, Ella 1931- CANR-35
Earlier sketch in CA 29-32R
See also CLC 19
See also DLBY 84
See also SATA 65
Leffler, Melvyn Paul 1945- 89-92
Lefkoe, Morty R. 1937- 29-32R
Lefkowitz, Annette S(ara) 1922- 17-20R
Lefkowitz, Bernard 1937- CANR-30
Earlier sketch in CA 29-32R
Lefkowitz, Joel M. 1940- 45-48
Lefkowitz, Mary Rosenthal 1935- CANR-19
Earlier sketch in CA 103
Lefkowitz, R(obert) J. 1942- 45-48
Leflar, Robert A(llen) 1901- 29-32R
Le Fleming, Christopher (Kaye)
1908-1985 Obituary 117
Lefler, Hugh Talmage 1901- 5-8R
Lefler, Irene (Whitney) 1917- CANR-1
Earlier sketch in CA 45-48
See also SATA 12
LeFlore, Ron(ald) 1948(?)- Brief entry 115
Le Fontaine, Joseph (Raymond) 1927- 106
le Fort, Gertrud (Petrea) von
1876-1971 ....CANR-31
Obituary 33-36R
Earlier sketch in CA 69-72
See also DLB 66
Lefranc, Pierre 1927- 41-44R
Lefrancois, Guy R(enald) 1940- CANR-18
Earlier sketches in CA 45-48, CANR-2
Lefton, Robert Eugene 1931- CANR-31
Earlier sketch in CA 49-52
Leftwich, James (Adolf) 1902- CANR-15
Earlier sketch in CA 41-44R
Leftwich, Joseph 1892-1983 ....5-8R
Obituary 109
Leftwich, Richard Henry 1920- CANR-5
Earlier sketch in CA 13-16R
LeGalley, Donald P(aul) 1901- CAP-2
Earlier sketch in CA 17-18
Le Gallienne, Eva 1899-1991 45-48
Obituary 134
See also SATA 9
See also SATO 68
Le Gallienne, Richard
1866-1947 Brief entry 107
See also DLB 4
Legare, Hugh Swinton
1797-1843 ....DLB 3, 59, 73
Legare, James Mathewes 1823-1859 ....DLB 3
Legaret, Jean 1913-1976 ....CAP-2
Earlier sketch in CA 29-32
Legarreta, Dorothy 1926- 118
Legat, Michael (Ronald) 1923- 122
Legault, Albert 1938- 53-56
Leger, (Marie-Rene) Alexis Saint-Leger
1887-1975 ....13-16R
Obituary 61-64
See also Perse, St.-John
See also CLC 11
See also MTCW
Leger, Antoine-J 1880-1950 ....DLB 88
Leger, Fernand 1881-1955 Brief entry 123
Leger, Saintleger
See Leger, (Marie-Rene) Alexis Saint-Leger
Legeza, (Ireneus) Laszlo 1934- CANR-32
Earlier sketch in CA 65-68
Legg, Sarah Martha Ross Bruggeman
....SATA 40
Legg, (Francis) Stuart 1910-1988 Obituary 126
Leggatt, Alexander (Maxwell) 1940- 97-100
Legge, Elisabeth Schwarzkopf
See Schwarzkopf-Legge, Elisabeth
Legge, J(ohn) D(avid) 1921- CANR-2
Earlier sketch in CA 1-4R
Legge, M(ary) Dominica
1905-1986 Obituary 121
Legge-Bourke, (Edward Alexander) Henry
1914-1973 ....CAP-1
Earlier sketch in CA 9-10
Leggett, B(obby) J(oe) 1938- 53-56
Leggett, Eric
See Rimel, Duane (Weldon)
Leggett, Glenn 1918- CANR-5
Earlier sketch in CA 13-16R
Leggett, John C. 1930- 25-28R
Leggett, John (Ward) 1917- CANR-2
Earlier sketch in CA 1-4R
Leggett, Linda 1941- 108
Leggett, Stephen 1949- 77-80
Leggitt, (Samuel) Hunter (Jr.) 1935- 65-68
Legh, Kathleen Louise Wood
See Wood-Legh, Kathleen Louise
Legler, Henry M. 1897- 97-100
Legler, Philip 1928- 9-12R
Legman, G(ershon) 1917- CANR-15
Earlier sketch in CA 21-24R
LeGrand
See Henderson, LeGrand
Legrand, Catherine Carlisle 1947- 126
Legrand, Lucien 1926- 5-8R
Legrand, Michel (Jean) 1932- Brief entry 114
Legters, Lyman H(oward) 1928- CANR-15
Earlier sketch in CA 33-36R
Le Guin, Ursula K(roeber) 1929- CANR-32
Earlier sketches in CA 21-24R, CANR-9
See also AAYA 9
See also AITN 1
See also CDALB 1968-1988
See also CLC 8, 13, 22, 45, 71
See also CLR 3, 28
See also DLB 8, 52
See also MAICYA
See also MTCW
See also SATA 4, 52
Legum, Colin 1919- CANR-4
Earlier sketch in CA 1-4R
See also SATA 10
Legvold, Robert 1940- 85-88
Lehan, Richard (D'Aubin Daniel) 1930- 21-24R
Lehane, Brendan 1936- CANR-26
Earlier sketches in CA 21-24R, CANR-10
Lehiste, Ilse 1922- 37-40R
Lehman, Anita Jacobs 1920- 21-24R
Lehman, Celia 1928- CANR-1
Earlier sketch in CA 49-52
Lehman, Chester K. 1895-1980 ....CANR-1
Earlier sketch in CA 1-4R
Lehman, Dale 1920- 9-12R
Lehman, David 1948- CANR-24
Earlier sketches in CA 57-60, CANR-8
Lehman, Ernest Paul 1915- 85-88
See also DLB 44
Lehman, F(rederick) K. 1924- 9-12R
Lehman, Godfrey 25-28R
Lehman, Harold D(aniel) 1921- 81-84
Lehman, John F(rancis) Jr. 1942- 13-16R
Lehman, Milton 1917-1966 ....CAP-1
Earlier sketch in CA 13-14
Lehman, Peter 1944- 115
Lehman, Sam 1899- 49-52
Lehman, Warren (Winfred Jr.) 1930- 21-24R
Lehman, Yvonne 1936- CANR-12
Earlier sketch in CA 29-32R
Lehmann, A(ndrew) George 1922- CANR-4
Earlier sketch in CA 1-4R
Lehmann, Arno 1901- CAP-2
Earlier sketch in CA 29-32
Lehmann, Geoffrey (John)
1940- Brief entry 107
Lehmann, Irving J(ack) 1927- 53-56
Lehmann, Johannes 1929- CANR-14
Earlier sketch in CA 37-40R
Lehmann, (Rudolph) John (Frederick)
1907-1987 ....CANR-8
Obituary 122
Earlier sketch in CA 9-12R
See also DLB 27, 100
Lehmann, Linda 1906- 85-88
Lehmann, Lotte 1888-1976 73-76
Obituary 69-72
Lehmann, Martin Ernest 1915- 5-8R
Lehmann, Michael Boas 1941- 119
Lehmann, Paul Louis 1906- 85-88
Lehmann, Peter 1938- 57-60
Lehmann, Robert A(rthur) 1932- 57-60
Lehmann, Rosamond (Nina)
1901-1990 ....CANR-8
Obituary 131
Earlier sketch in CA 77-80
See also CLC 5
See also DLB 15
Lehmann, Theo 1934- 41-44R
Lehmann, Wilhelm 1882-1968 ....DLB 56
Lehmann, Winfred P(hilipp) 1916- 33-36R
Lehmann-Haupt, Christopher (Charles Herbert)
1934- 109
Lehmann-Haupt, Hellmut (Emile)
1903-1992 ....9-12R
Obituary 137
Lehmberg, Paul 1946- 102
Lehmberg, Stanford Eugene 1931- CANR-2
Earlier sketch in CA 1-4R
Lehn, Cornelia 1920- CANR-12
Earlier sketch in CA 29-32R
See also SATA 46
Lehner, Christine (Reine) 1952- 109
Lehnert, Herbert (Hermann) 1925- 41-44R
Lehning, James R(obert) 1947- 105
Lehninger, Albert L(ester)
1917-1986 Obituary 119
Lehnus, Donald James 1934- CANR-9
Earlier sketch in CA 57-60
Lehnus, Opal (Hull) 1920- 9-12R
Lehovich, Eugenie Ouroussow
See Ouroussow, Eugenie
Lehr, Delores 1920- 17-20R
See also SATA 10
Lehr, Norma 1930- ....SATA 71
Lehr, Paul E(dwin) 1918- 65-68
Lehrer, Adrienne (Joyce) 1937- 29-32R
Lehrer, James (Charles) 1934- 114
Brief entry 109
Lehrer, Kate 1939- 138
Lehrer, Keith 1936- 17-20R
Lehrer, Robert N(athaniel) 1922- 61-64
Lehrer, Stanley 1929- CANR-2
Earlier sketch in CA 5-8R
Lehrer, Thomas Andrew 1928- 123
Lehrer, Tom
See Lehrer, Thomas Andrew
Lehrman, Harold Arthur
1911-1988 Obituary 127

Lehrman, Liza
See Williams, Liza
Lehrman, Nat 1929- 93-96
Lehrman, Robert L(awrence) 1921- CANR-7
Earlier sketch in CA 5-8R
Lehrman, Simon Maurice 1900- CAP-1
Earlier sketch in CA 9-10
Lehrmann, Chanan
See Lehrmann, Charles C(uno)
Lehrmann, Charles C(uno) 1905-1977 ....33-36R
Lehrmann, Cuno Chanan
See Lehrmann, Charles C(uno)
Leib, Amos Patten 1917-1977 45-48
Obituary 133
Leib, Franklin A(llen) 1944- 138
Leibbrand, Kurt 1914- 45-48
Leibel, Charlotte P(ollack) 1899- 33-36R
Leibenguth, Charla Ann
See Banner, Charla Ann Leibenguth
Leibenstein, Harvey 1922- 103
Leiber, Fritz (Reuter Jr.) 1910- CANR-2
Earlier sketch in CA 45-48
See also CLC 25
See also DLB 8
See also MTCW
See also SATA 45
Leiber, Justin Fritz 1938- CANR-39
Earlier sketches in CA 97-100, CANR-17
Leibert, Julius A(mos) 1888- CAP-2
Earlier sketch in CA 17-18
Leibold, Jay 1957- 123
See also SATA 52, 57
Leibold, (William) John 1926- 37-40R
Leibowitz, Herbert A. 1935- 25-28R
Leibowitz, Herschel W. 1925- CANR-8
Earlier sketch in CA 17-20R
Leibowitz, Irving 1922-1979 ....9-12R
Obituary 85-88
Leibowitz, Rene 1913-1972 Obituary 37-40R
Leibson, Jacob J.
1883(?)-1971 Obituary 33-36R
Leiby, Adrian C(oulter) 1904-1976 ....CAP-1
Obituary 65-68
Earlier sketch in CA 9-10
Leiby, James 1924- 33-36R
Leichman, Seymour 1933- 25-28R
See also SATA 5
Leichter, Otto 1898(?)-1973 Obituary 41-44R
Leiden, Carl 1922- 5-8R
Leider, Emily Wortis 1937- 81-84
Leider, Frida 1888-1975 Obituary 57-60
Leigh, Carolyn 1926-1983 Obituary 111
Leigh, Egbert Giles Jr. 1940- 57-60
Leigh, Eugene
See Seltzer, Leon E(ugene)
Leigh, James L(eighton) 1930- 9-12R
Leigh, Janet
See Morrison, Jeanette Helen
Leigh, Matthew Andrew
See Chervokas, John V(incent)
Leigh, Michael 1914- 13-16R
Leigh, Mike 1943- CANR-31
Earlier sketch in CA 109
Leigh, Palmer
See Palmer, Pamela Lynn
Leigh, Ralph Alexander
1915-1987 Obituary 124
Leigh, Spencer 1945- 102
Leigh, Stephen (W.) 1951- 135
Leigh, Susannah 1938- CANR-15
Earlier sketch in CA 81-84
Leigh, Tom 1947- ....SATA 46
Leigh Fermor, Patrick (Michael)
1915- CANR-35
Earlier sketch in CA 81-84
See also MTCW
Leigh-Pemberton, John 1911- 108
See also SATA 35
Leight, Robert L(ewis) 1932- 110
Leighton, Albert C(hester) 1919- 37-40R
Leighton, Alexander H(amilton) 1908- 41-44R
Leighton, Ann
See Smith, Isadore Leighton Luce
Leighton, Clare (Veronica Hope) 1899- 108
See also SATA 37
Leighton, David S(truan) R(obertson)
1928- CANR-2
Earlier sketch in CA 5-8R
Leighton, Frances Spatz CANR-30
Earlier sketch in CA 81-84
Leighton, Jack Richard 1918- 1-4R
Leighton, Lauren G(ray) 1934- 118
Leighton, Lee
See Overholser, Wayne D.
Leighton, Margaret (Carver) 1896-1987 ....9-12R
Obituary 123
See also SATA 1, 52
Leikind, Morris C. 1906(?)-1976 Obituary 65-68
Leimbach, Martha 1963- 130
See also Leimbach, Marti
Leimbach, Marti
See Leimbach, Martha
See also CLC 65
Leimbach, Patricia Penton 1927- 57-60
Leimberg, Stephan R(obert) 1943- 117
Leimert, Lucille 1895(?)-1983 Obituary 110
Leinbach, Esther V(ashti) 1924- 61-64
Leiner, Katherine 1949- 132
Leinfellner, Werner (Hubertus) 1921- CANR-5
Earlier sketch in CA 53-56
Leininger, Madeleine M. 1925- 33-36R
Leino, Eino
See Loennbohm, Armas Eino Leopold
See also TCLC 24
Leinsdorf, Erich 1912- 119
Brief entry 112
Leinster, Murray
See Jenkins, Will(iam) F(itzgerald)
See also DLB 8
Leinwand, Gerald 1921- CANR-9
Earlier sketch in CA 5-8R
Leip, Hans 1893-1983 Obituary 110
Leipart, Charles 1944- 108
Leiper, Henry Smith 1891-1975 Obituary 53-56
Leipold, L. Edmond 1902- 69-72
See also SATA 16
Leiris, Michel (Julien) 1901-1990 128
Obituary 132
Brief entry 119
See also CLC 61
Leiser, Burton M. 1930- CANR-12
Earlier sketch in CA 29-32R
Leiser, Erwin (Moritz) 1923- CANR-14
Earlier sketch in CA 29-32R
Leiserson, Michael 1939- 37-40R
Leisewitz, Johann Anton 1752-1806 ....DLB 94
Leishman, J(ames) Blair 1902-1963 ....CANR-6
Earlier sketch in CA 5-8R
Leishman, Thomas L.
1900-1978 Obituary 81-84
Leisk, David Johnson 1906-1975 ....9-12R
Obituary 57-60
See also MAICYA
See also SATA 1, 26, 30
Leiss, William 1939- 41-44R
Leister, Mary 1917- CANR-11
Earlier sketch in CA 65-68
See also SATA 29
Leistritz, F(redrick) Larry 1945- 104
Leisy, James (Franklin) 1927- CANR-20
Earlier sketches in CA 9-12R, CANR-4
Leitch, Adelaide 1921- 101
Leitch, D(avid) B(ruce) 1940- 57-60
Leitch, Maurice 1933- 102
See also DLB 14
Leitch, Patricia 1933- CANR-9
Earlier sketch in CA 61-64
See also SATA 11
Leitch, Vincent Barry 1944- 113
Leitenberg, Milton 1933- CANR-19
Earlier sketch in CA 101
Leiter, Louis (Henry) 1921- 37-40R
Leiter, Marcia 1942- 116
Leiter, Robert D(avid) 1922-1976 ....CANR-4
Obituary 69-72
Earlier sketch in CA 5-8R
Leiter, Samuel L(ouis) 1940- CANR-31
Earlier sketch in CA 93-96
Leiter, Sharon 1942- 57-60
Leites, Edmund 1939- 126
Leites, Nathan Constantin 1912-1987 126
Obituary 122
Leith, (James) Andrew 1931- CANR-20
Earlier sketch in CA 45-48
Leith, J(ames) Clark 1937- 57-60
Leith, John H. 1919- CANR-3
Earlier sketch in CA 5-8R
Leith, Linda 1949- 131
Leithauser, Brad 1953- CANR-27
Earlier sketch in CA 107
See also CLC 27
See also DLB 120
Leithauser, Gladys Garner 1925- CANR-27
Earlier sketch in CA 13-16R
Leith-Ross, Prudence 1922- 132
Leitmann, George 1925- 53-56
Leitner, Moses J. 1908- CAP-1
Earlier sketch in CA 13-16
Leitz, Robert C(harles) III 1944- 133
Leivick, H.
See Halpern, Leivick
Leivick, Halper
See Halpern, Leivick
Lekachman, Robert 1920-1989 Obituary 127
Brief entry 106
Lekai, J(ulius) Louis 1916- 33-36R
Lekis, Lisa 1917- 9-12R
Lekson, Stephen H(enry) 1950- 122
Leland, Charles G(odfrey)
1824-1903 Brief entry 118
See also DLB 11
Leland, Christopher Towne 1951- 108
Leland, Henry 1923- CANR-18
Earlier sketch in CA 89-92
Leland, Jeremy (Francis David) 1932- CANR-13
Earlier sketch in CA 33-36R
Leland, Timothy 1937- 102
Lelchuk, Alan 1938- CANR-1
Earlier sketch in CA 45-48
See also CLC 5
Lele, Uma 1941- 73-76
Leliaert, Richard Maurice 1940- 101
le Lievre, Audrey 1923- 132
Lelouch, Claude (Barruck Joseph)
1937- Brief entry 113
LeLoup, Lance T. 1949- 110
Lelyveld, Arthur J(oseph) 1913- 25-28R
Lelyveld, Joseph (Salem) 1937- 126
Brief entry 117
Lem, Stanislaw 1921- CANR-32
Earlier sketch in CA 105
See also CAAS 1
See also CLC 8, 15, 40
See also MTCW
Lemagny, Jean-Claude 1931- 136
LeMahieu, D(an) L(loyd) 1945- 69-72
LeMair, H(enriette) Willebeek
1889-1966 ....SATA 29
LeMaire, H. Paul 1933- 113
Lemaitre, Georges E(douard) 1898-1972 ....CAP-2
Obituary 37-40R
Earlier sketch in CA 25-28
Lemann, Bernard 1905- CANR-21
Earlier sketch in CA 41-44R
Lemann, Nancy 1956- 136
Brief entry 118
See also CLC 39
Lemann, Nicholas 1954- 138
Lemarchand, Elizabeth (Wharton)
1906- CANR-26
Earlier sketches in CA 25-28R, CANR-10
Lemarchand, Rene 1932- 13-16R
LeMaster, J(immie) R(ay) 1934- CANR-30
Earlier sketches in CA 33-36R, CANR-13
LeMaster, Leslie Jean 1943- 125
LeMay, Alan 1899-1964 Obituary 115
Lemay, Harding 1922- CANR-21
Earlier sketches in CA 45-48, CANR-1
Lemay, J(oseph) A(lberic) Leo 1935- CANR-24
Earlier sketches in CA 17-20R, CANR-9
Lemay, Pamphile 1837-1918 ....DLB 99
le May, Reginald Stuart 1885- 5-8R
Lembeck, Ruth (Louise) 1919- 105
Lembke, Janet (Nutt) 1933- 45-48
Lembo, Diana L.
See Spirt, Diana L(ouise)
Lembo, John M(ario) 1937- 29-32R
Lembourn, Hans Joergen 1923- 105
Lemelin, Roger 1919- ....DLB 88
Lemelle, Wilbert J. 1931- 45-48
Lemerle, Paul (Emile) 1903-1989 Obituary 129
Lemert, Charles C(lay) 1937- 111
Lemert, Edwin M(cCarty) 1912- 93-96
Lemert, James B(olton) 1935- 73-76
Lemert, Jim
See Lemert, James B(olton)
Lemesurier, Peter
See Britton, Peter Ewart
Lemieux, Joanne (Hero) 1946- 114
Lemieux, Lucien 1934- 41-44R
Lemieux, Marc 1948- 102
Lemir, Andre
See Rimel, Duane (Weldon)
Le Mire, Eugene D(ennis) 1929- 41-44R
Lemire, Robert A(rthur) 1933- 101
Lemish, John 1921- 5-8R
Lemke, Horst 1922- 107
See also SATA 38
Lemme, Janet E(llen) 1941- 29-32R
Lemmon, David (Hector) 1931- 131
Lemmon, Kenneth 1911- 65-68
Lemmon, Sarah McCulloh 1914- 21-24R
Lemmons, Thom 1955- 134
Lemoine, Ernest
See Roy, Ewell Paul
Le Moine, James MacPherson
1825-1912 ....DLB 99
LeMon, Cal 1945- 53-56
Lemon, James Thomas 1929- 37-40R
Lemon, Lee T(homas) 1931- 17-20R
LeMon, Lynn
See Wert, Lynette L(emon)
LeMond, Alan 1938- CANR-9
Earlier sketch in CA 61-64
Lemonnier, (Antoine Louis) Camille
1844-1913 Brief entry 121
See also TCLC 22
Lemons, J. Stanley 1938- 37-40R
Lemont, George 1927- 65-68
Lemos, Ramon M(arcelino) 1927- 37-40R
Le Moyne, Jean 1913- ....DLB 88
Lena, Dan 1955- 134
Lena, Marie
See Lena, Marie H(oward)
Lena, Marie H(oward) 1956- 134
Lenanton, Carola Mary Anima Oman
See Oman, Carola (Mary Anima)
Lenarcic, R(aymond) J(ames) 1942- 49-52
Lenard, Alexander 1910-1972 ....CANR-4
Obituary 89-92
Earlier sketch in CA 5-8R
See also SATA 21
Lenard, Yvone 1921- CANR-7
Earlier sketch in CA 53-56
Lenardon, Robert J(oseph) 1928- 33-36R
Lenburg, Greg 1956- 105
Lenburg, Jeff 1956- CANR-20
Earlier sketch in CA 104
Lenczowski, George 1915- CANR-4
Earlier sketch in CA 1-4R
Lendon, Kenneth Harry 1928- 9-12R
Lendvai, Paul 1929- CANR-33
Earlier sketches in CA 85-88, CANR-15
Lenehan, William T. 1930- 21-24R
L'Enfant, Julie 1944- 109
Lengel, Frances
See Trocchi, Alexander
Lengle, James I(rvin) 1949- 106
L'Engle, Madeleine (Camp Franklin)
1918- CANR-39
Earlier sketches in CA 1-4R, CANR-3, 21
See also AAYA 1
See also AITN 2
See also CLC 12
See also CLR 1, 14
See also DLB 52
See also MAICYA
See also MTCW
See also SATA 1, 27
Lengyel, Alfonz 1921- 116
Lengyel, Cornel Adam 1915- CANR-24
Earlier sketches in CA 1-4R, CANR-1
See also SATA 27
Lengyel, Emil 1895-1985 ....CANR-3
Obituary 115
Earlier sketch in CA 9-12R
See also SATA 3, 42
Lengyel, Jozsef 1896-1975 85-88
Obituary 57-60
See also CLC 7
Lengyel, Melchior 1879(?)-1974 Obituary 53-56
Lenhoff, Alan (Stuart) 1951- 73-76
Lenier, Sue 1957- 120
Lenihan, John (Howard) 1941- 105
Lenihan, Kenneth J. 1928- 97-100
Lenin, N.
See Lenin
Lenin, Nikolai
See Lenin
Lenin, V. I.
See Lenin
Lenin, Vladimir I.
See Lenin
Lenin, Vladimir Ilyich
See Lenin
Lenin 1870-1924 Brief entry 121
Lenn, Theodore I. 1914- 45-48
Lennard, John (Chevening) 1964- 137
Lennart, Isobel 1915-1971 Obituary 29-32R
See also DLB 44
Lenneberg, Eric H. 1921-1975 ....CANR-7
Obituary 57-60
Earlier sketch in CA 53-56
Lennig, Arthur 1933- 57-60
Lennon, Florence Becker (Tanenbaum)
1895- 13-16R
Lennon, Helen M.
See Goulart, Frances Sheridan
Lennon, John (Ono) 1940-1980 102
See also CLC 12, 35
Lennon, Joseph Luke 1919- 33-36R
Lennon, Nigey 1954- 109
Lennon, Sister M. Isidore 1901- 41-44R
Lennon, Thomas M. 1942- 125
Lennox, Charlotte Ramsay
1729(?)-1804 ....DLB 39
Lennox, Terry
See Harvey, John (Barton)
Lennox-Short, Alan 1913- 102
Lennox-Smith, Judith (Elizabeth) 1953- 134
Lens, Sidney 1912-1986 ....CANR-17
Obituary 119
Earlier sketches in CA 1-4R, CANR-1
See also SATA 13, 48
Lensen, George Alexander 1923-1980 ....CANR-2
Earlier sketch in CA 1-4R
Lensink, Judy Nolte 1948- 127
Lenski, Gerhard Emmanuel Jr. 1924- 1-4R
Lenski, Lois 1893-1974 ....CAP-1
Obituary 53-56
Earlier sketch in CA 13-14
See also CLR 26
See also DLB 22
See also MAICYA
See also SATA 1, 26
Lenson, David (Rollar) 1945- 73-76
Lent, Blair CANR-11
Earlier sketch in CA 21-24R
See also MAICYA
See also SATA 2
Lent, D(ora) Geneva 1904- 5-8R
Lent, Henry Bolles 1901-1973 73-76
See also SATA 17
Lent, John A(nthony) 1936- CANR-30
Earlier sketches in CA 29-32R, CANR-12
Lentfoehr, Therese 1902- 97-100
Lentilhon, Robert Ward 1925- 9-12R
Lentin, Antony 1941- 103
Lentner, Howard H(enry) 1931- 106
Lenton, Henry Trevor 1924- 103
Lentricchia, Frank (Jr.) 1940- CANR-19
Earlier sketch in CA 25-28R
See also CLC 34
Lentz, Donald A. 1910- 17-20R
Lentz, Harold H(erbert) 1910- 57-60
Lentz, Perry 1943- 21-24R
Lenz, Carolyn Ruth Swift
See Swift, Carolyn Ruth
Lenz, Frederick 1950- 97-100
Lenz, Hermann 1913- ....DLB 69
Lenz, J. M. R. 1751-1792 ....DLB 94
Lenz, Siegfried 1926- 89-92
See also CLC 27
See also DLB 75
Lenz, William E(rnest) 1950- 118
Leodhas, Sorche Nic
See Alger, Leclaire (Gowans)
LeoGrande, William M(ark) 1949- 122
Leokum, Arkady 1916(?)- 116
See also SATA 45
Leon, Frances
See Swadesh, Frances Leon
Leon, Henry Cecil 1902-1976 Obituary 115
Leon, Pierre R. 1926- CANR-17
Earlier sketches in CA 45-48, CANR-1
Leon, Vicki 1942- 132
Leonard, Alison 1944- 138
See also SATA 70
Leonard, Calista V(erne) 1919- 21-24R
Leonard, Charlene M(arie) 1928- 33-36R
Leonard, Constance (Brink) 1923- CANR-28
Earlier sketch in CA 49-52
See also SATA 40, 42
Leonard, Diana 1941- 137
Leonard, Edith Marian CAP-1
Earlier sketch in CA 13-16
Leonard, Elmore (John Jr.) 1925- CANR-28
Earlier sketches in CA 81-84, CANR-12
See also AITN 1
See also BEST 89:1, 90:4
See also CLC 28, 34, 71
See also MTCW

Leonard, Eugenie Andruss 1888-1980 ... CAP-2
Obituary ... 97-100
Earlier sketch in CA 17-18
Leonard, Frank G. 1935(?)-1974 Obituary ... 49-52
Leonard, George B(urr) 1923- ... CANR-20
Earlier sketches in CA 9-12R, CANR-3
Leonard, George E(dward) 1931- ... 21-24R
Leonard, George H. 1921- ... 65-68
Leonard, George (Jay) 1946- ... 112
Leonard, George K. Jr. 1915- ... 17-20R
Leonard, Gladys Osborne
1882-1968 Obituary ... 112
Leonard, Graham Douglas 1921- ... 103
Leonard, Hugh
See Byrne, John Keyes
See also DLB 13
Leonard, Irving A(lbert) 1896- ... CANR-5
Earlier sketch in CA 5-8R
Leonard, Jason
See Escott, Jonathan
Leonard, John 1939- ... CANR-12
Earlier sketch in CA 13-16R
Leonard, Jonathan N(orton) 1903-1975 ... 61-64
Obituary ... 57-60
See also SATA 36
Leonard, Joseph T. 1916- ... 9-12R
Leonard, Justin W(ilkinson) 1909- ... CAP-1
Earlier sketch in CA 19-20
Leonard, Lawrence ... 121
Leonard, Leo D(onald) 1938- ... CANR-5
Earlier sketch in CA 53-56
Leonard, Maurice 1939- ... 107
Leonard, Neil 1927- ... 1-4R
Leonard, Phyllis B. 1929- ... 117
Leonard, Phyllis G(rubbs) 1924- ... CANR-12
Earlier sketch in CA 69-72
Leonard, Richard Anthony
1900(?)-1979 Obituary ... 85-88
Leonard, Robert C(arl) 1928- ... 45-48
Leonard, Robert 1928-1984 Obituary ... 112
Leonard, Roger Ashley 1940- ... 25-28R
Leonard, Ruth S(haw) 1906- ... CAP-2
Earlier sketch in CA 23-24
Leonard, Thomas C(harles) 1944- ... 77-80
Leonard, Thomas M. 1937- ... 122
Leonard, Tom 1944- ... CANR-31
Earlier sketches in CA 77-80, CANR-13
Leonard, V. A. 1898- ... CANR-15
Earlier sketch in CA 37-40R
Leonard, William Ellery 1876-1944 ... DLB 54
Leonard, William N. 1912- ... 37-40R
Leonard, William Torbert 1918- ... 107
Leonardi, Susan J. 1946- ... 131
Leondes, Cornelius Thomas 1927- ... 17-20R
Leone, Bruno 1939- ... 110
Leone, Leonard 1914- ... 115
Leone, Mark P(aul) 1940- ... 93-96
Leone, Robert A. 1945- ... 122
Leone, Sergio 1929(?)-1989 ... 123
Obituary ... 128
Leong, Charles L. 1911(?)-1984 Obituary ... 112
Leong, Gor Yun
See Ellison, Virginia H(owell)
Leonhard, Charles 1915- ... 5-8R
Leonhardt, Fritz 1909- ... 123
Leonhardt, Rudolf Walter 1921- ... CANR-3
Earlier sketch in CA 9-12R
Leoni, Edgar (Hugh) 1925- ... CANR-38
Earlier sketch in CA 125
Leonov, Leonid (Maximovich) 1899- ... 129
See also MTCW
Leonowens, Anna 1834-1914 ... DLB 99
Leon-Portilla, Miguel 1926- ... CANR-32
Earlier sketches in CA 21-24R, CANR-11
See also HW
Leontiades, Milton 1932- ... 110
Leontief, Wassily 1906- ... CAP-1
Earlier sketch in CA 17-18
Leontyev, Lev Abramovich
1901-1974 Obituary ... 49-52
Leopold, A(ldo) Starker
1913-1983 Obituary ... 110
Leopold, Allison Kyle 1955- ... 112
Leopold, Carolyn Clugston 1923- ... 73-76
Leopold, Luna B(ergere) 1915- ... CANR-31
Earlier sketch in CA 49-52
Leopold, Nathan F. 1904-1971 ... CAP-1
Obituary ... 29-32R
Earlier sketch in CA 13-16
Leopold, Richard William 1912- ... CANR-2
Earlier sketch in CA 1-4R
Leopold, Werner F. 1896- ... 45-48
Leopold III 1901-1983 Obituary ... 110
Le Pan, Douglas (Valentine) 1914- ... 129
Brief entry ... 117
See also DLB 88
Le Patourel, John Herbert 1909-1981 ... CAP-1
Obituary ... 104
Earlier sketch in CA 9-10
Lepawsky, Albert 1908- ... 45-48
Le Pelley, Guernsey 1910- ... 81-84
Lepetit, Charles
See Sala, Charles
Lepidus, Henry 1916(?)-1983 Obituary ... 110
Lepko, E.
See Kopelev, Lev (Zinovievich)
Lepley, Jean Elizabeth 1934- ... 69-72
Lepley, Paul M(ichael) 1933- ... 53-56
Le Poer Trench, (William Francis) Brinsley
1911- Brief entry ... 116
Lepore, D(ominick) J(ames) 1911- ... 45-48
Le Poulain, Jean 1924-1988 Obituary ... 125
Lepovitz, Helena Waddy 1945- ... 135
Lepp, Henry 1922- ... 53-56
Leppmann, Peter K. 1931- ... 25-28R
Leppmann, Wolfgang Arthur 1922- ... CANR-37
Earlier sketch in CA 1-4R
Leppzer, Robert 1958- ... 105
Leprohon, Pierre 1903- ... CANR-1
Earlier sketch in CA 45-48
Leprohon, Rosanna Eleanor
1829-1879 ... DLB 99
Le Quesne, A(lfred) L(aurence) 1928- ... 116
Le Quesne, Laurence
See Le Quesne, A(lfred) L(aurence)
Le Queux, William (Tufnell)
1864-1927 Brief entry ... 109
See also DLB 70
Lerbinger, Otto 1925- ... 21-24R
Lerche, Charles O(lsen) Jr. 1918-1966 ... 5-8R
Le Reveler
See Artaud, Antonin
le Riche, William Harding 1916- ... 107
Lerman, Eleanor 1952- ... 85-88
See also CLC 9
Lerman, Leo 1914- ... 45-48
Lerman, Paul 1926- ... 97-100
Lerman, Rhoda 1936- ... 49-52
See also CLC 56
Lernat-Holenia, Alexander
1898(?)-1976 ... DLB 85
Lerner, Aaron Bunsen 1920- ... 108
See also SATA 35
Lerner, Abba P(tachya) 1903-1982 ... CANR-2
Obituary ... 108
Earlier sketch in CA 1-4R
Lerner, Alan Jay 1918-1986 ... CANR-31
Obituary ... 119
Earlier sketch in CA 77-80
Lerner, Andrea 1954- ... 134
Lerner, Arthur 1915- ... 102
Lerner, Carol 1927- ... 102
See also SAAS 12
See also SATA 33
Lerner, Daniel 1917-1980 ... CANR-6
Obituary ... 97-100
Earlier sketch in CA 1-4R
Lerner, Eugene Max 1928- ... 17-20R
Lerner, Gerda 1920- ... CANR-26
Earlier sketch in CA 25-28R
See also SATA 65
Lerner, Herbert J. 1933- ... 53-56
Lerner, I. Michael 1910- ... 41-44R
Lerner, Janet W(eiss) 1926- ... CANR-7
Earlier sketch in CA 57-60
Lerner, Joel J. 1936- ... 53-56
Lerner, Laurence (David) 1925- ... CANR-20
Earlier sketches in CA 5-8R, CANR-3
Lerner, Lily Gluck 1928- ... 117
Lerner, Linda ... 73-76
Lerner, Louis A. 1935-1984 Obituary ... 114
Lerner, Marguerite Rush 1924-1987 ... 13-16R
Obituary ... 122
See also SATA 11, 51
Lerner, Maura 1953- ... 97-100
Lerner, Max(well Alan) 1902- ... CANR-25
Obituary ... 137
Earlier sketch in CA 13-16R
See also AITN 1
See also DLB 29
Lerner, Michael G(ordon) 1943- ... 49-52
Lerner, Michael P(hillip) 1943- ... 45-48
Lerner, Richard E(dward) 1941- ... 73-76
Lerner, Richard M(artin) 1946- ... 93-96
Lerner, Robert E. 1940- ... CANR-8
Earlier sketch in CA 21-24R
Lerner, Sharon (Ruth) 1938-1982 ... CANR-3
Obituary ... 106
Earlier sketch in CA 5-8R
See also SATA 11, 29
Lerner, Warren 1929- ... 29-32R
Lernet-Holenia, Alexander
1898(?)-1976 Obituary ... 65-68
Lernoux, Penny (Mary) 1940-1989 ... 77-80
Obituary ... 129
Leroe, Ellen W(hitney) 1949- ... 116
See also SATA 51, 61
Le Roi, David (de Roche) 1905- ... CANR-3
Earlier sketch in CA 9-12R
Leroi-Gourhan, Andre (Georges Leandre)
1911-1986 Obituary ... 118
Le Rossignol, James 1866-1969 ... DLB 92
Leroux, Etienne
See Leroux, S(tephanus) P(etrus) D(aniel)
Leroux, Gaston 1868-1927 ... 136
Brief entry ... 108
See also SATA 65
See also TCLC 25
Leroux, S(tephanus) P(etrus) D(aniel)
1922- ... CANR-2
Earlier sketch in CA 49-52
Le Roy, Bruce Murdock 1920- Brief entry ... 106
LeRoy, Dave
See LeRoy, (Lemuel) David
LeRoy, (Lemuel) David 1920- ... 81-84
LeRoy, Douglas 1943- ... CANR-18
Earlier sketches in CA 49-52, CANR-3
LeRoy, Gaylord C. 1910- ... 37-40R
LeRoy, Gen ... 134
Brief entry ... 115
See also SATA 36, 52
Leroy, Maurice (A. L.) 1909- ... 25-28R
LeRoy, Mervyn 1900-1987 Obituary ... 123
Brief entry ... 108
Le Roy Ladurie, Emmanuel 1929- ... 113
Lerrigo, Marion Olive 1898-1968 Obituary ... 109
See also SATA 29
Lerro, Anthony Joseph 1932- ... 33-36R
Lerski, George Jan 1917- ... 73-76
Lerteth, Oban
See Fanthorpe, R(obert) Lionel
Lerude, Warren (Leslie) 1937- Brief entry ... 122
Le Sage, Laurent 1913- ... CANR-25
Earlier sketch in CA 1-4R
Lescarbot, Marc 1570-1642 ... DLB 99
Lesch, John E(mmett) 1945- ... 132
Leschak, Peter M. 1951- ... 126
Lescoe, Francis J(oseph) 1916- ... 61-64
Lescroart, John T. 1948- ... 122
Lesesne, J(oab) Mauldin 1899- ... CAP-2
Earlier sketch in CA 33-36
LeShan, Eda J(oan) 1922- ... CANR-21
Earlier sketch in CA 13-16R
See also CLR 6
See also SATA 21
LeShan, Lawrence L(ee) 1920- ... CANR-21
Earlier sketch in CA 17-20R
Le Shana, David C(harles) 1932- ... 29-32R
Lesher, Phyllis A(senath Bayers)
1912- ... CANR-17
Earlier sketch in CA 25-28R
Lesher, Stephan 1935- ... 103
LeSieg, Theo.
See Geisel, Theodor Seuss
Lesieur, Henry R(ichard) 1946- ... 77-80
Lesikar, Raymond Vincent 1922- ... CANR-2
Earlier sketch in CA 1-4R
Lesikin, Joan 1947- ... 93-96
Lesins, Knuts 1909- ... 73-76
Lesko, George 1932- ... 17-20R
Lesko, Leonard Henry 1938- ... CANR-8
Earlier sketch in CA 61-64
Lesko, Wendy
See Schaetzel, Wendy
Lesky, Albin (Hans) 1896- ... 85-88
Leslau, Wolf 1906- ... 104
Lesley, Blake
See Duckworth, Leslie Blakey
Lesley, Cole
See Cole, Leonard Leslie
Leslie, A. L.
See Lazarus, A(rnold) L(eslie)
Leslie, Aleen ... 5-8R
Leslie, Anita 1914-1985 ... CANR-32
Obituary ... 117
Earlier sketch in CA 49-52
Leslie, Anne
See Leslie, Anita
Leslie, Cecilie 1914- ... 17-20R
Leslie, Charles M. 1923- ... 5-8R
Leslie, Clare Walker 1947- ... 108
Leslie, Conrad 1923- ... 29-32R
Leslie, Desmond 1921- ... 9-12R
Leslie, Donald Daniel 1922- ... 102
Leslie, Doris
See Fergusson Hannay, Doris
Leslie, F(rederic) Andrew 1927- ... CANR-7
Earlier sketch in CA 17-20R
Leslie, Frank 1821-1880 ... DLB 43, 79
Leslie, Gerald R(onnell) 1925- ... 17-20R
Leslie, Jane
See Coade, Jessie
Leslie, John Andrew 1940- ... CANR-30
Earlier sketch in CA 112
Leslie, Josephine Aimee Campbell
1898-1979 ... 85-88
Leslie, Kenneth 1892-1974 ... 93-96
Obituary ... 53-56
Leslie, Michael 1952- ... 118
Leslie, O. H.
See Slesar, Henry
Leslie, Phil 1909(?)-1988 Obituary ... 126
Leslie, Robert B.
See Wooley, John (Steven)
Leslie, Robert C(ampbell) 1917- ... 33-36R
Leslie, Robert Franklin 1911- ... CANR-28
Earlier sketch in CA 49-52
See also SATA 7
Leslie, Rochelle
See Diamond, Graham
Leslie, Roy F. 1922- ... 41-44R
Leslie, S(amuel) Clement 1898- ... 85-88
Leslie, San
See Crook, Bette (Jean)
Leslie, Sarah
See McGuire, Leslie Sarah
Leslie, Seymour 1890(?)-1979 Obituary ... 89-92
Leslie, (John Randolph) Shane
1885-1971 Obituary ... 33-36R
Leslie, Sir Shane
See Leslie, (John Randolph) Shane
Leslie, Ward S.
See Ward, Elizabeth Honor (Shedden)
Leslie, Warren III 1927- ... 9-12R
Leslie-Melville, Betty 1929- ... 81-84
Leslie-Melville, Jock
See Leslie-Melville, John D.
Leslie-Melville, John D. 1933-1984 ... 81-84
Obituary ... 112
Lesly, Philip 1918- ... CANR-14
Earlier sketch in CA 81-84
Lesnoff-Caravaglia, Gari ... 41-44R
LeSourd, Catherine
See Marshall, (Sarah) Catherine (Wood)
LeSourd, Leonard (E.) 1919- ... 135
Lesowitz, Robert I(rwin) 1939- ... 57-60
Lesperance, John 1835(?)-1891 ... DLB 99
L'Esperance, Wilford L(ouis) III
1930-1982 ... CANR-27
Earlier sketch in CA 33-36R
Lessa, William A(rmand) 1908- ... 61-64
Lessac, Arthur 1910- Brief entry ... 110
Lessac, Frane 1954- ... 127
See also SATA 61
Lessard, Michel 1942- ... 104
Lessel, William M. 1906- ... CAP-2
Earlier sketch in CA 33-36
Lesser, Alexander 1902-1982 ... CANR-28
Obituary ... 107
Earlier sketch in CA 49-52
Lesser, Charles H(uber) 1944- ... 73-76
Lesser, Eugene (Bernard) 1936- ... 49-52
Lesser, Gerald S(amuel) 1926- ... 97-100
Lesser, Margaret 1899(?)-1979 Obituary ... 93-96
See also SATA 22
Lesser, Michael 1939- ... 102
Lesser, Milton
See Marlowe, Stephen
Lesser, R(oger) H(arold) 1928- ... CANR-14
Earlier sketch in CA 73-76
Lesser, Rika 1953- ... 118
See also SATA 53
Lesser, Robert C. 1933- ... 104
Lessere, Samuel E. 1892- ... CAP-2
Earlier sketch in CA 21-22
Lessing, Bruno 1870-1940 ... DLB 28
Lessing, Doris (May) 1919- ... CANR-33
Earlier sketch in CA 9-12R
See also CAAS 14
See also CDBLB 1960 to Present
See also CLC 1, 2, 3, 6, 10, 15, 22, 40
See also DLB 15
See also DLBY 85
See also MTCW
See also SSC 6
Lessing, Gotthold Ephraim 1729-1781 ... DLB 97
Lessiter, Mike (J.) 1969- ... 135
Lessler, Richard Sigmund 1924- ... 1-4R
Lessmann, Paul G. 1919- ... 17-20R
LesStrang, Jacques 1926- ... CANR-17
Earlier sketch in CA 65-68
Lester, Alison 1952- ... 125
See also SATA 50
Lester, Andrew D(ouglas) 1939- ... CANR-26
Earlier sketch in CA 109
Lester, Anthony 1936- ... 37-40R
Lester, David 1942- ... CANR-31
Earlier sketches in CA 33-36R, CANR-12
Lester, Frank
See Usher, Frank (Hugh)
Lester, Gene
See Mercer, Jean
Lester, Godfrey Allen 1943- ... CANR-28
Earlier sketch in CA 111
Lester, Helen 1936- ... CANR-38
Earlier sketch in CA 115
See also SATA 46
Lester, James
See Blake, L(eslie) J(ames)
Lester, James D. 1935- ... CANR-15
Earlier sketch in CA 89-92
Lester, James P(inkney) 1944- ... CANR-35
Earlier sketch in CA 114
Lester, John
See Werner, Vivian
Lester, Julius (Bernard) 1939- ... CANR-23
Earlier sketches in CA 17-20R, CANR-8
See also BW
See also CLR 2
See also MAICYA
See also SATA 12
Lester, Mark
See Russell, Martin
Lester, Reginald Mounstephens 1896- ... CAP-1
Earlier sketch in CA 9-10
Lester, Richard A. 1908- ... 102
Lester, Richard 1932- ... CLC 20
Lester, Robert C(arlton) 1933- ... 73-76
Lester, Tanya 1956- ... 138
Lester, William ... 57-60
Lester-Rands, A.
See Judd, Frederick Charles
LeStourgeon, Diana E. 1927- ... 13-16R
L'Estrange, Anna
See Ellerbeck, Rosemary (Anne L'Estrange)
Le Sueur, Lucille 1908(?)-1977 Obituary ... 111
Le Sueur, Meridel 1900- ... CANR-30
Earlier sketches in CA 49-52, CANR-2
See also SATA 6
LeSueur, Stephen C. 1952- ... 133
LeSueur, William Dawson 1840-1917 ... DLB 92
Lesure, Francois 1923- Brief entry ... 108
Lesure, Thomas B(arbour) 1923- ... 102
Leszlei, Marta
See Dosa, Marta Leszlei
L'Etang, Hugh J(oseph) C(harles) J(ames)
1917- ... 45-48
LeTarte, Clyde E(dward) 1938- ... 53-56
Leterman, Elmer G. 1897- ... 25-28R
Lethbridge, Rex
See Meyers, Roy (Lethbridge)
Lethbridge, Robert (David) 1947- ... 135
Lethbridge, T(homas) C(harles)
1901-1971 ... CAP-2
Earlier sketch in CA 29-32
Letiche, John M(arion) 1918- ... 49-52
Letley, Emma 1949- ... 131
Le Tord, Bijou 1945- ... CANR-31
Earlier sketch in CA 65-68
See also SATA 49
LeTourneau, Richard (Howard) 1925- ... CANR-23
Earlier sketches in CA 53-56, CANR-7
Letrusco
See Martini, Virgilio
Lettau, Reinhard 1929- ... CANR-9
Earlier sketch in CA 17-20R
See also DLB 75
Lette, Kathy 1958- ... 136
Letterman, Edward John 1926- ... 29-32R
Lettis, Richard 1928- ... 5-8R
Lettvin, Maggie 1927- ... 73-76
Letwin, Shirley Robin 1924- ... 17-20R
Letwin, William L(ouis) 1922- ... 9-12R
Leuba, Clarence J(ames) 1899- ... 37-40R
Leubsdorf, Carl P(hilipp) 1938- ... 73-76
Leuchtenburg, William E(dward)
1922- ... CANR-12
Earlier sketch in CA 5-8R

Leuci, Bob
See Leuci, Robert
Leuci, Robert 1940- 125
Leukel, Francis 1922- 53-56
Leung, John K(ong-cheong) 1949- 127
Leuthner, Stuart 1939- 125
Leuthold, David Allen 1932- 21-24R
Leutscher, Alfred (George) 1913- 73-76
See also SATA 23
Lev, Daniel S(aul) 1933- 41-44R
Levack, Brian P(aul) 1943- 53-56
Levai, Blaise 1919- 108
See also SATA 39
Levant, Howard 1929- 89-92
Levant, Oscar 1906-1972 Obituary 37-40R
Levant, Victor 1947- 126
Levantrosser, William F(rederick) 1925- 21-24R
Levanway, Russell W(ilford)
1919- Brief entry 107
Levarie, Siegmund 1914- 13-16R
Le Vay, David 1915- 89-92
Levell, Byrd 1911(?)-1979 Obituary 89-92
Levelt, Willem J(ohannes) M(aria) 1938- 133
Leven, Charles L(ouis) 1928- CANR-14
Earlier sketch in CA 41-44R
Leven, Jeremy 1941- 102
Levendosky, Charles (Leonard)
1936- CANR-12
Earlier sketch in CA 29-32R
Levene, Malcolm 1937- 45-48
Levenkron, Steven 1941- 109
Levenson, Alan Ira 1935- 45-48
Levenson, Christopher 1934- 29-32R
Levenson, Dorothy (Perkins) 1927- 9-12R
Levenson, Edgar A. 1924- 128
Brief entry 108
Levenson, J(acob) C(lavner) 1922- 25-28R
Levenson, Jordan 1936- CANR-23
Earlier sketches in CA 57-60, CANR-7
Levenson, Joseph Richmond
1920-1969 .... CANR-6
Earlier sketch in CA 1-4R
Levenson, Myron H(erbert) 1926-1974 53-56
Levenson, Sam(uel) 1911-1980 .... CANR-26
Obituary 101
Earlier sketch in CA 65-68
See also AITN 1
Levenson, William B. 1907- CAP-2
Earlier sketch in CA 25-28
Levenstein, Aaron 1910-1986 .... CAP-1
Obituary 119
Earlier sketch in CA 19-20
Levenstein, Harvey A(llan) 1938- 106
Levenstein, Sidney 1917- 9-12R
Leventhal, Albert Rice 1907-1976 65-68
Obituary 61-64
Leventhal, Bennett (L.) 1949- 135
Leventhal, Donald B(ecker) 1930- 45-48
Leventhal, Fred Marc 1938- Brief entry 109
Leventhal, Herbert 1941- 69-72
Leventhal, Lance A. 1945- CANR-27
Earlier sketch in CA 110
Leventman, Seymour 1930- CANR-1
Earlier sketch in CA 1-4R
Lever, Charles (James) 1806-1872 .... DLB 21
Lever, (Tresham) Christopher (Arthur Lindsay)
1932- 136
Lever, J(ulius) W(alter) 1913-1975 .... CAP-2
Obituary 61-64
Earlier sketch in CA 23-24
Lever, Janet 1946- 85-88
Lever, Judy 1947- 107
Lever, Katherine 1916- 17-20R
Lever, Tresham (Joseph Philip)
1900-1975 .... 13-16R
Obituary 57-60
Lever, Walter
See Lever, J(ulius) W(alter)
Leverence, William John 1946- 102
Leverich, Kathleen 1948- 137
Levering, Frank (Graham) 1952- 119
Levering, Ralph (Brooks) 1947- 85-88
Leverson, Ada 1865(?)-1936(?) Brief entry 117
See also Elaine
See also TCLC 18
LeVert, (William) John 1946- 122
See also SATA 55
Levertov, Denise 1923- CANR-29
Earlier sketches in CA 1-4R, CANR-3
See also CLC 1, 2, 3, 5, 8, 15, 28, 66
See also DLB 5
See also MTCW
Levesque, Rene 1922-1987 Obituary 125
Levey, Martin 1913-1970 .... CANR-10
Earlier sketch in CA 13-16R
Levey, Michael (Vincent) 1927- CANR-25
Earlier sketches in CA 5-8R, CANR-4
Levey, Samuel 1932- CANR-2
Earlier sketch in CA 45-48
Levi, Albert William 1911- Brief entry 107
Levi, Anthony H(erbert) T(igar) 1929- CANR-24
Earlier sketches in CA 13-16R, CANR-9
Levi, Carlo 1902-1975 .... CANR-10
Obituary 53-56
Earlier sketch in CA 65-68
Levi, Darrell E(rville) 1940- 131
Levi, Edward H(irsch) 1911- CANR-2
Earlier sketch in CA 49-52
Levi, Gershon
See Levi, S(amuel) Gershon
Levi, Hans 1935- 41-44R
Levi, Helen I(sabel) 1929- 117
Levi, Isaac 1930- 97-100
Levi, Julian (Edwin) 1900-1982 Obituary 106
Levi, Lennart 1930- CANR-8
Earlier sketch in CA 17-20R
Levi, Maurice 1945- 111
Levi, Peter (Chad Tigar) 1931- CANR-34
Earlier sketch in CA 5-8R
See also CLC 41
See also DLB 40
Levi, Primo 1919-1987 .... CANR-33
Obituary 122
Earlier sketches in CA 13-16R, CANR-12
See also CLC 37, 50
See also MTCW
Levi, S(amuel) Gershon
1908-1990 Obituary 131
Levi, Vicki Gold 1941- 101
Levi, Werner 1912- CANR-37
Earlier sketches in CA 25-28R, CANR-16
Levi, Y. Leo 1926- CANR-36
Earlier sketch in CA 114
Leviatin, David 1961- 130
Levi D'Ancona, Mirella
See D'Ancona, Mirella Levi
LeVie, Donn Jr. 1951- 134
Levien, Sonya
See Hovey, Sonya
See also DLB 44
Levin, Alexandra Lee 1912- 9-12R
Levin, Alfred 1908- 13-16R
Levin, Alvin Irving 1921- CANR-1
Earlier sketch in CA 45-48
Levin, Beatrice Schwartz 1920- CANR-18
Earlier sketches in CA 9-12R, CANR-3
Levin, Benjamin H. 49-52
Levin, Betty 1927- CANR-25
Earlier sketches in CA 65-68, CANR-9
See also SAAS 11
See also SATA 19
Levin, Bob
See Levin, Robert A.
Levin, Dan 1914- Brief entry 108
Levin, David 1924- CANR-8
Earlier sketch in CA 5-8R
Levin, Donna 1954- 134
Levin, Doron P. 1950- 130
Levin, Gail 1948- 102
Levin, Gerald H(enry) 1929- CANR-33
Earlier sketches in CA 33-36R, CANR-15
Levin, Harold L(eonard) 1929- 93-96
Levin, Harry (Tuchman) 1912- CANR-2
Earlier sketch in CA 1-4R
Levin, Harry 1925- 109
Levin, Harvey J(oshua) 1924- 9-12R
Obituary 137
Levin, Henry M(ordecai) 1938- 122
Levin, Ira 1929- CANR-17
Earlier sketch in CA 21-24R
See also CLC 3, 6
See also MTCW
See also SATA 66
Levin, Jack 1941- CANR-19
Earlier sketches in CA 53-56, CANR-4
Levin, James (Benesch) 1940- 111
Levin, Jane Whitbread 1914- Brief entry 106
Levin, Jenifer 1955- CANR-26
Earlier sketch in CA 108
Levin, John 1944- 107
Levin, Jonathan V(ictor) 1927- 9-12R
Levin, Kenneth 1944- Brief entry 115
Levin, Kim 73-76
Levin, Kristine Cox 1944- 65-68
Levin, Marcia Obrasky 1918- 13-16R
See also SATA 13
Levin, Marlin 1921- CANR-9
Earlier sketch in CA 65-68
Levin, Meyer 1905-1981 .... CANR-15
Obituary 104
Earlier sketch in CA 9-12R
See also AITN 1
See also CLC 7
See also DLB 9, 28
See also DLBY 81
See also SATA 21, 27
Levin, Michael Eric 1943- 131
Levin, Michael (Graubart) 1958- 135
Levin, Milton 1925- 25-28R
Levin, Molly Apple 61-64
Levin, N. Gordon Jr. 1935- 25-28R
Levin, Nora 1916-1989 .... 25-28R
Obituary 130
Levin, Richard Louis 1922- 1-4R
Levin, Robert A. 1942- 81-84
Levin, Robert J. 1921(?)-1976 Obituary 65-68
Levin, Saul 1921- 13-16R
Levin, William C. 1946- 105
Levine, A(aron) L(awrence) 1925- 21-24R
Levine, Abby 1943- 126
See also SATA 52, 54
Levine, Adeline 1925- 49-52
Levine, Allan 1956- 135
Levine, Andrew 1944- 65-68
Levine, Arthur E(lliott) 1948- 73-76
Levine, Barry B(ernard) 1941- 101
Levine, Bernard 1934- 29-32R
Levine, Betty K(rasne) 1933- 93-96
See also SATA 66
Levine, Bob
See Levine, Robert
Levine, Caroline Anne 1942- 89-92
Levine, Charles H(oward) 1939-1988 .... CANR-35
Obituary 126
Earlier sketches in CA 89-92, CANR-15
Levine, Daniel H(arris) 1942- 73-76
Levine, Daniel Urey 1935- 57-60
Levine, Daniel 1934- 13-16R
Levine, David O(scar) 1955- 124
Levine, David 1926- 116
Brief entry 113
See also SATA 35, 43
Levine, David 1928- 17-20R
Levine, Donald N(athan) 1931- 53-56
Levine, Edna S(imon) 85-88
See also SATA 35
Levine, Edward M(onroe) 1924- 21-24R
Levine, Edwin Burton 1920- 25-28R
Levine, Ellen 1939- CANR-22
Earlier sketch in CA 69-72
Levine, Erwin L(eon) 1926- 9-12R
Levine, Faye (Iris) 1944- CANR-3
Earlier sketch in CA 49-52
Levine, Frederick S(pencer) 1945- 120
Levine, Gary 1938- 61-64
Levine, Gene N(orman) 1930- 5-8R
Levine, George R. 1929- 21-24R
Levine, George 1931- CANR-20
Earlier sketch in CA 25-28R
Levine, Herbert S(amuel) 1928- 128
Brief entry 107
Levine, I(srael) E. 1923- CANR-1
Earlier sketch in CA 1-4R
See also SATA 12
Levine, Irving R(askin) 1922- 13-16R
Levine, Isaac Don 1892-1981 .... CANR-11
Obituary 103
Earlier sketch in CA 13-16R
Levine, Isidore N. 1909-1972 .... 41-44R
Levine, Israel 1893(?)-1988(?) Obituary 125
Levine, Joan Goldman 61-64
See also SATA 11
Levine, Joseph 1910- 108
See also SATA 33
Levine, Laurence William 1931- 103
Levine, Lawrence W(illiam)
1933- Brief entry 115
Levine, Lawrence 1916- 9-12R
Levine, Lois (Elaine) L. 1931- 106
Levine, Louis 1921- Brief entry 116
Levine, Mark Lee 1943- CANR-2
Earlier sketch in CA 49-52
Levine, Marvin J. 1930- CANR-21
Earlier sketch in CA 45-48
Levine, Maurice 1902-1971 85-88
Levine, Michael 1939- 133
Levine, Michael 1954- 89-92
Levine, Milton I(sra) 1902- 109
Levine, Miriam 1939- 116
Levine, Mortimer 1922- 17-20R
Levine, Murray 1928- CANR-29
Earlier sketch in CA 49-52
Levine, Norman D(ion) 1912- 85-88
Levine, Norman 1924- CANR-14
Earlier sketch in CA 73-76
See also CLC 54
See also DLB 88
Levine, Paul 1948- 137
Levine, Peter D. 1944- 126
Levine, Philip 1928- CANR-37
Earlier sketches in CA 9-12R, CANR-9
See also CLC 2, 4, 5, 9, 14, 33
See also DLB 5
Levine, Rhoda 73-76
See also SATA 14
LeVine, Robert A(lan) 1932- CANR-13
Earlier sketch in CA 21-24R
Levine, Robert M. 1910(?)-1981 Obituary 108
Levine, Robert M. 1941- CANR-11
Earlier sketch in CA 21-24R
Levine, Robert 1944- 121
Levine, Sarah 1970- 125
See also SATA 57
Levine, Saul V. 1938- 123
Levine, Sol 1914-1987 .... 9-12R
Obituary 124
Levine, Solomon B. 1920- 104
Levine, Stephen 1937- CANR-35
Earlier sketch in CA 45-48
Levine, Stuart (George) 1932- 17-20R
Levine, Suzanne Jill 1946- CANR-31
Earlier sketches in CA 49-52, CANR-13
LeVine, Victor T(heodore) 1928- 13-16R
Levine-Freidus, Gail
See Provost, Gail Levine
Levine-Shneidman, Conalee 1930- 119
Levinger, George 1927- CANR-2
Earlier sketch in CA 49-52
Levins, Richard 1930- 119
Levinsohn, Florence H(amlish) 1926- 132
Levinson, Boris M(ayer) 1907-1984 .... CANR-13
Obituary 112
Earlier sketch in CA 33-36R
Levinson, Charles 1920- CANR-21
Earlier sketch in CA 45-48
Levinson, Daniel Jacob 1920- 102
Levinson, Deirdre 1931- 73-76
See also CLC 49
Levinson, Harold M(yer) 1919- 21-24R
Levinson, Harry 1922- CANR-29
Earlier sketches in CA 1-4R, CANR-1
Levinson, Henry Samuel 1948- CANR-26
Earlier sketch in CA 109
Levinson, Horace C(lifford) 1895- CAP-1
Earlier sketch in CA 19-20
Levinson, Irene
See Zahava, Irene
Levinson, Leonard L.
1905(?)-1974 Obituary 45-48
Levinson, Leonard 1935- CANR-31
Earlier sketches in CA 77-80, CANR-14
Levinson, Marjorie 1951- 127
Levinson, Nancy Smiler 1938- CANR-23
Earlier sketch in CA 107
See also SATA 33
Levinson, Olga May 103
Levinson, Richard (Leighton)
1934-1987 .... CANR-13
Obituary 121
Earlier sketch in CA 73-76
Levinson, Riki CANR-37
Earlier sketch in CA 121
See also MAICYA
See also SATA 49, 52
Levinson, Robert E. 1925- 132
Levinthal, Charles F(rederick) 1945- 127
Levinthal, Israel Herbert 1888- 13-16R
Levis, Donald J(ames) 1936- 41-44R
Levis, Larry 1946- 77-80
See also DLB 120
Levison, Andrew 1948- 93-96
Levi-Strauss, Claude 1908- CANR-32
Earlier sketches in CA 1-4R, CANR-6
See also CLC 38
See also MTCW
Levit, Herschel 1912- 111
Levit, Martin 1918- 45-48
Levit, Rose 1922- 73-76
Levitan, Donald 1928- 104
Levitan, Max 1921- 53-56
Levitan, Sar A. 1914- CANR-3
Earlier sketch in CA 9-12R
Levitan, Tina (Nellie) 1928- 9-12R
Levitas, Gloria B(arach) 1931- CANR-21
Earlier sketch in CA 45-48
Levitas, Louise
See Henriksen, Louise Levitas
Levitas, Maurice 1917- 77-80
Levitch, Joel A. 1942- 37-40R
Levith, Murray J(ay) 1939- 81-84
Levitin, Sonia (Wolff) 1934- CANR-32
Earlier sketches in CA 29-32R, CANR-14
See also CLC 17
See also MAICYA
See also SAAS 2
See also SATA 4, 68
Levitine, George 1916- 41-44R
Levitsky, David A(aron) 1942- 116
Levitt, I(srael) M(onroe) 1908- 45-48
Levitt, Jesse 1919- 45-48
Levitt, Leonard 1941- 104
Levitt, Morris J(acob) 1938- CANR-15
Earlier sketch in CA 41-44R
Levitt, Mortimer 1907- 118
Levitt, Morton P(aul) 1936- 111
Levitt, Morton 1920- 61-64
Levitt, Saul 1911-1977 81-84
Obituary 73-76
Levitt, Sidney (Mark) 1947- .... SATA 68
Levitzky, Sergei A. 1909-1983 Obituary 110
Levon, Fred
See Ayvazian, L. Fred
Levon, O. U.
See Kesey, Ken (Elton)
Le Vot, Andre 1921- 130
Levoy, Myron CANR-18
Earlier sketch in CA 93-96
See also SATA 37, 49
Levtzion, Nehemia 1935- CANR-4
Earlier sketch in CA 53-56
Levy, Alan 1932- CANR-21
Earlier sketches in CA 9-12R, CANR-6
Levy, Babette May 1907-1977 81-84
Obituary 73-76
Levy, Benn W(olfe) 1900-1973 101
Obituary 45-48
See also DLB 13
See also DLBY 81
Levy, Bernard 1907- 61-64
Levy, Bernard-Henri 1949- 122
Levy, Bill
See Levy, William V.
Levy, Charles K(ingsley) 1924- 120
Levy, Claude 1924- 129
Levy, D(arryl) A(llen) 1942-1968 .... CAP-2
Earlier sketch in CA 19-20
Levy, Darline Gay Shapiro 1939- 102
Levy, David A(rthur) 1955- 108
Levy, David M(ordecai) 1892-1977 73-76
Obituary 69-72
Levy, David N(eil) L(aurence) 1945- 119
Levy, David W(illiam) 1937- 41-44R
Levy, David 1913- 13-16R
Levy, Elizabeth 1942- CANR-34
Earlier sketches in CA 77-80, CANR-15
See also MAICYA
See also SATA 31, 69
Levy, Emanuel 1947- CANR-26
Earlier sketch in CA 108
Levy, Eugene Donald 1933- 102
Levy, Faye 1951- 125
Levy, Fred D(avid) Jr. 1937- CANR-14
Earlier sketch in CA 37-40R
Levy, G(ertrude) Rachel 1883-1966 .... 5-8R
Levy, Harold B(ernard) 1918- 73-76
Levy, Harry L(ouis) 1906-1981 .... 33-36R
Obituary 103
Levy, Herta Hess
See Kahn, Herta Hess
Levy, Howard S(eymour) 1923- CANR-25
Earlier sketches in CA 17-20R, CANR-10
Levy, Hyman 1889-1975 Obituary 57-60
Levy, Isaac Jack 1928- 41-44R
Levy, Jack Steven 1948- 115
Levy, JoAnn 1941- 134
Levy, John 1954- 128
Levy, Jonathan 1935- CANR-10
Earlier sketch in CA 61-64
Levy, Joseph V(ictor) 1928- 106
Levy, Julien 1906-1981 Obituary 103
Levy, Leonard W(illiams) 1923- CANR-20
Earlier sketches in CA 1-4R, CANR-1
Levy, Lester S(tern) 1896- 61-64
Levy, Lillian (Rae Berliner) 1918-1986 .... 17-20R
Obituary 120
Levy, Lorelei
See Schwalberg, Carol(yn Ernestine Stein)

Levy, Marilyn 1937- ... 135
See also SATA 67
Levy, Marion Joseph Jr. 1918- ... 73-76
Levy, Michael E(rnst) 1929- ... CANR-2
Earlier sketch in CA 5-8R
Levy, Michael R(ichard) 1946- ... 77-80
Levy, Morton 1930- ... 77-80
Levy, Nathan 1945- ... SATA 63
Levy, Owen 1948- ... 118
Levy, Raphael 1900-1969 ... CAP-1
Earlier sketch in CA 13-16
Levy, Reynold 1945- ... 97-100
Levy, Richard C. 1947- ... 73-76
Levy, Robert Calmann
See Calmann-Levy, Robert
Levy, Robert J(oseph) 1931- ... 37-40R
Levy, Robert 1926- ... 77-80
Levy, Roger (P.) 1950- ... 134
Levy, Rosalie Marie 1889- ... CAP-1
Earlier sketch in CA 9-10
Levy, S Jay 1922- ... 108
Levy, Sidney Jay 1921- Brief entry ... 106
Levy, Stephen 1947- ... 105
Levy, Sue 1936- ... CANR-8
Earlier sketch in CA 57-60
Levy, Wilbert J. 1917- ... CANR-6
Earlier sketch in CA 57-60
Levy, William Turner 1922- ... 25-28R
Levy, William V. 1930- ... 9-12R
Levytskjy, Borys 1915- ... 65-68
Lewald, H(erald) Ernest 1922-1982 ... 21-24R
Obituary ... 114
Lewald, (Theo) Roon 1942- ... 93-96
Lewallen, John 1942- ... 69-72
Lewalski, Barbara Kiefer 1931- ... 104
Lewandowski, Dan 1947- ... 77-80
Lewandowski, Stephen 1947- ... 93-96
Lewanski, Richard C(asimir) 1918- ... 17-20R
LeWarne, Charles P(ierce) 1930- ... 57-60
Lewbin, Hyman J(oseph) 1894- ... 61-64
Lewcock, Ronald (B.) 1929- ... 121
Lewees, John
See Stockton, Francis Richard
Lewellen, T(ed) C(harles) 1940- ... CANR-6
Earlier sketch in CA 13-16R
Lewels, Francisco J(ose) Jr. 1944- ... 104
Lewenstein, Morris R. 1923- ... 13-16R
Lewes, George Henry 1817-1878 ... DLB 55
Lewes, Lettie
See Cleveland, Philip Jerome
Lewesdon, John
See Daniell, Albert Scott
Lewin, Bertram D(avid) 1896-1971 ... 65-68
Lewin, Betsy 1937- ... 104
See also SATA 32
Lewin, C. L.
See Brister, Richard
Lewin, Elsa ... 118
Lewin, Esther 1922- ... 61-64
Lewin, Hugh 1939- ... CANR-38
Earlier sketch in CA 113
See also CLR 9
See also MAICYA
See also SATA 40
Lewin, L.
See Lewin, Leonard
Lewin, Leonard C(ase) 1916- ... 17-20R
Lewin, Leonard 1919- ... CANR-28
Earlier sketch in CA 49-52
Lewin, Michael Zinn 1942- ... 73-76
Lewin, Nathan 1936- ... 101
Lewin, Rhoda G. 1929- ... 135
Lewin, (George) Ronald 1914-1984 ... CANR-13
Obituary ... 111
Earlier sketch in CA 25-28R
Lewin, Ted 1935- ... CANR-25
Earlier sketch in CA 69-72
See also SATA 21
Lewine, Richard 1910- ... 81-84
Lewing, Anthony Charles 1933- ... 81-84
Lewinson, Paul 1900-1988 Obituary ... 127
LeWinter, Oswald 1931- ... 1-4R
Lewis, A(rthur) J(ames) 1914- ... 5-8R
Lewis, A(drian) S(teven) 1945- ... 116
Lewis, Adele
See Corwin, Adele Beatrice Lewis
Lewis, Albert 1885(?)-1978 Obituary ... 77-80
Lewis, Alfred Allan 1929- ... CANR-15
Earlier sketch in CA 73-76
Lewis, Alfred E. 1912-1968 Obituary ... 111
See also SATA 32
Lewis, Alfred Henry 1857-1914 Brief entry ... 120
See also DLB 25
Lewis, Alice C. 1936- ... SATA 46
Lewis, Alice Hudson 1895(?)-1971 Obituary ... 109
See also SATA 29
Lewis, Allan 1905- ... 13-16R
Lewis, Alun 1915-1944 Brief entry ... 104
See also DLB 20
See also TCLC 3
Lewis, Anthony Carey 1915-1983 Obituary ... 110
Lewis, (Joseph) Anthony 1927- ... 9-12R
See also SATA 27
Lewis, Archibald Ross 1914-1990 ... 81-84
Obituary ... 130
Lewis, Arthur H. 1906- ... CANR-1
Earlier sketch in CA 1-4R
Lewis, Arthur O(rcutt) Jr. 1920- ... 9-12R
Lewis, Arthur William 1905-1970 ... CAP-1
Earlier sketch in CA 9-10
Lewis, Barbara 1928-1984 Obituary ... 113
Lewis, Benjamin F. 1918- ... 45-48
Lewis, Bernard 1916- ... 118
Brief entry ... 113
Lewis, Beth Irwin 1934- ... 33-36R
Lewis, Bill
See Lewis, William
Lewis, Bill H. 1927- ... 1-4R
Lewis, Brad (Alan) 1954- ... 127
Lewis, C. Day
See Day Lewis, C(ecil)
Lewis, C(larence) I(rving) 1883-1964 ... 5-8R
Lewis, C(live) S(taples) 1898-1963 ... CANR-33
Earlier sketch in CA 81-84
See also AAYA 3
See also CDBLB 1945-1960
See also CLC 1, 3, 6, 14, 27
See also CLR 3, 27
See also DLB 15, 100
See also MAICYA
See also MTCW
See also SATA 13
See also WLC
Lewis, Charles
See Dixon, Roger
Lewis, Charles Bertrand
1842-1924 Brief entry ... 114
See also DLB 11
Lewis, Claude A. 1934- ... 9-12R
Lewis, Claudia (Louise) 1907- ... CANR-6
Earlier sketch in CA 5-8R
See also SATA 5
Lewis, Clay(ton Wilson) 1936- ... 101
Lewis, Craig A. 1955- ... 132
Lewis, D. B.
See Bixby, Jerome Lewis
Lewis, D(ominic) B(evan) Wyndham
1894-1969 Obituary ... 25-28R
Lewis, Dave
See Lewis, David V.
Lewis, David B(enjamin) 1965- ... 111
Lewis, David Kellogg 1941- ... CANR-33
Earlier sketches in CA 81-84, CANR-15
Lewis, David L(anier) 1927- ... 69-72
Lewis, David L(evering) 1936- ... CANR-2
Earlier sketch in CA 45-48
Lewis, David Marshall
See Cook, Michael Lewis
Lewis, David T(revor) 1920- ... 45-48
Lewis, David V. 1923- ... 5-8R
Lewis, David 1909-1981 ... 104
Lewis, David 1922- ... 41-44R
Lewis, David 1942- ... CANR-12
Earlier sketch in CA 69-72
Lewis, Diane 1936- ... 129
Lewis, Donald Earle 1925- ... 5-8R
Lewis, Dorothy Roe 1904-1985 Obituary ... 115
Lewis, E. M. ... 69-72
See also SATA 20
Lewis, Edith 1882(?)-1972 Obituary ... 111
Lewis, Edward W(illiams)
1899-1986 Obituary ... 118
Lewis, Edwin C(lark) 1933- ... 25-28R
Lewis, Eils Moorhouse 1919- ... 106
Lewis, Elizabeth Foreman 1892-1958 ... 137
See also MAICYA
See also YABC 2
Lewis, Elliott (Bruce) 1917-1990 ... CANR-22
Obituary ... 131
Earlier sketch in CA 104
Lewis, Eugene 1940- ... CANR-4
Earlier sketch in CA 53-56
Lewis, (E.) Faye (Cashatt) 1896-1982 ... 25-28R
Obituary ... 135
Lewis, Felice (Elizabeth) Flanery 1920- ... 73-76
Lewis, Finlay 1938- ... 101
Lewis, Flora ... 127
Brief entry ... 119
Lewis, Francine
See Wells, Helen
Lewis, Francis Ames
See Ames-Lewis, Francis
Lewis, Freeman 1908-1976 Obituary ... 69-72
Lewis, Fulton Jr. 1903-1966 Obituary ... 89-92
Lewis, G(ranville) Douglass 1934- ... 106
Lewis, Gene D. 1931- ... 45-48
Lewis, Geoffrey (Lewis) 1920- ... 13-16R
Lewis, George H(allam) 1943- ... 53-56
Lewis, George L. 1916- ... CANR-3
Earlier sketch in CA 45-48
Lewis, George Q. 1916-1979 ... 21-24R
Obituary ... 135
Lewis, George 1941- ... 29-32R
Lewis, George 1943- ... 77-80
Lewis, Gordon R(ussell) 1926- ... CANR-25
Earlier sketches in CA 21-24R, CANR-10
Lewis, Grover Virgil 1934- ... 106
Lewis, H(ywel) D(avid) 1910- ... CANR-3
Earlier sketch in CA 9-12R
Lewis, H. Warren 1924- ... 29-32R
Lewis, Harold M. 1891(?)-1973 Obituary ... 45-48
Lewis, Harry 1917- ... 109
Lewis, Harry 1942- ... CANR-3
Earlier sketch in CA 49-52
Lewis, Helen (Lillian) Block 1913-1987 ... 110
Obituary ... 121
Lewis, Henry Clay 1825-1850 ... DLB 3
Lewis, Henry T(rickey) 1928- ... 73-76
Lewis, Herbert S(amuel) 1934- ... 17-20R
Lewis, Hilda (Winifred) 1896-1974 ... 93-96
Obituary ... 49-52
See also SATA 20
Lewis, Horacio D(elano) 1944- ... 57-60
Lewis, Howard R(obert) 1934- ... CANR-10
Earlier sketch in CA 25-28R
Lewis, Hunter 1947- ... 109
Lewis, I(oan) M(yrddin) 1930- ... CANR-21
Earlier sketches in CA 9-12R, CANR-5
Lewis, Ian
See Bensman, Joseph
Lewis, J. Patrick 1942- ... 138
See also SATA 69
Lewis, J. R.
See Lewis, (John) Roy(ston)
Lewis, Jack P(earl) 1919- ... CANR-34
Earlier sketch in CA 37-40R
See also SATA 65
Lewis, James Jr. 1930- ... CANR-12
Earlier sketch in CA 29-32R
Lewis, James 1935- ... 65-68
Lewis, Jan (Ellen) 1949- ... 115
Lewis, Janet 1899- ... CANR-29
Earlier sketches in CAP-1, CA 9-12R
See also Winters, Janet Lewis
See also CLC 41
See also DLBY 87
Lewis, Jean 1924- ... CANR-28
Earlier sketches in CA 21-24R, CANR-11
See also SATA 61
Lewis, Jerry 1926- ... 121
Brief entry ... 113
Lewis, John D(onald) 1905-1988 ... 65-68
Obituary ... 124
Lewis, John E(arl) 1931- ... CANR-21
Earlier sketches in CA 57-60, CANR-6
Lewis, (F.) John 1916- ... 133
Lewis, John (Noel Claude) 1912- ... CANR-19
Earlier sketch in CA 102
Lewis, John P(rior) 1921- ... 9-12R
Lewis, John Parry 1927- ... 107
Lewis, John W(ilson) 1930- ... 9-12R
Lewis, John 1889- ... CANR-5
Earlier sketch in CA 5-8R
Lewis, Joseph 1889-1968 ... CAP-1
Earlier sketch in CA 13-14
Lewis, Judith Mary 1921- ... 97-100
Lewis, June E(thelyn) 1905- ... CAP-2
Earlier sketch in CA 29-32
Lewis, Lange
See Brandt, Jane Lewis
Lewis, Larry L(ynn) 1935- ... 115
Lewis, Lawrence E(dwin) 1928- ... 69-72
Lewis, Leon Ray 1883- ... CAP-1
Earlier sketch in CA 9-10
Lewis, Leon 1904- ... CAP-1
Earlier sketch in CA 13-16
Lewis, Lesley 1909- ... 102
Lewis, Linda (Joy) 1946- ... 135
See also SATA 67
Lewis, Linda 1927- ... 93-96
Lewis, Lionel Stanley 1933- ... CANR-5
Earlier sketch in CA 53-56
Lewis, Lucia Z.
See Anderson, Lucia (Lewis)
Lewis, Margaret (B.) 1942- ... 135
Lewis, Margie M. 1923- ... 101
Lewis, Marianna Olmstead 1923- ... 9-12R
Lewis, Marjorie 1929- ... 108
See also SATA 35, 40
Lewis, Martha E(llen) 1941- ... CANR-10
Earlier sketch in CA 25-28R
Lewis, Marvin 1923-1971 ... CAP-2
Earlier sketch in CA 21-22
Lewis, Mary (Christianna)
1907(?)-1988 ... CANR-13
Obituary ... 125
Earlier sketch in CA 77-80
See also SATA 56, 64
Lewis, Mary F. W.
See Bond, Mary Fanning Wickham
Lewis, Matthew Gregory 1775-1818 ... DLB 39
Lewis, Maynah 1919- ... CANR-16
Earlier sketch in CA 25-28R
Lewis, Mervyn
See Frewer, Glyn (M.)
Lewis, Mervyn K(eith) 1941- ... 125
Lewis, Michael
See Untermeyer, Louis
Lewis, Michael Arthur 1890-1970 ... CANR-5
Obituary ... 29-32R
Earlier sketch in CA 5-8R
Lewis, Michael 1937- ... CANR-1
Earlier sketch in CA 45-48
Lewis, Michael 1960- ... BEST 90:2
Lewis, Mildred D. 1912- ... 13-16R
Lewis, Mort(imer) R(eis) 1908-1991 ... 105
Obituary ... 134
Lewis, Naphtali 1911- ... 110
Lewis, Nigel (Stephen) 1948- ... 116
Lewis, Nolan D(on) C(arpenter) 1889- ... 5-8R
Lewis, Norman 1912- ... CANR-3
Earlier sketch in CA 9-12R
Lewis, Norman 1918- ... 129
Brief entry ... 112
See also MTCW
Lewis, Norman 1940- ... 136
Lewis, Oren Ritter 1902-1983 Obituary ... 110
Lewis, Oscar 1893- ... 5-8R
Lewis, Oscar 1914-1970 ... CAP-1
Obituary ... 29-32R
Earlier sketch in CA 19-20
Lewis, Patricia Ann 1933- ... 112
Lewis, Paul
See Gerson, Noel Bertram
Lewis, Paul H. 1937- ... 73-76
Lewis, Peirce F(ee) 1927- ... 41-44R
Lewis, Peter
See Lewis, Peter Elvet (Elfed)
Lewis, Peter Elvet (Elfed) 1937- ... 133
Lewis, Peter 1922- ... 9-12R
Lewis, Peter 1938- ... CANR-21
Earlier sketch in CA 45-48
Lewis, Philip 1913- ... 1-4R
Lewis, R. Duffy 1908- ... CAP-1
Earlier sketch in CA 11-12
Lewis, R(ichard) W(arrington) B(aldwin)
1917- ... 102
See also DLB 111
Lewis, Ralph F(erguson) 1918-1979 ... 29-32R
Obituary ... 89-92
Lewis, Ralph L(oren) 1919- ... 117
Lewis, Richard S. 1916- ... CANR-9
Earlier sketch in CA 57-60
Lewis, Richard 1700(?)-1734 ... DLB 24
Lewis, Richard 1935- ... CANR-5
Earlier sketch in CA 9-12R
See also SATA 3
Lewis, Robert T(urner) 1923- ... 85-88
Lewis, Robert 1932- ... 97-100
Lewis, Roger
See Zarchy, Harry
Lewis, Ronello B. 1909- ... CAP-1
Earlier sketch in CA 17-18
Lewis, (Ernest Michael) Roy 1913- ... CANR-3
Earlier sketch in CA 5-8R
Lewis, (John) Roy(ston) 1933- ... 105
Lewis, Samella S(anders) 1924- Brief entry ... 112
Lewis, Sasha Gregory 1947- ... CANR-15
Earlier sketch in CA 85-88
Lewis, Saunders 1893-1985 Obituary ... 117
Lewis, Sean Day
See Day-Lewis, Sean (Francis)
Lewis, Selma S. 1921- ... 123
Lewis, Shari 1934- ... CANR-19
Earlier sketch in CA 89-92
See also SATA 30, 35
Lewis, (Harry) Sinclair 1885-1951 ... 133
Brief entry ... 104
See also CDALB 1917-1929
See also DLB 9, 102
See also DLBD 1
See also MTCW
See also TCLC 4, 13, 23, 39
See also WLC
Lewis, Stephen Richmond Jr. 1939- ... 41-44R
Lewis, Stephen 1947(?)-1981 Obituary ... 103
See also AITN 1
Lewis, Sylvan R.
See Aronson, Virginia
Lewis, T(heodore) G(yle) 1941- ... 111
Lewis, Ted
See Lewis, Edward W(illiams)
Lewis, Theophilus 1891-1974 ... 125
See also BW
Lewis, Therese 1912(?)-1984 Obituary ... 113
Lewis, Thomas A. 1942- ... 128
Lewis, Thomas P(arker) 1936- ... 29-32R
See also SATA 27
Lewis, Thomas S(pottswood) W(ellford)
1942- ... CANR-31
Earlier sketch in CA 49-52
Lewis, Tom 1940- ... 105
Lewis, Tony 1938- ... 122
Lewis, Voltaire
See Ritchie, Edwin
Lewis, W(illiam) Arthur 1915-1991 ... CANR-13
Obituary ... 134
Brief entry ... 111
Earlier sketch in CA 17-20R
Lewis, W(alter) David 1931- ... CANR-9
Earlier sketch in CA 13-16R
Lewis, Walker 1904- ... CAP-2
Earlier sketch in CA 19-20
Lewis, Warren 1940- ... 115
Lewis, William Hubert 1928- ... 13-16R
Lewis, William 1946- ... 120
Lewis, Willie Newbury 1891-1985 ... 93-96
Obituary ... 116
Lewis, Wilmarth Sheldon 1895-1979 ... CANR-15
Obituary ... 89-92
Earlier sketch in CA 65-68
Lewis, (Percy) Wyndham
1884(?)-1957 Brief entry ... 104
See also DLB 15
See also TCLC 2, 9
Lewisohn, Ludwig 1883-1955 Brief entry ... 107
See also DLB 4, 9, 28, 102
See also TCLC 19
Lewisohn, Mark 1958- ... 130
Lewiston, Robert R(ueben) 1909- ... CAP-2
Earlier sketch in CA 23-24
Lewis-Williams, J(ames) David 1934- ... 117
Lewiton, Mina 1904-1970 ... CAP-2
Obituary ... 29-32R
Earlier sketch in CA 23-24
See also SATA 2
Lewitt, Shariann (N.) 1954- ... 119
Lewittes, Mordecai Henry
See Lewittes, Morton H(enry)
Lewittes, Morton H(enry) 1911-1990 ... 25-28R
Obituary ... 133
Lewontin, Richard Charles 1929- ... 104
Lewontin, Timothy (Andrew) 1955- ... 130
Lewsen, Phyllis 1916- ... 109
Lewton-Brain, James 1923- ... 97-100
Lewty, Marjorie 1906- ... CAP-1
Earlier sketch in CA 9-10
Lewy, Guenter 1923- ... CANR-21
Earlier sketches in CA 9-12R, CANR-3
Lexau, Joan M. ... CANR-11
Earlier sketch in CA 17-20R
See also SATA 1, 36
Ley, Alice Chetwynd 1913- ... CANR-21
Earlier sketches in CA 13-16R, CANR-6
Ley, Arthur Gordon 1911-1968 Obituary ... 102
Ley, Charles David 1913- ... 9-12R
Ley, Ralph 1929- ... 41-44R
Ley, Robert Arthur
See Ley, Arthur Gordon
Ley, Sandra 1944- ... 57-60
Ley, Willy 1906-1969 ... 9-12R
Obituary ... 25-28R
See also SATA 2
Leyburn, Ellen Douglass 1907-1966 ... CAP-2
Earlier sketch in CA 25-28
Leyburn, James G(raham) 1902- ... 5-8R
Leyda, Jay 1910-1988 ... 108
Obituary ... 124

Leydet, Francois G(uillaume) 1927- ... 9-12R
Leydon, Rita (Floden) 1949- ... SATA 21
Leyhart, Edward
  See Edwards, Elwyn Hartley
Leyland, Eric (Arthur) 1911- ... SATA 37
Leyland, Mal(colm Rex) 1944- ... 108
Leyland, Winston 1940- ... 107
Leynard, Martin
  See Berger, Ivan (Bennett)
Leyner, Mark 1956- ... CANR-28
  Earlier sketch in CA 110
Leypoldt, Martha M. 1918-1975 ... CAP-2
  Earlier sketch in CA 23-24
Leys, Mary Dorothy Rose 1890- ... 5-8R
Leys, Simon
  See Ryckmans, Pierre
Leys, Wayne A(lbert) R(isser)
  1905-1973 ... CAP-1
  Earlier sketch in CA 17-18
Leyser, Karl Joseph 1920- ... 112
  Obituary ... 137
Leyton, Elliott (Hastings) 1939- ... 120
Leyton, Sophie
  See Walsh, Sheila
Leyva, Ricardo
  See Valdes, Nelson P.
Lezama Lima, Jose 1910-1976 ... 77-80
  See also CLC 4, 10
  See also DLB 113
  See also HW
Lezra, Grizzella Paull 1934- ... 61-64
Lhamon, W(illiam) T(aylor) Jr. 1945- ... 65-68
L'Heureux, Bill
  See L'Heureux, W(illard) J(oseph)
L'Heureux, John (Clarke) 1934- ... CANR-23
  Earlier sketch in CA 13-16R
  See also CLC 52
L'Heureux, W(illard) J(oseph) 1918- ... 5-8R
L'Hommedieu, Dorothy Keasley
  1885-1961 Obituary ... 109
  See also SATA 29
Li, C(hing) C(hun) 1912- ... 17-20R
Li, Chiang-Kwang 1915- ... 73-76
Li, Choh-Ming 1912- ... 1-4R
Li, David H(siang-fu) 1928- ... 13-16R
Li, Fang Kuei 1902- ... 112
Li, Hui-Lin 1911- ... CANR-15
  Earlier sketch in CA 85-88
Li, Shu Hua 1890(?)-1979 Obituary ... 89-92
Li, Tien-yi 1915- ... 37-40R
Li, Tze-chung 1927- ... CANR-14
  Earlier sketch in CA 41-44R
Li, Yao-wen 1924- ... 106
Liang, Chin-tung 1893- ... 81-84
Liang, Yen 1908- ... 5-8R
Liao, David C. E. 1925- ... 41-44R
Lias, Edward J(ohn) 1934- ... 120
Lias, Godfrey ... 5-8R
Libbey, Elizabeth 1947- ... 110
Libbey, James K(eith) 1942- ... 81-84
Libby, Anthony 1942- ... 118
Libby, Bill
  See Libby, William M.
Libby, Leona Marshall 1919-1986 ... 101
  Obituary ... 121
Libby, Ronald T(heodore) 1941- ... 135
Libby, Violet K(elway)
  1892(?)-1981 Obituary ... 105
Libby, Willard F(rank) 1908-1980 Obituary ... 113
Libby, William C(harles) ... 104
Libby, William M. 1927-1984 ... CANR-10
  Obituary ... 113
  Earlier sketch in CA 25-28R
  See also SATA 5, 39
Liberace
  See Liberace, Wladziu Valentino
Liberace, Wladziu Valentino
  1919-1987 ... CANR-22
  Obituary ... 121
  Earlier sketch in CA 89-92
Liberman, Alexander 1912- Brief entry ... 113
Liberman, Anatoly 1937- ... 116
Liberman, Evsei Grigorevich
  1897-1983 Obituary ... 109
Liberman, Judith 1929- ... 73-76
Liberman, M(yron) M(andell) 1921- ... 57-60
Liberman, Robert Paul 1937- ... CANR-22
  Earlier sketches in CA 61-64, CANR-7
Liberman, Yevsei Grigorevich
  See Liberman, Evsei Grigorevich
Libersat, Henry 1934- ... 53-56
Liberty, Gene 1924- ... CANR-8
  Earlier sketch in CA 5-8R
  See also SATA 3
Libin, Laurence (Elliot) 1944- ... 119
Liblit, Jerome ... 13-16R
Libman, Carol 1928- ... 113
Libo, Kenneth (Harold) 1937- ... 133
  Brief entry ... 109
Libo, Lester M(artin) 1923- ... 77-80
Librach, Jan 1904(?)-1973 Obituary ... 41-44R
LiBretto, Ellen V. 1947- ... 110
Lichello, Robert 1926- ... 13-16R
Lichine, Alexis 1913-1989 ... 9-12R
  Obituary ... 128
Licht, Fred (Stephen) 1928- ... 13-16R
Licht, Sidney Herman 1907-1979 Obituary ... 108
Lichtblau, Myron Ivor 1925- ... 17-20R
Lichten, Joseph I. 1906(?)-1987 Obituary ... 125
Lichtenberg, Elisabeth Jacoba 1913- ... 13-16R
Lichtenberg, Georg Christoph
  1742-1799 ... DLB 94
Lichtenberg, Jacqueline 1942- ... 73-76
Lichtenberg, Philip 1926- ... CANR-13
  Earlier sketch in CA 37-40R
Lichtenstadter, Ilse
  See Niklaus, Thelma (Jones)
Lichtenstadter, Ilse 1907- ... CANR-13
  Earlier sketch in CA 33-36R
Lichtenstein, Aharon 1933- ... 17-20R
Lichtenstein, Grace 1941- ... CANR-22
  Earlier sketches in CA 49-52, CANR-2
Lichtheim, George 1912-1973 Obituary ... 41-44R
Lichtman, Allan J. 1947- ... 124
Lichtman, Celia S(chmukler) 1932- ... 41-44R
Lichtman, Wendy 1946- ... 114
Lichty, George M(aurice) 1905-1983 ... 104
  Obituary ... 110
Lichty, Lawrence W(ilson) 1937- ... 53-56
Lichty, Ron 1950- ... CANR-18
  Earlier sketch in CA 101
Licklider, Roy E(ilers) 1941- ... 33-36R
Lickona, Thomas Edward 1943- ... 113
Lida, Denah (Levy) 1923- ... 21-24R
Lidchi, Maggi
  See Lidchi Grassi, Maggi
Lidchi Grassi, Maggi 1930- ... 132
Liddell, Brendan E(dwin) A(lexander)
  1927- ... 29-32R
Liddell, C. H.
  See Kuttner, Henry
Liddell, Kenneth 1912-1975 ... SATA 63
Liddell, (John) Robert 1908- ... 13-16R
Liddell Hart, Basil Henry 1895-1970 ... 103
  Obituary ... 89-92
Lidderdale, Halliday Adair 1917- ... 21-24R
Liddicoat, Richard T. Jr. 1918- ... 45-48
Liddle, Peter Hammond 1934- ... CANR-18
  Earlier sketch in CA 102
Liddle, William 1925- ... 77-80
Liddy, G(eorge) Gordon (Battle) 1930- ... 114
Liddy, James (Daniel Reeves) 1934- ... CANR-20
  Earlier sketches in CA 13-16R, CANR-5
  See also AITN 2
Lide, Mary ... 132
  Brief entry ... 127
Lidman, David 1905- ... 69-72
Lidoff, Joan (Ilene) 1944-1989 ... 115
  Obituary ... 130
Lidtke, Vernon L. 1930- ... 21-24R
Lidz, Theodore 1910- ... 29-32R
Lie, Jonas (Lauritz Idemil)
  1833-1908(?) Brief entry ... 115
  See also TCLC 5
Lie, Trygve (Halvdan) 1896-1968 Obituary ... 113
Lieb, Fred(erick George) 1888-1980 ... 69-72
  Obituary ... 97-100
Lieb, Irwin Chester 1925- Brief entry ... 105
Lieb, Michael 1940- ... 65-68
Lieb, Robert C. 1944- ... 37-40R
Lieb, Sandra ... 112
Liebenow, J. Gus 1925- ... 45-48
Lieber, Arnold L(ou) 1937- Brief entry ... 113
Lieber, Joel 1937-1971 ... 73-76
  Obituary ... 29-32R
  See also CLC 6
Lieber, Robert J(ames) 1941- ... CANR-30
  Earlier sketches in CA 29-32R, CANR-12
Lieber, Stanley Martin
  See Lee, Stan
Lieber, Todd M(ichael) 1944- ... 45-48
Lieberg, Owen S. 1896-1973 ... CAP-2
  Earlier sketch in CA 25-28
Lieberman, Arnold (Leo) 1903- ... CAP-1
  Earlier sketch in CA 19-20
Lieberman, Donald 1927- ... 111
Lieberman, E(dwin) James 1934- ... CANR-22
  Earlier sketch in CA 45-48
  See also SATA 62
Lieberman, Elias 1883- ... 5-8R
Lieberman, Fredric 1940- ... CANR-7
  Earlier sketch in CA 53-56
Lieberman, Gerald F. 1923-1986 ... 85-88
  Obituary ... 119
Lieberman, Herbert (Henry) 1933- ... CANR-19
  Earlier sketches in CA 9-12R, CANR-5
Lieberman, J. Ben 1914-1984 Obituary ... 113
Lieberman, Jethro K(oller) 1943- ... CANR-10
  Earlier sketch in CA 21-24R
Lieberman, Joseph I. 1942- ... 17-20R
Lieberman, Laurence (James) 1935- ... CANR-36
  Earlier sketches in CA 17-20R, CANR-8
  See also CLC 4, 36
Lieberman, Mark 1942- ... 29-32R
Lieberman, Mendel Halliday 1913- ... 106
Lieberman, Morton A(lexander) 1931- ... 41-44R
Lieberman, Myron 1919- ... CANR-8
  Earlier sketch in CA 5-8R
Lieberman, Philip 1934- ... 93-96
Lieberman, Robert (Howard) 1941- ... CANR-10
  Earlier sketch in CA 57-60
  See also AITN 1
Lieberman, Rosalie ... 9-12R
Lieberman, Samuel 1911-1981 ... 17-20R
  Obituary ... 134
Lieberman, Saul 1898-1983 Obituary ... 109
Liebers, Arthur 1913- ... CANR-3
  Earlier sketch in CA 5-8R
  See also SATA 12
Liebers, Ruth 1910- ... CAP-1
  Earlier sketch in CA 9-10
Lieberson, Goddard 1911- ... CAP-2
  Earlier sketch in CA 25-28
Lieberson, Jonathan
  1949(?)-1989 Obituary ... 128
Lieberson, Stanley 1933- ... CANR-38
  Earlier sketches in CA 1-4R, CANR-1, 17
Lieberstein, Stanley H. 1934- ... 105
Liebert, Burt 1925- ... 33-36R
Liebert, Doris 1934- ... 105
Liebert, Robert M. 1942- ... 41-44R
Liebert, Robert S. 1930-1988 Obituary ... 125
Lieberthal, Kenneth G. 1943- ... 130
Lieberthal, Milton M(orton) 1911- ... 117
Liebeschuetz, Hans
  1893(?)-1978(?) Obituary ... 85-88
Liebhafsky, Herbert Hugo 1919- ... 5-8R
Liebhafsky, Herman A(lfred) 1905- ... 53-56
Lieblich, Amia 1939- ... 93-96
Lieblich, Irene 1923- ... SATA 22
Liebling, A(bbott) J(oseph) 1904-1963 ... 104
  Obituary ... 89-92
  See also DLB 4
Liebman, Arthur 1926- ... CANR-6
  Earlier sketch in CA 57-60
Liebman, Charles S(eymour) 1934- ... 61-64
Liebman, Marcel 1930(?)-1986 Obituary ... 118
Liebman, Ron(ald S.) 1943- ... 120
Liebman, Seymour B(ertrand)
  1907-1986 ... CANR-7
  Obituary ... 120
  Earlier sketch in CA 17-20R
Liebow, Averill A(braham)
  1911-1978 Obituary ... 111
Liederbach, Clarence Andrew 1910- ... 93-96
Liederman, Judith 1927- ... 85-88
Liedholm, Carl (Edward) 1940- ... 41-44R
Liedloff, Jean ... 81-84
Liedtke, Kurt E(rnst) H(einrich) 1919- ... 17-20R
Lief, N. H.
  See Bayes, Ronald H(omer)
Lief, Nina R. 1907- ... 118
Lief, Philip 1947- ... 107
Liehm, Antonin J. 1924- ... 102
Lieksman, Anders
  See Haavikko, Paavo Juhani
Liem, Nguyen Dang 1936- ... 57-60
Lien, Arnold J. 1920-1979 ... 21-24R
  Obituary ... 122
Lienhard, John H(enry IV) 1930- ... CANR-4
  Earlier sketch in CA 53-56
Lientz, Bennet Price 1942- ... CANR-8
  Earlier sketch in CA 61-64
Liepolt, Werner 1944- ... 25-28R
Liers, Emil E(rnest) 1890-1975 ... 107
  See also SATA 37
Liesner, Hans Hubertus (Karl Kurt Otto)
  1929- ... 104
Lietaer, Bernard A(rthur) 1942- ... 33-36R
Lietaert Peerbolte, Maarten 1905- ... 102
Lietz, Gerald S. 1918- ... SATA 11
Lieuwen, Edwin 1923- ... CANR-5
  Earlier sketch in CA 1-4R
Liew, Kit Siong 1932- ... 77-80
Lifar, Serge 1905-1986 Obituary ... 121
Lifchitz, Boris 1895-1984 Obituary ... 114
Li Fei-kan 1904- ... 105
  See also CLC 18
Liffring, Joan Louise 1929- ... 17-20R
Lifshin, Lyn (Diane) 1944- ... CANR-25
  Earlier sketches in CA 33-36R, CANR-8
  See also CAAS 10
Lifson, David S. 1908- ... CANR-32
  Earlier sketch in CA 33-36R
Lifton, Betty Jean ... CANR-27
  Earlier sketches in CA 5-8R, CANR-12
  See also SATA 6
Lifton, Robert Jay 1926- ... CANR-27
  Earlier sketch in CA 17-20R
  See also CLC 67
  See also SATA 66
Lifton, Walter M. 1918- ... CANR-16
  Earlier sketch in CA 33-36R
Liggero, John 1921- ... 25-28R
Liggett, Clayton E(ugene) 1930- ... 29-32R
Liggett, Hunter
  See Paine, Lauran (Bosworth)
Liggett, John 1923- ... 57-60
Liggett, Thomas 1918- ... 5-8R
Light, Albert 1927- ... 93-96
Light, Ivan 1941- ... 73-76
Light, James F. 1921- ... CANR-1
  Earlier sketch in CA 1-4R
Light, Martin 1927- ... 53-56
Light, P(aul) H. 1947- ... 128
Light, Patricia Kahn 1939- ... 61-64
Lightbody, Charles Wayland 1904- ... 5-8R
Lightbody, Donna Mae 1920-1976 Obituary ... 110
Lightbown, Ronald William 1932- ... 104
Lightfoot, Alfred 1936- ... CANR-4
  Earlier sketch in CA 53-56
Lightfoot, Claude M. 1910- ... 123
  See also BW
Lightfoot, David (William) 1945- ... 116
Lightfoot, Gordon 1938- Brief entry ... 109
  See also CLC 26
Lightfoot, Neil R(oland) 1929- ... 81-84
Lightfoot, Paul 1946- ... 110
Lighthall, William Douw 1857-1954 ... DLB 92
Lightman, Bernard 1950- ... 116
Lightner, A. M.
  See Hopf, Alice (Martha) L(ightner)
Lightner, Alice
  See Hopf, Alice (Martha) L(ightner)
Lightner, Robert P(aul) 1931- ... CANR-37
  Earlier sketches in CA 49-52, CANR-1, 16
Lightner, Theodore 1893(?)-1981 Obituary ... 113
Lightwood, Martha B. 1923- ... 33-36R
Lignell, Lois 1911- ... SATA 37
Ligomenides, Panos A. 1928- ... 29-32R
Ligon, Ernest M(ayfield) 1897- ... CAP-1
  Earlier sketch in CA 9-10
Ligotti, Thomas 1953- ... 123
  See also CLC 44
Liguori, Frank E. 1917-1980 ... 21-24R
  Obituary ... 134
Lihani, John 1927- ... CANR-14
  Earlier sketch in CA 37-40R
Lihn, Enrique 1929-1988 ... CANR-32
  Earlier sketch in CA 104
  See also HW
Lijphart, Arend 1936- ... CANR-25
  Earlier sketches in CA 21-24R, CANR-10
Likeness, George C(lark) 1927- ... 17-20R
Likert, Rensis 1903- ... 93-96
Likhovski, Eliahou 1927- ... 45-48
Liles, Bruce (Lynn) 1934- ... 53-56
Liley, Helen Margaret Irwin 1928- ... 25-28R
Liliencron, (Friedrich Adolf Axel) Detlev von
  1844-1909 Brief entry ... 117
  See also TCLC 18
Lilienfeld, Abraham M(orris)
  1920-1984 Obituary ... 113
Lilienfeld, Robert Henry 1927- ... CANR-1
  Earlier sketch in CA 1-4R
Lilienthal, Alfred M(orton) 1913- ... 37-40R
Lilienthal, David E(li) 1899-1981 ... CANR-3
  Obituary ... 102
  Earlier sketch in CA 5-8R
Li Ling-Ai ... 77-80
Lilje, Hanns 1899-1977 Obituary ... 69-72
Lillard, Charles (Marion) 1944- ... CANR-8
  Earlier sketch in CA 61-64
Lillard, Paula Polk 1931- ... 73-76
Lillard, Richard G(ordon) 1909-1990 ... 21-24R
  Obituary ... 131
Lilley, Dorothy B(race) 1914- ... 113
Lilley, Peter 1943- ... 77-80
Lillibridge, G(eorge) D(onald) 1921- ... 13-16R
Lillich, Meredith Parsons 1932- Brief entry ... 105
Lillich, Richard B(onnot) 1933- ... 119
Lillie, Beatrice (Gladys)
  1894(?)-1989 Obituary ... 127
Lillie, Helen 1915- ... 65-68
Lillie, John Adam 1884-1983 Obituary ... 110
Lillie, Ralph D(ougall)
  1896-1979 Obituary ... 89-92
Lillie, William 1899- ... 5-8R
Lillington, Kenneth (James) 1916- ... CANR-3
  Earlier sketch in CA 5-8R
  See also SATA 39
Lillo, George 1691-1739 ... DLB 84
Lilly, Charles ... SATA 33
Lilly, Doris 1926-1991 ... CANR-11
  Obituary ... 135
  Earlier sketch in CA 29-32R
Lilly, Eli 1885-1977 Obituary ... 69-72
Lilly, John C(unningham) 1915- ... CANR-1
  Earlier sketch in CA 1-4R
Lilly, Mark 1950- ... 136
Lilly, Ray
  See Curtis, Richard (Alan)
Lim, Genny 1946- ... CANR-39
  Earlier sketch in CA 116
Lim, John 1932- ... 116
  See also SATA 43
Lim, Paul Stephen 1944- ... CANR-25
  Earlier sketch in CA 108
Lima, Carolyn W(omack) 1938- ... 118
Lima, Frank 1939- ... 73-76
Lima, Jose Lezama
  See Lezama Lima, Jose
Lima, Robert 1935- ... 9-12R
Lima Barreto, Afonso Henrique de
  1881-1922 Brief entry ... 117
  See also TCLC 23
Liman, Claude Gilbert 1943- ... 57-60
Liman, Ellen (Fogelson) 1936- ... CANR-13
  Earlier sketch in CA 61-64
  See also SATA 22
Limb, Sue 1946- ... CANR-37
  Earlier sketch in CA 115
Limbacher, James L. 1926- ... CANR-17
  Earlier sketches in CA 5-8R, CANR-2
Limburg, James 1935- ... 112
Limburg, Peter R(ichard) 1929- ... 33-36R
  See also SATA 13
Limentani, Uberto 1913-1989(?) ... 17-20R
  Obituary ... 129
Limerick, Jeffrey W. 1948- ... 102
Limmer, Ruth 1927- ... CANR-1
  Earlier sketch in CA 45-48
Limonov, Eduard ... CLC 67
Limonov, Edward 1944- ... 137
Limpert, John A. 1934- ... 77-80
Lin, Adet J(usu) 1923- ... 5-8R
Lin, Florence (Shen) ... CANR-12
  Earlier sketch in CA 61-64
Lin, Frank
  See Atherton, Gertrude (Franklin Horn)
Lin, Julia C(hang) 1928- ... 73-76
Lin, Nan 1938- ... 73-76
Lin, Robert K(wan-Hwan) 1937- ... CANR-10
  Earlier sketch in CA 65-68
Lin, San-su C(hen) 1916- ... 17-20R
Lin, Tai-yi 1926- ... 9-12R
Lin, Yu-sheng 1934- ... 89-92
Lin, Yutang 1895-1976 ... CANR-2
  Obituary ... 65-68
  Earlier sketch in CA 45-48
Linamen, Harold Frederick 1921- ... 17-20R
Lincicome, Bernard Wesley
  See Lincicome, Bernie
Lincicome, Bernie 1941- ... 136
Linck, Orville F. 1906- ... 5-8R
Lincke, Jack 1909- ... CAP-2
  Earlier sketch in CA 29-32
Lincoff, Gary Henry 1942- ... 112
Lincoln, Alan Jay 1945- ... 123
Lincoln, Bruce 1948- ... CANR-22
  Earlier sketch in CA 105
Lincoln, C(harles) Eric 1924- ... CANR-27
  Earlier sketches in CA 1-4R, CANR-1
  See also BW
  See also SATA 5
Lincoln, Edith Maas 1891-1977 Obituary ... 73-76

Lincoln, G(eorge) Gould
1880-1974 Obituary ... 113
See also AITN 1
Lincoln, George Arthur 1907-1975 ... 1-4R
Obituary ... 57-60
Lincoln, Harry B. 1922- ... 25-28R
Lincoln, Henry ... 110
Lincoln, James Finney 1883-1965 ... 1-4R
Lincoln, James H. 1916- ... 25-28R
Lincoln, Kenneth Robert 1943- ... CANR-36
Earlier sketch in CA 114
Lincoln, Les
See Swatridge, Charles (John)
Lincoln, Murray D. 1892-1966 ... CAP-2
Earlier sketch in CA 19-20
Lincoln, Roger J(ohn) 1942- ... 117
Lincoln, Victoria 1904-1981 ... CAP-1
Obituary ... 104
Earlier sketch in CA 17-18
Lincoln, W(illiam) Bruce 1938- ... CANR-29
Earlier sketch in CA 85-88
Lind, Alan R(obert) 1940- ... CANR-12
Earlier sketch in CA 61-64
Lind, Andrew W(illiam) 1901- ... CANR-21
Earlier sketch in CA 45-48
Lind, Jakov
See Landwirth, Heinz
See also CAAS 4
See also CLC 1, 2, 4, 27
Lind, L(evi) R(obert) 1906- ... CANR-4
Earlier sketch in CA 5-8R
Lind, Millard C. 1918- ... 115
Lind, Sidney Edmund 1914- ... 37-40R
Lind, William S(turgiss) 1947- ... 123
Lindaman, Edward B. 1920-1982 ... 77-80
Obituary ... 107
Lindars, Barnabas 1923-1991 ... CANR-27
Obituary ... 135
Earlier sketches in CA 25-28R, CANR-11
Lindauer, John Howard 1937- ... 21-24R
Lindauer, Lois Lyons 1933- ... CANR-35
Earlier sketch in CA 49-52
Lindauer, Martin 1918- ... 5-8R
Linday, Ryllis Elizabeth Paine 1919- ... 13-16R
Lindbeck, (K.) Assar (E.) 1930- ... 37-40R
Lindberg, Carter 1937- ... 112
Lindberg, David C. 1935- ... CANR-11
Earlier sketch in CA 69-72
Lindberg, Gary H(ans) 1941- ... 65-68
Lindberg, Gladys 1905(?)-1990 Obituary ... 131
Lindberg, Leon N. 1932- ... 33-36R
Lindberg, Lucile 1913- ... 37-40R
Lindberg, Paul M(artin) 1905- ... 5-8R
Lindberg, Richard 1953- ... CANR-27
Earlier sketch in CA 110
Lindberg, Stanley W(illiam) 1939- ... 112
Lindbergh, Anne
See Sapieyevski, Anne Lindbergh
Lindbergh, Anne (Spencer) Morrow
1906- ... CANR-16
Earlier sketch in CA 17-20R
See also MTCW
See also SATA 33
Lindbergh, Charles A(ugustus Jr.)
1902-1974 ... CANR-16
Obituary ... 53-56
Earlier sketch in CA 93-96
See also SATA 33
Lindberg-Seyersted, Brita 1923- ... 111
Lindblom, Charles E(dward) 1917- ... CANR-1
Earlier sketch in CA 1-4R
Lindblom, (Christian) Johannes
1882-1974 Obituary ... 53-56
Lindblom, Steven (Winther) 1946- ... CANR-23
Earlier sketch in CA 106
See also SATA 39, 42
Linde, Gunnel 1924- ... CANR-27
Earlier sketches in CA 21-24R, CANR-11
See also SATA 5
Linde, Shirley Motter 1929- ... CANR-18
Earlier sketches in CA 45-48, CANR-1
Lindeburg, Franklin Alfred 1918- ... 5-8R
Lindeman, Jack 1924- ... 21-24R
Lindemann, Albert S(hirk) 1938- ... 49-52
Lindemann, Constance 1923- ... 61-64
Lindemann, Herbert Fred 1909- ... 29-32R
Linden, Catherine 1939- ... 110
Linden, George William 1938- ... 65-68
Linden, Kathryn (Wolaver) 1925- ... 37-40R
Linden, Oliver
See Abrahams, Doris Caroline
Linden, Patricia
See Nutting, Patricia Fink
Linden, Sara
See Bartlett, Marie (Swan)
Lindenau, Judith Wood 1941- ... 77-80
Lindenberger, Herbert (Samuel) 1929- ... CANR-3
Earlier sketch in CA 5-8R
Lindenfeld, David Frank 1944- ... 106
Lindenfeld, Frank 1934- ... 33-36R
Lindenmeyer, Otto J. 1936- ... 77-80
Linder, Bertram L. 1931- ... CANR-2
Earlier sketch in CA 49-52
Linder, Bill R. 1937- ... 112
Linder, Darwyn E(llsworth) 1939- ... 57-60
Linder, Erich 1925(?)-1983 Obituary ... 109
Linder, Ivan H. 1894- ... CAP-1
Earlier sketch in CA 9-10
Linder, Leslie Obituary ... 41-44R
Linder, Mark 1944- ... 120
Linder, Norma West 1928- ... 97-100
Linder, Robert D(ean) 1933- ... 41-44R
Linder, Staffan B(urenstam)
1931- Brief entry ... 105
Linder, Steven 1953- ... 112
Linderman, Earl W. 1931- ... 33-36R
Linderman, Gerald F(loyd) 1934- ... 85-88
Linderman, Lawrence 1940- ... 128
Linderman, Winifred B. ... CAP-2
Earlier sketch in CA 25-28
Lindesmith, Alfred Ray 1905- ... CAP-1
Earlier sketch in CA 9-10
Lindey, Christine 1947- ... 126
Lindfors, Judith Wells 1937- ... 117
Lindfors, Viveca 1920- ... 128
Lindgren, Alvin J. 1917- ... CANR-8
Earlier sketch in CA 17-20R
Lindgren, Astrid (Ericsson) 1907- ... CANR-39
Earlier sketch in CA 13-16R
See also CLR 1
See also MAICYA
See also SATA 2, 38
Lindgren, Barbo 1937- ... CLR 20
See also SATA 46, 63
Lindgren, Ernest H. 1910-1973 ... CAP-1
Earlier sketch in CA 13-14
Lindgren, Ethel John
See Lindgren-Utsi, E(thel) J(ohn)
Lindgren, Henry Clay 1914- ... CANR-1
Earlier sketch in CA 1-4R
Lindgren, Torgny 1938- ... 136
Lindgren-Utsi, E(thel) J(ohn)
1905-1988 Obituary ... 125
Lindheim, Irma Levy 1886-1978 ... 5-8R
Obituary ... 77-80
Lindholdt, Paul J. 1954- ... 137
Lindholm, Charles T. 1946- ... 134
Lindholm, Richard W(adsworth) 1914- ... CANR-5
Earlier sketch in CA 1-4R
Lindley, Betty G(rimes)
1900(?)-1976 Obituary ... 65-68
Lindley, Denver 1904-1982 Obituary ... 106
Lindley, Erica
See Quigley, Aileen
Lindley, Ernest K(idder)
1899-1979 Obituary ... 89-92
Lindley, Hilda 1919(?)-1980 Obituary ... 102
Lindley, Kenneth (Arthur) 1928- ... CANR-10
Earlier sketch in CA 5-8R
Lindman, Maj (Jan) 1886-1972 ... SATA 43
Lindner, D. Berry
See Du Breuil, (Elizabeth) L(or)inda
Lindner, Edgar T(heodore) 1911- ... 57-60
Lindop, Audrey (Beatrice Noel) Erskine
See Erskine-Lindop, Audrey (Beatrice Noel)
Lindop, Christine (Robin) 1949- ... 128
Lindop, Edmund 1925- ... CANR-38
Earlier sketches in CA 5-8R, CANR-2, 17
See also SATA 5
Lindop, Grevel 1948- ... CANR-29
Earlier sketches in CA 61-64, CANR-13
Lindow, John Frederick 1946- ... 113
Lindow, Wesley 1910- ... 45-48
Lindquist, Donald 1930- ... 65-68
Lindquist, E(veret) F(ranklin)
1901-1978 Obituary ... 77-80
Lindquist, Emory Kempton
1908-1992 ... CANR-31
Obituary ... 136
Earlier sketch in CA 49-52
Lindquist, Jennie Dorothea 1899-1977 ... 73-76
Obituary ... 69-72
See also SATA 13
Lindquist, John H(enry) 1931- ... 41-44R
Lindquist, Mark 1959- ... 136
Lindquist, Ray (Irving) 1941- ... 45-48
Lindquist, Willis 1908- ... 73-76
See also SATA 20
Lindsay, Catherine Brown 1928- ... 21-24R
Lindsay, Cressida 1934- ... 21-24R
Lindsay, David 1878-1945 Brief entry ... 113
See also TCLC 15
Lindsay, Dorothy 1902(?)-1983 Obituary ... 110
Lindsay, Frank Whiteman 1909- ... 104
Lindsay, Harold Arthur 1900- ... 5-8R
Lindsay, Howard 1889-1968 Obituary ... 25-28R
Lindsay, Ian G(ordon) 1906-1966 ... CAP-1
Earlier sketch in CA 9-10
Lindsay, Inabel (Frances) B(urns)
1900-1983 Obituary ... 110
Lindsay, J(ohn) Robert 1925- ... 13-16R
Lindsay, Jack 1900-1990 ... CANR-11
Obituary ... 131
Earlier sketch in CA 9-12R
See also DLBY 84
Lindsay, James Martin 1924- ... 29-32R
Lindsay, Jean 1926- ... CANR-11
Earlier sketch in CA 25-28R
Lindsay, Jeanne Warren 1929- ... CANR-22
Earlier sketch in CA 106
Lindsay, John (Joseph)
1921-1988 Obituary ... 127
Lindsay, John Vliet 1921- ... 101
Lindsay, Kenneth C(lement) 1919- ... 112
Lindsay, Loelia (Mary) 1902- ... 133
Lindsay, Martin Alexander
1905-1981 Obituary ... 103
Lindsay, Mary
See Nonhebel, Clare
Lindsay, (John) Maurice 1918- ... CANR-22
Earlier sketches in CA 9-12R, CANR-6
Lindsay, Merrill K(irk) 1915-1985 ... 73-76
Obituary ... 115
Lindsay, Michael Francis Morris 1909- ... CANR-1
Earlier sketch in CA 45-48
Lindsay, Norman Alfred William 1879-1969 ... 102
See also CLR 8
See also SATA 67
Lindsay, Perry
See Dern, Erolie Pearl Gaddis
Lindsay, R(obert) Bruce 1900- ... CANR-8
Earlier sketch in CA 13-16R
Lindsay, Rae ... 109
Lindsay, Robert 1924- ... 77-80
Lindsay, Thomas Fanshawe 1910- ... 21-24R
Lindsay, (Nicholas) Vachel 1879-1931 ... 135
Brief entry ... 114
See also CDALB 1865-1917
See also DLB 54
See also SATA 40
See also TCLC 17
See also WLC
Lindsay, Zaidee 1923- ... 29-32R
Lindsell, Harold 1913- ... CANR-5
Earlier sketch in CA 13-16R
Lindsey, Alfred J. 1931- ... 41-44R
Lindsey, Almont 1906- ... 1-4R
Lindsey, Alton A(nthony) 1907- ... 131
Lindsey, David 1914- ... 9-12R
Lindsey, George R(oy) 1920- ... 65-68
Lindsey, Hal ... CANR-22
Earlier sketch in CA 104
Lindsey, Jim 1957- ... 65-68
Lindsey, (Helen) Johanna 1952- ... CANR-18
Earlier sketch in CA 73-76
Lindsey, Karen 1944- ... 73-76
Lindsey, Robert (Hughes) 1935- ... CANR-22
Earlier sketch in CA 97-100
Lindskoog, Kathryn (Ann) 1934- ... CANR-25
Earlier sketches in CA 65-68, CANR-10
Lindsley, Mary F(rances) ... CANR-30
Earlier sketches in CA 61-64, CANR-9
Lindstrom, Carl E(inar) 1896-1969 ... 1-4R
Obituary ... 103
Lindstrom, Naomi (Eva) 1950- ... CANR-30
Earlier sketch in CA 112
Lindstrom, Thais (Stakhy) 1917- ... 21-24R
Lindt, Gillian 1932- ... 107
Line, Les 1935- ... 73-76
See also SATA 27
Line, Maurice Bernard 1928- ... 107
Lineaweaver, Thomas H(astings) III
1926- ... 73-76
Lineback, Richard H(arold) 1936- ... CANR-31
Earlier sketch in CA 29-32R
Linebarger, J(ames) M(orris) 1934- ... CANR-2
Earlier sketch in CA 49-52
Linebarger, Paul M(yron) A(nthony)
1913-1966 ... CANR-6
Earlier sketch in CA 5-8R
See also Smith, Cordwainer
Lineberry, John H(arvey) 1926- ... 1-4R
Lineberry, Robert L(eon) 1942- ... CANR-18
Earlier sketch in CA 73-76
Linecar, Howard (Walter Arthur) 1912- ... 110
Linedecker, Clifford L. 1931- ... 73-76
Linen, James A. III 1912-1988 Obituary ... 124
Linenthal, Edward Tabor 1947- ... CANR-30
Earlier sketch in CA 112
Lines, Kathleen Mary 1902-1988 Obituary ... 127
See also SATA 61
Linet, Beverly 1929- ... CANR-22
Earlier sketch in CA 89-92
Linett, Deena 1938- ... 113
Linfield, Esther ... 112
See also SATA 40
Ling, Amy 1939- ... 137
Ling, Arthur (William) 1901- ... 5-8R
Ling, Cyril Curtis 1936- ... 17-20R
Ling, Dwight L(eroy) 1923- ... CANR-11
Earlier sketch in CA 21-24R
Ling, H(sien) C(hang) 1910- ... 57-60
Ling, Hung-hsun 1894(?)-1981 Obituary ... 105
Ling, Jack (Chieh Sheng) 1930- ... 25-28R
Ling, Mona ... 9-12R
Ling, Peter J(ohn) 1956- ... 135
Ling, Roger (John) 1942- ... CANR-19
Earlier sketch in CA 103
Ling, Trevor 1920- ... CANR-11
Earlier sketch in CA 21-24R
Lingard, Joan 1932- ... CANR-18
Earlier sketch in CA 41-44R
See also MAICYA
See also SAAS 5
See also SATA 8
Lingeman, Richard R(oberts) 1931- ... CANR-11
Earlier sketch in CA 17-20R
Lingenfelter, Richard Emery 1934- ... CANR-5
Earlier sketch in CA 13-16R
Lingenfelter, Sherwood Galen 1941- ... 53-56
Lingis, Alphonso Frank 1933- ... CANR-15
Earlier sketch in CA 37-40R
Lings, Martin 1909- ... 57-60
Linhart, Robert 1944- ... 130
Linington, (Barbara) Elizabeth
1921-1988 ... CANR-20
Obituary ... 125
Earlier sketch in CA 1-4R, CANR 1
Link, Arthur S(tanley) 1920- ... CANR-3
Earlier sketch in CA 1-4R
See also DLB 17
Link, Edwin A(lbert) 1904-1981 Obituary ... 108
Link, Eugene P(erry) 1907- ... 37-40R
Link, Frederick M(artin) 1930- ... CANR-4
Earlier sketch in CA 53-56
Link, (S.) Gordden 1907-1986 ... 120
Link, Howard Anthony 1934- ... 127
Link, John R(einhardt) 1907- ... 17-20R
Link, Mark J(oseph) 1924- ... CANR-20
Earlier sketches in CA 13-16R, CANR-5
Link, Martin 1934- ... 106
See also SATA 28
Link, (Eugene) Perry (Jr.) 1944- ... 105
Link, Robert G(rant) 1918-1984 Obituary ... 113
Link, Ruth 1923- ... 29-32R
Link, Theodore Carl 1905(?)-1974 Obituary ... 104
Link, William 1933- ... CANR-13
Earlier sketch in CA 73-76
Linke, Maria (Zeitner) 1908- ... 65-68
Linke-Poot
See Doeblin, Alfred
Linker, Robert White 1905- ... 104
Linklater, Eric (Robert Russell)
1899-1974 ... CAP-2
Obituary ... 53-56
Earlier sketch in CA 13-14
Linklater, Magnus (Duncan) 1942- ... 131
Linkletter, Art(hur Gordan) 1912- ... CANR-4
Earlier sketch in CA 9-12R
Linkletter, John A(ustin) 1923-1985 ... 69-72
Obituary ... 115
Links, J(oseph) G(luckenstein) 1904- ... 81-84
Linkugel, Wil(mer) A(lbert) 1929- ... CANR-13
Earlier sketch in CA 17-20R
Linley, John (William) 1916- ... 41-44R
Lin Mao
See Shen Congwen
Linn, Allen 1955- ... 126
Linn, Bill
See Linn, William J(oseph)
Linn, Charles F. 1930- ... 85-88
Linn, Edward Allen 1922- ... 97-100
Linn, John Blair 1777-1804 ... DLB 37
Linn, John Gaywood 1917- ... 25-28R
Linn, William J(oseph) 1943- ... 117
Linnell, Charles Lawrence Scruton 1915- ... 5-8R
Linnell, Robert H(artley) 1922- ... 53-56
Linneman, Robert E. 1928- ... 29-32R
Linneman, William R(ichard) 1926- ... 125
Brief entry ... 118
Linner, Birgitta 1920- ... CANR-10
Earlier sketch in CA 21-24R
Linney, Romulus 1930- ... 1-4R
See also CLC 51
Linowes, David F(rancis) 1917- ... 49-52
Lins, Osman 1924- Brief entry ... 105
Linscott, Gillian 1944- ... 128
Linsenmeyer, Helen Walker 1906- ... CANR-1
Earlier sketch in CA 45-48
Linsky, Leonard 1922- ... 134
Brief entry ... 112
Linsley, William A(llan) 1933- ... 25-28R
Linstone, Harold A(drian) 1924- ... 112
Linstrum, Derek 1925- ... 107
Linthicum, Robert Charles 1936- ... 65-68
Lintner, John (Virgil) 1916-1983 ... 104
Obituary ... 110
Linton, Barbara Leslie 1945- ... 33-36R
Linton, Calvin D(arlington) 1914- ... CANR-5
Earlier sketch in CA 13-16R
Linton, David (Hector) 1923- ... 9-12R
Linton, Eliza Lynn 1822-1898 ... DLB 18
Linton, James M(ichael) 1946- ... 123
Linton, Robert R. 1909(?)-1979 Obituary ... 89-92
Linton, Ron(ald) M. 1929- ... 41-44R
Linton, William James 1812-1897 ... DLB 32
Lintott, Andrew (William) 1936- ... 116
Lintz, Harry McCormick ... 1-4R
Linzee, David (Augustine Anthony) 1952- ... 73-76
Linzey, Donald Wayne 1939- ... CANR-13
Earlier sketch in CA 61-64
Lionberger, Herbert F(rederick) 1912- ... 73-76
Lionel, Robert
See Fanthorpe, R(obert) Lionel
Lionni, Leo(nard) 1910- ... CANR-38
Earlier sketch in CA 53-56
See also CLR 7
See also DLB 61
See also MAICYA
See also SATA 8
Liotta, P. H. 1956- ... 136
Lipe, Dewey 1933- ... 85-88
Lipetz, Ben-Ami 1927- ... 33-36R
Lipez, Richard 1938- ... CANR-18
Earlier sketch in CA 101
Lipham, James Maurice 1927- ... 81-84
Lipinsky de Orlov, Lino S. 1908- ... SATA 22
Lipkin, Gladys B(albus) 1925- ... CANR-2
Earlier sketch in CA 49-52
Lipkin, Mack Jr. 1943- ... CANR-18
Earlier sketch in CA 101
Lipkina, Lawrence (Irwin) 1934- ... 41-44R
Lipkind, William 1904-1974 ... 101
Obituary ... 53-56
See also SATA 15
Lipking, Lawrence 1934- ... 130
Lipman, Aaron 1925- ... 21-24R
Lipman, Burton E(llis) 1931- ... 109
Lipman, David 1931- ... 21-24R
See also SATA 21
Lipman, Elinor 1950- ... 136
Lipman, Eugene Jay 1919- ... 9-12R
Lipman, Ira A 1940- ... 65-68
Lipman, Jean ... CANR-28
Earlier sketches in CA 21-24R, CANR-10
Lipman, Marilyn 1938- ... 69-72
Lipman, Matthew 1923- ... CANR-32
Earlier sketches in CA 33-36R, CANR-13
See also SATA 14
Lipman, Samuel 1934- ... 77-80
Lipman, Vivian David 1921-1990 ... 9-12R
Obituary ... 131
Lipmann, Fritz Albert 1899-1986 Obituary ... 119
Lipp, Frederick (John) 1916- ... 106
Lipp, Martin R(obert) 1940- ... 106
Lipp, Solomon 1913- Brief entry ... 111
Lippard, Lucy R. 1937- ... CANR-20
Earlier sketch in CA 25-28R
Lipper, Arthur III 1931- ... 127
Lippert, Clarissa Start 1917- ... 77-80
Lipphard, William B(enjamin) 1886-1971 ... CAP-2
Earlier sketch in CA 29-32
Lippincott, Bertram 1898(?)-1985 Obituary ... 115
See also SATA 42
Lippincott, David (McCord) 1925- ... CANR-9
Earlier sketch in CA 61-64

Lippincott, Joseph W(harton) 1887-1976 73-76
Obituary 69-72
See also SATA 17
Lippincott, Sara Jane Clarke
1823-1904 Brief entry 120
See also DLB 43
Lippincott, Sarah Lee 1920- 17-20R
See also SATA 22
Lippitt, Gordon L(eslie) 1920- CANR-12
Earlier sketch in CA 29-32R
Lippitt, Ronald O. 1914- 37-40R
Lippman, Edward A. 1920- 122
Lippman, Leopold 1919- 49-52
Lippman, Peter J. 1936- CANR-26
Earlier sketch in CA 108
See also SATA 31
Lippman, Theo Jr. 1929- 33-36R
Lippmann, Walter 1889-1974 ....CANR-6
Obituary 53-56
Earlier sketch in CA 9-12R
See also AITN 1
See also DLB 29
See also MTCW
Lippy, Charles H(oward) 1943- 138
Lipschutz, Ilse Hempel 1923- 41-44R
Lipscomb, Commander F. W.
See Lipscomb, F(rank) W(oodgate)
Lipscomb, David M(ilton) 1935- CANR-1
Earlier sketch in CA 49-52
Lipscomb, Elizabeth J(ohnston) 1938- 115
Lipscomb, F(rank) W(oodgate)
1903-1983 ....29-32R
Obituary 126
Lipscomb, James 1926- 85-88
Lipsen, Charles B. 1925- 73-76
Lipset, David 1951- 129
Lipset, Seymour Martin 1922- CANR-1
Earlier sketch in CA 1-4R
Lipsett, Laurence Cline 1915- 9-12R
Lipsett, Suzanne 1943- 132
Lipsey, David (Lawrence) 1948- 130
Lipsey, Richard A(llan) 1930- CANR-23
Earlier sketch in CA 107
Lipsey, Richard G(eorge) 1928- CANR-17
Earlier sketch in CA 97-100
Lipsey, Robert E(dward) 1926- CANR-18
Earlier sketches in CA 5-8R, CANR-2
Lipsitz, George R(aymond) 1947- CANR-32
Earlier sketch in CA 113
Lipsitz, Lou 1938- CANR-18
Earlier sketch in CA 101
Lipska, Ewa 1945- 132
Lipski, Alexander 1919- CANR-28
Earlier sketch in CA 49-52
Lipsky, David Bruce 1939- 103
Lipsky, Eleazar 1911- Brief entry 115
Lipsky, Michael 1940- 61-64
Lipsky, Mortimer 1915- 73-76
Lipson, Charles 1948- 123
Lipson, Goldie 1905- 33-36R
Lipson, Harry A(aron Jr.) 1919- 61-64
Lipson, Leon Samuel 1921- 104
Lipson, Leslie (Michel) 1912- 106
Lipson, Milton 1913- 65-68
Lipson, Shelley 1948- 119
Lipstadt, Deborah E(sther) 1947- 111
Lipstein, Kurt 1909- 117
Lipstreu, Otis 1919-1970 ....CAP-1
Earlier sketch in CA 13-16
Lipsyte, Marjorie (Rubin) 1932- 105
Lipsyte, Robert (Michael) 1938- CANR-8
Earlier sketch in CA 17-20R
See also AAYA 7
See also CLC 21
See also CLR 23
See also MAICYA
See also SATA 5, 68
Lipton, David R(obert) 1947- 97-100
Lipton, Dean 1919- CANR-31
Earlier sketch in CA 29-32R
Lipton, Lawrence 1898-1975 93-96
Obituary 57-60
See also DLB 16
Lipton, Lenny 1940- 101
Lipton, Peter 1954- 138
Liptzin, Sol(omon) 1901- 9-12R
Liquori, Martin William Jr. 1949- 130
Liquori, Marty
See Liquori, Martin William Jr.
Liroff, Richard A(llan) 1948- CANR-11
Earlier sketch in CA 69-72
Lisagor, Peter 1915-1976 Obituary 69-72
Lisca, Peter 1925- 37-40R
Lischer, Richard 1943- 101
Lisci, Leonardo Ginori
See Ginori Lisci, Leonardo
Liscombe, R. M.
See Windsor-Liscombe, Rhodri
Liscombe, R. W.
See Windsor-Liscombe, Rhodri
Liscow, Christian Ludwig 1701-1760 .... DLB 97
Lish, Gordon (Jay) 1934- 117
Brief entry 113
See also CLC 45
Lishka, Gerald R 1949- 89-92
Lisi, Albert 1929- 25-28R
Lisio, Donald J(ohn) 1934- 124
Lisk, Jill 1938- 25-28R
Liska, Edward G. 1914(?)-1984 Obituary 113
Liska, George 1922- 104
Lisker, Sonia O. 1933- CANR-2
Earlier sketch in CA 49-52
See also SATA 44
Lisle, Janet Taylor 1947- ....SAAS 14
See also SATA 47, 59
Lisle, Laurie 1942- 133
Lisle, Seward D.
See Ellis, Edward S(ylvester)
Lison-Tolosana, Carmelo 1929- CANR-13
Earlier sketch in CA 21-24R
Lisowski, Gabriel 1946- 97-100
See also SATA 31, 47
Lispector, Clarice 1925-1977 Obituary 116
See also CLC 43
See also DLB 113
Liss, Howard 1922- CANR-16
Earlier sketch in CA 25-28R
See also SATA 4
Liss, Jerome 1938- 53-56
Liss, Peggy K(orn) 1927- 41-44R
Liss, Robert E. 1945(?)-1979 Obituary 115
Liss, Sheldon B. 1936- 21-24R
Lissak, Moshe (Avraham) 1928- 97-100
Lissim, Simon 1900-1981 Obituary 109
See also SATA 28
Lissitzyn, Oliver J(ames) 1912- 45-48
Lissner, Will 1908- 101
Lisson, Deborah 1941- ....SATA 71
List, Ilka Katherine 1935- 37-40R
See also SATA 6
List, Jacob Samuel 1896-1967 ....CAP-1
Earlier sketch in CA 19-20
List, Robert Stuart 1903-1983 Obituary 109
Lister, Eric 1926(?)-1988(?) Obituary 125
Lister, Hal
See Lister, Harold
Lister, Harold 1922- 73-76
Lister, Laurier L. 1907-1986 Obituary 120
Lister, R(ichard) P(ercival) 1914- CANR-5
Earlier sketch in CA 9-12R
Lister, Raymond (George) 1919- CANR-24
Earlier sketches in CA 13-16R, CANR-8
Listfield, Emily 1957- 127
Liston, Jack
See Maloney, Ralph Liston
Liston, Mary Dawn 1936- 53-56
Liston, Robert A. 1927- CANR-30
Earlier sketches in CA 17-20R, CANR-12
See also SATA 5
Listowel, Judith (de Marffy-Mantuano)
1904- 13-16R
Litan, Robert E(li) 1950- 131
Litchfield, Ada B(assett) 1916- CANR-10
Earlier sketch in CA 25-28R
See also SATA 5
Litchfield, Harry R(obert)
1898-1973 Obituary 41-44R
Litchfield, Robert O(rbin) Obituary 73-76
Lite, Jams
See Schneck, Stephen
Lithman, Yngve Georg 1943- 132
Lithwick, Norman Harvey 1938- 61-64
Litoff, Judy Barrett 1944- 85-88
Litowinsky, Olga (Jean) 1936- 81-84
See also SATA 26
Litsey, Sarah 5-8R
Littauer, Florence 1928- 115
Littauer, Raphael (Max) 1925- Brief entry 109
Littauer, Vladimir S. 1893-1989 Obituary 129
Littell, Eliakim 1797-1870 .... DLB 79
Littell, Franklin H(amlin) 1917- 134
Brief entry 112
Littell, Robert S. 1831-1896 .... DLB 79
Littell, Robert 1896-1963 Obituary 93-96
Littell, Robert 1935(?)- 112
Brief entry 109
See also CLC 42
Litten, Julian (William Sebastian) 1947- 136
Litterer, Joseph A(ugust) 1926- CANR-35
Earlier sketches in CA 9-12R, CANR-3
Littke, Lael J. 1929- CANR-33
Earlier sketches in CA 85-88, CANR-15
See also SATA 51
Little, A. Edward
See Klein, Aaron E.
Little, Alan M(acNaughton) G(ordon)
1901-1987 Obituary 124
Little, Bryan (Desmond Greenway)
1913- CANR-22
Earlier sketch in CA 104
Little, Charles E. 1931- 128
Little, David 1933- 29-32R
Little, Elbert L(uther) Jr. 1907- 57-60
Little, Elbert Payson 1912(?)-1983 Obituary 110
Little, Geraldine C(linton) 109
Little, Ian M(alcolm) D(avid) 1918- CANR-34
Earlier sketches in CA 21-24R, CANR-15
Little, Jack
See Little, John D(utton)
Little, Jane Sneddon 1942- Brief entry 113
Little, (Flora) Jean 1932- 21-24R
See also CLR 4
See also MAICYA
See also SATA 2, 68
Little, John D(utton) 1894- 65-68
Little, Kenneth
See Scotland, James
Little, Kenneth L(indsay) 1908- 17-20R
Little, Lawrence Calvin 1897-1976 ....CANR-3
Earlier sketch in CA 1-4R
Little, Lessie Jones 1906-1986 101
Obituary 121
See also SATA 50, 60
Little, Lester Knox 1935- 103
Little, Loyd (Harry) Jr. 1940- 81-84
Little, Malcolm 1925-1965 125
Obituary 111
See also Malcolm X
See also BW
See also MTCW
Little, Mary E. 1912- 105
See also SATA 28
Little, Nina Fletcher 1903- 127
Brief entry 106
Little, Paul E. 1928-1975 ....CAP-2
Earlier sketch in CA 21-22
Little, Paul H(ugo) 1915-1987 ....CANR-13
Obituary 122
Earlier sketch in CA 17-20R
Little, Paula
See Little, Paul H(ugo)
Little, Pippa 1958- 123
Little, Ray 1918(?)-1980 Obituary 102
Little, Richard 1944- 114
Little, Roger W(illiam) 1922- 29-32R
Little, Royal (D.) 1896-1989 106
Obituary 127
Little, S. George 1903-1974 Obituary 49-52
Little, Sara (Pamela) 1919- 116
Little, Stuart W. 1921- CANR-1
Earlier sketch in CA 45-48
Little, Thomas Russell 1911- 13-16R
Little, Tom
See Little, Thomas Russell
Little, William Alfred
See Little, Wm. A.
Little, Wm. A. 1929- 57-60
Littleboy, Sheila M.
See Ary, Sheila M(ary Littleboy)
Littledale, Freya (Lota) CANR-25
Earlier sketches in CA 21-24R, CANR-10
See also SATA 2
Littledale, Harold (Aylmer) 1927- 5-8R
Littlefair, Duncan (Elliot) 1912- 45-48
Littlefield, David Joseph 1928- 41-44R
Littlefield, James Edward 1932- 53-56
Littlejohn, (Cameron) Bruce 1913- 61-64
Littlejohn, David 1937- CANR-14
Earlier sketch in CA 41-44R
Littleton, C(ovington) Scott 1933- 21-24R
Littleton, Harvey K(line) 1922- 53-56
Littlewit, Humphrey Gent.
See Lovecraft, H(oward) P(hillips)
Littlewood, Joan (Maud) 1914- Brief entry 116
See also DLB 13
Littlewood, Robert Percy 1910- 5-8R
Littlewood, Thomas B. 1928- 29-32R
Littman, Robert J. 1943- 81-84
Litto, Fredric M. 1939- 25-28R
Litto, Gertrude 1929- 69-72
Litvag, Irving 1928- 57-60
Litvak, Isaiah A(llan) 1936- 13-16R
Litvinoff, Barnet 1917- 17-20R
Litvinoff, Emanuel 1915- 129
Brief entry 117
Litvinoff, Saul 1925- 41-44R
Litvinov, Ivy 1890(?)-1977 Obituary 69-72
Litvinov, Pavel 1940- 89-92
Litwack, Leon F(rank) 1929- CANR-1
Earlier sketch in CA 1-4R
Litwak, Eugene 1925- Brief entry 114
Litwak, Leo (E.) 1924- CANR-22
Earlier sketch in CA 5-8R
Litwos
See Sienkiewicz, Henryk (Adam Alexander Pius)
Litz, A(rthur) Walton (Jr.) 1929- 33-36R
Litzel, Otto 1901- 57-60
Litzinger, Boyd (A. Jr.) 1929- CANR-20
Earlier sketches in CA 13-16R, CANR-5
Liu, Aimee 1953- 89-92
Liu, Alan P(ing-) L(in) 1937- 61-64
Liu, Da 1910- 85-88
Liu, James J(o) Y(u) 1926- CANR-7
Earlier sketch in CA 5-8R
Liu, James T(zu) C(hien) 1919- 21-24R
Liu, Jung-Chao 1929- 29-32R
Liu, Leo Yueh-yun 1940- 41-44R
Liu, Sarah 1943- CANR-38
Earlier sketch in CA 115
Liu, Sydney (Chieh) 1920- 103
Liu, Tzu-chien
See Liu, James T(zu) C(hien)
Liu, William T(homas) 1930- CANR-13
Earlier sketch in CA 21-24R
Liu, Wu-chi 1907- CANR-25
Earlier sketches in CA 13-16R, CANR-10
Liu, Yong
See Liu, William T(homas)
Liu Binyan 1925- 136
Liu E 1857-1909 Brief entry 115
See also TCLC 15
Liu Zongren 1940- 116
Livant, Rose Adleman
1899(?)-1986 Obituary 120
Lively, Penelope (Margaret) 1933- CANR-29
Earlier sketch in CA 41-44R
See also CLC 32, 50
See also CLR 7
See also DLB 14
See also MAICYA
See also MTCW
See also SATA 7, 60
Lively, Walter
See Elliott, Bruce (Walter Gardner Lively Stacy)
Liverani, Giuseppe 1903- CANR-6
Earlier sketch in CA 5-8R
Liverani, Mary Rose 1939- 104
Livergood, Norman D(avid) 1933- 37-40R
Livermore, Jean
See Sanville, Jean
Livermore, Seward W.
1901(?)-1984 Obituary 112
Livermore, Shaw 1902- CAP-2
Earlier sketch in CA 19-20
Liversidge, (Henry) Douglas 1913- CAP-1
Earlier sketch in CA 9-10
See also SATA 8
Liversidge, Joan (Eileen Annie)
1915(?)-1984 103
Obituary 112
Liverton, Joan 1913- CAP-1
Earlier sketch in CA 9-10
Livesay, Dorothy (Kathleen) 1909- CANR-36
Earlier sketch in CA 25-28R
See also CAAS 8
See also AITN 2
See also CLC 4, 15
See also DLB 68
See also MTCW
Livesay, Florence Randal 1874-1953 ...... DLB 92
Livesey, Claire Warner 1927- 29-32R
Livgren, Kerry 1949- 114
Livia, Anna 1955- 119
Livie-Noble, Frederick Stanley
1899-1970 ....CAP-1
Earlier sketch in CA 9-10
Livingood, James W(eston) 1910- CANR-32
Earlier sketches in CA 17-20R, CANR-8
Livings, Henry 1929- 13-16R
See also DLB 13
Livingston, A(lfred) D(elano) 1932- CANR-13
Earlier sketch in CA 17-20R
Livingston, Anne Home 1763-1841 .... DLB 37
Livingston, Bernard 1911- 81-84
Livingston, Carole 1941- 105
See also SATA 42
Livingston, Dorothy Michelson 1906- 49-52
Livingston, Elizabeth J(ane) 1952- 113
Livingston, George Herbert 1916- 53-56
Livingston, Harold 1924- 1-4R
Livingston, J(oseph) A(rnold) 1905-1989 ....1-4R
Obituary 130
Livingston, James C(raig) 1930- CANR-21
Earlier sketch in CA 45-48
Livingston, Jane S(helton) 1944- 107
Livingston, Jayson 1965- 136
Livingston, Jon 1944- 49-52
Livingston, M. Jay
See Livingston, Myran Jabez Jr.
Livingston, Martha 1945- 115
Livingston, Myra Cohn 1926- CANR-33
Earlier sketches in CA 1-4R, CANR-1
See also CLR 7
See also DLB 61
See also MAICYA
See also SAAS 1
See also SATA 5, 68
Livingston, Myran Jabez Jr. 1934- CANR-22
Earlier sketch in CA 105
Livingston, Nancy 1935- 134
Livingston, Paisley 1951- 136
Livingston, Peter Van Rensselaer
See Townsend, James B(arclay) J(ermain)
Livingston, Richard R(oland) 1922- 45-48
See also SATA 8
Livingston, Robert B(urr) 1918- 97-100
Livingston, Robert Henry 1934- 134
Livingston, William S. 1920- CANR-3
Earlier sketch in CA 9-12R
Livingston, William 1723-1790 .... DLB 31
Livingstone, Angela 1934- 119
Livingstone, Bernard L.
1907(?)-1984 Obituary 112
Livingstone, Douglas (James) 1932- CANR-20
Earlier sketches in CA 13-16R, CANR-5
Livingstone, Harrison Edward 1937- 33-36R
Livingstone, J(ohn) Leslie 1932- 73-76
Livingstone, Leon 1912- 33-36R
Livingstone, Marco (Eduardo) 1952- CANR-24
Earlier sketch in CA 107
Livo, Norma J. 1929- 123
Livoni, Cathy 1956- 113
Livsey, Clara G(rabois) 1924- 107
Livson, Norman 1924- 49-52
Li Xueqin 1933- 136
Liyong, Taban lo 1938- 105
See also BW
Lizardi, Joseph 1941- 129
See also HW
Lizarraga, Sylvia S. 1925- .... DLB 82
Lizotte, Ken 1948- 126
Ljoka, Daniel J. 1935- 49-52
Llano, George A(lbert) 1911- 125
Lleo, Manuel Urrutia
See Urrutia Lleo, Manuel
Llerena, Mario 1913- 81-84
Llerena Aguirre, Carlos (Antonio) 1952- 77-80
See also SATA 19
Llewellyn, D(avid) W(illiam) Alun 1903- 57-60
Llewellyn, Edward
See Llewellyn-Thomas, Edward
Llewellyn, Richard
See Llewellyn Lloyd, Richard Dafydd Vivian
See also CLC 7
See also DLB 15
Llewellyn-Jones, Derek 1923- CANR-34
Earlier sketches in CA 37-40R, CANR-15
Llewellyn Lloyd, Richard Dafydd Vivian
1906-1983 ....CANR-7
Obituary 111
Earlier sketch in CA 53-56
See also Llewellyn, Richard
See also SATA 11, 37
Llewellyn-Thomas, Edward 1917- 104
Llewellyn-Williams, Hilary (Maria) 1951- 127
Llewelyn, T. Harcourt
See Hamilton, Charles (Harold St. John)
Llewelyn-Davies, Richard 1912-1981 ....13-16R
Obituary 105
Llewelyn-Owens, Joan (Margaret)
1919- CANR-36
Llorens, Vicente 1906-1979 Obituary 89-92
LLorens, Washington 1900- ....HW
Lloret, Antoni 1935- 29-32R

Llosa, (Jorge) Mario (Pedro) Vargas
See Vargas Llosa, (Jorge) Mario (Pedro)
Llosa, Ricardo Pau
See Pau-Llosa, Ricardo
Lloyd, Adrien
See Gelb, Alan Lloyd
Lloyd, Alan C(hester) 1915- CANR-1
Earlier sketch in CA 1-4R
Lloyd, Alan 1927- 128
Lloyd, Albert Lancaster
1908-1982 Obituary 107
Lloyd, Charles
See Birkin, Charles (Lloyd)
Lloyd, (Charles) Christopher
1906-1986 Obituary 119
Lloyd, Christopher 1921- 120
Lloyd, Craig 1940- 61-64
Lloyd, Cynthia B(rown) 1943- CANR-8
Earlier sketch in CA 61-64
Lloyd, David Demarest 1911-1962 .... CAP-1
Earlier sketch in CA 11-12
Lloyd, David 1946- 89-92
Lloyd, Dennis 1915- 13-16R
Lloyd, E. James
See James, Elizabeth
Lloyd, Errol 1943- 101
See also SATA 22
Lloyd, Francis V(ernon) Jr. 1908- CAP-2
Earlier sketch in CA 21-22
Lloyd, G(eoffrey) E(rnest) R(ichard)
1933- 57-60
Lloyd, Howell Arnold 1937- 103
Lloyd, Hugh
See Fitzhugh, Percy Keese
Lloyd, Hugh (Pughe) 1894-1981 Obituary 108
Lloyd, J. Ivester 1905- 13-16R
Lloyd, Jack Ivester
See Lloyd, J. Ivester
Lloyd, James
See James, Elizabeth
Lloyd, James Barlow 1945- 112
Lloyd, John Ivester
See Lloyd, J. Ivester
Lloyd, John S. B. Selwyn
See Selwyn-Lloyd, John S. B.
Lloyd, Margaret Glynne 1946- 130
Lloyd, Marjorie 1909- CANR-8
Earlier sketch in CA 5-8R
Lloyd, Norman 1909-1980 ....CANR-28
Obituary 101
Earlier sketch in CA 37-40R
See also SATA 23
Lloyd, (Mary) Norris 1908- CANR-1
Earlier sketch in CA 1-4R
See also SATA 10
Lloyd, Peter C(utt) 1927- CANR-11
Earlier sketch in CA 25-28R
Lloyd, Peter Edward 1938- 107
Lloyd, Robin 1925- 73-76
Lloyd, Ronald
See Friedland, Ronald Lloyd
Lloyd, Rosemary (Helen) 1949- 116
Lloyd, Seton (Howard Frederick) 1902- 132
Lloyd, Stephanie
See Golding, Morton J(ay)
Lloyd, Trevor (Owen) 1934- 25-28R
Lloyd Evans, Barbara 1924- CANR-37
Earlier sketch in CA 93-96
Lloyd Evans, Gareth 1923-1984 Obituary 117
Lloyd George (of Dwyor), Frances (Louise
Stevenson) 1888(?)-1972 Obituary 37-40R
Lloyd-Jones, Esther McDonald 1901- 13-16R
Lloyd-Jones, (Peter) Hugh (Jefferd)
1922- CANR-21
Earlier sketches in CA 5-8R, CANR-4
Lloyd-Jones, Robin 1934- 111
Lloyd Owen, David Lanyon 1917- 117
Lloyd-Thomas, Catherine 1917- 65-68
Lloyd Webber, Andrew 1948- Brief entry 116
See also Webber, Andrew Lloyd
See also AAYA 1
See also SATA 56
Llywelyn, Morgan 1937- CANR-16
Earlier sketch in CA 81-84
Llywelyn-Williams, Alun 1913- CAP-1
Earlier sketch in CA 9-10
Lo, Irving Yucheng 1922- 57-60
Lo, Ruth Earnshaw 1910- 106
Lo, Samuel E. 1931- 29-32R
Lo, Steven C. 1949- 132
Lo, Winston W. 1938- 133
Loader, William Reginald 1916- 1-4R
Loades, David Michael 1934- 17-20R
Loane, Marcus L(awrence) 1911- CANR-2
Earlier sketch in CA 1-4R
Loasby, Brian John 1930- 93-96
Lobb, Charlotte 1935- CANR-15
Earlier sketch in CA 65-68
Lobb, Ebenezer
See Upward, Allen
Lobdell, Helen 1919- 9-12R
Lobdell, Jared C(harles) 1937- CANR-28
Earlier sketch in CA 49-52
Lobel, Anita (Kempler) 1934- CANR-33
Earlier sketches in CA 53-56, CANR-9
See also MAICYA
See also SATA 6, 55
Lobel, Arnold (Stark) 1933-1987 ....CANR-33
Obituary 124
Earlier sketches in CA 1-4R, CANR-2
See also AITN 1
See also CLR 5
See also DLB 61
See also MAICYA
See also SATA 6, 54, 55
Lobel, Brana 1942- 97-100
Lobel, Edgar 1889-1982 Obituary 107
Lobel, Stanley 1937- 111
Lo Bello, Nino 1921- CANR-28
Earlier sketches in CA 29-32R, CANR-12
Loberg, Mary Alice 1943- 29-32R
Lobkowicz, Nicholas 1931- CANR-32
Earlier sketches in CA 21-24R, CANR-10
Lobley, Robert (John) 1934- CANR-29
Earlier sketch in CA 29-32R
Lobo, Anthony S(avio) 1937- 49-52
Lobsenz, Amelia 13-16R
See also SATA 12
Lobsenz, Norman M(itchell) 1919- CANR-4
Earlier sketch in CA 9-12R
See also SATA 6
Loch, Joice N(anKivell) 1893-1982 ....25-28R
Obituary 108
Lochak, Michele 1936- 106
See also SATA 39
Lochard, Metz T(ullus) P(aul)
1896-1984 Obituary 112
Lochbiler, Don 1908- 49-52
Locher, Dick
See Locher, Richard (Earl)
Locher, Frances C(arol) CANR-17
Earlier sketch in CA 97-100
Locher, Richard (Earl) 1929- CANR-16
Earlier sketch in CA 85-88
Lochhead, Douglas (Grant) 1922- CANR-39
Earlier sketches in CA 45-48, CANR-1, 16
Lochhead, Liz 1947- 81-84
Lochhead, Marion Cleland 1902-1985 101
Obituary 115
Lochlons, Colin
See Jackson, C(aary) Paul
Lochman, Jan Milic 1922- CANR-28
Earlier sketches in CA 29-32R, CANR-12
Lochnan, Katharine A. 1946- 127
Lochner, Louis P(aul) 1887-1975 65-68
Obituary 53-56
Lochridge, Betsy Hopkins
See Fancher, Betsy
Lochte, Dick
See Lochte, Richard S(amuel)
Lochte, Richard S(amuel) 1944- CANR-23
Earlier sketch in CA 105
LoCicero, Donald 1937- 25-28R
Lock, C(lara) B(eatrice) Muriel 1914- 49-52
Lock, Dennis (Laurence) 1929- CANR-32
Earlier sketches in CA 41-44R, CANR-14
Lock, F(rederick) P(eter) 1948- 118
Lock, Fred
See Lock, F(rederick) P(eter)
Lock, Joan 1933- 132
Lock, Margaret M. 1936- 126
Lockard, Craig Alan 1942- 122
Lockard, (Walter) Duane 1921- 17-20R
Lockard, Leonard
See Thomas, Theodore L.
Locke, Alain (Le Roy) 1886-1954 124
Brief entry 106
See also BW
See also DLB 51
See also TCLC 43
Locke, Charles O. 1896(?)-1977 Obituary 69-72
Locke, Clinton W. CANR-26
Earlier sketches in CAP-2, CA 19-20
See also SATA 1
Locke, David M(illard) 1929- 41-44R
Locke, David Ross 1833-1888 .... DLB 11, 23
Locke, Duane CANR-1
Earlier sketch in CA 49-52
Locke, Edwin A. III 1938- 13-16R
Locke, Elsie 1912- CANR-26
Earlier sketches in CA 25-28R, CANR-11
Locke, Frederick W. 1918- 13-16R
Locke, Hubert G. 1934- 29-32R
Locke, John 1632-1704 .... DLB 101
Locke, Louis G(lenn) 1912- 33-36R
Locke, Lucie 1904- 53-56
See also SATA 10
Locke, Martin
See Duncan, W(illiam) Murdoch
Locke, Michael (Stephen) 1943- 73-76
Locke, Peter
See McCutchan, J(ohn) Wilson
Locke, R. E.
See Raffelock, David
Locke, Ralph P(aul) 1949- 124
Locke, Richard Adams 1800-1871 .... DLB 43
Locke, Robert 1944- 129
See also SATA 63
Locke, Steven E(lliot) 1945- 127
Locke, Wende 1945- 33-36R
Locke-Elliott, Sumner
See Elliott, Sumner Locke
Locker, Thomas 1937- 128
See also CLR 14
See also MAICYA
See also SATA 59
Lockerbie, D(onald) Bruce 1935- CANR-14
Earlier sketch in CA 37-40R
Lockerbie, Jeanette W. Honeyman CANR-5
Earlier sketch in CA 9-12R
Lockerbie, Jeannie 1938- CANR-13
Earlier sketch in CA 73-76
Locker-Lampson, Frederick 1821-1895 .... DLB 35
Lockert, (Charles) Lacy (Jr.) 1888-1974 .... CAP-2
Earlier sketch in CA 25-28
Lockert, Lucia (Alicia Ungaro Fox)
1928- CANR-14
Earlier sketch in CA 73-76
Lockhart, (Jeanne) Aileene Simpson
1911- 13-16R
Lockhart, Freda Bruce 1909-1987 Obituary 124
Lockhart, Jack Herbert 1909-1985 Obituary 117
Lockhart, John Gibson
1794-1854 ....DLB 110, 116
Lockhart, Robert (Hamilton) Bruce
1886-1970 Obituary 89-92
Lockhart, Russell A(rthur) 1938- CANR-21
Earlier sketch in CA 45-48
Locklair, Wriston 1924(?)-1984 Obituary 112
Lockley, Lawrence Campbell 1899-1969 .... CAP-1
Earlier sketch in CA 11-12
Lockley, Ronald M(athias) 1903- CANR-22
Earlier sketches in CA 9-12R, CANR-5
Locklin, Gerald (Ivan) 1941- CANR-32
Earlier sketches in CA 37-40R, CANR-14
Locklin, (David) Philip 1897- 1-4R
Lockmann, Ronald F(rederick) 1942- 117
Lockmiller, David A(lexander) 1906- 77-80
Lockridge, Ernest (Hugh) 1938- 25-28R
See also AITN 1
Lockridge, Frances Louise Obituary 93-96
Lockridge, Hildegarde (Dolson)
1908-1981 ....CANR-3
Obituary 102
Earlier sketch in CA 5-8R
See also Dolson, Hildegarde
Lockridge, Kenneth A(lan) 1940- 134
Brief entry 107
Lockridge, Laurence S(hockley) 1942- 130
Lockridge, Norman
See Roth, Samuel
Lockridge, Richard 1898-1982 85-88
Obituary 107
Lockridge, Ross (Franklin) Jr.
1914-1948 Brief entry 108
See also DLBY 80
Lockspeiser, Edward 1905-1973 ....CANR-6
Earlier sketch in CA 5-8R
Lockwood, Allison 1920- 115
Lockwood, C. C. 1949- 117
Lockwood, Charles Andrews 1890-1967 ....1-4R
Lockwood, Douglas (Wright) 1918- 21-24R
Lockwood, Guy C. 1943- 65-68
Lockwood, Lee 1932- 37-40R
Lockwood, M(ichael) J(ohn) 1950- 128
Lockwood, Margo 1939- 117
Lockwood, Mary
See Spelman, Mary
Lockwood, Michael 1944- 122
Lockwood, Theodore Davidge 1924- CANR-1
Earlier sketch in CA 1-4R
Lockwood, W(illiam) B(urley) 1917- 29-32R
Lockwood, William W(irt) 1906- CAP-2
Earlier sketch in CA 23-24
Lockyer, Herbert 1888(?)-1984 Obituary 115
Lockyer, Judith 1949- 138
Lockyer, Roger 1927- CANR-12
Earlier sketch in CA 17-20R
Locre, Peter E.
See Cole, E(ugene) R(oger)
Lodder, Christina (Anne) 1948- 125
Lode, Rex
See Goldstein, William Isaac
Loden, Barbara (Ann) 1937-1980 Obituary 101
Loder, John 1898-1988 Obituary 128
Lodge, Bernard 1933- 107
See also SATA 33
Lodge, David (John) 1935- CANR-19
Earlier sketch in CA 17-20R
See also BEST 90:1
See also CLC 36
See also DLB 14
See also MTCW
Lodge, George Cabot
1873-1909 Brief entry 123
See also DLB 54
Lodge, George Cabot 1927- 17-20R
Lodge, Henry Cabot (Jr.) 1902-1985 53-56
Obituary 115
Lodge, Henry Cabot 1850-1924 .... DLB 47
Lodge, Oliver (Joseph)
1851-1940 Brief entry 117
Lodge, Orlan Robert 1917-1975 Obituary 57-60
Lodrick, Deryck O(scar) 1942- 106
Loeb, Benjamin S. 1914- 128
Loeb, Catherine (Roberta) 1949- 89-92
Loeb, Gerald M(artin) 1899-1974 .... CAP-1
Obituary 49-52
Earlier sketch in CA 13-16
Loeb, Harold A(lbert) 1891-1974 106
Obituary 45-48
See also DLB 4
Loeb, Jeffrey 1946- 123
See also SATA 57
Loeb, Madeleine H.
1905(?)-1974 Obituary 45-48
Loeb, Marshall Robert 1929- 21-24R
Loeb, Paul Rogat 1952- 109
Loeb, Robert F(rederick)
1895-1973 Obituary 45-48
Loeb, Robert H. Jr. 1917- CANR-12
Earlier sketch in CA 29-32R
See also SATA 21
Loeb, William 1905-1981 93-96
Obituary 104
Loebl, Eugen 1907-1987 Obituary 123
Loebl, Suzanne 69-72
Loefgren, Ulf 1931- CANR-16
Earlier sketch in CA 25-28R
See also SATA 3
Loefstedt, Bengt 1931- CANR-1
Earlier sketch in CA 45-48
Loehlin, John C(linton) 1926- 21-24R
Loemker, Leroy E(arl) 1900- 41-44R
Loengard, John 1934- 133
Loening, Grover C.
1889(?)-1976 Obituary 65-68
Loening, Sarah (Elizabeth) Larkin
1896-1988 ....CANR-21
Obituary 124
Earlier sketch in CA 45-48
Loennbohm, Armas Eino Leopold
1878-1926 Brief entry 123
See also Leino, Eino
Loeoef, Jan 1940- 81-84
Loeper, John J(oseph) 1929- CANR-12
Earlier sketch in CA 29-32R
See also SATA 10
Loertscher, David V. 1940- 126
Loesch, Juli(anne) 1951- 89-92
Loescher, Ann Dull 1942- CANR-9
Earlier sketch in CA 61-64
See also SATA 20
Loescher, Gil(burt Damian) 1945- CANR-9
Earlier sketch in CA 61-64
See also SATA 20
Loeschke, Maravene Sheppard 1947- 115
Loeser, Herta 1921- 57-60
Loeser, Katinka 1913-1991 ....17-20R
Obituary 133
Loesser, Francis Henry
1910-1969 Obituary 112
Loesser, Frank
See Loesser, Francis Henry
Loether, Herman J(ohn) 1930- 21-24R
Loetscher, Lefferts A(ugustine) 1904- 5-8R
Loevinger, Jane 1918- 41-44R
Loevinger, Lee 1913- CANR-15
Earlier sketch in CA 81-84
Loew, Ralph William 1907- CAP-1
Earlier sketch in CA 19-20
Loew, Sebastian 1939- CANR-19
Earlier sketch in CA 103
Loewald, Hans W. 1906- 101
Loewe, Michael 1922- 133
Loewe, Ralph E. 1923- 21-24R
Loewe, Raphael J(ames) 1919- 118
Loewen, James W. 1942- CANR-14
Earlier sketch in CA 37-40R
Loewenberg, Bert James 1905-1974 ....CANR-5
Earlier sketch in CA 9-12R
Loewenberg, Frank M(eyer) 1925- CANR-2
Earlier sketch in CA 45-48
Loewenberg, Gerhard 1928- CANR-9
Earlier sketch in CA 21-24R
Loewenberg, J(orn) Joseph 1933- 33-36R
Loewenberg, Peter J(acob) 1933- 109
Loewenberg, Robert J(ames)
1938- Brief entry 114
Loewenfeld, Claire 1899-1974 .... CAP-2
Earlier sketch in CA 23-24
Loewenstein, Bernice .... SATA 40
Loewenstein, Joseph 1952- 124
Loewenstein, Karl 1891-1973 Obituary 41-44R
Loewenstein, Louis Klee 1927- 37-40R
Loewenstein, Prince Hubertus (F. zu)
See
Loewenstein(-Wertheim-Freudenberg), Hubertus
Loewenstein, Rudolph M(aurice)
1898-1976 .... CAP-2
Obituary 65-68
Earlier sketch in CA 21-22
Loewenstein(-Wertheim-Freudenberg), Hubertus
(Friedrich Maria Johannes Leopold Ludwig)
1906-1984 ....CANR-29
Obituary 114
Earlier sketches in CA 5-8R, CANR-4
Loewenthal, L(eonard) J(oseph) A(lfonso)
..........61-64
Loewer, (Henry) Peter 1934- 136
Loewer, Peter 1934- 138
Loewinsohn, Ron(ald William) 1937- 25-28R
See also CLC 52
Loewith, Karl 1897-1973 Obituary 116
Loewy, Ariel G(ideon) 1925- 89-92
Loewy, Raymond Fernand 1893-1986 104
Obituary 119
Lofaro, Michael Anthony 1948- 89-92
Lofland, John (Franklin) 1936- CANR-12
Earlier sketch in CA 33-36R
Lofland, Lyn (Hebert) 1937- 61-64
Lofstedt, Bengt
See Loefstedt, Bengt
Loftas, Tony 1940- 21-24R
Lofthouse, Jessica 1916-1988 ....29-32R
Obituary 125
Lofthus, Myrna 1935- 115
Lofting, Hugh (John) 1886-1947 137
Brief entry 109
See also CLR 19
See also MAICYA
See also SATA 15
Loftis, Anne 1922- 45-48
Loftis, John (Clyde Jr.) 1919- CANR-3
Earlier sketch in CA 1-4R
Lofton, John (Marion) 1919- CANR-6
Earlier sketch in CA 9-12R
Lofts, Norah (Robinson) 1904-1983 ....CANR-6
Obituary 110
Earlier sketch in CA 5-8R
See also AITN 2
See also SATA 8, 36
Loftus, Elizabeth F. 1944- 105
Loftus, Ernest Achey 1884-1987 Obituary 123
Loftus, John (Joseph) 1950- 117
Loftus, Richard J. 1929- 13-16R
Logan, Albert Boyd 1909- 53-56
Logan, Daniel 1936- 25-28R
Logan, Don
See Crawford, William (Elbert)
Logan, Elizabeth D(ulaney) 1914- 61-64
Logan, F(rancis) Donald 1930- 45-48
Logan, Ford
See Newton, D(wight) B(ennett)
Logan, Frank A(nderson) 1924- 41-44R
Logan, Gene A(dams) 1922- CANR-7
Earlier sketch in CA 9-12R
Logan, George M(eredith) 1941- 131

Logan, Gerald E(lton) 1924- 73-76
Logan, Jake
See Knott, William C(ecil Jr.)
and Krepps, Robert W(ilson)
and Pearl, Jacques Bain
and Riefe, Alan
and Rifkin, Shepard
and Smith, Martin Cruz
Logan, James Phillips 1921- 37-40R
Logan, James 1674-1751 .... DLB 24
Logan, Jane
See Gardner, Virginia (Marberry)
Logan, John A(rthur) Jr. 1923- 1-4R
Logan, John (Burton) 1923-1987 77-80
Obituary 124
See also CLC 5
See also DLB 5
Logan, Joshua (Lockwood) 1908-1988 89-92
Obituary 126
See also AITN 1
Logan, Lillian M(ay) 1909- CANR-1
Earlier sketch in CA 1-4R
Logan, Rayford W(hittingham)
1897-1982 ....CANR-25
Obituary 108
Earlier sketches in CA 1-4R, CANR-1
See also BW
Logan, Sara
See Haydon, June
and Simpson, Judith H(olroyd)
Logan, Sister Mary Francis Louise 1928- 5-8R
Logan, Spencer 1912(?)-1980 Obituary 93-96
Logan, Terence P(atrick) 1936- 57-60
Logan, Virgil G(lenn) 1904- 21-24R
Logan, William 1950- 136
See also DLB 120
Loganbill, G. Bruce 1938- 37-40R
Logelin, Warren E. 1940(?)-1985 Obituary 117
Loggins, Vernon 1893-1968 ....5-8R
Loggins, William Kirk 1946- 77-80
Logsdon, John M(ortimer III)
1937- Brief entry 115
Logsdon, Joseph 1938- 25-28R
Logsdon, Richard Henry 1912- CANR-2
Earlier sketch in CA 5-8R
Logsdon, Thomas S(tanley) 1937- CANR-21
Earlier sketches in CA 57-60, CANR-6
Logsdon, Tom
See Logsdon, Thomas S(tanley)
Logue, Cal(vin McLeod) 1935- 127
Brief entry 105
Logue, Christopher 1926- CANR-3
Earlier sketch in CA 9-12R
See also DLB 27
See also SATA 23
Logue, Jeanne 1921- 89-92
Logue, John 1933- 126
Logue, William (Herbert) 1934- 45-48
Loh, Jules 1931- 33-36R
Loh, Pichon P(ei) Y(ung) 1928- 17-20R
Loh, Robert 1924- 17-20R
Lohafer, Susan 1942- CANR-37
Lohf, Kenneth A. 1925- CANR-3
Earlier sketch in CA 9-12R
Lohman, Joseph D(ean) 1910-1968 .... CAP-2
Earlier sketch in CA 23-24
Lohnes, Walter F. W. 1925- CANR-29
Earlier sketch in CA 49-52
Lohr, Thomas F. 1926- 77-80
Lohrer, M(ary) Alice 1907- 17-20R
Lohrli, Anne 1906- 111
Lohrman, Paul
See Fairman, Paul W.
Lohse, Eduard 1924- 107
Lois, George 1931- 127
Loisy, Alfred (Firmin) 1857-1940 Brief entry 120
Lo-Johansson, (Karl) Ivar 1901-1990 .....CANR-20
Obituary 131
Earlier sketch in CA 102
Loken, Newton Clayton 1919- 1-4R
See also SATA 26
Loki
See Pearson, Karl
Lokken, Roy N(orman) 1917- 53-56
Lokos, Lionel 1928- 25-28R
Loll, Leo M(arius) Jr. 1923-1968 .... CAP-2
Earlier sketch in CA 25-28
Lollar, Coleman Aubrey (Jr.) 1946- 49-52
Lolli, Giorgio 1905-1979 ....CANR-2
Obituary 85-88
Earlier sketch in CA 1-4R
Lollis, Lorraine 1911- CAP-2
Earlier sketch in CA 29-32
Lolos, Kimon 1917- 1-4R
Lomas, Charles W(yatt) 1907- CAP-1
Earlier sketch in CA 13-14
Lomas, Derek 1933- 29-32R
Lomas, Geoffrey (Robert) 1950- 93-96
Lomas, Peter 1923- 21-24R
Lomas, Steve
See Brennan, Joseph Lomas
Lomask, Milton (Nachman) 1909-1991 .....CANR-1
Obituary 135
Earlier sketch in CA 1-4R
See also SATA 20
Lomax, Alan 1915- CANR-1
Earlier sketch in CA 1-4R
Lomax, Bliss
See Drago, Harry Sinclair
Lomax, Derek W(illiam) 1933- 130
Obituary 137
Lomax, John A(lbert) 1930- 61-64
Lomax, Louis E(manuel) 1922-1970 .... CAP-2
Earlier sketch in CA 25-28
See also BW
Lomax, Marion 1953- 133
Lomax, Pearl
See Cleage, Pearl (Michelle)
Lombard, C(harles) M(orris) 1920- CANR-1
Earlier sketch in CA 49-52
Lombard, Helen
See Vischer, Helen (Cassin Lombard) Carusi
Lombard, Lawrence Brian 1944- 124
Lombard, Nap
See Johnson, Pamela Hansford
Lombardi, John V(incent) 1942- CANR-20
Earlier sketches in CA 53-56, CANR-5
Lombardi, Mary 1940- 61-64
Lombardo, Josef Vincent 1908- 5-8R
LoMedico, Brian T.
See Monteleone, Thomas F(rancis)
Lomer, Mary
See Lide, Mary
Lommasson, Robert C(urtis) 1917- 41-44R
Lomosia, Andrew
See Stern, Jay B(enjamin)
Lomperis, Timothy J. 1947- 126
Lomupo, Brother Robert 1939- 13-16R
London, Artur 1915-1986 ....CANR-12
Obituary 120
Earlier sketch in CA 65-68
London, Carolyn 1918- 57-60
London, Ephraim 1911-1990 Obituary 131
London, H(oyt) H(obson) 1900- 49-52
London, Hannah R. 1894- 29-32R
London, Herbert I(ra) 1939- CANR-12
Earlier sketch in CA 33-36R
London, Jack
See London, John Griffith
See also AITN 2
See also CDALB 1865-1917
See also DLB 8, 12, 78
See also SATA 18
See also SSC 4
See also TCLC 9, 15, 39
See also WLC
London, Jack 1915-1988 ....CANR-25
Obituary 126
Earlier sketch in CA 89-92
London, Jane
See Geis, Darlene Stern
London, Joan 1901-1971 .... CAP-2
Earlier sketch in CA 25-28
London, John Griffith 1876-1916 119
Brief entry 110
See also London, Jack
See also MAICYA
See also MTCW
London, Julius 1917- 118
London, Kurt L(udwig) 1900- CANR-6
Earlier sketch in CA 1-4R
London, Laura
See Curtis, Sharon
and Curtis, Thomas Dale
London, Mel 1923- CANR-24
Earlier sketch in CA 107
London, Perry 1931- 45-48
London, Roy 1946- 108
Londre, Felicia Hardison 1941- CANR-21
Earlier sketch in CA 105
Lonergan, Bernard J(oseph) F(rancis)
1904-1984 ....CANR-11
Obituary 114
Earlier sketch in CA 53-56
Lonergan, (Pauline) Joy (MacLean) 1909- 1-4R
See also SATA 10
Lonesome Cowboy
See White, John I(rwin)
Lone Star Ranger
See White, John I(rwin)
Lonette, Reisie (Dominee) 1924- .... SATA 43
Loney, Glenn (Meredith) 1928- CANR-14
Earlier sketch in CA 33-36R
Loney, Martin 1944- CANR-18
Earlier sketch in CA 102
Long, A(nthony) A(rthur) 1937- CANR-29
Earlier sketches in CA 33-36R, CANR-13
Long, Ann Marie
See Jensen, Pauline Marie (Long)
Long, Charles R(ussell) 1904- CAP-1
Earlier sketch in CA 11-12
Long, Charles 1938- 65-68
Long, Chester Clayton 1932- 25-28R
Long, Clayton
See Long, Chester Clayton
Long, Cynthia 1956- 126
Long, David E(dwin) 1937- 89-92
Long, David F(oster) 1917- CANR-8
Earlier sketch in CA 61-64
Long, David 1948- 127
Long, E(verette) B(each) 1919-1981 ....CANR-1
Obituary 103
Earlier sketch in CA 1-4R
Long, Earlene (Roberta) 1938- 126
See also SATA 50
Long, Edward LeRoy Jr. 1924- CANR-22
Earlier sketches in CA 5-8R, CANR-7
Long, Emmett
See Leonard, Elmore (John Jr.)
Long, Esmond R(ay) 1890-1979 Obituary 89-92
Long, Eugene Thomas (III) 1935- 25-28R
Long, Father Valentine W. 1902- 17-20R
Long, Fern CAP-2
Earlier sketch in CA 23-24
Long, Frank Belknap 1903- CANR-16
Earlier sketch in CA 81-84
Long, Franklin A. 1910- 127
Long, Frederick Lawrence 1917- 9-12R
Long, Haniel (Clark) 1888-1956 Brief entry 122
See also DLB 45
Long, Helen Beecher CANR-26
Earlier sketches in CAP-2, CA 19-20
See also SATA 1
Long, Howard Rusk 1906- CANR-3
Earlier sketch in CA 5-8R
Long, Huey P(ierce) 1893-1935 Brief entry 115
Long, J(ohn) C(uthbert) 1892- CAP-1
Earlier sketch in CA 9-10
Long, James M. 1907-1979 Obituary 85-88
Long, John D(ouglas) 1920- 17-20R
Long, John H(enderson) 1916- 13-16R
Long, John L(atham) 1932- 111
Long, Judith Elaine 1953- 65-68
See also SATA 20
Long, Judy
See Long, Judith Elaine
Long, Kim 1949- 129
See also SATA 69
Long, Laura Mooney 1892-1967 Obituary 109
See also SATA 29
Long, Lois 1901-1974 Obituary 104
Long, Louise 37-40R
Long, Lucile
See Brandt, Lucile (Long Strayer)
Long, Luman H(arrison) 1907-1971 108
Obituary 104
Long, M(olly) 1916- 21-24R
Long, Naomi Cornelia
See Madgett, Naomi Long
Long, Norton E. 1910- 45-48
Long, Priscilla 1943- 29-32R
Long, Ralph B(ernard) 1906- 5-8R
Long, Richard A(lexander) 1927- CANR-24
Earlier sketch in CA 37-40R
See also BW
Long, Robert Emmet 1934- 122
Long, Robert 1954- CANR-30
Earlier sketch in CA 110
Long, Steven 1944- 125
Long, T(heodore) Dixon 1933- 121
Brief entry 118
Long, Theodore E(dward) 1944- 126
Long, Thomas (Joseph) 1938- 119
Long, Wesley
See Smith, George O(liver)
Long, William Stuart
See Stuart, (Violet) Vivian (Finlay)
Longacre, Edward G(eorge) 1946- CANR-22
Earlier sketches in CA 53-56, CANR-5
Longacre, Robert E(dmondson)
1922- CANR-19
Earlier sketches in CA 53-56, CANR-4
Longacre, William A(tlas) II 1937- CANR-12
Earlier sketch in CA 29-32R
Longaker, Richard P(ancoast) 1924- CANR-1
Earlier sketch in CA 1-4R
Longbaugh, Harry
See Goldman, William (W.)
Longbeard, Frederick
See Longyear, Barry Brookes
Longeaux y Vasquex, Enriqueta 1930- 57-60
Longenbach, James 1959- 127
Longenecker, Justin G. 1917- CANR-1
Earlier sketch in CA 1-4R
Longenecker, Richard N(orman) 1930- 13-16R
Longest, George C(alvin) 1938- 107
Longfellow, Henry Wadsworth
1807-1882 .... CDALB 1640-1865
See also DLB 1, 59
See also SATA 19
Longfellow, Samuel 1819-1892 .... DLB 1
Longford, Elizabeth Harmon 1906- 5-8R
Longgood, William (Frank) 1917- CANR-17
Earlier sketch in CA 1-4R
Longhurst, Henry Carpenter 1909-1978 85-88
Obituary 81-84
Longino, Charles F(reeman) Jr. 1938- CANR-24
Earlier sketches in CA 53-56, CANR-7
Longland, Jean R(ogers) 1913- CANR-10
Earlier sketch in CA 21-24R
Longleigh, Peter J. Jr.
See Korges, James
Longley, John Lewis Jr. 1920- 5-8R
Longley, Lawrence D(ouglas) 1939- 41-44R
Longley, Michael 1939- 102
See also CLC 29
See also DLB 40
Longley, Richmond W(ilberforce) 1907- 73-76
Longley, W. B.
See Randisi, Robert J(oseph)
Longman, Harold S. 1919- 25-28R
See also SATA 5
Longman, Lester Duncan
1905-1987 Obituary 121
Longman, Mark Frederic Kerr
1916-1972 Obituary 37-40R
Longmate, Norman Richard 1925- CANR-28
Earlier sketches in CA 9-12R, CANR-6
Longmore, George 1793(?)-1867 .... DLB 99
Longmore, Laura 5-8R
Long-Neck Woman
See Cheatham, K(aryn) Follis
Longo, Lucas 1919- 25-28R
Longrigg, Jane Chichester 1929- 9-12R
Longrigg, Roger (Erskine) 1929- CANR-3
Earlier sketch in CA 1-4R
Longrigg, Stephen Hemsley
1893-1979 Obituary 89-92
Longstreet, Augustus Baldwin
1790-1870 ....DLB 3, 11, 74
Longstreet, Stephen 1907- CANR-7
Earlier sketch in CA 9-12R
Longstreet, Wilma S. 1935- 93-96
Longstreth, Edward 1894- CAP-1
Earlier sketch in CA 13-16
Longstreth, Richard 1946- 132
Longstreth, T(homas) Morris 1886- 5-8R
Longstreth, W(illiam) Thacher 1920- 134
Longsworth, Polly 1933- 106
See also SATA 28
Longsworth, Robert M. 1937- 21-24R
Longtemps, Kenneth 1933- .... SATA 17
Longway, A. Hugh
See Lang, Andrew
Longworth, Alice Lee (Roosevelt)
1884-1980 Obituary 93-96
Longworth, I(an) H(eaps) 1935- 120
Longworth, Philip 1933- CANR-28
Earlier sketches in CA 21-24R, CANR-10
Longworth, Richard C(ole) 1935- 85-88
Longyear, Barry Brookes 1942- 102
Longyear, Christopher R(udston) 1929- 105
Longyear, Marie Marcia Bernstein 1928- 115
Longyear, Rey M(organ) 1930- CANR-22
Earlier sketch in CA 45-48
Lonnbohm, Armas Eino Leopold
See Loennbohm, Armas Eino Leopold
Lonsdale, Adrian L. 1927- 13-16R
Lonsdale, Frederick 1881-1954 Brief entry 109
See also DLB 10
Lonsdale, Gordon Arnold
1923(?)-1970 Obituary 104
Lonsdale, Kathleen (Yardley) 1903-1971 ......5-8R
Obituary 33-36R
Lonsdale, Richard E. 1926- CANR-13
Earlier sketch in CA 21-24R
Lonsdale, Steven (Hancock) 1952- CANR-36
Earlier sketch in CA 114
Look, Al 1893- 57-60
Look, Dennis 1949- 73-76
Looker, Antonina (Hansell) 29-32R
Looker, (Reginald) Earle 1895-1976 .... CAP-2
Obituary 65-68
Earlier sketch in CA 29-32
Lookout
See Noble, John (Appelbe)
Lookstein, Haskel 1932- 119
Loomba, N(arendra) Paul 1927- 57-60
Loomes, Brian 1938- CANR-30
Earlier sketches in CA 69-72, CANR-12
Loomie, Albert Joseph 1922- 5-8R
Loomis, Albertine (G.) 1895-1985 93-96
Obituary 117
Loomis, Burdett A. 1945- 129
Loomis, Charles P(rice) 1905- CANR-13
Earlier sketch in CA 21-24R
Loomis, Chauncey C(hester) Jr. 1930- 33-36R
Loomis, Edward 1924- CANR-2
Earlier sketch in CA 1-4R
Loomis, Noel M(iller) 1905-1969 ....1-4R
Obituary 25-28R
Loomis, Rae
See Steger, Shelby
Loomis, Robert D. 17-20R
See also SATA 5
Loomis, Roger Sherman 1887-1966 ....CANR-8
Earlier sketch in CA 5-8R
Loomis, Stanley 1922-1972 .... CAP-1
Obituary 37-40R
Earlier sketch in CA 11-12
Loomis, Zona Kemp 1911- 45-48
Looney, Robert E(dward) 1941- 104
Loory, Stuart H. 1932- 25-28R
Loos, Anita 1893(?)-1981 ....CANR-26
Obituary 104
Earlier sketch in CA 21-24R
See also AITN 1
See also DLB 11, 26
See also DLBY 81
Loos, Mary ....AITN 1
Loose, Gerhard 1907- 45-48
Loose, H.
See Lourie, Dick
Loosley, William Robert
See Langford, David
Loots, Barbara Kunz 1946- 57-60
Loovis, David (Mactavish) 1926- CANR-1
Earlier sketch in CA 1-4R
Lopach, James J. 1942- 135
Lopata, Helena Znaniecka 1925- 104
Lopate, Carol
See Ascher, Carol
Lopate, Phillip 1943- 97-100
See also CLC 29
See also DLBY 80
Lopatin, Judy 1954- 124
Loper, William C. 1927- 13-16R
Lopes, Henri (Marie-Joseph) 1937- 132
Lopes, Michael 1943- 57-60
Lopez, Adalberto 1943- 103
Lopez, Andrew 1910-1986 Obituary 120
Lopez, Barry Holstun 1945- CANR-23
Earlier sketches in CA 65-68, CANR-7
See also AAYA 9
See also MTCW
See also SATA 67
Lopez, Cecilia L(uisa) 1941- 53-56
Lopez, Claude-Anne 1920- 104
Lopez, Diana 1948- ....HW
Lopez, Ella B. 1900(?)-1978 Obituary 81-84
Lopez, Enrique 1921(?)-1985 Obituary 117
Lopez, Felix Manuel Jr. 1917- 13-16R
Lopez, Laura 1957- 136
Lopez, Manuel Dennis 1934- CANR-22
Earlier sketch in CA 105
Lopez, Nancy (Marie) 1957- Brief entry 113
Lopez, Robert S(abatino)
1910-1986 Obituary 119
Brief entry 112
Lopez, Vincent (Joseph)
1895-1975 Obituary 61-64
Lopez-Morillas, Juan 1913- CANR-1
Earlier sketch in CA 1-4R
Lopez Portillo (y Pacheco), Jose 1920- 129
See also CLC 46
See also HW
Lopez-Rey, Jose 1905- 37-40R

Lopez-Rey (y Arrojo), Manuel
1902-1987 ....29-32R
Obituary 124
Lopez Suria, Violeta 1926- ....HW
Lopez y Fuentes, Gregorio 1897(?)-1966 131
See also CLC 32
See also HW
Lopez Y Rivas, Gilberto 1943- 97-100
LoPiccolo, Joseph 1943- CANR-15
Earlier sketch in CA 81-84
Lo Pinto, Maria 1900(?)-1970 Obituary 104
Lopreato, Joseph 1928- 33-36R
Lopresti, Robert 1954- 137
Lopshire, Robert M(artin) 1927- CANR-30
Earlier sketches in CA 5-8R, CANR-8
See also SATA 6
Lopukhov, Fyodor V(asilevich)
1886-1973 Obituary 41-44R
Lora, Josephine
See Alexander, Josephine
Lora, Ronald 1938- 41-44R
Lorac, E. C. R.
See Rivett, Edith Caroline
Loram, Ian Craig 1917- 5-8R
Loran, Martin
See Baxter, John
Lorand, (Alexander) Sandor
1893(?)-1987 ....CAP-1
Obituary 123
Earlier sketch in CA 9-10
Lorang, Ruth Mary
See Lorang, Sister Mary Corde
Lorang, Sister Mary Corde 1904- 49-52
Loranger, Jean-Aubert 1896-1942 ....DLB 92
Lorant, Stefan 1901- CANR-9
Earlier sketch in CA 5-8R
See also AITN 1
Lorayne, Harry 1926- 41-44R
Lorberg, Aileen Dorothy 1910- CANR-2
Earlier sketch in CA 5-8R
Lorca, Federico Garcia
See Garcia Lorca, Federico
Lorch, Edgar R(aymond)
1907-1990 Obituary 131
Lorch, Robert Stuart 1925- 73-76
Lord, Albert Bates 1912-1991 103
Obituary 135
Lord, Athena V. 1932- 109
See also SATA 39
Lord, Beman 1924-1991 ....33-36R
Obituary 135
See also SATA 5
See also SATO 69
Lord, Bette Bao 1938- 107
See also BEST 90:3
See also CLC 23
See also SATA 58
Lord, Chalfont
See Jones, (Alun) Arthur Gwynne
Lord, Clifford L(ee) 1912-1980 ....CANR-8
Obituary 102
Earlier sketch in CA 13-16R
Lord, Donald Charles 1930- 37-40R
Lord, Douglas
See Cooper, Douglas
Lord, (Doreen Mildred) Douglas 1904- CAP-1
Earlier sketch in CA 13-14
See also SATA 12
Lord, Eda 1907-1976 Obituary 104
Lord, Edith Elizabeth 1907- 41-44R
Lord, Eugene Hodgdon 1894- 1-4R
Lord, Francis A. 1911- 17-20R
Lord, Frederic Mather 1912- 37-40R
Lord, Gabrielle 1946- 106
Lord, George deF(orest) 1919- CANR-25
Earlier sketches in CA 65-68, CANR-10
Lord, Graham 1943- CANR-4
Earlier sketch in CA 53-56
Lord, Jeffrey
See Nelson, R(adell) Faraday
Lord, Jeremy
See Redman, Ben Ray
Lord, Jess R. 1911- 65-68
Lord, John Keast 1818-1872 ....DLB 99
Lord, John Vernon 1939- 53-56
See also SATA 21
Lord, M(ary) G(race) 1955- 127
Lord, Mary Stinson Pillsbury 1904-1978 85-88
Obituary 81-84
Lord, Nancy
See Titus, Eve
Lord, Patricia C. 1927-1988 ....SATA 58
Lord, Phillips H.
See Yolen, Will(iam Hyatt)
Lord, Priscilla Sawyer 1908- 9-12R
Lord, Robert (Needham) 1945- 61-64
Lord, Shirley
See Rosenthal, Shirley Lord
Lord, Vivian
See Strother, Pat Wallace
Lord, Walter 1917- CANR-22
Earlier sketches in CA 1-4R, CANR-5
See also SATA 3
Lord, William Jackson Jr. 1926- 5-8R
Lord Altrincham
See Grigg, John (Edward Poynder)
Lordan, (Ellenora) Beth 1948- 130
Lord Astor of Hever
See Astor, Gavin
Lord Auch
See Bataille, Georges
Lord Beveridge
See Beveridge, William (Henry)
Lord Blake
See Blake, Robert (Norman William)
Lord Boyle of Handsworth
See Boyle, Edward Charles Gurney
Lord Brooke
See Greville, Fulke
Lord Butler of Saffron Walden
See Butler, Richard Austen
Lord Byron
See Byron, George Gordon (Noel)
Lord Chalfont
See Jones, (Alun) Arthur Gwynne
Lord Crowther-Hunt
See Crowther-Hunt, Norman Crowther
Lord Denning
See Denning, Alfred Thompson
Lord Dunsany
See Dunsany, Edward John Moreton Drax Plunkett
See also TCLC 2
Lorde, Audre (Geraldine) 1934- CANR-26
Earlier sketches in CA 25-28R, CANR-16
See also BLC 2
See also BW
See also CLC 18, 71
See also DLB 41
See also MTCW
Lord Energlyn
See Evans, William David
Lord Evans of Hungershall
See Evans, Benjamin Ifor
Lord Francis Williams
See Williams, Edward Francis
Lord George-Brown
See George-Brown, George Alfred
Lord Hailsham of St. Marylebone
See Hogg, Quintin McGarel
Lord Home
See Home, Alexander Frederick
Lord Houghton
See Milnes, Richard Monckton
Lordi, Robert J(oseph) 1923- 89-92
Lord Jeffrey
See Jeffrey, Francis
Lord Kames
See Home, Henry
Lord Killanin
See Morris, Michael
Lord Mancroft
See Mancroft, Stormont Mancroft Samuel
Lord Moran
See Wilson, (Richard) John (McMoran)
Lord Mountbatten
See
Mountbatten, Louis (Francis Albert Victor Nicholas)
Lord Rhyl
See Birch, (Evelyn) Nigel (Chetwode)
Lord Rothschild
See Rothschild, Nathaniel Mayer Victor
Lord Snowdon
See Armstrong-Jones, Antony (Charles Robert)
Lord Strange
See Drummond, John
Lord Thomas
See Thomas, (William) Miles (Webster)
Lord Windlesham
See Hennessy, David James George
Loree, Kate (Lambie) 1920- 21-24R
Lorek, Daniel N. 1958(?)-1983 Obituary 110
Loren, Sophia 1934- Brief entry 111
Lorenz, Alfred Lawrence 1937- 45-48
Lorenz, J(ames) D(ouglas) 1938- 102
Lorenz, Konrad Zacharias 1903-1989 ....CANR-35
Obituary 128
Earlier sketch in CA 61-64
See also MTCW
Lorenz, Lee (Sharp) 1932- Brief entry 124
See also SATA 39
Lorenz, Sarah E.
See Winston, Sarah
Lorenzen, Coral Elsie 1925- 113
Lorenzen, David N(eal) 1940- 33-36R
Lorenzini, Carlo 1826-1890
See Collodi, Carlo
See also MAICYA
See also SATA 29
Lorenzo, Carol Lee 1939- 53-56
Lorenzo, Heberto Padilla
See Padilla (Lorenzo), Heberto
Loreto, Charles A. 1903(?)-1990 Obituary 132
Loria, Jeffrey H. 1940- 17-20R
Lorie, James Hirsch 1922- 103
Lorig, Kate R. 1942- 117
Lorimer, Frank 1894-1985 Obituary 116
Lorimer, George Horace 1867-1937 ....DLB 91
Lorimer, James 1942- 123
Lorimer, Janet 1941- ....SATA 60
Lorimer, Lawrence T(heodore) 1941- CANR-6
Earlier sketch in CA 57-60
Lorimer, Scat
See Fuentes, Martha Ayers
Loring, Ann 1915- 97-100
Loring, Emilie (Baker) 1864(?)-1951 ....SATA 51
Loring, J. M.
See Warner-Crozetti, R(uth G.)
Loring, Murray 1917- CANR-22
Earlier sketch in CA 45-48
Lorion, R(aymond) P(aul) 1946- 85-88
Loris
See Hofmannsthal, Hugo von
Loris, Joseph James 1943-1987 Obituary 125
Lornquest, Olaf
See Rips, Ervine M(ilton)
Lorrah, Jean CANR-19
Earlier sketch in CA 103
Lorraine, Walter (Henry) 1929- ....SATA 16
Lorrance, Arleen 1939- 85-88
Lorrimer, Claire
See Robins, Patricia (Denise)
Lorsch, Jay William 1932- 97-100
Lorsch, Susan E. 1950- 116
Lortie, Dan C(lement) 1926- 115
Lortz, Richard 1917-1980 ....CANR-11
Obituary 102
Earlier sketch in CA 57-60
Lorusso, Edward N. S. 1949- 133
Lorwin, Val Rogin 1907-1982 Obituary 111
Lory, Robert (Edward) 1936- CANR-10
Earlier sketch in CA 53-56
Los, George
See Amabile, George
Losang, Rato Khyongla Ngawang 1923- 81-84
Lose, M(argaret) Phyllis 1925- CANR-18
Earlier sketch in CA 101
Losev, S(ergei) A(ndreevich)
1927-1988 Obituary 126
Losey, Joseph (Walton)
1909-1984 Obituary 113
Loshak, David (Leslie Ivor) 1933- 41-44R
Losoncy, Lawrence J. 1941- CANR-32
Earlier sketches in CA 37-40R, CANR-14
Losoncy, Mary Jan 1942- 37-40R
los Rios, Francisco Giner de
See Giner de los Rios, Francisco
Loss, Joan 1933- ....SATA 11
Loss, Louis 1914- CANR-2
Earlier sketch in CA 5-8R
Loss, Richard (Archibald John) 1938- 65-68
Lossing, Benson J. 1813-1891 ....DLB 30
Lossky, Andrew 1917- 93-96
Lossy, Rella 1934- 81-84
Loth, Calder 1943- 73-76
Loth, David 1899-1988 ....CANR-1
Obituary 125
Earlier sketch in CA 1-4R
Lothar, Ernst 1890-1974 ....DLB 81
Lothian, John Maule 1896-1970 ....CAP-1
Earlier sketch in CA 9-10
Lothringen, Geza Louis Eusebius Gebhard Ralphael
Albert Maria
See von Habsburg-Lothringen, Geza Louis
Eusebius Gebhard Ralphael Albert Maria
Lothrop, Harriet Mulford Stone
1844-1924 ....DLB 42
See also SATA 20
Lothstein, Leslie Martin 1942- 126
Loti, Pierre
See Viaud, (Louis Marie) Julien
See also TCLC 11
Lott, Arnold S(amuel) 1912- 13-16R
Lott, Bret 1958- 126
Lott, Davis Newton 1913- CANR-10
Earlier sketch in CA 21-24R
Lott, Milton 1919- 17-20R
Lott, Monroe
See Howard, Edwin
Lott, Robert E(ugene) 1926- CANR-4
Earlier sketch in CA 5-8R
Lottich, Kenneth V(erne) 1904- 17-20R
Lottie
See Grimke, Charlotte L(ottie) Forten
Lottinville, Savoie 1906- 105
Lottman, Eileen 1927- CANR-30
Earlier sketches in CA 57-60, CANR-12
See also Mellors, Samantha
Lottman, Herbert R. 1927- 105
See also CAAS 12
Lotz, David W(alter) 1937- Brief entry 115
Lotz, James Robert 1929- CANR-14
Earlier sketches in CA 37-40R, CANR-31
Lotz, Jim
See Lotz, James Robert
Lotz, John 1913-1973 Obituary 45-48
Lotz, Wolfgang 1912-1981 ....CANR-34
Earlier sketch in CA 81-84
See also SATA 65
Lotze, Dieter P(aul) 1933- 132
Loubere, Leo A(lbert) 1923- 130
Louch, A(lfred) R(ichard) 1927- 17-20R
Louchheim, Kathleen 1903-1991 ....21-24R
Obituary 133
Louchheim, Katie
See Louchheim, Kathleen
Loucks, William Negele 1899- 1-4R
Loud, G(raham) A(nthony) 1953- 136
Loud, Pat(ricia Russell) 1926- Brief entry 114
Loud, Patricia C(ummings) 135
Louden, J(ames) Keith 1905- 132
Louden, Robert Stuart 1912- 5-8R
Loudon, Irvine 1924- 126
Lougee, Robert Wayne 1919- 5-8R
Loughary, John W(illiam) 1930- 41-44R
Loughery, John 1953- 138
Loughhead, LaRue A(lvin) 1927- 61-64
Loughlin, Caroline 1940- 126
Loughlin, Richard L(awrence) 1907- CANR-21
Earlier sketch in CA 45-48
Loughmiller, Campbell 1906- CANR-13
Earlier sketch in CA 77-80
Loughran, Bernice B(ingham) 1919- 5-8R
Loughran, Peter 1938- 25-28R
Lougy, Robert E. 1940- 118
Louie, Ai-Ling 1949- 112
See also SATA 34, 40
Louie, David Wong 1954- ....CLC 70
Louis, Arthur M(urray) 1938- 106
Louis, David
See Carroll, David L.
Louis, Debbie 1945- 29-32R
Louis, Father M.
See Merton, Thomas
Louis, J(ack) C(harles) Jr. 1949- 105
Louis, Joe
See Barrow, Joseph Louis
Louis, Murray 1926- 126
Louis, Pat
See Francis, Dorothy Brenner
Louis, Paul P(anickavede) 1918- CANR-12
Earlier sketch in CA 61-64
Louis, Pierre(-Felix) 1870-1925 Brief entry 105
Louis, Ray Baldwin 1949- 65-68
Louis, Tobi 1940- 57-60
Louisburgh, Sheila Burnford
See Burnford, Sheila (Philip Cochrane Every)
Louisell, David William 1913-1977 ....CANR-4
Obituary 73-76
Earlier sketch in CA 1-4R
Loukes, Harold 1912- 17-20R
Lounsberry, Barbara 1946- 138
Lounsbury, Myron O. 1940- 37-40R
Lounsbury, Thomas R. 1838-1915 ....DLB 71
Loup, Jacques 1942- 120
Lourdeaux, Lee 1951- 136
Louria, Donald B(ruce) 1928- 107
Lourie, Dick 1937- 33-36R
Lourie, Helen
See Storr, Catherine (Cole)
Lourie, Peter (King) 1952- 137
Lourie, Richard 1940- 131
Brief entry 125
Lousley, J(ob) E(dward)
1907-1976 Obituary 104
Louthan, Robert 1951- 109
Louviere, Vernon Ray 1920- 108
Louvish, Misha 1909- CANR-1
Earlier sketch in CA 45-48
Louvish, Simon 1947- 121
Louw, Nicholaas Petrus Van Wyk
1906-1970 Obituary 89-92
Loux, Michael Joseph 1942- 103
Louys, Pierre
See Louis, Pierre(-Felix)
Lovaas, O(le) Ivar 1927- CANR-22
Earlier sketch in CA 45-48
Lovasik, Lawrence George 1913- CANR-20
Earlier sketches in CA 1-4R, CANR-1
Lovatt, Edwin A(lbert) 1944- 119
Love, Alan C(arson) 1937- 53-56
Love, Barbara J. 1937- 37-40R
Love, Charles K.
See Swicegood, Thomas L. P.
Love, Charles (Ross) 1932- 25-28R
Love, Edmund G(eorge) 1912-1990 ....CANR-4
Obituary 132
Earlier sketch in CA 1-4R
Love, Glen A. 1932- 29-32R
Love, Iris Cornelia 1933- 29-32R
Love, Janet
See Ferrier, Janet Mackay
Love, Jean O. 1920- 29-32R
Love, Joseph L. (Jr.) 1938- 29-32R
Love, Katherine (Isabel) 1907- ....SATA 3
Love, Kennett 1924- 77-80
Love, Philip H(ampton) 1905-1977 77-80
Obituary 73-76
Love, Richard S. 1923- 81-84
Love, Sandra (Weller) 1940- CANR-11
Earlier sketch in CA 69-72
See also SATA 26
Love, Sydney F(rancis) 1923- 81-84
Love, Thomas Teel 1931- 13-16R
Love, William F. 1932- 132
Lovecraft, H(oward) P(hillips) 1890-1937 133
Brief entry 104
See also MTCW
See also SSC 3
See also TCLC 4, 22
Lovegrove, Philip
See Ray, John (Philip)
Lovehill, C. B.
See Beaumont, Charles
Lovejoy, Bahija Fattuhi 1914- 5-8R
Lovejoy, Clarence Earle 1894-1974 ....5-8R
Obituary 45-48
Lovejoy, David Sherman 1919- 103
Lovejoy, Elijah P(arish) 1940- 45-48
Lovejoy, Jack 1937- CANR-35
Earlier sketch in CA 114
Lovejoy, L(awrence) C(lark) 1893- 1-4R
Lovejoy, Paul E(llsworth) 1943- 115
Lovelace, Delos Wheeler 1894-1967 ....5-8R
Obituary 25-28R
See also SATA 7
Lovelace, Earl 1935- 77-80
See also CLC 51
See also MTCW
Lovelace, Linda
See Marchiano, Linda Boreman
Lovelace, Marc Hoyle 1920- 37-40R
Lovelace, Maud Hart 1892-1980 ....CANR-39
Obituary 104
Earlier sketch in CA 5-8R
See also MAICYA
See also SATA 2, 23
Lovelace, Richard Franz 1930- 101
Loveland, Anne C(arol) 1938- 126
Brief entry 114
Loveless, E(dward) E. 1919- 57-60
Lovell, Ann 1933- CANR-19
Earlier sketch in CA 97-100
Lovell, (Alfred Charles) Bernard 1913- CANR-6
Earlier sketch in CA 13-16R
Lovell, Colin Rhys 1917- 5-8R
Lovell, Ernest J(ames) Jr. 1918-1975 ....1-4R
Obituary 103
Lovell, Ingraham
See Bacon, Josephine Dodge (Daskam)
Lovell, John Jr. 1907-1974 ....CAP-2
Obituary 49-52
Earlier sketch in CA 33-36
Lovell, John P(hilip) 1932- CANR-15
Earlier sketch in CA 29-32R
Lovell, Marc
See McShane, Mark
Lovell, Mark 1934- CANR-8
Earlier sketch in CA 61-64

Lovell, Michael Christopher 1930- 33-36R
Lovell, Ronald P. 1937- CANR-13
Earlier sketch in CA 73-76
Lovell, Stanley P(latt) 1890- 5-8R
Lovelock, J. E.
See Lovelock, James (Ephraim)
Lovelock, James (Ephraim) 1919- 123
Loveman, Brian E(lliot) 1944- CANR-17
Earlier sketch in CA 89-92
Loveman, Samuel 1885(?)-1976 Obituary 65-68
Lovenstein, Meno 1909- CANR-3
Earlier sketch in CA 5-8R
Lovequist, Gwendlelynn
See Stafford, Linda (Crying Wind)
Loverde, Lorin (James Bell) 1943- 45-48
Loveridge, Ronald O. 1938- 33-36R
Lovering, Joseph Paul 1921- 104
Lovesey, Peter (Harmer) 1936- CANR-28
Earlier sketch in CA 41-44R
See also DLB 87
See also MTCW
Lovestrand, Harold 1925- 21-24R
Lovett, A(lbert) W(inston) 1944- 124
Lovett, Clara Maria 1939- CANR-16
Earlier sketch in CA 93-96
Lovett, Gabriel H(arry) 1921- 65-68
Lovett, Margaret (Rose) 1915- 61-64
See also SATA 22
Lovett, Robert W. 1913- 33-36R
Lovin, Clifford R(amsey) 1937- 37-40R
Lovin, Roger Robert 1941- CANR-6
Earlier sketch in CA 57-60
Loving, Jerome MacNeill 1941- CANR-30
Earlier sketch in CA 112
Lovins, Amory B(loch) 1947- CANR-32
Earlier sketch in CA 69-72
Lovoll, Odd Sverre 1934- CANR-7
Earlier sketch in CA 61-64
Lovoos, Janice
See Garbutt, Janice (D.) Lovoos
Low, Alfred D(avid) 1913- 33-36R
Low, Alice 1926- CANR-8
Earlier sketch in CA 61-64
See also SATA 11
Low, Ann Marie 1912- 118
Low, Anthony 1935- CANR-13
Earlier sketch in CA 37-40R
Low, D(onald) A(nthony) 1927- 73-76
Low, David (Alexander Cecil)
1891-1963 Obituary 89-92
Low, Dorothy Mackie
See Low, Lois Dorothea
Low, Elizabeth Hammond 1898- CAP-2
Earlier sketch in CA 19-20
See also SATA 5
Low, Francis 1893-1972 Obituary 115
Low, Gardner
See Rodda, Charles
Low, George M(ichael) 1926-1984 Obituary 113
Low, Ivy
See Litvinov, Ivy
Low, Joseph 1911- CANR-15
Earlier sketch in CA 85-88
See also MAICYA
See also SATA 14
Low, Lois Dorothea 1916- CANR-15
Earlier sketch in CA 37-40R
Low, Rachael 1923- 125
Low, Samuel 1765- ....DLB 37
Low, Victor N. 1931- CANR-1
Earlier sketch in CA 49-52
Lowance, Mason I(ra) Jr. 1938- 57-60
Lowbury, Edward (Joseph Lister)
1913- CANR-29
Earlier sketches in CA 29-32R, CANR-12
Lowden, Desmond 1937- 53-56
Lowder, Jerry 1932- 65-68
Lowder, Paul D(aniel) 1929- 93-96
Lowdermilk, W(alter) C(lay)
1888-1974 Obituary 49-52
Lowe, A(lfred) Mifflin 1948- 128
Lowe, Alfonso
See Loewenthal, L(eonard) J(oseph) A(lfonso)
Lowe, C(arrington) Marshall 1930- 29-32R
Lowe, Carl 1949- 125
Lowe, Corke
See Pepper, Choral
Lowe, David A(llan) 1948- CANR-29
Earlier sketch in CA 111
Lowe, David (Garrard) 1933- CANR-22
Earlier sketch in CA 104
Lowe, Donald M. 1928- 21-24R
Lowe, Gordon R(obb) 1928- 49-52
Lowe, Gustav E. 1901- CAP-2
Earlier sketch in CA 23-24
Lowe, Jay Jr.
See Loeper, John J(oseph)
Lowe, Jeanne R.
1924(?)-1972 Obituary 33-36R
Lowe, John (Evelyn) 1928- 123
Lowe, John W(esley) G(uinn) 1946- 121
Lowe, Judah
See Lyon, Christopher (Leslie)
Lowe, Marjorie G(riffiths) Lowe 1909- 1-4R
Lowe, Richard Barrett
1902-1972 Obituary 33-36R
Lowe, Richard G. 1942- 123
Lowe, Robert W. 1910- CAP-1
Earlier sketch in CA 13-14
Lowe, Roberta (Justine) 1940- CANR-24
Earlier sketches in CA 61-64, CANR-8
Lowe, Sam Jack
See Rummel, (Louis) Jack(son)
Lowe, Sue Davidson 1922- 118
Lowe, Victor (Augustus) 1907-1988 ....17-20R
Obituary 127
Lowe, Victoria Lincoln
See Lincoln, Victoria
Lowe, William T(ebbs) 1929- 73-76
Lowell, Amy 1874-1925 Brief entry 104
See also DLB 54
See also TCLC 1, 8
Lowell, C. Stanley 1909- CANR-6
Earlier sketch in CA 5-8R
Lowell, James Russell
1819-1891 ....CDALB 1640-1865
See also DLB 1, 11, 64, 79
Lowell, Jon 1938- 97-100
Lowell, Juliet 1901- CANR-1
Earlier sketch in CA 1-4R
Lowell, Mildred Hawksworth 1905-1974 ....CAP-2
Earlier sketch in CA 33-36
Lowell, Robert (Traill Spence Jr.)
1917-1977 ....CANR-26
Obituary 73-76
Earlier sketch in CA 9-12R
See also CABS 2
See also CLC 1, 2, 3, 4, 5, 8, 9, 11, 15, 37
See also DLB 5
See also MTCW
See also PC 3
See also WLC
Lowell, Susan 1950- 126
Lowell, Tex
See Turner, George E(ugene)
Lowen, Alexander 1910- 17-20R
Lowenfeld, Andreas F(rank) 1930- CANR-8
Earlier sketch in CA 61-64
Lowenfeld, Berthold 1901- 17-20R
Lowenfels, Walter 1897-1976 ....CANR-3
Obituary 65-68
Earlier sketch in CA 1-4R
See also DLB 4
Lowenfish, Lee (Elihu) 1942- 106
Lowenkopf, Shelly A(lan) 1931- CANR-4
Earlier sketch in CA 49-52
Lowens, Irving 1916-1983 ....CANR-11
Obituary 111
Earlier sketch in CA 17-20R
Lowenstein, Dyno 1914- 9-12R
See also SATA 6
Lowenstein, Ralph Lynn 1930- 17-20R
Lowenstein, Sharon R. 1937- 122
Lowenstein, Tom 1941- 93-96
Lowenthal, Abraham F(rederic) 1941- 127
Lowenthal, David 1923- 115
Lowenthal, Leo 1900- CANR-20
Earlier sketches in CA 1-4R, CANR-5
Lowenthal, Marjorie Fiske
See Fiske, Marjorie
Lower, Arthur R(eginald) M(arsden)
1889-1988 ....CANR-4
Obituary 124
Earlier sketch in CA 9-12R
Lower, J(oseph) Arthur 1907- 21-24R
Lowerre, Susan (K.) 1962- 134
Lowery, Bruce Arlie 1931- CANR-1
Earlier sketch in CA 1-4R
Lowery, Daniel L(orne) 1929- 113
Lowery, James L(incoln) Jr. 1932- 45-48
Lowery, Lynn 1949- 93-96
Lowery, Robert G. 1941- 130
Lowery, Thomas V(incent) 1919- 37-40R
Lowi, Theodore J(ay) 1931- 37-40R
Lowidski, Witt
See Clinton, (Lloyd) D(eWitt)
Lowing, Anne
See Geach, Christine
Lowinsky, Edward E(lias) 1908-1985 ....CAP-1
Obituary 117
Earlier sketch in CA 13-14
Lowith, Karl
See Loewith, Karl
Lowitz, Anson C. 1901(?)-1978 81-84
Obituary 73-76
See also SATA 18
Lowitz, Sadyebeth Heath 1901-1969 85-88
See also SATA 17
Lowman, Charles LeRoy
1880(?)-1977 Obituary 69-72
Lowman, Eleanor B(arry)
1906-1983 Obituary 110
Lowman, Josephine (Cherry)
1899(?)-1983 Obituary 110
Lowndes, Betty 1929- 61-64
Lowndes, George Alfred Norman 1897- 5-8R
Lowndes, Marie Adelaide (Belloc)
1868-1947 Brief entry 107
See also DLB 70
See also TCLC 12
Lowndes, Robert A(ugustine) W(ard) 1916- 128
Brief entry 113
Lowndes, William 1914- 13-16R
Lowney, Paul Benjamin 1922- CANR-17
Earlier sketch in CA 93-96
Lowrey, Janette Sebring 1892- 13-16R
See also SATA 43
Lowrey, Kathleen 1943- 57-60
Lowrey, P(errin) H(olmes) 1923-1965 ....CAP-1
Earlier sketch in CA 11-12
Lowrey, Sara 1897- 17-20R
Lowrie, Donald A(lexander) 1889-1974 ....5-8R
Obituary 53-56
Lowrie, Jean E(lizabeth) 1918- 45-48
Lowry, Albert J(ames) 1927- 129
Brief entry 118
Lowry, Bates 1923- CANR-1
Earlier sketch in CA 1-4R
Lowry, Beverly (Fey) 1938- 101
Lowry, Charles W(esley) 1905- 37-40R
Lowry, Fern 1896(?)-1983 Obituary 111
Lowry, Joan (Catlow) 1911- 13-16R
Lowry, Lois 1937- CANR-13
Earlier sketch in CA 69-72
See also AAYA 5
See also CLR 6
See also DLB 52
See also MAICYA
See also SAAS 3
See also SATA 23, 70
Lowry, (Clarence) Malcolm 1909-1957 131
Brief entry 105
See also CDBLB 1945-1960
See also DLB 15
See also MTCW
See also TCLC 6, 40
Lowry, Martin John Clement 1940- 107
Lowry, Mina Gertrude 1882-1966 113
See also Loy, Mina
Lowry, Nan
See MacLeod, Ruth
Lowry, Peter 1953- 49-52
See also SATA 7
Lowry, Ritchie P(eter) 1926- 17-20R
Lowry, Robert (James Collas) 1919- 61-64
Lowry, S(tanley) Todd 1927- 126
Lowry, Shirley Park 1933- 109
Lowry, Thomas P. 1932- 21-24R
Lowther, George F. 1913-1975 Obituary 57-60
See also SATA 30
Lowther, Kevin G(eorge) 1941- 81-84
Lowther, Pat 1935-1975 ....DLB 53
Lowther, William (Anthony) 1942- 136
Lowy, George 1924- 17-20R
Loxsmith, John
See Brunner, John (Kilian Houston)
Loxton, (Charles) Howard 1934- CANR-27
Earlier sketches in CA 25-28R, CANR-11
Loy, J(ohn) Robert 1918- Brief entry 108
Loy, Jane M.
See Rausch, Jane M(eyer)
Loy, Mina
See Lowry, Mina Gertrude
See also CLC 28
See also DLB 4, 54
Loy, Rosetta 1931- 138
Loyd, Marianne 1955- 115
Loye, David (Elliot) 1925- 33-36R
Loyn, H(enry) R(oyston) 1922- 117
Loyn, Henry
See Loyn, H(enry) R(oyston)
Loyn, Henry R.
See Loyn, H(enry) R(oyston)
Loyson-Bridet
See Schwob, (Mayer Andre) Marcel
Lozano, Wendy 1941- 102
Lozansky, Edward D. 1941- ....SATA 62
Lozeau, Albert 1878-1924 ....DLB 92
Lozier, Herbert 1915- 49-52
See also SATA 26
Lozowick, Louis 1892-1973 Obituary 107
Lu, David J(ohn) 1928- CANR-5
Earlier sketch in CA 9-12R
Lu, K'uan-yu
See Luk, Charles
Lu, Paul Hsien 1926- 41-44R
Luard, (David) Evan (Trant) 1926- CANR-1
Earlier sketch in CA 1-4R
Luard, Nicholas 1937- 85-88
Lubalin, Herb(ert Frederick)
1918-1981 Obituary 104
Lubans, John Jr. 1941- 57-60
Lubar, Joel F. 1938- 37-40R
Lubar, Robert 1920- 73-76
Lubbe, Catherine Case ....AITN 1
Lubbock, (Mary Katherine) Adelaide
1906- 29-32R
Lubbock, Mark Hugh 1898-1986 Obituary 121
Lubbock, Percy 1879-1965 85-88
Lubeck, Steven G. 1944- 29-32R
Lubell, Cecil 1912- CANR-4
Earlier sketch in CA 9-12R
See also SATA 6
Lubell, Harold 1925- 9-12R
Lubell, Samuel 1911-1987 ....13-16R
Obituary 123
Lubell, Winifred (A. Milius) 1914- CANR-4
Earlier sketch in CA 49-52
See also SATA 6
Lubenow, William (Cornelius)
1939- Brief entry 107
Luber, Philip 1948- 124
Lubetski, Edith 1940- 112
Lubetski, Meir 1938- 112
Lubin, Bernard 1923- CANR-9
Earlier sketch in CA 21-24R
Lubin, David M. 1950- 120
Lubin, Ernest 1916-1977 ....41-44R
Lubin, Isador 1896-1978 Obituary 77-80
Lubin, Leonard
See Lubin, Leonard B.
Lubin, Leonard B. 1943- CANR-38
Brief entry 115
Earlier sketch in CA 125
See also MAICYA
See also SATA 37, 45
Lubis, Mochtar 1922- 29-32R
Lubitz, Raymond 1937-1984 Obituary 113
Lubove, Roy 1934- 21-24R
Lubow, Robert E. 1932- 77-80
Lubowe, Irwin I(rville) 1905- 53-56
Lubrano, Linda L. 1943- 126
Brief entry 108
Lucas, Alec 1913- 101
Lucas, Barbara
See Wall, Barbara
Lucas, Bryan Keith
See Keith-Lucas, Bryan
Lucas, C. Payne 1933- 85-88
Lucas, Carol 1929- 17-20R
Lucas, Celia 1938- CANR-24
Earlier sketch in CA 107
Lucas, Christopher J(ohn) 1940- 25-28R
Lucas, Craig 1951- 137
See also CLC 64
Lucas, D(onald) W(illiam) 1905-1985 ....CAP-1
Obituary 116
Earlier sketch in CA 13-14
Lucas, Darrel B(laine) 1902- CAP-1
Earlier sketch in CA 9-10
Lucas, Dione (Narnona Margaris Wilson)
1909-1971 Obituary 104
Lucas, E(dna) Louise 1899-1970 ....CAP-2
Earlier sketch in CA 25-28
Lucas, E(dward) V(errall) 1868-1938 ....DLB 98
See also SATA 20
Lucas, F(rank) L(aurence) 1894-1967 ....CANR-4
Obituary 25-28R
Earlier sketch in CA 1-4R
Lucas, George 1944- CANR-30
Earlier sketch in CA 77-80
See also AAYA 1
See also CLC 16
See also SATA 56
Lucas, Hans
See Godard, Jean-Luc
Lucas, Henry C(ameron) Jr. 1944- CANR-28
Earlier sketch in CA 109
Lucas, J. K.
See Paine, Lauran (Bosworth)
Lucas, J(ames) R(aymond) 1950- 118
Lucas, J(ohn) R(andolph) 1929- CANR-35
Earlier sketches in CA 21-24R, CANR-11
Lucas, Jason 1904- CAP-1
Earlier sketch in CA 9-10
Lucas, Jeremy 1953- 108
Lucas, Jerry 1940- 108
See also SATA 33
Lucas, Jim Griffing 1914-1970 Obituary 104
Lucas, John 1937- CANR-32
Earlier sketches in CA 37-40R, CANR-14
Lucas, Joseph 1928- 69-72
Lucas, Joyce 1927- 57-60
Lucas, Lawrence E(dward) 1933- 65-68
Lucas, Marion B(runson) 1935- 81-84
Lucas, Martin 1944- 111
Lucas, N. B. C. 1901- 81-84
Lucas, Noah 1927- 57-60
Lucas, Robert Emerson Jr. 1937- 107
Lucas, Robert Harold 1933- 37-40R
Lucas, Robert 1904-1984 101
Obituary 111
Lucas, Russell 1930- 137
Lucas, Ruth (Baxendale) 1909- CAP-2
Earlier sketch in CA 19-20
Lucas, Scott 1937- 93-96
Lucas, Stephen E. 1946- 125
Lucas, T(homas) E(dward) 1919- 77-80
Lucas, Victoria
See Plath, Sylvia
Lucas, W(ilmer) F(rancis Jr.) 1927- 77-80
See also BW
Lucash, Frank S. 1938- 120
Lucas Phillips, C(ecil) E(rnest)
1897-1984 ....CANR-3
Obituary 112
Earlier sketch in CA 1-4R
Lucchesi, Aldo
See von Block, Bela W(illiam)
Luce, Celia (Geneva Larsen) 1914- 61-64
See also SATA 38
Luce, Clare Boothe 1903-1987 45-48
Obituary 123
Luce, Don 1934- CANR-12
Earlier sketch in CA 29-32R
Luce, Gay Gaer 1930- 103
Luce, Henry R(obinson) 1898-1967 104
Obituary 89-92
See also MTCW
Luce, J(ohn) V(ictor) 1920- 61-64
Luce, T(orry) James (Jr.) 1932- 129
Luce, Willard (Ray) 1914- 61-64
See also SATA 38
Luce, William (Aubert) 1931- CANR-25
Earlier sketches in CA 65-68, CANR-11
Lucente, Gregory L. 1948- 120
Lucentini, Mauro 1924- 69-72
Lucero, Roberto
See Meredith, Robert C(hidester)
Lucey, James D(ennis) 1923- 25-28R
Lu-ch'iao
See Wu, Nelson I(kon)
Luchins, Abraham S(amuel) 1914- CANR-11
Earlier sketch in CA 69-72
Luchins, Edith H(irsch) 1921- CANR-11
Earlier sketch in CA 17-20R
Luchsinger, Elaine King 1902- CAP-2
Earlier sketch in CA 17-18
Lucia, Ellis (Joel) 1922- CANR-22
Earlier sketches in CA 1-4R, CANR-4
Lucia, Salvatore Pablo 1901-1984 ....13-16R
Obituary 112
Luciani, Vincent 1906- 61-64
Lucid, Robert F(rancis) 1930- 25-28R
Lucie-Smith, (John) Edward (McKenzie)
1933- CANR-7
Earlier sketch in CA 13-16R
See also DLB 40
Lucini, Gian Pietro 1867-1914 ....DLB 114
Luciuk, Lubomyr Y(aroslav) 1953- 132
Luck, David Johnston 1912- CANR-4
Earlier sketch in CA 53-56
Luck, G(eorge) Coleman 1913- 13-16R
Luck, George Hans 1926- 5-8R
Luck, Thomas Jefferson 1922- 5-8R
Luckert, Karl W(ilhelm) 1934- 81-84

Luckett, Hubert Pearson 1916- ... 77-80
Luckett, Karen Beth 1944- ... 77-80
Luckey, Eleanore Braun 1915- ... 33-36R
Luckhardt, C(harles) Grant 1943- ... 93-96
Luckhardt, Mildred Corell 1898- ... 13-16R
See also SATA 5
Luckless, John
See Burkholz, Herbert
and Irving, Clifford Michael
Luckmann, Thomas 1927- ... CANR-19
Earlier sketch in CA 101
Luckock, Elizabeth 1914- ... 21-24R
Luckyj, George S(tephen) N(estor)
1919- ... CANR-21
Earlier sketch in CA 45-48
Ludden, Allen (Ellsworth)
1918(?)-1981 Obituary ... 104
See also SATA 27
Ludden, David 1948- ... 127
Ludel, Jacqueline 1945- ... 111
See also SATA 64
Luder, William Fay 1910- ... 29-32R
Ludington, (Charles) Townsend
1936- ... CANR-25
Earlier sketches in CA 45-48, CANR-9
Ludlam, Charles 1943-1987 ... 85-88
Obituary ... 122
See also CLC 46, 50
Ludlow, Geoffrey
See Meynell, Laurence Walter
Ludlow, George
See Kay, Ernest
Ludlow, Howard T(homas) 1921- ... 21-24R
Ludlow, James Minor
1917-1974 Obituary ... 53-56
Ludlum, Mabel Cleland
See Widdemer, Mabel Cleland
Ludlum, Robert P(hillips) 1909-1987 ... CAP-1
Obituary ... 122
Earlier sketch in CA 13-16
Ludlum, Robert 1927- ... CANR-25
Earlier sketch in CA 33-36R
See also BEST 89:1, 90:3
See also CLC 22, 43
See also DLBY 82
See also MTCW
Ludmerer, Kenneth M. 1947- ... CANR-27
Earlier sketch in CA 45-48
Ludovici, Anthony M(ario) 1882- ... CAP-1
Earlier sketch in CA 11-12
Ludovici, L. J.
See Ludovici, Lorenz James
Ludovici, Laurence James
See Ludovici, Lorenz James
Ludovici, Lorenz James 1910- ... CANR-10
Earlier sketch in CA 21-24R
Ludowyk, E(velyn) F(rederick) C(harles)
1906-1985 ... CAP-1
Obituary ... 117
Earlier sketch in CA 11-12
Ludtke, James Buren 1924- ... 1-4R
Ludvigsen, Karl (Eric) 1934- ... 73-76
Ludvigson, Susan 1942- ... CANR-7
Earlier sketch in CA 57-60
See also DLB 120
Ludwig, Charles Shelton 1918- ... CANR-20
Earlier sketches in CA 9-12R, CANR-5
Ludwig, Ed(ward William) 1920- ... 97-100
Ludwig, Eric
See Grunwald, Stefan
Ludwig, Frederic
See Grunwald, Stefan
Ludwig, Helen ... SATA 33
Ludwig, Jack 1922- ... CANR-1
Earlier sketch in CA 1-4R
See also DLB 60
Ludwig, Jerry 1934- ... 81-84
Ludwig, Ken ... CLC 60
Ludwig, Lyndell 1923- ... CANR-38
Earlier sketch in CA 115
See also SATA 63
Ludwig, Myles Eric 1942- ... 25-28R
Ludwig, Richard M(ilton) 1920- ... 17-20R
Ludwigson, Kathryn Romaine 1921- ... CANR-6
Earlier sketch in CA 53-56
Luebke, Frederick Carl 1927- ... CANR-12
Earlier sketch in CA 33-36R
Luecke, Janemarie 1924- ... CANR-21
Earlier sketch in CA 104
Lueders, Edward (George) 1923- ... CANR-5
Earlier sketch in CA 13-16R
See also SATA 14
Luedtke, Kurt (Mamre) 1939- ... 111
Brief entry ... 109
Lueker, Erwin L(ouis) 1914- ... CANR-23
Earlier sketches in CA 17-20R, CANR-8
Luellen, Valentina
See Polley, Judith (Anne)
Luening, Otto 1900- ... 102
Luenn, Nancy 1954- ... CANR-39
Earlier sketch in CA 116
See also SATA 51
Lueschen, Guenther R(udolf) 1930- ... CANR-4
Earlier sketch in CA 53-56
Luescher, Max 1923- ... 101
Luetgen, Kurt (Bodo Heinrich) 1911- ... 108
Luethi, Max 1909- ... 29-32R
Luetzelschwab, John (William) 1940- ... 121
Brief entry ... 118
Lufburrow, William 1931(?)-1986 Obituary ... 118
Luff, S(tanley) G(eorge) A(nthony) 1921- ... 9-12R
Lufkin, Raymond H. 1897- ... SATA 38
Luft, David Sheers 1944- ... 106
Lugard, Flora Louisa Shaw
1852-1929 ... SATA 21
Luger, Harriett Mandelay 1914- ... CANR-1
Earlier sketch in CA 45-48
See also SATA 23
Lugg, George Wilson 1902- ... 105
Lugo, Ariel E(milio) 1943- ... 41-44R
Lugo, James O. 1928- ... 29-32R
Lugones, Leopoldo 1874-1938 ... 131
Brief entry ... 116
See also HW
See also TCLC 15
Lugt, Herbert Vander
See Vander Lugt, Herbert
Luhr, William 1946- ... 106
Luhrmann, T(anya) M(arie) 1959- ... 130
Luhrmann, Winifred B(ruce) 1934- ... 61-64
See also SATA 11
Lu Hsun 1881-1936 ... TCLC 3
Luick, John F(rancis) 1920- ... 25-28R
Luis, Earlene W. 1929- ... 61-64
See also SATA 11
Luisada, Aldo A(ugusto)
1901-1987 Obituary ... 124
Luisi, Billie M(eisner) 1940- ... 73-76
Luk, Charles 1898- ... 9-12R
Luka, Ronald 1937- ... 61-64
Lukach, Joan M(ickelson) 1935- ... 118
Lukacher, Ned 1950- ... 120
Lukacs, George
See Lukacs, Gyorgy (Szegeny von)
See also CLC 24
Lukacs, Gyorgy (Szegeny von) 1885-1971 ... 101
Obituary ... 29-32R
See also Lukacs, George
Lukacs, John (Adalbert) 1923- ... CANR-17
Earlier sketches in CA 1-4R, CANR-1
Lukaczer, Moses 1911-1984 Obituary ... 112
Lukas, Charlotte Koplinka 1954- ... 93-96
Lukas, Ellen ... 97-100
Lukas, J(ay) Anthony 1933- ... CANR-19
Earlier sketches in CA 49-52, CANR-2
See also MTCW
Lukas, Mary ... 101
Lukas, Richard C. 1937- ... 33-36R
Lukas, Susan 1940- ... 53-56
Lukashevich, Stephen 1931- ... 33-36R
Luke, Hugh J(ay) 1932- ... 89-92
Luke, Mary M. 1919- ... CANR-14
Earlier sketch in CA 21-24R
Luke, Peter (Ambrose Cyprian) 1919- ... 81-84
See also CLC 38
See also DLB 13
Luke, Thomas
See Masterton, Graham
Lukenbill, Willis B(ernard) 1939- ... 103
Luker, Kristin Carol 1946- ... 61-64
Luker, Nicholas (John Lydgate) 1945- ... 130
Lukes, Steven (Michael) 1941- ... CANR-16
Earlier sketch in CA 93-96
Lukodianov, Isai (Borisovich) 1913- ... 101
Lukonin, Mikhail K.
1920(?)-1977 Obituary ... 69-72
Lum, Peter
See Crowe, Bettina Lum
Lumian, Norman C. 1928- ... 29-32R
Lumiansky, R(obert) M(ayer)
1913-1987 Obituary ... 122
Lumley, Brian 1937- ... 132
Brief entry ... 120
Lummis, Keith 1904- ... 104
Lumpkin, Angela 1950- ... CANR-32
Earlier sketch in CA 112
Lumpkin, Grace ... 69-72
Lumpkin, Henry H(ope) 1913- ... 122
Lumpkin, William Latane 1916- ... CANR-4
Earlier sketch in CA 1-4R
Lumsden, Charles J(ohn) 1949- ... CANR-29
Earlier sketch in CA 111
Lumsden, D(an) Barry 1939- ... CANR-21
Earlier sketch in CA 45-48
Lunan, Duncan (Alasdair) 1945- ... 107
Lunar, Dennis
See Mungo, Raymond
Lunch, Lydia 1959- ... CANR-38
Earlier sketch in CA 115
Lund, A. Morten 1926- ... 13-16R
Lund, Doris Herold 1919- ... 17-20R
See also SATA 12
Lund, Gerald N. 1939- ... CANR-13
Earlier sketch in CA 33-36R
Lund, Gilda E. 1909- ... 5-8R
Lund, Herb(ert Frederick) 1926- ... 45-48
Lund, James
See Stonehouse, John (Thomson)
Lund, Philip R(eginald) 1938- ... 57-60
Lund, Robert P. 1915- ... 1-4R
Lund, Robert T. 1924- ... 126
Lund, Thomas A. 1922- ... 33-36R
Lundahl, Gene 1933- ... 21-24R
Lundberg, Dan
See Lundberg, Daniel
Lundberg, Daniel 1912-1986 ... 114
Obituary ... 119
Lundberg, Donald E(mil) 1916- ... CANR-12
Earlier sketch in CA 33-36R
Lundberg, Erik F(ilip) 1907- ... CANR-38
Earlier sketches in CA 25-28R, CANR-17
Lundberg, (Edgar) Ferdinand 1905- ... CAP-1
Earlier sketch in CA 9-10
Lundberg, Margaret (Jessie) 1919- ... 61-64
Lundborg, Louis B(illings) 1906- ... 81-84
Lunde, Donald T(heodore) 1937- ... 101
Lunde, Karl (Roy) 1931- ... 122
Lunden, Walter A(lbin) 1899- ... 21-24R
Lundgren, Paul Arthur 1925-1981 Obituary ... 103
Lundgren, William R. 1918- ... 13-16R
Lundin, Robert W(illiam) 1920- ... 1-4R
Lundkvist, Artur (Nils) 1906- Brief entry ... 117
Lundman, Richard J. 1944- ... 138
Lundquist, James (Carl) 1941- ... 65-68
Lundqvist, Lennart J. 1939- ... 129
Lundsgaarde, Henry P(eder) 1938- ... CANR-14
Earlier sketch in CA 73-76
Lundsteen, Sara W. ... 109
Lundstrom, David E. 1929- ... 126
Lundwall, Sam J(errie) 1941- ... CANR-37
Earlier sketches in CA 49-52, CANR-1, 17
Lundy, Robert F(ranklin) 1937- ... 5-8R
Lunenfeld, Marvin C. 1934- ... 61-64
Lunin, Lois F(ranklin) ... 102
Lunn, Arnold 1888-1974 ... 81-84
Obituary ... 49-52
Lunn, Carolyn (Kowalczyk) 1960- ... 136
See also SATA 67
Lunn, Eugene 1941- ... 45-48
Lunn, Janet (Louise Swoboda) 1928- ... CANR-22
Earlier sketch in CA 33-36R
See also CLR 18
See also MAICYA
See also SAAS 12
See also SATA 4, 68
Lunn, John Edward 1930- ... 41-44R
Lunsford, Cin Forshay
See Forshay-Lunsford, Cin
Lunt, Elizabeth Graves 1922- ... 33-36R
Lunt, Horace G(ray) 1918- ... 134
Brief entry ... 107
Lunt, James D(oiran) 1917- ... CANR-3
Earlier sketch in CA 1-4R
Lunt, Lois
See Metz, Lois Lunt
Lunt, Richard D(eForest) 1933- ... 13-16R
Luoma, Jon R. 1951- ... 127
Luomala, Katharine 1907- ... 37-40R
Luongo, C. Paul 1930- ... 105
Luongo, Edward Parker
1912(?)-1989 Obituary ... 128
Luper, Harold L(ee) 1924- ... 17-20R
Lupo, Alan 1938- ... 41-44R
Lupoff, Dick
See Lupoff, Richard A(llen)
Lupoff, Richard A(llen) 1935- ... CANR-25
Earlier sketches in CA 21-24R, CANR-9
See also SATA 60
Lupul, Manoly R(obert) 1927- ... 127
Brief entry ... 106
Lurgan, Lester
See Knowles, Mabel Winifred
Luria, Alexander R(omanovich)
1902-1977 ... CANR-33
Obituary ... 73-76
Earlier sketch in CA 25-28R
See also MTCW
Luria, Maxwell Sidney 1932- ... 37-40R
Luria, S(alvador) E(dward) 1912-1991 ... 61-64
Obituary ... 133
Lurie, Alison 1926- ... CANR-17
Earlier sketches in CA 1-4R, CANR-2
See also CLC 4, 5, 18, 39
See also DLB 2
See also MTCW
See also SATA 46
Lurie, Edward 1927- ... CANR-7
Earlier sketch in CA 9-12R
Lurie, Harry L. 1892(?)-1973 Obituary ... 41-44R
Lurie, Jonathan 1939- ... 132
Lurie, Morris 1938- ... 133
Lurie, Nancy Oestreich 1924- ... CANR-16
Earlier sketch in CA 1-4R
Lurie, Ranan R(aymond) 1932- ... 57-60
Lurie, Richard G. 1919- ... 21-24R
Lurie, Toby 1925- ... 45-48
Luriya, Aleksander Romanovich
See Luria, Alexander R(omanovich)
Luschei, Eugene C(harles) 1928- ... 37-40R
Luscher, Max
See Luescher, Max
Luscombe, David Edward 1938- ... 41-44R
Luscombe, William 1912- ... 5-8R
Lusinchi, Victor 1912-1985 Obituary ... 115
Luskin, Bernard J(ay) 1937- ... 33-36R
Luskin, John 1908- ... 45-48
Lussier, (Joseph) Ernest 1911-1979 ... CANR-9
Earlier sketch in CA 57-60
Lussu, Joyce (Salvadori) 1912- ... CANR-14
Earlier sketch in CA 29-32R
Lust, John (Benedict) 1920- ... 116
Lust, Peter 1911- ... 103
Lustbader, Eric Van 1946- ... CANR-14
Earlier sketch in CA 85-88
See also BEST 90:2
Lustgarten, Edgar (Marcus)
1907-1978 ... CANR-22
Earlier sketch in CA 25-28R
Lustgarten, Karen 1944- ... 85-88
Lustick, Ian Steven 1949- ... 117
Lustig, Arnost 1926- ... 69-72
See also AAYA 3
See also CLC 56
See also SATA 56
Lustig, Loretta 1944- ... SATA 46
Lustig, R(ichard) Jeffrey 1943- ... 112
Lustig-Arecco, Vera 1942- ... 101
Lutes, Catherine Urell
1900(?)-1983 Obituary ... 110
Lutetius
See Stearns, Harold Edmund
Lutgen, Kurt
See Luetgen, Kurt (Bodo Heinrich)
Luthans, Fred 1939- ... 29-32R
Luther, Edward T(urner) 1928- ... 77-80
Luther, Frank 1905-1980 Obituary ... 102
See also SATA 25
Luther, James W(allace) 1940- ... 69-72
Luther, Jim
See Luther, James W(allace)
Luther, Ray
See Ley, Arthur Gordon
Luthi, Max
See Luethi, Max
Luthuli, A. J.
See Luthuli, Albert John
Luthuli, Albert John 1898(?)-1967 Obituary ... 113
Lutin, Michael 1940- ... 89-92
Luttbeg, Norman R. 1938- ... CANR-10
Earlier sketch in CA 25-28R
Luttrell, Guy L. 1938- ... 97-100
See also SATA 22
Luttrell, Ida (Alleene) 1934- ... CANR-27
Earlier sketch in CA 110
See also SATA 35, 40
Luttrell, Ida (Alleene) 1934- ... CANR-27
Luttrell, Mark H. 1914- ... 97-100
Luttwak, Edward N(icholae) 1942- ... CANR-11
Earlier sketch in CA 25-28R
Lutwack, Leonard 1917- ... 41-44R
Lutyens, (Agnes) Elisabeth
1906-1983 Obituary ... 109
Lutyens, Mary 1908- ... 25-28R
Lutz, Alma 1890-1973 ... CAP-1
Obituary ... 45-48
Earlier sketch in CA 9-10
Lutz, Charles P(aul) 1931- ... 115
Lutz, Cora Elizabeth 1906-1985 ... 102
Obituary ... 115
Lutz, Frank W. 1928- ... 33-36R
Lutz, Gertrude May 1899- ... 33-36R
Lutz, Harley L. 1882-1975 Obituary ... 53-56
Lutz, Jerry 1939- ... 89-92
Lutz, Jessie Gregory 1925- ... 13-16R
Lutz, John (Thomas) 1939- ... CANR-24
Earlier sketches in CA 65-68, CANR-9
Lutz, Paul E(ugene) 1934- ... 61-64
Lutz, William D. 1940- ... 33-36R
Lutz, William W(alter) 1919- ... 49-52
Lutze, Karl E(rnst) 1920- ... 89-92
Lutzer, Erwin W(esley) 1941- ... CANR-2
Earlier sketch in CA 45-48
Lutzker, Edythe 1904-1991 ... 37-40R
Obituary ... 135
See also SATA 5
Luvaas, Jay 1927- ... 13-16R
Luvaas, William 1945- ... 121
Lux, Jimmy
See Obrecht, Jas
Lux, Thomas 1946- ... 41-44R
Luxemburg, Rosa 1870(?)-1919 Brief entry ... 118
Luxenburg, Norman 1927- ... 41-44R
Luxton, Leonora Kathrine 1895- ... 85-88
Luxton, Richard (Neil) 1950- ... 110
Luyben, Helen L. 1932- ... 17-20R
Luytens, David (Edwin) Bulwer 1929- ... 13-16R
Luza, Radomir 1922- ... CANR-24
Earlier sketches in CA 9-12R, CANR-9
Luzbetak, Louis J(oseph) 1918- ... 33-36R
Luzi, Mario 1914- ... CANR-9
Earlier sketch in CA 61-64
See also CLC 13
Luzma
See Umpierre (Herrera), Luz Maria
Luzwick, Dierdre 1945- ... 65-68
Luzzati, Emanuele 1921- ... 29-32R
See also SATA 7
Luzzatto, Paola Caboara 1938- ... 112
See also SATA 38
Lyall, Gavin (Tudor) 1932- ... CANR-26
Earlier sketches in CA 9-12R, CANR-4
See also DLB 87
Lyall, Katharine Elizabeth 1928- ... CANR-7
Earlier sketch in CA 5-8R
Lyall, Leslie T(heodore) 1905- ... 13-16R
Lyandres, Yulian Semenovich 1931- ... CANR-35
See also Semenov, Julian Semenovich
Lycan, Gilbert L(ester) 1909- ... CAP-2
Earlier sketch in CA 33-36
Lyday, Leon F(aidherbee) III 1939- ... 33-36R
Lydecker, Beatrice 1938- ... 106
Lyden, Fremont J(ames) 1926- ... 25-28R
Lydenberg, John 1913- ... 37-40R
Lydolph, Paul E. 1924- ... 13-16R
Lydon, James G(avin) 1927- ... 126
Brief entry ... 105
Lydon, Michael 1942- ... 85-88
See also SATA 11
Lyfick, Warren
See Reeves, Lawrence F.
Lyford, Joseph Philip 1918- ... 37-40R
Lyford-Pike, Margaret (Prudence) 1911- ... 109
Lygre, David G(erald) 1942- ... 93-96
Lykiard, Alexis (Constantine) 1940- ... 81-84
Lykken, David Thoreson 1928- ... 105
Lyle, Albert Walter 1944- ... 124
Brief entry ... 117
Lyle, David 1927- ... 118
Lyle, Guy R(edvers) 1907- ... 61-64
Lyle, Jack 1929- ... 13-16R
Lyle, Jerolyn R(oss) 1937- ... 89-92
Lyle, Katie Letcher 1938- ... CANR-29
Earlier sketch in CA 49-52
See also SATA 8
Lyle, Sparky
See Lyle, Albert Walter
Lyles, Vina Honish 1935- ... 9-12R
Lyles, William H(using) 1946- ... 111
Lyle-Smythe, Alan 1914- ... 103
Lyly, John 1554(?)-1606 ... DLB 62
Lyman, Albert Robison 1880-1973 ... CAP-1
Earlier sketch in CA 13-16
Lyman, Francesca 1951- ... 133
Lyman, Helen (Lucille) Huguenor 1910- ... 65-68
Lyman, Howard B(urbeck) 1920- ... 41-44R

Lyman, Irene (Vera) Ponting 5-8R
Lyman, Lauren D(wight)
1891-1972 Obituary 89-92
Lyman, Marilyn F(lorence) 1925- 93-96
Lyman, Mary Ely 1887-1975 Obituary 53-56
Lyman, Stanford M(orris) 1933- CANR-32
Earlier sketches in CA 29-32R, CANR-12
Lyman, Susan Elizabeth
1906-1976 Obituary 69-72
Lymington, John
See Chance, John Newton
Lynch, B. Suarez
See Bioy Casares, Adolfo
and Borges, Jorge Luis
Lynch, Benito 1885-1951 ....HW
Lynch, Brian
See Liddy, James (Daniel Reeves)
Lynch, Charles B. 1919- 137
Lynch, David (K.) 1946- 129
Brief entry 124
See also CLC 66
Lynch, Edith M. (Carstensen) 1912-1986 105
Obituary 119
Lynch, Eric
See Bingley, David Ernest
Lynch, Etta Lee 1924- 69-72
Lynch, Frances
See Compton, D(avid) G(uy)
Lynch, Hayden Wood
1927(?)-1979 Obituary 89-92
Lynch, Henry T(homson) 1928- 89-92
Lynch, Hollis Ralph 1935- CANR-1
Earlier sketch in CA 45-48
Lynch, J(ohn) Joseph 1894-1987 Obituary 123
Lynch, James
See Andreyev, Leonid (Nikolaevich)
Lynch, James F. 1919(?)-1985 Obituary 117
Lynch, James J(oseph) 1938- 73-76
Lynch, James 1936- CANR-18
Earlier sketch in CA 101
Lynch, John 1927- 85-88
Lynch, Kathleen M(artha) 1898- 73-76
Lynch, Kevin (Andrew) 1918-1984 ....CANR-3
Obituary 112
Earlier sketch in CA 5-8R
Lynch, Lorenzo 1932- 29-32R
See also SATA 7
Lynch, Malcolm 1922- 119
Lynch, Marietta 1947- 106
See also SATA 29
Lynch, Marilyn 1938- 89-92
Lynch, Owen M(artin) 1931- CANR-11
Earlier sketch in CA 29-32R
Lynch, Patricia (Nora) 1898-1972 .... CAP-1
Earlier sketch in CA 11-12
See also SATA 9
Lynch, Patrick B(eavis) 1927- 9-12R
Lynch, Thomas Francis 1938- 45-48
Lynch, W(illiam) E(dward) 1930- CANR-10
Earlier sketch in CA 17-20R
Lynch, W. Ware 1914(?)-1989 Obituary 128
Lynch, William F. 1908-1987 ....CANR-3
Obituary 121
Earlier sketch in CA 1-4R
Lynch Davis, B.
See Bioy Casares, Adolfo
and Borges, Jorge Luis
Lynch-Fraser, Diane 1953- 111
Lynch-Watson, Janet 1936- 93-96
Lynd, Helen Merrell 1896-1982 Obituary 105
Lynd, Robert S. 1892-1970 Obituary 29-32R
Lynd, Robert 1879-1949 ....DLB 98
Lynd, Staughton (Craig) 1929- 133
Brief entry 112
Lynde, Stan 1931- 65-68
Lynden, Patricia 1937- 73-76
Lyndon, Amy
See Radford, Richard F(rancis) Jr.
Lyndon, Diana
See Anthony, Diana
Lynds, Dennis 1924- CANR-22
Earlier sketches in CA 1-4R, CANR-6
See also SATA 37, 47
Lyne, John Alexander 1909- 97-100
Lyneis, Richard George 1935- 81-84
Lynen, John Fairbanks 1924- CANR-2
Earlier sketch in CA 1-4R
Lynes, (Joseph) Russell (Jr.)
1910-1991 ....CANR-3
Obituary 135
Earlier sketch in CA 1-4R
Lyngseth, Joan
See Davies, Joan
Lyngstad, Alexandra Halina 1925- 37-40R
Lyngstad, Sverre 1922- CANR-37
Earlier sketches in CA 37-40R, CANR-16
Lynn
See Brown, Velma Darbo
Lynn, Arthur D(ellert) Jr. 1921- CANR-10
Earlier sketch in CA 25-28R
Lynn, Conrad J. 1908- CAP-2
Earlier sketch in CA 23-24
Lynn, David B(randon) 1925- 57-60
Lynn, Edward S(hird) 1919- 57-60
Lynn, Edwin Charles 1935- 45-48
Lynn, Elizabeth A. 1946- 81-84
Lynn, Frank
See Leisy, James (Franklin)
Lynn, Irene
See Rowland, D(onald) S(ydney)
Lynn, Janet
See Salomon, Janet Lynn (Nowicki)
Lynn, Jeannette Murphy 1905- CAP-2
Earlier sketch in CA 21-22
Lynn, (Dorcas) Joanne (Harley) 1951- 125
Lynn, Jonathan 1943- 104
Lynn, Kenneth S(chuyler) 1923- CANR-27
Earlier sketches in CA 1-4R, CANR-3
See also CLC 50
Lynn, Laurence Edwin Jr. 1937- 105
Lynn, Loretta (Webb) 1932(?)- 81-84
Lynn, Margaret
See Battye, Gladys Starkey
Lynn, Mary
See Brokamp, Marilyn
Lynn, Naomi B. 1933- 61-64
Lynn, Patricia
See Watts, Mabel Pizzey
Lynn, Richard 1930- 37-40R
Lynn, Roa 1937- 101
Lynn, Robert A(than) 1930- 17-20R
Lynn, Robert Wood 1925- 21-24R
Lynn, Ruth Nadelman 1948- 103
Lynne, Becky
See Zawadsky, Patience
Lynne, James Broom 1920- 77-80
Lynskey, Winifred 1904- CAP-2
Earlier sketch in CA 23-24
Lynton, Ann
See Rayner, Claire (Berenice)
Lynton, Harriet Ronken 1920- 73-76
Lynx
See West, Rebecca
Lyon, Bryce Dale 1920- 126
Brief entry 106
Lyon, Buck
See Paine, Lauran (Bosworth)
Lyon, Christopher (Leslie) 1949- 132
Brief entry 118
Lyon, E(lijah) Wilson 1904-1989 97-100
Obituary 128
Lyon, Elinor 1921- 25-28R
See also SATA 6
Lyon, Eugene 1929- 106
Lyon, George Ella 1949- 120
See also SATA 68
Lyon, Harold C(lifford) Jr. 1935- 41-44R
Lyon, James K(arl) 1934- CANR-1
Earlier sketch in CA 45-48
Lyon, Jeff(rey R.) 1943- 130
Lyon, Jessica
See DeLeeuw, Cateau
Lyon, John 1932- CANR-15
Earlier sketch in CA 41-44R
Lyon, Katherine
See Mix, Katherine Lyon
Lyon, Linda Gale
See Van Voorhis, Linda Lyon
Lyon, Lyman R.
See de Camp, L(yon) Sprague
Lyon, Matthew 1749-1822 ....DLB 43
Lyon, Melvin (Ernest) 1927- 33-36R
Lyon, Peter 1915- CANR-5
Earlier sketch in CA 5-8R
Lyon, Peyton V(aughan) 1921- CANR-3
Earlier sketch in CA 9-12R
Lyon, Quinter M(arcellus) 1898- CAP-1
Earlier sketch in CA 19-20
Lyon, Thomas Edgar Jr. 1939- 37-40R
Lyon, William Henry 1926- 13-16R
Lyon, Winston
See Woolfolk, William
Lyons, Albert S. 1912- 126
Lyons, Arthur (Jr.) 1946- CANR-35
Earlier sketches in CA 29-32R, CANR-12
Lyons, Augusta Wallace 85-88
Lyons, Barbara (Baldwin) 1912- 93-96
Lyons, Catherine 1944- 85-88
Lyons, Christine 1943- 136
Lyons, Daniel 1920- 41-44R
Lyons, David (Barry) 1935- 33-36R
Lyons, Delphine C.
See Smith, Evelyn E.
Lyons, Dorothy M(arawee) 1907- CANR-24
Earlier sketch in CA 1-4R
See also SATA 3
Lyons, Elena
See Fairburn, Eleanor
Lyons, Enid (Muriel) 1897-1981 ....21-24R
Obituary 108
Lyons, Eugene 1898-1985 ....9-12R
Obituary 114
Lyons, F(rancis) S(tewart) L(eland)
1923-1983 ....29-32R
Obituary 110
Lyons, Gene 1943- 126
Lyons, Grant 1941- CANR-15
Earlier sketch in CA 41-44R
See also SATA 30
Lyons, Ivan 1934- CANR-19
Earlier sketch in CA 101
Lyons, J. B. 1922- CANR-17
Earlier sketch in CA 97-100
Lyons, James
See Loewen, James W.
Lyons, John O(rmsby) 1927- 1-4R
Lyons, John T. 1926- 29-32R
Lyons, John 1932- 132
Lyons, Joseph 1918- 13-16R
Lyons, Len 1942- 93-96
Lyons, Leonard 1906-1976 Obituary 69-72
Lyons, Louis M. 1897-1982 Obituary 106
Lyons, Marcus
See Blish, James (Benjamin)
Lyons, Mark Joseph 1910- 5-8R
Lyons, Nan 1935- CANR-19
Earlier sketch in CA 101
Lyons, Nick 1932- CANR-4
Earlier sketch in CA 53-56
Lyons, Phyllis I. 1942- 126
Lyons, Richard D(aniel) 1928- 69-72
Lyons, Richard E(ugene) 1920- CANR-21
Earlier sketch in CA 45-48
Lyons, Sister Jeanne Marie 1904- CAP-1
Earlier sketch in CA 11-12
Lyons, Thomas Tolman 1934- CANR-3
Earlier sketch in CA 9-12R
Lyons, Timothy J(ames) 1944- 73-76
Lyons, Tom W(allace) 1943- 116
Ly-Qui, Chung 1940- 29-32R
Lyre, Pinchbeck
See Sassoon, Siegfried (Lorraine)
Lys, Daniel 1924- 21-24R
Lysaght, Averil M(argaret) 85-88
Lysaught, Jerome Paul 1930- CANR-6
Earlier sketch in CA 5-8R
Lysenko, T(rofim) D(enisovich)
1898-1976 Obituary 69-72
Lysons, Kenneth 1923- CANR-33
Earlier sketches in CA 85-88, CANR-15
Lystad, Mary (Hanemann) 1928- CANR-26
Earlier sketches in CA 65-68, CANR-10
See also SATA 11
Lystad, Robert A(rthur) 1920- 13-16R
Lyte, Charles 1935- 104
Lyte, Richard
See Whelpton, (George) Eric
Lytle, Andrew (Nelson) 1902- 9-12R
See also CLC 22
See also DLB 6
Lytle, Clifford M(erle) 1932- 93-96
Lytle, Guy Fitch (III) 1944- 118
Lytle, Ruby (Coker) 1917- CAP-1
Earlier sketch in CA 13-16
Lyttelton, George (William) 1883-1962 134
Lyttelton, Humphrey (Richard Adeane)
1921- 129
Brief entry 118
Lyttle, Charles Harold 1885(?)-1980 109
Obituary 97-100
Lyttle, G(erald) R(oland) 1908- CAP-1
Earlier sketch in CA 9-10
Lyttle, Jean
See Garrett, Eileen J(eanette)
Lyttle, Richard B(ard) 1927- CANR-13
Earlier sketch in CA 33-36R
See also SATA 23
Lytton, Edward G(eorge) E(arle) L(ytton) Bulwer-
Lytton Baron 1803-1873 ....SATA 23
Lytton, Edward Robert Bulwer
1831-1891 ....DLB 32
Lytton, Hugh 1921- 45-48
Lytton, Noel (Anthony Scawen)
1900-1985 ....CAP-1
Obituary 115
Earlier sketch in CA 9-10
Lytton-Sells, Iris (Esther) 1903- 29-32R
Lyudvinskaya, Tatyana
1885(?)-1976 Obituary 65-68

M

M
See Stone, Susan Berch
M. C.
See Cook, Mabel Collins
M. G.
See Giergielewicz, Mieczyslaw F.
Ma, John T(a-jen) 1920- CANR-31
Earlier sketch in CA 49-52
Ma, Nancy Chih 1919- CANR-10
Earlier sketch in CA 65-68
Ma, Pearl (Pik Chun)
1928(?)-1989 Obituary 130
Maakestad, William J(ohn) 1951- 126
Maar, Leonard (Frank Jr.) 1927- 106
See also SATA 30
Maas, Audrey Gellen 1936-1975 ....CAP-2
Obituary 57-60
Earlier sketch in CA 23-24
Maas, Henry 1929- 25-28R
Maas, Jeremy (Stephen) 1928- CANR-32
Earlier sketch in CA 29-32R
Maas, Peter 1929- 93-96
See also CLC 29
Maas, Selve 69-72
See also SATA 14
Maas, Virginia H(argrave) 1913- 105
Maas, Willard 1911-1971 ....CAP-1
Obituary 29-32R
Earlier sketch in CA 13-14
Maasarani, Aly Mohamed 1927- 49-52
Maass, Arthur 1917- Brief entry 105
Maass, Joachim 1901-1972 Obituary 37-40R
See also DLB 69
Maass, John 1918- Brief entry 108
Mabberley, D(avid) J(ohn) 1948- 122
Mabbett, I(an) W(illiam) 1939- 29-32R
Mabbott, John David 1898-1988 ....13-16R
Obituary 124
Mabee, Carleton 1914- CANR-21
Earlier sketch in CA 1-4R
Maberly, Allan 1922-1977 103
Maberly, Norman C(harles) 1926- 33-36R
Mabery, D. L. 1953- 121
See also SATA 53
Mabey, Richard (Thomas) 1941- CANR-26
Earlier sketches in CA 21-24R, CANR-9
Mabie, Hamilton Wright 1845-1916 ....DLB 71
Mabie, Margot C(auldwell) J(ones) 1944- 125
Mabley, Edward (Howe) 1906-1984 ....29-32R
Obituary 114
Mabley, Jack 1915- 105
Mabogunje, Akin(lawon) L(adipo)
1931- CANR-16
Earlier sketch in CA 77-80
Mabon, John Scott 1910(?)-1980 Obituary 104
Mabry, Bevars Dupre 1928- 45-48
Mabry, Donald J(oseph) 1941- CANR-37
Earlier sketch in CA 49-52
Mac
See Maccari, Ruggero
and MacManus, Seumas
Mac, Carm
See Armstrong, Keith F(rancis) W(hitfield)
MacAdam, Eve
See Leslie, Cecilie
MacAdam, Preston
See Preston, John
MacAdams, Lewis (Perry Jr.) 1944- 97-100
MacAfee, Norman 1943- 122
MacAgy, Douglas G(uernsey) 1913-1973 102
Macainsh, Noel Leslie 1926- 103
MacAlan, Peter
See Ellis, Peter Berresford
MacAlister, Ian
See Albert, Marvin H(ubert)
MacAlpin, Rory
See Mackinnon, Charles Roy
MacAlpine, Margaret H(esketh Murray)
1907- CAP-1
Earlier sketch in CA 11-12
Macan, T(homas) T(ownley) 1910- 107
MacAndrew, Elizabeth 1924-1983(?) 126
Macao, Marshall
See Tuleja, Thaddeus F(rancis)
MacAodhagain, Eamon
See Egan, E(dward) W(elstead)
MacApp, C. C.
See Capps, Carroll M.
Macarov, David 1918- CANR-28
Earlier sketches in CA 29-32R, CANR-12
MacArthur, Charles 1895-1956 Brief entry 108
See also DLB 7, 25, 44
MacArthur, D(avid) Wilson 1903- CANR-5
Earlier sketch in CA 9-12R
MacArthur, Douglas 1880-1964 Obituary 113
MacArthur, John F. Jr. 1939- 81-84
MacArthur, Robert H(elmer)
1930-1972 Obituary 37-40R
MacArthur-Onslow, Annette Rosemary
1933- 102
See also SATA 26
Macartney, (Carlile) Aylmer 1895-1978 ......17-20R
Obituary 125
Macaulay, Catherine 1731-1791 ....DLB 104
Macaulay, David (Alexander) 1946- CANR-34
Earlier sketches in CA 53-56, CANR-5
See also BEST 89:2
See also CLR 3, 14
See also DLB 61
See also MAICYA
See also SATA 27, 46
Macaulay, John (Ure) 1925- 107
Macaulay, Neill (Webster Jr.) 1935- 21-24R
Macaulay, Rose 1881-1958 Brief entry 104
See also DLB 36
See also TCLC 7, 44
Macaulay, Stewart 1931- 77-80
Macaulay, Susan Schaeffer 1941- 120
Macaulay, Thomas Babington
1800-1859 ....CDBLB 1832-1890
See also DLB 32, 55
Macauley, Robie Mayhew 1919- CANR-3
Earlier sketch in CA 1-4R
MaCauley, Stephen ....CLC 50
MacAusland, Earle R(utherford)
1893-1980 Obituary 101
MacAvoy, Paul W(ebster) 1934- 126
Brief entry 105
MacAvoy, Roberta Ann 1949- 113
MacBean, Dilla Whittemore 1895- 5-8R
MacBeth, George (Mann) 1932-1992 ....25-28R
Obituary 136
See also CLC 2, 5, 9
See also DLB 40
See also MTCW
See also SATA 4
See also SATO 70
Macbeth, Madge 1880-1965 ....DLB 92
Macbeth, Norman 1910- CAP-2
Earlier sketch in CA 33-36
MacBride, Robert O(liver) 1926- 17-20R
MacBride, Roger Lea 1929- 81-84
MacBride, Sean 1904-1988 Obituary 124
MacCaffrey, Isabel Gamble 1924-1978 81-84
Obituary 77-80
MacCaffrey, Wallace T(revethic) 1920- 134
Brief entry 112
MacCaig, Norman (Alexander) 1910- CANR-34
Earlier sketches in CA 9-12R, CANR-3
See also CLC 36
See also DLB 27
MacCall, Libby
See Machol, Libby
MacCallum Scott, John H. 1911- 25-28R
MacCampbell, James C(urtis) 1916- 9-12R
MacCann, Donnarae 1931- CANR-1
Earlier sketch in CA 45-48
MacCann, Richard Dyer 1920- CANR-5
Earlier sketch in CA 9-12R
MacCannell, Juliet Flower 1943- 127
Maccari, Ruggero 1919(?)-1989 Obituary 128
MacCarthy, (Sir Charles Otto) Desmond
1877-1952 ....TCLC 36
MacCarthy, Fiona 1940- 125
MacCarthy, J(oseph) A(idan) 1913- 107
MacCauley, Sister Rose Agnes 1911- 37-40R
Macciocchi, Maria Antoinetta 1922- 73-76

MacClintock, Dorcas 1932- CANR-6
Earlier sketch in CA 57-60
See also SATA 8
MacCloskey, Monro 1902- CANR-5
Earlier sketch in CA 9-12R
Maccoby, Eleanor E(mmons)
1917- Brief entry 113
Maccoby, Michael 1933- CANR-14
Earlier sketch in CA 33-36R
MacCollam, Joel A(llan) 1946- 105
MacCombie, John 1932- 37-40R
MacCorkle, Stuart A(lexander) 1903- 17-20R
MacCormac, Earl Ronald 1935- 85-88
MacCormack, Sabine G(abriele) 1941- 106
MacCormick, Austin H(arbutt)
1893-1979 Obituary 93-96
MacCormick, (Donald) Neil 1941- 129
MacCorquodale, Patricia (Lee) 1950- 101
MacCoun, Catherine 1953- 131
MacCracken, Calvin D(odd) 1919- 116
MacCracken, Henry Noble 1880-1970 ...... CAP-1
Obituary 29-32R
Earlier sketch in CA 19-20
MacCracken, Mary 1926- CANR-30
Earlier sketch in CA 49-52
MacCraig, Hugh
See Ward, Craig
MacCulloch, Diarmaid 1951- 125
MacCullum, Hugh R. 1928- 127
MacCurdy, Raymond R(alph Jr.) 1916- 41-44R
MacDermott, Mercia 1927- 106
MacDiarmid, Hugh
See Grieve, C(hristopher) M(urray)
See also CDBLB 1945-1960
See also CLC 2, 4, 11, 19, 63
See also DLB 20
MacDonagh, Donagh
1912-1968 Obituary 93-96
MacDonald, Aeneas
See Thomson, George Malcolm
Macdonald, Alastair (A.) 1920- 136
MacDonald, Amy 1951- 135
MacDonald, Anne Elizabeth Campbell Bard
See MacDonald, Betty
See also MAICYA
Macdonald, Anne L. 1920- 136
MacDonald, Anson
See Heinlein, Robert A(nson)
MacDonald, Bernell 1948- 113
MacDonald, Betty 1908-1958 136
See also MacDonald, Anne Elizabeth Campbell Bard
See also YABC 1
Macdonald, Blackie
See Emrich, Duncan (Black Macdonald)
MacDonald, Bonnie 1941- 117
MacDonald, Charles B(rown)
1922-1990 ....CANR-23
Obituary 133
Earlier sketches in CA 9-12R, CANR-6
Macdonald, Coll 1924- 17-20R
MacDonald, Craig 1949- CANR-9
Earlier sketch in CA 57-60
Macdonald, Cynthia 1928- CANR-4
Earlier sketch in CA 49-52
See also CLC 13, 19
See also DLB 105
Macdonald, David W(hyte) 1951- 106
MacDonald, Dennis Ronald 1946- 111
Macdonald, Douglas J. 1947- 138
Macdonald, Dwight 1906-1982 ....29-32R
Obituary 108
See also SATA 29, 33
MacDonald, Edgar E(dgeworth) 1919- 115
MacDonald, Edwin A(nderson) 1907- 41-44R
MacDonald, Eleanor 1910- CAP-1
Earlier sketch in CA 9-10
Macdonald, Elisabeth 1926- 65-68
Macdonald, Finlay J. 1925- 132
MacDonald, George 1824-1905 137
Brief entry 106
See also DLB 18
See also MAICYA
See also SATA 33
See also TCLC 9
Macdonald, Gerard 1940- 119
MacDonald, Golden
See Brown, Margaret Wise
Macdonald, Gordon A(ndrew)
1911-1978 ....CANR-15
Earlier sketch in CA 65-68
Macdonald, H(enry) Malcolm 1914- 17-20R
MacDonald, Hope 1928- 135
MacDonald, J. Fred(erick) 1941- 130
Brief entry 117
MacDonald, Jake (M.) 1949- 126
Macdonald, John
See Millar, Kenneth
Macdonald, John (Barfoot) 1918- CANR-1
Earlier sketch in CA 49-52
MacDonald, John D(ann) 1916-1986 .....CANR-19
Obituary 121
Earlier sketches in CA 1-4R, CANR-1
See also CLC 3, 27, 44
See also DLB 8
See also DLBY 86
See also MTCW
Macdonald, John M. CANR-2
Earlier sketch in CA 1-4R
Macdonald, John Ross
See Millar, Kenneth
Macdonald, Julie 1926- 17-20R
Macdonald, Kenneth 1905- 73-76
Macdonald, Malcolm
See Ross-Macdonald, Malcolm J(ohn)
MacDonald, Malcolm John 1901-1981 ....9-12R
Obituary 102
MacDonald, Malcolm M(urdoch) 1935- 41-44R
Macdonald, Marcia
See Hill, Grace Livingston
MacDonald, Margaret Read 1940- CANR-27
Earlier sketch in CA 110
Macdonald, Mary
See Gifford, Griselda
Macdonald, Nancy (Gardiner Rodman)
1910- 126
Macdonald, Neil (William) 1936- 89-92
Macdonald, Nina Hansell
See Looker, Antonina (Hansell)
MacDonald, Norman Malcolm 1927- 130
MacDonald, Philip 1896(?)-1980 81-84
See also DLB 77
Macdonald, R. Ross 1923(?)-1983 Obituary 110
Macdonald, Robert M(unro) 1923- 9-12R
Macdonald, Robert S. 1925- 13-16R
Macdonald, Robert W. 1922- 17-20R
Macdonald, Ronald St. John 1928- 103
Macdonald, Ross
See Millar, Kenneth
See also CLC 1, 2, 3, 14, 34, 41
See also DLBD 6
MacDonald, Ruby (DeAngelo Norton)
1930- 115
MacDonald, Sandy 1949- 103
Macdonald, Shelagh 1937- 97-100
See also SATA 25
MacDonald, Simon G(avin) G(eorge)
1923- 53-56
MacDonald, Suse 1940- 125
See also SATA 52, 54
MacDonald, Timothy I(gnatius) 1941- 121
MacDonald, William L. 1921- 21-24R
MacDonald, Wilson 1880-1967 .... DLB 92
Macdonald, Zillah K(atherine) 1885- CAP-1
Earlier sketch in CA 9-10
See also SATA 11
Macdonnell, James Edmond 1917- CANR-8
Earlier sketch in CA 5-8R
MacDonnell, Kevin 1919- CANR-31
Earlier sketch in CA 45-48
MacDonnell, Megan
See Stevens, Serita (Deborah)
MacDonogh, Giles 1955- 132
MacDouall, Robertson
See Mair, George Brown
MacDougal, John
See Blish, James (Benjamin)
MacDougall, A(llan) Kent 1931- CANR-29
Earlier sketch in CA 45-48
MacDougall, Curtis D(aniel)
1903-1985 ....CANR-29
Obituary 117
Earlier sketch in CA 53-56
MacDougall, (George) Donald (Alastair)
1912- 106
MacDougall, Fiona
See MacLeod, Robert F.
MacDougall, Malcolm D(ouglas)
1928- Brief entry 110
MacDougall, Mary Katherine CANR-12
Earlier sketch in CA 29-32R
MacDougall, Ruth Doan 1939- CANR-8
Earlier sketch in CA 17-20R
MacDowell, Douglas M(aurice) 1931- CANR-6
Earlier sketch in CA 5-8R
MacDowell, John
See Parks, Tim(othy Harold)
Mace, C(ecil) Alec 1894- CAP-1
Earlier sketch in CA 13-14
Mace, Carroll Edward 1926- 41-44R
Mace, David Robert 1907-1990 ....CANR-23
Obituary 133
Earlier sketches in CA 57-60, CANR-7
Mace, Don 1899(?)-1983 Obituary 109
Mace, Elisabeth 1933- CANR-23
Earlier sketch in CA 77-80
See also SATA 27
Mace, Elizabeth Rhoda 1943- CANR-38
Mace, Myles L(a Grange) 1911- Brief entry 110
Mace, Nancy L(awson) 1941- 119
Mace, Varian 1938- ....SATA 49
Mace, Vera C(hapman) 1902- 113
MacEachern, Diane 1952- 133
Macedo, Stephen 1957- 138
MacEoin, Gary 1909- CANR-2
Earlier sketch in CA 1-4R
Macer-Story, E(ugenia) 1945- CANR-23
Earlier sketch in CA 107
Macesich, George 1927- 13-16R
MacEwan, J(ohn) W(alter) Grant 1902- 41-44R
MacEwan, Paul W. 1943- CANR-7
Earlier sketch in CA 61-64
MacEwen, Gwendolyn (Margaret)
1941-1987 ....CANR-22
Obituary 124
Earlier sketches in CA 9-12R, CANR-7
See also CLC 13, 55
See also DLB 53
See also SATA 50, 55
MacEwen, Malcolm 1911- 110
Macey, Samuel L(awson) 1922- 102
Macfadden, Bernarr 1868-1955 .... DLB 25, 91
MacFall, Russell P(atterson) 1903-1983 .... CAP-1
Obituary 110
Earlier sketch in CA 11-12
Macfarlan, Allan A. 1892-1982 107
See also SATA 35
Macfarlane, (Robert) Gwyn 1907-1987 131
Obituary 122
MacFarlane, Iris 1922- 89-92
See also SATA 11
MacFarlane, James Douglas 1916- 132
MacFarlane, Kenneth
See Walker, Kenneth Macfarlane
Macfarlane, Leslie John 1924- 21-24R
MacFarlane, Louise
1917(?)-1979 Obituary 89-92
MacFarlane, Neil 1936- 127
MacFarlane, Stephen
See Cross, John Keir
MacFarquhar, Roderick 1930- CANR-13
Earlier sketch in CA 21-24R
MacFee, Maxwell
See Rennie, James Alan
MacGaffey, Wyatt 1932- 73-76
MacGibbon, Jean 1913- 97-100
MacGill, Patrick 1890(?)-1963 116
MacGillivray, John H(enry) 1899- CAP-2
Earlier sketch in CA 25-28
MacGorman, J(ohn) W(illiam) 1920- 102
MacGowan, Christopher (John) 1948- 133
Macgowan, Jonathan
See Thurlow, David (Michael)
Macgowan, Kenneth 1888-1963 Obituary 93-96
MacGregor, Alasdair Alpin (Douglas)
1899-1970 ....CAP-1
Obituary 29-32R
Earlier sketch in CA 11-12
MacGregor, Bruce (Alan) 1945- 77-80
MacGregor, David Roy 1925- 93-96
MacGregor, Ellen 1906-1954 137
Brief entry 111
See also MAICYA
See also SATA 27, 39
Macgregor, Frances Cooke CANR-1
Earlier sketch in CA 1-4R
MacGregor, (John) Geddes 1909- CANR-21
Earlier sketches in CA 1-4R, CANR-2
MacGregor, James G(rierson) 1905- CANR-10
Earlier sketch in CA 25-28R
Macgregor, James (Murdoch) 1925- CANR-5
Earlier sketch in CA 13-16R
MacGregor, John M. 1941- 133
MacGregor, Loren J. 1950- 126
MacGregor, Malcolm D(ouglas) 1945- 102
MacGregor, Robert Mercer
1911-1974 Obituary 104
MacGregor, T. J.
See Janeshutz, Patricia M(arie)
MacGregor-Hastie, Roy (Alasdhair Niall)
1929- CANR-20
Earlier sketches in CA 1-4R, CANR-2
See also SATA 3
Macgregor-Morris, Pamela 1925- CANR-25
Earlier sketch in CA 29-32R
MacGuigan, Mark R(udolph) 1931- 21-24R
Mach, Elyse (Janet) 1941- 131
Machado, Eduardo 1953- 131
See also HW
Machado, Manuel Anthony Jr. 1939- 29-32R
Machado, Manuel 1874-1947 .... DLB 108
Machado (y Ruiz), Antonio
1875-1939 Brief entry 104
See also DLB 108
See also TCLC 3
Machado de Assis, Joaquim Maria
1839-1908 Brief entry 107
See also BLC 2
See also TCLC 10
Machan, Tibor R(ichard) 1939- CANR-1
Earlier sketch in CA 45-48
Machann, Clinton (John) 1947- 131
Machar, Agnes Maule 1837-1927 .... DLB 92
MacHardy, Charles 1926- 104
Machen, Arthur
See Jones, Arthur Llewellyn
See also DLB 36
See also TCLC 4
Machetanz, Frederick 1908- .... SATA 34
Machetanz, Sara Burleson 1918- 1-4R
Machiavelli
See McCready, Warren T(homas)
Machin, G(eorge) Ian T(hom) 1937- 13-16R
Machin Goodall, Daphne (Edith) CANR-7
Earlier sketch in CA 5-8R
See also SATA 37
Machlin, Milton Robert 1924- CANR-2
Earlier sketch in CA 1-4R
Machlis, Joseph 1906- CANR-22
Earlier sketches in CA 1-4R, CANR-2
Machlowitz, Marilyn M(arcia) 1952- 101
Machlup, Fritz 1902-1983 ....CANR-6
Obituary 109
Earlier sketch in CA 1-4R
Machol, Libby 1916- 21-24R
Machol, Robert E(ngel) 1917- 37-40R
Macholtz, James Donald 1926- 53-56
MacHorton, Ian
See Machorton, Ian (Duncan)
Machorton, Ian (Duncan) 1923- CANR-8
Earlier sketch in CA 17-20R
Machotka, Otakar (Richard) 1899-1970 ..... CAP-1
Obituary 29-32R
Earlier sketch in CA 13-16
Macht, Joel 1938- 57-60
Machung, Anne 1947- 133
Macia, Rafael 1946- 97-100
Maciel, Judi(th Anne) 1942- 33-36R
MacInnes, Colin 1914-1976 ....CANR-21
Obituary 65-68
Earlier sketch in CA 69-72
See also CLC 4, 23
See also DLB 14
See also MTCW
MacInnes, Helen (Clark) 1907-1985 ......CANR-28
Obituary 117
Earlier sketches in CA 1-4R, CANR-1
See also CLC 27, 39
See also DLB 87
See also MTCW
See also SATA 22, 44
MacInnis, Donald E(arl) 1920- 41-44R
MacIntosh, J(ohn) J(ames) 1934- 37-40R
MacIntosh, Joan 1924- 107
MacIntosh, Keitha 1954- 112
MacIntosh, Robert 1923- 137
MacIntyre, Alasdair (Chalmers) 1929- 128
Brief entry 118
Macintyre, Angus (Donald) 1935- 118
MacIntyre, Christine Melba
1939-1987 Obituary 123
MacIntyre, Donald George (Frederick Wyville)
1904- 5-8R
MacIntyre, Elisabeth 1916- CANR-5
Earlier sketch in CA 9-12R
See also SATA 17
MacIntyre, Michael 1939- 131
MacIntyre, Rod(erick Peter) 1947- 132
Macintyre, Stuart (Forbes) 1947- 131
MacIre, Esor B.
See Ambrose, Eric (Samuel)
MacIsaac, David 1935- CANR-31
Earlier sketches in CA 77-80, CANR-14
MacIsaac, Sharon 57-60
Maciuszko, Jerzy J. 1913- 25-28R
Maciuszko, Kathleen L(ynn) 1947- 113
MacIver, Robert M(orrison) 1882-1970 ...... CAP-1
Obituary 25-28R
Earlier sketch in CA 11-12
Mack, Carol K. 130
Mack, Charles R. 1940- 126
Mack, Edward C. 1905(?)-1973 Obituary 45-48
Mack, Evalina
See McNamara, Lena Brooke
Mack, Gerstle 1894-1983 129
Obituary 109
Mack, J. A. 1906- 65-68
Mack, James D(ecker) 1916- 21-24R
Mack, Jerry
See Johnson, Jerry Mack
Mack, John E(dward) 1929- 106
Mack, Karin E(ileen) 1946- 97-100
Mack, Kirby
See McEvoy, Harry K(irby)
Mack, Marjorie
See Dixon, Marjorie (Mack)
Mack, Mary Peter 1927-1973 ....1-4R
Obituary 103
Mack, Max Noble 1916- 61-64
Mack, Maynard 1909- CANR-25
Earlier sketch in CA 9-12R
See also DLB 111
Mack, Raymond (Wright) 1927- 13-16R
Mack, Stan(ley) 85-88
See also SATA 17
Mack, Walter Staunton 1895- 109
Mack, William P. 1915- 127
Mackal, Roy P(aul) 1925- 73-76
Mackaman, Frank H(indes) II 1950- 111
Mackarness, Richard 1916- 103
Mackay, Alan L(indsay) 1926- 137
MacKay, Alfred F(arnum) 1938- 104
MacKay, Alistair McColl 1931- 81-84
Mackay, Barbara E. 1944- 77-80
Mackay, Claire 1930- CANR-22
Earlier sketch in CA 105
See also SATA 40
Mackay, Constance D'Arcy 102
MacKay, D(onald) I(ain) 1937- CANR-24
Earlier sketch in CA 29-32R
Mackay, Donald (Alexander) 1914- 136
MacKay, Donald M(acCrimmon)
1922-1987 ....CANR-13
Obituary 121
Earlier sketch in CA 29-32R
Mackay, Harvey (B.) 1933(?)- 130
See also BEST 89:3
MacKay, Isabel Ecclestone 1875-1928 .... DLB 92
Mackay, James (Alexander) 1936- CANR-23
Earlier sketches in CA 53-56, CANR-7
Mackay, John Alexander
1889-1983 Obituary 110
MacKay, Joy 1918- 65-68
Mackay, Malcolm George 1919- 108
Mackay, Mary 1855-1924 Brief entry 118
See also Corelli, Marie
Mackay, Mercedes (Isabelle) 1906- CAP-1
Earlier sketch in CA 11-12
MacKay, Robert A(lexander) 1894- 9-12R
Mackay, Ruddock F(inlay) 1922- 102
Mackay, Shena 1944- 104
MacKay, William 1943(?)- Brief entry 110
MacKaye, Benton 1879-1975 Obituary 61-64
MacKaye, Milton 1901-1979 93-96
Obituary 85-88
MacKaye, Percy (Wallace)
1875-1956 Brief entry 113
See also DLB 54
See also SATA 32
MacKaye, William Ross 1934- Brief entry 109
MacKeever, Maggie
See Clark, Gail
MacKeith, Ronald Charles
1908-1977 Obituary 77-80
MacKellar, William 1914- CANR-13
Earlier sketch in CA 33-36R
See also SATA 4
Mackelworth, R(onald) W(alter) 1930- 29-32R
Macken, Walter 1915-1967 ....CAP-1
Obituary 25-28R
Earlier sketch in CA 13-14
See also DLB 13
See also SATA 36
Mackendrick, John 1946- 81-84
MacKendrick, Paul Lachlan 1914- CANR-1
Earlier sketch in CA 1-4R
Mackensen, Heinz Friedrich
1921- Brief entry 107

Mackenzie, Alastair (Ian Folliott) 1933- ... 118
Mackenzie, Alexander 1763-1820 ... DLB 99
MacKenzie, Andrew (Carr) 1911- ... CANR-29
Earlier sketch in CA 49-52
Mackenzie, Basil William Sholto
1900-1983 Obituary ... 111
MacKenzie, Christine Butchart 1917- ... 13-16R
Mackenzie, Compton (Edward Montague)
1883-1972 ... CAP-2
Obituary ... 37-40R
Earlier sketch in CA 21-22
See also CLC 18
See also DLB 34, 100
MacKenzie, David 1927- ... 21-24R
MacKenzie, Donald 1918- ... CANR-21
Earlier sketch in CA 25-28R
MacKenzie, Fred 1905- ... CAP-2
Earlier sketch in CA 25-28
Mackenzie, Garry 1921- ... SATA 31
Mackenzie, Henry 1745-1831 ... DLB 39
MacKenzie, Jean 1928- ... 93-96
Mackenzie, (Daisy) Jeanne 1922-1986 ... 130
Obituary ... 120
MacKenzie, John P(ettibone) 1930- ... 65-68
Mackenzie, Kathleen Guy 1907- ... 5-8R
Mackenzie, Kenneth Donald 1937- ... 37-40R
Mackenzie, Kenneth (Ivo)
1913-1955 Brief entry ... 122
Mackenzie, Locke L.
1900(?)-1977 Obituary ... 69-72
Mackenzie, Louise (Wilks) 1920- ... 29-32R
Mackenzie, Manfred 1934- ... 65-68
MacKenzie, Norman H(ugh) 1915- ... 21-24R
MacKenzie, Norman (Ian) 1921- ... 130
MacKenzie, Ossian 1907-1980 ... 25-28R
Obituary ... 120
MacKenzie, R(oderick) A(ndrew) F(rancis)
1911- ... 5-8R
Mackenzie, R. Alec
See Mackenzie, Richard Alexander
MacKenzie, Rachel 1909-1980 ... 102
Obituary ... 97-100
Mackenzie, Richard Alexander 1923- ... 109
Mackenzie, Seaforth
See Mackenzie, Kenneth (Ivo)
Mackenzie, Suzanne 1950- ... 136
Mackenzie, W(illiam) J(ames) M(illar) 1909- ... 104
Mackenzie-Grieve, Averil (Salmond)
1903- ... 9-12R
Mackerras, Colin Patrick 1939- ... CANR-33
Earlier sketches in CA 85-88, CANR-15
Mackesy, Piers G(erald) 1924- ... CANR-3
Earlier sketch in CA 9-12R
MacKethan, Lucinda Hardwick 1945- ... 102
Mackey, Ernan
See McInerny, Ralph
Mackey, Helen T. 1918- ... 5-8R
Mackey, J(ames) P(atrick) 1934- ... CANR-9
Earlier sketch in CA 65-68
Mackey, Louis H(enry) 1926- ... 33-36R
Mackey, Mary 1945- ... CANR-15
Earlier sketch in CA 77-80
Mackey, Sandra 1937- ... 127
Mackey, William Francis 1918- ... 37-40R
Mackey, William J. Jr.
1902(?)-1972 Obituary ... 37-40R
Mackey, William Wellington 1937- ... 124
Brief entry ... 120
See also BW
See also DLB 38
Mackie, Alastair 1925- ... 17-20R
Mackie, Albert D(avid) 1904- ... CAP-1
Earlier sketch in CA 9-10
Mackie, J(ohn) L(eslie) 1917- ... CANR-7
Earlier sketch in CA 57-60
Mackie, (Benjamin) James 1932- ... 41-44R
Mackie, John
See Levinson, Leonard
Mackie, Margaret Davidson 1914- ... 102
Mackie, Maron
See McNeely, Jeannette
Mackie, Philip 1918-1985 ... 103
Obituary ... 118
Mackiewicz, Jozef 1902-1985 Obituary ... 116
MacKillop, James (John) 1939- ... 113
Mackin, Anita
See Donson, Cyril
Mackin, Catherine (Patricia) 1939-1982 ... 109
Obituary ... 108
Mackin, Cooper R(icherson) 1933- ... 41-44R
Mackin, Dorothy (May Mabee) 1917- ... 107
Mackin, Edward
See McInerny, Ralph
Mackin, Jeanne 1951- ... 134
Mackin, John H(oward) 1921- ... 33-36R
Mackin, Theodore 1922- ... 116
Mackinlay, Leila Antoinette Sterling
1910- ... CANR-24
Earlier sketches in CAP-1, CA 11-12
Mackinlock, Duncan
See Watts, Peter Christopher
MacKinnon, Bernie 1957- ... 137
See also SATA 69
MacKinnon, Catharine A. 1946- ... 132
Brief entry ... 128
Mackinnon, Charles Roy 1924- ... CANR-7
Earlier sketch in CA 9-12R
MacKinnon, Edward M(ichael) 1928- ... CANR-12
Earlier sketch in CA 61-64
MacKinnon, Frank 1919- ... 49-52
MacKinnon, John Ramsay 1947- ... 103
Mackinnon, Marianne 1925- ... 128
MacKinnon, Stephen Robert 1940- ... CANR-36
Earlier sketch in CA 107
MacKinnon Groomer, Vera 1915- ... SATA 57
MacKinstry, Elizabeth 1879-1956 ... SATA 42
Mackintosh, Athole S(palding) 1926-1977 ... 5-8R
Obituary ... 134
Mackintosh, Elizabeth
1896(?)-1952 Brief entry ... 110
See also Daviot, Gordon
and Tey, Josephine
MacKintosh, Graham (D.) 1951- ... 132
MacKintosh, Ian 1940- ... 73-76
Mackintosh, John (Pitcairn) 1929-1978 ... 103
Mackintosh, (John) Malcolm 1921- ... 5-8R
Mackintosh, N(icholas) J(ohn) 1935- ... 124
Mackintosh, Prudence 1944- ... 124
Mackle, Jeff
See McLeod, John F(reeland)
Mackler, Bernard 1934- ... 21-24R
Mackley, George 1900-1983 Obituary ... 109
Macklin, Barbara J(une) 1925- Brief entry ... 118
Macklin, Charles 1699-1797 ... DLB 89
Macklin, June
See Macklin, Barbara J(une)
MacKnight, Nancy (Margaret) 1940- ... 118
Mackowski, Richard M(artin) 1929- ... 106
Macksey, (Catherine Angela) Joan 1925- ... 65-68
Macksey, Kenneth J. 1923- ... CANR-30
Earlier sketches in CA 25-28R, CANR-11
Macksey, Major K. J.
See Macksey, Kenneth J.
Macksey, Richard (Alan) 1930- ... 101
Mack Smith, Denis 1920- ... CANR-39
Earlier sketches in CA 21-24R, CANR-17
Mackworth, Cecily ... 57-60
Mackworth, Jane F. 1917- ... 37-40R
Macky, Peter W(allace) 1937- ... 53-56
MacLachlan, James Angell 1891-1967 ... CAP-2
Earlier sketch in CA 19-20
Maclachlan, Lewis 1894-1980 ... CANR-6
Earlier sketch in CA 5-8R
MacLachlan, Patricia 1938- ... 136
Brief entry ... 118
See also CLR 14
See also MAICYA
See also SATA 42, 62
Maclagan, Bridget
See Borden, Mary
Maclagan, Michael 1914- ... 5-8R
MacLaine, Allan H(ugh) 1924- ... 13-16R
MacLaine, Shirley 1934- ... CANR-32
Earlier sketch in CA 103
MacLane, Jack
See Crider, (Allen) Bill(y)
MacLaren, A. Allan 1938- ... 106
Maclaren, Colin Shaw 1898-1985 Obituary ... 116
MacLaren, James
See Grieve, C(hristopher) M(urray)
MacLaren, Sherrill M. 1939- ... 124
Mac Laverty, Bernard 1942- ... 118
Brief entry ... 116
See also CLC 31
Maclay, George 1943- ... 45-48
Maclay, Joanna Hawkins 1938- ... 112
Maclean, Alasdair 1926- Brief entry ... 113
MacLean, Alistair (Stuart) 1922-1987 ... CANR-28
Obituary ... 121
Earlier sketch in CA 57-60
See also CLC 3, 13, 50, 63
See also MTCW
See also SATA 23, 50
Maclean, Arthur
See Tubb, E(dwin) C(harles)
MacLean, Barbara Anne Hutmacher
See Hutmacher (MacLean), Barbara Anne
Maclean, Charles 1946- ... 109
Maclean, Donald Duart
1913-1983 Obituary ... 109
Maclean, Fitzroy (Hew) 1911- ... CANR-31
Earlier sketches in CA 29-32R, CANR-14
MacLean, Harry N(orman) 1942- ... 130
See also BEST 90:3
MacLean, Jane 1935- ... 101
MacLean, Janet Rockwood 1917- ... 33-36R
MacLean, Katherine 1925- ... 33-36R
See also DLB 8
Maclean, Norman (Fitzroy) 1902-1990 ... 102
Obituary ... 132
Maclean, Una 1925- ... 69-72
MacLeish, Andrew 1923- ... 17-20R
MacLeish, Archibald 1892-1982 ... CANR-33
Obituary ... 106
Earlier sketch in CA 9-12R
See also CLC 3, 8, 14, 68
See also DLB 4, 7, 45
See also DLBY 82
See also MTCW
MacLeish, Kenneth 1917-1977 ... 81-84
Obituary ... 73-76
MacLeish, Rod(erick) 1926- ... 41-44R
MacLeish, William H(itchcock) 1928- ... 120
MacLennan, David Alexander
1903-1978 ... CANR-2
Earlier sketch in CA 1-4R
MacLennan, (John) Hugh 1907- ... CANR-33
Earlier sketch in CA 5-8R
See also CLC 2, 14
See also DLB 68
See also MTCW
MacLennan, Toby 1939- ... 115
Macleod, Alison 1920- ... 53-56
MacLeod, Alistair 1936- ... 123
See also CLC 56
See also DLB 60
MacLeod, Ann 1940- ... 138
MacLeod, Beatrice (Beach) 1910- ... CAP-1
Earlier sketch in CA 19-20
See also SATA 10
MacLeod, Celeste (Lipow) 1931- ... 105
MacLeod, Charlotte (Matilda Hughes)
1922- ... CANR-18
Earlier sketch in CA 21-24R
See also SATA 28
Macleod, David I(rving Jr.) 1943- ... 123
Macleod, Donald 1914- ... 17-20R
MacLeod, Doug 1959- ... 112
See also SATA 60
MacLeod, Duncan J(ohn) 1939- ... 61-64
MacLeod, Earle Henry 1907- ... CAP-1
Earlier sketch in CA 9-10
MacLeod, Ellen Jane (Anderson)
1916- ... CANR-3
Earlier sketch in CA 5-8R
See also SATA 14
MacLeod, Jay 1961- ... 126
MacLeod, Jean Sutherland 1908- ... CANR-3
Earlier sketch in CA 9-12R
Macleod, Jennifer Selfridge 1929- ... 102
Macleod, Joseph (Todd Gordon)
1903-1984(?) ... 65-68
Obituary ... 112
Macleod, Norman (Wicklund) 1906-1985 ... 73-76
Obituary ... 116
See also DLB 4
MacLeod, Robert
See Knox, William
MacLeod, Robert F. 1917- ... 77-80
MacLeod, Roderick 1892(?)-1984 Obituary ... 113
MacLeod, Ruth 1903- ... 93-96
Mac Liammhoir, Micheal
See Mac Liammoir, Micheal
Mac Liammhoir, Micheal
See Mac Liammoir, Micheal
Mac Liammoir, Micheal 1899-1978 ... CANR-3
Obituary ... 77-80
Earlier sketch in CA 45-48
Mac Low, Jackson 1922- ... 81-84
Maclure, (John) Stuart 1926- ... 61-64
MacLysaght, Edward Anthony
1887-1986 ... CANR-1
Obituary ... 118
Earlier sketch in CA 1-4R
Macmahon, Arthur W(hittier) 1890-1980 ... 17-20R
Obituary ... 135
MacMahon, Bryan (Michael) 1909- ... CANR-23
Earlier sketch in CA 41-44R
MacMahon, Candace W(addell) 1950- ... 112
Macmann, Elaine
See Willoughby, Elaine Macmann
MacManus, James
See MacManus, Seumas
MacManus, Seumas 1869-1960 ... 102
Obituary ... 93-96
See also SATA 25
Macmanus, Sheila 1946- ... 111
MacManus, Susan A(nn) 1947- ... 116
MacManus, Yvonne 1931- ... CANR-11
Earlier sketch in CA 25-28R
MacMaster, Eve (Ruth) B(owers) 1942- ... 112
See also SATA 46
MacMaster, Richard Kerwin 1935- ... 115
Mac Master, Robert E(llsworth) 1919- ... 33-36R
MacMillan, Annabelle
See Quick, Annabelle
Macmillan, C(harles) J(ames) B(arr)
1935- ... 21-24R
MacMillan, Cecile 1898(?)-1986 Obituary ... 120
Macmillan, David S(tirling) 1925- ... 113
MacMillan, Donald L(ee) 1940- ... 57-60
MacMillan, Gail 1944- ... 97-100
Macmillan, (Maurice) Harold 1894-1986 ... 128
Obituary ... 121
Brief entry ... 113
Macmillan, James
See Brown, Hamish M.
Macmillan, Maurice Victor
1921-1984 Obituary ... 112
Macmillan, Mona 1908- ... 33-36R
Macmillan, Norman 1892-1976 ... CAP-1
Obituary ... 69-72
Earlier sketch in CA 11-12
Macmillan, William Miller 1885-1974 ... CANR-9
Obituary ... 53-56
Earlier sketches in CAP-1, CA 11-12
MacMullan, Charles Walden Kirkpatrick
1889-1973 Obituary ... 89-92
MacMullen, Ramsay 1928- ... CANR-13
Earlier sketch in CA 21-24R
Macnab, Francis Auchline 1931- ... 25-28R
MacNab, P(eter) A(ngus) 1903- ... 33-36R
Macnab, Roy 1923- ... 65-68
MacNalty, Arthur (Salusbury)
1880-1969 ... CANR-5
Earlier sketch in CA 5-8R
MacNamara, Brinsley
See Weldon, John
See also DLB 10
Mac Namara, Donal E(oin) J(oseph)
1916- ... CANR-14
Earlier sketch in CA 33-36R
Macnamara, Ellen 1924- ... 103
Macnamara, John (Theodore) 1929- ... CANR-13
Earlier sketch in CA 21-24R
Macnaughton, William R(obert) 1939- ... 119
MacNeice, Jill 1956- ... 115
MacNeice, (Frederick) Louis 1907-1963 ... 85-88
See also CLC 1, 4, 10, 53
See also DLB 10, 20
See also MTCW
MacNeil, Duncan
See McCutchan, Philip (Donald)
Macneil, Ian R(oderick) 1929- ... 33-36R
MacNeil, Neil
See Ballard, (Willis) Todhunter
MacNeil, Neil 1891-1969 ... CAP-1
Obituary ... 29-32R
Earlier sketch in CA 19-20
MacNeil, Robert (Breckenridge Ware)
1931- ... 114
Brief entry ... 108
See also BEST 89:3
MacNeill, Alastair (John) 1960- ... 130
MacNeill, Dand
See Fraser, George MacDonald
MacNeill, Earl S(chwom)
1893-1972 Obituary ... 37-40R
Macneill, Janet
See McNeely, Jeannette
Macneill, Norma 1922- ... 117
MacNeish, Richard S(tockton) 1918- ... 37-40R
Macnell, James
See Macdonnell, James Edmond
MacNelly, C(larence) L(amont)
1920(?)-1986 Obituary ... 118
MacNelly, Jeff(rey Kenneth) 1947- ... 102
MacNib
See Mackie, Albert D(avid)
MacNicholas, John (Malcolm) 1943- ... 123
Brief entry ... 118
Macnicol, Eona K(athleen) Fraser 1910- ... 9-12R
MacNutt, Francis S. 1925- ... CANR-12
Earlier sketch in CA 73-76
Macomber, Daria
See Robinson, Patricia Colbert
Macomber, William (Butts Jr.) 1921- ... 61-64
Mac Orlan, Pierre
See Dumarchais, Pierre
MacPeek, Walter G. 1902-1973 ... CAP-2
Obituary ... 41-44R
Earlier sketch in CA 29-32
See also SATA 4, 25
Macphail, Andrew 1864-1938 ... DLB 92
MacPhearson, James
See Wright, John L.
Macpherson, C(rawford) Brough
1911-1987 ... CANR-2
Obituary ... 123
Earlier sketch in CA 5-8R
Macpherson, James (Campbell) 1942- ... 136
Macpherson, James 1736-1796 ... DLB 109
Macpherson, (Jean) Jay 1931- ... 5-8R
See also CLC 14
See also DLB 53
Macpherson, Jeanie 1884-1946 Brief entry ... 123
See also DLB 44
Macpherson, Kenneth
1903(?)-1971 Obituary ... 29-32R
MacPherson, Malcolm C(ook) 1943- ... CANR-24
Earlier sketch in CA 102
MacPherson, Margaret 1908- ... 49-52
See also SAAS 4
See also SATA 9
MacPherson, Thomas George
1915-1976 ... CANR-4
Earlier sketch in CA 1-4R
See also SATA 30
Macquarrie, Alan (Denis) 1954- ... 122
Macquarrie, Heath Nelson 1919- ... CANR-20
Earlier sketch in CA 41-44R
Macquarrie, John 1919- ... CANR-29
Earlier sketches in CA 1-4R, CANR-1
Macqueen, James G(alloway) 1932- ... 17-20R
MacQueen, John 1929- ... 133
MacQueen, Winifred (Wallace) 1928- ... 133
MacQuitty, William ... CANR-7
Earlier sketch in CA 17-20R
MacRae, C(hristopher) Fred(erick) 1909- ... 45-48
MacRae, Donald E. 1907- ... 93-96
MacRae, Donald G. 1921- ... 13-16R
MacRae, Duncan (Jr.) 1921- ... 21-24R
MacRae, George W(insor)
1928-1985 Obituary ... 117
Macrae, John Jr. 1898(?)-1983 Obituary ... 111
Macrae, Marjorie Knight Obituary ... 41-44R
Macrae, Norman 1923- ... CANR-22
Earlier sketch in CA 106
Macrae, Travis
See Feagles, Anita M(acRae)
Macridis, Roy C(onstantine) 1918-1991 ... 115
Obituary ... 136
Macro, Eric 1920- ... CANR-32
Earlier sketch in CA 29-32R
Macrorie, Ken(neth) 1918- ... 65-68
Macrow, Brenda G(race Joan) Barton
1916- ... 9-12R
MacShane, Denis 1948- ... 109
MacShane, Frank 1927- ... CANR-33
Earlier sketches in CA 9-12R, CANR-3
See also CLC 39
See also DLB 111
MacStiofain, Sean
See Stephenson, John Edward Drayton
MacSweeney, Barry 1948- ... CANR-20
Earlier sketch in CA 25-28R
MacTaggart, Morna Doris
See Brown, Morna Doris
MacThomais, Ruaraidh
See Thomson, Derick S(mith)
Macumber, Mari
See Sandoz, Mari(e Susette)
Macura, Paul 1924- ... CANR-8
Earlier sketch in CA 17-20R
MacVane, John (Franklin) 1912-1984 ... CANR-16
Obituary ... 111
Earlier sketch in CA 65-68
Macvaugh, Gilbert S(tillman)
1902-1990 Obituary ... 131
MacVeagh, Lincoln 1890-1972 Obituary ... 33-36R
MacVean, Jean ... 131
Macvey, John W(ishart) 1923- ... CANR-7
Earlier sketch in CA 17-20R

MacVicar, Angus 1908- CANR-30
Earlier sketches in CA 13-16R, CANR-10
Macy, Helen 1904(?)-1978 Obituary 81-84
Macy, Joanna Rogers 1929- 125
Macy, John W(illiams) Jr. 1917-1986 ....33-36R
Obituary 121
Macy, Mike 1951- 122
Madachy, Joseph S(teven) 1927- 5-8R
Madame Simone
See Porche, Simone (Benda)
Madan, T(riloki) N(ath) 1931- CANR-7
Earlier sketch in CA 17-20R
Madaras, Area 1969- 116
Madaras, Lynda 1947- 107
Madariaga, Isabel de
See de Madariaga, Isabel
Madariaga (Y Rojo), Salvador de
1886-1978 ....CANR-32
Obituary 81-84
Earlier sketches in CA 9-12R, CANR-6
See also HW
Maday, Bela C(harles) 1912- 41-44R
Madden, Arthur Gerard 1911- 1-4R
Madden, Betty I(senbarger) 1915- 57-60
Madden, Bill 1945- 133
Madden, Carl H(alford) 1920-1978 ....41-44R
Obituary 81-84
Madden, Cecil (Charles)
1902-1987 Obituary 122
Madden, Charles F(rank) 1921- 25-28R
Madden, Daniel Michael 1916- 65-68
Madden, (Jerry) David 1933- CANR-4
Earlier sketch in CA 1-4R
See also CAAS 3
See also CLC 5, 15
See also DLB 6
See also MTCW
Madden, Deirdre 1960- 133
Madden, Don 1927- 25-28R
See also SATA 3
Madden, Donald L(eo) 1937- CANR-4
Earlier sketch in CA 53-56
Madden, E(dward) S(tanislaus) 1919- 9-12R
Madden, Edward H. 1925- CANR-1
Earlier sketch in CA 1-4R
Madden, Henry Miller 1912-1982 Obituary 108
Madden, Myron C(rowson) 1918- 115
Madden, Peter 1939- 115
Madden, Richard Raymond 1924- 5-8R
Madden, Tara Roth 1942- 126
Madden, Warren
See Cameron, Kenneth Neill
Madden, William A. 1923- 21-24R
Maddern, Al(an)
See Ellison, Harlan
Madderom, Gary 1937- 45-48
Maddex, Jack P(endleton) Jr.
1941- Brief entry 111
Maddi, Salvatore R(ichard) 1933- 13-16R
Maddison, Angela Mary 1923- 53-56
See also Banner, Angela
See also SATA 10
Maddison, Angus 1926- CANR-10
Earlier sketch in CA 13-16R
Maddison, Carol Hopkins 1923- 17-20R
Maddock, Brent 1950- 81-84
Maddock, Kenneth Obituary 104
Maddock, Larry
See Jardine, Jack
Maddock, Mary (Denise Catharine Majdak)
1951- 116
Maddock, Reginald (Bertram) 1912- 81-84
See also SATA 15
Maddocks, Margaret (Kathleen Avern)
1906- 116
Maddocks, Morris Henry St. John 1928- 116
Maddow, Ben 1909- ....DLB 44
Maddox, Brenda 1932- CANR-22
Earlier sketch in CA 97-100
Maddox, Carl
See Tubb, E(dwin) C(harles)
Maddox, Conroy 1912- 101
Maddox, Gaynor 9-12R
Maddox, George L(amar) Jr. 1925- 17-20R
Maddox, James G(ray) 1907-1973 ....CAP-2
Obituary 45-48
Earlier sketch in CA 21-22
Maddox, Jerrold (Warren) 1932- 17-20R
Maddox, Lester (Garfield) 1915- Brief entry 112
Maddox, Marion Errol 1910- 21-24R
Maddox, Robert James 1931- 33-36R
Maddox, Russell W(ebber) Jr. 1921- 1-4R
Maddox, Sara Higgins Sturm
See Sturm-Maddox, Sara Higgins
Maddux, Rachel 1912- CANR-5
Earlier sketch in CA 1-4R
Madeleva, Sister Mary
See Wolff, Mary Evaline
Madelung, A. Margaret (Arent) 1926- 13-16R
Mader, (Stanley) Chris(topher Jr.)
1943(?)-1980 Obituary 103
Mader, Katherine 1948- 126
Madge, Charles Henry 1912- 97-100
Madge, John (Hylton) 1914-1968 ....CAP-1
Earlier sketch in CA 9-10
Madge, Nicola 1949- 130
Madge, Violet 1916- CAP-2
Earlier sketch in CA 21-22
Madgett, Naomi Long 1923- CANR-29
Earlier sketches in CA 33-36R, CANR-13
See also BW
See also DLB 76
Madgwick, P(eter) J(ames) 1925- CANR-24
Earlier sketch in CA 29-32R
Madhubuti, Haki R. 1942- CANR-24
Earlier sketch in CA 73-76
See also Lee, Don L.
See also BLC 2
See also BW
See also CLC 6
See also DLB 5, 41
See also DLBD 8
See also PC 5
Madian, Jon 1941- 61-64
See also SATA 9
Madigan, Marian East 1898- CAP-2
Earlier sketch in CA 19-20
Madigan, Mary Jean Smith 1941- 110
Madison, Alfreda Louise
1911-1989 Obituary 129
Madison, Arnold 1937- CANR-9
Earlier sketch in CA 21-24R
See also SATA 6
Madison, Charles A(llan) 1895- CANR-1
Earlier sketch in CA 1-4R
Madison, Frank
See Hutchins, Francis Gilman
Madison, Gary (Brent) 1940- 131
Madison, Hank
See Rowland, D(onald) S(ydney)
Madison, James H. 1944- 138
Madison, James 1751-1836 ....DLB 37
Madison, Jane
See Horne, Hugh Robert
Madison, Joyce
See Mintz, Joyce Lois
Madison, Peter 1918- 9-12R
Madison, Russ 1929- 25-28R
Madison, Thomas A(lvin) 1926- 57-60
Madison, Tom
See Madison, Thomas A(lvin)
Madison, Winifred 37-40R
See also SATA 5
Madle, Dorothy
See Madlee, Dorothy (Haynes)
Madlee, Dorothy (Haynes)
1917-1980 ....CANR-10
Earlier sketch in CA 17-20R
Madott, Darlene (Patrice) 1952- 123
Madow, Leo 1915- CANR-13
Earlier sketch in CA 33-36R
Madow, Pauline (Reichberg) 9-12R
See also CLC 1
Madrigal, Margarita 1912(?)-1983 Obituary 110
Madruga, Lenor 1942- 102
Madsen, Axel 1930- CANR-33
Earlier sketch in CA 25-28R
Madsen, Borge Gedso 1920- 1-4R
Madsen, Brigham Dwaine 1914- 103
Madsen, David Lawrence 1929- 21-24R
Madsen, (Mark) Hunter 1955- 133
Madsen, Richard (Paul) 1941- 123
Madsen, Roy Paul 1928- 89-92
Madsen, Truman Grant 1926- Brief entry 106
Madubuike, Ihechukwu (Chiedozie) 1943- 134
Maduell, Charles Rene Jr. 1918- 73-76
Mae, Eydie
See Hunsberger, Edith Mae
Maeder, Thomas 1951- 132
Maedke, Wilmer O(tto) 1922- 57-60
Maehl, William H(arvey) 1915- 89-92
Maehl, William Henry Jr. 1930- 21-24R
Maehlqvist, (Karl) Stefan 1943- CANR-24
Earlier sketch in CA 107
See also Mahlqvist, (Karl) Stefan
See also SATA 30
Maenchen, Otto John 1894-1969 Obituary 109
Maenchen-Helfen, Otto J.
See Maenchen, Otto John
Maend, Evald
See Mand, Ewald
Maepenn, Hugh
See Kuttner, Henry
Maepenn, K. H.
See Kuttner, Henry
Maeroff, Gene I(rving) 1939- 61-64
Maertz, Richard Charles 1935- 73-76
Maes-Jelinek, Hena 1929- 107
Maestro, Betsy C(rippen) 1944- CANR-37
Earlier sketches in CA 61-64, CANR-8, 23
See also MAICYA
See also SATA 30, 59
Maestro, Giulio 1942- CANR-37
Earlier sketches in CA 57-60, CANR-8, 23
See also MAICYA
See also SATA 8, 59
Maeterlinck, Maurice 1862-1949 136
Brief entry 104
See also SATA 66
See also TCLC 3
Maffei, Paolo 1926- CANR-25
Earlier sketch in CA 108
Magalaner, Marvin 1920- CANR-1
Earlier sketch in CA 1-4R
Magaret, Helene 1906- 1-4R
Magarshack, David 1899-1977 ....CANR-29
Earlier sketch in CA 5-8R
Magary, Alan 1944- CANR-8
Earlier sketch in CA 61-64
Magary, James F(rederick) 1933- 25-28R
Magary, Kerstin Fraser 1947- CANR-12
Earlier sketch in CA 61-64
Magdalany, Philip 1936(?)-1985 Obituary 117
Magdol, Edward 1918- CANR-9
Earlier sketch in CA 21-24R
Magee, Bryan 1930- CANR-2
Earlier sketch in CA 5-8R
Magee, David (Bickersteth) 1905-1977 81-84
Obituary 73-76
Magee, John 1901-1987 Obituary 122
Magee, Wes 1939- CANR-23
Earlier sketch in CA 107
See also SATA 64
Mager, George C(lyde) 1937- 49-52
Mager, Nathan H. 1912-1986 ....CANR-18
Earlier sketches in CA 45-48, CANR-2
Maggal, Moshe M(orris) 1908- CAP-2
Earlier sketch in CA 23-24
Maggin, Elliot S. 1950- 102
Maggio, Joe 1938- CANR-1
Earlier sketch in CA 45-48
Maggio, Rosalie 1943- 130
See also SATA 69
Maggiolo, Marcio E. Veloz
See Veloz Maggiolo, Marcio E.
Maggiolo, Walter A(ndrew) 1908- 85-88
Maggs, Peter B(lount) 1936- CANR-23
Earlier sketches in CA 17-20R, CANR-8
Maggs, Will(iam) Colston 1912- 13-16R
Magid, Ken(neth Marshall) 128
See also SATA 65
Magidoff, Robert 1905-1970 ....CAP-1
Earlier sketch in CA 19-20
Magidson, Herbert (Adolph)
1906-1986 Obituary 118
Magill, Frank N(orthen) 1907- CANR-6
Earlier sketch in CA 5-8R
Magill, Kathleen 1948- 116
Magill, Marcus
See Hill, Brian (Merrikin)
Magill, Robert S(amuel) 1941- 89-92
Maginn, William 1794-1842 ....DLB 110
Maginnis, Andrew Francis 1923- 45-48
Magister, Joseph
See Grant, Louis T(heodore)
Magloire-Saint-Aude, Clement 1912- 13-16R
Magnarella, Paul J(oseph) 93-96
Magner, James A. 1901- CAP-1
Earlier sketch in CA 13-14
Magner, James Edmund Jr. 1928- CANR-7
Earlier sketch in CA 17-20R
Magner, Thomas F(reeman) 1918- 17-20R
Magnin, Cyril I(saac) 1899-1988 107
Obituary 125
Magnus, Philip
See Magnus-Allcroft, Philip (Montefiore)
Magnus, Samuel Woolf 1910- CAP-1
Earlier sketch in CA 9-10
Magnus-Allcroft, Philip (Montefiore)
1906-1988 ....CAP-1
Obituary 127
Earlier sketch in CA 11-12
Magnuson, Don(ald Hammer)
1911-1979 Obituary 89-92
Magnuson, Edward F. 1926- 102
Magnuson, Keith (Arlen) 1947- 93-96
Magnuson, Paul Budd 1884-1968 Obituary 106
Magnuson, Paul 1939- 69-72
Magnuson, Warren G(rant) 1905- 85-88
Magnussen, Daniel Osar 1919- 65-68
Magnusson, Magnus 1929- CANR-23
Earlier sketch in CA 105
Magog, Paul Dowsey
See Dowsey-Magog, Paul
Magoon, Robert A(rnold) 1922- CANR-24
Earlier sketch in CA 107
Magorian, Christopher 1959- 111
Magorian, James 1942- CANR-18
Earlier sketch in CA 102
See also SATA 32
Magorian, Michelle 1947- 135
See also MAICYA
See also SATA 67
Magoun, F(rederick) Alexander 1896- CAP-2
Earlier sketch in CA 17-18
Magoun, Francis P(eabody) Jr.
1895-1979(?) 107
Magowan, Robin 1936- CANR-20
Earlier sketches in CA 9-12R, CANR-4
Magrath, C(laude) Peter 1933- 17-20R
Magrid, Henry M. 1918(?)-1979 Obituary 89-92
Magriel, Paul (David)
1906(?)-1990 Obituary 132
Magris, Claudio 1939- 133
Magruder, Jeb Stuart 1934- 101
Magsam, Charles Michael 1907- CAP-1
Earlier sketch in CA 13-16
Magubane, Bernard (Makhosezwe) 1930- 93-96
Maguen, David
See Markish, David
Maguinness, W(illiam) Stuart 1903-1982 ....CAP-1
Obituary 108
Earlier sketch in CA 13-16
Maguire, Anne
See Nearing, Penny
Maguire, Daniel Charles 1931- CANR-32
Earlier sketch in CA 49-52
Maguire, Francis T(homas)
1911-1976 Obituary 69-72
Maguire, Gregory 1954- 81-84
See also SATA 28
Maguire, Henry Pownall 1943- 111
Maguire, Jack 1920- 81-84
Maguire, John David 1932- CANR-9
Earlier sketch in CA 21-24R
Maguire, John T(homas) 1917- 1-4R
Maguire, Michael 1945- 104
Maguire, R(obert) A(ugustine) J(oseph)
1898- 5-8R
Maguire, Robert A(lan) 1930- 73-76
Magwood, John McLean 1912- 106
Mahaffey, Vicki 1952- 133
Mahajan, Vidya Dhar 1913- CANR-29
Earlier sketches in CA 25-28R, CANR-11
Mahajani, Usha 1933- 53-56
Mahan, Alfred Thayer 1840-1914 ....DLB 47
Mahan, Bill
See Mahan, William Allen
Mahan, Pat
See Wheat, Patte
Mahan, Patte Wheat
See Wheat, Patte
Mahan, William Allen 1930- CANR-15
Earlier sketch in CA 85-88
Mahapatra, Jayanta 1928- CANR-33
Earlier sketches in CA 73-76, CANR-15
See also CAAS 9
See also CLC 33
Mahar, J. Michael 1929- 13-16R
Mahdi, Muhsin S(ayyid) 1926- CANR-3
Earlier sketch in CA 1-4R
Maher, Brendan A(rnold) 1924- 25-28R
Maher, James T(homas) 1917- 65-68
Maher, John E. 1925- 17-20R
Maher, Ramona 1934- CANR-9
Earlier sketch in CA 21-24R
See also SATA 13
Maher, Robert F. 1922- 17-20R
Maher, Trafford P(atrick) 1914- 21-24R
Maheshwari, Shriram 1931- CANR-30
Earlier sketches in CA 21-24R, CANR-11
Maheux-Forcier, Louise 1929- ....DLB 60
Mahfouz, Naguib (Abdel Aziz Al-Sabilgi)
1911(?)- 128
See also Mahfuz, Najib
See also BEST 89:2
See also MTCW
Mahfuz, Najib
See Mahfouz, Naguib (Abdel Aziz Al-Sabilgi)
See also CLC 52, 55
See also DLBY 88
Mahin, John Lee 1902(?)-1984 Obituary 112
See also DLB 44
Mahindra, Indira 1926- 136
Mahl, George F(ranklin) 1917- 93-96
Mahl, Mary R. 1914- 25-28R
Mahlendorf, Ursula R. 1929- 49-52
Mahler, Gregory S. 1950- 123
Mahler, Jane Gaston 1906- 37-40R
Mahler, Margaret S(choenberger)
1897-1985 103
Obituary 117
Mahlqvist, (Karl) Stefan
See Maehlqvist, (Karl) Stefan
See also SATA 30
Mahmood, Mamdani 1946- 105
Maholick, Leonard T(homas) 1921- CANR-1
Earlier sketch in CA 1-4R
Mahon, Derek 1941- 128
Brief entry 113
See also CLC 27
See also DLB 40
Mahon, John K(eith) 1912- 17-20R
Mahon, Julia C(unha) 1916- 61-64
See also SATA 11
Mahon, Thomas (Cavan) 1944- 119
Mahoney, Irene 1921- 61-64
Mahoney, J. Daniel 1931- 61-64
Mahoney, John (Francis) 1929- 41-44R
Mahoney, John Leo 1928- CANR-14
Earlier sketch in CA 33-36R
Mahoney, John Thomas 1905-1981 ....CAP-1
Obituary 104
Earlier sketch in CA 11-12
Mahoney, Michael J(ohn) 1946- CANR-8
Earlier sketch in CA 53-56
Mahoney, Olivia 1952- 133
Mahoney, Patrick 1927- 81-84
Mahoney, Robert F. 1914- 13-16R
Mahoney, Rosemary 1961- 135
Mahoney, Thomas Arthur 1928- 1-4R
Mahoney, Thomas H(enry) D(onald)
1913- 13-16R
Mahoney, Tim 1947- 123
Mahoney, Tom
See Mahoney, John Thomas
Mahony, Devin (Adair) 1963- 130
Mahony, Elizabeth Winthrop 1948- 41-44R
See also SATA 8
Mahony, Patrick
See O'Mahony, Patrick
Mahony, Peter (Bernard) 1931- 118
Mahood, Kenneth 1930- 103
See also SATA 24
Mahood, Ruth I. 1908- CAP-1
Earlier sketch in CA 19-20
Mahrer, Alvin R(aymond) 1927- 21-24R
Mahy, Margaret 1936- CANR-38
Earlier sketches in CA 69-72, CANR-13, 30
See also AAYA 8
See also CLR 7
See also MAICYA
See also SATA 14, 69
Mai, Ludwig H(ubert) 1898- 73-76
Maibaum, Richard 1909-1991 102
Obituary 133
Maiden, Cecil (Edward) 1902-1981 73-76
See also SATA 52
Maidoff, Ilka
See List, Ilka Katherine
Maier, Charles S(teven) 1939- 69-72
Maier, Ernest L(ouis) 1938- 105
Maier, Howard 1906(?)-1983 Obituary 109
Maier, Joseph (Ben) 1911- 21-24R
Maier, Norman R(aymond) F(rederick)
1900-1977 ....CANR-4
Obituary 73-76
Earlier sketch in CA 1-4R
Maier, Paul L(uther) 1930- CANR-2
Earlier sketch in CA 5-8R
Maier, Pauline (Rubbelke) 1938- 37-40R
Maier, (Henry) William (Jr.) 1901- 1-4R

Maik, Henri
See Hecht, Henri Joseph
Mailer, Norman 1923- CANR-28
Earlier sketch in CA 9-12R
See also CABS 1
See also AITN 2
See also CDALB 1968-1988
See also CLC 1, 2, 3, 4, 5, 8, 11, 14, 28, 39
See also DLB 2, 16, 28
See also DLBD 3
See also DLBY 80, 83
See also MTCW
Maillard, Keith 1942- 93-96
Maillet, Adrienne 1885-1963 ....DLB 68
Maillet, Antonine 1929- 120
Brief entry 115
See also CLC 54
See also DLB 60
Mailloux, Steven 1950- CANR-25
Earlier sketch in CA 107
Mails, Thomas E. 1920(?)- 134
Brief entry 111
Maimon, Morton A. 1931- 33-36R
Maimonides, Moses 1138-1204 ....DLB 115
Main, Gloria (Jean) L(und) 1933- 112
Main, Jackson Turner 1917- CANR-1
Earlier sketch in CA 1-4R
Main, Mildred Miles 1898- CAP-1
Earlier sketch in CA 13-16
Maine, Charles Eric
See McIlwain, David
Maine, David
See Avice, Claude (Pierre Marie)
Maine, Trevor
See Catherall, Arthur
Maingot, Rodney 1893-1982 Obituary 105
Mainland, William Faulkner
1905-1988(?) Obituary 125
Mainprize, Don 1930- CANR-7
Earlier sketch in CA 17-20R
Mains, David R(andall) 1936- 93-96
Mainstone, Rowland J(ohnson) 1923- CANR-23
Earlier sketch in CA 107
Mainwaring, Daniel 1902-1977 ....DLB 44
Mainwaring, Marion CANR-3
Earlier sketch in CA 1-4R
Maiolo, Joseph 1938- 49-52
Maiorano, Robert 1946- 116
See also SATA 43
Mair, Alistair 1924- 9-12R
Mair, Charles 1838-1927 ....DLB 99
Mair, (Alexander) Craig 1948- 102
Mair, George Brown 1914- CANR-12
Earlier sketch in CA 13-16R
Mair, George F(isk) 1922-1978 Obituary 111
Mair, George L. 1929- 129
Mair, Lucy Philip 1901-1986 Obituary 119
Mair, Margaret
See Crompton, Margaret (Norah Mair)
Mair, Victor H(enry) 1943- CANR-32
Earlier sketch in CA 113
Mairowitz, David Zane 1943- 122
Mairs, Nancy 1943- 136
Mais, Roger 1905-1955 124
Brief entry 105
See also BW
See also MTCW
See also TCLC 8
Mais, S(tuart) P(etre) B(rodie) 1885-1975 69-72
Obituary 57-60
Maisel, Herbert 1930- 53-56
Maisel, Louis Sandy 1945- 117
Maisel, Sherman J(oseph) 1918- CANR-19
Earlier sketches in CA 5-8R, CANR-4
Maisels, Maxine S. 1939- 49-52
Maisky, Ivan (Mikhailovich) 1884-1975 65-68
Obituary 61-64
Maison, Della
See Katz, Bobbi
Maison, Margaret M(ary Bowles) 1920- 17-20R
Maissi, Elie 1911(?)-1983 Obituary 110
Maital, Sharone L(evow) 1947- 131
Maital, Shlomo 1942- CANR-25
Earlier sketch in CA 108
Maitland, Antony Jasper 1935- 101
See also SATA 25
Maitland, David J(ohnston) 1922- CANR-38
Earlier sketch in CA 116
Maitland, Derek 1943- CANR-23
Earlier sketch in CA 29-32R
Maitland, Margaret
See Du Breuil, (Elizabeth) L(or)inda
and Wallmann, Jeffrey M(iner)
Maitland, Sara (Louise) 1950- CANR-13
Earlier sketch in CA 69-72
See also CLC 49
Maitra, Priyatosh 1930- 107
Maizel, C. L.
See Maizel, Clarice Matthews
Maizel, Clarice Matthews 1919- 9-12R
Maizel, Leah
See Maizel, Clarice Matthews
Maja-Pearce, Adewale 1953- 126
Majault, Joseph 1916- 101
Majerus, Janet 1936- 65-68
Majeski, Bill
See Majeski, William
Majeski, William 1927- CANR-18
Earlier sketch in CA 25-28R
Majka, Linda C. 1947- 124
Majonica, Ernst 1920- 29-32R
Major, Alan P(ercival) 1929- CANR-7
Earlier sketch in CA 57-60
Major, Andre 1942- ....DLB 60
Major, Clarence 1936- CANR-25
Earlier sketches in CA 21-24R, CANR-13
See also CAAS 6
See also BLC 2
See also BW
See also CLC 3, 19, 48
See also DLB 33
Major, Geraldyn Hodges 1894-1984 85-88
Obituary 113
Major, Gerri
See Major, Geraldyn Hodges
Major, H. M.
See Jarvis, Sharon
Major, Henriette 1933- 109
Major, J(ames) Russell 1921- CANR-2
Earlier sketch in CA 5-8R
Major, Jean-Louis 1937- CANR-18
Earlier sketches in CA 49-52, CANR-2
Major, John M(cClellan) 1918- 13-16R
Major, Kevin (Gerald) 1949- CANR-38
Earlier sketches in CA 97-100, CANR-21
See also CLC 26
See also CLR 11
See also DLB 60
See also MAICYA
See also SATA 32
Major, Mabel 1893- 45-48
Major, Mark Imre 1923- 65-68
Major, Ralph Hermon 1884-1970 ....CAP-1
Earlier sketch in CA 9-10
Major, Reginald W. 1926- 29-32R
Major-General of Marsland
See Duncan, Ronald
Major-Poetzl, Pamela 1943- 116
Majumdar, R(amesh) C(handra) 1888- 33-36R
Majumder, Sanat K(umer) 1929- 33-36R
Makanowitzky, Barbara
See Norman, Barbara
Makarova, Marina 1942- 120
Makarova, Natalia 1940- 113
Makary
See Iranek-Osmecki, Kazimierz
Makeba, (Zensi) Miriam 1932- 104
See also BW
Makely, William O(rson) 1932- 53-56
Makemie, Francis 1658(?)-1708 ....DLB 24
Makepeace, Joanna
See York, Margaret Elizabeth
Makepeace, R(oyston) W(illiam) 1950- 116
Makerney, Edna Smith 1921- 61-64
Maki, James
See Ozu, Yasujiro
Maki, John M(cGilvrey) 1909- 109
Makie, Pam 1943- ....SATA 37
Makin, Peter (Julian) 1946- 93-96
Makino, Seiichi 1935- 113
Makins, Clifford 1924-1990 Obituary 132
Makins, Roger Mellor 1904- 111
Makkai, Adam 1935- CANR-10
Earlier sketch in CA 57-60
Makkreel, Rudolf A. 1939- 122
Makow, Henry 1949- 5-8R
Makower, Addie (Gertrude Leonaura)
1906- 65-68
Makower, Joel 1952- 124
Makowsky, Veronica A(nn) 1954- CANR-38
Earlier sketch in CA 116
Maksimov, Vladimir (Yemelyanovich)
See Maximov, Vladimir (Yemelyanovich)
Maktari, Abdulla M. A. 1936- 37-40R
Maktos, John 1902-1977 Obituary 69-72
Mal
See Hancock, Malcolm
Malabaila, Damiano
See Levi, Primo
Malabre, Alfred L(eopold) Jr. 1931- CANR-28
Earlier sketches in CA 65-68, CANR-12
Malamud, Bernard 1914-1986 ....CANR-28
Obituary 118
Earlier sketch in CA 5-8R
See also CABS 1
See also CDALB 1941-1968
See also CLC 1, 2, 3, 5, 8, 9, 11, 18, 27, 44
See also DLB 2, 28
See also DLBY 80, 86
See also MTCW
See also WLC
Malamud, Phyllis Carole 1938- 125
Malan, Rian 1954- 133
See also BEST 90:3
Malan, Roy Mark 1911- 41-44R
Maland, David 1929- 103
Malanga, Gerard (Joseph) 1943- 128
Brief entry 112
Malanos, George J(ohn) 1919-1962 ....1-4R
Obituary 103
Malarek, Victor 1948- 123
Malatesta, Peter J. 1932-1990 Obituary 130
Malavie, M. J. 1920- 29-32R
Malbin, Michael J(acob) 1943- CANR-17
Earlier sketch in CA 73-76
Malcolm, Andrew H(ogarth) 1943- 53-56
Malcolm, Andrew (Ian) 1927- 97-100
Malcolm, Dan
See Silverberg, Robert
Malcolm, Donald 1932(?)-1975 Obituary 104
Malcolm, Ian
See Malcolm, Andrew (Ian)
Malcolm, Janet 123
Malcolm, John
See Andrews, John Malcolm
Malcolm, Margaret
See Kuether, Edith Lyman
Malcolm, Norman (Adrian) 1911-1990 ......37-40R
Obituary 132
Malcolmson, Anne
See von Storch, Anne B.
Malcolmson, David 1899- 5-8R
See also SATA 6
Malcolmson, Robert W(illiam) 1943- CANR-19
Earlier sketch in CA 103
Malcolm X
See Little, Malcolm
See also BLC 2
Malcom, Robert E. 1933- 17-20R
Malcomson, R(osalie) M(ary) 1925- 119
Malcomson, Scott L. 1961- 137
Malcomson, William L. 1932- 25-28R
Malcoskey, Edna Walker 17-20R
Maldonado-Denis, Manuel 1933- 131
Brief entry 113
See also HW
Male, Belkis Cuza
See Cuza Male, Belkis
Male, David Arthur 1928- 57-60
Male, Roy R(aymond) 1919- 104
Malecki, Edward S(tanley) 1938- 41-44R
Malefakis, Edward E(manuel) 1932- 29-32R
Malefijt, Annemarie de Waal
See de Waal Malefijt, Annemarie
Malek, Frederic Vincent 1937- 81-84
Malek, James S(tanley) 1941- 57-60
Malenbaum, Wilfred 1913- CANR-1
Earlier sketch in CA 1-4R
Malerich, Edward P. 1940- 33-36R
Maleska, Eugene Thomas 1916- CANR-1
Earlier sketch in CA 1-4R
Malet, B(aldwyn) Hugh G(renville)
1928- 17-20R
Malgonkar, Manohar (Dattatray)
1913- CANR-18
Earlier sketches in CA 1-4R, CANR-1
Malherbe, Abraham J(ohannes) 1930- CANR-1
Earlier sketch in CA 49-52
Malherbe, Ernst Gideon 1895- CAP-1
Earlier sketch in CA 13-14
Malherbe, Janie Antonia (Nel) 1897- CAP-1
Earlier sketch in CA 13-16
Malhotra, Ashok Kumar 1940- 110
Malhotra, Inder 1930- 135
Mali, Jane Lawrence 1937- CANR-36
Earlier sketch in CA 114
See also SATA 44, 51
Mali, Paul 1926- CANR-8
Earlier sketch in CA 57-60
Malick, Terrence 1943- 101
Malick, Terry
See Malick, Terrence
Malickson, David L. 1928- 110
Malik, Charles Habib 1906-1987 ....CANR-7
Obituary 124
Earlier sketch in CA 45-48
Malik, Hafeez 1930- CANR-21
Earlier sketch in CA 77-80
Malik, Yogendra K(umar) 1929- 81-84
Malikin, David 1913- 77-80
Malimoto
See Puri, Shamlal
Malin, David (Frederick) 1941- 118
Malin, Irving 1934- CANR-6
Earlier sketch in CA 13-16R
Malin, James Claude 1893-1979 Obituary 113
Malin, Peter
See Conner, Patrick Reardon
Malina, Bruce J(ohn) 1933- 112
Malina, Frank J(oseph) 1912-1981 93-96
Obituary 108
Malina, Judith 1926- CANR-18
Earlier sketch in CA 102
Maling, Arthur (Gordon) 1923- CANR-22
Earlier sketches in CA 49-52, CANR-3
Malinin, Theodore I 1933- 93-96
Malino, Frances 1940- 115
Malinowski, Bronislaw (Kasper)
1884-1942 Brief entry 114
Malins, Edward (Greenway) 1910- 103
Malins, Penelope 1929- 126
Malipiero, Gian Francesco
1882-1973 Obituary 45-48
Malkiel, Burton Gordon 1932- CANR-31
Earlier sketch in CA 49-52
Malkiel, Yakov 1914- 25-28R
Malkiewicz, J(an) Kris 1931- 57-60
Malkin, Lawrence 1930- 126
Malkin, Maurice L. 1900- 49-52
Malkin, Michael R(obert) 1943- 129
Malkin, Sol(omon) M. 1910-1986 Obituary 118
Malkoff, Karl 1938- 17-20R
Malkus, Alida Wright 1899- 5-8R
Mall, E. Jane 1920- CANR-13
Earlier sketch in CA 21-24R
Mall, Viktor
See Beskow, Bo
Mallaby, (Howard) George
1902-1978 Obituary 108
Mallaby, Sebastian 1964- 138
Mallalieu, John Percival William 1908-1980 129
Obituary 97-100
Mallan, Lloyd 1914- 5-8R
Mallarme, Stephane 1842-1898 ....PC 4
Malle, Louis 1932- 101
Mallea, Eduardo 1903-1982(?) Obituary 114
See also HW
Mallen, Bruce E. 1937- CANR-14
Earlier sketch in CA 21-24R
Mallery, David 1923- 5-8R
Malleson, Andrew (Graeme)
1931- Brief entry 112
Malleson, Lucy Beatrice 1899-1973 97-100
Obituary 49-52
See also Gilbert, Anthony
Mallet-Joris, Francoise 1930- CANR-17
Earlier sketch in CA 65-68
See also CLC 11
See also DLB 83
Mallett, Anne 1913- 49-52
Malley, Ern
See McAuley, James Phillip
Mallin, Jay 1927- 17-20R
Mallin, Tom 1927(?)-1978 Obituary 89-92
Mallinson, George Greisen 1918- CANR-1
Earlier sketch in CA 1-4R
Mallinson, Jeremy (John Crosby)
1937- CANR-6
Earlier sketch in CA 57-60
Mallinson, Vernon 1910- 5-8R
Malliol, William
See McInenly, William T(homas)
Mallis, Jackie
See Mallis, Jacqueline
Mallis, Jacqueline 1922- 113
Malloch, Peter
See Duncan, W(illiam) Murdoch
Mallock, W. H. 1849-1923 ....DLB 18, 57
Mallon, Bill 1952- 119
Mallon, Thomas 1951- CANR-29
Earlier sketch in CA 110
Mallone, George 1944- 115
Mallone, Ronald Stephen 1916- CAP-1
Earlier sketch in CA 9-10
Mallonee, Richard C(arvel) II 1923- 109
Mallory, Bob F(ranklin) 1932- 89-92
Mallory, Enid Lorraine 1938- 105
Mallory, James Patrick 1945- 136
Mallory, Kenneth 1945- 124
Mallory, Mark
See Reynolds, Dallas McCord
Mallory, Walter Hampton 1892-1980 ....9-12R
Obituary 101
Mallough, Don 1914- 21-24R
Mallowan, Agatha Christie
See Christie, Agatha (Mary Clarissa)
Mallowan, Max (Edgar Lucien)
1904-1978 ....CANR-21
Obituary 81-84
Earlier sketch in CA 69-72
Mallows, (Edward) Wilfrid (Nassau) 1905- 119
Malloy, Ruth Lor 1932- CANR-22
Earlier sketch in CA 69-72
Malloy, Terry 1950- 69-72
Mally, E(mma) Louise 1908- 33-36R
Malm, F(inn) T(heodore) 1919- 17-20R
Malm, William P(aul) 1928- 9-12R
Malmberg, Carl 1904- 33-36R
See also SATA 9
Malmgren, Dallin 1949- 133
See also SATA 65
Malmgren, Harald B(ernard) 1935- CANR-27
Earlier sketch in CA 45-48
Malmo, Robert Beverley 1912- 61-64
Malmstroem, Vincent H(erschel)
See Malmstrom, Vincent H(erschel)
Malmstrom, Jean 1908- 53-56
Malmstrom, Vincent H(erschel) 1926- 112
Malo, John W. 1911- CANR-12
Earlier sketch in CA 33-36R
See also SATA 4
Malocsay, Zoltan 1946- 81-84
Malof, Joseph F(etler) 1934- 29-32R
Maloff, Chalda (Irene) 1946- 129
Maloff, Saul 1922- 33-36R
See also CLC 5
Malone, Bill C(harles) 1934- 65-68
Malone, Colonel Dick
See Malone, Richard S(ankey)
Malone, Dick
See Malone, Richard S(ankey)
Malone, Dumas 1892-1986 ....CANR-2
Obituary 121
Earlier sketch in CA 1-4R
See also DLB 17
Malone, Elmer Taylor Jr. 1943- CANR-17
Earlier sketches in CA 49-52, CANR-1
Malone, Joseph James
1924-1983 Obituary 111
Malone, Kemp 1889-1971 Obituary 89-92
Malone, Louis
See MacNeice, (Frederick) Louis
Malone, Margaret Gay 1939- 112
Malone, Mary CANR-2
Earlier sketch in CA 1-4R
Malone, Michael (Christopher) 1942- CANR-32
Earlier sketches in CA 77-80, CANR-14
See also CLC 43
Malone, Michael P. 1940- CANR-12
Earlier sketch in CA 29-32R
Malone, R. S.
See Malone, Richard S(ankey)
Malone, Richard S(ankey) 1909-1985 129
Obituary 116
Brief entry 107
Malone, Ruth 1918- 93-96
Malone, Ted
See Malone, Elmer Taylor Jr.
Malone, Wex S(mathers) 1906- 9-12R
Maloney, Frank E(dward) 1918-1980 73-76
Obituary 97-100
Maloney, George A(nthony) 1924- CANR-8
Earlier sketch in CA 21-24R
Maloney, J(oseph) J(ohn) 1940- 109
Maloney, Joan M(arie) 1931- 37-40R
Maloney, Pat
See Markun, Patricia Maloney
Maloney, Ralph Liston 1927-1973 ....CANR-3
Obituary 45-48
Earlier sketch in CA 1-4R
Maloney, Ray 1951- 133
Malony, H(enry) Newton 1931- 104

Malory, (Sir) Thomas
1410(?)-1471(?) ... CDBLB Before 1660
See also SATA 33, 59
Malouf, (George Joseph) David 1934- ... 124
See also CLC 28
Malouf, Pyrrha 1929- ... 117
Malpass, E(ric) L(awson) 1910- ... CANR-18
Earlier sketches in CA 9-12R, CANR-3
Malpass, Leslie F(rederick) 1922- ... CANR-8
Earlier sketch in CA 17-20R
Malpede, Karen (Sophia) 1945- ... CANR-26
Earlier sketch in CA 45-48
Malpott, Virgule
See Ghnassia, Maurice (Jean-Henri)
Malquiades
See Hayes, (Robert) Dennis
Malraux, (Georges-)Andre 1901-1976 ... CANR-34
Obituary ... 69-72
Earlier sketches in CAP-2, CA 21-22
See also CLC 1, 4, 9, 13, 15, 57
See also DLB 72
See also MTCW
Malraux, Clara (Goldschmidt)
1897(?)-1982 Obituary ... 108
Malraux-Goldschmidt, Clara
See Malraux, Clara (Goldschmidt)
Malta, Demetrio Aguilera
See Aguilera Malta, Demetrio
Maltby, Arthur 1935- ... CANR-10
Earlier sketch in CA 25-28R
Maltby, William S(aunders)
1940- Brief entry ... 113
Malten, William 1902- ... CAP-2
Earlier sketch in CA 23-24
Maltese, Michael 1909(?)-1981 Obituary ... 103
See also SATA 24
Malthus, Thomas Robert 1766-1834 ... DLB 107
Maltin, Leonard 1950- ... CANR-28
Earlier sketches in CA 29-32R, CANR-12
Maltman, Kim 1950- ... 112
Maltz, Albert 1908-1985 ... 41-44R
Obituary ... 115
See also DLB 102
Maltz, Maxwell 1899-1975 ... 65-68
Obituary ... 57-60
Maltz, Stephen 1932- ... 57-60
Maluf, Chafic 1905(?)-1976 Obituary ... 69-72
Malveaux, Julianne M(arie) 1953- ... CANR-23
Earlier sketch in CA 105
Malvern, Corinne 1905-1956 Brief entry ... 115
See also SATA 34
Malvern, Gladys ... 73-76
See also SATA 23
Malville, J. McKim
See Malville, John McKim
Malville, John McKim 1934- ... 120
Malville, Kim
See Malville, John McKim
Maly, Eugene H. 1920-1981 ... CANR-14
Earlier sketches in CA 21-24R
Malz, Betty 1929- ... CANR-32
Earlier sketch in CA 113
Malzberg, Barry N(athaniel) 1939- ... CANR-16
Earlier sketch in CA 61-64
See also CAAS 4
See also CLC 7
See also DLB 8
Malzberg, Benjamin 1893-1975 ... CAP-1
Obituary ... 57-60
Earlier sketch in CA 13-16
Mama G.
See Davis, Grania
Mamalakis, Markos J(ohn) 1932- ... CANR-27
Earlier sketch in CA 45-48
Maman, Andre 1927- ... 73-76
Mamatey, Victor S(amuel) 1917- ... 9-12R
Mamet, David (Alan) 1947- ... CANR-15
Earlier sketch in CA 81-84
See also CABS 3
See also AAYA 3
See also CLC 9, 15, 34, 46
See also DLB 7
See also MTCW
Mamis, Justin E. 1929- ... 9-12R
Mamleev, Yury
See Mamleyev, Yuri
Mamleyev, Yuri 1931- ... 85-88
Mamonova, Tatyana 1943- ... 114
Mamoulian, Rouben (Zachary)
1897-1987 ... 25-28R
Obituary ... 124
See also CLC 16
Man, Felix H.
See Baumann, Hans Felix S(iegismund)
Man, John 1941- ... CANR-16
Earlier sketch in CA 93-96
Manach, Jorge 1898(?)-1961 Obituary ... 111
Manard, Barbara Bolling 1945- ... 121
Manarin, Louis H(enry) 1932- ... 21-24R
Mana-Zucca
See Cassel, Mana-Zucca
Mancewicz, Bernice Winslow 1917- ... 37-40R
Manch, Joseph (Rodman) 1910- ... 53-56
Manchee, Fred B. 1903(?)-1981 Obituary ... 105
Manchel, Frank 1935- ... CANR-14
Earlier sketch in CA 37-40R
See also SATA 10
Manchester, Harland 1898-1977 ... 1-4R
Obituary ... 73-76
Manchester, Paul T(homas) 1893- ... 61-64
Manchester, William (Raymond)
1922- ... CANR-31
Earlier sketches in CA 1-4R, CANR-3
See also AITN 1
See also BEST 89:2
See also MTCW
See also SATA 65
Mancini, Anthony 1939- ... 73-76
Mancini, Pat McNees
See McNees, Pat
Mancke, Richard B(ell) 1943- ... 81-84
Mancroft, Stormont Mancroft Samuel
1914- ... CANR-28
Earlier sketch in CA 49-52
Mancusi-Ungaro, Harold R(aymond) Jr.
1947- ... 97-100
Mancuso, Joe
See Mancuso, Joseph R.
Mancuso, Joseph R. 1941- ... 93-96
Mand, Ewald 1906- ... 17-20R
Mandel, Adrienne Schizzano 1934- ... 37-40R
Mandel, Benjamin 1891(?)-1973 Obituary ... 45-48
Mandel, Bernard 1920- ... 1-4R
Mandel, Eli(as Wolf) 1922- ... CANR-15
Earlier sketch in CA 73-76
See also DLB 53
Mandel, Ernest 1923- ... CANR-15
Earlier sketch in CA 37-40R
Mandel, George 1920- ... 1-4R
Mandel, Jerome 1937- ... 37-40R
Mandel, Leon 1928- ... CANR-13
Earlier sketch in CA 77-80
Mandel, Loring 1928- ... 73-76
Mandel, Morris 1911- ... CANR-6
Earlier sketch in CA 5-8R
Mandel, Oscar 1926- ... CANR-21
Earlier sketches in CA 1-4R, CANR-2
Mandel, Ruth Blumenstock 1938- ... 105
Mandel, Sally Elizabeth 1944- ... 102
See also SATA 64
Mandel, Sheila 1930(?)-1987 Obituary ... 124
Mandel, Sidney Albert 1923- ... 93-96
Mandel, Siegfried 1922- ... CANR-20
Earlier sketches in CA 1-4R, CANR-5
Mandel, William M(arx) 1917- ... 9-12R
Mandela, Nelson R(olihlahla) 1918- ... 125
See also BW
Mandela, (Nomzamo) Winnie (Madikileza)
1936- ... 125
See also BW
Mandelbaum, Allen ... 111
Mandelbaum, Bernard 1922- ... 130
Mandelbaum, David G(oodman)
1911-1987 ... 41-44R
Obituary ... 122
Mandelbaum, Maurice (H.) 1908-1987 ... 131
Obituary ... 121
Brief entry ... 113
Mandelbaum, Michael 1946- ... 101
Mandelbaum, Seymour J. 1936- ... 17-20R
Mandelker, Daniel Robert 1926- ... CANR-20
Earlier sketches in CA 1-4R, CANR-5
Mandelkorn, Eugenia Miller 1916- ... 9-12R
Mandell, Arnold Joseph 1934- ... 101
Mandell, Betty Reid 1924- ... CANR-8
Earlier sketch in CA 61-64
Mandell, Fran Gare 1939- ... 115
Mandell, Gail Porter 1940- ... 123
Mandell, Maurice I(ra) 1925- ... CANR-11
Earlier sketch in CA 25-28R
Mandell, Mel 1926- ... 41-44R
Mandell, Muriel (Hortense Levin) 1921- ... 9-12R
See also SATA 63
Mandell, Richard Donald 1929- ... CANR-10
Earlier sketch in CA 25-28R
Mandelshtam, Nadezhda
See Mandelstam, Nadezhda (Yakovlevna)
Mandelstam, Nadezhda (Yakovlevna)
1899-1980 ... 110
Obituary ... 102
Mandelstam, Osip (Emilievich)
1891(?)-1938(?) Brief entry ... 104
See also TCLC 2, 6
Mandelstamm, Allan B(eryle) 1928- ... 41-44R
Mander, A(lfred) E(rnest) 1894- ... CAP-1
Earlier sketch in CA 11-12
Mander, Anica Vesel 1934- ... CANR-8
Earlier sketch in CA 61-64
Mander, Christine ... 136
Mander, Gertrud 1927- ... 93-96
Mander, (Mary) Jane 1877-1949 ... TCLC 31
Mander, Jerry 1936- ... 81-84
Mander, Raymond (Josiah Gale)
1911(?)-1983 ... 101
Obituary ... 111
Mander, Rosalie Grylls ... 5-8R
Mandeville, Bernard 1670-1733 ... DLB 101
Mandiargues, Andre Pieyre de
See Pieyre de Mandiargues, Andre
See also CLC 41
See also DLB 83
Mandino, Og 1923- ... 103
Mandler, George 1924- ... CANR-19
Earlier sketches in CA 1-4R, CANR-4
Mandler, Jean Matter 1929- ... CANR-19
Earlier sketch in CA 13-16R
Mandrake, Ethel Belle
See Thurman, Wallace (Henry)
Mandrepelias, Loizos
See Hartocollis, Peter
Mane, Robert 1926- ... 37-40R
Manella, Raymond L(awrence) 1917- ... 17-20R
Maner, Martin 1946- ... 135
Manes, Christopher 1957- ... 133
Manes, Stephen 1949- ... 97-100
See also SATA 40, 42
Manfred, Frederick (Feikema) 1912- ... CANR-25
Earlier sketches in CA 9-12R, CANR-5
See also DLB 6
See also SATA 30
Manfred, Freya 1944- ... 69-72
Manfred, Robert
See Marx, Erica Elizabeth
Manfredi, John Francis 1920- ... 109
Manfredi, V.
See Musciano, Walter A.
Mang, Karl 1922- ... 101
Mangalam, J(oseph) J(oseph) 1924- ... 37-40R
Mangan, James Thomas 1896- ... CAP-2
Earlier sketch in CA 19-20
Mangan, (John Joseph) Sherry
1904-1961 Obituary ... 112
See also DLB 4
Manganiello, Dominic 1951- ... 124
Mangat, J(agjit) S(ingh) 1937- ... 73-76
Mangin, Marie France 1940- ... SATA 59
Mangione, Jerre 1909- ... CANR-16
Earlier sketch in CA 13-16R
See also SATA 6
Mango, Cyril (Alexander) 1928- ... 109
Mango, Karin N. 1936- ... 123
See also SATA 52
Mangold, Tom 1934- ... 69-72
Manguel, Alberto 1948- ... 131
See also HW
Mangum, Garth L(eroy) 1926- ... 81-84
Mangurian, David 1938- ... CANR-10
Earlier sketch in CA 57-60
See also SATA 14
Manhattan, Avro 1914- ... CANR-30
Earlier sketches in CA 9-12R, CANR-5
Manheim, Emanuel 1897-1988 Obituary ... 125
Manheim, Jarol B(ruce) 1946- ... CANR-21
Earlier sketches in CA 57-60, CANR-6
Manheim, Leonard (Falk) 1902- ... CAP-2
Earlier sketch in CA 21-22
Manheim, Michael 1928- ... 81-84
Manheim, Ralph 1907(?)- Brief entry ... 115
Manheim, Sylvan D. 1897-1977 Obituary ... 73-76
Manheim, Theodore 1921- Brief entry ... 108
Manheim, Werner 1915- ... 53-56
Manhire, Bill 1946- ... CANR-20
Earlier sketch in CA 103
Manhoff, Bill
See Manhoff, Wilton
Manhoff, Wilton 1919-1974 Obituary ... 49-52
Maniates, Maria Rika 1937- ... 113
Maniaty, Anthony 1949- ... 119
Maniaty, Tony
See Maniaty, Anthony
Manicas, Peter T(heodore) 1934- ... 53-56
Maniere, J.-E.
See Giraudoux, (Hippolyte) Jean
Manifold, J(ohn) S(treeter) 1915- ... CANR-24
Earlier sketch in CA 69-72
Manigault, Edward 1897(?)-1983 Obituary ... 109
Manilla, James ... 97-100
Manis, Jerome G. 1917- ... 25-28R
Manis, Melvin 1931- ... 21-24R
Maniscalco, Joseph 1926- ... CANR-8
Earlier sketch in CA 5-8R
See also SATA 10
Manjon, Maite
See Manjon De Read, Maria Teresa
Manjon De Read, Maria Teresa
1931- ... CANR-38
Mank, Gregory William 1950- ... 89-92
Mankekar, D. R. 1910- ... CANR-13
Earlier sketch in CA 21-24R
Mankiewicz, Don M(artin) 1922- ... 13-16R
Mankiewicz, Frank (Fabian) 1924- ... 89-92
Mankiewicz, Herman (Jacob)
1897-1953 Brief entry ... 120
See also DLB 26
Mankiewicz, Joseph L(eo) 1909- ... 73-76
See also DLB 44
Mankiewicz, Thomas F. 1942- ... 128
Brief entry ... 124
Mankiewicz, Tom
See Mankiewicz, Thomas F.
Mankin, Paul A. 1924- ... 37-40R
Mankoff, Allan H. 1935- ... 45-48
Mankowitz, Wolf 1924- ... CANR-5
Earlier sketch in CA 5-8R
See also DLB 15
Mankowska, Joyce Kells Batten 1919- ... CAP-1
Earlier sketch in CA 9-10
Manley, Deborah 1932- ... CANR-22
Earlier sketch in CA 105
See also SATA 28
Manley, (Mary) Delariviere
1672(?)-1724 ... DLB 39, 80
Manley, Frank 1930- ... 5-8R
Manley, Joey 1965- ... 138
Manley, John F(rederick) 1939- ... 77-80
Manley, Lawrence (Gordon) 1949- ... 109
Manley, Michael Norman 1924- ... CANR-27
Earlier sketch in CA 85-88
Manley, Ruth Rodney King
1907(?)-1973 Obituary ... 41-44R
Manley, Seon 1921- ... 85-88
See also CLR 3
See also SAAS 2
See also SATA 15
Manley-Tucker, Audrie
1924(?)-1983(?) Obituary ... 108
Manlove, Colin Nicholas 1942- ... CANR-32
Earlier sketch in CA 113
Mann, A. Philo
See Ald, Roy A(llison)
Mann, Abby 1927- ... 109
See also DLB 44
Mann, Abel
See Creasey, John
Mann, (Francis) Anthony 1914- ... CAP-1
Earlier sketch in CA 9-10
Mann, Arthur 1922- ... 109
Mann, Avery
See Breetveld, Jim Patrick
Mann, Bob 1948- ... 61-64
Mann, Charles W. Jr. 1929- ... 41-44R
Mann, Chris(topher Michael Zithulele)
1948- ... 126
Mann, (Robert Francis) Christopher Stephen
1917- ... 89-92
Mann, D. J.
See Freeman, James Dillet
Mann, Dale 1938- ... 61-64
Mann, David Douglas 1934- ... CANR-28
Earlier sketch in CA 49-52
Mann, Dean Edson 1927- ... CANR-5
Earlier sketch in CA 9-12R
Mann, Deborah
See Bloom, Ursula
Mann, Donald Nathaniel
1920-1985 Obituary ... 114
Mann, Edward
See Fried, Emanuel
Mann, Edward Andrew 1932- ... 103
Mann, Emily 1952- ... 130
Mann, Erika 1905-1969 Obituary ... 25-28R
Mann, Esther Kingston
See Kingston-Mann, Esther
Mann, Floyd C(hristopher) 1917- ... 1-4R
Mann, Georg K(arl) F(riedrich) 1913- ... 1-4R
Mann, Golo 1909- ... 97-100
Mann, Harold W(ilson) 1925- ... 17-20R
Mann, (Luiz) Heinrich
1871-1950 Brief entry ... 106
See also DLB 66
See also TCLC 9
Mann, Heinrich 1871-1950 ... DLB 118
Mann, Horace 1796-1859 ... DLB 1
Mann, James
See Harvey, John (Barton)
Mann, Jessica ... CANR-24
Earlier sketches in CA 49-52, CANR-2
Mann, John H. 1928- ... 85-88
Mann, Josephine
See
Pullein-Thompson, Josephine (Mary Wedderburn)
Mann, Julia de Lacy 1891-1985 Obituary ... 116
Mann, Katharina 1883(?)-1980 Obituary ... 97-100
Mann, Kenneth Walker 1914- ... 29-32R
Mann, Klaus 1906-1949 ... DLB 56
Mann, Lucile Q.
See Mann, Lucile Quarry
Mann, Lucile Quarry 1897(?)-1986 Obituary ... 121
Mann, Marty 1904-1980 ... 103
Obituary ... 101
Mann, Michael K. 1943- ... 134
Brief entry ... 120
Mann, Michael 1919-1977 ... CANR-3
Obituary ... 69-72
Earlier sketch in CA 49-52
Mann, Milton B(ernard) 1937- ... 45-48
Mann, Patrick
See Waller, Leslie
Mann, Peggy ... CANR-27
Earlier sketches in CA 25-28R, CANR-10
See also Houlton, Peggy Mann
See also SATA 6
Mann, Peter (Clifford) 1948- ... 93-96
Mann, Peter H. 1926- ... CANR-12
Earlier sketch in CA 25-28R
Mann, Philip A(lan) 1934- ... 73-76
Mann, Ralph 1943- ... 112
Mann, Richard G(eorge) 1949- ... 124
Mann, Susan 1943- ... 128
Mann, (Paul) Thomas 1875-1955 ... 128
Brief entry ... 104
See also DLB 66
See also MTCW
See also SSC 5
See also TCLC 2, 8, 14, 21, 35, 44
See also WLC
Mann, W(illiam) Edward 1918- ... CANR-28
Earlier sketch in CA 49-52
Mann, William S(omervell) 1924-1989 ... 109
Obituary ... 129
Mann, Zane B. 1924- ... 101
Manne, Henry G. 1928- ... 33-36R
Mannello, George Jr. 1913- ... 33-36R
Mannering, Julia
See Bingham, Madeleine (Mary Ebel)
Manners, Alexandra
See Rundle, Anne
Manners, Ande Miller
1923(?)-1975 Obituary ... 57-60
Manners, David X. 1912- ... 106
Manners, Elizabeth (Maude) 1917- ... 49-52
Manners, Gerald 1932- ... 37-40R
Manners, John (Errol) 1914- ... 106
Manners, Julia
See Greenaway, Gladys
Manners, Robert A(lan) 1913- ... 33-36R
Manners, William 1907- ... 65-68
Mannes, Marya 1904-1990 ... CANR-3
Obituary ... 132
Earlier sketch in CA 1-4R
Mannetti, Lisa 1953- ... 125
See also SATA 51, 57
Manngian, Peter
See Monger, (Ifor) David
Mannheim, Grete (Salomon) 1909- ... 9-12R
See also SATA 10
Manniche, Lise 1943- ... CANR-25
Earlier sketch in CA 107
See also SATA 31
Mannin, Ethel (Edith) 1900-1984 ... CANR-8
Obituary ... 114
Earlier sketch in CA 53-56
Manning, Ambrose N(uel) 1922- ... 114
Manning, Bayless Andrew 1923- ... CANR-9
Earlier sketch in CA 13-16R
Manning, Beverley J(ane) 1942- ... 109
Manning, Clarence A(ugustus)
1893-1972 Obituary ... 37-40R

Manning, David
See Faust, Frederick (Shiller)
Manning, David John 1938- 103
Manning, Frank E(dward) 1944- CANR-7
Earlier sketch in CA 53-56
Manning, Frederic 1887(?)-1935 Brief entry 124
See also TCLC 25
Manning, Harvey (Hawthorne) 1925- CANR-30
Earlier sketch in CA 112
Manning, Helen Taft
1891(?)-1987 Obituary 121
Manning, Jack 1920- 69-72
Manning, Margaret Raymond
1921-1984 Obituary 114
Manning, Marie 1873(?)-1945 ....DLB 29
Manning, Marsha
See Grimstead, Hettie
Manning, Martin
See Smith, R(eginald) D(onald)
Manning, Mary Louise
See Cameron, Lou
Manning, Matthew 1955- Brief entry 111
Manning, Michael 1940- 65-68
Manning, Olivia 1915-1980 ....CANR-29
Obituary 101
Earlier sketch in CA 5-8R
See also CLC 5, 19
See also MTCW
Manning, Paul 1912- 107
Manning, Peter J. 1942- 125
Manning, Peter K(irby) 1940- CANR-34
Earlier sketches in CA 37-40R, CANR-14
Manning, Philip 1930(?)-1983 Obituary 110
Manning, Phyllis A(nne) Sergeant 1903- 5-8R
Manning, Reg(inald West)
1905-1986 Obituary 118
Manning, Robert (Joseph) 1919- 69-72
Manning, Roberta Thompson 1940- 130
Manning, Rosemary
See Cole, Margaret Alice
Manning, Rosemary (Joy) 1911-1988 ....CANR-25
Earlier sketches in CA 1-4R, CANR-1
See also SATA 10
Manning, Stanley Arthur 1921- 110
Manning, Sylvia 1943- 81-84
Manning, Thomas Davys 1898-1972 ....CAP-1
Earlier sketch in CA 19-20
Manning-Sanders, Ruth 1895(?)-1988 73-76
Obituary 126
See also MAICYA
See also SATA 15, 57
Mannion, John J(oseph) 1941- 73-76
Mannix, Edward 1928- 13-16R
Mannon, James M(onroe) 1942- 110
Mannon, Warwick
See Hopkins, (Hector) Kenneth
Mannoni, Octave 1899- 102
Mano, D. Keith 1942- CANR-26
Earlier sketch in CA 25-28R
See also CAAS 6
See also CLC 2, 10
See also DLB 6
Mano, M(oshe) Morris 1927- 103
Manocchia, Benito 1934- 69-72
Manoff, Robert Karl 1944- 126
Manogaran, Chelvadurai 1935- 124
Manolson, Frank 1925- 17-20R
Manoni, Mary H(allahan) 1924- CANR-4
Earlier sketch in CA 49-52
Manoogian, Haig P.
1916(?)-1980 Obituary 97-100
Manor, Jason
See Hall, Oakley (Maxwell)
Manos, Charley 1923-1985 ....29-32R
Obituary 116
Manosevitz, Martin 1938- 29-32R
Manross, William Wilson 1905- 57-60
Manry, Robert 1918-1971 ....CAP-2
Obituary 29-32R
Earlier sketch in CA 21-22
Mansbach, Richard W(allace) 1943- 53-56
Mansberg, Ruth 1924- 130
Mansbridge, Francis 1943- 133
Mansbridge, John 1901(?)-1981 Obituary 105
Manschreck, Clyde Leonard 1917- CANR-5
Earlier sketch in CA 9-12R
Mansell, Darrel (Lee Jr.) 1934- 57-60
Mansell, Gerard (Evelyn Herbert) 1921- 130
Manser, Martin H(ugh) 1952- 118
Mansergh, (Philip) Nicholas (Seton)
1910-1991 105
Obituary 133
Mansfield, Bruce Edgar 1926- 103
Mansfield, Comins 1896-1984 Obituary 112
Mansfield, Edwin 1930- CANR-18
Earlier sketches in CA 9-12R, CANR-3
Mansfield, Elizabeth
See Schwartz, Paula
Mansfield, Harold H. 1912- 17-20R
Mansfield, Harvey C(laflin) 1905-1988 ....1-4R
Obituary 125
Mansfield, Irving 1908(?)-1988 Obituary 126
Mansfield, John M(aurice) 1936- 29-32R
Mansfield, Katherine
See Beauchamp, Kathleen Mansfield
See also SSC 9
See also TCLC 2, 8, 39
See also WLC
Mansfield, Libby
See Schwartz, Paula
Mansfield, Norman
See Gladden, E(dgar) Norman
Mansfield, Peter 1928- 65-68
Mansfield, Roger (Ernest) 1939- CANR-11
Earlier sketch in CA 25-28R
Manship, David 1927- 25-28R
Manski, Charles F. 1948- 138
Manso, Peter 1940- 29-32R
See also CLC 39
Manson, Beverlie 1945- 113
See also SATA 44, 57
Manson, Richard 1939- 29-32R
Mansoor, Menahem 1911- CANR-15
Earlier sketch in CA 41-44R
Mansur, Ina 1910- CANR-38
Earlier sketch in CA 116
Mantague, John 1929- 9-12R
Mantecon, Juan Jimenez
See Jimenez (Mantecon), Juan Ramon
Mantel, Hilary (Mary) 1952- 125
Mantel, Samuel J(oseph) Jr. 1921- 13-16R
Mantell, Leroy H. 1919- 37-40R
Mantell, Martin E(den) 1936- 45-48
Manternach, Janaan 1927- 116
Mantey, Julius Robert 1890- CAP-1
Earlier sketch in CA 11-12
Mantle, Jonathan 1954- 129
Mantle, Mickey (Charles) 1931- 89-92
Mantle, Winifred (Langford) CANR-6
Earlier sketch in CA 13-16R
Manton, Jo
See Gittings, Jo (Grenville) Manton
Manton, Peter
See Creasey, John
Manuel, E(spiridion) Arsenio 1909- 118
See also CAAS 9
Manuel, Frank Edward 1910- CANR-29
Earlier sketches in CA 9-12R, CANR-6
Manuel, George 1921- 107
Manus, Mavis 1929- 116
Manus, Willard 1930- CANR-28
Earlier sketch in CA 108
Manushkin, Fran 1942- CANR-1
Earlier sketch in CA 49-52
See also SATA 7, 54
Manvell, (Arnold) Roger 1909-1987 ....CANR-23
Obituary 124
Earlier sketches in CA 1-4R, CANR-6
Manville, W(illiam) H(enry) 1930- 93-96
Manwell, Reginald D. 1897- 37-40R
Man Without a Spleen, A
See Chekhov, Anton (Pavlovich)
Man Xibo
See Porkert, Manfred (Bruno)
Many, Seth E(dward) 1939- 97-100
Manyan, Gladys 1911- 57-60
Manzalaoui, Mahmoud (Ali) 1924- CANR-12
Earlier sketch in CA 29-32R
Manzella, David (Bernard) 1924- 5-8R
Manzini, Gianna 1899-1974 Obituary 53-56
Manzoni, Pablo Michelangelo
1939- Brief entry 106
Mao, James C. T. 1925- 37-40R
Mao Tse-tung 1893-1976 73-76
Obituary 69-72
See also MTCW
Mapel, William 1902-1984 Obituary 112
Mapes, Arthur Franklin 1913-1986 Obituary 118
Mapes, Mary A.
See Ellison, Virginia H(owell)
Maple, Eric William 1915- CANR-6
Earlier sketch in CA 53-56
Maple, Terry 1946- CANR-1
Earlier sketch in CA 49-52
Maples, Evelyn Palmer 1919- CANR-17
Earlier sketches in CA 5-8R, CANR-2
Mapp, Alf J(ohnson) Jr. 1925- CANR-1
Earlier sketch in CA 1-4R
Mapp, Edward C(harles) 33-36R
Maquet, Jacques Jerome Pierre
1919- CANR-29
Earlier sketches in CA 61-64, CANR-8
Mara, Barney
See Roth, Arthur J(oseph)
Mara, Jeanette
See Cebulash, Mel
Mara, Sally
See Queneau, Raymond
Mara, Thalia 1911- 9-12R
Marable, Manning 1950- 110
Marahiman, Ismail 1934- 136
Marai, Sandor 1900-1989 Obituary 128
Maraini, Dacia 1936- CANR-11
Earlier sketch in CA 5-8R
Maraini, Fosco 1912- Brief entry 116
Marais, Josef 1905-1978 Obituary 77-80
See also SATA 24
Maran, Rene 1887-1960 125
Obituary 107
See also BW
Maran, Stephen P(aul) 1938- 57-60
Maranda, Elli Kongas 1932- Brief entry 107
Maranda, Pierre 1930- 37-40R
Maranell, Gary M. 1932- 37-40R
Marangell, Virginia J(ohnson) 1924- 93-96
Maras, Karl
See Bulmer, (Henry) Kenneth
Marasmus, Seymour
See Rivoli, Mario
Marath, Laurie
See Roberts, Suzanne
Marath, Sparrow
See Roberts, Suzanne
Maravich, Pete(r Press)
1947(?)-1988 Obituary 124
Marazzi, Rich(ard Thomas) 1943- 102
Marberry, M. M(arion) 1905-1968 ....CAP-2
Earlier sketch in CA 21-22
Marble, Harriet Clement 1903-1975 73-76
Marble, Samuel D(avey) 1915- 106
Marbrook, Del
See Marbrook, Djelloul
Marbrook, Djelloul 1934- 73-76
Marbut, F(rederick) B(rowning) 1905- 33-36R
Marc
See Boxer, (Charles) Mark (Edward)
Marc, David 1951- 138
Marcal, Annette B.
See Callaway, Bernice (Anne)
Marcatante, John 1930- CANR-10
Earlier sketch in CA 25-28R
Marceau, Felicien
See Carette, Louis
Marceau, LeRoy 1907- CAP-1
Earlier sketch in CA 19-20
Marceau, Marcel 1923- 85-88
Marcel, Gabriel Honore 1889-1973 102
Obituary 45-48
See also CLC 15
See also MTCW
Marcelin, Pierre 1908- 106
Marcelino
See Agnew, Edith J(osephine)
Marcell, David Wyburn 1937- 41-44R
Marcellino, Fred 1939- ....SATA 68
March, Andrew Lee 1932- 110
March, Anthony 1912-1973 Obituary 45-48
March, Bill
See March, William Joseph
March, Carl
See Fleischman, (Albert) Sid(ney)
March, Hilary
See Adcock, Almey St. John
March, James Gardner 1928- 13-16R
March, Jessica
See Africano, Lillian
March, Joseph 1899(?)-1977 Obituary 69-72
March, Josie
See Titchener, Louise
March, Robert H(erbert) 1934- 61-64
March, Valerie
See Beecher, Maureen Ursenbach
March, William
See Campbell, William Edward March
See also DLB 9, 86
March, William J. 1915- 13-16R
March, William Joseph 1941-1990 Obituary 132
Marchaj, C(zeslaw) A(ntony) 1918- CANR-5
Earlier sketch in CA 9-12R
Marchak, M(aureen) Patricia 1936- CANR-29
Earlier sketch in CA 111
Marchak, Maureen
See Marchak, M(aureen) Patricia
Marcham, Frederick George 1898- 13-16R
Marchand, C(harles) Roland
1933- Brief entry 110
Marchand, Leslie A(lexis) 1900- CANR-12
Earlier sketch in CA 65-68
See also DLB 103
Marchand, Philip (Edward) 1946- 130
Marchant, Anyda 1911- CANR-29
Earlier sketch in CA 13-16R
Marchant, Bessie 1862-1941 ....YABC 2
Marchant, Catherine
See Cookson, Catherine (McMullen)
Marchant, Herbert S(tanley) 106
Marchant, John H. 1951- 125
Marchant, Leslie R(onald) 1924- Brief entry 110
Marchant, Maurice P(eterson) 1927- 110
Marchant, R(ex) A(lan) 1933- 13-16R
Marchant, William 1923- 69-72
Marchbanks, Samuel
See Davies, (William) Robertson
Marchenko, Anatoly (Timofeevich)
1938-1986 ....25-28R
Obituary 121
Marcher, Marion Walden 1890- 1-4R
See also SATA 10
Marchessault, Jovette 1938- ....DLB 60
Marchetti, Albert 1947- 89-92
Marchetti, Victor Brief entry 108
Marchi, Giacomo
See Bassani, Giorgio
Marchiano, Linda Boreman 1949(?)- 129
Brief entry 114
Marchione, Margherita (Frances)
1922- CANR-15
Earlier sketch in CA 37-40R
Marciniak, Ed(ward) 1917- 29-32R
Marckwardt, Albert H(enry) 1903-1975 ....CANR-4
Obituary 61-64
Earlier sketch in CA 1-4R
Marco
See Mountbatten, Louis (Francis Albert Victor Nicholas)
Marco
See Charlier, Roger H(enri)
Marco, Anton N(icholas) 1943- 110
Marco, Barbara (Starkey) 1934- 9-12R
Marco, Guy A(nthony) 1927- 118
Marco, Lou
See Gottfried, Theodore Mark
Marcombe, Edith Marion
See Shiffert, Edith (Marcombe)
Marcos, Ferdinand E(dralin) 1917-1989 130
Marcosson, Isaac Frederick
1877-1961 Obituary 89-92
Marcovich, Miroslav 1919- 115
Marcson, Simon 1910- 49-52
Marcum, John A(rthur) 1927- CANR-14
Earlier sketch in CA 25-28R
Marcus, Aaron 1943- 53-56
Marcus, Adrianne 1935- CANR-1
Earlier sketch in CA 45-48
Marcus, Alfred A(llen) 1950- 118
Marcus, Anne M(ulkeen) 1927- 73-76
Marcus, Betty Blum 1923-1984 Obituary 113
Marcus, David 1926- 134
Brief entry 110
Marcus, Donald (Edwin) 1946- 134
Marcus, Edward 1918- CANR-14
Earlier sketch in CA 21-24R
Marcus, Ellis 1918(?)-1990 Obituary 132
Marcus, Frank 1928- CANR-2
Earlier sketch in CA 45-48
See also DLB 13
Marcus, Fred H(arold) 1921- 104
Marcus, Genevieve Grafe 1932- 111
Marcus, George E. 1946- 124
Marcus, George H. 1939- 120
Marcus, Greil (Gerstley) 1945- 122
Marcus, Harold G. 1936- 37-40R
Marcus, Irwin M. 1919- 45-48
Marcus, Jacob Rader 1896- CANR-28
Earlier sketch in CA 21-24R
Marcus, Jerry 1924- 97-100
Marcus, Joanna
See Andrews, Lucilla (Mathew)
Marcus, Joe 1933- 65-68
Marcus, Larry
See Marcus, Lawrence B.
Marcus, Laurence R. 1947- 135
Marcus, Lawrence B. 1925- 133
Marcus, Leonard S. 1950- 134
Marcus, Maeva 1941- Brief entry 108
Marcus, Martin 1933- 25-28R
Marcus, Mildred Rendl 1928- CANR-2
Earlier sketch in CA 1-4R
Marcus, Mordecai 1925- CANR-38
Earlier sketches in CA 77-80, CANR-17
Marcus, Morton 1936- 105
Marcus, Phillip L. 1941- 134
Brief entry 111
Marcus, Rebecca B(rian) 1907- CANR-1
Earlier sketch in CA 5-8R
See also SATA 9
Marcus, Robert D. 1936- Brief entry 110
Marcus, Ruth Barcan 1921- 41-44R
Marcus, Sheldon 1937- Brief entry 106
Marcus, Stanley 1905- 53-56
Marcus, Steven 1928- 41-44R
Marcuse, F(rederick) L(awrence) 1916- 9-12R
Marcuse, Herbert 1898-1979 Obituary 89-92
Marcuse, Ludwig 1894-1971 Obituary 33-36R
Marden, Charles F(rederick) 1902- 37-40R
Marden, William (Edward) 1947- 61-64
Marder, Arthur (Jacob) 1910-1980 105
Obituary 102
Marder, Daniel 1923- 21-24R
Marder, Herbert 1934- 69-72
Marder, Louis 1915- 5-8R
Mardock, Robert W(inston) 1921- 17-20R
Mardon, Michael (Claude) 1919- 13-16R
Mardor, Munya Meir 1913- 17-20R
Mardus, Elaine Bassler 1914- 9-12R
Mare, W(illiam) Harold 1918- 105
Marechal, Leopoldo 1900-1970 ....HW
Marei, Sayed (Ahmed) 1913- 73-76
Marein, Shirley 1926- CANR-1
Earlier sketch in CA 45-48
Marek, George R(ichard) 1902-1987 ....CANR-1
Obituary 121
Earlier sketch in CA 49-52
Marek, Hannelore M(arie) C(harlotte)
1926- 13-16R
Marek, Kurt W(illi) 1915-1972 ....CAP-2
Obituary 33-36R
Earlier sketch in CA 17-18
Marek, Margot L. 1934(?)-1987 Obituary 123
See also SATA 54
Marek, Richard (William) 1933- 126
Marelli, Leonard R(ussell) 1933-1973 ....CAP-1
Earlier sketch in CA 13-16
Maremaa, Thomas 1945- 85-88
Marenbon, John (Alexander) 1955- 131
Marenco, Ethne (Elsie) K(aplan) 1925- 103
Marer, Paul 1936- 105
Mares, F(rancis) H(ugh) 1925- 25-28R
Mares, Michael A. 1945- 138
Maresca, Thomas Edward 1938- 85-88
Mareth, Glenville
See Gilbert, Willie
Marett, Robert Hugh Kirk 1907- 25-28R
Marevna
See Vorobeva, Maria
Margadant, Ted W(inston) 1941- 93-96
Margalith, Pinhas Z(alman) 1926- 110
Margaret, Karla
See Andersdatter, Karla M(argaret)
Margenau, Henry 1901- CANR-14
Earlier sketch in CA 37-40R
Marger, Mary Ann 1934- 93-96
Margerson, David
See Davies, David Margerison
Margetson, Stella 1912- CANR-13
Earlier sketch in CA 33-36R
Marghieri, Clotilde 1901(?)-1981 Obituary 105
Margold, Stella 81-84
Margolies, Alan 1933- 125
Margolies, Edward 1925- CANR-11
Earlier sketch in CA 65-68
Margolies, Joseph A(aron)
1889-1982 Obituary 108
Margolies, Luise 1945- 102
Margolies, Marjorie 1942- CANR-13
Earlier sketch in CA 65-68
Margolin, Edythe 69-72
Margolin, Judith B(elle) 1946- 117
Margolin, Malcolm 1940- 57-60
Margolin, Victor 1941- 65-68
Margolis, Anne T(hrone) 1949- 128
Margolis, Diane Rothbard 1933- 97-100
Margolis, Ellen (Edelman) 1934- 1-4R
Margolis, Gary 1945- 73-76
Margolis, Howard 1932- 130
Margolis, Jack S 1934- 69-72

Margolis, John D(avid) 1941- 134
Brief entry 113
Margolis, Joseph 1924- 37-40R
Margolis, Julius 1920- Brief entry 109
Margolis, Maxine L(uanna) 1942- 53-56
Margolis, Michael (Stephen) 1940- 93-96
Margolis, Richard J(ules) 1929-1991 ....CANR-25
Obituary 134
Earlier sketch in CA 29-32R
See also SATA 4
See also SATO 67
Margolis, Susan Spector 1941- 81-84
Margolis, Susanna 1944- 107
Margolis, Vivienne 1922- ....SATA 46
Margolius, Sidney (Senier)
1911-1980 ....CANR-11
Obituary 93-96
Earlier sketch in CA 21-24R
Margon, Lester 1892- CAP-1
Earlier sketch in CA 13-16
Margoshes, Dave 1941- CANR-29
Earlier sketch in CA 111
Margroff, Robert E. 1930- 134
Margulies, Harry D.
1907(?)-1980 Obituary 97-100
Margulies, Herbert F(elix) 1928- 77-80
Margulies, Jimmy 1951- 133
Margulies, Leo 1900-1975 Obituary 61-64
Margulies, Newton 1932- 61-64
Margulis, Lynn 1938- CANR-4
Earlier sketch in CA 53-56
Margull, Hans J(ochen) 1925- 9-12R
Marhoefer, Barbara (McGeary) 1936- 61-64
Maria Del Rey, Sister 1908- 5-8R
Mariah, Paul 1937- CANR-4
Earlier sketch in CA 53-56
Mariana
See Foster, Marian Curtis
Mariani, John Francis 1945- 117
Mariani, Paul L(ouis) 1940- CANR-12
Earlier sketch in CA 29-32R
See also DLB 111
Mariano, Frank 1931(?)-1976 Obituary 69-72
Marias (Aguilera), Julian 1914- CANR-22
Earlier sketches in CA 9-12R, CANR-5
Marie, Beverly Sainte
See Sainte-Marie, Beverly
Marie, Buffy Sainte
See Sainte-Marie, Beverly
Marie, Geraldine 1949- 108
See also SATA 61
Marie, Jeanne
See Wilson, Marie B(eatrice)
Marie-Andre du Sacre-Coeur, Sister 1899- 5-8R
Marien, Michael 1938- CANR-16
Earlier sketches in CA 49-52, CANR-1
Marier, Captain Victor
See Griffith, D(avid Lewelyn) W(ark)
Marie Therese, Mother 1891- CAP-1
Earlier sketch in CA 13-14
Marie-Victorin, Frere 1885-1944 ....DLB 92
Maril, Nadja 1954- CANR-17
Earlier sketch in CA 85-88
Marill, Alvin H(erbert) 1934- CANR-12
Earlier sketch in CA 73-76
Marilla, E(smond) L(inworth) 1900- CAP-2
Earlier sketch in CA 23-24
Marilue
See Johnson, Marilue Carolyn
Marimow, William K. 1947- 93-96
Marin, A. C.
See Coppel, Alfred
Marin, Cheech
See Marin, Richard Anthony
Marin, Diego 1914- 17-20R
Marin, Luis Munoz
See Munoz Marin, Luis
Marin, Richard Anthony 1946- Brief entry 112
Marinacci, Barbara 1933- CANR-9
Earlier sketch in CA 21-24R
Marinaccio, Anthony 1912- 53-56
Marine, David 1880(?)-1976 Obituary 69-72
Marine, Gene 1926- 65-68
Marine, Nick
See Oursler, Will(iam Charles)
Marinelli, Peter V(incent) 1933- 41-44R
Mariner, David
See Smith, David MacLeod
Mariner, Scott
See Pohl, Frederik
Marinetti, Filippo Tommaso
1876-1944 Brief entry 107
See also DLB 114
See also TCLC 10
Maring, Joel M(arvin) 1935- 49-52
Maring, Norman H(ill) 1914- 17-20R
Marini, Frank N(ick) 1935- 45-48
Marino, Carolyn Fitch 1942- 110
Marino, Dorothy Bronson 1912- 73-76
See also SATA 14
Marino, John J. 1948- 106
Marino, Joseph D. 1912(?)-1983 Obituary 109
Marino, Trentino J(oseph) 1917- 65-68
Marinoni, Rosa Zagnoni 1888-1970 ....CAP-1
Earlier sketch in CA 13-14
Marion, Frances 1886-1973 Obituary 41-44R
See also DLB 44
Marion, Frieda 1912- CANR-8
Earlier sketch in CA 61-64
Marion, Henry
See del Rey, Lester
Marion, John Francis 1922- CANR-3
Earlier sketch in CA 5-8R
Marion, Robert W. 1952- 130
Mariotti, (Raffaello) Marcello 1938- 29-32R
Marique, Joseph M(arie-) F(elix) 1899- 33-36R
Maris, Roger (Eugene) 1934-1985 Obituary 118
Maris, Ron ....SATA 45, 71
Marisa
See Nucera, Marisa Lonette
Mariscal, Richard N(orth) 1935- 53-56
Maritain, Jacques 1882-1973 85-88
Obituary 41-44R
Maritano, Nino 1919- 13-16R
Marius, Richard (Curry) 1933- CANR-29
Earlier sketch in CA 25-28R
See also DLBY 85
Marjolin, Robert (Ernest)
1911-1986 Obituary 119
Marjoram, J.
See Mottram, R(alph) H(ale)
Mark, Charles Christopher 1927- CANR-1
Earlier sketch in CA 1-4R
Mark, David 1922- 1-4R
Mark, Edwina
See Fadiman, Edwin Jr.
Mark, Irving 1908-1987 ....CAP-1
Obituary 121
Earlier sketch in CA 19-20
Mark, Jan 1943- CANR-17
Earlier sketch in CA 93-96
See also CLR 11
See also MAICYA
See also SATA 22, 69
Mark, Joan 1937- 130
Mark, Jon
See Du Breuil, (Elizabeth) L(or)inda
Mark, Julius 1898-1977 81-84
Obituary 73-76
Mark, Matthew
See Babcock, Frederic
Mark, Max 1910- 73-76
Mark, Michael L(aurence) 1936- 93-96
Mark, Norman (Barry) 1939- 113
Mark, Pauline (Dahlin) 1913- CANR-7
Earlier sketch in CA 17-20R
See also SATA 14
Mark, Polly
See Mark, Pauline (Dahlin)
Mark, Robert 1930- 110
Mark, Shelley M(uin) 1922- CANR-1
Earlier sketch in CA 1-4R
Mark, Steven Joseph 1913- 17-20R
Mark, Ted
See Gottfried, Theodore Mark
Mark, Theonie Diakidis 1938- 69-72
Mark, Yudel 1897-1975 Obituary 61-64
Markandaya, Kamala
See Taylor, Kamala (Purnaiya)
See also CLC 8, 38
Markbreit, Jerry 1935- 49-52
Marke, Julius J(ay) 1913- 17-20R
Markel, Geraldine (Ponte) 1939- 108
Markel, Helen 1919(?)-1990 Obituary 130
Markel, Lester 1894-1977 ....37-40R
Obituary 73-76
Markels, Julian 1925- 25-28R
Marken, Jack W(alter) 1922- CANR-31
Earlier sketch in CA 49-52
Marker, Frederick (Joseph Jr.) 1936- CANR-39
Earlier sketches in CA 41-44R, CANR-16
Marker, Gary 1948- 125
Marker, Lise-Lone (Christensen)
1934- CANR-39
Earlier sketches in CA 61-64, CANR-8
Market Man
See Lake, Kenneth R(obert)
Markevitch, Igor 1912-1983 Obituary 109
Markey, Gene 1895-1980 ....CAP-1
Obituary 97-100
Earlier sketch in CA 11-12
Markfield, Wallace 1926- 69-72
See also CAAS 3
See also CLC 8
See also DLB 2, 28
Markgraf, Carl 1928- CANR-31
Earlier sketch in CA 49-52
Markham, Beryl 1902-1986 Obituary 119
Markham, Clarence M(atthew) Jr. 1911- 69-72
Markham, Dewey 1904-1981 Obituary 108
Markham, Edwin 1852-1940 ....DLB 54
Markham, Felix (Maurice Hippisley)
1908- CAP-1
Earlier sketch in CA 11-12
Markham, Gervase 1568(?)-1637 ....DLB 121
Markham, James M(orris IV) 1943-1989 93-96
Obituary 129
Markham, James W(alter) 1910-1972 ....CAP-2
Earlier sketch in CA 21-22
Markham, Jesse William 1916- 9-12R
Markham, Marion M. 1929- 129
See also SATA 60
Markham, Meeler 1914- CANR-12
Earlier sketch in CA 25-28R
Markham, Pigmeat
See Markham, Dewey
Markham, Reed 1957- 110
Markham, Robert
See MIS
Marki, Ivan 1934- 97-100
Markides, Kyriacos (Costa) 1942- 81-84
Markie, Peter J(oseph) 1950- 123
Markins, W. S.
See Jenkins, Marie M(agdalen)
Markish, David 1938- 69-72
Markle, Fletcher 1921- ....DLB 68
See also DLBY 91
Markle, Joyce B(onners) 1942- 69-72
Markle, Sandra L(ee) 1946- 111
See also SATA 41, 57
Markley, Kenneth A(lan) 1933- 61-64
Markley, R(ayner) W(are) 1934- 111
Markman, Howard (Joel) 1950- 69-72
Markman, Sherwin J. 1929- 104
Markman, Sidney David 1911- CAP-2
Earlier sketch in CA 33-36
Markmann, Charles Lam 1913- 13-16R
Marko, Katherine D(olores) CANR-15
Earlier sketch in CA 29-32R
See also SATA 28
Markoe, Karen 1942- 81-84
Markoosie
See Patsauq, Markoosie
See also CLR 23
Markov, Georgi 1929(?)-1978 Obituary 104
Markov, Vladimir 1920- 17-20R
Markova, Alicia 1910- CAP-2
Earlier sketch in CA 19-20
Markovic, Mihailo (M.) 1923- 131
Markovic, Miroslav
See Marcovich, Miroslav
Markovic, Vida E. 1916- 33-36R
Markovitz, Irving Leonard 1934- 33-36R
Markowitz, Norman Daniel 1943- 45-48
Marks, Alfred H(arding) 1920- CANR-23
Earlier sketch in CA 45-48
Marks, Barry A(lan) 1926- 17-20R
Marks, Bayly Ellen 1943- 115
Marks, Burton 1930- 107
See also SATA 43, 47
Marks, Charles 1922- CANR-5
Earlier sketch in CA 53-56
Marks, Claude (Mordecai) 1915-1991 61-64
Obituary 134
Marks, David (Francis) 1945- 132
Marks, Edith Bobroff 1924- 17-20R
Marks, Edward S(tanford) 1936- 45-48
Marks, Elaine 1930- CANR-23
Earlier sketches in CA 17-20R, CANR-7
Marks, Eli S(amplin) 1911-1991 85-88
Obituary 133
Marks, Frederick (William III) 1940- 97-100
Marks, Geoffrey 1906- 33-36R
Marks, Hannah K.
See Trivelpiece, Laurel
Marks, Henry S(eymour) 1933- 73-76
Marks, J
See Highwater, Jamake (Mamake)
Marks, J(ames) M(acdonald) 1921- 61-64
See also SATA 13
Marks, James R(obert) 1932- 17-20R
Marks, Jane (A. Steinberg) 1943- 113
Marks, John David 1909-1985 Obituary 117
Marks, John H(enry) 1923- 17-20R
Marks, John 1943- 110
Marks, Johnny
See Marks, John David
Marks, Laurie J. 1957- 135
See also SATA 68
Marks, (Amelia) Lee 1948- 137
Marks, Margaret L. 1911(?)-1980 Obituary 101
See also SATA 23
Marks, Marjorie
See Bitker, Marjorie M(arks)
Marks, Mickey Klar CANR-6
Earlier sketch in CA 1-4R
See also SATA 12
Marks, Norton E(lliott) 1932- 21-24R
Marks, Pat R.
See Feinman, Jeffrey
Marks, Paula Mitchell 1951- 135
Marks, Peter
See Smith, Robert Kimmel
Marks, Rita 1938- 106
See also SATA 47
Marks, Sally (Jean) 1931- 102
Marks, Sema 1942- 29-32R
Marks, Stan(ley) CANR-31
Earlier sketches in CA 29-32R, CANR-12
See also SATA 14
Marks, Stuart A. 1939- 69-72
Marks, Vic(tor James) 1955- 118
Marksberry, Mary Lee 13-16R
Marks-Highwater, J
See Highwater, Jamake (Mamake)
Markson, David M(errill) 1927- CANR-1
Earlier sketch in CA 49-52
See also CLC 67
Markstein, David L. 1920- 29-32R
Markstein, George 1929-1987 Obituary 121
Markun, Alan Fletcher 1925- 45-48
Markun, Patricia Maloney 1924- CANR-4
Earlier sketch in CA 5-8R
See also SATA 15
Markus, Julia 1939- 105
Markus, R(obert) A(ustin) 1924- CANR-16
Earlier sketch in CA 65-68
Marland, Christina
See Pemberton, Margaret
Marland, Edward Allen 1912- 17-20R
Marland, Michael 1934- 103
Marland, Sidney P(ercy Jr.) 1914- 53-56
Obituary 137
Marlatt, Daphne (Buckle) 1942- CANR-39
Earlier sketches in CA 25-28R, CANR-17
See also DLB 60
Marlborough
See Oaksey, John
Marley, Augusta Anne Obituary 41-44R
Marley, Bob
See Marley, Robert Nesta
See also CLC 17
Marley, Robert Nesta 1945-1981 107
Obituary 103
See also Marley, Bob
Marlin, Alice Tepper 1944- 123
Marlin, Henry
See Giggal, Kenneth
Marlin, Hilda
See Van Stockum, Hilda
Marlin, Jeffrey 1940- 45-48
Marlin, John Tepper 1942- 124
Marling, William 1951- 123
Marling, Yvonne Rodd
See Rodd-Marling, Yvonne
Marlo, John A. 1934- 29-32R
Marlor, Clark Strang 1922- 37-40R
Marlot, Raymond
See Angremy, Jean-Pierre
Marlow, Cecilia Ann 1952- 121
Marlow, David 1943- 107
Marlow, Edwina
See Huff, T(om) E.
Marlow, Joyce
See Connor, Joyce Mary
Marlow, Louis
See Wilkinson, Louis (Umfreville)
Marlowe, Alan Stephen 1937- 21-24R
Marlowe, Amy Bell CANR-26
Earlier sketches in CAP-2, CA 19-20
See also SATA 1, 67
Marlowe, Christopher
1564-1593 ....CDBLB Before 1660
See also DC 1
See also DLB 62
See also WLC
Marlowe, Dan J(ames) 1914- CANR-1
Earlier sketch in CA 1-4R
Marlowe, Derek 1938- CANR-11
Earlier sketch in CA 17-20R
Marlowe, Don 61-64
Marlowe, Hugh
See Patterson, Harry
Marlowe, Kenneth 1926- 13-16R
Marlowe, Stephen 1928- CANR-6
Earlier sketch in CA 13-16R
Marlowe, Webb
See McComas, J(esse) Francis
Marlyn, John 1912- 9-12R
See also DLB 88
Marmion, Harry A. 1931- 25-28R
Marmion, Shakerley 1603-1639 ....DLB 58
Marmon, William F. Jr. 1942- 77-80
Marmor, J(udd) 1910- CANR-12
Earlier sketch in CA 25-28R
Marmor, T(heodore) R(ichard) 1939- CANR-27
Earlier sketch in CA 29-32R
Marmur, Dow 1935- 121
Marmur, Jacland 1901- 9-12R
Marmur, Mildred 1930- 5-8R
Marnell, William H. 1907- 21-24R
Marney, (Leonard) Carlyle 1916-1978 57-60
Obituary 135
Marney, Dean 1952- CANR-28
Earlier sketch in CA 110
Marney, John 1933- 69-72
Marnham, Patrick 1943- 102
Marokvia, Artur 1909- ....SATA 31
Marokvia, Mireille (Journet) 1918- 29-32R
See also SATA 5
Marol, Jean-Claude 1946- 130
Maron, Margaret 122
Maroon, Fred J. 1924- 132
Marossi, Ruth
See Krefetz, Ruth
Marot, Marc
See Koch, Kurt E(mil)
Marple, Allen Clark 1901(?)-1968 Obituary 106
Marple, Hugo D(ixon) 1920- 53-56
Marples, William F(rank) 1907- CAP-1
Earlier sketch in CA 13-16
Marquand, John P(hillips) 1893-1960 85-88
See also CLC 2, 10
See also DLB 9, 102
Marquand, Josephine
See Gladstone, Josephine
Marquand, Robert 1957- 136
Marquard, Leo(pold) 1897- 5-8R
Marquardt, Dorothy Ann 1921- 13-16R
Marques, Rene 1919-1979 97-100
Obituary 85-88
See also DLB 113
See also HW
Marquess, Harlan E(arl) 1931- 49-52
Marquess, William Henry 1954- 126
Marquess of Anglesey
See Paget, George Charles Henry Victor
Marquez, Gabriel (Jose) Garcia
See Garcia Marquez, Gabriel (Jose)
See also CLC 68
Marquez, Robert 1942- 53-56
Marquis, Arnold 57-60
Marquis, Dave 1951- 113
Marquis, Don(ald Robert Perry)
1878-1937 Brief entry 104
See also DLB 11, 25
See also TCLC 7
Marquis, Donald G(eorge)
1908-1973 Obituary 45-48
Marquis, G(eorge) Welton 1916- 17-20R
Marquis, Max 136
Marr, David G(eorge) 1937- CANR-28
Earlier sketch in CA 33-36R
Marr, James Pratt 1898-1986 Obituary 121
Marr, John S(tuart) 1940- 81-84
See also SATA 48
Marranca, Bonnie 1947- CANR-9
Earlier sketch in CA 65-68
Marreco, Anne
See Wignall, Anne
Marric, J. J.
See Butler, William (Arthur) Vivian
and Creasey, John
Marrin, Albert 1936- CANR-30
Earlier sketch in CA 49-52
See also SATA 43, 53

Marriner, Ernest (Cummings)
1891-1983 ....CANR-28
Obituary 109
Earlier sketch in CA 37-40R
Marrington, Pauline 1921- CANR-10
Earlier sketch in CA 65-68
Marriott, Alice Lee 1910- 57-60
Obituary 137
See also SATA 31, 71
Marriott, (Joyce) Anne 1913- CANR-18
Earlier sketch in CA 102
See also DLB 68
Marriott, Pat(ricia) 1920- ....SATA 35
Marriott, William H. 1909(?)-1986 Obituary 118
Marriott-Watson, Nan 1899-1982 Obituary 107
Marris, Peter (Horsey) 1927- CANR-29
Earlier sketch in CA 111
Marris, Robin Lapthorn 1924- CANR-8
Earlier sketch in CA 5-8R
Marris, Ruth 1948- 106
Marrison, L(eslie) W(illiam) 1901- 29-32R
Marr-Johnson, Diana (Maugham) 1908- 13-16R
Marrocco, W(illiam) Thomas 1909- 9-12R
Marron, Kevin (Christopher Gerard) 1947- 127
Marrone, Robert 1941- 77-80
Marrone, Steven P(hillip) 1947- 130
Marroquin, Patricio
See Markun, Patricia Maloney
Marrow, Alfred J. 1905-1978 81-84
Obituary 77-80
Marrow, Bernard
See Moore, Brian
Marrow, Stanley B. 1931- CANR-26
Earlier sketches in CA 25-28R, CANR-10
Marrs, Edwin W(ilson) Jr. 1928- 25-28R
Marrus, Michael R(obert) 1941- CANR-12
Earlier sketch in CA 33-36R
Marryat, Frederick 1792-1848 ....DLB 21
Mars, Alastair 1915-1985 Obituary 116
Mars, Florence L. 1923- 101
Mars, Gerald 1933- 132
Mars, Jean Price
See Price-Mars, Jean
Mars, W. T.
See Mars, Witold Tadeusz J.
Mars, Witold Tadeusz J. 1912- 25-28R
See also SATA 3
Marsack, Robyn (Louise) 1953- 127
Marsano, Ramon
See Dinges, John (Charles)
Marsden, George (Mish) 1939- CANR-12
Earlier sketch in CA 73-76
Marsden, James
See Creasey, John
Marsden, John 1950- 135
See also SATA 66
Marsden, Lorna R(uth) 1942- 85-88
Marsden, Malcolm Morse 1922- 5-8R
Marsden, Peter (Richard Valentine)
1940- CANR-14
Earlier sketch in CA 77-80
Marsden, Philip Kitson 1916-1984 Obituary 113
Marsden-Smedley, Hester
1901-1982 Obituary 107
Marsden-Smedley, Philip 1961- 135
Marsh, Analyticus
See Morrison, Marsh
Marsh, Andrew
See O'Donovan, John
Marsh, Clifton E. 1946- 77-80
Marsh, Corinna (Reiman)
1891-1990 Obituary 132
Marsh, Dave 1950- CANR-17
Earlier sketch in CA 97-100
See also SATA 66
Marsh, David Charles 1917- 103
Marsh, Edwin
See Schorb, E(dwin) M(arsh)
Marsh, George Perkins 1801-1882 ....DLB 1, 64
Marsh, Henry
See Saklatvala, Beram
Marsh, Irving T. 1907-1982 ....9-12R
Obituary 107
Marsh, J. E.
See Marshall, Evelyn
Marsh, James 1794-1842 ....DLB 1, 59
Marsh, Jean
See Marshall, Evelyn
Marsh, Jeanne C(ay) 1948- 111
Marsh, Jeri 1940- 85-88
Marsh, John L(eslie) 1927- CANR-1
Earlier sketch in CA 45-48
Marsh, John 1904- CAP-1
Earlier sketch in CA 9-10
Marsh, John 1907- CAP-1
Earlier sketch in CA 13-16
Marsh, Leonard (Charles) 1906- 37-40R
Marsh, Leonard (George) 1930- CANR-13
Earlier sketch in CA 73-76
Marsh, Margaret Sammartino 1945- 106
Marsh, Mary Val 1925- CANR-26
Earlier sketches in CA 69-72, CANR-11
Marsh, Meredith 1946- 77-80
Marsh, (Edith) Ngaio 1899-1982 ....CANR-6
Earlier sketch in CA 9-12R
See also CLC 7, 53
See also DLB 77
See also MTCW
Marsh, Norman Stayner 1913- 117
Marsh, Patrick O(tis) 1928- 25-28R
Marsh, Paul
See Hopkins, (Hector) Kenneth
Marsh, Peter T(imothy) 1935- 33-36R
Marsh, Philip M(errill) 1893- 9-12R
Marsh, Rebecca
See Neubauer, William Arthur
Marsh, Robert C(harles) 1924- 13-16R
Marsh, Robert (Harrison) 1926-1979 ....17-20R
Obituary 134
Marsh, Robert M(ortimer) 1931- CANR-2
Earlier sketch in CA 1-4R
Marsh, Ronald (James) 1914- 13-16R
Marsh, Rosalind
See Marsh, Rosalind J(udith)
Marsh, Rosalind J(udith) 1950- 132
Marsh, Spencer 1931- 61-64
Marsh, Susan (Sherry Raymond) 1914- 9-12R
Marsh, U(lysses) Grant 1911- 57-60
Marsh, Willard 1922-1970 ....CAP-2
Earlier sketch in CA 25-28
Marshak, Robert Eugene 1916- 107
Marshak, Samuil Yakovlevich
1887-1964 Obituary 111
Marshall, Alan 1902- 85-88
Marshall, Alfred 1884-1965 ....5-8R
Marshall, Annie Jessie 1922- CAP-1
Earlier sketch in CA 9-10
Marshall, Anthony D(ryden) 1924- 29-32R
See also SATA 18
Marshall, (Charles) Arthur (Bertram)
1910-1989 Obituary 127
Marshall, Bill 1937- CANR-17
Earlier sketch in CA 65-68
Marshall, Bruce 1899-1987 ....5-8R
Obituary 123
Marshall, Burke 1922- 13-16R
Marshall, Byron K. 1936- 33-36R
Marshall, (Sarah) Catherine (Wood)
1914-1983 ....CANR-8
Obituary 109
Earlier sketch in CA 17-20R
See also SATA 2, 34
Marshall, Charles Burton 1908- 37-40R
Marshall, Charles Wheeler 1906- 110
Marshall, D(onald) Bruce 1931- 65-68
Marshall, David F(ranklin) 1938- 25-28R
Marshall, Don
See Marshall, Donovan
Marshall, Donald R. 1934- 93-96
Marshall, Donald S(tanley) 1919- 29-32R
Marshall, Donovan 1908- 117
Marshall, Dorothy 1900- CAP-1
Earlier sketch in CA 13-14
Marshall, Douglas
See McClintock, Marshall
Marshall, E(dmund) Jesse 1888- CAP-1
Earlier sketch in CA 11-12
Marshall, Edison 1894-1967 ....CAP-1
Obituary 29-32R
Earlier sketch in CA 9-10
See also DLB 102
Marshall, Edmund
See Hopkins, (Hector) Kenneth
Marshall, Edward 1932- ....DLB 16
Marshall, Emily
See Hall, Bennie Caroline (Humble)
Marshall, Evelyn 1897- CANR-18
Earlier sketches in CA 5-8R, CANR-2
See also SATA 11
Marshall, F(reddie) Ray 1928- CANR-8
Earlier sketch in CA 17-20R
Marshall, Garry 1934- 111
See also AAYA 3
See also CLC 17
See also SATA 60
Marshall, George C(atlett) Jr.
1880-1959 Brief entry 115
Marshall, George (Nichols) 1920- 77-80
Marshall, George O(ctavius) Jr. 1922- 17-20R
Marshall, H. H.
See Jahn, Joseph Michael
Marshall, Helen E(dith) 1899- 37-40R
Marshall, Helen Lowrie 1904-1975 103
Marshall, Herbert Hedley
1909(?)-1982 Obituary 112
Marshall, Herbert (Percival James)
1906- CANR-29
Earlier sketch in CA 25-28R
Marshall, Hermine H(alprin) 1935- CANR-14
Earlier sketch in CA 41-44R
Marshall, Howard D(rake) 1924-1972 ....CAP-2
Obituary 37-40R
Earlier sketch in CA 23-24
Marshall, Howard Wight 1944- 107
Marshall, Hubert (Ray) 1920- 21-24R
Marshall, I(an) Howard 1934- 122
Marshall, I. N. 1931- 134
Marshall, J(ohn) D(uncan) 1919- CANR-31
Earlier sketch in CA 73-76
Marshall, Jack 1937- 97-100
Marshall, James (Edward) 1942- CANR-38
Earlier sketch in CA 41-44R
See also CLR 21
See also DLB 61
See also MAICYA
See also SATA 6, 51
Marshall, James M(orse) 1924- 120
Marshall, James Vance
See Payne, Donald Gordon
Marshall, James Vance 1887-1964 ....CAP-1
Earlier sketch in CA 11-12
Marshall, James 1896-1986 ....41-44R
Obituary 120
Marshall, Jeff
See Laycock, George (Edwin)
Marshall, Joanne
See Rundle, Anne
Marshall, John David 1928- CANR-19
Earlier sketches in CA 9-12R, CANR-3
Marshall, John Ross 1912- 109
Marshall, John S(edberry) 1898- CAP-1
Earlier sketch in CA 19-20
Marshall, John 1905(?)-1985(?) Obituary 116
Marshall, John 1922- CANR-15
Earlier sketch in CA 89-92
Marshall, Joyce 1913- 102
See also DLB 88
Marshall, Kathryn 1951- 57-60
See also AITN 1
Marshall, Kim
See Marshall, Michael (Kimbrough)
Marshall, Lenore Guinzburg 1899-1971 ....CAP-2
Obituary 33-36R
Earlier sketch in CA 25-28
Marshall, Lovat
See Duncan, W(illiam) Murdoch
Marshall, Margaret Wiley 1908- CAP-1
Earlier sketch in CA 9-10
Marshall, Margaret 1901(?)-1974 Obituary 104
Marshall, Martin V(ivan) 1922- 1-4R
Marshall, Max Lawrence 1922- 17-20R
Marshall, Max S(kidmore) 1897- CAP-1
Earlier sketch in CA 13-14
Marshall, Megan 1954- 124
Marshall, Mel(vin D.) 1911- CANR-12
Earlier sketch in CA 29-32R
Marshall, Michael (Kimbrough) 1948- CANR-3
Earlier sketch in CA 49-52
See also SATA 37
Marshall, Muriel 106
Marshall, Natalie J(unemann) 1929- 41-44R
Marshall, Norman 1901-1980 Obituary 108
Marshall, Paule 1929- CANR-25
Earlier sketch in CA 77-80
See also BLC 3
See also BW
See also CLC 27, 72
See also DLB 33
See also MTCW
See also SSC 3
Marshall, Percy
See Young, Percy M(arshall)
Marshall, Peter 1902-1949 Brief entry 112
Marshall, Ray
See Marshall, F(reddie) Ray
Marshall, Raymond
See Raymond, Rene (Brabazon)
Marshall, Richard (D.) 1947- 125
Marshall, Robert G. 1919- 37-40R
Marshall, Robert L(ewis) 1939- 104
Marshall, Roderick 1903-1975 Obituary 53-56
Marshall, Ronald 1905- CAP-2
Earlier sketch in CA 33-36
Marshall, Rosalind Kay 1939- CANR-19
Earlier sketches in CA 53-56, CANR-4
Marshall, S(amuel) L(yman) A(twood)
1900-1977 81-84
Obituary 73-76
See also SATA 21
Marshall, Shirley E(velyn) 1925- 21-24R
Marshall, Sybil Mary (Edwards) 1913- CANR-1
Earlier sketch in CA 1-4R
Marshall, T(homas) H(umphrey) 1893-1981 109
Obituary 105
Marshall, Thomas Archibald 1938- CANR-38
Earlier sketches in CA 49-52, CANR-1, 17
See also Marshall, Tom
Marshall, Thomas F(rederic) 1908- CAP-2
Earlier sketch in CA 23-24
Marshall, Thomas R. 1949- 115
Marshall, Tom
See Marshall, Thomas Archibald
See also DLB 60
Marshall, Tyler 1941- 136
Marshall, William
See Marshall, William Leonard
Marshall, William H(arvey) 1925-1968 ....CAP-1
Earlier sketch in CA 11-12
Marshall, William Leonard 1944- 133
Brief entry 127
Marshall-Cornwall, James (Handyside)
1887-1985 107
Obituary 118
Marshburn, Joseph Hancock 1890-1975 109
Obituary 106
Marshner, Connaught Coyne 1951- CANR-16
Earlier sketch in CA 93-96
Marsilius of Padua 1275(?)-1342(?) ....DLB 115
Mars-Jones, Adam 1954- CANR-27
Earlier sketch in CA 109
Marsland, Amy 1924- CANR-19
Earlier sketch in CA 103
Marsoli, Lisa Ann 1958- 120
See also SATA 53
Marson, Philip 1892- 9-12R
Marsteller, Bill
See Marsteller, William A.
Marsteller, William A. 1914-1987 Obituary 123
Marsten, Richard
See Hunter, Evan
Marston, David W(eese) 1942- 125
Marston, Elsa 1933- CANR-32
Earlier sketch in CA 113
Marston, Hope Irvin 1935- 101
See also SATA 31
Marston, John E. 1911- 5-8R
Marston, John 1576-1634 ....DLB 58
Marston, Philip Bourke 1850-1887 ....DLB 35
Marston, Thomas Ewart
1904-1984 Obituary 112
Marszalek, John F(rancis Jr.) 1939- CANR-14
Earlier sketch in CA 37-40R
Martchenko, Michael 1942- ....SATA 50
Marteka, Vincent (James) 1936- 13-16R
Martel, Jane G. 1926- 57-60
Martel, Leon C. 1933- 125
Martell, James
See Bingley, David Ernest
Martell, Paul 1921(?)-1985 Obituary 116
Martellaro, Joseph A. 1924- 17-20R
Martelli, Leonard J. 1938(?)-1988 Obituary 125
Marten, Michael 1947- 132
Martens, Elmer A(rthur) 1930- 127
Martens, Kurt 1870-1945 ....DLB 66
Marter, Joan M. 1946- 124
Marth, Del 1925- 61-64
Martha, Henry
See Harris, Mark
Marti, Fritz 1894- 107
Martianoff, Nicholas 1893-1984 Obituary 112
Martignoni, Margaret E.
1908(?)-1974 Obituary 104
See also SATA 27
Marti-Ibanez, Felix
1912(?)-1972 Obituary 33-36R
Martin, Albert
See Mehan, Joseph Albert
and Nussbaum, Al(bert F.)
Martin, Albro 1921- 77-80
Martin, Alex 1953- 137
Martin, Alfred Manuel 1928-1989 108
Obituary 130
Martin, Alfred 1916- 117
Martin, Allie Beth 1914-1976 Obituary 65-68
Martin, Anamae 1919- 9-12R
Martin, Andre
See Jacoby, Henry
Martin, Andrew 1906-1985 137
Obituary 115
Martin, Andy
See Martin, Andrew
Martin, Ann Bodenhamer 1927- CANR-11
Earlier sketch in CA 69-72
Martin, Ann M(atthews) 1955- CANR-32
Earlier sketch in CA 111
See also AAYA 6
See also MAICYA
See also SATA 41, 44, 70
Martin, April
See Sherrill, Dorothy
Martin, Arlan Stone 1932- 69-72
Martin, Augustine 1935- 93-96
Martin, Barclay (Cluck) 1923- 73-76
Martin, Ben(jamin S.) 1921- 1-4R
Martin, Benjamin F(ranklin Jr.) 1947- 89-92
Martin, Bernard (Davis) 1897- CAP-1
Earlier sketch in CA 9-10
Martin, Bernard 1905- CAP-1
Earlier sketch in CA 11-12
Martin, Bernard 1928- CANR-4
Earlier sketch in CA 53-56
Martin, Betty
See Martin, Elizabeth DuVernet
Martin, Bill
See Martin, William Ivan
Martin, Bill Jr.
See Martin, William Ivan
See also SATA 67
Martin, Billy
See Martin, Alfred Manuel
Martin, Boyd A(rcher) 1911- 37-40R
Martin, Brian P(hilip) 1947- CANR-38
Earlier sketch in CA 116
Martin, Bruce
See Paine, Lauran (Bosworth)
Martin, C(arol) Dianne 1943- 113
Martin, C(harles) Leslie 1897- 5-8R
Martin, C. Lewis 1915- 25-28R
Martin, Calvin (L.) 1948- Brief entry 113
Martin, Carter W(illiams) 1933- 25-28R
Martin, Charles B(asil) 1930- 93-96
Martin, Charles Burton 1924- 25-28R
Martin, Charles E.
See Mastrangelo, Charles E.
See also SATA 69, 70
Martin, Charles 1906- 1-4R
Martin, Charles 1942- ....DLB 120
Martin, Charles-Noel 1923- 29-32R
Martin, Chip
See Martin, Stoddard (Hammond) Jr.
Martin, Christopher
See Hoyt, Edwin P(almer) Jr.
Martin, Chryssee (MacCasler) Perry 1940- 126
Martin, Claire 1914- ....DLB 60
Martin, Cort
See Sherman, Jory (Tecumseh)
Martin, Curtis 1915- 53-56
Martin, David Alfred 1929- 107
Martin, David C(lark) 1943- 102
Martin, David Grant 1939- 65-68
Martin, David L(incoln) 1947- 119
Martin, David (Lozell) 1946- CANR-27
Earlier sketch in CA 89-92
Martin, David Stone 1913- ....SATA 39
Martin, David 1915- CANR-24
Earlier sketch in CA 103
Martin, Don W. 1934- 126
Martin, Don 1931- 101
Martin, Donald Franklin 1944- 65-68
Martin, Donald L(loyd) 1939- 111
Martin, Dorothy L. 1921- 138
Martin, Dorothy 1921- CANR-6
Earlier sketch in CA 57-60
See also SATA 47
Martin, Douglas (Ivor) 1939- 133
Martin, Dwight 1921-1978 Obituary 77-80
Martin, E(rnest) W(alter) 1914- CANR-20
Earlier sketches in CA 9-12R, CANR-5
Martin, Earl S(auder) 1944- 102
Martin, Edward A(lexander) 1927- 120
Martin, Elizabeth A(nn) 1945- 132
Martin, Elizabeth DuVernet 1910- 103
Martin, Ellis
See Ryan, Marah Ellis
Martin, Emily 1944- CANR-27
Earlier sketch in CA 49-52

Martin, Esmond Bradley 1941- CANR-16
Earlier sketch in CA 93-96
Martin, Eugene CANR-26
Earlier sketches in CAP-2, CA 19-20
See also SATA 1
Martin, Eva M. 1939- 126
See also SATA 65
Martin, F(rancis) David 1920- 33-36R
Martin, F(rancis) X(avier) 1922- CANR-30
Earlier sketches in CA 21-24R, CANR-13
Martin, Frances M(cEntee) 1906- 61-64
See also SATA 36
Martin, Francis
See Reid, Charles (Stuart)
Martin, Frederick M(orris)
1923-1985 Obituary 115
Martin, Fredric
See Christopher, Matt(hew F.)
Martin, G(eoffrey) H(oward) 1928- 5-8R
Martin, Gary M. 1936- 89-92
Martin, Ged
See Martin, Gerald Warren
Martin, Geoffrey John 1934- CANR-14
Earlier sketch in CA 37-40R
Martin, George R(aymond) R(ichard)
1948- 81-84
Martin, George (Whitney) 1926- CANR-21
Earlier sketches in CA 9-12R, CANR-3
Martin, Gerald Warren 1945- CANR-38
Earlier sketches in CA 45-48, CANR-1, 17
Martin, Graham Dunstan 1932- CANR-23
Earlier sketch in CA 106
Martin, Greg
See Miller, George Louquet
Martin, Harold Clark 1917- 9-12R
Martin, Harold Harber 1910- CANR-7
Earlier sketch in CA 61-64
Martin, Harold S(heaffer) 1930- 57-60
Martin, Herbert Woodward 1933- CANR-27
Earlier sketch in CA 73-76
See also BW
Martin, Herbert 1913- 29-32R
Martin, Hubert M. Jr. 1932- 103
Martin, Ian Kennedy
See Kennedy-Martin, Ian
Martin, Ira Jay III 1911- 53-56
Martin, J(ohn) P(ercival) 1880(?)-1966 81-84
See also SATA 15
Martin, Jack
See Etchison, Dennis (William)
Martin, James Alfred Jr. 1917- 73-76
Martin, James Gilbert 1926- 9-12R
Martin, James J(oseph) 1916- CANR-8
Earlier sketch in CA 5-8R
Martin, James Kirby 1943- 125
Martin, James L. 1948- 81-84
Martin, James Perry 1923- 5-8R
Martin, James (Thomas) 1933- 134
Brief entry 112
Martin, James 1921- 119
Martin, Jane Roland 1929- 119
Martin, Janet
See Garfinkel, Bernard Max
Martin, Jay
See Golding, Morton J(ay)
Martin, Jay (Herbert) 1935- CANR-21
Earlier sketch in CA 5-8R
See also DLB 111
Martin, Jeremy
See Levin, Marcia Obrasky
Martin, John Bartlow 1915-1987 ....CANR-8
Obituary 121
Earlier sketch in CA 13-16R
Martin, John Hanbury 1892-1983 Obituary 109
Martin, John Henry 1915- 102
Martin, John Rupert 1916- 17-20R
Martin, John Sayre 1921- 103
Martin, John Stuart 1900-1977 ....9-12R
Obituary 69-72
Martin, John 1893-1985 Obituary 116
Martin, Jose L(uis) 1921- CANR-12
Earlier sketch in CA 61-64
See also HW
Martin, Joseph George 1915-1981 108
Obituary 102
Martin, Joy 1922- 57-60
Martin, Judith (Sylvia) 1938- CANR-12
Earlier sketch in CA 97-100
Martin, Julie (Breyer) 1938- 133
Martin, June Hall
See McCash, June Hall
Martin, Kathryn 1908- 108
Martin, Ken
See Hubbard, L(afayette) Ron(ald)
Martin, Kenneth R(obert) 1938- CANR-38
Earlier sketches in CA 45-48, CANR-1, 17
Martin, Kevin
See Pelton, Robert W(ayne)
Martin, (Basil) Kingsley 1897-1969 ....CANR-11
Obituary 25-28R
Earlier sketch in CA 5-8R
Martin, L(eslie) John 1921- CANR-22
Earlier sketches in CA 57-60, CANR-6
Martin, Laura C(oogle) 1952- 117
Martin, Laurence W(oodward) 1928- CANR-7
Earlier sketch in CA 5-8R
Martin, Lawrence 1895- CAP-1
Earlier sketch in CA 9-10
Martin, Lee
See Wingate, (Martha) Anne (Guice)
Martin, Lee Nicholson
1916(?)-1987 Obituary 124
Martin, Les
See Schulman, L(ester) M(artin)
Martin, Linda G. 1947- 128
Martin, Lucien
See Gabel, Joseph
Martin, Luis 1927- 131
See also HW
Martin, Luther H(oward) Jr. 1937- 124
Martin, Lynne 1923- 65-68
See also SATA 21
Martin, M(arilynn) Kay 1942- 65-68
Martin, Malachi 81-84
See also AITN 1
Martin, Marcia
See Levin, Marcia Obrasky
Martin, Margaret Joan 1928- 69-72
Martin, Marie-Louise 1912- 69-72
Martin, Mario Jr.
See Monteleone, Thomas F(rancis)
Martin, Marjorie 1942- 53-56
Martin, Marta San
See San Martin, Marta
Martin, Mary Steichen
See Calderone, Mary S(teichen)
Martin, Mary 1913(?)-1990 113
Obituary 132
Brief entry 111
Martin, Maurice 1946- 115
Martin, Michael L. 1932- 17-20R
Martin, Michael William 1946- 121
Martin, Michelle 1957- 119
Martin, Mike W.
See Martin, Michael William
Martin, Milward Wyatt 1895-1974 ....CAP-1
Earlier sketch in CA 19-20
Martin, Morgan 1921- 17-20R
Martin, Murray S(impson) 1928- 112
Martin, Nancy
See Salmon, Annie Elizabeth
Martin, Noah S(ensenig) 1940- 69-72
Martin, Norma F(rances) 1936- 113
Martin, Oliver
See Smith, R(eginald) D(onald)
Martin, Ovid A. 1904-1979 Obituary 89-92
Martin, Patricia Miles 1899-1986 ....CANR-37
Obituary 119
Earlier sketches in CA 1-4R, CANR-2
See also MAICYA
See also SATA 1, 43, 48
Martin, Paul
See Deale, Kenneth Edwin Lee
Martin, Paul Sidney 1899-1974 ....CANR-8
Earlier sketch in CA 5-8R
Martin, Pete
See Martin, William Thorton
Martin, Peter
See Chaundler, Christine
Martin, (Roy) Peter 1931- 125
Brief entry 120
Martin, Peter W(illiam) 1939- 89-92
Martin, Philip (John Talbot) 1931- CANR-24
Earlier sketches in CA 61-64, CANR-9
Martin, Phyllis Cook 1908- 5-8R
Martin, Phyllis R(odgers) 130
Martin, Quinn 1922-1987 Obituary 123
Martin, R. Johnson
See Mehta, Rustam Jehangir
Martin, R(ichard) M(ilton) 1916- CANR-15
Earlier sketch in CA 41-44R
Martin, Ralph C. 1924- 9-12R
Martin, Ralph G. 1920- 5-8R
Martin, Ralph P(hilip) CANR-9
Earlier sketch in CA 65-68
Martin, Ralph 1942- CANR-9
Earlier sketch in CA 57-60
Martin, Reginald 1956- 126
Martin, Rene 1891-1977 ....SATA 20, 42
Martin, Renee C(ohen) 1928- 49-52
Martin, Rhona 1922- 121
Brief entry 116
Martin, Richard
See Creasey, John
Martin, Richard 1946- 124
Martin, Robert A(llen) 1930- 110
Martin, Robert Bernard 1918- CANR-25
Earlier sketches in CA 1-4R, CANR-2
Martin, Robert K(essler) 1941- 102
Martin, Robert (Lee) 1908-1976 ....1-4R
Obituary 103
Martin, Robert Sidney 1949- 122
Martin, Robert W.
See Pelton, Robert W(ayne)
Martin, Roderick 1940- CANR-12
Earlier sketch in CA 29-32R
Martin, Roger H(arry) 1943- 132
Martin, Ron 1941- 122
Martin, Ronald E(dward) 1933- 17-20R
Martin, Roscoe C(oleman) 1903-1972 ......CAP-1
Obituary 33-36R
Earlier sketch in CA 19-20
Martin, Rupert (Claude) 1905- ....SATA 31
Martin, Ruth
See Rayner, Claire (Berenice)
Martin, Sam
See Moskowitz, Sam
Martin, Samuel Elmo 1924- Brief entry 105
Martin, Stefan 1936- ....SATA 32
Martin, Stella
See Heyer, Georgette
Martin, Steve 1945- CANR-30
Earlier sketch in CA 97-100
See also CLC 30
See also MTCW
Martin, Stoddard (Hammond) Jr. 1948- 117
Martin, Susan B(oyles) 1959- 128
Martin, Susan Ehrlich 1940- 124
Martin, Sylvia (Pass) 1913-1981 ....17-20R
Obituary 135
Martin, Taffy 1945- 125
Martin, Thom(as) Francis 1934- 5-8R
Martin, Thomas Lyle Jr. 1921- 9-12R
Martin, Timothy (Peter) 1950- 138
Martin, Tom
See Paine, Lauran (Bosworth)
Martin, Tony 1942- CANR-26
Earlier sketches in CA 57-60, CANR-6
See also BW
Martin, Valerie 1948- 85-88
See also BEST 90:2
Martin, Vance G(regory) 1949- 114
Martin, Vernon N(orthfleet) 1930- 45-48
Martin, Vicky
See Storey, Victoria Carolyn
Martin, Wallace 1933- 122
Martin, Walter Ralston 1928-1989 Obituary 129
Martin, Walter T(ilford) 1917- 9-12R
Martin, Warren Bryan 1925- CANR-20
Earlier sketch in CA 41-44R
Martin, Webber
See Silverberg, Robert
Martin, Wendy
See Martini, Teri
Martin, Wendy 1940- 37-40R
Martin, Wilfred B(enjamin) W(eldon) 1940- 116
Martin, William C. 1937- CANR-14
Earlier sketch in CA 77-80
Martin, William Ivan 1916- 130
Brief entry 117
See also Martin, Bill Jr.
See also MAICYA
See also SATA 40
Martin, William Keble 1877-1969 Obituary 104
Martin, William Thorton
1901(?)-1980 Obituary 102
Martinco, John P. 1917(?)-1986 Obituary 118
Martindale, Charles (Anthony) 1949- 124
Martindale, Colin (Eugene) 1943- 61-64
Martindale, Don (Albert) 1915- CANR-6
Earlier sketch in CA 13-16R
Martin du Gard, Roger
1881-1958 Brief entry 118
See also DLB 65
See also TCLC 24
Martine
See Woolfolk, Joanna Martine
Martine, James J(ohn) 1937- 57-60
Martineau, Gilbert CANR-17
Earlier sketch in CA 29-32R
Martineau, Harriet 1802-1876 ....DLB 21, 55
See also YABC 2
Martineau, James 1805-1900 Brief entry 122
Martineau, Robert Arnold Schurhoff 1913- 106
Martine-Barnes, Adrienne 1942- 110
Martinelli, Ricardo
See Brandon, Johnny
Martines, Julia
See O'Faolain, Julia
Martines, Lauro 1927- CANR-12
Earlier sketch in CA 25-28R
Martinet, Andre 1908- CAP-1
Earlier sketch in CA 11-12
Martinetti, Ronald 1945- 57-60
Martinetz, V(ivian) L. 1927- 61-64
Martinez, Al 1929- 57-60
Martinez, Elizabeth Sutherland 1925- 121
Martinez, Enrique Gonzalez
See Gonzalez Martinez, Enrique
Martinez, Jacinto Benavente y
See Benavente (y Martinez), Jacinto
Martinez, Julio A(ntonio) 1931- CANR-18
Earlier sketch in CA 101
See also HW
Martinez, Max(imiano) 1943- 131
See also DLB 82
See also HW
Martinez, Orlando 1924- 138
Martinez, Oscar J(aquez) 1943- 120
Martinez, Rafael Arevalo
See Arevalo Martinez, Rafael
Martinez, Rafael V. 1923- 9-12R
Martinez, Raymond J(oseph) 1889- 61-64
Martinez, S(ally) A. 1938- 81-84
Martinez, Tomas Eloy 131
See also HW
Martinez Moreno, Carlos 1917-1986 131
See also HW
Martinez Ruiz, Jose 1873-1967 93-96
See also Azorin
and Ruiz, Jose Martinez
See also HW
Martinez Sierra, Gregorio
1881-1947 Brief entry 115
See also TCLC 6
Martinez Sierra, Maria (de la O'LeJarraga)
1874-1974 Obituary 115
See also TCLC 6
Marting, Diane E. 1952- 138
Martini, Teri 1930- CANR-2
Earlier sketch in CA 5-8R
See also SATA 3
Martini, Therese
See Martini, Teri
Martini, Virgilio 1903- 37-40R
Martino, Bill 1933- 57-60
Martino, Joseph P(aul) 1931- 61-64
Martino, Rocco L(eonard) 1929- 13-16R
Martins, Maria Isabel Barreno de Faria
1939- 105
See also Barreno, Maria Isabel
Martins, Maria 1898(?)-1973 Obituary 41-44R
Martins, Peter 1946- 113
Martins, Wilson 1921- 17-20R
Martinsen, Ella Barbara Lung 1901-1977 103
Martinsen, Martin
See Follett, Ken(neth Martin)
Martinson, David (Keith) 1946- CANR-1
Earlier sketch in CA 45-48
Martinson, Floyd M(ansfield) 1916- 93-96
Martinson, Harry (Edmund)
1904-1978 ....CANR-34
Earlier sketch in CA 77-80
See also CLC 14
Martinson, Robert M. 1927- 41-44R
Martinson, Ruth A(lice) 1915- CANR-17
Earlier sketch in CA 25-28R
Martinson, Tom L. 1941- 77-80
Martinson, William D. 1924-1979 ....21-24R
Obituary 135
Martland, Thomas R(odolphe) 1926- 5-8R
Marton, Beryl M(itchell) 1922- CANR-11
Earlier sketch in CA 69-72
Marton, Endre 1910- 37-40R
Marton, George 1900- 29-32R
Martone, Michael 1955- 124
Brief entry 118
Martos, Borys 1879-1977 Obituary 73-76
Martos, Joseph (John) 1943- 105
Marty, Martin E(mil) 1928- CANR-21
Earlier sketch in CA 5-8R
Marty, Myron A. 1932- CANR-11
Earlier sketch in CA 25-28R
Marty, Sid 1944- 108
Martyn, Edward 1859-1923 ....DLB 10
Martyn, Howe 1906-1989 ....9-12R
Obituary 129
Martyn, J(ames) Louis 1925- 126
Brief entry 105
Martyn, Kenneth A(lfred) 1926- 21-24R
Martynov, Leonid (Nikolaevich)
1905- Brief entry 116
Martyr, Paula (Jane)
See Lawford, Paula Jane
See also SATA 57
Martz, John D(anhouse) 1934- CANR-1
Earlier sketch in CA 45-48
Martz, Lawrence J. 1933- 69-72
Martz, Linda 1939- 135
Martz, Louis L(ohr) 1913- CANR-5
Earlier sketch in CA 13-16R
Martz, William J. 1928- CANR-9
Earlier sketch in CA 21-24R
Maruki, Toshi 1912- ....CLR 19
Marut, Ret
See Traven, B.
Marut, Robert
See Traven, B.
Maruya, Saiichi 1925- 135
Maruyama, Masao 1914- 13-16R
Marvel, Tom 1901-1970 Obituary 104
Marvell, Andrew 1621-1678 .... CDBLB 1660-1789
See also WLC
Marvick, Elizabeth Wirth 1925- 117
Marvin, Burton Wright
1913-1979 Obituary 85-88
Marvin, David Keith 1921- 13-16R
Marvin, Dorothy Betts
1894(?)-1975 Obituary 57-60
Marvin, Garry 1952- 127
Marvin, Harold Myers 1893-1977 ....5-8R
Obituary 73-76
Marvin, John R(obert) 1923- 117
Marvin, John T. 1906- 17-20R
Marvin, Philip (Roger) 1916- CANR-13
Earlier sketch in CA 37-40R
Marvin, Richard
See Ellis, Julie
Marvin, Susan
See Ellis, Julie
Marvin, W. R.
See Cameron, Lou
Marvin X
See El Muhajir
See also DLB 38
Marwell, Gerald 1937- 41-44R
Marwick, Arthur 1936- CANR-30
Earlier sketches in CA 29-32R, CANR-13
Marwick, Helen
See Lillie, Helen
Marwick, Lawrence 1909-1981 Obituary 106
Marwick, M(axwell) G(ay) 1916- 37-40R
Marwil, Jonathan L(evy) 1940- CANR-35
Earlier sketch in CA 114
Marwood, William
See Morton, James (Severs)
Marx, Anne CANR-30
Earlier sketches in CA 29-32R, CANR-12
Marx, Arthur 1893-1964 Obituary 113
Marx, Arthur 1921- CANR-24
Earlier sketch in CA 81-84
Marx, Erica Elizabeth 1909-1967 ....CAP-1
Earlier sketch in CA 13-14
Marx, Gary T. 1938- CANR-32
Earlier sketches in CA 37-40R, CANR-14
Marx, Groucho
See Marx, Julius Henry
Marx, Harpo
See Marx, Arthur
Marx, Herbert L(ewis) Jr. 1922- CANR-6
Earlier sketch in CA 9-12R
Marx, Jenifer (Grant) 1940- 101
Marx, Jerry
See Bernstein, Jerry Marx
Marx, Julius Henry 1890-1977 81-84
Obituary 73-76
Marx, Kenneth S(amuel) 1939- 69-72
Marx, Leo 1919- 126
Marx, Melvin H(erman) 1919- CANR-6
Earlier sketch in CA 5-8R
Marx, Paul 1920- 37-40R
Marx, Robert F(rank) 1936- CANR-6
Earlier sketch in CA 9-12R
See also SATA 24
Marx, Samuel 1902- 103
Obituary 137
Marx, Werner 1910- 81-84

Marx, Wesley 1934- ... CANR-12
Earlier sketch in CA 21-24R
Marxhausen, Joanne G. 1935- ... 37-40R
Mary Agnes Therese, Sister 1910- ... 1-4R
Mary Francis, Mother
See Aschmann, Alberta
Mary Kay
See Ash, Mary Kay (Wagner)
Mary Madeleine, Sister 1916-1974 ... CAP-1
Earlier sketch in CA 13-16
Marzan, Julio 1946- ... 131
Brief entry ... 113
See also HW
Marzani, Carl (Aldo) 1912- ... 61-64
See also SATA 12
Marzials, Theo 1850-1920 ... DLB 35
Marzolf, Marion Tuttle 1930- ... 124
Brief entry ... 114
Marzollo, Jean 1942- ... CANR-15
Earlier sketch in CA 81-84
See also SATA 29
Masani, Shakuntala ... 112
Masani, Zareer 1947- ... 97-100
Masannat, George S. 1933- ... 25-28R
Masao, Maruyama 1914- ... 107
Masaoka Shiki
See Masaoka Tsunenori
See also TCLC 18
Masaoka Tsunenori 1867-1902 Brief entry ... 117
See also Masaoka Shiki
Masatsugu, Mitsuyuki 1924- ... 129
Mascall, Eric L(ionel) 1905- ... 5-8R
Mascott, Trina ... 81-84
Masefield, Geoffrey Bussell 1911- ... 5-8R
Masefield, John (Edward) 1878-1967 ... CANR-33
Obituary ... 25-28R
Earlier sketches in CAP-2, CA 19-20
See also CDBLB 1890-1914
See also CLC 11, 47
See also DLB 10
See also MTCW
See also SATA 19
Masefield, (John) Richard (William) 1943- ... 119
Maser, Chris 1938- ... 132
Maser, Edward A(ndrew) 1923-1988 ... CANR-28
Obituary ... 126
Earlier sketch in CA 45-48
Maser, Jack D(avid) 1937- ... 57-60
Masey, Mary Lou(ise) 1932-1991 ... 21-24R
Obituary ... 134
Masha
See Stern, Marie
Masheck, Joseph (Daniel) 1942- ... 105
Masia, Seth 1948- ... CANR-28
Earlier sketch in CA 110
Masini, Eleonora Barbieri 1928- ... 130
Masinton, Charles G(erald) 1938- ... 77-80
Maslach, Christina 1946- ... 111
Maslenikov, Oleg A(lexander)
1907-1972 Obituary ... 111
Maslin, Alice 1914(?)-1981 Obituary ... 104
Maslin, Bonnie L(ynn) 1947- ... 107
Maslow, Abraham H. 1908-1970 ... CANR-4
Obituary ... 29-32R
Earlier sketch in CA 1-4R
See also MTCW
Maslow, Jonathan Evan 1948- ... 126
Maslowski, Peter 1944- ... 97-100
Maslowski, Raymond M(arion) 1931- ... 93-96
Maslowski, Stanley 1937- ... 21-24R
Masnata, Albert 1900- ... 93-96
Maso, Carole ... CLC 44
Mason, A. E. W. 1865-1948 ... DLB 70
Mason, Alpheus Thomas 1899-1989 ... CANR-32
Obituary ... 130
Earlier sketch in CA 1-4R
Mason, Betty (Oxford) 1930- ... 37-40R
Mason, Bobbie Ann 1940- ... CANR-31
Earlier sketches in CA 53-56, CANR-11
See also AAYA 5
See also CLC 28, 43
See also DLBY 87
See also MTCW
See also SSC 4
Mason, Bruce B(onner) 1923- ... 9-12R
Mason, Bruce Edward George 1921-1982 ... 129
Obituary ... 110
Mason, Carola
See Zentner, Carola
Mason, Chuck
See Rowland, D(onald) S(ydney)
Mason, Clarence (Eugene) Jr. 1904- ... 57-60
Mason, David E(rnest) 1928- ... 21-24R
Mason, Douglas R(ankine) 1918- ... CANR-17
Earlier sketches in CA 49-52, CANR-1
Mason, Edmund (John) 1911- ... 103
Mason, Edward S(agendorph) 1899- ... 73-76
Obituary ... 137
Mason, Edwin A. 1905-1979 ... CAP-2
Obituary ... 89-92
Earlier sketch in CA 25-28
See also SATA 32
Mason, Ellsworth (Goodwin) 1917- ... 126
Mason, Ernst
See Pohl, Frederik
Mason, Eudo C(olecestra) 1901-1969 ... CAP-1
Earlier sketch in CA 9-10
Mason, F(rancis) van Wyck 1901-1978 ... CANR-8
Obituary ... 81-84
Earlier sketch in CA 5-8R
See also SATA 3, 26
Mason, Francis K(enneth) 1928- ... 103
Mason, Frank Earl 1893-1979 Obituary ... 89-92
Mason, Frank W.
See Mason, F(rancis) van Wyck
Mason, Gabriel Richard
1884-1979 Obituary ... 85-88
Mason, Gene (William) 1928- ... 89-92
Mason, George E(van) 1932- ... CANR-30
Earlier sketches in CA 29-32R, CANR-12
Mason, George Frederick 1904- ... 73-76
See also SATA 14
Mason, Haydn T(revor) 1929- ... CANR-3
Earlier sketch in CA 9-12R
Mason, Herbert Molloy Jr. 1927- ... CANR-6
Earlier sketch in CA 13-16R
Mason, Herbert Warren Jr. 1932- ... CANR-38
Earlier sketches in CA 85-88, CANR-16
Mason, James (Neville)
1909-1984 Obituary ... 113
Mason, John Brown 1904- ... 49-52
Mason, Joseph B(igsbee) 1903- ... 125
Mason, Julian D(ewey) Jr. 1931- ... 37-40R
Mason, Lee W.
See Malzberg, Barry N(athaniel)
Mason, Lowell Blake 1893-1983 Obituary ... 110
Mason, Madeline 1913- ... 9-12R
Mason, Mark 1955- ... 138
Mason, Michael Henry 1900-1982 Obituary ... 108
Mason, Michael 1939- ... 120
Mason, Mike 1952- ... 126
Mason, Miriam E(vangeline)
1900-1973 ... CANR-15
Obituary ... 103
Earlier sketch in CA 1-4R
See also SATA 2, 26
Mason, Nicholas (Charles Sheppard)
1938- ... CANR-24
Earlier sketch in CA 104
Mason, Nick 1945-
See Pink Floyd
See also CLC 35
Mason, Pamela 1918- Brief entry ... 105
Mason, Paul T(aylor) 1937- ... 33-36R
Mason, Peter (Geoffrey) 1914- ... CANR-35
Earlier sketch in CA 114
Mason, Philip (Parker) 1927- ... CANR-38
Earlier sketch in CA 17-20R
Mason, Philip 1906- ... CANR-3
Earlier sketch in CA 9-12R
Mason, R(ichard) A(nthony) 1932- ... 119
Mason, R(onald) A(lison) K(ells)
1905-1971 Obituary ... 89-92
Mason, Raymond 1926- ... 9-12R
Mason, Richard (Lakin) 1919- ... 9-12R
Mason, Robert C(averly) 1942- ... 134
Brief entry ... 128
Mason, Robert E(mmett) 1914- ... CANR-17
Earlier sketch in CA 1-4R
Mason, Ronald (Charles) 1912- ... CANR-24
Earlier sketch in CA 13-16R
Mason, Ronald M. 1949- ... 111
Mason, Ruth Fitch 1890-1974 Obituary ... 53-56
Mason, Tally
See Derleth, August (William)
Mason, Ted
See Mason, Theodore C(harles)
Mason, Theodore C(harles) 1921- ... 109
Mason, Thomas A(lexander) 1944- ... 120
Mason, Tyler
See Mason, Madeline
Mason, Van Wyck
See Mason, F(rancis) van Wyck
Mason, Will Edwin 1912- ... 5-8R
Masotti, Louis H(enry) 1934- ... 41-44R
Mass, Jeffrey P(aul) 1940- Brief entry ... 111
Mass, William
See Gibson, William
Massa, Ann 1940- ... 29-32R
Massa, Richard W(ayne) 1932- ... 57-60
Massanari, Jared (Dean) 1943- ... 65-68
Massaquoi, Hans J(urgen) 1926- ... 69-72
Massarik, Fred 1926- ... CANR-35
Earlier sketch in CA 1-4R
Massel, Mark S. 1910- ... CAP-1
Earlier sketch in CA 11-12
Masselink, Ben 1919- ... 17-20R
Masselman, George 1897-1971 ... 9-12R
See also SATA 19
Massengale, John (Edward) Montague
1951- ... 125
Masserman, Jules H(oman) 1905- ... 69-72
Massey, Ellen Gray 1921- ... 118
Massey, Erika 1900- ... 61-64
Massey, Floyd Jr. 1915- ... 65-68
Massey, Gerald J. 1934- ... 89-92
Massey, Gerald 1828-1907 ... DLB 32
Massey, Harrie Stewart Wilson
1908-1983 Obituary ... 111
Massey, Irving (Joseph) 1924- ... 77-80
Massey, James A(ldege) 1939- ... 121
Massey, James Earl 1930- ... CANR-12
Earlier sketch in CA 29-32R
Massey, Joseph Earl 1897- ... 29-32R
Massey, Mary Elizabeth 1915-197 (?) ... CAP-2
Earlier sketch in CA 23-24
Massey, Raymond (Hart) 1896-1983 ... 104
Obituary ... 110
Massey, Reginald 1932- ... 21-24R
Massialas, Byron G. 1929- ... CANR-8
Earlier sketch in CA 21-24R
Massie, Diane Redfield ... 81-84
See also SATA 16
Massie, Joseph Logan 1921- ... CANR-2
Earlier sketch in CA 1-4R
Massie, Robert K(inloch) 1929- ... CANR-14
Earlier sketch in CA 77-80
Massine, Leonide
See Myassin, Leonid Fedorovich
Massing, Hede 1899-1981 Obituary ... 108
Massinger, Philip 1583-1640 ... DLB 58
Massingham, Harold William 1932- ... 65-68
Massis, Henri 1886-1970 Obituary ... 29-32R
Massman, Patti 1945- ... 117
Massman, Virgil Frank 1929- ... 37-40R
Masson, Andre (Aime Rene)
1896-1987 Obituary ... 124
Masson, David I. 1915- ... 25-28R
Masson, Georgina
See Johnson, Marion Georgina Wikeley
Masson, J. Moussaieff
See Masson, Jeffrey Moussaieff
Masson, Jeffrey M.
See Masson, Jeffrey Moussaieff
Masson, Jeffrey Moussaieff 1941- ... 122
Masson, Loyes 1915-1969 ... CAP-1
Earlier sketch in CA 13-14
Massow, Rosalind ... 89-92
Massy, William F(rancis) 1934- ... 41-44R
Mast, Gerald 1940-1988 ... CANR-12
Obituary ... 126
Earlier sketch in CA 69-72
Mast, Russell L. 1915- ... 13-16R
Masterman, John Cecil 1891-1977 ... CANR-6
Obituary ... 69-72
Earlier sketch in CA 9-12R
Masterman-Smith, Virginia 1937- ... 110
Masters, Anthony ... 25-28R
Masters, Anthony 1948(?)-1985 Obituary ... 115
Masters, Brian 1939- ... 118
Masters, Dexter (Wright)
1908-1989 Obituary ... 127
Masters, Edgar Lee 1868-1950 ... 133
Brief entry ... 104
See also CDALB 1865-1917
See also DLB 54
See also MTCW
See also PC 1
See also TCLC 2, 25
Masters, Elaine 1932- ... 57-60
Masters, G(eorge) Mallary 1936- ... 25-28R
Masters, Hardin (Wallace)
1899(?)-1979 Obituary ... 89-92
Masters, Hilary 1928- ... CANR-13
Earlier sketch in CA 25-28R
See also CLC 48
Masters, John 1914-1983 ... 110
Brief entry ... 108
Masters, Kelly R. 1897- ... 1-4R
See also SATA 3
Masters, Mildred 1932- ... 110
See also SATA 42
Masters, Nicholas A. 1929- ... 13-16R
Masters, Olga 1919-1986 ... 121
Obituary ... 135
Masters, Roger D(avis) 1933- ... 21-24R
Masters, William
See Cousins, Margaret
Masters, William H(owell) 1915- ... CANR-34
Earlier sketch in CA 21-24R
See also AITN 1
Masters, Zeke
See Bensen, Donald R.
and Goulart, Ron(ald Joseph)
Masterson, Dan 1934- ... 81-84
Masterson, Dave 1951- ... 118
Masterson, J. B.
See Edmondson, G. C.
Masterson, James F(rancis) 1925- ... 69-72
Masterson, Patrick 1936- ... 73-76
Masterson, Thomas R(obert) 1915- ... 25-28R
Masterson, Whit
See Miller, (H.) Bill(y)
and Wade, Robert (Allison)
Masterson, William Henry 1914-1983 ... 123
Masterton, Elsie (Lipstein) 1914-1966 ... 5-8R
Masterton, Graham 1946- ... CANR-22
Earlier sketch in CA 105
Mastny, Vojtech 1936- ... CANR-29
Earlier sketches in CA 33-36R, CANR-13
Maston, T(homas) B(uford)
1897-1988 ... CANR-18
Obituary ... 128
Earlier sketches in CA 5-8R, CANR-2
Mastrangelo, Charles E. 1910- ... 113
See also Martin, Charles E.
Mastro, Susan (Duff) 1945- ... 69-72
Mastrosimone, William ... CLC 36
Masuda, Takeshi 1944- ... 123
See also Aska, Warabe
Masuda, Yoneji 1909- ... 109
Masur, Gerhard Strassman 1901-1975 ... CANR-4
Earlier sketch in CA 1-4R
Masur, Harold Q. 1909- ... CANR-13
Earlier sketch in CA 77-80
Masur, Jenny 1948- ... 65-68
Mata, Daya 1914- ... 77-80
Matanzo, Jane Brady 1940- ... 103
Matarazzo, James M. 1941- ... CANR-14
Earlier sketch in CA 37-40R
Matarazzo, Joseph D(ominic) 1925- ... 57-60
Matatu, Michael
See Puri, Shamlal
Matcha, Jack 1919- ... CANR-2
Earlier sketch in CA 1-4R
Matchett, William H(enry) 1923- ... 13-16R
Matchette, Katharine E. 1941- ... 53-56
See also SATA 38
Matczak, Sebastian A(lexander) 1914- ... 9-12R
Matejic, Mateja 1924- ... CANR-30
Earlier sketch in CA 112
Matejka, Ladislav 1919- ... 73-76
Matejko, Alexander J. 1924- ... CANR-22
Earlier sketches in CA 57-60, CANR-6
Matek, Ord 1922- ... 89-92
Matenko, Percy 1901- ... CANR-1
Earlier sketch in CA 45-48
Mateosian, S. Richard 1941- ... 111
Materer, Timothy (John) 1940- ... 89-92
Mates, Julian 1927- ... CANR-31
Earlier sketch in CA 1-4R
Matesky, Ralph 1913- ... 5-8R
Math, Irwin 1940- ... 112
See also SATA 42
Mathabane, Mark 1960- ... 125
See also AAYA 4
See also BW
Mathai, M. O. 1909-1981 Obituary ... 108
Mathay, Francis 1925- ... 57-60
Mathe, Albert
See Camus, Albert
Mather, Berkely
See Davies, John Evan Weston
Mather, Bertrand 1914- ... CAP-1
Earlier sketch in CA 9-10
Mather, Bob
See Mather, Robert E(dward)
Mather, Cotton 1663-1728 ... CDALB 1640-1865
See also DLB 24, 30
Mather, Eleanore Price 1910- ... 116
Mather, Increase 1639-1723 ... DLB 24
Mather, Jean 1946- ... 115
Mather, June 1924- ... 107
Mather, Kenneth 1911-1990 Obituary ... 131
Mather, Kirtley F(letcher) 1888-1978 ... CANR-35
Earlier sketch in CA 17-20R
See also SATA 65
Mather, Melissa
See Brown, Melissa Mather
Mather, Richard B(urroughs) 1913- ... 73-76
Mather, Richard 1596-1669 ... DLB 24
Mather, Robert E(dward) 1945- ... 115
Mathers, Michael 1945- ... 65-68
Mathers, Peter 1931- ... 130
Brief entry ... 116
Mathes, J(ohn) C(harles) 1931- ... 49-52
Mathes, W(illiam) Michael 1936- ... CANR-26
Earlier sketches in CA 61-64, CANR-8
Matheson, Ann 1940- ... 133
Matheson, Don(ald S.) 1948- ... 126
Matheson, Joan (Transue) 1924- ... 97-100
Matheson, John Ross 1917- ... CANR-23
Earlier sketch in CA 106
Matheson, Richard Burton 1926- ... 97-100
See also CLC 37
See also DLB 8, 44
Matheson, Sylvia A.
See Schofield, Sylvia Anne
Matheson, William H(oward) 1929- ... 21-24R
Matheus, John F(rederick) 1887-1983 ... 124
See also BW
See also DLB 51
Mathew, David 1902-1975 ... CAP-2
Earlier sketch in CA 25-28
Mathew, (Anthony) Gervase 1905- ... 9-12R
Mathew, Ray(mond Frank) 1929- ... 17-20R
Mathews, Anthony Stuart 1930- ... 93-96
Mathews, Arthur 1903(?)-1980 Obituary ... 102
Mathews, Cornelius 1817(?)-1889 ... DLB 3, 64
Mathews, Denise
See Mathews, Patricia J.
Mathews, Donald G. 1932- ... 17-20R
Mathews, Donald K(enneth) 1923- ... 57-60
Mathews, Eleanor Muth 1923- ... 13-16R
Mathews, Evelyn Craw 1906- ... CAP-2
Earlier sketch in CA 19-20
Mathews, F(rancis) X. 1935- ... 25-28R
Mathews, H(arry) Lee 1939- ... 37-40R
Mathews, Harry 1930- ... CANR-18
Earlier sketch in CA 21-24R
See also CAAS 6
See also CLC 6, 52
Mathews, J(oseph) Howard 1881-1970 ... 9-12R
Obituary ... 103
Mathews, Jackson 1907(?)-1978 Obituary ... 104
Mathews, Jane DeHart 1936- ... 21-24R
Mathews, Janet 1914- ... 115
See also SATA 41
Mathews, John Joseph 1895- ... CAP-2
Earlier sketch in CA 19-20
Mathews, Louise
See Tooke, Louise Mathews
Mathews, Marcia Mayfield ... 9-12R
Mathews, Mitford M(cLeod)
1891-1985 Obituary ... 115
Mathews, Patricia J. 1929(?)-1983 Obituary ... 109
Mathews, Richard (Barrett) 1944- ... CANR-1
Earlier sketch in CA 45-48
Mathews, Russell Lloyd 1921- ... 109
Mathews, Thomas G(eorge) 1925- ... 49-52
Mathews, Virginia H(opper) 1925- ... 121
Mathews, Walter M(ichael) 1942- ... 110
Mathewson, Rufus Wellington Jr.
1919(?)-1978 Obituary ... 81-84
Mathewson, William (Glen Jr.) 1940- ... 106
Mathias, Frank Furlong 1925- ... CANR-12
Earlier sketch in CA 61-64
Mathias, Peter 1928- ... 17-20R
Mathias, Roland (Glyn) 1915- ... CANR-19
Earlier sketch in CA 97-100
See also CLC 45
See also DLB 27
Mathiesen, Egon 1907-1976 Obituary ... 109
See also SATA 28
Mathiesen, Thomas J(ames) 1947- ... CANR-34
Earlier sketch in CA 113
Mathieson, John A(ndrew) 1949- ... 111
Mathieson, Theodore 1913- ... 9-12R
Mathieu, Beatrice 1904-1976 Obituary ... 65-68
Mathieu, Bertrand 1936- ... 73-76
Mathieu, Joe
See Mathieu, Joseph P.
Mathieu, Joseph P. 1949- ... 125
Brief entry ... 117
See also SATA 36, 43
Mathieu, Noel Jean 1916-1984 ... 130
Obituary ... 113
Mathis, (Byron) Claude 1927- ... 45-48

Mathis, Cleopatra 1947- ... 104
Mathis, (Luster) Doyle 1936- ... 45-48
Mathis, Edward 1927- ... 119
Mathis, F(erdinand) John 1941- ... 37-40R
Mathis, James L. 1925- ... 105
Mathis, June 1892-1927 ... DLB 44
Mathis, (Gerald) Ray 1937-1981 ... CANR-31
Obituary ... 113
Earlier sketch in CA 37-40R
Mathis, Sharon Bell 1937- ... 41-44R
See also BW
See also CLR 3
See also DLB 33
See also MAICYA
See also SAAS 3
See also SATA 7, 58
Mathison, Richard Randolph
1919-1980 ... CANR-3
Earlier sketch in CA 1-4R
Mathison, Stuart L. 1942- ... 29-32R
Mathur, Dinesh C(handra) 1918- ... 41-44R
Mathur, Y. B. 1930- ... 49-52
Matias, Waldemar 1934- ... 5-8R
Matilal, Bimal Krishna 1935-1991 ... CANR-30
Obituary ... 134
Earlier sketches in CA 21-24R, CANR-13
Matisoff, James A(lan) 1937- ... 103
Matisoff, Susan 1940- ... 104
Matisse, Henri (Emile Benoit)
1869-1954 Brief entry ... 122
Matlaw, Myron 1924- ... 33-36R
Matlaw, Ralph E. 1927-1990 Obituary ... 131
Matlin, Margaret White 1944- ... 119
Matloff, Maurice 1915- ... CANR-6
Earlier sketch in CA 13-16R
Matney, Bill
See Matney, William C. Jr.
Matney, William C. Jr. 1924- ... 69-72
Matos, Luis Pales
See Pales Matos, Luis
Matos Paoli, Francisco 1915- ... 131
See also Paoli, Francisco Matos
See also HW
Matossian, Mary Kilbourne 1930- ... 125
Matossian, Nouritza 1945- ... 124
Matrat, Jean 1915- ... 61-64
Matray, James I(rving) 1948- ... 135
Matschat, Cecile H.
1895(?)-1976 Obituary ... 65-68
Matsen, Herbert Stanley 1926- ... 57-60
Matson, Albert Thomas
1915(?)-1987 Obituary ... 124
Matson, Clive 1941- ... 129
Matson, Emerson N(els) 1926- ... 45-48
See also SATA 12
Matson, Floyd W(illiam) 1921- ... 13-16R
Matson, Theodore E. 1906- ... 1-4R
Matson, Virginia (Mae) Freeberg 1914- ... 33-36R
Matson, Wallace I(rving) 1921- ... 13-16R
Matsuba, Moshe 1917- ... 37-40R
Matsui, Tadashi 1926- ... 41-44R
See also SATA 8
Matsumoto, Toru 1914(?)-1979 Obituary ... 89-92
Matsumura, Takao 1942- ... 132
Matsunaga, Alicia 1936- ... 29-32R
Matsunaga, Daigan Lee 1941- ... 41-44R
Matsunaga, Spark M(asayuki) 1916-1990 ... 128
Obituary ... 131
Matsuno, Masako
See Kobayashi, Masako Matsuno
See also SATA 6
Matsuo Basho 1644-1694 ... PC 3
Matsushita, Konosuke 1894-1989 Obituary ... 128
Matsutani, Miyoko 1925- ... 69-72
Matt, Daniel C(hanan) 1950- ... 116
Matt, Paul R(obert) 1926- ... 33-36R
Mattam, Donald 1909- ... 45-48
Matte, (Encarnacion) L'Enc 1936- ... SATA 22
Matte, Robert G. Jr. 1948- ... CANR-16
Earlier sketch in CA 65-68
Matteo, P. B. Jr.
See Ringgold, Gene
Matter, Joseph Allen 1901- ... 29-32R
Mattera, John 1953- ... 131
Mattera, Philip 1953- ... 133
Mattersdorf, Leo 1903-1985 Obituary ... 117
Mattes, Merrill J(ohn) 1910- ... 41-44R
Matteson, Michael T(ownsend) 1943- ... CANR-16
Earlier sketch in CA 89-92
Mattessich, Richard V(ictor) 1922- ... CANR-9
Earlier sketch in CA 13-16R
Matthaei, Julie Ann 1951- ... 110
Mattheson, Rodney
See Creasey, John
Matthew, Christopher C(harles) F(orrest)
1939- ... 129
Brief entry ... 116
Matthew, Donald J(ames) A(lexander)
1930- ... CANR-15
Earlier sketch in CA 5-8R
Matthew, Henry Colin Gray 1941- ... 53-56
Matthews, Anthony
See Barker, Dudley
Matthews, Brad
See DeMille, Nelson
Matthews, Brander 1852-1929 ... DLB 71, 78
Matthews, C(onstance) M(ary) 1908- ... 25-28R
Matthews, Carola 1937- ... 25-28R
Matthews, Carole Smith 1943- ... 111
Matthews, Clayton (Hartley) 1918- ... CANR-25
Earlier sketches in CA 53-56, CANR-9
Matthews, Clyde 1917- ... 103
Matthews, (Robert) Curt(is Jr.) 1934- ... 73-76
Matthews, Denis (James) 1919-1988 ... 103
Obituary ... 127
Matthews, Desmond S. 1922- ... 21-24R
Matthews, Donald Rowe 1925- ... CANR-2
Earlier sketch in CA 1-4R
Matthews, Downs 1925- ... SATA 71
Matthews, Ellen
See Bache, Ellyn
Matthews, Ellen 1950- ... 89-92
See also SATA 28
Matthews, Elmora Messer 1925- ... 21-24R
Matthews, Gareth B(lanc) 1929- ... 135
Matthews, Geoffrey M. 1920-1984 Obituary ... 115
Matthews, Glenna C. 1938- ... 126
Matthews, Greg 1949- ... 135
See also CLC 45
Matthews, Harry G(len) 1939- ... 73-76
Matthews, Herbert Lionel 1900-1977 ... CANR-2
Obituary ... 73-76
Earlier sketch in CA 1-4R
Matthews, Honor 1901- ... CAP-2
Earlier sketch in CA 23-24
Matthews, J(ohn) H(erbert) 1930- ... CANR-20
Earlier sketches in CA 13-16R, CANR-5
Matthews, Jack
See Matthews, John H(arold)
See also DLB 6
Matthews, Jack 1917- ... 9-12R
Matthews, Jack 1925- ... CAAS 15
Matthews, Jacklyn Meek
See Meek, Jacklyn O'Hanlon
Matthews, Jessie 1907-1981 Obituary ... 108
Matthews, Joan E(thel) 1914- ... 21-24R
Matthews, John H(arold) 1925- ... CANR-15
Earlier sketch in CA 33-36R
See also Matthews, Jack
Matthews, John (Pengwerne) 1927- ... 118
Matthews, Kathy 1949- ... CANR-27
Earlier sketch in CA 110
Matthews, Kevin
See Fox, G(ardner) F(rancis)
Matthews, L(eonard) Harrison
1901-1986 ... CANR-4
Obituary ... 121
Earlier sketch in CA 53-56
Matthews, Patricia (Anne) 1927- ... CANR-25
Earlier sketches in CA 29-32R, CANR-9
See also MTCW
See also SATA 28
Matthews, Ralph 1904(?)-1978 ... 85-88
Obituary ... 81-84
Matthews, Richard K(evin) 1952- ... 117
Matthews, Robert J(ames) 1926- ... 65-68
Matthews, Roy A(nthony) 1927- ... CANR-13
Earlier sketch in CA 33-36R
Matthews, Roy T(homas) 1932- ... 109
Matthews, Rupert O(liver) 1961- ... 118
Matthews, Stanley G(oodwin) 1924- ... 21-24R
Matthews, Stanley 1915- ... 134
Brief entry ... 115
Matthews, T(homas) S(tanley)
1901-1991 ... CANR-18
Obituary ... 133
Earlier sketches in CAP-1, CA 11-12
Matthews, Tom
See Klewin, W(illiam) Thomas
Matthews, Victor Monroe 1921- ... 93-96
Matthews, Walter Robert 1881-1973 ... CAP-1
Earlier sketch in CA 13-14
Matthews, William Henry III 1919- ... 9-12R
See also SATA 28, 45
Matthews, William (Richard) 1905-1975 ... 61-64
Obituary ... 57-60
Matthews, William 1942- ... CANR-12
Earlier sketch in CA 29-32R
See also CLC 40
See also DLB 5
Matthews-Simonton, Stephanie 1947- ... 132
Matthias, Catherine 1945- ... 110
See also SATA 41
Matthias, John (Edward) 1941- ... 33-36R
See also CLC 9
Matthiessen, F. O. 1902-1950 ... DLB 63
Matthiessen, Peter 1927- ... CANR-21
Earlier sketch in CA 9-12R
See also AAYA 6
See also BEST 90:4
See also CLC 5, 7, 11, 32, 64
See also DLB 6
See also MTCW
See also SATA 27
Matthis, Raimund Eugen 1928- ... 37-40R
Mattick, Paul 1904-1981 Obituary ... 115
Mattil, Edward La Marr 1918- ... 127
Brief entry ... 106
Mattill, A(ndrew) J(acob) Jr. 1924- ... CANR-31
Earlier sketches in CA 37-40R, CANR-14
Mattingley, Christobel (Rosemary)
1931- ... CANR-20
Earlier sketch in CA 97-100
See also CLR 24
See also MAICYA
See also SATA 37
Mattingly, Garrett 1900-1962 Obituary ... 111
Mattingly, George E. 1950- ... 105
Mattingly, Paul H(avey) 1941- ... 129
Mattioli, Raffaele 1895-1973 Obituary ... 45-48
Mattis, George 1905- ... CAP-2
Earlier sketch in CA 29-32
Mattison, Alice 1942- ... 110
Mattison, Christopher 1949- ... 125
Mattison, Judith 1939- ... CANR-24
Earlier sketches in CA 61-64, CANR-8
Mattlin, Paula Plotnick
1934(?)-1981 Obituary ... 104
Mattson, George E(dward) 1937- ... 5-8R
Mattson, Lloyd 1923- ... CANR-17
Earlier sketch in CA 93-96
Matulay, Laszlo 1912- ... SATA 43
Matulka, Jan 1890-1972 ... SATA 28
Matura, Mustapha 1939- ... CANR-12
Earlier sketch in CA 65-68
Matura, Thaddee 1922- ... 132
Matus, Greta 1938- ... 93-96
See also SATA 12
Matus, Irvin Leigh 1941- ... 129
Matuszak, John (Daniel)
1950-1989 Obituary ... 130
Matute (Ausejo), Ana Maria 1925- ... 89-92
See also CLC 11
See also MTCW
Mau, Ernest E(ugene) 1945- ... 112
Mau, James A. 1935- ... 25-28R
Mauchline, Mary 1915- ... 53-56
Maud, John P. R.
See Redcliffe-Maud, John Primatt
Maud, John Primatt Redcliffe
See Redcliffe-Maud, John Primatt
Maud, Ralph (Noel) 1928- ... 129
Maude, George 1931- ... CANR-33
Earlier sketch in CA 113
Maude, H(enry) E(vans) 1906- ... 103
Maududi, Maulana Abdul Ala
1903(?)-1979 Obituary ... 89-92
Maue, Kenneth 1947- ... 97-100
Mauermann, Mary Anne 1927- ... 33-36R
Maugham, Diana
See Marr-Johnson, Diana (Maugham)
Maugham, Robert Cecil Romer
1916-1981 ... 9-12R
Obituary ... 103
Maugham, Robin
See Maugham, Robert Cecil Romer
Maugham, W. S.
See Maugham, W(illiam) Somerset
Maugham, W(illiam) Somerset 1874-1965 ... 5-8R
Obituary ... 25-28R
See also CDBLB 1914-1945
See also CLC 1, 11, 15, 67
See also DLB 10, 36, 77, 100
See also MTCW
See also SATA 54
See also SSC 8
See also WLC
Maugham, William Somerset
See Maugham, W(illiam) Somerset
Maughan, A(nne) M(argery) ... 53-56
Mauldin, Bill
See Mauldin, William Henry
Mauldin, William Henry 1921- Brief entry ... 111
Maule, Christopher J(ohn) 1934- ... 37-40R
Maule, Hamilton Bee 1915- ... CANR-3
Earlier sketch in CA 1-4R
Maule, Harry E(dward) 1886-1971 Obituary ... 104
Maule, Henry (Ramsay) 1915-1981 ... 133
Maule, Tex
See Maule, Hamilton Bee
Maultsby, Maxie C(larence) Jr. 1932- ... 81-84
Maund, Alfred (Thomas Jr.) 1923- ... 1-4R
Maunder, Elwood R(ondeau) 1917- ... 85-88
Maunder, W(illiam) J(ohn) 1932- ... 33-36R
Maung, Mya 1933- ... 37-40R
Maupassant, (Henri Rene Albert) Guy de
1850-1893 ... SSC 1
See also WLC
Maupin, Armistead 1944- ... 130
Brief entry ... 125
Maura, Sister
See Eichner, Maura
Maureen, Sister Mary 1924- ... 21-24R
Maurer, Armand A(ugustine) 1915- ... 21-24R
Maurer, Charles Benes 1933- ... 33-36R
Maurer, Daphne (Jean) 1946- ... 128
Maurer, David J(oseph) 1935- ... 102
Maurer, David W(arren) 1906-1981 ... 17-20R
Obituary ... 104
Maurer, Joan Howard 1927- ... 119
Maurer, John G. 1937- ... 37-40R
Maurer, Otto
See Mason, Eudo C(olecestra)
Maurer, Rose
See Somerville, Rose M(aurer)
Maurhut, Richard
See Traven, B.
Mauriac, Claude 1914- ... 89-92
See also CLC 9
See also DLB 83
Mauriac, Francois (Charles) 1885-1970 ... CAP-2
Earlier sketch in CA 25-28
See also CLC 4, 9, 56
See also DLB 65
See also MTCW
Maurice, David (John Kerr) 1899- ... CAP-1
Earlier sketch in CA 11-12
Maurice, Frederick Denison 1805-1872 ... DLB 55
Maurice, Roger
See Asselineau, Roger (Maurice)
Mauricio, Victoria Courtney 1928- ... 106
Maurina, Zenta 1897-1978 Obituary ... 85-88
Maurois, Andre 1885-1967 ... CAP-2
Obituary ... 25-28R
Earlier sketch in CA 21-22
See also DLB 65
See also MTCW
Mauron, Charles (Paul) 1899-1966 ... CAP-1
Earlier sketch in CA 9-10
Maury, Inez 1909- ... 61-64
Maury, James 1718-1769 ... DLB 31
Maury, Reuben 1899-1981 Obituary ... 103
Mauser, Ferdinand F. 1914- ... CANR-2
Earlier sketch in CA 1-4R
Mauser, Patricia Rhoads 1943- ... CANR-22
Earlier sketch in CA 106
See also SATA 37
Mauskopf, Seymour Harold 1938- ... 104
Mauss, Armand L(ind) 1928- ... 111
Mautner, Franz H(einrich) 1902- ... CANR-12
Earlier sketch in CA 61-64
Mauzey, Merritt 1897-1975 ... 102
Maves, Carl (Edwin) 1940- ... 69-72
Maves, Karl
See Maves, Carl (Edwin)
Maves, Mary Carolyn 1916- ... 49-52
See also SATA 10
Maves, Paul B(enjamin) 1913- ... CANR-17
Earlier sketches in CA 45-48, CANR-1
See also SATA 10
Mavin, John
See Rickword, (John) Edgell
Mavis, Walter Curry 1905- ... 5-8R
Mavor, Elizabeth (Osborne) 1927- ... 107
See also DLB 14
Mavor, Osborne Henry
1888-1951 Brief entry ... 104
See also Bridie, James
Mavrodes, George I(on) 1926- ... 21-24R
Mavrogordato, J(ohn) G(eorge)
1905-1987 Obituary ... 122
Mavrogordato, Jack G.
See Mavrogordato, J(ohn) G(eorge)
Mavrogordatos, George T(hemistocles)
1945- ... 115
Mawby, Janet
See Garton, Janet
Mawdsley, Norman
See Hargreaves-Mawdsley, W(illiam) Norman
Mawer, Ronald Knox
See Knox-Mawer, Ronald
Mawer, Ronnie Knox
See Knox-Mawer, Ronald
Mawicke, Tran 1911- ... SATA 15
Max
See Diop, Birago (Ismael)
Max, Nicholas
See Asbell, Bernard
Max, Peter 1939- ... 116
See also SATA 45
Maxa, Rudolph Joseph Jr. 1949- ... 65-68
Maxa, Rudy
See Maxa, Rudolph Joseph Jr.
Maxcy, Spencer J. 1939- ... 110
Maxey, Chester Collins 1890- ... CAP-1
Earlier sketch in CA 13-16
Maxey, David R(oy) 1936-1984 ... 73-76
Obituary ... 112
Maxfield, Doris Morris 1953- ... 129
Maxfield, Elizabeth
See Miller, Elizabeth Maxfield
Maxhim, Tristan
See Jones, (Max Him) Henri
Maxim, John R. 1937- ... 118
Maximov, Vladimir (Yemelyanovich) 1930- ... 104
Maxmen, Jerrold S(amuel) 1942- ... CANR-27
Earlier sketch in CA 106
Maxner, Joyce (Karen Leopold) 1929- ... 133
Maxon, Anne
See Best, (Evangel) Allena Champlin
Maxon, John 1916-1977 Obituary ... 69-72
Maxon, Lou R(ussell) 1900-1971 Obituary ... 116
Maxtone Graham, James Anstruther
1924- ... 69-72
Maxtone-Graham, John 1929- ... 69-72
Maxwell, A. E.
See Maxwell, Ann (Elizabeth)
Maxwell, A(lbert) E(rnest) 1916- ... 5-8R
Maxwell, Ann (Elizabeth) 1944- ... 105
Maxwell, Arthur S. 1896-1970 ... CAP-1
Earlier sketch in CA 9-10
See also SATA 11
Maxwell, Cassandre 1942- ... 117
Maxwell, Colin 1956- ... 132
Maxwell, D(esmond) E(rnest) S(tewart)
1925- ... 33-36R
Maxwell, Edith 1923- ... 49-52
See also SATA 7
Maxwell, Edward
See Allan, Ted
Maxwell, Elsa 1883-1963 Obituary ... 89-92
Maxwell, Gavin 1914-1969 ... 5-8R
Obituary ... 25-28R
See also MTCW
See also SATA 65
Maxwell, Gilbert 1910-1979 ... CAP-1
Obituary ... 93-96
Earlier sketch in CA 9-10
Maxwell, Grant
See Richardson, Gladwell
Maxwell, Grover (Edward) 1918-1981 ... CANR-9
Earlier sketch in CA 5-8R
Maxwell, Jack
See McKeag, Ernest L(ionel)
Maxwell, James A. 1912- ... 13-16R
Maxwell, John
See Freemantle, Brian Harry
Maxwell, Kenneth E(ugene) 1908- ... 73-76
Maxwell, Kenneth (Robert) 1941- ... CANR-33
Earlier sketches in CA 85-88, CANR-15
Maxwell, Margaret F(inlayson) 1927- ... 109
Maxwell, Maurice 1910-1982 Obituary ... 107
Maxwell, Neville (George Anthony)
1926- ... CANR-4
Earlier sketch in CA 49-52
Maxwell, Nicholas 1937- ... 132
Maxwell, Nicole (Hughes) ... 1-4R
Maxwell, Patricia 1942- ... CANR-28
Earlier sketches in CA 29-32R, CANR-12
Maxwell, Rhonda 1950- ... 112
Maxwell, Richard C(allender) 1919- ... 41-44R
Maxwell, (Ian) Robert 1923-1991 ... 9-12R
Obituary ... 135
Maxwell, Robert S(idney) 1911- ... 57-60
Maxwell, Ronald
See Smith, Ronald Gregor

Maxwell, Sister Mary 1913- 37-40R
Maxwell, Vicky
  See Worboys, Anne(tte Isobel) Eyre
Maxwell, W(illiam) David 1926- 61-64
Maxwell, William (Keepers Jr.) 1908- 93-96
  See also CLC 19
  See also DLBY 80
Maxwell-Hudson, (Rachel) Clare 1946- 69-72
Maxwell-Lefroy, Cecil Anthony 1907- CAP-1
  Earlier sketch in CA 13-16
May, Allan 1923- 85-88
May, Arthur James 1899-1968 .... CAP-1
  Earlier sketch in CA 11-12
May, Charles E(dward) 1941- 117
May, Charles Paul 1920- CANR-5
  Earlier sketch in CA 1-4R
  See also SATA 4
May, Clifford D. 1951- 136
May, Dean E(dward) 1944- 57-60
May, Derwent (James) 1930- CANR-28
  Earlier sketches in CA 25-28R, CANR-11
May, Edgar 1929- 9-12R
May, Elaine Tyler 1947- CANR-30
  Earlier sketch in CA 111
May, Elaine 1932- Brief entry 124
  See also CLC 16
  See also DLB 44
May, Elizabeth 1907- CAP-2
  Earlier sketch in CA 19-20
May, Ernest R(ichard) 1928- CANR-22
  Earlier sketches in CA 1-4R, CANR-6
May, Eugene 1906- 1-4R
May, Florissa
  See Green, Kay
May, Francis Barns 1915- 9-12R
May, George S(mith) 1924- 65-68
May, Georges Claude 1920- CANR-6
  Earlier sketch in CA 13-16R
May, Gerald G(ordon) 1940- Brief entry 112
May, Gita 1929- CANR-13
  Earlier sketch in CA 29-32R
May, H(enry) J(ohn) 1903- 13-16R
May, Henry F(arnham) 1915- 9-12R
May, Herbert Gordon 1904-1977 ....CANR-6
  Obituary 89-92
  Earlier sketch in CA 5-8R
May, Irvin M(arion) Jr. 1939- 123
May, J. C.
  See May, Julian
May, Jacques M. 1896-1975 Obituary 57-60
May, James Boyer 1904- CAP-1
  Earlier sketch in CA 11-12
May, John D(ickinson) 1932- 45-48
May, John R(ichard) 1931- CANR-18
  Earlier sketches in CA 45-48, CANR-2
May, Judy Gail 1943- 57-60
May, Julian 1931- CANR-6
  Earlier sketch in CA 1-4R
  See also SATA 11
May, Kenneth Ownsworth
  1915-1977 Obituary 73-76
May, Lary L. 1944- 130
May, Lawrence Alan 1948- 106
May, Philip Radford 1928- 45-48
May, Robert E(van) 1943- 57-60
May, Robert Lewis 1905-1976 Obituary 104
  See also SATA 27
May, Robert M(cCredie) 1936- 69-72
May, Robert Stephen 1929- CANR-30
  Earlier sketches in CA 29-32R, CANR-13
  See also SATA 46
May, Robin
  See May, Robert Stephen
May, Rollo (Reece) 1909- 111
May, Sophie
  See Clarke, Rebecca Sophia
May, Stephen 1946- 124
May, Thomas 1595(?)-1650 ....DLB 58
May, Timothy C(laude) 1940- 73-76
May, William E(ugene) 1928- CANR-14
  Earlier sketch in CA 41-44R
Mayakovski, Vladimir (Vladimirovich)
  1893-1930 Brief entry 104
  See also TCLC 4, 18
Mayall, David 1953- 119
Mayall, R(obert) Newton 1904- CAP-1
  Earlier sketch in CA 11-12
Maybaum, Ignaz 1897- CAP-1
  Earlier sketch in CA 9-10
Mayberry, Florence V(irginia) Wilson 9-12R
  See also SATA 10
Mayberry, Genevieve 1900- CAP-1
  Earlier sketch in CA 19-20
Maybray-King, Horace 1901-1986 ....29-32R
  Obituary 120
Maybury, Anne
  See Buxton, Anne (Arundel)
Maybury-Lewis, David H(enry) P(eter)
  1929- 17-20R
Maye, Patricia 1940- 53-56
Mayer, Adrian C(urtius) 1922- 1-4R
Mayer, Agatha
  See Maher, Ramona
Mayer, Albert Ignatius Jr.
  1906-1960 Obituary 109
  See also SATA 29
Mayer, Albert 1897-1981 73-76
  Obituary 105
Mayer, Alfred 1903(?)-1984 Obituary 114
Mayer, (Henri) Andre (Van Huysen) 1946- 110
Mayer, Ann M(argaret) 1938- 57-60
  See also SATA 14
Mayer, Arno J. 1926- 85-88
Mayer, Arthur L(oeb) 1886-1981 Obituary 108
Mayer, Bernadette 1945- 33-36R
Mayer, Bob 1959- 137
Mayer, Carl J. 1959- 122
Mayer, Charles Leopold 1881- CANR-6
  Earlier sketch in CA 1-4R
Mayer, Christa Charlotte
  See Thurman, Christa C(harlotte) Mayer
Mayer, Clara Woollie 1895- CAP-2
  Earlier sketch in CA 19-20
Mayer, Debby
  See Mayer, Deborah Anne
Mayer, Deborah Anne 1946- 109
Mayer, Ellen Moers
  See Moers, Ellen
Mayer, Fanny (Alice) Hagin 1899- 118
Mayer, Gary (Richard) 1945- 53-56
Mayer, Gerda (Kamilla) 1927- 106
Mayer, Hannelore Valencak 1929- 116
  See also Valencak, Hannelore
Mayer, Hans (Heinrich) 1907- 133
  Brief entry 113
Mayer, Harold M(elvin) 1916- 41-44R
Mayer, Harry F(rederick) 1912- 101
Mayer, Henry 1941- 122
Mayer, Herbert Carleton 1893-1978 ....41-44R
Mayer, Herbert T. 1922- 33-36R
Mayer, Jane Rothschild 1903- 9-12R
  See also SATA 38
Mayer, Jean 1920- 129
  Brief entry 117
Mayer, Lawrence C(lark) 1936- 97-100
Mayer, Leo V. 1936- 73-76
Mayer, Lynne Rhodes 1926- 73-76
Mayer, Marianna 1945- 93-96
  See also SATA 32
Mayer, Martin (Prager) 1928- 5-8R
Mayer, Mercer 1943- CANR-38
  Earlier sketch in CA 85-88
  See also CLR 11
  See also DLB 61
  See also MAICYA
  See also SATA 16, 32
Mayer, Michael F. 1917- 13-16R
Mayer, Milton (Sanford) 1908-1986 ....37-40R
  Obituary 119
Mayer, Musa 1943- 135
Mayer, Orlando Benedict 1818-1891 .... DLB 3
Mayer, Philip 1910- 49-52
Mayer, Ralph 1895-1979 ....CANR-28
  Obituary 89-92
  Earlier sketch in CA 29-32R
Mayer, Raymond Richard 1924- 1-4R
Mayer, Robert 1879-1985 Obituary 115
Mayer, Robert 1939- 136
Mayer, S(ydney) L(ouis) 1937- 103
Mayer, Sigrid 1933- 121
Mayer, Thomas 1927- CANR-9
  Earlier sketch in CA 21-24R
Mayer, Tom 1943- 9-12R
Mayers, Daniel E. 1933(?)-1988 Obituary 129
Mayers, David (Allan) 1951- 131
Mayers, Lewis 1890-1975 Obituary 61-64
Mayers, Marvin K(eene) 1927- 41-44R
Mayerson, Charlotte Leon 13-16R
  See also SATA 36
Mayerson, Evelyn Wilde 1935- 101
  See also SATA 55
Mayerson, Philip 1918- 41-44R
Mayer-Thurman, Christa C.
  See Thurman, Christa C(harlotte) Mayer
Mayes, Edythe Beam 1902- CANR-7
  Earlier sketch in CA 53-56
Mayes, Frances 81-84
Mayes, Herbert R(aymond) 1900-1987 105
  Obituary 124
Mayes, Stanley (Herbert) 1911- 1-4R
Mayes, Wendell 1919(?)-1992 103
  Obituary 137
  See also DLB 26
Mayeux, Peter E(dmond) 1942- 119
Mayfair, Bertha
  See Raborg, Frederick A(shton) Jr.
Mayfair, Franklin
  See Mendelsohn, Felix Jr.
Mayfield, Chris 1951- 107
Mayfield, Guy 1905-1976 ....5-8R
  Obituary 122
Mayfield, Jack
  See Cooper, Parley J(oseph)
Mayfield, James Bruce 1934- 69-72
Mayfield, John S. 1904-1983 Obituary 109
Mayfield, Julia
  See Hastings, Phyllis (Dora Hodge)
Mayfield, Julian (Hudson) 1928-1984 .....CANR-26
  Obituary 114
  Earlier sketch in CA 13-16R
  See also BW
  See also DLB 33
  See also DLBY 84
Mayfield, L(afayette) H(enry) II 1910- CAP-2
  Earlier sketch in CA 19-20
Mayfield, Marlys 1931- CANR-27
  Earlier sketches in CA 25-28R, CANR-10
Mayfield, Robert C(harles) 1928- 37-40R
Mayfield, Sara (Martin) 1905-1979 ....25-28R
  Obituary 85-88
Mayhall, Jane (Francis) 1921- CANR-8
  Earlier sketch in CA 17-20R
Mayhall, Mildred P(ickle) 1902- CANR-1
  Earlier sketch in CA 1-4R
Mayhar, Ardath 1930- CANR-19
  Earlier sketch in CA 103
  See also SATA 38
Mayhew, Christopher Paget
  1915- Brief entry 106
Mayhew, David R(aymond) 1937- 17-20R
Mayhew, Edgar deNoailles 1913- 37-40R
Mayhew, Elizabeth
  See Bear, Joan
Mayhew, Henry 1812-1887 .... DLB 18, 55
Mayhew, Jonathan 1720-1766 .... DLB 31
Mayhew, Lenore 1924- 49-52
Mayhew, Lewis B. 1917- CANR-4
  Earlier sketch in CA 1-4R
Mayhue, Richard L(ee) 1944- 116
Ma Yinchu 1882-1982 Obituary 110
Mayleas, William 1927- 120
Mayman, Martin 1924- 9-12R
Maynard, Alan (Keith) 1944- CANR-7
  Earlier sketch in CA 57-60
Maynard, Chris
  See Maynard, Christopher
Maynard, Christopher 1949- Brief entry 118
  See also SATA 43
Maynard, Fredelle (Bruser) 1922- 85-88
Maynard, Geoffrey W(alter) 1921- 5-8R
Maynard, Harold Bright 1902-1975 ....9-12R
  Obituary 103
Maynard, John (Rogers) 1941- 65-68
Maynard, Joyce 1953- 129
  Brief entry 111
  See also CLC 23
Maynard, Olga 1920- 114
  See also SATA 40
Maynard, Richard Allen 1942- 33-36R
Maynard, Robert C(lyve) 1937- 115
  Brief entry 110
Mayne, Richard (John) 1926- CANR-6
  Earlier sketch in CA 13-16R
Mayne, Seymour 1944- CANR-18
  Earlier sketch in CA 101
  See also DLB 60
Mayne, William (James Carter) 1928- CANR-37
  Earlier sketch in CA 9-12R
  See also CLC 12
  See also CLR 25
  See also MAICYA
  See also SAAS 11
  See also SATA 6, 68
Maynes, E(dwin) Scott 1922- CANR-30
  Earlier sketch in CA 45-48
Maynes, J. O. Rocky Jr.
  See Maynes, J. Oscar Jr.
Maynes, J. Oscar Jr. 1929- 115
  See also SATA 38
Mayo, Bernard 1902-1979 Obituary 89-92
Mayo, Charles G(eorge)
  1931-1985 Obituary 116
Mayo, E(dward) L(eslie) 1904- 97-100
Mayo, James
  See Coulter, Stephen
Mayo, Janet 1949- 121
Mayo, Jim
  See L'Amour, Louis (Dearborn)
Mayo, Lida (Smith) 1904-1978 Obituary 112
Mayo, Lucy Graves 1909-1963 ....5-8R
Mayo, Margaret (Mary) 1935- 107
  See also SATA 38
Mayo, Margot 1910- CAP-1
  Earlier sketch in CA 13-16
Mayo, Mark
  See Lane, Yoti
Mayo, Nick 1922-1983 103
  Obituary 110
Mayo, Patricia Elton 1915- 103
Mayo, William L. 1931- 17-20R
Mayor, A(lpheus) Hyatt 1901-1980 ....CANR-1
  Obituary 97-100
  Earlier sketch in CA 45-48
Mayor, Alfred Hyatt 1934- 65-68
Mayor, Archer
  See Mayor, Archer H(untington)
Mayor, Archer H(untington) 1950- 134
Mayor, Beatrice CAP-1
  Earlier sketch in CA 9-10
Mayor, Flora Macdonald 1872-1932 .... DLB 36
Mayor, Stephen (Harold) 1927- 21-24R
Mayoux, Jean-Jacques
  1901(?)-1987(?) Obituary 125
Mayr, Ernst 1904- CANR-2
  Earlier sketch in CA 5-8R
Mayrant, Drayton
  See Simons, Katherine Drayton Mayrant
Mayrocker, Friederike 1924- .... DLB 85
Mays, Benjamin E(lijah) 1894-1984 ....CANR-25
  Obituary 112
  Earlier sketch in CA 45-48
  See also BW
Mays, Buddy (Gene) 1943- CANR-30
  Earlier sketches in CA 73-76, CANR-12
Mays, Cedric Wesley 1907- 29-32R
Mays, James A(rthur) 1939- CANR-25
  Earlier sketch in CA 57-60
  See also BW
Mays, John Barron 1914-1987 Obituary 123
Mays, Lucinda L(a Bella) 1924- 101
  See also SATA 49
Mays, Spike
  See Mays, Cedric Wesley
Mays, (Lewis) Victor (Jr.) 1927- 25-28R
  See also SATA 5
Mays, Willie (Howard Jr.) 1931- 105
Mayshark, Cyrus 1926-1976 ....17-20R
  Obituary 134
Maysi, Kadra
  See Simons, Katherine Drayton Mayrant
Maysles, Albert 1926- 29-32R
  See also CLC 16
Maysles, David 1932- .... CLC 16
Maytham, Thomas N(orthrup) 1931- 103
Maza, Regino Sainz de la
  See Sainz de la Maza, Regino
Maze, Edward 1925- 5-8R
Mazer, Anne 1953- 135
  See also SATA 67
Mazer, Harry 1925- CANR-32
  Earlier sketch in CA 97-100
  See also AAYA 5
  See also CLR 16
  See also MAICYA
  See also SAAS 11
  See also SATA 31, 67
Mazer, Milton 1911- 85-88
Mazer, Norma Fox 1931- CANR-32
  Earlier sketches in CA 69-72, CANR-12
  See also AAYA 5
  See also CLC 26
  See also CLR 23
  See also MAICYA
  See also SAAS 1
  See also SATA 24, 67
Mazia, Marjorie
  See Guthrie, Marjorie (Greenblatt Mazia)
Maziarz, Edward A(nthony) 1915- 37-40R
Mazlish, Bruce 1923- CANR-2
  Earlier sketch in CA 5-8R
Mazmanian, Arthur B(arkev) 1931- 77-80
Mazmanian, Daniel (Aram) 1945- CANR-5
  Earlier sketch in CA 53-56
Mazo, Earl 1919- 37-40R
Mazo, Joseph H(enry) 1938- 69-72
Mazonowicz, Douglas 1920- 57-60
Mazour, Anatole G. 1900- 13-16R
Mazow, Julia Wolf 1937- 103
Mazrui, Ali A(l'Amin) 1933- CANR-13
  Earlier sketch in CA 21-24R
Mazumdar, Maxim 1952(?)-1988 Obituary 125
Mazur, Allan Carl 1939- 105
Mazur, Gail 1937- 77-80
Mazur, Paul M(yer) 1892-1979 102
  Obituary 89-92
Mazur, Ronald Michael 1934- 25-28R
Mazurkiewicz, Albert J. 1926- CANR-3
  Earlier sketch in CA 9-12R
Mazursky, Paul 1930- CANR-24
  Earlier sketch in CA 77-80
  See also DLB 44
Mazza, Adriana 1928- CANR-4
  Earlier sketch in CA 1-4R
  See also SATA 19
Mazza, Cris 1956- 132
Mazzaro, Jerome 1934- CANR-13
  Earlier sketch in CA 33-36R
Mazze, Edward M(ark) 1941- CANR-5
  Earlier sketch in CA 13-16R
Mazzei, George 1941- 117
Mazzeo, Guido E(ttore) 1914-1984 ....CANR-28
  Obituary 113
  Earlier sketch in CA 45-48
Mazzeo, Joseph Anthony 1923- 17-20R
Mazzetti, Lorenza 1933- 9-12R
Mazzotta, Giuseppe 1942- CANR-37
  Earlier sketches in CA 93-96, CANR-16
Mazzulla, Fred 1903- CAP-2
  Earlier sketch in CA 29-32
Mberi, Antar Sudan Katara 1949- 81-84
Mbiti, John S(amuel) 1931- CANR-11
  Earlier sketch in CA 21-24R
McAdam, Charles Vincent
  1892-1985 Obituary 116
McAdam, Doug 1951- 126
Mc Adam, Robert E(verett) 1920- 81-84
McAdoo, Henry Robert 1916- 107
McAfee, (James) Thomas 1928- CANR-1
  Earlier sketch in CA 45-48
McAfee, Ward M(erner) 1939- 57-60
McAleavey, David 1946- 65-68
McAleavy, Henry 1912-1968 .... CAP-2
  Earlier sketch in CA 21-22
McAleer, John J(oseph) 1923- CANR-13
  Earlier sketch in CA 21-24R
McAleer, Neil 1942- 119
McAlester, A(rcie) Lee 1933- 118
McAlester, Lee
  See McAlester, A(rcie) Lee
McAlester, Virginia 1943- 120
McAlindon, Thomas 1932- 97-100
McAlister, Luther Durwood 1927- 134
McAlister, Neil Harding 1952- 110
McAlister, W(alter) Robert 1930- 69-72
McAll, Christopher 1948- 137
McAllaster, Elva 1922- 33-36R
McAllister, Alister 1877-1943 Brief entry 121
McAllister, Amanda
  See Dowdell, Dorothy (Florence) Karns
  and Hager, Jean
  and Meaker, Eloise
McAllister, Annie Laurie
  See Cassiday, Bruce (Bingham)
McAllister, Bruce (Hugh) 1946- 33-36R
McAllister, Harry E(dward) 5-8R
McAllister, Ian 1950- 128
McAllister, Lester G(rover) 1919- 41-44R
McAlmon, Robert (Menzies)
  1895-1956 Brief entry 107
  See also DLB 4, 45
McAlpin, Heller 1955- 109
McAnally, Mary E(llen) 1939- CANR-21
  Earlier sketch in CA 105
McAndrew, John 1904-1978 Obituary 77-80
McAndrews, John
  See Steward, Samuel M(orris)
McAnelly, James R. 1932- 57-60
McArdle, Catherine
  See Kelleher, Catherine McArdle
McArdle, Hugh M(c Lure) 1905- 107
McArdle, Karen 1936- 129
McArdle, Phil 1939- 129
McArdle, William D(aniel) 1939- 110
McArthur, Charles C(ampbell) 1920- 41-44R
McArthur, Edwin Douglas 1907-1987 ....17-20R
  Obituary 121

McArthur, Harvey K(ing) 1912- 25-28R
McArthur, John
See Wise, Arthur
McArthur, Peter 1866-1924 .... DLB 92
McAulay, John D(avid) 1912- 13-16R
McAuley, James J(ohn) 1936- 77-80
McAuley, James Phillip 1917-1976 97-100
See also CLC 45
McAuley, Patricia Ann Calistro
See Calistro McAuley, Patricia Ann
McAuliffe, Clarence 1903- CAP-2
Earlier sketch in CA 19-20
McAuliffe, Kevin Michael 1949- 81-84
McAuliffe, Mary Sperling 1943- 81-84
McAvoy, Thomas T(imothy)
1903-1969 ....CANR-15
Earlier sketch in CA 1-4R
McBain, Donald J(ames) 1945- 45-48
McBain, Ed
See Hunter, Evan
McBain, Gordon D(uncan) III 1946- 106
McBain, John M(aurice) 1921- 41-44R
McBain, Laurie 1949- 97-100
McBath, James Harvey 1922- 17-20R
McBee, Mary Louise 1924- 103
McBrearty, James C(onnell)
1941- Brief entry 113
McBriar, Alan M(arne) 1918- 5-8R
McBride, Alfred 1928- CANR-6
Earlier sketch in CA 13-16R
McBride, (Mary) Angela Barron 1941- CANR-1
Earlier sketch in CA 49-52
McBride, Chris(topher James) 1941- 81-84
McBride, David P(aul) 1947- 116
McBride, Donald O(pie)
1903-1978 Obituary 77-80
McBride, Earl Duwain 1891- CAP-1
Earlier sketch in CA 13-14
McBride, James H(ubert) 1924- 25-28R
McBride, John Cosgrove
1911-1983 Obituary 110
McBride, John G. 1919- 9-12R
McBride, Joseph (Pierce) 1947- 41-44R
McBride, Katharine 1904-1976 Obituary 65-68
McBride, Mary Margaret 1899-1976 69-72
Obituary 65-68
McBride, Patricia
See Bartz, Patricia McBride
McBride, Richard William 1928- 17-20R
McBride, Robert H(enry) 1918-1983 107
Obituary 111
McBride, Robert 1941- Brief entry 116
McBride, Theresa Marie 1947- 112
McBride, William Leon 1938- CANR-6
Earlier sketch in CA 57-60
McBrien, Richard P(eter) 1936- CANR-10
Earlier sketch in CA 17-20R
McBrien, William Augustine 1930- 107
See also CLC 44
McBroom, R. Curtis 1910- CAP-2
Earlier sketch in CA 21-22
McBurney, James H(oward) 1905- 17-20R
McCabe, Bernard P(atrick) Jr. 1933- 53-56
McCabe, Cameron
See Borneman, Ernest
McCabe, Charles B. 1899-1970 Obituary 89-92
McCabe, Charles Raymond
1915-1983 Obituary 109
McCabe, Cynthia Jaffee 1943-1986 117
Obituary 120
McCabe, David Aloysius
1884(?)-1974 Obituary 45-48
McCabe, Herbert 1926- 13-16R
McCabe, James P(atrick) 1937- 101
McCabe, John Charles III 1920- CANR-1
Earlier sketch in CA 1-4R
McCabe, Joseph E. 1912- 17-20R
McCabe, Patrick 1955- 130
McCabe, Sybil Anderson 1902- CAP-1
Earlier sketch in CA 13-16
McCabe, Victoria 1948- 29-32R
McCafferty, Lawrence 25-28R
McCafferty, (Barbara) Taylor 1946- 134
McCaffery, Dan 1952- 129
McCaffery, Janet 1936- .... SATA 38
McCaffery, John K(erwin) M(ichael)
1914(?)-1983 Obituary 111
McCaffery, Larry 1946- 115
McCaffery, Margo (Smith) 1938- 37-40R
McCaffrey, Anne (Inez) 1926- CANR-35
Earlier sketches in CA 25-28R, CANR-15
See also AAYA 6
See also AITN 2
See also BEST 89:2
See also CLC 17
See also DLB 8
See also MAICYA
See also MTCW
See also SAAS 11
See also SATA 8, 70
McCaffrey, Donald W. 1926- Brief entry 114
McCaffrey, Joseph A. 1940- 37-40R
McCaffrey, Lawrence John 1925- 25-28R
McCaffrey, Mary
See Szudek, Agnes S(usan) P(hilomena)
McCaffrey, Phillip 1945- CANR-15
Earlier sketch in CA 77-80
McCagg, William O. Jr. 1930- 93-96
McCaghy, Charles H(enry) 1934- 25-28R
McCague, James (P.) 1909-1977 ....CANR-2
Earlier sketch in CA 1-4R
McCahill, Thomas 1907(?)-1975 Obituary 104
McCaig, Donald 1940- CANR-14
Earlier sketch in CA 104
McCaig, Robert Jesse 1907- CANR-1
Earlier sketch in CA 1-4R
McCaig, Snee
See McCaig, Donald
McCain, Murray (David Jr.)
1926-1981 ....CANR-15
Obituary 105
Earlier sketch in CA 1-4R
See also SATA 7, 29
McCaleb, Robert Bruce 1950- 111
McCaleb, Walter Flavius 1873-1967 .... CAP-1
Earlier sketch in CA 9-10
McCall, Dan (Elliott) 1940- 135
Brief entry 113
McCall, Daniel F(rancis) 1918- 17-20R
McCall, Dorothy Lawson 1889(?)-1982 109
Obituary 106
McCall, Edith (Sansom) 1911- CANR-19
Earlier sketches in CA 1-4R, CANR-4
See also SATA 6
McCall, George J(ohn) 1939- CANR-9
Earlier sketch in CA 21-24R
McCall, Grant 1943- 107
McCall, John Corey
See Morland, Nigel
McCall, John R(obert) 1920- CANR-1
Earlier sketch in CA 45-48
McCall, Marsh H(oward) Jr. 1939- 29-32R
McCall, Mary C(aldwell) Jr.
1904-1986 Obituary 118
McCall, Robert B(ooth) 1940- CANR-14
Earlier sketch in CA 33-36R
McCall, Storrs 1930- 9-12R
McCall, Thomas (Lawson)
1913-1983 Obituary 108
McCall, Thomas S(creven) 1936- CANR-1
Earlier sketch in CA 49-52
McCall, Tom
See McCall, Thomas (Lawson)
McCall, Vincent
See Morland, Nigel
McCall, Virginia Nielsen 1909- CANR-39
Earlier sketches in CA 1-4R, CANR-1, 17
See also SATA 13
McCall, Wendell
See Pearson, Ridley
McCall, William A(nderson) 1891- CAP-1
Earlier sketch in CA 19-20
McCalley, John W(allace) 1916-1983 110
McCallum, George E(dward) 1931- 37-40R
McCallum, Ian R(obert) M(ore)
1919-1987 ....13-16R
Obituary 124
McCallum, James Dow
1893-1971 Obituary 104
McCallum, John D(ennis) 1924-1988 ......CANR-4
Obituary 127
Earlier sketch in CA 53-56
McCallum, Neil 1916- 13-16R
McCallum, Phyllis 1911- CANR-4
Earlier sketch in CA 53-56
See also SATA 10
McCallum, Ronald Buchanan 1898-1973 ......5-8R
Obituary 89-92
McCamant, John F. 1933- 25-28R
McCammon, Robert R(ick) 1952- 81-84
McCampbell, James M. 1924- 49-52
McCamy, James L(ucian) 1906- 5-8R
McCandless, Hugh (Douglas) 1907- 5-8R
McCandless, Perry 1917- CANR-1
Earlier sketch in CA 49-52
McCandless, Ruth Strout 1909- 128
McCandlish, George E(dward)
1914-1975 65-68
Obituary 61-64
McCanles, Michael (Frederick) 1936- 69-72
McCann, Arthur
See Campbell, John W(ood Jr.)
McCann, Coolidge
See Fawcett, F(rank) Dubrez
McCann, Dennis P(atrick) 1945- 115
McCann, Eamonn 1943- Brief entry 117
McCann, Edson
See del Rey, Lester
and Pohl, Frederik
McCann, Francis Daniel Jr. 1938- 117
McCann, Frank D. Jr.
See McCann, Francis Daniel Jr.
McCann, Gerald 1916- .... SATA 41
McCann, Graham 1961- 134
McCann, Kevin 1904-1981 Obituary 103
McCann, Sean 1929- 134
Brief entry 115
McCann, Thomas 1934- 73-76
McCannon, Dindga 114
See also SATA 41
McCants, Olga 1901- CANR-14
Earlier sketch in CA 73-76
McCants, Sister Dorothea Olga
See McCants, Olga
McCardell, John (Malcolm Jr.) 1949- 101
McCardle, Carl W(esley) 1904(?)-1972 ......37-40R
McCardle, Dorothy Bartlett 1904-1978 85-88
Obituary 81-84
McCarey, Peter 1956- 138
McCargar, James (Goodrich) 1920- 137
McCarr, Ken(neth George) 1903-1977 109
Obituary 106
McCarrick, Earlean M. 1930- 103
McCarroll, Marion C(lyde)
1893(?)-1977 Obituary 73-76
McCarroll, Tolbert (Henry) 1931- 110
McCarry, Charles 1930- 103
McCarten, John (Bernard Francis James)
1916(?)-1974 Obituary 115
McCarter, Alan 1943- 107
McCarter, Neely Dixon 1929- 109
See also SATA 47
McCarter, P(ete) Kyle (Jr.) 1945- 105
McCarthy, Agnes 1933- 17-20R
See also SATA 4
McCarthy, Barry (Wayne) 1943- CANR-32
Earlier sketch in CA 113
McCarthy, Cavan 1943- 61-64
McCarthy, Charlene B(arbara) 1929- 41-44R
McCarthy, Clarence F. 1909- 29-32R
McCarthy, Cormac 1933- CANR-10
Earlier sketch in CA 13-16R
See also CLC 4, 57
See also DLB 6
McCarthy, Darry 1930- CANR-35
Earlier sketch in CA 5-8R
McCarthy, David (Edgar) 1925- 1-4R
McCarthy, David Seymour 1935- 115
McCarthy, Dennis John 1924- 21-24R
McCarthy, E(dmund) Jerome
1928- Brief entry 112
McCarthy, Edward V. Jr. 1924- 93-96
McCarthy, Emily J(eannette) 1945- CANR-32
Earlier sketch in CA 113
McCarthy, Eugene J(oseph) 1916- CANR-2
Earlier sketch in CA 1-4R
McCarthy, Gary 1943- CANR-22
Earlier sketch in CA 69-72
McCarthy, Harold T. 1920- 127
McCarthy, James J(erome) 1927- 41-44R
McCarthy, Joe
See McCarthy, Joseph Weston
McCarthy, John J(oseph) 1909- 130
McCarthy, John P(atrick) 1938- 97-100
McCarthy, John 1898- 45-48
McCarthy, Joseph M(ichael) 1940- 97-100
McCarthy, Joseph Raymond
1909-1957 Brief entry 111
McCarthy, Joseph Weston 1915-1980 .....CANR-1
Obituary 97-100
Earlier sketch in CA 1-4R
McCarthy, Kevin M. 1940- 120
McCarthy, Kyle 1954- 127
McCarthy, Martha M(ay) 1945- CANR-31
Earlier sketch in CA 111
McCarthy, Marvin 1902-1983 Obituary 110
McCarthy, Mary (Therese) 1912-1989 ......CANR-16
Obituary 129
Earlier sketch in CA 5-8R
See also CLC 1, 3, 5, 14, 24, 39, 59
See also DLB 2
See also DLBY 81
See also MTCW
McCarthy, Michael 1939- 127
McCarthy, Mignon 138
McCarthy, Patrick Joseph 1922- 9-12R
McCarthy, Paul Eugene 1921- 103
McCarthy, R. Delphina (Polley) 1894- CAP-1
Earlier sketch in CA 13-16
McCarthy, Ray 1920(?)-1984 Obituary 112
McCarthy, Richard D(ean Max) 1927- 41-44R
McCarthy, Shaun (Lloyd) 1928- CANR-6
Earlier sketch in CA 9-12R
McCarthy, Teresa
See Anderson, Teresa
McCarthy, Thomas N. 1927- 37-40R
McCarthy, Thomas P. 1920- 13-16R
McCarthy, Thomas 1954- 133
McCarthy, (Daniel) Todd 1950- 105
McCarthy, William E(dward) J(ohn)
1925- CANR-6
Earlier sketch in CA 9-12R
McCartney, Christine Maye 1949- 116
McCartney, James H(arold) 1925- 73-76
McCartney, Mike
See McCartney, Peter Michael
McCartney, (James) Paul 1942- .... CLC 12, 35
McCartney, Peter Michael 1944- 109
McCartney, Scott 1960- 138
McCarty, Clifford 1929- 17-20R
McCarty, Doran Chester 1931- CANR-31
Earlier sketches in CA 65-68, CANR-10
McCarty, Maclyn 1911- 120
McCarty, Norma
See Crandall, Norma
McCarty, Rega Kramer 1904- 5-8R
See also SATA 10
McCary, James Leslie 1919-1978 85-88
McCash, June Hall 1938- 37-40R
McCasland, S(elby) Vernon 1896- 5-8R
McCaslin, Nellie 1914- 33-36R
See also SATA 12
McCaughey, Ellen
See Koshland, Ellen
McCaughey, Robert A(nthony) 1939- 77-80
McCaughrean, Geraldine 1951- 117
McCauley, Carole Spearin 1939- CANR-25
Earlier sketches in CA 57-60, CANR-8
McCauley, Elfrieda B(abnick) 1915- 9-12R
McCauley, Leon 1908(?)-1984 Obituary 112
McCauley, Martin 1934- CANR-23
Earlier sketch in CA 107
McCauley, Michael F(rederick) 1947- CANR-9
Earlier sketch in CA 61-64
McCauley, Michael J. 1961- 138
McCauley, Stephen .... CLC 50
McCaull, M. E.
See Bohlman, (Mary) Edna McCaull
McCaw, Kenneth Malcolm 1907- 109
McCaw, Mabel Niedermeyer 1899- CAP-2
Earlier sketch in CA 19-20
McCay, Winsor 1871-1934 .... DLB 22
See also SATA 41
McChesney, Kathryn 1936- 115
McClain, Alva J. 1888-1968 65-68
McClain, Carl S. 1899- 37-40R
McClain, John O. 1942- CANR-30
Earlier sketch in CA 110
McClain, Leanita 1952(?)-1984 Obituary 112
McClain, Russell H(arding) 1910- CAP-2
Earlier sketch in CA 21-22
McClane, A(lbert) J(ules) 1922-1991 126
Obituary 136
Brief entry 106
McClane, Kenneth Anderson Jr.
1951- CANR-21
Earlier sketches in CA 57-60, CANR-6
McClary, Andrew 1927- 61-64
McClary, Ben Harris 1931- CANR-3
Earlier sketch in CA 9-12R
McClary, Jane Stevenson 1919-1990 ......CANR-1
Obituary 130
Earlier sketch in CA 1-4R
See also SATO 64
McClatchy, C. K. 1858-1936 .... DLB 25
McClatchy, Eleanor Grace
1895(?)-1980 Obituary 102
McClatchy, J(oseph) D(onald Jr.) 1945- 105
McClaurin, Irma Pearl 1952- 57-60
McClean, Joseph Lucius 1919- CAP-1
Earlier sketch in CA 9-10
McCleary, Elliott H(arold) 1927- 57-60
McCleary, Robert A(ltwig) 1923-1973 ......17-20R
Obituary 134
McCleary, William J(ames) 1938- 119
McCleery, William (Thomas) 1911- CANR-5
Earlier sketch in CA 1-4R
McClellan, A(rchibald) W(illiam) 1908- 77-80
McClellan, Albert (Alfred) 1922- 122
McClellan, Edwin 1925- Brief entry 115
McClellan, George Marion 1860-1934 125
See also BW
See also DLB 50
McClellan, Grant S(amuel)
1914- Brief entry 114
McClellan, James Edward Jr. 1922- 25-28R
McClellan, James (Paul) 1937- 21-24R
McClellan, Norris 1905-1984 Obituary 116
McClellan, Robert F. Jr. 1934- 33-36R
McClellan, Stephen T. 1942- 133
McClelland, Charles A. 1917- 85-88
McClelland, Charles E(dgar III) 1940- 33-36R
McClelland, David C(larence) 1917- 25-28R
McClelland, Diane Margaret 1931- 105
McClelland, Doug 1934- CANR-31
Earlier sketches in CA 41-44R, CANR-14
McClelland, Ivy Lilian 1908- 29-32R
McClelland, Lucille Hudlin 1920- 21-24R
McClelland, Vincent Alan 1933- 103
McClendon, James William Jr. 1924- CANR-5
Earlier sketch in CA 9-12R
McClendon, Sarah 1910- 73-76
McClennen, Sandra Elaine 1942- 103
McClintock, Barbara 1955- .... SATA 57
McClintock, Marshall 1906-1967 .... CAP-1
Earlier sketch in CA 9-10
See also SATA 3
McClintock, May Garelick
See Garelick, May
McClintock, Mike
See McClintock, Marshall
McClintock, Robert (Mills) 1909- CAP-2
Earlier sketch in CA 21-22
McClintock, Theodore 1902-1971 73-76
Obituary 33-36R
See also SATA 14
McClinton, Katharine Morrison 1899- CANR-5
Earlier sketch in CA 1-4R
McClinton, Leon 1933- 65-68
See also SATA 11
McClory, Robert J(oseph) 1932- CANR-13
Earlier sketch in CA 77-80
McCloskey, Donald N(ansen) 1942- CANR-31
Earlier sketches in CA 57-60, CANR-8
McCloskey, Eunice (Loncoske) 1906- 9-12R
McCloskey, H(enry) J(ohn) 1925- 110
McCloskey, Mark 1938- CANR-1
Earlier sketch in CA 45-48
McCloskey, Maxine E(laine) 1927- 33-36R
McCloskey, Patrick 1948- CANR-38
Earlier sketch in CA 115
McCloskey, Paul N. Jr. 1927- 37-40R
McCloskey, (John) Robert 1914- 9-12R
See also CLR 7
See also DLB 22
See also MAICYA
See also SATA 2, 39
McCloskey, William B(ertine) Jr. 1928- 101
McCloy, Helen (Worrell Clarkson) 1904- 25-28R
McCloy, James F(loyd) 1941- 103
See also SATA 59
McCloy, Shelby Thomas 1898- CAP-2
Earlier sketch in CA 23-24
McClung, Floyd Jr. 1945- 61-64
McClung, Nellie Letitia 1873-1951 .... DLB 92
McClung, Patricia A. 1950- 119
McClung, Robert M(arshall) 1916- CANR-21
Earlier sketches in CA 13-16R, CANR-6
See also AITN 2
See also CLR 11
See also MAICYA
See also SATA 2, 68
McClung, William Alexander 1944- 113
McClure, Arthur F(rederick) II 1936- CANR-10
Earlier sketch in CA 65-68
McClure, Charles R(obert) 1949- CANR-29
Earlier sketch in CA 111
McClure, Gillian Mary 1948- 103
See also SATA 31
McClure, Grace 1918- 123
McClure, Hal 1921- 81-84
McClure, James (Howe) 1939- 69-72
McClure, Joanna 1930- Brief entry 116
See also DLB 16
McClure, John A. 1945- 132

McClure, Larry 1941- CANR-26
Earlier sketch in CA 69-72
McClure, Michael (Thomas) 1932- CANR-17
Earlier sketch in CA 21-24R
See also CLC 6, 10
See also DLB 16
McClure, Ron 1941- 37-40R
McClure, Ruth Koonz 107
McClure, S. S. 1857-1949 ....DLB 91
McCluskey, John (A.) Jr. 1944- CANR-24
Earlier sketches in CA 57-60, CANR-7
See also BW
See also DLB 33
McCluskey, Neil Gerard 1921- CANR-12
Earlier sketch in CA 25-28R
McColgan, John (Joseph) 1946- 132
McCollam, James Graham 1913- CANR-4
Earlier sketch in CA 45-48
McCollam, Jim
See McCollam, James Graham
McColley, Diane Kelsey 1934- 130
McColley, Robert (McNair) 1933- 13-16R
McCollough, Albert W. 1917- 102
McCollough, Celeste 1926- 13-16R
McCollough, Charles R(andolph) 1934- 118
McCollum, Audrey T(almage) 1924- 107
McCollum, Elmer Verner 1879-1967 ....CAP-1
Earlier sketch in CA 13-14
McComas, Annette Peltz 1911- 109
McComas, J(esse) Francis
1911-1978 Obituary 104
McComb, David G(lendinning) 1934- CANR-28
Earlier sketches in CA 29-32R, CANR-12
McComb, K(atherine Woods) 1895- 13-16R
McCombs, Don 1948- 115
McCombs, Judith 1939- 102
McCombs, Maxwell E(lbert) 1938- CANR-31
Earlier sketches in CA 73-76, CANR-12
McCombs, Philip A(lgie) 1944- 49-52
McConagha, Alan 1932- 77-80
McConahay, John B. 1938- 110
McCondach, J. P. 1912- 117
McCone, R(obert) Clyde 1915- 77-80
McConica, James Kelsey 1930- CANR-13
Earlier sketch in CA 33-36R
McConkey, Clarence 1925- 29-32R
McConkey, Dale Durant 1928- 93-96
McConkey, James (Rodney) 1921- 17-20R
McConkie, Bruce R(edd)
1915-1985 Obituary 115
McConnel, Patricia 1931- 133
McConnell, Allen 1923- 77-80
McConnell, Campbell R(obertson) 1928- 5-8R
McConnell, Dorothy 1900(?)-1989 Obituary 129
McConnell, Frank D(eMay) 1942- 104
McConnell, Grant 1915- 65-68
McConnell, James Douglas Rutherford
1915-1988 ....CANR-22
Obituary 125
Earlier sketches in CA 9-12R, CANR-6
See also SATA 40, 56
McConnell, James V(ernon) 1925-1990 ....5-8R
Obituary 131
McConnell, Jean 1928- CANR-39
Earlier sketches in CA 85-88, CANR-16
McConnell, John Lithgow Chandos 1918- 53-56
McConnell, John W(ilkinson) 1907- 107
McConnell, Jon Patrick 1928- 21-24R
McConnell, Malcolm 1939- 106
McConnell, Raymond A(rnott)
1915-1979 Obituary 89-92
McConnell, Roland C(alhoun) 1910- 73-76
McConnell, T. R.
See McConnell, Thomas Raymond
McConnell, Terrance C(allihan) 1948- 110
McConnell, Thomas Raymond 1901- 118
McConnell, Virginia (McCorison) 1928- 13-16R
McConnell, William C 1917- ....DLB 88
McConnell, William T(ate) 1941- 115
McConnor, Vincent CANR-23
Earlier sketch in CA 106
McConville, Sean 1943- 137
McCord, Anne 1942- 109
See also SATA 41
McCord, Arline F(ujii) 1934- CANR-1
Earlier sketch in CA 45-48
McCord, David (Thompson Watson)
1897- CANR-38
Earlier sketch in CA 73-76
See also CLR 9
See also DLB 61
See also MAICYA
See also SATA 18
McCord, Guy
See Reynolds, Dallas McCord
McCord, Howard 1932- CANR-18
Earlier sketches in CA 9-12R, CANR-4
See also CAAS 9
McCord, James I(ley) 1919- 21-24R
McCord, James W(alter) Jr. 1918(?)- ....AITN 1
McCord, Jean 1924- 49-52
See also SATA 34
McCord, John H(arrison) 1934- CANR-17
Earlier sketch in CA 25-28R
McCord, Whip
See Norwood, Victor G(eorge) C(harles)
McCord, William Maxwell 1930- CANR-1
Earlier sketch in CA 1-4R
McCorduck, Pamela (Ann) 1940- CANR-36
Earlier sketches in CA 81-84, CANR-15
McCorison, Marcus Allen 1926- 33-36R
McCorkle, Chester O(liver) Jr. 1925- 110
McCorkle, Jill (Collins) 1958- 121
See also CLC 51
See also DLBY 87
McCorkle, Samuel Eusebius 1746-1811 ....DLB 37
McCormac, John W. 1926- 41-44R
McCormack, Arthur Gerard 1911- 5-8R
McCormack, Gavan Patrick 1937- CANR-22
Earlier sketch in CA 105
McCormack, Mark H(ume) 1930- CANR-17
Earlier sketch in CA 49-52
McCormack, S(usan) Allison 1943- 111
McCormack, William A. 1932- 25-28R
McCormick, Anne (Elizabeth) O'Hare
1882(?)-1954 Brief entry 118
See also DLB 29
McCormick, Brooks
See Adams, William Taylor
McCormick, Claire
See Labus, Marta Haake
McCormick, Dell J. 1892-1949 ....SATA 19
McCormick, Diana Festa
See Festa-McCormick, Diana
McCormick, (George) Donald (King)
1911- CANR-32
Earlier sketches in CA 73-76, CANR-14
See also SATA 14
McCormick, E(dward) Allen 1925- 107
McCormick, E(ric) H(all) 1906- 103
McCormick, Edgar L(indsley) 1914- 5-8R
McCormick, Edith (Joan) 1934- ....SATA 30
McCormick, Ernest J(ames) 1911- 93-96
McCormick, Jack (Sovern) 1929-1979 ....CANR-5
Obituary 85-88
Earlier sketch in CA 9-12R
McCormick, James P(atton)
1911-1988 Obituary 125
McCormick, James (Phillip) 1920- 25-28R
McCormick, John O(wen) 1918- 17-20R
McCormick, Mary
See McCormick, Sister Rose M(atthew)
McCormick, Merla Jean 1938- 97-100
McCormick, Mona 77-80
McCormick, Peter J(oseph) 1940- 112
McCormick, Richard Arthur 1922- CANR-22
Earlier sketch in CA 105
McCormick, Richard P(atrick) 1916- 9-12R
McCormick, Robert (K.) 1911-1985 115
Obituary 117
McCormick, Robert R. 1880-1955 ....DLB 29
McCormick, Scott Jr. 1929- 17-20R
McCormick, Sister Rose M(atthew)
1914- 21-24R
McCormick, Wilfred 1903- CANR-1
Earlier sketch in CA 1-4R
McCormmach, Russell (Keith) 1933- 118
Brief entry 112
McCorquodale, Barbara
See Cartland, Barbara (Hamilton)
McCorquodale, Robin (Hunt) 121
McCorry, Vincent P(atrick)
1909-1990 Obituary 131
McCourt, Edward (Alexander) 1907-1972 ....9-12R
Obituary 103
See also DLB 88
See also SATA 28
McCourt, James 1941- 57-60
See also CLC 5
McCowen, Alec
See McCowen, Alexander Duncan
McCowen, Alexander Duncan 1925- 129
McCowen, George S(mith) Jr. 1935- 89-92
McCown, James H. 1911- 89-92
McCown, Wayne (Gordon) 1942- 111
McCoy, Alfred W. 1945- CANR-17
Earlier sketch in CA 29-32R
McCoy, Andrew 117
McCoy, Arch
See Miller, Victor (Brooke)
McCoy, Charles A(llan) 1920- CANR-16
Earlier sketch in CA 65-68
McCoy, D(onald) E(dward) 1923- 37-40R
McCoy, Donald R(ichard) 1928- CANR-2
Earlier sketch in CA 5-8R
McCoy, Elaine 1945- 119
McCoy, Esther 1904-1989 Obituary 130
McCoy, F(lorence) N(ina) 1925- 65-68
McCoy, Horace (Stanley)
1897-1955 Brief entry 108
See also DLB 9
See also TCLC 28
McCoy, Iola Fuller 13-16R
See also SATA 3
McCoy, J(oseph) J(erome) 1917- CANR-6
Earlier sketch in CA 13-16R
See also SATA 8
McCoy, John P(leasant)
1906(?)-1974 Obituary 49-52
McCoy, Joseph A(loysius) 1911- 1-4R
McCoy, Kathleen 1945- CANR-22
Earlier sketch in CA 81-84
McCoy, Kathy
See McCoy, Kathleen
McCoy, Lois (Rich) 1941- CANR-22
Earlier sketch in CA 101
See also SATA 38
McCoy, Malachy
See Caulfield, Malachy Francis
McCoy, Marjorie Casebier
1934-1985 Obituary 114
McCoy, Maureen 1949- 119
McCoy, Ralph E(dward) 1915- 37-40R
McCoy, Ronald 1947- 81-84
McCoy, Roy 1935- 29-32R
McCoy, Samuel (Duff)
1882-1964 Obituary 93-96
McCoy, Tim(othy John Fitzgerald)
1891-1978 81-84
Obituary 77-80
McCracken, (James) David 1939- 119
McCracken, Esther 1902-1971 Obituary 33-36R
McCracken, George E(nglert) 1904- 17-20R
McCracken, Glenn 1908- 5-8R
McCracken, Harold 1894- 107
McCracken, J(ohn) L(eslie) 1914- 25-28R
McCracken, James (Eugene)
1926-1988 Obituary 126
McCracken, Karen Harden 1905- 122
McCracken, Kay
See McCracken, Karen Harden
McCracken, Kenneth David
1901-1983 Obituary 109
McCracken, Mary Lou 1943- 61-64
McCracken, Paul Winston 1915- CANR-6
Earlier sketch in CA 5-8R
McCracken, Samuel 111
McCrackin, Mark (Owens) 1949- 107
McCrady, Lady 1951- 93-96
See also SATA 16
McCrae, John 1872-1918 Brief entry 109
See also DLB 92
See also TCLC 12
McCrank, Lawrence J(oseph) 1945- CANR-29
Earlier sketch in CA 110
McCrary, (James) Peyton 1943- 85-88
McCraw, James Edward 1943- 101
McCraw, Louise Harrison 1893-1975 ....1-4R
Obituary 103
McCraw, Thomas K(incaid) 1940- CANR-17
Earlier sketch in CA 33-36R
McCray, Mike
See Preston, John
McCrea, James (Craig Jr.) 1920- CANR-8
Earlier sketch in CA 5-8R
See also SATA 3
McCrea, Joan Marie Ryan 1922- 57-60
McCrea, Ruth (Pirman) 1921- CANR-8
Earlier sketch in CA 5-8R
See also SATA 3
McCrea, William Hunter 1904- 107
McCreadie, Marsha A. 1943- 111
McCready, Jack
See Powell, Talmage
McCready, Warren T(homas) 1915- 21-24R
McCreary, Alf(red) 1940- CANR-31
Earlier sketch in CA 69-72
McCreary, W. Burgess 1894- CAP-1
Earlier sketch in CA 19-20
McCreery, Charles (Anthony Selby)
1942- 25-28R
McCreigh, James
See Pohl, Frederik
McCrimmon, Barbara (Smith) 1918- 108
McCrimmon, James M(cNab) 1908- 9-12R
McCrindle, Joseph F(eder) 1923- 29-32R
McCrohan, Donna 1947- 111
McCrone, Kathleen E. 1941- 130
McCrorey, Sanders
See Counselman, Mary Elizabeth
McCrory, Moy (Ellen) 1953- 130
McCroskey, James C(layborne)
1936- CANR-13
Earlier sketch in CA 77-80
McCrossen, V(incent) A(loysius) 1918- 53-56
McCrosson, Doris Ross 1923- 17-20R
McCrum, Robert 1953- 101
McCuaig, Ronald 1908- 114
McCue, George R(obert) 1910- 110
McCue, Lillian Bueno 1902- CANR-2
Earlier sketch in CA 1-4R
McCue, Lisa (Emiline) 1959- 136
See also SATA 65
McCuen, Jo Ray 1929- 85-88
McCuen, John J(oachim) 1926- 21-24R
McCullagh, Joseph B. 1842-1896 ....DLB 23
McCullagh, Sheila K(athleen) 1920- 110
McCullagh, Suzanne Folds 1951- 127
McCullar, Michael 1951- 122
McCullers, (Lula) Carson (Smith)
1917-1967 ....CANR-18
Obituary 25-28R
Earlier sketch in CA 5-8R
See also CABS 1, 3
See also CDALB 1941-1968
See also CLC 1, 4, 10, 12, 48
See also DLB 2, 7
See also MTCW
See also SATA 27
See also SSC 9
See also WLC
McCulley, Johnston 1883-1958 Brief entry 115
McCullin, Donald 1935- Brief entry 106
McCulloch, Alan McLeod 1907- 104
McCulloch, Derek (Ivor Breashur)
1897-1967 Obituary 109
See also SATA 29
McCulloch, Frank E(liot) 1898- 112
McCulloch, John I(rvin) B(eggs)
1909(?)-1983 Obituary 110
McCulloch, John Tyler
See Burroughs, Edgar Rice
McCulloch, Joseph 1908-1990 Obituary 131
McCulloch, Sarah
See Ure, Jean
McCulloch, Thomas 1776-1843 ....DLB 99
McCulloch, Warren S(turgis) 1898-1969 ....CAP-2
Earlier sketch in CA 21-22
McCulloh, William Ezra 1931- 49-52
McCullough, Bonnie Runyan 1944- CANR-18
Earlier sketch in CA 102
McCullough, Colleen 1938(?)- CANR-17
Earlier sketch in CA 81-84
See also CLC 27
See also MTCW
McCullough, Constance Mary 1912- CANR-5
Earlier sketch in CA 1-4R
McCullough, Dale Richard 1933- 125
McCullough, David (Gaub) 1933- CANR-31
Earlier sketches in CA 49-52, CANR-2
See also SATA 62
McCullough, Donald W. 1949- 130
McCullough, Edo
See McCullough, Edward Joseph Tilyou
McCullough, Edward Joseph Tilyou
1901(?)-1987 Obituary 123
McCullough, Frances Monson 1938- 41-44R
See also SATA 8
McCullough, John Gerard
1917-1984 Obituary 111
McCullough, Ken(neth Douglas)
1943- CANR-22
Earlier sketch in CA 45-48
McCullough, W. S.
See McCullough, W(illiam) Stewart
McCullough, W(illiam) Stewart
1902-1982 ....21-24R
Obituary 135
McCully, Emily Arnold
See Arnold, Emily
See also SAAS 7
See also SATA 5
McCully, Ethel Walbridge
1896-1980 Obituary 103
McCully, Helen 1902(?)-1977 81-84
Obituary 73-76
McCully, Robert (Stephen) 1921- 53-56
McCune, Shannon 1913- CANR-13
Earlier sketch in CA 77-80
McCunn, Ruthanne Lum 1946- 119
See also SATA 63
McCurdy, Charles Robert 1926- 5-8R
McCurdy, Frances Lea 1906- 41-44R
McCurdy, Harold Grier 1909- CANR-7
Earlier sketch in CA 17-20R
McCurdy, Howard E(arl) 1941- 81-84
McCurdy, Jack 1933- 69-72
McCurdy, Michael 1942- CANR-25
Earlier sketch in CA 69-72
See also SATA 13
McCurley, Foster R. Jr. 1937- 134
Brief entry 107
McCusker, John J(ames) 1939- 102
McCutchan, J(ohn) Wilson 1909- 5-8R
McCutchan, Philip (Donald) 1920- CANR-22
Earlier sketches in CA 9-12R, CANR-5
McCutchen, Samuel Proctor 1909-1966 ....CAP-1
Earlier sketch in CA 9-10
McCutcheon, Elsie (Mary Jackson) 1937- 133
See also SATA 60
McCutcheon, Hugh Davie-Martin
1909- CANR-5
Earlier sketch in CA 9-12R
McCutcheon, James
See Lundgren, Paul Arthur
McCutcheon, James M(iller) 1932- 45-48
McCutcheon, John Tinney Jr. 1917- 69-72
McCutcheon, Lynn E(llis) 1944- 57-60
McCutcheon, W(illiam) A(lan) 1934- 53-56
McCutcheon, W(illiam) J(ohn) 1928- 41-44R
McDade, Thomas M. 1907- CAP-1
Earlier sketch in CA 13-16
McDaniel, Becky Bring 1953- 117
See also SATA 61
McDaniel, C. Yates 1907(?)-1983 Obituary 109
McDaniel, David (Edward) 1939-1977 ....CANR-10
Earlier sketch in CA 21-24R
McDaniel, Elsiebeth 65-68
McDaniel, Eugene B(arker) 1931- 65-68
McDaniel, George William 1944- 116
McDaniel, Gerald G(reen) 1945- 122
McDaniel, Herman 1938- 111
McDaniel, John N(oble) 1941- 57-60
McDaniel, Joseph Milton Jr.
1902-1980 Obituary 97-100
McDaniel, Lurlene 1944- ....SATA 71
McDaniel, Roderick D. 1927- 37-40R
McDaniel, Ruel 1896- CAP-1
Earlier sketch in CA 13-14
McDaniel, Walton Brooks 1871-1978 77-80
Obituary 81-84
McDaniels, Carl 1930- 93-96
McDarrah, Fred W(illiam) 1926- CANR-24
Earlier sketch in CA 81-84
McDavid, John E. Jr. 1934- 37-40R
McDavid, John W(alter Jr.) 1933- 41-44R
McDavid, Raven I(oor) Jr. 1911-1984 ....41-44R
Obituary 114
McDavid, Virginia (Glenn) 1926- 37-40R
McDearmon, Kay CANR-11
Earlier sketch in CA 69-72
See also SATA 20
McDermott, A(gnes) Charlene Senape
1937- 77-80
McDermott, Alice 1953- 109
McDermott, Beatrice Schmulling 17-20R
McDermott, Beverly Brodsky 1941- CANR-16
Earlier sketch in CA 65-68
See also SATA 11
McDermott, Catherine 1952- 125
McDermott, Charles J(ames) 1905- CAP-1
Earlier sketch in CA 13-16
McDermott, Geoffrey (Lyster) 1912- 73-76
McDermott, Gerald 1941- 85-88
See also AITN 2
See also CLR 9
See also MAICYA
See also SATA 16
McDermott, John F(rancis) Jr.
1929- Brief entry 114
McDermott, John Francis (III)
1902-1981 ....CANR-6
Earlier sketch in CA 5-8R
McDermott, John J(oseph) 1932- 73-76
McDermott, John R(alph)
1921-1977 Obituary 69-72
McDermott, Robert
See Hawley, Donald Thomas

McDermott, Robert A(nthony) 1939- 57-60
McDermott, Sister Maria Concepta
1913- 17-20R
McDermott, Thomas J. 1915- 9-12R
McDermott, Walsh 1909-1981 Obituary 105
McDill, Edward L. 1930- 77-80
McDole, Carol
See Farley, Carol
McDollu, Michael A. 1946- .... DLBY 87
McDonagh, Don(ald Francis) 1932- CANR-1
Earlier sketch in CA 49-52
McDonagh, Enda 1930- 101
McDonagh, John Michael 1944- 109
McDonald, Alan (Patrick) 1949- 124
McDonald, Angus Henry
1904(?)-1990 Obituary 130
McDonald, Angus W(illiam) Jr. 1941- 105
McDonald, Archie P(hilip) 1935- CANR-15
Earlier sketch in CA 81-84
McDonald, Claude C(omstock) Jr.
1925- 29-32R
McDonald, David J(ohn) 1902-1979 45-48
Obituary 125
McDonald, Dianna
See Shomaker, Dianna
McDonald, Elvin 1937- CANR-34
Earlier sketches in CA 5-8R, CANR-8
McDonald, Erwin L(awrence) 1907- 73-76
McDonald, Eva (Rose) CANR-6
Earlier sketch in CA 13-16R
McDonald, Forrest 1927- CANR-5
Earlier sketch in CA 9-12R
See also DLB 17
McDonald, Frank J(ames) 1941- 97-100
McDonald, Gerald D(oan) 1905-1970 .... CAP-1
Earlier sketch in CA 11-12
See also SATA 3
McDonald, Gregory 1937- CANR-3
Earlier sketch in CA 5-8R
McDonald, Hugh C(hisholm) 1913- 65-68
McDonald, Hugh Dermot 1910- CANR-3
Earlier sketch in CA 9-12R
McDonald, Ian A(rchie) 1933- CANR-26
Earlier sketch in CA 29-32R
McDonald, Iverach 1908- 138
McDonald, James Robert 1934- 41-44R
McDonald, Jamie
See Heide, Florence Parry
McDonald, Jerry N(ealon) 1944- CANR-31
Earlier sketch in CA 105
McDonald, Jill (Masefield) 1927-1982 .... CANR-12
Obituary 105
Earlier sketch in CA 65-68
See also SATA 13, 29
McDonald, John D(ennis) 1906- CAP-2
Earlier sketch in CA 19-20
McDonald, Julie 1929- CANR-12
Earlier sketch in CA 29-32R
McDonald, Kay L(aureen) 1934- 57-60
McDonald, Lee Cameron 1925- 5-8R
McDonald, Linda 1939- CANR-4
Earlier sketch in CA 49-52
McDonald, Lucile Saunders 1898- CANR-18
Earlier sketches in CA 1-4R, CANR-4
See also SATA 10
McDonald, (Mary) Lynn 1940- 101
McDonald, Mary Reynolds 1888- CAP-1
Earlier sketch in CA 13-16
McDonald, Megan 1959- 135
See also SATA 67
McDonald, Nicholas 1923- 13-16R
McDonald, Paula 1939(?)- .... AITN 1
McDonald, Pauline 1907- 33-36R
McDonald, (Duncan) Peter 1962- 124
McDonald, Richard C. 1935(?)- .... AITN 1
McDonald, Robert 1943- 115
McDonald, Roger 1941- 101
McDonald, Stephen L(ee) 1924- 89-92
McDonald, Walter (Robert) 1934- CANR-31
Earlier sketches in CA 73-76, CANR-12
See also DLB 105
See also DLBD 9
McDonald, William Andrew 1913- 41-44R
McDonald, William Francis 1898-1976 .... 37-40R
McDonald, William U(lma) Jr. 1927- 17-20R
McDonnell, Christine 1949- CANR-23
Earlier sketch in CA 107
See also SATA 34
McDonnell, Helen M(argaret) 1923- CANR-13
Earlier sketch in CA 33-36R
McDonnell, Jinny
See McDonnell, Virginia B(leecker)
McDonnell, Kilian (Perry) 1921- CANR-34
Earlier sketch in CA 33-36R
McDonnell, Lois Eddy 1914- 5-8R
See also SATA 10
McDonnell, Rea 1942- 127
McDonnell, Robert F. 1928- 17-20R
McDonnell, Virginia B(leecker) 1917- CANR-8
Earlier sketch in CA 21-24R
McDonogh, Gary Wray 1952- 127
McDonough, George Edward 1924- 41-44R
McDonough, Jack 1944- 125
McDonough, James Lee 1934- 73-76
McDonough, Jerome 1946- CANR-27
Earlier sketch in CA 109
McDonough, Jerry
See McDonough, Jerome
McDonough, Nancy 1935- 57-60
McDonough, Peter 1939- 138
McDonough, Sheila 1928- 77-80
McDonough, Thomas E(dmund) 1929- 21-24R
McDonough, William K. 1900- CAP-1
Earlier sketch in CA 9-10
McDormand, Thomas Bruce 1904- CAP-1
Earlier sketch in CA 19-20

McDougal, Myres Smith 1906- CANR-6
Earlier sketch in CA 5-8R
McDougal, Stan
See Diamant, Lincoln
McDougal, Stuart Y(eatman) 1942- CANR-13
Earlier sketch in CA 73-76
McDougall, Anne 1926- 104
McDougall, Bonnie S. 1941- 127
McDougall, Colin 1917-1984 .... DLB 68
McDougall, Donald 1907- 81-84
McDougall, John Lorne 1900- 37-40R
McDougall, Joyce 1926- CANR-36
Earlier sketches in CA 25-28R, CANR-11
McDougall, Marina 1945- 97-100
McDougall, Walter A(llan) 1946- 126
Brief entry 121
McDow, Gerald
See Scortia, Thomas N(icholas)
McDowall, Robert William
1914-1987 Obituary 123
McDowell, (Ho)Bart (Kelliston Jr.) 1923- 25-28R
McDowell, Charles (Rice) Jr. 1926- 1-4R
McDowell, Crosby
See Freeman, John Crosby
McDowell, David 1918(?)-1985 Obituary 115
McDowell, Dimmes
1925(?)-1976 Obituary 69-72
McDowell, Edward Allison Jr. 1898- CAP-2
Earlier sketch in CA 21-22
McDowell, Edwin (Stewart) 1935- 9-12R
McDowell, Elizabeth Tibbals 1912- 5-8R
McDowell, Frank 1911- 53-56
McDowell, Frederick P(eter) W(oll)
1915- CANR-5
Earlier sketch in CA 1-4R
McDowell, John (Henry) 1942- 103
McDowell, John Holmes 1946- 97-100
McDowell, Margaret B(laine) 1923- 69-72
McDowell, Michael P(aul) Kube
See Kube-McDowell, Michael P(aul)
McDowell, Michael 1950- CANR-29
Earlier sketch in CA 93-96
McDowell, Robert Emmett 1914-1975 .... 1-4R
Obituary 103
McDowell, Robert 1953- 127
McDowell, Virginia (Duncan) H(ecker)
1933- 85-88
McEachern, Theodore 1928- 21-24R
McElaney, (Joseph) Paul 1922- 9-12R
McElderry, Bruce R. Jr. 1900-1970 .... CAP-1
Earlier sketch in CA 13-14
McEldowney, (Richard) Dennis 1926- 103
McEleney, Neil Joseph 1927- 115
McElfresh, (Elizabeth) Adeline 1918- 1-4R
McElhaney, James W(illson) 1937- 85-88
McElhanon, K(enneth) A(ndrew) 1939- CANR-5
Earlier sketch in CA 53-56
McEllhenney, John Galen 1934- 53-56
McElrath, Damian (Edmund)
1928- Brief entry 111
McElrath, Dennis Cornealius 1929- 45-48
McElrath, Joseph R(ichard) Jr. 1945- 65-68
McElrath, William N. 1932- CANR-35
Earlier sketch in CA 77-80
See also SATA 65
McElroy, Bernard (Patrick Jr.) 1938-1991 61-64
Obituary 136
McElroy, Colleen J(ohnson) 1935- CANR-38
Earlier sketches in CA 49-52, CANR-2, 17
See also BW
McElroy, Davis Dunbar 1917- 37-40R
McElroy, Elam E. 1922- 57-60
McElroy, John Alexander 1913- 17-20R
McElroy, Joseph 1930- 17-20R
See also CLC 5, 47
McElroy, Lee
See Kelton, Elmer
McElroy, Paul Simpson 1902- 5-8R
McElroy, Thomas P(arker) Jr. 1914- 73-76
McElvaine, Robert S(tuart) 1947- 114
McElwee, William (Lloyd) 1907-1979 57-60
Obituary 104
McEnery, John H. 1925- 134
McEnroe, Colin (Welles) 1954- 127
McEntee, Dorothy (Layng) 1902- .... SATA 37
McEvedy, Colin (Peter) 1930- 97-100
McEvoy, Dennis 1918- 73-76
McEvoy, Harry K(irby) 1910- 17-20R
McEvoy, Hubert 1899- 5-8R
McEvoy, James III 1940-1976 .... CAP-2
Earlier sketch in CA 33-36
McEvoy, Marjorie Harte CANR-18
Earlier sketches in CA 5-8R, CANR-2
McEwan, Ian (Russell) 1948- CANR-14
Earlier sketch in CA 61-64
See also BEST 90:4
See also CLC 13, 66
See also DLB 14
See also MTCW
McEwan, Jenny 1951- 124
McEwan, Keith 1926- 21-24R
McEwan, (John) Neil 1946- 130
McEwan, Peter J(ames) M(ichael)
1924- CANR-17
Earlier sketch in CA 25-28R
McEwen, Robert (Lindley)
1926-1980 Obituary 101
See also SATA 23
McFadden, Charles Joseph 1909- 77-80
McFadden, Cyra 1937- 77-80
McFadden, David 1940- 104
See also CLC 48
See also DLB 60
McFadden, Dorothy Loa 1902- 17-20R
McFadden, George 1916- 111
McFadden, James A. Jr. 1913- 17-20R

McFadden, Maggie
See McFadden, Margaret
McFadden, Margaret 1941- 115
McFadden, Robert D(ennis) 1937- CANR-15
Earlier sketch in CA 85-88
McFadden, Roy 1921- Brief entry 111
McFadden, Steven (S. H.) 1948- 138
McFadden, Thomas M(ore) 1935- 89-92
McFadyean, Melanie 1950- 127
McFague, Sallie 1933- CANR-11
Earlier sketch in CA 21-24R
McFall, Christie 1918- 5-8R
See also SATA 12
McFarlan, Donald M(aitland) 1915- CANR-10
Earlier sketch in CA 65-68
See also SATA 59
McFarlan, F. Warren 1937- 17-20R
McFarland, Andrew S(tuart) 1940- CANR-13
Earlier sketch in CA 25-28R
McFarland, C(harles) K(eith) 1934- 29-32R
McFarland, Carl 1904-1979 Obituary 85-88
McFarland, Dalton E(dward) 1919- CANR-2
Earlier sketch in CA 5-8R
McFarland, Dennis 1950- .... CLC 65
McFarland, Dorothy Tuck 1938- 9-12R
McFarland, Ernest W(illiam)
1894-1984 Obituary 114
McFarland, Gerald Ward 1938- 85-88
McFarland, John 1943- 116
McFarland, Keith D(onavon) 1940- 57-60
McFarland, Kenton D(ean) 1920- 61-64
See also SATA 11
McFarland, M(alcolm) Carter 1912- 85-88
McFarland, Marvin W(ilks)
1919-1985 Obituary 115
McFarland, Philip (James) 1930- CANR-12
Earlier sketch in CA 73-76
McFarland, Ron(ald Earl) 1942- CANR-32
Earlier sketch in CA 113
McFarland, Ross A(rmstrong) 1901- CAP-2
Earlier sketch in CA 21-22
McFarland, Thomas (Alfred Jr.) 1926- 41-44R
McFarlane, Brian 1931- 122
McFarlane, Bruce John 1936- CANR-16
Earlier sketch in CA 81-84
McFarlane, I(an) D(alrymple) 1915- 107
McFarlane, James Walter 1920- CANR-5
Earlier sketch in CA 1-4R
McFarlane, K. B. 1903-1966 Obituary 114
McFarlane, Leslie (Charles)
1902-1977 .... CANR-37
Earlier sketch in CA 112
See also DLB 88
See also MAICYA
See also SATA 31
McFate, Patricia Ann 1932- 103
McFather, Nelle 1936- CANR-4
Earlier sketch in CA 49-52
McFeat, Tom Farrar Scott 1919- 103
McFee, June King 1917- CANR-16
Earlier sketch in CA 81-84
McFee, Michael 1954- CANR-30
Earlier sketch in CA 112
McFee, Oonah 1922- 116
McFee, William (Morley Punshon)
1881-1966 Obituary 116
McFeely, Mary Drake 1932- CANR-27
Earlier sketch in CA 110
McFeely, William S(hield) 1930- CANR-15
Earlier sketch in CA 33-36R
McFerran, Ann
See Townsend, Doris McFerran
McFerran, Doris
See Townsend, Doris McFerran
McFerran, Douglass David 1934- 65-68
McGaa, Ed 1936- 97-100
McGaffin, William 1910-1975 .... CAP-2
Earlier sketch in CA 25-28
McGahern, John 1934- CANR-29
Earlier sketch in CA 17-20R
See also CLC 5, 9, 48
See also DLB 14
See also MTCW
McGahey, Michael J(oseph) 1948- 116
McGann, George T(homas) 1913- 93-96
McGann, Jerome J(ohn) 1937- CANR-14
Earlier sketches in CA 45-48, CANR-1
McGann, Thomas F. 1920- 13-16R
McGannon, J(ohn) Barry 1924- 13-16R
McGarey, Gladys T(aylor) 1920- 57-60
McGarey, William A. 1919- 57-60
McGarrigle, Francis Joseph 1888- 5-8R
McGarrity, Mark 1943- CANR-37
Earlier sketches in CA 45-48, CANR-1, 17
McGarry, Daniel D(oyle) 1907- CAP-1
Earlier sketch in CA 11-12
McGarry, Jean 1952- 126
McGarry, Kevin J(ohn) 1935- 102
McGarry, Michael B(rett) 1948- 102
McGarvey, Robert 1948- 113
McGaugh, James L(afayette) 1931- CANR-7
Earlier sketch in CA 57-60
McGaughey, (Florence) Helen 1904- 37-40R
McGavin, E(lmer) Cecil 1900- CAP-1
Earlier sketch in CA 11-12
McGavran, Donald (Anderson)
1897-1990(?) 13-16R
Obituary 132
McGaw, Charles James
1910-1978 Obituary 106
McGaw, Jessie Brewer 1913- 1-4R
See also SATA 10
McGaw, Naomi Blanche Thoburn 1920- 9-12R
McGaw, William C(ochran) 1914- 101
McGeachy, D(aniel) P(atrick) III 1929- CANR-8
Earlier sketch in CA 61-64

McGear, Mike
See McCartney, Peter Michael
McGee, Barbara 1943- 25-28R
See also SATA 6
McGee, (Doctor) Frank 1921-1974 105
Obituary 89-92
McGee, Harold 1951- 118
McGee, Mark
See McGee, Mark T(homas)
McGee, Mark T(homas) 1947- 134
McGee, Reece (Jerome) 1929- CANR-17
Earlier sketches in CA 5-8R, CANR-2
McGee, Robert W(illiam) 1947- 112
McGee, T. D.
See Savage, Teresa
McGee, T(erence) G(ary) 1936- CANR-10
Earlier sketch in CA 21-24R
McGee, Thomas D'Arcy 1825-1868 .... DLB 99
McGee, Victor (Errol) 1935- 41-44R
McGeehan, Robert 1933- 33-36R
McGeehan, W. O. 1879-1933 .... DLB 25
McGeeney, Patrick John 1918- 5-8R
McGeezer, Mark
See McGee, Mark T(homas)
McGehee, Ralph W(alter) 1928- 112
McGeown, Patrick 1897- CAP-2
Earlier sketch in CA 23-24
McGerr, Patricia 1917-1985 .... CANR-1
Obituary 116
Earlier sketch in CA 1-4R
See also AITN 1
McGhan, Barry (Robert) 1939- 69-72
McGhie, Andrew 1926- 97-100
McGiffert, Michael 1928- 13-16R
McGiffert, Robert C(arnahan) 1922- 49-52
McGiffin, (Lewis) Lee (Shaffer) 1908- CAP-1
Earlier sketch in CA 13-16
See also SATA 1
McGilchrist, Iain 1953- 132
McGill, Dan M(ays) 1919- 134
Brief entry 107
McGill, Ian
See Allegro, John Marco
McGill, Leonard J(ames) 1956- 115
McGill, Ormond 1913- CANR-2
Earlier sketch in CA 49-52
McGill, Ralph (Emerson) 1898-1969 .... 5-8R
Obituary 25-28R
See also DLB 29
McGill, Thomas E(merson) 1930- 17-20R
McGilligan, Patrick (Michael) 1951- CANR-10
Earlier sketch in CA 65-68
McGilvery, Laurence 1932- 33-36R
McGimsey, Charles Robert III 1925- 37-40R
McGinley, Patrick (Anthony) 1937- 127
Brief entry 120
See also CLC 41
McGinley, Phyllis 1905-1978 .... CANR-19
Obituary 77-80
Earlier sketch in CA 9-12R
See also CLC 14
See also DLB 11, 48
See also SATA 2, 24, 44
McGinn, Bernard John 1937- 113
McGinn, Donald Joseph 1905- CAP-2
Earlier sketch in CA 23-24
McGinn, John T. 1900(?)-1972 Obituary 33-36R
McGinn, Matt 1928-1977 106
McGinn, Maureen Ann
See Sautel, Maureen Ann
McGinn, Noel F(rancis) 1934- 73-76
McGinn, Richard 1939- 126
McGinnies, Elliott M(orse) 1921- 77-80
McGinnies, W(illiam) G(rovenor) 1899- CANR-7
Earlier sketch in CA 57-60
McGinnis, Bruce 1941- 97-100
McGinnis, Dorothy Jean 1920- 29-32R
McGinnis, Duane
See Niatum, Duane
McGinnis, K. K.
See Page, Grover Jr.
McGinnis, Lila S(prague) 1924- 93-96
See also SATA 44
McGinnis, Marilyn 1939- 57-60
McGinnis, Robert 1927- 45-48
McGinnis, Thomas C(harles) 1925-1987 65-68
Obituary 123
McGinniss, Joe 1942- CANR-26
Earlier sketch in CA 25-28R
See also AITN 2
See also BEST 89:2
See also CLC 32
McGirk, Tim(othy Stephen) 1952- 136
McGirt, James E. 1874-1930 .... DLB 50
McGivering, John H. 1923- 25-28R
McGivern, Maureen Daly
See Daly, Maureen
McGivern, William P(eter) 1922-1982 .... CANR-7
Obituary 108
Earlier sketch in CA 49-52
McGlade, Francis S(tanley) 1930- 41-44R
McGlamry, Beverly 1932- 119
McGlashan, Alan (Fleming) 1898- 41-44R
McGlennon, John J(oseph) 1949- 119
McGlinchee, Claire CAP-2
Earlier sketch in CA 23-24
McGlinn, Dwight
See Brannon, William T.
McGloin, John Bernard 1912- 33-36R
McGloin, Joseph T(haddeus) 1917- CANR-39
Earlier sketches in CA 1-4R, CANR-1, 18
McGlone, Edward Leon 1941- Brief entry 108
McGlothlin, William J(oseph) 1908- CAP-2
Earlier sketch in CA 19-20
McGlynn, Christopher
See Ginder, Richard

McGlynn, James V(incent) 1919-1973 ....1-4R
Obituary 103
McGoey, John Heck 1915- CANR-21
Earlier sketches in CA 9-12R, CANR-6
McGoldrick, Desmond Francis 1919- 17-20R
McGoldrick, Edward J. Jr. 1909-1967 ....CAP-1
Earlier sketch in CA 19-20
McGoldrick, Joseph D.
1901-1978 Obituary 97-100
McGoldstein, Paddy
See Page, William
McGonigle, Thomas 1944- 137
McGoon, Clifford D. 1939- 113
McGough, Elizabeth (Hemmes) 1934- 107
See also SATA 33
McGough, Roger 1937- 105
See also DLB 40
McGovern, Ann 1930- CANR-2
Earlier sketch in CA 49-52
See also MAICYA
See also SATA 8, 69, 70
McGovern, Arthur F(rancis) 1929- 116
McGovern, Constance M(adeline) 1938- 120
McGovern, George S(tanley) 1922- CANR-8
Earlier sketch in CA 45-48
McGovern, James R(ichard) 1928- 108
McGovern, James (Walter) 1923-1989 ....CANR-7
Obituary 129
Earlier sketch in CA 17-20R
McGovern, John P(hillip) 1921- CANR-13
Earlier sketch in CA 21-24R
McGovern, Robert 1927- CANR-28
Earlier sketch in CA 49-52
McGowan, Jack 1896(?)-1977 Obituary 69-72
McGowan, James A(lfred) 1932- 97-100
McGowan, Joe A. Jr.
See McGowan, Joseph A. Jr.
McGowan, John J. 1936(?)-1982 Obituary 106
McGowan, John P. 1953- 135
McGowan, Joseph A. Jr. 1931- 133
McGowan, Margaret M(ary) 69-72
McGowen, Charles H(ammond) 1936- 69-72
McGowen, Thomas 1927- CANR-25
Earlier sketches in CA 21-24R, CANR-8
See also SATA 2
McGowen, Tom
See McGowen, Thomas
McGrade, Arthur Stephen 1934- 25-28R
McGrady, Donald Lee 1935- 25-28R
McGrady, Mike 1933- CANR-2
Earlier sketch in CA 49-52
See also SATA 6
McGrady, Patrick M(ichael) Jr. 1932- CANR-12
Earlier sketch in CA 29-32R
McGrady, Patrick Michael Sr. 1908-1980 103
Obituary 97-100
McGrail, Joie 1922(?)-1977 Obituary 69-72
McGrane, Bernard 1947- 133
McGrath, Alice (Greenfield) 1917- 112
McGrath, Alister E(dgar) 1953- 134
McGrath, Doyle
See Schorb, E(dwin) M(arsh)
McGrath, Earl James 1902- CAP-1
Earlier sketch in CA 19-20
McGrath, Edward G(orham) 1917- 25-28R
McGrath, Francis E.
1903(?)-1976 Obituary 61-64
McGrath, J. H. 1923- 29-32R
McGrath, James Bernard Jr. 1917- 5-8R
McGrath, Joan Rosita (Torr)
1895(?)-1967 Obituary 116
McGrath, John (Peter) 1935- Brief entry 112
McGrath, Lee Parr 1933- 29-32R
McGrath, Patrick 1950- 136
See also CLC 55
McGrath, Robert L(ee) 1920- 97-100
McGrath, Roger D. 1947- 118
McGrath, Sean
See Douglas, John (Frederick James)
McGrath, Susan 1955- 121
McGrath, Sylvia Wallace 1937- 61-64
McGrath, Thomas (Matthew)
1916-1990 ....CANR-33
Obituary 132
Earlier sketches in CA 9-12R, CANR-6
See also CLC 28, 59
See also MTCW
See also SATA 41
See also SATO 66
McGrath, Tom 1940- 130
McGrath, William J(ames) 1937- 85-88
McGrath, William Thomas 1917- 103
McGratty, Arthur R. 1909-1975 Obituary 53-56
McGraw, Eloise Jarvis 1915- CANR-36
Earlier sketches in CA 5-8R, CANR-4, 19
See also MAICYA
See also SAAS 6
See also SATA 1, 67
McGraw, Harold Whittlesey Sr.
1890(?)-1970 Obituary 29-32R
McGraw, James (Paul) 1913-1977 ....1-4R
McGraw, James R. 1935- 93-96
McGraw, Walter John Jr.
1919(?)-1978 Obituary 81-84
McGraw, William Corbin 1916- CANR-36
Earlier sketch in CA 29-32R
See also SATA 3
McGreal, Elizabeth
See Yates, Elizabeth
McGreal, Ian Philip 1919- 77-80
McGreevey, William Paul 1938- CANR-11
Earlier sketch in CA 69-72
McGreevy, Susan Brown 1934- 126
McGregor
See Hurley, Doran
McGregor, Craig 1933- CANR-13
Earlier sketch in CA 21-24R
See also SATA 8
McGregor, Iona 1929- 105
See also SATA 25
McGregor, James H. 1946- 138
McGregor, John C(harles) 1905- CAP-1
Earlier sketch in CA 19-20
McGregor, Malcolm Francis 1910- 45-48
McGregor, Rob Roy Jr. 1929- 108
McGrew, William W. 1933- 122
McGrory, Mary 1918- 106
See also AITN 2
McGuane, Thomas (Francis III) 1939- CANR-24
Earlier sketches in CA 49-52, CANR-5
See also AITN 2
See also CLC 3, 7, 18, 45
See also DLB 2
See also DLBY 80
See also MTCW
McGuckian, Medbh 1950- ....CLC 48
See also DLB 40
McGuffey, Alexander Hamilton
1816-1896 ....SATA 60
McGuffey, William Holmes 1800-1873 ....DLB 42
McGuffie, Tom H(enderson) 1902- CAP-2
Earlier sketch in CA 19-20
McGuffin, Mark
See McGee, Mark T(homas)
McGuigan, Dorothy Gies 1914-1982 ....CANR-11
Earlier sketch in CA 21-24R
McGuigan, F(rank) J(oseph) 1924- CANR-8
Earlier sketch in CA 5-8R
McGuinness, Arthur E(dward) 1936- 25-28R
McGuire, E(dward) Patrick 1932- 25-28R
McGuire, Edna 1899- CANR-2
Earlier sketch in CA 5-8R
See also SATA 13
McGuire, Frances Margaret (Cheadle) CAP-1
Earlier sketch in CA 9-10
McGuire, James Dean 1936- 21-24R
McGuire, Jerry 1934- 93-96
McGuire, Joseph William 1925- 9-12R
McGuire, Leslie Sarah 1945- 107
See also SATA 45, 52
McGuire, Martin C. 1933- 37-40R
McGuire, Martin Rawson Patrick
1897-1969 Obituary 111
McGuire, Meredith Anne (Black) 1944- 118
McGuire, Michael Terrance 1929- 41-44R
McGuire, Richard L(en) 1940- 57-60
McGuire, Robert G. (III)
1938(?)-1975 Obituary 61-64
McGuire, Thomas G. 1950- 111
McGuire, Thomas (Vertin) 1945- 73-76
McGuirk, Bernard 1949- 129
McGurk, Patrick (Maurice) 1928- 118
McGurk, Slater
See Roth, Arthur J(oseph)
McGurn, Barrett 1914- CANR-1
Earlier sketch in CA 1-4R
McGurn, James (Edward) 1953- 136
McGurn, William 1958- 126
McGwire, Michael 1924- 128
McHale, John 1922-1978 ....CANR-17
Earlier sketch in CA 61-64
McHale, Philip John 1928- 103
McHale, Tom 1942(?)-1982 77-80
Obituary 106
See also AITN 1
See also CLC 3, 5
McHale, Vincent E(dward) 1939- 112
McHam, David 1933- 73-76
McHaney, Thomas L(afayette) 1936- CANR-24
Earlier sketches in CA 65-68, CANR-9
McHarg, Ian L(ennox) 1920- 29-32R
McHargue, Georgess 1941- CANR-24
Earlier sketch in CA 25-28R
See also CLR 2
See also SAAS 5
See also SATA 4
McHenry, Dean E(ugene) 1910- 109
McHenry, Paul G(raham) Jr. 1924- 61-64
McHugh, Arona 1924- 5-8R
McHugh, Edna 69-72
McHugh, (Berit) Elisabet 1941- CANR-32
Earlier sketch in CA 113
See also SATA 44, 55
McHugh, Heather 1948- CANR-28
Earlier sketches in CA 69-72, CANR-11
McHugh, John (Francis) 1927- 103
McHugh, Leroy 1891(?)-1975 Obituary 104
McHugh, Mary 1928- 85-88
McHugh, Maxine Davis
1899(?)-1978 Obituary 77-80
McHugh, P(atrick) J(oseph) 1922- 21-24R
McHugh, Roger Joseph 1908- 5-8R
McHugh, Roland 1945- CANR-10
Earlier sketch in CA 65-68
McHugh, Ruth Nelson
See Nelson, Ruth
McHugh, Stuart
See Rowland, D(onald) S(ydney)
McHugh, Thomas Cannell 1926- 103
McHugh, Tom
See McHugh, Thomas Cannell
McHugh, Vincent 1904-1983 Obituary 109
McIlhany, William H(erbert) II 1951- CANR-6
Earlier sketch in CA 57-60
McIlroy, Thad 1956- 122
McIlvaine, Betsy 1945- 123
McIlvaine, Jane
See McClary, Jane Stevenson
McIlvanney, William 1936- 25-28R
See also CLC 42
See also DLB 14
McIlwain, Charles Howard 1871-1968 102
McIlwain, David 1921- 109
McIlwain, William (Franklin Jr.) 1925- CANR-1
Earlier sketch in CA 1-4R
McIlwraith, Jean Newton 1859-1938 ....DLB 92
McIlwraith, Maureen Mollie Hunter
See Hunter, Mollie
See also SATA 2
McInenly, William T(homas) 1932- 124
McInerney, Jay 1955- 123
Brief entry 116
See also CLC 34
McInerney, Judith W(hitelock) 1945- 118
See also SATA 46, 49
McInerny, Dennis Q(uentin) 1936- 97-100
McInerny, Ralph 1929- CANR-34
Earlier sketches in CA 21-24R, CANR-12
McInnes, Edward 1935- 109
McInnes, Graham (Campbell)
1912-1970 ....CAP-2
Earlier sketch in CA 25-28
McInnes, Ian (Andrew Stuart Fraser)
1925- 25-28R
McInnes, Neil 1924- 77-80
McInnis, Edgar Wardwell 1899- 5-8R
McInnis, Noel F. 1936- CANR-14
Earlier sketch in CA 33-36R
McInnis, Raymond G(eorge) 1936- 110
McIntire, C(arl) T(homas) 1939- 130
McIntire, Roger W(arren) 1935- 53-56
McIntosh, Alexander 1947- CANR-2
Earlier sketch in CA 45-48
McIntosh, Carey 1934- 77-80
McIntosh, Christopher 1943- 33-36R
McIntosh, Donal W. 1919- 69-72
McIntosh, Douglas M. 1909- CAP-1
Earlier sketch in CA 13-14
McIntosh, E. 1894(?)-1970 Obituary 104
McIntosh, J. T.
See Macgregor, James (Murdoch)
McIntosh, James (Henry) 1934- 104
McIntosh, John 1930-1970 ....CAP-2
Earlier sketch in CA 21-22
McIntosh, Kinn Hamilton CANR-27
Earlier sketch in CA 25-28R
McIntosh, Louis
See Johnson, Christopher
McIntosh, Michael (Scott) 1945- 107
McIntosh, Peter Chisholm 1915- 102
McIntosh, Sandy
See McIntosh, Alexander
McInturff, Roy A(rthur) 1905- 53-56
McIntyre, Dennis 1943(?)-1990 Obituary 130
McIntyre, James 1827-1906 ....DLB 99
McIntyre, John A(rmin) 1920- 57-60
McIntyre, Kenneth E. 1918- CANR-9
Earlier sketch in CA 21-24R
McIntyre, Michael P(erry) 1921- 41-44R
McIntyre, O. O. 1884-1938 ....DLB 25
McIntyre, Thomas (Alfred) 1952- 120
McIntyre, Thomas J(ames)
1915- Brief entry 114
McIntyre, Vonda N(eel) 1948- CANR-34
Earlier sketches in CA 81-84, CANR-17
See also CLC 18
See also MTCW
McIntyre, W(illiam) David 1932- CANR-26
Earlier sketches in CA 21-24R, CANR-10
McIntyre, William (Alexander) 1916- 37-40R
McIver, J(ohn) R(abie) 1931- 25-28R
McIver, Ray 1913- 25-28R
McIver, Stuart B(etts) 1921- 69-72
McJimsey, George T(ilden) 1936- 93-96
McJimsey, Harriet Tilden 1902- 5-8R
McKain, David W. 1937- CANR-5
Earlier sketch in CA 9-12R
See also CAAS 14
McKale, Donald M(arshall) 1943- CANR-5
Earlier sketch in CA 53-56
McKane, William 1921- 117
McKay, Alexander G(ordon) 1924- 37-40R
McKay, (Herbert) Alwyn (Cochrane) 1913- 119
McKay, Arthur R(aymond) 1918- 5-8R
McKay, Claude
See McKay, Festus Claudius
See also DLB 4, 45, 51, 117
See also PC 2
See also TCLC 7, 41
McKay, Derek 1942- 81-84
McKay, Don(ald) 1932- 33-36R
McKay, Donald 1895- ....SATA 45
McKay, Douglas R(ich) 1936- CANR-7
Earlier sketch in CA 57-60
McKay, Ernest A. 1918- 21-24R
McKay, Festus Claudius 1889-1948 124
Brief entry 104
See also McKay, Claude
See also BW
See also MTCW
See also WLC
McKay, George Frederick
1899-1970 Obituary 106
McKay, Jim
See McManus, James Kenneth
McKay, John H(arvey) 1923- Brief entry 115
McKay, John P(atrick) 1938- 29-32R
McKay, Quinn G(unn) 1926- 57-60
McKay, Robert B(udge) 1919-1990 57-60
Obituary 132
McKay, Robert W. 1921- CANR-10
Earlier sketch in CA 13-16R
See also SATA 15
McKay, Vernon 1912- 5-8R
McKay, William Paul 1951- 116
McKeachie, Wilbert J(ames) 1921- 21-24R
McKeag, Ernest L(ionel) 1896- CAP-1
Earlier sketch in CA 13-16
McKean, Charles (Alexander) 1946- 137
McKean, Dayton D(avid) 1904- CAP-1
Earlier sketch in CA 19-20
McKean, Gil(bert S.) 1918- 5-8R
McKean, Hugh Ferguson 1908- 102
McKean, John (Maule) 1943- 107
McKean, John Richard 1939- 33-36R
McKean, Keith F. 1915- 37-40R
McKean, Margaret A(nne) 1946- 108
McKean, Robert B. 1943- 135
McKean, Robert C(laud) 1920- 13-16R
McKean, Roland N(eely) 1917- 33-36R
McKean, William V. 1820-1903 ....DLB 23
McKeating, Henry 1932- 37-40R
McKeay, Eileen
See McKeag, Ernest L(ionel)
McKechnie, Paul (Richard) 1957- 137
McKee, Alasdair 1963- 132
McKee, Alexander (Paul Charrier)
1918- CANR-11
Earlier sketch in CA 9-12R
McKee, Barbara H(astings) 1902- 57-60
McKee, Christopher (Fulton) 1935- 77-80
McKee, David (John) 1935- 137
See also MAICYA
McKee, David 1935- ....SATA 69, 70
McKee, Edwin D(inwiddie) 1906- 57-60
McKee, Eric
See McKee, J. E. G.
McKee, J. E. G. Obituary 111
McKee, John DeWitt 1919- 41-44R
McKee, Louis 1951- 110
McKee, Paul Gordon 1897- CAP-1
Earlier sketch in CA 11-12
McKeefery, William James
1918-1987 Obituary 123
McKeever, James Ross
1909(?)-1986 Obituary 120
McKeever, Marcia
See Laird, Jean E(louise)
McKelvey, Blake F. 1903- 17-20R
McKelvey, Carole A. 1942- 135
McKelvey, James Lee 1934- 45-48
McKelvey, John J(ay) Jr. 1917- CANR-8
Earlier sketch in CA 61-64
McKelvy, Natalie 1950- 138
McKelway, Alexander J(effery) 1932- 13-16R
McKelway, Benjamin M.
1895-1976 Obituary 69-72
McKelway, St. Clair 1905-1980 ....5-8R
Obituary 93-96
McKemy, Kay 1924- 29-32R
McKendrick, (Hector) Fergus 1933- 115
McKendrick, Melveena (Christine)
1941- CANR-37
Earlier sketches in CA 93-96, CANR-17
See also SATA 55
McKendry, John (Joseph)
1933-1975 Obituary 61-64
McKenna, A. Daniel
See Corson-Finnerty, Adam Daniel
McKenna, Evelyn
See Joscelyn, Archie L.
McKenna, F(rancis) E(ugene)
1921-1978 Obituary 85-88
McKenna, George 1937- CANR-14
Earlier sketch in CA 81-84
McKenna, J(ane) J(essica) 1945- 93-96
McKenna, J(ohn) W(illiam) 1938- 37-40R
McKenna, Marian Cecilia 1926- CANR-22
Earlier sketch in CA 1-4R
McKenna, Michael C(layton) 1947- 116
McKenna, Patricia
See Goedicke, Patricia (McKenna)
McKenna, Richard (Milton)
1913-1964 ....CANR-13
Earlier sketch in CA 5-8R
McKenna, Sister Margaret Mary 1930- 21-24R
McKenna, Sister Mary Lawrence
See McKenna, Sister Margaret Mary
McKenna, Stephen 1888-1967 ....CAP-1
Earlier sketch in CA 9-10
McKenna, Terry 1949- 109
McKenney, Kenneth 1929- 69-72
McKenney, Mary 1946- 61-64
McKenney, Ruth 1911-1972 93-96
Obituary 37-40R
McKennon, Joe
See McKennon, Joseph W(esley)
McKennon, Joseph W(esley) 1907- CANR-2
Earlier sketch in CA 49-52
Mc Kenny, Margaret 73-76
McKenzie, Barbara 1934- 21-24R
McKenzie, Dorothy Clayton
1910-1981 ....SATA 28
McKenzie, Doug
See Thomas, Dave
McKenzie, Garry D(onald) 1941- 41-44R
McKenzie, George W(ashington) 1939- 69-72
McKenzie, John L(awrence) 1910-1991 ....9-12R
Obituary 133
McKenzie, Leon R(oy) 1932- 29-32R
McKenzie, Michael 1954- 127
McKenzie, Paige
See Blood, Marje
McKenzie, Robert T(relford) 1917-1981 ....17-20R
Obituary 105
McKenzie, William P. 1954- 130
McKeon, Richard P(eter)
1900-1985 Obituary 115
McKeon, Zahava Karl 1927- 126
McKeown, James E(dward) 1919- 13-16R
McKeown, Thomas 1912-1988 Obituary 125
McKeown, Tom 1937- CANR-20
Earlier sketches in CA 45-48, CANR-2
McKercher, Berneth N(oble) 1915- 53-56
McKern, Leo
See McKern, Reginald

McKern, Reginald 1920- ... 134
McKern, Sharon S(mith) 1941- ... 37-40R
McKernan, John J(oseph) 1942- ... 110
McKerrow, Mary 1915- ... 132
McKersie, R. B.
See McKersie, Robert Bruce
McKersie, Robert Bruce 1929- Brief entry ... 116
McKhann, Charles Fremont 1930- ... 112
McKibben, Bill
See McKibben, William (Ernest)
McKibben, William (Ernest) 1960- ... 130
McKibbin, Alma E(stelle Baker)
1871-1974 ... CAP-1
Earlier sketch in CA 19-20
McKibbin, Frank L(owell) 1917- ... 65-68
McKibbin, Jean 1919- ... 65-68
McKie, Ronald (Cecil Hamlyn) 1909- ... CANR-6
Earlier sketch in CA 9-12R
McKillip, Patricia A(nne) 1948- ... CANR-18
Earlier sketches in CA 49-52, CANR-4
See also MTCW
See also SATA 30
McKillop, Alan D(ugald) 1892-1974 ... CAP-1
Obituary ... 53-56
Earlier sketch in CA 19-20
McKillop, Menzies 1929- ... 77-80
McKillop, Norman 1892-1974 ... 5-8R
McKillop, Susan Regan 1929- ... CANR-8
Earlier sketch in CA 61-64
McKim, Audrey Margaret 1909- ... CANR-4
Earlier sketch in CA 1-4R
See also SATA 47
McKim, Donald K(eith) 1950- ... CANR-17
Earlier sketch in CA 93-96
McKimmey, James 1923- ... CANR-22
Earlier sketch in CA 85-88
McKinlay, Brian John 1933- ... CANR-19
Earlier sketch in CA 103
McKinley, Daniel (Lawson) 1924- ... 25-28R
McKinley, David Hopwood 1906- ... CAP-2
Earlier sketch in CA 33-36
McKinley, James (Courtright) 1935- ... 69-72
McKinley, (Jennifer Carolyn) Robin
1952- ... CANR-31
Earlier sketch in CA 107
See also AAYA 4
See also CLR 10
See also DLB 52
See also MAICYA
See also SATA 32, 50
McKinnell, James 1933- ... CANR-12
Earlier sketch in CA 61-64
McKinnell, Robert Gilmore 1926- ... 102
McKinney, D. J.
See Cooper, Parley J(oseph)
McKinney, David Walter Jr. 1920- ... 37-40R
McKinney, Don(ald Lee) 1923- ... 73-76
McKinney, Donald 1909- ... CANR-7
Earlier sketch in CA 57-60
McKinney, Eleanor Ruth 1918- ... 33-36R
McKinney, Eugene 1922- ... CANR-15
Earlier sketch in CA 73-76
McKinney, Fred 1908-1981 ... 17-20R
Obituary ... 135
McKinney, Gene
See McKinney, Eugene
McKinney, George Dallas Jr. 1932- ... 5-8R
McKinney, George W(esley) Jr. 1922- ... 57-60
McKinney, Gordon B(artlett) 1943- ... 85-88
McKinney, H(enry) Lewis 1935- ... 41-44R
McKinney, John William 1908- ... 1-4R
McKinney, Virginia (Marie) 1940- ... 57-60
McKinney, William 1946- ... 121
McKinnon, Alastair Thomson 1925- ... 102
McKinnon, James 1932- ... 128
McKinnon, Robert Scott 1937- ... 37-40R
McKinnon, Ronald I(an) 1935- ... 131
McKinzie, Richard D. 1936- ... 77-80
McKisack, May 1900-1981 ... 107
Obituary ... 103
McKissack, Fredrick L(emuel) 1939- ... 120
See also SATA 53
McKissack, Patricia (L'Ann) C(arwell)
1944- ... CANR-38
Earlier sketch in CA 118
See also CLR 23
See also MAICYA
See also SATA 51
McKissick, Floyd Bixler 1922-1991 ... 49-52
Obituary ... 134
McKitrick, Eric Louis 1919- ... 21-24R
McKittrick, David 1938- ... 61-64
McKivigan, John R(aymond) 1949- ... 119
McKnight, Allan Douglas 1918- ... 104
McKnight, Brian Emerson 1938- ... 106
McKnight, C. A.
See Russell, Rosalind
McKnight, C(olbert) A(ugustus)
1916-1986 Obituary ... 120
McKnight, Edgar V(ernon) 1931- ... 21-24R
McKnight, Gerald 1919- ... 13-16R
McKnight, John P(roctor)
1908(?)-1987 Obituary ... 123
McKnight, Reginald ... 129
McKnight, Thomas Lee
See McKnight, Tom Lee
McKnight, Tom Lee 1928- ... CANR-5
Earlier sketch in CA 9-12R
McKowen, Clark 1929- ... 41-44R
McKown, Dave Ross 1895- ... 97-100
McKown, Robert 1908-1973 Obituary ... 104
McKown, Robin ... CANR-1
Earlier sketch in CA 1-4R
See also SATA 6
McKuen, Rod 1933- ... 41-44R
See also AITN 1
See also CLC 1, 3
McKusick, Marshall Bassford 1930- ... CANR-9
Earlier sketch in CA 13-16R
McLachlan, Alexander 1818-1896 ... DLB 99
McLachlan, Ian 1938- ... 69-72
McLaglen, John J.
See Harvey, John (Barton)
McLanathan, Richard 1916- ... 81-84
McLandress, Herschel
See Galbraith, John Kenneth
McLane, Charles B(ancroft) 1919- ... 25-28R
McLane, Helen J. ... CANR-4
Earlier sketch in CA 9-12R
McLane, John R. 1935- ... 97-100
McLane, Paul Elliott 1907- ... CAP-1
Earlier sketch in CA 9-10
McLaren, Colin Andrew 1940- ... CANR-27
Earlier sketch in CA 106
McLaren, Floris Clark 1904-1978 ... DLB 68
McLaren, Homer D. 1887- ... CAP-2
Earlier sketch in CA 29-32
McLaren, Ian A. 1928- ... 103
McLaren, Ian Francis 1912- ... CANR-24
Earlier sketch in CA 106
McLaren, John (David) 1932- ... 29-32R
McLaren, Moray (David Shaw) 1901-1971 ... 103
McLaren, N(orman) Loyall
1892(?)-1977 Obituary ... 73-76
McLaren, Robert Bruce 1923- ... 29-32R
McLarry, Newman R(ay) 1923- ... 13-16R
McLaughlin, Andree N.
See McLaughlin, Andree Nicola
McLaughlin, Andree Nicola 1948- ... 133
McLaughlin, Ann L. 1928- ... 135
McLaughlin, Arthur Leo 1921- ... 17-20R
McLaughlin, Bill
See Phillips, James W.
McLaughlin, Charles Bernard 1937- ... 61-64
McLaughlin, Curtis P. 1932- ... CANR-5
Earlier sketch in CA 53-56
McLaughlin, David J(ohn) 1936- ... 73-76
McLaughlin, Dean (Jr.) 1931- ... 9-12R
McLaughlin, Elizabeth Taylor 1923- ... 93-96
McLaughlin, Emma Maude 1901- ... 65-68
McLaughlin, Jack
See McLaughlin, John Joseph
McLaughlin, John Joseph 1926- ... 129
McLaughlin, Joseph F. Jr.
1919-1978 Obituary ... 77-80
McLaughlin, Joseph 1940- ... CANR-20
Earlier sketches in CA 45-48, CANR-4
McLaughlin, Kathleen 1898-1990 Obituary ... 132
McLaughlin, Lorrie (Bell) 1924-1971 ... CANR-5
Earlier sketch in CA 5-8R
McLaughlin, Mignon ... 9-12R
McLaughlin, Robert (Emmet) 1908-1973 ... 1-4R
Obituary ... 45-48
McLaughlin, Robert William 1900- ... 1-4R
McLaughlin, Samuel Clarke 1924- ... 89-92
McLaughlin, Sister Raymond 1897- ... 25-28R
McLaughlin, Ted J(ohn) 1921- ... 13-16R
McLaughlin, Terence (Patrick) 1928- ... 33-36R
McLaughlin, Virginia Yans
See Yans-McLaughlin, Virginia
McLaughlin, William (DeWitt) 1918- ... 107
McLaughlin, William Raffian Davidson
1908- ... CAP-1
Earlier sketch in CA 11-12
McLaurin, Anne 1953- ... 106
See also SATA 27
McLaurin, Melton A(lonza) 1941- ... CANR-28
Earlier sketch in CA 81-84
McLaurin, R(onald) D(e) 1944- ... CANR-17
Earlier sketch in CA 65-68
McLaverty, Michael 1904- ... CAP-1
Earlier sketch in CA 13-14
See also DLB 15
McLean, Albert F(orbes) Jr. 1928- ... 17-20R
McLean, Allan Campbell 1922- ... CANR-4
Earlier sketch in CA 1-4R
McLean, Anne (Julia) 1951- ... 120
McLean, Antonio (Maxwell) 1919- ... 130
McLean, Beth Bailey 1892- ... CAP-2
Earlier sketch in CA 19-20
McLean, Don(ald George) 1932- ... 122
McLean, Donald 1905-1975 ... CANR-4
Earlier sketch in CA 1-4R
McLean, George F(rancis) 1929- ... CANR-6
Earlier sketch in CA 13-16R
McLean, George 1905(?)-1983 Obituary ... 109
McLean, Gordon R(onald) 1934- ... CANR-2
Earlier sketch in CA 49-52
McLean, Hugh 1925- ... 65-68
McLean, Iain (S.) 1946- ... 135
McLean, J. Sloan
See Gillette, Virginia M(ary)
and Wunsch, Josephine (McLean)
McLean, Janice W(alker) 1944- ... 119
McLean, John R. 1848-1916 ... DLB 23
McLean, Joseph E(rigina)
1915-1985 Obituary ... 118
McLean, Kathryn (Anderson) 1909-1966 ... CAP-2
Obituary ... 25-28R
Earlier sketch in CA 21-22
See also SATA 9
McLean, Malcolm Dallas 1913- ... CANR-39
Earlier sketches in CA 93-96, CANR-16
McLean, Robert Colin 1927- ... 17-20R
McLean, Robert 1891-1980 Obituary ... 103
McLean, Ruari 1917- ... CANR-10
Earlier sketch in CA 21-24R
McLean, Sammy Kay 1929- ... 37-40R
McLean, Susan 1937- ... 106
McLean, William L. 1852-1931 ... DLB 25
McLeave, Hugh George 1923- ... CANR-27
Earlier sketches in CA 5-8R, CANR-6
McLeavy, Gus 1951- ... 105
McLees, Ainslie Armstrong 1947- ... 135
McLeish, Garen
See Stine, Whitney Ward
McLeish, John 1917- ... CANR-7
Earlier sketch in CA 57-60
McLeish, Kenneth 1940- ... CANR-13
Earlier sketch in CA 29-32R
See also SATA 35
McLellan, David S(tanley) 1924- ... 103
McLellan, David 1940- ... CANR-33
Earlier sketches in CA 33-36R, CANR-15
McLellan, Diana 1937- ... 114
McLellan, Robert 1907-1985 ... 41-44R
Obituary ... 115
McLemore, Richard Aubrey 1903-1976 ... 49-52
Obituary ... 103
McLemore, S(amuel) Dale 1928- ... 9-12R
McLendon, Gloria H(ouston) 1940- ... 112
McLendon, Gordon (Barton) 1921-1986 ... 133
Obituary ... 120
McLendon, James (Nelson) 1942-1982 ... 41-44R
Obituary ... 106
McLendon, Jonathon C(ollins)
1919-1977 ... 17-20R
Obituary ... 134
McLendon, Will L(oving) 1925- ... 9-12R
McLendon, Winzola Poole ... 93-96
McLenighan, Valjean 1947- ... 108
See also SATA 40, 46
McLennan, Barbara N(ancy) 1940- ... 85-88
McLennan, Will
See Wisler, G(ary) Clifton
McLennan, William 1856-1904 ... DLB 92
McLeod, Alan L(indsey) 1928- ... 9-12R
McLeod, Emilie Warren 1926-1982 ... 33-36R
Obituary ... 108
See also SATA 23, 31
McLeod, Enid (Devoge) 1896-1985 ... 134
Obituary ... 116
McLeod, Jack (T.) 1932- ... 129
McLeod, James R(ichard) 1942- ... 41-44R
McLeod, John F(reeland) 1917-1989 ... 69-72
Obituary ... 128
McLeod, Kirsty
See Hudson, (Margaret) Kirsty
McLeod, Malcolm Donald 1941- ... 110
McLeod, Margaret Vail
See Holloway, Teresa (Bragunier)
McLeod, Mary Alice 1937- ... 112
McLeod, Raymond Jr. 1932- ... CANR-19
Earlier sketches in CA 49-52, CANR-3
McLeod, Ross
See Feldman, Herbert (H. S.)
McLeod, Wallace (Edmond) 1931- ... CANR-31
Earlier sketches in CA 37-40R, CANR-14
McLerran, Alice 1933- ... 136
See also SATA 68
McLin, Jon (Blythe) 1938- ... 102
McLin, Ruth (Arlene) 1924- ... 61-64
McLoughlin, John C. 1949- ... 108
See also SATA 47
McLoughlin, R. B.
See Mencken, H(enry) L(ouis)
McLoughlin, William G. 1922- ... CANR-6
Earlier sketch in CA 13-16R
McLouth, Gary (Michael) 1944- ... 119
McLowery, Frank
See Keevill, Henry J(ohn)
McLuhan, (Thomas) Eric (Marshall) 1942- ... 130
McLuhan, (Herbert) Marshall
1911-1980 ... CANR-34
Obituary ... 102
Earlier sketches in CA 9-12R, CANR-12
See also CLC 37
See also DLB 88
See also MTCW
McLure, Charles E. Jr. 1940- ... CANR-28
Earlier sketches in CA 57-60, CANR-8
McMahan, Ian ... SATA 45
McMahon, Bob 1943- ... 111
McMahon, Bryan T(homas) 1950- ... CANR-35
Earlier sketch in CA 45-48
McMahon, Charles P.
1916(?)-1983 Obituary ... 109
McMahon, Dorothy 1912-1984 Obituary ... 112
McMahon, Ed(ward Leo Peter Jr.) 1923- ... 89-92
McMahon, Francis E(lmer)
1906-1987 Obituary ... 123
McMahon, Jeremiah 1919- ... 109
McMahon, Joseph H(enry) 1930-1987 ... 9-12R
Obituary ... 124
McMahon, Michael 1943- ... 69-72
McMahon, Pat
See Hoch, Edward D(entinger)
McMahon, Robert
See Weverka, Robert
McMahon, Robert J. 1949- ... 109
McMahon, Thomas (Arthur) 1943- ... CANR-15
Earlier sketch in CA 33-36R
McMahon, Thomas
1923(?)-1972 Obituary ... 37-40R
McManis, Douglas R. ... 69-72
McManners, (Joseph) Hugh 1952- ... 132
McManners, John 1916- ... CANR-14
Earlier sketch in CA 37-40R
McManus, Edgar J. 1924- ... 97-100
McManus, Frederick R(ichard) 1923- ... 1-4R
McManus, James Kenneth 1921- ... 85-88
McManus, James 1951- ... 117
McManus, Jason 1934- ... 125
McManus, Marjorie 1950- ... 73-76
McManus, Patrick (Francis) 1933- ... 105
See also SATA 46
McMaster, Beth 1935- ... CANR-30
Earlier sketch in CA 112
McMaster, John Bach 1852-1932 ... DLB 47
McMaster, Juliet 1937- ... 37-40R
McMath, Robert C(arroll) Jr. 1944- ... 129
McMeekin, Clark
See McMeekin, Isabel McLennan
McMeekin, Dorothy 1932- ... 125
McMeekin, Isabel McLennan 1895- ... 5-8R
See also SATA 3
McMenemey, William Henry 1905- ... CAP-1
Earlier sketch in CA 11-12
McMenemy, Nickie 1925- ... 97-100
McMichael, George 1927- ... 103
McMichael, James 1939- ... 69-72
McMichael, Joan K(atharine) 1906- ... 107
McMillan, Alan D. 1945- ... 130
McMillan, Bruce 1947- ... CANR-35
Earlier sketches in CA 73-76, CANR-13
See also MAICYA
See also SATA 22, 70
McMillan, Colin 1923- ... 29-32R
McMillan, Constance (VanBrunt Johnson)
1949- ... 85-88
McMillan, George 1913-1987 ... 102
Obituary ... 123
McMillan, Ian 1956- ... 132
McMillan, James B. 1907- ... 85-88
McMillan, James F(rancis) 1948- ... 122
McMillan, John 1951- ... 138
McMillan, Polly Miller 1920- ... 1-4R
McMillan, Priscilla Johnson 1928- ... 41-44R
McMillan, Roddy 1923-1979 Obituary ... 109
McMillan, Terry 1951- ... CLC 50, 61
McMillen, Howard 1938- ... 57-60
McMillen, Neil R(aymond) 1939- ... 33-36R
McMillen, S(im) I. (Socrates) 1898- ... 5-8R
McMillen, Sally G(regory) 1944- ... 133
McMillen, Wheeler 1893- ... 33-36R
McMillin, (Joseph) Laurence (Jr.) 1923- ... 33-36R
McMillin, (Harvey) Scott 1934- ... 126
McMillion, Bonner 1921- ... 13-16R
McMorran, Susan
See Beattie, Susan
McMorrow, Fred 1925- ... 57-60
McMullan, Frank (Alonzo) 1907- ... 5-8R
McMullan, Kate
See McMullan, Kate Hall
McMullan, Kate Hall 1947- ... 123
See also SATA 48, 52
McMullen, Jay L. 1921- ... 118
Obituary ... 137
Brief entry ... 114
McMullen, Jeremy (John) 1948- ... 103
McMullen, Lorraine 1926- ... 117
McMullen, Mary
See Reilly, Mary
McMullen, Roy 1911-1984 ... 25-28R
Obituary ... 113
McMullin, Ernan 1924- ... CANR-22
Earlier sketches in CA 13-16R, CANR-6
McMullin, Ruth R(oney) 1942- ... 61-64
McMurdie, Annie Laurie
See Cassiday, Bruce (Bingham)
McMurray, George R(ay) 1925- ... 103
McMurray, Nancy A(rmistead) 1936- ... 41-44R
McMurrin, Sterling M(oss) 1914- ... 29-32R
McMurry, James Burton 1941- ... 69-72
McMurry, Linda O. 1945- ... 106
McMurry, Richard M. 1939- ... 132
McMurry, Robert N(oleman) 1901- ... 17-20R
McMurry, Sarah L. 1944- ... 123
McMurtrey, Martin A(loysias) 1921- ... 69-72
See also SATA 21
McMurtry, Jo 1937- ... 89-92
McMurtry, Larry (Jeff) 1936- ... CANR-19
Earlier sketch in CA 5-8R
See also AITN 2
See also BEST 89:2
See also CDALB 1968-1988
See also CLC 2, 3, 7, 11, 27, 44
See also DLB 2
See also DLBY 80, 87
See also MTCW
McMurtry, R(obert) Gerald 1906-1988 ... CAP-1
Obituary ... 127
Earlier sketch in CA 11-12
McNab, Oliver
See Frede, Richard
McNab, Thomas 1933- ... 108
McNab, Tom
See McNab, Thomas
McNail, Eddie Gathings 1905- ... CANR-6
Earlier sketch in CA 57-60
McNair, Clement John 1915-1989 Obituary ... 129
McNair, Kate ... 17-20R
See also SATA 3
McNair, Malcolm P(errine) 1894-1985 ... CAP-1
Obituary ... 117
Earlier sketch in CA 11-12
McNair, Marie 1900(?)-1989 Obituary ... 130
McNair, Philip Murray Jourdan 1924- ... 21-24R
McNair, Sylvia 1924- ... 121
McNair Scott, Ronald (Guthrie) 1906- ... 111
McNairy, Philip F(rederick) 1911- ... 17-20R
McNall, P(reston) E(ssex) 1888-1981 ... 29-32R
Obituary ... 135
McNall, Scott G(rant) 1941- ... CANR-11
Earlier sketch in CA 25-28R
McNally, Curtis
See Birchall, Ian H(arry)
McNally, Dennis 1949- ... 103
McNally, Gertrude Bancroft
1908(?)-1985 Obituary ... 115
McNally, John 1914- ... 17-20R
McNally, Raymond T. 1931- ... CANR-14
Earlier sketch in CA 37-40R
McNally, Robert E(dward) 1917-1978 ... CANR-11
Earlier sketch in CA 21-24R
McNally, Robert 1946- ... 107

McNally, Terrence 1939- CANR-2
Earlier sketch in CA 45-48
See also CLC 4, 7, 41
See also DLB 7
McNally, Tom 1923- 85-88
McNamara, Brooks 1937- 25-28R
McNamara, Dennis L. 1945- 136
McNamara, Eugene (Joseph) 1930- CANR-26
Earlier sketches in CA 21-24R, CANR-10
McNamara, Jo Ann 1931- CANR-15
Earlier sketch in CA 85-88
McNamara, John J(oseph) Jr.
1932-1986 ....41-44R
Obituary 120
McNamara, John S.
1908(?)-1977 Obituary 69-72
McNamara, Kevin (John) 1926-1987 ....25-28R
Obituary 122
McNamara, Lena Brooke 1891- CAP-1
Earlier sketch in CA 11-12
McNamara, Margaret C(raig)
1915-1981 ....SATA 24
McNamara, Michael M.
1940-1979 Obituary 89-92
McNamara, Robert S(trange)
1916- Obituary 129
Brief entry 112
McNamara, Sister Marie Aquinas
See Schaub, Marilyn McNamara
McNamara, William E. 1926- CANR-4
Earlier sketch in CA 1-4R
McNamee, James 1904- 5-8R
McNamee, Lawrence F. 1917- 25-28R
McNamee, Maurice B(asil) 1909- 5-8R
McNamee, Thomas 1947- 125
McNamer, Deirdre 1950- ....CLC 70
McNaspy, Clement James 1915- CANR-2
Earlier sketch in CA 5-8R
McNaught, Brian Robert 1948- 105
McNaught, Harry 106
See also SATA 32
McNaught, Judith 1944- 138
McNaught, Kenneth (William Kirkpatrick)
1918- 29-32R
McNaughton, Arnold 1930- 57-60
McNaughton, Colin 1951- 112
See also SATA 39
McNaughton, Frank
1906(?)-1978 Obituary 81-84
McNaughton, Howard (Douglas) 1945- 57-60
McNaughton, Wayne L. 1902- 1-4R
McNaughton, William (Frank) 1933- 41-44R
McNeal, Robert H(atch) 1930- 9-12R
McNear, Robert 1930(?)-1985 Obituary 117
McNeely, Jeannette 1918- 41-44R
See also SATA 25
McNeely, Jerry Clark 1928- Brief entry 115
McNeer, May CANR-2
Earlier sketch in CA 5-8R
See also SATA 1
McNees, Pat 1940- CANR-7
Earlier sketch in CA 57-60
McNeil, Art 1944- 124
McNeil, Barbara L(aurie) 1951- 97-100
McNeil, Bill
See McNeil, William Russell
McNeil, Elton B(urbank) 1924-1974 ....CAP-2
Earlier sketch in CA 25-28
McNeil, Florence 1940- 116
See also DLB 60
McNeil, John 1939- 131
McNeil, Mary 134
McNeil, Maureen (Christena) 1948- 128
McNeil, William Russell 1924- 133
McNeile, Herman Cyril 1888-1937
See Sapper
See also DLB 77
McNeill, Anthony 1941- 97-100
McNeill, Donald P(aul) 1936- 107
McNeill, Elisabeth
See Taylor, Elisabeth (D.)
McNeill, Janet
See Alexander, Janet
See also SATA 1
McNeill, John J. 1925- 65-68
McNeill, John Thomas 1885-1975 ....CANR-10
Obituary 57-60
Earlier sketches in CAP-1, CA 11-12
McNeill, Robert B(lakely) 1915- 17-20R
McNeill, Stuart 1942- 65-68
McNeill, William H(ardy) 1917- CANR-2
Earlier sketch in CA 5-8R
McNeilly, Wilfred (Glassford) 1921- CANR-28
Earlier sketch in CA 29-32R
McNeir, Waldo F(orest) 1908- 17-20R
McNeish, James 1931- CANR-29
Earlier sketches in CA 69-72, CANR-12
McNelly, Theodore (Hart) 1919- 5-8R
McNelly, Willis E(verett) 1920- 107
McNew, Ben(nie) B(anks) 1931- CANR-3
Earlier sketch in CA 9-12R
McNickle, (William) D'Arcy 1904-1977 ....CANR-5
Obituary 85-88
Earlier sketch in CA 9-12R
See also SATA 22
McNicoll, Alan (Wedel Ramsay)
1908-1987 Obituary 124
McNicoll, Robert E. 1907- 37-40R
McNiece, Harold Francis
1923-1972 Obituary 37-40R
McNierney, Mary Alice 9-12R
McNiff, William John 1899-1987 Obituary 122
McNitt, Gale 1921- 57-60
McNiven, Malcolm A(lbert) 1929- 29-32R
McNown, John S(tephenson) 1916- 57-60
McNulty, Edward N. 1936- CANR-25
Earlier sketches in CA 65-68, CANR-10
McNulty, Faith 1918- CANR-25
Earlier sketches in CA 49-52, CANR-1
See also SATA 12
McNulty, James Edmund Jr. 1924-1965 ....1-4R
Obituary 103
McNulty, James Francis
1934-1979 Obituary 113
McNutt, Dan James 1938- 61-64
McNutt, James (Allen) 1944- 49-52
McOwan, Rennie 1933- CANR-37
Earlier sketch in CA 115
McPhail, David M(ichael) 1940- CANR-38
Earlier sketches in CA 85-88, CANR-22
See also MAICYA
See also SATA 32, 47
McPharlin, Paul 1903-1948 Brief entry 110
See also SATA 31
McPhaul, Jack
See McPhaul, John J.
McPhaul, John J. 1904-1983 ....9-12R
Obituary 110
McPhee, Arthur G(ene) 1945- Brief entry 116
McPhee, John (Angus) 1931- CANR-20
Earlier sketch in CA 65-68
See also BEST 90:1
See also CLC 36
See also MTCW
McPhee, Richard B(yron) 1934- 111
See also SATA 41
McPhee, William N(orvell) 1921- 17-20R
McPherson, Anna Talbott 1904- CANR-19
Earlier sketches in CA 1-4R, CANR-4
McPherson, Gertrude H(untington) 1923- 45-48
McPherson, Harry Cummings Jr. 1929- 104
McPherson, Holt 1907(?)-1979 Obituary 89-92
McPherson, Hugo (Archibald) 1921- 29-32R
McPherson, James Alan 1943- CANR-24
Earlier sketch in CA 25-28R
See also BW
See also CLC 19
See also DLB 38
See also MTCW
McPherson, James Lowell 1921- 13-16R
McPherson, James M(unro) 1936- CANR-31
Earlier sketch in CA 9-12R
See also MTCW
See also SATA 16
McPherson, John 1925- 119
McPherson, Sandra 1943- CANR-12
Earlier sketch in CA 29-32R
See also DLBY 86
McPherson, Thomas Herdman 1925- 17-20R
McPherson, William (Alexander)
1933- CANR-28
Earlier sketch in CA 69-72
See also CLC 34
McPherson, William 1939- 57-60
McPhie, Walter E(van) 1926- 29-32R
McPolk, Andre (Hans) 1935- CANR-25
Earlier sketch in CA 93-96
McQuade, Ann Aikman 1928- CANR-34
Earlier sketch in CA 1-4R
McQuade, De Rosset Morrissey
1934(?)-1978 Obituary 81-84
McQuade, Donald A(nthony) 1941- CANR-16
Earlier sketch in CA 65-68
McQuade, Walter 1922- 103
McQuaid, Kim 1947- CANR-24
Earlier sketch in CA 107
McQuaig, Jack Hunter 9-12R
McQuaig, Linda 1951- 127
McQueen, Cyrus B. 1951- 135
McQueen, Ian 1930- 104
McQueen, Lucinda ....SATA 48, 58
McQueen, Mildred Hark 1908- CAP-1
Earlier sketch in CA 9-10
See also SATA 12
McQueen, William A. 1926- 21-24R
McQuigg, R. Bruce 1927- 17-20R
McQuilkin, Frank 1936- CANR-13
Earlier sketch in CA 33-36R
McQuillan, Karin 1950- 133
McQuin, Susan Coultrap
See Coultrap-McQuin, Susan (M.)
McQuiston, Joanne W(orth)
1922(?)-1985 Obituary 117
McQuown, F(rederic) R(ichard) 1907- 9-12R
McQuown, Judith H(ershkowitz) 1941- 107
McQuown, Norman A(nthony) 1914- 126
Brief entry 106
McRae, Barry (Donald) 1935- 136
McRae, Hamish (Malcolm Donald) 1943- 57-60
McRae, Kenneth D(ouglas) 1925- CANR-17
Earlier sketch in CA 1-4R
McRae, Lindsay
See Sowerby, A(rthur) L(indsay) M(cRae)
McRae, Robert (Forbes) 1914- 77-80
McRae, Russell (William) 1934- 129
See also SATA 63
McRae, William John 1933- 106
McReynolds, David 1929- 29-32R
McReynolds, Edwin C(larence)
1890-1967 ....CAP-1
Earlier sketch in CA 19-20
McReynolds, Ronald W(eldon) 1934- 49-52
McRoberts, Agnesann
See Meek, Pauline Palmer
McRoberts, R(obert) Lewis 1944- 33-36R
McShan, James 1937- 69-72
McShane, Joseph M(ichael) 1949- 127
McShane, Mark 1930- CANR-22
Earlier sketches in CA 17-20R, CANR-7
McShane, Philip 1932- 69-72
McShean, Gordon 1936- 108
See also SATA 41
McSherry, Frank D(avid) Jr. 1927- CANR-23
Earlier sketch in CA 107
McSherry, James E(dward) 1920- CANR-28
Earlier sketch in CA 49-52
McShine, Kynaston
See McShine, Kynaston L(eigh)
McShine, Kynaston L(eigh) 1935- 134
Brief entry 115
McSorley, Jean Sarah 1958- 133
McSorley, Joseph 1874-1963 ....CAP-1
Earlier sketch in CA 13-16
McSweeney, Kerry ....CLC 34
McSweeny, Maxine 1905- 61-64
Mc Swigan, Marie 1907-1962 73-76
See also SATA 24
McTaggart, Fred 1939- 65-68
McTaggart, J. McT. Ellis
See McTaggart, John McTaggart Ellis
McTaggart, John McTaggart Ellis
1866-1925 Brief entry 120
McTaggart, Lynne (Ann) 1951- Brief entry 113
McTeer, Wilson 1905- 41-44R
McVay, Gordon 1941- 73-76
McVean, James
See Luard, Nicholas
McVeigh, Malcolm J(ames) 1931- 61-64
McVey, Ruth T(homas) 1930- 109
McVickar, Elinor Guthrie
1902(?)-1982 Obituary 106
McVicker, Charles (Taggart) 1930- ....SATA 39
McVicker, Chuck
See McVicker, Charles (Taggart)
McVicker, Daphne Alloway
1895-1979 Obituary 85-88
McWaters, Barry 1937- 108
McWhiney, Grady 1928- CANR-6
Earlier sketch in CA 5-8R
McWhinney, Edward Watson 1926- CANR-28
Earlier sketches in CA 29-32R, CANR-12
McWhinnie, Donald 1920-1987 Obituary 123
McWhirter, A(lan) Ross 1925-1975 ....17-20R
Obituary 61-64
See also SATA 31, 37
McWhirter, George 1939- CANR-13
Earlier sketch in CA 77-80
See also DLB 60
McWhirter, Glenna S. 1929- 89-92
McWhirter, Nickie
See McWhirter, Glenna S.
McWhirter, Norris Dewar 1925- 13-16R
See also SATA 37
McWilliam, Candia 1955- 136
McWilliams, Carey 1905-1980 ....CANR-2
Obituary 101
Earlier sketch in CA 45-48
McWilliams, John P(robasco) Jr.
1940- CANR-28
Earlier sketch in CA 49-52
McWilliams, Karen 1943- 133
See also SATA 65
McWilliams, Margaret (Ann Edgar)
1929- CANR-26
Earlier sketches in CA 17-20R, CANR-8
McWilliams, Peter 1949- 41-44R
McWilliams, Wilson Carey 1933- CANR-19
Earlier sketch in CA 103
Meacham, Ellis K. 1913- 25-28R
Meacham, Harry M(onroe) 1901-1975 ....CAP-2
Earlier sketch in CA 25-28
Meacham, Margaret 1952- 118
Meacham, Standish (Jr.) 1932- 135
Brief entry 110
Meacher, Michael Hugh 1939- 109
Mead, D(onald) Eugene 1934- 65-68
Mead, Edgar T(horn) Jr. 1922- 113
Mead, Frank Spencer 1898-1982 ....CANR-9
Obituary 107
Earlier sketches in CAP-1, CA 19-20
Mead, G(eorge) R(obert) S(tow)
1863-1933 Brief entry 122
Mead, Harold C(harles) H(ugh) 1910- CAP-1
Earlier sketch in CA 13-14
Mead, Jude 1919- 25-28R
Mead, Margaret 1901-1978 ....CANR-4
Obituary 81-84
Earlier sketch in CA 1-4R
See also AITN 1
See also CLC 37
See also MTCW
See also SATA 20
Mead, Matthew 1924- 101
See also CAAS 13
See also DLB 40
Mead, Peter (Willan) 1911- 116
Mead, Robert Douglas 1928-1983 ....41-44R
Obituary 110
Mead, Russell
See Koehler, Margaret (Hudson)
Mead, Russell (M. Jr.) 1935- 9-12R
See also SATA 10
Mead, (Edward) Shepherd 1914- 9-12R
Mead, Sidney E(arl) 1904- CAP-1
Earlier sketch in CA 9-10
Mead, Sidney Moko 1927- CANR-23
Earlier sketch in CA 106
Mead, Stella Obituary 103
See also SATA 27
Mead, Taylor 1931(?)- 126
Brief entry 116
See also DLB 16
Mead, Walter B(ruce) 1934- 37-40R
Mead, William B(owmar) 1934- CANR-32
Earlier sketches in CA 85-88, CANR-15
Mead, William Richard 1915- 103
Meade, Bill C.
See Rogers, Paul T(aylor)
Meade, Dorothy (Joan Sampson) 1923- 9-12R
Meade, Elizabeth Thomasina
1854(?)-1914(?) Brief entry 112
Meade, Ellen
See Roddick, Ellen
See also SATA 5
Meade, Everard 1914- 25-28R
Meade, James Edward 1907- CANR-2
Earlier sketch in CA 1-4R
Meade, L. T.
See Meade, Elizabeth Thomasina
Meade, Marion 1934- CANR-1
Earlier sketch in CA 49-52
See also SATA 23
Meade, Mary
See Church, Ruth Ellen (Lovrien)
Meade, Richard
See Haas, Ben(jamin) L(eopold)
Meade, Richard A(ndrew) 1911- 45-48
Meade, Robert Douthat 1903-197 (?) CAP-2
Earlier sketch in CA 25-28
Meader, Stephen W(arren) 1892- 5-8R
See also SATA 1
Meades, Jonathan (Turner) 1947- 130
Meadmore, Susan
See Sallis, Susan (Diana)
Meador, Roy 1929- CANR-11
Earlier sketch in CA 69-72
Meadow, Barry 1947- 125
Meadow, Charles T(roub) 1929- CANR-15
Earlier sketch in CA 29-32R
See also SATA 23
Meadow, Kathryn Pendleton 1929- CANR-7
Earlier sketch in CA 57-60
Meadowcroft, Enid LaMonte
See Wright, Enid Meadowcroft (LaMonte)
Meadowes, Alicia
See Burak, Linda (Gallina)
and Zieg, Joan (Gallina)
Meadows, A(rthur) J(ack) 1934- 137
Meadows, Eddie S(pencer) 1939- 109
Meadows, Edward 1944- 101
Meadows, Jack
See Meadows, A(rthur) J(ack)
Meadows, Paul 1913- 41-44R
Meadows, Peter
See Lindsay, Jack
Meagher, John C. 1935- CANR-11
Earlier sketch in CA 17-20R
Meagher, Paul Kevin 1907-1976 Obituary 69-72
Meagher, Robert E(mmett) 1943- CANR-10
Earlier sketch in CA 25-28R
Meagher, Robert F. 1927- 41-44R
Meaker, Eloise 1915- CANR-28
Earlier sketch in CA 105
Meaker, M. J.
See Meaker, Marijane (Agnes)
Meaker, Marijane (Agnes) 1927- CANR-37
Earlier sketch in CA 107
See also Kerr, M. E.
See also MAICYA
See also MTCW
See also SATA 20, 61
Meakin, David 1943- 69-72
Means, Florence Crannell 1891-1980 ....CANR-37
Obituary 103
Earlier sketch in CA 1-4R
See also MAICYA
See also SATA 1, 25
Means, Gardiner C(oit) 1896-1988 Obituary 124
Means, Gordon P(aul) 1927- 33-36R
Means, John Barkley 1939- 33-36R
Means, Louis Edgar 1902- CANR-2
Earlier sketch in CA 5-8R
Means, Marianne Hansen 1934- 9-12R
Means, Richard K(eith) 1929- CANR-17
Earlier sketches in CA 5-8R, CANR-2
Meany, George 1894-1980 Obituary 97-100
Meara, (Mary) Jane (Frances) Cavolina
1954- 120
Meara, Mary Jane Frances Cavolina
See Meara, (Mary) Jane (Frances) Cavolina
Meares, Ainslie Dixon 1910- CANR-11
Earlier sketch in CA 25-28R
Mearian, Judy Frank 1936- 101
See also SATA 49
Mearns, Barbara (Crawford) 1955- 132
Mearns, David Chambers 1899-1981 ....1-4R
Obituary 104
Mearns, Richard (James) 1950- 132
Mears, Brainerd Jr. 1921- 53-56
Mears, Richard Chase 1935- 101
Mears, Walter R(obert) 1935- 113
Brief entry 111
Mearsheimer, John J(oseph) 1947- 117
Measday, George
See Soderberg, Percy Measday
Measham, D(onald) C. 1932- 21-24R
Measures, (William) Howard 1894- CAP-1
Earlier sketch in CA 13-14
Meath, Michael
See Marquis, Max
Mebane, John (Harrison) 1909- 13-16R
Mebane, Mary E(lizabeth) 1933- CANR-30
Earlier sketch in CA 73-76
Mech, Dave
See Mech, L(ucyan) David
Mech, L(ucyan) David 1937- CANR-14
Earlier sketch in CA 33-36R
Mecham, John Lloyd 1893- 1-4R
Mechanic, David 1936- CANR-19
Earlier sketches in CA 5-8R, CANR-3
Mechanic, Sylvia (Gertrude) 1920- 69-72
Mechin, Jacques Benoist
See Benoist-Mechin, Jacques
Meckel, Richard A(lan) 1948- 135
Meckier, Jerome (Thomas) 1941- 33-36R
Meckler, Alan Marshall 1945- 57-60
Meckley, Richard F(rederick) 1928- 37-40R

Mecklin, John Martin
1918-1971 Obituary 33-36R
Meckstroth, Jacob A.
1887(?)-1985 Obituary 115
Meckstroth, Jake
See Meckstroth, Jacob A.
Medalia, Leon S. 1881- 85-88
Medary, Marjorie 1890- 73-76
See also SATA 14
Medawar, Jean 1913- 134
Medawar, Peter Brian 1915-1987 97-100
Obituary 123
Medd, Charles Leighton
1928-1989 Obituary 130
Medd, Patrick 1919- 25-28R
Meddaugh, Susan 1944- 106
See also SATA 29
Meddis, Ray 1944- 77-80
Medea, Andra 1953- 57-60
Medearis, Mary 1915- 69-72
See also SATA 5
Medeiros, Earl Caton 1933- 89-92
Medhin, Tsegaye (Kawessa) Gabre
See Gabre-Medhin, Tsegaye (Kawessa)
Medhurst, Joan
See Liverton, Joan
Medicus II
See Philipp, Elliot Elias
Medill, Joseph 1823-1899 .... DLB 43
Medina, Jeremy T(yler) 1942- CANR-11
Earlier sketch in CA 69-72
Medina, Robert C. 1924- .... HW
Medina, William A.
See Medina, William Antonio
Medina, William Antonio
1935-1985 Obituary 117
Medley, Anne
See Borchard, Ruth (Berendsohn)
Medley, (Rachel) Margaret 1918- 13-16R
Medley, Morris L(ee) 1942- 57-60
Medlicott, Alexander G(uild) Jr. 1927- 37-40R
Medlicott, Margaret P(aget) 1913- 29-32R
Medlicott, William Norton 1900-1987 .... 9-12R
Obituary 123
Medlin, Virgil D(ewain) 1943- 57-60
Mednick, Murray 1939- 21-24R
Medoff, Jeslyn 1951- 128
Medoff, Mark (Howard) 1940- CANR-5
Earlier sketch in CA 53-56
See also AITN 1
See also CLC 6, 23
See also DLB 7
Medsger, Betty (Louise) 1942- 113
Medsker, Leland L. 1905- CANR-2
Earlier sketch in CA 1-4R
Medved, Diane 1951- 132
Medved, Harry 1961(?)- 93-96
Medved, Michael 1948- CANR-11
Earlier sketch in CA 65-68
Medvedev, P. N.
See Bakhtin, Mikhail Mikhailovich
Medvedev, Roy (Alexandrovich) 1925- 81-84
Medvedev, Zhores A(leksandrovich)
1925- 69-72
Mee, Charles L. Jr. 1938- CANR-3
Earlier sketch in CA 45-48
See also SATA 8
Mee, Fiona 1946(?)-1978 Obituary 104
Mee, John F(ranklin) 1908- CAP-1
Earlier sketch in CA 9-10
Meechan, Hugh L(awrence) 1933- 17-20R
Meehan, Daniel Joseph
1930-1978 Obituary 77-80
Meehan, Danny
See Meehan, Daniel Joseph
Meehan, Eugene J(ohn) 1923- CANR-14
Earlier sketch in CA 37-40R
Meehan, Francis X(avier) 1937- 116
Meehan, Richard Lawrence 1939- 107
Meehan, Thomas Edward 1932- CANR-28
Earlier sketch in CA 29-32R
Meehl, Paul E(verett) 1920- 93-96
Meek, Alexander Beaufort 1814-1865 .... DLB 3
Meek, Forrest B(urns) 1928- 110
Meek, H(arold) A(lan) 1922- 129
Meek, Jacklyn O'Hanlon 1933- 77-80
See also SATA 34, 51
Meek, Jay 1937- CANR-25
Earlier sketch in CA 107
Meek, Lois Hayden
See Stolz, Lois Meek
Meek, Loyal George 1918- 73-76
Meek, Margaret
See Meek Spencer, Margaret (Diston)
Meek, Pauline Palmer 1917- 106
Meek, Ronald L(indley) 1917-1978 .... CANR-6
Earlier sketch in CA 9-12R
Meek, S(terner St.) P(aul) 1894-1972 .... 1-4R
Obituary 103
See also SATA 28
Meeke, Mary .... DLB 116
Meeker, Alice (MacCutcheon) 1904- CAP-2
Earlier sketch in CA 25-28
Meeker, Joseph W(arren) 1932- CANR-28
Earlier sketch in CA 49-52
Meeker, Mary Nacol 1928- 53-56
Meeker, Oden 1919(?)-1976 73-76
Obituary 65-68
See also SATA 14
Meeker, Richard Kilburn 1925- CAP-2
Earlier sketch in CA 19-20
Meeks, Esther MacBain 1-4R
See also SATA 1
Meeks, John E. 33-36R
Meeks, Linda A.
See Brower, Linda A.
Meeks, M(errill) Douglas 1941- 93-96
Meeks, Wayne A. 1932- CANR-28
Earlier sketches in CA 13-16R, CANR-5
Meek Spencer, Margaret (Diston)
1925- CANR-21
Earlier sketch in CA 105
Meen, Victor Ben 1910-1971 Obituary 106
Meenan, James F(rancis) 1910-1987 124
Meer, Fatima 1929- 73-76
Meerhaeghe, M(arcel) A(lfons) G(ilbert) Van
See Van Meerhaeghe, M(arcel) A(lfons) G(ilbert)
Meerloo, Joost A(braham) M(aurits)
1903-1976 .... CANR-4
Obituary 69-72
Earlier sketch in CA 1-4R
Meeropol, Abel 1903(?)-1986 Obituary 121
Meese, Elizabeth Ann 1943- 122
Meeter, Glenn 1934- CANR-12
Earlier sketch in CA 33-36R
Meeth, Louis Richard 1934- 17-20R
Meeuse, Bastiaan (Jacob Dirk) 1916- 119
Meezan, William 1947- 117
Megargee, Edwin I(nglee) 1937- CANR-7
Earlier sketch in CA 17-20R
Meged, Aharon
See Megged, Aharon
Meged, Aron
See Megged, Aharon
Megged, Aharon 1920- CANR-1
Earlier sketch in CA 49-52
See also CAAS 13
See also CLC 9
Meggendorfer, Lothar
1847-1925 Brief entry 115
See also SATA 36
Meggers, Betty J(ane) 1921- 17-20R
Meggitt, M(ervyn) J(ohn) 1924- 13-16R
Meggs, Brown (Moore) 1930- CANR-7
Earlier sketch in CA 61-64
Meggs, Philip B(axter) 1942- 116
Meggyesy, Dave
See Meggyesy, David M.
Meggyesy, David M. 1941- 33-36R
Megill, Kenneth Alden 1939- Brief entry 106
Meglin, Nick 1935- CANR-21
Earlier sketch in CA 69-72
Meglitsch, Paul A(llen) 1914- 53-56
Mego, Al
See Roberts, Arthur O.
Megrah, Maurice Henry
1896-1985 Obituary 116
Megson, Barbara 1930- 29-32R
Mehaffy, Robert E(ugene) 1935- 113
Mehan, Joseph Albert 1929- 101
Mehdevi, Alexander (Sinclair) 1947- 49-52
See also SATA 7
Mehdevi, Anne (Marie) Sinclair 1947- 5-8R
See also SATA 8
Mehdi, M(ohammed) T(aki) 1928- CANR-8
Earlier sketch in CA 17-20R
Mehegan, John (Francis) 1920(?)-1984 .... 5-8R
Obituary 112
Meher Baba
See Baba, Meher
Mehl, Roger 1912- CANR-21
Earlier sketches in CA 9-12R, CANR-6
Mehlinger, Howard D(ean) 1931- CANR-6
Earlier sketch in CA 9-12R
Mehlmann, Marilyn 1939- 119
Mehnert, Klaus 1906-1984 .... CANR-2
Obituary 111
Earlier sketch in CA 1-4R
Mehr, Joseph (John) 1941- Brief entry 113
Mehrabian, Albert 1939- 33-36R
Mehrens, William A(rthur) 1937- 37-40R
Mehring, Walter 1896-1981 Obituary 105
Mehrotra, S(ri) Ram 1931- CANR-8
Earlier sketch in CA 13-16R
Mehrtens, Susan E(mily) 1945- 53-56
Mehta, Gaganvihari L(allubhai)
1900-1974 Obituary 49-52
Mehta, J. L. 1912(?)-1988 Obituary 126
Mehta, Rustam Jehangir 1912- 9-12R
Mehta, Shahnaz 106
Mehta, Ved (Parkash) 1934- CANR-23
Earlier sketches in CA 1-4R, CANR-2
See also CLC 37
See also MTCW
Mei, Ko-Wang 1918- CANR-2
Earlier sketch in CA 45-48
Meiden, Walter 1907- CANR-8
Earlier sketch in CA 13-16R
Meier, August 1923- CANR-3
Earlier sketch in CA 9-12R
Meier, C(arl) A(lfred) 1905- 130
Meier, Gerald M(arvin) 1923- CANR-30
Earlier sketch in CA 112
Meier, Heinz K(arl) 1929- 61-64
Meier, Joel F(rancis) 1940- 109
Meier, Matt S(ebastian) 1917- CANR-14
Earlier sketch in CA 41-44R
Meier, Minta 1906- .... SATA 55
Meier, Paul D. 136
Meier, Richard L(ouis) 1920- 17-20R
Meierhenry, Wesley Carl 1915- 41-44R
Meiggs, Russell 1902-1989 103
Obituary 129
Meighan, Donald Charles 1929- CANR-24
Earlier sketch in CA 107
See also SATA 30
Meigs, Alexander James 1921- 104
Meigs, Cornelia Lynde 1884-1973 .... 9-12R
Obituary 45-48
See also MAICYA
See also SATA 6
Meigs, Mary 1917- 132
Meigs, Peveril 1903-1979 .... 37-40R
Obituary 133
Meigs, Walter B(erkeley) 1912- 21-24R
Meij, Jacob L(ouis) 1900- 5-8R
Meijer, M(arinus) J(ohan) 1912- 69-72
Meikle, Clive
See Brooks, Jeremy
Meikle, Jeffrey L(ee) 1949- 101
Meiklejohn, Alexander 1872-1964 Obituary 111
Meilach, Dona Z(weigoron) 1926- CANR-22
Earlier sketches in CA 9-12R, CANR-5
See also SATA 34
Meilach, Michael D(avid) 1932- CANR-2
Earlier sketch in CA 5-8R
Meilaender, Gilbert 1946- 109
Meilen, Bill 1932- 69-72
Meillassoux, Claude 1925- 25-28R
Mein, Margaret 61-64
Meine, Curt 1958- 126
Meiners, R(oger) K(eith) 1932- CANR-3
Earlier sketch in CA 5-8R
Meiners, Roger Evert 1948- 110
Meinig, Donald William 1924- 112
Meinke, Peter 1932- CANR-29
Earlier sketch in CA 25-28R
See also DLB 5
Meinkoth, Norman A(ugust) 1913- 113
Meintjes, Johannes 1923-1980 .... CANR-8
Earlier sketch in CA 17-20R
Meir, Golda 1898-1978 89-92
Obituary 81-84
Meiring, Desmond
See Rice, Desmond Charles
Meiring, Jane (Muriel) 1920- CANR-20
Earlier sketch in CA 103
Meisch, Lynn A. 1945- 105
Meisch, Richard A(lden) 1943- 33-36R
Meisel, Anthony C(lark) 1943- 105
Meisel, Gerald Stanley 1937- 9-12R
Meisel, John 1923- 17-20R
Meisel, Martin 1931- CANR-15
Earlier sketch in CA 5-8R
Meisel, Perry 1949- 102
Meisel, Tony
See Meisel, Anthony C(lark)
Meiselas, Susan 1948- 106
Meiselman, David I(srael) 1924- 13-16R
Meisenholder, Robert 1915- 37-40R
Meisler, Richard 1940- 124
Meisler, Stanley 1931- 73-76
Meisner, Maurice 1931- 21-24R
Meiss, Millard (Lazare) 1904-1975 61-64
Obituary 57-60
Meissner, Hans-Otto 1909- CANR-2
Earlier sketch in CA 49-52
Meissner, Kurt 1885-1976 .... CAP-2
Earlier sketch in CA 29-32
Meissner, W(illiam) W. 1931- CANR-29
Earlier sketches in CA 33-36R, CANR-13
Meister, Anton D(iderik) 1944- 118
Meister, Barbara 1932- 102
Meister, Richard J(ulius) 1938- 57-60
Meister, Robert 1926- CANR-9
Earlier sketch in CA 5-8R
Meixner, John A(lbert) 1925- 5-8R
Mejia, Arthur Jr. 1934- 81-84
Mejia Vallejo, Manuel 1923- .... DLB 113
Mekas, Jonas 1922- Brief entry 113
Meketa, Jacqueline
See Meketa, Jacqueline Dorgan
Meketa, Jacqueline Dorgan 1926- 125
Melady, John 1938- 122
See also SATA 49
Melady, Thomas Patrick 1927- CANR-5
Earlier sketch in CA 9-12R
Melahn, Martha 1924- 107
Melamid, Alexander 1914- 45-48
Melancon, Robert 1947- .... DLB 60
Meland, Bernard Eugene 1899- 17-20R
Melanson, Richard A(llen) 1944- 113
Melanter
See Blackmore, R(ichard) D(oddridge)
Melantzon, Ricardo Aguilar
See Aguilar Melantzon, Ricardo
Melaro, Constance L(oraine) 1929- 17-20R
Melas, Evi 1930- 65-68
Melber, Jehuda 1916- 29-32R
Melbin, Murray 1927- 45-48
Melbo, Irving Robert 1908- 49-52
Melby, Ernest O(scar) 1891-1987 Obituary 121
Melby, John Fremont 1913- Brief entry 106
Melcher, Daniel 1912-1985 .... 33-36R
Obituary 116
See also SATA 43
Melcher, Frederic Gershom
1879-1963 Obituary 89-92
See also SATA 22
Melcher, Marguerite Fellows 1879-1969 .... 5-8R
See also SATA 10
Melcher, Robert Augustus 1910- 17-20R
Melchert, Norman Paul 1933- 25-28R
Melchett, Sonia
See Sinclair, Sonia
Melchinger, Siegfried 1906- 81-84
Melchior, Ib (Jorgen) 1917- CANR-22
Earlier sketches in CA 45-48, CANR-2
Meldal-Johnsen, Trevor Bernard
1944- CANR-19
Earlier sketch in CA 101
Melden, A(braham) I(rving) 1910- 17-20R
Melder, Keith E(ugene) 1932- 81-84
Meldrum, James
See Broxholme, John Franklin
Mele, Alfred R. 1951- 138
Mele, Frank Michael 1935- 53-56
Mele, Jim 1950- 113
Melendez, Conchita
See Melendez (Ramirez), Concha
Melendez (Ramirez), Concha 1892- .... HW
Melendy, H(oward) Brett 1924- CANR-23
Earlier sketches in CA 17-20R, CANR-8
Meleski, Patricia F(erguson) 1935- 61-64
Melezh, Ivan 1921(?)-1976 Obituary 69-72
Melfi, Leonard 1935- 73-76
Melfi, Mary 1951- CANR-32
Earlier sketch in CA 113
Melford, Austin (Alfred)
1884-1971 Obituary 115
Melges, Buddy
See Melges, Harry C. Jr.
Melges, Harry C. Jr. 1930- 130
Melhem, D(iana) H(elen) CANR-2
Earlier sketch in CA 49-52
Melhorn, Charles M(ason) 1918-1983 57-60
Obituary 111
Melhuish, George (William Seymour)
1916-1985 Obituary 117
Melick, Arden Davis 1940- 106
Melikow, Loris
See Hofmannsthal, Hugo von
Melin, Grace Hathaway 1892-1973 .... CAP-2
Obituary 45-48
Earlier sketch in CA 21-22
See also SATA 10
Mell
See Lazarus, Mell
Mell, Donald C(harles) Jr. 1931- 115
Mell, Max 1882-1971 .... DLB 81
Mellaart, James 1925- Brief entry 118
Mellan, Eleanor 1905- 5-8R
Mellan, Ibert 1901- 5-8R
Mellanby, Kenneth 1908- 85-88
Mellander, Gustavo Adolfo 1935- 33-36R
Mellard, James Milton 1938- 105
Mellen, Ida M(ay) 1877- 5-8R
Mellen, Joan 1941- CANR-11
Earlier sketch in CA 65-68
Mellencamp, Virginia Lynn 1917- 9-12R
Meller, Norman 1913- 25-28R
Mellers, Wilfrid (Howard) 1914- CANR-4
Earlier sketch in CA 5-8R
Mellersh, H(arold) E(dward) L(eslie)
1897- CANR-9
Earlier sketch in CA 53-56
See also SATA 10
Mellert, Robert B(oros) 1937- 61-64
Mellichamp, Josephine 1923- 93-96
Mellin, Jeanne 1929- CANR-24
Earlier sketch in CA 49-52
Mellini, Peter 1935- 93-96
Mellinkoff, David 1914- 13-16R
Mellinkoff, Ruth 1924- CANR-14
Earlier sketch in CA 37-40R
Mellins, Thomas 1957- 122
Mellizo (Cuadrado), Carlos 1942- 130
See also HW
Mellon, Constance A. 1938- 123
Mellon, James R(oss) 1942- 69-72
Mellon, John C(raig) 1933- Brief entry 107
Mellon, Knox
See Mellon, William Knox Jr.
Mellon, Matthew T(aylor) 1897- 29-32R
Mellon, Stanley 1927- Brief entry 108
Mellon, William Knox Jr. 1925- 37-40R
Mellor, Anne Kostelanetz 1941- 45-48
Mellor, J(ohn) Leigh 1928- 17-20R
Mellor, John W(illiams) 1928- 33-36R
Mellor, William Bancroft 1906- 61-64
Mellors, John (Parkin) 1920- 65-68
Mellors, Samantha CANR-30
See also Lottman, Eileen
Mellow, James R(obert) 1926- CANR-29
Earlier sketch in CA 105
See also DLB 111
Mellown, Elgin W(endell Jr.) 1931- 17-20R
Mellows, Joan 77-80
Melly, Diana 1937- 130
Melly, George 1926- 81-84
Melman, Seymour 1917- CANR-4
Earlier sketch in CA 1-4R
Melmoth, Sebastian
See Wilde, Oscar (Fingal O'Flahertie Wills)
Melnick, Donald 1926-1977 Obituary 69-72
Melnick, Jack 1929- 89-92
Melnitz, William W(olf) 1900-1989 Obituary 127
Melnyk, Z(inowii) Lew 1928- 41-44R
Meloan, Taylor Wells 1919- CANR-29
Earlier sketch in CA 45-48
Melone, Albert P(hilip) 1942- CANR-27
Earlier sketch in CA 109
Melone, Joseph J(ames) 1931- 13-16R
Meloney, Franken
See Franken, Rose (Dorothy)
Meloney, William Brown
1905-1971 Obituary 104
Meloon, Marion 1921- 65-68
Melosh, Barbara 1950- 130
Melosi, Martin Victor 1947- CANR-13
Earlier sketch in CA 77-80
Melot, Michel 1943- 132
Melrose, Andrea La Sonde
See Anastos, Andrea La Sonde (Melrose)
Melsa, James L(ouis) 1938- 104
Melson, Robert 1937- 85-88
Melton, David 1934- CANR-22
Earlier sketch in CA 69-72
Melton, J(ohn) Gordon 1942- 110
Melton, John L. 1920- 9-12R
Melton, Julius W(emyss) Jr. 1933- 21-24R
Melton, William 1920- 37-40R
Meltsner, Arnold J(erry) 1931- 57-60
Meltsner, Michael (Charles)
1937- Brief entry 108
Meltzer, Allan H. 1928- CANR-39
Earlier sketches in CA 5-8R, CANR-3, 18
Meltzer, Bernard N(athan) 1916- 21-24R

Meltzer, David 1937- ... CANR-35
Earlier sketches in CA 9-12R, CANR-6
See also DLB 16
Meltzer, Jack 1921- ... 119
Meltzer, Milton 1915- ... CANR-38
Earlier sketch in CA 13-16R
See also AAYA 8
See also CLC 26
See also CLR 13
See also DLB 61
See also MAICYA
See also SAAS 1
See also SATA 1, 50
Meltzer, Morton F. 1930- ... 21-24R
Meltzer, Peter D. 1951- ... 120
Meltzoff, Julian 1921- ... 21-24R
Meltzoff, Nancy 1952- ... 93-96
Meluch, R(ebecca) M. 1956- ... 109
Melvill, Harald 1895- ... 5-8R
Melville, A(lan) D(avid) 1912- ... 137
Melville, Alan
See Caverhill, William Melville
Melville, Annabelle McConnell 1910- ... 5-8R
Melville, Anne
See Potter, Margaret (Newman)
Melville, Arabella 1948- ... 130
Melville, Charles (Peter) 1951- ... 138
Melville, Herman 1819-1891 ... CDALB 1640-1865
See also DLB 3, 74
See also SATA 59
See also SSC 1
See also WLC
Melville, J. Keith 1921- ... 53-56
Melville, James
See Martin, (Roy) Peter
Melville, Jennie
See Butler, Gwendoline Williams
Melville, Jock Leslie
See Leslie-Melville, John D.
Melville, John D. Leslie
See Leslie-Melville, John D.
Melville, Joy 1932- ... 85-88
Melville, Keith 1945- ... 41-44R
Melvin, A(rthur) Gordon 1894- ... 9-12R
Melvin, Ann (Patricia) Skene
See Skene-Melvin, Ann (Patricia)
Melvin, (Lewis) David (St. Columb) Skene
See Skene-Melvin, (Lewis) David (St. Columb)
Melvin, Herman 1819-1891 ... DLB 3
Melwani, Murli Das 1939- ... 61-64
Melwood, Mary
See Lewis, E. M.
Melzack, Ronald 1929- ... CANR-15
Earlier sketch in CA 41-44R
See also SATA 5
Melzer, John Henry 1908-1967 ... CAP-1
Earlier sketch in CA 13-14
Melzi, Robert C. 1915- ... 37-40R
Memling, Carl 1918-1969 ... CANR-4
Earlier sketch in CA 1-4R
See also SATA 6
Memmi, Albert 1920- ... CANR-32
Earlier sketches in CA 81-84, CANR-14
Mena, Janet Gonzalez
See Gonzalez-Mena, Janet
Menacker, Julius 1933- ... 41-44R
Menaker, Daniel 1941- ... 65-68
Menard, H(enry) William 1920-1986 ... 37-40R
Obituary ... 118
Menard, Jean 1930(?)-1977 Obituary ... 69-72
Menard, Orville D. 1933- ... 21-24R
Menard, Russell 1942- ... 126
Menasco, Norman
See Guin, Wyman (Woods)
Menashe, Louis 1935- ... 21-24R
Menashe, Samuel 1925- ... 115
Brief entry ... 111
See also CAAS 11
Mencher, Melvin 1927- ... 73-76
Menchin, Robert S(tanley) 1923- ... CANR-13
Earlier sketch in CA 21-24R
Mencken, H(enry) L(ouis) 1880-1956 ... 125
Brief entry ... 105
See also CDALB 1917-1929
See also DLB 11, 29, 63
See also MTCW
See also TCLC 13
Menczer, Bela 1902-1983 Obituary ... 110
Mendel, Arthur P(aul) 1927-1988 ... 13-16R
Obituary ... 124
Mendel, Arthur 1905-1979 ... CANR-29
Obituary ... 89-92
Earlier sketch in CA 41-44R
Mendel, Douglas H(eusted) Jr. 1921- ... 17-20R
Mendel, Jo
See Bond, Gladys Baker
and Gilbertson, Mildred Geiger
Mendel, Sydney 1925- Brief entry ... 109
Mendel, Werner M(ax) 1927- ... CANR-11
Earlier sketch in CA 21-24R
Mendele mocher seforim
See Abramowitz, Shalom Jacob
Mendell, Clarence W(hittlesey)
1883-1970 ... CAP-1
Earlier sketch in CA 19-20
Mendeloff, Henry 1917-1984 Obituary ... 113
Mendelowitz, Daniel M(arcus) 1905-1980 ... 9-12R
Obituary ... 135
Mendels, Joseph 1937- ... 29-32R
Mendels, Ora 1936- ... 124
Mendelsohn, Allan R(obert) 1928- ... 45-48
Mendelsohn, Everett (Irwin) 1931- ... CANR-28
Earlier sketches in CA 17-20R, CANR-11
Mendelsohn, Ezra 1940- ... 130
Mendelsohn, Felix Jr. 1906- ... 29-32R
Mendelsohn, Harold 1923- ... 49-52
Mendelsohn, Jack 1918- ... CANR-1
Earlier sketch in CA 1-4R
Mendelsohn, Martin 1935- ... CANR-13
Earlier sketch in CA 33-36R
Mendelsohn, Michael John 1931- ... 85-88
Mendelsohn, Oscar (Adolf)
1896-1978 ... CANR-22
Earlier sketch in CA 9-12R
Mendelsohn, Pamela 1944- ... 101
Mendelsohn, Robert S(aul)
1926-1988 Obituary ... 125
Mendelsohn, Stefan
1930(?)-1987(?) Obituary ... 122
Mendelson, Edward 1946- ... CANR-11
Earlier sketch in CA 65-68
Mendelson, Lee 1933- ... 33-36R
Mendelson, Mary Adelaide (Jones) 1917- ... 85-88
Mendelson, Morris 1922- ... CANR-2
Earlier sketch in CA 5-8R
Mendelson, Sara Heller 1947- ... 126
Mendelson, Wallace 1911- ... 1-4R
Mendelssohn, Kurt (Alfred Georg)
1906-1980 ... CANR-7
Obituary ... 105
Earlier sketch in CA 53-56
Mendelssohn, Moses 1729-1786 ... DLB 97
Mendenhall, Corwin (Guy Jr.) 1916- ... 134
Mendenhall, George E(mery) 1916- ... 33-36R
Mendenhall, James Edgar
1903-1971 Obituary ... 33-36R
Mendenhall, John D(ale)
1911(?)-1983 Obituary ... 110
Mendenhall, Ruth Dyar 1912-1989 ... 65-68
Obituary ... 128
Mendenhall, Thomas C(orwin II) 1910- ... 115
Mendes-France, Pierre 1907-1982 ... 81-84
Obituary ... 108
Mendez, Charlotte (Walker) 1935- ... 120
Mendez, Eugenio Fernandez
See Fernandez Mendez, Eugenio
Mendez, Raymond A. 1947- ... SATA 66
Mendez M., Miguel 1930- ... 131
See also DLB 82
See also HW
Mendl, Robert William Sigismund
1892-1983 Obituary ... 111
Mendlovitz, Saul H. 1925- ... 21-24R
Mendonca, Susan
See Smith, Susan Vernon
See also SATA 45
Mendonsa, Eugene L(ouis) 1942- ... 109
Mendoza, George 1934- ... 73-76
See also SAAS 7
See also SATA 39, 41
Mendoza, Manuel G. 1936- ... 53-56
Mendoza, Tony 1941- ... 128
Mendras, Henri 1927- ... CANR-13
Earlier sketch in CA 73-76
Mendus, Susan 1951- ... 123
Mendyk, Stan A. E. 1953- ... 135
Menen, (Salvator) Aubrey (Clarence)
1912-1989 ... CANR-2
Obituary ... 127
Earlier sketch in CA 1-4R
Menendez, Albert J(ohn) 1942- ... CANR-22
Earlier sketches in CA 53-56, CANR-7
Menendez Pidal, Ramon
1869-1968 Obituary ... 116
See also HW
Meneses, Enrique 1929- ... CANR-27
Earlier sketches in CA 25-28R, CANR-11
Meng, Heinz (Karl) 1924- ... 69-72
See also SATA 13
Meng, John J(oseph) 1906-1988 Obituary ... 124
Menges, Karl (Heinrich) 1908- ... 37-40R
Menhennet, Alan 1933- ... 97-100
Menikoff, Barry 1939- ... 37-40R
Menkiti, Ifeanyi 1940- ... 65-68
Menkus, Belden 1931- ... CANR-31
Earlier sketch in CA 17-20R
Mennel, Robert McKisson 1938- Brief entry ... 109
Mennell, Stephen (John) 1944- ... 107
Menning, J(ack) H(arwood) 1915-1973 ... 21-24R
Obituary ... 134
Menninger, Edwin A(rnold) 1896- ... CANR-29
Earlier sketch in CA 9-12R
Menninger, Karl (Augustus)
1893-1990 ... CANR-29
Obituary ... 132
Earlier sketch in CA 17-20R
See also MTCW
Menninger, W(illiam) Walter 1931- ... 111
Menninger, Walt
See Menninger, W(illiam) Walter
Menninger, William C(laire)
1899-1966 Obituary ... 25-28R
Mennis, Bernard 1938- ... 41-44R
Menolascino, Frenk J(oseph) 1930- ... 73-76
Menon, K(umara) P(admanabha) S(ivasankara)
1898-1982 ... CANR-5
Obituary ... 108
Earlier sketch in CA 5-8R
Menon, R(amakrishna) Rabindranath
1927- ... CANR-11
Earlier sketch in CA 65-68
Menotti, Gian Carlo 1911- ... 104
See also SATA 29
Menshikov, Marina
1928(?)-1979 Obituary ... 93-96
Mensoian, Michael G(eorge) Jr. 1927- ... 85-88
Menton, Seymour 1927- ... CANR-31
Earlier sketch in CA 45-48
Mentor
See Lake, Kenneth R(obert)
Mentschikoff, Soia 1915-1984 Obituary ... 113
Mentzer, Michael J(ohn) 1949- ... 118
Menuhin, Hephzibah 1920-1981 Obituary ... 108
Menuhin, Yehudi 1916- ... CANR-2
Earlier sketch in CA 45-48
See also SATA 40
Menut, Albert D(ouglas Bartlett)
1894-1981 ... 25-28R
Obituary ... 135
Menville, Douglas 1935- ... 57-60
See also SATA 64
Menyuk, Paula 1929- ... 37-40R
Menzel, Barbara Jean 1946- ... 114
See also SATA 63
Menzel, Donald H(oward) 1901-1976 ... CAP-2
Obituary ... 69-72
Earlier sketch in CA 21-22
Menzel, Johanna
See Meskill, Johanna Menzel
Menzel, Paul T(heodore) 1942- ... 53-56
Menzel, Roderich 1907- ... 93-96
Menzies, Edna O(live) 1921- ... 116
Menzies, Elizabeth G(rant) C(ranbrook)
1915- ... 17-20R
Menzies, Robert Gordon 1894-1978 ... 81-84
Obituary ... 77-80
Menzies, William W(atson)
1931- Brief entry ... 110
Meo, Lucy Dorothy 1920- ... 25-28R
Meras, Phyllis 1931- ... CANR-37
Earlier sketches in CA 41-44R, CANR-16
Merbaum, Michael 1933- ... 65-68
Mercatante, Anthony Stephen 1940- ... 41-44R
Mercer, Blaine (Eugene) 1921- ... CANR-2
Earlier sketch in CA 1-4R
Mercer, Cecil William 1885-1960 Obituary ... 114
See also Yates, Dornford
Mercer, Charles (Edward) 1917-1988 ... CANR-2
Obituary ... 127
Earlier sketch in CA 1-4R
See also SATA 16, 61
Mercer, Colin 1952- ... 117
Mercer, David 1928-1980 ... CANR-23
Obituary ... 102
Earlier sketch in CA 9-12R
See also CLC 5
See also DLB 13
See also MTCW
Mercer, Derrik 1944- ... 130
Mercer, James L(ee) 1936- ... CANR-30
Earlier sketch in CA 112
Mercer, Jane R. ... 45-48
Mercer, Jean 1941- ... CANR-13
Earlier sketch in CA 33-36R
Mercer, Jessie ... CANR-2
Earlier sketch in CA 1-4R
See also Shannon, Terry
Mercer, Joan Bodger 1923- ... 101
Mercer, John 1704-1768 ... DLB 31
Mercer, Johnny 1906-1976 Obituary ... 65-68
Mercer, Marilyn 1923- Brief entry ... 107
Mercer, Paul 1950- ... 111
Mercer, Virginia Fletcher 1916- ... 5-8R
Mercey, Arch Andrew 1906-1980 Obituary ... 102
Merchant, Carolyn 1936- ... 113
Merchant, Jane (Hess) 1919-1972 ... CANR-4
Obituary ... 33-36R
Earlier sketch in CA 1-4R
Merchant, Larry 1931- ... 102
Merchant, Paul
See Ellison, Harlan
Mercie, Jean-Luc Henri 1939- ... 49-52
Mercier, Jean Doyle 1916- ... 1-4R
Mercier, Vivian (Herbert Samuel)
1919-1989 ... 81-84
Obituary ... 130
Mercouri, Melina 1925- Brief entry ... 106
Mercury
See Allen, Cecil J(ohn)
Meredith, Anne
See Malleson, Lucy Beatrice
Meredith, Arnold
See Hopkins, (Hector) Kenneth
Meredith, Char(lotte) 1921- ... 106
Meredith, Christopher (Laurence) 1954- ... 126
Meredith, D(oris) R. 1944- ... 128
Meredith, David William
See Miers, Earl Schenck
Meredith, Dean
See Dean, Edith M(ae)
Meredith, Don 1938- ... 102
Meredith, George (Marlor) 1923- ... CANR-4
Earlier sketch in CA 9-12R
Meredith, George Patrick
1904-1978 Obituary ... 108
Meredith, George 1828-1909 Brief entry ... 117
See also CDBLB 1832-1890
See also DLB 18, 35, 57
See also TCLC 17, 43
Meredith, James Howard 1933- ... 77-80
Meredith, Joel L(yman) 1935- ... 116
Meredith, Joseph C(harlton) 1914- ... 53-56
Meredith, Nicolete
See Stack, Nicolete Meredith
Meredith, Owen
See Lytton, Edward Robert Bulwer
Meredith, Richard C(arlton) 1937- ... 85-88
Meredith, Robert C(hidester) 1921- ... 5-8R
Meredith, Robert (King) 1923- ... 5-8R
Meredith, Roy 1914(?)-1984 Obituary ... 111
Meredith, Scott 1923- ... CANR-3
Earlier sketch in CA 9-12R
Meredith, William (Morris) 1919- ... CANR-6
Earlier sketch in CA 9-12R
See also CAAS 14
See also CLC 4, 13, 22, 55
See also DLB 5
Merewitz, Leonard (Alan) 1943- ... 69-72
Merezhkovsky, Dmitry Sergeyevich
1865-1941 ... TCLC 29
Merezhkovsky, Zinaida
See Gippius, Zinaida (Nikolayevna)
Mergen, Bernard 1937- ... 112
Merick, Wendell S. 1928(?)-1988 Obituary ... 124
Merideth, Robert 1935- ... 49-52
Merillat, Herbert C(hristian) L(aing)
1915- ... 29-32R
Merimee, Prosper 1803-1870 ... DLB 119
See also SSC 7
Merin, Peter
See Bihalji-Merin, Oto
Meringoff, Laurene Krasny
See Brown, Laurene Krasny
Merino, Gustavo Gutierrez
See Gutierrez Merino, Gustavo
Meritt, Lucy Shoe 1906- ... 37-40R
Merivale, John Herman 1779-1844 ... DLB 96
Merivale, Patricia 1934- ... 29-32R
Meriwether, James B. 1928- ... 13-16R
Meriwether, Lee 1862-1966 Obituary ... 116
Meriwether, Louise 1923- ... 77-80
See also BW
See also DLB 33
See also SATA 31
Merk, Frederick 1887-1977 ... 41-44R
Obituary ... 73-76
Merkel, Miles Adair 1929- ... 53-56
Merkin, Daphne 1954- ... 123
See also CLC 44
Merkin, Donald H. 1945- ... 69-72
Merkin, Robert (Bruce) 1947- ... 109
Merkl, Peter H(ans) 1932- ... CANR-24
Earlier sketches in CA 5-8R, CANR-7
Merkle, Edgar A. 1900(?)-1984 Obituary ... 113
Merkle, Judith A(stria) ... 105
See also Riley, Judith (Astria) Merkle
Merklinghaus, Michele 1965- ... 116
Merle, Robert (Jean Georges) 1908- ... 93-96
Merleau-Ponty, Maurice 1908-1961 ... 114
Obituary ... 89-92
Merli, Frank J(ohn) 1929- Brief entry ... 113
Merlin, Arthur
See Blish, James (Benjamin)
Merlin, Christina
See Heaven, Constance
Merlin, David
See Moreau, David Merlin
Merlin, Jan 1925- ... 108
Merlin, Mark D(avid) ... 118
Merlin, Samuel 1910- ... 115
Merlis, George 1940- ... 33-36R
Merliss, Reuben 1915- ... 17-20R
Merman, Ethel
See Zimmermann, Ethel Agnes
Mermin, Samuel 1912- ... 53-56
Merne, Oscar James 1943- ... 102
Mernit, Susan 1953- ... 69-72
Meroff, Deborah 1948- ... 89-92
Meron, Theodor 1930- ... 138
Merrell, James H. 1953- ... 127
Merrell, James L(ee) 1930- ... 17-20R
Merrell, Jo Ann 1945- ... 113
Merrell, Karen Dixon 1936- ... CANR-6
Earlier sketch in CA 13-16R
Merrell, V(ictor) Dallas 1936- ... 9-12R
Merrens, H(arry) Roy 1931- ... 9-12R
Merrett, Robert James 1944- ... 111
Merriam, Alan P(arkhurst) 1923-1980 ... CANR-1
Earlier sketch in CA 1-4R
Merriam, Eve 1916- ... CANR-29
Obituary ... 137
Earlier sketch in CA 5-8R
See also CLR 14
See also DLB 61
See also MAICYA
See also SATA 3, 40
Merriam, Harold G(uy) 1883-1981 ... CANR-10
Earlier sketch in CA 61-64
Merriam, Robert E(dward) 1918- ... 5-8R
Merriam, Sharan B. 1943- ... 135
Merrick, Gordon 1916-1988 ... CANR-11
Obituary ... 125
Earlier sketch in CA 13-16R
Merrick, Hugh
See Meyer, H(arold) A(lbert)
Merrick, William 1916-1969 ... CAP-1
Earlier sketch in CA 11-12
Merril, Judith 1923- ... CANR-15
Earlier sketch in CA 13-16R
See also MTCW
Merrill, Antoinette June 1912- ... 45-48
Merrill, Arch 1895(?)-1974 Obituary ... 49-52
Merrill, Bob
See Merrill, Robert Alexander
Merrill, Boynton Jr. 1925- ... 69-72
Merrill, Christopher (Lyall) 1957- ... 130
Merrill, David W. 1928- ... 108
Merrill, Dean 1943- ... CANR-27
Earlier sketches in CA 61-64, CANR-8
Merrill, Dick
See Merrill, Henry Tindall
Merrill, Edward C(lifton) Jr. 1920- ... 21-24R
Merrill, Edward H. 1903- ... CAP-1
Earlier sketch in CA 13-16
Merrill, Francis E(llsworth) 1904-1969 ... CAP-1
Earlier sketch in CA 19-20
Merrill, Frederick Thayer
1905-1974 Obituary ... 53-56
Merrill, Gary (Franklin)
1915(?)-1990 Obituary ... 131
Merrill, Harwood F(erry)
1904-1984 Obituary ... 114
Merrill, Henry Tindall 1897-1982 Obituary ... 108

Merrill, James (Ingram) 1926- CANR-10
Earlier sketch in CA 13-16R
See also CLC 2, 3, 6, 8, 13, 18, 34
See also DLB 5
See also DLBY 85
See also MTCW
Merrill, James M(ercer) 1920- 9-12R
Merrill, Jane 1946- ....SATA 42
Merrill, Jean (Fairbanks) 1923- CANR-38
Earlier sketches in CA 1-4R, CANR-4
See also MAICYA
See also SATA 1
Merrill, John Calhoun 1924- CANR-13
Earlier sketch in CA 73-76
Merrill, John N(igel) 1943- CANR-22
Earlier sketch in CA 103
Merrill, M. David 1937- CANR-16
Earlier sketch in CA 41-44R
Merrill, P. J.
See Roth, Holly
Merrill, Phil
See Filstrup, Jane (Merrill)
Merrill, Robert Alexander 1958- 136
Merrill, Robert 1919- 81-84
Merrill, Robert 1944- 89-92
Merrill, Thomas F. 1932- 29-32R
Merrill, Toni
See Merrill, Antoinette June
Merrill, Walter M. 1915- CANR-13
Earlier sketch in CA 21-24R
Merrill, Wilfred K. 1903- 9-12R
Merrill, William C. 1934- 29-32R
Merriman, Alex
See Silverberg, Robert
Merriman, Ann Lloyd 1934- 77-80
Merriman, Beth
See Taylor, Demetria
Merriman, Jerry Johnson 1939- 25-28R
Merriman, John 1924-1974 Obituary 104
Merriman, Marion 1909- 133
Merriman, Pat
See Atkey, Philip
Merrit, Elizabeth
See Goudge, Eileen
Merritt, A.
See Merritt, Abraham (P.)
Merritt, Abraham (P.) 1884-1943 Brief entry 120
Merritt, Dixon Lanier
1879-1972 Obituary 33-36R
Merritt, Don 1945- CANR-22
Earlier sketch in CA 106
Merritt, E. B. CANR-30
See also Waddington, Miriam
Merritt, Helen Henry 1920- 17-20R
Merritt, James D. 1934- 33-36R
Merritt, LeRoy Charles 1912-1970 ....CAP-2
Earlier sketch in CA 33-36
Merritt, Miriam 1925- 17-20R
Merritt, Muriel 1905- 69-72
Merritt, Ray E(merson) Jr. 1948- 73-76
Merritt, Raymond H(arland) 1936- 85-88
Merritt, Richard L(awrence) 1933- 41-44R
Merritt, William E. 1945- 132
Merry, Henry J(ohn) 1908- 37-40R
Mersand, Joseph 1907- CANR-1
Earlier sketch in CA 1-4R
Mersereau, John Jr. 1925- CANR-2
Earlier sketch in CA 1-4R
Mersky, Roy M. 1925- 37-40R
Mersmann, James Frederick 1938- 61-64
Mertens, Lawrence E(dwin) 1929- 85-88
Mertens, Thomas R(obert) 1930- CANR-6
Earlier sketch in CA 57-60
Mertes, Kate 1955- 129
Mertins, Herman Jr. 1931- 41-44R
Mertins, (Marshall) Louis 1885-1973 ....41-44R
Merton, Andrew H(arris) 1944- 107
Merton, Giles
See Curran, Mona (Elisa)
Merton, Robert K(ing) 1910- CANR-31
Earlier sketch in CA 41-44R
Merton, Stephen 1912- 21-24R
Merton, Thomas 1915-1968 ....CANR-22
Obituary 25-28R
Earlier sketch in CA 5-8R
See also CLC 1, 3, 11, 34
See also DLB 48
See also DLBY 81
See also MTCW
Mertz, Barbara (Gross) 1927- CANR-36
Earlier sketches in CA 21-24R, CANR-11
See also BEST 90:4
See also SATA 49
Mertz, Richard R(olland) 1927- 21-24R
Merullo, Roland 1953- 136
Merwe, A. v.d.
See Geyl, Pieter (Catharinus Arie)
Merwin, Decie 1894-1961 Obituary 111
See also SATA 32
Merwin, Sam(uel Kimball) Jr. 1910- 131
Merwin, W(illiam) S(tanley) 1927- CANR-15
Earlier sketch in CA 13-16R
See also CLC 1, 2, 3, 5, 8, 13, 18, 45
See also DLB 5
See also MTCW
Mery, Fernand 1897-1984 ....CANR-29
Earlier sketch in CA 105
Merz, Charles 1893-1977 Obituary 73-76
Merzer, Meridee 1947- 102
Mesa-Lago, Carmelo 1934- CANR-26
Earlier sketches in CA 25-28R, CANR-10
Meserve, Walter Joseph Jr. 1923- CANR-1
Earlier sketch in CA 1-4R
Meshack, B(illie) A(ugusta) 1922- 93-96
Meshenberg, Michael J(ay) 1942- CANR-16
Earlier sketch in CA 93-96
Meske, Eunice Boardman 1926- CANR-4
Earlier sketch in CA 9-12R
Meskill, Johanna Menzel 1930- 17-20R
Meskill, Robert 1918(?)-1970 Obituary 104
Mesquita, Bruce James Bueno de
See Bueno de Mesquita, Bruce James
Messager, Charles 1882-1971 Obituary 93-96
Messdeck Annie
See Coade, Jessie
Messegue, Maurice 1921- 103
Messel, Harry 1922- CANR-21
Earlier sketch in CA 103
Messenger, Charles (Rynd Milles)
1941- CANR-31
Earlier sketches in CA 73-76, CANR-13
See also SATA 59
Messenger, Christian K(arl) 1943- 132
Messenger, Elizabeth Margery (Esson)
1908- CAP-1
Earlier sketch in CA 11-12
Messenger, Phyllis (E.) Mauch 1950- 132
Messent, Peter Ronald 1949- 106
Messer, Alfred A(mes) 1922- 29-32R
Messer, Donald E(dward) 1941- 138
Messer, Ronald Keith 1942- 57-60
Messer, Sarah Carlin
1924(?)-1984 Obituary 112
Messer, Thomas M. 1920- 111
Brief entry 106
Messerer, Asaf Mikhailovich 1903- 104
Obituary 137
Messerli, Douglas 1947- CANR-39
Earlier sketch in CA 116
Messerli, Jonathan C. 1926- 41-44R
Messick, Dale 1906- ....SATA 48, 64
Messick, Hank
See Messick, Henry H(icks)
Messick, Henry H(icks) 1922- CANR-2
Earlier sketch in CA 45-48
Messieres, Nicole de
See de Messieres, Nicole
Messing, Shep 1949- Brief entry 111
Messing, Simon D(avid) 1922- 57-60
Messinger, C. F. 1913- 21-24R
Messinger, Sheldon L(eopold) 1925- 25-28R
Messmer, Otto 1892(?)-1983 Obituary 111
See also SATA 37
Messner, Fred(rick) R(ichard) 1926- 13-16R
Messner, Gerald 1935- 29-32R
Messner, Johannes 1891-1984 Obituary 112
Messner, Michael A. 1952- 138
Messner, Reinhold 1944- CANR-35
Earlier sketches in CA 81-84, CANR-15
Messner, Stephen Dale 1936- 21-24R
Mesta, Perle 1893(?)-1975 Obituary 57-60
Mesthene, Emmanuel George 1920- 77-80
Meston, John 1915(?)-1979 Obituary 85-88
Meszaros, Istvan 1930- CANR-9
Earlier sketch in CA 57-60
Meszaros, Marta 1931- 127
Meta
See Tomkiewicz, Mina
Metalious, Grace (de Repentigny)
1924-1964 ....CAP-2
Earlier sketch in CA 21-22
Metaxas, B(asil) N(icolas) 1925- 37-40R
Metcalf, E(ugene) W(esley) 1945- 65-68
Metcalf, George R. 1914- 25-28R
Metcalf, John 1938- 113
See also CLC 37
See also DLB 60
Metcalf, Kenneth N(olan) 1923-1965 ....5-8R
Metcalf, Keyes DeWitt 1889-1983 ....17-20R
Obituary 111
Metcalf, Lawrence E(ugene) 1915- 21-24R
Metcalf, Paul 1917- CANR-39
Earlier sketches in CA 45-48, CANR-1, 17
Metcalf, Peter 116
Metcalf, Suzanne
See Baum, L(yman) Frank
Metcalf, Thomas R. 1934- 13-16R
Metcalf, Vicky 1901- 89-92
Metcalfe, John Wallace
1901-1982 Obituary 107
Metcalfe, Steve 1953- 108
Metereau, Rebecca Bell
See Bell-Metereau, Rebecca
Metesky, George
See Hoffman, Abbie
Method, Kenneth (Walter) 1931- CANR-32
Earlier sketch in CA 13-16R
Methvin, Eugene H. 1934- 29-32R
Metos, Thomas H(arry) 1932- 93-96
See also SATA 37
Metraux, Guy S(erge) 1917- 9-12R
Metraux, Rhoda 1914- 57-60
Metress, James F(rancis)
See Metress, Seamus P.
Metress, Seamus P. 1933- CANR-21
Earlier sketches in CA 57-60, CANR-6
Metropolis, Nicholas Constantine 1915- 110
Mets, David Raymond 1928- 118
Mettler, Bert(ram Milton) 1927- ....SATA 56
Mettler, George B(arry) 1934- 93-96
Metwally, M(okhtar) M(ohamed)
1939- CANR-15
Earlier sketch in CA 65-68
Metz, Don 1940- 135
Metz, Donald L(ehman) 1935- 21-24R
Metz, Donald S(hink) 1916- 45-48
Metz, Jerred 1943- CANR-22
Earlier sketch in CA 104
Metz, Leon C(laire) 1930- CANR-36
Earlier sketches in CA 45-48, CANR-1, 16
Metz, Lois Lunt 1906- CAP-1
Earlier sketch in CA 9-10
Metz, Mary Haywood 1939- CANR-15
Earlier sketch in CA 85-88
Metz, Mary (Seawell) 1937- 53-56
Metz, Robert (Henry) 1928- CANR-13
Earlier sketch in CA 61-64
Metz, William 1918- 77-80
Metzdorf, Robert F(rederic)
1912-1975 Obituary 57-60
Metzger, Barbara 1944- 110
Metzger, Bruce Manning 1914- CANR-4
Earlier sketch in CA 9-12R
Metzger, Charles R(eid) 1921- 25-28R
Metzger, Deena P. 1936- 130
Metzger, Erika A(lma) 1933- 33-36R
Metzger, H(owell) Peter 1931- Brief entry 107
Metzger, Michael M(oses) 1935- 21-24R
Metzger, Norman 1924- CANR-9
Earlier sketch in CA 53-56
Metzger, Philip W. 1931- 45-48
Metzger, Robert 1950- 117
Metzger, Stanley D. 1916- 9-12R
Metzger, Thomas A(lbert) 1933- 97-100
Metzger, Walter P. 1922- CANR-17
Earlier sketch in CA 61-64
Metzker, Isaac 1901- 45-48
Metzler, Ken(neth Theodore) 1929- CANR-4
Earlier sketch in CA 53-56
Metzler, Lloyd A(ppleton) 1913- 104
Metzler, Paul 1914- CANR-6
Earlier sketch in CA 57-60
Metzner, Ralph 1936- 69-72
Metzner, Seymour 1924- 21-24R
Meudt, Edna Kritz 1906- CANR-9
Earlier sketch in CA 13-16R
Meurant, Georges 1948- 135
Meurice, Blanca
See von Block, Bela W(illiam)
Meux, Milton O(tto) 1930- 45-48
Meves, Christa 1925- CANR-24
Earlier sketch in CA 93-96
Mew, Charlotte (Mary)
1870-1928 Brief entry 105
See also DLB 19
See also TCLC 8
Mewburn, Martin
See Hitchin, Martin Mewburn
Mewhinney, Bruce 1949- 118
Mews, Hazel 1909-1975 ....CAP-2
Earlier sketch in CA 29-32
Mews, Siegfried 1933- CANR-22
Earlier sketches in CA 57-60, CANR-7
Mewshaw, Michael 1943- CANR-7
Earlier sketch in CA 53-56
See also CLC 9
See also DLBY 80
Mey, Jacob Lovis
See Meij, Jacob L(ouis)
Meyen, Edward L. 1937- 33-36R
Meyendorff, John 1926- CANR-9
Obituary 138
Earlier sketch in CA 21-24R
Meyer, Agnes E(lizabeth Ernst)
1887-1970 Obituary 29-32R
Meyer, Albert Julius 1919-1983 Obituary 111
Meyer, Alfred George 1920- 17-20R
Meyer, Alfred (Herman) 1893- CAP-1
Earlier sketch in CA 13-14
Meyer, Anthony 1920- 134
Meyer, Armin Henry 1914- 85-88
Meyer, Ben F. 1927- CANR-14
Earlier sketch in CA 37-40R
Meyer, Bernard C. 1910- 73-76
Meyer, Bernard F. 1891(?)-1975 Obituary 57-60
Meyer, Carl S(tamm) 1907-1972 ....CAP-1
Earlier sketch in CA 13-16
Meyer, Carol H. 1924- CANR-13
Earlier sketch in CA 73-76
Meyer, Carolyn 1935- CANR-2
Earlier sketch in CA 49-52
See also MAICYA
See also SAAS 9
See also SATA 9, 70
Meyer, Charles R(obert) 1926- 69-72
Meyer, Charles R. 1920- 33-36R
Meyer, Clarence 1903- 97-100
Meyer, D. Swing 1938- 17-20R
Meyer, David R. 1943- 65-68
Meyer, Donald (Burton) 1923- 21-24R
Meyer, Donald H(arvey) 1935- Brief entry 113
Meyer, Doris (L.) 1942- CANR-33
Earlier sketch in CA 89-92
See also HW
Meyer, Duane Gilbert 1926- 5-8R
Meyer, E. Y. 1946- ....DLB 75
Meyer, Edith Patterson 1895- CANR-1
Earlier sketch in CA 1-4R
See also SATA 5
Meyer, Elizabeth C(ooper) 1958- 69-72
Meyer, Ellen Hope 1928- 119
Meyer, Erika 1904- 73-76
Meyer, Ernst Hermann
1905-1988(?) Obituary 127
Meyer, Eugene L. 1942- 135
Meyer, Eugene 1875-1959 ....DLB 29
Meyer, F(ranklyn) E(dward) 1932- 1-4R
See also SATA 9
Meyer, Frank S(traus) 1909-1972 ....CAP-1
Obituary 33-36R
Earlier sketch in CA 9-10
Meyer, Fred(erick Robert) 1922-1985 57-60
Obituary 117
Meyer, George H(erbert) 1928- 116
Meyer, Gladys (Eleanor)
1908-1986 Obituary 118
Meyer, H(arold) A(lbert) 1898-1980 ....CANR-4
Obituary 102
Earlier sketch in CA 5-8R
Meyer, H. K. Houston
See Meyer, Heinrich
Meyer, Harding 1928- 130
Meyer, Harold D(iedrich) 1892-1974(?) CAP-2
Earlier sketch in CA 19-20
Meyer, Harold G. 1909(?)-1986 Obituary 118
Meyer, Heinrich 1904-1977 49-52
Obituary 85-88
Meyer, Herbert W(alter) 1892- CAP-2
Earlier sketch in CA 33-36
Meyer, Herman 1911- 21-24R
Meyer, Howard N(icholas) 1914- 13-16R
Meyer, Jean Shepherd ....SATA 11
Meyer, Jerome Sydney 1895-1975 ....CANR-4
Obituary 57-60
Earlier sketch in CA 1-4R
See also SATA 3, 25
Meyer, Joachim-Ernst 1917- 57-60
Meyer, John Robert 1927- CANR-9
Earlier sketch in CA 13-16R
Meyer, June
See Jordan, June
Meyer, Karl E(rnest) 1928- CANR-1
Earlier sketch in CA 1-4R
Meyer, Kathleen Allan 1918- 123
See also SATA 46, 51
Meyer, Lawrence (Robert) 1941- CANR-34
Earlier sketch in CA 73-76
Meyer, Leonard B. 1918- 13-16R
Meyer, Lillian Nicholson
1917(?)-1983 Obituary 109
Meyer, Linda D(oreen) 1948- CANR-37
Earlier sketches in CA 93-96, CANR-16
Meyer, Louis A(lbert) 1942- 37-40R
See also SATA 12
Meyer, Mabel H. 1890(?)-1976 Obituary 61-64
Meyer, Marie-Louise 1936- 97-100
Meyer, Mary Keysor 1919- 102
Meyer, Michael A. 1937- 21-24R
Meyer, Michael C. 1935- CANR-10
Earlier sketch in CA 21-24R
Meyer, Michael (Leverson) 1921- CANR-13
Earlier sketch in CA 25-28R
Meyer, Nicholas 1945- CANR-7
Earlier sketch in CA 49-52
Meyer, Philip (Edward) 1930- CANR-10
Earlier sketch in CA 65-68
Meyer, Renate 1930- 53-56
See also SATA 6
Meyer, Robert H. 1934- 37-40R
Meyer, Ronald 1952- 135
Meyer, Roy W(illard) 1925- 17-20R
Meyer, Ruth F(ritz) 1910- CAP-2
Earlier sketch in CA 23-24
Meyer, Stewart (Martin) 1947- 118
Meyer, Susan E. 1940- CANR-19
Earlier sketches in CA 45-48, CANR-2
See also SATA 64
Meyer, Thomas 1947- CANR-1
Earlier sketch in CA 49-52
Meyer, William Eugene 1923- 45-48
Meyer, William R(obert) 1949- 77-80
Meyerhoff, Arthur E(dward)
1895-1986 Obituary 120
Meyerhoff, Howard A(ugustus) 1899- CAP-2
Earlier sketch in CA 19-20
Meyering, Ralph A. 1930- 29-32R
Meyer-Meyrink, Gustav
1868-1932 Brief entry 117
See also Meyrink, Gustav
Meyerowitz, Eva (Leonie) L(ewin-) R(ichter)
..........9-12R
Meyerowitz, Patricia 1933- 21-24R
Meyers, Albert L. 1904(?)-1981 Obituary 102
Meyers, Annette (Brafman) 1934- 132
Meyers, Bert(ram) 1928-1979 101
Meyers, Carlton R(oy) 1922- 57-60
Meyers, Carol L(yons) 1942- CANR-32
Earlier sketch in CA 113
Meyers, Carole Terwilliger 1945- 69-72
Meyers, Cecil H(arold) 1920- 29-32R
Meyers, David W. 1942- 29-32R
Meyers, Edward 1934- 101
Meyers, Eric M(ark) 1940- 110
Meyers, Gertrude Barlow 1902- 1-4R
Meyers, Jeffrey 1939- 73-76
See also CLC 39
See also DLB 111
Meyers, Joan Simpson 1927- CANR-14
Earlier sketch in CA 17-20R
Meyers, Lawrence Stanley 1943- 57-60
Meyers, Marvin 1921- Brief entry 108
Meyers, Mary Ann 1937- 116
Meyers, Michael Jay 1946- 65-68
Meyers, Nancy 1950- 138
Meyers, Robert Rex 1923- 17-20R
Meyers, Roy (Lethbridge) 1910-1974 ....CAP-2
Earlier sketch in CA 25-28
Meyers, Ruth S(chlaff) 1923- 117
Meyers, Susan
See Falk, Susan Meyers
Meyers, Susan 1942- CANR-13
Earlier sketch in CA 21-24R
See also SATA 19
Meyers, Walter E(arl) 1939- CANR-6
Earlier sketch in CA 53-56
Meyerson, Adam 1953- 128
Meyerson, Edward L(eon) 1904-1980 ....CANR-12
Earlier sketch in CA 61-64
Meyerson, Martin 1922- Brief entry 115
Meynell, Alice (Christina Gertrude Thompson)
1847-1922 Brief entry 104
See also DLB 19, 98
See also TCLC 6
Meynell, Alix (Hester M.) 1903- 128

Meynell, Francis Meredith Wilfrid
1891-1975 .... CAP-2
Obituary 57-60
Earlier sketch in CA 19-20
Meynell, Hugo A. 1936- 130
Meynell, Laurence Walter 1899-1989 .... CANR-15
Obituary 128
Earlier sketch in CA 81-84
See also SATA 61
Meyners, J. Robert 1922- 104
Meynier, Yvonne (Pollet) 1908- 73-76
See also SATA 14
Meyrink, Gustav
See Meyer-Meyrink, Gustav
See also DLB 81
See also TCLC 21
Meyrink, Gustav Meyer
See Meyer-Meyrink, Gustav
Meza, Pedro Thomas 1941- 37-40R
Mezerick, Avrahm G. 1901-1986 Obituary 119
Mezey, Michael L(loyd) 1943- 118
Mezey, Robert 1935- CANR-7
Earlier sketch in CA 57-60
See also SATA 33
Mezvinsky, Edward M. 1937- 103
Mezvinsky, Shirley
See Lauro, Shirley (Shapiro) Mezvinsky
Mezzrow, Mezz
See Mezzrow, Milton
Mezzrow, Milton 1890(?)-1972 .... 37-40R
Miall, Robert
See Burke, John (Frederick)
Mian, Mary (Lawrence Shipman)
1902- .... SATA 47
Micale, Albert 1913- .... SATA 22
Micallef, Benjamin A(nthony) 1925-1980 53-56
Obituary 103
Micallef, John 1923- 25-28R
Micaud, Charles Antoine 1910- 5-8R
Miceli, Frank 1932- 57-60
Miceli, Vincent P(eter) 1915- Brief entry 114
Michael, David J. 1944- 29-32R
Michael, Franz H(enry) 1907- CANR-4
Earlier sketch in CA 5-8R
Michael, George 1919- 41-44R
Michael, Henry N(athaniel) 1913- 33-36R
Michael, Ian (Lockie) 1915- 104
Michael, James
See Scagnetti, Jack
Michael, John A(rthur) 1921- 133
Michael, Judith .... BEST 90:2
Michael, Manfred
See Winterfeld, Henry
Michael, Paul Martin 1934- CANR-10
Earlier sketch in CA 17-20R
Michael, Phyllis C(allender) 1908- CANR-2
Earlier sketch in CA 5-8R
Michael, S(tanley) T(heodore) 1912- 13-16R
Michael, Thomas A. 1933- 33-36R
Michael, Tom
See Michael, Thomas A.
Michael, William B(urton) 1922- 45-48
Michael, Wolfgang F(riedrich) 1909- CANR-14
Earlier sketch in CA 41-44R
Michaeles, M. M.
See Golding, Morton J(ay)
Michaelides, Constantine E. 1930- 25-28R
Michaelis, David (Tead) 1957- 114
Michaelis, John U(dell) 1912- 69-72
Michaelis-Jena, Ruth
See Ratcliff, Ruth
Michaels, Barbara
See Mertz, Barbara (Gross)
Michaels, Carolyn Leopold
See Leopold, Carolyn Clugston
Michaels, Dale
See Rifkin, Shepard
Michaels, Fern
See Anderson, Roberta
and Kuczkir, Mary
Michaels, J. Ramsey 1931- CANR-38
Earlier sketch in CA 116
Michaels, Joanne Louise
See Teitelbaum, Michael
Michaels, Joanne 1950- CANR-23
Earlier sketch in CA 107
Michaels, Joe
See Saltzman, Joseph
Michaels, Kasey
See Seidick, Kathryn A(melia)
Michaels, Kristin
See Williams, Jeanne
Michaels, Leonard 1933- CANR-21
Earlier sketch in CA 61-64
See also CLC 6, 25
See also MTCW
Michaels, Lynn
See Strongin, Lynn
Michaels, Molly
See Untermeyer, Louis
Michaels, Neal
See Teitelbaum, Michael
Michaels, Norman 97-100
Michaels, Philip
See van Rjndt, Philippe
Michaels, Ralph
See Filicchia, Ralph
Michaels, Sidney R(amon) 1927- 17-20R
Michaels, Ski
See Pellowski, Michael (Joseph)
Michaels, Steve
See Avallone, Michael (Angelo, Jr)
Michaels, Steve 1955- .... SATA 71
Michaelson, L(ouis) W. 1917- CANR-14
Earlier sketch in CA 77-80
Michaely, Michael 1928- 103
Michalczyk, John Joseph 1941- 104
Michalopoulos, Andre 1897- CAP-2
Earlier sketch in CA 23-24
Michalos, Alex C. 1935- 37-40R
Michalowski, Kazimierz
1901-1981 Obituary 108
Michalski, John 1934- 25-28R
Michalson, Carl (Donald Jr.) 1915-1965 .... 1-4R
Michaud, Charles Regis 1910- CAP-2
Earlier sketch in CA 19-20
Michaud, Stephen G(age) 1948- 109
Michaux, Henri 1899-1984 85-88
Obituary 114
See also CLC 8, 19
Michaux, William W(hitehead) 1919- 41-44R
Miche, Giuseppe
See Bochenski, Joseph M.
Micheaux, Oscar 1884-1951 .... DLB 50
Micheels, Peter A. 1945- 132
Michel, Anna 1943- 85-88
See also SATA 40, 49
Michel, Beth
See Dubus, Elizabeth Nell
Michel, Georges 1926- CANR-31
Earlier sketch in CA 25-28R
Michel, Henri (Jules) 1907- CANR-19
Earlier sketches in CA 53-56, CANR-4
Michel, Joseph 1922- CANR-13
Earlier sketch in CA 25-28R
Michel, Michel Georges
See Georges-Michel, Michel
Michel, Pierre 1934- 57-60
Michel, Sandra (Seaton) 1935- 77-80
Michel, Sandy
See Michel, Sandra (Seaton)
Michel, (Milton) Scott 1916- 1-4R
Michel, Walter 1922- 81-84
Micheli, Lyle Joseph 1940- CANR-20
Earlier sketch in CA 97-100
Micheline, Jack 1929- 122
Brief entry 114
See also DLB 16
Michell, John (F.) 1933- CANR-23
Earlier sketch in CA 107
Michelman, Herbert 1913-1980 Obituary 102
Michelman, Irving S(imon) 1917- 69-72
Michelmore, Peter 1930- CANR-7
Earlier sketch in CA 5-8R
Michelon, L. C. 1918- CANR-1
Earlier sketch in CA 45-48
Michels, Caroll Chesy 1943- 117
Michelson, Edward J(ulias) 1915- 77-80
Michelson, Florence B. CAP-2
Earlier sketch in CA 21-22
Michelson, Peter 1937- CANR-1
Earlier sketch in CA 45-48
Michelson, Stephan 1938- 93-96
Michelson, William M. 1940- 33-36R
Michener, Charles D(uncan) 1918- 117
Michener, Charles Thomson 1940- 104
Michener, James A(lbert) 1907(?)- CANR-21
Earlier sketch in CA 5-8R
See also AITN 1
See also BEST 90:1
See also CLC 1, 5, 11, 29, 60
See also DLB 6
See also MTCW
Michie, Allan (Andrew)
1915-1973 Obituary 45-48
Michie, Donald 1923- 121
Michie, James 1927- Brief entry 116
Michie, Jonathan 1957- 132
Michman, Ronald D(avid) 1931- CANR-7
Earlier sketch in CA 57-60
Mickel, Emanuel John Jr. 1937- 37-40R
Mickelsen, A(nton) Berkeley 1920- 9-12R
Mickelsen, Olaf 1912- 17-20R
Mickelson, Sig 1913- 111
Micken, Charles M. 1918- 13-16R
Mickey, Paul A(lbert) 1937- CANR-1
Earlier sketch in CA 49-52
Mickiewicz, Ellen Propper 1938- CANR-24
Earlier sketches in CA 21-24R, CANR-9
Mickle, Shelley Fraser 1944- 132
Micklejohn, George 1717(?)-1818 .... DLB 31
Micklem, Nathaniel 1888-1976 103
Mickler, Ernest M(atthew)
1940(?)-1988 Obituary 127
Micklish, Rita 1931- 49-52
See also SATA 12
Mickolus, Edward F(rancis) 1950- 106
Micks, Marianne H(offman) 1923- CANR-12
Earlier sketch in CA 17-20R
Micucci, Charles (Patrick Jr.) 1959- 137
Micunovic, Veljko 1916-1982 109
Obituary 107
Midda, Sara 1951- 135
Middeldorf, Ulrich Alexander
1901-1983 Obituary 109
Middendorf, John Harlan 1922- 104
Middlebrook, David
See Rosenus, Alan (Harvey)
Middlebrook, Diane Wood 1939- CANR-15
Earlier sketch in CA 81-84
Middlebrook, Jonathan 1940- 65-68
Middlebrook, (Norman) Martin 1932- CANR-31
Earlier sketches in CA 37-40R, CANR-14
Middlekauff, Robert (Lawrence) 1929- 130
Brief entry 112
Middleman, Ruth J. Rosenbloom 1923- 104
Middlemas, Keith
See Middlemas, Robert Keith
Middlemas, Robert Keith 1935- CANR-12
Earlier sketch in CA 29-32R
Middlemiss, Robert (William) 1938- CANR-12
Earlier sketch in CA 73-76
Middleton, Bernard C(hester) 1924- 41-44R
Middleton, Christopher 1926- CANR-29
Earlier sketch in CA 13-16R
See also CLC 13
See also DLB 40
Middleton, David L. 1940- 37-40R
Middleton, Drew 1914(?)-1990 Obituary 130
Brief entry 110
Middleton, George 1880-1967 Obituary 25-28R
Middleton, Haydn 1955- 132
Middleton, Michael (Humfrey) 1917- 124
Middleton, Nigel (Gordon) 1918- CANR-25
Earlier sketch in CA 45-48
Middleton, O(sman) E(dward) 1925- 81-84
Middleton, Richard 1945- 109
Middleton, Roger 1955- 126
Middleton, Stanley 1919- CANR-21
Earlier sketch in CA 25-28R
See also CLC 7, 38
See also DLB 14
Middleton, Thomas 1580-1627 .... DLB 58
Middleton-Murry, Colin
See Middleton-Murry, John (Jr.)
Middleton-Murry, John (Jr.) 1926- CANR-3
Earlier sketch in CA 5-8R
Middleton Murry, Mary
See Murry, Mary Middleton
Midelfort, H(ans) C(hristian) Erik
1942- CANR-26
Earlier sketch in CA 45-48
Midgett, Elwin W. 1911- CAP-2
Earlier sketch in CA 29-32
Midgett, Wink
See Midgett, Elwin W.
Midgley, David A(lan) 1898- 17-20R
Midgley, E(rnest) B(rian) F(rancis) 1927- 93-96
Midgley, Graham 1923- 73-76
Midgley, Louis C(asper) 1931- 41-44R
Midgley, Mary 1919- CANR-20
Earlier sketch in CA 89-92
Midlarsky, Manus I(ssacher) 1937- 57-60
Midler, Bette 1945- 106
Midtlyng, Joanna 1927- 61-64
Midwinter, E(ric) C(lare) 1932- CANR-26
Earlier sketch in CA 29-32R
Mieczkowski, Bogdan 1924- 111
Miegel, Agnes 1879-1964 .... DLB 56
Miel, Alice Marie 1906- CANR-20
Earlier sketches in CA 1-4R, CANR-5
Mielke, Arthur W(illard) 1912-1978 .... CANR-4
Earlier sketch in CA 1-4R
Mielziner, Jo 1901-1976 45-48
Obituary 65-68
Miernyk, William Henry 1918- 17-20R
Miers, Earl Schenck 1910-1972 .... CANR-2
Obituary 37-40R
Earlier sketch in CA 1-4R
See also SATA 1, 26
Miers, Suzanne (Doyle) 1922- 61-64
Mierzenski, Stanislaw 1903-1964 .... 1-4R
Miesel, Sandra (Louise) 1941- 128
Miethe, Terry Lee 1948- 105
Miewald, Robert D(ale) 1938- 117
Migdal, Joel S(amuel) 1945- CANR-6
Earlier sketch in CA 57-60
Migdalski, Edward C(harles) 1918- CANR-4
Earlier sketch in CA 9-12R
Migel, Parmenia
See Ekstrom, Parmenia Migel
Migliore, R. Henry 1940- 110
Migliorini, Bruno 1896-1975 Obituary 116
Miglis, John 1950- CANR-20
Earlier sketch in CA 81-84
Mignani, Rigo 1921- 37-40R
Migueis, Jose Rodrigues 1901- .... CLC 10
Miguez-Bonino, Jose 1924- 49-52
Mihailovich, Vasa D. 1926- CANR-14
Earlier sketch in CA 41-44R
Mihajlov, Mihajlo 1934- 130
Brief entry 105
Mihalas, Dimitri M(anuel) 1939- CANR-4
Earlier sketch in CA 53-56
Mihaly, Mary E(llen) 1950- 97-100
Mihanovich, Clement Simon 1913- 5-8R
Mijuskovic, Ben Lazare 1937- 132
Mikan, Baron
See Barba, Harry
Mikdashi, Zuhayr 1933- CANR-39
Earlier sketches in CA 89-92, CANR-17
Mikes, George 1912-1987 .... CANR-6
Obituary 123
Earlier sketch in CA 9-12R
Mikesell, Arthur M. 1932- 13-16R
Mikesell, John L(ee) 1942- 102
Mikesell, Marvin Wray 1930- CANR-4
Earlier sketch in CA 1-4R
Mikesell, Raymond F(rech) 1913- CANR-19
Earlier sketches in CA 1-4R, CANR-4
Mikesell, Rufus Merrill 1893-1972 .... CAP-2
Earlier sketch in CA 25-28
Mikesell, William H(enry) 1887-1969 .... CAP-2
Earlier sketch in CA 19-20
Mikhail, E(dward) H(alim) 1926- CANR-31
Earlier sketches in CA 37-40R, CANR-14
Mikhailov, M.
See Mihajlov, Mihajlo
Mikhalkov, Sergei Vladimirovich
1913- Brief entry 116
Mikhalkov-Konchalovsky, Andrei (Sergeyevich)
1937- 127
Miki, Chihan
See Naruse, Mikio
Mikkelsen, Ejnar 1881(?)-1971 Obituary 29-32R
Miklowitz, Gloria D. 1927- CANR-26
Earlier sketches in CA 25-28R, CANR-10
See also AAYA 6
See also MAICYA
See also SATA 4, 68
Mikolaycak, Charles 1937- CANR-38
Earlier sketches in CA 61-64, CANR-8, 23
See also MAICYA
See also SAAS 4
See also SATA 9
Mikolyzk, Thomas A. 1953- 138
Mikszath, Kalman 1847-1910 .... TCLC 31
Mikulas, William Lee 1942- 53-56
Mikus, Joseph A(ugust) 1909- 61-64
Milano, Paolo 1904-1988 Obituary 125
Milberg, Warren H(oward) 1941- 109
Milbrath, Lester W(alter) 1925- CANR-4
Earlier sketch in CA 9-12R
Milburn, George 1906-1966 Obituary 109
Milburn, Josephine F(ishel) 1928- CANR-13
Earlier sketch in CA 21-24R
Milburn, Joyce 1953- 114
Milburn, Robert (Leslie Pollington) 1907- 130
Milch, Robert J(effrey) 1938- 25-28R
Milcsik, Margie 1950- 110
Mild, Warren (Paul) 1922- CANR-8
Earlier sketch in CA 21-24R
See also SATA 41
Mildner, Gerard C. S. 1959- 138
Mildo, Albert 1945- CANR-21
Earlier sketch in CA 73-76
Mileck, Joseph 1922- 107
Milenkovitch, Michael M. 1932- 37-40R
Milenski, Paul Edward 1942- 128
Miles, Angela R(ose) 1946- 122
Miles, Barry 1943- 134
Miles, (Louise) Bebe 1924-1980 .... CANR-9
Earlier sketch in CA 61-64
Miles, Bernard 1907- 133
Miles, Betty 1928- CANR-20
Earlier sketches in CA 1-4R, CANR-5
See also SAAS 9
See also SATA 8
Miles, Beverly Parkhurst 1940- 107
Miles, Charles 1894- 5-8R
Miles, David H(olmes) 1940- 57-60
Miles, Dorien K(lein) 1915- CANR-8
Earlier sketch in CA 61-64
Miles, Dudley (Robert Alexander) 1947- 131
Miles, Edwin A(rthur) 1926- 1-4R
Miles, Elliot
See Ludvigsen, Karl (Eric)
Miles, Elton (Roger) 1917- 37-40R
Miles, Gary Britten 1940- 102
Miles, George C(arpenter)
1904-1975 Obituary 61-64
Miles, Herbert J(ackson) 1907- 21-24R
Miles, Ian (Douglas) 1948- 115
Miles, John
See Bickham, Jack M(iles)
Miles, Josephine 1911-1985 .... CANR-2
Obituary 116
Earlier sketch in CA 1-4R
See also CLC 1, 2, 14, 34, 39
See also DLB 48
Miles, Joyce C(rudgington) 1927- 105
Miles, Judith Mary (Huhta) 1937- 65-68
Miles, Keith
See Tralins, S(andor) Robert
Miles, Leland (Weber 1924- 13-16R
Miles, Margaret R(uth) 1937- 117
Miles, Mary Lillian (Brown) 1908- 13-16R
Miles, Matthew B(ailey) 1926- CANR-36
Earlier sketches in CA 81-84, CANR-15
Miles, Michael W. 1945- 33-36R
Miles, Miska
See Martin, Patricia Miles
Miles, O. Thomas 1923- 21-24R
Miles, Patricia A.
See Martin, Patricia Miles
Miles, (Mary) Patricia 1930- CANR-27
Earlier sketches in CA 69-72, CANR-11
See also SATA 29
Miles, Peter
See Miles, Richard
Miles, Richard 1938- 105
Miles, Robert H. 1944- 118
Miles, Robert L(ee) 1939- 107
Miles, Russell Hancock 1895- CAP-1
Earlier sketch in CA 9-10
Miles, Stanley 1911-1987 Obituary 123
Miles, Sylva
See Miles, Dorien K(lein)
and Mularchyk, Sylva
Miles, T(homas) R(ichard) 1923- CANR-38
Earlier sketches in CA 49-52, CANR-1, 17
Milestone, Lewis 1895-1980 Obituary 101
Miletus, Rex
See Burgess, M(ichael) R(oy)
Milford, D(avid) S(umner)
1905-1984 Obituary 113
Milford, Nancy 1938- 29-32R
Milgate, Rodney Armour 1934- 107
Milgram, Gail Gleason 1942- 29-32R
Milgram, Morris 1916- 73-76
Milgram, Stanley 1933-1984 .... CANR-29
Obituary 114
Earlier sketch in CA 105
Milgrom, Harry 1912- CANR-3
Earlier sketch in CA 1-4R
See also SATA 25
Milgrom, Jacob 1923- 53-56
Milhaud, Darius 1892-1974 Obituary 49-52
Milhaven, John Giles 1927- 29-32R
Milhous, Judith 1946- 129
Milhous, Katherine 1894-1977 Obituary 104
See also SATA 15
Milhouse, Paul W(illiam) 1910- CANR-27
Earlier sketches in CA 25-28R, CANR-11
Mili, Gjon 1904-1984 Obituary 112
Milic, Louis T(onko) 1922- 21-24R

Milio, Nancy 1938- CANR-13
Earlier sketch in CA 29-32R
Militant
See Sandburg, Carl (August)
Militello, Pietro
See Natali, Alfred Maxim
Milius, John 1945- 101
See also DLB 44
Milkomane, George Alexis Milkomanovich
1903- CANR-20
Earlier sketch in CA 104
Milks, Harold Keith 1908-1979 108
Obituary 93-96
Mill, C. R.
See Crnjanski, Milos
Mill, James 1773-1836 .... DLB 107
Mill, John Stuart 1806-1873 .... CDBLB 1832-1890
See also DLB 55
Milland, Jack
See Milland, Ray
Milland, Ray 1908(?)-1986 Obituary 118
Brief entry 113
Millar, Barbara F. 1924- 25-28R
See also SATA 12
Millar, Fergus 1935- CANR-20
Earlier sketches in CA 13-16R, CANR-5
Millar, George Reid 1910- 73-76
Millar, Gilbert John 1939- 104
Millar, J(ohn) Halket 1899- 9-12R
Millar, James Primrose Malcolm 1893- CAP-1
Earlier sketch in CA 9-10
Millar, James R(obert) 1936- 29-32R
Millar, Jeff(ery Lynn) 1942- CANR-11
Earlier sketch in CA 69-72
Millar, (Minna Henrietta) Joy 1914- 93-96
Millar, Kenneth 1915-1983 ....CANR-16
Obituary 110
Earlier sketch in CA 9-12R
See also Macdonald, Ross
See also CLC 14
See also DLB 2
See also DLBD 6
See also DLBY 83
See also MTCW
Millar, Margaret (Ellis Sturm) 1915- CANR-16
Earlier sketch in CA 13-16R
See also SATA 61
Millar, Ronald (Graeme) 1919- 73-76
Millar, T(homas) B(ruce) CANR-26
Earlier sketch in CA 29-32R
Millard, A(lan) R(alph) 1937- CANR-11
Earlier sketch in CA 25-28R
Millard, Andre 1947- 136
Millard, Charles W(arren III)
1932- Brief entry 115
Millard, Gregory B. 1947(?)-1984 Obituary 114
Millard, Joe
See Millard, Joseph (John)
Millard, Joseph (John) 1908- 13-16R
Millay, E. Vincent
See Millay, Edna St. Vincent
Millay, Edna St. Vincent 1892-1950 130
Brief entry 104
See also CDALB 1917-1929
See also DLB 45
See also MTCW
See also TCLC 4
Millbank, Captain H. R.
See Ellis, Edward S(ylvester)
Millburn, Cynthia
See Brooks, Anne Tedlock
Milldyke, (John) William 1937-1983 77-80
Obituary 111
Millen, Clifford H. 1901(?)-1972 Obituary 104
Millender, Dharathula H(ood) 1920- 17-20R
Miller, Abraham H(irsh) 1940- 104
Miller, Al 1936- 65-68
Miller, Alan Robert 1929- 73-76
Miller, Alan W. 1926- 29-32R
Miller, Albert G(riffith) 1905-1982 ....CANR-1
Obituary 107
Earlier sketch in CA 1-4R
See also SATA 12, 31
Miller, Albert Jay 1928- CANR-1
Earlier sketch in CA 45-48
Miller, Alden D(ykstra)
1940(?)-1984 Obituary 113
Miller, Alden Holmes 1906-1965 Obituary 109
Miller, Alfred W. 1893(?)-1983 Obituary 111
Miller, Alice P(atricia McCarthy) CANR-26
Earlier sketch in CA 29-32R
See also SATA 22
Miller, Alicia (Metcalf) 1939- 127
Miller, Anita 1926- CANR-29
Earlier sketch in CA 111
Miller, Ann
See Collier, Lucille Ann
Miller, Arthur B(urton) 1922- 37-40R
Miller, Arthur R(aphael) 1934- Brief entry 114
Miller, Arthur S(elwyn) 1917-1988 ....CANR-11
Obituary 125
Earlier sketch in CA 69-72
Miller, Arthur 1915- CANR-30
Earlier sketches in CA 1-4R, CANR-2
See also CABS 3
See also AITN 1
See also CDALB 1941-1968
See also CLC 1, 2, 6, 10, 15, 26, 47
See also DC 1
See also DLB 7
See also MTCW
See also WLC
Miller, Barbara D(iane) 1948- CANR-23
Earlier sketch in CA 106
Miller, Barbara S(toler) 1940- CANR-27
Earlier sketches in CA 25-28R, CANR-11
Miller, Barry 1946- 33-36R
Miller, Benj.
See Loomis, Noel M(iller)
Miller, Benjamin F(rank) 1907-1971 ....CANR-4
Obituary 29-32R
Earlier sketch in CA 1-4R
Miller, Bernard S. 1920- 106
Miller, Beth 1941- 136
Miller, Beulah Montgomery 1917- 61-64
Miller, Bill D. 1936- 102
Miller, (H.) Bill(y) 1920-1961 108
Miller, Brent C(arlton) 1947- 112
Miller, (Harvey) Brown 1943- 101
Miller, Byron Strongman
1912(?)-1978 Obituary 77-80
Miller, C(larence) William 1914- 53-56
Miller, Calvin 1936- CANR-13
Earlier sketch in CA 21-24R
Miller, Caroline 1903- .... DLB 9
Miller, Carroll H(iram) 1907-197 (?) CAP-1
Earlier sketch in CA 19-20
Miller, Casey (Geddes) 1919- 69-72
Miller, Cecilia Parsons 1909- CANR-12
Earlier sketch in CA 21-24R
Miller, Cecille (Boyd) 1908- 9-12R
Miller, Char
See Miller, Frank L(ubbock) IV
Miller, Charles A. 1937- 29-32R
Miller, Charles D(avid) 1942- CANR-32
Earlier sketch in CA 69-72
Miller, Charles E. 1929- 33-36R
Miller, Charles Henderson 1905- CAP-2
Earlier sketch in CA 19-20
Miller, Charles Leslie 1908- 49-52
Miller, Charles 1918- 77-80
Miller, Christian 1920- 108
Miller, Clarence H(arvey) 1930- 102
Miller, Clarence J(ohn) 1916- CANR-13
Earlier sketch in CA 21-24R
Miller, Clement (Albin) 1915- 41-44R
Miller, Conrad
See Strung, Norman
Miller, D(ean) A(rthur) 1931- 21-24R
Miller, Daniel Adlai II 1918- 37-40R
Miller, Danny 1947- 126
Miller, Darlis A(nn) 1939- 125
Miller, David E(ugene) 1909-1978 45-48
Obituary 103
Miller, David Harry 1938- 57-60
Miller, David L(eroy) 1936- 49-52
Miller, David Lee 1951- 122
Miller, David (Leslie) 1946- 130
Miller, David Louis 1903-1986 ....21-24R
Obituary 118
Miller, David Merlin 1934- 93-96
Miller, David W. 1940- 49-52
Miller, Debbie (S.) 1951- 133
Miller, Deborah Uchill 1944- 116
See also SATA 61
Miller, Delbert C(harles) 1913- 25-28R
Miller, Don 1923- .... SATA 15
Miller, Donald C(urtis) 1933- CANR-6
Earlier sketch in CA 57-60
Miller, Donald Eugene 1929- CANR-24
Earlier sketch in CA 106
Miller, Donald George 1909- CANR-4
Earlier sketch in CA 5-8R
Miller, Donald L(ane) 1918- 17-20R
Miller, Donald 1893-1986 Obituary 119
Miller, Donald 1934- 97-100
Miller, Doris R.
See Mosesson, Gloria R(ubin)
Miller, Dorothy (Ryan)
See Ryan, Dorothy (Barger)
Miller, Douglas T(aylor) 1937- 21-24R
Miller, E. Ethelbert 1950- .... DLB 41
Miller, E. F.
See Pohle, Robert W(arren) Jr.
Miller, E(dwin) S(hepard) 1904- 45-48
Miller, E(ugene) Willard 1915- CANR-17
Earlier sketches in CA 5-8R, CANR-2
Miller, Ed(die) L(eRoy) 1937- 37-40R
Miller, Eddie
See Miller, Edward
Miller, Edna Anita 1920- 112
See also SATA 29
Miller, Edward 1905-1974 .... CAP-2
Earlier sketch in CA 25-28
See also SATA 8
Miller, Edwin Haviland 1918- 110
Miller, Elizabeth Kubota 1932- 13-16R
Miller, Elizabeth Maxfield 1910- 45-48
Miller, Elizabeth 1933- 117
See also SATA 41
Miller, Ella May 1915- CANR-11
Earlier sketch in CA 21-24R
Miller, Elwood E. 1925- 122
Miller, Ethel Prince 1893- CAP-1
Earlier sketch in CA 13-14
Miller, Eugene E. 1930- 135
Miller, Eugene 1925- 101
See also SATA 33
Miller, Eugenia
See Mandelkorn, Eugenia Miller
Miller, F(rederick) W(alter) G(ascoyne)
1904- CANR-11
Earlier sketch in CA 25-28R
Miller, Florence B. 1895(?)-1976 Obituary 69-72
Miller, Floyd C. 1912- CANR-2
Earlier sketch in CA 1-4R
Miller, Forrestt A. 1931- 25-28R
Miller, Frances A. 1937- 123
See also SATA 46, 52
Miller, Francis Pickens 1895-1978 69-72
Obituary 135
Miller, Frank
See Loomis, Noel M(iller)
Miller, Frank L(ubbock) IV 1951- CANR-34
Earlier sketch in CA 113
Miller, Frank 1925-1983 Obituary 109
Miller, Fred D. Jr. 1944- 129
Miller, G. R.
See Judd, Frederick Charles
Miller, Gabriel 1948- 115
Miller, Gary M(ichael) 1941- 113
Miller, Gene Edward 1928- 97-100
Miller, Genevieve 1914- 17-20R
Miller, Geoffrey Samuel 1945- 104
Miller, Geoffrey 1921-1984 Obituary 112
Miller, George A(rmitage) 1920- CANR-1
Earlier sketch in CA 1-4R
Miller, George (Eric) 1943- CANR-14
Earlier sketch in CA 73-76
Miller, George H(all) 1919- 33-36R
Miller, George Louquet 1934- 89-92
Miller, Gerald R(aymond) 1931- CANR-16
Earlier sketch in CA 93-96
Miller, Gerald 1928(?)-1970 Obituary 104
Miller, Glenn T(homas) 1942- Brief entry 110
Miller, Gordon W(esley) 1918- 89-92
Miller, Gus
See Miller, Gustavus Hindman
Miller, Gustavus Hindman
1857-1929 Brief entry 120
Miller, Hanson Orlo 1911- 138
Miller, Haskell M(orris) 1910- CAP-2
Earlier sketch in CA 23-24
Miller, Heather Ross 1939- CANR-5
Earlier sketch in CA 13-16R
See also DLB 120
Miller, Helen Hill 1899- 9-12R
Miller, Helen M(arkley) CANR-2
Earlier sketch in CA 1-4R
See also SATA 5
Miller, Helen Topping 1884-1960 Obituary 109
See also SATA 29
Miller, Henry Knight 1920- CANR-2
Earlier sketch in CA 1-4R
Miller, Henry (Valentine) 1891-1980 ....CANR-33
Obituary 97-100
Earlier sketch in CA 9-12R
See also CDALB 1929-1941
See also CLC 1, 2, 4, 9, 14, 43
See also DLB 4, 9
See also DLBY 80
See also MTCW
See also WLC
Miller, Herbert E(lmer) 1914- CANR-11
Earlier sketch in CA 17-20R
Miller, Hope Ridings 25-28R
Miller, Howard S(mith) 1936- 29-32R
Miller, Hubert John 1927- 37-40R
Miller, Hugh Milton 1908- 33-36R
Miller, Hugh 1897(?)-1979 Obituary 89-92
Miller, Hugh 1937- CANR-12
Earlier sketch in CA 61-64
Miller, Isabel
See Routsong, Alma
Miller, J(ohn) D(onald) B(ruce) 1922- CANR-13
Earlier sketch in CA 73-76
Miller, J. Dale 1923- 105
Miller, J(oseph) Hillis 1928- 85-88
See also DLB 67
Miller, J. Innes 1892-1976 .... CAP-2
Earlier sketch in CA 29-32
Miller, J(ames) Maxwell 1937- 110
Miller, J(ames) P. 1919- 25-28R
See also AITN 1, 2
Miller, J(ohn) Robert 1913- 45-48
Miller, Jake C. 1929- 126
Miller, James A. 1957- 126
Miller, James C(lifford) III 1942- CANR-10
Earlier sketch in CA 25-28R
Miller, James Edward 1945- 135
Miller, James Edwin (Jr.) 1920- CANR-1
Earlier sketch in CA 1-4R
Miller, James G(rier) 1916- 21-24R
Miller, James 1947- 137
Miller, Jane (Judith) 1925-1989 ....CANR-34
Earlier sketches in CA 77-80, CANR-13
See also SATA 15
Miller, Jason 1939(?)- 73-76
See also AITN 1
See also CLC 2
See also DLB 7
Miller, Jay W(ilson) 1893- CAP-1
Earlier sketch in CA 13-14
Miller, Jean Baker 1927- Brief entry 108
Miller, Jerome K. 1931- 105
Miller, Jim Wayne 1936- CANR-20
Earlier sketches in CA 49-52, CANR-1
See also CAAS 15
Miller, Joan (Irene) 1944- 117
Miller, Joan M(ary) 1941- 108
Miller, John
See Samachson, Joseph
Miller, John C. 1916(?)-1979 Obituary 89-92
Miller, John Chester 1907-1991 73-76
Obituary 136
Miller, John Grider 1935- 133
Miller, John Harold 1925- 5-8R
Miller, John (Laurence) 1947- 93-96
Miller, John N. 1933- 33-36R
Miller, John P(earse Jr.) 1943- CANR-27
Earlier sketch in CA 69-72
Miller, Johnny
See Miller, John (Laurence)
Miller, Jolonda 1945- 108
Miller, Jon (Gordon) 1921- 53-56
Miller, Jonathan (Wolfe) 1934- 115
Brief entry 110
Miller, Jordan Y(ale) 1919- CANR-2
Earlier sketch in CA 1-4R
Miller, Joseph C(alder) 1939- 93-96
Miller, Judi 1941- 106
Miller, Judith von Daler 1940- 69-72
Miller, Julian M. 1922-1976 Obituary 69-72
Miller, June 1923- 89-92
Miller, K(eith) Bruce 1927- 33-36R
See also AITN 1
Miller, Karl (Fergus Connor)
1931- Brief entry 107
Miller, Kenneth Dexter 1887- CAP-1
Earlier sketch in CA 13-14
Miller, Kenneth E(ugene) 1926- 21-24R
Miller, Kent S(amuel) 1927- Brief entry 109
Miller, Kerby A. 1944- 132
Miller, Lanora 1932- 61-64
Miller, Lenore 1924- 107
Miller, Leon Gordon 1917- 104
Miller, Levi 1944- 113
Miller, Lewis (Ames) 1928- 93-96
Miller, Liam 1924(?)-1987 Obituary 122
Miller, Libuse (Lukas) 1915-1973 ....1-4R
Obituary 103
Miller, Lillian B(eresnack) 1923- CANR-25
Earlier sketches in CA 21-24R, CANR-9
Miller, Lily Poritz 1938- 126
Miller, Linda B. 1937- 21-24R
Miller, Linda Lael 1949- CANR-30
Earlier sketch in CA 110
Miller, Linda Patterson 1946- 135
Miller, Luree 1926- 93-96
Miller, Lyle L. 1919- CANR-6
Earlier sketch in CA 13-16R
Miller, Lynn F(ieldman) 1938- 109
Miller, Lynn H(ellwarth) 1937- 37-40R
Miller, Lynne (Ellen) 1945- 89-92
Miller, M. Hughes 1913-1989 Obituary 130
Miller, Madelaine Hemingway 1904- 103
See also AITN 2
Miller, Madge 1918- 123
Brief entry 117
See also SATA 63
Miller, Mara (Jayne) 1944- 97-100
Miller, Marc S(cott) 1947- CANR-31
Earlier sketch in CA 105
Miller, Margaret J.
See Dale, Margaret J(essy) Miller
Miller, Margery
See Welles, Margery Miller
Miller, Marilyn (Jean) 1925- .... SATA 33
Miller, Marilyn McMeen
See Brown, Marilyn McMeen Miller
Miller, Marjorie M. 1922- 101
Miller, Marshall Lee 1942- CANR-9
Earlier sketch in CA 57-60
Miller, Martha
See Ivan, Martha Miller Pfaff
Miller, Martha Porter
1897(?)-1983 Obituary 109
Miller, Martin A. 1938- 65-68
Miller, Marvin 133
See also SATA 65
Miller, Mary
See Northcott, (William) Cecil
Miller, Mary Agnes
1888(?)-1973 Obituary 45-48
Miller, Mary Beth 1942- 61-64
See also SATA 9
Miller, Mary Britton 1883-1975 ....CANR-16
Obituary 57-60
Earlier sketch in CA 1-4R
Miller, Max (Carlton) 1899-1967 ....CANR-16
Obituary 25-28R
Earlier sketch in CA 1-4R
Miller, May 1899- .... DLB 41
Miller, Melvin H(ull) 1920- 13-16R
Miller, Merl Kem 1942- 111
Miller, Merle 1919-1986 ....CANR-4
Obituary 119
Earlier sketch in CA 9-12R
See also AITN 1
Miller, Merton Howard 1923- 134
Brief entry 109
Miller, Michael M. 1910(?)-1977 Obituary 73-76
Miller, Milt 1916- 117
Miller, Minnie M. 1899-1983 .... CAP-2
Obituary 110
Earlier sketch in CA 21-22
Miller, Miranda 1950- 132
Miller, Morris 1914- 17-20R
Miller, Muriel
See Minor, Muriel Miller
Miller, N(ewton) Edd 1920- 25-28R
Miller, Naomi 1928- 111
Miller, Natalie 1917-1976 .... SATA 35
Miller, Nathan 1927- CANR-4
Earlier sketch in CA 53-56
Miller, Neal E(lgar) 1909- 81-84
Miller, Nicole Puleo 1944- 49-52
Miller, Nina Hull 1894-1974 .... CAP-1
Earlier sketch in CA 9-10
Miller, Nolan 1912- 9-12R
Miller, Norman C(harles) 1934- 37-40R
Miller, Norman 1933- 37-40R
Miller, Nyle H. 1907- CAP-2
Earlier sketch in CA 23-24
Miller, Olga K(omarkova) 1908- 107
Miller, Orson K. Jr. 1930- 126
Brief entry 110
Miller, Osborn (Maitland)
1896(?)-1979 Obituary 89-92
Miller, Oscar J. 1913- 37-40R
Miller, Patrick Dwight Jr. 1935- 112
Miller, Paul Martin 1914- CANR-10
Earlier sketch in CA 17-20R
Miller, Paul R(ichard) 1929- 21-24R
Miller, Paul William 1926- 41-44R

Miller, Perry (Gilbert Eddy)
1905-1963 Obituary 93-96
See also DLB 17, 63
Miller, Peter G. 1945- 129
Miller, Peter M(ichael) 1942- CANR-25
Earlier sketch in CA 69-72
Miller, (Mitchell) Peter 1934- 37-40R
Miller, Philip L(ieson) 1906- CAP-1
Earlier sketch in CA 11-12
Miller, Phyllis (Steinfurth) 1920- 131
Miller, R(onald) Baxter 1948- 115
Miller, R. Craig 1946- 135
Miller, R(ay Stephans) June 1923- 65-68
Miller, R. S. 1936- 45-48
Miller, Randall Martin 1945- CANR-34
Earlier sketches in CA 81-84, CANR-15
Miller, Randolph Crump 1910- CANR-1
Earlier sketch in CA 1-4R
Miller, Raymond W(iley)
1895-1988 Obituary 124
Miller, Rene Fueloep
See Fueloep-Miller, Rene
Miller, Rene Fulop
See Fueloep-Miller, Rene
Miller, Rex 1929- CANR-30
Earlier sketch in CA 110
Miller, Richard
See Pietschmann, Richard John III
Miller, Richard (Connelly) 1925- CANR-26
Earlier sketch in CA 17-20R
Miller, Richard I(rwin) 1924- 41-44R
Miller, Richard Lawrence 1949- 134
Miller, Richard S(herwin) 1930- 21-24R
Miller, Richard Ulric 1932- CANR-17
Earlier sketch in CA 41-44R
Miller (Riis), Maurine 1910- 118
Miller, Rob(ert) Hollis 1944- 37-40R
Miller, Robert A(llen) 1932- 33-36R
Miller, Robert H(enry) 1889- 33-36R
Miller, Robert Henry 1938- 110
Miller, Robert Keith 1949- CANR-35
Earlier sketch in CA 114
Miller, Robert L. 1928- 25-28R
Miller, Robert Moats 1924- Brief entry 105
Miller, Robert Ryal 1923- 41-44R
Miller, Robin Feuer 1947- 130
Miller, Roger LeRoy 1943- Brief entry 107
Miller, Ron 1947- 117
Miller, Ronald E(ugene) 1933- 5-8R
Miller, Roy Andrew 1924- CANR-18
Earlier sketches in CA 5-8R, CANR-2
Miller, Ruby 1890(?)-1976 Obituary 65-68
Miller, Russell E(lliott) 1916- Brief entry 117
Miller, Russell 1938- 133
Miller, Ruth
See Jacobs, Ruth Harriet
Miller, Ruth White
See White, Ruth C.
Miller, Ruth 1921- Brief entry 106
Miller, S(eymour) M(ichael) 1922- 17-20R
Miller, Sally M. 1937- CANR-26
Earlier sketch in CA 45-48
Miller, Samuel Jefferson 1919- 53-56
Miller, Sandra (Peden) 1948- CANR-38
Earlier sketch in CA 115
See also Miller, Sandy
Miller, Sandy
See Miller, Sandra (Peden)
See also SATA 35, 41
Miller, Shane 1907- CAP-2
Earlier sketch in CA 21-22
Miller, Shirley 1920- 93-96
Miller, Sigmund Stephen 1917- CANR-4
Earlier sketch in CA 1-4R
Miller, Stanley L(loyd) 1930- 45-48
Miller, Stanley S. 1924- 13-16R
Miller, Stanley 1916(?)-1977 Obituary 69-72
Miller, Stephen J(ohn) 1936- 33-36R
Miller, Stuart Creighton 1927- 33-36R
Miller, Stuart 1937- 41-44R
Miller, Sue ....BEST 90:3
See also CLC 44
Miller, Susan 1944- 107
Miller, Teresa 1952- 105
Miller, Thomas Lloyd 1913- 25-28R
Miller, Timothy (Alan) 1944- 126
Miller, Tom 1947- CANR-14
Earlier sketch in CA 73-76
Miller, Tony
See Penrose, Antony
Miller, Vassar 1924- CANR-4
Earlier sketch in CA 9-12R
See also DLB 105
Miller, Victor (Brooke) 1940- 107
Miller, Wade
See Miller, (H.) Bill(y)
and Wade, Robert (Allison)
Miller, Walter James 1918- 81-84
Miller, Walter M(ichael Jr.) 1923- 85-88
See also CLC 4, 30
See also DLB 8
Miller, Warren E. 1924- CANR-11
Earlier sketch in CA 13-16R
Miller, Warren 1921-1966 Obituary 25-28R
Miller, Wayne Charles 1939- CANR-1
Earlier sketch in CA 45-48
Miller, Webb 1892-1940 ....DLB 29
Miller, William Alvin 1931- CANR-17
Earlier sketches in CA 49-52, CANR-1
Miller, William D. 1916- 13-16R
Miller, William Hugh 1905-1975 ....1-4R
Miller, William J. 1913(?)-1989 Obituary 128
Miller, William L. 1943- 130
Miller, William McElwee 1892- CANR-6
Earlier sketch in CA 57-60
Miller, William (Moseley) 1909-1989 81-84
Obituary 129
Miller, William Robert 1927-1970 ....CAP-1
Obituary 29-32R
Earlier sketch in CA 11-12
Miller, Wilma H(ildruth) 1936- CANR-30
Earlier sketches in CA 33-36R, CANR-12
Miller, Wright (Watts) 1903-1974 ....17-20R
Obituary 120
Miller, Zane L. 1934- CANR-27
Earlier sketches in CA 25-28R, CANR-12
Millerson, Geoffrey L. 1931- 17-20R
Millet, Stanton 1931- 25-28R
Millett, Allan R(eed) 1937- 21-24R
Millett, Fred B(enjamin)
1890-1976 Obituary 61-64
Millett, John (Antill) 1922- CANR-20
Earlier sketch in CA 103
Millett, John D(avid) 1912- 104
Millett, Kate 1934- CANR-32
Earlier sketch in CA 73-76
See also AITN 1
See also CLC 67
See also MTCW
Millett, Martin 1955- 133
Millett, Richard L(eroy) 1938- 117
Millezr, William Lee 1926- 127
Millgate, Jane 1937- 57-60
Millgate, Michael (Henry) 1929- CANR-28
Earlier sketch in CA 29-32R
Millgram, Abraham E(zra) 1901- 33-36R
Millham, C(harles) B(lanchard) 1936- 37-40R
Millhauser, Milton 1910- CAP-1
Earlier sketch in CA 13-16
Millhauser, Steven 1943- 111
Brief entry 110
See also CLC 21, 54
See also DLB 2
Millhiser, Marlys (Joy) 1938- 53-56
Millican, Arthenia Jackson Bates 1920- 105
See also BW
See also DLB 38
Millicent
See Jordan, Mildred Arlene
Millichap, Joseph R(obert) 1940- 116
Millies, Suzanne 1943- 49-52
Milligan, Edward Archibald 1903-1977 ....41-44R
Milligan, Spike
See Milligan, Terence Alan
Milligan, Terence Alan 1918- CANR-33
Earlier sketches in CA 9-12R, CANR-4
See also MTCW
See also SATA 29
Millikan, Ruth Garrett 1933- 128
Milliken, Ernest Kenneth 1899- 5-8R
Milliken, Stephen F(rederick) 1928- 93-96
Milliken, William Mathewson 1889- CAP-2
Earlier sketch in CA 23-24
Millimaki, Robert H. 1931- 57-60
Millin, Sarah Gertrude 1889-1968 102
Obituary 93-96
See also CLC 49
Millington, Ada
See Deyneka, Anita
Millington, Barry 1951- 119
Millington, Frances Ryan
1899-1977 Obituary 69-72
Millington, Patrick 1910-1982 Obituary 107
Millington, Roger 1939- 65-68
Million, Elmer M(ayse) 1912- 41-44R
Millis, Walter 1899-1968 ....CAP-1
Obituary 37-40R
Earlier sketch in CA 9-10
Millman, Joan (M.) 1931- 135
Millman, Lawrence 1946- CANR-38
Earlier sketches in CA 93-96, CANR-17
Millner, Cork 1931- 134
Millon, Henry (Armand) 1927- 97-100
Millon, Rene 1921- 116
Brief entry 113
Millon, Robert Paul 1932- 21-24R
Millon, Theodore 1929- 57-60
Mills, Alison 1951- 53-56
Mills, Barriss 1912- CANR-12
Earlier sketch in CA 25-28R
Mills, Belen Collantes 1930- 37-40R
Mills, Betty (Lidstrom) 1926- 9-12R
Mills, Brenda J. 1940- 120
Mills, C(harles) Wright 1916-1962 Obituary 107
Mills, Carley 1897-1962 ....1-4R
Obituary 103
Mills, Clarence A(lonzo) 1891-1974 ....CAP-1
Obituary 53-56
Earlier sketch in CA 13-16
Mills, Claudia 1954- CANR-27
Earlier sketch in CA 109
See also SATA 41, 44
Mills, Constance (Quinby)
1898-1987 Obituary 122
Mills, Daniel Quinn 1941- CANR-30
Earlier sketch in CA 112
Mills, David Harlow 1932- 104
Mills, Dorothy
See Howard, Dorothy Gray
Mills, Edward D(avid) 1915- CANR-19
Earlier sketches in CA 5-8R, CANR-4
Mills, G(len) E(arl) 1908- CAP-1
Earlier sketch in CA 13-14
Mills, Gary B(ernard) 1944- 81-84
Mills, George S(torginne) 1906- 97-100
Mills, Gordon H(arrison)
1914-1978 Obituary 117
Mills, Helen 1923- CANR-16
Earlier sketch in CA 97-100
Mills, Hilary (Paterson) 1950- 115
Mills, Irving 1894-1985 Obituary 115
Mills, J(anet) M(elanie) A(ilsa) 1894- 69-72
Mills, James R(obert) 1927- 85-88
Mills, Jeannie 1939- 93-96
Mills, John FitzMaurice 1917- 103
Mills, John W(illiam) 1933- 69-72
Mills, John 1908- 108
Mills, John 1930- 81-84
Mills, Kathi
See Mills, Kathleen Lorraine
Mills, Kathleen Lorraine 1948- 131
Mills, Leonard Russell 1917- 45-48
Mills, Liston O. 1928- 107
Mills, (William) Mervyn 1906- CAP-1
Earlier sketch in CA 11-12
Mills, Ralph J(oseph) Jr. 1931- CANR-39
Earlier sketches in CA 9-12R, CANR-3, 18
Mills, Richard W. 1945- Brief entry 112
Mills, Robert P(ark) 1920-1986 97-100
Obituary 118
Mills, Stephen (Paul) 1952- 130
Mills, Terry Kenneth 1949- 107
Mills, Theodore M(ason) 1920- 21-24R
Mills, Watson Early 1939- 57-60
Mills, William Donald 1925- 33-36R
Mills, William 1935- Brief entry 118
Mills, Yaroslava Surmach 1925- ....SATA 35
Millstead, Thomas E. 106
See also SATA 30
Millstein, Rose Silverman
1903(?)-1975 Obituary 61-64
Millum, Trevor 1945- CANR-21
Earlier sketch in CA 104
Millward, Celia M(cCullough) 1935- 53-56
Millward, Eric (Geoffrey William) 1935- 65-68
Millward, John S(candrett) 1924- 13-16R
Milman, Donald S. 1924- 134
Brief entry 111
Milman, Henry Hart 1796-1868 ....DLB 96
Milman, Miriam 1928- 112
Milne, A(lan) A(lexander) 1882-1956 133
Brief entry 104
See also CLR 1, 26
See also DLB 10, 77, 100
See also MAICYA
See also MTCW
See also TCLC 6
See also YABC 1
Milne, Antony 1942- 101
Milne, Christopher (Robin) 1920- CANR-27
Earlier sketches in CA 61-64, CANR-11
See also AITN 2
Milne, Edward James 1915-1983 Obituary 109
Milne, Evander Mackay 1920- 5-8R
Milne, (Charles) Ewart 1903-1987 ....CANR-16
Obituary 121
Earlier sketch in CA 97-100
Milne, (William) Gordon 1921- 21-24R
Milne, Jean (Killgrove) 1920- 17-20R
Milne, Lorus J. CANR-14
Earlier sketch in CA 33-36R
See also CLR 22
See also SATA 5
Milne, Margery CANR-14
Earlier sketch in CA 33-36R
See also CLR 22
See also SATA 5
Milne, Roseleen 1945- CANR-13
Earlier sketch in CA 73-76
Milne, Seumas 1958- 135
Milner, Christina 1942- 49-52
Milner, Clyde A. II 1948- CANR-26
Earlier sketch in CA 108
Milner, Esther 1918- 21-24R
Milner, Ian Frank George 1911- 104
Milner, Jay
See Morton, James (Severs)
Milner, Jay (Dunston) 1926- 1-4R
Milner, Lucille Bernheimer
1888(?)-1975 Obituary 61-64
Milner, Marion (Blackett) 1900- 9-12R
Milner, Michael
See Cooper, Saul
Milner, Murray Jr. 1935- 41-44R
Milner, Neal A(lan) 1941- Brief entry 112
Milner, Richard B(ruce) 1941- 49-52
Milner, Ron(ald) 1938- CANR-24
Earlier sketch in CA 73-76
See also AITN 1
See also BLC 3
See also BW
See also CLC 56
See also DLB 38
See also MTCW
Milnes, Eric Charles 1912-1984 Obituary 112
Milnes, Richard Monckton 1809-1885 ....DLB 32
Milns, R(obert) D(avid) 1938- 33-36R
Milo, Ronald D(mitri) 1935- 25-28R
Milonas, Rolf
See Myller, Rolf
Miloradovich, Milo
1901(?)-1972 Obituary 37-40R
Milosh, Joseph E(dmund) 1936- 21-24R
Miloslavsky, Nikolai Dimitrievich Tolstoy
See Tolstoy (-Miloslavsky), Nikolai (Dimitrievich)
Milosz, Czeslaw 1911- CANR-23
Earlier sketch in CA 81-84
See also CLC 5, 11, 22, 31, 56
See also MTCW
Milotte, Alfred G(eorge) 1904-1989 ....CAP-1
Obituary 128
Earlier sketch in CA 19-20
See also SATA 11, 62
Milotte, Elma (Moore)
1908(?)-1989 Obituary 128
Milsen, Oscar
See Mendelsohn, Oscar (Adolf)
Milson, Fred(erick William) 1912- 73-76
Milstead, Jessica L(ee) 1939- CANR-14
Earlier sketch in CA 33-36R
Milstead, John 1924- 49-52
Milsted, David 1954- 132
Milstein, Mike M(yron) 1937- 81-84
Milton, Arthur 1922- CANR-27
Earlier sketch in CA 109
Milton, Charles R(udolph) 1925- 53-56
Milton, David Scott 1934- CANR-13
Earlier sketch in CA 73-76
Milton, Hilary (Herbert) 1920- CANR-21
Earlier sketches in CA 57-60, CANR-6
See also SATA 23
Milton, Jack
See Kimbro, John M.
Milton, John R(onald) 1924- 33-36R
See also SATA 24
Milton, John 1608-1674 ....CDBLB 1660-1789
See also WLC
Milton, Joyce 1946- 106
See also SATA 41, 52
Milton, Mark
See Pelton, Robert W(ayne)
Milton, Oliver
See Hewitt, Cecil Rolph
Milunsky, Aubrey 1936- 103
Milverton, Charles A.
See Penzler, Otto
Milvy, Paul 1931-1989 Obituary 129
Milward, Alan S. 1935- 45-48
Milward, Peter 1925- 101
Mims, Forrest M(arion) III 1944- CANR-39
Earlier sketches in CA 97-100, CANR-16
Mims, George L. 1934- 129
Mims, Lambert C. 1930- 29-32R
Mims, Roddey Earl 1936(?)-1982 Obituary 108
Min, Tu-ki 1932- 138
Minadeo, Richard (William) 1929- 25-28R
Minahan, John 1933- CANR-2
Earlier sketch in CA 45-48
Minale, Marcello 1938- 108
Minar, David W(illiam) 1925-1973 Obituary 111
Minard, Rosemary 1939- ....SATA 63
Minarik, Else Holmelund 1920- 73-76
See also MAICYA
See also SATA 15
Minarik, John Paul 1947- CANR-13
Earlier sketch in CA 73-76
Mincer, Jacob 1922- Brief entry 114
Minchinton, W(alter) E(dward) 1921- CANR-29
Earlier sketches in CA 29-32R, CANR-12
Mincieli, Rose Laura 1912- CANR-4
Earlier sketch in CA 5-8R
Minckler, (Sherwood) Leon 1906- 57-60
Minczeski, John 1947- 137
Mindel, Eugene D. 1934- 41-44R
Mindell, Earl L(awrence) 1940- 105
Mindlin, Michael 1923- 133
Mindlin, Murray 1924(?)-1987 Obituary 122
Mindszenty, Jozsef 1892-1975 65-68
Obituary 57-60
Mindt, Heinz R. 1940- Brief entry 115
Minear, Paul Sevier 1906- CANR-3
Earlier sketch in CA 1-4R
Minear, Richard H(offman) 1938- 33-36R
Minehaha, Cornelius
See Wedekind, (Benjamin) Frank(lin)
Mineka, Francis Edward 1907- Brief entry 106
Miner, Caroline Eyring 1907- CANR-27
Earlier sketches in CA 25-28R, CANR-11
Miner, Charles S(ydney) 1906- CAP-1
Earlier sketch in CA 19-20
Miner, Dwight Carroll 1904-1978 Obituary 81-84
Miner, Earl (Roy) 1927- CANR-1
Earlier sketch in CA 1-4R
Miner, H. Craig 1944- CANR-16
Earlier sketches in CA 45-48, CANR-1
Miner, (Opal) Irene Sevrey (Frazine) 1906- 5-8R
Miner, Jane Claypool 1933- CANR-27
Earlier sketch in CA 106
See also SATA 37, 38
Miner, John B(urnham) 1926- CANR-20
Earlier sketches in CA 9-12R, CANR-5
Miner, Joshua L. 1920- 106
Miner, Lewis S. 1909- CAP-1
Earlier sketch in CA 11-12
See also SATA 11
Miner, Mary Green 1928- 69-72
Miner, Matthew
See Wallmann, Jeffrey M(iner)
Miner, Valerie 1947- 97-100
See also CLC 40
Miner, Ward L(ester) 1916- 9-12R
Mines, Jeanette (Marie) 1948- 119
See also SATA 61
Mines, Samuel 1909- CANR-1
Earlier sketch in CA 45-48
Mines, Stephanie 1944- 77-80
Minetree, Harry 1935- 93-96
Minford, John (Michael) 1946- 130
Mingay, G(ordon) E(dmund) 1923- CANR-11
Earlier sketch in CA 17-20R
Minge, Ward Alan 1924- 97-100
Minghi, Julian V(incent) 1933- 29-32R
Mingi, Akili
See Puri, Shamlal
Mingus, Charles 1922-1979 93-96
Obituary 85-88
Minhinnick, Robert 1952- 126
Minichiello, Sharon 126
Minick, Michael 1945- 65-68
Minier, Nelson
See Stoutenburg, Adrien (Pearl)
Minifie, James MacDonald 1900-1974 49-52
Minihan, Janet
See Oppenheim, Janet
Minimo, Duca
See D'Annunzio, Gabriele
Minio-Paluello, Lorenzo
1907-1986 Obituary 119

Minirth, Frank B. ...136
Minium, Edward W(headon) 1917- ...29-32R
Mink, JoAnna Stephens 1947- ...138
Mink, Louis Otto Jr. 1921-1983 ...104
  Obituary ...109
Mink, Nelson G. 1907- ...123
Minkovitz, Moshe
  See Shokeid, Moshe
Minkow, Rosalie 1927- ...135
Minnelli, Vincente 1913(?)-1986 Obituary ...119
  Brief entry ...117
Minney, R(ubeigh) J(ames) 1895- ...CANR-5
  Earlier sketch in CA 5-8R
Minnich, Helen Benton 1892- ...CAP-1
  Earlier sketch in CA 9-10
Minnick, Wayne C. 1915- ...25-28R
Minnigerode, Meade 1887-1967 Obituary ...116
Minnion, John (Lawrence) 1939- ...130
Minogue, Kenneth R(obert) 1930- ...5-8R
Minogue, Valerie Pearson 1931- ...132
Minor, Andrew Collier 1918- ...13-16R
Minor, Anthropopagus
  See Conniff, James C(lifford) G(regory)
Minor, Audax
  See Ryall, George (Francis Trafford)
Minor, Edward Orville 1920- ...9-12R
Minor, Marz 1928- ...103
Minor, Muriel Miller 1908-1987 Obituary ...122
Minor, Nono 1932- ...103
Minot, Stephen 1927- ...CANR-17
  Earlier sketch in CA 13-16R
Minot, Susan 1956- ...134
  See also CLC 44
Minott, Rodney G(lisan) 1928- ...9-12R
Minow, Martha 1954- ...137
Minow, Newton N(orman) 1926- ...13-16R
Minrath, William R(ichard) 1900-1971 ...CAP-1
  Obituary ...89-92
  Earlier sketch in CA 9-10
Minshall, Merlin (Theodore)
  1906-1987 Obituary ...123
Minshall, Vera (Wild) 1924- ...13-16R
Minshull, Evelyn 1929- ...37-40R
Minshull, Roger (Michael) 1935- ...21-24R
Minsky, Betty Jane (Toebe) 1932- ...5-8R
Minsky, Hyman P(hilip) 1919- ...85-88
Minsky, Marvin (Lee) 1927- ...21-24R
Minsky, Morton 1902-1987 ...135
  Obituary ...122
Minta, Stephen 1947- ...132
Minter, David L. 1935- ...CANR-12
  Earlier sketch in CA 25-28R
Minter, William 1942- ...124
Minters, Arthur Herman 1932- ...102
Minto-Cowen, Frances
  See Munthe, Frances
Minton, Henry L. 1934- ...138
Minton, Lynn ...107
Minton, Madge Rutherford 1920- ...45-48
Minton, Paula
  See Little, Paul H(ugo)
Minton, Robert 1918- ...57-60
Minton, Sherman A(nthony) Jr. 1919- ...45-48
Mintonye, Grace ...25-28R
  See also SATA 4
Minturn, Leigh 1928- ...21-24R
Minty, Judith 1937- ...CANR-21
  Earlier sketches in CA 49-52, CANR-2
Mintz, Barbara 1931- ...110
Mintz, Donald E(dward) 1932- ...17-20R
Mintz, Elizabeth E. 1913- ...73-76
Mintz, Joyce Lois 1933- ...65-68
Mintz, Lannon W. 1938-1988 ...126
Mintz, Leigh W(ayne) 1939- ...57-60
Mintz, Max M. 1919- ...33-36R
Mintz, Morton A. 1922- ...13-16R
Mintz, Norman N(elson) 1934- ...41-44R
Mintz, Ruth Finer 1919- ...13-16R
Mintz, Samuel I(saiah) 1923- ...5-8R
Mintz, Sidney W(ilfred) 1922- ...CANR-21
  Earlier sketches in CA 1-4R, CANR-5
Mintz, Steven (Harry) 1953- ...118
Mintz, Thomas 1931- ...108
Mintzberg, Henry 1939- ...CANR-1
  Earlier sketch in CA 45-48
Mintzer, Yvette 1947- ...77-80
Minus, Ed 1938- ...CLC 39
Minus, Paul M(urray Jr.) 1935- ...118
Minyard, John Douglas 1943- ...120
Miola, Robert S(teven) 1951- ...129
Mirabehn
  See Slade, Madeleine
Mirabelli, Eugene (Jr.) 1931- ...25-28R
Miracle, Gordon E. 1930- ...33-36R
Miracle, Marvin P(reston) 1933- ...17-20R
Miranda, Anne 1954- ...SATA 71
Miranda, Javier
  See Bioy Casares, Adolfo
Mirande, Alfredo M(anuel) 1940- ...115
Mireaux, Emile 1885(?)-1969 Obituary ...104
Mireles, Marina 1927(?)-1986 Obituary ...119
Mirelman, Victor A. 1943- ...136
Mirenburg, Barry (Leonard Steffan) 1952- ...101
Mirepoix, Camille 1926- ...105
Mirkin, Gabe 1935- ...129
Miro (Ferrer), Gabriel (Francisco Victor)
  1879-1930 Brief entry ...104
  See also TCLC 5
Miro, Joan 1893-1983 ...121
  Obituary ...111
Miron, Dan 1934- ...77-80
Miron, Gaston 1928- ...DLB 60
Miron, Murray S(amuel) 1932- ...81-84
Miron, Salvador Diaz
  See Diaz Miron, Salvador
Mirow, Kurt Rudolf 1936- ...130
Mirsky, Jeannette 1903-1987 ...CAP-2
  Obituary ...122
  Earlier sketch in CA 19-20
  See also SATA 8, 51
Mirsky, Mark Jay 1939- ...25-28R
Mirsky, Reba Paeff 1902-1966 ...1-4R
  See also SATA 1
Mirsky, Stanley 1929- ...110
Mirvish, Robert Franklin 1921- ...1-4R
MIS ...CANR-28
  Earlier sketches in CA 9-12R, CANR-8
  See also AITN 2
  See also CDBLB 1945-1960
  See also CLC 1, 2, 3, 5, 8, 13, 40, 44
  See also DLB 15, 27, 100
  See also MTCW
Miscall, Peter D(arwin) 1943- ...111
Misch, Robert J(ay) 1905- ...21-24R
Mische, Gerald F(rederick) 1926- ...97-100
Mische, Patricia M(ary) 1939- ...CANR-16
  Earlier sketch in CA 93-96
Mischke, Bernard Cyril 1926- ...13-16R
Mischke, Fridolin 1916- ...117
Mischke, Fritz
  See Mischke, Fridolin
Mises, Ludwig (Edler) von 1881-1973 ...CANR-19
  Obituary ...45-48
  Earlier sketch in CA 5-8R
Mises, Margit von 1896- ...CANR-19
  Earlier sketch in CA 89-92
Mish, Charles C(arroll) 1913- ...33-36R
Mishael, Bert
  See Mishael, Herbert Stanley
Mishael, Herbert Stanley
  1900(?)-1985 Obituary ...117
Mishan, E(zra) J(oshua) 1917- ...CANR-30
  Earlier sketches in CA 73-76, CANR-13
Misheiker, Betty Fairly 1919- ...9-12R
Mishima, Yukio
  See Hiraoka, Kimitake
  See also CLC 2, 4, 6, 9, 27
  See also DC 1
  See also SSC 4
Mishkin, Paul J. 1927- ...17-20R
Mishler, William (Thomas Earle II) 1947- ...125
Mishra, Vishwa Mohan 1937- ...61-64
Misiak, Henryk 1911- ...CANR-5
  Earlier sketch in CA 1-4R
Misiunas, Romuald John 1945- ...109
Miskimin, Harry A(lvin Jr.) 1932- Brief entry ...109
Miskovits, Christine 1939- ...53-56
  See also SATA 10
Misner, Arthur J(ack) 1921- ...21-24R
Misner, Paul 1936- ...138
Misra, Bankey Bihari 1909- ...104
Miss C. L. F.
  See Grimke, Charlotte L(ottie) Forten
Missen, Leslie R(obert)
  1897-1983 Obituary ...110
Miss Frances
  See Horwich, Frances R(appaport)
Missildine, (Whitney) Hugh 1915- ...77-80
Missinne, Leo E(miel) 1927- ...CANR-39
  Earlier sketch in CA 116
Missiroli, Mario 1886-1974 Obituary ...53-56
Miss Lou
  See Bennett-Coverley, Louise
Miss Manners
  See Martin, Judith (Sylvia)
Miss Read
  See Saint, Dora Jessie
Mister Rogers
  See Rogers, Fred McFeely
Mister X
  See Hoch, Edward D(entinger)
Mistral, Frederic 1830-1914 Brief entry ...122
Mistral, Gabriela
  See Godoy Alcayaga, Lucila
  See also TCLC 2
Mistry, Rohinton 1952- ...CLC 71
Mitcalfe, Barry 1930- ...110
Mitcham, Carl 1941- ...CANR-37
  Earlier sketches in CA 85-88, CANR-16
Mitcham, Gilroy
  See Newton, William Simpson
Mitcham, Samuel W(ayne) Jr. 1949- ...106
Mitchel, Jonathan 1624-1668 ...DLB 24
Mitchel, Adam
  See Pyle, Hilary
Mitchell, Adrian 1932- ...33-36R
  See also DLB 40
Mitchell, Alan 1922- ...CANR-27
  Earlier sketches in CA 57-60, CANR-8
Mitchell, Alexander Ross Kerr 1934- ...73-76
Mitchell, Allan 1933- ...102
Mitchell, Allison
  See Butterworth, W(illiam) E(dmund III)
Mitchell, Andrew W. 1953- ...124
Mitchell, Arnold 1918- ...131
Mitchell, Arthur A(ustin) 1926- ...9-12R
Mitchell, Austin (Vernon) 1934- ...CANR-12
  Earlier sketch in CA 25-28R
Mitchell, B(rian) R(edman) 1929- ...49-52
Mitchell, Barbara A. 1939- ...25-28R
Mitchell, Barbara 1941- ...117
Mitchell, Basil George 1917- ...104
Mitchell, Betty L(ou) 1947- ...110
Mitchell, Bonner 1929- ...25-28R
Mitchell, Breon 1942- ...112
Mitchell, Broadus 1892-1988 ...CANR-5
  Obituary ...125
  Earlier sketch in CA 1-4R
Mitchell, Burroughs 1914(?)-1979 ...129
  Obituary ...89-92
Mitchell, Carlton
  See Marshall, Mel(vin D.)
Mitchell, Charles 1912- ...9-12R
Mitchell, Clyde
  See Ellison, Harlan
    and Garrett, (Gordon) Randall (Phillip)
    and Silverberg, Robert
Mitchell, Colin W(are) 1927- ...73-76
Mitchell, Curtis Cornelius Jr. 1927- ...105
Mitchell, Cynthia 1922- ...106
  See also SATA 29
Mitchell, Daniel J(esse) B(rody) 1942- ...123
Mitchell, David (John) 1924- ...CANR-12
  Earlier sketch in CA 53-56
Mitchell, Don(ald Earl) 1947- ...CANR-14
  Earlier sketches in CA 33-36R, CANR-31
Mitchell, Donald (Charles Peter) 1925- ...103
Mitchell, Donald Grant 1822-1908 ...DLB 1
Mitchell, Edgar D(ean) 1930- ...53-56
Mitchell, Edward B. 1937- ...21-24R
Mitchell, Elizabeth P(ryse) 1946- ...101
Mitchell, (Sibyl) Elyne (Keith) 1913- ...CANR-21
  Earlier sketches in CA 53-56, CANR-5
  See also SATA 10
Mitchell, Emerson Blackhorse Barney
  1945- ...45-48
Mitchell, Erica
  See Posner, Richard
Mitchell, Ewan
  See Janner, Greville Ewan
Mitchell, Fay Langellier 1884-1964 ...5-8R
Mitchell, Frank
  See Mitchell, George Francis
Mitchell, Frank Vincent 1919- ...9-12R
Mitchell, Franklin D. 1932- Brief entry ...118
Mitchell, G(eoffrey) Duncan 1921- ...CANR-11
  Earlier sketch in CA 29-32R
Mitchell, George Francis 1912- ...77-80
Mitchell, Giles 1928- ...93-96
Mitchell, Gladys (Maude Winifred)
  1901-1983 ...CANR-9
  Obituary ...110
  Earlier sketch in CA 9-12R
  See also DLB 77
  See also SATA 35, 46
Mitchell, Greg 1947- ...73-76
Mitchell, Harold P(aton) 1900-1983 ...9-12R
  Obituary ...109
Mitchell, (Arthur) Harris 1916- ...119
Mitchell, Helen S(wift) 1895-1984 ...25-28R
  Obituary ...114
Mitchell, Henry (Clay II) 1923- ...130
Mitchell, Henry H(eywood) 1919- ...CANR-10
  Earlier sketch in CA 57-60
Mitchell, (William) Hobart 1908- ...119
Mitchell, Howard E(still) 1921- ...108
Mitchell, J(ames) Clyde 1918- ...CANR-9
  Earlier sketch in CA 13-16R
Mitchell, Jack 1925- ...9-12R
Mitchell, Jackson
  See Matcha, Jack
Mitchell, James (Alexander Hugh)
  1939-1985 Obituary ...115
Mitchell, James Leslie
  1901-1935 Brief entry ...104
  See also Gibbon, Lewis Grassic
  See also DLB 15
Mitchell, James 1926- ...CANR-12
  Earlier sketch in CA 13-16R
Mitchell, Jay
  See Roberson, Jennifer
Mitchell, Jeremy 1929- ...41-44R
Mitchell, Jerome 1935- ...25-28R
Mitchell, Jerry 1905(?)-1972 Obituary ...33-36R
Mitchell, Joan Cattermole 1920- ...CAP-1
  Earlier sketch in CA 9-10
Mitchell, John Ames 1845-1918 ...DLB 79
Mitchell, John D(avid) B(awden)
  1917-1980 Obituary ...105
Mitchell, John D(ietrich) 1917- ...49-52
Mitchell, John Howard 1921- ...9-12R
Mitchell, John J(oseph) 1941- ...CANR-1
  Earlier sketch in CA 45-48
Mitchell, Joni 1943- ...112
  See also CLC 12
Mitchell, Joseph B(rady) 1915- ...9-12R
Mitchell, Joseph (Quincy) 1908- ...77-80
Mitchell, Joyce Slayton 1933- ...CANR-15
  Earlier sketch in CA 65-68
  See also SATA 43, 46
Mitchell, Judith Paige ...CANR-18
  Earlier sketch in CA 85-88
Mitchell, (Charles) Julian (Humphrey)
  1935- ...CANR-39
  Earlier sketches in CA 5-8R, CANR-5
  See also DLB 14
Mitchell, Julie 1959- ...128
Mitchell, Juliet (Constance Wyatt)
  1940- ...CANR-29
  Earlier sketch in CA 45-48
Mitchell, K. L.
  See Lamb, Elizabeth Searle
Mitchell, Kathy 1948- ...SATA 59
Mitchell, Ken(neth Ronald) 1940- ...CANR-37
  Earlier sketches in CA 93-96, CANR-16
  See also DLB 60
Mitchell, Kenneth R. 1930- ...17-20R
Mitchell, Kerry
  See Wilkes-Hunter, R(ichard)
Mitchell, Kirk (John) 1950- ...128
Mitchell, Lane 1907- ...CAP-1
  Earlier sketch in CA 19-20
Mitchell, Langdon (Elwyn)
  1862-1935 Brief entry ...120
  See also DLB 7
Mitchell, Lee M(ark) 1943- ...CANR-1
  Earlier sketch in CA 49-52
Mitchell, Leeds 1912- ...89-92
Mitchell, Leonel Lake 1930- ...89-92
Mitchell, Leslie 1905-1985 Obituary ...118
Mitchell, Lionel H. 1942- ...106
Mitchell, Loften 1919- ...CANR-26
  Earlier sketch in CA 81-84
  See also BW
  See also DLB 38
Mitchell, Marcia L(ouise) 1942- ...113
Mitchell, Margaret (Munnerlyn) 1900-1949 ...125
  Brief entry ...109
  See also DLB 9
  See also MTCW
  See also TCLC 11
Mitchell, Margaretta K. 1935- ...CANR-14
  Earlier sketch in CA 29-32R
Mitchell, Marianne Helen 1937- ...85-88
Mitchell, Memory F(armer) 1924- ...37-40R
Mitchell, Otis C. 1935- ...CANR-13
  Earlier sketch in CA 37-40R
Mitchell, P(hilip) M(arshall) 1916- ...CANR-20
  Earlier sketch in CA 104
Mitchell, Paige
  See Mitchell, Judith Paige
Mitchell, Pamela Holsclaw 1940- ...CANR-6
  Earlier sketch in CA 57-60
Mitchell, Peggy
  See Mitchell, Margaret (Munnerlyn)
Mitchell, Peter M(cQuilkin) 1934- ...85-88
Mitchell, Richard H(anks) 1931- ...21-24R
Mitchell, Robert H(ughes) 1921- ...117
Mitchell, Roger (Sherman) 1935- ...25-28R
Mitchell, Ruth K. ...33-36R
Mitchell, S. Valentine
  See Gammell, Susanna Valentine Mitchell
Mitchell, S(ilas) Weir 1829-1914 ...TCLC 36
Mitchell, Sally 1937- ...110
Mitchell, Scott
  See Godfrey, Lionel (Robert Holcombe)
Mitchell, Sidney Alexander 1895-1966 ...5-8R
  Obituary ...134
Mitchell, Stephen A. 1946- ...133
Mitchell, Stephen Arnold
  1903-1974 Obituary ...49-52
Mitchell, Stephen O. 1930- ...13-16R
Mitchell, Thomas N(oel) 1939- ...103
Mitchell, W. J. T. 1942- ...CANR-14
  Earlier sketch in CA 81-84
Mitchell, W(illiam) O(rmond) 1914- ...CANR-15
  Earlier sketch in CA 77-80
  See also CLC 25
  See also DLB 88
Mitchell, William E(dward) 1927- ...81-84
Mitchell, William E. 1936- ...93-96
Mitchell, William Hamilton
  1907(?)-1982 Obituary ...107
Mitchell, Yvonne 1925-1979 ...CANR-10
  Obituary ...85-88
  Earlier sketch in CA 17-20R
  See also SATA 24
Mitchelson, Marvin M. 1928- ...104
Mitchenson, Francis Joseph Blackett ...101
Mitchenson, Joe
  See Mitchenson, Francis Joseph Blackett
Mitchison, (Sonja) Lois ...1-4R
Mitchison, Naomi Margaret (Haldane)
  1897- ...CANR-15
  Earlier sketch in CA 77-80
  See also SATA 24
Mitchison, Rosalind (Mary) 1919- ...33-36R
Mitchll, John
  See Slater, Patrick
Mitchner, Stuart 1938- ...61-64
Mitchnik, Helen 1901- ...117
  See also SATA 35, 41
Mitchum, Hank
  See Knott, William C(ecil Jr.)
    and Newton, D(wight) B(ennett)
    and Sherman, Jory (Tecumseh)
Mitelman, Bonnie Cossman 1941- ...111
Mitford, Jessica 1917- ...CANR-1
  Earlier sketch in CA 1-4R
Mitford, Mary Russell 1787-1855 ...DLB 110, 116
Mitford, Nancy 1904-1973 ...9-12R
  See also CLC 44
Mitgang, Herbert 1920- ...CANR-4
  Earlier sketch in CA 9-12R
Mitgang, Lee D. 1949- ...77-80
Mitrany, David 1888-1975 ...65-68
  Obituary ...61-64
Mitscherlich, Alexander Joseph
  1908-1982 Obituary ...107
Mitson, Eileen N(ora) 1930- ...25-28R
Mitsuhashi, Yoko ...SATA 33, 45
Mittelholzer, Edgar Austin 1909-1965 ...CAP-1
  Earlier sketch in CA 13-14
  See also BW
  See also DLB 117
Mittelman, James H(oward) 1944- ...CANR-13
  Earlier sketch in CA 73-76
Mitterer, Erika 1906- ...DLB 85
Mitterling, Philip Ira 1926- ...102
Mittermeyer, Helen (Hayton Monteith)
  1930- ...124
Mittlebeeler, Emmet V(aughn) 1915- ...57-60
Mitton, Bruce H(arold) 1950- ...108
Mitton, Charles Leslie 1907- ...CANR-4
  Earlier sketch in CA 1-4R
Mitton, Jacqueline 1948- ...97-100
  See also SATA 66
Mitton, Simon 1946- ...97-100
  See also SATA 66
Mittra, S(id) 1930- ...41-44R
Mitzman, Arthur Benjamin 1931- ...104
Mitzman, Max E. 1908- ...97-100
Miura, Akira 1927- ...117
Miura, Ayako 1922- ...73-76
Miura, Chizuko 1931- ...133
Mix, C(larence) Rex 1935- ...29-32R
Mix, Katherine Lyon ...53-56

Mix, Paul E(merson) 1934- 45-48
Mix, Susan Shank 1943- 29-32R
Mixter, Elisabeth W.
See Morss, Elisabeth W.
Mixter, Keith Eugene 1922- 41-44R
Mixter, Russell Lowell 1906- CAP-1
Earlier sketch in CA 13-16
Miyakawa, T(etsuo) Scott 1906- 17-20R
Miyamoto, Kazuo 1900- CAP-1
Earlier sketch in CA 11-12
Miyamoto, Yuriko 1899-1951 .... TCLC 37
Miyoshi, Masao 1928- 29-32R
Mizener, Arthur (Moore) 1907-1988 .... CANR-5
Obituary 124
Earlier sketch in CA 5-8R
See also DLB 103
Mizner, Elizabeth Howard 1907- 13-16R
See also SATA 27
Mizruchi, Ephraim H(arold) 1926- 41-44R
Mizruchi, Mark S(heldon) 1953- CANR-30
Earlier sketch in CA 110
Mizumura, Kazue 85-88
See also SATA 18
Mjelde, Michael Jay 1938- 69-72
Mnacko, Ladislav 1919- CANR-31
Earlier sketch in CA 29-32R
Mo, Timothy (Peter) 1950(?)- 117
See also CLC 46
See also MTCW
Moak, Lennox L. 1912- 21-24R
Moak, Samuel K(uhn) 1929- 37-40R
Moan, Terrence 1947- 97-100
Moat, John 1936- CANR-29
Earlier sketches in CA 33-36R, CANR-13
Moats, Alice-Leone 1908(?)-1989 .... CAP-1
Obituary 128
Earlier sketch in CA 13-16
Moberg, David O(scar) 1922- CANR-18
Earlier sketches in CA 1-4R, CANR-2
Moberg, (Carl Arthur) Vilhelm
1898-1973 97-100
Obituary 45-48
Moberly, R(obert) B(asil) 1920- 29-32R
Moberly, Walter (Hamilton) 1881-1974 .... CAP-2
Earlier sketch in CA 29-32
Moberly-Bell, Enid 1881- 5-8R
Mobley, Harris W(itsel) 1929- 37-40R
Mobley, Tony Allen 1938- 102
Mobley, Walt
See Burgess, M(ichael) R(oy)
Moche, Dinah (Rachel) L(evine) 1936- 89-92
See also SATA 40, 44
Mochi, Ugo (A.) 1889-1977 .... SATA 38
Mock, Edward J(oseph) 1934- 21-24R
Mocker, Donald W(ilbur) 1935- 102
Mockler, Anthony 1937- 69-72
Mockler, Mike 1945- 109
Mockler, Robert J. 1932- 33-36R
Mockridge, Norton 1915- Brief entry 110
Mocsy, Andras 1929- 65-68
Modak, Manorama Ramkrishna 1895- 97-100
Modarressi, Taghi (M.) 1931- 134
Brief entry 121
See also CLC 44
Mode, Heinz (Adolf) 1913- Brief entry 111
Model, Lisette 1906-1983 Obituary 109
Modell, Frank B. 1917- CANR-39
Earlier sketch in CA 116
See also SATA 36, 39
Modell, John 1941- 93-96
Modell, Judith Schachter 1941- 111
Modelski, George 1926- CANR-2
Earlier sketch in CA 49-52
Modert, (Betty) Jo 1921- 132
Modesitt, L(eland) E(xton) Jr. 1943- CANR-27
Earlier sketch in CA 109
Modgil, Celia 1937- 124
Modgil, Sohan (Lal) 1938- 124
Modiano, Patrick (Jean) 1945- CANR-17
Earlier sketch in CA 85-88
See also CLC 18
See also DLB 83
Modigliani, Andre 1940- 53-56
Modigliani, Jeanne 1918(?)-1984 Obituary 113
Modisane, Bloke
See Modisane, William
Modisane, William 1923-1986 Obituary 118
Modley, Rudolph 1906-1976 Obituary 69-72
Modras, Ronald E(dward) 1937- CANR-9
Earlier sketch in CA 21-24R
Moe, Barbara 1937- 69-72
See also SATA 20
Moe, Christian (Hollis) 1929- 41-44R
Moe, Edith Monroe 1896(?)-1987 Obituary 122
Moehlman, Arthur H(enry) 1907- 9-12R
Moehlmann, F. Herbert 1893- 93-96
Moelleken, Wolfgang W. 1934- 33-36R
Moeller, Charles 1912- 73-76
Moeller, Dade W. 1927- 138
Moeller, Dorothy W(ilson) 1902- 45-48
Moeller, Helen (Elaine) 1921- CANR-13
Earlier sketch in CA 21-24R
Moellering, Ralph L(uther) 1923- 13-16R
Moenkemeyer, Heinz 1914- 102
Moenssens, Andre A. 1930- 29-32R
Moeran, Brian 1944- 127
Moerck, Paal
See Roelvaag, O(le) E(dvart)
Moeri, Louise 1924- CANR-9
Earlier sketch in CA 65-68
See also SAAS 10
See also SATA 24
Moerk, Ernst L(orenz) 1937- 126
Moerman, Daniel E(llis) 1941- 105
Moerman, Michael (Harris) 1934- 25-28R
Moerner, Magnus 1924- 132
Moers, Ellen 1928-1979 .... 9-12R
Obituary 89-92
Moes, Joh(a)n E(rnst) 1926- 1-4R
Moeser, John V(ictor) 1942- 116
Moffat, Abbot Low 1901- 1-4R
Moffat, Alexander W(hite) 1891- 69-72
Moffat, Anne Simon 1947- 107
Moffat, Frances 1912- 97-100
Moffat, Gwen 1924- CANR-27
Earlier sketches in CA 13-16R, CANR-10
Moffat, John Lawrence 1916- 103
Moffat, Mary Jane 1933- CANR-17
Earlier sketch in CA 97-100
Moffatt, Doris 1919- 105
Moffatt, (Marston) Michael 1944- CANR-20
Earlier sketch in CA 85-88
Moffett, Eileen Flower 1928- 123
Moffett, George D(inwiddie) III 1943- 118
Moffett, Hugh (Oliver) 1910-1985 73-76
Obituary 115
Moffett, Judith 1942- CANR-14
Earlier sketch in CA 69-72
Moffett, Kenworth W(illiam)
1934- Brief entry 118
Moffett, Martha (Leatherwood) 1934- 37-40R
See also SATA 8
Moffett, Samuel Hugh 1916- CANR-5
Earlier sketch in CA 9-12R
Moffett, (Anthony) Toby 1944- 85-88
Moffitt, Donald (Anthony) 1936- Brief entry 111
Moffitt, John 1908- CANR-10
Earlier sketch in CA 25-28R
Moffitt, Peggy 1937- 138
Moffitt, Phillip 1946- 114
Brief entry 110
Moffitt, William J. 1930- 57-60
Mofolo, Thomas (Mokopu)
1875(?)-1948 Brief entry 121
See also BLC 3
See also TCLC 22
Mofsie, Louis B. 1936- .... SATA 33
Mogal, Doris P(ick) 1918- 69-72
Mogan, Joseph J(ohn) Jr. 1924- 49-52
Mogel, Leonard Henry 1922- 104
Moger, Allen W(esley) 1905- CAP-2
Earlier sketch in CA 25-28
Moger, Art 1911- 120
Moggach, Deborah 1948- CANR-18
Earlier sketch in CA 89-92
Moggridge, D(onald) E(dward) 1943- 29-32R
Moglen, Helene 1936- 65-68
Mogulof, Melvin B(ernard) 1926- 105
Mohammed Riza Pahlevi
See Pahlevi, Mohammed Riza
Mohan, Beverly Moffett 1918- 5-8R
Mohan, Brij 1939- CANR-29
Earlier sketch in CA 110
Mohan, Peter John 1930- CANR-10
Earlier sketch in CA 61-64
Mohan, Robert Paul 1920- 41-44R
Mohanti, Prafulla 1936- 134
Mohanty, Jitendra N(ath) 1928- 117
Moher, Francis Anthony Peter 1955- 133
Moher, Frank
See Moher, Francis Anthony Peter
Mohl, Raymond A(llen) 1939- CANR-30
Earlier sketches in CA 33-36R, CANR-13
Mohl, Ruth 1891- CAP-1
Earlier sketch in CA 13-16
Mohlenbrock, Robert H. 1931- CANR-5
Earlier sketch in CA 53-56
Mohler, Charles 1913- 29-32R
Mohler, James A(ylward) 1923- CANR-23
Earlier sketches in CA 21-24R, CANR-8
Mohn, Peter B(urnet) 1934- 106
See also SATA 28
Mohn, Viola Kohl 1914- .... SATA 8
Mohr, Charles (Henry) 1929-1989 Obituary 128
Mohr, Clarence L(ee) 1946- 137
Mohr, Gordon 1916- CANR-12
Earlier sketch in CA 25-28R
Mohr, Jack
See Mohr, Gordon
Mohr, James C(rail) 1943- 73-76
Mohr, Nicholasa 1935- CANR-32
Earlier sketches in CA 49-52, CANR-1
See also AAYA 8
See also CLC 12
See also CLR 22
See also HW
See also SAAS 8
See also SATA 8
Mohrenschildt, Dimitri Sergius Von
See Von Mohrenschildt, Dimitri Sergius
Mohrhardt, Foster E(dward) 1907- CAP-1
Earlier sketch in CA 13-16
Mohrmann, Christine A(ndrina) E(lisabeth) M(aria)
1903- CAP-1
Earlier sketch in CA 9-10
Mohrt, Michel 1914- 13-16R
Moir, Alfred 1924- CANR-24
Earlier sketches in CA 21-24R, CANR-9
Moir, Duncan Wilson 1930-1983 Obituary 110
Moir, John S(argent) 1926- 41-44R
Moir, May A(rstad) 1907- 111
Moir, Ronald Eugene 1928- 29-32R
Moise, Edwin E(variste) 1946- 130
Moise, Lotte E(lla) 1917- 103
Mojica, Jose 1896-1974 Obituary 53-56
Mojtabai, A(nn) G(race) 1938- 85-88
See also CLC 5, 9, 15, 29
Mok, Paul P. 1934- 9-12R
Mokashi-Punekar, Shankar 1925- 97-100
Mokgatle, (Monyadio Moreleba) Naboth
1911-1985 .... CAP-2
Obituary 115
Earlier sketch in CA 33-36
Mokgatle, Naboth Nyadioe
See Mokgatle, (Monyadio Moreleba) Naboth
Mokgatle, Nyadioe Naboth
See Mokgatle, (Monyadio Moreleba) Naboth
Mokres, James A(llen) 1945- 49-52
Mokyr, Joel 1946- 136
Mol, Hans
See Mol, J(ohannis) J(acob)
Mol, J(ohannis) J(acob) 1922- CANR-18
Earlier sketches in CA 49-52, CANR-2
Molan, Dorothy L(ennon) 1911- 9-12R
Molan, Pat Carlson 1941- 112
Molarsky, Osmond 1909- 25-28R
See also SATA 16
Moldafsky, Annie 1930- 61-64
Moldea, Dan E. 1950- 122
Moldenhauer, Hans 1906- CANR-3
Earlier sketch in CA 1-4R
Moldenhauer, Joseph J(ohn) 1934- 33-36R
Moldenhauer, Rosaleen 1926- 97-100
Moldon, Peter L(eonard) 1937- 121
See also SATA 49
Moldovsky, Joel S(amuel) 1939- 97-100
Mole, John 1941- CANR-18
Earlier sketch in CA 101
See also SATA 36
Mole, Robert L. 1923- 29-32R
Molen, Ronald Lowry 1929- 65-68
Molenaar, Dee 1918- 37-40R
Moler, Kenneth Lloyd 1938- 89-92
Molesworth, Charles 1941- CANR-18
Earlier sketch in CA 77-80
Molette, Barbara Jean 1940- CANR-26
Earlier sketch in CA 45-48
See also BW
Molette, Carlton W(oodard) II 1939- CANR-25
Earlier sketches in CA 45-48, CANR-1
See also BW
Moley, Raymond (Charles) 1886-1975 61-64
Molho, Anthony 1939- Brief entry 106
Moliere 1622-1673 .... WLC
Molin, Charles
See Mayne, William (James Carter)
Molin, Sven Eric 1929- 17-20R
Molina, Enrique 1910- .... HW
Molinaro, Julius A(rthur) 1918- 41-44R
Molinaro, Matie A. 1922- 128
Molinaro, Ursule 69-72
Moline, Jon Nelson 1937- 111
Moline, Mary 1932- CANR-7
Earlier sketch in CA 57-60
Molinsky, Joan Sandra 1933- 123
Brief entry 116
Moll, Elick 1907- CANR-2
Earlier sketch in CA 1-4R
Molland, Einar 1908- 53-56
Mollegen, Albert Theodore
1906-1984 Obituary 111
Mollegen, Anne Rush
See Smith, Anne Mollegen
Mollel, Tololwa M. 1952- 137
Mollenhoff, Clark R(aymond)
1921-1991 .... CANR-13
Obituary 133
Earlier sketch in CA 17-20R
Mollenkott, Virginia R(amey) 1932- CANR-12
Earlier sketch in CA 33-36R
Moller, Richard Jay 1952- 106
Mollinger, Robert N. 1945- 106
Mollo, Andrew 1940- CANR-15
Earlier sketch in CA 65-68
Mollo, Terry (Madeline) 1949- 102
Mollo, Victor 1909-1987 .... CANR-20
Obituary 123
Earlier sketches in CA 9-12R, CANR-5
Molloy, Anne Baker 1907- 13-16R
See also SATA 32
Molloy, John T. 1937(?)- 81-84
Molloy, Julia Sale 1905-1983 .... CANR-1
Obituary 110
Earlier sketch in CA 1-4R
Molloy, M(ichael) J(oseph) 1917- 103
Molloy, Paul (George) 1924- CANR-17
Earlier sketch in CA 1-4R
See also SATA 5
Molloy, Robert (William) 1906-1977 .... CAP-2
Obituary 69-72
Earlier sketch in CA 29-32
Molloy, Tom 1948- 107
Molnar, Ferenc 1878-1952 Brief entry 109
See also TCLC 20
Molnar, Imre
See Lakatos, Imre
Molnar, Maria 1910(?)-1985 Obituary 117
Molnar, Thomas 1921- CANR-19
Earlier sketches in CA 1-4R, CANR-3
Molody, Konan Trofimovich
See Lonsdale, Gordon Arnold
Molotch, Harvey L(uskin) 1940- CANR-15
Earlier sketch in CA 41-44R
Molotov, V.
See Molotov, Viacheslav Mikhailovich
Molotov, V. M.
See Molotov, Viacheslav Mikhailovich
Molotov, Viacheslav Mikhailovich
1890-1986 Obituary 121
Molt, Cynthia Marylee 1957- 138
Moltmann, Juergen 1926- 93-96
Molton, Stephen 1951- 127
Molumby, Lawrence E. 1932- 21-24R
Molz, (Redmond) Kathleen 1928- 49-52
Momaday, N(avarre) Scott 1934- CANR-34
Earlier sketches in CA 25-28R, CANR-14
See also CLC 2, 19
See also MTCW
See also SATA 30, 48
Momboisse, Raymond M. 1927- 29-32R
Momen, Moojan 1950- 122
Moment, David 1925- 9-12R
Momigliano, Arnaldo (Dante)
1908-1987 Obituary 123
Mommsen, Katharina 1925- 69-72
Mommsen, Wolfgang J(ustin) 1930- 101
Monaco, James 1942- CANR-33
Earlier sketches in CA 69-72, CANR-15
Monaco, Richard 1940- CANR-33
Earlier sketches in CA 65-68, CANR-15
Monad, Jacques 1910-1976 Obituary 65-68
Monagan, Charles A(ndrew) 1950- 109
Monagan, John S(tephen) 1911- 126
Monaghan, David (Mark) 1944- 133
Monaghan, E(dith) Jennifer 1933- 115
Monaghan, (James) Jay (IV) 1891-1981 .... 41-44R
Obituary 103
Monaghan, (Mary) Patricia 1946- CANR-23
Earlier sketch in CA 107
Monaghan, Patrick C.
1903(?)-1972 Obituary 37-40R
Monahan, Arthur P(atrick) 1928- 57-60
Monahan, Brent J(effrey) 1948- 93-96
Monahan, James (Henry Francis)
1912-1985 Obituary 118
Monahan, John
See Burnett, W(illiam) R(iley)
Monahan, Kaspar .... AITN 1
Monahan, William G(regory) 1927(?)- 132
Monas, Sidney 1924- 13-16R
Monaster, Nathan 1916(?)-1990 Obituary 131
Monath, Elizabeth 1907- 5-8R
Monbeck, Michael E(ugene) 1942- CANR-2
Earlier sketch in CA 49-52
Monbiot, George (Joshua) 1963- 132
Monclova, Lidio Cruz
See Cruz Monclova, Lidio
Moncreiffe, (Rupert) Iain (Kay)
1919-1985 Obituary 115
Moncrieff, David (William Hardy) Scott
See Scott-Moncrieff, David (William Hardy)
Moncrieff, Earnest
See Chi, Richard Hu See-Yee
Moncrieff, Martha Christian Scott
See Scott Moncrieff, Martha Christian
Moncure, Jane Belk 1926- CANR-6
Earlier sketch in CA 9-12R
See also SATA 23
Mondadori, Alberto
1914(?)-1976 Obituary 65-68
Mondadori, Arnoldo
1889-1971 Obituary 29-32R
Mondale, Joan Adams 1930- 41-44R
Mondale, Walter F(rederick) 1928- 65-68
Monday, James 1951- 61-64
Monday, Michael
See Ginder, Richard
Mondey, David (Charles) 1917- 93-96
Mondor, Henri 1885(?)-1962 Obituary 111
Monegal, Emir Rodriquez
See Rodriguez Monegal, Emir
Monelli, Paolo 1894(?)-1984 Obituary 114
Mones, Paul 138
Monesson, Harry S. 1935- 133
Monet, Dorothy 1927- 81-84
Monet, Jacques 1930- CANR-11
Earlier sketch in CA 65-68
Money, David Charles 1918- 107
Money, James (Henry) 1918- 133
Money, John (William) 1921- CANR-18
Earlier sketches in CA 45-48, CANR-1
Money, Keith 1935- 107
Moneyhon, Carl H. 1944- 120
Money-Kyrle, Roger (Ernie)
1898-1980 Obituary 101
Monfalcone, Wesley R. 1942- 109
Monfolo, Rodolpho
1899(?)-1976 Obituary 69-72
Monger, (Ifor) David 1908- 5-8R
Monguio, Luis 1908- 5-8R
Monheim, Leonard M.
1911-1971 Obituary 33-36R
Monhoff, June Hildegarde Flanner
1899-1987 Obituary 122
See also Flanner, Hildegarde
Monie, Willis J. 1945- 112
Monier-Williams, Randall Herbert
1892(?)-1984 Obituary 113
Monig, Christopher
See Crossen, Kendell Foster
Monjo, F(erdinand) N(icholas III)
1924-1978 .... CANR-37
Earlier sketch in CA 81-84
See also CLR 2
See also MAICYA
See also SATA 16
Monk, Alan
See Kendall, Willmoore
Monk, Galdo
See Riseley, Jerry B(urr Jr.)
Monk, Janice J(ones) 1937- 93-96
Monk, Lorraine (Althea Constance) 101
Monk, Raymond 1925- 136
Monk, Robert C(larence) 1930- 21-24R
Monka, Paul 1935- 29-32R
Monkhouse, Alan 1858-1936 .... DLB 10
Monkhouse, Francis John 1914-1975 .... CANR-10
Obituary 57-60
Earlier sketch in CA 13-16R
Monkkonen, Eric H(enry) 1942- 61-64
Monkman, Leslie
See Monkman, Leslie G.
Monkman, Leslie G. 1946- 125
Monmonier, Mark Stephen 1943- CANR-27
Earlier sketch in CA 109
Monnet, Jean (Omer Marie) 1888-1979 102
Monninger, Joseph 1953- 121

Monnow, Peter
See Croudace, Glynn
Monod, Jacques 1910-1976 69-72
Monod, Rene
See Koch, Kurt E(mil)
Monod, Sylvere 1921- 21-24R
Monod, (Andre) Theodore 1902- 65-68
Monongo
See Clytus, John
Monro, Gavin
See Monro-Higgs, Gertrude
Monro, Harold 1879-1932 .... DLB 19
Monro, Isabel S(tevenson) 1884- CAP-2
Earlier sketch in CA 19-20
Monro, Kate M. 1883- CAP-2
Earlier sketch in CA 19-20
Monroe, Alan D(ouglas) 1944- 57-60
Monroe, Alan Houston 1903- 5-8R
Monroe, Bill
See Monroe, William Blanc Jr.
Monroe, Carole 1944- 105
Monroe, Charles R(exford) 1905- 73-76
Monroe, Debra 1958- 134
Monroe, Elizabeth 1905-1986 .... 13-16R
Obituary 118
Monroe, Frank
See Chapman, Frank M(onroe)
Monroe, Harriet 1860-1936 Brief entry 109
See also DLB 54, 91
See also TCLC 12
Monroe, Jonathan B(eck) 1954- 126
Monroe, Keith 1917- CANR-2
Earlier sketch in CA 5-8R
Monroe, Lyle
See Heinlein, Robert A(nson)
Monroe, (Marilyn) Lynn Lee 1935- 53-56
Monroe, Margaret Ellen 1914- 5-8R
Monroe, Marilyn
See Baker, Norma Jean
Monroe, Marion
See Cox, Marion Monroe
See also SATA 34
Monroe, Ruskyn Y. (a pseudonym) 1958- 116
Monroe, William Blanc Jr. 1920- 108
Monro-Higgs, Gertrude 1905- 105
Monsarrat, Ann Whitelaw 1937- 73-76
Monsarrat, Nicholas (John Turney)
1910-1979 .... CANR-3
Earlier sketch in CA 1-4R
See also DLB 15
Monsell, Helen Albee 1895-1971 .... CAP-1
Earlier sketch in CA 9-10
See also SATA 24
Monsen, R(aymond) Joseph Jr. 1931- 9-12R
Monsey, Derek 1921-1979 .... CANR-2
Obituary 85-88
Earlier sketch in CA 1-4R
Monsky, Mark 1941- 65-68
Monsma, James E. 1929- 29-32R
Monsma, Stephen V(os) 1936- 33-36R
Monsman, Gerald Cornelius 1940- CANR-8
Earlier sketch in CA 21-24R
Monson, Charles H. Jr. 1924- 5-8R
Monson, Karen Ann 1945-1988 .... CANR-20
Obituary 124
Earlier sketch in CA 97-100
Monsour, Sally A. 1929- 21-24R
Montag, Thomas 1947- 103
Montag, Tom
See Montag, Thomas
Montagnes, Ian 1932- 45-48
Montagu, Ashley 1905- CANR-5
Earlier sketch in CA 5-8R
Montagu, Elizabeth 1917- 9-12R
Montagu, Ewen (Edward Samuel)
1901-1985 77-80
Obituary 116
Montagu, Ivor (Goldsmid Samuel)
1904-1984 .... 13-16R
Obituary 114
Montagu, Jeremy (Peter Samuel) 1927- 93-96
Montagu, Mary (Pierrepont) Wortley
1689-1762 .... DLB 95, 101
Montagu, Robert 1949- 128
Montague, Gene Bryan 1928- 93-96
Montague, George T(homas) 1929- 133
Montague, Jeanne
See Yarde, Jeanne Betty Frances
Montague, Joel B(enjamin) Jr. 1912- 5-8R
Montague, John (Patrick) 1929- CANR-9
Earlier sketch in CA 9-12R
See also CLC 13, 46
See also DLB 40
See also MTCW
Montague, Lisa
See Shulman, Sandra (Dawn)
Montague, Peter Gunn 1938- 85-88
Montague-Smith, Patrick Wykeham 1920- 107
Montagu of Beaulieu, Edward John Barrington
1926- CANR-6
Earlier sketch in CA 9-12R
Montaigne, Michel (Eyquem) de
1533-1592 .... WLC
Montaigne, Sanford H(oward) 1935- 65-68
Montalbano, William D(aniel) 1940- CANR-22
Earlier sketch in CA 105
Montale, Eugenio 1896-1981 .... CANR-30
Obituary 104
Earlier sketch in CA 17-20R
See also CLC 7, 9, 18
See also DLB 114
See also MTCW
Montana, Bob 1920-1975 Obituary 89-92
See also SATA 21
Montana, Patrick J(oseph) 1937- CANR-10
Earlier sketch in CA 25-28R
Montanari, A(delio) J(oseph) 1917- 104
Montandon, Pat 57-60
Montapert, Alfred Armand 1906- 108
Montapert, William D(avid) 1930- 107
Montclair, Dennis
See Sladen, Norman St. Barbe
Montecino, Marcel 1945- 137
Brief entry 131
Montefiore, Hugh (William) 1920- 133
Montefiore, Simon Sebag
See Sebag-Montefiore, Simon
Monteilhet, Hubert 1928- Brief entry 117
Monteiro, George 1932- CANR-7
Earlier sketch in CA 17-20R
Monteiro, Luis (Infante de la Cerda) de Sttau
1926- CANR-10
Earlier sketch in CA 13-16R
Monteith, Hayton
See Mittermeyer, Helen (Hayton Monteith)
Monteleone, Thomas F(rancis) 1946- 113
Brief entry 109
Montell, William Lynwood 1931- CANR-11
Earlier sketch in CA 29-32R
Monter, E. William 1936- 21-24R
Montero, Darrel Martin 1946- 101
Monterosso, Carlo 1921- 29-32R
Monterroso, Augusto 1921- .... HW
Montes, Antonio Llano 1924- CANR-14
Earlier sketch in CA 69-72
Montes de Oca, Marco Antonio 1932- 114
See also HW
Montesi, Albert Joseph 1921- 37-40R
Montessori, Maria 1870-1952 Brief entry 115
Monteux, Doris (Hodgkins) 1894-1984 .... CAP-2
Obituary 112
Earlier sketch in CA 19-20
Montey, Vivian M(arie) 1956- 105
Montfort, Auguste 1913- CANR-18
Earlier sketch in CA 101
Montgomerie, Norah (Mary) 1913- 105
See also SATA 26
Montgomery, Albert A. 1929- 13-16R
Montgomery, Bernard Law 1887-1976 69-72
Obituary 65-68
Montgomery, Brian (Frederick)
1903-1989 53-56
Obituary 128
Montgomery, (Robert) Bruce
1921-1978 Obituary 104
See also Crispin, Edmund
Montgomery, Charles F(ranklin)
1910-1978 81-84
Obituary 77-80
Montgomery, Constance
See Cappel, Constance
Montgomery, David Bruce 1938- 29-32R
Montgomery, David 1927- 81-84
Montgomery, Edward F(inley) 1918- 9-12R
Montgomery, Elizabeth
See Julesberg, Elizabeth Rider Montgomery
Montgomery, Elizabeth Rider
See Julesberg, Elizabeth Rider Montgomery
See also SATA 3, 34, 41
Montgomery, Elizabeth Wakefield
1891- 41-44R
Montgomery, Helen
See Gunn, Helen Montgomery
Montgomery, Herbert J. 1933- CANR-18
Earlier sketches in CA 49-52, CANR-3
Montgomery, Horace 1906- 9-12R
Montgomery, James 1771-1854 .... DLB 93
Montgomery, John D(ickey) 1920- CANR-18
Earlier sketches in CA 5-8R, CANR-3
Montgomery, John (McVey) 1919- 25-28R
See also DLB 16
Montgomery, John Warwick 1931- CANR-25
Earlier sketches in CA 21-24R, CANR-10
Montgomery, L(ucy) M(aud) 1874-1942 137
Brief entry 108
See also CLR 8
See also DLB 92
See also MAICYA
See also YABC 1
Montgomery, Marion H. Jr. 1925- CANR-3
Earlier sketch in CA 1-4R
See also AITN 1
See also CLC 7
See also DLB 6
Montgomery, Max
See Davenport, Guy (Mattison Jr.)
Montgomery, Michael B. 1950- 122
Montgomery, Nancy S(chwinn) 93-96
Montgomery, Raymond A. (Jr.) 1936- CANR-16
Earlier sketch in CA 97-100
See also SATA 39
Montgomery, Robert L(angford) Jr. 1927- 5-8R
Montgomery, Robert 1904-1981 Obituary 108
Montgomery, Ruth Shick CANR-17
Earlier sketches in CA 1-4R, CANR-2
See also AITN 1
Montgomery, Rutherford George 1894- 9-12R
See also SATA 3
Montgomery, Sy 1958- 135
Montgomery, Thomas (Andrew) 1925- 49-52
Montgomery, Tommie Sue 1942- 112
Montgomery, Vivian 102
See also SATA 36
Monthan, Doris Born 1924- CANR-37
Earlier sketch in CA 115
Montherlant, Henry (Milon) de 1896-1972 85-88
Obituary 37-40R
See also CLC 8, 19
See also DLB 72
See also MTCW
Monti, Laura V(irginia) 1930- 111
Monti, Nicolas 1956- 128
Montias, John Michael 1928- CANR-2
Earlier sketch in CA 1-4R
Monticone, Ronald Charles 1937- 73-76
Montigny, Louvigny de 1876-1955 .... DLB 92
Montini, Giovanni Battista (Enrico Antonio Maria)
See Paul VI, Pope
Montoya, Jose 1932- 131
See also HW
Montresor, Beni 1926- CANR-28
Earlier sketch in CA 29-32R
See also MAICYA
See also SAAS 4
See also SATA 3, 38
Montrose, Graham
See Mackinnon, Charles Roy
Montrose, James St. David
See Appleman, John Alan
Montross, David
See Backus, Jean L(ouise)
Monty, Jeanne R(uth) 1935- 49-52
Monty Python
See Chapman, Graham
and Cleese, John (Marwood)
and Gilliam, Terry (Vance)
and Idle, Eric
and Jones, Terence Graham Parry
and Palin, Michael (Edward)
See also AAYA 7
See also CLC 21
Mood, Alexander M(cFarlane) 1913- 53-56
Mood, John J(ordan) L(indemann) 1932- 57-60
Moodie, Graeme C(ochrane) 1924- CANR-2
Earlier sketch in CA 1-4R
Moodie, John Wedderburn Dunbar
1797-1869 .... DLB 99
Moodie, Susanna (Strickland)
1803-1885 .... DLB 99
Moodie, T(homas) Dunbar 1940- 77-80
Moody, Anne 1940- 65-68
See also BW
Moody, Dale 1915- 17-20R
Moody, Eric N(elson) 1946- 116
Moody, Ernest A(ddison) 1903-1975 .... 13-16R
Obituary 61-64
Moody, G. F.
See Hamel Peifer, Kathleen
Moody, Hiram F. III 1961- 138
Moody, J. Carroll 1934- 33-36R
Moody, Jess C. 1925- 21-24R
Moody, John (Henry) 1953- 138
Moody, Joseph Nestor 1904- CANR-1
Earlier sketch in CA 49-52
Moody, Joshua 1633(?)-1697 .... DLB 24
Moody, Paul Amos 1903- 53-56
Moody, Paul E(lliot) 1936- 118
Moody, Peter R(ichard Jr.) 1943- 130
Brief entry 107
Moody, R. Bruce 1933- 17-20R
Moody, Ralph Owen 1898- CAP-1
Earlier sketch in CA 9-10
See also SATA 1
Moody, Raymond Avery Jr. 1944- 93-96
Moody, Richard 1911- 33-36R
Moody, Ron 1924- 108
Moody, T(heodore) W(illiam) 1907- 13-16R
Moody, William Vaughn
1869-1910 Brief entry 110
See also DLB 7, 54
Mookini, Esther T. 1928- 135
Moolb, Leinad
See Bloom, Daniel Halevi
Moolson, Melusa
See Solomon, Samuel
Moomaw, Ira W. 1894- CAP-1
Earlier sketch in CA 13-14
Moon, Carl 1879-1948 Brief entry 111
See also SATA 25
Moon, Douglas Mark 1937- 17-20R
Moon, Elizabeth 1945- 134
Moon, G(eoff) J. H. 1915- 105
Moon, Grace Purdie
1877(?)-1947 Brief entry 113
See also SATA 25
Moon, Harold K(ay) 1932- 53-56
Moon, Henry Lee 1901-1985 Obituary 116
Moon, Michael E(lliott) 1948- 85-88
Moon, (Edward) Penderel
1905-1987 Obituary 122
Moon, Rexford G(eorge) Jr. 1922- 41-44R
Moon, Robert 1925- 73-76
Moon, Sheila (Elizabeth) 1910- 25-28R
See also SATA 5
Moon, Warren G. 1946- 125
Moonblood, Q.
See Stallone, Sylvester (Enzio)
Mooney, Bel 1946- 138
Mooney, Bill
See Mooney, William F.
Mooney, Booth 1912-1977 .... CANR-3
Obituary 69-72
Earlier sketch in CA 49-52
Mooney, Canice (Albert James)
1911-1963 .... 5-8R
Mooney, Chase C(urran) 1913-1972 .... CAP-2
Earlier sketch in CA 19-20
Mooney, Christopher F(rancis) 1925- CANR-14
Earlier sketch in CA 37-40R
Mooney, Edward 1951- 130
See also CLC 25
Mooney, Elizabeth C(omstock)
1918-1986 .... CANR-9
Obituary 119
Earlier sketch in CA 61-64
See also SATA 48
Mooney, Eugene F. 1930- 17-20R
Mooney, George A(ustin)
1911-1979 Obituary 89-92
Mooney, Harry J(ohn) Jr. 1927- 5-8R
Mooney, Michael M.
See Mooney, Michael Macdonald
Mooney, Michael Macdonald
1930-1985 .... CANR-21
Obituary 117
Earlier sketch in CA 65-68
Mooney, Patrick 1937- 115
Mooney, Ted
See Mooney, Edward
Mooney, William F. 1919(?)-1985 Obituary 116
Mooneyham, W(alter) Stanley
1926-1991 .... CANR-6
Obituary 134
Earlier sketch in CA 13-16R
Moonitz, Maurice 1910- CANR-2
Earlier sketch in CA 5-8R
Moonman, Eric 1929- 103
Mooradian, Karlen 1935- 97-100
Moorcock, Michael (John) 1939- CANR-38
Earlier sketches in CA 45-48, CANR-2, 17
See also CAAS 5
See also CLC 5, 27, 58
See also DLB 14
See also MTCW
Moore, Acel 1940- 69-72
Moore, Alan 1960- 123
Moore, Alice Ruth
See Nelson, Alice Ruth Moore Dunbar
Moore, Alma Chesnut 1901- CAP-1
Earlier sketch in CA 13-14
Moore, Amos
See Hubbard, George (Barron)
Moore, Andrew
See Binder, Frederick Moore
Moore, Anne Carroll 1871-1961 73-76
See also SATA 13
Moore, Archie Lee 1916- 33-36R
Moore, Arthur James 1888-1974 .... 5-8R
Obituary 49-52
Moore, Arthur 1906(?)-1977 Obituary 69-72
Moore, Austin
See Muir, (Charles) Augustus (Carlow)
Moore, Barbara
See Lee, Barbara (Moore)
Moore, Barrington Jr. 1913- 117
Moore, Basil John 1933- 21-24R
Moore, Bernard 1904- CANR-13
Earlier sketch in CA 69-72
Moore, Bidwell 1917- 33-36R
Moore, Bob 1948- 61-64
Moore, Brian 1921- CANR-25
Earlier sketches in CA 1-4R, CANR-1
See also CLC 1, 3, 5, 7, 8, 19, 32
See also MTCW
Moore, C(atherine) L(ucile) 1911- 104
See also DLB 8
Moore, Carey Armstrong 1930- 37-40R
Moore, Carl L(eland) 1921- CANR-15
Earlier sketch in CA 5-8R
Moore, Carman L(eroy) 1936- 61-64
Moore, Charles
See Moore, Reg(inald Charles Arthur)
Moore, Charles A(lexander)
1901-1967 .... CANR-3
Earlier sketch in CA 1-4R
Moore, Charles Garrett Ponsonby 1910- 108
Moore, Chauncey O. 1895-1965 .... CAP-1
Earlier sketch in CA 11-12
Moore, Christopher (Hugh) 1950- 119
Moore, Clayton
See Brandner, Gary
and Henderson, M(arilyn) R(uth)
Moore, Clement Clarke 1779-1863 .... DLB 42
See also MAICYA
See also SATA 18
Moore, Clyde B. 1886-1973 .... CANR-4
Earlier sketch in CA 1-4R
Moore, Colleen 1902(?)-1988 Obituary 124
Moore, Cora R. 1902- CAP-2
Earlier sketch in CA 25-28
Moore, Cory
See Sturgeon, Wina
Moore, Dan Tyler 1908- 5-8R
Moore, Daniel G(eorge) 1899-1977 57-60
Obituary 126
Moore, David G. 1918- CANR-2
Earlier sketch in CA 1-4R
Moore, David Moresby 1933- 112
Moore, Deborah Dash 1946- 108
Moore, Dick
See Moore, John Richard Jr.
Moore, Don W. 1905(?)-1986 Obituary 119
See also SATA 48
Moore, Donald Joseph 1929- 57-60
Moore, Dora Mavor 1888-1979 .... DLB 92
Moore, Doris Langley 1903(?)-1989 .... CANR-1
Obituary 128
Earlier sketch in CA 1-4R
Moore, Dorothea (Mary)
1881-1933 Brief entry 121
Moore, Dorothy N(elson) 1915- CANR-21
Earlier sketch in CA 89-92
Moore, Douglas Stuart 1893-1969 .... CAP-1
Earlier sketch in CA 13-16
Moore, E(velyn) Garth 1906- CAP-1
Earlier sketch in CA 11-12
Moore, Edmund A(rthur) 1903- 5-8R
Moore, Edward
See Muir, Edwin
Moore, Edward C(arter) 1917- CANR-5
Earlier sketch in CA 1-4R
Moore, Edward J(ames) 1935- 65-68
Moore, Edward M(umford) 1940- 57-60
Moore, Elizabeth
See Atkins, Meg Elizabeth
Moore, Ethel Pauline Perry 1902- CAP-1
Earlier sketch in CA 11-12

Moore, Eva 1942- 45-48
See also SATA 20
Moore, Everett T(homson) 1909- CAP-1
Earlier sketch in CA 11-12
Moore, Fenworth CANR-26
Earlier sketches in CAP-2, CA 19-20
Moore, Francis D(aniels) 1913- Brief entry 113
Moore, Francis Edward 1898- CAP-1
Earlier sketch in CA 9-10
Moore, Frank Harper 1920- 5-8R
Moore, Frank Ledlie 1923- 5-8R
Moore, Franklin G. 1905- 1-4R
Moore, G(ranville) Alexander Jr. 1937- 21-24R
Moore, Gary T(homas) 1945- CANR-15
Earlier sketch in CA 85-88
Moore, Gene D. 1919- 21-24R
Moore, Geoffrey H(oyt) 1914- CANR-19
Earlier sketch in CA 81-84
Moore, Geoffrey Herbert 1920- 109
Moore, George Augustus
1852-1933 Brief entry 104
See also DLB 10, 18, 57
See also TCLC 7
Moore, George Ellis 1916- 5-8R
Moore, Gerald 1899-1987 .... CANR-5
Obituary 122
Earlier sketch in CA 1-4R
Moore, Glover 1911- 107
Moore, (David) Harmon 1911- 13-16R
Moore, Harold A. 1913- 33-36R
Moore, Harris
See Harris, Alf(red)
Moore, Harry Estill 1897- CAP-1
Earlier sketch in CA 13-14
Moore, Harry T(hornton) 1908-1981 .... CANR-3
Obituary 103
Earlier sketch in CA 5-8R
Moore, Henry (Spencer) 1898-1986 126
Obituary 121
Moore, Honor 1945- 85-88
Moore, J(ohn) Preston 1906- 65-68
Moore, J(ohn) William 1928- 5-8R
Moore, Jack B(ailey) 1933- 33-36R
Moore, Jack L(ynne) 1920- 89-92
Moore, Jack (William) 1941- 112
See also SATA 32, 46
Moore, James R(ichard) 1947- CANR-22
Earlier sketch in CA 105
Moore, James T. III 1939- CANR-31
Earlier sketch in CA 29-32R
Moore, James Tice 1945- 73-76
Moore, James 1928- 97-100
Moore, Jane Ann 1931- 37-40R
Moore, Janet Gaylord 1905- 77-80
See also SATA 18
Moore, Jean S. 130
Moore, Jenny 1923-1973 Obituary 45-48
Moore, Jerome (Aaron) 1903- 81-84
Moore, Jerrold Northrup 1934- 104
Moore, Jessie Eleanor 1886- CAP-1
Earlier sketch in CA 19-20
Moore, Jim 1946- .... SATA 42
Moore, Jimmy
See Moore, James T. III
Moore, John A.
See Moore, John Allen
Moore, John A(lexander) 1915- CANR-26
Earlier sketch in CA 45-48
Moore, John A(ndrew)
1918-1972 Obituary 37-40R
Moore, John Allen 1912- 119
Moore, John C(lare) 1933- 49-52
Moore, John (Cecil) 1907- 5-8R
Moore, John H. 1935- 118
Moore, John Hammond 1924- 57-60
Moore, John Hebron 1920- 21-24R
Moore, John Michael 1935- 104
Moore, John Norton 1937- CANR-14
Earlier sketch in CA 37-40R
Moore, John R(obert) 1928- CANR-3
Earlier sketch in CA 1-4R
Moore, John Rees 1918- 33-36R
Moore, John Richard Jr. 1925- 17-20R
Moore, John Robert 1890-1973 .... CAP-1
Earlier sketch in CA 9-10
Moore, John Travers 1908- CANR-3
Earlier sketch in CA 5-8R
See also SATA 12
Moore, Julia A. (Davis)
1847-1920 Brief entry 116
Moore, Katharine 1898- CANR-20
Earlier sketch in CA 89-92
Moore, Katherine Davis 1915- 13-16R
Moore, Kay 1948- 130
Moore, Keith L(eon) 1925- 69-72
Moore, Kenneth Clark 1943- 102
Moore, Kenneth E(ugene) 1930- 73-76
Moore, Kenny
See Moore, Kenneth Clark
Moore, L(ittleton) Hugh 1935- 49-52
Moore, L. Silas (Jr.) 1936- 41-44R
Moore, Lamont 1909- .... SATA 29
Moore, Lander
See Fensch, Thomas
Moore, Lester L(ee) 1924- 33-36R
Moore, Lilian 1909- CANR-38
Earlier sketch in CA 103
See also CLR 15
See also MAICYA
See also SATA 52
Moore, Lillian 1917-1967 .... CANR-2
Earlier sketch in CA 1-4R
Moore, Linda Perigo 1946- CANR-28
Earlier sketch in CA 107
Moore, Lisa
See Chater, Elizabeth (Eileen)
Moore, Lorrie
See Moore, Marie Lorena
See also CLC 39, 45, 68
Moore, Louis 1946- 130
Moore, Madeline (Roberta) 1934- 124
Moore, Marcia 1928- CANR-13
Earlier sketch in CA 61-64
Moore, Margaret R(umberger) 1903- 9-12R
See also SATA 12
Moore, Marianne (Craig) 1887-1972 .... CANR-3
Obituary 33-36R
Earlier sketch in CA 1-4R
See also CDALB 1929-1941
See also CLC 1, 2, 4, 8, 10, 13, 19, 47
See also DLB 45
See also DLBD 7
See also MTCW
See also PC 4
See also SATA 20
Moore, Marie Drury 1926- 33-36R
Moore, Marie Lorena 1957- CANR-39
Earlier sketch in CA 116
See also Moore, Lorrie
Moore, Marna
See Reynolds, (Marjorie) Moira Davison
Moore, (Georgina) Mary (Galbraith)
1930- Brief entry 112
Moore, Maureen (Audrey) 1943- 135
Moore, (James) Mavor 1919- 132
See also DLB 88
Moore, Maxine 1927- 73-76
Moore, Michael
See Harris, Herbert
Moore, Nicholas 1918- 69-72
Moore, P(eter) G(erald) 1928- CANR-26
Earlier sketch in CA 45-48
Moore, Pamela 1937-1964 .... 1-4R
Moore, Patrick (Alfred) 1923- CANR-8
Earlier sketch in CA 13-16R
See also SAAS 8
See also SATA 39, 49
Moore, Paul Jr. 1919- 89-92
Moore, Paul L. 1917-1976 .... 1-4R
Obituary 103
Moore, Peter D(ale) 1942- 127
Moore, R(obert) Laurence 1940- 29-32R
Moore, Ray (S.) 1905(?)-1984 Obituary 111
See also SATA 37
Moore, Ray 1941(?)-1989 Obituary 127
Moore, Rayburn Sabatzky 1920- CANR-37
Earlier sketches in CA 1-4R, CANR-2, 17
Moore, Raylyn 1928- 29-32R
Moore, Raymond Arthur Jr. 1925- 5-8R
Moore, Raymond S. 1915- CANR-21
Earlier sketch in CA 29-32R
Moore, Reg(inald Charles Arthur) 1930- 104
Moore, Regina
See Dunne, Mary Collins
Moore, Richard B. 1893(?)-1978 Obituary 81-84
Moore, Richard H(arlan) 1945- 121
Moore, Richard R. 1934- 105
Moore, Richard (Thomas) 1927- CANR-20
Earlier sketch in CA 33-36R
See also DLB 105
Moore, Robert
See Williams, Robert Moore
Moore, Robert E(verett) 1914- 57-60
Moore, Robert Etheridge 1919- 61-64
Moore, Robert Hamilton
1913-1984 Obituary 114
Moore, Robert L(owell) Jr. 1925- 13-16R
See also AITN 1
Moore, Robert (Samuel) 1936- CANR-11
Earlier sketch in CA 25-28R
Moore, Robin
See Moore, Robert L(owell) Jr.
Moore, Robin 1950- 134
Moore, Roger George 1927- 109
Moore, Rosalie (Gertrude) 1910- CANR-3
Earlier sketch in CA 5-8R
See also Brown, Rosalie
Moore, Russell Franklin 1920- CANR-6
Earlier sketch in CA 9-12R
Moore, Ruth (Ellen) 1908-1989 .... CANR-6
Obituary 127
Earlier sketch in CA 1-4R
See also SATA 23
Moore, Ruth Nulton 1923- CANR-15
Earlier sketch in CA 81-84
See also SATA 38
Moore, S(arah) E. CANR-2
Earlier sketch in CA 49-52
See also SATA 23
Moore, Sally Falk 1924- CANR-6
Earlier sketch in CA 57-60
Moore, Samuel Taylor
1893-1974 Obituary 53-56
Moore, Sebastian 1917- 21-24R
Moore, Sonia 1902- CANR-2
Earlier sketch in CA 45-48
Moore, Steven 1951- 123
Moore, Susanna 1948- 109
Moore, T. Inglis
See Moore, Tom Inglis
Moore, T(homas) Sturge
1870-1944 Brief entry 118
See also DLB 19
Moore, Tara 1950- CANR-38
Earlier sketch in CA 116
See also SATA 61
Moore, Thomas Gale 1930- CANR-12
Earlier sketch in CA 29-32R
Moore, Thomas (William) 1940- 132
Moore, Thomas 1779-1852 .... DLB 96
Moore, Tom Inglis 1901-1978(?) 21-24R
Obituary 135
Moore, Tom 1950- CANR-18
Earlier sketch in CA 101
Moore, Trevor Wyatt 1924- CANR-12
Earlier sketch in CA 29-32R
Moore, Tui De Roy 1953- 107
Moore, Vardine (Russell) 1906- 41-44R
Moore, Virginia Dryden 1911- 17-20R
Moore, W(illiam) Glenn 1925- 49-52
Moore, Walter (John) 1918- 131
Moore, Walter Lane 1905- CAP-1
Earlier sketch in CA 19-20
Moore, Ward 1903-1978 .... CAP-2
Obituary 113
Earlier sketch in CA 29-32
See also DLB 8
Moore, Warren (M. Jr.) 1923- 25-28R
Moore, Wilbert E(llis) 1914- CANR-5
Earlier sketch in CA 1-4R
Moore, Wilfred George 1907- CANR-4
Earlier sketch in CA 9-12R
Moore, William Howard 1942- 73-76
Moore, William L(eonard Jr.) 1943- 93-96
Moore, Yvette 1958- 135
See also SATA 69, 70
Moorehead, Agnes 1906-1974 Obituary 49-52
Moorehead, Alan (McCrae) 1910-1983 .... CANR-6
Obituary 110
Earlier sketch in CA 5-8R
Moorehead, Caroline 1944- CANR-39
Earlier sketches in CA 101, CANR-18
Moore-Rinvolucri, Mina Josephine 1902- 107
Moores, Dick
See Moores, Richard (Arnold)
Moores, Richard (Arnold) 1909-1986 69-72
Obituary 119
See also SATA 48
Moorey, P(eter) R(oger) S(tuart) 1937- 132
Moorey, Roger
See Moorey, P(eter) R(oger) S(tuart)
Moorhead, Diana 1940- 105
Moorhead, Hugh S. 1922- 130
Moorhead, James H(owell) 1947- 124
Moorhead, Max L(eon) 1914-1981 .... 21-24R
Obituary 135
Moorhouse, Charles Edmund 1911- 108
Moorhouse, Frank 1938- 118
Moorhouse, Geoffrey 1931- 25-28R
Moorhouse, Hilda Vansittart CAP-1
Earlier sketch in CA 11-12
Moorman, Charles (Wickliffe)
1925- Brief entry 114
Moorman, John Richard Humpidge
1905- CANR-2
Earlier sketch in CA 1-4R
Moorshead, Henry
See Pine, Leslie Gilbert
Moorsom, Sasha 1931- CANR-14
Earlier sketch in CA 69-72
Moorsteen, Richard H.
1926(?)-1975 Obituary 57-60
Moos, Malcolm C(harles) 1916-1982 .... 37-40R
Obituary 105
Moos, Rudolf H. 1934- CANR-1
Earlier sketch in CA 49-52
Moosa, Matti 1924- 127
Moose, Ruth 1938- 101
Mooser, Stephen 1941- CANR-15
Earlier sketch in CA 89-92
See also SATA 28
Moote, A(lanson) Lloyd 1931- 33-36R
Moquin, Wayne (Francis) 1930- 33-36R
Mora, Carl J(ose) 1936- 109
Mora, George 1923- CANR-1
Earlier sketch in CA 45-48
Mora, Pat(ricia) 1942- 129
See also HW
Morabito, Rocco 1920- 134
Morace, Robert A(nthony) 1947- 113
Moraes, Dom(inic F.) 1938- 25-28R
Moraes, Frank Robert 1907-1974 .... CAP-1
Obituary 49-52
Earlier sketch in CA 13-14
Moraes, (Marcus) Vinicius (Cruz) de (Mello)
1913-1980 Obituary 101
Moraga, Cherrie 1952- 131
See also DLB 82
See also HW
Morain, Lloyd L. 1917- 69-72
Morais, Vamberto 1921- 69-72
Morales, Alejandro 1944- 131
See also DLB 82
See also HW
Morales, Angel Luis 1919- 49-52
See also HW
Morales, Jorge Luis 1930- .... HW
Morales, Rafael 1919- .... DLB 108
Morales Carrion, Arturo 1913-1989 131
Obituary 129
See also HW
Moramarco, Fred Stephen 1938- 57-60
Moran, Barbara B. 1944- 124
Moran, Charles McMoran Wilson
See Wilson, Charles McMoran
Moran, Emilio F(ederico) 1946- 117
Moran, Gabriel 1935- CANR-4
Earlier sketch in CA 53-56
Moran, George 1942- 115
Moran, Hugh Anderson
1881-1977 Obituary 73-76
Moran, James Sterling 1909- CANR-12
Earlier sketch in CA 9-12R
Moran, Jim
See Moran, James Sterling
Moran, John C(harles) 1942- CANR-27
Earlier sketch in CA 110
Moran, John 1930- 45-48
Moran, Michael G. 1947- 138
Moran, Mike
See Ard, William (Thomas)
Moran, Patrick Alfred Pierce 1917- 9-12R
Moran, Richard (Jerome) 1942- 121
Moran, Ronald (Wesson Jr.) 1936- 37-40R
Moran, Tom 1943- CANR-29
Earlier sketch in CA 111
See also SATA 60
Moran, William E(dward) Jr. 1916- 13-16R
Morand, Paul 1888-1976 Obituary 69-72
See also CLC 41
See also DLB 65
Morano, Donald V(ictor) 1934- 45-48
Morante, Elsa 1918-1985 .... CANR-35
Obituary 117
Earlier sketch in CA 85-88
See also CLC 8, 47
See also MTCW
Morantz, Regina Markell
See Morantz-Sanchez, Regina (Ann) Markell
Morantz-Sanchez, Regina (Ann) Markell
1943- 124
Morasky, Robert Louis 1940- 105
Moraud, Marcel I(an) 1917- 53-56
Moravia, Alberto
See Pincherle, Alberto
See also CLC 2, 7, 11, 27, 46
Morawetz, Thomas H(ubert) 1942- 101
Morawski, Stefan T(adeusz) 1921- 81-84
Moray, Helga 89-92
Moray, Neville (Peter) 1935- 29-32R
Moray Williams, Ursula 1911- CANR-26
Earlier sketch in CA 111
See also Williams, Ursula Moray
See also MAICYA
See also SAAS 9
Morcom, John Brian 1925- 5-8R
Mordden, Ethan (Christopher) 1947- 73-76
Mordecai, Pamela (Claire) 1942- 134
Mordechai, Ben
See Gerber, Israel J(oshua)
Mordock, John B. 1938- 61-64
Mordvinoff, Nicolas 1911-1973 73-76
Obituary 41-44R
See also SATA 17
More, Caroline
See Cone, Molly Lamken
and Strachan, Margaret Pitcairn
More, Daphne 1929- 65-68
More, Hannah 1745-1833 ...... DLB 107, 109, 116
More, Harry W(illiam) 1929- CANR-20
Earlier sketches in CA 53-56, CANR-4
More, Jasper 1907-1987 .... CAP-1
Obituary 124
Earlier sketch in CA 9-10
More, Kenneth 1914-1982 Obituary 107
Moreas, Jean
See Papadiamantopoulos, Johannes
See also TCLC 18
Moreau, Daniel 1949- 125
Moreau, David Merlin 1927- 93-96
Moreau, John Adam 1938- 37-40R
Moreau, Jules Laurence 1917-1971 .... 1-4R
Obituary 103
Moreau, Reginald E(rnest)
1897-1970 Obituary 104
Morecambe, Eric 1926-1984 Obituary 112
Morehead, Albert H(odges) 1909-1966 ...... CAP-1
Earlier sketch in CA 13-14
Morehead, Joe
See Morehead, Joseph H(yde) Jr.
Morehead, Joseph H(yde) Jr. 1931- CANR-27
Earlier sketches in CA 57-60, CANR-6
Morehouse, Clifford P(helps) 1904-1977 ..... 9-12R
Obituary 134
Morehouse, Laurence E(nglemohr)
1913- CANR-4
Earlier sketch in CA 9-12R
Morehouse, Thomas A(lvin) 1937- 124
Morehouse, Ward
1899(?)-1966 Obituary 25-28R
Morel, Dighton
See Warner, Kenneth (Lewis)
Moreland, Lois B. 45-48
Moreland, Richard C. 1953- 135
Morell, David 1939- 110
Morella, Joseph (James) 1949- 104
Morello, Karen Berger 1949- 126
Moremen, Grace E(llen Partin) 1930- CANR-1
Earlier sketch in CA 45-48
Moren, Sally M(oore) 1947- 97-100
Morency, Pierre 1942- .... DLB 60
Moreno, Antonio Elosequi 1918- 33-36R
Moreno, Baldomero Fernandez
See Fernandez Moreno, Baldomero
Moreno, Carlos Martinez
See Martinez Moreno, Carlos
Moreno, Cesar Fernandez
See Fernandez Moreno, Cesar
Moreno, Francisco Jose 1934- 29-32R
Moreno, Jacob L. 1892-1974 .... CAP-2
Obituary 49-52
Earlier sketch in CA 19-20
Moreno, Jose A. 1928- 25-28R
Moreno, Martin
See Swartz, Harry (Felix)
Moreno, Pedro R. 1947- 69-72
Morentz, Ethel Irene 29-32R
Morentz, Pat
See Morentz, Ethel Irene
Morenus, Constance Gay
1895(?)-1985 Obituary 117
Moreton, John
See Cohen, Morton N(orton)
Moreton, N. Edwina 1950- 135
Moretti, Marino 1885(?)-1979 Obituary 89-92
See also DLB 114

Morewedge, Parviz 1934- ... 93-96
Morey, Charles
See Fletcher, Helen Jill
Morey, Robert A(lbert) 1946- ... CANR-32
Earlier sketch in CA 113
Morey, Roy D. 1937- ... 17-20R
Morey, Walt(er Nelson) 1907-1992 ... CANR-31
Obituary ... 136
Earlier sketch in CA 29-32R
See also MAICYA
See also SAAS 9
See also SATA 3, 51
See also SATO 70
Morford, Mark P(ercy) O(wen)
1929- Brief entry ... 111
Morgan, Al(bert Edward) 1920- ... CANR-1
Earlier sketch in CA 45-48
Morgan, Alfred P(owell) 1889-1972 ... 107
See also SATA 33
Morgan, Alison Mary 1930- ... CANR-18
Earlier sketches in CA 49-52, CANR-1
See also SATA 30
Morgan, Alison 1959- ... 137
Morgan, Alyssa
See Delatush, Edith G.
Morgan, Angela
See Paine, Lauran (Bosworth)
Morgan, Ann Lee 1941- ... 125
Morgan, Anne Hodges 1940- ... 117
Morgan, Arlene
See Paine, Lauran (Bosworth)
Morgan, Arthur Ernest 1878-1975 ... CANR-3
Obituary ... 61-64
Earlier sketch in CA 5-8R
Morgan, Austen 1949- ... 130
Morgan, B(ayard) Q(uincy) 1883-1967 ... CAP-1
Earlier sketch in CA 11-12
Morgan, Barton 1889- ... CAP-1
Earlier sketch in CA 9-10
Morgan, Berry 1919- ... 49-52
See also CLC 6
See also DLB 6
Morgan, Bill 1949- ... CANR-30
Earlier sketch in CA 110
Morgan, Brian 1919- ... 5-8R
Morgan, Bryan S(tanford) 1923-1976 ... CANR-9
Earlier sketch in CA 5-8R
Morgan, Cary
See Cutler, Roland
Morgan, Charles Jr. 1930- ... CANR-13
Earlier sketch in CA 17-20R
Morgan, Charles H(ill) 1902-1984 ... 37-40R
Obituary ... 112
Morgan, Charles 1894-1958 ... DLB 34, 100
Morgan, Chester A(lan) 1914- ... 17-20R
Morgan, Christopher 1952- ... 105
Morgan, Claire
See Highsmith, (Mary) Patricia
Morgan, Clifford T(homas) 1915-1976 ... CANR-4
Obituary ... 65-68
Earlier sketch in CA 1-4R
Morgan, Dale L. 1914-1971 Obituary ... 104
Morgan, Dan 1925- ... CANR-14
Earlier sketch in CA 37-40R
Morgan, Daniel C(roxton) Jr. 1931- ... 17-20R
Morgan, Darold H. 1924- ... 21-24R
Morgan, Davd (Rhys) 1937- ... 45-48
Morgan, David P(age) 1927- ... 123
Brief entry ... 118
Morgan, David T(aft Jr.) 1937- ... 69-72
Morgan, Dewi (Lewis) 1916- ... CANR-1
Earlier sketch in CA 1-4R
Morgan, Donald G(rant) 1911- ... 17-20R
Morgan, Donn F(arley) 1943- ... 113
Morgan, Edmund S(ears) 1916- ... CANR-4
Earlier sketch in CA 9-12R
See also DLB 17
Morgan, Edward James Ranembe
1900-1978 Obituary ... 108
Morgan, Edward P. 1910- ... CAP-1
Earlier sketch in CA 19-20
Morgan, Edwin (George) 1920- ... CANR-3
Earlier sketch in CA 5-8R
See also CLC 31
See also DLB 27
Morgan, Elaine (Neville) 1920- ... 41-44R
Morgan, Elizabeth 1947- ... 108
Morgan, Ellen
See Bumstead, Kathleen Mary
Morgan, Emanuel
See Bynner, Witter
Morgan, Fidelis 1952- ... 127
Morgan, Frank
See Paine, Lauran (Bosworth)
Morgan, Fred Bruce Jr. 1919-1975 ... 65-68
Obituary ... 61-64
Morgan, Fred Troy 1926- ... 89-92
Morgan, (George) Frederick 1922- ... CANR-21
Earlier sketch in CA 17-20R
See also CLC 23
Morgan, G. J.
See Rowland, D(onald) S(ydney)
Morgan, Geoffrey 1916- ... 21-24R
See also SATA 46
Morgan, Gerald 1925- ... 41-44R
Morgan, Glenn G(uy) 1926- ... 9-12R
Morgan, Gwen ... 101
Morgan, Gwyneth
See Beal, Gwyneth
Morgan, H(oward) Wayne 1934- ... CANR-18
Earlier sketches in CA 5-8R, CANR-2
Morgan, Hal
See Morgan, Henry A.
Morgan, Harriet
See Mencken, H(enry) L(ouis)
Morgan, Helen (Gertrude Louise) 1921- ... 57-60
See also SATA 29
Morgan, Henry
See von Ost, Henry Lerner
Morgan, Henry A. 1954- ... 112
Morgan, Hilda Campbell
1892-1985 Obituary ... 118
Morgan, Irvonwy 1907-1982 Obituary ... 107
Morgan, J(ill) M(eredith) 1946- ... 137
Morgan, James N(ewton) 1918- ... 21-24R
Morgan, Jane
See Cooper, James Fenimore
and Moren, Sally M(oore)
Morgan, Janet 1945- ... 65-68
See also CLC 39
Morgan, Jean (Werner) 1922- ... 102
Morgan, (Walter) Jefferson 1940- ... CANR-29
Earlier sketches in CA 73-76, CANR-12
Morgan, Jim 1950- ... 45-48
Morgan, Joan 1905- ... 5-8R
Morgan, Joe Warner 1912- ... 9-12R
Morgan, John
See Paine, Lauran (Bosworth)
Morgan, John A(ndrew) Jr. 1935- ... 49-52
Morgan, John S. 1921- ... 13-16R
Morgan, Joy Elmer 1889-1986 Obituary ... 119
Morgan, Judith A(dams) 1939- ... 49-52
Morgan, Kathryn L. ... 117
Morgan, Kay Summersby
1909-1975 Obituary ... 53-56
Morgan, Kenneth Owen 1934- ... CANR-23
Earlier sketches in CA 13-16R, CANR-7
Morgan, Kenneth R(emsen) 1916- ... 13-16R
Morgan, Lady 1776(?)-1859 ... DLB 116
Morgan, Lael 1936- ... CANR-5
Earlier sketch in CA 53-56
Morgan, Lenore H. 1908-1976 ... CAP-2
Earlier sketch in CA 33-36
See also SATA 8
Morgan, Louise ... 9-12R
Morgan, Lucy 1940- ... 108
Morgan, M(argaret) Ruth
1942(?)-1983 Obituary ... 109
Morgan, Marabel 1937- ... CANR-2
Earlier sketch in CA 49-52
See also AITN 1
Morgan, Marion (Nora Eluned) 1942- ... 120
Morgan, Marjorie
See Chibnall, Marjorie (McCallum)
Morgan, Mark
See Overholser, Wayne D.
Morgan, Mary 1943- ... 132
Morgan, McKayla
See Basile, Gloria Vitanza
Morgan, Memo
See Avallone, Michael (Angelo, Jr)
Morgan, Meredith
See Morgan, J(ill) M(eredith)
Morgan, Michael Croke 1911- ... 93-96
Morgan, Michaela
See Basile, Gloria Vitanza
Morgan, Murray 1916- ... 107
Morgan, Neil 1924- ... CANR-2
Earlier sketch in CA 5-8R
Morgan, Nicholas
See Morgan, Thomas Bruce
Morgan, Patricia 1944- ... 89-92
Morgan, Patrick M. 1940- ... 37-40R
Morgan, Paul 1928- ... 61-64
Morgan, (Colin) Pete(r) 1939- ... 133
Morgan, Peter F(rederick) 1930- ... 113
Morgan, Raleigh Jr. 1916- ... 41-44R
Morgan, Rebecca
See Forrest, Richard (Stockton)
Morgan, Richard E(rnest) 1937- ... CANR-15
Earlier sketch in CA 41-44R
Morgan, Robert
See Turner, Robert (Harry)
Morgan, Robert (R.) 1944- ... CANR-21
Earlier sketch in CA 33-36R
See also DLB 120
Morgan, Robert 1921- ... CANR-20
Earlier sketch in CA 103
Morgan, Roberta 1953- ... CANR-15
Earlier sketch in CA 93-96
Morgan, Robin 1941- ... CANR-29
Earlier sketch in CA 69-72
See also CLC 2
See also MTCW
Morgan, Roger P(earce) 1932- ... CANR-12
Earlier sketch in CA 17-20R
Morgan, Rosemarie (Anne Louise) ... 131
Morgan, Roy A(mos) 1916- ... 41-44R
Morgan, Ruth P. 1934- ... 37-40R
Morgan, Sally (Jane) 1951- ... 134
Morgan, Sarah (Nicola) 1959- ... 136
See also SATA 68
Morgan, Sarah (Williams) 1901- ... CAP-1
Earlier sketch in CA 9-10
Morgan, Scott
See Kuttner, Henry
Morgan, Seth 1949(?)-1990 Obituary ... 132
See also CLC 65
Morgan, Sharon A(ntonia) 1951- ... 61-64
Morgan, Shirley
See Kiepper, Shirley Morgan
See also SATA 10
Morgan, Speer 1946- ... 97-100
Morgan, Stanley 1929- ... 69-72
Morgan, Steven Michael 1942- ... 115
Morgan, Susan 1943- ... 137
Morgan, Ted 1932- ... CANR-3
See also CAAS 4
Morgan, (Joseph) Theodore 1910- ... 17-20R
See also CAAS 3
Morgan, Thomas (Bruce)
1885(?)-1972 Obituary ... 37-40R
Morgan, Thomas Bruce 1926- ... 13-16R
Morgan, Tom 1942- ... 108
See also SATA 42
Morgan, Valerie
See Paine, Lauran (Bosworth)
Morgan, Virginia
See Mundis, Hester
Morgan, Wesley
See Bennett, Isadora
Morgan, William 1944- ... 109
Morgan-Grenville, Gerard (Wyndham)
1931- ... 57-60
Morgan Witts, Max 1931- ... 29-32R
Morgello, Clemente Frank 1923- ... 103
Morgenroth, Barbara Brief entry ... 117
See also SATA 36
Morgenstein, Gary 1952- ... 116
Morgenstern, Christian
1871-1914 Brief entry ... 105
See also TCLC 8
Morgenstern, Dan (Michael) 1929- ... 127
Brief entry ... 111
Morgenstern, Julian 1881-1976 ... CAP-1
Obituary ... 89-92
Earlier sketch in CA 19-20
Morgenstern, Oskar 1902-1977 ... CANR-5
Obituary ... 73-76
Earlier sketch in CA 9-12R
Morgenstern, S.
See Goldman, William (W.)
Morgenstern, Soma
1891(?)-1976 Obituary ... 65-68
Morgenthau, Hans Joachim 1904-1980 ... 9-12R
Obituary ... 101
Morgenthau, Henry Jr. 1891-1967 Obituary ... 116
Morghen, Raffaello 1896-1983 Obituary ... 109
Morgner, Irmtraud 1933- ... DLB 75
Morgulas, Jerrold 1934- ... CANR-13
Earlier sketch in CA 21-24R
Morhaim, Victoria Kelrich 1937- ... 1-4R
Mori, Kyozo 1907(?)-1984 Obituary ... 112
Mori, Toshio 1910- Brief entry ... 116
Moriarty, Alice Marie Ewell 1917- ... 21-24R
Moriarty, Christopher 1936- ... 81-84
Moriarty, Florence Jarman ... 104
Moriarty, Frederick Leo 1913- ... CANR-2
Earlier sketch in CA 5-8R
Moriarty, Tim 1923- ... 61-64
Morice, Anne
See Shaw, Felicity
Morice, Dave 1946- ... 109
Morich, Stanton
See Griffith-Jones, George Chetwynd
Morick, Harold 1933- ... 25-28R
Moricz, Zsigmond 1879-1942 ... TCLC 33
Morier, James Justinian 1782(?)-1849 ... DLB 116
Morin, Claire
See Dore, Claire (Morin)
Morin, Edgar 1921- ... 107
Morin, Paul 1889-1963 ... DLB 92
Morin, Relman George 1907-1973 ... CANR-4
Obituary ... 41-44R
Earlier sketch in CA 1-4R
Morin, William J(ames) 1939- ... 111
Morine, Hoder
See Conroy, John Wesley
Moringstar, Mildred 1912- ... 127
Morini, Simona 1932- ... 110
Mori Ogai
See Mori Rintaro
See also TCLC 14
Mori Rintaro 1862-1922 Brief entry ... 110
See also Mori Ogai
Morisey, A. Alexander
1913-1979 Obituary ... 89-92
Morison, David Lindsay 1920- ... 13-16R
Morison, Samuel Eliot 1887-1976 ... CANR-4
Obituary ... 65-68
Earlier sketch in CA 1-4R
See also DLB 17
Morisseau, James J(oseph) 1929- ... 41-44R
Morita, James R. 1931- ... 103
Morita, Yuzo 1940- ... CANR-1
Earlier sketch in CA 45-48
Moritz, A(lbert) F(rank) 1947- ... 110
Moritz, Charles Fredric 1917- ... 118
Moritz, Karl Philipp 1756-1793 ... DLB 94
Moritz, Theresa
See Moritz, Theresa Anne
Moritz, Theresa Anne 1948- ... 127
Morken, Lucinda Oakland 1906- ... 61-64
Morkovin, Bela V.
See Morkovin, Boris V(ladimir)
Morkovin, Boris V(ladimir) 1882-1968 ... CAP-1
Earlier sketch in CA 19-20
Morlan, George K(olmer) 1904- ... 29-32R
Morlan, John E(dmund) 1930- ... 9-12R
Morlan, Robert L(oren) 1920-1985 ... 17-20R
Obituary ... 118
Morland, Dick
See Hill, Reginald (Charles)
Morland, Howard 1942- ... 107
Morland, (John) Kenneth 1916- ... 41-44R
Morland, Nigel 1905-1986 ... 53-56
Obituary ... 119
Morland, Peter Henry
See Faust, Frederick (Shiller)
Morle, Albert Henry George 1919- ... 5-8R
Morley, Christopher (Darlington)
1890-1957 Brief entry ... 112
See also DLB 9
Morley, David 1923- ... 108
Morley, Don 1937- ... 108
Morley, Felix M. 1894-1982 Obituary ... 106
Morley, Frank V(igor) 1899-1980 ... 105
Obituary ... 102
Morley, (John) Geoffrey (Nicholson)
1905-1983 Obituary ... 109
Morley, Hugh 1908(?)-1978 Obituary ... 77-80
Morley, James William 1921- ... 13-16R
Morley, John(athan) David 1948- ... 126
Morley, John F(rancis) 1936- ... 132
Morley, John 1838-1923 ... DLB 57
Morley, Patricia (Ann) 1929- ... 73-76
Morley, R.
See Morley, Robert (Adolph Wilton)
Morley, Robert (Adolph Wilton) 1908- ... 130
Obituary ... 137
Brief entry ... 113
Morley, S(ylvanus) Griswold 1878- ... 5-8R
Morley, Samuel A. 1934- ... 37-40R
Morley, Sheridan 1941- ... 29-32R
Morley, Steve 1953- ... 132
Morley, Susan
See Cross, John Keir
Morley, Wilfred Owen
See Lowndes, Robert A(ugustine) W(ard)
Morman, Jean Mary 1925- ... 61-64
Morn, Frank T(homas) 1937- ... 107
Morneau, Robert Fealey 1938- ... 113
Mornell, Pierre 1935- ... 131
Morner, Magnus
See Moerner, Magnus
Morningstar, Connie 1927- ... 69-72
Morningstar, Mildred 1912- ... SATA 61
Moro, Cesar 1903-1956 ... 131
See also HW
Moroney, John R. 1939- ... CANR-17
Earlier sketch in CA 41-44R
Morowitz, Harold Joseph 1927- ... 104
Morpurgo, J(ack) E(ric) 1918- ... CANR-4
Earlier sketch in CA 9-12R
Morra, Marion Eleanor ... 104
Morra, Umberto Obituary ... 105
Morrah, Dave
See Morrah, David Wardlaw Jr.
Morrah, David Wardlaw Jr. 1914-1991 ... 1-4R
Obituary ... 134
See also SATA 10
Morrah, Dermot (Michael Macgregor)
1896-1974 ... CAP-2
Obituary ... 53-56
Earlier sketch in CA 29-32
Morrall, John B. 1923- ... 25-28R
Morray, Joseph Parker 1916- ... 5-8R
Morreale, Ben 1924- ... 57-60
Morrell, David C. 1929- ... 81-84
Morrell, David 1943- ... CANR-7
Earlier sketch in CA 57-60
Morrell, Robert E(llis) 1930- ... 121
Morrell, William Parker 1899- ... CANR-1
Earlier sketch in CA 1-4R
Morren, Theophil
See Hofmannsthal, Hugo von
Morressy, John 1930- ... CANR-28
Earlier sketches in CA 21-24R, CANR-8
See also SATA 23
Morrice, J(ames) K(enneth) W(att) 1924- ... 118
Morrice, Ken
See Morrice, J(ames) K(enneth) W(att)
Morrie
See Turner, Morris
Morrill, Allen C(onrad) 1904- ... 101
Morrill, Claire 1900(?)-1981 Obituary ... 103
Morrill, Eleanor D(unlap) 1907- ... 101
Morrill, George Percival 1920- ... 33-36R
Morrill, John S. 1946- ... 130
Morrill, Leslie H(olt) 1934- ... MAICYA
See also SATA 33, 48
Morrill, Richard
See Schreck, Everett M.
Morrill, Richard L(eland) 1934- ... CANR-35
Earlier sketch in CA 29-32R
Morris, A(ndrew) J(ames) A(nthony)
1936- ... CANR-12
Earlier sketch in CA 73-76
Morris, Adalaide K(irby) 1942- ... 57-60
Morris, Aldyth V. 1901- ... 29-32R
Morris, Alton C(hester) 1903- ... 13-16R
Morris, Ben(jamin Stephen) 1910-1990 ... 113
Obituary ... 132
Morris, Berenice Robinson
1909(?)-1990 Obituary ... 132
Morris, Bernadine (Taub) 1925- ... 102
Morris, Bertram 1908- ... CANR-18
Earlier sketch in CA 1-4R
Morris, Brian 1930- ... CANR-18
Earlier sketch in CA 29-32R
Morris, Bruce R(obert) 1909- ... 5-8R
Morris, C(harles) R(ichard)
1898-1990 Obituary ... 131
Morris, Celia 1935- ... 138
Morris, Charles Lee 1943(?)-1986 Obituary ... 118
Morris, Charles (William) 1901-1979 ... 13-16R
Obituary ... 135
Morris, Chris(topher Crosby) 1946- ... 133
See also SATA 66
Morris, Christopher 1938- ... 21-24R
Morris, Clyde M(cMahon) 1921- ... 93-96
Morris, (Edward) Craig 1939- ... 123
Morris, Cynthia Taft 1928- ... 25-28R
Morris, Dan (H.) 1912- ... 21-24R
Morris, David Brown 1942- ... CANR-22
Earlier sketch in CA 105
Morris, David 1945- ... 85-88
Morris, Desmond (John) 1928- ... CANR-38
Earlier sketches in CA 45-48, CANR-2, 18
See also MTCW
See also SATA 14
Morris, Donald R. 1924- ... 17-20R
Morris, Edgar Poe
See Kinnaird, Clark
Morris, Edita (deToll) ... CANR-1
Earlier sketch in CA 1-4R
Morris, Edmund 1940- ... 89-92

Morris, (Murrell) Edward 1935- CANR-31
Earlier sketches in CA 69-72, CANR-14
Morris, Edwin Bateman
1881-1971 Obituary 112
Morris, Eric 1940- 81-84
Morris, Everett B. 1899-1967 ....CAP-1
Earlier sketch in CA 9-10
Morris, Freda 1933- CANR-4
Earlier sketch in CA 53-56
Morris, George Pope 1802-1864 .... DLB 73
Morris, Gilbert (Leslie) 1929- 117
Morris, Grant Harold 1940- 29-32R
Morris, Gregory L(ynn) 1950- 119
Morris, Harry (Caesar) 1924- 9-12R
Morris, Harvey 1946- 134
Morris, Helen 1909- CANR-18
Earlier sketch in CA 101
Morris, Henry M(adison Jr.) 1918- CANR-29
Earlier sketches in CA 37-40R, CANR-13
Morris, Herbert 1928- CANR-1
Earlier sketch in CA 1-4R
Morris, Ira (Victor) 1903- 9-12R
Morris, Ivan (Ira Esme) 1925-1976 ....CANR-11
Obituary 65-68
Earlier sketch in CA 9-12R
Morris, J(ohn) H(umphrey) C(arlile) 1910- 5-8R
Morris, J(ames) Kenneth 1896- 5-8R
Morris, J. R. 1914(?)-1977 Obituary 73-76
Morris, Jackson E(dgar) 1918- 17-20R
Morris, James A(lvin) 1938- 120
Morris, James E(lliot) 1942- 112
Morris, James (Humphrey)
See Morris, Jan
Morris, James M(atthew) 1935- 89-92
Morris, Jan 1926- CANR-1
Earlier sketch in CA 1-4R
See also MTCW
Morris, Jane
See Ardmore, Jane Kesner
Morris, Janet (Ellen) 1946- CANR-35
Earlier sketches in CA 73-76, CANR-13
See also SATA 66
Morris, (Margaret) Jean 1924- Brief entry 116
Morris, Jerrold 1911- CANR-11
Earlier sketch in CA 21-24R
Morris, Joan 1901- 45-48
Morris, Joe A(lex) 1904-1990 65-68
Obituary 130
Morris, Joe Alex Jr. 1927- 73-76
Morris, John
See Hearne, John (Edgar Caulwell)
Morris, John D(avid) 1946- 111
Morris, John N(elson) 1931- 33-36R
See also CAAS 13
Morris, John O(sgood) 1918- 41-44R
Morris, John W(esley) 1907- CANR-6
Earlier sketch in CA 13-16R
Morris, John 1895-1980 Obituary 102
Morris, Jonas 1933- 117
Morris, Judy K. 1936- 116
See also SATA 61
Morris, Julian
See West, Morris L(anglo)
Morris, Katharine CAP-1
Earlier sketch in CA 13-16
Morris, Kenneth Earl 1955- 127
Morris, Kenneth T(hompson) 1941- 57-60
Morris, Kevin L. 1954- 129
Morris, Leon (Lamb) 1914- CANR-20
Earlier sketches in CA 9-12R, CANR-4
Morris, Lewis 1833-1907 .... DLB 35
Morris, Loverne Lawton 1896- 5-8R
Morris, M.
See Thibaudeau, Colleen
Morris, Margaret Francine 1938- 57-60
Morris, Margaret 1891-1980 Obituary 97-100
Morris, Mary (Elizabeth Davis) 1913-1986 53-56
Obituary 121
Morris, Mary Lee 120
Morris, Mary 1947- 132
Morris, Max 1913- 109
Morris, Mel (Merrill) 1930- 69-72
Morris, Michael (Spence Lowdell)
1940- CANR-23
Earlier sketch in CA 107
Morris, Michael 1914- CANR-5
Earlier sketch in CA 5-8R
Morris, Michelle 1941- 108
Morris, Milton D(onald) 1939- 57-60
Morris, Monica B. 1928- Brief entry 113
Morris, Nobuko
See Albery, Nobuko
Morris, Norman S. 1931- 33-36R
Morris, Norval 1923- 37-40R
Morris, Phyllis Sutton 1931- 104
Morris, Phyllis 1894-1982 Obituary 106
Morris, R(oger) J(ohn) B(owring) 1946- 93-96
Morris, Raymond N. 1936- 25-28R
Morris, Raymond Philip 1904- 45-48
Morris, Richard B(randon) 1904-1989 ......CANR-2
Obituary 128
Earlier sketch in CA 49-52
See also DLB 17
Morris, Richard J(ules) 1942- CANR-16
Earlier sketch in CA 89-92
Morris, Richard K(nowles) 1915- 21-24R
Morris, Richard (Ward) 1939- CANR-39
Earlier sketches in CA 45-48, CANR-1, 18
Morris, Robert A(da) 1933- 49-52
See also SATA 7
Morris, Robert C. 1942- 135
Morris, Robert Kerwin 1933- 33-36R
Morris, Robert (Lyle) 1942- Brief entry 116
Morris, Robert 1910- CANR-16
Earlier sketch in CA 89-92
Morris, Ruby Turner 1908- CANR-1
Earlier sketch in CA 1-4R
Morris, Ruth
See Webb, Ruth Enid Borlase Morris
Morris, Sara
See Burke, John (Frederick)
Morris, Sarah M(iller) 1906- 81-84
Morris, Scot 1942- 101
Morris, Stephen 1935- CANR-20
Earlier sketch in CA 103
Morris, Steveland Judkins
1950(?)- Brief entry 111
See also Wonder, Stevie
Morris, Suzanne 1944- CANR-17
Earlier sketch in CA 89-92
Morris, T(homas) B(aden) 1900- CANR-2
Earlier sketch in CA 5-8R
Morris, Taylor 1923- 103
Morris, Terry Lesser 1914- 9-12R
Morris, Thomas D(ean) 1938- Brief entry 112
Morris, Thomas Victor 1952- 120
Morris, Tina 1941- CANR-12
Earlier sketch in CA 29-32R
Morris, W. R. 1936- 77-80
Morris, William E(dgar) 1926- 9-12R
Morris, William O. 1922- 37-40R
Morris, William T(homas) 1928- 17-20R
Morris, William 1834-1896 ..... CDBLB 1832-1890
See also DLB 18, 35, 57
Morris, William 1913- CANR-12
Earlier sketch in CA 17-20R
See also SATA 29
Morris, Willie 1934- CANR-13
Earlier sketch in CA 17-20R
See also AITN 2
See also DLBY 80
Morris, Wright 1910- CANR-21
Earlier sketch in CA 9-12R
See also CLC 1, 3, 7, 18, 37
See also DLB 2
See also DLBY 81
See also MTCW
Morrisey, George L(ewis) 1926- CANR-14
Earlier sketch in CA 73-76
Morris-Goodall, Vanne 1909- 29-32R
Morrish, (Ernest) Ivor (James) 1914- 33-36R
Morris-Jones, W(yndraeth) H(umphreys)
1918- CANR-11
Earlier sketch in CA 21-24R
Morrison, Arnold Telford 1928- 110
Morrison, Arthur 1863-1945 Brief entry 120
See also DLB 70
Morrison, Bill 1935- 135
Brief entry 115
See also SATA 37, 66
Morrison, (Philip) Blake 1950- 138
Morrison, Bruce 1904(?)-1983 Obituary 109
Morrison, Carl V(incent) 1908- 93-96
Morrison, Charles Clayton
1874-1966 Obituary 89-92
See also DLB 91
Morrison, Cheryl 1947- 107
Morrison, Chloe Anthony Wofford
See Morrison, Toni
Morrison, Claudia C(hristopherson)
1936- 29-32R
Morrison, Clinton (Dawson Jr.) 1924- 13-16R
Morrison, David (Douglas) 1940- CANR-30
Earlier sketch in CA 112
Morrison, Denton E(dward) 1932- CANR-6
Earlier sketch in CA 57-60
Morrison, Donald George 1938- 85-88
Morrison, Dorothy Nafus CANR-24
Earlier sketches in CA 61-64, CANR-8
See also SATA 29
Morrison, Edward
See Humphrey, Paul
Morrison, Eleanor S(helton) 1921- CANR-1
Earlier sketch in CA 49-52
Morrison, Eula Atwood 1911- 25-28R
Morrison, Frank G. 1894(?)-1983 Obituary 111
Morrison, Frank M. 1914- 37-40R
Morrison, Fred L. 1939- Brief entry 112
Morrison, Gertrude W. CANR-26
Earlier sketches in CAP-2, CA 19-20
Morrison, G.F.
See Bernstein, Gerry
Morrison, Hobe 1904- 77-80
Morrison, Howard A(lexander) 1955- 118
Morrison, Ida Edith 1-4R
Morrison, J. S.
See Morrison, John (Sinclair)
Morrison, Jack 1912- 105
Morrison, James Douglas 1943-1971 73-76
See also Morrison, Jim
Morrison, James F(rederic) 1937- 25-28R
Morrison, James (Harris) 1918- 73-76
Morrison, James L(unsford) Jr. 1923- 57-60
Morrison, James R(oy) 1940- 123
Brief entry 118
Morrison, James (Ryan) 1924- 105
Morrison, Jeanette Helen 1927- 134
Morrison, Jim
See Morrison, James Douglas
See also CLC 17
Morrison, Joan 1922- 133
See also SATA 65
Morrison, John Gordon 1904- 103
Morrison, John (Sinclair) 1913- 122
Morrison, John 1949- 137
Morrison, Joseph L(ederman) 1918-1970 ....5-8R
Obituary 122
Morrison, Kristin (Diane) 1934- CANR-14
Earlier sketch in CA 37-40R
Morrison, Lester M(arvin) 1907-1991 .... CAP-1
Obituary 134
Earlier sketch in CA 13-16
Morrison, Lillian 1917- CANR-22
Earlier sketches in CA 9-12R, CANR-7
See also SATA 3
Morrison, Lucile Phillips 1896- .... SATA 17
Morrison, Margaret Mackie Obituary 41-44R
Morrison, Marsh 1902- CANR-10
Earlier sketch in CA 61-64
Morrison, N(ancy Agnes) Brysson (Inglis)
....13-16R
Obituary 118
Morrison, Paul Fix 1902-1983 Obituary 111
Morrison, Peggy
See Morrison, Margaret Mackie
Morrison, Perry 1959- 134
Morrison, Philip 1915- Brief entry 106
Morrison, Phylis 1927- 117
Morrison, R(obert) H(ay) 1915- 135
Morrison, Richard
See Lowndes, Robert A(ugustine) W(ard)
Morrison, Robert
See Lowndes, Robert A(ugustine) W(ard)
Morrison, Robert H(aywood) 1927- 5-8R
Morrison, Robert S(tanley) 1909- 65-68
Morrison, Roberta
See Webb, Jean Francis
Morrison, Susan Dudley 1949- 119
Morrison, Theodore 1901-1988 ....CANR-1
Obituary 127
Earlier sketch in CA 1-4R
Morrison, Toni 1931- CANR-27
Earlier sketch in CA 29-32R
See also AAYA 1
See also BLC 3
See also BW
See also CDALB 1968-1988
See also CLC 4, 10, 22, 55
See also DLB 6, 33
See also DLBY 81
See also MTCW
See also SATA 57
Morrison, Tony 1936- 81-84
Morrison, Van 1945- Brief entry 116
See also CLC 21
Morrison, Velma Ford 1909- 9-12R
See also SATA 21
Morrison, Victor
See Glut, Donald F(rank)
Morrison, Wilbur Howard 1915- CANR-1
Earlier sketch in CA 1-4R
See also SATA 64
Morrison, William
See Samachson, Joseph
Morrison, William R(obert) 1942- 124
Morrison-Reed, Mark D(ouglas) 1949- 116
Morriss, Frank 1923- CANR-3
Earlier sketch in CA 5-8R
Morriss, James E(dward) 1932- 57-60
See also SATA 8
Morriss, J.-H.
See Ghnassia, Maurice (Jean-Henri)
Morriss, Mack 1920(?)-1976 Obituary 65-68
Morrissette, Bruce A(rcher) 1911- 17-20R
Morrissey, Charles Thomas 1933- 108
Morrissey, L(eroy) J(ohn) 1935- CANR-1
Earlier sketch in CA 49-52
Morrissey, Leonard E. Jr. 1925- 9-12R
Morrissey, Stephen 1950- 115
Morris-Suzuki, Tessa 1951- 123
Morritt, Hope 1930- CANR-16
Earlier sketch in CA 97-100
Morrow, Ann Patricia 130
Morrow, Baker H(arrison) 1946- 127
Morrow, Betty
See Bacon, Elizabeth
Morrow, Bradford 1951- CANR-32
Earlier sketch in CA 113
Morrow, Charlotte
See Kirwan, Molly (Morrow)
Morrow, Dennis 1952- 132
Morrow, E(verett) Frederic 1909- CANR-2
Earlier sketch in CA 5-8R
See also BW
Morrow, Felix 1906- 107
Morrow, Glenn R(aymond) 1895-197 (?) CAP-1
Earlier sketch in CA 19-20
Morrow, James 1947- 108
Morrow, John Howard Jr. 1944- 113
Morrow, John Howard 1910- 25-28R
Morrow, Lance 1939- Brief entry 119
Morrow, Mable 1892-1977 Obituary 106
Morrow, Mary Lou 1926- 61-64
Morrow, Patrick David 1940- CANR-8
Earlier sketch in CA 61-64
Morrow, Skip
See Morrow, Dennis
Morrow, Stephen 1939- 73-76
Morrow, William L(ockhart) 1935- 33-36R
Mors, Victor
See Roeseler, W(olfgang) G(uenter)
Mors, Wallace P. 1911- 17-20R
Morsberger, Katharine M. 1931- 105
Morsberger, Robert Eustis 1929- CANR-3
Earlier sketch in CA 5-8R
Morscher, Betsy 1939- 115
Morse, A. Reynolds 1914- CANR-7
Earlier sketch in CA 17-20R
Morse, Anne Christensen 1915- 1-4R
Morse, Arthur David
1920-1971 Obituary 29-32R
Morse, B. J. Obituary 73-76
Morse, Carol
See Yeakley, Marjory Hall
Morse, Chandler 1906- 5-8R
Morse, Charles A. 1898- CAP-1
Earlier sketch in CA 19-20
Morse, David 1940- 37-40R
Morse, Donald E. 1936- 37-40R
Morse, Donald R(oy) 1931- CANR-21
Earlier sketch in CA 105
Morse, Dorothy B(ayley) 1906-1979 ...... SATA 24
Morse, Edward Lewis 1942- CANR-7
Earlier sketch in CA 57-60
Morse, Flo 1921- 106
See also SATA 30
Morse, Grant W(esley) 1926- 17-20R
Morse, H(enry) Clifton IV 1924- 9-12R
Morse, Harold Marston
1892-1977 Obituary 69-72
Morse, Hermann Nelson
1887-1977 Obituary 73-76
Morse, J(osiah) Mitchell 1912- 65-68
Morse, James Herbert 1841-1923 .... DLB 71
Morse, Jedidiah 1761-1826 .... DLB 37
Morse, John D. 1906- 104
Morse, John T. Jr. 1840-1937 .... DLB 47
Morse, L(arry) A(lan) 1945- 107
Morse, Peter 1935- CANR-14
Earlier sketch in CA 73-76
Morse, Philip M(cCord) 1903-1985 108
Obituary 117
Morse, Richard M(cGee) 1922- CANR-10
Earlier sketch in CA 13-16R
Morse, Roger A(lfred) 1927- CANR-23
Earlier sketches in CA 57-60, CANR-8
Morse, Samuel French 1916- CANR-4
Earlier sketch in CA 9-12R
Morse, Theresa Adler 1901-1980 89-92
Obituary 97-100
Morse, Thomas S(purr) 1925- 109
Morse, Wayne (Lyman)
1900-1974 Obituary 49-52
Morse-Boycott, Desmond (Lionel)
1892-1979 107
Obituary 104
Morsey, Royal J(oseph) 1910- 73-76
Morshead, Ian 1922- 111
Morshiel, George
See Shiels, George
Morson, Gary S(aul) 1948- 121
Morss, Elisabeth W. 1918- 41-44R
Morsy, Magali 1933- 132
Mort, Vivian
See Cromie, Alice Hamilton
Mortensen, Ben(jamin) F. 1928- 104
Mortensen, C. David 1939- 37-40R
Morthland, John 1947- 129
Mortimer, Anthony 1936- 116
Mortimer, Armine Kotin 1943- 117
Mortimer, Chapman
See Chapman-Mortimer, William Charles
Mortimer, John (Clifford) 1923- CANR-21
Earlier sketch in CA 13-16R
See also CDBLB 1960 to Present
See also CLC 28, 43
See also DLB 13
See also MTCW
Mortimer, John L(ynn) 1908-1977 69-72
Obituary 135
Mortimer, Mary H.
See Coury, Louise Andree
Mortimer, Penelope (Ruth) 1918- 57-60
See also CLC 5
Mortimer, Peter
See Roberts, Dorothy James
Mortimore, Olive 1890- 49-52
Mortman, Doris Brief entry 129
See also BEST 89:4
Mortmane, J. D.
See Kiefer, Louis Sr.
Morton, A(rthur) L(eslie) 1903-1987 ....9-12R
Obituary 124
Morton, A(ndrew) Q(ueen) 1919- 105
Morton, Adam 1945- 128
Morton, Alexander C(lark) 1936- CANR-12
Earlier sketch in CA 25-28R
Morton, Anthony
See Creasey, John
Morton, C(lement) Manly 1884-1976 .... CAP-2
Earlier sketch in CA 29-32
Morton, Carlos 1947- CANR-32
Earlier sketch in CA 73-76
See also HW
Morton, Desmond 1937- CANR-32
Earlier sketches in CA 29-32R, CANR-15
Morton, Donald E(dward) 1938- 57-60
Morton, Frederic 1924- CANR-20
Earlier sketches in CA 1-4R, CANR-3
Morton, Gregory 1911-1986 102
Obituary 118
Morton, H(enry Canova) V(ollam)
1892-1979 103
Obituary 89-92
Morton, Harry 1925- CANR-15
Earlier sketch in CA 81-84
Morton, Henry W(alter) 1929- 13-16R
Morton, James (Severs) 1938- 133
Morton, Jane 1931- 93-96
See also SATA 50
Morton, Jocelyn 1912- 73-76
Morton, John (Cameron Andrieu) Bingham (Michael)
1893-1979 93-96
Obituary 85-88
Morton, Joseph
See Richmond, Al
Morton, Lee Jack Jr. 1928- .... SATA 32
Morton, Lena Beatrice 1901- 17-20R
Morton, Leopold 1922- 110
Morton, Louis 1913-1976 ....CANR-21
Obituary 65-68
Earlier sketch in CA 69-72
Morton, Lucie T. 1950- 118
Morton, Lynne 1952- 106
Morton, Marcia Colman 1927- 73-76
Morton, Marian J(ohnson) 1937- 77-80

Morton, Miriam 1918(?)-1985 ....CANR-2
Obituary 117
Earlier sketch in CA 49-52
See also SATA 9, 46
Morton, Nathaniel 1613-1685 ....DLB 24
Morton, Newton 1901-1967 ....CAP-1
Earlier sketch in CA 19-20
Morton, Patricia
See Golding, Morton J(ay)
Morton, Phyllis Digby Obituary 113
Morton, R(obert) S(teel) 1917- 49-52
Morton, Richard (Everett) 1930- 37-40R
Morton, Richard Lee 1889-1974 ....CANR-16
Obituary 53-56
Earlier sketch in CA 1-4R
Morton, Robert L(ee) 1889-1976 45-48
Obituary 134
Morton, Robert 1934- 69-72
Morton, Sarah Wentworth 1759-1846 ....DLB 37
Morton, Stanley
See Freedgood, Morton
Morton, T(homas) Ralph 1900- 29-32R
Morton, Thomas 1579(?)-1647(?) ....DLB 24
Morton, W(illiam) L(ewis) 1908- CAP-1
Earlier sketch in CA 19-20
Morton, W(illiam) Scott 1908- 81-84
Morton, Ward McKinnon 1907- 1-4R
Morton, William C(uthbert) 1875-1971 ....CAP-2
Earlier sketch in CA 25-28
Morwood, James 1943- 124
Mosby, Aline 1922- 130
Moscati, Sabatino 1922- 77-80
Mosco, Vincent 1948- CANR-35
Earlier sketch in CA 114
Moscotti, Albert D(ennis) 1920- 65-68
Moscovitch, Allan 1946- 111
Moscovitz, Judy 1942- 123
Moscow, Alvin 1925- CANR-4
Earlier sketch in CA 1-4R
See also SATA 3
Moscow, Henry (I.) 1904(?)-1983 Obituary 108
Moscow, Warren 1908- 21-24R
Moscowitz, Raymond 1938- 111
Mosel, Arlene (Tichy) 1921- 49-52
See also SATA 7
Mosel, Tad 1922- 73-76
Moseley, David (Victor) 1939- 97-100
Moseley, Edward H(olt) 1931- 132
Moseley, Edwin M(aurice) 1916-1978 ....CANR-8
Earlier sketch in CA 5-8R
Moseley, George (V. H. III) 1931- 49-52
Moseley, J(oseph) Edward 1910-1973 ....37-40R
Moseley, James G(wyn) 1946- CANR-38
Earlier sketch in CA 116
Moseley, Ray 1932- 85-88
Moseley, Spencer A(ltemont) 1925- 93-96
Moseley, Virginia D(ouglas) 1917- 21-24R
Mosely, Philip Edward
1905-1972 Obituary 33-36R
Moser, Barry 1940- ....MAICYA
See also SATA 56
Moser, Charles A. 1935- 29-32R
Moser, Don(ald Bruce) 1932- 106
See also SATA 31
Moser, Lawrence E. 1939- 33-36R
Moser, Mary Beck 1924- 122
Moser, Norman Calvin 1931- CANR-10
Earlier sketch in CA 57-60
Moser, Reta C(arol) 1936- 13-16R
Moser, Shia 1906- CAP-2
Earlier sketch in CA 25-28
Moser, Thomas (Colborn) 1923- 5-8R
Moses, Anna Mary Robertson
1860-1961 Obituary 93-96
Moses, Claire Goldberg 1941- 113
Moses, Elbert R(aymond) Jr. 1908- CAP-1
Earlier sketch in CA 13-16
Moses, Gerald Robert 1938- 57-60
Moses, Grandma
See Moses, Anna Mary Robertson
Moses, Joel C(harles) 1944- CANR-10
Earlier sketch in CA 65-68
Moses, Robert 1888-1981 45-48
Obituary 104
Moses, W(illiam) R(obert) 1911- 9-12R
Moses, Wilson Jeremiah 1942- 85-88
Mosesson, Gloria R(ubin) 41-44R
See also SATA 24
Mosey, Anne Cronin 1938- 49-52
Moshe, David
See Winkelman, Donald M.
Mosher, Arthur Theodore 1910- 85-88
Mosher, Frederick C(amp) 1913-1990 ....37-40R
Obituary 131
Mosher, Howard Frank ....CLC 62
Mosher, Ralph Lamont 1928- CANR-7
Earlier sketch in CA 17-20R
Mosher, Steven W(estley) 1948- 116
Mosher, (Christopher) Terry 1942- 93-96
Moshier, W(illiam) Franklyn 1929- 97-100
Mosiman, Billie Sue (Stahl) 1947- 119
Mosk
See Moskowitz, Gene
Moskin, J(ohn) Robert 1923- 17-20R
Moskin, Marietta D(unston) 1928- CANR-13
Earlier sketch in CA 73-76
See also SATA 23
Moskof, Martin Stephen 1930- 29-32R
See also SATA 27
Moskos, Charles C. 1934- CANR-26
Earlier sketches in CA 25-28R, CANR-10
Moskow, Michael H. 1938- CANR-14
Earlier sketch in CA 37-40R
Moskow, Shirley Blotnick 1935- 127
Moskowitz, Gene 1921(?)-1982 Obituary 108
Moskowitz, Ira 1912- 102
Moskowitz, Moses 1911(?)-1990 Obituary 131
Brief entry 114
Moskowitz, Robert 1946- 109
Moskowitz, Sam 1920- CANR-4
Earlier sketch in CA 5-8R
Moskvitin, Jurij 1938- 93-96
Mosley, Diana 1910- 106
Mosley, Francis 1957- ....SATA 57
Mosley, J(ohn) Brooke (Jr.)
1915-1988 Obituary 125
Mosley, Jean Bell 1913- 9-12R
Mosley, Leonard O(swald) 1913- 109
Brief entry 108
Mosley, Nicholas 1923- 69-72
See also CLC 43, 70
See also DLB 14
Mosley, Oswald (Ernald) 1896-1980 ....CAP-2
Obituary 102
Earlier sketch in CA 25-28
Mosley, Philip 1947- 130
Mosley, Steven 1952- 133
Moss, Arthur 1889-1969 Obituary 112
See also DLB 4
Moss, Barbara 1946- 116
Moss, Bernard H(aym) 1943- Brief entry 115
Moss, Bobby Gilmer 1932- 49-52
Moss, C(laude) Scott 1924- CANR-8
Earlier sketch in CA 17-20R
Moss, Cynthia J(ane) 1940- CANR-12
Earlier sketch in CA 65-68
Moss, Don(ald) 1920- ....SATA 11
Moss, Elaine (Dora) 1924- Brief entry 110
See also SATA 31, 57
Moss, Frank Edward 1911- CANR-13
Earlier sketch in CA 61-64
Moss, Gordon E(rvin) 1937- 57-60
Moss, Howard 1922-1987 ....CANR-1
Obituary 123
Earlier sketch in CA 1-4R
See also CLC 7, 14, 45, 50
See also DLB 5
Moss, J. Joel 1922- 45-48
Moss, James A(llen) 1920- 33-36R
Moss, John 1940- CANR-17
Earlier sketch in CA 97-100
Moss, Leonard (Jerome) 1931- 25-28R
Moss, Marissa 1959- ....SATA 71
Moss, Michael (Stanley) 1947- 108
Moss, Nancy
See Moss, Robert (Alfred)
Moss, Norman 1928- 49-52
Moss, (Victor) Peter (Cannings) 1921- CANR-2
Earlier sketch in CA 49-52
Moss, Ralph W(alter) 1943- 101
Moss, Robert (Alfred) 1903- CAP-1
Earlier sketch in CA 11-12
Moss, Robert F. 1942- CANR-20
Earlier sketch in CA 81-84
Moss, Robert (John) 1946- Brief entry 118
Moss, Roberta
See Moss, Robert (Alfred)
Moss, Roger 1951- 124
Moss, Rosalind (Louisa Beaufort)
1890-1990 Obituary 131
Moss, Rose 1937- 49-52
Moss, Sanford Alexander III 1939- 118
Moss, Sidney P(hil) 1917- 5-8R
Moss, Stanley 1925- 97-100
Moss, Stephen Joseph 1935- 103
Moss, Stirling 1929- 5-8R
Moss, Thylias 1954- ....DLB 120
Moss, Walter (Gerald) 1938- 65-68
Mosse, George L(achmann) 1918- CANR-28
Earlier sketches in CA 5-8R, CANR-12
Mosse, Werner E(ugen Emil) 1918- 9-12R
Mossiker, Frances (Sanger) 1906-1985 ....9-12R
Obituary 116
Mossman, Dow 1943- 45-48
Mossman, Frank H(omer) 1915- CANR-5
Earlier sketch in CA 1-4R
Mossman, Jennifer 1944- CANR-38
Earlier sketches in CA 97-100, CANR-17
Mossner, Ernest C(ampbell) 1907-1986 123
Obituary 120
Mossop, D(eryk) J(oseph) 1919- 1-4R
Mossop, Irene
See Swatridge, Irene Maude (Mossop)
Most, Bernard 1937- CANR-27
Earlier sketch in CA 104
See also SATA 40, 48
Most, Glenn W(arren) 1952- 112
Most, William G(eorge) 1914- 49-52
Mostel, Kate
See Mostel, Kathryn Harkin
Mostel, Katherine Harkin
See Mostel, Kathryn Harkin
Mostel, Kathryn Harkin 1918-1986 81-84
Obituary 118
Mostel, Samuel Joel 1915-1977 89-92
Mostel, Zero
See Mostel, Samuel Joel
Mosteller, (Charles) Frederick 1916- CANR-23
Earlier sketches in CA 17-20R, CANR-7
Mostert, Noel 1929- 105
Mostofsky, David I(saac) 1931- 17-20R
Mostyn, Trevor 1946- 129
Mota, Avelino Teixeira da
See Teixeira da Mota, Avelino
Mother Mary Anthony
See Weinig, Jean Maria
Mothershead, Harmon Ross 1931- 33-36R
Motherwell, Cathryn 1957- 132
Mothner, Ira S(anders) 1932- CANR-13
Earlier sketch in CA 21-24R
Motion, Andrew 1952- ....CLC 47
See also DLB 40
Motley, Arthur H(arrison)
1900-1984 Obituary 112
See also AITN 2
Motley, John Lothrop 1814-1877 ....DLB 1, 30, 59
Motley, Mary
See De Reneville, Mary Margaret Motley Sheridan
Motley, Mary Penick 1920- 73-76
Motley, Red
See Motley, Arthur H(arrison)
Motley, Willard (Francis) 1912-1965 117
Obituary 106
See also BW
See also CLC 18
See also DLB 76
Motley, Wilma E(lizabeth) 1912- 41-44R
Motmot, Snik P.
See Tompkins, Everett Thomas
Motoyama, Hiroshi 1925- 110
Mott, Frank Luther 1886-1964 ....1-4R
Mott, George Fox 1907-1987 ....13-16R
Obituary 123
Mott, Michael (Charles Alston) 1930- CANR-29
Earlier sketches in CA 5-8R, CANR-7
See also CAAS 7
See also CLC 15, 34
Mott, N(evill) F(rancis) 1905- 129
Mott, Paul E. 103
Mott, Sir Nevill
See Mott, N(evill) F(rancis)
Mott, Stephen Charles 1940- CANR-38
Earlier sketch in CA 116
Mott, Vincent Valmon 1916- 41-44R
Motta, Dick 1931- 134
Brief entry 111
Mottahedeh, Roy Parviz 1940- CANR-21
Earlier sketch in CA 104
Motter, Alton M(yers) 1907- CAP-1
Earlier sketch in CA 11-12
Motteux, Peter Anthony 1663-1718 ....DLB 80
Motto, Anna Lydia 41-44R
Motto, Carmine J. 1914- 33-36R
Mottram, Anthony John 1920- 5-8R
Mottram, (Vernon) Henry 1882- CAP-1
Earlier sketch in CA 11-12
Mottram, R(alph) H(ale) 1883-1971 108
Obituary 29-32R
See also DLB 36
Mottram, Tony
See Mottram, Anthony John
Motz, Lloyd 1909- CANR-4
Earlier sketch in CA 9-12R
See also SATA 20
Mouat, Kit 1920- 113
Mould, Daphne D(esiree) C(harlotte) Pochin
1920- CANR-4
Earlier sketch in CA 9-12R
Mould, George 1894- 57-60
Moule, C(harles) F(rancis) D(igby)
1908- CANR-5
Earlier sketch in CA 1-4R
Moulier, (Antoine) Fernand 1913- 81-84
Moult, Edward (Walker)
1926-1986 Obituary 120
Moult, Ted
See Moult, Edward (Walker)
Moult, Thomas 1895-1974 Obituary 89-92
Moulton, Edward C. 1936- 77-80
Moulton, Eugene R(ussell)
1916-1981 ....CANR-11
Earlier sketch in CA 21-24R
Moulton, Gary E(van) 1942- 115
Moulton, Harland B. 1925- 37-40R
Moulton, J(ames) L(ouis) 1906- 21-24R
Moulton, Nancy 1946- 116
Moulton, Phillips P(rentice) 1909- 37-40R
Moulton, William G(amwell) 1914- 9-12R
Mouly, George J(oseph) 1915- CANR-17
Earlier sketch in CA 1-4R
Mounce, R(obert H.) 1921- CANR-2
Earlier sketch in CA 1-4R
Mount, Charles Merrill 1928- 13-16R
Mount, Elisabeth
See Dougherty, Betty
Mount, Ellis 1921- CANR-39
Earlier sketch in CA 116
Mount, (William Robert) Ferdinand
1939- CANR-11
Earlier sketch in CA 21-24R
Mount, Marshall Ward 1927- 73-76
Mountain, Julian
See Cowie, Donald
Mountain, Marian
See Wisberg, Marian Aline
Mountain, Robert
See Montgomery, Raymond A. (Jr.)
Mountbatten, Louis (Francis Albert Victor Nicholas)
1900-1979 133
Obituary 113
Mountbatten, Richard
See Wallmann, Jeffrey M(iner)
Mountfield, David
See Grant, Neil
Mountfield, Stuart 1903(?)-1984 Obituary 115
Mountfort, Guy 1905- 17-20R
Mountjoy, Roberta Jean
See Sohl, Jerry
Mountsier, Robert
1888(?)-1972 Obituary 37-40R
Mourant, John A(rthur) 1903- CAP-1
Earlier sketch in CA 9-10
Moure, Erin 1955- 113
See also DLB 60
Mourelatos, Alexander P(hoebus) D(ionysiou)
1936- 29-32R
Mourier, Marguerite
See Boulton, Marjorie
Moursund, David G. 1936- CANR-30
Earlier sketches in CA 25-28R, CANR-12
Moursund, Janet (Peck) 1936- CANR-30
Earlier sketch in CA 45-48
Moussa, Pierre L(ouis) 1922- 13-16R
Moussard, Jacqueline 1924- CANR-8
Earlier sketch in CA 61-64
See also SATA 24
Mouton, Jane Srygley 1930- 123
Moutoux, John T. 1901(?)-1979 Obituary 89-92
Mouzelis, Nicos P. 1939- 33-36R
Mouzon, Olin T(errell) 1912- 5-8R
Mow, Anna Beahm 1893- CANR-3
Earlier sketch in CA 9-12R
Mowat, C(harles) L(och) 1911-1970 ....CAP-1
Earlier sketch in CA 13-16
Mowat, Claire (Angel Wheeler) 1933- 131
Mowat, David 1943- 77-80
Mowat, Farley (McGill) 1921- CANR-24
Earlier sketches in CA 1-4R, CANR-4
See also AAYA 1
See also CLC 26
See also CLR 20
See also DLB 68
See also MAICYA
See also MTCW
See also SATA 3, 55
Mowat, R(obert) C(ase) 1913- 29-32R
Mowatt, Ian 1948- 41-44R
Mowitz, Robert J(ames) 1920- CANR-3
Earlier sketch in CA 5-8R
Mowrer, Edgar Ansel 1892-1977 ....CAP-1
Obituary 69-72
Earlier sketch in CA 13-16
See also DLB 29
Mowrer, Lilian Thomson 1889(?)-1990 65-68
Obituary 132
Mowrer, O(rval) Hobart 1907- CANR-1
Earlier sketch in CA 1-4R
Mowrer, Paul Scott 1887-1971 ....CANR-4
Obituary 29-32R
Earlier sketch in CA 5-8R
See also DLB 29
Mowry, George E(dwin) 1909-1984 ....CANR-17
Earlier sketch in CA 1-4R
Mowry, Jess 1960- 133
Mowshowitz, Abbe 1939- 109
Moxham, Robert Morgan
1919-1978 Obituary 77-80
Moyano, Daniel 1930- 131
See also HW
Moye, Catherine 1960- 136
Moyer, Carolyn
See Swayze, Carolyn (Norma)
Moyer, Claire B. (Inch) 1905- CAP-2
Earlier sketch in CA 19-20
Moyer, Elgin Sylvester 1890- 5-8R
Moyer, Kenneth E(van) 1919- CANR-13
Earlier sketch in CA 33-36R
Moyer, Kermit 1943- 136
Moyers, Bill 1934- CANR-31
Earlier sketch in CA 61-64
See also AITN 2
Moyes, John Stoward 1884- CAP-1
Earlier sketch in CA 13-14
Moyes, Norman Barr 1931- 37-40R
Moyes, Patricia 1923-
See Haszard, Patricia Moyes
See also SATA 63
Moyler, Alan (Frank Powell) 1926- ....SATA 36
Moyles, R(obert) Gordon 1939- CANR-17
Earlier sketch in CA 65-68
Moynahan, John F. 1912-1985 Obituary 115
Moynahan, Julian (Lane) 1925- CANR-1
Earlier sketch in CA 1-4R
Moynahan, Molly 1957- 133
Moyne, Ernest J(ohn) 1916-1976 ....CAP-2
Earlier sketch in CA 25-28
Moynihan, Daniel P(atrick) 1927- 5-8R
Moynihan, John Dominic 1932- 103
Moynihan, Maurice (Gerard) 1902- 107
Moynihan, Ruth B(arnes) 1933- 117
Moynihan, William T. 1927- 21-24R
Moyse-Bartlett, Hubert
1902(?)-1973(?) Obituary 104
Moyser, George H. 1945- 134
Mozley, Charles 1915- ....SATA 32, 43
Mphahlele, Es'kia
See Mphahlele, Ezekiel
Mphahlele, Ezekiel 1919- CANR-26
Earlier sketch in CA 81-84
See also BLC 3
See also BW
See also CLC 25
Mqhayi, S(amuel) E(dward) K(rune Loliwe)
1875-1945 ....BLC 3
See also TCLC 25
Mr. Cleveland
See Seltzer, Louis B(enson)
Mr. Kenneth
See Marlowe, Kenneth
Mr. Martin
See Burroughs, William S(eward)
Mr. McGillicuddy
See Abisch, Roslyn Kroop
Mr. Metropolitan Opera
See Robinson, Francis (Arthur)
Mr. Sniff
See Abisch, Roslyn Kroop
Mr. Wizard
See Herbert, Don(ald Jeffrey)
Mrabet, Mohammed
See el Hajjam, Mohammed ben Chaib
Mrazek, James E(dward) 1914- 33-36R
Mrosovsky, Kitty 128
Mrozek, Donald J(ohn) 1945- 107

Mrozek, Slawomir 1930- CANR-29
Earlier sketch in CA 13-16R
See also CAAS 10
See also CLC 3, 13
See also MTCW
Mrs. Belloc-Lowndes
See Lowndes, Marie Adelaide (Belloc)
Mrs. Bishop
See Bishop, Isabella Lucy (Bird)
Mrs. Fairstar
See Horne, Richard Henry
Mrs. G.
See Griffiths, Kitty Anna
Mrs. Miggy
See Krentel, Mildred White
Mrs. R.F.D.
See Peden, Rachel (Mason)
M'Taggart, John M'Taggart Ellis
See McTaggart, John McTaggart Ellis
M'Timkulu, Donald (Guy Sidney) 1910- 97-100
Mtwa, Percy .... CLC 47
Mu, Yang
See Wang, C(hing) H(sien)
Mucha, Jiri 1915-1991 .... CANR-26
Obituary 134
Earlier sketches in CA 21-24R, CANR-11
Muchnic, Helen (Lenore) 1903- CANR-5
Earlier sketch in CA 1-4R
Mudd, Emily Hartshorne 1898- 13-16R
Mudd, Harvey (Seeley II) 1940- 130
Mudd, Roger H(arrison) 1928- 105
Mudd, Stuart 1893-1975 .... 9-12R
Obituary 57-60
Muddiman, John 1947- 136
Mude, O.
See Gorey, Edward (St. John)
Mudge, Jean McClure 1933- CANR-6
Earlier sketch in CA 5-8R
Mudge, Lewis Seymour 1929- 89-92
Mudgeon, Apeman
See Mitchell, Adrian
Mudgett, Herman W.
See White, William A(nthony) P(arker)
Mudie, Ian (Mayelston) 1911-1976 .... 25-28R
Obituary 135
Mudrick, Marvin 1921- CANR-20
Earlier sketch in CA 25-28R
Muecke, D(ouglas) C(olin) 1919- 53-56
Muehl, Lois Baker 1920- CANR-18
Earlier sketch in CA 1-4R
Muehl, (Ernest) William 1919- 45-48
Muehlen, Norbert 1909-1981 69-72
Obituary 104
Muehsam, Gerd 1913(?)-1979 Obituary 93-96
Muelder, Walter George 1907- CAP-1
Earlier sketch in CA 13-14
Mueller, Amelia 1911- 57-60
Mueller, Barbara R(uth) 1925- 9-12R
Mueller, Charles S(teinkamp) 1929- CANR-20
Earlier sketches in CA 13-16R, CANR-5
Mueller, Claus 1941- CANR-31
Earlier sketch in CA 65-68
Mueller, David L. 1929- 29-32R
Mueller, Dennis C(ary) 1940- CANR-39
Earlier sketch in CA 116
Mueller, Dorothy 1901- 102
Mueller, Dorothy 1949(?)-1989 Obituary 130
Mueller, Erwin W. 1911-1977 Obituary 69-72
Mueller, Gerald F(rancis) 1927- 13-16R
Mueller, Gerhard G(ottlob) 1930- CANR-36
Earlier sketches in CA 25-28R, CANR-12
Mueller, Gerhard O. W. 1926- CANR-20
Earlier sketches in CA 1-4R, CANR-5
Mueller, Gerhardt
See Bickers, Richard Leslie Townshend
Mueller, Gustav Emil 1898- CANR-7
Earlier sketch in CA 17-20R
Mueller, James R. 1951- 138
Mueller, James W(illiam) 1941- 57-60
Mueller, Janel M(ulder) 1938- 132
Mueller, Joerg 1942- 136
See also SATA 67
Mueller, John E(rnest) 1937- CANR-14
Earlier sketch in CA 37-40R
Mueller, Kate Hevner 1898- 41-44R
Mueller, Klaus Andrew 1921- CANR-4
Earlier sketch in CA 49-52
Mueller, Lisel 1924- 93-96
See also CLC 13, 51
See also DLB 105
Mueller, M(ax) G(erhard) 1925- 17-20R
Mueller, Maler 1749-1825 .... DLB 94
Mueller, Marlies K(uhfuss) 1937- 114
Mueller, Merrill 1916-1980 Obituary 103
Mueller, Red
See Mueller, Merrill
Mueller, Reuben Herbert
1897-1982 Obituary 107
Mueller, Robert E(mmett) 1925- 1-4R
Mueller, Robert Kirk 1913- CANR-12
Earlier sketch in CA 73-76
Mueller, Virginia 1924- CANR-27
Earlier sketches in CA 65-68, CANR-10
See also SATA 28
Mueller, Wilhelm 1794-1827 .... DLB 90
Mueller, Willard Fritz 1925- 17-20R
Mueller, William R(andolph) 1916- CANR-2
Earlier sketch in CA 1-4R
Mueller-Vollmer, Kurt 1928- 126
Muenchen, Al(fred) 1917- 49-52
Muesing, Edith E(lizabeth)
See Muesing-Ellwood, Edith E(lizabeth)
Muesing-Ellwood, Edith E(lizabeth) 1947- 114
Muffett, D(avid) J(oseph) M(ead) 1919- 45-48
Muggeridge, Malcolm (Thomas)
1903-1990 .... CANR-33
Earlier sketch in CA 101
See also AITN 1
See also MTCW
Muggeson, Margaret Elizabeth 1942- 103
Muhajir, Nazzam Al Fitnah
See El Muhajir
Muheim, Harry Miles 1920- 85-88
Muhlen, Norbert
See Muehlen, Norbert
Muhlenfeld, Elisabeth 1944- CANR-24
Earlier sketch in CA 108
Muhlhausen, John Prague 1940- 61-64
Muhlstein, Anka 1935- 114
Mui, Hoh-cheung 1916- 45-48
Mui, Lorna H(olbrook) 1915- 133
Muileman, Kathryn Saltzman 1946- 85-88
Muilenburg, Grace (Evelyn) 1913- 61-64
Muir, (Charles) Augustus (Carlow)
1893(?)-1989 .... 13-16R
Obituary 128
Muir, Barbara K(enrick Gowing) 1908- 9-12R
Muir, Dexter
See Gribble, Leonard (Reginald)
Muir, Edwin 1887-1959 Brief entry 104
See also DLB 20, 100
See also TCLC 2
Muir, Frank (Herbert) 1920- CANR-29
Earlier sketch in CA 81-84
See also SATA 30
Muir, Helen 1911(?)- .... AITN 2
Muir, Helen 1937- 130
See also DLB 14
See also SATA 65
Muir, Jane
See Petrone, Jane Muir
Muir, Jean 1906-1973 .... CAP-2
Obituary 41-44R
Earlier sketch in CA 29-32
Muir, John 1838-1914 .... TCLC 28
Muir, Kenneth (Arthur) 1907- CANR-4
Earlier sketch in CA 1-4R
Muir, Lynette R(oss) 1930- 122
Muir, Malcolm Jr. 1915-1984 Obituary 113
Muir, Malcolm 1885-1979 93-96
Obituary 85-88
Muir, Marie 1904- CANR-5
Earlier sketch in CA 1-4R
Muir, Percival H(orace) 1894-1979 .... CANR-5
Obituary 97-100
Earlier sketch in CA 9-12R
Muir, Percy H.
See Muir, Percival H(orace)
Muir, Richard 1943- CANR-23
Earlier sketch in CA 106
Muir, William Ker Jr. 1931- 53-56
Muirhead, Ian A(dair) 1913- 13-16R
Muirhead, Thorburn 1899- 5-8R
Mujica, Barbara 1943- 138
Mujica Lainez, Manuel 1910-1984 .... CANR-32
Obituary 112
Earlier sketch in CA 81-84
See also Lainez, Manuel Mujica
See also CLC 31
See also HW
Mukerji, Chandra 1945- 113
Mukerji, Dhan Gopal 1890-1936 136
Brief entry 119
See also CLR 10
See also MAICYA
See also SATA 40
Mukerji, Kshitimohon 1920- 17-20R
Mukherjee, Bharati 1940- 107
See also BEST 89:2
See also CLC 53
See also DLB 60
See also MTCW
Mukherjee, Meenakshi 1937- 65-68
Mukherjee, Ramkrishna 1919- CANR-7
Earlier sketch in CA 57-60
Mulac, Margaret E(lizabeth) 1912- CANR-2
Earlier sketch in CA 5-8R
Mulaisho, Dominic (Chola) 1933- 97-100
Mularchyk, Sylva 93-96
Mulay, Larry L. 1904(?)-1987 Obituary 122
Mulcahy, Lucille Burnett 5-8R
See also SATA 12
Mulchrone, Vincent
1919(?)-1977 Obituary 73-76
Mulder, John M(ark) 1946- Brief entry 112
Muldoon, Paul 1951- 129
Brief entry 113
See also CLC 32, 72
See also DLB 40
Muldoon, Roland W. 1941- 105
Muldowny, John 1931- 127
Mule, Marty 1944- 108
Mulesko, Angelo
See Oglesby, Joseph
Mulford, David Campbell 1937- 9-12R
Mulford, Philippa G(reene) 1948- 116
See also SATA 43
Mulgan, Catherine 1931- CANR-11
Earlier sketch in CA 25-28R
See also Gough, Catherine
Mulgrew, Peter David 1927- 13-16R
Mulhauser, Ruth (Elizabeth)
1913-1980 .... CANR-7
Earlier sketch in CA 5-8R
Mulhearn, John 1932- 65-68
Mulholland, Jim 1949- 61-64
Mulholland, John F(ield) 1903- 41-44R
Mulholland, John 1898-1970 .... 5-8R
Obituary 89-92
Mulisch, Harry 1927- CANR-26
Earlier sketches in CA 9-12R, CANR-6
See also CLC 42
Mulkeen, Anne
See Marcus, Anne M(ulkeen)
Mulkeen, Thomas P(atrick) 1923- 85-88
Mulkerne, Donald James Dennis 1921- 9-12R
Mull, Martin 1943- 105
See also CLC 17
Mullally, Frederic 1920- CANR-1
Earlier sketch in CA 1-4R
Mullaly, Edward (Joseph) 1941- 41-44R
Mullan, Bob 1947- 123
Mullan, David George 1951- 130
Mullan, Fitzhugh 1942- 69-72
Mullaney, Marie Marmo 1953- 112
Mullaney, Thomas E. 1922(?)-1978 93-96
Obituary 81-84
Mullard, Chris(topher Paul)
1944- Brief entry 112
Mullarky, Taylor 1922- CANR-26
Earlier sketch in CA 103
Mullen, Barbara 1914-1979 Obituary 85-88
Mullen, C.J.J.
See Mullen, Cyril J.
Mullen, Cyril J. 1908- 61-64
Mullen, Dore
See Mullen, Dorothy
Mullen, Dorothy 1933- 104
Mullen, Edward John Jr. 1942- CANR-17
Earlier sketches in CA 49-52, CANR-2
Mullen, Harris H. 1924- 69-72
Mullen, James H. 1924- 1-4R
Mullen, Michael 1937- CANR-39
Earlier sketch in CA 116
Mullen, Robert R(odolph) 1908- CAP-1
Earlier sketch in CA 19-20
Mullen, Thomas J(ames) 1934- CANR-5
Earlier sketch in CA 9-12R
Mullen, William Charles 1944- 73-76
Mullenbach, Philip 1912-1989 Obituary 128
Mullendore, William Clinton
1892-1983 Obituary 111
Muller, Alexander V(ilhelm) 1932- 45-48
Muller, Billex
See Ellis, Edward S(ylvester)
Muller, Charles G(eorge Geoffrey)
1897- CANR-2
Earlier sketch in CA 1-4R
Muller, Charles Geoffrey
See Muller, Charles G(eorge Geoffrey)
Muller, Dorothy
See Mueller, Dorothy
Muller, Edward John 1916- 57-60
Muller, Gilbert H(enry) 1941- CANR-14
Earlier sketch in CA 41-44R
Muller, H(erman) J(oseph)
1890-1967 Obituary 106
Muller, Herbert J(oseph) 1905- CANR-1
Earlier sketch in CA 1-4R
Muller, Herman J(oseph) 1909- 73-76
Muller, Hilgard 1914-1985 Obituary 117
Muller, James W(aldemar) 1953- 132
Muller, John E.
See Fanthorpe, R(obert) Lionel
Muller, John P(aul) 1940- 103
Muller, Jorg
See Mueller, Joerg
Muller, Leo C. Jr. 1924- 5-8R
Muller, Marcia 1944- 81-84
Muller, Peter O. 1942- 110
Muller, Priscilla E(lkow) 1930- 61-64
Muller, Robert George 1923- 103
Muller, (Lester) Robin 1953- 127
Muller, Ronald E(rnst) 1939- 107
Muller, Siegfried H(ermann) 1902-1965 .... CAP-1
Earlier sketch in CA 11-12
Mulligan, Hugh A. 1925- CANR-11
Earlier sketch in CA 21-24R
Mulligan, James J. 1936- 45-48
Mulligan, John Joseph 1918- 33-36R
Mulligan, Raymond A(lexander) 1914- 37-40R
Mulligan, Robert S(mith) 1941- 65-68
Mulliken, Robert Sanderson 1896-1986 109
Obituary 120
Mullin, Chris(topher John) 1947- 132
Mullin, Michael 1944- 103
Mullin, Robert N(orville) 1893- 89-92
Mullin, Willard 1902-1978 Obituary 89-92
Mullings, Llewellyn M. 1932- 37-40R
Mullins, (George) Aloysius 1910- CAP-1
Earlier sketch in CA 13-14
Mullins, Ann
See Dally, Ann Mullins
Mullins, Carolyn J(ohns) 1940- CANR-10
Earlier sketch in CA 65-68
Mullins, Claud 1887-1968 .... CAP-1
Earlier sketch in CA 13-14
Mullins, Edward S(wift) 1922- 17-20R
See also SATA 10
Mullins, Edwin (Brandt) 1933- CANR-22
Earlier sketches in CA 53-56, CANR-4
Mullins, Helene 1899- 77-80
Mullins, June B(onner) 1927- 126
Mullins, Larry E(dward) 1935- 117
Mullins, Nicholas C(reed) 1939- 33-36R
Mullins, Pat(rick Joseph) 1923- 128
Mullins, Vera (Annie) Cooper 1903- 61-64
Mulloy, Elizabeth D(ibert) 1945- 93-96
Mulock, Dinah Maria
See Craik, Dinah Maria (Mulock)
Multhauf, Robert P(hilip) 1919- 93-96
Mulvaney, Robert J(oseph) 1937- 126
Mulvanity, George 1903(?)-1976 Obituary 69-72
Mulvey, Ruth Watt
See Harmer, Ruth Mulvey
Mulvihill, Edward Robert 1917- 9-12R
Mulvihill, Maureen E. 1944- 135
Mulvihill, William Patrick 1923- 1-4R
See also SATA 8
Mulville, Frank 1924- 107
Mumey, Glen A(llen) 1933- 73-76
Mumford, Bob 1930- 103
Mumford, Emily (Hamilton) 1920(?)-1987 57-60
Obituary 123
Mumford, Erika 1935(?)-1988 Obituary 126
Mumford, Lewis 1895-1990 .... CANR-5
Obituary 130
Earlier sketch in CA 1-4R
See also DLB 63
Mummery, David R. 1932- 21-31-4R
Mumms, Hardee
See McLellan, Diana
Mun
See Leaf, (Wilbur) Munro
Munari, Bruno 1907- CANR-38
Earlier sketch in CA 73-76
See also CLR 9
See also MAICYA
See also SATA 15
Munby, A(lan) N(oel) L(atimer)
1913-1974 Obituary 53-56
Munby, Arthur Joseph 1828-1910 .... DLB 35
Munby, D(enys) L(awrence)
1919-1976 .... CANR-2
Earlier sketch in CA 1-4R
Munce, Ruth Hill 1898- CAP-1
Earlier sketch in CA 9-10
See also SATA 12
Munch, Peter A(ndreas) 1908-1984 .... 29-32R
Obituary 111
Munch, Theodore W(illiam) 1919- 57-60
Muncy, Raymond Lee 1928- 49-52
Mund, Vernon A(rthur) 1906- CANR-20
Earlier sketch in CA 1-4R
Munday, Anthony 1560-1633 .... DLB 62
Mundel, Marvin E(verett) 1916- 21-24R
Mundell, Robert A(lexander) 1932- CANR-2
Earlier sketch in CA 45-48
Mundell, William Daniel 1913- 73-76
Mundis, Hester 1938- CANR-34
Earlier sketches in CA 69-72, CANR-15
Mundis, Jerrold 1941- CANR-11
Earlier sketch in CA 69-72
Mundlak, Max 1899- CAP-1
Earlier sketch in CA 9-10
Mundy, John Hine 1917- 45-48
Mundy, Max
See Schofield, Sylvia Anne
Mundy, Simon (Andrew James Hainault)
1954- 128
See also SATA 64
Munford, Robert 1737(?)-1783 .... DLB 31
Munford, W(illiam) A(rthur) 1911- 116
Mungello, David Emil 1943- 110
Munger, Al
See Unger, Maurice Albert
Munger, Frank James 1929-1981 .... CANR-1
Obituary 116
Earlier sketch in CA 1-4R
Munger, Hortense Roberta
See Roberts, Hortense Roberta
Munger, Robert Boyd 1910- 77-80
Mungo, Raymond 1946- CANR-2
Earlier sketch in CA 49-52
See also CLC 72
Munholland, John K(im) 1934- CANR-25
Earlier sketch in CA 29-32R
Munir, Muhammad 1895-1981 Obituary 108
Munitz, Milton K(arl) 1913- CANR-36
Earlier sketches in CA 93-96, CANR-16
Muniz, Angelina 1936- 131
See also HW
Munk, Arthur W. 1909- CANR-7
Earlier sketch in CA 13-16R
Munk, Christian
See Weisenborn, Guenther
Munk, Erika 1939- 17-20R
Munker, Dona 1945- 138
Munn, Geoffrey C(harles) 1953- 118
Munn, Glenn (Gaywaine)
1890(?)-1977 Obituary 73-76
Munn, H(arold) Warner 1903-1981 .... CANR-11
Earlier sketch in CA 21-24R
Munn, Hart
See Hardy, C. Colburn
Munnecke, Wilbur C(heney)
1906-1984 Obituary 112
Munnell, Alicia H(aydock) 1942- CANR-30
Earlier sketches in CA 73-76, CANR-13
Munonye, John 1929- 103
See also DLB 117
Munowitz, Ken 1935-1977 .... SATA 14
Munoz, Braulio 1946- 110
Munoz, Heraldo 1948- 111
Munoz, William 1949- .... SATA 42
Munoz Marin, Luis 1898-1980 Obituary 97-100
See also HW
Munro, Alice 1931- CANR-33
Earlier sketch in CA 33-36R
See also AITN 2
See also CLC 6, 10, 19, 50
See also DLB 53
See also MTCW
See also SATA 29
See also SSC 3
Munro, Bertha 1887-1983 45-48
Munro, C. K.
See MacMullan, Charles Walden Kirkpatrick
Munro, Dana Gardner 1892-1990 .... 1-4R
Obituary 131
Munro, David
See Devine, D(avid) M(cDonald)
Munro, Donald J(acques) 1931- 133

Munro, Duncan H.
See Russell, Eric Frank
Munro, Eleanor 1928- ... 1-4R
See also SATA 37
Munro, H(ector) H(ugh) 1870-1916 ... 130
Brief entry ... 104
See also Saki
See also CDBLB 1890-1914
See also DLB 34
See also MTCW
See also WLC
Munro, Hector H.
See Munro, H(ector) H(ugh)
Munro, (Macfarlane) Hugh ... 9-12R
Munro, Ian S. ... 29-32R
Munro, James
See Cave, Roderick (George James Munro) and Mitchell, James
Munro, Jane 1943- ... 112
Munro, John (Henry Alexander) 1938- ... 41-44R
Munro, John M(urchinson) 1932- ... CANR-11
Earlier sketch in CA 69-72
Munro, Leslie Knox 1901-1974 Obituary ... 49-52
Munro, Mary
See Howe, Doris Kathleen
Munro, Roxie 1945- ... SATA 58
Munro, Thomas 1897-1974 ... CANR-3
Earlier sketch in CA 5-8R
Munroe, Elizabeth L(ee) 1900- ... CANR-2
Earlier sketch in CA 17-20R
Munroe, John A(ndrew) 1914- ... 49-52
Munroe, Kirk 1850-1930 Brief entry ... 123
See also DLB 42
Munrow, David John 1942-1976 ... 103
Obituary ... 106
Munsch, Robert (Norman) 1945- ... CANR-37
Earlier sketch in CA 121
See also CLR 19
See also MAICYA
See also SATA 48, 50
Munsell, F(loyd) Darrell 1934- ... 129
Munsey, Cecil (Richard Jr.) 1935- ... CANR-17
Earlier sketch in CA 41-44R
Munsey, Frank A(ndrew)
1854-1925 Brief entry ... 116
See also DLB 25, 91
Munshi, Kiki Skagen 1943- ... CANR-15
Earlier sketch in CA 37-40R
Munshi, Shehnaaz
See Munshi, Kiki Skagen
Munshower, Suzanne 1945- ... 97-100
Munsinger, Harry 1935- ... 45-48
Munsinger, Lynn 1951- ... SATA 33
Munslow, Barry 1950- ... 117
Munson, Amelia H. Obituary ... 33-36R
Munson, Byron Edwin 1921- ... 41-44R
Munson, Charlie E(llis) 1877-1975 ... 57-60
Obituary ... 134
Munson, Don 1908-1978 ... 73-76
Obituary ... 133
Munson, Fred C(aleb) 1928- ... 33-36R
Munson, Gorham B(ert) 1896-1969 ... CAP-1
Earlier sketch in CA 11-12
Munson, Harold L(ewis) 1923- ... 29-32R
Munson, Henry (Lee) Jr. 1946- ... 115
Munson, James (Edward Bradbury) 1944- ... 124
Munson, Kenneth (George) 1929- ... 127
Brief entry ... 111
Munson, Lou
See Munson, Mary Lou (Easley)
Munson, Mary Lou (Easley) 1935- ... 9-12R
Munson, Thomas N(olan) 1924- ... CANR-20
Earlier sketch in CA 1-4R
Munson, Thurman (Lee) 1947-1979 ... 108
Obituary ... 89-92
Munson-Benson, Tunie 1946- ... 77-80
See also SATA 15
Munsterberg, Hugo 1916- ... CANR-2
Earlier sketch in CA 5-8R
Munsterhjelm, Erik 1905- ... 49-52
Munter, Robert (L.) 1926- ... 21-24R
Munthe, Adam John 1946- ... 107
Munthe, Frances 1915- ... 9-12R
Munthe, Malcolm Grane 1920- ... 5-8R
Munthe, Nelly 1947- ... 117
See also SATA 53
Munting, Roger 1945- ... 127
Munton, Alan (Guy) 1945- ... CANR-24
Earlier sketch in CA 107
Muntyan, Miodrag 1914-1985 Obituary ... 117
Muntz, (Isabelle) Hope 1907- ... 13-16R
Muntz, James
See Crowcroft, Peter
Munves, James (Albert) 1922- ... CANR-3
Earlier sketch in CA 5-8R
See also SATA 30
Munz, Peter 1921- ... 13-16R
Munz, Philip Alexander 1892- ... 5-8R
Munzer, Martha E. 1899- ... CANR-4
Earlier sketch in CA 1-4R
See also SATA 4
Mura, David (Alan) 1952- ... 138
Murad, Anatol 1904- ... 73-76
Murad, Gauhar-i
See Sa'Idi, Ghulam Husayn
Murari, Timeri N(upendra) 1941- ... 102
Murat, Ines 1939- ... 130
Murata, Kiyoaki 1922- ... 130
Muravchik, Joshua 1947- ... 136
Muravin, Victor 1929- ... 85-88
Murawski, Benjamin J(oseph) 1926- ... 45-48
Murbarger, Nell Lounsberry 1909- ... CAP-1
Earlier sketch in CA 13-16
Murch, Edward (William Lionel) 1920- ... 61-64
Murch, James DeForest 1892-1973 ... CANR-4
Earlier sketch in CA 5-8R
Murchie, Guy 1907- ... CANR-27
Earlier sketch in CA 1-4R
Murchison, Thomas Moffat
1907-1984 Obituary ... 111
Murchland, Bernard 1929- ... 112
Murden, Forrest D(ozier) Jr.
1921-1977 Obituary ... 73-76
Murdick, Robert Gordon 1920- ... CANR-6
Earlier sketch in CA 5-8R
Murdin, Paul 1942- ... CANR-23
Earlier sketch in CA 106
Murdoch, (Henry) Derrick 1909-1985 ... 89-92
Obituary ... 116
Murdoch, (Jean) Iris 1919- ... CANR-8
Earlier sketch in CA 13-16R
See also CDBLB 1960 to Present
See also CLC 1, 2, 3, 4, 6, 8, 11, 15, 22, 31, 51
See also DLB 14
See also MTCW
Murdoch, Joseph S(impson) F(erguson)
1919- ... 102
Murdoch, (Keith) Rupert 1931- Brief entry ... 111
Murdock, Eugene C(onverse) 1921- ... CANR-13
Earlier sketch in CA 33-36R
Murdock, George Peter 1897- ... CAP-1
Earlier sketch in CA 13-14
Murdock, Kenneth Ballard 1895-1975 ... 65-68
Obituary ... 61-64
Murdock, Laurette P. 1900- ... 101
Murdock, M(elinda) S(eabrooke)
1947- ... CANR-32
Earlier sketch in CA 113
Murdock, Myrtle Cheney
1886(?)-1980 Obituary ... 97-100
Murdy, Louise Baughan 1935- ... 33-36R
Mure, David (William Alexander)
1912-1986 ... 134
Obituary ... 120
Mure, G(eoffrey) R(eginald) G(ilchrist)
1893-1979 ... 107
Murena, H. A.
See Alvarez Murena, Hector Alberto
Murena, Hector Alberto Alvarez
See Alvarez Murena, Hector Alberto
Murfin, James Vernon
1930(?)-1987 Obituary ... 122
Murfin, Ross C. 1948- ... 125
Murfree, Mary Noailles
1850-1922 Brief entry ... 122
See also DLB 12, 74
Murie, Margaret Elizabeth 1902- ... 110
Murnau, Friedrich Wilhelm
See Plumpe, Friedrich Wilhelm
Murnion, Philip (Joseph) 1938- ... 116
Muro, Amado (Jesus)
See Seltzer, Chester E.
See also DLB 82
Muro, Diane Patricia 1940- ... 65-68
Muro, James J(oseph) 1934- ... 33-36R
Murphet, Howard 1906- ... 61-64
Murphey, Murray Griffin 1928- ... CANR-6
Earlier sketch in CA 5-8R
Murphey, Rhoads 1919- ... 33-36R
Murphey, Robert W(entworth) 1916- ... 13-16R
Murphy, Agnes Louise Keating 1912- ... 1-4R
Murphy, Arthur Lister 1906- ... 77-80
Murphy, Arthur Richard Jr.
1915-1987 Obituary ... 123
Murphy, Arthur 1727-1805 ... DLB 89
Murphy, Barbara Beasley 1933- ... CANR-20
Earlier sketch in CA 41-44R
See also SATA 5
Murphy, Beatrice M. 1908- ... CANR-9
Obituary ... 137
Earlier sketch in CA 53-56
See also DLB 76
Murphy, Brenda C(arol) 1950- ... 120
Murphy, Brian (Michael) 1931- ... CANR-13
Earlier sketch in CA 21-24R
Murphy, Brian 1939- ... 108
Murphy, Buck
See Whitcomb, Ian
Murphy, C. L.
See Murphy, Charlotte A(lice) and Murphy, Lawrence A(gustus)
Murphy, Charles J(ohn) V(incent)
1904-1987 Obituary ... 124
Murphy, Charlotte A(lice) 1924- ... 105
Murphy, Cornelius Francis Jr. 1933- ... 89-92
Murphy, Dervla (Mary) 1931- ... CANR-21
Earlier sketch in CA 103
Murphy, Dorothy Dey
1911(?)-1983 Obituary ... 110
Murphy, E(mmett) Jefferson 1926- ... 25-28R
See also Murphy, Pat
See also SATA 4
Murphy, Earl Finbar 1928- ... 13-16R
Murphy, Ed
See Murphy, Edward Francis
Murphy, Edward Francis 1914- ... 102
Murphy, Edward J. 1927- ... 37-40R
Murphy, Emily 1868-1933 ... DLB 99
Murphy, Emmy Lou Osborne 1910- ... 5-8R
Murphy, Francis 1932- ... CANR-7
Earlier sketch in CA 13-16R
Murphy, Frank Hughes 1940- ... 61-64
Murphy, Fred P. 1889-1979 Obituary ... 89-92
Murphy, Gardner 1895-1979 ... 93-96
Obituary ... 85-88
Murphy, George E(dward) Jr. 1948- ... CANR-13
Earlier sketch in CA 77-80
Murphy, George G(regory) S(tanislaus)
1924- ... 21-24R
Murphy, George Lloyd 1902- ... 45-48
Murphy, Geraldine (Joanne)
1920-1990 Obituary ... 131
Murphy, Grace E. Barstow
1888-1975 Obituary ... 57-60
Murphy, Haughton
See Duffy, James H(enry)
Murphy, Hazel
See Thurston, Hazel (Patricia)
Murphy, Herta A(lbrecht) 1908- ... 49-52
Murphy, Irene L(yons) 1920- ... 53-56
Murphy, J(ohn) Carter 1921- ... 13-16R
Murphy, James F(redrick) 1943- ... CANR-8
Earlier sketch in CA 61-64
Murphy, James J(erome) 1923- ... CANR-27
Earlier sketches in CA 33-36R, CANR-12
Murphy, James M(artin) 1917- ... 29-32R
Murphy, James M(aurice) 1932-1966(?) ... CAP-1
Earlier sketch in CA 11-12
Murphy, James S. 1934- ... 134
Murphy, Jane Brevoort Walden
1902(?)-1980 Obituary ... 97-100
Murphy, Jeffrie G(uy) 1940- Brief entry ... 118
Murphy, Jill 1949- ... 105
See also MAICYA
See also SATA 37, 70
Murphy, Jim 1947- ... 111
See also SATA 32, 37
Murphy, John
See Grady, Ronan Calistus Jr.
Murphy, John L(awrence) 1924- ... CANR-20
Earlier sketch in CA 1-4R
Murphy, John W(illiam) 1948- ... CANR-30
Earlier sketch in CA 112
Murphy, Joseph E. Jr. 1930- ... 133
See also SATA 65
Murphy, Karen A(lee) 1945- ... 115
Murphy, Larry
See Murphy, Lawrence R(ichard)
Murphy, Lawrence A(gustus) 1924- ... 104
Murphy, Lawrence R(ichard) 1942- ... 105
Murphy, Lois Barclay 1902- ... CANR-19
Earlier sketches in CA 1-4R, CANR-4
Murphy, Louis J.
See Hicks, Tyler Gregory
Murphy, Mario
See Edmondson, G. C.
Murphy, Marion Fisher 1902- ... 53-56
Murphy, Martha W(atson) 1951- ... 136
Murphy, (Gavin) Martin (Hedd) 1934- ... 132
Murphy, Michael 1930- ... 73-76
Murphy, N(orman) T. P. 1933- ... 125
Murphy, Nonie Carol
See Caroll, Nonie
Murphy, P(eter) J(ohn) 1946- ... 136
Murphy, Pat ... 137
See also Murphy, E(mmett) Jefferson
Murphy, Patrick T(homas) 1939- ... 108
Murphy, Patrick V(incent) 1920- ... 105
Murphy, Paul J(ames) 1943- ... 112
Murphy, Paul L(loyd) 1923- ... CANR-7
Earlier sketch in CA 17-20R
Murphy, Paul 1917(?)-1983 Obituary ... 111
Murphy, Raymond E(dward) 1898- ... 41-44R
Murphy, Reg 1934- ... 33-36R
Murphy, Richard T. A. 1908- ... CANR-1
Earlier sketch in CA 1-4R
Murphy, Richard 1927- ... 29-32R
See also CLC 41
See also DLB 40
Murphy, Robert Cushman 1887-1973 ... CAP-2
Obituary ... 41-44R
Earlier sketch in CA 23-24
Murphy, Robert D(aniel) 1894-1978 ... CAP-1
Obituary ... 73-76
Earlier sketch in CA 9-10
Murphy, Robert F(rancis) 1924- ... 118
Murphy, Robert (William) 1902-1971 ... CAP-1
Obituary ... 29-32R
Earlier sketch in CA 9-10
See also SATA 10
Murphy, Roland Edmund 1917- ... CANR-6
Earlier sketch in CA 5-8R
Murphy, Romaine 1941- ... 77-80
Murphy, Sharon M. 1940- ... 77-80
Murphy, Shirley Rousseau 1928- ... CANR-29
Earlier sketches in CA 21-24R, CANR-13
See also MAICYA
See also SATA 36, 70, 71
Murphy, Sylvia 1937- ... 121
See also CLC 34
Murphy, Terrence J. 1921- ... 5-8R
Murphy, Thomas Basil Jr. 1935- ... CANR-11
Earlier sketch in CA 69-72
Murphy, Thomas (Bernard) 1935- ... 101
See also CLC 51
Murphy, Thomas P(atrick) 1931- ... CANR-16
Earlier sketch in CA 41-44R
Murphy, Tom
See Murphy, Thomas Basil Jr.
Murphy, Vi 1924(?)-1987 Obituary ... 124
Murphy, Walter F(rancis) 1929- ... CANR-2
Earlier sketch in CA 1-4R
Murphy, Warren B. 1933- ... CANR-31
Earlier sketches in CA 33-36R, CANR-13
Murphy, William Francis 1906- ... 17-20R
Murphy, William M(ichael) 1916- ... 85-88
Murphy-O'Connor, Jerome James
1935- ... CANR-5
Earlier sketch in CA 13-16R
Murra, John V(ictor) 1916- ... CANR-1
Earlier sketch in CA 45-48
Murrah, David Joe 1941- ... 106
Murray, Adrian
See Curran, Mona (Elisa)
Murray, Albert L. 1916- ... CANR-26
Earlier sketch in CA 49-52
See also BW
See also DLB 38
Murray, Andrew Evans 1917- ... 25-28R
Murray, Beatrice
See Posner, Richard
Murray, Bruce C(hurchill) 1931- ... 103
Murray, Christopher 1940- ... 117
Murray, Clara Elizabeth 1894- ... CAP-1
Earlier sketch in CA 9-10
Murray, Cromwell
See Morgan, Murray
Murray, D. Stark
See Murray, David Stark
Murray, Daniel E(dward) 1925- ... 45-48
Murray, David (J.) 1945- ... 133
Murray, David Stark 1900-1977 Obituary ... 111
Murray, Dick 1924- ... 106
Murray, Donald M(orison) 1924- ... CANR-17
Earlier sketch in CA 1-4R
Murray, Dorothy Garst 1915- ... 21-24R
Murray, Edmund P(atrick) 1930- ... 81-84
Murray, Edna
See Rowland, D(onald) S(ydney)
Murray, Edward J(ames) 1928- ... 13-16R
Murray, Edward (James Jr.) 1928- ... CANR-1
Earlier sketch in CA 49-52
Murray, Elwood 1897- ... 73-76
Murray, Eugene Bernard 1927- ... 104
Murray, Frances
See Booth, Rosemary Frances
Murray, G(erald) E(dward Jr.) 1945- ... CANR-5
Earlier sketch in CA 53-56
Murray, (Jesse) George 1909- ... 17-20R
Murray, George (McIntosh) 1900-1970 ... CAP-1
Earlier sketch in CA 13-14
Murray, (George) Gilbert (Aime)
1866-1957 Brief entry ... 110
See also DLB 10
Murray, Hallard T(homas) Jr. 1937- ... 17-20R
Murray, Henry A(lexander)
1893-1988 Obituary ... 125
Brief entry ... 116
Murray, Irene
See Witherspoon, Irene Murray
Murray, J(ohn) Alex ... 41-44R
Murray, J. Harley 1910(?)-1977 Obituary ... 73-76
Murray, J(ohn) Joseph 1915- ... CANR-4
Earlier sketch in CA 5-8R
Murray, James Patrick 1919- ... CANR-34
Earlier sketches in CA 65-68, CANR-15
Murray, James 1946- ... CANR-1
Earlier sketch in CA 49-52
Murray, Jean Shaw 1927(?)-1985 Obituary ... 116
Murray, Jerome T(homas) 1928- ... 33-36R
Murray, Jim
See Murray, James Patrick
Murray, Joan E. 1941- ... 81-84
Murray, Joan 1943- ... 124
Murray, Joan 1945- ... 77-80
Murray, Jocelyn (Margaret) 1929- ... 113
Murray, John A. 1954- ... 138
Murray, John Bernard 1915- ... 41-44R
Murray, John Courtney 1904-1967 Obituary ... 106
Murray, John E(dward) Jr. 1932- ... CANR-31
Earlier sketch in CA 45-48
Murray, John F(rancis) 1923-1977 ... CAP-2
Obituary ... 69-72
Earlier sketch in CA 29-32
Murray, John L(arry) 1937- ... 108
Murray, John MacDougall 1910- ... 33-36R
Murray, John 1923- ... CANR-19
Earlier sketches in CA 5-8R, CANR-4
See also SATA 39
Murray, Judith Sargent 1751-1820 ... DLB 37
Murray, K. F.
See Carlisle, Fred
Murray, K(atherine) M(aud) Elisabeth
1909- ... 77-80
Murray, Keith A. 1910- ... CAP-2
Earlier sketch in CA 33-36
Murray, Ken
See Turner, Robert (Harry)
Murray, Ken 1903-1988 Obituary ... 126
Murray, Les(lie) A(llan) 1938- ... CANR-27
Earlier sketches in CA 21-24R, CANR-11
See also CLC 40
Murray, Lieutenant
See Ballou, Maturin Murray
Murray, Linda Charlton
1936(?)-1986 Obituary ... 118
Murray, Lois Smith 1906- ... 37-40R
Murray, Margaret Alice 1863-1963 ... 5-8R
Murray, Marguerite 1917- ... SATA 63
Murray, Marian ... 41-44R
See also SATA 5
Murray, Martin J(ulius) 1945- ... 132
Murray, Mary (Morrison) 1925- ... 25-28R
Murray, Maynard 1911(?)-1983 Obituary ... 110
Murray, Merrill G. 1900(?)-1976 Obituary ... 69-72
Murray, Michael
See McLaren, Moray (David Shaw)
Murray, Michael V(ivian) 1906- ... 5-8R
Murray, (Judith) Michele (Freedman)
1933-1974 ... 49-52
See also SATA 7
Murray, Ossie 1938- ... SATA 43
Murray, (Anna) Pauli(ne) 1910-1985 ... 125
Obituary ... 116
See also BW
See also DLB 41
Murray, Peter (John) 1920- ... CANR-10
Obituary ... 137
Earlier sketch in CA 13-16R
Murray, Philip 1924- ... 65-68
Murray, Ralph L(a Verne) 1921- ... 13-16R
Murray, Rebecca (Jean) 1936- ... 57-60
Murray, Robert A. 1929- ... 29-32R
Murray, Robert Keith 1922- ... 53-56
Murray, Robin 1940- ... 126
Murray, Roger N(icholas) 1932- ... 21-24R

Murray, Ruth Lovell 1900- 103
Murray, Sister Mary Verona 1909- 17-20R
Murray, Sonia Bennett 1936- 65-68
Murray, Thomas J(oseph) 1943- 77-80
Murray, W(illiam) H(utchison) 1913- CANR-4
Earlier sketch in CA 9-12R
Murray, Walter I(saiah) 1910-1978 85-88
Obituary 73-76
Murray, William Cotter 1929- 53-56
Murray, William J(oseph) III 1946- 110
Murray-Brown, Jeremy 1932- 77-80
Murray-Smith, Stephen 1922- 103
Murrell, Elsie Kathleen Seth-Smith 1883- CAP-1
Earlier sketch in CA 9-10
Murrell, Jim
See Murrell, Vernon James
Murrell, K(eith) F(rank) H(ywel)
1908(?)-1984 Obituary 112
Murrell, Vernon James 1934- 132
Murren, Doug(las) 1951- 136
Murrett, John Charles 1892- 1-4R
Murrow, Casey 1945- 97-100
Murrow, Edward R(oscoe) 1908-1965 103
Obituary 89-92
Murry, J. Middleton
See Murry, John Middleton
Murry, John Middleton
1889-1957 Brief entry 118
See also TCLC 16
Murry, Katherine Middleton 1925- 133
Murry, Mary Middleton 1897-1983 Obituary 110
Murstein, Bernard I(rving) 1929- CANR-3
Earlier sketch in CA 9-12R
Murtagh, John M(artin) 1911-1976 17-20R
Obituary 61-64
Murtagh, William J. 1923- 25-28R
Murton, Jessie Wilmore 5-8R
Murton, Mary 1933- 117
Murton, Thomas O'Rhelius
1929-1990 Obituary 132
Murton, Tom
See Murton, Thomas O'Rhelius
Musa, Mark 1934- 13-16R
Musaeus, Johann Karl August
1735-1787 DLB 97
Musafir
See Tagore, Amitendranath
Musaphia, Joseph 1935- CANR-17
Earlier sketch in CA 97-100
Musarurwa, Willie 1928(?)-1990 Obituary 131
Muscat, Robert J. 1931- 17-20R
Muscatine, Charles 1920- 21-24R
Muscatine, Doris (Corn) 1926- 9-12R
Muschamp, Thomas
See Lloyd-Thomas, Catherine
Muschenheim, Carl 1905-1977 Obituary 69-72
Muschenheim, William (Emil) 1902-1990 CAP-1
Obituary 130
Earlier sketch in CA 13-16
Muschg, Adolf 1934- DLB 75
Musciano, Walt
See Musciano, Walter A.
Musciano, Walter A. 1922- 121
Muse, Beatriz de Regil
1901(?)-1983 Obituary 109
Muse, Benjamin 1898- CANR-1
Earlier sketch in CA 1-4R
Muse, Clarence 1889-1979 Obituary 104
Muse, Daphne P. 1944- 112
Muse, Ken 1925- 111
Muse, Patricia (Alice) 1923- 69-72
Muses, C. A.
See Muses, Charles Arthur
Muses, Charles Arthur 1919- 135
Brief entry 115
Musetto, Andrew P(aul) 1945- 111
Musgrave, Barbara S(tewart) 1913- 5-8R
Musgrave, Clifford 1904-1982 Obituary 107
Musgrave, Florence 1902- CAP-1
Earlier sketch in CA 13-14
See also SATA 3
Musgrave, Richard Abel 1910- 113
Musgrave, Susan 1951- 69-72
See also CLC 13, 54
Musgraves, Don 1935- 65-68
Musgrove, Frank 1922- CANR-6
Earlier sketch in CA 13-16R
Musgrove, Margaret Wynkoop 1943- 65-68
See also SATA 26
Musgrove, Philip 1940- CANR-11
Earlier sketch in CA 29-32R
Musgrove, Stanley (E.) 1924-1986 108
Obituary 118
Mushabac, Jane 1944- 108
Mushkat, Jerome 1931- 81-84
Mushkat, Mari'on 1919- 120
Mushkin, Selma J. 1913-1979 Obituary 93-96
Musial, Joe 1905(?)-1977 Obituary 69-72
Musial, Stan(ley Frank) 1920- 93-96
Musicant, Elke (Alice) 1919- 107
Musicant, Tobias (Ted) 1921- 108
Musiker, Reuben 1931- 57-60
Musil, Robert (Edler von)
1880-1942 Brief entry 109
See also DLB 81
See also TCLC 12
Muske, Carol
See Muske-Dukes, Carol (Anne)
Muske, Irmgard (Gertrud) 1912- CANR-18
Earlier sketch in CA 25-28R
Muske-Dukes, Carol (Anne) 1945- CANR-32
Earlier sketch in CA 65-68
Muskie, Edmund S(ixtus) 1914- CANR-2
Earlier sketch in CA 49-52
Musmanno, Michael A(ngelo) CAP-1
Earlier sketch in CA 9-10
Musolf, Lloyd D(aryl) 1919- CANR-9
Earlier sketch in CA 17-20R
Musselman, George Paul
1895-1987 Obituary 123
Musselman, Vernon A(rmor) 1912- 37-40R
Mussen, Paul Henry 1922- Brief entry 114
Musser, Joe
See Musser, Joseph L.
Musser, Joseph L. 1936- CANR-12
Earlier sketch in CA 29-32R
Mussey, Virginia Howell
See Ellison, Virginia H(owell)
Mussey, Virginia T.H.
See Ellison, Virginia H(owell)
Mussi, Mary 1907- CANR-6
Earlier sketch in CA 53-56
Mussoff, Lenore 1927- 21-24R
Mussolini, Benito (Amilcare Andrea)
1883-1945 Brief entry 116
Mussolini, Rachele Guidi
1890-1979 Obituary 111
Mussulman Joseph A(gee) 1928- 37-40R
Mustafa, Zaki 1934- 41-44R
Muste, John M(artin) 1927- 21-24R
Musteikis, Antanas 1914- 45-48
Musto, Barry 1930- 106
Musto, David Franklin 1936- 104
Musto, Michael 1955- 132
Musto, Ronald G. 1948- 127
Musurillo, Herbert (Anthony Peter)
1917-1974 CAP-1
Obituary 49-52
Earlier sketch in CA 13-14
Mutchler, David E(dward) 1941- 33-36R
Muth, John F(raser) 1930- 13-16R
Muth, Richard F(erris) 1927- 13-16R
Mutharika, B(rightson) W(ebster) T(hom)
1934- 41-44R
Muthesius, Stefan 1939- 61-64
Mutis, Alvaro 1923- HW
Mutke, Peter H(ans) C(hristoph) 1927- 93-96
Muto, Susan Annette 1942- CANR-29
Earlier sketch in CA 110
Mutton, Alice F. A. 1908- 5-8R
Mutz
See Kuenstler, Morton
Muus, Bent J(oergen) 1926- 103
Muus, Flemming B(ruun)
1907-1982 Obituary 110
Muuss, Rolf E(duard Helmut) 1924- 9-12R
Muzumdar, Ammu Menon 1919- 21-24R
Myassin, Leonid Fedorovich 1895-1979 97-100
Obituary 85-88
My Brother's Brother
See Chekhov, Anton (Pavlovich)
Mycue, Edward 1937- CANR-4
Earlier sketch in CA 53-56
Mydans, Carl 97-100
Mydans, Shelley Smith 1915- Brief entry 105
Myddleton, Robert
See Hebblethwaite, Peter
Myer, Dillon S(eymour) 1891-1982 CAP-2
Obituary 116
Earlier sketch in CA 29-32
Myer, John Colby 1912- 45-48
Myer, John Randolph 1927- 5-8R
Myerhoff, Barbara G.
1936(?)-1985 Obituary 114
Myers, A(lexander) J(ohn) William 1877- CAP-1
Earlier sketch in CA 11-12
Myers, Albert M(orris) 1917- 118
Myers, Alec Reginald
See Myers, Alexander Reginald
Myers, Alexander Reginald
1912-1980 CANR-10
Earlier sketch in CA 13-16R
Myers, Alonzo F(ranklin)
1895-1970 Obituary 104
Myers, Andrew Breen 1920- 61-64
Myers, Arthur Sim 1928-1984 Obituary 113
Myers, Arthur 1922- CANR-7
Earlier sketch in CA 17-20R
See also SATA 35
Myers, Bernard S(amuel) 1908- 65-68
Myers, Bernice CANR-8
Earlier sketch in CA 61-64
See also SATA 9
Myers, Bettye (Blanche) 1926- Brief entry 107
Myers, C. F.
See Fairbanks, Carol
Myers, C(hauncie) Kilmer
1916-1981 Obituary 108
Myers, Carol Fairbanks
See Fairbanks, Carol
Myers, Caroline Elizabeth Clark
1887-1980 29-32R
Obituary 134
See also SATA 28
Myers, Charles A(ndrew) 1913- 85-88
Myers, Charles B(ennett) 1939- 57-60
Myers, David G. 1942- CANR-22
Earlier sketch in CA 106
Myers, (Eugene Victor) Debs
1911-1971 Obituary 104
Myers, Desaix B. III 1945- 104
Myers, Edward 1950- 116
Myers, Elisabeth P(erkins) 1918- CANR-3
Earlier sketch in CA 5-8R
See also SATA 36
Myers, Eugene A(braham) 1910- 45-48
Myers, Francis Milton 1917- 5-8R
Myers, Gail E(ldridge) 1923- CANR-1
Earlier sketch in CA 49-52
Myers, Garry Cleveland 1884-1971 CAP-2
Earlier sketch in CA 29-32
Myers, Gay Nagle 1943- 102
Myers, George (Francis) Jr. 1953- 119
Myers, Gerald E(ugene) 1923- 29-32R
Myers, Gustavus 1872-1942 Brief entry 123
See also DLB 47
Myers, Harriet Kathryn
See Whittington, Harry (Benjamin)
Myers, (Mary) Hortense (Powner)
1913-1987 CANR-2
Obituary 123
Earlier sketch in CA 1-4R
See also SATA 10
Myers, Irma A(shley) 1924- 112
Myers, J(ohn) N(owell) L(inton)
1902-1989 Obituary 129
Myers, J(ohn) William 1919- CANR-30
Earlier sketches in CA 33-36R, CANR-12
Myers, (Elliott) Jack 1941- 73-76
Myers, Jacob M(artin) 1904- 17-20R
Myers, John Bernard
1920(?)-1987 Obituary 123
Myers, John H(olmes) 1915- 9-12R
Myers, John Myers 1906- CANR-1
Earlier sketch in CA 1-4R
Myers, Katherine 1952- CANR-28
Earlier sketch in CA 110
Myers, L. H. 1881-1944 DLB 15
Myers, L(ouis) M(cCorry) 1901- 21-24R
Myers, Lonny 1922- 65-68
Myers, Lou(is) 1915- 136
Myers, M(arvin) Scott 1922- 69-72
Myers, Martin 1927- CANR-20
Earlier sketch in CA 29-32R
Myers, Mary Ruth 1947- CANR-16
Earlier sketch in CA 85-88
Myers, Minor Jr. 1942- 133
Myers, Neil 1930- 105
Myers, Norma 1929- 61-64
Myers, Norman 1934- CANR-20
Earlier sketches in CA 49-52, CANR-1
Myers, Patricia 1929- 37-40R
Myers, Paul 1932- 123
Myers, R(obert) E(ugene) 1924- CANR-23
Earlier sketch in CA 77-80
Myers, Ramon H. 1929- 113
Myers, Raymond E(dward) 1902- CAP-1
Earlier sketch in CA 13-16
Myers, Robert J(ohn) 1924- CANR-27
Earlier sketch in CA 107
Myers, Robert J(ulius) 1912- CANR-6
Earlier sketch in CA 13-16R
Myers, Robert Manson 1921- 37-40R
Myers, Rollo Hugh 1892-1984(?) 17-20R
Obituary 115
Myers, Samuel 1897(?)-1983 Obituary 109
Myers, Vernon C. 1911-1990 Obituary 130
Myers, Walter Dean 1937- CANR-20
Earlier sketch in CA 33-36R
See also AAYA 4
See also BLC 3
See also BW
See also CLC 35
See also CLR 4, 16
See also DLB 33
See also MAICYA
See also SAAS 2
See also SATA 27, 41, 70, 71
Myers, Walter M.
See Myers, Walter Dean
Myers, Wayne A(lan) 1931- 138
Myers, William 1939- 132
Myerscough-Walker, Raymond
1912-1984 Obituary 113
Myerson, Bess 1924- 108
Myerson, Joel 1945- CANR-19
Earlier sketch in CA 102
Myerson, Michael 1940- 73-76
Myhers, John 1921- 105
Obituary 137
Myhill, Henry (James) 1925-1977 103
Mykle, Agrar 1915- 13-16R
Mylander, Maureen 1937- CANR-5
Earlier sketch in CA 53-56
Myler, Joseph L. 1905(?)-1973 Obituary 41-44R
Myles, Eugenie Louise (Butler) 1905- CAP-1
Earlier sketch in CA 11-12
Myles, Symon
See Follett, Ken(neth Martin)
Myller, Rolf 1926- CANR-8
Earlier sketch in CA 5-8R
See also SATA 27
Mylonas, George Emmanuel
1898-1988 Obituary 125
Mynors, Roger A(ubrey) B(askerville)
1903-1989 5-8R
Obituary 129
Myra, Harold L(awrence) 1939- CANR-8
Earlier sketch in CA 61-64
See also SATA 42, 46
Myrdal, Alva Reimer 1902-1986 69-72
Obituary 118
Myrdal, (Karl) Gunnar 1898-1987 CANR-4
Obituary 122
Earlier sketch in CA 9-12R
Myrdal, Jan 1927- 132
Brief entry 117
Myrer, Anton 1922- CANR-3
Earlier sketch in CA 1-4R
Myres, J(ohn) N(owell) L(inton) 1902- 123
Myres, Sandra Lynn 1933- CANR-14
Earlier sketch in CA 33-36R
Myrick, David F. CANR-6
Earlier sketch in CA 13-16R
Myrick, Robert D(eWayne) 1935- CANR-17
Earlier sketch in CA 41-44R
Myrick, William J(ennings Jr.) 1932- 73-76
Myrland, Doug 1952- 117
Myron, Robert 1926- 13-16R
Myrsiades, Kostas J. 1940- CANR-27
Earlier sketch in CA 109
Myrus, Donald (Richard) 1927- CANR-4
Earlier sketch in CA 1-4R
See also SATA 23
Mysak, Edward D(amien)
1930-1989 Obituary 130

N

Naamani, Israel T(arkow) 1913(?)- 124
Brief entry 106
Naar, Jon 1920- 102
Nabbes, Thomas 1605(?)-1641 DLB 58
Nabholtz, John R(obert) 1931- 65-68
Nabl, Franz 1883-1974 DLB 81
Nabokov, Dmitri 1934- 132
Nabokov, Nicolas 1903-1978 85-88
Obituary 77-80
Nabokov, Peter (Francis) 1940- CANR-27
Earlier sketches in CA 21-24R, CANR-9
Nabokov, Vladimir (Vladimirovich)
1899-1977 CANR-20
Obituary 69-72
Earlier sketch in CA 5-8R
See also CDALB 1941-1968
See also CLC 1, 2, 3, 6, 8, 11, 15, 23, 44, 46, 64
See also DLB 2
See also DLBD 3
See also DLBY 80, 91
See also MTCW
See also WLC
Nacci, Chris (Natale) 1909- 41-44R
Nachbar, Herbert
1930(?)-1980 Obituary 97-100
Nachbar, Jack 1941- 53-56
Nachman, Gerald 1938- CANR-37
Earlier sketches in CA 65-68, CANR-16
Nachtigal, Paul M. 1930- 112
Nachtigall, Lila Ehrenstein
1934- Brief entry 105
Nachtmann, Francis Weldon
1913-1982 37-40R
Obituary 133
Nadan, Paul 1933(?)-1978 Obituary 104
Naddor, Eliezer 1920- 21-24R
Nadeau, Maurice 1911- 49-52
Nadeau, R(aymond) E(rnest)
1913- Brief entry 107
Nadeau, Ray E.
See Nadeau, R(aymond) E(rnest)
Nadeau, Remi A(llen) 1920- CANR-2
Earlier sketch in CA 1-4R
Nadeau, Roland 1928- CANR-4
Earlier sketch in CA 53-56
Nadel, Frances 1905(?)-1977 Obituary 69-72
Nadel, Gerald H. 1944-1977 81-84
Obituary 73-76
Nadel, Ira Bruce 1943- CANR-39
Earlier sketches in CA 102, CANR-18
Nadel, Mark V(ictor) 1943- 33-36R
Nadel, Norman (Sanford) 1915- 106
Nadelhoffer, Hans (L.) 1940-1988 137
Nader, George Albert 1940- 111
Nader, George 1921- Brief entry 109
Nader, Laura 1930- CANR-7
Earlier sketch in CA 17-20R
Nader, Ralph 1934- 77-80
Nadich, Judah 1912- 127
Nadler, Harvey 1933- 13-16R
Nadler, Leonard 1922- CANR-20
Earlier sketches in CA 53-56, CANR-5
Nadler, Paul S(tephen) 1930- 25-28R
Nadler, Susan
See Gantry, Susan Nadler
Nadler, Zeace 1925- 121
Naef, Weston J(ohn) 1942- Brief entry 111
Naeslund, Erik 1948- 103
Naess, Harald Sigurd 1925- 41-44R
Naether, Carl (Albert) 1892- 25-28R
Nafziger, E(stel) Wayne 1938- 85-88
Nafziger, George F(rancis) 1949- 132
Nag
See Grauer, Neil A(lbert)
Nag, Moni 1925- 41-44R
Nagai Berthrong, Evelyn 1946- 115
Nagai Kafu
See Nagai Sokichi
Nagai Sokichi 1879-1959 Brief entry 117
Nagara, Susumu 1932- CANR-3
Earlier sketch in CA 45-48
Nagatsu, Toshiharu 1930- 107
Nagatsuka, Ryuji 1924- Brief entry 125
na gCopaleen, Myles
See O Nuallain, Brian
Nagel, Andreas Fischer
See Fischer-Nagel, Andreas
Nagel, Ernest 1901-1985 93-96
Obituary 117
Nagel, Heiderose Fischer
See Fischer-Nagel, Heiderose
Nagel, James (Edward) 1940- CANR-27
Earlier sketch in CA 29-32R
Nagel, Otto 1894-1967 Obituary 106
Nagel, Paul C(hester) 1926- CANR-22
Earlier sketches in CA 9-12R, CANR-5
Nagel, Shirley 1922- 93-96
Nagel, Stuart S(amuel) 1934- CANR-33
Earlier sketches in CA 33-36R, CANR-14
Nagel, Thomas 1937- CANR-4
Earlier sketch in CA 53-56

Nagel, William G(eorge) 1916- 49-52
Nagenda, Musa
See Howard, Moses L(eon)
Nagera, Humberto 1927- 57-60
Nagi, Mostafa H. 1934- 33-36R
Nagi, Saad Z. 1925- 29-32R
Nagle, James J. 1909-1978 85-88
Obituary 81-84
Naglee, David Ingersoll 1930- 53-56
Nagler, Alois Maria 1907- CANR-19
Earlier sketch in CA 103
Nagler, Barney 1912-1990 ....17-20R
Obituary 132
Nagler, Michael N(icholas) 1937- CANR-13
Earlier sketch in CA 73-76
na Gopaleen, Myles
See O Nuallain, Brian
Nagorski, Andrew 1947- 93-96
Nagorski, Zygmunt Jr. 1912- 73-76
Nagorski, Zygmunt
1885(?)-1973 Obituary 41-44R
Nagourney, Peter (Jon) 1940- 37-40R
Naguib, Mohammed 1902(?)-1984 Obituary 113
Nagy, Ferenc 1903-1979 Obituary 89-92
Nagy, Gil D. 1933- 25-28R
Nagy, Gregory 1942- 102
Nagy, Imre 1895(?)-1958 Brief entry 118
Nagy, Laszlo 1925-1978 129
Obituary 112
See also CLC 7
Nagy-Talavera, Nicholas M(anuel)
1929- 33-36R
Naha, Ed 1950- 109
Nahal, Chaman 1927- CANR-17
Earlier sketch in CA 37-40R
Nahas, Gabriel G(eorges) 1920- CANR-17
Earlier sketches in CA 49-52, CANR-1
Nahas, Rebecca 1946- 69-72
Nahem, Joseph 1917- 113
Nahm, Milton C(harles) 1903-1991 ....13-16R
Obituary 133
Nahum, Lucien 1930(?)-1983 Obituary 111
Naidis, Mark 1918- 33-36R
Naidoo, Beverley 1943- ....SATA 63
Naifeh, Steven Woodward 1952- 102
Naik, Madhukar Krishna 1926- CANR-25
Earlier sketches in CA 21-24R, CANR-10
Naim, C(houdhri) M(ohammed)
1936- Brief entry 112
Naiman, Arthur 1941- CANR-29
Earlier sketch in CA 108
Naimy, Mikhail 1889-1988 Obituary 124
Naipaul, Shiva(dhar Srinivasa)
1945-1985 ....CANR-33
Obituary 116
Brief entry 110
Earlier sketch in CA 112
See also CLC 32, 39
See also DLBY 85
See also MTCW
Naipaul, V(idiadhar) S(urajprasad)
1932- CANR-33
Earlier sketches in CA 1-4R, CANR-1
See also CDBLB 1960 to Present
See also CLC 4, 7, 9, 13, 18, 37
See also DLBY 85
See also MTCW
Nairn, Ian (Douglas) 1930-1983 Obituary 110
Nairn, Ronald C(harles) 1922- 21-24R
Nairne, Katharine Davina 1949- 128
Nairne, Kathy
See Nairne, Katharine Davina
Naisawald, L. Van Loan 1920- CANR-6
Earlier sketch in CA 5-8R
Naisbitt, John 1929- 128
Brief entry 113
See also BEST 90:3
Naismith, Grace (Akin) 1904-1983 ....CANR-20
Obituary 111
Earlier sketch in CA 65-68
Naismith, Helen 1929- 69-72
Naismith, Horace
See Helmer, William J(oseph)
Naismith, James 1861-1939 Brief entry 118
Naismith, Marion (Overend) 1922- 29-32R
Naismith, Robert J. 1916- 121
Najafi, Najmeh 25-28R
Najarian, Nevart 1901(?)-1985 Obituary 117
Najder, Zdzislaw 1930- 17-20R
Najemy, John Michael 1943- 118
Nakadate, Neil Edward 1943- 115
Nakae, Noriko 1940- 49-52
See also SATA 59
Nakamura, Hajime 1912- CANR-10
Earlier sketch in CA 53-56
Nakamura, James I. 1919- 21-24R
Nakamura, Yasuo 1919- 45-48
Nakanishi, Don T(oshiaki) 1949- 114
Nakanishi, Marsha
See Hirano-Nakanishi, Marsha J(oyce)
Nakanishi, Marsha J(oyce) Hirano
See Hirano-Nakanishi, Marsha J(oyce)
Nakano, Desmond 134
Nakano, Hirotaka 1942- 33-36R
Nakarai, Toyozo W(ada) 1898- 41-44R
Nakashima, George Katsutoshi 1905- 106
Nakatani, Chiyoko 1930-1981 77-80
See also SATA 40, 55
Nakayama, Shigeru 1928- 29-32R
Nakdimon, Shlomo 1936- 128
Nakhleh, Emile A. 1938- 77-80
Nakhnikian, George 1920- CANR-2
Earlier sketch in CA 1-4R
Nakos, Lilika 1899(?)- ....CLC 29
Nalder, Eric C(hristopher) 1946- 89-92
Nale, Sharon Anne 1944- 108
Nall, Hiram Abiff 1950- 57-60
Nall, T(orney) Otto 1900- 17-20R
Nallin, Walter E. 1917(?)-1978 Obituary 77-80
Nalty, Bernard Charles 1931- CANR-18
Earlier sketch in CA 102
Nam, Charles B(enjamin) 1926- CANR-10
Earlier sketch in CA 65-68
Nam, Koon Woo 1928- 61-64
Namath, Joe
See Namath, Joseph William
Namath, Joseph William 1943- 89-92
Namba, Toshio 1910-1987 Obituary 124
Nambiar, O. K. 1910- 13-16R
Nameroff, Rochelle 1943- 41-44R
Namias, June 1941- 81-84
Namier, Julia 1893-1977 61-64
Obituary 120
Namier, Lewis Bernstein
1888-1960 Obituary 113
Namikawa, Banri 1931- CANR-8
Earlier sketch in CA 53-56
Namikawa, Ryo 1905- 93-96
Namioka, Lensey 1929- CANR-27
Earlier sketches in CA 69-72, CANR-11
See also SATA 27
Namir, Mordecai 1897-1975 Obituary 57-60
Namjoshi, Suniti 1941- 113
Namora, Ferando (Goncalves)
1919-1989 Obituary 127
Namovicz, Gene Inyart 1927- 17-20R
See also Inyart, Gene
Nanassy, Louis C(harles) 1913- CANR-19
Earlier sketches in CA 53-56, CANR-4
Nance, Guinevera Ann 1939- 106
Nance, James Clark 1893(?)-1984 Obituary 113
Nance, John J. 1946- 137
Nance, Joseph Milton 1913- CANR-1
Earlier sketch in CA 1-4R
Nanda, B(al) R(am) 1917- CANR-23
Earlier sketches in CA 13-16R, CANR-7
Nandakumar, Prema 1939- 9-12R
Nandy, Pritish 1947- CANR-12
Earlier sketch in CA 65-68
Nangia, Sudesh 1942- CANR-22
Earlier sketches in CA 53-56, CANR-4
NanKivell, Joice M.
See Loch, Joice N(anKivell)
Nannes, Caspar Harold 1906-1978 ....9-12R
Obituary 81-84
Nanogak Agnes 1925- ....SATA 61
Nanry, Charles (Anthony) 1938- 73-76
Nanus, Burt 1936- 115
Napier, B(unyan) Davie 1915- CANR-4
Earlier sketch in CA 1-4R
Napier, Bill 1940- 130
Napier, Geraldine
See Glemser, Bernard
Napier, Mark
See Laffin, John (Alfred Charles)
Napier, Mary
See Wright, (Mary) Patricia
Napier, Priscilla 1908- 21-24R
Napier, William
See Seymour, William Napier
Napjus, Alice James 1913- 21-24R
Napjus, James
See Napjus, Alice James
Napley, David 1915- 129
Napley, Sir David
See Napley, David
Napoleon, Art
See Sudhalter, Richard M(errill)
Napolitan, Joseph 1929- 37-40R
Napolitane, Catherine A(nn) Durrum
1936- 85-88
Narain, Jai Prakash
See Narayan, Jayaprakash
Narang, Gopi Chand 1931- CANR-31
Earlier sketches in CA 29-32R, CANR-14
Narasimhachar, K. T.
See Narasimha Char, K. T.
Narasimha Char, K. T. 1903- CANR-5
Earlier sketch in CA 53-56
Narasimhan, Chakravarthi V. 1915- 17-20R
Narayan, Jayaprakash 1902-1979 97-100
Obituary 89-92
Narayan, Ongkar 1926- 103
Narayan, R(asipuram) K(rishnaswami)
1906- CANR-33
Earlier sketch in CA 81-84
See also CLC 7, 28, 47
See also MTCW
See also SATA 62
Narayn, Deane 1929- 1-4R
Nardi, James B. 1948- 127
Nardin, Terry 1942- 41-44R
Narell, Irena 1923- CANR-1
Earlier sketch in CA 1-4R
Naremore, James 1941- CANR-11
Earlier sketch in CA 69-72
Naroll, Raoul 1920-1985 ....33-36R
Obituary 116
Narrache, Jean 1893-1970 ....DLB 92
Narramore, Stanley Bruce 1941- 57-60
Naruse, Mikio 1905-1969 118
Narveson, Jan F(redric) 1936- CANR-24
Earlier sketches in CA 21-24R, CANR-9
Nasatir, A(braham) P(hineas) 1904- CANR-5
Earlier sketch in CA 9-12R
Nasatir, David 1934- 41-44R
Nasaw, David 1945- 116
Nasaw, Jonathan Lewis 1947- 61-64
Nasby, A(sher Gordon)
1909-1983 Obituary 109
Nasby, Petroleum Vesuvius
See Locke, David Ross
Nash, Alanna 1950- 129
Nash, Allan N(ylin) 1932- 41-44R
Nash, Bruce M(itchell) 1947- CANR-15
Earlier sketch in CA 85-88
See also SATA 34
Nash, Daniel
See Loader, William Reginald
Nash, David T(heodore) 1929- 93-96
Nash, Eno
See Stevens, Austin N(eil)
Nash, Ethel Miller 1909- CAP-1
Earlier sketch in CA 13-16
Nash, Father Stephen
See Kavanaugh, James J(oseph)
Nash, Gary B. 1933- 37-40R
Nash, George (E.) 1948- 138
Nash, Gerald D(avid) 1928- CANR-8
Earlier sketch in CA 21-24R
Nash, Howard P(ervear) Jr. 1900-1981 73-76
Obituary 133
Nash, Isabel
See Eberstadt, Isabel
Nash, J(essie) Madeleine 1943- 69-72
Nash, James E(dward) 1933- 29-32R
Nash, Jay Robert 1937- 21-24R
Nash, June (Caprice) 1927- 29-32R
Nash, (Cyril) Knowlton 1927- 135
Nash, Lee (Marten) 1927- 41-44R
Nash, Linell
See Smith, Linell Nash
Nash, Manning 1924- 17-20R
Nash, Mary (Hughes) 1925- 5-8R
See also SATA 41
Nash, N. Richard 1913- CANR-14
Earlier sketch in CA 85-88
Nash, Nancy 1943- 21-24R
Nash, Newlyn
See Howe, Doris Kathleen
Nash, (Fredric) Ogden 1902-1971 ....CANR-34
Obituary 29-32R
Earlier sketches in CAP-1, CA 13-14
See also CLC 23
See also DLB 11
See also MAICYA
See also MTCW
See also SATA 2, 46
Nash, Padder
See Sewart, Alan
Nash, Paul 1924- 17-20R
Nash, Ralph (Lee) 1925- 17-20R
Nash, Ray 1905-1982 Obituary 106
Nash, Robert 1902- CAP-1
Earlier sketch in CA 9-10
Nash, Roderick 1939- 17-20R
Nash, Ronald H. 1936- CANR-23
Earlier sketches in CA 5-8R, CANR-8
Nash, Simon
See Chapman, Raymond
Nash, William (Wray) Jr. 1928- 85-88
Naske, Claus-M(ichael) 1935- CANR-31
Earlier sketches in CA 77-80, CANR-13
Naslund, Erik
See Naeslund, Erik
Nason, Alvin 1919-1978 Obituary 77-80
Nason, Donna 1944- 97-100
Nason, Leonard H(astings)
1895-1970 Obituary 114
Nason, Leslie J. 5-8R
Nason, Tema 138
Nasr, Seyyed Hossein 1933- CANR-10
Earlier sketch in CA 21-24R
Nass, Elyse (Linda) 1947- 111
Nass, Stanley 1940- 115
Nassaar, Christopher S(uhayl) 1944- 97-100
Nassar, Eugene Paul 1935- 33-36R
Nassau, Wilhelmina Helena Pauline Maria
1880-1962 Obituary 113
Nassauer, Rudolf 1924- 105
Nasser, Gamal Abdel 1918-1970 Obituary 113
Nassivera, John 1950- 109
Nassour, Ellis (Michael) 1941- 119
Nast, Conde 1873-1942 ....DLB 91
Nast, Elsa Ruth
See Watson, Jane Werner
Nast, Thomas 1840-1902 Brief entry 112
See also SATA 33, 51
Nastick, Sharon 1954- 114
See also SATA 41
Natale, Samuel M(ichael) 1943- 116
Natali, Alfred Maxim 1915- 57-60
Natanson, George 1928- 73-76
Natanson, Maurice (Alexander) 1924- CANR-12
Earlier sketch in CA 17-20R
Natchez, Gladys W. 1915- CANR-4
Earlier sketch in CA 9-12R
Natella, Arthur A(ristides) Jr. 1941- CANR-15
Earlier sketch in CA 89-92
Nathan, Adele (Gutman) 1900(?)-1986 73-76
Obituary 119
See also SATA 48
Nathan, Andrew J(ames) 1943- 65-68
Nathan, Daniel
See Dannay, Frederic
Nathan, David 1926- CANR-12
Earlier sketch in CA 29-32R
Nathan, Dorothy (Goldeen) 81-84
See also SATA 15
Nathan, George Jean
1882-1958 Brief entry 114
See also Hatteras, Owen
See also TCLC 18
Nathan, Hans 1910- CANR-1
Earlier sketch in CA 1-4R
Nathan, James A. 1942- CANR-16
Earlier sketch in CA 85-88
Nathan, Jean
See Levinsohn, Florence H(amlish)
Nathan, Joan 1943- 61-64
Nathan, Joe 1948- 115
Nathan, Leonard E(dward) 1924- CANR-7
Earlier sketch in CA 5-8R
Nathan, Norman 1915- CANR-1
Earlier sketch in CA 1-4R
Nathan, Otto 1893-1987 Obituary 121
Nathan, Paul S. 1913- Brief entry 116
Nathan, Peter E. 1935- 73-76
Nathan, Richard P(erle) 1935- CANR-7
Earlier sketch in CA 57-60
Nathan, Robert (Gruntal) 1894-1985 ....CANR-6
Obituary 116
Earlier sketch in CA 13-16R
See also DLB 9
See also SATA 6, 43
Nathan, Robert Stuart 1948- 81-84
Nathanson, Carol (Edna) 1922- 132
Nathanson, Jerome 1908-1975 Obituary 57-60
Nathanson, Laura Walther 1941- 123
See also SATA 57
Nathanson, Leonard 1933- 21-24R
Nathanson, Nathaniel L(ouis) 1908-1983 89-92
Obituary 111
Nathanson, Yale S(amuel) 1895- 77-80
Nations, Opal (Louis) 1941- 112
Natkin, Rick 1952- 129
Natoli, Joseph
See Natoli, Joseph P.
Natoli, Joseph P. 1943- 132
Natow, Annette 1933- 114
Natsume, Kinnosuke 1867-1916 Brief entry 104
See also Natsume, Soseki
Natsume, Soseki
See Natsume, Kinnosuke
See also TCLC 2, 10
Natta, Giulio 1903-1979 Obituary 113
Natti, (Mary) Lee 1919- CANR-2
Earlier sketch in CA 5-8R
See also Kingman, Lee
Natti, Susanna 1948- ....SATA 32
Natusch, Sheila (Ellen) 1926- CANR-20
Earlier sketch in CA 103
Natwar-Singh, K. 1931- 13-16R
Nau, Erika S(chwager) 1918- 65-68
Nau, Henry R(ichard) 1941- 135
Naude, (Aletta) Adele da Fonseca-Wollheim
1910- 9-12R
Nauer, Barbara Joan 1932- Brief entry 105
Naughton, Bill
See Naughton, William John (Francis)
Naughton, James Franklin 1957- 132
Naughton, Jim
See Naughton, James Franklin
Naughton, John 1933- 57-60
Naughton, William John (Francis)
1910-1992 ....CANR-36
Obituary 136
Earlier sketch in CA 105
See also DLB 13
See also MTCW
Naugle, Helen Harrold 1920- 53-56
Naugle, John E(arl) 1923- 65-68
Nauheim, Ferd(inand Alan) 1909- CANR-16
Earlier sketches in CA 49-52, CANR-1
Nauman, St. Elmo Jr. 1935- 53-56
Naumann, Anthony Frank 1921-1971 ....21-24R
Obituary 89-92
Naumann, Marina 1938- 93-96
Naumann, Oscar E(dward) 1912- 77-80
Naumann, Rose 1919- 65-68
Naumburg, Margaret 1890-1983 Obituary 109
Naumoff, Lawrence 1946- 128
Nauticus
See Waltari, Mika (Toimi)
Nava, Gregory 1949- 131
See also HW
Nava, Julian 1927- 61-64
See also HW
Nava, Michael 1954- 124
Nava, Roberto 1906(?)-1983 Obituary 111
Navarra, Fernand Jean 1915- 108
Navarra, John Gabriel 1927- 41-44R
See also SATA 8
Navarre, Yves (Henri Michel) 1940- 133
Navarro, Antonio 1922- 107
Navarro (Gerassi), Marysa 1934- 106
Navarro, Peter 1949- 118
Navas, Deborah 1943- 112
Navasky, Victor S. 1932- CANR-10
Earlier sketch in CA 21-24R
Navas-Ruiz, Ricardo 1932- Brief entry 107
Navone, John J(oseph) 1930- CANR-28
Earlier sketches in CA 21-24R, CANR-10
Navrozov, Lev 1928- 61-64
Naydler, Merton 1920- 45-48
Naylor, Chris(topher Michael) 1947- 118
Naylor, Eric W(oodfin) 1936- 45-48
Naylor, Gloria 1950- CANR-27
Earlier sketch in CA 107
See also AAYA 6
See also BLC 3
See also BW
See also CLC 28, 52
See also MTCW
Naylor, Harriet H. 1915- CANR-9
Earlier sketch in CA 21-24R
Naylor, James C(harles) 1932- CANR-1
Earlier sketch in CA 45-48
Naylor, John 1920- 93-96
Naylor, Margot Ailsa (Lodge) 1907-1972 ....9-12R
Obituary 134
Naylor, Penelope 1941- 37-40R
See also SATA 10

Naylor, Phyllis (Reynolds) 1933- ... CANR-24
Earlier sketches in CA 21-24R, CANR-8
See also AAYA 4
See also CLR 17
See also MAICYA
See also SAAS 10
See also SATA 12, 66
Nazareth, Peter 1940- ... 101
Nazarian, Nikki
See Nichols, Cecilia Fawn
Nazaroff, Alexander I. 1898- ... 33-36R
See also SATA 4
Nazzaro, Anthony M. 1927- Brief entry ... 106
Neagle, Anna 1904-1986 Obituary ... 119
Neagley, Ross Linn 1907- ... 106
Neagoe, Anna (Frankel)
1885(?)-1986 Obituary ... 120
Neagoe, Peter 1881-1960 ... 105
See also DLB 4
Neal, Alfred C. 1912- ... 121
Neal, Ann Parker 1934- Brief entry ... 114
Neal, Arminta Pearl 1921- ... 85-88
Neal, Bruce W(alter) 1931- ... 21-24R
Neal, Charles Dempsey 1908- ... CANR-5
Earlier sketch in CA 5-8R
Neal, Emily Gardiner ... CANR-3
Earlier sketch in CA 5-8R
Neal, Ernest G(ordon) 1911- ... 13-16R
Neal, Fred Warner 1915- ... CANR-2
Earlier sketch in CA 5-8R
Neal, Harry
See Bixby, Jerome Lewis
Neal, Harry Edward 1906- ... CANR-2
Earlier sketch in CA 5-8R
See also SATA 5
Neal, Helen Keating 1907-1987 ... 124
Obituary ... 122
Neal, Hilary
See Norton, Olive (Claydon)
Neal, James M(adison) 1925- ... 73-76
Neal, James T(homas) 1936- ... 57-60
Neal, John 1793-1876 ... DLB 1, 59
Neal, Joseph C. 1807-1847 ... DLB 11
Neal, Julia 1905- ... 69-72
Neal, Larry
See Neal, Lawrence (P.)
See also DLB 38
Neal, Lawrence (P.) 1937-1981 ... 81-84
Obituary ... 102
See also Neal, Larry
See also BW
Neal, Marie Augusta 1921- ... CANR-35
Earlier sketches in CA 114, CANR-32
Neal, Michael
See Teitelbaum, Michael
Neal, Nelson 1921(?)-1983 Obituary ... 109
Neal, Patsy 1938- ... 61-64
Neal, W(illiam) Keith 1905-1990 Obituary ... 131
Neale, Gay Weeks 1935- ... 113
Neale, John E(rnest) 1890-1975 ... 65-68
Obituary ... 61-64
Neale, Robert George 1919- Brief entry ... 108
Neale, Walter Castle 1925- ... CANR-7
Earlier sketch in CA 5-8R
Neale-Silva, Eduardo 1905- Brief entry ... 106
Nealon, Eleanor ... 103
Nealon, Thomas E. 1933- ... 33-36R
Neaman, Judith S(ilverman) 1936- ... 61-64
Neame, Alan John 1924- ... CANR-2
Earlier sketch in CA 1-4R
Nearing, Guy 1890-1986 Obituary ... 118
Nearing, Helen K(nothe) 1904- ... CANR-11
Earlier sketch in CA 29-32R
Nearing, Penny 1916- ... 81-84
See also SATA 42, 47
Nearing, Scott 1883-1983 ... CANR-11
Obituary ... 110
Earlier sketch in CA 41-44R
Neary, John (Anthony Jr.) 1937- Brief entry ... 107
Neatby, H(erbert) Blair 1924- Brief entry ... 111
Neatby, Leslie Hamilton 1902- ... CANR-3
Earlier sketch in CA 5-8R
Neate, Frank Anthony 1928- ... 105
Neave, Airey (Middleton Sheffield)
1916-1979 ... 85-88
Neavles, Janet Talmadge 1919- ... 5-8R
Nebel, Gustave E. ... SATA 33, 45
Nebel, Mimouca
See Nebel, Gustave E.
Nebenzahl, Kenneth 1927- ... 111
Brief entry ... 109
Nebrensky, Alex
See Cooper, Parley J(oseph)
Nebylitsyn, Vladimir Dmitrievich
1930(?)-1972 Obituary ... 37-40R
Necheles, Ruth F. 1936- ... 41-44R
Necker, Claire (Kral) 1917- ... 33-36R
Nederhood, Joel H(oman) 1930- ... 29-32R
Nee, Brett de Bary 1943- ... 101
Nee, Kay Bonner ... CANR-31
Earlier sketches in CA 49-52, CANR-2
See also SATA 10
Needham, David C. 1929- ... 118
Needham, (Noel) Joseph (Terence Montgomery)
1900- ... CANR-34
Earlier sketches in CA 9-12R, CANR-5
Needham, Richard (John) 1912- ... 101
Needham, Rodney 1923- ... CANR-15
Earlier sketch in CA 81-84
Needham, (Amy) Violet
1876-1967 Obituary ... 116
Needle, Jan 1943- ... CANR-28
Earlier sketch in CA 106
See also SATA 30
Needleman, Jacob 1934- ... CANR-12
Earlier sketch in CA 29-32R
See also SATA 6
Needleman, Morriss H. 1907- ... 25-28R
Needler, Howard I(an) 1937- ... 111
Needler, Martin C(yril) 1933- ... CANR-18
Earlier sketches in CA 5-8R, CANR-2
Needles, Robert Johnson 1903- ... CAP-1
Earlier sketch in CA 11-12
Neef, Elton T.
See Fanthorpe, R(obert) Lionel
Neel, (Louis) Boyd 1905-1981 Obituary ... 108
Neel, Janet
See Cohen, Janet
Neel, Joanne Loewe 1920- ... 25-28R
Neely, Bill 1930- ... CANR-28
Earlier sketches in CA 33-36R, CANR-13
Neely, Carol Thomas 1939- ... 128
Brief entry ... 107
Neely, James C. 1926- ... 109
Neely, Mark E(dward) Jr. 1944- ... CANR-25
Earlier sketch in CA 106
Neely, Martina 1939- ... 61-64
Neely, Richard (Forlani) 1941- ... CANR-28
Earlier sketch in CA 107
Neenan, William B(raunger) 1929- ... 41-44R
Neeper, Carolyn 1937- ... 57-60
Neeper, Cary
See Neeper, Carolyn
Neerskov, Hans Kristian 1932- ... 65-68
Nef, Evelyn Stefansson 1913- ... CANR-20
Earlier sketch in CA 49-52
Nef, John Ulric 1899-1988 ... CANR-20
Obituary ... 127
Earlier sketch in CA 1-4R
Neff, Alan (Henry) 1949- ... 117
Neff, Donald (Lloyd) 1930- ... CANR-28
Earlier sketch in CA 77-80
Neff, Emery E. 1892-1983 ... 5-8R
Obituary ... 109
Neff, H(arry) Richard 1933- ... 33-36R
Neff, Hildegard
See Knef, Hildegard
Neff, John C. 1913- ... 17-20R
Neff, Miriam 1945- ... 115
Neff, Renfreu (de St. Laurence) 1938- ... 29-32R
Neff, Robert W(ilbur) 1936- ... 106
Neff, Walter S(cott) 1910- ... CAP-2
Earlier sketch in CA 25-28
Neff, William Lee 1906-1973 ... 1-4R
Obituary ... 103
Neft, David S(amuel) 1937- ... 41-44R
Negandhi, A(nant) R(anchoddas) 1933- ... 33-36R
Neggers, Carla A(malia) 1955- ... CANR-30
Earlier sketch in CA 112
Negley, Glenn (Robert) 1907-1988 ... 17-20R
Obituary ... 125
Negri, Ada 1870-1945 ... DLB 114
Negri, Rocco 1932- ... SATA 12
Negroponte, Nicholas Peter 1943- ... 29-32R
Negus, Arthur George 1903-1985 Obituary ... 116
Negus, Kenneth George 1927- ... 17-20R
Nehamas, Alexander 1946- ... 126
Neher, Andre 1914- ... CANR-26
Earlier sketch in CA 109
Neher, Clark D(umont) 1938- ... 118
Neher, Jack 1918- ... 118
Nehrling, Arno H. 1886-1974 ... 9-12R
Obituary ... 53-56
Nehrling, Irene Dahlberg 1900- ... 9-12R
Nehrt, Lee Charles 1926- ... CANR-13
Earlier sketch in CA 21-24R
Nehru, Jawaharlal 1889-1964 ... CANR-34
Earlier sketch in CA 85-88
See also MTCW
Neiburg, Gladys Eudas 1898- ... 61-64
Neider, Charles 1915- ... CANR-24
Earlier sketch in CA 17-20R
Neiderman, Andrew 1940- ... CANR-13
Earlier sketch in CA 33-36R
Neidermyer, Dan 1947- ... CANR-24
Earlier sketch in CA 45-48
Neidhardt, W(ilfried) S(teffen) 1941- ... 65-68
Neidpath, James
See Charteris, James Donald
Neier, Aryeh 1937- ... 57-60
See also SATA 59
Neighbour, Ralph W(ebster) 1906- ... CANR-1
Earlier sketch in CA 1-4R
Neighbour, Rhona M.
See Martin, Rhona
Neighbours, Kenneth Franklin 1915- ... 61-64
Neigoff, Anne ... 41-44R
See also SATA 13
Neigoff, Mike 1920- ... CANR-2
Earlier sketch in CA 5-8R
See also SATA 13
Neihardt, John Gneisenau 1881-1973 ... CAP-1
Earlier sketch in CA 13-14
See also CLC 32
See also DLB 9, 54
Neikirk, William (Robert) 1938- ... 117
Neil, Hugh Michael 1930- Brief entry ... 109
Neil, J. Meredith 1937- ... 33-36R
Neil, Randolph L. 1941- ... 93-96
Neil, Randy
See Neil, Randolph L.
Neil, William 1909-1979 ... CANR-6
Obituary ... 93-96
Earlier sketch in CA 9-12R
Neilan, Sarah ... 69-72
Neilands, J(ohn) B(rian) 1921- ... 97-100
Neill, A(lexander) S(utherland) 1883-1973 ... 101
Obituary ... 45-48
Neill, Christopher Harry Douglas 1955- ... 117
Neill, Stephen Charles 1900-1984 ... CANR-7
Obituary ... 113
Earlier sketch in CA 9-12R
Neill, Thomas Patrick 1915-1970 ... CANR-3
Earlier sketch in CA 5-8R
Neilson, Andrew 1946- ... CANR-27
Earlier sketch in CA 110
Neilson, Frances Fullerton (Jones) 1910- ... 73-76
See also SATA 14
Neilson, James Warren 1933- ... 1-4R
Neilson, Marguerite
See Tompkins, Julia (Marguerite Hunter Manchee)
Neilson, Melany 1958- ... 132
Neilson, N(eils) P. 1895- ... CANR-2
Earlier sketch in CA 5-8R
Neiman, David 1921- ... 69-72
Neiman, Fraser 1911- ... 25-28R
Neiman, Morris 1910(?)-1989 Obituary ... 130
Neimark, Anne E. 1935- ... CANR-36
Earlier sketches in CA 29-32R, CANR-16
See also SATA 4
Neimark, Edith D(eborah) 1928- ... 41-44R
Neimark, Paul G. 1934- ... 135
Brief entry ... 115
See also SATA 37
Neipris, Janet
See Wille, Janet Neipris
Neisser, Hans P(hilip) 1895-1975 ... CAP-1
Obituary ... 53-56
Earlier sketch in CA 13-16
Neisser, Ulric 1928- ... CANR-26
Earlier sketch in CA 108
Nekrasov, Viktor (Platonovich)
1911-1987 Obituary ... 123
Nekrich, Aleksandr M(oisei) 1920- ... 81-84
Neligan, David 1899- ... CAP-2
Earlier sketch in CA 29-32
Nelkin, Dorothy 1933- ... CANR-31
Earlier sketches in CA 41-44R, CANR-14
Nell
See Hanna, Nell(ie L.)
Nell, Edward John 1935- ... 65-68
Nell, Victor 1935- ... 136
Nelles, Henry Vivian 1942- ... 103
Nelli, Humbert S(teven) 1930- ... CANR-14
Earlier sketch in CA 41-44R
Nelligan, Emile 1879-1941 Brief entry ... 114
See also DLB 92
See also TCLC 14
Nellis, Muriel ... 102
Nellist, John B(owman) 1923- ... 25-28R
Nelms, C(larice) E. 1919- ... 25-28R
Nelms, Henning C(unningham)
1900-1986 Obituary ... 119
Nelsen, Anne Kusener 1942- ... 97-100
Nelsen, Hart M(ichael) 1938- ... CANR-8
Earlier sketch in CA 53-56
Nelson, A(ndrew) Thomas 1933- ... 5-8R
Nelson, Alan H(olm) 1938- ... 104
Nelson, Alice Fray 1911(?)-1983 Obituary ... 110
Nelson, Alice Ruth Moore Dunbar
1875-1935 ... 124
Brief entry ... 122
See also BW
See also DLB 50
See also MTCW
Nelson, Alvin F(redolph) 1917-1973 ... CAP-2
Earlier sketch in CA 25-28
Nelson, Amirtharaj 1934- ... 57-60
Nelson, Andrew N(athaniel)
1893-1975 ... CANR-3
Earlier sketch in CA 5-8R
Nelson, Anne 1954- ... 123
Nelson, Antonya 1961- ... 138
Nelson, Benjamin N(athaniel) 1935- ... CANR-1
Earlier sketch in CA 1-4R
Nelson, Benjamin N. 1911-1977 ... CANR-28
Obituary ... 73-76
Earlier sketch in CA 81-84
Nelson, Beth
See Nelson, Mary Elizabeth
Nelson, Betty Palmer 1938- ... 134
Nelson, C(arl) Ellis 1916- ... 108
Nelson, Carl Leroy 1910- ... 104
Nelson, Carnot E(dward) 1941- ... 37-40R
Nelson, Cary (Robert) 1946- ... 49-52
Nelson, Charles Lamar 1917- ... 69-72
Nelson, Charles R(owe) 1942- ... 37-40R
Nelson, Cholmondeley M. 1903- ... 5-8R
Nelson, Clifford Ansgar 1906- ... CAP-1
Earlier sketch in CA 11-12
Nelson, Conny E(dwin) 1933- Brief entry ... 108
Nelson, Cordner (Bruce) 1918- ... 29-32R
See also SATA 29, 54
Nelson, Dalmas H(ildor) 1925- ... 119
Nelson, Daniel 1941- ... 25-28R
Nelson, David Moir 1920- ... CANR-38
Earlier sketches in CA 1-4R, CANR-17
Nelson, Donald F. 1929- ... 37-40R
Nelson, E(ugene) Clifford 1911- ... 13-16R
Nelson, Edna Deu Pree ... 5-8R
Nelson, Elof G. 1924- ... CANR-35
Earlier sketch in CA 21-24R
Nelson, Eric Hilliard 1940-1985 Obituary ... 118
Nelson, Esther L. 1928- ... CANR-28
Earlier sketches in CA 69-72, CANR-11
See also SATA 13
Nelson, Ethel Florence 1913- ... CANR-6
Earlier sketch in CA 53-56
Nelson, Eugene 1929- ... 61-64
Nelson, F(rancis) William 1922- ... 13-16R
Nelson, Geoffrey K(enneth) 1923- ... CANR-24
Earlier sketch in CA 29-32R
Nelson, George (Carl) E(dward)
1900-1982 ... CANR-24
Earlier sketch in CA 45-48
Nelson, George (H.) 1908-1986 ... 81-84
Obituary ... 118
Nelson, Gideon E(dmund Jr.) 1924- ... 53-56
Nelson, Harold A(lfred) 1932- ... 114
Nelson, Harold L(ewis) 1917- ... 93-96
Nelson, Herbert B(enjamin) 1903- ... CAP-2
Earlier sketch in CA 19-20
Nelson, Howard 1947- ... 136
Nelson, Indiana 1940- ... 97-100
Nelson, J. Bryan 1932- ... CANR-10
Earlier sketch in CA 25-28R
Nelson, J(oseph) Raleigh
1873-1961 Obituary ... 110
Nelson, J(ohn) Robert 1920- ... CANR-19
Earlier sketches in CA 9-12R, CANR-3
Nelson, Jack
See Nelson, John Howard
Nelson, Jack L. 1932- ... CANR-10
Earlier sketch in CA 25-28R
Nelson, Jacquelyn S. 1950- ... 137
Nelson, James B(ruce) 1930- ... CANR-17
Earlier sketches in CA 49-52, CANR-1
Nelson, James C(ecil) 1908- ... CANR-13
Earlier sketch in CA 77-80
Nelson, James G(raham) 1929- ... 9-12R
Nelson, Jan Alan 1935- ... 41-44R
Nelson, Jane Armstrong 1927- Brief entry ... 105
Nelson, Janet 1930- ... 115
Nelson, Jean Erichsen
See Erichsen-Nelson, Jean
Nelson, John Charles 1925- ... 49-52
Nelson, John Howard 1929- ... 29-32R
Nelson, John Oliver 1909-1990 ... 37-40R
Obituary ... 131
Nelson, Joseph Schieser 1937- ... 73-76
Nelson, June Kompass 1920- ... 73-76
Nelson, Katherine Shaw 1926- ... 110
Nelson, Kay Shaw
See Nelson, Katherine Shaw
Nelson, Keith L(ebahn) 1932- Brief entry ... 113
Nelson, Kent 1943- ... 77-80
Nelson, L(ester) Ivar 1941- ... 119
Nelson, Lawrence E(rnest) 1928-1977 ... 53-56
Obituary ... 103
See also SATA 28
Nelson, Lawrence Emerson 1893-1978 ... 17-20R
Obituary ... 134
Nelson, Lois (Ney) 1930- ... 61-64
Nelson, Lowry Jr. 1926- ... CANR-39
Earlier sketch in CA 5-8R
Nelson, Malcolm A. 1934- ... 45-48
Nelson, Marg (Raibley) 1899- ... CANR-2
Earlier sketch in CA 1-4R
Nelson, Marguerite
See Floren, Lee
Nelson, Marion Harvey 1925- ... 9-12R
Nelson, Martha 1923- ... 29-32R
Nelson, Mary Carroll 1929- ... CANR-16
Earlier sketches in CA 49-52, CANR-1
See also SATA 23
Nelson, Mary Elizabeth 1926- ... 93-96
Nelson, Michael Harrington 1921- ... CANR-2
Earlier sketch in CA 5-8R
Nelson, Nina
See Nelson, Ethel Florence
Nelson, O. Terry 1941- ... SATA 62
Nelson, Oliver W(endell) 1904- ... 29-32R
Nelson, Oswald George 1907-1975 ... 93-96
Obituary ... 57-60
Nelson, Ozzie
See Nelson, Oswald George
Nelson, Paul David 1941- ... 120
Nelson, Peter
See Solow, Martin
Nelson, Peter 1940- ... CANR-12
Earlier sketch in CA 61-64
Nelson, Philip Bradford 1951- ... 113
Nelson, R(adell) Faraday 1931- ... CANR-26
Earlier sketch in CA 69-72
Nelson, Rachel W(est) 1955- ... 117
Nelson, Ralph C(arl) 1927- ... 53-56
Nelson, Ralph 1916-1987 ... 49-52
Obituary ... 124
Nelson, Randy F(ranklin) 1948- ... 125
Brief entry ... 110
Nelson, Ray
See Nelson, R(adell) Faraday
Nelson, Raymond S(tanley) 1921- ... CANR-36
Earlier sketches in CA 45-48, CANR-1, 16
Nelson, Richard K(ing) 1941- ... CANR-30
Earlier sketches in CA 29-32R, CANR-12
See also SATA 65
Nelson, Richard R(obinson) 1930- ... CANR-16
Earlier sketch in CA 97-100
Nelson, Richard 1950- ... 129
Brief entry ... 123
Nelson, Rick
See Nelson, Eric Hilliard
Nelson, Ricky
See Nelson, Eric Hilliard
Nelson, Robert James 1925- ... CANR-8
Earlier sketch in CA 5-8R
Nelson, Rosanne E(ierdanz) 1939- ... 49-52
Nelson, Rowland Whiteway
1902-1979 Obituary ... 105
Nelson, Roy Paul 1923- ... CANR-22
Earlier sketches in CA 17-20R, CANR-7
See also SATA 59
Nelson, Ruben F(rederick) W(erthenbach)
1939- ... CANR-31
Earlier sketch in CA 112
Nelson, Ruth Youngdahl
1904(?)-1984 Obituary ... 112
Nelson, Ruth 1914- ... 41-44R
Nelson, Severing E. 1896- ... 5-8R
Nelson, Sharon H. 1948- ... 113
Nelson, Stanley 1933- ... CANR-39
Earlier sketches in CA 49-52, CANR-1, 18
Nelson, Thomas P. 1925(?)-1983 Obituary ... 110

Nelson, Truman (John Seymour)
1911-1987 .... CANR-1
Obituary 123
Earlier sketch in CA 1-4R
Nelson, W(esley) Dale 1927- 77-80
Nelson, Walter Henry 1928- CANR-7
Earlier sketch in CA 13-16R
Nelson, Warren L. 1940- 89-92
Nelson, William R(ichard) 1924- 25-28R
Nelson, William Rockhill 1841-1915 .... DLB 23
Nelson, William 1908-1978 49-52
Obituary 103
See also DLB 103
Nelson, Willie 1933- 107
See also CLC 17
Nelton, Sharon (Lee) 1937- 123
Nemanic, Gerald Carl 1941- 107
Nemec, David 1938- CANR-2
Earlier sketch in CA 49-52
Nemerov, Howard (Stanley)
1920-1991 .... CANR-27
Obituary 134
Earlier sketches in CA 1-4R, CANR-1
See also CABS 2
See also CLC 2, 6, 9, 36
See also DLB 6
See also DLBY 83
See also MTCW
Nemeshegyi, Peter 1923- 130
Nemeth, Laszlo 1901-1975 93-96
Obituary 57-60
Nemir, Alma 1902-1971 .... CAP-2
Earlier sketch in CA 29-32
Nemiro, Beverly Anderson 1925- CANR-5
Earlier sketch in CA 53-56
Nemiroff, Robert Brief entry 116
See also AITN 2
Nemirow, Steven 1949- 110
Nemmers, Erwin Esser 1916- 9-12R
Nemoianu, Virgil (Petre) 1940- 130
Nemow, A.
See Neznansky, Friedrich
Nemser, Cindy 1937- 61-64
Nenni, Pietro 1891-1980 Obituary 105
Nerbovig, Marcella H. 1919- 89-92
Nere, Jacques 1917- 57-60
Nerhood, Harry W(arren) 1910- 29-32R
Nerlich, Graham 73-76
Nerlove, Marc L(eon) 1933- 104
Nerlove, Miriam 1959- 121
See also SATA 49, 53
Neruda, Pablo 1904-1973 .... CAP-2
Obituary 45-48
Earlier sketch in CA 19-20
See also CLC 1, 2, 5, 7, 9, 28, 62
See also HW
See also MTCW
See also PC 4
See also WLC
Nerval, Gaston
See Diez de Medina, Raul
Nervi, Pier Luigi 1891-1979 Obituary 113
Nervo, (Jose) Amado (Ruiz de) 1870-1919 131
Brief entry 109
See also HW
See also TCLC 11
Nesbin, Esther W(inter) 1910- 41-44R
Nesbit, E(dith) 1858-1924 137
Brief entry 118
See also CLR 3
See also MAICYA
See also YABC 1
Nesbit, Robert C(arrington) 1917- 45-48
Nesbit, Troy
See Folsom, Franklin (Brewster)
Nesbitt, Cathleen 1888-1982 Obituary 107
Nesbitt, Elizabeth 1897(?)-1977 Obituary 73-76
Nesbitt, George L(yman) 1903- 41-44R
Nesbitt, Paul H(omer) 1904- 77-80
Nesbitt, Ralph Beryl
1891(?)-1975 Obituary 61-64
Nesbitt, Rosemary (Sinnett) 1924- 81-84
Neshamith, Sara
See Dushnitzky-Shner, Sara
Nesmith, Robert I. 1891-1972 .... CANR-15
Obituary 103
Earlier sketch in CA 1-4R
Nesovich, Peter
See Naumoff, Lawrence
Nespojohn, Katherine V(eronica) 1912- 37-40R
See also SATA 7
Ness, Evaline (Michelow) 1911-1986 .... CANR-37
Obituary 120
Earlier sketches in CA 5-8R, CANR-5
See also CLR 6
See also DLB 61
See also MAICYA
See also SAAS 1
See also SATA 1, 26, 49
Ness, Gayl D(eForrest) 1929- 29-32R
Ness, John H. Jr. 1919- 21-24R
Nessen, (Lewis) Robert 1932- 107
Nessen, Ron(ald Harold) 1934- Brief entry 106
Nessi, Pio Baroja y
See Baroja (y Nessi), Pio
Nestle, John Francis 1912- 89-92
Nestor, William P(rodromos) 1947- CANR-26
Earlier sketch in CA 109
See also SATA 49
Nesvadba, Josef 1926- 97-100
Netanyahu, Benzion 1910- 61-64
Netanyahu, Jonathan
1946(?)-1976 Obituary 114
Netanyahu, Yonatan
See Netanyahu, Jonathan
Netboy, Anthony 1906- CANR-7
Earlier sketch in CA 17-20R
Neter, John 1923- 53-56
Netherclift, Beryl (Constance) 1911- 93-96
Nethercot, Arthur H(obart) 1895- CANR-28
Earlier sketch in CA 1-4R
Netland, Dwayne 1932- 110
Neto, Antonio Agostinho 1922-1979 101
Obituary 89-92
Nettel, Reginald 1899- 13-16R
Nettelbeck, F(red) A(rthur) 1950- 118
Nettell, Richard (Geoffrey) 1907- CAP-2
Earlier sketch in CA 25-28
Nettels, Curtis Putnam 1898- CANR-1
Earlier sketch in CA 1-4R
Nettels, Elsa 1931- 77-80
Netter, (Jean) Patrick 1952- 119
Netting, Robert M(cCorkle) 1934- 61-64
Nettis, Joseph 1928- 9-12R
Nettl, Bruno 1930- 17-20R
Nettl, J(ohn) P(eter) 1926-1968 .... CAP-2
Earlier sketch in CA 23-24
Nettl, Paul 1889-1972 .... CAP-1
Obituary 33-36R
Earlier sketch in CA 9-10
Nettleford, Rex M. 37-40R
Nettler, Gwynn 1913- 33-36R
Nettles, Thomas Julian 1946- 117
Nettles, Tom
See Nettles, Thomas Julian
Netzer, Dick 1928- Brief entry 112
Netzer, Lanore A. 1916- 17-20R
Neu, Charles E. 1936- 21-24R
Neu, Jerome 1947- 138
Neubauer, Alex(ander) 1959- 135
Neubauer, David William 1944- 65-68
Neubauer, John 1933- 101
Neubauer, William Arthur 1916- 9-12R
Neubeck, Gerhard 1918- 41-44R
Neuberger, Egon 1925- CANR-30
Earlier sketch in CA 25-28R
Neuberger, Julia 1950- 135
Neuberger, Richard Lewis
1912-1960 Obituary 89-92
Neubert, Christopher J. 1948- 106
Neuburg, Paul 1939- 45-48
Neuburg, Victor E. 1924- 33-36R
Neuenschwander, John A.
1941- Brief entry 113
Neufeld, John (Arthur) 1938- CANR-37
Earlier sketches in CA 25-28R, CANR-11
See also CLC 17
See also MAICYA
See also SAAS 3
See also SATA 6
Neufeld, Maurice Frank 1910- 1-4R
Neufeld, Peter Lorenz 1931- 25-28R
Neufeld, Rose 1924- 29-32R
Neufelder, Jerome M(ichael) 1929- 115
Neufeldt, Leonard N(ick) 1937- 108
Neufer Emswiler, Sharon
See Emswiler, Sharon Neufer
Neuffer, Claude Henry 1911- 41-44R
Neuffer, Irene LaBorde 1919- 61-64
Neugeboren, Jay (Michael) 1938- CANR-21
Earlier sketch in CA 17-20R
See also DLB 28
Neuharth, Allen .... AITN 2
Neuhaus, Richard (John) 1936- 33-36R
Neuhaus, Ruby (Hart) 1932- 103
Neulinger, John 1924-1991 .... CANR-16
Obituary 134
Earlier sketch in CA 41-44R
Neuls-Bates, Carol 1939- 114
Neuman, Abraham A(aron)
1890-1970 Obituary 104
Neuman, Betty Mavine 1924- 33-36R
Neuman, E(rnst) Jack 1921- Brief entry 127
Neuman, Fredric (Jay) 1934- CANR-20
Earlier sketch in CA 97-100
Neuman, Ladd A. 1942- 97-100
Neuman, Shirley Carol 1946- 121
Neuman, William Frederick
1919-1981 Obituary 103
Neumann, Alfred 1895-1952 .... DLB 56
Neumann, Emanuel 1893-1980 Obituary 105
Neumann, Gareth William 1930- 61-64
Neumann, Gerhard 1917- 132
Neumann, John von
See von Neumann, John
Neumann, Jonathan 1950- 85-88
Neumann, Robert G(erhard) 1916- 5-8R
Neumann, Robert 1897-1975 103
Obituary 89-92
Neumann, William Louis 1915-1971 .... CAP-1
Obituary 33-36R
Earlier sketch in CA 11-12
Neumeyer, Alfred
1900(?)-1973 Obituary 41-44R
Neumeyer, Ken(neth Walter) 1953- 107
Neumeyer, M(artin) Henry 1892- CAP-2
Earlier sketch in CA 19-20
Neumeyer, Peter F(lorian) 1929- CANR-30
Earlier sketch in CA 33-36R
See also SATA 13
Neurath, Marie (Reidemeister) 1898- 13-16R
See also SATA 1
Neurath, Otto 1882-1945 Brief entry 117
Neuschel, Richard F(rederick) 1915- 13-16R
Neuschuetz, Karin 1946- 116
Neuschutz, Karin
See Neuschuetz, Karin
Neuse, Erna Kritsch 1923- 105
Neusner, Jacob 1932- CANR-22
Earlier sketches in CA 13-16R, CANR-7
See also SATA 38
Neustadt, Bertha C(ummings)
1921(?)-1984 Obituary 112
Neustadt, Egon 1898(?)-1984 Obituary 112
Neustadt, Richard E(lliott) 1919- CANR-27
Earlier sketch in CA 9-12R
Neustadt, Richard M(itchells) 1948- CANR-27
Earlier sketch in CA 45-48
Neutra, Richard Joseph 1892-1970 .... CANR-5
Obituary 29-32R
Earlier sketch in CA 5-8R
Neutrelle, Dale 1937- 61-64
Neuville, H(enry) Richmond Jr. 1937- 21-24R
Neve, Herbert T(heodore) 1931- 25-28R
Neve, Lloyd 1923- 53-56
Nevell, Dick
See Nevell, Richard (William Babcock)
Nevell, Richard (William Babcock) 1947- 102
Nevelson, Louise 1900(?)-1988 108
Obituary 125
Neveux, Georges 1900-1982 Obituary 108
Nevill, Barry St-John 1941- 119
Neville, Anna
See Fairburn, Eleanor
Neville, B(arbara) Alison (Boodson)
1925- CANR-11
Earlier sketch in CA 5-8R
Neville, Charles
See Bodsworth, (Charles) Fred(erick)
Neville, Emily Cheney 1919- CANR-37
Earlier sketches in CA 5-8R, CANR-3
See also CLC 12
See also MAICYA
See also SAAS 2
See also SATA 1
Neville, Gwen Kennedy 1938- CANR-35
Earlier sketch in CA 114
Neville, Heather Buckley
See Buckley Neville, Heather
Neville, James Edmund Henderson
1897-1982 Obituary 107
Neville, Jill 1932- 21-24R
Neville, Joyce 115
Neville, Kris (Ottman) 1925-1980 132
Obituary 117
Neville, Mary
See Woodrich, Mary Neville
Neville, Pauline 1924- 29-32R
Neville, Richard F. 1931- 85-88
Neville, Robert C(ummings) 1939- CANR-29
Earlier sketches in CA 25-28R, CANR-11
Neville, Robert 1905-1970 Obituary 104
Neville, Susan 1951- 119
Nevin, David 1927- 121
Nevin, Evelyn C. 1910- 17-20R
Nevins, Albert J. 1915- CANR-19
Earlier sketches in CA 5-8R, CANR-5
See also SATA 20
Nevins, (Joseph) Allan 1890-1971 .... CANR-30
Obituary 29-32R
Earlier sketch in CA 5-8R
See also DLB 17
Nevins, Deborah 1947- 105
Nevins, Edward M(ichael) 1938- 29-32R
Nevins, Francis M(ichael) Jr. 1943- CANR-16
Earlier sketch in CA 41-44R
Nevinson, C(hristopher) R(ichard) W(ynne)
1889-1946 Brief entry 120
Nevitt, H(enry) J(ohn) Barrington
1908- CANR-14
Earlier sketch in CA 37-40R
Nevius, Blake (Reynolds) 1916- 17-20R
Nevo, Ruth 1924- 61-64
New, Anthony (Sherwood Brooks)
1924- CANR-23
Earlier sketch in CA 107
New, Christopher 116
New, William Herbert 1938- Brief entry 114
Newall, Christopher 1951- 128
Newall, Venetia 1935- 37-40R
Newberry
See Vellacott, Jo
Newberry, Clare Turlay 1903-1970 .... CAP-2
Earlier sketch in CA 19-20
See also SATA 1, 26
Newberry, Lida 1909- 97-100
Newberry, Vellacott
See Vellacott, Jo
Newberry, Wilma (Jean) 1927- 73-76
Newbery, John 1713-1767 .... MAICYA
See also SATA 20
Newbigin, (James Edward) Lesslie
1909- CANR-26
Earlier sketches in CA 13-16R, CANR-10
Newbill, James Guy 1931- 61-64
Newbold, H(erbert) L(eon Jr.) 1921- CANR-5
Earlier sketch in CA 1-4R
Newbold, Robert T(homas Jr.) 1920- 89-92
Newbold, Stokes
See Adams, Richard N(ewbold)
Newbolt, Henry (John)
1862-1938 Brief entry 118
See also DLB 19
Newborn, Jud 1952- 125
Newbound, Bernard Slade 1930- 81-84
See also Slade, Bernard
Newbury, Colin (Walter) 1929- CANR-8
Earlier sketch in CA 5-8R
Newbury, Will 1912- 45-48
Newby, Eric 1919- 5-8R
Newby, I(dus) A. 1931- 17-20R
Newby, James R(ichard) 1949- 112
Newby, Leroy Winfred 1921- 114
Newby, P(ercy) H(oward) 1918- CANR-32
Earlier sketch in CA 5-8R
See also CLC 2, 13
See also DLB 15
See also MTCW
Newcomb, Benjamin H. 1938- 45-48
Newcomb, Charles King 1820-1894 .... DLB 1
Newcomb, Covelle 1908- CAP-2
Earlier sketch in CA 19-20
Newcomb, Duane G(raham) 1929- CANR-5
Earlier sketch in CA 53-56
Newcomb, Ellsworth
See Kenny, Ellsworth Newcomb
Newcomb, Franc(es Lynette) J(ohnson)
1887- 17-20R
Newcomb, John (Robert) 1937- 123
Newcomb, Kerry 1946- CANR-10
Earlier sketch in CA 65-68
Newcomb, Norma
See Neubauer, William Arthur
Newcomb, Richard F(airchild) 1913- 1-4R
Newcomb, Robert N(orman) 1925- 21-24R
Newcomb, Simon 1835-1909 Brief entry 108
Newcomb, Theodore Mead 1903-1984 .... 33-36R
Obituary 114
Newcomb, Wilburn Wendell 1935- 17-20R
Newcomb, William W(ilmon) Jr. 1921- 102
Newcombe, Eugene A. 1923-1990 113
Obituary 130
See also Newcombe, Jack
Newcombe, Jack
See Newcombe, Eugene A.
See also SATA 33, 45
Newcombe, John (David) 1944- CANR-25
Earlier sketch in CA 69-72
Newcombe, Park Judson 1930- 106
Newcomer, James (William) 1912- CANR-15
Earlier sketch in CA 41-44R
Newell, Allen 1927- 104
Newell, Arlo F(rederic) 1926- 114
Newell, Barbara Warne 1929- 1-4R
Newell, Crosby
See Bonsall, Crosby Barbara (Newell)
Newell, D. A.
See Musciano, Walter A.
Newell, David McCheyne
1898(?)-1986 Obituary 120
Newell, Edythe W(eatherford) 1910- 65-68
See also SATA 11
Newell, Fred D(elmer) 1912- 97-100
Newell, Gordon 1913- CANR-20
Earlier sketches in CA 9-12R, CANR-4
Newell, Helen M(arie) 1909- 93-96
Newell, Homer E(dward) 1915-1983 97-100
Obituary 110
Newell, Hope Hockenberry 1896-1965 73-76
See also SATA 24
Newell, Kenneth B(ernard) 1930- 41-44R
Newell, Norman Dennis 1909- CANR-21
Earlier sketch in CA 104
Newell, Peter F(rancis) 1915- 13-16R
Newell, Peter (Sheaf Hersey)
1862-1924 Brief entry 122
See also DLB 42
Newell, Richard S. 1933- 134
Brief entry 112
Newell, Robert Henry
1836-1901 Brief entry 111
See also DLB 11
Newell, Rosemary 1922- 49-52
Newell, William H(are) 1922- 103
Newell, William T(hrift) 1929- 37-40R
Newey, Vincent 1943- 132
Newfeld, Frank 1928- 105
See also SATA 26
Newfield, Jack 1939- CANR-13
Earlier sketch in CA 21-24R
Newhafer, Richard L. 1922- 13-16R
Newhall, Beaumont 1908- 9-12R
Newhall, Nancy 1908-1974 Obituary 49-52
Newhall, Richard A.
1888-1973 Obituary 41-44R
Newhouse, Edward 1911- 97-100
Newhouse, Joseph P. 1942- 111
Newhouse, Neville H. 1919- 21-24R
Newhouse, Norman N(athan)
1906-1988 Obituary 127
Newhouse, Samuel I(rving)
1895-1979 Obituary 89-92
Newick, John 1919- CAP-1
Earlier sketch in CA 11-12
Newkirk, Glen A. 1931- 37-40R
Newland, Kathleen 1951- 97-100
Newland, T. Ernest 1903- 105
Newlands, George (McLeod) 1941- 129
Newley, Anthony (George) 1931- 105
Newlin, Dika 1923- 107
Newlin, Margaret Rudd 1925- CANR-1
Earlier sketch in CA 49-52
Newlon, (Frank) Clarke 1905(?)-1982 .... CANR-10
Obituary 108
Earlier sketch in CA 49-52
See also SATA 6, 33
Newlove, Donald 1928- CANR-25
Earlier sketch in CA 29-32R
See also CLC 6
Newlove, John (Herbert) 1938- CANR-25
Earlier sketches in CA 21-24R, CANR-9
See also CLC 14
Newlyn, Walter T(essier) 1915- 21-24R
Newman, Adrien Ann 1941- 102
Newman, Albert H. 1913(?)-1987 Obituary 122
Newman, Alyse 1953- 107
Newman, Andrea 1938- 73-76
Newman, Arnold 1941- 137
Newman, Arthur J. 1939- 117
Newman, Aubrey N(orris) 1927- CANR-25
Earlier sketch in CA 29-32R
Newman, Barbara
See Newman, Mona Alice Jean
Newman, Barbara (Pollock) 1939- 132
Newman, Barclay M. Jr. 1931- CANR-9
Earlier sketch in CA 17-20R

Newman, Bernard (Charles) 1897-1968 97-100
Obituary 25-28R
Newman, Charles L. 1923- CANR-6
Earlier sketch in CA 13-16R
Newman, Charles 1900-1989 Obituary 129
Newman, Charles 1938- 21-24R
See also CLC 2, 8
Newman, Christina McCall 1935- 112
Newman, Coleman J. 1935- 77-80
Newman, Daisy 1904- 37-40R
See also SATA 27
Newman, David 1937- 102
See also DLB 44
Newman, E. J. 1943- 61-64
Newman, Edwin (Harold) 1919- CANR-5
Earlier sketch in CA 69-72
See also AITN 1
See also CLC 14
Newman, Elmer S(imon) 1919- 106
Newman, Eric P. 1911- 5-8R
Newman, Ernest
See Roberts, William
Newman, Frances 1883(?)-1928 Brief entry 110
See also DLBY 80
Newman, Frank
See Abrams, Sam(uel)
Newman, G(ordon) F. 1942- 104
Newman, George 1936- 106
Newman, Gerald 1939- 101
See also SATA 42, 46
Newman, Greatrex 1892-1984(?) Obituary 112
Newman, Harold 1899- CANR-10
Earlier sketch in CA 65-68
Newman, Harold 1927- 53-56
Newman, Herbert Ellis 1914- 25-28R
Newman, Howard 1911-1977 57-60
Obituary 73-76
Newman, Jacob 1914- 9-12R
Newman, Jay Hartley 1951- CANR-9
Earlier sketch in CA 65-68
Newman, Jeremiah Joseph 1926- CANR-8
Earlier sketch in CA 5-8R
Newman, John Henry
1801-1890 .....DLB 18, 32, 55
Newman, John Kevin 1928- 123
Newman, Jon O(rmond) 1932- 21-24R
Newman, Joseph W(illiam) 1918- 37-40R
Newman, Joseph 1912- CANR-17
Earlier sketch in CA 89-92
Newman, Judie 1950- 117
Newman, Katharine D. 1911- 37-40R
Newman, Kim (James) 1959- 119
Newman, L(eonard) Hugh 1909- 9-12R
Newman, Lea Bertani Vozar 1926- 120
Newman, Lee Scott 1953- CANR-15
Earlier sketch in CA 65-68
Newman, Leslea 1955- 126
See also SATA 71
Newman, Loretta Marie 1911- 45-48
Newman, Louis Israel 1893-1972 .....CAP-1
Obituary 33-36R
Earlier sketch in CA 19-20
Newman, Matthew (Harrison) 1955- .....SATA 56
Newman, Michael 1946- 116
Newman, Mona Alice Jean CANR-31
Earlier sketch in CA 102
Newman, Oscar 1935- 102
Newman, P(aul) B(aker) 1919- 33-36R
Newman, Parley Wright 1923- Brief entry 106
Newman, Peter C(harles) 1929- CANR-29
Earlier sketches in CA 9-12R, CANR-3
Newman, Peter (Kenneth) 1928- 17-20R
Newman, Philip L(ee) 1931- 17-20R
Newman, Phyllis 1933- 134
Newman, Ralph Abraham 1892- CANR-6
Earlier sketch in CA 1-4R
Newman, Ralph G(eoffrey) 1911- CANR-25
Earlier sketch in CA 45-48
Newman, Randolph H.
1904-1975 Obituary 61-64
Newman, Richard (Alan) 1930- 110
Newman, Robert Chapman 1941- 115
Newman, Robert D(ouglas) 1951- 120
Newman, Robert (Howard)
1909-1988 .....CANR-19
Obituary 127
Earlier sketches in CA 1-4R, CANR-4
See also SATA 4, 60
Newman, Robert P(reston) 1922- 1-4R
Newman, Robert S. 1935- 65-68
Newman, Ruth (May) G(allert) 1914- 105
Newman, Sharan 1949- CANR-25
Earlier sketch in CA 106
Newman, Shirlee Petkin 1924- 5-8R
See also SATA 10
Newman, Shirley S. 1924- 123
Newman, Stephen A(aron) 1946- 97-100
Newman, Stephen L. 1952- 132
Newman, Stewart A(lbert) 1907- CAP-2
Earlier sketch in CA 23-24
Newman, Terence 1927- 5-8R
Newman, Terry
See Newman, Terence
Newman, Thelma R(ita) 1925-1978 .....CANR-7
Obituary 81-84
Earlier sketch in CA 13-16R
Newman, Walter (Brown) 1920- Brief entry 110
Newman, William H(erman) 1909- CANR-19
Earlier sketches in CA 5-8R, CANR-3
Newman, William Mark 1943- 57-60
Newman, William S(tein) 1912- CANR-3
Earlier sketch in CA 1-4R
Newmar, Rima
See Wagman, Naomi
Newmark, Joseph 1943- 53-56
Newmark, Leonard 1929- 17-20R
Newmyer, R. Kent 1930- 77-80
Newport, John P(aul) 1917- CANR-29
Earlier sketches in CA 33-36R, CANR-13
Newport, John Paul Jr. 1954- 135
Newquist, Jerreld L. 1919-1976 .....17-20R
Obituary 134
Newquist, Roy 1925- 13-16R
Newsham, Ian (Alan) 1953- 115
Newsham, Wendy (Elizabeth) 1952- 117
Newsom, Carol 1948- .....SATA 40
Newsom, Carroll V(incent) 1904-1990 .....CAP-2
Obituary 130
Earlier sketch in CA 17-18
Newsom, Doug(las Ann) 1934- 73-76
Newsome, Arden J(eanne) 1932- 29-32R
Newsome, David Hay 1929- CANR-17
Earlier sketch in CA 89-92
Newsome, Effie Lee 1885-1979 .....DLB 76
Newsome, George L(ane) Jr. 1923- 29-32R
Newsome, Walter L(ee) 1941- 105
Newson, Elizabeth (Palmer) 1929- CANR-5
Earlier sketch in CA 9-12R
Newson, John 1925- 9-12R
Newson, Tony 1953- 124
Newth, Rebecca 1940- 33-36R
Newton, Brian 1928- 49-52
Newton, Byron Louis 1913- 53-56
Newton, D(wight) B(ennett) 1916- CANR-17
Earlier sketches in CA 5-8R, CANR-2
Newton, David C.
See Chance, John Newton
Newton, David E(dward) 1933- 135
See also SATA 67
Newton, Derek A(rnold) 1930- 120
Newton, Douglas 1920- 104
Newton, Earle Williams 1917- 41-44R
Newton, Eric 1893-1965 .....CAP-1
Earlier sketch in CA 13-16
Newton, Ethel (de la Bete) 1921- 101
Newton, Francis
See Hobsbawm, Eric J(ohn Ernest)
Newton, Huey P(ercy) 1942-1989 Obituary 129
Brief entry 114
Newton, Ian 1940- 123
Newton, Ivor 1892-1981 Obituary 108
Newton, James R(obert) 1935- 101
See also SATA 23
Newton, Kenneth 1940- CANR-16
Earlier sketch in CA 29-32R
Newton, Macdonald
See Newton, William Simpson
Newton, Maxwell 1929- 126
Newton, Michael 1951- 108
Newton, Norman (Lewis) 1929- 9-12R
Newton, Norman Thomas 1898- 104
Newton, Peter A(nthony)
1935-1987 Obituary 124
Newton, Peter 1906- CAP-1
Earlier sketch in CA 9-10
Newton, Ray C(lyde) 1935- 77-80
Newton, Robert (Henry) G(erald) 1903- CAP-1
Earlier sketch in CA 9
Newton, Robert P(arr) 1929- 113
Newton, Roy 1904(?)-1974 Obituary 104
Newton, Stu
See Whitcomb, Ian
Newton, Suzanne 1936- CANR-14
Earlier sketch in CA 41-44R
See also CLC 35
See also SATA 5
Newton, Virgil Miller Jr. 1904-1977 .....1-4R
Obituary 103
Newton, William Simpson 1923- CANR-7
Earlier sketch in CA 53-56
Nexo, Martin Andersen 1869-1954 .....TCLC 43
Ney, James W(alter) 1932- CANR-15
Earlier sketch in CA 41-44R
Ney, John 1923- 115
See also SATA 33, 43
Ney, Patrick
See Bolitho, (Henry) Hector
Ney, Richard 1917(?)- .....AITN 1
Ney, Virgil 1905-1979 Obituary 85-88
Neyland, James (Elwyn) 1939- 103
Neyman, Jerzy 1899-1981 Obituary 108
Neyrey, Jerome H(enry) 1940- 126
Neznansky, Friedrich 1932- 128
Nezval, Vitezslav 1900-1958 Brief entry 123
See also TCLC 44
Ng, David 1934- 115
Ng, Larry K. Y. 1940- CANR-9
Earlier sketch in CA 17-20R
Ngagoyeanes, Nicholas 1939- 49-52
Ngara, Emmanuel 1947- 109
Ngema, Mbongeni 1955- .....CLC 57
Ngoc, Nguyen Huy
See Nguyen Ngoc Huy
Ngubane, Jordan K(hush) 1917- 121
Ngugi, James T(hiong'o)
See Ngugi wa Thiong'o
See also CLC 3, 7, 13
Ngugi wa Thiong'o 1938- CANR-27
Earlier sketch in CA 81-84
See also Ngugi, James T(hiong'o)
See also BLC 3
See also BW
See also CLC 36
See also MTCW
Nguyen, Dinh Hoa 1924- CANR-10
Earlier sketch in CA 21-24R
Nguyen, Vuong Hung
1922(?)-1985 Obituary 118
Nguyen Ngoc Bich 1937- CANR-15
Earlier sketch in CA 81-84
Nguyen Ngoc Huy 1924- 126
Niall, Sean
See Mangan, (John Joseph) Sherry
Nias, D(avid) K(enneth) B(oydell) 1940- 105
Niatum, Duane 1938- CANR-21
Earlier sketch in CA 41-44R
Niblett, W(illiam) R(oy) 1906- CANR-3
Earlier sketch in CA 1-4R
Niccolini, Dianora 1936- 113
Nice, Jill 1940- 138
Nicely, Thomas S(hryock) Jr. 1939- 93-96
Nicely, Tom
See Nicely, Thomas S(hryock) Jr.
Nichelson, F(loyd) Patrick 1942- 33-36R
Nichol, B(arrie) P(hillip) 1944-1988 53-56
See also CLC 18
See also DLB 53
See also SATA 66
Nichol, John Thomas 1928- 17-20R
Nicholas, Anna Katherine 1917- 93-96
Nicholas, Barry 1919- 5-8R
Nicholas, David M(ansfield) 1939- 49-52
Nicholas, Donald 1909- 5-8R
Nicholas, Elizabeth 1915-1985 Obituary 117
Nicholas, Herbert George 1911- CANR-26
Earlier sketch in CA 1-4R
Nicholas, John (Morton) 1944- 118
Nicholas, Leslie 1913- 81-84
Nicholas, Robert L(eon) 1937- 53-56
Nicholas, Ted
See Peterson, Ted Nicholas
Nicholas, Tracy (Christine) 1952- 121
Nicholas, William
See Thimmesch, Nicholas Palen
Nicholas of Cusa 1401-1464 .....DLB 115
Nicholds, Elizabeth (Beckwith) CAP-1
Earlier sketch in CA 11-12
Nicholl, Louise Townsend 1890(?)-1981 97-100
Obituary 105
Nicholls, C(hristine) S(tephanie) 1943- 133
Nicholls, David 1948- 97-100
Nicholls, F(rederick) F(rancis) 1926- 5-8R
Nicholls, Judith (Ann) 1941- 121
See also SATA 61
Nicholls, Mark
See Frewin, Leslie Ronald
Nicholls, Peter (Douglas) 1939- 105
Nicholls, (C. G.) William 1921- 17-20R
Nichols, Adelaide
See Baker, Adelaide N(ichols)
Nichols, Albert L. 1951- 122
Nichols, (John) Beverley 1898-1983 .....CANR-17
Obituary 110
Earlier sketch in CA 93-96
Nichols, Bill
See Nichols, William James
Nichols, Cecilia Fawn 1906- CAP-1
Earlier sketch in CA 13-16
See also SATA 12
Nichols, Charles H(arold) 1919- CANR-6
Earlier sketch in CA 53-56
See also BW
Nichols, Dale (William) 1904- CAP-2
Earlier sketch in CA 17-18
Nichols, Dave
See Frost, Helen
Nichols, David A(llen) 1939- 104
Nichols, David 1956- 133
Nichols, Dudley 1895-1960 Obituary 89-92
See also DLB 26
Nichols, Edward J(ay) 1900- 5-8R
Nichols, Eve K(aufman) 1952- 128
Nichols, Fred Joseph 1939- 114
Nichols, Frederick Adams
1907-1983 Obituary 111
Nichols, Harold 1903- CAP-1
Earlier sketch in CA 13-16
Nichols, Irby C(oghill) Jr. 1926- 41-44R
Nichols, J(ohn) G(ordon) 1930- 33-36R
See also CAAS 2
Nichols, Jack 1938- 41-44R
Nichols, James Hastings 1915- Brief entry 114
Nichols, James R(ichard) 1938- 105
Nichols, Janet (Louise) 1952- 135
See also SATA 67
Nichols, Jeannette Paddock 1890-1982 .....9-12R
Obituary 107
Nichols, Jeannette 1931- 77-80
Nichols, John (Treadwell) 1940- CANR-6
Earlier sketch in CA 9-12R
See also CAAS 2
See also CLC 38
See also DLBY 82
Nichols, Joseph C. 1905(?)-1984 Obituary 114
Nichols, K(enneth) D(avid) 1907- 126
Nichols, Leigh
See Koontz, Dean R(ay)
Nichols, Lewis 1903-1982 Obituary 106
Nichols, Maggie
See Nichols, Margaret
Nichols, Margaret 1931- 81-84
Nichols, Marie Hochmuth 1908-1978 103
Nichols, Marion 1921- 102
Nichols, Mary Sargeant (Neal) Gove
1810-1884 .....DLB 1
Nichols, Nina (Marianna) da Vinci
1932- CANR-14
Earlier sketch in CA 73-76
Nichols, Paul D(yer) 1938- 109
Nichols, Peter
See Youd, (Christopher) Samuel
Nichols, Peter (Richard) 1927- CANR-33
Earlier sketch in CA 104
See also CLC 5, 36, 65
See also DLB 13
See also MTCW
Nichols, Peter 1928-1989 Obituary 127
Nichols, R(oy) Eugene 1914- 29-32R
Nichols, Robert (Molise Bowyer) 1919- 93-96
Nichols, Roger L(ouis) 1933- CANR-5
Earlier sketch in CA 13-16R
Nichols, Roger 1939- 108
Nichols, Roy F(ranklin) 1896-1973 .....CANR-3
Obituary 37-40R
Earlier sketch in CA 5-8R
See also DLB 17
Nichols, (Joanna) Ruth 1948- CANR-37
Earlier sketches in CA 25-28R, CANR-16
See also DLB 60
See also SATA 15
Nichols, Scott
See Scortia, Thomas N(icholas)
Nichols, Stephen G(eorge Jr.) 1936- CANR-31
Earlier sketch in CA 45-48
Nichols, Sue 9-12R
Nichols, Victoria (Sorensen) 1944- 132
Nichols, William James 1942- 93-96
Nichols, William Thomas 1927- 41-44R
Nicholsen, Margaret E(sther) 1904- 29-32R
Nicholson, Arnold 1902- CAP-2
Earlier sketch in CA 19-20
Nicholson, Ben 1894-1982 Obituary 110
Nicholson, C(harles) A. III 1922- 41-44R
Nicholson, Charles (Edward) 1946- 136
Nicholson, Dorothy Nelis 1923- Brief entry 109
Nicholson, Geoff 1953- 130
Nicholson, Geoffrey (George) 1929- CANR-8
Earlier sketch in CA 5-8R
Nicholson, Gerald W(illiam) L(ingen)
1902-1980 101
Nicholson, Hubert 1908- 13-16R
Nicholson, Jack 1937(?)- Brief entry 116
Nicholson, Jane
See Steen, Marguerite
Nicholson, Joe
See Nicholson, Joseph Hugh Jr.
Nicholson, John Greer 1929- 45-48
Nicholson, Joseph Hugh Jr. 1943- 81-84
Nicholson, Joyce Thorpe 1919- CANR-5
Earlier sketch in CA 9-12R
See also SATA 35
Nicholson, (Edward) Max 1904- Brief entry 106
Nicholson, Norman (Cornthwaite)
1914-1987 .....CANR-24
Obituary 122
Earlier sketches in CA 9-12R, CANR-3
See also DLB 27
Nicholson, Norman L(eon) 1919- CANR-3
Earlier sketch in CA 9-12R
Nicholson, Patrick J(ames) 1920- 120
Nicholson, Paul (Joseph) Jr. 1937- 73-76
Nicholson, Ranald (George) 1931- 37-40R
Nicholson, Robert Lawrence 1908-1985 53-56
Obituary 117
Nicholson, Shirley J. 1925- CANR-26
Earlier sketch in CA 29-32R
Nicholson, Simon 1934- 114
Nicholson, W(illiam) G(eorge) 1935- 93-96
Nichter, Rhoda 1926- 81-84
Nichtern, Sol 1920-1988 .....17-20R
Obituary 126
Ni Chuilleanain, Eilean 1942- 126
See also DLB 40
Nickel, Herman 1928- 73-76
Nickel, Mildred L(ucille) 1912- 108
Nickell, Joe 1944- 110
Nickell, Lesley J(acqueline) 1944- 103
Nickels, William G(eorge) 1939- 108
Nickelsburg, George W(illiam) E(lmer) Jr.
1934- CANR-19
Earlier sketches in CA 53-56, CANR-5
Nickelsburg, Janet 1893- 65-68
See also SATA 11
Nickerson, Betty 1922- 77-80
See also Nickerson, Elizabeth
Nickerson, Clarence B(entley) 1906- 5-8R
Nickerson, Elizabeth
See Nickerson, Betty
See also SATA 14
Nickerson, Jan 1-4R
Nickerson, Jane Soames (Bon)
1900-1988 .....CANR-28
Obituary 124
Earlier sketch in CA 77-80
Nickerson, John Mitchell 1937- 53-56
Nickerson, Joseph 1914-1990 Obituary 131
Nickerson, Roy 1927- CANR-35
Earlier sketch in CA 114
Nickerson, Sheila B(unker) 1942- 118
Nickerson, William (Ernest) 1908- 1-4R
Nickl, Barbara (Elisabeth) 1939-
See Schroeder, Binette
See also SATA 56
Nicklanovich, Michael David 1941- 107
Nicklaus, Carol .....SATA 33, 62
Nicklaus, (Charles) Frederick 1936- 37-40R
Nicklaus, Jack (William) 1940- CANR-39
Earlier sketches in CA 89-92, CANR-16
Nickle, Keith Fullerton 1933- 115
Nickless, Will 1902- 81-84
See also SATA 66
Nickson, J. Richard 1917- 129
Niclas, Yolla 1900- 25-28R
Nic Leodhas, Sorche
See Alger, Leclaire (Gowans)
Nicol, Abioseh
See Nicol, Davidson (Sylvester Hector Willoughby)
Nicol, Ann
See Turnbull, Ann (Christine)
Nicol, Charles (David) 1940- 115
Nicol, D(onald) M(acGillivray) 1923- CANR-4
Earlier sketch in CA 53-56
Nicol, Davidson (Sylvester Hector Willoughby)
1924- CANR-26
Earlier sketch in CA 61-64
See also BW

Nicol, Eric (Patrick) 1919- CANR-36
Earlier sketches in CA 49-52, CANR-1, 16
See also DLB 68
Nicol, Jean 1919- 21-24R
Nicola, Andree
See McLaughlin, Andree Nicola
Nicolaeff, Ariadne 1915- 57-60
Nicolai, Friedrich 1733-1811 .... DLB 97
Nicolas
See Mordvinoff, Nicolas
Nicolas, Claire
See White, Claire Nicolas
Nicolas, F. R. E.
See Freeling, Nicolas
Nicolay, Helen 1866-1954 Brief entry 121
See also YABC 1
Nicolay, John G(eorge)
1832-1901 Brief entry 122
See also DLB 47
Nicolaysen, Bruce 1934- 105
Nicole, Christopher Robin 1930- 13-16R
See also SATA 5
Nicoll, (John Ramsay) Allardyce
1894-1976 ....CANR-5
Obituary 65-68
Earlier sketch in CA 9-12R
Nicoll, Bruce H. 1913(?)-1983 Obituary 111
Nicoll, Helen 1937- 122
Nicolle, Jacques Maurice Raoul 1901- 9-12R
Nicoloff, Philip Loveless 1926- 1-4R
Nicolson, (Lionel) Benedict 1914-1978 ....CANR-6
Earlier sketch in CA 13-16R
Nicolson, Catherine 121
Nicolson, Harold George 1886-1968 .... CAP-1
Earlier sketch in CA 13-16
See also DLB 100
Nicolson, I(an) F(erguson) 1921- 29-32R
Nicolson, James R(obert) 1934- CANR-9
Earlier sketch in CA 65-68
Nicolson, Marjorie Hope 1894-1981 ....9-12R
Obituary 103
Nicolson, Nigel 1917- 101
Nicosia, Francesco M(ichael) 1933- 81-84
Nicosia, Franco M.
See Nicosia, Francesco M(ichael)
Nicosia, Gerald (Martin) 1949- 115
Nida, Eugene A(lbert) 1914- CANR-17
Earlier sketches in CA 1-4R, CANR-1
Nidditch, Peter (Harold)
1928-1983 Obituary 109
Niddrie, David Lawrence 1917- 25-28R
Nideffer, Robert M(orse) 1942- CANR-9
Earlier sketch in CA 65-68
Nidetch, Jean 1923- 89-92
Nie, Norman H. 1943- CANR-15
Earlier sketch in CA 65-68
Niebuhr, H(elmut) Richard
1894-1962 Obituary 116
Niebuhr, Reinhold 1892-1971 ....41-44R
Obituary 29-32R
See also DLB 17
Niebuhr, Richard R. 1926- 77-80
Niebuhr, Ursula 1907- 89-92
Nieburg, H(arold) L. 1927- 9-12R
Niedecker, Lorine 1903-1970 .... CAP-2
Earlier sketch in CA 25-28
See also CLC 10, 42
See also DLB 48
Niederauer, David J(ohn) 1924- 45-48
Niederhoffer, Arthur 1917-1981 Obituary 103
Niederland, William G(ugliemo) 1904- 81-84
Niedzielski, Henri 1931- 49-52
Nieh, Hualing 1925- 81-84
Niehans, Juerg 1919- 133
Niehans, Jurg
See Niehans, Juerg
Niehoff, Arthur H. 1921- 21-24R
Nielander, William Ahlers 1901- 5-8R
Nield, Howard (Kingsley) 1949- 135
Nielsen, Aage Rosendal 1921- 25-28R
Nielsen, Aldon Lynn 1950- 136
Nielsen, Dulcimer 1943- 93-96
Nielsen, Eduard 1923- 29-32R
Nielsen, Gary (Elton) 1939- 97-100
Nielsen, Helen Berniece 1918- CANR-1
Earlier sketch in CA 1-4R
Nielsen, Jean Sarver 1922- 5-8R
Nielsen, Kay (Rasmus) 1886-1957 .... CLR 16
See also MAICYA
See also SATA 16
Nielsen, Knut Schmidt
See Schmidt-Nielsen, Knut
Nielsen, Margaret A(nne) 105
Nielsen, Niels Christian Jr. 1921- CANR-3
Earlier sketch in CA 9-12R
Nielsen, Niels Juel
See Juel-Nielsen, Niels
Nielsen, Oswald 1904- CAP-2
Earlier sketch in CA 19-20
Nielsen, Robert F. 1937- 122
Nielsen, Sven Sigurd 1901-1976 Obituary 104
Nielsen, Torben 1918- Brief entry 114
Nielsen, Veneta Leatham 1909- 89-92
Nielsen, Virginia
See McCall, Virginia Nielsen
Nielsen, Waldemar August 1917- 103
Nielssen, Eric
See Ludvigsen, Karl (Eric)
Nieman, Egbert William 1909- CAP-1
Earlier sketch in CA 11-12
Nieman, Lucius W. 1857-1935 .... DLB 25
Niemann, Linda (Grant) 1946- 133
Niemeier, Jean (Gilbreath) 1912- 25-28R
Niemeyer, Eberhardt Victor Jr. 1919- 102
Niemeyer, Gerhart 1907- CANR-30
Earlier sketch in CA 1-4R
Niemeyer, Roy K(urt) 1922- 1-4R
Niemi, Albert (William) Jr. 1942- 73-76
Niemi, John A. 1932- 77-80
Niemi, Richard G(ene) 1941- 41-44R
Niemoeller, (Friedrich Gustav Emil) Martin
1892-1984 Obituary 112
Niemoller, Ara
See Llerena, Mario
Niemoller, (Friedrich Gustav Emil) Martin
See Niemoeller, (Friedrich Gustav Emil) Martin
Nienhauser, William H. Jr. 1943- 125
Nierenberg, Gerard I. 1923- 25-28R
Nierman, M. Murray 1918- 1-4R
Nies, Judith 1941- 77-80
Niesewand, Peter 1944-1983 101
Obituary 109
Niess, Robert Judson 1911- CAP-2
Earlier sketch in CA 29-32
Niethammer, Carolyn 1944- 85-88
Nietz, John Alfred 1888- 1-4R
Nietzke, Ann 1945- 105
Nietzsche, Friedrich (Wilhelm) 1844-1900 121
Brief entry 107
See also TCLC 10, 18
Nievergelt, Jurg 1938- CANR-26
Earlier sketch in CA 29-32R
Niewyk, Donald L. 1940- 33-36R
Nigg, Joe
See Nigg, Joseph E(ugene)
Nigg, Joseph E(ugene) 1938- CANR-35
Earlier sketch in CA 114
Niggli, Josefina (Maria) 1910- CANR-32
Earlier sketches in CAP-2, CA 23-24R
See also DLBY 80
See also HW
Nightingale, Anne Redmon 1943- 103
See also Redmon, Anne
Nightingale, Benedict 1939- 132
Nightingale, Earl (Clifford)
1921-1989 Obituary 128
Nightingale, Elena O(ttolenghi) 1932- 123
Nightingale, Sir Geoffrey (Slingsby)
1904- CAP-1
Earlier sketch in CA 13-14
Nightrate, Emil
See Spielmann, Peter James
Nigro, Felix A(nthony) 1914- CANR-14
Earlier sketch in CA 37-40R
Nihal Singh, Surendra 1929- 93-96
Nihilo, Arthur X. 1938- 105
Niizaka, Kazuo 1943- 77-80
Nijinska, Bronislava 1891-1972 117
Nijinsky, Romola Flavia
1891-1978 Obituary 81-84
Nijinsky, Vaslav (Fomitch)
1890-1950 Brief entry 115
Nikelly, Arthur G(eorge) 1927- 17-20R
Niklas, Gerald R. 1933- 118
Niklaus, Robert 1910- 9-12R
Niklaus, Thelma (Jones) 1912-1970 ....9-12R
Obituary 134
Nikolaev, Vsevolod A(postolov) 1909- 130
Nikola-Lisa, W. 1951- .... SATA 71
Nikolay, Michael 1941- 97-100
Nikolic, Mile
See Djilas, Milovan
Nik.T.O.
See Annensky, Innokenty Fyodorovich
Niland, D'Arcy Francis 1920-1967 ....CANR-3
Earlier sketch in CA 1-4R
Niland, Deborah 1951- 106
See also SATA 27
Niland, Powell 1919- 21-24R
Nile, Dorothea
See Avallone, Michael (Angelo, Jr)
Niles, D(aniel) T(hambyrajah)
1908-1970 Obituary 29-32R
Niles, Gwendolyn 1914- 9-12R
Niles, Hezekiah 1777-1839 .... DLB 43
Niles, John D(eWitt) 1945- 125
Niles, John Jacob 1892-1980 ....CANR-33
Obituary 97-100
Earlier sketch in CA 41-44R
Nill, Michael 1942- 124
Nilles, Jack M(athias) 1932- 108
Nilsen, Alleen Pace 1936- 112
Nilsen, Don L(ee) F(red) 1934- CANR-15
Earlier sketch in CA 41-44R
Nilsson, Birgit (Marta) 1918- 129
Nilsson, Usha Saksena 1930- 41-44R
Nimble, Jack B.
See Burgess, M(ichael) R(oy)
Nimeth, Albert J. 1918-1984 ....25-28R
Obituary 114
Nimitz, Chester W(illiam)
1885-1966 Obituary 113
Nimmer, Melville B(ernard) 1923-1985 49-52
Obituary 117
Nimmo, Dan D(ean) 1933- CANR-7
Earlier sketch in CA 13-16R
Nimmo, Derek (Robert) 1933- CANR-28
Earlier sketch in CA 109
Nimmo, Jenny 1942- 108
Nimnicht, Nona 1930- 73-76
Nimocks, Walter 1930- 41-44R
Nimoy, Leonard 1931- CANR-25
Earlier sketch in CA 57-60
Nims, Charles F(rancis) 1906-1988 ....17-20R
Obituary 127
Nims, John Frederick 1913- CANR-35
Earlier sketches in CA 13-16R, CANR-6
See also DLB 5
Nin, Anais 1903-1977 ....CANR-22
Obituary 69-72
Earlier sketch in CA 13-16R
See also AITN 2
See also CLC 1, 4, 8, 11, 14, 60
See also DLB 2, 4
See also MTCW
See also SSC 10
Nineham, Dennis (Eric) 1921- 85-88
Nininger, H(arvey) H(arlow) 1887-1986 ....21-24R
Obituary 118
Ninkovich, Thomas 1943- 137
Ninkovich, Tom
See Ninkovich, Thomas
Nioche, Brigitte 109
Niosi, Jorge 1945- 129
See also HW
Nir, Yehuda 1930- 107
Nirenberg, Jesse S(tanley) 1921- 69-72
Nirmala-Kumara, V
See Bose, N(irmal) K(umar)
Nirodi, Hira 1930- 5-8R
Nisbet, Ada Blanche 1907- 41-44R
Nisbet, Robert A(lexander) 1913- CANR-17
Earlier sketch in CA 25-28R
Nisbet, Stanley (Donald) 1912- CAP-1
Earlier sketch in CA 13-14
Nisbett, (Thomas) Alec 1930- CANR-22
Earlier sketch in CA 81-84
Nisbett, Richard E. 1941- 37-40R
Nisetich, Frank Joseph 1942- 97-100
Nish, Ian Hill 1926- CANR-17
Earlier sketch in CA 21-24R
Nishihara, Masashi 1937- CANR-12
Earlier sketch in CA 69-72
Nishio, Suehiro 1891-1981 Obituary 108
Nishiwaki, Junzaburo 1894-1982 Obituary 107
Nishiyama, Chiaki 1924- Brief entry 110
Niskanen, William Arthur Jr. 1933- 41-44R
Nissen, Lowell A(llen) 1932- 33-36R
Nissenbaum, Stephen 1941- 77-80
Nissenson, Hugh 1933- CANR-27
Earlier sketch in CA 17-20R
See also CLC 4, 9
See also DLB 28
Nissman, Albert 1930- 37-40R
Nissman, Blossom S. 1928- CANR-19
Earlier sketch in CA 37-40R
Nist, John (Albert) 1925-1981 ....CANR-11
Earlier sketch in CA 21-24R
Nitchie, George W(ilson) 1921- 9-12R
Nitske, W(illiam) Robert 1909- CANR-5
Earlier sketch in CA 13-16R
Nittler, Alan H(opkins) 1918- CANR-13
Earlier sketch in CA 61-64
Nityanandan, P(erumpilavil) M(adhava Menon)
1926- 9-12R
Nitzsche, Jane Chance 1945- CANR-8
Earlier sketch in CA 57-60
Niven, Alastair 1944- CANR-16
Earlier sketch in CA 81-84
Niven, Alexander Curt 1920- CANR-2
Earlier sketch in CA 5-8R
Niven, (James) David (Graham)
1910-1983 ....CANR-31
Obituary 110
Earlier sketch in CA 77-80
Niven, Frederick John 1878-1944 .... DLB 92
Niven, John 1921- 65-68
Niven, Larry
See Niven, Laurence Van Cott
See also CLC 8
See also DLB 8
Niven, Laurence Van Cott 1938- CANR-14
Earlier sketch in CA 21-24R
See also Niven, Larry
See also CAAS 12
See also MTCW
Niven, Marian
See Alston, Mary Niven
Niven, (Cecil) Rex 1898- 120
Niven, Vern
See Grier, Barbara G(ene Damon)
Nivens, Beatryce 1948- 114
Niver, Garry 1938- 138
Nivison, David Shepherd 1923- 103
Niwa, Tamako 1922- Brief entry 106
Niwano, Nikkyo 1906- 130
Nixon, Agnes Eckhardt 1927- 110
See also CLC 21
Nixon, Allan 1918- 17-20R
Nixon, Clarence H. Jr.
1908(?)-1990 Obituary 130
Nixon, Edna (Mary) 5-8R
Nixon, George 1924- 49-52
Nixon, Hershell Howard 1923- 89-92
See also SATA 42
Nixon, Howard Millar 1909-1983 Obituary 109
Nixon, Ivor Gray 1905- CAP-2
Earlier sketch in CA 29-32
Nixon, Joan Lowery 1927- CANR-38
Earlier sketches in CA 9-12R, CANR-7, 24
See also CLR 24
See also MAICYA
See also SAAS 9
See also SATA 8, 44
Nixon, John Erskine 1917- 101
Nixon, K.
See Nixon, Kathleen Irene (Blundell)
Nixon, Kathleen Irene (Blundell)
1894-1988(?) 73-76
Obituary 126
See also SATA 14, 59
Nixon, Lucille M. 1908-1963 ....5-8R
Nixon, Marion 1930- 49-52
Nixon, Richard M(ilhous) 1913- CANR-33
Earlier sketch in CA 73-76
See also BEST 90:3
See also MTCW
Nixon, Robert E(arl Jr.) 1918- 5-8R
Nixon, St. John Cousins 1885- 5-8R
Nixon, William R(ussell) 1918- 29-32R
Nixson, Frederick Ian 1943- CANR-20
Earlier sketch in CA 104
Nizan, Paul 1905-1940 .... DLB 72
See also TCLC 40
Nizer, Louis 1902- 53-56
Njururi, Ngumbu 1930- 17-20R
Nketia, J(oseph) H(anson) Kwabena
1921- CANR-7
Earlier sketch in CA 9-12R
Nkosi, Lewis 1936- CANR-27
Earlier sketch in CA 65-68
See also BLC 3
See also BW
See also CLC 45
Nkrumah, Kwame 1909-1972 132
Obituary 113
Noad, Frederick (McNeill) 1929- CANR-4
Earlier sketch in CA 9-12R
Noah, Harold J(ulius) 1925- CANR-30
Earlier sketches in CA 33-36R, CANR-13
Noah, Joseph W(atson) 1928- 81-84
Noakes, Jeremy 1941- 101
Noakes, Vivien 1937- 65-68
Noall, Roger 1935- 9-12R
Nobbs, David 1935- 138
Nobile, Umberto 1885-1978 Obituary 81-84
Noble, Allen G(eorge) 1930- 116
Noble, Charles
See Pawley, Martin Edward
Noble, David Watson 1925- CANR-1
Earlier sketch in CA 49-52
Noble, Dudley (Henry)
1893(?)-1970 Obituary 104
Noble, Elizabeth Marian 1945- CANR-9
Earlier sketch in CA 65-68
Noble, G(eorge) Bernard 1892-1972 .... CAP-2
Obituary 37-40R
Earlier sketch in CA 33-36
Noble, Iain (Andrew) 1949- 128
Noble, Iris (Davis) 1922-1986 ....CANR-2
Obituary 120
Earlier sketch in CA 1-4R
See also SATA 5, 49
Noble, J(ames) Kendrick Jr. 1928- 17-20R
Noble, J(ames) Kendrick
1896(?)-1978 Obituary 104
Noble, Jeanne L(aveta) 1926- Brief entry 112
Noble, John (Appelbe) 1914- CANR-1
Earlier sketch in CA 45-48
Noble, John Wesley 1913- 9-12R
Noble, John 1923- 45-48
Noble, Joseph Veach 1920- 61-64
Noble, June (Solveig) 1924-1984 ....CANR-18
Earlier sketch in CA 97-100
Noble, Marguerite (Buchanan) 1910- 105
Noble, Stanley R(odman)
1904(?)-1977 Obituary 104
Noble, Trinka Hakes Brief entry 116
See also SATA 37
Noble, William Charles 1935- 107
Noble, William P(arker) 1932- CANR-39
Earlier sketches in CA 101, CANR-18
Nochlin, Linda Weinberg 1931- CANR-6
Earlier sketch in CA 9-12R
Nock, Albert Jay 1870(?)-1945 Brief entry 122
Nock, Francis J. 1905-1969 .... CAP-1
Earlier sketch in CA 13-14
Nock, O(swald) S(tevens) 1905- CANR-16
Earlier sketch in CA 85-88
Nockolds, Harold 1907-1982 Obituary 108
Noddings, Nel 1929- 115
Noddings, Thomas C. 1933- CANR-2
Earlier sketch in CA 49-52
Nodel, Sol 1912-1976 Obituary 107
Nodier, (Jean) Charles (Emmanuel)
1780-1844 .... DLB 119
Nodset, Joan L.
See Lexau, Joan M.
Noe, Thomas R. 1947- 112
Noe, Tom
See Noe, Thomas R.
Noel, Christopher 1960- 127
Noel, Daniel C(alhoun) 1936- 101
Noel, Hilda Bloxton Jr.
See Schroetter, Hilda Noel
Noel, John
See Bird, Dennis L(eslie)
Noel, John V(avasour) Jr. 1912- CANR-15
Earlier sketch in CA 21-24R
Noel, Roden 1834-1894 .... DLB 35
Noel, Ruth (Swycaffer) 1947- 69-72
Noel, Sterling 1903-1984 Obituary 114
Noel, Thomas Jacob 1945- CANR-24
Earlier sketch in CA 107
Noel-Baker, Philip John
1889-1982 Obituary 108
Noel Hume, Ivor 1927- CANR-12
Earlier sketch in CA 13-16R
See also SATA 65
Noer, Thomas John 1944- 102
Noestlinger, Christine 1936- CANR-38
Brief entry 115
Earlier sketch in CA 123
See also Nostlinger, Christine
See also CLR 12
See also MAICYA
See also SATA 37, 64
Noether, Emiliana P. 101
Nof, Shimon Y. 1946- 135
Nofi, Albert A(urelio) 1944- 112

Nofziger, Margaret 1946- CANR-30
Earlier sketch in CA 110
Nogee, Joseph Lippman 1929- 17-20R
Noggle, Burl L. 1924- 134
Brief entry 107
Noguere, Suzanne 1947- 107
See also SATA 34
Nohl, Frederick 1927- CANR-3
Earlier sketch in CA 5-8R
Nohrnberg, James (Carson) 1941- 69-72
Nojiri, Kiyohiko 1897-1973 93-96
Obituary 41-44R
Nokes, Gerald Dacre 1899-1971 Obituary 104
Nolan, Alan T. 1923- 1-4R
Nolan, Albert 1934- 117
Nolan, Bob 1908(?)-1980 Obituary 101
Nolan, Brian
See O Nuallain, Brian
Nolan, Carroll A(nthony) 1906- 17-20R
Nolan, Christopher 1965- 111
See also CLC 58
Nolan, Chuck
See Edson, J(ohn) T(homas)
Nolan, David (Joseph) 1946- 132
Nolan, Dennis 1945- CANR-32
Earlier sketch in CA 112
See also SATA 34, 42
Nolan, Edward Francis 1915- Brief entry 108
Nolan, James 1947- CANR-5
Earlier sketch in CA 53-56
Nolan, Jeannette Covert 1897-1974 ....CANR-4
Obituary 53-56
Earlier sketch in CA 5-8R
See also SATA 2, 27
Nolan, Keith W(illiam) 1964- CANR-36
Earlier sketch in CA 114
Nolan, Madeena Spray 1943- 89-92
Nolan, Michael 1940- 126
Nolan, Paul T(homas) 1919- CANR-2
Earlier sketch in CA 5-8R
See also SATA 48
Nolan, Richard Thomas 1937- CANR-10
Earlier sketch in CA 25-28R
Nolan, Tom 1948- 77-80
Nolan, William F(rancis) 1928- CANR-1
Earlier sketch in CA 1-4R
See also CAAS 16
See also DLB 8
See also SATA 28
Nolan, Winefride (Bell) 1913- 13-16R
Noland, C. F. M. 1810(?)-1858 .... DLB 11
Noland, Ronald G(ene) 1936- 41-44R
Nolde, O(tto) Frederick 1899-1972 .... CAP-2
Obituary 37-40R
Earlier sketch in CA 29-32
Nolen, Barbara 1902- 104
Nolen, Claude H. 1921- 21-24R
Nolen, William A(nthony) 1928-1986 ......CANR-15
Obituary 121
Earlier sketch in CA 77-80
Nolin, Bertil 1926- 65-68
Noling, A(lfred) W(ells) 1899- CAP-2
Earlier sketch in CA 29-32
Noll, Bink
See Noll, Lou Barker
Noll, Lou Barker 1927- 5-8R
Noll, Mark A(llan) 1946- CANR-38
Earlier sketch in CA 115
Noll, Martin
See Buxbaum, Martin (David)
Noll, Richard 1959- 134
Noll, Roger G(ordon) 1940- CANR-27
Earlier sketches in CA 53-56, CANR-8
Nollau, Gunther 1911- 5-8R
Nollen, Stanley D(ale) 1940- 110
Nolte, Carl William 1933- 77-80
Nolte, Elleta 1919- 61-64
Nolte, M(ervin) Chester 1911- 9-12R
Nolte, William H(enry) 1928- 33-36R
Nolting, Frederick (Ernest Jr.)
1911-1989 Obituary 130
Nolting, Orin F(rederyc) 1903- 29-32R
Noltingk, B(ernard) E(dward) 1918- 17-20R
Noma, Koremichi 1938(?)-1987 Obituary 122
Nomad, Max 1880(?)-1973 Obituary 41-44R
Noma Shoichi 1911-1984 Obituary 113
Nonas, Elisabeth 1949- 119
Nonet, Philippe 1939- 57-60
Nonhebel, Clare 1953- 119
Noon, Brian 1919- 49-52
Noon, William T(homas) 1912-1975 65-68
Obituary 53-56
Noonan, John Ford 1943- 85-88
Noonan, John T(homas) Jr. 1926- CANR-13
Earlier sketch in CA 13-16R
Noonan, Julia 1946- 33-36R
See also SATA 4
Noonan, Lowell G(erald) 1922- 29-32R
Noonan, Michael John 1921- 21-24R
Noonan, Peggy 1950- 132
See also BEST 90:3
Noone, Edwina
See Avallone, Michael (Angelo, Jr)
Noone, John 1936- Brief entry 109
See also DLB 14
Noone, Richard 1918(?)-1973 Obituary 104
Noorbergen, Rene 1928- 77-80
Nooteboom, Cees 1933- 130
Brief entry 124
Nora, James Jackson 1928- CANR-20
Earlier sketch in CA 104
Norall, Frank 1918- 133
Norback, Craig T(homas) 1943- 113
Norbeck, Edward 1915- CANR-1
Earlier sketch in CA 1-4R
Norberg-Schulz, Christian 1926- 81-84
Norbu, Thubten Jigme
See Thubten Sigme Norbu
Norcross, John
See Conroy, John Wesley
Norcross, Lisabet
See Gladstone, Arthur M.
Norcutt, Bill
See Norcutt, William E.
Norcutt, William E. 1946- Brief entry 118
Nord, Ole C. 1935- 13-16R
Nord, Paul 1900(?)-1981 Obituary 103
Nord, Walter R(obert) 1939- 37-40R
Nordan, Lewis 1939- 117
Nordberg, H(arold) Orville 1916- 1-4R
Nordberg, Robert B. 1921- 13-16R
Nordby, Vernon James 1945- 57-60
Nordell, (Hans) Roderick 1925- 104
Norden, Albert 1904-1982 Obituary 107
Norden, Charles
See Durrell, Lawrence (George)
Norden, Denis 1922- CANR-29
Earlier sketch in CA 104
Norden, Heinz 1905- 53-56
Norden, Helen Brown
See Lawrenson, Helen
Nordham, George Washington 1929- CANR-23
Earlier sketch in CA 106
Nordhaus, William D(awbney) 1941- 97-100
Nordhoff, Charles (Bernard)
1887-1947 Brief entry 108
See also DLB 9
See also SATA 23
See also TCLC 23
Nordholm, Harriet 1912- 29-32R
Nordicus
See Snyder, Louis L(eo)
Nordin, D(ennis) Sven 1942- 61-64
Nordland, Gerald John 1927- 104
Nordland, Rod(ney Lee) 1949- 118
Nordlicht, Lillian 105
See also SATA 29
Nordlinger, Eric A. 1939- 77-80
Nordloh, David J(oseph) 1942- 137
Nordmann, Joseph (Behrens) 1922- 25-28R
Nordness, Lee 1924- 9-12R
Nordoff, Paul 1909-1977 102
Nordquist, Barbara K(ay) 1940- 77-80
Nordskog, John Eric 1893-1974 ....1-4R
Obituary 120
Nordstrom, Ursula 1910-1988 ....13-16R
Obituary 126
See also SATA 3, 57
Nordtvedt, Matilda 1926- 124
See also SATA 67
Nordyke, Eleanor C(ole) 1927- 107
Nordyke, James W(alter) 1930- 49-52
Noreen, Robert Gerald 1938- 77-80
Norelli, Martina R(oudabush) 1942- 73-76
Noren, Catherine (Hanf) 1938- CANR-16
Earlier sketch in CA 65-68
Noren, Paul Harold Andreas 1910- CAP-1
Earlier sketch in CA 11-12
Norfleet, Barbara P. 1926- Brief entry 107
Norfleet, Mary Crockett 1919- 1-4R
Norgate, Matthew 1901- 103
Norgay, Tenzing 1914-1986 Obituary 119
Nori, Claude 1949- CANR-18
Earlier sketch in CA 101
Norinsky, Marvin 1927- 130
Norland, Howard Bernett 1932- 49-52
Norling, Bernard 1924- 29-32R
Norling, Jo(sephine Stearns) 1-4R
Norling, Rita 61-64
Norman, Adrian R(oger) D(udley)
1938- CANR-26
Earlier sketch in CA 29-32R
Norman, Alexander Vesey Bethune
1930- CANR-9
Earlier sketch in CA 21-24R
Norman, Barbara 33-36R
Norman, Bruce 1936- 61-64
Norman, C. J.
See Barrett, Norman (S.)
Norman, Cecilia 1927- CANR-23
Earlier sketches in CA 57-60, CANR-7
Norman, Charles 1904- 107
See also DLB 111
See also SATA 38
Norman, Diana 1935- 135
Norman, Dor(ald) Cleveland
1909(?)-1979 Obituary 89-92
Norman, Donald A(rthur) 1935- CANR-1
Earlier sketch in CA 49-52
Norman, Dorothy 1905- 25-28R
Norman, E. D.
See Goodwin, Bennie Eugene II
Norman, Edward (Robert) 1938- CANR-27
Earlier sketches in CA 17-20R, CANR-10
Norman, Frank 1930-1980 ....CANR-6
Obituary 102
Earlier sketch in CA 1-4R
Norman, Geraldine (Lucia) 1940- 93-96
Norman, Greg(ory John) 1955- 133
Norman, Hilary 126
Norman, Howard
See Norman, Howard A.
Norman, Howard A. 1949- 137
Brief entry 129
Norman, James
See Schmidt, James Norman
Norman, Jillian 1940- 25-28R
Norman, Joe
See Heard, J(oseph) Norman
Norman, John
See Lange, John Frederick Jr.
Norman, John 1912- 17-20R
Norman, Joyce Ann 1937- 65-68
Norman, Kerry
See Le Pelley, Guernsey
Norman, Lilith 1927- CANR-1
Earlier sketch in CA 45-48
Norman, Lloyd (Henry) 1913-1987 102
Obituary 124
Norman, Louis
See Whittemore, Don
Norman, Marc 1941- 49-52
Norman, Marsha 1947- 105
See also CABS 3
See also CLC 28
See also DLBY 84
Norman, Mary 1931- .... SATA 36
Norman, Maxwell H(erbert) 1917- 29-32R
Norman, Michael 1947- 129
Norman, Nicole
See Cudlipp, Edythe
Norman, Rick (J.) 1954- 137
Norman, Ruth 1903(?)-1977 Obituary 73-76
Norman, Steve
See Pashko, Stanley
Norman, Sylva 1901- CAP-1
Earlier sketch in CA 13-14
Norman, Theodore 1910-1987 124
Obituary 122
Norman, Vesey
See Norman, Alexander Vesey Bethune
Norman, W. S.
See Wilson, N(orman) Scarlyn
Norman, Yvonne
See Seely, Norma
Normyx
See Douglas, (George) Norman
Norodom Sihanouk (Varman), Samdech Preah
1922- 129
Brief entry 106
Norquest, Carrol 1901-1981 ....41-44R
Obituary 133
Norquist, Richard F(ranklin) 1933- 113
Norrie, Ian 1927- CANR-23
Earlier sketch in CA 106
Norris, Benjamin Franklin Jr.
1870-1902 Brief entry 110
See also Norris, Frank
See also TCLC 24
Norris, Charles G(ilman Smith)
1881-1945 Brief entry 118
See also DLB 9
Norris, Christopher (Charles) 1947- CANR-29
Earlier sketch in CA 111
Norris, Christopher Neil Foxley
See Foxley-Norris, Christopher Neil
Norris, Clarence 1912-1989 Obituary 127
Norris, Donald F(ranklin) 1942- CANR-2
Earlier sketch in CA 49-52
Norris, Dorothy E. Koch 1907- CAP-2
Earlier sketch in CA 21-22
Norris, Edgar Poe
See Kinnaird, Clark
Norris, Francis Hubert 1909- 5-8R
Norris, Frank
See Norris, Benjamin Franklin Jr.
See also CDALB 1865-1917
See also DLB 12, 71
Norris, Frank C(allan)
1907-1967 Obituary 25-28R
Norris, Gunilla Brodde 1939- 93-96
See also SATA 20
Norris, Harold 1918- 108
Norris, Hoke 1913-1977 ....9-12R
Obituary 73-76
Norris, J(ames) A(lfred) 1929- 25-28R
Norris, James Donald 1930- 17-20R
Norris, Joan 1943- 73-76
Norris, John 1925- 9-12R
Norris, Kathleen (Thompson)
1880-1966 Obituary 25-28R
Norris, Kathleen 1947- 33-36R
Norris, Katrin 17-20R
Norris, Ken 1951- 113
Norris, Kenneth S(tafford) 1924- 77-80
Norris, Leslie 1921- CANR-14
Earlier sketches in CAP-1, CA 11-12
See also CLC 14
See also DLB 27
Norris, Louanne 1930- CANR-20
Earlier sketch in CA 53-56
Norris, Louis William 1906- CAP-1
Earlier sketch in CA 9-10
Norris, Maureen
See Cudlipp, Edythe
Norris, Nigel (Harold) 1943- 65-68
Norris, Pippa 1953- 134
Norris, Richard A(lfred) Jr. 1930- 17-20R
Norris, Ronald V. 1940- 116
Norris, Ruby Turner
See Morris, Ruby Turner
Norris, Russell Bradner (Jr.) 1942- 53-56
Norris, Theo L. 1926- 21-24R
Norse, Harold (George) 1916- CANR-4
Earlier sketch in CA 53-56
See also DLB 16
Norst, Joel
See Mitchell, Kirk (John)
North, Alvin J(ohn) 1917- 49-52
North, Andrew
See Norton, Andre
North, Anthony
See Koontz, Dean R(ay)
North, Captain George
See Stevenson, Robert Louis (Balfour)
North, Carol S. 1954- 128
North, Charles W.
See Bauer, Erwin A.
North, Christopher
See Wilson, John
North, Christopher R(ichard)
1888-1975 Obituary 61-64
North, Colin
See Bingley, David Ernest
North, Edmund H(all) 1911-1990 121
Obituary 132
North, Eleanor B(eryl) 1898- 49-52
North, Elizabeth 1932- 81-84
North, Gary 1942- CANR-38
Earlier sketches in CA 65-68, CANR-16
North, Gil
See Horne, Geoffrey
North, Helen Florence 1921- 104
North, Joan 1920- 13-16R
See also SATA 16
North, John (Francis Allen) 1894-1973 107
Obituary 104
North, Joseph 1904-1976 ....CANR-4
Obituary 69-72
Earlier sketch in CA 1-4R
North, Mark
See Miller, Wright (Watts)
North, Milou
See Erdrich, Louise
North, Morgan 1915(?)-1978 Obituary 104
North, Robert
See Withers, Carl A.
North, Robert Carver 1914- CANR-4
Earlier sketch in CA 5-8R
North, Robert Grady 1916- 17-20R
North, Sara
See Bonham, Barbara Thomas
and Hager, Jean
North, Sterling 1906-1974 ....5-8R
Obituary 53-56
See also MAICYA
See also SATA 1, 26, 45
North, Wheeler James 1922- 101
Northam, Ray M(ervyn) 1929- 73-76
Northart, Leo J(oseph) 1929- 69-72
Northcote, Peter
See Cotes, Peter
Northcott, (William) Cecil 1902-1987 ....9-12R
Obituary 124
See also SATA 55
Northcott, Kenneth J(ames) 1922- CANR-29
Earlier sketch in CA 45-48
Northcutt, Wayne 1944- 138
Northedge, Frederick Samuel 1918-1985 104
Obituary 115
Northen, Helen 1914- CANR-13
Earlier sketch in CA 33-36R
Northen, Henry T(heodore) 1908-1979 97-100
Northen, Rebecca Tyson 1910- 105
Northgrave, Anne
See Tibble, Anne
Northmore, Elizabeth Florence
1906-1974 .... CAP-2
Earlier sketch in CA 19-20
Northouse, Cameron (George) 1948- 81-84
Northrop, Filmer S(tuart) C(uckow)
1893- CANR-17
Earlier sketch in CA 1-4R
Northrop, J. H.
See Northrop, John H(oward)
Northrop, John H(oward)
1891-1987 Obituary 123
Northrup, B. A.
See Hubbard, L(afayette) Ron(ald)
Northrup, Herbert Roof 1918- 9-12R
North Staffs
See Hulme, T(homas) E(rnest)
Northumbrian Gentleman, The
See Tegner, Henry (Stuart)
Northway, Mary L(ouise) 1909- 45-48
Northwood, Lawrence K(ing) 1917- 13-16R
Norton, Alan (Lewis) 1926- CANR-15
Earlier sketch in CA 81-84
Norton, Alden H(olmes) 1903- 101
Norton, Alice Mary
See Norton, Andre
See also MAICYA
See also SATA 1, 43
Norton, Alice 1926- 33-36R
Norton, Andre 1912- CANR-31
Earlier sketches in CA 1-4R, CANR-2
See also Norton, Alice Mary
See also CLC 12
See also DLB 8, 52
See also MTCW
Norton, Andrews 1786-1853 .... DLB 1
Norton, Augustus Richard 1946- 113
Norton, Bess
See Norton, Olive (Claydon)
Norton, Bettina A(ntonia) 1936- 93-96
Norton, Boyd 1936- 37-40R
Norton, Bram
See Bramesco, Norton J.
Norton, Browning
See Norton, Frank R. B(rowning)
Norton, Caroline 1808-1877 .... DLB 21
Norton, Charles A(lbert) 1920- 109
Norton, Charles Eliot 1827-1908 .... DLB 1, 64
Norton, David Fate 1937- 107
Norton, David L. 1930- 37-40R
Norton, (William) Elliot 1903- Brief entry 109
Norton, Frank R. B(rowning) 1909- 61-64
See also SATA 10
Norton, Frederick H. 1896- 61-64
Norton, Glyn P(eter) 1941- 122
Norton, Herman A. 1921- CANR-7
Earlier sketch in CA 5-8R
Norton, Howard Melvin 1911- CANR-3
Earlier sketch in CA 1-4R
Norton, Hugh S(tanton) 1921- 9-12R
Norton, John 1606-1663 .... DLB 24
Norton, Joseph L(ouis) 1918- 29-32R

Norton, Lucy 1902-1989 Obituary 129
Norton, M. D. Herter
See Crena de Iongh, Mary (Dows Herter Norton)
Norton, Mary Beth 1943- CANR-5
Earlier sketch in CA 49-52
Norton, Mary E(lizabeth) 1913- 41-44R
Norton, Mary 1903- 97-100
See also CLR 6
See also MAICYA
See also SATA 18, 60
Norton, Olive (Claydon) 1913-1973 ....9-12R
Norton, Paul Foote 1917- 41-44R
Norton, Perry L. 1920- 13-16R
Norton, Peter (John) 1913- 13-16R
Norton, Roger C(ecil) 1921- 114
Norton, Thomas Elliot 1942- 61-64
Norton, Thomas 1532-1584 ....DLB 62
Norton, Victor 1906-1983 Obituary 109
Norton, Wesley 1923- 114
Norton-Smith, John 1931-1988 107
Obituary 127
Norton-Taylor, Duncan 1904-1982 102
Obituary 107
Norvil, Manning
See Bulmer, (Henry) Kenneth
Norville, Warren 1923- 73-76
Norwak, Mary 1929- 109
Norway, Kate
See Norton, Olive (Claydon)
Norway, Nevil Shute 1899-1960 102
Obituary 93-96
See also Shute, Nevil
Norwich, John Julius (Cooper) 1929- CANR-29
Earlier sketches in CA 49-52, CANR-5
Norwood, Fred W(ayland) 1920- Brief entry 112
Norwood, Frederick Abbott 1914- CANR-20
Earlier sketches in CA 1-4R, CANR-5
Norwood, Gilbert 1880-1954 Brief entry 116
Norwood, John
See Stark, Raymond
Norwood, Paul
See Nettl, J(ohn) P(eter)
Norwood, Robert 1874-1932 ....DLB 92
Norwood, Robin 128
Norwood, Victor G(eorge) C(harles)
1920- CANR-10
Earlier sketch in CA 21-24R
Norwood, Warren C. 1945- 112
Nosanow, Barbara Shissler 1931- CANR-28
Earlier sketch in CA 29-32R
Nosco, Peter 1950- 93-96
Nosille, Nabrah
See Ellison, Harlan
Noss, John Boyer 1896- 85-88
Noss, Luther (Melancthon) 1907- 5-8R
Nossack, Hans Erich 1901-1978 93-96
Obituary 85-88
See also CLC 6
See also DLB 69
Nossal, Frederick (Christian) 1927-1979 ....5-8R
Obituary 89-92
Nossal, Gustav Joseph Victor 1931- 109
Nossiter, Bernard D(aniel) 1926- 41-44R
Obituary 138
Nostlinger, Christine
See Noestlinger, Christine
See also CLR 12
See also SATA 37
Nostrand, Howard Lee 1910- 9-12R
Nostwich, T(heodore) D. 127
Nosu, Chuji
See Ozu, Yasujiro
Notar, Stephen 1926- 119
Notarius
See Martin, Andrew
Notehelfer, F(red) G(eorge) 1939- 81-84
Notestein, Frank Wallace
1902-1983 Obituary 109
Notestein, Wallace 1878-1969 ....CAP-1
Earlier sketch in CA 9-10
Noth, Martin D. 1902-1968 ....CAP-2
Earlier sketch in CA 21-22
Nothing Venture
See Finney, Humphrey S.
Notlep, Robert
See Pelton, Robert W(ayne)
Notley, Alice 1945- Brief entry 124
Noto, Lore(nzo) 1923- 134
Nott, David 1928- 45-48
Nott, Kathleen Cecilia CANR-3
Earlier sketch in CA 1-4R
Notterman, Joseph M(elvin) 1923- 17-20R
Nottingham, Elizabeth K. 1900- 93-96
Nottingham, William Jesse 1927- 25-28R
Notz, Rebecca Love 1888-1974 Obituary 104
Nourie, Alan (Raymond) 1942- 138
Nourie, Barbara (Livingston) 1947- 138
Nourissier, Francois 1927- 81-84
Nourse, Alan E(dward) 1928- CANR-21
Earlier sketches in CA 1-4R, CANR-3
See also DLB 8
See also SATA 48
Nourse, Edwin G(riswold)
1883-1974 Obituary 49-52
Nourse, Hugh O(liver) 1933- Brief entry 107
Nourse, James G(regory) 1947- 105
Nourse, Joan Thellusson 1921- 9-12R
Nourse, Mary Augusta
1880(?)-1971 Obituary 33-36R
Nourse, Robert Eric Martin 1938- 21-24R
Nouveau, Arthur
See Whitcomb, Ian
Nouwen, Henri J(osef Machiel) 1932- 73-76
Nova, Craig 1945- CANR-2
Earlier sketch in CA 45-48
See also CLC 7, 31
Novack, Evelyn Reed
1906(?)-1979 Obituary 85-88
Novack, George (Edward) 1905- 49-52
Novak, Barbara 97-100
Novak, Bogdan C(yril) 1919- 33-36R
Novak, David 1941- 93-96
Novak, Jane Dailey 1917- 105
Novak, Joe
See Novak, Joseph
Novak, Joseph
See Kosinski, Jerzy (Nikodem)
Novak, Joseph 1898- CAP-1
Earlier sketch in CA 11-12
Novak, Lorna 1927- 17-20R
Novak, Matt 1962- 125
See also SATA 52, 60
Novak, Maximillian E(rwin) 1930- CANR-12
Earlier sketch in CA 33-36R
Novak, Michael Paul 1935- 49-52
Novak, Michael 1933- CANR-30
Earlier sketches in CA 1-4R, CANR-1
Novak, Robert
See Levinson, Leonard
Novak, Robert D(avid) 1931- CANR-12
Earlier sketch in CA 13-16R
Novak, Rose 1940- CANR-22
Earlier sketch in CA 105
Novak, Stephen R(obert) 1922- 85-88
Novak, William (Arnold) 1948- CANR-26
Earlier sketch in CA 93-96
Novalis 1772-1801 ....DLB 90
Novaro, Mario 1868-1944 ....DLB 114
Novarr, David 1917- 17-20R
Novas Calvo, Lino 1905-1983 ....HW
Nove, Alec 1915- CANR-3
Earlier sketch in CA 1-4R
Novelli, Florence 1931- 112
Novelli, Luca 1947- ....SATA 61
Novello, Don 1943- 107
Noventa, Giacomo 1898-1960 ....DLB 114
Nover, Barnet 1899-1973 Obituary 41-44R
Noverr, Douglas A(rthur) 1942- 102
Novick, David 1906- 33-36R
Novick, Julius Lerner 1939- 103
Novick, Marian 1951- 123
Novick, Paul 1891-1989 Obituary 130
Novik, Mary 1945- 61-64
Novins, Stuart 1914(?)-1989 Obituary 130
Novitski, Joseph (W. D.) 1940- 124
Novitz, Charles R. 1934- 69-72
Novo, Salvador 1904-1974 131
Obituary 110
See also HW
Novoa, John David Bruce
See Bruce-Novoa, Juan D.
Novoa, Juan Bruce
See Bruce-Novoa, Juan D.
Novogrod, R(eevan) Joseph 1916- 29-32R
Novomesky, Ladislav
1904-1976 Obituary 69-72
Novotny, Ann M. 1936-1982 ....25-28R
Obituary 108
Novotny, Fritz 1903- CANR-18
Earlier sketch in CA 65-68
Novotny, Louise Miller 1889- CAP-2
Earlier sketch in CA 23-24
Novy, Marianne (Lucille) 1945- 118
Nowacki, Walenty 1906- 37-40R
Nowak, Mariette 1941- 102
Nowakowski, Marek 1935- 119
Nowell, Elizabeth Cameron CANR-1
Earlier sketch in CA 1-4R
See also SATA 12
Nowlan, Alden (Albert) 1933-1983 ....CANR-5
Earlier sketch in CA 9-12R
See also CLC 15
See also DLB 53
Nowlan, James Dunlap 1941- Brief entry 105
Nowlan, Philip Francis
1888-1940 Brief entry 108
Nowlan, Robert Anthony Jr. 1934- CANR-32
Earlier sketch in CA 113
Nowlis, Helen H(oward) 1913- Brief entry 111
Noxon, James Herbert 1924- 85-88
Noyce, Gaylord B. 1926- CANR-29
Earlier sketches in CA 37-40R, CANR-13
Noyes, Alfred 1880-1958 Brief entry 104
See also DLB 20
See also TCLC 7
Noyes, Charles Edmund 1904-1972 ....37-40R
Noyes, Crosby S(tuart) 1921-1988 Obituary 125
Noyes, Crosby S. 1825-1908 ....DLB 23
Noyes, David 1898(?)-1981 Obituary 104
Noyes, Henry (Halsey) 1910- 133
Noyes, James H(oyt) 1927- 118
Noyes, Jeanice W. 1914- 25-28R
Noyes, Joan 1935- 115
Noyes, Kathryn Johnston 1930- 17-20R
Noyes, Morgan Phelps 1891-1972 ....CAP-1
Obituary 37-40R
Earlier sketch in CA 11-12
Noyes, Nell Braly 1921- 37-40R
Noyes, Nicholas 1647-1717 ....DLB 24
Noyes, Peter R. 1930- 49-52
Noyes, Russell 1901- 25-28R
Noyes, Stanley 1924- CANR-35
Earlier sketches in CA 45-48, CANR-1
Noyes, Theodore W. 1858-1946 ....DLB 29
Noyes-Kane, Dorothy 1906- CAP-1
Earlier sketch in CA 13-14
Noyle, Ken(neth Alfred Edward) 1922- 85-88
Nozick, Martin 1917- 37-40R
Nozick, Robert 1938- 61-64
Nriagu, Jerome O. 1942- 135
Nsarkoh, J. K(wasi) 1931- 13-16R
Nucera, Marisa Lonette 1959- 17-20R
Nuchtern, Jean 1939- 25-28R
Nuckolls, James L(awton)
1938-1987 Obituary 123
Nudel, Adele Rice 1927- 124
Nudel, Ida 1931- 134
Nudelman, Jerrold 1942- 33-36R
Nuechterlein, Donald Edwin 1925- CANR-1
Earlier sketch in CA 1-4R
Nuelle, Helen S(hearman) 1923- CANR-12
Earlier sketch in CA 61-64
Nuernberger, Phil 1942- CANR-35
Earlier sketch in CA 114
Nuessel, Frank H(enry) 1943- CANR-31
Earlier sketch in CA 111
Nuetzel, Charles (Alexander) 1934- 105
Nugent, Bruce
See Nugent, Richard Bruce
Nugent, Donald G(ene) 1930- 45-48
Nugent, Elliott (John) 1899-1980 ....5-8R
Obituary 101
Nugent, Frances Roberts 1904-1964(?) 5-8R
Nugent, Frank 1908-1965 ....DLB 44
Nugent, Jeffrey B(ishop) 1936- 93-96
Nugent, John Peer 1930- 13-16R
Nugent, Nancy 1938- CANR-16
Earlier sketch in CA 65-68
Nugent, Neill 1947- 133
Nugent, Richard Bruce 1906(?)- 125
See also BW
See also DLB 51
Nugent, Robert 1920- 61-64
Nugent, Tom 1943- 49-52
Nugent, Vincent Joseph 1913- 41-44R
Nugent, Walter T(erry) K(ing) 1935- CANR-5
Earlier sketch in CA 5-8R
Null, Gary CANR-17
Earlier sketch in CA 65-68
Nulman, Macy 1923- 57-60
Nulty, William H(arry) 1932- 136
Numbers, Ronald L(eslie) 1942- CANR-18
Earlier sketch in CA 101
Numeroff, Laura Joffe 1953- 106
See also SATA 28
Nummi, Seppo (Antero Yrjoepoika)
1932-1981 Obituary 108
Nunan, Desmond J. 1927- 17-20R
Nunes, Claude 1924- 134
Brief entry 112
Nunes, Rhoda (Gwylleth) 1938- Brief entry 113
Nunez, Ana Rosa 1926- CANR-14
Earlier sketch in CA 69-72
Nunis, Doyce B(lackman) Jr. 1924- CANR-19
Earlier sketches in CA 5-8R, CANR-3
Nunley, Maggie Rennert
See Rennert, Maggie
Nunn, Frederick M. 1937- 33-36R
Nunn, G(odfrey) Raymond 1918- CANR-13
Earlier sketch in CA 33-36R
Nunn, Henry L(ightfoot)
1878-1972 Obituary 37-40R
Nunn, John 1955- 115
Nunn, Kem ....CLC 34
Nunn, Marshall E(arl) 1928- 112
Nunn, Walter (Harris) 1942- CANR-23
Earlier sketch in CA 45-48
Nunn, William Curtis 1908- CANR-1
Earlier sketch in CA 1-4R
Nunnerley, (Gould) David 1947- 45-48
Nuquist, Andrew E(dgerton)
1905-1975 Obituary 61-64
Nuraini
See Sim, Katharine (Thomasset)
Nurcombe, Barry 1933- 65-68
Nurenberg, Thelma
See Greenhaus, Thelma Nurenberg
Nurge, Ethel 1920- 33-36R
Nurmi, Martin Karl 1920- CANR-17
Earlier sketch in CA 1-4R
Nurnberg, Maxwell 1897-1984 ....CANR-2
Obituary 114
Earlier sketch in CA 5-8R
See also SATA 27, 41
Nurnberg, Walter 1907- 13-16R
Nurse, Malcolm Ivan Meredith
1903-1959 Brief entry 119
Nurse, Peter H(arold) 1926- 9-12R
Nusbaum, N. Richard
See Nash, N. Richard
Nusbaum, Rosemary 1907- 113
Nussbaum, Aaron 1910-1981 49-52
Obituary 104
Nussbaum, Al(bert F.) 1934- 85-88
Nussbaum, Martha Craven 1947- 134
Nussbaumer, Paul (Edmund) 1934- 93-96
See also SATA 16
Nusser, J(ames) L(ivingston) 1925- 1-4R
Nute, Grace Lee 1895-1990 Obituary 131
Nutini, Hugo G(ino) 1928- Brief entry 109
Nutt, Grady 1934- 97-100
Nuttall, A(nthony) D(avid) 1937- CANR-11
Earlier sketch in CA 21-24R
Nuttall, Geoffrey Fillingham 1911- CANR-25
Earlier sketches in CA 13-16R, CANR-10
Nuttall, Jeff 1933- CANR-14
Earlier sketch in CA 29-32R
Nuttall, Kenneth 1907- 17-20R
Nuttall-Smith, Margaret Emily Noel 1919- 104
See also Fortnum, Peggy
Nutter, G(ilbert) Warren 1923-1979 ....CANR-2
Obituary 85-88
Earlier sketch in CA 1-4R
Nuttgens, Patrick 1930- 128
Nutting, (Harold) Anthony 1920- CANR-7
Earlier sketch in CA 5-8R
Nutting, Patricia Fink 1926- 129
Nutting, Willis D(wight) 1900-1975 ....CAP-2
Earlier sketch in CA 25-28
Nutzle, Futzie
See Kleinsmith, Bruce John
Nuwer, Hank
See Nuwer, Henry
Nuwer, Henry 1946- 128
Nwankwo, Nkem 1936- 65-68
Nwoauau, Edwin Ifeanyichukwu 1933- 17-20R
Nyabongo, Akiki K. 1905-1975 Obituary 61-64
Nyad, Diana 1949- 136
Brief entry 111
Nyagumbo, Maurice (Tapfumaneyi)
1924-1989 Obituary 128
Nyanaponika 1901- CAP-1
Earlier sketch in CA 9-10
Nybakken, Elizabeth I. 1940- 114
Nybakken, Oscar Edward 1904- 93-96
Nyberg, David (Alan) 1943- 107
Nyberg, Kathleen Neill 1919- 21-24R
Nyberg, (Everett Wayne) Morgan 1944- 127
Nyce, (Nellie) Helene von Strecker
1885-1969 ....SATA 19
Nyce, Vera 1862-1925 ....SATA 19
Nye, Bill
See Nye, Edgar Wilson
See also DLB 11
Nye, Doug(las Charles) 1945- Brief entry 114
Nye, Edgar Wilson 1850-1896
See Nye, Bill
See also DLB 23
Nye, F(rancis) Ivan 1918- CANR-21
Earlier sketches in CA 9-12R, CANR-6
Nye, Hermes 1908- CAP-2
Earlier sketch in CA 19-20
Nye, Joseph S(amuel) Jr. 1937- CANR-35
Earlier sketches in CA 25-28R, CANR-12
Nye, Loyal 1921- 106
Nye, Miriam (Maurine Hawthorn) Baker
1918- 85-88
Nye, Naomi Shihab 1952- ....DLB 120
Nye, Nelson C(oral) 1907- CANR-4
Earlier sketch in CA 5-8R
Nye, Robert D(onald) 1934- 73-76
Nye, Robert Evans 1911- CANR-1
Earlier sketch in CA 1-4R
Nye, Robert 1939- CANR-29
Earlier sketch in CA 33-36R
See also CLC 13, 42
See also DLB 14
See also MTCW
See also SATA 6
Nye, Russel B(laine) 1913- CANR-4
Earlier sketch in CA 1-4R
Nye, Simon (Beresford) 1958- 131
Nye, Vernice Trousdale 1913- CANR-1
Earlier sketch in CA 1-4R
Nye, Wilbur S. 1898-1970 ....CANR-15
Obituary 103
Earlier sketch in CA 1-4R
Nyenhuis, Jacob E(ugene)
1935- Brief entry 117
Nyerere, Julius K(ambarage) 1922- 125
Brief entry 105
See also BW
Nygaard, Anita 1934- 65-68
Nygaard, Norman E. 1897-1971 ....CANR-2
Earlier sketch in CA 1-4R
Nygard, Roald 1935- 103
Nygren, Anders T(heodor) S(amuel)
1890- 9-12R
Nyhart, Nina 1934- 135
Nykoruk, Barbara (Christine)
1949- Brief entry 115
Nylander, Carl 1932- 33-36R
Nynych, Stephanie J.
See Caulder, Colline
Nyquist, Ewald B(erger) 1914- Brief entry 113
Nyquist, Thomas E. 1931- 41-44R
Nyren, Dorothy Elizabeth 1927- CANR-5
Earlier sketch in CA 1-4R
Nyren, Karl 1922(?)-1988 Obituary 126
Nyro, Laura 1947- ....CLC 17
Nystrom, Carolyn 1940- CANR-37
Earlier sketch in CA 114
See also SATA 67
Nzimiro, Ikenna 1927- CANR-2
Earlier sketch in CA 45-48

O

O(rdonez), Jaime E(dmundo) Rodriguez
See Rodriguez O(rdonez), Jaime E(dmundo)
Oak, Liston M. 1895-1970 Obituary 104
Oakes, James 1953- 107
Oakes, John Bertram 1913- 13-16R
Oakes, Philip (Barlow) 1928- CANR-29
Earlier sketches in CA 53-56, CANR-4
Oakes, Urian 1631(?)-1681 ....DLB 24
Oakes, Vanya 1909-1983 ....33-36R
Obituary 111
See also SATA 6, 37
Oakeshott, Michael (Joseph)
1901-1990 ....CANR-27
Obituary 133
Earlier sketch in CA 1-4R
Oakeshott, Walter (Fraser) 1903-1987 ....13-16R
Obituary 123
Oakie, Jack
See Offield, Lewis Delaney
Oakland, Thomas David 1939- 53-56
Oakley, Allen 1943- 126

Oakley, Ann (Rosamund) 1944- CANR-25
Earlier sketches in CA 57-60, CANR-6
Oakley, Barry K(ingham) 1931- 104
Oakley, Charles Allen 1900- 108
Oakley, Don(ald G.) 1927- 29-32R
See also SATA 8
Oakley, Eric Gilbert 1916- 9-12R
Oakley, Francis (Christopher) 1931- 13-16R
Oakley, Giles (Francis) 1946- 103
Oakley, Graham 1929- CANR-38
Earlier sketch in CA 106
See also CLR 7
See also MAICYA
See also SATA 30
Oakley, Helen (McKelvey) 1906- 17-20R
See also SATA 10
Oakley, J. Ronald 1941- 121
Oakley, Josephine
1903(?)-1978 Obituary 81-84
Oakley, K. P.
See Oakley, Kenneth Page
Oakley, Kenneth P.
See Oakley, Kenneth Page
Oakley, Kenneth Page 1911-1981 122
Obituary 108
Oakley, Mary Ann B. 1940- 45-48
Oakley, Stewart P(hilip) 1931- 21-24R
Oakman, Barbara F(rances) 1931- 57-60
Oaks, Dallin H(arris) 1932- 25-28R
Oaksey, John 1929- 105
Oana, Katherine 1929- 108
See also SATA 37, 53
Oates, Jeannette 1912(?)-1984 Obituary 112
Oates, John F. 1934- 17-20R
Oates, John (Frederick) 1944- 69-72
Oates, Joyce Carol 1938- CANR-25
Earlier sketch in CA 5-8R
See also AITN 1
See also BEST 89:2
See also CDALB 1968-1988
See also CLC 1, 2, 3, 6, 9, 11, 15, 19, 33, 52
See also DLB 2, 5
See also DLBY 81
See also MTCW
See also SSC 6
See also WLC
Oates, Stephen B. 1936- CANR-26
Earlier sketches in CA 9-12R, CANR-4
See also SATA 59
Oates, Wallace Eugene 1937- CANR-14
Earlier sketch in CA 37-40R
Oates, Wayne Edward 1917- 85-88
Oates, Whitney J(ennings) 1904-1973 .....CANR-3
Obituary 45-48
Earlier sketch in CA 5-8R
Oathout, John D(avid) 1913- 111
Oatley, Keith 1939- 45-48
Oatman, Eric F(urber) 1939- CANR-19
Earlier sketch in CA 103
Oatts, Balfour
See Oatts, Lewis Balfour
Oatts, Henry Augustus 1898-1980 ....5-8R
Obituary 103
Oatts, Lewis Balfour 1902- 110
Obach, Robert 1939- 106
Obaldia, Rene de 1918- 133
Brief entry 116
O'Ballance, Edgar 1918- CANR-7
Earlier sketch in CA 5-8R
O'Banion, Terry 1936- 33-36R
O'Bannon, Dan(iel Thomas) 1946- 138
O'Barr, William M(cAlston) 1942- 49-52
O'Beirne, T(homas) H(ay) 1915-1982 ....17-20R
Obituary 120
Obele, Norma Taylor 1933- 104
Obenchain, Anne DeCroes
1914(?)-1984 Obituary 112
Obenhaus, Victor 1903- CAP-1
Earlier sketch in CA 13-14
Ober, Stuart Alan 1946- 103
Ober, Warren U(pton) 1925- 13-16R
Oberdorf, Charles (Donnell) 1941- 126
Oberdorfer, Don 1931- 129
Oberg, Alcestis R. 1949- 128
Oberg, Arthur K. 1938-1977 Obituary 112
Oberg, James E(dward) 1944- CANR-26
Earlier sketch in CA 108
Oberhansli, Trudi
See Schlapbach-Oberhansli, Trudi
Oberhelman, Harley D(ean) 1928- 53-56
Oberholtzer, Ellis Paxton 1868-1936 .... DLB 47
Oberholtzer, Peter
See Brannon, William T.
Oberholtzer, W(alter) Dwight 1939- 101
Oberholzer, Emil Jr. 1926(?)-1981 Obituary 102
Oberle, Joseph 1958- 136
See also SATA 69
Oberman, Heiko Augustinus 1930- CANR-25
Earlier sketches in CA 5-8R, CANR-7
Obermann, C. Esco 1904- 53-56
Obermayer, Herman J. 1924- 65-68
Obermeyer, Barrett John 1937- 5-8R
Obermeyer, Henry 1899- CAP-2
Earlier sketch in CA 29-32
Obermeyer, Marion Barrett 5-8R
Oberschall, Antony R. 1936- 97-100
Obert, John C. 1924-1987 Obituary 122
Oberth, Hermann Julius
1894-1979(?) Obituary 113
Obey, Andre 1892-1975 97-100
Obituary 57-60
Obichere, Boniface Ihewunwa 1932- 41-44R
Obiechina, Emmanuel Nwanonye
1933- CANR-15
Earlier sketch in CA 41-44R
O'Biso, Carol (Anne) 1953- 133
Obligado, Lilian (Isabel) 1931- 134
See also SATA 45, 61
Oboe, Peter
See Jacobs, Walter Darnell
Obojski, Robert 1929- CANR-24
Earlier sketch in CA 108
Obolensky, Dimitri 1918- CANR-25
Earlier sketch in CA 45-48
Oboler, Arch 1909(?)-1987 Obituary 122
Brief entry 105
Oboler, Eli M(artin) 1915-1983 ....CANR-6
Obituary 110
Earlier sketch in CA 57-60
Obourn, Ellsworth Scott 1897- CAP-2
Earlier sketch in CA 17-18
O'Brady, Frederic Michel Maurice
1903- CANR-3
Earlier sketch in CA 9-12R
Obrant, Susan 1946- .... SATA 11
O'Brawes, Tarnel
See La Barre, Weston
Obrecht, James Carlton
See Obrecht, Jas
Obrecht, Jas 1952- 135
Obregon, Mauricio 1921- CANR-1
Earlier sketch in CA 45-48
O'Brian, Frank
See Garfield, Brian (Wynne)
O'Brian, Jack 1921- 103
O'Brian, John Lord 1874-1973 Obituary 41-44R
O'Briant, Walter H(erbert) 1937- 25-28R
O'Brien, Andrew William 1910- CANR-17
Earlier sketch in CA 25-28R
O'Brien, Andy
See O'Brien, Andrew William
O'Brien, Anne Sibley 1952- 122
See also SATA 48, 53
O'Brien, Conor Cruise 1917- 65-68
O'Brien, Cyril C(ornelius) 1906- 53-56
O'Brien, Darcy 1939- CANR-8
Earlier sketch in CA 21-24R
O'Brien, David J(oseph) 1938- 25-28R
O'Brien, Dean D.
See Binder, Otto O(scar)
O'Brien, Des(mond John) 1930- 114
O'Brien, E. G.
See Clarke, Arthur C(harles)
O'Brien, Edna 1936- CANR-6
Earlier sketch in CA 1-4R
See also CDBLB 1960 to Present
See also CLC 3, 5, 8, 13, 36, 65
See also DLB 14
See also MTCW
See also SSC 10
O'Brien, Edward C.
See Schrodt, Philip A(ndrew)
O'Brien, Elmer 1911- 17-20R
O'Brien, Esse Forrester
1895(?)-1975 Obituary 61-64
See also SATA 30
O'Brien, Fitz-James 1828-1862 .... DLB 74
O'Brien, Flann
See O Nuallain, Brian
See also CLC 1, 4, 5, 7, 10, 47
O'Brien, Frances (Kelly) 1906- CAP-2
Earlier sketch in CA 17-18
O'Brien, Francis J(oseph) 1903- 81-84
O'Brien, Geoffrey 1948- 106
O'Brien, George Dennis 1931- 103
O'Brien, George 1945- 131
O'Brien, Gregory (C. Jr.) 1945- 117
O'Brien, J(ohn) W(ilfrid) 1931- 13-16R
O'Brien, Jacqueline Robin 1949- 105
O'Brien, James A(loysius) 1936- Brief entry 110
O'Brien, James J. 1929- CANR-9
Earlier sketch in CA 17-20R
O'Brien, John Anthony 1893-1980 ....CANR-1
Obituary 97-100
Earlier sketch in CA 1-4R
O'Brien, John J(oseph) 1937- 111
O'Brien, John 1953- 132
O'Brien, Justin (McCortney)
1906-1968 ....CANR-5
Earlier sketch in CA 5-8R
O'Brien, K.
See O'Brien, Katherine
O'Brien, Kate 1897-1974 93-96
Obituary 53-56
See also DLB 15
O'Brien, Katherine 1915-1982 Obituary 118
O'Brien, Kevin P. 1922- 53-56
O'Brien, Lawrence Francis 1917- 57-60
O'Brien, Lee 1948- 61-64
O'Brien, Marian P(lowman) 1915- 53-56
O'Brien, Michael J. 1920- 25-28R
O'Brien, Michael 1943- 126
O'Brien, Michael 1948- 121
O'Brien, (William Joseph) Pat(rick)
1899-1983 Obituary 111
O'Brien, Patrick 1932- 21-24R
O'Brien, Richard 1934- 73-76
O'Brien, Richard 1942- 124
See also CLC 17
O'Brien, Robert C.
See Conly, Robert Leslie
See also AAYA 6
See also CLR 2
O'Brien, Robert W(illiam) 1907- CANR-25
Earlier sketch in CA 45-48
O'Brien, Saliee
See Janas, Frankie-Lee
O'Brien, Sister Mary Celine 1922- 21-24R
O'Brien, Thomas C(lement) 1938- 106
See also SATA 29
O'Brien, Tim 1946- 85-88
See also CLC 7, 19, 40
See also DLBD 9
See also DLBY 80
O'Brien, Vincent 1916- 9-12R
O'Brien, William V(incent) 1923- 13-16R
O'Broin, Leon 1902- CANR-8
Earlier sketch in CA 61-64
O'Brynt, Jon
See Barnum, W(illiam) Paul
Observer
See Velikovsky, Immanuel
Obst, Frances Melanie 17-20R
Obstfeld, Raymond 1952- 116
Obstfelder, Sigbjoern
1866-1900 Brief entry 123
See also TCLC 23
Oca, Marco Antonio Montes de
See Montes de Oca, Marco Antonio
O'Callaghan, Denis F(rancis) 1931- 17-20R
O'Callaghan, Joseph F(rancis) 1928- 81-84
O'Callaghan, Julie 1954- 117
Ocampo, Silvina 1906- 131
See also HW
Ocampo, Victoria 1891-1979 105
Obituary 85-88
See also HW
O'Carroll, Ryan
See Markun, Patricia Maloney
O'Casey, Eileen (Reynolds) 1903- 133
Brief entry 112
O'Casey, Sean 1880-1964 89-92
See also CDBLB 1914-1945
See also CLC 1, 5, 9, 11, 15
See also DLB 10
See also MTCW
O'Cathasaigh, Donal
See Casey, Daniel J(oseph)
O'Cathasaigh, Sean
See O'Casey, Sean
Occomy, Marita Bonner 1899-1971 .... DLB 51
Ocean, Julian
See de Mesne, Eugene (Frederick Peter Cheshire)
O Ceithearnaigh, Seumas
See Carney, James (Patrick)
Ochester, Ed(win Frank) 1939- CANR-25
Earlier sketch in CA 45-48
Ochiltree, Thomas H 1912- 77-80
Ochojski, Paul M(aximilian)
1916-1983 ....CANR-20
Earlier sketch in CA 25-28R
Ochorowicz, Julian 1850-1917 Brief entry 114
Ochs, Adolph S(imon)
1858-1935 Brief entry 118
See also DLB 25
Ochs, Carol (Rebecca) 1939- CANR-36
Earlier sketch in CA 114
Ochs, Donovan J(oseph) 1938- 45-48
Ochs, Michael 1943- 119
Ochs, Phil 1940-1976 Obituary 65-68
See also CLC 17
Ochs, Robert J. 1930- 29-32R
Ochs, Vanessa (L.) 1953- 134
Ochse, Orpha Caroline 1925- 93-96
Ochsenschlager, Edward L(loyd) 1932- 17-20R
Ochsner, (Edward William) Alton
1896-1981 ....17-20R
Obituary 105
Ochsner, Jeffrey Karl 1950- 111
Ockenga, Harold John 1905-1985 ....CANR-1
Obituary 115
Earlier sketch in CA 1-4R
Ockenga, Starr 1938- 134
Ockham, William of 1285(?)-1347 .... DLB 115
O'Clair, Robert M. 1923- 77-80
O'Clery, Helen (Gallagher) 1910- 9-12R
O'Collins, Gerald Glynn 1931- CANR-34
Earlier sketches in CA 85-88, CANR-15
O'Connell, Brian (Vincent) J(ohn)
1923- Brief entry 113
O'Connell, Daniel Patrick 1924-1979 .....CANR-25
Obituary 89-92
Earlier sketch in CA 29-32R
O'Connell, David 1940- 102
O'Connell, Frank 1892- 5-8R
O'Connell, Jack 1959- 137
O'Connell, Jeffrey 1928- CANR-11
Earlier sketch in CA 25-28R
O'Connell, Jeremiah Joseph 1932- CANR-7
Earlier sketch in CA 13-16R
O'Connell, John James III
1921-1982 Obituary 107
O'Connell, Margaret F(orster) 1935-1977 73-76
See also SATA 30, 49
O'Connell, Marvin R(ichard) 1930- 134
Brief entry 111
O'Connell, Maurice R. 1922- 17-20R
O'Connell, Michael (William) 1943- 101
O'Connell, Peg
See Ahern, Margaret McCrohan
O'Connell, Richard L(eo) Jr. 1912-1975 ....41-44R
O'Connell, Timothy E(dward) 1943- CANR-12
Earlier sketch in CA 73-76
O'Connell, Walter E(dward) 1925- 41-44R
O'Conner, Bert
See Paine, Lauran (Bosworth)
O'Conner, Clint
See Paine, Lauran (Bosworth)
O'Conner, R(ay) L. 1928- 17-20R
O'Connor, A(nthony) M(ichael) 1939- CANR-11
Earlier sketch in CA 21-24R
O'Connor, Alan 1955- 133
O'Connor, Anthony Obituary 109
O'Connor, Daniel William 1925- 33-36R
O'Connor, David 1949- 110
O'Connor, Dick 1930- 97-100
O'Connor, Edward Dennis 1922- 41-44R
O'Connor, Edwin (Greene) 1918-1968 93-96
Obituary 25-28R
See also CLC 14
O'Connor, Egan 1937- 119
O'Connor, Elizabeth (Anita) 1921- CANR-30
Earlier sketch in CA 25-28R
O'Connor, (Mary) Flannery 1925-1964 .....CANR-3
Earlier sketch in CA 1-4R
See also AAYA 7
See also CDALB 1941-1968
See also CLC 1, 2, 3, 6, 10, 13, 15, 21, 66
See also DLB 2
See also DLBY 80
See also MTCW
See also SSC 1
See also WLC
O'Connor, Francine M(arie) 1930- 111
O'Connor, Francis V(alentine) 1937- CANR-13
Earlier sketch in CA 21-24R
O'Connor, Frank
See O'Donovan, Michael John
See also CLC 23
See also SSC 5
O'Connor, Garry 1938- CANR-20
Earlier sketch in CA 89-92
O'Connor, Harvey 1897-1987 ....5-8R
Obituary 123
O'Connor, Jack
See O'Connor, John Woolf
O'Connor, James I(gnatius) 1910-1988 ..... CAP-1
Obituary 126
Earlier sketch in CA 13-16
O'Connor, Jane 1947- 124
See also SATA 47, 59
O'Connor, John E. 1943- 127
Brief entry 109
O'Connor, John J(oseph) 1918- 73-76
O'Connor, John Joseph
1904-1978 Obituary 77-80
O'Connor, John (Morris) 1937- 29-32R
O'Connor, John P. 1892-1986 Obituary 119
O'Connor, John Woolf 1902-1978 ....CANR-3
Obituary 77-80
Earlier sketch in CA 5-8R
O'Connor, June (Elizabeth) 1941- 114
O'Connor, Karen 1938- CANR-28
Earlier sketch in CA 89-92
See also SATA 34
O'Connor, Liam
See Liddy, James (Daniel Reeves)
O'Connor, Lillian M. 1894(?)-1987 Obituary 122
O'Connor, M.
See O'Connor, Michael Patrick
O'Connor, Mark 1945- CANR-31
Earlier sketches in CA 65-68, CANR-11
O'Connor, Marty 1924(?)-1990 Obituary 131
O'Connor, Mary 1947- 133
O'Connor, Michael Patrick 1950- 113
O'Connor, Patricia Walker 1931- CANR-38
Earlier sketches in CA 37-40R, CANR-17
O'Connor, Patrick
See Wibberley, Leonard (Patrick O'Connor)
O'Connor, Patrick 77-80
O'Connor, Patrick J(oseph) 1947- 113
O'Connor, Patrick Joseph 1924- 53-56
O'Connor, Patrick 1949- 130
O'Connor, Philip F(rancis) 1932- CANR-28
Earlier sketch in CA 33-36R
O'Connor, Philip Marie Constant Bancroft
1916- 9-12R
O'Connor, Raymond G(ish) 1915- CANR-4
Earlier sketch in CA 5-8R
O'Connor, Richard 1915-1975 61-64
Obituary 57-60
See also SATA 21
O'Connor, Robert F. 1943- 128
O'Connor, Rory 1951- 109
O'Connor, Sister Mary Catharine CAP-2
Earlier sketch in CA 17-18
O'Connor, Thomas Henry 1922- 33-36R
O'Connor, Ulick 1928- CANR-4
Earlier sketch in CA 9-12R
O'Connor, William E(dmund) 1922- 37-40R
O'Connor, William P. Jr. 1916- 9-12R
O'Connor, William Van 1915-1966 ....CANR-1
Obituary 25-28R
Earlier sketch in CA 1-4R
O'Connor Howe, Josephine (Mary) 1924- 119
O'Conor, John F(rancis) 1918- 33-36R
October, John
See Portway, Christopher (John)
Octopus
See Drachman, Julian M(oses)
Ocvirk, Otto G(eorge) 1922- 61-64
Odaga, Asenath (Bole) 1937- 124
See also BW
See also MAICYA
See also SATA 67
Odahl, Charles Matson 1944- 37-40R
Odajnyk, Walter 1938- 13-16R
O'Daly, William 1951- 137
O Danachair, Caoimhin
See Danaher, Kevin
O'Daniel, Janet 1921- 29-32R
See also SATA 24
O'Daniel, Therman B(enjamin)
1908-1986 45-48
Obituary 133
See also BW
O'Day, Cathy
See Crane, Barbara (Joyce)
O'Day, Edward Francis 1925- 29-32R
O'Day, Rey 1947- 105
Odd, Gilbert E(dward) 1902- 110
Oddner, Georg 1923- 129
Oddo, Gilbert L. 1922- CANR-1
Earlier sketch in CA 1-4R

Oddo, Sandra (Schmidt) 1937- ... 65-68
O'Dea, Agnes C. 1911- ... 124
O'Dea, Thomas F(rancis) 1915-1974 ... CAP-2
Obituary ... 53-56
Earlier sketch in CA 23-24
Odean, Kathleen 1953- ... 128
Odegaard, Charles Edwin 1911- Brief entry ... 106
Odegard, Douglas Andrew 1935- ... 108
Odegard, Holtan Peter 1923- ... 61-64
O'Dell, Andrew C(harles) 1909-1966 ... CAP-1
Earlier sketch in CA 13-16
Odell, Gill
See Gill, Traviss
Odell, Jonathan 1737-1818 ... DLB 31, 99
Odell, Ling Chung 1945- ... 45-48
O'Dell, M(ary) E(lise) ... 9-12R
Odell, Peter R(andon) 1930- ... 97-100
Odell, Rice 1928- ... 77-80
Odell, Robin 1935- ... CANR-12
Earlier sketch in CA 73-76
O'Dell, Scott 1898-1989 ... CANR-30
Obituary ... 129
Earlier sketches in CA 61-64, CANR-12
See also AAYA 3
See also CLC 30
See also CLR 1, 16
See also DLB 52
See also MAICYA
See also SATA 12, 60
O'Dell, William F(rancis) 1909- ... CANR-12
Earlier sketch in CA 25-28R
Odem, J.
See Rubin, Jacob A.
Oden, Clifford 1916- ... 65-68
Oden, Gloria (Catherine) 1923- ... CANR-25
Earlier sketch in CA 108
Oden, Marilyn Brown 1937- ... 33-36R
Oden, Thomas C(lark) 1931- ... CANR-19
Earlier sketches in CA 9-12R, CANR-5
Oden, William E(ugene) 1923- ... 37-40R
Odenwald, Robert P(aul) 1899-1965 ... 1-4R
See also SATA 11
Odescalchi, Esther Kando 1938- ... 69-72
Odets, Clifford 1906-1963 ... 85-88
See also CLC 2, 28
See also DLB 7, 26
See also MTCW
Odgers, Merle Middleton
1900-1983 Obituary ... 110
Odier, Daniel 1945- ... CANR-29
Earlier sketch in CA 29-32R
Odiorne, George Stanley 1920-1992 ... CANR-1
Obituary ... 136
Earlier sketch in CA 1-4R
Odishaw, Hugh 1916-1984 Obituary ... 112
Odle, Joe T(aft) 1908-1980 ... 33-36R
Obituary ... 97-100
Odling-Smee, John (Charles) 1943- ... 112
Odlum, Doris Maude 1890-1985 ... CAP-1
Obituary ... 118
Earlier sketch in CA 13-14
O'Doherty, Brian 1934- ... 105
O'Doherty, E(amonn) F(elchin) 1918- ... 37-40R
O'Doire, Annraoi
See Beechhold, Henry F(rank)
Odom, William E(ldridge) 1932- ... 73-76
O'Donnell, Bernard 1929-1983 ... 41-44R
Obituary ... 133
O'Donnell, Cyril 1900- ... CAP-1
Earlier sketch in CA 11-12
O'Donnell, Dick
See Lupoff, Richard A(llen)
and Thompson, Don(ald Arthur)
O'Donnell, Donat
See O'Brien, Conor Cruise
O'Donnell, Elliott 1872-1965 ... CAP-1
Earlier sketch in CA 13-16
O'Donnell, Francis Obituary ... 114
O'Donnell, Harry J(ames)
1914-1985 Obituary ... 117
O'Donnell, James H(owlett) III 1937- ... CANR-27
Earlier sketch in CA 45-48
O'Donnell, James J(oseph Jr.) 1950- ... CANR-16
Earlier sketch in CA 89-92
O'Donnell, James Kevin 1951- ... CANR-6
Earlier sketch in CA 57-60
O'Donnell, James P(reston)
1917-1990 Obituary ... 131
O'Donnell, Jim
See O'Donnell, James Kevin
O'Donnell, John A. 1916- ... 17-20R
O'Donnell, John P. 1923- ... 17-20R
O'Donnell, K. M.
See Malzberg, Barry N(athaniel)
O'Donnell, Kenneth P.
See O'Donnell, (Philip) Kenneth
O'Donnell, (Philip) Kenneth 1924-1977 ... 81-84
Obituary ... 73-76
O'Donnell, Kevin Jr. 1950- ... CANR-23
Earlier sketch in CA 106
O'Donnell, Lawrence
See Kuttner, Henry
and Moore, C(atherine) L(ucile)
O'Donnell, Lawrence F(rancis) Jr. 1951- ... 117
O'Donnell, Lillian Udvardy 1926- ... CANR-18
Earlier sketches in CA 5-8R, CANR-3
O'Donnell, Margaret Jane 1899- ... 5-8R
O'Donnell, Mark 1954- ... CANR-21
Earlier sketch in CA 104
O'Donnell, Patrick (James) 1948- ... 114
O'Donnell, Peadar 1893-1986 ... 135
Obituary ... 119
O'Donnell, Peter 1920- ... 117
Brief entry ... 114
See also DLB 87
O'Donnell, Red
See O'Donnell, Francis
O'Donnell, Thomas Francis 1915- ... CANR-1
Earlier sketch in CA 1-4R
O'Donnell, Thomas J(oseph) 1918- ... 65-68
O'Donnell, William H. 1940- ... 128
O'Donnevan, Finn
See Sheckley, Robert
O'Donoghue, Bernard 1945- ... 137
O'Donoghue, Bryan 1921- ... 77-80
O'Donoghue, Gregory 1951- ... 114
Brief entry ... 109
O'Donoghue, Joseph 1931- ... 21-24R
O'Donoghue, Michael 1940- ... 128
O'Donovan, John 1921- ... CANR-11
Earlier sketch in CA 25-28R
O'Donovan, Katherine 1942- ... 123
O'Donovan, Michael John 1903-1966 ... 93-96
See also O'Connor, Frank
See also CLC 14
Odor, Ruth Shannon 1926- ... 120
See also SATA 44
O'Dowd, Liam 1947- ... 116
O'Driscoll, Dennis 1954- ... 127
O'Driscoll, Gerald P(atrick) Jr. 1947- ... 133
O'Driscoll, Robert 1938- ... CANR-35
Earlier sketch in CA 53-56
O'Dwyer, James F. 1939- ... 33-36R
O'Dwyer, Paul 1907- ... 97-100
Odysseus
See Johnson, Donald McI(ntosh)
Oe, Kenzaburo 1935- ... CANR-36
Earlier sketch in CA 97-100
See also CLC 10, 36
See also MTCW
Oechsli, Kelly 1918- ... CANR-16
Earlier sketch in CA 97-100
See also SATA 5
Oehmke, T(homas) H(arold) 1947- ... CANR-11
Earlier sketch in CA 65-68
Oehser, Paul H(enry) 1904- ... CANR-12
Earlier sketch in CA 29-32R
Oeksenholt, Svein 1925- Brief entry ... 106
Oenslager, Donald (Mitchell) 1902-1975 ... 61-64
Obituary ... 57-60
Oepik, Ernst Julius 1893-1985 Obituary ... 118
Oerkeny, Istvan
See Orkeny, Istvan
Oerum, Poul (Erik) 1919- ... CANR-32
Earlier sketches in CA 65-68, CANR-13
Oesterle, John A(rthur) 1912- ... 5-8R
Oesterreicher, John M(aria) 1904- ... CANR-26
Earlier sketch in CA 29-32R
Oettinger, Anthony Gervin 1929- ... CANR-31
Earlier sketch in CA 1-4R
Oettinger, Elmer R(osenthal Jr.) 1913- ... 29-32R
O'Faolain, Julia 1932- ... CANR-12
Earlier sketch in CA 81-84
See also CAAS 2
See also CLC 6, 19, 47
See also DLB 14
See also MTCW
O'Faolain, Sean 1900-1991 ... CANR-12
Obituary ... 134
Earlier sketch in CA 61-64
See also CLC 1, 7, 14, 32, 70
See also DLB 15
See also MTCW
Ofari, Earl 1945- ... 41-44R
O'Farrell, Patrick (James) 1933- ... CANR-20
Earlier sketch in CA 103
Ofek, Uriel 1926- ... CANR-18
Earlier sketch in CA 101
See also CLR 28
See also SATA 36
Offen, Karen (Marie Stedtfeld) 1939- ... CANR-34
Earlier sketch in CA 113
Offen, Neil 1946- ... 49-52
Offen, Ron 1930- ... 45-48
Offer, Daniel 1930- ... CANR-11
Earlier sketch in CA 21-24R
Offerle, Mildred 1912- ... 77-80
Offield, Lewis Delaney 1903-1978 Obituary ... 111
Offiong, Daniel A(sukwo) 1942- ... 118
Offit, Avodah K(omito) 1931- ... CANR-13
Earlier sketch in CA 77-80
Offit, Sidney 1928- ... CANR-1
Earlier sketch in CA 1-4R
See also SATA 10
Offner, Arnold A. 1937- ... 25-28R
Offner, Eric D(elmonte) 1928- ... CANR-9
Earlier sketch in CA 17-20R
Offord, Carl Ruthven 1910- ... DLB 76
Offord, Lenore Glen 1905- ... 77-80
Offutt, Andrew J(efferson V) 1934(?)- ... CANR-15
Earlier sketch in CA 41-44R
O Fiaich, Tomas (Seamus) 1923-1990 ... 103
Obituary ... 131
O'Finn, Thaddeus
See McGloin, Joseph T(haddeus)
O'Flaherty, James C(arneal) 1914- ... 21-24R
O'Flaherty, Liam 1896-1984 ... CANR-35
Obituary ... 113
Earlier sketch in CA 101
See also CLC 5, 34
See also DLB 36
See also DLBY 84
See also MTCW
See also SSC 6
O'Flaherty, Louise 1920- ... CANR-6
Earlier sketch in CA 57-60
O'Flaherty, Terrence 1917- ... 73-76
O'Flaherty, Wendy Doniger 1940- ... CANR-23
Earlier sketch in CA 65-68
O'Flynn, Peter
See Fanthorpe, R(obert) Lionel
Ofomata, G(odfrey) E(zediaso) K(ingsley)
1936- ... 93-96
Ofosu-Appiah, L(awrence) H(enry)
1920- ... 33-36R
See also SATA 13
Ofshe, Richard 1941- ... 89-92
Og, Liam
See O'Neill, William
O'Gallagher, Liam 1917- ... 45-48
Ogan, George F. 1912- ... CANR-4
Earlier sketch in CA 9-12R
See also SATA 13
Ogan, M. G.
See Ogan, George F.
and Ogan, Margaret E. (Nettles)
Ogan, Margaret E. (Nettles)
1923-1979 ... CANR-4
Earlier sketch in CA 9-12R
See also SATA 13
O'Gara, James Vincent Jr. 1918-1979 ... 69-72
Obituary ... 85-88
Ogata, Sadako (Nakamura) 1927- ... CANR-9
Earlier sketch in CA 17-20R
Ogawa, Dennis Masaaki 1943- ... 37-40R
Ogawa, Tetsuro 1912-1978 ... 41-44R
Ogbu, John U(zor) 1939- ... 93-96
Ogburn, Charlton (Jr.) 1911- ... CANR-3
Earlier sketch in CA 5-8R
See also SATA 3
Ogburn, W. F.
See Ogburn, William Fielding
Ogburn, William F.
See Ogburn, William Fielding
Ogburn, William Fielding
1886-1959 Brief entry ... 122
Ogden, Chris 1945- ... 133
Ogden, Daniel M(iller) Jr. 1922- ... 9-12R
Ogden, Dunbar H. ... 53-56
Ogden, Gina 1935- ... 81-84
Ogden, Howard
See Winokur, Jon
Ogden, Margaret Sinclair 1909- Brief entry ... 107
Ogden, (John) Michael (Hubert) 1923- ... 13-16R
Ogden, Samuel R(obinson) 1896- ... 29-32R
Ogden, Schubert Miles 1928- ... CANR-21
Earlier sketch in CA 104
Ogden, Scott 1957- ... 138
Ogg, Oscar (John) 1908-1971 ... CAP-1
Obituary ... 33-36R
Earlier sketch in CA 11-12
Ogilvie, Elisabeth May 1917- ... CANR-19
Earlier sketch in CA 103
See also SATA 29, 40
Ogilvie, Gordon (Bryant) 1934- ... CANR-8
Earlier sketch in CA 61-64
Ogilvie, Lloyd John 1930- ... 73-76
Ogilvie, Mardel 1910- ... CANR-29
Earlier sketch in CA 1-4R
Ogilvie, Robert Maxwell 1932-1981 ... CANR-6
Obituary ... 105
Earlier sketch in CA 13-16R
Ogilvie, William G(eorge) 1899- ... 130
Ogilvy, C(harles) Stanley 1913- ... CANR-4
Earlier sketch in CA 5-8R
Ogilvy, David Mackenzie 1911- Brief entry ... 105
Ogilvy, Gavin
See Barrie, J(ames) M(atthew)
Ogilvy, Stewart Marks
1914-1985(?) Obituary ... 118
Oglanby, Elva
See Clairmont, Elva
Ogle, James Lawrence 1911- ... 5-8R
Ogle, Jim
See Ogle, James Lawrence
Ogle, Lucille Edith 1904-1988 ... SATA 59
Ogle, Robert 1926(?)-1984 Obituary ... 112
Oglesby, Joseph 1931- ... CANR-17
Earlier sketch in CA 97-100
Oglesby, Richard E(dward) 1931- ... CANR-6
Earlier sketch in CA 9-12R
Oglesby, William B(arr) Jr. 1916- ... 25-28R
Ogletree, Earl Joseph 1930- ... CANR-10
Earlier sketch in CA 65-68
Ogletree, Thomas W(arren) 1933- ... 17-20R
Ognall, Leopold Horace 1908-1979 ... CANR-12
Earlier sketch in CA 9-12R
Ognibene, Peter J(ohn) 1941- ... 110
O'Gorman, Edward Charles 1929- ... 81-84
O'Gorman, Frank 1940- ... 61-64
O'Gorman, Gerald 1916- ... 21-24R
O'Gorman, Hubert J(oseph)
1925-1990 Obituary ... 131
O'Gorman, James F(rancis) 1933- ... 53-56
O'Gorman, John
See MacGill, Patrick
O'Gorman, Ned
See O'Gorman, Edward Charles
O'Gorman, Richard F. 1928- ... 37-40R
O'Gorman, Samuel F.
See Cusack, Michael J(oseph)
O'Grada, Sean
See O'Grady, John (Patrick)
O'Grady, Anne ... 53-56
O'Grady, Desmond (James Bernard)
1935- ... CANR-38
Earlier sketches in CA 25-28R, CANR-14
See also DLB 40
O'Grady, Francis Dominic 1909- ... CAP-1
Earlier sketch in CA 9-10
O'Grady, Frank
See O'Grady, Francis Dominic
O'Grady, John F(rancis) 1939- ... 93-96
O'Grady, John (Patrick) 1907- ... 104
O'Grady, Joseph P(atrick) 1934- ... 41-44R
O'Grady, Rohan
See Skinner, June O'Grady
O'Grady, Ron 1930- ... 114
O'Grady, Standish James
1846-1928 Brief entry ... 104
See also TCLC 5
O'Grady, Timothy 1951- ... 138
See also CLC 59
Ogram, Ernest W(illiam) Jr. 1928- ... 57-60
O'Green, Jennifer
See Roberson, Jennifer
Ogul, Morris S(amuel) 1931- ... 13-16R
Oh, John Kie-chiang 1930- ... 29-32R
O'Hagan, Caroline 1946- ... 111
See also SATA 38
O'Hagan, Howard 1902-1982 ... 1-4R
See also DLB 68
O'Hagan, Joan 1926- ... 132
O'Hair, Madalyn (Mays) Murray 1919- ... CANR-12
Earlier sketch in CA 61-64
O'Hallion, Sheila
See Allen, Sheila Rosalynd
O'Halpin, Eunan 1954- ... 128
O'Hanlon, Daniel John 1919- ... 61-64
O'Hanlon, Jacklyn
See Meek, Jacklyn O'Hanlon
O'Hanlon, Redmond (Douglas) 1947- ... 123
O'Hanlon, Thomas J(oseph) 1933- ... 61-64
Ohanneson, Joan 1930- ... 130
O'Hara, Charles E. 1912-1984 ... 29-32R
Obituary ... 125
O'Hara, Dale
See Gillese, John Patrick
O'Hara, Frank 1926-1966 ... CANR-33
Obituary ... 25-28R
Earlier sketch in CA 9-12R
See also CLC 2, 5, 13
See also DLB 5, 16
See also MTCW
O'Hara, Frederic James 1917- ... 103
O'Hara, Georgina 1956- ... 126
O'Hara, John (Henry) 1905-1970 ... CANR-31
Obituary ... 25-28R
Earlier sketch in CA 5-8R
See also CDALB 1929-1941
See also CLC 1, 2, 3, 6, 11, 42
See also DLB 9, 86
See also DLBD 2
See also MTCW
O'Hara, Kenneth
See Morris, (Margaret) Jean
O'Hara, Kevin
See Cumberland, Marten
O'Hara, Marjorie (Doreen) 1928- ... 135
O'Hara, Mary
See Alsop, Mary O'Hara
Ohashi, Wataru 1944- ... 73-76
O'Hayre, John 1923-1986 Obituary ... 121
O'hearn, Peter J(oseph) T(homas)
1917- ... 17-20R
O'Heffernan, Patrick 1944- ... 117
O Hehir, Diana 1922- ... 93-96
See also CLC 41
O hEithir, Breandan 1930-1990 Obituary ... 132
O'Higgins, Donal Peter 1922-1984 ... 77-80
Obituary ... 112
O'Higgins, Paul 1927- ... 130
Ohira, Masayoshi 1910-1980 Obituary ... 105
Ohkawa, Kazushi 1908- ... 85-88
Ohl, (Mary) Suzanne Sickler 1923- ... 69-72
Ohles, John Ford 1920- ... 57-60
Ohlig, Karl-Heinz 1938- ... CANR-13
Earlier sketch in CA 69-72
Ohlin, Bertil 1899(?)-1979 Obituary ... 89-92
Ohlin, Lloyd E(dgar) 1918- ... 104
Ohlinger, Gustavus 1877-1972 Obituary ... 37-40R
Ohlsen, Merle M(arvel) 1914- ... CANR-15
Earlier sketch in CA 37-40R
Ohlsson, Ib 1935- ... SATA 7
Ohman, Jack 1960- ... 110
Brief entry ... 108
Ohmann, Carol Burke
1929(?)-1989 Obituary ... 129
Ohmann, Richard (Malin) 1931- ... 13-16R
Ohmer, Merlin M(aurice) 1923- ... 57-60
Ohon
See Barba, Harry
Ohsberg, H(arry) Oliver 1926- ... 114
Ohtomo, Yasuo 1946- ... SATA 37
Oinas, Felix J(ohannes) 1911- ... CANR-29
Earlier sketches in CA 33-36R, CANR-13
Oiwa, Keibo ... 138
Oja, Carol J. 1953- ... 135
Ojany, Francis Frederick 1935- ... 77-80
Ojo, G. J. Afolabi 1930- ... 25-28R
Oka, Takashi 1924- ... 135
Okada, Sumie 1940- ... 132
Okamoto, Shumpei 1932- ... 29-32R
Okara, Gabriel Imomotimi Gbaingbain
1921- ... 105
See also BW
Okasha, Elisabeth 1942- ... 45-48
Oke, Janette 1935- ... 111
O'Keefe, Bernard J(oseph) 1919-1989 ... 120
Obituary ... 129
O'Keefe, Daniel Lawrence
1928- Brief entry ... 116
O'Keefe, M(aurice) Timothy 1943- ... 77-80
O'Keefe, Patrick E.
See Grace, John Patrick
O'Keefe, Paul 1900(?)-1976 Obituary ... 65-68
O'Keefe, Richard R(obert) 1934- ... 57-60
O'Keefe, Sister Maureen 1917- ... 5-8R
O'Keeffe, Georgia 1887-1986 ... 110
Obituary ... 118
O'Keeffe, John 1747-1833 ... DLB 89
O'Keeffe, Laurence 1931- ... 122
Okeke, Uchefuna 1933- ... 97-100
O'Kelley, Mattie Lou 1908- ... 116
See also SATA 36

O'Kelly, Charlotte G. 1946- ... 111
O'Kelly, Elizabeth 1915- ... CANR-20
Earlier sketch in CA 103
Oken, Alan C(harles) 1944- ... 45-48
O'Key
See Radwanski, Pierre A(rthur)
Okigbo, Christopher (Ifenayichukwu) 1932-1967 ... 77-80
See also BLC 3
See also BW
See also CLC 25
See also MTCW
Okigbo, P(ius) N(wabufo) C. 1924- ... 17-20R
Okihiro, Gary Y(ukio) 1945- ... 120
Okimoto, Jean Davies 1942- ... CANR-37
Earlier sketches in CA 97-100, CANR-16
See also SATA 34
Okin, Susan Moller 1946- ... 93-96
Oklahoma Peddler
See Gilles, Albert S(imeon) Sr.
Okner, Benjamin A. 1936- ... 21-24R
Okonjo, Chukuka 1928- ... 29-32R
Okpaku, Joseph (Ohiomogben) 1943- ... 29-32R
See also BW
Okpewho, Isidore 1941- ... CANR-3
Earlier sketch in CA 49-52
Okrent, Daniel 1948- ... CANR-22
Earlier sketch in CA 105
Okri, Ben 1959- ... 138
Brief entry ... 130
Oksenberg, Michel Charles 1938- ... 111
Oksenholt, Svein
See Oeksenholt, Svein
Okubo, Genji 1915- ... 25-28R
Okudzhava, Bulat Shalvovich 1924- ... 129
Brief entry ... 116
Okun, Arthur M. 1928-1980 ... CANR-11
Obituary ... 97-100
Earlier sketch in CA 61-64
Okun, Lawrence E(ugene) 1929- ... 101
Olafson, Frederick A(rlan) 1924- ... 17-20R
Olan, Ben 1923- ... 111
Olan, Levi Arthur 1903- ... 109
O'Laoghaire, Liam
See O'Leary, Liam
Olbricht, Thomas H. 1929- ... 33-36R
Olby, Robert C(ecil) 1933- ... 21-24R
Olcheski, Bill 1925- ... CANR-8
Earlier sketch in CA 61-64
Olcott, Anthony 1950- ... 106
Olcott, Frances Jenkins 1872(?)-1963 ... SATA 19
Olcott, Henry Steel 1832-1907 Brief entry ... 118
Olcott, Jack 1932- ... 53-56
Old, Bruce S(cott) 1913- ... CANR-17
Earlier sketch in CA 1-4R
Old Boy
See Hughes, Thomas
Oldenburg, Carl
See Oldenburg, Ray
Oldenburg, Claes (Thure) 1929- ... 121
Brief entry ... 117
Oldenburg, E(gbert) William 1936-1974 ... 105
See also SATA 35
Oldenburg, Ray 1932- ... 132
Older, Fremont 1856-1935 ... DLB 25
Older, Julia 1941- ... CANR-14
Earlier sketch in CA 73-76
Olderman, Murray 1922- ... CANR-1
Earlier sketch in CA 45-48
Olderman, Raymond M. 1937- ... 41-44R
Old Fag
See Bell, Robert S(tanley) W(arren)
Oldfeld, Peter
See Bartlett, Vernon
Oldfield, A(rthur) Barney 1909- ... 105
Oldfield, James E(dmund) 1921- ... 89-92
Oldfield, Margaret J(ean) 1932- ... SATA 56
Oldfield, Michael 1950- ... 135
Oldfield, Mike
See Oldfield, Michael
Oldfield, R(ichard) C(harles) 1909-1972 ... CAP-2
Earlier sketch in CA 25-28
Oldfield, Ruth L(atzer) 1922- ... 13-16R
Oldham, Frank 1903- ... 9-12R
Oldham, John (M.) 1940- ... 138
Oldham, June ... 138
See also SATA 70
Oldham, Mary 1944- ... 109
See also SATA 65
Oldham, Perry (Donald) 1943- ... 107
Oldham, W(illiam) Dale 1903- ... 9-12R
Old Jowett
See Fantoni, Barry (Ernest)
Oldman, Oliver 1920- ... 33-36R
Oldroyd, Harold 1913- ... 77-80
Olds, Elizabeth Fagg 1913- ... 123
Olds, Elizabeth 1896-1991 ... 5-8R
Obituary ... 133
See also SATA 3
See also SATO 66
Olds, Helen Diehl 1895-1981 ... CANR-3
Obituary ... 103
Earlier sketch in CA 1-4R
See also SATA 9, 25
Olds, Sally Wendkos 1933- ... CANR-39
Earlier sketches in CA 45-48, CANR-1, 18
Olds, Sharon 1942- ... CANR-18
Earlier sketch in CA 101
See also CLC 32, 39
See also DLB 120
Oldsey, Bernard 1923- ... CANR-7
Earlier sketch in CA 5-8R
Oldson, William O(rville) 1940- ... 53-56
Old Stager
See Gore, John Francis
Oldstyle, Jonathan
See Irving, Washington
Olea, Maria Florencia Varas 1938- ... 105
O'Leary, Brian (Todd) 1940- ... CANR-20
Earlier sketch in CA 33-36R
See also SATA 6
O'Leary, Chester F.
See Kuehnelt-Leddihn, Erik (Maria) Ritter von
O'Leary, Frank(lin) J. 1922- ... 5-8R
O'Leary, K. Daniel 1940- ... 41-44R
O'Leary, Liam 1910- ... 109
O'Leary, Patrick 1920- ... 134
O'Leary, Thomas V(incent) 1910- ... 5-8R
Oleck, Howard L(eoner) 1911- ... CANR-4
Earlier sketch in CA 9-12R
Oleksy, Walter 1930- ... CANR-17
Earlier sketches in CA 45-48, CANR-1
Olen, Jeffrey 1946- ... 112
Olendorf, William 1924- ... 117
Olesha, Yuri (Karlovich) 1899-1960 ... 85-88
See also CLC 8
Oleszek, Walter J(oseph) 1941- ... 120
O'Levenson, Jordan
See Levenson, Jordan
Oleyar, Rita Balkey
See Balkey, Rita
Olford, Stephen F(rederick) 1918- ... 17-20R
Olfson, Lewy 1937- ... 93-96
Olgyay, Victor 1910-1970 ... 5-8R
Obituary ... 103
Oliansky, Joel 1935- ... 133
Olien, Diana Davids 1943- ... CANR-32
Earlier sketch in CA 113
Olien, Michael D(avid) 1937- ... CANR-3
Earlier sketch in CA 49-52
Olien, Roger M. 1938- ... 113
Olin, John C(harles) 1915- ... 126
Olin, Spencer C(arl) Jr. 1937- ... 93-96
Olin, William 1929- ... 106
Oliner, Samuel P. 1930- ... 129
Olins, Wally 1930- ... 120
Oliphant, B. J.
See Tepper, Sheri S.
Oliphant, J(ames) Orin 1894-1979 Obituary ... 85-88
Oliphant, Laurence 1829(?)-1888 ... DLB 18
Oliphant, Margaret (Oliphant Wilson) 1828-1897 ... DLB 18
Oliphant, Patrick (Bruce) 1935- ... 101
Oliphant, Robert (Thompson) 1924- ... 102
Oliva, L(awrence) Jay 1933- ... 13-16R
Oliva, Leo E. 1937- ... CANR-24
Earlier sketches in CA 21-24R, CANR-9
Oliva, Pavel 1923- ... 132
Olivares, Julian (Jr.) 1940- ... 118
Oliveira, Antonio Ramos
See Ramos-Oliveira, Antonio
Oliveira Salazar, Antonio de
See Salazar, Antonio de Oliveira
Olivella, Manuel Zapata
See Zapata Olivella, Manuel
Olivelle, Patrick 1942- ... 138
Oliven, John F. 1915(?)-1975 Obituary ... 53-56
Oliver, A. Richard 1912- ... 13-16R
Oliver, Amy Roberta
See Ruck, Amy Roberta
Oliver, Andrew 1906-1981 ... 109
Obituary ... 105
Oliver, Anthony 1923- ... CANR-20
Earlier sketch in CA 103
Oliver, Bernard John Jr. 1918-1966 ... 5-8R
Oliver, Burton
See Burt, Olive Woolley
Oliver, Carl Russell 1941- ... 106
Oliver, Chad
See Oliver, Symmes C(hadwick)
Oliver, Chad 1928- ... DLB 8
Oliver, Covey T(homas) 1913- ... 111
Oliver, Dawn 1942- ... 123
Oliver, Douglas Llewellyn 1913- ... 97-100
Oliver, E(dward) J(ames) 1911- ... 9-12R
Oliver, Egbert S(amuel) 1902- ... 103
Oliver, G(uillaume) Raymond 1909- ... CAP-2
Earlier sketch in CA 25-28
Oliver, H(arold) J(ames) 1916-1982 Obituary ... 111
Oliver, Herman 1885- ... CAP-1
Earlier sketch in CA 11-12
Oliver, James A(rthur) 1914-1981 Obituary ... 106
Oliver, James Henry 1905- ... CANR-17
Earlier sketch in CA 1-4R
Oliver, Jane
See Rees, Helen Christina Easson (Evans)
Oliver, John Edward 1933- ... 33-36R
See also SATA 21
Oliver, Kenneth A(rthur) 1912- ... 53-56
Oliver, Mark
See Tyler-Whittle, Michael Sidney
Oliver, Mary Hempstone 1885(?)-1973 Obituary ... 41-44R
Oliver, Mary 1935- ... CANR-9
Earlier sketch in CA 21-24R
See also CLC 19, 34
See also DLB 5
Oliver, Paul (Hereford) 1927- ... CANR-1
Earlier sketch in CA 1-4R
Oliver, R(ichard) A(lexander) C(avaye) 1904- ... CAP-1
Earlier sketch in CA 11-12
Oliver, Raymond (Davies) 1936- ... CANR-26
Earlier sketch in CA 109
Oliver, Raymond (Guillaume) 1909-1990 Obituary ... 132
Oliver, Revilo P(endleton) 1910- ... 121
Oliver, Richard (Bruce) 1942-1985 ... 116
Oliver, Robert (Shelton) 1934- ... 105
Oliver, Robert T(arbell) 1909- ... CANR-19
Earlier sketches in CA 5-8R, CANR-4
Oliver, Robert W. 1922- ... 135
Oliver, Roland Anthony 1923- ... CANR-12
Earlier sketch in CA 73-76
Oliver, Rupert
See Matthews, Rupert O(liver)
Oliver, Smith Hempstone 1912- ... 25-28R
Oliver, Symmes C(hadwick) 1928- ... 113
Oliver, (McWhorter) Thomas 1950- ... 127
Oliver, W. Andrew 1941- ... 37-40R
Oliver, William Irvin 1926- ... 17-20R
Olivera, Otto 1919- ... 49-52
Oliveri, Mario 1944- ... 107
Olivier, Charles P(ollard) 1884-1975 Obituary ... 61-64
Olivier, Laurence (Kerr) 1907-1989 Obituary ... 129
Brief entry ... 111
See also CLC 20
Olivier, Robert L(ouis) 1903- ... 93-96
Olivova, Vera 1926- ... 81-84
Olkes, Cheryl 1948- ... 127
Olkowski, Helga 1931- ... 85-88
Olkowski, William 1941- ... 97-100
Ollard, Richard (Laurence) 1923- ... CANR-20
Earlier sketch in CA 93-96
Oller, John W(illiam) Jr. 1943- ... CANR-5
Earlier sketch in CA 53-56
Ollerenshaw, Kathleen (Mary) 1912- Brief entry ... 107
Ollestad, Norman (Tennyson) 1935- ... 21-24R
Olli, John B. 1893(?)-1984 Obituary ... 112
Ollier, Claude 1922- ... DLB 83
Ollier, Cliff(ord) David 1931- ... 61-64
Ollif, Lorna (Anne) 1918- ... 93-96
Olliff, Donathan C(ames) 1933- ... 115
Ollman, Bertell 1935- ... CANR-16
Earlier sketch in CA 85-88
Olm, Kenneth W(illiam) 1924- ... 21-24R
Olmstead, Alan H. 1907(?)-1980 Obituary ... 101
Olmstead, Andrea (Louise) 1948- ... 127
Olmstead, Clifton Earl 1926-1962 ... 1-4R
Olmstead, Earl P. 1920- ... 137
Olmstead, Robert 1954- ... 129
Olmsted, Charlotte
See Kursh, Charlotte Olmsted
Olmsted, Frederick Law 1822-1903 Brief entry ... 120
Olmsted, John Charles 1942- ... 93-96
Olmsted, Lorena Ann 1890- ... 29-32R
See also SATA 13
Olmsted, Robert W(alsh) 1936- ... 41-44R
Olmsted, Sterling P(itkin) 1915- ... 25-28R
Olney, James 1933- ... 77-80
Olney, Ross R. 1929- ... CANR-7
Earlier sketch in CA 13-16R
See also SATA 13
Olorunsola, Victor A. 1939- ... CANR-7
Earlier sketch in CA 57-60
O'Loughlin, Carleen ... CAP-2
Earlier sketch in CA 25-28
Olowu, (Claudius) Dele 1952- ... 135
Olscamp, Paul James 1937- ... 104
Olschewski, Alfred 1920- ... 41-44R
See also SATA 7
Olschki, G. Cesare 1890-1971 Obituary ... 104
Olsen, Alfa-Betty 1947- ... 103
Olsen, Alfred Johannes Jr. 1884-1956 Brief entry ... 113
Olsen, Bob
See Olsen, Alfred Johannes Jr.
Olsen, Donald J(ames) 1929- ... 13-16R
Olsen, Edward G(ustave) 1908- ... CANR-11
Earlier sketches in CAP-1, CA 9-10
Olsen, Hans Christian Jr. 1929- Brief entry ... 106
Olsen, Ib Spang 1921- ... CANR-37
Earlier sketches in CA 49-52, CANR-3
See also MAICYA
See also SATA 6
Olsen, Jack
See Olsen, John Edward
Olsen, James 1933- ... 49-52
Olsen, John Edward 1925- ... CANR-29
Earlier sketches in CA 17-20R, CANR-9
Olsen, Larry Dean 1939- ... 69-72
Olsen, Marvin E(lliott) 1936- ... CANR-26
Earlier sketch in CA 29-32R
Olsen, Otto H(arald) 1925- ... 33-36R
Olsen, R(obert) Arthur 1910- ... CAP-2
Earlier sketch in CA 23-24
Olsen, Richard E(llison) 1941- ... 81-84
Olsen, Stein Haugom 1946- ... 128
Olsen, T(heodore) V(ictor) 1932- ... CANR-39
Earlier sketches in CA 1-4R, CANR-3, 18
Olsen, Tillie 1913- ... CANR-1
Earlier sketch in CA 1-4R
See also CLC 4, 13
See also DLB 28
See also DLBY 80
See also MTCW
Olsen, V(iggo) Norskov 1916- ... 53-56
Olsen, Violet (Mae) 1922-1991 ... 113
Obituary ... 134
See also SATA 58
Olsen, William 1954- ... 128
Olshaker, Bennett 1921- Brief entry ... 108
Olshaker, Mark 1951- ... 73-76
Olshaker, Thelma ... 114
Olshan, Joseph 1956- ... 128
Olshan, Neal H(ugh) 1947- ... 119
Olshen, Barry N(eil) 1944- ... 89-92
Olshewsky, Thomas M(ack) 1934- ... 37-40R
Olson, Alan M(elvin) 1939- ... CANR-8
Earlier sketch in CA 61-64
Olson, Alison Gilbert 1931- Brief entry ... 109
Olson, (Elizabeth) Ann 1953- ... 126
Olson, Arielle North 1932- ... 134
See also SATA 67
Olson, Arnold O(rville) 1917- ... 45-48
Olson, Bernhard Emanuel 1910-1975 ... CANR-24
Obituary ... 61-64
Earlier sketch in CA 45-48
Olson, Carl 1941- ... CANR-36
Earlier sketch in CA 114
Olson, Charles (John) 1910-1970 ... CANR-35
Obituary ... 25-28R
Earlier sketches in CAP-1, CA 13-16
See also CABS 2
See also CLC 1, 2, 5, 6, 9, 11, 29
See also DLB 5, 16
See also MTCW
Olson, Clair C(olby) 1901-1972 ... 41-44R
Olson, (Carl Bernard) David 1904- ... 61-64
Olson, David F. 1938- ... 49-52
Olson, David John 1941- ... 53-56
Olson, David R(ichard) 1935- ... 33-36R
Olson, Donald 1938- ... 65-68
Olson, Elder (James) 1909- ... CANR-31
Earlier sketches in CA 5-8R, CANR-6
See also CAAS 12
See also DLB 48, 63
Olson, Eric 1944- ... 53-56
Olson, Everett C. 1910- ... 53-56
Olson, Gene 1922- ... 106
See also SATA 32
Olson, Harry E(dwin) Jr. 1932- ... 61-64
Olson, Harry F(erdinand) 1901- ... 37-40R
Olson, Harvey S(tuart) 1908-1985 ... CANR-1
Obituary ... 118
Earlier sketch in CA 1-4R
Olson, Helen Kronberg ... CANR-12
Earlier sketch in CA 29-32R
See also SATA 48
Olson, Herbert Waldo 1927- ... 1-4R
Olson, James C(lifton) 1917- ... 37-40R
Olson, James R(obert) 1938- ... 49-52
Olson, Jane Virginia 1916- ... 89-92
Olson, Keith W(aldemar) 1931- ... 49-52
Olson, Ken(neth John) 1930- ... 97-100
Olson, Lawrence Alexander 1918- Obituary ... 137
Brief entry ... 110
Olson, Lois Ellen 1941- ... 105
Olson, Mancur Jr. 1932- ... 13-16R
Olson, McKinley C(lar) 1931- ... 110
Olson, Mildred Thompson 1922- ... 21-24R
Olson, Paul R(ichard) 1925- ... 21-24R
Olson, Philip G(ilbert) 1934- ... 9-12R
Olson, Richard G(eorge) 1940- ... CANR-17
Earlier sketch in CA 89-92
Olson, Richard Paul 1934- ... CANR-24
Earlier sketches in CA 61-64, CANR-8
Olson, Robert G(oodwin) 1924- ... 29-32R
Olson, Robert W(illiam) 1940- ... 136
Olson, Sidney 1908- ... CAP-1
Earlier sketch in CA 11-12
Olson, Sigurd F(erdinand) 1899-1982 ... CANR-1
Obituary ... 105
Earlier sketch in CA 1-4R
Olson, Stanley 1948-1989 ... 89-92
Obituary ... 130
Olson, Ted
See Olson, Theodore B.
Olson, Theodore B. 1899- ... 49-52
Olson, Toby 1937- ... CANR-31
Earlier sketches in CA 65-68, CANR-9
See also CLC 28
Olson, Walter K. 1954- ... 135
Olson, Willard Clifford 1899-1978 Obituary ... 111
Olsson, Axel Adolf 1889-1977 Obituary ... 73-76
Olsson, Karl A(rthur) 1913- ... CANR-4
Earlier sketch in CA 5-8R
Olsson, Nils 1909- ... 73-76
Olstad, Charles (Frederick) 1932-1976 ... 17-20R
Obituary ... 134
Olthuis, James H(erman) 1938- ... 61-64
Oltmans, Willem L(eonard) 1925- ... 57-60
Olton, Charles S(haw) 1938- Brief entry ... 108
Olton, Roy 1922- ... 103
Oludhe-Macgoye, Marjorie 1928- ... 133
Olugebefola, Ademole 1941- ... SATA 15
Olyesha, Yuri
See Olesha, Yuri (Karlovich)
Olzendam, Roderic Marble 1892-1986 Obituary ... 121
O'Mahoney, Rich
See Warner-Crozetti, R(uth G.)
O'Mahony, Patrick 1911- ... 13-16R
O'Malley, Brian (Jack Morgan) 1918(?)-1980 Obituary ... 101
O'Malley, Charles Donald 1907-1970 Obituary ... 109
O'Malley, Frank
See O'Rourke, Frank
O'Malley, J(ohn) Steven 1942- ... 53-56
O'Malley, John W(illiam) 1927- Brief entry ... 114
O'Malley, Joseph James 1930- ... 37-40R
O'Malley, Kevin
See Hossent, Harry
O'Malley, Mary Brief entry ... 110
O'Malley, Mary Dolling (Sanders) 1889-1974 ... 65-68
O'Malley, Michael (Anthony) ... 1-4R
O'Malley, Patrick
See O'Rourke, Frank
O'Malley, Richard K(ilroy) 1911- ... 97-100
O'Malley, Suzanne 1951- ... 110
O'Malley, William J(ohn) 1931- ... CANR-31
Earlier sketches in CA 73-76, CANR-12
Oman, Carola (Mary Anima) 1897-1978 ... CANR-4
Earlier sketch in CA 5-8R
See also SATA 35
Oman, Charles Chichele 1901-1982 ... 103
Obituary ... 105
Oman, Julia Trevelyan 1930- ... 126
Omang, Joanne (Brenda) 1943- ... 135

Omansky, Dorothy Linder
1905(?)-1977 Obituary 73-76
O Maolain, Ciaran 1958- 123
O'Maonaigh, Cainneach
See Mooney, Canice (Albert James)
Omari, T(hompson) Peter 1930- 29-32R
O'Marie, Carol Anne 1933- 136
Omarr, Sydney Brief entry 116
O'Meally, Robert G(eorge) 1948- 130
O'Meara, John J. 1915- CANR-3
Earlier sketch in CA 1-4R
O'Meara, Patrick 1938- 113
O'Meara, Thomas F(ranklin) 1935- 110
O'Meara, Walter (Andrew) 1897-1989 ....13-16R
Obituary 129
See also SATA 65
Omer, Garth St.
See St. Omer, Garth
Ommanney, F(rancis) D(ownes)
1903-1980 ....CANR-7
Obituary 101
Earlier sketch in CA 13-16R
See also SATA 23
O'More, Peggy
See Blocklinger, Peggy O'More
O'Morrison, Kevin CANR-9
Earlier sketch in CA 53-56
O Mude
See Gorey, Edward (St. John)
O'Mullane, Tess De Araugo
See De Araugo, Tess (S.)
Onacewicz, Wlodzimierz
1893(?)-1986 Obituary 120
Onadipe, (Nathaniel) Kola(wole) 1922- 101
O'Nair, Mairi
See Evans, Constance May
Onate, Andres David 1940- Brief entry 112
Ondaatje, Christopher 1933- 49-52
Ondaatje, Michael 1943- 77-80
See also CLC 14, 29, 51
See also DLB 60
O'Neal, Bill
See O'Neal, John W(illiam)
O'Neal, Charles E. 1904- CAP-2
Earlier sketch in CA 19-20
O'Neal, Cothburn M(adison) 1907- 1-4R
Oneal, Elizabeth 1934- CANR-28
Earlier sketch in CA 106
See also Oneal, Zibby
See also MAICYA
See also SATA 30
O'Neal, Forest Hodge 1917- 5-8R
O'Neal, Glenn (Franklin) 1919- 49-52
O'Neal, Hank 1940- 134
O'Neal, John W(illiam) 1942- 89-92
O'Neal, William B(ainter) 1907- 73-76
Oneal, Zibby
See Oneal, Elizabeth
See also AAYA 5
See also CLC 30
See also CLR 13
O'Neil, Daniel J. 1936- 89-92
O'Neil, Dennis 1939- 97-100
O'Neil, Eric
See Barnum, W(illiam) Paul
O'Neil, Isabel MacDonald
1908(?)-1981 Obituary 105
O'Neil, Paul E. 1909(?)-1988 Obituary 124
O'Neil, Robert M(archant) 1934- 106
O'Neil, Terry 1949- 61-64
O'Neil, W(illiam) M(atthew) 1912- CANR-32
Earlier sketch in CA 113
O'Neil, Will(iam Daniel III) 1938- 101
O'Neill, Archie
See Henaghan, Jim
O'Neill, Barbara Powell 1929- 17-20R
O'Neill, Carlota 1918- 101
O'Neill, Carlotta Monterey
1888-1970 Obituary 29-32R
O'Neill, Charles Edwards 1927- CANR-9
Earlier sketch in CA 21-24R
O'Neill, Cherry Boone 1954- 112
O'Neill, Daniel Joseph 1905- Brief entry 106
O'Neill, David P(atrick) 1918- 17-20R
O'Neill, Dennis (Bernard) 1947- 114
O'Neil, E. Bard 1941- 85-88
O'Neill, Egan
See Linington, (Barbara) Elizabeth
O'Neill, Eugene (Gladstone) 1888-1953 132
Brief entry 110
See also AITN 1
See also CDALB 1929-1941
See also DLB 7
See also MTCW
See also TCLC 1, 6, 27
See also WLC
O'Neill, Eugene 1922- 77-80
O'Neill, Frank F. 1926(?)-1983 Obituary 109
O'Neill, Frank (Quale) 1943- 120
O'Neill, George 1921(?)-1980 Obituary 102
See also AITN 1
O'Neill, Gerard K(itchen) 1927- CANR-21
Obituary 137
Earlier sketch in CA 93-96
See also SATA 65
O'Neill, Gerard (Michael) 1942- 69-72
O'Neill, James E(dward) 1929-1987 117
Obituary 121
O'Neill, John Joseph 1920- 21-24R
O'Neill, John 1933- 53-56
O'Neill, Joseph Harry 1915- 13-16R
O'Neill, Judith (Beatrice) 1930- CANR-26
Earlier sketch in CA 109
See also SATA 34
O'Neill, Mary L(e Duc) 1908(?)-1990 ....CANR-4
Obituary 130
Earlier sketch in CA 5-8R
See also SATA 2
See also SATO 64
O'Neill, Michael J. 104
O'Neill, Michael J(ames) 1922- 112
Brief entry 108
O'Neill, Michael J. 1913- 13-16R
O'Neill, Michael 1953- 133
O'Neill, Nena ....AITN 1
O'Neill, Olivia
See Barstow, Phyllida
O'Neill, Patrick Geoffrey 1924- 21-24R
O'Neill, Paul 1928- 107
O'Neill, Reginald F. 1915- 1-4R
O'Neill, Richard W(inslow)
1925- Brief entry 107
O'Neill, Robert J(ohn) 1936- 25-28R
O'Neill, Shane
See O'Neill, William
O'Neill, Terence Marne 1914- 108
O'Neill, Tim 1918- 1-4R
O'Neill, Timothy P. 1941- 85-88
O'Neill, Timothy R. 1943- 128
O'Neill, William F. 1931- 29-32R
O'Neill, William L. 1935- CANR-34
Earlier sketches in CA 21-24R, CANR-12
O'Neill, William 1927- 37-40R
O'Neill Of The Maine, Baron of Ahoghill
See O'Neill, Terence Marne
O'Nell, Carl William 1925- 73-76
Onetti, Juan Carlos 1909- CANR-32
Earlier sketch in CA 85-88
See also CLC 7, 10
See also DLB 113
See also HW
See also MTCW
Ong, Walter J(ackson) 1912- CANR-21
Earlier sketches in CA 1-4R, CANR-4
Ongaro, Alberto 1925- 25-28R
O'Niell, C. M.
See Wilkes-Hunter, R(ichard)
Onions, Charles Talbut
1873-1965 Obituary 107
Onley, David C(harles) 1950- 112
Onlooker
See Grange, Cyril
Ono, Chiyo 1941- CANR-12
Earlier sketch in CA 29-32R
Onoda, Hiroo 1922(?)- Brief entry 108
Onofri, Arturo 1885-1928 ....DLB 114
O'Nolan, Brian
See O Nuallain, Brian
Onopa, Robert 1943- 112
Onorato, Richard James 1933- Brief entry 108
Onslow, Annette Rosemary MacArthur
See MacArthur-Onslow, Annette Rosemary
Onslow, John 1906-1985 Obituary 118
See also SATA 47
Onstott, Kyle 1887-1966 ....5-8R
Obituary 126
O Nuallain, Brian 1911-1966 ....CAP-2
Obituary 25-28R
Earlier sketch in CA 21-22
See also O'Brien, Flann
Onyeama, (Charles) Dillibe 1951- 125
See also BW
Ooi Jin-Bee 1931- 73-76
Ooiman, Jo Ann
See Robinson, Jo Ann Ooiman
Oost, Stewart Irvin 1921-1981 ....29-32R
Obituary 135
Oosterman, Gordon 1927- 49-52
Oosterwal, Gottfried 1930- 93-96
Oosthuizen, G(erhardus) C(ornelis)
1922- CANR-27
Earlier sketch in CA 29-32R
Oparin, Aleksandr (Ivanovich)
1894-1980 Obituary 108
Opdahl, Keith Michael 1934- 61-64
Opdahl, Richard D(ean) 1924- 21-24R
Opgenoorth, Winfried 1939- ....SATA 50
Ophuls, Max 1902-1957 Brief entry 113
Ophuls, Patrick 1934- 135
Ophuls, William
See Ophuls, Patrick
Opie, Amelia 1769-1853 ....DLB 116
Opie, Iona 1923- 61-64
See also SAAS 6
See also SATA 3, 63
Opie, John 1934- 29-32R
Opie, Peter (Mason) 1918-1982 ....CANR-2
Obituary 106
Earlier sketch in CA 5-8R
See also SATA 3, 28, 63
Opie, Redvers 1900-1984 Obituary 112
Opik, E.
See Oepik, Ernst Julius
Opik, Ernst
See Oepik, Ernst Julius
Opik, Ernst J.
See Oepik, Ernst Julius
Opik, Ernst Julius
See Oepik, Ernst Julius
Opitz, Edmund A. 1914- 29-32R
Opland, Jeff 1943- 106
Opler, Marvin K(aufmann) 1914-1981 ....21-24R
Obituary 133
Opler, Morris E(dward) 1907- CANR-29
Earlier sketch in CA 45-48
Opotowsky, Stan 1923- CANR-1
Earlier sketch in CA 1-4R
Oppen, George 1908-1984 ....CANR-8
Obituary 113
Earlier sketch in CA 13-16R
See also CLC 7, 13, 34
See also DLB 5
Oppen, Mary 1908-1990 119
Obituary 131
Oppenheim, A(dolph) Leo
1904-1974 Obituary 49-52
Oppenheim, E(dward) Phillips
1866-1946 Brief entry 111
See also DLB 70
See also TCLC 45
Oppenheim, Felix E(rrera) 1913- 1-4R
Oppenheim, Frank Mathias 1925- 116
Oppenheim, Irene 1928- 77-80
Oppenheim, James 1882-1932 ....DLB 28
Oppenheim, Janet 1948- 117
Oppenheim, Joanne 1934- CANR-25
Earlier sketches in CA 21-24R, CANR-9
See also SATA 5
Oppenheim, Michael 1940- 138
Oppenheim, Paul 1885(?)-1977 Obituary 69-72
Oppenheim, Philip 1956- 138
Oppenheim, S(aul) Chesterfield
1897-1988 Obituary 124
Oppenheim, Shulamith (Levey) 1930- 73-76
Oppenheimer, Evelyn 1907- CANR-3
Earlier sketch in CA 1-4R
Oppenheimer, George 1900-1977 ....13-16R
Obituary 73-76
Oppenheimer, Harold L. 1919- 17-20R
Oppenheimer, J(ulius) Robert
1904-1967 ....CANR-34
Earlier sketch in CA 103
See also MTCW
Oppenheimer, Jess 1913(?)-1988 Obituary 127
Oppenheimer, Joan L(etson) 1925- CANR-37
Earlier sketches in CA 37-40R, CANR-17
See also SATA 28
Oppenheimer, Joe A(llan) 1941- 111
Oppenheimer, Joel (Lester)
1930-1988 ....CANR-21
Obituary 126
Earlier sketches in CA 9-12R, CANR-4
See also DLB 5
Oppenheimer, Martin 1930- 29-32R
Oppenheimer, Max Jr. 1917- 17-20R
Oppenheimer, Paul 1939- 21-24R
Oppenheimer, Samuel P(hilip) 1903- 33-36R
Opper, F.
See Opper, Frederick (Burr)
Opper, Frederick (Burr)
1857-1937 Brief entry 118
See also AITN 1
Opper, Jacob 1935- 49-52
Opperby, Preben 1924- 110
Oppersdorff, Tony 1945- 113
Oppitz, Rene 1905(?)-1976 Obituary 65-68
Oppong, Christine 1940- CANR-7
Earlier sketch in CA 57-60
Optic, Oliver
See Adams, William Taylor
and Stratemeyer, Edward L.
Opton, Edward M. Jr. 1936- CANR-11
Earlier sketch in CA 21-24R
Opuls, Max
See Ophuls, Max
O'Quill, Scarlett
See Mossman, Dow
O'Quinn, Garland 1935- 21-24R
O'Quinn, Hazel Hedick 37-40R
Orage, A(lfred) R(ichard)
1873-1934 Brief entry 122
Oraison, Marc 1914- 85-88
Oram, Hiawyn 1946- 106
See also SATA 56
Oram, Malcolm 1944(?)-1976 Obituary 104
O'Ramus, Seamus
See O'Neill, William
O'Rand, Angela M(etropulos) 1945- 104
Oras, Ants 1900- CAP-1
Earlier sketch in CA 13-16
Orbaan, Albert F. CANR-8
Earlier sketch in CA 5-8R
Orbach, Ruth Gary 1941- 65-68
See also SATA 21
Orbach, Susie 1946- CANR-19
Earlier sketch in CA 85-88
Orbach, William W(olf) 1946- 73-76
Orben, Robert 1927- CANR-31
Earlier sketch in CA 81-84
Orbis, Victor
See Powell-Smith, Vincent (Walter Francis)
Orcutt, Georgia 1949- 112
Orczy, Emma Magdalena Rosalia Maria Josefa Barbara
1865-1947 Brief entry 104
See also Orczy, Emmuska
See also DLB 70
Orczy, Emmuska
See Orczy, Emma Magdalena Rosalia Maria
Josefa Barbara
See also SATA 40
Ord, John E. 1917- 81-84
Orde, A. J.
See Tepper, Sheri S.
Orde, Lewis 1943- CANR-28
Earlier sketch in CA 109
Ord-Hume, Arthur W. J. G. 101
Ordish, (Francis) George 1908(?)-1991 ....CANR-9
Obituary 133
Earlier sketch in CA 61-64
Ordover, Sondra T. 1929-1988 Obituary 127
Ordway, Frederick I(ra) III 1927- CANR-20
Earlier sketches in CA 5-8R, CANR-5
Ordway, Sally 1939- 57-60
O'Regan, Richard Arthur 1919- 73-76
O'Reilly, Don 1913- 111
O'Reilly, Jane 1936- CANR-31
Earlier sketch in CA 73-76
O'Reilly, John (Thomas) 1945- 29-32R
O'Reilly, Montagu
See Andrews, Wayne
O'Reilly, Robert P. 1936- 29-32R
O'Reilly, Timothy 1954- CANR-23
Earlier sketch in CA 106
Orel, Harold 1926- CANR-19
Earlier sketches in CA 5-8R, CANR-3
Orellana, Sandra L. 1941- 126
O'Relley, Z(oltan) Edward 1940- 119
Orem, R(eginald) C(alvert) 1931- 17-20R
Oren, Dan A. 1958- 138
Oren, Uri 1931- 65-68
Orengo, Charles 1913(?)-1974 Obituary 104
Orenstein, Denise Gosliner 1950- 110
Orenstein, Frank (Everett) 1919- CANR-30
Earlier sketch in CA 111
Orenstein, Gloria Feman 1938- 65-68
Orenstein, Henry 1924- 13-16R
Orent, Norman B. 1920- 17-20R
Oreshnik, A. F.
See Nussbaum, Al(bert F.)
Oresick, Peter (Michael) 1955- CANR-30
Earlier sketches in CA 73-76, CANR-13
Orest
See Bedrij, Orest (John)
Orewa, George Oka 1928- 5-8R
Orfalea, Gregory (M.) 1949- 128
Orff, Carl 1895-1982 Obituary 106
Orfield, Olivia 1922- 103
Orga, Ates 1944- 93-96
Organ, John 1925- CANR-7
Earlier sketch in CA 5-8R
Organ, Troy Wilson 1912- 37-40R
Organski, A(bramo) F(imo) K(enneth)
1923- 103
Orgel, Doris 1929- CANR-2
Earlier sketch in CA 45-48
See also AITN 1
See also SATA 7
Orgel, Joseph Randolph 1902-1987 ....CAP-1
Obituary 123
Earlier sketch in CA 11-12
Orgel, Stephen (Kitay) 1933- CANR-14
Earlier sketch in CA 73-76
Orgill, Douglas 1922-1984 ....CANR-29
Earlier sketch in CA 81-84
Orgill, Michael (Thomas) 1946- 61-64
Orians, George H(arrison) 1900- 49-52
Orians, Gordon H(owell) 1932- CANR-30
Earlier sketch in CA 45-48
Oriard, Michael (Vincent) 1948- 110
Origo, Iris (Margaret Cutting) 1902- 105
O'Riley, Warren
See Richardson, Gladwell
Oring, Elliott 1945- 111
Oriolo, Joe
See Oriolo, Joseph D.
Oriolo, Joseph D. 1913-1985 Obituary 118
See also SATA 46
Orion
See Naylor, John
O'Riordan, Robert (Garrett) 1943- 119
Orjuela, Hector H(ugo) 1930- CANR-32
Earlier sketches in CA 45-48, CANR-2
See also HW
Orkeny, Istvan 1912-1979 103
Obituary 89-92
Orkin, Harvey 1918(?)-1975 Obituary 61-64
Orkin, Ruth 1921-1985 119
Obituary 114
Orlando, Guido 1908(?)-1988 Obituary 126
Orlans, Harold 1921- CANR-15
Earlier sketch in CA 33-36R
Orlean, Susan 1955- 134
Orleans, Ilo 1897-1962 ....CANR-15
Earlier sketch in CA 1-4R
See also SATA 10
Orleans, Leo A(nton) 1924- CANR-32
Earlier sketches in CA 41-44R, CANR-15
Orledge, Robert (Nicholas) 1948- 113
Orlen, Steve 1942- 101
Orlev, Uri 1931- CANR-34
Earlier sketch in CA 101
See also SATA 58
Orlich, Donald C(harles) 1931- CANR-22
Earlier sketches in CA 13-16R, CANR-7
Orlick, Terrance D(ouglas) 1945- CANR-21
Earlier sketches in CA 57-60, CANR-6
Orlick, Terry
See Orlick, Terrance D(ouglas)
Orlicky, Joseph A. 1922- 25-28R
Orlier, Blaise
See Sylvestre, (Joseph Jean) Guy
Orlinsky, Harry M(eyer) 1908- 85-88
Obituary 137
Orlob, Helen Seaburg 1908- 5-8R
Orlock, Carol (Ellen) 1947- 122
Orloff, Ed(gar Sam) 1923-1983 69-72
Obituary 110
Orloff, Max
See Crowcroft, Peter
Orlofsky, Myron 1928(?)-1976 Obituary 69-72
Orloski, Richard J(ohn) 1947- 97-100
Orlova, Alexandra (Anatol'evna) 1911- 133
Orlova, R.
See Orlova-Kopelev, Raissa (Davydovna)
Orlova, R. D.
See Orlova-Kopelev, Raissa (Davydovna)
Orlova, Raisa
See Orlova-Kopelev, Raissa (Davydovna)
Orlova-Kopelev, Raissa (Davydovna) 1918- 123

Orlovitz, Gil 1918-1973 ... 77-80
Obituary ... 45-48
See also CLC 22
See also DLB 2, 5
Orlovsky, Peter 1933- ... CANR-9
Earlier sketch in CA 13-16R
See also DLB 16
Orlow, Dietrich 1937- ... 65-68
Ormai, Stella ... SATA 48, 57
Orme, Antony R(onald) 1936- ... CANR-35
Earlier sketch in CA 73-76
Ormerod, Jan(ette Louise) 1946- ... CANR-35
Earlier sketch in CA 113
See also CLR 20
See also MAICYA
See also SATA 44, 55, 70
Ormerod, Roger 1920- ... CANR-35
Earlier sketches in CA 77-80, CANR-15
Ormes, Jackie
See Ormes, Zelda J.
Ormes, Robert M. 1904- ... CAP-1
Earlier sketch in CA 11-12
Ormes, Robert Verner 1921-1984 Obituary ... 112
Ormes, Zelda J. 1914-1986 Obituary ... 118
See also SATA 47
Ormesson, Jean (Bruno Waldemar Francois-de-Paule Lefevre) d'
See d'Ormesson, Jean (Bruno Waldemar Francois-de-Paule Lefevre)
Ormesson, Wladimir d'
1888-1973 Obituary ... 45-48
Ormiston, Roberta
See Fletcher, Adele (Whitely)
Ormond, (Willard) Clyde 1906-1985 ... CANR-36
Obituary ... 115
Earlier sketch in CA 9-12R
Ormond, Frederic
See Dey, Frederic (Merrill) Van Rensselaer
Ormond, John 1923- ... CANR-32
Earlier sketch in CA 65-68
See also DLB 27
Ormond, Leonee (Jasper) 1940- ... 85-88
Ormond, Richard (Louis) 1939- ... CANR-35
Earlier sketches in CA 41-44R, CANR-15
Ormondroyd, Edward 1925- ... 73-76
See also SATA 14
Ormont, Louis Robert 1918- ... CANR-35
Earlier sketch in CA 13-16R
Ormrod, Richard (James) 1946- ... 119
Ormsbee, David
See Longstreet, Stephen
Ormsby, Frank 1947- ... CANR-23
Earlier sketch in CA 107
Ormsby, Virginia H(aire) ... 9-12R
See also SATA 11
Ormsby, William (George) 1921- ... 73-76
Orna, Mary Virginia 1934- ... 29-32R
Ornati, Oscar A(braham) 1922-1991 ... CANR-14
Obituary ... 136
Earlier sketch in CA 37-40R
Ornis
See Winchester, Clarence
Ornitz, Samuel (Badisch)
1890-1957 Brief entry ... 117
See also DLB 28, 44
Ornstein, Allan C(harles) 1941- ... CANR-4
Earlier sketch in CA 53-56
Ornstein, Dolph 1947- ... 77-80
Ornstein, J. L.
See Ornstein-Galicia, J(acob) L(eonard)
Ornstein, Jack H(ervey) 1938- ... 103
Ornstein, Norman J(ay) 1948- ... 93-96
Ornstein, Robert E. 1942- ... CANR-35
Earlier sketch in CA 53-56
Ornstein, Robert 1925- ... 1-4R
Ornstein-Galicia, J(acob) L(eonard)
1915- ... 93-96
Oropeza, Renato Prada
See Prada Oropeza, Renato
O'Rourke, Andrew P(atrick) 1933- ... 126
O'Rourke, Edward William 1917- ... 112
O'Rourke, Frank 1916-1989 ... 118
Obituary ... 128
Brief entry ... 114
O'Rourke, John James Joseph 1926- ... 33-36R
O'Rourke, John T(homas)
1900-1983 Obituary ... 111
O'Rourke, Lawrence Michael 1938- ... CANR-35
Earlier sketch in CA 69-72
O'Rourke, P. J. 1947- ... CANR-13
Earlier sketch in CA 77-80
O'Rourke, Terrence James 1932-1992 ... 41-44R
Obituary ... 136
O'Rourke, Timothy G(erald) 1949- ... 111
O'Rourke, William (Andrew) 1945- ... CANR-35
Earlier sketches in CA 45-48, CANR-1
Orozco, Olga 1920- ... HW
Orpaz, Yitzhak 1923- ... 101
Orpen, Eve 1926(?)-1978 Obituary ... 104
Orpen, Neil D.
See Orpen, Neil (Newton D'Arcy)
Orpen, Neil (Newton D'Arcy) 1913- ... 120
Orr, Bobby
See Orr, Robert Gordon
Orr, Daniel 1933- ... 29-32R
Orr, David 1929- ... 33-36R
Orr, Gregory 1947- ... CANR-22
Earlier sketch in CA 105
Orr, Helen Frances Burton
1913-1989 Obituary ... 129
Orr, J(ames) Edwin 1912- ... CANR-4
Earlier sketch in CA 9-12R
Orr, John Boyd 1880-1971 Obituary ... 113
Orr, Linda 1943- ... CANR-35
Earlier sketch in CA 97-100
Orr, Mary
See Denham, Mary Orr
Orr, Mary E. E. McCombe 1917- ... 5-8R
Orr, Oliver H(amilton) Jr. 1921- ... 1-4R
Orr, Robert Gordon 1948- ... 112
Orr, Robert R(ichmond) 1930- ... 25-28R
Orr, Robert T. 1908- ... 33-36R
Orr, William F(ridell) 1907- ... 108
Orrell, John (Overton) 1934- ... CANR-35
Earlier sketches in CA 37-40R, CANR-15
Orris
See Ingelow, Jean
Orrmont, Arthur 1922- ... CANR-35
Earlier sketches in CA 1-4R, CANR-4
Orsborn, Carol 1948- ... 124
Orsini, Gian Napoleone Giordano 1903- ... 5-8R
Orsini, Joseph E(mmanuel) 1937- ... 37-40R
Orso, Kathryn Wickey 1921-1979 ... 57-60
Obituary ... 85-88
Orsy, Ladislas M. 1921- ... 25-28R
Orszagh, Laszlo 1907-1984 Obituary ... 112
Ort, Ana
See Andrews, Arthur (Douglas Jr.)
Ortega y Gasset, Jose 1883-1955 ... 130
Brief entry ... 106
See also HW
See also MTCW
See also TCLC 9
Ortego, Philip D.
See Ortego y Gasca, Philip D.
Ortego y Gasca, Philip D. 1926- ... 131
See also HW
Orth, Charles D. III 1921- ... 5-8R
Orth, Penelope 1938- ... 45-48
Orth, Ralph H(arry) 1930- ... 21-24R
Orth, Richard
See Gardner, Richard (M.)
Orthwine, Rudolf 1900(?)-1970 Obituary ... 104
Ortiz, Adalberto 1914- ... 131
See also HW
Ortiz, Alfonso A(lex) 1939- ... 29-32R
Ortiz, Elisabeth Lambert 1928- ... CANR-35
Earlier sketch in CA 97-100
Ortiz, Simon J(oseph) 1941- ... 134
See also CLC 45
See also DLB 120
Ortiz, Victoria 1942- ... 107
Ortiz y Pino, Jose III 1932- ... 112
Ortlund, Anne 1923- ... 106
Ortlund, Raymond C(arl) 1923- ... 114
Ortman, E(lmore) Jan 1884- ... CAP-2
Earlier sketch in CA 25-28
Ortman, Elmer John
See Ortman, E(lmore) Jan
Ortner, Donald John 1938- ... 117
Ortner, Robert 1927- ... 135
Ortner, Sherry B(eth) 1941- ... 130
Ortner-Zimmerman, Toni 1941- ... CANR-19
Earlier sketches in CA 53-56, CANR-5
Orton, Alvin E. 1906-1987 Obituary ... 122
Orton, Barry 1949- ... 111
Orton, Harold 1898-1975 Obituary ... 57-60
Orton, Joe
See Orton, John Kingsley
See also CDBLB 1960 to Present
See also CLC 4, 13, 43
See also DLB 13
Orton, John Kingsley 1933-1967 ... CANR-35
Earlier sketch in CA 85-88
See also Orton, Joe
See also MTCW
Orton, Lawrence D(wayne)
1941- Brief entry ... 118
Orton, Vrest (Teachout) 1897-1986 ... CANR-35
Obituary ... 121
Earlier sketch in CA 33-36R
Ortzen, Len
See Ortzen, Leonard Edwin
Ortzen, Leonard Edwin 1912-1979 ... 118
Brief entry ... 114
Orum, Anthony M(endl) 1939- ... 41-44R
Orvell, Miles 1944- ... 41-44R
Orwell, George
See Blair, Eric (Arthur)
See also CDBLB 1945-1960
See also DLB 15, 98
See also TCLC 2, 6, 15, 31
See also WLC
Orwell, Sonia 1919(?)-1980 Obituary ... 102
Orwen, (Phillips) Gifford ... 37-40R
Ory, Edward 1886-1973 Obituary ... 41-44R
Ory, Kid
See Ory, Edward
Orzeck, Arthur Z(alman) 1921- ... CANR-1
Earlier sketch in CA 45-48
Osanka, Franklin Mark 1936- ... 5-8R
Osaragi, Jiro
See Nojiri, Kiyohiko
Osbeck, Kenneth W. 1924- ... CANR-19
Earlier sketches in CA 1-4R, CANR-3
Osbey, Brenda Marie 1957- ... DLB 120
Osbon, B. S. 1827-1912 ... DLB 43
Osborn, Albert D. 1896(?)-1972 Obituary ... 104
Osborn, Alex(ander) F(aickney)
1888-1966 Obituary ... 106
Osborn, Arthur W(alter) 1891- ... 21-24R
Osborn, Barbara M(onroe)
See Henkel, Barbara Osborn
Osborn, Carolyn 1934- ... 93-96
Osborn, Catherine B. 1914- ... 29-32R
Osborn, David (D.) 1923- ... 134
Brief entry ... 109
Osborn, Eric (Francis) 1922- ... 65-68
Osborn, Frederic J(ames) 1885-1978 ... CANR-5
Earlier sketch in CA 5-8R
Osborn, Frederick (Henry) 1889-1981 ... 25-28R
Obituary ... 102
Osborn, George C(oleman)
1904-1982 ... CANR-19
Earlier sketch in CA 25-28R
Osborn, James M(arshall) 1906-1976 ... CAP-2
Obituary ... 69-72
Earlier sketch in CA 25-28
Osborn, John Jay Jr. 1945- ... CANR-6
Earlier sketch in CA 57-60
Osborn, Lois D(orothy) 1915- ... 116
See also SATA 61
Osborn, Mary Elizabeth 1898- ... 5-8R
Osborn, Merton B(idwell) 1908- ... 25-28R
Osborn, Paul 1901-1988 ... 112
Obituary ... 125
Brief entry ... 108
Osborn, Percy George
1899(?)-1972 Obituary ... 104
Osborn, Robert (Chesley) 1904- ... 13-16R
Osborn, Robert T(appan) 1926- ... 21-24R
Osborn, Ronald E(dwin) 1917- ... 13-16R
Osborn, Stella Brunt
See Osborn, Stellanova
Osborn, Stellanova 1894-1988 Obituary ... 125
Osborn, Thomas Noel II 1940- ... 114
Osborne, Adam 1939- ... 109
Osborne, (Reginald) Arthur 1906-1970 ... 17-20R
Obituary ... 125
Osborne, Betsy
See Boswell, Barbara (S.)
Osborne, C(harles) H(umfrey) C(aufeild)
1891- ... 5-8R
Osborne, Cecil G. 1904- ... CANR-1
Earlier sketch in CA 45-48
Osborne, Charles 1927- ... CANR-34
Earlier sketches in CA 13-16R, CANR-13
See also SATA 59
Osborne, Chester G(orham) 1915- ... CANR-35
Earlier sketches in CA 21-24R, CANR-9
See also SATA 11
Osborne, Dan 1948(?)-1983 Obituary ... 110
Osborne, David
See Silverberg, Robert
Osborne, Dorothy (Gladys) Yeo 1917- ... 9-12R
Osborne, Elsie L(etitia) 1924- ... 118
Osborne, Ernest (Glenn) 1903-1963 ... 5-8R
Osborne, G(erald) S(tanley) 1926- ... 21-24R
Osborne, Geoffrey 1930- ... 110
Osborne, George
See Silverberg, Robert
Osborne, George E(dward) 1893- ... CAP-2
Earlier sketch in CA 23-24
Osborne, Harold W(ayne) 1930- ... 57-60
Osborne, Harold 1905-1987 ... CANR-6
Obituary ... 122
Earlier sketch in CA 13-16R
Osborne, Helena
See Moore, (Georgina) Mary (Galbraith)
Osborne, J(ulius) K(enneth) 1941- ... 33-36R
Osborne, John (Franklin) 1907-1981 ... CANR-10
Obituary ... 108
Earlier sketch in CA 61-64
Osborne, John (James) 1929- ... CANR-21
Earlier sketch in CA 13-16R
See also CDBLB 1945-1960
See also CLC 1, 2, 5, 11, 45
See also DLB 13
See also MTCW
See also WLC
Osborne, John W(alter) 1927- ... 33-36R
Osborne, Juanita Tyree 1916- ... CANR-23
Earlier sketches in CA 61-64, CANR-8
Osborne, Lawrence 1958- ... CLC 50
Osborne, Leone Neal 1914- ... 21-24R
See also SATA 2
Osborne, Linda Barrett 1949- ... 65-68
Osborne, Maggie
See Osborne, Margaret Ellen
Osborne, Margaret Ellen 1941- ... CANR-18
Earlier sketch in CA 102
Osborne, Margaret 1909- ... 13-16R
Osborne, Martha Lee 1928- ... 113
Osborne, Mary Pope 1949- ... CANR-29
Earlier sketch in CA 111
See also SATA 41, 55
Osborne, Maureen 1924- ... 109
Osborne, Milton Edgeworth 1936- ... CANR-9
Earlier sketch in CA 13-16R
Osborne, Richard Horsley 1925- ... 21-24R
Osborne, Richard 1943- ... 123
Osborne, Will 1949- ... 132
Osborne, William A(udley) 1919- ... 61-64
Osborne, William S(tewart) 1923- ... 53-56
Osborne, William (Terry Jr.) 1934- ... 25-28R
Osbourn, R(ichard) A(lton) 1930- ... 120
Osbourne, Ivor Livingstone 1951- ... 108
Osburn, Charles B(enjamin) 1939- ... CANR-13
Earlier sketch in CA 33-36R
Osceola
See Blixen, Karen (Christentze Dinesen)
Osen, Lynn M(oses) 1920- ... 65-68
Osenenko, John 1918-1983 Obituary ... 109
Oser, Jacob 1915- ... CANR-2
Earlier sketch in CA 5-8R
Osgood, Charles
See Wood, Charles Osgood III
Osgood, Charles E(gerton) 1916- ... 17-20R
Osgood, Charles Grosvenor
1871-1964 ... CANR-4
Earlier sketch in CA 5-8R
Osgood, Cornelius 1905-1985 Obituary ... 114
Osgood, David William 1940- ... 89-92
Osgood, Don(ald W.) 1930- ... CANR-11
Earlier sketch in CA 61-64
Osgood, Ernest S(taples) 1888- ... CAP-1
Earlier sketch in CA 11-12
Osgood, Herbert L(evi)
1855-1918 Brief entry ... 122
See also DLB 47
Osgood, Lawrence 1929- ... 85-88
Osgood, Robert Endicott 1921-1986 ... CANR-3
Obituary ... 121
Earlier sketch in CA 1-4R
Osgood, Samuel M(aurice) 1920-1975 ... 33-36R
Osgood, William E(dward) 1926- ... 33-36R
See also SATA 37
O'Shaughnessy, Arthur 1844-1881 ... DLB 35
O'Shaughnessy, Brian 1925- ... 132
O'Shea, (Martin) Lester 1938- ... 108
O'Shea, (Catherine) Pat(ricia Shiels)
1931- ... CLR 18
O'Shea, Sean
See Tralins, S(andor) Robert
Osherow, Jacqueline 1956- ... 137
Oshima, Nagisa 1932- ... 121
Brief entry ... 116
See also CLC 20
Osiek, Betty Tyree 1931- ... 45-48
Osing, Gordon T. 1937- ... 136
O Siochain, P(adraig) A(ugustine) 1905- ... CAP-2
Earlier sketch in CA 17-18
Osipow, Samuel H(erman) 1934- ... CANR-1
Earlier sketch in CA 49-52
Osis, Karlis 1917- ... 85-88
Oskam, Bob
See Oskam, Robert T(heo)
Oskam, Robert T(heo) 1945- ... 108
Oskamp, Stuart 1930- ... CANR-12
Earlier sketch in CA 29-32R
Oski, Frank A(ram) 1932- ... 119
Oskison, John M(ilton) 1874-1947 ... TCLC 35
Osler, Margaret Jo 1942- ... 126
Osler, Robert Willard 1911-1984 ... CANR-17
Obituary ... 114
Earlier sketch in CA 1-4R
Osley, A(rthur) S(idney) 1917-1987 ... 125
Osman, Betty B(arshad) 1929- ... CANR-35
Earlier sketch in CA 93-96
Osman, Jack D(ouglas) 1943- ... CANR-35
Earlier sketches in CA 61-64, CANR-11
Osman, John 1907(?)-1978 Obituary ... 77-80
Osmanczyk, Edmund Jan
1913-1989 Obituary ... 130
Osmer, Margaret ... 93-96
Osmond, Andrew 1938- ... 25-28R
Osmond, Edward 1900- ... CAP-1
Earlier sketch in CA 13-14
See also SATA 10
Osmond, Humphrey (Fortescue)
1917- ... CANR-28
Earlier sketch in CA 21-24R
Osmond, Marie 1959- ... 134
Brief entry ... 112
Osmond-Smith, David 1946- ... 120
Osmun, Mark 1952- ... 93-96
Osmunson, Robert Lee 1924- ... 9-12R
Osofsky, Gilbert 1935-1974 ... 65-68
Obituary ... 53-56
Osserman, Richard A. 1930- ... 29-32R
Osslinger, Kurt
See Allen, Bob
Ossman, David (H.) 1936- ... 9-12R
Ossoli, Sarah Margaret (Fuller marchesa d')
1810-1850
See Fuller, Margaret
See also SATA 25
Ossorgin, Mikhail
See Ilyin, Mikhail Andreyevich
Ossowska, Maria 1896- ... 29-32R
Ossowski, Stanislaw 1897-1963 ... CAP-1
Earlier sketch in CA 13-14
Ost, David H(arry) 1940- ... CANR-6
Earlier sketch in CA 53-56
Ost, John William Philip 1931- ... 37-40R
Osten, Gar 1923- ... 65-68
Ostendorf, (Arthur) Lloyd (Jr.) 1921- ... CANR-6
Earlier sketch in CA 1-4R
See also SATA 65
Ostenso, Martha 1900-1963 ... CAP-1
Earlier sketch in CA 13-16
See also DLB 92
Oster, Jerry 1943- ... CANR-35
Earlier sketch in CA 77-80
Oster, Ludwig (Friedrich) 1931- ... 53-56
Oster, Patrick (Ralph) 1944- ... 131
Osterburg, James W(illiam) 1917- ... 45-48
Ostergaard, G(eoffrey) N(ielsen)
1926-1990 ... 25-28R
Obituary ... 131
Osterhaven, M(aurice) Eugene 1915- ... 49-52
Osterhoudt, Robert G(erald) 1942- ... CANR-35
Earlier sketch in CA 53-56
Osterlund, Steven 1943- ... 77-80
Osterritter, John F. 1923- ... 45-48
Osterweis, Rollin G(ustav)
1907-1982(?) ... 41-44R
Obituary ... 106
Ostheimer, John 1938- ... 41-44R
Ostle, Bernard 1921- ... 5-8R
Ostlere, Gordon (Stanley) 1921- ... 107
Ostling, Richard N(eil) 1940- ... CANR-35
Earlier sketch in CA 53-56
Ostow, Mortimer 1918- ... CANR-35
Earlier sketch in CA 49-52
Ostrander, Gilman Marston 1923- ... 65-68
Ostriker, Alicia (Suskin) 1937- ... CANR-30
Earlier sketches in CA 25-28R, CANR-10
See also DLB 120
Ostrinsky, Meir Simha 1906- ... CAP-2
Earlier sketch in CA 29-32
Ostroff, Anthony J(ames) 1923-1978 ... CANR-3
Obituary ... 77-80
Earlier sketch in CA 5-8R

Ostrom, Alan (Baer) 1925- 21-24R
Ostrom, John Ward 1903- 1-4R
Ostrom, Thomas M. 1936- 37-40R
Ostrom, Vincent (Alfred) 1919- Brief entry 113
Ostrov, Eric 1941- CANR-34
Earlier sketch in CA 113
Ostrow, Joanna 1938- 29-32R
Ostrow, Ronald J. 1931- 130
Ostrower, Alexander 1901-1979 ....17-20R
Obituary 120
Ostrowsky
See Holmquist, Anders
Ostry, Sylvia 1927- CANR-15
Earlier sketch in CA 41-44R
Ostwald, Martin 1922- CANR-35
Earlier sketch in CA 33-36R
Ostwald, Peter F. 1928- 17-20R
O Suilleabhain, Sean 1903- CANR-18
Earlier sketch in CA 25-28R
O'Sullivan, Gerry 1959- 135
O'Sullivan, Joan (D'Arcy) 77-80
O'Sullivan, John J. 1939- Brief entry 114
O'Sullivan, John 1942- 132
O'Sullivan, Judith 1942- 120
O'Sullivan, P. Michael 1940- 93-96
O'Sullivan, Sean
See O Suilleabhain, Sean
O'Sullivan, Vincent (Gerard) 1937- CANR-35
Earlier sketch in CA 97-100
Osusky, Stefan 1889-1973 Obituary 45-48
Oswald, Eleazer 1755-1795 ....DLB 43
Oswald, Ian 1929- CANR-13
Earlier sketch in CA 17-20R
Oswald, J(oseph) Gregory 1922- 104
Oswald, Russell G. 1908- 45-48
Oswalt, John N(ewell) 1940- 117
Oswalt, Sabine
See MacCormack, Sabine G(abriele)
Oswalt, Wendell H(illman) 1927- CANR-35
Earlier sketches in CA 17-20R, CANR-12
Otake, Sadao 1913(?)-1983 Obituary 109
Otchis, Ethel (Herberg) 1920- 13-16R
Otero, Blas de 1916- 89-92
See also CLC 11
Otero, Miguel Antonio (II) 1859-1944 ....DLB 82
See also HW
Otfinoski, Steven 1949- ....SATA 56
Otis, George
See Mellen, Ida M(ay)
Otis, Jack 1923- 1-4R
Otis, James
See Kaler, James Otis
Otis, James Jr. 1725-1783 ....DLB 31
O'Toole, James (Joseph) 1945- 126
O'Toole, Rex
See Tralins, S(andor) Robert
O'Toole, Thomas 1941- ....SATA 71
O'Trigger, Sir Lucius
See Horne, Richard Henry
Ott, Attiat F(arag) 1935- CANR-10
Earlier sketch in CA 21-24R
Ott, David Jackson 1934-1975 ....CANR-8
Earlier sketch in CA 5-8R
Ott, Maggie Glen
See Ott, Virginia
Ott, Peter
See von Hildebrand, Dietrich
Ott, Thomas O(liver) III 1938- 49-52
Ott, Virginia 1917- 77-80
Ott, William Griffith 1909- CANR-1
Earlier sketch in CA 1-4R
Ottemiller, John H(enry) 1916-1968 ....CAP-2
Earlier sketch in CA 17-18
Otten, Anna 21-24R
Otten, C. Michael 1934- 33-36R
Otten, Charlotte F(ennema) 1926- 131
Otten, Charlotte M(arie) 1915- CANR-35
Earlier sketch in CA 29-32R
Otten, Terry (Ralph) 1938- CANR-35
Earlier sketches in CA 37-40R, CANR-15
Ottenberg, Miriam 1914-1982 ....CANR-10
Obituary 108
Earlier sketch in CA 5-8R
Ottenberg, Simon 1923- CANR-35
Earlier sketch in CA 33-36R
Ottendorfer, Oswald 1826-1900 Brief entry 123
See also DLB 23
Otter, Anthony 1896-1986 Obituary 118
Otterbein, Keith Frederick 1936- CANR-35
Earlier sketch in CA 21-24R
Ottersen, (John) Ottar 1918- 33-36R
Ottesen, Thea Tauber 1913- 5-8R
Otteson, Schuyler Franklin
1917- Brief entry 106
Ottley, Reginald Leslie 1909-1985 ....CANR-34
Earlier sketch in CA 93-96
See also MAICYA
See also SATA 26
Ottley, Roi (Vincent) 1906-1960 Obituary 89-92
Ottlik, Geza 1912-1990 ....CANR-39
Obituary 132
Earlier sketch in CA 17-20R
Ottman, Robert W(illiam) 1914- CANR-3
Earlier sketch in CA 1-4R
Otto, Calvin P. 1930- 29-32R
Otto, Henry J. 1901- CAP-2
Earlier sketch in CA 13-16
Otto, Herbert Arthur 1922- CANR-1
Earlier sketch in CA 45-48
Otto, Lon 1948- 130
Otto, Luther B(enedict) 1937- 133
Otto, Margaret Glover
1909-1976 Obituary 61-64
See also SATA 30
Otto, Svend
See Soerensen, Svend Otto
Otto, Wayne (R.) 1931- CANR-11
Earlier sketch in CA 29-32R
Otto, Whitney 1955- ....CLC 70
Ottum, Bob
See Ottum, Robert K. Jr.
Ottum, Robert K. Jr. 1925(?)-1986 Obituary 119
Otway, Thomas 1652-1685 ....DLB 80
Otway-Ruthven, Jocelyn
1909-1989 Obituary 128
Otwell, John H(erbert) 1915- 73-76
Ouchi, William G(eorge) 1943- 129
Oudaii, Hashmi el
See McGirk, Tim(othy Stephen)
Ouellette, Fernand 1930- CANR-17
Earlier sketches in CA 49-52, CANR-2
See also CAAS 13
See also DLB 60
Oughton, Frederick 1923- CANR-29
Earlier sketch in CA 1-4R
Ouida
See De La Ramee, (Marie) Louise
See also DLB 18
See also TCLC 43
Ouimette, Victor 1944- 73-76
Oulahan, Richard 1918-1985 ....CANR-36
Obituary 117
Earlier sketch in CA 33-36R
Oulanoff, Hongor 1929- 25-28R
Ouologuem, Yambo 1940- Brief entry 111
Ouroussoff, Peter Sergeivich
1900(?)-1984 Obituary 114
Ouroussow, Eugenie 1908-1975 Obituary 53-56
Oursler, Fulton Jr. 1932- Brief entry 116
Oursler, (Charles) Fulton
1893-1952 Brief entry 108
Oursler, Will(iam Charles) 1913-1985 ....CANR-35
Obituary 115
Earlier sketches in CA 5-8R, CANR-2
Ousby, Ian (Vaughan Kenneth) 1947- CANR-35
Earlier sketch in CA 89-92
Ousley, Odille 1896- CAP-1
Earlier sketch in CA 11-12
See also SATA 10
Ousmane, Sembene 1923- 125
Brief entry 117
See also BLC 3
See also BW
See also CLC 66
See also MTCW
Ouston, Philip (Anfield)
1924(?)-1988(?) Obituary 125
Outerbridge, David E(ugene) 1933- CANR-38
Earlier sketches in CA 93-96, CANR-16
Outhwaite, Leonard 1892- 53-56
Outhwaite, (Richard) William 1949- 130
Outka, Gene 1937- 41-44R
Outland, Charles 1910- 9-12R
Outler, Albert C(ook) 1908- CANR-1
Earlier sketch in CA 1-4R
Outram, Dorinda 1949- 132
Ouverson, Marlin D(ean) 1952- 111
Ovard, Glen F. 1928- 33-36R
Overacker, Louise 1891- CAP-2
Earlier sketch in CA 29-32
Overall, Christine (Dorothy) 1949- 138
Overbeck, Pauletta 1915- 97-100
Overbeek, J(ohannes) 1932- 73-76
Overberg, Kenneth R(ichard) 1944- CANR-35
Earlier sketch in CA 114
Overbury, Stephen 1954- 119
Overgard, William (Thomas Jr.) 1926-1990 138
Obituary 131
Overholser, Stephen 1944- CANR-16
Earlier sketch in CA 97-100
Overholser, Wayne D. 1906- CANR-16
Earlier sketches in CA 5-8R, CANR-2
Overholt, William H. 1945- 117
Overman, Michael 1920- 108
Overstreet, Bonaro (Wilkinson)
1902-1985 Obituary 117
Overstreet, Harry Allen 1875-1970 ....CAP-1
Obituary 29-32R
Earlier sketch in CA 13-16
Overton, Jenny (Margaret Mary) 1942- 57-60
See also SATA 36, 52
Overton, Richard Cleghorn 1907- 108
Overton, Robert
See Knox-Mawer, Ronald
Overy, Paul 1940- CANR-35
Earlier sketch in CA 29-32R
Overy, R(ichard) J(ames) 1947- 119
Ovesen, Ellis
See Smith, Shirley M(ae)
Ovid 43 - ....PC 2
Ovstedal, Barbara 130
Owen, Alan Robert George 1919- 9-12R
Owen, Alun (Davies) 1925- CANR-34
Earlier sketch in CA 5-8R
Owen, Bob
See Geis, Richard E(rwin)
Owen, Bruce M(anning) 1943- CANR-35
Earlier sketch in CA 57-60
Owen, Caroline Dale
See Snedeker, Caroline Dale (Parke)
Owen, Charles A(braham) Jr. 1914- CANR-36
Earlier sketch in CA 53-56
Owen, Clifford
See Hamilton, Charles (Harold St. John)
Owen, D(enis) F(rank) 1931- CANR-35
Earlier sketches in CA 53-56, CANR-4
Owen, David (Anthony Llewellyn) 1938- 129
Owen, David E(lystan) 1912-1987 124
Owen, David (Edward) 1898-1968 ....CANR-36
Earlier sketches in CAP-1, CA 13-16
Owen, David Lanyon Lloyd
See Lloyd Owen, David Lanyon
Owen, Dilys
See Gater, Dilys
Owen, Dolores B(ullock) CANR-34
Earlier sketch in CA 53-56
Owen, Douglas David Roy 1922- CANR-35
Earlier sketch in CA 89-92
Owen, Edmund
See Teller, Neville
Owen, (Benjamin) Evan 1918-1984 109
See also SATA 38
Owen, Frank 1907(?)-1979 Obituary 85-88
Owen, G(ail) L(ee) 1937- 45-48
Owen, G(eorge) Vale
1869-1931 Brief entry 119
Owen, Gail R.
See Owen-Crocker, Gail R(edfern)
Owen, Gareth 1936- ....SAAS 14
Owen, George Earle 1908- 77-80
Owen, Guy (Jr.) 1925-1981 ....CANR-36
Obituary 104
Earlier sketches in CA 1-4R, CANR-3
See also DLB 5
Owen, Gwilym Ellis Lane
1922-1982 Obituary 107
Owen, (William) Harold 1897-1971 ....13-16R
Obituary 89-92
Owen, Henry 1920- Brief entry 111
Owen, Hugh
See Faust, Frederick (Shiller)
Owen, Irvin 1910- 97-100
Owen, Jack 1929- CANR-37
Earlier sketch in CA 33-36R
Owen, Jennifer 1936- CANR-38
Earlier sketch in CA 116
Owen, John E. 1919- CANR-4
Earlier sketch in CA 9-12R
Owen, John 1564-1622 ....DLB 121
Owen, Lewis J(ames) 1925- Brief entry 116
Owen, Lewis 1915- 29-32R
Owen, Marsha
See Stanford, Sally
Owen, Norman G. 1944- 126
Owen, Oliver S. 1920- 104
Owen, Philip
See Philips, Judson (Pentecost)
Owen, Reginald 1887-1972 Obituary 37-40R
Owen, Richard 1947- 127
Owen, Robert N.
See Geis, Richard E(rwin)
Owen, Robert 1771-1858 ....DLB 107
Owen, Roderic
See Fenwick-Owen, Roderic (Franklin Rawnsley)
Owen, Roderic (Franklin Rawnsley) Fenwick
See Fenwick-Owen, Roderic (Franklin Rawnsley)
Owen, Roger C(orey) 1928- CANR-37
Earlier sketch in CA 77-80
Owen, Thomas Richard 1918- CANR-10
Earlier sketch in CA 21-24R
Owen, Tobias Chant 1936- CANR-29
Earlier sketch in CA 111
Owen, Tom
See Watts, Peter Christopher
Owen, W(arwick) J(ack) B(urgoyne) 1916- 134
Brief entry 111
Owen, Wilfred 1893-1918 Brief entry 104
See also CDBLB 1914-1945
See also DLB 20
See also TCLC 5, 27
See also WLC
Owen, Wilfred 1912- CANR-36
Earlier sketch in CA 37-40R
Owen, William Vern 1894- CAP-2
Earlier sketch in CA 17-18
Owen, Wyn F(oster) 1923- Brief entry 115
Owen-Crocker, Gail R(edfern) 1947- 128
Owendoff, Robert S(cott) 1945- 17-20R
Owens, Agnes 1926- 128
Owens, Bill 1938- 73-76
Owens, Carole (Ehrlich) 1942- 116
Owens, Carolyn 1946- 109
Owens, Craig 1950-1990 Obituary 132
Owens, Edgar (Leonard)
1924-1987 Obituary 124
Owens, Gail 1939- ....SATA 54
Owens, Gary 1936- 97-100
Owens, Jesse 1913-1980 110
Owens, John R(obert) 1926- 77-80
Owens, Joseph 1908- CANR-20
Earlier sketches in CA 5-8R, CANR-5
Owens, Louis (D.) 1948- 137
Owens, Pat(rick) J. 1929- 73-76
Owens, Richard Meredith 1944- CANR-37
Earlier sketch in CA 61-64
Owens, Robert Goronwy 1923- CANR-28
Earlier sketch in CA 29-32R
Owens, Rochelle 1936- CANR-39
Earlier sketch in CA 17-20R
See also CAAS 2
See also CLC 8
Owens, Thelma 1905- 69-72
Owens, Virginia Stem 1941- CANR-14
Earlier sketch in CA 81-84
Owens, William A. 1905-1990 ....CANR-36
Obituary 133
Earlier sketch in CA 9-12R
Ower, John 1942- 77-80
Owings, Loren C(lyde) 1928- 37-40R
Owings, Mark (Samuel) 1945- Brief entry 114
Owings, Nathaniel Alexander
1903-1984 ....CANR-35
Obituary 113
Earlier sketch in CA 61-64
Owl, Grey
See Belaney, Archibald Stansfeld
See also DLB 92
Owomoyela, Oyekan 1938- 112
Owsley, Frank L(awrence)
1890-1956 Brief entry 116
See also DLB 17
Owsley, Harriet Chappell 1901- 81-84
Oxenbury, Helen 1938- CANR-35
Earlier sketch in CA 25-28R
See also CLR 22
See also MAICYA
See also SATA 3, 68
Oxenham, Elsie J.
See Dunkerley, Elsie Jeanette
Oxenhandler, Neal 1926- CANR-6
Earlier sketch in CA 13-16R
Oxenhorn, Harvey 1952(?)-1990 Obituary 131
Oxley, Dorothy (Anne) 1948- 116
Oxley, William 1939- 73-76
Oxnam, Robert B(romley) 1942- CANR-5
Earlier sketch in CA 53-56
Oxnard, Charles (Ernest) 1933- CANR-16
Earlier sketches in CA 45-48, CANR-1
Oxorn, Harry 1920- 111
Oxtoby, Willard Gurdon 1933- CANR-37
Earlier sketch in CA 49-52
Oyle, Irving 1925- CANR-6
Earlier sketch in CA 57-60
Oyler, Philip (Tom) 1879- CAP-1
Earlier sketch in CA 9-10
Oy-Vik
See Holmvik, Oyvind
Oz, Amos 1939- CANR-27
Earlier sketch in CA 53-56
See also CLC 5, 8, 11, 27, 33, 54
See also MTCW
Oz, Frank (Richard) 1944- ....SATA 60
Ozaki, Robert S(higeo) 1934- CANR-35
Earlier sketch in CA 49-52
Ozawa, Terutomo 1935- CANR-34
Earlier sketch in CA 85-88
Ozbudun, Ergun 1937- 126
Ozer, Jerome S. 1927- 107
See also SATA 59
Ozer, Mark N(orman) 1932- CANR-30
Earlier sketch in CA 112
Ozick, Cynthia 1928- CANR-23
Earlier sketch in CA 17-20R
See also BEST 90:1
See also CLC 3, 7, 28, 62
See also DLB 28
See also DLBY 82
See also MTCW
Ozinga, James Richard 1932- CANR-37
Earlier sketch in CA 97-100
Ozment, Robert V. 1927- 17-20R
Ozment, Steven E(dgar) 1939- CANR-35
Earlier sketch in CA 108
Ozmon, Howard A. 25-28R
Ozu, Yasujiro 1903-1963 112
See also CLC 16
Ozy
See Rosset, B(enjamin) C(harles)

P

P. L. K.
See Kirk-Greene, Anthony (Hamilton Millard)
P. Q.
See Quennell, Peter (Courtney)
P. W.
See Strasser, Bernard Paul
Paak, Carl Erich 1922- 106
Paananen, Eloise (Katherine) 1923- CANR-18
Earlier sketches in CA 1-4R, CANR-2
See also Engle, Eloise
Paananen, Victor Niles 1938- 73-76
Paarlberg, Don 1911- 21-24R
Paasche, Carol L(evine) 1937- 5-8R
Paauw, Douglas Seymour 1921- 103
Pab
See Blooman, Percy A.
Paca, Lillian Grace (Baker) 1883- CAP-1
Earlier sketch in CA 11-12
Pacaut, Marcel 1920- 29-32R
Pace, C(harles) Robert 1912- 81-84
Pace, David 1944- 130
Pace, Denny F. 1925- 49-52
Pace, Donald Metcalf 1906-1982 Obituary 108
Pace, Eric 1936- 45-48
Pace, J. Blair 1916- 69-72
Pace, Mildred Mastin 1907- CANR-5
Earlier sketch in CA 5-8R
See also SATA 29, 46
Pace, Nathaniel 1925- 110
Pace, Peter
See Burnett, David (Benjamin Foley)
Pace, R(alph) Wayne 1931- CANR-1
Earlier sketch in CA 45-48
Pace, Robert Lee 1924- 1-4R
Pacernick, Gary 1941- 73-76
Pacey, (William Cyril) Desmond
1917-1975 ....CANR-4
Earlier sketch in CA 5-8R
See also DLB 88
Pachai, Bridglal 1927- CANR-17
Earlier sketch in CA 93-96
Pacheco, C.
See Pessoa, Fernando (Antonio Nogueira)
Pacheco, Catherine Chapman 1927- 130
Pacheco, Ferdie 1927- 81-84
Pacheco, Henricus Luis 1947-
See Pacheco, Henry L.
See also HW

Pacheco, Henry L.
See Pacheco, Henricus Luis
See also HW
Pacheco, Henry L(uis) 1947- 49-52
Pacheco, Jose Emilio 1939- 131
Brief entry 111
See also HW
Pa Chin
See Li Fei-kan
Pachmuss, Temira 1927- CANR-20
Earlier sketches in CA 9-12R, CANR-4
Pachter, Hedwig ....SATA 63
Pachter, Henry M(aximillian) 1907- 9-12R
Pachter, Josh 1951- 132
Pacifici, Sergio 1925- CANR-3
Earlier sketch in CA 1-4R
Pacifico, Carl 1921- 21-24R
Pack, Robert 1929- CANR-3
Earlier sketch in CA 1-4R
See also CLC 13
See also DLB 5
Pack, Roger A(mbrose) 1907- CAP-1
Earlier sketch in CA 13-16
Pack, S(tanley) W(alter) C(roucher)
1904-1977 ....13-16R
Obituary 125
Packard, Andrew 1929- 1-4R
Packard, Cindy
See Richmond, Cindy Packard
Packard, Edward 1931- 114
See also SATA 47
Packard, Frederick Clifton Jr.
1899-1985 Obituary 116
Packard, George R(andolph) III 1932- 127
Brief entry 112
Packard, Jerrold M(ichael) 1943- CANR-23
Earlier sketch in CA 106
Packard, Karl 1911(?)-1977 Obituary 69-72
Packard, Reynolds 1903-1976 73-76
Obituary 69-72
Packard, Robert G(eorge) 1933- 57-60
Packard, Robert 1916- 134
Packard, Rosa Covington 1935- 97-100
Packard, Rosalie 1-4R
Packard, Russell C. 1946- 119
Packard, Sidney R(aymond) 1893- 61-64
Packard, Vance (Oakley) 1914- CANR-7
Earlier sketch in CA 9-12R
See also AITN 1
Packard, William 1933- CANR-7
Earlier sketch in CA 13-16R
Packenham, Robert Allen 1937- 73-76
Packer, Arnold H. 1935- 37-40R
Packer, B(arbara) L(ee) 1947- 133
Packer, Bernard J(ules) 1934- CANR-19
Earlier sketch in CA 65-68
Packer, David W(illiam) 1937- 9-12R
Packer, Herbert L(eslie) 1925-1972 ....37-40R
Packer, J(ames) I(nnell) 1926- CANR-37
Earlier sketches in CA 49-52, CANR-1, 16
Packer, Joy (Petersen) 1905-1977 ....CANR-3
Earlier sketch in CA 1-4R
Packer, Lady
See Packer, Joy (Petersen)
Packer, Nancy Huddleston 1925- 65-68
Packer, Rod Earle 1931- 109
Packer, Vin
See Meaker, Marijane (Agnes)
Packman, David 1949- 123
Pacosz, Christina V(ivian) 1946- 77-80
Pacyga, Dominic A. 1949- 128
Pad, Peter
See Stratemeyer, Edward L.
Padberg, Daniel I(van) 1931- 33-36R
Padberg, John W(illiam) 1926- 25-28R
Padden, R(obert) C(harles) 1922- 21-24R
Paddison, Ronan 1945- 117
Paddleford, Clementine Haskin
1900-1967 Obituary 89-92
Paddock, John 1918- 17-20R
Paddock, Paul (Ezekiel Jr.) 1907-1975 ....CAP-2
Obituary 61-64
Earlier sketch in CA 21-22
Paddock, William (Carson) 1921- 21-24R
Pade, Victoria 1953- 113
Padel, Ruth 1946- 134
Paden, William D(oremus Jr.) 1941- 124
Padev, Michael Alexander
1915-1989 Obituary 128
Padfield, Harland (Irvine) 1926- Brief entry 112
Padfield, Peter 1932- CANR-26
Earlier sketch in CA 101
Padgett, Desmond
See von Block, Bela W(illiam)
Padgett, Dora 1893(?)-1976 Obituary 61-64
Padgett, Lewis
See Kuttner, Henry
and Moore, C(atherine) L(ucile)
Padgett, Ron 1942- CANR-30
Earlier sketches in CA 25-28R, CANR-12
See also DLB 5
Padilla, Genaro M(iguel) 1949- 128
Padilla (Lorenzo), Heberto 1932- 131
Brief entry 123
See also AITN 1
See also CLC 38
See also HW
Padilla, Raymond V. 1944- 130
See also HW
Padilla, Victoria 1907-1986 103
Obituary 120
Padley, Walter Ernest 1916-1984 Obituary 112
Padmore, George
See Nurse, Malcolm Ivan Meredith
Padovano, Anthony T(homas) 1934- CANR-22
Earlier sketches in CA 17-20R, CANR-7
Padover, Saul K(ussiel) 1905-1981 ....CANR-2
Obituary 103
Earlier sketch in CA 49-52
Padwick, E(ric) W(illiam) 1923- 119
Paetro, Maxine 1946- 123
Paffard, Michael Kenneth 1928- 103
Pafford, John Henry Pyle 1900- CANR-21
Earlier sketch in CA 104
Pagan Ferrer, Gloria M. 1921-
See Palma, Marigloria
See also HW
Pagden, Anthony 1945- 101
Page, Benjamin I(ngrim) 1940- 112
Page, Carole Gift 1942- 117
Page, Charles H(unt) 1909-1992 ....CANR-4
Obituary 136
Earlier sketch in CA 5-8R
Page, Christopher H. 1952- 137
Page, Curtis C(arling) 1914- 21-24R
Page, Diana (Preuthun) 1946- 126
Page, Drew 1905- 105
Page, Eileen
See Heal, Edith
Page, Eleanor
See Coerr, Eleanor (Beatrice)
Page, Ellis Batten 1924- 13-16R
Page, Emma
See Tirbutt, Honoria
Page, Evelyn 1902- 5-8R
Page, G. S.
See Galbraith, Georgie Starbuck
Page, Geoff(rey Donald) 1940- 133
Page, Gerald W(ilburn) 1939- 93-96
Page, Grover Jr. 1918- 17-20R
Page, Harry Robert 1915- 9-12R
Page, Homer (Gordon) 1918-1985 Obituary 117
Page, Jake
See Page, James K(eena) Jr.
Page, James A(llen) 1918- 107
Page, James D. 1910- 73-76
Page, James K(eena) Jr. 1936- CANR-35
Earlier sketch in CA 97-100
Page, Jimmy 1944- ....CLC 12
Page, Joseph A(nthony) 1934- CANR-14
Earlier sketch in CA 81-84
Page, Katherine Hall 1947- 136
Page, Kathy 1958- 133
Page, Lorna
See Rowland, D(onald) S(ydney)
Page, Lou Williams 1912- CANR-5
Earlier sketch in CA 5-8R
See also SATA 38
Page, Louise 1955- ....CLC 40
Page, Malcolm 1935- CANR-31
Earlier sketch in CA 45-48
Page, Marian 69-72
Page, Martin 1938- CANR-12
Earlier sketch in CA 17-20R
Page, Mary
See Heal, Edith
Page, Norman 1930- CANR-31
Earlier sketches in CA 61-64, CANR-8
Page, P(atricia) K(athleen) 1916- CANR-22
Earlier sketches in CA 53-56, CANR-4
See also CLC 7, 18
See also DLB 68
See also MTCW
Page, Robert Collier 1908-1977 Obituary 73-76
Page, Robert J(effress) 1922- 17-20R
Page, Robert Morris 1903- CAP-2
Earlier sketch in CA 17-18
Page, Robin 1943- 103
Page, Roch 1939- 33-36R
Page, Russell 1906-1985 Obituary 114
Page, Stanton
See Fuller, Henry Blake
Page, Thomas Nelson
1853-1922 Brief entry 118
See also DLB 12, 78
Page, Thomas 1942- 81-84
Page, Thornton (Leigh) 1913- CANR-2
Earlier sketch in CA 5-8R
Page, Vicki
See Avey, Ruby
Page, Walter Hines 1855-1918 ....DLB 71, 91
Page, Warren (Kempton)
1910-1977 Obituary 111
Page, William Roberts 1904- 21-24R
Page, William 1929- CANR-35
Earlier sketch in CA 114
Page, William 1946- 115
Pagel, Walter T. U. 1898-1983 129
Obituary 109
Pagels, Elaine Hiesey 1943- CANR-24
Earlier sketches in CA 45-48, CANR-2
Pagels, Heinz R(udolf) 1939-1988 ....CANR-23
Obituary 126
Earlier sketch in CA 107
Pages, Pedro
See Alba, Victor
Paget, George Charles Henry Victor
1922- 17-20R
Paget, John
See Aiken, John (Kempton)
Paget, Julian 1921- 21-24R
Paget, Margaret
See Medlicott, Margaret P(aget)
Paget, Violet 1856-1935 Brief entry 104
See also Lee, Vernon
Paget-Fredericks, Joseph E. P. Rous-Marten
1903-1963 ....SATA 30
Paget-Lowe, Henry
See Lovecraft, H(oward) P(hillips)
Paglia, Camille 1947- ....CLC 68
Paglin, Morton 1922- 97-100
Pagnol, Marcel (Paul) 1895-1974 128
Obituary 49-52
See also MTCW
Pagter, Carl R(ichard) 1934- 127
Paher, Stanley W(illiam) 1940- 29-32R
Pahl, R(aymond) E(dward) 1935- 25-28R
Pahlavi, Mohammed Riza
See Pahlevi, Mohammed Riza
Pahlen, Kurt 1907- CANR-7
Earlier sketch in CA 13-16R
Pahlevi, Mohammed Riza
1919-1980 Obituary 106
Pahz, (Anne) Cheryl Suzanne 1949- CANR-8
Earlier sketch in CA 53-56
See also SATA 11
Pahz, James Alon 1943- CANR-8
Earlier sketch in CA 53-56
See also SATA 11
Pai, Anna C(hao) 1935- 89-92
Pai, Young 1929- 33-36R
Paice, Eric 1927(?)-1989 Obituary 129
Paice, Margaret 1920- CANR-20
Earlier sketch in CA 29-32R
See also SATA 10
Paier, Robert (David) 1943- 89-92
Paiewonsky, Michael 1939- 137
Paige, Connie 1945- 130
Paige, David
See Whittingham, Richard
Paige, Glenn D(urland) 1929- 25-29R
Paige, Harry W(orthington) 1922- CANR-32
Earlier sketch in CA 113
See also SATA 35, 41
Paige, Leo
See Cochrane, William E.
Paige, Leroy Robert 1907(?)-1982 Obituary 107
Paige, Richard
See Koontz, Dean R(ay)
Paige, Richard E(aton) 1904-1988 111
Obituary 126
Paige, Satchel
See Paige, Leroy Robert
Paikeday, Thomas M. 1926- 128
Pailin, David A. 1936- 129
Pain, Barry (Eric Odell)
1864-1928 Brief entry 109
Pain, Philip ....DLB 24
Paine, Albert Bigelow
1861-1937 Brief entry 108
Paine, J. Lincoln
See Kramish, Arnold
Paine, Lauran (Bosworth) 1916- CANR-31
Earlier sketches in CA 45-48, CANR-7
Paine, Philbrook 1910- CAP-1
Earlier sketch in CA 11-12
Paine, R(ussell) Howard 1922- 5-8R
Paine, Robert Treat Jr. 1773-1811 ....DLB 37
Paine, Roberta M. 1925- 33-36R
See also SATA 13
Paine, Roger W(arde) III 1942- 65-68
Paine, Stephen William 1908- 1-4R
Paine, Thomas 1737-1809 ....CDALB 1640-1865
See also DLB 31, 43, 73
Painter, Charlotte CANR-3
Earlier sketch in CA 1-4R
Painter, Daniel
See Burgess, M(ichael) R(oy)
Painter, George D(uncan) 1914- 101
Painter, Helen W(elch) 1913- 33-36R
Painter, Nell Irvin 1942- CANR-19
Earlier sketch in CA 65-68
See also BW
Painter, Pamela 1941- 122
Pairault, Pierre 1922- 53-56
Pais, Abraham 1918- 109
Paish, F(rank) W(alter) 1898-1988 ....17-20R
Obituary 125
Paisley, Tom 1932- CANR-15
Earlier sketch in CA 61-64
See also Bethancourt, T. Ernesto
Paisner, Milton 1915- 113
Pak Chong-Hui
See Park Chung Hee
Pakenham, Antonia
See Fraser, Antonia (Pakenham)
Pakenham, Edward Arthur Henry
1902-1961 Obituary 114
Pakenham, Francis Aungier 1905- 109
Pakenham, Frank Sevent
See Pakenham, Francis Aungier
Pakenham, Simona Vere 1916- CANR-3
Earlier sketch in CA 1-4R
Pakenham, Thomas (Frank Dermot) 1933- 109
Pakula, Alan J(ay) 1928- 130
Brief entry 124
Pakula, Marion Broome 1926- CANR-7
Earlier sketch in CA 57-60
Pal, Pratapaditya 1935- 37-40R
Palamas, Kostes 1859-1943 Brief entry 105
See also TCLC 5
Palamountain, Joseph Cornwall Jr.
1920-1987 45-48
Obituary 124
Palandri, Angela (Chin-ying) Jung 1926- 37-40R
Palange, Anthony (Jr.) 1942- 37-40R
Palau, Luis (Jr.) 1934- CANR-39
Earlier sketch in CA 116
Palazzeschi, Aldo 1885-1974 89-92
Obituary 53-56
See also CLC 11
See also DLB 114
Palazzo, Anthony D.
See Palazzo, Tony
Palazzo, Tony 1905-1970 ....CANR-4
Obituary 29-32R
Earlier sketch in CA 5-8R
See also SATA 3
Palder, Edward L. 1922- ....SATA 5
Palecek, Josef 1932- ....SATA 56
Paleckis, Justas (Ignovich)
1899-1980 Obituary 105
Palen, J(oseph) John 1939- CANR-15
Earlier sketch in CA 41-44R
Palen, Jennie M. 5-8R
Palermo, David Stuart 1929- 17-20R
Pales Matos, Luis 1898-1959 ....HW
Palestrant, Simon S. 1907- CAP-1
Earlier sketch in CA 9-10
Paley, Alan L(ouis) 1943- 69-72
Paley, Grace 1922- CANR-13
Earlier sketch in CA 25-28R
See also CLC 4, 6, 37
See also DLB 28
See also MTCW
See also SSC 8
Paley, Maggie 1939- 121
Paley, Morton D(avid) 1935- CANR-13
Earlier sketch in CA 33-36R
Paley, Nicholas M(iroslav) 1911- CANR-15
Earlier sketch in CA 41-44R
Paley, Vivian Gussin 1929- CANR-30
Earlier sketch in CA 93-96
Paley, William S(amuel) 1901-1990 110
Obituary 132
Palffy-Alpar, Julius 1908- CAP-2
Earlier sketch in CA 23-24
Palfrey, John Gorham 1796-1881 ....DLB 1, 30
Palfrey, Thomas R(ossman) 1895- 61-64
Palgrave, Francis Turner 1824-1897 ....DLB 35
Palin, Michael (Edward) 1943- CANR-35
Earlier sketch in CA 107
See also Monty Python
See also CLC 21
See also SATA 67
Palinchak, Robert S(tephen) 1942- 49-52
Palinurus
See Connolly, Cyril (Vernon)
Palisca, Claude V. 1921- 17-20R
Palkovic, Mark 1954- 137
Pall, Ellen Jane 1952- 93-96
Palladini, David (Mario) 1946- ....MAICYA
See also SATA 32, 40
Pallas, Dorothy Constance
1933-1971 Obituary 33-36R
Pallas, Norvin 1918- CANR-3
Earlier sketch in CA 1-4R
See also SATA 23
Pallavera, Franco
See Soldati, Mario
Palle, Albert 1916- 13-16R
Pallenberg, Corrado 1912- 13-16R
Palley, Julian I(rving) 1925- 73-76
Palley, Marian Lief 1939- CANR-8
Earlier sketch in CA 61-64
Palli, Pitsa
See Hartocollis, Peter
Pallidini, Jodi
See Robbin, (Jodi) Luna
Pallis, Alexander (Anastasius)
1883-1975 Obituary 61-64
Palliser, Charles 1947- 136
See also CLC 65
Pallister, Janis L(ouise) 1926- CANR-14
Earlier sketch in CA 41-44R
Pallister, John C(lare) 1891-1980 ....5-8R
Obituary 103
See also SATA 26
Pallone, Nathaniel John 1935- CANR-29
Earlier sketches in CA 21-24R, CANR-10
Palm, Goeran 1931- 29-32R
Palm, Goran
See Palm, Goeran
Palm, John Daniel 1924- Brief entry 106
Palma, Marigloria
See Pagan Ferrer, Gloria M.
See also HW
Palma, Ricardo 1833-1919 ....TCLC 29
Palmatier, Robert Allen 1926- 37-40R
Palmedo, Roland 1895-1977 53-56
Obituary 69-72
Palmer, Alan Warwick 1926- CANR-6
Earlier sketch in CA 13-16R
Palmer, Archie M(acInnes) 1896-1985 ....13-16R
Obituary 116
Palmer, Arnold (Daniel) 1929- 85-88
Palmer, B. C.
See Schmidt, Laura M(arie)
Palmer, Bernard 1914- CANR-12
Earlier sketches in CA 57-60, CANR-7
See also SATA 26
Palmer, Brooks 1900(?)-1974 Obituary 45-48
Palmer, Bruce (Hamilton) 1932- CANR-3
Earlier sketch in CA 1-4R
Palmer, C(yril) Everard 1930- 41-44R
See also BW
See also SATA 14
Palmer, C(edric) King 1913- 13-16R
Palmer, (Ruth) Candida 1926- 61-64
See also SATA 11
Palmer, (John) Carey (Bowden) 1943- 103
Palmer, Charles Earl 1919- 13-16R
Palmer, (Thomas) Cruise 1917- 69-72
Palmer, Dave Richard 1934- CANR-1
Earlier sketch in CA 45-48
Palmer, David (Walter) 1928- CANR-28
Earlier sketch in CA 21-24R
Palmer, Don
See Benson, Mildred (Augustine Wirt)
Palmer, Donald C. 1934- 53-56
Palmer, Dorothy Ann 1935- 57-60
Palmer, E(dgar) P(oole) Jr. 1938- 116
Palmer, Earl Frank 1931- 113
Palmer, Edgar Z(avitz) 1898-1977 ....21-24R
Obituary 135

Palmer, Edward L. 1938- 101
Palmer, Elsie Pavitt 1922- 5-8R
Palmer, Eve 1916- 21-24R
Palmer, Everett W(alter) 1906-1970 ....CAP-2
Earlier sketch in CA 17-18
Palmer, Frank R. 1922- 17-20R
Palmer, Gabrielle G. 1938- 128
Palmer, George E. 1908- 1-4R
Palmer, George Herbert
1842-1933 Brief entry 121
Palmer, George 1915(?)-1986 Obituary 119
Palmer, Gerald Eustace Howell
1904-1984 Obituary 112
Palmer, (James) Gregory 1938- 121
Palmer, Hap 1942- 136
See also SATA 68
Palmer, Heidi 1948- ....SATA 15
Palmer, Helen H. 1911- 21-24R
Palmer, Helen Marion
See Geisel, Helen
Palmer, Henry R(obinson) Jr. 1911- 21-24R
Palmer, (Nathaniel) Humphrey 1930- CANR-31
Earlier sketches in CA 29-32R, CANR-12
Palmer, James B. 1929- 25-28R
Palmer, Jerome Robert 1904- 45-48
Palmer, Jim
See Palmer, James B.
Palmer, John A(lfred)
See Lacey, Douglas R(aymond)
Palmer, John A(lfred) 1926-1982 ....29-32R
Palmer, John L(ogan) 1943- 73-76
Palmer, John (Leslie)
1885-1944 Brief entry 121
Palmer, Joseph (Mansergh) 1912- 5-8R
Palmer, Juliette 1930- 81-84
See also SATA 15
Palmer, Kenneth T. 1937- 77-80
Palmer, L(eonard) R(obert) 1906-1984 ....25-28R
Obituary 114
Palmer, Larry Garland 1938- 17-20R
Palmer, Laura
See Schmidt, Laura M(arie)
Palmer, Lilli
See Peiser, Maria Lilli
Palmer, Lynn
See Palmer, Pamela Lynn
Palmer, Madelyn 1910- 103
Palmer, Marian 1930- 53-56
Palmer, Marjorie 1919- CANR-12
Earlier sketch in CA 57-60
Palmer, Michael D. 1933- 37-40R
Palmer, Michael (Stephen) 1942- CANR-35
Earlier sketch in CA 114
Palmer, Nicholas 1950- CANR-15
Earlier sketch in CA 89-92
Palmer, Norman D(unbar) 1909- CANR-19
Earlier sketches in CA 1-4R, CANR-3
Palmer, Pamela Lynn 1951- CANR-4
Earlier sketch in CA 53-56
Palmer, Parker J. 1939- CANR-38
Earlier sketch in CA 115
Palmer, Pete
See Palmer, E(dgar) P(oole) Jr.
Palmer, Peter
See Palmer, Elsie Pavitt
Palmer, Peter John 1932- CANR-20
Earlier sketch in CA 103
Palmer, R(obert) R(oswell) 1909- 13-16R
Palmer, Ralph Simon 1914- 73-76
Palmer, Raymond A. 1910-1977 Obituary 111
Palmer, Raymond Edward 1927- 77-80
Palmer, Richard Edward 1933- CANR-1
Earlier sketch in CA 45-48
Palmer, Richard Phillips 1921- 57-60
Palmer, Richard 1904- 97-100
Palmer, Robert C(harles) 1947- 113
Palmer, Robert E(verett) A(llen)
1932- Brief entry 114
Palmer, Robert (Franklin Jr.) 1945- 128
Brief entry 121
Palmer, Robin 1911- 109
See also SATA 43
Palmer, Roy (Ernest) 1932- CANR-23
Earlier sketches in CA 61-64, CANR-8
Palmer, Spencer J(ohn) 1927- CANR-10
Earlier sketch in CA 61-64
Palmer, Stanley H. 1944- 135
Palmer, Stuart 1924- CANR-3
Earlier sketch in CA 1-4R
Palmer, Susann(a Louisa) 1923- 132
Palmer, Thomas (Coryell) 1955- CANR-39
Earlier sketch in CA 109
Palmer, Tim 1948- 121
Palmer, Tobias
See Weathers, Winston
Palmer, Tony 1941- Brief entry 111
Palmer, William J. 1943- 134
Palmer, Winthrop Bushnell 1899-1988 65-68
Obituary 126
Palmieri, Anthony Francis 1920- 114
Palmore, Erdman B. 1930- 37-40R
Palms, Roger C(urtis) 1936- CANR-38
Earlier sketches in CA 93-96, CANR-17
Paloczi-Horvath, George 1908-1973 ....5-8R
Obituary 37-40R
Palombo, Stanley R(obert) 1934- 122
Palomo, G(aspar) J(esus) 1952- 61-64
Palovic, Clara Lora 1918- 25-28R
Paltenghi, Madeleine
See Anderson, Madeleine Paltenghi
Paltock, Robert 1697-1767 ....DLB 39
Paltrowitz, Donna (Milman) 1950- 119
See also SATA 50, 61
Paltrowitz, Stuart 1946- 118
See also SATA 50, 61
Paludan, (Stig Henning) Jacob (Puggaard)
1896-1975 Obituary 115
Paludan, Phillip S(haw) 1938- 73-76
Paluello, Lorenzo Minio
See Minio-Paluello, Lorenzo
Palumbo, Dennis J(ames) 1929- CANR-28
Earlier sketch in CA 29-32R
Palusci, Larry 1916- 29-32R
Paluszny, Maria Janina 1939- 103
Palyi, Melchior 1892(?)-1970 Obituary 104
Pan, Peter
See Bartier, Pierre
Pan, Stephen C(hao) Y(ing) 1915- 45-48
Panagopoulos, Epaminondas Peter
1915- 13-16R
Panama, Norman 1920- 104
See also DLB 26
Panassie, Hugues (Louis Marie Henri)
1912-1974 97-100
Obituary 53-56
Panati, Charles 1943- 81-84
See also SATA 65
Pancake, Breece Dexter 1952-1979 123
Obituary 109
See also Pancake, Breece D'J
Pancake, Breece D'J
See Pancake, Breece Dexter
See also CLC 29
Pancake, John S(ilas) 1920- 53-56
Pandey, B(ishwa) N(ath) 1929-1982 ....CANR-20
Obituary 108
Earlier sketch in CA 25-28R
Pandit, Vijaya Lakshmi 1900- 104
Panek, LeRoy Lad 1943- CANR-32
Earlier sketch in CA 113
Panella, Vincent 1939- 97-100
Panero, Leopoldo 1909-1962 ....DLB 108
Panetta, George 1915-1969 81-84
See also SATA 15
Panetta, Leon Edward 1938- 101
Pang, May 1950- 118
Pangborn, Edgar 1909-1976 ....CANR-4
Earlier sketch in CA 1-4R
See also DLB 8
Panger, Daniel 1926- 93-96
Panglaykim, J(usuf Pangestu) 1922- CANR-15
Earlier sketch in CA 21-24R
Pangle, Thomas L(ee) 1944- CANR-1
Earlier sketch in CA 49-52
Pangrazzi, Arnaldo 1947- 115
Paniagua Bermudez, Domingo
1880(?)-1973 Obituary 41-44R
Panichas, George A(ndrew) 1930- CANR-25
Earlier sketches in CA 25-28R, CANR-10
Paniker, Raimundo
See Panikkar, Raimundo
Panikkar, K(avalam) Madhava
1895-1963 ....CAP-1
Earlier sketch in CA 13-16
Panikkar, Raimundo 1918- CANR-25
Earlier sketch in CA 81-84
Panikkar, Raymond
See Panikkar, Raimundo
Panin, Dimitri (Mikhailovich)
1911-1987 Obituary 124
Panitch, Leo (Victor) 1945- 119
Panitt, Merrill 1917- 106
Panitz, Esther L(eah) 116
Pankey, Eric 1959- 120
Pankhurst, Emmeline (Goulden)
1858-1928 Brief entry 116
Pankhurst, Richard (Keir Pethick)
1927- CANR-21
Earlier sketches in CA 9-12R, CANR-6
Pankin, Robert M. 1935- 114
Pannabecker, Samuel Floyd 1896- 65-68
Pannell, Anne Gary 1910- CAP-2
Earlier sketch in CA 23-24
Pannenberg, Wolfhart (Ulrich) 1928- CANR-11
Earlier sketch in CA 25-28R
Panneton, Philippe
See Ringuet
Pannick, David 1956- 130
Panning, Anne 1966- 138
Pannor, Reuben 1922- 61-64
Pannwitz, Rudolf 1881-1969 Obituary 89-92
Pano, Nicholas C(hristopher) 1934- 37-40R
Panofsky, Erwin 1892-1968 117
Obituary 113
Panos, Chris(tos) 1935- 65-68
Panos, Louis G. 1925- 136
Panov, Valery (Shulman) 1938- 102
Panova, Vera (Fedorovna) 1905-1973 102
Obituary 89-92
See also MTCW
Panowski, Eileen Thompson 1920- 5-8R
See also SATA 49
Panshin, Alexei 1940- 57-60
See also DLB 8
Panshin, Cory (Seidman) 1947- Brief entry 112
Pansy
See Alden, Isabella (Macdonald)
Pantell, Dora (Fuchs) 111
See also SATA 39
Panter, Carol 1936- 49-52
See also SATA 9
Panter, Gideon G. 1935- 77-80
Panter-Downes, Mollie Patricia 1906- 101
Panting, Phyllis
See Morton, Phyllis Digby
Panzarella, Andrew 1940- 25-28R
Panzarella, Joseph John Jr. 1919- 85-88
Panzer, Pauline (Richman)
1911(?)-1972 Obituary 37-40R
Pao, Ping-Nie 1922- 103
Paoletti, John T(homas) 1939- 112
Paoli, Francisco Matos
See Matos Paoli, Francisco
See also HW
Paoli, Pia 1930- 25-28R
Paolini, Gilberto 1928- CANR-22
Earlier sketch in CA 45-48
Paolucci, Anne 73-76
Paolucci, Henry 1921- 102
Paone, Anthony J(oseph) 1913- 5-8R
Paor, Richard de
See Power, Richard
Papachristou, Judy 1930- 93-96
Papadiamantis, Alexandros
1851-1911 ....TCLC 29
Papadiamantopoulos, Johannes
1856-1910 Brief entry 117
See also Moreas, Jean
Papaleo, Joseph 1925- 25-28R
Papandreou, Andreas G(eorge) 1919- 37-40R
Papandreou, Margaret C. 1923- 29-32R
Papanek, Ernst 1900-1973 ....CANR-4
Earlier sketch in CA 1-4R
Papanek, Gustav F(ritz) 1926- CANR-1
Earlier sketch in CA 45-48
Papas, William 1927- CANR-12
Earlier sketch in CA 25-28R
See also SATA 50
Papashvily, George 1898-1978 81-84
Obituary 77-80
See also SATA 17
Papashvily, Helen (Waite) 1906- 81-84
See also SATA 17
Papazian, Dennis R(ichard) 1931- 45-48
Papazoglou, Orania 1951- 126
Pape, D. L.
See Pape, Donna (Lugg)
Pape, Donna (Lugg) 1930- CANR-25
Earlier sketches in CA 21-24R, CANR-9
See also SATA 2
Pape, Gordon 1936- CANR-25
Earlier sketch in CA 105
Pape, Greg 1947- 113
Papenfuse, Edward C(arl) Jr. 1943- CANR-8
Earlier sketch in CA 57-60
Paper, Herbert H(arry) 1925- CANR-1
Earlier sketch in CA 45-48
Paper, Lewis J(ay) 1946- Brief entry 114
Paperny, Myra (Green) 1932- 69-72
See also SATA 33, 51
Papert, Emma N. 1926- 101
Papi, G(iuseppe) Ugo 1893- 25-28R
Papich, Stephen 1925- 69-72
Papier, Judith Barnard 1932- 21-24R
Papin, Joseph 1914- 65-68
Papineau, David 1947- 130
Papini, Giovanni 1881-1956 Brief entry 121
See also TCLC 22
Papp, Charles Steven 1917- CANR-15
Earlier sketch in CA 41-44R
Pappageotes, George C(hristos)
1926-1963 ....CANR-2
Earlier sketch in CA 1-4R
Pappas, George 1929- 29-32R
Pappas, Lou Seibert 1930- CANR-23
Earlier sketches in CA 61-64, CANR-8
Pappworth, M(aurice) H(enry) 1910- 21-24R
Paprika
See Holmvik, Oyvind
Papus
See Encausse, Gerard (Anaclet Vincent)
Paquet, Alfons 1881-1944 ....DLB 66
Paradeise, Catherine 1946- 138
Paradis, Adrian A(lexis) 1912- CANR-18
Earlier sketches in CA 1-4R, CANR-3
See also SAAS 8
See also SATA 1, 67
Paradis, James G(ardiner) 1942- 93-96
Paradis, Marjorie Bartholomew
1886(?)-1970 73-76
Obituary 29-32R
See also SATA 17
Paradis, Suzanne 1936- ....DLB 53
Paradise, Louis V(incent) 1946- 114
Paradise, Paul R. 1950- 137
Parakh, Jal Sohrab 1932- Brief entry 105
Parandowski, Jan 1895- CAP-1
Earlier sketch in CA 11-12
Parasol, Peter
See Stevens, Wallace
Parasuram, T(attamangalam) V(iswanatha Iyer)
1923- 106
Paratore, Angela 1912- 13-16R
Parchman, William E(ugene) 1936- 93-96
Pardee, Michael 1945- 113
Pardey, Larry
See Pardey, Lawrence Fred
Pardey, Lawrence Fred 1939- 93-96
Pardey, (Mary) Lin 1944- 93-96
Paredes, Americo 1915- 37-40R
See also HW
Pareek, Udai (Narain) 1925- CANR-28
Earlier sketches in CA 21-24R, CANR-11
Parelius, Ann Parker 1943- 81-84
Parelius, Robert J. 1941- 81-84
Parens, Henri 1928- 89-92
Parent, David J(oseph) 1931- CANR-9
Earlier sketch in CA 57-60
Parent, Gail 1940- 101
Parent, Ronald 1937-1982 Obituary 107
Parent, William A. 1944- 127
Parente, Pascal P(rosper) 1890-1971 ....CAP-1
Obituary 33-36R
Earlier sketch in CA 17-18
Parente, Sarah (Eleanor) 1913- CANR-16
Earlier sketch in CA 41-44R
Parenteau, Shirley Laurolyn 1935- CANR-33
Earlier sketches in CA 85-88, CANR-15
See also SATA 40, 47
Parenti, Michael 1933- 73-76
Pares, Marion (Stapylton) 1914- CANR-12
Earlier sketch in CA 17-20R
Paret, Peter 1924- Brief entry 114
Paretsky, Sara 1947- 129
Brief entry 125
See also BEST 90:3
Paretti, Sandra CANR-7
Earlier sketch in CA 53-56
Parezo, Nancy Jean 1951- 114
Parfenie, Maria
See Codrescu, Andrei
Parfit, Michael 1947- 119
Parfitt, George (Albert Ekins) 1939- CANR-26
Earlier sketch in CA 109
Parfitt, Tudor (Vernon) 1944- 123
Pargeter, Edith Mary 1913- CANR-24
Earlier sketches in CA 1-4R, CANR-4
See also MTCW
Parham, Joseph Byars 1919-1980 65-68
Obituary 135
Parham, Robert Randall 1943- 57-60
Parham, William Thomas 1913- CANR-20
Earlier sketch in CA 103
Parham, William 1914- 103
Parini, Jay (Lee) 1948- CANR-32
Earlier sketch in CA 97-100
See also CAAS 16
See also CLC 54
Parins, James William 1939- 109
Paris, Arthur E. 127
Paris, Bernard J. 1931- CANR-7
Earlier sketch in CA 17-20R
Paris, Erna 1938- 105
Paris, Ginette 1946- 123
Paris, Jeanne 1918- 1-4R
Paris, Michael 1949- 135
Paris, Mike
See Paris, Michael
Parise, Goffredo 1929-1986 132
Obituary 120
Pariseau, Earl J(oseph) 1928- 9-12R
Parish, Charles 1927- 25-28R
Parish, David 1932- CANR-14
Earlier sketch in CA 73-76
Parish, Helen Rand 1912- Brief entry 115
Parish, James Robert 1944- CANR-37
Earlier sketch in CA 33-36R
Parish, James 1904-1973 Obituary 114
Parish, Margaret Cecile 1927-1988 ....CANR-38
Obituary 127
Earlier sketches in CA 73-76, CANR-18
See also Parish, Peggy
See also MAICYA
Parish, Margaret Holt
See Holt, Margaret
Parish, Peggy
See Parish, Margaret Cecile
See also CLR 22
See also SATA 17, 59
Parish, Peter J(oseph) 1929- 57-60
Parish, Townsend
See Pietschmann, Richard John III
Parisi, Joseph 1944- 93-96
Parizeau, Alice 1930- ....DLB 60
Park, Barbara 1947- 113
See also SATA 35, 40
Park, Bert Edward 1947- 128
Park, Bill
See Park, W(illiam) B(ryan)
See also SATA 22
Park, Charles F(rederick) Jr. 1903- 57-60
Park, Clara Claiborne 1923- CANR-39
Earlier sketch in CA 21-24R
Park, D. U.
See Woods, Clee
Park, David 1919- 105
Park, Ed 1930- 73-76
Park, Edwards 1917- 123
Park, Elm
See Dunbar, Charles Stuart
Park, George 1925- 77-80
Park, James (Robert) 1956- 120
Park, James William 1936- 121
Park, Joe 1913- 21-24R
Park, Jordan
See Kornbluth, C(yril) M.
and Pohl, Frederik
Park, Joseph H. 1890(?)-1979 Obituary 89-92
Park, Maeva
See Dobner, Maeva Park
Park, O'Hyun 1940- 53-56
Park, Paul (Claiborne) 1954- 128
Park, Peter 1929- 29-32R
Park, Richard L(eonard) 1920- 77-80
Park, Robert E(zra) 1864-1944 Brief entry 122
Park, Robert L. 1932- 89-92
Park, (Rosina) Ruth 105
See also SATA 25
Park, Sung-Bae 1933- 115
Park, W(illiam) B(ryan) 1936- CANR-39
Earlier sketches in CA 97-100, CANR-17
See also Park, Bill
See also SATA 22
Park, William John 1930- 49-52
Park Chung Hee 1917-1979 ....CANR-10
Obituary 97-100
Earlier sketch in CA 61-64
Parke, Herbert William 1903- 105
Parke, John 1754-1789 ....DLB 31
Parke, Margaret Bittner 1901- 89-92
Parke, Richard H. 1909(?)-1989 Obituary 128
Parke, Ross D(uke) 1938- CANR-38
Earlier sketches in CA 45-48, CANR-1, 16
Parker, Adrian David 1947- 103
Parker, Alexander A(ugustine) 1908- CANR-16
Earlier sketch in CA 21-24R
Parker, Alfred Browning 1916- 17-20R

Parker, Ann
See Neal, Ann Parker
Parker, Arthur C(aswell)
1881-1955 Brief entry 115
Parker, Barry (Richard) 1935- CANR-31
Earlier sketch in CA 112
Parker, Beatrice
See Huff, T(om) E.
Parker, Bert
See Ellison, Harlan
Parker, Bertha Morris 1890-1980 ....CANR-5
Obituary 102
Earlier sketch in CA 5-8R
Parker, Betty June 1929- CANR-22
Earlier sketches in CA 57-60, CANR-7
Parker, Beulah 1912- 81-84
Parker, Brant Julian 1920- Brief entry 114
Parker, Brother Michael
See Parker, Kenneth L(eroy)
Parker, Clifford S(tetson) 1891- 5-8R
Parker, Clyde A. 1927- 41-44R
Parker, David B. 1956- 135
Parker, David L(ambert) 1935- 108
Parker, David Marshall 1929- 77-80
Parker, David 1941- 132
Parker, Dee
See Parker, David L(ambert)
Parker, (William George) Derek 1932- CANR-23
Earlier sketch in CA 29-32R
Parker, Don(ald) H(enry) 1912- CANR-6
Earlier sketch in CA 5-8R
Parker, Donald Dean 1899-1983 ....CANR-34
Earlier sketch in CA 37-40R
Parker, Donn B(lanchard) 1929- CANR-9
Earlier sketch in CA 65-68
Parker, Dorothy Mills CANR-11
Earlier sketch in CA 21-24R
Parker, Dorothy (Rothschild) 1893-1967 .... CAP-2
Obituary 25-28R
Earlier sketch in CA 19-20
See also CLC 15, 68
See also DLB 11, 45, 86
See also MTCW
See also SSC 2
Parker, Dorothy 1922- 93-96
Parker, Douglas Hugh 1926- 1-4R
Parker, Edna Jean 1935- 101
Parker, Edwin B(urke) 1932- 13-16R
Parker, Elinor Milnor 1906- CANR-3
Earlier sketch in CA 1-4R
See also SATA 3
Parker, Elliott S(evern) 1939- 103
Parker, Francis H(oward) 1920- 21-24R
Parker, Frank J(oseph) 1940- 49-52
Parker, Frank R. 1940- 136
Parker, Franklin D(allas) 1918- 13-16R
Parker, Franklin 1921- CANR-22
Earlier sketches in CA 33-36R, CANR-7
Parker, Gail Thain 1943- 104
Parker, Geoffrey 1933- 49-52
Parker, Gilbert 1860-1932 ....DLB 99
Parker, Gordon 1940- 103
Parker, H(enry) M(ichael) D(enne)
1896(?)-1971 Obituary 104
Parker, Harold T(albot) 1907- CANR-9
Earlier sketch in CA 21-24R
Parker, Hershel 1935- CANR-30
Earlier sketches in CA 33-36R, CANR-13
Parker, Howard J(ohn) 1948- 57-60
Parker, J(ohn) Carlyle 1931- CANR-24
Earlier sketches in CA 57-60, CANR-7
Parker, Jack Horace 1914- 113
Parker, James
See Newby, Eric
Parker, James Reid 1909-1984 Obituary 111
Parker, James 1714(?)-1770 ....DLB 43
Parker, Jean
See Sharat Chandra, G(ubbi) S(hankara Chetty)
Parker, Joan H. 1932- 85-88
Parker, John
See Wyatt, John
Parker, (Herbert) John (Harvey)
1906-1987 ....CANR-34
Obituary 124
Earlier sketch in CA 5-8R
Parker, John Thomas 1950- 118
Parker, John 1923- CANR-5
Earlier sketch in CA 5-8R
Parker, Julia (Louise) 1932- CANR-23
Earlier sketch in CA 101
Parker, Kenneth L(eroy) 1954- 132
Parker, Kristy 1957- 126
See also SATA 59
Parker, Laura
See Castoro, Laura A(nn)
Parker, Lois M(ay) 1912- CANR-39
Earlier sketches in CA 69-72, CANR-11
See also SATA 30
Parker, Margot M. 1937- 122
See also SATA 52
Parker, Marsha Zurich 1952- 107
Parker, Mary Jessie 1948- ....SATA 71
Parker, Nancy Winslow 1930- CANR-22
Earlier sketches in CA 49-52, CANR-1
See also MAICYA
See also SATA 10, 69
Parker, Nathan Carlyle 1960- 102
Parker, Pat 1944- 57-60
Parker, Percy Spurlark 1940- 53-56
Parker, Peter (Robert Nevill) 1954- 136
Parker, Richard 1915- 73-76
See also SATA 14
Parker, Robert
See Boyd, Waldo T.
Parker, Robert Allerton
1889(?)-1970 Obituary 29-32R
Parker, Robert B(rown) 1932- CANR-26
Earlier sketches in CA 49-52, CANR-1
See also BEST 89:4
See also CLC 27
See also MTCW
Parker, Robert Miles 1939- 118
Parker, Robert Stewart 1915- 103
Parker, Robert 1920- CANR-13
Earlier sketch in CA 77-80
Parker, Rolland (Sandau) 1928- CANR-2
Earlier sketch in CA 45-48
Parker, Ron
See Parker, Ronald B(ruce)
Parker, Ronald B(ruce) 1932- 117
Parker, Ronald K(eith) 1939- 108
Parker, Rowland 1912-1989 ....CANR-10
Obituary 128
Earlier sketch in CA 65-68
Parker, Sanford S.
1919(?)-1980 Obituary 97-100
Parker, Scott 1950- 113
Parker, Stanley R(obert) 1927- CANR-19
Earlier sketch in CA 103
Parker, Stephen Jan 1939- 118
Parker, (James) Stewart 1941-1988 ....CANR-32
Obituary 127
Earlier sketch in CA 103
Parker, T(homas) H(enry) L(ouis)
1916- CANR-6
Earlier sketch in CA 5-8R
Parker, Theodore 1810-1860 ....DLB 1
Parker, Thomas F(rancis) 1932- 73-76
Parker, Thomas Maynard 1906- CAP-2
Earlier sketch in CA 17-18
Parker, Tom
See Parker, John Thomas
Parker, Tom 1943- 130
Parker, W(illiam) H(enry) 1912- CANR-13
Earlier sketch in CA 33-36R
Parker, W(ilford) Oren 1911- 41-44R
Parker, Watson 1924- 106
Parker, William Riley 1906-1968 ....CAP-2
Earlier sketch in CA 17-18
See also DLB 103
Parker, Willie J. 1924- 77-80
Parker, Wyman W(est) 1912- 13-16R
Parkerson, John 1885(?)-1978 Obituary 77-80
Parkes, Colin Murray 1928- 81-84
Parkes, Graham 1949- 127
Parkes, Henry B. 1904-1972 Obituary 33-36R
Parkes, James William 1896-1981 Obituary 104
Parkes, K. Stuart 1943- 127
Parkes, Lucas
See Harris, John (Wyndham Parkes Lucas) Beynon
Parkes, (Grahem) Roger 1933- 53-56
Parkes, Terence 1927- 104
Parket, I(rwin) Robert 1931- 114
Parkhill, Forbes 1892- 1-4R
Parkhill, John
See Cox, William R(obert)
Parkhill, Wilson 1901- 5-8R
Parkhurst, Helen 1887-1973 Obituary 41-44R
Parkhurst, Louis Gifford Jr. 1946- 113
Parkhurst, Winthrop 1892(?)-1983 Obituary 110
Parkin, Alan 1934- 29-32R
Parkin, David 1940- CANR-30
Earlier sketches in CA 25-28R, CANR-13
Parkin, Frank 1940- ....CLC 43
Parkin, G(eorge) Raleigh
1896-1977(?) Obituary 106
Parkin, Molly 1932- 104
Parkin, Peter Hubert 1917-1984 Obituary 113
Parkinson, C(yril) Northcote 1909- CANR-5
Earlier sketch in CA 5-8R
Parkinson, (Frederick) Charles Douglas
1916- CAP-1
Earlier sketch in CA 11-12
Parkinson, Claire L(ucille) 1948- 120
Parkinson, Cornelia M. 1925- CANR-15
Earlier sketch in CA 81-84
Parkinson, Ethelyn M(inerva) 1906- CANR-1
Earlier sketch in CA 49-52
See also SATA 11
Parkinson, J(ohn) R(ichard) 1922- 102
Parkinson, Kathryn N. 1954- 120
See also Parkinson, Kathy
Parkinson, Kathy
See Parkinson, Kathryn N.
See also SATA 71
Parkinson, Michael 1944- CANR-27
Earlier sketch in CA 29-32R
Parkinson, Roger 1939-1978 106
Parkinson, Thomas (Francis)
1920-1992 ....CANR-3
Obituary 136
Earlier sketch in CA 5-8R
Parkinson, Thomas P(aul) 102
Parkinson, Tom
See Parkinson, Thomas P(aul)
Parkman, Francis Jr. 1823-1893 ....DLB 1, 30
Parks, Aileen Wells 1901- 5-8R
Parks, Arva Moore 1939- 103
Parks, David 1944- 25-28R
Parks, Douglas R(ichard) 1942- 111
Parks, Edd Winfield 1906-1968 ....5-8R
See also SATA 10
Parks, Edmund 1911- 69-72
Parks, Edna D(orintha) 1910- 13-16R
Parks, Gordon (Alexander Buchanan)
1912- CANR-26
Earlier sketch in CA 41-44R
See also AITN 2
See also BLC 3
See also BW
See also CLC 1, 16
See also DLB 33
See also SATA 8
Parks, Joseph Howard 1903- 1-4R
Parks, Lloyd Clifford 1922- 57-60
Parks, Michael 1943- 126
Parks, Pat 1918- 61-64
Parks, Robert James 1940- 65-68
Parks, Stephen Robert 1940- 65-68
Parks, Tim(othy Harold) 1954- 131
Brief entry 126
Parks, Van Dyke 1943- ....SATA 62
Parks, William 1698(?)-1750 ....DLB 43
Parksmith, George
See Bush, George S(idney)
Parlakian, Nishan 1925- 133
Parlato, Salvatore J(oseph) Jr. 1936- 73-76
Parlett, David (Sidney) 1939- CANR-20
Earlier sketch in CA 103
Parley, Peter
See Goodrich, Samuel Griswold
Parlin, Bradley W(illiam) 1938- 69-72
Parlin, John
See Graves, Charles Parlin
Parma, Clemens
See Menzel, Roderich
Parman, Donald L(ee) 1932- 65-68
Parmelee, Alice 1903- CAP-2
Earlier sketch in CA 21-22
Parmenter, Ross 1912- 17-20R
Parmer, J(ess) Norman 1925- 5-8R
Parmet, Herbert S. 1929- CANR-11
Earlier sketch in CA 21-24R
Parmet, Robert D(avid) 1938- 77-80
Parmet, Simon 1897- CAP-1
Earlier sketch in CA 13-14
Parnaby, Owen Wilfred 1921- 9-12R
Parnall, Peter 1936- 81-84
See also MAICYA
See also SAAS 11
See also SATA 16, 69
Parnas, Raymond I. 1937- 33-36R
Parnell, (David) Michael 1934- 130
Parnell, Thomas 1679-1718 ....DLB 94
Parnes, Herbert S(aul) 1919- CANR-34
Earlier sketches in CA 41-44R, CANR-15
Parnes, Sidmore 1928-1984 Obituary 113
Parnes, Sidney J. 1922- CANR-10
Earlier sketch in CA 21-24R
Paroissien, David (Harry) 1939- 111
Parot, Joseph (John) 1940- 126
Parque, Richard (Anthony) 1935- 124
Parr, A. H.
See Parr, Adolf Henry
Parr, Adolf Henry 1900-1990 Obituary 132
Parr, Charles McKew 1884- CAP-1
Earlier sketch in CA 11-12
Parr, James A(llan) 1936- 49-52
Parr, John (Lloyd) 1928- 102
Parr, Letitia (Evelyn) 1906- 103
See also SATA 37
Parr, Lucy 1924- 29-32R
See also SATA 10
Parr, Michael 1927- 17-20R
Parra, Nicanor 1914- CANR-32
Earlier sketch in CA 85-88
See also CLC 2
See also HW
See also MTCW
Parramore, Thomas C(ustis) 1932- 112
Parrinder, E(dward) Geoffrey 1910- CANR-10
Earlier sketch in CA 21-24R
Parrinder, (John) Patrick 1944- 127
Parrington, Vernon L(ouis)
1871-1929 Brief entry 113
See also DLB 17, 63
Parrini, Carl P. 1933- Brief entry 107
Parrino, John J(oseph) 1942- 101
Parrino, Michael 1915(?)-1976 Obituary 65-68
Parriott, Sara 1953- 107
Parris, Addison W(ilson) 1923-1975 ....CAP-2
Earlier sketch in CA 25-28
Parris, Guichard 1903-1990 81-84
Obituary 133
Parris, Judith (Ann) H(eimlich) 1939- 57-60
Parris, Matthew (Francis) 1949- 134
Parrish, Anne 1888-1957 Brief entry 115
See also SATA 27
Parrish, Bernard P. 1936- 103
Parrish, Bernie
See Parrish, Bernard P.
Parrish, Carl (George) 1904-1965 ....5-8R
Parrish, Eugene
See Harding, Donald Edward
Parrish, John A(lbert) 1939- 37-40R
Parrish, Louis 1927- Brief entry 107
Parrish, Mary
See Cousins, Margaret
Parrish, Mary Frances
See Fisher, M(ary) F(rances) K(ennedy)
Parrish, (Frederick) Maxfield
1870-1966 ....SATA 14
Parrish, Michael E. 1942- 29-32R
Parrish, Patt
See Bucheister, Patt
Parrish, Robert (Reese) 1916- 81-84
Parrish, Stephen Maxfield 1921- 104
Parrish, Thomas (Douglas) 1927- 93-96
Parrish, Wayland Maxfield 1887- CAP-2
Earlier sketch in CA 23-24
Parrish, Wendy (Louise) 1950-1977 73-76
Obituary 133
Parrish, William E(arl) 1931- CANR-3
Earlier sketch in CA 1-4R
Parrott, Bruce 1945- 128
Parrott, Cecil (Cuthbert) 1909-1984 103
Obituary 113
Parrott, Fred J(ames) 1913- 41-44R
Parrott, Ian 1916- CANR-2
Earlier sketch in CA 5-8R
Parrott, (Alonzo) Leslie 1922- 97-100
Parrott, Lindesay 1901-1987 Obituary 123
Parrott, Lora Lee 1923- 25-28R
Parry, Albert 1901- CANR-6
Earlier sketch in CA 1-4R
Parry, Caroline (Balderston) 1945- 128
Parry, Clive 1917-1982 Obituary 107
Parry, David 1908- 113
Parry, Ellwood C(omly) III 1941- 93-96
Parry, Hugh J(ones) 1916- 13-16R
Parry, J(ohn) H(orace) 1914- CANR-6
Earlier sketch in CA 5-8R
Parry, John
See Whelpton, (George) Eric
Parry, Linda (Alberta) 1945- 111
Parry, Marian 1924- 41-44R
See also SATA 13
Parry, Michael Patrick 1947- 101
Parry, Thomas H. 1904-1985 Obituary 116
Parry-Jones, Daniel 1891- 13-16R
Parseghian, Ara (Raoul) 1923- Brief entry 105
Parsegian, V(ozcan) Lawrence 1908- 57-60
Parsifal
See Curl, James Stevens
Parsloe, Guy Charles 1900- CAP-1
Earlier sketch in CA 13-14
Parson, Mary Jean 1934- 133
Parson, Ruben L(eRoy) 1907- 13-16R
Parson Lot
See Kingsley, Charles
Parsons, C(hristopher) J(ames) 1941- 103
Parsons, Charles (Dacre) 1933- 45-48
Parsons, Charles H(enry III) 1940- 134
Parsons, Coleman O(scar) 1905-1991 ....CAP-1
Obituary 134
Earlier sketch in CA 13-16
Parsons, Cynthia 1926- CANR-21
Earlier sketch in CA 45-48
Parsons, Denys 1914- CANR-12
Earlier sketch in CA 13-16R
Parsons, Ellen
See Dragonwagon, Crescent
Parsons, Elmer E. 1919- 25-28R
Parsons, Frances M. 1923- 129
Parsons, Geoffrey 1908-1981 Obituary 105
Parsons, Harriet Oettinger
1906(?)-1983(?) Obituary 108
Parsons, Howard L(ee) 1918- CANR-17
Earlier sketches in CA 49-52, CANR-1
Parsons, Ian (Macnaghten) 1906-1980 97-100
Obituary 102
Parsons, Jack 1920- 104
Parsons, James Bunyan 1921- 29-32R
Parsons, John (Anthony) 1938- 120
Parsons, Kermit Carlyle 1927- 29-32R
Parsons, Kitty 13-16R
Obituary 120
Parsons, Louella (Oettinger) 1881-1972 93-96
Obituary 37-40R
Parsons, Malcolm Barningham
1919- Brief entry 108
Parsons, Martin 1907- 53-56
Parsons, Paul 1952- 132
Parsons, R(ichard) A(ugustus) 101
Parsons, Stanley B. Jr. 1927- CANR-21
Earlier sketch in CA 45-48
Parsons, Talcott 1902-1979 ....CANR-35
Obituary 85-88
Earlier sketches in CA 5-8R, CANR-4
See also MTCW
Parsons, Thornton H(arris) 1921- 73-76
Parsons, Tom
See MacPherson, Thomas George
Parsons, William Edward Jr. 1936- 21-24R
Parsons, William T(homas) 1923- 65-68
Partain, Floydene 1924- 114
Partch, Virgil Franklin II 1916-1984 108
Obituary 113
See also SATA 39, 45
Partington, F. H.
See Yoxall, Harry W(aldo)
Partington, Martin 1944- 124
Partington, Susan Trowbridge 1924- 9-12R
Partlow, Vern 1910(?)-1987 Obituary 121
Partner, Peter (David) 1924- 85-88
Parton, Anthony 1959- 133
Parton, James 1822-1891 ....DLB 30
Parton, Margaret 1915- 97-100
Parton, Sara Payson Willis
1811-1872 ....DLB 43, 74
Partridge, Anthony
See Oppenheim, E(dward) Phillips
Partridge, Astley Cooper 1901- 103
Partridge, Benjamin W(aring) Jr. 1915- 25-28R
See also SATA 28
Partridge, Derek 1945- 135
Partridge, Edward B(ellamy) 1916- 65-68
Partridge, Elinore Hughes 1937- 115
Partridge, Eric (Honeywood)
1894-1979 ....CANR-3
Obituary 85-88
Earlier sketch in CA 1-4R
Partridge, Ernest 1935- 115
Partridge, Frances (Catherine) 1900- CANR-30
Earlier sketch in CA 29-32R
Partridge, Jenny (Lilian) 1947- CANR-26
Earlier sketch in CA 109
See also SATA 37, 52
Partridge, Larry (Harold) 1949- 114
Partridge, William L(ee) 1944- CANR-1
Earlier sketch in CA 45-48
Parulski, George R(ichard) Jr. 1954- CANR-17
Earlier sketch in CA 97-100
Parvin, Betty 1916- CANR-17
Earlier sketch in CA 97-100
Parx, C. C.
See Gilmore, Christopher Cook

Parzen, Herbert 1896- 25-28R
Pasachoff, Jay M(yron) 1943- 117
Pasamanik, Luisa 1930- 101
Pasarell, Emilio J(ulio) 1891- ....HW
Pascal, Anthony H(enry) 1933- CANR-16
Earlier sketch in CA 29-32R
Pascal, David 1918- 9-12R
See also SATA 14
Pascal, Francine 1938- CANR-39
Brief entry 115
Earlier sketch in CA 123
See also AAYA 1
See also CLR 25
See also MAICYA
See also SATA 37, 51
Pascal, Gerald Ross 1907-1984 ....37-40R
Obituary 133
Pascal, John Robert 1932(?)-1981 Obituary 102
Pascal, Paul 1925- 21-24R
Pascal, Roy 1904-1980 ....CANR-6
Earlier sketch in CA 5-8R
Pascale, Richard Tanner 1938- CANR-25
Earlier sketch in CA 53-56
Pascarella, Perry (James) 1934- 93-96
Paschal, George H. Jr. 1925- 29-32R
Paschal, Nancy
See Trotter, Grace V(iolet)
Paschall, H. Franklin 1922- 25-28R
Pascoe, Elaine 1946- 124
Pascoe, Elizabeth Jean 69-72
Pascoe, John (Dobree) 1908-1972 ....CAP-1
Earlier sketch in CA 13-14
Pascoe, Peggy 1954- 136
Pascoli, Giovanni 1855-1912 ....TCLC 45
Pascu, Stefan 1914- 117
Pascudniak, Pascal
See Lupoff, Richard A(llen)
Pasewark, William R(obert) 1924- CANR-35
Earlier sketches in CA 33-36R, CANR-15
Pashko, Stanley 1913- 97-100
See also SATA 29
Pasick, Robert 1946- 134
Pasinetti, P(ier-) M(aria) 1913- 73-76
Pask, Gordon 1928- 111
Pask, Raymond (Frank) 1944- CANR-22
Earlier sketch in CA 105
Paskowicz, Patricia
See Molan, Pat Carlson
Pasley, Virginia Schmitz
1905-1986 Obituary 119
Pasmanik, Wolf 1924- 101
Pasolini, Pier Paolo 1922-1975 93-96
Obituary 61-64
See also CLC 20, 37
See also MTCW
Pasqua, Thomas M(ario) Jr. 1938- 131
Pasqua, Tom
See Pasqua, Thomas M(ario) Jr.
Pasquier, Marie-Claire 1933- 29-32R
Pasquini
See Silone, Ignazio
Pass, Gail 1940- 65-68
Passage, Charles Edward 1913-1983 ....33-36R
Obituary 110
Passailaigue, Thomas E.
See Paisley, Tom
Passantino, Gretchen 1953- 110
Passantino, Robert Louis 1951- 108
Passel, Anne W(onders) 1918- CANR-11
Earlier sketch in CA 29-32R
Passell, Peter 1944- CANR-2
Earlier sketch in CA 45-48
Passerin D'Entreves, Alessandro 1902- 69-72
Passeron, Rene (Jean) 1920- CANR-17
Earlier sketch in CA 97-100
Passes(-Pazolski), Alan 1943- 85-88
Passin, Herbert 1916- CANR-20
Earlier sketches in CA 45-48, CANR-1
Passman, Brian 1934- 25-28R
Passmore, John (Arthur) 1914- CANR-6
Earlier sketch in CA 13-16R
Passmore, Richard E. Obituary 107
Passonneau, Joseph Russell 1921- 17-20R
Passow, A(aron) Harry 1920- CANR-3
Earlier sketch in CA 1-4R
Passwater, Richard (Albert) 1937- CANR-19
Earlier sketch in CA 97-100
Past, Ray(mond Edgar) 1918- 29-32R
Pastan, Linda (Olenik) 1932- CANR-18
Earlier sketch in CA 61-64
See also CLC 27
See also DLB 5
Pasternack, Stefan Alan 1939- Brief entry 108
Pasternak, Boris (Leonidovich) 1890-1960 127
Obituary 116
See also CLC 7, 10, 18, 63
See also MTCW
See also WLC
Pasternak, Burton 1933- 127
Brief entry 109
Pasternak, Velvel 1933- 73-76
Pastine, Maureen (Diane) 1944- CANR-8
Earlier sketch in CA 57-60
Paston, Herbert S. 1928- 49-52
Pastor, Robert (Alan) 1947- 105
Pastore, Arthur R(alph) Jr. 1922- 17-20R
Pastore, Nicholas 1916- 29-32R
Pastorius, Francis Daniel 1651-1720(?) ....DLB 24
Pastor X
See Johnson, Merle Allison
Pastos, Spero 1940- 126
Paszkowski, Jan Krok
See Krok-Paszkowski, Jan
Patai, Daphne 1943- CANR-33
Earlier sketch in CA 113
Patai, Raphael 1910- CANR-33
Earlier sketches in CA 29-32R, CANR-20
Pataky, Denes 1921- 13-16R
Patanne, Maria
See La Pietra, Mary
Patapoff, Elizabeth 1917- 29-32R
Patchen, Kenneth 1911-1972 ....CANR-35
Obituary 33-36R
Earlier sketches in CA 1-4R, CANR-3
See also CLC 1, 2, 18
See also DLB 16, 48
See also MTCW
Patchen, Martin 1932- 57-60
Patchett, Mary (Osborne) Elwyn 1897- CANR-3
Earlier sketch in CA 5-8R
Pate, Billie 1932- 61-64
Pate, Martha B. Lucas 1912-1983 Obituary 110
Patel, Harshad C(hhotabhia) 1934- 53-56
Patel, I(ndraprasad) G(ordhanbhai) 1924- 126
Pateman, Carole 1940- 85-88
Pateman, Kim
See Levin, Kim
Pateman, Trevor 1947- 49-52
Patent, Dorothy Hinshaw 1940- CANR-24
Earlier sketches in CA 61-64, CANR-9
See also CLR 19
See also MAICYA
See also SAAS 13
See also SATA 22, 69
Pater, Walter (Horatio)
1839-1894 ....CDBLB 1832-1890
See also DLB 57
Paterson, A(ndrew) B(arton)
1864-1941 ....TCLC 32
Paterson, Alistair (Ian Hughes) 1929- 107
Paterson, Allen P(eter) 1933- 93-96
Paterson, Ann 1916- 33-36R
Paterson, Barbara (Olive) 1933- 112
Paterson, Diane (R. Cole) 1946- 101
See also SATA 33, 59
Paterson, George W(illiam) 1931- 103
Paterson, Hugh
See Bower, Ursula Violet Graham
Paterson, Huntley
See Ludovici, Anthony M(ario)
Paterson, John Harris 1923- CANR-6
Earlier sketch in CA 5-8R
Paterson, John 1887- CAP-1
Earlier sketch in CA 13-14
Paterson, Judith
See Jones, Judith Paterson
Paterson, Katherine (Womeldorf)
1932- CANR-28
Earlier sketch in CA 21-24R
See also AAYA 1
See also CLC 12, 30
See also CLR 7
See also DLB 52
See also MAICYA
See also MTCW
See also SATA 13, 53
Paterson, (James Edmund) Neil 1916- 13-16R
Paterson, R(onald) W(illiam) K(eith)
1933- 33-36R
Paterson, Thomas G(raham) 1941- CANR-16
Earlier sketches in CA 45-48, CANR-1
Paterson, William E(dgar) 1941- CANR-13
Earlier sketch in CA 61-64
Paterson-Jones, Judith
See Jones, Judith Paterson
Patinkin, Don 1922- CANR-10
Earlier sketch in CA 17-20R
Patinkin, Mark 1953- 133
Patka, Frederick 1922- 9-12R
Patman, (John William) Wright 1893-1976 109
Obituary 107
Patmore, Coventry Kersey Dighton
1823-1896 ....DLB 35, 98
Patmore, Derek Coventry 1908-1972 ....5-8R
Obituary 103
Patmore, John Allan 1931- 104
Patner, Andrew 1959- 128
Paton, Alan (Stewart) 1903-1988 ....CANR-22
Obituary 125
Earlier sketches in CAP-1, CA 13-16
See also CLC 4, 10, 25, 55
See also MTCW
See also SATA 11, 56
See also WLC
Paton, David Macdonald 1913- 114
Paton, George (Whitecross) 1902- CAP-1
Earlier sketch in CA 11-12
Paton, Herbert James 1887-1969 ....CAP-1
Earlier sketch in CA 13-14
Paton, Jane (Elizabeth) 1934- ....SATA 35
Paton, Joseph Noel 1821-1901 ....DLB 35
Paton, Steven C. 1928(?)-1980 Obituary 97-100
Paton Walsh, Gillian 1939- CANR-38
See also Walsh, Jill Paton
See also MAICYA
See also SAAS 3
See also SATA 4
Paton Walsh, Jill
See Paton Walsh, Gillian
Patoski, Margaret (Nancy Pearson) 1930- 69-72
Patra, Atul Chandra 1915- 57-60
Patras, Louis 1931- CANR-15
Earlier sketch in CA 85-88
Patrice, Ann
See Galbraith, Georgie Starbuck
Patrick, Alison (Mary Houston) 1921- 49-52
Patrick, Clarence H(odges) 1907- 33-36R
Patrick, Cuthbert Melvin
1914-1985 Obituary 116
Patrick, Douglas Arthur 1905- 17-20R
Patrick, Hugh 1930- 41-44R
Patrick, J(ohn) Max 1911- CANR-5
Earlier sketch in CA 5-8R
Patrick, James (Arthur) 1933- CANR-20
Earlier sketch in CA 104
Patrick, John 1905- 89-92
See also DLB 7
Patrick, Johnstone G(illespie) 1918- CANR-2
Earlier sketch in CA 5-8R
Patrick, Leal
See Stone, Patti
Patrick, Lilian
See Keogh, Lilian Gilmore
Patrick, Martha 1956- 109
Patrick, Maxine
See Maxwell, Patricia
Patrick, Q.
See Wheeler, Hugh (Callingham)
Patrick, Rembert Wallace 1909-1967 ....5-8R
Obituary 134
Patrick, Robert 1937- CANR-30
Earlier sketches in CA 45-48, CANR-1
See also AITN 2
Patrick, Vincent 1935- CANR-22
Earlier sketch in CA 104
Patrick, Walton Richard 1909- 37-40R
Patrides, C(onstantinos) A(postolos)
1930- CANR-20
Earlier sketches in CA 13-16R, CANR-5
Patrikeyev
See
Healey-Kay, (Sydney Francis) Patrick (Chippendall)
Patrouch, Joseph F(rancis) Jr. 1935- 49-52
Patsauq, Markoosie 1942- 101
See also Markoosie
Patsouras, Louis
See Patras, Louis
Pattee, Fred Lewis 1863-1950 ....DLB 71
Pattee, Howard Hunt Jr. 1926- Brief entry 109
Pattemore, Arnel W(ilfred) 1934- 53-56
Patten, Bebe H(arrison) 1913- 61-64
Patten, Brian 1946- 25-28R
See also SATA 29
Patten, Lewis B(yford) 1915-1981 ....CANR-21
Obituary 103
Earlier sketch in CA 25-28R
Patten, Nigel 1940- 25-28R
Patten, Priscilla C(arla) 1950- 117
Patten, (Bebe) Rebecca 1950- 117
Patten, Robert L(owry) 1939- 109
Patten, Thomas H. Jr. 1929- 21-24R
Patterson, A(lfred) Temple 1902-1983 103
Obituary 111
Patterson, Alicia Brooks
1906-1963 Obituary 89-92
Patterson, Barbara 1944- 110
Patterson, Benton Rain 1929- 122
Patterson, Bradley H. Jr. 1921- 136
Patterson, C(ecil) H(olden) 1912- CANR-16
Earlier sketch in CA 21-24R
Patterson, Carolyn Bennett 1921- 106
Patterson, Charles D(arold) 1928- 122
Patterson, Charles E(dwin) Jr. 1934- 41-44R
Patterson, Charles H(enry) 1896- 37-40R
Patterson, Charles 1935- 117
See also SATA 59
Patterson, Charlotte (Buist) 1942- 29-32R
Patterson, Craig E(ugene) 1945- 93-96
Patterson, David S(ands) 1937- 65-68
Patterson, Edwin W(ilhite) 1889-1965 ....CANR-27
Earlier sketch in CA 1-4R
Patterson, Eleanor Medill
1881(?)-1948 Brief entry 118
See also DLB 29
Patterson, Elinor Josephine
See Patterson, Eleanor Medill
Patterson, Elizabeth C. 29-32R
Patterson, Emma L. 1904-1984 ....CAP-2
Obituary 135
Earlier sketch in CA 25-28
Patterson, Eric James 1891-1972 ....CAP-1
Earlier sketch in CA 11-12
Patterson, Evelyn Roelofs 1917- 5-8R
Patterson, Frank Harmon 1912- Brief entry 109
Patterson, Frank M(organ) 1931- CANR-25
Earlier sketch in CA 45-48
Patterson, Franklin (Kessel) 1916- 45-48
Patterson, Gardner 1916- Brief entry 106
Patterson, Geoffrey 1943- 103
See also SATA 44, 54
Patterson, George N(eilson) 1920- 137
Patterson, Gerald R. 1926- 41-44R
Patterson, Harriet-Louise H(olland)
1903- CAP-1
Earlier sketch in CA 13-16
Patterson, Harry 1929- CANR-33
Earlier sketch in CA 13-16R
See also Higgins, Jack
Patterson, Henry
See Patterson, Harry
Patterson, James (B.) 1947- 133
Patterson, James (Tyler) 1935- 21-24R
Patterson, Jane
See Britton, Mattie Lula Cooper
Patterson, Janet McFadden 1915- 89-92
Patterson, Jefferson 1891-1977 Obituary 115
Patterson, Jerry E(ugene) 1931- Brief entry 107
Patterson, John McCready
1913-1983 Obituary 109
Patterson, Joseph Medill
1879-1946 Brief entry 118
See also DLB 29
Patterson, June (Marie) 1924- 126
Patterson, K(arl) David 1941- 65-68
Patterson, Kevin 1956(?)-1988 Obituary 126
Patterson, L(loyd) G(eorge) Jr. 1929- 41-44R
Patterson, L(yman) Ray 1929- 33-36R
Patterson, Lawrence Thomas II 1937- 104
Patterson, Letha L(emon) 1913- 5-8R
Patterson, Lillie G. 73-76
See also SATA 14
Patterson, Lindsay 1942- 77-80
See also BW
Patterson, Margaret C(leveland) 1923- CANR-7
Earlier sketch in CA 57-60
Patterson, Mary H(agelin)
1928-1973 Obituary 37-40R
Patterson, Michael 1939- 111
Patterson, (James) Milton 1927- 53-56
Patterson, Olive
See Rowland, D(onald) S(ydney)
Patterson, (Horace) Orlando (Lloyd)
1940- CANR-27
Earlier sketch in CA 65-68
See also BW
Patterson, (Leighton) Paige 1942- CANR-10
Earlier sketch in CA 25-28R
Patterson, Paul 1909- 85-88
Patterson, Peter
See Terson, Peter
Patterson, Raymond R. 1929- 29-32R
Patterson, Rebecca Elizabeth Coy
1911-1975 103
Patterson, Richard North 1947- 85-88
Patterson, Richard
1908(?)-1976 Obituary 69-72
Patterson, Robert B(enjamin) 1934- 73-76
Patterson, Robert Leet 1893- 17-20R
Patterson, Ruth P(olk) 1930- 119
Patterson, Samuel C(harles) 1931- CANR-22
Earlier sketches in CA 17-20R, CANR-7
Patterson, Samuel White 1883-1975 ....CAP-2
Obituary 61-64
Earlier sketch in CA 17-18
Patterson, Sheila Caffyn 1918- 9-12R
Patterson, Sylvia W(iese) 1940- 61-64
Patterson, Tom 1920- 128
Patterson, Virginia 1931- 102
Patterson, W. M(acLean)
1912(?)-1976 Obituary 69-72
Patterson, W. Morgan 1925- 65-68
Patterson, Walter C(ram) 1936- CANR-20
Earlier sketch in CA 103
Patterson, Ward L(amont) 1933- CANR-23
Earlier sketches in CA 57-60, CANR-8
Patterson, Wayne 1946- CANR-16
Earlier sketch in CA 85-88
Patterson, Webster T. 1920- 25-28R
Patterson, William Dudley
1910-1986 Obituary 119
Patterson, William L(orenzo) 1890-1980 ....41-44R
Obituary 97-100
Patti, Archimedes L(eonida) A(ttilio) 1913- 106
Patti, Ercole 1904(?)-1976 Obituary 69-72
Patti, Paul 1956- 136
Pattie, Alice 1906- CAP-2
Earlier sketch in CA 29-32
Pattillo, Henry 1726-1801 ....DLB 37
Pattillo, James W(ilson) 1937- CANR-11
Earlier sketch in CA 17-20R
Pattillo, Manning M. Jr. 1919- 21-24R
Pattinson, Nancy Evelyn Brief entry 117
Pattison, O(live) R(uth) B(rown) 1916- 29-32R
Pattison, Robert 1945- 129
Pattison, Walter Thomas 1903- 81-84
Patton, Alva Rae 1908- 5-8R
Patton, Arch 1908- CAP-1
Earlier sketch in CA 13-16
Patton, Bobby R(ay) 1935- CANR-17
Earlier sketches in CA 45-48, CANR-1
Patton, Brian (Lee) 1943- 123
Patton, Frances Gray 1906- 101
Patton, Frank
See Palmer, Raymond A.
Patton, Gerald W(ilson) 1947- 112
Patton, James W(elch) 1900- CAP-1
Earlier sketch in CA 11-12
Patton, Kenneth L(eo) 1911- CANR-7
Earlier sketch in CA 17-20R
Patton, Oliver B(eirne) 1920- 81-84
Patton, Phil 1952- 133
Patton, Rob(ert Warren) 1943- 37-40R
Pattullo, George 1879-1967 Obituary 115
Patty, C. Robert 1925- CANR-10
Earlier sketch in CA 25-28R
Patty, Ernest N(ewton) 1894-1976 ....CAP-2
Earlier sketch in CA 25-28
Patty, James S(ingleton) 1925- 53-56
Paturi, Felix R.
See Mindt, Heinz R.
Pauck, Wilhelm 1901-1981 ....CANR-28
Obituary 104
Earlier sketch in CA 81-84
Pauk, Walter 1914- CANR-39
Earlier sketches in CA 5-8R, CANR-2, 18
Pauker, Guy J(ean) 1916- CANR-1
Earlier sketch in CA 45-48
Pauker, John 1920-1991 ....25-28R
Obituary 133
Pauker, Samuel L. 1948- 127
Pauker, Ted
See Conquest, (George) Robert (Acworth)
Paul, Aileen 1917- CANR-19
Earlier sketch in CA 41-44R
See also SATA 12
Paul, (John) Anthony 1941- 77-80
Paul, Anthony (Marcus) 1937- 77-80
Paul, Auren
See Uris, Auren
Paul, Barbara
See Ovstedal, Barbara
Paul, Barbara 1931- 132
Paul, Charles B. 1931- 105
Paul, Charlotte 1916-1989 ....CANR-7
Obituary 129
Earlier sketch in CA 5-8R

Paul, Daniel
See Kessel, Lipmann
Paul, Danielle
See Mittermeyer, Helen (Hayton Monteith)
Paul, David (Tyler) 1934-1988 Obituary 125
See also SATA 56
Paul, David W(arren) 1944- 107
Paul, Elizabeth
See Crow, Donna Fletcher
Paul, Elliot (Harold) 1891-1958 Brief entry 107
See also DLB 4
Paul, Emily
See Eicher, (Ethel) Elizabeth
Paul, F. W.
See Fairman, Paul W.
Paul, Florrie 1928- 61-64
Paul, Geoffrey John 1921-1983 Obituary 110
Paul, Gordon L. 1935- CANR-7
Earlier sketch in CA 17-20R
Paul, Grace 1908- 17-20R
Paul, Hugo
See Little, Paul H(ugo)
Paul, I(rving) H. 1928- 103
Paul, James 1936- ....SATA 23
Paul, Jordan 1936- 97-100
Paul, Judith Edison 1939- CANR-16
Earlier sketch in CA 29-32R
Paul, Leslie (Allen) 1905-1985 ....CANR-3
Obituary 117
Earlier sketch in CA 1-4R
Paul, Louis
See Placet, Leroi
Paul, Margaret 1939- 97-100
Paul, Norman L(eo) 1926- 61-64
Paul, Raymond 1940- 106
Paul, Robert
See Roberts, John G(aither)
Paul, Robert S(idney) 1918- CANR-3
Earlier sketch in CA 1-4R
Paul, Rodman Wilson 1912-1987 ....CANR-3
Obituary 122
Earlier sketch in CA 1-4R
Paul, Roland A(rthur) 1937- 41-44R
Paul, Sheri
See Resnick, Sylvia (Safran)
Paul, Sherman 1920- CANR-3
Earlier sketch in CA 5-8R
Paul, William
See Eicher, (Ethel) Elizabeth
Paulden, Sydney (Maurice) 1932- CANR-12
Earlier sketch in CA 29-32R
Paulding, James Kirke
1778-1860 ....DLB 3, 59, 74
Pauley, Barbara Anne 1925- 89-92
Pauley, Bruce F. 1937- 41-44R
Pauley, (Margaret) Jane 1950- 106
Paulhan, Jean 1884-1968 Obituary 25-28R
Pauli, Hertha (Ernestine) 1909-1973 ....CANR-2
Obituary 41-44R
Earlier sketch in CA 1-4R
See also SATA 3, 26
Paulin, Thomas Neilson 1949- 128
Brief entry 123
See also Paulin, Tom
Paulin, Tom
See Paulin, Thomas Neilson
See also CLC 37
See also DLB 40
Pauling, Linus (Carl) 1901- 116
Brief entry 110
See also MTCW
Paull, Grace A. 1898- ....SATA 24
Paull, Raymond Allan 1906-1972 ....CAP-1
Earlier sketch in CA 9-10
Pau-Llosa, Ricardo 1954- 111
See also HW
Paulon, Flavia 1907(?)-1987 Obituary 122
Paulos, John Allen 1945- 136
Brief entry 128
See also BEST 89:3
Pauls, John P. 1916- 45-48
Paulsell, William Oliver 1935- 111
Paulsen, F(rank) Robert 1922- 21-24R
Paulsen, Gary 1939- CANR-30
Earlier sketch in CA 73-76
See also AAYA 2
See also CLR 19
See also MAICYA
See also SATA 22, 50, 54
Paulsen, Lois (Thompson) 1905- CAP-2
Earlier sketch in CA 19-20
Paulsen, Wolfgang 1910- CANR-11
Earlier sketch in CA 17-20R
Paulson, Belden 1927- 21-24R
Paulson, Jack
See Jackson, C(aary) Paul
Paulson, Morton C. 1923- 111
Paulson, Ronald (Howard) 1930- CANR-33
Earlier sketches in CA 17-20R, CANR-15
Paulson, Terry L. 1945- 136
Paulsson, Bjoern 1932- 61-64
Paulsson, Thomas A(lfred) 1923- 9-12R
Paulston, Christina Bratt CANR-10
Earlier sketch in CA 65-68
Paulston, Rolland G(lenn) 1929- CANR-13
Earlier sketch in CA 33-36R
Paulu, Burton 1910- 13-16R
Paulus, John Douglas 1917- 69-72
Paul VI, Pope 1897-1978 ....CANR-30
Obituary 77-80
Earlier sketch in CA 81-84
Pauly, Thomas H(arry) 1940- 115
Paun, Maggie
See Voysey, Margaret
Pauquet, Gina Ruck
See Ruck-Pauquet, Gina
Paustovsky, Konstantin (Georgievich)
1892-1968 93-96
Obituary 25-28R
See also CLC 40
Pautler, Albert J. Jr. 1935- 33-36R
Pauw, Berthold Adolf 1924- 9-12R
Pauwels, Louis 1920- Brief entry 111
Pavalko, Ronald M(ichael) 1934- 57-60
Pavarotti, Luciano 1935- Brief entry 112
Pavel, Frances 1907- 21-24R
See also SATA 10
Pavenstedt, Eleanor 1903- 21-24R
Pavese, Cesare 1908-1950 Brief entry 104
See also TCLC 3
Pavey, Don 1922- 107
Pavic, Milorad 1929- 136
See also CLC 60
Pavitranda, Swami
1896(?)-1977 Obituary 73-76
Pavlakis, Christopher 1928- 73-76
Pavletich, Aida 101
Pavlik, Evelyn Marie 1954- 97-100
Pavlov, Ivan Petrovich
1849-1936 Brief entry 118
Pavlowitch, Stevan K. 1933- CANR-29
Earlier sketches in CA 33-36R, CANR-13
Pavord, Anna 1940- CANR-37
Earlier sketch in CA 115
Pawel, Ernst 1920- 131
Pawelczynska, Anna 1922- 101
Pawle, Gerald Strachan 1913-1991 ....5-8R
Obituary 135
Pawley, Bernard C(linton) 1911-1981 ....25-28R
Obituary 105
Pawley, Martin Edward 1938- 101
Pawley, Thomas Desire III 1917- 29-32R
Pawlick, Thomas F(rancis) 1941- 119
Pawlicki, T(homas) B(ert) 1930- 109
Pawlikowski, John T. 1940- CANR-24
Earlier sketches in CA 21-24R, CANR-9
Pawlowicz, Sala Kaminska 1925- 5-8R
Pawlowski, Gareth L. 1939- 29-32R
Pawson, G(eoffrey) P(hilip) H(enry) 1904- 5-8R
Pax, Clyde 1928- 49-52
Paxman, Jeremy Dickson 1950- 108
Paxson, Ethel 1885- 25-28R
Paxton, Dr. John
See Lawton, Sherman P(axton)
Paxton, Jack
See Lawton, Sherman P(axton)
Paxton, Jack 1939-1985 Obituary 117
Paxton, John 1911-1985 Obituary 114
See also DLB 44
Paxton, John 1923- 129
Paxton, Lois
See Low, Lois Dorothea
Paxton, Mary Jean Wallace 1930- 109
Paxton, Robert O(wen) 1932- 73-76
Paxton, Thomas R. 1937- 105
See also Paxton, Tom
Paxton, Tom
See Paxton, Thomas R.
See also SATA 70
Payack, Paul J. J. 1950- CANR-31
Earlier sketch in CA 69-72
Paye, Robert
See Campbell, (Gabrielle) Margaret (Vere)
Payelle, Raymond-Gerard
1898-1971 Obituary 33-36R
Payer, Cheryl Ann 1940- 61-64
Payer, Lynn (Jeanine) 1945- 128
Payes, Rachel C(osgrove) 1922- CANR-16
Earlier sketches in CA 49-52, CANR-1
Payn, James 1830-1898 ....DLB 18
Payne, A. J.
See Payne, Anthony
Payne, Alan
See Jakes, John (William)
Payne, Alma Smith
See Ralston, Alma (Smith Payne)
Payne, Anthony 1952- 125
Payne, B(en) Iden 1888-1976 73-76
Obituary 65-68
Payne, Basil 1928- 81-84
Payne, Bernal C. Jr. 1941- ....SATA 60
Payne, Bruce 1911- 9-12R
Payne, Charles 1909- 103
Payne, David A(llen) 1935- 25-28R
Payne, Donald Gordon 1924- CANR-24
Earlier sketches in CA 13-16R, CANR-9
See also SATA 37
Payne, Emmy
See West, Emily Govan
Payne, Eric Francis Jules 1895- 57-60
Payne, Ernest A(lexander) 1902-1980 ......CANR-9
Obituary 105
Earlier sketch in CA 9-12R
Payne, F(rances) Anne 1932- 73-76
Payne, J(ohn) Barton 1922- CANR-3
Earlier sketch in CA 1-4R
Payne, J(ames) Gregory 1949- 123
Payne, Jack 1926- 33-36R
Payne, James L. 1939- 33-36R
Payne, Joan Balfour Obituary 41-44R
Payne, John Howard 1791-1852 ....DLB 37
Payne, John 1842-1916 ....DLB 35
Payne, Karen 1951- 111
Payne, Ladell 1933- 134
Brief entry 111
Payne, Laurence 1919- 5-8R
Payne, LaVeta Maxine 1916- 37-40R
Payne, Leanne 1932- CANR-37
Earlier sketch in CA 115
Payne, Michael 1941- CANR-12
Earlier sketch in CA 29-32R
Payne, Mildred Y(ounger) 1906- 41-44R
Payne, Peggy 1949- 128
Payne, Richard A. 1934- 97-100
Payne, Robert O. 1924- 97-100
Payne, (Pierre Stephen) Robert
1911-1983 ....CANR-31
Obituary 109
Earlier sketch in CA 25-28R
Payne, Ronald 1926- 97-100
Payne, Stanley G(eorge) 1934- CANR-3
Earlier sketch in CA 1-4R
Paynter, David H. 1921- 135
Paynter, Will(iam) 1903-1984 Obituary 115
Paynter, William Henry 1901- 13-16R
Paynton, Clifford T. 1929- 37-40R
Payro, Roberto J(orge) 1867-1928 ....HW
Payson, Dale 1943- CANR-3
Earlier sketch in CA 49-52
See also SATA 9
Payson, Herb(ert III) 1927- 115
Payzant, Charles ....SATA 18
Paz, A.
See Pahz, James Alon
Paz, Carlos F(ernando) 1937- 109
Paz, Gil
See Lugones, Leopoldo
Paz, Octavio 1914- CANR-32
Earlier sketch in CA 73-76
See also CLC 3, 4, 6, 10, 19, 51, 65
See also DLBY 90
See also HW
See also MTCW
See also PC 1
See also WLC
Paz, Zan
See Pahz, (Anne) Cheryl Suzanne
Pazder, Lawrence Henry 1936- 107
p'Bitek, Okot 1931-1982 124
Obituary 107
See also BLC 3
See also BW
See also MTCW
Peabody, Barbara 1933- 122
Peabody, Elizabeth Palmer 1804-1894 ....DLB 1
Peabody, Oliver William Bourn
1799-1848 ....DLB 59
Peabody, Robert Lee 1931- 9-12R
Peabody, Velton 1936- 53-56
Peace, Richard (Arthur) 1933- 131
Peace, Richard 1938- CANR-14
Earlier sketch in CA 25-28R
Peace, Roger Craft 1899-1968 Obituary 89-92
Peach, Lawrence du Garde 1890-1974 101
Peach, William Bernard 1918- 127
Peach, William Nelson 1912- 21-24R
Peacher, Georgiana M(elicent) 1919- 25-28R
Peachey, Laban 1927- 17-20R
Peacock, Alan T(urner) 1922- CANR-3
Earlier sketch in CA 1-4R
Peacock, Basil 1898- 103
Peacock, Carlos (Charles Hanbury) 132
Peacock, D(avid) P(hilip) S(pencer) 1939- 123
Peacock, Daniel J. 1919- 125
Peacock, Dick
See Peacock, Richard
Peacock, James Craig
1888(?)-1977 Obituary 73-76
Peacock, James L(owe) 1937- Brief entry 113
Peacock, L(elon) J(ames) 1928- 21-24R
Peacock, Mary Reynolds (Bradshaw)
1916- 57-60
Peacock, Mary (Willa) 1942- 69-72
Peacock, Molly 1947- 103
See also CLC 60
See also DLB 120
Peacock, Richard 1933- 107
Peacock, Ronald 1907- CANR-5
Earlier sketch in CA 53-56
Peacock, Thomas Love
1785-1866 ....DLB 96, 116
Peacock, Wilbur Scott
1915(?)-1979 Obituary 89-92
Peacocke, A(rthur) R(obert) 1924- 41-44R
Peacocke, Christopher 1950- 124
Peacocke, Isabel Maud
1881-1973 Obituary 116
Pead, Deuel ....DLB 24
Peairs, Lillian Gehrke 1925- 103
Peairs, Richard Hope 1929- Brief entry 105
Peak, David 1953- 133
Peake, C(harles) H. 1920(?)-1988 Obituary 124
Peake, Lilian (Margaret) 1924- Brief entry 115
Peake, Mervyn 1911-1968 ....CANR-3
Obituary 25-28R
Earlier sketch in CA 5-8R
See also CLC 7, 54
See also DLB 15
See also MTCW
See also SATA 23
Peake, Miriam Morrison 1901- 57-60
Peaker, G(ilbert) F.
1903(?)-1983(?) Obituary 109
Peale, Norman Vincent 1898- CANR-29
Earlier sketch in CA 81-84
See also AITN 1
See also MTCW
See also SATA 20
Peale, Ruth Stafford 1906- CANR-29
Earlier sketch in CA 73-76
Pear, Lillian Myers 73-76
Pearce, Ann Philippa
See Christie, (Ann) Philippa
Pearce, Arthur Williams
1913(?)-1983 Obituary 111
Pearce, Brian Louis 1933- CANR-19
Earlier sketch in CA 103
Pearce, Charles A. 1906-1970 Obituary 104
Pearce, David (Robert) 1937- 126
Pearce, Dick
See Pearce, Richard Elmo
Pearce, Donald R(oss) 1917- 119
Pearce, Donn 1928- 13-16R
Pearce, Frank 1909- 109
Pearce, J(ohn) Kenneth 1898- 45-48
Pearce, J. Winston 1907- 130
Brief entry 106
Pearce, Janice 1931- 61-64
Pearce, John Kingston 1925- 118
Pearce, Kenneth 1921- 120
Pearce, Mary E(mily) 1932- CANR-31
Earlier sketch in CA 69-72
Pearce, Moira 103
Pearce, Philippa
See Christie, (Ann) Philippa
See also CLC 21
See also CLR 9
See also MAICYA
See also SATA 1, 67
Pearce, Richard Elmo 1909- 1-4R
Pearce, Richard 1932- 41-44R
Pearce, Roy Harvey 1919- CANR-3
Earlier sketch in CA 1-4R
Pearce, Thomas Matthews 1902- CANR-7
Earlier sketch in CA 17-20R
Pearce, William M(artin) 1913- 9-12R
Pearcy, G(eorge) Etzel 1905-1980 ....CANR-3
Earlier sketch in CA 1-4R
Peardon, Thomas Preston
1899-1985 Obituary 116
Peare, Catherine Owens 1911- 5-8R
See also SATA 9
Pearl, Arthur 1922- 13-16R
Pearl, Chaim 1919- 49-52
Pearl, Cyril (Altson) 1906-1987(?) Obituary 122
Pearl, David 1944- 133
Pearl, Eric
See Elman, Richard
Pearl, Esther Elizabeth
See Ritz, David
Pearl, Hal 1914(?)-1975 Obituary 61-64
Pearl, Jack
See Pearl, Jacques Bain
Pearl, Jacques Bain 1923- CANR-23
Earlier sketch in CA 5-8R
Pearl, Joseph L. 1886(?)-1974 Obituary 53-56
Pearl, Leon 1922- 5-8R
Pearl, Leonard 1911- CAP-2
Earlier sketch in CA 33-36
Pearl, Minnie
See Cannon, Sarah Ophelia Colley
Pearl, Ralph 1910- 73-76
Pearl, Richard M(axwell) 1913- CANR-3
Earlier sketch in CA 9-12R
Pearl, Virginia L(ou) 1930- 61-64
Pearlman, Daniel (David) 1935- CANR-24
Earlier sketches in CA 61-64, CANR-9
Pearlman, Maurice 1911- CANR-6
Earlier sketch in CA 5-8R
Pearlman, Mickey 1938- 134
Pearlman, Moshe
See Pearlman, Maurice
Pearlstein, Howard J. 1942- 57-60
Pearman, Jean R(ichardson) 1915- 49-52
Pears, Charles 1873-1958 Brief entry 114
See also SATA 30
Pears, David Francis 1921- 65-68
Pears, Iain (George) 1955- 130
Pearsall, Derek (Albert) 1931- CANR-24
Earlier sketch in CA 107
Pearsall, (F.) Paul 126
Pearsall, Robert Brainard 1920- CANR-2
Earlier sketch in CA 45-48
Pearsall, Ronald 1927- CANR-31
Earlier sketches in CA 21-24R, CANR-14
Pearsall, Thomas E. 1925- 25-28R
Pearsall, William Harold
1891-1964 Obituary 106
Pearse, Peter H(ector) 1932- 138
Pearson, Andrew Russell 1897-1969 ....CANR-6
Obituary 25-28R
Earlier sketch in CA 5-8R
See also MTCW
Pearson, B(enjamin) H(arold) 1893- 65-68
Pearson, Bill
See Pearson, William Harrison
Pearson, Bruce L. 1932- 73-76
Pearson, Carol Lynn 1939- 133
Pearson, Carol 1944- 57-60
Pearson, David E. 1953- 127
Pearson, Diane
See McClelland, Diane Margaret
Pearson, Drew
See Pearson, Andrew Russell
Pearson, Frederic S(tephen) 1944- 113
Pearson, Gayle 1947- 122
See also SATA 53
Pearson, (Edward) Hesketh (Gibbons)
1887-1964 ....5-8R
Pearson, James Larkin 1879-1981 Obituary 104
Pearson, Jim Berry 1924- 17-20R
Pearson, John 1934- CANR-4
Earlier sketch in CA 49-52
Pearson, Karl 1857-1936 Brief entry 119
Pearson, Kit 1947- ....CLR 26
Pearson, Lester B(owles) 1897-1972 121
Obituary 37-40R
Pearson, (Edith) Linnea 1942- 65-68
Pearson, Lionel (Ignatius Cusack)
1908-1988 ....1-4R
Obituary 126
Pearson, Lon
See Pearson, Milo Lorentz
Pearson, M(ichael) N(aylor)
1941- Brief entry 118
Pearson, Michael 102

Pearson, Milo Lorentz 1939- ... 73-76
Pearson, Neville P(ershing) 1917- ... 45-48
Pearson, Norman Holmes 1909-1975 ... CAP-1
Obituary ... 61-64
Earlier sketch in CA 13-16
Pearson, R(obert) A(rthur) 1945- ... 128
Pearson, Richard Joseph 1938- ... 65-68
Pearson, Ridley 1953- ... 135
Pearson, Robert Paul 1938- ... 65-68
Pearson, Ronald Hooke 1915- ... 13-16R
Pearson, Roy 1914- ... 1-4R
Pearson, Scott Roberts 1938- ... CANR-11
Earlier sketch in CA 29-32R
Pearson, Susan 1946- ... CANR-14
Earlier sketch in CA 65-68
See also SATA 27, 39
Pearson, T(homas) R(eid) 1956- ... 130
Brief entry ... 120
See also CLC 39
Pearson, Thomas S(pencer) 1949- ... 132
Pearson, Tracey Campbell 1956- ... SATA 64
Pearson, William Harrison 1922- ... 57-60
Peary, Dannis 1949- ... CANR-27
Earlier sketch in CA 109
Peary, Danny
See Peary, Dannis
Peary, Marie Ahnighito
See Kuhne, Marie (Ahnighito Peary)
Peascod, Bill
See Peascod, William
Peascod, William 1920(?)-1985 Obituary ... 116
Pease, Dorothy Wells 1896- ... 5-8R
Pease, Howard 1894-1974 ... 5-8R
Obituary ... 106
See also MAICYA
See also SATA 2, 25
Pease, Jane H(anna) 1929- ... CANR-4
Earlier sketch in CA 9-12R
Pease, Victor Philip 1938- ... 107
Pease, William H(enry) 1924- ... CANR-4
Earlier sketch in CA 9-12R
Peaston, Monroe 1914- ... 49-52
Peat, F. David 1938- ... 132
Peate, Iorwerth C.
See Peate, Iorwerth Cyfeiliog
Peate, Iorwerth Cyfeiliog 1901-1982 ... 120
Obituary ... 108
Peate, Patricia Flynn
1911(?)-1983 Obituary ... 111
Peatman, John Gray 1904- ... 5-8R
Peattie, Donald Culross 1898-1964 ... 102
Peattie, Lisa Redfield 1924- ... CANR-10
Earlier sketch in CA 25-28R
Peattie, Mark R(obert) 1930- ... CANR-8
Earlier sketch in CA 61-64
Peavler, Terry J. 1942- ... 135
Peavy, Charles D(ruery) 1931- ... 25-28R
Peavy, John W(esley) III 1944- ... 119
Peavy, Linda 1943- ... CANR-31
Earlier sketch in CA 109
See also SATA 54
Pebworth, Ted-Larry 1936- ... 121
Peccei, Aurelio 1908-1984 Obituary ... 112
Peccorini, Francisco L(etona) 1915- ... CANR-25
Earlier sketch in CA 45-48
Pech, Stanley Z. 1924- ... 33-36R
Pechel, Peter (Rudolf) 1920- ... 135
Pechman, Joseph A(aron) 1918-1989 ... 85-88
Obituary ... 129
Pechter, Edward 1941- ... 85-88
Peck, Abe 1945- ... 73-76
Peck, Anne Merriman 1884- ... 77-80
See also SATA 18
Peck, David W(arner) 1902-1990 ... 1-4R
Obituary ... 132
Peck, Ellen 1942- Brief entry ... 113
Peck, Frederic Taylor
1920(?)-1983 Obituary ... 110
Peck, George W(ilbur)
1840-1916 Brief entry ... 115
See also DLB 23, 42
Peck, George (Willis) 1931-1990 Obituary ... 130
Peck, Harry Thurston 1856-1914 ... DLB 71, 91
Peck, Helen E(stelle) 1910- ... 5-8R
Peck, Ira 1922- ... 77-80
Peck, Jane Cary 1932-1990 Obituary ... 132
Peck, John B. 1918(?)-1973 Obituary ... 104
Peck, John 1941- ... CANR-3
Earlier sketch in CA 49-52
See also CLC 3
Peck, Kathryn Blackburn 1904-1975 ... CAP-2
Earlier sketch in CA 25-28
Peck, Leonard
See Hardy, C. Colburn
Peck, M(organ) Scott 1936- ... CANR-20
Earlier sketch in CA 89-92
See also BEST 89:2
Peck, Merton J(oseph) 1925- ... 13-16R
Peck, Paula 1927(?)-1972 Obituary ... 104
Peck, Ralph H(arold-Henry) 1926- ... CANR-22
Earlier sketch in CA 69-72
Peck, Richard E(arl) 1936- ... CANR-31
Earlier sketch in CA 81-84
Peck, Richard (Wayne) 1934- ... CANR-38
Earlier sketches in CA 85-88, CANR-19
See also AAYA 1
See also CLC 21
See also MAICYA
See also SAAS 2
See also SATA 18, 55
Peck, Robert F. 1919- ... 13-16R
Peck, Robert McCracken 1952- ... 112
Peck, Robert Newton 1928- ... CANR-31
Earlier sketch in CA 81-84
See also AAYA 3
See also CLC 17
See also MAICYA
See also SAAS 1
See also SATA 21, 62
Peck, Russell A(lbert) 1933- ... 108
Peck, Ruth L. 1915- ... 29-32R
Peck, Seymour 1917-1985 Obituary ... 114
Peck, Sidney M. 1926- ... 5-8R
Peck, Stacey 1925- ... 123
Peck, Sylvia 1953- ... 135
Peck, Theodore P(arker) 1924- ... 103
Peckenpaugh, Angela J(ohnson) 1942- ... 104
Peckham, Howard Henry 1910- ... 9-12R
Peckham, James O. 1903(?)-1984 Obituary ... 113
Peckham, Lawton (Parker Greenman)
1904-1979 Obituary ... 89-92
Peckham, Morse 1914- ... CANR-1
Earlier sketch in CA 1-4R
Peckham, Richard
See Holden, Raymond (Peckham)
Peckinpah, (David) Sam(uel) 1925-1984 ... 109
Obituary ... 114
See also CLC 20
Pecsok, Mary Bodell 1919- ... 5-8R
Peden, Margaret Sayers 1927- ... CANR-14
Earlier sketch in CA 37-40R
Peden, Rachel (Mason) 1901- ... 110
Peden, William (Harwood) 1913- ... 21-24R
Pedersen, Elsa Kienitz 1915- ... CANR-2
Earlier sketch in CA 1-4R
Pedersen, (Thelma) Jean J(orgenson)
1934- ... CANR-21
Earlier sketches in CA 57-60, CANR-6
Pedersen, Knut 1859-1952 ... 119
Brief entry ... 104
See also Hamsun, Knut
See also MTCW
Pedersen, Paul B(odholdt) 1936- ... 41-44R
Pederson, Kern O(wen) 1910- ... 102
Pedicord, Harry William 1912- ... 33-36R
Pedler, Christopher Magnus Howard
1927- ... 97-100
Pedler, Frederick Johnson 1908-1991 ... 107
Obituary ... 134
Pedler, Kit
See Pedler, Christopher Magnus Howard
Pedleton, Don
See Jagninski, Tom
Pedley, Robin 1914-1988 ... 9-12R
Obituary ... 127
Pedoe, Daniel 1910- ... 65-68
Pedolsky, Andrea 1951- ... CANR-38
Earlier sketch in CA 115
Pedrick, Jean 1922- ... CANR-6
Earlier sketch in CA 57-60
Pedrosa, Carmen Navarro 1941- ... 128
Peebles, Anne
See Galloway, Priscilla
Peebles, Dick 1918-1980 ... 77-80
Obituary ... 97-100
Peek, Bertrand Meigh 1891-1964 Obituary ... 111
Peek, Merle 1938- ... CANR-22
Earlier sketch in CA 105
See also SATA 39
Peek, Walter W(illiam) 1922- ... 45-48
Peel, Bruce Braden 1916- ... 17-20R
Peel, Colin D(udley) 1936- ... 119
Peel, Edwin A(rthur) 1911- ... 13-16R
Peel, H(azel) M(ary) 1930- ... CANR-4
Earlier sketch in CA 9-12R
Peel, J(ohn) D(avid) Y(eadon) 1941- ... 33-36R
Peel, John Donald 1908- ... 33-36R
Peel, Kendal J(ohn) 1940- ... 116
Peel, Malcolm Lee 1936- ... 29-32R
Peel, Norman Lemon
See Hirsch, Phil
Peel, Robert 1909-1992 ... 77-80
Obituary ... 136
Peel, Ronald Francis (Edward Waite)
1912-1985 Obituary ... 117
Peel, Wallis
See Peel, H(azel) M(ary)
Peele, David A(rnold) 1929-1985 ... 102
Obituary ... 118
Peele, George 1556-1596 ... DLB 62
Peele, Stanton 1946- ... 57-60
Peelor, Harry N. 1922- ... 17-20R
Peeples, Edwin A(ugustus Jr.) 1915- ... 9-12R
See also SATA 6
Peer, Lyndon A. 1899(?)-1977 Obituary ... 73-76
Peerbolte, Maarten Lietaert
See Lietaert Peerbolte, Maarten
Peerce, Jan 1904-1984 ... 101
Obituary ... 114
Peerman, Dean G(ordon) 1931- ... 13-16R
Peers, William R(aymond) 1914-1984 ... 13-16R
Obituary ... 112
Peery, Paul D(enver) 1906- ... CAP-2
Earlier sketch in CA 29-32
Peeslake, Gaffer
See Durrell, Lawrence (George)
Peet, Bill
See Peet, William Bartlett
See also CLR 12
Peet, C(harles) Donald Jr. 1927- ... 13-16R
Peet, Creighton B. 1899-1977 ... 106
Obituary ... 69-72
See also SATA 30
Peet, Louise Jenison 1885- ... 5-8R
Peet, William Bartlett 1915- ... CANR-38
Earlier sketch in CA 17-20R
See also Peet, Bill
See also MAICYA
See also SATA 2, 41
Peffer, Randall S(cott) 1948- ... 101
Pegge, C(ecil) Denis 1902- ... CAP-1
Earlier sketch in CA 13-16
Pegis, Anton Charles 1905- Brief entry ... 106
Pegis, Jessie Corrigan 1907- ... CAP-1
Earlier sketch in CA 13-14
Pegler, (James) Westbrook 1894-1969 ... 103
Obituary ... 89-92
Pegram, Marjorie Anne (Dykes) 1925- ... 9-12R
Pegrum, Dudley F(rank) 1898- ... 33-36R
Pegues, Franklin J(ohnson) 1924- ... 5-8R
Peguy, Charles Pierre
1873-1914 Brief entry ... 107
See also TCLC 10
Pehnt, Wolfgang 1931- ... CANR-24
Earlier sketch in CA 107
Pehrson, Justine Davis Randers
See Randers-Pehrson, Justine Davis
Pei, Mario A(ndrew) 1901-1978 ... CANR-5
Obituary ... 77-80
Earlier sketch in CA 5-8R
Peierls, Rudolf E.
See Peierls, Rudolf (Ernst)
Peierls, Rudolf (Ernst) 1907- ... 128
Peifer, Claude J(ohn) 1927- ... 17-20R
Peifer, Kathleen Hamel
See Hamel Peifer, Kathleen
Peikoff, Leonard 1933- ... 108
Peil, Margaret 1929- ... CANR-8
Earlier sketch in CA 61-64
Peirce, J(ames) F(ranklin) 1918- ... 41-44R
Peirce, Neal R. 1932- ... CANR-21
Earlier sketch in CA 25-28R
Peirce, Waldo 1884-1970 ... SATA 28
Peiris, Denzil 1918(?)-1985 Obituary ... 116
Peiser, Maria Lilli 1914-1986 ... 116
Obituary ... 118
Brief entry ... 110
Peissel, Michel (Francois) 1937- ... CANR-30
Earlier sketches in CA 25-28R, CANR-12
Peitchinis, Stephen G(abriel) 1925- ... CANR-24
Earlier sketch in CA 45-48
Pejovich, Svetozar 1931- ... CANR-12
Earlier sketch in CA 17-20R
Pejovich, Ted
See Pejovich, Theodore Peter
Pejovich, Theodore Peter 1945- ... 131
Pekarik, Andrew J(oseph) 1946- ... 112
Pekic, Borislav 1930- ... 69-72
Peladeau, Marius B(eaudoin) 1935- ... 73-76
Pelaez, Jill 1924- ... 33-36R
See also SATA 12
Pelavin, Cheryl 1946- ... 106
Pelecanos, George P. 1957- ... 138
Pelenski, Jaroslaw 1929- Brief entry ... 111
Pelfrey, William 1947- ... 33-36R
Pelger, Lucy J. 1913-1971 ... CAP-2
Earlier sketch in CA 21-22
Pelham, David 1938- ... 138
See also SATA 70
Peli, Pinchas H(acohen)
1930(?)-1989 Obituary ... 128
Pelikan, Jaroslav Jan 1923- ... CANR-1
Earlier sketch in CA 1-4R
Pelissier, Anthony 1912-1988 Obituary ... 125
Pelissier, Roger 1924-1972 ... CAP-2
Obituary ... 37-40R
Earlier sketch in CA 23-24
Pell, Arthur R. 1920- ... CANR-26
Earlier sketches in CA 29-32R, CANR-11
Pell, Claiborne (de Borda) 1918- ... 49-52
Pell, Derek 1947- ... 77-80
Pell, Eve 1937- ... 33-36R
Pell, John (Howland Gibbs)
1904-1987 Obituary ... 123
Pell, Olive Bigelow 1886-1980 Obituary ... 103
Pell, Robert
See Hagberg, David J(ames)
Pell, Walden II 1902-1983 Obituary ... 109
Pella, Milton O(rville) 1914- ... 17-20R
Pellegreno, Ann Holtaren ... 33-36R
Pellegrini, Angelo M. 1904- ... 17-20R
See also CAAS 11
Pellegrini, Anthony D(avid) 1949- ... 117
Pellegrino, Charles R. 1953- ... 136
Pellegrino, Victoria Y(urasits) 1944- ... 107
Peller, Sigismund 1890-1985 Obituary ... 116
Pellerano, Maria B. 1957- ... 133
Pelletier, Ingrid 1912- ... 29-32R
Pelletier, Kenneth R. 1946- ... CANR-29
Earlier sketches in CA 69-72, CANR-11
Pelletier, Nancy 1923- ... 136
Pelletreau, John 1925(?)-1983 Obituary ... 111
Pellew, Jill (Hosford) 1942- ... 109
Pelli, Moshe 1936- ... 132
Pellicer, Carlos 1900(?)-1977 Obituary ... 69-72
See also HW
Pelling, Henry Mathison 1920- ... 61-64
Pellow, Deborah 1945- ... CANR-13
Earlier sketch in CA 73-76
Pellowski, Anne 1933- ... CANR-9
Earlier sketch in CA 21-24R
See also SATA 20
Pellowski, Michael (Joseph) 1949- ... CANR-29
Earlier sketch in CA 110
See also SATA 48
Pells, Richard Henry 1941- ... 53-56
Pelly, David F. 1948- ... 124
Pelshe, Arvid Yanovich
1899-1983 Obituary ... 109
Pelta, Kathy 1928- ... 85-88
See also SATA 18
Peltason, J(ack) W(alter) 1923- ... CANR-4
Earlier sketch in CA 1-4R
Peltier, Leslie C(opus) 1900- ... 17-20R
See also SATA 13
Pelto, Bert
See Pelto, Pertti J(uho)
Pelto, Pertti J(uho) 1927- ... 97-100
Pelton, Barry C(lifton) 1935- ... 61-64
Pelton, Beverly Jo 1939- ... 49-52
Pelton, Joseph N(eal) 1943- ... 107
Pelton, Robert D(oane) 1935- ... 103
Pelton, Robert Stuart 1921- ... 5-8R
Pelton, Robert W(ayne) 1934- ... CANR-28
Earlier sketch in CA 29-32R
Pelton, Warren J. 1923- ... 133
Peltz, Mary Ellis 1896-1981 ... 85-88
Obituary ... 105
Peluso, Joseph L(ouis) 1929- ... 97-100
Pelz, Lotte A(uguste) Hensl 1924- ... 9-12R
Pelz, Stephen Ernest 1942- ... 114
Brief entry ... 110
Pelz, Werner 1921- ... 9-12R
Peman, Jose Maria 1897-1981 Obituary ... 104
Pemberton, John E(dward) 1930- ... 33-36R
Pemberton, John Leigh
See Leigh-Pemberton, John
Pemberton, Madge
188 (?)-1970 Obituary ... 29-32R
Pemberton, Margaret 1943- ... CANR-38
Earlier sketches in CA 93-96, CANR-17
Pemberton, Max 1863-1950 Brief entry ... 120
See also DLB 70
Pemberton, Nan
See Pykare, Nina
Pemberton, William Baring 1897- ... 5-8R
Pemberton, William E(rwin) 1940- ... 97-100
Pembrook, Linda 1942- ... 61-64
Pembrooke, Kenneth
See Page, Gerald W(ilburn)
Pembury, Bill
See Groom, Arthur William
Pempel, T. J. 1942- ... CANR-30
Earlier sketch in CA 112
Pen, Jan 1921- ... CANR-17
Earlier sketch in CA 1-4R
Pena, Humberto J(ose) 1928- ... 73-76
Pena, Ramon del Valle y
See Valle-Inclan, Ramon (Maria) del
Pendar, Kenneth 1906-1972 Obituary ... 37-40R
Pendarvis, China Clark
See Clark-Pendarvis, China
Pendell, Elmer 1894- ... CAP-1
Earlier sketch in CA 11-12
Pendennis, Arthur Esquir
See Thackeray, William Makepeace
Pender, Lex
See Pendower, Jacques
Pender, Lydia Podger 1907- ... CANR-2
Earlier sketch in CA 5-8R
See also SATA 61
Pender, Marilyn
See Pendower, Jacques
Pendergast, Charles 1950- ... 65-68
Pendergast, Chuck
See Pendergast, Charles
Pendergast, Richard J. 1927- ... 93-96
Penderwhistle, Judith (Blair) 1952- ... CANR-22
Earlier sketch in CA 81-84
Pendery, Rosemary (Schmitz) ... 53-56
See also SATA 7
Pendle, Alexy 1943- ... SATA 29
Pendle, George 1906-1977 ... 5-8R
Obituary ... 103
See also SATA 28
Pendlebury, B(evis) J(ohn) 1898- ... CAP-2
Earlier sketch in CA 33-36
Pendleton, Conrad
See Kidd, Walter E.
Pendleton, Don
See Garside, (Clifford) Jack
and Obstfeld, Raymond
Pendleton, Don(ald Eugene) 1927- ... 33-36R
Pendleton, James D(udley) 1930- ... 107
Pendleton, Mary ... 65-68
Pendleton, Winston K. 1910- ... CAP-1
Earlier sketch in CA 13-16
Pendo, Stephen 1947- ... 65-68
Pendower, Jacques 1899-1976 ... 9-12R
Obituary ... 89-92
Pendray, Edward
See Pendray, George Edward
Pendray, G. Edward
See Pendray, George Edward
Pendray, George Edward
1901-1987 Obituary ... 123
Penelope
See Boyden, Sarah B.
Penfield, Thomas 1903- ... 5-8R
Penfield, Wilder (Graves) 1891-1976 ... CANR-3
Obituary ... 65-68
Earlier sketch in CA 5-8R
Pengelley, Eric T. 1919- ... 89-92
Penick, James (Lal) Jr. 1932- ... 33-36R
Penn, Anne
See Pendower, Jacques
Penn, Arthur (Hiller) 1922- ... 130
Brief entry ... 112
Penn, Asher 1908(?)-1979 Obituary ... 93-96
Penn, Audrey 1950- ... CANR-13
Earlier sketch in CA 77-80
See also Zellan, Audrey Penn
Penn, Christopher
See Lawlor, Patrick Anthony
Penn, David
See Balsiger, David (Wayne)
Penn, John
See Harcourt, Palma
Penn, Margaret Obituary ... 105
Penn, Ruth Bonn
See Rosenberg, Ethel (Clifford)
Penn, William 1644-1718 ... DLB 24

Penna, Sandro 1906-1977 .... DLB 114
Pennage, E. M.
See Finkel, George (Irvine)
Pennar, Jaan 1924- Brief entry 115
Pennekamp, John (David)
1897-1978 Obituary 89-92
See also AITN 2
Penner, Fred (Ralph Cornelius) 1946- 136
See also SATA 67
Penner, Jonathan 1940- CANR-39
Earlier sketches in CA 97-100, CANR-17
See also DLBY 83
Penner, Peter 1925- 129
Penney, Annette Culler 1916- 45-48
Penney, Edmund F. 1926- 132
Penney, Grace Jackson 1904- 5-8R
See also SATA 35
Penney, J(ames) C(ash)
1875-1971 Obituary 29-32R
Penney, Jennifer 1946- 122
Pennick, Nigel Campbell 1946- CANR-28
Earlier sketch in CA 110
Pennie, Hester
See Taylor, Elisabeth (D.)
Penniman, Clara 1914- Brief entry 111
Penniman, Howard R(ae) 1916- CANR-12
Earlier sketch in CA 13-16R
Penniman, Thomas Kenneth
1896(?)-1977 Obituary 69-72
Penninger, F(rieda) Elaine 1927- 57-60
Penningroth, Paul W(illiam) 1901-1974 49-52
Obituary 103
Penning-Rowsell, Edmund 1913- 127
Pennington, Albert Joe 1950- 57-60
Pennington, Anne (Elizabeth)
1934-1981 Obituary 114
Pennington, Chester Arthur 1916- 104
Pennington, Donald Henshaw 1919- 5-8R
Pennington, Eunice 1923- 57-60
See also SATA 27
Pennington, Howard (George) 1923- 49-52
Pennington, John Selman
1924(?)-1980 Obituary 102
Pennington, Lee 1939- CANR-31
Earlier sketch in CA 69-72
See also DLBY 82
Pennington, Lillian Boyer 1904- .... SATA 45
Pennington, Lucinda 1945- 117
Pennington, M. (Robert John) Basil
1931- CANR-37
Earlier sketches in CA 93-96, CANR-16
Pennington, Penny
See Galbraith, Georgie Starbuck
Pennington, Robert (Roland) 1927- 73-76
Pennington, Stuart
See Galbraith, Georgie Starbuck
Pennington, W(eldon) J(erry)
1919-1985 Obituary 115
Pennink, (John Jacob) Frank 1913- 5-8R
Pennock, J(ames) Roland 1906- CANR-29
Earlier sketches in CA 33-36R, CANR-13
Penny, J. Leith 1955- 127
Penny, Julie 1945- 117
Penny, Prudence
See Goldberg, Hyman
Penny, Ruthanna (Merrick) 1914- 17-20R
Pennycuick, John 1943- 97-100
Penrod, James 1934- 77-80
Penrose, Antony 1947- 137
Penrose, Boies 1902-1976 Obituary 65-68
Penrose, Edith Tilton 1914- 25-28R
Penrose, Gordon 1925- 127
See also SATA 66
Penrose, Harald CANR-21
Earlier sketches in CA 13-16R, CANR-6
Penrose, Margaret CANR-27
Earlier sketches in CAP-2, CA 19-20
Penrose, Roger 1931- .... BEST 90:2
Penrose, Roland (Algernon) 1900-1984 85-88
Obituary 112
Penslar, Derek J(onathan) 1958- 136
Pentecost, Edward C(lyde) 1917- 57-60
Pentecost, Hugh
See Philips, Judson (Pentecost)
Pentecost, J(ohn) Dwight 1915- CANR-2
Earlier sketch in CA 5-8R
Pentecost, Martin
See Hearn, John
Pentony, DeVere Edwin 1924- CANR-8
Earlier sketch in CA 5-8R
Pentreath, A(rthur Godolphin) Guy C(arleton)
1902-1985 .... CAP-1
Obituary 118
Earlier sketch in CA 13-14
Pentz, Croft Miner CANR-9
Earlier sketch in CA 5-8R
Pentz, Lundy H(urd) 1951- 116
Penuel, Arnold M(cCoy) 1936- 57-60
Penuelas, Marcelino C. 1916- 25-28R
Penzel, Frederick 1948- 85-88
Penzik, Irena
See Narell, Irena
Penzl, Herbert 1910- CANR-24
Earlier sketch in CA 45-48
Penzler, Otto 1942- CANR-35
Earlier sketch in CA 81-84
See also SATA 38
Peoples, Morgan D. 1919- 133
Pepe, John Frank 1920- 9-12R
Pepe, Phil(ip) 1935- CANR-18
Earlier sketch in CA 25-28R
See also SATA 20
PEPECE
See Prado (Calvo), Pedro
Pepelasis, Adam(antios) A. 1923- CANR-2
Earlier sketch in CA 1-4R
Peper, George Frederick 1950- CANR-25
Earlier sketch in CA 108
Pepin, Jacques (Georges) 1935- CANR-25
Earlier sketch in CA 103
Pepinsky, Harold E(ugene) 1945- 119
Pepitone, Albert (Davison) 1923- 9-12R
Pepitone, Joe 1940- Brief entry 109
Pepitone, Joseph Anthony
See Pepitone, Joe
Peppard, Murray B(isbee) 1917-1974 .... CAP-2
Obituary 53-56
Earlier sketch in CA 21-22
Peppe, Rodney 1934- 33-36R
See also MAICYA
See also SAAS 10
See also SATA 4
Pepper, Adeline 41-44R
Pepper, Art(hur Edward)
1925-1982 Obituary 107
Pepper, Choral 1918- 25-28R
Pepper, Claude Denson
1900-1989 Obituary 128
Pepper, Curtis Bill
See Pepper, Curtis G.
Pepper, Curtis G. 1920- CANR-10
Earlier sketch in CA 21-24R
Pepper, Frank S. 1910-1988 Obituary 127
See also SATA 61
Pepper, Joan
See Wetherell-Pepper, Joan Alexander
Pepper, John 1942- 117
Pepper, Martin
See Krich, John
Pepper, Stephen C(oburn)
1891-1972 .... CANR-32
Obituary 103
Earlier sketch in CA 1-4R
Pepper, Thomas 1939- CANR-16
Earlier sketch in CA 97-100
Pepper, William M(ullin) Jr. 1903-1975 97-100
Obituary 57-60
Peppercorn, David 1931- 118
Peppercorn, Lisa M(argot) 1913- 138
Peppiatt, Michael 1941- 118
Peppin, Brigid (Mary) 1941- 65-68
Peppler, Alice Stolper 1934- 53-56
Pepys, Samuel 1633-1703 .... CDBLB 1660-1789
See also DLB 101
See also WLC
Peradotto, John Joseph 1933- 41-44R
Perceval-Maxwell, M(ichael) 1933- 53-56
Percival, Alicia C(onstance) 1903- 9-12R
Percival, John 1927- 33-36R
Percival, Walter 1896- CAP-1
Earlier sketch in CA 11-12
Percy, Charles H(arting) 1919- 65-68
Percy, Charles Henry
See Smith, Dorothy Gladys
Percy, Douglas Cecil 1914- CANR-3
Earlier sketch in CA 5-8R
Percy, Herbert R(oland) 1920- 5-8R
Percy, Rachel 1930- .... SATA 63
Percy, Thomas 1729-1811 .... DLB 104
Percy, Walker 1916-1990 .... CANR-23
Obituary 131
Earlier sketches in CA 1-4R, CANR-1
See also CLC 2, 3, 6, 8, 14, 18, 47, 65
See also DLB 2
See also DLBY 80, 90
See also MTCW
Percy, William A. Jr. 1933- 29-32R
Perdue, Charles L. Jr. 1930- 135
Perdue, Theda 1949- CANR-16
Earlier sketch in CA 93-96
Perdurabo, Frater
See Crowley, Edward Alexander
Perec, Georges 1936-1982 .... CLC 56
See also DLB 83
Pereda (y Sanchez de Porrua), Jose Maria de
1833-1906 Brief entry 117
See also TCLC 16
Pereda y Porrua, Jose Maria de
See Pereda (y Sanchez de Porrua), Jose Maria de
Peregoy, George Weems
See Mencken, H(enry) L(ouis)
Peregrine
See Deutscher, Isaac
Pereira, Harold Bertram 1890- 9-12R
Pereira, Sam 1949- 111
Pereira, W(ilfred) D(ennis) 1921- CANR-20
Earlier sketch in CA 104
Pereira Carneiro, Maurina
1899(?)-1983 Obituary 111
Perel, William M. 1927- 33-36R
Perella, Nicholas James 1927- 73-76
Perelman, Chaim 1912- 103
Perelman, Lewis J(oel) 1946- 73-76
Perelman, Michael 1939- 111
Perelman, S(idney) J(oseph)
1904-1979 .... CANR-18
Obituary 89-92
Earlier sketch in CA 73-76
See also AITN 1, 2
See also CLC 3, 5, 9, 15, 23, 44, 49
See also DLB 11, 44
See also MTCW
Perenyi, Eleanor (Spencer Stone) 1918- 133
Brief entry 113
Perera, Gretchen G(ifford) 1940- 93-96
Perera, Thomas Biddle 1938- CANR-21
Earlier sketch in CA 37-40R
See also SATA 13
Perera, Victor 1934- 29-32R
Peres, Richard 1947- 93-96
Peres, Shimon 1923- 85-88
Peret, Benjamin 1899-1959 Brief entry 117
See also TCLC 20
Peretti, Frank E. 1951- 136
Peretz, Don 1922- CANR-19
Earlier sketches in CA 9-12R, CANR-4
Peretz, Isaac Loeb
1851(?)-1915 Brief entry 109
See also TCLC 16
Peretz, Yitzkhok Leibush
See Peretz, Isaac Loeb
Pereyra, Lillian A(nita) 1920- 21-24R
Perez, Joseph F(rancis) 1930- CANR-36
Earlier sketches in CA 29-32R, CANR-16
Perez, Louis A. Jr. 1943- 121
Perez, Louis C(elestino) 1923- 77-80
Perez de Ayala, Ramon
1881-1962 Obituary 93-96
Perez-Firmat, Gustavo (Francisco) 1949- 123
Perez Galdos, Benito
1843-1920 Brief entry 125
See also HW
See also TCLC 27
Perez-Gomez, Alberto 1949- 130
See also HW
Perez Lopez, Francisco 1916- 49-52
Perez-Marchand, Monelisa L(ina) 1918- .... HW
Perham, Margery (Freda) 1895-1982 .... CANR-1
Obituary 106
Earlier sketch in CA 1-4R
Pericoli, Ugo 1923- 97-100
Perigoe, J. Rae 1910- 61-64
Perillo, Joseph M. 1933- 17-20R
Perin, Constance 29-32R
Perin, Roberto 1948- 133
Perinbanayagam, Robert S(idharthan)
1934- 109
Perino, Joseph 1946- 106
Perino, Sheila C. 1948- 106
Peripatus
See Whittington-Egan, Richard
Peri Rossi, Cristina 1941- 131
See also HW
Peristiany, John G(eorge) 1911-1987 .... 17-20R
Obituary 124
Peritz, Rene 1933- 45-48
Perkes, Dan 1931- CANR-21
Earlier sketch in CA 69-72
Perkin, Harold (James) 1926- CANR-14
Earlier sketch in CA 77-80
Perkin, J(ames) R(ussell) C(onway) 1928- 113
Perkin, Joan 1926- 131
Perkin, Robert L(yman)
1914-1978 Obituary 77-80
Perkins, Agnes (Regan) 1926- CANR-10
Earlier sketch in CA 57-60
Perkins, Al(bert Rogers) 1904-1975 107
Obituary 57-60
See also SATA 30
Perkins, Ann (Louise) 1915- Brief entry 113
Perkins, Bradford 1925- 1-4R
Perkins, Carl (Lee) 1932- 102
Perkins, David (Lee) 1939- CANR-13
Earlier sketch in CA 73-76
Perkins, David 1928- 77-80
Perkins, Dexter 1889-1984 .... 5-8R
Obituary 113
Perkins, Dwight Heald 1934- CANR-22
Earlier sketches in CA 17-20R, CANR-7
Perkins, E(rnest) Benson 1881-1964 .... 5-8R
Obituary 134
Perkins, Edward A. Jr. 1928- CANR-14
Earlier sketch in CA 21-24R
Perkins, Edwin Judson 1939- 106
Perkins, Eugene 1932- .... DLB 41
Perkins, Faith
See Bramer, Jennie (Perkins)
Perkins, George (Burton Jr.) 1930- 13-16R
Perkins, Hugh V(ictor) 1918-1988 93-96
Obituary 124
Perkins, James Alfred 1911- 108
Perkins, James Ashbrook 1941- 73-76
Perkins, James Oliver Newton 1924- 9-12R
Perkins, James S(cudday) 1899- 89-92
Perkins, John Allen 1919- 114
Perkins, John Bryan Ward
See Ward-Perkins, John Bryan
Perkins, John (William) 1935- CANR-13
Earlier sketch in CA 73-76
Perkins, Ken 1926- 137
Perkins, Lawrence A.
1917(?)-1979 Obituary 89-92
Perkins, Lucy Fitch 1865-1937 137
Brief entry 122
See also MAICYA
Perkins, (Richard) Marlin 1905-1986 103
Obituary 119
See also SATA 21, 48
Perkins, Merle Lester 1919- 45-48
Perkins, Michael 1942- CANR-8
Earlier sketch in CA 17-20R
Perkins, Newton Stephens 1925- 49-52
Perkins, Ralph 1913- 13-16R
Perkins, Robert L(ee) 1930- 25-28R
Perkins, Rollin M(orris) 1889- 53-56
Perkins, Steve
See Perkins, Newton Stephens
Perkins, Van L. 1930- Brief entry 106
Perkins, Virginia Chase 1902- CAP-2
Earlier sketch in CA 33-36
Perkins, Whitney Trow 1921- 106
Perkins, William H(ughes) 1923- 53-56
Perkins, Wilma Lord 1897-1976 Obituary 104
Perkinson, Henry J(oseph) 1930- CANR-12
Earlier sketch in CA 17-20R
Perkoff, Stuart Z. 1930-1974 Obituary 113
See also DLB 16
Perkowski, Jan Louis 1936- CANR-2
Earlier sketch in CA 45-48
Perl, Arnold 1914-1971 Obituary 33-36R
Perl, Jeffrey M(ichael) 1952- 138
Perl, Lila 33-36R
See also SATA 6
Perl, Ruth June 1929- 25-28R
Perl, Susan 1922-1983 .... CANR-11
Obituary 110
Earlier sketch in CA 17-20R
See also SATA 22, 34
Perl, Teri (Hoch) 1926- CANR-19
Earlier sketch in CA 93-96
Perl, William R. 1906- 126
Perlberg, Deborah 1948- 118
Perlberg, Mark 1929- 37-40R
Perle, George 1915- CANR-3
Earlier sketch in CA 1-4R
Perles, Alfred 1897-1990(?) Obituary 130
Perles, Benjamin Max 1922- 45-48
Perley, Michael 1946- 114
Perley, Moses Henry 1804-1862 .... DLB 99
Perlin, John 1944- 134
Perlin, Seymour 1925- 121
Perlinski, Jerome 1940- 112
Perlis, Vivian 1928- 85-88
Perlman, Bennard B(loch) 1928- 89-92
Perlman, Helen Harris 1905- CANR-3
Earlier sketch in CA 1-4R
Perlman, Janice E(laine) 1943- 61-64
Perlman, Jess 1891- 89-92
Perlman, John N(iels) 1946- CANR-12
Earlier sketch in CA 33-36R
Perlman, Mark 1923- CANR-19
Earlier sketches in CA 1-4R, CANR-3
Perlman, Samuel 1905-1975 .... CAP-2
Earlier sketch in CA 33-36
Perlmutter, Emanuel
1907(?)-1986 Obituary 118
Perlmutter, Jerome H. 1924- 17-20R
Perlmutter, Nathan 1923-1987 .... 13-16R
Obituary 123
Perlmutter, O(scar) William 1920-1975 57-60
See also SATA 8
Perlmutter, Ruth Ann 1924- 109
Perlo, Victor 1912- CANR-2
Earlier sketch in CA 5-8R
Perloff, Harvey S(tephen) 1915-1983 129
Obituary 110
Perloff, Marjorie G(abrielle) 1931- CANR-22
Earlier sketches in CA 57-60, CANR-7
Perlongo, Bob 1933- 112
Perls, Eugenia Soderberg
1904(?)-1973 Obituary 37-40R
Perls, Frederick S(alomon) 1893-1970 101
Perls, Fritz
See Perls, Frederick S(alomon)
Perls, Hugo 1886(?)-1977 Obituary 73-76
Perlstein, Gary R(obert) 1940- 57-60
Perman, Dagmar Horna
1926(?)-1978 Obituary 77-80
Perman, Michael 1942- Brief entry 113
Pern, Stephen (Antony Nigel) 1950- 128
Pernet, A(nn) 1940- 107
Perniciaro, Tony 1917- 41-44R
Pernick, Martin S(teven) 1948- 128
Pernoud, Regine 1909- 102
Peroff, Nicholas C(arl) 1944- 113
Peron, Juan (Domingo)
1895-1974 Obituary 49-52
Perosa, Sergio 1933- CAP-1
Earlier sketch in CA 13-16
Peroutka, Ferdinand
1895(?)-1978 Obituary 77-80
Perowne, Barry
See Atkey, Philip
Perowne, Stewart Henry 1901-1989 .... CANR-3
Obituary 128
Earlier sketch in CA 1-4R
Perrault, Charles 1628-1703 .... MAICYA
See also SATA 25
Perreard, Suzanne Louise Butler
1919- .... SATA 29
Perreault, John 1937- CANR-1
Earlier sketch in CA 45-48
Perreault, William D(aniel) Jr. 1948- 110
Perrella, Robert 1917- 61-64
Perrenod, Virginia Marion (Lacy) 1928- 117
Perret, Gene 1937- 117
Brief entry 114
Perrett, Bryan 1934- CANR-20
Earlier sketch in CA 29-32R
Perrett, Geoffrey 1940- CANR-4
Earlier sketch in CA 53-56
Perriam, Wendy 1940- 136
Perrigo, Lynn I(rwin) 1904- 33-36R
Perrin, Blanche Chenery 1894-1973 .... 5-8R
Obituary 41-44R
Perrin, Gail 1938- 136
Perrin, Noel 1927- CANR-31
Earlier sketch in CA 13-16R
Perrin, (Horace) Norman 1920-1976 .... CANR-11
Earlier sketch in CA 13-16R
Perrin, Porter Gale 1896-1962 Obituary 113
Perrin, Robert G(eorge) 1945- 111
Perrin, Robert 1939- 97-100
Perrin, Ursula 1935- 101
Perrine, Laurence 1915- CANR-3
Earlier sketch in CA 1-4R
Perrine, Mary 1913- 25-28R
See also SATA 2
Perrin Jassy, Marie-France 1942- 93-96
Perrins, Lesley 1953- 123
See also SATA 56
Perrone, Charles A. 1951- 132
Perrottet, Philippe (Louis Gaston)
1921-1982 .... 25-28R
Obituary 122
Perroy, Edouard (Marie Joseph)
1901-1974 Obituary 53-56

Perrucci, Robert 1931- CANR-34
Earlier sketches in CA 85-88, CANR-15
Perruchot, Henri 1917-1967 .... CAP-1
Earlier sketch in CA 9-10
Perry, Anne 1938- CANR-22
Earlier sketch in CA 101
Perry, Barbara Fisher
See Fisher, Barbara
Perry, Ben Edwin 1892-1968 .... CAP-2
Earlier sketch in CA 23-24
Perry, Bernard (Berenson)
1910-1985 Obituary 117
Perry, Bliss 1860-1954 .... DLB 71
Perry, Brighton
See Sherwood, Robert E(mmet)
Perry, Carmen ....AITN 2
Perry, Charles Edward ....AITN 2
Perry, Charles 1941- 124
Perry, Charner M(arquis)
1902-1985 Obituary 117
Perry, Collin 1949- 108
Perry, David L. 1931- 33-36R
Perry, David Thomas 1946- 37-40R
Perry, Dick 1922- 13-16R
Perry, Edgar C(loud) 1900- 117
Perry, Eleanor (Rosenfeld Bayer)
1915(?)-1981 111
Obituary 103
See also DLB 44
Perry, Elisabeth Israels 1939- 111
Perry, Elizabeth Jean 1948- 104
Perry, Erma (Jackson McNeil) 89-92
Perry, Gaylord (Jackson) 1938- Brief entry 113
Perry, George 1935- CANR-26
Earlier sketch in CA 103
Perry, Gordon Arthur 1914- 108
Perry, Grace 1927- CANR-20
Earlier sketch in CA 102
Perry, Henry Ten Eyck 1890-1973 .... CAP-2
Earlier sketch in CA 19-20
Perry, Huey 1936- 49-52
Perry, James M(oorhead) 1927- 13-16R
Perry, Jim (Angelo) 1942- 53-56
Perry, John Curtis 1930- 104
Perry, John D(elbert) Jr. 1940- 25-28R
Perry, John Oliver 1929- 93-96
Perry, John 1914- CANR-6
Earlier sketch in CA 5-8R
Perry, Joseph M(cGarity) 1936- 37-40R
Perry, Kenneth F(rederick) 1902-1974 ...... CAP-2
Earlier sketch in CA 19-20
Perry, Kenneth I. 1929- 29-32R
Perry, Kenneth W(ilbur) 1919- 57-60
Perry, Lewis (Curtis) 1938- CANR-1
Earlier sketch in CA 45-48
Perry, Linette (Purbi) 108
Perry, Lloyd M(erle) 1916- CANR-9
Earlier sketch in CA 21-24R
Perry, Louis B(arnes) 1918- CAP-1
Earlier sketch in CA 13-14
Perry, Margaret 1933- 89-92
See also BW
Perry, Michael (Charles) 1933- 101
Perry, Milton F(reeman) 1926- 13-16R
Perry, Nicolette E. 1949- 119
Perry, Octavia Jordan 1894- CAP-1
Earlier sketch in CA 13-14
Perry, Patricia 1949- 106
See also SATA 30
Perry, Peter John 1937- 49-52
Perry, Phillip M. 1948- 29-32R
Perry, Phyllis J. 1933- ....SATA 60
Perry, Ralph Barton 1876-1957 Brief entry 123
Perry, Regenia (Alfreda) 1941- 126
Perry, Richard 41-44R
Perry, Richard S. 1924- 13-16R
Perry, Richard 1944- 115
See also BW
Perry, Ritchie (John Allen) 1942- CANR-21
Earlier sketches in CA 45-48, CANR-1
Perry, Robin 1917- 65-68
Perry, Roger 1933- CANR-14
Earlier sketch in CA 77-80
See also SATA 27
Perry, Rosalie Sandra 1945- 53-56
Perry, Rufus
See Gibson, Walter B(rown)
Perry, Ruth (Fuller) 1892- 131
Perry, Ruth 1943- 118
Perry, Shauneille 1930- 113
Perry, Stewart E(dmond) 1928- 17-20R
Perry, (Charles) Stuart 1908- 107
Perry, Susan
See Perry, Susan M.
Perry, Susan M. 1950- 124
Perry, T. Anthony 1938- 81-84
Perry, Thomas Brief entry 123
Perry, Thomas Whipple 1925- 9-12R
Perry, Thomas 1947- 130
Perry, Troy D(eroy) 1940- Brief entry 109
Perry, Walter (Laing Macdonald) 1921- 113
Perry, Will 1933- 65-68
Perry, William E(dward) 1931- 111
Perry, Wilma I. 1912- 105
Perse, Saint-John
See Leger, (Marie-Rene) Alexis Saint-Leger
Perse, St.-John
See Leger, (Marie-Rene) Alexis Saint-Leger
See also CLC 4, 11, 46
Pershall, Mary K. 1951- 138
See also SATA 70
Pershing, Marie
See Schultz, Pearle Henriksen
Persichetti, Vincent 1915-1987 Obituary 124
Persico, Joseph E(dward) 1930- CANR-21
Earlier sketch in CA 93-96
Persinger, Michael A. 1945- 69-72
Persis
See Haime, Agnes Irvine Constance (Adams)
Perske, Robert 1927- 106
See also SATA 57
Persky, Mordecai 1931- 81-84
Persky, Mort
See Persky, Mordecai
Persky, Stan 1941- CANR-39
Earlier sketches in CA 101, CANR-18
Person, Amy L. 1896- CAP-2
Earlier sketch in CA 23-24
Person, Bernard 1895(?)-1981 Obituary 103
Person, Peter P. 1889- CAP-1
Earlier sketch in CA 11-12
Persons, Robert H(odge) Jr. 1922- CANR-13
Earlier sketch in CA 17-20R
Persons, Stow Spaulding 1913- 103
Pertinax
See Geraud, (Charles Joseph) Andre
and Haws, Duncan
Pertschuk, Michael 1933- CANR-26
Earlier sketch in CA 109
Pertwee, Michael (Henry Roland)
1916- Brief entry 124
Pertwee, Roland 1885-1963 Obituary 93-96
Perutz, Kathrin 1939- CANR-3
Earlier sketch in CA 1-4R
Perutz, Leo 1882-1957 .... DLB 81
Pervin, Lawrence A. 1936- CANR-8
Earlier sketch in CA 21-24R
Pescadero, Joey
See Obrecht, Jas
Pescadero, Julia
See Obrecht, Jas
Peschel, Enid Rhodes 1943- 110
Pescow, Jerome K(enneth) 1929- 45-48
Peseenz, Tulio F.
See Lopez y Fuentes, Gregorio
Pesek, Boris P(eter) 1926- 21-24R
Pesek, Ludek 1919- 29-32R
Pesetsky, Bette 1932- 133
See also CLC 28
Peshkin, Alan 1931- 81-84
Peshkov, Alexei Maximovich
1868-1936 Brief entry 105
See also Gorky, Maxim
Pesin, Harry 1919- 29-32R
Peskin, Allan 1933- Brief entry 109
Pesnot, Patrick 1943- 101
Pessen, Beth 1943- 97-100
Pessen, Edward 1920- CANR-14
Earlier sketch in CA 37-40R
Pessina, Giorgio 1902(?)-1977 Obituary 73-76
Pessino, Clara Park 1899(?)-1985 Obituary 116
Pesso, Albert 1929- 73-76
Pessoa, Fernando (Antonio Nogueira)
1888-1935 Brief entry 125
See also TCLC 27
Pestalozzi, Johann Heinrich 1746-1827 .... DLB 94
Pestelli, Giorgio 1938- 124
Pestieau, Phyllis Smith 1946- 97-100
Petacco, Arrigo 1929- CANR-21
Earlier sketch in CA 103
Petacque, Art 1924- 136
Petaja, Emil (Theodore) 1915- 25-28R
Peter
See Stratemeyer, Edward L.
Peter, Armistead (III)
1896(?)-1983 Obituary 111
Peter, James (Fletcher) 1919- 17-20R
Peter, John (Desmond) 1921- CANR-3
Earlier sketch in CA 1-4R
Peter, Laurence J(ohnston)
1919-1990 ....CANR-17
Obituary 130
Earlier sketch in CA 17-20R
See also DLB 53
Peterfreund, Sheldon P(aul) 1917- 21-24R
Peterfreund, Stuart (Samuel) 1945- CANR-30
Earlier sketches in CA 33-36R, CANR-13
Peterkiewicz, Jerzy 1916- CANR-5
Earlier sketch in CA 5-8R
Peterkin, Julia Mood 1880-1961 102
See also CLC 31
See also DLB 9
Peterman, Michael A(lan) 1942- 111
Peterman, Ruth 1924- 57-60
Peter of Spain 1205(?)-1277 .... DLB 115
Peters, Alexander
See Hollander, Zander
Peters, Arthur Anderson
1913-1979 Obituary 93-96
Peters, Arthur King 1919- 104
Peters, Barney
See Bauer, Erwin A.
Peters, Caroline
See Betz, Eva Kelly
Peters, Catherine 1930- 127
Peters, Charles (Given Jr.) 1926- 122
Brief entry 116
Peters, Christina 1942- 85-88
Peters, Daniel (James) 1948- CANR-39
Earlier sketches in CA 85-88, CANR-15
Peters, David A(lexander) 1923- 25-28R
Peters, Donald L. 1925- 21-24R
Peters, Edward (Murray) 1936- CANR-18
Earlier sketch in CA 101
Peters, Elizabeth
See Mertz, Barbara (Gross)
Peters, Ellis
See Pargeter, Edith Mary
Peters, Eugene H(erbert) 1929- 41-44R
Peters, F(rancis) E(dward) 1927- CANR-12
Earlier sketch in CA 73-76
Peters, Frederick George 1935- 104
Peters, Fritz
See Peters, Arthur Anderson
Peters, Geoffrey
See Palmer, Madelyn
Peters, George W(illiam) 1907- CANR-24
Earlier sketch in CA 45-48
Peters, H. Frederick 1910- 73-76
Peters, J. Ross 1936- 29-32R
Peters, Jean (Rae) 1935- 116
Peters, Joan K. 1945- .... CLC 39
Peters, Ken(neth Walter) 1929- 17-20R
Peters, Lane
See Lapidus, Elaine
Peters, Lawrence
See Davies, L(eslie) P(urnell)
Peters, Lenrie (Wilfred Leopold) 1932- 108
See also BW
See also DLB 117
Peters, Leslie
See Peters, Donald L.
Peters, Linda
See Catherall, Arthur
Peters, Ludovic
See Brent, Peter (Ludwig)
Peters, Marcia
See Gouled, Vivian G(loria)
Peters, Margaret Evelyn 1936- 53-56
Peters, Margot 1933- CANR-12
Earlier sketch in CA 73-76
Peters, Maureen 1935- 33-36R
Peters, Max S(tone) 1920- 57-60
Peters, Michael
See Hornsby-Smith, Michael P(eter)
Peters, Michael Bartley 1943- 110
Brief entry 108
Peters, Mike
See Peters, Michael Bartley
Peters, Natasha
See Cleaver, Anastasia N.
Peters, R(ichard) S(tanley) 1919- CANR-16
Earlier sketch in CA 21-24R
Peters, Richard Dorland
1910-1984 Obituary 114
Peters, Robert Anthony 1926- 49-52
Peters, Robert L(ouis) 1924- 13-16R
See also CAAS 8
See also CLC 7
See also DLB 105
Peters, Ronald M. Jr. 1947- 85-88
Peters, Ruth Marie 1913(?)-1978 Obituary 104
Peters, S. H.
See Porter, William Sydney
and Proffitt, Nicholas (Charles)
Peters, S. T.
See Brannon, William T.
Peters, Stephen 1907(?)-1990 Obituary 130
Peters, Steven
See Geiser, Robert L(ee)
Peters, Ted
See Peters, Theodore F(rank)
Peters, Theodore F(rank) 1941- 81-84
Peters, Thomas J. 1942- 135
Brief entry 123
See also Peters, Tom
Peters, Tom
See Peters, Thomas J.
See also BEST 89:1
Peters, Victor 1915- 17-20R
Peters, Virginia Bergman 1918- 93-96
Peters, William 1921- CANR-20
Earlier sketches in CA 9-12R, CANR-3
Petersen, Arnold 1885-1976 Obituary 65-68
Petersen, Carol Otto 1914- 57-60
Petersen, Clarence G. 1933- 77-80
Petersen, David M(uir) 1939- 41-44R
Petersen, David 1946- ....SATA 62
Petersen, Donald 1928- 13-16R
Petersen, E. Allen 1903(?)-1987 Obituary 122
Petersen, Gwenn Boardman 1924- CANR-2
Earlier sketch in CA 45-48
See also Boardman, Gwenn R.
See also SATA 61
Petersen, James R(eeve) 1948- 114
Petersen, Karen Daniels 1910- 73-76
Petersen, Mark E. 1900-1984 132
Obituary 111
Petersen, Melba F(rances) Runtz 1919- 5-8R
Petersen, P(eter) J(ames) 1941- CANR-30
Earlier sketch in CA 112
See also MAICYA
See also SATA 43, 48
Petersen, Peter (Barron) 1932- 57-60
Petersen, Sigurd Damskov 1904- 9-12R
Petersen, William J. 1929- CANR-9
Earlier sketch in CA 21-24R
Petersen, William John 1901- 5-8R
Petersen, William 1912- CANR-3
Earlier sketch in CA 1-4R
Petersham, Maud (Sylvia Fuller)
1890-1971 ....CANR-29
Obituary 33-36R
Earlier sketch in CA 73-76
See also CLR 24
See also DLB 22
See also MAICYA
See also SATA 17
Petersham, Miska 1888-1960 ....CANR-29
Earlier sketch in CA 73-76
See also CLR 24
See also DLB 22
See also MAICYA
See also SATA 17
Peterson, A(lexander) D(uncan) C(ampbell)
1908-1988 108
Obituary 126
Peterson, Agnes F(ischer) 1923- 29-32R
Peterson, Arthur L(aVerne) 1926- 9-12R
Peterson, Audrey 131
Peterson, Brent D(an) 1942- 120
Peterson, Carl 1896(?)-1983 Obituary 110
Peterson, Carolyn Sue 1938- CANR-12
Earlier sketch in CA 73-76
Peterson, Carroll V(alleen) 1929- 45-48
Peterson, Charles Jacobs 1819-1887 ...... DLB 79
Peterson, Charles S. 1927- 49-52
Peterson, Charles 1900(?)-1976 Obituary 69-72
Peterson, Christmas
See Christmas, Joyce
Peterson, Dale 1944- 109
Peterson, Donald R(obert) 1923- 25-28R
Peterson, Donald 1956- 135
Peterson, Douglas L(ee) 1924- 41-44R
Peterson, Edward N(orman) 1925- 29-32R
Peterson, Edwin (Lewis)
1904-1972 Obituary 37-40R
Peterson, Edwin Loose 1915- 5-8R
Peterson, Eldridge
1905(?)-1977 Obituary 73-76
Peterson, Eleanor M. 1912- 25-28R
Peterson, Elmer 1930- 37-40R
Peterson, Esther (Allen) 1934- CANR-16
Earlier sketch in CA 89-92
See also SATA 35
Peterson, Evan T(ye) 1925- 45-48
Peterson, F. Ross 1941- 97-100
Peterson, Forrest H(arold) 1912- CANR-25
Earlier sketch in CA 45-48
Peterson, Franklynn 1938- CANR-37
Earlier sketch in CA 110
Peterson, Frederick Alvin 1920- 49-52
Peterson, Gilbert Allan 1935- CANR-35
Earlier sketch in CA 114
Peterson, Hans 1922- CANR-1
Earlier sketch in CA 49-52
See also SATA 8
Peterson, Harold F(erdinand) 1900- 5-8R
Peterson, Harold L(eslie) 1922-1978 ......CANR-4
Obituary 73-76
Earlier sketch in CA 1-4R
See also SATA 8
Peterson, Harold 1939- 29-32R
Peterson, Helen Stone 1910- 37-40R
See also SATA 8
Peterson, Houston 1897-1981 107
Obituary 103
Peterson, James
See Zeiger, Henry A(nthony)
Peterson, James Alfred 1913- 104
Obituary 137
Peterson, James Allan 1932- 29-32R
Peterson, Jeanne Whitehouse
See Whitehouse, Jeanne
Peterson, Jim
See Crawford, William (Elbert)
Peterson, John Eric 1933- 53-56
Peterson, John J. 1918- 53-56
Peterson, John W(illard) 1921- 97-100
Peterson, Kenneth G(erard) 1927- 33-36R
Peterson, Len 1917- .... DLB 88
Peterson, Levi S(avage) 1933- CANR-26
Earlier sketch in CA 109
Peterson, Linda H(aenlein) 1948- 121
Peterson, Lloyd R(ichard) 1922- Brief entry 107
Peterson, Lorraine 1940- 113
See also SATA 44, 56
Peterson, Louis 1922- .... DLB 76
Peterson, M(ildred) Jeanne 1937- 103
Peterson, Marilyn Ann 1933- 57-60
Peterson, Martin Severin 1897- CANR-3
Earlier sketch in CA 1-4R
Peterson, Mendel (Lazear) 1918- 73-76
Peterson, Merrill D(aniel) 1921- CANR-19
Earlier sketches in CA 1-4R, CANR-3
Peterson, Nancy L(ee) 1939- 105
Peterson, Norma Lois 1922- 13-16R
Peterson, Ottis 1907- 21-24R
Peterson, Owen M. 1924- CANR-26
Earlier sketch in CA 108
Peterson, Paul E(lliott) 1940- CANR-24
Earlier sketch in CA 45-48
Peterson, R(odney) D(elos) 1932- 41-44R
Peterson, Reona 1941- 73-76
Peterson, Richard A(ustin) 1932- 25-28R
Peterson, Richard F(rank) 1939- 128
Peterson, Richard H(ermann) 1942- 137
Peterson, Richard S(cot) 1938- 133
Peterson, Robert E(ugene) 1928- 13-16R
Peterson, Robert W. 1925- 33-36R
Peterson, Robert 1924- CANR-17
Earlier sketch in CA 25-28R
Peterson, Roger Tory 1908- CANR-1
Earlier sketch in CA 1-4R
Peterson, Russell Arthur 1922- 33-36R
Peterson, Simone
See Thomson, Daisy H(icks)
Peterson, Steven A. 1947- 138
Peterson, Susan (Annette) H(arnly)
1925- 57-60
Peterson, Ted Nicholas 1934- 121
Peterson, Theodore (Bernard) 1918- 9-12R
Peterson, Trudy H(uskamp) 1945- 116
Peterson, Virgil W(allace)
1904-1989 Obituary 127
Peterson, Virgilia 1904-1966 Obituary 25-28R
Peterson, Wallace Carroll 1921- 5-8R
Peterson, Walter Scott 1944- 21-24R
Peterson, Wilferd Arlan 1900- CANR-6
Earlier sketch in CA 9-12R
Peterson, Willard James 1938- 103
Peterson, William R. 1943-1990 Obituary 132
Peterson, William S(amuel) 1939- CANR-11
Earlier sketch in CA 29-32R
Petersson, Robert T. 1918- 45-48
Peterzell, Jay 1952- 118

Petesch, Natalie L(evin) M(aines)
1924- ...CANR-21
Earlier sketches in CA 57-60, CANR-6
See also CAAS 12
Petgen, Dorothea 1903(?)-1985 Obituary ...115
Petgen, Dorothy
See Petgen, Dorothea
Pethybridge, Roger 1934- ...5-8R
Petie, Haris
See Petty, Roberta
See also SATA 10
Petievich, Gerald 1944- ...105
Petiot, Henri Jules Charles
1901-1965 Obituary ...114
Petit, Gaston 1930- ...73-76
Petitclair, Pierre 1813-1860 ...DLB 99
Petitclerc, Denne Bart 1929- ...93-96
Petite, Irving (Laurence) 1920- Brief entry ...113
Petitfils, Pierre (Robert) 1908- ...137
Petkas, Peter (James) 1945- ...37-40R
Petmecky, Ben (Joe) 1922- ...1-4R
Peto
See White, Stanley
Peto, James
See White, Stanley
Petrakis, Harry Mark 1923- ...CANR-30
Earlier sketches in CA 9-12R, CANR-4
See also CLC 3
Petranek, Stephen Lynn 1944- ...133
Petras, James Frank 1937- ...CANR-22
Earlier sketches in CA 61-64, CANR-7
Petras, John W. 1940- ...29-32R
Petrement, Simone 1907- ...77-80
Petres, Robert E(van) 1939- ...104
Petric, Vlada
See Petric, Vladimir
Petric, Vladimir 1928- ...129
Petrich, Patricia Barrett 1942- ...61-64
Petrides, Avra ...123
Petrides, George Athan 1916- Brief entry ...106
Petrides, Heidrun 1944- ...SATA 19
Petrie, Alexander 1881- ...CAP-1
Earlier sketch in CA 13-16
Petrie, Asenath 1914- ...21-24R
Petrie, Catherine 1947- ...109
See also SATA 41, 52
Petrie, Charles (Alexander) 1895-1977 ...CANR-8
Obituary ...89-92
Earlier sketch in CA 17-20R
Petrie, Mildred McClary 1912- ...21-24R
Petrie, Paul J(ames) 1928- ...CANR-18
Earlier sketches in CA 9-12R, CANR-3
Petrie, Rhona
See Buchanan, Marie
Petrie, Sidney 1923- ...21-24R
Petrinovich, Lewis 1930- ...41-44R
Petro, Nicolai N. 1958- ...135
Petro, Sylvester 1917- ...1-4R
Petrocelli, Orlando R(alph) 1930- ...CANR-1
Earlier sketch in CA 45-48
Petrone, Jane Muir 1929- ...5-8R
Petroni, Frank A. 1936- ...85-88
Petropulos, John A(nthony) 1929- ...25-28R
Petroski, Catherine (Ann Groom)
1939- ...CANR-22
Earlier sketch in CA 106
See also SATA 48
Petrou, David Michael 1949- ...73-76
Petrov, Evgeny
See Kataev, Evgeny Petrovich
See also TCLC 21
Petrov, Fyodor 1877(?)-1973 Obituary ...41-44R
Petrov, Michel
See Visson, Lynn
Petrov, Victor P. 1907- ...CANR-26
Earlier sketches in CA 21-24R, CANR-10
Petrov, Vladimir 1915- ...21-24R
Petrova, Olga 1884(?)-1977 Obituary ...73-76
Petrovich, Michael B(oro) 1922- ...108
See also SATA 40
Petrovska, Marija 1926- ...107
Petrovskaya, Kyra
See Wayne, Kyra Petrovskaya
Petrovsky, Boris
See Beauchamp, Kathleen Mansfield
Petrovsky, N.
See Poltoratzky, N(ikolai) P(etrovich)
Petrucci, Kenneth R(occo) 1947- ...57-60
Petruccio, Steven James 1961- ...SATA 67
Petry, Alice Hall 1951- ...130
Petry, Ann (Lane) 1908- ...CANR-4
Earlier sketch in CA 5-8R
See also CAAS 6
See also BW
See also CLC 1, 7, 18
See also CLR 12
See also DLB 76
See also MAICYA
See also MTCW
See also SATA 5
Petry, Carl Forbes 1943- ...106
Petry, R(ay) C. 1903- ...5-8R
Pettas, Mary 1918- ...25-28R
Pettee, George S(awyer)
1904(?)-1989 Obituary ...130
Petterson, Henry William 1922- ...9-12R
Petterson, Steve D. 1948- ...138
Petterssen, Sverre 1898-1974 Obituary ...53-56
Pettersson, Karl-Henrik 1937- ...65-68
Pettes, Dorothy E. ...CANR-12
Earlier sketch in CA 25-28R
Pettifer, Julian 1935- ...136
Pettigrew, Thomas Fraser 1931- ...CANR-30
Earlier sketches in CA 33-36R, CANR-13
Pettingill, Amos
See Harris, William Bliss
Pettingill, Olin Sewall Jr. 1907- ...CANR-1
Earlier sketch in CA 45-48
Pettit, Arthur G. 1938-1977 ...53-56
Obituary ...135
Pettit, Clyde Edwin 1932- ...65-68
Pettit, Henry (Jewett) 1906- ...1-4R
Pettit, Lawrence K. 1937- ...33-36R
Pettit, Michael (Edwin) 1950- ...114
Pettit, Norman 1929- ...17-20R
Pettit, Philip 1945- ...CANR-37
Earlier sketches in CA 97-100, CANR-17
Pettitt, George A(lbert) 1901-1976 ...CAP-2
Earlier sketch in CA 29-32
Pettoello, Decio (Egberto Saadi)
1886-1984 Obituary ...113
Petty, Anne C(otton) 1945- ...115
Petty, Mary 1899-1976 Obituary ...65-68
Petty, Norman 1927(?)-1984 Obituary ...113
Petty, Roberta 1915- ...CANR-10
Earlier sketch in CA 61-64
See also Petie, Haris
Petty, Walter T. 1918- ...CANR-9
Earlier sketch in CA 21-24R
Petty, William Henry 1921- ...65-68
Petuchowski, Jakob Josef 1925-1991 ...CANR-18
Obituary ...136
Earlier sketches in CA 1-4R, CANR-3
Petulla, Joseph M. 1932- ...CANR-9
Earlier sketch in CA 21-24R
Petzinger, Thomas Jr. 1955- ...136
Petzold, Paul 1940- ...CANR-9
Earlier sketch in CA 61-64
Petzoldt, Paul Kiesow 1908- ...57-60
Petzoldt, Richard 1907-1974 Obituary ...111
Peukert, Detlev
See Peukert, Detlev J(ulio) K.
Peukert, Detlev J(ulio) K. 1950- ...133
Pevsner, Nikolaus (Bernhard Leon)
1902-1983 ...CANR-7
Obituary ...110
Earlier sketch in CA 9-12R
See also MTCW
Pevsner, Stella ...CANR-27
Earlier sketch in CA 57-60
See also SAAS 14
See also SATA 8
Peyo
See Culliford, Pierre
Peyre, Henri (Maurice) 1901-1988 ...CANR-3
Obituary ...127
Earlier sketch in CA 5-8R
Peyrefitte, Alain Antoine 1925- ...85-88
Peyrefitte, (Pierre) Roger 1907- ...65-68
Peyser, Joan 1931- Brief entry ...112
Peyton, K. M.
See Peyton, Kathleen Wendy
See also CLR 3
Peyton, Karen (Hansen) 1897-196 (?) ...CAP-1
Earlier sketch in CA 9-10
Peyton, Kathleen Wendy 1929- ...CANR-32
Earlier sketch in CA 69-72
See also Peyton, K. M.
See also MAICYA
See also SATA 15, 62
Peyton, Myron A(lvin) 1909- Brief entry ...114
Peyton, Patrick J(oseph) 1909- ...CAP-2
Obituary ...137
Earlier sketch in CA 23-24
Pezzullo, Ralph 1951- ...135
Pezzulo, Ted 1936(?)-1979 Obituary ...89-92
Pezzuti, Thomas Alexander 1936- ...61-64
Pfadt, Robert Edward 1915- ...73-76
Pfaff, Daniel W. 1940- ...136
Pfaff, Richard W(illiam) 1936- ...128
Pfaff, William (Wendle III) 1928- ...CANR-24
Earlier sketch in CA 5-8R
Pfaffenberger, Bryan 1949- ...118
Pfaffenberger, Clarence J. 1889-1967 ...CAP-1
Earlier sketch in CA 13-14
Pfahl, John K(erch) 1927- ...CANR-1
Earlier sketch in CA 1-4R
Pfaltz, Marilyn 1933- ...103
Pfaltzgraff, Robert L. Jr. 1934- ...CANR-24
Earlier sketches in CA 21-24R, CANR-9
Pfanner, Helmut Franz 1933- ...57-60
Pfanner, (Anne) Louise 1955- ...136
See also SATA 68
Pfanz, Harry W. 1921- ...128
Pfarrer, Donald 1934- ...111
Pfatteicher, Philip H(enry) 1935- ...114
Pfau, Hugo 1908- ...29-32R
Pfau, Richard Anthony 1942- ...120
Pfeffer, J(ay) Alan 1907- ...CANR-3
Earlier sketch in CA 1-4R
Pfeffer, Jeffrey 1946- ...109
Pfeffer, Leo 1910- ...CANR-22
Earlier sketches in CA 13-16R, CANR-7
Pfeffer, Rose 1908-1985 Obituary ...115
Pfeffer, Susan Beth 1948- ...CANR-31
Earlier sketch in CA 29-32R
See also CLR 11
See also SATA 4
Pfefferle, Seth 1955- ...128
Pfeffermann, Guy 1941- ...25-28R
Pfeifer, Carl J(ames) 1929- ...49-52
Pfeifer, Luanne 1928- ...CANR-16
Earlier sketch in CA 89-92
Pfeiffer, Bruce Brooks 1930- ...121
Pfeiffer, C(urtis) Boyd 1937- ...57-60
Pfeiffer, Carl Curt 1908- ...101
Pfeiffer, Charles F. 1919-1976 ...CANR-4
Obituary ...65-68
Earlier sketch in CA 1-4R
Pfeiffer, Eric 1935- ...CANR-10
Earlier sketch in CA 13-16R
Pfeiffer, John E(dward) 1914- ...101
Pfeiffer, Karl G(raham) ...1-4R
Pfeiffer, Marcella
See Syracuse, Marcella Pfeiffer
Pfeil, (John) Fred(erick) 1949- ...133
Pfeilschifter, Boniface 1900- ...CAP-2
Earlier sketch in CA 19-20
Pferd, William (III) 1922(?)-1987 Obituary ...121
Pfiffner, John M(cDonald) 1893- ...5-8R
Pfingston, Roger 1940- ...CANR-20
Earlier sketch in CA 104
Pfister, Arthur 1949- ...45-48
Pflanze, Otto (Paul) 1918- ...5-8R
Pflaum, Irving Peter 1906-1985 ...13-16R
Obituary ...115
Pflaum, Melanie L(oewenthal) 1909- ...CANR-6
Earlier sketch in CA 13-16R
Pflaum, Susanna Whitney 1937- ...110
Brief entry ...106
Pflaum-Connor, Susanna
See Pflaum, Susanna Whitney
Pflieger, Elmer F. 1908- ...17-20R
Pflum, John (Edward) 1934- Brief entry ...107
Pfordresher, John 1943- ...65-68
Pfouts, Ralph W(illiam) 1920- ...41-44R
Pfoutz, Shirley Eclov 1922- ...1-4R
Pfriem, John E. 1923(?)-1983 Obituary ...110
Pfuetze, Paul E(ugene) 1904-1985 ...1-4R
Obituary ...118
Phair, Judith Turner 1946- ...61-64
Phalle, Thibaut de Saint
See de Saint Phalle, Thibaut
Phan, Peter C(ho) 1943- ...114
Phares, Donald 1942- ...81-84
Phares, Ross (Oscar) 1908- ...CAP-1
Earlier sketch in CA 11-12
Phares, Timothy B. 1954- ...97-100
Pharr, Emory Charles
1896(?)-1981 Obituary ...104
Pharr, Robert Deane 1916- ...CANR-27
Obituary ...137
Earlier sketch in CA 49-52
See also BW
See also DLB 33
Pharr, Susan J(ane) 1944- ...105
Phelan, Francis (Joseph) 1925- ...CANR-36
Earlier sketch in CA 5-8R
Phelan, James Pius X 1951- ...CANR-35
Earlier sketch in CA 114
Phelan, John Leddy 1924-1976 ...CANR-12
Earlier sketch in CA 21-24R
Phelan, John Martin 1932- ...73-76
Phelan, Josephine 1905- ...SATA 30
Phelan, Mary Kay 1914- ...CANR-4
Earlier sketch in CA 1-4R
See also SATA 3
Phelan, Mary Michenfelder 1936- ...97-100
Phelan, Nancy 1913- ...101
Phelan, Shane 1956- ...137
Phelan, Terry Wolfe 1941- ...97-100
See also SATA 56
Phelge, Nanker
See Richards, Keith
Phelps, Arthur Warren 1909- ...49-52
Phelps, Ashton 1913-1983 Obituary ...109
Phelps, D(udley) Maynard 1897- ...CAP-2
Earlier sketch in CA 25-28
Phelps, Digger
See Phelps, Richard
Phelps, Donald (Norman) 1929- ...CANR-25
Earlier sketch in CA 45-48
Phelps, Elizabeth Stuart 1844-1911 ...DLB 74
Phelps, Ethel Johnston 1914- ...106
See also SATA 35
Phelps, Frederic
See McCulley, Johnston
Phelps, Gilbert (Henry Jr.) 1915- ...CANR-26
Earlier sketches in CA 5-8R, CANR-7
Phelps, Humphrey 1927- ...111
Phelps, J(oseph) Alfred 1927- ...135
Phelps, Jack 1926- ...29-32R
Phelps, O(rme) Wheelock 1906- ...1-4R
Phelps, Phelps 1897-1981 Obituary ...104
Phelps, Richard ...103
Phelps, Robert 1922-1989 ...CANR-19
Obituary ...129
Earlier sketch in CA 17-20R
Phelps, Roger P(aul) 1920- ...49-52
Phelps, Thomas Ross 1929- ...61-64
Phenix, Philip Henry 1915- ...5-8R
Pheto, Molefe 1935- ...118
Phialas, Peter George 1914- ...25-28R
Phibbs, Brendan (Pearse) 1916- ...33-36R
Phifer, Kenneth G. 1915- ...17-20R
Philbrick, Allen Kellogg 1914- ...117
Philbrick, Charles (Horace) II
1922-1971 ...CANR-4
Earlier sketch in CA 1-4R
Philbrick, Helen L. 1910- ...103
Philbrick, Joseph Lawrence 1927- ...45-48
Philbrook, Clem(ent E.) 1917- ...104
See also SATA 24
Philby, Harold Adrian Russell
1912-1988 Obituary ...125
Philby, Kim
See Philby, Harold Adrian Russell
Philip, Cynthia Owen 1928- ...49-52
Philip, J(ames) A(llenby) 1901- ...CAP-2
Earlier sketch in CA 23-24
Philip, John Robert 1927- ...108
Philip, Leila 1961- ...137
Philip, Lotte Brand
See Foerster, Lotte B(rand)
Philipp, Elliot Elias 1915- ...CANR-3
Earlier sketch in CA 9-12R
Philippatos, George Crito 1938- Brief entry ...106
Philippe, Charles-Louis 1874-1909 ...DLB 65
Philippi, Donald L. 1930- ...108
Philips, Cyril Henry 1912- ...103
Philips, G(eorge) Edward 1926- ...41-44R
Philips, John 1676-1708 ...DLB 95
Philips, Judson (Pentecost)
1903-1989 ...CANR-14
Obituary ...128
Earlier sketch in CA 89-92
See also AITN 1
Philips, Michael 1942- ...125
Philips, Thomas
See Davies, L(eslie) P(urnell)
Philipson, Morris H. 1926- ...CANR-4
Earlier sketch in CA 1-4R
See also CLC 53
Philipson, Susan Sacher 1934- ...9-12R
Philliber, William W(esley) 1943- ...111
Phillifent, John Thomas
1916-1976 Obituary ...102
Phillippi, Wendell Crane 1918- ...136
Phillips, Aileen Paul
See Paul, Aileen
Phillips, Alan
See Stauderman, Albert P(hilip)
Phillips, Alan Meyrick Kerr 1916- ...5-8R
Phillips, Alice H(erz) 1909- ...114
Phillips, Allen
See Allen, (Evelyn) Elizabeth
Phillips, Almarin 1925- ...CANR-1
Earlier sketch in CA 1-4R
Phillips, Anne G(arvey) 1929- ...73-76
Phillips, (Elizabeth Margaret Ann) Barty
1933- ...CANR-24
Earlier sketches in CA 61-64, CANR-8
Phillips, Beeman N(oal) 1927- ...122
Phillips, Bernard S. 1931- ...CANR-12
Earlier sketch in CA 25-28R
Phillips, Bernice Maxine 1925- ...45-48
Phillips, Betty Lou
See Phillips, Elizabeth Louise
Phillips, Billie M(cKindra) 1925- ...102
Phillips, Bluebell
See Phillips, Bluebell Stewart
Phillips, Bluebell S.
See Phillips, Bluebell Stewart
Phillips, Bluebell Stewart 1904- ...131
Phillips, Bob 1940- ...69-72
Phillips, C(ecil) E(rnest) Lucas
See Lucas Phillips, C(ecil) E(rnest)
Phillips, Cabell (Beverly Hatchett)
1904-1975 ...97-100
Obituary ...61-64
Phillips, Carla Rahn 1943- ...128
Phillips, Carole 1938- ...108
Phillips, Cecil R(andolph) 1933- ...13-16R
Phillips, Celeste R(ose Nagel) 1933- ...110
Phillips, Charles F(ranklin) Jr. 1934- ...CANR-2
Earlier sketch in CA 5-8R
Phillips, Charles F(ranklin Jr.) 1910- ...85-88
Phillips, Claude S. Jr. 1923- ...9-12R
Phillips, Clifton J(ackson) 1919- ...37-40R
Phillips, (Preswly) Craig 1922- ...9-12R
Phillips, D(ennis) J(ohn Andrew)
1924- ...CANR-10
Earlier sketch in CA 13-16R
Phillips, David Atlee 1922-1988 ...CANR-12
Obituary ...126
Earlier sketch in CA 69-72
Phillips, David Graham
1867-1911 Brief entry ...108
See also DLB 9, 12
See also TCLC 44
Phillips, Debora R(othman) 1939- ...93-96
Phillips, Derek L(ee) 1934- ...CANR-18
Earlier sketch in CA 33-36R
Phillips, Dewi Zephaniah 1934- ...CANR-25
Earlier sketches in CA 17-20R, CANR-9
Phillips, Dorothy S(anborn)
1893-1972 Obituary ...37-40R
Phillips, Dorothy W. 1906-1977 Obituary ...73-76
Phillips, E(lmo) Bryant 1905-1975 ...CANR-6
Earlier sketch in CA 5-8R
Phillips, E(wing) Lakin 1915- ...37-40R
Phillips, E(ugene) Lee 1941- ...115
Phillips, Edward O. 1931- ...124
Phillips, Edwin A(llen) 1915- ...53-56
Phillips, Elizabeth C(row) 1906- ...41-44R
Phillips, Elizabeth Louise ...SATA 48, 58
Phillips, Emma Julia 1900- ...CAP-1
Earlier sketch in CA 13-14
Phillips, Frances Lucas
1896-1986 Obituary ...119
Phillips, Frank
See Nowlan, Philip Francis
Phillips, Gene D(aniel) 1935- ...CANR-38
Earlier sketches in CA 45-48, CANR-1, 17
Phillips, George H(oward) 1907- ...112
Phillips, Gerald M. 1928- ...CANR-29
Earlier sketches in CA 33-36R, CANR-13
Phillips, Gordon Lewis 1911-1982 Obituary ...108
Phillips, Herbert P. 1929- ...13-16R
Phillips, Hiram Stone 1912(?)-1979 ...85-88
Phillips, Irv(ing W.) 1905- ...CANR-31
Earlier sketch in CA 65-68
See also SATA 11
Phillips, J(ohn) B(ertram) 1906-1982 ...106
Obituary ...108
Phillips, Jack
See Sandburg, Carl (August)
Phillips, James E(merson Jr.)
1912-1979 Obituary ...89-92
Phillips, James Emerson Jr. 1912-1979 ...101
Phillips, James M(cJunkin) 1929- ...106
Phillips, James W. 1922- ...33-36R
Phillips, Jayne Anne 1952- ...CANR-24
Earlier sketch in CA 101
See also CLC 15, 33
See also DLBY 80
See also MTCW

Phillips, Jerome C.
See Cleveland, Philip Jerome
Phillips, Jewell Cass 1900- CAP-2
Earlier sketch in CA 33-36
Phillips, Jill (Meta) 1952- CANR-39
Earlier sketches in CA 65-68, CANR-14
Phillips, John A(llen) 1949- 133
Phillips, John L(awrence) Jr. 1923- 33-36R
Phillips, Josephine E(lvira Frye)
1896-1975 ....5-8R
Obituary 61-64
Phillips, Julien L(ind) 1945- 77-80
Phillips, Kathleen C(oleman) 1920- CANR-39
Earlier sketch in CA 116
Phillips, Keith W(endall) 1946- 102
Phillips, Kevin Price 1940- 65-68
Phillips, Klaus (Peter) 1947- 116
Phillips, L(ouis) C(hristopher) 1939- 57-60
Phillips, Laughlin 1924- 102
Phillips, Leon
See Gerson, Noel Bertram
Phillips, Leona Rasmussen 1925- CANR-14
Earlier sketch in CA 65-68
Phillips, Lois (Elisabeth) 1926- Brief entry 114
Phillips, Loretta (Hosey) 1893- CAP-1
Earlier sketch in CA 13-16
See also SATA 10
Phillips, Louis 1942- CANR-20
Earlier sketches in CA 49-52, CANR-3
See also SATA 8
Phillips, Mac
See Phillips, Maurice J(ack)
Phillips, Margaret Mann 1906-1987 ....13-16R
Obituary 123
Phillips, Margaret McDonald
1910(?)-1978 Obituary 77-80
Phillips, Margaret 1892(?)-1985 Obituary 116
Phillips, Marjorie (Fell) 5-8R
Phillips, Mark
See Garrett, (Gordon) Randall (Phillip)
and Janifer, Laurence M(ark)
Phillips, Mary Geisler 1881-1964 ....5-8R
See also SATA 10
Phillips, Mary L. 1930- 116
Phillips, Maurice J(ack) 1914-1976 ....5-8R
Obituary 103
Phillips, Michael
See Nolan, William F(rancis)
Phillips, Michael Joseph 1937- CANR-18
Earlier sketches in CA 49-52, CANR-3
Phillips, Michael R(ay) 1946- 114
Phillips, Michael 1938- 108
Phillips, (Holly) Michelle 1944- 137
Phillips, Mickey
See Phillips, Alan Meyrick Kerr
Phillips, Mike
See Phillips, Michael R(ay)
Phillips, O(wen) Hood 1907- CANR-2
Earlier sketch in CA 5-8R
Phillips, O(wen) M(artin) 1930- 89-92
Phillips, Osborne
See Barcynski, Leon Roger
Phillips, Patricia 1935- 103
Phillips, Paul T(homas) 1942- 138
Phillips, Paul 1938- CANR-14
Earlier sketch in CA 73-76
Phillips, Pauline (Esther Friedman)
1918- CANR-19
Earlier sketch in CA 1-4R
Phillips, Prentice 1894- CAP-1
Earlier sketch in CA 13-16
See also SATA 10
Phillips, R. Hart
See Phillips, Ruby Hart
Phillips, Rachel 1934- 49-52
Phillips, Ray C. 1922- CANR-10
Earlier sketch in CA 25-28R
Phillips, Richard
See Dick, Philip K(indred)
Phillips, Richard C(laybourne) 1934- 65-68
Phillips, Robert L(eRoy) Jr. 1940- 77-80
Phillips, Robert (Schaeffer) 1938- CANR-8
Earlier sketch in CA 17-20R
See also CAAS 13
See also CLC 28
See also DLB 105
Phillips, Roderick (Goler) 1947- 131
Phillips, Ruby Hart 1902-1985 Obituary 117
Phillips, Samantha
See Gelles-Cole, Sandi
Phillips, Stella 1927- CANR-11
Earlier sketch in CA 21-24R
Phillips, Stephen 1864-1915 Brief entry 111
See also DLB 10
Phillips, Steve
See Whittington, Harry (Benjamin)
Phillips, Steven 1947- 103
Phillips, Tom
See Drotning, Phillip T(homas)
Phillips, Tom 1937- 128
Phillips, Ulrich B. 1877-1934 .... DLB 17
Phillips, Velma 1894- CAP-2
Earlier sketch in CA 19-20
Phillips, Vic 1941- 128
Phillips, Ward
See Lovecraft, H(oward) P(hillips)
Phillips, Warren (Henry) 1926- 107
Phillips, Wendell 1921-1975 .... CAP-2
Obituary 61-64
Earlier sketch in CA 23-24
Phillips, Willard 1784-1873 .... DLB 59
Phillips, William CANR-35
Earlier sketch in CA 29-32R
Phillips, William G. 1924(?)-1990 Obituary 130
Phillips-Birt, Douglas Hextall Chedzey
1920-1977 ....CANR-1
Earlier sketch in CA 1-4R
Phillips-Jones, Linda 1943- CANR-26
Earlier sketch in CA 109
Phillipson, David W(alter) 1942- 107
Phillipson, David 1930- 57-60
Phillipson, Michael 1940- 133
Phillpotts, (Mary) Adelaide Eden
1896- CANR-37
Earlier sketch in CA 115
Phillpotts, Eden 1862-1960 102
Obituary 93-96
See also DLB 10, 70
See also SATA 24
Philmus, Robert M. 1943- 33-36R
Philomythes
See Dewart, Leslie
Philp, Howard Littleton 1902- 5-8R
Philp, Kenneth R(oy) 1941- 65-68
Philp, (Dennis Alfred) Peter 1920- 5-8R
Philp, Richard Nilson 1943- CANR-11
Earlier sketch in CA 69-72
Philpott, David G(oodwin) 1927- 123
Philpott, Kent 1942- 61-64
Phin
See Thayer, Ernest Lawrence
Phipps, Christine 1945- 123
Phipps, Frances (Lucille Walker)
1924(?)-1986 Obituary 119
Phipps, Grace May Palk 1901- CANR-4
Earlier sketch in CA 9-12R
Phipps, Joyce 1942- 49-52
Phipps, Nicholas 1913-1980 Obituary 97-100
Phipps, William E(ugene) 1930- CANR-30
Earlier sketches in CA 29-32R, CANR-12
Phipson, Joan
See Fitzhardinge, Joan Margaret
See also CLR 5
See also SAAS 3
Phiz
See Browne, Hablot Knight
Phleger, Fred B. 1909- CANR-21
Earlier sketch in CA 1-4R
See also SATA 34
Phleger, Marjorie Temple 1908(?)-1986 ......9-12R
Obituary 118
See also SATA 1, 47
Phoenix, John
See Derby, George Horatio
Phoenix, Pat
See Pilkington, Pat
Phypers, David (John) 1939- 114
Physick, John Frederick 1923- 114
Phythian, B(rian) A(rthur) 1932- CANR-10
Earlier sketch in CA 21-24R
Piaf, Edith 1915-1963 Obituary 113
Piaget, Jean 1896-1980 ....CANR-31
Obituary 101
Earlier sketch in CA 21-24R
See also MTCW
See also SATA 23
Pian, Rulan Chao 1922- 21-24R
Piano, Celeste
See Lykiard, Alexis (Constantine)
Piasecki, Bruce 1955- CANR-12
Earlier sketch in CA 69-72
Piatigorsky, Alexander 1929- 124
Piatigorsky, Gregor 1903-1976 Obituary 69-72
Piatti, Celestino 1922- 73-76
See also SATA 16
Piazza, Ben 1934- 9-12R
Picano, Felice 1944- CANR-27
Earlier sketches in CA 69-72, CANR-11
See also CAAS 13
Picard, Barbara Leonie 1917- CANR-2
Earlier sketch in CA 5-8R
See also MAICYA
See also SAAS 10
See also SATA 2
Picard, Robert G(eorge) 1951- 127
Picasso, Pablo (Ruiz) 1881-1973 97-100
Obituary 41-44R
Picazo, Jose 1910- CAP-1
Earlier sketch in CA 13-14
Piccard, Auguste 1884-1962 Obituary 113
Piccard, Betty
See Piccard, Elizabeth J(ane)
Piccard, Elizabeth J(ane) 1925- 65-68
Piccard, Jacques 1922- 65-68
Piccard, Joan Russell 29-32R
Picchio, Riccardo 1923- CANR-24
Earlier sketch in CA 45-48
Piccolo, Lucio 1901-1969 97-100
See also CLC 13
See also DLB 114
Pichaske, David Richard 1943- CANR-1
Earlier sketch in CA 45-48
Pichois, Claude 1925- 132
Pick, J(ohn) B(arclay) 1921- CANR-5
Earlier sketch in CA 1-4R
Pick, John 1911- CAP-2
Earlier sketch in CA 33-36
Pick, (Frederick) Michael 1949- 123
Pick, Robert 1898-1978 ....CANR-8
Obituary 77-80
Earlier sketch in CA 17-20R
Pickard, Charles 1932- ....SATA 36
Pickard, Dorothea Wilgus 1902- 21-24R
Pickard, John Benedict 1928- 1-4R
Pickard, Tom 1946- 81-84
See also DLB 40
Pickell, Charles N(orman) 1927- 17-20R
Pickem, Peter
See Stearns, Harold Edmund
Picken, Mary Brooks
1886(?)-1981 Obituary 103
Picken, Stuart D(onald) B(lair) 1942- 106
Pickens, Donald Kenneth 1934- 53-56
Pickens, Robert S.
1900(?)-1978 Obituary 81-84
Pickens, Roy 1939- 57-60
Picker, Fred 1927- 81-84
Picker, Ingrid 1932- 25-28R
Picker, Martin 1929- CANR-7
Earlier sketch in CA 17-20R
Pickerell, Albert G(eorge) 1912- 25-28R
Pickerill, Don 1928- 77-80
Pickering, Ernest 1893(?)-1974 Obituary 53-56
Pickering, Frederick Pickering 1909- 105
Pickering, George W. 1937- 136
Pickering, George (White) 1904-1980 73-76
Obituary 105
Pickering, James H(enry) 1937- CANR-29
Earlier sketches in CA 33-36R, CANR-13
Pickering, James Sayre 1897-1969 ....CANR-16
Obituary 103
Earlier sketch in CA 1-4R
See also SATA 28, 36
Pickering, Jerry V(ane) 1931- 57-60
Pickering, Paul 1952- 138
Pickering, Percival
See
Stirling, Anna Maria Diana Wilhelmina (Pickering)
Pickering, R(obert) E(aston) 1934- 21-24R
Pickering, Samuel Francis Jr. 1941- 104
Pickering, Stephen 1947- 57-60
Pickersgill, J(ohn) W(hitney) 1905- 45-48
Pickett, Calder M. 1921- 53-56
Pickett, Carla 1944- 37-40R
Pickett, J(arrell) Waskom 1890- CAP-1
Earlier sketch in CA 13-16
Pickett, Robert S. 1931- 33-36R
Pickford, Cedric Edward 1926-1983 107
Obituary 109
Pickford, Mary 1893-1979 Obituary 85-88
Pickle, Hal B(rittain) 1929- CANR-21
Earlier sketches in CA 57-60, CANR-6
Pickles, (Maud) Dorothy 1903- 77-80
Pickles, M(abel) Elizabeth 1902- CAP-1
Earlier sketch in CA 9-10
Pickles, Wilfred 1904-1978(?) 108
Pickoff, David 1930(?)-1986 Obituary 118
Pickrel, Paul (Murphy) 1917- 9-12R
Pickthall, Marjorie L(owry) C(hristie)
1883-1922 Brief entry 107
See also DLB 92
See also TCLC 21
Pickthorn, Helen 1927- 25-28R
Pico, Rafael 1912- 45-48
Picon, Molly 1898- 104
Picott, J(ohn) Rupert
1916(?)-1989 Obituary 129
Picou, Alphonse
See Ghnassia, Maurice (Jean-Henri)
Picoult, Jodi 1966- 138
Picton, Bernard
See Knight, Bernard
Pidal, Ramon Menendez
See Menendez Pidal, Ramon
Pidgeon, Mary E. 1890(?)-1979 Obituary 89-92
Piechocki, Joachim von Lang
See von Lang-Piechocki, Joachim
Piediscalzi, Nicholas 1931- 122
Brief entry 112
Pied Piper
See Mallalieu, John Percival William
Piehl, Mel (Willis) 1946- 111
Piehler, Paul 1929- Brief entry 111
Piekalkiewicz, Jaroslaw A. 1926- 81-84
Piel, Gerard 1915- 57-60
Pielmeier, John 1949- 132
Brief entry 125
Pienkowski, Jan (Michal) 1936- CANR-38
Earlier sketches in CA 65-68, CANR-11
See also CLR 6
See also MAICYA
See also SATA 6, 58
Pieper, Josef 1904- 119
Piepkorn, Arthur Carl 1907-1973 ....41-44R
Pier, Arthur Stanhope
1874(?)-1966 Obituary 25-28R
Pierard, Richard Victor 1934- CANR-38
Earlier sketches in CA 29-32R, CANR-17
Pieratt, Asa B. 1938- 77-80
Pierce, Arthur Dudley 1897-1967 ....1-4R
Obituary 103
Pierce, Bessie Louise
1888-1974 Obituary 53-56
Pierce, E(ugene) 1924- 13-16R
Pierce, Edith Gray 1893-1977 61-64
See also SATA 45
Pierce, Edward T. 1917(?)-1978 Obituary 77-80
Pierce, George Gilbert 1923- 5-8R
Pierce, Gerald S(wetnam) 1933- 45-48
Pierce, Glenn
See Dumke, Glenn S.
Pierce, James Smith 1930- 21-24R
Pierce, Janis V(aughn) 1934- 45-48
Pierce, Joe E. 1924- 33-36R
Pierce, John Leonard Jr. 1921- 9-12R
Pierce, John Robinson 1910- 17-20R
Pierce, Katherine
See St. John, Wylly Folk
Pierce, Lawrence C(olman) 1936- 85-88
Pierce, Meredith Ann 1958- CANR-26
Earlier sketch in CA 108
See also CLR 20
See also MAICYA
See also SATA 48, 67
Pierce, Milton Plotz 1933- 106
Pierce, Ovid Williams 1910- CANR-4
Earlier sketch in CA 1-4R
Pierce, Patricia (May) 1943- 120
Pierce, Paul 1910- 69-72
Pierce, Philip E(arly) 1912- 110
Pierce, Richard A(ustin) 1918- CANR-2
Earlier sketch in CA 5-8R
Pierce, Robert N(ash) 1931- 104
Pierce, Roy 1923- 37-40R
Pierce, Ruth (Ireland) 1936- 29-32R
See also SATA 5
Pierce, Tamora 1954- 118
See also SATA 49, 51
Pierce, Willard Bob 1914- 13-16R
Piercy, Josephine Ketcham 1895- CAP-1
Earlier sketch in CA 13-16
Piercy, Marge 1936- CANR-13
Earlier sketch in CA 21-24R
See also CAAS 1
See also CLC 3, 6, 14, 18, 27, 62
See also DLB 120
See also MTCW
Pierik, Robert 1921- 37-40R
See also SATA 13
Pierman, Carol J 1947- 77-80
Pierotti, John 1911-1987 133
Obituary 122
Pierpoint, Robert (Charles) 1925- 107
Pierre, Andrew J. 1934- CANR-1
Earlier sketch in CA 45-48
Pierre, Clara 1939- 65-68
Pierrot, George Francis 1898-1980 ....5-8R
Obituary 103
See also AITN 2
Piers, Maria W(eigl) 1911- CANR-8
Earlier sketch in CA 21-24R
Piers, Robert
See Anthony, Piers
Piersen, William D. 1942- 126
Pierson, Frank
See Pierson, Frank R(omer)
Pierson, Frank R(omer) 1925- 123
Brief entry 114
Pierson, G(eorge) W(ilson) 1904- CANR-3
Earlier sketch in CA 9-12R
Pierson, Howard 1922- 49-52
Pierson, Jan 1937- 112
Pierson, John H(erman) G(roesbeck)
1906- CANR-4
Earlier sketch in CA 9-12R
Pierson, Paul Everett 1927- 108
Pierson, Peter O'Malley 1932- 97-100
Pierson, Robert H. 1911- 21-24R
Pierson, Stanley 1925- 85-88
Pierson, William H(arvey) Jr. 1911- 122
Piet, John H(enry) 1914- 29-32R
Pietri, Arturo Uslar
See Uslar Pietri, Arturo
Pietri, Pedro (Juan) 1943- CANR-32
Earlier sketch in CA 97-100
See also HW
Pietrofesa, John J(oseph) 1940- 57-60
Pietropinto, Anthony 1938- 89-92
Pietrusza, David 1949- 135
Pietsch, Paul Andrew 1929- 104
Pietschmann, Richard John III 1940- 69-72
Pieyre de Mandiargues, Andre
1909-1991 ....CANR-22
Obituary 136
Earlier sketch in CA 103
See also Mandiargues, Andre Pieyre de
Pifer, Alan J(ay Parrish) 1921- 127
Pifer, Ellen 1942- CANR-23
Earlier sketch in CA 106
Pig, Edward
See Gorey, Edward (St. John)
Piggott, C. M.
See Guido, (Cecily) Margaret
Piggott, (Alan) Derek 1923- CANR-37
Earlier sketch in CA 115
Piggott, Stuart 1910- 134
Pigman, William Ward
1910-1977 Obituary 73-76
Pigney, Joseph Pape 1908- 1-4R
Pihera, Larry 1933- CANR-1
Earlier sketch in CA 45-48
Pihl, Marshall R(alph) 1933- 49-52
Pijewski, John 1952- 111
Piji
See Williams, Ann Jr.
Pike, Albert 1809-1891 .... DLB 74
Pike, Burton 1930- CANR-33
Earlier sketch in CA 1-4R
Pike, Charles R.
See Bulmer, (Henry) Kenneth
and Harknett, Terry
Pike, Christopher 136
See also SATA 68
Pike, Dag 1933- 69-72
Pike, Diane Kennedy 1938- 37-40R
Pike, E(dgar) Royston 1896-1980 ....9-12R
Obituary 125
See also SATA 22, 56
Pike, Eunice V(ictoria) 1913- CANR-20
Earlier sketch in CA 97-100
Pike, James A(lbert) 1913-1969 ....CANR-4
Obituary 25-28R
Earlier sketch in CA 1-4R
Pike, Kenneth Lee 1912- 120
Pike, Margaret (Prudence) Lyford
See Lyford-Pike, Margaret (Prudence)
Pike, Nelson C. 1930- Brief entry 111
Pike, Norman 1901- CAP-2
Earlier sketch in CA 25-28
Pike, Robert E(vording) 1905- 5-8R
Pike, Robert L.
See Fish, Robert L.
Pike, Ruth 1931- 134
Brief entry 112
Pike, William H. 1943- 115
Pikelny, Philip S. 1951- 107
Pikoulis, John 1941- 115

Pikunas, Justin 1920- 25-28R
Pilapil, Vicente R. 1941- 37-40R
Pilarski, Laura 1926- 29-32R
See also SATA 13
Pilat, O. R.
See Pilat, Oliver (Ramsay)
Pilat, Oliver (Ramsay) 1903-1987 .... 5-8R
Obituary 123
Pilbrow, Richard (Hugh) 1933- 29-32R
Pilcer, Sonia 1949- CANR-13
Earlier sketch in CA 89-92
Pilch, John J(oseph) 1936- CANR-25
Earlier sketch in CA 108
Pilch, Judah 1902- CANR-6
Earlier sketch in CA 5-8R
Pilcher, George William 1935- 105
Pilcher, Rosamunde 1924- CANR-27
Earlier sketch in CA 57-60
See also BEST 89:1, 90:4
See also MTCW
Pilcher, William W. 1930- 45-48
Pilditch, James (George Christopher)
1929- 9-12R
Pile, John F(rederick) 1924- CANR-36
Earlier sketches in CA 93-96, CANR-16
Pileggi, Nicholas 1933- 124
Pilgrim, Anne
See Allan, Mabel Esther
Pilgrim, David
See Palmer, John (Leslie)
and Saunders, Hilary Aidan St. George
Pilgrim, David 1950- 120
Pilgrim, Geneva Hanna 1914- 25-28R
Pilgrim, Walter E(dward) 1934- 113
Piliawsky, Monte 1944- 111
Pilinszky, Janos 1921-1981 Obituary 104
Pilio, Gerone
See Whitfield, John Humphreys
Pilisuk, Marc 1934- 29-32R
Pilk, Henry
See Campbell, Ken
Pilkey, Dav 1966- 136
See also SATA 68
Pilkey, Orrin H. 1934- 97-100
Pilkington, Betty 69-72
Pilkington, Cynthia
See Horne, Cynthia Miriam
Pilkington, E(dward) C(ecil) A(rnold)
1907- CAP-2
Earlier sketch in CA 25-28
Pilkington, Francis Meredyth 1907- CAP-2
Earlier sketch in CA 25-28
See also SATA 4
Pilkington, John Jr. 1918- 17-20R
Pilkington, Pat 1923-1986 123
Obituary 120
Pilkington, Roger (Windle) 1915- CANR-5
Earlier sketch in CA 1-4R
See also SATA 10
Pilkington, Walter Obituary 109
Pilkington, William T(homas Jr.) 1939- CANR-8
Earlier sketch in CA 61-64
Pill, Erastes
See Madsen, (Mark) Hunter
Pill, Virginia 1922- 61-64
Pillai, Karnam Chengalvaroya 1901- 5-8R
Pillar, James Jerome 1928- 13-16R
Pillin, William 1910-1985 .... 9-12R
Obituary 116
Pilling, Arnold R(emington) 1926- CANR-3
Earlier sketch in CA 1-4R
Pilling, Christopher Robert 1936- CANR-19
Earlier sketch in CA 101
Pillinger, Douglass 1906(?)-1983 Obituary 111
Pillon, Nancy Bach 1917- 110
Pilnyak, Boris
See Vogau, Boris Andreyevich
See also TCLC 23
Pilo, Giuseppe Maria 1929- CANR-5
Earlier sketch in CA 9-12R
Pilon, Jean-Guy 1930- .... DLB 60
Pilon, Juliana Geran 1947- 97-100
Pilou
See Bardot, Louis
Pilpel, Harriet F(leischl) CAP-2
Earlier sketch in CA 21-22
Pilpel, Robert H(arry) 1943- CANR-9
Earlier sketch in CA 65-68
Pimsleur, Meira Goldwater
1905(?)-1979 .... 13-16R
Obituary 89-92
Pimsleur, Paul 1927-1976 .... CAP-2
Obituary 65-68
Earlier sketch in CA 33-36
Pina, Laura Obituary 113
Pina, Leslie A. 1947- 138
Pina-Cabral, Joao de 1954- 136
Pinar, William 1947- 57-60
Pinard, (J. L.-M.) Maurice 1929- 41-44R
Pincher, H(enry) Chapman 1914- CANR-34
Earlier sketches in CA 13-16R, CANR-12
Pincherle, Alberto 1907-1990 .... CANR-33
Obituary 132
Earlier sketch in CA 25-28R
See also Moravia, Alberto
See also CLC 11, 18
See also MTCW
Pincherle, Marc 1888-1974 Obituary 49-52
Pinchin, Jane Lagoudis 1942- 69-72
Pinchot, Ann (Kramer) CANR-4
Earlier sketch in CA 1-4R
Pinchot, David 1914(?)-1983 Obituary 109
See also SATA 34
Pinckney, Catherine L(arkum) 17-20R
Pinckney, Cathey
See Pinckney, Catherine L(arkum)
Pinckney, Edward R(obert) 1924- 17-20R
Pinckney, Josephine (Lyons Scott)
1895-1957 Brief entry 107
See also DLB 6
Pincus, Edward R. 1938- CANR-12
Earlier sketch in CA 33-36R
Pincus, Gregory Goodwin
1903-1967 Obituary 113
Pincus, Harriet 1938- 102
See also SATA 27
Pincus, Joseph 1919- 25-28R
Pincus, Lily 1898-1981 .... CANR-5
Obituary 105
Earlier sketch in CA 53-56
Pindar, Peter
See Wolcot, John
Pindell, Terry 1947- 133
Pinder, John H(umphrey) M(urray) CANR-39
Earlier sketches in CA 9-12R, CANR-3, 18
Pinder, Leslie Hall
See Hall, Leslie
Pindyck, Robert (Stephen) 1945- 89-92
Pine, Leslie Gilbert 1907-1987 .... 13-16R
Obituary 122
Pine, Robert 1928- 129
Pine, Theodore
See Petaja, Emil (Theodore)
Pine, Tillie S(chloss) 1896- 69-72
See also SATA 13
Pine, William
See Harknett, Terry
Pineau, Roger 1916- 25-28R
Pineda, Cecile 1942- 118
See also CLC 39
Pinera, Virgilio 1912- 131
See also HW
Pinero, Arthur Wing 1855-1934 Brief entry 110
See also DLB 10
See also TCLC 32
Pinero, Miguel (Antonio Gomez)
1946-1988 .... CANR-29
Obituary 125
Earlier sketch in CA 61-64
See also CLC 4, 55
See also HW
Pines, Maya 13-16R
Pines, Paul (Andre) 1941- 112
Ping, Charles J. 1930- 17-20R
Pinget, Robert 1919- 85-88
See also CLC 7, 13, 37
See also DLB 83
Pinion, F(rancis) B(ertram) 1908- CANR-28
Earlier sketches in CA 25-28R, CANR-12
Pink Floyd
See Barrett, (Roger) Syd
and Gilmour, David
and Mason, Nick
and Waters, Roger
and Wright, Rick
See also CLC 35
Pinka, Patricia G(arland) 1935- 126
Pinkerton, Edward C(askin) 1911- 108
Pinkerton, James R(onald) 1932- CANR-24
Earlier sketch in CA 45-48
Pinkerton, Jan 1934- Brief entry 112
Pinkerton, Joan Trego 1928- 107
Pinkerton, Kathrene Sutherland (Gedney)
1887-1967 .... 1-4R
Obituary 103
See also SATA 26
Pinkerton, Marjorie Jean 1934- 45-48
Pinkerton, Robert E(ugene)
1882-1970 Obituary 29-32R
Pinkerton, Todd 1917- 69-72
Pinkerton, W. Anson
See Steele, Henry
Pinkett, Harold T(homas) 1914- 29-32R
Pinkham, Mary Ellen 101
Pinkney, Alphonso 1929- 25-28R
Pinkney, David H(enry) 1914- 9-12R
Pinkney, Jerry 1939- .... MAICYA
See also SAAS 12
See also SATA 32, 41, 71
Pinkowski, Edward 1916- 9-12R
Pinkston, Joe M. 1931- 5-8R
Pinkus, Oscar 1927- CANR-27
Earlier sketch in CA 5-8R
Pinkus, Philip 1922- Brief entry 113
Pinkwater, Daniel Manus 1941- CANR-38
Earlier sketches in CA 29-32R, CANR-12
See also Pinkwater, Manus
See also AAYA 1
See also CLC 35
See also CLR 4
See also MAICYA
See also SAAS 3
See also SATA 46
Pinkwater, Manus
See Pinkwater, Daniel Manus
See also SATA 8
Pinna, Giovanni 1939- CANR-4
Earlier sketch in CA 49-52
Pinner, David 1940- CANR-19
Earlier sketch in CA 25-28R
Pinner, Erna 1896- CAP-1
Earlier sketch in CA 11-12
Pinner, Joma
See Werner, Herma
Pinney, Lucy (Catherine) 1952- 136
Pinney, Peter (Patrick) 1922- 25-28R
Pinney, Roy 1911- CANR-6
Earlier sketch in CA 5-8R
Pinney, Thomas 1932- CANR-21
Earlier sketch in CA 85-88
Pinney, Wilson G(ifford) 1929- 45-48
Pino, E.
See Wittermans, Elizabeth (Pino)
Pino, Jose Ortiz y III
See Ortiz y Pino, Jose III
Pinoak, Justin Willard
See Prosser, H(arold) L(ee)
Pinsdorf, Marion K(atheryn) 1932- 124
Pinsent, Arthur 1888- CAP-2
Earlier sketch in CA 29-32
Pinsent, Gordon (Edward) 1930- 106
Pinsker, Sanford 1941- CANR-31
Earlier sketches in CA 33-36R, CANR-12
Pinsky, Robert 1940- 29-32R
See also CAAS 4
See also CLC 9, 19, 38
See also DLBY 82
Pinson, William M(eredith) Jr. 1934- CANR-9
Earlier sketch in CA 17-20R
Pinta, Harold
See Pinter, Harold
Pintak, Larry 1955- 132
Pintauro, Joseph 1930- 81-84
Pintel, Gerald 1922- CANR-4
Earlier sketch in CA 49-52
Pinter, Harold 1930- CANR-33
Earlier sketch in CA 5-8R
See also CDBLB 1960 to Present
See also CLC 1, 3, 6, 9, 11, 15, 27, 58
See also DLB 13
See also MTCW
See also WLC
Pinter, Walter S. 1928- 102
Pintner, Walter McKenzie 1931- 21-24R
Pinto, David 1937- 61-64
Pinto, Edward Henry 1901-1972 .... CAP-1
Earlier sketch in CA 13-14
Pinto, John A. 1948- 127
Pinto, Peter
See Berne, Eric (Lennard)
Pinto, Vivian de Sola 1895-1969 .... CANR-10
Earlier sketch in CA 5-8R
Pintoff, Ernest 1931- 17-20R
Pintoro, John 1947- 103
Pinxten, Rik 1947- 131
Pioneer
See Yates, Raymond F(rancis)
Piontek, Heinz 1925- CANR-34
Earlier sketches in CA 25-28R, CANR-13
See also DLB 75
Piore, Michael J(oseph) 1940- 130
Piotrow, Phyllis Tilson 1933- 122
Piotrowski, Andrew 1939- 131
Piovene, Guido 1907-1974 97-100
Obituary 53-56
Piowaty, Kim Kennelly 1957- 115
See also SATA 49
Piozzi, Hester Lynch (Thrale)
1741-1821 .... DLB 104
Pipa, Arshi 1920- CANR-10
Earlier sketch in CA 25-28R
Piper, Anson C(onant) 1918- 41-44R
Piper, Don Courtney 1932- CANR-15
Earlier sketch in CA 41-44R
Piper, Eileen 1906- 122
Piper, H(enry) Beam 1904-1964 117
Obituary 110
See also DLB 8
Piper, H(erbert) W(alter) 1915- 5-8R
Piper, Henry Dan 1918- 17-20R
Piper, Jim 1937- 97-100
Piper, Otto A. 1891- 5-8R
Piper, Roger
See Fisher, John (Oswald Hamilton)
Piper, Watty 137
See also DLB 22
See also MAICYA
Piper, William Bowman 1927- CANR-12
Earlier sketch in CA 61-64
Pipes, Richard (Edgar) 1923- 21-24R
Pippert, Wesley Gerald 1934- 53-56
Pippett, (Winifred) Aileen 1895- CAP-1
Earlier sketch in CA 13-14
Pippin, Frank Johnson 1906-1968 .... CAP-2
Earlier sketch in CA 19-20
Pippin, Robert B. 1948- 130
Pipping, Ella (Geologica) 1897- 61-64
Piquet, Howard S(amuel) 1903-1983 .... CANR-16
Obituary 111
Earlier sketches in CAP-2, CA 19-20
Piquet-Wicks, Eric 1915- 5-8R
Pirages, Dennis (Clark) 1942- 116
Pirandello, Luigi 1867-1936 Brief entry 104
See also TCLC 4, 29
See also WLC
Pires, Joe
See Stout, Robert Joe
Pirie, David (Tarbat) 1946- CANR-21
Earlier sketch in CA 97-100
Pirie, N(orman) W(ingate) 1907- 29-32R
Pirie-Gordon, (Charles) Harry (Clinton)
1883(?)-1969 Obituary 104
Pirmantgen, Pat
See Pirmantgen, Patricia H.
Pirmantgen, Patricia H. 1933- 45-48
Piro, Richard 1934- 49-52
See also SATA 7
Pirogov, Peter A. 1920-1987 Obituary 121
Pirone, Pascal P(ompey) 1907- 9-12R
Pirosh, Robert 1910-1989 Obituary 130
Pirsig, Robert M(aynard) 1928- 53-56
See also CLC 4, 6
See also MTCW
See also SATA 39
Pirson, Sylvain J. 1905- 5-8R
Pirtle, Caleb (Jackson) III 1941- CANR-26
Earlier sketches in CA 69-72, CANR-11
Pisano, Ronald G(eorge) 1948- CANR-20
Earlier sketch in CA 102
Pisar, Samuel 1929- CANR-27
Earlier sketch in CA 29-32R
See also DLBY 83
Piserchia, Doris (Elaine) 1928- 125
Brief entry 107
Pishkin, Vladimir 1931- CANR-24
Earlier sketch in CA 45-48
Pisk, Paul A(madeus) 1893- CAP-1
Earlier sketch in CA 13-14
Pismire, Osbert
See Hivnor, Robert
Pisor, Robert (Louis) 1939- 109
Pistole, Elizabeth (Smith) 1920- CANR-8
Earlier sketch in CA 17-20R
Piston, Walter 1894-1976 Obituary 69-72
Pitavy, Francois L(ouis) 1934- 73-76
Pitcairn, Frank
See Cockburn, (Francis) Claud
Pitcairn, Leonora 1912- 21-24R
Pitcher, Caroline (Nell) 1948- 132
Pitcher, Evelyn G(oodenough) 1915- 17-20R
Pitcher, George (Willard) 1925- 21-24R
Pitcher, Gladys 1890- CAP-1
Earlier sketch in CA 9-10
Pitcher, Harvey (John) 1936- CANR-3
Earlier sketch in CA 45-48
Pitcher, Robert W(alter) 1918- 29-32R
Pitchford, Kenneth S(amuel) 1931- 104
Pitkin, Dorothy (Horton)
1899(?)-1972 Obituary 37-40R
Pitkin, Hanna Fenichel 1931- 122
Brief entry 111
Pitkin, Thomas M(onroe) 1901- 17-20R
Pitkin, Timothy 1766-1847 .... DLB 30
Pitkin, Walter Jr. 1913- 13-16R
Pitman, (Isaac) James 1901-1985 .... CAP-2
Obituary 117
Earlier sketch in CA 29-32
See also SATA 46
Pitrone, Jean Maddern 1920- CANR-8
Earlier sketch in CA 17-20R
See also SATA 4
Pitseolak, Peter 1902-1973 93-96
Pitsula, James (Michael) 1950- 137
Pitt, Barrie (William Edward) 1918- CANR-20
Earlier sketch in CA 5-8R
Pitt, David C(harles) 1938- CANR-37
Earlier sketches in CA 29-32R, CANR-16
Pitt, David G(eorge) 1921- 126
Pitt, Jeremy
See Wynne-Tyson, (Timothy) Jon (Lyden)
Pitt, Peter (Clive Crawford) 1933- 33-36R
Pitt, Valerie Joan 1925- 5-8R
Pitt-Aikens, Tom 1940- 131
Pittenger, W(illiam) Norman 1905- CANR-20
Earlier sketches in CA 1-4R, CANR-5
Pitter, Ruth 1897- CAP-1
Obituary 137
Earlier sketch in CA 13-14
See also DLB 20
Pitt-Kethley, Fiona 1954- 129
Pittman, David J(oshua) 1927- CANR-6
Earlier sketch in CA 5-8R
Pittman, Helena Clare 1945- .... SATA 71
Pittock, Joan (Hornby) 1930- CANR-26
Earlier sketch in CA 107
Pittock, Murray (G. H.) 1962- 138
Pitt-Rivers, Julian Alfred 1919- 101
Pitts, Denis 1930- 65-68
Pitts, Robert F. 1908-1977 Obituary 69-72
Pitz, Henry C(larence) 1895-1976 .... CANR-9
Obituary 69-72
Earlier sketch in CA 9-12R
See also SATA 4, 24
Pitzer, Sara 1938- 107
Pivar, David J. 1933- 45-48
Piven, Frances Fox 1932- 49-52
Piver, M. Steven 1934- 138
Pix, Mary (Griffith) 1666-1709 .... DLB 80
Pixley, Jorge V. 1937- CANR-37
Earlier sketches in CA 45-48, CANR-1, 16
Pizarro, Agueda 1941- 131
See also HW
Pizer, Donald 1929- 9-12R
Pizer, Harry F(rancis) 1947- 101
Pizer, Vernon 1918- CANR-4
Earlier sketch in CA 1-4R
See also SATA 21
Pizzat, Frank J(oseph) 1924- 49-52
Pizzey, Erin 1939- 81-84
Pizzo, Peggy 1946- 118
Pjerrou, Mary 1945- 137
Pla, Josep 1897-1981 Obituary 103
Place, Irene Magdaline (Glazik) 1912- CANR-1
Earlier sketch in CA 1-4R
Place, Janey Ann 1946- 73-76
Place, Marian T(empleton) 1910- CANR-20
Earlier sketches in CA 1-4R, CANR-5
See also SATA 3
Place, Robin (Mary) 1926- .... SATA 71
Placere, Morris N.
See Gupta, S(ushil) (Kumar)
Placet, Leroi 1901-1970 Obituary 29-32R
Placksin, Sally 1948- 111
Placzek, Adolf Kurt 1913- 112
Plagemann, (William) Bentz
1913-1991 .... CANR-4
Obituary 134
Earlier sketch in CA 1-4R
Plagens, Peter (L.) 1941- Brief entry 107
Plager, Sheldon J. 1931- 25-28R
Plaidy, Jean
See Hibbert, Eleanor Burford
Plain, Belva 1919- CANR-29
Earlier sketches in CA 81-84, CANR-14
See also BEST 89:4
See also SATA 62

Plaine, Alfred R. 1898(?)-1981 Obituary 105
See also SATA 29
Plaister, Theodore H. 1923- Brief entry 113
Plaja, Guillermo Diaz
See Diaz Plaja, Guillermo
Plamenatz, John Petrov 1912-1975 ....CANR-5
Earlier sketch in CA 13-16R
Planck, Carolyn H(eine) 1910- 73-76
Planck, Charles Evans 1896-1987 73-76
Obituary 121
Planck, Max (Karl Ernst Ludwig)
1858-1947 Brief entry 115
Plank, Emma N(uschi) 1905- CAP-2
Earlier sketch in CA 33-36
Plank, Robert 1907-1983 ....CANR-12
Earlier sketch in CA 25-28R
Plano, Jack Charles 1921- CANR-39
Earlier sketches in CA 5-8R, CANR-2, 17
Plant, Marcus L. 1911- 1-4R
Plant, Raymond 1945- CANR-21
Earlier sketch in CA 29-32R
Plant, Robert 1948- .... CLC 12
Plante, David (Robert) 1940- CANR-36
Earlier sketches in CA 37-40R, CANR-12
See also CLC 7, 23, 38
See also DLBY 83
See also MTCW
Plante, (Joseph) Jacques (Omer)
1929-1986 Obituary 118
Brief entry 108
Plante, Julian G(erard) 41-44R
Plantinga, Alvin C. 1932- CANR-11
Earlier sketch in CA 21-24R
Plantinga, Leon B(rooks) 1935- 21-24R
Planz, Allen 1937- 53-56
Plaskow, Judith (Ellen) 1947- 126
Brief entry 108
Plastaras, James C(onstantine) 1931- 21-24R
Plate, Andrea Darvi
See Plate, Andrea
Plate, Andrea 1952- 130
Plate, Robert 1918- 17-20R
Plate, Thomas 1944- CANR-23
Earlier sketch in CA 69-72
Platen, August von 1796-1835 .... DLB 90
Plater, Alan (Frederick) 1935- 85-88
Plater, William M(armaduke) 1945- 85-88
Plath, David W(illiam) 1930- CANR-3
Earlier sketch in CA 9-12R
Plath, Sylvia 1932-1963 ....CANR-34
Earlier sketches in CAP-2, CA 19-20
See also CDALB 1941-1968
See also CLC 1, 2, 3, 5, 9, 11, 14, 17, 50, 51, 62
See also DLB 5, 6
See also MTCW
See also PC 1
See also WLC
Platig, E(mil) Raymond 1924- 37-40R
Platonov, Andrei
See Klimentov, Andrei Platonovich
See also TCLC 14
Platov, Mariquita (Villard) 1905- 5-8R
Platt, Anthony M. 1942- 25-28R
Platt, Charles 1945- CANR-24
Earlier sketch in CA 21-24R
Platt, Christopher
See Platt, D(esmond) C(hristopher St.) M(artin)
Platt, D(esmond) C(hristopher St.) M(artin)
1934-1989 Obituary 129
Brief entry 109
Platt, Eugene Robert 1939- CANR-3
Earlier sketch in CA 49-52
Platt, Frederick 1946- 61-64
Platt, Gerald M. 1933- CANR-17
Earlier sketch in CA 97-100
Platt, Harlan D. 1950- 123
Platt, Harrison Gray 1902- 41-44R
Platt, Jennifer (Ann) 1937- 29-32R
Platt, John (Rader) 1918- 17-20R
Platt, John Rader 1918-1992 Obituary 138
Platt, Kin 1911- CANR-11
Earlier sketch in CA 17-20R
See also CLC 26
See also SATA 21
Platt, Lyman De 1943- 102
Platt, Michael 1942- 122
Platt, Rutherford 1894-1975 Obituary 61-64
Platt, Washington 1890-1965 ....1-4R
Obituary 120
Platten, Thomas George 1899- CAP-1
Earlier sketch in CA 11-12
Platts, Beryl 1918- 61-64
Plauger, P(hillip) J(ames) 1944- 57-60
Plaut, Allene Talmey 1903-1986 Obituary 118
Plaut, Thomas F(ranz) A(lfred) 1925- 25-28R
Plaut, W(olf) Gunther 1912- CANR-17
Earlier sketches in CA 5-8R, CANR-2
Plawin, Paul 1938- 89-92
Player, Gary (Jim) 1935- 101
Player, Ian 1927- 49-52
Playfair, Giles 1910- 133
Playfair, Guy Lyon 1935- CANR-23
Earlier sketch in CA 106
Playfellow, Robin
See Ellis, Edward S(ylvester)
Playsted, James
See Wood, James Playsted
Pleasants, Henry Jr. 1884-1963 ....1-4R
Pleasants, Henry 1910- 107
Pleasants, Samuel A(ugustus III) 1918- 77-80
Pleck, Elizabeth
See Pleck, Elizabeth Hafkin
Pleck, Elizabeth H.
See Pleck, Elizabeth Hafkin
Pleck, Elizabeth Hafkin 1945- 129
Brief entry 115
Pleck, Joseph H(ealy) 1946- CANR-23
Earlier sketches in CA 57-60, CANR-7
Plekker, Robert J(ohn) 1929- 69-72
Plendello, Leo
See Saint, Andrew (John)
Plender, Richard O(wen) 1945- 101
Plenzdorf, Ulrich 1934- .... DLB 75
Plessen, Elisabeth 1944- .... DLB 75
Plesset, Isabel R(osahoff) 1912- 103
Plesur, Milton 1927-1987 ....CANR-24
Earlier sketch in CA 45-48
Pletcher, Barbara A. 1946- 123
Pletcher, David M(itchell) 1920- 1-4R
Pletcher, Eldon L(ee) 1922- 133
Pletsch, Carl (Erich) 1943- 137
Pleydell, Susan
See Senior, Isabel J(anet Couper Syme)
Plick et Plock
See Simenon, Georges (Jacques Christian)
Plievier, Theodor 1892-1955 .... DLB 69
Plimmer, Charlotte 1916- 104
Plimmer, Denis 1914- 104
Plimpton, George (Ames) 1927- CANR-32
Earlier sketch in CA 21-24R
See also AITN 1
See also CLC 36
See also MTCW
See also SATA 10
Plimpton, Ruth Talbot 1916- 13-16R
Plischke, Elmer 1914- CANR-18
Earlier sketches in CA 1-4R, CANR-2
Plochmann, George Kimball 1914- 5-8R
Ploeg, Johannes P(etrus) M(aria) van der
See van der Ploeg, Johannes P(etrus) M(aria)
Plog, Fred (Thomas III) 1944- CANR-12
Earlier sketch in CA 25-28R
Plog, Stanley C. 1930- CANR-15
Earlier sketch in CA 41-44R
Ploghoft, Milton E(rnest) 1923- 104
Plomer, William Charles Franklin
1903-1973 ....CANR-34
Earlier sketches in CAP-2, CA 21-22
See also CLC 4, 8
See also DLB 20
See also MTCW
See also SATA 24
Plomley, Roy 1914-1985 Obituary 116
Brief entry 107
Plommer, (William) Hugh Obituary 109
Plopper, Julie Jynelle 1916- 69-72
Ploscowe, Morris 1904-1975 ....CANR-2
Obituary 61-64
Earlier sketch in CA 45-48
Ploss, Sidney I. 1932- 13-16R
Plossl, George W. 1918- 21-24R
Plotnick, Alan R(alph) 1926- 17-20R
Plotnick, Charles K(eith) 1931- 114
Plotnicov, Leonard 1930- 21-24R
Plotnik, Arthur 1937- CANR-20
Earlier sketch in CA 69-72
Plotz, Helen Ratnoff 1913- CANR-8
Earlier sketch in CA 9-12R
See also SATA 38
Plowden, Alison 1931- CANR-15
Earlier sketch in CA 33-36R
Plowden, David 1932- 33-36R
See also SATA 52
Plowden, G(eoffrey) F(rank) C(hichele)
1929- 116
Plowden, Gene 1906-1985 ....21-24R
Obituary 117
Plowhead, Ruth Gipson 1877-1967 .... SATA 43
Plowman, E(dward) Grosvenor 1899- 13-16R
Plowman, Edward E(arl) 1931- 37-40R
Plowman, Piers
See Kavanagh, Patrick (Joseph)
Plowman, Stephanie 1922- CANR-5
Earlier sketch in CA 53-56
See also SATA 6
Pluckrose, Henry (Arthur) 1931- 33-36R
See also SATA 13
Pluff, Barbara Littlefield 1926- 5-8R
Plum, J.
See Wodehouse, P(elham) G(renville)
Plum, Jennifer
See Kurland, Michael (Joseph)
Plum, Lester Virgil 1906-1972 ....1-4R
Obituary 37-40R
Plumb, Barbara Louise Brown 1934- CANR-15
Earlier sketch in CA 89-92
Plumb, Beatrice
See Hunzicker, Beatrice Plumb
Plumb, Charles P. 1900(?)-1982 Obituary 105
See also SATA 29
Plumb, Charlie
See Plumb, Joseph Charles Jr.
Plumb, J(ohn) H(arold) 1911- CANR-3
Earlier sketch in CA 5-8R
Plumb, Joseph Charles Jr. 1942- CANR-3
Earlier sketch in CA 49-52
Plume, Ilse .... SATA 43
Plumly, Stanley (Ross) 1939- 110
Brief entry 108
See also CLC 33
See also DLB 5
Plumme, Don E.
See Katz, Bobbi
Plummer, Alfred 1896- 29-32R
Plummer, Ben
See Bingley, David Ernest
Plummer, Beverly J. 1918- 29-32R
Plummer, Catharine 1922- 21-24R
Plummer, Clare (Emsley) 1912- 25-28R
Plummer, Kenneth 1946- 73-76
Plummer, L. Gordon 1904- CAP-2
Earlier sketch in CA 33-36
Plummer, Margaret 1911- CAP-2
Earlier sketch in CA 25-28
See also SATA 2
Plummer, Mark A(llen) 1929- 37-40R
Plummer, William (Halsey Jr.) 1945- 102
Plummer, William J(oseph) 1927- 53-56
Plumpe, Friedrich Wilhelm
1888-1931 Brief entry 112
Plumpp, Sterling D(ominic) 1940- CANR-24
Earlier sketch in CA 45-48
See also BW
See also DLB 41
Plumptre, Arthur Fitzwalter Wynne
1907-1977 109
Obituary 106
Plumstead, A(rthur) William 1933- CANR-11
Earlier sketch in CA 25-28R
Plunket, Robert 1945- 115
Plunkett, James
See Kelly, James Plunkett
See also DLB 14
Plunkett, Thomas J. 1921- 33-36R
Plutchik, Robert 1927- CANR-11
Earlier sketch in CA 21-24R
Pluto, Terry 1955- 107
Plutonius
See Mehta, Rustam Jehangir
Plutschow, Herbert Eugen 1939- CANR-18
Earlier sketch in CA 102
Plutzik, Roberta Ann 1948- 110
Plymell, Charles 1935- CANR-11
Earlier sketch in CA 21-24R
See also CAAS 11
See also DLB 16
Plympton, Bill
See Plympton, William M.
Plympton, William M. 1946- 110
Poag, James F(itzgerald) 1934- Brief entry 107
Poage, Godfrey Robert 1920- 5-8R
Poage, Scott T(abor) 1931- 53-56
Poague, Leland A(llen) 1948- CANR-6
Earlier sketch in CA 57-60
Pobo, Kenneth 1954- 104
Pochin, Edward (Eric) 1909-1990 Obituary 130
Pochmann, Henry A(ugust) 1901-1973 ......37-40R
Pochmann, Ruth Fouts 1903- CAP-2
Earlier sketch in CA 25-28
Pocius, Gerald L(ewis) 1950- 137
Pocock, Douglas C. D. 1935- 129
Pocock, H(ugh) R(aymond) S(pilsbury)
1904- 25-28R
Pocock, Nick 1934- 53-56
Pocock, Thomas Allcot Guy 1925- CANR-23
Earlier sketch in CA 103
Pocock, Tom
See Pocock, Thomas Allcot Guy
Podbielski, Gisele 1918- 53-56
Podell, Janet 1954- 124
Podendorf, Illa (E.) 1903(?)-1983 ....CANR-28
Obituary 110
Earlier sketch in CA 81-84
See also SATA 18, 35
Podeschi, John B(attista) 1942- 110
Podhajsky, Alois 1898-1973 69-72
Podhoretz, Norman 1930- CANR-7
Earlier sketch in CA 9-12R
Podhradsky, Gerhard 1929- 21-24R
Podlecki, Anthony J(oseph) 1936- CANR-3
Earlier sketch in CA 49-52
Podmarsh, Rollo
See Salter, Donald P. M.
Podoliak, Boris
See Kostiuk, Hryhory
Podro, Michael (Isaac) 1931- 132
Podulka, Fran 1933- 49-52
Poduschka, Walter 1922- 107
Poe, Charlsie 1909- CAP-2
Earlier sketch in CA 23-24
Poe, Edgar Allan 1809-1849 .... CDALB 1640-1865
See also DLB 3, 59, 73, 74
See also PC 1
See also SATA 23
See also SSC 1
See also WLC
Poe, James 1921-1980 113
Obituary 93-96
See also DLB 44
Poen, Monte Mac 1930- 107
Poern, Ingmar 1935- 33-36R
Poesch, Jessie (J.) 1922- 128
Poetker, Frances Jones 1912- 85-88
Poet of Titchfield Street, The
See Pound, Ezra (Weston Loomis)
Poetzl, Pamela Major
See Major-Poetzl, Pamela
Poewe, Karla 1941- 124
Poganski, Donald J(ohn) 1928- 25-28R
Pogany, Andras H(enrik) 1919- 21-24R
Pogany, Hortenzia Lers 21-24R
Pogany, William Andrew 1882-1955
See Pogany, Willy
See also SATA 44
Pogany, Willy
See Pogany, William Andrew
See also SATA 30
Poggi, Emil J. 1928- 29-32R
Poggi, Gianfranco 1934- 85-88
Poggi, Jack
See Poggi, Emil J.
Poggie, John J(oseph) Jr. 1937- Brief entry 107
Poggioli, Renato 1907-1963 ....CANR-2
Earlier sketch in CA 1-4R
Pogrebin, Letty Cottin 1939- CANR-33
Earlier sketches in CA 29-32R, CANR-15
Pogue, Bill
See Pogue, William R.
Pogue, Forrest Carlisle 1912- CANR-3
Earlier sketch in CA 5-8R
Pogue, William R. 1930- 137
Poh, Caroline (Anne) 1938- 61-64
Pohl, Frederick Julius 1889- CANR-27
Earlier sketches in CA 1-4R, CANR-5
Pohl, Frederik 1919- CANR-37
Earlier sketches in CA 61-64, CANR-11
See also CAAS 1
See also CLC 18
See also DLB 8
See also MTCW
See also SATA 24
Pohle, Linda C(arol) 1947- 45-48
Pohle, Robert W(arren) Jr. 1949- 81-84
Pohlman, Edward 1933- 33-36R
Pohlmann, Lillian (Grenfell) 1902- 9-12R
See also SATA 11
Pohndorf, Richard Henry
1916-1977 Obituary 73-76
Pohrt, Tom .... SATA 67
Poignant, Raymond 1917- 29-32R
Poincelot, Raymond P. 1944- 122
Poindexter, Clarence Albert
1902(?)-1984 Obituary 111
Poindexter, David 1929- 29-32R
Poindexter, Hally Beth Walker
1927- Brief entry 110
Poindexter, Marian J(ean) 1929- 29-32R
Poinsett, Alex(ander) Ceasar 1926- 29-32R
Pointer, Larry 1940- 101
Pointer, Michael 1927- 57-60
Pointer, Richard W(ayne) 1955- 131
Pointon, Marcia R(achel) 1943- 33-36R
Pointon, Robert
See Rooke, Daphne (Marie)
Poirier, Frank E(ugene) 1940- CANR-3
Earlier sketch in CA 49-52
Poirier, Louis 1910- 126
Brief entry 122
See also Gracq, Julien
Poirier, Normand 1928(?)-1981 Obituary 102
Poirier, Philip P(atrick) 1920-1979 133
Brief entry 113
Poirier, Richard 1925- CANR-3
Earlier sketch in CA 1-4R
Pois, Joseph 1905- CAP-1
Earlier sketch in CA 13-16
Poitier, Sidney 1927- 117
See also BW
See also CLC 26
Pok Chong-Hui
See Park Chung Hee
Pokrovsky, Boris Aleksandrovich
1912- Brief entry 109
POLA
See Watson, Pauline
Polach, Jaroslav G(eorge) 1914- 9-12R
Polack, Albert Isaac 1892- CAP-1
Earlier sketch in CA 9-10
Polak, Ada Buch 1914- Brief entry 111
Polak, Jacques Jacobus 1914- 104
Polakoff, Keith Ian 1941- 49-52
Polakoff, Murray Emanuel 1922- Brief entry 114
Polakow, Valerie (Suransky) 1950- 111
Polanco, Vicente Geigel
See Geigel Polanco, Vicente
Poland, Dorothy (Elizabeth Hayward)
1937- CANR-20
Earlier sketch in CA 103
Poland, Larry 1939- 101
Polanski, Roman 1933- 77-80
See also CLC 16
Polansky, Norman A. 1918- 85-88
Polanyi, Michael 1891-1976 ....CANR-28
Obituary 65-68
Earlier sketch in CA 81-84
See also DLB 100
Polatnick, Florence T. 1923- 29-32R
See also SATA 5
Polcher, Egon
See Anschel, Eugene
Polder, Markus
See Kruess, James
Poldervaart, Arie 1909-1969 ....1-4R
Obituary 103
Pole, J(ack) R(ichon) 1922- CANR-8
Earlier sketch in CA 17-20R
Polebaum, Elliot E(dward) 1950- 107
Poleman, Thomas T(heobald) 1928- 13-16R
Polenberg, Richard 1937- 21-24R
Polese, Carolyn 1947- 127
See also SATA 58
Polese, Marcia Ann 1949- 65-68
Polette, Nancy (Jane) 1930- CANR-21
Earlier sketches in CA 57-60, CANR-6
See also SATA 42
Polevoi, Boris
See Kampov, Boris Nikolayevich
Polhamus, Jean Burt 1928- 103
See also SATA 21
Polhemus, Robert M(ackinlay) 1935- 130
Poli, Bernard 1929- 21-24R
Poliakoff, Michael B. 1953- 127
Poliakoff, Stephen 1952- 106
See also CLC 38
See also DLB 13
Poliakov, Leon 1910- 104
The Police
See Copeland, Stewart (Armstrong)
and Summers, Andrew James
and Sumner, Gordon Matthew
See also CLC 26
Polidori, John William 1795-1821 .... DLB 116
Polier, Justine Wise 1903-1987 104
Obituary 123
Polin, Raymond 1918- 37-40R

Poling, Daniel Alfred 1884-1968 Obituary 93-96
Poling, David 1928- 85-88
Poling(-Kempes), Lesley 1954- 136
Polinger, Elliot Hirsch 1898-1970 Obituary 104
Polis, A(lbert) Richard 1937- CANR-6
Earlier sketch in CA 57-60
Polisensky, Josef V. 1915- Brief entry 107
Polish, David 1910- 13-16R
Polishook, Irwin H. 1935- 21-24R
Polite, Carlene Hatcher 1932- CANR-25
Earlier sketch in CA 21-24R
See also BW
See also DLB 33
Polite, Frank (C.) 1936- 125
Politella, Dario 1921- 13-16R
Politella, Joseph 1910- CAP-2
Earlier sketch in CA 21-22
Politi, Leo 1908- CANR-13
Earlier sketch in CA 17-20R
See also MAICYA
See also SATA 1, 47
Politicus
See Kulski, Wladyslaw W(szebor)
Politzer, Heinrich 1910-1978 ....CANR-3
Obituary 81-84
Earlier sketch in CA 5-8R
Politzer, Heinz
See Politzer, Heinrich
Politzer, Robert L. 1921- 5-8R
Polivy, Janet 1951- 115
Poljanski, Hristo Andonov
See Andonov-Poljanski, Hristo
Polk, Cara Saylor 1945- CANR-38
Earlier sketch in CA 116
Polk, Dora (Beale) 1923- 49-52
Polk, Edwin Weiss 1916- 37-40R
Polk, James R. 1937- 69-72
Polk, James 1939- CANR-23
Earlier sketch in CA 105
Polk, Judd (Knox) 1913(?)-1975 Obituary 57-60
Polk, Kenneth 1935- CANR-1
Earlier sketch in CA 1-4R
Polk, Mary 1898- CAP-1
Earlier sketch in CA 11-12
Polk, Noel E(arl) 1943- 123
Polk, Ralph Lane Jr. 1940-1985 Obituary 118
Polk, Ralph Weiss 1890-1978 ....37-40R
Obituary 77-80
Polk, Stella Gipson 1901- CANR-16
Earlier sketch in CA 93-96
Polk, William R(oe) 1929- 25-28R
Polking, Kirk 1925- CANR-30
Earlier sketches in CA 29-32R, CANR-12
See also SATA 5
Polkinghorn, Anne T(oogood) 1937- 109
Poll, Richard Douglas 1918- 101
Pollack, Cecelia 1909- 29-32R
Pollack, Dale 1950- 130
Pollack, Eileen 1956- 138
Pollack, Ervin H(arold) 1913-1972 ....CAP-1
Earlier sketch in CA 13-16
Pollack, (Wilburt) Erwin 1935- 49-52
Pollack, Harvey 1913- 5-8R
Pollack, Herman 1907- 69-72
Pollack, Jack H(arrison)
1915(?)-1984 Obituary 113
Pollack, Merrill S. 1924-1988 ....5-8R
Obituary 124
See also SATA 55
Pollack, Norman 1933- 13-16R
Pollack, Peter 1911-1978 81-84
Obituary 77-80
Pollack, Reginald 1924- 37-40R
Pollack, Robert H(arvey) 1927- 49-52
Pollack, Sandra (Barbara) 1937- 119
Pollack, Seymour V(ictor) 1933- 25-28R
Pollak, Felix 1909- CANR-10
Earlier sketch in CA 25-28R
Pollak, Kurt 1919- 29-32R
Pollak, Louis Heilprin 1922- 17-20R
Pollak, Michael 1918- 122
Pollak, Richard 1934- Brief entry 111
Pollak, Vivian R. 1938- 136
Polland, Barbara K(ay) 1939- 73-76
See also SATA 44
Polland, Madeleine A(ngela Cahill)
1918- CANR-37
Earlier sketches in CA 5-8R, CANR-3
See also MAICYA
See also SAAS 8
See also SATA 6, 68
Pollard, A(nthony) J(ames) 1941- 132
Pollard, David 1942- 123
Pollard, Edward A. 1832-1872 ....DLB 30
Pollard, (Henry) Graham
1903-1976 Obituary 69-72
Pollard, Jack 1926- CANR-30
Earlier sketch in CA 29-32R
Pollard, James E(dward) 1894-1979 ....CAP-1
Obituary 89-92
Earlier sketch in CA 13-16
Pollard, John (Richard Thornhill) 1914- 5-8R
Pollard, Percival 1869-1911 ....DLB 71
Pollard, Sidney 1925- CANR-13
Earlier sketch in CA 17-20R
Pollard, T(homas) E(van) 1921- 29-32R
Pollard, William G(rosvenor) 1911- CANR-6
Earlier sketch in CA 13-16R
Polley, Judith (Anne) 1938- 129
Polley, Robert L. 1933- 17-20R
Pollin, Burton R. 1916- 129
Pollinger, Kenneth Joseph 1933- 57-60
Pollini, Francis 1930- CANR-1
Earlier sketch in CA 1-4R
Pollio, Howard R. 1937- 37-40R
Pollitt, Jerome J(ordan) 1934- 21-24R
Pollitt, Katha 1949- 122
Brief entry 120
See also CLC 28
See also MTCW
Pollitt, Ronald 1939- 122
Pollitz, Edward A(llan) Jr. 1937- 127
Pollock, Bruce 1945- CANR-23
Earlier sketches in CA 57-60, CANR-7
See also SATA 46
Pollock, David H(arold) 1922- 49-52
Pollock, George 1938- 61-64
Pollock, Harry 1920- 89-92
Pollock, James K(err) 1898-1968 ....CAP-2
Obituary 29-32R
Earlier sketch in CA 21-22
Pollock, John (Charles) 1923- CANR-18
Earlier sketches in CA 5-8R, CANR-2
Pollock, John L(eslie) 1940- 37-40R
Pollock, Linda A(nne) 1955- CANR-39
Earlier sketch in CA 116
Pollock, Mary
See Blyton, Enid (Mary)
Pollock, Norman H(all) Jr. 1909- CAP-2
Earlier sketch in CA 33-36
Pollock, Penny 1935- 101
See also SATA 42, 44
Pollock, Robert 1930- 45-48
Pollock, Seton 1910- 5-8R
Pollock, Sharon 1936- ....CLC 50
See also DLB 60
Pollock, Ted 1929- 85-88
Pollock, Thomas Clark 1902-1988 ....CAP-2
Obituary 125
Earlier sketch in CA 21-22
Pollock, William 1899-1982 Obituary 110
Pollowitz, Melinda Kilborn 1944- CANR-13
Earlier sketch in CA 77-80
See also SATA 26
Polmar, Norman 1938- 49-52
Polnaszek, Frank P(aul) 1947- 107
Polner, Murray 1928- CANR-23
Earlier sketches in CA 13-16R, CANR-5
See also SATA 64
Poloma, Margaret Mary 1943- CANR-30
Earlier sketch in CA 111
Polome, Edgar (Ghislain) C(harles)
1920- CANR-13
Earlier sketch in CA 29-32R
Polon, Linda Beth 1943- CANR-20
Earlier sketch in CA 103
Polonsky, Abraham (Lincoln) 1910- 104
See also DLB 26
Polonsky, Antony Barry 1940- 73-76
Polonsky, Arthur 1925- ....SATA 34
Polony, Raymond
See Machan, Tibor R(ichard)
Polos, Nicholas C(hristopher) 1917- 17-20R
Pols, Edward 1919- 9-12R
Polsby, Nelson W(oolf) 1934- CANR-23
Earlier sketches in CA 53-56, CANR-5
Polselli, Joseph 1950- 122
Polseno, Jo 81-84
See also SATA 17
Polsky, Abe 1935- 109
Polsky, Howard W. 1928- 25-28R
Polsky, Ned 1928- 25-28R
Poltawska, Wanda (Wiktoria) 1921- 136
Poltoratzky, N(ikolai) P(etrovich) 1921- 73-76
Poltroon, Milford
See Bascom, David
Polukhina, Valentina 1936- 135
Polunin, Nicholas (Vladimir) 1909- 65-68
Polunin, Oleg 1914-1985 85-88
Obituary 117
Polya, George 1887-1985 Obituary 117
Polya, Gyorgy
See Polya, George
Pomada, Elizabeth 1940- CANR-8
Earlier sketch in CA 61-64
Pomerance, Bernard 1940- 101
See also CLC 13
Pomerans, Arno
See Pomerans, Arnold J(ulius)
Pomerans, Arnold J(ulius) 1920- 129
Pomerantz, Charlotte 1930- CANR-38
Earlier sketches in CA 85-88, CANR-16
See also SATA 20
Pomerantz, Edward 1934- 65-68
Pomerantz, Joel 1930- 29-32R
Pomerantz, Sidney I(rving)
1909-1975 Obituary 61-64
Pomeranz, Virginia E. 1925(?)-1986 134
Obituary 120
Pomerleau, Cynthia S(todola) 1943- 73-76
Pomerleau, Ovide F(elix) 1940- CANR-13
Earlier sketch in CA 73-76
Pomeroy, Charles A. 1930- 25-28R
Pomeroy, Earl 1915- 17-20R
Pomeroy, Elizabeth W(right) 1938- CANR-32
Earlier sketch in CA 113
Pomeroy, Florence Mary
See Powley, Florence Mary Pomeroy
Pomeroy, Hub(bard)
See Claassen, Harold
Pomeroy, John H(oward)
1918-1985 Obituary 115
Pomeroy, Kenneth B(rownridge)
1907-1975 Obituary 61-64
Pomeroy, Pete
See Roth, Arthur J(oseph)
Pomeroy, Sarah B(erman) 1938- 65-68
Pomeroy, Wardell B. 1913- CANR-1
Earlier sketch in CA 1-4R
Pomeroy, William J(oseph) 1916- 85-88
Pomfret, Baron
See Dame, Lawrence
Pomfret, John Edwin 1898-1981 ....CANR-3
Obituary 105
Earlier sketch in CA 1-4R
Pomfret, Richard 1948- 112
Pommer, Henry F(rancis) 1918- CANR-20
Earlier sketch in CA 1-4R
Pommer, Richard 1930- 137
Pommery, Jean 1932- 101
Pomorska, Krystyna 1928-1986 ....CANR-31
Earlier sketch in CA 41-44R
Pompa, Leon 1933- CANR-7
Earlier sketch in CA 57-60
Pomper, Gerald M(arvin) 1935- CANR-19
Earlier sketches in CA 9-12R, CANR-5
Pomper, Philip 1936- 77-80
Pompian, Richard O(wen) 1935- CANR-11
Earlier sketch in CA 29-32R
Pompidou, Georges (Jean Raymond)
1911-1974 Obituary 49-52
Pomrenke, Norman E. 1930- 21-24R
Pomroy, Martha 1943- 101
Ponce, Juan Garcia
See Garcia Ponce, Juan
Ponce de Leon, Jose Luis S. 1931- 49-52
Pond, Alonzo W(illiam) 1894- CANR-1
Earlier sketch in CA 1-4R
See also SATA 5
Pond, Elizabeth (Ann) 129
Pond, Grace (Isabelle) 1910- CANR-5
Earlier sketch in CA 13-16R
Pond, L. W.
See Chute, Robert M.
Ponder, Catherine 1927- CANR-17
Earlier sketches in CA 1-4R, CANR-1
Ponder, James A(lton) 1933- 69-72
Ponder, Patricia
See Maxwell, Patricia
Pondrom, Cyrena N(orman)
1938- Brief entry 111
Poneman, Daniel 1956- 130
Ponge, Francis (Jean Gaston Alfred)
1899-1988 85-88
Obituary 126
See also CLC 6, 18
Poniatowska, Elena 1933- CANR-32
Earlier sketch in CA 101
See also DLB 113
See also HW
Ponicsan, Darryl 1938- CANR-21
Earlier sketch in CA 29-32R
Ponnamperuma, Cyril A. 1923- 101
Pons, Maurice 1927- CANR-5
Earlier sketch in CA 53-56
Ponsonby, D(oris) A(lmon) CANR-2
Earlier sketch in CA 5-8R
Ponsonby, Frederick Edward Neuflize
1913- 13-16R
Ponsot, Marie Birmingham 9-12R
Pont, Clarice Holt 1907- 5-8R
Ponte, Lowell (Alton) 1946- 57-60
Ponte, Pierre Viansson
See Viansson-Ponte, Pierre
Pontes, Paulo 1941(?)-1976 Obituary 69-72
Pontiero, Giovanni 1932- 29-32R
Pontiflet, Ted 1932- 105
See also SATA 32
Ponting, Kenneth 1913-1983 Obituary 109
Pontney, Jack A(rthur) 1931- 21-24R
Pontoppidan, Henrik 1857-1943 ....TCLC 29
Ponty, Maurice Merleau
See Merleau-Ponty, Maurice
Pool, David de Sola
1885-1970 Obituary 29-32R
Pool, Elizabeth 1914- 114
Pool, Eugene (Hillhouse) 1943- 85-88
Pool, Ithiel de Sola 1917-1984 ....CANR-14
Obituary 112
Earlier sketch in CA 17-20R
Pool, Phoebe Dorothy 1913- 5-8R
Pool, Tamar de Sola
1891(?)-1981 Obituary 104
Poole, Ernest 1880-1950 Brief entry 109
See also DLB 9
Poole, Frederick King 1934- 25-28R
Poole, Gary Thomas 1931- 107
Poole, Gray Johnson 1906- CANR-6
Earlier sketch in CA 5-8R
See also SATA 1
Poole, Herbert Edmund
1912-1984 Obituary 115
Poole, Herbert (Leslie) 103
Poole, Josephine
See Helyar, Jane Penelope Josephine
See also CLC 17
See also SAAS 2
See also SATA 5
Poole, Lynn 1910-1969 ....5-8R
See also SATA 1
Poole, Peggy 1925- CANR-24
Earlier sketch in CA 107
See also SATA 39
Poole, Peter A(ndrews) 113
Poole, Richard 1945- 135
Poole, Robert W(illiam) Jr. 1944- 112
Poole, Roger 1939- 102
Poole, Seth
See Riemer, George
Poole, Susan 1926- 114
Poole, Victoria (Simes) 1927- 102
Pooler, Victor H(erbert) Jr. 1924- 13-16R
Pooley, Beverley J(ohn) 1934- 45-48
Pooley, Robert C(ecil) 1898-1978 ....CANR-7
Earlier sketch in CA 5-8R
Pooley, Roger 1947- 115
Poolla, Tirupati Raju
See Raju, Poolla Tirupati
Poor, Harold Lloyd 1935- 45-48
Poor, Henry Varnum
1914(?)-1972 Obituary 37-40R
Poore, Benjamin Perley 1820-1887 ....DLB 23
Poore, Charles (Graydon)
1902-1971 Obituary 29-32R
Poorman, Paul Arthur 1930-1992 106
Obituary 136
Poortvliet, Rien 1932- 136
See also SATA 37, 65
Poots-Booby, Edna
See Larsen, Carl
Poovey, W(illiam) A(rthur) 1913- CANR-10
Earlier sketch in CA 21-24R
Popa, Vasko 1922- Brief entry 112
See also CLC 19
Pope, Alexander 1688-1744 ....CDBLB 1660-1789
See also DLB 95, 101
See also WLC
Pope, Arthur Upham
1881-1969 Obituary 25-28R
Pope, Carl 1945- 113
Pope, Clifford Hillhouse 1899-1974 ....1-4R
Obituary 103
Pope, Daniel 1946- 111
Pope, Deborah 136
Pope, Dudley (Bernard Egerton) 1925- CANR-2
Earlier sketch in CA 5-8R
Pope, Edwin 1928- 73-76
Pope, Elizabeth Marie 1917- 49-52
See also SATA 36, 38
Pope, Generoso Paul Jr.
1927-1988 Obituary 126
Pope, Harrison (Graham) Jr. 1947- 41-44R
Pope, James S. Sr. 1900(?)-1985 Obituary 118
Pope, John Alexander 1906-1982 Obituary 107
Pope, Joya 1943- 124
Pope, Katherine Victoria 1939- 111
Pope, Maurice (Wildon Montague) 1926- 69-72
Pope, Michael James 1940- 101
Pope, Phyllis Ackerman
1894(?)-1977 Obituary 69-72
Pope, Ray 1924- 29-32R
Pope, Richard Martin 1916- 17-20R
Pope, Robert G(ardner) 1936- 29-32R
Pope, Robert H. 1925- 33-36R
Pope, Thomas Harrington 1913- 73-76
Pope, Whitney 1935- 69-72
Pope, Willard Bissell 1903-1988 Obituary 127
Pope-Hennessy, James 1916-1974 97-100
Obituary 45-48
Pope-Hennessy, John W(yndham)
1913- CANR-35
Earlier sketches in CA 1-4R, CANR-1
Popenoe, David 1932- CANR-28
Earlier sketches in CA 29-32R, CANR-12
Popenoe, Paul (Bowman) 1888- CANR-27
Earlier sketch in CA 1-4R
Popescu, Christine 1930- CANR-20
Earlier sketches in CA 13-16R, CANR-7
See also Pullein-Thompson, Christine
Popescu, D. R.
See Popescu, Dumitru Radu
Popescu, Dumitru Radu 1935- Brief entry 122
Popescu, Julian (John Hunter) 1928- CANR-20
Earlier sketches in CA 1-4R, CANR-1
Popham, Arthur Ewart 1889-1970 Obituary 111
Popham, Estelle I. 1906- CANR-5
Earlier sketch in CA 1-4R
Popham, Hugh 1920- CANR-6
Earlier sketch in CA 5-8R
Popham, Margaret Evelyn
1895(?)-1982 Obituary 106
Popham, Melinda 1944- 49-52
Popham, Peter (Nicholas Home) 1952- 121
Popiel, Elda S(taver) 1915- 57-60
Popkin, Debra 1944- 118
Popkin, Jeremy D(avid) 1948- 102
Popkin, John William 1909- CAP-1
Earlier sketch in CA 13-14
Popkin, Richard H(enry) 1923- 77-80
Popkin, Roy 1921- 25-28R
Popkin, Zelda F. 1898-1983 ....25-28R
Obituary 109
Poploff, Michelle 1956- 135
See also SATA 67
Popov, Dusko 1912(?)-1981 Obituary 105
Popov, Haralan (Ivanov) 1907-1988 ....21-24R
Obituary 127
Popovic, Nenad D(ushan) 1909- CAP-2
Earlier sketch in CA 29-32
Popovic, Tanya
See Popovic, Tatyana (Vladana)
Popovic, Tatyana (Vladana) 1928- 130
Popovsky, Mark 1922- CANR-19
Earlier sketch in CA 102
Popowski, Bert (John) 1904- CANR-17
Earlier sketch in CA 1-4R
Poppe, Fred C(hristoph) 1923- CANR-35
Earlier sketch in CA 114
Poppe, Nicholas N. 1897- 73-76
Poppel, Hans 1942- ....SATA 71
Popper, Frank J. 1944- CANR-12
Earlier sketch in CA 29-32R
Popper, Karl R(aimund) 1902- CANR-20
Earlier sketches in CA 5-8R, CANR-3
See also MTCW
Popperwell, Ronald Obituary 111
Poppino, Rollie E(dward) 1922- 13-16R
Popple, James 1927- 107
Poppleton, Marjorie 1895- CAP-1
Earlier sketch in CA 13-14
Popplewell, Jack 1911- 9-12R
Porada, Edith 1912- 103
Porath, Jonathan David 1944- 118
Porcari, Constance Kwolek 1933- 33-36R
Porch, Douglas 1944- 107

Porche, Simone (Benda)
  1877(?)-1985 Obituary 118
Porcher, Mary F. Wickham
  See Bond, Mary Fanning Wickham
Porcino, Jane 1923- 116
Pore, Renate (Elfriede) 1943- 113
Porell, Bruce 1947- 102
Porges, Paul Peter 1927- 124
Poriss, Martin 1948- 81-84
Poritz, Lily
  See Miller, Lily Poritz
Porkert, Manfred (Bruno) 1933- 131
Porlock, Martin
  See MacDonald, Philip
Porosky, P. H. 45-48
Porqueras-Mayo, Alberto 1930- CANR-24
  Earlier sketch in CA 45-48
Porsche, Ferdinand 1909- 89-92
Porsche, Ferry
  See Porsche, Ferdinand
Port, M(ichael) H. 1930- 69-72
Port, Wymar
  See Judy, Will(iam Lewis)
Portal, Colette 1936- 53-56
  See also SATA 6
Portal, Ellis
  See Powe, Bruce
Portal, Francis Spencer
  1903-1984 Obituary 114
Porte, Barbara Ann .... SATA 45, 57
Porte, Joel (Miles) 1933- CANR-24
  Earlier sketches in CA 17-20R, CANR-8
Porten, Bezalel 1931- CANR-11
  Earlier sketch in CA 25-28R
Porteous, (Leslie) Crichton 1901- 5-8R
Porter, A(nthony) P(eyton) 1945- 136
  See also SATA 68
Porter, Alan
  See Clark, Ruth C(ampbell)
Porter, Alan L(eslie) 1945- 115
Porter, Albert Wright 1923- 107
Porter, Alvin
  See Rowland, D(onald) S(ydney)
Porter, Andrew 1928- CANR-23
  Earlier sketches in CA 53-56, CANR-5
Porter, Anna 130
Porter, Anna Maria 1780-1832 .... DLB 116
Porter, Arthur T(homas) 1924- 5-8R
Porter, Bern(ard Harden) 1911- CANR-24
  Earlier sketches in CA 21-24R, CANR-9
Porter, Bernard (John) 1941- CANR-24
  Earlier sketch in CA 107
Porter, Brian (Ernest) 1928- 25-28R
Porter, Bruce 1938- 124
Porter, Burton F(rederick) 1936- 106
Porter, C(edric) L(ambert) 1905- CAP-2
  Earlier sketch in CA 23-24
Porter, Carolyn (Jane) 1946- 131
Porter, Charles A(llan) 1932- 21-24R
Porter, Cole 1893-1964 Obituary 93-96
Porter, Connie 1960- .... CLC 70
Porter, Darwin (Fred) 1937- CANR-30
  Earlier sketches in CA 69-72, CANR-13
Porter, David L(indsey) 1941- CANR-24
  Earlier sketch in CA 107
Porter, David T. 1928- 17-20R
Porter, Donald Clayton
  See Gerson, Noel Bertram
Porter, Donald 1939- CANR-19
  Earlier sketch in CA 103
Porter, Edward A. 1936- 21-24R
Porter, Eleanor H(odgman)
  1868-1920 Brief entry 108
  See also DLB 9
Porter, Elias H(ull) 1914- 9-12R
Porter, Eliot (Furness) 1901-1990 .... 5-8R
  Obituary 132
Porter, Ernest Graham 1889- 1-4R
Porter, Ethel K. 1901- CAP-2
  Earlier sketch in CA 21-22
Porter, Fairfield 1907-1975 Obituary 61-64
Porter, Frank W(illiam) III 1947- 97-100
Porter, Gareth 1942- 130
Porter, Gene L. 1935- 25-28R
Porter, Gene(va Grace) Stratton
  1863(?)-1924 Brief entry 112
  See also TCLC 21
Porter, George 1920- 107
Porter, Glenn 1944- 73-76
Porter, H(arry) Boone 1923- CANR-8
  Earlier sketch in CA 5-8R
Porter, H(arry) C(ulverwell) 1927- 33-36R
Porter, Hal 1911-1984 .... CANR-3
  Obituary 114
  Earlier sketch in CA 9-12R
Porter, Henry .... DLB 62
Porter, J(ene) M(iles) 1937- CANR-21
  Earlier sketch in CA 103
Porter, J(oshua) R(oy) 1921- CANR-5
  Earlier sketch in CA 53-56
Porter, Jack Nusan 1944- CANR-20
  Earlier sketch in CA 41-44R
Porter, James A(rmer) Jr. 1922- 121
Porter, Jane 1776-1850 .... DLB 116
Porter, Janice Lee 1953- .... SATA 68
Porter, Joe Ashby 1942- CANR-12
  Earlier sketch in CA 73-76
Porter, John 1919- 21-24R
Porter, Jonathan 1938- 77-80
Porter, Joseph C(harles) 1946- 116
Porter, Joyce 1924-1990 .... CANR-8
  Obituary 133
  Earlier sketch in CA 17-20R
Porter, Judith D(eborah) R(evitch) 1940- 81-84
Porter, Katherine Anne 1890-1980 .... CANR-1
  Obituary 101
  Earlier sketch in CA 1-4R
  See also AITN 2
  See also CLC 1, 3, 7, 10, 13, 15, 27
  See also DLB 4, 9, 102
  See also DLBY 80
  See also MTCW
  See also SATA 23, 39
  See also SSC 4
Porter, Kathryn
  See Swinford, Betty (June Wells)
Porter, Kenneth Wiggins 1905- CANR-2
  Earlier sketch in CA 5-8R
Porter, Laurence M(inot) 1936- CANR-23
  Earlier sketch in CA 107
Porter, Lyman W(illiam) 1930- 21-24R
Porter, M. Gilbert 1937- 129
Porter, Margaret Eudine 1905-1975 .... CANR-8
  Earlier sketch in CA 57-60
Porter, Mark
  See Cox, James Anthony
    and Leckie, Robert (Hugh)
Porter, McKenzie 1911- 69-72
Porter, Melinda Camber 1953- 127
Porter, Michael E. 1947- CANR-22
  Earlier sketch in CA 105
Porter, Michael Leroy 1947- 118
Porter, Monica 1952- 107
Porter, Peter (Neville Frederick) 1929- 85-88
  See also CLC 5, 13, 33
  See also DLB 40
Porter, Philip W(iley) 1900-1985 69-72
  Obituary 116
Porter, R(obert) Russell
  1908-1986 Obituary 120
Porter, Raymond J(ames) 1935- 85-88
Porter, Richard C(orbin) 1931- 9-12R
Porter, Robert 1946- 122
Porter, Roger B. 1946- 108
Porter, Sheena 1935- 81-84
  See also SAAS 10
  See also SATA 24
Porter, Sue
  See Limb, Sue
Porter, Sylvia F(ield) 1913-1991 81-84
  Obituary 134
Porter, Theodore M(ark) 1953- 123
Porter, Thomas E. 1928- 29-32R
Porter, W(alter) Thomas Jr. 1934- 29-32R
Porter, Willard H(all) 1920- 57-60
Porter, William E. 1918- CANR-13
  Earlier sketch in CA 69-72
Porter, William Sydney 1862-1910 131
  Brief entry 104
  See also Henry, O.
  See also CDALB 1865-1917
  See also DLB 12, 78, 79
  See also MTCW
  See also YABC 2
Porter, William Trotter 1809-1858 .... DLB 3, 43
Porterfield, Amanda 1947- 138
Porterfield, Bruce 1925- 21-24R
Porterfield, Nolan 1936- 33-36R
Portes, Alejandro 1944- CANR-36
  Earlier sketches in CA 93-96, CANR-16
Porteus, Stanley D(avid) 1883- CANR-17
  Earlier sketch in CA 1-4R
Portillo (y Pacheco), Jose Lopez
  See Lopez Portillo (y Pacheco), Jose
Portillo Trambley, Estela 1936- CANR-32
  See also HW
Portis, Charles (McColl) 1933- CANR-1
  Earlier sketch in CA 45-48
  See also DLB 6
Portisch, Hugo 1927- CANR-36
  Earlier sketch in CA 21-24R
Portlock, Rob 1952- 128
Portman, David N(athan) 1937- 45-48
Portnoy, Howard N. 1946- 81-84
Portoghesi, Paolo 1931- 108
Portteus, Eleanora Marie Manthei .... SATA 36
Portugal, Franklin H. 1940- Brief entry 116
Portuges, Paul 1945- 77-80
Portway, Christopher (John) 1923- 57-60
Porush, David H(illel) 1952- CANR-17
  Earlier sketch in CA 93-96
Porzelt, Paul 1902- 108
Posell, Elsa Z. CANR-20
  Earlier sketches in CA 1-4R, CANR-4
  See also SATA 3
Posen, Barry R. 1952- 137
Posener, Georges (Henri)
  1906-1988 Obituary 125
Posey, Carl A(lfred Jr.) 1933- CANR-30
  Earlier sketch in CA 111
Posey, Sam 1944- 93-96
Posey, Walter B(rownlow) 1900- CAP-1
  Earlier sketch in CA 13-16
Posin, Daniel Q. 1909- CAP-1
  Earlier sketch in CA 13-14
Posin, Jack A. 1900- 13-16R
Posnack, Emanuel R. 1897-1989 Obituary 128
Posner, Alice
  See Fins, Alice
Posner, Barry Z(ane) 1949- 111
Posner, David Louis 1938-1985 106
  Obituary 117
Posner, Donald 1931- Brief entry 115
Posner, Ernst (Maximilian) 1892-1980 .... 41-44R
  Obituary 97-100
Posner, Mitchell Jay 1949- 110
Posner, Richard A. 1939- 135
Posner, Richard 1944- CANR-20
  Earlier sketches in CA 53-56, CANR-5
Posner, Steve 1953- 127
Pospelov, Pyotr Nikolayevich
  1898-1979 Obituary 85-88
Pospesel, Howard Andrew 1937- 73-76
Pospielovsky, Dimitry V. 1935- 29-32R
Pospisil, J(aroslav) Leopold 1923- 13-16R
Possony, Stefan T(homas)
  1913- Brief entry 117
Post, Austin 1922- 85-88
Post, C(harles) Gordon 1903- CAP-1
  Earlier sketch in CA 11-12
Post, Elizabeth L(indley) 1920- 49-52
Post, Emily Price 1873-1960 103
  Obituary 89-92
Post, Felix 1913- 21-24R
Post, Gaines Jr. 1937- CANR-12
  Earlier sketch in CA 73-76
Post, Gaines 1902- CAP-1
  Earlier sketch in CA 13-14
Post, Henry 1948- 61-64
Post, Homer A(very) 1888- CAP-2
  Earlier sketch in CA 25-28
Post, J(eremiah) B(enjamin) 1937- 97-100
Post, John F(rederic) 1936- 127
Post, Jonathan F(rench) S(cott)
  1947- CANR-37
  Earlier sketch in CA 115
Post, Joyce A(rnold) 1939- CANR-8
  Earlier sketch in CA 61-64
Post, Marie J. 1919- 111
Post, Melville Davisson
  1869-1930 Brief entry 110
  See also TCLC 39
Post, Steve(n A.) 1944- 103
Postal, Bernard 1905-1981 .... CANR-2
  Obituary 103
  Earlier sketch in CA 5-8R
Postan, Michael Moissey
  1899-1981 Obituary 105
Posten, Margaret L(ois) 1915- 29-32R
  See also SATA 10
Poster, Carol 1956- 118
Poster, Cyril D(ennis) 1924- CANR-7
  Earlier sketch in CA 13-16R
Poster, John B. 1939- 29-32R
Poster, Mark 1941- 33-36R
Posteuca, Vasile 1912-1972 Obituary 37-40R
Postgate, Raymond (William)
  1896-1971 .... CANR-3
  Obituary 89-92
  Earlier sketch in CA 5-8R
Posthumus, Cyril 1918- 104
Postlethwait, S(amuel) N(oel) 1918- CANR-8
  Earlier sketch in CA 17-20R
Postma, Johannes Menne 1935- 135
Postma, Lidia 1952- 101
Postma, Magdalena Jacomina 1908- 65-68
Postma, Minnie
  See Postma, Magdalena Jacomina
Postman, Neil 102
Poston, Larry (A.) 1952- 138
Poston, Richard W(averly) 1914- 65-68
Poston, Ted
  See Poston, Theodore Roosevelt Augustus Major
  See also DLB 51
Poston, Theodore Roosevelt Augustus Major
  1906-1974 125
  Obituary 104
  See also Poston, Ted
  See also BW
Posvar, Wesley W(entz) 1925- 17-20R
Posy, Arnold 1894- 9-12R
Potash, Betty 1933- 122
Potash, Robert A(aron) 1921- CANR-19
  Earlier sketch in CA 102
Poteet, G(eorge) Howard 1935- CANR-29
  Earlier sketches in CA 33-36R, CANR-13
Pothan, Kap 1929- 29-32R
Potholm, Christian Peter II 1940- 29-32R
Potichnyj, Peter J(oseph) 1930- 41-44R
Potiphar
  See Hern, (George) Anthony
Potok, Chaim 1929- CANR-35
  Earlier sketches in CA 17-20R, CANR-19
  See also AITN 1, 2
  See also CLC 2, 7, 14, 26
  See also DLB 28
  See also MTCW
  See also SATA 33
Potoker, Edward M(artin) 1931- 33-36R
Pottebaum, Gerald A. 1934- CANR-5
  Earlier sketch in CA 9-12R
Potter, A(lfred) Neal 1915- 13-16R
Potter, Beatrice
  See Webb, (Martha) Beatrice (Potter)
  See also MAICYA
Potter, (Helen) Beatrix 1866-1943 137
  Brief entry 108
  See also CLR 1, 19
  See also YABC 1
Potter, Beverly A(nn) 1944- 119
Potter, Carole A. 1940- 123
Potter, Charles E(dward) 1916-1979 61-64
  Obituary 135
Potter, Clare J. 1946- 122
Potter, Dan (Scott) 1932- 33-36R
Potter, David Morris 1910-1971 108
  See also DLB 17
Potter, David 1915- 29-32R
Potter, Dennis (Christopher George)
  1935- CANR-33
  Earlier sketch in CA 107
  See also CLC 58
  See also MTCW
Potter, E. B. 1908- 37-40R
Potter, Eloise Fretz 1931- CANR-21
  Earlier sketch in CA 105
Potter, Faith
  See Toperoff, Sam
Potter, Frank N(ewton) 1911- 130
Potter, G(eorge) W(illiam Jr.) 1930- 1-4R
Potter, Gail M(ac Leod) 1914- 25-28R
Potter, George Richard 1900- 5-8R
Potter, J(im) 1922- 21-24R
Potter, Jack M(ichael) 1936- 41-44R
Potter, James Gerrard 1944- 97-100
Potter, James H(arry)
  1912-1978 Obituary 77-80
Potter, James L(ane) 1922- 107
Potter, (Ronald) Jeremy 1922- CANR-30
  Earlier sketch in CA 53-56
Potter, John Mason 1907- CAP-1
  Earlier sketch in CA 11-12
Potter, Joy Hambuechen 1935- 123
Potter, Karl Harrington 1927- 5-8R
Potter, Kathleen Jill 1932- 104
Potter, Kathleen 1929(?)-1987 Obituary 122
Potter, Lois 1941- CANR-15
  Earlier sketch in CA 41-44R
Potter, Loren D(avid) 1918- 121
Potter, M(aurice) David 1900- CAP-2
  Earlier sketch in CA 23-24
Potter, Margaret (Newman) 1926- CANR-21
  Earlier sketches in CA 13-16R, CANR-6
  See also SATA 21
Potter, Marian 1915- CANR-1
  Earlier sketch in CA 49-52
  See also SATA 9
Potter, Miriam Clark 1886-1965 .... 5-8R
  See also SATA 3
Potter, Philip 1907-1988 Obituary 125
Potter, Robert Alonzo 1934- CANR-1
  Earlier sketch in CA 45-48
Potter, Robert D(ucharme)
  1905-1978 Obituary 77-80
Potter, Simeon 1898-1976 .... CANR-4
  Earlier sketch in CA 5-8R
Potter, Stephen 1900-1969 101
  Obituary 25-28R
  See also MTCW
Potter, Sulamith Heins 1944- 81-84
Potter, Van Rensselaer 1911- 37-40R
Potter, Vincent G. 1928- 25-28R
Potter, William Hotchkiss 1914- 1-4R
Potterton, Gerald 1931- 49-52
Potterton, Homan 1946- CANR-25
  Earlier sketch in CA 108
Pottker, Janice Marie 1948- 118
Pottle, Frederick A(lbert) 1897-1987 .... CANR-3
  Obituary 122
  Earlier sketch in CA 5-8R
  See also DLB 103
  See also DLBY 87
Potts, Albert M(intz) 1914- 116
Potts, Charles 1943- 105
Potts, E(li) Daniel 1930- 25-28R
Potts, Eve 1929- 103
Potts, George Chapman 1898- CAP-1
  Earlier sketch in CA 11-12
Potts, Jean 1910- CANR-2
  Earlier sketch in CA 5-8R
Potts, Paul (Hugh Patrick Howard)
  1911-1990 Obituary 132
Potts, Ralph Bushnell 1901- 57-60
Potts, Richard 1938- 103
Potts, Willard (Charles) 1929- 123
Potvin, Denis (Charles) 1953- Brief entry 113
Potvin, Georges C. 1928- 45-48
Potvin, Raymond H(erve) 1924- 21-24R
Pou, Genevieve Long 1919- Brief entry 114
Poucher, William Arthur 1891- CAP-1
  Earlier sketch in CA 11-12
Pough, Frederick Harvey 1906- 81-84
Pouillon, Fernand 1912- 29-32R
Poulakidas, Andreas K. 1934- 45-48
Poulet, Georges 1902- 13-16R
Poulin, A(lfred A.) Jr. 1938- CANR-32
  Earlier sketches in CA 21-24R, CANR-12
Poulin, Jacques 1937- .... DLB 60
Poulin, Stephane 1961- .... CLR 28
Poullada, Leon B(aqueiro)
  1913-1987 Obituary 123
Poulos, Constantine 1916(?)-1986 Obituary 119
Poulter, S(cott) L(arry) 1943- 49-52
Poulton, Edith Eleanor (Diana) Chloe
  1903- 85-88
Poulton, Helen Jean 1920-1971 .... CAP-2
  Earlier sketch in CA 33-36
Poulton, Richard (Christopher) 1938- 107
Pound, Arthur 1884-1966 Obituary 89-92
Pound, Ezra (Weston Loomis) 1885-1972 .... 5-8R
  Obituary 37-40R
  See also CDALB 1917-1929
  See also CLC 1, 2, 3, 4, 5, 7, 10, 13, 18, 34, 48, 50
  See also DLB 4, 45, 63
  See also MTCW
  See also PC 4
  See also WLC
Pound, Merritt B(loodworth) 1898-1970 .... CAP-2
  Earlier sketch in CA 19-20
Pound, Omar S(hakespear) 1926- CANR-16
  Earlier sketches in CA 49-52, CANR-1
Pound, Roscoe 1870-1964 Obituary 111
Pounds, Norman John Greville 1912- CANR-4
  Earlier sketch in CA 1-4R
Pounds, Ralph Linnaeus 1910- 5-8R
Pournelle, Jerry (Eugene) 1933- CANR-30
  Earlier sketch in CA 77-80
  See also SATA 26
Poussaint, Alvin F(rancis) 1934- 53-56
Povenmire, (Edward) King(sley) 1904- 61-64
Poverman, C. E. 1944- Brief entry 115
Povey, John F. 1929- 85-88
Povich, Maury 1939- 138

Povod, Reinaldo 1959- 136
See also CLC 44
Pow, Tom 1950- 134
Powdermaker, Hortense 1900-1970 .... CAP-1
Obituary 29-32R
Earlier sketch in CA 13-14
Powe, B(ruce) W. 1955- 133
Powe, Bruce 1925- 53-56
Powell, A. M.
See Morgan, Alfred P(owell)
Powell, Adam Clayton Jr. 1908-1972 102
Obituary 33-36R
See also BLC 3
See also BW
Powell, Ann 1951- .... SATA 51
Powell, Anthony (Dymoke) 1905- CANR-32
Earlier sketches in CA 1-4R, CANR-1
See also CDBLB 1945-1960
See also CLC 1, 3, 7, 9, 10, 31
See also DLB 15
See also MTCW
Powell, Barbara 1929- 119
Powell, Barry B. 1942- 136
Powell, Brian S(harples) 1934- 25-28R
Powell, Cecil Frank 1903-1969 Obituary 113
Powell, Clarence Alva 1905- CAP-1
Earlier sketch in CA 11-12
Powell, Clilan B. 1894-1977 Obituary 73-76
Powell, (John) Craig 1940- 77-80
Powell, Dawn 1897-1965 ....5-8R
See also CLC 66
Powell, Donald M. 1914- 13-16R
Powell, Dorothy Baden
See Baden-Powell, Dorothy
Powell, Dorothy M. 1914- 106
Powell, (Drexel) Dwane (Jr.) 1944- 89-92
Powell, Elwin H(umphreys) 1925- 81-84
Powell, Eric F(rederick) W(illiam) 1899- CANR-6
Earlier sketch in CA 5-8R
Powell, Evan Arnold 1937- CANR-21
Earlier sketch in CA 69-72
Powell, Fern 1942- 25-28R
Powell, G. Bingham Jr. 1942- CANR-11
Earlier sketch in CA 29-32R
Powell, Geoffrey Stewart 1914- 61-64
Powell, Gordon (George) 1911- 1-4R
Powell, Grosvenor (Edward) 1932- 129
Powell, Ivor 1910- CANR-38
Earlier sketches in CA 1-4R, CANR-17
Powell, J(ohn) Enoch 1912- 97-100
Powell, James M(atthew) 1930- CANR-8
Earlier sketch in CA 5-8R
Powell, James V(irgil) 1938- 104
Powell, James 1932- 107
Powell, John Roland 1889- CAP-1
Earlier sketch in CA 13-14
Powell, L(awrence) F(itzroy)
1881-1975 Obituary 57-60
Powell, Larson Merrill 1932- 103
Powell, Lawrence Clark 1906- CANR-25
Earlier sketches in CA 21-24R, CANR-8
Powell, Lawrence N(elson) 1943- 104
Powell, Lily
See Froissard, Lily Powell
Powell, Marcia (Leonora) 108
Powell, Margaret 1907(?)-1984 ....CANR-15
Obituary 112
Earlier sketch in CA 29-32R
Powell, Marvin 1924- CANR-8
Earlier sketch in CA 21-24R
Powell, Meredith (Ann) 1936- 37-40R
Powell, Michael (Latham)
1905-1990 Obituary 130
Powell, Milton Bryan 1934- 21-24R
Powell, Neil
See Innes, Brian
Powell, Neil 1948- CANR-34
Earlier sketches in CA 85-88, CANR-15
Powell, (Caryll) Nicolas (Peter) 1920- CANR-12
Earlier sketch in CA 61-64
Powell, Norman J(ohn) 1908-1974 .... CAP-2
Obituary 49-52
Earlier sketch in CA 21-22
Powell, Padgett 1952- 126
See also CLC 34
Powell, Paul W. 1933- 116
Powell, Peter John 1928- 33-36R
Powell, Peter 1908-1985 Obituary 116
Powell, Philip Wayne 1913- 85-88
Powell, Ralph L. 1917-1975 Obituary 57-60
Powell, Raymond P(ark)
1922-1980 Obituary 97-100
Powell, Reed M(adsen) 1921- 29-32R
Powell, Richard (Pitts) 1908- CANR-4
Earlier sketch in CA 1-4R
Powell, Richard Stillman
See Barbour, Ralph Henry
Powell, Robert (Stephenson Smyth) Baden
See Baden-Powell, Robert (Stephenson Smyth)
Powell, Robert Richard 1909- 5-8R
Powell, Ronald R(owe) 1944- 114
Powell, Shirley 1931- 106
Powell, Sidney W. 5-8R
Powell, Sumner Chilton 1924- 5-8R
Powell, Talmage 1920- CANR-2
Earlier sketch in CA 5-8R
Powell, Terry 1949- 103
Powell, Theodore 1919- 1-4R
Powell, Thomas F. 1933- 25-28R
Powell, Victor M(organ) 1919- 45-48
Powell, Violet Georgiana 1912- 103
Powell, William S(tevens) 1919- 69-72
Powell-Smith, Vincent (Walter Francis)
1939- CANR-30
Earlier sketch in CA 25-28R
Powelson, John Palen 1920- CANR-19
Earlier sketches in CA 1-4R, CANR-4
Power, Arthur
See Dudden, Arthur P(ower)
Power, Catherine
See Du Breuil, (Elizabeth) L(or)inda
Power, Edward John 1921- CANR-2
Earlier sketch in CA 5-8R
Power, Francis C. 1909(?)-1987 Obituary 124
Power, John 1927- 61-64
Power, Jonathan 1941- 107
Power, M(aurice) S(tephen) 1935- 130
Power, Margaret 1950- 127
Power, Michael 1933- CAP-1
Earlier sketch in CA 11-12
Power, Norman S(andiford) 1916- CANR-10
Earlier sketch in CA 65-68
Power, Paul F(rederick) 1925- 41-44R
Power, Richard 1928-1970 .... CAP-1
Earlier sketch in CA 9-10
Power, Tyrone
See Guthrie, (William) Tyrone
Power, (Patrick) Victor 1930- CANR-13
Earlier sketch in CA 77-80
Power-Ross, Robert W. 1922- 102
Powers, Andy 1896- CANR-6
Earlier sketch in CA 57-60
Powers, Anne
See Schwartz, Anne Powers
Powers, Barbara Hudson
See Dudley, Barbara Hudson
Powers, Bill 1931- 77-80
See also SATA 31, 52
Powers, Bob
See Powers, Robert L(eroy)
and Repp, William
Powers, David Guy 1911-1967 .... CAP-2
Earlier sketch in CA 19-20
Powers, Doris Cooper 1918- 105
Powers, Edward A(lvin) 1941- 77-80
Powers, Edward Alton 1927- 53-56
Powers, Edward D(oyle) 1900- 45-48
Powers, Edwin 1896- 73-76
Powers, Francis Gary 1929-1977 Obituary 109
Powers, George
See Infield, Glenn (Berton)
Powers, Helen 1925- 97-100
Powers, J(ames) F(arl) 1917- CANR-2
Earlier sketch in CA 1-4R
See also CLC 1, 4, 8, 57
See also MTCW
See also SSC 4
Powers, Jeffrey W(ells) 1950- 61-64
Powers, John J(ames) 1945- 69-72
See also Powers, John R.
Powers, John R.
See Powers, John J(ames)
See also CLC 66
Powers, Joseph M(ichael) 1926- 85-88
Powers, Lyall H(arris) 1924- Brief entry 115
Powers, M. L.
See Tubb, E(dwin) C(harles)
Powers, Mala 1931- 129
Powers, Margaret
See Heal, Edith
Powers, Mark James 1940- 110
Powers, Nora
See Pykare, Nina
Powers, Patrick W(illiam) 1924- 13-16R
Powers, Richard M. Gorman 1921- 21-24R
Powers, Robert L(eroy) 1924- 93-96
Powers, Robert M(aynard) 1942- CANR-14
Earlier sketch in CA 77-80
Powers, Ron(ald Dean) 1941- 97-100
Powers, Thomas (Moore) 1940- CANR-17
Earlier sketch in CA 37-40R
Powers, Tim 1952- 134
Powers, William Edwards 1902- CAP-2
Earlier sketch in CA 19-20
Powers, William K(eegan) 1934- 25-28R
Powers, William T(reval) 1926- 111
Powers, William 1930- 45-48
Powers, Willow Roberts 1943- 127
Powerscourt, Sheila
See Wingfield, Sheila (Claude)
Power-Waters, Alma Shelley
1896-1983 ....CANR-18
Earlier sketch in CA 1-4R
Power-Waters, Brian 1922- CANR-18
Earlier sketch in CA 93-96
Powicke, Michael Rhys 1920- CANR-8
Earlier sketch in CA 5-8R
Powledge, Fred 1935- CANR-27
Earlier sketches in CA 21-24R, CANR-9
See also SATA 37
Powley, Edward Barzillai 1887-1968 .... CAP-1
Earlier sketch in CA 13-14
Powley, Florence Mary Pomeroy 1892- CAP-1
Earlier sketch in CA 13-16
Powling, Chris 1943- 121
Pownall, David 1938- 89-92
See also CLC 10
See also DLB 14
Powrie, Peter James 1927- 21-24R
Powys, John Cowper 1872-1963 85-88
See also CLC 7, 9, 15, 46
See also DLB 15
See also MTCW
Powys, Llewelyn 1884-1939 .... DLB 98
Powys, T(heodore) F(rancis)
1875-1953 Brief entry 106
See also DLB 36
See also TCLC 9
Poyer, David 1949- CANR-30
Earlier sketch in CA 111
Poyer, Joe
See Poyer, Joseph John (Jr.)
Poyer, Joseph John (Jr.) 1939- CANR-17
Earlier sketches in CA 49-52, CANR-1
Poynter, Dan(iel Frank) 1938- CANR-24
Earlier sketch in CA 89-92
Poynter, Margaret 1927- CANR-36
Earlier sketches in CA 93-96, CANR-16
See also SATA 27
Poynter, Nelson 1903-1978 Obituary 77-80
Pozner, Vladimir 1934- 136
See also BEST 90:3
Pozzetta, George Enrico 1942- CANR-29
Earlier sketch in CA 111
Prabhavananda, Swami 1893-1976 ....CANR-8
Obituary 65-68
Earlier sketch in CA 17-20R
Prabhu, Pandharinath H. 1911- CANR-7
Earlier sketch in CA 13-16R
Prabhupada, A. C. Bhaktivedanta Swami
See Prabhupada, A. C. Bhaktivedanta
Prabhupada, A. C. Bhaktivedanta
1896-1977 ....CANR-14
Earlier sketch in CA 73-76
Prada, Manuel Gonzalez
See Gonzalez Prada, Manuel
Prada Oropeza, Renato 1937- CANR-32
Earlier sketch in CA 41-44R
See also HW
Prado, C(arlos) G(onzalez) 1937- CANR-27
Earlier sketch in CA 110
Prado (Calvo), Pedro 1886-1952 131
See also HW
Prados, John 1951- 106
Praed, Winthrop Mackworth 1802-1839 .... DLB 96
Prager, Arthur CANR-12
Earlier sketch in CA 29-32R
See also SATA 44
Prager, Emily 1952- .... CLC 56
Prager, Jonas 1938- 105
Prager, Karsten 1936- 73-76
Prago, Albert 1911- 29-32R
Prain, Ronald (Lindsay) 1907- 109
Prall, Stuart E(dward) 1929- 21-24R
Pramoedya Ananta Toer 1925- 134
Prance, Claude A(nnett) 1906- CANR-20
Earlier sketch in CA 89-92
Prance, June E(lizebeth) 1929- 69-72
Prandy, K(en) 1938- 117
Prange, Erwin (Edward) 1917- 113
Prange, Gordon W(illiam)
1910-1980 Obituary 97-100
Pranger, Robert J(ohn) 1931- CANR-10
Earlier sketch in CA 25-28R
Prantera, Amanda 1942- 130
Earlier sketch in CA 126
Prasad, S(rinivas) Benjamin 1929- CANR-5
Earlier sketch in CA 53-56
Prassel, Frank Richard 1937- CANR-1
Earlier sketch in CA 49-52
Prater, Donald A(rthur) 1918- 128
Prather, Hugh 1938- CANR-2
Earlier sketch in CA 45-48
Prather, Richard S(cott) 1921- CANR-5
Earlier sketch in CA 1-4R
Pratley, Gerald 1923- 112
Pratney, William Alfred 1944- 124
Pratney, Winkie
See Pratney, William Alfred
Pratson, Frederick John 1935- 101
Pratt, Allan D(aniel) 1933- 112
Pratt, Charles 1926-1976 ....CANR-21
Obituary 65-68
Earlier sketch in CA 69-72
Pratt, Chris (James) 1950- 118
Pratt, (Mildred) Claire 1921- 103
Pratt, Dallas 1914- 106
Pratt, Edwin John 1883-1964 Obituary 93-96
See also CLC 19
See also DLB 92
Pratt, (Murray) Fletcher
1897-1956 Brief entry 113
Pratt, J(oseph) Gaither 1910-1979 ....CANR-6
Obituary 89-92
Earlier sketch in CA 9-12R
Pratt, James Norwood 1942- 112
Pratt, Jane 1963(?)- 138
See also AAYA 9
Pratt, John Clark 1932- CANR-17
Earlier sketch in CA 13-16R
Pratt, John Lowell 1906-1968 ....CANR-3
Earlier sketch in CA 1-4R
Pratt, John 1931- CANR-1
Earlier sketch in CA 1-4R
Pratt, Julius W(illiam) 1888- CAP-1
Earlier sketch in CA 11-12
Pratt, Keith L(eslie) 1938- 29-32R
Pratt, Norman T(wombly) Jr. 1911- 118
Pratt, Robert Cranford 1926- 101
Pratt, Samuel Jackson 1749-1814 .... DLB 39
Pratt, Theodore 1901-1969 ....CANR-4
Earlier sketch in CA 1-4R
Pratt, William C(rouch Jr.) 1927- CANR-6
Earlier sketch in CA 13-16R
Pratt, Willis Winslow 1908- Brief entry 105
Pratt-Butler, Grace Kipp 1916- 103
Pratte, Richard (Norman) 1929- 93-96
Prattis, Percival L. 1895-1980 Obituary 97-100
Prawer, Joshua 1917- 41-44R
Prawer, S(iegbert) S(alomon) 1925- CANR-29
Earlier sketch in CA 103
Pray, Lawrence M. 1947- 113
Praz, Mario 1896-1982 101
Obituary 106
Prchal, Mildred 1895-1983 Obituary 109
Prebble, John Edward Curtis 1915- CANR-3
Earlier sketch in CA 5-8R
Prebble, Marjorie Mary Curtis 1912- CANR-15
Earlier sketch in CA 17-20R
Prebish, Charles S(tuart) 1944- 57-60
Preble, Duane 1936- 61-64
Preble, Robert Curtis 1897-1983 Obituary 111
Predmore, Michael P. 1938- CANR-34
Earlier sketch in CA 45-48
Predmore, Richard L. 1911- 17-20R
Preece, Harold 1906- 5-8R
Preece, Rod(ney John) 1939- 113
Preedy, George
See Campbell, (Gabrielle) Margaret (Vere)
Preeg, Ernest H. 1934- 33-36R
Prefontaine, Yves 1937- .... DLB 53
Pregel, Boris 1893-1976 Obituary 106
Preger, Paul D(aniel) Jr. 1926- 49-52
Preheim, Marion Keeney 1934- 25-28R
Preil, Gabriel 1911- CANR-1
Earlier sketch in CA 49-52
Preiser, Wolfgang F(riedrich) E(rnst)
1941- CANR-7
Earlier sketch in CA 57-60
Preiss, Byron (Cary) CANR-14
Earlier sketch in CA 69-72
See also SATA 42, 47
Preiss, David (Lee) 1935- 69-72
Prelinger, Ernst 1926- 9-12R
Prelutsky, Jack 1940- CANR-38
Earlier sketch in CA 93-96
See also CLR 13
See also DLB 61
See also MAICYA
See also SATA 22, 66
Prem, Dhani 1904(?)-1979 Obituary 93-96
Premacanda
See Srivastava, Dhanpat Rai
Premack, Ann J(ames) 1929- 57-60
Premack, David 1925- 126
Premchand
See Srivastava, Dhanpat Rai
See also TCLC 21
Prem Chand, Munshi
See Srivastava, Dhanpat Rai
Premchand, Munshi
See Srivastava, Dhanpat Rai
Preminger, Alex 1915- 13-16R
Preminger, Erik Lee 1944- 132
Preminger, Marion Mill
1913-1972 Obituary 33-36R
Preminger, Otto (Ludwig) 1906(?)-1986 134
Obituary 119
Brief entry 110
Premont, Brother Jeremy
See Willett, Brother Franciscus
Prendergast, Alan 1956- 124
Prendergast, Karen A(nn) 1951- 117
Prentice, Amy
See Kaler, James Otis
Prentice, Ann E(thelynd) 1933- CANR-6
Earlier sketch in CA 57-60
Prentice, Charlotte
See Platt, Charles
Prentice, George D. 1802-1870 .... DLB 43
Prentice, P(ierrepont) I(sham)
1899-1989 Obituary 127
Prenting, Theodore O(tto) 1933- 57-60
Prentis, Steve Obituary 122
Prentiss, Augustin M.
1890-1977 Obituary 69-72
Presberg, Miriam Goldstein 1919-1978 ....CANR-3
Earlier sketch in CA 1-4R
See also SATA 38
Prescott, Allen 1904(?)-1978 Obituary 73-76
Prescott, Caleb
See Bingley, David Ernest
Prescott, Casey
See Morris, Chris(topher Crosby)
Prescott, David M(arshall) 1926- 127
Brief entry 113
Prescott, J(ohn) R(obert) V(ictor)
1931- CANR-23
Earlier sketch in CA 107
Prescott, Jack
See Preston, John
Prescott, John Brewster 1919- 5-8R
Prescott, Kenneth W(ade) 1920- CANR-8
Earlier sketch in CA 57-60
Prescott, Orville 1906- 41-44R
Prescott, Peter S(herwin) 1935- CANR-14
Earlier sketch in CA 37-40R
Prescott, William Hickling
1796-1859 ....DLB 1, 30, 59
Preshing, W(illiam) A(nthony) 1929- 85-88
Preslan, Kristina 1945- 106
Presland, John
See Bendit, Gladys Williams
Presley, Delma E(ugene) 1939- CANR-31
Earlier sketch in CA 112
Presley, James (Wright) 1930- CANR-10
Earlier sketch in CA 21-24R
Presnell, Robert (Jr.)
1915(?)-1986 Obituary 119
Press, (Otto) Charles 1922- CANR-6
Earlier sketch in CA 13-16R
Press, Frank 1924- 130
Press, John (Bryant) 1920- CANR-3
Earlier sketch in CA 9-12R
Press, Simone Juda 1943- 111
Press, Toni 1949- 108
Pressau, Jack Renard 1933- 77-80
Pressburger, Emeric 1902-1988 104
Obituary 124
Presseisen, Ernst L(eopold) 1928- 13-16R
Presser, (Gerrit) Jacob 1899-1970 .... CAP-2
Earlier sketch in CA 25-28
Presser, Janice 1946- CANR-24
Earlier sketch in CA 107
Pressly, Thomas J(ames) 1919- 17-20R
Pressman, David 1937- 89-92
Pressman, Jeffrey L(eonard) 1943- CANR-3
Earlier sketch in CA 45-48

Prest, Alan Richmond 1919-1985 93-96
Obituary 115
Prest, Wilfred 1907-1985 111
Obituary 117
Prest, Wilfrid R(obertson) 1940- 112
Prestbo, John A(ndrew) 1941- CANR-2
Earlier sketch in CA 49-52
Prestera, Hector A(nthony) 1932- 65-68
Presthus, Robert 1917- CANR-20
Earlier sketches in CA 1-4R, CANR-5
Prestidge, Pauline 1922- 103
Preston, Dickson J(oseph) 1914-1985 ....CANR-8
Obituary 114
Earlier sketch in CA 61-64
Preston, Edna Mitchell 111
See also SATA 40
Preston, Edward
See Guess, Edward Preston
Preston, Florence (Margaret) 1905- 103
Preston, Frances I(sabella) 1898- 61-64
Preston, Harry 1923- CANR-23
Earlier sketch in CA 57-60
Preston, Ivan L. 1931- 57-60
Preston, Ivy (Alice) Kinross 1914- CANR-30
Earlier sketches in CAP-1, CA 9-10, CANR-12
Preston, James
See Unett, John
Preston, James J(ohn) 1941- CANR-27
Earlier sketch in CA 109
Preston, James 1913- CAP-1
Earlier sketch in CA 9-10
Preston, John Hyde 1906-1980 Obituary 102
Preston, John 1945- 130
Preston, Lee E. 1930- CANR-11
Earlier sketch in CA 21-24R
Preston, Lillian Elvira 1918- 108
See also SATA 47
Preston, Michael B. 1933- 126
Preston, Nathaniel Stone 1928- 29-32R
Preston, Ralph C(lausius) 1908- CANR-6
Earlier sketch in CA 13-16R
Preston, Richard
See Lindsay, Jack
Preston, Richard Arthur 1910- CANR-18
Earlier sketches in CA 5-8R, CANR-3
Preston, Richard (McCann) 1954- 128
Preston, Thomas A(rthur) 1933- 112
Preston, Thomas R(onald)
1936- Brief entry 109
Preston, Thomas 1537-1598 ....DLB 62
Preston, William L(ee) 1949- 105
Prestwich, Menna 1917- 21-24R
Prestwich, Michael (Charles) 1943- 134
Pretorius, Hertha
See Kouts, Hertha Pretorius
Preto-Rodas, Richard (Anthony) 1936- 49-52
Prettyman, E(lijah) Barrett Jr. 1925- 9-12R
Preus, Anthony 1936- 49-52
Preus, Herman Amberg 1896- 85-88
Preus, Jacob A(all) O(ttesen) 1920- 33-36R
Preus, Johan Carl Keyser
1881-1983 Obituary 111
Preus, Robert 1924- 33-36R
Preuss, Paul 1942- 130
Preussler, Otfried 1923- 77-80
See also CLC 17
See also SATA 24
Prevelakis, Pandelis 1909-1986 Obituary 118
Prevert, Jacques (Henri Marie)
1900-1977 ....CANR-29
Obituary 69-72
Earlier sketch in CA 77-80
See also CLC 15
See also MTCW
See also SATA 30
Previn, Andre (George) 1929- 115
Previn, Dor(oth)y (Langan) 1929(?)- 111
Prevost, Alain 1930(?)-1971 Obituary 33-36R
Prevost, Marcel 1862-1941 Brief entry 116
Prevots, Naima 135
Prewitt, Kenneth 1936- CANR-12
Earlier sketch in CA 29-32R
Preziosi, Donald 1941- 93-96
Prezzolini, Giuseppi 1882-1982 Obituary 107
Pribam, Karl 1878(?)-1973 Obituary 41-44R
Pribichevich, Stoyan
1905(?)-1976 Obituary 65-68
Price, Alfred 1936- CANR-24
Earlier sketches in CA 21-24R, CANR-9
Price, Anthony 1928- CANR-33
Earlier sketches in CA 77-80, CANR-15
Price, Archibald Grenfell 1892-1977 ....9-12R
Obituary 125
Price, Arnold H(ereward) 1912- 45-48
Price, Barbara Anne Ellvinger
1946(?)-1987 Obituary 122
Price, Barbara Pradal 103
Price, Beverley Joan 1931- CANR-24
Earlier sketch in CA 106
Price, Bruce D(eitrick) 1941- 25-28R
Price, Byron 1891-1981 Obituary 104
Price, Cecil (John Layton) 1915- 21-24R
Price, Charles C(oale) 1913- 107
Price, Charles P(hilip) 1920- 115
Price, Charles 1925- 9-12R
Price, Christine (Hilda) 1928-1980 ....CANR-4
Obituary 93-96
Earlier sketch in CA 5-8R
See also SATA 3, 23
Price, Daniel O('Haver) 1918- 21-24R
Price, David Deakins 1902-1983 Obituary 110
Price, (Paul) David 1940- 130
Price, Derek (John) de Solla
1922-1983 ....CANR-3
Obituary 110
Earlier sketch in CA 1-4R
Price, Don C(ravens) 1937- 81-84
Price, Don K(rasher Jr.) 1910- 73-76
Price, E(dgar) Hoffmann (Trooper)
1898-1988 ....CANR-10
Obituary 125
Earlier sketch in CA 61-64
Price, Emerson 1902(?)-1977 Obituary 104
Price, Eugenia 1916- CANR-18
Earlier sketches in CA 5-8R, CANR-2
See also BEST 89:4
Price, Evadne 1896-1985 Obituary 116
Price, Frances Brown 1895- 49-52
Price, Francis Wilson 1895-1974 ....CAP-1
Earlier sketch in CA 13-14
Price, Frank James 1917- 104
Price, Frank W.
See Price, Francis Wilson
Price, Garrett 1896-1979 Obituary 85-88
See also SATA 22
Price, George (Henry) 1910- CAP-1
Earlier sketch in CA 13-14
Price, George R(ennie) 1909- CANR-4
Earlier sketch in CA 1-4R
Price, George 1901- 103
Price, Glanville 1928- 132
Price, Glenn W(arren) 1918- 21-24R
Price, Harry 1881-1948 Brief entry 119
Price, Henry Habberley
1899-1984 Obituary 114
Price, J(oseph) H(enry) 1924- 25-28R
Price, Jacob M(yron) 1925- CANR-1
Earlier sketch in CA 45-48
Price, James Ligon Jr. 1915- 1-4R
Price, Jennifer
See Hoover, Helen (Drusilla Blackburn)
Price, Jimmie
See White, John I(rwin)
Price, Joan 1931- 111
Price, John A(ndrew) 1933- CANR-7
Earlier sketch in CA 57-60
Price, John Valdimir 1937- 17-20R
Price, Jonathan (Reeve) 1941- CANR-19
Earlier sketches in CA 45-48, CANR-3
See also SATA 46
Price, Kenneth M(arsden) 1954- CANR-38
Earlier sketch in CA 115
Price, Kingsley Blake 1917- 21-24R
Price, Larkin B(url) 1927- Brief entry 112
Price, Leo 1941- 77-80
Price, Lucie Locke
See Locke, Lucie
Price, Margaret (Evans)
1888-1973 Obituary 109
See also SATA 28
Price, Marion E(lizabeth) 1947- 111
Price, Marjorie 1929- 53-56
Price, Martin 1920- CANR-13
Earlier sketch in CA 17-20R
Price, Miles O(scar) 1890-1968 ....CAP-1
Earlier sketch in CA 13-16
Price, Molly 1903(?)-1984 Obituary 114
Price, Morgan Philips 1885-1973 ....CAP-1
Earlier sketch in CA 13-14
Price, (Lilian) Nancy (Bache)
1880-1970 Obituary 111
Price, Nelson Lynn 1931- CANR-24
Earlier sketches in CA 61-64, CANR-8
Price, Olive 1903- 41-44R
See also SATA 8
Price, Paul 1912(?)-1985 Obituary 116
Price, R(onald) F(rancis) 1926- CANR-26
Earlier sketch in CA 29-32R
Price, R(ichard) G(eoffrey) G(eorge)
1910- CAP-1
Earlier sketch in CA 13-14
Price, Ray Glenn 1903- CANR-2
Earlier sketch in CA 5-8R
Price, Ray(mond John) 1931- 25-28R
Price, Raymond (Kissam Jr.) 1930- 105
Price, (Edward) Reynolds 1933- CANR-37
Earlier sketches in CA 1-4R, CANR-1
See also CLC 3, 6, 13, 43, 50, 63
See also DLB 2
Price, Rhys
See Price, George (Henry)
Price, Richard 1941- CANR-27
Earlier sketch in CA 105
Price, Richard 1949- CANR-3
Earlier sketch in CA 49-52
See also CLC 6, 12
See also DLBY 81
Price, Robert W. 1925(?)-1979 Obituary 89-92
Price, Robert 1900- 33-36R
Price, Roger (David) 1944- CANR-35
Earlier sketch in CA 107
Price, Roger 1921- 9-12R
Price, S(eymour) Stephen 1919- 25-28R
Price, Sally 1943- CANR-27
Earlier sketch in CA 106
Price, Stanley 1931- 13-16R
Price, Steven D(avid) 1940- CANR-37
Earlier sketches in CA 49-52, CANR-1, 16
Price, Susan 1955- 105
See also SATA 25
Price, V(incent) B(arrett) 1940- 69-72
Price, Victor 1930- 9-12R
Price, Vincent 1911- 89-92
Price, Walter K(leber) 1924- CANR-7
Earlier sketch in CA 17-20R
Price, Willadene Anton 1914- 5-8R
Price, Willard 1887-1983 ....CANR-1
Earlier sketch in CA 1-4R
See also SATA 38, 48
Price, William 1938- 37-40R
Price, Wilson T(itus) 1931- 37-40R
Price-Mars, Jean 1875-1969 Obituary 112
Prichard, Caradog 1904-1980 103
Obituary 97-100
Prichard, Doris (Smith) 1947- 116
Prichard, James W(illiam) 1925- 13-16R
Prichard, Katharine Susannah
1883-1969 ....CANR-33
Earlier sketches in CAP-1, CA 11-12
See also CLC 46
See also MTCW
See also SATA 66
Prichard, Nancy S(awyer) 1924- 29-32R
Prichard, Robert Williams 1923- 89-92
Prichard, Susan Perez 1953- 108
Prickett, (Alexander Thomas) Stephen
1939- CANR-29
Earlier sketch in CA 29-32R
Priddy, Fran(ces Rosaleen) 1931- CANR-17
Earlier sketch in CA 1-4R
Pride, Cletis 1925- 41-44R
Pride, J(ohn) B(ernard) 1929- Brief entry 110
Prideaux, James 1935- 138
Prideaux, Tom 1908- 108
See also SATA 37
Pridham, Geoffrey 1942- CANR-38
Earlier sketches in CA 97-100, CANR-17
Pridham, Radost 1922- 21-24R
Pries, Nancy R(uth) 1944- 118
Priesand, Sally J(ane) 1946- 65-68
Priest, Alice L. 1931- 102
Priest, Christopher 1943- 33-36R
See also DLB 14
Priest, Harold Martin 1902- 73-76
Priest, Robert 1951- 118
Priestley, Barbara 1937- 33-36R
Priestley, Brian 1946- 129
Priestley, F(rancis) E(thelbert) L(ouis)
1905- 21-24R
Priestley, Harold E(dford) 1901- 73-76
Priestley, J(ohn) B(oynton)
1894-1984 ....CANR-33
Obituary 113
Earlier sketch in CA 9-12R
See also CDBLB 1914-1945
See also CLC 2, 5, 9, 34
See also DLB 10, 34, 77, 100
See also DLBY 84
See also MTCW
Priestley, Lee (Shore) 1904- CANR-2
Earlier sketch in CA 5-8R
See also SATA 27
Priestley, Mary 1925- 61-64
Priestley, Philip 1939- 123
Priestman, Martin 1949- 135
Prieto, Mariana Beeching 1912- CANR-5
Earlier sketch in CA 5-8R
See also SATA 8
Prigmore, Charles S(amuel) 1919- CANR-25
Earlier sketch in CA 45-48
Prigogine, Ilya 1917- 131
Priley, Margaret Hubbard 1909- 1-4R
Prill, Felician 1904- 103
Primack, Joel (Robert) 1945- 61-64
Primavera, Elise 1954- ....SATA 48, 58
Prime, Benjamin Young 1733-1791 ....DLB 31
Prime, C(ecil) T(homas) 1909-1979 ....CANR-3
Earlier sketch in CA 49-52
Prime, Derek (James) 1931- CANR-25
Earlier sketch in CA 108
See also SATA 34
Primeau, Ronald 1946- 108
Primeaux, Walter J(oseph) Jr. 1928- 41-44R
Primm, Brother Orrin
See Willett, Brother Franciscus
Primm, James Neal 1918- 45-48
Primmer, Phyllis (Cora Griesbach) 1926- 5-8R
Primo, Albert T. 1935- 73-76
Primrose, William 1904-1982 116
Obituary 106
Prince, Alison (Mary) 1931- CANR-26
Earlier sketch in CA 29-32R
See also SATA 28
Prince, Carl E. 1934- CANR-14
Earlier sketch in CA 21-24R
Prince, (Peter) Derek 1915- CANR-34
Earlier sketch in CA 113
Prince, Don 1905(?)-1983 Obituary 110
Prince, F(rank) T(empleton) 1912- 101
See also CLC 22
See also DLB 20
Prince, Gary Michael 1948- 89-92
Prince, Gerald (Joseph) 1942- 57-60
Prince, J(ack) H(arvey) 1908- 81-84
See also SATA 17
Prince, Melvin 1932- 116
Prince, Morton 1854-1929 Brief entry 121
Prince, Suzan D(enise) 1957- 111
Prince, Thomas Richard 1934- 13-16R
Prince, Thomas 1687-1758 ....DLB 24
Prince 1958(?)- ....CLC 35
Prince Ibis
See Randi, James
Prince Kropotkin
See Kropotkin, Peter (Aleksieevich)
Princess Grace
See Kelly, Grace (Patricia)
Prindl, A(ndreas) R(obert) 1939- 69-72
Pring, Julian Talbot 1913- 5-8R
Pring, Martin J(ohn) 1943- 111
Pringle, David (William) 1950- 134
Pringle, J(ohn) M(artin) Douglas 1912- 13-16R
Pringle, Laurence P. 1935- CANR-14
Earlier sketch in CA 29-32R
See also CLR 4
See also MAICYA
See also SAAS 6
See also SATA 4, 68
Pringle, Mia (Lilly) Kellmer 1920(?)-1983 65-68
Obituary 109
Pringle, Peter 1940- CANR-27
Earlier sketch in CA 69-72
Pringle, Terrence Michael 1947- 136
Pringle, Terry
See Pringle, Terrence Michael
Pring-Mill, Robert D(uguid) F(orrest)
1924- 9-12R
Printz, Peggy 1945- 73-76
Prinz, Joachim 1902- CAP-1
Earlier sketch in CA 11-12
Priolo, Pauline Pizzo 1907- 1-4R
Prior, A(rthur) N(orman) 1914-1969 ....CANR-3
Earlier sketch in CA 1-4R
Prior, Allan 1922- CANR-10
Earlier sketch in CA 65-68
Prior, Andrew 1940- 112
Prior, Ann 1949- 25-28R
Prior, Kenneth Francis William 1926- 17-20R
Prior, Matthew 1664-1721 ....DLB 95
Prisco, Michele 1920- 53-56
Prisco, Salvatore III 1943- CANR-12
Earlier sketch in CA 61-64
Prising, Robin 1933- 57-60
Pritchard, Arnold 1949- 97-100
Pritchard, J(ohn) Harris 1923- 21-24R
Pritchard, James Bennett 1909- 5-8R
Pritchard, John Paul 1902-1976 ....9-12R
Obituary 126
Pritchard, John Wallace 1912- 81-84
Pritchard, Leland J(ames) 1908- CAP-1
Earlier sketch in CA 11-12
Pritchard, Melissa 1948- 128
Pritchard, Norman Henry II 1939- 77-80
Pritchard, R(onald) E(dward) 1936- 37-40R
Pritchard, R(obert) John 1945- 116
Pritchard, Sheila (Edwards) 1909- CAP-1
Earlier sketch in CA 13-16
Pritchard, William H(arrison) 1932- CANR-23
Earlier sketch in CA 65-68
See also CLC 34
See also DLB 111
Pritchett, C(harles) Herman 1907- CANR-18
Earlier sketches in CA 1-4R, CANR-3
Pritchett, Elaine H(illyer) 1920- 108
See also SATA 36
Pritchett, John Perry 1902- 1-4R
Pritchett, Kay 1946- 135
Pritchett, Price 1941- 123
Pritchett, V(ictor) S(awdon) 1900- CANR-31
Earlier sketch in CA 61-64
See also CLC 5, 13, 15, 41
See also DLB 15
See also MTCW
Pritchett, W(illiam) Kendrick 1909- 97-100
Pritikin, Nathan 1915-1985 ....CANR-27
Obituary 114
Earlier sketch in CA 89-92
Pritikin, Robert C(harles) 1929- 104
Prittie, Terence Cornelius Farmer
1913-1985 ....CANR-4
Obituary 116
Earlier sketch in CA 1-4R
Private 19022
See Manning, Frederic
Privateer, Paul Michael 1946- 135
Priyamvada, Usha
See Nilsson, Usha Saksena
Prizzia, Ross 1942- 119
Probert, Walter 1925- 77-80
Probst, Leonard 1921-1982 65-68
Obituary 106
Probst, Mark 1925- 130
See also CLC 59
Prochazkova, Iva 1953- 135
See also SATA 68
Prochnau, William W. 1937- 33-36R
Prochnow, Herbert V(ictor) Jr. 1931- 110
Prochnow, Herbert V. 1897- CANR-4
Earlier sketch in CA 1-4R
Procktor, Richard (Edward Christopher)
1933- 53-56
Procopio, Mariellen
See Grutz, Mariellen Procopio
Procter, Adelaide Anne 1825-1864 ....DLB 32
Procter, Ben H. 1927- CANR-9
Earlier sketch in CA 5-8R
Procter, Bryan Waller 1787-1874 ....DLB 96
Procter, Maurice 1906-1973 ....5-8R
Obituary 122
Proctor, Charles S(heridan) 1925- 29-32R
Proctor, (Philip) Dennis
1905-1983 Obituary 110
Proctor, Dorothea Hardy 1910- 61-64
Proctor, E(velyn) E(mma) S(tefanos)
1897-1980 103
Obituary 97-100
Proctor, Elsie 1902- 29-32R
Proctor, Everitt
See Montgomery, Rutherford George
Proctor, Lillian Cummins 1900- CAP-2
Earlier sketch in CA 23-24
Proctor, Priscilla 1945- 65-68
Proctor, Raymond L(ambert) 1920- 45-48
Proctor, Robert N. 1954- 138
Proctor, Samuel D(eWitt) 1921- 133
Brief entry 118
Proctor, Samuel 1919- CANR-3
Earlier sketch in CA 9-12R
Proctor, Thelwall 1912- 29-32R
Proctor, William (Gilbert Jr.) 1941- CANR-16
Earlier sketch in CA 37-40R
Prodan, Mario 1911- 9-12R
Proeysen, Alf 1914-1970 136
See also Proysen, Alf
See also CLR 24
Proface, Dom
See Sheehy, Maurice S(tephen)

Proffer, Carl R(ay) 1938-1984 ....41-44R
Obituary 113
Proffer, Ellendea 1944- CANR-1
Earlier sketch in CA 45-48
Proffitt, Charles G. 1896-1982 Obituary 108
Proffitt, Nicholas (Charles)
1943- Brief entry 131
Profumo, David 1955- 137
Proger, Samuel (Herschel)
1906- Brief entry 106
Progoff, Ira 1921- 133
Prohias, Antonio 1921- 104
Prokasy, William F(rederick) 1930- 49-52
Prokhovnik, Simon Jacques 1920- 107
Prokofiev, Aleksandr Andreyevich
1900-1971 Obituary 33-36R
Prokofiev, Camilla Gray
1938(?)-1971 Obituary 33-36R
Prokofiev, Sergei (Sergeevich)
1891-1953 Brief entry 112
Prokop, Phyllis Stillwell 1922- CANR-9
Earlier sketch in CA 21-24R
Prokopczyk, Czeslaw 1935- 108
Prokosch, Frederic 1908-1989 73-76
Obituary 128
See also CLC 4, 48
See also DLB 48
Prole, Lozania
See Bloom, Ursula
Pronin, Alexander 1927- 49-52
Pronko, Leonard Cabell 1927- CANR-1
Earlier sketch in CA 1-4R
Pronko, N(icholas) Henry 1908- 9-12R
Pronzini, Bill 1943- CANR-32
Earlier sketches in CA 49-52, CANR-1, 14
Proosdii, Cornelis Van
See Van Proosdy, Cornelis
Propes, Stephen Charles 1942- CANR-1
Earlier sketch in CA 49-52
Propes, Steve
See Propes, Stephen Charles
Prophet, The
See Dreiser, Theodore (Herman Albert)
Propper, Dan 1937- 104
See also DLB 16
Prosch, Harry 1917- 13-16R
Prose, Francine 1947- 112
Brief entry 109
See also CLC 45
Proske, Beatrice (Irene) Gilman 1899- CAP-1
Earlier sketch in CA 9-10
Proskouriakoff, Tatiana (Avenirovna)
1909-1985 Obituary 117
Prosper, John (joint pseudonym)
See Farrar, John C(hipman)
Prosper, Lincoln
See Cannon, Helen
Prosser, Eleanor 1922- 1-4R
Prosser, H(arold) L(ee) 1944- CANR-33
Earlier sketches in CA 77-80, CANR-15
Prosser, Michael H. 1936- CANR-17
Earlier sketch in CA 25-28R
Prostano, Emanuel Theodore Jr. 1931- 29-32R
Prostano, Joyce S. 126
Prosterman, Roy L. 1935- 57-60
Prothero, R(alph) Mansell 1924- 41-44R
Prothro, Edwin Terry 1919- 53-56
Prothro, James W(arren) 1922- CANR-8
Earlier sketch in CA 5-8R
Protopapas, George 1917- 57-60
Prou, Suzanne (Marcelle Henriette)
1920- CANR-20
Earlier sketch in CA 33-36R
Proud, Robert 1728-1813 ....DLB 30
Proudfoot, J(ohn) J(ames) 1918- 21-24R
Proudhon
See Cunha, Euclides (Rodrigues Pimenta) da
Proujan, Carl 1929- 81-84
Proussis, Costas M(ichael) 1911- CANR-15
Earlier sketch in CA 41-44R
Proust, (Valentin-Louis-George-Eugene-)Marcel
1871-1922 120
Brief entry 104
See also DLB 65
See also MTCW
See also TCLC 7, 13, 33
See also WLC
Prout, W(illiam) Leslie 1922- 9-12R
Prouty, L. Fletcher 1917- 45-48
Prouty, Morton D(ennison) Jr. 1918- CANR-28
Earlier sketch in CA 1-4R
Prouty, Olive Higgins 1882(?)-1974 ....9-12R
Obituary 49-52
Prouvost, Jean 1885-1978 Obituary 89-92
Provan, Jill E(llen) 1948- 117
Provence, Marcel
See Jouhandeau, Marcel Henri
Provence, Sally
See Provence, Sally A(nn)
Provence, Sally A(nn) 1916- 128
Provensen, Alice 1918- CANR-5
Earlier sketch in CA 53-56
See also CLR 11
See also MAICYA
See also SATA 9, 70
Provensen, Martin (Elias) 1916-1987 ....CANR-5
Obituary 122
Earlier sketch in CA 53-56
See also CLR 11
See also MAICYA
See also SATA 9, 51, 70
Provenzo, Eugene (F. Jr.) 1949- 135
Provist, d'Alain
See Diop, Birago (Ismael)
Provo, Frank 1913(?)-1975 Obituary 61-64
Provost, Gail Levine 1944- 127
See also SATA 65
Provost, Gary (Richard) 1944- 133
See also SATA 66
Provus, Malcolm M. 1928- Brief entry 108
Prowe, Diethelm (Manfred-Hartmut)
1941- 57-60
Prowler, Don(ald) 1950- 121
Prowler, Harley
See Masters, Edgar Lee
Prown, Jules David 1930- 29-32R
Proxmire, William 1915- CANR-31
Earlier sketch in CA 29-32R
Proysen, Alf
See Proeysen, Alf
See also SATA 67
Prpic, George J(ure) 1920- CANR-38
Earlier sketches in CA 25-28R, CANR-17
Prucha, Francis Paul 1921- CANR-38
Earlier sketches in CA 5-8R, CANR-2, 17
Prudden, Bonnie 1914- CANR-14
Earlier sketch in CA 77-80
Prude, Agnes George de Mille 1905- CANR-30
Earlier sketch in CA 65-68
Pruden, (James) Wesley Jr. 1935- 17-20R
Prueitt, Melvin L(ewis) 1932- 118
Pruett, John H(aywood) 1947- 102
Pruett, Kyle D(ean) 1943- 131
Prugh, Jeff(ery Douglas) 1939- 41-44R
Pruitt, Evelyn L(ord) 1918- 5-8R
Pruitt, Ida 1888-1985 Obituary 116
Pruitt, William O(badiah) Jr. 1922- 21-24R
Pruner, Leonora 1931- 114
Prunty, Merle C(harles) 1917-1983 ....37-40R
Obituary 109
Prunty, (Eugene) Wyatt 1947- 110
Prusek, Jaroslav 1906- 129
Brief entry 117
Prusina, Katica 1935- 69-72
Pruter, Robert 1944- 137
Pruthi, Surinder P(aul) S(ingh) 1934- 61-64
Pruyser, Paul W(illem) 1916- CANR-9
Earlier sketch in CA 21-24R
Prybyla, Jan S(tanislaw) 1927- 21-24R
Pryce, Roy 1928- 29-32R
Pryce-Jones, David 1936- CANR-14
Earlier sketch in CA 13-16R
Pryde, Philip Rust 1938- 61-64
Pryer, Pauline
See Roby, Mary Linn
Prynne, J(eremy) H(alvard) 1936- CANR-39
Earlier sketch in CA 97-100
See also DLB 40
Pryor, Adel
See Wasserfall, Adel
Pryor, Bonnie H. 1942- 130
See also SATA 69
Pryor, Frederic L(eRoy) 1933- CANR-2
Earlier sketch in CA 5-8R
Pryor, Helen Brenton 1897-1972 ....CAP-2
Earlier sketch in CA 33-36
See also SATA 4
Pryor, Karen 1932- 119
Pryor, Larry
See Pryor, Lawrence A(llderdice)
Pryor, Lawrence A(llderdice) 1938- 85-88
Pryor, Richard (Franklin Lenox Thomas)
1940- Brief entry 122
See also CLC 26
Pryor, Vanessa
See Yarbro, Chelsea Quinn
Prys-Jones, Arthur Glyn 1888- 104
Przybyszewski, Stanislaw 1868-1927 ....DLB 66
See also TCLC 36
Psathas, George 1929- 21-24R
Pseudo-Dionysius the Areopagite ....DLB 115
Pteleon
See Grieve, C(hristopher) M(urray)
Puccetti, Roland (Peter) 1924- 93-96
Pucci, Albert John 1920- ....SATA 44
Pucciani, Oreste F(rancesco) 1916- 21-24R
Puche, Jose Luis Castillo
See Castillo Puche, Jose Luis
Puck, Wolfgang 1949- 124
Puck, Y. U.
See Andre, (Kenneth) Michael
Puckett, Lute
See Masters, Edgar Lee
Puckett, Robert Hugh 1935- 41-44R
Puckett, (William) Ronald 1936- 33-36R
Puckett, Ruby Parker 1932- 57-60
Puckey, Walter (Charles) 1899-1983 ....CAP-2
Obituary 111
Earlier sketch in CA 29-32
Pudaite, Rochunga 1927- 120
Puddepha, Derek (Noel) 1930- 61-64
Pudney, John (Sleigh) 1909-1977 ....CANR-5
Obituary 77-80
Earlier sketch in CA 9-12R
See also SATA 24
Pudovkin, V(sevolod) I(llarionovich)
1893-1953 Brief entry 112
Puechner, Ray 1935- 25-28R
Puette, William J(oseph) 1946- 77-80
Puffer, K(enneth) Hart 1910- 5-8R
Pugh, Anthony (Roy) 1931- 53-56
Pugh, Charles 1948- 81-84
Pugh, Ellen (Tiffany) 1920- 49-52
See also SATA 7
Pugh, Griffith T(hompson) 1908- 5-8R
Pugh, J(ohn) W(ilbur) 1912- 21-24R
Pugh, John Charles 1919- 110
Pugh, L(eslie) P(enrhys)
1895-1983 Obituary 110
Pugh, Ralph B(ernard) 1910-1982 ....CANR-28
Obituary 108
Earlier sketch in CA 25-28R
Pugh, Rod(erick) W(ellington) 1919- 45-48
Pugh, Samuel F(ranklin) 1904- CAP-1
Earlier sketch in CA 13-14
Pugh, Wynette 1942- Brief entry 111
Pugin, A. Welby 1812-1852 ....DLB 55
Pugliese, Anthony J(ulian)
1912-1985 Obituary 117
Pugsley, Clement H. 1908- CAP-1
Earlier sketch in CA 13-14
Pugsley, John A. 1934- CANR-19
Earlier sketch in CA 103
Puharich, Henry (Andrija) Karl 1918- 85-88
Puhvel, Jaan 1932- CANR-31
Earlier sketch in CA 29-32R
Puig, Manuel 1932-1990 ....CANR-32
Earlier sketches in CA 45-48, CANR-2
See also CLC 3, 5, 10, 28, 65
See also DLB 113
See also HW
See also MTCW
Pulaski, Mary Ann Spencer 1916- CANR-10
Obituary 137
Earlier sketch in CA 25-28R
Pulay, George 1923-1981 45-48
Obituary 135
Puleo, Nicole
See Miller, Nicole Puleo
Pulgram, Ernst 1915- 49-52
Puligandla, Ramakrishna 1930- CANR-7
Earlier sketch in CA 61-64
Pulis, Clifford A(lton) 1916- 116
Pulitzer, Joseph Jr. 1885-1955 ....DLB 29
Pulitzer, Joseph 1847-1911 Brief entry 114
See also DLB 23
Pulitzer, Roxanne 1951- 128
Pulkingham, Betty (Jane) 1928- CANR-26
Earlier sketches in CA 61-64, CANR-8
Pulkingham, W(illiam) Graham 1926- 53-56
Pullapilly, Cyriac K(alapura) 1932- 61-64
Pullar, Philippa 1935- Brief entry 116
Pullein-Thompson, Christine
See Popescu, Christine
See also SATA 3
Pullein-Thompson, Denis
See Cannan, Denis
Pullein-Thompson, Diana
See Farr, Diana (Pullein-Thompson)
See also SATA 3
Pullein-Thompson, Joanna Maxwell
1898-1961 106
Pullein-Thompson, Josephine (Mary Wedderburn)
....CANR-20
Earlier sketches in CA 5-8R, CANR-7
See also SATA 3
Pullen, John James 1913- 17-20R
Pulliam, Eugene C(ollins)
1889-1975 Obituary 89-92
See also AITN 2
Pulliam, H(oward) Ronald 1945- 114
Pulliam, Myrta 1947- 97-100
Pullias, Earl V(ivon) 1907- CAP-1
Earlier sketch in CA 11-12
Pulling, Albert Van Siclen 1891-1980 53-56
Obituary 135
Pulling, Christopher Robert Druce 1893- CAP-1
Earlier sketch in CA 13-14
Pulling, Pierre
See Pulling, Albert Van Siclen
Pullman, Philip 1946- 127
See also CLR 20
See also MAICYA
See also SATA 65
Pullum, Geoffrey K(eith) 1945- 138
Pulman, Jack 1928(?)-1979 Obituary 85-88
Pulman, Michael Barraclough 1933- 33-36R
Pulos, William L(eroy) 1920- 45-48
Pulsford, Petronella 1946- 133
Pulsipher, Gerreld L(ewis) 1939- 101
Pulver, Mary Monica
See Kuhfeld, Mary Pulver
Pulzer, Peter George Julius 1929- 13-16R
Pumphrey, H(enry) George 1912- 13-16R
Pumroy, Donald K(eith) 1925- 49-52
Punch, Maurice 1941- 65-68
Pundeff, Marin 1921- 9-12R
Pundt, Helen Marie 5-8R
Punekar, Shankar Mokashi
See Mokashi-Punekar, Shankar
Puner, Helen W(alker) 1915-1989 ....CANR-2
Obituary 129
Earlier sketch in CA 5-8R
See also SATA 37, 63
Puner, Morton 1921- 73-76
Punnett, R(obert) M(alcolm) 1936- 25-28R
Purcal, John T(homas) 1931- 33-36R
Purcell, Arthur Henry 1944- 102
Purcell, Donald 1916- 122
Purcell, Gillis Philip 1904-1987 Obituary 124
Purcell, H(ugh) D(ominic) 1932- CANR-17
Earlier sketch in CA 25-28R
Purcell, Mary 1906- CANR-2
Earlier sketch in CA 5-8R
Purcell, Roy E(verett) 1936- CANR-6
Earlier sketch in CA 57-60
Purcell, Sally 1944- 49-52
Purcell, Susan Kaufman 1942- Brief entry 114
Purcell, Theodore V(incent) 1911-1984 ....41-44R
Obituary 112
Purcell, Victor 1896-1965 ....5-8R
Purdom, Charles B(enjamin) 1883-1965 ....CAP-1
Earlier sketch in CA 9-10
Purdom, P(aul) Walton 1917- 57-60
Purdom, Thomas E. 1936- 13-16R
Purdom, Tom
See Purdom, Thomas E.
Purdon, Eric (Sinclaire) 1913-1989 93-96
Obituary 130
Purdue, A(rthur) W(illiam) 1941- 124
Purdue, Bill
See Purdue, A(rthur) W(illiam)
Purdy, A(lfred) W(ellington) 1918- 81-84
See also Purdy, Al
See also CLC 3, 6, 14, 50
Purdy, Al
See Purdy, A(lfred) W(ellington)
See also DLB 88
Purdy, Alexander 1890-1976 Obituary 65-68
Purdy, Anne S. 1902(?)-1987 Obituary 122
Purdy, (Charles) Anthony 1932- 17-20R
Purdy, Captain Jim
See Gillelan, G(eorge) Howard
Purdy, Carol 1943- 136
See also SATA 66
Purdy, Dwight H(illiard) 1941- 131
Purdy, James (Amos) 1923- CANR-19
Earlier sketch in CA 33-36R
See also CAAS 1
See also CLC 2, 4, 10, 28, 52
See also DLB 2
See also MTCW
Purdy, John David 1946- 122
Purdy, Ken W(illiam)
1913-1972 Obituary 37-40R
Purdy, Laura M. 1946- 137
Purdy, Richard Little 1904-1990 Obituary 132
Purdy, Susan Gold 1939- CANR-10
Earlier sketch in CA 13-16R
See also SATA 8
Purdy, Theodore Martindale
1903-1979 Obituary 89-92
Pure, Simon
See Swinnerton, Frank Arthur
Puri, Shamlal 1951- 130
Purkey, Roy (Delbert) 1905- CAP-2
Earlier sketch in CA 23-24
Purkey, William Watson 1929- 29-32R
Purkis, John 1933- 97-100
Purkiser, W(estlake) T(aylor) 1910- CAP-1
Earlier sketch in CA 13-16
Purl, Sandy M. 1953- 122
Purnell, Idella 1901- 61-64
Purpel, David E(dward) 1932- 49-52
Purrington, Robert Daniel 1936- 122
Purscell, Phyllis 1934- 25-28R
See also SATA 7
Pursell, Carroll W(irth) Jr. 1932- 77-80
Purser, John Whitley 1942- 103
Purser, Philip John 1925- CANR-21
Earlier sketch in CA 104
Purtill, Richard L. 1931- CANR-29
Earlier sketch in CA 37-40R
See also SATA 53
Purton, Rowland W(illiam Crisby)
1925- CANR-4
Earlier sketch in CA 53-56
Purves, Alan C(arroll) 1931- CANR-9
Earlier sketch in CA 21-24R
Purves, Libby 1950- 130
Purvis, Charles C. 1902(?)-1985 Obituary 115
Puryear, Alvin N(elson) 1937- Brief entry 115
Puryear, Edgar F. Jr. 1930- 115
Pusey, Edward Bouverie 1800-1882 ....DLB 55
Pusey, Merlo John 1902-1985 ....9-12R
Obituary 117
Pusey, Nathan Marsh 1907- 109
Pushkarev, Boris S. 1929- CANR-6
Earlier sketch in CA 5-8R
Pushkarev, Sergei Germanovich 1888- CANR-6
Earlier sketch in CA 5-8R
Pushkin, Alexander (Sergeyevich)
1799-1837 ....SATA 61
See also WLC
Pustay, John S(tephen) 1931- 17-20R
Putcamp, Luise jr. 1924- 29-32R
Puthoff, Harold E(dward) 1936- Brief entry 113
Putnam, Alice 1916- 112
See also SATA 61
Putnam, Arnold Oscar 1922- 9-12R
Putnam, Arthur Lee
See Alger, Horatio Jr.
Putnam, Carleton 1901- 65-68
Putnam, Donald F(ulton) 1903- CAP-2
Earlier sketch in CA 29-32
Putnam, George Palmer 1814-1872 ....DLB 3, 79
Putnam, George Palmer
1887-1950 Brief entry 109
Putnam, Hilary 1926- 61-64
Putnam, J. Wesley
See Drago, Harry Sinclair
Putnam, Jackson K(eith) 1929- 29-32R
Putnam, John
See Beckwith, Burnham Putnam
Putnam, John Fay 1924(?)-1982 Obituary 106
Putnam, Michael Courtney Jenkins 1933- 105
Putnam, Peter B(rock) 1920- 85-88
See also SATA 30
Putnam, Robert D(avid) 1941- CANR-10
Earlier sketch in CA 65-68
Putnam, Robert E. 1933- CANR-19
Earlier sketches in CA 53-56, CANR-5
Putnam, Roy Clayton 1928- 69-72
Putnam, Samuel Whitehall
1892-1950 Brief entry 107
See also DLB 4
Putney, Gail J.
See Fullerton, Gail Jackson
Putra, Kerala
See Panikkar, K(avalam) Madhava
Putt, Robert C. 1938- 120
Putt, S(amuel) Gorley 1913- CANR-6
Earlier sketch in CA 5-8R
Putter, Irving 1917- 65-68
Putter, Polly
See Adomeit, Ruth E(lizabeth)
Putterman, Ron 1946- 108

Puttfarken, Thomas 1943- 122
Putz, Louis J. 1909- CAP-1
Earlier sketch in CA 13-14
Putzar, Edward (David) 1930- 41-44R
Putzel, Max 1910- 9-12R
Putzel, Michael 1942- 73-76
Puxon, Grattan 1939- 81-84
Puzo, Mario 1920- CANR-4
Earlier sketch in CA 65-68
See also CLC 1, 2, 6, 36
See also DLB 6
See also MTCW
Pybus, Rodney 1938- 107
Pye, (John) David 1932- 25-28R
Pye, Jack
See Morton, James (Severs)
Pye, Lloyd (Anthony Jr.) 1946- 77-80
Pye, Lucian W(ilmot) 1921- 21-24R
Pye, Norman 1913- 109
Pyk, Ann Phillips 1937- 77-80
Pykare, Nina 1932- 130
Pyke, David (Alan) 1921- 138
Pyke, Helen Godfrey 1941- 29-32R
Pyke, Magnus 1908- CANR-6
Earlier sketch in CA 13-16R
Pyle, A(lbert) M(offett) 1945- 123
Pyle, Ernest Taylor 1900-1945 Brief entry 115
See also Pyle, Ernie
Pyle, Ernie
See Pyle, Ernest Taylor
See also DLB 29
Pyle, (William) Fitzroy 1907- CAP-2
Earlier sketch in CA 29-32
Pyle, Hilary 1936- 77-80
Pyle, Howard 1853-1911 137
Brief entry 109
See also CLR 22
See also DLB 42
See also MAICYA
See also SATA 16
Pyle, Katharine 1863-1938 .... SATA 66
Pyles, Aitken
See McDavid, Raven I(oor) Jr.
Pyles, Thomas 1905-1980 ....13-16R
Obituary 133
Pylyshyn, Zenon W(alter) 1937- 29-32R
Pym, Barbara (Mary Crampton)
1913-1980 ....CANR-34
Obituary 97-100
Earlier sketches in CAP-1, CA 13-14, CANR-13
See also CLC 13, 19, 37
See also DLB 14
See also DLBY 87
See also MTCW
Pym, Christopher 1929- 13-16R
Pym, Denis 1936- 25-28R
Pym, Dora Olive (Ivens) 1890- CAP-1
Earlier sketch in CA 13-14
Pym, Michael 1890(?)-1983 Obituary 109
Pym, Peter and Delores
See Sandlin, Tim
Pynchon, Thomas (Ruggles Jr.)
1937- CANR-22
Earlier sketch in CA 17-20R
See also BEST 90:2
See also CLC 2, 3, 6, 9, 11, 18, 33, 62, 72
See also DLB 2
See also MTCW
See also WLC
Pyne, Mable Mandeville 1903-1969 ....1-4R
Obituary 103
See also SATA 9
Pyne, Stephen J(oseph) 1949- 106
Pynn, Ronald 1942- 85-88
Pyrnelle, Louise-Clarke 1850-1907 .... DLB 42
Pyros, John 1931- 77-80
Pytchely, R. F. St. B.
See Cowie, Donald

Q

Q
See Quiller-Couch, Arthur Thomas
Qadar, Basheer
See Alexander, (Charles) K(halil)
Qazzaz, Ayad (Sayyid Ali) Al
See Al-Qazzaz, Ayad (Sayyid Ali)
Qian Hao 1925- 111
Qian Zhongshu
See Ch'ien Chung-shu
Qoboza, Percy 1938-1988 Obituary 124
Qroll
See Dagerman, Stig (Halvard)
Quackenbush, Margery (Carlson) 1943- 73-76
Quackenbush, Robert M(ead) 1929- CANR-38
Earlier sketches in CA 45-48, CANR-2, 17
See also MAICYA
See also SAAS 7
See also SATA 7, 70
Quad, M.
See Lewis, Charles Bertrand
Quade, E(dward) S(chaumberg)
1908-1988 Obituary 125
Quade, Quentin Lon 1933- Brief entry 106
Quaife, Darlene Barry 1948- 136
Quaife, Milo Milton 1880-1959 Brief entry 114
Quain, Edwin A. 1906(?)-1975 Obituary 61-64
Quale, G(ladys) Robina 1931- 21-24R
Qualey, Carlton C(hester) 1904- 77-80
Qualter, Terence H(all) 1925- 37-40R
Quammen, David 1948- CANR-28
Earlier sketch in CA 29-32R
See also SATA 7
Quanbeck, Philip A. 1927- 25-28R
Quandt, B. Jean 1932- 33-36R
Quandt, Richard E(meric) 1930- CANR-29
Earlier sketch in CA 45-48
Quandt, William B. 1941- CANR-35
Earlier sketch in CA 29-32R
Quantrill, Malcolm 1931- CANR-35
Earlier sketch in CA 13-16R
Quarles, Benjamin 1904- CANR-16
Earlier sketches in CA 1-4R, CANR-1
See also BW
See also SATA 12
Quarles, John R(hodes) Jr. 1935- CANR-15
Earlier sketch in CA 65-68
Quarm, Daisy 1948- 122
Quarmby, Arthur 1934- 45-48
Quarrie, Bruce (Roy Bryant) 1947- 103
Quarrington, Paul (Lewis) 1953- 129
See also CLC 65
Quarry, Nick
See Albert, Marvin H(ubert)
Quartermain, James
See Lynne, James Broom
Quartermain, Peter (Allan) 1934- 117
Quasimodo, Salvatore 1901-1968 .... CAP-1
Obituary 25-28R
Earlier sketch in CA 13-16
See also CLC 10
See also DLB 114
See also MTCW
Quastel, J. H.
See Quastel, Juda Hirsch
Quastel, Juda Hirsch 1899-1987 Obituary 123
Quasten, Johannes 1900- 9-12R
Quatermass, Martin
See Carpenter, John (Howard)
Quay, Herbert C. 1927- CANR-33
Earlier sketch in CA 13-16R
Quayle, (John) Anthony
1913-1989 Obituary 130
Quayle, Eric 1921- CANR-36
Earlier sketch in CA 21-24R
Qubain, Fahim I(ssa) 1924- 1-4R
Quebedeaux, Richard (Anthony)
1944- CANR-30
Earlier sketches in CA 73-76, CANR-12
Queen, Ellery
See Dannay, Frederic
and Davidson, Avram
and Lee, Manfred B(ennington)
and Sturgeon, Theodore (Hamilton)
and Vance, John Holbrook
See also CLC 3, 11
Queen, Ellery Jr.
See Dannay, Frederic
and Holding, James (Clark Carlisle Jr.)
and Lee, Manfred B(ennington)
Queen, Stuart Alfred 1890- 21-24R
Queen Wilhelmina
See Nassau, Wilhelmina Helena Pauline Maria
Quelch, John A(nthony) 1951- CANR-29
Earlier sketch in CA 112
Queller, Donald E(dward) 1925- CANR-4
Earlier sketch in CA 53-56
Queneau, Raymond 1903-1976 ....CANR-32
Obituary 69-72
Earlier sketch in CA 77-80
See also CLC 2, 5, 10, 42
See also DLB 72
See also MTCW
Quenelle, Gilbert 1914- 25-28R
Quennell, Marjorie Courtney 1884-1972 73-76
See also SATA 29
Quennell, Peter (Courtney) 1905- 115
Brief entry 113
Quentin, Patrick
See Wheeler, Hugh (Callingham)
Querry, Ronald B(urns) 1943- 117
Query, William T(heodore) Jr. 1929- 41-44R
Quesnel, Joseph 1746-1809 .... DLB 99
Quesnell, John G(eorge) 1936- CANR-1
Earlier sketch in CA 45-48
Quesnell, Quentin 1927- 120
Quest, Linda (Gerber) 1935- 77-80
Quest, (Edna) Olga W(ilbourne) Hall
See Hall-Quest, (Edna) Olga W(ilbourne)
Quest, Rodney CAP-2
Earlier sketch in CA 29-32
Quester, George H. 1936- CANR-34
Earlier sketches in CA 25-28R, CANR-10
Queston, Joanna (Marie) 1951- 131
Quezada, Abel 1920(?)-1991 ....5-8R
Obituary 133
Quichot, Dona
See Tomkiewicz, Mina
Quick, Annabelle 1922- 21-24R
See also SATA 2
Quick, Armand James
1894-1978 Obituary 73-76
Quick, Barbara 1954- 133
Quick, Philip
See Strage, Mark
Quick, Richard (John Worth) 1944- 127
Quick, Thomas L(ee) 1929- CANR-34
Earlier sketch in CA 41-44R
Quick, William K(ellon) 1933- 137
Quickel, Stephen (Woodside) 1936- 73-76
Quie, Gretchen 1927- 117
Quiery, William H. 1926- 21-24R
Quigg, Jane (Hulda) Obituary 120
See also SATA 49
Quigg, Philip W. 1920- CANR-35
Earlier sketch in CA 9-12R
Quigless, Helen Gordon 1944- Brief entry 105
Quigley, Aileen 1930- 124
Brief entry 104
Quigley, Austin E(dmund) 1942- 101
Quigley, Carroll 1910-1977 ....CANR-27
Obituary 69-72
Earlier sketch in CA 37-40R
Quigley, Eileen Elliott
See Vivers, Eileen Elliott
Quigley, Ellen 1955- 111
Quigley, Harold Scott 1889-1968 ....1-4R
Obituary 103
Quigley, Joan 29-32R
See also BEST 90:3
Quigley, John M(ichael) 1942- 110
Brief entry 107
Quigley, John 1927- 17-20R
Quigley, Martin (Peter) 1913- CANR-18
Earlier sketch in CA 17-20R
Quigley, Martin (Schofield) Jr. 1917- CANR-38
Earlier sketches in CA 1-4R, CANR-17
Quilici, Folco 1930- 105
Quill
See Grange, Cyril
Quill, Barnaby
See Brandner, Gary
Quill, Monica
See McInerny, Ralph
Quiller, Andrew
See Bulmer, (Henry) Kenneth
Quiller-Couch, Arthur Thomas
1863-1944 Brief entry 118
Quilligan, Maureen 1944- CANR-16
Earlier sketch in CA 89-92
Quilty, Rafe
See Witcombe, R(ick) T(rader)
Quimber, Mario
See Alexander, (Charles) K(halil)
Quimby, George Irving 1913- CANR-34
Earlier sketch in CA 57-60
Quimby, Myron J. 25-28R
Quimby, Myrtle 1891- CAP-2
Earlier sketch in CA 25-28
Quin, Ann (Marie) 1936-1973 ....9-12R
Obituary 45-48
See also CLC 6
See also DLB 14
Quin, Mike
See Ryan, Paul William
Quinan, Jack
See Quinan, John F.
Quinan, John F. 1939- 125
Quince, Peter
See Day, George Harold
Quince, Peter Lum
See Ritchie, (Harry) Ward
Quincunx, Ramona J.
See Borgmann, Dmitri A(lfred)
Quincy, Samuel 1734-1789 .... DLB 31
Quinderpunte, Raoul (Cornelius)
1907- CANR-15
Earlier sketch in CA 85-88
Quindlen, Anna 1953- 138
Quine, W. V.
See Quine, Willard Van Orman
Quine, Willard V.
See Quine, Willard Van Orman
Quine, Willard Van Orman 1908- CANR-37
Earlier sketches in CA 1-4R, CANR-1, 16
Quin-Harkin, Janet 1941- CANR-33
Earlier sketches in CA 81-84, CANR-15
See also AAYA 6
See also SATA 18
Quinlan, Red
See Quinlan, Sterling C(arroll)
Quinlan, Sterling C(arroll) 1916- CANR-8
Earlier sketch in CA 5-8R
Quinley, Harold E(arl) 1942- 61-64
Quinn, A(lexander) James 1932- 29-32R
Quinn, Anthony (Rudolph Oaxaca)
1915- Brief entry 111
See also HW
Quinn, Arthur 1942- 110
Quinn, (Mary) Bernetta 1915- 105
Quinn, C(osmas) Edward
1926-1989 Obituary 129
Quinn, Charles (Nicholas) 1930- 123
Brief entry 110
Quinn, Daniel 1935- 137
Quinn, David B(eers) 1909- CANR-15
Earlier sketch in CA 77-80
Quinn, Edward 1932- 77-80
Quinn, Elisabeth 1881-1962 .... SATA 22
Quinn, Esther Casier 1922- CANR-35
Earlier sketch in CA 5-8R
Quinn, Francis X. 1932- CANR-4
Earlier sketch in CA 9-12R
Quinn, Herbert F(urlong) 1910- CAP-1
Earlier sketch in CA 19-20
Quinn, James Brian 1928- CANR-35
Earlier sketch in CA 13-16R
Quinn, James 1919- 13-16R
Quinn, Jane Bryant 1939- 93-96
Quinn, John Francis 1925- Brief entry 115
Quinn, John M(ichael) 1922- 45-48
Quinn, John Paul 1943- 33-36R
Quinn, John R. 1938- 97-100
Quinn, Kenneth (Fleming) 1920- CANR-17
Earlier sketch in CA 25-28R
Quinn, Martin
See Smith, Martin Cruz
Quinn, Michael A(lan) 1945- CANR-25
Earlier sketch in CA 45-48
Quinn, Niall 1943- CANR-37
Earlier sketch in CA 108
Quinn, R(obert) M(acLean) 1920- 21-24R
Quinn, Sally 1941- CANR-27
Earlier sketch in CA 65-68
See also AITN 2
Quinn, Seabury (Grandin) 1889-1969 108
Obituary 104
Quinn, Simon
See Smith, Martin Cruz
Quinn, Sister Bernetta
See Quinn, (Mary) Bernetta
Quinn, Susan 1940- 103
See also Jacobs, Susan
Quinn, Terry 1945- CANR-18
Earlier sketch in CA 101
Quinn, Theodora K.
See Kroeber, Theodora (Kracaw)
See also SATA 1
Quinn, Vernon
See Quinn, Elisabeth
Quinn, Vincent 1926- 21-24R
Quinn, William Arthur 1920- 5-8R
Quinn, Zdenka (Hodbodova) 1942- 33-36R
Quinnett, Paul G(uthrie) 1939- 114
Quinney, Richard 1934- CANR-9
Earlier sketch in CA 57-60
Quinones, Ricardo J(oseph)
1935- Brief entry 112
Quinsey, Mary Beth 1948- 132
Quint, Barbara Gilder 1928- 103
Quint, Bert 1930- 69-72
Quint, Howard H. 1917- 97-100
Quint, Jeanne
See Benoliel, Jeanne Quint
Quintal, Claire 1930- 13-16R
Quintana, Bertha B(eatrice)
1924- Brief entry 113
Quintana, Frances
See Swadesh, Frances Leon
Quintana, Leroy V. 1944- 131
See also DLB 82
See also HW
Quintana, Ricardo (Beckwith) 1898- 25-28R
Quintanilla, Maria Aline Griffith y Dexter Condes
1921- 9-12R
Quintero, Jose (Benjamin) 1924- ....HW
Quinto, Leon 1926- 37-40R
Quinton, Anthony Meredith 1925- CANR-10
Earlier sketch in CA 21-24R
Quirarte, Jacinto 1931- CANR-32
Earlier sketch in CA 45-48
See also HW
Quirin, G(eorge) David 1931- CANR-9
Earlier sketch in CA 21-24R
Quirin, William L(ouis) 1942- 93-96
Quirk, James P(atrick) 1926- CANR-7
Earlier sketch in CA 57-60
Quirk, John E(dward) 1920- 5-8R
Quirk, Lawrence J. 1923- CANR-27
Earlier sketches in CA 25-28R, CANR-12
Quirk, Paul J. 1949- 108
Quirk, Randolph 1920- CANR-2
Earlier sketch in CA 5-8R
Quirk, Robert E. 1918- 1-4R
Quirk, Thomas Vaughan 1946- 122
Quirk, Tom
See Quirk, Thomas Vaughan
Quiroga, Horacio (Sylvestre) 1878-1937 131
Brief entry 117
See also HW
See also MTCW
See also TCLC 20
Quispel, Gilles 1916- 89-92
Quist, Susan 1944- 57-60
Quitslund, Sonya A(ntoinette) 1935- CANR-1
Earlier sketch in CA 49-52
Quixley, Jim 1931- .... SATA 56
Quoirez, Francoise 1935- CANR-39
Earlier sketches in CA 49-52, CANR-6
See also Sagan, Francoise
See also CLC 9
See also MTCW
Quoist, Michel 1921- 65-68
Quong, Rose Lanu
1879(?)-1972 Obituary 37-40R
Qureshi, Hazel 1949- 138
Qureshi, Ishtiaq Husain 1903- CAP-1
Earlier sketch in CA 11-12

R

R
See Rees, (Morgan) Goronwy
R. R.
See
Iyengar, K(odaganallur) R(amaswami) Srinivasa
Ra, Jong Oh 1945- 85-88
Raab, Lawrence 1946- 65-68
Raab, Menachem 1923- 114
Raab, Robert Allen 1924- 29-32R
Raab, Selwyn 1934- 73-76
Raabe, Wilhelm 1831-1910 .... TCLC 45
Raack, R(ichard) C(harles) 1928- 41-44R
Ra'Anan, Gavriel D. 1954(?)-1983 Obituary 110
Ra'Anan, H. F. Frischwasser
See Ra'Anan, Uri
Ra'Anan, Uri 1926- CANR-25
Earlier sketch in CA 108
Raat, W(illiam) Dirk 1939- CANR-23
Earlier sketch in CA 106
Rabalais, Maria 1921- 61-64
Raban, Jonathan 1942- CANR-17
Earlier sketch in CA 61-64

Rabassa, Gregory 1922- CANR-26
Earlier sketches in CA 45-48, CANR-2
See also CAAS 9
See also HW
Rabasseire, Henri
See Pachter, Henry M(aximillian)
Rabb, Theodore K. 1937- CANR-10
Earlier sketch in CA 21-24R
Rabbie
See Towers, Maxwell
Rabbitt, Thomas 1943- 57-60
Rabdau, Marianne
See Bakker-Rabdau, Marianne K(atherine)
Rabe, Berniece (Louise) 1928- CANR-1
Earlier sketch in CA 49-52
See also SAAS 10
See also SATA 7
Rabe, David (William) 1940- 85-88
See also CABS 3
See also CLC 4, 8, 33
See also DLB 7
Rabe, Olive H(anson) CAP-2
Earlier sketch in CA 19-20
See also SATA 13
Rabe, Stephen G(eorge) 1948- 108
Rabelais, Francois 1483-1553 WLC
Raben, Joseph 1924- CANR-12
Earlier sketch in CA 69-72
Rabi, I(sidor) I(saac) 1898-1988 Obituary 125
Rabie, Jan 1920- 29-32R
Rabikovitz, Dalia 1936- Brief entry 108
Rabikowitz, Dalyah
See Rabikovitz, Dalia
Rabil, Albert Jr. 1934- CANR-10
Earlier sketch in CA 25-28R
Rabin, A(lbert) I(srael) 1912- CANR-19
Earlier sketches in CA 53-56, CANR-4
Rabin, Chaim 1915- 105
Rabin, Edward H(arold) 1937- 49-52
Rabin, Yitzhak 1922- Brief entry 111
Rabinovich, Abraham 1933- 61-64
Rabinovich, Isaiah 1904-1972 CAP-2
Earlier sketch in CA 25-28
Rabinovitch, Sholem 1859-1916 Brief entry 104
See also Aleichem, Sholom
Rabinovitz, Rubin 1938- 21-24R
Rabinow, Paul 1944- CANR-13
Earlier sketch in CA 61-64
Rabinowich, Ellen 1946- 106
See also SATA 29
Rabinowicz, Mordka Harry 1919- 5-8R
Rabinowitch, Alexander 1934- 21-24R
Rabinowitch, Eugene 1901-1973 77-80
Obituary 41-44R
Rabinowitz, Alan 1927- CANR-27
Earlier sketch in CA 29-32R
Rabinowitz, Ezekiel 1892- 25-28R
Rabinowitz, Howard Neil 1942- 105
Rabinowitz, Isaac 1909-1988 Obituary 126
Rabinowitz, Louis Isaac
1906-1984 Obituary 113
Rabinowitz, Paula 1951- 127
Rabinowitz, Peter MacGarr 1956- 104
Rabinowitz, Sandy 1954- 103
See also SATA 39, 52
Rabinowitz, Solomon
See Rabinovitch, Sholem
Rabins, Peter V(incent) 1947- 109
Rabkin, Brenda 1945- 101
Rabkin, Eric S. 1946- CANR-4
Earlier sketch in CA 49-52
Rabkin, Gerald Edward 1930- Brief entry 105
Rabkin, Norman C. 1930- CANR-4
Earlier sketch in CA 1-4R
Rabkin, Richard 1932- 33-36R
Rable, George C(alvin) 1950- 116
Raboff, Ernest Lloyd SATA 37
Raborg, Frederick A(shton) Jr. 1934- CANR-20
Earlier sketch in CA 103
Rabow, Gerald 1928- 25-28R
Raboy, Marc 1948- 135
Rabushka, Alvin 1940- Brief entry 116
Rabuzzi, Kathryn Allen 1938- 113
Raby, Derek Graham 1927- 103
Raby, William L(ouis) 1927- CANR-23
Earlier sketches in CA 17-20R, CANR-8
Race, Jeffrey 1943- 37-40R
Race, Robert Russell 1907-1984 Obituary 113
Racevskis, Karlis 1939- 117
Rachleff, Owen S(pencer) 1934- CANR-14
Earlier sketch in CA 21-24R
Rachlin, Carol K(ing) 1919- 57-60
See also SATA 64
Rachlin, Harvey (Brant) 1951- CANR-26
Earlier sketch in CA 107
See also SATA 47
Rachlin, Nahid CANR-14
Earlier sketch in CA 81-84
See also SATA 64
Rachlis, Eugene (Jacob) 1920-1986 5-8R
Obituary 121
See also SATA 50
Rachman, David Jay 1928- 57-60
Rachman, Stanley Jack 1934- 89-92
Rachow, Louis A(ugust) 1927- 57-60
Racina, Thom
See Raucina, Thomas Frank
Racine, Michel 1942- 136
Rack, Henry D(enman) 1931- 13-16R
Racker, Efraim 1913- 89-92
Rackham, Arthur 1867-1939 MAICYA
See also SATA 15
Rackham, John
See Phillifent, John Thomas
Rackham, Thomas W(illiam) 1919- 25-28R
Rackin, Phyllis 1933- 85-88
Rackman, Emanuel 1910- 29-32R
Rackowe, Alec 1897- 25-28R
Rad, Gerhard von
See von Rad, Gerhard
Radan, G. T.
See Radan, George T(ivadar)
Radan, George T(ivadar) 1923- CANR-39
Earlier sketch in CA 116
Radbill, Samuel X. 1901- 49-52
Radcliff, Alan L(awrence) 1920- 49-52
Radcliff, Peter (Edward Jr.) 1932- 21-24R
Radcliffe, Ann (Ward) 1764-1823 DLB 39
Radcliffe, Donnie
See Radcliffe, Redonia
Radcliffe, George L.
1878(?)-1974 Obituary 53-56
Radcliffe, Janette
See Roberts, Janet Louise
Radcliffe, Lynn J. 1896- 1-4R
Radcliffe, Philip (Fitzhugh)
1905-1986 Obituary 120
Radcliffe, Redonia 132
Radcliffe, Virginia
See Hurst, Virginia Radcliffe
Radcliffe-Brown, A(lfred) R(eginald)
1881-1955 Brief entry 114
Radcliff-Umstead, Douglas 1944- CANR-13
Earlier sketch in CA 33-36R
Raddall, Thomas Head 1903- CANR-28
Earlier sketch in CA 1-4R
See also DLB 68
Raddysh, Garry
See Radison, Garry
Radel, John J(oseph) 1934- 29-32R
Radelet, Louis A(ugust) 1917- 89-92
Rader, Benjamin G(ene) 1935- 21-24R
Rader, Dotson 1942- CANR-11
Earlier sketch in CA 61-64
Rader, Melvin (Miller) 1903-1981 CANR-5
Earlier sketch in CA 13-16R
Rader, Ralph Wilson 1930- 13-16R
Rader, Randall R(ay) 1949- 121
Rader, Rosemary 1931- 112
Rader, (John) Trout (III) 1938- 37-40R
Radest, Howard B(ernard) 1928- 41-44R
Radford, Edwin Isaac 1891- 104
Radford, John 1901-1967 CAP-2
Earlier sketch in CA 21-22
Radford, Richard F(rancis) Jr. 1939- CANR-20
Earlier sketch in CA 104
Radford, Ruby L(orraine) 1891-1971 CANR-4
Earlier sketch in CA 1-4R
See also SATA 6
Radha, Sivananda 1911- CANR-36
Earlier sketch in CA 114
Radha, Swami Sivananda
See Radha, Sivananda
Radhakrishnan, C(hakkorayil) 1939- 57-60
Radhakrishnan, Sarvepalli 1888-1975 CAP-1
Obituary 57-60
Earlier sketch in CA 13-16
Radice, Barbara 133
Radice, Betty 1912-1985 CANR-12
Obituary 115
Earlier sketch in CA 25-28R
Radice, Giles 1936- CANR-17
Earlier sketch in CA 25-28R
Radiguet, Raymond 1903-1923 DLB 65
See also TCLC 29
Radimsky, Ladislaw
1898-1970 Obituary 29-32R
Radin, Edward D(avid) 1909-1966 Obituary 114
Radin, George 1896-1981 Obituary 102
Radin, Paul 1883-1959 Brief entry 120
Radin, Ruth Yaffe 1938- 124
See also SATA 52, 56
Radison, Garry 1949- 117
Radji, Parviz C(amran) 1936- 131
Radke, Don 1940- 57-60
Radl, Shirley L(ouise) 1935- CANR-12
Earlier sketch in CA 69-72
Radlauer, David 1952- 106
See also SATA 28
Radlauer, Edward 1921- CANR-30
Earlier sketches in CA 69-72, CANR-13
See also SATA 15
Radlauer, Ruth Shaw 1926- CANR-30
Earlier sketches in CA 81-84, CANR-13
See also SATA 15
Radler, D(on) H. 1926- 13-16R
Radley, Eric John 1917- 109
Radley, Gail 1951- CANR-16
Earlier sketch in CA 89-92
See also SATA 25
Radley, Paul John 1962- 121
Radley, Sheila
See Robinson, Sheila Mary
Radley, Virginia L. 1927- 25-28R
Radner, Gilda 1946-1989 129
Obituary 128
See also BEST 89:4
Radner, Roy 1927- 49-52
Radnoti, Miklos 1909-1944 Brief entry 118
See also TCLC 16
Rado, Alexander
See Rado, Sandor
Rado, James 1939- 105
See also CLC 17
Rado, Sandor 1900-1981 109
Obituary 105
Radoff, Morris L(eon) 1905-1978 85-88
Obituary 81-84
Radom, Matthew 1905- 57-60
Radosh, Ronald 1937- 101
Radtke, Guenter 1920- 110
Radtke, Gunter
See Radtke, Guenter
Radvanyi, Janos 1922- 41-44R
Radvanyi, Netty 1900-1983 85-88
Obituary 110
See also Seghers, Anna
Radwanski, Pierre A(rthur) 1903- CAP-2
Earlier sketch in CA 23-24
Radwanski-Szinagel, Dr. Pierre A.
See Radwanski, Pierre A(rthur)
Radway, Ann
See Geis, Richard E(rwin)
Radway, Janice A(nne) 1949- 121
Radyr, Tomos
See Haldane-Stevenson, James Patrick
Radzinowicz, Leon 1906- CANR-26
Earlier sketch in CA 106
Rae, Daphne 1933- 109
Rae, (Margaret) Doris 1907- CANR-15
Earlier sketches in CAP-1, CA 11-12
Rae, Douglas W(hiting) 1939- 77-80
Rae, Evonne 1928-1974 Obituary 104
Rae, Gwynedd 1892-1977 65-68
See also SATA 37
Rae, Hugh C(rauford) 1935- CANR-29
Earlier sketches in CA 17-20R, CANR-8
Rae, John B(ell) 1911- 13-16R
Rae, John Malcolm 1931- CANR-4
Earlier sketch in CA 1-4R
Rae, Milford Andersen 1946- CANR-8
Earlier sketch in CA 61-64
Rae, Nicol C(ursiter) 1960- 131
Rae, Rusty
See Rae, Milford Andersen
Rae, Walter 1916- 57-60
Rae, Wesley D(ennis) 1932- 21-24R
Raebeck, Lois 1921- 13-16R
See also SATA 5
Raeburn, Antonia 1934- 101
Raeburn, John (Hay) 1941- 57-60
See also CLC 34
Raeburn, Michael 1940- 107
Raeburn, Michael 1943- 103
Raef, Laura (Gladys) C(auble) CANR-11
Earlier sketch in CA 29-32R
Raeff, Marc 1923- 61-64
Rael, Leyla 1948- 106
Raelin, Joseph A(lan) 1948- 125
Raeper, William 1959- 131
Raeschild, Sheila 1936- CANR-22
Earlier sketch in CA 105
Rafael, Gideon 1913- 129
Brief entry 106
RAF Casualty
See Gleave, T(om) P.
Rafe, Stephen C. 1937- 132
Rafelson, Bob 1933(?)- 128
Brief entry 112
Raffa, Frederick Anthony 1944- 53-56
Raffaele, Joseph A(ntonio) 1916- CANR-8
Earlier sketch in CA 5-8R
Raffel, Burton 1928- CANR-30
Earlier sketches in CA 9-12R, CANR-7
See also CAAS 9
Raffelock, David 1897- CAP-2
Earlier sketch in CA 25-28
See also AITN 1
Rafferty, Kathleen Kelly
1915-1981 Obituary 103
Rafferty, Max L. 1917-1982 CANR-1
Obituary 107
Earlier sketch in CA 1-4R
Rafferty, Milton 1932- 101
Rafferty, S.S.
See Hurley, John J(erome)
Raffi
See Cavoukian, Raffi
Raffini, James O. 1941- 117
Rafroidi, Patrick (Pierre) 1930-1989 132
Raftery, Gerald (Bransfield) 1905- CAP-1
Earlier sketch in CA 13-14
See also SATA 11
Ragan, David 1925- 65-68
Ragan, Sam(uel Talmadge) 1915- 13-16R
Ragan, William Burk 1896-1973 CANR-2
Earlier sketch in CA 1-4R
Ragaway, Martin A(rnold)
1928(?)-1989 CANR-12
Obituary 128
Earlier sketch in CA 61-64
Ragen, Joseph E(dward) 1897-1971 CAP-2
Obituary 33-36R
Earlier sketch in CA 21-22
Ragen, Naomi 1949- 130
Raghavan, Manayath D. 1892- CAP-2
Earlier sketch in CA 19-20
Ragins, Sanford 117
Raglan, Baron
See Raglan, FitzRoy
Raglan, FitzRoy 1885-1964 5-8R
Ragni, Gerome 1942-1991 105
Obituary 134
See also CLC 17
Rago, Henry Anthony 1915-1969 CAP-2
Earlier sketch in CA 25-28
Rago, Louis J(oseph von) 1924- 9-12R
Ragosta, Millie J(ane) 1931- CANR-12
Earlier sketch in CA 73-76
Ragsdale, Ray W(aldo) 1909- 45-48
Ragsdale, W(arner) B(ernice) 1898-1986 73-76
Obituary 121
Raguin, Yves (Emile) 1912- 81-84
Ragusa, Olga (M.) 1922- 122
Raham, (R.) Gary 1946- 136
Rahill, Peter J(ames) 1910- 5-8R
Rahim, Enayetur 1938- 107
Rahl, James A(ndrew) 1917- 77-80
Rahm, David A. 1931- 57-60
Rahman, Abdul
See Wayman, Tony Russell
Rahman, F.
See Rahman, Fazlur
Rahman, Fazlur 1919-1988 Obituary 126
Rahn, Joan Elma 1929- CANR-13
Earlier sketch in CA 37-40R
See also SATA 27
Rahner, Karl 1904-1984 109
Obituary 112
Rahner, Raymond M. 101
Rahsepar
See Yar-Shater, Ehsan O(llah)
Rahtjen, Bruce D(onald) 1933- 21-24R
Rahv, Betty T(homas) 1931- 105
Rahv, Philip
See Greenberg, Ivan
See also CLC 24
Rai, Kul B(husan) 1937- 105
Rai, Navab
See Srivastava, Dhanpat Rai
Raia, Anthony P(aul) 1928- 61-64
Raible, Alton (Robert) 1918- SATA 35
Raiff, Stan 1930- 61-64
See also SATA 11
Railton, Esther P(auline) 1929- 101
Raimi, Sam(uel M.) 1959- 123
Raimond, C. E.
See Robins, Elizabeth
Raimund, Ferdinand Jakob 1790-1836 DLB 90
Raimy, Eric 1942- 93-96
Raimy, Victor 1913- 81-84
Rainbird, George (Meadus) 1905-1986 133
Obituary 120
Rainbow-Wind, Shandor
See Weiss, (Paul) Shandor
Raine, Craig 1944- CANR-29
Earlier sketch in CA 108
See also CLC 32
See also DLB 40
Raine, Kathleen (Jessie) 1908- 85-88
See also CLC 7, 45
See also DLB 20
See also MTCW
Raine, Norman Reilly
1895-1971 Obituary 33-36R
Raine, Richard
See Sawkins, Raymond H(arold)
Rainer, George
See Greenburger, Ingrid Elisabeth
Rainer, Julia
See Goode, Ruth
Rainer, Yvonne 1934- 133
Raines, Howell (Hiram) 1943- 73-76
Raines, Jeff 1958- 127
Raines, John C. 1933- 73-76
Raines, Robert A(rnold) 1926- CANR-7
Earlier sketch in CA 13-16R
Raines, Shirley (Carol) 1945- 113
Raines, Theron 1925- 127
Rainey, Bill G. 1926- 89-92
Rainey, Buck
See Rainey, Bill G.
Rainey, Gene E(dward) 1934- 25-28R
Rainey, Homer Price 1896-1985 Obituary 118
Rainey, Patricia Ann 1937- 49-52
Rainey, W. B.
See Blassingame, Wyatt Rainey
Rainham, Thomas
See Barren, Charles (MacKinnon)
Rainis, Janis 1865-1929 TCLC 29
Rains, Rob 1956- 138
Rainsberger, Todd J(effrey) 1951- 106
Rainsford, George Nichols 1928- 49-52
Raintree, Lee
See Sellers, Con(nie Leslie Jr.)
Rainwater, (Mary) Catherine 1953- 119
Rainwater, Dorothy T(hornton) 1918- CANR-1
Earlier sketch in CA 45-48
Rainwater, Lee 1928- 53-56
Raistrick, Arthur 1896- CANR-3
Earlier sketch in CA 9-12R
Raisz, Erwin J(osephus) 1893-1968 1-4R
Obituary 103
Raitt, A(lan) W(illiam) 1930- 29-32R
Raizis, M(arios) Byron 1931- 41-44R
Raizner, Bernard I. 1945- 127
Rajan, Balachandra 1920- 69-72
Rajan, M(annarswamighala) S(reeranga)
1920- CANR-13
Earlier sketch in CA 13-16R
Rajan, Tilottama 1951- 107
Rajanen, Aini 109
Rajaram
See
Iyengar, K(odaganallur) R(amaswami) Srinivasa
Rajasekharaiah, T(umkur) R(udraradhya)
1926- 33-36R
Rajec, Elizabeth M(olnar) 1931- 109
Rajic, Negovan 1923- 130
Rajneesh, Acharya 1931-1990 93-96
Obituary 130
Rajneesh, Bhagwan Shree
See Rajneesh, Acharya
Rajski, Raymond B. 1917- 21-24R
Raju, Poolla Tirupati 1904- 33-36R
Rakel, Robert E(dwin) 1932- CANR-26
Earlier sketch in CA 107
Raknes, Ola 1887-1975 CAP-2
Earlier sketch in CA 29-32
Rako, Susan Mandell 1939- 117
Rakoff, Alvin 1927- 102
Rakosi, Carl
See Rawley, Callman
See also CAAS 5
See also CLC 47
Rakosi, Matyas 1892-1971 Obituary 29-32R
Rakove, Jack N(orman) 1947- 93-96

Rakove, Milton L(eon) 1918-1983 ....CANR-15
Obituary 111
Earlier sketch in CA 65-68
Rakowski, James Peter 1945- 105
Rakowski, John 1922- 106
Rakstis, Ted J(ay) 1932- 101
Ralbovsky, Martin Paul 1942- 49-52
Rale, Nero
See Burgess, M(ichael) R(oy)
Ralegh, Sir Walter
1554(?)-1618 .... CDBLB Before 1660
Raleigh, Donald J(oseph) 1949- 125
Raleigh, John Henry 1920- CANR-3
Earlier sketch in CA 1-4R
Raleigh, Richard
See Lovecraft, H(oward) P(hillips)
Raley, Harold (Cecil) 1934- 41-44R
Raley, Patricia E(ward) 1940- 73-76
Raley, Rowena
See McCulley, Johnston
Rallentando, H. P.
See Sayers, Dorothy L(eigh)
Ralph, David Clinton 1922- CANR-2
Earlier sketch in CA 5-8R
Ralph, Elizabeth K(ennedy) 1921- 33-36R
Ralph, Julian 1853-1903 .... DLB 23
Ralph, Margaret Nutting 1941- 121
Ralphs, Sheila 1923- 106
Ralston, Alma (Smith Payne) CANR-11
Earlier sketch in CA 17-20R
Ralston, Gilbert A(lexander) 1912- CANR-2
Earlier sketch in CA 45-48
Ralston, James Kenneth 1896- 49-52
Ralston, Jan
See Dunlop, Agnes M. R.
Ralston, Leonard F. 1925- 45-48
Ralston, Melvin B. 1937- 49-52
Ram, Immanuel
See Velikovsky, Immanuel
Rama
See Gupta, Ram Chandra
Rama, Swami
See Swami Rama
Ramacharaka, Yogi
See Atkinson, William Walker
Ramage, Edwin S(tephen) 1929- 65-68
Ramage, James A(lfred) 1940- 61-64
Ramal, Walter
See de la Mare, Walter (John)
Ramamurty, K(otamraju) Bhaskara 1924- 53-56
Raman, Chandrasekhara Venkata
1888-1970 Obituary 113
Ramanujan, A(ttipat) K(rishnaswami)
1929- CANR-24
Earlier sketches in CA 17-20R, CANR-8
Ramanujan, Molly 1932- CANR-24
Earlier sketch in CA 29-32R
Ramanujan, Shouri
See Ramanujan, Molly
Rama Rau, Dhanvanthi (Handoo)
1893-1987 Obituary 123
Brief entry 106
Rama Rau, Santha
See Wattles, Santha Rama Rau
Ramaswamy, Mysore 1902- CAP-1
Earlier sketch in CA 13-14
Ramati, Alexander 1921- CANR-7
Earlier sketch in CA 13-16R
Ramati, Yohanan (Joseph) 1921- 111
Ramazani, Rouhollah K(aregar)
1928- CANR-26
Earlier sketches in CA 13-16R, CANR-10
Rambam, Cyvia
See Rambert, Marie
Rambam, Myriam
See Rambert, Marie
Rambeau, James (Morris) 1938- 117
Ramberg, Bennett 1946- 111
Rambert, Marie 1888-1982 103
Obituary 107
Rambo, Lewis Ray 1943- 109
Ramdin, Ron(ald Andrew) 1942- 131
Rame, David
See Divine, Arthur Durham
Rameh, Clea 1927- 53-56
Ramenofsky, Ann F. 1942- 125
Ramey, James W(alter) 1928- 112
Ramey, Mary Ann 1947- 125
Ramge, Sebastian Victor 1930- 9-12R
Ramirez, Carolyn H(olmes) 1933- CANR-2
Earlier sketch in CA 5-8R
Ramirez, Susan E(lizabeth) 1946- 130
See also HW
Ramirez de Arellano, Diana (T. Clotilde)
1919- CANR-32
Earlier sketch in CA 45-48
See also HW
Ramirez de Arellano, Rafael W(illiam)
1884- ....HW
Ramis, Harold (Allen) 1944- 128
Brief entry 124
Ramke, Bin 1947- CANR-31
Earlier sketches in CA 81-84, CANR-14
See also DLB 120
Ramler, Karl Wilhelm 1725-1798 .... DLB 97
Ramm, Bernard L(awrence)
1916- Brief entry 112
Rammelkamp, Julian S(turtevant) 1917- ...17-20R
Ramo, Simon 1913- Brief entry 111
Ramon, Juan
See Jimenez (Mantecon), Juan Ramon
Ramond, Charles K(night) 1930- 101
Ramos, Graciliano 1892-1953 .... TCLC 32
Ramos, Suzanne 1942- 101
Ramos-Oliveira, Antonio
1907-1973 Obituary 104
Ramp, Eugene A(ugust) 1942- 49-52

Rampa, Tuesday Lobsang
See Hoskin, Cyril Henry
Rampersad, Arnold 1941- 133
Brief entry 127
See also CLC 44
See also DLB 111
Rampling, Anne
See Rice, Anne
Ramquist, Grace (Bess) Chapman
1907- CANR-3
Earlier sketch in CA 9-12R
Ramrus, Al 1930- 105
Rams, Edwin M(arion) 1922- 17-20R
Ramsaur, Ernest Edmondson Jr. 1915- 41-44R
Ramsay, Allan 1684(?)-1758 .... DLB 95
Ramsay, David 1749-1815 .... DLB 30
Ramsay, J(ames) A(rthur)
1909-1988 Obituary 124
Ramsay, Jay 1958- 135
Ramsay, Raymond (Henry) 1927- 77-80
Ramsay, William M(cDowell) 1922- CANR-12
Earlier sketch in CA 13-16R
Ramsbottom, John 1885-1974 Obituary 53-56
Ramsdell, Kristin (Romeis) 1940- 125
Ramsden, E. H. 102
Ramsden, Herbert 1927- CANR-25
Earlier sketch in CA 108
Ramsden, John Andrew 1947- 108
Ramsell, Donald 1926(?)-1983 Obituary 110
Ramsett, David E. 1942- 29-32R
Ramsey, Charles E(ugene) 1923- 13-16R
Ramsey, Dan(ny Clarence) 1945- 101
Ramsey, Doug(las A.) 1934- 132
Ramsey, Eric
See Hagberg, David J(ames)
Ramsey, (Charles) Frederic Jr. 1915- 5-8R
Ramsey, G(ordon) C(lark) 1941- CANR-9
Earlier sketch in CA 21-24R
Ramsey, George Wilson 1937- 113
Ramsey, Ian T(homas) 1915-1972 ....CANR-4
Earlier sketch in CA 5-8R
Ramsey, Jackson E. 1938- 122
Ramsey, Jarold 1937- 33-36R
Ramsey, John F(raser) 1907- 49-52
Ramsey, Lee C(arter) 1935- 120
Ramsey, (Arthur) Michael 1904-1988 ......CANR-14
Obituary 125
Earlier sketch in CA 77-80
Ramsey, (Robert) Paul 1913-1988 ....CANR-1
Obituary 124
Earlier sketch in CA 1-4R
Ramsey, Paul W. 1905-1976 Obituary 69-72
Ramsey, Paul 1924- 41-44R
Ramsey, Robert D. 1934- 25-28R
Ramsey, Roy S. 1920(?)-1976 Obituary 65-68
Ramsey, Russell W. 1935- 124
Ramseyer, John A(lvin) 1908-1968 ....CANR-4
Earlier sketch in CA 5-8R
Ramseyer, Lloyd L. 1899- CAP-2
Earlier sketch in CA 19-20
Ramskill, Valerie Patricia Roskams CAP-1
Earlier sketch in CA 9-10
Ramsland, Katherine 1953- 136
Ramson, W(illiam) S(tanley) 1933- 45-48
Ramundo, Bernard A. 1925- 21-24R
Ramuz, Charles-Ferdinand 1878-1947 ..... TCLC 33
Rana, J.
See Bhatia, Jamunadevi
Ranadive, Gail 1944- 53-56
See also SATA 10
Rance, Patrick 1918- 138
Rancour-Laferriere, Daniel 138
Rand, Ann (Binkley) 106
See also SATA 30
Rand, Austin Loomer 1905- 89-92
Rand, Ayn 1905-1982 ....CANR-27
Obituary 105
Earlier sketch in CA 13-16R
See also CLC 3, 30, 44
See also MTCW
See also WLC
Rand, Brett
See Norwood, Victor G(eorge) C(harles)
Rand, Christopher 1912-1968 77-80
Rand, Clayton (Thomas) 1891-1971 ....5-8R
Obituary 29-32R
Rand, Earl (James) 1933- 21-24R
Rand, Frank Prentice 1889- CAP-1
Earlier sketch in CA 11-12
Rand, Harry 1947- 137
Rand, J. H.
See Holland, James R.
Rand, James S.
See Attenborough, Bernard George
Rand, Paul 1914- 21-24R
See also SATA 6
Rand, Peter 1942- 77-80
Rand, Willard J. Jr. 1913- 9-12R
Randal, Beatrice (a pseudonym) 1916- 61-64
Randal, Vera 1922- 9-12R
Randall, Belle 1940- 118
Randall, Bob 1937- 106
Randall, Charles Edgar 1897- 41-44R
Randall, Charles H(enry) 1920- 133
Randall, Clarence Belden 1891-1967 .... CAP-1
Earlier sketch in CA 13-14
Randall, Clay
See Adams, Clifton
Randall, Dale B(ertrand) J(onas) 1929- CANR-2
Earlier sketch in CA 5-8R
Randall, David A(nton)
1905-1975 Obituary 57-60
Randall, Deborah 1957- 131
Randall, Diane
See Ross, W(illiam) E(dward) D(aniel)
Randall, Donald A. 1933- 61-64

Randall, Dudley (Felker) 1914- CANR-23
Earlier sketch in CA 25-28R
See also BLC 3
See also BW
See also CLC 1
See also DLB 41
Randall, Florence Engel 1917- 41-44R
See also SATA 5
Randall, Francis Ballard 1931- 9-12R
Randall, Henry S. 1811-1876 .... DLB 30
Randall, J. G.
See Randall, James Garfield
Randall, James G.
See Randall, James Garfield
See also DLB 17
Randall, James Garfield
1881-1953 Brief entry 118
See also Randall, James G.
Randall, Janet
See Young, Janet Randall
and Young, Robert W(illiam)
Randall, Jo Anne Yarus 1942- 118
Randall, John E(rnest Jr.) 1924- 65-68
Randall, John Herman Jr. 1899-1980 ......CANR-1
Obituary 102
Earlier sketch in CA 1-4R
Randall, John L(eslie) 1933- 107
Randall, Joseph Hungerford 1897- 1-4R
Randall, Julia (Sawyer) 1923- 33-36R
Randall, Laura 1935- 37-40R
Randall, Lillian M. C. 1931- 21-24R
Randall, Margaret 1936- 41-44R
Randall, Marta 107
Randall, Mary
See Colver, Alice Mary (Ross)
Randall, Mercedes M. 1895-1977 ....13-16R
Obituary 69-72
Randall, Monica 1944- 97-100
Randall, Randolph C. 1900- 17-20R
Randall, Robert
See Garrett, (Gordon) Randall (Phillip)
and Silverberg, Robert
Randall, Ruth (Elaine) Painter 1892-1971 .....1-4R
Obituary 103
See also SATA 3
Randall, Steven
See Andrews, Clarence A(delbert)
Randall, Willard Sterne 1942- 69-72
Randall-Mills, Elizabeth West 1906- 13-16R
Randazzo, Mary Callahan 1950- 127
Randazzo, Renee
See Randazzo, Mary Callahan
Randel, William (Peirce) 1909- 13-16R
Randell, Beverley
See Price, Beverley Joan
Randell, John Bulmer 1918-1982 109
Obituary 106
Randers-Pehrson, Justine Davis 1910- 111
Randhawa, M(ohinder) S(ingh)
1909-1986 ....CANR-28
Earlier sketch in CA 29-32R
Randi, James 1928- 117
Randisi, Robert J(oseph) 1951- 116
Randles, Anthony V(ictor) Jr. 1942- 65-68
Randles, Slim
See Randles, Anthony V(ictor) Jr.
Randoll, Anthony
See Blacking, John (Anthony Randoll)
Randolph, A(sa) Philip 1889-1979 125
Obituary 85-88
See also BW
Randolph, Arthur C.
See Greene, A(lvin) C(arl)
Randolph, Boynton M.D.
See Ellis, Edward S(ylvester)
Randolph, David James 1934- CANR-3
Earlier sketch in CA 49-52
Randolph, (Mary) Elizabeth 1930- 135
Randolph, Ellen
See Ross, W(illiam) E(dward) D(aniel)
Randolph, Geoffrey
See Ellis, Edward S(ylvester)
Randolph, Georgiana Ann
1908-1957 Brief entry 116
Randolph, Gordon
See von Block, Bela W(illiam)
and von Block, Sylvia
Randolph, J. H.
See Ellis, Edward S(ylvester)
Randolph, John 1915- 45-48
Randolph, Lieutenant J. H.
See Ellis, Edward S(ylvester)
Randolph, Marion
See Rodell, Marie F(reid)
Randolph, Melanie
See Ragosta, Millie J(ane)
Randolph, Nancy
See Robb, Inez (Callaway)
Randolph, Thomas 1605-1635 .... DLB 58
Randolph, Vance 1892- 105
Random, Alan
See Kay, Ernest
Random, Alex
See Rowland, D(onald) S(ydney)
Rands, William Brighty 1823-1882 .... SATA 17
Ranelagh, John (O'Beirne) 1947- 128
Ranga, N. G. 1900- 29-32R
Ranganathan, S(hiyali) R(amamrita)
1892-1972 ....CANR-5
Earlier sketch in CA 5-8R
Range, Willard Edgar Allen 1910- 1-4R
Rangel, Carlos 1929-1988 104
Obituary 124
Rangell, Leo 1913- 105
Ranger, Ken
See Creasey, John
Ranger, Paul 1933- 37-40R

Ranger, T(erence) O(sborn) 1929- CANR-19
Earlier sketch in CA 25-28R
Ranis, Gustav 1929- CANR-3
Earlier sketch in CA 9-12R
Ranis, Peter 1935- 41-44R
Ranjee
See Shahani, Ranjee
Rank, Benjamin (Keith) 1911- 109
Rank, Hugh (Duke) 1932- CANR-12
Earlier sketch in CA 73-76
Rank, Maureen Joy 1947- 117
Ranke-Heinemann, Uta (Johanna Ingrid)
1927- 137
Ranki, Gyoergy 1930-1988 Obituary 124
Rankin, Daniel S(tanislaus) 1895-1972 ...... CAP-1
Earlier sketch in CA 13-16
Rankin, David J. 1945- 108
Rankin, Herbert David 1931- 103
Rankin, Hugh F(ranklin) 1913- CANR-1
Earlier sketch in CA 1-4R
Rankin, Jeannette 1880-1973 Obituary 41-44R
Rankin, Judith Torluemke 1945- Brief entry 107
Rankin, Judy
See Rankin, Judith Torluemke
Rankin, Karl Lott 1898- CAP-1
Earlier sketch in CA 13-16
Rankin, Paula C(lark) 1945- CANR-21
Earlier sketch in CA 104
Rankin, Robert Harry 1909-1990 Obituary 131
Rankin, Robert P(arks) 1912- 77-80
Rankin, Robert 1915- 126
Brief entry 108
Rankin, Ruth (DeLone) I(rvine) 1924- 61-64
Rankine, John
See Mason, Douglas R(ankine)
Rankine, Paul Scott 1909(?)-1983 Obituary 109
Ranly, Ernest W. 1930- 37-40R
Ranney, Agnes V. 1916- 5-8R
See also SATA 6
Ranney, (Joseph) Austin 1920- 77-80
Rannit, Aleksis 1914-1985 Obituary 114
Brief entry 109
Ranous, Charles A. 1912- 13-16R
Ransel, David L(orimer) 1939- 73-76
Ransford, Oliver 1914- CANR-10
Earlier sketch in CA 21-24R
Ransley, Peter 1931- CANR-21
Earlier sketch in CA 69-72
Ransohoff, Paul M(artin) 1948- 103
Ransom, Bill 1945- CANR-19
Earlier sketch in CA 101
Ransom, Candice F. 1952- 121
See also SATA 49, 52
Ransom, Harry Howe 1922- 9-12R
Ransom, Jay Ellis 1914- CANR-20
Earlier sketches in CA 9-12R, CANR-3
Ransom, John Crowe 1888-1974 ....CANR-34
Obituary 49-52
Earlier sketches in CA 5-8R, CANR-6
See also CLC 2, 4, 5, 11, 24
See also DLB 45, 63
See also MTCW
Ransom, William Michael 1945- Brief entry 108
Ransom, William R.
1876-1973 Obituary 37-40R
Ransome, Arthur (Michell) 1884-1967 73-76
See also CLR 8
See also MAICYA
See also SATA 22
Ransome, Eleanor 1915- 93-96
Ransome, Stephen
See Davis, Frederick C(lyde)
Ransome-Davies, Basil
See Colley, Iain
Ransone, Coleman B(ernard) Jr. 1920- 45-48
Rant, Tol E.
See Longyear, Barry Brookes
Ranum, Orest Allen 1933- CANR-8
Earlier sketch in CA 9-12R
Ranum, Patricia M(cGroder) 1932- 45-48
Ranz, James 1921- 9-12R
Ranz, Jim
See Ranz, James
Ranzini, Addis Durning 1909-1983 Obituary 110
Rao, B. Shiva 1900(?)-1975 Obituary 61-64
Rao, C. H. Hanumantha 1929- CANR-7
Earlier sketch in CA 17-20R
Rao, K(oneru) Ramakrishna 1932- 130
Rao, R(anganatha) P(admanabha)
1924- 13-16R
Rao, Raja 1909- 73-76
See also CLC 25, 56
See also MTCW
Raoul, Anthony
See Wilmot, Anthony
Rapaport, Herman 1947- CANR-35
Earlier sketch in CA 114
Rapaport, Ionel F.
1909(?)-1972 Obituary 37-40R
Rapaport, Stella F(read) 1-4R
Raper, Arthur F(ranklin) 1899-1979 ....CANR-12
Obituary 89-92
Earlier sketch in CA 61-64
Raper, J(ulius) R(owan) 1938- 33-36R
Raper, Jack
See Raper, J(ulius) R(owan)
Raphael, Bertram 1936- 97-100
Raphael, Beverley 1934- 117
Raphael, Chaim 1908- CANR-16
Earlier sketch in CA 85-88
Raphael, Dan 1952- 104
Raphael, Dana 61-64
Raphael, David D(aiches) 1916- CANR-20
Earlier sketches in CA 5-8R, CANR-2
Raphael, Elaine
See Bolognese, Elaine Raphael (Chionchio)
See also SATA 23

Raphael, Frederic (Michael) 1931- CANR-1
Earlier sketch in CA 1-4R
See also CLC 2, 14
See also DLB 14
Raphael, Jay
See Josephs, Ray
Raphael, Lev 1954- 134
Raphael, Marc Lee 1942(?)- Brief entry 113
Raphael, Phyllis 1940- 45-48
Raphael, Rick 1919- CANR-10
Earlier sketch in CA 21-24R
Raphael, Robert 1927- 45-48
Raphael, Sandra (Joan) 1939- 104
Raphaelson, Elliot 1937- 124
Raphaelson, Samson 1896-1983 65-68
Obituary 110
See also DLB 44
Rapkin, Chester 1918- 17-20R
Rapoport, Alan M. 1942- 134
Rapoport, Amos 1929- 65-68
Rapoport, Anatol 1911- 41-44R
Rapoport, Janis 1946- CANR-18
Earlier sketch in CA 101
Rapoport, Judith L. ....BEST 89:3
Rapoport, Louis (Harvey) 1942- 117
Rapoport, Rhona (Ross) 1927- CANR-8
Earlier sketch in CA 61-64
Rapoport, Robert Norman 1924- CANR-39
Earlier sketches in CA 5-8R, CANR-2, 17
Rapoport, Roger 1946- 33-36R
Rapoport, Ron 1940- 89-92
Raposo, Joseph Guilherme
1938-1989 Obituary 127
See also SATA 61
Rapp, Doris Jean 1929- CANR-21
Earlier sketch in CA 37-40R
Rapp, George (Robert) Jr. 1930- 130
Rapp, Joel ....AITN 1
Rapp, Lynn ....AITN 1
Rappaport, Alfred 1932- Brief entry 110
Rappaport, Armin H. 1916- Brief entry 111
Rappaport, David 1907- CAP-2
Earlier sketch in CA 19-20
Rappaport, Eva 1924- 29-32R
See also SATA 6
Rappaport, Julian 1942- Brief entry 112
Rappaport, Roy A(braham) 1926- 41-44R
Rappaport, Sheldon R(aphael) 1926- 29-32R
Rappaport, Steve 1948- 134
Rappole, John H(ilton) 1946- 123
Rappoport, David Steven 1957- 133
Rappoport, Ken 1935- CANR-20
Earlier sketches in CA 53-56, CANR-4
Rappoport, Leon 1932- 41-44R
Rapson, Richard L(awrence) 1937- CANR-10
Earlier sketch in CA 21-24R
Rarick, Carrie 1911- 115
See also SATA 41
Rasberry, Robert W. 1945- 110
Rasberry, Salli 1940- CANR-23
Earlier sketch in CA 107
Rasch, Sunna Cooper 1925- 105
Raschke, Carl A(llan) 1944- 104
Rascoe, Jesse Ed
See Bartholomew, Ed(ward Ellsworth)
Rascoe, Judith 1941(?)- 107
Rascovich, Mark 1918(?)-1976 Obituary 69-72
Rasey, Ruth M.
See Simpson, Ruth Mary Rasey
Rash, Dora Eileen Agnew (Wallace)
1897- CANR-2
Earlier sketch in CA 5-8R
Rash, J(esse) Keogh 1906- 93-96
Rash, Nancy 1940- CANR-37
Rashad, Johari M(ahasin) 1951- 138
Rashidof, Sharif Rashidovich
See Rashidov, Sharaf Rashidovich
Rashidov, Sharaf Rashidovich
1917(?)-1983 Obituary 111
Rashke, Richard L. 1936- CANR-24
Earlier sketch in CA 107
Raskin, A(braham) H(enry) 1911- 104
Raskin, Barbara 1935- 129
Brief entry 126
Raskin, Edith Lefkowitz 1908- CANR-3
Earlier sketch in CA 9-12R
See also SATA 9
Raskin, Ellen 1928-1984 ....CANR-37
Obituary 113
Earlier sketch in CA 21-24R
See also CLR 1, 12
See also DLB 52
See also MAICYA
See also SATA 2, 38
Raskin, Eugene 1909- 33-36R
Raskin, Herbert A(lfred) 1919-1979 ....29-32R
Obituary 122
Raskin, Jonah 1942- 81-84
Raskin, Joseph 1897-1982 ....CANR-13
Obituary 105
Earlier sketch in CA 33-36R
See also SATA 12, 29
Raskin, Marcus G. 1934- 37-40R
Rasky, Frank (John) 1923- Brief entry 107
Rasky, Harry 1928- CANR-31
Earlier sketch in CA 105
Rasmusen, Henry N(eil) 1909- 5-8R
Rasmussen, David (William) 1942- 53-56
Rasmussen, Douglas B(ruce) 1948- 119
Rasmussen, John Peter 1933- Brief entry 110
Rasmussen, Knud Johan Victor
1879-1933 Brief entry 113
See also SATA 34
Rasmussen, Larry L. 1939- 118
Rasmussen, Louis J(ames Jr.) 1921- 73-76
Rasmussen, R. Kent 1943- 93-96
Rasmussen, Steen Eiler
1898-1990 Obituary 132
Rasmussen, Wayne D(avid) 1915- 33-36R
Rasof, Henry 1946- 113
Rasor, Eugene L(atimer) 1936- 89-92
Raspberry, William J(ames) 1935- 122
Brief entry 110
See also BW
Rasponi, Lanfranco 1914-1983 ....17-20R
Obituary 109
Rasputin, Maria
See Bern, Maria Rasputin Soloviev
Rasputin, Valentin (Grigorevich) 1937- 127
Brief entry 108
Rass, Rebecca 1936- 105
Rast, Walter E(mil) 1930- 73-76
Ratch, Jerry 1944- 118
Ratcliff, Carter 1941- CANR-13
Earlier sketch in CA 61-64
Ratcliff, John Drury 1903-1973 108
Obituary 106
Ratcliff, Ruth 1905- 121
Ratcliffe, Barrie M(ichael) 1940- 114
Ratcliffe, F(rederick) W(illiam) 1927- 125
Ratcliffe, James M(axwell) 1925- 21-24R
Ratcliffe, James P.
See Mencken, H(enry) L(ouis)
Ratcliffe, T(om) A(rundel) 1910- CAP-2
Earlier sketch in CA 25-28
Ratermanis, J(anis) B(ernhards) 1904- 9-12R
Rath, Frederick L(ouis) Jr. 1913- 41-44R
Rath, Patricia M(ink) 17-20R
Rath, R. John 1910- 37-40R
Rath, Sara 1941- 108
Rathbone, Julian 1935- CANR-34
Earlier sketch in CA 101
See also CLC 41
Rathbone, Lucy 1896- 5-8R
Rathbone, Ouida Bergere
1886(?)-1974 Obituary 53-56
Rathbone, Robert Reynolds 1916- 21-24R
Rathe, Alex W(erner) 1912- 17-20R
Rathe, Gustave 1921- 138
Rathenau, Walther 1867-1922 Brief entry 121
Rather, Dan (Irvin) 1931- CANR-9
Earlier sketch in CA 53-56
See also AITN 1
Rather, L(elland) J(oseph) 1913- 77-80
Rathjen, Carl Henry 1909- CANR-2
Earlier sketch in CA 5-8R
See also SATA 11
Rathjen, Frederick W(illiam) 1929- 41-44R
Rathlesberger, James (H.)
1948- Brief entry 114
Rathmell, J(ohn) C. A. 1935- 9-12R
Rathmell, Neil 1947- 104
Ratigan, Eleanor Eldridge 1916- 5-8R
Ratigan, William 1910- 29-32R
Ratiu, Ion 1917- 5-8R
Ratliff, Charles Edward Jr. 1926- CANR-1
Earlier sketch in CA 1-4R
Ratliff, Gerald Lee 1944- 107
Ratliff, Richard C(harles) 1922- 65-68
Ratliffe, Sharon A(nn) 1939- 61-64
Ratner, Joseph 1901(?)-1979 Obituary 85-88
Ratner, Leonard G(ilbert) 1916- 21-24R
Ratner, Lorman 1932- CANR-10
Earlier sketch in CA 25-28R
Ratner, Marc L. 1926- 45-48
Ratner, Rochelle 1948- CANR-12
Earlier sketch in CA 33-36R
Ratner, Sidney 1908- 21-24R
Ratner, Stanley C(harles) 1925- 13-16R
Rattenbury, Arnold (Foster) 1921- 29-32R
Rattenbury, Ken(neth Miller) 1920- 134
Ratti, John 1933- 73-76
Ratti, Oscar 41-44R
Rattigan, Terence (Mervyn) 1911-1977 85-88
Obituary 73-76
See also CDBLB 1945-1960
See also CLC 7
See also DLB 13
See also MTCW
Rattner, David S(amuel) 1916- 69-72
Rattray, Everett T(ennant) 1932-1980 89-92
Obituary 97-100
Rattray, Simon
See Trevor, Elleston
Ratushinskaya, Irina 1954- 129
See also CLC 54
Ratzan, Scott C. 1962- 124
Rau, Dhanvanthi (Handoo) Rama
See Rama Rau, Dhanvanthi (Handoo)
Rau, Margaret 1913- CANR-8
Earlier sketch in CA 61-64
See also CLR 8
See also SATA 9
Rauch, Basil 1908-1986 ....CAP-2
Obituary 119
Earlier sketch in CA 19-20
Rauch, Constance 1937- 57-60
Rauch, Earl Mac 1950(?)- Brief entry 118
Rauch, Georg Von
See Von Rauch, Georg
Rauch, Irmengard 1933- CANR-11
Earlier sketch in CA 21-24R
Rauch, Joseph B(rian) 1965- 131
Rauch, Leo 1927- 110
Rauch, Mabel Thompson 1888-1972 ....5-8R
Obituary 103
See also SATA 26
Rauch, Rufus William Jr.
1929-1977 Obituary 113
Raucher, Alan R(ichard) 1939- 118
Raucher, Herman 1928- CANR-29
Earlier sketch in CA 29-32R
See also SATA 8
Raucina, Thomas Frank 1946- CANR-29
Earlier sketches in CA 73-76, CANR-12
Raudive, Konstantin 1909-1974 ....29-32R
Obituary 126
Rauf, Abdur 1924- CANR-13
Earlier sketch in CA 73-76
Rauf, Muhammad Abdul
See Abdul-Rauf, Muhammad
Raulston, J(ames) Leonard 1905- 89-92
Rault, Walter
See Gorham, Maurice Anthony Coneys
Rauner, Robert M(cKenzie) 1925- CANR-1
Earlier sketch in CA 1-4R
Raunikar, Robert 1931- 124
Raup, H(allock) F(loyd) 1901- 37-40R
Raup, Robert 1888(?)-1976 Obituary 65-68
Rausch, Edward N. 1919- CANR-7
Earlier sketch in CA 13-16R
Rausch, Jane M(eyer) 1940- 119
Rauschenberg, Roy A(nthony) 1929- 45-48
Rauscher, Donald J. 1921- 9-12R
Rauschning, Hermann 1887-1982 Obituary 109
Raush, Harold L(ester) 1921- Brief entry 110
Raushenbush, Esther (Mohr) 1898- CAP-1
Earlier sketch in CA 13-16
Ravel, Aviva 1928- 119
Raven, Frithjof Andersen 1907-1966 ....CAP-1
Earlier sketch in CA 13-16
Raven, J(ohn) E(arle) 1914-1980 103
Obituary 97-100
Raven, Ninette Helene Jeanty
1903-1990 Obituary 132
Raven, Ronald William 1904-1991 ....CANR-23
Obituary 136
Earlier sketch in CA 107
Raven, Simon (Arthur Noel) 1927- 81-84
See also CLC 14
Ravenal, Earl C(edric) 1931- 33-36R
Ravenel, Shannon 1938- CANR-27
Earlier sketch in CA 108
Ravenna, Roger
See Horbach, Michael
Ravenscroft, Arthur 1924- CANR-29
Earlier sketch in CA 110
Ravetch, Irving 1915(?)- Brief entry 110
Ravetz, Alison 1930- 116
Ravetz, Jerome R(aymond) 1929- 97-100
Ravetz, Jerry
See Ravetz, Jerome R(aymond)
Ravich, Robert A(lan) 1920- Brief entry 113
Ravielli, Anthony 1916- CANR-11
Earlier sketch in CA 29-32R
See also SATA 3
Ravikovitch, Dahlia
See Rabikovitz, Dalia
Ravikovitz, Dalia
See Rabikovitz, Dalia
Ravin, Neil 1947- 105
Ravindra, Ravi 1939- CANR-35
Earlier sketch in CA 114
Ravitch, Diane 1938- CANR-31
Earlier sketches in CA 53-56, CANR-4
See also MTCW
Ravitch, Mark M(itchell)
1910-1989 Obituary 128
Ravitch, Norman 1936- 37-40R
Ravitz, Abe Carl 1927- 9-12R
Ravitz, Shlomo 1885-1980 Obituary 103
Ravvin, Norman 1963- 138
Raw, Isaias 1927- 57-60
Rawcliffe, (John) Michael 1934- 115
Rawding, F(rederick) W(illiam) 1930- ....SATA 55
Rawford, W. C.
See Crawford, William (Elbert)
Rawick, George P(hilip) 1929- 61-64
Rawitch, Robert Joe 1945- 133
Rawlence, Christopher 1945- 136
Rawles, Beverly A(rcher) 1930- 107
Rawley, Callman 1903- CANR-32
Earlier sketches in CA 21-24R, CANR-12
See also Rakosi, Carl
Rawley, James A. 1916- 21-24R
Rawling, Thomas Jackson 1916- 114
Rawling, Tom
See Rawling, Thomas Jackson
Rawlings, Hunter Ripley III 1944- 103
Rawlings, John 1930(?)-1981(?) Obituary 102
Rawlings, Louisa
See Baumgarten, Sylvia
Rawlings, Marjorie Kinnan 1896-1953 137
Brief entry 104
See also DLB 9, 22, 102
See also MAICYA
See also TCLC 4
See also YABC 1
Rawlings, Maurice S(kaggs) 1922- 108
Rawlins, Clive Leonard 1940- CANR-22
Earlier sketch in CA 105
Rawlins, Dennis 1937- 45-48
Rawlins, Eustace Robert
See Barton, Eustace Robert
Rawlins, Jack P. 1946- 57-60
Rawlins, Jennie Brown 1910- CAP-2
Earlier sketch in CA 23-24
Rawlins, Winifred 1907- 9-12R
Rawlinson, A(rthur) R(ichard)
1894-1984 Obituary 113
Rawlinson, Dick
See Rawlinson, A(rthur) R(ichard)
Rawlinson, Jane 1947- 138
Rawls, Eugene S. 1927- 9-12R
Rawls, James J(abus) 1945- 112
Rawls, John Bordley 1921- Brief entry 114
Rawls, Philip
See Levinson, Leonard
Rawls, Walter Cecil Jr. 1928- 111
Rawls, Walton (Hendry) 1933- 121
Rawls, Wendell L(ee) Jr. 1941- CANR-22
Earlier sketch in CA 73-76
Rawls, (Woodrow) Wilson 1913- CANR-5
Earlier sketch in CA 1-4R
See also AITN 1
See also SATA 22
Rawlyk, George Alexander 1935- CANR-26
Earlier sketch in CA 109
See also SATA 64
Raworth, Thomas Moore 1938- 29-32R
See also Raworth, Tom
Raworth, Tom
See Raworth, Thomas Moore
See also CAAS 11
See also DLB 40
Rawski, Conrad H(enry) 1914- 73-76
Rawski, Evelyn S(akakida) 1939- 89-92
Rawson, Beryl 1933- 121
Rawson, C(laude) J(ulien) 1935- 25-28R
Rawson, Clayton 1906-1971 ....CANR-4
Obituary 29-32R
Earlier sketch in CA 5-8R
Rawson, Elizabeth (Donata)
1934-1988 Brief entry 115
Rawson, Margaret B(yrd) 1899- 25-28R
Rawson, Philip Stanley 1924- CANR-21
Earlier sketches in CA 5-8R, CANR-6
Rawson, Wyatt Trevelyan Rawson
1894-1980 ....5-8R
Obituary 103
Ray, Ann 1937- 114
Ray, Arthur J. 1941- 127
Ray, Carl 1943-1978 ....SATA 63
Ray, Cyril 1908-1991 ....CANR-21
Obituary 135
Earlier sketches in CA 5-8R, CANR-5
Ray, D(avid) Michael 1935- CANR-9
Earlier sketch in CA 17-20R
Ray, David 1932- CANR-5
Earlier sketch in CA 9-12R
See also CAAS 7
See also DLB 5
Ray, Deborah
See Kogan Ray, Deborah
See also SATA 8
Ray, Delia 1963- 138
See also SATA 70
Ray, Dixy Lee 1914- 134
Ray, Dorothy Jean 1919- CANR-12
Earlier sketch in CA 25-28R
Ray, George McNeill 1910- 1-4R
Ray, Gordon N(orton) 1915-1986 57-60
Obituary 121
See also DLB 103
Ray, H(enrietta) Cordelia 1849(?)-1916 124
Brief entry 122
See also BW
See also DLB 50
Ray, Irene
See Sutton, Margaret Beebe
Ray, JoAnne 1935- 61-64
See also SATA 9
Ray, John B(ernard) 1930- 61-64
Ray, John (Philip) 1929- CANR-11
Earlier sketch in CA 25-28R
Ray, John R(obert) 1921- 37-40R
Ray, Joseph M(alchus) 1907- 41-44R
Ray, (Suzanne) Judy 1939- 111
Ray, Karen 1956- 108
Ray, Kenneth Clark 1901- CAP-2
Earlier sketch in CA 19-20
Ray, Man 1890-1976 ....CANR-29
Obituary 69-72
Earlier sketch in CA 77-80
Ray, Mary (Eva Pedder) 1932- CANR-12
Earlier sketch in CA 29-32R
See also SATA 2
Ray, Michele S. 1938- 25-28R
Ray, N(ancy) L(ouise) 1918- CANR-26
Earlier sketch in CA 109
Ray, Oakley S(tern) 1931- 45-48
Ray, Paul C(harles) 1926- 104
Ray, Philip A(lexander) 1911-1970 ....CAP-2
Earlier sketch in CA 23-24
Ray, Robert H. 1940- 135
Ray, Robert J. 1935- 126
Ray, Russell
See Strait, Raymond
Ray, Satyajit 1921- 114
Obituary 137
See also CLC 16
Ray, Sibnarayan 1921- CANR-15
Earlier sketch in CA 21-24R
Ray, Talton F. 1939- 29-32R
Ray, Trevor 1934- 107
Ray, Wesley
See Gaulden, Ray
Ray, Wilbert S(cott) 1901- CAP-2
Earlier sketch in CA 25-28
Rayback, Joseph G(eorge) 1914- 5-8R
Rayburn, James Chalmers III 1945- 121
Rayburn, Jim III
See Rayburn, James Chalmers III
Rayburn, Robert G(ibson) 1915- 25-28R
Raycraft, Donald R(obert) 1942- 41-44R
Rayfield, David 1940- 45-48
Rayfield, (Patrick) Donald 1942- 103
Rayfield, Stanley C.
1901(?)-1983(?) Obituary 108
Raygor, Alton Lamon 1922- 49-52
Rayman, Paula Marian 1947- 107
Raymond, Agnes G. 1916- 25-28R
Raymond, Alex(ander Gillespie)
1909-1956 Brief entry 112
Raymond, Charles
See Koch, Charlotte
and Koch, Raymond

Raymond, Diana (Joan) 1916- 89-92
Raymond, Ellsworth (Lester) 1912- 37-40R
Raymond, Ernest 1888-1974 Obituary 89-92
Raymond, E.V.
See Gallun, Raymond Z(inke)
Raymond, Father M.
See Flanagan, Joseph David Stanislaus
Raymond, G. Alison
See Lanier, Alison Raymond
Raymond, Harold 1887-1975 Obituary 104
Raymond, Henry J. 1820-1869 .... DLB 43, 79
Raymond, James (Charles) 1940- 119
Raymond, James Crossley
1917-1981 Obituary 105
See also SATA 29
Raymond, Janice G. 1943- 89-92
Raymond, Joseph H.
See Le Fontaine, Joseph (Raymond)
Raymond, Lee
See Hill, Mary Raymond
Raymond, Margaret E(lmendorf) 1912- 104
Raymond, Mary
See Keegan, Mary Heathcott
Raymond, P. L.
See Gibson, Walter B(rown)
Raymond, Patrick (Ernest) 1924- 102
Raymond, Rene (Brabazon) 1906-1985 126
Obituary 115
Raymond, Robert
See Alter, Robert Edmond
Raymond, Steve 1940- 49-52
Raymond, Walter J(ohn) 1930- 53-56
Raymond, William O. 1880-1970 .... CAP-2
Earlier sketch in CA 19-20
Raymond de Jesus, Mother
See Dion, Sister Anita
Raynal, Paul 1885(?)-1971 Obituary 33-36R
Rayne, Alan
See Tobin, James Edward
Rayner, Claire (Berenice) 1931- CANR-13
Earlier sketch in CA 21-24R
Rayner, E(dgar) G(eoffrey) 1927- CANR-10
Earlier sketch in CA 21-24R
Rayner, John Desmond 1924- 103
Rayner, Mary 1933- CANR-29
Earlier sketches in CA 69-72, CANR-12
See also SATA 22
Rayner, Ray
See Rahner, Raymond M.
Rayner, Richard
See McIlwain, David
Rayner, William 1929- 77-80
See also SATA 36, 55
Raynor, David R(alph) 1948- 111
Raynor, Dorka 106
See also SATA 28
Raynor, Henry (Broughton) 1917- 85-88
Rayside, Betty 1931- 57-60
Rayson, Paul
See Jennings, Leslie Nelson
Rayson, Steven 1932- 106
See also SATA 30
Rayward, W(arden) Boyd 1939- 102
Raywid, Mary Anne 5-8R
Raz, Joseph 1939- 125
Razaf, Andy 1895-1973 Obituary 41-44R
Razik, Taher A. 1924- CANR-19
Earlier sketch in CA 25-28R
Razin, Assaf 1941- 136
Razor Saltboy
See Louis, Ray Baldwin
Razran, Gregory 1901-1973 .... 41-44R
Obituary 45-48
Razzell, Arthur (George) 1925- 85-88
See also SATA 11
Razzi, James 1931- CANR-5
Earlier sketch in CA 53-56
See also SATA 10
Re, Edward D(omenic) 1920- CANR-12
Earlier sketch in CA 21-24R
Rea, Frederick B(eatty) 1908- 9-12R
Rea, Gardner 1892-1966 Obituary 93-96
Rea, K(enneth) J(ohn) 1932- Brief entry 107
Rea, Kenneth Wesley 1944- 107
Rea, Robert R(ight) 1922- CANR-28
Earlier sketch in CA 1-4R
Reach, Angus 1821-1856 .... DLB 70
Reach, James 1910(?)-1970 Obituary 29-32R
Read, Al 1919-1987 Obituary 123
Read, Anthony 1935- 107
Read, Bill 1917- 13-16R
Read, Brian (Ahier) 1927- 108
Read, Cecil B(yron) 1901-1972 .... CAP-1
Earlier sketch in CA 13-16
Read, David Haxton Carswell 1910- CANR-3
Earlier sketch in CA 1-4R
Read, Donald 1930- CANR-1
Earlier sketch in CA 1-4R
Read, Elfreida 1920- CANR-25
Earlier sketches in CA 21-24R, CANR-9
See also SATA 2
Read, Forrest 1926-1980 Obituary 112
Read, Gardner 1913- CANR-6
Earlier sketch in CA 13-16R
Read, Hadley 1918- 81-84
Read, Helen Appleton
1887(?)-1974 Obituary 53-56
Read, Herbert Edward 1893-1968 85-88
Obituary 25-28R
See also CLC 4
See also DLB 20
Read, Jan
See Read, John Hinton
Read, John Hinton 1917- CANR-32
Earlier sketches in CA 77-80, CANR-15
Read, Kenneth E(yre) 1917- 101
Read, Leonard Edward 1898-1983 .... CANR-11
Obituary 109
Earlier sketch in CA 17-20R
Read, Maureen Hay 1937- 113
Read, Opie 1852-1939 .... DLB 23
Read, Piers Paul 1941- CANR-38
Earlier sketch in CA 21-24R
See also CLC 4, 10, 25
See also DLB 14
See also SATA 21
Read, R. B. 1916-1982 .... CANR-13
Earlier sketch in CA 61-64
Read, Ritchard 1914- 57-60
Read, Sylvia Joan 103
Read, William M(erritt) 1901- 33-36R
Reade, B(rian) Edmund 1913- 21-24R
Reade, Charles 1814-1884 .... DLB 21
Reade, Deborah 1949- .... SATA 69
Reade, Hamish
See Gray, Simon (James Holliday)
Reade, Lang
See Carter, David C(harles)
Reader, Dennis Joel 1939- 106
Reader, Dennis 1929- .... SATA 71
Reader, Desmond H. 1920- 21-24R
Reader, W(illiam) J(oseph)
1920-1990 .... CANR-39
Obituary 132
Earlier sketches in CA 37-40R, CANR-16
Reading, Peter 1946- 103
See also CLC 47
See also DLB 40
Ready, Kirk L(ewis) 1943- 114
See also SATA 39
Ready, William B(ernard) 1914-1981 .... CANR-22
Earlier sketch in CA 25-28R
Reagan, Charles E(llis) 1942- 53-56
Reagan, Michael D(aniel) 1927- 49-52
Reagan, Nancy (Davis) 1923- CANR-33
Earlier sketch in CA 110
See also BEST 90:1
Reagan, Patricia Ann
See Davis, Patti
Reagan, Ronald 1911- 85-88
See also BEST 90:1
Reagan, Sydney C(handler) 1916- 41-44R
Reagan, Thomas (James) B(utler)
1916- 37-40R
Reagen, Edward P(aul) 1924- 49-52
Reagen, Michael V. 1942- 81-84
Reagin, Ewell Kerr 1900- 41-44R
Reaman, George Elmore 1889-1969 .... CAP-1
Earlier sketch in CA 11-12
Reamer, Judy 1940- 125
Reams, Bernard D(insmore) Jr. 1943- CANR-16
Earlier sketch in CA 93-96
Reamy, Tom 1935-1977 81-84
Reaney, James 1926- 41-44R
See also CAAS 15
See also CLC 13
See also DLB 68
See also SATA 43
Rearden, Jim 1925- 65-68
Reardon, B(ernard) M(orris) G(arvin)
1914- CANR-2
Earlier sketch in CA 5-8R
Reardon, Dennis J(oseph) 1944- 113
Brief entry 110
Reardon, Joan 1930- 116
Reardon, John J(oseph) 1926- 61-64
Reardon, William R. 1920- CANR-2
Earlier sketch in CA 1-4R
Rearick, Charles Walter 1942- 102
Reaske, Christopher R(ussell) 1941- 21-24R
Reason, James T(ootle) 1938- 104
Reasoner, Harry 1923-1991 111
Obituary 135
See also AITN 1
Reaver, Chap 1935- 137
See also SATA 69
Reaver, Herbert R.
See Reaver, Chap
Reaver, J(oseph) Russell 1915- 33-36R
Reaves, Philip
See Kiester, Edwin Jr.
Reaves, Wendy Wick 1950- 114
Reavey, George 1907-1976 Obituary 69-72
Reavey, Jean (Bullowa)
1917(?)-1987 Obituary 123
Reavis, Dick J. 1945- 133
Reb, Paul 1924- 49-52
Rebatet, Lucien 1903-1972 Obituary 37-40R
Rebay, Luciano 1928- 45-48
Rebbot, Olivier 1951(?)-1981 Obituary 103
Rebelsky, Freda Gould 1931- 41-44R
Rebert, M. Charles 1920- 53-56
Rebeta-Burditt, Joyce 81-84
Rebholz, Ronald A(lexander) 1932- 111
Rebischung, James A. 1928- 53-56
Rebora, Clemente 1885-1957 .... DLB 114
Rebreanu, Liviu 1885-1944 .... TCLC 28
Rebuffat, Gaston (Louis Simon)
1921-1985 .... 21-24R
Obituary 116
Receveur, Betty Layman 1930- 130
Rechcigl, Miloslav Jr. 1930- CANR-12
Earlier sketch in CA 17-20R
Rechy, John (Francisco) 1934- CANR-32
Earlier sketches in CA 5-8R, CANR-6
See also CAAS 4
See also CLC 1, 7, 14, 18
See also DLBY 82
See also HW
Reck, Alma Kehoe 1901- 1-4R
Reck, Andrew J(oseph) 1927- CANR-6
Earlier sketch in CA 13-16R
Reck, David 1935- 73-76
Reck, Franklin Mering 1896-1965 Obituary 109
See also SATA 30
Reck, Rima Drell 1933- 21-24R
Reck, W(aldo) Emerson 1903- 61-64
Recker, Colane 1940- 113
Reckless, Walter Cade 1899- 37-40R
Reckord, Barry 77-80
Record, Cy Wilson 1916- 9-12R
Record, Jane Cassels 1915-1981 .... CANR-5
Earlier sketch in CA 13-16R
Rector, Frank 106
Reday, Ladislaw 1913- 112
Red Butterfly
See Lauritsen, John (Phillip)
Redcam, Tom 1870-1933 .... TCLC 25
Redcliffe-Maud, John
See Redcliffe-Maud, John Primatt
Redcliffe-Maud, John Primatt 1906-1982 129
Obituary 108
Redcliffe-Maud, Lord
See Redcliffe-Maud, John Primatt
Redd, (Newton) Lawrence 1941- 57-60
Reddan, Harold J. 1926- 13-16R
Reddaway, (Arthur Frederick) John
1916-1990 Obituary 132
Reddaway, Peter (Brian) 1939- CANR-10
Earlier sketch in CA 21-24R
Reddaway, W(illiam) Brian 1913- 17-20R
Redden, James Erskine 1928- 41-44R
Redder, George
See Drummond, Jack
Reddick, DeWitt Carter 1904- 5-8R
Reddick, L(awrence) D(unbar) 1910- 61-64
Reddin, Keith .... CLC 67
Reddin, W(illiam) J(ames) 1930- 29-32R
Redding, Bud
See Redding, Edward C.
Redding, David A. 1923- CANR-3
Earlier sketch in CA 1-4R
Redding, Edward C. 1917-1984 Obituary 113
Redding, Robert Hull 1919- CANR-28
Earlier sketches in CA 21-24R, CANR-11
See also SATA 2
Redding, (Jay) Saunders 1906-1988 .... CANR-26
Obituary 124
Earlier sketches in CA 1-4R, CANR-5
See also BW
See also DLB 63
Reddish, Bessie Braid 1905-1974 .... 25-28R
Reddy, John F. X. 1912(?)-1975 Obituary 53-56
Reddy, Maureen T. 1955- 130
Reddy, Michael 1933- 61-64
Reddy, T. J. 1945- 45-48
Reddy, T(hammaiahgari) Ramakrishna
1937- 45-48
Redekop, Calvin Wall 1925- CANR-26
Earlier sketches in CA 25-28R, CANR-10
Redekop, John Harold 1932- 21-24R
Redekopp, Elsa 127
See also SATA 61
Reder, Philip 1924-1983 Obituary 110
Redfern, George B. 1910- 9-12R
Redfern, W(alter) D(avid) 1936- 21-24R
Redfield, Alden 1941- 77-80
Redfield, Alfred Clarence
1890-1983 Obituary 109
Redfield, Clark
See McMorrow, Fred
Redfield, Jennifer
See Hoskins, Robert
Redfield, Malissa
See Elliott, Malissa Childs
Redfield, Margaret Park
1899(?)-1977 Obituary 69-72
Redfield, Robert 1897-1958 Brief entry 121
Redfield, William 1927-1976 Obituary 69-72
Redford, Emmette Shelburn 1904- 112
Redford, Polly 1925-1972 .... CAP-2
Earlier sketch in CA 33-36
Redford, (Charles) Robert (Jr.) 1937- 107
Red Fox, William 1871(?)-1976 Obituary 65-68
Redgate, John
See Kennedy, Adam
Redgrave, Lady
See Kempson, Rachel
Redgrave, Michael (Scudamore)
1908-1985 Obituary 115
Redgrave, Paul 1920- 5-8R
Redgrove, Peter (William) 1932- CANR-39
Earlier sketches in CA 1-4R, CANR-3
See also CLC 6, 41
See also DLB 40
Redhead, Brian 1928- 128
Redinger, Ruby V(irginia) 1915-1981 65-68
Obituary 120
Redish, Bessie Braid 1905-1974 .... CAP-2
Earlier sketch in CA 25-28
Redkey, Edwin S(torer) 1931- 29-32R
Redlich, Frederick Carl 1910- Brief entry 106
Redman, Ben Ray 1896-1961 Obituary 93-96
Redman, Eric 1948- 49-52
Redman, L(ister) A(ppleton) 1933- 108
Redmayne, John
See Wood, Herbert Fairlie
Redmayne, Paul (Brewis) 1900- 5-8R
Redmon, Anne
See Nightingale, Anne Redmon
See also CLC 22
See also DLBY 86
Redmond, Eugene B. 1937- CANR-25
Earlier sketches in CA 25-28R, CANR-12
See also BW
See also DLB 41
Redmond, Gerald 1934- 37-40R
Redmond, Howard A(lexander) 1925- 13-16R
Redmond, Juanita
See Hipps, Juanita Redmond
Redmont, Bernard Sidney 1918- 73-76
Redmont, Dennis Foster 1942- 77-80
Redner, Harry 1937- 110
Redon, Joel 1961- 131
Redpath, Alan (Ogle) 1907-1989 Obituary 128
Redpath, (Robert) Theodore (Holmes)
1913- 104
Redpath, William 1893(?)-1985 Obituary 116
Redstone, Louis G(ordon) 1903- CANR-2
Earlier sketch in CA 49-52
Redway, Ralph
See Hamilton, Charles (Harold St. John)
Redway, Ridley
See Hamilton, Charles (Harold St. John)
Redwood, Alec
See Milkomane, George Alexis Milkomanovich
Redwood, John (Alan) 1951- CANR-19
Earlier sketch in CA 102
Ree, Jonathan 1948- 57-60
Reece, Benny R(amon) 1930- 41-44R
Reece, Jack Eugene 1941- 101
Reece, Robert D(enton) 1939- 128
Reeck, Darrell (Lauren) 1939- 104
Reed, A(lfred) H(amish) 1875-1975 .... CANR-4
Obituary 57-60
Earlier sketch in CA 9-12R
Reed, A(lexander) W(yclif) 1908-1979 .... CANR-4
Earlier sketch in CA 9-12R
Reed, Alison Touster 1952- 105
Reed, Barry
See Reed, Barry C(lement)
Reed, Barry C(lement) 1927- CANR-23
Earlier sketch in CA 29-32R
Reed, Betty Jane 1921- 29-32R
See also SATA 4
Reed, Bobbie (Butler) 1944- 77-80
Reed, Carroll E(dward) 1914- 103
Reed, Daniel 1892(?)-1978 Obituary 77-80
Reed, Don C(harles) 1945- 106
Reed, Donald A(nthony) 1935- 103
Reed, Douglas 1895-1976 103
Obituary 89-92
Reed, E.
See Evans, Mari
Reed, Edward W(ilson) 1913- 29-32R
Reed, Eliot
See Ambler, Eric
Reed, Elizabeth Liggett 1895-1978 77-80
Obituary 133
Reed, Elizabeth Stewart 1914- 1-4R
Reed, Emmett X.
See King, Florence
Reed, Evelyn 1905-1979 102
Reed, Graham 1923- CANR-24
Earlier sketch in CA 45-48
Reed, Gwendolyn E(lizabeth) 1932- 25-28R
See also SATA 21
Reed, H(erbert) Owen 1910- CANR-19
Earlier sketches in CA 53-56, CANR-4
Reed, Harold W(illiam) 1909- 118
Reed, Harrison Merrick Jr. 1898- 1-4R
Obituary 134
Reed, Henry Clay 1899-1972 Obituary 111
Reed, Henry 1808-1854 .... DLB 59
Reed, Henry 1914-1986 104
Obituary 121
See also DLB 27
Reed, Howard Alexander 1920- 13-16R
Reed, Ishmael 1938- CANR-25
Earlier sketch in CA 21-24R
See also BLC 3
See also BW
See also CLC 2, 3, 5, 6, 13, 32, 60
See also DLB 2, 5, 33
See also DLBD 8
See also MTCW
Reed, J(ames) D(onald) 1940- 33-36R
Reed, James F(red) 1909- CAP-1
Earlier sketch in CA 11-12
Reed, James Wesley 1944- 112
Reed, James 1922- 102
Reed, John F(ord) 1911- 13-16R
Reed, John L(incoln) 1938- 57-60
Reed, John P(lume) 1921- 65-68
Reed, John Q(uincy) 1918-1978 45-48
Obituary 103
Reed, John R(obert) 1938- CANR-8
Earlier sketch in CA 17-20R
Reed, John Shelton (Jr.) 1942- CANR-5
Earlier sketch in CA 53-56
Reed, John (Silas) 1887-1920 Brief entry 106
See also TCLC 9
Reed, John 1909- 125
Reed, Joseph Verner
1902-1973 Obituary 45-48
Reed, Joseph W(ayne) Jr. 1932- 37-40R
Reed, Kenneth T(errence) 1937- 73-76
Reed, Kenneth 1944- 57-60
Reed, Kit CANR-36
Earlier sketches in CA 1-4R, CANR-1, 16
See also SATA 34
Reed, Lawrence
See Reday, Ladislaw
Reed, Linda 1955- 137
Reed, Lou
See Firbank, Louis
See also CLC 21
Reed, Louis S(chultz)
1902-1975 Obituary 61-64
Reed, Luther D(otterer) 1873- 5-8R
Reed, M(athilda) N(ewman) 1905- 1-4R
Obituary 134
Reed, Macon Jr. 1911(?)-1986 Obituary 121
Reed, Marcia 1929- 120
Reed, Mark D(ouglas) Morrison
See Morrison-Reed, Mark D(ouglas)
Reed, Mark L(afayette) III 1935- 93-96

Reed, Mary Jane (Pobst) 1920- 25-28R
Reed, Michael 1930- 123
Reed, (Fred) Mort(on) 1912- 61-64
Reed, Nelson A. 1926- 9-12R
Reed, Paul 1956- 113
Reed, Peter J. 1935- 53-56
Reed, Philip G. 1908- ....SATA 29
Reed, Rex (Taylor) 1938- CANR-27
Earlier sketches in CA 53-56, CANR-9
See also AITN 1
Reed, Robert C(arroll) 1937- CANR-10
Earlier sketch in CA 65-68
Reed, Robert Rentoul Jr. 1911- 33-36R
Reed, Robert 1956- 127
Reed, Ronald F. 1945- 116
Reed, S(amuel) Kyle 1922- 41-44R
Reed, Sampson 1800-1880 .... DLB 1
Reed, Thomas Harrison
1881-1971 Obituary 110
Reed, Thomas (James) 1947- 103
See also SATA 34
Reed, Thomas Thornton 1902- 107
Reed, Victor (Brenner) 1926- 33-36R
Reed, Walter Logan 1943- 102
Reed, William Maxwell 1871-1962 .... SATA 15
Reed, Willis 1942- 104
Reeder, Carolyn 1937- 135
See also SATA 66
Reeder, Colonel Red
See Reeder, Russell P. Jr.
Reeder, John P. Jr. 1937- 101
Reeder, Russell P. Jr. 1902- CANR-5
Earlier sketch in CA 1-4R
See also SATA 4
Reedstrom, Ernest Lisle 1928- 89-92
Reedy, George E(dward) 1917- 29-32R
Reedy, Jerry Edward 1936- 119
Reedy, John Louis 1925-1983 Obituary 111
Reedy, William A. 1916(?)-1975 Obituary 61-64
Reedy, William James 1921- 13-16R
Reedy, William Marion 1862-1920 .... DLB 91
Reefe, Thomas Q(uentin) 1943- 123
Brief entry 116
Reel, A(dolf) Frank 1907- 93-96
Reeman, Douglas Edward 1924- CANR-3
Earlier sketch in CA 1-4R
See also SATA 28, 63
Reems, Harry 1947- 61-64
Reens, Mary
See Singleton, Betty
Reep, Edward 1918- 33-36R
Rees, Alan M(axwell) 1929- 106
Rees, Albert (Everett) 1921- CANR-12
Earlier sketch in CA 29-32R
Rees, Barbara (Elizabeth) 1934- CANR-9
Earlier sketch in CA 53-56
Rees, Brian 1929- 133
Rees, Clair (Francis) 1938- 117
Rees, David Bartlett 1936- 105
See also MAICYA
See also SAAS 5
See also SATA 36, 69
Rees, David Morgan 1904- 104
Rees, David 1928- CANR-11
Earlier sketch in CA 9-12R
Rees, Dilwyn
See Daniel, Glyn (Edmund)
Rees, Ennis (Samuel Jr.) 1925- CANR-2
Earlier sketch in CA 1-4R
See also SATA 3
Rees, (Morgan) Goronwy 1909- CANR-3
Earlier sketch in CA 45-48
Rees, Helen Christina Easson (Evans)
1903-1970 ....5-8R
Obituary 89-92
Rees, Henry 1916- 107
Rees, Ioan Bowen 1929- 29-32R
Rees, Jean A(nglin) 1912- CANR-1
Earlier sketch in CA 1-4R
Rees, Joan Alice Gladys
See Rees, Joan
Rees, Joan 1927- CANR-29
Earlier sketches in CA 25-28R, CANR-12
Rees, (George) Leslie (Clarence)
1905- CANR-26
Earlier sketch in CA 104
Rees, Lucy 1943- 107
Rees, Margaret A(nn) 1933- CANR-39
Earlier sketches in CA 101, CANR-18
Rees, Meriel
See Lambot, Isobel
Rees, Nigel (Thomas) 1944- 132
Rees, Paul Stromberg 1900- 5-8R
Rees, Richard (Lodowick Edward Montagu)
1900-1970 ....CANR-4
Obituary 89-92
Earlier sketch in CA 5-8R
Rees, Robert A(lvin) 1935- 81-84
Rees, (Margaret) Una 1920- 124
Rees, William 1887-1978(?) 5-8R
Obituary 104
Reese, Alexander 1881-1969 97-100
Reese, Algernon B(everly)
1896-1981 Obituary 105
Reese, Bob
See Reese, Robert A.
Reese, Carolyn Johnson 1938- 112
See also Reese, Lyn
Reese, Curtis W(illiford)
1887-1961 Obituary 110
Reese, Edward Jr. 1928- 113
Reese, Francesca Gardner 1940- 65-68
Reese, Gustave 1899-1977 Obituary 73-76
Reese, Heloise (Bowles) 1919-1977 ....9-12R
Obituary 73-76
Reese, Jim E(anes) 1912-1976 ....13-16R
Obituary 134
Reese, John (Henry) 102
Reese, Lizette Woodworth 1856-1935 ..... DLB 54
Reese, Lyn
See Reese, Carolyn Johnson
See also SATA 64
Reese, M(ax) M(eredith) 1910-1987 ....CANR-3
Obituary 123
Earlier sketch in CA 9-12R
Reese, Mason 1966- 97-100
Reese, Robert A. 1938- 114
See also SATA 53, 60
Reese, Sammy
See Reese, Samuel Pharr
Reese, Samuel Pharr 1930-1985 49-52
Obituary 117
Reese, (John) Terence 1913- 109
See also SATA 59
Reese, Thomas J(oseph) 1945- 106
Reese, Thomas R.
1890(?)-1974 Obituary 53-56
Reese, Thomas 1742-1796 .... DLB 37
Reese, Trevor Richard 1929- 9-12R
Reese, William Lewis 1921- CANR-8
Earlier sketch in CA 17-20R
Reese, William S(herman) 1955- 111
Reese, Willis L(ivingston) M(esier) 1913- 57-60
Reesink, Maryke 1919- 25-28R
Reeve, Agnesa B. 1927- 138
Reeve, Clara 1729-1807 .... DLB 39
Reeve, F(ranklin) D(olier) 1928- 77-80
Reeve, Frank D(river) 1899-1967 .... CAP-1
Earlier sketch in CA 11-12
Reeve, G. Joan (Price) 1901- 13-16R
Reeve, Joel
See Cox, William R(obert)
Reeve, Richard M(ark) 1935- 37-40R
Reeve, Wilfred D. 1895- CAP-1
Earlier sketch in CA 13-14
Reeve, William Charles 1943- 93-96
Reeves, Alexander Stuart Frere
See Frere-Reeves, Alexander Stuart
Reeves, Amber
See Blanco White, Amber
Reeves, (Richard) Ambrose
1899-1980 Obituary 105
Reeves, Bruce Douglas 1940- CANR-11
Earlier sketch in CA 21-24R
Reeves, Charles Everand 1889- 5-8R
Reeves, Donald 1952- 37-40R
Reeves, Dorothea D(resser) 1901- CAP-1
Earlier sketch in CA 11-12
Reeves, Earl J(ames Jr.) 1933- 61-64
Reeves, Elton T(raver) 1912- 29-32R
Reeves, Fionnuala 1943- 112
Reeves, Floyd (Wesley)
1890-1979 Obituary 89-92
Reeves, Gareth 1947- 119
Reeves, Gene (Arthur) 1933- 61-64
Reeves, Gregory Shaw 1950- 77-80
Reeves, Hubert 1932- 132
Reeves, James 1909- 5-8R
See also SATA 15
Reeves, Joan Wynn 1910-1972 .... CAP-2
Earlier sketch in CA 21-22
Reeves, John K(night) 1907- CAP-2
Earlier sketch in CA 25-28
Reeves, John 1926- 113
See also DLB 88
Reeves, Joyce 1911- CANR-12
Earlier sketch in CA 73-76
See also SATA 17
Reeves, Lawrence F. 1926- 105
See also SATA 29
Reeves, Marjorie E(thel) 1905- CANR-20
Earlier sketches in CA 13-16R, CANR-5
Reeves, Martha Emilie 1941- 65-68
Reeves, Mavis Mann 1921- CANR-25
Earlier sketch in CA 45-48
Reeves, Nancy 1913- 33-36R
Reeves, Paschal 1917-1976 81-84
Reeves, Patricia Houts 1947- 126
Reeves, Richard 1936- CANR-28
Earlier sketch in CA 69-72
Reeves, Rosser 1910-1984 89-92
Obituary 111
Reeves, Ruth Ellen
See Ranney, Agnes V.
Reeves, Thomas C(harles) 1936- CANR-9
Earlier sketch in CA 57-60
Reeves, Thomas Carl 1939- 33-36R
Reeves, Trish
See Reeves, Patricia Houts
Reff, Theodore Franklin 1930- 89-92
Refregier, Anton 1905- 5-8R
Regalado, Nancy Freeman 1935- 17-20R
Regan, Brad
See Norwood, Victor G(eorge) C(harles)
Regan, Cronan 1925- 45-48
Regan, Donald T(homas) 1918- 127
Brief entry 106
Regan, Geoffrey 1946- 129
Regan, John J. 1929- 131
Regan, Richard Joseph 1930- 5-8R
Regan, Robert (Charles) 1930- 17-20R
Regan, Thomas Howard 1938- 104
Regan, Tom
See Regan, Thomas Howard
Regardie, (Francis) Israel 1907- 85-88
Regehr, Lydia 1903- 45-48
See also SATA 37
Regelski, Thomas A(dam) 1941- 57-60
Regenstein, Lewis 1943- 57-60
Regensteiner, Else (Friedsam)
1906- Brief entry 111
Reger, Roger 1933- 21-24R
Reggiani, Renee 1925- CANR-36
Earlier sketch in CA 85-88
See also SATA 18
Reghaby, Heydar 1932- 29-32R
Regin, Deric (Wagenvort) 37-40R
Reginald
See Burgess, M(ichael) R(oy)
Reginald, R(obert)
See Burgess, M(ichael) R(oy)
Regis, Ed
See Regis, Edward Jr.
Regis, Edward Jr. 1944- 132
Regis, Sister Mary 1908- CAP-1
Earlier sketch in CA 13-14
Register, Cheri
See Register, Cheryl Lynn
Register, Cheryl Lynn 1945- 126
Register, Willie Raymond 1937- 45-48
Regnery, Henry 1912- 101
Regoli, Robert M. 1950- 116
Regosin, Richard L(loyd) 1937- Brief entry 109
Regueiro, Helen 1943- 104
Rehak, Peter (Stephen) 1936- 77-80
Rehder, Helmut 1905-1977 ....CANR-4
Earlier sketch in CA 5-8R
Rehder, Jessie Clifford 1908-1967 .... CAP-1
Earlier sketch in CA 9-10
Rehfeld, Barry J. 1946- 132
Rehfuss, John Alfred 1934- 85-88
Rehrauer, George 1923- 53-56
Reibel, Paula
See Schwartz, Paula
Reich, Ali
See Katz, Bobbi
Reich, Bernard 1941- CANR-32
Earlier sketches in CA 81-84, CANR-14
Reich, Charles Alan 1928- 108
Reich, Deborah 1960- 130
Reich, Edward 1903(?)-1983 Obituary 109
Reich, Ilse Ollendorff 1909- 49-52
Reich, John Theodore 1906-1988 Obituary 124
Reich, Kenneth 1938- 69-72
Reich, Nancy B(assen) 126
Reich, Peter M(aria) 1929- 85-88
Reich, Sheldon 1931- 112
Reich, Steve 1936- CANR-8
Earlier sketch in CA 61-64
Reich, Tova Rachel 1942- 103
Reich, Walter 1943- 129
Reichard, Gary Warren 1943- CANR-26
Earlier sketches in CA 61-64, CANR-10
Reichard, Robert S. 1923- 21-24R
Reichardt, Jasia 1933- CANR-2
Earlier sketch in CA 5-8R
Reichart, Elisabeth 1953- 132
Reichart, Walter A(lbert) 1903- 5-8R
Reiche, Reimut 1941- 41-44R
Reichek, Morton A(rthur) 1924- 85-88
Reichel, Aaron I(srael) 1950- 130
Reichel, Mary 1946- 125
Reichel, O. Asher 1921- 45-48
Reichel, Sabine 1946- 132
Reichenbach, Bruce R. 1943- 33-36R
Reichenberger, Arnold G(ottfried)
1903- 17-20R
Reichert, Edwin C(lark)
1909-1988 Obituary 126
See also SATA 57
Reichert, Herbert W(illiam)
1917-1978 ....CANR-24
Earlier sketch in CA 45-48
Reichert, Mickey Zucker
See Zucker, Miriam S.
Reichert, Victor Emanuel 1897- 13-16R
Reichl, Ernst 1900-1980 Obituary 102
Reichl, Ruth 1948- 61-64
Reichler, Joseph Lawrence 1915-1988 103
Obituary 127
Reichley, (Anthony) James 1929- 1-4R
Reichmann, Felix 1899- 104
Reicke, Bo I(var) 1914- 13-16R
Reid, Alan 1915(?)-1987 Obituary 123
Reid, Alastair 1926- CANR-3
Earlier sketch in CA 5-8R
See also DLB 27
See also SATA 46
Reid, Albert Clayton 1894- 53-56
Reid, Alfred S(andlin) 1924-1976 ....CANR-2
Earlier sketch in CA 45-48
Reid, Anthony 1916- 29-32R
Reid, B(enjamin) L(awrence)
1918-1990 ....17-20R
Obituary 133
See also DLB 111
Reid, Barbara 1922- CANR-12
Earlier sketch in CA 25-28R
See also SATA 21
Reid, Charles K(er) II 1912- CAP-1
Earlier sketch in CA 19-20
Reid, Charles L(loyd) 1927- 37-40R
Reid, Charles R(obert) 1926- 114
Reid, Charles (Stuart) 1900-1987 101
Obituary 121
Reid, Christopher 1949- .... CLC 33
See also DLB 40
Reid, Clyde H. 1928- CANR-12
Earlier sketch in CA 25-28R
Reid, Daniel P. (Jr.) 1948- 125
Reid, Desmond
See McNeilly, Wilfred (Glassford)
and Moorcock, Michael (John)
Reid, Donald (Matthew) 1952- 124
Reid, Dorothy M(arion) Obituary 109
See also SATA 29
Reid, E. Emmet 1872-1973 Obituary 45-48
Reid, Ela 1907-1982 Obituary 107
Reid, Escott (Meredith) 1905- CANR-20
Earlier sketch in CA 101
Reid, Esmond 1945- 123
Reid, Eugenie Chazal 1924- 13-16R
See also SATA 12
Reid, Frances P(ugh) 1910- CANR-2
Earlier sketch in CA 5-8R
Reid, H. 1925- 17-20R
Reid, Helen Rogers 1882-1970 Obituary 115
See also DLB 29
Reid, Hilda (Stewart) 1898-1982 Obituary 106
Reid, Ian 1915-1984 Obituary 113
Reid, Inez Smith 49-52
Reid, J(ohn) C(owie) 1916-1972 ....9-12R
Obituary 103
Reid, James ....DLB 31
Reid, James Macarthur 1900-1970 .... CAP-1
Earlier sketch in CA 9-10
Reid, James Malcolm 1902-1982 ....5-8R
Obituary 107
Reid, James W. 1912-197 (?) CAP-2
Earlier sketch in CA 25-28
Reid, Jan 1945- 61-64
Reid, Jim 1929- 61-64
Reid, John Calvin CANR-11
Earlier sketch in CA 25-28R
See also SATA 21
Reid, John Kelman Sutherland 1910- CANR-3
Earlier sketch in CA 1-4R
Reid, John Phillip 1930- CANR-19
Earlier sketch in CA 25-28R
Reid, John T(urner) 1908-1978 81-84
Reid, Leslie Hartley 1895- CAP-1
Earlier sketch in CA 13-14
Reid, Loren (Dudley) 1905- CANR-1
Earlier sketch in CA 1-4R
Reid, Louis Arnaud 1895- CAP-1
Earlier sketch in CA 13-14
Reid, Malcolm 1941- 53-56
Reid, Margaret (Isabel) 1925- 130
Reid, (Thomas) Mayne 1818-1883 .... DLB 21
See also SATA 24
Reid, Meta Mayne 13-16R
See also SATA 36, 58
Reid, Michaela (Ann) 1933- 128
Reid, Mildred I. 1908- 21-24R
Reid, P(atrick) R(obert)
1910-1990 Obituary 131
Reid, Pat
See Reid, P(atrick) R(obert)
Reid, Philip
See Ingrams, Richard (Reid)
and Osmond, Andrew
Reid, R(obert) W(illiam) 1933-1990(?) 29-32R
Obituary 132
Reid, Randall 1931- 25-28R
Reid, Robert G(eorge) B(urnside) 1939- 119
Reid, Seerley 1909(?)-1972 Obituary 37-40R
Reid, Sue Titus 1939- CANR-31
Earlier sketches in CA 37-40R, CANR-14
Reid, Tim
See Reid, Timothy E. H.
Reid, Timothy E. H. 1936- 17-20R
Reid, Vic(tor Stafford) 1913- CANR-16
Earlier sketch in CA 65-68
See also BW
Reid, W(illiam) Stanford 1913- CANR-18
Earlier sketches in CA 49-52, CANR-1
Reid, Whitelaw 1837-1912 .... DLB 23
Reid, William H(oward) 1945- CANR-37
Earlier sketches in CA 93-96, CANR-16
Reid, William J(ames) 1928- CANR-39
Earlier sketches in CA 77-80, CANR-17
Reid, William 1926- 85-88
Reida, Bernice 1915- 93-96
Reid Banks, Lynne 1929- CANR-38
Earlier sketches in CA 1-4R, CANR-6, 22
See also Banks, Lynne Reid
See also CLR 24
See also MAICYA
See also SATA 22
Reidel, Carl Hubert 1937- 107
Reidel-Geubtner, Virginia 1921- 116
Reidenbaugh, Lowell (Henry) 1919- 121
Reidy, John Patrick 1930- 17-20R
Reidy, Joseph 1920- 53-56
Reierson, Gary B(ruce) 1948- CANR-36
Earlier sketch in CA 114
Reif, Rita 1929- 41-44R
Reifen, David 1911- 93-96
Reiff, Henry 1899-1983 Obituary 110
Reiff, Robert (Frank) 1918-1982 ....17-20R
Obituary 135
Reiff, Stephanie Ann 1948- 93-96
See also SATA 28, 47
Reiffel, Leonard 1927- 101
Reifler, Samuel 1939- 93-96
Reifsnyder, William E(dward) 1924- 65-68
Reig, June 1933- 105
See also SATA 30
Reigelman, Milton Monroe 1942- 65-68
Reiger, George (Wesley) 1939- CANR-18
Earlier sketch in CA 101
Reiger, John F(ranklin) 1943- 57-60
Reiger, Kurt (Edward) 1956- 116
Reigle, Donald W(ayne) Jr. 1938- 61-64
Reigot, Betty Polisar 1924- 111
See also SATA 41, 55
Reigstad, Paul (Matthew) 1921- 81-84
Reik, Theodor 1888-1969 ....CANR-5
Obituary 25-28R
Earlier sketch in CA 5-8R
Reile, Louis 1925- 29-32R
Reill, Peter Hanns 1938- 101
Reilly, Catherine W(inifred) 1925- 118
Reilly, Christopher T(homas) 1924- 101

Reilly, D(avid) Robin 1928- ... CANR-8
Earlier sketch in CA 5-8R
Reilly, Edward R(andolph) 1929- ... 93-96
Reilly, Edwin David Jr. 1932- ... 111
Reilly, Esther H(untington) 1917- ... 33-36R
Reilly, Francis E(agan) 1922- ... 29-32R
Reilly, Harold J. 1895(?)-1987 Obituary ... 123
Reilly, John H(urford) 1934- ... 77-80
Reilly, John M(arsden) 1933- ... 104
Reilly, Judith G(ladding) 1935- ... 61-64
Reilly, Mary Lonan 1926- ... 33-36R
Reilly, Mary 1920- ... 128
Brief entry ... 114
Reilly, Michael (Francis)
1910(?)-1973 Obituary ... 41-44R
Reilly, Patrick D.
See Rogers, Peter D(amien)
Reilly, Patrick 1932- ... CANR-37
Earlier sketch in CA 115
Reilly, Paul 1912-1990 ... 125
Obituary ... 132
Reilly, Robert Thomas 1922- ... CANR-2
Earlier sketch in CA 5-8R
Reilly, Robin 1928- ... CANR-5
Earlier sketch in CA 53-56
Reilly, William J(ohn) 1899- ... CAP-2
Earlier sketch in CA 19-20
Reilly, William K.
See Creasey, John
Reiman, Donald H(enry) 1934- ... CANR-31
Earlier sketches in CA 33-36R, CANR-14
Reiman, Jeffrey H. 1942- ... 93-96
Reimann, Brigitte 1933-1973 ... DLB 75
Reimann, Guenter Hans 1904- ... 25-28R
Reimann, Lewis C. 1890-1961 Obituary ... 113
Reimann, Viktor 1915- ... 69-72
Reimer, Bennett 1932- ... CANR-3
Earlier sketch in CA 45-48
Reimers, David 1931- ... 115
Rein, Irving J. 1937- ... CANR-28
Earlier sketch in CA 25-28R
Rein, Martin 1928- ... 93-96
Rein, Mercedes ... 131
See also HW
Rein, Richard
See Smith, Richard Rein
Reina, Ruben E. 1924- ... 49-52
Reinach, Jacquelyn (Krasne) 1930- ... CANR-22
Earlier sketch in CA 105
See also SATA 28
Reincheld, Bill 1946- ... 57-60
Reindorp, George E(dmund) 1911- ... CANR-5
Earlier sketch in CA 5-8R
Reindorp, Reginald C(arl) 1907- ... 25-28R
Reinecke, Ian 1945- ... 117
Reinemer, Vic 1923- ... 21-24R
Reiner, Carl 1922- ... 138
Brief entry ... 112
Reiner, Joseph H. 1912(?)-1983 Obituary ... 111
Reiner, Laurence E(rwin) ... 102
Reiner, Max
See Caldwell, (Janet Miriam) Taylor (Holland)
Reiner, Rob(ert) 1945- ... 138
Reiner, William B(uck) 1910-1976 ... CANR-3
Obituary ... 61-64
Earlier sketch in CA 45-48
See also SATA 30, 46
Reinerman, Alan J(erome) 1935- ... 114
Reinert, Paul C(lare) 1910- ... 85-88
Reines, Alvin J. 1926- ... 53-56
Reinfeld, Fred 1910-1964 ... CAP-1
Earlier sketch in CA 9-10
See also SATA 3
Reinhard, David W(illiam) 1952- ... 118
Reinhard, Ernst
See Frank, Rudolf
Reinhardt, Ad(olph Frederick)
1913-1967 Obituary ... 111
Reinhardt, Gottfried 1913- ... 93-96
Reinhardt, James Melvin 1894-1974 ... CANR-4
Obituary ... 49-52
Earlier sketch in CA 1-4R
Reinhardt, Jon M(c Ewen) 1936- ... 41-44R
Reinhardt, Kurt F(rank) 1896- ... CANR-1
Earlier sketch in CA 1-4R
Reinhardt, Richard W. 1927- ... CANR-31
Earlier sketches in CA 25-28R, CANR-13
Reinhart, Bruce Aaron 1926- ... 5-8R
Reinhart, Charles (Franklin) 1946- ... 104
Reinhart, Peter 1950- ... 136
Reinhart, Theodore R(ussell) 1938- ... 125
Reinhartz, Dennis 1944- ... 123
Reinharz, Jehuda 1944- ... CANR-24
Earlier sketches in CA 65-68, CANR-9
Reinharz, Shulamit 1946- ... 138
Reinhold, Meyer 1909- ... CANR-26
Earlier sketches in CA 5-8R, CANR-5
Reinhold, Robert 1941- ... 133
Reiniger, Lotte 1899-1981 Obituary ... 108
See also SATA 33, 40
Reining, Conrad C(opeland) 1918-1984 ... 21-24R
Obituary ... 114
Reinisch, June M(achover) 1943- ... 138
Reinitz, Richard (Martin) 1934- ... 89-92
Reinke, William A(ndrew) 1928- ... CANR-24
Earlier sketch in CA 45-48
Reinmuth, Oscar William 1900- ... 37-40R
Reinsmith, Richard
See Smith, Richard Rein
Reis, Claire Raphael 1889-1978 Obituary ... 77-80
Reis, Ricardo
See Pessoa, Fernando (Antonio Nogueira)
Reis, Richard H(erbert) 1930- ... 41-44R
Reisch, Walter 1903-1983 Obituary ... 109
See also DLB 44
Reischauer, August Karl 1879-1971 ... CAP-2
Earlier sketch in CA 19-20
Reischauer, Edwin O(ldfather)
1910-1990 ... 17-20R
Obituary ... 132
Reiser, Martin 1927- ... 53-56
Reiser, Morton F(rancis) 1919- ... 124
Reiser, Oliver Leslie 1895-1974 ... CANR-4
Obituary ... 49-52
Earlier sketch in CA 1-4R
Reiser, William (Edward) 1943- ... 114
Reisfeld, Bert 1906- ... 112
Reising, Robert W(illiam) 1933- ... 89-92
Reisinger, William M. 1957- ... 138
Reisman, Arnold 1934- ... CANR-12
Earlier sketch in CA 33-36R
Reisman, George Gerald 1937- ... 104
Reisman, John M(ark) 1930- ... CANR-8
Earlier sketch in CA 21-24R
Reisner, George
See Ben-Ephraim, Gavriel
Reisner, Robert George 1921-1974 ... 9-12R
Obituary ... 135
Reisner, Thomas Andrew 1935- ... 113
Reiss, Albert J(ohn) Jr. 1922- ... CANR-24
Earlier sketches in CA 21-24R, CANR-9
Reiss, Alvin H(erbert) 1930- ... 81-84
Reiss, Alvin 1932- ... 61-64
Reiss, Barbara Eve 1941- ... CANR-15
Earlier sketch in CA 41-44R
Reiss, David S. 1953- ... 108
Reiss, Edmund (Allan) 1934- ... CANR-10
Earlier sketch in CA 21-24R
Reiss, Ira L(eonard) 1925- ... 13-16R
Reiss, James 1941- ... 33-36R
Reiss, Johanna (de Leeuw) 1929(?)- ... 85-88
See also CLR 19
See also SATA 18
Reiss, John J. ... 106
See also SATA 23
Reiss, Stephen (Charles) 1918- ... 57-60
Reiss, Timothy James 1942- ... 107
Reissig, Herman F. 1899(?)-1985 Obituary ... 116
Reissig, Julio Herrera y
See Herrera y Reissig, Julio
Reissman, Leonard 1921-1975 ... CANR-4
Obituary ... 53-56
Earlier sketch in CA 5-8R
Reister, Floyd Nester 1919- ... 69-72
Reit, Seymour (V.) 1918- ... CANR-16
Earlier sketch in CA 93-96
See also SATA 21
Reit, Sy
See Reit, Seymour (V.)
Reitan, E(arl) A(aron) 1925- ... 17-20R
Reitci, John G(eorge) 1922-1983 Obituary ... 109
Reitci, Rita Krohne 1930- ... 5-8R
Reitemeyer, John Reinhart
1898-1979 Obituary ... 85-88
Reiter, Charles Jules 1928- ... 25-28R
Reiter, Robert E. 1932- ... 25-28R
Reiter, Seymour 1921- ... 101
Reiterman, Carl 1921- ... 49-52
Reiterman, Tim 1947- ... 109
Reith, Charles C. 1953- ... 122
Reith, J.C.W.
See Reith, John Charles Walsham
Reith, John Charles Walsham
1889-1971 Obituary ... 113
Reither, Joseph 1903- ... 109
Reitlinger, Gerald R. 1900(?)-1978 Obituary ... 104
Reitmeister, Louis Aaron 1903-1975 ... 49-52
Obituary ... 61-64
Reitsch, Hanna 1912(?)-1979 Obituary ... 89-92
Reitz, Donald J(oseph) 1932- ... 25-28R
Reitze, Arnold W(infred) Jr. 1938- ... 49-52
Rejai, Mostafa 1931- ... CANR-13
Earlier sketch in CA 37-40R
Rejaunier, Jeanne 1934- ... 29-32R
Rekai, Kati 1921- ... 105
Rekers, George A(lan) 1948- ... 119
Relf, Patricia 1954- ... SATA 71
Relgis, Eugene 1895- ... 81-84
Relis, Harry
See Endore, (Samuel) Guy
Rella, Ettore 1907(?)-1988 Obituary ... 126
Relyea, Suzanne 1945- ... 77-80
Remak, Henry H. H. 1916- ... 17-20R
Remak, Joachim 1920- ... CANR-3
Earlier sketch in CA 1-4R
Remarque, Erich Maria 1898-1970 ... 77-80
Obituary ... 29-32R
See also CLC 21
See also DLB 56
See also MTCW
Rembar, Charles 1915- ... 25-28R
Remen, (Rachelle) Naomi 1938- ... 122
Brief entry ... 118
Remenih, Maurine 1916(?)-1985 Obituary ... 118
Remer, Theodore G. 1899- ... CAP-1
Earlier sketch in CA 13-16
Remi, Georges 1907-1983 ... CANR-31
Obituary ... 109
Earlier sketch in CA 69-72
See also Herge
See also SATA 13, 32
Remington, Ella-Carrie 1914- ... 69-72
Remington, Frederic 1861-1909 Brief entry ... 108
See also DLB 12
See also SATA 41
Remington, Mark
See Bingley, David Ernest
Remington, Robin Alison 1938- ... CANR-12
Earlier sketch in CA 33-36R
Remini, Robert V(incent) 1921- ... CANR-20
Earlier sketches in CA 9-12R, CANR-3
Remizov, A.
See Remizov, Aleksei (Mikhailovich)
Remizov, A. M.
See Remizov, Aleksei (Mikhailovich)
Remizov, Aleksei (Mikhailovich) 1877-1957 ... 133
Brief entry ... 125
See also TCLC 27
Remley, David A. 1931- ... 45-48
Remley, Mary L(ouise) 1930- ... 102
Remmers, H(ermann) H(enry) 1892-1969 ... 1-4R
Obituary ... 103
Remmling, Gunter W(erner) 1929- ... 41-44R
Remoff, Heather T(rexler) 1938- ... 117
Remonda-Ruibal, Jorge Silvestre 1928- ... 108
Remsberg, Bonnie K(ohn) 1937- ... 69-72
Remsberg, Charles A(ndruss) 1936- ... CANR-7
Earlier sketch in CA 57-60
Remson, Irwin 1923- ... 53-56
Remy
See Renault, Gilbert (Leon Etienne Theodore)
Remy, Georges
See Remi, Georges
Remy, Pierre-Jean
See Angremy, Jean-Pierre
Remy, Richard C. 1942- ... CANR-29
Earlier sketch in CA 111
Rena, Sally
See Rena, Sarah Mary
Rena, Sarah Mary 1941- ... 103
Renan, Sheldon (Jackson) 1941- ... CANR-14
Earlier sketch in CA 21-24R
Renard, Alexandre Charles
1906-1983 Obituary ... 111
Renard, Jules 1864-1910 Brief entry ... 117
See also TCLC 17
Renaud, Bernadette 1945- ... 134
See also SATA 66
Renaud, Jacques 1943- ... DLB 60
Renauer, Albin (J.) 1959- ... 133
Renault, Gilbert (Leon Etienne Theodore)
1904-1984 Obituary ... 113
Renault, Mary
See Challans, Mary
See also CLC 3, 11, 17
See also DLBY 83
Renault, Rick
See Wallmann, Jeffrey M(iner)
Renay, Liz 1926- ... 33-36R
Rendall, Ted S. ... 101
Rendel, George William 1889-1979 ... 5-8R
Obituary ... 103
Rendel, John 1906(?)-1978 Obituary ... 104
Rendell, Joan ... CANR-23
Earlier sketches in CA 61-64, CANR-7
See also SATA 28
Rendell, Ruth (Barbara) 1930- ... CANR-32
Earlier sketch in CA 109
See also Vine, Barbara
See also CLC 28, 48
See also DLB 87
See also MTCW
Render, Sylvia Lyons 1913- ... CANR-15
Earlier sketch in CA 41-44R
Rendina, Laura (Jones) Cooper 1902- ... 9-12R
See also SATA 10
Rendleman, Danny L(ee) 1945- ... 65-68
Rendon, Armando B. 1939- ... 37-40R
Rene, Leon (T.) 1902-1982 Obituary ... 107
Rene, Natalia 1908(?)-1977 Obituary ... 69-72
Renehan, Robert (Francis Xavier)
1935- Brief entry ... 108
Renetzky, Alvin 1940- ... 101
Renfield, Richard L. 1932- ... 29-32R
Renfrew, Jane Margaret 1942- ... 49-52
Renfroe, Martha Kay 1938- ... CANR-9
Earlier sketch in CA 65-68
Renich, Fred C. 1916-1979 ... 115
Renich, Jill 1916- ... 25-28R
Renick, Marion (Lewis) 1905- ... CANR-1
Earlier sketch in CA 1-4R
See also SATA 1
Renier, Elizabeth
See Baker, Betty D(oreen Flook)
Renken, Aleda 1907- ... CANR-12
Earlier sketch in CA 21-24R
See also SATA 27
Renkiewicz, Frank 1935- ... CANR-26
Earlier sketch in CA 45-48
Renlie, Frank H. 1936- ... SATA 11
Renn, Casey
See Crim, Keith R(enn)
Renn, Ludwig
See Vieth von Golssenau, Arnold Friedrich
Renn, Thomas E(dward) 1939- ... 29-32R
Renne, Roland Roger 1905- ... 1-4R
Renner, Al G. 1912- ... 89-92
Renner, Beverly Hollett 1929- ... 85-88
Renner, Bruce 1944- ... 33-36R
Renner, John Wilson 1924- ... 41-44R
Renner, K(enneth) Edward 1936- ... 101
Renner, Thomas C(hoate) 1928-1990 ... 73-76
Obituary ... 130
Renner, Tom
See Renner, Thomas C(hoate)
Rennert, Maggie 1922- ... CANR-13
Earlier sketch in CA 61-64
Rennert, Richard Scott 1956- ... 135
See also SATA 67
Rennick, Robert M(orris) 1932- ... 122
Rennie, Christopher
See Ambrose, Eric (Samuel)
Rennie, Eric 1947- ... 45-48
Rennie, James Alan 1899-1969 ... CAP-1
Earlier sketch in CA 11-12
Rennie, Ysabel Fisk 1918- ... CANR-2
Earlier sketch in CA 5-8R
Reno, Clint
See Ballard, (Willis) Todhunter
Reno, Dawn E. 1953- ... 125
Reno, Marie R(oth) ... CANR-10
Earlier sketch in CA 65-68
Reno, Ottie W(ayne) 1929- ... 41-44R
Reno, Philip 1913-1981 Obituary ... 111
Renoir, Alain 1921- ... 77-80
Renoir, Jean 1894-1979 ... 129
Obituary ... 85-88
See also CLC 20
Renouf, Alan 1919- ... 108
Rensberger, Boyce 1942- ... 81-84
Rensch, Bernhard (Carl Emmanuel) 1900- ... 102
Renshaw, Domeena C(ynthia) 1929- ... 89-92
Renshaw, Patrick (Richard George)
1936- ... 21-24R
Renshaw, Samuel 1892-1981 ... 77-80
Obituary ... 133
Renshon, Stanley Allen 1943- Brief entry ... 109
Rensie, Willis
See Eisner, Will(iam Erwin)
Renton, Cam
See Armstrong, Richard
Renton, Julia
See Cole, Margaret Alice
Rentschler, Eric 1949- ... 118
Renvoize, Jean ... 41-44R
See also SATA 5
Renwick, Ethel Hulbert 1910- ... 5-8R
Renwick, Fred B(lackwell) 1930- ... 33-36R
Renzulli, L(ibero) Marx Jr. 1934- Brief entry ... 108
Repetto, Robert C. ... 129
Replansky, Naomi 1918- ... 33-36R
Repp, Arthur C(hristian) 1906- ... CAP-1
Earlier sketch in CA 13-16
Repp, Ed Earl 1900(?)-1979 Obituary ... 85-88
Repp, William 1936- ... 110
Reps, John W(illiam) 1921- ... CANR-39
Earlier sketches in CA 45-48, CANR-1, 18
Reps, (Saladin) Paul 1895-1990 ... CANR-6
Obituary ... 132
Earlier sketch in CA 5-8R
ReQua, Eloise Gallup 1902- ... CAP-1
Earlier sketch in CA 13-16
Resch, John Phillips 1940- Brief entry ... 108
Rescher, Nicholas 1928- ... CANR-12
Earlier sketch in CA 21-24R
Rescoe, A(ntoine) Stan(ley) 1910- ... 5-8R
Reshetar, John S(tephen) Jr. 1924- ... 5-8R
Reshevsky, Samuel Herman 1911- ... 65-68
Resick, Matthew C(larence) 1916- ... 57-60
Reske, Hermann 1911- ... 45-48
Reskind, John
See Wallmann, Jeffrey M(iner)
Resnais, Alain 1922- ... CLC 16
Resnick, H(arvey) L(ewis) P(aul) 1930- ... 21-24R
Resnick, Marvin D. 1933- ... 21-24R
Resnick, Michael D(iamond) 1942- ... CANR-24
Earlier sketch in CA 107
See also SATA 38
Resnick, Mike
See Resnick, Michael D(iamond)
Resnick, Nathan 1910-1977 ... CAP-2
Obituary ... 73-76
Earlier sketch in CA 19-20
Resnick, Patricia 1953- ... 135
Resnick, Rose ... 61-64
Resnick, Seymour 1920- ... 73-76
See also SATA 23
Resnick, Sylvia (Safran) 1927- ... CANR-30
Earlier sketch in CA 93-96
Resnik, H(arvey) L(ewis) P(aul) 1930- ... CANR-10
Earlier sketch in CA 21-24R
Resnik, Hank
See Resnik, Henry S.
Resnik, Henry S. 1940- ... CANR-29
Earlier sketch in CA 29-32R
Resnik, Michael D(avid) 1938- ... 116
Resposo, Epifania R. Castro
1922-1974 Obituary ... 113
Ressler, Alice 1918- ... 53-56
Ressner, Phil(ip) 1922- ... 13-16R
Rest, Friedrich Otto 1913- ... CANR-38
Earlier sketches in CA 5-8R, CANR-2, 17
Rest, Karl H(einrich) A(lbert) 1908- ... 5-8R
Restak, Richard M(artin) 1942- ... CANR-24
Earlier sketches in CA 61-64, CANR-8
Restany, Pierre 1930- ... 130
Restivo, Sal 1940- ... 112
Restle, Frank (Joseph) 1927-1982(?) ... 41-44R
Obituary ... 133
Reston, James B(arrett) Jr. 1941- ... CANR-31
Earlier sketch in CA 37-40R
Reston, James (Barrett) 1909- ... CANR-31
Earlier sketch in CA 65-68
See also AITN 1, 2
Reston, Jody ... AITN 2
Reston, Richard ... AITN 2
Retamar, Roberto Fernandez
See Fernandez Retamar, Roberto
Retla, Robert
See Alter, Robert Edmond
Retner, Beth A.
See Brown, Beth
Rettig, Edward B(ertram) 1940- ... 57-60
Rettig, Jack L(ouis) 1925- ... 57-60
Reuben, David 1933- ... 41-44R
See also AITN 1
Reuben, Shelly 1945- ... 127
Reuber, Grant L(ouis) 1927- ... CANR-3
Earlier sketch in CA 49-52
Reul, R(ose) Myrtle 1919- ... 21-24R
Reuman, Robert E(verett) 1923- ... 37-40R
Reumann, John 1927- ... CANR-5
Earlier sketch in CA 1-4R
Reuss, Carl F(rederick) 1915- ... 41-44R
Reuss, Frederick G(ustav) 1904- ... CAP-1
Earlier sketch in CA 11-12

Reuss, Henry S(choellkopf) 1912- CANR-6
Earlier sketch in CA 9-12R
Reuss-Ianni, Elizabeth 1946- 130
Reuter, Bjarne (B.) 1950- 137
See also SATA 68
Reuter, Carol (Joan) 1931- 21-24R
See also SATA 2
Reuter, Frank T. 1926- 21-24R
Reuter, Gabriele 1859-1941 .... DLB 66
Reuther, David L(ouis) 1946- CANR-31
Earlier sketch in CA 112
Reuther, Ruth E. 1917- CANR-12
Earlier sketch in CA 33-36R
Reuther, Victor G(eorge) 1912- 77-80
Reutter, Mark 1950- 129
Rev, B.
See Eisner, Betty Grover
Reval, Jacques
See Laver, James
Revankar, Ratna G. 1937- 33-36R
Revard, Stella Purce 1933- 97-100
Reve, Karel van het
See van het Reve, Karel
Revel, Jean-Francois 1924- 127
Brief entry 109
Reveley, Edith 1930- 123
Reveley, W(alter) Taylor III 1943- 126
Revell, Donald 1954- CANR-39
Earlier sketch in CA 116
Revell, J(ohn) R(obert) S(tephen)
1920- CANR-26
Earlier sketches in CA 25-28R, CANR-11
Revell, Jack
See Revell, J(ohn) R(obert) S(tephen)
Revell, Peter 1929-1983 ....CANR-13
Earlier sketch in CA 29-32R
ReVelle, Charles S. 1938- 45-48
ReVelle, Penelope 1941- 49-52
Revena
See Wright, Betty Ren
Reventlow, Franziska Graefin zu
1871-1918 .... DLB 66
Reverdy, Pierre 1889-1960 97-100
Obituary 89-92
See also CLC 53
Reverend Mandju
See Su Chien
Reves, Emery 1904-1981 Obituary 105
Rewald, John 1912- CANR-5
Earlier sketch in CA 9-12R
Rewoldt, Stewart H(enry) 1922- 37-40R
Rex, Barbara (Clayton) 1904- 77-80
Rex, John A(rderne) 1925- CANR-24
Earlier sketches in CA 5-8R, CANR-6
Rex, Walter E(dwin) 1927- 45-48
Rexine, John E(fstratios) 1929- CANR-15
Earlier sketch in CA 37-40R
Rexroth, Kenneth 1905-1982 ....CANR-34
Obituary 107
Earlier sketches in CA 5-8R, CANR-14
See also CDALB 1941-1968
See also CLC 1, 2, 6, 11, 22, 49
See also DLB 16, 48
See also DLBY 82
See also MTCW
Rey, H(ans) A(ugusto) 1898-1977 ....CANR-6
Obituary 73-76
Earlier sketch in CA 5-8R
See also CLR 5
See also DLB 22
See also MAICYA
See also SATA 1, 26, 69
Rey, Margret (Elisabeth) 1906- CANR-38
Earlier sketch in CA 105
See also CLR 5
See also MAICYA
See also SATA 26
Rey, Michael Stephan 1946- 113
Reyam
See Mayer, Charles Leopold
Reybold, Malcolm 1911(?)-1988 Obituary 124
Reyburn, Wallace (Macdonald) 1913- CANR-1
Earlier sketch in CA 49-52
Reyes, Alfonso 1889-1959 131
See also HW
See also TCLC 33
Reyes, Carlos Jose 1941- ....HW
Reyes, Carlos 1935- CANR-3
Earlier sketch in CA 49-52
Reyes y Basoalto, Ricardo Eliecer Neftali
See Neruda, Pablo
Reyher, Becky
See Reyher, Rebecca Hourwich
Reyher, Rebecca Hourwich
1897-1987 Obituary 121
See also SATA 18, 50
Reyles, Carlos 1868-1938 ....HW
Reymont, Wladyslaw (Stanislaw)
1868(?)-1925 Brief entry 104
See also TCLC 5
Reynolds, Alan 1942- 61-64
Reynolds, Ann
See Bly, Carol(yn)
Reynolds, Anne
See Steinke, Ann E(lizabeth)
Reynolds, Barbara (Ann) 1942- 73-76
Reynolds, Barbara 1914- CANR-29
Earlier sketch in CA 9-12R
Reynolds, Barrie (Gordon Robert)
1932- 13-16R
Reynolds, Bart
See Emblen, D(onald) L(ewis)
Reynolds, Bede 1893(?)-1989 Obituary 130
Reynolds, Bertha Capen 1885- CAP-2
Earlier sketch in CA 19-20
Reynolds, Charles O. 1921- 9-12R
Reynolds, (Alfred) Christopher 1911- 104
Reynolds, Clark G(ilbert) 1939- CANR-27
Earlier sketches in CA 25-28R, CANR-12
Reynolds, Clark Winton 1934- CANR-8
Earlier sketch in CA 21-24R
Reynolds, Dallas McCord 1917- CANR-9
Earlier sketch in CA 5-8R
See also Reynolds, Mack
Reynolds, David K(ent) 1940- CANR-25
Earlier sketches in CA 65-68, CANR-9
Reynolds, David S(pencer) 1948- 124
Reynolds, Dickson
See Reynolds, Helen Mary Greenwood Campbell
Reynolds, Donald E. 1931- 33-36R
Reynolds, Elizabeth
See Steinke, Ann E(lizabeth)
Reynolds, Ernest (Randolph) 1910- CANR-6
Earlier sketch in CA 3-16R
Reynolds, Frank 1923-1983 114
Obituary 109
Reynolds, G. Scott 1925- 29-32R
Reynolds, G. W. M. 1814-1879 .... DLB 21
Reynolds, (Arthur) Graham 1914- CANR-17
Earlier sketch in CA 13-16R
Reynolds, Graham 1944- 138
Reynolds, Harry W. Jr. 1924- 13-16R
Reynolds, Helen Mary Greenwood Campbell
1884-1969 ....5-8R
Obituary 103
See also SATA 26
Reynolds, Jack
See Jones, Jack
Reynolds, Joe
See Steward, Samuel M(orris)
Reynolds, John
See Whitlock, Ralph
Reynolds, John Hamilton 1794-1852 ...... DLB 96
Reynolds, John J(oseph) 1924- 37-40R
Reynolds, John 1901- 9-12R
Reynolds, Jonathan 1942- CANR-28
Earlier sketch in CA 65-68
See also CLC 6, 38
Reynolds, Joshua 1723-1792 .... DLB 104
Reynolds, Julia Louise
1883(?)-1980 Obituary 102
Reynolds, Kenyon L.
See Reynolds, Bede
Reynolds, Kimberley (Griffith) 1955- 135
Reynolds, Larry T(homas) 1938- 134
Brief entry 107
Reynolds, Lloyd George 1910- CANR-15
Earlier sketch in CA 21-24R
Reynolds, Louis B. 1917- 41-44R
Reynolds, Mack
See Reynolds, Dallas McCord
See also DLB 8
Reynolds, Madge
See Whitlock, Ralph
Reynolds, Malvina 1900-1978 114
Obituary 105
See also SATA 24, 44
Reynolds, Marie E. 1912- 17-20R
Reynolds, Marjorie Harris 1903- 5-8R
Reynolds, Mary Trackett 1914- 109
Reynolds, Michael Shane 1937- CANR-9
Earlier sketch in CA 65-68
See also CLC 44
Reynolds, (Marjorie) Moira Davison
1915- CANR-21
Earlier sketch in CA 105
Reynolds, Morgan O(wen) 1942- 117
Reynolds, Pamela 1923- 103
See also SATA 34
Reynolds, Paul Davidson 1938- CANR-12
Earlier sketch in CA 33-36R
Reynolds, Paul R(evere) 1904-1988 102
Obituary 125
Reynolds, Peter C(arlton) 1943- 105
Reynolds, Philip Alan 1920- CANR-3
Earlier sketch in CA 5-8R
Reynolds, Quentin (James) 1902-1965 73-76
Reynolds, Robert Leonard 1902-1966 ....1-4R
Obituary 103
Reynolds, Roger 1934- 53-56
Reynolds, Ruth Sutton
1890(?)-1977 Obituary 69-72
Reynolds, Susan (Mary Grace) 1929- 117
Reynolds, Terry S(cott) 1946- 117
Reynolds, Timothy (Robin) 1936- CANR-8
Earlier sketch in CA 9-12R
Reynolds, Valrae 1944- 93-96
Reynolds, Vernon 1935- 132
Reynolds, William Howard
1922-1972 Obituary 107
Reynolds, William J. 1956- 123
Reynolds, William Jensen 1920- CANR-7
Earlier sketch in CA 5-8R
Rey-Rosa, Rodrigo 1958- 131
Rezits, Joseph 1925- 107
Rezler, Julius 1911- 25-28R
Rezmerski, John Calvin 1942- CANR-27
Earlier sketch in CA 29-32R
Rezneck, Samuel 1897-1983 ....CANR-24
Obituary 110
Earlier sketch in CA 45-48
Reznikoff, Charles 1894-1976 .... CAP-2
Obituary 61-64
Earlier sketch in CA 33-36
See also CLC 9
See also DLB 28, 45
Rezny, Arthur A(dolph) 1910- CAP-2
Earlier sketch in CA 19-20
Rezzori (d'Arezzo), Gregor von 1914- 136
Brief entry 122
See also CLC 25
Rhea, Claude H(iram) Jr. 1927- 103
Rhea, Nicholas
See Walker, Peter N.
Rhees, Rush 1905(?)-1989(?) Obituary 129
Rhein, Francis Bayard 1915- 17-20R
Rhein, Phillip H(enry) 1923- 81-84
Rheinstein, Max 1899-1977 Obituary 73-76
Rhenisch, Harold (Arthur) 1958- 113
Rhett, Robert Barnwell 1800-1876 .... DLB 43
Rhie, Schi-Zhin 1936- 77-80
Rhine, J(oseph) B(anks) 1895-1980 ....CANR-4
Obituary 93-96
Earlier sketch in CA 5-8R
Rhine, Louisa (Weckesser) E. 1891- CANR-4
Earlier sketch in CA 1-4R
Rhine, Richard
See Silverstein, Alvin
Rhinehart, Luke
See Cockcroft, George Powers
Rhinehart, Susan Oneacre 1938- 1-4R
Rhoades, Jonathan
See Olsen, John Edward
Rhoades, Judith G(rubman) 1935- 97-100
Rhoads, Dorothy M(ary) 1895- CAP-2
Earlier sketch in CA 19-20
Rhoads, Edward J(ohn) M(ichael)
1938- 33-36R
Rhoads, Jonathan E(vans) 1907- 104
Rhode, Austen
See Francis, Basil (Hoskins)
Rhode, Eric 1934- 21-24R
Rhode, Irma 1900-1982 Obituary 106
Rhode, John 1884-1964 .... DLB 77
Rhode, Robert B(artlett) 1916- 17-20R
Rhode, Robert D(avid) 1911- 93-96
Rhode, Winslow
See Roe, F(rederic) Gordon
Rhodehamel, Josephine DeWitt 1901- 61-64
Rhodes, Albert 1916-1977 ....CANR-14
Earlier sketch in CA 21-24R
Rhodes, Anthony (Richard Ewart) 1916- 9-12R
Rhodes, Arnold Black 1913- 13-16R
Rhodes, Bennie (Loran) 1927- 108
See also SATA 35
Rhodes, Carolyn Hodgson 1925- 122
Rhodes, Clifford Oswald 1911-1985 65-68
Obituary 118
Rhodes, David 1946- 57-60
Rhodes, Dennis Everard 1923- 13-16R
Rhodes, Ernest Lloyd 1915- 119
Rhodes, Evan H. 1929- CANR-10
Earlier sketch in CA 57-60
Rhodes, Frank Harold Trevor 1926- 107
See also SATA 37
Rhodes, Hari 1932- 17-20R
Rhodes, Irwin Seymour 1901- 73-76
Rhodes, James Allen 1909- Brief entry 105
Rhodes, James Ford 1848-1927 .... DLB 47
Rhodes, James M. 1940- 89-92
Rhodes, John J(acob) 1916- 103
Rhodes, Laura
See Robinson, Lisa
Rhodes, Leland
See Paine, Lauran (Bosworth)
Rhodes, Margaret 1915- 45-48
Rhodes, Philip 1922- 107
Rhodes, Richard (Lee) 1937- CANR-20
Earlier sketches in CA 45-48, CANR-1
See also BEST 90:1
Rhodes, Robert E(dward) 1927- 122
Rhodes, Robert Hunt 1937- 136
Rhodes, Robert I. 1942- 69-72
Rhodes, William C(onley) 1918- 81-84
Rhodes James, Robert (Vidal) 1933- CANR-14
Earlier sketch in CA 101
Rhodin, Eric Nolan 1916- CANR-3
Earlier sketch in CA 1-4R
Rhone, Trevor (Dave) 1940- 127
See also BW
Rhue, Morton
See Strasser, Todd
Rhydderch, Ieuan
See Jones, Evan David
Rhymer, Joseph 1927- CANR-9
Earlier sketch in CA 21-24R
Rhyne, Nancy 1926- 133
See also SATA 66
Rhys, Frank
See Rees, Clair (Francis)
Rhys, Ioan
See Rees, Ioan Bowen
Rhys, J(ohn) Howard W(inslow) 1917- 17-20R
Rhys, Jean 1890(?)-1979 ....CANR-35
Obituary 85-88
Earlier sketch in CA 25-28R
See also CDBLB 1945-1960
See also CLC 2, 4, 6, 14, 19, 51
See also DLB 36, 117
See also MTCW
Rhys, Kate
See Donald, Anabel
Rhys, Keidrych 1915-1987 Obituary 122
Riad, Mahmoud 1917-1992 131
Obituary 136
Riasanovsky, Nicholas V(alentine)
1923- CANR-3
Earlier sketch in CA 5-8R
Ribal, Joseph E(dward) 1931- 61-64
Ribalow, Harold U(riel) 1919-1982 ....CANR-2
Obituary 108
Earlier sketch in CA 5-8R
Ribar, Joe 1943- 77-80
Ribbons, Ian 1924- 108
See also SAAS 3
See also SATA 30, 37
Ribeiro, Aileen 1944- 124
Ribeiro, Darcy 1922- 33-36R
See also CLC 34
Ribeiro, Joao Ubaldo (Osorio Pimentel)
1941- 81-84
See also CLC 10, 67
Ribera Chevremont, Evaristo 1896-1976 ....HW
Ribicoff, Abraham (Alexander) 1910- 108
Ribman, Ronald (Burt) 1932- 21-24R
See also CLC 7
Ribner, Irving 1921-1972 ....CANR-3
Obituary 37-40R
Earlier sketch in CA 1-4R
Riboud, Barbara (Dewayne Tosi) Chase
See Chase-Riboud, Barbara (Dewayne Tosi)
Ribuffo, Leo P(aul) 1945- 118
Ricardo, David 1772-1823 .... DLB 107
Ricardo, Harry R(alph) 1885-1974 Obituary 114
Ricardo-Campbell, Rita CANR-26
Earlier sketches in CA 57-60, CANR-8
Ricardou, Jean 1932- .... DLB 83
Ricart, Josep Gudiol i
See Gudiol i Ricart, Josep
Riccards, Michael P(atrick) 1944- 61-64
Ricchiuti, Paul B(urton) 1925- 107
Ricci, Larry J. 1948- 109
Ricci, Nino 1959- 137
See also CLC 70
Ricciardi, Lorenzo 1930- 109
Ricciuti, Edward R(aphael) 1938- 41-44R
See also SATA 10
Rice, A(lbert) Kenneth 1908- 5-8R
Rice, Albert
See Leventhal, Albert Rice
Rice, Alice (Caldwell) Hegan
1870-1942 .... SATA 63
Rice, Allan Lake 1905-1984 ....CANR-27
Earlier sketch in CA 37-40R
Rice, Anne 1941- CANR-36
Earlier sketches in CA 65-68, CANR-12
See also AAYA 9
See also BEST 89:2
See also CLC 41
Rice, Arnold Sanford 1928- 113
Rice, Berkeley 1937- 21-24R
Rice, C(harles) David 1941- 118
Rice, C(harles) Duncan 1942- CANR-10
Earlier sketch in CA 57-60
Rice, Charles D(uane) 1910-1971 Obituary 104
See also SATA 27
Rice, Charles E. 1931- CANR-1
Earlier sketch in CA 1-4R
Rice, Charles L(ynvel) 1936- 65-68
Rice, Craig
See Randolph, Georgiana Ann
Rice, Cy 1905-1971 .... CAP-1
Obituary 33-36R
Earlier sketch in CA 11-12
Rice, Dale R(ichard) 1948- 116
See also SATA 42
Rice, David G(ordon) 1938- 101
Rice, David Talbot 1903-1972 ....CANR-5
Earlier sketch in CA 9-12R
Rice, Desmond Charles 1924- CANR-21
Earlier sketches in CA 9-12R, CANR-5
Rice, Donald L. 1938- CANR-14
Earlier sketch in CA 37-40R
Rice, Dorothy Mary 1913- 9-12R
Rice, Edmund C. 1910(?)-1982 Obituary 106
Rice, Edward E(arl) 1909- 41-44R
Rice, Edward E. 1918- CANR-1
Earlier sketch in CA 49-52
See also BEST 90:4
See also SATA 42, 47
Rice, Elinor
See Hays, Elinor Rice
Rice, Elizabeth 1913- 21-24R
See also SATA 2
Rice, Elmer (Leopold) 1892-1967 .... CAP-2
Obituary 25-28R
Earlier sketch in CA 21-22
See also CLC 7, 49
See also DLB 4, 7
See also MTCW
Rice, Eugene F(ranklin) Jr. 1924- 29-32R
Rice, Eve (Hart) 1951- CANR-4
Earlier sketch in CA 53-56
See also SATA 34
Rice, Frank M(artin) 1908- 45-48
Rice, George H(all) Jr. 1923- 53-56
Rice, Grantland 1880-1954 Brief entry 114
See also DLB 29
Rice, Helen Steiner 1900(?)-1981 133
Rice, Homer C(ranston) 1927- 73-76
Rice, Inez 1907- 29-32R
See also SATA 13
Rice, James 1934- CANR-8
Earlier sketch in CA 61-64
See also SATA 22
Rice, John R(ichard) 1895-1980 ....CANR-5
Earlier sketch in CA 5-8R
Rice, Joseph Peter 1930- 29-32R
Rice, Julius 1923- 41-44R
Rice, Keith A(lan) 1954- 109
Rice, Lawrence D. 1929- 33-36R
Rice, Martin P(aul) 1938- 57-60
Rice, Max M(cGee) 1928- 93-96
Rice, Michael 1928- 137
Rice, Mitchell F. 1948- 138
Rice, Otis K(ermit) 1919- CANR-27
Earlier sketch in CA 29-32R
Rice, R. B.
See Chapman, Frank M(onroe)
Rice, Ross R(ichard) 1922- 45-48
Rice, Stan 1942- CANR-36
Earlier sketch in CA 77-80
Rice, Tamara (Abelson) Talbot
1904- Brief entry 111
Rice, Thomas Jackson 1945- CANR-18
Earlier sketch in CA 101

Rice, Tim 1944- ... 103
See also CLC 21
Rice, Wayne 1945- ... 89-92
Rice, William C(arroll) 1911- ... 9-12R
Rice, William (Edward) 1938- ... 118
Rich, Adrienne (Cecile) 1929- ... CANR-20
Earlier sketch in CA 9-12R
See also CLC 3, 6, 7, 11, 18, 36
See also DLB 5, 67
See also MTCW
See also PC 5
Rich, Alan 1924- ... 9-12R
Rich, Barbara
See Graves, Robert (von Ranke)
Rich, Bennett M(ilton) 1909-1984 ... 134
Rich, Daniel Catton 1904-1976 ... 73-76
Obituary ... 69-72
Rich, Doris L. 1920- ... 138
Rich, Edwin Ernest 1904-1979 Obituary ... 89-92
Rich, Elaine Sommers 1926- ... CANR-24
Earlier sketches in CA 17-20R, CANR-9
See also SATA 6
Rich, Elizabeth 1935- ... 29-32R
Rich, (Ora) Everett 1900- ... CAP-1
Earlier sketch in CA 11-12
Rich, Frank 1949- ... 73-76
Rich, Gerry
See Brandon, Johnny
Rich, (David) Gibson 1936- ... 57-60
Rich, Joe 1935- ... 57-60
Rich, John H. Jr. 1917- ... 81-84
Rich, John Martin 1931- ... 21-24R
Rich, Josephine Bouchard 1912- ... 5-8R
See also SATA 10
Rich, Louise Dickinson 1903-1991 ... 73-76
Obituary ... 134
See also SATA 54
See also SATO 67
Rich, Mark J. 1948- ... SATA 53
Rich, Michael B(enjamin) 1935- ... 29-32R
Rich, Norman 1921- ... 45-48
Rich, Paul B(enjamin) 1950- ... 124
Rich, Robert
See Trumbo, Dalton
Rich, Russell R(ogers) 1912- ... 101
Richard, Adrienne 1921- ... 29-32R
See also SAAS 9
See also SATA 5
Richard, Arthur Windsor
See Windsor-Richards, Arthur (Bedlington)
Richard, Betty Byrd 1922- ... 106
Richard, James Robert
See Bowen, Robert Sydney
Richard, John 1954- ... 106
Richard, Keith
See Richards, Keith
Richard, Lee
See Le Pelley, Guernsey
Richard, Lionel (Camille Paul) 1938- ... 93-96
Richard, Lucien J(oseph) 1931- ... 105
Richard, Marthe 1889-1982 Obituary ... 110
Richard, Michel Paul 1933- ... 45-48
Richard, Olga 1914- ... 103
Richard-Amato, Patricia (Abbott) 1940- ... 126
Richards, Alayna
See Posner, Richard
Richards, Alfred (Luther) 1939- ... 45-48
Richards, Allen
See Rosenthal, Richard A.
Richards, Alun 1929- ... CANR-17
Earlier sketch in CA 65-68
Richards, Arlene Kramer 1935- ... CANR-11
Earlier sketch in CA 65-68
Richards, Audrey I(sabel) 1899-1984 ... CANR-27
Obituary ... 113
Earlier sketch in CA 21-24R
Richards, Blair P(atton) 1940- ... 69-72
Richards, Cara E(lizabeth) 1927- ... CANR-1
Earlier sketch in CA 49-52
Richards, Carl Edward Jr. 1933- ... CANR-24
Earlier sketch in CA 45-48
Richards, Caroline 1939- ... 77-80
Richards, Charles
See Marvin, John T.
Richards, Clare
See Titchener, Louise
Richards, Clay
See Crossen, Kendell Foster
Richards, David
See Bickers, Richard Leslie Townshend
Richards, David Adams 1950- ... 93-96
See also CLC 59
See also DLB 53
Richards, Denis (George) 1910- ... 9-12R
Richards, Dennis L(ee) 1938- ... 102
Richards, Dorothy B(urney) 1894- ... 85-88
Richards, Duane
See Hurley, Vic
Richards, E. B.
See Bayley, Edwin Richard
Richards, Frank
See Hamilton, Charles (Harold St. John)
Richards, Fred
See Richards, Alfred (Luther)
Richards, George 1760(?)-1814 ... DLB 37
Richards, Guy 1905-1979 ... CANR-11
Obituary ... 81-84
Earlier sketch in CA 61-64
Richards, H(arold) M(arshall) S(ylvester)
1894-1985 ... CAP-2
Obituary ... 116
Earlier sketch in CA 23-24
Richards, Hilda
See Hamilton, Charles (Harold St. John)
Richards, Horace G(ardiner) 1906- ... 5-8R
Richards, Hubert J. 1921- ... 128
Richards, I(vor) A(rmstrong)
1893-1979 ... CANR-34
Obituary ... 89-92
Earlier sketch in CA 41-44R
See also CLC 14, 24
See also DLB 27
Richards, J(ohn) Howard 1916- ... CANR-18
Earlier sketches in CA 45-48, CANR-2
Richards, J(ames) M(aude) 1907- ... CANR-25
Earlier sketches in CA 5-8R, CANR-5
Richards, Jack W(esley) 1933- ... 33-36R
Richards, James O(lin) 1936- ... 37-40R
Richards, Jane 1934- ... 33-36R
Richards, Janet Radcliffe 1944- ... 133
Richards, Jeffrey (Michael) 1945- ... CANR-13
Earlier sketch in CA 73-76
Richards, Jock 1918- ... 107
Richards, Joe 1909-1992 ... CAP-1
Obituary ... 136
Earlier sketch in CA 9-10
Richards, John F(olsom) 1938- ... 115
Richards, John Marvin 1929- ... 13-16R
Richards, John 1939- ... 57-60
Richards, Kathleen
See Dale, Kathleen
Richards, Kay
See Baker, Susan (Catherine)
Richards, Keith 1943- ... 107
Richards, Kenny
See Broderick, Richard L(awrence)
Richards, Kent David 1938- ... 104
Richards, Larry
See Richards, Lawrence O.
Richards, Laura E(lizabeth Howe)
1850-1943 ... 137
Brief entry ... 120
See also DLB 42
See also MAICYA
See also YABC 1
Richards, Lawrence O. 1931- ... CANR-20
Earlier sketch in CA 29-32R
Richards, Lewis A(lva) 1925- ... 45-48
Richards, M(ary) C(aroline) 1916- ... 108
Richards, Mark
See Ra'Anan, Uri
Richards, Martin P(aul) M(eredith)
1940- ... CANR-23
Earlier sketches in CA 61-64, CANR-8
Richards, Max D(eVoe) 1923- ... CANR-16
Earlier sketch in CA 21-24R
Richards, Nat
See Richardson, James Nathaniel
Richards, Norman 1932- ... CANR-31
Earlier sketch in CA 112
See also SATA 48
Richards, Owain Westmacott
1901-1984 Obituary ... 114
Richards, Pamela Spence 1941- ... 111
Richards, Peter
See Monger, (Ifor) David
Richards, Peter Godfrey 1923-1987 ... 108
Obituary ... 123
Richards, Phyllis
See Auty, Phyllis
Richards, R(onald) C(harles) W(illiam)
1923- ... CANR-26
Earlier sketches in CA 21-24R, CANR-10
See also SATA 43, 59
Richards, Stanley 1918-1980 ... 25-28R
Obituary ... 101
Richards, Susan 1948- ... 135
Richards, Todd
See Sutphen, Richard Charles
Richards, Victor 1918- ... 57-60
Richards, Walter Alden (Jr.)
1907-1988 Obituary ... 125
See also SATA 56
Richards, William Carey 1818-1892 ... DLB 73
Richardson, Alan 1923- ... 29-32R
Richardson, Ann 1942- ... 119
Richardson, Anne
See Roiphe, Anne Richardson
Richardson, Arleta 1923- ... CANR-36
Earlier sketches in CA 93-96, CANR-16
Richardson, Beth
See Gutcheon, Beth R(ichardson)
Richardson, Betty 1935- ... 53-56
Richardson, Bonham C. 1939- ... 135
Richardson, Bradley M. 1928- ... 49-52
Richardson, C.
See Munsey, Cecil (Richard Jr.)
Richardson, Carol 1932- ... SATA 58
Richardson, Cecil Antonio 1928-1991 ... 121
Obituary ... 136
Brief entry ... 115
Richardson, Charles E(verett) 1928- ... 57-60
Richardson, Charles F. 1851-1913 ... DLB 71
Richardson, Cyril Charles 1909-1976 ... 37-40R
Obituary ... 69-72
Richardson, Don(ald MacNaughton)
1935- ... CANR-9
Earlier sketch in CA 65-68
Richardson, Donald P(orter) 1932- ... 119
Richardson, Dorothy Lee 1900-1986 ... 106
Obituary ... 121
Richardson, Dorothy Miller
1873-1957 Brief entry ... 104
See also DLB 36
See also TCLC 3
Richardson, Dorsey 1896-1981 Obituary ... 105
Richardson, (Robert) Douglas
1893-1989 Obituary ... 128
Richardson, Edgar Preston 1902-1985 ... 110
Obituary ... 115
Richardson, Elliot L(ee) 1920- Brief entry ... 111
Richardson, Elmo (R.) 1930- ... CANR-11
Earlier sketch in CA 13-16R
Richardson, Ethel Florence (Lindesay)
1870-1946 Brief entry ... 105
See also Richardson, Henry Handel
Richardson, Evelyn M(ay Fox) 1902- ... CAP-1
Earlier sketch in CA 13-14
Richardson, Frank Howard
1882-1970 Obituary ... 104
See also SATA 27
Richardson, Frank McLean 1904- ... CANR-20
Earlier sketch in CA 103
Richardson, Gayle E(lwin) 1911- ... 9-12R
Richardson, George Barclay 1924- ... 1-4R
Richardson, Gladwell 1903-1980 ... 123
Richardson, Grace Lee
See Dickson, Naida
Richardson, H(arold) Edward 1929- ... CANR-15
Earlier sketch in CA 29-32R
Richardson, Harry V(an Buren) 1901- ... 69-72
Richardson, Harry W(ard) 1938- ... CANR-27
Earlier sketch in CA 29-32R
Richardson, Henrietta
See Richardson, Ethel Florence (Lindesay)
Richardson, Henry Handel
See Richardson, Ethel Florence (Lindesay)
See also TCLC 4
Richardson, Henry V(okes) M(ackey)
1923- ... 25-28R
Richardson, Howard (Dixon) 1917-1984 ... 41-44R
Obituary ... 114
Richardson, Isla Paschal 1886-1971 ... CAP-1
Earlier sketch in CA 9-10
Richardson, Ivan L(eRoy) 1920- ... 101
Richardson, Ivor Lloyd Morgan 1930- ... 9-12R
Richardson, J. G.
See Richardson, Jacques (Gabriel)
Richardson, Jack (Carter) 1935- ... 5-8R
See also DLB 7
Richardson, Jacques (Gabriel) 1924- ... 125
Richardson, James F(rancis) 1931- ... 29-32R
Richardson, James L(ongden) 1933- ... 21-24R
Richardson, James Nathaniel 1942- ... 53-56
Richardson, James R. 1911- ... 1-4R
Richardson, James 1950- ... 77-80
Richardson, Jean (Mary) ... 127
See also SATA 59
Richardson, Jeremy John 1942- ... CANR-27
Earlier sketch in CA 29-32R
Richardson, Joanna ... CANR-26
Earlier sketches in CA 13-16R, CANR-10
Richardson, Joe M(artin) 1934- ... CANR-26
Earlier sketch in CA 45-48
Richardson, John Adkins 1929- ... 57-60
Richardson, John Martin Jr. 1938- ... CANR-12
Earlier sketch in CA 33-36R
Richardson, John 1796-1852 ... DLB 99
Richardson, Justin
1900(?)-1975 Obituary ... 61-64
Richardson, Kenneth Ridley 1934- ... 29-32R
Richardson, Laurel 1938- ... 111
Richardson, Laurence E(aton) 1893- ... CAP-1
Earlier sketch in CA 11-12
Richardson, (Stewart) Lee (Jr.) 1940- ... CANR-9
Earlier sketch in CA 21-24R
Richardson, Leopold John Dixon
1893-1979(?) Obituary ... 104
Richardson, Malcolm 1947- ... 120
Richardson, Midge Turk 1930- ... 33-36R
Richardson, Miles (Edward) 1932- ... 33-36R
Richardson, Mozelle Groner 1914- ... 33-36R
Richardson, Neil R(yan) 1944- ... 103
Richardson, Nola 1936- ... 57-60
See also BW
Richardson, (George) Peter 1935- ... 114
Richardson, R(alph) Daniel 1931- ... 109
Richardson, Richard C(olby) Jr.
1933- ... CANR-13
Earlier sketch in CA 77-80
Richardson, Richard Judson 1935- ... 29-32R
Richardson, Robert D(ale) Jr. 1934- ... CANR-29
Earlier sketches in CA 29-32R, CANR-12
Richardson, Robert Galloway 1926- ... CANR-7
Earlier sketch in CA 13-16R
Richardson, Robert S(hirley) 1902- ... 49-52
See also SATA 8
Richardson, Rupert Norval 1891- ... 17-20R
Richardson, Ruth 1951- ... 136
Richardson, S(tanley) D(ennis) 1925- ... CANR-28
Earlier sketches in CA 21-24R, CANR-10
Richardson, Samuel
1689-1761 ... CDBLB 1660-1789
See also DLB 39
See also WLC
Richardson, Stephen A. 1920- ... 61-64
Richardson, Thomas Dow 1887- ... 5-8R
Richardson, Tony
See Richardson, Cecil Antonio
Richardson, Vokes
See Richardson, Henry V(okes) M(ackey)
Richardson, W(alter) C(ecil) 1902- ... CANR-1
Earlier sketch in CA 1-4R
Richardson, William John 1920- ... 21-24R
Richardson, Willis 1889-1977 ... 124
See also BW
See also DLB 51
See also SATA 60
Richason, Benjamin F(ranklin Jr.) 1922- ... 41-44R
Richberg, Donald R(andall)
1881-1960 Obituary ... 113
Riche, Pierre 1921- ... 123
Riche, Robert 1925- ... 108
Riche, William Harding le
See le Riche, William Harding
Richelieu, Peter
See Robinson, P. W.
Richelson, Geraldine 1922- ... 106
See also SATA 29
Richelson, Jeffrey T(albot) 1949- ... 119
Richens, Richard Hook
1919-1984 Obituary ... 114
Riches, David 1947- ... 128
Riches, John (Kenneth) 1939- ... 117
Riches, Pierre 1927- ... 118
Richette, Lisa Aversa 1928- ... 25-28R
Richetti, John J(oseph) 1938- ... 110
Richey, David 1939- ... CANR-10
Earlier sketch in CA 57-60
Richey, Dorothy Hilliard ... CANR-6
Earlier sketch in CA 9-12R
Richey, Elinor 1920- ... 45-48
Richey, Margaret Fitzgerald
1883(?)-1974 Obituary ... 53-56
Richey, Robert W(illiam) 1912-1978 ... CANR-17
Obituary ... 116
Earlier sketch in CA 25-28R
Richey, Russell Earle 1941- ... 69-72
Richie, Donald (Steiner) 1924- ... CANR-24
Earlier sketches in CA 17-20R, CANR-8
Richland, W(ilfred) Bernard 1909- ... 102
Richler, Daniel 1956- ... 137
Richler, Mordecai 1931- ... CANR-31
Earlier sketch in CA 65-68
See also AITN 1
See also CLC 3, 5, 9, 13, 18, 46, 70
See also CLR 17
See also DLB 53
See also MAICYA
See also MTCW
See also SATA 27, 44
Richman, Barry M(artin) 1936-1978 ... CANR-17
Earlier sketch in CA 21-24R
Richman, Milton (Saul) 1922-1986 ... 69-72
Obituary ... 119
Richman, Phyllis C. 1939- ... 89-92
Richman, Robert (Maxwell)
1914-1987 Obituary ... 124
Richman, Saul 1917(?)-1979 Obituary ... 85-88
Rich-McCoy, Lois
See McCoy, Lois (Rich)
Richmond, Al 1913-1987 ... 41-44R
Obituary ... 124
Richmond, Anthony H(enry) 1925- ... 21-24R
Richmond, Cindy Packard 1948- ... 112
Richmond, Dick 1933- ... 61-64
Richmond, Douglas W(ertz) 1946- ... 111
Richmond, Grace
See Marsh, John
Richmond, H(ugh) M(acrae) 1932- ... CANR-3
Earlier sketch in CA 9-12R
Richmond, Ian Archibald
1902-1965 Obituary ... 111
Richmond, John C(hristopher) B(lake)
1909- Brief entry ... 106
Richmond, Julius B(enjamin) 1916- ... 29-32R
Richmond, Lee J(oyce) 1934- ... 113
Richmond, Lee 1943- ... 49-52
Richmond, Leigh (Tucker) 1911- ... 21-24R
Richmond, Roaldus Frederick 1910- ... 114
Richmond, Robert P. 1914- ... 21-24R
Richmond, Robert W(illiam) 1927- ... 53-56
Richmond, Rod
See Glut, Donald F(rank)
Richmond, Roe
See Richmond, Roaldus Frederick
Richmond, Samuel B(ernard) 1919- ... 41-44R
Richmond, Sandra 1948- ... 117
Richmond, (John) Stanley 1906- ... 45-48
Richmond, Velma E. B(ourgeois) 1931- ... 61-64
Richmond, W(illiam) Kenneth 1910- ... CANR-10
Earlier sketch in CA 25-28R
Richmond, Walt(er F.) 1922-1977 ... 21-24R
Obituary ... 117
Richoux, Pat(ricia) 1927- ... 25-28R
See also SATA 7
Richstatter, Thomas 1939- ... 112
Richter, Alice 1941- ... 105
See also SATA 30
Richter, C(harles) F(rancis)
1900-1985 Obituary ... 117
Richter, Conrad (Michael) 1890-1968 ... CANR-23
Obituary ... 25-28R
Earlier sketch in CA 5-8R
See also CLC 30
See also DLB 9
See also MTCW
See also SATA 3
Richter, David H. 1945- ... 101
Richter, Derek 1907- ... 101
Richter, Dorothy 1906- ... 29-32R
Richter, Gerard R(ichard) 1905- ... 5-8R
Richter, Gisela M(arie) A(ugusta)
1882-1972 ... CANR-4
Earlier sketch in CA 5-8R
Richter, Hans Peter 1925- ... CANR-2
Earlier sketch in CA 45-48
See also CLR 21
See also MAICYA
See also SAAS 11
See also SATA 6
Richter, Hans Werner 1908- ... 97-100
See also DLB 69
Richter, Hans 1888-1976 ... 73-76
Obituary ... 65-68
Richter, Harvena 1919- ... CANR-3
Earlier sketch in CA 5-8R
Richter, Horst-Eberhard 1923- ... CANR-20
Earlier sketches in CA 53-56, CANR-5
Richter, Irving 1911- ... 57-60
Richter, J. H(ans) 1901- ... CAP-1
Earlier sketch in CA 13-16
Richter, Joan 1930- ... 101
Richter, Johann Paul Friedrich
1763-1825 ... DLB 94
Richter, Lin 1936- ... 73-76
Richter, Linda K. 1942- ... 117

Richter, Maurice N(athaniel) Jr. 1930- 49-52
Richter, Melvin 1921- Brief entry 110
Richter, Valentin
See Pick, Robert
Richter, Vernon
See Hutchcroft, Vera
Richter, William L. 1942- 126
Rickard, Bob
See Rickard, Robert J(ohn) M(oberley)
Rickard, Graham 1949- ....SATA 71
Rickard, Robert J(ohn) M(oberley) 1945- 106
Rickards, Colin (William) 1937- 25-28R
Rickards, Maurice 1919- 103
Rickel, Annette U. 1941- 123
Rickels, Karl 1924- CANR-1
Earlier sketch in CA 45-48
Rickels, Milton H. 1920- 5-8R
Rickenbacker, Eddie
See Rickenbacker, Edward Vernon
Rickenbacker, Edward Vernon 1890-1973 101
Obituary 41-44R
Ricker, George Marvin 1922- CANR-20
Earlier sketch in CA 89-92
Rickert, Corinne Holt
See Sawyer, Corinne Holt
Rickert, John E(arl) 1923- CANR-24
Earlier sketch in CA 45-48
Rickett, Frances 1921- 107
Rickett, Harold William 1896- 17-20R
Ricketts, C(arl) E(verett) 1906- 57-60
Ricketts, Mac Linscott 1930- 130
Ricketts, Ralph Robert 1902- 116
Ricketts, Viva Leone (Harris) 1900- CAP-1
Earlier sketch in CA 11-12
Rickey, Don Jr. 1925- CANR-9
Earlier sketch in CA 5-8R
Rickey, George Warren 1907- 65-68
Rickey, Mary Ellen 1929- 21-24R
Rickford, John R(ussell) 1949- 126
Ricklefs, Roger 1940- 127
Rickman, Geoffrey (Edwin) 1932- 29-32R
Rickman, H(ans) P(eter) 1918- CANR-32
Earlier sketches in CA 17-20R, CANR-14
Rickover, H. G.
See Rickover, Hyman George
Rickover, Hyman George
1900-1986 Obituary 119
Ricks, Chip
See Ricks, Nadine
Ricks, Christopher (Bruce) 1933- CANR-23
Earlier sketches in CA 9-12R, CANR-7
Ricks, David F(rank) 1927- CANR-10
Earlier sketch in CA 21-24R
Ricks, David Trulock 1936- 25-28R
Ricks, Don(ald) M(ax) 1936- 25-28R
Ricks, Nadine 1925- CANR-29
Earlier sketches in CA 77-80, CANR-13
Rickword, (John) Edgell 1898-1982 ......CANR-36
Obituary 106
Earlier sketch in CA 101
See also DLB 20
Rico, Don(ato) 1917-1985 ....CANR-28
Obituary 115
Earlier sketch in CA 81-84
See also SATA 43
Rico, Gabriele Lusser 1937- 110
Ricoeur, Paul 1913- CANR-10
Earlier sketch in CA 61-64
Ricou, Laurence (Rodger) 1944- CANR-25
Earlier sketches in CA 61-64, CANR-8
Riday, George E(mil) 1912- 13-16R
Riddel, Frank S(tephen) 1940- 85-88
Riddel, Joseph N(eill) 1931- CANR-5
Earlier sketch in CA 9-12R
Riddell, Alan 1927- 104
Riddell, J. H. 1832-1906 ....TCLC 40
Ridder, Bernard J. 1913-1983 Obituary 110
Ridder, Joseph B(ernard)
1920-1989 Obituary 127
Ridder, Marie 1925- 73-76
Ridderbos, Herman N(icolaas) 1909- 57-60
Riddle, Donald H(usted) 1921- 9-12R
Riddle, John M(arion) 1937- 45-48
Riddle, Kenneth Wilkinson 1920- 1-4R
Riddle, Maxwell 1907- CANR-3
Earlier sketch in CA 5-8R
Riddle, Thomas Wilkinson
1886-1983 Obituary 110
Riddleberger, Patrick Williams 1915- 21-24R
Riddy, Felicity (Jacqueline) 1940- 128
Ridenour, Fritz 1932- CANR-25
Earlier sketch in CA 108
Ridenour, George M(eyer) 1928- 93-96
Ridenour, Ron 1939- 69-72
Rider, Alice Damon 1895- 69-72
Rider, (Arthur) Fremont
1885-1962 Obituary 89-92
Rider, John R. 1923- 25-28R
Ridge, Antonia (Florence) 9-12R
Obituary 104
See also SATA 7, 27
Ridge, George Ross 1931- 1-4R
Ridge, Julie 1956- 120
Ridge, Lola 1873-1941 ....DLB 54
Ridge, Martin 1923- 121
See also SATA 43
Ridgely, Beverly S(ellman) 1920- CANR-17
Earlier sketch in CA 25-28R
Ridgely, Joseph Vincent 1921- 5-8R
Ridgeway, James Fowler 1936- 106
Ridgeway, Jason
See Marlowe, Stephen
Ridgeway, Marian E(lizabeth) 1913- 33-36R
Ridgeway, Rick 1949- 93-96
Ridgway, Brunilde Sismondo 1929- CANR-1
Earlier sketch in CA 45-48
Ridgway, John M. 1938- 25-28R
Ridgway, Judith 1939- CANR-26
Earlier sketch in CA 109
Ridgway, Judy
See Ridgway, Judith
Ridgway, Ronald S(idney) 1923- 45-48
Ridgway, Whitman H(awley) 1941- 101
Riding, Alan 1943- 122
Riding, Laura
See Jackson, Laura (Riding)
See also CLC 3, 7
Ridle, Julia Brown 1923- 1-4R
Ridler, Anne Barbara 1912- CANR-3
Earlier sketch in CA 5-8R
See also DLB 27
Ridley, Anthony 1933- 107
Ridley, Arnold 1896-1984 Obituary 112
Ridley, B(rian) K(idd) 1931- 104
Ridley, Charles P(rice) 1933- 73-76
Ridley, Jasper (Godwin) 1920- CANR-22
Earlier sketches in CA 13-16R, CANR-6
Ridley, Mark 1956- 133
Ridley, Nat Jr. CANR-26
Earlier sketches in CAP-2, CA 19-20
Ridlon, Marci
See Balterman, Marcia Ridlon
See also SATA 22
Ridout, Albert K(ilburn) 1905- CAP-2
Earlier sketch in CA 19-20
Ridout, Ronald 1916- CANR-20
Earlier sketch in CA 103
Ridpath, Ian (William) 1947- 77-80
Ridruejo, Dionisio 1913(?)-1975 Obituary 57-60
See also DLB 108
Rieber, Alfred J(oseph) 1931- 9-12R
Rieber, R(obert) W(olff) 1932- CANR-3
Earlier sketch in CA 45-48
Riede, David G(eorge) 1951- 131
Riedel, Eunice 1931(?)-1986 Obituary 120
Riedel, Richard Langham 1908-1988 .... CAP-2
Obituary 127
Earlier sketch in CA 29-32
Riedel, Walter E(rwin) 1936- CANR-24
Earlier sketch in CA 45-48
Riedesel, C(lark) Alan 1930- 25-28R
Riedl, John O(rth) 1905- CAP-2
Earlier sketch in CA 21-22
Riedman, Sarah R(egal) 1902- CANR-37
Earlier sketches in CA 1-4R, CANR-1
See also SATA 1
Riefe, Alan 1925- CANR-9
Earlier sketch in CA 61-64
Riefe, Barbara
See Riefe, Alan
Riefenstahl, Berta Helene Amalia 1902- 108
See also Riefenstahl, Leni
Riefenstahl, Leni
See Riefenstahl, Berta Helene Amalia
See also CLC 16
Rieff, Philip 1922- 49-52
Riegel, Robert Edgar 1897- 5-8R
Rieger, James H(enry) 1936- 93-96
Rieger, Shay 1929- 29-32R
Riegert, Eduard Richard 1932- 69-72
Riegert, Ray 1947- 105
Riel, Louis 1844-1885 ....DLB 99
Riely, John (Cabell) 1945- CANR-32
Earlier sketch in CA 113
Riemer, George 1920-1973 ....CAP-2
Obituary 41-44R
Earlier sketch in CA 25-28
Riemer, Neal 1922- 21-24R
Rienits, Rex 1909-1971 ....CAP-1
Obituary 29-32R
Earlier sketch in CA 13-14
Rienow, Leona Train 1903(?)-1983 111
Rienow, Robert 1909-1989 ....CANR-36
Earlier sketch in CA 21-24R
Rienstra, Ellen Walker 1940- 123
Riepe, Dale (Maurice) 1918- 37-40R
Ries, Al 1929- 120
Ries, Estelle H. 1896- 25-28R
Ries, John C(harles) 1930- 13-16R
Ries, Lawrence R(obert) 1940- 65-68
Riese, Walther 1890- 49-52
Rieseberg, Harry E(arl) 1892- 5-8R
Rieselbach, Leroy N(ewman) 1934- CANR-24
Earlier sketches in CA 21-24R, CANR-9
Riesenberg, Felix Jr. 1913-1962 101
See also SATA 23
Riesenberg, Saul H(erbert) 1911- 49-52
Rieser, Dolf 1898-1983 Obituary 109
Riesman, David 1909- CANR-34
Earlier sketch in CA 5-8R
Riesman, Evelyn Thompson 1912- 21-24R
Riess, Claudia 1937- 110
Riess, Oswald George Lorenz 1896- 5-8R
Riess, Steven A(llan) 1947- 112
Riess, Walter 1925- 17-20R
Riessen, Martin Clare 1941- 41-44R
Riessman, Frank 1924- CANR-6
Earlier sketch in CA 1-4R
Riesterer, Berthold P(hillip) 1935- 41-44R
Rieth, Marian
See Amft, M(arian) J(anet)
Rietz, Sandra A. 1943- 123
Rieu, E(mile) V(ictor) 1887-1972 ....CANR-15
Obituary 103
Earlier sketch in CA 1-4R
See also SATA 26, 46
Riewald, J(acobus) G(erhardus)
1910- CANR-21
Earlier sketches in CA 57-60, CANR-6
Rifaat, Alifa
See Rifaat, Fatma Abdallah
Rifaat, Fatma Abdallah 1930- 123
Rifbjerg, Klaus (Thorvald) 1931- 137
Brief entry 124
Rife, J(ohn) Merle 1895- 61-64
Rife, Joanne 1932- 110
Rife, Rosemary
See Nusbaum, Rosemary
Riffaterre, Michael 1924- .... DLB 67
Riffe, Ernest
See Bergman, (Ernst) Ingmar
Riffel, Herman H(arold) 1916- 112
Rifkin, Jeremy 1945- 129
Brief entry 121
Rifkin, Paul 1942- 127
Rifkin, Shepard 1918- CANR-1
Earlier sketch in CA 1-4R
Rifkind, Carole 1935- 85-88
Rifkind, Simon H(irsch) 1901- 109
Rift, Valerie
See Bartlett, Marie (Swan)
Riga, Frank P(eter) 1936- 89-92
Riga, Peter J(ohn) 1933- CANR-37
Earlier sketch in CA 5-8R
Rigault, Andre 1922- 45-48
Rigby, Andrew 1944- 61-64
Rigby, Ida Katherine 1944- CANR-10
Earlier sketch in CA 65-68
Rigby, Paul H(erbert) 1924- 17-20R
Rigby, T(homas) H(enry Richard)
1925- CANR-36
Earlier sketches in CA 17-20R, CANR-10
Rigden, John S. 1934- 127
Rigdon, Raymond M. 1919- 29-32R
Rigdon, Walter 1930- 13-16R
Rigelhof, T(errance) F(rederick) 1944- 112
Rigg, A(rthur) G(eorge) 1937- 37-40R
Rigg, H(enry Hemmingway) K(ilburn)
1911-1980 ....29-32R
Obituary 93-96
Rigg, John Linton 1894- 5-8R
Rigg, Robinson P(eter) 1918- 33-36R
Riggan, (John) Rob(inson) 1943- 115
Riggan, William (Edward Jr.) 1946- 103
Riggio, Thomas P(asquale) 1943- 109
Riggs, David (Ramsey) 1941- 133
Riggs, Dionis Coffin 1898- CAP-2
Earlier sketch in CA 29-32
Riggs, Fred(erick) W(arren) 1917- CANR-16
Earlier sketch in CA 25-28R
Riggs, James (Lear) 1929- 33-36R
Riggs, John R(aymond) 1945- CANR-37
Earlier sketch in CA 115
Riggs, Robert E. 1927- CANR-8
Earlier sketch in CA 13-16R
Riggs, Sidney Noyes 1892-1975 ....1-4R
Obituary 103
See also SATA 28
Riggs, William (George) 1938- 61-64
Righter, Carroll (Burch) 1900-1988 93-96
Obituary 125
Righter, James H(aslam)
1916-1984 Obituary 113
Righter, Robert Willms 1933- 108
Right Honourable Lord Denning
See Denning, Alfred Thompson
Rightmire, G. Philip 1942- 135
Rigoni, Orlando (Joseph) 1897- CANR-11
Earlier sketch in CA 13-16R
Rigsby, Howard 1909- 9-12R
Rigutti, Mario 1926- 131
Riha, Thomas 1929- 9-12R
Riis, Jacob A(ugust) 1849-1914 Brief entry 113
See also DLB 23
Riis, Sharon 1947- 136
Riker, John H. 1943- 111
Riker, Leigh 1941- 119
Riker, Tom L. 1936- 104
Riker, William H(arrison) 1920- CANR-24
Earlier sketch in CA 1-4R
Rikhoff, James C. 1931- 13-16R
Rikhoff, Jean 1928- 61-64
See also SATA 9
Rikhye, Indar Jit 1920- CANR-17
Earlier sketch in CA 93-96
Rikki
See Ducornet, Erica
Rikon, Irving 1931- 29-32R
Riley, Barry 1942- 136
Riley, Carroll L(averne) 1923- CANR-10
Earlier sketch in CA 25-28R
Riley, Clara (Mae Deatherage) 1931- 25-28R
Riley, Dan 1946- 135
Riley, Dick 1946- 101
Riley, E(dward) C(alverley) 1923- 9-12R
Riley, G. Micheal 1934- 45-48
Riley, Glenda 1938- CANR-23
Earlier sketch in CA 106
Riley, James C. 1943- 133
Riley, James F(rederic) 1912-1985 ....29-32R
Obituary 134
Riley, James Whitcomb 1849-1916 137
Brief entry 118
See also MAICYA
See also SATA 17
Riley, Jeannie C(arolyn Stepehnson) 1945- 129
Riley, Jocelyn (Carol) 1949- CANR-39
Earlier sketch in CA 115
See also SATA 50, 60
Riley, John 1937-1978 ....DLB 40
Riley, Judith (Astria) Merkle 1942- CANR-35
Earlier sketch in CA 105
See also Merkle, Judith A(stria)
Riley, Lawrence 1897(?)-1975 Obituary 61-64
Riley, Lee
See Vare, Ethlie Ann
Riley, Madeleine 1933- 25-28R
Riley, Matilda White 1911- 132
Brief entry 114
Riley, Miles O'Brien 1937- CANR-21
Earlier sketch in CA 104
Riley, (Thomas) Nord 1914- 13-16R
Riley, R. David 1944(?)-1983 Obituary 111
Riley, (Hugh) Ridge(ly Jr.) 1907-1976 101
Riley, Roy Jr. 1943(?)-1977 Obituary 73-76
Riley, Sam G. 1939- 136
Riley, Sandra 1938- 104
Riley, Tex
See Creasey, John
Riley, Thomas J. 1901(?)-1977 Obituary 73-76
Riley, Tim 1960- 129
Riley-Smith, Jonathan (Simon Christopher)
1938- 21-24R
Riling, Raymond L. J.
1896(?)-1974 Obituary 53-56
Rilke, Rainer Maria 1875-1926 132
Brief entry 104
See also DLB 81
See also MTCW
See also PC 2
See also TCLC 1, 6, 19
Rilla, Wolf 1925- 49-52
Rils
See Bohr, R(ussell) L(eRoi)
Rima, I(ngrid) H(ahne) 1925- 21-24R
Rimanoczy, Richard Stanton 1902- 73-76
Rimbaud, (Jean Nicolas) Arthur
1854-1891 ....PC 3
See also WLC
Rimberg, John 1929- 57-60
Rimel, Duane (Weldon) 1915- 29-32R
Rimer, Barbara K. 1949- 136
Rimer, J. Thomas 130
Rimington, Critchell 1907-1976 Obituary 61-64
Rimland, Bernard 1928- CANR-6
Earlier sketch in CA 13-16R
Rimland, Ingrid 1936- 61-64
Rimlinger, Gaston V. 1926- 37-40R
Rimmer, C(harles) Brandon 1918- CANR-12
Earlier sketch in CA 61-64
Rimmer, Douglas 1927- 111
Rimmer, Robert H(enry) 1917- CANR-20
Earlier sketches in CA 9-12R, CANR-4
See also CAAS 10
Rimmer, W. J.
See Rowland, D(onald) S(ydney)
Rimmington, Gerald T(horneycroft)
1930- 17-20R
Rinaldi, Ann 1934- 111
See also SATA 50, 51
Rinaldi, Nicholas M. 1934- CANR-22
Earlier sketch in CA 104
Rinaldini, Angiolo
See Battisti, Eugenio
Rinard, Judith E(llen) 1947- 97-100
See also SATA 44
Rinchen, Byambyn
1905(?)-1977 Obituary 69-72
Rinder, Walter (Murray) 1934- CANR-11
Earlier sketch in CA 69-72
Rindfleisch, Norval (William) 1930- 65-68
Rinehart, Frederick Roberts
1903(?)-1981 Obituary 104
Rinehart, Mary Roberts
1876-1958 Brief entry 108
Rinehart, Stanley Marshall Jr.
1897-1969 Obituary 29-32R
Ring, Alfred A. 1905- 29-32R
Ring, Daniel F(rank) 1945- 113
Ring, Douglas
See Prather, Richard S(cott)
Ring, Elizabeth 1912- 103
Ring, Malvin E. 1919- 120
Ring, Raymond H. 1949- 128
Ringdalh, Mark
See Longyear, Barry Brookes
Ringe, Donald A(rthur) 1923- 1-4R
Ringenbach, Paul T(homas) 1936- CANR-25
Earlier sketch in CA 45-48
Ringer, Alexander L(othar) 1921- CANR-24
Earlier sketch in CA 45-48
Ringer, Barbara Alice 1925- 9-12R
Ringer, Fritz (Franz) K(laus) 1934- 73-76
Ringer, Robert J. 81-84
Ringgold, Faith 1930- ....SATA 71
Ringgold, Gene 1918- 25-28R
Ringgren, (Karl Vilhelm) Helmer 1917- CANR-3
Earlier sketch in CA 5-8R
Ringi, Kjell (Arne Soerensen) 1939- CANR-1
Earlier sketch in CA 45-48
See also SATA 12
Ringkamp, Jonathan 1929-1986 Obituary 120
Ringler, William A(ndrew) Jr.
1912-1987(?) 5-8R
Obituary 121
Ringmaster, The
See Mencken, H(enry) L(ouis)
Ringo, Johnny
See Keevill, Henry J(ohn)
Ringold, Clay
See Hogan, (Robert) Ray
Ringold, May Spencer 1914- 21-24R
Ringrose, David R. 1938- 53-56
Ringuet 1895-1960 ....DLB 68
Ringwald, Donald C(harles)
1917-1987 ....CANR-36
Obituary 122
Earlier sketch in CA 21-24R
Ringwood, Gwen(dolyn Margaret) Pharis
1910-1984 Obituary 112
See also CLC 48
See also DLB 88
Rinhart, Floyd (Lincoln) 1915- CANR-10
Earlier sketch in CA 25-28R
Rinhart, Marion (Hutchinson) 1916- CANR-10
Earlier sketch in CA 25-28R
Rink, Oliver A(lbert) 1947- 125

Rinker, Rosalind Beatrice 1906- CANR-5
Earlier sketch in CA 5-8R
Rinkoff, Barbara Jean (Rich) 1923-1975 .... CAP-2
Obituary 57-60
Earlier sketch in CA 19-20
See also SATA 4, 27
Rinpoche
See Chogyam Trungpa
Rinser, Luise 1911- .... DLB 69
Rintels, David 1939- 73-76
Rinvolucri, Mario (Francesco Giuseppe)
1940- CANR-26
Earlier sketches in CA 21-24R, CANR-10
Rinvolucri, Mina Josephine Moore
See Moore-Rinvolucri, Mina Josephine
Rinzema, Jakob 1931- 102
Rinzler, Alan 1938- CANR-12
Earlier sketch in CA 21-24R
Rinzler, Carol Ann 1937- 135
Rinzler, Carol Eisen (Gene) 1941-1990 49-52
Obituary 133
Rio, Michel ....CLC 43
Riols, Noreen 1926- 124
Riopelle, Arthur J. 1920- 37-40R
Riordan, J. W.
See Feist, Gene
Riordan, James 1936- CANR-11
Earlier sketch in CA 69-72
See also SATA 28
Riordan, James 1949- 111
Riordan, Mary Marguerite 1931- 106
Riordan, Michael 1946- CANR-37
Earlier sketch in CA 106
Riordon, Michael 1944- 133
Rios, Alberto (Alvaro) 1952- CANR-34
Earlier sketch in CA 113
Rios, Francisco Giner de los
See Giner de los Rios, Francisco
Rios, Isabella
See Lopez, Diana
Rios, Tere
See Versace, Marie Teresa Rios
Riotte, Louise 1909- 57-60
Riotto, Guy Michael 1943- 73-76
Riou, Roger 1909- 61-64
Ripa, Karol 1895-1983 Obituary 109
Ripley, Alexandra 1934- CANR-38
Earlier sketch in CA 119
Ripley, Arthur 1895-1961 .... DLB 44
Ripley, (Sidney) Dillon 1913- 57-60
Ripley, Elizabeth Blake 1906-1969 ....CANR-3
Earlier sketch in CA 1-4R
See also SATA 5
Ripley, Francis Joseph 1912- CANR-39
Earlier sketches in CA 1-4R, CANR-3, 18
Ripley, George 1802-1880 ....DLB 1, 64, 73
Ripley, Jack
See Wainwright, John
Ripley, Michael David 1952- 130
Ripley, Mike
See Ripley, Michael David
Ripley, Randall B(utler) 1938- CANR-19
Earlier sketches in CA 53-56, CANR-5
Ripley, Sheldon N(ichols) 1925- 5-8R
Ripley, Stephens 1901(?)-1984 Obituary 111
Ripley, Theresa M(argaret) 1944- 85-88
Ripley, (William Young) Warren 1921- CANR-33
Earlier sketches in CA 33-36R, CANR-15
Rippa, S(ol) Alexander 1925- 53-56
Ripper, Charles L(ewis) 1929- CANR-1
Earlier sketch in CA 1-4R
See also SATA 3
Ripper, Chuck
See Ripper, Charles L(ewis)
Ripperger, Helmut Lothar
1897-1974 Obituary 53-56
Ripperger, Henrietta
See Hawley, Henrietta Ripperger
Rippey, Mari 1939- 112
Rippey, Robert (Max) 1926- 45-48
Ripple, Paula 112
Ripple, Richard E. 1931- CANR-22
Earlier sketch in CA 33-36R
Rippley, La Vern J. 1935- 33-36R
Rippon, Angela 1944- 126
Rippon, Marion E(dith) 1921- CANR-1
Earlier sketch in CA 49-52
Rippy, Frances (Marguerite) Mayhew
1929- 89-92
Rips, Ervine M(ilton) 1921- 101
Rips, Geoffrey 1950- 108
Rips, Rae Elizabeth 1914-1970 Obituary 104
Riq
See Atwater, Richard (Tupper)
Riquelme, John Paul 1946- 119
Risatti, Howard A(nthony) 1943- 133
Rischin, Moses 1925- CANR-3
Earlier sketch in CA 9-12R
Risebero, Bill 1938- 130
Riseley, Jerry B(urr Jr.) 1920- CANR-13
Earlier sketch in CA 21-24R
Riseling, John J. W.
1888(?)-1977 Obituary 73-76
Risenhoover, Morris 1940- 65-68
Riser, Wayne H. 1909- CAP-1
Earlier sketch in CA 13-14
Risjord, Norman K. 1931- CANR-22
Earlier sketches in CA 17-20R, CANR-7
Riskin, Robert 1897-1955 .... DLB 26
Riskind, Mary 1944- CANR-26
Earlier sketch in CA 108
See also SATA 60
Riss, Richard 1952- 81-84
Risse, Heinz 1898- .... DLB 69
Rissi, Mathias 1920- 45-48
Rissman, Art
See Sussman, Susan
Rissman, Susan
See Sussman, Susan
Rissover, Fredric 1940- 33-36R
Rist, John M(ichael) 1936- CANR-18
Earlier sketch in CA 101
Rist, Ray C(harles) 1944- CANR-3
Earlier sketch in CA 49-52
Ristaino, Marcia R. 1939- 127
Rist Arnold, Elisabeth 1950- 65-68
Riste, Olav 1933- CANR-12
Earlier sketch in CA 29-32R
Ristic, Dragisha N. 1909- CAP-2
Earlier sketch in CA 21-22
Ristow, Walter W(illiam) 1908- 17-20R
Ritcheson, Charles R(ay) 1925- Brief entry 112
Ritchey, John A(rthur) 1919- 21-24R
Ritchie, Andrew Carnduff
1907-1978 Obituary 81-84
Ritchie, (John) Andrew 1943- 85-88
Ritchie, Anna Cora (Ogden) Mowatt
1819-1870 .... DLB 3
Ritchie, Anne Thackeray 1837-1919 .... DLB 18
Ritchie, Barbara Gibbons 73-76
See also SATA 14
Ritchie, Bill
See Edgar, Frank Terrell Rhoades
Ritchie, C(icero) T(heodore) 1914- 9-12R
Ritchie, Donald A(rthur) 1945- 122
Brief entry 106
Ritchie, Donald D(irk) 1914- 112
Ritchie, Edwin 1921- CANR-35
Earlier sketch in CA 29-32R
Ritchie, Elisavietta (Yurievna Artamonoff)
....CANR-2
Earlier sketch in CA 49-52
Ritchie, G(eorge) Stephen 1914- 13-16R
Ritchie, Jack
See Reitci, John G(eorge)
Ritchie, James McPherson 1927- 25-28R
Ritchie, James T. R. 1908- CAP-2
Earlier sketch in CA 19-20
Ritchie, John C(ollins) 1927- 49-52
Ritchie, M(iller) A(lfred) F(ranklin) 1909- CAP-2
Earlier sketch in CA 29-32
Ritchie, Paul 1923- 21-24R
Ritchie, Rita
See Reitci, Rita Krohne
Ritchie, Ruth 1900- CANR-2
Earlier sketch in CA 1-4R
Ritchie, Simon
See Fodden, Simon R.
Ritchie, Thomas 1778-1854 .... DLB 43
Ritchie, (Harry) Ward 1905- CANR-22
Earlier sketches in CA 57-60, CANR-7
Ritchie, William A(ugustus) 1903- CANR-24
Earlier sketch in CA 45-48
Ritchie-Calder, Peter Ritchie
1906-1982 ....CANR-4
Obituary 105
Earlier sketch in CA 1-4R
Ritner, Peter Vaughn 1927(?)-1976 77-80
Obituary 69-72
Ritschl, Dietrich 1929- CANR-24
Earlier sketches in CA 21-24R, CANR-9
Ritsos, Giannes
See Ritsos, Yannis
Ritsos, Yannis 1909-1990 ....CANR-39
Obituary 133
Earlier sketch in CA 77-80
See also CLC 6, 13, 31
See also MTCW
Rittenhouse, Mignon 1904- 41-44R
Ritter, Alan 1937- 117
Brief entry 113
Ritter, Ed 1917- 17-20R
Ritter, Erika 1948(?)- .... CLC 52
Ritter, Felix
See Kruess, James
Ritter, Gerhard 1888-1967 Obituary 111
Ritter, Henry Jr. 1920- 93-96
Ritter, Jess(e P. Jr.) 1930- 37-40R
Ritter, Lawrence S(tanley) 1922- CANR-22
Earlier sketch in CA 21-24R
See also SATA 58
Ritter, Naomi 1937- 138
Ritterbush, Philip C. 1936- CANR-6
Earlier sketch in CA 9-12R
Ritts, Paul 1920(?)-1980 Obituary 102
See also SATA 25
Ritvala, M.
See Waltari, Mika (Toimi)
Ritvo, Harriet 1946- 124
Ritz, Charles 1891-1976 Obituary 65-68
Ritz, David 1943- 85-88
Ritz, Jean-Georges 1906- 5-8R
Ritz, Joseph P. 1929- 21-24R
Ritzenthaler, Pat 1914- 25-28R
Ritzer, George 1940- CANR-20
Earlier sketches in CA 53-56, CANR-5
Rivard, Adjutor 1868-1945 .... DLB 92
Rivas, Gilberto Lopez y
See Lopez Y Rivas, Gilberto
Rive, Richard (Moore) 1931-1989 ....CANR-27
Obituary 128
Earlier sketch in CA 13-16R
See also BW
Rivel, Isade
See Cuevas, Clara
Rivenburgh, Viola K(leinke) 1897- 17-20R
Rivera, Feliciano (Moreno) 1932- CANR-24
Earlier sketch in CA 45-48
Rivera, Geraldo (Miguel) 1943- CANR-32
Earlier sketch in CA 108
See also HW
See also SATA 28, 54
Rivera, Jose Eustasio 1889-1928 ....HW
See also TCLC 35
Rivera, Tomas 1935-1984 ....CANR-32
Earlier sketch in CA 49-52
See also DLB 82
See also HW
Rivere, Alec
See Nuetzel, Charles (Alexander)
Rivero, Eliana Suarez 1942- 41-44R
Rivers, Caryl 1937- CANR-22
Earlier sketches in CA 49-52, CANR-4
Rivers, Clarence Joseph 1931- 77-80
Rivers, Conrad Kent 1933-1968 85-88
See also BW
See also CLC 1
See also DLB 41
Rivers, Elfrida
See Bradley, Marion Zimmer
Rivers, Elias L(ynch) 1924- 17-20R
Rivers, Francine (Sandra) 1947- 130
Rivers, Joan
See Molinsky, Joan Sandra
Rivers, Julian Alfred Pitt
See Pitt-Rivers, Julian Alfred
Rivers, Larry 1923- 124
Brief entry 117
Rivers, Patrick 1920- 131
Rivers, William L. 1925- CANR-7
Earlier sketch in CA 17-20R
Rivers-Coffey, Rachel 1943- 73-76
Riverside, John
See Heinlein, Robert A(nson)
Rives, Leigh
See Seward, William W(ard) Jr.
Rives, Stanley G(ene) 1930- CANR-11
Earlier sketch in CA 21-24R
Rives, William T. 1911(?)-1983 Obituary 111
Rivet, A(lbert) L(ionel) F(rederick)
1915- CANR-24
Earlier sketches in CA 21-24R, CANR-9
Rivett, Carol
See Rivett, Edith Caroline
Rivett, Edith Caroline
1894-1958 Brief entry 110
Rivett, Rohan (Deakin) 1917-1977 ....25-28R
Obituary 135
Rivett-Carnac, Charles Edward 1901- CAP-2
Earlier sketch in CA 19-20
Rivette, Marc 1916- 5-8R
Riviere, Bill
See Riviere, William Alexander
Riviere, Claude 1932- 102
Riviere, Peter Gerard 1934- 103
Riviere, William Alexander 1916- CANR-8
Earlier sketch in CA 5-8R
Rivington, James 1724(?)-1802 .... DLB 43
Rivkin, Allen (Erwin) 1903-1990 ....CANR-28
Obituary 130
Earlier sketches in CA 65-68, CANR-11
See also DLB 26
Rivkin, Ann 1920- 112
See also SATA 41
Rivkin, Arnold 1919-1968 ....CANR-3
Earlier sketch in CA 1-4R
Rivkin, Ellis 1918- 33-36R
Rivlin, Alice M(itchell) 1931- 33-36R
Rivlin, Harry N. 1904- 17-20R
Rivoire, Jean 1929- CANR-21
Earlier sketches in CA 9-12R, CANR-5
Rivoli, Mario 1943-
See Koutoukas, H. M.
See also SATA 10
Rix, Donna
See Rowland, D(onald) S(ydney)
Rizkalla, John 1935- 129
Rizzo, Betty 1926- 111
Rizzo, Mario 1948- 124
Rizzoli, Andrea 1914-1983 Obituary 109
Rizzoli, Angelo 1889-1970 Obituary 104
Rizzuto, Anthony 1937- 106
Rizzuto, James J(oseph) 1939- 107
Rizzuto, Jim
See Rizzuto, James J(oseph)
Roa (y Garcia), Raul 1908-1982 Obituary 107
Roa Bastos, Augusto (Antonio) 1917- 131
See also CLC 45
See also DLB 113
See also HW
Roach, Helen P(auline) 1903- CAP-1
Earlier sketch in CA 11-12
Roach, Hildred 1937- 57-60
Roach, Jack L. 1925- Brief entry 109
Roach, James P. 1907-1978 Obituary 77-80
Roach, Joyce Gibson 1935- CANR-18
Earlier sketch in CA 101
Roach, Marilynne K(athleen) 1946- CANR-12
Earlier sketch in CA 57-60
See also SATA 9
Roach, Marion 1956- 120
Roach, Mary Ellen 1921- 17-20R
Roach, Portia
See Takakjian, Portia
Roadarmel, Gordon 1932-1972 Obituary 104
Roadarmel, Paul 1942- 93-96
Roaden, Arliss L. 1930- 37-40R
Roadstrum, William H(enry) 1915- 25-28R
Roalfe, William R(obert) 1896- 93-96
Roam, Pearl (Sovern) 1920- 1-4R
Roark, Albert E(dward) 1933- 85-88
Roark, Dallas M(organ) 1931- 37-40R
Roark, Garland 1904-1985 ....CANR-1
Obituary 115
Earlier sketch in CA 1-4R
Roark, James L. 1941- CANR-19
Earlier sketch in CA 85-88
Roazen, Paul 1936- 25-28R
Roback, A(braham) A(aron) 1890-1965 ....5-8R
Robacker, Earl Francis 1904- CANR-37
Earlier sketch in CA 53-56
Robana, Abderrahman 1938- 65-68
Robard, Jackson
See Wallmann, Jeffrey M(iner)
Robards, Karen 1954- 122
Robards, Sherman M(arshall) 1939- CANR-37
Earlier sketch in CA 61-64
Robards, Terry
See Robards, Sherman M(arshall)
Robathan, Dorothy M(ae) 1898- 41-44R
Robb, Brian 1913-1979 113
Robb, David M(etheny)
1903-1990 Obituary 131
Brief entry 113
See also AITN 1
Robb, (George) Douglas
1899-1974 Obituary 114
Robb, Frank Thomson 1908- 57-60
Robb, Graham 1958- 136
Robb, Inez (Callaway) 1901(?)-1979 97-100
Obituary 85-88
Robb, J(ohn) Wesley 1919- 5-8R
Robb, James H(arding) 1920- 9-12R
Robb, James Willis 1918- 41-44R
Robb, Mary K(unkle) 1908- CAP-2
Earlier sketch in CA 19-20
Robb, Nesca A(deline) 1905- 9-12R
Robbe-Grillet, Alain 1922- CANR-33
Earlier sketch in CA 9-12R
See also CLC 1, 2, 4, 6, 8, 10, 14, 43
See also DLB 83
See also MTCW
Robben, John 1930- 93-96
Robbert, Louise Buenger 1925- 41-44R
Robbin, (Jodi) Luna 1936- 103
Robbins, Anthony J. 1960- 126
Robbins, Brother Gerald 1940- 13-16R
Robbins, Caroline 1903- 107
Robbins, Ceila Dame 1943- 118
Robbins, Daniel 1933- CANR-3
Earlier sketch in CA 45-48
Robbins, Frank 1917- 109
See also SATA 32, 42
Robbins, Glaydon Donaldson 1908- 5-8R
Robbins, Harold 1916- CANR-26
Earlier sketch in CA 73-76
See also CLC 5
See also MTCW
Robbins, Henry 1928(?)-1979 Obituary 89-92
Robbins, Horace 1909-1982 Obituary 107
Robbins, Ira A(braham) 1954- 123
Robbins, J(ohn) Albert 1914- 17-20R
Robbins, Jane (Borsch) 1939- CANR-38
Robbins, Jane Marla 1943- 134
Robbins, June 61-64
Robbins, Kay
See Hooper, Kay
Robbins, Keith (Gilbert) 1940- CANR-28
Earlier sketches in CA 25-28R, CANR-11
Robbins, Ken .... SATA 53
Robbins, Kenneth 1944- 128
Robbins, Lionel (Charles)
1898-1984 Obituary 112
Robbins, Martin 1931- CANR-12
Earlier sketch in CA 29-32R
Robbins, Marty
See Robinson, Martin David
Robbins, Matthew 129
Brief entry 110
Robbins, Mildred Brown CAP-2
Earlier sketch in CA 33-36
Robbins, Millie
See Robbins, Mildred Brown
Robbins, Paul R(ichard) 1930- CANR-35
Earlier sketch in CA 114
Robbins, Raleigh
See Hamilton, Charles (Harold St. John)
Robbins, Richard G. Jr. 1939- 53-56
Robbins, Rossell Hope 1912-1990 ....CANR-2
Obituary 131
Earlier sketch in CA 45-48
Robbins, Roy M(arvin) 1904-1981 ....CANR-36
Earlier sketch in CA 65-68
Robbins, Ruth 1917(?)- 73-76
See also SATA 14
Robbins, S(allie) A(nn) 1940- 21-24R
Robbins, Sam
See Potter, Carole A.
Robbins, Thomas Eugene 1936- CANR-29
Earlier sketch in CA 81-84
See also Robbins, Tom
See also MTCW
Robbins, Tom
See Robbins, Thomas Eugene
See also BEST 90:3
See also CLC 9, 32, 64
See also DLBY 80
Robbins, Tony
See Pashko, Stanley
Robbins, Trina 1938- 128
See also CLC 21
Robbins, Vesta O(rdelia) 1891- 53-56
Robbins, Wayne
See Cox, William R(obert)
Robbins-Carter, Jane
See Robbins, Jane (Borsch)
Robe, Stanley L(inn) 1915- CANR-6
Earlier sketch in CA 5-8R
Robeck, Mildred C(oen) 1915- 57-60
Roberge, Earl 1918- 85-88
Roberson, (Charles) Ed(win) 1939- 77-80
Roberson, Jennifer 1953- 117
Roberson, John R(oyster) 1930- 129
See also SATA 53
Roberson, Marie
See Hamm, Marie Roberson
Roberson, Ricky James 1956- 101
Roberson, William H(oward) 1952- 110

Robert, Adrian
See St. John, Nicole
Robert, Marc 1927- 114
Robert, Marika Barna 9-12R
Robert, Paul A.
See Roubiczek, Paul (Anton)
Robert, Paul 1911(?)-1980 Obituary 101
Robertiello, Richard C. 1923- CANR-3
Earlier sketch in CA 9-12R
Roberto, Brother
See Mueller, Gerald F(rancis)
Roberts, (Edward) Adam 1940- CANR-9
Earlier sketch in CA 21-24R
Roberts, Allen 1914- 29-32R
Roberts, Andrew 1963- 135
Roberts, Anthony
See Watney, John B(asil)
Roberts, Archibald Edward 1915- CANR-6
Earlier sketch in CA 57-60
Roberts, Arthur O. 1923- 25-28R
Roberts, Arthur Sydney 1905(?)-1978 85-88
Obituary 81-84
Roberts, Ben
See Eisenberg, Benjamin
Roberts, Benjamin Charles 1917- 102
Roberts, Bill 1914(?)-1978 Obituary 81-84
Roberts, Bleddyn J(ones) 1906- CAP-1
Earlier sketch in CA 13-14
Roberts, Brian 1930- CANR-12
Earlier sketch in CA 29-32R
Roberts, Bruce (Stuart) 1930- CANR-6
Earlier sketch in CA 9-12R
See also SATA 39, 47
Roberts, C(atherine) 1917- 21-24R
Roberts, Carey 1935- 106
Roberts, Carlos A.
See Avila, Charles
Roberts, Carol A. 1933- 37-40R
Roberts, Cecil (Edric Mornington)
1892-1976 ....CAP-2
Obituary 69-72
Earlier sketch in CA 29-32
Roberts, Chalmers M(cGeagh) 1910- 41-44R
Roberts, Charles G(eorge) D(ouglas)
1860-1943 Brief entry 105
See also DLB 92
See also SATA 29
See also TCLC 8
Roberts, Charles Wesley 1916-1992 ....17-20R
Obituary 136
Roberts, (Ray) Clayton 1923- 21-24R
Roberts, Clete 1910(?)-1984 Obituary 113
Roberts, Colette Jacqueline
1910-1971 Obituary 115
Roberts, Colin H(enderson) 1909-1990 132
Roberts, Dan
See Ross, W(illiam) E(dward) D(aniel)
Roberts, Daniel (Frank) 1922- CANR-6
Earlier sketch in CA 9-12R
Roberts, David
See Cox, John Roberts
Roberts, David Arthur 1924-1987 134
Obituary 122
Roberts, David D(ion) 1943- 101
Roberts, David S(tuart) 1943- 33-36R
Roberts, Dell
See Fendell, Bob
Roberts, Dennis W(ayne) 1947- 109
Roberts, Denys Kilham
1904(?)-1976 Obituary 65-68
Roberts, Denys (Tudor Emil) 1923- CAP-1
Earlier sketch in CA 9-10
Roberts, Derrell C(layton) 1927- 29-32R
Roberts, Donald Alfred
1897-1978 Obituary 77-80
Roberts, Donald Frank Jr. 1939- 107
Roberts, Doreen 1922- 108
Roberts, Dorothy James 1903-1990 ....CAP-1
Obituary 131
Earlier sketch in CA 13-14
Roberts, Dorothy 1906- ....DLB 88
Roberts, Edgar V. 1928- 21-24R
Roberts, Edward B(aer) 1935- CANR-9
Earlier sketch in CA 21-24R
Roberts, Edward Barry 1900-1972 ....CAP-2
Earlier sketch in CA 19-20
Roberts, Edward Dryhurst
1904-1989 Obituary 129
Roberts, Edwin A(lbert) Jr. 1932- 21-24R
Roberts, Elizabeth H. 1913- 61-64
Roberts, Elizabeth Madox
1886-1941 Brief entry 111
See also DLB 9, 54, 102
See also SATA 27, 33
Roberts, Elizabeth (Allan) Mauchline
1936- Brief entry 114
Roberts, Ellen Elizabeth Mayhew
1946- CANR-26
Earlier sketch in CA 108
Roberts, Elliott B. 1899-1988 ....1-4R
Obituary 126
Roberts, Eric 1914- 5-8R
Roberts, Estelle (Wills) 1889-1970 Obituary 112
Roberts, Eugene (L. Jr.) 1932- 97-100
Roberts, Evelyn Lutman 1917- 65-68
Roberts, F(rederick) David 1923- 5-8R
Roberts, Florence Bright 1941- 65-68
Roberts, Frances C(abaniss) 1916- 9-12R
Roberts, Francis Warren 1916- 13-16R
Roberts, Geoffrey R(ansford) 1924- 101
Roberts, Grant
See Wallmann, Jeffrey M(iner)
Roberts, Harold S(elig) 1911-1970 ....CAP-2
Earlier sketch in CA 23-24
Roberts, Harold 1896(?)-1982 Obituary 108
Roberts, Henry L(ithgow)
1916-1972 Obituary 37-40R
Roberts, Hortense Roberta 89-92
Roberts, Howard R(adclyffe) 1906- 109
Roberts, I.
See Roberts, Irene
Roberts, I(olo) F(rancis) 1925- 29-32R
Roberts, I. M.
See Roberts, Irene
Roberts, Irene 1925- CANR-21
Earlier sketches in CA 13-16R, CANR-6
Roberts, Ivor
See Roberts, Irene
Roberts, J(ohn) A(lexander) Fraser
1899-1987 Obituary 121
Roberts, J(ohn) Kimberley 1935- 117
Roberts, J. R.
See Randisi, Robert J(oseph)
Roberts, James Deotis 1927- CANR-15
Earlier sketch in CA 33-36R
Roberts, James Hall
See Duncan, Robert L(ipscomb)
Roberts, Jane
See Butts, Jane Roberts
Roberts, Janet Louise 1925- CANR-13
Earlier sketch in CA 61-64
Roberts, Jason
See Bock, Fred
Roberts, Jeanne Addison 89-92
Roberts, Jim
See Bates, Barbara S(nedeker)
Roberts, Joan Ila 1935- 29-32R
Roberts, Joe
See Saltzman, Joseph
Roberts, John
See Bingley, David Ernest
Roberts, John G(aither) 1913- 49-52
See also SATA 27
Roberts, John M(ilton) 1916- 37-40R
Roberts, John M(orris) 1928- CANR-16
Earlier sketch in CA 85-88
Roberts, John R. 1934- CANR-12
Earlier sketch in CA 33-36R
Roberts, John Storm 1936- CANR-12
Earlier sketch in CA 25-28R
Roberts, Joseph B(oxley) Jr. 1918- 41-44R
Roberts, Julian
See Bardens, Dennis (Conrad)
Roberts, K.
See Lake, Kenneth R(obert)
Roberts, Kate 1891-1985 107
Obituary 116
See also CLC 15
Roberts, Keith (John Kingston) 1935- 25-28R
See also CLC 14
Roberts, Keith 1937(?)-1979 Obituary 85-88
Roberts, Ken
See Lake, Kenneth R(obert)
Roberts, Kenneth H(arris) 1930- 33-36R
Roberts, Kenneth (Lewis)
1885-1957 Brief entry 109
See also DLB 9
See also TCLC 23
Roberts, Kevin E(rnest) A(lbert) 1940- 113
Roberts, Lee
See Martin, Robert (Lee)
Roberts, Len
See Roberts, Leonard
Roberts, Leonard W(ard) 1912-1983 ....CANR-28
Earlier sketch in CA 33-36R
Roberts, Leonard 1947- CANR-32
Earlier sketch in CA 113
Roberts, Les 1937- 128
Roberts, Leslie 1896-1980 103
Roberts, Lionel
See Fanthorpe, R(obert) Lionel
Roberts, Lisa
See Turner, Robert (Harry)
Roberts, MacLennan
See Terrall, Robert
Roberts, Marguerite 1905(?)-1989 Obituary 128
Roberts, Mary D(uffy) 1925- 1-4R
Roberts, Mervin F(rancis) 1922- CANR-24
Earlier sketches in CA 65-68, CANR-9
Roberts, Michael 1945- 69-72
Roberts, Michele (B.) 1949- 115
See also CLC 48
Roberts, Myron 1923- CANR-31
Earlier sketch in CA 29-32R
Roberts, Nancy Correll 1924- CANR-6
Earlier sketch in CA 9-12R
See also SATA 28, 52
Roberts, Nora 1950- 123
Roberts, Oral 1918- 41-44R
Roberts, (Thomas) Patrick 1920- 61-64
Roberts, Paul Craig 1939- CANR-22
Earlier sketch in CA 33-36R
Roberts, Paul McHenry 1917-1967 ....1-4R
Obituary 103
Roberts, Percival R(udolph) III 1935- 41-44R
Roberts, Philip Davies 1938- CANR-26
Earlier sketch in CA 109
Roberts, Phyllis Barzillay 1932- 41-44R
Roberts, Rachel 1927-1980 Obituary 115
Roberts, Rand
See Parham, Robert Randall
Roberts, Randy (W.) 1951- 134
Roberts, Richard J(erome) 1928- 5-8R
Roberts, Richard W. 1935-1978 Obituary 73-76
Roberts, Rinalda
See Cudlipp, Edythe
Roberts, Robert B. 1911- 117
Roberts, Robert C(ampbell) 1942- CANR-31
Earlier sketches in CA 69-72, CANR-14
Roberts, Ron E. 1939- 33-36R
Roberts, Roy Allison 1887-1967 Obituary 89-92
Roberts, Rufus Putnam 1926- 1-4R
Roberts, Sally
See Jones, Sally Roberts
Roberts, Sheila 1942- 102
Roberts, Spencer Eugene 1920- 89-92
Roberts, Steven V(ictor) 1943- 61-64
Roberts, Susan F. 1919- 104
Roberts, Suzanne 1931- 106
Roberts, Sydney (Castle) 1887-1966 ....CAP-1
Earlier sketch in CA 13-16
Roberts, Terence
See Sanderson, Ivan T(erence)
Roberts, Theodore Goodridge
1877-1953 ....DLB 92
Roberts, Thom(as Sacra) 1940- CANR-15
Earlier sketch in CA 81-84
Roberts, Thomas J(ohn) 1925- 41-44R
Roberts, Tom
See Thomas, R(obert) Murray
Roberts, Trev
See Trevathan, Robert E.
Roberts, Vera Mowry 1918- 17-20R
Roberts, Virginia
See Dean, Nell Marr
Roberts, Walter Orr 1915- 131
Roberts, Walter R(onald) 1916- CANR-1
Earlier sketch in CA 49-52
Roberts, Warren Aldrich 1901- CAP-1
Earlier sketch in CA 11-12
Roberts, Warren (Errol) 1933- 73-76
Roberts, Wayne
See Overholser, Wayne D.
Roberts, William P(utnam) 1931- CANR-32
Earlier sketch in CA 113
Roberts, William 1868-1959 Brief entry 122
Roberts, Willo Davis 1928- CANR-19
Earlier sketches in CA 49-52, CANR-3
See also MAICYA
See also SAAS 8
See also SATA 21, 70
Roberts, Willow
See Powers, Willow Roberts
Robertshaw, (James) Denis 1911- 65-68
Robertson, Alec
See
Robertson, Alexander Thomas Parke Anthony Cecil
Robertson, Alexander Thomas Parke Anthony Cecil
1892-1982 104
Obituary 105
Robertson, Andrew (Beaumont) 1921-1986 134
Obituary 120
Robertson, Arthur Henry 1913-1984 ....9-12R
Obituary 113
Robertson, Barbara (Anne) 1931- 25-28R
See also SATA 12
Robertson, Brian 1951- 101
Robertson, Carol P. 1934- 123
Robertson, Charles L(angner) 1927- 21-24R
Robertson, Charles Martin 1911- 104
Robertson, Colin 1906- 9-12R
Robertson, Constance (Pierrepont Noyes)
1896(?)-1985 ....29-32R
Obituary 116
Robertson, Cordelia Biddle
1898(?)-1984 Obituary 114
Robertson, D(onald) J(ames)
1926-1970 ....CANR-10
Earlier sketch in CA 5-8R
Robertson, D(urant) W(aite) Jr. 1914- CANR-9
Earlier sketch in CA 61-64
Robertson, Dale 1923- Brief entry 107
Robertson, David (Allan Jr.) 1915- 81-84
Robertson, Dede 1927- 114
Robertson, Don 1929- CANR-23
Earlier sketches in CA 9-12R, CANR-7
See also SATA 8
Robertson, Donald S. 1918- 123
Robertson, Dorothy Lewis 1912- 25-28R
See also SATA 12
Robertson, Dougal 1924-1991 61-64
Obituary 135
Robertson, Durant Waite Jr. 1914- 109
Robertson, E(smonde) M(anning)
1923-1987 ....29-32R
Obituary 121
Robertson, Edith Anne (Stewart) 1883- CAP-1
Earlier sketch in CA 11-12
Robertson, Edwin (Hanton) 1912- 130
Robertson, Elizabeth Chant 1899- 49-52
Robertson, Ellis
See Ellison, Harlan
and Silverberg, Robert
Robertson, Eric Desmond
1914-1987 Obituary 122
Robertson, Frank C(hester) 1890-1969 ....CANR-4
Earlier sketch in CA 1-4R
Robertson, H(ector) M(enteith)
1905-1984 Obituary 113
Robertson, Heather Margaret 1942- CANR-37
Earlier sketches in CA 93-96, CANR-17
Robertson, Howard Stephen 1931- 41-44R
Robertson, Ian (Campbell) 1928- 132
Robertson, James Douglas 1904- 5-8R
Robertson, James (Irvin) Jr. 1930- CANR-6
Earlier sketch in CA 9-12R
Robertson, James Louis 1907- CAP-2
Earlier sketch in CA 29-32
Robertson, James Oliver 1932- 111
Brief entry 106
Robertson, James Wilson 1899-1983 109
Obituary 110
Robertson, James 1911- 5-8R
Robertson, Janet (E.) 1935- 137
See also SATA 68
Robertson, Jean (K.) 1913-1990 Obituary 132
Robertson, Jennifer Sinclair 1942- CANR-5
Earlier sketch in CA 53-56
See also SATA 12
Robertson, Jenny
See Robertson, Jennifer Sinclair
Robertson, John (Charles) 1951- 124
Robertson, Keith (Carlton)
1913-1991 ....CANR-37
Obituary 135
Earlier sketch in CA 9-12R
See also MAICYA
See also SATA 1
See also SATO 69
Robertson, Leon S(purgeon) 1936- 41-44R
Robertson, M(arion) G(ordon) 1930- 111
Robertson, Marian 1921- 111
Robertson, Martin
See Robertson, Charles Martin
Robertson, Mary D(emmond) 1927- 102
Robertson, Mary Elsie 1937- CANR-33
Earlier sketches in CA 81-84, CANR-15
Robertson, Nan 1926- 121
Robertson, Olivia (Melian) 1917- 9-12R
Robertson, Pat
See Robertson, M(arion) G(ordon)
Robertson, Patrick 1940- 61-64
Robertson, Priscilla (Smith) 1910-1989 ....CAP-2
Obituary 130
Earlier sketch in CA 23-24
Robertson, Roland 1938- 29-32R
Robertson, Stephen
See Walker, Robert W(ayne)
Robertson, Thomas Anthony 1897- CAP-1
Earlier sketch in CA 13-16
Robertson, Wally
See Robertson, Walter
Robertson, Walter 1892-1983 Obituary 109
Robertson, Wilfrid 1892- 5-8R
Robertson, William 1721-1793 ....DLB 104
Roberts-Wray, Kenneth (Owen) 1899- CAP-2
Earlier sketch in CA 25-28
Robeson, Gerald B(yron) 1938- 65-68
Robeson, Kenneth
See Dent, Lester
and Goulart, Ron(ald Joseph)
Robeson, Paul (Leroy Bustill) 1898-1976 124
Obituary 109
See also BW
Robey, Daniel 1944- 111
Robey, Edward George (Haydon)
1900-1983 Obituary 109
Robey, Harriet 1900- 107
Robey, Ralph W(est)
1899-1972 Obituary 37-40R
Robhs, Dwight
See Monaco, Richard
Robichaud, Gerald A(laric)
1912-1979 Obituary 85-88
Robichaud, Gerard 1908- CAP-2
Earlier sketch in CA 17-18
Robichon, Jacques 1920- 101
Robie, Edward H(odges) 1886- CAP-2
Earlier sketch in CA 19-20
Robilliard, Eileen Dorothy 1921- 21-24R
Robilliard, St. John Anthony 1953- 124
Robin
See Roberts, Eric
Robin, Arthur de Quetteville 1929- 104
Robin, Leo 1900(?)-1984 Obituary 114
Robin, Ralph 1914- 65-68
Robin, Richard S(hale) 1926- 21-24R
Robinet, Harriette Gillem 1931- 69-72
See also SATA 27
Robinett, Betty Wallace 1919- 41-44R
Robinett, Stephen (Allen) 1941- 101
Robinette, Joseph A. 1939- 131
Robinowitz, Carolyn B. 1938- 136
Robins, Corinne 1934- 118
Robins, Denise (Naomi)
1897(?)-1985 ....CANR-19
Obituary 116
Earlier sketches in CA 65-68, CANR-10
Robins, Dorothy B.
See Robins-Mowry, Dorothy B(ernice)
Robins, Eli 1921- 109
Robins, Elizabeth 1862(?)-1952 Brief entry 116
Robins, Harry Franklin 1915- 5-8R
Robins, Lee N(elken) 1922- CANR-14
Earlier sketch in CA 21-24R
Robins, Michael H(arvey) 1941- 133
Robins, Natalie S. 1938- 17-20R
Robins, Patricia (Denise) 1921- CANR-19
Earlier sketch in CA 89-92
Robins, Robert Henry 1921- 5-8R
Robins, Rollo Jr.
See Ellis, Edward S(ylvester)
Robins, Seelin
See Ellis, Edward S(ylvester)
Robins-Mowry, Dorothy B(ernice) 1921- 25-28R
Robinson, A(ntony) M(eredith) Lewin
1916- CANR-9
Earlier sketch in CA 21-24R
Robinson, A(rthur) N(apoleon) R(aymond)
1926- 33-36R
Robinson, Abby 1947- 117
Robinson, Adjai 1932- 45-48
See also SATA 8
Robinson, Alan R(onald) 1920- CAP-1
Earlier sketch in CA 11-12
Robinson, Albert J(ohn) 1926- 53-56
Robinson, Alice Gram
1896(?)-1984 Obituary 111
Robinson, Alice M(erritt) 1920-1983 108
Obituary 109
Robinson, Anthony (Christopher)
1931- CANR-1
Earlier sketch in CA 1-4R
Robinson, Archie W.
1906(?)-1987 Obituary 123
Robinson, B(asil) W(illiam) 1912- CANR-3
Earlier sketch in CA 5-8R

Robinson, Barbara Webb 1927- ... 1-4R
See also SATA 8
Robinson, Barry (James) 1938- ... 25-28R
Robinson, Betsy Julia 1951- ... 109
Robinson, Bill
See Robinson, William Wheeler
Robinson, Blackwell P(ierce) 1916- ... CANR-24
Earlier sketch in CA 45-48
Robinson, Brooks (Calbert Jr.) 1937- ... 116
Robinson, Bruce 1946- ... 131
Robinson, Budd
See Robinson, David
Robinson, C(harles) A(lexander) Jr. 1900-1965 ... CANR-4
Earlier sketch in CA 1-4R
See also SATA 36
Robinson, Casey 1903-1979 ... DLB 44
Robinson, Cecil 1921- ... 13-16R
Robinson, Cervin 1928- ... 61-64
Robinson, Chaille Howard (Payne) ... 13-16R
Robinson, Charles E(dward) 1941- ... CANR-13
Earlier sketch in CA 77-80
Robinson, Charles Knox (Jr.) 1909-1980 ... 103
Obituary ... 97-100
Robinson, Charles M. III 1949- ... 120
Robinson, Charles 1870-1937 ... SATA 17
Robinson, Charles 1931- ... CANR-2
Earlier sketch in CA 49-52
See also SATA 6
Robinson, Corinne H(ogden) 1909- ... 93-96
Robinson, Daniel N. 1937- ... 33-36R
Robinson, Daniel Sommer 1888-1977 ... 29-32R
Obituary ... 125
Robinson, David A. 1925- ... 17-20R
Robinson, David 1915- ... 81-84
Robinson, Dean (Stewart) 1946- ... CANR-36
Earlier sketch in CA 114
Robinson, Derek 1932- ... 77-80
Robinson, Donald H(oy) 1910- ... CAP-2
Earlier sketch in CA 33-36
Robinson, Donald L(eonard) 1936- ... 41-44R
Robinson, Donald W(ittmer) 1911-1980 ... CANR-12
Earlier sketch in CA 21-24R
Robinson, Donald 1913-1991 ... 25-28R
Obituary ... 135
Robinson, Dorothy W. 1929- ... SATA 54
Robinson, Douglas Hill 1918- ... CANR-8
Earlier sketch in CA 5-8R
Robinson, Earl (Hawley) 1910-1991 ... CANR-2
Obituary ... 135
Earlier sketch in CA 45-48
Robinson, Edgar Eugene 1887-1977 Obituary ... 73-76
Robinson, Edward G. 1893-1973 Obituary ... 45-48
Robinson, Edward L(ouis) 1921- ... 41-44R
Robinson, Edwin Arlington 1869-1935 ... 133
Brief entry ... 104
See also CDALB 1865-1917
See also DLB 54
See also MTCW
See also PC 1
See also TCLC 5
Robinson, Elwyn B(urns) 1905- ... CAP-2
Earlier sketch in CA 19-20
Robinson, Eric 1924- ... 49-52
Robinson, Forrest G(len) 1940- ... 41-44R
Robinson, Francis (Arthur) 1910-1980 Obituary ... 97-100
Robinson, Francis (Christopher Rowland) 1944- ... 112
Robinson, Frank M(alcolm) 1926- ... CANR-19
Earlier sketches in CA 49-52, CANR-3
Robinson, Frank M(elvin) Jr. 1928- ... 57-60
Robinson, Frank S(teven) 1947- ... 97-100
Robinson, Fred Colson 1930- ... 37-40R
Robinson, Fred Miller 1942- ... 107
Robinson, Godfrey Clive 1913- ... 13-16R
Robinson, Gustavus H. 1881-1972 Obituary ... 37-40R
Robinson, H(enry) Basil 1919- ... 131
Robinson, Haddon W. 1931- ... 73-76
Robinson, Halbert B(enefiel) 1925-1981 ... CANR-9
Earlier sketch in CA 17-20R
Robinson, Harlow (Loomis) 1950- ... 128
Robinson, Helen Caister 1899- ... CANR-16
Earlier sketch in CA 93-96
Robinson, Helen Mansfield 1906- ... 13-16R
Robinson, Helene M. ... 13-16R
Robinson, Henry Crabb 1775-1867 ... DLB 107
Robinson, Henry Morton 1898-1961 Obituary ... 116
Robinson, Herbert Spencer ... 93-96
Robinson, Horace W(illiam) 1909- ... 93-96
Robinson, Howard 1885- ... CAP-1
Earlier sketch in CA 13-14
Robinson, Hubbell 1905-1974 Obituary ... 53-56
Robinson, Ira E(dwin) 1927- ... 81-84
Robinson, J(ohn) Lewis 1918- ... 107
Robinson, J(ohn) W(illiam) 1934- ... 17-20R
Robinson, James A(rthur) 1932- ... 17-20R
Robinson, James Harvey 1863-1936 ... DLB 47
Robinson, James K(eith) 1916- ... 17-20R
Robinson, James M(cConkey) 1924- ... 13-16R
Robinson, Jan M. 1933- ... 61-64
See also SATA 6
Robinson, Jancis (Mary) 1950- ... 128
Robinson, Janet O(live) 1939- ... 33-36R
Robinson, Janice S(tevenson) 1941- ... 111
Robinson, Jay (Luke) 1932- ... 41-44R
Robinson, Jean O. 1934- ... 29-32R
See also SATA 7
Robinson, Jeffrey 1945- ... CANR-37
Earlier sketch in CA 121
Robinson, Jerry 1922- Brief entry ... 112
See also SATA 34
Robinson, Jill 1936- ... 102
See also CLC 10
Robinson, Jo Ann Ooiman 1942- ... 111
Robinson, Joan (Mary) G(ale Thomas) 1910- ... CANR-5
Earlier sketch in CA 5-8R
See also SATA 7
Robinson, Joan (Violet) 1903-1983 ... CANR-6
Obituary ... 110
Earlier sketch in CA 9-12R
See also MTCW
Robinson, John A(rthur) T(homas) 1919-1983 ... CANR-6
Obituary ... 111
Earlier sketch in CA 5-8R
Robinson, John W(esley) 1929- ... CANR-2
Earlier sketch in CA 49-52
Robinson, Joseph Frederick 1912- ... 13-16R
Robinson, Joseph William 1908- ... CAP-2
Earlier sketch in CA 25-28
Robinson, Joseph 1927- ... 45-48
Robinson, Karl Frederic 1904-1967 ... CANR-5
Earlier sketch in CA 5-8R
Robinson, Kathleen
See Robinson, Chaille Howard (Payne)
Robinson, Kenneth Ernest 1914- ... 5-8R
Robinson, Kim Stanley 1952- ... 126
See also CLC 34
Robinson, L(eonard) W(allace) 1912- ... 69-72
Robinson, (Esme Stuart) Lennox 1886-1958 Brief entry ... 120
See also DLB 10
Robinson, Leonard A. 1904(?)-1980 ... 97-100
Robinson, Lisa 1936- ... 93-96
Robinson, Lloyd
See Silverberg, Robert
Robinson, Logan Gilmore 1949- ... 108
Robinson, Louie Jr. 1926- ... 107
Robinson, Lytle W(ebb) 1913- ... 61-64
Robinson, Mabel Louise 1874-1962 Obituary ... 113
See also DLB 22
Robinson, Mairi 1945- ... 123
Robinson, Margaret A(twood) 1937- ... 107
Robinson, Marguerite S. 1935- ... 49-52
Robinson, Marileta 1942- ... 101
See also SATA 32
Robinson, Marilynne 1944- ... 116
See also CLC 25
Robinson, Martin David 1925-1982 Obituary ... 108
Robinson, Matt(hew) 1937- ... 45-48
Robinson, Maudie Millian Oller 1914- ... CANR-8
Earlier sketch in CA 61-64
See also SATA 11
Robinson, Maurice R(ichard) 1895-1982 Obituary ... 106
See also SATA 29
Robinson, Max (C.) 1939-1988 ... 124
Obituary ... 127
Brief entry ... 110
See also BW
Robinson, Michael J(ay) 1945- ... 113
Robinson, Nancy K(onheim) 1942- ... CANR-24
Earlier sketch in CA 106
See also SATA 31, 32
Robinson, Nancy (Lou) M(ayer) 1930- ... 61-64
Robinson, Norman H(amilton) G(alloway) 1912- ... 13-16R
Robinson, O(liver) Preston 1903- ... 13-16R
Robinson, (Frances) Olvis 1923- ... 53-56
Robinson, P. W. 1893- ... 103
Robinson, Patricia
See Goedicke, Patricia (McKenna)
Robinson, Patricia Colbert 1923- ... 77-80
Robinson, Paul 1940- ... 81-84
Robinson, Philip (Bedford) 1926- ... CANR-16
Earlier sketch in CA 21-24R
Robinson, Philip (Samuel) 1946- ... 129
Robinson, Ras 1935- ... 105
Robinson, Ray Charles 1932- Brief entry ... 115
Robinson, Ray(mond Kenneth) 1920- ... 77-80
See also SATA 23
Robinson, Raymond Henry 1927- ... 41-44R
Robinson, Richard Dunlop 1921- ... 5-8R
Robinson, Richard 1945- ... CANR-13
Earlier sketch in CA 57-60
Robinson, Robert H(ouston) 1936- ... CANR-6
Earlier sketch in CA 5-8R
Robinson, Robert (Reginald) 1922- ... CANR-14
Earlier sketch in CA 41-44R
Robinson, Robert 1886-1975 Obituary ... 113
Robinson, Robert 1927- ... 9-12R
Robinson, Roland Inwood 1907- ... CANR-1
Earlier sketch in CA 1-4R
Robinson, Rollo S(mith) 1915- ... 41-44R
Robinson, Rose ... 77-80
Robinson, Roxana (Barry) ... 128
Robinson, Selma 1899(?)-1977 Obituary ... 73-76
Robinson, Shari
See McGuire, Leslie Sarah
Robinson, Sheila Mary 1928- ... 131
Brief entry ... 126
Robinson, Sidney K. 1943- ... CANR-33
Earlier sketch in CA 113
Robinson, Sister Marian Dolores 1916- ... 9-12R
Robinson, Smokey
See Robinson, William Jr.
See also CLC 21
Robinson, Sondra Till 1931- ... CANR-7
Earlier sketch in CA 53-56
Robinson, Spider 1948- ... CANR-11
Earlier sketch in CA 65-68
Robinson, T(homas) H(eath) 1869-1950 ... SATA 17
Robinson, T(homas) M(ore) 1936- ... 29-32R
Robinson, Terry 1916- ... 108
Robinson, Therese 1797-1870 ... DLB 59
Robinson, Thomas W. 1935- ... 33-36R
Robinson, Trevor 1929- ... 53-56
Robinson, Vaughan 1957- ... 132
Robinson, (Wanda) Veronica 1926- ... 105
See also SATA 30
Robinson, Vince
See Newton, Michael
Robinson, Virgil E. 1908- ... 21-24R
Robinson, W(illiam) Gordon 1903-1977 ... CANR-5
Earlier sketch in CA 5-8R
Robinson, W(illiam) Heath 1872-1944 ... SATA 17
Robinson, W(illiam) R(onald) 1927- ... 21-24R
Robinson, W. Stitt
See Robinson, W(alter) Stitt Jr.
Robinson, W(alter) Stitt Jr. 1917- ... 126
Brief entry ... 105
Robinson, Wayne A(ustin) 1937- ... 73-76
Robinson, Wayne 1916- ... 1-4R
Robinson, Wilhelmena S(impson) 1912- ... 25-28R
Robinson, Willard B(ethurem) 1935- ... 57-60
Robinson, William Jr. 1940- Brief entry ... 116
See also Robinson, Smokey
Robinson, William Childs 1897-1982 ... 1-4R
Obituary ... 116
Robinson, William F(rank) 1946- ... 118
Robinson, William H(enry) 1922- ... CANR-25
Earlier sketch in CA 37-40R
See also BW
Robinson, William H. 1912-1984 Obituary ... 111
Robinson, William I. 1959- ... 127
Robinson, William P(owell) 1910- ... 5-8R
Robinson, William Wheeler 1918- ... CANR-18
Earlier sketches in CA 5-8R, CANR-3
Robison, Bonnie 1924- ... 57-60
See also SATA 12
Robison, David V. 1911(?)-1978 ... 93-96
Obituary ... 81-84
Robison, Mabel Otis 1891- ... CAP-1
Earlier sketch in CA 11-12
Robison, Mary 1949- ... 116
Brief entry ... 113
See also CLC 42
Robison, Nancy L(ouise) 1934- ... 93-96
See also SATA 32
Robison, Sophia Moses 1888-1969 ... 5-8R
Obituary ... 103
Robitscher, Jonas B(ondi Jr.) 1920-1981 ... CANR-19
Obituary ... 103
Earlier sketch in CA 21-24R
Robles, Emmanuel 1914- ... 81-84
See also DLB 83
Robles, Mireya 1934- ... 81-84
See also HW
Robley, Grace 1918- ... 61-64
Robley, Rob
See Robley, Wendell
Robley, Wendell 1916- ... 61-64
Robo, Etienne 1879- ... CAP-1
Earlier sketch in CA 11-12
Robock, Stefan H. 1915- ... 17-20R
Robottom, John 1934- ... CANR-38
Earlier sketches in CA 29-32R, CANR-16
See also SATA 7
Robsjohn-Gibbings, Terence Harold 1905-1976 Obituary ... 69-72
Robson, B(rian) T(urnbull) 1939- ... 29-32R
Robson, D(erek) I(an) 1935- ... 25-28R
Robson, Dirk
See Robinson, Derek
Robson, E(manuel) W(alter) 1897- ... 65-68
Robson, Elizabeth 1942- ... 101
Robson, Ernest (Mack) 1902- ... CANR-24
Earlier sketch in CA 45-48
Robson, James 1890- ... 5-8R
Robson, Jeremy 1939- ... CANR-4
Earlier sketch in CA 5-8R
Robson, John M(ercel) 1927- ... CANR-28
Earlier sketch in CA 29-32R
Robson, L(eslie) L(loyd) 1931-1990 ... 132
Robson, Lucia St. Clair 1942- ... CANR-27
Earlier sketch in CA 108
Robson, Marion M. 1908- ... 89-92
Robson, William Alexander 1895-1980 ... 103
Obituary ... 97-100
Robson, William N. ... AITN 1
Roby, Kinley E. 1929- ... 77-80
Roby, Mary Linn ... CANR-7
Earlier sketch in CA 13-16R
Roby, Pamela A. 1942- ... 29-32R
Roby, Robert C(urtis) 1922- ... 5-8R
Robyns, Gwen 1917- ... 93-96
Roca-Pons, Josep 1914- ... 49-52
Roccapriore, Marie 1933- ... 115
Roccatagliata Ceccardi, Ceccardo 1871-1919 ... DLB 114
Roch, John H(enry) 1916- ... 102
Rocha, Guy Louis 1951- ... 128
Rocha, Rina Garcia
See Garcia Rocha, Rina
Rochard, Henri
See Charlier, Roger H(enri)
Rochberg-Halton, Eugene 1950- ... 111
Roche, A. K.
See Abisch, Roslyn Kroop and Kaplan, Boche
Roche, Alphonse Victor 1895- ... 104
Roche, Daniel(-Robert) 1935- ... 128
Roche, Douglas J. 1929- ... 101
Roche, George Charles III 1935- ... 29-32R
Roche, J. Jeffrey 1916(?)-1975 Obituary ... 61-64
Roche, John
See Le Roi, David (de Roche)
Roche, John P(earson) 1923- ... 69-72
Roche, Kennedy Francis 1911- ... 61-64
Roche, Orion 1948- ... 61-64
Roche, Owen I. A. 1911(?)-1973 Obituary ... 41-44R
Roche, P(atricia) K. 1935- Brief entry ... 112
See also SATA 34, 57
Roche, Paul 1928- ... CANR-4
Earlier sketch in CA 5-8R
Roche, T(homas) W(illiam) E(dgar) 1919-197 (?) ... CAP-2
Earlier sketch in CA 21-22
Roche, Terry
See Poole, Peggy
Roche, Thomas P(atrick) Jr. 1931- ... 106
Rochelle, Jay C. 1938- ... 53-56
Rocher, Guy 1924- ... CANR-24
Earlier sketch in CA 45-48
Rocher, Ludo 1926- Brief entry ... 106
Rochester, Devereaux 1917- ... 105
Rochester, Harry A(rthur) 1897(?)-1983 Obituary ... 109
Rochester, J. Martin 1945- ... 37-40R
Rochester, Jack B. 1944- ... 122
Rochlin, Doris 1932- ... 128
Rochlin, Gregory 1912- ... 49-52
Rochlin, Harriet 1924- ... 117
Rochmis, Lyda N(onne) 1912- ... 29-32R
Rock, David (Peter) 1945- ... CANR-19
Earlier sketch in CA 101
Rock, Gail Brief entry ... 111
See also SATA 32
Rock, Irvin 1922- ... CANR-10
Earlier sketch in CA 21-24R
Rock, James M(artin) 1935- ... 102
Rock, John 1890-1984 Obituary ... 114
Rock, Maxine 1940- ... 113
Rock, Milton L(ee) 1921- ... 49-52
Rock, Phillip 1927- ... 101
Rock, Richard
See Mainprize, Don
Rock, Stanley A(rthur) 1937- ... 101
Rock, William R(ay) 1930- ... 41-44R
Rockas, Leo 1928- ... 13-16R
Rockcastle, Verne N(orton) 1920- ... 73-76
Rocke, Russell 1945- ... 33-36R
Rockefeller, John D(avison Sr.) 1839-1937 Brief entry ... 116
Rockefeller, John Davison III 1906-1978 ... 81-84
Obituary ... 77-80
Rockefeller, John William Jr. 1899(?)-1987 Obituary ... 122
Rocker, Fermin 1907- ... SATA 40
Rockingham, Montague
See Nye, Nelson C(oral)
Rockland, Mae Shafter 1937- ... 65-68
Rockland, Michael Aaron 1935- ... CANR-32
Earlier sketch in CA 37-40R
Rockley, L(awrence) E(dwin) 1916- ... CANR-27
Earlier sketch in CA 29-32R
Rocklin, Ross Louis 1913- ... 61-64
Rocklynne, Ross
See Rocklin, Ross Louis
Rockmore, Tom 1942- ... 127
Rockne, Dick 1939- ... 61-64
Rockowitz, Murray 1920- ... 25-28R
Rocks, Lawrence 1933- ... 85-88
Rockwell, Anne (F.) 1934- ... CANR-22
Earlier sketch in CA 21-24R
See also MAICYA
See also SATA 33, 71
Rockwell, F(rederick) F(rye) 1884-1976 ... 49-52
Obituary ... 103
Rockwell, Gail ... SATA 36
Rockwell, Harlow 1910-1988 ... CANR-22
Obituary ... 125
Earlier sketch in CA 109
See also SATA 33, 56
Rockwell, Jane 1929- ... 65-68
Rockwell, John (Sargent) 1940- ... 126
Brief entry ... 114
Rockwell, Kiffin Ayres 1917- ... 37-40R
Rockwell, Matt
See Rowland, D(onald) S(ydney)
Rockwell, Norman (Percevel) 1894-1978 ... 89-92
Obituary ... 81-84
See also SATA 23
Rockwell, Thomas 1933- ... 29-32R
See also CLR 6
See also MAICYA
See also SATA 7, 70
Rockwell, Wilson (Miller) 1909- ... CAP-2
Earlier sketch in CA 19-20
Rockwood, Joyce 1947- ... CANR-6
Earlier sketch in CA 57-60
See also SATA 39
Rockwood, Louis G. 1925- ... 45-48
Rockwood, Roy ... CANR-27
Earlier sketches in CAP-2, CA 19-20
See also SATA 1, 67
Rodahl, Kaare 1917- ... 9-12R
Rodale, J(erome) I(rving) 1898-1971 Obituary ... 29-32R
Rodale, Robert (David) 1930-1990 ... 53-56
Obituary ... 132
Rodan, Paul N. Rosenstein
See Rosenstein-Rodan, Paul N.
Rodari, Gianni 1920-1980 ... CLR 24
Rodaway, Angela 1918- ... 120
Rodberg, Leonard S(idney) 1932- ... CANR-24
Earlier sketch in CA 45-48
Rodberg, Lillian 1936- ... 29-32R
Rodd, Kathleen Tennant
See Rodd, Kylie Tennant
See also SATA 55, 57

Rodd, Kylie Tennant 1912-1988 ....CANR-26
Obituary 124
Earlier sketches in CA 5-8R, CANR-5
See also Rodd, Kathleen Tennant and Tennant, Kylie
See also MTCW
Rodda, Charles 1891- 5-8R
Rodda, Peter (Gordon) 1937- 81-84
Rodden, John (Gallagher) 1956- 131
Roddenberry, Eugene Wesley 1921-1991 ....CANR-37
Obituary 135
Earlier sketch in CA 110
See also Roddenberry, Gene
See also SATA 45
Roddenberry, Gene
See Roddenberry, Eugene Wesley
See also AAYA 5
See also CLC 17
See also SATO 69
Roddick, Alan (Melven) 1937- CANR-15
Earlier sketch in CA 77-80
Roddick, Ellen 1936- 41-44R
See also Meade, Ellen
Roddis, Louis Harry 1887- 5-8R
Roddis, Roland J. 1908- 5-8R
Rodd-Marling, Yvonne 1912-1982 Obituary 107
Roddy, Lee 1921- 123
See also SATA 57
Rodefer, Stephen 1940- CANR-23
Earlier sketch in CA 107
Rodell, Fred 1907-1980 Obituary 97-100
Rodell, Marie F(reid) 1912-1975 Obituary 61-64
Rodenberg, Julius 1884-1970 Obituary 104
Roder, Wolf 1932- 17-20R
Roderus, Frank 1942- CANR-38
Earlier sketches in CA 89-92, CANR-17
Rodes, John E(dward) 1923- 13-16R
Rodes, Robert Emmet Jr. 1927- 112
Rodewyk, Adolf 1894- 65-68
Rodger, Alec
See Rodger, Thomas Alexander
Rodger, Anne 1910-1983 Obituary 111
Rodger, Ian (Graham) 1926- CANR-4
Earlier sketch in CA 5-8R
Rodger, Thomas Alexander 1907-1982 Obituary 106
Rodgers, Betsy (Aikin-Sneath) 1907- CAP-1
Earlier sketch in CA 13-14
Rodgers, Betty June (Flint) 1921- 9-12R
Rodgers, Brian 1910- 29-32R
Rodgers, Buck
See Rodgers, Francis G.
Rodgers, Carolyn M(arie) 1945- CANR-27
Earlier sketches in CA 45-48, CANR-2
See also CAAS 13
See also BW
See also DLB 41
Rodgers, Daniel T(racy) 1942- 124
Rodgers, Dorothy F(einer) 1909- 89-92
Rodgers, Eugene 1939- 132
Rodgers, Francis G. 1926- 123
Rodgers, Frank
See Infield, Glenn (Berton)
Rodgers, Frank P(eter) 1924- 9-12R
Rodgers, Frank 1944- ....SATA 69
Rodgers, Frank 1944- 137
Rodgers, Franklin C. 1931- 133
Rodgers, Harrell R(oss) Jr. 1939- CANR-25
Earlier sketches in CA 53-56, CANR-7
Rodgers, Joann Ellison 1941- 77-80
Rodgers, John (Charles) 1906- CAP-1
Earlier sketch in CA 11-12
Rodgers, Mary 1931- CANR-8
Earlier sketch in CA 49-52
See also CLC 12
See also CLR 20
See also MAICYA
See also SATA 8
Rodgers, Pepper
See Rodricks, Daniel J.
Rodgers, Raboo 1945- 119
Rodgers, Richard (Charles) 1902-1979 89-92
Rodgers, Stanley 1928-1977 Obituary 106
Rodgers, W(illiam) R(obert) 1909-1969 85-88
See also CLC 7
See also DLB 20
Rodgers, William H. 1918- 17-20R
Rodgers, William Henry 1947- 101
Rodick, Burleigh Cushing 1889- 5-8R
Rodimer, Eva 1895- CAP-2
Earlier sketch in CA 21-22
Rodimstev, Aleksandr 1905(?)-1977 Obituary 69-72
Rodin, Alvin E(li) 1926- 119
Rodin, Arnold W. 1917- 89-92
Rodini, Robert J(oseph) 1936- 29-32R
Rodinson, Maxime 1915- CANR-4
Earlier sketch in CA 53-56
Roditi, Edouard Herbert 1910- 101
Obituary 137
See also CAAS 14
Rodli, Agnes Sylvia 1921- 9-12R
Rodman, Bella (Kashin) 1903- CAP-2
Earlier sketch in CA 19-20
Rodman, Emerson
See Ellis, Edward S(ylvester)
Rodman, Eric
See Silverberg, Robert
Rodman, F(rancis) Robert 1934- 122
Brief entry 117
Rodman, Howard 1920(?)-1985 Obituary 118
See also CLC 65
Rodman, Hyman 1931- CANR-25
Earlier sketches in CA 17-20R, CANR-8
Rodman, Maia
See Wojciechowska, Maia (Teresa)
Rodman, Selden 1909- CANR-25
Earlier sketches in CA 5-8R, CANR-5
See also SATA 9
Rodney, Bob
See Rodrigo, Robert
Rodney, Robert M(orris) 1911- 77-80
Rodney, Walter 1942-1980 125
Rodney, William 1923- 25-28R
Rodnick, David 1908- 33-36R
Rodnitzky, Jerome Leon 1936- 41-44R
Rodolph, Utto
See Ouologuem, Yambo
Rodowsky, Colby (F.) 1932- CANR-23
Earlier sketch in CA 69-72
See also SATA 21
Rodricks, Daniel J. 1954- 133
Rodrigo, Robert 1928- 13-16R
Rodrigues, Jose Honorio 1913- CANR-13
Earlier sketch in CA 29-32R
Rodriguez, Claudio 1934- ....CLC 10
Rodriguez, Judith Green 1936- CANR-23
Earlier sketch in CA 107
Rodriguez, Mario 1922- 17-20R
Rodriguez, Richard 1944- 110
See also DLB 82
See also HW
Rodriguez-Alcala, Hugo (Rosendo) 1917- CANR-14
Earlier sketch in CA 21-24R
See also HW
Rodriguez-Alcala, Sally 1938- 21-24R
Rodriguez Cepeda, Enrique 1939- 45-48
Rodriguez Delgado, Jose M(anuel)
See Delgado, Jose Manuel R(odriguez)
Rodriguez Monegal, Emir 1921-1985 131
Obituary 117
Brief entry 115
See also HW
Rodriguez O(rdonez), Jaime E(dmundo) 1940- 110
See also HW
Rodway, Allan 1919- 13-16R
Rodwin, Lloyd 1919- CANR-19
Earlier sketches in CA 5-8R, CANR-4
Rodwin, Victor G(eorge) 1950- 120
Rodzinski, Halina 1904- 69-72
Roe, Anne 1904- 17-20R
Roe, Daphne A(nderson) 1923- 93-96
Roe, Derek A(rthur) 1937- CANR-23
Earlier sketch in CA 107
Roe, Dorothy
See Lewis, Dorothy Roe
Roe, F(rederic) Gordon 1894-1985 ....9-12R
Obituary 115
Roe, Gerald 1940- 117
Roe, Harry Mason CANR-26
Earlier sketches in CAP-2, CA 19-20
Roe, SirJohn 1581-1608 ....DLB 121
Roe, Kathleen Robson 1910- 93-96
Roe, Keith E. 1937- 127
Roe, Richard L(ionel) 1936- CANR-15
Earlier sketch in CA 65-68
Roe, W(illiam) G(ordon) 1932- 21-24R
Roe, William Henry 1918- 5-8R
Roeber, Edward C(harles) 1913-1969 ....CANR-5
Earlier sketch in CA 5-8R
Roebuck, Carl Angus 1914- Brief entry 105
Roebuck, Derek 1935- CANR-29
Earlier sketch in CA 111
Roebuck, Janet 1943- 49-52
Roebuck, Julian B(aker) 1920- 101
Roebuck, Peter (Michael) 1956- 119
Roeburt, John 1909(?)-1972 Obituary 33-36R
Roecker, W(illiam) A. 1942- 61-64
Roeder, Bill 1922-1982 Obituary 107
Roeder, Ralph Leclerq 1890-1969 Obituary 104
Roehr, George L. 1931(?)-1983 Obituary 110
Roehrig, Catharine H. 1949- 134
See also SATA 67
Roehrs, Walter R(obert) 1901- 103
Roeiker, Nancy Lyman 1915- 9-12R
Roelofs, H. Mark 1923- 111
Roelvaag, O(le) E(dvart) 1876-1931 Brief entry 117
See also DLB 9
See also TCLC 17
Roemer, Joan (Phylis Akre) 1933- 132
Roemer, Kenneth Morrison 1945- CANR-32
Earlier sketch in CA 112
Roemer, Lawrence John 1916(?)-1989 Obituary 129
Roemer, Michael 1937- 111
Roemer, Milton I(rwin) 1916- CANR-21
Earlier sketches in CA 57-60, CANR-6
Roemer, Norma H. 1905-1973 ....CAP-2
Earlier sketch in CA 19-20
Roemer, William F. Jr. 1926- 132
Roeming, Robert Frederick 1911- 29-32R
Roepke, Wilhelm (Theodor) 1899-1966 ....CAP-1
Earlier sketch in CA 9-10
Roer, Berniece Marie 9-12R
Roes, Nicholas A. 1952- 124
Roes, Nicholas 1926- 29-32R
Roesch, Roberta F(leming) 1919- CANR-2
Earlier sketch in CA 5-8R
Roesch, Ronald 1947- 106
Roeseler, Robert O. 1882- CAP-2
Earlier sketch in CA 17-18
Roeseler, W(olfgang) G(uenter) 1925- 111
Roesler, Robert Harry 1927- 120
Roessel-Waugh, C. C.
See Waugh, Carol-Lynn Roessel and Waugh, Charles G(ordon)
Roessler, Carl (Fred) 1933- 117
Roethenmund, Robert 1956- 103
Roethke, Theodore (Huebner) 1908-1963 81-84
See also CABS 2
See also CDALB 1941-1968
See also CLC 1, 3, 8, 11, 19, 46
See also DLB 5
See also MTCW
Roett, Riordan Joseph Allenby III 1938- 57-60
Roetter, Charles Frederick 1919- 61-64
Roetzel, Calvin J. 1931- 112
Roever, J(oan) M(arilyn) 1935- 105
See also SATA 26
Rofe, (Fevzi) Husein 1922- CAP-1
Earlier sketch in CA 9-10
Rofes, Eric Edward 1954- 106
See also SATA 52
Roff, William R(obert) 1929- 57-60
Roffey, Maureen 1936- 108
See also SATA 33
Roffman, Howard 1953- 61-64
Roffman, Roger A. 1942- 110
Roffman, Sara
See Hershman, Morris
Rogal, Samuel J. 1934- CANR-39
Earlier sketches in CA 25-28R, CANR-17
Rogaly, (Henry) Joseph 1935- 104
Rogan, Barbara 1951- 124
Rogan, Donald L(ynn) 1930- 29-32R
Rogan, Johnny 1953- 130
Rogasky, Barbara 1933- 130
Roger
See Sanchez Flores, Daniel
Roger, Mae Durham 57-60
Rogers, A(mos) Robert 1927- CANR-8
Earlier sketch in CA 61-64
Rogers, Agnes
See Allen, Agnes Rogers
Rogers, (Thomas) Alan (Stinchcombe) 1937- CANR-18
Earlier sketch in CA 25-28R
See also SATA 2
Rogers, Alan 1933- CANR-28
Earlier sketches in CA 21-24R, CANR-11
Rogers, Augustus James III 1929- 33-36R
Rogers, Barbara 1945- CANR-17
Earlier sketch in CA 65-68
Rogers, Berto 1903-1974 ....CAP-2
Earlier sketch in CA 29-32
Rogers, Bruce 1870-1957 Brief entry 123
Rogers, Carl R(ansom) 1902-1987 ....CANR-18
Obituary 121
Earlier sketches in CA 1-4R, CANR-1
See also MTCW
Rogers, (Grenville) Cedric (Harry) 1915- CANR-1
Earlier sketch in CA 1-4R
Rogers, Charles B. 1911- 89-92
Rogers, Clara Coltman
See Vyvyan, C(lara) C(oltman Rogers)
Rogers, Cyril A(lfred) 1923- 5-8R
Rogers, Cyril H(arold) 1907- CANR-20
Earlier sketches in CA 9-12R, CANR-5
Rogers, Dale Evans 1912- 103
Rogers, David C(harles) D(rummond) 1931- CANR-5
Earlier sketch in CA 9-12R
Rogers, David 1930- 29-32R
Rogers, Donald I(rwin) 1918-1980 57-60
Obituary 102
Rogers, Dorothy 1914-1986 ....CANR-1
Obituary 118
Earlier sketch in CA 1-4R
Rogers, Douglass Marcel 1925- 127
Rogers, Edith R(andam) 1924- 117
Rogers, Elizabeth F(rances) 1892-1974 ....5-8R
Obituary 53-56
Rogers, Elyse M(acFadyen) 1932- 102
Rogers, Florence K(atherine) 1936- 101
Rogers, Floyd
See Spence, William John Duncan
Rogers, Frances 1888-1974 ....5-8R
See also SATA 10
Rogers, Francis M(illet) 1914- CANR-1
Earlier sketch in CA 1-4R
Rogers, Franklin R(obert) 1921- 1-4R
Rogers, Fred B(aker) 1926- 109
Rogers, Fred McFeely 1928- 107
See also SATA 33
Rogers, Garet 1-4R
Rogers, Gayle 1923- 69-72
Rogers, George Calvin Jr. 1922- CANR-1
Earlier sketch in CA 1-4R
Rogers, George W(illiam) 1917- CANR-1
Earlier sketch in CA 1-4R
Rogers, H(ugh) C(uthbert) Basset 1905- CANR-14
Earlier sketch in CA 73-76
Rogers, Helen Spelman 1913(?)-1990 Obituary 132
Rogers, Henry C. 1914- 102
Rogers, Ingrid 1951- 116
Rogers, Jack 1934- 93-96
Rogers, James Allen 1929- 13-16R
Rogers, James T(racy) 1921- 45-48
Rogers, Jane 1952- 113
Rogers, Jean 1919- 115
See also SATA 47, 55
Rogers, Jeanne F. 1926(?)-1984 Obituary 113
Rogers, JoAnn V. 1940- 89-92
Rogers, Joel Townsley 1896-1984 Obituary 114
Rogers, John 1906- 5-8R
Rogers, Josephine 1925- 61-64
Rogers, Kate Ellen 1920- 13-16R
Rogers, Katharine M(unzer) 1932- CANR-8
Earlier sketch in CA 21-24R
Rogers, Kenneth Paul 1940- 53-56
Rogers, Kenneth Ray 85-88
Rogers, Kenny
See Rogers, Kenneth Ray
Rogers, Linda (Hall) 1944- 77-80
Rogers, Matilda 1894-1976 ....CAP-2
Earlier sketch in CA 29-32
See also SATA 5, 34
Rogers, Max Gray 1932- 53-56
Rogers, Michael (A.) 1950- CANR-28
Earlier sketches in CA 49-52, CANR-1
Rogers, Mick
See Glut, Donald F(rank)
Rogers, Millard F(oster) Jr. 1932- 101
Rogers, Neville William 1908- 108
Rogers, Pamela 1927- CANR-4
Earlier sketch in CA 49-52
See also SATA 9
Rogers, Pat 1938- 85-88
Rogers, Pattiann 1940- CANR-26
Earlier sketch in CA 109
See also DLB 105
Rogers, Paul (Patrick) 1900- 41-44R
Rogers, Paul T(aylor) 1936-1984 119
Obituary 113
Rogers, Paul 1950- 123
See also SATA 54
Rogers, Peter D(amien) 1942- CANR-38
Earlier sketch in CA 116
Rogers, Peter 1934- 101
Rogers, Raymond A(rthur) 1911- 21-24R
Rogers, Robert
See Hamilton, Charles (Harold St. John)
Rogers, Rolf E(rnst) 1931- 57-60
Rogers, Rosemary 1932- CANR-23
Earlier sketches in CA 49-52, CANR-3
See also AITN 1
See also MTCW
Rogers, Roy 1912- 112
Rogers, Rutherford D(avid) 1915- Brief entry 109
Rogers, Samuel 1763-1855 ....DLB 93
Rogers, Sarah F. 1923(?)-1976 Obituary 69-72
Rogers, Thomas Hunton 1927- 89-92
See also CLC 57
Rogers, Timothy (John Godfrey) 1927- CANR-1
Earlier sketch in CA 45-48
Rogers, (George) Truett 1931- 69-72
Rogers, Tyler Stewart 1895-1967 ....5-8R
Obituary 134
Rogers, Vincent R(obert) 1926- Brief entry 115
Rogers, W(illiam) G(arland) 1896-1978 ....9-12R
Obituary 77-80
See also SATA 23
Rogers, Wade
See Madlee, Dorothy (Haynes)
Rogers, Warren
See Brucker, Roger W(arren)
Rogers, Warren (Joseph Jr.) 1922- CANR-13
Earlier sketch in CA 77-80
Rogers, Will(iam Penn Adair) 1879-1935 Brief entry 105
See also DLB 11
See also TCLC 8
Rogers, William C(ecil) 1919- 17-20R
Rogers, William D(ill) 1927- 41-44R
Rogers, William Elford 1944- 113
Rogers, William R(aymond) 1932- 104
Rogers, William Warren 1929- 127
Brief entry 112
Rogerson, J(ohn) W(illiam) 1935- CANR-38
Earlier sketch in CA 115
Rogerson, John
See Rogerson, J(ohn) W(illiam)
Rogg, Eleanor H(ertha) Meyer 1942- 57-60
Rogg, Sanford G. 1917-1976 ....17-20R
Obituary 134
Rogge, Oetje John 1903-1981 ....1-4R
Obituary 103
Rogin, Gilbert 1929- CANR-15
Earlier sketch in CA 65-68
See also CLC 18
Rogin, Michael Paul 1937- 101
Roginski, J(ames) W. 1945- 119
Roginski, Jim
See Roginski, J(ames) W.
Rogler, Lloyd H(enry) 1930- 17-20R
Roglieri, John Louis 1939- 105
Rogness, Alvin N. 1906- CANR-8
Earlier sketch in CA 21-24R
Rogness, Michael 1935- 101
Rogo, D. Scott 1950- CANR-28
Earlier sketches in CA 33-36R, CANR-13
Rogoff, Barbara 1950- 118
Rogoff, Harry 1882-1971 Obituary 33-36R
Rogosin, (William) Donn 1947- 123
Rogovin, Anne 1918- 97-100
Rogow, Arnold Austin 1924- CANR-1
Earlier sketch in CA 1-4R
Rogowski, Ronald (Lynn) 1944- 125
Roh, Jae Min 1927- 117
Rohan, Koda
See Koda Shigeyuki
See also TCLC 22
Rohan, Zina 1946- 137
Rohatyn, Dennis 1949- 69-72
Rohatyn, Felix G(eorge) 1928- 118
Rohen, Edward 1931- CANR-4
Earlier sketch in CA 53-56
Rohlen, Tom 1940- 85-88
Rohmer, Eric
See Scherer, Jean-Marie Maurice
See also CLC 16
Rohmer, Harriet 1938- ....SATA 56
Rohmer, Richard 1924- CANR-19
Earlier sketch in CA 103

Rohmer, Sax
See Ward, Arthur Henry Sarsfield
See also DLB 70
See also TCLC 28
Rohn, Arthur H(enry Jr.) 1929- ...CANR-25
Earlier sketch in CA 45-48
Rohner, Ronald P(reston) 1935- ...CANR-32
Earlier sketch in CA 37-40R
Rohr, John A. 1934- ...33-36R
Rohrbach, Peter Thomas 1926- ...CANR-1
Earlier sketch in CA 1-4R
Rohrbaugh, Joanna Bunker 1943- ...101
Rohrberger, Mary 1929- ...CANR-1
Earlier sketch in CA 45-48
Rohrbough, Malcolm J(ustin) 1932- ...29-32R
Rohrer, Alyce Stevens 1922- ...123
Rohrer, Daniel M(organ) 1941- ...33-36R
Rohrer, Norman B(echtel) 1929- ...CANR-16
Earlier sketch in CA 93-96
Rohrer, Wayne C(urry) 1920- ...21-24R
Rohrl, Vivian J. (Lober) ...110
Rohrlich, Chester 1900(?)-1974 Obituary ...53-56
Rohrlich, George F(riedrich) 1914- ...CANR-14
Earlier sketch in CA 37-40R
Rohrlich, Ruby ...CANR-5
Earlier sketch in CA 53-56
Rohrlich-Leavitt, Ruby
See Rohrlich, Ruby
Rohrlick, Paula 1955- ...111
Rohrman, Nicholas L(eroy) 1937- ...29-32R
Rohwer, Juergen 1924- ...65-68
Rohwer, Jurgen
See Rohwer, Juergen
Roider, Karl A(ndrew) Jr. 1943- ...111
Roiphe, Anne Richardson 1935- ...89-92
See also CLC 3, 9
See also DLBY 80
Rojan
See Rojankovsky, Feodor Stepanovich
Rojankovsky, Feodor Stepanovich
1891-1970 ...77-80
See also SATA 21
Rojas, A. R.
See Rojas, Arnold R.
Rojas, Arnold R. 1896(?)-1988 ... DLB 82
See also HW
Rojas, Carlos 1928- ...CANR-22
Earlier sketches in CA 17-20R, CANR-7
Rojas, Guillermo 1938- ...HW
Rojas (Sepulveda), Manuel 1896-1973 ...HW
Rojko, Anthony J. 1918(?)-1978 Obituary ...77-80
Rojo, Ricardo 1923- ...25-28R
Rokeach, Milton 1918-1988 ...CANR-5
Obituary ...127
Earlier sketch in CA 1-4R
Rokeby-Thomas, Anna E(lma) 1911- ...77-80
See also SATA 15
Rokes, Willis Park 1926- ...25-28R
Roland, Albert 1925- ...61-64
See also SATA 11
Roland, Betty 1903- ...103
Roland, Charles P(ierce) 1918- ...41-44R
Roland, Mary
See Lewis, Mary (Christianna)
Roland, Nicholas
See Walmsley, Arnold Robert
Roland Smith, Gordon 1931- ...102
Rolant, Rene
See Fanthorpe, R(obert) Lionel
Roldos Aguilera, Jaime
1940-1981 Obituary ...108
Roleder, George 1928- ...CANR-21
Earlier sketch in CA 105
Rolerson, Darrell A(llen) 1946- ...49-52
See also SATA 8
Rolf, David 1938- ...130
Rolfe, Bari 1916- ...CANR-32
Earlier sketch in CA 113
Rolfe, Eugene (Edward Musgrave)
1914- ...13-16R
Rolfe, Franklin P(rescott)
1902-1985 Obituary ...117
Rolfe, Frederick (William Serafino Austin Lewis
Mary) 1860-1913 Brief entry ...107
See also DLB 34
See also TCLC 12
Rolfe, Lionel (Menuhin) 1942- ...CANR-28
Earlier sketch in CA 110
Rolfe, Sheila Constance 1935- ...102
Rolfe, Sidney 1921-1976 ...69-72
Obituary ...65-68
Rolfsrud, Erling Nicolai 1912- ...65-68
Roll, Charles W(eissert) Jr. 1928- ...CANR-1
Earlier sketch in CA 45-48
Roll, Eric 1907- ...102
Roll, Richard J(effrey) 1952- ...124
Roll, Samuel 1942- ...124
Roll, William George Jr. 1926- ...81-84
Roll, Winifred 1909- ...49-52
See also SATA 6
Rolland, Barbara J(une) 1929- ...77-80
Rolland, Romain 1866-1944 Brief entry ...118
See also DLB 65
See also TCLC 23
Rolle, Andrew Frank 1922- ...CANR-3
Earlier sketch in CA 1-4R
Roller, David C(harles) 1937- ...107
Roller, Duane H(enry) D(uBose) 1920- ...61-64
Rolleston, James Lancelot 1939- ...85-88
Rollin, Bernard Elliot 1943- ...108
Rollin, Betty 1936- ...CANR-22
Earlier sketches in CA 13-16R, CANR-7
Rollin, Roger Best 1930- ...CANR-8
Earlier sketch in CA 17-20R
Rollini, Arthur 1912- ...127
Rollins, Alfred Brooks Jr. 1921- ...5-8R
Rollins, Bryant 1937- ...49-52
Rollins, C(alvin) D(wight) 1918- ...41-44R
Rollins, Charlemae Hill 1897-1979 ...9-12R
Obituary ...104
See also BW
See also SATA 3, 26
Rollins, Judith ...122
Rollins, Kelly (a pseudonym) 1924- ...106
Rollins, Peter C(ushing) 1942- ...CANR-26
Earlier sketch in CA 108
Rollins, Richard M(eryl) 1945- ...121
Rollins, Royce
See Pepper, Choral
Rollins, Steed 1916-1985 Obituary ...118
Rollins, Wayne G(ilbert) 1929- ...CANR-3
Earlier sketch in CA 9-12R
Rollison, William D(ewey) 1897-1971 ... CAP-2
Earlier sketch in CA 19-20
Rollo, Vera Foster 1924- ...81-84
Rollock, Barbara T(herese) 1924- ... SATA 64
Rolls, Anthony
See Vulliamy, Colwyn Edward
Rolls, Charles J(ubilee) 1887- ...107
Rolls, Eric C(harles) 1923- ...CANR-13
Earlier sketch in CA 33-36R
Rollyson, Carl
See Rollyson, Carl E(dmund) Jr.
Rollyson, Carl E(dmund) Jr. 1948- ...129
Rolo, Charles J(acques) 1916-1982 ...101
Obituary ...108
Rolo, Paul Jacques Victor 1917- ...21-24R
Roloff, Leland Harold 1927- ...49-52
Roloff, Michael 1937- ...130
Rolph, C. H.
See Hewitt, Cecil Rolph
Rolph, Earl R(obert) 1910- ... CAP-2
Earlier sketch in CA 23-24
Rolston, Holmes III 1932- ...CANR-32
Earlier sketch in CA 113
Rolston, Holmes 1900-1977 ...CANR-3
Earlier sketch in CA 1-4R
Rolt, Francis 1955- ...127
Rolt, L(ionel) T(homas) C(aswall)
1910-1974 ...CANR-1
Earlier sketch in CA 1-4R
Rolt-Wheeler, Francis William
1876-1960 Obituary ...89-92
Rolvaag, O(le) E(dvart)
See Roelvaag, O(le) E(dvart)
Rom, M. Martin 1946- ...81-84
Romagnoli, G(ian) Franco 1926- ...73-76
Romagnoli, Margaret O'Neill 1922- ...73-76
Romain Arnaud, Saint
See Aragon, Louis
Romaine, Lawrence B. 1900- ... CAP-1
Earlier sketch in CA 13-14
Romaine, Paul
See Bleamer, Burton
Romains, Jules 1885-1972 ...CANR-34
Earlier sketch in CA 85-88
See also CLC 7
See also DLB 65
See also MTCW
Roman, Daniel (David) 1921- ...41-44R
Roman, Eric 1926- ...CANR-1
Earlier sketch in CA 1-4R
Roman, Howard (Edgar)
1916(?)-1988 Obituary ...127
Roman, Murray 1920-1984 Obituary ...112
Roman, Stephen B(oleslav)
1921- Brief entry ...112
Romanell, Patrick 1912- ...21-24R
Romanelli, Charles S. 1930- ...13-16R
Romano, Clare 1922- ...CANR-24
Earlier sketch in CA 41-44R
See also Ross, Clare
Romano, Deane Louis 1927- ...25-28R
Romano, Don
See Turner, Robert (Harry)
Romano, John 1948- ...133
Romano, Louis G. 1921- ...CANR-8
Earlier sketch in CA 17-20R
See also SATA 35
Romano, Octavio I. 1932- ...HW
Romanoff, Alexis Lawrence
1892-1980 ...CANR-5
Earlier sketch in CA 9-12R
Romanoff, Harry 1892(?)-1970 Obituary ...104
Romanow, Roy (John) 1939- ...132
Romanowski, Patricia
See Bashe, Patricia Ann Romanowski
Romans, J(ohn) Thomas 1933- ...13-16R
Romanucci-Ross, Lola 1928- ...CANR-18
Earlier sketch in CA 101
Romanus, Charles Franklin 1915-1983 ...21-24R
Obituary ...111
Romanyshyn, Robert Donald 1942- ...118
Romasco, Albert U(go) 1930- ...110
Romberger, Judy 1940- ...106
Rome, Anthony
See Albert, Marvin H(ubert)
Rome, Beatrice K(aufman) 1913- ...13-16R
Rome, Florence 1910- ...33-36R
Romein, J. M.
See Romein, Jan (Marius)
Romein, Jan (Marius) 1893-1962 Obituary ...111
Romer, Alfred 1906- ...37-40R
Romer, (Louis) John 1941- ...110
Romer, Stephen 1957- ...125
Romero, George A. 1940(?)- Brief entry ...116
Romero, Gerry
See Neyland, James (Elwyn)
Romero, Jose Ruben 1890-1952 ...131
Brief entry ...114
See also HW
See also TCLC 14
Romero, Luis 1916- Brief entry ...111
Romero, Orlando 1945- ...69-72
See also DLB 82
See also HW
Romero, Patricia W. 1935- ...CANR-31
Romerstein, Herbert 1931- ...9-12R
Romey, Bill
See Romey, William D(owden)
Romey, William D(owden) 1930- ...57-60
Romig, Edna Davis 1889-1978 ...45-48
Obituary ...103
Romig, Walter 1903-1977 Obituary ...110
Romijn, Johanna Maria Kooyker
See Kooyker-Romijn, Johanna Maria
Romm, Ethel Grodzins 1925- ...33-36R
Romm, Sharon 1942- ...118
Rommel, (Mimi) Dayton ...5-8R
Rommetveit, Ragnar 1924- ...57-60
Romney, George W(ilcken)
1907- Brief entry ...106
Romney, Rodney Ross 1931- ...102
Romney, Ronna 1943- ...116
Romney, Steve
See Bingley, David Ernest
Romo, Ricardo 1943- ...111
Romoser, George K(enneth) 1929- ...41-44R
Rompkey, Ronald (George) 1943- ...CANR-37
Earlier sketch in CA 118
Romtvedt, David 1950- ...125
Romulo, Carlos P(ena) 1899(?)-1985 ...CANR-10
Obituary ...118
Earlier sketch in CA 13-16R
Romyn, Johanna Maria Kooyker
See Kooyker-Romijn, Johanna Maria
Rona, Peter A(rnold) 1934- ...108
Ronald, Ann 1939- ...124
Ronald, David William 1937- ...65-68
Ronald, Hugh 1912(?)-1983 Obituary ...109
Ronalds, Mary Teresa 1946- ...25-28R
Ronaldson, Agnes S. 1916- ...17-20R
Ronan, Colin A(listair) 1920- ...CANR-6
Earlier sketch in CA 5-8R
Ronan, Frank 1963- ...138
Ronan, Georgia
See Crampton, Georgia Ronan
Ronan, Margaret 1918- ...102
Ronan, Thomas Matthew 1907- ... CAP-1
Earlier sketch in CA 9-10
Ronan, Tom
See Ronan, Thomas Matthew
Ronan, William W. 1917- ...33-36R
Ronay, Gabriel Ernest 1930- ...85-88
Roncalli, Angelo Giuseppe
See John XXIII, Pope
Ronck, Ronn 1946- ...121
Ronda, James P(aul) 1943- ...134
Brief entry ...113
Rondell, Florence 1907- ...57-60
Ronder, Paul 1940(?)-1977 Obituary ...73-76
Rondinelli, Dennis A(ugust) 1943- ...111
Rondthaler, Edward 1905- ...13-16R
Ronell, Avital 1956- ...133
Ronen, Dov 1933- ...CANR-28
Earlier sketches in CA 57-60, CANR-10
Roney, Ruth Anne
See McMullin, Ruth R(oney)
Rongen, Bjoern 1906- ... CAP-2
Earlier sketch in CA 29-32
See also SATA 10
Rongen, Bjorn
See Rongen, Bjoern
Rongione, Louis Anthony 1912- ...57-60
Ronken, Harriet
See Lynton, Harriet Ronken
Ronne, Finn 1899-1980 ...CANR-1
Obituary ...97-100
Earlier sketch in CA 1-4R
Ronnie, Art(hur William) 1931- ...41-44R
Ronning, C. Neale 1927- ...5-8R
Ronning, Chester A. 1894-1984 Obituary ...114
Ronns, Edward
See Aarons, Edward S(idney)
Ronsheim, Sally B(ober) 1917(?)-1990 ...57-60
Obituary ...133
Ronsin, Jean
See Rodinson, Maxime
Ronsley, Joseph 1931- ...CANR-10
Earlier sketch in CA 25-28R
Ronsman, M. M.
See Nowak, Mariette
Ronson, Mark
See Alexander, Marc
Rood, Allan 1894- ... CAP-1
Earlier sketch in CA 13-14
Rood, John (Hiram) 1902-1974 ...5-8R
Obituary ...120
Rood, Karen Lane 1946- ...102
Rood, Robert Thomas 1942- ...107
Rood, Ronald (N.) 1920- ...CANR-24
Earlier sketches in CA 21-24R, CANR-9
See also SATA 12
Roodenburg, Nancy McKee
1909-1972 Obituary ...104
Roof, Wade Clark 1939- ...114
Rook, (William) Alan 1909- ...97-100
Rook, Earnest Robert 1917- ...104
Rook, Tony 1932- ...69-72
Rooke, Constance 1942- ...126
Rooke, Daphne (Marie) 1914- ...53-56
See also SATA 12
Rooke, Leon 1934- ...CANR-23
Earlier sketch in CA 25-28R
See also CLC 25, 34
Rooke, P(atricia) T. 1938- ...127
Rookmaaker, Hendrik Roelof
1922-1977 ...CANR-26
Earlier sketch in CA 57-60
Rooks, George (M.) 1951- ...CANR-22
Earlier sketch in CA 105
Room, Adrian 1933- ...CANR-16
Earlier sketch in CA 97-100
Roome, Katherine Ann Davis 1952- ...85-88
Rooney, Andrew A(itken) 1919- ...CANR-9
Earlier sketch in CA 5-8R
See also MTCW
Rooney, Andy
See Rooney, Andrew A(itken)
Rooney, David Douglas 1924- ...CANR-11
Earlier sketch in CA 21-24R
Rooney, Elmo
See Perry, Charles
Rooney, James R(owell) 1927- ...61-64
Rooney, James 1938- ...101
Rooney, Jim
See Rooney, James
Rooney, John F(rancis) Jr. 1939- ...101
Rooney, Lucy 1926- ...135
Rooney, Miriam Theresa ...81-84
Rooney, Patrick C. 1937- ...29-32R
Rooney, William Richard 1938- ...102
Roop, Connie
See Roop, Constance Betzer
Roop, Constance Betzer 1951- ...122
See also SATA 49, 54
Roop, Peter (G.) 1951- ...122
See also SATA 49, 54
Roorbach, Bill 1953- ...137
Roos, Audrey (Kelley) 1912-1982 ...128
Obituary ...108
Roos, Charles A. 1914(?)-1974 Obituary ...53-56
Roos, Hans
See Meissner, Hans-Otto
Roos, Hans Dietrich 1919- ...17-20R
Roos, Kelley
See Roos, Audrey (Kelley)
Roos, Leslie L(eon) Jr. 1940- ...33-36R
Roos, Murphre (joint pseudonym)
See Mele, Jim
Roos, Noralou P(reston) 1942- ...33-36R
Roos, Stephen (Kelley) 1945- ...CANR-31
Earlier sketch in CA 112
See also SATA 41, 47
Roosa, Robert V(incent) 1918- ...25-28R
Roose, Ronald 1945- ...81-84
Roose-Evans, James 1927- ...CANR-35
Earlier sketch in CA 29-32R
See also SATA 65
Roosen, William (James) 1940- ...117
Roosenburg, Henriette
1920-1972 Obituary ...37-40R
Roosevelt, Archibald Bulloch Jr.
1918-1990 ...127
Obituary ...131
Roosevelt, Archie
See Roosevelt, Archibald Bulloch Jr.
Roosevelt, Edith Kermit 1926- ...69-72
Roosevelt, (Anna) Eleanor
1884-1962 Obituary ...89-92
See also SATA 50
Roosevelt, Elliott 1910-1990 ...105
Obituary ...132
See also AITN 1
Roosevelt, Felicia Warburg 1927- ...57-60
Roosevelt, Franklin Delano
1882-1945 Brief entry ...116
Roosevelt, James 1907-1991 ...CANR-12
Obituary ...135
Earlier sketch in CA 69-72
Roosevelt, Nicholas 1893-1982 Obituary ...106
Roosevelt, Selwa 1929- ...134
Roosevelt, Theodore
1858-1919 Brief entry ...115
See also DLB 47
Root, Deane L(eslie) 1947- ...CANR-23
Earlier sketch in CA 107
Root, E(dward) Merrill 1895-1973 ... CAP-1
Earlier sketch in CA 13-16
Root, Franklin Russell 1923- ...5-8R
Root, Judith C(arol) ...65-68
Root, Lin (Segal) ...69-72
Root, Oren 1911- ...85-88
Root, Phyllis 1949- ...123
See also SATA 48, 55
Root, Shelton L. Jr. 1923-1986 ... SATA 51
Root, Waverley (Lewis) 1903-1982 ...CANR-29
Obituary ...108
Earlier sketch in CA 25-28R
See also DLB 4
Root, William Pitt 1941- ...CANR-12
Earlier sketch in CA 25-28R
See also CAAS 11
See also DLB 120
Root-Bernstein, Robert Scott 1953- ...132
Rooth, Gerhard Theodore
1898(?)-1983 Obituary ...110
Rootham, Jasper (St. John) 1910- ...CANR-19
Earlier sketches in CA 5-8R, CANR-4
Roots, Clive (George) 1935- Brief entry ...111
Roots, Ivan Alan 1921- ...9-12R
Roots, John McCook
1904(?)-1988 Obituary ...126
Rooze, Gene E(dward) 1934- ...120
Rope, Henry Edward George 1880-1978 ...5-8R
Obituary ...103
Roper, Gayle G(ordinier) 1940- ...97-100
Roper, H(ugh) R(edwald) Trevor
See Trevor-Roper, H(ugh) R(edwald)
Roper, John Herbert 1948- ...128
Roper, John Stephen
1924(?)-1980 Obituary ...102
Roper, Lanning 1912-1983 Obituary ...109
Roper, Laura Wood 1911- ...57-60
See also SATA 34
Roper, Robert 1946- ...73-76

Roper, Ronnalie J. 1936- 41-44R
Roper, Steve 1941- 103
Roper, Susan Bonthron 1948- 81-84
Roper, William L(eon) 1897-1990 ....33-36R
Obituary 130
Ropke, Wilhelm (Theodor)
See Roepke, Wilhelm (Theodor)
Ropp, Theodore 1911- 5-8R
Roppolo, Joseph Patrick 1913- 13-16R
Rops, Daniel
See Petiot, Henri Jules Charles
Roquebrune, Robert 1889-1978 .... DLB 68
Roquelaure, A. N.
See Rice, Anne
Roquemore, Kathleen (Ann) 1941- 61-64
Rorabaugh, William Joseph 1945- 101
Rorem, Ned 1923- CANR-32
Earlier sketch in CA 17-20R
Roripaugh, A(lan) Robert 1930- 13-16R
Rorke, Margaret (Curry) 1915- 110
Rorty, Amelie Oksenberg 1932- 107
Rorty, James 1891(?)-1973 Obituary 41-44R
Rorty, Richard M(cKay) 1931- CANR-9
Earlier sketch in CA 21-24R
Rorty, Winifred Raushenbush
1894(?)-1979 Obituary 93-96
Rorvik, David M(ichael) 1946- CANR-38
Earlier sketch in CA 85-88
Rosa, Alexis Gomez
See Gomez Rosa, Alexis
See also HW
Rosa, Alfred F(elix) 1942- 41-44R
Rosa, Joao Guimaraes
1908-1967 Obituary 89-92
See also CLC 23
See also DLB 113
Rosa, Joseph G. 1932- 13-16R
Rosa, Nicholas 1926- 110
Rosage, David E. 1913- CANR-21
Earlier sketches in CA 13-16R, CANR-6
Rosaldo, Michelle Z(imbalist) 1944-1981 101
Obituary 108
Rosaldo, Renato I(gnacio) Jr. 1941- 89-92
Rosales, Francisco A(rturo) 1942- 131
See also HW
Rosand, David 1938- 111
Rosa-Nieves, Cesareo 1901-1974 57-60
See also HW
Rosario Green (de Heller), Maria del 1941- 130
See also HW
Rosbottom, Ronald C(arlisle) 1942- 61-64
Rosca, Ninotchka 127
Roscoe, A(drian) A(lan) 1939- 49-52
Roscoe, Charles
See Rowland, D(onald) S(ydney)
Roscoe, D(onald) T(homas) 1934- 113
See also SATA 42
Roscoe, Edwin Scott 1896-1978 ....5-8R
Obituary 103
Roscoe, George B(oggs) 1907- 65-68
Rosdail, Jesse Hart
1914(?)-1977 Obituary 73-76
Rose, A(rthur) James 1927- 17-20R
Rose, Ada Campbell
1902(?)-1976 Obituary 65-68
Rose, Al 1916- 97-100
Rose, Alan Henry 1938- 93-96
Rose, Albert H(enry) 1903- 41-44R
Rose, Alvin E(manuel) 1903-1983 Obituary 109
Rose, Andrew (Wyness) 1944- 136
Rose, Anna Perrott
See Wright, Anna (Maria Louisa Perrott) Rose
Rose, Anne CANR-2
Earlier sketch in CA 49-52
See also SATA 8
Rose, Anthony Lewis 1939- 101
Rose, Arnold M(arshall) 1918-1968 ....5-8R
Rose, Arnold 1916-1983 Obituary 109
Rose, Barbara E. 1937- Brief entry 111
Rose, Betsy
See Rose, Elizabeth
Rose, Billy 1899-1966 Obituary 116
Rose, Brian Waldron 1915- 97-100
Rose, Camille Davied 1893- CAP-2
Earlier sketch in CA 21-22
Rose, Carl 1903-1971 Obituary 29-32R
See also SATA 31
Rose, Clarkson 1890-1968 ....5-8R
Rose, Clive (Martin) 1921- 121
Rose, Constance Hubbard 1934- CANR-16
Earlier sketch in CA 29-32R
Rose, Daniel M. 1940- 33-36R
Rose, David S. 1947- 121
Rose, Deborah Lee 1955- .... SATA 71
Rose, Elinor K(iess) 1920- 29-32R
Rose, Elizabeth (Jane Pretty) 1933- CANR-9
Earlier sketch in CA 5-8R
See also SATA 28, 68
Rose, Elizabeth 1915- 73-76
Rose, (Edward) Elliot 1928- 65-68
Rose, Ernst A(ndreas) G(ottlieb) 1899- CANR-4
Earlier sketch in CA 5-8R
Rose, Florella
See Carlson, Vada F.
Rose, Frank 1949- 103
Rose, Gerald (Hembdon Seymour)
1935- CANR-9
Earlier sketch in CA 65-68
See also SATA 30, 68
Rose, Gilbert J(acob) 1923- 103
Rose, (Arthur) Gordon 1920-1975 ....CANR-4
Earlier sketch in CA 1-4R
Rose, Grace B(erne) 1914- 108
Rose, Hannah T. 1909(?)-1976 Obituary 69-72
Rose, Harold Wickliffe 1896- CAP-1
Earlier sketch in CA 9-10
Rose, Harold 1921-1967 ....5-8R
Obituary 103
Rose, Helen 1904(?)-1985 Obituary 117
Rose, Hilary
See Mackinnon, Charles Roy
Rose, Homer C. 1909-1967 .... CAP-1
Earlier sketch in CA 13-16
Rose, James M. 1941- 102
Rose, Jeanne 1940- CANR-16
Earlier sketch in CA 93-96
Rose, Jennifer
See Weber, Nancy
Rose, Jerome G. 1926- CANR-8
Earlier sketch in CA 13-16R
Rose, Jerry D. 1933- 33-36R
Rose, Joel 1948- 129
Rose, Kenneth Jon 1954- CANR-38
Earlier sketch in CA 115
Rose, Kenneth (Vivian) 1924- 128
Brief entry 123
Rose, Leo E. 1926- 85-88
Rose, Lisle A(bbott) 1936- CANR-10
Earlier sketch in CA 65-68
Rose, Lynn Edmondson 1934- Brief entry 105
Rose, Marcia
See Kamien, Marcia
and Novak, Rose
Rose, Margaret A. 1947- 138
Rose, Marilyn Gaddis 1930- 33-36R
Rose, Mark 1939- CANR-10
Earlier sketch in CA 25-28R
Rose, Michael (Simon) 1937- 133
Rose, Nancy A.
See Sweetland, Nancy A(nn)
Rose, Nancy (Ann) 1934- 37-40R
Rose, Norman Anthony 1934- 104
Rose, Paul (Bernard) 1935- 103
Rose, Pete(r Edward) 1942- Brief entry 113
Rose, Peter I(saac) 1933- CANR-5
Earlier sketch in CA 13-16R
Rose, Phyllis
See Thompson, Phyllis Hoge
Rose, Phyllis 1942- 135
Rose, R(obert) B(arrie) 1929- 61-64
Rose, Ralph 1911(?)-1984 Obituary 112
Rose, Reginald 1920- 73-76
See also DLB 26
Rose, Richard 1933- CANR-27
Earlier sketches in CA 21-24R, CANR-10
Rose, Stephen C. 1936- 129
Rose, Stuart 1899(?)-1975 Obituary 61-64
Rose, Susan (Phyllida) 1938- 111
Rose, Thomas 1938- 33-36R
Rose, Wendy 1948- CANR-5
Earlier sketch in CA 53-56
See also SATA 12
Rose, Will(iam Palen) 1889-1977 57-60
Obituary 134
Rose, William 1920(?)-1987 Obituary 121
Rose, Willie Lee (Nichols) 1927- 13-16R
Rose-Ackerman, Susan 1942- 111
Roseberry, Cecil R. 1902- 21-24R
Roseboom, Eugene Holloway 1892- 5-8R
Roseboro, John 1933- 102
Rosebrock, Ellen Fletcher 1947- CANR-10
Earlier sketch in CA 57-60
Rosebury, Theodor 1904-1976 .... CAP-2
Obituary 69-72
Earlier sketch in CA 25-28
Rosecrance, Francis Chase 1897- 5-8R
Rosecrance, Richard (Newton)
1930- Brief entry 111
Rosedale, Valerie
See Harron, Don(ald)
Rosefielde, Steven 1942- CANR-25
Earlier sketch in CA 45-48
Rosei, Peter 1946- .... DLB 85
Roseliep, Raymond 1917- CANR-6
Earlier sketch in CA 9-12R
Roselle, Daniel 1920- 13-16R
Roseller, David
See Timms, E(dward) V(ivian)
Roseman, Ellen Barbara 1947- 124
Roseman, Kenneth David 1939- 110
Rosemeyer, Nita (Mary) 1907- 119
Rosemond, John K(irk) 1947- 110
Rosemont, Henry Jr. 1934- 41-44R
Rosen, Barbara 1929- 37-40R
Rosen, Barry 1944- 136
Rosen, Benson 1942- 120
Rosen, Carol (Cynthia) 1950- 119
Rosen, Charles (Welles) 1927- 126
Rosen, Corey 1948- 138
Rosen, Dorothy 1916- 119
Rosen, Edward 1906-1985 ....21-24R
Obituary 115
Rosen, Elliot A(lfred) 1928- 93-96
Rosen, Frederick 1938- 120
Rosen, George 1910-1977 ....CANR-31
Obituary 73-76
Earlier sketch in CA 81-84
Rosen, George 1920- 57-60
Rosen, Gerald 1938- 33-36R
Rosen, Haiim B(aruch) 1922- CANR-20
Earlier sketch in CA 1-4R
Rosen, Hjalmar 1922- 17-20R
Rosen, Ira 1954- 114
Rosen, James Alan
1908(?)-1972 Obituary 37-40R
Rosen, Joe
See Rosen, Joseph
Rosen, Joseph 1937- CANR-9
Earlier sketch in CA 65-68
Rosen, Laura 1948- 116
Rosen, Lawrence R(onald) 1938- 57-60
Rosen, Leonard 1954- 125
Rosen, Lillian (Diamond) 1928- 108
See also SATA 63
Rosen, Martin Meyer
See Rosen, Moishe (Martin)
Rosen, Marvin J(erold) 1929- 69-72
Rosen, Michael J(oel) 1954- 132
Rosen, Michael 1946- CANR-32
Earlier sketches in CA 25-28R, CANR-15
See also SATA 40, 48
Rosen, Moishe (Martin) 1932- CANR-4
Earlier sketch in CA 49-52
Rosen, Mortimer (Gilbert) 1931- 101
Rosen, Norma (Gangel) 1925- 33-36R
See also DLB 28
Rosen, Paul L(yon) 1939- 61-64
Rosen, Richard (Dean) 1949- 77-80
See also CLC 39
Rosen, Robert C(harles) 1947- 106
Rosen, Ruth (E.) 1945- 125
Rosen, S. McKee 1902(?)-1978 Obituary 77-80
Rosen, Sam 1920- 5-8R
Rosen, Samuel 1897-1981 Obituary 108
Rosen, Seymour Michael 1924- 33-36R
Rosen, Sheldon 1943- 109
Rosen, Shirley 1933- 105
Rosen, Sidney 1916- 9-12R
See also SATA 1
Rosen, Stanley H. 1929- 25-28R
Rosen, Stephen 1934- 65-68
Rosen, Trix 1947- 116
Rosen, Winifred 1943- CANR-32
Earlier sketch in CA 29-32R
See also SATA 8
Rosenak, Charles B. 1927- 134
Rosenak, Chuck
See Rosenak, Charles B.
Rosenak, Jan(ice M.) 1930- 134
Rosenast, Eleanor S(trauss) 1929- 97-100
Rosenau, Helen 101
Rosenau, James N(athan) 1924- CANR-18
Earlier sketches in CA 1-4R, CANR-2
Rosenauer, Johnnie L(ee) 1951- 110
Rosenbaum, Alan S(helby) 1941- 124
Brief entry 106
Rosenbaum, Alvin 1945- 113
Rosenbaum, Bernard L. 1937- 107
Rosenbaum, Eileen 1936- 21-24R
Rosenbaum, Ernest H. 1929- 97-100
Rosenbaum, H. Jon 1941- 41-44R
Rosenbaum, Jean 1927- 17-20R
Rosenbaum, Jonathan 1943- 130
Rosenbaum, Kurt 1926- 13-16R
Rosenbaum, Maurice 1907- 17-20R
See also SATA 6
Rosenbaum, Max 1923- 41-44R
Rosenbaum, Nathan 1897- CAP-2
Earlier sketch in CA 23-24
Rosenbaum, Patricia L(eib) 1932- 105
Rosenbaum, Peter S. 1940- CANR-14
Earlier sketch in CA 21-24R
Rosenbaum, S(tanford) P(atrick) 1929- 13-16R
Rosenbaum, Samuel R(awlins)
1888-1972 Obituary 37-40R
Rosenbaum, Veryl 1936- CANR-1
Earlier sketch in CA 49-52
Rosenbaum, Walter A(nthony) 1937- 21-24R
Rosenberg, Alexander 1946- 132
Rosenberg, Arthur D(onald) 1939- 61-64
Rosenberg, Betty 1916- 113
Rosenberg, Bruce A(lan) 1934- 29-32R
Rosenberg, Charles E(rnest) 1936- 97-100
Rosenberg, Claude N(ewman) Jr.
1928- CANR-5
Earlier sketch in CA 1-4R
Rosenberg, David A(aron) 1940- 93-96
Rosenberg, Dorothy 1906- CANR-18
Earlier sketches in CA 45-48, CANR-2
See also SATA 40
Rosenberg, Edgar 1925- 13-16R
Rosenberg, Ellis Howard
1936(?)-1986 Obituary 121
Rosenberg, Emily S(chlaht) 1944- 108
Rosenberg, Ethel (Clifford) 1915- CANR-16
Earlier sketch in CA 29-32R
See also SATA 3
Rosenberg, George S(tanley) 1930- 29-32R
Rosenberg, Harold 1906-1978 ....CANR-39
Obituary 77-80
Earlier sketch in CA 21-24R
Rosenberg, Harry E. 1932- 57-60
Rosenberg, Isaac 1890-1918 Brief entry 107
See also DLB 20
See also TCLC 12
Rosenberg, Israel 1909- 49-52
Rosenberg, J(ehiol) Mitchell 1906- 37-40R
Rosenberg, Jakob 1893-1980 Obituary 97-100
Rosenberg, James L. 1921- 13-16R
Rosenberg, Jane 1949- 121
See also SATA 58
Rosenberg, Janet 1930- 117
Rosenberg, Jerome Roy 1926- 104
Rosenberg, Jerry M. 1935- CANR-24
Earlier sketches in CA 21-24R, CANR-9
Rosenberg, Jessie 1941- 21-24R
Rosenberg, Joel 1954- 115
Rosenberg, John D(avid) 1929- CANR-5
Earlier sketch in CA 1-4R
Rosenberg, John J.
See Ramati, Yohanan (Joseph)
Rosenberg, Joseph
See Ramati, Yohanan (Joseph)
Rosenberg, Judith K(aren) 1945- 57-60
Rosenberg, Kenyon Charles 1933- 57-60
Rosenberg, Marvin 1912- 1-4R
Rosenberg, Maurice 1919- 81-84
Rosenberg, Maxine B(erta) 1939- 117
See also SATA 47, 55
Rosenberg, Morris 1922- CANR-2
Earlier sketch in CA 5-8R
Rosenberg, Nancy (Sherman) 1931- CANR-22
Earlier sketches in CA 1-4R, CANR-5
See also SATA 4
Rosenberg, Nathan 1927- Brief entry 113
Rosenberg, Neil V. 1939- 122
Rosenberg, Norman J(ack) 1930- 57-60
Rosenberg, Norman L(ewis) 1942- 122
Rosenberg, Philip 1942- 103
Rosenberg, Rosalind 1946- 108
Rosenberg, Samuel 1912- 53-56
Rosenberg, Sharon 1942- CANR-10
Earlier sketch in CA 57-60
See also SATA 8
Rosenberg, Shirley Sirota 1925- CANR-12
Earlier sketch in CA 21-24R
Rosenberg, Stephen N(icholas) 1941- 111
Rosenberg, Stuart E. 1922-1990 ....CANR-9
Obituary 131
Earlier sketch in CA 5-8R
Rosenberg, Tina 1960- 136
Rosenberg, William Gordon 1938- 61-64
Rosenberg, Wolfgang 1915- CANR-9
Earlier sketch in CA 65-68
Rosenberger, Francis Coleman
1915- CANR-15
Earlier sketch in CA 41-44R
Rosenberger, Harleigh M. 1913- 21-24R
Rosenberger, Homer Tope 1908- CANR-8
Earlier sketch in CA 17-20R
Rosenblatt, Arthur
See Rosenblatt, Arthur S.
Rosenblatt, Arthur S. 1938- 134
See also SATA 45, 68
Rosenblatt, Bernard A. 1886- CAP-1
Earlier sketch in CA 13-14
Rosenblatt, Fred 1914- 41-44R
Rosenblatt, Gary 1947- 77-80
Rosenblatt, Jason P. 1941- 137
Rosenblatt, Joe
See Rosenblatt, Joseph
See also CLC 15
Rosenblatt, Jon M(ichael) 1947- 89-92
Rosenblatt, Joseph 1933- 89-92
See also Rosenblatt, Joe
Rosenblatt, Louise M(ichelle) 1904- 49-52
Rosenblatt, Milton B.
1908(?)-1975 Obituary 53-56
Rosenblatt, Roger 1940- CANR-34
Earlier sketch in CA 85-88
Rosenblatt, Samuel 1902- 53-56
Rosenblatt, Stanley M. 1936- 29-32R
Rosenblatt, Suzanne Maris 1937- 69-72
Rosenblith, Judy F(rancis) 1921- 25-28R
Rosenbloom, Bert 1944- 109
Rosenbloom, David H(arry) 1943- 73-76
Rosenbloom, David L. 1944- 45-48
Rosenbloom, Jerry S(amuel) 1939- 129
Brief entry 110
Rosenbloom, Joseph R. 1928- 29-32R
Rosenbloom, Joseph 1928- CANR-21
Earlier sketches in CA 57-60, CANR-6
See also SATA 21
Rosenbloom, Noah H. 1915- CANR-14
Earlier sketch in CA 37-40R
Rosenblum, Art 1927- 57-60
Rosenblum, Davida 1927- 93-96
Rosenblum, Gershen 1924- 41-44R
Rosenblum, Helen Faye 1941- 121
Rosenblum, Joseph 1947- 111
Rosenblum, Leonard A. 1936- CANR-11
Earlier sketch in CA 57-60
Rosenblum, Marc J. 1936- 29-32R
Rosenblum, Martin J(ack) 1946- CANR-18
Earlier sketches in CA 45-48, CANR-2
See also CAAS 11
Rosenblum, Mort 1943- 73-76
Rosenblum, Nancy L. 1947- 133
Rosenblum, Richard 1928- CANR-9
Earlier sketch in CA 65-68
See also SATA 11
Rosenblum, Robert H. 1927- CANR-5
Earlier sketch in CA 1-4R
Rosenbluth, Gideon 1921- 61-64
Rosenburg, John M. 1918- 21-24R
See also SATA 6
Rosenburg, Robert K(emper) 1920- CANR-4
Earlier sketch in CA 5-8R
Rosendall, Betty 1916- 49-52
Rosenfarb, Chawa 1923- 53-56
Rosenfeld, Albert (Hyman) 1920- CANR-11
Earlier sketch in CA 65-68
Rosenfeld, Alvin H(irsch) 1938- CANR-24
Earlier sketches in CA 49-52, CANR-4
Rosenfeld, Alvin 1919- 73-76
Rosenfeld, Arnold (Solomon) 1933- 65-68
Rosenfeld, Edward J(ulius) 1943- 41-44R
Rosenfeld, Harry M(orris) 1929- 69-72
Rosenfeld, Harvey 1939- 110
Rosenfeld, Isaac 1918-1956 .... DLB 28
Rosenfeld, Isadore 1926- 81-84
Rosenfeld, Jeffrey P(hilip) 1946- 115
Rosenfeld, Lulla 1914- 85-88
Rosenfeld, Marthe 1928- 45-48
Rosenfeld, Sam 1920- 9-12R
Rosenfeld, Samuel 1896-1963 Obituary 89-92
See also Tzara, Tristan
Rosenfeld, Sybil (Marion) 1903- 119
Rosenfield, Isadore 1893-1980 Obituary 97-100
Rosenfield, Israel 1939- 128
Rosenfield, James A(lexander) 1943- 49-52
Rosenfield, John M(ax) 1924- CANR-14
Earlier sketch in CA 21-24R
Rosenfield, Leonora Cohen 1909-1982 ....41-44R
Obituary 105
Rosengart, Oliver A. 1941- 49-52

Rosengarten, Frank 1927- 73-76
Rosengarten, Frederic (Jr.) 1916- 118
Rosengarten, Herbert (J.) 1940- 138
Rosengarten, Theodore 1944- 103
Rosengren, William R(udolph)
1929- Brief entry 114
Rosenhaupt, Hans 1911-1985 Obituary 116
Rosenheim, Edward W(eil) Jr. 1918- 25-28R
Rosenheim, Lucile G. 1902-1990 Obituary 132
Rosenhouse, Archie 1878- CAP-2
Earlier sketch in CA 21-22
Rosenkrantz, Linda 1934- CANR-11
Earlier sketch in CA 25-28R
Rosenkranz, Richard S. 1942- 37-40R
Rosenman, John B(rown) 1941- 106
Rosenman, Ray H(arold) 1920- 97-100
Rosenman, Samuel I(rving)
1896-1973 Obituary 41-44R
Rosenmeyer, Thomas Gustav 1920- 111
Rosenn, Keith S(amuel) 1938- 111
Rosenof, Theodore 1943- CANR-10
Earlier sketch in CA 65-68
Rosenow, John E(dward) 1949- 97-100
Rosenquist, Carl M(artin) 1895-1973 .... CAP-2
Earlier sketch in CA 29-32
Rosenrauch, Heinz Erich
See Rosen, Haiim B(aruch)
Rosensaft, Menachem Z. 1948- 21-24R
Rosenstein-Rodan, Paul N. 1902-1985 107
Obituary 116
Rosenstiel, Annette 1911- 115
Rosenstiel, Leonie 1947- 85-88
Rosenstock, (Patricia) Janet (Stearns)
1933- 108
Rosenstock-Huessy, Eugen 1888-1973 ...... CAP-1
Obituary 41-44R
Earlier sketch in CA 13-16
Rosenstone, Robert A(llan) 1936- CANR-28
Earlier sketch in CA 29-32R
Rosenstone, Steven J(ay) 1952- 104
Rosenthal, A(braham) M(ichael)
1922- CANR-27
Earlier sketch in CA 21-24R
Rosenthal, Alan 1936- 105
Rosenthal, Albert H(arold) 1914- 21-24R
Rosenthal, Andrew
1918(?)-1979 Obituary 89-92
Rosenthal, Bernard G(ordon) 1922- CANR-11
Earlier sketch in CA 29-32R
Rosenthal, Bernice (Glatzer) 1938- 121
Rosenthal, David 1916- 41-44R
Rosenthal, Donald B. 1937- CANR-14
Earlier sketch in CA 37-40R
Rosenthal, Douglas E(urico) 1940- 57-60
Rosenthal, Earl E(dgar) 1921- 41-44R
Rosenthal, Edwin Stanley 1914- 77-80
Rosenthal, Eric 1905- CANR-6
Earlier sketch in CA 9-12R
Rosenthal, Erwin Isak Jacob 1904- 102
Rosenthal, F(rank) F(ranz)
1911(?)-1979 Obituary 89-92
Rosenthal, Harold (David) 1917-1987 ....5-8R
Obituary 122
Rosenthal, Harold 1914- 111
See also SATA 35
Rosenthal, Harry F(rederick) 1927- 65-68
Rosenthal, Harry Kenneth 1941- 57-60
Rosenthal, Henry Moses
1906-1977 Obituary 73-76
Rosenthal, Joe
See Rosenthal, Joseph J.
Rosenthal, Joel T(homas) 1934- 57-60
Rosenthal, Joseph J. 1911- 69-72
Rosenthal, Jules M. 1924- 17-20R
Rosenthal, M(acha) L(ouis) 1917- CANR-4
Earlier sketch in CA 1-4R
See also CAAS 6
See also CLC 28
See also DLB 5
See also SATA 59
Rosenthal, Mark A(lan) 1946- .... SATA 64
Rosenthal, Mark 1945- 130
Rosenthal, Mitchell S(tephen) 1935- 104
Rosenthal, Peggy 1944- 121
Rosenthal, Renee Obituary 57-60
Rosenthal, Richard A. 1925- 1-4R
Rosenthal, Ricky 1930(?)-1984 Obituary 114
Rosenthal, Robert 1933- CANR-16
Earlier sketch in CA 41-44R
Rosenthal, Shirley Lord 1934- CANR-27
Earlier sketches in CA 65-68, CANR-11
Rosenthal, Stuart 1934- 117
Rosenthal, Sylvia 1911- CANR-27
Earlier sketch in CA 109
Rosenus, Alan (Harvey) 1940- 73-76
Rosenwald, Henry M(artin) 1905- 33-36R
Rosenwasser, Dorothy Eckmann 1917- 1-4R
Rosenzweig, Michael L(eo) 1941- 101
Rosenzweig, Norman 1924- CANR-6
Earlier sketch in CA 57-60
Rosenzweig, Robert Myron 1931- 113
Rosenzweig, Roy 1950- CANR-35
Earlier sketch in CA 113
Rosett, Arthur (Irwin) 1934- 69-72
Rosette, Bennetta Jules
See Jules-Rosette, Bennetta (Washington)
Roseveare, Helen Margaret 1925- 73-76
Rosewell, Paul Truman 1926- 17-20R
Roseyear, John 1936- 21-24R
Roshco, Bernard 1929- 5-8R
Rosher, Grace Obituary 111
Roshwalb, Irving 1924- 45-48
Roshwald, Mordecai Marceli 1921- 1-4R
Rosi, Eugene J(oseph) 1931- 61-64
Rosichan, Richard H(arry) 1941- 45-48
Rosie, George 1941- 120
Rosier, Bernard 1931- CANR-12
Earlier sketch in CA 29-32R
Rosier, James L(ouis) 1932- CANR-22
Earlier sketch in CA 1-4R
Rosillo-Calle, Francisco 1945- 121
Rositzke, Harry A(ugust) 1911- CANR-29
Earlier sketch in CA 45-48
Roskamp, Karl Wilhelm 1923- 13-16R
Roske, Ralph Joseph 1921- 122
Roskies, David G(regory) 1948- 120
Roskies, Ethel 1933- CANR-25
Earlier sketch in CA 45-48
Roskill, Mark W(entworth) 1933- CANR-6
Earlier sketch in CA 5-8R
Roskill, Stephen W(entworth)
1903-1982 ....CANR-6
Obituary 108
Earlier sketch in CA 13-16R
Rosko, Milt 1930- 41-44R
Roskolenko, Harry 1907-1980 ....CANR-17
Obituary 101
Earlier sketch in CA 13-16R
Roslavleva, Natalia
See Rene, Natalia
Rosman, Abraham 1930- 89-92
Rosmond, Babette 1921- CANR-6
Earlier sketch in CA 5-8R
Rosner, David K(arl) 1947- 112
Rosner, Fred 1935- CANR-32
Earlier sketch in CA 113
Rosner, Joseph 1914- 57-60
Rosner, Lynn 1944- 61-64
Rosner, Stanley 1928- 41-44R
Rosnow, Ralph L(eon) 1936- CANR-28
Earlier sketches in CA 21-24R, CANR-10
Rosochacki, Daniel 1942- 45-48
Rosoff, Sidney D. 1924- 1-4R
Rosovsky, Henry 1927- Brief entry 105
Rosow, Irving 1921- 85-88
Rosow, Jerome M(orris) 1919- 81-84
Rosowski, Susan J(ean) 1942- CANR-29
Earlier sketch in CA 111
Ross, Alan
See Warwick, Alan R(oss)
Ross, Alan O(tto) 1921- 41-44R
Ross, Alan Strode Campbell 1907-1980 .....9-12R
Obituary 102
Ross, Alan 1922- CANR-21
Earlier sketches in CA 9-12R, CANR-6
Ross, Albert
See Jarrett, Philip (Martin)
Ross, Alec 1926- 29-32R
Ross, Alex(ander) 1909- .... SATA 29
Ross, Alf (Niels Christian Hansen) 1899- 53-56
Ross, Angus
See Giggal, Kenneth
Ross, Angus 1911- 21-24R
Ross, Barnaby
See Dannay, Frederic
Ross, Bernard H(arvey) 1934- 102
Ross, Bernard L.
See Follett, Ken(neth Martin)
Ross, Bette M. 1932- 106
Ross, Betty 69-72
Ross, Bill D. 1921- 123
Ross, Billy I(rvan) 1925- 57-60
Ross, Brian (Elliot) 1948- 126
Brief entry 119
Ross, Caroline
See Nicolson, Catherine
Ross, Catherine
See Beaty, Betty
Ross, Charles (Derek)
1924(?)-1986 Obituary 118
Ross, Charlotte (Brand) 1921- 117
Ross, Clare
See Romano, Clare
See also SATA 48
Ross, Clarissa
See Ross, W(illiam) E(dward) D(aniel)
Ross, Colin
See Roskolenko, Harry
Ross, Corinne Madden 1931- 106
Ross, Dallas
See Reynolds, Dallas McCord
Ross, Dan
See Ross, W(illiam) E(dward) D(aniel)
Ross, Dana
See Ross, W(illiam) E(dward) D(aniel)
Ross, Dana Fuller
See Gerson, Noel Bertram
Ross, Dave
See Ross, David
See also SATA 32
Ross, David O(liver) Jr. 1936- Brief entry 117
Ross, David P(reston) Jr.
1908-1984 Obituary 112
Ross, David 1896-1975 65-68
Obituary 61-64
See also SATA 20, 49
Ross, David 1949- 111
See also Ross, Dave
Ross, Davis R. B. 1934- 33-36R
Ross, Diana
See Denney, Diana
Ross, Donald K. 1943- 49-52
Ross, Dorothy 1936- 137
Ross, Elizabeth Irvin 1942- 121
Ross, Emory 1887-1973 Obituary 41-44R
Ross, Eric (De Witt) 1929- 29-32R
Ross, Eulalie Steinmetz 1910-1975 ....17-20R
Obituary 134
Ross, Eva J(eany) 1903-1969 .... CAP-2
Earlier sketch in CA 23-24
Ross, Floyd H(iatt) 1910- 73-76
Ross, Frances Aileen 1909- CAP-1
Earlier sketch in CA 9-10
Ross, Frank E. 1925- 17-20R
Ross, Frank (Xavier) Jr. 1914- CANR-16
Earlier sketch in CA 93-96
See also SATA 28
Ross, Gary 1948- CANR-38
Earlier sketch in CA 115
Ross, George
See Morgan-Grenville, Gerard (Wyndham)
Ross, H(ugh) Laurence 1934- CANR-13
Earlier sketch in CA 77-80
Ross, Hal 1941- 65-68
Ross, Harold Raymond 1904- CAP-2
Earlier sketch in CA 19-20
Ross, Harold W(allace)
1892-1951 Brief entry 119
Ross, Helaine
See Daniels, Dorothy
Ross, Helen 1890(?)-1978 85-88
Obituary 81-84
Ross, Ian
See Rossmann, John F(rancis)
Ross, Ian Simpson 1930- CANR-3
Earlier sketch in CA 45-48
Ross, Irwin 1919- 97-100
Ross, Ishbel 1897-1975 93-96
Obituary 61-64
Ross, Ivan T.
See Rossner, Robert
Ross, J. H.
See Lawrence, T(homas) E(dward)
Ross, James Davidson 1924- 49-52
Ross, James F(rancis) 1931- CANR-11
Earlier sketch in CA 21-24R
Ross, James Frederick Stanley 1886- 9-12R
Ross, James S(tiven)
1892-1975 Obituary 57-60
Ross, Janet 1914- 37-40R
Ross, Joel E(lmore Jr.) 1922- 29-32R
Ross, John A(ddison) 1919- 17-20R
Ross, John Munder 1945- 127
Ross, John O'C(onnell) 1916- 25-28R
Ross, John 1921- 108
See also SATA 45
Ross, Jonathan
See Rossiter, John
Ross, Joseph
See Wrzos, Joseph Henry
Ross, Judith Wilson 1937- 114
Ross, Judy 1942- .... SATA 54
Ross, K. G. M. Obituary 116
Ross, Katherine
See Walter, Dorothy Blake
Ross, Kenneth Lynn 1940- 125
Ross, Kenneth (Michael Andrew) 1941- 107
Ross, Kenneth N(eedham) 1908-1970 .....CANR-5
Earlier sketch in CA 5-8R
Ross, Lanson Clifford Jr. 1936- 120
Ross, Laura
See Mincieli, Rose Laura
Ross, Leah
See Webb, Mary H(aydn)
Ross, Leonard
See Rosten, Leo C(alvin)
Ross, Leonard M(ichael) 1945-1985 ......CANR-29
Obituary 116
Earlier sketch in CA 29-32R
Ross, Leonard Q.
See Rosten, Leo C(alvin)
Ross, Lillian 1927- 9-12R
Ross, Lola Romanucci
See Romanucci-Ross, Lola
Ross, Lynne Nannen
See Ross-Robertson, Lynne Nannen
Ross, Mabel (Irene) H(ughes) 1909- 81-84
Ross, Malcolm
See Ross-Macdonald, Malcolm J(ohn)
Ross, Marc H(ansen) 1928- 114
Ross, Marilyn
See Ross, W(illiam) E(dward) D(aniel)
Ross, Marilyn (Ann) Heimberg 1939- CANR-31
Earlier sketches in CA 81-84, CANR-14
Ross, Marjorie Drake Rhoades 1901- 1-4R
Ross, Martha 1951- 103
Ross, Martin J. 1912- 53-56
Ross, Marvin C(hauncey) 1904-1977 .... CAP-2
Obituary 69-72
Earlier sketch in CA 19-20
Ross, Mary Adelaide Eden
See Phillpotts, (Mary) Adelaide Eden
Ross, Michael W(allis) 1952- 118
Ross, Michael 1905- 85-88
Ross, Mitchell S(cott) 1953- 81-84
Ross, Murray George 1912- 17-20R
Ross, Nancy
See DeRoin, Nancy
Ross, Nancy Wilson 1910-1986 97-100
Obituary 118
Ross, Nathaniel 1904- 21-24R
Ross, Pat(ricia Kienzle) 1943- 128
See also SATA 48, 53
Ross, Patricia
See Baxter, Patricia E. W.
Ross, Paul
See Crawford, William (Elbert)
Ross, Philip 1939- 69-72
Ross, Phyllis (Freedman) 1926-1970 .... CAP-2
Earlier sketch in CA 17-18
Ross, Prudence Leith
See Leith-Ross, Prudence
Ross, Ralph 1911- 13-16R
Ross, Ramon R(oyal) 1930- .... SATA 62
Ross, Raymond S(amuel) 1925- CANR-27
Earlier sketches in CA 21-24R, CANR-8
Ross, Robert H(enry) Jr. 1916- 13-16R
Ross, Robert Horace 106
Ross, Robert S(amuel) 1940- 57-60
Ross, Robert W.
See Power-Ross, Robert W.
Ross, Russell M. 1921- 21-24R
Ross, Ruth 1930(?)-1986 Obituary 119
Ross, Sam 1912- 13-16R
Ross, Sheila Muriel 1925- 106
Ross, (James) Sinclair 1908- 73-76
See also CLC 13
See also DLB 88
Ross, Stanley R(obert) 1921- CANR-7
Earlier sketch in CA 17-20R
Ross, Stanley Ralph 1940- CANR-20
Earlier sketch in CA 97-100
Ross, Stephen David 1935- CANR-39
Earlier sketches in CA 41-44R, CANR-17
Ross, Steven Thomas 1937- 41-44R
Ross, Sutherland
See Callard, Thomas Henry
Ross, T(heodore) J(ohn) 1924- 57-60
Ross, Terrence 1947- 103
Ross, Thomas B. 1929- 29-32R
Ross, Thomas W(ynne) 1923- 41-44R
Ross, Timothy A(rrowsmith) 1936- 57-60
Ross, Tony 1938- CANR-35
Earlier sketch in CA 77-80
See also MAICYA
See also SATA 17, 65
Ross, Veronica 1946- 113
Ross, W(illiam) E(dward) D(aniel)
1912- CANR-32
Earlier sketches in CA 81-84, CANR-14
Ross, W(illiam) Gordon 1900- 45-48
Ross, W. W. E. 1894-1966 .... DLB 88
Ross, Wilda 1915- 85-88
See also SATA 39, 51
Ross, William
See Dewart, Leslie
Ross, William B. 1915- 25-28R
Ross, Z. H.
See Ross, Zola Helen
Ross, Zola Helen 1912-1989 53-56
Obituary 130
Rossabi, Morris 1941- 102
Rossant, Murray J(oseph)
1923-1988 Obituary 125
Rossbach, Richard M.
1915(?)-1987 Obituary 123
Rossbacher, Lisa A(nn) 1952- 117
Rossberg, Robert H. 1926- 45-48
Rosse, Ian
See Straker, J(ohn) F(oster)
Rosse, Susanna
See Connolly, Vivian
Rossel, Seymour 1945- CANR-21
Earlier sketches in CA 53-56, CANR-5
See also SATA 28
Rossel, Sven H(akon) 1943- CANR-22
Earlier sketch in CA 105
Rossellini, Roberto 1906-1977 Obituary 69-72
Rossel-Waugh, C. C.
See Waugh, Carol-Lynn Roessel
Rossen, Robert 1908-1966 Obituary 113
See also DLB 26
Rosser, Neill A(lbert) 1916-1973 .... CAP-1
Earlier sketch in CA 13-16
Rosset, B(enjamin) C(harles) 1910-1974 .....9-12R
Obituary 103
Rosset, Barnet Lee Jr. 1922- 97-100
Rosset, Barney
See Rosset, Barnet Lee Jr.
Rossetti, Christina (Georgina)
1830-1894 .... DLB 35
See also MAICYA
See also SATA 20
See also WLC
Rossetti, Dante Gabriel
1828-1882 .... CDBLB 1832-1890
See also DLB 35
See also WLC
Rossetti, Minerva
See Rowland, D(onald) S(ydney)
Rossi, Aga
See Agarossi, Elena
Rossi, Alfred 1935- 29-32R
Rossi, Alice S(chaerr) 1922- CANR-17
Earlier sketches in CA 45-48, CANR-1
Rossi, Bruno
See Levinson, Leonard
Rossi, Cristina Peri
See Peri Rossi, Cristina
Rossi, Ernest Lawrence 1933- CANR-14
Earlier sketch in CA 37-40R
Rossi, Ino 89-92
Rossi, Lino 1923- 104
Rossi, Mario 1916- CANR-8
Earlier sketch in CA 5-8R
Rossi, Nicholas Louis Jr. 1924- CANR-6
Earlier sketch in CA 13-16R
Rossi, Nick
See Rossi, Nicholas Louis Jr.
Rossi, Paul A. 1929- Brief entry 110
Rossi, Peter Henry 1921- CANR-19
Earlier sketches in CA 1-4R, CANR-4
Rossi, Philip Joseph 1943- 115
Rossi, Sanna Morrison Barlow 1917- 93-96
Rossi, William A(nthony) 1916- 65-68
Rossie, Jonathan Gregory
1935- Brief entry 106
Rossi-Landi, Ferruccio 1921- 114
Rossini, Frederick A(nthony) 1939- CANR-12
Earlier sketch in CA 73-76
Rossit, Edward A. 1921- 17-20R
Rossiter, Clare
See Dawson, Janis
Rossiter, Clinton (Lawrence)
1917-1970 Obituary 25-28R
Rossiter, Frank R(aymond) 1937- 61-64

Rossiter, Ian
See Ross Williamson, Hugh
Rossiter, Jane
See Ross, W(illiam) E(dward) D(aniel)
Rossiter, John 1916- ... 33-36R
Rossiter, Margaret W(alsh) 1944- ... CANR-13
Earlier sketch in CA 77-80
Rossiter, Sarah 1942- ... 136
Rossiter, (Percival) Stuart (Bryce) 1923- ... 85-88
Rosskam, Edwin 1903(?)-1985 Obituary ... 115
Rosskopf, Myron Frederick 1907-1973 ... CANR-5
Obituary ... 41-44R
Earlier sketch in CA 5-8R
Ross-Macdonald, Malcolm J(ohn)
1932- ... CANR-13
Earlier sketch in CA 65-68
Rossman, Charles Raymond 1938- ... CANR-34
Earlier sketch in CA 113
Rossman, Evelyn
See Rothchild, Sylvia
Rossman, Jack E(ugene) 1936- ... 49-52
Rossman, Marlene L. 1948- ... 124
Rossman, Michael Dale 1939- ... 101
Rossman, (George) Parker 1919- ... 69-72
Rossmann, John F(rancis) 1942- ... 101
Rossner, Judith (Perelman) 1935- ... CANR-18
Earlier sketch in CA 17-20R
See also AITN 2
See also BEST 90:3
See also CLC 6, 9, 29
See also DLB 6
See also MTCW
Rossner, Robert 1932- ... CANR-1
Earlier sketch in CA 1-4R
Rossoff, Martin 1910- ... 9-12R
Rossomando, Frederic William 1924- ... 49-52
Ross-Robertson, Lynne Nannen
1936- ... CANR-25
Earlier sketch in CA 107
Ross Williamson, Hugh 1901-1978 ... CANR-8
Earlier sketch in CA 17-20R
Rostand, Edmond (Eugene Alexis)
1868-1918 ... 126
Brief entry ... 104
See also MTCW
See also TCLC 6, 37
Rostand, J.
See Rostand, Jean
Rostand, Jean 1894-1977 ... 126
Brief entry ... 124
Rostand, Robert
See Hopkins, Robert S(ydney)
Rosten, Leo C(alvin) 1908- ... CANR-6
Earlier sketch in CA 5-8R
See also DLB 11
Rosten, Norman 1914- ... CANR-21
Earlier sketch in CA 77-80
Rostenberg, Leona 1908- ... CANR-5
Earlier sketch in CA 5-8R
Rostkowski, Margaret I. 1945- ... 127
See also SATA 59
Roston, Murray 1928- ... CANR-5
Earlier sketch in CA 53-56
Rostow, Eugene Victor 1913- ... 5-8R
Rostow, Walt W(hitman) 1916- ... CANR-8
Earlier sketch in CA 13-16R
Rostvold, Gerhard N(orman) 1919- ... CANR-10
Earlier sketch in CA 21-24R
Roszak, Betty 1933- ... 29-32R
Roszak, Theodore 1933- ... 77-80
Rota, Gian-Carlo 1932- ... 126
Rotarius
See Kerekes, Tibor
Rotberg, Robert I. 1935- ... CANR-21
Earlier sketches in CA 13-16R, CANR-6
Rotblat, Joseph 1908- ... CANR-26
Earlier sketch in CA 109
Rotchstein, Janice 1944- ... CANR-25
Earlier sketch in CA 106
Rote, Kyle 1928- ... 21-24R
Rotella, Guy Louis 1947- ... 115
Rotenstreich, Nathan 1914- ... CANR-23
Earlier sketches in CA 61-64, CANR-8
Roth, Alexander
See Dunner, Joseph
Roth, Andrew 1919- ... 53-56
Roth, Arlen 1952- ... 103
Roth, Arnold 1929- ... 21-24R
See also SATA 21
Roth, Arthur J(oseph) 1925- ... CANR-7
Earlier sketch in CA 53-56
See also SAAS 11
See also SATA 28, 43
Roth, Arthur 1920- ... 1-4R
Roth, Audrey J. 1927- ... 21-24R
Roth, Cecil 1899-1970 ... CANR-13
Obituary ... 25-28R
Earlier sketch in CA 9-12R
Roth, Charles E(dmund) 1934- ... 111
Roth, Claire Jarett 1923- ... 5-8R
Roth, David F(rancisco) 1939- ... 41-44R
Roth, David M(orris) 1935- ... 57-60
Roth, David M. 1874(?)-1971 Obituary ... 104
Roth, David 1940- ... 106
See also SATA 36
Roth, Don A. 1927- ... 25-28R
Roth, Ernst 1896-1971 ... CAP-2
Earlier sketch in CA 25-28
Roth, Eugen 1895-1976 Obituary ... 65-68
Roth, Geneen 1951- ... 111
Roth, Gerhard 1942- ... DLB 85
Roth, Hal 1927- ... 37-40R
Roth, Harold ... SATA 49
Roth, Harold L(eo) 1919-1982 Obituary ... 108
Roth, Harry 1903(?)-1976 Obituary ... 65-68
Roth, Henry 1906- ... CANR-38
Earlier sketches in CAP-1, CA 11-12
See also CLC 2, 6, 11
See also DLB 28
See also MTCW
Roth, Herbert (Otto) 1917- ... 61-64
Roth, Herrick S. 1916- ... 77-80
Roth, Holly 1916-1964 ... CANR-6
Earlier sketch in CA 1-4R
Roth, Jack J(oseph) 1920- ... 21-24R
Roth, John K(ing) 1940- ... CANR-26
Earlier sketches in CA 25-28R, CANR-10
Roth, Joseph 1894-1939 ... DLB 85
See also TCLC 33
Roth, Julius A(lfred) 1924- ... 21-24R
Roth, June (Doris Spiewak)
1926-1990 ... CANR-19
Obituary ... 132
Earlier sketches in CA 9-12R, CANR-5
Roth, Leland M(artin) 1943- ... CANR-16
Earlier sketch in CA 93-96
Roth, (Hyam) Leon 1896-1963 Obituary ... 106
Roth, Lillian 1910-1980 Obituary ... 97-100
Roth, Mark J(oseph) 1941- ... 77-80
Roth, Martin 1924- ... 134
Roth, Marty
See Roth, Martin
Roth, Mary Jane ... 21-24R
Roth, Michael S. 1957- ... 127
Roth, Moira 1933- ... 121
Roth, Peggy (Meehan) Obituary ... 104
Roth, Philip (Milton) 1933- ... CANR-36
Earlier sketches in CA 1-4R, CANR-1, 22
See also BEST 90:3
See also CDALB 1968-1988
See also CLC 1, 2, 3, 4, 6, 9, 15, 22, 31, 47, 66
See also DLB 2, 28
See also DLBY 82
See also MTCW
See also WLC
Roth, Richard H(enry) 1949- ... 77-80
Roth, Robert Howard 1933- ... CANR-14
Earlier sketch in CA 41-44R
Roth, Robert J. 1920- ... 17-20R
Roth, Robert Paul 1919- ... 61-64
Roth, Samuel 1894-1974 Obituary ... 49-52
Roth, Sister Mary Augustine 1926- ... CANR-3
Earlier sketch in CA 9-12R
Roth, Sol 1927- ... 65-68
Roth, Theodore W(illiam) 1916- ... 57-60
Roth, (Vanceburg), Martha 1938- ... 137
Roth, William 1942- ... 101
Roth, Wolfgang M(ax) W(ilhelm) 1930- ... 41-44R
Rotha, Paul 1907-1984 ... 9-12R
Obituary ... 112
Rothafel, Roxy
See Rothafel, Samuel L(ionel)
Rothafel, Samuel L(ionel)
1881(?)-1936(?) Brief entry ... 123
Rothbard, Murray N(ewton) 1926- ... CANR-22
Earlier sketches in CA 5-8R, CANR-6
Rothbart, Harold A(rthur) 1917- ... 111
Rothbaum, Melvin 1926- ... 5-8R
Rothberg, Abraham 1922- ... 33-36R
See also SATA 59
Rothblatt, Ben 1924- ... 25-28R
Rothblatt, Donald N(oah) 1935- ... CANR-23
Earlier sketches in CA 61-64, CANR-8
Rothblatt, Henry B(arnett) 1916-1985 ... CANR-19
Obituary ... 117
Earlier sketch in CA 25-28R
Rothchild, Donald (Sylvester) 1928- ... CANR-14
Earlier sketches in CA 41-44R, CANR-31
Rothchild, Sylvia 1923- ... 77-80
Rothel, David 1936- ... CANR-10
Earlier sketch in CA 65-68
Rothenberg, Alan B(aer)
1907-1977 Obituary ... 73-76
Rothenberg, Albert 1930- ... CANR-25
Earlier sketches in CA 57-60, CANR-8
Rothenberg, B(arbara) Annye 1940- ... 107
Rothenberg, Diane Brodatz 1932- ... 115
Rothenberg, Gunther Eric 1923- ... CANR-8
Earlier sketch in CA 21-24R
Rothenberg, Jerome 1924- ... 29-32R
Rothenberg, Jerome 1931- ... CANR-1
Earlier sketch in CA 45-48
See also CLC 6, 57
See also DLB 5
Rothenberg, Joshua 1911- ... 37-40R
Rothenberg, Lillian 1922- ... 9-12R
Rothenberg, Marc 1949- ... 115
Rothenberg, Polly 1916- ... 85-88
Rothenberg, Randall 1956- ... 118
Rothenberg, Robert E(dward) 1908- ... 37-40R
Rothenstein, John K(newstub) M(aurice)
1901- ... CANR-1
Earlier sketch in CA 1-4R
Rothermere, Viscount
See Harmsworth, Esmond Cecil
Rothery, Brian 1934- ... CANR-1
Earlier sketch in CA 49-52
Rothfork, John 1946- ... 110
Rothkopf, Carol Z. 1929- ... 25-28R
See also SATA 4
Rothman, Barbara Katz 1948- ... CANR-29
Earlier sketch in CA 111
Rothman, Charles Warren 1952- ... 120
Rothman, Chuck
See Rothman, Charles Warren
Rothman, David B. 1956- ... 111
Rothman, David J. 1937- ... 33-36R
Rothman, Esther P. 1919- ... 37-40R
Rothman, Hal (K.) 1958- ... 130
Rothman, Joel 1938- ... 37-40R
See also SATA 7
Rothman, Judith
See Peters, Maureen
Rothman, Milton A. 1919- ... 41-44R
Rothman, Stanley 1927- ... 93-96
Rothman, Theodore 1907- ... CAP-2
Earlier sketch in CA 29-32
Rothman, Tony 1953- ... CANR-33
Earlier sketches in CA 85-88, CANR-15
Rothmuller, Aron Marko 1908- ... 73-76
Rothrock, George A(bel) 1932- ... 61-64
Rothschild, Alfred 1894(?)-1972 ... 37-40R
Rothschild, Fritz A(lexander)
1919- Brief entry ... 106
Rothschild, Guy de
See de Rothschild, Guy (Edward Alphonse Paul)
Rothschild, J(acquard) H(irshorn) 1907- ... CAP-2
Earlier sketch in CA 17-18
Rothschild, Joseph 1931- ... CANR-3
Earlier sketch in CA 9-12R
Rothschild, Kurt Wilhelm 1914- ... CANR-23
Earlier sketch in CA 102
Rothschild, Lincoln 1902-1983 ... CANR-12
Obituary ... 109
Earlier sketch in CA 45-48
Rothschild, Nathaniel Mayer Victor
1910-1990 Obituary ... 131
Rothschild, Norman 1913- ... 103
Rothschild, Richard Charles
1895-1986 Obituary ... 118
Rothstein, Arthur 1915-1985 ... CANR-6
Obituary ... 117
Earlier sketch in CA 57-60
Rothstein, Edward 1952- ... 136
Rothstein, Eric 1936- ... 73-76
Rothstein, Samuel
1902(?)-1978 Obituary ... 77-80
Rothstein, Samuel 1921- ... 61-64
Rothstein, Stanley William 1929- ... 120
Rothstein, William G(ene) 1937- ... 73-76
Rothweiler, Paul Roger 1931- ... CANR-10
Earlier sketch in CA 65-68
Rothwell, Bruce 1923(?)-1984 Obituary ... 114
Rothwell, Kenneth J(ames) 1925- ... CANR-14
Earlier sketch in CA 21-24R
Rothwell, Kenneth S(prague) 1921- ... 33-36R
Rothwell, Talbot (Nelson Conn)
1916-1981 Obituary ... 103
Rothwell, V(ictor) H(oward) 1945- ... 37-40R
Rotimi, E. G. O.
See Rotimi, (Emmanuel Gladstone) Ola(wale)
Rotimi, (Emmanuel Gladstone) Ola(wale)
1938(?)- ... 124
See also BW
Rotimi, Olawale
See Rotimi, (Emmanuel Gladstone) Ola(wale)
Rotkin, Charles E. 1916- ... 5-8R
Rotmans, Elmer A. 1896- ... 5-8R
Rotondi, Cesar 1926- ... 97-100
Rotsler, William 1926- ... CANR-4
Earlier sketch in CA 53-56
Rotstein, Abraham 1929- ... 104
Rottenberg, Dan(iel) 1942- ... CANR-19
Earlier sketch in CA 102
Rottenberg, Isaac C. 1925- ... 13-16R
Rottensteiner, Franz 1942- ... CANR-33
Earlier sketches in CA 81-84, CANR-15
Rotter, Julian B(ernard) 1916- ... 33-36R
Rotter, Marion 1940(?)-1973 Obituary ... 104
Roubiczek, Paul (Anton)
1898-1972 Obituary ... 115
Roubinek, Darrell L(eRoy) 1935- ... 57-60
Roucek, Joseph S(labey) 1902- ... CANR-32
Earlier sketch in CA 9-12R
Roud, Richard 1929-1989 Obituary ... 127
Roudiez, Leon S(amuel) 1917- ... 37-40R
Roudybush, Alexandra (Brown) 1911- ... 65-68
Roueche, Berton 1911- ... CANR-1
Earlier sketch in CA 1-4R
See also SATA 28
Roueche, John E(dward) 1938- ... 49-52
Rougemont, Denis de
See de Rougemont, Denis
Roughsey, Dick 1921(?)- ... 109
See also SATA 35
Rougier, Louis (Auguste Paul)
1889-1982 ... CANR-13
Earlier sketch in CA 29-32R
Rougier, Nicole 1929- ... 29-32R
Rouhani, Fuad 1907- ... 37-40R
Roukes, Nicholas 1925- ... 25-28R
Roulac, Stephen E. 1945- ... 104
Rouleau, Raymond (Edgard Marie)
1904-1981 Obituary ... 108
Roulston, Marjorie Hillis
1890-1971 Obituary ... 104
Roumain, Jacques (Jean Baptiste)
1907-1944 ... 125
Brief entry ... 117
See also BLC 3
See also BW
See also TCLC 19
Rounds, David 1930-1983 Obituary ... 111
Rounds, Glen (Harold) 1906- ... CANR-22
Earlier sketches in CA 53-56, CANR-7
See also MAICYA
See also SATA 8, 70
Rouner, Arthur A(cy) Jr. 1929- ... CANR-5
Earlier sketch in CA 9-12R
Rouner, Leroy S(tephens) 1930- ... 73-76
Rountree, Owen
See Kittredge, William
and Krauzer, Steven M(ark)
Rountree, Owen
See Krauzer, Steven M(ark)
Rountree, Thomas J. 1927- ... 25-28R
Rourke, Constance (Mayfield)
1885-1941 Brief entry ... 107
See also TCLC 12
See also YABC 1
Rourke, Francis E(dward) 1922- ... CANR-6
Earlier sketch in CA 1-4R
Rous, Stanley (Ford) 1895- ... 108
Rousculp, Charles G(ene) 1923- ... 29-32R
Rouse, (Hubert) Blair 1912- ... 1-4R
Rouse, (Benjamin) Irving (Jr.) 1913- ... 9-12R
Rouse, John E(dward) Jr. 1942- ... 89-92
Rouse, John E(vans) 1892- ... 73-76
Rouse, Parke (Shepherd) Jr. 1915- ... 17-20R
Rouse, Richard H(unter) 1933- ... 29-32R
Rouse, Russell 1913(?)-1987 Obituary ... 123
Rouse Jones, Lewis 1907- ... CAP-1
Earlier sketch in CA 13-14
Roush, Barbara 1940- ... 109
Roush, John H. Jr. 1923- ... 37-40R
Rousmaniere, John 1944- ... CANR-38
Earlier sketches in CA 93-96, CANR-17
Rousseau, George Sebastian 1941- ... CANR-11
Earlier sketch in CA 29-32R
Rousseau, Jean-Jacques 1712-1778 ... WLC
Rousseau, Richard W(ilfred) 1924- ... 110
Roussel, Raymond 1877-1933 Brief entry ... 117
See also TCLC 20
Rousselle, Aline 1939- ... 130
Roussin, Andre (Jean Paul Marie)
1911-1987 Obituary ... 124
Rout, Leslie B(rennan) Jr. 1936-1987 ... 57-60
Obituary ... 122
Routh, C(harles) R(ichard) N(airne)
1896- ... CAP-1
Earlier sketch in CA 13-14
Routh, Donald K(ent) 1937- ... 57-60
Routh, Francis John 1927- ... 13-16R
Routh, Jonathan ... 110
Routh, Porter W(roe) 1911- ... 77-80
Routhier, Adolphe-Basile 1839-1920 ... DLB 99
Routier, Simone 1901-1987 ... DLB 88
Routley, Erik (Reginald) 1917-1982 ... CANR-5
Obituary ... 108
Earlier sketch in CA 1-4R
Routsong, Alma 1924- ... 49-52
Routt, Mary Patterson
1890(?)-1986 Obituary ... 119
Routtenberg, Max Jonah 1909- ... 77-80
Rouverol, Jean
See Butler, Jean Rouverol
Roux, Edward R(udolph) 1903- ... 13-16R
Roux, Georges 1914- ... 17-20R
Roux, Willan Charles 1902- ... CAP-2
Earlier sketch in CA 17-18
Rover, Constance (Mary) 1910- ... 21-24R
Rovere, Richard H(alworth) 1915-1979 ... CANR-3
Obituary ... 89-92
Earlier sketch in CA 49-52
Rovin, Ben
See Clevenger, Ernest Allen Jr.
Rovin, Jeff 1951- ... 77-80
Rovit, Earl (Herbert) 1927- ... CANR-12
Earlier sketch in CA 5-8R
See also CLC 7
Rowan, Andrew N(icholas) 1946- ... 124
Rowan, Carl Thomas 1925- ... 89-92
See also BW
Rowan, Dan (Hale) 1922-1987 Obituary ... 125
Rowan, Deirdre
See Williams, Jeanne
Rowan, Ford 1943- ... CANR-29
Earlier sketch in CA 69-72
Rowan, Helen 1927(?)-1972 Obituary ... 37-40R
Rowan, Hester
See Robinson, Sheila Mary
Rowan, Richard Lamar 1931- ... 9-12R
Rowan, Stephen A(nthony) 1928- ... 45-48
Rowan, Steven William 1943- ... 116
Rowans, Virgina
See Tanner, Edward Everett III
Rowat, Donald C(ameron) 1921- ... CANR-20
Earlier sketches in CA 9-12R, CANR-5
Rowatt, G(eorge) Wade Jr. 1943- ... 126
Rowbotham, David (Harold)
1924- Brief entry ... 112
Rowbotham, Sheila 1943- ... 101
Rowdon, Maurice 1922- Brief entry ... 110
Rowe, A(lbert) W(ard) 1915- ... CANR-14
Earlier sketch in CA 21-24R
Rowe, C(hristopher) J(ames) 1944- ... 132
Rowe, Clarence J(ohn) Jr. 1916- ... 104
Rowe, David Knox 1924(?)-1989 ... 77-80
Obituary ... 129
Rowe, David Nelson 1905- ... CANR-2
Earlier sketch in CA 5-8R
Rowe, Elizabeth Singer 1674-1737 ... DLB 39, 95
Rowe, Erna (Dirks) 1926- ... 93-96
Rowe, Frank (A.) 1921-1985 ... 130
Obituary ... 115
Rowe, Frederick William 1912- ... 101
Rowe, G(ail) S(tuart) 1936- ... 112
Rowe, George E(rnest) Jr. 1947- ... 93-96
Rowe, H. Edward 1927- ... 69-72
Rowe, James L(ester) Jr. 1948- ... 69-72
Rowe, James N(icholas) 1938-1989 ... 37-40R
Obituary ... 128
Rowe, Jeanne A. 1938- ... 29-32R
Rowe, John Carlos 1945- ... CANR-36
Earlier sketch in CA 114
Rowe, John L(eroy) 1914-1975(?) ... 17-20R
Obituary ... 135
Rowe, John (Seymour) 1936- ... CANR-28
Earlier sketch in CA 109
Rowe, Margaret (Kevin) 1920- ... 13-16R
Rowe, Mary Budd 1925- ... 113
Rowe, Nicholas 1674-1718 ... DLB 84
Rowe, Robert 1920- ... 17-20R

Rowe, Terry ... AITN 2
Rowe, Viola Carson 1903-1969 ... 1-4R
Obituary ... 103
See also SATA 26
Rowe, Vivian C(laud) 1902-1978 ... CANR-2
Earlier sketch in CA 1-4R
Rowe, William D(avid) 1930- ... 114
Rowe, William L. 1931- Brief entry ... 108
Rowe, William (Neil) 1942- ... 131
Rowell, Galen 1940- ... CANR-18
Earlier sketch in CA 65-68
Rowell, (Douglas) Geoffrey 1943- ... 129
Rowell, George (Rignall) 1923- ... CANR-39
Earlier sketches in CA 5-8R, CANR-2, 18
Rowell, Henry T(hompson) 1904- ... CAP-1
Earlier sketch in CA 13-14
Rowell, John W(illiam) 1914- ... 33-36R
Rowen, Betty (Jane Rose) 1920- ... 127
Brief entry ... 109
Rowen, Henry S(tanislaus) 1925- ... 123
Brief entry ... 118
Rowen, Herbert H(arvey) 1916- ... CANR-3
Earlier sketch in CA 9-12R
Rowen, Hobart 1918- ... 9-12R
Rowen, Lilian 1925- ... 108
Rowen, Ruth Halle 1918- ... 33-36R
Rowes, Barbara Gail ... 101
Rowett, Colin 1952- ... 128
Rowland, Arthur R(ay) 1930- ... CANR-21
Earlier sketches in CA 13-16R, CANR-6
Rowland, Benjamin Jr.
1904-1972 Obituary ... 37-40R
Rowland, Beryl ... 89-92
Rowland, Christopher (Charles) 1947- ... 116
Rowland, Claude K. 1943- ... 112
Rowland, D(onald) S(ydney) 1928- ... 21-24R
Rowland, Diana 1950- ... 122
Rowland, Florence Wightman 1900- ... CANR-5
Earlier sketch in CA 5-8R
See also SATA 8
Rowland, Iris
See Roberts, Irene
Rowland, J(ohn) R(ussell) 1925- ... 101
Rowland, Judith 1944- ... 124
Rowland, Peter (Kenneth) 1938- ... 25-28R
Rowland, Robin F. 1950- ... 136
Rowland, Stanley J. Jr. 1928- ... 13-16R
Rowland, Virgil K(enneth) 1909- ... 5-8R
Rowland-Entwistle, (Arthur) Theodore (Henry)
1925- ... CANR-24
Earlier sketch in CA 107
See also SATA 31
Rowlands, John Robert 1947- ... 109
Rowlands, Peter
See Lovell, Mark
Rowlands, Samuel 1570(?)-1630 ... DLB 121
Rowlandson, Mary 1635(?)-1678(?) ... DLB 24
Rowlatt, Mary 1908- ... 5-8R
Rowley, Ames Dorrance
See Lovecraft, H(oward) P(hillips)
Rowley, Anthony 1939- ... 61-64
Rowley, Brian A(lan) 1923- ... 5-8R
Rowley, Charles (Dunford) 1906-1985 ... 103
Obituary ... 117
Rowley, Peter T(empleton)
1929- Brief entry ... 112
Rowley, Peter 1934- ... 65-68
Rowley, (Richard) Trevor 1942- ... 131
Rowley, William Dean 1939- ... 112
Rowley, William 1585(?)-1626 ... DLB 58
Rowling, Marjorie A(lice Thexton) 1900- ... 5-8R
Rowlingson, Donald T(aggart) 1907- ... CANR-6
Earlier sketch in CA 1-4R
Rowney, Don Karl 1936- ... 108
Rowse, A(lfred) L(eslie) 1903- ... CANR-1
Earlier sketch in CA 1-4R
See also CAAS 8
Rowsome, Frank (Howard) Jr. 1914-1983 ... 112
See also SATA 36
Rowson, Susanna Haswell
1762(?)-1824 ... DLB 37
Rowthorn, Anne W(heeler) 1939- ... 113
Roxas, Savina A. ... 37-40R
Roxborough, Henry Hall 1891- ... 5-8R
Roxon, Lillian 1933(?)-1973 Obituary ... 111
Roy, Archibald Edmiston 1924- ... 102
Roy, Archie E.
See Roy, Archibald Edmiston
Roy, Camille 1870-1943 ... DLB 92
Roy, David Tod 1933- ... 41-44R
Roy, Emil L. 1933- ... 25-28R
Roy, Ewell Paul 1929- ... 9-12R
Roy, G(eorge) Ross 1924- ... 77-80
Roy, Gabrielle 1909-1983 ... CANR-5
Obituary ... 110
Earlier sketch in CA 53-56
See also CLC 10, 14
See also DLB 68
See also MTCW
Roy, Gregor 1929- ... 21-24R
Roy, Jack
See Dangerfield, Rodney
Roy, James A(lexander) 1884- ... CAP-1
Earlier sketch in CA 11-12
Roy, Jessie Hailstalk 1895-1986 Obituary ... 121
See also SATA 51
Roy, Joaquin 1943- ... 77-80
Roy, John (Flint) 1913- ... 93-96
Roy, Jules 1907- ... DLB 83
Roy, Katherine (Morris) 1906- ... 1-4R
Roy, Liam
See Scarry, Patricia (Murphy)
Roy, Michael 1913-1976 ... CANR-10
Obituary ... 65-68
Earlier sketch in CA 61-64
Roy, Mike
See Roy, Michael
Roy, Patricia E. ... 137
Roy, Reginald H(erbert) 1922- ... 49-52
Roy, Robert L(ouis) 1947- ... 106
Roy, Robin 1946- ... CANR-36
Earlier sketch in CA 114
Roy, Ron(ald) 1940- ... 114
See also SATA 35, 40
Roy, Rustum 1924- ... 113
Royal, Claudia Smith 1904- ... 5-8R
Royal, D.
See Du Breuil, (Elizabeth) L(or)inda
Royal, Denise 1935- ... 25-28R
Royal, William Robert 1905- ... 101
Royale, A.
See Gibson, Arthur
Royall, Anne 1769-1854 ... DLB 43
Royall, Vanessa
See Hinkemeyer, Michael T(homas)
Royalton-Kisch, Martin (Bruce) 1952- ... 128
Royce, Anya Peterson 1940- ... 101
Royce, James E(mmet) 1914- ... CANR-34
Earlier sketch in CA 1-4R
Royce, Kenneth
See Gandley, Kenneth Royce
Royce, Patrick M(ilan) 1922- ... 13-16R
Royce, R(ussell) Joseph 1921- ... CANR-9
Earlier sketch in CA 21-24R
Royds, Caroline 1953- ... 123
See also SATA 55
Royer, Fanchon 1902- ... 5-8R
Royko, Mike 1932- ... CANR-26
Earlier sketch in CA 89-92
Roylance, William H(erbert) 1927- ... 61-64
Royle, Edward 1944- ... 61-64
Royle, Selena 1904-1983 Obituary ... 109
Royle, Trevor 1945- ... CANR-31
Earlier sketch in CA 112
Royster, Charles 1944- ... 101
Royster, Philip M. 1943- ... CANR-13
Earlier sketch in CA 65-68
Royster, Salibelle 1895-1975 ... CAP-2
Earlier sketch in CA 25-28
Royster, Vermont (Connecticut) 1914- ... 21-24R
Royston, Angela 1945- ... 128
Royston, Olive 1904- ... 102
Rozakis, Gregory 1943(?)-1989 Obituary ... 129
Rozeboom, William W(arren) 1928- ... 17-20R
Rozek, Evalyn Robillard 1941- ... 61-64
Rozensztroch, Daniel 1944- ... 128
Rozental, Alek A(ron) 1920- ... 33-36R
Rozewicz, Tadeusz 1921- ... CANR-36
Earlier sketch in CA 108
See also CLC 9, 23
See also MTCW
Rozhdestvensky, Vsevolod A.
1895(?)-1977 Obituary ... 73-76
Rozier, John W(iley) 1918- ... 107
Rozin, Skip 1941- ... 89-92
Rozman, Deborah 1949- ... 115
Rozman, Gilbert Friedell 1943- ... CANR-26
Earlier sketch in CA 109
Rozovsky, Lorne Elkin 1942- ... CANR-24
Earlier sketch in CA 108
Rozwenc, Edwin C(harles) 1915-1974 ... CAP-1
Earlier sketch in CA 13-14
Ruane, Gerald P(atrick) 1934- ... 69-72
Ruano, Argimiro 1924- ... 33-36R
Ruano, Nazario
See Ruano, Argimiro
Ruark, Gibbons 1941- ... CANR-31
Earlier sketches in CA 33-36R, CANR-14
See also CLC 3
See also DLB 120
Ruark, Robert (Chester) 1915-1965 ... CAP-2
Obituary ... 25-28R
Earlier sketch in CA 19-20
Ruas, Charles (Edward) 1938- ... 124
Rubadeau, Duane O. 1927- ... 29-32R
Rubashov, Schneor Zalman
See Shazar, (Schneor) Zalman
Rubashov, Zalman
See Shazar, (Schneor) Zalman
Rubbra, Edmund 1901-1986 Obituary ... 119
Rubel, Arthur J. 1924- ... CANR-15
Earlier sketch in CA 41-44R
Rubel, Marc (Reid) 1949- ... 123
Rubel, Maximilien 1905- ... CAP-1
Earlier sketch in CA 11-12
Rubel, Nicole 1953- ... 125
See also SATA 18
Rubel, Paula G(licksman) 1933- ... 89-92
Ruben, Brent David 1944- ... 41-44R
Ruben, Harvey L. 1941- ... 119
Rubens, Bernice (Ruth) 1923- ... CANR-33
Earlier sketch in CA 25-28R
See also CLC 19, 31
See also DLB 14
See also MTCW
Rubens, Jeff(rey Peter) 1941- ... CANR-39
Earlier sketches in CA 25-28R, CANR-17
Rubenson, Sven (Abel) 1921- ... 115
Rubenstein, Boris B.
1907(?)-1974 Obituary ... 53-56
Rubenstein, Joshua 1949- ... 103
Rubenstein, Richard E(dward) 1938- ... CANR-32
Earlier sketch in CA 29-32R
Rubenstein, Richard L(owell) 1924- ... CANR-17
Earlier sketch in CA 21-24R
Rubenstein, (Clarence) Robert 1926- ... 21-24R
Rubenstein, Roberta 1944- ... 89-92
Rubenstone, Jessie 1912- ... 69-72
Rubia Barcia, Jose 1914- ... CANR-19
Earlier sketch in CA 103
Rubicam, Harry Cogswell Jr. 1902- ... CAP-2
Earlier sketch in CA 17-18
Rubicon
See Lunn, Arnold
Rubin, Alan (Michael) 1936- ... 113
Rubin, Amy Kateman 1945- ... 106
Rubin, Arnold P(erry) 1946- ... 69-72
Rubin, Barry (M.) 1950- ... CANR-32
Earlier sketch in CA 108
Rubin, Benny 1899-1986 Obituary ... 119
Rubin, Charles J. 1950- ... 101
Rubin, Cynthia Elyce 1944- ... 97-100
Rubin, David Lee 1939- ... CANR-33
Earlier sketches in CA 41-44R, CANR-15
Rubin, David M. 1945- ... 77-80
Rubin, Dorothy 1932- ... CANR-19
Earlier sketch in CA 101
Rubin, Duane R(oger) 1931- ... 57-60
Rubin, Eli Z(under) 1922- ... 17-20R
Rubin, Ernest 1915-1978 Obituary ... 81-84
Rubin, Eva Johanna 1925- ... SATA 38
Rubin, Eva R(edfield) 1926- ... 113
Rubin, Frederick 1926- ... 33-36R
Rubin, Ida Ely 1923- ... 107
Rubin, Isadore 1912-1970 ... CAP-1
Obituary ... 29-32R
Earlier sketch in CA 13-16
Rubin, Israel 1923- ... 37-40R
Rubin, Jacob A. 1910-1972 ... CAP-1
Obituary ... 37-40R
Earlier sketch in CA 11-12
Rubin, James Henry 1944- ... 106
Rubin, Jerry 1938- ... 69-72
Rubin, Joan 1932- ... 102
Rubin, Julia Danielle 1944- ... 113
Rubin, Larry (Jerome) 1930- ... 5-8R
Rubin, Leona G(reenstone) 1920- ... 49-52
Rubin, Lillian B(reslow) 1924- ... CANR-37
Earlier sketch in CA 65-68
Rubin, Louis D(ecimus) Jr. 1923- ... CANR-21
Earlier sketches in CA 1-4R, CANR-6
Rubin, Mann 1927- ... 119
Rubin, Mark 1946- ... CANR-9
Earlier sketch in CA 53-56
Rubin, Michael 1935- ... CANR-1
Earlier sketch in CA 1-4R
Rubin, Morris H(arold) 1911-1980 Obituary ... 101
Rubin, Morton 1923- ... 41-44R
Rubin, Nancy 1944- ... 129
Rubin, Stanley 1928- ... 107
Rubin, Steven Jay 1951- ... 110
Rubin, Steven Joel 1943- ... 107
Rubin, Theodore Isaac 1923- ... 110
Brief entry ... 108
See also AITN 1
Rubin, Vera (Dourmashkin)
1911-1985 Obituary ... 115
Rubin, Vitalii 1923-1981 ... 69-72
Obituary ... 105
Rubin, William 1927- ... 77-80
Rubin, Zick 1944- ... CANR-1
Earlier sketch in CA 49-52
Rubinfeld, William A.
1914(?)-1984 Obituary ... 113
Rubington, Earl 1923- ... 73-76
Rubinoff, (M.) Lionel 1930- ... 25-28R
Rubinow, Sol (Isaac) 1923-1981 Obituary ... 103
Rubins, Harriett 1942- ... 120
Rubins, Jack L(awrence) 1916-1982 ... 85-88
Obituary ... 107
Rubinstein, Alvin Zachary 1927- ... CANR-39
Earlier sketches in CA 9-12R, CANR-3, 18
Rubinstein, Amnon 1931- ... CANR-7
Earlier sketch in CA 13-16R
Rubinstein, Arthur 1887(?)-1982 ... 113
Obituary ... 108
Rubinstein, Daryl Reich
1938(?)-1981 Obituary ... 102
Rubinstein, David H(ugh) 1915- ... 109
Rubinstein, David M(ichael) 1942- ... 93-96
Rubinstein, E(lliott) 1936- ... 41-44R
Rubinstein, Erna F(erber) 1922- ... 120
Rubinstein, Gillian (Margaret) 1942- ... 136
See also SATA 68
Rubinstein, H(arold) F(rederick)
1891-1975 Obituary ... 115
Rubinstein, Helena 1871(?)-1965 Obituary ... 113
Rubinstein, Helge 1929- ... 134
Rubinstein, Hilary 1926- ... 57-60
Rubinstein, Moshe F(ajwel) 1930- ... 57-60
Rubinstein, Paul (Arthur) ... CANR-7
Earlier sketch in CA 61-64
Rubinstein, Robert E(dward) 1943- ... 106
See also SATA 49
Rubinstein, S(amuel) Leonard 1922- ... 45-48
Rubinstein, Stanley (Jack) 1890-1975 ... CAP-2
Earlier sketch in CA 29-32
Rubinstein, W(illiam) D(avid) 1946- ... 114
Rublowsky, John M(artin) 1928- ... 17-20R
See also SATA 62
Rubsamen, Walter H. 1911- ... 13-16R
Rubulis, Aleksis 1922- ... 37-40R
Ruby, Jay 1935- ... 136
Ruby, Kathryn 1947- ... 65-68
Ruby, Lois F. 1942- ... CANR-39
Earlier sketches in CA 97-100, CANR-18
See also SATA 34, 35
Ruby, Robert Holmes 1921- ... CANR-7
Earlier sketch in CA 17-20R
Ruchames, Louis 1917-1976 ... CANR-2
Obituary ... 65-68
Earlier sketch in CA 1-4R
Ruchelman, Leonard I. 1933- ... CANR-28
Earlier sketch in CA 29-32R
Ruchlis, Hy(man) 1913- ... CANR-2
Earlier sketch in CA 1-4R
See also SATA 3
Ruchwarger, Gary 1949- ... 128
Ruck, Amy Roberta 1878-1978 ... CANR-5
Earlier sketch in CA 5-8R
Ruck, Berta
See Ruck, Amy Roberta
Ruck, Carl A(nton) P(aul) 1935- ... 25-28R
Ruck, Peter F(rederick) Carter
See Carter-Ruck, Peter F(rederick)
Rucker, Bryce W(ilson) 1921- ... 9-12R
Rucker, (Egbert) Darnell 1921- ... 41-44R
Rucker, Frank Warren 1886-1975 ... 1-4R
Obituary ... 103
Rucker, Helen (Bornstein) ... 1-4R
Rucker, Rudolf v(on) B(itter) 1946- ... 124
Brief entry ... 119
Rucker, Rudy
See Rucker, Rudolf v(on) B(itter)
Rucker, W(infred) Ray 1920- ... 13-16R
Ruckman, Ivy 1931- ... 111
See also SATA 37
Ruck-Pauquet, Gina 1931- ... 122
Brief entry ... 116
See also SATA 37, 40
Rudd, Enid ... 108
Rudd, Hughes (Day) 1921- ... 73-76
Rudd, Margaret
See Newlin, Margaret Rudd
Rudd, Margaret T(homas) 1907- ... 17-20R
Rudd, Robert D(ean) 1924- ... 93-96
Rudd, Robert L. 1921- ... 117
Rudd, Steele
See Davis, Arthur Hoey
Ruddell, Robert B(yron) 1937- ... 93-96
Rudder, Robert S(ween) 1937- ... CANR-5
Earlier sketch in CA 53-56
Rudder, Virginia L. 1941- ... 65-68
Ruddick, Sara 1935- ... 77-80
Ruddock, Ralph 1913- ... 53-56
Ruddy, Frank C.
See Frank, Rudolf
Ruddy, T(homas) Michael 1946- ... 124
Rude, George F. E(lliot) 1910- ... CANR-24
Earlier sketches in CA 5-8R, CANR-5
Rudeen, Kenneth Brief entry ... 117
See also SATA 36
Rudel, Hans-Ulrich 1916-1982 Obituary ... 110
Rudelius, William 1931- ... CANR-29
Earlier sketch in CA 45-48
Rudensky, Morris "Red"
See Friedman, Max Motel
Rudenstine, Neil Leon 1935- Brief entry ... 105
Ruder, William 1921- ... 17-20R
Rudhart, Alexander 1930- ... 61-64
Rudhyar, Dane 1895-1985 ... CANR-21
Obituary ... 117
Earlier sketch in CA 29-32R
Rudin, Jacob Philip 1902-1982 Obituary ... 107
Rudin, Marcia Ruth 1940- ... 102
Rudinsky, Joseph F(rancis) 1891- ... 5-8R
Rudis, Al 1943- ... 77-80
Rudisill, D(orus) P(aul) 1902-1978 ... 45-48
Obituary ... 135
Rudkin, (James) David 1936- ... 89-92
See also CLC 14
See also DLB 13
Rudley, Stephen 1946- ... 106
See also SATA 30
Rudloe, Jack 1943- ... 97-100
Rudman, Mark 1948- ... 119
Rudman, Masha Kabakow 1933- ... CANR-27
Earlier sketch in CA 110
Rudnick, Hans H(einrich) 1935- ... 41-44R
Rudnick, Lois Palken 1944- ... 121
Rudnick, Milton Leroy 1927- ... CANR-3
Earlier sketch in CA 1-4R
Rudnik, Raphael 1933- ... 29-32R
See also CLC 7
Rudofsky, Bernard 1905-1988 ... 17-20R
Obituary ... 125
Rudolf, Anthony 1942- ... CANR-24
Earlier sketches in CA 61-64, CANR-9
Rudolph, Albert
See Frank, Rudolf
Rudolph, Donna Keyse 1934- ... 33-36R
Rudolph, Erwin Paul 1916- ... 33-36R
Rudolph, Frederick 1920- ... 9-12R
Rudolph, L(avere) C(hristian) 1921- ... CANR-2
Earlier sketch in CA 5-8R
Rudolph, Lee (Norman) 1948- ... CANR-7
Earlier sketch in CA 57-60
Rudolph, Lloyd I(rving) 1927- ... 57-60
Rudolph, Marguerita 1908- ... CANR-13
Earlier sketch in CA 33-36R
See also SATA 21
Rudolph, Nancy 1923- ... 57-60
Rudolph, Richard (H.) 1940- ... 128
Rudolph, Robert S. 1937- ... 41-44R
Rudolph, Susanne Hoeber 1930- ... 25-28R
Rudomin, Esther
See Hautzig, Esther Rudomin
Rudrum, Alan (William) 1932- ... CANR-36
Earlier sketch in CA 25-28R
Rudwick, Elliot M. 1927-1986(?) ... 104
Obituary ... 118
Rudy, Ann 1927- ... 101
Rudy, Peter 1922- ... 53-56
Rudy, Willis 1920- ... 37-40R
Rudyerd, SirBenjamin 1572-1658 ... DLB 121
Rue, John E. 1924- ... 21-24R
Rue, Leonard Lee III 1926- ... CANR-1
Earlier sketch in CA 1-4R
See also SATA 37
Rue, Leslie W(aits) 1944- ... 110
Rue, Nancy Naylor 1951- ... 122
Ruebsaat, Helmut J(ohannes) 1920- ... 61-64
Ruechelle, Randall C(ummings) 1920- ... 41-44R
Rueckert, William H(owe) 1926- ... 21-24R
Ruedi, Norma Paul
See Ainsworth, Norma
Ruef, John S. 1927- ... 37-40R

Rueff, Jacques (Leon) 1896-1978 .... CANR-12
Obituary 77-80
Earlier sketch in CA 65-68
Ruege, Klaus 1934- CANR-11
Earlier sketch in CA 65-68
Ruehle, Juergen 1924- 25-28R
Ruehlmann, William 1946- 105
Ruell, Patrick
See Hill, Reginald (Charles)
Ruesch, Hans 1913- 13-16R
Ruesch, Jurgen 1909- 73-76
Rueschemeyer, Marilyn 1938- 122
Rueschhoff, Phil H. 1924- 29-32R
Ruether, Rosemary Radford 1936- CANR-39
Earlier sketch in CA 97-100
Rueveni, Uri 1933- 102
Ruff, Ann 1930- 120
Ruff, Howard J. CANR-36
Earlier sketch in CA 93-96
Ruffell, Ann 1941- CANR-23
Earlier sketch in CA 107
See also SATA 30
Ruffell, Thomas
See Laslett, Peter
Ruffian, M.
See Hasek, Jaroslav (Matej Frantisek)
Ruffin, C(aulbert) Bernard III 1947- CANR-27
Earlier sketch in CA 109
Ruffin, Josephine St. Pierre 1842-1924 .... DLB 79
Ruffini, (Jacopo) Remo 1942- 57-60
Ruffins, Reynold 1930- 112
See also MAICYA
See also SATA 41
Ruffle, The
See Tegner, Henry (Stuart)
Ruffner, Budge
See Ruffner, Lester Ward
Ruffner, Lester Ward 1918- 89-92
Ruffo, Vinnie 25-28R
Ruffridge, Frank(lin James) 1931- CANR-27
Earlier sketches in CA 25-28R, CANR-12
Rugel, Miriam 1911- 101
Rugg, Dean S(prague) 1923- 41-44R
Ruggiero, Guido 1944- 118
Ruggiers, Paul G(eorge) 1918- CANR-24
Earlier sketch in CA 25-28R
Ruggles, Eleanor 1916- 5-8R
Ruggles, Henry Joseph 1813-1906 .... DLB 64
Ruggles, Joanne Beaule 1946- 73-76
Ruggles, Philip (Kent) 1944- 73-76
Rugh, Belle Dorman 1908- CAP-1
Earlier sketch in CA 13-16
Rugh, Roberts 1903-1978 93-96
Obituary 81-84
Rugoff, Milton 1913- 21-24R
See also SATA 30
Ruhen, Olaf 1911- CANR-20
Earlier sketches in CA 1-4R, CANR-5
See also SATA 17
Ruhlen, Merritt 1944- 122
Ruibal, Jorge Silvestre Remonda
See Remonda-Ruibal, Jorge Silvestre
Ruihley, Glenn Richard 107
Ruitenbeek, Hendrik M(arinus)
1928-1983 .... CANR-8
Obituary 109
Earlier sketch in CA 5-8R
Ruiz, Jose Martinez
See Martinez Ruiz, Jose
See also CLC 11
Ruiz, Ramon Eduardo 1921- CANR-11
Earlier sketch in CA 25-28R
See also HW
Ruiz, Ricardo Navas
See Navas-Ruiz, Ricardo
Ruiz, Roberto 1925- 41-44R
Ruiz, Vicki Lynn 1955- 127
Ruiz-De-Conde, Justina (Malaxechevarria)
1909- 73-76
Ruiz-Fornells, Enrique 1925- CANR-36
Earlier sketch in CA 33-36R
Ruja, Harry 1912- 41-44R
Rukeyser, Louis 1933- CANR-36
Earlier sketch in CA 65-68
Rukeyser, Merryle Stanley 1897-1988 .... CAP-2
Obituary 127
Earlier sketch in CA 23-24
Rukeyser, Muriel 1913-1980 .... CANR-26
Obituary 93-96
Earlier sketch in CA 5-8R
See also CLC 6, 10, 15, 27
See also DLB 48
See also MTCW
See also SATA 22
Rukeyser, William Simon 1939- CANR-37
Earlier sketch in CA 69-72
Ruksenas, Algis 1942- 49-52
Ruland, Richard (Eugene) 1932- CANR-36
Earlier sketch in CA 21-24R
Ruland, Vernon Joseph 1931- 17-20R
Rule, Ann 1935- .... BEST 90:2
Rule, Gordon Wade 1906-1982 Obituary 107
Rule, James B(ernard) 1943- 73-76
Rule, Jane (Vance) 1931- CANR-12
Earlier sketch in CA 25-28R
See also CLC 27
See also DLB 60
Rulfo, Juan 1918-1986 .... CANR-26
Obituary 118
Earlier sketch in CA 85-88
See also CLC 8
See also DLB 113
See also HW
See also MTCW
Rulon, Philip Reed 1934- CANR-14
Earlier sketch in CA 37-40R
Rumaker, Michael 1932- CANR-2
Earlier sketch in CA 1-4R
See also DLB 16
Rumanes, George N(icholas) 1925- 45-48
Rumbelow, Donald 1940- 49-52
Rumberger, Russell W(illiam) 1949- CANR-26
Earlier sketch in CA 109
Rumble, Adrian 1945- 137
Rumble, Thomas C(lark) 1919- 13-16R
Rumble, Wilfrid E. Jr. 1931- 25-28R
Rumbold-Gibbs, Henry St. John Clair
1913- CANR-3
Earlier sketch in CA 1-4R
Rumens, Carol(-Ann) 1944- 131
See also DLB 40
Rummel, J(osiah) Francis 1911- 17-20R
Rummel, (Louis) Jack(son) 1950- 132
Rummel, R(udolph) J(oseph) 1932- 65-68
Rumpleforeskin
See Krassner, Paul
Rumscheidt, H(ans) Martin 1935- CANR-36
Earlier sketch in CA 57-60
Rumsey, Marian (Barritt) 1928- 21-24R
See also SATA 16
Runcie, Robert A. K.
See Runcie, Robert (Alexander Kennedy)
Runcie, Robert (Alexander Kennedy)
1921- CANR-28
Earlier sketch in CA 108
Runciman, (James Cochran) Steven(son)
1903- CANR-3
Earlier sketch in CA 1-4R
Rundell, Walter Jr. 1928- CANR-3
Earlier sketch in CA 9-12R
Rundle, Anne CANR-12
Earlier sketch in CA 57-60
Runes, Dagobert D(avid) 1902-1982 .... CANR-26
Obituary 108
Earlier sketch in CA 25-28R
Runge, C(arlisle) Ford 1953- 122
Runge, William H(arry) 1927- 1-4R
Runia, Klaas 1926- CANR-20
Earlier sketches in CA 5-8R, CANR-5
Runkel, Philip J(ulian) 1917- CANR-11
Earlier sketch in CA 29-32R
Runkle, Gerald 1924- CANR-14
Earlier sketch in CA 37-40R
Runnels, Curtis 1950- 126
Running, Leona Glidden 1916- 89-92
Runte, Alfred 1947- CANR-19
Earlier sketch in CA 102
Runyan, Harry (John) 1913- CAP-2
Earlier sketch in CA 23-24
Runyan, John
See Palmer, Bernard
Runyan, Thora J. 1931- 69-72
Runyon, A(lfred) Milton
1905-1983 Obituary 109
Runyon, Catherine 1947- 61-64
See also SATA 62
Runyon, Charles W. 1928- 17-20R
Runyon, (Alfred) Damon
1884(?)-1946 Brief entry 107
See also DLB 11, 86
See also TCLC 10
Runyon, Daniel V. 1954- 120
Runyon, John H(arold) 1945- 33-36R
Runyon, Richard P(orter) 1925- CANR-3
Earlier sketch in CA 45-48
Ruoff, James E. 1925- 41-44R
Ruotolo, Andrew K(eogh) 1926(?)-1979 103
Obituary 89-92
Ruotolo, Lucio P(eter) 1927- 41-44R
Rupert, Hoover 1917- CANR-3
Earlier sketch in CA 1-4R
Rupert, James C(layton) II 1957- 136
Rupert, Raphael Rudolph 1910- CAP-2
Earlier sketch in CA 19-20
Ruple, Wayne Douglas 1950- 53-56
Rupp, E. G.
See Rupp, E(rnest) Gordon
Rupp, E(rnest) Gordon 1910-1986 124
Brief entry 113
Rupp, Gordon
See Rupp, E(rnest) Gordon
Rupp, Leila J(ane) 1950- 81-84
Rupp, Richard H(enry) 1934- 29-32R
Ruppenthal, Karl M. 1917- 17-20R
Ruppersburg, Hugh Michael 1950- 124
Ruppli, Michel 1934- 101
Ruprecht, Mary M(argaret Wyant) 1934- 118
Rus, Vladimir 1931- 17-20R
Rusalem, Herbert 1918- 41-44R
Rusbridger, Alan 1953- 125
Rusbridger, James 1928- CANR-39
Earlier sketch in CA 134
Rusch, Hermann G. 1907- 61-64
Rusch, John J(ay) 1942- 106
Rusco, Elmer R(itter) 1928- 65-68
Ruscoe, (Steuart) James (Bailey) 1947- 116
Ruse, Gary Alan 1946- CANR-12
Earlier sketch in CA 61-64
Ruse, Michael E. 1940- 107
Rush, Alison 1951- 115
See also SATA 41
Rush, Anne Kent 1945- CANR-8
Earlier sketch in CA 61-64
Rush, Benjamin 1746-1813 .... DLB 37
Rush, Christopher 1944- 122
Rush, Elizabeth 1918- 115
Rush, James J. 1929- 120
Rush, Joseph H(arold) 1911- 5-8R
Rush, Joshua
See Pearlstein, Howard J.
Rush, Michael (David) 1937- 61-64
Rush, Myron 1922- 45-48
Rush, N(ixon) Orwin 1907- CANR-25
Earlier sketch in CA 45-48
Rush, Norman 1933- 126
Brief entry 121
See also CLC 44
Rush, Peter 1937- 111
See also SATA 32
Rush, Philip
See Lardner, Ring(gold Wilmer) Jr.
Rush, Philip 1908- 104
Rush, Ralph E(ugene) 1903-1965 .... 5-8R
Rush, Richard Henry 1915- CANR-6
Earlier sketch in CA 5-8R
Rush, Robert
See Barber, D(ulan) F(riar Whilberton)
Rush, Theressa Gunnels 1945- 104
Rushbrook Williams, L(aurence) F(rederic)
1890-1978 97-100
Rushdie, (Ahmed) Salman 1947- CANR-33
Brief entry 108
Earlier sketch in CA 111
See also BEST 89:3
See also CLC 23, 31, 55
See also MTCW
Rushdoony, R(ousas) J(ohn) 1916- 93-96
Rusher, William A(llen) 1923- CANR-28
Earlier sketch in CA 103
Rushford, Patricia H(elen) 1943- CANR-37
Earlier sketch in CA 115
Rushforth, Peter (Scott) 1945- 101
See also CLC 19
Rushing, Francis W(illard) 1939- CANR-31
Earlier sketch in CA 112
Rushing, Jane Gilmore 1925- 49-52
Rushing, William A. 1930- 81-84
Rushmer, Robert F(razer) 1914- 134
Brief entry 111
Rushmore, Helen 1898- 25-28R
See also SATA 3
Rushmore, Robert (William) 1926-1986 .... 25-28R
Obituary 120
See also SATA 8, 49
Rusholm, Peter
See Powell, Eric F(rederick) W(illiam)
Rushton, J(ohn) Philippe 1943- 111
Rushton, Julian (Gordon) 1941- 132
Rushton, William Faulkner 1947- CANR-22
Earlier sketch in CA 101
Rusinek, Alla 1949- 45-48
Rusinko, Susan 1922- 133
Rusinow, Dennison I. 1930- 85-88
Rusk, Howard A(rchibald) 1901-1989 103
Obituary 130
Rusk, Ralph Leslie 1888-1962 .... 5-8R
See also DLB 103
Rusk, Richard (Geary) 1946- 138
Ruskay, Joseph A. 1910- CAP-2
Earlier sketch in CA 29-32
Ruskay, Sophie 1887-1980 69-72
Obituary 97-100
Ruskin, Ariane
See Batterberry, Ariane Ruskin
Ruskin, John 1819-1900 129
Brief entry 114
See also CDBLB 1832-1890
See also DLB 55
See also SATA 24
See also TCLC 20
Ruskin, Ronald 1944- 115
Ruslanov, Sviatoslav
See Krasnov, Vladislav Georgievich
Russ, Joanna 1937- CANR-31
Earlier sketches in CA 25-28R, CANR-11
See also CLC 15
See also DLB 8
See also MTCW
Russ, Laurence 1943- 114
Russ, Lavinia (Faxon) 1904-1992 .... 25-28R
Obituary 137
Russ, Martin 1931- 106
Russ, William Adam Jr. 1903- 1-4R
Russak, Ben 1912-1988 Obituary 127
Russek, Henry I(rving) 1911-1990 Obituary 131
Russel, Robert R(oyal) 1890- 13-16R
Russell, Albert
See Bixby, Jerome Lewis
Russell, Allan Melvin 1930- 122
Russell, Amanda
See Feldman, Ellen (Bette)
Russell, Andy 1915- CANR-26
Earlier sketches in CA 21-24R, CANR-10
Russell, Annie V(est)
1880(?)-1974 Obituary 49-52
Russell, Arthur (Wolseley) 1908- CANR-16
Earlier sketches in CAP-1, CA 13-14
Russell, (Muriel) Audrey
1906(?)-1989(?) Obituary 129
Russell, Benjamin 1761-1845 .... DLB 43
Russell, Bertrand (Arthur William)
1872-1970 .... CAP-1
Obituary 25-28R
Earlier sketch in CA 13-16
See also DLB 100
See also MTCW
Russell, Bill
See Russell, William Felton
Russell, C(harles) Allyn 1920- 65-68
Russell, Carroll Mason
1898(?)-1983 Obituary 111
Russell, Charles Edward 1860-1941 .... DLB 25
Russell, Charles 1944- 111
Russell, Charlotte
See Rathjen, Carl Henry
Russell, Claude Vivian 1919- 17-20R
Russell, Clifford S(pringer) 1938- CANR-12
Earlier sketch in CA 73-76
Russell, Colin Archibald 1928- 45-48
Russell, Conrad 1937- 33-36R
Russell, D(avid) S(yme) 1916- 13-16R
Russell, Daniel 1937- 41-44R
Russell, Diana E(lizabeth) H(amilton)
1938- CANR-34
Earlier sketches in CA 61-64, CANR-8
Russell, Diarmuid 1902(?)-1973 Obituary 45-48
Russell, Don(ald Bert) 1899-1986 .... CANR-1
Obituary 118
Earlier sketch in CA 1-4R
See also SATA 47
Russell, Donald Andrew (Frank Moore)
1920- 110
Russell, Dora (Winifred Black) 1894-1986 125
Obituary 119
Russell, Douglas A(ndrew) 1927- CANR-16
Earlier sketch in CA 41-44R
Russell, Edward (Frederick Langley)
1895-1981 107
Obituary 103
Russell, Eric Frank 1905-1978 124
Obituary 102
Russell, Foster Meharry 1907- 111
Russell, Francis 1910-1989 .... 25-28R
Obituary 128
Russell, Frank D. 1923- 126
Russell, Franklin (Alexander) 1926- CANR-11
Earlier sketch in CA 17-20R
See also SATA 11
Russell, Frederick Stratten
1897-1984 Obituary 113
Russell, George William
1867-1935 Brief entry 104
See also A. E.
See also CDBLB 1890-1914
Russell, Gertrude Barrer
See Barrer-Russell, Gertrude
Russell, (Sydney) Gordon 1892- CAP-2
Earlier sketch in CA 29-32
Russell, Gordon 1930(?)-1981 Obituary 102
Russell, H. Diane 1936- 110
Russell, Harold (John) 1914- 129
Russell, Helen Ross 1915- 33-36R
See also SATA 8
Russell, Howard Lewis 1962- 136
Russell, Howard S(ymmes) 1887-1980 105
Russell, I(saac) Willis 1903-1985 118
Russell, Ivy E(thel Southern) 1909- 5-8R
Russell, J.
See Bixby, Jerome Lewis
Russell, J(effrey) P(eter) 1954- 112
Russell, James
See Harknett, Terry
Russell, James E. 1916-1975 Obituary 57-60
Russell, James 1933- .... SATA 53
Russell, Jeffrey Burton 1934- CANR-28
Earlier sketches in CA 25-28R, CANR-11
Russell, Jeremy Longmore 1935- 110
Russell, Jim
See Russell, James
Russell, Joan Mercedes 1921- 102
Russell, John David 1928- 9-12R
Russell, John L(eonard) 1906- 13-16R
Russell, John L(owry) Jr. 1921- 9-12R
Russell, John 1919- CANR-34
Earlier sketch in CA 13-16R
Russell, Josiah Cox 1900- 41-44R
Russell, (Henry) Ken(neth Alfred) 1927- 105
See also CLC 16
Russell, Ken(neth Victor) 1929- CANR-11
Earlier sketch in CA 25-28R
Russell, Letty M(andeville) 1929- CANR-8
Earlier sketch in CA 57-60
Russell, Lois Ann 1931- 113
Russell, Mariann Barbara 1935- 109
Russell, Mark 1932- 113
Brief entry 108
Russell, Martin 1934- 73-76
Russell, Maud 1893(?)-1989 Obituary 130
Russell, Maurin
See Russell, Maurine (Fletcher)
Russell, Maurine (Fletcher) 1899- CAP-1
Earlier sketch in CA 9-10
Russell, Norma Hull Lewis 1902- 5-8R
Russell, Norman H(udson) Jr. 1921- 49-52
Russell, O(live) Ruth 1897-1979 57-60
Obituary 133
Russell, P(eggy) J(ean) 1934- 97-100
Russell, Pamela Redford 1950- 81-84
Russell, Patrick
See Sammis, John
Russell, Paul (Gary) 1942- .... SATA 57
Russell, Paul 1956- 133
Russell, (Irwin) Peter 1921- 97-100
Russell, Ray 1924- CANR-6
Earlier sketch in CA 1-4R
Russell, Robert W(illiam) 1924- CANR-34
Earlier sketch in CA 1-4R
Russell, Ronald (Stanley) 1904-1974 .... CAP-1
Earlier sketch in CA 11-12
Russell, Ronald 1924- 102
Russell, Rosalind 1911-1976 116
Obituary 111
Russell, Ross 1909- CANR-34
Earlier sketch in CA 1-4R
Russell, Roy 1918- CANR-26
Earlier sketch in CA 107
Russell, Russell
See Meades, Jonathan (Turner)
Russell, Sarah
See Laski, Marghanita
Russell, Shane
See Norwood, Victor G(eorge) C(harles)
Russell, Solveig Paulson 1904- CANR-5
Earlier sketch in CA 1-4R
See also SATA 3
Russell, Thomas 1902(?)-1984 Obituary 114

Russell, Victor L. 1948- 117
Russell, William F(rank) 1945- 126
Russell, William Felton 1934- 108
Russell, William H. 1911- 61-64
Russell, Willy 1947- ....CLC 60
Russell-Smith, Enid (Mary Russell)
1903-1989 Obituary 129
Russell Taylor, Elisabeth 1930- CANR-34
Earlier sketches in CA 81-84, CANR-15
Russell-Wood, A(nthony) J(ohn) R(ussell)
1939- CANR-7
Earlier sketch in CA 57-60
Russett, Bruce M(artin) 1935- CANR-2
Earlier sketch in CA 5-8R
Russett, Cynthia Eagle 1937- 21-24R
Russman, Thomas A. 1944- 128
Russo, Anthony 1933- 61-64
Russo, Giuseppe Luigi 1884- CAP-1
Earlier sketch in CA 9-10
Russo, John Paul 1944- 41-44R
Russo, Joseph Louis
See Russo, Giuseppe Luigi
Russo, Richard Paul 1954- 129
Russo, Richard 1949- 133
Brief entry 127
Russo, Sarett Rude
1918(?)-1976 Obituary 65-68
Russo, Susan 1947- 106
See also SATA 30
Russo, Vito 1946- 107
Russon, Allien R. 1905- 105
Russon, L(eslie) J(ohn) 1907- 17-20R
Rust, Brian Arthur Lovell 1922- CANR-2
Earlier sketch in CA 45-48
Rust, Claude 1916- 109
Rust, Doris (Dibblin) 13-16R
Rust, Eric C(harles) 1910- 13-16R
Rust, Richard Dilworth 1937- 29-32R
Rusticus
See Martin, Brian P(hilip)
Rustin, Bayard 1910(?)-1987 ....CANR-25
Obituary 123
Earlier sketch in CA 53-56
See also BW
Rustomji, Nari Kaikhosru 1919- 101
Rustow, Dankwart A(lexander) 1924- CANR-1
Earlier sketch in CA 1-4R
Ruta, Suzanne 1940- 127
Rutberg, Sidney 1924- 69-72
Rutenber, Culbert G(erow) 1909- CAP-2
Earlier sketch in CA 17-18
Rutgers van der Loeff, An
See
Rutgers van der Loeff-Basenau, An(na) Maria
Rutgers van der Loeff-Basenau, An(na) Maria Margaretha
1910- CANR-7
Earlier sketch in CA 9-12R
See also SATA 22
Ruth, Babe
See Ruth, George Herman (Jr.)
Ruth, Claire (Merritt) 1900-1976 Obituary 69-72
Ruth, George Herman (Jr.)
1895-1948 Brief entry 116
Ruth, John L(andis) 1930- 73-76
Ruth, Kent Ringelman 1916- CANR-2
Earlier sketch in CA 5-8R
Ruth, Rod 1912- ....SATA 9
Rutherford, Andrew 1929- CANR-9
Earlier sketch in CA 5-8R
Rutherford, Douglas
See McConnell, James Douglas Rutherford
Rutherford, Malcolm 1939- 119
Rutherford, Margaret
1882-1972 Obituary 33-36R
Rutherford, Mark
See White, William Hale
See also DLB 18
See also TCLC 25
Rutherford, Meg 1932- 29-32R
See also SATA 34
Rutherford, Michael (Andrew) 1946- CANR-26
Earlier sketch in CA 45-48
Rutherford, Phillip Roland 1939- 37-40R
Rutherford, Ward 1927- CANR-14
Earlier sketch in CA 77-80
Ruthin, Margaret ....SATA 4
Ruthstrom, Dorotha 1936- 107
Ruthven, K(enneth) K(nowles) 1936- CANR-26
Earlier sketch in CA 25-28R
Rutkoff, Peter M. 1942- CANR-39
Earlier sketch in CA 116
Rutkowski, Edwin H(enry) 1923- 37-40R
Rutland, Dodge
See Singleton, Betty
Rutland, Robert A(llen) 1922- CANR-2
Earlier sketch in CA 45-48
Rutledge, Aaron L(eslie) 1919- 45-48
Rutledge, Albert J(ohn) 1934- 33-36R
Rutledge, Archibald (Hamilton)
1883-1973 ....CANR-5
Obituary 45-48
Earlier sketch in CA 5-8R
Rutledge, Brett
See Paul, Elliot (Harold)
Rutledge, Dom Denys
See Rutledge, Edward William
Rutledge, Edward William 1906- 5-8R
Rutledge, Harley Dean 1926- 107
Rutledge, Howard Elmer
1929(?)-1984 Obituary 113
Rutman, Darrett B(ruce) 1929- CANR-6
Earlier sketch in CA 13-16R
Rutman, Gilbert L(ionel) 1935- 25-28R
Rutman, Leo 1935- 45-48
Rutsala, Vern 1934- CANR-20
Earlier sketches in CA 9-12R, CANR-6
Rutstein, David D(avis) 1909-1986 ....33-36R
Obituary 118
Rutstein, Harry Sidney 1929- 108
Rutstein, Nat(han) 1930- 53-56
Rutstrum, Calvin 1895-1982 ....CANR-1
Obituary 106
Earlier sketch in CA 1-4R
Rutt, M. E.
See Shah, Amina
Rutt, Richard 1925- CANR-6
Earlier sketch in CA 9-12R
Ruttan, Vernon W(esley) 1924- 41-44R
Ruttenberg, Joseph 1889-1983 Obituary 109
Ruttenberg, Stanley H(arvey) 1917- 33-36R
Rutter, Barbara A. 1943- 118
Rutter, Eileen Joyce 1945- CANR-10
Earlier sketch in CA 61-64
Rutter, Michael (Llewellyn) 1933- CANR-29
Earlier sketch in CA 109
Ruttkowski, Wolfgang Victor 1935- CANR-15
Earlier sketch in CA 41-44R
Ruttle, Lee 1909- 81-84
Rutz, Viola Larkin 1932- 21-24R
See also SATA 12
Rutzebeck, Hjalmar 1889- 9-12R
Ruud, Charles A(rthur) 1933- 121
Ruud, Josephine Bartow 1921- 73-76
Ruuth, Marianne 1937- CANR-21
Earlier sketches in CA 57-60, CANR-6
Ruxin, Robert H(arris) 1953- 110
Ruyerson, James Paul
See Rothweiler, Paul Roger
Ruyslinck, Ward
See Belser, Reimond Karel Maria de
Ruz, Fidel Castro
See Castro (Ruz), Fidel
Ruzic, Neil P. 1930- CANR-39
Earlier sketches in CA 17-20R, CANR-8
Ruzicka, Rudolph 1883-1978 Obituary 81-84
See also SATA 24
Ryall, Edward W(illiam) 1902- 61-64
Ryall, George (Francis Trafford)
1887(?)-1979 103
Obituary 89-92
Ryalls, Alan 1919- 102
Ryals, Clyde de L(oache) 1928- 21-24R
Ryan, Alan 1940- 29-32R
Ryan, Allan A(ndrew) Jr. 1945- 124
Ryan, Alvan Sherman 1912- 17-20R
Ryan, Bernard Jr. 1923- CANR-6
Earlier sketch in CA 5-8R
Ryan, Betsy
See Ryan, Elizabeth (Anne)
Ryan, Bob 1946- CANR-4
Earlier sketch in CA 49-52
Ryan, Bryce F(inley) 1911- 81-84
Ryan, Charles W(illiam) 1929- 57-60
Ryan, Charles W(illiam) 1932- 93-96
Ryan, Cheli Duran 102
See also SATA 20
Ryan, Claude 1925- Brief entry 111
Ryan, Cornelius (John) 1920-1974 ....CANR-38
Obituary 53-56
Earlier sketch in CA 69-72
See also CLC 7
Ryan, Desmond 1893-1964 Obituary 113
Ryan, Desmond 1943- 130
Ryan, Dorothy (Barger) 1942- CANR-13
Earlier sketch in CA 73-76
Ryan, Edwin 1916- 5-8R
Ryan, Elizabeth (Anne) 1943- CANR-7
Earlier sketch in CA 61-64
See also SATA 30
Ryan, Herbert J(oseph) 1931- 41-44R
Ryan, James H(erbert) 1928- 53-56
Ryan, Jeanette Mines
See Mines, Jeanette (Marie)
Ryan, Jessica Cadwalader
1915(?)-1972 Obituary 33-36R
Ryan, John Barry 1933- CANR-7
Earlier sketch in CA 57-60
Ryan, John Fergus 1931- 73-76
Ryan, John (Gerald Christopher)
1921- CANR-16
Earlier sketches in CA 49-52, CANR-1
See also SATA 22
Ryan, John J. 1922(?)-1977 Obituary 69-72
Ryan, John Julian 1898- 73-76
Ryan, John K(enneth) 1897-1981 ....CANR-16
Earlier sketch in CA 13-16R
Ryan, Joseph A. 1920- 138
Ryan, Joseph J. 1910(?)-1976 Obituary 69-72
Ryan, Juanita 1949- 120
Ryan, Kathryn Morgan 1925- 102
Ryan, Kevin 1932- CANR-12
Earlier sketch in CA 29-32R
Ryan, Lawrence Vincent 1923- 5-8R
Ryan, Leonard Eames 1930- 9-12R
Ryan, Marah Ellis 1866(?)-1934 Brief entry 122
Ryan, Marleigh Grayer 1930- 17-20R
Ryan, Mary E(lizabeth) 1953- ....SATA 61
Ryan, Mary P(atricia) 1945- 134
Brief entry 113
Ryan, Maureen Jones
See Jones-Ryan, Maureen
Ryan, Michael 1946- 49-52
See also CLC 65
See also DLBY 82
Ryan, Milo 1907- 5-8R
Ryan, Neil Joseph 1930- 13-16R
Ryan, Oscar 1904- ....DLB 68
Ryan, Pat M(artin) 1928- CANR-13
Earlier sketch in CA 33-36R
Ryan, Patrick J. 1902- CAP-1
Earlier sketch in CA 11-12
Ryan, Paul B(rennan) 1913- CANR-15
Earlier sketch in CA 81-84
Ryan, Paul William 1906-1947 Brief entry 114
Ryan, Peter Allen 1923- 109
Ryan, Peter (Charles) 1939- 61-64
See also SATA 15
Ryan, Regina (Claire) 1938- 118
Ryan, Regina S(ara) 1945- 119
Ryan, Robert Michael 1934- 29-32R
Ryan, Sister Joseph Eleanor 61-64
Ryan, T. Antoinette 1924- 41-44R
Ryan, Thomas Arthur 1911- 41-44R
Ryan, Thomas Richard 1897-1981 ....29-32R
Obituary 122
Ryan, Tim
See Dent, Lester
Ryan, Tom 1938- CANR-10
Earlier sketch in CA 57-60
Ryan, William H. 1928(?)-1986 Obituary 121
Ryan, William (Howard) 1914- 104
Ryan, William M(artin) 1918- 33-36R
Ryan, William (Michael) 1948- 122
Ryans, David Garriott 1909- 5-8R
Ryans, John K(elley) Jr. 1932- 61-64
Ryavec, Karl W(illiam) 1936- 137
Ryback, Eric 1952- 37-40R
Rybak, Nathan 1913-1978(?) Obituary 81-84
Rybakov, Anatoli (Naumovich) 1911- 135
Brief entry 126
See also CLC 23, 53
Rybalka, Michel 1933- 41-44R
Rybczynski, Witold (Marian) 1943- CANR-29
Earlier sketch in CA 110
Rybka, Edward F(rank) 1928- 33-36R
Rybolt, Thomas R(oy) 1954- ....SATA 62
Rybot, Doris
See Ponsonby, D(oris) A(lmon)
Rychlak, Joseph F(rank) 1928- CANR-14
Earlier sketch in CA 37-40R
Ryckmans, Pierre 1935- CANR-16
Earlier sketch in CA 85-88
Rycroft, Charles (Frederick) 1914- CANR-11
Earlier sketch in CA 21-24R
Rydberg, Ernest E(mil) 1901- 13-16R
See also SATA 21
Rydberg, Lou(isa Hampton) 1908- 69-72
See also SATA 27
Rydel, Christine A(nn) 1944- 118
Rydell, Forbes
See Forbes, DeLoris (Florine) Stanton
Rydell, Robert W(illiam) 1952- 126
Rydell, Wendell
See Rydell, Wendy
Rydell, Wendy 33-36R
See also SATA 4
Ryden, Ernest Edwin 1886-1981 Obituary 102
Ryden, Hope CANR-14
Earlier sketch in CA 33-36R
See also SATA 8
Rydenfelt, Sven 1911- 132
Ryder, A(rthur) J(ohn) 1913- 21-24R
Ryder, Eileen 1908- 117
Ryder, Ellen 1913- 29-32R
Ryder, Frank G(lessner) 1916- 5-8R
Ryder, Joanne (Rose) 1946- 133
Brief entry 112
See also MAICYA
See also SATA 34, 65
Ryder, John 1917- CANR-5
Earlier sketch in CA 5-8R
Ryder, Jonathan
See Ludlum, Robert
Ryder, M(ichael) L(awson) 1927- 102
Ryder, Meyer S. 1909- 21-24R
Ryder, Norman B(urston) 1923- 37-40R
Ryder, Ron 1904- 61-64
Ryder, Rowland (Vint) 1914- 85-88
Ryder, T(homas) A(rthur) 1902- 5-8R
Ryder, Thom
See Harvey, John (Barton)
Ryding, William W. 1924- 77-80
Rye, Anthony
See Youd, (Christopher) Samuel
Rye, Bjoern Robinson 1942- 61-64
Ryerson, Margery (Austin)
1886-1989 Obituary 128
Ryerson, Martin 1907- CANR-8
Earlier sketch in CA 13-16R
Ryf, Robert S. 1918-1985 ....17-20R
Obituary 117
Ryga, George 1932-1987 101
Obituary 124
See also CLC 14
See also DLB 60
Ryken, Leland 1942- CANR-28
Earlier sketches in CA 29-32R, CANR-12
Rykwert, Joseph 1926- CANR-11
Earlier sketch in CA 69-72
Ryland, Lee
See Arlandson, Leone
Rylant, Cynthia 1954- 136
See also CLR 15
See also MAICYA
See also SAAS 13
See also SATA 44, 50
Ryle, Anthony 1927- 107
Ryle, Gilbert 1900-1976 73-76
Obituary 69-72
Ryle, Martin (H.) 1918-1984 133
Ryle, Michael 1927- 133
Rylski, Aleksander Scibor
See Scibor-Rylski, Aleksander
Ryman, Geoff(rey Charles) 1951- 134
Rymer, Alta May 1925- CANR-1
Earlier sketch in CA 49-52
See also SATA 34
Rymer, Thomas 1643(?)-1713 ....DLB 101
Rymes, Thomas Kenneth 1932- 37-40R
Ryn, Claes G. 1943- 129
Rynearson, Edward H(arper)
1901-1987 Obituary 121
Rynew, Arden N. 1943- 37-40R
Ryrie, Charles C(aldwell) 1925- CANR-39
Earlier sketches in CA 9-12R, CANR-3, 18
Ryskamp, Charles (Andrew) 1928- 104
Ryskind, Morrie 1895-1985 Obituary 117
Brief entry 109
See also DLB 26
Rystrom, Kenneth 1932- 110
Rywell, Martin 1905-1971 ....CAP-2
Earlier sketch in CA 19-20
Rywkin, Michael 1925- 13-16R
Ryzl, Milan 1928- 29-32R
Rzepka, Charles J(ulian) 1949- 127
Rzhevsky, Leonid 1905- CANR-14
Earlier sketch in CA 41-44R
Rzhevsky, Nicholas 1943- 115

S

S. L. C.
See Clemens, Samuel Langhorne
S. S.
See Sassoon, Siegfried (Lorraine)
S. S. E.
See Sperry, (Sally) Baxter
S., Svend Otto
See Soerensen, Svend Otto
Saab, E(velyn) Ann Pottinger 1934- 107
Saab, Edouard 1929-1976 Obituary 65-68
Saadawi, Nawal El
See El Saadawi, Nawal
Saal, Jocelyn
See Sachs, Judith
Saalman, Howard 1928- CANR-1
Earlier sketch in CA 1-4R
Saar, James 1949- 131
Saarinen, Aline B(ernstein Louchheim)
1914-1972 Obituary 37-40R
Saarinen, Eero 1910-1961 Obituary 113
Saatkamp, Herman J(oseph) Jr. 1942- 126
Saaty, Thomas L(orie) 1926- CANR-8
Earlier sketch in CA 57-60
Saavedra, Luis Spota
See Spota Saavedra, Luis
Saba, Umberto 1883-1957 ....DLB 114
See also TCLC 33
Sabais, Heinz Winfried 1922-1981 Obituary 114
Sabaliunas, Leonas 1934- 61-64
Sabar, Yona 1939- CANR-30
Earlier sketch in CA 112
Sabaroff, Rose Epstein 1918- 85-88
Sabatier, Robert 1923- CANR-39
Earlier sketches in CA 102, CANR-18
Sabato, Ernesto (R.) 1911- CANR-32
Earlier sketch in CA 97-100
See also CLC 10, 23
See also HW
See also MTCW
Sabato, Larry (J.) 1952- CANR-27
Earlier sketch in CA 108
Sabbag, Robert 1946- 101
Sabbah, Hassan i
See Butler, William Huxford
Sabel, Charles F(rederick) 1947- 129
Saberhagen, Fred(erick Thomas)
1930- CANR-33
Earlier sketches in CA 57-60, CANR-7, 27
See also DLB 8
See also MTCW
See also SATA 37
Sabiad
See White, Stanhope
Sabin, Edwin L(egrand) 1870-1952 ....YABC 2
Sabin, Francene CANR-11
Earlier sketch in CA 69-72
See also SATA 27
Sabin, Katharine Cover 1910- 57-60
Sabin, Lou
See Sabin, Louis
Sabin, Louis 1930- CANR-11
Earlier sketch in CA 69-72
See also SATA 27
Sabin, Mark
See Fox, Norman A(rnold)
Sabine, B(asil) E. V. 1914- CANR-28
Earlier sketch in CA 97-100
Sabine, Ellen S. (Borcherding) 1908- CAP-1
Earlier sketch in CA 17-18
Sabine, Gordon Arthur 1917- 117
Sabine, Waldo
See Sabine, William H(enry) W(aldo)
Sabine, William H(enry) W(aldo) 1903- CANR-4
Earlier sketch in CA 53-56
Sabines, Jaime 1925(?)- ....HW
Sabini, John Anthony 1921- 9-12R
Sabisch, Christian 1955- 129
Sabki, Hisham M. 1934- Brief entry 106
Sable, Martin Howard 1924- CANR-29
Earlier sketches in CA 33-36R, CANR-12
Sabloff, Jeremy A(rac) 1944- CANR-8
Earlier sketch in CA 61-64
Sablosky, Irving L. 1924- 124
Sabom, Michael Bruce 1944- 109
Sabourin, Anne Winifred 1910- 101
Sabourin, Justine
See Sabourin, Anne Winifred
Sabourin, Leopold 1919- CANR-11
Earlier sketch in CA 65-68

Sabre, Dirk
  See Laffin, John (Alfred Charles)
Sabri-Tabrizi, Gholam-Reza 1934- 61-64
Sacastru, Martin
  See Bioy Casares, Adolfo
Saccio, Peter (Churchill) 1941- 61-64
Sach, Nathan
  See Zach, Nathan
Sachar, Abram Leon 1899- 97-100
Sachar, Emily 1958- 135
Sachar, Howard Morley 1928- CANR-6
  Earlier sketch in CA 5-8R
Sachar, Louis 1954- CANR-33
  Earlier sketches in CA 81-84, CANR-15
  See also CLR 28
  See also SATA 50, 63
Sacharoff, Shanta Nimbark 1945- 61-64
Sachdev, Paul 115
Sachem, E. B.
  See Creel, Stephen Melville
Sacher, Jack Jr. 1931- 57-60
Sacher-Masoch, Alexander
  1902(?)-1972 Obituary 37-40R
Sachs, Albert Louis 1935- CANR-14
  Earlier sketch in CA 21-24R
Sachs, Albie
  See Sachs, Albert Louis
Sachs, Alexander 1893-1973 Obituary 41-44R
Sachs, Elizabeth-Ann 1946- 111
  See also SATA 48
Sachs, Georgia
  See Adams, Georgia Sachs
Sachs, (Stewart) Harvey 1946- 85-88
Sachs, Herbert L. 1929- 25-28R
Sachs, Judith 1947- 122
  See also SATA 51, 52
Sachs, Lewis Benjamen 1938- 61-64
Sachs, Margaret 1948- Brief entry 115
Sachs, Marianne 1945- 114
Sachs, Marilyn (Stickle) 1927- CANR-13
  Earlier sketch in CA 17-20R
  See also AAYA 2
  See also CLC 35
  See also CLR 2
  See also MAICYA
  See also SAAS 2
  See also SATA 3, 68
Sachs, Mary P(armly) K(oues)
  1882(?)-1973 Obituary 45-48
Sachs, Mendel 1927- CANR-12
  Earlier sketch in CA 29-32R
Sachs, Michael L(eo) 1951- CANR-37
  Earlier sketch in CA 115
Sachs, Murray 1924- CANR-14
  Earlier sketch in CA 37-40R
Sachs, Nelly 1891-1970 .... CAP-2
  Obituary 25-28R
  Earlier sketch in CA 17-18
  See also CLC 14
Sachse, William L(ewis) 1912- 25-28R
Sack, James J(ohn) 1944- 101
Sack, John 1930- CANR-14
  Earlier sketch in CA 21-24R
Sack, Saul 1912- 53-56
Sackerman, Henry
  See Kahm, H(arold) S.
Sackett, L(eyland) H(ugh) 1928- 119
Sackett, S(amuel) J(ohn) 1928- CANR-6
  Earlier sketch in CA 1-4R
  See also SATA 12
Sackett, Susan 1943- CANR-22
  Earlier sketch in CA 106
Sackett, Theodore Alan 1940- 89-92
Sackett, Walter W(allace) Jr. 1905-1985 ...... 5-8R
  Obituary 117
Sackheim, Maxwell 1890-1982 Obituary 108
Sackler, Howard (Oliver) 1929-1982 ...... CANR-30
  Obituary 108
  Earlier sketch in CA 61-64
  See also CLC 14
  See also DLB 7
Sackman, Harold 1927- CANR-12
  Earlier sketch in CA 21-24R
Sackrey, Charles 1936- 77-80
Sacks, Benjamin 1903- CAP-2
  Earlier sketch in CA 23-24
Sacks, Claire
  See Sprague, Claire S(acks)
Sacks, Karen 1941- CANR-26
  Earlier sketch in CA 109
Sacks, Norman P(aul) 1914- 45-48
Sacks, Oliver (Wolf) 1933- CANR-28
  Earlier sketch in CA 53-56
  See also CLC 67
  See also MTCW
Sacks, Peter
  See Sacks, Peter M.
Sacks, Peter M. 1950- 124
Sacks, Sheldon 1930-1979 .... 17-20R
  Obituary 122
Sackson, Sid 1920- CANR-12
  Earlier sketch in CA 69-72
  See also SATA 16
Sackton, Alexander H(art) 1911- 37-40R
Sackville, Thomas 1536-1608 .... DLB 62
Sackville-West, V(ictoria Mary) 1892-1962 104
  Obituary 93-96
  See also DLB 34
  See also MTCW
(el-)Sadat, Anwar 1918-1981 101
  Obituary 104
Sadd, Susan 1951- 103
Saddhatissa, Hammalawa 1914- CANR-17
  Earlier sketch in CA 97-100
Saddlemyer, E(leanor) Ann 1932- 17-20R
Saddler, Allen
  See Richards, R(onald) C(harles) W(illiam)
Saddler, K. Allen
  See Richards, R(onald) C(harles) W(illiam)
Sadecky, Petr Milos 1943- 41-44R
Sadeh, Pinhas 1929- CANR-34
  Earlier sketches in CA 25-28R, CANR-13
Sadick, Neil (S.) 1951- 138
Sadie, Stanley (John) 1930- CANR-9
  Earlier sketch in CA 17-20R
  See also SATA 14
Sadiq, Muhammad 1898-1984 .... CANR-18
  Earlier sketch in CA 17-20R
Sadker, Myra Pollack 1943- CANR-22
  Earlier sketches in CA 53-56, CANR-5
Sadler, Arthur Lindsay 1882- 5-8R
Sadler, Barry 1940- 129
Sadler, Catherine Edwards 1952- .... SATA 45
Sadler, Christine 1908-1983 .... CAP-1
  Obituary 110
  Earlier sketch in CA 11-12
Sadler, Ella Jo 1942- 57-60
Sadler, Glenn Edward 1935- 97-100
Sadler, Julius Trousdale Jr. 1923- 65-68
Sadler, Mark
  See Lynds, Dennis
Sadler, William A(lan) Jr. 1931- 25-28R
Sadlier, Mary Anne 1820-1903 .... DLB 99
Sadock, Benjamin James 1933- Brief entry 105
Sadoff, Ira 1945- CANR-21
  Earlier sketches in CA 53-56, CANR-5
  See also CLC 9
  See also DLB 120
Sadun, Elvio H. 1918(?)-1974 Obituary 49-52
Saenz, Dalmiro
  See Saenz, Dalmiro A.
Saenz, Dalmiro A. 1926- .... HW
Saerchinger, Cesar 1884-1971 Obituary 33-36R
Saetone
  See Camus, Albert
Safa, Helen M. Icken 1930- CANR-30
  Earlier sketches in CA 45-48, CANR-1
Safarian, Albert Edward 1924- 105
Safarik, Allan 1948- 114
Safdie, Moshe 1938- 69-72
Safer, Daniel J. 1934- CANR-11
  Earlier sketch in CA 69-72
Safer, Elaine Berkman 1937- 41-44R
Safer, Morley 1931- 93-96
  See also AITN 2
Saffell, David C(lyde) 1941- CANR-11
  Earlier sketch in CA 61-64
Saffin, John 1626(?)-1710 .... DLB 24
Saffron, Morris Harold 1905- 45-48
Saffron, Robert 1918(?)-1985 Obituary 114
Safian, Jill
  See Bharti, Ma Satya
Safilios-Rothschild, Constantina
  1936- CANR-31
  Earlier sketch in CA 45-48
Safir, Leonard 1921- 109
Safire, William 1929- CANR-31
  Earlier sketch in CA 17-20R
  See also CLC 10
  See also AITN 2
Safran, Claire 1930- 101
Safran, Nadav 1925- 5-8R
Safran, William 1930- CANR-32
  Earlier sketch in CA 113
Sagall, Elliot L. 1918- 29-32R
Sagalyn, Lynne B. 1947- 134
Sagan, Carl (Edward) 1934- CANR-36
  Earlier sketches in CA 25-28R, CANR-11
  See also AAYA 2
  See also CLC 30
  See also MTCW
  See also SATA 58
Sagan, Dorion 1959- 131
Sagan, Eli 1927- 124
Sagan, Francoise
  See Quoirez, Francoise
  See also CLC 3, 6, 9, 17, 36
  See also DLB 83
Sagan, Leonard A. 1928- 49-52
Sagan, Miriam 1954- 77-80
Sagar, Keith (Milsom) 1934- CANR-14
  Earlier sketch in CA 21-24R
Sagarin, Edward 1913- CANR-4
  Earlier sketch in CA 5-8R
Sagarin, Mary 1903- 81-84
Sagarra, Eda 1933- CANR-11
  Earlier sketch in CA 65-68
Sage, George Harvey 1929- 61-64
Sage, Joe
  See Sage, Joseph
Sage, Jonathan 1953- 129
Sage, Joseph 1921-1987 Obituary 122
Sage, Juniper
  See Brown, Margaret Wise
Sage, Leland L(ivingston) 1899- 61-64
Sage, Robert 1899-1962 106
  See also DLB 4
Sagel, Jim 1947- 131
  See also DLB 82
  See also HW
Sagendorf, Bud
  See Sagendorf, Forrest C(owles)
Sagendorf, Forrest C(owles)
  1915- Brief entry 112
Sagendorph, Robb Hansell 1900-1970 ...... CANR-7
  Obituary 29-32R
  Earlier sketch in CA 5-8R
Sager, Clifford J. 1916- CANR-12
  Earlier sketch in CA 29-32R
Sager, Samuel 1923- 123
Sageser, A(delbert) Bower 1902- 29-32R
Saggs, Henry W(illiam) F(rederick) 1920- 5-8R
Saghir, Marcel T(awfic) 1937- 49-52
Sagne, Thierry (Bright) 1946- 53-56
Sagsoorian, Paul 1923- .... SATA 12
Sagstetter, Karen 1941- 105
Sahagun, Carlos 1938- .... DLB 108
Sahakian, Lucille 1894- 53-56
Sahakian, Mabel Lewis 1921- 21-24R
Sahakian, William S(ahak) 1921- CANR-8
  Earlier sketch in CA 17-20R
Sahgal, Nayantara (Pandit) 1927- CANR-11
  Earlier sketch in CA 9-12R
  See also CLC 41
Sahl, Hans 1902- .... DLB 69
Sahl, Mort(on Lyon) 1927- Brief entry 113
Sahlins, Marshall
  See Sahlins, Marshall D(avid)
Sahlins, Marshall D(avid) 1930- 133
  Brief entry 114
Sahn, Seung 1927- 113
Sahni, Balbir S. 1934- CANR-3
  Earlier sketch in CA 45-48
Sahni, Chaman L. 1933- 128
Said, Abdul Aziz 1930- 81-84
Said, Edward W. 1935- 21-24R
  See also DLB 67
Saida
  See LeMair, H(enriette) Willebeek
Saidel, Rochelle G. 1942- 121
Sa'Idi, Ghulam Husayn 1936-1985 Obituary 119
Saidy, Anthony Fred 1937- 89-92
Saidy, Fareed Milhem 1907-1982 Obituary 106
Saidy, Fred M.
  See Saidy, Fareed Milhem
Saiki, Jessica K(awasuna) 1928- 138
Saiko, George 1892-1962 .... DLB 85
Sail, Lawrence (Richard) 1942- 132
Sailor, Charles 1947- 97-100
Sailor, Merlin F(orrest) 1906- CAP-1
  Earlier sketch in CA 13-16
Saine, Thomas P(rice) 1941- 41-44R
Sainer, Arthur 1924- CANR-3
  Earlier sketch in CA 49-52
Saini, B(alwant) S(ingh) 1930- 107
Sainsbury, Eric (Edward) 1925- CANR-13
  Earlier sketch in CA 33-36R
Sainsbury, John A. 1946- 127
Sainsbury, Maurice Joseph 1927- 108
Saint, Andrew (John) 1946- 65-68
Saint, Dora Jessie 1913- CANR-22
  Earlier sketches in CA 13-16R, CANR-7
  See also SATA 10
Saint, H(arry) F. 1941- 127
  See also CLC 50
Saint, Phil(ip) 1912- 61-64
St. Andre, Lucien
  See Mott, Vincent Valmon
St. Angelo, Douglas 1931- 45-48
St. Antoine, Theodore J(oseph) 1929- 41-44R
St. Aubin de Teran, Lisa 1953- 126
  Brief entry 118
  See also Teran, Lisa St. Aubin de
St. Aubyn, F(rederic) C(hase) 1921- 25-28R
St. Aubyn, Fiona 1952- CANR-23
  Earlier sketch in CA 106
St. Aubyn, Giles 1925- CANR-19
  Earlier sketches in CA 5-8R, CANR-4
St. Bruno, Albert Francis 1909- CAP-1
  Earlier sketch in CA 9-10
St. Clair, (Howard) Barry 1945- 120
St. Clair, Byrd Hooper 1905-1976 .... 1-4R
  Obituary 103
  See also SATA 28
St. Clair, Clovis
  See Skarda, Patricia Lyn
St. Clair, David 1932- 33-36R
St. Clair, Elizabeth
  See Cohen, Susan
St. Clair, Katherine
  See Huff, T(om) E.
St. Clair, Leonard 1916-1986 101
  Obituary 118
St. Clair, Margaret 1911- 49-52
  See also CAAS 8
St. Clair, Philip
  See Howard, Munroe
St. Clair, Robert James 1925- 9-12R
St. Clair, William 77-80
St. Cyr, Cyprian
  See Berne, Eric (Lennard)
St. Cyr, Margaret 1920- 29-32R
Saint-Denis, Michel Jacques 1897-1971 ...... CAP-2
  Obituary 33-36R
  Earlier sketch in CA 19-20
Saint Dorliae
  See Dorliae, Peter Gondro
Saint-Eden, Dennis
  See Foster, Don(ald)
Sainte-Marie, Beverly 1941- 107
Sainte-Marie, Buffy
  See Sainte-Marie, Beverly
Saint-Exupery, Antoine (Jean Baptiste Marie Roger) de
  1900-1944 132
  Brief entry 108
  See also CLR 10
  See also DLB 72
  See also MAICYA
  See also MTCW
  See also SATA 20
  See also TCLC 2
  See also WLC
Saint-Gall, Auguste Amedee de
  See Strich, Christian
St. George, Arthur
  See Paine, Lauran (Bosworth)
St. George, David
  See Markov, Georgi
St. George, Edith
  See Delatush, Edith G.
St. George, George 1904- 25-28R
St. George, Judith 1931- CANR-14
  Earlier sketch in CA 69-72
  See also AAYA 7
  See also SAAS 12
  See also SATA 13
St. George, Margaret
  See Osborne, Margaret Ellen
St. George, Noel
  See Green, Jonathon
St. Germain, Gregory
  See Wallmann, Jeffrey M(iner)
St. Hereticus
  See Brown, Robert McAfee
Saint-Jacques, Bernard 1928- CANR-37
  Earlier sketches in CA 41-44R, CANR-16
St. James, Bernard
  See Treister, Bernard W(illiam)
St. James, Blakely
  See Gottfried, Theodore Mark
    and Platt, Charles
St. John, Beth
  See John, Elizabeth Beaman
St. John, Bob (J.) 1937- Brief entry 122
St. John, Bruce (Carlisle) 1923- 107
St. John, David
  See Hunt, E(verette) Howard Jr.
St. John, Elizabeth
  See John, Elizabeth Beaman
St. John, Henry 1678-1751 .... DLB 101
St. John, John 1917-1988 .... CANR-5
  Obituary 127
  Earlier sketch in CA 5-8R
St. John, Leonie
  See Bayer, William
    and Jenkins, Nancy (Harmon)
St. John, Lisa
  See Sanford, Annette
St. John, Nicole CANR-32
  See also Johnston, Norma
  See also SAAS 7
St. John, Patricia Mary 1919- CANR-3
  Earlier sketch in CA 5-8R
St. John, Philip
  See del Rey, Lester
St. John, Primus 1939- 113
  See also BW
St. John, Robert 1902- CANR-5
  Earlier sketch in CA 1-4R
St. John, Wylly Folk 1908-1985 .... 21-24R
  Obituary 117
  See also SATA 10, 45
Saint-John Perse
  See Leger, (Marie-Rene) Alexis Saint-Leger
St. Johns, Adela Rogers 1894-1988 108
  Obituary 126
  See also AITN 1
  See also DLB 29
St. John-Stevas, Norman Anthony Francis
  1929- CANR-4
  Earlier sketch in CA 49-52
St. John Thomas, David
  See Thomas, David St. John
St. Max, E. S.
  See Ellis, Edward S(ylvester)
St. Meyer, Ned
  See Stratemeyer, Edward L.
St. Mox, E. A.
  See Ellis, Edward S(ylvester)
St. Myer, Ned
  See Stratemeyer, Edward L.
St. Omer, Garth 73-76
  See also DLB 117
Saint Phalle, Thibaut de
  See de Saint Phalle, Thibaut
St. Pierre, Dorothy
  See Nyren, Dorothy Elizabeth
Saint Pierre, Michel de 1916-1987 .... DLB 83
St. Pierre, Paul 1923- 113
Saintsbury, George (Edward Bateman)
  1845-1933 .... DLB 57
  See also TCLC 31
St. Tamara
  See Kolba, St. Tamara
St. Vivant, M.
  See Bixby, Jerome Lewis
Sainty, John Christopher 1934- 93-96
Sainz, Gustavo 1940- 131
  See also HW
Sainz de la Maza, Regino
  1896-1981 Obituary 108
Saisselin, Remy G(ilbert) 1925- 9-12R
Sait Faik
  See Abasiyanik, Sait Faik
  See also TCLC 23
Saito, Fred
  See Saito, Hiroyuki
Saito, Hiroyuki 1917- 61-64
Saito, Michiko
  See Fujiwara, Michiko
Sakamaki, Shunzo 1906-1973 .... 1-4R
  Obituary 103
Sakamoto, Yoshikazu 1927- 133
Sakell, Achilles Nicholas 1906-1987 .... 1-4R
  Obituary 123
Sakers, Don 1958- 127
Sakers, George 1950- 108
Sakharnov, S.
  See Sakharnov, Svyatoslav (Vladimirovich)
Sakharnov, Svyatoslav (Vladimirovich)
  1923- 133
  See also SATA 65
Sakharov, Andrei D(mitrievich) 1921-1989 128
  Obituary 130
  Brief entry 105
Saki
  See Munro, H(ector) H(ugh)
  See also TCLC 3

Saklatvala, Beram 1911-1976 ... 89-92
Sakoian, Frances 1912- ... 65-68
Sakol, Jeannie 1928- ... CANR-11
Earlier sketch in CA 5-8R
Sakran, Frank Charles
1895(?)-1983 Obituary ... 111
Saks, Elmer Eliot
See Fawcett, F(rank) Dubrez
Saks, Katia 1939- ... 29-32R
Sala, Charles 1924- ... 116
Salaam, Kalamu ya 1947- ... 126
See also DLB 38
Saladino, Salvatore 1922- ... 33-36R
Salaff, Janet W. 1940- ... 112
Salama, Hannu 1936- ... CLC 18
Salaman, Esther 1900- ... 61-64
Salaman, Nicholas 1936- Brief entry ... 116
Salamanca, J(ack) R(ichard) 1922- ... 25-28R
See also CLC 4, 15
Salamanca, Lucy
See del Barco, Lucy Salamanca
Salamatullah
See Ullah, Salamat
Salamon, Julie 1953- ... 136
Salamon, Lester M(ilton) 1943- ... 89-92
Salant, Nathan N(athaniel) 1955- ... 106
Salant, Walter S. 1911- ... CANR-2
Earlier sketch in CA 5-8R
Salas, Floyd Francis 1931- ... 119
See also DLB 82
See also HW
Salas, Rafael M(ontinola) 1928-1987 ... 129
Obituary ... 121
Salassi, Otto R(ussell) 1939- ... 106
See also SATA 38
Salazar, Antonio de Oliveira
1889-1970 Obituary ... 113
Salazar, Fred A. 1942- ... 21-24R
Salazar, Rachel 1954- ... 123
Salazar, Ruben 1928-1970 Obituary ... 115
Salazar Bondy, Sebastian 1924-1965 ... HW
Salber, Eva J. 1916- ... 125
Saldutti, Denise 1953- ... SATA 39
Sale, J. Kirkpatrick
See Sale, Kirkpatrick
Sale, Kirkpatrick 1937- ... CANR-10
Earlier sketch in CA 13-16R
See also CLC 68
Sale, Larry L(owell) 1939- Brief entry ... 113
Sale, Richard (Bernard) 1911- ... 9-12R
Sale, Roger 1932- ... CANR-33
Earlier sketch in CA 21-24R
Sale, William (Merritt III) 1929- ... 45-48
Saleh, Dennis 1942- ... CANR-13
Earlier sketch in CA 33-36R
Salem, Elie Adib 1930- ... 49-52
Salem, James M. 1937- ... 21-24R
Salemme, Lucia (Autorino) 1919- ... 89-92
Salemson, Harold J(ason) 1910-1988 ... 110
Obituary ... 126
Brief entry ... 108
See also DLB 4
Salerno, Lynn M(cCormick) 1926- ... 119
Sales, Grover 1919- ... 65-68
Sales, Jane M(agorian) 1931- ... 49-52
Sales, M(ary) E(ileen) 1936- ... 29-32R
Sales, M(illard) Vance 1929- ... 53-56
Saletore, Bhasker Anand 1900- ... 5-8R
Salgado, Gamini 1929- ... 102
Salgado, Maria Antonia 1933- ... 41-44R
Saliba, John A. 1937- ... CANR-35
Earlier sketch in CA 114
Saliers, Don E(arl) 1937- ... 119
Salih, H(alil) Ibrahim 1939- ... 93-96
Salin, Mary Wolff
See Wolff-Salin, Mary
Salinas, Luis Omar 1937- ... 131
See also DLB 82
See also HW
Salinas (y Serrano), Pedro
1891(?)-1951 Brief entry ... 117
See also TCLC 17
Saline, Carol 1939- ... 128
Salinger, Herman 1905- ... CAP-1
Earlier sketch in CA 13-14
Salinger, J(erome) D(avid) 1919- ... CANR-39
Earlier sketch in CA 5-8R
See also AAYA 2
See also CDALB 1941-1968
See also CLC 1, 3, 8, 12, 55, 56
See also CLR 18
See also DLB 2, 102
See also MAICYA
See also MTCW
See also SATA 67
See also SSC 2
See also WLC
Salinger, Margaretta 1908(?)-1985 Obituary ... 115
Salinger, Pierre (Emil George) 1925- ... CANR-14
Earlier sketch in CA 17-20R
Salisbury, Carola (Isobel Julien) 1943- ... 89-92
Salisbury, Charlotte Y. 1914- ... 129
Salisbury, Dorothy (Kendall Cleveland)
1891(?)-1976 Obituary ... 69-72
Salisbury, Edward J(ames) 1886- ... CAP-1
Earlier sketch in CA 13-14
Salisbury, Frank B(oyer) 1926- ... CANR-8
Earlier sketch in CA 17-20R
Salisbury, Frank 1930- ... 108
Salisbury, Harrison E(vans) 1908- ... CANR-30
Earlier sketches in CA 1-4R, CANR-3
See also CAAS 15
See also MTCW
Salisbury, John
See Caute, David
Salisbury, Joyce E(llen) 1944- ... 135
Salisbury, Mike 1942- ... 136
Salisbury, Ralph 1926- ... CANR-15
Earlier sketch in CA 41-44R
Salisbury, Ray(mond Eric) 1942- ... CANR-31
Earlier sketch in CA 110
Salisbury, Richard Frank 1926- ... CANR-9
Earlier sketch in CA 5-8R
Salisbury, Robert H(olt) 1930- ... 9-12R
Salisbury, Ruth 1921- ... 73-76
Salisbury-Jones, Guy 1896-1985 Obituary ... 115
Salivarova, Zdena
See Skvorecka, Zdena Salivarova
Salk, Erwin Arthur 1918- ... 81-84
Salk, Jonas Edward 1914- ... 49-52
Salk, Lee 1926- ... 104
Obituary ... 137
See also AITN 1
Salkeld, Robert J(ohn) 1932- ... CANR-31
Earlier sketch in CA 29-32R
Salkever, Louis R(omov) 1914- ... 17-20R
Salkey, (Felix) Andrew (Alexander)
1928- ... CANR-27
Earlier sketches in CA 5-8R, CANR-13
See also BW
See also SATA 35
Sallada, Logan Henry 1942-1987 Obituary ... 123
Sallaska, Georgia 1933- ... 25-28R
Sallaway, George H(enry) 1930- ... 21-24R
Sallis, James 1944- ... 33-36R
Sallis, John C(leveland) 1938- ... 41-44R
Sallis, Susan (Diana) 1929- ... SATA 55
Sallnow, Michael (Julian)
1949-1990 Obituary ... 131
Salls, Betty Ruth 1926- ... 49-52
Salm, Peter 1919-1990 ... 41-44R
Obituary ... 132
Salma, Abu
See Karmi, Abdul Karim
Salmen, Walter (Heinrich) 1926- ... 132
Salmon, Annie Elizabeth 1899- ... CANR-12
Earlier sketch in CA 69-72
See also SATA 13
Salmon, Charles Gerald 1930- ... 49-52
Salmon, Edward T(ogo) 1905- ... CANR-2
Earlier sketch in CA 5-8R
Salmon, H. Morrey 1892(?)-1985 Obituary ... 116
Salmon, J(ohn) B(rynmor) 1942- ... 118
Salmon, J(ohn) H(earsey) M(cMillan)
1925- ... 25-28R
Salmon, James F(rancis) 1925- ... 111
Salmon, John Tenison 1910- ... 13-16R
Salmon, Margaret Belais 1921- ... CANR-8
Earlier sketch in CA 17-20R
Salmon, Nathan Ucuzoglu 1951- ... CANR-27
Earlier sketch in CA 109
Salmon, Tim(othy) 1942- ... 128
Salmon, Wesley C(harles) 1925- ... CANR-23
Earlier sketches in CA 17-20R, CANR-8
Salmond, John A(lexander) 1937- ... 114
Salmonson, Jessica Amanda 1950- ... CANR-36
Earlier sketch in CA 114
Salmonson, R(oland) F(rank) 1922- ... CANR-17
Earlier sketch in CA 25-28R
Saloma, John S. III 1935(?)-1983 Obituary ... 110
Salomon, Albert 1891-1966 ... 5-8R
Salomon, Herman Prins 1930- ... 41-44R
Salomon, I(sidore) L(awrence)
1899-1985 ... 73-76
Obituary ... 116
Salomon, Irving 1897-1979 Obituary ... 85-88
Salomon, Janet Lynn (Nowicki) 1953- ... 61-64
Salomon, Julian Harris 1896-1987 Obituary ... 123
Salomon, Roger Blaine 1928- ... 1-4R
Salomon, Sir Walter
See Salomon, Walter (Hans)
Salomon, Walter (Hans)
1906-1987 Obituary ... 123
Salomone, A(rcangelo) William
1915-1989 ... 13-16R
Obituary ... 127
Salop, Lynne
See Hawes, Lynne Gusikoff Salop
Salot, Lorraine 1914- ... 17-20R
Saloutos, Theodore 1910- ... 9-12R
Salper, Roberta Linda 1940- ... 115
Salpeter, Eliahu (Arnost) 1927- ... 93-96
Salpukas, Agis 1939- ... 128
Salsbury, Barbara G(race) 1937- ... 121
Brief entry ... 118
Salsbury, Edith Colgate 1907-1971 ... CAP-2
Earlier sketch in CA 17-18
Salsbury, Kathryn H(errick) 1924- ... 107
Salsbury, Stephen 1931- ... CANR-11
Earlier sketch in CA 21-24R
Salsini, Paul E(dward) 1935- ... 77-80
Salt, Beryl (Winifred) 1931- ... 110
Salt, Waldo 1914-1987 ... 111
Obituary ... 121
See also DLB 44
Salten, Felix
See Salzmann, Siegmund
Salter, Cedric
See Knight, Francis Edgar
Salter, Charles A. 1947- ... 127
Salter, Donald P. M. 1942- ... 93-96
Salter, Elizabeth 1918-1981 ... CANR-9
Obituary ... 103
Earlier sketch in CA 53-56
Salter, Elizabeth 1925-1980 ... 105
Obituary ... 97-100
Salter, James 1925- ... 73-76
See also CLC 7, 52, 59
Salter, Lionel (Paul) 1914- ... CANR-3
Earlier sketch in CA 5-8R
Salter, Margaret Lennox
See Donaldson, Margaret
Salter, Mary D.
See Ainsworth, Mary D(insmore) Salter
Salter, Mary Jo 1954- ... 119
See also DLB 120
Salter, Paul Sanford 1926- ... 61-64
Salter, Robbie
See Salter, Robina
Salter, Robina ... 123
Salter, Stefan 1908(?)-1985 Obituary ... 115
Salter, W(illiam) H(enry)
1880-1970 Obituary ... 112
Salter-Mathieson, Nigel Cedric Stephen
1932- ... 1-4R
Salthe, Stanley N(orman) 1930- ... 53-56
Saltman, Jack 1936- ... 129
Saltman, Judith 1947- ... 126
See also SATA 64
Saltman, Juliet 1923- ... 101
Saltonstall, Richard Jr. 1937-1981 ... 33-36R
Obituary ... 103
Saltonstall, William G(urdon)
1905(?)-1989 Obituary ... 130
Saltus, Edgar (Everton)
1855-1921 Brief entry ... 105
See also TCLC 8
Saltz, Donald 1933- ... 102
Saltz, Eli 1926- Brief entry ... 108
Saltzgaber, Jan M. 1933- ... 115
Saltzman, Arthur M(ichael) 1953- ... 136
Saltzman, Joe
See Saltzman, Joseph
Saltzman, Joseph 1939- ... 81-84
Saltzman, Marvin L(ouis) 1922- ... 85-88
Salu, Mary 1919- ... 93-96
Salusinszky, Imre 1955- ... 126
Salutin, Rick 1942- ... 131
Salvadori, Joyce
See Lussu, Joyce (Salvadori)
Salvadori, Mario (George) 1907- ... 108
See also SATA 40
Salvadori, Massimo
See Salvadori-Paleotti, Massimo
Salvadori, Max (William)
See Salvadori-Paleotti, Massimo
Salvadori-Paleotti, Massimo 1908- ... CANR-7
Obituary ... 138
Earlier sketch in CA 9-12R
Salvan, Jacques-Leon 1898- ... 1-4R
Salvato, Larry 1948- ... 118
Salvato, Sharon 1938- ... CANR-15
Earlier sketch in CA 65-68
Salvatore, Nicholas 1943- ... CANR-32
Earlier sketch in CA 109
Salvatore, Nick
See Salvatore, Nicholas
Salvendy, Gavriel 1938- ... 49-52
Salverson, Laura Goodman 1890-1970 ... DLB 92
Salwak, Dale (Francis) 1947- ... 137
Salzano, F(rancisco) M(auro) 1928- ... CANR-12
Earlier sketch in CA 29-32R
Salzberg, Allen 1953- ... 137
Salzer, Felix 1904-1986 ... 109
Obituary ... 120
Salzer, L. E.
See Wilson, Lionel
Salzer, Linda P(arsons) 1951- ... 122
Salzinger, Kurt 1929- ... 136
Brief entry ... 107
Salzman, Eric 1933- ... CANR-13
Earlier sketch in CA 25-28R
Salzman, Jack 1937- ... CANR-11
Earlier sketch in CA 25-28R
Salzman, Mark (Joseph) 1959- ... 136
Salzman, Paul 1953- ... 125
Salzman, Yuri ... SATA 42
Salzmann, Siegmund 1869-1945 ... 137
Brief entry ... 108
See also MAICYA
See also SATA 25
Salzmann, Zdenek 1925- ... CANR-36
Earlier sketches in CA 97-100, CANR-16
Samachson, Dorothy (Mirkin) 1914- ... 9-12R
See also SATA 3
Samachson, Joseph 1906-1980 ... 17-20R
Obituary ... 122
See also SATA 3, 52
Samarakis, Antonis 1919- ... CANR-36
Earlier sketch in CA 25-28R
See also CAAS 16
See also CLC 5
Samarin, William J. 1926- ... 93-96
Samartha, S(tanley) J(edidiah) 1920- ... CAP-1
Earlier sketch in CA 11-12
Samay, Sebastian 1926- ... 37-40R
Sambrook, Arthur James 1931- ... 13-16R
Sambrot, William 1920- ... 25-28R
Samek, Hana 1953- ... 126
Samelson, William 1928- ... CANR-37
Earlier sketches in CA 25-28R, CANR-17
Samenow, Stanton E(than) 1941- ... 129
Sametz, Arnold W(illiam) 1919- ... CANR-1
Earlier sketch in CA 1-4R
Samford, Clarence D(ouglas) 1905- ... CAP-2
Earlier sketch in CA 19-20
Samford, Doris E. 1923- ... 21-24R
Samhaber, Ernst Marzell 1901-1974 ... 9-12R
Obituary ... 122
Samigli, E.
See Schmitz, Aron Hector
Samkange, S. J. T.
See Samkange, Stanlake (John Thompson)
Samkange, Stanlake (John Thompson)
1922-1988 ... CANR-28
Obituary ... 125
Earlier sketch in CA 29-32R
Samli, A. Coskun 1931- ... CANR-22
Earlier sketch in CA 105
Sammartino, Peter 1904- ... CANR-7
Obituary ... 137
Earlier sketch in CA 57-60
Sammis, John 1942- ... 29-32R
See also SATA 4
Sammons, David 1938- ... 73-76
Sammons, Jeffrey L(eonard) 1936- ... CANR-19
Earlier sketch in CA 21-24R
Samoiloff, Louise Cripps
See Cripps, L(ouise) L(ilian)
Samolin, William 1911- ... 61-64
Samora, Julian 1920- ... 37-40R
See also HW
Samore, Theodore 1924- Brief entry ... 108
Sampedro, Jose Luis 1917- ... CANR-11
Earlier sketch in CA 21-24R
Sampford, Michael 1924(?)-1983 Obituary ... 109
Sampley, Arthur M(cCullough)
1903-1975 ... 41-44R
Sampley, J(ohn) Paul 1935- ... 105
Sampson, A(lwin) A(rthur) 1926- ... 117
Sampson, Anthony 1926- ... CANR-3
Earlier sketch in CA 1-4R
Sampson, Edward C(oolidge) 1920- ... 57-60
Sampson, Edward E. 1934- ... CANR-14
Earlier sketch in CA 37-40R
Sampson, Emma (Keats) Speed
1868-1947 ... 135
See also SATA 68
Sampson, Fay (Elizabeth) 1935- ... CANR-18
Earlier sketch in CA 101
See also SATA 40, 42
Sampson, Geoffrey 1944- ... 97-100
Sampson, H(erbert) Grant 1932- ... 45-48
Sampson, Henry T(homas) 1934- ... 117
Sampson, R(obert) Neil 1938- ... CANR-31
Earlier sketch in CA 106
Sampson, R(onald) V(ictor) 1918- ... CANR-5
Earlier sketch in CA 9-12R
Sampson, Richard Henry
See Hull, Richard
Sampson, Robert C. 1909- ... 21-24R
Sampson, Roy J(ohnson) 1919- ... CANR-1
Earlier sketch in CA 1-4R
Samra, Cal 1931- ... 37-40R
Sams, David R. 1958- ... 138
Sams, Eric 1926- ... 123
Sams, Jonathan Carter 1942- Brief entry ... 110
Samsell, R(ay) L(ane) 1925- ... 69-72
Samson, Anne S(tringer) 1933- ... 25-28R
See also SATA 2
Samson, Jack
See Samson, John G(adsden)
Samson, (Thomas) Jim 1946- ... 129
Samson, Joan 1937-1976 ... 73-76
See also SATA 13
Samson, John G(adsden) 1922- ... 134
Brief entry ... 109
Samsonov, Leon
See Maximov, Vladimir (Yemelyanovich)
Samstag, Nicholas 1903-1968 ... 5-8R
Obituary ... 25-28R
Samter, Linda Bantel
See Bantel, Linda
Samtur, Susan J(oy) 1944- ... 97-100
Samuel, Alan E(douard) 1932- ... CANR-37
Earlier sketches in CA 73-76, CANR-17
Samuel, Athanasius Y.
See Samuel, Yeshue
Samuel, Dorothy T(ucker) 1918- ... 45-48
Samuel, Edwin Herbert 1898-1978 ... CANR-2
Earlier sketch in CA 1-4R
Samuel, Irene 1915-1991 ... 17-20R
Obituary ... 134
Samuel, Maurice 1895-1972 ... 102
Obituary ... 33-36R
Samuel, Yeshue 1907- ... CAP-2
Earlier sketch in CA 21-22
Samuels, Charles Thomas 1936-1974 ... 41-44R
Obituary ... 49-52
Samuels, Charles 1902-1982 ... CANR-5
Obituary ... 106
Earlier sketch in CA 1-4R
See also SATA 12
Samuels, Cynthia K(alish) 1946- ... 135
Samuels, E. A.
See Tiffany, E. A.
Samuels, Ernest 1903- ... CAP-1
Earlier sketch in CA 11-12
See also DLB 111
Samuels, Gertrude ... CANR-6
Earlier sketch in CA 9-12R
See also SATA 17
Samuels, Harold 1917- ... 93-96
Samuels, Harry 1893- ... 13-16R
Samuels, Lesser 1894(?)-1980 Obituary ... 102
Samuels, M(ichael) L(ouis) 1920- ... 41-44R
Samuels, Peggy 1922- ... 97-100
Samuels, Warren J. 1933- ... CANR-14
Earlier sketch in CA 21-24R
Samuelson, Arnold 1912(?)-1981 Obituary ... 116
Samuelson, Paul A(nthony) 1915- ... 5-8R
Samway, Patrick H(enry) 1939- ... CANR-21
Earlier sketch in CA 105
Sanborn, B. X.
See Ballinger, William Sanborn
Sanborn, Duane 1914- ... CANR-1
Earlier sketch in CA 1-4R
See also SATA 38
Sanborn, Franklin Benjamin 1831-1917 ... DLB 1
Sanborn, Margaret 1915- ... CANR-4
Earlier sketch in CA 53-56
Sanborn, Patricia F. 1937- ... 25-28R
Sanborn, Ruth Cummings 1917- ... 29-32R
Sancha, Sheila 1924- ... CANR-11
Earlier sketch in CA 69-72
See also SATA 38

Sanchez, Federico
See Semprun, Jorge
Sanchez, Florencio 1875-1910 ....HW
See also TCLC 37
Sanchez, Jose M(ariano) 1932- 9-12R
Sanchez, Luis Rafael 1936- 128
See also CLC 23
See also HW
Sanchez, Oscar Arias
See Arias Sanchez, Oscar
Sanchez, Ramiro Guerra y
See Guerra y Sanchez, Ramiro
Sanchez, Ricardo 1941- CANR-32
Earlier sketch in CA 73-76
See also DLB 82
See also HW
Sanchez, Sonia 1934- CANR-24
Earlier sketch in CA 33-36R
See also BLC 3
See also BW
See also CLC 5
See also CLR 18
See also DLB 41
See also DLBD 8
See also MAICYA
See also MTCW
See also SATA 22
Sanchez, Thomas 1944- CANR-32
Earlier sketches in CA 45-48, CANR-2
See also BEST 90:1
See also HW
Sanchez (y Sanchez), George I(sidore)
1906-1972 ....HW
Sanchez Albornoz (y Mediuna), Claudio
1893-1984 127
Obituary 113
Sanchez Flores, Daniel
1960(?)-1990 Obituary 132
Sanchez-Hidalgo, Efrain Sigisfredo
1918-1974 57-60
Sanchez-Korrol, Virginia 131
See also HW
Sanchez-Scott, Milcha 131
See also HW
Sanchez-Silva, Jose Maria 1911- 73-76
See also CLR 12
See also MAICYA
See also SATA 16
Sanctuary, Gerald 1930- CANR-12
Earlier sketch in CA 29-32R
Sand, George X. 13-16R
See also SATA 45
Sand, George 1804-1876 ....DLB 119
See also WLC
Sand, Margaret 1932- 85-88
Sand, Richard E(ugene) 1924- 33-36R
Sandak, Cass R(obert) 1950- 108
See also SATA 37, 51
Sandars, N(ancy) K(atharine) 1914- 61-64
Sandbach, Francis Henry 1903-1991 93-96
Obituary 135
Sandbach, Mary (Warburton) 1901- 25-28R
Sandberg, (Karin) Inger 1930- CANR-26
Earlier sketches in CA 65-68, CANR-11
See also SATA 15
Sandberg, John H(ilmer) 1930- 49-52
Sandberg, Karl C. 1931- 49-52
See also SATA 35
Sandberg, Larry 1944- 77-80
Sandberg, Lars G(unnarsson) 1939- 53-56
Sandberg, Lasse (E. M.) 1924- ....SATA 15
Sandberg, Margaret M(ay) 1919- 61-64
Sandberg, Peter Lars 1934- CANR-24
Earlier sketches in CA 61-64, CANR-9
Sandbrook, K(eith) R(ichard) J(ames)
1943- CANR-36
Earlier sketches in CA 97-100, CANR-16
Sandburg, Carl (August) 1878-1967 ......CANR-35
Obituary 25-28R
Earlier sketch in CA 5-8R
See also CDALB 1865-1917
See also CLC 1, 4, 10, 15, 35
See also DLB 17, 54
See also MAICYA
See also MTCW
See also PC 2
See also SATA 8
See also WLC
Sandburg, Charles
See Sandburg, Carl (August)
Sandburg, Charles A.
See Sandburg, Carl (August)
Sandburg, Helga 1918- CANR-5
Earlier sketch in CA 1-4R
See also SAAS 10
See also SATA 3
Sande, Theodore Anton 1933- CANR-12
Earlier sketch in CA 65-68
Sandeen, Ernest (Emanuel) 1908- 13-16R
Sandeen, Ernest Robert 1931- CANR-1
Earlier sketch in CA 45-48
Sandelowski, Margarete J. 1946- 116
Sander, (Jane) Ellen 1944- 41-44R
Sander, Joseph Lincoln 1926- Brief entry 108
Sander, Volkmar 1929- 113
Sanderlin, David 1943- 123
Sanderlin, George 1915- 13-16R
See also SATA 4
Sanderlin, Owenita (Harrah) 1916- CANR-7
Earlier sketch in CA 17-20R
See also SATA 11
Sanders, Albert
See Davidson, David
Sanders, Ann(a Pearl Goodman) 1935- 5-8R
Sanders, Bill 1951- 137
Sanders, Buck
See Frentzen, Jeffrey
Sanders, Byrne Hope
See Sperry, Byrne Hope
Sanders, Charles L. 1932(?)-1990 Obituary 132
Sanders, Charles 1935- 25-28R
Sanders, D(onald) G(len) 1899- 85-88
Sanders, Daphne
See Randolph, Georgiana Ann
Sanders, (Franklin) David 1934- 41-44R
Sanders, David (Scott Jr.) 1926- 25-28R
Sanders, Dennis 1949- 108
Sanders, Donald H. 1932- CANR-10
Earlier sketch in CA 25-28R
Sanders, Donald 1915(?)-1979 Obituary 89-92
Sanders, Dorothy Lucie 1917- 33-36R
Sanders, (James) Ed(ward) 1939- CANR-13
Earlier sketch in CA 13-16R
See also CLC 53
See also DLB 16
Sanders, Ed Parish 1937- 105
Sanders, Frederick K(irkland) 1936- 65-68
Sanders, Gerald D(eWitt) 1895- CAP-1
Earlier sketch in CA 13-14
Sanders, Gladys (Shultz)
1919(?)-1988 Obituary 125
Sanders, Harland 1890-1980 114
Obituary 102
Sanders, Herbert H(arvey) 1909- 13-16R
Sanders, Ivan 1944- 119
Sanders, J(ohn) Oswald 1902- CANR-21
Earlier sketches in CA 13-16R, CANR-6
Sanders, Jack T(homas) 1935- 37-40R
Sanders, Jacquin 1922- 1-4R
Sanders, James A(lvin) 1927- CANR-14
Earlier sketch in CA 21-24R
Sanders, James Bernard 1924- 41-44R
Sanders, James Edward 1911- 103
Sanders, Jeanne
See Rundle, Anne
Sanders, Jennings B(ryan) 1901- CAP-2
Earlier sketch in CA 25-28
Sanders, Joan Allred 1924- 9-12R
Sanders, Joseph Lee 1940- 105
Sanders, Kent
See Wilkes-Hunter, R(ichard)
Sanders, Lawrence 1920- CANR-33
Earlier sketch in CA 81-84
See also BEST 89:4
See also CLC 41
See also MTCW
Sanders, Leonard 1929- CANR-3
Earlier sketch in CA 9-12R
Sanders, Leslie Catherine 1944- 129
Sanders, Margaret 5-8R
Sanders, Marion K. 1905-1977 ....33-36R
Obituary 73-76
Sanders, Marlene 1931- 65-68
Sanders, Noah
See Blount, Roy (Alton) Jr.
Sanders, Norman (Joseph) 1929- 9-12R
Sanders, Peter B(asil) 1938- 105
Sanders, Pieter 1912- CANR-12
Earlier sketch in CA 29-32R
Sanders, (Charles) Richard 1904- 53-56
Sanders, Ronald 1932-1991 ....CANR-20
Obituary 133
Earlier sketch in CA 21-24R
Sanders, Scott Russell 1945- CANR-35
Earlier sketches in CA 85-88, CANR-15
See also SATA 56
Sanders, Sol (Witner) 1926- CANR-2
Earlier sketch in CA 49-52
Sanders, Stephen (Jesse Jr.) 1919- 29-32R
Sanders, Thomas E. 1926- 21-24R
Sanders, Thomas Griffin 1932- 9-12R
Sanders, Tobi Gillian
See Hammes, Tobi Gillian Sanders
Sanders, William B(rauns) 1944- CANR-10
Earlier sketch in CA 65-68
Sanders, William T(imothy) 1926- CANR-3
Earlier sketch in CA 45-48
Sanders, Winston P.
See Anderson, Poul (William)
Sanderson, Irma 1912- 135
See also SATA 66
Sanderson, Isabel S(aunders)
1913-1987 Obituary 123
Sanderson, Ivan T(erence) 1911-1973 ......37-40R
Obituary 41-44R
See also SATA 6
Sanderson, James L(ee) 1926- Brief entry 111
Sanderson, Jayne 1943- 21-24R
Sanderson, Margaret Love
See Keats, Emma
and Sampson, Emma (Keats) Speed
Sanderson, (John) Michael 1939- 127
Sanderson, Milton W(illiam) 1910- CANR-9
Earlier sketch in CA 9-12R
Sanderson, Peter (Crawshaw) 1929- 33-36R
Sanderson, Ruth (L) 1951- ....SATA 41
Sanderson, Sabina W(arren) 1931- CANR-3
Earlier sketch in CA 9-12R
Sanderson, Stewart (Forson) 1924- 108
Sanderson, Warren 1931- 105
Sandford, Cedric Thomas 1924- CANR-32
Earlier sketch in CA 113
Sandford, Christopher 1902-1983 Obituary 109
Sandford, John Loren 1929- CANR-36
Earlier sketch in CA 101
Sandford, Nell Mary 1936- 81-84
Sandford, Paula 1931- CANR-36
Earlier sketch in CA 101
Sandford, William P(hillips) 1896-1975 ......CAP-2
Earlier sketch in CA 17-18
Sandhaus, Paul 1923- 25-28R
Sandifer, Durward Valdamir
1900-1981 Obituary 108
Sandifer, Linda P(rophet) 1951- 120
Sandin, Joan 1942- ....SATA 12
Sandin, Robert T(heodore) 1927- 111
Sandison, Alan 1932- 21-24R
Sandison, Janet
See Cameron, Elizabeth Jane
Sandle, Floyd Leslie 1913- Brief entry 106
Sandler, Benjamin P.
1902(?)-1979 Obituary 85-88
Sandler, Irving (Harry) 1925- CANR-31
Earlier sketch in CA 29-32R
Sandler, Lucy Freeman 1930- CANR-31
Brief entry 113
Sandler, Stanley Lawrence 1937- 113
Sandlin, Joann S(chepers) De Lora
1935- CANR-4
Earlier sketch in CA 53-56
Sandlin, John L(ewis) 1908- CANR-4
Earlier sketch in CA 1-4R
Sandlin, Tim 1950- 126
Sandman, Peter M(ark) 1945- 25-28R
Sandmel, Samuel 1911-1979 ....CANR-2
Earlier sketch in CA 1-4R
Sando, Joe S. 1923- 123
Sandom, J. Gregory 1956- 137
Sandon, Henry 1928- 81-84
Sandon, J. D.
See Harvey, John (Barton)
Sandor, Bela I(mre) 1935- 102
Sandor, Gyorgy 108
Sandoz, (George) Ellis (Jr.) 1931- CANR-14
Earlier sketch in CA 37-40R
Sandoz, Mari(e Susette) 1896-1966 ......CANR-17
Obituary 25-28R
Earlier sketch in CA 1-4R
See also CLC 28
See also DLB 9
See also MTCW
See also SATA 5
Sandrof, Ivan 1912(?)-1979 93-96
Obituary 85-88
Sandroff, Ronni 1943- 102
Sandrow, Edward T. 1906-1975 Obituary 61-64
Sands, Donald B. 1920- 13-16R
Sands, Dorothy 1893-1980 Obituary 102
Sands, Edith Sylvia (Abeloff) 1912- 21-24R
Sands, John Edward 1930- 13-16R
Sands, Kathleen M.
See Sands, Kathleen Mullen
Sands, Kathleen Mullen 118
Sands, Leo G(eorge) 1912-1984 ....CANR-29
Obituary 114
Earlier sketch in CA 17-20R
Sands, Martin
See Burke, John (Frederick)
Sands, Melissa 1949- 109
Sandusky, Annie Lee
1900(?)-1976 Obituary 69-72
Sandved, Arthur O. 1931- 33-36R
Sandweiss, Martha A(nn) 1954- 136
Sandwell, B. K. 1876-1954 ....DLB 92
Sandy, Max
See Saunders, Carl Maxon
Sandy, Stephen 1934- CANR-22
Earlier sketches in CA 49-52, CANR-5
Sandys, Elspeth (Somerville) 1940- CANR-26
Earlier sketch in CA 108
Sandys, George 1578-1644 ....DLB 24, 121
Saner, Reg(inald Anthony) 1931- 65-68
See also CLC 9
Sanfield, Steve 1937- 124
Sanfilip, Thomas 1952- 57-60
Sanford, Agnes (White) 1897-1976 ....17-20R
See also SATA 61
Sanford, Annette 1929- 130
Sanford, Charles B(elding) 1920- 113
Sanford, Charles Le Roy 1920- 5-8R
Sanford, David (Boyer) 1943- Brief entry 114
Sanford, Doris 1937- 138
See also SATA 69
Sanford, Fillmore H(argrave) 1914-1967 ......1-4R
Obituary 103
Sanford, George 1943- 118
Sanford, Harry Allen 1929- 1-4R
Sanford, Jack D(onald) 1925- 5-8R
Sanford, John A. 1929- CANR-10
Earlier sketch in CA 25-28R
Sanford, John B.
See Sanford, John
Sanford, John 1904- 123
Brief entry 117
Sanford, Leda 1933- CANR-12
Earlier sketch in CA 65-68
Sanford, Terry 1917- 17-20R
Sanford, Thomas K(yle) Jr. 1921-1977 73-76
Sanger, Andrew 1948- 123
Sanger, Clyde 1928- CANR-36
Earlier sketch in CA 114
Sanger, David E. 1960- 136
Sanger, Elliott M(axwell)
1897-1989 Obituary 129
Sanger, Margaret (Higgins)
1883-1966 Obituary 89-92
Sanger, Marjory Bartlett 1920- 37-40R
See also SATA 8
Sanger, Richard H.
1905(?)-1979 Obituary 85-88
Sangiuliano, Iris (Agatha) 1923- Brief entry 114
Sangrey, Dawn 1942- CANR-15
Earlier sketch in CA 85-88
Sangster, Charles 1822-1893 ....DLB 99
Sangster, Ian 1934- 61-64
Sangster, Jimmy 1927- CANR-14
Earlier sketch in CA 21-24R
Sangster, Margaret E(lizabeth)
1894-1981 Obituary 105
Sanguinetti, Elise Ayers 1926- CANR-1
Earlier sketch in CA 1-4R
Saniel, Josefa M. 1925- 13-16R
Sanjian, Avedis K(rikor) 1921- 33-36R
San Juan, Epifanio Jr. 1938- CANR-10
Earlier sketch in CA 25-28R
Sankar, D(evarakonda) V(enkata) Siva
1927- 53-56
Sankey, Alice (Ann-Susan) 1910- 61-64
See also SATA 27
Sankhala, Kailash S. 1925- 101
San Martin, Marta 1942- 102
Sann, Paul 1914-1986 ....CANR-5
Obituary 120
Earlier sketch in CA 13-16R
Sannebeck, Norvelle 1909- 97-100
Sanoff, Alvin P. 1941- 136
Sansom, Arthur B(aldwin) 1920-1991 112
Obituary 134
Sansom, Clive 1910- 104
Sansom, Peter 1958- 133
Sansom, William 1912-1976 ....5-8R
Obituary 65-68
See also CLC 2, 6
See also MTCW
Sansone, Sam J(ohn) 1915- 115
San Souci, Robert D. 1946- 108
See also SATA 40
Sansweet, Stephen Jay 1945- 61-64
Sant, Thomas 1948- 136
Santa Cruz (Gamarra), Nicomedes 1925- ....HW
Santa Maria
See Powell-Smith, Vincent (Walter Francis)
Santas, Joan Foster 1930- 17-20R
Santayana, George 1863-1952 Brief entry 115
See also DLB 54, 71
See also TCLC 40
Santee, Ross 1889(?)-1965 108
Santesson, Hans Stefan 1914(?)-1975 93-96
Obituary 57-60
See also SATA 30
Santi, Enrico Mario 1950- 116
Santiago, Danny
See James, Daniel (Lewis)
See also CLC 33
Santini, Rosemarie 81-84
Santmire, H(arold) Paul 1935- 53-56
Santmyer, Helen Hooven 1895-1986 .....CANR-33
Obituary 118
Earlier sketches in CA 1-4R, CANR-15
See also CLC 33
See also DLBY 84
See also MTCW
Santoli, Al 1949- 105
Santoni, Georges V. 1938- 103
Santoni, Ronald E(rnest) 1931- 5-8R
Santos, Bienvenido N(uqui) 1911- CANR-19
Earlier sketch in CA 101
See also CLC 22
Santos, Eduardo 1888-1974 Obituary 89-92
Santos, Sherod (A.) 1948- 132
Santostefano, Sebastiano 1929- 41-44R
Santrey, Louis
See Sabin, Louis
Sanville, Jean 1918- 89-92
Sanwal, B(hairava) D(at) 1917- 17-20R
Saperstein, Alan 103
Saperstein, David 1937- 130
Saphier, Michael 1911- 25-28R
Saphire, Saul 1896(?)-1974 Obituary 53-56
Sapia, Yvonne (V.) 1946- 126
Sapiets, Janis 1921-1983(?) Obituary 109
Sapieyevski, Anne Lindbergh 1940- 115
Brief entry 113
See also Feydy, Anne Lindbergh
See also SATA 35
Sapinsley, Alvin 1921- CANR-21
Earlier sketch in CA 104
Sapinsley, Barbara 137
Sapir, Edward 1884-1939 ....DLB 92
Sapir, Richard (Ben) 1936-1987 ....CANR-13
Obituary 121
Earlier sketch in CA 69-72
Sapiro, Virginia 1951- 126
Sapori, Armando 1892- 33-36R
Saporta, Marc(el) 1923- 21-24R
Saporta, Sol 1925- 17-20R
Saposnik, Irving Seymour 1936- 97-100
Saposs, David Joseph 1886-1968 ....CANR-15
Obituary 103
Earlier sketch in CA 1-4R
Sapp, Phyllis Woodruff 1908- CANR-1
Earlier sketch in CA 1-4R
Sappell, Joel 1953- 133
Sapper
See McNeile, Herman Cyril
See also TCLC 44
Sapper, Laurence Joseph
1922-1989 Obituary 129
Sappho ....PC 5
Sappington, Roger E(dwin) 1929- 13-16R
Sara
See Blake, Sally Mirliss
Sara, Dorothy 1897(?)-1976 Obituary 69-72
Sarac, Roger
See Caras, Roger A(ndrew)
Saracevic, Tefko 1930- 37-40R
Sarah, Duchess of York
See Ferguson, Sarah (Margaret)
Sarah, Robyn 1949- CANR-31
Earlier sketch in CA 112
Saran, Parmatma 1943- 129
Sarano, Jacques 1920- 29-32R
Sarant, P(eter) C. 1933(?)-1979 Obituary 89-92
Sarasin, Jennifer
See Sachs, Judith
Sarason, Seymour Bernard 1919- 120
Sarasy, Phyllis Powell 1930- 13-16R
Sarat, Austin Dean 1947- 106

SarDesai, D(amodar) R. 1931- CANR-11
Earlier sketch in CA 25-28R
Sardeson, Charles T. 1921- 5-8R
Sarducci, Father Guido
See Novello, Don
Sarduy, Severo 1937- 89-92
See also CLC 6
See also DLB 113
See also HW
Sarett, Alma (Johnson) 1908- CAP-2
Earlier sketch in CA 17-18
Sarett, Morton R(euben) 1916- 93-96
Sarf, Wayne M(ichael) 1957- 114
Sarg, Anthony Frederick
See Sarg, Tony
Sarg, Tony 1880-1942 ....YABC 1
Sargant, Norman 1909-1982 Obituary 107
Sargant, William (Walters) 1907- 65-68
Sargeant, Howland H(ill)
1911-1984 Obituary 112
Sargeant, Winthrop 1903-1986 ....29-32R
Obituary 120
Sargent, Alice G(oldstein) 1939-1988 110
Obituary 125
Sargent, Alvin 121
Brief entry 111
Sargent, Ben 1948- 118
Brief entry 113
Sargent, Brian (Lawrence) 1927- 97-100
Sargent, Daniel 1890-1987 Obituary 121
Sargent, David R(utledge) 1920- 93-96
Sargent, Frederic O(berlin) 1919- 41-44R
Sargent, Jean Vieth 1918- 106
Sargent, John Richard 1925- 13-16R
Sargent, Lyman Tower 1940- CANR-15
Earlier sketch in CA 29-32R
Sargent, Pamela CANR-8
Earlier sketch in CA 61-64
See also DLB 8
See also SATA 29
Sargent, Ralph M(illard) 1904-1985 ....37-40R
Obituary 116
Sargent, Robert 1933- 21-24R
See also SATA 2
Sargent, Ruth (Sexton) 1920- 112
Sargent, Sarah 1937- 106
See also SATA 41, 44
Sargent, Shirley 1927- CANR-2
Earlier sketch in CA 1-4R
See also SATA 11
Sargent, (Francis) William (Jr.) 1946- 106
Sargent, Wyn 49-52
Sargeson, Frank 1903-1982 ....CANR-38
Obituary 106
Earlier sketch in CA 25-28R
See also CLC 31
Sarhan, Samir 1941- 103
Sari
See Fleur, Anne
Saricks, Ambrose 1915- 17-20R
Sariego, Patricia Treece
See Treece, Patricia
Sariola, Sakari 1919- 41-44R
Sarjeant, William A(ntony) S(within) 1935- 105
Sarkar, Asoke 1911(?)-1983 Obituary 109
Sarkar, (Anvil) Kumar 1912- 37-40R
Sarkesian, Sam C(harles) 1927- 57-60
Sarlos, Robert Karoly 1931- 109
Sarma, G. V. L. N. 1925- 17-20R
Sarmiento, Felix Ruben Garcia
1867-1916 Brief entry 104
See also Dario, Ruben
Sarna, Jonathan D(aniel) 1955- CANR-27
Earlier sketch in CA 109
Sarna, Nahum M(attathias) 1923- 17-20R
Sarnat, Marshall 1929- CANR-26
Earlier sketches in CA 21-24R, CANR-10
Sarndal, Carl Erik 1937- 105
Sarner, Harvey 1934- 17-20R
Sarno, Arthur D. 1921(?)-1982 Obituary 106
Sarno, Ronald A(nthony) 1941- CANR-27
Earlier sketches in CA 29-32R, CANR-12
Sarnoff, David 1891-1971 Obituary 113
Sarnoff, Dorothy 1917- 33-36R
Sarnoff, Irving 1922- CANR-8
Earlier sketch in CA 17-20R
Sarnoff, Jane 1937- CANR-9
Earlier sketch in CA 53-56
See also SATA 10
Sarnoff, Paul 1918- CANR-18
Earlier sketches in CA 5-8R, CANR-2
Sarnoff, Stanley Jay 1917-1990 Obituary 131
Sarnoff, Suzanne 1928- 97-100
Saroyan, Aram 1943- CANR-30
Earlier sketch in CA 21-24R
See also CAAS 5
Saroyan, Arshalyus 1923-1974 Obituary 53-56
Saroyan, William 1908-1981 ....CANR-30
Obituary 103
Earlier sketch in CA 5-8R
See also CLC 1, 8, 10, 29, 34, 56
See also DLB 7, 9, 86
See also DLBY 81
See also MTCW
See also SATA 23, 24
See also WLC
Sarrantonio, Al 1952- 120
Sarratt, Reed 1918(?)-1986 Obituary 118
Sarraute, Nathalie 1900- CANR-23
Earlier sketch in CA 9-12R
See also CLC 1, 2, 4, 8, 10, 31
See also DLB 83
See also MTCW
Sarrazin, Albertine 1937-1967 ....DLB 83
Sarre, Winifred Turner 1931- 29-32R
Sarri, Rosemary C(onzemius) 1926- 111
Sarris, Andrew 1928- 21-24R
Sarsfield, C. P.
See Marshner, Connaught Coyne
Sartain, Aaron Quinn 1905- 1-4R
Sarti, Roland 1937- 37-40R
Sarto, Ben
See Fawcett, F(rank) Dubrez
Sarton, (Eleanor) May 1912- CANR-34
Earlier sketches in CA 1-4R, CANR-1
See also CLC 4, 14, 49
See also DLB 48
See also DLBY 81
See also MTCW
See also SATA 36
Sartor, Margaret 1959- 125
Sartori, Giovanni 1924- CANR-38
Earlier sketches in CA 5-8R, CANR-2, 17
Sartre, Jean-Paul 1905-1980 ....CANR-21
Obituary 97-100
Earlier sketch in CA 9-12R
See also CLC 1, 4, 7, 9, 13, 18, 24, 44, 50, 52
See also DLB 72
See also MTCW
See also WLC
Sarvepalli, Gopal 1923- 81-84
Sarver, Hannah
See Nielsen, Jean Sarver
Sasaki, R. A. 1952- 136
Sasaki, Tazu 1932- CANR-10
Earlier sketch in CA 25-28R
Saseen, Sharon (Dillon) 1949- ....SATA 59
Sasek, Lawrence A(nton) 1923- CANR-1
Earlier sketch in CA 1-4R
Sasek, Miroslav 1916-1980 73-76
Obituary 101
See also CLR 4
See also SATA 16, 23
Saslow, Helen 1926- 105
Sasnett, Martena T(enney) 1908- 53-56
Saso, Michael R. 1930- 112
Sass, Lorna Janet 1945- 102
Sass, Steven A(rthur) 1949- 116
Sasser, Charles W(ayne) 1942- 122
Sasson, Sarah Diane Hyde 1946- 125
Sassoon, Beverly Adams 65-68
Sassoon, Rosemary 1931- 118
Sassoon, Siegfried (Lorraine)
1886-1967 ....CANR-36
Obituary 25-28R
Earlier sketch in CA 104
See also CLC 36
See also DLB 20
See also MTCW
Sassoon, Vidal 1928- CANR-15
Earlier sketch in CA 65-68
Sasuly, Richard 1913- 109
Satchidananda, Swami
See Dharmi, Santana
Satchwell, John ....SATA 49
Sater, William F(rederick) 1937- 118
Sather, Julia Coley Duncan 1940- 106
Satin, Joseph 1922- 9-12R
Satin, Mark 1946- 41-44R
Satir, Virginia (Mildred) 1916-1988 Obituary 126
Satiricus
See Roetter, Charles Frederick
Sato, Esther Masako Tateishi 1915- 108
Satprem 1923- CANR-35
Earlier sketches in CA 85-88, CANR-15
Satran, Pamela Redmond 1953- 110
Sattelmeyer, Robert 1946- 125
Satterfield, Archie 1933- CANR-14
Earlier sketch in CA 57-60
Satterfield, Charles
See del Rey, Lester
and Pohl, Frederik
Satterlund, Donald R(obert) 1928- 53-56
Satterly, Weston
See Sunners, William
Satterthwait, Walter 1946- 127
Sattin, Anthony (Neil) 1956- 126
Sattler, Helen Roney 1921- CANR-31
Earlier sketches in CA 33-36R, CANR-14
See also CLR 24
See also SATA 4
Sattler, Henry V(ernon) 1917- CANR-7
Earlier sketch in CA 5-8R
Sattler, Jerome M(urray) 1931- 49-52
Sattler, Warren 1934- 65-68
Sattley, Helen R(owland) 1-4R
Satyamurti, Carole 1939- 127
Satz, Paul 1932- 61-64
Satz, Ronald Norman 1944- CANR-8
Earlier sketch in CA 61-64
Saucy, Robert L(loyd) 1930- 123
Brief entry 118
Sauer, Carl Ortwin 1889-1975 ....CANR-9
Earlier sketch in CA 61-64
Sauer, Julia Lina 1891-1983 81-84
See also SATA 32, 36
Sauer, Muriel Stafford 13-16R
Sauer, Val John Jr. 1938- 107
Sauerhaft, Stan 1926- 85-88
Sauerlaender, Willibald 1924- 118
Sauerlander, Willibald
See Sauerlaender, Willibald
Sauers, Richard James 1930- 53-56
Sauers, Wendy 1958- 116
Saul, George Brandon 1901-1986 ....CANR-6
Obituary 120
Earlier sketch in CA 13-16R
Saul, John Ralston 1947- 133
Saul, John (W. III) 1942- CANR-16
Earlier sketch in CA 81-84
See also BEST 90:4
See also CLC 46
Saul, Leon J(oseph) 1901- CANR-10
Earlier sketch in CA 21-24R
Saul, Mary 105
Saul, Nigel Edward 1952- 117
Saul, Norman E(ugene) 1932- 53-56
Saul, Oscar
See Halpern, Oscar Saul
Saul, (Ellen) Wendy 1946- 114
See also SATA 42
Saulnier, Raymond Joseph 1908- 5-8R
Sauls, Roger 1944- 33-36R
Saum, Karen 1935- 137
Saunders, Allen 1899-1986 69-72
Obituary 118
Saunders, Ann Loreille 1930- 103
Saunders, Aretas (Andrews) 1884- CAP-1
Earlier sketch in CA 11-12
Saunders, B(ernard) C(harles)
1903-1983 Obituary 115
Saunders, Beatrice 49-52
Saunders, Blanche 1906- CAP-1
Earlier sketch in CA 13-14
Saunders, Caleb
See Heinlein, Robert A(nson)
Saunders, Carl Maxon
1890-1974 Obituary 89-92
Saunders, Charles B(askerville) Jr. 1928- 61-64
Saunders, Christopher T(homas) 1907- 119
Saunders, David
See Sontup, Dan(iel)
Saunders, Doris E(vans) 1921- 77-80
Saunders, E. Dale 1919- 5-8R
Saunders, Ernest 1901(?)-1983 Obituary 109
Saunders, Francis J. 1927- 131
Saunders, Frank
See Saunders, Francis J.
Saunders, Helen E(lizabeth) 1912- 25-28R
Saunders, Hilary Aidan St. George
1898-1951 Brief entry 121
Saunders, Ione
See Cole, Margaret Alice
Saunders, J(ohn) W(hiteside) 1920- CANR-39
Earlier sketch in CA 116
Saunders, James (Arthur) 1925- Brief entry 124
See also DLB 13
Saunders, Jason Lewis 1922- Brief entry 106
Saunders, Jean 1932- CANR-19
Earlier sketch in CA 102
Saunders, John Monk 1897-1940 ....DLB 26
Saunders, John Turk 1929-1974 ....CAP-2
Earlier sketch in CA 21-22
Saunders, Keith 1910- 57-60
See also SATA 12
Saunders, Margaret Marshall
1861-1947 ....DLB 92
Saunders, Peter 1950- CANR-36
Earlier sketch in CA 114
Saunders, Richard 1947- CANR-21
Earlier sketch in CA 105
Saunders, Roy 1911- CAP-1
Earlier sketch in CA 11-12
Saunders, Rubie (Agnes) 1929- 49-52
See also SATA 21
Saunders, Sally Love 1940- 125
Saunders, Susan 1945- 106
See also SATA 41, 46
Saunders, Thomas 1909- CANR-12
Earlier sketch in CA 73-76
Saura (Atares), Carlos 1932- 131
Brief entry 114
See also CLC 20
See also HW
Sauro, Regina Calderone 1924- 9-12R
Sause, George G(abriel) 1919- 41-44R
Sauser-Hall, Frederic 1887-1961 ....CANR-36
Obituary 93-96
Earlier sketch in CA 102
See also CLC 18
See also MTCW
Saussure, Eric de
See de Saussure, Eric
Sautel, Maureen Ann 1951- 61-64
Sauter, Edwin Charles Scott Jr. 1930- 13-16R
Sauter, Eric 1948- 117
Sauter, Van Gordon 1935- 73-76
Sauvage, Franck
See Horn, Maurice
Sauvage, Leo 1913(?)-1988 Obituary 127
Sauvage, Roger 1917-1977 Obituary 73-76
Sauvageau, Juan 1917- CANR-11
Earlier sketch in CA 65-68
Sauvain, Philip Arthur 1933- CANR-21
Earlier sketch in CA 104
Sauvant, Karl P(eter) 1944- 77-80
Sauvy, Jean (Maurice Paul) 1916- 65-68
Sauvy, Simonne 1922- 65-68
Sava, George
See Milkomane, George Alexis Milkomanovich
Savacool, John K(enneth) 1917- 45-48
Savage, Blake
See Goodwin, Harold L(eland)
Savage, Brian 1933- 41-44R
Savage, Candace (M.) 1949- 123
Savage, Carlton Raymond
1897-1990 Obituary 131
Savage, Catharine
See Brosman, Catharine Savage
Savage, Charles 1918- 53-56
Savage, Christina
See Newcomb, Kerry
and Schaefer, Frank
Savage, Christopher I(vor) 1924-1969 ....CANR-6
Earlier sketch in CA 5-8R
Savage, D(ouglas) J(oseph) 1950- 118
Savage, D(erek) S(tanley) 1917- 104
Savage, Elizabeth Fitzgerald 1918- CANR-1
Earlier sketch in CA 1-4R
Savage, Ernest 1918- 112
Savage, Frances Higginson (Fuller)
1898- CAP-1
Earlier sketch in CA 19-20
Savage, (Leonard) George (Gimson)
1909- CANR-5
Earlier sketch in CA 9-12R
Savage, Georgia 138
Savage, Helen 1915- 97-100
Savage, Henry Jr. 1903- CAP-2
Earlier sketch in CA 25-28
Savage, James F(rancis) 1939- 73-76
Savage, James 1784-1873 ....DLB 30
Savage, Jon
See Sage, Jonathan
Savage, Joseph P.
1895(?)-1977 Obituary 69-72
Savage, Katharine James 1905-1989 ....13-16R
Obituary 128
See also SATA 61
Savage, Lee 1928- 101
Savage, Leonard J(immie) 1917-1971 ....CAP-2
Obituary 33-36R
Earlier sketch in CA 17-18
Savage, Marc 1945- 65-68
Savage, Marmion 1803(?)-1872 ....DLB 21
Savage, Michael D(onald) 1946- 101
Savage, Mildred (Spitz) 1919- 9-12R
Savage, Minot Judson
1841-1918 Brief entry 115
Savage, Richard 1697(?)-1743 ....DLB 95
Savage, Robert L(ynn) 1939- 109
Savage, Roth
See Kehrer, Daniel M(ark)
Savage, Teresa 1950- 113
Savage, Thomas Gerard 1926- 49-52
Savage, Thomas 1915- 132
Brief entry 126
See also CAAS 15
See also CLC 40
Savage, W(illiam) Sherman 1890- 69-72
Savage, William W(oodrow) Jr. 1943- 57-60
Savage, William W(oodrow) 1914- 37-40R
Savain, Petion Obituary 41-44R
Savan, Bruce (Sheldon) 1927-1987 ....5-8R
Obituary 122
Savan, Glenn ....CLC 50
Savard, Felix-Antoine 1896-1982 ....DLB 68
Savarese, Julia 37-40R
Savarin
See Courtine, Robert
Savary, Louis M(ichael) 1936- CANR-24
Earlier sketches in CA 21-24R, CANR-9
Savas, E(manuel) S(tephen) 1931- 17-20R
Saveland, Robert N(elson) 1921- 41-44R
Savell, Don P(atrick) 1939- 119
Savelle, Max(well) 1896- 21-24R
Saven, Glenn ....CLC 50
Savery, Constance (Winifred) 1897- CANR-7
Earlier sketch in CA 9-12R
See also SATA 1
Savery, Ranald 1903(?)-1974 Obituary 104
Saveson, John E(dward) 1923- 41-44R
Saveth, Edward N(orman) 1915- 21-24R
Saville, Eugenia (Curtis) 1913- 41-44R
Saville, Lloyd (Blackstone) 1913- 21-24R
Saville, (Leonard) Malcolm 1901-1982 101
Obituary 107
See also SATA 23, 31
Savin, Marc 1948- 106
Saviozzi, Adriana
See Mazza, Adriana
Savitch, Jessica 1948-1983 108
Obituary 110
Savitt, Ronald 1939- 33-36R
Savitt, Sam CANR-17
Earlier sketches in CA 1-4R, CANR-1
See also SATA 8
Savitt, Todd Lee 1943- 102
Savitz, Harriet May 1933- CANR-32
Earlier sketches in CA 41-44R, CANR-14
See also MAICYA
See also SAAS 9
See also SATA 5
Savitz, Leonard D. 1926- CANR-8
Earlier sketch in CA 21-24R
Savoie, Donald J(oseph) 1947- 112
Savoie, Paul 1946- 113
Savory, Alan Forsyth 1905- 9-12R
Savory, Hubert Newman 1911- CANR-26
Earlier sketches in CA 25-28R, CANR-10
Savory, Jerold 1933- CANR-10
Earlier sketch in CA 25-28R
Savory, Teo 1907-1989 ....CANR-31
Earlier sketch in CA 29-32R
Savory, Theodore Horace 1896-1980 ....CANR-6
Earlier sketch in CA 5-8R
Savours, Ann (Margaret) 1927- 57-60
Savoy, Mark
See Turner, Robert (Harry)
Sawai, Gloria Ostrem 113
Saward, Michael 1932- 97-100
Sawatsky, Harry Leonard 1931- 89-92
Sawer, Geoffrey 1910- 17-20R
Sawey, Orlan (Lester) 1920- CANR-12
Earlier sketch in CA 29-32R
Sawhill, Isabel V(an Devanter) 1937- 130
Sawicki, Marianne 1950- CANR-36
Earlier sketch in CA 114
Sawin, Martica 1927- 124
Sawin, Philip 1933- 137
Sawkins, Raymond H(arold) 1923- 103
Sawyer, Albert E(rnest) 1898- 5-8R
Sawyer, Charles 1887-1979 ....CAP-2
Obituary 85-88
Earlier sketch in CA 25-28
Sawyer, Corinne Holt 17-20R

Sawyer, Diane K. 1946(?)- 115
Brief entry 109
Sawyer, (Frederick) Don(ald) 1947- 133
Sawyer, Jack 1931- 61-64
Sawyer, Jesse O. 1918- 17-20R
Sawyer, John
See Foley, (Cedric) John
Sawyer, Mark
See Greenhood, (Clarence) David
Sawyer, P(eter) H(ayes) 1928- CANR-6
Earlier sketch in CA 9-12R
Sawyer, R(obert) McLaran 1929- 45-48
Sawyer, Ralph Alanson
1895-1978 Obituary 81-84
Sawyer, Roger 1931- 123
Sawyer, Ruth 1880-1970 ....CANR-37
Earlier sketch in CA 73-76
See also DLB 22
See also MAICYA
See also SATA 17
Sawyer, W(alter) W(arwick) 1911- 53-56
Sawyer-Laucanno, Christopher 1951- CANR-36
Earlier sketch in CA 114
Sawyerr, Harry (Alphonso Ebun)
1909-1986 ....37-40R
Obituary 120
Sax, Gilbert 1930- 21-24R
Sax, Joseph L. 1936- 33-36R
Sax, Karl 1892-1973 Obituary 45-48
Sax, Richard 1949- 125
Sax, Saville 1924- 97-100
Saxberg, Borje O(svald) 1928- 41-44R
Saxby, (Henry) Maurice 1924- ....SATA 71
Saxe, Isobel
See Rayner, Claire (Berenice)
Saxe, Richard W(arren) 1923- 49-52
Saxe, Thomas E. Jr. 1903-1975 Obituary 61-64
Saxon, A(rthur) H(artley) 1935- CANR-37
Earlier sketches in CA 25-28R, CANR-16
Saxon, Alex
See Pronzini, Bill
Saxon, Antonia
See Sachs, Judith
Saxon, Bill
See Wallmann, Jeffrey M(iner)
Saxon, Charles D(avid)
1920-1988 Obituary 127
Brief entry 118
Saxon, Gladys Relyea 5-8R
Saxon, Grant Tracy
See Raucina, Thomas Frank
Saxon, John
See Rumbold-Gibbs, Henry St. John Clair
Saxon, Lyle 1891-1946 Brief entry 119
Saxon, Peter
See McNeilly, Wilfred (Glassford)
Saxon, Van
See Henderson, M(arilyn) R(uth)
Saxon, William
See Mayleas, William
Saxton, Alexander P(laisted) 1919- 105
Saxton, Josephine (Mary) 1935- 29-32R
Saxton, Judith 1936- 105
Saxton, Lloyd 1919- 29-32R
Saxton, Mark 1914-1988 93-96
Obituary 124
Saxton, Martha 1945- 81-84
Say, Allen 1937- CANR-30
Earlier sketch in CA 29-32R
See also CLR 22
See also MAICYA
See also SATA 28, 69
Saya, Peter
See Peterson, Robert E(ugene)
Sayce, Richard Anthony 1917- 61-64
Saydah, J. Roger 1939-1976 ....25-28R
Obituary 120
Saye, Albert B(erry) 1912- CANR-5
Earlier sketch in CA 5-8R
Sayeed, Khalid B. 1926- 25-28R
Sayegh, Fayez A(bdullah) 1922-1980 ....9-12R
Obituary 102
Sayer, Angela 1935- 89-92
Sayer, Paul 1955- 132
Sayers, Dorothy L(eigh) 1893-1957 119
Brief entry 104
See also CDBLB 1914-1945
See also DLB 10, 36, 77, 100
See also MTCW
See also TCLC 2, 15
Sayers, Frances Clarke 1897-1989 ....17-20R
Obituary 129
See also SATA 62, 3
Sayers, Gale 1943- 73-76
Sayers, Janet 1945- 134
Sayers, Peig 1873-1958 Brief entry 113
Sayers, Raymond S. 1912- CANR-10
Earlier sketch in CA 25-28R
Sayers, Richard Sidney
1908-1989 Obituary 128
Sayers, Valerie 1952- 134
See also CLC 50
Sayles, E(dwin) B(ooth) 1892- CAP-2
Earlier sketch in CA 25-28
Sayles, George O(sborne) 1901- CANR-4
Earlier sketch in CA 53-56
Sayles, John Thomas 1950- 57-60
See also CLC 7, 10, 14
See also DLB 44
Sayles, Leonard Robert 1926- CANR-1
Earlier sketch in CA 1-4R
Sayles, Nettie Leitch Major
1903(?)-1984 Obituary 113
Sayles, Ted
See Sayles, E(dwin) B(ooth)
Saylor, David J(onathan) 1945- 89-92
Saylor, Irene 1932- 33-36R
Saylor, J(ohn) Galen 1902- CANR-9
Earlier sketch in CA 17-20R
Saylor, Neville 1922- 61-64
Sayre, Anne 1923- 61-64
Sayre, Eleanor Axson 1916- 25-28R
Sayre, Henry M(arshall) 1948- 119
Sayre, J(ohn) Woodrow 1913- CANR-5
Earlier sketch in CA 9-12R
Sayre, Joel 1900-1979 Obituary 89-92
Sayre, John L(eslie) 1924- 53-56
Sayre, Kenneth Malcolm 1928- CANR-3
Earlier sketch in CA 9-12R
Sayre, Leslie C. 1907- CAP-1
Earlier sketch in CA 11-12
Sayre, Nora 1932- 118
Sayre, Robert F(reeman) 1933- 9-12R
Sayre, Wallace S. 1905-1972 Obituary 33-36R
Sayres, Alfred Nevin 1893- CAP-1
Earlier sketch in CA 17-18
Sayres, William C(ortlandt) 1927- 17-20R
Sayrs, Henry John 1904- 5-8R
Saywell, John T(upper) 1929- 13-16R
Sazer, Nina 1949- 69-72
See also SATA 13
Sbarbaro, Camillo 1888-1967 ....DLB 114
Scabrini, Janet 1953- ....SATA 13
Scacco, Anthony M. Jr. 1939- 109
Scaduto, Anthony 104
Scaduto, Tony
See Scaduto, Anthony
Scaer, David P(aul) 1936- CANR-12
Earlier sketch in CA 33-36R
Scaglione, Aldo D(omenico) 1925- CANR-21
Earlier sketches in CA 13-16R, CANR-6
Scaglione, Cecil F(rank) 1934- 81-84
Scagnetti, Jack 1924- CANR-4
Earlier sketch in CA 49-52
See also SATA 7
Scala, James 1934- 124
Scalapino, Leslie 1947- 123
Scalapino, Robert A(nthony) 1919- CANR-18
Earlier sketches in CA 1-4R, CANR-2
Scales, James Ralph 1919- 120
Scales, Junius Irving 1920- 126
Scales, Pat(sy) R. 1944- 122
Scali, John (Alfred) 1918- 65-68
Scalia, Toni 1939- 133
Scally, M. A.
See Scally, Sister (Mary) Anthony
Scally, Robert James 1937- 61-64
Scally, Sister (Mary) Anthony 1905- 110
Scally, Sister Mary Anthony
See Scally, Sister (Mary) Anthony
Scalzo, Joe 1941- 49-52
Scamehorn, H(oward) Lee 1926- 69-72
Scammell, Michael ....CLC 34
Scammell, William McConnell 1920- CANR-6
Earlier sketch in CA 5-8R
Scammon, John H(umphrey) 1905- 53-56
Scammon, Richard M(ontgomery) 1915- 61-64
Scandura, Joseph M(ichael) 1931- CANR-5
Earlier sketch in CA 53-56
Scanlan, James P(atrick) 1927- 9-12R
Scanlan, Michael 1931- CANR-23
Earlier sketches in CA 57-60, CANR-7
Scanlan, Patrick F. 1895(?)-1983 Obituary 109
Scanlan, Thomas J. 1934- 114
Scanlon, David G. 1921-1990 ....13-16R
Obituary 132
Scanlon, James Edward 1940- 125
Scanlon, Kathryn I(da) 1909- CAP-1
Earlier sketch in CA 11-12
Scanlon, Marion Stephany 5-8R
See also SATA 11
Scannell, Francis P. 1915-1988 Obituary 125
Scannell, Frank
See Scannell, Francis P.
Scannell, Vernon 1922- CANR-24
Earlier sketches in CA 5-8R, CANR-8
See also CLC 49
See also DLB 27
See also SATA 59
Scanzoni, John H. 1935- CANR-24
Earlier sketches in CA 21-24R, CANR-9
Scanzoni, Letha Dawson 1935- CANR-14
Earlier sketch in CA 57-60
Scarberry, Alma Sioux 1899-1990 Obituary 131
Scarborough, Alma May C. 1913- 5-8R
Scarborough, Elizabeth (Ann) 1947- 120
Scarborough, John 1940- CANR-15
Earlier sketch in CA 41-44R
Scarborough, Ruth 1904- 115
Scarborough, William Kauffman 1933- 17-20R
Scarbrough, George (Addison) 1915- CANR-38
Earlier sketches in CA 77-80, CANR-16
Scardino, Albert (James) 1948- 129
Brief entry 119
Scaretti, Marjorie Obituary 107
Scarf, Maggi
See Scarf, Maggie
Scarf, Maggie 1932- CANR-22
Earlier sketch in CA 29-32R
See also SATA 5
Scarfe, Allan (John) 1931- CANR-13
Earlier sketch in CA 25-28R
Scarfe, Francis Harold 1911-1986 Obituary 118
Scarfe, Wendy (Elizabeth) 1933- CANR-13
Earlier sketch in CA 25-28R
Scargall, Jeanne Anna 1928- 93-96
Scargill, (David) Ian 1935- CANR-12
Earlier sketch in CA 61-64
Scarisbrick, J(ohn) J(oseph) 1928- CANR-18
Earlier sketch in CA 25-28R
Scarlett, Roger
See Page, Evelyn
Scarlett, Susan
See Streatfeild, (Mary) Noel
Scarne, John 1903-1985 Obituary 116
Scarpitti, Frank R(oland) 1936- CANR-14
Earlier sketch in CA 41-44R
Scarr, Dee 1948- 122
Scarr, Deryck (Antony) 1939- 132
Scarr(-Salapatek), Sandra (Wood) 1936- 126
Scarrott, Michael
See Fisher, A(rthur) Stanley T(heodore)
Scarrow, Howard A(lbert) 1928- 110
Scarry, Elaine (Margaret) 1946- 137
Scarry, Huck
See Scarry, Richard McClure Jr.
Scarry, Patricia (Murphy) 1924- 17-20R
See also SATA 2
Scarry, Patsy
See Scarry, Patricia (Murphy)
Scarry, Richard McClure Jr. 1953- 130
See also SATA 35
Scarry, Richard (McClure) 1919- CANR-39
Earlier sketches in CA 17-20R, CANR-18
See also CLR 3
See also DLB 61
See also MAICYA
See also SATA 2, 35
Scavullo, Francesco 1929- 102
Schaaf, C(arl) Hart 1912- 5-8R
Schaaf, Martha Eckert 1911- CANR-1
Earlier sketch in CA 1-4R
Schaaf, Peter 1942- 106
Schaafsma, Polly 1935- 57-60
Schaal, John H. 1908- 73-76
Schaap, Dick
See Schaap, Richard J(ay)
Schaap, James C(alvin) 1948- 118
Schaap, Richard J(ay) 1934- CANR-5
Earlier sketch in CA 9-12R
Schaar, John H(omer) 1928- CANR-31
Earlier sketch in CA 1-4R
Schaarwaechter, Georg 1929- 25-28R
Schabert, Kyrill S. 1909(?)-1983 Obituary 109
Schachner, Nat(han) 1895-1955 Brief entry 120
Schacht, Al(exander)
1894(?)-1984 Obituary 113
Schacht, Hjalmar (Horace Greeley)
1877-1970 Obituary 113
Schacht, Richard (Lawrence) 1941- CANR-31
Earlier sketch in CA 29-32R
Schachtel, Ernest G(eorge) 1903-1975 ....37-40R
Schachtel, Hyman Judah 1907- 49-52
Schachtel, Roger (Bernard) 1949- 106
See also SATA 38
Schachter, Gustav 1926- 17-20R
Schachter, Michael 1941- 102
Schachter, Oscar 1915- 65-68
Schachter, Stanley 1922- 37-40R
Schachterle, Nancy (Lange) 1925- 101
Schachtman, Max 1903-1972 Obituary 37-40R
Schack, William 1898-1988 Obituary 128
Schackne, Stewart 1905-1975 Obituary 61-64
Schad, Jasper G(ripper) 1932- 110
Schad, Wilhelm
See Reichert, Herbert W(illiam)
Schaechter, Mordkhe 1927- 41-44R
Schaedel, Richard P. 1920- 45-48
Schaef, Anne Wilson 1934- 118
Schaefer, Charles E. 1933- 37-40R
Schaefer, Claude 1913- 33-36R
Schaefer, Frank 1936- CANR-10
Earlier sketch in CA 65-68
Schaefer, Jack (Warner) 1907-1991 ....CANR-15
Obituary 133
Earlier sketches in CAP-1, CA 19-20R
See also SATA 3, 66
See also SATO 65
Schaefer, John H(arrison) 1937- 57-60
Schaefer, John 1958- 126
Schaefer, Josephine O'Brien 1929- 37-40R
Schaefer, Leah Cahan 1920- 49-52
Schaefer, Nicola Caroline 1939- 104
Schaefer, Ted 1939- 77-80
Schaefer, Vincent J(oseph) 1906- 120
Schaefer, Walter Erich
1901-1982(?) Obituary 106
Schaefer, William D. 1928- 134
Schaeffer, Albrecht 1885-1950 ....DLB 66
Schaeffer, Claude Frederic Armand
1898-1982 Obituary 108
Schaeffer, Edith (Seville) 1914- 77-80
Schaeffer, Elizabeth 1939- 45-48
Schaeffer, Francis A(ugust) 1912-1984 77-80
Obituary 112
Schaeffer, K(laus) H(eymann) 1921- 61-64
Schaeffer, Mead 1898- ....SATA 21
Schaeffer, Neil 1940- 107
Schaeffer, Norma 1924-1985 119
Schaeffer, Susan Fromberg 1941- CANR-18
Earlier sketch in CA 49-52
See also CLC 6, 11, 22
See also DLB 28
See also MTCW
See also SATA 22
Schaeffer-Forrer, Claude F. A.
See Schaeffer, Claude Frederic Armand
Schaeling, Marianne
See Amft, M(arian) J(anet)
Schaeper, Thomas J(erome) 1948- 109
Schaeren, Beatrix 1941- 29-32R
Schaerf, Carlo 1935- 133
Schaetzel, J(oseph) Robert 1917- 65-68
Schaetzel, Wendy 1950- 136
Schafer, Charles (Louis) 1916- 61-64
Schafer, Edward Hetzel 1913- CANR-1
Earlier sketch in CA 1-4R
Schafer, Grant C. 1926- 21-24R
Schafer, R(aymond) Murray 1933- 77-80
Schafer, Robert 1942- 108
Schafer, Stephen 1911-1976 ....37-40R
Schafer, Violet (Christine) 1910- 61-64
Schafer, William J. 1937- 49-52
Schaff, Adam 1913- CANR-12
Earlier sketch in CA 25-28R
Schaff, David 1943- 33-36R
Schaffer, (Benjamin) Bernard
1925-1984 Obituary 113
Schaffer, Daniel 1950- 114
Schaffer, Frank 1910- 103
Schaffer, Jeff(rey P.) 1943- CANR-22
Earlier sketch in CA 105
Schaffer, Lewis A(dam) 1934- 101
Schaffer, Marion 1931- 111
Schaffer, Ulrich 1942- CANR-31
Earlier sketch in CA 69-72
Schaffner, Cynthia V. A. 1947- 121
Schaffner, Kenneth 1939- 45-48
Schaffner, Nicholas 1953-1991 ....CANR-15
Obituary 135
Earlier sketch in CA 85-88
Schaffner, Val(entine) 1951- 107
Schaflander, Gerald M(aurice) 1920- 37-40R
Schagrin, Morton L(ouis) 1930- 25-28R
Schaie, K(laus) Warner 1928- CANR-34
Earlier sketches in CA 41-44R, CANR-15
Schakne, Robert 1926-1989 65-68
Obituary 129
Schakovskoy, Zinaida 1908- CANR-8
Earlier sketch in CA 17-20R
Schaldenbrand, Mary 1922- 49-52
Schaleben, Arville Orman 1907- CANR-1
Earlier sketch in CA 1-4R
Schalk, Adolph F(rancis) 1923- 33-36R
Schalk, David L(ouis) 1936- 89-92
Schall, James V(incent) 1928- CANR-20
Earlier sketches in CA 9-12R, CANR-6
Schaller, George B(eals) 1933- CANR-9
Earlier sketch in CA 5-8R
See also SATA 30
Schaller, Lyle E(dwin) 1923- 131
Schaller, Michael 1947- 126
Brief entry 110
Schalm, Bernard 1928-1974 ....1-4R
Obituary 103
Scham, Alan (Myron) 1937- 29-32R
Schama, Simon (Michael) 1945- CANR-39
Earlier sketch in CA 105
See also BEST 89:4
Schanberg, Sydney H(illel) 1934- 69-72
Schanche, Don A. 1926- CANR-6
Earlier sketch in CA 5-8R
Schandler, Herbert Y(ale) 1928- 69-72
Schang, Frederick C. 1893- CANR-13
Earlier sketch in CA 33-36R
Schank, Roger C(arl) 1946- 132
Schanz, John P(hilip) 1924- 107
Schanzer, George O(swald) 1914- 41-44R
Schaper, Edzard 1908-1984 ....DLB 69
Schapiro, J(acob) Salwyn 1879-1973 ....CANR-5
Obituary 45-48
Earlier sketch in CA 5-8R
Schapiro, Leonard (Bertram)
1908-1983 ....CANR-13
Obituary 111
Earlier sketch in CA 65-68
Schapiro, Meyer 1904- 97-100
Schapper, Beatrice Aronson 1906-1974 ....9-12R
Obituary 45-48
Schappes, Morris U(rman) 1907- 49-52
Schapsmeier, Edward L(ewis) 1927- 29-32R
Schapsmeier, Frederick H(erman)
1927- 29-32R
Schara, Ron 1942- 69-72
Scharbach, (John) Alexander 1909- 114
Scharbach, J. Alexander
See Scharbach, (John) Alexander
Scharf, Bertram 1931- 53-56
Scharf, J. Thomas 1843-1898 ....DLB 47
Scharfenberg, Doris 1925- 108
Scharff, Edward E. 1946- 123
Scharfstein, Ben-Ami 1919- 101
Scharfstein, Zevi 1884-1972 Obituary 37-40R
Scharine, Richard (G.) 1938- Brief entry 118
Scharine, Richard G. 1938- 123
Scharlatt, Hal 1936(?)-1974 Obituary 104
Scharlemann, Dorothy Hoyer 1912- 65-68
Scharlemann, Martin H(enry) 1910- 13-16R
Scharlemann, Robert Paul 1929- 9-12R
Scharnhorst, Gary (Francis) 1950- 119
Scharper, Phillip (Jenkins) 1919-1985 73-76
Obituary 116
Schary, Dore 1905-1980 ....CANR-1
Obituary 101
Earlier sketch in CA 1-4R
Schary, Jill
See Robinson, Jill
Schatell, Brian 124
See also SATA 47, 66
Schatkin, Margaret 1944- 118
Schatkin, Sidney B. 1903- 25-28R
Schatt, Stanley 1943- CANR-26
Earlier sketch in CA 69-72
Schatten, Fritz (Max Robert) 1930- 13-16R
Schatten, Robert 1911-1977 Obituary 73-76
Schatz, Mark N(orton) 1929- 113
Schatz, Ronald W. 1949- 125
Schatz, Sayre P(erry) 1922- 41-44R
Schatzki, Walter 1899- ....SATA 31
Schau, Michael 1945- 85-88
Schaub, Marilyn McNamara 1928- 17-20R
Schaub, Thomas Hill 1947- 105
Schauer, Frederick Franklin 1946- 112
Schauf, George Edward 1925- 41-44R
Schaufele, William E. Jr. 1923- 111
Scheader, Catherine 1932- 85-88
Schealer, John M(ilton) 1920- 5-8R

Schechner, Richard 1934- ...CANR-17
Earlier sketches in CA 45-48, CANR-1
Schechter, A(bel) A(lan)
1907-1989 Obituary ...128
Schechter, Alan H(enry) 1936- ...9-12R
Schechter, Betty (Goodstein) 1921- ...5-8R
See also SATA 5
Schechter, Harold 1948- ...108
Schechter, Ruth Lisa 1927- ...33-36R
Schechter, William 1934- ...21-24R
Schechtman, Joseph B. 1891-1970 ...CANR-3
Earlier sketch in CA 1-4R
Schecter, Jerrold L. 1932- ...21-24R
Scheel, J(oergen) D(itlev) 1918- ...9-12R
Scheele, Adele M. 1938- ...CANR-18
Earlier sketch in CA 97-100
Scheele, Carl H(arry) 1928- ...85-88
Scheer, George F(abian) 1917- ...13-16R
Scheer, Julian (Weisel) 1926- ...49-52
See also SATA 8
Scheer, Robert 1936- ...106
Scheer, Wilbert E. 1909- ...CANR-17
Earlier sketch in CA 25-28R
Scheff, Thomas Joel 1929- ...105
Scheffer, Nathalie P.
1890(?)-1981 Obituary ...105
Scheffer, Victor B(lanchard) 1906- ...CANR-11
Earlier sketch in CA 29-32R
See also SATA 6
Scheffler, Harold W(alter) 1932- ...17-20R
Scheffler, Israel 1923- ...CANR-1
Earlier sketch in CA 1-4R
Scheflen, Albert E. 1920-1980 ...CANR-3
Obituary ...101
Earlier sketch in CA 45-48
Schefter, Jim 1940- ...89-92
Scheibe, Karl E(dward) 1937- ...CANR-11
Earlier sketch in CA 29-32R
Scheiber, Harry N(oel) 1935- ...CANR-1
Earlier sketch in CA 1-4R
Scheiber, Jane L(ang) 1937- ...93-96
Scheibla, Shirley 1919- ...41-44R
Scheick, William J(oseph) 1941- ...CANR-38
Earlier sketches in CA 49-52, CANR-1, 17
Scheid, Francis J(ames) 1920- ...17-20R
Scheidler, Joseph M. 1927- ...122
Scheier, Ivan Henry 1926- ...CANR-7
Earlier sketch in CA 5-8R
Scheier, Libby 1946- ...136
Scheier, Michael 1943- ...CANR-36
Earlier sketch in CA 115
See also SATA 36, 40
Scheimann, Eugene 1897- ...33-36R
Schein, Clarence J(acob) 1918- ...65-68
Schein, James Arns 1920(?)-1983 Obituary ...110
Schein, Jerome D(aniel) 1923- ...118
Schein, Muriel
See Dimen, Muriel
Scheiner, Seth M(ordecai) 1933- ...17-20R
Scheinfeld, Aaron 1899-1970 ...CAP-2
Earlier sketch in CA 29-32
Scheinfeld, Amram 1897-1979 ...17-20R
Obituary ...89-92
Scheingold, Stuart A(llen) 1931- ...53-56
Scheleen, Joseph C(arl)
1904-1985 Obituary ...116
Schell, Bunny
See Schell, Rolfe F(inch)
Schell, Edgar T(homas) 1931- ...45-48
Schell, Herbert S(amuel) 1899- ...CANR-21
Earlier sketch in CA 1-4R
Schell, Jonathan 1943- ...CANR-12
Earlier sketch in CA 73-76
See also CLC 35
Schell, Maximilian 1930- Brief entry ...116
Schell, Mildred 1922- ...113
See also SATA 41
Schell, Orville H. 1940- ...25-28R
See also SATA 10
Schell, Rolfe F(inch) 1916- ...CANR-7
Earlier sketch in CA 57-60
Schellenberg, Helene Chambers ...13-16R
Schellenberg, James A. 1932- ...37-40R
Schellenberg, Theodore R. 1903- ...CAP-1
Earlier sketch in CA 17-18
Schellie, Don 1932- ...101
See also SATA 29
Schelling, Friedrich Wilhelm Joseph von
1775-1854 ...DLB 90
Schelling, Thomas Crombie 1921- ...1-4R
Schelly, William 1951- ...114
Schemering, (Crien) Christopher 1956- ...123
Schemm, Mildred Walker 1905- ...CANR-1
Earlier sketch in CA 1-4R
See also SATA 21
Schemmer, Benjamin Franklin 1932- ...61-64
Schemmer, Kenneth E(dwin) 1936- ...110
Schenck, Anita A(llen) 1909- ...89-92
Schenck, Janet Daniels
1883(?)-1976 Obituary ...69-72
Schendler, Sylvan 1925- ...25-28R
Schenk, H(ans) G(eorg) 1912- ...21-24R
Schenkar, Joan 1946- ...133
Schenken, Howard 1904(?)-1979 ...93-96
Obituary ...85-88
Schenker, Alexander M(arian) 1924- ...33-36R
Schenker, Dona 1947- ...135
See also SATA 68
Schenker, Eric 1931- ...37-40R
Schenkkan, Robert (Frederic Jr.) 1953- ...132
Scheper, Nancy
See Scheper-Hughes, Nancy
Scheper-Hughes, Nancy 1944- ...89-92
Schepers, Maurice B. 1928- ...13-16R
Scheps, Clarence 1915- ...33-36R
Scher, Helene L(enz) 1935- ...123
Scher, Helene Lenz 1935- Brief entry ...118
Scher, Les 1946- ...101
Scher, Paula 1948- ...115
See also SATA 47
Scher, Steven Paul 1936- ...CANR-3
Earlier sketch in CA 49-52
Schere, Monroe 1913- ...85-88
Scherer, F(rederic) M(ichael) 1932- ...CANR-12
Earlier sketch in CA 29-32R
Scherer, Frances Schlosser 1912- ...69-72
Scherer, Jack F(ranklin) 1939- ...69-72
Scherer, Jacqueline Rita 1931- ...53-56
Scherer, Jean-Marie Maurice 1920- ...110
See also Rohmer, Eric
Scherer, Joanna Cohan 1942- ...107
Scherer, Klaus R(ainer) 1943- ...101
Scherer, Lester B(uryl) 1931- ...132
Scherer, Paul (Ehrman) 1892-1969 ...5-8R
Obituary ...134
Scherer, Priscilla 1948- ...119
Scherer, Raymond Lewis 1919- ...104
Scherer, William F(rederick) 1939- ...41-44R
Scherf, Margaret 1908-1979 ...CANR-6
Earlier sketch in CA 5-8R
See also SATA 10
Scherle, Victor 1935- ...25-28R
Scherman, Bernadine Kielty
1890(?)-1973 Obituary ...45-48
Scherman, David E(dward) 1916- ...102
Scherman, Katharine 1915- ...CANR-27
Earlier sketches in CA 5-8R, CANR-11
Scherman, Thomas K(ielty)
1917-1979 Obituary ...106
Schermer, Judith (Denise) 1941- ...106
See also SATA 30
Schermerhorn, Richard A(lonzo) 1903- ...37-40R
Scherr, George Harry 1920- ...114
Scherr, Max 1916(?)-1981 Obituary ...105
Schertenleib, Charles
1905-1972 Obituary ...37-40R
Schertle, Alice 1941- ...CANR-23
Earlier sketch in CA 107
See also SATA 36
Scherzer, Carl John 1901- ...1-4R
Scheub, Harold 1931- ...61-64
Scheuer, Joseph F(rancis)
1918-1975 Obituary ...61-64
Scheuer, Philip K(atz) 1902-1985 Obituary ...115
Scheuerle, William H(oward) 1930- ...33-36R
Scheuerman, Richard D(ean) 1951- ...CANR-27
Earlier sketch in CA 57-60
Scheuring, Lyn 1937- ...73-76
Scheuring, Tom 1942- ...73-76
Schevill, James (Erwin) 1920- ...5-8R
See also CAAS 12
See also CLC 7
Schevitz, Jeffrey M(orrie) 1941- ...65-68
Scheyer, Ernst 1900- ...13-16R
Schiaparelli, Elsa 1890-1973 Obituary ...113
Schiappa, Barbara D(ublin) 1943- ...109
Schiavone, James 1933- ...CANR-9
Earlier sketch in CA 5-8R
Schick, Alice 1946- ...CANR-15
Earlier sketch in CA 81-84
See also SATA 27
Schick, Eleanor 1942- ...CANR-19
Earlier sketches in CA 49-52, CANR-4
See also SATA 9
Schick, Frank L(eopold) 1918- ...132
Schick, George B(aldwin Powell) 1903- ...41-44R
Schick, Joel 1945- ...107
See also SATA 30, 31
Schickel, Julia Whedon 1936- ...49-52
Schickel, Richard (Warren) 1933- ...CANR-34
Earlier sketches in CA 1-4R, CANR-1
See also AITN 1
Schickele, Peter 1935- ...85-88
Schickele, Rene 1883-1940 ...DLB 66
Schiddel, Edmund 1909-1982 ...5-8R
Obituary ...107
Schiefelbusch, Richard L. 1918- ...CANR-11
Earlier sketch in CA 25-28R
Schieffer, Bob 1937- ...69-72
Schier, Donald (Stephen) 1914- ...29-32R
Schier, Ernest L. 1918- ...77-80
Schier, Flint 1954(?)-1988 Obituary ...126
Schiff, Dorothy 1903-1989 ...121
Obituary ...129
Brief entry ...114
Schiff, Harold (Irvin) 1923- ...89-92
Schiff, Irwin A(llan) 1928- ...CANR-25
Earlier sketch in CA 65-68
Schiff, Jacqui Lee 1934- ...37-40R
Schiff, Ken(neth Roy) 1942- ...49-52
See also SATA 7
Schiff, Michael 1915- ...13-16R
Schiffer, Irvine 1917- Brief entry ...114
Schiffer, Michael B(rian) 1947- ...CANR-27
Earlier sketch in CA 110
Schiffer, Michael 1948- ...106
Schifferes, Justus J(ulius) 1907- ...CANR-5
Earlier sketch in CA 5-8R
Schiffhorst, Gerald J. 1940- ...CANR-38
Earlier sketch in CA 17-20R
Schiffman, Jack 1921- ...49-52
Schiffman, Joseph Harris 1914- ...17-20R
Schiffrin, Harold Z. 1922- ...29-32R
Schiler, Marc (Eugene) 1951- ...106
Schillaci, Anthony
See Schillaci, Peter Paul
Schillaci, Peter Paul 1929- ...29-32R
Schillebeeckx, Edward (Cornelis Florentius Alfons)
1914- ...127
Brief entry ...111
Schiller, A. Arthur 1902-1977 ...CANR-28
Obituary ...73-76
Earlier sketch in CA 37-40R
Schiller, Andrew 1919- ...41-44R
See also SATA 21
Schiller, Barbara (Heyman) 1928- ...17-20R
See also SATA 21
Schiller, Bob
See Schiller, Robert Achille
Schiller, Bradley R(obert) 1943- ...57-60
Schiller, Craig 1951- ...81-84
Schiller, Dan(iel T.) 1951- ...131
Schiller, Dorothea E.
1898(?)-1987 Obituary ...123
Schiller, Friedrich 1759-1805 ...DLB 94
Schiller, Herbert I(rving) 1919- ...29-32R
Schiller, Jerome P(aul) 1934- ...25-28R
Schiller, Justin G. 1943- Brief entry ...110
See also SATA 31
Schiller, Lee Virginia Chambers
See Chambers-Schiller, Lee Virginia
Schiller, Mayer
See Schiller, Craig
Schiller, Robert Achille 1918- ...123
Brief entry ...118
Schiller, Rose Leiman
See Goldemberg, Rose Leiman
Schilling, Betty 1925- ...106
Schilling, S. Paul 1904- ...CANR-16
Earlier sketches in CA 1-4R, CANR-1
Schilling, Warner R(oller) 1925- Brief entry ...112
Schilpp, Madelon Golden ...117
Schilpp, Paul A(rthur) 1897- ...CANR-19
Earlier sketches in CA 1-4R, CANR-4
Schilz, Thomas F. 1950- ...125
Schimel, John L(ouis) 1916- ...25-28R
Schimmel, Annemarie (Brigitte) 1922- ...132
Brief entry ...120
Schimmel, Herbert D(avid) 1927- ...117
Schimmels, Cliff 1937- ...115
Schimpff, Jill Wagner 1945- ...135
Schinagl, Mary S(onora) 1914- ...17-20R
Schindeler, Fred(erick) Fernand 1934- ...41-44R
Schindelman, Joseph 1923- ...SATA 32, 67
Schindler, Marvin Samuel 1932- Brief entry ...106
Schindler, S(tephen) D. ...SATA 50
Schinhan, Jan Philip 1887-1975 ...CAP-2
Obituary ...61-64
Earlier sketch in CA 23-24
Schinto, Jeanne 1951- ...133
Schioetz, Aksel 1906-1975 Obituary ...111
Schiotz, Aksel
See Schioetz, Aksel
Schipf, Robert G(eorge) 1923- ...61-64
Schirmer, Daniel B(oone) 1915- ...41-44R
Schirmer, Gregory A(lan) 1944- ...117
Schirmer, Henry W. 1922- ...107
Schirmer, Jennifer G(ay) 1947- ...113
Schirmerhorn, Clint
See Riemer, George
Schirokauer, Conrad M(ax) 1929- ...107
Schisgal, Murray (Joseph) 1926- ...21-24R
See also CLC 6
Schisgall, Oscar 1901-1984 ...CANR-9
Obituary ...112
Earlier sketch in CA 53-56
See also SATA 12, 38
Schivelbusch, Wolfgang 1941- ...105
Schjeldahl, Peter 1942- Brief entry ...113
Schkade, Lawrence L. 1930- ...CANR-7
Earlier sketch in CA 17-20R
Schlabach, Theron F(rederick) 1933- ...25-28R
Schlabrendorff, Fabian von
See von Schlabrendorff, Fabian
Schlachter, Gail Ann 1943- ...CANR-31
Earlier sketches in CA 77-80, CANR-14
Schlachter, Susan
See Thaler, Susan
Schlaf, Johannes 1862-1941 ...DLB 118
Schlafly, Phyllis 1924- ...CANR-26
Earlier sketch in CA 25-28R
See also AITN 1
See also MTCW
Schlain, Bert H(oward) 1898- ...17-20R
Schlamm, William S(iegmund) 1904-1978 ...93-96
Obituary ...81-84
Schlanger, Henry 1918(?)-1984 Obituary ...113
Schlant, Ernestine 1935- ...81-84
Schlapbach-Oberhansli, Trudi 1944- ...21-24R
Schlatter, Richard 1912-1987 ...21-24R
Obituary ...123
Schlauch, Margaret 1898-1986 ...CAP-1
Obituary ...119
Earlier sketch in CA 13-14
Schlayer, Mary Elizabeth 1915-1987 ...129
Schlebecker, John T(homas) 1923- ...9-12R
Schleck, Charles A. 1925- ...CANR-6
Earlier sketch in CA 5-8R
Schlee, Ann 1934- ...CANR-29
Earlier sketch in CA 101
See also CLC 35
See also SATA 36, 44
Schlee, Guenther 1951- ...135
Schlee, Gunther
See Schlee, Guenther
Schlee, Susan 1940- ...93-96
Schlegel, August Wilhelm von
1767-1845 ...DLB 94
Schlegel, Dorothea 1763-1839 ...DLB 90
Schlegel, Dorothy B(adders) 1910- ...37-40R
Schlegel, Friedrich 1772-1829 ...DLB 90
Schlegel, Richard 1913- ...65-68
Schlegel, Stuart A(llen) 1932- ...61-64
Schlegelmann, V. E.
See Hartz, Fred R.
Schleh, Eugene 1939- ...137
Schleicher, Charles P. 1907- ...9-12R
Schleier, Curt 1944- ...89-92
Schleier, Gertrude 1933- ...1-4R
Schleiermacher, Friedrich 1768-1834 ...DLB 90
Schleifer, James T(homas) 1942- ...97-100
Schleifer, Ronald 1948- ...118
Schlein, Miriam 1926- ...CANR-2
Earlier sketch in CA 1-4R
See also SATA 2
Schleiner, Winfried 1938- ...29-32R
Schlem
See Prevost, Marcel
Schlender, William E(lmer) 1920- ...CANR-14
Earlier sketch in CA 17-20R
Schlenker, Elizabeth D. (Wallace)
1912- ...17-20R
Schlenther, Boyd (Stanley) 1936- ...41-44R
Schlepp, Wayne Allen 1931- ...29-32R
Schlereth, Howard (Hewitt) 1936- ...57-60
Schlereth, Thomas J(ohn) 1941- ...97-100
Schlesinger, Alfred Cary 1900- ...CAP-1
Earlier sketch in CA 13-14
Schlesinger, Arthur M(eier) Jr. 1917- ...CANR-28
Earlier sketches in CA 1-4R, CANR-1
See also AITN 1
See also DLB 17
See also MTCW
See also SATA 61
Schlesinger, Arthur Meier 1888-1965 ...CANR-5
Obituary ...25-28R
Earlier sketch in CA 5-8R
Schlesinger, Benjamin 1928- ...CANR-22
Earlier sketches in CA 17-20R, CANR-7
Schlesinger, Bruno Walter 1876-1962 ...116
Obituary ...111
Schlesinger, Elizabeth Bancroft
1886-1977 Obituary ...69-72
Schlesinger, Hilde S(tephanie) ...CANR-6
Earlier sketch in CA 53-56
Schlesinger, Joseph A(braham) 1922- ...61-64
Schlesinger, Lawrence E(rwin) 1921- ...41-44R
Schlesinger, Leonard A. 1952- ...126
Schlesinger, Marian Cannon 1912- ...89-92
Schlesinger, Roger 1943- ...126
Schlesinger, Stephen C(annon)
1942- ...CANR-28
Earlier sketch in CA 57-60
Schlesinger, Thomas O(tto) 1925- ...41-44R
Schlessinger, Philip J. 1914- ...5-8R
Schleunes, Karl A(lbert) 1937- ...29-32R
Schley, Jim 1956- ...118
Schlichting, Harold E(ugene Jr.) 1926- ...112
Schlimbach, Alice (Paula) 1898- ...CAP-1
Earlier sketch in CA 13-16
Schlink, Frederick John 1891- ...65-68
Schlink, Klara 1904- ...101
Schlink, M. Basilea
See Schlink, Klara
Schlink, Mother Basilea
See Schlink, Klara
Schlissel, Lillian 1930- ...CANR-29
Earlier sketches in CA 25-28R, CANR-13
Schlitzer, Albert Lawrence 1902- ...1-4R
Schloat, G. Warren Jr. 1914- ...21-24R
See also SATA 4
Schlobin, Roger Clark 1944- ...CANR-18
Earlier sketch in CA 102
Schlosberg, H. J.
See May, H(enry) J(ohn)
Schloss, Arthur David
See Waley, Arthur (David)
Schlossberg, Dan 1948- ...CANR-19
Earlier sketch in CA 101
Schlossberg, Edwin (Arthur)
1945- Brief entry ...112
Schlossberg, Herbert 1935- ...111
Schlossman, Beryl 1955- ...124
Schlossman, Steven L(awrence)
1947- ...CANR-16
Earlier sketch in CA 81-84
Schlossstein, Steven 1941- ...122
Schlueter, June 1942- ...CANR-32
Earlier sketch in CA 101
Schlueter, Paul (George) 1933- ...CANR-32
Earlier sketches in CA 13-16R, CANR-11
Schlumberger, Daniel
1904-1972 Obituary ...37-40R
Schlumberger, Jean 1877-1968 Obituary ...116
See also DLB 65
Schmacher, Evelyn A(nn) 1919- ...130
Schmalenbach, Werner 1920- ...CANR-29
Earlier sketches in CA 73-76, CANR-13
Schmandt, Henry J. 1918- ...CANR-9
Earlier sketch in CA 5-8R
Schmandt, Raymond H(enry Jr.) 1925- ...9-12R
Schmandt-Besserat, Denise 1933- ...CANR-20
Earlier sketch in CA 69-72
Schmeck, Harold M(arshall) Jr. 1923- ...17-20R
Schmeidler, Gertrude Raffel 1912- ...37-40R
Schmeiser, Douglas Albert 1934- ...CANR-3
Earlier sketch in CA 9-12R
Schmeling, Gareth L(on) 1940- ...73-76
Schmeling, Marianne 1930- ...101
Schmeltz, Susan Alton ...111
Schmeltz, Susan M.
See Schmeltz, Susan Alton
Schmeltz, William Frederick 1924- ...41-44R
Schmemann, Alexander 1921-1983 ...117
Obituary ...111
Schmemann, Serge 1945- ...136
Schmertz, Herb(ert) 1930- ...120
Schmid, A. Allan 1935- ...37-40R
Schmid, Carlo 1896-1979 Obituary ...97-100
Schmid, Carol L(ouise) 1946- ...105
Schmid, Claus-Peter 1942- ...61-64
Schmid, Eduard 1890-1966 Obituary ...113
See also Edschmid, Kasimir
Schmid, Elenore 1939- ...CANR-21
Earlier sketches in CA 53-56, CANR-5
See also SATA 12
Schmid, John 1926- ...133

Schmid, Mark J(oseph) 1901- CAP-1
Earlier sketch in CA 13-14
Schmiderer, Dorothy 1940- 85-88
See also SATA 19
Schmidgall, Gary 1945- 77-80
Schmidhauser, John R(ichard) 1922- CANR-1
Earlier sketch in CA 45-48
Schmidt, Albert J(ohn) 1925- 37-40R
Schmidt, Alexander 1956- 125
Schmidt, Alice M(ahany) 1925- 65-68
Schmidt, Alvin J(ohn) 1932- CANR-1
Earlier sketch in CA 45-48
Schmidt, Annie M. G. 1911- 135
See also CLR 22
See also SATA 67
Schmidt, Arno (Otto) 1914-1979 128
Obituary 109
See also CLC 56
See also DLB 69
Schmidt, Charles T. Jr. 1934- 25-28R
Schmidt, Claire Harman 1957- 109
Schmidt, Dana Adams 1915- 9-12R
Schmidt, Diane 1953- .... SATA 70
Schmidt, Dolores Barracano 1931- 41-44R
Schmidt, Dorothea
See Wender, Dorothea
Schmidt, Elizabeth 1915- .... SATA 15
Schmidt, Emerson Peter
1899-1976 Obituary 111
Schmidt, Fred H(artz) 1918- 85-88
Schmidt, Frederick G. 1924- 49-52
Schmidt, George P. 1894(?)-1989 Obituary 130
Schmidt, Hans 1938- 61-64
Schmidt, Helmut Dan 1915- 9-12R
Schmidt, Hubert (Glasgow)
1905-1980 Obituary 112
Schmidt, J(akob) E(dward) 1906- 13-16R
Schmidt, James Norman 1912- CANR-1
Earlier sketch in CA 1-4R
See also SATA 21
Schmidt, James W. 1947- 121
Schmidt, Jerry A(rthur) 1945- CANR-28
Earlier sketch in CA 69-72
Schmidt, Joel (Paul Armand) 1937- 130
Schmidt, John 1905-1969 .... CAP-1
Earlier sketch in CA 19-20
Schmidt, Karl M. (Jr.) 1917- 13-16R
Schmidt, Laura M(arie) 1952- CANR-16
Earlier sketch in CA 65-68
Schmidt, Leigh Eric 1961- 133
Schmidt, Lyle D(arrel) 1933- 61-64
Schmidt, Margaret Fox 1925-1979 65-68
Obituary 125
Schmidt, Marlene 133
Schmidt, Michael Jack 1949- 126
Schmidt, Michael Norton 1947- CANR-2
Earlier sketch in CA 49-52
See also DLB 40
Schmidt, Mike
See Schmidt, Michael Jack
Schmidt, Nancy Jeanne 1936- CANR-7
Earlier sketch in CA 57-60
Schmidt, Paul Frederic 1925- CANR-1
Earlier sketch in CA 1-4R
Schmidt, Peggy Jeanne 1951- 109
Schmidt, Rick
See Schmidt, William R(ichard) III
Schmidt, Robert Milton 1930- 5-8R
Schmidt, Royal Jae (Jr.) 1915- 41-44R
Schmidt, Sandra
See Oddo, Sandra (Schmidt)
Schmidt, Stanley (Albert) 1944- CANR-24
Earlier sketches in CA 61-64, CANR-8
Schmidt, Steven (Thomas) 1927- 33-36R
Schmidt, Warren H(arry) 1920- CANR-1
Earlier sketch in CA 45-48
Schmidt, Werner Felix 1923- 9-12R
Schmidt, Werner H. 1935- 131
Schmidt, William E. 1947- 73-76
Schmidt, William R(ichard) III 1949- 110
Schmidt, Wilson Emerson 1927- 103
Schmidtbonn, Wilhelm August
1876-1952 .... DLB 118
Schmidt-Nielsen, Knut 1915- 106
Schmiechen, James A. 1940- 126
Schmier, Louis Eugene 1940- 112
Schmit, Patricia Brady
See Brady, Patricia
Schmithals, Walter 1923- CANR-9
Earlier sketch in CA 65-68
Schmitt, Abraham 1927- CANR-17
Earlier sketch in CA 97-100
Schmitt, Albert R(ichard) 1929- 73-76
Schmitt, Bernadotte Everly 1886-1969 .... 1-4R
Obituary 103
Schmitt, Charles 1934(?)-1986 Obituary 119
Schmitt, David (Edward) 1940- 53-56
Schmitt, Gladys 1909-1972 .... CANR-2
Obituary 37-40R
Earlier sketch in CA 1-4R
Schmitt, Hans A. 1921- CANR-5
Earlier sketch in CA 1-4R
Schmitt, Heinrich 1894-1976 Obituary 115
Schmitt, Karl Michael 1922- 41-44R
Schmitt, Marshall L. 1919- 13-16R
Schmitt, Martin (Ferdinand) 1917-1978 .... CANR-9
Earlier sketch in CA 53-56
Schmitt, Raymond L(ouis) 1936- 93-96
Schmitt, Richard 1927- 118
Schmitter, Dean Morgan 1917- 41-44R
Schmitter, Phillipe Charles 1936- 115
Schmitthoff, Clive M(acmillan)
1903-1990 .... CANR-18
Obituary 132
Earlier sketches in CA 5-8R, CANR-3
Schmittroth, John (William) Jr. 1949- CANR-19
Earlier sketch in CA 97-100
Schmittroth, John 1924-1988 49-52
Obituary 125
Schmitz, Aron Hector 1861-1928 122
Brief entry 104
See also Svevo, Italo
See also MTCW
Schmitz, Carl August 1920-1966 Obituary 116
Schmitz, Charles Henry 1904- 5-8R
Schmitz, David F. 1956- 132
Schmitz, Dennis 1937- 29-32R
Schmitz, James H(enry) 1911- 103
See also DLB 8
Schmitz, Joseph William 1905-1966 .... 5-8R
Schmitz, Michael J. 1934- 21-24R
Schmitz, Virginia
See Pasley, Virginia Schmitz
Schmokel, Wolfe W(illiam) 1933- 9-12R
Schmoller, Hans 1916-1985 Obituary 117
Schmook, Kathy Grizzard 1947- 127
Schmookler, Andrew Bard 1946- 135
Schmuck, Richard A(llen) 1936- 13-16R
Schmucke, Anne
See Strich, Christian
Schmuhl, Robert (Philip) 1948- 135
Schmuller, Aaron 1910- 53-56
Schnabel, Billie H(agen)
1944(?)-1980 Obituary 101
Schnabel, Truman Gross Jr. 1919- 105
Schnacke, Dick
See Schnacke, Richard N(ye)
Schnacke, Richard N(ye) 1919- 61-64
Schnackenberg, Gjertrud 1953- Brief entry 116
See also CLC 40
See also DLB 120
Schnackenburg, Rudolf 1914- CANR-12
Earlier sketch in CA 29-32R
Schnall, Maxine (Swartz) 1934- 17-20R
Schnapper, Dominique 1934- 130
Schnaubelt, Franz Joseph 1914- 65-68
Schneck, Jerome M. 1920- 17-20R
Schneck, Stephen 1933- CANR-10
Earlier sketch in CA 13-16R
Schneebaum, Tobias 1921- CANR-15
Earlier sketch in CA 29-32R
Schneede, Uwe M(ax) 1939- Brief entry 111
Schneewind, Elizabeth Hughes 1940- CANR-2
Earlier sketch in CA 45-48
Schneewind, J(erome) B(orges) 1930- 25-28R
Schneidau, Herbert N. 1935- 29-32R
Schneider, Andrew (J.) 1942- 132
Brief entry 127
Schneider, Anna
See Sequoia, Anna
Schneider, Ben Ross Jr. 1920- 37-40R
Schneider, Benjamin 1938- 41-44R
Schneider, Carl D(avid) 1942- 69-72
Schneider, Clement J(oseph)
1927-1972 .... 41-44R
Schneider, Daniel J(ohn) 1927- 61-64
Schneider, David M(urray)
1918- Brief entry 112
Schneider, David 1918- 114
Schneider, Delwin Byron 1926- 37-40R
Schneider, Dick
See Schneider, Richard H(enry)
Schneider, Duane 1937- 103
Schneider, Elisabeth Wintersteen 1897- CAP-1
Earlier sketch in CA 11-12
Schneider, Elizabeth (Susan) 1943- CANR-36
Earlier sketches in CA 93-96, CANR-16
Schneider, Hans J(uergen) 1935- 73-76
Schneider, Harold K(enneth) 1925- 33-36R
Schneider, Herbert Wallace 1892-1984 ..... 13-16R
Obituary 114
Schneider, Herman 1905- CANR-16
Earlier sketch in CA 29-32R
See also SATA 7
Schneider, Howie .... AITN 2
Schneider, Isidor 1896-1977 .... CAP-1
Obituary 73-76
Earlier sketch in CA 13-14
Schneider, John C(harles) 1945- 102
Schneider, Joyce Anne 1942- 107
Schneider, Kenneth Ray 1927- 49-52
Schneider, Lambert 1900-1970 Obituary 104
Schneider, Laurence Allen 1937- 81-84
Schneider, Laurie
See Adams, Laurie
Schneider, Leo 1916- 5-8R
Schneider, Leonard Alfred 1925-1966 89-92
See also Bruce, Lenny
Schneider, Louis 1915-1979 .... CANR-13
Earlier sketch in CA 57-60
Schneider, Myles J(ay) 1943- 116
Schneider, Myra 1936- CANR-24
Earlier sketch in CA 107
Schneider, Nicholas A. 1930- 25-28R
Schneider, Nina 1913- CANR-15
Earlier sketch in CA 29-32R
See also SATA 2
Schneider, Rex 1937- 122
See also SATA 44
Schneider, Richard H(enry) 1922- 97-100
Schneider, Robert G. 1930- 112
Schneider, Robert T(homas) 1925- 5-8R
Schneider, Robert W. 1933- 13-16R
Schneider, Rolf 1932- 130
Brief entry 112
Schneider, Ronald M(ilton) 1932- 53-56
Schneider, Stanley D(ale) 1921- 17-20R
Schneider, Stephen H(enry) 1945- CANR-12
Earlier sketch in CA 69-72
Schneider, Steven A. 1952- 120
Schneider, Susan Weidman 1944- 118
Schneider, William Jr. 1941- CANR-19
Earlier sketch in CA 29-32R
Schneiderman, Beth Kline 97-100
Schneiderman, Harry
1885-1975 Obituary 61-64
Schneiderman, L(awrence) J(erome)
1932- 57-60
Schneiderman, Stuart (Alan) 1943- 114
Schneiders, Alexander A(loysius)
1909-1968 .... CAP-1
Earlier sketch in CA 17-18
Schneier, Edward V(incent) Jr. 1939- 29-32R
Schneir, Miriam 1933- 77-80
Schnell, George A(dam) 1931- CANR-27
Earlier sketches in CA 29-32R, CANR-12
Schnell, R(odolph) L(eslie) 1931- 113
Schnell, William J(acob) 5-8R
Schnelle, Kenneth E(dward) 1914- 21-24R
Schnepper, Jeff A(lan) 1947- CANR-21
Earlier sketch in CA 85-88
Schneps, Maurice 1917- 1-4R
Schnessel, S. Michael 1947- CANR-14
Earlier sketch in CA 73-76
Schneyder, J. F.
See Taylor, (Frank Herbert) Griffin
Schnirel, James R. 1931- 69-72
See also SATA 14
Schnitzer, Martin C(olby) 1925- 134
Brief entry 110
Schnitzler, Arthur 1862-1931 Brief entry 104
See also DLB 81, 118
See also TCLC 4
Schnore, Leo F(rancis) 1927- 17-20R
Schnurre, Wolfdietrich 1920-1989 Obituary 129
See also DLB 69
See also SATA 63
Schob, David Eugene 1941- 61-64
Schochet, Gordon J(oel) 1937- 45-48
Schochet, J(acob) Immanuel 1935- CANR-1
Earlier sketch in CA 45-48
Schock, Pauline 1928- 111
See also SATA 45
Schocken, Theodore 1914-1975 Obituary 104
Schodek, Daniel L(ewis) 1941- 127
Schoder, Raymond V(ictor) 1916-1987 .... CANR-1
Obituary 122
Earlier sketch in CA 1-4R
Schodt, Frederick L(owell) 1950- 132
Schoebaum, S(amuel) 1927- CANR-28
Schoeck, Richard J(oseph) 1920- CANR-5
Earlier sketch in CA 1-4R
Schoeffler, Oscar E(dmund) 1899-1979 73-76
Obituary 85-88
Schoeman, Karel 1939- 101
Schoemperlen, Diane 1954- 133
Schoen, Barbara 1924- 21-24R
See also SATA 13
Schoen, Elin 1945- 101
Schoen, Juliet P. 1923- 69-72
Schoenbach, Carrie 1928- 120
Schoenbaum, S(amuel) 1927- 107
Schoenbaum, Thomas John 1939- 104
Schoenberg, Arnold 1874-1951 Brief entry 109
Schoenberg, B(ernhardt) Mark 1928- 97-100
Schoenberg, Bernard 1927-1979 .... CANR-2
Obituary 85-88
Earlier sketch in CA 45-48
Schoenberg, Ronald 1942- 126
Schoenberg, Wilfred Paul 1915- 9-12R
Schoenberger, Guido L.
1891-1974 Obituary 53-56
Schoenberger, Nancy 1950- 126
Schoenberger, Walter Smith 1920- 29-32R
Schoenberner, Franz 1892-1970 Obituary 104
Schoenbohm, Wilko B. 1913- 17-20R
Schoenbrun, David (Franz) 1915-1988 ..... CANR-3
Obituary 125
Earlier sketch in CA 49-52
Schoendoerffer, Pierre 1928- Brief entry 111
Schoenewolf, Gerald 1941- 136
Schoenfeld, Clarence Albert 1918- CANR-6
Earlier sketch in CA 1-4R
Schoenfeld, David 1923- CANR-12
Earlier sketch in CA 17-20R
Schoenfeld, Eugene 1935- Brief entry 118
Schoenfeld, Hanns Martin W(alter)
1928- CANR-6
Earlier sketch in CA 57-60
Schoenfeld, Maxwell Philip 1936- 33-36R
Schoenfield, Allen 1896(?)-1979 Obituary 85-88
Schoenherr, John (Carl) 1935- 136
See also MAICYA
See also SAAS 13
See also SATA 37, 66
Schoenherr, Karl 1867-1943 .... DLB 118
Schoenherr, Richard Anthony 1935- CANR-21
Earlier sketch in CA 29-32R
Schoenholtz, Larry 1948- 57-60
Schoenman, Ralph 1935- 25-28R
Schoenstein, Paul 1902-1974 Obituary 89-92
Schoenstein, Ralph 1933- 13-16R
Schoenwald, Richard L. 1927- 17-20R
Schoep, Arthur Paul 1920- 53-56
Schoepfer, Virginia B. 1934- 33-36R
Schoepflin, George A. 1939- 29-32R
Schoeps, Hans-Joachim 1909- Brief entry 106
Schoeps, Karl-Heinz 1935- CANR-24
Earlier sketch in CA 107
Schoer, Lowell A(ugust) 1931- 29-32R
Schoeser, Mary 1950- 133
Schoettle, Lynn 49-52
Schofer, Lawrence 1940- 77-80
Schoffman, Nachum 1930- 137
Schofield, B(rian) B(etham) 1895-1984 ..... 21-24R
Obituary 114
Schofield, (Edward) Guy
1902-1990 Obituary 131
Schofield, J(ohn) N(oel)
1899-1986 Obituary 120
Schofield, Jonathan
See Streib, Dan(iel Thomas)
Schofield, Mary Anne 1948- 124
Schofield, Michael 1919- CANR-14
Earlier sketch in CA 41-44R
Schofield, Paul
See Tubb, E(dwin) C(harles)
Schofield, Sylvia Anne 1918- CANR-13
Earlier sketch in CA 73-76
Schofield, W(ilfred) B(orden) 1927- 134
Schofield, William G(reenough) 1909- CANR-2
Earlier sketch in CA 5-8R
Schofield, William 1921- 9-12R
Scholastica, Sister Mary
See Jenkins, Marie M(agdalen)
Scholberg, Henry 1921- 77-80
Scholderer, Victor 1880-1971 Obituary 104
Scholefield, A. T.
See Scholefield, Alan
Scholefield, Alan 1931- CANR-34
Earlier sketch in CA 97-100
See also SATA 66
Scholefield, Edmund O.
See Butterworth, W(illiam) E(dmund III)
Scholem, Gershom (Gerhard)
1897-1982 .... CANR-39
Obituary 106
Earlier sketch in CA 45-48
Scholer, David M(ilton) 1938- 101
Scholes, Katherine 1959- 123
Scholes, Marie V(ielmetti) 1916- 29-32R
Scholes, Robert (Edward) 1929- CANR-14
Earlier sketch in CA 9-12R
Scholes, Walter V(inton) 1916-1975 .... CAP-2
Earlier sketch in CA 29-32
Scholey, Arthur 1932- 93-96
See also SATA 28
Scholl, John 1922- 9-12R
Scholl, Lisette 1945- 89-92
Scholl, Sharon L. 1932- 41-44R
Scholl, William M(athias)
1882-1968 Obituary 113
Scholt, Grayce 1925- 104
Scholtz, William 1916- 5-8R
Scholz, Albert A(ugust) 1899- CAP-2
Earlier sketch in CA 29-32
Scholz, Carter 1953- 119
Scholz, Jackson Volney 1897-1986 .... 5-8R
Obituary 120
See also SATA 49
Scholz, William 1916- 5-8R
Schom, Alan 1937- 128
Schomaker, Mary Zimmeth 1928- 108
Schomp, Gerald 1937- 29-32R
Schon, Donald A(lan) 1930- 17-20R
Schon, Isabel 1940- 110
See also HW
Schonberg, Arnold
See Schoenberg, Arnold
Schonberg, Harold C(harles) 1915- 112
Schonberg, Rosalyn Krokover
1913(?)-1973 Obituary 41-44R
Schonberger, Richard J. 1937- 110
Schonborg, Virginia 1913- 77-80
Schone, Virginia 97-100
See also SATA 22
Schonell, Fred(erick) Joyce 1900-1969 .... CANR-2
Earlier sketch in CA 1-4R
Schonfeld, William R(ost) 1942- CANR-17
Earlier sketch in CA 37-40R
Schonfield, Hugh J(oseph) 1901-1988 .... 9-12R
Obituary 124
Schongut, Emanuel 1936- .... SATA 36, 52
Schooler, Carmi 1933- 114
Schooler, (Seward) Dean Jr. 1941- 73-76
Schoolfield, George C(larence) 1925- CANR-6
Earlier sketch in CA 1-4R
Schoolland, Marian M(argaret) 1902- CANR-2
Earlier sketch in CA 5-8R
Schoonhoven, Calvin R(obert) 1931- 21-24R
Schoonmaker, Alan N. 1936- 25-28R
Schoonmaker, Ann 1928- 73-76
Schoonmaker, Frank 1905-1976 Obituary 61-64
Schoonover, Frank (Earle) 1877-1972 106
See also SATA 24
Schoonover, Jason 1946- 129
Schoonover, Lawrence Lovell
1906-1980 .... CANR-4
Obituary 97-100
Earlier sketch in CA 1-4R
Schoonover, Melvin E(ugene)
1926- Brief entry 114
Schoonover, Shirley 1936- 77-80
Schoonover, Thelma I(rene) 1907- 41-44R
Schoonover, Thomas D(avid) 1936- 120
Schoor, Gene 1921- CANR-29
Earlier sketch in CA 29-32R
See also SATA 3
Schopenhauer, Arthur 1788-1860 .... DLB 90
Schopenhauer, Johanna 1766-1838 .... DLB 90
Schopf, J(ames) William 1941- 133
Schopflin, George A.
See Schoepflin, George A.
Schor, Amy 1954- 105
Schor, Lynda 1938- 73-76
Schor, Naomi 1943- CANR-16
Earlier sketch in CA 89-92
Schor, Sandra (M.) 1932(?)-1990 Obituary 132
See also CLC 65
Schorb, E(dwin) M(arsh) 1940- 61-64
Schorer, Mark 1908-1977 .... CANR-7
Obituary 73-76
Earlier sketch in CA 5-8R
See also CLC 9
See also DLB 103
Schorr, Alan Edward 1945- 85-88

Schorr, Alvin L. 1921- CANR-15
Earlier sketch in CA 29-32R
Schorr, Daniel (Louis) 1916- 65-68
See also AITN 2
Schorr, Jerry 1934- 29-32R
Schorr, Lisbeth B. 1931- 136
Schorr, Mark 1953- 122
Schorsch, Ismar 1935- Brief entry 115
Schorske, Carl E(mil) 1915- 85-88
Schosberg, Paul A. 1938- 13-16R
Schossberger, Emily Maria
1905-1979 Obituary 104
Schott, Jeffrey J. 1949- 126
Schott, John R(obert) 1936- CANR-7
Earlier sketch in CA 57-60
Schott, Penelope Scambly 1942- 77-80
Schott, Richard Lockwood 1939- 117
Schott, Webster 1927- 49-52
Schottenfeld, Barbara 134
Schottland, Charles Irwin 1906- 13-16R
Schouler, James 1839-1920 .... DLB 47
Schowalter, John E(rwin) 1936- 109
Schoyer, B. Preston
1912(?)-1978 Obituary 77-80
Schrader, Constance 1933- CANR-18
Earlier sketch in CA 101
Schrader, George A(lfred) Jr. 1917- 21-24R
Schrader, Paul Joseph 1946- 37-40R
See also CLC 26
See also DLB 44
Schrader, Richard James 1941- 85-88
Schrader, Robert F(ay) 1931- 119
Schraff, Anne E(laine) 1939- CANR-39
Earlier sketches in CA 49-52, CANR-1, 17
See also SATA 27
Schraff, Francis Nicholas 1937- 101
Schraffenberger, Nancy 1933- CANR-16
Earlier sketch in CA 93-96
Schrag, Adele Frisbie 1921- 105
Schrag, Calvin Orville 1928- CANR-1
Earlier sketch in CA 1-4R
Schrag, Oswald O. 1916- 49-52
Schrag, Peter 1931- CANR-8
Earlier sketch in CA 13-16R
Schrag, Philip G(ordon) 1943- 102
Schrager, Jeanne Hart 1919- 127
Schram, Martin 1942- CANR-13
Earlier sketch in CA 69-72
Schram, Stuart R(eynolds) 1924- 97-100
Schramm, David N(orman) 1945- 135
Schramm, Percy Ernst 1894-1970 Obituary 104
Schramm, Richard (Howard) 1934- 41-44R
Schramm, Sarah Slavin 1942- 93-96
Schramm, Wilbur (Lang) 1907-1987 .... CANR-22
Obituary 124
Earlier sketch in CA 105
Schrank, Jeffrey 1944- 29-32R
Schrank, Joseph 1900-1984 .... CANR-20
Obituary 112
Earlier sketch in CA 5-8R
See also SATA 38
Schreck, Alan (Edward) 1951- 124
Schreck, Everett M. 1897- CAP-2
Earlier sketch in CA 33-36
Schrecker, John (Ernest) 1937- Brief entry 112
Schreiber, Daniel 1909-1981 .... CAP-1
Obituary 103
Earlier sketch in CA 13-14
Schreiber, Elizabeth Anne (Ferguson)
1947- 69-72
See also SATA 13
Schreiber, Flora Rheta 1918-1988 .... CANR-11
Obituary 127
Earlier sketch in CA 53-56
See also AITN 1
Schreiber, Georges 1904-1977 Obituary 109
See also SATA 29
Schreiber, Hermann (Otto Ludwig)
1920- CANR-36
Earlier sketch in CA 25-28R
Schreiber, Jan 1941- 65-68
Schreiber, Jean-Jacques Servan
See Servan-Schreiber, Jean-Jacques
Schreiber, Le Anne 1945- .... BEST 90:2
Schreiber, Mark 1960- 116
Schreiber, Michael 1937- 116
Schreiber, Ralph W(alter) 1942- 69-72
See also SATA 13
Schreiber, Ron 1934- 41-44R
Schreiber, Ted
See Schreiber, V. Theodore
Schreiber, V. Theodore 1905-1986 124
Schreiber, Vernon R(oy) 1925- 61-64
Schreiber-Wicke, Edith 1943- 123
Schreider, Frank(lin David) 1924- 5-8R
Schreiner, George F(rederic) 1949- 117
Schreiner, Lee
See Schreiner, George F(rederic)
Schreiner, Olive (Emilie Albertina)
1855-1920 Brief entry 105
See also DLB 18
See also TCLC 9
Schreiner, Samuel A(gnew) Jr. 1921- CANR-26
Earlier sketches in CA 65-68, CANR-9
See also SATA 70
Schreiner-Mann, Joan 1939- 45-58
Schreiter, Rick 1936- 21-24R
Schreivogel, Paul A. 1930- 25-28R
Schrepfer, Susan R(ita) 1941- 117
Schreuder, D(eryck) M(arshall) 1942- 120
Schreyer, George M(aurice) 1913- 5-8R
Schriber, Mary Suzanne 1938- 126
Schrier, Arnold 1925- 49-52
Schrier, Nettie Vander
See Vander-Schrier, Nettie
Schrier, William 1900-1973 .... 41-44R
Schrift, Shirley 1922(?)- 113
Brief entry 110
Schriftgiesser, Karl (John) 1903-1988 .... CAP-1
Obituary 126
Earlier sketch in CA 11-12
Schrire, Theodore 1906- 21-24R
Schrock, Simon 1938- 113
Schroder, Amund A. Schulze 1925- CANR-5
Earlier sketch in CA 13-16R
Schroder, John Henry Erle 1895- CAP-1
Earlier sketch in CA 13-14
Schrodinger, Erwin
See Schroedinger, Erwin
Schrodt, Philip A(ndrew) 1951- 111
Schroedel, Jean Reith 1951- 122
Schroeder, Alan 1961- 133
See also SATA 66
Schroeder, Albert H(enry) 1914- CANR-14
Earlier sketch in CA 41-44R
Schroeder, Andreas (Peter) 1946- CANR-37
Earlier sketches in CA 93-96, CANR-16
See also DLB 53
Schroeder, Binette
See Nickl, Barbara (Elisabeth)
See also SATA 56
Schroeder, David 1924- 21-24R
Schroeder, Eric 1904- CAP-1
Earlier sketch in CA 13-14
Schroeder, Fred E(rich) H(arald) 1932- 41-44R
Schroeder, Frederick W(illiam) 1896- 1-4R
Schroeder, Henry A(lfred) 1906-1975 .... CAP-2
Earlier sketch in CA 25-28
Schroeder, John H(erman) 1943- 49-52
Schroeder, Manfred (Robert) 1926- 138
Schroeder, Mary 1903- 73-76
Schroeder, Oliver Charles Jr. 1916- CANR-30
Earlier sketch in CA 110
Schroeder, Paul Walter 1927- 5-8R
Schroeder, Ted 1931(?)-1973 .... SATA 20
Schroeder, W(illiam) Widick
1928- Brief entry 111
Schroedinger, Erwin 1887-1961 Obituary 113
Schroeter, James 1927- 21-24R
Schroeter, Louis C(larence) 1929- 29-32R
Schroetter, Hilda Noel 1917- 29-32R
Schroll, Herman T(heodore III) 1946- 33-36R
Schruben, Francis W(illiam) 1918- 45-48
Schruth, Peter Elliott 1917-1979 Obituary 89-92
Schubart, Christian Friedrich Daniel
1739-1791 .... DLB 97
Schubart, Mark Allen 1918- 105
Schubel, J(erry) R(obert) 1936- 126
Schubert, Delwyn George 1919- 9-12R
Schubert, Dieter 1947- CANR-28
Earlier sketch in CA 111
See also SATA 62
Schubert, Glendon 1918- CANR-21
Earlier sketches in CA 5-8R, CANR-6
Schubert, Gotthilf Heinrich 1780-1860 .... DLB 90
Schubert, Kurt 1923- 5-8R
Schubert-Gabrys, Ingrid 1953- CANR-28
Earlier sketch in CA 111
See also SATA 62
Schuberth, Christopher J. 1933- CANR-18
Earlier sketch in CA 25-28R
Schuchman, Joan 1934- 101
Schuck, Peter H. 129
Schudson, Charles B(enjamin) 1950- 130
Schudson, Michael 1946- CANR-19
Earlier sketch in CA 101
Schueler, Donald G(ustave) 1929- 106
Schuerer, Ernst 1933- CANR-37
Earlier sketches in CA 45-48, CANR-1, 17
Schuessler, Hermann E.
1929(?)-1975 Obituary 61-64
Schuessler, Karl F(rederick) 1915- 105
Schuettinger, Robert Lindsay 1936- 33-36R
Schuetz, John Howard 1933- 97-100
Schuetze, Armin William 1917- 57-60
Schug, Willis E(rvin) 1924- 49-52
Schuh, Dwight R(aymond) 1945- 101
Schuh, G(eorge) Edward 1930- CANR-30
Earlier sketch in CA 29-32R
Schuker, Stephen Alan 1939- 69-72
Schul, Bill D(ean) 1928- CANR-8
Earlier sketch in CA 61-64
Schulberg, Budd (Wilson) 1914- CANR-19
Earlier sketch in CA 25-28R
See also CLC 7, 48
See also DLB 6, 26, 28
See also DLBY 81
Schulberg, Herbert C(harles) 1934- CANR-8
Earlier sketch in CA 61-64
Schulberg, Stuart 1922-1979 Obituary 89-92
Schulder, Diane Blossom 1937- 37-40R
Schuler, Carol Ann 1946- 106
Schuler, Edgar A(lbert) 1905- CAP-2
Earlier sketch in CA 23-24
Schuler, Stanley Carter 1915- CANR-5
Earlier sketch in CA 5-8R
Schulian, John 1945- 129
Schulke, Flip Phelps Graeme 1930- CANR-22
Earlier sketch in CA 105
See also SATA 57
Schulkind, Eugene (Walter) 1923- 97-100
Schull, (John) Joseph 1916-1980 .... CANR-8
Earlier sketch in CA 53-56
Schuller, Gunther 1925- CANR-28
Earlier sketch in CA 69-72
Schuller, Robert (Harold) 1926- CANR-14
Earlier sketch in CA 9-12R
Schullery, Paul (David) 1948- CANR-30
Earlier sketch in CA 111
Schulman, Arnold 1925- 103
Schulman, Bob
See Schulman, Robert
Schulman, Grace 65-68
Schulman, Helen 1961- 128
Schulman, Ivan A(lbert) 1931- 131
Schulman, J(oseph) Neil 1953- 89-92
Schulman, Janet 1933- 101
See also SATA 22
Schulman, L(ester) M(artin) 1934- CANR-12
Earlier sketch in CA 33-36R
See also SATA 13
Schulman, Michael D. 1948- 137
Schulman, Robert 1916- 77-80
Schulman, Rosalind 1914- 41-44R
Schulman, Sam 1924- 45-48
Schulman, Sarah 1958- 118
Schulman, Tom 1951(?)- 133
Schulmerich, Alma 1902(?)-1985 Obituary 115
Schulte, Elaine L(ouise) 1934- CANR-28
Earlier sketches in CA 73-76, CANR-12
See also SATA 36
Schulte, Henry F(rank) 1924- 25-28R
Schulte, Paul C(larence)
1890-1984 Obituary 112
Schulte, Rainer 21-24R
Schultes, Richard Evans 1915- CANR-25
Earlier sketch in CA 108
Schultheis, Rob 1943- 111
Schulthess, Emil 1913- 65-68
Schults, Raymond L. 1926- 105
Schultz, Barbara A. 117
Schultz, Barbara 1923- 21-24R
Schultz, Dodi 1930- CANR-36
Earlier sketches in CA 45-48, CANR-1, 16
Schultz, Donald O. 1939- CANR-17
Earlier sketch in CA 25-28R
Schultz, Duane P(hilip) 1934- 29-32R
Schultz, Ed 1933- 45-48
Schultz, Edna Moore 1912- 13-16R
Schultz, Edward W(illiam) 1936- CANR-1
Earlier sketch in CA 45-48
Schultz, George F(ranklin) 1908- CAP-2
Earlier sketch in CA 19-20
Schultz, George J(oseph) 1932- Brief entry 109
Schultz, Gerard 1902-1974 Obituary 110
Schultz, Gladys Denny
1896(?)-1984 Obituary 113
Schultz, Gwendolyn 65-68
See also SATA 21
Schultz, Harold John 1923- 103
Schultz, Harry D. CANR-14
Earlier sketch in CA 21-24R
Schultz, James Willard
1859-1947 Brief entry 121
See also YABC 1
Schultz, John (Ludwig) 1932- CANR-15
Earlier sketch in CA 41-44R
Schultz, Joseph P(enn) 1928- 113
Schultz, Mark 1935- 116
Schultz, Mort(on) J(oel) 1930- CANR-28
Earlier sketches in CA 73-76, CANR-12
Schultz, Pearle Henriksen 1918- CANR-1
Earlier sketch in CA 49-52
See also SATA 21
Schultz, Philip 1945- 104
Schultz, Samuel J(acob) 1914- CANR-12
Earlier sketch in CA 25-28R
Schultz, Sigrid (Lillian)
1893-1980 Obituary 97-100
Schultz, Stanley K(enton) 1938- Brief entry 116
Schultz, Terri 1946- CANR-10
Earlier sketch in CA 65-68
Schultz, Theodore William 1902- 85-88
Schultz, Vernon B(urdette) 1924- 9-12R
Schultze, Charles L(ouis) 1924- Brief entry 114
Schultze, William Andrew 1937- 37-40R
Schulz, Ann Tibbitts 1938- 116
Schulz, Anne Markham 1938- 121
Schulz, Bruno 1892-1942 123
Brief entry 115
See also TCLC 5
Schulz, Charles M(onroe) 1922- CANR-6
Earlier sketch in CA 9-12R
See also CLC 12
See also SATA 10
Schulz, Clare Elmore 1924- 13-16R
Schulz, David A. 1933- CANR-30
Earlier sketch in CA 29-32R
Schulz, Ernst B(ernhard) 1896- 73-76
Schulz, Florence 1908- CAP-2
Earlier sketch in CA 21-22
Schulz, James Henry 1936- 89-92
Schulz, John E. 1939- 29-32R
Schulz, Juergen 1927- 41-44R
Schulz, Max F(rederick) 1923- 5-8R
Schulz, Phillip Stephen 1946- 123
Schulz-Behrend, George 1913- 45-48
Schulze, Franz 1927- 125
Schulze, Gene 1912- 85-88
Schulze, Hertha 1935- 122
Schulzinger, Robert D(avid) 1945- 61-64
Schumacher, Alvin J. 1928- 13-16R
Schumacher, Ernst Friedrich
1911-1977 .... CANR-34
Obituary 73-76
Earlier sketch in CA 81-84
Schumacher, John N(orbert Jr.) 1927- 131
Schuman, Ben N. 1923- 17-20R
Schuman, David Feller 1942- CANR-17
Earlier sketch in CA 97-100
Schuman, Frederick Lewis 1904-1981 45-48
Obituary 135
Schuman, Howard 1928- 124
Schuman, Patricia Glass 1943- CANR-14
Earlier sketch in CA 33-36R
Schumann, Elizabeth Creighton 1907- CAP-1
Earlier sketch in CA 11-12
Schumann, Paul L. 1955- 112
Schumm, Ruth Frances
1921-1988 Obituary 125
Schuon, Frithjof 1907- CANR-13
Earlier sketch in CA 73-76
Schuon, Karl Albert 1913-1984 .... 13-16R
Obituary 114
Schur, Edwin M(ichael) 1930- CANR-7
Earlier sketch in CA 13-16R
Schur, Maxine
See Schur, Maxine Rose
Schur, Maxine Rose 1948- 129
See also SATA 49, 53
Schur, Norman W(arren) 1907- CANR-37
Earlier sketches in CA 41-44R, CANR-17
Schurer, Ernst
See Schuerer, Ernst
Schurer, Leopold (Sidney) Launitz Jr.
See Launitz-Schurer, Leopold (Sidney) Jr.
Schurfranz, Vivian 1925- 61-64
See also SATA 13
Schurke, Paul 1955- 126
Schurmacher, Emile C.
1903(?)-1976 Obituary 69-72
Schurman, D(onald) M. 1924- 37-40R
Schurr, Cathleen 9-12R
Schurz, Carl 1829-1906 .... DLB 23
Schuschnigg, Kurt von
See von Schuschnigg, Kurt
Schusky, Ernest L(ester) 1931- CANR-8
Earlier sketch in CA 17-20R
Schuster, George 1873-1972 Obituary 37-40R
Schuster, George 1881-1982 Obituary 107
Schuster, Louis A. 1916- 13-16R
Schuster, Max Lincoln
1897-1970 Obituary 29-32R
Schutte, William Metcalf 1919- 5-8R
Schutz, Anton Friedrich Joseph
1894-1977 81-84
Obituary 73-76
Schutz, Benjamin Merrill 1949- 107
Schutz, John Adolph 1919- 5-8R
Schutz, John Howard
See Schuetz, John Howard
Schutz, Susan Polis 1944- 105
Schutz, Wallace J. 1908- 135
Schutz, Wilhelm Wolfgang 1911- 25-28R
Schutz, William C(arl) 1925- CANR-10
Earlier sketch in CA 25-28R
Schutze, Gertrude 1917- 17-20R
Schutze, Jim 1946- 123
Schutzer, A. I. 1922- 25-28R
See also SATA 13
Schutzman, Steven 1947- 114
Schuyler, David 1950- 126
Schuyler, George Samuel 1895-1977 81-84
Obituary 73-76
See also BW
See also DLB 29, 51
Schuyler, James Marcus 1923-1991 101
Obituary 134
See also CLC 5, 23
See also DLB 5
Schuyler, Jane 1943- 65-68
Schuyler, Joseph B(ernard) 1921- 1-4R
Schuyler, Judy
See Eshbach, Lloyd Arthur
Schuyler, Keith C. 1919- CANR-12
Earlier sketch in CA 29-32R
Schuyler, Pamela R. 1948- 106
See also SATA 30
Schuyler, Philippa Duke 1934-1967 .... 5-8R
See also BW
Schuyler, Robert Livingston 1883-1966 .... CAP-1
Earlier sketch in CA 11-12
Schvaneveldt, Jay D. 1937- 103
Schvey, Henry I(van) 1948- 133
Schwab, Arnold T. 1922- 9-12R
Schwab, George 1931- CANR-37
Earlier sketches in CA 45-48, CANR-1, 16
Schwab, James C. 1949- 128
Schwab, Jim
See Schwab, James C.
Schwab, John J. 1923- 85-88
Schwab, Joseph J(ackson) 1909- CANR-5
Earlier sketch in CA 5-8R
Schwab, Paul Josiah 1894-1966 .... 5-8R
Obituary 103
Schwab, Peter 1940- CANR-14
Earlier sketch in CA 41-44R
Schwabacher, Ethel K(remer)
1903-1984 Obituary 114
Schwabe, William
See Cassidy, William L(awrence Robert)
Schwaber, Paul 1936- 13-16R
Schwadron, Abraham A(be)
1925-1987 Obituary 123
Schwalberg, Carol(yn Ernestine Stein)
1930- 69-72
Schwaller, John Frederick 1948- 126
Schwamm, Ellen 1934- 122
Schwandt, Stephen (William) 1947- 126
See also SATA 61
Schwardberg, Guenther 1926- 130
Schwark, Mary Beth 1954- .... SATA 51
Schwartz, Al(bert) 1911(?)-1988 Obituary 125
Schwartz, Alfred 1922- 17-20R
Schwartz, Alvin 1927- CANR-24
Obituary 137
Earlier sketches in CA 13-16R, CANR-7
See also CLR 3
See also MAICYA
See also SATA 4, 56, 71
Schwartz, Amy 1954- CANR-29
Earlier sketch in CA 110
See also CLR 25
See also SATA 41, 47
Schwartz, Anna J(acobson) 1915- 125

Schwartz, Anne Powers 1913- CANR-1
Earlier sketch in CA 1-4R
See also SATA 10
Schwartz, Arthur Nathaniel 1922- CANR-28
Earlier sketches in CA 61-64, CANR-8
Schwartz, Audrey James 1928- 89-92
Schwartz, Barry N. 1942- 33-36R
Schwartz, Barry 1938- 77-80
Schwartz, Benjamin I. 1916- 13-16R
Schwartz, Bernard (Sherman) 1945- 106
Schwartz, Bernard 1923- Brief entry 117
Schwartz, Bertie G.
1901(?)-1976 Obituary 69-72
Schwartz, Betty 1927- 93-96
Schwartz, Charles 73-76
Schwartz, Charles W(alsh) 1914- 13-16R
See also SATA 8
Schwartz, Daniel (Bennet) 1929- ....SATA 29
Schwartz, David C. 1939- 37-40R
Schwartz, David (E.) 1916-1989 Obituary 130
Schwartz, David J(oseph) Jr. 1927- CANR-13
Earlier sketch in CA 17-20R
Schwartz, David M(artin) 1951- 118
See also SATA 59
Schwartz, Delmore (David)
1913-1966 ....CANR-35
Obituary 25-28R
Earlier sketches in CAP-2, CA 17-18
See also CLC 2, 4, 10, 45
See also DLB 28, 48
See also MTCW
Schwartz, Donald E(dward)
1930-1988 Obituary 127
Schwartz, Douglas W(right) 1929- CANR-17
Earlier sketch in CA 25-28R
Schwartz, Eleanor Brantley 1937- 57-60
Schwartz, Eli 1921- CANR-34
Earlier sketch in CA 1-4R
Schwartz, Elias 1923- 41-44R
Schwartz, Elizabeth Reeder 1912- 13-16R
See also SATA 8
Schwartz, Elkanah 1937- 21-24R
Schwartz, Elliott S. 1936- 13-16R
Schwartz, Emanual K. 1912-1973 ....37-40R
Obituary 41-44R
Schwartz, Ernst
See Ozu, Yasujiro
Schwartz, Eugene M. 1927- 13-16R
Schwartz, Gail Garfield 117
Schwartz, George Leopold
1891-1983 Obituary 109
Schwartz, George R. 1942- CANR-17
Earlier sketch in CA 97-100
Schwartz, George 1908-1974 Obituary 104
Schwartz, Gerald 1932- 120
Schwartz, Harry W. 1903(?)-1984 Obituary 114
Schwartz, Helen 1935- 111
Schwartz, Helene E(nid) 1941- 65-68
Schwartz, Hillel 1948- CANR-20
Earlier sketch in CA 102
Schwartz, Howard 1945- CANR-22
Earlier sketches in CA 49-52, CANR-5
Schwartz, Israel J(acob)
1885-1971 Obituary 33-36R
Schwartz, Jerome
See Lawrence, Jerome
Schwartz, Joel L. 1940- 121
See also SATA 51, 54
Schwartz, John Burnham 1965- 132
See also CLC 59
Schwartz, Jonathan 1938- 97-100
See also DLBY 82
Schwartz, Joseph 1925- 33-36R
Schwartz, Julius 1907- 109
See also SATA 45
Schwartz, K(arlene) V. 1936- 104
Schwartz, Kessel 1920- CANR-6
Earlier sketch in CA 1-4R
Schwartz, Larry 1922- 53-56
Schwartz, Laurens R. 1951- 127
Schwartz, Leon 1922- 113
Schwartz, Lester J(erome) 1927- 113
Schwartz, Lewis M(arvin) 1935- 45-48
Schwartz, Lita Linzer 1930- 29-32R
Schwartz, Lloyd 1941- 112
Schwartz, Lois C. 1935- 33-36R
Schwartz, Loretta 1943- 97-100
Schwartz, Louis B. 1913- 21-24R
Schwartz, Lynne Sharon 1939- 103
See also CLC 31
Schwartz, Martin D(avid) 1945- 118
Schwartz, Michael 1942- 113
Schwartz, Mildred A(nne) 1932- CANR-9
Earlier sketch in CA 21-24R
Schwartz, Morris S. 1916- 17-20R
Schwartz, Mortimer (Donald) 1922- 116
Schwartz, Muriel A.
See Eliot, T(homas) S(tearns)
Schwartz, Murray M. 1942- 116
Schwartz, Nancy Lynn 1952-1978 107
Schwartz, Ned 1948- 107
Schwartz, Norman B(oris) 1932- 111
Schwartz, Paula 1925- CANR-18
Earlier sketch in CA 85-88
Schwartz, Pedro 1935- CANR-24
Earlier sketch in CA 107
Schwartz, Pepper 1945- 33-36R
Schwartz, Richard B. 1941- CANR-15
Earlier sketch in CA 85-88
Schwartz, Richard D(erecktor) 1925- CANR-6
Earlier sketch in CA 1-4R
Schwartz, Ronald 1937- 65-68
Schwartz, S.
See Starr, S(tephen) Frederick
Schwartz, Selwyn S.
1907(?)-1988 Obituary 125
Schwartz, Sheila (Ruth) 1929- CANR-30
Earlier sketches in CA 25-28R, CANR-11
See also SATA 27
Schwartz, Shloime
See Schwartz, Selwyn S.
Schwartz, Stephan A(ndrew) 1942- 130
Schwartz, Stephen (Lawrence) 1948- 85-88
See also SATA 19
Schwartz, Steven 1950- 118
Schwartz, Stuart B. 1940- 126
Brief entry 108
Schwartz, William 1916-1982 Obituary 107
Schwartzberg, Julie 1943- 29-32R
Schwartzman, Aaron
1900(?)-1981 Obituary 102
Schwartzman, David 1924- 41-44R
Schwartzman, Edward 1927- 73-76
Schwartzman, Sylvan D(avid) 1913- CANR-21
Earlier sketch in CA 41-44R
Schwartzmann, Mischa 1919- 29-32R
Schwarz, Alfred 1925- Brief entry 118
Schwarz, Boris 1906-1983 ....CANR-29
Obituary 111
Earlier sketch in CA 37-40R
Schwarz, Daniel R(oger) 1941- 131
Schwarz, Egon 1922- 57-60
Schwarz, Fred(erick) Charles 1913- CANR-32
Earlier sketch in CA 1-4R
Schwarz, Hans 1939- 41-44R
Schwarz, Henry G(uenter) 1928- 37-40R
Schwarz, Jack
See Schwarz, Jacob
Schwarz, Jacob 1924- 103
Schwarz, Jordan A(braham) 1937- 105
Schwarz, Karen 1957- 138
Schwarz, Leo W(alder) 1906-1967 ....5-8R
Schwarz, Liese O'Halloran 1963- 133
Schwarz, Richard W(illiam) 1925- CANR-12
Earlier sketch in CA 29-32R
Schwarz, Robert 1921- 77-80
Schwarz, Solomon M.
1882(?)-1973 Obituary 45-48
Schwarz, Ted
See Schwarz, Theodore R. Jr.
Schwarz, Theodore R. Jr. 1945- CANR-26
Earlier sketches in CA 65-68, CANR-10
Schwarz, Walter 1930- 13-16R
Schwarz, Wilhelm Johannes 1929- 65-68
Schwarz-Bart, Andre 1928- 89-92
See also CLC 2, 4
Schwarz-Bart, Simone 1938- 97-100
See also CLC 7
Schwarzenberger, Georg 1908- 13-16R
Schwarzenegger, Arnold 1947- CANR-21
Earlier sketch in CA 81-84
Schwarzkopf, LeRoy C(arl) 1920- CANR-38
Earlier sketch in CA 115
Schwarzkopf-Legge, Elisabeth 1915- 109
Schwarzschild, Bettina 1925- 29-32R
Schwarzschild, Stuart 1918- 5-8R
Schwarzweller, Harry K(arl) 1929- 37-40R
Schwebel, Milton 1914- 17-20R
Schwebel, Stephen M(yron) 1929- 77-80
Schwebell, Gertrude C(lorius) 9-12R
Schwed, Peter 1911- CANR-31
Earlier sketches in CA 57-60, CANR-13
Schweickart, Patrocinio P. 1942- 138
Schweid, Eliezer 1929- CANR-18
Earlier sketches in CA 45-48, CANR-1
Schweid, Richard M. 1946- 106
Schweik, Robert C(harles) 1927- CANR-31
Earlier sketch in CA 45-48
Schweikart, Larry (Earl) 1951- 134
Schweitzer, Albert 1875-1965 Obituary 93-96
Schweitzer, Arthur 1905- 9-12R
Schweitzer, Byrd Baylor
See Baylor, Byrd
Schweitzer, Christoph E(ugen)
1922- Brief entry 107
Schweitzer, Darrell 1952- CANR-39
Earlier sketch in CA 116
Schweitzer, George K(eene) 1924- 17-20R
Schweitzer, Gertrude 1909- 85-88
Schweitzer, Iris Brief entry 117
See also SATA 36, 59
Schweitzer, Jerome William 1908- 41-44R
Schweitzer, John C. 1934- 17-20R
Schweizer(-Hanhart), Eduard 1913- CANR-20
Earlier sketches in CA 13-16R, CANR-5
Schweizer, Karl W. 1946- 136
Schwendeman, J(oseph) R(aymond)
1897- 81-84
Schweninger, Ann 1951- 107
See also SATA 29
Schweninger, Loren (Lance) 1941- 101
Schwerin, Doris H(alpern) 1922- CANR-9
Earlier sketch in CA 65-68
See also SATA 64
Schwerin, Kurt 1902- 45-48
Schwerner, Armand 1927- 9-12R
Schwertfeger, Ruth 1941- 132
Schwiebert, Ernest G(eorge) 1895- CAP-1
Earlier sketch in CA 13-16
Schwieder, Dorothy 1933- 89-92
Schwimmer, Walter 1903-1989 Obituary 129
Schwitzgebel, Robert L. 1934- 41-44R
Schwob, (Mayer Andre) Marcel
1867-1905 Brief entry 117
See also TCLC 20
Schwoerer, Lois G(reen) 1927- CANR-15
Earlier sketch in CA 77-80
Schydlowsky, Daniel M(oses) 1940- CANR-27
Earlier sketch in CA 45-48
Scialiano, Robert (G.) 1925- 9-12R
Sciascia, Leonardo 1921-1989 ....CANR-35
Obituary 130
Earlier sketch in CA 85-88
See also CLC 8, 9, 41
See also MTCW
Scibetta, Barbara Smith 1949- 129
Scibor-Rylski, Aleksander
1927(?)-1983 Obituary 109
Scicluna, Hannibal Publius
1880-1981(?) Obituary 106
Scieszka, Jon 1954- 135
See also CLR 27
See also SATA 68
Scifres, Bill(y N.) 1925- 103
Scimecca, Joseph A. 1940- 129
Scioscia, Mary (Hershey) 1926- ....SATA 63
Scipio
See Watson, (John Hugh) Adam
Scire
See Gardner, G(erald) B(rosseau)
Scism, Carol K. 1931- 41-44R
Scithers, George H(arry) 1929- 57-60
Scitovsky, Tibor 1910- 104
Scivener, Michael (Henry) 1948- 130
Scliar, Moacyr 1937- 136
Scoales, William 1933- 33-36R
Scobel, Donald N. 1929- 122
Scobey, Joan 1927- CANR-7
Earlier sketch in CA 57-60
Scobey, Mary-Margaret 1915- CANR-1
Earlier sketch in CA 1-4R
Scobie, James R(alston) 1929-1981 ....CANR-6
Obituary 104
Earlier sketch in CA 9-12R
Scobie, Stephen 1943- 111
Scoby, Donald R(ay) 1931- 33-36R
Scofield, Jonathan
See Levinson, Leonard
and Rothweiler, Paul Roger
and Toombs, John
Scofield, Martin (Paul) 1945- 132
Scofield, Norma Margaret Cartwright 1924- 103
Scofield, Penrod 1933- ....SATA 62
Scofield, William H. 1915- 17-20R
Scoggin, Margaret C(lara)
1905-1968 ....SATA 28, 47
Scoggins, James (Lawrence) 1934- 21-24R
Scoles, Eugene F(rancis) 1921- CANR-15
Earlier sketch in CA 37-40R
Scollan, E. A.
See O'Grady, Anne
Scolnick, Sylvan 1930(?)-1976 Obituary 69-72
Scopes, John T. 1900-1970 Obituary 29-32R
Scoppettone, Sandra 1936- 5-8R
See also CLC 26
See also SATA 9
Scorer, Richard 1919- 77-80
Scorsese, Martin 1942- 114
Brief entry 110
See also CLC 20
Scortia, Thomas N(icholas) 1926-1986 .....CANR-6
Obituary 119
Earlier sketch in CA 1-4R
Scorza, Manuel 1928-1983 131
Obituary 113
See also HW
Scorza, Thomas J. 1948- 132
Scot, Chesman
See Bulmer, (Henry) Kenneth
Scotford, John Ryland 1888-1976 ....5-8R
Obituary 103
Scotland, Andrew 1905- 5-8R
Scotland, James 1917-1983 ....CANR-36
Obituary 110
Earlier sketch in CA 33-36R
Scotland, Jay
See Jakes, John (William)
Scotson, John L(loyd) 1928-1980 ....21-24R
Obituary 134
Scotson, Linda 1945- 128
Scott
See Charlier, Roger H(enri)
Scott, A(dolphe) C(larence) 1909- CANR-2
Earlier sketch in CA 5-8R
Scott, Alastair
See Allen, Kenneth S.
Scott, Alexander 1920- 105
Scott, Allan
See Shiach, Allan G.
Scott, Allen John 1938- 97-100
Scott, Amoret (Scudamore) 1930- CANR-10
Earlier sketch in CA 21-24R
Scott, Andrew M(acKay) 1922- 17-20R
Scott, Ann Herbert 1926- 21-24R
See also SATA 29, 56
Scott, Anne Firor 1921- 33-36R
Scott, Anthony
See Dresser, Davis
Scott, Anthony Dalton 1923- CANR-29
Earlier sketches in CA 65-68, CANR-11
Scott, Arthur Finley 1907- CANR-18
Earlier sketches in CA 5-8R, CANR-2
Scott, Arthur L(incoln) 1914- 21-24R
Scott, Austin (Wakeman)
1885(?)-1981 Obituary 103
Scott, Beth (Bailey) 1922- 132
Scott, Bill
See Scott, William N(eville)
Scott, Bill 1920(?)-1985 Obituary 117
See also SATA 46
Scott, Bonnie Kime 1944- 119
Scott, C(atharine) A(my) Dawson
See Dawson-Scott, C(atharine) A(my)
Scott, C(ecil) Winfield 1905- 5-8R
Scott, Casey
See Kubis, Pat
Scott, Cecil Alexander
1902(?)-1981 Obituary 104
Scott, Charles R(alph) Jr. 1914- CANR-16
Earlier sketch in CA 89-92
Scott, Charles T. 1932- 21-24R
Scott, Charles W(esley) 1932- 116
Scott, Christopher 1930- 21-24R
Scott, Claudia 1948-1979 Obituary 114
Scott, Clinton Lee 1890- CAP-2
Earlier sketch in CA 19-20
Scott, Cora Annett (Pipitone) 1931- 17-20R
See also SATA 11
Scott, Cyril (Meir) 1879-1970 Obituary 111
Scott, Dan
See Barker, S. Omar
Scott, Dan CANR-27
Earlier sketches in CAP-2, CA 19-20
Scott, Dana
See Robertson, Constance (Pierrepont Noyes)
Scott, David (Aubrey) 1919- 109
Scott, David (Henry Tudor) 1948- 127
Scott, David W(infield) 1916- 109
Scott, Denise 114
Scott, Derek B. 1950- 137
Scott, Dixon 1881-1915 ....DLB 98
Scott, Donald F(letcher) 1930- 89-92
Scott, Dorothea Hayward 93-96
Scott, Duncan Campbell
1862-1947 Brief entry 104
See also DLB 92
See also TCLC 6
Scott, Edward M. 1919- 33-36R
Scott, Elaine 1940- CANR-21
Earlier sketch in CA 105
See also SATA 36
Scott, Eleanor 1921- 61-64
Scott, Ellis L(averne) 1915- 49-52
Scott, Eve
See Rodgers, Joann Ellison
Scott, Evelyn 1893-1963 104
Obituary 112
See also CLC 43
See also DLB 9, 48
Scott, F(rancis) R(eginald) 1899-1985 101
Obituary 114
See also CLC 22
See also DLB 88
Scott, Frances V.
See Wing, Frances (Scott)
Scott, Frank
See Scott, F(rancis) R(eginald)
Scott, Franklin D(aniel) 1901- CANR-5
Earlier sketch in CA 5-8R
Scott, Frederick George 1861-1944 ....DLB 92
Scott, Gail 1945- 127
Scott, Gavin 1936- 77-80
Scott, Geoffrey 1952- 106
Scott, George (Edwin) 1925-1988 ....29-32R
Obituary 127
Scott, George Walton 1921- 21-24R
Scott, Harold George 1925- 61-64
Scott, Harold Richard 1887- 5-8R
Scott, Harold W(illiam) 1906- 118
Scott, Harvey W. 1838-1910 ....DLB 23
Scott, Helen G. 1915(?)-1987 Obituary 124
Scott, Herbert 1931- CANR-6
Earlier sketch in CA 53-56
Scott, Hilda 1915- 124
Scott, Ira O(scar) Jr. 1918- 17-20R
Scott, J(ohn) D(ick) 1917-1980 77-80
Obituary 97-100
Scott, J(ames) M(aurice) 1906-1986 105
Obituary 118
Scott, Jack B(rown) 1928- 77-80
Scott, Jack Denton 1915- 108
See also CLR 20
See also MAICYA
See also SAAS 14
See also SATA 31
Scott, Jack S.
See Escott, Jonathan
Scott, James A. 1946- 123
Scott, James B(urton) 1926- 85-88
Scott, James C(ampbell) 1936- 29-32R
Scott, James Frazier 1934- CANR-22
Earlier sketch in CA 77-80
Scott, Jane
See McElfresh, (Elizabeth) Adeline
Scott, Jane (Harrington) 1931- ....SATA 55
Scott, Jay 1949- 133
Scott, Jean
See Muir, Marie
Scott, Jeffrey
See Usher, Shaun
Scott, Jeremy
See Dick, Kay
Scott, Joanna 1960- 126
See also CLC 50
Scott, Jody 81-84
Scott, John A. 1948- 135
Scott, John Anthony 1916- CANR-23
Earlier sketches in CA 9-12R, CANR-6
See also SATA 23
Scott, John Irving E(lias) 73-76
Obituary 133
Scott, John M(artin) 1913- CANR-25
Earlier sketches in CA 65-68, CANR-10
See also SATA 12
Scott, John (Peter) 1949- 126
Scott, John 1912-1976 ....CANR-6
Obituary 69-72
Earlier sketch in CA 5-8R
See also SATA 14
Scott, Johnie Harold 1946- CANR-14
Earlier sketch in CA 33-36R
Scott, Jonathan 1958- 132
Scott, (Henry) Joseph 1917- 57-60

Scott, Joseph Reid 1926- 41-44R
Scott, Judith Unger 1916- 5-8R
Scott, Justin CANR-26
Earlier sketch in CA 104
Scott, Kenneth J. 1933(?)-1983 Obituary 111
Scott, Kenneth 1900- CANR-26
Earlier sketches in CA 69-72, CANR-11
Scott, Lalla (McIntosh) 1893- CAP-2
Earlier sketch in CA 21-22
Scott, Latayne Colvett 1952- CANR-17
Earlier sketch in CA 97-100
Scott, Lauren
See Frentzen, Jeffrey
Scott, Laurence Prestwich
1909-1983 Obituary 110
Scott, Lloyd
See Turner, George E(ugene)
Scott, Lloyd F. 1926- 21-24R
Scott, Louise Binder 1910- CANR-4
Earlier sketch in CA 1-4R
Scott, Marcia (Adele Morse) 1943- 97-100
Scott, Margaret B(rodie) Obituary 61-64
Scott, Martin
See Gehman, Richard (Boyd)
Scott, Marvin B(ailey) 1944- Brief entry 118
Scott, Mary Jane W(ittstock) 1949- 129
Scott, Mel(lier Goodin) 1906- 29-32R
Scott, (Guthrie) Michael 1907-1983 130
Obituary 110
Scott, Michael 1924(?)-1989 Obituary 129
Scott, (Robert James) Munroe 1927- 130
Scott, Natalie Anderson 1906- CAP-2
Earlier sketch in CA 23-24
Scott, Nathan A(lexander) Jr. 1925- CANR-20
Earlier sketches in CA 9-12R, CANR-5
See also BW
Scott, Nerissa
See Ring, Elizabeth
Scott, Norford
See Rowland, D(onald) S(ydney)
Scott, Otto J. 1918- 85-88
Scott, Owen Le Grand 1898-1985 Obituary 117
Scott, P. T.
See Poage, Scott T(abor)
Scott, Patrick (Greig) 1945- 112
Scott, Paul (Mark) 1920-1978 .... CANR-33
Obituary 77-80
Earlier sketch in CA 81-84
See also CLC 9, 60
See also DLB 14
See also MTCW
Scott, Peter Dale 1929- CANR-9
Earlier sketch in CA 21-24R
Scott, Peter Graham
See Graham Scott, Peter
Scott, Peter (Markham) 1909-1989 101
Obituary 129
Scott, R(obert) B(algarnie) Y(oung)
1899-1987 Obituary 124
Scott, Rachel (Ann) 1947- 103
Scott, Ralph S(amuel) 1927- 41-44R
Scott, Rebecca J(arvis) 1950- 128
Scott, Richard
See Rennert, Richard Scott
Scott, Richard A(llen) 1931- 25-28R
Scott, Robert A. 1936- 89-92
Scott, Robert Adrian
1901(?)-1972 Obituary 37-40R
Scott, Robert E(dwin) 1923- CANR-1
Earlier sketch in CA 1-4R
Scott, Robert F(alcon)
1868-1912 Brief entry 115
Scott, Robert Garth 1957- 137
Scott, Robert Haney 1927- 17-20R
Scott, Robert Ian 1931- 106
Scott, Robert Lee Jr. 1908- CAP-1
Earlier sketch in CA 11-12
Scott, Robert Lee 1928- CANR-3
Earlier sketch in CA 5-8R
Scott, Robin
See Wilson, Robin Scott
Scott, Roger (Dennis) 1939- 97-100
Scott, Ronald Bodley 1906-1982 109
Obituary 106
Scott, Ronald (Guthrie) McNair
See McNair Scott, Ronald (Guthrie)
Scott, Roney
See Gault, William Campbell
Scott, Roy Vernon 1927- CANR-1
Earlier sketch in CA 1-4R
Scott, Sally (Elisabeth) 1948- 125
See also SATA 44
Scott, Sally 1909-1978 116
See also SATA 43
Scott, Sarah 1723-1795 .... DLB 39
Scott, Sheila (Christine) 1927-1988 53-56
Obituary 126
Scott, Stanley
See Fagerstrom, Stan
Scott, Stephen E. 1948- 119
Scott, Steve
See Crawford, William (Elbert)
Scott, Stuart
See Aitken, W(illiam) R(ussell)
Scott, Tirsa Saavedra 1920- 13-16R
Scott, Tom 1918- 9-12R
See also DLB 27
Scott, Valerie
See Rowland, D(onald) S(ydney)
Scott, Virgil (Joseph) 1914- CANR-2
Earlier sketch in CA 5-8R
Scott, Virginia M(uhleman) 1945- 121
Scott, W(illiam) E(dgar) Jr. 1929- 49-52
Scott, W. N.
See Scott, William N(eville)
Scott, W(illiam) Richard 1932- 17-20R
Scott, Walter 1771-1832 .... CDBLB 1789-1832
See also DLB 93, 107, 116
See also WLC
See also YABC 2
Scott, Warwick
See Trevor, Elleston
Scott, Willard H. Jr. 1934- 109
Scott, William Abbott 1926- CANR-9
Earlier sketch in CA 5-8R
Scott, William B(utler) 1945- 126
Scott, William Bell 1811-1890 .... DLB 32
Scott, William C(lyde) 1937- 119
Scott, William G(eorge) 1926- CANR-11
Earlier sketch in CA 21-24R
Scott, William Henry 1921- 132
Scott, William N(eville) 1923- 132
Scott, William R(alph) 1918-1992 101
Obituary 136
Scott, William R(eese) 1907- 77-80
Scott, Wilson L(udlow) 1909-1983 .... CANR-34
Obituary 111
Earlier sketch in CA 45-48
Scott, Winfield H(arker) 1932-1992 .... 21-24R
Obituary 136
Scott, Winfield Townley 1910-1968 .... CANR-7
Obituary 25-28R
Earlier sketch in CA 5-8R
Scott-Giles, C(harles) W(ilfred)
1893-1982(?) Obituary 106
Scott-Heron, Gil 1949- CANR-24
Earlier sketch in CA 45-48
See also BW
See also DLB 41
Scotti, Paul C(arl) 1943- 118
Scotti, R. A. 1946- 122
Scott-James, Anne Eleanor 1913- 105
Scott-Moncrieff, David (William Hardy)
1907-1987 Obituary 123
Scott-Moncrieff, George (Irving) 1910- CAP-1
Earlier sketch in CA 11-12
Scott Moncrieff, Martha Christian 1897- 61-64
Scotto, Robert M(ichael) 1942- 57-60
Scott-Stokes, Henry J. M. 128
Brief entry 117
Scott-Taggart, John 1897-1979 Obituary 104
Scott Thorn, Ronald
See Wilkinson, Ronald
Scouten, Arthur Hawley 1910- CANR-11
Earlier sketches in CAP-1, CA 13-14
Scovel, Myra (Scott) 1905- CANR-2
Earlier sketch in CA 5-8R
Scovell, Brian (Souter) 1935- 130
Scovell, E(dith) J(oy) 1907- 136
Scovell, Jane (Frances) 1934- 116
Scoville, Herbert Jr. 1915-1985 .... 29-32R
Obituary 116
Scoville, James G(riffin) 1940- 29-32R
Scoville, Warren Candler 1913-1969 .... CANR-2
Earlier sketch in CA 1-4R
Scowcroft, Richard P(ingree) 1916- 9-12R
Scraton, Phil 1949- 128
Scriabine, Helen (Gorstrine) 1906- CANR-14
Earlier sketch in CA 21-24R
Scribner, Charles Jr. 1921- 69-72
See also SATA 13
Scribner, Charles III 1951- 126
Scribner, Joanne L. 1949- .... SATA 33
Scribner, Kimball 1917- .... SATA 63
Scribner, Sylvia 1923- 133
Scrimgeour, Gary J(ames) 1934- 108
Scrimshaw, Nevin Stewart 1918- 89-92
Scrimsher, Lila Gravatt 1897-1974 .... 1-4R
Obituary 103
See also SATA 28
Scripps, E(dward) W(yllis)
1854-1926 Brief entry 118
See also DLB 25
Scripps, James G. 1911-1986 Obituary 121
Scriven, Michael (John) 1928- CANR-14
Earlier sketch in CA 21-24R
Scriver, Bob
See Scriver, Robert MacFie
Scriver, Robert MacFie 1914- 115
Scrivner, Wilma Possien 1915- 107
Scroggins, Daniel C(oy) 1937- 33-36R
Scroggs, Robin (Jerome) 1930- 116
Scruggs, C(harles) Eugene 1937- 113
Scrum, R.
See Crumb, R(obert)
Scruton, Roger 1944- CANR-39
Earlier sketches in CA 89-92, CANR-16
Scudamore, Pauline 1936- 129
Scudder, C(leo) W(ayne) 1915- CANR-3
Earlier sketch in CA 1-4R
Scudder, Horace E(lisha)
1838-1902 Brief entry 119
See also DLB 42, 71
Scudder, Kenyon J. 1890-1977 Obituary 73-76
Scudder, Mildred Lee 1908- 9-12R
See also Lee, Mildred
Scudder, Rogers V(aughn) 1912- 17-20R
Scudder, Thayer 1930- 126
Brief entry 106
Scudder, Townsend (III)
1900-1988 Obituary 126
Scudder, Vida Dutton 1861-1954 .... DLB 71
Sculatti, (Eu)Gene 1947- 110
Scull, Andrew 1947- CANR-33
Earlier sketches in CA 81-84, CANR-15
Scull, Florence Doughty 1905- CAP-1
Earlier sketch in CA 11-12
Scullard, Howard Hayes 1903-1983 .... CANR-3
Obituary 109
Earlier sketch in CA 9-12R
Sculley, John 1939- 127
Scully, Frank 1892-1964 .... 5-8R
Scully, Gerald William 1941- 65-68
Scully, James 1937- CANR-11
Earlier sketch in CA 25-28R
Scully, Julia S(ilverman) 1929- 103
Scully, Vincent (Joseph Jr.)
1920- Brief entry 113
Scum
See Crumb, R(obert)
Scumbag, Little Bobby
See Crumb, R(obert)
Scuorzo, Herbert E(rnest) 1928- 21-24R
Scupham, John Peter 1933- CANR-9
Earlier sketch in CA 65-68
See also DLB 40
Scuro, Vincent 1951- CANR-5
Earlier sketch in CA 53-56
See also SATA 21
Scutt, Ronald 1916- 97-100
Seaberg, Stanley 1929- 21-24R
Seaborg, Glenn T(heodore) 1912- CANR-2
Earlier sketch in CA 49-52
Seabough, Ed(ward Ellis) 1932- 29-32R
Seabrook, Jeremy 1939- 108
Seabrook, John
See Hubbard, L(afayette) Ron(ald)
Seabrook, William B(uehler)
1886-1945 Brief entry 107
See also DLB 4
Seabrooke, Brenda 1941- 107
See also SATA 30
Seabury, Paul 1923-1990 Obituary 132
Brief entry 115
Seabury, Samuel 1729-1796 .... DLB 31
Seagears, Clayton B.
1902(?)-1983 Obituary 110
Seager, Allan 1906-1968 .... 5-8R
Obituary 25-28R
Seager, Ralph William 1911- CANR-6
Earlier sketch in CA 9-12R
Seager, Robert II 1924- CANR-6
Earlier sketch in CA 5-8R
Seager, Walter H(arold) T(ennant) 1938- 120
Seagle, Janet 1924- 102
Seagle, William 1898-1977 .... 5-8R
Obituary 73-76
Seagoe, May V(iolet) 1906-1980 .... CANR-10
Earlier sketch in CA 13-16R
Seagrave, Sterling 1937- 135
Brief entry 125
Seagroatt, Margaret 1920- CANR-13
Earlier sketch in CA 73-76
Seagull, Louis Martin 1941- 112
Seal, Anil 1938- 25-28R
Seal, Basil
See Kavanagh, Dan(iel)
Seale, Bobby
See Seale, Robert George
Seale, Ervin 1910(?)-1990 Obituary 130
Seale, Patrick 1930- 97-100
Seale, Robert George 1936- 110
See also BW
Seale, William 1939- CANR-7
Earlier sketch in CA 17-20R
Sealey, Bruce
See Sealey, D(onald) Bruce
Sealey, D(onald) Bruce 1929- 121
Sealey, Danguole 1931- 33-36R
Sealey, Leonard (George William) 1923- 103
Sealey, (Bertram) Raphael (Izod) 1927- 65-68
Sea-Lion
See Bennett, Geoffrey (Martin)
Sealock, Richard Burl 1907- CAP-2
Earlier sketch in CA 23-24
Sealts, Merton M(iller) Jr. 1915- 13-16R
Sealy, I(rwin) Allan 1951- 136
Sealy, I. Allan 1951- .... CLC 55
Seaman, Augusta Huiell
1879-1950 Brief entry 110
See also SATA 31
Seaman, Barbara 1935- 29-32R
Seaman, (A.) Barrett 1945- 73-76
Seaman, Don F(erris) 1935- 77-80
Seaman, Donald (Peter) 1922- Brief entry 114
Seaman, Elizabeth Cochrane
See Cochrane, Elizabeth
Seaman, Gerald Roberts 1934- 25-28R
Seaman, John E(ugene) 1932- 89-92
Seaman, L(ewis) C(harles) B(ernard)
1911- 57-60
Seaman, Sylvia S(ybil) CAP-2
Earlier sketch in CA 23-24
Seaman, William M(illard) 1907- 41-44R
Seamands, John Thompson 1916- 9-12R
Seamands, Ruth 1916- 45-48
See also SATA 9
Sear, Frank 1944- 121
Seara Vazquez, M(odesto) 1931- CANR-14
Earlier sketch in CA 17-20R
Search, Alexander
See Pessoa, Fernando (Antonio Nogueira)
Search-Light
See Frank, Waldo (David)
Searcy, Margaret Zehmer 1926- 81-84
See also SATA 39, 54
Seare, Nicholas
See Whitaker, Rod
Searight, Mary W(illiams) 1918- 29-32R
See also SATA 17
Searing, Helen E. 1933- 111
Searing, Susan Ellis 1950- 122
Searle, Humphrey 1915-1982 .... 9-12R
Obituary 106
Searle, John R(ogers) 1932- CANR-26
Earlier sketch in CA 25-28R
Searle, Kathryn Adrienne 1942- 29-32R
See also SATA 10
Searle, Leroy F(rank) 1942- 73-76
Searle, Mark 1941- 114
Searle, Ronald (William Fordham)
1920- CANR-25
Earlier sketch in CA 9-12R
See also MAICYA
See also SATA 42, 70
Searle, Verna (Ruth) 1919- 132
Searles, (William) Baird 1934- 123
Searles, Herbert L(eon) 1891- 45-48
Searls, Hank
See Searls, Henry Hunt Jr.
Searls, Henry Hunt Jr. 1922- CANR-28
Earlier sketch in CA 13-16R
Sears, David O'Keefe 1935- 29-32R
Sears, Deane
See Rywell, Martin
Sears, Donald A(lbert) 1923- CANR-6
Earlier sketch in CA 5-8R
Sears, Edward I. 1819(?)-1876 .... DLB 79
Sears, Francis W. 1898-1975 Obituary 61-64
Sears, Hal D(on) 1942- 122
Sears, Paul Bigelow 1891- 17-20R
Sears, Paul M(cCutcheon) 1920- 1-4R
Sears, Pauline Snedden 1908- 29-32R
Sears, Peter 1937- 110
Sears, Robert R(ichardson) 1908-1989 .... 17-20R
Obituary 128
Sears, Sallie 1932- 41-44R
Sears, Stephen W. 1932- 33-36R
See also SATA 4
Sears, Val 1927- 73-76
Sears, William P(aul) Jr.
1902-1976 Obituary 61-64
Seary, E(dgar) R(onald) 1908- 41-44R
Seashore, Stanley E. 1915- CANR-24
Earlier sketch in CA 33-36R
Seasoltz, R(obert) Kevin 1930- 9-12R
Seasongood, Murray 1878-1983 Obituary 109
Seat, William R(obert) Jr. 1920- 13-16R
Seaton, Beryl
See Platts, Beryl
Seaton, Don Cash(ius) 1902- CAP-1
Earlier sketch in CA 9-10
Seaton, Douglas P(aul) 1947- 107
Seaton, Frederick Andrew
1909-1974 Obituary 89-92
Seaton, George 1911-1979 105
Obituary 89-92
See also DLB 44
Seaton, Mary Ethel Obituary 53-56
Seaton, William Winston 1785-1866 .... DLB 43
Seaver, George (Fenn) 1890- CAP-1
Earlier sketch in CA 13-14
Seaver, Paul S(iddall) 1932- 29-32R
Seay, James 1939- 29-32R
Seay, Thomas A(ustin) 1942- 97-100
Sebag Montefiore, Simon
See Sebag-Montefiore, Simon
Sebag-Montefiore, Simon 1965- 136
Sebald, Hans 1929- 73-76
Sebald, William J(oseph) 1901-1980 .... CAP-1
Obituary 101
Earlier sketch in CA 13-16
Sebastian, Jeanne
See Newsome, Arden J(eanne)
Sebastian, Lee
See Silverberg, Robert
Sebastian, Margaret
See Gladstone, Arthur M.
Sebastian Owl
See Thompson, Hunter S(tockton)
Sebba, Anne (Marietta) 1951- 127
Sebenthall, R(oberta) E(lizabeth) 1917- 33-36R
Sebeok, Thomas A(lbert) 1920- 9-12R
Seberg, Jean 1938-1979 Obituary 89-92
Sebes, Joseph (Schobert)
1915-1990 Obituary 131
Sebesta, Sam L(eaton) 1930- 85-88
Sebestyen, Gyorgy 1930- CANR-6
Earlier sketch in CA 9-12R
Sebestyen, Ouida 1924- 107
See also AAYA 8
See also CLC 30
See also CLR 17
See also MAICYA
See also SAAS 10
See also SATA 39
Seboldt, Roland H(enry) A(ugust) 1924- 5-8R
Sebree, Charles 1914-1985 Obituary 117
Sebrey, Mary Ann 1951- 116
See also SATA 62
Secher, Bjorn 1929- 33-36R
Sechrest, Lee 1929- 17-20R
Sechrist, Elizabeth Hough 1903- 5-8R
See also SATA 2
Seckel, Al 1958- 122
Seckler, David William 1935- 115
Secombe, Harry (Donald) 1921- 57-60
Secondari, John Hermes 1919-1975 61-64
Obituary 57-60
Second Duke of Buckingham
See Villiers, George
Secor, Robert 1939- CANR-15
Earlier sketch in CA 89-92
Secrest, Meryle
See Beveridge, Meryle Secrest
Secretan, Lance H. K. 1939- 130
Secrist, Margaret C(rystal) 1905- 111
Secunda, Sholom 1894-1974 Obituary 49-52
Sedaka, Neil 1939- 103
Sederberg, Arelo Charles 1930- 37-40R
Sederberg, Peter C(arl) 1943- 65-68
Sedges, John
See Buck, Pearl S(ydenstricker)
Sedgwick, Alexander 1930- 17-20R
Sedgwick, Arthur George 1844-1915 .... DLB 64
Sedgwick, Catharine Maria
1789-1867 .... DLB 1, 74

Sedgwick, Ellery 1872-1960 Obituary 89-92
See also DLB 91
Sedgwick, Jeffrey Leigh 1951- 116
Sedgwick, Michael Carl 1926-1983 89-92
Obituary 111
Sedgwick, Peter 1934-1983 Obituary 110
Sedgwick, Walter (Bradbary) 1885- CAP-1
Earlier sketch in CA 13-14
Sedlacek, William E(dward) 1939- 69-72
Sedler, Robert Allen 1935- 41-44R
Seduro, Vladimir 1910- 41-44R
Sedwick, B(enjamin) Frank 1924- 9-12R
Sedych, Andrei
See Zwibak, Jacques
See, Carolyn (Penelope) 1934- CANR-25
Earlier sketch in CA 29-32R
See, (Nadine) Ingram 1904- 112
See, Lisa
See Kendall, Lisa See
See, Ruth Douglas 1910- CANR-35
Earlier sketches in CA 1-4R, CANR-1
Seeber, Edward Derbyshire 1904- 13-16R
Seeber, Gerd Christian 1941- 113
Seebohm, Caroline 1940- 102
Seebord, G. R.
See Soderberg, Percy Measday
Seed, Cecil Eugenie 1930- CANR-26
Seed, Cecile Eugenie 1930- CANR-10
Earlier sketch in CA 21-24R
See also Seed, Jenny
Seed, Jenny
See Seed, Cecile Eugenie
See also SATA 8
Seed, Sheila Turner
1937(?)-1979 Obituary 89-92
See also SATA 23
Seedman, Albert A. 1918- Brief entry 112
Seeger, Alan 1888-1916 .... DLB 45
Seeger, Charles Louis 1886-1979 101
Obituary 85-88
Seeger, Elizabeth 1889-1973 Obituary 45-48
See also SATA 20
Seeger, Pete(r R.) 1919- CANR-33
Earlier sketch in CA 69-72
See also SATA 13
Seegers, Kathleen Walker 1915- 21-24R
Seeley, John R(onald) 1913- 25-28R
Seeley, Laura L. 1958- .... SATA 71
Seelhammer, Ruth 1917- 41-44R
Seelig, Sharon Cadman 1941- 119
Seely, Gordon M. 1930- 37-40R
Seely, Norma 1942- 113
Seely, Rebecca Z(ahm) 1935- 104
Seelye, H(ugh) Ned 1934- 102
Seelye, John (Douglas) 1931- 97-100
Seelye, John 1931- ....CLC 7
Seeman, Bernard 1911- 21-24R
Seeman, Elizabeth (Brickel) 1904- CAP-1
Earlier sketch in CA 19-20
Seeman, Ernest Albright 1887- 85-88
Seers, Dudley 1920-1983 129
Obituary 109
Seese, Ethel Gray 1903- 89-92
Seese, June Akers 1935- 134
Seever, R.
See Reeves, Lawrence F.
Seferiades, Giorgos Stylianou
1900-1971 ....CANR-36
Obituary 33-36R
Earlier sketches in CA 5-8R, CANR-5
See also Seferis, George
See also MTCW
Seferis, George
See Seferiades, Giorgos Stylianou
See also CLC 5, 11
Sefler, George Francis 1945- 81-84
Sefton, Catherine
See Waddell, Martin
Sefton, James E(dward) 1939- 21-24R
Segal, Abraham 1911(?)-1977 Obituary 69-72
Segal, Alan F(ranklin) 1945- 119
Segal, Bernice G. 1929-1989 Obituary 128
Segal, Charles Paul 1936- CANR-39
Earlier sketches in CA 41-44R, CANR-16
Segal, David I. 1928(?)-1970 Obituary 104
Segal, David R(obert) 1941- CANR-28
Earlier sketch in CA 111
Segal, Elliot A(lan) 1938- 93-96
Segal, Erich (Wolf) 1937- CANR-36
Earlier sketches in CA 25-28R, CANR-20
See also BEST 89:1
See also CLC 3, 10
See also DLBY 86
See also MTCW
Segal, Fred 1924(?)-1976 69-72
Obituary 65-68
Segal, Gerald 1953- 117
Segal, Geraldine R(osenbaum) 1908- 113
Segal, Hanna M(aria) 1918- 101
Segal, Harold S. 1903- 29-32R
Segal, Harriet 1931- 123
Segal, Harvey H(irst) 1922- 1-4R
Segal, Henry 1901(?)-1985 Obituary 116
Segal, Jeanne (Sandra) 1939- 108
Segal, Joyce 1940- 101
See also SATA 35
Segal, Julius 1924- Brief entry 112
Segal, Lore (Groszmann) 1928- CANR-5
Earlier sketch in CA 13-16R
See also SAAS 11
See also SATA 4, 66
Segal, Lynne 1943- 133
Segal, Marilyn 1927- CANR-23
Earlier sketches in CA 17-20R, CANR-8
Segal, Martin CANR-1
Earlier sketch in CA 1-4R
Segal, Melvin J(ames) 1910- 37-40R
Segal, Mendel 1914- 49-52
Segal, Muriel 1913- 121
Segal, Naomi (Dinah) 1949- 128
Segal, Robert M(ilton) 1925- CANR-32
Earlier sketch in CA 29-32R
Segal, Ronald (Michael) 1932- CANR-14
Earlier sketch in CA 21-24R
Segal, S(tanley) S. 1919- 25-28R
Segalan, Martine 1940- 130
Segalman, Ralph 1916- 106
Segar, E(lzie) C(risler) 1894-1938 .... SATA 61
Segel, Harold B(ernard) 1930- 21-24R
Segel, Thomas D(onald) 1931- 93-96
Seger, Bob 1945- ....CLC 35
Segerberg, Osborn Jr. 1924- 115
Segger, Sydney Walter 1902- CAP-1
Earlier sketch in CA 13-16
Seghers
See Radvanyi, Netty
Seghers, Anna
See Radvanyi, Netty
See also CLC 7
See also DLB 69
Segler, Franklin Morgan 1907- 17-20R
Segovia, Andres 1893(?)-1987 Obituary 122
Brief entry 111
See also SATA 52
Segrave, Edmond 1904-1971 Obituary 29-32R
Segraves, Kelly L(ee) 1942- CANR-13
Earlier sketch in CA 61-64
Segre, Claudio Giuseppe 1937- 53-56
Segre, Dan V(ittorio) 1922- 104
Segre, Emilio (Gino) 1905-1989 ....CANR-13
Obituary 128
Earlier sketch in CA 33-36R
Segundo, Bart
See Rowland, D(onald) S(ydney)
Segy, Ladislas 1904- CANR-30
Earlier sketch in CA 45-48
Seib, Kenneth Allen 1938- 29-32R
Seib, Philip 1949- 129
Seibel, C(lifford) W(inslow) 1890- CAP-2
Earlier sketch in CA 25-28
Seibel, Hans Dieter 1941- CANR-29
Earlier sketches in CA 65-68, CANR-11
Seid, Ruth 1913- 5-8R
See also Sinclair, Jo
Seide, Diane 1930- CANR-31
Earlier sketches in CA 73-76, CANR-14
Seide, Michael 1911- 111
Seidel, Frederick (Lewis) 1936- CANR-8
Earlier sketch in CA 13-16R
See also CLC 18
See also DLBY 84
Seidel, George J(oseph) 1932- 13-16R
Seidel, Ina 1885-1974 Obituary 116
See also DLB 56
Seidel, Kathleen G(illes) 1951- 112
Seidel, Michael Alan 1943- 93-96
Seidelman, James Edward 1926- 25-28R
See also SATA 6
Seiden, Art(hur) ....SATA 42
Seiden, Martin H. 1934- 13-16R
Seiden, Morton Irving 1921- 17-20R
Seidenbaum, Art(hur David) 1930-1990 .....29-32R
Obituary 132
Seidenberg, Robert 1920- 25-28R
Seidenberg, Roderick
1890(?)-1973 Obituary 45-48
Seidensticker, Edward G. 1921- 89-92
Seidick, Kathryn A(melia) 1943- 108
Seidler, Ann (G.) 1925- 25-28R
Seidler, Grzegorz Leopold 1913- CANR-28
Earlier sketches in CA 29-32R, CANR-12
Seidler, Lee J. 1935- 73-76
Seidler, Murray Benjamin 1924- 5-8R
Seidler, Tor 1952- 123
See also SATA 46, 52
Seidlin, Oskar 1911- 41-44R
Seidman, Ann (Willcox) 1926- 81-84
Seidman, Harold 1911- 29-32R
Seidman, Hugh 1940- CANR-35
Earlier sketch in CA 29-32R
Seidman, Jerome M(artin) 1911- 45-48
Seidman, Joel 1906- CANR-9
Earlier sketch in CA 5-8R
Seidman, Laurence Ivan 1925- 77-80
See also SATA 15
Seidman, Robert J(erome) 1941- 73-76
Seidmann, Ginette
See Spanier, Ginette
Seidner, Diane
See Seide, Diane
Seiferheld, Alfredo M. 1950-1988 Obituary 125
Seifert, Anne 1943- 105
Seifert, Elizabeth
See Gasparotti, Elizabeth Seifert
Seifert, Harvey (J.D.) 1911- CANR-3
Earlier sketch in CA 9-12R
Seifert, Jaroslav 1901-1986 127
See also CLC 34, 44
See also MTCW
Seifert, Shirley L(ouise) 1888-1971 ....CANR-2
Obituary 33-36R
Earlier sketch in CA 1-4R
Seifman, Eli 1936- 37-40R
Seigel, Jerrold (Edward) 1936- 85-88
Seigel, Jules 1931- 93-96
Seigel, Kalman 1917- 25-28R
See also SATA 12
Seigenthaler, John (Lawrence)
1927- Brief entry 113
Seignobosc, Francoise 1897-1961 73-76
See also SATA 21
Seignolle, Claude 1917- 21-24R
Seiler, John A(ndrew) 1927- 21-24R
Seiler, Robert E. 1925- 17-20R
Seilhamer, Frank Henry 1933- 85-88
Seim, Richard K(nudt) 1928- 102
Seimer, Stanley J(ames) 1918- CANR-28
Earlier sketch in CA 1-4R
Seinfel, Ruth
See Goode, Ruth
Seip, Terry Lee 1944- 113
Seitlin, Charlotte 1907(?)-1979 Obituary 89-92
Seitz, Georg J(osef) 1920- 13-16R
Seitz, Jacqueline 1931- ....SATA 50
Seitz, Nick 1939- 97-100
Seitz, William Chapin 1914-1974 ....CANR-2
Obituary 53-56
Earlier sketch in CA 1-4R
Seixas, Judith S. 1922- 85-88
See also SATA 17
Sejima, Yoshimasa 1913- 33-36R
See also SATA 8
Sejour, Victor 1817-1874 .... DLB 50
Sejour Marcou et Ferrand, Juan Victor
See Sejour, Victor
Sekaxsu Petakwonexnajunkis 1950- 133
Sekers, Simone 1945- 119
Sekler, Eduard F(ranz) 1920- 69-72
Sekora, John 1939- Brief entry 106
Selavy, Rrose
See Duchamp, (Henri-Robert) Marcel
Selberg, Ingrid (Maria) 1950- 136
See also SATA 68
Selbourne, David 1937- CANR-38
Earlier sketches in CA 89-92, CANR-16
Selby, Bettina 1934- 117
Selby, Curt
See Piserchia, Doris (Elaine)
Selby, Donald Joseph 1915- CANR-24
Earlier sketch in CA 1-4R
Selby, Edward B(urford) Jr. 1938- 45-48
Selby, Hazel Barrington 1889-1972 .... CAP-2
Earlier sketch in CA 17-18
Selby, Henry A. 1934- 37-40R
Selby, Hubert Jr. 1928- CANR-33
Earlier sketch in CA 13-16R
See also CLC 1, 2, 4, 8
See also DLB 2
Selby, James Winford III 1947- 108
Selby, John (Allen) 1897-1980 ....1-4R
Obituary 97-100
Selby, John M(illin) 1905- 25-28R
Selcamm, George
See Machlis, Joseph
Selcher, Wayne A(lan) 1942- CANR-10
Earlier sketch in CA 65-68
Selden, George
See Thompson, George Selden
See also CLR 8
See also DLB 52
Selden, Mark 1938- 81-84
Selden, Neil R(oy) 1931- 106
See also SATA 61
Selden, Raman 1937-1991 127
Obituary 134
Selden, Samuel 1899-1979 ....CANR-3
Earlier sketch in CA 1-4R
Selden, William K(irkpatrick) 1911- 1-4R
Seldes, George (Henry) 1890- CANR-2
Earlier sketch in CA 5-8R
Seldes, Gilbert (Vivian) 1893-1970 ....5-8R
Obituary 29-32R
Seldes, Marian (Hall) 1928- CANR-19
Earlier sketch in CA 85-88
Seldin, Maury 1931- CANR-34
Earlier sketches in CA 29-32R, CANR-15
Seldis, Henry 1925-1978 Obituary 77-80
Seldon, Anthony 1953- 136
Seldon, James R(alph) 1944- 112
Seldon, Mary Elisabeth 1921- 37-40R
Seldon-Truss, Leslie 1892- 5-8R
Selegen, Galina V(assily) 1899- 41-44R
Selement, George Joseph 1946- 113
Self, Carolyn Shealy 1931- CANR-16
Earlier sketch in CA 93-96
Self, Edwin F(orbes) 1920- 69-72
Self, Huber 1914- 73-76
Self, Jerry M(arvin) 1938- 61-64
Self, Margaret Cabell 1902- CANR-3
Earlier sketch in CA 5-8R
See also SATA 24
Self, Peter J(ohn) O(tter) 1919- 120
Self, William L(ee) 1932- 122
Selg, Herbert 1935- 69-72
Selig, Elaine Booth 1935- 104
Selig, Sylvie 1942- ....SATA 13
Seligman, Barnard 1923- 113
Seligman, Ben B(aruch) 1912-1970 ....CANR-2
Obituary 29-32R
Earlier sketch in CA 1-4R
Seligman, Daniel 1924- Brief entry 113
Seligman, Edwin R. A. 1861-1939 .... DLB 47
Seligman, Eustace
1889(?)-1976 Obituary 69-72
Seligman, Germain 1893-1978 Obituary 77-80
Seligman, Lester George 1918- 13-16R
Seligman, Linda H(elen Goldberg) 1944- 114
Seligman, Susan Meilach 1950- 105
Seligmann, G(ustav) L(eonard) Jr. 1934- 45-48
Seligmann, Herbert J(acob)
1891-1984 Obituary 112
Seligmann, Nancy 1948- 57-60
Seligson, Mitchell A(llan) 1945- 119
Seligson, Tom 1946- 33-36R
Selimovic, Mehmed 1910-1982 Obituary 108
Selimovic, Mesa
See Selimovic, Mehmed
Selkirk, Jane
See Chapman, John Stanton Higham
Sell, Betty (Marie) H(aas) 1928- 102
Sell, Charles M(urray) 1933- 113
Sell, DeWitt E(llsworth) 1915- 1-4R
Sell, Francis Edmund 1902- 5-8R
Sell, Henry Blackman
1889-1974 Obituary 89-92
Sell, Joseph
See Haley, William (John)
Sell, Kenneth D(aniel) 1928- 102
Sell, Roger D(avid) 1944- 116
Sell, Ted 1928-1989 69-72
Obituary 128
Sellars, Wilfrid Stalker 1912-1989 Obituary 129
Sellen, Robert W(alker) 1930- 45-48
Seller, Maxine Schwartz 1935- 104
Sellers, Bettie M(ixon) 1926- 77-80
Sellers, Charles Coleman 1903-1980 .....CANR-11
Earlier sketch in CA 17-20R
Sellers, Con(nie Leslie Jr.)
1922-1992 ....CANR-37
Obituary 136
Earlier sketch in CA 97-100
Sellers, James Earl 1926- 113
Sellers, Naomi
See Flack, Naomi John White
Sellers, Robert Victor 1894-1973 .... CAP-1
Obituary 89-92
Earlier sketch in CA 13-14
Sellers, Ronnie 1948- 115
Sellery, C. Morley 1894- CAP-2
Earlier sketch in CA 21-22
Sellew, Gladys 1887- CAP-1
Earlier sketch in CA 11-12
Sellin, Eric 1933- CANR-22
Earlier sketches in CA 17-20R, CANR-7
Sellin, Paul R(oland) 1930- 45-48
Sellings, Arthur
See Ley, Arthur Gordon
Sellman, Hunton Dade 1900- 5-8R
Sellman, Roger R(aymond) 1915- CANR-1
Earlier sketch in CA 1-4R
Sells, Arthur Lytton 1895- CANR-6
Earlier sketch in CA 5-8R
Sells, Iris (Esther) Lytton
See Lytton-Sells, Iris (Esther)
Sells, S(aul) B. 1913- CANR-19
Earlier sketches in CA 1-4R, CANR-4
Selltiz, Claire (Alice) 1914- 5-8R
Selman, LaRue W. 1927- ....SATA 55
Selmark, George
See Seldon-Truss, Leslie
Selness, Craig A(lan) 1955- 119
Selormey, Francis 1927- 21-24R
See also BW
Selsam, Howard 1903-1970 Obituary 29-32R
Selsam, Millicent Ellis 1912- CANR-38
Earlier sketches in CA 9-12R, CANR-5
See also CLR 1
See also MAICYA
See also SATA 1, 29
Seltzer, Alvin J(ay) 1939- 65-68
Seltzer, Chester E. 1915-1971 131
See also Muro, Amado (Jesus)
See also HW
Seltzer, Daniel 1933-1980 89-92
Obituary 97-100
Seltzer, David 1920(?)- Brief entry 110
Seltzer, George 1924- 73-76
Seltzer, Leon E(ugene) 1918-1988 89-92
Obituary 124
Seltzer, Leon F(rancis) 1940- 33-36R
Seltzer, Louis B(enson)
1897-1980 Obituary 97-100
Seltzer, Meyer 1932- ....SATA 17
Seltzer, Richard (Warren Jr.) 1946- 105
See also SATA 41
Selver, (Percy) Paul 1888-1970 .... CAP-2
Earlier sketch in CA 29-32
Selvin, David F(rank) 1913- 25-28R
Selvin, Hanan C(harles) 1921- 9-12R
Selvin, Joel 1950- 133
Selvon, Sam
See Selvon, Samuel (Dickson)
Selvon, Samuel (Dickson) 1923- 128
Brief entry 117
See also MTCW
Selwyn-Clarke, Selwyn
1893-1976 Obituary 65-68
Selwyn-Lloyd, John S. B.
1904-1978 Obituary 110
Selye, Hans 1907-1982 ....CANR-2
Obituary 108
Earlier sketch in CA 5-8R
Selz, Peter (Howard) 1919- CANR-29
Earlier sketch in CA 1-4R
Selzer, Joae Graham 1926- 53-56
Selzer, Michael (I.) 1940- CANR-9
Earlier sketch in CA 53-56
Selzer, Richard 1928- CANR-14
Earlier sketch in CA 65-68
Selznick, David O(liver)
1902-1965 Obituary 110
Selznick, Irene Mayer 1907-1990 Obituary 132
Semaan, Khalil I. H. 1920- 37-40R
Sembene, Ousmane
See Ousmane, Sembene
Semchyshyn, Stefan 1940- 134
Semeiks, Jonna Gormely 1944- 109
Semenov, Julian Semenovich 1931- 85-88
See also Lyandres, Yulian Semenovich
Semenov, Yulian
See Lyandres, Yulian Semenovich
Semkiw, Virlyana
See Bishop, Tania Kroitor
Semler, H. Eric 1965- 125
Semloh
See Holmes, Peggy
Semmel, Bernard 1928- 77-80

Semmelroth, Otto 1912-1979 .... CANR-10
Earlier sketch in CA 13-16R
Semmens, James P(ike) 1919- 61-64
Semmler, Clement (William) 1914- CANR-14
Earlier sketch in CA 21-24R
Semonche, John E(rwin) 1933- CANR-30
Earlier sketch in CA 45-48
Sempell, Charlotte 1909- 41-44R
Semple, Gordon
See Neubauer, William Arthur
Semple, Lorenzo Jr. 129
Brief entry 125
Semprun, Jorge 1920(?)- Brief entry 111
Semyonov, Julian
See Lyandres, Yulian Semenovich
Semyonov, Yulian
See Lyandres, Yulian Semenovich
Sen, Ela
See Reid, Ela
Sen, Sudhir 1906-1989 .... 33-36R
Obituary 129
Sena, John F(rancis) 1940- 110
Senancour, Etienne Pivert de
1770-1846 .... DLB 119
Sencourt, Robert
See George, Robert Esmonde Gordon
Sencourt, Robert Esmonde
See George, Robert Esmonde Gordon
Sendak, Jack 77-80
See also SATA 28
Sendak, Maurice (Bernard) 1928- CANR-39
Earlier sketches in CA 5-8R, CANR-11
See also CLR 1, 17
See also DLB 61
See also MAICYA
See also MTCW
See also SATA 1, 27
Sender, Ramon (Jose) 1902-1982 .... CANR-8
Obituary 105
Earlier sketch in CA 5-8R
See also CLC 8
See also HW
See also MTCW
Sender, Ruth M(insky) 1926- .... SATA 62
Sender Barayon, Ramon 1934- 130
See also HW
Sendler, David A. 1938- 65-68
Sendrey, A(ladar) Alfred 1884- 13-16R
Sendy, Jean 1910-1978 .... CANR-12
Earlier sketch in CA 53-56
Senecal, Eva 1905- .... DLB 92
Senelick, Laurence P(hilip) 1942- CANR-22
Earlier sketch in CA 106
Senesh, Hannah 1921-1944 Brief entry 119
Senesi, Mauro 1931- 17-20R
Seng, Peter J. 1922- 17-20R
Senghor, Leopold Sedar 1906- 125
Brief entry 116
See also BLC 3
See also BW
See also CLC 54
See also MTCW
Sengler, Johanna 1924- .... SATA 18
Sengstacke, John H(erman Henry) 1912- 101
See also BW
Sen Gupta, Pranati 1938- 102
Sen Gupta, Rajeswar 1908- CAP-1
Earlier sketch in CA 9-10
Senick, Gerard J(oseph) 1953- 97-100
Senior, Clarence (Ollson) 1903-1974 65-68
Obituary 53-56
Senior, Donald 1940- CANR-29
Earlier sketches in CA 77-80, CANR-13
Senior, Isabel J(anet Couper Syme) CANR-9
Earlier sketch in CA 5-8R
Senior, Michael 1940- 103
Senior, Nancy 1941- 119
Senkevitch, Anatole Jr. 1942- CANR-19
Earlier sketch in CA 101
Senn, Alfred Erich 1932- 134
Brief entry 112
Senn, Frank C(olvin) 1943- CANR-39
Earlier sketch in CA 115
Senn, Fritz 1928- 41-44R
Senn, Milton J(ohn) E(dward) 1902- 81-84
Senn, Peter R(ichard) 1923- 33-36R
Senn, Steve 1950- 105
See also SATA 48, 60
Senna, Carl 1944- CANR-19
Earlier sketches in CA 49-52, CANR-4
Sennett, Richard 1943- 73-76
Sennett, Ted 1928- CANR-38
Earlier sketch in CA 33-36R
Sennholz, Hans F. 1922- 120
Brief entry 118
Sensabaugh, George Frank 1906- CAP-1
Earlier sketch in CA 13-14
Senser, Robert A(nton) 1921- 5-8R
Senter, Florence H.
See Ellis, Florence Hawley
Senter, Sylvia 1921- 113
Sentner, David P. 1898-1975 Obituary 57-60
Sentner, Mary Steele
1900(?)-1983 Obituary 110
Seoane, Rhoda 1905- CAP-2
Earlier sketch in CA 25-28
Sepetys, Jonas 1901- 57-60
Sepheriades, Georgios
See Seferiades, Giorgos Stylianou
Sepia
See Holmvik, Oyvind
Sequoia, Anna 109
Serafian, Michael
See Martin, Malachi
Serafini, Anthony Louis 1945- 112
Serage, Nancy 1924- 65-68
See also SATA 10
Serb, Ann Toland 1937- 81-84
Serban, George 1926- 129
Serban, William M(ichael) 1949- 102
Serebryakova, Galina Iosifovna
1905-1980 Obituary 102
Seredy, Kate 1899-1975 .... 5-8R
Obituary 57-60
See also CLR 10
See also DLB 22
See also MAICYA
See also SATA 1, 24
Sereni, Vittorio 1913-1983 Obituary 109
Sereny, Gitta
See Serenyi, Gitta
Serenyi, Gitta 1923- 119
Serenyi, Peter 1931- 61-64
Serfaty, Simon 1940- CANR-26
Earlier sketches in CA 25-28R, CANR-10
Sergeant, Harriet 1954- 132
Sergeant, (Herbert) Howard
1914-1987 .... CANR-20
Obituary 121
Earlier sketches in CA 5-8R, CANR-5
Sergel, Ruth
See Perry, Ruth (Fuller)
Sergent, Bernard 1946- 133
Sergievsky, Orest 1911-1984 Obituary 114
Sergio, Elisa 1905-1989 61-64
Obituary 129
Sergio, Lisa
See Sergio, Elisa
Seriel, Jerome
See Vallee, Jacques F.
Serif, Med 1924- 17-20R
Serig, Beverly J. 1934- 101
Serle, (Alan) Geoffrey 1922- 13-16R
Serling, Robert J(erome) 1918- CANR-1
Earlier sketch in CA 45-48
Serling, (Edward) Rod(man) 1924-1975 65-68
Obituary 57-60
See also AITN 1
See also CLC 30
See also DLB 26
Serna, Ramon Gomez de la
See Gomez de la Serna, Ramon
Serna-Maytorena, Manuel Antonio
1932- CANR-3
Earlier sketch in CA 45-48
Sernett, Milton C(harles) 1942- 61-64
Seroff, Victor I(lyitch) 1902-1979 .... 25-28R
Obituary 85-88
See also SATA 12, 26
Seroka, James H. 1950- 124
Seroka, Jim
See Seroka, James H.
Serpieres
See Guillevic, (Eugene)
Serra, Diana
See Cary, Peggy-Jean Montgomery
Serraillier, Ian (Lucien) 1912- CANR-1
Earlier sketch in CA 1-4R
See also CLR 2
See also MAICYA
See also SAAS 3
See also SATA 1
Serrano, Lucienne J. 1936- 131
Serrano, Miguel 1917- 132
Serrano, Napoleon Diestro Valeriano
See Valeriano, Napoleon D(iestro)
Serrano Plaja, Arturo 1909-1979 .... CANR-13
Earlier sketch in CA 29-32R
Serrifile, F. O. O.
See Holmes, William Kersley
Serron, Luis A(ugusto) 1930- 102
Sert, Josep Lluis 1902-1983 Obituary 109
Servadio, Gaia 1938- CANR-11
Earlier sketch in CA 25-28R
Servan-Schreiber, Jean-Jacques 1924- 102
Servello, Joe 1932- .... SATA 10
Serventy, Vincent (Noel) CANR-27
Earlier sketches in CA 65-68, CANR-10
Service, Alastair (Stanley Douglas) 1933- 130
Service, Elman Rogers 1915- 112
Service, John S(tewart) 1909- Brief entry 113
Service, Pamela F. 1945- 120
See also SATA 64
Service, Robert
See Service, Robert W(illiam)
See also DLB 92
Service, Robert W(illiam)
1874(?)-1958 Brief entry 115
See also Service, Robert
See also SATA 20
See also TCLC 15
See also WLC
Servin, Manuel P(atrick) 1920- 37-40R
Serviss, Garrett P(utnam)
1851-1929 Brief entry 119
Serwadda, W(illiam) Moses 1931- 107
See also SATA 27
Serwer, Blanche L. 1910- 65-68
See also SATA 10
Serwicher, Kurt 1912-1979 Obituary 89-92
Seskin, Eugene P(aul) 1948- 89-92
Sesonske, Alexander 1917- 13-16R
Sessions, Kyle Cutler 1934- Brief entry 106
Sessions, Roger Huntington 1896-1985 93-96
Obituary 115
Sessions, Will 1905- 1-4R
Sessoms, H(anson) Douglas 1931- 41-44R
Sesti, Giuseppe Maria 1942- 137
Seth, Ronald (Sydney) 1911-1985 106
Obituary 115
Seth, Vikram 1952- 127
Brief entry 121
See also CLC 43
See also DLB 120
Sethi, Narendra Kumar 1935- CANR-14
Earlier sketch in CA 37-40R
Sethi, S. Prakash 1934- 41-44R
Sethna, Jehangir Minocher 1941- 37-40R
Sethna, Minocher Jehangirji 1911- 9-12R
Seth-Smith, Elsie K.
See Murrell, Elsie Kathleen Seth-Smith
Seth-Smith, Leslie James 1923- 104
Seth-Smith, Michael 1928- CANR-16
Earlier sketch in CA 29-32R
Setien, Miguel Delibes
See Delibes Setien, Miguel
Seton, Anya 1904(?)-1990 .... 17-20R
Obituary 133
See also SATA 3
See also SATO 66
Seton, Cynthia Propper 1926-1982 .... CANR-7
Obituary 108
Earlier sketch in CA 5-8R
See also CLC 27
Seton, Ernest (Evan) Thompson
1860-1946 Brief entry 109
See also DLB 92
See also SATA 18
See also TCLC 31
Seton, Marie 1910- 105
Seton-Thompson, Ernest
See Seton, Ernest (Evan) Thompson
Seton-Watson, Christopher 1918- CANR-11
Earlier sketch in CA 21-24R
Seton-Watson, (George) Hugh (Nicholas)
1916-1984 117
Obituary 114
Settel, Gertrude S. 17-20R
Settel, Irving 1916- 17-20R
Settel, Trudy S.
See Settel, Gertrude S.
Settle, Edith
See Andrews, (William) Linton
Settle, Mary Lee 1918- 89-92
See also CAAS 1
See also CLC 19, 61
See also DLB 6
Setton, Kenneth M. 1914- CANR-39
Earlier sketches in CA 9-12R, CANR-3, 18
Setzekorn, William David 1935- 65-68
Setzler, Frank M(aryl)
1902-1975 Obituary 57-60
Seufert, Karl Rolf 1923- CANR-28
Earlier sketch in CA 9-12R
Seuling, Barbara 1937- CANR-26
Earlier sketches in CA 61-64, CANR-8
See also SATA 10
Seume, Johann Gottfried 1763-1810 .... DLB 94
Seung, Thomas Kaehao 1930- CANR-36
Earlier sketch in CA 108
Seuphor, Michel
See Arp, Jean
Seuren, Pieter A. M. 1934- 49-52
Seuss, Dr.
See Geisel, Theodor Seuss
See also CLR 9
Sevareid, (Arnold) Eric 1912- 69-72
See also AITN 1
Sevela, Efraim 1928- CANR-30
Earlier sketch in CA 69-72
Severin, Mark (Fernand) 1906- 107
Severin, (Giles) Timothy 1940- CANR-10
Earlier sketch in CA 21-24R
Severino, Alexandrino E(usebio) 1931- 41-44R
Severn, Bill
See Severn, William Irving
Severn, David
See Unwin, David S(torr)
Severn, Sue 1918- 5-8R
Severn, William Irving 1914- CANR-36
Earlier sketches in CA 1-4R, CANR-1, 16
See also SATA 1
Severo, Richard 1932- 73-76
Severs, Jerome
See Wooley, John (Steven)
Severs, Vesta-Nadine 1935- CANR-15
Earlier sketch in CA 89-92
Severson, John H(ugh) 1933- 13-16R
Sewall, Joseph 1688-1769 .... DLB 24
Sewall, Marcia 1935- CANR-18
Earlier sketches in CA 45-48, CANR-1
See also MAICYA
See also SATA 37, 69
Sewall, Mary Franklin 1884- CAP-2
Earlier sketch in CA 21-22
Sewall, Richard B(enson) 1908- 93-96
See also DLB 111
Sewall, Samuel 1652-1730 .... DLB 24
Seward, Desmond 1935- Brief entry 114
Seward, Jack
See Seward, John Neil
Seward, James H(odson) 1928- 65-68
Seward, John Neil 1924- CANR-8
Earlier sketch in CA 21-24R
Seward, Prudence 1926- .... SATA 16
Seward, William W(ard) Jr. 1913- 9-12R
Sewart, Alan 1928- CANR-25
Earlier sketch in CA 108
Sewel, John 1946- 103
Sewell, Anna 1820-1878 .... CLR 17
See also MAICYA
See also SATA 24
Sewell, Brocard 1912- 107
Sewell, (Margaret) Elizabeth 1919- 49-52
Sewell, Helen (Moore) 1896-1957 137
Brief entry 123
See also MAICYA
See also SATA 38
Sewell, J. Leslie 1923- 21-24R
Sewell, James Patrick 1930- 73-76
Sewell, Richard H(erbert) 1931- Brief entry 117
Sewell, W. R. Derrick 1931- CANR-9
Earlier sketch in CA 21-24R
Sewell, William H(amilton) 1909- 45-48
Sewell, Winifred 1917- 102
Sewny, Kathryn Wiehe 1909- CAP-1
Earlier sketch in CA 13-16
Sewter, Albert Charles 1912- 89-92
Sexton, A(da) Jeanette 1924- 65-68
Sexton, Anne (Harvey) 1928-1974 .... CANR-36
Obituary 53-56
Earlier sketches in CA 1-4R, CANR-3
See also CABS 2
See also CDALB 1941-1968
See also CLC 2, 4, 6, 8, 10, 15, 53
See also DLB 5
See also MTCW
See also PC 2
See also SATA 10
See also WLC
Sexton, James D(ean) 1942- 113
Sexton, Linda Gray 1953- CANR-36
Earlier sketch in CA 101
Sexton, Michael J(oseph) 1939- 45-48
Sexton, Richard J(oseph) 1912- 45-48
Sexton, Virgil Wesley 1918- 33-36R
Sexton, Virginia Staudt 1916- 29-32R
Sexton, William C(ottrell) 1928- 133
Seybolt, Peter J(ordan) 1934- CANR-35
Earlier sketch in CA 53-56
Seydel, Mildred Woolley 1890(?)-1988 .... 37-40R
Obituary 124
Seydell, Mildred
See Seydel, Mildred Woolley
Seydor, Paul 1947- 97-100
Seyer, Philip C. 1941- 119
Seyersted, Brita Lindberg
See Lindberg-Seyersted, Brita
Seyersted, Per 1921- CANR-15
Earlier sketch in CA 29-32R
Seyfert, Carl K(eenan) 1938- 57-60
Seyler, Dorothy U(pton) 1938- 109
Seymour, A(rthur) J(ames) 1914- CANR-29
Earlier sketch in CA 97-100
Seymour, Alan 1927- 53-56
Seymour, Alta Halverson CAP-1
Earlier sketch in CA 11-12
See also SATA 10
Seymour, Anne
See Morton, Phyllis Digby
Seymour, Charles Jr. 1912-1977 .... 9-12R
Obituary 69-72
Seymour, Digby G. 1923- 17-20R
Seymour, Dorothy Jane Z(ander) 1928- 89-92
Seymour, Emery W. 1921- 13-16R
Seymour, Forrest W. 1905-1983 Obituary 111
Seymour, (William Herschel Kean) Gerald
1941- 101
Seymour, Harold 1910- 138
Seymour, Henry
See Hartmann, Helmut Henry
Seymour, John 1914- CANR-9
Earlier sketch in CA 13-16R
Seymour, Miranda
See Sinclair, Miranda
Seymour, Raymond B(enedict) 1912- CANR-13
Earlier sketch in CA 73-76
Seymour, Rogers James 1942- 110
Seymour, Stephan A(ndrew) 1920- 21-24R
Seymour, W(illiam) Douglas 1910- 49-52
Seymour, Whitney North Jr. 1923- CANR-14
Earlier sketch in CA 81-84
Seymour, William Kean 1887-1975 .... 9-12R
Obituary 126
Seymour, William Napier 1914- 77-80
Seymour-Smith, Martin 1928- 5-8R
Seymour-Ure, Colin K. 1938- CANR-18
Earlier sketch in CA 25-28R
Seyton, Marion
See Saxon, Gladys Relyea
Seznec, Jean J. 1905-1983 Obituary 111
Sgroi, Peter Philip 1936- 57-60
Sgroi, Suzanne M(ary) 1943- 108
Shaaban, Bouthaina 1953- 137
Shaaber, M. A.
See Shaaber, Matthias A(dam)
Shaaber, Matthias A(dam)
1897-1979 Obituary 111
Shaara, Michael (Joseph Jr.)
1929-1988 Obituary 125
Shaara, Michael (Joseph Jr.) 1929-1988 102
See also AITN 1
See also CLC 15
See also DLBY 83
Shabad, Theodore 1922-1987 .... CANR-10
Obituary 122
Earlier sketch in CA 25-28R
Shachtman, Tom 1942- 89-92
See also SATA 49
Shack, William A(lfred) 1923- 113
Shackelford, Jean 1946- 105
Shacket, Sheldon R(ubin) 1941- 102
Shackford, Martha Hale 1875-1963 .... 1-4R
Shackford, R(oland) H(erbert) 1908- 1-4R
Shackle, G(eorge) L(ennox) S(harman)
1903- CANR-2
Obituary 137
Earlier sketch in CA 5-8R
Shackleford, Bernard L. 1889-1975 .... CAP-2
Earlier sketch in CA 29-32
Shackleford, Ruby P(aschall) 1913- 57-60
Shackleton, C. C.
See Aldiss, Brian W(ilson)
Shackleton, Doris (Cavell) 1918- 93-96
Shackleton, Edward Arthur Alexander
1911- 13-16R
Shackleton, Ernest Henry
1874-1922 Brief entry 118

Shackleton, Keith Hope 1923- 5-8R
Shackleton, Philip 1923- 101
Shackleton, Robert 1919-1986 ....1-4R
Obituary 120
Shackleton Bailey, D(avid) R(oy)
1917- CANR-19
Earlier sketches in CA 5-8R, CANR-3
Shackley, Myra (Lesley) 1949- 115
Shackley, Theodore (George Jr.)
1927- Brief entry 117
Shacochis, Bob
See Shacochis, Robert G.
See also CLC 39
Shacochis, Robert G. 1951- 124
Brief entry 119
See also Shacochis, Bob
Shadbolt, Maurice (Francis Richard)
1932- CANR-5
Earlier sketch in CA 13-16R
See also CAAS 3
Shade, Rose (Marian) 1927- 57-60
Shade, William G(erald) 1939- 41-44R
Shade, William L(eonard) 1945- Brief entry 113
Shadegg, Stephen C. 1909-1990 ....13-16R
Obituary 131
Shadi, Dorothy Clotelle Clarke 1908- 13-16R
Shadily, Hassan 1920- 105
Shadlick, Harold (Ernest) 1902- 41-44R
Shadoian, Jack 1940- 105
Shadowitz, Albert 1915- 69-72
Shadwell, Thomas 1641(?)-1692 ....DLB 80
Shaearman, John 1931- 13-16R
Shaevitz, Marjorie Hansen 1943- 101
Shaevitz, Morton H(erbert) 1935- 102
Shafarevich, Igor Rostislavovich 1923- 105
Shafer, Boyd Carlisle 1907- 17-20R
Shafer, D. Michael 1953- 134
Shafer, Neil 1933- 33-36R
Shafer, Robert E(ugene) 1925- CANR-10
Earlier sketch in CA 57-60
See also SATA 9
Shafer, Robert Jones 1920- 37-40R
Shafer, Ronald G. 1939- CANR-10
Earlier sketch in CA 65-68
Shafer, Thomas 1910(?)-1986 Obituary 119
Shaff, Albert L(averne) 1937- 29-32R
Shaffer, Anthony (Joshua) 1926- 116
Brief entry 110
See also CLC 19
See also DLB 13
Shaffer, Betty
See Shaffer, Elizabeth (Nickerson)
Shaffer, Dale Eugene 1929- 37-40R
Shaffer, Elizabeth (Nickerson) 1925- 113
Shaffer, Harry George 1919- CANR-6
Earlier sketch in CA 5-8R
Shaffer, Helen B. 1909(?)-1978 85-88
Obituary 81-84
Shaffer, Jerome A(rthur) 1929- 37-40R
Shaffer, K(atherine) Stevenson 1902- CAP-2
Earlier sketch in CA 17-18
Shaffer, Karen A. 1947- 127
Shaffer, Kenneth R(aymond) 1914- 5-8R
Shaffer, Laurance Frederic
1903-1976 Obituary 65-68
Shaffer, Peter (Levin) 1926- CANR-25
Earlier sketch in CA 25-28R
See also CDBLB 1960 to Present
See also CLC 5, 14, 18, 37, 60
See also DLB 13
See also MTCW
Shaffer, Rosalind Keating
1896-1990 Obituary 131
Shaffer, Samuel 1910- 104
Shaffer, Thomas Lindsay 1934- 37-40R
Shaffer, Wilma L. 1916- 17-20R
Shafir, Michael 1944- 129
Shafritz, Jay M(ichael) 1944- 117
Shaftel, Oscar 1912- 57-60
Shaftner, Dorothy 1918- 25-28R
Shagan, Steve 1927- CANR-6
Earlier sketch in CA 53-56
Shaginyan, Marietta (Sergeyevna)
1888-1982 129
Obituary 106
Shah, A(ruind) M(anilal) 1931- 73-76
Shah, Amina 1918- 49-52
Shah, Diane K(iver) 1945- 73-76
Shah, (Sayed) Idries 1924- CANR-22
Earlier sketches in CA 17-20R, CANR-7
Shah, Krishna B. 1933- 17-20R
Shaha, Rishikesh 1925- 69-72
Shahan, Lynn 1941- 106
Shahane, Vasant Anant 1923- CANR-12
Earlier sketch in CA 25-28R
Shahani, Ranjee 1904-1968 ....CANR-2
Earlier sketch in CA 1-4R
Shahar, David 1926- 65-68
Shaheen, Jack G(eorge) 1935- 124
Shaheen, Naseeb 1931- CANR-34
Earlier sketch in CA 65-68
Shahn, Ben(jamin) 1898-1969 121
Obituary 89-92
See also SATA 21
Shahn, Bernarda Bryson
See Bryson, Bernarda
Shah Of Iran
See Pahlevi, Mohammed Riza
Shain, Henry 1941- 57-60
Shain, Merle 1935- 61-64
See also AITN 1
Shain, Yossi 1956- 131
Shainberg, Lawrence 1936- 137
Brief entry 131
Shainmark, Eliezer L. 1900-1976 Obituary 104
Shainmark, Lou
See Shainmark, Eliezer L.
Shairp, (Alexander) Mordaunt
1887-1939 Brief entry 110
See also DLB 10
Shakabpa, Tsepon W(angchuk) D(eden)
1907-1989 ....CAP-2
Obituary 128
Earlier sketch in CA 23-24R
Sha'Ked, Ami 1945- 101
Shaked, Gershon 1929- 131
Shaked, Haim 1939- 130
Shakesby, Paul S(tewart) 1946- 57-60
Shakespeare, Geoffrey (Hithersay)
1893-1980 Obituary 105
Shakespeare, William
1564-1616 ....CDBLB Before 1660
See also DLB 62
See also WLC
Shakey, Bernard
See Young, Neil
Shakow, David 1901-1981 Obituary 108
Shalamov, Varlam (Tikhonovich)
1907(?)-1982 129
Obituary 105
See also CLC 18
Shale, Richard 1947- 89-92
Shales, Thomas William 1948- 112
Brief entry 110
Shales, Tom
See Shales, Thomas William
Shalett, Anita Effron 1917(?)-1984 Obituary 112
Shalhope, Robert E. 1941- 85-88
Shallcrass, John James 1922- CANR-20
Earlier sketch in CA 103
Shallow, Robert
See Atkinson, Frank
Shaloff, Stanley 1939- 29-32R
Shalom, Stephen Rosskamm 1948- 112
Shalvey, Thomas (Joseph) 1937- 105
Shamburger, (Alice) Page 9-12R
Shames, Laurence 1951- 124
Shamlu, Ahmad 1925- ....CLC 10
Shammas, Anton 1951- ....CLC 55
Shamon, Albert Joseph 1915- 13-16R
Shan, Yeh
See Wang, C(hing) H(sien)
Shanahan, Eileen 1924- 102
Shanahan, William J. 1935- 29-32R
Shands, Harley Cecil 1916-1981 109
Obituary 105
Shane, Alex M(ichael) 1933- 45-48
Shane, C(harles) Donald
1895-1983 Obituary 109
Shane, Don (Graves) 1933- 53-56
Shane, Harold Gray 1914- CANR-21
Earlier sketches in CA 9-12R, CANR-3
See also SATA 36
Shane, John
See Durst, Paul
Shane, Mark
See Norwood, Victor G(eorge) C(harles)
Shane, Maxwell 1905(?)-1983 Obituary 111
Shane, Rhondo
See Norwood, Victor G(eorge) C(harles)
Shaner, Madeleine 1932- 73-76
Shanes, Eric 1944- 134
Shanet, Howard (Stephen) 1918- 130
Shange, Ntozake 1948- CANR-27
Earlier sketch in CA 85-88
See also CABS 3
See also AAYA 9
See also BLC 3
See also BW
See also CLC 8, 25, 38
See also DLB 38
See also MTCW
Shank, Alan 1936- 53-56
Shank, David Arthur 1924- 29-32R
Shank, Joseph E(lmer) 1892- CAP-2
Earlier sketch in CA 25-28
Shank, Margarethe Erdahl 1910- CAP-2
Earlier sketch in CA 19-20
Shank, Theodore
See Shank, Theodore J(unior)
Shank, Theodore J(unior) 1929- 129
Shankel, George Edgar 1894- CAP-2
Earlier sketch in CA 23-24
Shankland, Peter Macfarlane 1901- CANR-16
Earlier sketches in CAP-1, CA 11-12
Shankle, Ralph O(tis) 1933- 9-12R
Shanklin, William L(eslie) 1941- 120
Shankman, Arnold M(ichael) 1945- 129
Shankman, Florence V(ogel) 1912- 41-44R
Shankman, Paul (Andrew) 1943- 93-96
Shanks, Ann Zane (Kushner) 53-56
See also SATA 10
Shanks, Bob 1932- 101
Shanks, Bruce ....AITN 1
Shanks, Hershel 1930- 126
Brief entry 106
Shanks, Michael (James) 1927-1984 ....CANR-8
Obituary 111
Earlier sketch in CA 5-8R
Shanley, John Patrick 1950- 133
Brief entry 128
Shann, Renee 1907(?)-1979 Obituary 89-92
Shannon, David Allen 1920- 1-4R
Shannon, Dell
See Linington, (Barbara) Elizabeth
Shannon, Doris 1924- CANR-23
Earlier sketches in CA 61-64, CANR-8
Shannon, Edgar F(inley) Jr. 1918- 9-12R
Shannon, Ellen 1927- 77-80
Shannon, Foster (Houts) 1930- 106
Shannon, Fred Albert 1893-1963 Obituary 111
Shannon, George (William Bones)
1952- CANR-23
Earlier sketch in CA 106
See also SATA 35
Shannon, Jacqueline ....SATA 63
Shannon, Jasper Berry 1903-1984 ....1-4R
Obituary 114
Shannon, John 1943- 57-60
Shannon, Lyle William 1920- 61-64
Shannon, M.
See Geddie, John
Shannon, Mike 1951- 127
Shannon, Monica 1905(?)-1965 Obituary 109
See also SATA 28
Shannon, Richard 1945- 73-76
Shannon, Robert
See Wieder, Robert S(hannon)
Shannon, Robert C. 1930- 13-16R
Shannon, Robert L(eroy) 1926- 93-96
Shannon, Terry
See Mercer, Jessie
See also SATA 21
Shannon, Thomas A(nthony) 1940- CANR-20
Earlier sketches in CA 53-56, CANR-5
Shannon, William H(enry) 1917- 45-48
Shannon, William V(incent) 1927-1988 ....CANR-6
Obituary 126
Earlier sketch in CA 9-12R
Shanor, Donald Read 1927- CANR-30
Earlier sketches in CA 61-64, CANR-12
Shanwa
See Haarer, Alec Ernest
Shao, Stephen P(inyee) 1924- CANR-11
Earlier sketch in CA 21-24R
Shapard, Robert (Perry) 1942- 126
Shapcott, Jo 1958- 135
Shapcott, Thomas William 1935- 69-72
See also CLC 38
Shapell, Nathan 1922- 49-52
Shapere, Dudley 1928- 17-20R
Shapiro, Alan E(lihu) 1942- 128
Shapiro, Alan 1952- 125
Shapiro, Barbara J(une) 1934- 130
Shapiro, Cecile 85-88
Shapiro, Charles K. 1926- 5-8R
Shapiro, David (Joel) 1947- 13-16R
Shapiro, David S(idney) 1923-1983 ....CANR-1
Obituary 109
Earlier sketch in CA 1-4R
Shapiro, Deborah 1923- 106
Shapiro, Dolph
See Sharp, Dolph
Shapiro, Edward 1920- 17-20R
Shapiro, Elizabeth Klein
See Klein, Elizabeth
Shapiro, Fred(eric) C(harles) 1931- 17-20R
Shapiro, Harold I(srael) 1931- 45-48
Shapiro, Harold T(afler) 1935- 132
Shapiro, Harry L(ionel) 1902- 49-52
Shapiro, Harvey 1924- CANR-34
Earlier sketches in CA 41-44R, CANR-15
Shapiro, Henry D(avid) 1937- CANR-3
Earlier sketch in CA 9-12R
Shapiro, Herbert 1929- 37-40R
Shapiro, Herman 1922- 13-16R
Shapiro, Howard I(ra) 1937- 73-76
Shapiro, Irving 1917- 29-32R
Shapiro, Irwin 1911- 81-84
See also SATA 32
Shapiro, James E(arnest) 1946- 108
Shapiro, Jane P.
See Zacek, Jane Shapiro
Shapiro, Jim
See Shapiro, James E(arnest)
Shapiro, Joan Hatch 1928- 33-36R
Shapiro, Julian L.
See Sanford, John
Shapiro, Karl (Jay) 1913- CANR-36
Earlier sketches in CA 1-4R, CANR-1
See also CAAS 6
See also CLC 4, 8, 15, 53
See also DLB 48
See also MTCW
Shapiro, Kenneth A(llan) 1942- 118
Shapiro, Lillian L(adman) 1913- 102
Shapiro, Linda Gaye 1953- 65-68
Shapiro, Marianne (Goldner) 1940- 123
Brief entry 118
Shapiro, Martin M(athew) 1933- 102
Shapiro, Max 1912(?)-1981 Obituary 105
Shapiro, Mel 1937- 101
Shapiro, Milton J. 1926- 81-84
See also SATA 32
Shapiro, Nat(haniel M.) 1922-1983 ....CANR-15
Obituary 111
Earlier sketch in CA 29-32R
Shapiro, Norman R(ichard) 1930- 93-96
Shapiro, Paulett
See Tumay, Paulett
Shapiro, Robert 1935- 113
Shapiro, Samuel 1927- CANR-1
Earlier sketch in CA 1-4R
Shapiro, Sidney 1915- 136
Shapiro, Stanley 1925-1990 Obituary 132
Shapiro, Stuart C(harles) 1944- 127
Shapiro, Sue A. 1947- 109
Shapiro, William E. 1934- CANR-20
Earlier sketch in CA 25-28R
Shaplen, June Herman
1924(?)-1982 Obituary 108
Shaplen, Robert (Modell) 1917-1988 ....9-12R
Obituary 125
Shapley, Fern Rusk 1890-1984 ....41-44R
Obituary 114
Shapley, Harlow 1885-1972 Obituary 37-40R
Shapley, John 1890(?)-1978 Obituary 81-84
Shapo, Marshall S(chambelan) 1936- CANR-15
Earlier sketch in CA 41-44R
Shapp, Charles M(orris) 1906-1989 57-60
Obituary 127
See also SATA 61
Shapp, Martha Glauber 1910- CANR-2
Earlier sketch in CA 1-4R
See also SATA 3
Shappiro, Herbert (Arthur) 1899(?)-1975 ....CAP-2
Obituary 57-60
Earlier sketch in CA 21-22
Sharabi, H(isham) B(ashir) 1927- CANR-2
Earlier sketch in CA 5-8R
Sharat Chandra, G(ubbi) S(hankara Chetty)
1938- 53-56
Sharfman, Amalie 73-76
See also SATA 14
Sharif, M(ohammad) Nawaz 1942- CANR-36
Earlier sketch in CA 114
Sharif, Omar
See Chalhoub, Michael
Sharkansky, Ira 1938- 29-32R
Sharkawi, A(bdel)-R(ahman)
1920-1987 Obituary 125
Sharkey, Bernarda 1934- 33-36R
Sharkey, Jack
See Sharkey, John Michael
Sharkey, John Michael 1931- CANR-3
Earlier sketch in CA 1-4R
Sharkey, Olive (Margaret Mary) 1954- 128
Sharkey, (Neil) Owen 1917- 61-64
Sharlet, Robert (Stewart) 1935- 37-40R
Sharlin, Harold I(ssadore) 1925- 9-12R
Sharma, Chandradhar 1920- 13-16R
Sharma, Govind Narain 1927- 45-48
Sharma, Jagdish Prasad 1934- 81-84
Sharma, Partap 1939- CANR-14
Earlier sketch in CA 77-80
See also SATA 15
Sharma, Ravindra N(ath) 1944- 110
Sharma, Shripad Rama 1879- CAP-2
Earlier sketch in CA 29-32
Sharma, Sohan L(al) 1927- 128
Sharman, Alison
See Leonard, Alison
Sharman, Maisie
See Bolton, Maisie Sharman
Sharman, Miriam
See Bolton, Maisie Sharman
Sharmat, Marjorie Weinman 1928- CANR-39
Earlier sketches in CA 25-28R, CANR-12
See also MAICYA
See also SATA 4, 33
Sharmat, Mitchell 1927- 104
See also SATA 33
Sharon, Donna Haye
See Scharlemann, Dorothy Hoyer
Sharon, Rose
See Merril, Judith
Sharon, Sylvia
See Little, Paul H(ugo)
Sharot, Stephen 1943- 109
Sharouni, Yusuf
See Al Sharouni, Youssef
Sharp, Aaron John 1904- 9-12R
Sharp, Alan 1934- 13-16R
Sharp, Andrew 1906-1974 ....CANR-3
Earlier sketch in CA 1-4R
Sharp, Ann Margaret 1942- 81-84
Sharp, Ansel M(iree) 1924- 77-80
Sharp, Buchanan 1942- 105
Sharp, Clifford Henry 1922- 108
Sharp, Daniel A(sher) 1932- 49-52
Sharp, Dolph 1914- 29-32R
Sharp, Donald Bruce 1938- 29-32R
Sharp, Doreen Maud 1920- CANR-25
Earlier sketch in CA 108
Sharp, Dorothea Elizabeth 21-24R
Sharp, Edith Lambert 1917- 5-8R
Sharp, Ernest Jack
See Sharpsteen, Ernest Jack
Sharp, Francis Michael 1941- 106
Sharp, Hal
See Sharp, Harold W(ilson)
Sharp, Harold S(pencer) 1909- CANR-3
Earlier sketch in CA 9-12R
Sharp, Harold W(ilson) 1914- 93-96
Sharp, Helen
See Paine, Lauran (Bosworth)
Sharp, James
See Kinghorn, A(lexander) M(anson)
Sharp, James Roger 1936- 29-32R
Sharp, John Kean 1892-1979 Obituary 93-96
Sharp, John R. 1921- 17-20R
Sharp, Laure M(etzger) 1921- 29-32R
Sharp, Margery 1905-1991 ....CANR-18
Obituary 134
Earlier sketch in CA 21-24R
See also CLR 27
See also MAICYA
See also SATA 1, 29
See also SATO 67
Sharp, Martin 1900(?)-1987 Obituary 124
Sharp, Paula 1957- 128
Sharp, Roger (William) 1935-1986 73-76
Obituary 119
Sharp, Ronald A(llan) 1945- 123
Sharp, Saundra 1942- 45-48
See also BW
Sharp, Shirley I. 1934- 45-48
Sharp, Sister Mary Corona 1922- 13-16R
Sharp, William 1855-1905 ....TCLC 39
Sharp, Zerna A. 1889-1981 Obituary 104
See also SATA 27
Sharpe, Genell J(ackson) Subak
See Subak-Sharpe, Genell J(ackson)
Sharpe, Grant W(illiam) 1925- 69-72

Sharpe, J(ames) A(nthony) 1946- 117
Sharpe, Jon
See Knott, William C(ecil Jr.)
Sharpe, Kevin 1949- 136
Sharpe, Lawrence A(lbright) 1920- 49-52
Sharpe, Lucretia
See Burgess, M(ichael) R(oy)
Sharpe, Mitchell R(aymond) 1924- 29-32R
See also SATA 12
Sharpe, Myron E(manuel) 1928- 136
Sharpe, Roger Carter 1948- 93-96
Sharpe, Susan 1946- ....SATA 71
Sharpe, Thomas Ridley 1928- 122
Brief entry 114
See also Sharpe, Tom
Sharpe, Tom
See Sharpe, Thomas Ridley
See also CLC 36
See also DLB 14
Sharpe, William D(onald) 1927- 17-20R
Sharpes, Donald K(enneth) 1934- CANR-1
Earlier sketch in CA 45-48
Sharples, Win(ston S.) Jr. 1932- 45-48
Sharpless, F(rancis) Parvin 1929- 25-28R
Sharpsteen, Ernest Jack
1880-1976 Obituary 110
Sharpton, Robert E(arl) 1936- 104
Sharrock, Roger (Ian) 1919-1991(?) CANR-2
Obituary 133
Earlier sketch in CA 5-8R
Sharwood Smith, Bryan Evers
1899-1983 ....CAP-2
Obituary 111
Earlier sketch in CA 29-32
Shatto, Gloria M. 1931- 41-44R
Shattock, Ernest (Henry) 1904- 102
Shattuck, Charles H(arlen) 1910- CANR-2
Earlier sketch in CA 5-8R
Shattuck, George C. 1927- 137
Shattuck, Roger (Whitney) 1923- CANR-7
Earlier sketch in CA 5-8R
See also SATA 64
Shatzkin, Leonard 1919- 109
Shaughnessy, Alfred (James) 1916- 134
Shaughnessy, Edward J(oseph Jr.) 1934- 110
Shaughnessy, Edward L(awrence) 1932- 130
Shaul, Frank
See Rowland, D(onald) S(ydney)
Shaull, (Millard) Richard 1919- CANR-11
Earlier sketch in CA 21-24R
Shave, Gordon A(shton) 1922- 101
Shavelson, Melville 1917- CANR-4
Earlier sketch in CA 53-56
Shaver, James P. 1933- CANR-7
Earlier sketch in CA 17-20R
Shaver, Phillip (Robert) 1944- 130
Shaver-Crandell, Anne (Elizabeth) 1941- 113
Shaver-Crandell, Annie
See Shaver-Crandell, Anne (Elizabeth)
Shavin, Norman 1926- 81-84
Shaw, Alan George Lewers 1916- CANR-9
Earlier sketch in CA 21-24R
Shaw, Albert 1857-1947 ....DLB 91
Shaw, Alison 1957- 130
Shaw, Arnold 1909-1989 ....CANR-1
Obituary 129
Earlier sketch in CA 1-4R
See also SATA 4, 63
Shaw, B(iswanath) N. 1923- 37-40R
Shaw, Barton C(arr) 1947- 123
Shaw, Bernard
See Shaw, George Bernard
See also TCLC 45
Shaw, Bernard 1940- 119
Brief entry 109
See also BW
Shaw, Bob 1931- CANR-19
Earlier sketches in CA 49-52, CANR-1
Shaw, Brian
See Tubb, E(dwin) C(harles)
Shaw, Bruce 1941- 119
Shaw, Bruno 1905-1984 Obituary 114
Shaw, Bynum (Gillette) 1923- CANR-4
Earlier sketch in CA 1-4R
Shaw, Carleton Ford 1908- CAP-1
Earlier sketch in CA 13-16
Shaw, Carolyn Hagner
1903(?)-1977 Obituary 69-72
Shaw, Charles (Green) 1892-1974 ....CAP-1
Earlier sketch in CA 17-18
See also SATA 13
Shaw, Charles R(aymond) 1921- CANR-14
Earlier sketch in CA 21-24R
Shaw, Chester Lee 1898(?)-1985 Obituary 118
Shaw, David 1943- 49-52
Shaw, Dawn
See Shaw, Thelma
Shaw, Donald Lewis 1936- 61-64
Shaw, Earl Bennett 1889- CAP-1
Earlier sketch in CA 17-18
Shaw, Edward P(ease) 1911-1986 ....21-24R
Obituary 118
Shaw, Elizabeth
See Prance, June E(lizebeth)
Shaw, Ellen Torgerson
See Torgerson Shaw, Ellen
Shaw, Evelyn S. 1927- 104
See also SATA 28
Shaw, Felicity 1918- 104
Shaw, Flora Louisa
See Lugard, Flora Louisa Shaw
Shaw, Fred Obituary 104
Shaw, Frederick W. 1916(?)-1983 Obituary 111
Shaw, Frederick 1912- CANR-1
Earlier sketch in CA 45-48
Shaw, G. Bernard
See Shaw, George Bernard
Shaw, Gaylord 1942- 81-84
Shaw, George
See Bickham, Jack M(iles)
Shaw, George Bernard 1856-1950 128
Brief entry 104
See also Shaw, Bernard
See also CDBLB 1914-1945
See also DLB 10, 57
See also MTCW
See also TCLC 3, 9, 21
See also WLC
Shaw, Graham 1944- 118
Shaw, Harold 1916(?)-1986 Obituary 118
Shaw, Harry Edmund 1946- 114
Shaw, Harry (Lee Jr.) 1905- 81-84
Shaw, Helen 1913-1985 ....CANR-20
Earlier sketch in CA 103
Shaw, Henry I(var) Jr. 1926- 33-36R
Shaw, Henry Wheeler 1818-1885 ....DLB 11
Shaw, Howard 1934- 106
Shaw, Irene
See Roberts, Irene
Shaw, Irwin 1913-1984 ....CANR-21
Obituary 112
Earlier sketch in CA 13-16R
See also AITN 1
See also CDALB 1941-1968
See also CLC 7, 23, 34
See also DLB 6, 102
See also DLBY 84
See also MTCW
Shaw, J(oseph) Thomas 1919- 17-20R
Shaw, Janet Beeler
See Shaw, Janet
Shaw, Janet 1937- 127
See also SATA 61
Shaw, John Bennett 1913- 21-24R
Shaw, John Mackay 1897-1984 ....CANR-13
Earlier sketch in CA 29-32R
Shaw, Lau
See Shu Ch'ing-ch'un
Shaw, Lawrence H(ugh) 1940- 69-72
Shaw, Leroy R(obert) 1923- 13-16R
Shaw, Linda 1938- CANR-23
Earlier sketch in CA 106
Shaw, Luci N(orthcote) 1928- CANR-39
Earlier sketches in CA 101, CANR-17
Shaw, Malcolm Edwin 1926- CANR-1
Earlier sketch in CA 1-4R
Shaw, Margret 1940- 136
See also SATA 68
Shaw, Marvin E(vert) 1919- 21-24R
Shaw, Maxine 1945- 57-60
Shaw, Murray 1908- 134
Shaw, Nancy Stoller 1942- 57-60
Shaw, Nancy 1946- ....SATA 71
Shaw, Peter 1936- CANR-9
Earlier sketch in CA 65-68
Shaw, Priscilla Washburn 1930- 13-16R
Shaw, Ralph R(obert)
1907-1972 Obituary 37-40R
Shaw, Ray 33-36R
See also SATA 7
Shaw, Richard 1923- 37-40R
See also SATA 12
Shaw, Robert B. 1947- ....DLB 120
Shaw, Robert B. 1947- 137
Shaw, Robert Byers 1916- 37-40R
Shaw, Robert 1927-1978 ....CANR-4
Obituary 81-84
Earlier sketch in CA 1-4R
See also AITN 1
See also CLC 5
See also DLB 13, 14
Shaw, Ronald D. M. 1883- CAP-1
Earlier sketch in CA 13-14
Shaw, Ronald E. 1923- 17-20R
Shaw, Russell B(urnham) 1935- CANR-3
Earlier sketch in CA 1-4R
Shaw, Stanford Jay 1930- CANR-6
Earlier sketch in CA 5-8R
Shaw, Steven John 1918- 17-20R
Shaw, T. D. W.
See Shaw, Thelma
Shaw, T. E.
See Lawrence, T(homas) E(dward)
Shaw, Thelma 25-28R
Shaw, Thurstan 1914- 103
Shaw, Timothy Milton 1945- CANR-30
Earlier sketch in CA 112
Shaw, Vivian
See Seldes, Gilbert (Vivian)
Shaw, W. David 1937- 29-32R
Shaw, (Harold) Watkins 1911- 1-4R
Shaw, Wayne E(ugene) 1932- 53-56
Shaw, William Harlan 1922- CANR-15
Earlier sketch in CA 41-44R
Shawchuck, Norman 1935- 126
Shawcross, John T. 1924- 13-16R
Shawcross, William 1946- 105
Shawhan, Ralph 1903(?)-1990 Obituary 130
Shawn, Edwin Meyers
1891-1972 Obituary 33-36R
Shawn, Frank S.
See Goulart, Ron(ald Joseph)
Shawn, Ted
See Shawn, Edwin Meyers
Shawn, Wallace 1943- 112
See also CLC 41
Shawn, William 1907- 108
Shay, Arthur 1922- 33-36R
See also SATA 4
Shay, Lacey
See Shebar, Sharon Sigmond
Shayne, Gordon
See Winter, Bevis (Peter)
Shayon, Robert Lewis 49-52
Shayon, Samuel 1904(?)-1984 Obituary 112
Shazar, Rachel
See Katznelson-Shazar, Rachel
Shazar, (Schneor) Zalman 1889-1974 101
Obituary 53-56
Shea, Donald F(rancis) 1925- 73-76
Shea, George E. Jr.
1902-1980 Obituary 97-100
Shea, George 1940- 108
See also SATA 42, 54
Shea, James J. 1890(?)-1977 Obituary 69-72
Shea, John Gerald 1906- 9-12R
Shea, John Gilmary 1824-1892 ....DLB 30
Shea, John S. 1933- 21-24R
Shea, John 1941- 73-76
Shea, Michael (Sinclair MacAuslan) 1938- 130
Shea, Michael 1946- 112
Shea, Patrick 1908- 130
Shea, Robert (Joseph) 1933- 101
Shea, Shirley 1924- 121
Sheaffer, Louis
See Slung, Louis Sheaffer
See also DLB 103
Sheaffer, Robert M(errill) 1949- 106
Sheagren, Thomas G(eorge) 1949- 118
Sheahan, John 1923- 17-20R
Sheahan, Richard T(homas) 1942- CANR-15
Earlier sketch in CA 65-68
Shealy, C(lyde) Norman 1932- CANR-7
Earlier sketch in CA 57-60
Shean, Glenn (Daniel) 1939- 53-56
Sheard, Kevin 1916- 41-44R
Shearer, John 1947- 125
See also SATA 27, 43
Shearer, Ronald A(lexander) 1932- 77-80
Shearer, Ted 1919- ....SATA 43
Shearing, Joseph
See Campbell, (Gabrielle) Margaret (Vere)
See also DLB 70
Shearman, Hugh (Francis) 1915- 13-16R
Shearman, John 1931- 13-16R
Shears, Billie
See Watson, O(scar) Michael
Sheats, Mary Boney 1918- 13-16R
Sheats, Paul Douglas 1932- 101
Shebar, Sharon Sigmond 1945- CANR-19
Earlier sketch in CA 103
See also SATA 36
Shebbeare, John 1709-1788 ....DLB 39
Shebl, James M(ichael) 1942- CANR-23
Earlier sketches in CA 61-64, CANR-8
Shechner, Mark E. 1940- 124
Sheckley, Robert 1928- CANR-2
Earlier sketch in CA 1-4R
See also DLB 8
Shecter, Ben 1935- 81-84
See also SATA 16
Shecter, Leonard 1926-1974 Obituary 45-48
Shedd, Charlie W. 1915- 17-20R
Shedd, Clarence Prouty
1887-1973 Obituary 45-48
Shedd, Margaret Cochran
1900-1986 Obituary 118
Shedd, William G. T. 1820-1894 ....DLB 64
Shedley, Ethan I.
See Beizer, Boris
Sheean, Diana 1915(?)-1987 Obituary 124
Sheean, (James) Vincent 1899-1975 61-64
Sheed, F. J.
See Sheed, Francis Joseph
Sheed, Francis J.
See Sheed, Francis Joseph
Sheed, Francis Joseph 1897-1981 129
Obituary 105
Sheed, Frank
See Sheed, Francis Joseph
Sheed, Frank J.
See Sheed, Francis Joseph
Sheed, Wilfrid (John Joseph) 1930- CANR-30
Earlier sketch in CA 65-68
See also CLC 2, 4, 10, 53
See also DLB 6
See also MTCW
Sheedy, Alexandra Elizabeth 1962- 85-88
See also SATA 19, 39
Sheehan, Arthur 1910(?)-1975 Obituary 61-64
Sheehan, Bernard W(illiam) 1934- 41-44R
Sheehan, Donald Henry 1917-1974 ....CANR-2
Earlier sketch in CA 1-4R
Sheehan, Ethna 1908- 61-64
See also SATA 9
Sheehan, George (Augustine) 1918- CANR-13
Earlier sketch in CA 73-76
Sheehan, James J(ohn) 1937- CANR-11
Earlier sketch in CA 17-20R
Sheehan, John F(rancis) X(avier) 1933- 122
Brief entry 118
Sheehan, Joseph Green
1918-1983 Obituary 111
Sheehan, Margaret A(nne) 1956- 111
Sheehan, Neil 1936- 29-32R
See also BEST 89:2
Sheehan, Patrick Augustine
See O Siochain, P(adraig) A(ugustine)
Sheehan, Paul V(incent) 1904- 33-36R
Sheehan, Sister Helen 1904- CAP-1
Earlier sketch in CA 17-18
Sheehan, Susan 1937- CANR-12
Earlier sketch in CA 21-24R
Sheehan, Thomas 1941- 122
Sheehan, Valerie Harms
See Harms, Valerie
Sheehy, Eugene P(aul) 1922- 9-12R
Sheehy, Gail 1937- CANR-33
Earlier sketches in CA 49-52, CANR-1
See also MTCW
Sheehy, Helen 1948- 133
Sheehy, Jeanne 1939- 110
Sheehy, Maurice S(tephen)
1898-1972 Obituary 111
Sheekman, Arthur 1901-1978 81-84
Obituary 73-76
Sheen, Fulton J(ohn) 1895-1979 ....CANR-5
Obituary 89-92
Earlier sketch in CA 5-8R
See also MTCW
Sheeran, James Jennings 1932- 65-68
Sheerin, John Basil 1906-1992 ....CANR-4
Obituary 136
Earlier sketch in CA 1-4R
Sheets, Elva (Darah) 1898- 57-60
Sheets, John R(ichard) 1922- 25-28R
Sheets, Kenneth Ray 1936- 136
Sheets, Millard (Owen) 1907-1989 Obituary 128
Sheets, Robin Lauterbach 1943- 131
Sheetz, Ann Kindig 1934- 101
Shefelman, Janice Jordan 1930- 120
See also SATA 58
Shefelman, Tom (Whitehead) 1927- ....SATA 58
Sheffer, H. R.
See Abels, Harriette S(heffer)
Sheffer, Isaiah 1935- 17-20R
Sheffield, James Rockwell
1936- Brief entry 106
Sheffield, Janet N. 1926- 65-68
See also SATA 26
Sheffy, Lester Fields 1887- CAP-1
Earlier sketch in CA 13-14
Sheftell, Fred D. 1941- 137
Shefter, Harry 1910- 9-12R
Shefter, Martin 1943- 136
Shefts, Joelle ....SATA 49
Shehan, Lawrence Joseph 1898-1984 117
Shein, Brian 1947- 110
Shein, Louis J(ulius) 1914- 25-28R
Sheiness, (Lee) Marsha 1940- CANR-15
Earlier sketch in CA 89-92
Sheinwold, Alfred 1912- 61-64
Sheinwold, Patricia
See Fox-Sheinwold, Patricia
Shek, Ben-Zion 1927- 110
Shekerjian, Regina Tor ....SATA 16
Shelbourne, Cecily
See Goodwin, Suzanne
Shelby, Brit
See Grady, James (Thomas)
Shelby, Carroll Hall 1923- 17-20R
Shelby, Graham 1940- 102
Shelby, Susan
See Kinnicutt, Susan Sibley
Sheldon, Alan 1933- 114
Sheldon, Alice Hastings Bradley
1915(?)-1987 ....CANR-34
Obituary 122
Earlier sketch in CA 108
See also Tiptree, James Jr.
See also MTCW
Sheldon, Ann CANR-27
Earlier sketches in CAP-2, CA 19-20
See also SATA 1, 67
Sheldon, Aure 1917-1976 61-64
See also SATA 12
Sheldon, Charles Harvey 1929- 107
Sheldon, Charles S(tuart) II
1917-1981 Obituary 105
Sheldon, Deyan 53-56
Sheldon, Edward 1886-1946 ....DLB 7
Sheldon, Eleanor Bernert 1920- 85-88
Sheldon, Esther K. 1906- 37-40R
Sheldon, George E.
See Stahl, Le Roy
Sheldon, John
See Bloch, Robert (Albert)
Sheldon, Lee
See Lee, Wayne C.
Sheldon, Michael 1918- 17-20R
Sheldon, Muriel 1926- CANR-18
Earlier sketch in CA 101
See also SATA 39, 45
Sheldon, Peter 1922- 25-28R
Sheldon, Raccoona
See Sheldon, Alice Hastings Bradley
Sheldon, Richard (Robert) 1932- 33-36R
Sheldon, Roy ....AITN 1
Sheldon, Roy
See Tubb, E(dwin) C(harles)
Sheldon, Scott
See Wallmann, Jeffrey M(iner)
Sheldon, Sidney 1917- CANR-33
Earlier sketch in CA 29-32R
See also AITN 1
See also BEST 89:1
See also MTCW
Sheldon, Suzanne Eaton
1928(?)-1985 Obituary 117
Sheldon, Walt
See Sheldon, Walter J.
Sheldon, Walter J. 1917- CANR-10
Earlier sketch in CA 25-28R
See also AITN 1
Sheldon, William Denley 1915- 17-20R
Sheldon, William (Herbert) 1898-1977 ....25-28R
Obituary 116
Sheldrake, Rupert 1942- 127
Sheldrick, Daphne 1934- CANR-3
Earlier sketch in CA 49-52
Shell, Ellen Ruppel 1952- 138
Shell, Virginia Law 1923- 21-24R
Shelley, Bruce L(eon) 1927- CANR-9
Earlier sketch in CA 21-24R
Shelley, Dolores 1937- 122
Shelley, Florence D(ubroff) 1921- 65-68
Shelley, Frances
See Wees, Frances Shelley

Shelley, Lillian
See Koppel, Lillian
and Koppel, Shelley R(uth)
Shelley, Louise I(sabel) 1952- 108
Shelley, Mack Clayton II 1950- 126
Shelley, Mary Wollstonecraft (Godwin)
1797-1851 .... CDBLB 1789-1832
See also DLB 110, 116
See also SATA 29
See also WLC
Shelley, Noreen 1920- 104
Shelley, Percy Bysshe
1792-1822 .... CDBLB 1789-1832
See also DLB 96, 110
See also WLC
Shelley, Rebecca 1887(?)-1984 Obituary 111
Shelly, (Michael) Bruce 1929- 57-60
Shelly, Judith A(llen) 1944- CANR-38
Earlier sketch in CA 115
Shelly, Maynard W(olfe) 1928- CANR-7
Earlier sketch in CA 13-16R
Shelly, Peter
See Dresser, Davis
Shelmerdine, Cynthia Wright 1949- 117
Shelnutt, Eve (Brown) 1941- 132
See also CAAS 14
Shelp, Earl E(dward) 1947- 116
Shelton, Barrett C(linton)
1903(?)-1984 Obituary 112
Shelton, (Austin) Jess(e) Jr. 1926- CANR-25
Earlier sketch in CA 1-4R
Shelton, Kathleen J. 1946-1990 Obituary 131
Shelton, Lola
See Klaue, Lola Shelton
Shelton, Mark L(ogan) 1958- 135
Shelton, Regina Maria 1927- 112
Shelton, Richard 1933- CANR-13
Earlier sketch in CA 33-36R
Shelton, Suzanne
See Buckley, Suzanne Shelton
Shelton, William Roy 1919- CANR-11
Earlier sketch in CA 5-8R
See also AITN 1
See also SATA 5
Shemie, Bonnie (Jean Brenner) 1949- 133
Shemin, Margaretha (Hoeneveld) 1928- 13-16R
See also SATA 4
Shen, James C. H. 1909- 126
Shen, Peter 110
Shen Congwen 1902-1988 Obituary 125
Shengold, Leonard 1925- 136
Shenk, David W(itmer) 1937- 106
Shenk, Lois (Landis) 1944- 114
Shenk, Marcia Ann 1953- 73-76
Shenk, Wilbert R. 1935- 21-24R
Shenkin, Elizabeth Shoemaker Obituary 61-64
Shennan, Joseph Hugh 1933- 103
Shenon, Philip 1959- 136
Shenoy, B(ellikoth) R(aghunath) 1905- 77-80
Shenstone, William 1714-1763 .... DLB 95
Shenton, Edward H(eriot) 1932- CANR-17
Earlier sketch in CA 25-28R
Shenton, Edward 1895-1977 .... SATA 45
Shenton, James P(atrick) 1925- CANR-2
Earlier sketch in CA 5-8R
Shen Tong 1968- 135
Shepard, David W. 1922- 93-96
Shepard, Elaine (Elizabeth) 1923- 21-24R
Shepard, Ernest Howard 1879-1976 ....CANR-23
Obituary 65-68
Earlier sketch in CA 9-12R
See also CLR 27
See also MAICYA
See also SATA 3, 24, 33
Shepard, Francis P(arker) 1897- 13-16R
Shepard, Gary 1939- 97-100
Shepard, Jean H(eck) 1930- 49-52
Shepard, Jim 1956- 137
See also CLC 36
Shepard, Jon M(ax) 1939- CANR-7
Earlier sketch in CA 57-60
Shepard, Leslie (Alan) 1917- CANR-8
Earlier sketch in CA 17-20R
Shepard, Leslie Albert 1929- 29-32R
Shepard, Lucius Brief entry 128
See also CLC 34
Shepard, Martin 1934- 33-36R
Shepard, Mary
See Knox, (Mary) Eleanor Jessie
Shepard, Odell 1884-1967 ....CANR-3
Obituary 25-28R
Earlier sketch in CA 5-8R
Shepard, Paul (Howe) 1925- CANR-10
Earlier sketch in CA 21-24R
Shepard, Richard F. 1922- 115
Shepard, Richmond 1929- 29-32R
Shepard, Sam 1943- CANR-22
Earlier sketch in CA 69-72
See also CABS 3
See also AAYA 1
See also CLC 4, 6, 17, 34, 41, 44
See also DLB 7
See also MTCW
Shepard, Thomas I 1604(?)-1649 .... DLB 24
Shepard, Thomas II 1635-1677 .... DLB 24
Shepard, Thomas Rockwell Jr. 1918- 105
Shepardson, Mary (Thygeson) 1906- 29-32R
Shephard, Esther 1891-1975 .... CAP-2
Obituary 57-60
Earlier sketch in CA 25-28
See also SATA 5, 26
Shephard, John (Brownlow) 1900- CAP-1
Earlier sketch in CA 13-14
Shephard, Roy J(esse) 1929- CANR-11
Earlier sketch in CA 29-32R
Shepherd, David Gwynne 1924- 5-8R
Shepherd, (Richard) David 1931- 65-68
Shepherd, Donald (Lee) 1932- 61-64
Shepherd, Elizabeth 33-36R
See also SATA 4
Shepherd, Geoffrey (Seddon) 1898- CANR-20
Earlier sketch in CA 1-4R
Shepherd, George W. Jr. 1926- CANR-6
Earlier sketch in CA 1-4R
Shepherd, Gordon
See Brook-Shepherd, (Frederick) Gordon
Shepherd, J(ohn) Barrie 1935- CANR-29
Earlier sketch in CA 111
Shepherd, Jack 1937- 57-60
Shepherd, James L(eftwich) III 1921- 21-24R
Shepherd, Jean (Parker) 1929- 77-80
See also AITN 2
Shepherd, Joan
See Buchanan, Betty (Joan)
Shepherd, John
See Ballard, (Willis) Todhunter
Shepherd, L. P. 53-56
Shepherd, Massey H. Jr.
See Shepherd, Massey Hamilton Jr.
Shepherd, Massey Hamilton
See Shepherd, Massey Hamilton Jr.
Shepherd, Massey Hamilton Jr. 1913- 122
Shepherd, Michael
See Ludlum, Robert
Shepherd, Nan 1893- 105
Shepherd, Neal
See Morland, Nigel
Shepherd, Robert Henry Wishart
1888-1971 .... CAP-1
Earlier sketch in CA 13-14
Shepherd, Robert 1949- 136
Shepherd, Simon 1951- 120
Shepherd, Walter Bradley 1904- 105
Shepherd, William C(hauncey) 1942- CANR-18
Earlier sketch in CA 25-28R
Shepley, James R(obinson)
1917-1988 Obituary 127
Brief entry 112
Sheppard, Anne
See Sheppard, Anne D(eborah) R(aphael)
Sheppard, Anne D(eborah) R(aphael)
1951- 128
Sheppard, Barry 1937- 61-64
Sheppard, Cynthia A(nne) 1955- 108
Sheppard, David Stuart 1929- 103
Sheppard, Don(ald D.) 1930- 138
Sheppard, Eugenia (Benbow) 1900(?)-1984 103
Obituary 114
Sheppard, Francis Henry Wollaston
1921- 21-24R
Sheppard, Harold L(loyd) 1922- CANR-1
Earlier sketch in CA 45-48
Sheppard, Joseph 1930- CANR-23
Earlier sketches in CA 61-64, CANR-8
Sheppard, Lancelot C(apel) 1906- CANR-5
Earlier sketch in CA 5-8R
Sheppard, Lila (Brooks) 1906- CAP-1
Earlier sketch in CA 13-14
Sheppard, Mary 29-32R
Sheppard, Roger 1939- 77-80
Sheppard, Sally 1917- 69-72
Sheppard, Stephen 1945- 105
Sheppard, Thomas F(rederick) 1935- 73-76
Sheppard, Walter Lee Jr. 1911- 69-72
Sheppard-Jones, Elisabeth 1920- 13-16R
Shepperson, Wilbur Stanley 1919- CANR-6
Earlier sketch in CA 1-4R
Sheps, Cecil G(eorge) 1913- 9-12R
Sheps, Mindel (Cherniack)
1913-1973 Obituary 37-40R
Sher, Barbara 1935- 132
Sher, Eva CAP-2
Earlier sketch in CA 23-24
Sher, Gerson S(amuel) 1947- 81-84
Sher, Jack 1913-1988 Obituary 126
Sher, Zelig 1888-1971 Obituary 104
Shera, Jesse Hauk 1903-1982 ....CANR-2
Obituary 106
Earlier sketch in CA 5-8R
Sherar, Mariam G(hose) 1924- 45-48
Sherashevski, Boris
See Brown, John J.
Sheraton, Mimi 1926- 126
Sheraton, Neil
See Smith, Norman Edward Mace
Sheratsky, Rodney E(arl) 1933- 25-28R
Sherbo, Arthur 1918- Brief entry 113
Sherburne, Donald W(ynne) 1929- 1-4R
Sherburne, James (Robert) 1925- 33-36R
Sherburne, Zoa (Morin) 1912- CANR-37
Earlier sketches in CA 1-4R, CANR-3
See also CLC 30
See also MAICYA
See also SATA 3
Sherby, Linda B(arbara) 1946- 108
Shercliff, Jose 1902(?)-1985 Obituary 115
Sherdeman, Ted 1910(?)-1987 Obituary 123
Shere, Dennis 1940- 77-80
Sherek, Henry 1900-1967 .... CAP-1
Earlier sketch in CA 13-16
Sherer, Mary Louise 1901- 101
Sherer, Michael W. 1952- 127
Sherer, Robert G(lenn Jr.) 1940- 69-72
Sherer, Rene (Dundee) 1933- 29-32R
Sherfey, Mary Jane 1933-1983 Obituary 109
Shergold, N(orman) D(avid) 1925- 25-28R
Sheridan, Adora
See Hong, Jane Fay
and Pavlik, Evelyn Marie
Sheridan, Anne-Marie 1948- 85-88
Sheridan, Dorothy Elizabeth 1948- 116
Sheridan, Eugene Robert 1945- CANR-23
Earlier sketch in CA 107
Sheridan, Frances 1724-1766 .... DLB 39, 84
Sheridan, James E(dward) 1922- 21-24R
Sheridan, James F(rancis) Jr. 1927- 29-32R
Sheridan, Jane
See Winslow, Pauline Glen
Sheridan, John V. 1915- CANR-3
Earlier sketch in CA 9-12R
Sheridan, L(ionel) A(stor) 1927- CANR-9
Earlier sketch in CA 21-24R
Sheridan, Lane
See Winslow, Pauline Glen
Sheridan, Lee
See Lee, Elsie
Sheridan, Marion Campbell 17-20R
Sheridan, Martin 1914- 104
Sheridan, Polly
See Oates, Jeannette
Sheridan, Richard B. 1918- 45-48
Sheridan, Richard Brinsley
1751-1816 .... CDBLB 1660-1789
See also DC 1
See also DLB 89
See also WLC
Sheridan, Thomas L. 1926- 37-40R
Sheridan, Thomas 1938- 61-64
Sherif, Carolyn W(ood) 1922- 17-20R
Sherif, Muzafer 1906-1988 .... CAP-1
Obituary 126
Earlier sketch in CA 13-14
Sheriff, John K(eith) 1944- 120
Sherlock, John 1932- CANR-3
Earlier sketch in CA 9-12R
Sherlock, Patti .... SATA 71
Sherlock, Philip Manderson 1902- CANR-6
Earlier sketch in CA 5-8R
Sherlock, Richard 1947- 126
Sherman, A(lan) Robert 1942- 57-60
Sherman, Allan 1924-1973 101
Obituary 45-48
Sherman, Arnold 1932- CANR-14
Earlier sketch in CA 33-36R
Sherman, Arthur W(esley) Jr. 1917- CANR-21
Earlier sketch in CA 1-4R
Sherman, Barbara H(ayes) 1942- 25-28R
Sherman, Bernard 1929- 29-32R
Sherman, Cecil E(dwin) 1927- 127
Brief entry 110
Sherman, Charles Bezalel 1896-1971 ....1-4R
Obituary 103
Sherman, Charlotte A.
See Sherman, Jory (Tecumseh)
Sherman, Claire Richter 1930- 106
Sherman, Constance D(enise) 1909- 45-48
Sherman, D(enis) R(onald) 1934- CANR-8
Earlier sketch in CA 13-16R
See also SATA 29, 48
Sherman, Dan(iel Michael) 1950- 77-80
Sherman, Diane (Finn) 1928- CANR-5
Earlier sketch in CA 9-12R
See also SATA 12
Sherman, Eileen Bluestone 1951- 119
Sherman, Eleanor Rae 1929- 13-16R
Sherman, Elizabeth
See Friskey, Margaret (Richards)
Sherman, Eric 1947- 69-72
Sherman, Francis 1871-1926 .... DLB 92
Sherman, Franklin (Eugene) 1928- 57-60
Sherman, G(eorge) W(itters) 1903- 117
Sherman, Harold (Morrow) 1898- 77-80
See also SATA 37
Sherman, (Marcus) Harvey 1917-1985 ....21-24R
Obituary 114
Sherman, Howard J. 1931- CANR-10
Earlier sketch in CA 13-16R
Sherman, Ingrid 1919- 103
Sherman, James E(dward) 1939- 25-28R
Sherman, Jane 1908- CANR-12
Earlier sketch in CA 73-76
Sherman, Jerry 1924- 97-100
Sherman, Joan
See Dern, Erolie Pearl Gaddis
Sherman, Joe 1945- 137
Sherman, Jonathan Marc .... CLC 55
Sherman, Jory (Tecumseh) 1932- CANR-28
Earlier sketches in CA 69-72, CANR-11
Sherman, Josepha 127
Sherman, Julia A(nn) 1934- 37-40R
Sherman, Kenneth 1950- 117
Sherman, L. L.
See Armentrout, Fred S(herman)
Sherman, Lawrence W(illiam) 1949- CANR-7
Earlier sketch in CA 57-60
Sherman, Lynn
See Obrecht, Jas
Sherman, Martin 1941(?)- 123
Brief entry 116
See also CLC 19
Sherman, Michael
See Lowndes, Robert A(ugustine) W(ard)
Sherman, Michele 1945- CANR-36
Earlier sketch in CA 114
Sherman, Murray H(erbert) 1922- 17-20R
Sherman, Nancy
See Rosenberg, Nancy (Sherman)
Sherman, Patrick 1928- 103
Sherman, Peter Michael
See Lowndes, Robert A(ugustine) W(ard)
Sherman, Philip M(artin) 1930- 29-32R
Sherman, Ray W(esley)
1884-1971 Obituary 33-36R
Sherman, Richard B. 1929- 29-32R
Sherman, Richard M(orton)
1928- Brief entry 107
Sherman, Robert B(ernard)
1925- Brief entry 108
Sherman, Roger 1930- 37-40R
Sherman, Spencer E. 1936- 112
Sherman, Steve (Barry) 1938- 37-40R
Sherman, Susan Jean 1939- 1-4R
Sherman, T. P. 1917-1976 .... CAP-2
Earlier sketch in CA 29-32
Sherman, Theodore A(llison)
1901-1981 ....17-20R
Obituary 134
Sherman, William David 1940- CANR-21
Earlier sketch in CA 105
Sherman, William Lewis 1927- 105
Shero, Fred (Alexander) 1925- 105
Sherover, Charles M. 25-28R
Sherr, Lynn Beth 1942- Brief entry 109
Sherr, Paul C(linton) 1920- 77-80
Sherraden, Michael (Wayne) 1948- 137
Sherrard, Philip (Owen Arnould) 1922- CANR-7
Earlier sketch in CA 13-16R
Sherriff, R(obert) C(edric) 1896-1975 85-88
Obituary 61-64
See also DLB 10
Sherriffs, Ronald E(verett)
1934- Brief entry 112
Sherrill, Dorothy 1901- 69-72
Sherrill, Elizabeth 1928- 110
Sherrill, Henry Knox
1890-1980 Obituary 97-100
Sherrill, John L. 1923- 110
Sherrill, Robert G(lenn) 1925- CANR-15
Earlier sketch in CA 21-24R
Sherrill, Suzanne
See Woods, Sherryl
Sherrin, Edward George 1931- CANR-15
Earlier sketch in CA 21-24R
Sherrin, Ned
See Sherrin, Edward George
Sherrington, Richard (Wallace) 1940-1977 108
Sherrod, Blackie .... AITN 2
Sherrod, Drury 1943- 109
Sherrod, Jane
See Singer, Jane Sherrod
Sherrod, Robert (Lee) 1909- 77-80
Sherry, James 1946- 112
Sherry, John E(rnest) H(orwath)
1932- CANR-37
Earlier sketches in CA 89-92, CANR-16
Sherry, John (Olden) 1923- 119
Sherry, Michael S(tephen) 1945- 73-76
Sherry, Norman 1925- CANR-34
Earlier sketch in CA 49-52
See also BEST 89:4
Sherry, Patrick 1938- 138
Sherry, Pearl Andelson 1899- 109
Sherry, (Dulcie) Sylvia 1932- CANR-34
Earlier sketch in CA 49-52
See also SATA 8
Sherry, Vincent B(ernard) Jr. 1948- CANR-39
Earlier sketch in CA 116
Shershow, Scott Cutler 1953- 123
Shertzer, Bruce E(ldon) 1928- CANR-3
Earlier sketch in CA 9-12R
Sherwan, Earl 1917- 5-8R
See also SATA 3
Sherwin, Byron L(ee) 1946- 123
Sherwin, Judith Johnson 1936- CANR-34
Earlier sketch in CA 25-28R
See also CLC 7, 15
Sherwin, Martin J(ay) 1937- Brief entry 110
Sherwin, Oscar 1902-1976 ....1-4R
Obituary 65-68
Sherwin, Richard E(lliott) 1933- 69-72
Sherwin, Sidney 1920- 65-68
Sherwin, Sterling
See Hagen, John Milton
Sherwin-White, A(drian) N(icholas) 1911- 119
Sherwood, Debbie
See Sherwood, Deborah
Sherwood, Deborah 25-28R
Sherwood, Dolly 138
Sherwood, Frank Persons 1920- CANR-9
Earlier sketch in CA 5-8R
Sherwood, Hugh C. 1928- 29-32R
Sherwood, John C(ollingwood) 1918- 13-16R
Sherwood, John (Herman Mulso)
1913- CANR-21
Earlier sketches in CA 5-8R, CANR-6
Sherwood, John J(oseph) 1933- 29-32R
Sherwood, Martin (Anthony) 1942- CANR-19
Earlier sketch in CA 102
Sherwood, Michael 1938-1976 .... CAP-2
Earlier sketch in CA 29-32
Sherwood, Morgan B(ronson) 1929- CANR-6
Earlier sketch in CA 13-16R
Sherwood, Nelson
See Bulmer, (Henry) Kenneth
Sherwood, Robert D(an) 1949- 118
Sherwood, Robert E(mmet)
1896-1955 Brief entry 104
See also DLB 7, 26
See also TCLC 3
Sherwood, William Robert 1929- 21-24R
Shesgreen, Sean N(icholas) 1939- 45-48
Shestack, Alan 1938- 33-36R
Shestack, Jerome J(oseph) 1925- 118
Shestack, Melvin (Bernard) 1931- 120
Sheth, Jagdish N(anchand) 1938- CANR-11
Earlier sketch in CA 61-64
Shetter, William Z(eiders Jr.) 1927- 81-84
Shetterly, Will(iam Howard) 1955- 119
Shettles, Landrum Brewer 1909- CANR-13
Earlier sketch in CA 77-80
Shetty, C(handrashekar) M(ajur)
1927- CANR-10
Earlier sketch in CA 13-16R
Shetty, Sharat 1940- 73-76
Shev, Edward E(lmer) 1919- 93-96
Shevchenko, A. N.
See Shevchenko, Arkady N(ikolaevich)
Shevchenko, Arkady N(ikolaevich) 1930- 129

Shevchuk, Tetiana
See Bishop, Tania Kroitor
Shevelove, Burt 1915-1982 Obituary ... 106
Shevin, David (Avram) 1951- ... 77-80
Shevrin, Aliza 1931- ... 129
Shew, E(dward) Spencer 1908-1977 ... CANR-3
Obituary ... 69-72
Earlier sketch in CA 1-4R
Shewbridge, Edythe A(nne) 1943- ... 41-44R
Shewell-Cooper, W(ilfred) E(dward)
1900- ... CANR-7
Earlier sketch in CA 9-12R
Shewmaker, Kenneth E. 1936- ... 33-36R
Shewring, Walter Hayward (Francis)
1906(?)-1990 Obituary ... 132
Shi, David Emory 1951- ... CANR-28
Earlier sketch in CA 106
Shiach, Allan G. 1941- ... 136
Shiarella, Robert 1936- ... 57-60
Shibles, Warren 1933- ... CANR-12
Earlier sketch in CA 29-32R
Shibutani, Tamotsu 1920- ... 17-20R
Shideler, John C(lement) 1949- ... 118
Shideler, Mary McDermott 1917- ... 25-28R
Shidle, Norman G(lass) 1895- ... 17-20R
Shiefman, Vicky 1942- ... 57-60
See also SATA 22
Shieh, Francis S(hih-hoa) 1926- ... 37-40R
Shiel, M(atthew) P(hipps)
1865-1947 Brief entry ... 106
See also TCLC 8
Shield, Renee Rose 1948- ... 115
Shields, Allan (Edwin) 1919- ... 65-68
Shields, Brenda Desmond (Armstrong)
1914- ... 5-8R
See also SATA 37
Shields, Carol 1935- ... 81-84
Shields, Charles 1944- ... SATA 10
Shields, Currin Vance 1918- ... 1-4R
Shields, David 1956- ... 124
Shields, Donald J(ames) 1937- ... 53-56
Shields, Gerald R. 1925- ... 110
Shields, Joyce Farley 1930- Brief entry ... 109
Shields, Laurie 1922(?)-1989 Obituary ... 128
Shiels, Barbara
See Adams, Barbara Johnston
Shiels, Frederick L(ambert) 1949- ... 118
Shiels, George 1886-1949 Brief entry ... 111
See also DLB 10
Shiels, W(illiam) Eugene 1897- ... CAP-1
Earlier sketch in CA 9-10
Shiers, George 1908- ... 73-76
Shiff, Nathan A. 1914- ... 25-28R
Shiffert, Edith (Marcombe) 1916- ... CANR-6
Earlier sketch in CA 13-16R
Shifflett, Crandall A(vis) 1938- ... 135
Shiffrin, Nancy 1944- ... 81-84
Shiflet, Kenneth E(lwood) 1918-1978 ... CANR-2
Obituary ... 81-84
Earlier sketch in CA 1-4R
Shiflett, Lee
See Shiflett, Orvin Lee
Shiflett, Orvin Lee 1947- ... 115
Shiga, Naoya 1883-1971 ... 101
Obituary ... 33-36R
See also CLC 33
Shigley, Forrest Dwight 1930- ... 1-4R
Shih, Chung-wen ... 81-84
Shih, Vincent Y(u) C(hung) 1903- ... 77-80
Shih Hsio-Yen 1933- ... 119
Shikes, Ralph E. 1912- ... CANR-12
Obituary ... 137
Earlier sketch in CA 29-32R
Shillaber, Benjamin Penhallow
1814-1890 ... DLB 1, 11
Shiller, Jack G(erald) 1928- ... 73-76
Shiller, Robert J. 1946- ... 136
Shilling, Dana 1953- ... CANR-29
Earlier sketch in CA 109
Shilling, N(ed) 1924- ... 29-32R
Shillinglaw, Gordon 1925- ... CANR-7
Earlier sketch in CA 17-20R
Shillingsburg, Miriam J.
See Shillingsburg, Miriam (Carolyn) Jones
Shillingsburg, Miriam (Carolyn) Jones
1943- ... 130
Shillony, Ben-Ami 1937- ... 73-76
Shiloh, Ailon 1924- ... 33-36R
Shils, Edward B. 1915- ... CANR-6
Earlier sketch in CA 5-8R
Shilton, Lance(lot) R(upert) 1921- ... 5-8R
Shilts, Randy 1951- ... 127
Brief entry ... 115
Shimazaki Haruki 1872-1943 ... 134
Brief entry ... 105
See also Shimazaki Toson
Shimazaki Toson
See Shimazaki Haruki
See also TCLC 5
Shimberg, Benjamin 1918- ... 45-48
Shimberg, Elaine Fantle 1937- ... CANR-31
Earlier sketch in CA 112
Shimer, Dorothy Blair 1911- ... 45-48
Shimin, Symeon 1902- ... 81-84
See also MAICYA
See also SATA 13
Shimkin, Michael B(oris)
1912-1989 Obituary ... 127
Shimoniak, Wasyl 1923- Brief entry ... 108
Shimota, Helen
See Gross, Helen Shimota
Shinagel, Michael 1934- ... 25-28R
Shindell, Sidney 1923- ... 13-16R
Shinder, Jason (Scott) 1955- ... 133
Shine, Deborah 1932- ... 110
See also SATA 71
Shine, Frances L(ouise) 1927- ... 25-28R
Shine, Ted 1931- ... CANR-24
Earlier sketches in CA 77-80, CANR-13
See also BW
See also DLB 38
Shiner, Larry (Ernest) 1934- ... 21-24R
Shiner, Roger A(lfred) 1940- Brief entry ... 109
Shingleton, John D. ... CANR-37
Earlier sketch in CA 115
Shingleton, Royce (Gordon Sr.)
1935- ... CANR-12
Earlier sketch in CA 29-32R
Shinichi, Kano
See Jackson, G. Mark
Shinkle, James D. 1897(?)-1973 Obituary ... 104
Shinkle, Tex
See Shinkle, James D.
Shinn, Everett 1876-1953 ... SATA 21
Shinn, Larry Dwight 1942- ... 107
Shinn, Roger L(incoln) 1917- ... CANR-18
Earlier sketch in CA 1-4R
Shinnie, Peter Lewis 1915- ... 103
Shinoda, Minoru 1915- ... 5-8R
Shinwell, Emanuel 1884-1986 Obituary ... 119
Ship, Reuben 1915-1975 ... DLB 88
Shipler, David K(arr) 1942- ... CANR-21
Earlier sketch in CA 103
Shiplett, June Lund 1930- ... CANR-36
Earlier sketches in CA 81-84, CANR-16
Shipley, David
See Holden, David (Shipley)
Shipley, David O. 1925- ... 37-40R
Shipley, Joseph T(wadell) 1893-1988 ... CANR-9
Obituary ... 125
Earlier sketch in CA 13-16R
Shipley, Nan (Sommerville) ... 9-12R
Shipley, Peter (Samuel) 1946- ... CANR-20
Earlier sketch in CA 103
Shipley, (Howard) Thorne 1927- ... 5-8R
Shipman, David 1932- ... CANR-30
Earlier sketches in CA 29-32R, CANR-12
Shipman, Harry L(ongfellow) 1948- ... CANR-32
Earlier sketches in CA 65-68, CANR-10
Shipp, Nelson 1892- ... 57-60
Shipp, Thomas J. 1918- ... 13-16R
Shippen, Katherine B(inney) 1892-1980 ... 5-8R
Obituary ... 93-96
See also SATA 1, 23
Shipper, Frank M(artin) 1945- ... 119
Shippey, Frederick Alexander 1908- ... CAP-1
Earlier sketch in CA 13-14
Shippey, (Henry) Lee
1884-1969 Obituary ... 89-92
Shippey, Thomas Alan 1943- ... 108
Shipps, Jan (Barnett) 1929- ... 127
Shippy, Richard W. 1927- ... 81-84
Shipton, Clifford K(enyon) 1902-1973 ... CAP-2
Earlier sketch in CA 17-18
Shipton, Eric Earle 1907-1977 ... 65-68
Obituary ... 69-72
See also SATA 10
Shipway, George 1908- ... 25-28R
Shirakawa, Yoshikazu 1935- ... CANR-14
Earlier sketch in CA 73-76
Shiratori, Rei 1937- ... 133
Shire, Helena (Mary) Mennie
1912-1991 ... CANR-27
Obituary ... 136
Earlier sketch in CA 29-32R
Shirer, William L(awrence) 1904- ... CANR-7
Earlier sketch in CA 9-12R
See also DLB 4
See also MTCW
See also SATA 45
Shires, Henry M(illis) 1913-1980 ... 17-20R
Obituary ... 134
Shires, Linda M(arguerite) 1950- ... 118
Shirk, Evelyn Urban 1918- ... 17-20R
Shirk, George H(enry) 1913- ... 17-20R
Shirk, Susan L(ee) 1945- ... 108
Shirkey, Albert P(atterson) 1904-1990 ... CAP-2
Obituary ... 133
Earlier sketch in CA 17-18
Shirley, Dennis 1955- ... 137
Shirley, Frances A(nn) 1931- ... CANR-2
Earlier sketch in CA 5-8R
Shirley, Glenn 1916- ... 89-92
Shirley, Hardy L(omax) 1900- ... 37-40R
Shirley, James 1596-1666 ... DLB 58
Shirley, Jean 1919- ... 138
See also SATA 70
Shirley, John William 1908- ... 126
Brief entry ... 114
Shirley, John 1953- ... 126
Shirley, Ralph 1865-1946 Brief entry ... 117
Shirley-Smith, Hubert 1901-1981 Obituary ... 113
Shirreffs, Gordon D(onald) 1914- ... CANR-21
Earlier sketches in CA 13-16R, CANR-6
See also SATA 11
Shirts, Morris A(lpine) 1922- ... 73-76
See also SATA 63
Shissler, Barbara Johnson
See Nosanow, Barbara Shissler
Shivanandan, Mary 1932- ... CANR-12
Earlier sketch in CA 73-76
Shively, Donald H(oward) 1921- Brief entry ... 115
Shively, George Jenks
1893(?)-1980 Obituary ... 97-100
Shivers, Alfred Samuel 1929- ... 41-44R
Shivers, Frank R(emer) Jr. 1924- ... 130
Shivers, Jay S(anford) 1930- ... CANR-27
Earlier sketches in CA 33-36R, CANR-12
Shivers, Louise 1929- ... 136
Shivers, Samuel A.
See Shivers, Alfred Samuel
Shivpuri, Gopi Krishna 1903-1984 ... 101
Obituary ... 113
Shklovsky, Iosif Samuilovitch
1916-1985 Obituary ... 115
Shklovsky, Viktor Borisovich
1893-1984 Obituary ... 114
Shlaim, Avi 1945- ... 136
Shlemon, Barbara Leahy 1936- ... CANR-31
Earlier sketch in CA 112
Shlonsky, Abraham
1898(?)-1973 Obituary ... 41-44R
Shmueli, Adi 1941- ... CANR-1
Earlier sketch in CA 45-48
Shnayerson, Michael 1954- ... 132
Shneerson, Grigory Mikhailovich
1901-1982 Obituary ... 106
Shneiderman, Ben A. 1947- ... 115
Shneiderman, Samuel L(oeb) 1906- ... 97-100
Shneidman, Conalee Levine
See Levine-Shneidman, Conalee
Shneidman, Edwin S. 1918- ... CANR-36
Earlier sketch in CA 29-32R
Shneidman, J(erome) Lee 1929- ... 37-40R
Shneidman, N(oah) N(orman) 1924- ... 136
Shneour, Elie A(lexis) 1925- ... 37-40R
Shoaf, Richard Allen 1948- ... 119
Shoales, Ian
See Kessler, Merle (Bruce)
Shoben, Edward Joseph Jr. 1918- ... 21-24R
Shober, Joyce Lee 1932- ... 1-4R
Shoberg, Lore 1949- ... 33-36R
Shobin, David 1945- ... CANR-20
Earlier sketch in CA 104
Shoblad, Richard H(anson) 1937- ... 41-44R
Shock, Julian
See Williamson, Gerald Neal
Shock, Nathan W(etherill) 1906-1989 ... 5-8R
Obituary ... 130
Shockley, Ann Allen 1927- ... CANR-1
Earlier sketch in CA 49-52
See also BW
See also DLB 33
Shockley, Donald G(rady) 1937- ... 103
Shockley, William (Bradford)
1910-1989 Obituary ... 129
Brief entry ... 113
Shoe, Lucy T.
See Meritt, Lucy Shoe
Shoemaker, Don(ald) C(leavenger)
1912- ... 97-100
Shoemaker, Donald J(ay) 1927- ... 37-40R
Shoemaker, Leonard Calvin 1881- ... CAP-1
Earlier sketch in CA 13-16
Shoemaker, Lloyd R. 1921- ... 133
Shoemaker, Lynn Henry 1939- ... CANR-9
Earlier sketch in CA 65-68
Shoemaker, Richard H(eston)
1907-1970 ... CAP-1
Earlier sketch in CA 11-12
Shoemaker, Robert John 1919- ... 13-16R
Shoemaker, Robin 1949- ... 108
Shoemaker, Sarah
See Wolf, Sarah (Elizabeth)
Shoemaker, William H(utchinson) 1902- ... 13-16R
Shoemaker, William Lee 1931- Brief entry ... 115
Shoemaker, Willie
See Shoemaker, William Lee
Shoenight, Aloise 1914- ... 77-80
Shoesmith, Kathleen A(nne) 1938- ... CANR-17
Earlier sketches in CA 49-52, CANR-1
Shofner, Jerrell H(arris) 1929- ... 57-60
Shofner, Robert D(ancey) 1933- ... 57-60
Shokeid, Moshe 1936- ... CANR-16
Earlier sketch in CA 41-44R
Sholinsky, Jane 1943- ... 89-92
Sholokhov, Mikhail (Aleksandrovich)
1905-1984 ... 101
Obituary ... 112
See also CLC 7, 15
See also MTCW
See also SATA 36
Shomaker, Dianna 1934- ... 109
Shomon, Joseph James 1914- ... 73-76
Shomroni, Reuven
See von Block, Bela W(illiam)
Shone, Patric
See Hanley, James
Shone, Robert 1906- ... 109
Shone, Ronald 1946- ... CANR-20
Earlier sketch in CA 103
Shonfield, Andrew (Akiba) 1917-1981 ... 105
Obituary ... 102
Shontz, Franklin C(urtis) 1926- ... 17-20R
Shook, Karel 1920-1985 Obituary ... 117
Shook, Laurence K(ennedy) 1909- ... 73-76
Shook, Robert L. 1938- ... CANR-23
Earlier sketches in CA 61-64, CANR-8
Shoolbred, C(laude) F(rederick) 1901- ... CAP-2
Earlier sketch in CA 25-28
Shooter, James (Charles) 1951- ... 136
Shooter, Jim
See Shooter, James (Charles)
Shor, Elizabeth N(oble) 1930- ... 110
Shor, Franc(is Marion Luther)
1914-1974 Obituary ... 111
Shor, Ira 1945- ... 126
Shor, Joel 1919- ... 89-92
Shor, Pekay 1923- ... 45-48
Shor, Ronald (Edwin) 1930- ... 61-64
Shorb, Wil(bert Hanson Jr.) 1938- ... 45-48
Shore, Anne
See Sanford, Annette
Shore, Bernard (Alexander Royle)
1896-1985 Obituary ... 116
Shore, Jane 1947- ... 77-80
Shore, June Lewis ... 105
See also AITN 1
See also SATA 30
Shore, Norman
See Smith, Norman Edward Mace
Shore, Paul J(ohn) 1956- ... 118
Shore, Philippa
See Holbeche, Philippa Jack
Shore, Robert 1924- ... SATA 39
Shore, Sidney 1921-1981 Obituary ... 103
Shore, William B(urton) 1925- ... 53-56
Shore, Wilma 1913- ... 13-16R
Shores, David L(ee) 1933- ... 123
Brief entry ... 118
Shores, Louis 1904-1981 ... CANR-8
Obituary ... 104
Earlier sketch in CA 13-16R
Shorris, Earl 1936- ... CANR-34
Earlier sketches in CA 65-68, CANR-10
Shorrock, William I(rwin) 1941- ... 65-68
Short, Alan Lennox
See Lennox-Short, Alan
Short, Alison 1920- ... 61-64
Short, Bobby
See Short, Robert Waltrip
Short, Brian (Michael) 1944- ... 136
Short, (Charles) Christopher (Dudley) ... CANR-2
Earlier sketch in CA 1-4R
Short, Clarice 1910-1977 ... 45-48
Obituary ... 103
Short, Edmund C(oen) 1931- ... 25-28R
Short, Howard E(lmo) 1907- ... 61-64
Short, Jackson ... 53-56
Short, James F(ranklin Jr.) 1924- ... CANR-25
Earlier sketches in CA 5-8R, CANR-8
Short, James R. 1922(?)-1980 Obituary ... 103
Short, K(enneth) R(ichard) M(acDonald)
1936- ... 131
Short, Luke
See Glidden, Frederick D(illey)
Short, Michael 1937- ... 117
See also SATA 65
Short, Philip 1945- ... 105
Short, Robert L(ester) 1932- ... 77-80
Short, Robert Stuart 1938- ... 29-32R
Short, Robert Waltrip 1924(?)- Brief entry ... 107
Short, Roger
See Arkin, Alan (Wolf)
Short, Roger Jr.
See Eyen, Tom
Short, Roy Hunter 1902- ... 120
Short, Ruth Gordon ... CANR-6
Earlier sketch in CA 1-4R
Short, Thayne R(edford) 1929- ... 108
Short, Wayne 1926- ... 9-12R
Shortall, Leonard W. ... 81-84
See also SATA 19
Shorter, Aylward 1932- ... 81-84
Shorter, Carl
See Schwalberg, Carol(yn Ernestine Stein)
Shorter, Edward 1941- ... 73-76
Shorter, Frank C(harles) 1947- ... 132
Shorthouse, Joseph Henry
1834-1903 Brief entry ... 121
See also DLB 18
Shorto, Harry L(eonard) 1919- ... 5-8R
Shortridge, James R. 1944- ... 136
Shortt, Terence Michael 1911- ... 77-80
Shostak, Arthur B. 1937- ... 108
Shostak, Jerome 1913- ... CANR-7
Earlier sketch in CA 17-20R
Shostak, Stanley 1938- ... 117
Shostakovich, Dmitri 1906-1975 Obituary ... 113
Shosteck, Robert 1910-1979 ... CANR-11
Obituary ... 85-88
Earlier sketch in CA 61-64
Shotwell, Louisa Rossiter 1902- ... CANR-4
Earlier sketch in CA 1-4R
See also SATA 3
Shouksmith, George A. 1931- ... 49-52
Shoumatoff, Alex(ander) 1946- ... CANR-9
Earlier sketch in CA 53-56
Shoup, Carl S(umner) 1902- ... 49-52
Shoup, Laurence H(enry) 1943- ... 102
Shoup, Paul Snedden 1929- ... 106
Shover, John L. 1927- ... 21-24R
Showalter, Dennis 1942- ... 89-92
Showalter, Elaine 1941- ... 57-60
See also DLB 67
Showalter, English Jr. 1935- ... 53-56
Showalter, Jean B(reckinridge) ... 21-24R
See also SATA 12
Showalter, Ronda Kerr 1942- ... 37-40R
Showell, Ellen Harvey 1934- ... 85-88
See also SATA 33
Showers, Paul C. 1910- ... CANR-38
Earlier sketches in CA 1-4R, CANR-4
See also CLR 6
See also MAICYA
See also SAAS 7
See also SATA 21
Showers, Renald E(dward) 1935- ... CANR-13
Earlier sketch in CA 77-80
Showers, Victor 1910- ... 53-56
Shoy, Lee Ang
See Sheridan, L(ionel) A(stor)
Shrady, Maria 1924- ... 49-52
Shragin, Boris 1926-1990 ... 102
Obituary ... 132
Shrake, Bud
See Shrake, Edwin
Shrake, Edwin 1931- Brief entry ... 116
Shreffler, Philip A. 1948- ... 138
Shreve, L(evin) G(ale) 1910- ... 101
Shreve, Susan Richards 1939- ... CANR-38
Earlier sketches in CA 49-52, CANR-5
See also CAAS 5
See also CLC 23
See also MAICYA
See also SATA 41, 46

Shriber, Ione Sandberg
1911-1987 Obituary 121
Shrimpton, Gordon Spencer 1941- 115
Shrimsley, Anthony 1934-1984 Obituary 114
Shrimsley, Bernard 1931- 103
Shrivastava, Paul 1951- 133
Shriver, Donald W(oods) Jr. 1927- CANR-1
Earlier sketch in CA 45-48
Shriver, George H(ite) Jr. 1931- 21-24R
Shriver, Harry C(lair) 1904- CANR-10
Earlier sketch in CA 65-68
Shriver, Lionel 1957- 134
Shriver, Peggy (Ann) L(eu) 1931- 107
Shriver, Phillip Raymond 1922- 13-16R
Shriver, Rosalia (Oliver) 1927-1987 115
Obituary 135
Shroder, Maurice Z(orensky) 1933- 1-4R
Shrodes, Caroline 1908- CANR-4
Earlier sketch in CA 1-4R
Shropshire, W(alter) Jr. 1932- 118
Shrosbree, Colin (John) 1938- 130
Shrout, Thomas R(euben) 1919- 41-44R
Shroyer, Frederick B(enjamin)
1916-1983 ..... CANR-13
Earlier sketch in CA 13-16R
Shryock, (Edwin) Harold 1906- CANR-8
Earlier sketch in CA 21-24R
Shryock, Richard Harrison 1893-1972 ..... CAP-2
Obituary 33-36R
Earlier sketch in CA 17-18
Shtainmets, Leon 105
See also SATA 32
Shtemenko, Sergei Matveyevich
1907-1976 103
Shternfeld, Ari A(bramovich)
1905-1980 Obituary 105
Shtromas, Alexander 1931- 132
Shu, Austin Chi-wei 1915- 29-32R
Shub, Beth
See Pessen, Beth
Shub, David 1887-1973 Obituary 41-44R
Shub, Elizabeth CANR-15
Earlier sketch in CA 41-44R
See also SATA 5
Shubik, Martin 1926- CANR-2
Earlier sketch in CA 5-8R
Shubin, Seymour 1921- 1-4R
Shucard, Alan R(obert) 1935- CANR-26
Earlier sketch in CA 61-64
Shu Ch'ing-ch'un 1899-1966 Obituary 109
Shuchman, Abraham
1919-1978 Obituary 77-80
Shue, Larry 1946-1985 Obituary 117
See also CLC 52
Shuffelton, Frank 1940- CANR-38
Earlier sketch in CA 115
Shuford, Cecil Eugene 1907- 13-16R
See also AITN 1
Shuford, Gene
See Shuford, Cecil Eugene
Shugrue, Michael F(rancis) 1934- 21-24R
Shu-Jen, Chou 1881-1936 Brief entry 104
See also Hsun, Lu
Shukert, Elfrieda Berthiaume 1948- 129
Shukman, Harold 1931- 53-56
Shukshin, V.
See Shukshin, Vasily (Makarovich)
Shukshin, V. M.
See Shukshin, Vasily (Makarovich)
Shukshin, Vasily (Makarovich) 1929-1974 135
Shula, Don(ald Francis) 1930- Brief entry 106
Shulberg, Alan
See Wilkes-Hunter, R(ichard)
Shuldinger, Herbert 1929- 130
Shuler, Linda Lay 128
Shulevitz, Uri 1935- CANR-3
Earlier sketch in CA 9-12R
See also CLR 5
See also DLB 61
See also MAICYA
See also SATA 3, 50
Shull, Fremont Adam Jr. 1924- CANR-1
Earlier sketch in CA 1-4R
Shull, Margaret Anne Wyse 1940- 77-80
Shull, Peg
See Shull, Margaret Anne Wyse
Shulman, Albert M(aimon) 1902- 49-52
Shulman, Alix Kates 1932- 29-32R
See also CLC 2, 10
See also SATA 7
Shulman, Arnold 1914- 29-32R
Shulman, Bernard H. 1922- 108
Shulman, Charles E. 1904-1968 ..... CAP-1
Earlier sketch in CA 13-14
Shulman, David Dean 1949- 102
Shulman, Fay Grissom Stanley
1925(?)-1990 Obituary 133
Shulman, Frank Joseph 1943- CANR-30
Earlier sketches in CA 29-32R, CANR-12
Shulman, Harry Manuel 1899- 1-4R
Shulman, Harry 1903-1955 Brief entry 112
Shulman, Irving 1913- CANR-6
Earlier sketch in CA 1-4R
See also SATA 13
Shulman, Marshall Darrow 1916- 1-4R
Shulman, Max 1919-1988 89-92
Obituary 126
See also DLB 11
See also SATA 59
Shulman, Milton 1913- 103
Shulman, Morton 1925- CANR-14
Earlier sketch in CA 21-24R
See also AITN 1
Shulman, Neil B(arnett) 1945- CANR-26
Earlier sketches in CA 65-68, CANR-9
Shulman, Sandra (Dawn) 1944- CANR-9
Earlier sketch in CA 21-24R
Shultz, George P(ratt) 1920- 104
Shultz, Gladys Denny 1895- 49-52
Shultz, William J(ohn) 1902-1970 ..... CANR-16
Obituary 103
Earlier sketch in CA 1-4R
Shulvass, Moses A. 1909- 13-16R
Shumaker, Wayne 1910- 5-8R
Shuman, Bruce A(lan) 1941- 110
Shuman, James B(urrow) 1932- 61-64
Shuman, Nicholas R(oman) 1921- 109
Shuman, R(obert) Baird 1929- CANR-4
Earlier sketch in CA 1-4R
Shuman, Samuel I(rving) 1925- CANR-3
Earlier sketch in CA 9-12R
Shumsky, Zena
See Hampson, Zena
Shumway, Floyd M(allory Jr.) 1917- CANR-29
Earlier sketch in CA 29-32R
Shumway, George (Alfred Jr.) 1928- 9-12R
Shumway, Mary L. 1926- CANR-7
Earlier sketch in CA 17-20R
Shupe, Anson 1948- 129
Shupp, Mike 1946- 121
Shura, Mary Francis
See Craig, Mary (Francis) Shura
Shurden, Walter B(yron) 1937- CANR-21
Earlier sketch in CA 69-72
Shurkin, Joel N. 1938- CANR-14
Earlier sketch in CA 69-72
Shurr, William H(oward) 1932- CANR-18
Earlier sketch in CA 41-44R
Shurter, Robert L(e Fevre) 1907-1974 ..... CANR-2
Earlier sketch in CA 1-4R
Shurtleff, Malcolm C. Jr. 1922- 5-8R
Shurtleff, Michael 1930- 41-44R
Shurtleff, William 1941- CANR-16
Earlier sketch in CA 93-96
Shuseki, Hayashi
See Hubbell, Lindley Williams
Shuster, Albert H. Jr. 1917- 17-20R
Shuster, Alvin 1930- Brief entry 113
Shuster, E. G. 1932- 138
Shuster, George Nauman 1894-1977 77-80
Obituary 69-72
Shuster, Joe 1914- ..... CLC 21
Shuster, Ronald L(owell) 1927- 45-48
Shusterman, David 1912- 25-28R
Shusterman, Neal 1962- 133
Shusterman, Richard (M.) 1949- 136
Shute, Alberta V(an Horn) 1906- CANR-7
Earlier sketch in CA 57-60
Shute, Gary Brana
See Brana-Shute, Gary
Shute, Henry A. 1856-1943 ..... DLB 9
Shute, Jenefer 1956- 138
Shute, Nerina 101
Shute, Nevil
See Norway, Nevil Shute
See also CLC 30
Shute, R(eginald) Wayne 1933- 29-32R
Shute, Wallace B. 1911- 29-32R
Shute, Wilfred Eugene 1907- 105
Shuttle, Penelope (Diane) 1947- CANR-39
Earlier sketch in CA 93-96
See also CLC 7
See also DLB 14, 40
Shuttlesworth, Dorothy Edwards CANR-4
Earlier sketch in CA 1-4R
See also SATA 3
Shuttleworth, John 1937- ..... AITN 1
Shuval, Judith T(annenbaum) 1925- CANR-25
Earlier sketch in CA 45-48
Shuy, Roger W(ellington) 1931- CANR-13
Earlier sketch in CA 61-64
Shwadran, Benjamin 1907- CANR-20
Earlier sketches in CA 13-16R, CANR-5
Shwartz, Susan Martha 1949- 109
Shwayder, David S(amuel) 1926- 106
Shy, John W(illard) 1931- CANR-3
Earlier sketch in CA 5-8R
Shyer, Charles (Richard) 1941- 138
Shyer, Marlene Fanta CANR-11
Earlier sketch in CA 69-72
See also SATA 13
Shyne, Ann W(entworth) 1914- 115
Shyre, Paul 1929(?)-1989 103
Obituary 130
Siano, Mary M(artha) 1924- 77-80
Siberell, Anne 104
See also SATA 29
Siberry, (Jane) Elizabeth 1957- 122
Sibley, Agnes M(arie) 1914- 61-64
Sibley, Celestine 1917- 85-88
Sibley, Don 1922- ..... SATA 12
Sibley, Elbridge 1903- CAP-1
Earlier sketch in CA 13-14
Sibley, Marilyn McAdams 1923- 21-24R
Sibley, Mulford Quickert 1912- CANR-6
Earlier sketch in CA 5-8R
Sibley, Patricia (Hayles) 1928- 97-100
Sibley, Susan
See Kinnicutt, Susan Sibley
Sibly, John 1920- 1-4R
Sices, David 1933- 25-28R
Sichel, Peter M(ax) F(erdinand) 1922- 65-68
Sichel, Pierre (Laugier) 1915- 1-4R
Sichel, Werner 1934- CANR-23
Earlier sketches in CA 21-24R, CANR-8
Sicherman, Carol 1937- 135
Sichol, Marcia W. 1940- 135
Sichov, Vladimir 1945- 108
Sicignano, Robert 1946- 116
Siciliano, Vincent Paul 1911- CAP-2
Earlier sketch in CA 29-32
Sicinski, Andrzej 1924- 115
Sickels, Robert J(udd) 1931- 41-44R
Sicker, Philip 1951- 103
Sickles, William Russell 1913- 57-60
Sickman, Laurence C(halfant) S(tevens)
1906-1988 ..... CAP-1
Obituary 125
Earlier sketch in CA 11-12
Siculan, Daniel 1922- ..... SATA 12
Siddall, William R(ichard) 1928- 41-44R
Siddiqi, Akhtar Husain 1925- 61-64
Siddiqui, Ashraf (Hossain) 1927- CANR-2
Earlier sketch in CA 5-8R
Siddons, (Sybil) Anne Rivers 1936- CANR-33
Earlier sketch in CA 101
See also BEST 89:2
See also MTCW
Siddons, Robert 1952- 119
Sidel, Victor W(illiam) 1931- CANR-9
Earlier sketch in CA 65-68
Sider, Don 1933- 77-80
Sider, Robert Dick 1932- CANR-16
Earlier sketch in CA 37-40R
Sider, Ronald J(ames) 1939- CANR-39
Earlier sketches in CA 93-96, CANR-17
Siders, Ellis L(eroy) 1920- 17-20R
Sidetracked Home Executives
See Jones, Peggy
and Young, Pam
Sidey, Hugh (Swanson) 1927- 124
Brief entry 111
Sidgwick, Henry 1838-1900 Brief entry 120
Sidhwa, Bapsy (N.) 1938- CANR-25
Earlier sketch in CA 108
Sidhwa, Keki R(attanshah) 1926- 69-72
Sidjakov, Nicolas 1924- ..... SATA 18
Sidley, Nathan T(heodore) 1929- 113
Sidnell, Michael John 1935- 113
Sidney, Frank
See Warwick, Alan R(oss)
Sidney, Jonathan
See Cooper, Emmanuel
Sidney, Kathleen M(arion) 1944- 103
Sidney, Margaret
See Lothrop, Harriet Mulford Stone
Sidney, Neilma
See Gantner, Neilma
Sidney, Sir Philip
1554-1586 ..... CDBLB Before 1660
Sidney-Fryer, Donald 1934- 45-48
Sidowski, Joseph B(oleslaus) 1925- 21-24R
Sidran, Ben H. 1943- 102
Sidransky, Ruth 1929- 135
Siebel, Fritz (Frederick) 1913- ..... SATA 44
Siebenheller, Norma 1937- 107
Siebenschuh, William R(obert) 1942- 89-92
Sieber, Joan E. 1937- CANR-35
Earlier sketch in CA 114
Sieber, Roy 1923- 102
Sieber, Sam Dixon 1931- 13-16R
Siebert, Fred(rick) Seaton 1901- 21-24R
Siedel, Frank 1914- 25-28R
Siedel, James M. 1937- 25-28R
Siegal, Aranka 1930- 112
See also AAYA 5
See also SATA 37
Siegal, Diana Laskin 1931- 127
Siegal, Harvey A. 1945- 127
Siegal, Mordecai 1934- 102
Siegal, Sanford (Sherwin) 1928- 105
Siegan, Bernard H(erbert) 1924- 65-68
Siegel, Adrienne 1936- CANR-12
Earlier sketch in CA 61-64
Siegel, Beatrice CANR-18
Earlier sketch in CA 101
See also SATA 36
Siegel, Ben 1925- 77-80
Siegel, Benjamin 1914-1991 ..... CANR-4
Obituary 135
Earlier sketch in CA 1-4R
Siegel, Bernie S(hepard) 1932- 123
See also BEST 89:4
Siegel, Bertram M. 1936- 25-28R
Siegel, Dorothy (Schainman) 1932- 9-12R
Siegel, Eli 1902-1978 ..... CANR-9
Obituary 81-84
Earlier sketch in CA 17-20R
Siegel, Ernest 1922- 73-76
Siegel, Esther 1949- 102
Siegel, Frederick F(ein) 1945- 133
Siegel, Gonnie McClung 1928- 110
Siegel, Helen
See Siegl, Helen
Siegel, Irving H(erbert) 1914-1988 ..... CANR-9
Obituary 125
Earlier sketch in CA 21-24R
Siegel, Jack
See Siegel, Jacob
Siegel, Jacob 1913- 17-20R
Siegel, James T. 1937- Brief entry 113
Siegel, Jerome 1914- Brief entry 116
See also CLC 21
Siegel, Jerry
See Siegel, Jerome
Siegel, June 1929- 77-80
Siegel, Lee 1945- 126
Siegel, Marcia B. 1932- CANR-37
Earlier sketch in CA 69-72
Siegel, Mark Richard 1949- CANR-29
Earlier sketch in CA 110
Siegel, Martin 1933- 33-36R
Siegel, Mary-Ellen
See Siegel, Mary-Ellen Kulkin
Siegel, Mary-Ellen Kulkin 1932- 116
Siegel, Max 1904-1972 Obituary 104
Siegel, Maxwell E(dward) 1933- 101
Siegel, Paul N. 1916- 37-40R
Siegel, Richard L(ewis) 1940- 73-76
Siegel, Robert (Harold) 1939- CANR-21
Earlier sketches in CA 53-56, CANR-5
See also SATA 39
Siegel, Seymour 1927-1988 Obituary 124
Siegel, Stanley E(lliott) 1928- 41-44R
Siegel-Gorelick, Bryna 1954- 115
Siegelman, James Howard 1951- 81-84
Siegelman, Jim
See Siegelman, James Howard
Siegener, Ray(mond) 1931- 123
Brief entry 118
Sieghart, (Henry Laurence) Paul (Alexander)
1927-1988 Obituary 127
Siegl, Helen 1924- ..... SATA 34
Siegle, Bernard A(ndrew) 1914- 89-92
Siegler, Frederick Adrian 1932- 49-52
Siegler, Ilene C. 1946- 114
Siegman, Gita 1939- CANR-31
Earlier sketch in CA 112
Siegmeister, Elie 1909-1991 ..... CANR-1
Obituary 133
Earlier sketch in CA 1-4R
Siegner, C(larence) Vernon Jr. 1920- 1-4R
Sielaff, Theodore J. 1920- 13-16R
Sieller, William Vincent 1917- 29-32R
Siemanowski, Richard F.
1922(?)-1981 Obituary 104
Siemens, Reynold Gerrard 1932- 41-44R
Siemon, James Ralph 1948- 121
Siemon, Jeff 1950- 103
Sienkiewicz, Henryk (Adam Alexander Pius)
1846-1916 134
Brief entry 104
See also TCLC 3
Sienkiewicz-Mercer, Ruth 1950- 136
Sienko, Michell J. 1923-1983 Obituary 111
Siepmann, Charles Arthur 1899-1985 ..... 1-4R
Obituary 115
Sierra, Gregorio Martinez
See Martinez Sierra, Gregorio
Sierra, Judy 1945- 128
Sierra, Maria (de la O'LeJarraga) Martinez
See Martinez Sierra, Maria (de la O'LeJarraga)
Sies, Luther F(rank) 1927- 111
Siev, Asher 1913- 57-60
Sievers, Allen M. 1918- 89-92
Sievers, Harry J(oseph) 1920-1977 ..... 25-28R
Obituary 73-76
Sievers, W(ieder) David 1919-1966 ..... 1-4R
Obituary 103
Siewert, Frances E. (Cornelius) 1881- CAP-1
Earlier sketch in CA 11-12
Sifakis, G(regory) M(ichael) 1935- 25-28R
Siffert, Robert S(pencer) 1918- 109
Sifford, (Charles) Darrell 1931- CANR-15
Earlier sketch in CA 77-80
Sifton, Claire 1897(?)-1980 Obituary 93-96
Sifton, Paul F. 1893(?)-1972 Obituary 33-36R
Sigal, Clancy 1926- 1-4R
See also CLC 7
Sigal, Leon V(ictor) 1942- Brief entry 114
Sigband, Norman Bruce 1920- CANR-17
Earlier sketches in CA 5-8R, CANR-2
Sigel, Efrem 1943- 121
Sigelschiffer, Saul 1902- 81-84
Siger of Brabant 1240(?)-1284(?) ..... DLB 115
Sigler, Jay A(drian) 1933- 25-28R
Sigler, John W(illiam) 1946- 127
Sigler, William F. 128
Sigmund, Paul E(ugene) 1929- CANR-39
Earlier sketches in CA 5-8R, CANR-2, 18
Signoret, Simone 1921-1985 135
Obituary 117
Sigourney, Andre R. 132
Sigourney, Lydia Howard (Huntley)
1791-1865 ..... DLB 1, 42, 73
Sigurjonsson, Johann 1880-1919 ..... TCLC 27
Sigworth, Oliver F(rederic) 1921- 13-16R
Sihanouk, Norodom
See Norodom Sihanouk (Varman), Samdech Preah
Siirala, Aarne 1919- 13-16R
Sik, Endre 1891-1978 Obituary 77-80
Sikelianos, Angelos 1884-1951 ..... TCLC 39
Sikes, Herschel Moreland 1928- 17-20R
Sikes, Walter W(allace) 1925- 57-60
Sikora, Frank J(oseph) 1936- 115
Sikora, Joseph (John) 1932-1967 ..... CAP-2
Earlier sketch in CA 17-18
Sikora, Stefan
See Rey, Michael Stephan
Sikorsky, Igor (Ivan) 1889-1972 Obituary 113
Siks, Geraldine Brain 1912- 25-28R
Sikula, Andrew F(rank) 1944- CANR-2
Earlier sketch in CA 49-52
Silangan, Manuel
See Yabes, Leopoldo Y(abes)
Silbajoris, Frank
See Silbajoris, Rimvydas
Silbajoris, Rimvydas 1926- 25-28R
Silber, Diana 1936- 134
Silber, Evelyn (Ann) 1949- 124
Silber, Irwin 1925- 9-12R
Silber, Joan 1945- CANR-20
Earlier sketch in CA 104
Silber, Kate 1902- 77-80
Silber, Mark 1946- 45-48
Silber, Norman I. 1951- 114
Silber, William L. 1942- CANR-29
Earlier sketch in CA 29-32R
Silberg, Moshe 1900-1975 Obituary 61-64
Silberg, Richard 1942- 21-24R
Silberger, Julius 1929- CANR-21
Earlier sketch in CA 105
Silberkleit, Louis Horace
1905-1986 Obituary 118
Silberman, Arlene 133

Silberman, Charles E(liot) 1925- CANR-7
Earlier sketch in CA 9-12R
Silberman, James H(enry) 1927- 133
Silberman, Jerome 1935(?)- Brief entry 116
Silberman, Neil Asher 1950- 108
Silbermann, Eileen Z(ieget) 1925- 114
Silbersack, John (Walter) 1954- CANR-33
Earlier sketch in CA 107
Silberschlag, Eisig 1903- CANR-17
Earlier sketches in CA 1-4R, CANR-1
Silberschmidt, Max 1899- 65-68
Silberstang, Edwin 1930- CANR-3
Earlier sketch in CA 49-52
Silberstein, Gerard Edward 1926- 37-40R
Silberstein, Howard E.
1907(?)-1984 Obituary 112
Silberstein, Warren P(aul) 1948- 110
Silberstein-Storfer, Muriel (Rosoff) 111
Silbey, Joel H. 1933- 21-24R
Silbiger, Alexander 1935- 136
Silcock, Sara Lesley 1947- ....SATA 12
Silcock, Thomas H(enry) 1910- 9-12R
Silcox, David Phillips 1937- 109
Silen, Juan Angel 1938- 33-36R
Silesky, Barry 1949- 135
Silet, Charles L(oring) P(rovine)
1942- CANR-17
Earlier sketch in CA 93-96
Silitch, Clarissa MacVeagh 1930- CANR-31
Earlier sketch in CA 112
Silk, Andrew 1953(?)-1981 Obituary 106
Silk, Dennis (Peter) 1928- 132
Silk, Gerald 1947- 133
Silk, Leonard S(olomon) 1918- CANR-4
Earlier sketch in CA 1-4R
Silkin, Jon 1930- 5-8R
See also CAAS 5
See also CLC 2, 6, 43
See also DLB 27
Silko, Leslie Marmon 1948- 122
Brief entry 115
See also CLC 23
Sill, Geoffrey M(ichael) 1944- 111
Sill, Gertrude Grace 69-72
Sill, Sterling Welling 1903- CANR-6
Earlier sketch in CA 57-60
Sillanpaa, Frans Eemil 1888-1964 129
Obituary 93-96
See also CLC 19
See also MTCW
Sillem, Edward 1916-1964 ....5-8R
Sillen, Samuel 1911(?)-1973 Obituary 41-44R
Sillery, Anthony 1903-1976 ....CANR-5
Obituary 65-68
Earlier sketch in CA 5-8R
Silliman, Ron(ald Glenn) 1946- 45-48
Silliphant, Stirling (Dale) 1918- CANR-14
Earlier sketch in CA 73-76
See also DLB 26
Sillitoe, Alan 1928- CANR-26
Earlier sketches in CA 9-12R, CANR-8
See also CAAS 2
See also AITN 1
See also CDBLB 1960 to Present
See also CLC 1, 3, 6, 10, 19, 57
See also DLB 14
See also MTCW
See also SATA 61
Sillman, Leonard (Dexter)
1908-1982 Obituary 105
Sills, Beverly 1929- 89-92
Sills, David Lawrence 1920- 33-36R
Sills, Frank D(reyer) 1914- 1-4R
Sills, Jennifer
See Lewis, Stephen
Sills, Leslie (Elka) 1948- 130
Sills, Ruth C(urtis) 29-32R
Silly, E. S.
See Kraus, Robert
Silman, Roberta 1934- 101
See also DLB 28
Silone, Ignazio 1900-1978 ....CANR-34
Obituary 81-84
Earlier sketches in CAP-2, CA 25-28
See also CLC 4
See also MTCW
Siluriensis, Leolinus
See Jones, Arthur Llewellyn
Silva, Beverly 1935- 131
See also HW
Silva, Eduardo Neale
See Neale-Silva, Eduardo
Silva, Joseph
See Goulart, Ron(ald Joseph)
Silva, Julian 1927- 115
Silva, Julio A(lberto) 1933- 17-20R
Silva, Ruth C. 13-16R
Silvanus
See Strasser, Bernard Paul
Silvaroli, Nicholas J. 1930- CANR-12
Earlier sketch in CA 29-32R
Silver, A(aron) David 1941- 124
Silver, A(aron) Henry 1891-1986 Obituary 121
Silver, Abba Hillel 1893-1963 ....1-4R
Silver, Alain (Joel) 1947- CANR-10
Earlier sketch in CA 57-60
Silver, Alfred 1951- CANR-15
Earlier sketch in CA 85-88
Silver, Carole G(reta) 1937- 132
Silver, Daniel Jeremy 1928-1989 ....CANR-3
Obituary 130
Earlier sketch in CA 5-8R
Silver, Gary (Thomas) 1944- 89-92
Silver, Gerald A(lbert) 1932- CANR-30
Earlier sketches in CA 33-36R, CANR-13
Silver, Harold 1928- CANR-10
Earlier sketch in CA 21-24R
Silver, Isidore 1934- 53-56
Silver, James W(esley) 1907-1988 ....9-12R
Obituary 126
Silver, Joan Micklin 1935- 121
Brief entry 114
See also CLC 20
Silver, Jody 1942- 109
Silver, Marjorie A. 1948- 93-96
Silver, Nathan 1936- CANR-11
Earlier sketch in CA 21-24R
Silver, Nicholas
See Faust, Frederick (Shiller)
Silver, Philip Warnock 1932- 106
Silver, Richard
See Bulmer, (Henry) Kenneth
Silver, Rollo G(abriel) 1909- CAP-1
Earlier sketch in CA 19-20
Silver, Roy R. 1918-1979 Obituary 89-92
Silver, Ruth
See Chew, Ruth
Silver, Samuel M. 1912- CANR-11
Earlier sketch in CA 21-24R
Silver, Samuel 1915(?)-1976 Obituary 69-72
Silver, Warren A. 1914- 65-68
Silvera, Alain 1930- 21-24R
Silverberg, Robert 1935- CANR-36
Earlier sketches in CA 1-4R, CANR-1, 20
See also CAAS 3
See also CLC 7
See also DLB 8
See also MAICYA
See also MTCW
See also SATA 13
Silverlock, Anne
See Titchener, Louise
Silverman, Al 1926- 9-12R
Silverman, Alvin Michaels 1912- 9-12R
Silverman, Burt(on Philip) 1928- 103
Silverman, Corinne 1930- 5-8R
Silverman, David 1907- CAP-2
Earlier sketch in CA 21-22
Silverman, Gerry 1938- 133
Silverman, Harold M(artin) 1945- 112
Silverman, Hillel E. 1924- CANR-11
Earlier sketch in CA 21-24R
Silverman, Hirsch Lazaar 1915- 45-48
Silverman, Hugh J(erald) 1945- 118
Silverman, Jason H(oward) 1952- 110
Silverman, Jerry 1931- CANR-7
Earlier sketch in CA 13-16R
Silverman, Jonathan 1955- 138
Silverman, Joseph H(erman) 1924- 104
Silverman, Judith 1933- 103
Silverman, Kaja 1947- 132
Silverman, Kenneth 1936- CANR-17
Earlier sketch in CA 57-60
See also DLB 111
Silverman, Mel(vin Frank) 1931-1966 ....5-8R
See also SATA 9
Silverman, Milton J. 1944- 108
Silverman, Morris 1894-1972 Obituary 33-36R
Silverman, Oscar Ansell
1903-1977 Obituary 69-72
Silverman, Robert A(llan) 1943- 57-60
Silverman, Robert E(ugene) 1924- 41-44R
Silverman, Robert J(ay) 1940- 101
Silverman, Rose
See Millstein, Rose Silverman
Silverman, S(ol) Richard 1911- 107
Silverman, Samuel ....AITN 1
Silverman, Stephen M. 1951- 135
Silverman, Sydel 1933- 77-80
Silverman, William B. 1913- 49-52
Silvern, Leonard C. 1919- CANR-7
Earlier sketch in CA 17-20R
Silvers, Phil
See Silversmith, Philip
Silvers, Vicki 1941- 93-96
Silversmith, Philip 1912-1985 Obituary 117
Brief entry 111
Silverstein, Alvin 1933- CANR-2
Earlier sketch in CA 49-52
See also CLC 17
See also CLR 25
See also MAICYA
See also SATA 8, 69
Silverstein, Charles 1935- 73-76
Silverstein, Josef 1922- CANR-31
Earlier sketches in CA 37-40R, CANR-14
Silverstein, Mel(vin Jerome) 1940- 101
Silverstein, Norman 1922-1974 ....37-40R
Obituary 49-52
Silverstein, Shel(by) 1932- 107
See also CLR 5
See also MAICYA
See also SATA 27, 33
Silverstein, Theodore 1904- 106
Silverstein, Virginia B(arbara Opshelor)
1937- CANR-2
Earlier sketch in CA 49-52
See also CLC 17
See also CLR 25
See also MAICYA
See also SATA 8, 69
Silverstone, Lou 1928- 108
Silverstone, Paul H. 1931- 21-24R
Silvert, Kalman H(irsch) 1921-1976 ....CANR-6
Obituary 65-68
Earlier sketch in CA 13-16R
Silverthorn, J(ames) E(dwin) 1906- CAP-1
Earlier sketch in CA 13-16
Silverthorne, Elizabeth 1930- 89-92
See also SATA 35
Silverton, Michael 1935- 65-68
Silverwood, Jane
See Titchener, Louise
Silvester, Frank
See Bingley, David Ernest
Silvester, P(eter) P. 1935- 135
Silvester, Peter (John) 1934- 133
Silvester, Victor CAP-1
Earlier sketch in CA 13-14
Silvestri, Richard 1944- 81-84
Silving, Helen 1906- 41-44R
Silvis, Randall 1950- 136
Silvius, G(eorge) Harold 1908-1981 ....CANR-3
Obituary 104
Earlier sketch in CA 5-8R
Sim, Georges
See Simenon, Georges (Jacques Christian)
Sim, John Cameron 1911-1990 ....25-28R
Obituary 132
Sim, Katharine (Thomasset) 1913- 13-16R
Sim, Myre 1915- 61-64
Sim, Yawsoon 1937- 108
Simak, Clifford D(onald) 1904-1988 ....CANR-35
Obituary 125
Earlier sketches in CA 1-4R, CANR-1
See also CLC 1, 55
See also DLB 8
See also MTCW
See also SATA 56
Simard, Real 1951- 129
Simbari, Nicola 1927- CANR-1
Earlier sketch in CA 1-4R
Simckes, L(azarre) S(eymour) 1937- 9-12R
Simcoe, Elizabeth 1762-1850 ....DLB 99
Simcox, Carroll E(ugene) 1912- 132
Simcox, George Augustus 1841-1905 ....DLB 35
Sime, Jessie Georgina 1868-1958 ....DLB 92
Sime, Mary 1911- 53-56
Simenon, Georges (Jacques Christian)
1903-1989 ....CANR-35
Obituary 129
Earlier sketch in CA 85-88
See also CLC 1, 2, 3, 8, 18, 47
See also DLB 72
See also DLBY 89
See also MTCW
Simeon, Mother Mary 1888- CAP-1
Earlier sketch in CA 13-14
Simeon, Richard 1943- CANR-9
Earlier sketch in CA 61-64
Simeone, Diane A. 1953(?)-1983 Obituary 109
Simic, Andrei 1930- 93-96
Simic, Charles 1938- CANR-33
Earlier sketches in CA 29-32R, CANR-12
See also CAAS 4
See also CLC 6, 9, 22, 49, 68
See also DLB 105
Simini, Joseph Peter 1921- CANR-8
Earlier sketch in CA 17-20R
Simirenko, Alex 1931- 13-16R
Simis, Konstantin 1919- 130
Simister, Florence Parker 1913- CANR-2
Earlier sketch in CA 5-8R
Simkin, C(olin) G(eorge) F(rederick)
1915- 29-32R
Simkin, Penny 1938- 116
Simkin, Tom 1933- 132
Simkin, William E(dward) 1907- 45-48
Simkins, Lawrence D(avid) 1933- 41-44R
Simley, Anne 1891- 5-8R
Simmel, Edward C(lemens) 1932- CANR-31
Earlier sketch in CA 45-48
Simmel, Johannes M(ario) 1924- 81-84
See also DLB 69
Simmel, Marianne L(enore) 1923- 21-24R
Simmie, James Martin 1941- CANR-38
Earlier sketch in CA 115
Simmonds, A(ndrew) J(effrey) 1943- 81-84
Simmonds, George W. 1929- 21-24R
Simmonds, James D(udley) 1933- 104
Simmonds, John 1942- 135
Simmonds, Posy ....CLR 23
Simmonds, Walter H(enry) C(live) 1917- 118
Simmons, A(lan) John 1950- 106
Simmons, Anthony 1922- 103
Simmons, Billy E. 1931- CANR-10
Earlier sketch in CA 21-24R
Simmons, Blake
See Wallmann, Jeffrey M(iner)
Simmons, Charles (Paul) 1924- 89-92
See also CLC 57
Simmons, D(avid) R(oy) 1930- CANR-28
Earlier sketch in CA 110
Simmons, Dan 138
See also CLC 44
Simmons, David
See Gold, Alan R(obert)
Simmons, Dawn Langley 29-32R
Simmons, Edwin Howard 1921- 89-92
Simmons, Ernest J(oseph) 1903-1972 ....CANR-3
Earlier sketch in CA 1-4R
See also DLB 103
Simmons, Geoffrey 1943- 104
Simmons, Gloria Mitchell 1932- 37-40R
Simmons, Henry T. 1927(?)-1986 Obituary 120
Simmons, Herbert A(lfred) 1930- 1-4R
See also BW
See also DLB 33
Simmons, Ian 1937- 106
Simmons, J(oseph) Edgar (Jr.) 1921- 21-24R
Simmons, J(erry) L(aird) 1933- 29-32R
Simmons, Jack 1915- CANR-38
Earlier sketches in CA 5-8R, CANR-2
Simmons, James E(dwin) 1923- 41-44R
Simmons, James (Stewart Alexander)
1933- 105
See also CLC 43
See also DLB 40
Simmons, James W(illiam) 1936- CANR-12
Earlier sketch in CA 17-20R
Simmons, Jerold L. 1941- 129
Simmons, John Edwards
1918-1986 Obituary 121
Simmons, Joseph Larry 1935- 65-68
Simmons, Judy Dothard 1944- 77-80
Simmons, Mabel Clark 1899-1988 Obituary 124
Simmons, Marc 1937- CANR-26
Earlier sketches in CA 25-28R, CANR-10
Simmons, Mary Kay 1933- 81-84
Simmons, Matty 1926- 29-32R
Simmons, Merle Edwin 1918- CANR-2
Earlier sketch in CA 5-8R
Simmons, Michael 1935- 128
Simmons, Otis D(avis) 1928- 57-60
Simmons, Ozzie Gordon 1919-1988 ....9-12R
Obituary 127
Simmons, Patricia A. 1930- 93-96
Simmons, Paul D(ewayne) 1936- CANR-31
Earlier sketch in CA 45-48
Simmons, Robert R. 1940- 97-100
Simmons, S. H.
See Simmons, Sylvia
Simmons, Sylvia 49-52
Simmons, William S(cranton) 1938- 121
Simms, D(enton) Harper 1912- 29-32R
Simms, Eric Arthur 1921- 101
Simms, George (Otto) 1910-1991 ....CANR-25
Obituary 136
Earlier sketch in CA 108
Simms, Peter (F. J.) 1925- 21-24R
Simms, Ruth P. 1937- 17-20R
Simms, Willard S. 1943- 29-32R
Simms, William Gilmore
1806-1870 ....DLB 3, 30, 59, 73
Simon, Alfred (Edward) 1907-1991 ....41-44R
Obituary 134
Simon, Andre (Louis)
1877-1970 Obituary 29-32R
Simon, Anne W(ertheim) 1914- 105
Simon, Arthur 1930- 33-36R
Simon, Bennett 1933- 101
Simon, Boris-Jean
1913(?)-1972 Obituary 33-36R
Simon, Carl P(aul) 1945- 107
Simon, Carly 1945- 105
See also CLC 26
Simon, Charlie May
See Fletcher, Charlie May Hogue
Simon, Christopher Fitz
See Fitz-Simon, Christopher
Simon, Claude 1913- CANR-33
Earlier sketch in CA 89-92
See also CLC 4, 9, 15, 39
See also DLB 83
See also MTCW
Simon, David 1960- 136
Simon, Disney 1927- 21-24R
Simon, Eckehard 1939- 61-64
Simon, Edith 1917- 13-16R
Simon, George T(homas) 1912- CANR-17
Earlier sketch in CA 25-28R
Simon, Henry W(illiam) 1901-1970 ....CANR-4
Obituary 29-32R
Earlier sketch in CA 5-8R
Simon, Herbert A(lexander) 1916- CANR-9
Earlier sketch in CA 13-16R
Simon, Herbert 1898(?)-1974 Obituary 53-56
Simon, Hilda Rita 1921- 77-80
See also SATA 28
Simon, Howard 1903-1979 ....33-36R
Obituary 89-92
See also SATA 21, 32
Simon, Hubert K. 1917- 13-16R
Simon, James E(dward) 1954- 119
Simon, James F. 1939- 134
Simon, Jo Ann 1946- 106
Simon, Joan L. 1921- 13-16R
Simon, Joe
See Simon, Joseph H.
Simon, John G. 1928- 37-40R
Simon, John (Ivan) 1925- 21-24R
Simon, John Y. 1933- CANR-29
Earlier sketches in CA 25-28R, CANR-12
Simon, Joseph H. 1913- 29-32R
See also SATA 7
Simon, Julian L. 1932- 33-36R
Simon, Kate (Grobsmith) 1912-1990 127
Obituary 130
Brief entry 115
See also MTCW
Simon, Leonard 1922- 9-12R
Simon, Linda 1946- CANR-13
Earlier sketch in CA 73-76
Simon, Lorena Cotts 1897- 5-8R
Simon, Louis M(ortimer) 1906- 77-80
Simon, Marcia L. 1939- 93-96
Simon, Martin P(aul William) 1903-1969 ......CAP-1
Earlier sketch in CA 11-12
See also SATA 12
Simon, Mary of the Angels
1897(?)-1985 Obituary 116
Simon, Matila 1908- 17-20R
Simon, Michael A(rthur) 1936- CANR-13
Earlier sketch in CA 33-36R
Simon, Mina Lewiton
See Lewiton, Mina
Simon, Morton J. 1913- 17-20R
Simon, (Marvin) Neil 1927- CANR-26
Earlier sketch in CA 21-24R
See also AITN 1
See also CLC 6, 11, 31, 39, 70
See also DLB 7
See also MTCW
Simon, Norma (Feldstein) 1927- CANR-21
Earlier sketches in CA 5-8R, CANR-6
See also MAICYA
See also SATA 3, 68

Simon, Paul 1928- 81-84
Simon, Paul 1942(?)- Brief entry 116
See also CLC 17
Simon, Pierre-Henri
1903-1972 Obituary 37-40R
Simon, Rita James 1931- CANR-8
Earlier sketch in CA 21-24R
Simon, Robert
See Musto, Barry
Simon, Robert A. 1897(?)-1981 Obituary 103
Simon, Robin (John Hughes) 1947- 128
Simon, Roger David 1943- 109
Simon, Roger L(ichtenberg) 1943- 137
Simon, Samuel A(lan) 1945- 117
Simon, Seymour 1931- CANR-29
Earlier sketches in CA 25-28R, CANR-11
See also CLR 9
See also MAICYA
See also SATA 4
Simon, Sheldon W(eiss) 1937- CANR-26
Earlier sketches in CA 25-28R, CANR-10
Simon, Shirley (Schwartz) 1921- CANR-16
Earlier sketches in CA 1-4R, CANR-1
See also SATA 11
Simon, Sidney B(lair) 1927- 101
Simon, Solomon 1895-1970 Obituary 104
See also SATA 40
Simon, (Edward) Ted 1931- 105
Simon, Tony 1921- 5-8R
Simon, Ulrich E(rnst) 1913- 29-32R
Simon, Walter G(old) 1924- 17-20R
Simon, William E(dward) 1927- 81-84
Simon, William 1927- 9-12R
Simonds, John Ormsbee 1913- 77-80
Simonds, Roger (Tyrrell) 1929- 93-96
Simonds, Rollin Head 1910- 1-4R
Simonds, William Adams 1887- CAP-1
Earlier sketch in CA 11-12
Simone
See Porche, Simone (Benda)
Simone, Albert Joseph 1935- 17-20R
Simone, Charles B(rian) 1949- 116
Simonelli, Maria Picchio 1921- 49-52
Simonet, Thomas Solon 1942- 116
Simonetta, Linda 1948- 77-80
See also SATA 14
Simonetta, Sam 1936- 77-80
See also SATA 14
Simonhoff, Harry 1891- 5-8R
Simoni, John Peter 1911- Brief entry 106
Simonin, Albert (Charles)
1905-1980 Obituary 104
Simonini, R(inaldo) C(harles) Jr.
1922-1967 .... CAP-1
Earlier sketch in CA 11-12
Simonon, Paul 1956(?)-
See The Clash
See also CLC 30
Simonov, Konstantin (Kirill) Mikhailovich
1915-1979 Obituary 89-92
Simons, Barbara B(rooks) 1934- 108
See also SATA 41
Simons, Beverley 1938- 104
Simons, David G(oodman) 1922- 17-20R
Simons, Donald L. 1945- 138
Simons, Elwyn LaVerne 1930- CANR-22
Earlier sketch in CA 105
Simons, Eric N(orman) 1896- 13-16R
Simons, Hans 1893-1972 Obituary 33-36R
Simons, Harry 1912- 1-4R
Simons, Howard 1929-1989 65-68
Obituary 128
Simons, James Marcus 1939- 106
Simons, Jim
See Simons, James Marcus
Simons, John D(onald) 1935- 41-44R
Simons, Joseph 1933- 81-84
Simons, Katherine Drayton Mayrant
1892(?)-1969 ....9-12R
Obituary 112
See also DLBY 83
Simons, Lewis M(artin) 1939- 128
Brief entry 123
Simons, Myron (Bud) 1920- 113
Simons, Robin 1951- 65-68
Simons, Thomas G(erald) 1950- 111
Simons, Thomas W(inston) Jr. 1938- 134
Simons, William Edward 1927- 17-20R
Simonson, Conrad 1931- 49-52
Simonson, Harold P(eter) 1926- 33-36R
Simonson, Lee 1888-1967 ....9-12R
Simonson, Mary Jane
See Wheeler, Mary Jane
Simonson, Solomon S. 1914- 21-24R
Simont, Marc 1915- CANR-38
Earlier sketch in CA 61-64
See also MAICYA
See also SATA 9
Simonton, Dean Keith 1948- 119
Simonton, Stephanie
See Matthews-Simonton, Stephanie
Simoons, Frederick J. 1922- CANR-23
Earlier sketch in CA 1-4R
Simos, Miriam 1951- 104
Simper, Robert 1937- CANR-23
Earlier sketches in CA 61-64, CANR-8
Simpich, Frederick Jr. 1911-1975 61-64
Obituary 57-60
Simpkin, Richard E(velyn) 1921-1986 124
Simpson, A(lfred) W. Brian 1931- 5-8R
Simpson, Alan 1912- CANR-30
Earlier sketch in CA 1-4R
Simpson, Cedric Keith 1907-1985 111
Obituary 117
Simpson, Claude M(itchell) Jr. 1910-1976 .....5-8R
Obituary 65-68
Simpson, Colin 1908- CANR-5
Earlier sketch in CA 53-56
See also SATA 14
Simpson, Craig M(ichael) 1942- 119
Simpson, D(avid) P(enistan) 1917- 9-12R
Simpson, Dick 1940- CANR-30
Earlier sketches in CA 33-36R, CANR-13
Simpson, Dorothy 1933- CANR-30
Earlier sketch in CA 107
See also MTCW
Simpson, E(rvin) P(eter) Y(oung) 1911- 17-20R
Simpson, Elizabeth Alice Hilts
1921-1989 Obituary 130
Simpson, Elizabeth Leonie 33-36R
Simpson, Ethel 1937- 117
Simpson, (John) Evan 1940- 97-100
Simpson, George E(dward) 1944- 101
Simpson, George Eaton 1904- 77-80
Simpson, George Gaylord 1902-1984 .....CANR-16
Obituary 114
Earlier sketches in CAP-1, CA 19-20
See also MTCW
Simpson, Harold Brown 1917- CANR-4
Earlier sketch in CA 9-12R
Simpson, Harriette
See Arnow, Harriette (Louisa) Simpson
Simpson, Hassell A(lgernon) 1930- 41-44R
Simpson, Helen 134
Simpson, Helen (De Guerry)
1897-1940 Brief entry 109
See also DLB 77
Simpson, Hilary 1954- 131
Simpson, Howard Russell 1925- CANR-1
Earlier sketch in CA 1-4R
Simpson, Ian J(ames) 1895- CAP-1
Earlier sketch in CA 13-14
Simpson, Ida Harper 1928- 17-20R
Simpson, Jacqueline (Mary) 1930- CANR-5
Earlier sketch in CA 13-16R
Simpson, Jacynth Hope
See Hope Simpson, Jacynth
Simpson, James B(easley) 1926- CANR-9
Earlier sketch in CA 5-8R
Simpson, Jean I(rwin) 1896- 5-8R
Simpson, Jerry H(oward Jr.) 1925- 138
Simpson, Joan Murray
1918-1977 Obituary 89-92
Simpson, John (Andrew) 1953- 122
Simpson, John L(iddle) 9-12R
Simpson, Judith H(olroyd) 1941- 110
Simpson, Kemper 1893- CAP-1
Earlier sketch in CA 11-12
Simpson, Kirke L(arue)
1882(?)-1972 Obituary 37-40R
Simpson, Leo 1934- 101
See also AITN 2
Simpson, Lewis P(earson) 1916- CANR-8
Earlier sketch in CA 17-20R
Simpson, Louis (Aston Marantz) 1923- CANR-1
Earlier sketch in CA 1-4R
See also CAAS 4
See also CLC 4, 7, 9, 32
See also DLB 5
See also MTCW
Simpson, Matt(hew William) 1936- 131
Simpson, Michael Andrew 1944- 89-92
Simpson, Mona (Elizabeth) 1957- 135
Brief entry 122
See also CLC 44
Simpson, Myrtle L(illias) 1931- CANR-11
Earlier sketch in CA 21-24R
See also SATA 14
Simpson, N(orman) F(rederick) 1919- 13-16R
See also CLC 29
See also DLB 13
Simpson, Norman T.
1919(?)-1988 Obituary 125
Simpson, O(renthal) J(ames) 1947- 103
Simpson, R(onald) A(lbert) 1929- CANR-14
Earlier sketch in CA 77-80
Simpson, Ray H. 1907- 1-4R
Simpson, Richard L(ee) 1929- 9-12R
Simpson, Robert H. 1912- 108
Simpson, Robert (Wilfred Levick) 1921- 103
Simpson, Robert 1924- 49-52
Simpson, Ruth Mary Rasey 1902- CANR-1
Earlier sketch in CA 1-4R
Simpson, Ruth 1926- 73-76
Simpson, (Robert) Smith 1906- CAP-2
Earlier sketch in CA 21-22
Simpson, Stanhope Rowton 1903- 73-76
Simpson, Thomas W(illiam) 1957- 137
Simpson, W. W.
See Simpson, William Wynn
Simpson, William Hays 1903- 41-44R
Simpson, William Kelly 1928- 105
Simpson, William Wynn
1907-1987 Obituary 123
Sims, Bernard John 1915- 13-16R
Sims, Bobbi 1931- 117
Sims, Charles A(gustus)
1901-1983 Obituary 111
Sims, Edward H. 1923- CANR-6
Earlier sketch in CA 1-4R
Sims, Edward J(ames) 1927- 41-44R
Sims, George (Frederick Robert)
1923- CANR-12
Earlier sketch in CA 25-28R
See also DLB 87
Sims, George R. 1847-1922 .... DLB 35, 70
Sims, Harold D(ana) 1935- 41-44R
Sims, James H(ylbert) 1924- 1-4R
Sims, Janet L.
See Sims-Wood, Janet L(ouise)
Sims, Lois Dorothy Lang
See Lang-Sims, Lois Dorothy
Sims, Mary Sophia Stephens
1886-1976 Obituary 65-68
Sims, Naomi (Ruth) 1949- CANR-26
Earlier sketch in CA 69-72
Sims, Norman (Howard) 1948- 132
Sims, Patsy 1938- 135
Brief entry 110
Sims, Patterson 1947- 124
Sims, Phillip L(eon) 1940- 105
Simson, Eve 1937- 73-76
Simsova, Sylva 1931- CANR-12
Earlier sketch in CA 29-32R
Sims-Wood, Janet L(ouise) 1945- 108
Simundsson, Elva 1950- .... SATA 63
Sinai, I(saac) Robert 1924- CANR-10
Earlier sketch in CA 21-24R
Sinclair, Andrew (Annandale) 1935- CANR-38
Earlier sketches in CA 9-12R, CANR-14
See also CAAS 5
See also CLC 2, 14
See also DLB 14
See also MTCW
Sinclair, Bennie Lee 1939- CANR-1
Earlier sketch in CA 49-52
Sinclair, Bertrand William 1881-1972 ...... DLB 92
Sinclair, Bruce A. 1929- 126
Brief entry 106
Sinclair, Clive (John) 1948- 127
Sinclair, Clover
See Gater, Dilys
Sinclair, Donna 1943- CANR-23
Earlier sketch in CA 106
Sinclair, Emil
See Hesse, Hermann
Sinclair, (Allan) Gordon 1900-1984 102
Obituary 112
See also AITN 1
Sinclair, Grace
See Wallmann, Jeffrey M(iner)
Sinclair, Grant
See Drago, Harry Sinclair
Sinclair, Harold (Augustus) 1907-1966 ....5-8R
Sinclair, Heather
See Johnston, William
Sinclair, Iain MacGregor
See Sinclair, Iain
Sinclair, Iain 1943- 132
Sinclair, Ian
See Foley, (Cedric) John
Sinclair, Irene
See Griffith, D(avid Lewelyn) W(ark)
Sinclair, James
See Staples, Reginald Thomas
Sinclair, Jo
See Seid, Ruth
See also DLB 28
Sinclair, John L(eslie) 1902- 105
Sinclair, Julian
See Sinclair, Mary Amelia St. Clair
Sinclair, Keith 1922- 17-20R
Sinclair, Lister (Shedden) 1921- 105
See also DLB 88
Sinclair, Marjorie (Jane) 1913- 132
Sinclair, Mary Amelia St. Clair
1865(?)-1946 Brief entry 104
See also Sinclair, May
Sinclair, Max 1945- 113
Sinclair, May
See Sinclair, Mary Amelia St. Clair
See also DLB 36
See also TCLC 3, 11
Sinclair, Michael
See Shea, Michael (Sinclair MacAuslan)
Sinclair, Miranda 1948- 77-80
Sinclair, Murray 1950- 108
Sinclair, Olga 1923- CANR-26
Earlier sketches in CA 61-64, CANR-11
Sinclair, Rose
See Smith, Susan Vernon
Sinclair, Roy
See Griffith, D(avid Lewelyn) W(ark)
Sinclair, Sandra 1940- 120
Sinclair, Sonia 1928- 126
Sinclair, Upton (Beall) 1878-1968 ....CANR-7
Obituary 25-28R
Earlier sketch in CA 5-8R
See also CDALB 1929-1941
See also CLC 1, 11, 15, 63
See also DLB 9
See also MTCW
See also SATA 9
See also WLC
Sinclair-Stevenson, Christopher 1939- 102
Sincoff, Michael Z(olman) 1943- 85-88
Sinden, Donald (Alfred) 1923- 132
Sindermann, Carl J(ames) 138
Sindler, Allan Paul 1928- 97-100
Sinel, Allen 1936- 45-48
Siner, Howard W(alter) 1946- 117
Sinfield, Alan 1941- CANR-32
Earlier sketch in CA 113
Singal, Daniel Joseph 1944- 129
Singe, (Edmund) J(ohn) M(illington)
1871-1909 ....WLC
Singer, Adam
See Karp, David
Singer, Amanda
See Brooks, Janice Young
Singer, Armand Edwards 1914- CANR-14
Earlier sketch in CA 41-44R
Singer, Arthur 1917-1990 .... SATA 64
Singer, Benjamin D. 1931- 37-40R
Singer, Beth J(udith) 1927- 113
Singer, Burns
See Singer, James Hyman
Singer, C(harles) Gregg 1910- CANR-12
Earlier sketch in CA 73-76
Singer, David L(in) 1937- 73-76
Singer, Fred J. 1931- 21-24R
Singer, Irving 1925- 21-24R
Singer, Isaac
See Singer, Isaac Bashevis
Singer, Isaac Bashevis 1904-1991 ....CANR-39
Obituary 134
Earlier sketches in CA 1-4R, CANR-1
See also AITN 1, 2
See also CDALB 1941-1968
See also CLC 1, 3, 6, 9, 11, 15, 23, 38, 69
See also CLR 1
See also DLB 6, 28, 52
See also DLBY 91
See also MAICYA
See also MTCW
See also SATA 3, 27
See also SATO 68
See also SSC 3
See also WLC
Singer, Israel Joshua 1893-1944 .... TCLC 33
Singer, J(oel) David 1925- CANR-6
Earlier sketch in CA 1-4R
Singer, Jack W(olfe) 1942- 104
Singer, James Hyman 1928-1964 102
Obituary 89-92
Singer, Jane Sherrod 1917-1985 ....CANR-17
Obituary 115
Earlier sketch in CA 25-28R
See also SATA 4, 42
Singer, Jerome L(eonard) 1924- 132
Singer, Joe
See Singer, Joseph
Singer, Joseph I.
See Singer, Joseph
Singer, Joseph 1923- CANR-2
Earlier sketch in CA 45-48
Singer, Joy Daniels 1928- 29-32R
Singer, Judith 1926- 61-64
Singer, Julia 1917- 65-68
See also SATA 28
Singer, June Flaum 1933- 106
Singer, June (Kurlander) 1918- CANR-10
Earlier sketch in CA 41-44R
Singer, Kurt D(eutsch) 1911- CANR-2
Earlier sketch in CA 49-52
See also SATA 38
Singer, Marcus George 1926- CANR-3
Earlier sketch in CA 1-4R
Singer, Marilyn 1948- CANR-39
Earlier sketches in CA 65-68, CANR-9
See also MAICYA
See also SAAS 13
See also SATA 38, 48
Singer, Mark 1950- 138
Singer, Marshall R. 1932- 41-44R
Singer, Michael A(lan) 1947- 57-60
Singer, Milton Borah 1912- CANR-23
Earlier sketch in CA 105
Singer, Neil M(ichael) 1939- 93-96
Singer, Norman 1925- 41-44R
Singer, Peter (Albert David) 1946- CANR-8
Earlier sketch in CA 57-60
Singer, Phylis
See Morrison, Phylis
Singer, Ray 1916- 105
Singer, Richard G. 1943- 89-92
Singer, (Dennis) Robert 1931- 49-52
Singer, Robert N. CANR-25
Earlier sketches in CA 53-56, CANR-5
Singer, Rochelle 1939- CANR-20
Earlier sketch in CA 104
Singer, S(iegfried) Fred 1924- Brief entry 118
Singer, Samuel L(oewenberg) 1911- 65-68
Singer, Sarah 1915- 81-84
Singer, Shelley
See Singer, Rochelle
Singer, Sholom A. 1924-1987 Obituary 123
Singer, Susan (Mahler) 1941- 61-64
See also SATA 9
Singerman, Robert 1942- 110
Singh, Ajit 1940- 109
Singh, Amritjit 1945- 102
Singh, Arjan 1917- 49-52
Singh, Avtar 1929- 65-68
Singh, Baliit 1929- 41-44R
Singh, Bawa Satinder 1932- 101
Singh, Chetan 1955- 138
Singh, Darshan 1921- 133
Singh, G(han Shyam) 1926- CANR-20
Earlier sketches in CA 9-12R, CANR-5
Singh, Harbans 1921- 17-20R
Singh, Karan 1931- 13-16R
Singh, Khushwant 1915- CANR-6
Earlier sketch in CA 9-12R
See also CAAS 9
See also CLC 11
Singh, Lalita Prasad 1936- 21-24R
Singh, Madanjeet 1924- 17-20R
Singh, Nagendra 1914- CANR-7
Earlier sketch in CA 17-20R
Singh, R. K. Janmeja 1932- 37-40R
Singh, St. Nihal 1884- 105
Singh, Surender 1932- 49-52
Singh, Surendra Nihal
See Nihal Singh, Surendra
Singh, Vijai Pratap 1939- Brief entry 106
Singhal, D(amodar) P(rasad) 1925- 49-52
Singher, Martial (Jean-Paul)
1904-1990 Obituary 131
Singing Nun, The
See Deckers, Jeanine
Singletary, Otis Arnold Jr. 1921- 45-48
Singleton, Betty 1910- CAP-2
Earlier sketch in CA 25-28

Singleton, Charles S(outhward)
  1909-1985 Obituary 117
  Brief entry 113
Singleton, Frederick Bernard 1926- 89-92
Singleton, Ira C(uster) 1920- 5-8R
Singleton, Jack 1911- 13-16R
Singleton, John 1930- 138
  Earlier sketch in CA 21-24R
Singleton, M(arvin) K(enneth) 1933- 1-4R
Singleton, Mary Ann 1934- 57-60
Singleton, Ralph Herbert 1900- 13-16R
Singleton, Rebecca (Jane) 1948- 121
Singleton, Rupert
  See Pitt-Kethley, Fiona
Singleton, V(ernon) L(eRoy) 1923- 25-28R
Singmaster, Elsie 1879-1958 Brief entry 110
  See also DLB 9
Sinha, Krishna N(andan) 1924- 13-16R
Sinha, Phulgenda 1924- 130
Sinha, Sasadhar 1901- 17-20R
Sinibaldi, Fosco
  See Kacew, Romain
Sinick, Daniel 1913- 45-48
Sinicropi, Giovanni Andrea 1924- 45-48
Sinisgalli, Leonardo 1908-1981 Obituary 103
  See also DLB 114
Sinjohn, John
  See Galsworthy, John
Sinjun
  See John, Elizabeth Beaman
Sinkankas, John 1915- CANR-6
  Earlier sketch in CA 1-4R
Sinkler, George 1927- 85-88
Sinnema, John R(alph) 1911- 41-44R
Sinnen, Jeanne 1926-1976 Obituary 104
Sinnette, Elinor Des Verney 1925- 132
Sinnigen, William G. 1928- 13-16R
Sinning, Wayne E. 1931- 77-80
Sinofsky, Esther R. 1951- 126
Sinopoli, Richard C. 1956- 138
Sinor, Denis 1916- CANR-6
  Earlier sketch in CA 1-4R
Sinor, John 1930- CANR-11
  Earlier sketch in CA 69-72
Sinyavsky, Andrei (Donatevich) 1925- 85-88
  See also CLC 8
Siodmak, Curt 1902- 113
  Brief entry 111
  See also DLB 44
Sionil Jose, F(rancisco) 1924- CANR-10
  Earlier sketch in CA 21-24R
Sions, Harry 1906-1974 Obituary 104
Siotis, Jean 1931- 25-28R
Sippl, Charles J. 1924- CANR-18
  Earlier sketch in CA 21-24R
Sipress, David 1947- 130
Siracusa, Joseph M(arcus) 1944- CANR-12
  Earlier sketch in CA 73-76
Siracusa, Joseph 1929- CANR-1
  Earlier sketch in CA 45-48
Sirageldin, Ismail A(bdel-Hamid)
  1930- CANR-16
  Earlier sketch in CA 29-32R
Sirc, Ljubo 1920- 103
Sire, James W(alter) 1933- CANR-28
  Earlier sketches in CA 29-32R, CANR-11
Siri, Giuseppe 1906-1989 Obituary 128
Sirica, John J(oseph) 1904- 110
Sirin, V.
  See Nabokov, Vladimir (Vladimirovich)
Siris, Peter 1944- 117
Sirius
  See Beuve-Mery, Hubert
Sirjamaki, John 1911- 13-16R
Sirkin, Gerald 1920- 25-28R
Sirkis, Nancy 1936- 102
Sirluck, Ernest 1918- 25-28R
Sirof, Harriet 1930- CANR-20
  Earlier sketch in CA 104
  See also SATA 37
Sirrom, Wes
  See Weiss, Morris S(amuel)
Sis, Peter 1949- 128
  See also SATA 67
Sisco, John I(sodore) 1931- 41-44R
Sisk, Dorothy Poole 1897-1983 Obituary 111
Sisk, Frank A. Jr. 1915-1985 Obituary 115
Sisk, Henry L(ybran) 1914- 49-52
Sisk, John P(aul) 1914- 29-32R
Siskel, Eugene Kal 1946- 113
  Brief entry 110
Siskel, Gene
  See Siskel, Eugene Kal
Sisler, Harry Hall 1917- 109
Sisler, Rebecca 1932- 104
Sisley, Emily L(ucretia) 1930- Brief entry 113
Sissle, Noble 1889-1975 Obituary 112
Sissman, L(ouis) E(dward) 1928-1976 ....CANR-13
  Obituary 65-68
  Earlier sketch in CA 21-24R
  See also CLC 9, 18
  See also DLB 5
Sisson, A(lbert) F(ranklin) 1901- 5-8R
Sisson, C(harles) H(ubert) 1914- CANR-3
  Earlier sketch in CA 1-4R
  See also CAAS 3
  See also CLC 8
  See also DLB 27
Sisson, Rosemary Anne 1923- CANR-29
  Earlier sketches in CA 13-16R, CANR-12
  See also SATA 11
Sister Carol Anne O'Marie
  See O'Marie, Carol Anne
Sister Luc-Gabrielle
  See Deckers, Jeanine
Sister M. Victoria
  See Maria Del Rey, Sister
Sister Magdeleine de Jesus
  See Hutin, Magdeleine
Sister Mary Annette
  See Buttimer, Anne
Sister Mary Jeremy
  See Finnegan, Mary Jeremy
Sister Mary Terese
  See Donze, Mary Terese
Sister Maura
  See Eichner, Maura
Sister Smile
  See Deckers, Jeanine
Sister Teresa Margaret
  See Rowe, Margaret (Kevin)
Sisyphus
  See Barthelmes, (Albert) Wes(ley Jr.)
Sitaram, K(ondavagil) S(urya) 1935- 69-72
Sitarz, Paula (Gaj) 1955- 122
Sitchin, Zecharia 1920- CANR-22
  Earlier sketch in CA 69-72
Sites, James N(eil) 1924- 1-4R
Sites, Paul 1926- 53-56
Sithole, Ndabaningi 1920- Brief entry 110
Sitomer, Harry 1903- 101
  See also SATA 31
Sitomer, Mindel 1903- 101
  See also SATA 31
Sitter, John E(dward) 1944- 130
  Brief entry 114
Sittler, Joseph 1904-1987 Obituary 124
Sitton, Claude (Fox) 1925- Brief entry 122
Sitwell, Dame Edith 1887-1964 ....CANR-35
  Earlier sketch in CA 9-12R
  See also CDBLB 1945-1960
  See also CLC 2, 9, 67
  See also DLB 20
  See also MTCW
  See also PC 3
Sitwell, (Francis) Osbert (Sacheverell)
  1892-1969 ....CAP-2
  Obituary 25-28R
  Earlier sketch in CA 21-22
  See also DLB 100
Sitwell, Sacheverell 1897-1988 ....21-24R
  Obituary 126
Sitzfleisch, Vladimir
  See Spirer, Herbert F(rederick)
Siu, Helen 1950- 114
Siu, R(alph) G(un) H(oy) 1917- CANR-10
  Earlier sketch in CA 25-28R
Sive, Helen R(obinson) 1951- 107
  See also SATA 30
Sive, Mary Robinson 1928- CANR-10
  Earlier sketch in CA 65-68
Siverson, Randolph M. 1940- 138
Siviero, Rodolpho 1912(?)-1983 Obituary 111
Sivulich, Sandra (Jeanne) Stroner 1941- 61-64
  See also SATA 9
Siwek, Manuel 1908-1976 Obituary 65-68
Siwundhla, Alice Msumba 1928- 45-48
Sixsmith, Eric Keir Gilborne 1904-1986 ....33-36R
  Obituary 118
Siy, Robert Y(oung) Jr. 1955- 119
Sizemore, Burlan A. 1933- 45-48
Sizemore, Chris(tine) Costner 1927- 81-84
Sizemore, Christine Wick 1945- 134
Sizemore, Deborah Lightfoot 1956- 138
Sizemore, Margaret D(avidson) CAP-2
  Earlier sketch in CA 19-20
Sizer, John 1938- CANR-12
  Earlier sketch in CA 29-32R
Sizer, Nancy F(aust) 1935- 45-48
Sizer, Theodore R(yland) 1932- CANR-13
  Earlier sketch in CA 33-36R
Sjoeberg, Leif 1925- 65-68
Sjoewall, Maj 1935- 65-68
  See also CLC 7
Sjowall, Maj
  See Sjoewall, Maj
Skaar, Grace Brown 1903- 69-72
Skaer, Peter M(acKall) 1953- 103
Skagen, Kiki
  See Munshi, Kiki Skagen
Skaggs, David Curtis (Jr.) 1937- 41-44R
Skaggs, Jimmy M(arion) 1940- CANR-39
  Earlier sketches in CA 45-48, CANR-1
Skaggs, Merrill Maguire 1937- 45-48
Skala, John J. 1923- 17-20R
Skaldaspillir, Sigfridur
  See Broxon, Mildred Downey
Skallerup, Harry R(obert) 1927- 73-76
Skard, Sigmund 1903- CANR-22
  Earlier sketches in CA 17-20R, CANR-7
Skarda, Patricia Lyn 1946- 106
Skardal, Dorothy Burton 1922- 61-64
Skardon, Alvin W(ilson Jr.) 1912- 53-56
Skarmeta, Antonio 1940- 131
  See also HW
  See also SATA 57
Skarsaune, Oskar 1946- 136
Skarsten, Malvin O. 1892- CAP-1
  Earlier sketch in CA 13-16
Skartvedt, Dan (L.) 1945- 77-80
Skates, John R(ay) 1934- 97-100
Skeaping, John Rattenbury 1901-1980 108
  Obituary 97-100
Skeaping, Mary 1902-1984 Obituary 112
Skedgell, Marian Jay 1921- CANR-14
  Earlier sketch in CA 17-20R
Skeel, Dorothy J(une) CANR-8
  Earlier sketch in CA 61-64
Skeen, Carl Edward 1937- 113
Skegg, P(eter) D(onald) G(raham) 1944- 127
Skehan, James W(illiam) 1923- 57-60
Skei, Allen B(ennet) 1935-1985 ....CANR-31
  Earlier sketch in CA 108
Skellings, Edmund 1932- 77-80
Skelly, James R(ichard) 1927- 85-88
  See also SATA 17
Skelly, Madge 1903- 41-44R
Skelton, Barbara 1918- 136
Skelton, Eugene (Lamar) 1914- CANR-1
  Earlier sketch in CA 45-48
Skelton, Geoffrey (David) 1916- CANR-18
  Earlier sketches in CA 49-52, CANR-1
Skelton, John E. 1934- 37-40R
Skelton, Peter 1928- 13-16R
Skelton, Red 1913- 104
Skelton, Robin 1925- CANR-28
  Earlier sketch in CA 5-8R
  See also CAAS 5
  See also AITN 2
  See also CLC 13
  See also DLB 27, 53
Skelton, Roger
  See Horn, Peter (Rudolf Gisela)
Skemp, Joseph Bright 1910- 106
Skemp, Richard R(owland) 1919- 107
Skendi, Stavro 1906- 25-28R
Skene-Melvin, Ann (Patricia) 1936- 108
Skene-Melvin, (Lewis) David (St. Columb)
  1936- 108
Skibbe, Eugene M(oritz) 1930- 21-24R
Skidelsky, Robert 1939- CANR-11
  Earlier sketch in CA 25-28R
Skidmore, Ian 1929- CANR-10
  Earlier sketch in CA 61-64
Skidmore, Max J(oseph Sr.) 1933- CANR-12
  Earlier sketch in CA 29-32R
Skidmore, Rex A(ustin) 1914- 13-16R
Skidmore, Thomas E. 1932- 21-24R
Skiles, Jacqueline D(ean) 1937- 108
Skilken, Patricia S(tout) 1943- 119
Skilling, H(arold) Gordon 1912- CANR-7
  Earlier sketch in CA 13-16R
Skillings, R(oger) D(eering) 1937- 61-64
Skilliter, S(usan) A. 1931(?)-1985 Obituary 117
Skilton, John H. 1906- 37-40R
Skimin, Robert (Elwayne) 1929- 108
Skinner, Ainslie
  See Gosling, Paula
Skinner, B(urrhus) F(rederic)
  1904-1990 ....CANR-18
  Obituary 132
  Earlier sketch in CA 9-12R
  See also MTCW
Skinner, Charles Edward 1891- CAP-1
  Earlier sketch in CA 17-18
Skinner, Constance Lindsay 1882-1939 ....DLB 92
  See also YABC 1
Skinner, Cornelia Otis 1901-1979 ....17-20R
  Obituary 89-92
  See also SATA 2
Skinner, Elliott P(ercival) 1924- 13-16R
Skinner, G(eorge) William 1925- CANR-2
  Earlier sketch in CA 49-52
Skinner, Gordon S(weetland) 1924- 13-16R
Skinner, Jeffrey 1949- 126
Skinner, John Emory 1925- 5-8R
Skinner, John Stuart 1788-1851 ....DLB 73
Skinner, June O'Grady 1922- 5-8R
Skinner, Knute (Rumsey) 1929- CANR-24
  Earlier sketches in CA 17-20R, CANR-9
Skinner, Michael 1953- 134
Skinner, Rulon Dean 1931- 61-64
Skinner, Thomas Edward 1909- 109
Skinner, Tom 1942- 25-28R
Skiold, Birgit Obituary 107
Skipp, Victor (Henry Thomas) 1925- 123
  Brief entry 118
Skipper, Betty
  See Barr, Betty
Skipper, G. C. 1939- CANR-14
  Earlier sketch in CA 77-80
  See also SATA 38, 46
Skipper, James K(inley) Jr. 1934- CANR-12
  Earlier sketch in CA 17-20R
Skipsey, Joseph 1832-1903 ....DLB 35
Skipwith, Sofka 1907- 29-32R
Skira, Albert 1904-1973 Obituary 104
Skirpa, Kazys 1895(?)-1979 Obituary 89-92
Skjei, Eric William 1947- 97-100
Sklansky, Morris Aaron 1919- 17-20R
Sklar, Dusty 1928- 65-68
Sklar, George 1908-1988 ....1-4R
  Obituary 125
Sklar, Kathryn Kish 1939- CANR-18
  Earlier sketches in CA 45-48, CANR-3
Sklar, Lawrence 1938- 105
Sklar, Michael Joel 1945(?)-1984 Obituary 112
Sklar, Morty 1935- CANR-13
  Earlier sketch in CA 77-80
Sklar, Richard L(awrence) 1930- 9-12R
Sklar, Robert 1936- CANR-8
  Earlier sketch in CA 21-24R
Sklar, Scott 1950- 131
Sklare, Arnold B(eryl) 1924- 17-20R
Sklare, Marshall 1921- CANR-12
  Obituary 137
  Earlier sketch in CA 21-24R
Sklarew, Myra 1934- CANR-30
  Earlier sketch in CA 109
Sklarewitz, Norman 1924- 69-72
Skocpol, Theda Ruth 1947- Brief entry 105
Skofield, James ....SATA 44
Skoglund, Elizabeth 1937- CANR-34
  Earlier sketches in CA 41-44R, CANR-15
Skoglund, Goesta 1904- 65-68
Skoglund, John Egnar 1912- 9-12R
Skold, Betty Westrom 1923- 112
  See also SATA 41
Skolimowski, Jerzy 1938- 128
  See also CLC 20
Skolnick, Jerome H(erbert)
  1931- Brief entry 114
Skolnik, Alfred 1920(?)-1977 Obituary 69-72
Skolnik, Peter L(aurence) 1944- 57-60
Skolnikoff, Eugene B. 1928- 21-24R
Skolsky, Sidney 1905-1983 103
  Obituary 109
Skornia, Harry J(ay) 1910- CAP-2
  Earlier sketch in CA 17-18
Skorpen, Liesel Moak 1935- 25-28R
  See also SATA 3
Skotheim, Robert Allen 1933- 21-24R
Skou-Hansen, Tage 1925- CANR-6
  Earlier sketch in CA 13-16R
Skousen, Mark 104
Skousen, W(illard) Cleon 1913- CANR-5
  Earlier sketch in CA 5-8R
Skowronski, JoAnn 108
Skoyles, John 1949- 104
Skrade, Carl 1935- 65-68
Skram, Amalie (Bertha) 1847-1905 ....TCLC 25
Skrivanek, John M(arion) 1913- 49-52
Skrzynecki, Peter 1945- 128
Skulicz, Matthew V. 1944- 37-40R
Skulsky, Harold Lawrence 1935- 107
Skura, Meredith Anne 1944- 117
Skurdenis, Juliann V.
  See Skurdenis-Smircich, Juliann V(eronica)
Skurdenis-Smircich, Juliann V(eronica)
  1942- 77-80
Skurnik, W. A. E. 1926- 41-44R
Skurzynski, Gloria (Joan) 1930- CANR-30
  Earlier sketches in CA 33-36R, CANR-13
  See also SAAS 9
  See also SATA 8
Skutch, Alexander F(rank) 1904- CANR-21
  Earlier sketch in CA 33-36R
Skutch, Margaret F. 1932- 105
Skutsch, Otto 1906- 126
Skvorecka, Zdena Salivarova 1933- 41-44R
Skvorecky, Josef (Vaclav) 1924- CANR-34
  Earlier sketches in CA 61-64, CANR-10
  See also CAAS 1
  See also CLC 15, 39, 69
  See also MTCW
Sky, Kathleen
  See Goldin, Kathleen Mckinney
Skye, Maggie
  See Werner, Herma
Skyrms, Brian 1938- CANR-26
  Earlier sketch in CA 108
Slaatte, Howard A(lexander) 1919- CANR-31
  Earlier sketches in CA 41-44R, CANR-14
Slabbert, F(rederik) Van Zyl 1940- 133
Slaby, Andrew Edmund 1942- CANR-7
  Earlier sketch in CA 57-60
Slack, Adrian (Charles) 104
Slack, Charles W(illiam) 1929- 61-64
Slack, Kenneth 1917-1987 Obituary 123
Slack, Robert C(harles) 1914- 81-84
Slack, Walter H. 1932- 21-24R
Slackman, Charles B. 1934- ....SATA 12
Slade, Afton 1919- 89-92
Slade, Bernard
  See Newbound, Bernard Slade
  See also CAAS 9
  See also CLC 11, 46
  See also DLB 53
Slade, Caroline (Beach)
  1886-1975 Obituary 61-64
Slade, Jack
  See Ballard, (Willis) Todhunter
    and Germano, Peter B.
Slade, Joseph W(arren) 1941- 89-92
Slade, Madeleine 1892-1982 Obituary 115
Slade, Peter 1912- 13-16R
Slade, Richard 1910-1971 ....CAP-2
  Earlier sketch in CA 23-24
  See also SATA 9
Slade, Tony 1936- 33-36R
Sladek, John 1937- 25-28R
Sladen, Kathleen 1904- 69-72
Sladen, Norman St. Barbe CAP-1
  Earlier sketch in CA 13-14
Slaght, Lawrence T(ownsend) 1912- 73-76
Slakter, Malcolm J(ulian) 1929- 41-44R
Slamecka, Vladimir 1928- 5-8R
Slaney, George Wilson 1884- CAP-1
  Earlier sketch in CA 13-14
Slappey, Sterling G(reene) 1917- 65-68
Slate, Joseph (Frank) 1928- 110
  See also SATA 38
Slate, Joseph 1927- 45-48
Slate, Sam J(ordan) 1909- 49-52
Slaten, Yeffe Kimball
  1914(?)-1978 Obituary 77-80
Slater, Charlotte (Wolpers) 1944- 65-68
Slater, Eliot (Trevor Oakeshott) 1904- 53-56
Slater, Ian 1941- CANR-34
  Earlier sketch in CA 85-88
Slater, James (Derrick)
  See Slater, Jim
Slater, Jerome N(orman) 1935- 17-20R
Slater, Jim 1929- Brief entry 112
  See also SATA 34
Slater, Layton Ernest Alfred
  1916-1984 Obituary 114
Slater, Leonard 1920- 13-16R
Slater, Lydia (Elizabeth) Pasternak
  1902-1989 Obituary 128
Slater, Mariam K(reiselman) 1922- 123
  Brief entry 118
Slater, Mary Louise 1923- 29-32R
Slater, Maya 1941- 119
Slater, Miriam 1931- 120
Slater, Niall W. 126

Slater, Nigel 1944- CANR-18
Earlier sketch in CA 102
Slater, Patrick 1880-1951 ....DLB 68
Slater, Peter Gregg 1940- 81-84
Slater, Philip E(lliot) 1927- 21-24R
Slater, Ralph P(hipps) 1915- 21-24R
Slater, Robert (Henry) Lawson 1896- CAP-1
Earlier sketch in CA 13-14
Slater, Robert 1943- 119
Slater, Veronica
See Sullivan, Victoria
Slatin, John M. 1952- 126
Slatkin, Charles Eli 1907-1977 Obituary 73-76
Slatoff, Walter J(acob) 1922-1991 ....9-12R
Obituary 133
Slatta, Richard W(ayne) 1947- 133
Slattery, Marty 1938- 134
Slattery, Timothy Patrick 1911- 25-28R
Slattery, William J(ames) 1930- 101
Slatzer, Robert F(ranklin) 1927- Brief entry 113
Slaughter, Carolyn 1946- 85-88
See also CLC 56
Slaughter, Eugene Edward 1909- 37-40R
Slaughter, Frank G(ill) 1908- CANR-5
Earlier sketch in CA 5-8R
See also AITN 2
See also CLC 29
Slaughter, Howard K(ey) 1927- 45-48
Slaughter, Jane M(undy) 1908- 73-76
Slaughter, Jean
See Doty, Jean Slaughter
Slaughter, Jim
See Paine, Lauran (Bosworth)
Slaughter, M(ary) M(artina) 1940- 131
Slavens, Thomas P(aul) 1928- CANR-22
Earlier sketch in CA 104
Slavet, Joseph S. 1920- 61-64
Slavic, Rosalind Welcher
See Welcher, Rosalind
Slavick, William H(enry) 1927- 104
Slavin, Arthur Joseph 1933- CANR-3
Earlier sketch in CA 9-12R
Slavin, Morris 1913- 118
Slavin, Stephen L(oren) 1939- 111
Slavitt, David R. 1935- 21-24R
See also CAAS 3
See also CLC 5, 14
See also DLB 5, 6
Slavson, Samuel R(ichard) 1891- 17-20R
Slavutych, Yar 1918- CANR-38
Earlier sketches in CA 45-48, CANR-2, 17
Slawson, Ron(ald L.) 1932- 128
Slawson, William David 1931- 110
Slaymaker, R(edsecker) Samuel II 1923- 65-68
Slayton, Mariette (Elizabeth) Paine 1908- 65-68
Sleator, William (Warner III) 1945- 29-32R
See also AAYA 5
See also MAICYA
See also SATA 3, 68
Sledd, James Hinton 1914- 17-20R
Sledge, Linda Ching 1944- 108
Sleeper, James A. 1947- 133
Sleeper, Jim
See Sleeper, James A.
Sleigh, Barbara 1906-1982 ....CANR-6
Obituary 106
Earlier sketch in CA 13-16R
See also SATA 3, 30
Sleigh, Burrows Willcocks Arthur
1821-1869 ....DLB 99
Sleigh, (Brocas) Linwood 1902- 5-8R
Sleigh, Robert Collins Jr. 1932- 37-40R
Sleight, Robert B(enton) 1922- 41-44R
Slepian, Jan(ice B.) 1921- 136
See also MAICYA
See also SAAS 8
See also SATA 45, 51
Slesar, Henry 1927- CANR-1
Earlier sketch in CA 1-4R
Slesin, Suzanne 1944- 123
Slesinger, Doris P(eyser) 1927- 113
Slesinger, Reuben E. 1916- 5-8R
Slesinger, Tess 1905-1945 Brief entry 107
See also DLB 102
See also TCLC 10
Slesinger, Warren 1933- 33-36R
Slesser, Malcolm 1926- 17-20R
Slessor, Kenneth 1901-1971 102
Obituary 89-92
See also CLC 14
Sletholt, Erik 1919- 77-80
Slezak, Walter 1902-1983 Obituary 109
Slicer, Margaret O. 1920- 25-28R
See also SATA 4
Slide, Anthony 1944- CANR-29
Earlier sketches in CA 33-36R, CANR-12
Slim, William Joseph 1891-1970 Obituary 107
Slimming, John 1927-1979 ....25-28R
Obituary 89-92
Slitor, Richard Eaton 1911- CANR-32
Earlier sketch in CA 45-48
Slive, Seymour 1920- 103
Sliwa, Curtis 1954- 111
Sljivic-Simsic, Biljana 1933- 41-44R
Sloan, Alfred P(ritchard) Jr.
1875-1966 Obituary 113
Sloan, Allan 1944- 118
Sloan, Anthony
See Feist, Gene
Sloan, Carolyn 1937- 127
See also SATA 58
Sloan, Edward William III 1931- 37-40R
Sloan, Harold Stephenson 1887- CAP-1
Earlier sketch in CA 17-18
Sloan, Irving J. 1924- CANR-7
Earlier sketch in CA 17-20R
Sloan, James Park (Jr.) 1944- 29-32R
Sloan, Kay 1951- 108
Sloan, Michael 1946- 130
Sloan, Pat(rick Alan) 1908- 65-68
Sloan, Phillip R(eid) 1938- 109
Sloan, Raymond Paton 1893-1983 ....CAP-1
Obituary 109
Earlier sketch in CA 19-20
Sloan, Ruth Catherine
1898(?)-1976 Obituary 65-68
Sloan, Stephen 1936- 33-36R
Sloan, Thomas 1928- 93-96
Sloan, William Wilson 1901- 1-4R
Sloane, Arthur A(llan) 1931- 33-36R
Sloane, Eric 1910(?)-1985 108
Obituary 115
See also SATA 42, 52
Sloane, Eugene A(nthony) 1926- 65-68
Sloane, Howard N(orman) 1932- 81-84
Sloane, Joseph C(urtis) 1909- CAP-1
Earlier sketch in CA 11-12
Sloane, Leonard 1932- 21-24R
Sloane, Martin 1940- 132
Sloane, Peter J(ames) 1942- 108
Sloane, R(obert) Bruce 1923- 53-56
Sloane, Sara
See Bloom, Ursula
Sloane, Thomas O. 1929- 37-40R
Sloane, William M. 1906-1974 Obituary 53-56
Sloat, Teri 1948- 138
See also SATA 70
Sloate, Daniel 1931- CANR-32
Earlier sketch in CA 113
Slobin, Dan Isaac 1939- CANR-11
Earlier sketch in CA 65-68
Slobin, Mark 1943- 93-96
Slobodin, Richard 1915- 102
Slobodkin, Florence Gersh 1905- 1-4R
See also SATA 5
Slobodkin, Lawrence (B.) 1928- 137
Slobodkin, Louis 1903-1975 ....13-16R
Obituary 57-60
See also MAICYA
See also SATA 1, 26
Slobodkina, Esphyr 1908- CANR-1
Earlier sketch in CA 1-4R
See also SAAS 8
See also SATA 1
Slochower, Harry 1900-1991 ....CANR-2
Obituary 134
Earlier sketch in CA 49-52
Slocum, Bill
See Slocum, William J(oseph Michael) Jr.
Slocum, Donald Barclay
1911-1983 Obituary 110
Slocum, Frank 1925- 136
Slocum, John W(esley) Jr. 1940- 112
Slocum, Michael
See Slocum, William J(oseph Michael) Jr.
Slocum, Milton Jonathan 1905- 126
Slocum, Robert Bigney 1922- 9-12R
Slocum, Walter L(ucius) 1910- 21-24R
Slocum, William J(oseph Michael) Jr.
1912(?)-1974 Obituary 53-56
Sloggatt, Arthur H(astings)
1917(?)-1975 Obituary 61-64
Sloggett, Nellie 1851-1923 ....SATA 44
Sloma, Richard Stanley 1929- CANR-19
Earlier sketch in CA 103
Sloman, Albert Edward 1921- 5-8R
Sloman, Larry 1948- CANR-20
Earlier sketch in CA 81-84
Slomovitz, Philip 1896- 81-84
Slone, Dennis 1930-1982 Obituary 106
Slone, Verna Mae 1914- 89-92
Slonim, Marc 1894-1976 Obituary 65-68
Slonim, Morris J(ames) 1909- 1-4R
Slonim, Reuben 1914- 97-100
Slonim, Ruth 1918- 17-20R
Slonimski, Antoni 1895-1976 Obituary 65-68
Slonimsky, Nicolas 1894- 17-20R
Slonimsky, Yuri 1902-1978 Obituary 77-80
Slosberg, Mike 1934- 69-72
Slosberg, Myron
See Slosberg, Mike
Slosser, Bob G(ene) 1929- CANR-10
Earlier sketch in CA 65-68
Slosson, Preston (William) 1892- CANR-8
Earlier sketch in CA 61-64
Slote, Alfred 1926- ....CLR 4
See also MAICYA
See also SATA 8
Slote, Bernice D. 1915(?)-1983 Obituary 109
Slote, Michael A(nthony) 1941- 61-64
Slote, Stanley J(ames) 1917- 61-64
Slotkin, Richard S. 1942- 102
Slotnick, Daniel L(eonid)
1931-1985 Obituary 117
Slovenko, Ralph 1926- 17-20R
Slowikowski, M. Z. Rygor
1896-1989(?) Obituary 129
Sloyan, Gerard Stephen 1919- CANR-18
Earlier sketches in CA 5-8R, CANR-2
Sluckin, W(ladyslaw) 1919-1985 ....21-24R
Obituary 116
Slung, Louis Sheaffer 1912- 53-56
See also Sheaffer, Louis
Slung, Michele (Beth) 1947- 102
Slusher, Howard S. 1937- 25-28R
Slusser, Dorothy M. 1922- 33-36R
Slusser, George Edgar 1939- CANR-13
Earlier sketch in CA 69-72
Slusser, Gerald H(erbert) 1920- 13-16R
Slusser, Robert M(elville) 1916- CANR-3
Earlier sketch in CA 1-4R
Slye, Leonard
See Rogers, Roy
Small, Bertrice 1937- CANR-29
Earlier sketches in CA 77-80, CANR-13
Small, David 1937- CANR-39
Earlier sketch in CA 108
Small, David 1945- ....SATA 46, 50
Small, Dwight Hervey 1919- CANR-8
Earlier sketch in CA 61-64
Small, Ernest
See Lent, Blair
Small, Gary W. 1951- 127
Small, George L(eroy) 1924- 85-88
Small, George Raphael 1918- 57-60
Small, Kenneth A(lan) 1945- 112
Small, Melvin 1939- CANR-30
Earlier sketches in CA 29-32R, CANR-12
Small, Miriam Rossiter 1899- 1-4R
Small, Norman M. 1944- 41-44R
Small, William
See Eversley, D(avid) E(dward) C(harles)
Smallenburg, Harry W. 1907- CAP-1
Earlier sketch in CA 13-14
Smalley, Barbara Martin 1926- 105
Smalley, Beryl 1905-1984 103
Obituary 112
Smalley, Donald (Arthur) 1907- 17-20R
Smalley, Ruth E(lizabeth) 1903- CAP-2
Earlier sketch in CA 21-22
Smalley, Stephen Stewart 1931- 103
Smalley, William A. 1923- CANR-1
Earlier sketch in CA 45-48
Smallwood, Carol 1939- 122
Smallwood, Frank(lin) 1927- 123
Brief entry 118
Smallwood, James (Milton) 1944- 115
Smallwood, Joseph R(oberts) 1900- 105
Smallwood, Norah (Evelyn)
1910(?)-1984 Obituary 114
See also SATA 41
Smaridge, Norah (Antoinette) 1903- 37-40R
See also SATA 6
Smart, (Peter) Alastair (Marshall) 1922- 37-40R
Smart, Albert Davis 1931(?)-1989 Obituary 130
Smart, Barry 1946- 117
Smart, Carol 1948- CANR-37
Earlier sketches in CA 73-76, CANR-16
Smart, Carolyn (Alexandra) 1952- CANR-38
Earlier sketch in CA 116
Smart, Charles Allen 1904-1967 ....CAP-1
Earlier sketch in CA 11-12
Smart, Christopher 1722-1771 ....DLB 109
Smart, Elizabeth 1913-1986 81-84
Obituary 118
See also CLC 54
See also DLB 88
Smart, Graydon F. 1906(?)-1984 Obituary 111
Smart, Harold R(obert) 1892- CAP-1
Earlier sketch in CA 9-10
Smart, J(ohn) J(amieson) C(arswell)
1920- CANR-36
Earlier sketches in CA 13-16R, CANR-7
Smart, James D(ick) 1906-1982 ....CANR-8
Obituary 105
Earlier sketch in CA 57-60
Smart, Mollie S(tevens) 1916- 61-64
Smart, (Roderick) Ninian 1927- CANR-30
Earlier sketches in CA 29-32R, CANR-12
Smart, William (Edward Jr.) 1933- CANR-7
Earlier sketch in CA 13-16R
Smartt, J(oseph) 1931- 138
Smead, (Edwin) Howard 1953- 124
Smedes, Lewis B. 1921- CANR-36
Earlier sketches in CA 69-72, CANR-11
Smedley, Hester Marsden
See Marsden-Smedley, Hester
Smedley, Philip Marsden
See Marsden-Smedley, Philip
Smeds, Dave 1955- 118
Smee, John (Charles) Odling
See Odling-Smee, John (Charles)
Smeed, J. W. 1926- 127
Smeeton, Miles (Richard) 1906-1988 ....13-16R
Obituary 126
Smellie, Jim 1955- 133
Smellie, K.
See Smellie, Kingsley Bryce (Speakman)
Smellie, K. B.
See Smellie, Kingsley Bryce (Speakman)
Smellie, Kingsley Bryce (Speakman)
1897-1987 ....5-8R
Obituary 124
Smelser, Marshall 1912-1978 ....17-20R
Obituary 135
Smelser, Neil J(oseph) 1930- CANR-8
Earlier sketch in CA 17-20R
Smelser, William T. 1924- 29-32R
Smeltzer, C(larence) H(arry) 1900- CANR-15
Earlier sketch in CA 1-4R
Smelyakov, Yaroslav
1913(?)-1972 Obituary 37-40R
Smerk, George M(artin) 1933- 107
Smertenko, Johan J.
1897(?)-1983 Obituary 109
Smerud, Warren D(ouglas) 1928- 49-52
Smetana, Josette 1928- 93-96
Smethurst, Mae J. 1935- 133
Smethurst, William (Knowles) 1945- 117
Smidt, Kristian 1916- 17-20R
Smigel, Erwin O. 1917-1973 ....41-44R
Obituary 45-48
Smil, Vaclav 1943- CANR-30
Earlier sketch in CA 112
Smiles, Samuel 1812-1904 ....DLB 55
Smiley, Charles W(esley) 1940- 113
Smiley, David L(eslie) 1921- 5-8R
Smiley, Jane (Graves) 1949- CANR-30
Earlier sketch in CA 104
See also CLC 53
Smiley, Sam Max 1931- 105
Smiley, Virginia Kester 1923- CANR-28
Earlier sketches in CA 29-32R, CANR-12
See also SATA 2
Smirnov, Sergei Sergeevich
1915-1976 Obituary 65-68
Smith, A(nthony) C(harles) H(ockley) 1935- 119
Brief entry 116
Smith, A(lexander) G(raham) Cairns
See Cairns-Smith, A(lexander) G(raham)
Smith, A(lbert) H(ugh) 1903- 5-8R
Smith, A(lbert) J(ames) 1924-1991 65-68
Obituary 136
Smith, A(rthur) J(ames) M(arshall)
1902-1980 ....CANR-4
Obituary 102
Earlier sketch in CA 1-4R
See also CLC 15
See also DLB 88
Smith, A. Robert 1925- 73-76
Smith, A. Weston 1900(?)-1975 Obituary 57-60
Smith, Abbot E(merson)
1906-1983 Obituary 109
Smith, Ada Beatrice Queen Victoria Louisa Virginia
1894-1984 Obituary 111
Smith, Adam
See Goodman, George J(erome) W(aldo)
Smith, Adam 1723-1790 ....DLB 104
Smith, Alan M(cKinley) 1937- 41-44R
Smith, Alexander 1829-1867 ....DLB 32, 55
Smith, Alfred Edward 1895-1969 ....CAP-1
Earlier sketch in CA 11-12
Smith, Alfred G(oud) 1921- CANR-4
Earlier sketch in CA 9-12R
Smith, Alice K(imball) 1907- 138
Smith, Alice Upham 1908- 45-48
Smith, Allen William 1938- 61-64
Smith, Alson Jesse 1908-1965 ....1-4R
Obituary 103
Smith, Alton E. 1917- 17-20R
Smith, Angel
See Masterton, Graham
Smith, Anna Deavere 1950- 133
Smith, Anna H(ester) 1912- CANR-6
Earlier sketch in CA 57-60
Smith, Anna Piszczan-Czaja 1920- 110
Smith, Anne Mollegen 1940- 81-84
Smith, Anne Warren 1938- 111
See also SATA 34, 41
Smith, Anthony D(avid) 1939- 101
Smith, Anthony (John Francis) 1926- CANR-3
Earlier sketch in CA 9-12R
Smith, Anthony Peter 1912-1980 Obituary 105
Smith, Anthony 1938- CANR-10
Earlier sketch in CA 53-56
Smith, Arnold Cantwell 1915- 109
Smith, Arthur C. 1916- 21-24R
Smith, Arthur L(ee)
See Asante, Molefi K(ete)
Smith, Arthur L(ee) Jr. 1927- 37-40R
Smith, Arthur M(umford) 1903- CAP-2
Earlier sketch in CA 17-18
Smith, Arthur 1948- 120
Smith, Audrey D(owling) 1930- 119
Smith, Barbara Clark 1951- 124
Smith, Barbara Herrnstein 1932- 13-16R
Smith, Bardwell L(eith) 1925- 41-44R
Smith, Barry D(ecker) 1940- 29-32R
Smith, Beatrice S(chillinger) CANR-10
Earlier sketch in CA 57-60
See also SATA 12
Smith, Ben A(rwood) 1916- 1-4R
Smith, Benjamin Franklin 1902- 41-44R
Smith, Bernard (William) 1916- CANR-17
Earlier sketches in CA 1-4R, CANR-1
Smith, Bert Kruger 1915- CANR-11
Earlier sketch in CA 13-16R
Smith, Betsy Covington 1937- 111
See also SATA 43, 55
Smith, Betty (Wehner) 1896-1972 ....5-8R
Obituary 33-36R
See also CLC 19
See also DLBY 82
See also SATA 6
Smith, Beulah Fenderson 1915- 13-16R
Smith, Bobbi
See Walton, Bobbi Smith
Smith, Bonnie G(ene) 1940- CANR-25
Earlier sketch in CA 108
Smith, Boyd M. 1888(?)-1973 Obituary 41-44R
Smith, Bradford 1909-1964 ....CANR-16
Earlier sketch in CA 1-4R
See also SATA 5
Smith, Bradley F. 1931- 108
Smith, Bradley 1910- CANR-19
Earlier sketches in CA 5-8R, CANR-2
Smith, Brian C(ive) 1938- CANR-30
Earlier sketch in CA 110
Smith, Brian R. 1939- 129
Smith, Bromley K(eables)
1911-1987 Obituary 121
Smith, Bruce 1949- 108
Smith, Bryan Evers Sharwood
See Sharwood Smith, Bryan Evers
Smith, C. Busby
See Smith, John (Charles)
Smith, C. Pritchard
See Hoyt, Edwin P(almer) Jr.
Smith, C. Ray 1929-1988 ....CANR-28
Obituary 126
Earlier sketch in CA 109
Smith, C(lifford) T(horpe) 1924- 21-24R
Smith, C(hristopher) U(pham) M(urray)
1930- 33-36R
Smith, C. U. 1901- 41-44R
Smith, C(harles) W(illiam) 1940- 61-64
Smith, C. Willard 1899(?)-1979 Obituary 89-92

Smith, Caesar
See Trevor, Elleston
Smith, Cameron Mitchell 1935- 133
Smith, Carleton 1910-1984 Obituary 112
Smith, Carlton
See Rocklin, Ross Louis
Smith, Carmichael
See Linebarger, Paul M(yron) A(nthony)
Smith, Carol H(ertzig) 1929- 5-8R
Smith, Carol Sturm 1938- CANR-25
Earlier sketch in CA 25-28R
See also DLBY 81
Smith, Carole 1935- 101
Smith, (Charles) Carter (Jr.) 1930- 107
Smith, Catherine C. 1929- 29-32R
Smith, Cecil (Howard III) 1917- 69-72
Smith, Celina Janson
See Janson-Smith, Celina
Smith, Chard Powers 1894-1977 ....5-8R
Obituary 73-76
Smith, Charles E(dward)
1904-1970 Obituary 29-32R
Smith, Charles Harvard Gibbs
See Gibbs-Smith, Charles Harvard
Smith, Charles Henry
1826-1903 Brief entry 119
See also DLB 11
Smith, Charles Merrill Obituary 115
Smith, Charles W(illiam) (Frederick)
1905- 13-16R
Smith, Charlotte (Turner)
1749-1806 ....DLB 39, 109
Smith, Cherry 1931- 120
Smith, Clagett G. 1930- 37-40R
Smith, Clark Ashton 1893-1961 ....CLC 43
Smith, Clifford Neal 1923- 41-44R
Smith, Clodus R(ay) 1928- CANR-8
Earlier sketch in CA 21-24R
Smith, (Christopher) Colin 1927- 102
Smith, Constance Babington
See Babington Smith, Constance
Smith, Cordelia Titcomb 1902- CAP-1
Earlier sketch in CA 11-12
Smith, Cordwainer
See Linebarger, Paul M(yron) A(nthony)
See also DLB 8
Smith, Cornelius C(ole Jr.) 1913- CANR-22
Earlier sketch in CA 21-24R
Smith, Courtland L(ester) 1939- 81-84
Smith, Craig R(alph) 1944- 81-84
Smith, Curt 1951- 81-84
Smith, Curtis C. 1939- 127
Smith, Cynthia S. 1924- 106
Smith, Cyril James 1909-1974 Obituary 53-56
Smith, Cyril 1928- 109
Smith, D(avid) Howard 1900-1987 ....25-28R
Obituary 123
Smith, D. MacLeod
See Smith, David MacLeod
Smith, D(wight) Moody Jr. 1931- CANR-20
Earlier sketch in CA 41-44R
Smith, D(onald) V(incent) 1933-1978 ....25-28R
Obituary 117
Smith, D(avid) W(arner) 1932- CANR-12
Earlier sketch in CA 17-20R
Smith, Dale O(rville) 1911- 73-76
Smith, Dan Throop 1908-1982 Obituary 106
Smith, Dana Prom 1927- 49-52
Smith, Daniel M(alloy) 1922-1976 ....CANR-8
Earlier sketch in CA 17-20R
Smith, Darren L. 1958- 124
Smith, Datus C(lifford) Jr. 1907- CANR-11
Earlier sketches in CAP-1, CA 11-12
See also SATA 13
Smith, Dave
See Smith, David (Jeddie)
See also CAAS 7
See also CLC 22, 42
See also DLB 5
Smith, David (Anthony) 1943- 128
Smith, David C(layton) 1929- 49-52
Smith, David C. 1931- 69-72
Smith, David C. 1952- 120
Smith, David Elvin 1939- 29-32R
Smith, David Fay 1939- 112
Smith, David H. 1939- 93-96
Smith, David Horton 1939- CANR-7
Earlier sketch in CA 57-60
Smith, David (Jeddie) 1942- CANR-1
Earlier sketch in CA 49-52
See also Smith, Dave
Smith, David M(arshall) 1936- CANR-12
Earlier sketch in CA 29-32R
Smith, David MacLeod 1920- CANR-5
Earlier sketch in CA 53-56
Smith, David Osmond
See Osmond-Smith, David
Smith, David Shiverick 1918- 108
Smith, David T. 1935- 53-56
Smith, David W. 1921-1981 110
Obituary 108
Smith, David 1906-1965 Obituary 113
Smith, Dean E(llis) 1923- CANR-4
Earlier sketch in CA 9-12R
Smith, Delos Owen 1905-1973 Obituary 41-44R
Smith, Denison Langley 1924- 13-16R
Smith, Dennis 1940- CANR-10
Earlier sketch in CA 61-64
Smith, Desmond 1927- 103
Smith, Dian G. 1946- 120
Smith, Diana Kappel
See Kappel-Smith, Diana
Smith, Dick King
See King-Smith, Dick
Smith, Dick 1908-1974 ....CAP-1
Earlier sketch in CA 19-20
Smith, Dinitia 1945- 136
Smith, Dodie
See Smith, Dorothy Gladys
Smith, Don(ald Taylor) 1909- 49-52
Smith, Don Ian 1918- 45-48
Smith, Donal Ian Bryce 1934- 41-44R
Smith, Donald Eugene 1927- 9-12R
Smith, Donald G. 1927- 13-16R
Smith, Doris Buchanan 1934- CANR-11
Earlier sketch in CA 69-72
See also DLB 52
See also MAICYA
See also SAAS 10
See also SATA 28
Smith, Doris E(dna Elliott) 1919- CANR-18
Earlier sketch in CA 25-28R
Smith, Dorothy Gladys 1896-1990 ....CANR-37
Obituary 133
See also MAICYA
See also SATO 65
Smith, Dorothy Stafford 1905- 21-24R
See also SATA 6
Smith, Dorothy Valentine 1908- 29-32R
Smith, Douglas 1918- 73-76
Smith, Douglas 1949- 113
Smith, Duane A(llan) 1937- CANR-23
Earlier sketches in CA 21-24R, CANR-8
Smith, Dwight C(hichester) Jr. 1930- 77-80
Smith, Dwight L. 1918- CANR-24
Earlier sketch in CA 33-36R
Smith, Dwight R. 1921- 106
Smith, E(lmer) Boyd 1860-1943 ....YABC 1
Smith, E(dric) Brooks 1917- 5-8R
See also SATA 40
Smith, E(ric) D(avid) 1923- 118
Smith, E. E.
See Smith, Edward Elmer
Smith, E. E. "Doc"
See Smith, Edward Elmer
Smith, Edgar H(erbert) 1934- 25-28R
Smith, Edna Hopkins
1932(?)-1979 Obituary 89-92
Smith, Edward Conrad 1891- 45-48
Smith, Edward E.
See Smith, Edward Elmer
Smith, Edward E. "Doc"
See Smith, Edward Elmer
Smith, Edward Ellis 1921- 25-28R
Smith, Edward Elmer 1890-1965 118
Obituary 102
See also DLB 8
Smith, Edward W(illiam)
1920-1975 Obituary 57-60
Smith, Edwin H. 1920- 13-16R
Smith, Elbert B(enjamin) 1920- 21-24R
Smith, Eleanor Touhey 1910- 25-28R
Smith, Elihu Hubbard 1771-1798 ....DLB 37
Smith, Elinor Goulding 1917- CANR-3
Earlier sketch in CA 1-4R
Smith, Eliot Fremont
See Fremont-Smith, Eliot
Smith, Elizabeth A(ngele) T(aft) 1958- 133
Smith, Elizabeth Oakes (Prince)
1806-1893 ....DLB 1
Smith, Elliott Dunlap
1890(?)-1976 Obituary 61-64
Smith, Elsdon C(oles) 1903- CANR-6
Earlier sketch in CA 1-4R
Smith, Elske v(an)P(anhuys) 1929- 77-80
Smith, Elton E(dward) 1915- CANR-14
Earlier sketch in CA 13-16R
Smith, Elva Sophronia 1871-1965 Obituary 107
See also SATA 31
Smith, Elwyn Allen 1919- CANR-9
Earlier sketch in CA 5-8R
Smith, Emma 1923- 73-76
See also SATA 36, 52
Smith, Ernest A(llyn) 1911-1977 ....1-4R
Obituary 103
Smith, Ethel Sabin 1887- CAP-1
Earlier sketch in CA 13-16
Smith, Eugene L(ewis) 1912-1986 ....21-24R
Obituary 118
Smith, Eugene Waldo 1905- CAP-1
Earlier sketch in CA 9-10
Smith, (Katherine) Eunice (Young)
1902- CANR-2
Earlier sketch in CA 5-8R
See also SATA 5
Smith, Evelyn E. 1927- Brief entry 113
Smith, F(rederick) G(eorge) Walton
1909-1989 45-48
Obituary 130
Smith, F. Joseph 1925- CANR-2
Earlier sketch in CA 45-48
Smith, Fay Jackson 1912- 25-28R
Smith, Florence Margaret 1902-1971 ....CANR-35
Obituary 29-32R
Earlier sketches in CAP-2, CA 17-18
See also Smith, Stevie
See also CLC 8
See also MTCW
Smith, Frances C(hristine) 1904- CANR-1
Earlier sketch in CA 1-4R
See also SATA 3
Smith, Frances Scott Fitzgerald Lanahan
1921-1986 Obituary 119
Smith, Frank (Arthur) 1917- 69-72
Smith, Frank E(llis) 1918- 17-20R
Smith, Frank E. 1919-1984 Obituary 114
Smith, Frank Kingston 1919- CANR-18
Earlier sketch in CA 102
Smith, Frank O. M. Obituary 109
Smith, Frank Seymour 1898-1972 ....9-12R
Obituary 89-92
Smith, (David) Fred(erick)
1898(?)-1976 Obituary 69-72
Smith, Frederick E(screet) 1922- CANR-19
Earlier sketches in CA 5-8R, CANR-3
Smith, Frederick W(illiam) 1920- 73-76
Smith, Frederick William Robin
1936-1985 Obituary 115
Smith, Frederick Winston Furneaux
1907-1975 65-68
Obituary 57-60
Smith, Fredrika Shumway
1877-1968 Obituary 109
See also SATA 30
Smith, G(eorge) E(verard) Kidder 1913- 9-12R
Smith, Gaddis 1932- 21-24R
Smith, Garry (Van Dorn) 1933- 5-8R
Smith, Gary (Milton) 1943- 97-100
Smith, Gary R. 1932- 69-72
See also SATA 14
Smith, Gary V(incent) 1943- 101
Smith, Gene 1924- 77-80
Smith, Gene 1929- 81-84
Smith, Genevieve Love 1917- 21-24R
Smith, Geoffrey (Francis) Hattersley
See Hattersley-Smith, Geoffrey (Francis)
Smith, Geoffrey (John) 1943- 120
Smith, Geoffrey Sutton 1941- 49-52
Smith, George E. 1938- 37-40R
Smith, George Harmon 1920- 49-52
See also SATA 5
Smith, George (Henry) 1922- 103
Smith, George Ivan 1915- 121
Smith, George O(liver) 1911-1981 ....CANR-28
Obituary 103
Earlier sketch in CA 97-100
See also DLB 8
Smith, George P(atrick) II 1939- 131
Smith, Gerald A(lfred) 1921- 37-40R
Smith, Gerald B. 1909- CAP-2
Earlier sketch in CA 25-28
Smith, Gerald L(yman) K(enneth)
1898-1976 Obituary 65-68
Smith, Gerald Stanton 1938- 123
Smith, Glenn C. 1924- 123
Smith, Godfrey 1926- 9-12R
Smith, Goldwin (Albert) 1912- 41-44R
Smith, Goldwin 1823-1910 ....DLB 99
Smith, Gordon Roland
See Roland Smith, Gordon
Smith, Gordon Ross 1917- 5-8R
Smith, Grahame 1933- 25-28R
Smith, Gretchen L. Obituary 104
Smith, Grover C(leveland) 1923- 33-36R
Smith, Gudmund J(ohn) W(ilhelm) 1920- 102
Smith, Guy-Harold 1895- CAP-2
Earlier sketch in CA 19-20
Smith, H(arry) Allen 1907-1976 ....CANR-5
Obituary 65-68
Earlier sketch in CA 5-8R
See also AITN 2
See also DLB 11, 29
See also SATA 20
Smith, H(arold) Wendell 1923- 111
Smith, Hale G(illiam) 1918- 61-64
Smith, Hallett (Darius) 1907- 21-24R
Smith, Harmon L. 1930- 29-32R
Smith, Harold Ivan 1947- 121
Smith, Harold L(ester) 1942- 125
Smith, Harris (Gordon) 1921- 49-52
Smith, (Oliver) Harrison
1888-1971 Obituary 29-32R
Smith, Harry E(dmund) 1928- 25-28R
Smith, Harry W(illiam) 1937- 112
Smith, Harry 1936- CANR-29
Earlier sketches in CA 77-80, CANR-13
Smith, Harvey K(ennedy) 1904-1968 ....CAP-1
Earlier sketch in CA 13-14
Smith, Hedrick (Laurence) 1933- CANR-11
Earlier sketch in CA 65-68
Smith, Helen Zenna
See Price, Evadne
Smith, Henry
See Smith, Henry DeWitt II
Smith, Henry Clay 1913- 1-4R
Smith, Henry DeWitt II 1940- 119
Smith, Henry Lee Jr.
1913-1972 Obituary 37-40R
Smith, Henry Nash 1906-1986 ....CANR-2
Obituary 119
Earlier sketch in CA 1-4R
Smith, Henry Peter 1910-1968 ....1-4R
Obituary 103
Smith, Henry 1905-1988 Obituary 124
Smith, Herbert F. A. 1915-1969 ....CAP-1
Earlier sketch in CA 13-16
Smith, Herbert F(rancis) 1922- CANR-30
Earlier sketches in CA 77-80, CANR-13
Smith, Hermon Dunlap 1900-1983 Obituary 109
Smith, Hilda Worthington
1889(?)-1984 Obituary 112
Smith, Hobart M(uir) 1912- CANR-9
Earlier sketch in CA 65-68
Smith, Hope M(ayhew) 1916- 1-4R
Smith, Horatio (Horace)
1779-1849 ....DLB 96, 116
Smith, Howard E(verett) Jr. 1927- CANR-21
Earlier sketch in CA 25-28R
See also SATA 12
Smith, Howard K(ingsbury) 1914- CANR-2
Earlier sketch in CA 45-48
Smith, Howard R(oss) 1917- 1-4R
Smith, Howard Van 1910(?)-1986 ....5-8R
Obituary 120
Smith, Hubert Shirley
See Shirley-Smith, Hubert
Smith, Hugh L(etcher) 1921-1968 ....CAP-2
Earlier sketch in CA 25-28
See also SATA 5
Smith, Huston (Cummings) 1919- 61-64
Smith, I(rving) Norman 1909- 107
Smith, Iain Crichton 1928- 21-24R
See also CLC 64
See also DLB 40
Smith, Imogene Henderson 1922- 5-8R
See also SATA 12
Smith, Irene 1903- 73-76
Smith, Irving H(arold) 1932- 49-52
Smith, Irwin 1892-1977 ....5-8R
Obituary 73-76
Smith, Isadore Leighton Luce 1901-1985 101
Obituary 118
Smith, J. Allen 1860-1924 ....DLB 47
Smith, J(ohn) Holland 1932- 17-20R
Smith, J(ames) L(eonard) B(rierley)
1897-1968 ....CAP-1
Earlier sketch in CA 13-14
Smith, J(ohn) Malcolm 1921- 49-52
Smith, J(oseph) Russell 1874-1966 ....CAP-1
Earlier sketch in CA 13-14
Smith, J(oe) W(illiam) Ashley 1914- 5-8R
Smith, Jack (Clifford) 1916- CANR-12
Earlier sketch in CA 69-72
Smith, Jack Prescott 1945- 127
Smith, Jackie M. 1930- 93-96
Smith, Jackson Algernon 1917- Brief entry 105
Smith, Jacqueline B. 1937- ....SATA 39
Smith, James A. 1914- CANR-39
Earlier sketch in CA 21-24R
Smith, James D(ale) 1940- 121
Smith, James L(eslie Clarke) 1936- 25-28R
Smith, James Morton 1919- 103
Smith, James R. 1941- 101
Smith, James Roy 1920- 21-24R
Smith, James 1775-1839 ....DLB 96
Smith, James 1904-1972 85-88
Smith, Jane F(rances) 1916- 123
Brief entry 117
Smith, Jane I(dleman) 1937- 107
Smith, Jane S. 1947- 118
Smith, Janet (Buchanan) Adam
See Adam Smith, Janet (Buchanan)
Smith, Janice Lee 1949- ....SATA 54
Smith, J.C.S.
See Smith, Jane S.
Smith, Jean
See Smith, Frances C(hristine)
Smith, Jean DeMouthe 1949- 65-68
Smith, Jean Edward 1932- 37-40R
Smith, Jean Pajot 1945- 53-56
See also SATA 10
Smith, Jeff Allen
See Smith, Jeff(rey Alan)
Smith, Jeff(rey Alan) 1958- 132
Smith, Jerome F(ranken) 1928- 107
Smith, Jessica 1895- CANR-2
Earlier sketch in CA 49-52
Smith, Jessie
See Kunhardt, Edith
Smith, Jessie Carney 1930- CANR-39
Earlier sketches in CA 89-92, CANR-17
Smith, Jessie Willcox 1863-1935 ....MAICYA
See also SATA 21
Smith, Jim 1920- Brief entry 115
See also SATA 36
Smith, Joan K(aren) 1939- 93-96
Smith, Joan (Mary) 1933- ....SATA 46, 54
Smith, Joan 1935- 61-64
Smith, Joanmarie 1932- CANR-16
Earlier sketch in CA 85-88
Smith, Jody Brant 1943- 113
Smith, John
See Herrick, Marvin Theodore
Smith, John Chabot 1915- 69-72
Smith, John (Charles) 1924- 103
Smith, John Coventry 1903-1984 115
Smith, John David 1949- CANR-30
Earlier sketch in CA 111
Smith, John Edwin 1921- 103
Smith, John F(erris) 1934- 81-84
Smith, John H(azel) 1928- 9-12R
Smith, John Norton
See Norton-Smith, John
Smith, John 1580(?)-1631 ....DLB 24, 30
Smith, Johnston
See Crane, Stephen (Townley)
Smith, Jon R(ichard) 1946- 77-80
Smith, Jordan 1954- 110
Smith, Joseph B(urkholder) 1921- 65-68
Smith, Joseph Fielding
1876-1972 Obituary 37-40R
Smith, Joseph H(enry) 1913-1981 Obituary 105
Smith, Josiah 1704-1781 ....DLB 24
Smith, Julia Floyd 1914- 85-88
Smith, Julia Frances 1911-1989 Obituary 128
Smith, Julian W. 1901- 13-16R
Smith, Julian 1937- 61-64
Smith, Julie 1944- CANR-32
Earlier sketch in CA 112
Smith, K(ermit) Wayne 1938- 29-32R
Smith, Karl U(lrich) 1907- CANR-9
Earlier sketch in CA 61-64
Smith, Kate
See Smith, Kathryn Elizabeth
Smith, Kathleen J(oan) 1929- 103
Smith, Kathryn Elizabeth
1907(?)-1986 Obituary 119
Smith, Kay
See Smith, Catherine C.
Smith, Kay Nolte 1932- CANR-18
Earlier sketch in CA 101
Smith, Keith V(an) 1937- 112
Smith, Ken(neth Danforth) 1902- CANR-1
Earlier sketch in CA 45-48
Smith, Ken(neth John) 1938- CANR-39
Earlier sketch in CA 33-36R
See also DLB 40

Smith, Kenneth Lee 1925- 77-80
Smith, Kenneth M(anley)
1892-1981 Obituary 108
Smith, L(eonard) Glenn 1939- 93-96
Smith, Lacey Baldwin 1922- CANR-6
Earlier sketch in CA 5-8R
Smith, Lafayette
See Higdon, Hal
Smith, Larry 1940- 49-52
Smith, Laura I(vory) 1902- 17-20R
Smith, Laurence D. 1950- 123
Smith, Lavon B(enson) 1921- 21-24R
Smith, Lawrence Berk 1939- CANR-13
Earlier sketch in CA 73-76
Smith, Lawrence R(ichard) 1945- 117
Smith, Lee
See Albion, Lee Smith
Smith, Lee L. 1930- 29-32R
Smith, Lee 1937- 73-76
Smith, Lee 1944- 119
Brief entry 114
See also CLC 25
See also DLBY 83
Smith, Lena (Kennedy) 1914- 93-96
Smith, Lendon H(oward) 1921- 81-84
See also SATA 64
Smith, LeRoi Tex 1934- 29-32R
Smith, Leslie F(rancis) 1901- CAP-1
Earlier sketch in CA 19-20
Smith, Leslie James Seth
See Seth-Smith, Leslie James
Smith, Leslie R(aymond) 1904- 1-4R
Smith, Lew
See Floren, Lee
Smith, Lillian (Eugenia) 1897-1966 ....CAP-2
Obituary 25-28R
Earlier sketch in CA 17-18
Smith, Lillian H(elena) 1887-1983 Obituary 111
See also SATA 32
Smith, Linell Nash 1932- 5-8R
See also SATA 2
Smith, Liz 1923- 65-68
Smith, Logan Pearsall 1865-1946 ....DLB 98
Smith, Lou 1918- 73-76
Smith, Louis
See Barzini, Luigi (Giorgio Jr.)
Smith, Louis M(ilde) 1929- 17-20R
Smith, Lucia B. 1943- 108
See also SATA 30
Smith, Lynnette 1951- 116
Smith, M(ahlon) Brewster 1919- 61-64
Smith, M. Estellie 1935- CANR-8
Earlier sketch in CA 61-64
Smith, M. Weston
See Weston-Smith, M.
Smith, Malcolm 1938- 97-100
Smith, Malcom N(orman)
1919(?)-1985 Obituary 116
Smith, Manuel (Juan) 1934- 105
Smith, Marcus J(oel) 1918- 73-76
Smith, Margaret Chase 1897- 73-76
Smith, Margaret Emily Noel Nuttall
See Nuttall-Smith, Margaret Emily Noel
Smith, Margaret F(oltz) 1915- 102
Smith, Margaret Mary 1916- 108
Smith, Margaret Ruth 1902- CAP-1
Earlier sketch in CA 19-20
Smith, Margarita G. 1923(?)-1983 Obituary 109
Smith, Marie D. 13-16R
Smith, Marilyn Cochran
See Cochran-Smith, Marilyn
Smith, Marion Hagens 1913- 17-20R
See also SATA 12
Smith, Marion Jaques 1899- CANR-11
Earlier sketch in CA 69-72
See also SATA 13
Smith, Mark (Richard) 1935- CANR-10
Earlier sketch in CA 13-16R
See also DLBY 82
Smith, Marny 1932- 108
Smith, Martin
See Smith, Martin Cruz
Smith, Martin Cruz 1942- CANR-23
Earlier sketches in CA 85-88, CANR-6
See also BEST 89:4
See also CLC 25
Smith, Mary Ann 1934- 126
Smith, Mary Benton 1903- CAP-2
Earlier sketch in CA 17-18
Smith, Mary Elizabeth 1932- 41-44R
Smith, Mary Ellen 69-72
See also SATA 10
Smith, Mary-Ann Tirone 1944- 136
Brief entry 118
See also CLC 39
Smith, Mason McCann 1952- 108
Smith, Maxwell A(ustin) 1894- 37-40R
Smith, (Albert) Merriman 1913-1970 ....CANR-2
Obituary 29-32R
Earlier sketch in CA 1-4R
Smith, Merritt Roe 1940- 77-80
Smith, Michael A(nthony) 1942- 102
Smith, Michael P(eter) 1942- 65-68
Smith, Michael Stephen 1944- 103
Smith, Michael (Townsend) 1935- CANR-11
Earlier sketch in CA 21-24R
Smith, Michael 1698-1771(?) ....DLB 31
Smith, Michael 1946- 132
Smith, Mike
See Smith, Mary Ellen
Smith, Mildred C(atharine) 1891-1973 101
Obituary 45-48
Smith, Mildred Nelson 1918- 69-72
Smith, Mitchell 1935- 136
Smith, Mortimer B(rewster) 1906-1981 107
Obituary 104
Smith, Morton Howison 1923- 45-48
Smith, Morton 1915-1991 ....CANR-6
Obituary 134
Earlier sketch in CA 5-8R
Smith, Murphy D(ewitt) 1920- CANR-13
Earlier sketch in CA 37-40R
Smith, Murray G(ordon) 1952- 120
Smith, Myron J(ohn) Jr. 1944- CANR-38
Earlier sketches in CA 45-48, CANR-1, 16
Smith, N(orman) J(ames) 1930- CANR-20
Earlier sketch in CA 103
Smith, N. V.
See Smith, Neil(son Voyne)
Smith, Nancy Covert 1935- CANR-10
Earlier sketch in CA 57-60
See also SATA 12
Smith, Nancy Taylor 57-60
Smith, Neil Homer
1909(?)-1972 Obituary 37-40R
Smith, Neil(son Voyne) 1939- 133
Smith, Nicholas D. 1949- 137
Smith, Nigel J(ohn) H(arwood) 1949- 109
Smith, Nila Banton 1890-1976 ....21-24R
Obituary 120
Smith, Nina Slingsby 1928- 119
Smith, Norman Edward Mace 1914- 103
Smith, Norman F. 1920- 29-32R
See also SATA 5, 70
Smith, Norman Lewis 1941- 77-80
Smith, Norris Kelly 1917- 21-24R
Smith, Ophia D(elilah) Smith 1891- 5-8R
Smith, Oswald J(effrey)
1889-1986 Obituary 119
Smith, P(eter) J(ohn) 1931- 41-44R
Smith, (Charles) Page 1917- CANR-2
Earlier sketch in CA 1-4R
Smith, Patricia Jean Adam
See Adam-Smith, Patricia Jean
Smith, Patrick D(avis) 1927- 77-80
Smith, Patrick J(ohn) 1932- 41-44R
Smith, Patrick Wykeham Montague
See Montague-Smith, Patrick Wykeham
Smith, Patrick 1936- 77-80
Smith, Patti 1946- 93-96
See also CLC 12
Smith, Pattie Sherwood
1909(?)-1974 Obituary 53-56
Smith, Paul CANR-2
Earlier sketch in CA 1-4R
Smith, Paul B(rainerd) 1921- CANR-28
Earlier sketches in CA 13-16R, CANR-10
Smith, Paul C. 1908-1976 Obituary 65-68
Smith, Paul F. 1919- 57-60
Smith, Paul H(ubert) 1931- 89-92
Smith, Paul Jordan
See Jordan-Smith, Paul
Smith, Paul Julian 1956- 138
Smith, Pauline C(oggeshall) 1908- 29-32R
See also SATA 27
Smith, Pauline (Urmson) 1882-1959 ....TCLC 25
Smith, Percival Gardner
See Gardner-Smith, Percival
Smith, Perry McCoy 1934- 29-32R
Smith, Peter C(harles Horstead)
1940- CANR-30
Earlier sketches in CA 57-60, CANR-7
Smith, Peter H(opkinson) 1940- 41-44R
Smith, Peter J(ohn) 1931- 114
Smith, Peter 1897-1982 Obituary 107
Smith, Philip Chadwick Foster 1939- 77-80
Smith, Philip E(dward II) 1943- 25-28R
Smith, Philip L. 1943- 108
Smith, Philip Warren 1936- ....SATA 46
Smith, R(ichard) A(lbert) N(ewton) 1908- 9-12R
Smith, R(eginald) C(harles) 1907- 65-68
Smith, R(eginald) D(onald) 1914- 117
Smith, R(obert) Philip 1907- 81-84
Smith, R(ichard) Selby 1914- 108
Smith, Ralph Alexander 1929- 77-80
Smith, Ralph B. 1894(?)-1985 Obituary 115
Smith, Ralph (Bernard) 1939- 33-36R
Smith, Ralph Carlisle 1910- 124
Smith, Ralph Lee 1927- CANR-1
Earlier sketch in CA 1-4R
Smith, Ray Winfield 1897-1982 Obituary 110
Smith, Ray 1915- CANR-11
Earlier sketch in CA 13-16R
Smith, Ray 1941- CANR-18
Earlier sketch in CA 101
Smith, Red
See Smith, Walter W(ellesley)
See also DLB 29
Smith, Rex Alan 1921- 61-64
Smith, Rhea Marsh 1907- CAP-1
Earlier sketch in CA 17-18
Smith, Richard A(ustin) 1911- 17-20R
Smith, Richard C(hristopher) 1948- 81-84
Smith, Richard Harris 1946- 41-44R
Smith, Richard Joseph 1944- CANR-20
Earlier sketch in CA 97-100
Smith, Richard K(ent) 1936- 41-44R
Smith, Richard M(ills) 1946- 73-76
Smith, Richard N. 1937- 21-24R
Smith, Richard P(aul) 1949- CANR-30
Earlier sketch in CA 111
Smith, Richard Rein 1930- 97-100
See also Davis, Jim
Smith, Richard 1941- 81-84
Smith, Robert A(rthur) 1944- 69-72
Smith, Robert Allan 1909-1980 Obituary 105
Smith, Robert C(harles) 1947- 111
Smith, Robert C(hester)
1912-1975 Obituary 114
Smith, Robert Charles 1938- 65-68
Smith, Robert D. 1937- 37-40R
Smith, Robert Dickie 1928- 9-12R
Smith, Robert Eliot 1899- 37-40R
Smith, Robert Ellis 1940- CANR-16
Earlier sketch in CA 89-92
Smith, Robert Freeman 1930- CANR-1
Earlier sketch in CA 1-4R
Smith, Robert G(illen) 1913- 45-48
Smith, Robert G(ordon) 1947- 102
Smith, Robert Griffin Jr. 1920- 41-44R
Smith, Robert Houston 1931- 105
Smith, Robert J(ohn) 1927- 53-56
Smith, Robert Kimmel 1930- CANR-8
Earlier sketch in CA 61-64
See also SATA 12
Smith, Robert Lee 1928- 111
Smith, Robert Paul 1915-1977 73-76
Obituary 69-72
See also SATA 30, 52
Smith, Robert S(idney) 1904-1969 ....CAP-1
Earlier sketch in CA 13-16
Smith, Robert W(ayne) 1926- 45-48
Smith, Robert W(illiam) 1926- 13-16R
Smith, Robin Baird
See Baird-Smith, Robin
Smith, Rockwell Carter 1908- 53-56
Smith, Rodney P(ennell) Jr. 1930- 29-32R
Smith, Roger H(askell) 1932-1980 69-72
Obituary 101
Smith, Roger Montgomery
1915(?)-1975 Obituary 57-60
Smith, Rogers M(ood) 1953- 120
Smith, Roland B(eatcher) 1909- 1-4R
Smith, Rolando (R.) Hinojosa
See Hinojosa(-Smith), Rolando (R.)
Smith, Ronald Gregor 1913-1968 ....CAP-1
Earlier sketch in CA 9-10
Smith, Ronald L(ande) 1952- CANR-36
Earlier sketch in CA 110
Smith, Rosamond
See Oates, Joyce Carol
Smith, Roswell 1829-1892 ....DLB 79
Smith, Rowland (James) 1938- 45-48
Smith, Roy C(yrus) 1896- 124
Smith, Roy H(armon) III 1936- 25-28R
Smith, Russell E. 1932- 77-80
Smith, Russell F. W.
1915(?)-1975 Obituary 61-64
Smith, Ruth Leslie 1902- CAP-2
Earlier sketch in CA 29-32
See also SATA 2
Smith, Ruth Schluchter 1917- CANR-26
Earlier sketches in CA 69-72, CANR-11
Smith, S(idney) G(erald) Denis 1932- 103
Smith, Sally Liberman 1929- CANR-11
Earlier sketch in CA 21-24R
Smith, Sam(uel Frederic Houston) 1937- 73-76
Smith, Samantha 1972-1985 Obituary 117
See also SATA 45
Smith, Samuel Harrison 1772-1845 ....DLB 43
Smith, Samuel Stanhope 1751-1819 ....DLB 37
Smith, Samuel 1904- CANR-11
Earlier sketch in CA 29-32R
Smith, Sandra 1940- 122
Smith, Sarah Stafford
See Smith, Dorothy Stafford
Smith, Sarah 1832-1911 Brief entry 112
Smith, Scottie
See Smith, Frances Scott Fitzgerald Lanahan
Smith, Scottie Fitzgerald
See Smith, Frances Scott Fitzgerald Lanahan
Smith, Seba 1792-1868 ....DLB 1, 11
Smith, Sharon 1947- 77-80
Smith, Sheila Kaye
See Kaye-Smith, Sheila
Smith, Shelley
See Bodington, Nancy H(ermione)
and Shelley, Dolores
and Smith, Sandra
Smith, Sherry L. 1951- 133
Smith, Sherwin 1924(?)-1985 Obituary 116
Smith, Shirley M(ae) 1923- CANR-4
Earlier sketch in CA 53-56
Smith, Stan(ley Roger) 1946- 85-88
Smith, Stan(ley William) 1943- 120
Smith, Stanley H. 1920- 138
Smith, Stephen Murray
See Murray-Smith, Stephen
Smith, Steve(n R.) 1947- 118
Smith, Steven A(lbert) 1939- 57-60
Smith, Steven Phillip 1943- CANR-10
Earlier sketch in CA 57-60
Smith, Stevie
See Smith, Florence Margaret
See also CLC 3, 8, 25, 44
See also DLB 20
Smith, Susan Carlton 1923- ....SATA 12
Smith, Susan M. 1942- 137
Smith, Susan Mathias 1950- 114
See also SATA 35, 43
Smith, Susan Vernon 1950- CANR-19
Earlier sketch in CA 102
See also Mendonca, Susan
See also SATA 48
Smith, Susy 1911- CANR-6
Earlier sketch in CA 5-8R
Smith, Sydney Goodsir 1915-1975 101
Obituary 57-60
See also DLB 27
Smith, Sydney 1771-1845 ....DLB 107
Smith, T(ed) C. 1915- 49-52
Smith, T(homas) E(dward) 1916- 13-16R
Smith, T(homas) Lynn 1903- 5-8R
Smith, Talbot 1899- CAP-1
Earlier sketch in CA 11-12
Smith, Terence (Fitzgerald) 1938- 73-76
Smith, Terrence L(ore) 1942-1988 Obituary 127
Smith, Terri McFerrin 1954- 129
Smith, Thomas B(ell) 1923- 122
Smith, Thomas G. 1945- 123
Smith, Thomas Malcolm 1921- Brief entry 106
Smith, Tilman R(ay) 1903- 113
Smith, Timothy Dudley
See Dudley-Smith, Timothy
Smith, Timothy L(awrence) 1924- 116
Smith, Toby 1946- 119
Smith, Tony 93-96
Smith, Tony
See Smith, Anthony Peter
Smith, Ursula 1934- ....SATA 54
Smith, V(incent) Kerry 1945- 111
Smith, Varrel Lavere 1925- 29-32R
Smith, Verla Lee 1927(?)-1982 Obituary 106
Smith, Vernon Lomax 1927- CANR-6
Earlier sketch in CA 1-4R
Smith, Vesta (Henderson) 1933- 5-8R
Smith, Vian (Crocker) 1920-1969 ....CANR-3
Earlier sketch in CA 1-4R
See also SATA 11
Smith, Victor C(lyde) 1902- 5-8R
Smith, Vincent E(dward)
1915-1972 Obituary 33-36R
Smith, Virginia Carlson 1944- 49-52
Smith, Virginia Masterman
See Masterman-Smith, Virginia
Smith, Vivian (Brian) 1933- CANR-23
Earlier sketches in CA 61-64, CANR-8
Smith, W(illiam) David 1928- 77-80
Smith, W. Eugene 1918(?)-1978 Obituary 81-84
Smith, Walter W(ellesley) 1905-1982 ....CANR-36
Obituary 105
Earlier sketch in CA 77-80
See also Smith, Red
Smith, Wanda VanHoy 1926- 133
See also SATA 65
Smith, Ward
See Goldsmith, Howard
Smith, Warren L(ounsbury) 1914-1972 ....CAP-2
Earlier sketch in CA 21-22
Smith, Warren Sylvester 1912- 21-24R
Smith, Warren T(homas) 1923-1986 117
Obituary 119
Smith, Webster
See Coleman, Clayton W(ebster)
Smith, Wendell I(rving) 1921- 13-16R
Smith, Wendell 1914-1972 Obituary 104
Smith, Wendy 1956- 138
Smith, Wesley D(ale) 1930- Brief entry 111
Smith, Wesley E. 1938- 29-32R
Smith, Whitney Jr. 1940- 97-100
Smith, Wilbur A(ddison) 1933- CANR-7
Earlier sketch in CA 13-16R
See also CLC 33
See also MTCW
Smith, Wilbur M(oorehead) 17-20R
Smith, Wilda M(axine) 1924- 137
Smith, Wilford E(mery) 1916- 49-52
Smith, Wilfred Cantwell 1916- CANR-7
Earlier sketch in CA 13-16R
Smith, Wilfred R(obert) 1915- 13-16R
Smith, Willard L(aurence) 1927- 5-8R
Smith, William A. 1918- ....SATA 10
Smith, William A. 1929- 45-48
Smith, William Allen 1904- 45-48
Smith, William C(harles)
1881-1972 Obituary 111
Smith, William Dale 1929- 49-52
Smith, William E(rnest) 1892- 5-8R
Smith, William Frank 1925- 103
Smith, William Gardner 1926-1974 65-68
Obituary 53-56
See also BW
See also DLB 76
Smith, William I. 1932- 29-32R
Smith, William J. 1907(?)-1986 Obituary 118
Smith, William Jay 1918- 5-8R
See also CLC 6
See also DLB 5
See also MAICYA
See also SATA 2, 68
Smith, William Martin 1911- 105
Smith, William S. 1917- 13-16R
Smith, William Scott 1926- 117
Smith, William Stevenson 1907-1969 ....CAP-2
Earlier sketch in CA 21-22
Smith, William 1727-1803 ....DLB 31
Smith, William 1728-1793 ....DLB 30
Smith, (Francis) Wilson 1922- 81-84
Smith, Winsome 1935- 115
See also SATA 45
Smith, Woodrow Wilson
See Kuttner, Henry
Smith, Woodruff D(onald) 1946- 85-88
Smith, Z. Z.
See Westheimer, David
Smith Brindle, Reginald 1917- 89-92
Smithdas, Robert Joseph 1925- 17-20R
Smithells, Roger (William) 1905- CAP-1
Earlier sketch in CA 13-14
Smither, Elizabeth 1941- 107
Smitherman, Geneva 1940- 130
Smitherman, P(hilip) H(enry) 1910- 21-24R
Smithers, Don LeRoy 1933- 45-48
Smithers, Peter Henry Berry Otway
1913- 29-32R
Smithgall, Elizabeth
See Watts, Elizabeth (Bailey) Smithgall
Smithies, Arthur 1907-1981 Obituary 104
Smithies, Edward (Draper) 1941- 132
Smithies, Richard H(ugo) R(ipman)
1936- 21-24R
Smithson, Alison (Margaret) 1928- CANR-5
Earlier sketch in CA 25-28R
Smithson, Norman 1931- 33-36R
Smithson, Peter (Denham) 1923- CANR-5
Earlier sketch in CA 53-56
Smithson, Rulon N(ephi) 1927- 45-48

Smithyman, (William) Kendrick 1922- 101
Smits, Teo
See Smits, Theodore R(ichard)
Smits, Theodore R(ichard) 1905- 77-80
See also SATA 28, 45
Smitten, Jeffrey Roger 1941- 105
Smitten, Richard 1940- 136
Smoke, Jim 109
Smoke, Richard 1944- CANR-10
Earlier sketch in CA 65-68
Smolansky, Oles M. 1930- CANR-1
Earlier sketch in CA 45-48
Smolar, Boris (Ber) 1897-1986 ....41-44R
Obituary 118
Smolich, Yurik K. 1899(?)-1976 Obituary 69-72
Smolin, C. Roger 1948- 110
Smoll, Frank L(ouis) 1941- 115
Smolla, Rodney A(lan) 1953- 121
Smoller, Bruce M. 1944- 113
Smoller, Sanford J(erome) 1937- 57-60
Smollett, Tobias (George)
1721-1771 .... CDBLB 1660-1789
See also DLB 39, 104
Smoluchowski, Louise 1922- 126
Smooha, Sammy 1941- 101
Smoot, Dan 1913- CANR-1
Earlier sketch in CA 1-4R
Smothers, Frank A(lbert)
1901-1981 Obituary 104
Smout, T(homas) C(hristopher) 1933- CANR-9
Earlier sketch in CA 21-24R
Smucker, Barbara (Claassen) 1915- CANR-23
Earlier sketch in CA 106
See also CLR 10
See also MAICYA
See also SAAS 11
See also SATA 29
Smucker, Leonard 1928- 21-24R
Smullyan, Arthur Francis 1912- 1-4R
Smullyan, Raymond
See Smullyan, Raymond M(errill)
Smullyan, Raymond M(errill) 1919- 125
Brief entry 120
Smurl, James F(redrick) 1934- 45-48
Smurr, John Welling 1922- 1-4R
Smurthwaite, Ronald 1918-1975 ....CAP-2
Earlier sketch in CA 21-22
Smyer, Richard 1935- 102
Smykay, Edward W(alter) 1924- CANR-12
Earlier sketch in CA 17-20R
Smylie, James H(utchinson) 1925- CANR-14
Earlier sketch in CA 37-40R
Smylie, Mark A. 1954- 111
Smyllie, J. S.
See Smellie, Jim
Smyrl, Frank H(erbert) 1938- 113
Smyser, Adam A(lbert) 1920- 77-80
Smyser, H(amilton) M(artin) 1901- CAP-1
Earlier sketch in CA 13-16
Smyser, Jane Worthington 1914-1975 65-68
Obituary 61-64
Smyth, Alice M.
See Hadfield, Alice M(ary)
Smyth, David 1929- CANR-12
Earlier sketch in CA 61-64
Smyth, H. D.
See Smyth, Henry DeWolf
Smyth, H(arriet) Rucker (Crowell) 1926- 1-4R
Smyth, Henry DeWolf 1898-1986 Obituary 120
Smyth, Howard McGaw
1901-1975 Obituary 61-64
Smyth, Jacqui (Marie) 1960- 124
Smyth, John (George) 1893-1983 ....CANR-11
Obituary 109
Earlier sketch in CA 61-64
Smyth, Paul 1944- CANR-8
Earlier sketch in CA 61-64
Smyth, R(obert) L(eslie) 1922- CANR-10
Earlier sketch in CA 9-12R
Smyth, William J. 1949- 135
Smythe, Colin 1942- CANR-16
Earlier sketch in CA 97-100
Smythe, Daniel Webster 1908- 13-16R
Smythe, David Mynders 1915- 1-4R
Smythe, Donald 1927- 41-44R
Smythe, Hugh H(eyne) 1913-1977 ....9-12R
Obituary 69-72
Smythe, Mabel M(urphy) 1918- 37-40R
Smythe, Reginald 1918(?)- ....AITN 1
Smythe, Ted Curtis 1932- 101
Smythies, J(ohn) R(aymond) 1922- 37-40R
Snadowsky, Alvin M. 1938- 61-64
Snailham, (George) Richard 1930- 37-40R
Snaith, Norman Henry 1898-1982 Obituary 106
Snaith, William Theodore 1908-1974 110
Obituary 106
Snape, H(enry) Currie 1902- 9-12R
Snape, R(ichard) H(al) 1936- 29-32R
Snapes, Joan 1925- 107
Snavely, Adam A. 1930- 25-28R
Snavely, Ellen Bartow 1910- CAP-2
Earlier sketch in CA 21-22
Snavely, Guy Everett 1881-1974 ....5-8R
Obituary 49-52
Snavely, Tipton Ray 1890- 17-20R
Snavely, William P(ennington) 1920- 17-20R
Snead, Rodman Eldredge 1931- 73-76
Snead, Sam(uel Jackson) 1912- Brief entry 114
Snedeker, Bonnie 1947- 119
Snedeker, Caroline Dale (Parke)
1871-1956 ....YABC 2
Sneed, Joseph Donald 1938- 49-52
Sneed, Joseph Tyree 1920- 21-24R
Sneider, Vern(on) John 1916-1981 ....CANR-13
Obituary 103
Earlier sketch in CA 5-8R
Snell, Bruno 1896- CAP-1
Earlier sketch in CA 13-16
Snell, David 1936- 77-80
Snell, Foster Dee 1898-1980 Obituary 108
Snell, Frank 1920- 1-4R
Snell, George Davis 1903- 106
Snell, John Leslie Jr. 1923-1972 ....CANR-3
Obituary 33-36R
Earlier sketch in CA 5-8R
Snell, John Nicholas Blashford
See Blashford-Snell, John Nicholas
Snell, Nigel (Edward Creagh) 1936- 111
See also SATA 40, 57
Snell, Tee Loftin 1922- 105
Sneller, Delwyn Lee 1945- 111
Snellgrove, David L(lewellyn)
1920- Brief entry 115
Snellgrove, L(aurence) E(rnest)
1928- CANR-23
Earlier sketches in CA 9-12R, CANR-3
See also SATA 53
Snellgrove, Louis 1928- 45-48
Snelling, Lois 5-8R
Snelling, O(swald) F(rederick) 1916- 17-20R
Snelling, W(illiam) Rodman 1931- 93-96
Snellings, Rolland
See Toure, Askia Muhammad Abu Bakr el
Snepp, Frank (Warren III) 1943- 105
Snetsinger, John (Goodall) 1941- 73-76
Snetsinger, Robert 1928- 107
Sneve, Virginia Driving Hawk 1933- CANR-3
Earlier sketch in CA 49-52
See also CLR 2
See also SATA 8
Snider, Delbert A(rthur) 1914- 1-4R
Snider, Lewis W. 119
Sniderman, Florence (Lama) 1915- 33-36R
Snipes, Wilson Currin 1924- 29-32R
Snively, Susan 1945- 117
Snively, W(illiam) D(aniel) Jr. 1911- 29-32R
Snodgrass, A(nthony) M(cElrea)
1934- CANR-10
Earlier sketch in CA 21-24R
Snodgrass, Donald R(ay) 1935- 112
Snodgrass, Joan Gay 1934- 77-80
Snodgrass, Jon 1941- 113
Snodgrass, Milton M(oore) 1931- 29-32R
Snodgrass, Quentin Curtius
See Clemens, Samuel Langhorne
Snodgrass, Thomas Jefferson
See Clemens, Samuel Langhorne
Snodgrass, William D(e Witt) 1926- CANR-36
Earlier sketches in CA 1-4R, CANR-6
See also CLC 2, 6, 10, 18, 68
See also DLB 5
See also MTCW
Snoek, J(aap) Diedrick 1931- 49-52
Snoke, Albert W(aldo) 1907- 125
Snook, Barbara (Lillian) 1913-1976 109
See also SATA 34
Snook, I(van) A(ugustine) 1933- CANR-14
Earlier sketch in CA 77-80
Snook, John B. 1927- 106
Snortum, Niel K(lendenon) 1928- 21-24R
Snow, C(harles) P(ercy) 1905-1980 ....CANR-28
Obituary 101
Earlier sketch in CA 5-8R
See also CDBLB 1945-1960
See also CLC 1, 4, 6, 9, 13, 19
See also DLB 15, 77
See also MTCW
Snow, Charles Ernest 1910-1967 Obituary 116
Snow, D(avid) W(illiam) 1924- 65-68
Snow, Davis W. 1913(?)-1975 Obituary 61-64
Snow, Donald Clifford 1917- 85-88
See also SATA 16
Snow, Donald M(erritt) 1943- CANR-27
Earlier sketch in CA 106
Snow, Donald 1951- 138
Snow, Dorothea J(ohnston) 1909- CANR-27
Earlier sketches in CA 1-4R, CANR-3
See also SATA 9
Snow, Dorothy Mary Barter 1897- CAP-1
Earlier sketch in CA 13-14
Snow, Edgar Parks 1905-1972 ....CANR-38
Obituary 33-36R
Earlier sketch in CA 81-84
Snow, Edward Rowe 1902-1982 ....CANR-6
Obituary 106
Earlier sketch in CA 9-12R
Snow, Frances Compton
See Adams, Henry (Brooks)
Snow, George (D'Oyly) 1903- 5-8R
Snow, Helen Foster 1907- 57-60
Snow, John Hall 1924- 37-40R
Snow, Karen (a pseudonym) 1923- 120
Snow, Kathleen 1944- 81-84
Snow, Keith Ronald 1943- 110
Snow, Lois Wheeler 1920- 57-60
Snow, Lucy
See Aubert, Rosemary
Snow, Peter G(ordon) 1933- 21-24R
Snow, Philip (Albert) 1915- CANR-28
Earlier sketch in CA 9-12R
Snow, Philip 1952- 130
Snow, Richard F(olger) 1947- 106
See also SATA 37, 52
Snow, Roslyn 1936- CANR-9
Earlier sketch in CA 21-24R
Snow, Russell E(lwin) 1938- 65-68
Snow, Sinclair 1909-1972 ....CAP-2
Earlier sketch in CA 25-28
Snow, Vernon F. 1924- 37-40R
Snow, (Charles) Wilbert 1884-1977 ....9-12R
Obituary 73-76
Snow, William George Sinclair 1908- 5-8R
Snowden, Frank M(artin) Jr. 1911- 41-44R
Snowdon
See Armstrong-Jones, Antony (Charles Robert)
Snowman, Daniel 1938- CANR-33
Earlier sketches in CA 53-56, CANR-4
Snukal, Robert (Martin) 1942- 45-48
Snyder, Anne 1922- CANR-14
Earlier sketch in CA 37-40R
See also SATA 4
Snyder, Bernadette McCarver 1930- CANR-37
Earlier sketch in CA 115
Snyder, Carl Dean 1921- Brief entry 113
Snyder, Carol 1941- 85-88
See also SATA 35
Snyder, Cecil K. Jr. 1927- 29-32R
Snyder, Charles M. 1909- 49-52
Snyder, Charles Royce 1924- 105
Snyder, Chuck 1933- 122
Snyder, Don J. 1950- 126
Snyder, E(ugene) V(incent) 1943- 41-44R
Snyder, Eldon E. 1930- 49-52
Snyder, Eloise C(olleen) 1928- 29-32R
Snyder, Francis Gregory 1942- CANR-22
Earlier sketches in CA 17-20R, CANR-7
Snyder, Fred A. 1931- 37-40R
Snyder, Gary (Sherman) 1930- CANR-30
Earlier sketch in CA 17-20R
See also CLC 1, 2, 5, 9, 32
See also DLB 5, 16
Snyder, George Sergeant 1952- 122
Snyder, Gerald S(eymour) 1933- CANR-12
Earlier sketch in CA 61-64
See also SATA 34, 48
Snyder, Glenn Herald 1924- CANR-18
Earlier sketch in CA 1-4R
Snyder, Graydon F. 1930- 13-16R
Snyder, Guy (Eugene Jr.) 1951- 57-60
Snyder, Henry Leonard 1929- 41-44R
Snyder, Howard A(lbert) 1940- CANR-34
Earlier sketch in CA 113
Snyder, James E(dward) 1928-1990 123
Obituary 132
Brief entry 117
Snyder, Jane McIntosh 1943- 130
Snyder, Jerome 1916-1976 Obituary 65-68
See also SATA 20
Snyder, Joan 1943- 41-44R
Snyder, John P(arr) 1926- CANR-31
Earlier sketch in CA 41-44R
Snyder, John William 1924- 1-4R
Snyder, Laura (Lillie) 1940- 120
Snyder, Leslie 1945- 114
Snyder, Louis L(eo) 1907- CANR-34
Earlier sketches in CA 1-4R, CANR-2
Snyder, Marilyn 1936- 120
Snyder, (Donald) Paul 1933- CANR-1
Earlier sketch in CA 45-48
Snyder, Rachel 1924- 9-12R
Snyder, Richard C(arlton) 1916- 61-64
Snyder, Robert Edward 1943- 120
Snyder, Robert L. 1928- 25-28R
Snyder, Solomon H(albert) 1938- CANR-14
Earlier sketch in CA 37-40R
Snyder, Susan 1934- 93-96
Snyder, Tom 1936- 121
Brief entry 109
Snyder, William P(aul) 1928- 13-16R
Snyder, William S(tover) 1927- 123
Brief entry 118
Snyder, William 1951- 104
Snyder, Zilpha Keatley 1927- CANR-38
Earlier sketch in CA 9-12R
See also CLC 17
See also MAICYA
See also SAAS 2
See also SATA 1, 28
Snyderman, Reuven K. 1922- 29-32R
See also SATA 5
Soames, Jane
See Nickerson, Jane Soames (Bon)
Soames, Mary 1922- 111
Soares, Anthony T(homas) 1923- 45-48
Soares, Bernardo
See Pessoa, Fernando (Antonio Nogueira)
Sobel, B. Z. 1933- 77-80
Sobel, Bernard 1887-1964 ....5-8R
Sobel, Brian M. 1954- 107
Sobel, Harold W(illiam) 1933- 61-64
Sobel, Irwin Philip 1901-1991 45-48
Obituary 134
Sobel, Lester A(lbert) 1919- CANR-9
Earlier sketch in CA 21-24R
Sobel, Michael I. 1939- 128
Sobel, Robert 1931- CANR-31
Earlier sketches in CA 5-8R, CANR-8
Sobell, Morton 1917- 53-56
Sober, Elliott (Reuben) 1948- 132
Soberman, Richard M. 1937- CANR-10
Earlier sketch in CA 25-28R
Sobh, A.
See Shamlu, Ahmad
Sobieski, Carol (O'Brien) 1939-1990 129
Obituary 132
Brief entry 124
Sobiloff, Hy(man J.)
1912-1970 Obituary 29-32R
See also DLB 48
Sobin, A. G.
See Sobin, Anthony
Sobin, Anthony 1944- 116
Sobin, Gustaf 1935- CANR-38
Earlier sketch in CA 115
Sobin, Julian M(elvin) 1920- 132
Soble, Alan 1947- 122
Soble, Jennie
See Cavin, Ruth (Brodie)
Sobol, Donald J. 1924- CANR-38
Earlier sketches in CA 1-4R, CANR-1, 18
See also CLR 4
See also MAICYA
See also SATA 1, 31
Sobol, Harriet Langsam 1936- CANR-8
Earlier sketch in CA 61-64
See also SATA 34, 47
Sobol, Joshua ....CLC 60
Sobol, Louis 1896-1986 ....CAP-2
Obituary 118
Earlier sketch in CA 29-32
Sobol, Rose 1931- 101
Sobolev, Leonid (Sergeevich)
1898-1971 Obituary 29-32R
Sobosan, Jeffrey G. 1946- 126
Soboul, Albert Marius 1914-1982 Obituary 107
Sobrino, Josephine 1915- CANR-36
Earlier sketch in CA 45-48
Soby, James Thrall 1906-1979 103
Socarides, Charles W(illiam)
1922- Brief entry 118
Sochen, June 1937- CANR-14
Earlier sketch in CA 41-44R
Sockman, Ralph W(ashington) 1889-1970 ....5-8R
Obituary 89-92
Socolofsky, Homer E(dward) 1922- CANR-1
Earlier sketch in CA 1-4R
Socolow, Robert H(arry) 1937- 37-40R
Sodaro, Craig 1948- CANR-18
Earlier sketch in CA 101
Soderberg, Hjalmar 1869-1941 ....TCLC 39
Soderberg, Paul Stephen 1949- CANR-19
Earlier sketch in CA 103
Soderberg, Percy Measday 1901-1969 ....CAP-1
Earlier sketch in CA 9-10
Sodergran, Edith (Irene)
See Soedergran, Edith (Irene)
Soderholm, Marjorie Elaine 1923- 13-16R
Soderlind, Arthur E(dwin) 1920- 69-72
See also SATA 14
Soderlund, Jean Ruth 1947- 127
Soderstrom, Edward Jonathan 1954- CANR-30
Earlier sketch in CA 111
Sodowsky, Roland (E.) 1938- 134
Soedergran, Edith (Irene) 1892-1923 ....TCLC 31
Soedjatmoko 1922-1989 Obituary 130
Soekarno
See Sukarno, (Ahmed)
Soelle, Dorothee 1929- CANR-11
Earlier sketch in CA 69-72
Soerensen, Svend Otto 1916- 132
See also SATA 67
Soeur Sourire
See Deckers, Jeanine
Sofen, Edward 1919- 9-12R
Sofer, Cyril 1921- 5-8R
Soffer, Reba N(usbaum) 1934- 85-88
Soffici, Ardengo 1879-1964 ....DLB 114
Softly, Barbara Frewin 1924- CANR-2
Earlier sketch in CA 5-8R
See also SATA 12
Softly, Edgar
See Lovecraft, H(oward) P(hillips)
Softly, Edward
See Lovecraft, H(oward) P(hillips)
Soglow, Otto 1900-1975 93-96
Obituary 57-60
See also SATA 30
Sohl, Frederic J(ohn) 1916- 21-24R
See also SATA 10
Sohl, Jerry 1913- CANR-15
Earlier sketch in CA 81-84
Sohl, Robert (Allen) 1941- 103
Sohn, David A. 1929- CANR-6
Earlier sketch in CA 9-12R
Sohn, Louis B(runo) 1914- 101
Sokel, Walter H(erbert) 1917- CANR-6
Earlier sketch in CA 5-8R
Sokil, Ya.
See Sokolyszyn, Aleksander
Sokol, Anthony E. 1897- 37-40R
Sokol, Bill
See Sokol, William
Sokol, David M(artin) 1942- CANR-16
Earlier sketches in CA 49-52, CANR-1
Sokol, William 1923- ....SATA 37
Sokoloff, Alice Hunt 1912- 25-28R
Sokoloff, Boris Theodore 1889- 89-92
Sokoloff, Kiril 1947- 108
Sokoloff, Natalie B.
See Scott, Natalie Anderson
Sokoloff, Natalie J(ean) 1944- 113
Sokolov, Alexander V(sevolodovich)
1943- 73-76
Sokolov, Kirill 1930- ....SATA 34
Sokolov, Raymond 1941- 85-88
See also CLC 7
Sokolov, Sasha
See Sokolov, Alexander V(sevolodovich)
Sokolov, Valentin 1925(?)-1984 Obituary 114
Sokolow, Jayme Aaron 1946- 113
Sokolowski, Robert (Stanley) 1934- 89-92
Sokolski, Alan 1931- 13-16R
Sokolsky, George Ephraim
1893-1962 Obituary 89-92
Sokolyszyn, Aleksander 1914- 132
Solano, Solita 1888-1975 117
Obituary 61-64
See also DLB 4
Solaun, Mauricio 1935- 138
Brief entry 106
Solberg, Carl Edward 1940- 61-64
Solberg, Carl 1915- CANR-12
Earlier sketch in CA 73-76
Solberg, Gunard 1932- 29-32R

Solberg, Richard W. 1917- CANR-3
Earlier sketch in CA 9-12R
Solberg, S(ammy) E(dward) 1930- 21-24R
Solberg, Winton U(dell) 1922- 41-44R
Solbert, Romaine G. 1925- 29-32R
See also SATA 2
Solbert, Ronni
See Solbert, Romaine G.
Solbrig, Otto T(homas) 1930- CANR-9
Earlier sketch in CA 21-24R
Soldati, Mario 1906- 108
Soldo, John J(oseph) 1945- CANR-14
Earlier sketch in CA 77-80
Soldofsky, Robert Melvin 1920- CANR-1
Earlier sketch in CA 1-4R
Sole, Carlos A(lberto) 1938- 53-56
Solecki, Ralph S(tefan) 1917- Brief entry 109
Solem, (George) Alan 1931- 57-60
Solensten, John M(artin) 1929- CANR-28
Earlier sketch in CA 110
Soleri, Paolo 1919- 106
Soliday, Gerald Lyman 1939- CANR-12
Earlier sketch in CA 61-64
Solinger, Dorothy J(ane) 1945- CANR-32
Earlier sketch in CA 113
Solkoff, Joel 1947- 133
Soll, Ivan 1938- 29-32R
Sollberger, Edmond (Albert)
1920-1989 Obituary 129
Solle, Dorothee
See Soelle, Dorothee
Sollers, Philippe 1936- ....DLB 83
Solley, Charles Marion Jr. 1925- 1-4R
Sollors, Werner 1943- 119
Solman, Paul 1944- Brief entry 119
Solmi, Sergio 1899-1981 ....DLB 114
Solmon, Lewis C(alvin) 1942- 41-44R
Solmsen, Friedrich (Rudolf Heinrich)
1904-1989 53-56
Obituary 127
Solnick, Bruce B. 1933- 29-32R
Solnit, Albert J. 1919- 103
Solo, Jay
See Ellison, Harlan
Solo, Robert A(lexander) 1916- CANR-37
Earlier sketches in CA 45-48, CANR-1, 17
Sologub, Fyodor
See Teternikov, Fyodor Kuzmich
See also TCLC 9
Solomon, Barbara H. 1936- CANR-13
Earlier sketch in CA 73-76
Solomon, Barbara Probst 1928- 5-8R
Solomon, Bernard S(imon) 1924- 61-64
Solomon, (Neal) Brad(ley) 1945- 103
Solomon, Brad 1945- 101
Solomon, Carl 1928- 21-24R
See also DLB 16
Solomon, Charles J.
1906(?)-1975 Obituary 61-64
Solomon, Daniel 1933- 9-12R
Solomon, David J. 1925- 17-20R
Solomon, Deborah 1957- 127
Solomon, Dorothy Allred 1949- 119
Solomon, Esther Riva 1921-1969 ....5-8R
Obituary 135
Solomon, Ezra 1920- CANR-17
Earlier sketch in CA 85-88
Solomon, Flora 1895(?)-1984 Obituary 114
Solomon, George 1940- 45-48
Solomon, Goody L(ove) 57-60
Solomon, Henry A. 1937- 123
Solomon, Irving I. 1922- CANR-16
Earlier sketch in CA 21-24R
Solomon, Janis Little 1938- CANR-15
Earlier sketch in CA 41-44R
Solomon, Jay 1960- 135
Solomon, Joan 1930- CANR-28
Earlier sketch in CA 109
See also SATA 40, 51
Solomon, Kenneth Ira 1942- 49-52
Solomon, Leonard 1930- 45-48
Solomon, Margaret C(laire) 1918- 29-32R
Solomon, Maynard (Elliott) 1930- 41-44R
Solomon, Michael M(aurice) 1909- 97-100
Solomon, Morris J. 1919- 13-16R
Solomon, Neil 1932- CANR-27
Earlier sketch in CA 65-68
Solomon, Norman 1951- CANR-9
Earlier sketch in CA 57-60
Solomon, Richard H(arvey) 1937- 103
Solomon, Robert C(harles) 1942- CANR-32
Earlier sketches in CA 41-44R, CANR-15
Solomon, Robert 1921- 108
Solomon, Ruth (Freeman) 1908- 21-24R
Solomon, Samuel 1904-1988 53-56
Obituary 126
Solomon, Shirl 1928- 93-96
Solomon, Stanley J. 1937- 41-44R
Solomon, Stephen D(avid) 1950- 69-72
Solomon, Steve 1942- 117
Solomons, David 1912- 13-16R
Solomons, Ikey Esquir
See Thackeray, William Makepeace
Solon, Gregory Kent
1923(?)-1985 Obituary 117
Solonevich, George 1915- ....SATA 15
Solorzano, Carlos 1922- ....HW
Solot, Mary Lynn 1939- 49-52
See also SATA 12
Solotaroff, Robert David 1937- 57-60
Solotaroff, Ted
See Solotaroff, Theodore
See also CAAS 2
Solotaroff, Theodore 1928- CANR-8
Earlier sketch in CA 9-12R
See also Solotaroff, Ted
Soloukhin, Vladimir (Alekseevich)
1924- Brief entry 111
Solow, Martin 1920-1991 81-84
Obituary 135
Soloway, Richard Allen 1934- 118
Solt, Mary Ellen (Bottom) 1920- 17-20R
Soltau, T(heodore) Stanley 1890- 5-8R
Soltis, Andrew (Eden Jr.) 1947- CANR-4
Earlier sketch in CA 49-52
Soltis, Andy
See Soltis, Andrew (Eden Jr.)
Soltis, Jonas F(rancis) 1931- CANR-31
Earlier sketches in CA 37-40R, CANR-14
Soltow, James H(arold) 1924- 109
Soltow, Lee 1923- 108
Soltow, Martha-Jane 1924- 110
Solway, David 1941- 112
See also DLB 53
Solwoska, Mara
See French, Marilyn
Solyn, Paul 1951- 77-80
Solzhenitsyn, Aleksandr I(sayevich)
1918- 69-72
See also AITN 1
See also CLC 1, 2, 4, 7, 9, 10, 18, 26, 34
See also MTCW
See also WLC
Soma, Daniel
See Lange, Martin
Soman, Alfred 1934- CANR-36
Earlier sketch in CA 45-48
Soman, Jean Powers 1949- 122
Soman, Shirley Camper CANR-3
Earlier sketch in CA 9-12R
Somekh, Emile 1915- 53-56
Somer, John (Laddie) 1936- 37-40R
Somerlott, Robert 1928- 105
See also SATA 62
Somers, Albert B(ingham) 1939- 115
Somers, Gerald G(eorge) 1922-1977 ....CANR-5
Earlier sketch in CA 13-16R
Somers, Herman Miles 1911-1991 ....CANR-1
Obituary 134
Earlier sketch in CA 1-4R
Somers, Jane
See Lessing, Doris (May)
Somers, Paul
See Winterton, Paul
Somers, Robert H(ough) 1929- 45-48
Somers, Suzanne
See Daniels, Dorothy
Somerset, FitzRoy Richard
See Raglan, FitzRoy
Somerset, Henry Hugh Arthur FitzRoy
1900-1984 Obituary 112
Somerset Fry, (Peter George Robin) Plantagenet
1931- 104
Somerville, (James) Hugh (Miller) 1922- 9-12R
Obituary 137
Somerville, James 1947- 128
Somerville, John (P. M.) 1905- 45-48
Somerville, (Henry) Lee 1915- 69-72
Somerville, Mollie CANR-12
Earlier sketch in CA 29-32R
Somerville, Rose M(aurer) 1908- 45-48
Somerville-Large, Peter 1928- CANR-20
Earlier sketch in CA 97-100
Somit, Albert 1919- 81-84
Somkin, Fred 1924- 25-28R
Sommer, Angela
See Sommer-Bodenburg, Angela
Sommer, Elyse 1929- CANR-2
Earlier sketch in CA 49-52
See also SATA 7
Sommer, Joellen 1957- 45-48
Sommer, John 1941- 29-32R
Sommer, Richard J(erome) 1934- CANR-1
Earlier sketch in CA 45-48
Sommer, Robert 1929- CANR-18
Earlier sketches in CA 9-12R, CANR-3
See also SATA 12
Sommer, Scott 1951- 106
See also CLC 25
Sommer-Bodenburg, Angela 1948- 132
See also SATA 63
Sommerfeld, Ray(nard) M(atthias)
1933- CANR-28
Earlier sketch in CA 105
Sommerfeld, Richard Edwin 1928- 13-16R
Sommerfeldt, John R(obert) 1933- CANR-3
Earlier sketch in CA 49-52
Sommerfelt, Aimee 1892- 37-40R
See also SATA 5
Sommerness, Martin David 1954- 116
Sommers, David
See Smith, Howard Van
Sommers, Fred(eric Tamler) 1923- 113
Sommers, Jay 1917(?)-1985 Obituary 117
Sommers, Joseph 1924-1979 ....CANR-29
Earlier sketch in CA 25-28R
Sommers, Lawrence M(elvin) 1919- 126
Sommers, Tish 1914(?)-1985 Obituary 117
Sommerville, C(harles) John 1938- 137
Sommerville, John (P.M.) 1905- CANR-29
Somorjai, Gabor Arpad 1935- 105
Somtow, S. P.
See Sucharitkul, Somtow
See also CLC 30, 39
Sondak, Norman E(dward) 1931- 112
Sondermann, Fred A. 1923- 49-52
Sonders, Scott 1953- 132
Sondheim, Stephen (Joshua) 1930- 103
See also CLC 30, 39
Sondrup, Steven P(reece) 1944- 103
Sonenberg, Maya 1960- 131
Sonenblick, Jerry 1931- 104
Sonenblum, Sidney 1924- 29-32R
Sonenscher, Michael 1947- 118
Sonero, Devi
See Pelton, Robert W(ayne)
Song, Ben (Chunho) 1937- 37-40R
Song, C(hoan-)S(eng) 1929- 115
Songe, Alice Heloise 1914- 102
Sonkin, Robert 1911(?)-1980 Obituary 97-100
Sonneborn, Harry L(ee) 1919- 77-80
Sonneborn, Ruth (Cantor) 1899-1974 ....CAP-2
Obituary 49-52
Earlier sketch in CA 21-22
See also SATA 4, 27
Sonneborn, Tracy Morton
1905-1981 Obituary 108
Sonnenfeld, Marion (Wilma) 1928- 37-40R
Sonnenschein, Allan 1941- 133
Sonneveld, A.
See Stolk, Anthonie
Sonnichsen, C. L. 1901- CANR-39
Earlier sketches in CA 1-4R, CANR-2, 17
Sonntag, Jacob 1905-1984 Obituary 113
Sono, Ayako
See Miura, Chizuko
Son of the Soil
See Fletcher, J(oseph) S(mith)
Sons, Raymond W(illiam) 1926- 136
Sonstegard, Manford Aldrich 1911- CANR-2
Earlier sketch in CA 49-52
Sonstroem, David 1936- 29-32R
Sontag, Alan 1946- 85-88
Sontag, Frederick (Earl) 1924- CANR-1
Earlier sketch in CA 1-4R
Sontag, Frederick H(erman) 1924- 81-84
Sontag, Raymond J(ames)
1897-1972 Obituary 37-40R
Sontag, Susan 1933- CANR-25
Earlier sketch in CA 17-20R
See also CLC 1, 2, 10, 13, 31
See also DLB 2, 67
See also MTCW
Sontheimer, Morton 101
Sontup, Dan(iel) 1922- 1-4R
Soong Ching-ling 1890-1981 Obituary 108
Soper, Alexander Coburn 1904- 105
Soper, Donald Oliver 1903- 109
Soper, Eileen A(lice) 1905-1990(?) 9-12R
Obituary 131
Soper, Eileen Louise 1900- 103
Soper, Fred L. 1894(?)-1977 Obituary 69-72
Soper, Paul L(eon) 1906- 5-8R
Soper, Tony 1939- CANR-22
Earlier sketch in CA 105
Sopher, Sharon Isabel 1945- 101
Sophocles 496 (?)-406 (?) ....DC 1
Sopko, Eugen 1949- ....SATA 58
Sorauf, Francis Joseph 1928- 9-12R
Sorauf, Frank J.
See Sorauf, Francis Joseph
Sorden, L(eland) G(eorge) 1898- CANR-1
Earlier sketch in CA 1-4R
Sorel, Byron
See Yatron, Michael
Sorel, Edward 1929- CANR-33
Earlier sketch in CA 9-12R
See also SATA 37, 65
Sorel, Georges 1847-1922 Brief entry 118
Sorel, Julia
See Drexler, Rosalyn
Sorel, Nancy Caldwell 1934- 37-40R
Sorel-Cameron, James (Robert) 1948- 136
Sorell, Walter 1905- 21-24R
Sorensen, Andrew Aaron 1938- 65-68
Sorensen, Chris 1942- 107
Sorensen, Jacki 1942- 110
Sorensen, Robert C(haikin) 1923- 45-48
Sorensen, Svend Otto
See Soerensen, Svend Otto
Sorensen, Theodore C(haikin) 1928- CANR-2
Earlier sketch in CA 45-48
Sorensen, Thomas C. 1926- 21-24R
Sorensen, Virginia 1912- CANR-22
Earlier sketch in CA 13-16R
See also MAICYA
See also SATA 2
Sorenson, Herbert 1898- 21-24R
Sorenson, Jane 1926- ....SATA 63
Sorenson, Marian 1925-1968 ....CAP-1
Earlier sketch in CA 11-12
Sorestad, Glen (Allan) 1937- CANR-31
Earlier sketch in CA 112
Sorge, Reinhard Johannes 1892-1916 ....DLB 118
Sorgman, Mayo 1912- 13-16R
Soria, Regina 1911- 126
Sorin, Gerald 1940- CANR-31
Earlier sketch in CA 77-80
Sorine, Stephanie Riva 1954- 105
Sorkin, Alan Lowell 1941- CANR-31
Earlier sketches in CA 41-44R, CANR-14
Sorley, Lewis 1934- 117
Sorley Walker, Kathrine CANR-6
Earlier sketch in CA 5-8R
See also SATA 41
Sorokin, Boris 1922- 116
Sorokin, Elena 1894(?)-1975 Obituary 61-64
Sorokin, Pitirim A(lexandrovitch)
1889-1968 ....CANR-5
Obituary 25-28R
Earlier sketch in CA 5-8R
Sorrell, Alan 1904-1974 93-96
Sorrell, J(ohn) E(dward) 1954- 137
Sorrells, Dorothy C. 9-12R
Sorrells, Helen 1908- 37-40R
Sorrells, Robert T. 1932- 127
Sorrentino, Gilbert 1929- CANR-33
Earlier sketches in CA 77-80, CANR-14
See also CLC 3, 7, 14, 22, 40
See also DLB 5
See also DLBY 80
Sorrentino, Joseph N. 1937- CANR-3
Earlier sketch in CA 49-52
See also SATA 6
Sorsby, Arnold 1900- 85-88
Sortor, June Elizabeth 1939- 61-64
See also SATA 12
Sortor, Toni
See Sortor, June Elizabeth
Sorum, Paul Clay 1943- 103
Sosa, Ernest 1940- 53-56
Sosa, Roberto 1930- 131
See also HW
Sosa de Quesada, Aristides V. 1908- 53-56
Soskice, Janet Martin 1951- 124
Soskin, V.H.
See Ellison, Virginia H(owell)
Sosna, Morton 1945- 102
Sosnick, Stephen H(oward) 1930- 45-48
Sosnow, Eric 1910-1987 Obituary 121
Sossaman, Stephen 1944- 77-80
Soth, Lauren (Kephart) 1910- CAP-1
Earlier sketch in CA 17-18
Sotheby, William 1757-1833 ....DLB 93
Soto, Gary 1952- 125
Brief entry 119
See also CLC 32
See also DLB 82
See also HW
Soto, Pedro Juan 1928- 131
Brief entry 114
See also HW
Soto, Shirlene A(nn) 1947- 131
See also HW
Sotomayor, Antonio 1902- 73-76
See also SATA 11
Sotter, Fred
See Lake, Kenneth R(obert)
Souci, Robert D. San
See San Souci, Robert D.
Soucie, Gary (Arnold) 1937- 127
Soucy, Robert J(oseph) 1933- CANR-30
Earlier sketch in CA 45-48
Soudley, Henry
See Wood, James Playsted
Souerwine, Andrew H(arry) 1924- CANR-19
Earlier sketch in CA 81-84
Souhami, Diana 1940- 130
Souhuk, James R(udolph) 1928- 9-12R
Soule, Gardner (Bosworth) 1913- CANR-2
Earlier sketch in CA 5-8R
See also SATA 14
Soule, George (Alan) 1930- 57-60
Soule, George (Henry Jr.) 1887-1970 ....CAP-2
Obituary 29-32R
Earlier sketch in CA 21-22
Soule, Isabel Walker
1898(?)-1972 Obituary 37-40R
Soule, Jean Conder 1919- 5-8R
See also SATA 10
Soule, Sandra W(olf) 1946- 137
Soupault, Philippe 1897-1990 Obituary 131
Brief entry 116
See also CLC 68
Soupcoff, Murray 1943- 101
Souper, Patrick Charles 1928- 110
Sour, Robert B(andler) 1905-1985 Obituary 115
Sourian, Peter 1933- 1-4R
Souritz, Elizabeth 1923- 135
Sourkes, Theodore L(ionel) 1919- 17-20R
Sours, John Appling 1931-1983 ....CANR-9
Obituary 110
Earlier sketch in CA 21-24R
Sousa, Marion 1941- 65-68
Soustelle, Jacques (Emile)
1912-1990 Obituary 132
Souster, (Holmes) Raymond 1921- CANR-29
Earlier sketches in CA 13-16R, CANR-13
See also CAAS 14
See also CLC 5, 14
See also DLB 88
See also SATA 63
South, Clark
See Swain, Dwight V(reeland)
South, Cris 1950- 118
South, Grace
See Clark, Gail
South, Malcolm Hudson 1937- 107
Southall, Aidan (William) 1920- 77-80
Southall, Ivan (Francis) 1921- CANR-7
Earlier sketch in CA 9-12R
See also CLR 2
See also MAICYA
See also SAAS 3
See also SATA 3, 68
Southam, B(rian) C(harles) 1931- CANR-26
Earlier sketches in CA 13-16R, CANR-10
Southard, Frank Allan Jr. 1907- 107
Southard, Helen Fairbairn 1906- 5-8R
Southard, Samuel 1925- CANR-3
Earlier sketch in CA 1-4R
Southerington, F(rank) R(odney) 1938- 57-60
Southerland, Ellease 1943- 107
See also BW
See also DLB 33
Southern, David W. 1938- 25-28R
Southern, Eileen 1920- CANR-31
Earlier sketches in CA 37-40R, CANR-14
Southern, Richard William 1912- 9-12R
Southern, Richard 1903-1989 Obituary 129
Southern, Terry 1926- CANR-1
Earlier sketch in CA 1-4R
See also CLC 7
See also DLB 2
Southerne, Thomas 1660-1746 ....DLB 80
Southey, Caroline Anne Bowles
1786(?)-1854 ....DLB 116

Southey, Robert 1774-1843 .... DLB 93, 107
See also SATA 54
Southgate, Minoo S. 132
Southgate, Vera 109
See also SATA 54
Southgate, W(yndham) M(ason) 1910- CAP-2
Earlier sketch in CA 23-24
Southwell, Eugene A. 1928- 17-20R
Southwell, Samuel B(eall) 1922- 17-20R
Southwick, Charles H(enry) 1928- 65-68
Southworth, Herbert Rutledge 1908- 85-88
Southworth, Horton C. 1926- 17-20R
Southworth, James G(ranville) 1896- CAP-2
Earlier sketch in CA 33-36
Southworth, John Van Duyn
1904-1986 .... CANR-6
Obituary 118
Earlier sketch in CA 5-8R
Southworth, Louis
See Grealey, Thomas Louis
Southworth, Warren H(ilbourne) 1912- 37-40R
Soutter, Fred
See Lake, Kenneth R(obert)
Souvarine, Boris
See Lifchitz, Boris
Souza, Ernest
See Scott, Evelyn
Souza, Raymond D(ale) 1936- CANR-30
Earlier sketches in CA 69-72, CANR-13
See also HW
Souza, Steven M. 1953- 49-52
Souza Filho, Henrique de
1945(?)-1988 Obituary 124
Sovik, E(dward) A(nders) 1918- Brief entry 112
Sowards, J(esse) K(elley) 1924- 73-76
Sowden, Lewis 1905-1974 .... CAP-1
Earlier sketch in CA 9-10
Sowell, Mike 1948- 131
Sowell, Thomas 1930- CANR-26
Earlier sketch in CA 41-44R
See also BW
Sowerby, A(rthur) L(indsay) M(cRae)
1899- CAP-1
Earlier sketch in CA 9-10
Sowerby, E(mily) Millicent 1883-1977 .... CAP-2
Obituary 73-76
Earlier sketch in CA 25-28
Sowers, Miriam R. 1922- 89-92
Sowers, Robert (Watson) 1923- 17-20R
Sowers, Sidney Gerald Jr. 1935- 17-20R
Sowter, Nita .... SATA 69
Sox, (Harold) David 1936- 124
Soyer, Raphael 1899-1987 81-84
Obituary 124
Soyinka, Wole 1934- CANR-39
Earlier sketches in CA 13-16R, CANR-27
See also BLC 3
See also BW
See also CLC 3, 5, 14, 36, 44
See also DC 2
See also MTCW
See also WLC
Spaak, Paul-Henri 1899-1972 Obituary 37-40R
Spaatz, Carl A(ndrew)
1891-1974 Obituary 49-52
Spach, John Thom 1928- 29-32R
Spache, Evelyn B(ispham) 1929- CANR-30
Earlier sketch in CA 29-32R
Spache, George D(aniel) 1909- CANR-6
Earlier sketch in CA 5-8R
Spackman, Doc
See Spackman, Robert R. Jr.
Spackman, Robert R. Jr. 1917-1984 .... 13-16R
Obituary 111
Spackman, W(illiam) M(ode) 1905-1990 81-84
Obituary 132
See also CLC 46
Spacks, Barry 1931- CANR-33
Earlier sketch in CA 29-32R
See also CLC 14
See also DLB 105
Spacks, Patricia Meyer 1929- CANR-1
Earlier sketch in CA 1-4R
Spada, James 1950- CANR-28
Earlier sketches in CA 57-60, CANR-7
Spade, Mark
See Balchin, Nigel (Marlin)
Spade, Rupert
See Pawley, Martin Edward
Spaeth, Anthony 1955- 133
Spaeth, David A(nthony) 1941- 119
Spaeth, Eloise O'Mara 1904- 104
Spaeth, Gerold 1939- CANR-24
Earlier sketches in CA 65-68, CANR-9
See also Spath, Gerold
See also DLB 75
Spaeth, Harold J(oseph) 1930- CANR-32
Earlier sketch in CA 45-48
Spaeth, Robert L(ouis) 1935- 119
Spaeth, Sigmund 1885-1965 .... 5-8R
Spahn, Mary Attea 1929- CANR-7
Earlier sketch in CA 57-60
Spain, Daphne 1949- 111
Spain, David H. 1939- 57-60
Spain, James W(illiam) 1926- 5-8R
Spain, John
See Adams, Cleve F(ranklin)
Spain, Rufus B(uin) 1923- 21-24R
Spake, Amanda 1947- 77-80
Spalatin, Christopher 1909- 49-52
Spalding, Frances 1950- CANR-26
Earlier sketch in CA 104
Spalding, Graydon (Edward) 1911- 89-92
Spalding, Henry D(aniel) 1915- CANR-11
Earlier sketch in CA 25-28R
Spalding, Jack 1913- 69-72
Spalding, Linda 1943- 128
Spalding, Lucile
See Spalding, Ruth
Spalding, P(hilip) A(nthony) 1911- 5-8R
Spalding, (Billups) Phinizy 1930- CANR-39
Earlier sketches in CA 41-44R, CANR-16
Spalding, R(onald) W(olcott) 1904- 81-84
Spalding, Ruth 104
Spalek, John M. 1928- 104
Spalter, Max 1929- 21-24R
Spanfeller, James J(ohn) 1930-
See Spanfeller, Jim
See also MAICYA
See also SATA 19
Spanfeller, Jim
See Spanfeller, James J(ohn)
See also SAAS 8
Spangenberg, Judith Dunn 1942- CANR-12
Earlier sketch in CA 29-32R
See also SATA 5
Spangler, Earl 1920- CANR-5
Earlier sketch in CA 5-8R
Spanidou, Irini 1946- .... CLC 44
Spanier, David 1932- CANR-39
Earlier sketches in CA 101, CANR-18
Spanier, Ginette 1904-1987 Obituary 125
Spanier, John W(inston) 1930- CANR-2
Earlier sketch in CA 1-4R
Spann, Edward K(enneth) 1931- 45-48
Spann, Gloria Carter 1926-1990 77-80
Obituary 131
Spann, Meno H. 1903-1991 .... CANR-21
Obituary 136
Earlier sketch in CA 1-4R
Spann, Philip O. 1941- 128
Spann, Weldon O(ma) 1924- 17-20R
Spano, Charles 1948- 93-96
Spanos, William V(aios) 1925- CANR-11
Earlier sketch in CA 21-24R
Spar, Jerome 1918- 25-28R
See also SATA 10
Sparano, Vin(cent) T(homas) 1934- CANR-22
Earlier sketch in CA 45-48
Sparer, Joyce
See Adler, Joyce Sparer
Spargo, John 1876-1966 Obituary 89-92
Spark, Debra (Alison) 1962- 122
Spark, Muriel (Sarah) 1918- CANR-36
Earlier sketches in CA 5-8R, CANR-12
See also CDBLB 1945-1960
See also CLC 2, 3, 5, 8, 13, 18, 40
See also DLB 15
See also MTCW
See also SSC 10
Sparke, (George) Archibald 1871-1970 ..... CAP-2
Earlier sketch in CA 21-22
Sparkes, Ivan G(eorge) 1930- CANR-38
Earlier sketch in CA 115
Sparkia, Roy (Bernard) 1924- 77-80
Sparkman, Brandon B(uster) 1929- CANR-13
Earlier sketch in CA 61-64
Sparkman, G(rady) Temp 1932- CANR-15
Earlier sketch in CA 89-92
Sparkman, William
See Roper, William L(eon)
Sparks, Asa H(oward) 1937- CANR-19
Earlier sketch in CA 97-100
Sparks, Beatrice Mathews 1918- 97-100
See also SATA 28, 44
Sparks, Bertel M(ilas) 1918- 21-24R
Sparks, Donald B. 1931- 124
Sparks, Edgar H(erndon) 1908- 13-16R
Sparks, Fred 1916(?)-1981 Obituary 103
Sparks, Jack Norman 1928- 102
Sparks, James Allen 1933- 109
Sparks, Jared 1789-1866 .... DLB 1, 30
Sparks, John 1939- 103
Sparks, Mary W. 1920- .... SATA 15
Sparks, Merla Jean
See McCormick, Merla Jean
Sparks, Merrill 1922- 21-24R
Sparks, Will (R.) 1924-1987 .... 37-40R
Obituary 124
Sparrow, (John Walter) Gerald 1903- 49-52
Sparrow, John (Hanbury Angus) 1906- 103
Sparrow, Phil
See Steward, Samuel M(orris)
Sparrow, Philip
See Steward, Samuel M(orris)
Sparse Grey Hackle
See Miller, Alfred W.
Sparshott, F. E.
See Sparshott, Francis (Edward)
Sparshott, Francis (Edward) 1926- CANR-26
Earlier sketches in CA 25-28R, CANR-10
See also CAAS 15
See also DLB 60
Spartacus, Deutero
See Fanthorpe, R(obert) Lionel
Spartacus, Tertius
See Burgess, M(ichael) R(oy)
Spate, O(skar) H(ermann) K(hristian)
1911- CANR-29
Earlier sketches in CA 25-28R, CANR-10
Spater, George (Alexander)
1909-1984 Obituary 113
Spath, Gerold
See Spaeth, Gerold
See also DLB 75
Spatz, (Kenneth) Chris(topher Jr.)
1940- 37-40R
Spatz, Jonas 1935- 29-32R
Spaulding, Dayton M(athewson) 1922- 61-64
Spaulding, Douglas
See Bradbury, Ray (Douglas)
Spaulding, Leonard
See Bradbury, Ray (Douglas)
Spaulding, Robert K(ilburn) 1898- 5-8R
Spaulding, William E(llsworth)
1898-1979 Obituary 93-96
Spaull, Hebe (Fanny Lily) 1893- 9-12R
Speaight, George Victor 1914- CANR-12
Earlier sketch in CA 29-32R
Speaight, Robert (William) 1904-1976 .... CANR-12
Earlier sketch in CA 13-16R
Speakes, Larry (Melvin) 1939- 137
Spear, Allan Henry 1937- 21-24R
Spear, Benjamin
See Henisch, Heinz K.
Spear, George E(lliott) 1925- 102
Spear, Hilda D(oris) 1926- CANR-23
Earlier sketch in CA 107
Spear, (Thomas George) Percival
1901-1982 106
Obituary 108
Spear, Richard E(dmund) 1940- 45-48
Spear, Roberta 1948- 113
Speare, Elizabeth George 1908- 1-4R
See also CLR 8
See also MAICYA
See also SATA 5, 62
Spearing, Judith (Mary Harlow) 1922- CANR-3
Earlier sketch in CA 49-52
See also SATA 9
Spearman, Arthur Dunning 1899- CAP-2
Earlier sketch in CA 21-22
Spearman, Walter (Smith) 1908- CAP-2
Earlier sketch in CA 29-32
Spears, Betty (Mary) 1918- CANR-6
Earlier sketch in CA 1-4R
Spears, Dorothea (Johnson) 1901- CAP-1
Earlier sketch in CA 13-14
Spears, Edward (Louis) 1886-1974 .... CAP-2
Obituary 45-48
Earlier sketch in CA 23-24
Spears, Jack 1919- 29-32R
Spears, Monroe K(irk) 1916- CANR-2
Earlier sketch in CA 5-8R
Spears, Richard A(lan) 1939- CANR-21
Earlier sketch in CA 104
Spears, Ross 1947- 122
Spears, Woodridge 1913- 13-16R
Specht, Ernst Konrad 1926- 29-32R
Specht, Harry 1929- CANR-8
Earlier sketch in CA 53-56
Specht, Robert 1928- 103
Specht, Walter F(rederick) 1912- 97-100
Speck, Gordon 1898- CAP-2
Earlier sketch in CA 17-18
Speck, Ross V(ictor) 1927- 125
Brief entry 107
Specking, Inez 1890-196(?) 5-8R
See also SATA 11
Spectator
See Popovic, Nenad D(ushan)
Spector, Debra 1953- 109
Spector, Irwin 1916- 45-48
Spector, Ivar 1898- 1-4R
Spector, Jack J. 1925- 29-32R
Spector, Leonard S. 1945- 122
Spector, Marshall 1936- 45-48
Spector, Robert Donald 1922- 13-16R
Spector, Ronald (Harvey) 1943- 57-60
Spector, Samuel I(ra) 1924- 77-80
Spector, Sherman David 1927- CANR-22
Earlier sketch in CA 1-4R
Spector, Shushannah 1903- 9-12R
Spector, Stanley 1924- 9-12R
Spector, Stephen 1946- 138
Spectorsky, A(uguste) C(omte)
1910-1972 .... CAP-2
Obituary 33-36R
Earlier sketch in CA 17-18
Spedding, C(olin) R(aymond) W(illiam)
1925- 53-56
Speed, Eric CANR-27
Earlier sketches in CAP-2, CA 19-20
Speed, F(rederick) Maurice 1912- 107
Speed, Frank Warren 104
Speed, (Herbert) Keith 1934- 115
Speed, Nell
See Keats, Emma
and Sampson, Emma (Keats) Speed
Speed, Nell (Ewing) 1878-1913 135
See also SATA 68
Speelman, Arlene 1916- 41-44R
Speer, Albert 1905-1981 65-68
Obituary 104
Speer, David G(ordon) 1913- 45-48
Speer, Laurel 1940- 132
Speer, Michael L. 1934- 93-96
Speeth, Kathleen Riordan 1937- 89-92
Spehar, Betty M. 1924- 45-48
Speicher, Helen Ross S(mith) 1915- CANR-4
Earlier sketch in CA 5-8R
See also SATA 8
Speicher, John 1934(?)-1986 Obituary 119
Speidel, Hans 1897-1984 133
Obituary 114
Speidel, Michael P(aul) 1937- 108
Speier, Hans 1905-1990 .... CANR-9
Obituary 131
Earlier sketch in CA 21-24R
Speight, Harold 1916- 5-8R
Speight, Johnny 1921(?)- Brief entry 117
Speirs, John (Hastie) 1906- 61-64
Speirs, Logan 1938- 37-40R
Speirs, Russell 1901-1975 .... CANR-4
Obituary 61-64
Earlier sketch in CA 45-48
Speiser, Jean 69-72
Speiser, Stuart Marshall 1923- Brief entry 106
Speitel, H. H.
See Speitel, Hans(-Henning)
Speitel, Hans(-Henning) 1937- 123
Speizman, Morris 1905- 77-80
Spekke, Arnolds 1887-1972 Obituary 37-40R
Spelios, Thomas 1930- 25-28R
Spellman, Alfred B. 1935- 97-100
See also BW
See also DLB 41
Spellman, Cathy Cash 1941- 121
Spellman, Francis Cardinal
See Spellman, Francis (Joseph)
Spellman, Francis (Joseph)
1889-1967 Obituary 113
Spellman, John W(illard) 1934- 13-16R
See also SATA 14
Spellman, Roger G.
See Cox, William R(obert)
Spelman, Mary 1934- CANR-13
Earlier sketch in CA 77-80
See also SATA 28
Spelvin, George
See Phillips, David Atlee
Spence, Bill
See Spence, William John Duncan
Spence, Clark C(hristian) 1923- CANR-6
Earlier sketch in CA 1-4R
Spence, Donald P(ond) 1926- Brief entry 109
Spence, Duncan
See Spence, William John Duncan
Spence, Eleanor (Rachel) 1928- CANR-3
Earlier sketch in CA 49-52
See also CLR 26
See also SATA 21
Spence, Gerald Leonard 1929- 118
Spence, Geraldine 1931- .... SATA 47
Spence, Gerry
See Spence, Gerald Leonard
Spence, Gordon William 1936- 25-28R
Spence, Hartzell 1908- 5-8R
Spence, J. A. D.
See Eliot, T(homas) S(tearns)
Spence, J(ohn) E(dward) 1931- 25-28R
Spence, James R(obert) 1927- 25-28R
Spence, Jonathan D(ermot) 1936- CANR-23
Earlier sketch in CA 21-24R
See also BEST 90:4
Spence, (James) Lewis (Thomas Chalmers)
1874-1955 Brief entry 115
Spence, Mary Lee 1927- 45-48
Spence, Vernon Gladden 1924- 37-40R
Spence, William John Duncan 1923- CANR-20
Earlier sketch in CA 103
Spencer
See Herz, Jerome Spencer
Spencer, Ann 1918- 29-32R
See also SATA 10
Spencer, Anne 1882-1975 .... DLB 51, 54
Spencer, Benjamin T(ownley) 1904- 124
Spencer, (Charles) Bernard
1909-1963 Obituary 115
Spencer, Bonnell 1909- 106
Spencer, Charles 1920- 49-52
Spencer, Christopher 1930- 13-16R
Spencer, Colin 1933- CANR-12
Earlier sketch in CA 21-24R
Spencer, Cornelia
See Yaukey, Grace S(ydenstricker)
Spencer, Dale R(ay) 1925- 57-60
Spencer, Donald D(ean) 1931- 108
See also SATA 41
Spencer, Edgar Winston 1931- 41-44R
Spencer, Elizabeth 1921- CANR-32
Earlier sketch in CA 13-16R
See also CLC 22
See also DLB 6
See also MTCW
See also SATA 14
Spencer, Harold (Edwin) 1920- CANR-23
Earlier sketch in CA 45-48
Spencer, Herbert 1820-1903 .... DLB 57
Spencer, J(oseph) E(arle) 1907-1984 ..... CANR-22
Earlier sketch in CA 45-48
Spencer, James 1932- 109
Spencer, Jean E(lizabeth) 1933- 17-20R
Spencer, Jeffry Withers B(urress) 1927- 45-48
Spencer, John Hall 1928- 5-8R
Spencer, John Hathaway 1907- 112
Spencer, John (Walter) 1922- 9-12R
Spencer, LaVyrle 1943- CANR-34
Earlier sketch in CA 102
See also BEST 89:3
Spencer, Leonard G.
See Garrett, (Gordon) Randall (Phillip)
and Silverberg, Robert
Spencer, Lloyd Neville 1955- 121
Spencer, Margaret 1916- 21-24R
Spencer, Metta Wells 1931- 69-72
Spencer, Michael (Clifford) 1936- 57-60
Spencer, Milton Harry 1926- CANR-6
Earlier sketch in CA 1-4R
Spencer, Raine 132
Spencer, Robert Allan 1920- 5-8R
Spencer, Robert F(rancis) 1917- Brief entry 108
Spencer, Ross (Harrison) 1921- 101
Spencer, Scott 1945- 113
See also CLC 30
See also DLBY 86
Spencer, Sharon Dougherty 1933- CANR-13
Earlier sketch in CA 5-8R
Spencer, Sidney 5-8R
Spencer, Steven M. 1905- CAP-1
Earlier sketch in CA 13-14
Spencer, Stewart 1949- 121
Spencer, Terence (John Bew)
1915-1978 Obituary 77-80
Spencer, Warren F(rank) 1923- 29-32R
Spencer, William Browning 1946- 133

Spencer, William 1922- CANR-23
Earlier sketches in CA 17-20R, CANR-8
See also SATA 9
Spencer, Zane A(nn) 1935- 89-92
See also SATA 35
Spencer-Churchill, Laura
1915-1990 Obituary 131
Spender, Dale 1943- 125
Brief entry 120
Spender, J. A. 1862-1942 ....DLB 98
Spender, Lynne 1946- 119
Spender, Stephen (Harold) 1909- CANR-31
Earlier sketch in CA 9-12R
See also CDBLB 1945-1960
See also CLC 1, 2, 5, 10, 41
See also DLB 20
See also MTCW
Spengemann, William Charles 1932- 102
Spengler, Edwin H(arold)
1906-1981 Obituary 104
Spengler, Oswald (Arnold Gottfried)
1880-1936 Brief entry 118
See also TCLC 25
Spenser, Edmund
1552(?)-1599 ....CDBLB Before 1660
See also WLC
Sperber, A(nn) M. 126
Sperber, Al E(lias) 1916- 65-68
Sperber, Manes 1905-1984 124
Obituary 112
Sperber, Murray A(rnold) 1940- CANR-12
Earlier sketch in CA 61-64
Sperber, Perry Arthur 1907- 37-40R
Sperber, Philip 1944- CANR-26
Earlier sketch in CA 109
Spergel, Irving A. 1924- CANR-11
Earlier sketch in CA 21-24R
Sperka, Joshua S. 1905- 49-52
Sperlich, Peter W. 1934- 37-40R
Sperling, Dan(iel Lee) 1949- 112
See also SATA 65
Sperling, John G(len) 1921- 49-52
Sperling, Milton M. 1912-1988 Obituary 126
Spero, Sterling D. 1896-1976 65-68
Obituary 61-64
Speroni, Charles 1911-1984 93-96
Obituary 113
Sperry, Armstrong W. 1897-1976 ....CAP-1
Obituary 107
Earlier sketch in CA 9-10
See also MAICYA
See also SATA 1, 27
Sperry, (Sally) Baxter 1914- CANR-16
Earlier sketches in CA 49-52, CANR-1
Sperry, Byrne Hope 1902- 69-72
Sperry, J. E.
See Eisenstat, Jane Sperry
Sperry, Kip 1940- CANR-19
Earlier sketch in CA 101
Sperry, Len 1943- CANR-12
Earlier sketch in CA 61-64
Sperry, Margaret 1905- 37-40R
Sperry, Ralph A(ddison) 1944- 106
Sperry, Raymond
See Garis, Howard R(oger)
Sperry, Raymond Jr. CANR-26
Earlier sketches in CAP-2, CA 19-20
See also SATA 1
Sperry, Stuart M(ajor) 1929- 49-52
Speshock, Phyllis (Nieboer) 1925- 17-20R
Spewack, Bella 1899-1990 Obituary 131
Spewack, Samuel 1899-1971 Obituary 33-36R
Spice, Marjorie Davis 1924- 9-12R
Spicehandler, Daniel 1923- 1-4R
Spicer, Bart 1918- 103
Spicer, Dorothy Gladys CANR-4
Earlier sketch in CA 1-4R
See also SATA 32
Spicer, Jack 1925-1965 85-88
See also CLC 8, 18, 72
See also DLB 5, 16
Spicer, James 1928(?)-1979 Obituary 85-88
Spicer, Michael 1943- 135
Spicker, Stuart Francis 1937- CANR-30
Earlier sketch in CA 65-68
Spidle, Jake Wilton Jr. 1941- 127
Spiegel, Don(ald Elwin) 1926- 41-44R
Spiegel, Henry William 1911- 1-4R
Spiegel, John P(aul) 1911-1991 103
Obituary 135
Spiegel, Joseph 1928- 9-12R
Spiegel, Richard Alan 1947- CANR-30
Earlier sketch in CA 104
Spiegel, Robert H. 1922- 81-84
Spiegel, Shalom 1899-1984 Obituary 112
Spiegel, Steven L(ee) 1941- 77-80
Spiegel, Ted 1934- Brief entry 105
Spiegelberg, Herbert 1904-1990 ....9-12R
Obituary 132
Spiegelman, Art 1948- 125
Spiegelman, J(oseph) Marvin 1926- 57-60
Spiegelman, Judith M. 21-24R
See also SATA 5
Spiegelman, Judith 1942- 101
Spiegler, Charles G. 1911- CANR-3
Earlier sketch in CA 9-12R
Spiegler, Michael D(avid) 1943- 61-64
Spiel, Hilde (Maria) 1911-1990 ....CANR-14
Obituary 133
Earlier sketches in CAP-1, CA 9-10
Spielberg, Peter 1929- CANR-4
Earlier sketch in CA 5-8R
See also CLC 6
See also DLBY 81
Spielberg, Steven 1947- CANR-32
Earlier sketch in CA 77-80
See also AAYA 8
See also CLC 20
See also SATA 32
Spielberger, Charles D(onald) 1927- 102
Spielberger, Walter Jakob 1925- CANR-16
Earlier sketch in CA 21-24R
Spielman, Patrick E. 1936- CANR-22
Earlier sketches in CA 13-16R, CANR-7
Spielmann, Peter James 1952- 97-100
Spier, Peter (Edward) 1927- 5-8R
See also CLR 5
See also DLB 61
See also MAICYA
See also SATA 4, 54
Spier, Robert F(orest) G(ayton) 1922- 41-44R
Spier, William H. 1907(?)-1973 Obituary ..41-44R
Spierenburg, Pieter (Cornelis) 1948- 132
Spiering, Frank 1938- CANR-10
Earlier sketch in CA 25-28R
Spiers, Edward M(ichael) 1947- 119
Spies, Werner 1937- 37-40R
Spigel, Irwin M(yron) 1926- 17-20R
Spigelgass, Leonard 1908-1985 103
Obituary 115
Spike, Paul 1947- 120
Spikes, Brian S. J. 101
Spilhaus, Athelstan (Frederick) 1911- CANR-31
Earlier sketch in CA 17-20R
See also SATA 13
Spilka, Arnold 1917- 49-52
See also SATA 6
Spilka, Mark 1925- CANR-31
Earlier sketch in CA 81-84
Spilke, Francine S. 101
Spillane, Frank Morrison 1918- CANR-28
Earlier sketch in CA 25-28R
See also Spillane, Mickey
See also MTCW
See also SATA 66
Spillane, John D(avid)
1909(?)-1985 Obituary 117
Spillane, Mickey
See Spillane, Frank Morrison
See also CLC 3, 13
Spillard, Anne 1932- 128
Spiller, Burton L(owell) 1886- 5-8R
Spiller, Earl A(lexander) Jr. 1934- 21-24R
Spiller, Gene A(lan) 1927- 133
Spiller, Robert E. 1896- CANR-4
Earlier sketch in CA 5-8R
Spillmann, Betty Evelyn 1920- 53-56
Spilman, Richard 1946- 132
Spilsbury, Richard J(oy) 1919-1984 104
Obituary 113
Spina, Tony 1914- 69-72
Spinage, Clive A(lfred) 1933- 13-16R
Spindler, Arthur 1918- 104
Spindler, George Dearborn 1920- 21-24R
Spindler, Louise Schaubel 1917- 49-52
Spindler, Michael (James) 1948- 116
Spinelli, Altiero 1907-1986 ....CANR-16
Obituary 119
Earlier sketch in CA 21-24R
Spinelli, Eileen 1942- 107
See also SATA 38
Spinelli, Jerry 1941- CANR-30
Earlier sketch in CA 111
See also CLR 26
See also MAICYA
See also SATA 39, 71
Spinelli, Marcos 1904-1970 Obituary 29-32R
Sping, Dan
See Spalding, Henry D(aniel)
Spingarn, Lawrence P(erreira) 1917- CANR-23
Earlier sketches in CA 1-4R, CANR-6
Spingarn, Natalie Davis 1922- 85-88
Spinifex
See Martin, David
Spink, Ian 1932- Brief entry 113
Spink, John Stephenson
1909-1985 Obituary 116
Spink, Reginald (William) 1905- CANR-19
Earlier sketches in CA 53-56, CANR-4
See also SATA 11
Spink, Walter M. 1928- 61-64
Spinka, Matthew 1890-1972 ....CANR-2
Obituary 37-40R
Earlier sketch in CA 1-4R
Spinks, G(eorge) Stephens 1903- CAP-2
Earlier sketch in CA 23-24
Spinks, John William Tranter 1908- 109
Spinner, Stephanie 1943- CANR-32
Earlier sketch in CA 45-48
See also SATA 38
Spinner, Thomas J(ohn) Jr. 1929- 45-48
Spinney, David
See Spinney, J(ohn) D(avid)
Spinney, J(ohn) D(avid) 1912- 29-32R
Spinossimus
See White, William Jr.
Spinrad, Norman (Richard) 1940- CANR-20
Earlier sketch in CA 37-40R
See also CLC 46
See also DLB 8
Spinrad, William 1917- 29-32R
Spira, Ruth Rodale 1928- 61-64
Spirer, Herbert F(rederick) 1925- CANR-16
Earlier sketch in CA 93-96
Spires, Elizabeth 1952- CANR-28
Earlier sketch in CA 106
See also DLB 120
See also SATA 71
Spires, Robert C(ecil) 1936- 125
Spiro, Edward 1908- 25-28R
Spiro, Herbert J(ohn) 1924- CANR-6
Earlier sketch in CA 1-4R
Spiro, Herzl Robert 1935- 104
Spiro, Howard M(arget) 1924- 125
Spiro, Jack D. 1933- CANR-6
Earlier sketch in CA 9-12R
Spiro, Melford E(lliot) 1920- CANR-1
Earlier sketch in CA 45-48
Spirt, Diana L(ouise) 1925- 17-20R
Spisak, James W(illiam) 1951- 117
Spit, Sam
See Schneck, Stephen
Spittel, Richard Lionel 1881-1969 ....CAP-1
Earlier sketch in CA 13-14
Spitteler, Carl (Friedrich Georg)
1845-1924 Brief entry 109
See also TCLC 12
Spitz, A. Edward 1923- 73-76
Spitz, Allan A(ugust) 1928- 13-16R
Spitz, David 1916-1979 ....41-44R
Obituary 85-88
Spitz, Lewis W(illiam) 1922- CANR-32
Earlier sketches in CA 1-4R, CANR-6
Spitz, Mark (Andrew) 1950- Brief entry 115
Spitzer, Abe 1912(?)-1984 Obituary 112
Spitzer, E(rwin) E(dwin) 1910- CAP-2
Earlier sketch in CA 21-22
Spitzer, Herbert Frederick 1906- CAP-1
Earlier sketch in CA 13-14
Spitzer, John 1956- CANR-18
Earlier sketch in CA 102
Spitzer, Leo 1939- 61-64
Spitzer, Lyman (Jr.) 1914- 116
Spitzer, Morton Edward 41-44R
Spitzer, Robert J(ames) 1953- CANR-30
Earlier sketch in CA 112
Spitzer, Robert S(idney) 1926- 61-64
Spivack, Charlotte K(esler) 1926- 21-24R
Spivack, Ellen Sue 1937- 106
Spivack, George 1927- Brief entry 109
Spivack, Kathleen (Romola Drucker)
1938- 49-52
See also CLC 6
Spivack, Robert (Gerald)
1915-1970 Obituary 104
Spivak, Gayatri Chakravorty
1942- Brief entry 110
Spivak, John L(ouis) 1897-1981 Obituary 105
Spivak, Mel 1937- 57-60
Spivak, Talbot 1937- 77-80
Spivakovsky, Erika 1909- 49-52
Spivey, Richard L. 1937- 115
Spivey, Robert Atwood 1931- Brief entry 106
Spivey, Ted R(ay) 1927- 105
Splane, Richard B. 1916- 17-20R
Splaver, Sarah 85-88
See also SATA 28
Spletter, Mary 1946- 111
Spock, Benjamin (McLane) 1903- CANR-35
Earlier sketch in CA 21-24R
See also AITN 1
See also MTCW
Spodek, Bernard 1931- CANR-22
Earlier sketches in CA 17-20R, CANR-7
Spoehr, Alexander 1913- 109
Spoelstra, Nyle (Ray) 1939- 29-32R
Spofford, Harriet Prescott 1835-1921 ......DLB 74
Spofford, Walter O(smon) Jr. 1936- 107
Spollen, Christopher 1952- ....SATA 12
Spolsky, Bernard 1932- CANR-1
Earlier sketch in CA 45-48
Spolsky, Ellen 1943- 119
Spong, John Shelby 1931- 104
Spooner, Frank (Clyffurde) 1924- 85-88
Spooner, Frederick Percy 1898- CAP-1
Earlier sketch in CA 13-14
Spooner, Jane R(oss) 1922- 5-8R
Spooner, John D. 1937- 21-24R
Spooner, (Glenda) Victoria Maude (Graham)
1897- CAP-1
Earlier sketch in CA 9-10
Spores, Ronald 1931- 21-24R
Spot, Ryhen
See Post, Henry
Spota, Luis
See Spota Saavedra, Luis
Spota Saavedra, Luis 1925-1985 Obituary 114
See also HW
Spotnitz, Hyman 1908- CANR-6
Earlier sketch in CA 1-4R
Spoto, Donald 1941- CANR-11
Earlier sketch in CA 65-68
See also CLC 39
Spotte, Stephen 1942- CANR-1
Earlier sketch in CA 45-48
Spottiswoode, Raymond J.
1913-1970 Obituary 104
Spotts, Charles D(ewey) 1899-1974(?) CAP-2
Earlier sketch in CA 19-20
Spotts, Frederic 1930- 101
Spradley, James P(hillip) 1933-1982 .....CANR-13
Earlier sketch in CA 29-32R
Spradling, Mary Elizabeth Mace 1911- 104
Spragens, Thomas A(rthur) Jr. 1942- 85-88
Spragens, William C(lark) 1925- 41-44R
Spraggett, Allen (Frederick) 1932- CANR-18
Earlier sketch in CA 25-28R
Sprague, Arthur Colby 1895- 89-92
Sprague, Carter
See Merwin, Sam(uel Kimball) Jr.
Sprague, Charles Arthur
1887-1969 Obituary 89-92
Sprague, Claire S(acks) 1926- 25-28R
Sprague, Gretchen (Burnham) 1926- 13-16R
See also SATA 27
Sprague, Howard B(ennet) 1898- 41-44R
Sprague, Irvine H(enry Jr.) 1921- 123
Sprague, Ken 1945- 108
Sprague, Marshall 1909- CANR-1
Earlier sketch in CA 1-4R
Sprague, Richard E. 1921- 29-32R
Sprague, Rosamond Kent 1922- CANR-2
Earlier sketch in CA 5-8R
Sprague, Rosemary 17-20R
Sprague, W. D.
See von Block, Bela W(illiam)
and von Block, Sylvia
Spraos, John 1926- 5-8R
Spratt, Hereward Philip 1902- 5-8R
Spray, Pauline 1920- CANR-10
Earlier sketch in CA 25-28R
Spray, Sherrad L(ee) 1935- 104
Spreiregen, Paul D. 1931- 21-24R
Sprengel, Donald P(hilip) 1938- 53-56
Spriegel, William R(obert) 1893- 5-8R
Sprigel, Olivier
See Avice, Claude (Pierre Marie)
Sprigg, C(hristopher) St. John
1907-1937 Brief entry 120
Sprigg, June 1953- 65-68
Sprigge, Elizabeth (Miriam Squire)
1900-1974 ....13-16R
See also SATA 10
Sprigge, Timothy L(auro) S(quire) 1932- ...57-60
Sprinchorn, Evert Manfred 1923- 107
Spring, Bob
See Spring, Robert W(alton)
Spring, David 1918- 81-84
Spring, Gerald M(ax) 1897- 61-64
Spring, (Robert) Howard 1889-1965 ....CAP-1
Earlier sketch in CA 9-10
See also SATA 28
Spring, Ira L. 1918- CANR-7
Earlier sketch in CA 57-60
Spring, Joel Henry 1940- CANR-3
Earlier sketch in CA 49-52
Spring, Norma 1917- 61-64
Spring, Robert W(alton) 1918- CANR-7
Earlier sketch in CA 57-60
Springborg, Robert 1944- 119
Springer, Axel 1912-1985 Obituary 117
Springer, Bernhard J.
1907(?)-1970 Obituary 29-32R
Springer, E(ustace) Laurence 1903- 21-24R
Springer, Haskell S(aul) 1939- CANR-29
Earlier sketch in CA 111
Springer, John L(awrence) 1915- CANR-25
Earlier sketch in CA 1-4R
Springer, John 1916- 53-56
Springer, L(ois) Elsinore 1911- 69-72
Springer, Marilyn Harris 1931- CANR-9
Earlier sketch in CA 21-24R
See also SATA 47
Springer, Marlene Ann 1937- 107
Springer, Mary Doyle 1918- 116
Springer, Nancy 1948- CANR-18
Earlier sketch in CA 101
See also SATA 65
Springer, Nelson P(aul) 1915- 115
Springer, Nesha Bass 1930-1990 81-84
Obituary 132
Springer, Otto 1905- CAP-1
Earlier sketch in CA 13-14
Springer, Sally P(earl) 1947- 108
Springfield
See Kelly, Maurice Anthony
Springfield, David
See Lewis, (John) Roy(ston)
Springs, Nadia
See Obrecht, Jas
Springsted, Eric Osmon 1951- 113
Springsteen, Bruce (F.) 1949- 111
See also CLC 17
Springstubb, Tricia 1950- CANR-21
Earlier sketch in CA 105
See also SATA 40, 46
Sprinkel, Beryl W(ayne) 1923- 9-12R
Sprinker, Michael 1950- 129
Sprinkle, Patricia Houck 1943- 133
Sprinthall, Richard C(lark) 1930- 45-48
Sproat, John G(erald) 1921- 25-28R
Sproston, John
See Scott, Peter Dale
Sprott, W(alter) John Herbert
1897-1971 ....CANR-16
Obituary 103
Earlier sketch in CA 1-4R
Sproul, Barbara Chamberlain 1945- 105
Sproul, Dorothy Noyes
See Noyes-Kane, Dorothy
Sproul, R(obert) C(harles) 1939- CANR-30
Earlier sketch in CA 111
Sprouse, Mary L. 1948- 108
Sprout, Harold 1901-1980 ....CANR-6
Obituary 102
Earlier sketch in CA 1-4R
Spruch, Grace Marmor 1926- 57-60
Spruch, Larry 1923- 102
Sprug, Joseph W(illiam) 1922- 21-24R
Spruill, Charles R(ay) 1946- 117
Spruill, Steven G(regory) 1946- 73-76
Sprunger, Keith L(a Verne) 1935- 41-44R
Sprunt, Alexander Jr.
1898-1973 Obituary 37-40R
Spuhler, J(ames) N(orman) 1917- CANR-3
Earlier sketch in CA 1-4R
Spulber, Nicolas 1915- CANR-3
Earlier sketch in CA 9-12R
Spuler, Bertold 1911- 81-84
Spungen, Deborah 1937- 119
Spurling, Hilary 1940- CANR-25
Earlier sketch in CA 104
See also CLC 34

Spurling, John 1936- ... CANR-25
Earlier sketches in CA 45-48, CANR-1
Spurr, Clinton
See Rowland, D(onald) S(ydney)
Spurr, David Anton 1949- ... 118
Spurr, Stephen Hopkins 1918- ... 81-84
Spurr, William A(lfred) 1905- ... 5-8R
Spurrier, William A(twell) 1916- ... 53-56
Spyers-Duran, Peter 1932- ... CANR-23
Earlier sketches in CA 17-20R, CANR-8
Spyker, John Howland 1918- ... 101
Spykman, E(lizabeth) C(hoate) 1896-1965 ... 101
See also SATA 10
Spyri, Johanna (Heusser) 1827-1901 ... 137
See also CLR 13
See also MAICYA
See also SATA 19
Spyridakis, Stylianos 1937- ... 89-92
Squibob
See Derby, George Horatio
Squier, Charles L(a Barge) 1931- ... 17-20R
Squier, Susan Merrill 1950- ... 120
Squire, Elizabeth 1919- ... 13-16R
Squire, Jason E(dward) 1948- ... CANR-23
Earlier sketch in CA 45-48
Squire, Norman 1907- ... CANR-3
Earlier sketch in CA 9-12R
Squire, Robin 1937- ... 105
Squire, Russel Nelson 1908- ... 1-4R
Squire, Susan 1950- ... 112
Squires, Eric
See Ball, Sylvia Patricia
Squires, James (David) 1943- ... 119
Squires, James Duane 1904- ... 5-8R
Squires, Michael (George) 1941- ... 61-64
Squires, Patricia
See Ball, Sylvia Patricia
Squires, Phil
See Barker, S. Omar
Squires, Radcliffe 1917- ... CANR-21
Earlier sketches in CA 1-4R, CANR-6
See also CLC 51
Sraffa, Piero 1898-1983 ... CANR-27
Obituary ... 110
Earlier sketch in CA 45-48
Srere, Benson M. 1928- ... 77-80
S-Ringi, Kjell
See Ringi, Kjell (Arne Soerensen)
Srivastava, Dhanpat Rai
1880(?)-1936 Brief entry ... 118
See also Premchand
Srivastava, Jane Jonas 1941- ... 119
See also SATA 37
Srivastava, Ramesh K(umar) 1940- ... 127
Srole, Leo 1908- ... 125
Brief entry ... 107
Staaf, Robert J(ames) 1939- ... 93-96
Staal, Cyril 1912- Brief entry ... 113
Staal, J(ohan) F(rederik) 1930- ... 45-48
Staal, Julius D(irk) W(illem)
1917-1986 Obituary ... 120
Staar, Richard F(elix) 1923- ... CANR-38
Earlier sketches in CA 1-4R, CANR-1, 16
Staats, Arthur (Wilbur) 1924- ... 13-16R
Stabb, Martin S(anford) 1928- ... 21-24R
Stabile, Toni ... 85-88
Stableford, Brian (Michael) 1948- ... CANR-29
Earlier sketch in CA 57-60
Stablein, Marilyn 1946- ... 120
Stabler, Arthur P(hillips) 1919- ... CANR-14
Earlier sketch in CA 41-44R
Stabley, Fred(erick) W(illiam) 1915- ... 112
Stace, Christopher 1942- ... 97-100
Stace, Walter Terence 1886-1967 ... CANR-2
Earlier sketch in CA 1-4R
Stacey, C(harles) P(erry) 1906- ... CANR-19
Earlier sketch in CA 101
Stacey, Frank Arthur 1923-1977 ... 57-60
Obituary ... 135
Stacey, Judith 1943- ... 125
Stacey, Margaret 1922- ... CANR-38
Earlier sketches in CA 29-32R, CANR-17
Stacey, Nicholas Anthony Howard 1920- ... 5-8R
Stacey, Roy 1919- ... 9-12R
Stacey, Susannah
See Staynes, Jill
Stacey, Thomas Charles Gerard
1930- ... CANR-21
Earlier sketch in CA 9-12R
Stacey, Tom
See Stacey, Thomas Charles Gerard
Stachow, Hasso G(ert) 1924- ... 109
Stachys, Dimitris
See Constantelos, Demetrios J.
Stack, Edward M(acGregor) 1919- ... CANR-28
Earlier sketch in CA 1-4R
Stack, Frank H(untington) 1937- ... CANR-9
Earlier sketch in CA 61-64
Stack, George J. 1931- ... 37-40R
Stack, Herbert James 1893-1967 ... CANR-3
Earlier sketch in CA 1-4R
Stack, Nicolete Meredith 1896- ... 13-16R
Stackhouse, Max L. 1935- ... 21-24R
Stackhouse, Reginald 1925- ... 21-24R
Stackpole, Edouard Alexander 1903- ... CANR-16
Earlier sketches in CA 1-4R, CANR-1
Stackpole, Edward J(ames) 1894-1967 ... 1-4R
Obituary ... 103
Stacks, John F(ultz) 1942- ... 113
Stacton, David (Derek) 1925-1968 ... CANR-6
Obituary ... 25-28R
Earlier sketch in CA 5-8R
Stacy, Bruce
See Elliott, Bruce (Walter Gardner Lively Stacy)
Stacy, Donald
See Pohl, Frederik
Stacy, Donald L. 1925- ... 29-32R
Stacy, Jan 1948(?)-1989 Obituary ... 129
Stacy, Pat(ricia A.) 1941- ... 118
Stacy, R(obert) H(arold) 1919- ... 73-76
Stacy, Walter
See Elliott, Bruce (Walter Gardner Lively Stacy)
Stade, George 1933- ... 29-32R
Stadelman, S(ara) L(ee) 1917- ... 81-84
Stadler, Karl R(udolph) 1913- ... 21-24R
Stadley, Pat (Anna May Gough)
1918- Brief entry ... 114
Stadt, Ronald W(ilmer) 1935- ... CANR-16
Earlier sketch in CA 93-96
Stadter, Philip A(ustin) 1936- ... 104
Stadtfeld, Curtis K(arl) 1935- ... 49-52
Stadtler, Bea 1921- ... 65-68
See also SATA 17
Stadtman, Verne A. 1926- ... 29-32R
Staebler, Edna ... 101
Staebler, Neil 1905- ... 77-80
Staebler, Warren 1912- ... 45-48
Staehle, Albert 1899-1974 ... AITN 1
Stael, Germaine de
See Stael-Holstein, Anne Louise Germaine Necker Baronn
See also DLB 119
Stael-Holstein, Anne Louise Germaine Necker
Baronn 1766-1817
See Stael, Germaine de
Staender, Gilbert F(rank) 1930- ... 104
Staender, Vivian 1923- ... 97-100
Staff, Adrienne 1947- ... 123
Staff, Frank 1908- ... 25-28R
Staffel, Megan 1952- ... 128
Stafford, Caroline
See Watjen, Carolyn L. T.
Stafford, David Alexander Tetlow
1942- ... CANR-21
Earlier sketch in CA 104
Stafford, David (Christopher) 1943- ... 103
Stafford, Edward Peary 1918- ... 135
Stafford, Fiona (Jane) 1960- ... 131
Stafford, Gilbert Wayne 1938- ... CANR-31
Earlier sketch in CA 112
Stafford, Irvin G. 1936- ... 114
Stafford, Jean 1915-1979 ... CANR-3
Obituary ... 85-88
Earlier sketch in CA 1-4R
See also CLC 4, 7, 19, 68
See also DLB 2
See also MTCW
See also SATA 22
Stafford, Kenneth R(ay) 1922- ... 17-20R
Stafford, Kim R(obert) 1949- ... CANR-22
Earlier sketch in CA 69-72
Stafford, Linda (Crying Wind) 1943- ... 108
Stafford, Muriel
See Sauer, Muriel Stafford
Stafford, Peter
See Tabori, Paul
Stafford, Robert A(ndrew) 1953- ... 133
Stafford, Tim ... 135
Stafford, William B(utler) 1931- ... 53-56
Stafford, William (Edgar) 1914- ... CANR-22
Earlier sketches in CA 5-8R, CANR-5
See also CAAS 3
See also CLC 4, 7, 29
See also DLB 5
Stafford, William T(almadge) 1924- ... CANR-25
Earlier sketch in CA 1-4R
Stafford-Clark, David 1916- ... 21-24R
Staffordshire Knot
See Wrottesley, A(rthur) J(ohn) F(rancis)
Stageberg, Norman C(lifford) 1905- ... CAP-1
Earlier sketch in CA 11-12
Stage Door Jimmy
See Starr, James (A.)
Stagg, Albert 1903- ... 85-88
Stagg, Evelyn 1914- ... 85-88
Stagg, Frank 1911- ... CANR-18
Earlier sketches in CA 1-4R, CANR-1
Stagg, James Martin 1900-1975 Obituary ... 61-64
Stagg, Paul L. 1914- ... 21-24R
Stagge, Jonathan
See Wheeler, Hugh (Callingham)
Stagner, Lloyd Ernest 1923- ... 101
Stagner, Ross 1909- ... CANR-5
Earlier sketch in CA 5-8R
Stahl, Ben(jamin) 1910-1987 ... 29-32R
Obituary ... 123
See also SATA 5, 54
Stahl, Donald 1935- ... 25-28R
Stahl, Fred Alan 1944- ... 45-48
Stahl, Gustav Richard
1888(?)-1978 Obituary ... 81-84
Stahl, Hilda 1938- ... 116
See also SATA 48
Stahl, Le Roy 1908- ... CAP-1
Earlier sketch in CA 11-12
Stahl, Lesley R(ene) 1941- ... 107
See also AITN 2
Stahl, Nancy 1937- ... 104
Stahl, Norman 1931- ... 85-88
Stahl, O(scar) Glenn 1910- ... CANR-14
Earlier sketch in CA 41-44R
Stahl, William Harris 1908-1969 Obituary ... 111
Stahlecker, Lotar V(ictor) 1915- ... 21-24R
Stahlman, James Geddes
1893-1976 Obituary ... 89-92
Stahnke, Arthur A(llan) 1935- ... 65-68
Stahnke, Astrida B. 1935- ... 123
Stahr, John W. 1904-1981 Obituary ... 104
Staib, Bjorn O. 1938- ... 17-20R
Staicar, Thomas Edward 1946- ... 108
Staicar, Tom
See Staicar, Thomas Edward
Staiger, Janet 1946- ... 123
Stainback, Susan Bray 1947- ... CANR-31
Earlier sketches in CA 57-60, CANR-7, 14
Stainback, William (Clarence) 1943- ... CANR-31
Earlier sketches in CA 77-80, CANR-14
Staines, David 1946- ... 125
Staines, Trevor
See Brunner, John (Kilian Houston)
Stainsby, Charles 1925-1985 Obituary ... 118
Stair, Gobin (John) 1912- ... SATA 35
Stairs, Denis (Winfield) 1939- Brief entry ... 114
Stairs, Gordon
See Austin, Mary (Hunter)
Stalder, Valerie ... 41-44R
See also SATA 27
Staley, Allen 1935- Brief entry ... 115
Staley, Charles E(arl) 1927- ... 45-48
Staley, (Alvah) Eugene 1906- ... 77-80
Staley, Thomas F(abian) 1935- ... CANR-30
Earlier sketches in CA 77-80, CANR-13
Stalker, John 1939- ... 127
Stall, Katharine 1950- ... 127
Stallard, John (Richard) 1935-1985 ... 49-52
Obituary ... 116
Stalley, Rodney E(dward) 1930- ... 116
Stalley, Roger 1945- ... 101
Stallibrass, (Helen) Alison 1916- ... 104
Stallings, Constance L(ee) 1932- ... CANR-17
Earlier sketch in CA 97-100
Stallings, James O. 1938- ... CANR-19
Earlier sketch in CA 103
Stallings, Laurence 1894-1968 Obituary ... 89-92
See also DLB 7, 44
Stallman, Robert Wooster 1911- ... CANR-3
Earlier sketch in CA 1-4R
Stallone, Sylvester (Enzio) 1946- ... 77-80
Stallworth, Anne Nall 1935- ... 85-88
Stallworthy, Jon (Howie) 1935- ... CANR-8
Earlier sketch in CA 9-12R
See also DLB 40
Stallybrass, Oliver (George Weatherhead)
1925-1978 ... CANR-24
Earlier sketch in CA 29-32R
Stalvey, Lois Mark 1925- ... CANR-14
Earlier sketch in CA 29-32R
Stam, James H(enry) 1937- ... 49-52
Stam, Robert 1941- ... 115
Stamaty, Mark Alan 1947- ... CANR-15
Earlier sketch in CA 61-64
See also SATA 12
Stambaugh, Joan 1932- ... 89-92
Stambaugh, Sara 1936- ... 119
Stamberg, Susan 1938- ... 103
Stambler, Helen
See Latner, Helen (Stambler)
Stambler, Irwin 1924- ... CANR-2
Earlier sketch in CA 5-8R
See also SATA 5
Stambolian, George 1938-1991 ... 41-44R
Obituary ... 136
Stambuk, George 1927- ... 5-8R
Stames, Ward
See Steward, Samuel M(orris)
Stamey, Sara (Lucinda) 1953- ... 126
Stamm, Keith R(oman) 1941- ... 116
Stamm, Martin L. 1917- ... CANR-19
Earlier sketch in CA 37-40R
Stammers, Neil 1950- ... 119
Stamp, L(aurence) Dudley 1898-1966 ... CAP-1
Earlier sketch in CA 13-14
Stamp, Robert M(iles) 1937- ... 126
Stamper, Alexander
See Kent, Arthur William Charles
Stampfer, Judah (Leon) 1923- ... 25-28R
Stampfle, Felice 1912- ... 105
Stampp, Kenneth M. 1912- ... 13-16R
See also DLB 17
Stanbury, David 1933- ... 104
Stanbury, Walter A. 1910-1976 Obituary ... 65-68
Stancliffe, Michael (Staffurth) 1916-1987 ... 124
Stancu, Zaharia 1902-1974 ... 97-100
Obituary ... 53-56
Standard, William L.
1900(?)-1978 Obituary ... 77-80
Stander, Siegfried 1935- ... CANR-19
Earlier sketches in CA 9-12R, CANR-4
Standiford, Lester A(lan) 1945- ... 77-80
Standing, Edwin (Mortimer) 1887- ... CAP-1
Earlier sketch in CA 9-10
Standing, Sue 1952- ... 119
Standing Bear, Luther
1868(?)-1939(?) Brief entry ... 113
Standish, Buck
See Paine, Lauran (Bosworth)
Standish, Carole
See Koehler, Margaret (Hudson)
Standish, Robert 1898(?)-1981 Obituary ... 105
Standley, Fred L(loyd) 1932- ... 41-44R
Standon, Anna (Slater) 1929- ... 17-20R
Standring, Gillian 1935- ... 69-72
Stanek, Carolyn 1951- ... 107
Stanek, Lou Willett 1931- ... SATA 63
Stanek, Muriel (Novella) 1915- Brief entry ... 112
See also SATA 34
Stanev, Emilian
See Stanev, Nikola (Stoyanov)
Stanev, Nikola (Stoyanov) 1907-1979 ... 108
Stanfield, Nancy Fisher Clay 1905- ... CAP-1
Earlier sketch in CA 9-10
Stanfield, Vernon Latrelle 1920- ... 97-100
Stanford, Alfred (Boller) 1900-1985 ... CAP-1
Obituary ... 115
Earlier sketch in CA 17-18
Stanford, Ann 1916-1987 ... CANR-32
Obituary ... 123
Earlier sketches in CA 9-12R, CANR-4
See also DLB 5
Stanford, Barbara Dodds 1943- ... 37-40R
Stanford, Derek 1918- ... 9-12R
Stanford, Don
See Stanford, Donald E(lwin)
Stanford, Don(ald Kent) 1918- ... 53-56
Stanford, Donald E(lwin) 1913- ... CANR-28
Earlier sketches in CA 13-16R, CANR-5
Stanford, Edward V(alentine) 1897-1966 ... 5-8R
Stanford, Gene 1944- ... 37-40R
Stanford, J(ohn) K(eith) 1892- ... 5-8R
Stanford, Melvin Joseph 1932- ... CANR-16
Earlier sketch in CA 89-92
Stanford, Miles J(oseph) 1914- ... 65-68
Stanford, Neal 1906(?)-1988 Obituary ... 127
Stanford, Quentin Hunt 1935- ... 45-48
Stanford, Sally 1903-1982 Obituary ... 105
Stanford, William Bedell 1910-1984 ... 85-88
Obituary ... 115
Stanforth, Deirdre 1924- ... 102
Stang, Ivan 1949- ... 129
Stang, Judit 1921-1977 ... CANR-8
Earlier sketch in CA 5-8R
See also SATA 29
Stang, Judy
See Stang, Judit
Stang, Sondra J. 1928- ... 131
Stange, G(eorge) Robert 1919- ... 21-24R
Stanger, Frank Bateman 1914- ... 109
Stanger, Ila (Ann) 1940- ... 65-68
Stangerup, Helle 1939- ... 132
Stangl, (Mary) Jean 1928- ... 136
See also SATA 67
Stanhope, Eric
See Hamilton, Charles (Harold St. John)
Stanhope, Philip Dormer 1694-1773 ... DLB 104
Stanier, Maida Euphemia Kerr 1909- ... 101
Staniforth, (John Hamilton) Maxwell
1893- ... CAP-2
Earlier sketch in CA 25-28
Stanislavsky, Constantin (Sergeivich)
1863(?)-1938 Brief entry ... 118
Stanislawski, Dan 1903- ... CANR-3
Earlier sketch in CA 5-8R
Stanislawski, Michael 1952- ... 119
Stanke, Alain 1934- ... 81-84
Stanke, Don E(dward) 1929- ... 61-64
Stankevich, Boris 1928- ... 21-24R
See also SATA 2
Stankiewicz, Edward 1920- ... 45-48
Stankiewicz, Marketa Goetz
See Goetz-Stankiewicz, Marketa
Stankiewicz, W(ladyslaw) J(ozef)
1922- ... CANR-1
Earlier sketch in CA 45-48
Stanko, Elizabeth Anne 1950- ... CANR-38
Earlier sketch in CA 116
Stanley, Alexander O. 1910- ... 5-8R
Stanley, Bennett
See Hough, S(tanley) B(ennett)
Stanley, C(laude) Maxwell 1904-1984 ... 114
Stanley, Carol
See White, Carol
Stanley, Dave
See Dachs, David
Stanley, David T(aylor) 1916- Brief entry ... 107
Stanley, David 1944- ... CANR-39
Earlier sketch in CA 115
Stanley, Diana 1909- ... SATA 30
Stanley, Diane 1943- ... CANR-32
Earlier sketch in CA 112
See also SATA 32, 37
Stanley, Fay Grissom
See Shulman, Fay Grissom Stanley
Stanley, George Edward 1942- ... CANR-39
Earlier sketches in CA 97-100, CANR-17
See also SATA 53
Stanley, George F(rancis) G(ilman)
1907- ... CANR-15
Earlier sketch in CA 41-44R
Stanley, George 1934- Brief entry ... 114
Stanley, John L(angley) 1937- ... 45-48
Stanley, John 1940- ... 21-24R
Stanley, Julian C(ecil) Jr. 1918- ... CANR-8
Earlier sketch in CA 21-24R
Stanley, Leo Leonidas 1886- ... 69-72
Stanley, Liz 1947- ... 119
Stanley, Marge
See Weinbaum, Stanley Grauman
Stanley, Nora Kathleen Begbie Strange
1885- ... CAP-1
Earlier sketch in CA 11-12
Stanley, Patricia H. ... 138
Stanley, Peter (Alan) 1956- ... 118
Stanley, Phil
See Ind, Allison
Stanley, Robert
See Hamilton, Charles (Harold St. John)
Stanley, Robert Henry 1940- ... 101
Stanley, Roy M. II 1936- ... 114
Stanley, Steven M(itchell) 1941- ... 109
Stanley, Timothy Wadsworth 1927- ... 77-80
Stanley, Warwick
See Hilton, John Buxton
Stanley, William O(liver) Jr. 1902- ... CANR-1
Earlier sketch in CA 1-4R
Stanley-Brown, Katherine (Oliver)
1893(?)-1972 Obituary ... 33-36R
Stanley-Jones, D(ouglas) 1905- ... 9-12R
Stanley-Wrench, Margaret 1916- ... 9-12R
Stanli, Sue
See Meilach, Dona Z(weigoron)
Stanlis, Peter J(ames) 1919- ... 101
Stanmeyer, William A(nthony) 1934- ... 118
Stann, Francis E. 1912(?)-1987 Obituary ... 124
Stannard, David E(dward) 1941- ... 65-68
Stannard, Martin ... CLC 44
Stannard, Neville (George) 1949- ... 118
Stannard, Una 1927- ... 73-76

Stanner, W(illiam) E(dward) H(anley)
1905-1981 Obituary 108
Stannus, (James) Gordon (Dawson)
1902- 65-68
Stannus (James) Gordon (Dawson)
1902-1989 Obituary 129
Stanovich, Betty Jo 1954- 118
See also SATA 51
Stans, Maurice H(ubert) 1908- Brief entry 113
Stansberger, Richard 1950- CANR-18
Earlier sketch in CA 101
Stansbury, Donald L. 1929- 37-40R
Stansfield, Richard Habberton 1921- 107
Stansky, Peter (David Lyman) 1932- CANR-12
Earlier sketch in CA 17-20R
Stanstead, John
See Groom, Arthur William
Stanton, Dorothy
See Kaumeyer, Dorothy
Stanton, Edward F(eagler) 1942- 89-92
Stanton, Elizabeth Cady 1815-1902 .... DLB 79
Stanton, Frank L. 1857-1927 .... DLB 25
Stanton, Gerald B(arry) 1918- 9-12R
Stanton, Graham N(orman) 1940- 61-64
Stanton, Jessie Earl 1887-1976 Obituary 65-68
Stanton, Marietta (P.) 1948- 134
Stanton, Maura 1946- CANR-15
Earlier sketch in CA 89-92
See also CLC 9
See also DLB 120
Stanton, Paul
See Beaty, (Arthur) David
Stanton, Peggy Smeeton 1939- 61-64
Stanton, Phoebe B(aroody) 1914- 37-40R
Stanton, Royal (Waltz) 1916- 37-40R
Stanton, Schuyler
See Baum, L(yman) Frank
Stanton, Vance
See Avallone, Michael (Angelo, Jr)
Stanton, Will 1918- 85-88
Stanton, William J(ohn Jr.)
1919- Brief entry 115
Stanton, William 1925- 1-4R
Stanwood, Brooks
See Kaminsky, Susan Stanwood
Stanwood, Brooks
See Kaminsky, Howard
and Kaminsky, Susan Stanwood
Stanwood, P(aul) G(rant) 1933- 49-52
Stanyer, Jeffrey 1936- 61-64
Staph, C. C.
See Carroll, Bob
Stapledon, (William) Olaf
1886-1950 Brief entry 111
See also DLB 15
See also TCLC 22
Stapler, Harry (Bascom) 1919- CANR-13
Earlier sketch in CA 61-64
Staples, Reginald Thomas 1911- CANR-14
Earlier sketch in CA 69-72
Staples, Robert (Eugene) 1942- CANR-2
Earlier sketch in CA 49-52
Staples, Suzanne Fisher 1945- 132
See also SATA 70
Stapleton, Constance 1930- 104
Stapleton, G(eorge) Brian 1922- 25-28R
Stapleton, Jean 1942- 69-72
Stapleton, (Katharine) Laurence 1911- 17-20R
Stapleton, Margaret (Lucy) 1903- 57-60
Stapleton, Marjorie (Winifred) 1932- 106
See also SATA 28
Stapleton, Richard John 1940- 89-92
Stapleton, Ruth Carter 1929-1983 81-84
Obituary 110
Stapp, Arthur D(onald) 1906-1972 ....CANR-2
Obituary 33-36R
Earlier sketch in CA 1-4R
See also SATA 4
Stapp, William B. 1929- CANR-22
Earlier sketches in CA 45-48, CANR-2
Stappenbeck, Herb(ert) Louis (Jr.) 1935- 65-68
Star, Angel
See Quigley, Joan
Star, Cima 1939- 110
Star, Jack 1920- 73-76
Star, Max 1890(?)-1986 Obituary 121
Star, Shirley A(nn) 1918-1976 ....41-44R
Obituary 65-68
Starbird, Kaye 1916- CANR-38
Earlier sketch in CA 17-20R
See also MAICYA
See also SATA 6
Starbuck, George (Edwin) 1931- CANR-23
Earlier sketch in CA 21-24R
See also CLC 53
Starbuck, William H(aynes) 1934- CANR-7
Earlier sketch in CA 57-60
Starch, Daniel 1883-1979 ....37-40R
Obituary 133
Starchild, Adam (Aristotle) 1946- 123
Starchuk, Orest 1915- 5-8R
Stardust, Alvin 1942- 123
Stare, Fredrick J(ohn) 1910- 132
Starenko, Ronald C(harles) 1930- 93-96
Starer, Robert 1924- 125
Stargell, Willie
See Stargell, Wilver Dornel
Stargell, Wilver Dornel 1941- Brief entry 118
Starhawk
See Simos, Miriam
Stark, Bradford 1948-1979 ....CANR-3
Earlier sketch in CA 49-52
Stark, Claude Alan 1935-1980 57-60
Obituary 134
Stark, Cruce 1942- 137
Stark, Freya (Madeline) 1893- CANR-5
Earlier sketch in CA 5-8R
Stark, Gary Duane 1948- CANR-21
Earlier sketch in CA 105
Stark, George Washington
1884-1966 Obituary 89-92
Stark, Harry 1895- 1-4R
Stark, Irwin 1912- 9-12R
Stark, Jack
See Stark, John H.
Stark, James
See Goldston, Robert (Conroy)
Stark, John
See Godwin, John
Stark, John H. 1914- 49-52
Stark, John Olsen 1939- CANR-5
Earlier sketch in CA 53-56
Stark, Joshua
See Olsen, T(heodore) V(ictor)
Stark, Michael
See Lariar, Lawrence
Stark, Paul C. 1891(?)-1974 Obituary 53-56
Stark, R. J.
See Kikel, Rudy (John)
Stark, Raymond 1919- 73-76
Stark, Richard
See Westlake, Donald E(dwin)
Stark, Werner 1909- CANR-10
Earlier sketch in CA 21-24R
Starke, Aubrey (Harrison)
1905(?)-1972 Obituary 37-40R
Starke, Catherine Juanita 1913- 37-40R
Starke, J(oseph) G(abriel) 1911- 115
Starke, Roland 53-56
Starkey, Lycurgus M(onroe) Jr. 1928- 5-8R
Starkey, Marion L(ena) 1901- CANR-1
Earlier sketch in CA 1-4R
See also SATA 13
Starkie, Enid 1903(?)-1970 ....CANR-2
Obituary 29-32R
Earlier sketch in CA 1-4R
Starkie, Walter F(itzwilliam) 1894-1976 77-80
Obituary 69-72
Starkins, Edward 1946- 120
Starkloff, Carl F. 1933- 53-56
Starkman, Miriam K(osh) 1916- 65-68
Starkman, Moshe 1906-1975 Obituary 57-60
Starks, Richard 1947- 113
Starkweather, David 1935- 97-100
See also DLB 7
Starling, Thomas
See Hayton, Richard Neil
Star-Man's Padre
See Patrick, Johnstone G(illespie)
Starn, Randolph 1939- CANR-32
Earlier sketch in CA 45-48
Starnes, Richard 1922- Brief entry 114
Starobin, Joseph R(obert) 1913-1976 45-48
Obituary 69-72
Starobin, Rosalind Gould
1912(?)-1983 Obituary 111
Starobinski, Jean 1920- 131
Starr, Anne
See Sanford, Annette
Starr, Cecile 1921- 65-68
Starr, Chauncey 1912- 109
Starr, Chester G. 1914- CANR-36
Earlier sketches in CA 1-4R, CANR-1, 16
Starr, Edward Caryl 1911- 13-16R
Starr, Frank 1938- 69-72
Starr, Henry
See Bingley, David Ernest
Starr, Herbert F(rederick) 1932- 116
Starr, Isidore 1911- CANR-7
Earlier sketch in CA 13-16R
Starr, James (A.) 1904(?)-1990 Obituary 132
Starr, Jerold M. 1941- 77-80
Starr, Jimmy
See Starr, James (A.)
Starr, John
See Counselman, Mary Elizabeth
Starr, John A.
See Gillese, John Patrick
Starr, John Bryan 1939- 77-80
Starr, John 1914(?)-1980 Obituary 101
Starr, Judy
See Gelfman, Judith S(chlein)
Starr, Kevin 1940- 120
Starr, Louis M(orris) 1917-1980 53-56
Obituary 97-100
Starr, Mark 1894-1985 Obituary 116
See also AITN 1
Starr, Martin Kenneth 1927- CANR-8
Earlier sketch in CA 17-20R
Starr, Paul (Elliot) 1949- 127
Brief entry 123
Starr, Penelope
See Gelles-Cole, Sandi
Starr, Raymond 1937- 65-68
Starr, Roger 1918- CANR-11
Earlier sketch in CA 21-24R
Starr, Roland
See Rowland, D(onald) S(ydney)
Starr, S(tephen) Frederick 1940- CANR-17
Earlier sketch in CA 85-88
Starr, Stephen Z. 1909-1985 ....CANR-17
Earlier sketch in CA 37-40R
Starr, William Thomas 1910- 41-44R
Starr, Wilmarth Holt 1913- 17-20R
Starratt, Alfred B(yron) 1914- 17-20R
Starret, William
See McClintock, Marshall
Starrett, (Charles) Vincent (Emerson)
1886-1974 ....CANR-31
Obituary 45-48
Earlier sketch in CA 73-76
Starrs, James E(dward) 1930- 118
Starry, Donn Albert 1925- 109
Start, Clarissa
See Lippert, Clarissa Start
Stasch, Stanley F. 1931- 41-44R
Stasheff, Christopher 1944- CANR-26
Earlier sketches in CA 65-68, CANR-10
Stasheff, (Adolph) Edward 1909- 5-8R
Stashower, Daniel (Meyer) 1960- 131
Stasiak, Krystyna ....SATA 49
Stasio, Marilyn L(ouise) 1940- 33-36R
Stassinopoulos, Arianna
See Huffington, Arianna Stassinopoulos
Stasz, Clarice CANR-7
Earlier sketch in CA 61-64
Staten, Patricia S. 1945- 53-56
Statera, Gianni 1943- CANR-8
Earlier sketch in CA 57-60
States, Bert O(len) 1929- 73-76
Statham, Frances P(atton) 1931- 101
Statham, Jane 1917- 13-16R
Statler, Oliver Hadley 1915- 5-8R
Staton, Knofel L. 1934- CANR-35
Earlier sketch in CA 114
Staton, Thomas Felix 1917- 5-8R
Staub, August W(illiam) 1931- CANR-2
Earlier sketch in CA 45-48
Staub, Ervin 1938- 133
Staubach, Charles N(eff) 1906- CANR-4
Earlier sketch in CA 5-8R
Staubach, Roger (Thomas) 1942- 104
Staudacher, Joseph M. 1914- 25-28R
Staudacher, Rosemarian V(alentiner)
1918- 5-8R
Staudenraus, P(hilip) J(ohn) 1928-1971 ....1-4R
Obituary 103
Stauder, Jack 1939- 37-40R
Stauderman, Albert P(hilip) 1910- CANR-39
Earlier sketches in CA 77-80, CANR-18
Staudinger, Hermann 1881-1965 Obituary 113
Staudt, Virginia
See Sexton, Virginia Staudt
Stauffer, Don
See Berkebile, Fred D(onovan)
Stauffer, Donald Barlow 1930- 57-60
Stauffer, Helen Winter 1922- CANR-30
Earlier sketch in CA 109
Staum, Martin Sheldon 1943- 103
Staunton, Schuyler
See Baum, L(yman) Frank
Staupers, Mabel Keaton
1890-1989 Obituary 129
Stauter, (Justin) Jay 1907-1986 Obituary 118
Stave, Bruce M(artin) 1937- CANR-12
Earlier sketch in CA 29-32R
Staveacre, Tony 1942- 130
Staveley, Gaylord L(ee) 1931- 37-40R
Stavenhagen, Lee 1933- 104
Stavenhagen, Rodolfo 1932- CANR-12
Earlier sketch in CA 29-32R
Stavis, Barrie 1906- 49-52
Stavis, Ben(edict) 1941- 29-32R
Stavrianos, Leften Stavros 1913- CANR-6
Earlier sketch in CA 5-8R
Stavros, Niko
See King, Florence
Stavrou, Theofanis G. 1934- 45-48
Stayer, James M(entzer) 1935- CANR-26
Earlier sketch in CA 45-48
Staynes, Jill 133
Stead, Christian Karlson 1932- CANR-6
Earlier sketch in CA 57-60
Stead, Christina (Ellen) 1902-1983 ....CANR-33
Obituary 109
Earlier sketch in CA 13-16R
See also CLC 2, 5, 8, 32
See also MTCW
Stead, Philip John 1916- 108
Stead, Robert J. C. 1880-1959 ....DLB 92
Stead, Thistle Yolette 1902- 107
Steadman, David (Wilton) 1936- 107
Steadman, John M(arcellus III) 1918- 25-28R
Steadman, Mark 1930- 37-40R
See also DLB 6
Steadman, Ralph (Idris) 1936- CANR-29
Earlier sketch in CA 107
See also SATA 32
Steahly, Vivian Eugenia Emrick 1915- 61-64
Steakley, John 1951- 120
Stealingworth, Slim
See Wesselmann, Tom
Steamer
See Nason, Leonard H(astings)
Steamer, Robert J(ulius) 1920- 41-44R
Steane, J(ohn) B(arry) 1928- 9-12R
Steanson, Karen E(lizabeth) 1942- 116
Stearn, Gerald E. 1934(?)-1982 Obituary 108
Stearn, Jess 97-100
Stearns, Harold Edmund
1891-1943 Brief entry 107
See also DLB 4
Stearns, Marshall Winslow
1908-1966 Obituary 110
Stearns, Martha Genung 1886- 9-12R
Stearns, Monroe (Mather) 1913-1987 ......CANR-2
Obituary 124
Earlier sketch in CA 5-8R
See also SATA 5, 55
Stearns, Pamela Fujimoto 1935- 65-68
Stearns, Peter N. 1936- CANR-28
Earlier sketches in CA 21-24R, CANR-10
Stearns, Raymond Phineas 1904-1970 ...... CAP-1
Earlier sketch in CA 11-12
Stebbins, G(eorge) Ledyard 1906- 45-48
Stebbins, Richard P(oate) 1913- CANR-2
Earlier sketch in CA 5-8R
Stebbins, Robert A(lan) 1938- CANR-30
Earlier sketches in CA 29-32R, CANR-12
Stebbins, Robert C(yril) 1915- 49-52
Stebbins, Theodore Ellis Jr. 1938- 89-92
Stebel, S(idney) L(eo) 1924- 29-32R
Steber, A. R.
See Palmer, Raymond A.
Steber, Rick 1946- 128
Stecher, Miriam B(rodie) 1917- 106
Stechow, Wolfgang 1896-1974 ....CANR-9
Obituary 53-56
Earlier sketch in CA 65-68
Steck, James S(perow) 1911- 41-44R
Steckel, William Reed 1915- 17-20R
Steckler, Arthur 1921-1985 108
See also SATA 65
Steckler, Doug(las) 1948- 107
Steckler, Phyllis B. (Schwartzbard) 1933- 9-12R
Stedman, Edmund Clarence 1833-1908 ..... DLB 64
Stedman, James Murphy 1938- 77-80
Stedman, Jane W(inifred) 1920- 37-40R
Stedman, Murray S(alisbury) Jr. 1917- 17-20R
Stedman, R(aymond) William 1930- 29-32R
Stedman, Ray C. 1917- 104
Stedman Jones, Gareth 1942- CANR-31
Earlier sketch in CA 45-48
Stedmond, John Mitchell 1916- 103
Stedwell, Paki 1945- 103
Steed, Gitel P. 1914-1977 ....41-44R
Steed, Thomas Jefferson
1904-1983 Obituary 110
Steed, Tom
See Steed, Thomas Jefferson
Steedman, Marguerite Couturier 1908- CANR-1
Earlier sketch in CA 1-4R
Steefel, Lawrence D. 1894- CAP-2
Earlier sketch in CA 21-22
Steeger, Henry 1903-1990 ....41-44R
Obituary 133
Steeger, Henry 1929(?)-1978 Obituary 77-80
Steegmuller, Francis 1906- CANR-2
Earlier sketch in CA 49-52
See also DLB 111
Steel, Anthony Bedford 1900-1973 ....5-8R
Obituary 89-92
Steel, Byron
See Steegmuller, Francis
Steel, Danielle (Fernande) 1947- CANR-36
Earlier sketches in CA 81-84, CANR-19
See also BEST 89:1, 90:4
See also MTCW
See also SATA 66
Steel, Edward M(arvin) Jr. 1918- 9-12R
Steel, Eric M. 1904- 89-92
Steel, Flora Annie (Webster)
1847-1929 Brief entry 116
Steel, Ronald (Lewis) 1931- CANR-7
Earlier sketch in CA 9-12R
Steel, Tex
See Ross, W(illiam) E(dward) D(aniel)
Steele, A(rchibald) T(rojan) 1903- CAP-2
Obituary 137
Earlier sketch in CA 19-20
Steele, Addison II
See Lupoff, Richard A(llen)
Steele, Alan 1905-1985 Obituary 115
Steele, Allen 1958- 136
Steele, Arthur R(obert) 1916- 9-12R
Steele, Chester K. CANR-26
Earlier sketches in CAP-2, CA 19-20
Steele, Colin Robert 1944- 104
Steele, Curtis
See Davis, Frederick C(lyde)
Steele, Dale
See Glut, Donald F(rank)
Steele, Dirk
See Plawin, Paul
Steele, Elizabeth 1921- 45-48
Steele, Erskine
See Henderson, Archibald
Steele, Fletcher 1885-1971 .... CAP-1
Earlier sketch in CA 13-14
Steele, Frank 1935- 37-40R
Steele, Fred I(rving) 1938- CANR-17
Earlier sketches in CA 45-48, CANR-2
Steele, Fritz
See Steele, Fred I(rving)
Steele, George P(eabody II) 1924- 1-4R
Steele, Gordon (Charles) 1892-1981 105
Obituary 102
Steele, Harwood R(obert) E(lmes) 1897- CAP-1
Earlier sketch in CA 13-16
Steele, Henry 1931- 41-44R
Steele, I(an) K(enneth) 1937- 45-48
Steele, Jack 1914-1980 109
Obituary 102
Steele, James B(ruce Jr.) 1943- 115
Brief entry 110
Steele, Mary Q(uintard Govan) 1922- CANR-22
Earlier sketches in CA 1-4R, CANR-6
See also MAICYA
See also SATA 3, 51
Steele, (Henry) Max(well) 1922- 25-28R
See also DLBY 80
See also SATA 10
Steele, Michael Rhoads 1945- 111
Steele, Peter (R.) 1935- 108
Steele, Phillip W(ayne) 1934- 61-64
Steele, R. David 1931- 135
Steele, Richard W(illiam) 1934- 134
Brief entry 107
Steele, Richard 1672-1729 ..... CDBLB 1660-1789
See also DLB 84, 101
Steele, Robert (Scott) 1917- 49-52
Steele, Thomas J(oseph) 1933- 61-64
Steele, Timothy (Reid) 1948- CANR-16
Earlier sketch in CA 93-96
See also CLC 45
See also DLB 120

Steele, Tommy
See Hicks, Thomas
Steele, Valerie (Fahnestock) 1955- 138
Steele, Wilbur Daniel 1886-1970 109
Obituary 29-32R
See also DLB 86
Steele, William O(wen) 1917-1979 ....CANR-2
Earlier sketch in CA 1-4R
See also MAICYA
See also SATA 1, 27, 51
Steelman, Robert J(ames) 1914- CANR-28
Earlier sketches in CA 69-72, CANR-11
Steely, John E(dward) 1922- 37-40R
Steen, Edwin B. 1901- 101
Steen, Frank
See Felstein, Ivor
Steen, John Warren Jr. 1925- 13-16R
Steen, Malcolm Harold 1928-1983 ....29-32R
Obituary 135
Steen, Marguerite 1894-1975 97-100
Obituary 61-64
Steen, Mike
See Steen, Malcolm Harold
Steen, Sara Jayne 1949- 106
Steenberg, Sven 1905- 37-40R
Steene, Birgitta 1928- 85-88
Steensma, Robert Charles 1930- 41-44R
Steenson, Gary P(aul) 1944- 107
Steer, Alfred G(ilbert) Jr. 1913- 45-48
Steer, Charlotte
See Hunter, Maud L(ily)
Steere, Daniel C(onrad) 1938- 93-96
Steere, Douglas V(an) 1901- 13-16R
Steere, Richard 1643(?)-1721 ....DLB 24
Steers, J(ames) A(lfred) 1899-1987 124
Steese, Edward 1902-1981 Obituary 105
Steese, Peter B(echler) 1933- 17-20R
Steeves, Frank Leslie 1921- 13-16R
Steeves, Harrison R(oss)
1881-1981 Obituary 104
Stefanelli, Vladimir Clain
See Clain-Stefanelli, Vladimir
Stefanics, Charlotte L(ouise) 1927- 116
Stefanik, Alfred T. 1939- ....SATA 55
Stefanile, Felix 1920- CANR-1
Earlier sketch in CA 45-48
Stefansson, Evelyn
See Nef, Evelyn Stefansson
Stefansson, Thorsteinn 1912- CANR-29
Earlier sketch in CA 77-80
Steffan, Alice Kennedy 1907- 5-8R
Steffan, Jack
See Steffan, Alice Kennedy
Steffan, Siobhan R.
See Goulart, Frances Sheridan
Steffan, Truman Guy 1910- 29-32R
Steffanson, Con
See Cassiday, Bruce (Bingham)
and Goulart, Ron(ald Joseph)
Steffek, Edwin F(rancis) 1912-1985 89-92
Obituary 118
Steffen, Albert 1884-1963 Obituary 93-96
Steffen, Jerome O(rville) 1942- 112
Steffen, Jonathan 1958- 135
Steffens, (Joseph) Lincoln
1866-1936 Brief entry 117
See also TCLC 20
Steffensmeier, Darrell J. 1942- 123
Stefferud, Alfred (Daniel) 1903- CAP-1
Earlier sketch in CA 13-16
Steffler, John 1947- CANR-33
Earlier sketch in CA 110
Steffre, Buford 1916- 5-8R
Stegall, Carrie Coffey 1908- CAP-2
Earlier sketch in CA 25-28
Stegeman, Janet Allais 1923- 128
See also Britton, Kate
See also SATA 49, 53
Stegeman, John F(oster) 1918- 17-20R
Stegenga, James A. 1937- 25-28R
Steger, Shelby 1906- 49-52
Steglich, W(infred) G(eorge) 1921- CANR-30
Earlier sketch in CA 45-48
Stegman, Michael A(llen) 1940- 41-44R
Stegner, Page 1937- CANR-10
Earlier sketch in CA 21-24R
Stegner, Wallace (Earle) 1909- CANR-21
Earlier sketches in CA 1-4R, CANR-1
See also CAAS 9
See also AITN 1
See also BEST 90:3
See also CLC 9, 49
See also DLB 9
See also MTCW
Stehling, Kurt R(ichard) 1919- Brief entry 110
Stehr, Hermann 1864-1940 ....DLB 66
Steible, Daniel J(oseph) 1912-1976 45-48
Obituary 103
Steichen, Edward 1879-1973 Obituary 41-44R
Steichen, Joanna T(aub) 1933- 132
Steichen, Paula 1943- 25-28R
Steig, Irwin 1901-1977 Obituary 73-76
Steig, William 1907- CANR-21
Earlier sketch in CA 77-80
See also AITN 1
See also CLR 2, 15
See also DLB 61
See also MAICYA
See also SATA 18, 70
Steiger, Andrew Jacob 1900- 5-8R
Steiger, Brad (E.) 1936- CANR-21
Earlier sketch in CA 33-36R
Steiger, Paul E(rnest) 1942- 77-80
Steigman, Benjamin
1889(?)-1974 Obituary 53-56
Steiman, Sidney 1922- 5-8R
Steimle, Edmund A(ugustus) 1907- 121
Stein, Aaron Marc 1906-1985 ....CANR-6
Obituary 117
Earlier sketch in CA 9-12R
Stein, Arnold (Sidney) 1915- Brief entry 114
Stein, Arthur (Benjamin) 1937- 29-32R
Stein, Ben
See Stein, Benjamin
Stein, Benjamin 1944- 106
Stein, Bob 1920- 37-40R
Stein, Bruno 1930- 37-40R
Stein, Calvert 1903-1982 ....29-32R
Obituary 125
Stein, Charles
See Schwalberg, Carol(yn Ernestine Stein)
Stein, Charles S. 1940- 21-24R
Stein, Charles W(arner) 1918- 116
Stein, Dona 77-80
Stein, Edward V(incent) 1920- 13-16R
Stein, Emanuel 1908-1985 Obituary 114
Stein, George P(hilip) 1917- 65-68
Stein, Gertrude 1874-1946 132
Brief entry 104
See also CDALB 1917-1929
See also DLB 4, 54, 86
See also MTCW
See also TCLC 1, 6, 28
See also WLC
Stein, Harry 1938- 61-64
Stein, Harry 1948- 128
Brief entry 120
Stein, Harve 1904- ....SATA 30
Stein, Herb 1928- 65-68
Stein, Herbert 1916- 106
Stein, Herman D(avid) 1917- CANR-30
Earlier sketch in CA 1-4R
Stein, Jack M(adison) 1914-1976 ....CANR-15
Obituary 103
Earlier sketch in CA 1-4R
Stein, Jan
See Hegeler, Sten
Stein, Jane Jacobson 1937- 97-100
Stein, Janice Gross 1943- 127
Stein, Jerome L(eon) 1928- 81-84
Stein, Jess 1914-1984 Obituary 113
Stein, Joseph 1912- CANR-31
Earlier sketch in CA 13-16R
Stein, Leo Daniel 1872-1947 Brief entry 107
See also DLB 4
Stein, Leon 1910- 17-20R
Stein, Leon 1912-1990 ....CANR-7
Obituary 130
Earlier sketch in CA 17-20R
Stein, Louis 1917- 138
Stein, M(eyer) L(ewis) 1920- CANR-13
Earlier sketch in CA 17-20R
See also SATA 6
Stein, Mark (Avrum) 1951- 118
Stein, Martha L(inda) 1942- 53-56
Stein, Maurice Robert 1926- 49-52
Stein, Michael B. 1940- CANR-32
Earlier sketch in CA 45-48
Stein, Mini 29-32R
See also SATA 2
Stein, Morris I(saac) 1921- CANR-1
Earlier sketch in CA 1-4R
Stein, Peter (Gonville) 1926- 21-24R
Stein, Philip L(awrence) 1939- 61-64
Stein, R(ichard) Conrad 1937- CANR-22
Earlier sketch in CA 41-44R
See also SATA 31
Stein, Rita F. 1922- Brief entry 106
Stein, Robert H(arry) 1935- 101
Stein, Robert 1924- 49-52
Stein, Roger B(reed) 1932- CANR-2
Earlier sketch in CA 45-48
Stein, Sandra Kovacs 1939- 106
Stein, Sara Bonnett ....SATA 34
Stein, Sol 1926- CANR-2
Earlier sketch in CA 49-52
See also AITN 1
Stein, Stanley J. 1920- Brief entry 108
Stein, Susan M. 1942- CANR-14
Earlier sketch in CA 37-40R
Stein, Thomas A. 1924- 45-48
Stein, Toby 1935- 5-8R
Stein, Walter 1924- 25-28R
Stein, William B. 1915- 104
Stein, William W(arner) 1921- 1-4R
Steinbach, Alexander Alan 1894-1978 85-88
Obituary 81-84
Steinbach, Meredith 1949- 107
Steinbeck, John (Ernst) 1902-1968 ....CANR-35
Obituary 25-28R
Earlier sketches in CA 1-4R, CANR-1
See also CDALB 1929-1941
See also CLC 1, 5, 9, 13, 21, 34, 45
See also DLB 7, 9
See also DLBD 2
See also MTCW
See also SATA 9
See also WLC
Steinberg, Aaron Zacharovich
1891-1975 Obituary 61-64
Steinberg, Alfred 1917- CANR-9
Earlier sketch in CA 5-8R
See also SATA 9
Steinberg, Charles S(ide) 1913-1978 ....CANR-4
Earlier sketch in CA 49-52
Steinberg, Danny D(avid Charles)
1931- CANR-14
Earlier sketch in CA 37-40R
Steinberg, David Joel 1937- 25-28R
Steinberg, Eleanor B(usick) 1936- 65-68
Steinberg, Erwin R(ay) 1920- CANR-12
Earlier sketch in CA 29-32R
Steinberg, Fannie 1899- 115
See also SATA 43
Steinberg, Fred J. 1933- 37-40R
See also SATA 4
Steinberg, Harriet 1954- 127
Steinberg, Israel 1903(?)-1983 Obituary 109
Steinberg, J(ay) Leonard 1930- 57-60
Steinberg, Jeffrey 1947(?)-1981 Obituary 104
Steinberg, Jonathan 1934- 21-24R
Steinberg, Joseph L(awrence) 1928- 25-28R
Steinberg, Judah 1861-1908 Brief entry 106
Steinberg, Leo 1920- CANR-17
Earlier sketches in CA 45-48, CANR-1
Steinberg, M. W. 1918- 127
Steinberg, Phillip Orso 1921- CANR-2
Earlier sketch in CA 5-8R
See also SATA 34
Steinberg, Rafael (Mark) 1927- CANR-9
Earlier sketch in CA 61-64
See also SATA 45
Steinberg, Rolf 1929- 132
Steinberg, S(igrid) H(enry) 1899-1969 ....CAP-1
Earlier sketch in CA 9-10
Steinberg, Saul 1914- 89-92
See also SATA 67
Steinbergh, Judith W(olinsky) 1943- CANR-1
Earlier sketch in CA 45-48
Steinbicker, Paul G(eorge) 1906- CAP-2
Earlier sketch in CA 19-20
Steinbreder, Harry John Jr.
1930-1985 Obituary 117
Steinbreder, Sandy
See Steinbreder, Harry John Jr.
Steinbrueck, Victor 1911- 13-16R
Steinbruner, John David 1941- 77-80
Steinbrunner, (Peter) Chris(tian) 1933- CANR-1
Earlier sketch in CA 45-48
Steincrohn, Peter J(oseph)
1899-1986 Obituary 118
Brief entry 112
Steinem, Gloria 1934- CANR-28
Earlier sketch in CA 53-56
See also CLC 63
See also MTCW
Steiner, Barbara A(nnette) 1934- CANR-30
Earlier sketches in CA 73-76, CANR-13
See also SAAS 13
See also SATA 13
Steiner, Barry H(oward) 1942- 137
Steiner, Barry R(aymond) 115
Steiner, Charlotte 1900-1981 ....SATA 45
Steiner, Claude 1935- 97-100
Steiner, Frederick 1949- CANR-39
Earlier sketch in CA 116
Steiner, Gary A(lbert) 1931-1966 ....9-12R
Obituary 103
Steiner, George A(lbert) 1912- CANR-7
Earlier sketch in CA 13-16R
Steiner, George 1929- CANR-31
Earlier sketch in CA 73-76
See also CLC 24
See also DLB 67
See also MTCW
See also SATA 62
Steiner, Gerolf 1908- 29-32R
Steiner, Gilbert Y(ale) 1924- Brief entry 115
Steiner, H. Arthur 1905- 5-8R
Steiner, Irene Hunter 1920- 97-100
Steiner, Joerg 1930- CANR-29
Earlier sketch in CA 108
See also SATA 35
Steiner, Jorg
See Steiner, Joerg
Steiner, Kurt 1912- CANR-7
Earlier sketch in CA 17-20R
Steiner, Lee R. 1901- CAP-1
Earlier sketch in CA 13-14
Steiner, Paul CANR-37
Earlier sketches in CA 9-12R, CANR-4
Steiner, Peter O(tto) 1922- CANR-14
Earlier sketch in CA 37-40R
Steiner, Ralph 1899-1986 Obituary 119
Brief entry 113
Steiner, Roger J(acob) 1924- CANR-32
Earlier sketch in CA 45-48
Steiner, Rudolf 1861-1925 Brief entry 107
See also TCLC 13
Steiner, Shari 1941- 73-76
Steiner, Stan(ley) 1925-1987 ....CANR-39
Obituary 121
Earlier sketches in CA 45-48, CANR-1, 16
See also SATA 14, 50
Steiner, Susan Clemmer 1947- 115
Steiner, Thomas R(obert) 1934- 45-48
Steiner, Vera P(olgar) John
See John-Steiner, Vera P(olgar)
Steiner, Wendy 1949- CANR-14
Earlier sketch in CA 81-84
Steiner, Zara S(hakow) 1928- 129
Steiner-Prag, Hugo 1880-1945 ....SATA 32
Steinert, Marlis G(ertrud) 81-84
Steinfels, Peter (Francis) 1941- Brief entry 116
Steingold, Fred S(aul) 1936- 109
Steinhardt, Anne Elizabeth 1941- 104
Steinhardt, Herschel S. 1910- CAP-2
Earlier sketch in CA 23-24
Steinhardt, Milton 1909- 77-80
Steinhardt, Nancy Shatzman 1954- 135
Steinhart, Carol E(lder) 1935- 57-60
Steinhauer, Harry 1905- CANR-1
Earlier sketch in CA 1-4R
Steinhaus, Arthur H. 1897-1970 ....CAP-1
Earlier sketch in CA 19-20
Steinhaus, John Edward 1917- 127
Steinheimer, Richard (V.) 1929- 123
Steinhoff, Dan 1911- 77-80
Steinhoff, William (Richard) 1914- 85-88
Steinitz, Kate T(rauman) 1889-1975 ....CAP-2
Earlier sketch in CA 23-24
Steinitz, Paul 1909- 104
Steinke, Ann E(lizabeth) 1946- CANR-32
Earlier sketch in CA 113
Steinke, Peter L(ouis) 1938- 29-32R
Steinkraus, Warren E(dward) 1922- 21-24R
Steinle, John G(erard) 1916-1990 ....9-12R
Obituary 132
Steinle, Paul (Michael) 1939- 77-80
Steinman, Lisa Malinowski 1950- 69-72
Steinman, Michael 1952- 134
Steinmann, Anne G. 1906(?)-1987 Obituary 121
Steinmann, Martin Jr. 1915- CANR-26
Earlier sketch in CA 1-4R
Steinmetz, Eulalie
See Ross, Eulalie Steinmetz
Steinmetz, Lawrence L(eo) 1938- CANR-11
Earlier sketch in CA 21-24R
Steinmetz, Leon 136
Steinmetz, Paul B. 1928- 135
Steinmetz, Rollin C. 1912(?)-1986 Obituary 121
Steinmetz, Urban G. 1920- CANR-10
Earlier sketch in CA 25-28R
Steintrager, James A(lvin) 1936- 93-96
Steinwedel, Louis William 1943- 37-40R
Steirman, Hy 1921- 29-32R
Steiss, Alan Walter 1937- CANR-28
Earlier sketches in CA 29-32R, CANR-12
Steitz, Edward S(tephen) 1920-1990 69-72
Obituary 131
Stekert, Ellen J(ane) 1935- 33-36R
Stekler, Herman O. 1932- 17-20R
Stell, Aaron 1911- 57-60
Stell, Geoffrey (Percival) 1944- 124
Stellingwerf, Steve(n Lee) 1962- 138
Stellman, Jeanne M(ager) 1947- 102
Stellman, Steven D(ale) 1945- 85-88
Steltenkamp, Michael F(rancis) 1950- 112
Stelter, Gilbert Arthur 1933- CANR-15
Earlier sketch in CA 41-44R
Steltzer, Ulli 1923- 104
Stelzer, Dick 1950- 107
Stelzig, Eugene Louis 1943- 81-84
Stem, Thad(deus Garland) Jr.
1916-1980 97-100
Obituary 101
Stember, Charles Herbert 1916-1982 ....21-24R
Obituary 135
Stemp, Isay 1922- 29-32R
Stemp, Robin (Jenniver Pamela) 1944- 107
Stempel, Guido H(ermann) III 1928- 77-80
Stempel, John Dallas 1938- 110
Stempel, Thomas Ritter 1941- 110
Stempel, Tom
See Stempel, Thomas Ritter
Sten, Christopher (W.) 1944- 137
Stenberger, Marten 1898- CANR-5
Earlier sketch in CA 5-8R
Stendahl, Krister 1921- CANR-12
Earlier sketch in CA 17-20R
Stendhal 1783-1842 ....DLB 119
See also WLC
Stene, Edwin O(tto) 1900- CAP-2
Earlier sketch in CA 21-22
Steneck, Nicholas H. 1940- 106
Steneman, Shep 1945- 107
Stenerson, Douglas C. 1920- 37-40R
Stengel, Richard 1955- 136
Stenhouse, David 1932- 89-92
Stenius, George
See Seaton, George
Stensboel, Ottar 1930- 69-72
Stenson, Frederick 1951- 113
Stent, Gunther S(iegmund) 1924- 29-32R
Stenton, Doris Mary (Parsons)
1894-1971 Obituary 104
Stenus
See Huxley, Herbert H(enry)
Stenzel, Anne K(atherine) 1911- 57-60
Stenzel, George 1910- 45-48
Stepanchev, Stephen 1915- CANR-7
Earlier sketch in CA 17-20R
Stepanian, Michael 1939- 45-48
Stephan, John J(ason) 1941- 41-44R
Stephan, Leslie (Bates) 1933- CANR-24
Earlier sketches in CA 21-24R, CANR-9
Stephan, Ruth 1910- 5-8R
Stephen, David 1910- 106
Stephen, George 1926- 102
Stephen, Jan 1933- 1-4R
Stephen, Leslie 1832-1904 Brief entry 123
See also DLB 57
See also TCLC 23
Stephen, Martin 1949- 135
Stephen, Parel Lukose 1898- CAP-1
Earlier sketch in CA 9-10
Stephen, R. J.
See Barrett, Norman (S.)
Stephen, Sid 1942- 105
Stephen, Sir Leslie
See Stephen, Leslie
Stephen, Virginia
See Woolf, (Adeline) Virginia
Stephens, A. Ray 1932- CANR-13
Earlier sketch in CA 77-80
Stephens, Alan 1925- 17-20R
Stephens, Alexander H. 1812-1883 ....DLB 47
Stephens, Alice Barber 1858-1932 ....SATA 66
Stephens, Ann Sophia (Winterbotham)
1810-1886 ....DLB 3, 73
Stephens, C(harles) Ralph 1943- 122
Stephens, Casey
See Wagner, Sharon B.
Stephens, Charles
See Goldin, Stephen
Stephens, Charles Asbury
1844(?)-1931 ....DLB 42
Stephens, Donald G. 1931- 21-24R

Stephens, Edna Buell 1903- CANR-14
Earlier sketch in CA 37-40R
Stephens, Edward Carl 1924- 21-24R
Stephens, Eve
See
Ward-Thomas, Evelyn Bridget Patricia Stephens
Stephens, Frances
See Bentley, Margaret
Stephens, Henrietta Henkle
1909-1983 .... CANR-6
Obituary 109
Earlier sketch in CA 9-12R
See also Buckmaster, Henrietta
Stephens, Ian Melville 1903-1984 Obituary 112
Stephens, J(ohn) M(ortimer) 1901- 13-16R
Stephens, Jack Edward (Jr.) 1955- 133
Stephens, James Charles 1915- CANR-3
Earlier sketch in CA 5-8R
Stephens, James 1882(?)-1950 Brief entry 104
See also DLB 19
See also TCLC 4
Stephens, Jeanne
See Hager, Jean
Stephens, Joyce 1941- 69-72
Stephens, Lester D(ow) 1933- CANR-32
Earlier sketch in CA 45-48
Stephens, M(ichael) G(regory) 1946- CANR-3
Earlier sketch in CA 49-52
Stephens, Martha (Thomas) 1937- 77-80
Stephens, Mary Jo 1935- 37-40R
See also SATA 8
Stephens, Meic 1938- 65-68
Stephens, Michael D(awson) 1936- CANR-22
Earlier sketches in CA 57-60, CANR-7
Stephens, Mitchell 1949- 136
Stephens, Otis H(ammond) Jr. 1936- 65-68
Stephens, Reed
See Donaldson, Stephen R.
Stephens, Robert O(ren) 1928- 25-28R
Stephens, Rockwell R(ittenhouse) 1900- 53-56
Stephens, Rosemary 1924- 77-80
Stephens, Thomas M. 1931- 29-32R
Stephens, W(illiam) P(eter) 1934- CANR-28
Earlier sketches in CA 29-32R, CANR-12
Stephens, W(illiam) Richard 1932- 29-32R
Stephens, Wade C. 1932- 21-24R
Stephens, Will Beth 1918- 37-40R
Stephens, William M(cLain) 1925- 57-60
See also SATA 21
Stephens, William N(ewton) 1927- CANR-1
Earlier sketch in CA 1-4R
Stephenson, Alan M. G. Obituary 113
Stephenson, Andrew M(ichael) 1946- 124
Brief entry 118
Stephenson, David 1947- 118
Stephenson, Gilbert T(homas)
1884-1972 .... CAP-1
Obituary 37-40R
Earlier sketch in CA 17-18
Stephenson, Howard 1893-1978 .... 37-40R
Stephenson, Jean 1892-1979 Obituary 85-88
Stephenson, John B(ell) 1937- 61-64
Stephenson, John Edward Drayton
1928- Brief entry 112
Stephenson, Matthew A(rnold) 1935- 45-48
Stephenson, Maureen 1927- CANR-38
Earlier sketches in CA 85-88, CANR-16
Stephenson, Neal 1959- 122
Stephenson, (William) Ralph (Ewing)
1910- 17-20R
Stephenson, Richard M(anning) 1918- 109
Stephenson, Wendell Holmes
1899-1970 .... CANR-3
Earlier sketch in CA 1-4R
Stepka, Milan
See Benes, Jan
Stepp, Ann 1935- 106
See also SATA 29
Stepto, Michele 1946- 128
See also SATA 61
Stepto, Robert B(urns) 1945- 101
See also BW
Steptoe, John (Lewis) 1950-1989 .... CANR-26
Obituary 129
Earlier sketches in CA 49-52, CANR-3
See also BW
See also CLR 2, 12
See also MAICYA
See also SATA 8, 63
Steptoe, Lydia
See Barnes, Djuna
Steptoe, Patrick C(hristopher)
1913-1988 Obituary 125
Sterba, Gunther Hans Wenzel 1922- 5-8R
Sterba, Richard F(rancis) 1898- 124
Sterchi, Beat 1949- .... CLC 65
Stercho, Peter George 1919- 49-52
Sterland, E(rnest) G(eorge) 1919- 65-68
Sterling, Anthony
See Caesar, (Eu)Gene (Lee)
Sterling, Brett
See Bradbury, Ray (Douglas)
and Hamilton, Edmond
and Samachson, Joseph
Sterling, Bruce 1954- 119
See also CLC 72
Sterling, Chandler W(infield) 1911- 21-24R
Sterling, Claire 1919(?)- 123
Sterling, Donald J(ustus) Jr. 1927- 77-80
Sterling, Dorothy 1913- CANR-28
Earlier sketches in CA 9-12R, CANR-5
See also CLR 1
See also MAICYA
See also SAAS 2
See also SATA 1
Sterling, George 1869-1926 Brief entry 117
See also DLB 54
See also TCLC 20
Sterling, Helen
See Watts, Helen L. Hoke
Sterling, James 1701-1763 .... DLB 24
Sterling, John 1806-1844 .... DLB 116
Sterling, Maria Sandra
See Floren, Lee
Sterling, Philip 1907-1989 49-52
Obituary 129
See also SATA 8, 63
Sterling, Richard W(hitney) 1922- 45-48
Sterling, Robert R. 1931- CANR-28
Earlier sketch in CA 29-32R
Sterling, Sandra
See Floren, Lee
Sterling, Theodor D(avid) 1923- 25-28R
Stermer, Bill 1947- 110
Stern, Alfred 1899- 53-56
Stern, Barbara L.
See Lang, Barbara
Stern, Bill 1907-1971 Obituary 89-92
Stern, Boris 1892-1984 .... CAP-2
Obituary 113
Earlier sketch in CA 17-18
Stern, Carl 1937- 97-100
Stern, Catherine B(rieger)
1894-1973 Obituary 37-40R
Stern, Clarence A. 1913- 17-20R
Stern, Curt 1902-1981 Obituary 105
Stern, Daniel N. 1934- 136
Stern, Daniel 1928- CANR-5
Earlier sketch in CA 5-8R
Stern, David 1949- 138
Stern, Donald A. 1928(?)-1975 Obituary 57-60
Stern, E. Mark 1929- 37-40R
Stern, Edith Mendel 1901-1975 Obituary 57-60
Stern, Edward Severin 1924- 53-56
Stern, Elizabeth
See Uhr, Elizabeth
Stern, Ellen Norman 1927- CANR-14
Earlier sketch in CA 37-40R
See also SATA 26
Stern, Frances Meritt 1938- 112
Stern, Frederick Curtis 1929- 108
Stern, Frederick M.
1890(?)-1977 Obituary 69-72
Stern, Fritz 1926- CANR-1
Earlier sketch in CA 1-4R
Stern, G(ladys) B(ertha)
1890-1973 Obituary 45-48
Stern, George G(ordon) 1923-1974 .... CAP-2
Earlier sketch in CA 29-32
Stern, Gerald M(ann) 1937- 69-72
Stern, Gerald 1925- CANR-28
Earlier sketch in CA 81-84
See also CLC 40
See also DLB 105
Stern, Geraldine 1907- 101
Stern, Gerd Jacob 1928- Brief entry 106
Stern, Guy 1922- 41-44R
Stern, Harold P. 1922-1977 Obituary 69-72
Stern, Harold S. 1923(?)-1976 Obituary 65-68
Stern, Harry Joshua 1897- 69-72
Stern, Henry L. 1899- 97-100
Stern, J(ulius) David 1886-1971 Obituary 104
Stern, J(oseph) P(eter Maria)
1920-1991 .... CANR-10
Obituary 136
Earlier sketch in CA 21-24R
Stern, James 1904- 21-24R
Stern, Jane 1946- CANR-10
Earlier sketch in CA 61-64
Stern, Jay B(enjamin) 1929- CANR-18
Earlier sketch in CA 25-28R
Stern, Jean Gordon 1904(?)-1985 Obituary 117
Stern, Karl 1906-1975 .... CANR-12
Obituary 61-64
Earlier sketch in CA 9-12R
Stern, Laurence (Marcus) 1929-1979 85-88
Obituary 89-92
Stern, Louis William 1935- CANR-18
Earlier sketch in CA 25-28R
Stern, Madeleine B(ettina) 1912- CANR-22
Earlier sketches in CA 17-20R, CANR-7
See also SATA 14
Stern, Madeleine B. 1912- .... DLB 111
Stern, Malcolm H(enry) 1915- 73-76
Stern, Marie 1909- 45-48
Stern, Martha Eccles Dodd
1908-1990 Obituary 132
Stern, Michael 1910- CAP-2
Earlier sketch in CA 23-24
Stern, Milton R(alph) 1928- CANR-15
Earlier sketch in CA 41-44R
Stern, Nancy (B.) 1944- CANR-28
Earlier sketch in CA 110
Stern, Paula 1945- 102
Stern, Philip M(aurice) 1926- 104
Obituary 137
Stern, Philip Van Doren 1900-1984 .... CANR-6
Obituary 113
Earlier sketch in CA 5-8R
See also SATA 13, 39
Stern, Richard (Gustave) 1928- CANR-25
Earlier sketches in CA 1-4R, CANR-1
See also CLC 4, 39
See also DLBY 87
Stern, Richard Martin 1915- CANR-18
Earlier sketches in CA 1-4R, CANR-2
Stern, Robert A. M. 1939- CANR-25
Earlier sketch in CA 29-32R
Stern, Robert M. 1927- CANR-10
Earlier sketch in CA 21-24R
Stern, Rudi 1936- Brief entry 115
Stern, S. M.
See Stern, Samuel Miklos
Stern, Samuel Miklos 1920-1969 Obituary 111
Stern, Sheila (Frances) 1922- 136
Stern, Simon 1943- 89-92
See also SATA 15
Stern, Steve 1947- 132
Brief entry 126
Stern, Stewart 1922- Brief entry 113
See also DLB 26
Stern, Stuart
See Rae, Hugh C(rauford)
Stern, Susan (Tanenbaum)
1943-1976 Obituary 65-68
Stern, Sydney Ladensohn 1947- 134
Stern, Tracy 1953- 129
Stern, William B(ernhard) 1910-1972 .... CAP-1
Earlier sketch in CA 13-16
Stern, Wilma 1940- 138
Stern, Zelda 1949- 116
Sternberg, Cecilia 1908-1983 .... CANR-39
Obituary 111
Earlier sketch in CA 73-76
Sternberg, Jacques 1923- Brief entry 111
Sternberg, Josef von 1894-1969 81-84
See also CLC 20
Sternberg, Martin L(eo) A(ltar) 1925- 107
Sternberg, Patricia 1930- 118
Sternberg, Robert J(effrey) 1949- 126
Brief entry 119
Sternberg, Vernon (Arthur)
1915-1979 Obituary 104
Sternberger, Dolf 1907- 104
Sterne, Emma Gelders 1894- CANR-5
Earlier sketch in CA 5-8R
See also SATA 6
Sterne, Laurence
1713-1768 .... CDBLB 1660-1789
See also DLB 39
See also WLC
Sterne, Richard S(tephen) 1921- 13-16R
Sterner, Lewis George 1894- 5-8R
Sterner, R. Eugene 1912- CANR-3
Earlier sketch in CA 9-12R
Sternfeld, Robert 1917- 81-84
Sternfield, Allen 1930- 53-56
Sternheim, (William Adolf) Carl
1878-1942 Brief entry 105
See also DLB 56, 118
See also TCLC 8
Sternlicht, Sanford 1931- CANR-26
Earlier sketches in CA 25-28R, CANR-10
Sternlieb, George 1928- CANR-25
Earlier sketches in CA 21-24R, CANR-8
Sternsher, Bernard 1925- 9-12R
Sterry, Rick 1938- 25-28R
Stertz, Eda 1921- 104
Stessin, Lawrence 1911- 9-12R
Stetler, Charles E(dward) 1927- 65-68
Stetler, Russell (Dearnley Jr.) 1945- 41-44R
Stetson, Damon 1915- 85-88
Stetson, Erlene 108
Stettler, Howard Frederic 1919- 5-8R
Stettner, Irving 1922- CANR-37
Earlier sketches in CA 77-80, CANR-16
Steurt, Marjorie Rankin 1888- 13-16R
See also SATA 10
Steven, Hugh 1931- CANR-14
Earlier sketch in CA 41-44R
Stevens, Anita 1911- Brief entry 110
Stevens, Anthony (George) 1933- 110
Stevens, Ardis 1921- 45-48
Stevens, Art 1935- 124
Stevens, (John) Austin 53-56
Stevens, Austin N(eil) 1930- 104
Stevens, Bernice A. 37-40R
Stevens, Blaine
See Whittington, Harry (Benjamin)
Stevens, Bryna 1924- 136
See also SATA 65
Stevens, Carl
See Obstfeld, Raymond
Stevens, Carla M(cBride) 1928- CANR-12
Earlier sketch in CA 69-72
See also SATA 13
Stevens, Cat
See Georgiou, Steven Demetre
Stevens, Charles W. 1955- 136
Stevens, Christopher
See Tabori, Paul
Stevens, Christopher 1948- 119
Stevens, Clifford 1926- CANR-6
Earlier sketch in CA 9-12R
Stevens, Clysle
See Wade, John Stevens
Stevens, Dan J.
See Overholser, Wayne D.
Stevens, David Harrison 1884-1980 77-80
Obituary 93-96
Stevens, Denis William 1922- CANR-3
Earlier sketch in CA 9-12R
Stevens, Diane 1944- 65-68
Stevens, E. S.
See Drower, E(thel) S(tefana May)
Stevens, Edmund William 1910- 109
Obituary 137
Stevens, Edward 1928- CANR-11
Earlier sketch in CA 29-32R
Stevens, Edwin L(ockwood) 1913-1987 .... 21-24R
Obituary 122
Stevens, Eleanour V(irginia) 1926- 29-32R
Stevens, Elisabeth (Goss) 1929- 110
Stevens, Fae Hewston
See Stevens, Frances Isted
Stevens, Frances Isted 1907- CAP-1
Earlier sketch in CA 9-10
Stevens, Franklin 1933- 29-32R
See also SATA 6
Stevens, George (Cooper) Jr. 1932- 125
Brief entry 118
Stevens, George Putnam 1918- 45-48
Stevens, George 1904(?)-1985 Obituary 116
Stevens, Georgiana G(erlinger) 1904- CAP-1
Earlier sketch in CA 17-18
Stevens, Gerald 1909- 5-8R
Stevens, Graeme R(oy) 1932- 118
Stevens, Gwendolyn 1944- 104
See also SATA 33
Stevens, Halsey 1908-1989 .... 25-28R
Obituary 127
Stevens, Harold 1917- 89-92
Stevens, Harvey A(lonzo) 1913- 89-92
Stevens, Holly 1924- 25-28R
Obituary 137
Stevens, J. D.
See Rowland, D(onald) S(ydney)
Stevens, James F. 1892-1971 Obituary 33-36R
Stevens, James (Richard) 1940- CANR-16
Earlier sketch in CA 93-96
Stevens, Jane Greengold 1945- 108
Stevens, Joan 1908- CANR-2
Earlier sketch in CA 5-8R
Stevens, John
See Tubb, E(dwin) C(harles)
Stevens, Joseph C(harles) 1929- 17-20R
Stevens, Joseph E. 1956- 128
Stevens, Kathleen 1936- CANR-39
Earlier sketch in CA 116
See also SATA 49
Stevens, L(ewell) Robert 1932- 111
Stevens, Laird 1953- 128
Stevens, Lauren R(ogers) 1938- 5-8R
Stevens, Lee
See Leigh, Stephen (W.)
Stevens, Leonard A. 1920- CANR-12
Earlier sketch in CA 17-20R
See also SATA 67
Stevens, Lucile Vernon 1899- 61-64
See also SATA 59
Stevens, Mark 1951- 122
See also CLC 34
Stevens, Martin 1927- 13-16R
Stevens, Michael 1919- 53-56
Stevens, Norma Young 1927- 21-24R
Stevens, Pam
See Gilbert, George
Stevens, Patricia Bunning 1931- 53-56
See also SATA 27
Stevens, Paul 1946- 123
Stevens, Peter
See Geis, Darlene Stern
Stevens, Peter S(mith) 1936- 53-56
Stevens, Peter 1927- 93-96
Stevens, R(obert) B(ocking) 1933- CANR-9
Earlier sketch in CA 21-24R
Stevens, R. L.
See Hoch, Edward D(entinger)
Stevens, Richard P. 1931- CANR-10
Earlier sketch in CA 21-24R
Stevens, Robert D(avid) 1921- 112
Stevens, Robert Tyler
See Staples, Reginald Thomas
Stevens, Robert Warren 1918-1987 .... CANR-1
Obituary 122
Earlier sketch in CA 45-48
Stevens, Roger (Bentham)
1906-1980 Obituary 105
Stevens, Rolland E(lwell) 1915- 81-84
Stevens, Rosemary (Anne) 1935- 85-88
Stevens, S. P.
See Palestrant, Simon S.
Stevens, S(tanley) S(mith)
1906-1973 Obituary 116
Stevens, Serita (Deborah) 1949- 119
See also SATA 70
Stevens, Shane 1941- 21-24R
Stevens, Sharon 1949- 77-80
Stevens, Shira
See Stevens, Serita (Deborah)
Stevens, Suzanne H. 1938- 136
Stevens, Sylvester K(irby) 1904-1974 .... CAP-1
Obituary 45-48
Earlier sketch in CA 13-16
Stevens, Thomas Terry Hoar
1911-1990 Obituary 130
Stevens, Tricia
See Pearl, Jacques Bain
Stevens, Trisha
See Pearl, Jacques Bain
Stevens, Wallace 1879-1955 124
Brief entry 104
See also CDALB 1929-1941
See also DLB 54
See also MTCW
See also TCLC 3, 12, 45
See also WLC
Stevens, William W(ilson) 1914- 37-40R
Stevens, William 1925- 21-24R
Stevens-Arroyo, Antonio M. 1941- 120
Stevenson, Adlai E(wing) 1900-1965 .... CAP-1
Earlier sketch in CA 13-16
Stevenson, Anna (M.) 1905- .... SATA 12
Stevenson, Anne (Katharine) 1933- CANR-33
Earlier sketches in CA 17-20R, CANR-9
See also CAAS 9
See also CLC 7, 33
See also DLB 40
See also MTCW
Stevenson, Augusta 1869(?)-1976 .... 1-4R
Obituary 65-68
See also SATA 2, 26
Stevenson, (William) Bruce 1906- 49-52

Stevenson, Burton Egbert 1872-1962 102
Obituary 89-92
See also SATA 25
Stevenson, Carol Dornfeld 1931- 5-8R
Stevenson, Charles
1908(?)-1979 Obituary 85-88
Stevenson, Christopher Sinclair
See Sinclair-Stevenson, Christopher
Stevenson, David Lloyd 1910-1975 .... CAP-2
Obituary 57-60
Earlier sketch in CA 23-24
Stevenson, David 1942- CANR-28
Earlier sketch in CA 109
Stevenson, Dorothy E(mily) 1892-1973 ..... CAP-1
Obituary 49-52
Earlier sketch in CA 13-16
Stevenson, Drew 1947- ....SATA 60
Stevenson, Dwight E(shelman) 1906- CANR-1
Earlier sketch in CA 1-4R
Stevenson, Elizabeth 1919- CANR-26
Earlier sketch in CA 1-4R
Stevenson, Florence CANR-16
Earlier sketch in CA 97-100
Stevenson, George J(ames) 1924- 9-12R
Stevenson, Gloria 1945- 61-64
Stevenson, Grace Thomas 1900- 37-40R
Stevenson, Harold W(illiam) 1921- 25-28R
Stevenson, Henry M(iller) 1914- 77-80
Stevenson, Herbert Frederick 1906- CANR-2
Earlier sketch in CA 5-8R
Stevenson, Hugh A(lexander) 1935- 112
Stevenson, Ian (Pretyman)
1918- Brief entry 115
Stevenson, Ian Ralph 1943- 102
Stevenson, J. P.
See Haldane-Stevenson, James Patrick
Stevenson, James Patrick
See Haldane-Stevenson, James Patrick
Stevenson, James 1929- 115
See also CLR 17
See also MAICYA
See also SATA 34, 42, 71
Stevenson, Janet 1913- CANR-29
Earlier sketch in CA 13-16R
See also SATA 8
Stevenson, John Albert
1890(?)-1979 Obituary 89-92
Stevenson, John P.
See Grierson, Edward
Stevenson, L(eland) W(ells) 1916- 107
Stevenson, Laura Caroline 1946- 120
Stevenson, Leslie (Forster) 1943- 65-68
Stevenson, (Arthur) Lionel 1902-1973 103
Obituary 45-48
Stevenson, Michael Ian 1953- 103
Stevenson, Randall 1953- 128
Stevenson, Richard
See Lipez, Richard
Stevenson, Robert Louis (Balfour)
1850-1894 .... CDBLB 1890-1914
See also CLR 10, 11
See also DLB 18, 57
See also MAICYA
See also WLC
See also YABC 2
Stevenson, Robert (Murrell) 1916- CANR-1
Earlier sketch in CA 1-4R
Stevenson, Robert 1905-1986 Obituary 120
Stevenson, Suzanne Silvercruys
1898(?)-1973 Obituary 41-44R
Stevenson, T(homas) H(ulbert) 1919- 61-64
Stevenson, Tom 1899(?)-1982 Obituary 106
Stevenson, Vera Kemp 1920- 57-60
Stevenson, Victoria F.
1878(?)-1973 Obituary 41-44R
Stevenson, W(illiam) Taylor 1928- CANR-18
Earlier sketch in CA 25-28R
Stevenson, (Stanley) Warren 1933- 41-44R
Stevenson, William 1925- 13-16R
Stevermer, C. J.
See Stevermer, Caroline
Stevermer, Caroline 1955- 136
Stevick, Philip T. 1930- 132
Steward, F(rederick) C(ampion) 1904- 41-44R
Steward, Hal D(avid) 1922- 69-72
Steward, Julian H. 1902-1972 Obituary 33-36R
Steward, Samuel M(orris) 1909- 112
Stewart, A(gnes) C(harlotte) 77-80
See also SATA 15
Stewart, A(nthony) T(erence) Q(uincey)
1929- 25-28R
Stewart, (John) Allan 1939- 1-4R
Stewart, Allegra 1899- 45-48
Stewart, Angus (J. M.) 1936- 106
Stewart, Bertie Ann Gardner 1912- 5-8R
Stewart, Bill 1942(?)-1979 Obituary 89-92
Stewart, Charles
See Zurhorst, Charles (Stewart Jr.)
Stewart, Charles J(oseph) 1936- 41-44R
Stewart, Charles T(odd) Jr. 1922- 101
Stewart, Christina Duff 1926- 65-68
Stewart, Cochrane
See Stewart, Kenneth
Stewart, D(avid) H(ugh) 1926- 21-24R
Stewart, Daniel K(enneth) 1925- 29-32R
Stewart, David
See Politella, Dario
Stewart, Desmond (Stirling)
1924-1981 ....CANR-30
Obituary 104
Earlier sketch in CA 37-40R
Stewart, Donald Charles 1930- 37-40R
Stewart, Donald H(enderson) 1911- 29-32R
Stewart, Donald Ogden 1894-1980 81-84
Obituary 101
See also DLB 4, 11, 26
Stewart, Dorothy Mary 1917-1965 Obituary 104
Stewart, Douglas (Alexander) 1913- 81-84
Stewart, Edgar I(rving) 1900- 5-8R
Stewart, Edith Hamilton 1883- CAP-1
Earlier sketch in CA 11-12
Stewart, Elbert Wilton 1916- 37-40R
Stewart, Eleanor
See Porter, Eleanor H(odgman)
Stewart, Elizabeth Grey
See Reed, Elizabeth Stewart
Stewart, Elizabeth Laing 1907- 49-52
See also SATA 6
Stewart, Ella Winter 1898-1980 Obituary 101
Stewart, Eve
See Napier, Priscilla
Stewart, Frank 1946- CANR-20
Earlier sketch in CA 104
Stewart, Fred Mustard 1936- 37-40R
Stewart, Garrett (Fitzgerald) 1945- 93-96
Stewart, George Jr. 1848-1906 .... DLB 99
Stewart, George Rippey 1895-1980 ......CANR-3
Obituary 101
Earlier sketch in CA 1-4R
See also DLB 8
See also SATA 3, 23
Stewart, George 1892-1972 Obituary 33-36R
Stewart, Hal D(ouglas) 1899- CAP-1
Earlier sketch in CA 13-16
Stewart, Harold C. 1891(?)-1976 Obituary 69-72
Stewart, Harold Frederick 1916- 69-72
Stewart, Harris B(ates) Jr. 1922- CANR-35
Earlier sketch in CA 45-48
Stewart, Hilary 1924- CANR-16
Earlier sketch in CA 93-96
Stewart, Horace Floyd Jr. 1928- 49-52
Stewart, J(ohn) I(nnes) M(ackintosh)
1906- 85-88
See also CAAS 3
See also CLC 7, 14, 32
See also MTCW
Stewart, James Alexander 1948- 113
Stewart, James Brewer 1940- CANR-32
Earlier sketch in CA 29-32R
Stewart, James S(tuart) 1896-1990 ....9-12R
Obituary 132
Stewart, Jean
See Newman, Mona Alice Jean
Stewart, Jim
See Stewart, James Alexander
Stewart, John B(enjamin) 1924- 9-12R
Stewart, John G(ilman) 1935- Brief entry 112
Stewart, John (William) 1920- 33-36R
See also SATA 14
Stewart, John 1904(?)-1985 Obituary 116
Stewart, John 1933- CANR-37
Earlier sketches in CA 97-100, CANR-16
Stewart, John 1941- 97-100
Stewart, Judith
See Polley, Judith (Anne)
Stewart, Judith Anne
See Maciel, Judi(th Anne)
Stewart, K(athleen) Alison Clarke
See Clarke-Stewart, K(athleen) Alison
Stewart, Katharine Jeanne (Dark) 1914- 9-12R
Stewart, Kaye
See Howe, Doris Kathleen
Stewart, Kenneth N. 1901-1978 Obituary 77-80
Stewart, Kenneth 1918-1985 Obituary 118
Stewart, Kerry
See Stewart, Linda
Stewart, Lawrence D(elbert) 1926- 89-92
Stewart, Lawrence H(oyle) 1922- 17-20R
Stewart, Linda 101
Stewart, Margaret 1912- CANR-18
Earlier sketch in CA 25-28R
Stewart, Marie M(cCaffery) 1899- 5-8R
Stewart, Mark Armstrong 1929- 89-92
Stewart, Mary (Florence Elinor) 1916- CANR-1
Earlier sketch in CA 1-4R
See also CLC 7, 35
See also SATA 12
Stewart, Mary Rainbow
See Stewart, Mary (Florence Elinor)
Stewart, Maxwell S(lutz)
1900-1990 Obituary 131
Stewart, (Robert) Michael (Maitland)
1906-1990 ....CANR-22
Obituary 131
Earlier sketch in CA 106
Stewart, Michael 1924(?)-1987 Obituary 123
Stewart, Michael 1933- 116
Stewart, Michael 1945- 138
Stewart, Natacha
See Ullman, Natacha
Stewart, Oliver 1895-1980 ....CANR-5
Earlier sketch in CA 5-8R
Stewart, Omer C(all) 1908- 127
Stewart, Pat(ricia) 1944- 97-100
Stewart, Paul D(ekker) 1918- 1-4R
Stewart, Philip Robert 1940- 29-32R
Stewart, Phyllis Langton 1933- Brief entry 106
Stewart, Ramona 1922- CANR-6
Earlier sketch in CA 1-4R
Stewart, Randall 1896-1964 ....CANR-1
Earlier sketch in CA 1-4R
See also DLB 103
Stewart, Rex William 1907-1967 Obituary 110
Stewart, Rhea Talley 1915- 41-44R
Stewart, Robert G(ordon) 1931- 65-68
Stewart, Robert Neil 1891- 9-12R
See also SATA 7
Stewart, Robert T. 1920(?)-1977 Obituary 73-76
Stewart, Robert Wilson 1935- 49-52
Stewart, Rosemary (Gordon) CANR-15
Earlier sketch in CA 37-40R
Stewart, Sam
See Stewart, Linda
Stewart, Scott
See Zaffo, George J.
Stewart, Seumas 1919- 61-64
Stewart, Shelia 1928- 21-24R
Stewart, Stanley N(ordahl) 1931- 17-20R
Stewart, Suzanne 61-64
Stewart, Vincent (Astor Jr.) 1939- 29-32R
Stewart, W(illiam) A(lexander) Campbell
1915- 13-16R
Stewart, W(alter) P. 1924- .... SATA 53
Stewart, Walter Bingham 1913- CANR-16
Earlier sketch in CA 85-88
Stewart, Walter 1931- 129
Stewart, Will
See Williamson, John Stewart
Stewart, William Stanley 1938- 89-92
Stewart, William T(homas) 1934- 127
Stewart, Wynn 1934-1985 Obituary 116
Stewart, Zeph 1921- 41-44R
Stewig, John Warren 1937- CANR-32
Earlier sketches in CA 81-84, CANR-14
See also SATA 26
Steyaert, Thomas A(dolph) 1930- 37-40R
Steyer, Wesley W. 1923- 29-32R
Steyermark, Julian A(lfred)
1909-1988 ....CANR-17
Obituary 126
Earlier sketches in CAP-1, CA 13-14
Stibbs, Alan M(arshall) 1901- CANR-2
Earlier sketch in CA 1-4R
Stich, Stephen P(eter) 1943- 41-44R
Stick, David 1919- CANR-17
Earlier sketch in CA 97-100
Stickells, Austin T. 1914- 41-44R
Stickgold, Bob 1945- 104
Stickland, Caroline (Amanda) 1955- 127
Stickney, Benjamin D. 1940- 135
Stickney, Trumbull 1874-1904 .... DLB 54
Stidworthy, John 1943- .... SATA 63
Stieber, Jack 1919- CANR-6
Earlier sketch in CA 1-4R
Stiehm, Judith 1935- 61-64
Stierlin, Helm 1926- 29-32R
Stierwell, Jay
See Swicegood, Thomas L. P.
Stiff, Robert M(artin) 1931- 132
Stiffel, Frank 1916- 117
Stigger, Judith A. 1949- 111
Stigler, George J(oseph) 1911-1991 ....41-44R
Obituary 136
Stigler, Stephen M(ack) 1941- 125
Stigum, Marcia (Lee) 1934- CANR-8
Earlier sketch in CA 61-64
Stigwood, Robert C. 1934- 102
Stiles, Ezra 1727-1795 .... DLB 31
Stiles, John R. 1916(?)-1976 Obituary 65-68
Stiles, Joseph 1903- CAP-2
Earlier sketch in CA 17-18
Stiles, Lindley Joseph 1913- CANR-3
Earlier sketch in CA 5-8R
Stiles, Martha Bennett 37-40R
See also SATA 6
Stiles, Merritt N. 1899-1975 Obituary 57-60
Stiles, Ned B. 1932- 17-20R
Stiles, Norman B. 1942- 114
See also SATA 36
Stilgoe, John R. 109
Still, C. Henry 1920- 9-12R
Still, Edgar
See Garber, Joseph R(ene)
Still, James 1906- CANR-26
Earlier sketches in CA 65-68, CANR-10
See also CLC 49
See also DLB 9
See also SATA 29
Still, Richard R(alph) 1921- CANR-1
Earlier sketch in CA 1-4R
Still, William N(orwood) Jr. 1932- CANR-18
Earlier sketch in CA 25-28R
Stiller, Brian C(arl) 1942- 117
Stillerman, Robbie 1947- .... SATA 12
Stilley, Frank 1918- 61-64
See also SATA 29
Stillinger, Jack 1931- CANR-1
Earlier sketch in CA 1-4R
Stillman, Damie 1933- CANR-36
Earlier sketch in CA 45-48
Stillman, Edmund O. 1924-1983 Obituary 111
Stillman, Frances (Jennings) 1910-1975 .... CAP-1
Obituary 57-60
Earlier sketch in CA 13-16
Stillman, Irwin M(axwell) 1895-1975 49-52
Obituary 61-64
Stillman, Myra Stephens 1915- CANR-6
Earlier sketch in CA 5-8R
Stillman, Nathan 1914- 5-8R
Stillman, Noam
See Stillman, Norman A(rthur)
Stillman, Norman A(rthur) 1945- 136
Stillman, Richard J. 1917- CANR-34
Earlier sketches in CA 37-40R, CANR-14
Stillwell, Margaret Bingham 1887-1984 ....41-44R
Obituary 112
Stillwell, Norma Jamieson 1894- CAP-1
Earlier sketch in CA 13-16
Stillwell, Paul (Lewis) 1944- 126
Stillwell, Richard 1899-1982 Obituary 111
Stilson, Max 1919- 9-12R
Stilwell, William E(arle) III 1936- 107
Stimmel, Barry 1939- CANR-11
Earlier sketch in CA 69-72
Stimpson, Catherine R(oslyn) 1936- 41-44R
Stimson, Dorothy 1890-1988 Obituary 126
Stimson, Robbe Pierce 1948- 136
Stimson, William 1946- 122
Stinchcombe, Arthur L. 1933- CANR-23
Earlier sketches in CA 13-16R, CANR-8
Stinchcombe, William 1937- 105
Stine, G(eorge) Harry 1928- CANR-30
Earlier sketches in CA 65-68, CANR-9
See also SATA 10
Stine, Hank
See Stine, Henry Eugene
Stine, Henry Eugene 1945- 133
Stine, Jovial Bob
See Stine, R(obert) L(awrence)
Stine, R(obert) L(awrence) 1943- CANR-22
Earlier sketch in CA 105
See also SATA 31
Stine, Whitney Ward 1930- CANR-7
Earlier sketch in CA 57-60
See also AITN 1
Stineman, Esther F. 1947- CANR-17
Earlier sketch in CA 97-100
Stinetorf, Louise (Allender) 1900- 9-12R
See also SATA 10
Sting
See Sumner, Gordon Matthew
Stinger, Charles L(ewis) 1944- 77-80
Stini, William A(rthur Anthony) 1930- 127
Brief entry 107
Stinnett, Caskie 1911- 5-8R
Stinnett, Nick 1942- 110
Stinnett, Ronald F. 1929- 21-24R
Stinnett, Tim Moore 1901-1985 ....CANR-13
Obituary 115
Earlier sketch in CA 17-20R
Stinnette, Charles R(oy) Jr. 1914- 77-80
Stinson, James Emerson Jr. 1937- 119
Stinson, Jim
See Stinson, James Emerson Jr.
Stinson, Kathy 1952- 113
Stinson, Robert William 1941- 111
Stinton, T(homas) C(harles) W(arren)
1925-1985 Obituary 117
Stipe, Robert Edwin 1928- 49-52
Stirling, Alfred (Thorpe) 1902-1981 110
Obituary 108
Stirling, Anna Maria Diana Wilhelmina (Pickering)
1865-1965 .... CAP-1
Earlier sketch in CA 9-10
Stirling, Arthur
See Sinclair, Upton (Beall)
Stirling, Betty Rutledge 1923- 9-12R
Stirling, (Thomas) Brents 1904- CAP-2
Earlier sketch in CA 25-28
Stirling, Jessica
See Coghlan, Margaret M.
and Rae, Hugh C(rauford)
Stirling, Jessica
See Rae, Hugh C(rauford)
Stirling, Lilla (May Elderkin) 1902- 107
Stirling, Matthew Williams
1896-1975 Obituary 53-56
Stirling, Monica 1916-1983 81-84
Obituary 111
Stirling, Nora B(romley) 1900- CANR-3
Earlier sketch in CA 5-8R
See also SATA 3
Stirnweis, Shannon 1931- .... SATA 10
Stitelman, Leonard (Arnold) 1932- 41-44R
Stites, Francis N(oel) 1938- 41-44R
Stites, Raymond S(omers) 1899-1974 65-68
Obituary 53-56
Stith, John E(dward) 1947- 117
Stith, William 1707-1755 .... DLB 31
Stitskin, Leon D. 1910-1978 ....CANR-1
Earlier sketch in CA 1-4R
Stitt, Milan 1941- 69-72
See also CLC 29
Stitt, Peter 1940- 123
Stitzel, Thomas E(dward) 1936- 93-96
Stivens, Dal(las George) 1911- CANR-14
Earlier sketch in CA 69-72
Stiver, Mary Weeden 1909- CAP-1
Earlier sketch in CA 13-14
Stivers, Robert L(loyd) 1940- 69-72
Stjernberg, Lloyd A(rmand) 1937- 25-28R
St-John Nevill, Barry
See Nevill, Barry St-John
Stoan, Stephen K(uzman) 1942- 111
Stob, Ralph 1894-1965 ....1-4R
Obituary 103
Stobart, Thomas Ralph 1914- 13-16R
Stobaugh, Robert B. (Jr.) 1927- 101
Stobbs, John L(ouis) N(ewcombe)
1921- 13-16R
Stobbs, William 1914- 81-84
See also SATA 17
Stock, A(my) G(eraldine)
1902-1988 Obituary 126
Stock, Barbara R(uth) 1942- CANR-19
Earlier sketch in CA 112
Stock, Brian 1939- 41-44R
Stock, Catherine 1952- 119
See also SATA 65
Stock, Claudette 1934- 65-68
Stock, Ernest 1924- 21-24R
Stock, Guy 1933- 124
Stock, Irvin 1920- 25-28R
Stock, Phyllis H(artman) 1930- 85-88
Stock, R(obert) D(ouglas) 1941- CANR-14
Earlier sketch in CA 41-44R
Stockanes, Anthony E(dward) 1935- 109
Stockard, James Wright Jr. 1935- 13-16R
Stockard, Jimmy
See Stockard, James Wright Jr.
Stockdale, Eric 1929- 25-28R
Stocker, Margarita 1955- 121
Stocker, Mark (Andrew) 1956- 131
Stockham, Peter (Alan) 1928- .... SATA 57
Stockhammer, Morris 1904- 13-16R
Stocking, David M(ackenzie) 1919- 25-28R
Stocking, George W(ard) Jr. 1928- 73-76

Stocking, George Ward
1892-1975 Obituary 61-64
Stocking, Hobart E(bey) 1906- 101
Stocking, Kathleen 1945- 135
Stocking, Marion Kingston 1922- 25-28R
Stocking, S(usan) Holly 1945- 117
Stockman, David A(llen) 1946- 123
Stocks, Mary (Danvers Brinton)
1891-1975 ....13-16R
Obituary 118
Stockton, Adrian James 1935-1981 ....29-32R
Obituary 134
Stockton, Bayard 1930- 134
Stockton, Francis Richard 1834-1902 137
Brief entry 108
See also Stockton, Frank R.
See also MAICYA
See also SATA 44
Stockton, Frank R.
See Stockton, Francis Richard
See also DLB 42, 74
See also SATA 32
Stockton, J. Roy 1893(?)-1972 Obituary 37-40R
Stockton, Jim
See Stockton, Adrian James
Stockton, John R(obert) 1903- 13-16R
Stockton, Ronald R. 1940- 118
Stockwell, Edward G(rant) 1933- 21-24R
Stockwell, John R(obert) 1937- 104
Stockwell, Robert P(aul) 1925- 17-20R
Stockwin, (James) Arthur (Ainscow) 1935- 103
Stockwood, (Arthur) Mervyn
1913- Brief entry 117
Stoddard, Charles
See Kuttner, Henry
Stoddard, Edward G. 1923- 9-12R
See also SATA 10
Stoddard, Ellwyn R(eed) 1927- CANR-38
Earlier sketches in CA 45-48, CANR-1, 17
Stoddard, George Dinsmore
1897-1981 Obituary 106
Stoddard, Hope 1900- 49-52
See also SATA 6
Stoddard, Richard Henry
1825-1903 Brief entry 114
See also DLB 3, 64
Stoddard, Richard 1942- 102
Stoddard, Robert H. 1928- 133
Stoddard, Sandol 1927- CANR-8
Earlier sketch in CA 5-8R
See also Warburg, Sandol Stoddard
Stoddard, Solomon 1643-1729 ....DLB 24
Stoddard, Tom 1933- 37-40R
Stoddard, Whitney Snow 1913- 109
Stoddart, Jack Elliott 1916-1988 Obituary 124
Stodelle, Ernestine 1912- 117
Stoeckle, John D(uane) 1922- 128
Stoehr, C(arl) Eric 1945- 65-68
Stoessinger, John G. 1927- CANR-9
Earlier sketch in CA 13-16R
Stoetzer, O(tto) Carlos (Enrique)
1921- CANR-28
Earlier sketch in CA 109
Stoff, Joshua 1958- 136
Stoff, Sheldon (Ptaschevitch) 1930- 21-24R
Stoffel, Albert Law 1909- 65-68
Stoffel, Betty W. 1922- 17-20R
Stoffel, Ernest Lee 1923- 114
Stoffel, Lester L(enneth Jr.) 1920- 45-48
Stoffle, Carla J(oy) 1943- CANR-7
Earlier sketch in CA 61-64
Stofflet, Mary 1942- 127
Stogdill, Ralph M(elvin) 1904- CANR-1
Earlier sketch in CA 1-4R
Stohl, Michael (Steven) 1947- CANR-25
Earlier sketch in CA 107
Stohlman, Martha Lou Lemmon 1913- 65-68
Stoianovich, Trajan 1921- 21-24R
Stoiber, Rudolph M(aria) 1925- 1-4R
Stoiko, Michael 1919- 9-12R
See also SATA 14
Stoil, Michael Jon 1950- 53-56
Stojanovic, Svetozar 1931- 134
Brief entry 112
Stok, T.
See Stolk, Anthonie
Stokely, James R(orex) Jr. 1913-1977 ....9-12R
Obituary 69-72
Stoker, Abraham 1847-1912 Brief entry 105
See also Stoker, Bram
See also SATA 29
Stoker, Alan 1930- CANR-24
Earlier sketches in CA 21-24R, CANR-9
Stoker, Bram
See Stoker, Abraham
See also CDBLB 1890-1914
See also DLB 36, 70
See also TCLC 8
See also WLC
Stoker, H(oward) Stephen 1939- CANR-8
Earlier sketch in CA 61-64
Stokes, Adrian Durham 1902-1972 ....CANR-5
Obituary 89-92
Earlier sketch in CA 13-16R
Stokes, Bob
See Wilkening, Howard (Everett)
Stokes, Bruce 1948- 130
Stokes, Carl B(urton) 1927- 69-72
Stokes, Cedric
See Beardmore, George
Stokes, Charles (Herbert) 1932- 103
Stokes, Charles J(unius) 1922- CANR-10
Earlier sketch in CA 25-28R
Stokes, Daniel M. J. 1950- 57-60
Stokes, Donald Elkinton 1927- CANR-1
Earlier sketch in CA 1-4R
Stokes, Donald (Hubert)
1913-1986 Obituary 119
Stokes, Donald W. 1947- 132
Stokes, Doris 1919-1987 Obituary 122
Brief entry 115
Stokes, Edward 1922- 128
Stokes, Eric (Thomas) 1924-1981 107
Obituary 103
Stokes, Geoffrey 1940- CANR-36
Earlier sketch in CA 69-72
Stokes, Henry J. M. Scott
See Scott-Stokes, Henry J. M.
Stokes, Jack (Tilden) 1923- 29-32R
See also SATA 13
Stokes, Martin 1958- 127
Stokes, Olivia Pearl 1916- 37-40R
See also SATA 32
Stokes, Peg (Lee Ewing) 1-4R
Stokes, Robert
See Wilkening, Howard (Everett)
Stokes, Roy Eliot CANR-26
Earlier sketches in CAP-2, CA 19-20
Stokes, Roy 1915- 17-20R
Stokes, Simpson
See Fawcett, F(rank) Dubrez
Stokes, Thomas L. 1898-1958 ....DLB 29
Stokes, William Lee 1915- CANR-20
Earlier sketch in CA 41-44R
Stokesbury, James L(awton) 1934- CANR-38
Earlier sketches in CA 93-96, CANR-17
Stokesbury, Leon 1945- CANR-21
Earlier sketch in CA 69-72
See also DLB 120
Stokke, Baard Richard 1937- 25-28R
Stokoe, William C(larence) Jr. 1919- 41-44R
Stokstad, Marilyn 1929- CANR-15
Earlier sketch in CA 37-40R
Stolberg, Christian Graf zu 1748-1821 .....DLB 94
Stolberg, Friedrich Leopold Graf zu
1750-1819 ....DLB 94
Stoler, Ann Laura 1949- 119
Stoler, Peter (Robert) 1935- 97-100
Stolk, Anthonie 1916- 131
Stoll, Clarice Stasz
See Stasz, Clarice
Stoll, Clifford 1950- 136
See also BEST 90:3
Stoll, Dennis G(ray) 1912-1987 ....13-16R
Obituary 124
Stoll, Irma 1929- 135
Stoll, John E(dward) 1933- 49-52
Stoller, Robert J(esse) 1924-1991 Obituary 135
Brief entry 117
Stollnitz, Fred 1939- 45-48
Stoloff, Carolyn 1927- CANR-9
Earlier sketch in CA 65-68
Stolorow, Robert D(avid) 1942- 102
Stolper, Wolfgang F(riedrich) 1912- 21-24R
Stolten, Jane (Henry) 97-100
Stoltenberg, Donald Hugo 1927- 89-92
Stoltzfus, Ben Franklin 1927- 103
Stoltzfus, (Mary) Louise 1952- 138
Stolz, Lois Meek 1891- CAP-2
Earlier sketch in CA 21-22
Stolz, Mary (Slattery) 1920- CANR-13
Earlier sketch in CA 5-8R
See also AAYA 8
See also AITN 1
See also CLC 12
See also MAICYA
See also SAAS 3
See also SATA 10, 70, 71
Stolzenbach, Norma Frizzell 1904- 41-44R
Stolzenberg, Mark 1950- 102
Stonberg, Selma F(ranks) 69-72
Stone, Alan
See Svenson, Andrew E(dward)
See also SATA 1
Stone, Alan A(braham) 1929- 17-20R
Stone, Albert E. Jr.
See Stone, Albert E(dward)
Stone, Albert E(dward) 1924- CANR-8
Earlier sketch in CA 17-20R
Stone, Alfred R. 1926- 17-20R
Stone, Alma 1908- 77-80
Stone, Barbara Haskins
1924(?)-1979 Obituary 89-92
Stone, Betty E. 1926- 9-12R
Stone, Bonnie (M.) Domrose 1941- 133
Stone, Brian 1919- 13-16R
Stone, Charles Sumner Jr. 1924- 77-80
Stone, Christopher D(avid) 1937- 53-56
Stone, Chuck
See Stone, Charles Sumner Jr.
Stone, Clarence N. 1935- CANR-30
Earlier sketch in CA 112
Stone, Clifford A. 1951-1986 Obituary 118
Stone, David (Anthony) 1929- 5-8R
Stone, David K(arl) 1922- 85-88
See also SATA 9
Stone, David U. 1927- CANR-7
Earlier sketch in CA 17-20R
Stone, Deborah
See Navas, Deborah
Stone, Donald (Adelbert) Jr. 1937- 29-32R
Stone, Donald D(avid) 1942- 81-84
Stone, Doris (Mary) 1918- 117
Stone, Doris (Zemurray) 1909- 105
Stone, Edward 1913- 37-40R
Stone, Elaine Murray 1922- CANR-38
Earlier sketches in CA 89-92, CANR-17
Stone, Elizabeth W(enger) 1918- CANR-25
Earlier sketch in CA 107
Stone, Ellery W(heeler)
1894-1981 Obituary 105
Stone, Elna CANR-5
Earlier sketch in CA 13-16R
Stone, Eugenia 1879-1971 ....9-12R
See also SATA 7
Stone, Ferdinand Fairfax
1908-1989 Obituary 129
Stone, Frank A(ndrews) 1929- CANR-8
Earlier sketch in CA 61-64
Stone, Gene
See Stone, Eugenia
Stone, George Winchester Jr. 1907- CANR-6
Earlier sketch in CA 5-8R
Stone, Gerald (Charles) 1932- 104
Stone, Grace Zaring 1891-1991 ....CAP-2
Obituary 135
Earlier sketch in CA 25-28
Stone, Gregory P(rentice) 1921-1981 ......CANR-1
Obituary 116
Earlier sketch in CA 49-52
Stone, Hampton
See Stein, Aaron Marc
Stone, Harris B. 1934- 57-60
Stone, Harry 1926- 130
Stone, Harry 1928- 13-16R
Stone, Helen V(irginia) 25-28R
See also SATA 6
Stone, Howard W. 1942- 124
Stone, Hoyt E(dward) 1935- 101
Stone, I(sidor) F(einstein) 1907-1989 61-64
Obituary 129
Stone, Idella Purnell
See Purnell, Idella
Stone, Ikey
See Purnell, Idella
Stone, Irving 1903-1989 ....CANR-23
Obituary 129
Earlier sketches in CA 1-4R, CANR-1
See also CAAS 3
See also AITN 1
See also CLC 7
See also MTCW
See also SATA 3
See also SATO 64
Stone, James Champion 1916- 17-20R
Stone, James H(erbert) 1918- 41-44R
Stone, Jerry 1942(?)-1987 Obituary 124
Stone, Joan 1930- CANR-13
Earlier sketch in CA 77-80
Stone, Joel 1931- 138
Stone, John H(enry) 1936- 89-92
Stone, John (Timothy Jr.) 1933- 102
Stone, Jon 1931- 107
See also SATA 39
Stone, Josephine Rector
See Dixon, Jeanne
Stone, Julius 1907-1985 ....CANR-5
Obituary 117
Earlier sketch in CA 53-56
Stone, Justin (Federman) 1916- 116
Stone, L(awrence) Joseph
1912-1975 Obituary 61-64
Stone, Lawrence 1919- 13-16R
Stone, Louis 1910(?)-1985 Obituary 115
Stone, Lucy 1818-1893 ....DLB 79
Stone, Margaret N.
See Dresser, Norine
Stone, Marvin Lawrence 1924- 69-72
Stone, Melville 1848-1929 ....DLB 25
Stone, Merlin 1931- CANR-39
Earlier sketches in CA 101, CANR-17
Stone, Michael E(dward) 1938- 132
Stone, Mildred Fairbanks 1902- CAP-1
Earlier sketch in CA 11-12
Stone, Nancy (Young) 1925- 49-52
Stone, Natalie
See Goldenbaum, Sally
and Staff, Adrienne
Stone, Oliver 1946- 110
Stone, Patti 1926- 5-8R
Stone, Peter 1930- CANR-7
Earlier sketch in CA 9-12R
See also SATA 65
Stone, Philip James III 1936- 21-24R
Stone, Ralph A. 1934- 37-40R
Stone, Raymond CANR-26
Earlier sketches in CAP-2, CA 19-20
See also SATA 1
Stone, Reynolds 1909-1979 Obituary 89-92
Stone, Richard
See Delaney, Jack J(ames)
Stone, Richard H. CANR-26
Earlier sketches in CAP-2, CA 19-20
Stone, Robert (Anthony) 1937- CANR-23
Earlier sketch in CA 85-88
See also CLC 5, 23, 42
See also MTCW
Stone, Robert B. 1916- CANR-31
Earlier sketch in CA 29-32R
Stone, Roger D. 1934- 119
Stone, Ronald H. 1939- CANR-16
Earlier sketch in CA 77-80
Stone, Rosetta
See Geisel, Theodor Seuss
Stone, Rufus
See Cowie, Donald
Stone, Ruth 1915- CANR-2
Earlier sketch in CA 45-48
See also DLB 105
Stone, Samuel 1602-1663 ....DLB 24
Stone, Scott C(linton) S(tuart) 1932- CANR-18
Earlier sketch in CA 25-28R
Stone, Shelley C(lyde Jr.) 1928- 61-64
Stone, Shepard 1908-1990 Obituary 131
Stone, Susan Berch 1944- 61-64
Stone, Thomas H.
See Harknett, Terry
Stone, Vernon A(lfred) 1929- 65-68
Stone, Wilfred (Healey) 1917- 21-24R
Stone, William F(rank) 1931- 41-44R
Stone, William Sidney 1928- 13-16R
Stone, Zachary
See Follett, Ken(neth Martin)
Stoneburner, (Charles Joseph) Tony
1926- 41-44R
Stonehouse, Bernard 1926- CANR-19
Earlier sketches in CA 49-52, CANR-2
See also SATA 13
Stonehouse, John (Thomson) 1925- 112
Stonehouse, Merlin 1911- 13-16R
Stoneman, Elvyn Arthur 1919- 17-20R
Stoneman, Paul 1947- 115
Stoneman, Richard (John) 1951- 130
Stoneman, William H(arlan)
1904-1987 Obituary 122
Stonequist, Everett Verner
1901-1979 Obituary 85-88
Stoner, Carol Hupping 1949- 53-56
Stones, E(dgar) 1922- CANR-15
Earlier sketch in CA 37-40R
Stones, E(dward) L(ionel) G(regory)
1914-1987 Obituary 121
Stonesifer, Richard James 1922- 13-16R
Stong, Clair L. 1902(?)-1975 Obituary 61-64
Stong, Phil(ip Duffield) 1899-1957 ....SATA 32
Stong, Red
See Stong, Clair L.
Stonier, Tom (Ted) 1927- 5-8R
Stonor, Oliver 1903- CAP-1
Earlier sketch in CA 13-16
Stonum, Gary Lee 1947- 89-92
Stoodley, Bartlett Hicks 1907-1978 ....1-4R
Obituary 103
Stookey, Richard 1938- 93-96
Stookey, Robert W(ilson) 1917- CANR-14
Earlier sketch in CA 81-84
Stoop, David 1937- 119
Stoop, Norma McLain 65-68
Stoops, Emery 1902- CANR-17
Earlier sketches in CA 1-4R, CANR-1
Stoops, John A(lbert) 1925- 29-32R
Stopelman, Francis
See Stoppelman, Frans
Stopes, M. C.
See Stopes, Marie (Charlotte) Carmichael
Stopes, Marie C.
See Stopes, Marie (Charlotte) Carmichael
Stopes, Marie (Charlotte) Carmichael
1880-1958 Brief entry 115
Stopford, Robert Wright 1901- CAP-1
Earlier sketch in CA 13-14
Stopp, Elisabeth (Charlotte Vellar-Etscheit)
1911- 5-8R
Stoppard, Miriam 1937- 120
Stoppard, Tom 1937- CANR-39
Earlier sketch in CA 81-84
See also CDBLB 1960 to Present
See also CLC 1, 3, 4, 5, 8, 15, 29, 34, 63
See also DLB 13
See also DLBY 85
See also MTCW
See also WLC
Stoppelman, Francis
See Stoppelman, Frans
Stoppelman, Frans 1921- CAP-1
Earlier sketch in CA 9-10
Storch, Margaret 1941- 137
Storer, Doug(las) 1899-1985 57-60
Obituary 118
Storer, J(ames) D(onald) 1928- CANR-23
Earlier sketch in CA 107
Storer, Norman W(illiam) 1930- 41-44R
Storer, Tracy I(rwin) 1889-1973 ....13-16R
Obituary 126
Storey, Anthony 1928- CANR-2
Earlier sketch in CA 49-52
See also DLB 14
Storey, Arthur 1915- 45-48
Storey, David (Malcolm) 1933- CANR-36
Earlier sketch in CA 81-84
See also CLC 2, 4, 5, 8
See also DLB 13, 14
See also MTCW
Storey, Edward J. 1901- 89-92
Storey, Edward 1930- 97-100
Storey, John W(oodrow) 1938- 121
Storey, Margaret 1926- CANR-1
Earlier sketch in CA 49-52
See also SATA 9
Storey, R(obin) L(indsay) 1927- CANR-11
Earlier sketch in CA 21-24R
Storey, Robert F(ranklin) 1945- 85-88
Storey, Victoria Carolyn 1945- 33-36R
See also SATA 16
Storey, W(illiam) George 1923- CANR-6
Earlier sketch in CA 5-8R
Storfer, Muriel (Rosoff) Silberstein
See Silberstein-Storfer, Muriel (Rosoff)
Storing, Herbert James
1928-1977 Obituary 73-76
Storke, Thomas More
1876-1971 Obituary 89-92
Storm, Christopher
See Olsen, T(heodore) V(ictor)
Storm, Hester G(lory) 1903- 9-12R
Storm, Hyemeyohsts 1935- 81-84
See also CLC 3
Storm, Lesley
See Clark, Mabel Margaret (Cowie)
Storm, Mallory
See Fairman, Paul W.
Storm, Marian 1892(?)-1975 Obituary 61-64
Storm, Russell
See Williams, Robert Moore
Storm, Virginia
See Swatridge, Irene Maude (Mossop)

Storme, Peter
See Stern, Philip Van Doren
Stormer, John A. 1928- 25-28R
Storni, Alfonsina 1892-1938 131
Brief entry 104
See also HW
See also TCLC 5
Storr, Anthony 1920- CANR-17
Earlier sketch in CA 97-100
Storr, Catherine (Cole) 1913- CANR-23
Earlier sketch in CA 13-16R
See also SATA 9
Storrer, Carol Marchal 1949- 112
Storrow, H(ugh) A(lan) 1926- 21-24R
Storrow, James J. Jr. 1917-1984 Obituary 111
Storry, Richard 1914(?)-1982 Obituary 106
Storsve, LaVaughn (Ernestine Kipena)
1921- 1-4R
Story, E(ugenia) Macer
See Macer-Story, E(ugenia)
Story, Edward M. 1921- 29-32R
Story, G(eorge) M(orley) 1927- CANR-9
Earlier sketch in CA 21-24R
Story, Gertrude 1929- 129
Story, Jack Trevor 1917-1991 ....29-32R
Obituary 136
Story, Josephine
See Loring, Emilie (Baker)
Story, Ronald (D.) 1946- CANR-11
Earlier sketch in CA 65-68
Story, Thomas 1670(?)-1742 .... DLB 31
Story, William Wetmore 1819-1895 .... DLB 1
Stotland, Ezra 1924- 17-20R
Stott, D(enis) H(erbert) 1909-1988 ....CANR-8
Obituary 124
Earlier sketch in CA 13-16R
Stott, Dorothy (M.) 1958- 134
See also SATA 67
Stott, Dot
See Stott, Dorothy (M.)
Stott, Douglas W(ayne) 1948- 109
Stott, Jane 1940- 85-88
Stott, John R. W. 1921- CANR-18
Earlier sketches in CA 5-8R, CANR-2
Stott, Leland H. 1897- 25-28R
Stott, Mary 1907- 104
Stott, Mike 1944- 104
Stott, Raymond Toole
See Toole Stott, Raymond
Stott, William (Merrell) 1940- 61-64
Stotts, Herbert Edward 1916- CANR-1
Earlier sketch in CA 1-4R
Stotts, Jack L. 1932- 49-52
Stotz, Charles Morse 1898-1985 Obituary 115
Stouck, David (Hamilton) 1940- 61-64
Stoudemire, Sterling A(ubrey) 1902- 37-40R
Obituary 137
Stoudt, John Joseph 1911- 49-52
Stough, Furman C(harles) 1928- Brief entry 107
Stoughton, Clarence Charles
1895-1975 Obituary 61-64
Stoughton, Gertrude K. 1901- CAP-2
Earlier sketch in CA 25-28
Stoughton, William 1631-1701 .... DLB 24
Stout, Alan Ker 1900-1983 Obituary 110
Stout, David 1942- 136
Stout, Gardner Dominick
1903-1984 Obituary 111
Stout, George L(eslie) 1897-1978 81-84
Obituary 77-80
Stout, Glenn 1958- 138
Stout, Irving Wright 1903-1972 ....CANR-3
Earlier sketch in CA 1-4R
Stout, James (Harvey) 1954- 119
Stout, Jeffrey Lee 1950- 106
Stout, Joseph A(llen) Jr. 1939- CANR-2
Earlier sketch in CA 45-48
Stout, Nancy 1942- 137
Stout, Neil Ralph 1932- 97-100
Stout, Rex (Todhunter) 1886-1975 61-64
See also AITN 2
See also CLC 3
Stout, Robert Joe 1936- 65-68
Stout, Russell Jr. 1932- CANR-18
Earlier sketch in CA 101
Stout, Ruth 1884-1980 ....33-36R
Obituary 120
Stout, Wesley Winans
1889-1971 Obituary 89-92
Stout, William 1949- 126
Stoutamire, Albert 1921- 41-44R
Stoutenburg, Adrien (Pearl) 1916- 5-8R
See also SATA 3
Stovall, Floyd 1896- 9-12R
Stove, D. C.
See Stove, David (Charles)
Stove, David (Charles) 1927- 136
Stover, Allan C(arl) 1938- CANR-12
Earlier sketch in CA 69-72
See also SATA 14
Stover, Bill
See Stover, W(illiam) H(arrison) M(owbray)
Stover, Jo Ann 1931- 37-40R
Stover, John F(ord) 1912- CANR-1
Earlier sketch in CA 1-4R
Stover, Leon E(ugene) 1929- CANR-2
Earlier sketch in CA 49-52
Stover, Marjorie Filley 1914- CANR-31
Earlier sketch in CA 45-48
See also SATA 9
Stover, W(illiam) H(arrison) M(owbray)
1898-1980 103
Obituary 97-100
Stover, Webster 1902- 53-56

Stow, (Julian) Randolph 1935- CANR-33
Earlier sketch in CA 13-16R
See also CLC 23, 48
See also MTCW
Stowe, Charles E(dwin) Hambrick
See Hambrick-Stowe, Charles E(dwin)
Stowe, David M. 1919- 9-12R
Stowe, Harriet (Elizabeth) Beecher
1811-1896 .... CDALB 1865-1917
See also DLB 1, 12, 42, 74
See also MAICYA
See also WLC
See also YABC 1
Stowe, James L(ewis) 1950- 89-92
Stowe, Leland 1899- 77-80
See also DLB 29
See also SATA 60
Stowe, Noel James 1942- 106
Stowe, Richard S(cribner) 1925- 73-76
Stowe, Rosetta
See Ogan, George F.
and Ogan, Margaret E. (Nettles)
Stowe, William McFerrin 1913- 5-8R
Stowell, Joseph M(ishael) 1944- 119
Stowers, Carlton 1942- CANR-14
Earlier sketches in CA 81-84, CANR-31
Stoy, R(ichard) H(ugh) 1910- 57-60
Strabolgi, Bartolomeo
See Tucci, Niccolo
Strachan, Hew (Francis Anthony) 1949- 61-64
Strachan, J(ohn) George 1910- 107
Strachan, Margaret Pitcairn 1908- 5-8R
See also SATA 14
Strachan, T(ony) S(impson) 1920- 13-16R
Strachan, W. J.
See Strachan, Walter John
Strachan, Walter John 1903- 120
Strachan, Winona Peacock 1918- 5-8R
Strachey, Alix 1892-1973 133
Strachey, Barbara
See Halpern, Barbara Strachey
Strachey, Isobel 1907-1987 Obituary 122
Strachey, James 1888-1967 128
Brief entry 124
Strachey, (Evelyn) John (St. Loe)
1901-1963 Obituary 93-96
Strachey, (Giles) Lytton
1880-1932 Brief entry 110
See also TCLC 12
Strackbein, O(scar) R(obert) 1900- 21-24R
Straczynski, J(oseph) Michael 1954- 109
Strader, June (Sellers) 1925- 97-100
Stradley, Mark
See Smith, Richard Rein
Stradling, Leslie Edward 1908- 104
Strage, Mark 1927- 81-84
Strahan, Randall (W.) 1954- 136
Strahl, Leonard E. 1926- 29-32R
Strahlem, Richard E(arl) 1909- 37-40R
Straight, Michael Whitney 1916- CANR-7
Earlier sketch in CA 5-8R
Strain, Dudley 1909- CAP-1
Earlier sketch in CA 11-12
Strain, Frances Bruce CAP-2
Earlier sketch in CA 29-32
Strain, Lucille Brewton 69-72
Strainchamps, Ethel (Reed) 1912- 53-56
Strait, Raymond 1924- CANR-4
Earlier sketch in CA 53-56
Strait, Treva Adams 1909- 97-100
See also SATA 35
Straiton, E(dward) C(ornock) 1917- CANR-19
Earlier sketches in CA 45-48, CANR-3
Straiton, Eddie
See Straiton, E(dward) C(ornock)
Straiton, John S(eal) 1922- 136
Straka, Gerald Milton 1931- CANR-2
Earlier sketch in CA 5-8R
Straker, J(ohn) F(oster) 1904- CANR-11
Earlier sketch in CA 13-16R
Strakosch, Avery
See Denham, Avery Strakosch
Straley, John A(lonzo) 1894-1966 ....1-4R
Obituary 103
Strand, Kenneth A(lbert) 1927- CANR-3
Earlier sketch in CA 9-12R
Strand, Mark 1934- 21-24R
See also CLC 6, 18, 41, 71
See also DLB 5
See also SATA 41
Strand, Paul E.
See Palestrant, Simon S.
Strand, Paul 1890-1976 Obituary 65-68
Strand, Thomas 1944- 65-68
Strand, William K. 1931- 29-32R
Strandberg, Victor H(ugo) 1935- CANR-16
Earlier sketch in CA 89-92
Strane, Susan 1944- 136
Strang, Barbara M(ary) H(ope)
1925-1982 ....37-40R
Obituary 106
Strang, Gerald 1908- CAP-2
Earlier sketch in CA 25-28
Strang, Ruth May 1895-1971 ....CANR-2
Earlier sketch in CA 1-4R
Strange, Dillon
See Norwood, Victor G(eorge) C(harles)
Strange, Jack Roy 1921- 17-20R
Strange, James F(rancis) 1938- 117
Strange, K(athleen) H(aidee) 1904- 113
Strange, Maureen 1948- 89-92
Strange, N. Blair
See Sargent, Brian (Lawrence)
Strange, Nora K.
See Stanley, Nora Kathleen Begbie Strange
Strange, Philippa
See Coury, Louise Andree

Strange, Susan 1923- 49-52
Stranger, Joyce
See Wilson, Joyce M(uriel Judson)
Strankay, Sam J(ames) 1905- 57-60
Strasberg, Lee 1901-1982 ....CANR-29
Obituary 106
Earlier sketch in CA 13-16R
Strasberg, Susan (Elizabeth)
1938- Brief entry 120
Strasburger, Victor C. 1949- 112
Strassels, Paul N. 109
Strasser, Bernard Paul 1895- CAP-1
Earlier sketch in CA 9-10
Strasser, Marland K(eith) 1915- CANR-6
Earlier sketch in CA 5-8R
Strasser, Otto (Johann Maximilian)
1897-1974 Obituary 53-56
Strasser, Stephan 1905- 133
Strasser, Susan 1948- CANR-24
Earlier sketch in CA 107
Strasser, Todd 1950- 123
Brief entry 117
See also AAYA 2
See also CLR 11
See also MAICYA
See also SATA 41, 45, 71
Strassfeld, Michael J. 1950- 120
Strassfeld, Sharon M(arcia) 1950- 107
Strassmann, W(olfgang) Paul 1926- 41-44R
Strassova, Helena 1924- 49-52
Stratemeyer, Edward L. 1862-1930 ....CANR-27
Earlier sketches in CAP-2, CA 19-20
See also DLB 42
See also MAICYA
See also SATA 1, 67
Stratford, H. Philip
See Bulmer, (Henry) Kenneth
Stratford, Philip 1927- CANR-5
Earlier sketch in CA 9-12R
See also SATA 47
Strathern, Andrew (Jamieson) 1939- CANR-19
Earlier sketches in CA 49-52, CANR-2
Strathern, Ann Marilyn 1941- CANR-3
Earlier sketch in CA 49-52
Strati, Saverio 1924- CANR-23
Earlier sketches in CA 17-20R, CANR-7
Stratman, Carl J(oseph) 1917-1972 .... CAP-2
Earlier sketch in CA 19-20
Straton, Hillyer H(awthorne) 1905- CAP-1
Earlier sketch in CA 9-10
Stratton, Arthur M.
1910(?)-1975 Obituary 61-64
Stratton, George Malcolm
1865-1957 Brief entry 112
Stratton, Henry
See Nelson, Michael Harrington
Stratton, J(ohn) T(heodore) 61-64
Stratton, John R(ay) 1935- 45-48
Stratton, Porter Andrew 1918- 37-40R
Stratton, Rebecca Brief entry 115
Stratton, Roy (Olin) CAP-2
Earlier sketch in CA 21-22
Stratton, Ted
See Stratton, J(ohn) T(heodore)
Stratton, Thomas
See Coulson, Robert S(tratton)
and DeWeese, Thomas Eugene
Stratton, William David 1896- CAP-1
Earlier sketch in CA 9-10
Stratton-Porter, Gene(va Grace)
1863-1924 137
Stratton-Porter, Gene 1863-1924 .... MAICYA
See also SATA 15
Stratyner, Barbara Naomi Cohen
See Cohen-Stratyner, Barbara Naomi
Straub, Gerard Thomas 1947- 126
Straub, Peter (Francis) 1943- CANR-28
Earlier sketch in CA 85-88
See also BEST 89:1
See also CLC 28
See also DLBY 84
See also MTCW
Straubing, Harold (Elk) 1918- 126
Strauch, Carl F(erdinand) 1908- 41-44R
Strauch, Judith V(ivian) 1942- 107
Strauch, Katina (Parthemos) 1946- 105
Straughan, Robert P(aul) L(ouis) 1924- 49-52
Straughn, Charles (Thomas II) 1933- 117
Straumann, Heinrich 1902- 13-16R
Straus, Dennis CANR-23
Earlier sketch in CA 105
Straus, Dorothea 1916- 37-40R
Straus, Murray A(rnold) 1926- CANR-10
Earlier sketch in CA 21-24R
Straus, Nathan 1889-1961 Obituary 89-92
Straus, Richard 1925-1986 ....CANR-22
Earlier sketch in CA 1-4R
Straus, Robert 1923- CANR-6
Earlier sketch in CA 57-60
Straus, Roger A(ustin) 1948- 109
Strauss, Albrecht B(enno) 1921- 37-40R
Strauss, Anselm L(eonard)
1916- Brief entry 114
Strauss, Bert(ram) Wiley 1901- 13-16R
Strauss, Botho 1944- .... CLC 22
Strauss, David 1937- 89-92
Strauss, Diane Wheeler 1943- 128
Strauss, Elaine Mandle
1916(?)-1982 Obituary 107
Strauss, Erich 1911-1981 ....13-16R
Obituary 135
Strauss, Frances Goetzmann 1904-1991 .... CAP-2
Obituary 134
Earlier sketch in CA 29-32
Strauss, Gerald 1922- CANR-33
Earlier sketch in CA 9-12R
Strauss, Hans 1898(?)-1977 Obituary 69-72

Strauss, Harold 1907-1975 Obituary 104
Strauss, Helen M(arion)
1904(?)-1987 Obituary 122
Strauss, Herbert A(rthur) 1918- 133
Brief entry 121
Strauss, Joyce 1936- 93-96
See also SATA 53
Strauss, Leo 1899-1973 101
Obituary 45-48
Strauss, Lewis Lichtenstein
1896-1974 Obituary 45-48
Strauss, (Mary) Lucille Jackson 1908- CAP-1
Earlier sketch in CA 11-12
Strauss, Maurice B(enjamin) 1904-1974 ..... CAP-2
Earlier sketch in CA 25-28
Strauss, Patricia (Frances O'Flynn)
1909-1987 Obituary 123
Strauss, Richard (Georg)
1864-1949 Brief entry 118
Strauss, Richard L(ehman) 1933- CANR-36
Earlier sketches in CA 49-52, CANR-1, 16
Strauss, Victor 1907(?)-1979 Obituary 89-92
Strauss, W(allace) Patrick 1923- 41-44R
Strauss, Walter A(dolf) 1923- 81-84
Strauss, Walter L(eopold) 1922-1988 .....CANR-28
Obituary 124
Earlier sketch in CA 81-84
Strauss, Werner 1930- 29-32R
Strauss, William Louis 1914- 61-64
Strausz-Hupe, Robert 1903- 9-12R
Stravinski, Igor Fedorovich
See Stravinsky, Igor Fedorovich
Stravinsky, Igor Fedorovich 1882-1971 107
Obituary 29-32R
Stravinsky, Vera 1888-1982 106
Obituary 107
Strawinsky, Igor Fedorovich
See Stravinsky, Igor Fedorovich
Strawson, Galen (John) 1952- 133
Strawson, John 1921- CANR-12
Earlier sketch in CA 29-32R
Strawson, P(eter) F(rederick) 1919- 25-28R
Strax, Philip 1909- 61-64
Strayer, Barry L. 1932- 29-32R
Strayer, E. Ward
See Stratemeyer, Edward L.
Strayer, Joseph Reese 1904-1987 103
Obituary 123
Strayer, Sara Barker
1896(?)-1986 Obituary 118
Strean, Herbert S(amuel) 1931- CANR-19
Earlier sketch in CA 103
Streano, Vince(nt Catello) 1945- 53-56
See also SATA 20
Streatfeild, (Mary) Noel 1895(?)-1986 .....CANR-31
Obituary 120
Earlier sketch in CA 81-84
See also CLC 21
See also CLR 17
See also MAICYA
See also SATA 20, 48
Streebeck, Nancy 1934- 118
Street, Alicia (Kumpula) 1911- 5-8R
Street, Arthur George 1892-1966 .... CAP-1
Earlier sketch in CA 13-14
Street, Brian Jeffrey 1955- 133
Street, Cecil John Charles
See Rhode, John
Street, Harry 1919-1984 Obituary 112
Street, James H(arry) 1915-1988 ....CANR-4
Obituary 125
Earlier sketch in CA 53-56
Street, Jay
See Slesar, Henry
Street, Julia Montgomery 1898- CANR-2
Earlier sketch in CA 5-8R
See also SATA 11
Street, Lee
See Hampton, Kathleen
Street, Leslie
See Freemantle, Brian Harry
Street, Lucie 13-16R
Street, Margaret M(ary) 1907- 65-68
Street, Mattie (Waters) 1896- CAP-1
Earlier sketch in CA 13-16
Street, Pamela 1921- CANR-27
Earlier sketch in CA 45-48
Street, Robert
See Thomas, Gordon
Streeten, Paul Patrick 1917- CANR-28
Earlier sketches in CA 25-28R, CANR-11
Streeter, Edward 1891-1976 ....CANR-2
Obituary 65-68
Earlier sketch in CA 1-4R
See also DLB 11
Streeter, Herbert Andrus 1918- 5-8R
Streeter, James (Jr.) 61-64
Strehlow, Theodor (George Heinrich)
1908- Brief entry 106
Strehlow, Theodor George Henry
See Strehlow, Theodor (George Heinrich)
Streib, Dan(iel Thomas) 1928- 106
Streib, Gordon F(ranklin) 1918- 112
Streiker, Lowell D(ean) 1939- 49-52
Streit, Clarence Kirshman 1896-1986 ....1-4R
Obituary 119
Streithorst, Tom 1932(?)-1981 Obituary 103
Strelka, Joseph P(eter) 1927- CANR-26
Earlier sketches in CA 61-64, CANR-8
Strelsky, Katharine (Anderson) 108
Strempek, Carol Campbell 37-40R
Stren, Patti 1949- 124
Brief entry 117
See also CLR 5
See also SATA 41
Streng, Frederick J(ohn) 1933- CANR-27
Earlier sketch in CA 21-24R

Streng, William D(ietrich) 1909- CANR-1
Earlier sketch in CA 1-4R
Streng, William Paul 1937- Brief entry 108
Streshinsky, Shirley G. 1934- CANR-20
Earlier sketch in CA 85-88
Strete, Craig Kee 1950- 114
See also SATA 44
Stretton, Barbara (Humphrey) 1936- CANR-39
Earlier sketch in CA 116
See also SATA 35, 43
Stretton, Charles
See Dyer, Charles (Raymond)
Stretton, Hesba
See Smith, Sarah
Stretton, Hugh 1924- 104
Stretton, Renshaw
See Dyer, Charles (Raymond)
Stribling, T(homas) S(igismund)
1881-1965 Obituary 107
See also CLC 23
See also DLB 9
Strich, Christian 1930- 109
Strick, Ivy 1952- 85-88
Strick, Philip 1939- Brief entry 109
Stricker, George 1936- CANR-14
Earlier sketch in CA 37-40R
Strickland, Arvarh E(unice) 1930- 21-24R
Strickland, (William) Brad(ley) 1947- 130
Strickland, Charles E(verett) 1930- 77-80
Strickland, Cowles
1903(?)-1971 Obituary 33-36R
Strickland, D. A.
See Strickland, Donald A(llen)
Strickland, Donald A(llen) 1934- Brief entry 109
Strickland, Dorothy S(alley) 1933- 108
Strickland, Glenn G. 1917- 97-100
Strickland, Joshua 1896- 81-84
Strickland, Margaret 1930- 116
Strickland, Margot 1927- CANR-10
Earlier sketch in CA 65-68
Strickland, Phil D. 1941- 29-32R
Strickland, Rennard (James) 1940- 21-24R
Strickland, Rex W(allace) 1897- 45-48
Strickland, Ron(ald Gibson) 1943- 122
Strickland, Ruth Gertrude 1898- CANR-5
Earlier sketch in CA 5-8R
Strickland, Samuel 1804-1867 ....DLB 99
Strickland, Stephen P(arks) 1933- CANR-3
Earlier sketch in CA 45-48
Strickler, Susan (Elizabeth) 1952- 124
Strickon, Arnold 1930- 127
Brief entry 108
Strieber, Whitley 1945- CANR-12
Earlier sketch in CA 81-84
Strieby, Irene Macy 1894- CAP-1
Earlier sketch in CA 11-12
Strieder, Peter (Adolf) 1913- 131
Strietelmeier, John (Henry) 1920- 25-28R
Stright, Hayden Leroy 1898-1975 ....37-40R
Strike, Jeremy
See Renn, Thomas E(dward)
Striker, Cecil Leopold 1932- 109
Striker, Susan 1942- ....SATA 63
Strimple, Earl O. 1938- 97-100
Strindberg, (Johan) August 1849-1912 135
Brief entry 104
See also TCLC 1, 8, 21
See also WLC
Stringer, Arthur 1874-1950 ....DLB 92
See also TCLC 37
Stringer, David
See Roberts, Keith (John Kingston)
Stringer, Lorene A(dair) 1908- 37-40R
Stringer, Ruth M(arjorie) Pearson 1905- 5-8R
Stringer, William Henry
1908-1976 Obituary 65-68
Stringfellow, (Frank) William
1928-1985 ....CANR-9
Obituary 115
Earlier sketch in CA 5-8R
Stringfield, Leonard H(arry) 1920- 85-88
Strittmatter, Erwin 1912- ....DLB 69
Strobel, Margaret 1946- 124
Strober, Gerald S. 1935- 85-88
Strobos, Robert Julius 1921- 102
Strobridge, Truman R(ussell) 1927- 41-44R
Strodach, George Kleppinger 1905- 5-8R
Strode, Hudson 1892-1976 ....CANR-8
Obituary 69-72
Earlier sketch in CA 13-16R
Strodtbeck, Fred L(ouis) 1919- 5-8R
Stroeyer, Poul 1923- CANR-14
Earlier sketch in CA 77-80
See also SATA 13
Stroh, Guy W(eston) 1931- 49-52
Stroh, Thomas F. 1924- CANR-11
Earlier sketch in CA 21-24R
Strohm, John
See Strohm, John L(ouis)
Strohm, John L(ouis) 1912-1987 Obituary 124
Strohmeyer, John 1924- 128
Brief entry 125
Strom, Deborah 1947- 123
Strom, Ingrid Mathilda 1912- 13-16R
Strom, Leslie Winter
See Winter, Leslie
Strom, Robert D(uane) 1935- CANR-10
Earlier sketch in CA 25-28R
Stroman, Duane F(rederick) 1934- 104
Stromberg, Gustaf (Benjamin)
1882-1962 Obituary 112
Stromberg, Roland N(elson) 1916- CANR-21
Earlier sketches in CA 5-8R, CANR-6
Strommen, Merton P. 1919- CANR-5
Earlier sketch in CA 9-12R
Strong, Anna Louise
1885-1970 Obituary 29-32R
Strong, Charles
See Epstein, Beryl (M. Williams)
and Epstein, Samuel
Strong, Charles Olen 1925- 5-8R
Strong, David
See McGuire, Leslie Sarah
Strong, Donald Stuart 1912- 41-44R
Strong, Douglas H(illman) 1935- 117
Brief entry 111
Strong, Eithne 1923- 97-100
Strong, Harrington
See McCulley, Johnston
Strong, J. J.
See Strong, Jeremy
Strong, Jeremy 1949- 108
See also SATA 36
Strong, John S. 1956- 138
Strong, John W. 1930- 37-40R
Strong, John William 1935- 37-40R
Strong, Jonathan 1944- 37-40R
Strong, June 1928- 126
Strong, Kenneth William Dobson
1900-1982 104
Obituary 105
Strong, Leah A(udrey) 1922- 21-24R
Strong, Lennox
See Grier, Barbara G(ene Damon)
Strong, Pat
See Hough, Richard (Alexander)
Strong, Patience
See Cushing, Winifred
Strong, Philip Nigel Warrington 1899-1983 109
Obituary 110
Strong, Roy (Colin) 1935- CANR-21
Earlier sketches in CA 49-52, CANR-1
Strong, Rupert 1911- 13-16R
Strong, Solange
See Hertz, Solange (Strong)
Strong, Susan
See Rees, Joan
Strong, Tracy B(urr) 1943- 93-96
Strong, William S. 1951- 124
Strongblood, Casper
See Webster, David Endicott
Strongin, Lynn 1939- CANR-1
Earlier sketch in CA 49-52
Strongman, K(enneth) T(homas)
1940- CANR-10
Earlier sketch in CA 61-64
Stroop, Helen E.
See Witty, Helen E. S(troop)
Strother, David B(oyd) 1928- 25-28R
Strother, David Hunter 1816-1888 ....DLB 3
Strother, Elsie (Frances Warmoth Weitzel)
1912- CANR-28
Earlier sketches in CA 65-68, CANR-11
Strother, Horatio Theodore 1930- 5-8R
Strother, Pat Wallace 1929- CANR-29
Earlier sketches in CA 65-68, CANR-9
Strother, Patricia
See Strother, Pat Wallace
Stroube, Hal 1921(?)-1983 Obituary 110
Stroud, Joe H(inton) 1936- 103
Stroud, Kandy (Andrea) 108
Stroud, Patricia Tyson 1932- 138
Stroup, Herbert H(ewitt) 1916- 13-16R
Stroup, Thomas B(radley) 1903- 25-28R
Strouse, Jean 1945- 103
See also DLB 111
Strousse, Flora G. 1897(?)-1974 Obituary 49-52
Strout, (Sewall) Cushing (Jr.) 1923- 13-16R
Strout, Richard L(ee) 1898-1990 69-72
Obituary 132
Strover, Dorothea 9-12R
Stroyen, William Basil 1925- 25-28R
Stroyer, Poul
See Stroeyer, Poul
Stroynowski, Juliusz 1919- 132
Strozier, Charles B(urnett) 1944- CANR-24
Earlier sketch in CA 107
Struble, Mitch 1945- 93-96
Struble, Virginia
See Burlingame, Virginia (Struble)
Struever, Stuart McKee 1931- 104
Strugatskii, Arkadii (Natanovich) 1925-1991 106
Obituary 135
See also CLC 27
Strugatskii, Boris (Natanovich) 1933- 106
See also CLC 27
Struglia, Erasmus Joseph 1915- 13-16R
Struik, Dirk Jan 1894- CANR-6
Earlier sketch in CA 5-8R
Struk, Danylo 1940- 57-60
Strum, Philippa 1938- 61-64
Strummer, Joe 1953(?)-
See The Clash
See also CLC 30
Strumpen-Darrie, Robert L. 1912- 13-16R
Strung, Norman 1941- CANR-14
Earlier sketch in CA 41-44R
Strunk, (William) Oliver 1901-1980 105
Strunk, Oliver 1901-1980 Obituary 97-100
Strunk, Orlo Jr. 1925- CANR-1
Earlier sketch in CA 1-4R
Strunk, William Jr. 1869-1946 Brief entry 118
Strupp, Hans H(ermann) 1921- CANR-2
Earlier sketch in CA 1-4R
Strutt, Malcolm 1936- 115
Strutton, William Harold 1918- 77-80
Strutz, Henry 1932- CANR-24
Earlier sketches in CA 5-8R, CANR-7
Struve, Walter 1935- 49-52
Struyk, Raymond J(ay) 1944- 134
Brief entry 107
Stryjkowski, Julian 1905- CANR-30
Earlier sketches in CA 49-52, CANR-3
Stryk, Dan 1951- 120
Stryk, Lucien 1924- CANR-28
Earlier sketches in CA 13-16R, CANR-10
Stryker, Daniel
See Morris, Chris(topher Crosby)
and Stump, Jane Barr
Stryker, (Philip) David 1916- 45-48
Stryker, Perrin 1908- 5-8R
Stryker, Sheldon 1924- 9-12R
Stryker-Rodda, Harriet 1905- 81-84
Stryker-Rodda, Kenn 1903-1990 73-76
Obituary 132
Stuart, Aimee 1886(?)-1981 Obituary 103
Stuart, Alex
See Stuart, (Violet) Vivian (Finlay)
Stuart, Alice V(andockum) 1899- 13-16R
Stuart, Anthony
See Hale, Julian A(nthony) S(tuart)
Stuart, Charles
See Mackinnon, Charles Roy
and Reid, Charles (Stuart)
Stuart, Clay
See Whittington, Harry (Benjamin)
Stuart, Colin 1910- 104
Stuart, Dabney 1937- CANR-8
Earlier sketch in CA 17-20R
See also DLB 105
Stuart, David
See Hoyt, Edwin P(almer) Jr.
Stuart, Don A.
See Campbell, John W(ood Jr.)
Stuart, Douglas (Keith) 1943- 115
Stuart, Forbes 1924- 69-72
See also SATA 13
Stuart, Francis 1902- 13-16R
Stuart, Graham H. 1887- CAP-1
Earlier sketch in CA 13-14
Stuart, Ian
See MacLean, Alistair (Stuart)
Stuart, Ian 1927- CANR-30
Earlier sketches in CA 73-76, CANR-13
Stuart, Irving R. 1916- CANR-14
Earlier sketch in CA 41-44R
Stuart, (Jessica) Jane 1942- CANR-31
Earlier sketch in CA 41-44R
Stuart, Jay Allison
See Tait, Dorothy
Stuart, Jesse (Hilton) 1906-1984 ....CANR-31
Obituary 112
Earlier sketch in CA 5-8R
See also CLC 1, 8, 11, 14, 34
See also DLB 9, 48, 102
See also DLBY 84
See also SATA 2, 36
Stuart, Kenneth
See Cox, P(atrick) Brian
See also DLB 9
Stuart, Leslie
See Marlowe, Kenneth
Stuart, Lyle 1922- 81-84
Stuart, Margaret
See Paine, Lauran (Bosworth)
Stuart, Monroe
See Shapiro, Max
Stuart, Reginald (Charles) 1943- CANR-38
Earlier sketch in CA 116
Stuart, Richard Bernard 1933- 41-44R
Stuart, Sarah Payne 1952- 136
Stuart, Sheila
See Baker, Mary Gladys Steel
Stuart, Sidney
See Avallone, Michael (Angelo, Jr)
Stuart, Simon (Walter Erskine) 1930- 29-32R
Stuart, V. A.
See Stuart, (Violet) Vivian (Finlay)
Stuart, Virginia (Elaine) 1953- 128
Stuart, (Violet) Vivian (Finlay) 1914- CANR-12
Earlier sketch in CA 13-16R
Stuart, W. J.
See MacDonald, Philip
Stuart, Warren
See MacDonald, Philip
Stuart-Clark, Christopher (Anthony)
1940- CANR-24
Earlier sketch in CA 107
See also SATA 32
Stuart-Jones, Edwyn Henry 1895- CAP-1
Earlier sketch in CA 13-16
Stub, Holger R(ichard) 1922- 41-44R
Stubbings, Hilda Uren
See U'Ren-Stubbings, Hilda
Stubblebine, James H(arvey)
1920-1987 97-100
Obituary 121
Stubblefield, Harold W. 1934- 17-20R
Stubbs, Harry C(lement) 1922- CANR-26
Earlier sketches in CA 13-16R, CANR-7
See also Clement, Hal
Stubbs, Jean 1926- 5-8R
Stubbs, Joanna 1940- ....SATA 53
Stubbs, John C(aldwell) 1936- 29-32R
Stubbs, P(eter) C(harles) 1937- 117
Stuber, Florian (Cy) 1947- CANR-24
Earlier sketch in CA 106
Stuber, Stanley I(rving) 1903-1985 ....CAP-1
Obituary 116
Earlier sketch in CA 13-14
Stubis, Talivaldis 1926- ....SATA 5
Stubley, Trevor (Hugh) 1932- ....SATA 22
Stuckenschmidt, H(ans) H(einz)
1901-1988 ....CANR-18
Obituary 126
Earlier sketch in CA 25-28R
Stuckey, Elma 1907(?)-1988 Obituary 126
Stuckey, Gilbert B. 1912- 65-68
Stuckey, Sterling 1932- 101
Stuckey, William Joseph 1923- 41-44R
Stucki, Curtis W(illiam) 1928- 13-16R
Stucky, Solomon 1923- 117
Stucky, Steven 1949- 109
Stucley, Elizabeth
See Northmore, Elizabeth Florence
Studd, Stephen (Allen) 1946- 116
Studdert-Kennedy, (William) Gerald 1933- 131
Studebaker, J. W.
See Studebaker, John W(ard)
Studebaker, John W(ard)
1887-1989 Obituary 129
Studer, Gerald C. 1927- 65-68
Studlar, Donley T(rent) 1947- 120
Stueart, Robert D. 1935- 105
Stuebing, (Arthur) Douglas 1913- 25-28R
Stueck, William Whitney Jr. 1945- 105
Stuempke, Harald
See Steiner, Gerolf
Stuermann, Walter E(arl) 1919-1965 ....5-8R
Stuermer, Nina Roberta 1933- 104
Stuerup, Georg Kristoffer 1905- 25-28R
Stuewe, Paul 1943- 130
Stuhlmann, Gunther 1927- 25-28R
Stuhlmueller, Carroll 1923- CANR-24
Earlier sketches in CA 13-16R, CANR-9
Stulman, Julius 1906- 118
Stultifer, Morton
See Curtis, Richard (Alan)
Stultz, Newell M(aynard) 1933- 29-32R
Stump, Jane Barr 1936- 133
Stumpf, Samuel Enoch 1918- 41-44R
Stumpf, Stephen A(lan) 1949- CANR-34
Earlier sketch in CA 111
Stumpke, Harald
See Steiner, Gerolf
Stunkard, Albert J(ames) 1922- 117
Stunkel, Kenneth Reagan 1931- 127
Stuntz, Albert Edward
1902-1976 Obituary 65-68
Stuntz, Laurance F(itzhugh) 1908- 61-64
Stupak, Ronald J(oseph) 1934- 29-32R
Stupples, Peter (Cecil) 1936- 133
Sturcken, Frank 1929- 135
Sturdivant, Frederick D(avid) 1937- 41-44R
Sturgeon, Foolbert
See Stack, Frank H(untington)
Sturgeon, Theodore (Hamilton)
1918-1985 ....CANR-32
Obituary 116
Earlier sketch in CA 81-84
See also Queen, Ellery
See also CLC 22, 39
See also DLB 8
See also DLBY 85
See also MTCW
Sturgeon, Wina 85-88
Sturges, Patricia P(atterson) 1930- 69-72
Sturges, Preston 1898-1959 Brief entry 114
See also DLB 26
Sturges, Robert S(tuart) 1953- 138
Sturgill, Claude C(arol) 1933- CANR-9
Earlier sketch in CA 13-16R
Sturgis, James L(averne) 1936- 37-40R
Sturm, Ernest 1932- 65-68
Sturm, John E. 1927- 37-40R
Sturm, Rudolf 1912- Brief entry 109
Sturm, Sara
See Sturm-Maddox, Sara Higgins
Sturmey, S(tanley) G(eorge) 1924- 9-12R
Sturm-Maddox, Sara Higgins
1938- Brief entry 108
Sturmthal, Adolf F(ox) 1903-1986 ....9-12R
Obituary 119
Sturrock, Jeremy
See Healey, Ben (James)
Stursberg, Peter 1913- 101
Sturt, Mary 1896- CAP-2
Earlier sketch in CA 23-24
Sturtevant, Catherine Obituary 104
Sturtevant, David Reeves 1926- 104
Sturtevant, Peter M(ann) Jr. 1943- 69-72
Sturton, Hugh
See Johnston, H(ugh) A(nthony) S(tephen)
Sturtzel, Howard A(llison) 1894- CANR-6
Earlier sketch in CA 1-4R
See also SATA 1
Sturtzel, Jane Levington 1903- CANR-6
Earlier sketch in CA 1-4R
See also SATA 1
Sturup, Georg Kristoffer
See Stuerup, Georg Kristoffer
Stutler, Boyd B. 1889-1970 ....CAP-2
Earlier sketch in CA 23-24
Stutz, Robert Michael 1941- Brief entry 110
Stutzman, Esther M. Friesner
See Friesner-Stutzman, Esther M.
Styan, J(ohn) L(ouis) 1923- CANR-6
Earlier sketch in CA 5-8R
Stycos, J(oseph) Mayone 1927- 13-16R
Styles, Jimmie C(arter) 1931- 41-44R
Styles, (Frank) Showell 1908- CANR-21
Earlier sketches in CA 1-4R, CANR-6
See also SATA 10
Stylianos, Andrew John 1956- 138
Stylla, Joanne
See Branden, Victoria (Fremlin)
Styron, Rose (Burgunder) 1928- 17-20R
Styron, William 1925- CANR-33
Earlier sketches in CA 5-8R, CANR-6
See also BEST 90:4
See also CDALB 1968-1988
See also CLC 1, 3, 5, 11, 15, 60
See also DLB 2
See also DLBY 80
See also MTCW
Styx, Marguerite (Salzer)
1908(?)-1975 Obituary 53-56
Suares, Guy 1932- 103

Suarez, Mario 1925- ... DLB 82
Suarez, Virgil 1962- ... 131
See also HW
Suarez Lynch, B.
See Borges, Jorge Luis
Suarez Lynch, B.
See Bioy Casares, Adolfo
and Borges, Jorge Luis
Suba, Susanne ... 29-32R
See also SATA 4
Subak-Sharpe, Genell J(ackson)
1936- ... CANR-31
Earlier sketch in CA 112
Subbiah, B(ommireddi) V(enkata)
1917-1975 ... 41-44R
Subilia, Vittorio 1911- ... CANR-4
Earlier sketch in CA 9-12R
Sublette, Edith Blanche 1909- ... 17-20R
Sublette, Walter (Edwards) 1940- ... 124
Brief entry ... 117
Subond, Valerie
See Grayland, Valerie (Merle Spanner)
Such, Peter 1939- ... DLB 60
Sucharitkul, Somtow 1952- ... 118
Sucher, Dorothy 1933- ... 128
Sucher, Harry V(ictor) 1915- ... 89-92
Su Chien 1884-1918 Brief entry ... 123
See also Su Man-shu
Suchlicki, Jaime 1939- ... CANR-29
Earlier sketch in CA 29-32R
Suchman, Edward A(llen) 1915-197 (?) ... CAP-1
Earlier sketch in CA 13-14
Suchocki, Marjorie Hewitt 1933- ... 109
Suchoff, Benjamin 1918- ... CANR-11
Earlier sketch in CA 69-72
Suckiel, Ellen Kappy 1943- ... 127
Suckling, John 1609-1642 ... DLB 58
Suckow, Ruth 1892-1960 Obituary ... 113
See also DLB 9, 102
Sucre, Guillermo 1933- ... HW
Suda, Zdenek (Ludvik) 1920- ... CANR-31
Earlier sketch in CA 29-32R
Sudbery, Rodie 1943- ... 104
See also SATA 42
Sudermann, Hermann
1857-1928 Brief entry ... 107
See also DLB 118
See also TCLC 15
Sudhalter, Richard M(errill) 1938- ... 101
Sudman, Seymour 1928- ... CANR-15
Earlier sketch in CA 41-44R
Sue, Eugene 1804-1857 ... DLB 119
Sue, Judy
See Epstein, Judith Sue
Suedfeld, Peter 1935- ... 41-44R
Sueflow, August R(obert) 1922- ... 9-12R
Sueltz, Arthur Fay 1928- ... CANR-2
Earlier sketch in CA 49-52
Suenens, Leon Joseph 1904- ... 61-64
Sueskind, Patrick 1949- ... CLC 44
Sueyoshi, Akiko 1942- ... 132
Suffling, Mark
See Rowland, D(onald) S(ydney)
Sufrin, Sidney Charles 1910- ... CANR-17
Earlier sketches in CA 5-8R, CANR-2
Sugano, Takuo 1931- ... 123
Sugar, Bert Randolph 1937- ... CANR-9
Earlier sketch in CA 65-68
Sugarman, Daniel A(rthur) 1931- ... 21-24R
Sugarman, Joan G. 1917- ... SATA 64
Sugarman, Tracy 1921- ... 21-24R
See also SATA 37
Sugden, John 1947- ... 120
Sugden, Mark 1902-1990 ... CAP-1
Obituary ... 130
Earlier sketch in CA 13-14
Sugerman, Danny 1954- ... 137
Sugerman, Shirley 1919- ... 65-68
Sugg, Joyce (Marie) 1926- ... 131
Sugg, Redding S(tancill) Jr. 1922- ... CANR-2
Earlier sketch in CA 45-48
Sugg, Richard P(eter) 1941- ... 131
Suggs, George G(raham) Jr. 1929- ... 41-44R
Suggs, M(arion) Jack 1924- ... CANR-3
Earlier sketch in CA 1-4R
Suggs, Robert Carl 1932- ... 9-12R
Suggs, Willie Kathryn 1950- ... 77-80
Sugimoto, Yoshio 1939- ... 130
Sugita, Yutaka 1930- ... 115
See also SATA 36
Sugiyama, Shinya 1949- ... 132
Sugnet, Charles (Joseph) 1944- ... 109
Suh, Dae-Sook 1931- ... 21-24R
Suhl, Benjamin ... 49-52
Suhl, Yuri (Menachem) 1908-1986 ... CANR-38
Obituary ... 121
Earlier sketches in CA 45-48, CANR-2
See also CLR 2
See also MAICYA
See also SAAS 1
See also SATA 8, 50
Suhor, Charles 1935- ... CANR-10
Earlier sketch in CA 25-28R
Suhr, Elmer George 1902-1976 ... 9-12R
Obituary ... 65-68
Su Hsuan-ying
See Su Chien
Su Hsuean-ying
See Su Chien
Suid, Lawrence Howard 1938- ... 101
Suid, Murray 1942- ... CANR-30
Earlier sketch in CA 97-100
See also SATA 27
Suinn, Richard M(ichael) 1933- ... 29-32R
Suits, Daniel B(urbidge) 1918- ... 29-32R
Sujata, Anagarika 1948- ... 65-68
Suk, Julie ... CANR-38
Earlier sketch in CA 115
Sukarno, (Ahmed) 1901-1970 Obituary ... 113
Sukenick, Ronald 1932- ... CANR-32
Earlier sketch in CA 25-28R
See also CAAS 8
See also CLC 3, 4, 6, 48
See also DLBY 81
Sukhotin-Tolstoy, Tatyana
See Tolstoy, Tatyana (Sukhotin)
Sukhwal, Bheru Lal 1929- ... 57-60
Sukiennik, Adelaide Weir 1938- ... 126
Suknaski, Andrew 1942- ... 101
See also CLC 19
See also DLB 53
Suleiman, Ezra N. 1941- ... 85-88
Suleiman, Michael W(adie) 1934- ... CANR-9
Earlier sketch in CA 21-24R
Suleiman, Susan Rubin ... CANR-28
Earlier sketch in CA 109
Suleri, Sara 1953- ... 136
Sulimirski, Tadeusz Joseph
1898-1983 Obituary ... 110
Sulitzer, Paul-Loup 1946- ... 126
Brief entry ... 122
Sulkin, Sidney 1918- ... CANR-17
Earlier sketches in CA 5-8R, CANR-2
Sullens, Idelle 1921- ... 21-24R
Sullivan, A(loysius) M(ichael) 1896-1980 ... CAP-2
Obituary ... 97-100
Earlier sketch in CA 29-32
Sullivan, Alan 1868-1947 ... DLB 92
Sullivan, Alvin 1942- ... 29-32R
Sullivan, Anita T. 1942- ... 123
Sullivan, Barry
See Sullivan, Matthew Barry
Sullivan, C(harles) Gardner
1886(?)-1965 Obituary ... 113
See also DLB 26
Sullivan, Chester L(amar) 1939- ... 53-56
Sullivan, Clara K(atherine) 1915- ... 21-24R
Sullivan, Colleen (M.) 1950-1991 ... 117
Obituary ... 133
Sullivan, D(ale) H(owill) 1936- ... 61-64
Sullivan, Dan(iel Joseph) 1935- ... 135
Sullivan, Denis G(artland) 1929- ... 103
Sullivan, Donald 1942(?)-1989 Obituary ... 130
Sullivan, Dulcie Turner 1895-1969 ... CAP-2
Earlier sketch in CA 25-28
Sullivan, Earl L. 1942- ... 124
Sullivan, Ed(ward Vincent)
1902(?)-1974 Obituary ... 89-92
Sullivan, Edmund V(incent) 1938- ... 61-64
Sullivan, Edward A(nthony) 1936- ... 115
Sullivan, Edward Daniel 1913- ... 5-8R
Sullivan, Eleanor (Regis) 1928- Brief entry ... 112
Sullivan, Elizabeth L.
1904(?)-1985 Obituary ... 115
Sullivan, Faith 1933- ... 134
Sullivan, Francis John 1892-1976 ... CAP-2
Obituary ... 65-68
Earlier sketch in CA 25-28
See also Sullivan, Frank
Sullivan, Francis (Patrick) 1929- ... CANR-7
Earlier sketch in CA 57-60
Sullivan, Frank
See Sullivan, Francis John
See also DLB 11
Sullivan, Frank 1912-1975 ... 65-68
Obituary ... 61-64
Sullivan, George Edward 1927- ... 13-16R
See also SATA 4
Sullivan, J(ohn) P(atrick) 1930- ... CANR-26
Earlier sketches in CA 25-28R, CANR-10
Sullivan, Jack 1946- ... 119
Sullivan, James L(enox) 1910- ... 29-32R
Sullivan, Jerry 1938- ... 115
Sullivan, John L. 1908- ... 21-24R
Sullivan, Judy 1936- ... 53-56
See also AITN 1
Sullivan, Kevin 1918(?)-1987 ... CANR-34
Obituary ... 122
Earlier sketch in CA 1-4R
Sullivan, Larry E. 1944- ... 136
Sullivan, Louis (Graydon) 1951- ... 134
Sullivan, Marion F. 1899- ... 37-40R
Sullivan, Mark W(ilbur) 1927- ... 25-28R
Sullivan, Martin (Gloster) 1910-1980 ... 107
Obituary ... 104
Sullivan, Martin (Richard Preece) 1934- ... 29-32R
Sullivan, Mary Ann 1954- ... 125
See also SATA 63
Sullivan, Mary B(arrett) 1918- ... 13-16R
Sullivan, Mary W(ilson) 1907- ... CANR-12
Earlier sketch in CA 73-76
See also SATA 13
Sullivan, Matthew Barry 1915- ... 132
Sullivan, Maurice William 1925- ... CANR-2
Earlier sketch in CA 5-8R
Sullivan, Michael B. 1938- ... 77-80
Sullivan, (Donovan) Michael 1916- ... CANR-3
Earlier sketch in CA 5-8R
Sullivan, Nancy 1929- ... 17-20R
Sullivan, Navin 1929- ... 5-8R
Sullivan, Pat
See Messmer, Otto
Sullivan, Paul (Robert) 1951- ... 133
Sullivan, Peggy (Anne) 1929- ... CANR-12
Earlier sketch in CA 29-32R
Sullivan, Prescott 1904(?)-1985 Obituary ... 116
Sullivan, Richard E(ugene)
1921- Brief entry ... 115
Sullivan, Richard 1908-1981 ... 77-80
Obituary ... 104
Sullivan, Robert E(rtel) 1947- ... 135
Sullivan, Roger J. 1928- ... 132
Sullivan, Rosemary 1947- ... 97-100
Sullivan, Ruth Christ 1924- ... 57-60
Sullivan, Sean Mei
See Sohl, Jerry
Sullivan, Sheila 1927- ... CANR-14
Earlier sketch in CA 77-80
Sullivan, Sister Bede 1915- ... 25-28R
Sullivan, Stanislaus 1930- ... 127
Sullivan, Thomas Joseph Jr. 1947- ... 81-84
See also SATA 16
Sullivan, Thomas (William) 1940- ... 127
Sullivan, Tom
See Sullivan, Thomas Joseph Jr.
Sullivan, Tony
See Sullivan, Stanislaus
Sullivan, Vernon
See Vian, Boris
Sullivan, Victoria 1943- ... 65-68
Sullivan, Vincent F. 1899- ... CAP-2
Earlier sketch in CA 29-32
Sullivan, Walter (Laurence) 1924- ... 41-44R
Sullivan, Walter Seager 1918- ... CANR-2
Earlier sketch in CA 1-4R
Sullivan, Walter 1906- ... 13-16R
Sullivan, William H(ealy) 1922- ... 133
Sullivan, William M. 1945- ... 109
Sullivant, Robert S(cott) 1925- ... 1-4R
Sulloway, Alison G. 1917- Brief entry ... 111
Sulloway, Frank J(ones) 1947- ... 124
Brief entry ... 118
Sully, (Lionel Henry) Francois
1927-1971 ... CAP-2
Obituary ... 29-32R
Earlier sketch in CA 25-28
Sully, Kathleen M. 1910- ... 13-16R
Sully, Nina (Rosemary) 1948- ... 110
Sully Prudhomme 1839-1907 ... TCLC 31
Sultan, Arne 1925-1986 Obituary ... 118
Sultan, Stanley 1928- ... CANR-26
Earlier sketches in CA 13-16R, CANR-10
Sultana, Donald Edward 1924- ... 103
Sulte, Benjamin 1841-1923 ... DLB 99
Sulzberger, Arthur Hays
1891-1968 Obituary ... 89-92
Sulzberger, C(yrus) L(eo II) 1912- ... CANR-23
Earlier sketches in CA 53-56, CANR-7
Sulzberger, Iphigene (Bertha) Ochs
1892-1990 Obituary ... 131
Sulzberger, Marina Tatiana
1919(?)-1976 Obituary ... 111
Su Man-shu
See Su Chien
See also TCLC 24
Sumichrast, Jozef 1948- ... SATA 29
Sumichrast, Michael M. 1921- ... CANR-21
Earlier sketch in CA 104
Sumida, Jon Tetsuro 1949- ... 124
Sumiko
See Davies, Sumiko
Summer, Brian
See Du Breuil, (Elizabeth) L(or)inda
Summer, Charles Edgar 1923- ... 81-84
Summerfield, Harry L. 1940- ... 37-40R
Summerfield, Jack
See Summerfield, John D(udley)
Summerfield, Joanne 1940- ... 117
Summerfield, John D(udley) 1927- ... 21-24R
Summerfield, Lin(da Victoria) 1952- ... 132
Summerfield, Margie 1949- ... 89-92
Summerfield, Penny 1951- ... 119
Summerforest, Ivy B.
See Kirkup, James
Summerhayes, Victor Samuel
1897(?)-1974 Obituary ... 53-56
Summerhill, J. K.
See Schere, Monroe
Summerlin, Sam(uel A.) 1928- ... CANR-34
Earlier sketch in CA 45-48
Summers, Andrew James 1942-
See The Police
See also CLC 26
Summers, Andy
See Summers, Andrew James
Summers, Anthony (Bruce) 1942- ... CANR-23
Earlier sketch in CA 69-72
Summers, Clyde Wilson 1918- ... 109
Summers, Essie
See Summers, Ethel Snelson
Summers, Ethel Snelson 1912- Brief entry ... 116
Summers, Festus P(aul) 1895- ... CAP-1
Earlier sketch in CA 11-12
Summers, Gene F(ranklin) 1936- ... CANR-12
Earlier sketch in CA 29-32R
Summers, Gordon
See Hornby, John (Wilkinson)
Summers, Hal
See Summers, Henry Forbes
Summers, Harrison B(oyd) 1894- ... 13-16R
Summers, Harry G(lenn) Jr. 1932- ... 123
Summers, Henry Forbes 1911- ... 109
Summers, Hollis (Spurgeon Jr.) 1916- ... CANR-3
Earlier sketch in CA 5-8R
See also CLC 10
See also DLB 6
Summers, Ian 1939- ... 105
Summers, James L(evingston)
1910-1973 ... 13-16R
See also SATA 28, 57
Summers, JoAn 1943- ... 106
Summers, John A.
See Lawson, H(orace) L(owe)
Summers, Joseph H(olmes) 1920- ... 41-44R
Summers, Lionel M(organ) 1905-1975 ... 45-48
Obituary ... 103
Summers, Merna 1933- ... 131
Summers, (Alphonsus Joseph-Mary Augustus) Montague
1880-1948 Brief entry ... 118
See also TCLC 16
Summers, Ray 1910- ... 13-16R
Summers, Robert E. 1918- ... 25-28R
Summers, Robert S(amuel) 1933- ... CANR-11
Earlier sketch in CA 69-72
Summers, Robert 1922- ... 77-80
Summers, Rowena
See Saunders, Jean
Summerscales, William 1921- ... 29-32R
Summersell, Charles Grayson 1908- ... CANR-19
Earlier sketches in CA 1-4R, CANR-3
Summerskill, Edith 1901-1980 Obituary ... 93-96
Summerson, John (Newenham)
1904- Brief entry ... 117
Summerson, Rachel (Elizabeth) 1944- ... 107
Summerville, James 1947- ... 119
Sumner, Cid Ricketts 1890-1970 ... 5-8R
Obituary ... 29-32R
Sumner, Colin 1949- ... 111
Sumner, David (W. K.) 1937- ... 57-60
Sumner, Eldon
See Bruno, James Edward
Sumner, Gordon Matthew 1951-
See The Police
See also CLC 26
Sumner, Lloyd Quinton 1943- ... 103
Sumner, Richard (William) 1949- ... 69-72
Sumption, Jonathan (Philip Chadwick)
1948- ... 136
Sumwalt, Martha Murray 1924- ... 69-72
Sun, Ruth Q(uinlan) 1907- ... 57-60
Sunagel, Lois A(nn) 1926- ... 93-96
Sund, Robert B(ruce) 1926- ... CANR-36
Earlier sketch in CA 29-32R
Sundarananda
See Nakashima, George Katsutoshi
Sunday, Billy
See Sunday, William Ashley
Sunday, William Ashley
1862(?)-1935 Brief entry ... 120
Sundberg, Trudy James 1925- ... 17-20R
Sundell, Roger H(enry) 1936- ... 21-24R
Sunder, Shyam 1944- ... 118
Sunderland, Eric 1930- ... CANR-21
Earlier sketch in CA 103
Sunderland, Glenn W. 1925- ... 25-28R
Sunderland, Lane V(on) 1945- ... 97-100
Sunderlin, Sylvia 1911- ... 73-76
See also SATA 28
Sunderman, James F. 1919- ... 17-20R
Sunderman, Lloyd Frederick
1905-1983 Obituary ... 109
Sundgaard, Arnold (Olaf) 1909- ... CANR-2
Earlier sketch in CA 45-48
Sundman, Per Olof 1922- Brief entry ... 111
Sundquist, Eric J. 1952- ... 129
Sundquist, James L(loyd) 1915- ... 29-32R
Sundquist, Ralph Roger Jr.
1922- Brief entry ... 106
Sung, Betty Lee ... CANR-10
Earlier sketch in CA 25-28R
See also SATA 26
Sung, P. M.
See Chun, Jinsie K(yung) S(hien)
Sungolowsky, Joseph 1931- ... 41-44R
Sunley, Margaret 1921-1990 ... 134
Sunners, William 1903-1988 ... CAP-1
Obituary ... 125
Earlier sketch in CA 9-10
Sunoo, Harold Hak-Won 1918- ... 41-44R
Sunseri, Alvin R(aymond) 1925- ... 93-96
Sunshine, John 1897(?)-1987 Obituary ... 123
Sunstein, Emily W(eisberg) 1924- ... 53-56
Suny, Ronald Grigor 1940- ... CANR-29
Earlier sketch in CA 111
Sun Yat-sen, Madame
See Soong Ching-ling
Sun Yefang 1908-1983 Obituary ... 109
Super, Donald E(dwin) 1910- ... CANR-3
Earlier sketch in CA 1-4R
Super, R(obert) H(enry) 1914- ... 13-16R
Super Santa
See Berman, Ed
Supervielle, Jules 1884-1960 Obituary ... 114
Suponev, Michael 1923- ... 65-68
Suppe, Frederick (Roy) 1940- ... 41-44R
Suppes, Patrick (Colonel) 1922- ... CANR-20
Earlier sketches in CA 1-4R, CANR-4
Suppon, Charles 1949-1989 Obituary ... 128
Supraner, Robyn 1930- ... CANR-26
Earlier sketch in CA 69-72
See also SATA 20
Supree, Burt(on) 1941- ... 65-68
Obituary ... 137
Surace, Samuel J. 1919- ... 21-24R
Suran, Bernard G(regory) 1939- ... 81-84
Suransky, Valerie Polakow
See Polakow, Valerie (Suransky)
Suret-Canale, Jean 1921- ... CANR-1
Earlier sketch in CA 49-52
Surette, (Philip) Leon 1938- ... 110
Surface, Bill
See Surface, William E.
Surface, William E. 1935-1980(?) ... CANR-13
Earlier sketch in CA 5-8R
Surge, Frank 1931- ... 69-72
See also SATA 13
Suria, Violeta Lopez
See Lopez Suria, Violeta
Surkin, Marvin 1938- ... 61-64
Surkov, Alexei Aleksandrovich
1899-1983 Obituary ... 110
Surles, Lynn 1917- ... 13-16R
Surman, Charles Edward 1901- ... 5-8R
Surmelian, Leon (Zaven) 1907- ... CAP-2
Earlier sketch in CA 25-28
Surplus, Robert W. 1923- ... 5-8R
Surrey, (Arthur) John 1933- ... 117

Surrey, Peter J. 1928- 106
Surrey, Stanley Sterling
1910-1984 Obituary 113
Surtees, Robert Smith 1803-1864 ..... DLB 21
Surtz, Edward 1910(?)-1973 Obituary 41-44R
Susac, Andrew 1929- 49-52
See also SATA 5
Susan
See Graham, (Maude Fitzgerald) Susan
Susann, Jacqueline 1921-1974 65-68
Obituary 53-56
See also AITN 1
See also CLC 3
See also MTCW
Suskind, Patrick
See Sueskind, Patrick
Suskind, Richard 1925- CANR-9
Earlier sketch in CA 13-16R
Suslov, Alexander 1950- 105
Suslov, Mikhail Andreyevich
1902-1982 Obituary 105
Susman, Warren (Irving)
1927-1985 Obituary 116
Suss, Elaine 102
Susser, Mervyn (Wilfred) 1921- CANR-1
Earlier sketch in CA 45-48
Susser, Samuel S. 1910- 97-100
Susskind, Charles 1921- CANR-15
Earlier sketch in CA 85-88
Sussman, Aaron 1903- Brief entry 116
Sussman, Barry 1934- 53-56
Sussman, Cornelia Silver 1914- CANR-13
Earlier sketch in CA 5-8R
See also SATA 59
Sussman, Gerald 1933(?)-1989 Obituary 130
Sussman, Henry 1947- 111
Sussman, Herbert L. 1937- 25-28R
Sussman, Irving 1908- CANR-13
Earlier sketch in CA 77-80
See also SATA 59
Sussman, Leonard R(ichard) 1920- CANR-4
Earlier sketch in CA 53-56
Sussman, Marvin B(ernard) 1918- CANR-19
Earlier sketches in CA 9-12R, CANR-4
Sussman, Susan 1942- CANR-30
Earlier sketch in CA 111
See also SATA 48
Sutch, Richard C(harles) 1942- CANR-34
Earlier sketch in CA 107
Sutcliff, Rosemary 1920- CANR-37
Earlier sketch in CA 5-8R
See also CLC 26
See also CLR 1
See also MAICYA
See also SATA 6, 44
Sutcliffe, Anthony (Richard) 1942- CANR-34
Earlier sketch in CA 106
Suter, Ronald 1930- 41-44R
Sutermeister, Robert Arnold 1913- 5-8R
Suther, Marshall E(dward) Jr. 1918- 1-4R
Sutherland, Allan T(homas) 1950- 132
Sutherland, Arthur Eugene Jr.
1902-1973 ..... CAP-1
Obituary 41-44R
Earlier sketch in CA 19-20
Sutherland, C(arol) Humphrey V(ivian)
1908- 13-16R
Sutherland, Daniel E(llyson) 1946- CANR-26
Earlier sketch in CA 109
Sutherland, Donald W(ayne) 1931- 9-12R
Sutherland, Donald 1915- 37-40R
Sutherland, Douglas 1919- 21-24R
Sutherland, Earl Wilbur
1915-1974 Obituary 49-52
Sutherland, Efua (Theodora Morgue) 1924- 105
See also BW
See also DLB 117
See also SATA 25
Sutherland, Elizabeth
See Martinez, Elizabeth Sutherland
Sutherland, Elizabeth 1926- 85-88
Sutherland, Fraser 1946- 102
Sutherland, Gordon (Brims Black McIvor)
1907-1980 Obituary 108
Sutherland, H(erbert) W(arren)
1917-1981 ..... 13-16R
Obituary 134
Sutherland, James (Edward) 1948- CANR-2
Earlier sketch in CA 49-52
Sutherland, John (Anthony) 1933- CANR-16
Earlier sketch in CA 93-96
Sutherland, John P(atrick) 1920-1988 ..... 21-24R
Sutherland, John (Patrick)
1920-1988 Obituary 125
Sutherland, John 1919-1956 ..... DLB 68
Sutherland, Jon Nicholas 1941-1977 ..... CANR-32
Earlier sketch in CA 41-44R
Sutherland, Lucy Stuart 1903-1980 ..... CAP-1
Obituary 105
Earlier sketch in CA 13-14
Sutherland, Margaret 1941- CANR-14
Earlier sketch in CA 77-80
See also SATA 15
Sutherland, N(icola) M(ary) 1925- 49-52
Sutherland, R(ussell) Galbraith 1924- CAP-1
Earlier sketch in CA 9-10
Sutherland, Robert D(onald) 1937- 37-40R
Sutherland, Roger
See Hicks, Roger W(illiam)
Sutherland, Ronald 1933- 25-28R
Sutherland, (Norman) Stuart 1927- 65-68
Sutherland, (William) Temple (Gairdner)
1906- CAP-1
Earlier sketch in CA 9-10
Sutherland, Zena Bailey 1915- 102
See also SATA 37
Suthinee
See Ambhanwong, Suthilak
Suthren, Victor (James Henry) 1942- CANR-23
Earlier sketch in CA 107
Sutin, Lawrence 1951- 135
Sutnar, Ladislav 1897-1976 Obituary 104
Sutphen, Dick
See Sutphen, Richard Charles
Sutphen, Richard Charles 1937- CANR-28
Earlier sketches in CA 25-28R, CANR-11
Sutphin, Winfield Blair
1919(?)-1990 Obituary 131
Sutphin, Wyn Blair
See Sutphin, Winfield Blair
Sutro, Alfred 1863-1933 Brief entry 105
See also DLB 10
See also TCLC 6
Sutro, John 1903(?)-1985 Obituary 117
Sutryn, Barbara M(ay) 1927- 120
Sutter, Franz
See Strich, Christian
Sutter, Frederic Koehler 1938- 107
Sutter, Ruth E(laine) 1935- 45-48
Suttles, Gerald 1932- 85-88
Suttles, Shirley (Smith) 1922- 13-16R
See also SATA 21
Suttmeier, Richard Peter 1942- CANR-6
Earlier sketch in CA 57-60
Sutton, Ann (Livesay) 1923- CANR-10
Earlier sketch in CA 5-8R
See also SATA 31
Sutton, Antony C. 1925- 97-100
Sutton, Barry 1919-1988 Obituary 125
Sutton, Carol 1933-1985 Obituary 115
Sutton, Caroline 1953- 106
Sutton, Christine 1950- 120
Sutton, David (John) 1944- 116
Sutton, David 1947- 101
Sutton, Denys (Miller) 1917-1991 ..... CANR-20
Obituary 133
Earlier sketches in CA 53-56, CANR-5
Sutton, Eve(lyn Mary) 1906- CANR-10
Earlier sketch in CA 65-68
See also SATA 26
Sutton, Felix 1910(?)- 77-80
See also SATA 31
Sutton, George Miksch 1898-1982 107
Obituary 109
Sutton, Gordon 1910- 21-24R
Sutton, Henry
See Slavitt, David R.
Sutton, Horace (Ashley) 1919-1991 ..... CANR-10
Obituary 135
Earlier sketch in CA 13-16R
Sutton, Howard 1930- 65-68
Sutton, Jane 1950- 89-92
See also SATA 43, 52
Sutton, Jeff
See Sutton, Jefferson (Howard)
Sutton, Jefferson (Howard)
1913-1979 ..... CANR-10
Earlier sketch in CA 21-24R
Sutton, John L(awrence) 1917- 105
Sutton, L(aurence) P(aul) Elwell
See Elwell-Sutton, L(aurence) P(aul)
Sutton, Larry M(atthew) 1931- CANR-14
Earlier sketch in CA 37-40R
See also SATA 29
Sutton, Margaret Beebe 1903- 1-4R
See also SATA 1
Sutton, Maurice Lewis 1927- 13-16R
Sutton, Max Keith 1937- 93-96
Sutton, Myron Daniel 1925- 107
See also SATA 31
Sutton, Penny
See Wood, Christopher (Hovelle)
Sutton, Peter C. 1949- 132
Sutton, Remar 1941- 126
Sutton, Robert M(ize) 1915- 77-80
Sutton, Roberta Briggs 1899- 5-8R
Sutton, S(tephanne) B(arry) 1940- 29-32R
Sutton, Stack
See Sutton, Maurice Lewis
Sutton, Tony C.
See Sutton, Antony C.
Sutton, Walter 1916- 85-88
Sutton, William A(lfred) 1915- 61-64
Sutton-Smith, Brian 1924- CANR-17
Earlier sketch in CA 29-32R
Sutton-Vane, Vane Hunt
See Vane, (Vane Hunt) Sutton
Suttor, T(imothy) L(achlan) 1926- 21-24R
Suvin, Darko (Ronald) 1932- CANR-38
Earlier sketches in CA 89-92, CANR-16
Suvorov, Viktor (a pseudonym) 116
Suyin, Han
See Han, Suyin
Su Yuan-ying
See Su Chien
Su Yuean-ying
See Su Chien
Suzanne, Jamie
See Hawes, Louise
Suzuki, D. T.
See Suzuki, Daisetz Teitaro
Suzuki, Daisetz T.
See Suzuki, Daisetz Teitaro
Suzuki, Daisetz Teitaro 1870-1966 121
Obituary 111
See also MTCW
Suzuki, Teitaro
See Suzuki, Daisetz Teitaro
Suzuki, Tessa Morris
See Morris-Suzuki, Tessa
Svajian, Stephen G.
1906(?)-1977 Obituary 73-76
Svanstrom, Ragnar 1904(?)-1988 Obituary 127
Svareff, Count Vladimir
See Crowley, Edward Alexander
Svarlien, Oscar 1906- CAP-1
Earlier sketch in CA 13-16
Svartvik, Jan 1931- 21-24R
Svejda, George J. 1927- 41-44R
Svendsen, Hanne Marie 1933- 134
Svenson, Andrew E(dward)
1910-1975 ..... CANR-27
Obituary 61-64
Earlier sketch in CA 5-8R
See also Stone, Alan
See also SATA 2, 26
Svensson, Arne 1929- 49-52
Sverdlin, Hannah Grad
1911(?)-1989 Obituary 127
Svestka, Oldrich 1922-1983 Obituary 110
Svevo, Italo
See Schmitz, Aron Hector
See also TCLC 2, 35
Svirsky, Grigori 1921- 69-72
Svoboda, Frederic Joseph 1949- 116
Swaan, Wim 1927- CANR-18
Earlier sketch in CA 25-28R
Swabey, Marie Collins 1890-1966 ..... CANR-16
Earlier sketch in CA 1-4R
Swadesh, Frances Leon 1917- 120
Swadley, Elizabeth 1929- 21-24R
Swados, Elizabeth 1951- 97-100
See also CLC 12
Swados, Harvey 1920-1972 ..... CANR-6
Obituary 37-40R
Earlier sketch in CA 5-8R
See also CLC 5
See also DLB 2
Swaffer, Hannen 1879-1962 Obituary 112
Swaim, Alice Mackenzie 1911- CANR-6
Earlier sketch in CA 9-12R
Swaim, Joan (Hewatt) 1934- 138
Swaim, Lawrence 1942- 69-72
Swain, Bruce M(cArthur) 1943- 101
Swain, Charles 1801-1874 ..... DLB 32
Swain, Donald C(hristie) 1931- 29-32R
Swain, Dwight V(reeland) 1915- CANR-37
Earlier sketches in CA 17-20R, CANR-7
Swain, Frank G. 1893(?)-1975 Obituary 53-56
Swain, James E(dgar) 1897-1975 ..... CAP-2
Earlier sketch in CA 25-28
Swain, Joseph P(eter) 1955- 136
Swain, Joseph Ward 1891-1971 ..... CAP-2
Earlier sketch in CA 21-22
Swain, Margaret (Helen) 1909- 53-56
Swain, Mark
See Latimer, Dean
Swain, Marshall (William) 1940- 124
Brief entry 117
Swain, Martha H(elen) 1929- 85-88
Swain, Olive 1896- 5-8R
Swain, Raymond Charles 1912- 9-12R
Swain, Roger (Bartlett) 1949- 102
Swain, Su Zan (Noguchi) 1916- CANR-6
Earlier sketch in CA 5-8R
See also SATA 21
Swainson, Donald 1938- CANR-30
Earlier sketch in CA 109
Swainson, Eleanor Frances 111
Swale, Rose 1947- Brief entry 116
Swale, Rosie
See Swale, Rose
Swales, Martin 1940- 81-84
Swallow, Alan 1915-1966 ..... CANR-16
Obituary 25-28R
Earlier sketch in CA 1-4R
Swallow, Mark (Richard Crawley) 1963- 134
Swallow, Norman 1921- 21-24R
Swami Rama 1925- 119
Swamy, Subramanian 1939- 49-52
Swan, Berta W(aterhouse) 1928- 29-32R
Swan, Bradford Fuller
1908(?)-1976 Obituary 65-68
Swan, Carroll J. 1914-1984 Obituary 112
Swan, Christopher C(ushing) 1946- 103
Swan, Gladys 1934- CANR-39
Earlier sketches in CA 101, CANR-17
See also CLC 69
Swan, Jon 1929- 89-92
Swan, Marie
See Bartlett, Marie (Swan)
Swan, Susan 1944- ..... SATA 22
Swanberg, W(illiam) A(ndrew) 1907- CANR-8
Earlier sketch in CA 5-8R
See also CAAS 13
See also DLB 103
Swander, Mary 1950- 122
Swanger, David 1940- 49-52
Swann, Brian (Stanley Frank) 1940- CANR-31
Earlier sketch in CA 37-40R
Swann, Donald (Ibrahim) 1923- CANR-16
Earlier sketch in CA 21-24R
Swann, Francis 1913- CANR-4
Earlier sketch in CA 9-12R
Swann, Ingo 1933- 57-60
Swann, Lois 1944- CANR-12
Earlier sketch in CA 65-68
Swann, Peggy
See Geis, Richard E(rwin)
Swann, Peter C(harles) 1921- 5-8R
Swann, Thomas Burnett Jr. 1928-1976 ..... CANR-4
Earlier sketch in CA 5-8R
Swansea, Charleen 1932- CANR-16
Earlier sketch in CA 103
Swansen, Vern 1916- 49-52
Swanson, Arlene Collyer 1913- 5-8R
Swanson, Austin D. 1930- 25-28R
Swanson, Bert E(lmer) 1924- 29-32R
Swanson, Carl P(ontius) 1911- 45-48
Swanson, Don R(ichard) 1924- 13-16R
Swanson, Donald Roland 1927- 41-44R
Swanson, Edward I. 1923- 29-32R
Swanson, Gloria Borseth 1927- 77-80
Swanson, Gloria 1899(?)-1983 Obituary 109
Swanson, Gustav A(dolph) 1910- CANR-14
Earlier sketch in CA 77-80
Swanson, H(arold) N(orling) 1899- 132
Swanson, Harold B(urdette) 1917- 37-40R
Swanson, Heather (Crichton) 1949- 135
Swanson, Neil H(armon)
1896-1983 Obituary 109
Swanson, Roy Arthur 1925- 17-20R
Swanson, (Karl) Thor (Waldemar)
1922- CANR-22
Earlier sketch in CA 45-48
Swanson, Walter S. J. 1917- 29-32R
Swanson, Wayne 1951- 130
Swanton, Ernest William 1907- CANR-18
Earlier sketches in CA 5-8R, CANR-2
Swanwick, Michael 1950- 119
Swarbrick, Andrew 1955- 120
Sward, Robert (Stuart) 1933- CANR-23
Earlier sketches in CA 5-8R, CANR-5
See also CAAS 13
Swardson, Harold Roland Jr. 1925- 1-4R
Swarthout, Doris L(ouise) 1931- 77-80
Swarthout, Glendon (Fred) 1918- CANR-1
Earlier sketch in CA 1-4R
See also CLC 35
See also SATA 26
Swarthout, Kathryn 1919- 41-44R
See also SATA 7
Swartley, David Warren 1950- 102
Swartley, Willard M(yers) 1936- 117
Swartz, Harry (Felix) 1911- CANR-6
Earlier sketch in CA 57-60
Swartz, Jon D(avid) 1934- CANR-39
Earlier sketch in CA 69-72
Swartz, Marc J(erome) 1931- 21-24R
Swartz, Marvin 1941- 101
Swartz, Mary I(sabelle) 1942- 97-100
Swartz, Melvin Jay 1930- 97-100
Swartz, Norman (Manuel) 1939- 127
Swartz, Paul 1927- 5-8R
Swartz, Robert D(avid) 1937- 41-44R
Swartz, Robert J(ason) 1936- 17-20R
Swartz, Willis George 1902-1965 ..... 1-4R
Swartzlow, Ruby Johnson 1903- CAP-1
Earlier sketch in CA 13-16
Swarzenski, Hanns (Peter Theophil)
1903-1985 Obituary 116
Swatridge, Charles (John) CANR-34
Earlier sketches in CA 13-16R, CANR-7
Swatridge, Irene Maude (Mossop) CANR-34
Earlier sketches in CA 29-32R, CANR-7
Sway, Marlene 1950- 129
Swaybill, Roger E(lliot) 1943-1991 105
Obituary 133
Swayne, Geoffrey
See Campion, Sidney R(onald)
Swayne, Sam(uel F.) 1907- ..... SATA 53
Swayne, Zoa (Lourana) 1905- ..... SATA 53
Swayze, (Sarah) Beulah G(arland) 1907- 5-8R
Swayze, Carolyn (Norma) 1945- 127
Swayze, E(rnest) Harold 1930- 1-4R
Swayze, John Cameron 1906- 102
Swearengen, Thomas F. 1924- 17-20R
Swearer, Donald K(eeney) 1934- 37-40R
Swearingen, Arthur Rodger 1923- CANR-10
Earlier sketch in CA 5-8R
Sweat, Lynn 1934- ..... SATA 57
Sweazey, George E. 1905- CANR-4
Earlier sketch in CA 1-4R
Swedburg, Wilma Adeline 5-8R
Swede, George 1940- CANR-32
Earlier sketch in CA 113
See also SATA 67
Sweeney, Amin 1938- 105
Sweeney, Barry
See Hand, G(eoffrey) J(oseph Philip Macaulay)
Sweeney, (Roderick) Charles (Hinton)
1922- CANR-16
Earlier sketch in CA 21-24R
Sweeney, Earl M. 1937- 112
Sweeney, Francis 1916- 5-8R
Sweeney, Henry Whitcomb 1898-1967 ..... CAP-2
Earlier sketch in CA 17-18
Sweeney, James B(artholomew)
1910- CANR-12
Earlier sketch in CA 29-32R
See also SATA 21
Sweeney, James Johnson 1900-1986 ..... CANR-6
Obituary 119
Earlier sketch in CA 5-8R
Sweeney, Joyce (Kay) 1955- CANR-35
Earlier sketch in CA 116
See also SATA 65, 68
Sweeney, Karen O'Connor
See O'Connor, Karen
Sweeney, (Charles) Leo 1918- CANR-34
Earlier sketches in CA 37-40R, CANR-15
Sweeney, R. C. H.
See Sweeney, (Roderick) Charles (Hinton)
Sweeney, Robert Dale 1939- 45-48
Sweeney, Thomas J(ohn) 1936- 41-44R
Sweeney, William J(oseph) III 1922- 45-48
Sweeney, William J(oseph) III 1922- CANR-33
Sweeny, Mary K. 1923- 126
Sweet, Donald H(erbert) 1925- 112
Sweet, Franklyn Haley 1916- 9-12R
Sweet, Frederick A(rnold) 1903- CAP-2
Earlier sketch in CA 17-18
Sweet, George Elliott 1904- 45-48
Sweet, J(ohn) P(hilip) M(cMurdo) 1927- 119
Sweet, James Stouder 1918- 41-44R
Sweet, Jeffrey 1950- 81-84
Sweet, Leonard Ira 1947- 97-100

Sweet, Muriel W. 1888-1977 ... 106
Sweet, Paul R(obinson) 1907- ... 77-80
Sweet, Robert Burdette 1930- ... 85-88
Sweet, Sarah C.
See Jewett, (Theodora) Sarah Orne
Sweet, Waldo Earle 1912- ... 1-4R
Sweeting, George 1924- ... CANR-11
Earlier sketch in CA 65-68
Sweetkind, Morris 1898- ... 13-16R
Sweetland, Nancy A(nn) 1934- ... SATA 48
Sweetland, Richard C. 1931- ... 119
Sweetman, Jack 1940- ... CANR-26
Earlier sketches in CA 25-28R, CANR-10
Sweetman, Rosita (Anne) 1948- ... 124
Brief entry ... 118
Sweets, John Frank 1945- ... 89-92
Sweetser, Mary (Chisholm) 1894- ... 41-44R
Sweetser, Ted
See Sweetser, Mary (Chisholm)
Sweetser, Thomas P(atrick) 1939- ... 112
Sweetser, Wesley D(uaine) 1919- ... 37-40R
Sweezy, Alan Richardson 1907- ... 41-44R
Sweezy, Paul M(arlor) 1910- ... CANR-5
Earlier sketch in CA 1-4R
Sweigard, Lulu E. Obituary ... 53-56
Swell, Lila ... 97-100
Sweney, Fredric 1912- ... 1-4R
Swenson, Allan A(rmstrong) 1933- ... 77-80
See also SATA 21
Swenson, Clifford H(enrik) Jr. 1926- ... 45-48
Swenson, Judy Harris 1947- ... 120
Swenson, Karen 1936- ... 53-56
See also CAAS 13
Swenson, Loyd S(ylvan) Jr. 1932- ... CANR-15
Earlier sketch in CA 41-44R
Swenson, May 1919-1989 ... CANR-36
Obituary ... 130
Earlier sketch in CA 5-8R
See also CLC 4, 14, 61
See also DLB 5
See also MTCW
See also SATA 15
Swenson, Peggy
See Geis, Richard E(rwin)
Swenson, Peggye 1933- ... 73-76
Swensson, Paul S. 1907- ... 77-80
Swerdlow, Amy (Miriam) G(alstuck) 1923- ... 105
Swerling, Jo 1897- ... DLB 44
Swetman, Glenn R(obert) 1936- ... CANR-4
Earlier sketch in CA 53-56
Swetnam, Evelyn (Frances) 1919- ... 93-96
Swets, John A(rthur) 1928- ... CANR-9
Earlier sketch in CA 21-24R
Swetz, Frank J. 1937- ... 135
Swezey, Kenneth M.
1905(?)-1972 Obituary ... 33-36R
Swicegood, Thomas L. P. 1930- ... 53-56
Swick, Clarence 1883(?)-1979 Obituary ... 89-92
Swick, Kevin J(ames) 1943- ... 111
Swick, Marly 1949- ... 135
Swick, Thomas 1952- ... 138
Swidler, Ann 1944- ... 132
Swidler, Arlene (Anderson) 1929- ... CANR-12
Earlier sketch in CA 61-64
Swidler, Leonard 1929- ... CANR-7
Earlier sketch in CA 17-20R
Swierenga, Robert P. 1935- ... 25-28R
Swift, Augustus
See Lovecraft, H(oward) P(hillips)
Swift, Benjamin
See McKimmey, James
Swift, Bryan
See Knott, William C(ecil Jr.)
Swift, Carolyn Ruth 1928- ... 107
Swift, Clive 1936- ... 129
Swift, David
See Kaufmann, John
Swift, E(dward) M(cKelvy) 1951- ... 107
Swift, Edd
See Swift, Edward
Swift, Edward 1943- ... 37-40R
Swift, George B. 1902(?)-1983 Obituary ... 110
Swift, Graham 1949- ... 122
Brief entry ... 117
See also CLC 41
Swift, Helen C(ecilia) 1920- ... 117
Swift, Helen Miller 1914- ... 1-4R
Swift, Hildegarde Hoyt
1890(?)-1977 Obituary ... 69-72
See also SATA 20
Swift, Howard W. 1908- ... CAP-1
Earlier sketch in CA 9-10
Swift, Joan 1926- ... 115
Swift, Jonathan 1667-1745 ... CDBLB 1660-1789
See also DLB 39, 95, 101
See also SATA 19
See also WLC
Swift, Kate 1923- ... 69-72
Swift, Marshall S(tefan) 1936- ... 53-56
Swift, Mary Grace 1927- ... 29-32R
Swift, Merlin
See Leeming, Joseph
Swift, Patrick 1927-1983 Obituary ... 110
Swift, Richard N(ewton) 1924- ... CANR-34
Earlier sketch in CA 1-4R
Swift, W. Porter 1914- ... 29-32R
Swigart, Rob 1941- ... CANR-28
Earlier sketches in CA 69-72, CANR-11
Swiger, Elinor Porter 1927- ... 37-40R
See also SATA 8
Swigg, Richard 1938- ... 103
Swihart, Altman K 1903- ... 1-4R
Swihart, Thomas L(ee) 1929- ... 107
Swinburne, Algernon Charles
1837-1909 Brief entry ... 105
See also CDBLB 1832-1890
See also DLB 35, 57
See also TCLC 8, 36
See also WLC
Swinburne, Laurence (Joseph) 1924- ... CANR-15
Earlier sketch in CA 61-64
See also SATA 9
Swinburne, Richard 1934- ... CANR-28
Earlier sketches in CA 25-28R, CANR-10
Swindell, Larry (Nolan) 1929- ... 25-28R
Swindells, Robert (Edward) 1939- ... CANR-21
Earlier sketch in CA 97-100
See also MAICYA
See also SAAS 14
See also SATA 34, 50
Swinden, Patrick 1941- ... 49-52
Swindler, William F(inley) 1913-1984 ... 13-16R
Obituary ... 112
Swindoll, Luci 1932- ... 112
Swineford, Ada 1917- ... 61-64
Swineshead, Richard ... DLB 115
Swinfen, Ann ... CLC 34
Swinfen, D(avid) B(erridge) 1936- ... 37-40R
Swinford, Betty (June Wells) 1927- ... CANR-7
Earlier sketch in CA 5-8R
See also SATA 58
Swinford, Bob
See Swinford, Betty (June Wells)
Swing, Raymond Gram
1887-1968 Obituary ... 89-92
Swing, Thomas Kaehao 1930- ... 9-12R
Swingle, Paul G(eorge) 1937- ... 41-44R
Swinglehurst, Edmund 1917- ... CANR-28
Earlier sketches in CA 57-60, CANR-8
Swinnerton, A(rnold) R(eber) 1912- ... 106
Swinnerton, Frank Arthur
1884-1982 Obituary ... 108
See also CLC 31
See also DLB 34
Swinnerton, James Guilford
1875-1974 Obituary ... 93-96
Swinson, Arthur 1915-1970 ... CAP-2
Earlier sketch in CA 17-18
Swint, Henry L(ee) 1909- ... 37-40R
Swinton, George 1917- ... 85-88
Swinton, John 1939- ... 111
Swinton, Stanley M(itchell)
1919-1982 Obituary ... 107
Swinton, William E(lgin) 1900- ... 13-16R
Swinyard, Alfred W(ilbur) 1915- ... 9-12R
Swire, Otta F(lora Macdonald Lois)
1898-1973 ... CAP-1
Earlier sketch in CA 13-14
Swisher, Carl Brent 1897-1968 ... CANR-16
Obituary ... 103
Earlier sketch in CA 1-4R
Swisher, (Frank) Earl 1902- ... CAP-2
Earlier sketch in CA 29-32
Swisher, Robert K. Jr. 1947- ... 61-64
Swisher, Viola Hegyi
1904(?)-1990 Obituary ... 131
Swisshelm, Jane Grey 1815-1884 ... DLB 43
Swithen, John
See King, Stephen (Edwin)
Switzer, David Karl 1925- ... 57-60
Switzer, Ellen 1923- ... CANR-2
Earlier sketch in CA 45-48
See also SATA 48
Switzer, (Perry) Richard 1925- ... CANR-18
Earlier sketch in CA 25-28R
Swivett, R. G. O.
See Trippett, Frank
Swomley, John M. Jr. 1915- ... 9-12R
Swope, George S(teel) 1915- ... 29-32R
Swope, Herbert Bayard 1882-1958 ... DLB 25
Swor, Chester E(ugene) 1907- ... 9-12R
Sword, Randall S(tanford) 1942- ... 114
Sword, Wiley 1937- ... 85-88
Swords, James ... DLB 73
Swords, Thomas 1763-1843 ... DLB 73
Swortzell, Lowell (Stanley) 1930- ... CANR-1
Earlier sketch in CA 49-52
Swycaffer, Jefferson P(utnam) 1956- ... 119
Swyhart, Barbara Ann DeMartino 1942- ... 61-64
Syberberg, Hans-Juergen 1935- ... 93-96
Sybesma, Jetske
See Ironside, Jetske
Syburg, Jane 1927- ... 29-32R
Sydenham, Michael J(ohn) 1923- ... 17-20R
Sydney, C.
See Tralins, S(andor) Robert
Sydney, Frank
See Warwick, Alan R(oss)
Sydnor, Charles W(right) Jr. 1943- ... 77-80
Sydnor, James Rawlings 1911- ... 5-8R
Sydnor, (Charles) William 1911- ... 112
Syed, Anwar H(ussain) 1926- ... 102
Syers, Ed
See Syers, William Edward
Syers, William Edward 1914- ... CANR-4
Earlier sketch in CA 1-4R
Sykes, (Richard) Adam 1940- ... 29-32R
Sykes, Alrene ... 77-80
Sykes, Christopher (Hugh) 1907-1986 ... 29-32R
Obituary ... 121
Sykes, Gerald 1903-1984 ... 134
Obituary ... 113
Sykes, Jay G(ilbert) 1922- ... 45-48
Sykes, John 1918- ... 17-20R
Sykes, Roosevelt 1906-1983 Obituary ... 110
Sylva, Carmen
See Elisabeth (Ottilie Luise), Queen (Pauline)
Sylvander, Carolyn W(edin) 1939- ... 117
Sylvester, A(lbert) J(ames) 1889- ... 101
Sylvester, Arline 1914- ... 65-68
Sylvester, Bob
See Sylvester, Robert (McPherson)
Sylvester, Dorothy 1906- ... 29-32R
Sylvester, Edward J(oseph) 1942- ... 118
Sylvester, Janet Hart 1917-1987 Obituary ... 123
Sylvester, Josuah 1562(?)-1618 ... DLB 121
Sylvester, Kathryn F.
1901(?)-1983 Obituary ... 111
Sylvester, Natalie G(abry) 1922- ... 97-100
See also SATA 22
Sylvester, Richard Standish
1926-1978 ... CANR-2
Obituary ... 77-80
Earlier sketch in CA 1-4R
Sylvester, Robert (McPherson)
1907-1975 ... 61-64
Obituary ... 57-60
Sylvester, William (Arthur) 1918- ... CANR-34
Earlier sketch in CA 45-48
Sylvestre, (Joseph Jean) Guy 1918- ... 61-64
Sylvia
See Ashton-Warner, Sylvia (Constance)
Sylvin, Francis
See Seaman, Sylvia S(ybil)
Symanski, Richard 1941- ... 111
Symcox, Geoffrey Walter 1938- ... 112
Syme, (Neville) Ronald 1913- ... CANR-6
Earlier sketch in CA 9-12R
See also SATA 2
Syme, Ronald 1903-1989 Obituary ... 129
Symeonoglou, Sarantis 1937- ... 126
Symington, David 1904-1984 ... CAP-2
Obituary ... 113
Earlier sketch in CA 29-32
Symmes, Robert Edward
See Duncan, Robert (Edward)
Symmons-Symonolewicz, Konstantin
1909- ... 37-40R
Symonds, Craig L. 1946- ... 126
Symonds, Helen Sanford 1899- ... 5-8R
Symonds, John ... 105
Symonds, John Addington 1840-1893 ... DLB 57
Symonds, (John) Richard (Charters)
1918- ... 21-24R
Symons, Allene 1944- ... 110
Symons, Arthur 1865-1945 Brief entry ... 107
See also DLB 19, 57
See also TCLC 11
Symons, (Dorothy) Geraldine 1909- ... 85-88
See also SATA 33
Symons, Julian (Gustave) 1912- ... CANR-33
Earlier sketches in CA 49-52, CANR-3
See also CAAS 3
See also CLC 2, 14, 32
See also DLB 87
See also MTCW
Symons, Leslie John 1926- ... CANR-26
Earlier sketch in CA 109
Symons, R(obert) D(avid) 1898-1973 ... 41-44R
Symons, (H. B.) Scott 1933- ... 77-80
See also DLB 53
Symser, H(amilton) M(artin) 1901- ... 13-16R
Synan, Edward A(loysius) 1918- ... 17-20R
Synan, (Harold) Vinson 1934- ... CANR-14
Earlier sketch in CA 37-40R
Synge, (Edmund) J(ohn) M(illington)
1871-1909 Brief entry ... 104
See also CDBLB 1890-1914
See also DC 2
See also DLB 10, 19
See also TCLC 6, 37
Synge, (Phyllis) Ursula 1930- ... CANR-1
Earlier sketch in CA 49-52
See also SATA 9
Synnestvedt, Sig(fried T.) 1924-1977 ... 37-40R
Syntax, John
See Dennett, Herbert Victor
Sypher, Francis Jacques Jr. 1941- ... CANR-10
Earlier sketch in CA 57-60
Sypher, Lucy Johnston 1907- ... CANR-2
Earlier sketch in CA 45-48
See also SATA 7
Sypher, Wylie 1905- ... CANR-3
Earlier sketch in CA 1-4R
Syracuse, Marcella Pfeiffer 1930- ... 21-24R
Syrdal, Rolf A(rthur) 1902- ... 25-28R
Syred, Celia 1911- ... CANR-12
Earlier sketch in CA 29-32R
Syrett, David 1939- Brief entry ... 106
Syrett, Harold Coffin 1913-1984 Obituary ... 113
Syrkin, Marie 1899-1989 ... CANR-6
Obituary ... 127
Earlier sketch in CA 9-12R
Syrop, Konrad 1914- ... CANR-5
Earlier sketch in CA 9-12R
Syruc, J.
See Milosz, Czeslaw
Sysyn, Frank E. 1946- ... 126
Syvertsen, Edythe 1921- ... 73-76
Syverud, Genevieve Wold 1914- ... 21-24R
Szabo, Denis 1929- ... CANR-20
Earlier sketch in CA 89-92
Szabolcsi, Bence 1899-1973 Obituary ... 116
Szajkowski, Zosa
See Frydman, Szajko
Szancer, Henryk Obituary ... 61-64
Szaniawski, Jerzy 1886-1970 Obituary ... 29-32R
Szanto, George H. 1940- ... 41-44R
Szanton, Peter L(oeb) 1930- ... CANR-11
Earlier sketch in CA 69-72
Szasz, Ferenc Morton 1940- ... 125
Szasz, Kathleen 1912- ... 25-28R
Szasz, Margaret Connell 1935- ... 97-100
Szasz, Suzanne (Shorr) 1915- ... CANR-18
Earlier sketches in CA 5-8R, CANR-3
See also SATA 13
Szasz, Thomas (Stephen) 1920- ... CANR-9
Earlier sketch in CA 17-20R
Szathmary, Louis (Istvan) II 1919- ... 81-84
Szaz, Zoltan Michael 1930- ... CANR-3
Earlier sketch in CA 1-4R
Szczesniak, Boleslaw (B.) 1908- ... 9-12R
Szczypiorski, Andrzej 1924- ... 133
Szechter, Szymon 1920(?)-1983 Obituary ... 110
Szekely, Endre 1922- ... 17-20R
Szekeres, Cyndy 1933- ... 137
See also MAICYA
See also SAAS 13
See also SATA 5, 60
Szent-Gyoergyi, Albert (von Nagyrapolt)
1893-1986 Obituary ... 120
Brief entry ... 112
Szent-Gyorgyi, Albert (von Nagyrapolt)
See Szent-Gyoergyi, Albert (von Nagyrapolt)
Szep
See Szep, Paul (Michael)
Szep, Paul (Michael) 1941- ... 128
Brief entry ... 110
Szeplaki, Joseph 1932- ... 73-76
Szerlip, Barbara 1949- ... CANR-3
Earlier sketch in CA 49-52
Szigeti, Joseph 1892-1973 ... CAP-1
Earlier sketch in CA 9-10
Szilard, Leo 1898-1964 Obituary ... 113
Szirtes, George 1948- ... CANR-27
Earlier sketch in CA 109
See also CLC 46
Szittya, Ruth Outland 1910- ... 112
Szoeverffy, Joseph 1920- ... CANR-17
Earlier sketch in CA 65-68
Szogyi, Alex 1929- ... CANR-35
Earlier sketch in CA 45-48
Szporluk, Roman 1933- ... CANR-1
Earlier sketch in CA 45-48
Szpur, Mary 1956- ... 128
Szudek, Agnes S(usan) P(hilomena)
... SATA 49, 57
Szulc, Tad 1926- ... CANR-23
Earlier sketches in CA 9-12R, CANR-4
See also SATA 26
Szumigalski, Anne 1922- ... CANR-36
Earlier sketches in CA 49-52, CANR-1, 16
Szumski, Bonnie 1958- ... 122
Szwarc, Josef 1947- ... 118
Szydlow, Jarl
See Szydlowski, Mary Vigliante
Szydlowski, Mary Vigliante 1946- ... 104
Szydlowski, Roman 1918(?)-1983 Obituary ... 111
Szyliowicz, Joseph S. 1931- ... 41-44R
Szymanski, Albert (John)
1942(?)-1985 Obituary ... 115
Szymanski, Richard
See Symanski, Richard

T

T. B. D.
See James, William Milbourne
T. V. Vet
See Straiton, E(dward) C(ornock)
Taaffe, Edward James 1921- ... 85-88
Taaffe, James G. 1932- ... 17-20R
Taaffe, Michael
See Maguire, R(obert) A(ugustine) J(oseph)
Taagepera, Rein 1933- ... 109
Tabachnik, Abraham B(er)
1902-1970 Obituary ... 29-32R
Taback, Simms 1932- Brief entry ... 115
See also SATA 36, 40
Tabak, Israel 1904- Brief entry ... 105
Tabard, Geoffrey
See McNelly, Willis E(verett)
Tabard, Peter
See Blake, L(eslie) J(ames)
Tabb, Jay Yanai 1907-1976 ... CAP-2
Earlier sketch in CA 29-32
Taber, Anthony Scott 1944- ... 105
Taber, George M(cCaffrey) 1942- ... 65-68
Taber, Gladys (Bagg) 1899-1980 ... CANR-4
Obituary ... 97-100
Earlier sketch in CA 5-8R
See also SATA 22
Taber, Julian Ingersoll 1929- Brief entry ... 106
Taber, Robert ... 17-20R
Taber, Robert W(illiam) 1921- ... 73-76
Tabler, Edward C. 1916- ... 5-8R
Tablet, Hilda
See Swann, Donald (Ibrahim)
Tabor, Paul
See Tabori, Paul
Tabor, Stephen 1951- ... 127
Tabori, George 1914- ... CANR-4
Earlier sketch in CA 49-52
See also CLC 19
Tabori, Paul 1908-1974 ... CANR-5
Obituary ... 53-56
Earlier sketch in CA 5-8R
Taborsky, Edward (Joseph) 1910- ... CANR-3
Earlier sketch in CA 1-4R
Tabouis, Genevieve 1892-1985 Obituary ... 117
Tabrah, Ruth Milander 1921- ... CANR-28
Earlier sketches in CA 13-16R, CANR-10
See also SATA 14
Tacey, William S(anford) 1904- ... 37-40R
Tachau, Frank 1929- ... 127
Brief entry ... 111
Tachau, Mary K(atherine) Bonsteel 1926- ... 85-88

Tache, Joseph-Charles 1820-1894 ... DLB 99
Tacheron, Donald Glen 1928- ... 21-24R
Tack, Alfred 1906- ... 104
Tadlock, Max R. 1919- ... 17-20R
Tadrack, Moss
See Caryl, Warren
Taegel, William S(tephens) 1940- ... 45-48
Taetzsch, Lyn 1941- ... CANR-8
Earlier sketch in CA 57-60
Taeuber, Alma Ficks 1933- ... 17-20R
Taeuber, Conrad 1906- ... CANR-28
Earlier sketch in CA 45-48
Taeuber, Irene Barnes 1906-1974 Obituary ... 106
Taeuber, Karl E(rnst) 1936- ... CANR-28
Earlier sketch in CA 17-20R
Tae-yong, Ro
See Rutt, Richard
Tafel, Edgar Allen 1912- ... 89-92
Taffy
See Llewellyn, D(avid) W(illiam) Alun
Tafolla, (Mary) Carmen 1951- ... 131
See also DLB 82
See also HW
Taft, Charles P(helps II)
1897-1983 Obituary ... 110
Brief entry ... 105
Taft, John (Thomas) 1950- ... 133
Taft, Pauline Dakin 1891- ... CAP-1
Earlier sketch in CA 13-16
Taft, Philip 1902-1976 Obituary ... 69-72
Taft, Ronald 1920- ... 21-24R
Taft, William H(oward) 1915- ... 13-16R
Tafti, H. B. Dehqani
See Dehqani-Tafti, H. B.
Tafuri, Manfredo 1935- ... CANR-26
Earlier sketch in CA 69-72
Tafuri, Nancy 1946- ... 118
See also MAICYA
See also SAAS 14
See also SATA 39
Tager, Jack 1936- ... 118
Tageson, Carroll W(illiam) 1925- ... 53-56
Taggard, Genevieve 1894-1948 ... DLB 45
Taggart, Dorothy T(rekell) 1917- ... 102
Taggart, (Paul) John 1942- ... CANR-1
Earlier sketch in CA 45-48
Taggart, John Scott
See Scott-Taggart, John
Taggart, Joseph Herman
1902-1984 Obituary ... 112
Taggart, Robert (III) 1945- Brief entry ... 111
Tagiuri, Renato 1919- ... 77-80
Tagliabue, John 1923- ... 21-24R
Tagliaferri, Aldo 1931- ... 77-80
Tagliavia, Sheila 1936- ... 104
Tagore, Amitendranath 1922- ... 61-64
Tagore, Rabindranath 1861-1941 ... 120
Brief entry ... 104
See also MTCW
See also TCLC 3
Taha, Hamdy A(bdelaziz) 1937- ... 37-40R
Taha, Karen T(erry) 1942- ... 120
See also SATA 71
Tahara, Mildred Machiko 1941- ... 104
Taheri, Amir 1942- ... 136
Tahir, Abe M(ahmoud) Jr. 1931- ... 69-72
Tahir, Kemal 1910(?)-1973 Obituary ... 45-48
Tahlaquah, David
See LeMond, Alan
Tahtinen, Dale R(udolph) 1945- ... 65-68
Tai, Hung-chao 1929- ... 73-76
Taibo, Paco Ignacio II 1949- ... 131
See also HW
Taichert, Louise C(ecile) 1925- ... 89-92
Taikeff, Stanley 1940- ... 109
Taines, Beatrice (Green) 1923- ... CANR-14
Earlier sketch in CA 73-76
Taira, Koji 1926- ... 41-44R
Taishoff, Sol J(oseph) 1904-1982 ... 73-76
Obituary ... 107
Tait, Alan A(nderson) 1934- ... CANR-10
Earlier sketch in CA 21-24R
Tait, Dorothy 1902(?)-1972 Obituary ... 33-36R
Tait, Douglas 1944- ... SATA 12
Tait, George E(dward) 1910- ... 5-8R
Tait, Katharine 1923- ... 65-68
Tait, L(eslie) Gordon 1926- ... 45-48
Taitz, Emily 1937- ... 85-88
Takacs, Carol Addison 1926- ... 124
Takagi, Akimitsu 1920- Brief entry ... 108
Takahashi, Akira 1932- ... 29-32R
Takahashi, Yasundo 1912- ... CANR-14
Earlier sketch in CA 41-44R
Takaki, Ronald T(oshiyuki) 1939- ... 37-40R
Takakjian, Portia 1930- ... SATA 15
Takashima, Shizuye 1928- ... 45-48
See also SATA 13
Takayama, Akira 1932- ... CANR-2
Earlier sketch in CA 49-52
Takeshita, Thomas Kohachiro
1891(?)-1973 Obituary ... 45-48
Takeuchi, Yoshinori 1913- ... 132
Taki
See Theodoracopulos, Taki
Taktsis, Costas 1927-1988 ... 21-24R
Obituary ... 126
Talafous, Don (Francis) 1926- ... 113
Talamantes, Florence Williams 1931- ... CANR-6
Earlier sketch in CA 57-60
Talamini, John T(homas) 1940- ... 126
Brief entry ... 113
Talarico, Ross 1945- ... 73-76
Talbert, Ansel Edward (McLaurine)
1912-1987 Obituary ... 124
Talbert, Charles Gano 1912- ... 5-8R
Talbert, Charles H(arold) 1934- ... CANR-31
Earlier sketches in CA 41-44R, CANR-14
Talbert, Marc 1953- ... 136
See also SATA 68
Talbot, Alice-Mary 1939- ... 112
Talbot, Allan R. 1934- ... CANR-10
Earlier sketch in CA 21-24R
Talbot, Carol Terry 1913- ... 13-16R
Talbot, Charlene Joy 1928- ... CANR-8
Earlier sketch in CA 17-20R
See also SATA 10
Talbot, Edward Hugh Frederick Chetwynd
See Chetwynd-Talbot, Edward Hugh Frederick
Talbot, Godfrey (Walker) 1908- ... 107
Talbot, Gordon (Gray) 1928- ... CANR-14
Earlier sketch in CA 69-72
Talbot, Hugh
See Chetwynd-Talbot, Edward Hugh Frederick
Talbot, Kay
See Rowland, D(onald) S(ydney)
Talbot, Lawrence
See Bryant, Edward (Winslow Jr.)
Talbot, Michael 1953- ... 119
Obituary ... 137
Talbot, Nathan B(ill) 1909- ... 104
Talbot, Norman (Clare) 1936- ... CANR-9
Earlier sketch in CA 21-24R
Talbot, Ross B. 1919- ... 17-20R
Talbot, Toby 1928- ... CANR-29
Earlier sketch in CA 21-24R
See also Josephs, Rebecca
See also SATA 14
Talbot Rice, David
See Rice, David Talbot
Talbot Rice, Tamara (Abelson)
See Rice, Tamara (Abelson) Talbot
Talbott, Basil 1899-1985 Obituary ... 117
Talbott, Hudson 1949- ... 128
Talbott, John E(dwin) 1940- ... 25-28R
Talbott, Robert D(ean) 1928- ... 57-60
Talbott, Strobe 1946- ... 93-96
See also AITN 1
Talcott, Dudley Vaill 1899-1986 Obituary ... 119
Talese, Gay 1932- ... CANR-9
Earlier sketch in CA 1-4R
See also AITN 1
See also CLC 37
See also MTCW
Talker, T.
See Rands, William Brighty
Talkin, Gil
See Rosenthal, Alan
Talkington, Virginia Savage
See McAlester, Virginia
Tall, Deborah 1951- ... CANR-22
Earlier sketch in CA 105
Tall, Stephen
See Crook, Compton Newby
Talland, George A(lexander) 1917- ... CAP-2
Earlier sketch in CA 25-28
Tallcott, Emogene ... 29-32R
See also SATA 10
Tallent, Elizabeth (Ann) 1954- ... 117
See also CLC 45
Tallent, Norman 1921- ... 17-20R
Talleur, Richard W(iley) 1931- ... 97-100
Talley-Morris, Neva B(ennett) 1909- ... 57-60
Tallman, Albert 1902- ... 53-56
Tallon, Robert 1939- ... CANR-8
Earlier sketch in CA 9-12R
See also SATA 28, 43
Tally, Ted 1952- ... 124
Brief entry ... 120
See also CLC 42
Talmadge, Marian ... SATA 14
Talmage, Anne
See Powell, Talmage
Talmage, Frank (Ephraim) 1938- ... 97-100
Talmey, Allene
See Plaut, Allene Talmey
Talmon, Jacob L(aib) 1916-1980 ... 13-16R
Obituary ... 101
Talmon, Shemaryahu 1920- ... CANR-28
Earlier sketches in CA 29-32R, CANR-12
Talpalar, Morris 1900- ... 73-76
Talvi
See Robinson, Therese
Talvj
See Robinson, Therese
Tamaki, Norio 1940- ... 128
Tamar, Erika 1934- ... SATA 62
Tamari, Meier 1927- ... 127
Tamarin, Alfred H. 1913-1980 ... CANR-4
Obituary ... 102
Earlier sketch in CA 29-32R
See also SATA 13
Tamasi, Aron 1897-1966 Obituary ... 114
Tambasco, Anthony J(oseph) 1939- ... 117
Tambi
See Tambimuttu, Thurairajah
Tambiah, S. J.
See Tambiah, Stanley Jeyaraja
Tambiah, Stanley Jeyaraja 1929- ... 123
Tambimuttu, Thurairajah
1915(?)-1983 Obituary ... 110
Tambling, Jeremy (Charles Richard) 1948- ... 128
Tambs, Lewis Arthur 1927- ... CANR-4
Earlier sketch in CA 53-56
Tamburine, Jean 1930- ... 9-12R
See also SATA 12
Tamburri, Anthony Julian 1949- ... 138
Tamedly, Elisabeth L. 1931- ... 29-32R
Tames, Richard (Lawrence) 1946- ... 103
See also SATA 67
Tamir, Max Mordecai 1912- ... 29-32R
Tamir, Vicki 1924- ... 29-32R
Tammaro, Thom(as Michael) 1951- ... 109
Tammeus, William David 1945- ... 136
Tamminga, Frederick W(illiam) 1934- ... 135
Tamminga, Frederick (William) 1934- ... SATA 66
Tammsaare, A(nton) H(ansen)
1878-1940 ... TCLC 27
Tammuz, Benjamin 1919-1989 ... CANR-36
Obituary ... 129
Earlier sketch in CA 85-88
See also SATA 63
Tamny, Martin 1941- ... 37-40R
Tampion, John 1937- ... 73-76
Tam'si, Tchicaya U
See Tchicaya, Gerald Felix
Tamsin
See Summers, Ethel Snelson
Tamulaitis, Vytas 1913- ... 17-20R
Tamuno, Tekena N. 1932- ... 21-24R
Tan, Amy 1952- ... 136
See also AAYA 9
See also BEST 89:3
See also CLC 59
Tan, Fred 1955(?)-1990 Obituary ... 131
Tana, Tomoe (Hayashima) 1913- ... 21-24R
Tanahashi, Kazuaki 1933- ... 122
Tanaka, Beatrice 1932- ... 115
Tanaka, Hideyuki 1940- ... 132
Tanaquil, Paul
See Le Clercq, Jacques Georges Clemenceau
Tanay, Emanuel 1928- ... 93-96
Tanchuck, Nathaniel 1912- ... 13-16R
Tancock, John (Leon) 1942- ... 105
Tancredi, Laurence R(ichard) 1940- ... CANR-39
Earlier sketch in CA 116
Tandem, Felix
See Spitteler, Carl (Friedrich Georg)
Tandon, Prakash 1911- ... 93-96
Tandy, Clifford Ronald Vivien
1919(?)-1981 Obituary ... 104
Tanenbaum, Jan Karl 1936- ... 61-64
Tanenbaum, Robert ... 128
Brief entry ... 116
Tang, Peter Shen-Hao 1919- ... 1-4R
Tang, Victor 1942- ... 138
Tang, You-Shan 1946- ... SATA 53
Tang, Yungmei 1940- ... 129
Tangerman, Elmer John 1907- ... CANR-23
Earlier sketch in CA 106
Tangri, Shanti S. 1928- ... 25-28R
Tangye, Nigel (Trevithick)
1909-1988 Obituary ... 125
Brief entry ... 117
Tanham, George K(ilpatrick) 1922- ... CANR-1
Earlier sketch in CA 1-4R
Tania B.
See Blixen, Karen (Christentze Dinesen)
Taniguchi, Kazuko 1946- ... 93-96
Taniguchi, Masaharu 1893-1985 Obituary ... 116
Tanikawa, Shuntaro 1931- ... 121
Tanis, James (Robert) 1928- ... 118
Tanis, Norman Earl 1929- ... 110
Tanizaki, Jun'ichiro 1886-1965 ... 93-96
Obituary ... 25-28R
See also CLC 8, 14, 28
Tank, Herbert 1922(?)-1982 Obituary ... 108
Tank, Ronald W(arren) 1929- ... 49-52
Tankard, Alice (Doumanian) 1926- ... 117
Tankard, James William Jr. 1941- ... 73-76
Tanksley, Perry 1928- ... 37-40R
Tann, Jennifer 1939- ... 103
Tannahill, Reay 1929- ... CANR-2
Earlier sketch in CA 49-52
Tannehill, Robert C(ooper) 1934- ... CANR-26
Earlier sketch in CA 45-48
Tannen, Deborah F(rances) 1945- ... 118
Tannen, Jack 1907-1991 ... 114
Obituary ... 136
Tannen, Mary 1943- ... 105
See also SATA 37
Tannenbaum, Arnold S(herwood) 1925- ... 17-20R
Tannenbaum, Arthur C. 1941- ... 123
Tannenbaum, Beulah Goldstein 1916- ... CANR-7
Earlier sketch in CA 5-8R
See also SATA 3
Tannenbaum, D(onald) Leb 1948- ... 115
See also SATA 42
Tannenbaum, Edward R(obert) 1921- ... 17-20R
Tannenbaum, Frank 1893-1969 ... 9-12R
Tannenbaum, Harold E. 1914- ... 5-8R
Tannenbaum, Percy Hyman
1927- Brief entry ... 106
Tannenbaum, Robert 1915- ... 21-24R
Tanner, Adam 1964- ... 127
Tanner, C(harles) Kenneth 1938- ... 53-56
Tanner, Clara L(ee) 1905- ... 41-44R
Tanner, Daniel 1926- ... 17-20R
Tanner, Edward Everett III 1921-1976 ... 73-76
Obituary ... 69-72
Tanner, Helen Hornbeck 1916- ... 61-64
Tanner, Henry 1918- ... 73-76
Tanner, James M(ourilyan) 1920- ... CANR-5
Earlier sketch in CA 13-16R
Tanner, James T(homas) F(ontenot)
1937- ... 41-44R
Tanner, John
See Matcha, Jack
Tanner, John (Ian) 1927- ... 103
Tanner, John S. 1950- ... 138
Tanner, Louise S(tickney) 1922- ... 69-72
See also SATA 9
Tanner, Nancy Makepeace
1933-1989 Obituary ... 129
Tanner, Paul O(ra) W(arren) 1917- ... 61-64
Tanner, Roy L(ynn) 1947- ... 118
Tanner, Stephen L. 1938- ... 123
Tanner, Terence A(rthur) 1948- ... 135
Tanner, Thomas 1936- ... 128
Tanner, Tony 1935- ... 85-88
Tanner, William
See MIS
Tanner-Rutherford, C.
See Winchester, Clarence
Tanobe, Miyuki 1937- ... 69-72
See also SATA 23
Tanous, Peter (Joseph) 1938- ... CANR-7
Earlier sketch in CA 61-64
Tanselle, G(eorge) Thomas 1934- ... CANR-28
Earlier sketches in CA 21-24R, CANR-11
Tansill, Charles Callan 1890-1964 ... 1-4R
Tanter, Raymond 1938- ... CANR-25
Earlier sketch in CA 45-48
Tantrist
See Cox, P(atrick) Brian
Tanyzer, Harold Joseph 1929- ... 9-12R
Tanzer, Lester 1929- ... 17-20R
Tanzer, Michael David 1935- ... 57-60
Tanzi, Vito 1935- ... CANR-5
Earlier sketch in CA 53-56
Tao Lao
See Storni, Alfonsina
Tao Mulian
See Totten, George Oakley III
Tapia, Ralph J(ohn) 1925- ... 41-44R
Tapio, Pat Decker
See Kines, Pat Decker
Tapley, Caroline 1934- ... 97-100
Taplin, Glen W(illiam) 1917- ... 107
Taplin, Oliver 1943- ... 102
Taplin, Walter 1910- ... CAP-1
Earlier sketch in CA 9-10
Taplinger, Cecily Lent 1943-1983 Obituary ... 110
Taplinger, Richard Jacques
1911-1973 Obituary ... 41-44R
Taplinger, Terry
See Taplinger, Cecily Lent
Tapp, Jack Thomas 1934- ... 49-52
Tapp, June Louin 1929- ... 41-44R
Tapp, Kathy Kennedy 1949- ... CANR-39
Earlier sketch in CA 116
See also SATA 50
Tapp, Robert B(erg) 1925- ... 41-44R
Tappan, Paul Wilbur 1911-1964 ... 5-8R
Tappert, Theodore G(erhardt)
1904-1973 ... CANR-2
Earlier sketch in CA 1-4R
Tapply, William G(eorge) 1940- ... 118
Tapply H(orace) G(ardner) 1910- ... 13-16R
Tapscott, Stephen (J.) 1948- ... CANR-17
Earlier sketch in CA 89-92
Tapsell, R(obert) F(rederick) 1936- ... 21-24R
Taradash, Daniel 1913- ... 101
See also DLB 44
Taranovsky, Kiril 1911- ... 114
Taranow, Gerda ... 37-40R
Tarascio, Vincent J(oseph) 1930- ... 45-48
Tarassoff, Lev
See Troyat, Henri
Tarassuk, Leonid (Ilyich) 1925-1990 ... 130
Obituary ... 132
Tarazaga, Santiago Genoves
See Genoves Tarazaga, Santiago
Tarbell, Ida M(inerva)
1857-1944 Brief entry ... 122
See also DLB 47
See also TCLC 40
Tarbert, Gary C(harles) 1937- ... 101
Tarcher, Martin 1921- ... 17-20R
Tardat, Claude 1949- ... 136
Tardieu, Jean 1903- Brief entry ... 116
Tardiff, Olive 1916- ... 73-76
Tardivel, Jules-Paul 1851-1905 ... DLB 99
Tardy, Gaye 1929(?)-1982 Obituary ... 108
Targ, Harry R. 1940- ... 118
Targ, Russell 1934- ... 104
Targ, William 1907- ... 61-64
Targan, Barry 1932- ... CANR-17
Earlier sketch in CA 73-76
Target, G(eorge) W(illiam) 1924- ... CANR-7
Earlier sketch in CA 5-8R
Tarica, Ralph 1932- ... 113
Tarkenton, Fran(cis Asbury) 1940- ... 103
Tarkington, (Newton) Booth
1869-1946 Brief entry ... 110
See also DLB 9, 102
See also SATA 17
See also TCLC 9
Tarkovsky, Andrei (Arsenyevich)
1932-1986 ... 127
Tarling, (Peter) Nicholas 1931- ... 21-24R
Tarlock, A(nthony) Dan 1940- ... CANR-37
Earlier sketches in CA 97-100, CANR-16
Tarlov, I. M. 1905(?)-1977 Obituary ... 69-72
Tarlton, Gillian Leigh 1953- ... 119
Tarn, John Nelson 1934- ... 41-44R
Tarn, Nathaniel 1928- ... CANR-30
Earlier sketches in CA 9-12R, CANR-5
See also CAAS 16
Tarnawski, Wit(old) 1894-1988 Obituary ... 126
Tarnawsky, Ostap 1917- ... 73-76
Tarnopol, Lester 1913- ... 77-80
Tarnower, Herman 1910-1980 ... 89-92
Obituary ... 97-100
Tarpey, Elizabeth (Pinscher)
1880-1979 ... CANR-4
Earlier sketch in CA 5-8R
Tarpey, Lawrence Xavier 1928- ... 21-24R
Tarpley, Fred 1932- ... 41-44R
Tarpy, Roger M(aynard) 1941- ... 93-96
Tarr, Herbert 1929- ... 13-16R
Tarr, Joel A(rthur) 1934- ... CANR-38
Earlier sketches in CA 37-40R, CANR-14
Tarr, Judith 1955- ... 120
See also SATA 64
Tarr, Rodger L(eRoy) 1941- ... 110
Tarr, Yvonne Young 1929- ... CANR-8
Earlier sketch in CA 61-64
Tarrance, V(ernon) Lance Jr. 1940- ... 37-40R

Tarrant, Desmond 1924- 21-24R
Tarrant, John
See Egleton, Clive (Frederick)
Tarrant, John J(oseph) 1924- CANR-19
Earlier sketches in CA 53-56, CANR-4
Tarrant, Wilma
See Sherman, Jory (Tecumseh)
Tarrok, Peer
See Zwerenz, Gerhard
Tarry, Ellen 1906- 73-76
See also BW
See also CLR 26
See also SATA 16
Tarsaidze, Alexandre 1901-1978 .... 37-40R
Obituary 77-80
Tarshis, Jerome 1936- 61-64
See also SATA 9
Tarsis, Valery Yakovlevich
1906-1983 Obituary 109
Tarski, Alfred 1901(?)-1983 Obituary 111
Tarsky, Sue 1946- CANR-31
Earlier sketch in CA 112
See also SATA 41
Tart, Charles T(heodore) 1937- 29-32R
Tarter, Donald E(dward) 1938- 112
Tartre, Raymond S. 1901-1975 .... CAP-2
Earlier sketch in CA 21-22
Tarver, Ben 1927- 113
Tasca, Henry J. 1912-1979 Obituary 89-92
Tasca, Jules 1938- CANR-26
Earlier sketch in CA 109
See also AITN 1
Tasch, Peter A(nthony) 1933- 73-76
Taschdjian, Claire L(ouise) 1914- 73-76
Tashjian, Dickran (Levon) 1940- 61-64
Tashjian, Virginia A. 1921- 29-32R
See also SATA 3
Tashlin, Frank 1913-1972 113
Obituary 110
See also DLB 44
Tasker, James 1908- 49-52
See also SATA 9
Tasker, Joe 1948-1982 129
Obituary 108
Tassin, Myron Jude 1933- 61-64
Tassin, Ray(mond Jean) 1926- 53-56
Tatar, Maria M. 1945- 85-88
Tatarka, Dominik 1913-1989 Obituary 128
Tatarkiewicz, Wladyslaw 1886-1980 103
Obituary 97-100
Tatchell, Peter 1952- 125
Tate, (John Orley) Allen 1899-1979 .... CANR-32
Obituary 85-88
Earlier sketch in CA 5-8R
See also CLC 2, 4, 6, 9, 11, 14, 24
See also DLB 4, 45, 63
See also MTCW
Tate, B. H.
See Boyer, Bruce Hatton
Tate, Claudia C. 1946- 121
Tate, Edward
See Dransfield, Michael (John Pender)
Tate, Eleanora E(laine) 1948- CANR-25
Earlier sketch in CA 105
See also SATA 38
Tate, Ellalice
See Hibbert, Eleanor Burford
Tate, Gary 1930- 21-24R
Tate, George T(homas) 1931- 21-24R
Tate, Jackson R. 1899(?)-1978 Obituary 81-84
Tate, James (Vincent) 1943- CANR-29
Earlier sketch in CA 21-24R
See also CLC 2, 6, 25
See also DLB 5
Tate, Joan 1922- CANR-1
Earlier sketch in CA 49-52
See also SATA 9
Tate, Marilyn Freeman 1921- 13-16R
Tate, Mary Anne
See Hale, Arlene
Tate, Merle W(esley) 1903- CAP-1
Earlier sketch in CA 17-18
Tate, Merze 17-20R
Tate, Nahum 1652(?)-1715 .... DLB 80
Tate, Richard
See Masters, Anthony
Tate, Robin
See Fanthorpe, R(obert) Lionel
Tate, Velma 1913- 21-24R
Tatelbaum, Judith Ann 1938- 104
Tatelbaum, Judy
See Tatelbaum, Judith Ann
Tatem, Moira (Phillips) 1928- 133
Tatford, Brian F(rederick) B(arrington)
1927- CAP-1
Earlier sketch in CA 9-10
Tatford, Frederick Albert 1901- CANR-10
Earlier sketch in CA 13-16R
Tatgenhorst, John 1938- 65-68
Tatham, Andrew Francis 1949- 125
Tatham, C. Ernest 1905- CAP-1
Earlier sketch in CA 9-10
Tatham, Campbell
See Elting, Mary
Tatham, David 1932- 138
Tatham, Laura (Esther) 1919- 13-16R
Tati, Jacques
See Tatischeff, Jacques
Tatischeff, Jacques 1908-1982 Obituary 108
Tatlow, Antony 1935- 122
Taton, Rene 1915- 9-12R
Tatray, Istvan
See Rupert, Raphael Rudolph
Tattersall, Ian (Michael) 1945- 115
Tattersall, (Honor) Jill 1931- CANR-10
Earlier sketch in CA 25-28R
Tattersall, Lawrence H(olmes) 1933- 29-32R
Tattersall, M(uriel Joyce) 1931- CAP-1
Earlier sketch in CA 9-10
Tatu, Michel 1933- 25-28R
Tatum, Arlo 1923- 25-28R
Tatum, Billy Joe 1933- 61-64
Tatum, Charles M(ichael) 1943- CANR-29
Earlier sketch in CA 111
Tatum, Edward Lawrie 1909-1975 Obituary 113
Tatum, Jack
See Tatum, John David
Tatum, John David 1948- 104
Taub, Harald (Jay) 1918- 110
Taube, Evert 1890-1976 Obituary 61-64
Taube, Lester S. 1920- 69-72
Taubenfeld, Howard J(ack) 1924- 13-16R
Tauber, Abraham 1915(?)-1977 Obituary 69-72
Tauber, Edward S(anford)
1908-1988 Obituary 124
Tauber, Gerald E(rich) 1922- 89-92
Tauber, Gilbert 1935- CANR-9
Earlier sketch in CA 21-24R
Tauber, Kurt P(hilip) 1922- 21-24R
Tauber, Maurice F(alcolm) 1908-1980 105
Obituary 102
Tauber, Peter 1947- 37-40R
Taubert, Sigfred 1914- 120
Taubert, William H(owland) 1934- 103
Taubes, Frederic 1900-1981 .... CANR-9
Obituary 104
Earlier sketch in CA 17-20R
Taubes, Susan
See Feldmann, Susan Judith
Taubman, Jane A. 1942- 130
Taubman, William 1941- 21-24R
Taubr, Paul Raymond 1937- 29-32R
Taunton, Eric
See Westcott-Jones, K(enneth)
Tauranac, John 1939- 124
Ta Van Tai 1938- 133
Tavard, George H(enry) 1922- CANR-37
Earlier sketches in CA 1-4R, CANR-1, 16
Tave, Stuart M(alcolm) 1923- 104
Tavel, Ronald 1940- CANR-33
Earlier sketch in CA 21-24R
See also CLC 6
Taverne, Dick 1928- 85-88
Tavernier, Bertrand 1941- 123
Taves, Ernest H(enry) 1916- 93-96
Taves, Isabella 1915- CANR-8
Earlier sketch in CA 21-24R
See also SATA 27
Taviss, Irene
See Thomson, Irene Taviss
Tavo, Gus
See Ivan, Martha Miller Pfaff
Tavor, Eve
See Bannet, Eve Tavor
Tavuchis, Nicholas 1934- 57-60
Tavy, Peter
See Hemery, Eric
Tawa, Nicholas E. 1923- 136
Tawney, R(ichard) H(enry)
1880-1962 Obituary 93-96
Tax, Sol 1907- 5-8R
Taydo
See McDonald, Erwin L(awrence)
Tayler, Irene 136
Taylor, A(lan) J(ohn) P(ercivale)
1906-1990 .... CANR-32
Obituary 132
Earlier sketch in CA 5-8R
See also MTCW
Taylor, Alan Carey 1905-1975 Obituary 114
Taylor, Alan R(os) 1926- 109
Taylor, Alastair M(acDonald) 1915- 17-20R
Taylor, Albert E(dward) 1908- 89-92
Taylor, Alec Clifton
See Clifton-Taylor, Alec
Taylor, Alfred 1896-1973 105
Taylor, Alice J. 1909-1969 .... CAP-2
Earlier sketch in CA 25-28
Taylor, Alice L(ouise) 1911-1985 61-64
Obituary 116
Taylor, Alison 1927- 21-24R
Taylor, Alix 1921- 5-8R
Taylor, Allegra 1940- 136
Taylor, Andrew (John Robert) 1951- CANR-28
Earlier sketch in CA 110
See also SATA 70
Taylor, Andrew (McDonald) 1940- CANR-27
Earlier sketches in CA 69-72, CANR-11
Taylor, Andrew 1944-1988 126
Taylor, Anique 1946- 109
Taylor, Ann
See Smith, Richard Rein
Taylor, Ann 1782-1866 .... SATA 35, 41
Taylor, Anna 1944- 25-28R
Taylor, Anne (Gary) Pannell
1910-1984 Obituary 112
Taylor, Apirana 1956- 128
Taylor, Archer 1890-1973 Obituary 107
Taylor, Arnold H. 1929- 33-36R
Taylor, Art
See Taylor, Arthur (Stephen)
Taylor, Arthur Samuel 1894-1963 .... 1-4R
Obituary 103
Taylor, Arthur (Stephen) 1929- 122
Taylor, Audilee Boyd 1931- .... SATA 59
Taylor, Barbara G. 1942- 25-28R
Taylor, Barbara J. 1927- 53-56
See also SATA 10
Taylor, Bayard 1825-1878 .... DLB 3
Taylor, Benjamin J. 1934- 21-24R
Taylor, Bernard 1934- CANR-24
Earlier sketch in CA 69-72
Taylor, Bert Leston 1866-1921 Brief entry 117
See also DLB 25
Taylor, Betty Jo 1933- 13-16R
Taylor, Beverly (White) 1947- 132
Taylor, Bob L(eslie) 1923- 33-36R
Taylor, Brad
See Smith, Richard Rein
Taylor, Bron Raymond 1955- 138
Taylor, Carl 1937- 69-72
See also SATA 14
Taylor, Cecil Philip 1929-1981 .... 25-28R
Obituary 105
See also CLC 27
Taylor, Charlene M(ae) 1938- 33-36R
Taylor, Charles Alfred 1922- 109
Taylor, Charles D(oonan) 1938- CANR-37
Earlier sketches in CA 101, CANR-17
Taylor, Charles H. 1846-1921 .... DLB 25
Taylor, Charles Lewis 1935- CANR-13
Earlier sketch in CA 77-80
Taylor, Charles 1931- CANR-27
Earlier sketches in CA 13-16R, CANR-11
Taylor, Clyde R(ussell) 1931- 45-48
Taylor, Clyde Willis 1904-1988 Obituary 125
Taylor, Constance Lindsay 1907- 106
Taylor, Cora (Lorraine) 1936- 124
See also SATA 64
Taylor, Cora Sibal 1941(?)-1987 Obituary 123
Taylor, D. J. 1960- 122
Taylor, Dalmas A(rnold) 1933- 57-60
Taylor, David Alan 1943- 108
Taylor, David (Conrad) 1934- 105
Taylor, David 1900-1965 .... 1-4R
See also SATA 10
Taylor, Dawson 1916- CANR-25
Earlier sketch in CA 13-16R
Taylor, Day
See Parkinson, Cornelia M.
and Salvato, Sharon
Taylor, Dayna
See Parkinson, Cornelia M.
Taylor, (Joseph) Deems
1885-1966 Obituary 89-92
Taylor, Delores 138
Taylor, Demetria 1903-1977 Obituary 73-76
Taylor, (Edmund) Dennis 1940- 119
Taylor, Desmond 1930- 37-40R
Taylor, Don(ald) 1910- 13-16R
Taylor, Donald L(avor) 1916- 17-20R
Taylor, Donald Stewart 1924- Brief entry 106
Taylor, Donna June 1949- 37-40R
Taylor, Duncan (Burnett) 1912- 25-28R
Taylor, Duncan Norton
See Norton-Taylor, Duncan
Taylor, Dwight 1902-1986(?) Obituary 121
Taylor, Earl Aulick 1904-1965 .... CAP-1
Earlier sketch in CA 13-14
Taylor, Edith 1913- 45-48
Taylor, Edward 1642(?)-1729 .... DLB 24
Taylor, Eleanor Ross 1920- 81-84
See also CLC 5
Taylor, Elisabeth (D.) 1931- 135
Taylor, Elisabeth Russell
See Russell Taylor, Elisabeth
Taylor, Elizabeth Tebbetts 101
Taylor, Elizabeth 1912-1975 .... CANR-9
Earlier sketch in CA 13-16R
See also CLC 2, 4, 29
See also MTCW
See also SATA 13
Taylor, Ethel Stoddard
1895(?)-1975 Obituary 57-60
Taylor, Eugene Jackson
1913-1978 Obituary 81-84
Taylor, Florance Walton 37-40R
See also SATA 9
Taylor, Florence M(arian Tompkins)
1892- 13-16R
See also SATA 9
Taylor, Frank J. 1894-1972 .... CAP-1
Obituary 37-40R
Earlier sketch in CA 13-14
Taylor, Fred James 1919- 107
Taylor, (George) Frederick 1928- 77-80
Taylor, G(eorge) Jeffrey 1944- 116
Taylor, George
See Parulski, George R(ichard) Jr.
Taylor, George A(lbert) 1942- 102
Taylor, George E(dward) 1905- CANR-22
Earlier sketch in CA 1-4R
Taylor, Gordon O(verton) 1938- 25-28R
Taylor, Gordon Rattray 1911-1981 85-88
Obituary 105
Taylor, (Frank Herbert) Griffin 1917- 65-68
Taylor, H. Baldwin
See Waugh, Hillary Baldwin
Taylor, H. Kerr 1891(?)-1977 Obituary 73-76
Taylor, Harold L(awrence) 1934- 110
Taylor, Harold McCarter 1907- 109
Taylor, Harold S. 1901(?)-1985 Obituary 116
Taylor, Harold 1914- 25-28R
Taylor, Harry
See Granick, Harry
Taylor, Harry H. 1926- 57-60
Taylor, Helen 1947- 133
Taylor, Henry J(unior) 1902-1984 .... CAP-2
Obituary 112
Earlier sketch in CA 23-24
Taylor, Henry (Splawn) 1942- CANR-31
Earlier sketch in CA 33-36R
See also CAAS 7
See also CLC 44
See also DLB 5
Taylor, Henry 1800-1886 .... DLB 32
Taylor, Herb(ert Norman Jr.) 1942-1987 97-100
Obituary 123
See also SATA 22, 54
Taylor, Howard F(rancis) 1939- 110
Taylor, Hugh A(lexander) 1920- 115
Taylor, Hugh 1917(?)-1987 Obituary 123
Taylor, Ian 1944- 77-80
Taylor, Ina (Margaret Kathleen) 1949- 119
Taylor, Irving A. 1925- 61-64
Taylor, J. Thomas 1930- 107
Taylor, Jack W(ilson) 1915- 9-12R
Taylor, James B(entley) 1930- 37-40R
Taylor, James C(hapman) 1937- 77-80
Taylor, James R(owe) 1907- CAP-2
Earlier sketch in CA 17-18
Taylor, James Spear
1897(?)-1979 Obituary 85-88
Taylor, James Stephen 1935- 121
Taylor, Jane 1783-1824 .... SATA 35, 41
Taylor, Janelle (Diane Williams) 1944- 124
Brief entry 118
Taylor, (Samuel) Jared 1951- 122
Taylor, Jed H(arbottle) 1902- CAP-1
Earlier sketch in CA 13-16
Taylor, Jennifer (Evelyn) 1935- 128
Taylor, Jenny 1910- 105
Taylor, Jeremy F. 1952- 137
Taylor, Jeremy James 1948- 128
Taylor, Jerome 1918- CANR-1
Earlier sketch in CA 1-4R
Taylor, Jerry D(uncan) 1938- 115
See also SATA 47
Taylor, Jesse
See Amidon, Bill (Vincent)
Taylor, Jim 1937- 119
Taylor, Joan du Plat Obituary 109
Taylor, Joe Gray 1920- CANR-6
Earlier sketch in CA 57-60
Taylor, John (Alfred) 1931- 61-64
Taylor, John F(rank) A(dams) 1915- 17-20R
Taylor, John G(erald) 1931- 29-32R
Taylor, John H(ilton) 1958- 138
Taylor, John Laverack 1937- CANR-1
Earlier sketch in CA 45-48
Taylor, John M(axwell) 1930- 25-28R
Taylor, John Randolph 1929- 1-4R
Taylor, John Robert
See Taylor, Andrew (John Robert)
Taylor, John Russell 1935- CANR-37
Earlier sketch in CA 5-8R
Taylor, John Vernon 1914- CANR-21
Earlier sketches in CA 9-12R, CANR-5
Taylor, John W(illiam) R(ansom) 1922- 49-52
Taylor, John 1577(?)-1653 .... DLB 121
Taylor, John 1916- 93-96
Taylor, John 1921- CANR-16
Earlier sketch in CA 21-24R
Taylor, John 1925- 81-84
Taylor, John 1955- 124
Taylor, Joshua Charles 1917-1981 104
Taylor, Judy
See Hough, Judy Taylor
Taylor, Kamala (Purnaiya) 1924- 77-80
See also Markandaya, Kamala
Taylor, Karen
See Malpede, Karen (Sophia)
Taylor, Karl K. 1938- 41-44R
Taylor, Katharine Whiteside 1897- CAP-2
Earlier sketch in CA 25-28
Taylor, Keith Weller 1946- 111
Taylor, Ken 1922- 108
Taylor, Kenneth N(athaniel) 1917- CANR-8
Earlier sketch in CA 17-20R
See also AITN 2
See also SATA 26
Taylor, (Paul) Kent 1940- CANR-9
Earlier sketch in CA 17-20R
Taylor, L(aurie) A(ylma) 1939- CANR-30
Earlier sketch in CA 111
Taylor, L(ester) B(arbour) Jr. 1932- CANR-26
Earlier sketches in CA 57-60, CANR-11
See also SATA 27
Taylor, Larissa J(uliet) 1952- 138
Taylor, Laurie
See Taylor, L(aurie) A(ylma)
Taylor, Lawrence 1942- 105
Taylor, (M.) Lee 1930- 41-44R
Taylor, Lester D(ean) 1938- 17-20R
Taylor, Lisa (Suter) 1933-1991 128
Obituary 134
Taylor, Liz McNeill
See Taylor, Elisabeth (D.)
Taylor, Lloyd A(ndrew) 1921- 41-44R
Taylor, Lloyd C(hamberlain) Jr. 1923- 57-60
Taylor, Lois Dwight Cole
See Cole, Lois Dwight
Taylor, Lord
See Taylor, Stephen James Lake
Taylor, Louis 1900- CANR-2
Earlier sketch in CA 5-8R
Taylor, Louise Todd 1939- 115
See also SATA 47
Taylor, Malcolm Gordon 1915- 109
Taylor, Margaret
See Burroughs, Margaret Taylor (Goss)
Taylor, Margaret
See Burroughs, Margaret Taylor (Goss)
Taylor, Margaret Stewart 89-92
Taylor, Marion Ansel 1904- 13-16R
Taylor, Mark C. 1945- 125
Taylor, Mark 1927- 108
See also SATA 28, 32
Taylor, Mary Ann 1912- 97-100
Taylor, Maxwell D(avenport)
1901-1987 Obituary 122
Brief entry 111
Taylor, Michael J(ohn) H(addrick)
1949- CANR-34
Earlier sketches in CA 77-80, CANR-14
Taylor, Michael J. 1924- CANR-7
Earlier sketch in CA 17-20R
Taylor, Michael M. 1944- 97-100

Taylor, Mildred D. CANR-25
Earlier sketch in CA 85-88
See also BW
See also CLC 21
See also CLR 9
See also DLB 52
See also MAICYA
See also SAAS 5
See also SATA 15, 70
Taylor, Morris F. 1915- 37-40R
Taylor, Norman 1883-1967 ....CAP-2
Earlier sketch in CA 23-24
Taylor, Owen Reece
1912(?)-1983 Obituary 111
Taylor, P(hilip) A. M. 1920- 136
Taylor, Pat Ellis 1941- 111
Taylor, Paul B(eekman) 1930- 81-84
Taylor, Paul S(chuster) 1895-1984 ....CANR-29
Obituary 112
Earlier sketch in CA 81-84
Taylor, Paul W(arren) 1923- CANR-21
Earlier sketch in CA 1-4R
Taylor, Paul 1948- 121
Taylor, Paula (Wright) 1942- 122
Brief entry 111
See also SATA 33, 48
Taylor, Peggy 1946- 120
Taylor, Peter (Hillsman) 1917- CANR-9
Earlier sketch in CA 13-16R
See also CLC 1, 4, 18, 37, 44, 50, 71
See also DLBY 81
See also MTCW
See also SSC 10
Taylor, Philip Elbert 1908-1975 Obituary 61-64
Taylor, Phoebe Atwood
1909-1976 Obituary 61-64
Taylor, Phoebe Jean
1921(?)-1979 Obituary 89-92
Taylor, Ransom Theodore 1913- 45-48
Taylor, Ray J. 1918(?)-1977 Obituary 69-72
Taylor, Ray Ward 1908- CAP-2
Earlier sketch in CA 19-20
Taylor, Rebe Prestwich 1911- 13-16R
Taylor, Rex 1921- 13-16R
Taylor, Richard K(night) 1933- CANR-39
Earlier sketches in CA 101, CANR-18
Taylor, Richard S(helley) 1912- CANR-38
Earlier sketch in CA 115
Taylor, Richard W(arren) 1924- CANR-19
Earlier sketches in CA 5-8R, CANR-3
Taylor, Richard 1919- 17-20R
Taylor, Robert Jr. 1941- 118
Taylor, Robert B(artley) 1926- 81-84
Taylor, Robert Brown 1936- CANR-12
Earlier sketch in CA 61-64
Taylor, Robert Lewis 1912- CANR-3
Earlier sketch in CA 1-4R
See also CLC 14
See also SATA 10
Taylor, Robert Martin 1909- CAP-2
Earlier sketch in CA 25-28
Taylor, Robert R(atcliffe) 1939- 53-56
Taylor, Robert 1925- 81-84
Taylor, Roland 1907- CAP-1
Earlier sketch in CA 13-14
Taylor, Ron(ald) W(illiam) 1922- CAP-1
Earlier sketch in CA 11-12
Taylor, Ronald (Jack) 1924- CANR-26
Earlier sketch in CA 93-96
Taylor, Ronald L(ee) 1938- 77-80
Taylor, Ross McLaury
1909(?)-1977 Obituary 69-72
Taylor, Rupert (Maurice) 1946- 45-48
Taylor, Ruth Mattson 1922- 101
Taylor, Samuel (Albert) 1912- 25-28R
Taylor, Samuel (Woolley) 1907- CANR-28
Earlier sketch in CA 73-76
Taylor, Sandra C. 1936- 123
Taylor, Stephen
See Taylor, Stephen James Lake
Taylor, Stephen James Lake
1910-1988 Obituary 124
Taylor, Stephen 1948- 133
Taylor, Sybil (Renee) 1933- 122
Taylor, Sydney (Brenner)
1904(?)-1978 ....CANR-4
Obituary 77-80
Earlier sketch in CA 5-8R
See also MAICYA
See also SATA 1, 26, 28
Taylor, T(homas) F(is) 1913- 136
Taylor, T. G.
See Taylor, T(homas) Geoffrey
Taylor, T(homas) Geoffrey
1918-1987 Obituary 123
Taylor, Telford 1908- CANR-16
Earlier sketch in CA 25-28R
See also MTCW
Taylor, Theodore Brewster 1925- 102
Taylor, Theodore W(alter) 1913- 119
Taylor, Theodore 1921- CANR-38
Earlier sketches in CA 21-24R, CANR-9, 25
See also AAYA 2
See also MAICYA
See also SAAS 4
See also SATA 5, 54
Taylor, Thomas 1934- 21-24R
Taylor, Tim 1920-1974 45-48
Obituary 53-56
Taylor, Tom
See Taylor, J. Thomas
Taylor, Valerie
See Tate, Velma
Taylor, Vernon L. 1922- 33-36R
Taylor, Verta 1948- 114
Taylor, W(illiam) H(odge)
1904-1984 Obituary 113
Taylor, Walter Fuller 1900-1966 ....1-4R
Taylor, Walter W(illard) 1913- 61-64
Taylor, Warren 1903- 21-24R
Taylor, Weldon J. 1908- 1-4R
Taylor, Welford Dunaway 1938- 37-40R
Taylor, Wendell H(ertig) 1905- 102
Taylor, William David Jr.
1902-1975 Obituary 107
Taylor, William E(dwards) 1920- CANR-10
Earlier sketch in CA 25-28R
Taylor, William Ewart Jr. 1927- 126
Taylor, William L. 1937- 29-32R
Taylor, William R(obert) 1922- 138
Taylor, William 1930- CANR-15
Earlier sketch in CA 81-84
Taylor, Zack 1927- 65-68
Taylor-Gooby, Peter 1947- 118
Taylor-Olson, Clara Mae
1899(?)-1988 Obituary 124
Tazewell, Charles 1900-1972 Obituary 37-40R
Tazieff, Haroun 1914- Brief entry 113
Tchaadaieff
See Sorokin, Pitirim A(lexandrovitch)
Tchekhov, Anton
See Chekhov, Anton (Pavlovich)
Tchernichovski, Saul (Gutmanovich)
1875-1943 Brief entry 116
Tchicaya, Gerald Felix 1931-1988 129
Obituary 125
Tchicaya U Tam'si
See Tchicaya, Gerald Felix
Tchividjian, Gigi Graham 1945- 108
Tchobanoglous, George 1935- 102
Tchudi, Stephen N. 1942- CANR-22
Earlier sketch in CA 89-92
See also SATA 55
Teachout, Terry 1956- 133
Tead, Ordway 1891-1973 Obituary 45-48
Teaford, Jon C(hristian) 1946- CANR-10
Earlier sketch in CA 65-68
Teague, Bob
See Teague, Robert
Teague, Kathleen 1937- 97-100
Teague, Mark (Christopher) 1963- 136
See also SATA 68
Teague, Michael 1932- 109
Teague, Robert 1929- 106
See also SATA 31, 32
Teal, G. Donn 1932- 33-36R
Teal, John J(erome) Jr.
1921-1982 Obituary 110
Teal, Val(entine M.) 1903- 61-64
See also SATA 10
Teale, Edwin Way 1899-1980 ....CANR-2
Obituary 102
Earlier sketch in CA 1-4R
See also SATA 7, 25
Teasdale, Sara 1884-1933 Brief entry 104
See also DLB 45
See also SATA 32
See also TCLC 4
Tebbel, John (William) 1912- CANR-29
Earlier sketch in CA 85-88
See also SATA 26
Tebbel, Robert E(verett) 1924- 5-8R
Tebbetts-Taylor, Elizabeth
See Taylor, Elizabeth Tebbetts
Tebbit, Norman 1931- 138
Tebeau, Charlton Watson 1904- 110
Tebelak, John-Michael
1949(?)-1985 Obituary 115
Tec, Leon 1919- 97-100
Tec, Nechama 1931- CANR-23
Earlier sketch in CA 9-12R
Teck, Alan 1934- 25-28R
Tedder, Arthur William 1890-1967 ....CAP-2
Earlier sketch in CA 23-24
Tedder, Lord
See Tedder, Arthur William
Teddy, Paul
See Aldrich, Jonathan
Tedeschi, (Theodore) James Jr. 1928- 41-44R
Tedlock, E(rnest) W(arnock) Jr. 1910- CAP-2
Earlier sketch in CA 17-18
Tedone, David A. 1953- 132
Tedrow, R. L.
See Tedrow, Richard L(ove)
Tedrow, Richard L(ove)
1913(?)-1987 Obituary 121
Tee, John
See Meades, Jonathan (Turner)
Teece, David J(ohn) 1948- 138
Teegen, Otto John 1899-1983 Obituary 109
Teer, Frank 1934- 53-56
Teeter, Don E(l) 1934- 73-76
Teeter, Karl V(an Duyn) 1929- 17-20R
Teeters, Negley K(ing) 1896-1971 ....CAP-2
Obituary 33-36R
Earlier sketch in CA 23-24
Teetor, Paul R(aymond) 1919- 113
Teets, Bruce E. 1914- 37-40R
Teets, John Phillip 1948- 132
Tee-Van, Helen Damrosch 1893-1976 49-52
Obituary 65-68
See also SATA 10, 27
Teevan, Richard C(ollier) 1919- CANR-4
Earlier sketch in CA 1-4R
Teffeteller, Gordon Lamar 1931- 115
Tefft, Bess H(agaman)
1915(?)-1977 Obituary 110
Tega, Vasile 1921- CANR-18
Earlier sketch in CA 102
Tegenfeldt, Herman G(ustaf) 1913- 73-76
Tegerdine, Maria
See Morsy, Magali
Tegner, Bruce 1928- CANR-8
Earlier sketch in CA 61-64
See also SATA 62
Tegner, Henry (Stuart) 1901- CANR-12
Earlier sketch in CA 13-16R
Tehan, Arline Boucher 1930- 130
Teich, Albert H(arris) 1942- CANR-25
Earlier sketch in CA 45-48
Teicher, Morton I(rving) 1920- CANR-11
Earlier sketch in CA 69-72
Teichgraeber, Richard F. III 1950- 125
Teichman, Jenny 1930- 127
Teichmann, Howard (Miles)
1916-1987 ....CANR-17
Obituary 123
Earlier sketch in CA 69-72
Teikmanis, Arthur L. 1914- 13-16R
Teilhard de Chardin, (Marie Joseph) Pierre
1881-1955 Brief entry 105
See also TCLC 9
Teiser, Ruth 1915- 109
Teissier du Cros, Janet 1906- CAP-2
Earlier sketch in CA 17-18
Teitelbaum, Harry 1930- 21-24R
Teitelbaum, Michael 1953- 121
See also SATA 59
Teitelbaum, Myron 1929- 13-16R
Teitelman, Robert 1954- 135
Teixeira, Bernardo 1926- 108
Teixeira da Mota, Avelino Obituary 106
Tejima 1931- ....CLR 20
Tekeyan, Charles 1927- 29-32R
Telander, Richard F(orster) 1948- 65-68
Teleki, Geza 1943- CANR-19
Earlier sketches in CA 49-52, CANR-3
See also SATA 45
Telemaque, Eleanor Wong 1934- 104
See also SATA 43
Telescope, Tom
See Newbery, John
Telfer, Dariel (Doris) 1905-1987 ....CAP-2
Obituary 122
Earlier sketch in CA 25-28
Telfer, R(oss) 1937- 106
Telfer, William 1886-1968 ....CAP-1
Earlier sketch in CA 13-14
Telford, Charles W(itt) 1903- 65-68
Tell, Jack 1909(?)-1979 Obituary 89-92
Teller, Edward 1908- CANR-33
Earlier sketches in CAP-1, CA 13-14
See also MTCW
Teller, James D(avid) 1906- 41-44R
Teller, Judd L. 1912-1972 Obituary 33-36R
Teller, Neville 1931- CANR-23
Earlier sketch in CA 103
Teller, Walter (Magnes) 1910- CANR-2
Earlier sketch in CA 5-8R
Telles, Lygia Fagundes 1924- ....DLB 113
Tello, Carlos 1938- 112
Telser, Lester G(reenspan) 1931- 33-36R
Temianka, Henri 1906- 45-48
Temin, Peter 1937- 13-16R
Temkin, Pauline B. 1919- 25-28R
Temkin, Sara Anne Schlossberg 1913- 1-4R
See also SATA 26
Temko, Allan 1924- 136
Temko, Florence CANR-37
Earlier sketches in CA 49-52, CANR-1, 17
See also SATA 13
Temmer, Mark J. 1922- Brief entry 107
Temp, George (Edward) 1929- 45-48
Temperley, Howard 1932- 85-88
Temperley, Nicholas 1932- 107
Tempest, Jan
See Swatridge, Irene Maude (Mossop)
Tempest, Margaret Mary
1892-1982 Obituary 108
See also SATA 33
Tempest, Sarah
See Ponsonby, D(oris) A(lmon)
Tempest, Theresa
See Kent, Louise Andrews
Tempest, Victor
See Philipp, Elliot Elias
Templar, Maurice
See Groom, Arthur William
Temple, Ann
See Mortimer, Penelope (Ruth)
Temple, Arthur
See Northcott, (William) Cecil
Temple, Cliff 1947- 111
Temple, Dan
See Newton, D(wight) B(ennett)
Temple, Herbert 1919- ....SATA 45
Temple, Joe 1917- 97-100
Temple, Nigel (Hal Longdale) 1926- 29-32R
Temple, Paul
See McConnell, James Douglas Rutherford
Temple, Paul
See Durbridge, Francis (Henry)
Temple, Philip (Robert) 1939- CANR-22
Earlier sketch in CA 104
Temple, Robert (Kyle Grenville)
1945- CANR-16
Earlier sketch in CA 89-92
Temple, Robert M(ickler) Jr.
1935- Brief entry 107
Temple, Ruth Z(abriskie) 1908- 61-64
Temple, Wayne C(alhoun) 1924- CANR-17
Earlier sketches in CA 1-4R, CANR-1
Temple, Willard H. 1912- 1-4R
Temple, William 1628-1699 ....DLB 101
Temple, William 1881-1944 Brief entry 120
Templeman, Eleanor Lee (Reading)
1906-1990 Obituary 131
Templeton, Charles B. 1915- 101
Templeton, Edith 1916- 53-56
Templeton, Janet
See Hershman, Morris
Templeton, John J(oseph) Jr. 1928- 25-28R
Tenax
See Lean, Garth Dickinson
ten Boom, Corrie 1892-1983 111
Obituary 109
Tendryakov, Vladimir Fyodorovich
1923-1984(?) 104
Obituary 113
Tenenbaum, Frances 1919- CANR-12
Earlier sketch in CA 73-76
Tenenbaum, Shea 1910- CANR-1
Earlier sketch in CA 49-52
Tener, Robert L(awrence) 1924- 110
Teng, S(su)-Y(u) 1906- CANR-22
Earlier sketch in CA 13-16R
Tengbom, Mildred 1921- CANR-39
Earlier sketches in CA 97-100, CANR-17
Tenggren, Gustaf 1896-1970 ....SATA 18, 26
Ten Harmsel, Henrietta 1921- 106
Ten Hoor, Elvie (Marie Mortensen)
1900-1984 ....9-12R
Obituary 112
TenHouten, Warren David
1939- Brief entry 108
Tenhula, John 1951- 135
Tenison, Marika Hanbury
See Hanbury-Tenison, Marika
Tenison, Robin Hanbury
See Hanbury-Tenison, (Airling) Robin
Tenn, Ada N(ina) 1915- CANR-11
Earlier sketch in CA 25-28R
Tenn, William 1919- ....DLB 8
Tennant, Alan 1943- 108
Tennant, Emma (Christina) 1937- CANR-38
Earlier sketches in CA 65-68, CANR-10
See also CAAS 9
See also CLC 13, 52
See also DLB 14
Tennant, Ivo (S.) 1955- 128
Tennant, Kylie
See Rodd, Kylie Tennant
See also SATA 6
Tennant, Nora Jackson 1915- CANR-4
Earlier sketch in CA 9-12R
Tennant, (Charles) Roger 1919- 106
Tennant, Stephen (James Napier)
1906-1987 Obituary 122
Tennant, Veronica 1947- 103
See also SATA 36
Tennen, Howard 1948- 138
Tennenbaum, Silvia 1928- CANR-21
Earlier sketch in CA 77-80
Tenneshaw, S. M.
See Beaumont, Charles
and Garrett, (Gordon) Randall (Phillip)
and Silverberg, Robert
Tenness, George
See Delk, Robert Carlton
Tenney, H(orace) Kent 1892-1982 Obituary 107
Tenney, Merrill C(hapin) 1904-1985 ....CANR-4
Obituary 115
Earlier sketch in CA 1-4R
Tenney, Tabitha Gilman 1762-1837 ....DLB 37
Tenniel, John 1820-1914 Brief entry 111
See also CLR 18
See also MAICYA
See also SATA 27
Tennien, Mark A. 1900(?)-1983 Obituary 108
Tennies, Arthur C(ornelius) 1931- 53-56
Tennison, Patrick Joseph 1928- CANR-23
Earlier sketch in CA 106
Tennissen, Anthony C(ornelius) 1920-1982 114
Tennov, Dorothy 1928- 41-44R
Tennyson, Alfred
1809-1892 ....CDBLB 1832-1890
See also DLB 32
See also WLC
Tennyson, Charles (Bruce Locker)
1879-1977 ....CANR-29
Obituary 73-76
Earlier sketch in CA 81-84
Tennyson, Frederick 1807-1898 ....DLB 32
Tennyson, G(eorg) B(ernhard) 1930- CANR-9
Earlier sketch in CA 21-24R
Tenpas, Margaret (Susan Lyon) 1923- 85-88
Tensen, Ruth M(arjorie) 5-8R
Tent, Ned
See Dennett, Herbert Victor
TePaske, John J(ay) 1929- 117
Teplitz, Paul V(ictor) 1940- 111
Tepper, Albert 1928- 25-28R
Tepper, Michael 1941- CANR-12
Earlier sketch in CA 73-76
Tepper, Sheri S. 1929- 137
Tepper, Terri P(atricia) 1942- 107
Teran, Lisa St. Aubin de
See St. Aubin de Teran, Lisa
See also CLC 36
Terayama, Shuji 1936-1983 Obituary 109
Terban, Marvin 1940- ....SATA 45, 54
Terborgh, George (Willard) 1897-1989 ....CAP-2
Obituary 128
Earlier sketch in CA 23-24
Terbovich, John B. 1933-1969 ....CAP-2
Earlier sketch in CA 21-22
Terchek, Ronald John 1936- 49-52
Terdiman, Richard 1941- 73-76
Terenzio, Stephanie 1932- 118
Teresi, Judith M.
See Goldberger, Judith M.
ter Haar, Jaap 1922- 37-40R
See also Haar, Jaap ter
See also SATA 6
terHorst, J(erald) F(ranklin) 1922- 107
See also AITN 1

ter Horst, Robert 1929- 116
Terhune, Albert Payson 1872-1942 136
Brief entry 111
See also DLB 9
See also MAICYA
See also SATA 15
Terhune, William B(arclay) 1893-1987 61-64
Obituary 122
Terich, Thomas A. 1943- 125
Terkel, Louis 1912- CANR-18
Earlier sketch in CA 57-60
See also Terkel, Studs
See also MTCW
Terkel, Studs
See Terkel, Louis
See also AITN 1
See also CLC 38
Terkel, Susan N(eiburg) 1948- CANR-38
Earlier sketch in CA 115
See also SATA 59
Terlecki, Tymon Tadeusz J(ulian) 1905- 132
Terlouw, Jan (Cornelis) 1931- 108
See also SATA 30
Terman, Douglas 1933- 136
Brief entry 112
Terman, Sibyl 1902(?)-1975 Obituary 57-60
Terme, Hilary
See Hay, Jacob
Terner, Janet 1938- 102
Terni-Cialente, Fausta 1900- CANR-5
Earlier sketch in CA 5-8R
Terpstra, Vern 1927- CANR-11
Earlier sketch in CA 21-24R
Terr, Lenore (C.) 1936- 134
Terr, Leonard B(rian) 1946- 73-76
Terrace, Edward L. B.
1936(?)-1973 Obituary 45-48
Terrace, Herbert S(ydney) 1936- 102
Terrace, Vincent 1948- CANR-25
Earlier sketches in CA 65-68, CANR-9
Terraine, John (Alfred) 1921- CANR-13
Earlier sketch in CA 5-8R
Terrall, Robert 1914- 102
Terras, Victor 1921- 128
Brief entry 113
Terrell, Carroll F(ranklin) 1917- CANR-20
Earlier sketch in CA 102
Terrell, Donna McManus 1908- 57-60
Terrell, John Upton 1900-1988 ....29-32R
Obituary 127
See also SATA 60
Terrell, Robert L(ouis) 1943- CANR-17
Earlier sketch in CA 41-44R
Terres, John K(enneth) 1905- CANR-5
Earlier sketch in CA 5-8R
Terrien, Samuel Lucien 1911- 81-84
Terrill, Ross 1938- CANR-35
Earlier sketch in CA 25-28R
Terrill, Tom E(dward) 1935- 41-44R
Terris, Susan 1937- CANR-12
Earlier sketch in CA 29-32R
See also SATA 3
Terris, Virginia R(inaldy) 1917- 65-68
Terry, Arthur 1927- 85-88
Terry, Bill 1931- 118
Terry, C. V.
See Slaughter, Frank G(ill)
Terry, Carol
See Talbot, Carol Terry
Terry, Charles S. 1926(?)-1982 Obituary 107
Terry, Doug(las) 1950- 120
Terry, Edith (Buchanan) 1952- 120
Terry, Edward D(avis) 1927- 29-32R
Terry, Luther L(eonidas) 1911-1985 ....CAP-2
Obituary 115
Earlier sketch in CA 33-36
See also SATA 11, 42
Terry, Margaret
See Dunnahoo, Terry
Terry, Mark 1947- 37-40R
Terry, Marshall 1931- 1-4R
Terry, Megan 1932- 77-80
See also CABS 3
See also CLC 19
See also DLB 7
Terry, Michael 1899-1981 104
Terry, Robert H(arold) 1935- 29-32R
Terry, Robert Meredith 1939- 41-44R
Terry, Robert W(illiam) 1937- 37-40R
Terry, Sarah Meiklejohn 1937- 111
Terry, Saralee
See Kaye, Marvin (Nathan)
Terry, Walter 1913-1982 ....CANR-10
Obituary 107
Earlier sketch in CA 21-24R
See also SATA 14
Terry, William
See Harknett, Terry
Terry-Thomas
See Stevens, Thomas Terry Hoar
Terson, Peter 1932- 104
See also DLB 13
Terstegge, Mabel Alice 1905- 93-96
Tertis, Lionel 1876-1975 93-96
Obituary 57-60
Tertz, Abram
See Sinyavsky, Andrei (Donatevich)
Terwilliger, Robert E(lwin) 1917-1991 65-68
Obituary 134
Terzani, Tiziano 1938- CANR-14
Earlier sketch in CA 77-80
Terzian, James P. 1915- 13-16R
See also SATA 14
Terzian, Kathryn
See Cramer, Kathryn
Terzian, Pierre 1948- 136
Terzian, Yervant 1939- 125
TeSelle, Eugene (Arthur Jr.) 1931- 37-40R
TeSelle, Sallie McFague
See McFague, Sallie
Tesich, Steve 1943(?)- 105
See also CLC 40, 69
See also DLBY 83
Teslik, Kennan Lee 1952- 113
Tessa, Delio 1886-1939 ....DLB 114
Tessier, (Ernst) M(aurice) 1885-1973 ....CANR-3
Earlier sketch in CA 5-8R
Tessler, Mark A(rnold) 1941- CANR-37
Earlier sketches in CA 45-48, CANR-1, 16
Tessler, Stephanie Gordon 1940- 124
See also SATA 64
Tester, Sylvia Root 1939- CANR-8
Earlier sketch in CA 9-12R
See also SATA 37, 64
Teta, Jon (Anthony) 1933- 25-28R
Tetel, Julie 1950- 118
Tetel, Marcel 1932- 21-24R
Tetens, Tete Harens
1899(?)-1976 Obituary 65-68
Teternikov, Fyodor Kuzmich
1863-1927 Brief entry 104
See also Sologub, Fyodor
Tether, (Cynthia) Graham 1950- CANR-6
Earlier sketch in CA 57-60
See also SATA 36, 46
Tetlow, Edwin 1905- 17-20R
Tetreault, Wilfred F. 1927- 106
Teubal, Savina J. 1926- 132
Teune, Henry 1936- CANR-3
Earlier sketch in CA 49-52
Teunissen, John James 1933- 112
Teuscher, Robert H(erman) 1934- 77-80
Teveth, Shabtai (Amotz)
1926(?)- Brief entry 117
Tevis, Walter 1928-1984 113
See also CLC 42
Tewkesbury, Joan 1936- 101
Texon, Meyer 1909- 124
Tey, Josephine
See Mackintosh, Elizabeth
See also DLB 77
See also TCLC 14
Teynac, Francoise (Dolores Dupuis) 123
Teyte, Maggie 1888-1976 Obituary 65-68
Tezla, Albert 1915- CANR-31
Earlier sketches in CA 37-40R, CANR-14
Thacher, Alida McKay 1951- CANR-11
Earlier sketch in CA 69-72
Thacher, James 1754-1844 ....DLB 37
Thacher, Mary McGrath 1933- ....SATA 9
Thacher, Russell 1919(?)-1990 Obituary 132
Thackara, James 1944- 129
Thacker, Eric (Lee) 1923- Brief entry 107
Thacker, Ernest W(ichman) 1914- 13-16R
Thacker, Thomas William
1911-1984 Obituary 113
Thackeray, Milton G. 1914- 13-16R
Thackeray, William Makepeace
1811-1863 ....CDBLB 1832-1890
See also DLB 21, 55
See also SATA 23
See also WLC
Thackray, Arnold 1939- 49-52
Thackray, Derek V(incent) 1926- 103
Thackrey, Russell I. 1904- 37-40R
Thackrey, Ted Jr. 1918- 132
Thaddeus, Janice Farrar 1933- 13-16R
Thaden, Edward Carl 1922- 17-20R
Thain, Chris 1937- 127
Thain, Donald H(ammond) 1928- CANR-25
Earlier sketch in CA 1-4R
Thakur, Shivesh Chandra 1936- 29-32R
Thakura, Ravindranatha
See Tagore, Rabindranath
Thalacker, Donald W(illiam) 1939-1987 127
Brief entry 108
Thalberg, Irving (Grant Jr.) 1930-1987 ....41-44R
Obituary 123
Thale, Jerome 1927- 13-16R
Thaler, Alwin 1891- CAP-1
Earlier sketch in CA 11-12
Thaler, M. N.
See Kerner, Fred
Thaler, Michael C. 1936- 124
See also SATA 47, 56
Thaler, Mike
See Thaler, Michael C.
Thaler, Susan 1939- 21-24R
Thalheimer, Ross 1905-1977 ....41-44R
Thalia
See Bokum, Fanny Butcher
Thalmann, Rita Renee Line 1926- CANR-19
Earlier sketches in CA 53-56, CANR-4
Thamer, Katie 1955- ....SATA 42
Thames, C. H.
See Marlowe, Stephen
Thames, Jack
See Ryan, John Fergus
Thamm, Robert 1933- 89-92
Thampi, Parvathi (Menon) 1925- 5-8R
Thane, (Lillian) Adele 1904- 25-28R
Thane, Elswyth 1900- 5-8R
See also SATA 32
Thanet, Neil
See Fanthorpe, R(obert) Lionel
Thant, U 1909-1974 Obituary 108
Thapar, Romesh 1922- 133
Tharaud, Lucien Rostaing Jr. 1953- 69-72
Tharaud, Ross
See Tharaud, Lucien Rostaing Jr.
Tharoor, Shashi 1956- ....CLC 70
Tharp, Louise (Marshall) Hall 1898- CANR-33
Earlier sketch in CA 1-4R
See also SATA 3
Tharpe, Jac Lyndon 1928-1985 ....CANR-7
Obituary 117
Earlier sketch in CA 57-60
't Hart, Maarten 1944- 129
Thass-Thienemann, Theodore 1900- 25-28R
Thatcher, David 1922- 77-80
Thatcher, Dora (Fickling) 1912- 13-16R
Thatcher, Dorothy Southwell 1903- CAP-1
Earlier sketch in CA 13-14
Thatcher, Floyd W(ilson) 1917- 102
Thatcher, Joan (Claire) 1934- 106
Thatcher, Julia
See Bensen, Donald R.
Thaxton, John 1949- 127
Thaxton, Ralph 1944- 114
Thayer, Charles Wheeler 1910-1969 ....CANR-26
Obituary 103
Earlier sketch in CA 1-4R
Thayer, Emma R(edington) Lee
1874-1973 ....CAP-1
Obituary 45-48
Earlier sketch in CA 9-10
Thayer, Ernest Lawrence
1863-1940 Brief entry 119
See also SATA 60
Thayer, Frederick C(lifton) Jr. 1924- CANR-12
Earlier sketch in CA 73-76
Thayer, George (Chapman Jr.)
1933-1973 ....CAP-2
Obituary 45-48
Earlier sketch in CA 25-28
Thayer, Geraldine
See Daniels, Dorothy
Thayer, H(orace) S(tandish) 1923- CANR-27
Earlier sketch in CA 45-48
Thayer, James Stewart 1949- 73-76
Thayer, Jane
See Woolley, Catherine
Thayer, Lee
See Thayer, Emma R(edington) Lee
Thayer, Lee (Osborne) 1927- CANR-18
Earlier sketches in CA 49-52, CANR-3
Thayer, Marjorie Brief entry 116
See also SATA 37
Thayer, Mary Van Rensselaer
1903(?)-1983 97-100
Obituary 111
Thayer, Molly
See Thayer, Mary Van Rensselaer
Thayer, Nathaniel B(owman) 1929- 45-48
Thayer, Peter
See Wyler, Rose
Thayer, Theodore 1904-1981 Obituary 103
Thayer, V(ivian) T(row) 1886-1979 ....CAP-2
Obituary 89-92
Earlier sketch in CA 17-18
Thayler, Carl 1933- 37-40R
See also CAAS 11
Thayne, Emma Lou 1924- 65-68
Thayne, Miria Greenwood 1907- 21-24R
Theakston, Kevin 1958- 127
Theall, Donald Francis 1928- 105
Thebaud, Jo 1914- 49-52
Theberge, James D.
See Theberge, James Daniel
Theberge, James Daniel 1930-1988 ....25-28R
Obituary 124
Thede, Marion Draughon 1903- CAP-2
Earlier sketch in CA 25-28
Thee, Marek 1918- 101
The Ear
See McLellan, Diana
Theen, Rolf H(einz) W(ilhelm) 1937- 41-44R
The Fourth Brother
See Aung, (Maung) Htin
The Gallerite
See Bason, Frederick (Thomas)
The Great Comte
See Hawkesworth, Eric
The Great Merlini
See Rawson, Clayton
Theil, Henri 1924- CANR-22
Earlier sketches in CA 17-20R, CANR-7
Theiner, George (Fredric) 1927-1988 ....CANR-27
Earlier sketch in CA 29-32R
Theis, John William 1911- Brief entry 109
Theis, Paul A(nthony) 1923- 41-44R
Theisen, Jerome Paul 1930- 113
Theissen, Gerd 1943- 117
Thekaekara, Matthew P(othen)
1914-1976 77-80
Obituary 69-72
Thelen, David P(aul) 1939- 134
Brief entry 110
Thelen, Gil 1938- 73-76
Thelen, Herbert Arnold 1913- 108
Thelin, John R(obert) 1947- CANR-11
Earlier sketch in CA 69-72
Thelle, Notto R(eidar) 1941- 125
Thelwall, John 1764-1834 ....DLB 93
Thelwell, Michael Miles 1939- 101
See also CLC 22
Thelwell, Norman 1923- CANR-4
Earlier sketch in CA 5-8R
See also SATA 14
Themerson, Stefan 1910-1988 ....CANR-28
Obituary 126
Earlier sketches in CA 65-68, CANR-9
See also SATA 65
Theo, Ion
See Theodorescu, Ion N.
Theobald, Lewis Jr.
See Lovecraft, H(oward) P(hillips)
Theobald, Robert 1929- 37-40R
Theocharis, Reghinos D(emetrios)
1929- CANR-11
Earlier sketch in CA 13-16R
Theodoracopulos, Taki 1937- 129
Theodorakis, Michalis 1925- Brief entry 105
Theodorakis, Mikis
See Theodorakis, Michalis
Theodorakopoulos, Ioannis
1900-1981 Obituary 108
Theodoratus, Robert J(ames) 1928- 41-44R
Theodore, Athena 1919- 41-44R
Theodore, Chris A(thanasios) 1920- 13-16R
Theodore, Sister Mary 1907- 5-8R
Theodorescu, Ion N. 1880-1967 Obituary 116
Theodorson, George A. 1924- 29-32R
Theoharis, Athan G(eorge) 1936- CANR-30
Earlier sketches in CA 29-32R, CANR-12
The Old Settler
See Lyman, Albert Robison
The Prophet
See Dreiser, Theodore (Herman Albert)
Theriault, Albert A(ugustine) Jr. 1928- 53-56
Theriault, Yves 1915-1983 102
See also DLB 88
Therio, Adrien 1925- ....DLB 53
Thernstrom, Abigail M. 1936- 127
Thernstrom, Stephan (Albert) 1934- 13-16R
Theroux, Alexander (Louis) 1939- CANR-20
Earlier sketch in CA 85-88
See also CLC 2, 25
Theroux, Joseph (Peter) 1953- 133
Theroux, Paul (Edward) 1941- CANR-20
Earlier sketch in CA 33-36R
See also BEST 89:4
See also CLC 5, 8, 11, 15, 28, 46
See also DLB 2
See also MTCW
See also SATA 44
Theroux, Peter (Christopher Sebastian)
1956- 132
Theroux, Phyllis 1939- 110
Thersites
See Bram, Christopher
Thesen, Hjalmar Peter 1925- 107
Thesen, Sharon 1946- ....CLC 56
Thesiger, Wilfred (Patrick) 1910- CAP-2
Earlier sketch in CA 17-18
Thesing, William B(arney) 1947- CANR-32
Earlier sketch in CA 113
Theunissen, Michael 1932- 132
Thevenin, Denis
See Duhamel, Georges
Thevoz, Michel 1936- 132
Thewlis, P(eter) J(ohn) 1944- 127
Thibaudeau, Colleen 1925- 113
See also DLB 88
Thibaudeau, May Murphy 1908- 131
Thibault, Jacques Anatole Francois
1844-1924 127
Brief entry 106
See also France, Anatole
See also MTCW
Thibault, John C(rowell) 1922- 77-80
Thiebaud, Wayne 1920- 45-48
Thiebaux, Marcelle 1931- 122
Brief entry 110
Thieda, Shirley Ann 1943- 69-72
See also SATA 13
Thiele, Colin (Milton) 1920- CANR-28
Earlier sketches in CA 29-32R, CANR-12
See also CLC 17
See also CLR 27
See also MAICYA
See also SAAS 2
See also SATA 14
Thiele, Edwin R(ichard) 1895- CAP-1
Earlier sketch in CA 19-20
Thiele, Margaret Rossiter 1901- 21-24R
Thielen, Benedict 1903-1965 ....DLB 102
Thielen, Thoraf Theodore 1921- 5-8R
Thielens, Wagner P. Jr. 1925- 1-4R
Thielicke, Helmut 1908-1986 ....CANR-11
Obituary 118
Earlier sketch in CA 69-72
Thiem, E(zra) George 1897-1987 134
Obituary 123
Thiem, George
See Thiem, E(zra) George
Thien-An, Thich 1926- 57-60
Thier, Herbert D(avid) 1932- 29-32R
Thierauf, Robert J(ames) 1933- CANR-12
Earlier sketch in CA 29-32R
Thiesenhusen, William C. 1936- 21-24R
Thiessen, Jack 1931- CANR-34
Earlier sketches in CA 41-44R, CANR-15
Thiessen, John
See Thiessen, Jack
Thiessen, John C(aldwell) 1890- 5-8R
Thiher, Allen 1941- CANR-31
Earlier sketches in CA 41-44R, CANR-14
Thiman, Eric Harding 1900- CAP-1
Earlier sketch in CA 13-14
Thimblethorpe, June Sylvia
1926- Brief entry 117
Thimm, Alfred L. 1923- CANR-8
Earlier sketch in CA 61-64
Thimmesch, Nicholas Palen
1927-1985 ....CANR-28
Obituary 116
Earlier sketch in CA 13-16R
Thimmesch, Nick
See Thimmesch, Nicholas Palen
Thirgood, J(ack) V(incent) 1924- 127
Thirion, Andre 1907- 101
Thirkell, Angela (Margaret)
1890-1961 Obituary 93-96
Thirkell, John Henry 1913- CANR-10
Earlier sketch in CA 13-16R
Thirlwall, John C(onnop Jr.) 1904- 69-72
Thirsk, (Irene) Joan 1922- 25-28R

Thiry, Joan (Marie) 1926- 121
See also SATA 45
Thisby
See Turner, Dona M.
Thistle, Mel(ville William) 1914- 53-56
Thistlethwaite, Miles 1945- ....SATA 12
Thistlethwaite, Susan (Brooks) 1948- 127
Thoby-Marcelin, (Emile) Philippe
1904-1975 125
Obituary 61-64
See also BW
Thody, Philip 1928- CANR-9
Earlier sketch in CA 5-8R
Thoene, Alma E(vans) 1903- 49-52
Thoene, Peter
See Bihalji-Merin, Oto
Thoger, Marie 1923- CANR-11
Earlier sketch in CA 25-28R
Tholfsen, Trygve R(ainone) 1924- 134
Brief entry 108
Thollander, Earl 1922- CANR-18
Earlier sketch in CA 101
See also SATA 22
Thom, Alexander 1894-1985 133
Thom, James Alexander 1933- CANR-15
Earlier sketch in CA 77-80
Thom, Mary 1944- 128
Thom, Robert Anderson 1915- 61-64
Thom, Robert 1929-1979 ....21-24R
Obituary 85-88
Thom, Valerie M(acLaren) 1929- 124
Thoma, Henry F. 1909(?)-1983 Obituary 110
Thoma, Ludwig 1867-1921 ....DLB 66
Thoma, Richard 1902- ....DLB 4
Thomae, Betty Kennedy 1920- 61-64
Thoman, Richard S(amuel) 1919- 65-68
Thomaneck, J(uergen) K. A. 1941- 132
Thomas, A(rthur) J(oshua) Jr.
1918-1982 ....CANR-10
Earlier sketch in CA 5-8R
Thomas, A(ndrew) R(owland) B(enedick)
1904- 65-68
Thomas, Abraham V(azhayil) 1934- 61-64
Thomas, Alan (Cedric) 1933- 81-84
Thomas, Alan G. 1911- 25-28R
Thomas, Alexander 1914- 103
Thomas, Andrea
See Hill, Margaret (Ohler)
Thomas, Ann Van Wynen 1919- CANR-10
Earlier sketch in CA 5-8R
Thomas, Anna (Irena) 1948- CANR-24
Earlier sketch in CA 41-44R
Thomas, Annabel 1929- 106
Thomas, Arline 1913-1989 49-52
Obituary 128
Thomas, Armstrong
1909(?)-1975 Obituary 57-60
Thomas, Art(hur Lawrence) 1952- 105
See also SATA 38, 48
Thomas, Audrey (Callahan) 1935- CANR-36
Earlier sketch in CA 21-24R
See also AITN 2
See also CLC 7, 13, 37
See also DLB 60
See also MTCW
Thomas, Ben Bowen 1899-1977 Obituary 108
Thomas, Bill 1934- CANR-8
Earlier sketch in CA 61-64
Thomas, Bob
See Thomas, Robert J(oseph)
Thomas, Bruce 134
Thomas, Bruce
See Paine, Lauran (Bosworth)
Thomas, Carl H.
See Doerffler, Alfred
Thomas, (Antony) Charles 1928- 119
Thomas, Charles W(ellington) 1943- 65-68
Thomas, Charles W.
1903-1973 Obituary 41-44R
Thomas, Claire Sherman 1923- 108
Thomas, Clara (McCandless) 1919- 25-28R
Thomas, Conrad Ward 1914- 37-40R
Thomas, Craig (David) 1942- 112
Brief entry 108
Thomas, Cullen
See Kimes, Beverly Rae
Thomas, D(onald) M(ichael) 1935- CANR-17
Earlier sketch in CA 61-64
See also CAAS 11
See also CDBLB 1960 to Present
See also CLC 13, 22, 31
See also DLB 40
See also MTCW
Thomas, D(avid) O(swald) 1924- 117
Thomas, Dan
See Sanders, Leonard
Thomas, Daniel B.
See Bluestein, Daniel Thomas
Thomas, Daniel H(arrison) 1904- 13-16R
Thomas, Dante 1922- 53-56
Thomas, Dave 1949(?)- Brief entry 115
Thomas, David A(rthur) 1925- 13-16R
Thomas, David H(urst) 1945- 108
Thomas, David St. John 1929- CANR-30
Earlier sketch in CA 112
Thomas, David Winton 1901-1970 .... CAP-1
Earlier sketch in CA 9-10
Thomas, David 1931- 103
Thomas, Denis 1922- CANR-34
Earlier sketches in CA 77-80, CANR-15
Thomas, Dian 1945- CANR-10
Earlier sketch in CA 65-68
Thomas, Diane Renee
1946(?)-1985 Obituary 117
Thomas, Donald F. 1913- 29-32R
Thomas, Donald Roff 1924-1979 Obituary 111
Thomas, Donald 1926- 49-52
Thomas, Dorothy Swaine 1899-1977 .... CAP-2
Obituary 69-72
Earlier sketch in CA 17-18
Thomas, Dwight (Rembert) 1944- 127
Thomas, Dylan (Marlais) 1914-1953 120
Brief entry 104
See also CDBLB 1945-1960
See also DLB 13, 20
See also MTCW
See also PC 2
See also SATA 60
See also SSC 3
See also TCLC 1, 8, 45
See also WLC
Thomas, E(ric) H(ubert) Gwynne
See Gwynne-Thomas, E(ric) H(ubert)
Thomas, Earl W(esley) 1915- 53-56
Thomas, Edison H(ugh) 1912- 85-88
Thomas, Edward Llewellyn
See Llewellyn-Thomas, Edward
Thomas, (Philip) Edward
1878-1917 Brief entry 106
See also DLB 19
See also TCLC 10
Thomas, Edwin J(ohn) 1927- 21-24R
Thomas, Egbert S.
See Ellis, Edward S(ylvester)
Thomas, Elizabeth Ann 1952- 85-88
Thomas, Elizabeth Marshall 1931- 17-20R
Thomas, Emory M. 1939- 97-100
Thomas, Ernest Lewys 1904- CANR-1
Earlier sketch in CA 1-4R
Thomas, Estelle Webb 1899- 21-24R
See also SATA 26
Thomas, Evangeline 1904- 117
Thomas, F(ranklin) Richard 1940- CANR-29
Earlier sketches in CA 77-80, CANR-13
Thomas, Frances 1943- 130
Thomas, Frank P(atrick) 1916- 119
Thomas, G. K.
See Davies, L(eslie) P(urnell)
Thomas, George Finger
1899-1977 Obituary 73-76
Thomas, George I. 1915- 25-28R
Thomas, George Leicester Jr. 1907- CAP-1
Earlier sketch in CA 11-12
Thomas, (Thomas) George 1909- 126
Thomas, Gilbert (Oliver) 1891- 5-8R
Thomas, Gordon L. 1914- 37-40R
Thomas, Gordon 1933- 9-12R
Thomas, Graham Stuart 1909- CANR-19
Earlier sketches in CA 9-12R, CANR-4
Thomas, Gwyn 1913-1981 ....CANR-9
Obituary 103
Earlier sketch in CA 65-68
See also DLB 15
Thomas, H. C.
See Keating, Lawrence A.
Thomas, Harold Becken
1888-1971 Obituary 104
Thomas, Heather Smith 1944- CANR-6
Earlier sketch in CA 57-60
Thomas, Helen A. 1920- 101
Thomas, Helen Shirley 1931-1968 ....5-8R
Obituary 103
Thomas, Henri (Joseph Marie) 1912- CAP-1
Earlier sketch in CA 9-10
Thomas, Henry 1886-1970 Obituary 29-32R
Thomas, Hugh Swynnerton 1931- CANR-5
Earlier sketch in CA 9-12R
Thomas, I(saac) D(avid) E(llis) 1921- 65-68
Thomas, Ianthe 1951- ....CLR 8
See also SATA 42
Thomas, Isaiah 1750-1831 ....DLB 43, 73
Thomas, Ivo Herbert Christopher 1912- 5-8R
Thomas, J(eremy) A(mbler) 1947- 118
Thomas, J. C. 57-60
Thomas, J(ames) D(avid) 1910- CANR-31
Earlier sketches in CA 57-60, CANR-6
Thomas, J. James 1933- 53-56
Thomas, J. W. 1917- 101
Thomas, Jack Ray 1931- 41-44R
Thomas, Jack W(illiam) 1930- CANR-16
Earlier sketches in CA 49-52, CANR-1
Thomas, James H(arold) 1943- 119
Thomas, Jane Resh 1936- CANR-24
Earlier sketch in CA 106
See also SATA 38
Thomas, Jeannette Grise 1935- 101
Thomas, Jim
See Reagan, Thomas (James) B(utler)
Thomas, Joan Gale
See Robinson, Joan (Mary) G(ale Thomas)
Thomas, John Allen Miner
1900-1932 Brief entry 107
See also DLB 4
Thomas, John Hunter 1928- 57-60
Thomas, John Lawrence 1910-1991 ....5-8R
Obituary 134
Thomas, John 1890- 49-52
Thomas, Joyce Carol 1938- 116
Brief entry 113
See also BW
See also CLC 35
See also CLR 19
See also DLB 33
See also MAICYA
See also MTCW
See also SAAS 7
See also SATA 40
Thomas, K. H.
See Kirk, T(homas) H(obson)
Thomas, Keith (Vivian) 1933- CANR-34
Earlier sketches in CA 37-40R, CANR-15
Thomas, Kenneth Bryn Obituary 81-84
Thomas, Kurt 1956- Brief entry 114
Thomas, Latta R(oosevelt) 1927- 65-68
Thomas, Lawrence L(eslie) 1924- 45-48
Thomas, Lee
See Floren, Lee
Thomas, Lee 1918- CANR-1
Earlier sketch in CA 1-4R
Thomas, Leslie (John) 1931- CANR-22
Earlier sketch in CA 13-16R
Thomas, Lewis H(erbert) 1917-1983 ......CANR-13
Earlier sketch in CA 73-76
Thomas, Lewis 1913- CANR-38
Earlier sketch in CA 85-88
See also CLC 35
See also MTCW
Thomas, Lionel H(ugh) C(hristopher)
1922(?)-1978 Obituary 104
Thomas, Liz
See Thomas, Elizabeth Ann
Thomas, Lorenzo 1944- CANR-25
Earlier sketch in CA 73-76
See also BW
See also DLB 41
Thomas, Lowell Jackson Jr. 1923- 85-88
See also SATA 15
Thomas, Lowell (Jackson) 1892-1981 .....CANR-3
Obituary 104
Earlier sketch in CA 45-48
See also AITN 1, 2
Thomas, M(ilton) Halsey 1903-1977 ....25-28R
Obituary 73-76
Thomas, Mack
See Womack, Thomas Hale
Thomas, Mack 1928- 9-12R
Thomas, Maria
See Worrick, Roberta
Thomas, Mary Martha Hosford 1927- 53-56
Thomas, Mason P(age) Jr. 1928- CANR-22
Earlier sketch in CA 25-28R
Thomas, Mervyn
See Curran, Mona (Elisa)
Thomas, Michael
See Wilks, Michael Thomas
Thomas, (William) Miles (Webster)
1897-1980 Obituary 105
Thomas, Nicholas (Jeremy) 1960- 135
Thomas, Norman C(arl) 1932- 17-20R
Thomas, Norman L(ee) 1925- 41-44R
Thomas, Norman (Mattoon) 1884-1968 101
Obituary 25-28R
Thomas, Owen Clark 1922- 9-12R
Thomas, Patricia J. 1934- 37-40R
See also SATA 51
Thomas, Paul
See Mann, (Paul) Thomas
Thomas, Paul 1908- CANR-22
Earlier sketches in CAP-1, CA 9-10
Thomas, Peter Wynne
See Wynne-Thomas, Peter
Thomas, Peter 1928- 37-40R
Thomas, Phillip Drennon 1938- 124
Thomas, Phyllis 1935- 119
Thomas, Piri 1928- 73-76
See also CLC 17
See also HW
Thomas, R(ichard) Hinton 1912-1983 ......CANR-5
Obituary 110
Earlier sketch in CA 5-8R
Thomas, R(obert) Murray 1921- CANR-22
Earlier sketches in CA 17-20R, CANR-7
Thomas, R(onald) S(tuart) 1913- CANR-30
Earlier sketch in CA 89-92
See also CAAS 4
See also CDBLB 1960 to Present
See also CLC 6, 13, 48
See also DLB 27
See also MTCW
Thomas, Richard (Earl) 1951- 107
Thomas, Robert C(harles) 1925- 101
Thomas, Robert J(oseph) 1922- CANR-13
Earlier sketch in CA 77-80
Thomas, Robert 1930- 25-28R
Thomas, Rollin G. 1896- CAP-1
Earlier sketch in CA 13-16
Thomas, Rosalind 1959- 132
Thomas, Rosie 1947- 133
Brief entry 126
Thomas, Ross (Elmore) 1926- CANR-22
Earlier sketch in CA 33-36R
See also CLC 39
Thomas, S(idney) Claudewell 1932- 17-20R
Thomas, Sara (Sally)
1911(?)-1982 Obituary 106
Thomas, Sewell 1884- CAP-1
Earlier sketch in CA 9-10
Thomas, Sherilyn 1948- CANR-13
Earlier sketch in CA 73-76
Thomas, Sherry
See Thomas, Sherilyn
Thomas, Shirley 5-8R
Thomas, Stanley 1933- 21-24R
Thomas, Stephen N(aylor) 1942- 89-92
Thomas, T. M(athai) 1933- 53-56
Thomas, Ted
See Thomas, Theodore L.
Thomas, Theodore L. 1920- 29-32R
Thomas, Thom 1940- 108
Thomas, (Philip) Thomas 1878-1917 ...... DLB 98
Thomas, Tony 1947- 61-64
Thomas, Vaughan 1934- 81-84
Thomas, Vernon (Arthur) 1934- .... SATA 56
Thomas, Victoria
See DeWeese, Thomas Eugene
and Kugi, Constance Todd
Thomas, Virginia Castleton
See Castleton, Virginia
Thomas, W(illiam) A(rthur) 1937- 127
Thomas, W(alter) Ian 1914- 17-20R
Thomas, William E(dward) 1942- 111
Thomas, William F. 1924- 69-72
Thomas, William G(ordan) 1931- 93-96
Thomas, William L(eRoy Jr.) 1920- 41-44R
Thomas, William 1906- 73-76
Thomasma, David Charles 1939- CANR-21
Earlier sketch in CA 104
Thomason, A(lan) Mims
1910-1985 Obituary 117
Thomason, Burke C(urtis) 1943- 113
Thomason, Tommy 1949- 73-76
Thometz, Carol Estes 1938- 9-12R
Thomey, Tedd 1920- CANR-2
Earlier sketch in CA 5-8R
Thomis, Malcolm I(an) 1936- Brief entry 118
Thomis, Wayne 1907-1988 Obituary 126
Thomison, Dennis 1937- 53-56
Thomlinson, Ralph 1925- 41-44R
Thommen, George S. 1896- CAP-1
Earlier sketch in CA 13-16
Thompson, A(lbert) Gray 1928- 41-44R
Thompson, A(rthur) L(eonard) B(ell)
1917-1975 ....CANR-5
Obituary 61-64
Earlier sketch in CA 53-56
Thompson, Alan Eric 1924- 109
Thompson, Anne Armstrong 1939- 85-88
Thompson, Anne Hall Whitt 1930- 119
Thompson, Arthur A. Jr. 1940- 85-88
Thompson, Arthur W(illiam) 1920-1966 ....1-4R
Thompson, Bard 1925-1987 ....CANR-1
Obituary 123
Earlier sketch in CA 1-4R
Thompson, Betty A(nne) 1926- 111
Thompson, Blanche Jennings 5-8R
Thompson, Brenda 1935- 106
See also SATA 34
Thompson, Brian 1935- 109
Thompson, Buck
See Paine, Lauran (Bosworth)
Thompson, C(lara) Mildred
1881-1975 Obituary 57-60
Thompson, Caroline 1956- 110
Thompson, Charles Lowell 1937- CANR-3
Earlier sketch in CA 49-52
Thompson, Charles Waters Jr.
See Thompson, Toby
Thompson, China
See Lewis, Mary (Christianna)
Thompson, Claude Holmes 1908- CAP-1
Earlier sketch in CA 11-12
Thompson, Corrie 1887- 61-64
Thompson, Craig 1907-1986 Obituary 121
Thompson, Daniel (Calbert) 1916- 13-16R
Thompson, David (Bradford) 1938- 57-60
Thompson, David H(ugh) 1941- 81-84
See also SATA 17
Thompson, David 1770-1857 ....DLB 99
Thompson, David 1953- 127
Thompson, Dennis F(rank) 1940- 53-56
Thompson, Dennis L. 1935- 41-44R
Thompson, (Arthur) Denys (Halstead)
1907-1988 ....CANR-4
Obituary 124
Earlier sketch in CA 9-12R
Thompson, Don(ald Arthur) 1935- 53-56
Thompson, Donald Eugene 1913- 109
Thompson, Donald L(ambert) 1930- 49-52
Thompson, Donald Neil 1939- 37-40R
Thompson, Donnis Stark 1928- 21-24R
Thompson, Dorothy 1894-1961 Obituary 89-92
See also DLB 29
Thompson, Duane G(len) 1933- 73-76
Thompson, Earl 1931(?)-1978 85-88
Obituary 81-84
Thompson, Edgar T(ristram) 1900- 17-20R
Thompson, Edward Thorwald 1928- CANR-21
Earlier sketch in CA 105
Thompson, Eileen
See Panowski, Eileen Thompson
Thompson, Elizabeth Allen 1914-1984 119
Thompson, Era Bell 1905-1986 89-92
Obituary 121
Thompson, Eric
See Thompson, J(ohn) Eric S(idney)
Thompson, (Richard) Ernest 1949- 123
Brief entry 115
Thompson, Ernest Trice 1894-1985 ....1-4R
Obituary 115
Thompson, Eugene Allen 1924- CANR-26
Earlier sketch in CA 104
Thompson, Evelyn Wingo 1921- 21-24R
Thompson, Ewa M(ajewska) 1937- 49-52
Thompson, Flora (Jane Timms)
1877(?)-1947 Brief entry 123
Thompson, Frances C(lements) 1906- CAP-1
Earlier sketch in CA 9-10
Thompson, Francis Clegg
See Mencken, H(enry) L(ouis)
Thompson, Francis George 1931- CANR-23
Earlier sketch in CA 106
Thompson, Francis Joseph
1859-1907 Brief entry 104
See also CDBLB 1890-1914
See also DLB 19
See also TCLC 4
Thompson, Frank H. Jr. 1926- 25-28R
Thompson, Fred Dalton 1942- 69-72
Thompson, Fred P(riestly) Jr. 1917- 89-92
Thompson, Fred 1900-1987 Obituary 121
Thompson, G(ary) R(ichard) 1937- CANR-2
Earlier sketch in CA 45-48
Thompson, Gene
See Thompson, Eugene Allen
Thompson, George Clifford 1920- 104
Thompson, George G(reene) 1914- 21-24R
Thompson, George H(yman) 1923- 125
Brief entry 117

Thompson, George Selden
1929-1989 ... CANR-37
Obituary ... 130
Earlier sketches in CA 5-8R, CANR-21
See also Selden, George
See also MAICYA
See also SATA 4, 63
Thompson, Gerald E(verett) 1924- ... 53-56
Thompson, Gertrude Caton
See Caton-Thompson, Gertrude
Thompson, Grant P(helps) 1940- ... 111
Thompson, Harlan (Howard) 1894-1987 ... CAP-1
Obituary ... 123
Earlier sketch in CA 9-10
See also SATA 10, 53
Thompson, Harry C.
1921(?)-1980 Obituary ... 97-100
Thompson, (Harry) Harwood 1894- ... 65-68
Thompson, Helen M. (Smith) 1903- ... CAP-1
Earlier sketch in CA 13-14
Thompson, Henry O(rrin) 1931- ... CANR-25
Earlier sketch in CA 45-48
Thompson, Hilary 1943- ... 127
See also SATA 49, 56
Thompson, Hildegard (Steerstedter)
1901- ... 17-20R
Thompson, Hunter S(tockton) 1939- ... CANR-23
Earlier sketch in CA 17-20R
See also BEST 89:1
See also CLC 9, 17, 40
See also MTCW
Thompson, Ian B(entley) 1936- ... 37-40R
Thompson, Irene 1919- ... 110
Thompson, Isabel
See Kelsay, Isabel Thompson
Thompson, J(ohn) Eric S(idney)
1898-1975 ... 65-68
Obituary ... 61-64
Thompson, J(esse) J(ackson) 1919- ... 5-8R
Thompson, Jack Maynard 1924- ... 41-44R
Thompson, Jacqueline 1945- ... CANR-38
Earlier sketches in CA 97-100, CANR-17
Thompson, James Clay 1943- ... 127
Thompson, James D(avid) 1920-1973 ... CAP-2
Earlier sketch in CA 21-22
Thompson, James H.
See Freeman, G(raydon) L(a Verne)
Thompson, James W. 1935- ... 105
Thompson, James 1902-1983 Obituary ... 109
Thompson, James 1932- ... 73-76
Thompson, Jean 1950- ... 136
Thompson, Jim 1906-1976 ... CLC 69
Thompson, Joan Berengild 1915- ... 17-20R
Thompson, Joan 1943- ... 97-100
Thompson, Joanna Maxwell Pullein
See Pullein-Thompson, Joanna Maxwell
Thompson, Joe Allen 1936- ... 37-40R
Thompson, John (Anderson) 1918- ... 5-8R
Thompson, John Leslie 1917- ... 5-8R
Thompson, John M(eans) 1926- ... 129
Thompson, John Reuben 1823-1873 ... DLB 3, 73
Thompson, John 1938-1976 ... DLB 60
Thompson, Josiah 1935- ... 41-44R
Thompson, Judith ... CLC 39
Thompson, Julian F(rancis) 1927- ... CANR-30
Earlier sketch in CA 111
See also AAYA 9
See also CLR 24
See also MAICYA
See also SAAS 13
See also SATA 40, 55
Thompson, Julius Eric 1946- ... 49-52
Thompson, Karl F. 1917- ... 37-40R
Thompson, Kay 1912(?)- ... 85-88
See also CLR 22
See also MAICYA
See also SATA 16
Thompson, Ken D(avid) 1926- ... 65-68
Thompson, Kenneth W(infred) 1921- ... CANR-29
Earlier sketches in CA 9-12R, CANR-5
Thompson, Kent 1936- ... 49-52
Thompson, Kristin 1950- ... CANR-25
Earlier sketch in CA 108
Thompson, Laura (Maud) 1905- ... 53-56
Thompson, Laurence C(assius) 1926- ... CANR-7
Earlier sketch in CA 5-8R
Thompson, Laurence G(raham) 1920- ... 37-40R
Thompson, Lawrance (Roger)
1906-1973 ... CANR-10
Obituary ... 41-44R
Earlier sketch in CA 5-8R
See also DLB 103
Thompson, Lawrence Sidney
1916-1986 ... CANR-5
Obituary ... 121
Earlier sketch in CA 9-12R
Thompson, Leonard Monteath 1916- ... CANR-16
Earlier sketches in CA 1-4R, CANR-1
Thompson, Lewis
1915(?)-1972 Obituary ... 37-40R
Thompson, Lloyd A(rthur) 1932- ... 137
Thompson, Loring M(oore) 1918- ... 45-48
Thompson, Luther Joe 1918- ... 21-24R
Thompson, M(ichael) W(elman) 1928- ... 128
Thompson, Marian Spitzer
1899(?)-1983 Obituary ... 110
Thompson, Mark L. 1945- ... 137
Thompson, Mary Wolfe 1886- ... 107
Thompson, Maurice 1844-1901 ... DLB 71, 74
Thompson, Mel(vin R.) 1929- ... 73-76
Thompson, Morris Mordecai 1912- ... 109
Thompson, Neil 1929- ... 108
Thompson, Neville 1938- ... 37-40R
Thompson, Noel W. 1951- ... 123
Thompson, Paul (Richard) 1935- ... CANR-38
Earlier sketches in CA 21-24R, CANR-16
Thompson, Paul 1943- ... CANR-32
Earlier sketches in CA 77-80, CANR-14
Thompson, Phyllis Hoge 1926- ... CANR-36
Earlier sketches in CA 29-32R, CANR-13
Thompson, (William) Ralph 1910- ... 53-56
Thompson, Ralph 1904-1979 Obituary ... 89-92
Thompson, Randall 1899-1984 Obituary ... 113
Thompson, Richard A(rlen) 1930- ... 61-64
Thompson, Richard 1924- ... 9-12R
Thompson, Robert Elliott 1921- ... 77-80
See also AITN 2
Thompson, Robert Farris 1932- ... 103
Thompson, Robert (Grainger Ker) 1916- ... 49-52
Thompson, Robert Norman 1914- ... 106
Thompson, Robert Sidney 1918- ... 111
Thompson, Roger Francis 1933- ... CANR-13
Earlier sketch in CA 73-76
Thompson, Roy Anton 1897- ... CAP-2
Earlier sketch in CA 29-32
Thompson, Russ
See Paine, Lauran (Bosworth)
Thompson, Ruth Plumly 1891-1976 ... 134
Obituary ... 113
See also DLB 22
See also SATA 66
Thompson, Samuel M(artin)
1902-1983 Obituary ... 110
Thompson, Sandra (Jean) 1943- ... 121
Thompson, Stanbury Dugard 1905- ... CAP-1
Earlier sketch in CA 11-12
Thompson, Steven L(ynn) 1948- ... 114
Thompson, Stith 1885-1976 ... CANR-5
Obituary ... 61-64
Earlier sketch in CA 5-8R
See also SATA 20, 57
Thompson, Susan (Ayers) 1946- ... 132
Thompson, Susan L. 1945- ... 114
Thompson, Susan O(tis) 1931- ... 85-88
Thompson, Sylvia
See Thompson, Sylvia Vaughn (Sheekman)
Thompson, Sylvia Vaughn (Sheekman)
1935- ... CANR-26
Earlier sketch in CA 5-8R
Thompson, Thomas Kirkland 1914- ... 13-16R
Thompson, Thomas Phillips 1843-1933 ... DLB 99
Thompson, Thomas 1933-1982 ... CANR-14
Obituary ... 108
Earlier sketch in CA 65-68
Thompson, Toby 1944- ... 65-68
Thompson, Travis I. 1937- ... 37-40R
Thompson, Victor A(lexander) 1912- ... 25-28R
Thompson, Virginia
See Adloff, Virginia Thompson
Thompson, Virginia 1937- ... 108
Thompson, Vivian L(aubach) 1911- ... CANR-1
Earlier sketch in CA 1-4R
See also SATA 3
Thompson, W(illard) Scott 1942- ... CANR-12
Earlier sketch in CA 25-28R
Thompson, Wayne C(urtis) 1943- ... 109
Thompson, Wayne N. 1914- ... 21-24R
Thompson, Wilbur R(ichard) 1923- ... 13-16R
Thompson, Willa 1916- ... 9-12R
Thompson, Willard Mead 1913- ... 5-8R
Thompson, William A(ncker) 1931- ... 77-80
Thompson, William Bernard 1914- ... CAP-1
Earlier sketch in CA 9-10
Thompson, William C. L.
See Edwards, William B(ennett)
Thompson, William D. 1929- ... 17-20R
Thompson, William E(llison) Jr. 1923- ... 13-16R
Thompson, William Fletcher Jr. 1929- ... 1-4R
Thompson, William Irwin 1938- ... CANR-9
Earlier sketch in CA 21-24R
Thompson, William N. 1940- ... 135
Thompson, William Tappan
1812-1882 ... DLB 3, 11
Thompson, Wolfe
See Thompson, Mary Wolfe
Thompson-Frey, Nancy 1955- ... 127
Thoms, Herbert 1885-1972 Obituary ... 110
Thomsen, Harry 1928- ... 5-8R
Thomsen, Moritz 1915- ... 29-32R
Thomsen, Robert 1915(?)-1983 Obituary ... 117
Thomsen, Russel J(ohn) 1941- ... 37-40R
Thomsett, Michael C. 1948- ... 119
Thomson, Arthur Alexander (Malcolm)
1894-1969 ... CAP-1
Earlier sketch in CA 11-12
Thomson, Basil (Home)
1861-1939 Brief entry ... 110
Thomson, Beatrix 1900-1986 Obituary ... 120
Thomson, Betty Flanders 1913- ... 9-12R
Thomson, C(harles) Leslie 1914- ... 9-12R
Thomson, Daisy H(icks) 1918- ... CANR-20
Earlier sketch in CA 103
Thomson, Dale C(airns) 1923- ... 25-28R
Thomson, David (Robert Alexander)
1914-1988 ... CANR-24
Obituary ... 124
Earlier sketch in CA 107
See also SATA 40, 55
Thomson, David 1912-1970 ... CANR-2
Obituary ... 29-32R
Earlier sketch in CA 1-4R
Thomson, Derick S(mith) 1921- ... CANR-12
Earlier sketch in CA 25-28R
Thomson, Douglas Ferguson Scott
1919- ... 41-44R
Thomson, Edward
See Tubb, E(dwin) C(harles)
Thomson, Edward William 1849-1924 ... DLB 92
Thomson, Elizabeth
See Thomson, Elizabeth M.
Thomson, Elizabeth M. 1957- ... 127
Thomson, F(rancis) P(aul) 1914- ... 21-24R
Thomson, Frank S(elee) 1881-1975 ... 57-60
Thomson, Garry 1925- ... 109
Thomson, George Derwent
1903-1987 Obituary ... 121
Thomson, George H(enry) 1924- ... 21-24R
Thomson, George Malcolm 1899- ... 9-12R
Thomson, George Paget 1892-1975 ... CANR-4
Obituary ... 61-64
Earlier sketch in CA 5-8R
Thomson, (George) Ian F(alconer)
1912-1987 ... 9-12R
Obituary ... 122
Thomson, Irene Taviss 1941- ... 29-32R
Thomson, James C(laude) Jr. 1931- ... CANR-32
Earlier sketch in CA 29-32R
Thomson, James C(utting) 1909- ... 61-64
Thomson, James Miln 1921- ... 109
Thomson, James 1700-1748 ... DLB 95
Thomson, James 1834-1882 ... DLB 35
Thomson, Joan
See Charnock, Joan
Thomson, John A(idan) F(rancis) 1934- ... 132
Thomson, John (Edward Palmer) 1936- ... 109
Thomson, John W(illiam) 1940- ... 125
Thomson, Jonathan H.
See Thomson, Daisy H(icks)
Thomson, June (Valerie) 1930- ... CANR-21
Earlier sketch in CA 81-84
Thomson, Keith 1912- ... 29-32R
Thomson, Liz
See Thomson, Elizabeth M.
Thomson, Mortimer 1831-1875 ... DLB 11
Thomson, Peggy 1922- ... 85-88
See also SATA 31
Thomson, Peter (William) 1938- ... 108
Thomson, Peter 1913- ... 5-8R
Thomson, Randall J(oseph) 1946- ... 109
Thomson, Robert (James) 1961- ... 127
Thomson, Robert W(illiam) 1934- ... CANR-21
Earlier sketch in CA 104
Thomson, Robert 1921- ... 25-28R
Thomson, Robert 1943- ... 122
Thomson, Ronald William 1908- ... 25-28R
Thomson, Roy Herbert
1894-1976 Obituary ... 69-72
Thomson, S(amuel) Harrison
1895-1975 ... 41-44R
Obituary ... 61-64
Thomson, Virgil (Garnett) 1896-1989 ... 41-44R
Obituary ... 129
Thomson, William A(rchibald) R(obson)
1906-1983 ... 103
Obituary ... 111
Thomson, William A.
1879-1971 Obituary ... 33-36R
Thomy, Al(fred Marshall) ... 69-72
Thon, Melanie Rae 1957- ... 134
Thonssen, Lester 1904- ... 5-8R
Thorat, Sudhakar S. 1935- ... CANR-29
Earlier sketch in CA 45-48
Thorburn, David 1940- ... CANR-7
Earlier sketch in CA 53-56
Thorburn, Hugh G(arnet) 1924- ... 13-16R
Thorburn, John
See Goldsmith, John Herman Thorburn
Thoreau, Henry David
1817-1862 ... CDALB 1640-1865
See also DLB 1
See also WLC
Thorelli, Hans B(irger) 1921- ... CANR-6
Earlier sketch in CA 13-16R
Thoren, Arne 1927- ... 69-72
Thorer, Konrad
See Greve, Felix Paul (Berthold Friedrich)
Thoresen, Carl E. 1933- ... 57-60
Thorez, Maurice 1900-1964 Obituary ... 113
Thorlby, Anthony K. 1928- ... 25-28R
Thorman, Donald J. 1924-1977 ... 17-20R
Obituary ... 73-76
Thorman, Richard 1924- ... 105
Thorn, Barbara
See Paine, Lauran (Bosworth)
Thorn, John 1947- ... CANR-17
Earlier sketch in CA 97-100
See also SATA 59
Thorn, Richard S(emour) 1929- ... 17-20R
Thorn, Ronald Scott
See Wilkinson, Ronald
Thorn, William E. 1923- ... 9-12R
Thornber, Jean H(ewitt) 1919- ... 61-64
Thornbrook, Bill
See Turnbaugh, William A(rthur)
Thornbrough, Emma Lou ... 25-28R
Thornburg, Hershel D(ean)
1936-1987 ... CANR-14
Obituary ... 121
Earlier sketch in CA 37-40R
Thornburg, Newton K(endall) 1930- ... CANR-9
Earlier sketch in CA 21-24R
Thorndike, A.
See Thorndike, A(nthony) E(dward)
Thorndike, A(nthony) E(dward) 1941- ... 117
Thorndike, E. L.
See Thorndike, Edward L(ee)
Thorndike, Edward L(ee)
1874-1949 Brief entry ... 121
Thorndike, Joseph J(acobs) Jr.
1913- Brief entry ... 117
Thorndike, (Everett) Lynn
1882-1965 Obituary ... 111
Thorndike, Robert Ladd 1910-1990 ... CANR-1
Obituary ... 132
Earlier sketch in CA 1-4R
Thorndike, (Arthur) Russell
1885-1972 Obituary ... 37-40R
Thorndike, Susan 1944- ... 41-44R
Thorndike, Tony
See Thorndike, A(nthony) E(dward)
Thorndyke, Helen Louise ... CANR-27
Earlier sketches in CAP-2, CA 19-20
See also SATA 1, 67
Thorne, Alice Dunn 1910-1973 Obituary ... 45-48
Thorne, Bliss K(irby) 1916- ... 17-20R
Thorne, Bradley D.
See Glut, Donald F(rank)
Thorne, Christopher 1934- ... CANR-29
Obituary ... 137
Earlier sketches in CA 21-24R, CANR-11
Thorne, Edouard
See Greve, Felix Paul (Berthold Friedrich)
Thorne, Florence Calvert
1878(?)-1973 Obituary ... 41-44R
Thorne, Hart
See Carhart, Arthur Hawthorne
Thorne, Ian
See May, Julian
Thorne, Jean Wright
See May, Julian
Thorne, Jim 1922- ... CANR-1
Earlier sketch in CA 1-4R
Thorne, John (H.) 1943- ... 136
Thorne, Nicola
See Ellerbeck, Rosemary (Anne L'Estrange)
Thorne, Ramsay
See Cameron, Lou
Thorne, Sabina 1927- ... 106
Thorne, Sterling
See Fuller, Dorothy Mason
Thorne, William James 1898- ... 5-8R
Thornhill, Alan 1907(?)-1988 Obituary ... 127
Thorning, Joseph F(rancis) 1896-1985 ... CAP-1
Obituary ... 115
Earlier sketch in CA 9-10
Thornley, Richard 1950- ... 117
Thornton, Big Mama
See Thornton, Willie Mae
Thornton, Emma Shore 1908- ... 114
Thornton, Francis John 1938- ... 85-88
Thornton, Gene ... 93-96
Thornton, Hall
See Silverberg, Robert
Thornton, J(onathan) Mills III 1943- ... 77-80
Thornton, James W. Jr. 1908- ... CANR-1
Earlier sketch in CA 1-4R
Thornton, Jerry
See Thornton, Emma Shore
Thornton, John Leonard 1913- ... CANR-4
Earlier sketch in CA 9-12R
Thornton, John W(illiam) Jr. 1948- ... 106
Thornton, John W(illiam) 1922- ... 106
Thornton, Lawrence 1937- ... 132
Thornton, Lee 1944- ... 73-76
Thornton, Martin (Stuart Farrin) 1915- ... 9-12R
Thornton, Michael 1941- ... 105
Thornton, Peter Kai 1925- ... CANR-20
Earlier sketch in CA 102
Thornton, R(obert) K(elsey) R(ought) 1938- ... 119
Thornton, Ralph 1922(?)-1989 Obituary ... 129
Thornton, Richard C. 1936- ... 81-84
Thornton, Thomas Perry 1931- ... 9-12R
Thornton, W. B.
See Burgess, Thornton Waldo
Thornton, Weldon 1934- ... 25-28R
Thornton, Willie Mae 1926-1984 Obituary ... 113
Thornton, Willis 1900- ... CAP-1
Earlier sketch in CA 13-16
Thorp, Duncan Roy 1914- ... 13-16R
Thorp, Edward O. 1932- ... 21-24R
Thorp, John 1947- ... 133
Thorp, Margaret Farrand
1891-1970 Obituary ... 104
Thorp, Roderick Mayne Jr. 1936- ... CANR-6
Earlier sketch in CA 1-4R
Thorp, Willard Long 1899- ... CANR-28
Obituary ... 137
Earlier sketch in CA 1-4R
Thorp, Willard 1899-1990 ... CANR-3
Obituary ... 130
Earlier sketch in CA 5-8R
Thorpe, Adam 1956- ... 129
Thorpe, D. R. 1943- ... 129
Thorpe, Donald W(illiam) 1928- ... 29-32R
Thorpe, E(ustace) G(eorge) 1916- ... 9-12R
See also SATA 21
Thorpe, Earl(ie) E(ndris) 1924- ... 61-64
Thorpe, Elliott R(aymond) 1897-1989 ... 65-68
Obituary ... 129
Thorpe, George P. 1913(?)-1983 Obituary ... 110
Thorpe, J. K.
See Nathanson, Laura Walther
Thorpe, James 1915- ... CANR-17
Earlier sketches in CA 5-8R, CANR-2
Thorpe, Lewis (Guy Melville)
1913-1977 ... CANR-10
Earlier sketch in CA 9-12R
Thorpe, Louis P(eter) 1893- ... CANR-20
Earlier sketch in CA 1-4R
Thorpe, Michael 1932- ... CANR-8
Earlier sketch in CA 21-24R
Thorpe, Peter 1932- ... 57-60
Thorpe, Sylvia
See Thimblethorpe, June Sylvia
Thorpe, Thomas Bangs 1815-1878 ... DLB 3, 11
Thorpe, Trebor
See Fanthorpe, R(obert) Lionel
Thorpe, Trevor
See Fanthorpe, R(obert) Lionel
Thorpe, William Homan 1902-1986 ... CANR-2
Obituary ... 119
Earlier sketch in CA 5-8R
Thorsell, Richard Lawrence 1938- ... 89-92
Thorsley, Peter L(arsen) Jr. 1929- ... 5-8R
Thorson, Thomas Landon 1934- ... 17-20R
Thorstad, David 1941- ... 57-60

Thorstein, Eric
See Merril, Judith
Thorup, Kirsten 1942- 127
Brief entry 125
Thorvall, Kerstin 1925- CANR-13
Earlier sketch in CA 17-20R
See also SATA 13
Thorvall-Falk, Kerstin
See Thorvall, Kerstin
Thorwald, Juergen 1916- CANR-21
Earlier sketches in CA 49-52, CANR-1
Thouless, Robert H(enry) 1894-1984 77-80
Obituary 114
Thrapp, Dan Lincoln 1913- CANR-4
Earlier sketch in CA 9-12R
Thrasher, Crystal (Faye) 1921- CANR-8
Earlier sketch in CA 61-64
See also SATA 27
Threlkeld, Richard 1937- 65-68
Thresher, B(rainard) Alden
1896-1984 Obituary 111
Thribb, E. J.
See Fantoni, Barry (Ernest)
Thring, M(eredith) W(ooldridge) 1915- 130
Throckmorton, Burton Hamilton Jr. 1921- 5-8R
Throckmorton, Peter 1928-1990 ....17-20R
Obituary 131
Throneberry, Jimmy B. 1933- 89-92
Throneburg, James 5-8R
Thrower, Norman J(oseph) W(illiam)
1919- 41-44R
Thrower, Percy John 1913-1988 ....CANR-4
Obituary 125
Earlier sketch in CA 9-12R
Thruelsen, Richard (Delmar)
1908-1989 Obituary 129
Thubron, Colin (Gerald Dryden)
1939- CANR-29
Earlier sketches in CA 25-28R, CANR-12
Thubten Sigme Norbu 1922- Brief entry 109
Thuemmel, Moritz August von
1738-1817 ....DLB 97
Thuesen, Gerald J(organ) 1938- 37-40R
Thuillier, Jacques 1928- CANR-7
Earlier sketch in CA 9-12R
Thulstrup, Niels 1924- CANR-26
Earlier sketches in CA 21-24R, CANR-10
Thum, Gladys 1920- 41-44R
See also SATA 26
Thum, Marcella CANR-21
Earlier sketches in CA 9-12R, CANR-6
See also SATA 3, 28
Thumm, Garold W(esley) 1915- 13-16R
Thuna, Lee
See Thuna, Leonora
Thuna, Leonora 1929- CANR-16
Earlier sketch in CA 21-24R
Thundercloud, Katherine
See Witt, Shirley Hill
Thundy, Zacharias Pontian 1936- 102
Thundyil, Zacharias Pontian
See Thundy, Zacharias Pontian
Thurber, Helen (Wismer)
1902(?)-1986 Obituary 121
Thurber, James (Grover) 1894-1961 ....CANR-39
Earlier sketches in CA 73-76, CANR-17
See also CDALB 1929-1941
See also CLC 5, 11, 25
See also DLB 4, 11, 22, 102
See also MAICYA
See also MTCW
See also SATA 13
See also SSC 1
Thurber, Walter A(rthur) 1908- CANR-12
Earlier sketch in CA 21-24R
Thurian, Max 1921- 129
Thurkettle, James 1929- 69-72
Thurley, Geoffrey John 1936- CANR-13
Earlier sketch in CA 61-64
Thurley, Jon (Mark) 118
Thurlow, David (Michael) 1932- 134
Thurman, Christa C(harlotte) Mayer
1934- CANR-2
Earlier sketch in CA 49-52
Thurman, Howard 1900-1981 ....CANR-25
Obituary 103
Earlier sketch in CA 97-100
See also BW
Thurman, Judith 1946- CANR-1
Earlier sketch in CA 49-52
See also SATA 33
Thurman, Kelly 1914- 57-60
Thurman, Mark (Gordon Ian) 1948- 131
See also SATA 63
Thurman, Wallace (Henry) 1902-1934 124
Brief entry 104
See also BLC 3
See also BW
See also DLB 51
See also TCLC 6
Thurman, Wayne L(averne) 1923- 49-52
Thurmond, Nancy Moore 1946- 132
Brief entry 114
Thurmond, (J.) Strom 1902- 89-92
Thurow, Lester C(arl) 1938- 81-84
Thursby, Vincent Victor 1918- 41-44R
Thurstan, Violetta CAP-1
Earlier sketch in CA 13-16
Thurston, Carol (M.) 126
Thurston, David B. 1918- CANR-6
Earlier sketch in CA 5-8R
Thurston, Elliott Ladd
1895-1975 Obituary 89-92
Thurston, Harry 1950- CANR-32
Earlier sketch in CA 113
Thurston, Hazel (Patricia) 1906- 57-60
Thurston, Jarvis 1914- 13-16R
Thurston, Lorrin P. 1900(?)-1984 Obituary 114
Thurston, Robert (Donald) 1936- CANR-15
Earlier sketch in CA 85-88
Thut, I(saac) N(oah) CAP-1
Earlier sketch in CA 13-16
Thwaite, Ann (Barbara Harrop) 1932- 5-8R
See also SATA 14
Thwaite, Anthony (Simon) 1930- 5-8R
See also DLB 40
Thwaite, M(ary) F. (Austin) 21-24R
Thwaites, Michael 1915- 77-80
Thwaites, Reuben Gold 1853-1913 ....DLB 47
Thwing, Leroy (L.) 1879- 5-8R
Thygerson, Alton L(uie) 1940- CANR-39
Earlier sketches in CA 45-48, CANR-1, 18
Thynn, Alexander (George) 1932- 132
Thynne, Alexander
See Thynn, Alexander (George)
Tiant, Luis 1940- 73-76
(al-)Tibawi, A(bdul-)L(atif) 1910-1981 ....CANR-24
Obituary 105
Earlier sketch in CA 25-28R
Tibber, Robert
See Friedman, (Eve) Rosemary (Tibber)
Tibber, Rosemary
See Friedman, (Eve) Rosemary (Tibber)
Tibbets, Albert B. 1888- 5-8R
Tibbetts, Arnold M(acLean) 1927- CANR-16
Earlier sketch in CA 93-96
Tibbetts, Charlene 1921- 93-96
Tibbetts, John C(arter) 1946- 89-92
Tibbetts, John W(esley) 1928- 25-28R
Tibbetts, Norris L. 1892(?)-1983 Obituary 108
Tibbetts, Orlando L(ailer) Jr. 1919- CANR-11
Earlier sketch in CA 29-32R
Tibbetts, William
See Brannon, William T.
Tibble, Anne 1912-1980 ....CANR-10
Obituary 102
Earlier sketch in CA 9-12R
Tibbs, Ben 1907- 61-64
Tibbs, Virginia M.
See Scott, Virginia M(uhleman)
Tiber, Elliot 1935- 129
Tibi, Bassam 1944- 130
Tibo, Gilles 1951- 136
See also SATA 67
Tiburzi, Bonnie 1948- 136
See also SATA 65
Tice, George A(ndrew) 1938- CANR-12
Earlier sketch in CA 61-64
Ticheburn, Cheviot
See Ainsworth, William Harrison
Tichenor, Tom 1923- 29-32R
See also SATA 14
Tichi, Cecelia 1942- 104
Tichy, H(enrietta) J. 1912- 21-24R
Tichy, Susan (Elizabeth) 1952- 123
Tichy, William 1924- 107
See also SATA 31
Tickell, Renee Oriana Haynes
See Haynes, Renee (Oriana Tickell)
Tickle, P(hyllis) A(lexander) 1934- CANR-24
Earlier sketches in CA 65-68, CANR-9
Tickner, Fred(erick James) 1902- CAP-1
Earlier sketch in CA 9-10
Tickner, Lisa 1944- 128
Ticknor, George 1791-1871 ....DLB 1, 59
Tidball, Derek J(ohn) 1948- 120
Tidy, Michael 1943- 113
Tidyman, Ernest 1928-1984 ....CANR-29
Obituary 113
Earlier sketch in CA 73-76
Tieck, (Johann) Ludwig 1773-1853 ....DLB 90
Tiede, Tom (Robert) 1937- 25-28R
Tiedt, Iris M(cClellan) 1928- CANR-24
Earlier sketches in CA 13-16R, CANR-7
Tiedt, Sidney W(illis) 1927- CANR-24
Earlier sketch in CA 13-16R
Tiegreen, Alan F. 1935- ....SATA 36
Tiempo, Edith (Lopez) 1919- 104
Tien, H. Yuan 1926- 49-52
Tien, Hung-Mao 1938- 73-76
Tierney, Brian 1922- 103
Tierney, Frank M. 1930- ....SATA 54
Tierney, Gene 1920- Brief entry 116
Tierney, John Lawrence 1892-1972 ....CAP-2
Earlier sketch in CA 21-22
Tierney, Kevin (Hugh) 1942- CANR-26
Earlier sketch in CA 29-32R
Tierney, M. Leo 1932(?)-1986 Obituary 118
Tierney, Michael 1894-1975 Obituary 114
Tierney, Paul Ambrose
1895(?)-1979 Obituary 85-88
Tierney, Richard L(ouis) 1936- 111
Tierney, Tom 1928- CANR-23
Earlier sketches in CA 57-60, CANR-8
Tiersky, Ronald S. 1944- 118
Tietjens, Eunice 1884-1944 ....DLB 54
Tietze, Andreas 1914- 49-52
Tietze, Christopher 1908-1984 Obituary 112
Tiffany, Donald Wayne 1930- Brief entry 108
Tiffany, E. A. 1911- 103
Tiffany, Phyllis G. 1932- 37-40R
Tiffany, William R(obert) 1920- 5-8R
Tiffin, Joseph 1905- 17-20R
Tifft, Ellen CANR-1
Earlier sketch in CA 49-52
Tifft, Susan E. 1951- 135
Tifton, Leo
See Page, Gerald W(ilburn)
Tigar, Michael E(dward) 1941- 77-80
Tigay, Alan M(errill) 1947- 124
Tiger, Derry
See Ellison, Harlan
Tiger, Jack
See Puechner, Ray
Tiger, John
See Wager, Walter H(erman)
Tiger, Lionel 1937- CANR-14
Earlier sketch in CA 25-28R
Tiger, Virginia Marie 1940- Brief entry 106
Tigerman, Stanley 1930- CANR-36
Earlier sketch in CA 114
Tiger of the Snows
See Norgay, Tenzing
Tighe, Donald J. 1928- 29-32R
Tighe, Thomas B. 1907(?)-1983 Obituary 109
Tignor, Robert L(ee) 1933- 134
Brief entry 109
Tigue, Ethel Erkkila 1918- 21-24R
Tikhonov, Nikolai Semyonovich
1896-1979 Obituary 85-88
Tikhonov, Valentin
See Payne, (Pierre Stephen) Robert
Tikku, Girdhari L(al) 1925- 45-48
Tiktin, Carl 1930- CANR-13
Earlier sketch in CA 73-76
Tilden, Freeman 1884(?)-1980 97-100
Tiles, J. E. 1944- 128
Tilghman, Benjamin R(oss) 1927- 134
Brief entry 107
Tilghman, Christopher 1948(?)- ....CLC 65
Till, Barry 1923- 49-52
Till, Geoffrey 1945- 132
Tillard, Jean-M(arie) Roger 1927- CANR-28
Earlier sketch in CA 45-48
Tillema, Herbert K(endall) 1942- 45-48
Tilleman, William Arthur 1932- 53-56
Tiller, Carl W(illiam) 1915- 108
Tiller, Ted
See Tiller, Theodore II
Tiller, Terence (Rogers) 1916-1987 101
Obituary 124
Tiller, Theodore II 1913(?)-1988 Obituary 126
Tilles, Solomon 1932- Brief entry 108
Tillett, Bill G(lenn) 1942- 118
Tillett, Gregory J. 1950- 110
Tilley, Ethel 1894- CAP-1
Earlier sketch in CA 9-10
Tilley, Patrick 1928- 106
Tilley, (William) Roger (Montgomerie)
1905-1971 ....CAP-2
Earlier sketch in CA 25-28
Tillich, Hannah 1896-1988 73-76
Obituary 127
Tillich, Paul (Johannes) 1886-1965 ....CANR-33
Obituary 25-28R
Earlier sketch in CA 5-8R
See also MTCW
Tillinghast, B(urette) S(tinson) Jr. 1930- 65-68
Tillinghast, Pardon E(lisha) 1920- 9-12R
Tillinghast, Richard (Williford) 1940- CANR-26
Earlier sketch in CA 29-32R
See also CLC 29
Tillion, Diana (Rutzebeck) 1928- Brief entry 110
Tillion, Germaine Marie Rosine 1907- 104
Tillman, Barrett 1948- 132
Tillman, Rollie Jr. 1933- 21-24R
Tillman, Seth Phillip 1930- 1-4R
Tillman, Stephen Frederick
1900(?)-1977 Obituary 69-72
Tillotson, G(iles) H(enry) R(upert) 1960- 126
Tillotson, Geoffrey 1905-1969 ....CAP-1
Earlier sketch in CA 13-14
Tilly, Charles 1929- CANR-20
Earlier sketch in CA 103
Tilly, Louise A(udino) 1930- 120
Tilly, Nancy 1935- 120
See also SATA 62
Tilly, Richard H(ugh) 1932- 17-20R
Tillyard, E(ustace) M(andeville) W(etenhall)
1889-1962 Obituary 93-96
Tilman, Harold William 1898-1978 103
Tilman, Robert O(liver) 1929- CANR-1
Earlier sketch in CA 45-48
Tilson, Everett 1923- 41-44R
Tiltman, Hessell 1897(?)-1976 Obituary 69-72
Tiltman, Ronald Frank 1901- CAP-1
Earlier sketch in CA 9-10
Tilton, Alice
See Taylor, Phoebe Atwood
Tilton, Eleanor M(arguerite)
1913- Brief entry 110
Tilton, John W(ightman) 1928-1983 122
Brief entry 118
Tilton, Madonna Elaine 1929- CANR-36
Earlier sketch in CA 114
See also SATA 41
Tilton, Rafael
See Tilton, Madonna Elaine
Tilton, Timothy Alan 1942- 61-64
Timasheff, Nicholas S. 1886-1970 ....1-4R
Obituary 29-32R
Timberlake, Carolyn
See Dresang, Eliza (Carolyn Timberlake)
Timberlake, Charles E(dward) 1935- 41-44R
Timberlake, Richard Henry Jr. 1922- 21-24R
Timerman, Jacobo 1923- CANR-32
Brief entry 109
Earlier sketch in CA 120
See also HW
Timko, Michael 1925- 17-20R
Timlett, Peter Valentine 1933- Brief entry 111
Timm, Uwe 1940- 130
Timmen, Fritz 1918- 53-56
Timmerman, Joan 1938- 118
Timmerman, John H(ager) 1945- CANR-29
Earlier sketch in CA 111
Timmerman, John Johnson 1908- 111
Timmermans, Claire 1938- 104
Timmers, J(an) Joseph M(arie) 1907- CAP-1
Earlier sketch in CA 13-14
Timmins, Lois Fahs 1914- CANR-27
Earlier sketch in CA 45-48
Timmins, William F(rederick) ....SATA 10
Timmis, John Henry III 1934- 104
Timmons, Bascom N(olly) 1890-1987 104
Obituary 122
Timmons, Bonnie 1951- 120
Timmons, Jeffry A. 1941- 108
Timms, Arthur W(arren) 1940- 120
Timms, David 1946- 109
Timms, E(dward) V(ivian)
1895-1960 Brief entry 112
Timms, Kathleen 1943- 122
Timms, Noel 1927- CANR-16
Earlier sketch in CA 13-16R
Timoney, Francis 1938- 61-64
Timoshenko, Stephen P.
1878-1972 Obituary 33-36R
Timothy, Hamilton B(aird) 1913- 102
Timothy, Peter 1725(?)-1782 ....DLB 43
Timpe, Eugene Frank 1926- 77-80
Timperley, Rosemary Kenyon 1920- CANR-17
Earlier sketch in CA 97-100
Timrod, Henry 1828-1867 ....DLB 3
Tinbergen, Jan 1903- CANR-2
Earlier sketch in CA 5-8R
Tinbergen, Niko(laas) 1907-1988 108
Obituary 127
See also SATA 60
Tindall, George Brown 1921- 85-88
Tindall, Gillian 1938- CANR-11
Earlier sketch in CA 21-24R
See also CLC 7
Tindall, Kenneth (Thomas) 1937- 29-32R
Tindall, P(eggy) E(leanor) N(ancy)
1927- 29-32R
Tindall, William York 1903-1981 ....CANR-16
Obituary 104
Earlier sketch in CA 1-4R
Tiner, John Hudson 1944- CANR-18
Earlier sketch in CA 101
See also SATA 32
Tiner, Ralph W. Jr. 1948- 124
Ting
See Tingley, Merle R(andolph)
Ting, Jan C(hing-an) 1948- 37-40R
Ting, Walasse 1929- 21-24R
Tingay, Lance 1915-1990 101
Obituary 131
Tingle, Dolli 1920- CANR-10
Earlier sketch in CA 25-28R
Tingley, Donald F(red) 1922- CANR-10
Earlier sketch in CA 25-28R
Tingley, Elizabeth 1955- 114
Tingley, Merle R(andolph) 1921- 129
Tingsten, Herbert 1896-1973 Obituary 45-48
Tinic, Seha M(ehmet) 1941- 37-40R
Tinkelman, Murray 1933- ....SATA 12
Tinker, Beamish
See Jesse, F(ryniwyd) Tennyson
Tinker, Ben (Hill) 1903- 102
Tinker, Edward Larocque 1881-1968 ....CAP-1
Earlier sketch in CA 13-14
Tinker, Hugh (Russell) 1921- CANR-3
Earlier sketch in CA 5-8R
Tinker, Jack 1938- 132
Tinker, Miles Albert 1893-1977 ....CANR-4
Earlier sketch in CA 5-8R
Tinker, Spencer Wilkie 1909- 41-44R
Tinkham, Ace
See Tinkham, Harley
Tinkham, Harley 1923-1990 Obituary 132
Tinkle, (Julien) Lon 1906-1980 104
See also SATA 36
Tinling, Ted 1910-1990 Obituary 131
Tinling, Teddy
See Tinling, Ted
Tinne, Dorothea
See Strover, Dorothea
Tinne, E. D.
See Strover, Dorothea
Tinnin, David B(ruce) 1930- 49-52
Tinniswood, Peter 1936- 25-28R
Tinsley, Ernest John 1919- 5-8R
Tinsley, James Robert 1921- 13-16R
Tinsley, Jim Bob
See Tinsley, James Robert
Tinsley, (John) Russell 1932- 17-20R
Tinterow, Gary 1953- 109
Tintner, Adeline R. 1912- 123
Tio (y Nazario de Figueroa), Aurelio 1907- ....HW
Tiomkin, Dimitri 1899-1979 Obituary 93-96
Tippett, James S(terling) 1885-1958 135
See also SATA 66
Tippett, Michael (Kemp) 1905- CANR-27
Earlier sketch in CA 109
Tippette, Giles 1934- CANR-37
Earlier sketches in CA 65-68, CANR-17
Tipping, Marjorie Jean 1917- 122
Tippit, Sammy 1947- 104
Tipple, John Ord 1916- 9-12R
Tipton, Charles Leon 1932- 41-44R
Tipton, David 1934- Brief entry 111
Tipton, James 1942- CANR-8
Earlier sketch in CA 57-60
Tiptree, James Jr.
See Sheldon, Alice Hastings Bradley
See also CLC 48, 50
See also DLB 8
Tirbutt, Honoria CANR-22
Earlier sketch in CA 106
Tirro, Frank (Pascale) 1935- 81-84
Tiryakian, Edward A(shod) 1929- CANR-19
Earlier sketches in CA 5-8R, CANR-2
Tischler, Barbara L. 1949- 123
Tischler, Hans 1915- CANR-6
Earlier sketch in CA 1-4R

Tischler, Nancy Marie (Patterson) 1931- 5-8R
Tischner, Rudolf (E.) 1879-1961 Obituary 112
Tisdale, Celes 1941- 57-60
Tisdell, Clement Allan 1939- CANR-15
Earlier sketch in CA 25-28R
Tise, Larry Edward 1942- 102
Tish-Tash
See Tashlin, Frank
Tisserand, Jacques
See Barnes, Jim
Titchener, James Lampton 1922- 45-48
Titchener, Louise 1941- 122
Titcomb, Margaret 1891- CANR-5
Earlier sketch in CA 5-8R
Titler, Dale M(ilton) 1926- 81-84
See also SATA 28, 35
Titley, David Paul 1929- 110
Titley, E. Brian 1945- 128
Titley, Norah M(ary) 1920- 118
Titmarsh, Michael Angelo
See Thackeray, William Makepeace
Titmuss, Richard M(orris) 1907-1973 109
Obituary 107
Tito, Josip Broz 1892-1980 Obituary 97-100
Tito, Marshal
See Tito, Josip Broz
Titon, Jeff Todd 1943- CANR-37
Earlier sketches in CA 89-92, CANR-16
Titra, Stephen Andrew 1945- 97-100
Titterton, Ernest William 1916- 109
Tittle, Charles R(ay) 1939- CANR-15
Earlier sketch in CA 41-44R
Tittler, Jonathan (Paul) 1945- 119
Tittler, Robert 1942- CANR-15
Earlier sketch in CA 81-84
Tittmann, George Fabian 1915-1978 ......5-8R
Obituary 81-84
Titunik, Irwin R(obert) 1929- 126
Titus, A(lice) Costandina 1950- 127
Titus, Barry J(oseph) 1938- 1-4R
Titus, Charles 1942- 45-48
Titus, David Anson 1934- 97-100
Titus, Edward William 1870-1952 ...... DLB 4
Titus, Eve 1922- CANR-30
Earlier sketch in CA 29-32R
See also SATA 2
Titus, Harold H(opper) 1896- 5-8R
Titus, Warren Irving 1921- 17-20R
Tiusanen, Timo 1936-1985 85-88
Obituary 117
Tjader, Marguerite 1901- 17-20R
Tjepkema, Sandra L(ynn) 1953- 114
Tjernagel, Neelak S(erawlook) 1906- 17-20R
Tkacik, Arnold J(ohn) 1919- 81-84
Toan, Arthur B(enjamin) Jr. 1915- 25-28R
Tobach, Ethel 1921- 81-84
Toback, James 1944- 41-44R
Tobe, John Harold 1907-1979 ......CANR-1
Earlier sketch in CA 1-4R
Tobey, George B. Jr. 1917- 49-52
Tobey, Kathrene McLandress 1908- CAP-2
Earlier sketch in CA 29-32
Tobey, Mark 1890-1976 Obituary 65-68
Tobey, Ronald C(harles) 1942- 73-76
Tobias, Andrew P. 1947- CANR-14
Earlier sketch in CA 37-40R
Tobias, Henry J(ack) 1925- 41-44R
Tobias, J(ohn) J(acob) 1925- 53-56
Tobias, Katherine
See Gottfried, Theodore Mark
Tobias, Phillip V. 1925- CANR-15
Earlier sketch in CA 37-40R
Tobias, Richard C(lark) 1925- 29-32R
Tobias, Ronald B(enjamin) 1948- CANR-28
Earlier sketch in CA 111
Tobias, Sheila 1935- 93-96
Tobias, Tobi 1938- CANR-16
Earlier sketch in CA 29-32R
See also CLR 4
See also SATA 5
Tobin, James Edward 1905-1968 ...... CAP-2
Earlier sketch in CA 23-24
Tobin, James 1918- CANR-5
Earlier sketch in CA 53-56
Tobin, Jean Holloway
1917(?)-1989 Obituary 130
Tobin, Kay 1930- 37-40R
Tobin, Richard J. 1946- 137
Tobin, Richard Lardner 1910- CANR-1
Earlier sketch in CA 1-4R
Tobin, Sheldon S(idney) 1931- 134
Brief entry 110
Tobin, Terence 1938- 53-56
Toby, Liz
See Minsky, Betty Jane (Toebe)
Toby, Mark 1913(?)-1972 Obituary 37-40R
Toch, Hans (Herbert) 1930- CANR-23
Earlier sketches in CA 17-20R, CANR-7
Toch, Henry 1923- CANR-21
Earlier sketches in CA 9-12R, CANR-6
Toczek, Nick 1950- 106
Tod, Ian J. 1945- 103
Tod, Osma Gallinger 1898-1982(?) CAP-1
Obituary 108
Earlier sketch in CA 9-10
Todd, Alden 1918- CANR-6
Earlier sketch in CA 1-4R
Todd, Ann 1909- 129
Todd, Anne Ophelia
See Dowden, Anne Ophelia
Todd, Barbara Euphan 1890-1976 104
Todd, Barbara K(eith) 1917- 61-64
See also SATA 10
Todd, Burbank L. CANR-26
Earlier sketches in CAP-2, CA 19-20
Todd, Clark 1945(?)-1983 Obituary 110
Todd, Edgeley W(oodman)
1914- Brief entry 109
Todd, Edward N. 1931- 53-56
Todd, Frances 1910- 13-16R
Todd, Frederick Porter
1903-1977 Obituary 73-76
Todd, Galbraith Hall 1914- 1-4R
Todd, Herbert Eatton 1908-1988 ......CANR-30
Earlier sketches in CAP-1, CA 9-10, CANR-12
See also SATA 11
Todd, Hollis N(elson) 1914- 57-60
Todd, Ian A(lexander) 1941- CANR-31
Earlier sketch in CA 112
Todd, Ian Menzies 1923- 69-72
Todd, Janet M(argaret) 1942- CANR-28
Earlier sketches in CA 49-52, CANR-1
Todd, Jerry D(ale) 1941- 53-56
Todd, John M(urray) 1918- 9-12R
Todd, Karen (Iris) Rohne (Pritchett)
1936- Brief entry 111
Todd, Leonard 1940- 65-68
Todd, Loreto 1942- 107
See also SATA 30
Todd, Louise
See Sandweiss, Martha A(nn)
Todd, Malcolm 1939- 101
Todd, Paul
See Posner, Richard
Todd, Peter
See Hamilton, Charles (Harold St. John)
Todd, R. Larry 1952- 128
Todd, Richard (Killingworth) 1949- 125
Todd, Ruth Van Dorn
1889(?)-1976 Obituary 65-68
Todd, Ruthven 1914- 81-84
Todd, Virgil H. 1921- Brief entry 106
Todd, Vivian Edmiston 1912- 17-20R
Todd, William Burton 1919- 41-44R
Todd, William Mills III 1944- 65-68
Todman, Bill
See Todman, William S.
Todman, William S. 1916-1979 Obituary 89-92
Todorov, Nikolai (Todorov) 1921- 132
Todorov, Tzvetan 1939- 73-76
Todrank, Gustave H(erman) 1924- 41-44R
Todrin, Boris 1915- 61-64
Todsicher, J(ohn) Edgar 1926- CANR-31
Earlier sketches in CA 29-32R, CANR-14
Toekes, Rudolf L(eslie) 1935- 21-24R
Toepfer, Ray Grant 1923- 21-24R
Toeplitz, Jerzy 1909- 65-68
Toernqvist, (Per) Egil 1932- 29-32R
Tofani, Loretta 1953- 116
Brief entry 113
Toffler, Alvin 1928- CANR-15
Earlier sketch in CA 13-16R
See also MTCW
Toft, (Eric) John 1933- 103
Tofte, Arthur 1902-1980 73-76
Obituary 103
Togliatti, Palmiro 1893(?)-1964 133
Obituary 113
Tohata, Seiichi 1899-1983 Obituary 110
Toka, Salchak Kalbakkhoreviich
1901-1973 Obituary 41-44R
Tokayer, Marvin 1936- 102
Toker, Franklin K(arl) B(enedict) S(erchuk)
1944- CANR-15
Earlier sketch in CA 81-84
Tokes, Rudolf L(eslie) 1935- Brief entry 114
Toklas, Alice B(abette) 1877-1967 81-84
Obituary 25-28R
See also DLB 4
Tokmakoff, George 1928- 123
Tolan, Stephanie S. 1942- CANR-34
Earlier sketches in CA 77-80, CANR-15
See also SATA 38
Toland, John (Willard) 1912- CANR-23
Earlier sketches in CA 1-4R, CANR-6
See also MTCW
See also SATA 38
Tolbert, E(lias) L(ake) 1915- CANR-3
Earlier sketch in CA 1-4R
Tolbert, Francis Xavier 1912-1984 ......CANR-16
Obituary 111
Earlier sketch in CA 1-4R
Tolbert, Frank X.
See Tolbert, Francis Xavier
Tolbert, Malcolm O(liver) 1924- 65-68
Tolbert, Mary Ann 1947- 116
Tolby, Arthur
See Infield, Glenn (Berton)
Tolchin, Martin 1928- 120
Toldson, Ivory L. 1943- 114
Toledano, Ralph de 1916- CANR-31
Earlier sketch in CA 9-12R
See also AITN 1
Toledano, Roulhac (Bunkley) 1938- 101
Tolegian, Aram 1909- CANR-6
Earlier sketch in CA 1-4R
Toles, Thomas G. 1951- 126
Toles, Tom
See Toles, Thomas G.
Tolf, Robert W(alter) 1929- 73-76
Tolischus, Otto D(avid)
1890-1967 Obituary 93-96
Toliver, George
See Masselink, Ben
Toliver, Harold E(arl) 1932- CANR-34
Earlier sketch in CA 21-24R
Toliver, Raymond F. 1914- CANR-35
Earlier sketch in CA 17-20R
Tolkien, J(ohn) R(onald) R(euel)
1892-1973 ......CANR-36
Obituary 45-48
Earlier sketches in CAP-2, CA 17-18
See also AITN 1
See also CDBLB 1914-1945
See also CLC 1, 2, 3, 8, 12, 38
See also DLB 15
See also MAICYA
See also MTCW
See also SATA 2, 24, 32
See also WLC
Tolkin, Michael 1950- 137
Toll, Robert C(harles) 1938- 53-56
Toll, Seymour I. 1925- 29-32R
Toll, William 1941- 114
Toller, Ernst 1893-1939 Brief entry 107
See also TCLC 10
Toller, Kate Caffrey
See Caffrey, Kate
Tollers, Vincent L(ouis) 1939- 57-60
Tolles, Frederick B(arnes) 1915-1975 ......5-8R
Obituary 103
Tolles, Martha 1921- 49-52
See also SATA 8
Tollet, Elizabeth 1694-1754 ...... DLB 95
Tolley, A(rnold) T(revor) 1927- 123
Tolley, Howard B(oyd) Jr. 1943- 53-56
Tolley, Kemp 1908- 45-48
Tolley, William Pearson 1900- 93-96
Tolliver, Ruby C(hangos) 1922- 111
See also SATA 41, 55
Tolman, Newton F. 1908-1986 ......1-4R
Obituary 120
Tolmie, Kenneth Donald 1941- 69-72
See also SATA 15
Tolnai, Karoly
See De Tolnay, Charles Erich
Tolnai, Vagujhelyi Karoly
See De Tolnay, Charles Erich
Tolson, M. B.
See Tolson, Melvin B(eaunorus)
Tolson, Melvin B(eaunorus) 1898(?)-1966 124
Obituary 89-92
See also BLC 3
See also BW
See also CLC 36
See also DLB 48, 76
Tolstaya, Tatyana 1951- 130
Tolstoi, Aleksei Nikolaevich
See Tolstoy, Alexey Nikolaevich
Tolstoy, Alexandra L(vovna) 1884-1979 65-68
Obituary 89-92
Tolstoy, Alexey Nikolaevich
1882-1945 Brief entry 107
See also TCLC 18
Tolstoy, Count Leo
See Tolstoy, Leo (Nikolaevich)
Tolstoy, Dimitry 1912- 29-32R
Tolstoy, Leo (Nikolaevich) 1828-1910 123
Brief entry 104
See also SATA 26
See also SSC 9
See also TCLC 4, 11, 17, 28, 44
See also WLC
Tolstoy, Mary Koutouzov
1884(?)-1976 Obituary 69-72
Tolstoy (-Miloslavsky), Nikolai (Dimitrievich)
1935- 81-84
Tolstoy, Tatyana (Sukhotin)
1864-1950 Brief entry 117
Tolzmann, Don Heinrich 1945- CANR-38
Earlier sketches in CA 49-52, CANR-2, 17
Toma, Dave
See Toma, David
Toma, David 1933- 118
Tomalin, Claire 1933- 89-92
Tomalin, Nicholas 1931-1973 Obituary 45-48
Tomalin, Ruth CANR-29
Earlier sketches in CA 13-16R, CANR-13
See also SATA 29
Toman, Walter 1920- 5-8R
Tomas, Andrew Paul 73-76
Tomasek, Robert D(ennis) 1928- 17-20R
Tomaselli, Sylvana 1957- 137
Tomasevic, Nebojsa 1929- 81-84
Tomashevich, George Vid 1927- 133
Tomasi, Silvano M(ario) 1940- 115
Tomasic, D(inko) A(nthony) 1902- CAP-1
Earlier sketch in CA 19-20
Tomasi di Lampedusa, Giuseppe
1896-1957 Brief entry 111
See also Lampedusa, Giuseppe (Tomasi) di
Tomasson, Katherine 1895- CAP-1
Earlier sketch in CA 9-10
Tomasson, Richard F(inn) 1928- CANR-1
Earlier sketch in CA 45-48
Tomb, David A(lan) 1944- 117
Tomek, Ivan 1939- 120
Tomes, Margot (Ladd) 1917-1991 ...... MAICYA
See also SATA 27, 36, 70
See also SATO 69
Tomeski, Edward Alexander 1930- 37-40R
Tomfool
See Farjeon, Eleanor
Tomikel, John 1928- CANR-4
Earlier sketch in CA 53-56
Tomin, Zdena 1941- 123
Tomkiewicz, Mina 1917-1975 ...... CAP-2
Earlier sketch in CA 29-32
Tomkins, Calvin 1925- CANR-8
Earlier sketch in CA 13-16R
Tomkins, Jasper
See Batey, Tom
Tomkins, Mary E(ileen) 1914- 61-64
Tomkinson, Constance
See Weeks, Constance Tomkinson
Tomkinson, Michael 1940- CANR-22
Earlier sketch in CA 93-96
Tomlan, Michael A. 1947- 137
Tomlin, E(ric) W(alter) F(rederick)
1913-1988(?) CANR-3
Obituary 124
Earlier sketch in CA 5-8R
Tomlin, Lily
See Tomlin, Mary Jean
See also CLC 17
Tomlin, Mary Jean 1939(?)- Brief entry 117
See also Tomlin, Lily
Tomlins, Jack E(dward) 1929- 25-28R
Tomlinson, (Alfred) Charles 1927- CANR-33
Earlier sketch in CA 5-8R
See also CLC 2, 4, 6, 13, 45
See also DLB 40
Tomlinson, Edward
1891(?)-1973 Obituary 45-48
Tomlinson, Gerald (Arthur) 1933- 85-88
Tomlinson, H(enry) M(ajor)
1873-1958 Brief entry 118
See also DLB 36, 100
Tomlinson, Harry 1943- 135
Tomlinson, Jill 1931-1976 ...... CAP-2
Earlier sketch in CA 29-32
See also SATA 3, 24
Tomlinson, Kenneth Y(oung) 1944- 65-68
Tomlinson, Reginald R(obert)
1885-1979(?) Obituary 104
See also SATA 27
Tomlinson, T(homas) B(rian) 1925- 9-12R
Tomlinson-Keasey, Carol 1942- 101
Tommeraasen, Miles 1923- 21-24R
Tompert, Ann 1918- CANR-11
Earlier sketch in CA 69-72
See also SATA 14
Tompkins, C(linton) David 1937- 41-44R
Tompkins, Dorothy (Campbell) 1908- 17-20R
Tompkins, E(dwin) Berkeley 1935- 29-32R
Tompkins, Everett Thomas 1931- 107
Tompkins, J(oyce) M(arjorie) S(anxter)
1897-1986 Obituary 121
Tompkins, Jane P(arry) 1940- CANR-39
Earlier sketches in CA 29-32R, CANR-17
Tompkins, Jerry R(obert) 1931- 17-20R
Tompkins, Julia (Marguerite Hunter Manchee)
1909- 29-32R
Tompkins, Kathleen Burns 1934- 93-96
Tompkins, Peter 1919- CANR-12
Earlier sketch in CA 9-12R
Tompkins, Richard A.
1896(?)-1977 Obituary 73-76
Tompkins, Stuart R(amsay) 1886-1977 ......37-40R
Tompkins, Tom
See Tompkins, Everett Thomas
Tompkins, Walker A. 1909- 5-8R
Tompson, Benjamin 1642-1714 ...... DLB 24
Toms, Bernard 1931- 17-20R
Tomson, Bernard 1909-1978 Obituary 77-80
Ton, Mary Ellen 1933- 112
Tonashi
See Harrington, Mark Raymond
Tone, Teona 1944- 112
Toner, Raymond John 1908- 5-8R
See also SATA 10
Toney, Albert (Livingston Jr.) 1933- 120
Toney, Anthony 1913- CANR-9
Earlier sketch in CA 17-20R
Tong, Gary S. 1942- 135
See also SATA 66
Tong, Raymond 1922- CANR-2
Earlier sketch in CA 5-8R
Tong, Te-kong 1920- CANR-8
Earlier sketch in CA 9-12R
Tongren, Sally S(tetson) 1926- 118
Tonkin, Humphrey 1939- CANR-38
Earlier sketches in CA 41-44R, CANR-16
Tonkin, Peter (Francis) 1950- 101
Tonkinson, Robert 1928- 77-80
Tonks, A. Ronald 1934- 125
Tonks, Rosemary (D. Boswell) 89-92
See also DLB 14
Tonn, Martin H. 1921- 5-8R
Tonquedec, Joseph de
1868-1962 Obituary 112
Tonson, Jacob
See Bennett, (Enoch) Arnold
Tonsor, Stephen (John) 1923- Brief entry 114
Toobin, Jerome 1920(?)-1984 Obituary 111
Toohey, Catherine 1949- 109
Toohey, Robert E(ugene) 1935- 89-92
Took, Belladonna
See Chapman, Vera
Tooke, Ann (Mary Margaret) Hales
See Hales-Tooke, Ann (Mary Margaret)
Tooke, Louise Mathews 1950- 105
See also SATA 38
Tooke, Thomas (Renshaw) 1947- 73-76
Tooker, Elisabeth (Jane) 1927- 49-52
Toole, John Kennedy 1937-1969 104
See also CLC 19, 64
See also DLBY 81
Toole, K(enneth) Ross 1920- Brief entry 112
Toole, Rex
See Tralins, S(andor) Robert
Toole, William Bell III 1930- 21-24R
Toole Stott, Raymond 1910-1982 Obituary 105
Tooley, M. J.
See Tooley, Michael J(ohn)
Tooley, Michael J(ohn) 1942- CANR-24
Earlier sketch in CA 106
Tooley, R(onald) Vere 1898-1986 ......9-12R
Obituary 120
Toomay, Patrick J(ay) 1948- 65-68
Toombs, John 1927- 106

Toombs, Lawrence Edmund 1919- CANR-8
Earlier sketch in CA 5-8R
Toomer, Derek 1946- 65-68
Toomer, Jean 1894-1967 85-88
See also BLC 3
See also BW
See also CDALB 1917-1929
See also CLC 1, 4, 13, 22
See also DLB 45, 51
See also MTCW
See also SSC 1
Toon, Peter 1939- CANR-30
Earlier sketch in CA 112
Toona, Elin(-Kai) 1937- CANR-15
Earlier sketch in CA 81-84
Toonder, Martin
See Groom, Arthur William
Toothaker, Roy Eugene 1928- 65-68
See also SATA 18
Tooze, Ruth (Anderson) 1892- 5-8R
See also SATA 4
Topaz, Jacqueline
See Hyman, Jackie (Diamond)
Topel, L(ouis) John 1934- 118
Toperoff, Sam 1933- CANR-30
Earlier sketch in CA 45-48
Topitsch, Ernst 1919- 136
Topkins, Katharine 1927- 49-52
Topkins, Richard 1925- 25-28R
Toplin, Robert Brent 1940- CANR-15
Earlier sketch in CA 77-80
Topol, Allan 1941- 93-96
Topolski, Daniel 1945- CANR-28
Earlier sketch in CA 110
Topolski, Feliks 1907- Brief entry 112
Topor, Tom 1938- 105
Topper, Suzanne 1939- 128
Toppin, Edgar A(llan) 1928- 21-24R
Topping, Anne Marie 25-28R
Topping, Audrey R(onning) 1928- 41-44R
See also SATA 14
Topping, C(oral) W(esley) 1889- 41-44R
Topping, Donald M(edley) 1929- 53-56
Topping, Seymour 1921- 49-52
Topping, Wesley
See Topping, C(oral) W(esley)
Topsfield, L(eslie) T(homas)
1920-1981 ....CANR-9
Obituary 105
Earlier sketch in CA 61-64
Tor, Regina
See Shekerjian, Regina Tor
Torack, Richard M(aurice) 1927- 106
Torberg, Friedrich
See Kantor-Berg, Friedrich
See also DLB 85
Torbert, Floyd James 1922- 105
See also SATA 22
Torbert, William Rockwell 1944- 41-44R
Torbet, Laura 1942- CANR-16
Earlier sketch in CA 69-72
Torbet, Robert G(eorge) 1912- 9-12R
Torbett, Harvey Douglas Louis 1921- 9-12R
Torchiana, Donald T(hornhill) 1923- 17-20R
Torchio, Menico 1932- 61-64
Torday, Ursula 97-100
See also CABS 28
Tordoff, William 1925- 120
Toren, Heller 77-80
Torgersen, Don Arthur 1934- 111
See also SATA 41, 55
Torgersen, Eric 1943- 37-40R
Torgersen, Paul Ernest 1931- 81-84
Torgerson, Dial 1928- 53-56
Torgerson Shaw, Ellen
1929(?)-1983 Obituary 109
Torgoff, Martin 1952- 109
Torgovnick, Marianna 1949- 115
Torley, Luke
See Blish, James (Benjamin)
Torme, Mel(vin Howard) 1925- Brief entry 118
Tormey, John Connolly 1942- 61-64
Tornabene, Lyn 1930- 69-72
Torney, Judith V.
See Torney-Purta, Judith V(ollmar)
Torney-Purta, Judith V(ollmar) 1937- CANR-10
Earlier sketch in CA 65-68
Tornimparte, Alessandra
See Ginzburg, Natalia
Torok, Lou 1927- 49-52
Torr, Iain
See Mackinnon, Charles Roy
Torrance, E. Paul 1915- CANR-18
Earlier sketches in CA 1-4R, CANR-3
Torrance, Thomas F(orsythe) 1913- CANR-29
Earlier sketches in CA 9-12R, CANR-5
Torre, Jose de la
See de la Torre, Jose
Torre, Raoul della
See Mencken, H(enry) L(ouis)
Torre-Bueno, Lillian de la
See McCue, Lillian Bueno
Torregian, Sotere 1941- CANR-3
Earlier sketch in CA 45-48
Torrence, Ridgely 1874-1950 .... DLB 54
Torrens, Duncan
See Ripley, Michael David
Torrens, Robert George Obituary 105
Torrents, Nissa 1937- 128
Torres, Andres Segovia
See Segovia, Andres
Torres, Edwin 111
Torres, Emmanuel 1932- 97-100
Torres, Jose Acosta 1925- CANR-32
Earlier sketch in CA 57-60
See also HW
Torres, Sergio
See Torres Gonzalez, Sergio A(ntonio)
Torres, Tereska
See Torres-Levin, Tereska (Szwarc)
Torres Bodet, Jaime 1902-1974 ....CANR-32
Obituary 49-52
Earlier sketch in CA 101
See also HW
See also MTCW
Torres Gonzalez, Sergio A(ntonio) 1929- 117
Torres-Levin, Tereska (Szwarc) CANR-15
Earlier sketch in CA 5-8R
Torres-Rioseco, Arturo 1897-1971 .... CAP-1
Earlier sketch in CA 9-10
Torrey, E(dwin) Fuller 1937- 119
See also CLC 34
Torrey, Gordon H(oward) 1919- 9-12R
Torrey, Norman Lewis 1894-1980 ....1-4R
Obituary 102
Torrey, Therese von Hohoff
1898(?)-1974 Obituary 45-48
Torrey, Volta (Wray) 1905- 69-72
Torrie, James H(iram) 1908- 73-76
Torrie, Malcolm
See Mitchell, Gladys (Maude Winifred)
Torro, Pel
See Fanthorpe, R(obert) Lionel
Tors, Ivan (Lawrence) 1916-1983 103
Obituary 110
Torsney, Cheryl B. 1955- 135
Torsvan, Ben Traven
See Traven, B.
Torsvan, Benno Traven
See Traven, B.
Torsvan, Berick Traven
See Traven, B.
Torsvan, Berwick Traven
See Traven, B.
Torsvan, Bruno Traven
See Traven, B.
Torsvan, Traven
See Traven, B.
Tortolano, William 1930- 77-80
Tortora, Daniel F(rancis) 1947- CANR-13
Earlier sketch in CA 73-76
Toscano, Peter Ralph 1920- 45-48
Tosches, Nick 1949- 81-84
Tosi, Henry L(ouis) Jr. 1936- 125
Tosics, Ivan 1952- 138
Toson
See Shimazaki Haruki
Tosti, Donald Thomas 1935- 49-52
Toth, Charles W(illiam) 1919- CANR-10
Earlier sketch in CA 65-68
Toth, Emily 1944- 101
Toth, Lazlo
See Novello, Don
Toth, Robert Charles 1928- 102
Toth, Stephen Jr. 1950- 69-72
Toth, Susan Erickson Allen 1940- 105
See also DLBY 86
Totham, Mary
See Breinburg, Petronella
Totman, Conrad 1934- CANR-38
Earlier sketches in CA 101, CANR-17
Totten, George Oakley III 1922- CANR-21
Earlier sketches in CA 9-12R, CANR-5
Totten, Martha Wescoat 1957- 118
Totten, Sam(uel) 1949- 118
Totten, W. Fred 1905- 37-40R
Tough, Allen (MacNeill) 1936- 108
Touliatos, John 1944- 93-96
Toulmin, Stephen Edelston 1922- CANR-20
Earlier sketches in CA 9-12R, CANR-5
Toulouse-Lautrec, Marie-Pierre (Mapie) de
1901-1972 Obituary 37-40R
Toulson, Shirley 1924- CANR-38
Earlier sketches in CA 101, CANR-17
Touraine, Alain 1925- 85-88
Toure, Askia Muhammad
See Toure, Askia Muhammad Abu Bakr el
See also DLB 41
Toure, Askia Muhammad Abu Bakr el
1938- 124
See also Toure, Askia Muhammad
See also BW
Tourgee, Albion W. 1838-1905 .... DLB 79
Tourneur, Cyril 1580(?)-1626 .... DLB 58
Tourneur, Dina-Kathelijn 1934- 108
Tourney, Garfield 1927- 57-60
Tournier, Michel (Edouard) 1924- CANR-36
Earlier sketches in CA 49-52, CANR-3
See also CLC 6, 23, 36
See also DLB 83
See also MTCW
See also SATA 23
Tournier, Paul 1898-1986 ....CANR-29
Obituary 120
Earlier sketch in CA 81-84
Tournimparte, Alessandra
See Ginzburg, Natalia
Tours, Hugh Berthold 1910- CAP-1
Earlier sketch in CA 9-10
Tourtellot, Arthur Bernon 1913-1977 ......CANR-4
Obituary 73-76
Earlier sketch in CA 5-8R
Tourtellot, Jonathan B. 1946- 111
Tourville, Elsie A(lma) 1926- 57-60
Tousley, Clare M. 1889(?)-1985 Obituary 114
Toussaint, Stanley D. 1928- 115
Touster, Alison
See Reed, Alison Touster
Touval, Saadia E. 1932- CANR-35
Earlier sketch in CA 45-48
Touw, Kathleen 1949- 109
Tovey, Doreen Evelyn 1918- 104
Tovo, Jerome 1936- 45-48
Towber, Chaim 1902(?)-1972 Obituary 33-36R
Towell, Julie E. 1953- 122
Tower, Ann
See Straubing, Harold (Elk)
Tower, Diana
See Smith, Richard Rein
Tower, Don
See Bower, Donald E(dward)
Tower, John G(oodwin) 1925- Brief entry 106
Tower, Margene 1939- 37-40R
Towers, Ivar
See Kornbluth, C(yril) M.
Towers, Maxwell 1909- 57-60
Towers, Regina
See Pykare, Nina
Towers, (Augustus) Robert 1923- 132
Towey, Cyprian 1912- 21-24R
Towle, Joseph W(alter) 1909- CAP-1
Earlier sketch in CA 13-14
Towle, Philip 1945- 117
Towle, Tony 1939- 37-40R
Towler, Juby Earl 1913- 13-16R
Town, Glenn P(atrick) 1949- 118
Town, Harold (Barling) 1924- CANR-15
Earlier sketch in CA 41-44R
Towne, Anthony 1928-1980 ....25-28R
Obituary 117
Towne, Benjamin 1740(?)-1793 .... DLB 43
Towne, Mary
See Spelman, Mary
Towne, Peter
See Nabokov, Peter (Francis)
Towne, Robert (Burton) 1936(?)- 108
See also DLB 44
Towne, Stuart
See Rawson, Clayton
Towner, Donald (Chisholm) 1903-1985 ..... CAP-1
Obituary 117
Earlier sketch in CA 19-20
Towner, Jason
See Smith, Harold Ivan
Towner, W. Sibley
See Towner, Wayne Sibley
Towner, Wayne Sibley 1933- Brief entry 118
Townley, Ralph 1923- 21-24R
Townley, Rod
See Townley, Roderick
Townley, Roderick 1942- CANR-29
Earlier sketches in CA 57-60, CANR-12
Towns, Elmer L(eon) 1932- CANR-2
Earlier sketch in CA 45-48
Towns, James E(dward) 1942- CANR-23
Earlier sketches in CA 61-64, CANR-8, 21
Towns, Jim
See Towns, James E(dward)
Townsend, Charles Bud 1929- 53-56
Townsend, Charles E(dward) 1932- 41-44R
Townsend, Charles R(ay) 1929- 69-72
Townsend, Doris McFerran 1914- CANR-19
Earlier sketch in CA 103
Townsend, Elsie Doig 1908- 29-32R
Townsend, Harry 1925- 25-28R
Townsend, Irving 1920- 101
Townsend, J(ames) Benjamin 1918- 21-24R
Townsend, J(acob) David 1888- 5-8R
Townsend, James B(arclay) J(ermain)
1910- 49-52
Townsend, Janet (Elizabeth) 1925- 107
Townsend, John Rowe 1922- 37-40R
See also CLR 2
See also MAICYA
See also SAAS 2
See also SATA 4, 68
Townsend, Larry 1935- 136
Townsend, Mark
See Wallmann, Jeffrey M(iner)
Townsend, Peter (Wooldridge) 1914- CANR-28
Earlier sketch in CA 29-32R
Townsend, Ralph M.
1901(?)-1976 Obituary 65-68
Townsend, Reginald T.
1890-1977 Obituary 73-76
Townsend, Richard E.
1897(?)-1975 Obituary 61-64
Townsend, Robert 1920- 45-48
Townsend, Sue 1946- 127
Brief entry 119
See also CLC 61
See also MTCW
See also SATA 48, 55
Townsend, Thomas L. 1944- 127
See also SATA 59
Townsend, Tom
See Townsend, Thomas L.
Townsend, William Cameron
1896-1982 Obituary 106
Townsend, William H(enry)
1890-1964 Obituary 111
Townshend, Aurelian 1583(?)-1651(?) .... DLB 121
Townshend, Peter (Dennis Blandford)
1945- 107
See also CLC 17, 42
Townshend, Richard
See Bickers, Richard Leslie Townshend
Townson, Hazel CANR-18
Earlier sketch in CA 97-100
Toy, Henry Jr. 1915- 37-40R
Toye, Clive 1933(?)- ....SATA 30
Toye, John Francis 1883-1964 .... CAP-1
Earlier sketch in CA 9-10
Toye, William Eldred 1926- CANR-4
Earlier sketch in CA 1-4R
See also SATA 8
Toynbee, Arnold J(oseph) 1889-1975 .....CANR-36
Obituary 61-64
Earlier sketch in CA 5-8R
See also AITN 2
Toynbee, Jocelyn M(ary) C(atherine)
1897-1985 ....37-40R
Obituary 118
Toynbee, (Theodore) Philip 1916-1981 ....CANR-4
Obituary 104
Earlier sketch in CA 1-4R
Toynbee, Polly (Mary Louisa) 1946- CANR-9
Earlier sketch in CA 21-24R
Tozer, Mary (Christine) 1947- 101
Tozzi, Federigo 1883-1920 .... TCLC 31
Trabasso, Tom 1935- CANR-11
Earlier sketch in CA 21-24R
Trace, Arther Storrey Jr. 1922- CANR-20
Earlier sketch in CA 1-4R
Tracey, Hugh (Travers) 1903-1977 .... CAP-2
Obituary 77-80
Earlier sketch in CA 29-32
Tracey, Patricia Cleland 1932- 5-8R
Trachman, Muriel Karlin CANR-15
Earlier sketch in CA 85-88
Trachte, Don(ald) 1915- 89-92
Trachtenberg, Inge 1923- 77-80
Trachtenberg, Marvin (Lawrence) 1939- 65-68
Trachtenberg, Paul 1948- 112
Trachtenberg, Stanley 119
Traci, Philip (Joseph) 1934-1984 ....41-44R
Obituary 133
Tracy, Aloise
See Shoenight, Aloise
Tracy, Ann B(laisdell) 1941- 107
Tracy, Charles (William) 1938- 128
Tracy, Clarence 1908- 9-12R
Tracy, David W. 1939- 101
Tracy, Don(ald Fiske) 1905-197 (?) CANR-2
Earlier sketch in CA 1-4R
Tracy, Doris 1925- 61-64
Tracy, Honor (Lilbush Wingfield)
1913-1989 ....CANR-24
Obituary 128
Earlier sketches in CA 61-64, CANR-8
See also DLB 15
Tracy, Jack W. 1945- 105
Tracy, James D. 1938- 102
Tracy, John A(lvin) 1934- 53-56
Tracy, L(ee) Jack 1926- 9-12R
Tracy, Leland
See Tralins, S(andor) Robert
Tracy, Lorna 1934- 132
Tracy, Louise Treadwell
1896-1983 Obituary 114
Tracy, Michael 1932- 13-16R
Tracy, Powers
See Ward, Don(ald G.)
Tracy, Robert E. 1928- 89-92
Tracy, Susan
See Marino, Carolyn Fitch
Tracy, Theodore J(ames) 1916- 29-32R
Tracy, Thomas Henry 1900- CAP-2
Earlier sketch in CA 17-18
Tracz, Richard Francis 1944- CANR-17
Earlier sketch in CA 29-32R
Trader Vic
See Bergeron, Victor (Jules Jr.)
Traer, James Frederick 1938- 102
Trafzer, Clifford Earl 1949- CANR-26
Earlier sketch in CA 109
Trager, Frank N(ewton) 1905-1984 ....CANR-9
Obituary 113
Earlier sketch in CA 17-20R
Trager, George L(eonard) 1906- 41-44R
Trager, Helen G. 1910- 69-72
Trager, James 1925- CANR-34
Earlier sketches in CA 37-40R, CANR-15
Tragle, Henry Irving 1914- 37-40R
Trahan, Ronald 1950- 106
Traherne, Michael
See Watkins-Pitchford, Denys James
Trahey, Jane 1923- CANR-17
Earlier sketch in CA 17-20R
See also SATA 36
Traill, Catharine Parr 1802-1899 .... DLB 99
Train, Arthur (Cheney)
1875-1945 Brief entry 112
See also DLB 86
Train, Arthur K(issam)
1902(?)-1981 Obituary 104
Train, John 1928- CANR-30
Earlier sketch in CA 106
Traina, Richard P(aul) 1937- 25-28R
Trainer, David 1947- CANR-20
Earlier sketch in CA 25-28R
Trainer, Jennifer 1956- 108
Trainer, Orvel 1925- 45-48
Trainor, Richard
See Tralins, S(andor) Robert
Traister, Aaron 1904(?)-1976 Obituary 65-68
Trakas, Pedro N(icholas) 1923- 104
Trakl, Georg 1887-1914 Brief entry 104
See also TCLC 5
Tralbaut, Mark-Edo 1902-1976 .... CAP-2
Earlier sketch in CA 29-32
Tralins, Bob
See Tralins, S(andor) Robert
Tralins, Robert S.
See Tralins, S(andor) Robert
Tralins, S(andor) Robert 1926- CANR-14
Earlier sketch in CA 21-24R
Trambley, Estela Portillo 1936- 77-80
Trani, Eugene P(aul) 1939- CANR-29
Earlier sketch in CA 25-28R
Transtroemer, Tomas (Goesta) 1931- 129
Brief entry 117
See also CLC 52, 65
Transtromer, Tomas Gosta
See Transtroemer, Tomas (Goesta)
Transue, Jacob
See Matheson, Joan (Transue)

Transue, Joan
  See Matheson, Joan (Transue)
Tranter, John Ernest 1943- 110
Tranter, Nigel (Godwin) 1909- CANR-20
  Earlier sketches in CA 9-12R, CANR-5
Trantino, Tommy 1938- 65-68
Trapido, Barbara 1941- 123
Trapier, Elizabeth du Gue
  1893(?)-1974 Obituary 53-56
Trapp, E(dward) Philip 1923- 45-48
Trapp, Frank Anderson 1922- 57-60
Trapp, Maria Augusta von
  See von Trapp, Maria Augusta
  See also SATA 16
Traschen, Isadore 1915- 25-28R
Trask, David F(rederic) 1929- CANR-17
  Earlier sketches in CA 1-4R, CANR-1
Trask, John Jacquelin
  1904(?)-1977 Obituary 69-72
Trask, Jonathan
  See Levinson, Leonard
Trask, Margaret Pope 1907- 1-4R
Trask, Roger R(eed) 1930- 41-44R
Trask, Willard (Ropes)
  1900(?)-1980 Obituary 101
Trasler, Gordon (Blair) 1929- CANR-3
  Earlier sketch in CA 1-4R
Trattner, Walter I(rwin) 1936- CANR-13
  Earlier sketch in CA 37-40R
Traube, Ruy
  See Tralins, S(andor) Robert
Traube, Shepard 1907-1983 Obituary 111
Traubel, Horace
  See Traubel, Horace L(ogo)
Traubel, Horace L(ogo)
  1858-1919 Brief entry 123
Traudl
  See Flaxman, Traudl
Trauger, Wilmer K(ohl) 1898- CAP-1
  Earlier sketch in CA 9-10
Traugott, Elizabeth Closs 1939- 41-44R
Traupman, John C. 1923- 41-44R
Traut, Dennis 1953- 111
Trautman, Donald T. 1924- 37-40R
Trautman, Ray 1907- 45-48
Trautmann, Frederic 1936- 132
Trautmann, Thomas R(oger) 1940- 131
Travell, Janet (Graeme) 1901- CAP-2
  Earlier sketch in CA 29-32
Traven, B. CAP-2
  Obituary 25-28R
  Earlier sketch in CA 19-20
  See also CLC 8, 11
  See also DLB 9, 56
  See also MTCW
Traven, Beatrice
  See Goldemberg, Rose Leiman
Traver, Robert
  See Voelker, John D(onaldson)
Travers, Ben 1886-1980 133
  Obituary 102
  See also DLB 10
Travers, Kenneth
  See Hutchin, Kenneth Charles
Travers, Louise Allderdice 1891- CAP-1
  Earlier sketch in CA 9-10
Travers, P(amela) L(yndon) 1906- CANR-30
  Earlier sketch in CA 33-36R
  See also CLR 2
  See also MAICYA
  See also SAAS 2
  See also SATA 4, 54
Travers, Paul J(oseph) 1951- 138
Travers, Robert J. 1911(?)-1974 Obituary 49-52
Travers, Robert M(orris) W(illiam)
  1913- CANR-2
  Earlier sketch in CA 5-8R
Travers, Scott A(ndrew) 1961- 125
Travers, Virginia
  See Coigney, Virginia
Travers, Will
  See Rowland, D(onald) S(ydney)
Traversi, Derek A(ntona) 1912- 77-80
Travis, Charles S. 1943- 37-40R
Travis, Dempsey J. 1920- CANR-15
  Earlier sketch in CA 85-88
Travis, Elizabeth (Frances Chandler) 1920- 134
Travis, Frederick F. 1942- 135
Travis, Gerry
  See Trimble, Louis P(reston)
Travis, Gretchen A. 103
Travis, John T. 1935- 25-28R
Travis, Neal 1939(?)- 103
Travis, Stephen H(enry) 1944- 106
Travis, Walter Earl 1926- 21-24R
Travis, William 1924- 25-28R
Travlos, John 1908(?)-1985 Obituary 118
Trawick, Buckner Beasley 1914- 5-8R
Trawick, Leonard M. 1933- 137
Traxler, Arthur E(dwin) 1900- CAP-2
  Earlier sketch in CA 21-22
Traylor, Ellen Gunderson 1946- 122
Traylor, W. L. 1929- 37-40R
Traynor, Alex
  See Lagerwall, Edna
TRB
  See Strout, Richard L(ee)
Treacy, William 1919- 61-64
Treadgold, Donald W(arren) 1922- 9-12R
Treadgold, Mary 1910- 13-16R
  See also SATA 49
Treadway, John D(avid) 1950- 128
Treadway, Terry
  See Treadway, Theresa
Treadway, Theresa 1941- 107
Treadwell, Sandy 1946- 124
Treahearne, Elizabeth
  See Maxwell, Patricia
Treanor, John Holland
  1903(?)-1978 Obituary 77-80
Treanor, Oliver 1949- 128
Trease, (Robert) Geoffrey 1909- CANR-38
  Earlier sketches in CA 5-8R, CANR-7, 22
  See also MAICYA
  See also SAAS 6
  See also SATA 2, 60
Treaster, Joseph B. 1941- 128
Treasure, G(eoffrey) R(ussell) R(ichards)
  1929- 77-80
Treat, Ida
  See Bergeret, Ida Treat
Treat, John Whittier 1953- 128
Treat, Lawrence 1903- 49-52
  See also SATA 59
Treat, Payson J(ackson)
  1879-1972 Obituary 37-40R
Trebach, Arnold S. 1928- CANR-12
  Earlier sketch in CA 9-12R
Trebing, Harry M(artin) 1926- CANR-31
  Earlier sketch in CA 29-32R
Trecker, Harleigh B(radley) 1911- CANR-5
  Earlier sketch in CA 5-8R
Trecker, Janice Law 1941- CANR-9
  Earlier sketch in CA 65-68
Tredennick, (George) Hugh (Percival Phair)
  1899-1981 109
  Obituary 105
Tredez, Alain 1926- 85-88
  See also SATA 17
Tredez, Denise 1930- CANR-8
  Earlier sketch in CA 5-8R
  See also SATA 50
Tredgold, Nye
  See Tranter, Nigel (Godwin)
Tredgold, Roger F(rancis) 1911-1975 ...... CANR-5
  Earlier sketch in CA 5-8R
Tree, Christina 1944- CANR-12
  Earlier sketch in CA 73-76
Tree, Cornelia
  See Nichols, Nina (Marianna) da Vinci
Tree, Gregory
  See Bardin, John Franklin
Tree, Michael (John) 1926- 9-12R
Tree, Ronald 1897-1976 69-72
  Obituary 65-68
Treece, Henry 1912-1966 .... CANR-6
  Obituary 25-28R
  Earlier sketch in CA 1-4R
  See also CLR 2
  See also MAICYA
  See also SATA 2
Treece, Patricia 1938- 110
Trefethen, Florence 1921- 29-32R
Trefethen, James B(yron Jr.)
  1916-1976 .... CANR-11
  Obituary 69-72
  Earlier sketch in CA 21-24R
Treffert, Darold A(llen) 1933- 131
Trefflich, Henry (Herbert Frederick)
  1908-1978 .... CAP-2
  Obituary 77-80
  Earlier sketch in CA 23-24
Trefftzs, Kenneth Lewis 1911- 13-16R
Trefil, James S. 1938- CANR-27
  Earlier sketch in CA 101
Trefor, Eirlys
  See Williams, Eirlys O(lwen)
Trefousse, Hans Louis 1921- CANR-14
  Earlier sketch in CA 37-40R
Tregarthen, Enys
  See Sloggett, Nellie
Tregaskis, Hugh 1905(?)-1983 Obituary 110
Tregaskis, Richard 1916-1973 .... CANR-2
  Obituary 45-48
  Earlier sketch in CA 1-4R
  See also SATA 3, 26
Tregear, Thomas R(efoy) 1897- 21-24R
Treger, Harvey 1924- 61-64
Treggiari, Susan (Mary) 1940- 61-64
Tregidgo, Philip Sillince 1926- 105
Treglown, Jeremy (Dickinson) 1946- 114
  Brief entry 111
Tregoe, Benjamin B. Jr. 1927- 125
Tregonning, Kennedy Gordon 1923- 9-12R
Trehey, Harold F. 1902(?)-1978 Obituary 77-80
Treichler, Jessie C(ambron)
  1906(?)-1972 Obituary 37-40R
Treister, Bernard W(illiam) 1932- 101
Treitel, Jonathan 1959- .... CLC 70
Trejo, Arnulfo D(uenes) 1922- CANR-32
  Earlier sketch in CA 57-60
  See also HW
Trejos, Carlota 1920- 49-52
Trekell, Harold E(verett) 1910- 49-52
Trelawny, Edward John
  1792-1881 .... DLB 110, 116
Trelease, Allen William 1928- 108
Trelease, James J(oseph) 1941- 112
Trelease, Jim
  See Trelease, James J(oseph)
Trelford, Donald Gilchrist 1937- 111
Trell, Bluma L(ee) 1903- 77-80
Trell, Max 1900- 41-44R
  See also SATA 14
Treloar, Dorothy 1920(?)-1983 Obituary 111
Treloar, James A(rthur) 1933- 45-48
Trelos, Tony
  See Crechales, Anthony George
Tremain, Rose 1943- 97-100
  See also CLC 42
  See also DLB 14
Tremain, Ruthven 1922- 85-88
  See also SATA 17
Tremaine, Jennie
  See Chesney, Marion
Tremayne, Jonathan
  See Forrest-Webb, Robert
Tremayne, Ken(neth Eugene Jr.) 1933- 17-20R
Tremayne, Peter
  See Ellis, Peter Berresford
Tremayne, Sydney (Durward) 1912- CANR-5
  Earlier sketch in CA 5-8R
Tremblay, Bill
  See Tremblay, William Andrew
Tremblay, Marc-Adelard 1922- 41-44R
Tremblay, Michel 1942- 128
  Brief entry 116
  See also CLC 29
  See also DLB 60
  See also MTCW
Tremblay, William Andrew 1940- 89-92
Tremble, Freda B. 1894- 73-76
Tremens, Del
  See MacDonald, Amy
Treml, Vladimir G(uy) 1929- 25-28R
Tremmel, William Calloley 1918- 97-100
Trench, (William Francis) Brinsley Le Poer
  See Le Poer Trench, (William Francis) Brinsley
Trench, Richard 1949- 133
Trendall, Arthur Dale 1909- CANR-22
  Earlier sketches in CA 53-56, CANR-5
Treneer, Anne 1891- CAP-1
  Earlier sketch in CA 9-10
Trenerry, Walter N. 1917- 135
Trengove, Alan Thomas 1929- 108
Trenhaile, John (Stevens) 1949- 110
Trenholm, Virginia Cole 1902- 13-16R
Trenker, Alois Franz 1892-1990 Obituary 131
Trenker, Luis
  See Trenker, Alois Franz
Trennert, Robert A. Jr. 1937- 57-60
Trensky, Paul I. 1929- 93-96
Trent, James W(illiam) 1933- 21-24R
Trent, Jimmie Douglas 1933- 49-52
Trent, May Wong 1939- 57-60
Trent, Olaf
  See Fanthorpe, R(obert) Lionel
Trent, Robbie 1894- CAP-1
  Earlier sketch in CA 9-10
  See also SATA 26
Trent, Timothy
  See Malmberg, Carl
Trent, William P(eterfield)
  1862-1939 Brief entry 122
  See also DLB 47, 71
Trent, William 1919- CANR-3
  Earlier sketch in CA 1-4R
Trento, Joseph John 1947- 45-48
Trento, Salvatore Michael 1952- 101
Trepp, Leo 1913- CANR-18
  Earlier sketches in CA 5-8R, CANR-2
Trepper, Leopold Leib
  1904-1982(?) Obituary 105
Tresch, John William Jr. 1937- Brief entry 106
Trescot, William Henry 1822-1898 .... DLB 30
Trescott, Paul B(arton) 1925- CANR-2
  Earlier sketch in CA 1-4R
Trese, Leo J(ohn) 1902- 5-8R
Treseder, Terry Walton 1956- .... SATA 68
Tresemer, David 1948- 108
Treshow, Michael 1926- 57-60
Tresidder, Argus John 1907- CANR-5
  Earlier sketch in CA 5-8R
Tresilian, Liz 1940- 25-28R
Tresilian, (Cecil) Stuart 1891- .... SATA 40
Tress, Arthur 1940- 101
Tresselt, Alvin 1916- CANR-1
  Earlier sketch in CA 49-52
  See also MAICYA
  See also SATA 7
Tressidy, Jim
  See Norwood, Victor G(eorge) C(harles)
Tressilian, Charles
  See Atcheson, Richard
Tressler, Donald K(iteley) 1894-1981 ...... CANR-4
  Obituary 103
  Earlier sketch in CA 45-48
Trethowan, K(enneth) Illtyd 1907- CANR-3
  Earlier sketch in CA 1-4R
Tretick, Stanley 1921- 103
Trettel, (Mario) Efrem 1921- 69-72
Treuenfels, Peter 1926- 37-40R
Treuer, Robert 1926- 69-72
Trevanian (a pseudonym) 1930(?)- 108
  See also CLC 29
Trevaskis, G(erald) K(ennedy) N(icholas)
  1915-1990 Obituary 131
Trevaskis, John 1911-1968 .... CAP-1
  Obituary 33-36R
  Earlier sketch in CA 9-10
Trevaskis, Sir Kennedy
  See Trevaskis, G(erald) K(ennedy) N(icholas)
Trevathan, Robert E. 1925- CANR-6
  Earlier sketch in CA 1-4R
Trevelyan, George Macaulay 1876-1962 89-92
Trevelyan, Humphrey 1905-1985 .... 37-40R
  Obituary 115
Trevelyan, Julian O(tto) 1910-1988 .... 9-12R
  Obituary 126
Trevelyan, Katharine 1908- CAP-1
  Earlier sketch in CA 11-12
Trevelyan, Raleigh 1923- CANR-22
  Earlier sketches in CA 13-16R, CANR-6
Trevelyan, Robert
  See Forrest-Webb, Robert
Trever, John C(ecil) 1915- 17-20R
Treverton, Gregory F(rye) 1947- 118
Treves, Ralph 1906- 13-16R
Trevino, Elizabeth B(orton) de 1904- CANR-9
  Earlier sketch in CA 17-20R
  See also MAICYA
  See also SAAS 5
  See also SATA 1, 29
Trevino, Lee (Buck) 1939- 113
Trevor, Elleston 1920- 5-8R
  See also SATA 28
Trevor, Glen
  See Hilton, James
Trevor, (Lucy) Meriol 1919- CANR-16
  Earlier sketches in CA 1-4R, CANR-1
  See also SATA 10
Trevor, William 1928-
  See Cox, William Trevor
  See also CLC 7, 9, 14, 25, 71
  See also DLB 14
Trevor-Roper, H(ugh) R(edwald) 1914- 101
Trew, Antony (Francis) 1906- CANR-2
  Earlier sketch in CA 45-48
Trewin, Ion (Courtenay Gill) 1943- 69-72
Trewin, J(ohn) C(ourtenay)
  1908-1990 Obituary 131
  Brief entry 112
Treyz, Russell 1940- 132
Trez, Alain
  See Tredez, Alain
Trez, Denise
  See Tredez, Denise
Trezise, Percy (James) 1923- 132
Trezise, Philip Harold 1912- 109
Trezza, Alphonse F(iore) 1920- 118
Triana, Jose 1932(?)- 131
  See also HW
Triandis, Harry C(haralambos) 1926- 41-44R
Tribbe, Frank C(alvert) 1914- 117
Tribble, Edwin 1907-1986 Obituary 119
Tribble, Harold Wayland
  1899-1986 Obituary 121
Tribe, David (Harold) 1931- 25-28R
Tribe, Ivan M(athews) 1940- 122
Tribe, Laurence H(enry) 1941- 133
Tribich, Susan 1945(?)-1985 Obituary 115
Tribune
  See Armstrong, Douglas Albert
Trice, Borough
  See Allen, A(rthur) B(ruce)
Trice, Harrison M. 1920- 21-24R
Tricker, B(rian) J(ohn) K(ingsbury)
  1937- 25-28R
Trickett, Joyce 1915- CANR-34
  Earlier sketch in CA 105
Trickett, Mabel Rachel 1923- 101
Triegel, Linda (Jeanette) 1942- 117
Triem, Eve 1902- CANR-9
  Earlier sketch in CA 17-20R
Triere, Lynette 1941- 108
Trieschman, Albert E(well) 1931-1984 ...... 29-32R
  Obituary 113
Triffin, Robert 1911- CANR-3
  Earlier sketch in CA 1-4R
Trifonov, Yuri (Valentinovich) 1925-1981 126
  Obituary 103
  See also CLC 45
  See also MTCW
Trigg, Harry Davis 1927- 61-64
Trigg, Joseph Wilson 1949- 118
Trigg, Roger (Hugh) 1941- 49-52
Trigg, Yolanda Lillian 1926- 61-64
Trigger, Bruce G(raham) 1937- CANR-29
  Earlier sketches in CA 21-24R, CANR-9
Triggs, Tony D. 1946- 138
  See also SATA 70
Trigoboff, Joseph 1947- 81-84
Trillin, Calvin 1935- CANR-20
  Earlier sketch in CA 85-88
  See also AITN 1
  See also MTCW
Trilling, Diana (Rubin) 1905- CANR-10
  Earlier sketch in CA 5-8R
  See also MTCW
Trilling, Lionel 1905-1975 .... CANR-10
  Obituary 61-64
  Earlier sketch in CA 9-12R
  See also CLC 9, 11, 24
  See also DLB 28, 63
  See also MTCW
Trilussa 1871-1950 .... DLB 114
Trimball, W. H.
  See Mencken, H(enry) L(ouis)
Trimble, Barbara Margaret 1921- 132
Trimble, Jacquelyn W(hitney) 1927- 13-16R
Trimble, John F(elix) 1925- 97-100
Trimble, Louis P(reston) 1917- CANR-6
  Earlier sketch in CA 13-16R
Trimble, Marshall I(ra) 1939- 77-80
Trimble, Martha Scott 1914- 29-32R
Trimble, Vance H(enry) 1913- 49-52
Trimble, William Raleigh 1913- 9-12R
Trimby, Elisa 1948- 122
  See also SATA 40, 47
Trimingham, J(ohn) Spencer 1904- CANR-3
  Earlier sketch in CA 1-4R
Trimmer, Ellen McKay 1915- 9-12R
Trimmer, Eric J. 1923- 9-12R
Trimmer, Joseph F(rancis) 1941- CANR-13
  Earlier sketch in CA 77-80
Tring, A. Stephen
  See Meynell, Laurence Walter
Trinidad, Corky
  See Trinidad, Francisco D. Jr.
Trinidad, Francisco D. Jr. 1939- 69-72
Trinkaus, Charles (Edward) 1911- 29-32R
Trinklein, Frederick E(rnst) 1924- 41-44R
Trinkner, Charles L. 1920- 29-32R
Trinquier, Roger Paul 1908- CANR-5
  Earlier sketch in CA 9-12R

Triola, Mario F(rank) 1944- ... 57-60
Triolet, Elsa 1896-1970 Obituary ... 25-28R
See also DLB 72
Triplehorn, Charles A(lbert) 1927- ... 130
Triplett, Kenneth E(arl) 1926- ... 57-60
Triplett, Raymond (Francis) 1921- ... 117
Tripodi, Tony 1932- ... CANR-12
Earlier sketch in CA 29-32R
Tripp, C(larence) A(rthur) 1919- ... 73-76
Tripp, Eleanor B(aldwin) 1936- ... 29-32R
See also SATA 4
Tripp, John
See Moore, John Travers
Tripp, John 1927- ... 97-100
See also DLB 40
Tripp, Karen 1923- ... 53-56
Tripp, L(ouis) Reed 1913- ... 5-8R
Tripp, Miles (Barton) 1923- ... CANR-28
Earlier sketches in CA 13-16R, CANR-12
Tripp, Paul 1916- ... 21-24R
See also SATA 8
Tripp, Wallace (Whitney) 1940- ... CANR-23
Earlier sketch in CA 106
See also SATA 31
Tripp, Wendell Jr. 1928- ... 114
Trippett, Frank 1926- ... 21-24R
Trisco, Robert Frederick 1929- ... 41-44R
Triska, Jan Francis 1922- ... CANR-7
Earlier sketch in CA 5-8R
Trisler, Hank 1937- ... 121
Tristan
See Gomez de la Serna, Ramon
Tristram
See Housman, A(lfred) E(dward)
Tritel, Barbara
See Quick, Barbara
Triton, A. N.
See Barclay, Oliver R(ainsford)
Tritt, Robert E(arl) 1921- ... 21-24R
Trittschuh, Travis Edward 1920- ... 5-8R
Trivas, A(lexander) Victor 1894-1970 ... CAP-1
Obituary ... 29-32R
Earlier sketch in CA 19-20
Trivelpiece, Laurel 1926- ... 123
See also SATA 46, 56
Trivers, Howard 1909-1987 ... 73-76
Obituary ... 122
Trivett, Daphne Harwood 1940- ... 97-100
See also SATA 22
Trnka, Jiri 1912-1969 Obituary ... 111
See also MAICYA
See also SATA 32, 43
Trobian, Helen R(eed) 1918- ... 5-8R
Trobisch, Ingrid (Hult) 1926- ... CANR-28
Earlier sketch in CA 97-100
Trocchi, Alexander 1925-1984 ... 9-12R
Obituary ... 112
See also DLB 15
Trocme, Etienne 1924- ... 49-52
Troeger, Thomas H(enry) 1945- ... CANR-34
Earlier sketches in CA 89-92, CANR-15
Troelstrup, Arch William 1901- ... 17-20R
Troen, Selwyn K. 1940- ... 104
Trofimenkoff, Susan Mann 1941- ... 73-76
Trogdon, William (Lewis) 1939- ... 119
Brief entry ... 115
See also Heat-Moon, William Least
Trohan, Walter (Joseph) 1903- ... 81-84
Troiden, Richard (Russell) 1946- ... 89-92
Troise, Joe 1942- ... 103
Troisgros, Jean (Georges)
1926-1983 Obituary ... 110
Troitsky, Artemy 1955- ... 136
Trojan, Judith 1947- ... 131
Trojanowicz, John M.
See Troyanovich, John M(ichael)
Trojanowicz, Robert C(hester) 1941- ... CANR-31
Earlier sketch in CA 45-48
Trojanski, John 1943- ... 45-48
Trolander, Judith Ann 1942- ... 61-64
Trollope, Anthony
1815-1882 ... CDBLB 1832-1890
See also DLB 21, 57
See also SATA 22
See also WLC
Trollope, Frances 1779-1863 ... DLB 21
Trollope, Joanna 1943- ... 101
Troman, Morley 1918- ... 13-16R
Tromanhauser, Edward (Downer) 1932- ... 41-44R
Trombley, Charles C(yprian) 1928- ... 65-68
Trombley, Stephen 1954- ... 129
Tromp, S. W.
See Tromp, Solco Walle
Tromp, Solco W.
See Tromp, Solco Walle
Tromp, Solco Walle 1909-1983 Obituary ... 116
Tronchin-James, (Robert) Nevil 1916- ... CAP-1
Earlier sketch in CA 9-10
Trooboff, Peter D(ennis) 1942- ... 65-68
Troop, Elizabeth 1931- Brief entry ... 116
See also DLB 14
Troop, Miriam 1917- ... 13-16R
Tropp, Martin 1945- ... 65-68
Trost, Cathy 1951- ... 125
Trost, Lucille W(ood) 1938- ... CANR-9
Earlier sketch in CA 61-64
See also SATA 12
Trotman, Jack H(arry) ... 129
Trotsky, Leon 1879-1940 Brief entry ... 118
See also TCLC 22
Trott, Susan 1937- ... 97-100
Trotta, John 1936- ... 45-48
Trotta, Maurice S. 1907-1976 Obituary ... 111
Trotter (Cockburn), Catharine
1679-1749 ... DLB 84
Trotter, Grace V(iolet) 1900- ... CANR-1
Earlier sketch in CA 1-4R
See also SATA 10
Trotter, Jesse McLane Obituary ... 110
Trotter, Patrick C. 1935- ... 126
Trotter, Robert J(oseph) 1943- ... 120
Trotter, Sallie (W. B.) 1915- ... 29-32R
Trotti, John H. 1936- ... 118
Trotti, Lamar 1898-1952 ... DLB 44
Trottier, Pierre 1925- ... DLB 60
Troughton, Joanna (Margaret) 1947- ... CANR-26
Earlier sketch in CA 109
See also SATA 37
Trouncer, Margaret (Lahey)
1903-1982 ... CANR-10
Obituary ... 108
Earlier sketch in CA 5-8R
Troup, Cornelius V. 1902- ... CAP-1
Earlier sketch in CA 9-10
Troupe, Quincy (Thomas Jr.) 1943- ... 124
Brief entry ... 113
See also BW
See also DLB 41
Trout, Charles Hathaway 1935- ... 113
Trout, Kilgore
See Farmer, Philip Jose
Troutman, Charles (Henry) 1914- ... 69-72
Trouve, Roger 1882(?)-1984 Obituary ... 112
Trow, George W. S. 1943- ... 126
See also CLC 52
Trow, M(eirion) J(ames) 1949- ... 120
Trow, Martin A. 1926- ... 112
Trow, W(illiam) Clark 1894- ... CANR-6
Earlier sketch in CA 5-8R
Trowbridge, Clinton W(hiting) 1928- ... CANR-10
Earlier sketch in CA 65-68
Trowbridge, Keith W(ayne) 1937- ... 108
Trowbridge, Leslie Walter 1920- ... CANR-13
Earlier sketch in CA 77-80
Trowell, Kathleen Margaret 1904- ... 65-68
Troxell, Eugene A(nthony) 1937- ... 73-76
Troxell, Mary D(earborn) 1907- ... 37-40R
Troy, George F(rancis) Jr. 1909-1969 ... 1-4R
Obituary ... 103
Troy, Katherine
See Buxton, Anne (Arundel)
Troy, Lawrence M. 1928- ... 21-24R
Troy, Nancy J. 1952- ... CANR-37
Earlier sketch in CA 115
Troy, Una 1913- ... CANR-3
Earlier sketch in CA 1-4R
Troy, William 1903-1961 Obituary ... 89-92
Troyanovich, John M(ichael) 1936- ... CANR-31
Earlier sketch in CA 49-52
Troyat, Henri 1911- ... CANR-33
Earlier sketches in CA 45-48, CANR-2
See also CLC 23
See also MTCW
Troyer, Byron L(eRoy) 1909- ... 65-68
Troyer, Johannes 1902-1969 ... SATA 40
Troyer, Warner 1932- ... 101
Troyka, Lynn Quitman 1938- ... 37-40R
Troyna, Barry 1951- ... 117
Truax, Carol 1900- ... CANR-5
Earlier sketch in CA 5-8R
Truax, Charles B. 1933-197 (?) ... CANR-13
Earlier sketches in CAP-2, CA 21-22
Truax, R. Hawley 1889(?)-1978 Obituary ... 81-84
Trubitt, Allen R(oy) 1931- ... 77-80
Trubo, Richard 1946- ... CANR-11
Earlier sketch in CA 61-64
Trubowitz, Sidney 1926- ... 21-24R
Truby, J(ohn) David 1938- ... CANR-24
Earlier sketches in CA 53-56, CANR-4
Truch, Stephen 1947- ... 115
Trudeau, G(arretson) B(eekman)
1948- ... CANR-31
Earlier sketch in CA 81-84
See also Trudeau, Garry B.
See also SATA 35
Trudeau, Garry B.
See Trudeau, G(arretson) B(eekman)
See also AITN 2
See also CLC 12
Trudeau, Margaret (Joan) 1948- ... 93-96
Trudeau, Noah Andre 1949- ... 132
Trudeau, (Joseph Philippe) Pierre (Yves) Elliott
1919- ... CANR-3
Earlier sketch in CA 45-48
Trudel, Marcel 1917- ... 104
Trudix, Marty
See Truman, Ruth
True, Dan 1924- ... 117
True, Michael (D.) 1933- ... CANR-37
Earlier sketches in CA 41-44R, CANR-17
Trueblood, Alan Stubbs 1917- ... 103
Trueblood, D(avid) Elton 1900- ... 41-44R
Trueblood, Paul Graham 1905- ... CANR-12
Earlier sketches in CAP-1, CA 17-18
Trueblood, Ted Whitaker
1913-1982 Obituary ... 111
Trueheart, Charles 1951- ... 45-48
Truemper, David G(eorge) 1939- ... 112
Truesdale, C(alvin) W(illiam) 1929- ... CANR-30
Earlier sketch in CA 29-32R
Truesdell, Leon E. 1881(?)-1979 Obituary ... 85-88
Truesdell, Sue
See Truesdell, Susan G.
Truesdell, Susan G. ... SATA 45
Truett, Fred M(oore) 1899- ... CAP-2
Earlier sketch in CA 21-22
Truett, Joe C(lyde) 1941- ... 118
Truffaut, Francois 1932-1984 ... CANR-34
Obituary ... 113
Earlier sketch in CA 81-84
See also CLC 20
Truillier-Lacombe, Joseph-Patrice
1807-1863 ... DLB 99
Truitt, Deborah H(unsberger) 1945- ... 45-48
Truitt, Evelyn Mack 1931- ... 57-60
Truitt, Gloria A(nn) 1939- ... CANR-30
Earlier sketch in CA 111
Truitt, John O(liver) 1934- ... 117
Truitt, Willis H(arrison) 1936- ... 57-60
Truman, Harry S 1884-1972 ... 106
Obituary ... 37-40R
Truman, Jill 1934- ... 128
Truman, (Mary) Margaret 1924- ... CANR-29
Earlier sketch in CA 105
See also BEST 90:1
See also MTCW
Truman, Ruth 1931- ... 53-56
Trumbo, Dalton 1905-1976 ... CANR-10
Obituary ... 69-72
Earlier sketch in CA 21-24R
See also CLC 19
See also DLB 26
Trumbull, Benjamin 1735-1820 ... DLB 30
Trumbull, John 1750-1831 ... DLB 31
Trumbull, Robert 1912- ... CANR-5
Earlier sketch in CA 9-12R
Trump, Donald J.
See Trump, Donald J(ohn)
See also BEST 89:1
Trump, Donald J(ohn) 1946- ... 130
See also Trump, Donald J.
Trump, Fred(erick Leonard) 1924- ... 13-16R
Trump, Richard F. 1912- ... 126
Trumpener, Ulrich 1930- ... 25-28R
Trumper, Hubert Bagster 1902- ... CAP-1
Earlier sketch in CA 9-10
Trundlett, Helen B.
See Eliot, T(homas) S(tearns)
Trungpa, Chogyam
See Chogyam Trungpa
Trunk, Isaiah Elezer 1905-1981 ... 89-92
Obituary ... 108
Truong, Thanh-Dam 1949- ... 136
Trupin, James E. 1940- ... 37-40R
Trupp, Beverly Ann 1937- ... 105
Truscott, Alan (Fraser) 1925- ... 25-28R
Truscott, Lucian K(ing) IV 1947- ... 89-92
Truscott, Robert Blake 1944- ... 77-80
Truse, Kenneth (Philip) 1946- ... 105
Truss, Jan 1925- ... 102
See also SATA 35
Truss, Seldon
See Seldon-Truss, Leslie
Trussell, C(harles) P(rescott)
1892-1968 Obituary ... 89-92
Trussler, Simon 1942- ... CANR-28
Earlier sketches in CA 25-28R, CANR-12
Trustman, Alan Robert 1930- Brief entry ... 111
Truumaa, Aare 1926- ... 49-52
Truzzi, Marcello 1935- ... 41-44R
Tryon, Darrell Trevor 1942- ... 111
Tryon, Georgiana Shick 1945- ... 116
Tryon, Ruth Wilson 1892(?)-1987 Obituary ... 123
Tryon, Thomas 1926-1991 ... CANR-32
Obituary ... 135
Earlier sketch in CA 29-32R
See also AITN 1
See also CLC 3, 11
See also MTCW
Tryon, Tom
See Tryon, Thomas
Tryon, W(arren) S(tenson) 1901-1989 ... CAP-1
Obituary ... 129
Earlier sketch in CA 11-12
Trypanis, C(onstantine) A(thanasius)
1909- ... CANR-24
Earlier sketches in CA 5-8R, CANR-7
Trythall, Anthony John 1927- ... 77-80
Trythall, J(ohn) W(illiam) D(onald)
1944- ... 29-32R
Tsadick, Marta Gabre
See Gabre-Tsadick, Marta
Tsai, Shih-shan Henry 1940- ... 125
Tsambassis, Alexander N(icholas)
1919- ... 21-24R
Tsatsos, Jeanne 1909- ... CANR-13
Earlier sketch in CA 29-32R
Tschachbasov, Nahum 1899-1984 Obituary ... 112
Tschebotarioff, Gregory P. 1899- ... 13-16R
Tschichold, Jan 1902(?)-1974 Obituary ... 53-56
Tschudy, James Jay 1925- ... 13-16R
Tschumi, Raymond Robert 1924- ... CANR-3
Earlier sketch in CA 5-8R
Tse, K. K. 1948- ... 125
Tsegaye, Gabre-Medhin (Kawessa)
See Gabre-Medhin, Tsegaye (Kawessa)
Tseng Wen-Shing 1935- ... CANR-35
Earlier sketch in CA 114
Tshiamala, Kabasele Obituary ... 109
Tsien, Tsuen-hsuin 1909- ... CANR-23
Earlier sketches in CA 17-20R, CANR-7
Tsiolkovsky, Konstantin Eduardovich
1857-1935 Brief entry ... 119
Tsipis, Kosta 1934- ... 110
Tsongas, Paul Efthemios 1941- ... 108
Tsou, Tang 1918- ... CANR-8
Earlier sketch in CA 5-8R
Tso Yiu-kam 1918(?)-1983 Obituary ... 110
Tsukahira, Toshio George 1915- ... 21-24R
Tsukinabe, Isao
See Vermeule, Cornelius Clarkson III
Tsukui, Nobuko 1938- ... 133
Tsuneishi, Warren M(ichio) 1921- ... 17-20R
Tsurumi, Shunsuke 1922- ... 138
Tsurutani, Taketsugu 1935- ... 104
Tsushima, Shuji 1909-1948 Brief entry ... 107
See also Dazai, Osamu
Tsutsui, Yoriko 1945- ... 132
Tsuzuki, Chushichi 1926- ... CANR-3
Earlier sketch in CA 1-4R
Tsvetaeva (Efron), Marina (Ivanovna)
1892-1941 ... 128
Brief entry ... 104
See also MTCW
See also TCLC 7, 35
Tu, Wei-ming 1940- ... 65-68
Tuan, Yi-Fu 1930- ... CANR-37
Earlier sketches in CA 93-96, CANR-16
Tuann, Lucy H(siu-mei) C(hen) 1938- ... 85-88
Tubb, E(dwin) C(harles) 1919- ... CANR-21
Earlier sketch in CA 101
Tubb, Ernest (Dale) 1914-1984 Obituary ... 114
Tubbs, Stewart L(ee) 1943- ... CANR-6
Earlier sketch in CA 57-60
Tubby, I. M.
See Kraus, Robert
Tucci, Giuseppe 1894-1984 Obituary ... 112
Tucci, Niccolo 1908- ... 81-84
Tuccille, Jerome 1937- ... CANR-12
Earlier sketch in CA 29-32R
Tuchinsky, Joseph S. 1937- ... CANR-10
Earlier sketch in CA 25-28R
Tuchman, Barbara W(ertheim)
1912-1989 ... CANR-24
Obituary ... 127
Earlier sketches in CA 1-4R, CANR-3
See also BEST 89:1
See also MTCW
Tuchman, Gaye 1943- ... 85-88
Tuchman, Maurice 1936- ... CANR-27
Earlier sketches in CA 49-52, CANR-4
Tuchman, Phyllis 1947- ... 114
Tuchock, Wanda 1898(?)-1985 Obituary ... 115
Tucholsky, Kurt 1890-1935 ... DLB 56
Tuck, (John) Anthony 1940- ... 124
Tuck, Dorothy
See McFarland, Dorothy Tuck
Tuck, James A(lexander) 1940- ... 37-40R
Tuck, Lily 1938- ... CLC 70
Tuck, Lon 1938(?)-1987 ... 133
Obituary ... 122
Tuck, Susan H. 1947- ... 118
Tucker, Ann
See Giudici, Ann Couper
Tucker, Anne 1945- ... CANR-19
Earlier sketch in CA 102
Tucker, Anthony 1924- ... 104
Tucker, Archibald Norman
1904(?)-1980 Obituary ... 101
Tucker, Audrie Manley
See Manley-Tucker, Audrie
Tucker, Bob
See Tucker, (Arthur) Wilson
Tucker, Carll 1951- ... 133
Tucker, Caroline
See Nolan, Jeannette Covert
Tucker, Cynthia Grant 1941- ... 135
Tucker, David M(ilton) 1937- ... 101
Tucker, Edward L(lewellyn) 1921- ... 17-20R
Tucker, Ernest E(dward) 1916-1969 ... 61-64
Tucker, Eva 1929- ... 17-20R
Tucker, Frank H(ammond) 1923- ... CANR-10
Earlier sketch in CA 25-28R
Tucker, Gabe
See Tucker, Gaylord B(ob)
Tucker, Gaylord B(ob) 1915- ... 110
Tucker, Gene M(ilton) 1935- ... CANR-15
Earlier sketch in CA 37-40R
Tucker, George 1775-1861 ... DLB 3, 30
Tucker, Georgina P. 1911- ... 97-100
Tucker, Gina
See Tucker, Georgina P.
Tucker, Glenn (Irving) 1892-1976 ... 5-8R
Obituary ... 69-72
Tucker, Graham Harold 1925- ... 113
Tucker, Harry Jr. 1921- ... 41-44R
Tucker, Helen 1926- ... CANR-11
Earlier sketch in CA 29-32R
Tucker, Irwin St. John 1886-1982 Obituary ... 105
Tucker, James 1929- ... CANR-9
Earlier sketch in CA 21-24R
Tucker, Jonathan B(rin) 1954- ... 109
Tucker, Lael
See Wertenbaker, Lael (Tucker)
Tucker, Link
See Bingley, David Ernest
Tucker, Marcia 1940- ... 65-68
Tucker, Martin 1928- ... 17-20R
Tucker, Melvin J(ay) 1931- ... 113
Tucker, Michael R(ay) 1941- ... CANR-12
Earlier sketch in CA 61-64
Tucker, Nathaniel Beverley 1784-1851 ... DLB 3
Tucker, Nicholas 1936- ... CANR-11
Earlier sketch in CA 65-68
Tucker, Patricia 1912- ... 65-68
Tucker, Paul Hayes 1950- ... 110
Tucker, Robert C(harles) 1918- ... CANR-3
Earlier sketch in CA 1-4R
Tucker, Robert W(arren) 1924- ... 134
Tucker, Robin 1950- ... 53-56
Tucker, Ruth A(nne) 1945- ... 117
Tucker, St. George 1752-1827 ... DLB 37
Tucker, Susan (Norris) 1950- ... 130
Tucker, Wallace H. 1939- ... 121
Tucker, William E(dward) 1932- ... CANR-3
Earlier sketch in CA 9-12R
Tucker, William R(ayburn) 1923- ... 61-64
Tucker, (Arthur) Wilson 1914- ... 17-20R
Tucker-Fettner, Ann
See Giudici, Ann Couper
Tuckerman, Henry Theodore
1813-1871 ... DLB 64
Tuckey, John S(utton) 1921- ... CANR-7
Earlier sketch in CA 5-8R

Tuckman, Bruce W(ayne) 1938- CANR-11
 Earlier sketch in CA 25-28R
Tuckman, Howard P(aul) 1941- CANR-10
 Earlier sketch in CA 57-60
Tuckner, Howard 1932(?)-1980 Obituary 101
Tudhope, Richard
 See Rodda, Peter (Gordon)
Tudor, Andrew Frank 1942- 107
Tudor, Dean 1943- CANR-8
 Earlier sketch in CA 61-64
Tudor, Nancy (Patricia Rice)
 1943- Brief entry 109
Tudor, Tasha 1915- 81-84
 See also CLR 13
 See also MAICYA
 See also SATA 20, 69
Tudor-Craig, Pamela 1928- 124
Tudyman, Al 1914- 21-24R
Tuell, Jack Marvin 1923- 29-32R
Tueni, Nadia (Hamade)
 1935-1983 Obituary 110
Tuerck, David G(eorge) 1941- CANR-14
 Earlier sketch in CA 21-24R
Tuerk, Hanne 1951- 118
 See also SATA 71
Tufail, Muhammad 1921(?)-1984 Obituary 113
Tuffnell, Everett S(pencer) 1917- CANR-7
 Earlier sketch in CA 5-8R
Tuffs, J(ack) Elsden 1922- 5-8R
Tufte, Edward R(olf) 1942- CANR-1
 Earlier sketch in CA 49-52
Tufte, Virginia J(ames) 1918- 125
 Brief entry 106
Tufts, Eleanor (May) 1927-1991 77-80
 Obituary 136
Tufty, Barbara 1923- 37-40R
Tufty, Esther Van Wagoner
 1896-1986 Obituary 119
Tugay, Emine Foat
 See Foat Tugay, Emine
Tugend, Harry 1898(?)-1989 Obituary 129
Tugendhat, Christopher Samuel 1937- 89-92
Tuggle, Ann Montgomery 1942- 125
Tuggy, Joy Turner 1922- 21-24R
Tugwell, Franklin 1942- 57-60
Tugwell, Rexford Guy 1891-1979 85-88
 Obituary 89-92
Tulasiewicz, J(an) B(runo) 1913- 41-44R
Tulchin, Joseph S(amuel) 1939- 37-40R
Tulchin, Lewis 1905-1971 ....CAP-1
 Earlier sketch in CA 19-20
Tuleja, Tad
 See Tuleja, Thaddeus F(rancis)
Tuleja, Thaddeus F(rancis) 1944- 108
Tulis, Jeffrey K. 1950- CANR-30
 Earlier sketch in CA 111
Tull, Charles Joseph 1931- 17-20R
Tull, Delena 1950- 125
Tull, Donald S(tanley) 1924- 81-84
Tull, James E. 1913- CANR-13
 Earlier sketch in CA 77-80
Tullett, James Stuart 1912- 106
Tullis, F. LaMond 1935- 81-84
Tulloch, G(ertrude) Janet 1924- 65-68
Tullock, Gordon 1922- CANR-3
 Earlier sketch in CA 1-4R
Tullos, Allen 1950- 132
Tully, Andrew (Frederick Jr.) 1914- 17-20R
Tully, Gordon F(rederick) 1935- 106
Tully, Grace George 1900-1984 Obituary 113
Tully, John (Kimberley) 1923- CANR-28
 Earlier sketches in CA 69-72, CANR-12
 See also SATA 14
Tully, (William) Mark 1935- 136
Tully, Mary Jo 1937- CANR-22
 Earlier sketch in CA 105
Tuma, Elias H. 1928- Brief entry 115
Tumay, Paulett 1945- 128
Tumelty, James J.
 1921(?)-1979(?) Obituary 104
Tumin, Melvin M(arvin) 1919- 45-48
Tumpson, Helen ....AITN 1
Tung, Ling
 See Tung, William L(ing)
Tung, Shih-tsin (Shih-chin) 1900- 5-8R
Tung, William L(ing) 1907- 85-88
Tunick, Irve 1912-1987 Obituary 123
Tunick, Stanley B(loch) 1900- CAP-1
 Earlier sketch in CA 17-18
Tunink, Wilfrid Bernard 1920- 5-8R
Tunis, Edwin (Burdett) 1897-1973 ....CANR-7
 Obituary 45-48
 Earlier sketch in CA 5-8R
 See also CLR 2
 See also MAICYA
 See also SATA 1, 24, 28
Tunis, John R(oberts) 1889-1975 61-64
 See also CLC 12
 See also DLB 22
 See also MAICYA
 See also SATA 30, 37
Tunley, Roul 1912- 13-16R
Tunnadine, Prudence 1928- 129
Tunnard, Christopher 1910-1979 ....CANR-6
 Obituary 85-88
 Earlier sketch in CA 5-8R
Tunnell, Doug(las Alan) 1949- 97-100
Tunner, William H(enry) 1906-1983 ....CAP-1
 Obituary 109
 Earlier sketch in CA 13-16
Tunney, Gene
 See Tunney, James Joseph
Tunney, James Joseph
 1898(?)-1978 Obituary 111
Tunney, John V(arick) 1934- 61-64
Tunney, Kieran 1922- 117
Tunnicliffe, C(harles) F(rederick) 1901- 104
 See also SATA 62
Tunstall, (Cuthbert) Jeremy 1934- CANR-20
 Earlier sketches in CA 5-8R, CANR-4
Tunstall, Shana Barrett
 See Tunstall, Velma
Tunstall, Velma 1914- 53-56
Tunyogi, Andrew C(sapo) 1907- CAP-2
 Earlier sketch in CA 29-32
Tuohy, Frank
 See Tuohy, John Francis
 See also CLC 37
 See also DLB 14
Tuohy, John Francis 1925- CANR-3
 Earlier sketch in CA 5-8R
 See also Tuohy, Frank
Tuohy, William Klaus 1926- 104
Tuohy, William S. 1938- 41-44R
Tuohy, William 1941- 37-40R
Tuplin, W(illiam) A(lfred)
 1902-1975 Obituary 111
Tupper, Margo (Browne) 1919- 17-20R
Tupper, Martin F. 1810-1889 ....DLB 32
Turabian, Kate L(arimore)
 1893-1987 Obituary 123
Turan, Kenneth 1946- 132
Turbayne, Colin Murray 1916- CANR-24
 Earlier sketch in CA 1-4R
Turbyfill, Mark 1896- 108
 See also DLB 45
Turchin, Valentin F(yodorovich) 1931- 101
Turco, Lewis (Putnam) 1934- CANR-24
 Earlier sketch in CA 13-16R
 See also CLC 11, 63
 See also DLBY 84
Turco, Richard (Peter) 1943- 135
Turell, Saul J. 1921-1986 Obituary 120
Turetzky, Bertram Jay 1933- 57-60
Turgenev, Ivan 1818-1883 ....SSC 7
 See also WLC
Turgeon, Charlotte Snyder 1912- CANR-3
 Earlier sketch in CA 5-8R
Turgeon, Lynn 1920- 5-8R
Turiel, Isaac 1941- 122
Turing, John (Ferrier) 1908- CAP-2
 Earlier sketch in CA 25-28
Turing, Penelope (Anne Tryon) 1925- 132
Turk, Frances (Mary) 1915- CAP-1
 Earlier sketch in CA 9-10
Turk, Hanne
 See Tuerk, Hanne
Turk, Herman 1929- 45-48
Turk, Laurel H(erbert) 1903- 21-24R
Turk, Midge
 See Richardson, Midge Turk
Turk, Rudy H(enry) 1927- 97-100
Turkel, Christopher 1955(?)-1983 Obituary 110
Turkel, Pauline
 See Kesselman-Turkel, Judi
Turkel, Robin R. 1929(?)-1984 Obituary 113
Turkevich, Ludmilla Buketoff 1909- 5-8R
Turki, Fawaz 1940- 41-44R
Turkle, Brinton 1915- 25-28R
 See also SATA 2
Turkle, Sherry 1948- 102
Turkus, Burton B. 1902-1982 Obituary 108
Turley, Gerald H. 1931- 136
Turley, William S(tephen) 1943- CANR-21
 Earlier sketch in CA 105
Turlington, Bayly 1919-1977 ....29-32R
 Obituary 122
 See also SATA 5, 52
Turlington, Catherine (Isabel) Hackett
 1900(?)-1978 Obituary 77-80
Turlington, Henry E. 1918- 21-24R
Turnage, Anne Shaw 1927- 77-80
Turnage, Mac(lyn) N(eil) 1927- 77-80
Turnbaugh, William A(rthur) 1948- CANR-31
 Earlier sketch in CA 112
Turnbull, Agnes Sligh 1888-1982 ....CANR-2
 Obituary 105
 Earlier sketch in CA 1-4R
 See also SATA 14
Turnbull, Andrew Winchester
 1921-1970 ....CANR-3
 Obituary 25-28R
 Earlier sketch in CA 1-4R
 See also DLB 103
Turnbull, Ann (Christine) 1943- 65-68
 See also SATA 18
Turnbull, Bob 1936- CANR-14
 Earlier sketch in CA 37-40R
Turnbull, Colin M(acmillan) 1924- CANR-3
 Earlier sketch in CA 1-4R
 See also AITN 1
Turnbull, Gael Lundin 1928- CANR-10
 Earlier sketch in CA 65-68
 See also CAAS 14
 See also DLB 40
Turnbull, John G. 1913- 1-4R
Turnbull, Patrick Edward Xenophon
 1908- CANR-6
 Earlier sketch in CA 5-8R
Turnbull, Peter (John) 1950- 130
Turnbull, Stephen (Richard) 1948- CANR-20
 Earlier sketch in CA 104
Turnell, (George) Martin 1908-1979 45-48
 Obituary 103
Turner, A(lmon) Richard 1932- 17-20R
Turner, Alberta Tucker 1919- CANR-17
 Earlier sketches in CA 49-52, CANR-1
Turner, Alice K. 1940- 53-56
 See also SATA 10
Turner, Amedee E. 1929- 9-12R
Turner, Ann W(arren) 1945- CANR-31
 Earlier sketches in CA 69-72, CANR-14
 See also SATA 14
Turner, (Henry) Arlin 1909-1980 ....CANR-6
 Obituary 97-100
 Earlier sketch in CA 5-8R
 See also DLB 103
Turner, Arnella K. 1917- 138
Turner, Arthur C(ampbell) 1918- 17-20R
Turner, Bessye Tobias 1917- 53-56
Turner, Bill
 See Turner, W(illiam) Price
Turner, Bruce (Malcolm) 1922- 132
Turner, Bryan S(tanley) 1945- 115
Turner, Charles (Tennyson) 1808-1879 ....DLB 32
Turner, Charles W(ilson) 1916- CANR-30
 Earlier sketches in CA 37-40R, CANR-13
Turner, Clair (Elsmere) 1890- CAP-1
 Earlier sketch in CA 9-10
Turner, Clay
 See Ballard, (Willis) Todhunter
Turner, D(avid) Harold 1912- 117
Turner, Daniel F(rank) 1947- 97-100
Turner, Darwin T(heodore Troy)
 1931-1991 ....CANR-11
 Obituary 133
 Earlier sketch in CA 21-24R
 See also BW
Turner, David R(euben) 1915- 57-60
Turner, Dean (Edson) 1927- 29-32R
Turner, Dennis C(lair) 1948- 61-64
Turner, Dona M. 1951- 103
Turner, E(rnest) S(ackville) 1909- 113
Turner, Edward R(euben) A(rthur) 1924- 81-84
Turner, Elizabeth 1774-1846 ....YABC 2
Turner, Eloise Fain 1906- 5-8R
Turner, Eric Gardner 1911-1983 Obituary 109
Turner, Ethel (Sybil) 1872-1958 Brief entry 111
Turner, Florence (Hayes) 1919- 128
Turner, Francis Joseph (Michael)
 1929- CANR-22
 Earlier sketch in CA 69-72
Turner, Frederick C(lair) 1938- CANR-28
 Earlier sketch in CA 25-28R
Turner, Frederick Jackson
 1861-1932 Brief entry 113
 See also DLB 17
Turner, Frederick (William III) 1937- CANR-34
 Earlier sketches in CA 37-40R, CANR-15
Turner, Frederick 1943- CANR-30
 Earlier sketches in CA 73-76, CANR-12
 See also CAAS 10
 See also CLC 48
 See also DLB 40
Turner, George Allen 1908- CANR-10
 Earlier sketch in CA 13-16R
Turner, George E(ugene) 1925- CANR-5
 Earlier sketch in CA 53-56
Turner, George (Reginald) 1916- CANR-21
 Earlier sketch in CA 103
Turner, George W(illiam) 1921- CANR-24
 Earlier sketch in CA 104
Turner, Gladys T(ressia) 1935- CANR-13
 Earlier sketch in CA 77-80
Turner, Glennette Tilley 1933- 133
 See also SATA 71
Turner, Graham 1932- CANR-14
 Earlier sketch in CA 21-24R
Turner, Gwenda 1947- 118
Turner, H(arold) W(alter) 1911- CANR-10
 Earlier sketch in CA 21-24R
Turner, Henry Andrew Jr. 1919- 9-12R
Turner, Henry Ashby Jr. 1932- 49-52
Turner, Henry Dicken 1919- 61-64
Turner, Henry Ernest William 1907- CAP-1
 Earlier sketch in CA 9-10
Turner, Herbert Snipes 1891-1976 ....41-44R
Turner, Howard M(oore) Jr. 1918- 13-16R
Turner, John Elliot 1917- CANR-3
 Earlier sketch in CA 5-8R
Turner, John F(reeland) 1942- 97-100
Turner, John Frayn 1923- CANR-3
 Earlier sketch in CA 9-12R
Turner, John H(enry) 1938- 77-80
Turner, Jonathan H. 1942- CANR-14
 Earlier sketches in CA 37-40R, CANR-32
Turner, Joseph Addison 1826-1868 ....DLB 79
Turner, Josie
 See Crawford, Phyllis
Turner, Judy
 See Saxton, Judith
Turner, Justin G(eorge) 1898-1976 ....CANR-32
 Earlier sketch in CA 41-44R
Turner, Katharine Charlotte 1910- CAP-2
 Earlier sketch in CA 23-24
Turner, Kathleen J. 1952- 138
Turner, Kay 1932- 69-72
Turner, Kermit 1936- 104
Turner, L(eonard) C(harles) F(rederick)
 1914- 29-32R
Turner, Len
 See Floren, Lee
Turner, Lloyd 1924- 103
Turner, Louis (Mark) 1942- CANR-34
 Earlier sketches in CA 37-40R, CANR-15
Turner, Lowell 1947- 138
Turner, Lynn Warren 1906- 5-8R
Turner, Martha Anne (Bonner) 1904-1985 134
 Obituary 117
Turner, Mary
 See Lambot, Isobel
Turner, Mason 1914- 123
Turner, Merfyn (Lloyd) 1915-1991 104
 Obituary 135
Turner, Morrie
 See Turner, Morris
Turner, Morris 1923- CANR-15
 Earlier sketch in CA 29-32R
Turner, Myron 1935- 112
Turner, Paul Digby Lowry 1917- 105
Turner, Paul R(aymond) 1929- 45-48
Turner, Peter Paul
 See Jeffery, Grant
Turner, Philip (William) 1925- CANR-27
 Earlier sketches in CA 25-28R, CANR-11
 See also SAAS 6
 See also SATA 11
Turner, Ralph H(erbert) 1919- 37-40R
Turner, Ralph Lilley 1888-1983 ....5-8R
 Obituary 109
Turner, Ralph V(ernon) 1939- 77-80
Turner, Ralph 1936- Brief entry 107
Turner, Richard E(ugene) 1920- 29-32R
Turner, Robert C(lemens) 1908- 77-80
Turner, Robert Edward III 1938(?)- 120
Turner, Robert F(oster) 1944- CANR-30
 Earlier sketches in CA 77-80, CANR-13
Turner, Robert (Harry) 1915- CANR-1
 Earlier sketch in CA 45-48
Turner, Robert Kean Jr. 1926- 17-20R
Turner, Robert Y(ongue) 1927- Brief entry 110
Turner, Roger (Humphrey George) 1943- 123
Turner, Roland 1943- 106
Turner, Ronald Cordell 1939- 41-44R
Turner, Sheila
 See Rowbotham, Sheila
Turner, Sheila R.
 See Seed, Sheila Turner
Turner, Sheila 1906- CAP-1
 Earlier sketch in CA 13-14
Turner, Silvie 1946- 117
Turner, Stansfield 1923- 124
 Brief entry 118
Turner, Stephen P. 1951- 122
Turner, Steve
 See Turner, Stephen P.
Turner, (Clarence) Steven 1923- 29-32R
Turner, Susan 1952- 106
Turner, T. H. D. 1946- 122
Turner, Ted
 See Turner, Robert Edward III
Turner, Thomas B(ourne) 1902- 41-44R
Turner, Thomas Coleman 1927- 5-8R
Turner, Thomas N(oel) 1940- 113
Turner, Tom
 See Turner, T. H. D.
Turner, Tom 1942- 136
Turner, Victor Witter 1920-1983 ....CANR-3
 Obituary 111
 Earlier sketch in CA 5-8R
Turner, Violet Bender
 1902(?)-1990 Obituary 130
Turner, W(illiam) Price 1927- CANR-16
 Earlier sketch in CA 21-24R
Turner, Wallace 1921- 17-20R
Turner, William F. 1936(?)-1989 Obituary 130
Turner, William O(liver) 1914- CANR-3
 Earlier sketch in CA 1-4R
 See also AITN 1
Turner, William W. 1927- CANR-12
 Earlier sketch in CA 25-28R
Turney, Alfred (Walter) 1916- 73-76
Turney, Catherine 1906- 101
Turngren, Annette 1902(?)-1980 ....9-12R
 Obituary 101
 See also SATA 23
Turngren, Ellen 5-8R
 See also SATA 3
Turnill, Reginald 1915- CANR-15
 Earlier sketch in CA 37-40R
Turnock, David 1938- 109
Turock, Betty J(ane) CANR-30
 Earlier sketch in CA 110
Turow, Joseph G(regory) 1950- CANR-30
 Earlier sketch in CA 111
Turow, Rita P(astron) 1919- 101
Turow, Scott 1949- 73-76
 See also BEST 90:3
Turpin, James W(esley) 1927- 21-24R
Turpin, Lorna 1950- 107
Turpin, Waters Edward 1910-1968 125
 See also BW
 See also DLB 51
Turska, Krystyna (Zofia) 1933- 106
 See also SATA 27, 31
Tursun-Zade, Mirzo 1911-1977 Obituary 104
Turton, Godfrey (Edmund) 1901- 21-24R
Turton, James
 See Crace, Jim
Turton-Jones, Edith Constance (Bradshaw)
 1904-1968 ....CAP-1
 Earlier sketch in CA 9-10
Turville-Petre, Edward Oswald Gabriel
 1908-1978 ....9-12R
 Obituary 77-80
Turyn, Alexander 1900-1981 Obituary 104
Tusa, John (Jr.) 1936- 127
Tusan, Stan 1936- 105
 See also CLC 22
Tushingham, A(rlotte) Douglas 1914- 41-44R
Tushnet, Leonard 1908-1973 ....CAP-1
 Obituary 45-48
 Earlier sketch in CA 13-16
Tushnet, Mark V. 1945- 126
Tusiani, Joseph 1924- CANR-20
 Earlier sketches in CA 9-12R, CANR-5
 See also SATA 45
Tuska, Jon 1942- CANR-13
 Earlier sketch in CA 73-76
Tussing, A(ubrey) Dale 1935- 17-20R
Tutaev, David 1916- 21-24R
Tute, Warren (Stanley) 1914- CANR-1
 Earlier sketch in CA 1-4R
Tuten, Frederic 1936- 37-40R
Tuthill, John Wills 1910- 108
Tutin, Thomas Gaskell 1908-1987 Obituary 123
Tutko, Thomas A(rthur) 1931- 69-72

Tutorow, Norman E. 1934- ... CANR-29
Earlier sketch in CA 25-28R
Tuttle, Alva M(aurice) 1900- ... 5-8R
Tuttle, Day
See Tuttle, (Frank) Day Jr.
Tuttle, (Frank) Day Jr. 1902- ... 116
Tuttle, Frank W(aldo) 1896- ... 61-64
Tuttle, Howard Nelson 1935- ... 41-44R
Tuttle, Lisa 1952- ... 126
Tuttle, Russell (Howard) 1939- ... 77-80
Tuttle, W(ilbur) C(oleman) 1883- ... CAP-2
Earlier sketch in CA 21-22
Tuttle, William M. Jr. 1937- ... CANR-11
Earlier sketch in CA 29-32R
Tuttleton, James Welsey 1934- ... 41-44R
Tutu, Desmond M(pilo) 1931- ... 125
See also BLC 3
See also BW
Tutuola, Amos 1920- ... CANR-27
Earlier sketch in CA 9-12R
See also BLC 3
See also BW
See also CLC 5, 14, 29
See also MTCW
Tuve, Merle Antony 1901-1982 Obituary ... 106
Tuve, Rosemond 1903-1964 ... CAP-1
Earlier sketch in CA 9-10
Tuveson, Ernest (Lee) 1915- ... 17-20R
Tuwhare, Hone 1922- ... 103
Tuzin, Donald F(rancis) 1945- ... 106
Tvardovsky, Alexandr Trifonovich
1910-1971 ... 102
Obituary ... 33-36R
Twaddell, W(illiam) F(reeman)
1906-1982 ... CANR-32
Earlier sketch in CA 81-84
Twaddle, Andrew C. 1938- ... 120
Twain, Mark
See Clemens, Samuel Langhorne
See also DLB 11, 12, 23, 64, 74
See also SSC 6
See also TCLC 6, 12, 19, 36
See also WLC
Twark, Allan J(oseph) 1931- ... 49-52
Twedt, Dik Warren 1920-1985 ... CANR-14
Obituary ... 115
Earlier sketch in CA 37-40R
Tweed, Stephen C. 1949- ... 133
Tweed, Thomas A. 1954- ... 137
Tweedale, Douglas 1958(?)-1990 Obituary ... 132
Tweedale, J.
See Bickle, Judith Brundrett
Tweedale, Violet (Chambers)
1862-1936 Brief entry ... 116
Tweedie, Donald F(erguson) Jr. 1926- ... 13-16R
Tweeten, Luther 1931- ... 89-92
Twelveponies, Mary
See Cleveland, Mary
Twemlow, Stuart W(est) 1941- ... 128
Twersky, Isadore 1930- ... 120
Twersky, Jacob 1920- ... 49-52
Tweton, D. Jerome 1933- ... SATA 48
Twichell, Chase 1950- ... 127
Twigg, Alan (Robert) 1952- ... 125
Twiggy
See Hornby, Leslie
Twin, Stephanie L. 1948- ... 101
Twiname, Eric 1942(?)-1980 Obituary ... 102
Twining, Nathan F(arragut)
1897-1982 Obituary ... 106
Twining, William (Lawrence) 1934- ... 123
Twisleton-Wykeham-Fiennes, Richard Nathaniel
1909- ... CANR-11
Earlier sketch in CA 21-24R
Twiss, Sumner B(arnes) Jr.
1944- Brief entry ... 114
Twist, Ananias
See Nunn, William Curtis
Twitchell, James B(uell) 1943- ... 118
Twitchell, Paul 1908(?)-1971 ... 132
Obituary ... 111
Twitchett, Carol Cosgrove 1943- ... CANR-26
Earlier sketch in CA 29-32R
Twitchett, Denis Crispin 1925- Brief entry ... 106
Twohig, Elizabeth Shee 1946- ... 132
Twombly, Robert C(harles) 1940- ... 85-88
Twombly, Wells A. 1935-1977 ... 41-44R
Obituary ... 69-72
Tworkov, Jack 1900-1982 Obituary ... 107
See also SATA 31, 47
Twyman, Gib
See Twyman, Gilbert Oscar III
Twyman, Gilbert Oscar III 1943- ... 109
Ty-Casper, Linda 1931- ... CANR-24
Earlier sketch in CA 107
Tyde, Eddie
See Meades, Jonathan (Turner)
Tydeman, William (Marcus) 1935- ... 119
Tydings, Joseph D(avies) 1928- ... 29-32R
Tyerman, Hugo 1880-1977 Obituary ... 77-80
Tygiel, Jules 1949- ... 132
Tyl, Noel 1936- ... 93-96
Tylden-Wright, David 1923- ... 25-28R
Tylecote, Mabel (Phythian) 1896-1987 ... CAP-1
Obituary ... 121
Earlier sketch in CA 13-14
Tylecote, R(onald) F(rank)
1916-1990 Obituary ... 132
Tyler, A. E.
See Armstrong, (Annette) Elizabeth
Tyler, Anne 1941- ... CANR-33
Earlier sketches in CA 9-12R, CANR-11
See also BEST 89:1
See also CLC 7, 11, 18, 28, 44, 59
See also DLB 6
See also DLBY 82
See also MTCW
See also SATA 7
Tyler, Converse 1903(?)-1978 Obituary ... 81-84
Tyler, David B(udlong) 1899- ... 77-80
Tyler, Elias S. 1904(?)-1977 Obituary ... 73-76
Tyler, Gus 1911- ... 130
Tyler, Hamilton A(lden) 1917- ... CANR-5
Earlier sketch in CA 9-12R
Tyler, J. Allen 1924- ... 101
Tyler, John Ecclesfield ... CAP-1
Earlier sketch in CA 9-10
Tyler, Leona E(lizabeth) 1906- ... 17-20R
Tyler, Linda
See Tyler, Linda W(agner)
Tyler, Linda W(agner) 1952- ... 136
See also SATA 65
Tyler, Moses Coit 1835-1900 ... DLB 47, 64
Tyler, Parker 1907-1974 ... CANR-5
Obituary ... 49-52
Earlier sketch in CA 5-8R
Tyler, Patrick (Edward) 1951- ... 125
Tyler, (John) Poyntz 1907-1971 ... 1-4R
Obituary ... 103
Tyler, Ralph Winfred 1902- ... 109
Tyler, Richard W(illis) 1917- ... CANR-24
Earlier sketch in CA 41-44R
Tyler, Robert L(awrence) 1922- ... 13-16R
Tyler, Rodney 1943- ... 127
Tyler, Ron(nie) C(urtis) 1941- ... CANR-28
Earlier sketches in CA 29-32R, CANR-12
Tyler, Royall 1757-1826 ... DLB 37
Tyler, S(amuel) Lyman 1920- ... 77-80
Tyler, Stephen A(lbert) 1932- ... 29-32R
Tyler, Tom R(ichard) 1950- ... 135
Tyler, Varro Eugene 1926- ... 110
Tyler, Vicki 1952- ... 121
See also SATA 64
Tyler, W. T.
See Hamrick, Samuel J. Jr.
Tyler, William R(oyall) 1910- ... 37-40R
Tyler, Zeke
See Marshall, Mel(vin D.)
Tyler-Whittle, Michael Sidney 1927- ... CANR-4
Earlier sketch in CA 5-8R
Tylor, Edward Burnett
1832-1917 Brief entry ... 123
See also DLB 57
Tymchuk, Alexander J(ames) 1942- ... 57-60
Tymeson, Mildred McClary
See Petrie, Mildred McClary
Tymieniecka, Anna-Teresa ... CANR-9
Earlier sketch in CA 61-64
Tymms, Ralph Vincent 1913-1987 Obituary ... 123
Tymn, Marshall (Benton) 1937- ... 107
Tymon, Dorothy ... 85-88
Tynan, Katharine 1861-1931 Brief entry ... 104
See also TCLC 3
Tynan, Kathleen ... 97-100
Tynan, Kenneth (Peacock)
1927-1980 ... CANR-22
Obituary ... 101
Earlier sketch in CA 13-16R
See also MTCW
Tyre, Nedra ... 104
Tyrell, Donald J(ohn) 1929- Brief entry ... 110
Tyrmand, Leopold 1920-1985 ... CANR-5
Obituary ... 115
Earlier sketch in CA 49-52
Tyrone, Paul
See Norwood, Victor G(eorge) C(harles)
Tyrrell, Bernard (James) 1933- ... 57-60
Tyrrell, Francis M(artin) 1916- Brief entry ... 107
Tyrrell, Joseph M(orten) 1927- ... 41-44R
Tyrrell, R(obert) Emmett Jr. 1943- ... CANR-25
Earlier sketch in CA 85-88
Tyrrell, Robert 1929- ... 41-44R
Tyrrell, William Blake 1940- ... 125
Tyrwhitt, (Mary) Jacqueline
1905-1983(?) Obituary ... 109
Tyrwhitt, Janice 1928- ... 97-100
Tysdahl, B(joern) J(ohan) 1933- ... 25-28R
Tysliava, Valerie 1914(?)-1984 Obituary ... 112
Tyson, Alan (Walker) 1926- ... 128
Tyson, Joseph B(lake) 1928- ... CANR-38
Earlier sketches in CA 37-40R, CANR-14
Tyson, Nancy Jane 1949- ... 117
Tyson, Remer (Hoyt) 1934- ... 131
Tyson, Richard 1944- ... 69-72
Tysse, Agnes N. 1904- ... 101
Tytell, John 1939- ... 29-32R
See also CLC 50
Tytler, Graeme (Douglas Colville) 1934- ... 117
Tzannes, Nicolaos S(tamatios) 1937- ... 57-60
Tzara, Tristan
See Rosenfeld, Samuel
See also CLC 47
Tzitsikas, Helene 1926- ... 45-48
Tzonis, Alexander 1937- ... 101

U

Ubbelohde, Carl (William Jr.) 1924- ... CANR-6
Earlier sketch in CA 1-4R
Ubell, Earl 1926- ... 37-40R
See also SATA 4
Uble, T(homas) R(alph) O(bermeyer)
1931- ... CANR-29
Earlier sketches in CA 29-32R, CANR-13
Ucelay, Margarita 1916- ... 21-24R
Uchida, Tadao 1939- ... 65-68
Uchida, Yoshiko 1921- ... CANR-22
Earlier sketches in CA 13-16R, CANR-6
See also CLR 6
See also MAICYA
See also MTCW
See also SAAS 1
See also SATA 1, 53
Ucko, Barbara 1945- ... 136
Udall, Jan Beaney 1938- ... CANR-35
Earlier sketch in CA 65-68
See also SATA 10
Udall, Morris K(ing) 1922- ... CANR-1
Earlier sketch in CA 45-48
Udall, Nicholas 1504-1556 ... DLB 62
Udall, Stewart L(ee) 1920- ... 69-72
Ude, Wayne 1946- ... CANR-13
Earlier sketch in CA 77-80
Udell, Jon G(erald) 1935- ... CANR-37
Earlier sketches in CA 45-48, CANR-1, 16
Udelson, Joseph H. 1943- ... 125
Uden, (Bernard Gilbert) Grant 1910- ... 102
See also SATA 26
Udo, Reuben Kenrick 1935- ... CANR-35
Earlier sketch in CA 77-80
Udoff, Yale M(aurice) 1935- ... CANR-12
Earlier sketch in CA 57-60
Udolf, Roy 1926- ... CANR-4
Earlier sketch in CA 53-56
Udovitch, Abraham Labe 1933- Brief entry ... 105
Udry, J(oe) Richard 1928- ... 33-36R
Udry, Janice May 1928- ... CANR-6
Earlier sketch in CA 5-8R
See also SATA 4
Udy, Stanley Hart Jr. 1928- Brief entry ... 106
Ueda, Makoto 1931- ... CANR-34
Earlier sketch in CA 21-24R
Uehling, Carl Theodore 1927- ... 29-32R
Uehling, Theodore Edward Jr. 1935- ... CANR-20
Earlier sketch in CA 104
Ueno, Noriko
See Nakae, Noriko
Uffelman, F. C.
See Gehman, Richard (Boyd)
Uffenbeck, Lorin A(rthur) 1924- ... 61-64
Ugama, LeRoi
See Smith, LeRoi Tex
Ugarte, Francisco 1910-1969 ... CAP-1
Earlier sketch in CA 9-10
Ugarte, Michael 1949- ... 114
Ugboajah, (Francis) Okwu 1945- ... 93-96
Ugresic, Dubravka 1949- ... 136
Uhalley, Stephen Jr. 1930- Brief entry ... 106
Uhl, Alexander H. 1899(?)-1976 Obituary ... 69-72
Uhl, Melvin John 1915- ... CANR-34
Earlier sketch in CA 5-8R
Uhlan, Edward 1912-1988 Obituary ... 127
Uhland, Ludwig 1787-1862 ... DLB 90
Uhlfelder, Myra L. 1923- Brief entry ... 109
Uhlin, Donald M(acbeth) 1930- ... 49-52
Uhlinger, Susan J. 1942-1980 ... CANR-34
Obituary ... 120
Earlier sketch in CA 57-60
Uhlman, Fred 1901-1985(?) ... CANR-34
Obituary ... 116
Earlier sketch in CA 105
Uhnak, Dorothy 1933- ... CANR-29
Earlier sketch in CA 81-84
See also AITN 1
Uhr, Carl George 1911- ... 81-84
Uhr, Elizabeth 1929- ... 25-28R
Uhr, Leonard (Merrick) 1927- ... CANR-7
Earlier sketch in CA 5-8R
Uhry, Alfred 1936- ... 133
Brief entry ... 127
See also CLC 55
Uitti, Karl David 1933- ... CANR-10
Earlier sketch in CA 17-20R
Ujfalussy, Jozsef 1920- Brief entry ... 114
Ujse, Bodo 1904-1963 ... DLB 69
Ulam, Adam B(runo) 1922- ... CANR-26
Earlier sketches in CA 13-16R, CANR-7
Ulam, S(tanislaw) M(arcin)
1909-1984 ... CANR-34
Obituary ... 112
Earlier sketch in CA 61-64
See also SATA 51
Ulanoff, Stanley M(elvin) 1922- ... CANR-23
Earlier sketches in CA 17-20R, CANR-7
Ulanov, Ann Belford 1938- ... CANR-38
Earlier sketches in CA 49-52, CANR-16
Ulanov, Barry 1918- ... CANR-38
Earlier sketches in CA 1-4R, CANR-16
Ulbricht, Walter 1893-1973 Obituary ... 113
Ulc, Otto 1930- ... CANR-13
Earlier sketch in CA 77-80
Ulene, Art(hur Lawrence) 1936- ... CANR-30
Earlier sketch in CA 103
Ulett, George A(ndrew) 1918- ... 21-24R
Ulevich, Neal Hirsch 1946- ... 108
Ulf, Haerved
See Strindberg, (Johan) August
Ulf, Harved
See Strindberg, (Johan) August
Ulibarri, Sabine R(eyes) 1919- ... 131
See also HW
Ulibarri, Sabine Reyes 1919- Brief entry ... 105
See also DLB 82
Ulica, Jorge 1870-1926 ... DLB 82
Ulich, Robert 1890(?)-1977 Obituary ... 69-72
Ullah, Najib 1914- ... 13-16R
Ullah, Salamat 1913- ... 13-16R
Ulle, Robert F. 1948- ... 117
Ullendorff, Edward 1920- ... CANR-18
Earlier sketches in CA 1-4R, CANR-2
Ullian, Joseph S(ilbert) 1930- ... 41-44R
Ullman, Allan 1909(?)-1982 Obituary ... 106
Ullman, Barbara
See Schwalberg, Carol(yn Ernestine Stein)
Ullman, Edward L(ouis) 1912-1976 ... 45-48
Obituary ... 125
Ullman, Elwood 1903(?)-1985 Obituary ... 117
Ullman, James Ramsey 1907-1971 ... CANR-3
Obituary ... 29-32R
Earlier sketch in CA 1-4R
See also SATA 7
Ullman, Leslie 1947- ... 104
Ullman, Michael (Alan) 1945- ... 103
Ullman, Montague 1916- ... CANR-28
Earlier sketch in CA 41-44R
Ullman, Natacha 1929(?)-1986 Obituary ... 119
Ullman, Pierre L(ioni) 1929- ... 33-36R
Ullman, Richard Henry 1933- ... CANR-3
Earlier sketch in CA 1-4R
Ullmann, John E(manuel) 1923- ... CANR-34
Earlier sketch in CA 17-20R
Ullmann, Leonard P(aul) 1930- ... 17-20R
Ullmann, Liv 1939- ... 102
Ullmann, Stephen 1914-1976 ... CANR-4
Obituary ... 65-68
Earlier sketch in CA 5-8R
Ullmann, Walter 1910-1983 ... CANR-10
Obituary ... 108
Earlier sketch in CA 21-24R
Ullrich, Helen D(enning) 1922- ... CANR-28
Earlier sketch in CA 109
Ullstein, Hermann 1875(?)-1943 Brief entry ... 116
Ullyot, Joan 1940- ... 73-76
Ulm, Robert 1934-1977 ... SATA 17
Ulman, William A. 1908(?)-1979 ... 103
Obituary ... 89-92
Ulmer, (Roland) Curtis 1923- ... 103
Ulmer, Diane K. 1943- ... 122
Ulmer, Gregory L(eland) 1944- ... 136
Ulmer, Louise 1943- ... 113
See also SATA 53
Ulmer, Melville J(ack) 1911- ... 21-24R
Ulmer, S(hirley) Sidney 1923- ... 41-44R
Ulph, Owen 1914- ... 133
Ulrich, Betty Garton 1919- ... 29-32R
Ulrich, Carolyn F. 1881(?)-1970 Obituary ... 104
Ulrich, Heinz 1927(?)-1980 Obituary ... 97-100
Ulrich, (John) Homer 1906-1987 ... CANR-36
Obituary ... 124
Earlier sketches in CA 5-8R, CANR-2
Ulrich, Louis E. Jr. 1918- ... 13-16R
Ulrich, Roger E(lwood) 1931- ... 41-44R
Ultan, Lloyd 1929- ... 117
Ultee, (J.) Maarten 1949- ... 109
Ulyanov, V. I.
See Lenin
Ulyanov-Lenin
See Lenin
Ulyatt, Kenneth 1920- ... CANR-8
Earlier sketch in CA 61-64
See also SATA 14
Umen, Samuel 1917(?)-1990 Obituary ... 132
Umland, Craig (Owen) 1947- ... 61-64
Umphlett, Wiley Lee 1931- ... CANR-34
Earlier sketches in CA 49-52, CANR-1
Umpierre (Herrera), Luz Maria 1947- ... HW
Umstead, William Lee 1921- ... 81-84
Unada
See Gliewe, Unada (Grace)
Unamuno (y Jugo), Miguel de 1864-1936 ... 131
Brief entry ... 104
See also DLB 108
See also HW
See also MTCW
See also TCLC 2, 9
Unbegaun, Boris Ottokar
1898-1973 Obituary ... 41-44R
Uncle Gordon
See Roe, F(rederic) Gordon
Uncle Gus
See Rey, H(ans) A(ugusto)
Uncle Mac
See McCulloch, Derek (Ivor Breashur)
Uncle Ray
See Coffman, Ramon Peyton
Uncle Shelby
See Silverstein, Shel(by)
Undercliffe, Errol
See Campbell, (John) Ramsey
Underdown, David (Edward) 1925- ... CANR-26
Earlier sketches in CA 5-8R, CANR-11
Underhill, Alice Mertie (Waterman)
1900-1971 ... 1-4R
Obituary ... 103
See also SATA 10
Underhill, Charles
See Hill, Reginald (Charles)
Underhill, Hal
See Underhill, Harold
Underhill, Harold 1926-1972 ... CAP-2
Earlier sketch in CA 25-28
Underhill, Liz 1948- ... 121
See also SATA 49, 53
Underhill, Miriam E.
1898(?)-1976 Obituary ... 61-64
Underhill, Peter
See Soderberg, Percy Measday
Underhill, Ruth Murray 1884-1984 ... CANR-39
Obituary ... 114
Earlier sketches in CA 1-4R, CANR-3
Underwood, Aggie
See Underwood, Agness May Wilson
Underwood, Agness May Wilson
1902-1984 Obituary ... 113
Underwood, Barbara 1952- ... 101

Underwood, Benton J. 1915- CANR-34
Earlier sketch in CA 101
Underwood, (Mary) Betty 1921- 37-40R
Underwood, Gary Neal 1940- Brief entry 113
Underwood, Jane H(ammons) 1931- 61-64
Underwood, Jeffery S(cott) 1954- 137
Underwood, John Weeden 1932- CANR-35
Earlier sketch in CA 17-20R
Underwood, Laura (Drew) 1963- 129
Underwood, Lewis Graham
See Wagner, C(harles) Peter
Underwood, Mavis Eileen 1916- Brief entry 108
Underwood, Michael
See Evelyn, (John) Michael
Underwood, Miles
See Glassco, John
Underwood, Norman
1878(?)-1974 Obituary 53-56
Underwood, Paul S(taats) 1915-1985 77-80
Obituary 118
Underwood, Peter 1923- CANR-21
Earlier sketch in CA 104
Underwood, Sam J(esse) 1922- CANR-2
Earlier sketch in CA 45-48
Underwood, Ted Leroy 1935- 115
Underwood, Tim (Edward) 1948- CANR-24
Earlier sketch in CA 105
Undine, P. F.
See Paine, Lauran (Bosworth)
Undset, Sigrid 1882-1949 129
Brief entry 104
See also MTCW
See also TCLC 3
See also WLC
Undy, R(oger) 1938- 115
Unett, John 13-16R
Ungar, Frederick 1898-1988 Obituary 127
Ungar, Sanford J. 1945- CANR-29
Earlier sketches in CA 37-40R, CANR-13
Ungar, Steven (Ronald) 1945- 126
Ungaretti, Giuseppe 1888-1970 .... CAP-2
Obituary 25-28R
Earlier sketch in CA 19-20
See also CLC 7, 11, 15
See also DLB 114
Ungaro, Harold R(aymond) Mancusi Jr.
See Mancusi-Ungaro, Harold R(aymond) Jr.
Ungaro, Susan Kelliher 1953- 103
Ungaro, Arthur 1924- 1-4R
Unger, Barbara 1932- CANR-13
Earlier sketch in CA 77-80
Unger, Craig 1949- 128
Unger, David 1950- ....HW
Unger, Douglas 1952- 130
See also CLC 34
Unger, Friederike Helene 1741-1813 .... DLB 94
Unger, Hans 1915- 17-20R
Unger, Henry F. 1912- 13-16R
Unger, Irwin 1927- CANR-7
Earlier sketch in CA 9-12R
Unger, J(ames) Marshall 1947- 126
Unger, Jim 1937- CANR-13
Earlier sketch in CA 61-64
See also SATA 67
Unger, Len
See Unger, Leonard
Unger, Leonard 1916- CANR-34
Earlier sketch in CA 5-8R
Unger, Leonard 1934- 69-72
Unger, Marion
See Thede, Marion Draughon
Unger, Marvin H. 1936- 29-32R
Unger, Maurice Albert 1917- CANR-3
Earlier sketch in CA 9-12R
Unger, Merrill F. 1909- CANR-6
Earlier sketch in CA 1-4R
Unger, Peter K(enneth) 1942- 136
Brief entry 109
Unger, Richard (Lawrence) 1939- CANR-15
Earlier sketch in CA 65-68
Unger, Richard W. 1942- 121
Unger, Walter P(eter) 1939- Brief entry 115
Ungerer, Jean Thomas 1931- 41-44R
See also Ungerer, Tomi
See also MAICYA
See also SATA 5, 33
Ungerer, Miriam 1929- 117
Ungerer, Tomi
See Ungerer, Jean Thomas
See also CLR 3
Unger-Hamilton, Clive (Wolfgang)
1942- CANR-19
Earlier sketch in CA 101
Ungermann, Kenneth Armistead 1916- 9-12R
Ungs, Thomas D(ale) 1928- 81-84
Unkelbach, Kurt 1913- CANR-8
Earlier sketch in CA 21-24R
See also SATA 4
Unkovic, Charles M. 1922- 45-48
Unnerstad, Edith Totterman 1900- CANR-6
Earlier sketch in CA 5-8R
See also SATA 3
Unrau, Ruth 1922- 61-64
See also SATA 9
Unrau, William E. 1929- 37-40R
Unruh, Adolph 1908- 49-52
Unruh, Fritz von
See Von Unruh, Fritz
See also DLB 118
Unruh, Glenys Grace (Green) 1910- 29-32R
Unruh, John D. Jr. 1938(?)-1976 Obituary 105
Unser, Bobby
See Unser, Robert William
Unser, Robert William 1934- 97-100

Unstead, R(obert) J(ohn) 1915-1988 .....CANR-23
Obituary 125
Earlier sketches in CA 9-12R, CANR-7
See also SATA 12, 56
Unsworth, Barry (Forster) 1930- CANR-30
Earlier sketch in CA 25-28R
Unsworth, Mair 1909- CANR-10
Earlier sketch in CA 25-28R
Unsworth, Walt(er) 1928- CANR-38
Earlier sketches in CA 29-32R, CANR-17
See also SATA 4
Unterberger, Betty Miller 1923- 25-28R
Unterbrink, Mary 1937- 113
Unterecker, John (Eugene)
1922-1989 ....CANR-34
Obituary 127
Earlier sketch in CA 17-20R
Untereiner, Raymond Edward
1898-1983 Obituary 110
Unterman, Alan 1942- 97-100
Unterman, Issar Y(ehuda)
1886-1976 Obituary 61-64
Untermeyer, Bryna Ivens 1909-1985 ......CANR-31
Earlier sketches in CA 5-8R, CANR-3
See also SATA 61
Untermeyer, Jean Starr
1886-1970 Obituary 29-32R
Untermeyer, Louis 1885-1977 ....CANR-31
Obituary 73-76
Earlier sketch in CA 5-8R
See also SATA 2, 26, 37
Unthank, Luisa-Teresa 33-36R
Unthank, Tessa Brown
See Unthank, Luisa-Teresa
Unwalla, Darab B. 1928- 25-28R
Unwin, David S(torr) 1918- CANR-6
Earlier sketch in CA 9-12R
See also SATA 14
Unwin, Derick (James) 1931- 21-24R
Unwin, Nora S(picer) 1907-1982 ....21-24R
Obituary 120
See also SATA 3, 49
Unwin, Rayner S(tephens) 1925- 1-4R
Unwin, Stanley 1884-1968 ....5-8R
Upchurch, Boyd (Bradfield) 1919- CANR-27
Earlier sketch in CA 25-28R
See also Boyd, John
Updike, David (H.) 1957- 128
Updike, John (Hoyer) 1932- CANR-33
Earlier sketches in CA 1-4R, CANR-4
See also CABS 1
See also CDALB 1968-1988
See also CLC 1, 2, 3, 5, 7, 9, 13, 15, 23, 34, 43, 70
See also DLB 2, 5
See also DLBD 3
See also DLBY 80, 82
See also MTCW
See also WLC
Updike, L(eRoy) Wayne 1916- 49-52
Updyke, James
See Burnett, W(illiam) R(iley)
Upfield, Arthur W(illiam)
1888-1964 Obituary 114
Upgren, Arthur P. 1897-1986 Obituary 120
Uphaus, Robert W(alter) 1942- 57-60
Uphaus, Willard Edwin 1890-1983 ....CAP-1
Obituary 111
Earlier sketch in CA 19-20
Uphoff, Norman T(homas) 1940- CANR-11
Earlier sketch in CA 29-32R
Uphoff, Walter H. 1913- CANR-14
Earlier sketch in CA 25-28R
Upits, Andrejs 1877-1970 Obituary 104
Upjohn, Everard M(iller) 1903-1978 ....CAP-1
Obituary 81-84
Earlier sketch in CA 13-14
Uppal, Jogindar S. 1927- CANR-1
Earlier sketch in CA 45-48
Uppman, Jean Seward 1922- 136
Upright, Diane W(arner) 1947- 120
Upshaw, Margaret Mitchell
See Mitchell, Margaret (Munnerlyn)
Upson, Norma 1919- CANR-8
Earlier sketch in CA 61-64
Upson, William Hazlett 1891-1975 ....5-8R
Obituary 57-60
Upton, Albert 1897- CAP-2
Earlier sketch in CA 23-24
Upton, Anthony F. 1929- 17-20R
Upton, Arvin 1914- 81-84
Upton, Bertha (Hudson)
1849-1912 Brief entry 121
Upton, Charles 1948- Brief entry 116
See also DLB 16
Upton, Dell 1949- 123
Upton, Joseph C(heshire) N(ash) 1946- 81-84
Upton, L(eslie) F(rancis) S(tokes)
1931-1980 61-64
Obituary 125
Upton, Lee 1953- 123
Upton, Mark
See Sanders, Lawrence
Upton, Monroe 1898- CAP-2
Earlier sketch in CA 17-18
Upton, Robert CANR-29
Earlier sketches in CA 73-76, CANR-13
Upward, Allen 1863-1926 Brief entry 117
See also DLB 36
Upward, Edward (Falaise) 1903- 77-80
Urbach, Reinhard 1939- Brief entry 113
Urban, Michael E(dward) 1947- CANR-29
Earlier sketch in CA 111
Urban, Wilbur Marshall
1873-1952 Brief entry 119
Urban, William L(awrence) 1939- CANR-18
Earlier sketches in CA 45-48, CANR-2
Urbanek, Mae 1903- 77-80

Urbano, Victoria (Eugenia) 1926- CANR-2
Earlier sketch in CA 45-48
Urbanska, Wanda (Marie) 1956- 124
Urbanski, Edmund Stefan
See Urbanski, Edmund Stephen
Urbanski, Edmund Stephen 1909- CANR-23
Earlier sketch in CA 45-48
Urbanski, Marie M. Olesen 1922- 102
Urch, Elizabeth 1921- 103
Urda, Nicholas 1922- 21-24R
Urdang, Constance (Henriette) 1922- CANR-24
Earlier sketches in CA 21-24R, CANR-9
See also CLC 47
Urdang, Laurence 1927- CANR-17
Earlier sketch in CA 89-92
Ure, Jean 125
See also MAICYA
See also SAAS 14
See also SATA 48
Ure, Peter 1919-1969 .... CAP-1
Earlier sketch in CA 11-12
Uren, Hilda
See U'Ren-Stubbings, Hilda
U'Ren, Hilda
See U'Ren-Stubbings, Hilda
U'Ren-Stubbings, Hilda 1914- 29-32R
Uretsky, Myron 1940- 53-56
Urey, Harold C(layton) 1893-1981 Obituary 102
Uri, Pierre Emmanuel 1911- 97-100
Uri, Pierre (Emmanuel) 1911-1992 Obituary 138
Uriel, Henry
See Faust, Frederick (Shiller)
Uris, Auren 1913- CANR-22
Earlier sketch in CA 17-20R
Uris, Dorothy CANR-9
Earlier sketch in CA 61-64
Uris, Leon (Marcus) 1924- CANR-1
Earlier sketch in CA 1-4R
See also AITN 1, 2
See also BEST 89:2
See also CLC 7, 32
See also MTCW
See also SATA 49
Urista, Alberto H. 1947- CANR-2
Earlier sketches in CA 45-48, CANR-32
See also Alurista
See also HW
Urkowitz, Steven 1941- 111
Urmson, J(ames) O(pie) 1915- 25-28R
Urmuz
See Codrescu, Andrei
Urness, Carol 1936- Brief entry 111
Uroff, Margaret Dickie 1935- 93-96
Urofsky, Melvin I. 1939- CANR-31
Earlier sketches in CA 37-40R, CANR-14
Urquhart, Alvin W. 1931- 13-16R
Urquhart, Brian (Edward) 1919- CANR-26
Earlier sketch in CA 105
Urquhart, Caroline 1940- 118
Urquhart, Colin 1940- CANR-37
Earlier sketch in CA 115
Urquhart, Fred(erick Burrows) 1912- CANR-21
Earlier sketches in CA 9-12R, CANR-6
Urquhart, Guy
See McAlmon, Robert (Menzies)
Urquhart, Jane 1949- CANR-32
Earlier sketch in CA 113
Urquhart, Judy 1942- 123
Urrutia Lleo, Manuel 1901-1981 Obituary 104
Urry, David (Laurence) 1931- 85-88
Urry, John 1946- 122
Urry, W(illiam) G(eorge)
1913-1981 Obituary 103
Ursini, James 1947- 61-64
Urvater, Michele 1946- 102
Urwick, Lyndall Fownes 1891-1983 ....CAP-1
Obituary 111
Earlier sketch in CA 13-14
Urwin, Gregory J(ohn) W(illiam)
1955- CANR-36
Earlier sketch in CA 114
Ury, William L(anger) 1953- CANR-27
Earlier sketch in CA 109
Ury, Zalman F. 1924- CANR-17
Earlier sketch in CA 65-68
Urzidil, Johannes 1896-1970 Obituary 29-32R
See also DLB 85
Us
See Deal, Borden
Usborne, Richard Alexander 1910- 104
Usco
See Stern, Gerd Jacob
Usdin, Gene (Leonard) 1922- 37-40R
Useem, Michael 1942- 61-64
Usher, Dan 1934- CANR-12
Earlier sketch in CA 29-32R
Usher, Frank (Hugh) 1909-1976 ....CANR-5
Earlier sketch in CA 5-8R
Usher, George 1930- 109
Usher, Margo Scegge
See McHargue, Georgess
Usher, Shaun 1937- 77-80
Usher, Stephen 1931- 29-32R
Usher-Wilson, Rodney N.
1908(?)-1983 Obituary 109
Usherwood, Elizabeth (Ada) 1923- 123
Usherwood, Stephen Dean 1907- CANR-19
Earlier sketches in CA 5-8R, CANR-3
Usigli, Rodolfo 1905-1979 131
See also HW
Usikota
See Brinitzer, Carl
Uslaner, Eric M(ichael) 1947- 111
Uslar Pietri, Arturo 1906- ....DLB 113
See also HW
Usmiani, Renate 1931- 113
Usry, Milton F. 1931- 17-20R

Ussher, (Percival) Arland 1899-1980 .....CANR-10
Obituary 102
Earlier sketches in CAP-1, CA 13-14
Ussher, Percy Arland
See Ussher, (Percival) Arland
Ustinov, D(mitri) F(edorovich) 1908-1984 133
Obituary 114
Ustinov, Peter (Alexander) 1921- CANR-25
Earlier sketch in CA 13-16R
See also AITN 1
See also CLC 1
See also DLB 13
Uston, Ken(neth Senzo) 1935-1987 108
Obituary 123
See also SATA 65
U Tam'si, Gerald Felix Tchicaya
See Tchicaya, Gerald Felix
U Tam'si, Tchicaya
See Tchicaya, Gerald Felix
Utechin, S(ergei) V(asilievich) 1921- 9-12R
Utgard, Russell O(liver) 1933- 49-52
Utke, Allen R(ay) 1936- 81-84
Utlee, (J.) Maarten 1949- CANR-37
Utley, Francis Lee 1907-1974 ....CANR-2
Obituary 49-52
Earlier sketch in CA 1-4R
Utley, Freda 1898-1978 81-84
Obituary 77-80
Utley, (Clifton) Garrick 1939- 69-72
Utley, Jonathan G. 1942- 129
Utley, Ralph
See Cairns, Huntington
Utley, Robert M(arshall) 1929- CANR-2
Earlier sketch in CA 5-8R
Utley, T(homas) E(dwin)
1921-1988 Obituary 125
Utt, Richard H. 1923- CANR-7
Earlier sketch in CA 9-12R
Utt, Walter C(harles) 1921- 21-24R
Uttley, Alice Jane (Taylor) 1884-1976 ......CANR-7
Obituary 65-68
Earlier sketch in CA 53-56
See also SATA 3, 26
Uttley, Alison
See Uttley, Alice Jane (Taylor)
Uttley, John 1914- 21-24R
Utton, Albert Edgar 1931- CANR-1
Earlier sketch in CA 45-48
Utz, Lois (Marie) 1932-1986 ....25-28R
Obituary 121
See also SATA 5, 50
Utz, Robert T(homas) 1934- 53-56
Uu, David
See Harris, David W.
Uveges, Joseph A(ndrew) Jr. 1938- 41-44R
Uvezian, Sonia CANR-9
Earlier sketch in CA 57-60
Uviller, H. Richard 1929- 129
Uyl, Douglas J(ohn) Den
See Den Uyl, Douglas J(ohn)
Uys, Errol Lincoln 1943- 136
Uz, Johann Peter 1720-1796 ....DLB 97
Uzgiris, Ina Cepenas 1937- Brief entry 108
Uzzell, J(ohn) Douglas 1937- 93-96

V

v
See Chekhov, Anton (Pavlovich)
V., Nina
See Vickers, Antoinette L.
Vac, Bertrand 1914- ....DLB 88
Vacca, Roberto 1927- CANR-1
Earlier sketch in CA 49-52
Vaccaro, Ernest B.
1905(?)-1979 Obituary 89-92
Vaccaro, Joseph P(ascal) 1935- 104
Vaccaro, Louis C(harles) 1930- CANR-1
Earlier sketch in CA 45-48
Vaccaro, Tony
See Vaccaro, Ernest B.
Vachek, Josef 1909- 132
Vachell, Horace Annesley
1861-1955 Brief entry 120
Vachon, Brian 1941- 41-44R
Vachon, Mary L. S. 1945- 127
Vachss, Andrew H(enry) 1942- 118
Vaculik, Ludvik 1926- 53-56
See also CLC 7
Vaczek, Louis 1913-1983 ....CANR-21
Obituary 111
Earlier sketch in CA 9-12R
Vadakin, James C(harles) 1924-1981 ....29-32R
Obituary 134
Vadney, Thomas E(ugene) 1939- 45-48
Vaeth, J(oseph) Gordon 1921- 5-8R
See also SATA 17
Vaggi, Gianni 1947- 127
Vago, Bela Adalbert 1922- 93-96
Vagts, Alfred (Hermann Friedrich) 1892- 5-8R
Vagts, Detlev F(rederick) 1929- 25-28R
Vagts, Miriam Beard 1901-1983 Obituary 110
Vahanian, Gabriel (Antoine) 1927- CANR-22
Earlier sketches in CA 1-4R, CANR-6
Vaid, Krishna Baldev 1927- CANR-8
Earlier sketch in CA 61-64
Vaidon, Lawdom
See Woolman, David S.
Vaihinger, Hans 1852-1933 Brief entry 116
Vail, (Marilyn) Elaine 1948- 109

Vail, Laurence 1891-1968 Obituary 112
See also DLB 4
Vail, Priscilla L. 1931- 101
Vail, Robert William 1921- CANR-12
Earlier sketch in CA 17-20R
Vaill, George D. 1911(?)-1986 Obituary 119
Vaillancourt, Jean-Guy 1937- CANR-21
Earlier sketch in CA 105
Vaillancourt, Pauline M(ariette) 104
Vailland, Roger (Francois) 1907-1965 103
Obituary 89-92
See also DLB 83
Vaillant, George E. 1934- CANR-13
Earlier sketch in CA 77-80
Vaillant, Janet G. 1937- 136
Vairo, Philip Dominic 1933- 102
Vaizey, John 1929-1984 ....CANR-4
Obituary 113
Earlier sketch in CA 5-8R
Vaizey, Marina 1938- 116
Vajda, Ernest 1887-1954 Brief entry 122
See also DLB 44
Vajda, Stephan 1926-1987 ....CANR-27
Earlier sketch in CA 29-32R
Vajk, J(oseph) Peter 1942- 117
Vakar, N(icholas) P(latonovich)
1897-1970 ....CANR-20
Obituary 103
Earlier sketch in CA 1-4R
Valaskakis, Kimon Plato 1941- 89-92
Valbonne, Jean
See Leprohon, Pierre
Valbuena-Briones, Angel (Julian)
1928- CANR-3
Earlier sketch in CA 45-48
Valcarcel, Emilio Diaz
See Diaz Valcarcel, Emilio
Valcoe, H. Felix
See Swartz, Harry (Felix)
Valdemi, Maria L. 1947- 114
Valdes, Donald M(anuel) 1922- 21-24R
Valdes, Ivy 1921- 105
Valdes, Joan 1931- 49-52
Valdes, Mario J. 1934- CANR-21
Earlier sketches in CA 13-16R, CANR-6
Valdes, Nelson P. 1945- CANR-38
Earlier sketch in CA 33-36R
Valdez, Luis (Miguel) 1940- CANR-32
Earlier sketch in CA 101
See also HW
Valdez, Paul
See Yates, A(lan) G(eoffrey)
Valdman, Albert 1931- 103
Vale, C(orwyn) P(hilip) 1921- 49-52
Vale, (Henry) Edmund (Theodoric)
1888-1969 .... CAP-1
Earlier sketch in CA 9-10
Vale, Eugene 1916- CANR-12
Earlier sketch in CA 57-60
Vale, Juliet (Elizabeth) 1952- 132
Vale, Lewis
See Oglesby, Joseph
Vale, Malcolm Graham Allan
1942- Brief entry 109
Valen, Nanine 1950- 65-68
See also SATA 21
Valencak, Hannelore
See Mayer, Hannelore Valencak
See also SATA 42
Valency, Maurice 1903- CANR-26
Earlier sketches in CA 25-28R, CANR-10
Valens, Amy 1946- 138
See also SATA 70
Valens, E(vans) G. Jr. 1920- CANR-3
Earlier sketch in CA 5-8R
See also SATA 1
Valens, Evans G. CANR-14
Earlier sketch in CA 81-84
Valenstein, Elliot S(piro) 1923- 132
Valenstein, Suzanne G(ebhart) 1928- 77-80
Valente, Jose Angel 1929- ....DLB 108
Valente, Michael F(eeney) 57-60
Valenti, Jack 1921- 73-76
Valentin, Thomas 1922-1981 Obituary 103
Valentine, Alan (Chester) 1901-1980 ....CANR-2
Obituary 101
Earlier sketch in CA 5-8R
Valentine, Charles A. 1929- 25-28R
Valentine, Charles Wilfrid
1879-1964 Obituary 107
Valentine, D(onald) G(raham) 1929- 5-8R
Valentine, David
See Ludovici, Anthony M(ario)
Valentine, Douglas
See Williams, (George) Valentine
Valentine, Foy (Dan) 1923- CANR-10
Earlier sketch in CA 17-20R
Valentine, Helen
See Valentine, Sister Mary Hester
Valentine, Helen (Lachman)
1893-1986 Obituary 121
Valentine, James W(illiam) 1926- 126
Valentine, Jean 1934- CANR-34
Earlier sketch in CA 65-68
Valentine, Jo
See Armstrong, Charlotte
Valentine, Lloyd Magnus 1922- Brief entry 110
Valentine, Roger
See Duke, Donald Norman
Valentine, Sister Mary Hester 1909- CAP-2
Earlier sketch in CA 23-24
Valentine, Steven Richards 1956- 113
Valentine, Tom 1935- CANR-22
Earlier sketch in CA 45-48
Valentiñe, William Alexander 1905- 57-60
Valenzuela, Arturo A. 1944- 101
Valenzuela, Luisa 1938- CANR-32
Earlier sketch in CA 101
See also CLC 31
See also DLB 113
See also HW
Valeo, Francis Ralph 1916- Brief entry 108
Valeran, A. B.
See Starr, S(tephen) Frederick
Valera y Alcala-Galiano, Juan
1824-1905 Brief entry 106
See also TCLC 10
Valeriani, Richard (Gerard) 1932- CANR-12
Earlier sketch in CA 65-68
Valeriano, Napoleon D(iestro)
1917(?)-1975 Obituary 53-56
Valery, Bernard 1913(?)-1984 Obituary 113
Valery, (Ambroise) Paul (Toussaint Jules)
1871-1945 122
Brief entry 104
See also MTCW
See also TCLC 4, 15
Vales, Robert L(ee) 1933- 53-56
Valett, Robert E. 1927- CANR-22
Earlier sketches in CA 17-20R, CANR-7
Valette, Rebecca M(arianne Loose)
1938- CANR-8
Earlier sketch in CA 21-24R
Valgardson, W(illiam) D(empsey)
1939- CANR-38
Earlier sketch in CA 41-44R
See also DLB 60
Valgemae, Mardi 1935- 41-44R
Vali, Ferenc Albert 1905-1984 ....CANR-37
Obituary 114
Earlier sketches in CA 1-4R, CANR-3
Valiani, Leo 1909- CANR-18
Earlier sketch in CA 101
Valin, Jonathan Louis 1948- CANR-38
Earlier sketch in CA 101
Valin, Martial (Henry) 1898-1980 Obituary 105
Valis, Noel M(aureen Ritter) 1945- 110
Valkenier, Elizabeth Kridl 1926- 119
Vall, Seymour 1925(?)-1987 Obituary 124
Vallance, Elizabeth (Mary) 1945- 102
Valleau, Emily 1925- ....SATA 51
Vallee, Hubert P(rior) 1901-1986 ....CANR-2
Obituary 119
Earlier sketch in CA 1-4R
Vallee, Jacques F. 1939- CANR-10
Earlier sketch in CA 17-20R
Vallee, Lillian (Bozenna) 1949- 135
Vallee, Rudy
See Vallee, Hubert P(rior)
Valle-Inclan, Ramon (Maria) del
1866-1936 Brief entry 106
See also TCLC 5
Vallejo, Antonio Buero
See Buero Vallejo, Antonio
Vallejo, Cesar (Abraham)
1892-1938 Brief entry 105
See also HW
See also TCLC 3
Vallen, Jerome J(ay) 1928- 93-96
Vallentine, John F(ranklin) 1931- CANR-19
Earlier sketches in CA 53-56, CANR-4
Valle Y Pena, Ramon del
See Valle-Inclan, Ramon (Maria) del
Valmaggia, Juan S. 1895-1980 Obituary 97-100
Valsan, E. H. 1933- 29-32R
Valtz, Robert C. K. 1936- 13-16R
Value, Barbara Ann 1932-1986 Obituary 120
Valverde, Jose Maria 1926- ....DLB 108
Vambe, Lawrence (Chinyani) 1917- 110
Vamos, Mara (Miriam) 1927- Brief entry 114
Vamplew, Wray 1943- CANR-20
Earlier sketch in CA 103
Van Abbe, Derek Maurice 1916- 57-60
Van Abbe, Salaman 1883-1955 ....SATA 18
Van Allsburg, Chris 1949- CANR-38
Brief entry 113
Earlier sketch in CA 117
See also CLR 5, 13
See also DLB 61
See also MAICYA
See also SATA 37, 53
Van Alstyne, Richard W(arner) 1900- CANR-39
Earlier sketch in CA 9-12R
Van Anda, Carr 1864-1945 ....DLB 25
Van Anrooy, Francine 1924- 21-24R
See also SATA 2
Van Anrooy, Frans
See Van Anrooy, Francine
van Appledorn, Mary Jeanne 1927- CANR-26
Earlier sketches in CA 25-28R, CANR-10
Vanardy, Varick
See Dey, Frederic (Merrill) Van Rensselaer
Van Arsdel, Rosemary T(horstenson)
1926- 108
Van Ash, Cay 1918- ....CLC 34
Van Atta, Winfred 1910- CANR-1
Earlier sketch in CA 1-4R
Vanauken, Sheldon 1914- CANR-35
Earlier sketches in CA 85-88, CANR-15
Vanbalen, A.
See Stolk, Anthonie
van Beeck, Frans Jozef 1930- 115
Vanberg, Bent J(arl) 1915- 118
VanBibber, Max A(rnold)
1913(?)-1981 Obituary 103
Van Briggle, Margaret F(rances) Jessup
1917- 9-12R
Van Brocklin, Norm(an Mack)
1926-1983 Obituary 109
Vanbrugh, Sir John 1664-1726 ....DLB 80
Van Brunt, H. L.
See Van Brunt, (Howell) Lloyd
Van Brunt, (Howell) Lloyd 1936- CANR-35
Earlier sketch in CA 49-52
See also CAAS 15
Van Buitenen, J(ohannes) A(drian) B(ernard)
1928(?)-1979 103
Obituary 89-92
Van Buren, Abigail
See Phillips, Pauline (Esther Friedman)
Van Buren, James G(eil) 1914- 57-60
van Buren, Paul (Matthews) 1924- CANR-11
Earlier sketch in CA 61-64
Van Buren, Raeburn 1891- CANR-39
Earlier sketch in CA 103
Van Caenegem, R(aoul) C(harles)
1927- CANR-23
Earlier sketch in CA 45-48
Van Campen, Karl
See Campbell, John W(ood Jr.)
Van Caspel, Venita 1922- 104
Vance, A. D.
See Vane-Wright, R(ichard) I(rwin)
Vance, Adrian 1936- 77-80
Vance, Barbara Jane 1934- 57-60
Vance, Bruce 1931- 33-36R
Vance, Cyrus R(oberts) 1917- 121
Vance, Edgar
See Ambrose, Eric (Samuel)
Vance, Eleanor Graham 1908- 9-12R
See also SATA 11
Vance, Ethel
See Stone, Grace Zaring
Vance, Eugene 1934- 126
Vance, Gerald
See Garrett, (Gordon) Randall (Phillip)
and Silverberg, Robert
Vance, Jack
See Vance, John Holbrook
See also CLC 35
See also DLB 8
Vance, John Holbrook 1916- CANR-17
Earlier sketch in CA 29-32R
See also Queen, Ellery
and Vance, Jack
See also MTCW
Vance, Lawrence L(ee) 1911- CANR-39
Earlier sketch in CA 49-52
Vance, Louis Joseph 1879-1933 Brief entry 112
Vance, Marguerite 1889-1965 Obituary 109
See also SATA 29
Vance, (Robert) Norman (Colbert) 1950- 122
Vance, Rupert B(ayless)
1899-1975 Obituary 61-64
Vance, Samuel 1939- 29-32R
Vance, Stanley 1915- CANR-3
Earlier sketch in CA 1-4R
Vance, William E. 1911-1986 105
Obituary 119
Vance, William L(ynn) 1934- 132
Vanceburg, Martha
See Roth (Vanceburg), Martha
Vancil, Richard F(ranklin) 1931- CANR-8
Earlier sketch in CA 5-8R
Van Cise, Jerrold G(ordon) 1910- 114
Van Cleef, Eugene 1887-1973 Obituary 107
Van Cleve, John Walter 1950- 122
Van Cleve, Thomas Curtis 1888-1976 ......41-44R
Obituary 65-68
Van Coevering, Jack
See Van Coevering, Jan Adrian
Van Coevering, Jan Adrian 1900- CAP-1
Earlier sketch in CA 9-10
van Corstanje, Auspicius
See van Corstanje, Charles
van Corstanje, Charles 1913- 107
van Croonenburg, Engelbert J(ohannes)
1909- 37-40R
Van Dahm, Thomas E(dward) 1924- 65-68
Van Dalen, Deobold B(ertrude) 1911- CANR-20
Earlier sketch in CA 1-4R
Van Dam, Ine 1947- 109
van Dam, J.
See Presser, (Gerrit) Jacob
Vande Kieft, Ruth Marguerite 1925- 17-20R
Van D'Elden, Karl H. 1923- 45-48
Vandeman, George E(dward)
1916- Brief entry 114
Vandenberg, Arthur Hendrick
1884-1951 Brief entry 120
Vandenberg, Donald 1931- 29-32R
Vandenberg, Philipp 1941- CANR-23
Earlier sketches in CA 61-64, CANR-8
Vandenberg, T. F. 1941- 25-28R
van den Berghe, Pierre L. 1933- CANR-5
Earlier sketch in CA 9-12R
Van Den Bogarde, Derek Jules Gaspard Ulric Niven
1921- 77-80
See also Bogarde, Dirk
Vandenbosch, Amry 1894- 61-64
Vandenbosch, Robert 1922-1978 Obituary 107
VandenBroeck, Andre 1923- 128
Vandenburg, Mary Lou 1943- 73-76
See also SATA 17
Vandenburgh, Jane ....CLC 59
Vandenburgh, Mildred 1898- 97-100
Vandenbusche, Duane (Lee) 1937- CANR-24
Earlier sketch in CA 45-48
van den Bussche, Henri O(mer) A(ntoine)
See Bussche, Henri O(mer) A(ntoine) Van den
van den Haag, Ernest 1914- CANR-26
Earlier sketches in CA 5-8R, CANR-6
van den Heuvel, Albert H(endrik) 1932- 17-20R
van den Heuvel, Cornelisz A. 1931- 13-16R
vanden Heuvel, Katrina 1959- 133
Van De Pitte, Frederick P. 1932- 45-48
Vander, Harry J(oseph) III 1913- CAP-2
Earlier sketch in CA 25-28
VanDerBeets, Richard 1932- CANR-35
Earlier sketch in CA 29-32R
van der Bent, Ans J(oachim) 1924- 131
Vanderbilt, Amy 1908-1974 ....CANR-3
Obituary 53-56
Earlier sketch in CA 1-4R
Vanderbilt, Arthur T. II 1950- 122
Vanderbilt, Cornelius Jr. 1898-1974 .... CAP-1
Obituary 49-52
Earlier sketch in CA 9-10
See also AITN 1
Vanderbilt, Gloria (Laura Morgan)
1924- CANR-22
Earlier sketch in CA 89-92
Vander Boom, Mae M. ....SATA 14
Vanderburgh, R(osamond) M(oate) 1926- 105
Vander-Els, Betty 1936- ....SATA 63
Vander Goot, Mary 1947- 112
Vandergriff, (Lola) Aola 1920-1989 ....CANR-18
Obituary 128
Earlier sketch in CA 89-92
Vanderhaar, Gerard A(nthony) 1931- 125
Vanderhaeghe, Guy 1951- 113
See also CLC 41
van der Heyden, A(ntonius) A(lphonsus) M(aria)
1922- CANR-7
Earlier sketch in CA 57-60
Vander Hill, C(harles) Warren 1937- 33-36R
VanDerhoof, Jack W(arner) 1921- 53-56
Van der Horst, Brian 1944- 41-44R
Vander Kooi, Ronald C(harles) CANR-2
Earlier sketch in CA 45-48
van der Kroef, Justus M(aria) 1925- CANR-14
Earlier sketch in CA 41-44R
Vanderlip, D(odava) George 1926- CANR-15
Earlier sketch in CA 77-80
Vander Lugt, Herbert 1920- CANR-18
Earlier sketch in CA 101
van der Marck, Jan 1929- 119
van der Merwe, Nikolaas J(ohannes)
1940- CANR-35
Earlier sketch in CA 41-44R
van der Meulen, Daniel 1894- 117
VanderMolen, Robert 1947- CANR-36
Earlier sketch in CA 57-60
van der Plas, Rob(ert) 1938- 138
van der Ploeg, Johannes P(etrus) M(aria)
1909- CANR-15
Earlier sketches in CAP-1, CA 9-10
van der Poel, Cornelius J(ohannes)
1921- CANR-4
Earlier sketch in CA 53-56
Vanderpool, Harold Y(oung) 1936- 53-56
Vanderpool, James A(lbert)
1916-1983 Obituary 109
van der Post, Laurens (Jan) 1906- CANR-35
Earlier sketch in CA 5-8R
See also CLC 5
Van Dersal, William R(ichard) 1907-1990 77-80
Obituary 131
Vander-Schrier, Nettie 1922- 114
Vandersee, Charles (Andrew) 1938- CANR-29
Earlier sketch in CA 41-44R
Van Der Slik, Jack R(onald) 1936- CANR-30
Earlier sketch in CA 29-32R
van der Smissen, Betty
See van der Smissen, Margaret Elisabeth
van der Smissen, Margaret Elisabeth
1927- CANR-9
Earlier sketch in CA 17-20R
Van der Spiel, Luigi 1920- 102
van der Vat, Dan(iel Francis Jeroen)
1939- CANR-28
Earlier sketch in CA 109
Vanderveen, Bareld Harmannus 1932- 103
Vanderveen, Bart H.
See Vanderveen, Bareld Harmannus
Van der Veer, Judy 1912-1982 ....33-36R
Obituary 108
See also SATA 4, 33
Vandervelde, Marjorie (Mills) 1908- CANR-10
Earlier sketch in CA 21-24R
Van der Veldt, James
1893(?)-1977 Obituary 73-76
Van der Veur, Paul W. 1921- 21-24R
Van Der Voort, Richard Lee 1936- 37-40R
Vanderwall, Francis W(illiam) 1946- CANR-26
Earlier sketch in CA 108
Van der Wee, Herman (Frans Anna) 1928- 133
Vanderwerken, David L(eon) 1945- 119
Vanderwerth, W(illiam) C(onnor) 1904- 73-76
Vanderwood, Paul J(oseph) 1929- CANR-28
Earlier sketch in CA 29-32R
Vander Zanden, James Wilfrid 1930- CANR-19
Earlier sketches in CA 13-16R, CANR-5
van der Zee, Henri (Antony)
1934- Brief entry 114
Van Der Zee, James (Augustus Joseph)
1886-1983 104
Obituary 109
van der Zee, John 1936- CANR-32
Earlier sketches in CA 21-24R, CANR-15
Vanderzell, John H. 1924- 45-48
VanderZwaag, Harold J. 1929- CANR-23
Earlier sketch in CA 45-48
van Deurs, George 1901- 25-28R
van Deursen, A. Th. 1931- 138
Van Deusen, Dayton G(roff) 1914- 9-12R
Van Deusen, Glyndon Garlock 1897- CANR-1
Earlier sketch in CA 1-4R
Van Deusen, L. Marshall 1922- 61-64
Van Deusen, Ruth B(rown) 1907- 5-8R
Van De Vall, Mark 1923- CANR-30
Earlier sketches in CA 29-32R, CANR-12
Van Devander, Charles W(ood)
1902-1986 Obituary 121
Van Devanter, Lynda (Margaret) 1947- 117

Van de Vate, Dwight Jr. 1928- 61-64
Vande Velde, Vivian 1951- ....SATA 62
Van Deventer, David E(arl)
 1937- Brief entry 115
Van Deventer, Fred 1903-1971 ....CAP-1
 Earlier sketch in CA 13-16
VanDeventer, Robert 105
Van de Water, Frederic F(ranklyn)
 1890-1968 Obituary 110
van de Wetering, Janwillem 1931- CANR-4
 Earlier sketch in CA 49-52
 See also CLC 47
Van Dine, S. S.
 See Wright, Willard Huntington
 See also TCLC 23
Vandiver, Edward P(inckney) Jr. 1902- CAP-1
 Earlier sketch in CA 13-14
Vandiver, Frank E(verson) 1925- CANR-7
 Earlier sketch in CA 5-8R
Vandivert, Rita (Andre) 1905- CANR-6
 Earlier sketch in CA 5-8R
 See also SATA 21
Van Domelen, John E(mory) 1935- 130
Van Dommelen, David B. 1929- CANR-35
 Earlier sketch in CA 5-8R
van Dooren, Ingrid 1949- 114
Van Dooren, L(eonard) A(lfred) T(heophile)
 1912- CANR-19
 Earlier sketches in CA 5-8R, CANR-3
Van Doren, Carl (Clinton)
 1885-1950 Brief entry 111
 See also TCLC 18
Van Doren, Charles L. 1926- CANR-4
 Earlier sketch in CA 5-8R
Van Doren, Dorothy Graffe 1896- 1-4R
Van Doren, Irita 1891-1966 Obituary 89-92
Van Doren, Mark 1894-1972 ....CANR-3
 Obituary 37-40R
 Earlier sketch in CA 1-4R
 See also CLC 6, 10
 See also DLB 45
 See also MTCW
Van Dorne, R.
 See Wallmann, Jeffrey M(iner)
Vandour, Cyril
 See Surmelian, Leon (Zaven)
Van Druten, John (William)
 1901-1957 Brief entry 104
 See also DLB 10
 See also TCLC 2
Van Dusen, Albert E(dward) 1916- CANR-3
 Earlier sketch in CA 5-8R
Van Dusen, Clarence Raymond 1907- 5-8R
Van Dusen, Henry P(itney) 1897-1975 ....CANR-3
 Obituary 57-60
 Earlier sketch in CA 1-4R
Van Dusen, Robert LaBranche 1929- 41-44R
Van Duyn, Janet 1910- 69-72
 See also SATA 18
Van Duyn, Mona (Jane) 1921- CANR-38
 Earlier sketches in CA 9-12R, CANR-7
 See also CLC 3, 7, 63
 See also DLB 5
Van Duzee, Mabel 1895- 5-8R
Van Dyk, Jere
 See Van Dyk, Wilmer Jerald
Van Dyk, Wilmer Jerald 1945- 131
Van Dyke, Carolynn 1947- 116
Van Dyke, Dick 1925- Brief entry 112
Van Dyke, Henry 1852-1933 ....DLB 71
Van Dyke, Henry 1928- CANR-25
 Earlier sketch in CA 49-52
 See also BW
 See also DLB 33
Van Dyke, Jon M. 1943- 29-32R
Van Dyke, Lauren A. 1906- 29-32R
Van Dyke, Vernon Brumbaugh 1912- CANR-23
 Earlier sketch in CA 1-4R
Van Dyne, Edith
 See Baum, L(yman) Frank
  and Sampson, Emma (Keats) Speed
  and van Zantwijk, Rudolf (Alexander Marinus)
Vane, Brett
 See Kent, Arthur William Charles
Vane, Michael
 See Humphries, Sydney Vernon
Vane, Roland
 See McKeag, Ernest L(ionel)
Vane, (Vane Hunt) Sutton
 1888-1963 Obituary 113
 See also DLB 10
Van Eerde, Katherine S(ommerlatte)
 1920- 61-64
Van Egmond, Peter (George) 1937- 61-64
Vanek, Jaroslav 1930- 103
Van Engen, John H. 1947- 117
Van Ermengem, Frederic
 1881-1972 Obituary 33-36R
Van Erven, Eugene 1955- 138
Van Ess, Dorothy 1885(?)-1975 Obituary 61-64
Van Ettinger, Jan 1902- CANR-21
 Earlier sketch in CA 1-4R
Van Every, Dale 1896-1976 ....CANR-3
 Earlier sketch in CA 1-4R
Vane-Wright, R(ichard) I(rwin) 1942- 121
Van Fossen, Richard W(aight) 1927- CANR-6
 Earlier sketch in CA 5-8R
van Fraassen, Bastiaan Cornelis CANR-14
 Earlier sketch in CA 37-40R
van Geert, Paul 1950- 132
Van Geil, Mercury E. C. L.
 See McGilvery, Laurence
van Gelder, Dora 1904- Brief entry 116
Van Gelder, Lindsy 1944- 97-100
Van Gelder, Richard George 1928- 73-76
Vangelisti, Paul 1945- CANR-31
 Earlier sketches in CA 77-80, CANR-14
Vangen, Roland Dean 1935- 105
Vanger, Milton Isadore 1925- CANR-34
 Earlier sketch in CA 13-16R
Van Goethem, Larry 1934- 101
van Gulik, Robert Hans 1910-1967 ....CANR-3
 Obituary 25-28R
 Earlier sketch in CA 1-4R
VanGundy, Arthur B(oice) Jr. 1946- CANR-29
 Earlier sketch in CA 110
Van Haaften, Julia 1946- 109
Van Hassen, Amy
 See Wiles, Domini
Van Hattum, Rolland J(ames) 1924- CANR-21
 Earlier sketch in CA 105
Van Hecke, B(resee) C(oleman) 1926- 29-32R
Van Heijenoort, Jean 1912-1986 Obituary 120
Van Helden, Albert 1940- 125
Van Herik, Judith 1947- 108
van Herk, Aritha 1954- 101
van het Reve, Karel 1921- 49-52
van Heyningen, Christina 1900- 17-20R
van Heyningen, William Edward 1911- 112
Van Hise, Della 1955- 121
Van Hoesen, Walter H.
 1898(?)-1977 Obituary 69-72
Van Hook, Roger Eugene 1943- 29-32R
Van Hoose, William H. 1927- 89-92
Van Horn, Richard L. 1932- 53-56
Van Horn, William 1939- 115
 See also SATA 43
Van Horne, Harriet 1920- Brief entry 113
Van Houten, Lois 1918- CANR-34
 Earlier sketch in CA 77-80
Van Huss, Wayne D(aniel) 1917- 61-64
van Inwagen, Peter (Jan) 1942- CANR-39
 Earlier sketch in CA 116
van Itallie, Jean-Claude 1936- CANR-1
 Earlier sketch in CA 45-48
 See also CAAS 2
 See also CLC 3
 See also DLB 7
Van Itallie, Philip H. 1899- CAP-1
 Earlier sketch in CA 9-10
Van Iterson, S(iny) R(ose) 102
 See also SATA 26
van Jaarsveld, Floris Albertus 1922- CANR-7
 Earlier sketch in CA 5-8R
van Kaam, Adrian (L) 1920- CANR-26
 Earlier sketches in CA 17-20R, CANR-10
Van Kampen, Vlasta 1943- ....SATA 54
Van Kleek, Peter Eric 1929- CANR-35
 Earlier sketch in CA 53-56
Van Krevelen, Alice 1914- 45-48
van Lawick, Hugo 1937- 85-88
van Lawick-Goodall, Jane
 See Goodall, Jane
Vanleer, Jay
 See Williams, June Vanleer
Van Leeuwen, Jean 1937- CANR-28
 Earlier sketches in CA 25-28R, CANR-11
 See also SAAS 8
 See also SATA 6
Van Lente, Charles R(obert) 1941- 65-68
van Lhin, Erik
 See del Rey, Lester
Van Lierde, John 1907- CAP-1
 Earlier sketch in CA 9-10
Van Lierde, Peter Canisius
 See Van Lierde, John
van Lint, June 1928- 65-68
van Loon, Gerard Willem 1911- 45-48
Van Loon, Hendrik Willem
 1882-1944 Brief entry 117
 See also SATA 18
Van Meerhaeghe, M(arcel) A(lfons) G(ilbert)
 1921- CANR-13
 Earlier sketch in CA 77-80
Van Melsen, Andreas G(erardus) M(aria)
 1912- CANR-34
 Earlier sketches in CA 1-4R, CANR-4
Vann, J(erry) Don 1938- 29-32R
Vann, James Allen 1939- 110
Vann, Richard T(ilman) 1931- 21-24R
Vann, Robert L. 1879-1940 ....DLB 29
Vannatta, Dennis 1946- 138
Vanneman, Reeve 1945- 127
Van Ness, Peter 1933- 29-32R
Van Niel, Cornelius B(ernardus)
 1897-1985 Obituary 115
Vannier, Maryhelen 1915- CANR-22
 Earlier sketches in CA 1-4R, CANR-6
van Nieuwenhuijze, C(hristoffel) A(nthonie) O(livier)
 1920- 25-28R
Van Nimmen, (Carol) Jane 1937- 125
Van Nooten, Barend A(drian) 1932- 45-48
Van Noppen, Ina (Faye) W(oestemeyer)
 1906-1980 ....5-8R
 Obituary 103
Vannorsdall, John Warren 1924- 113
Van Nostrand, A(lbert) D(ouglass)
 1922- CANR-16
 Earlier sketch in CA 41-44R
Vannoy, Russell (Columbus) 1933- 119
Vano, Gerard S. 1943- 112
Vanocur, Edith C. 1924(?)-1975 Obituary 57-60
Vanocur, Sander 1928- 120
 Brief entry 109
van Oort, Jan 1921- CANR-31
 Earlier sketch in CA 29-32R
Van Orden, M(erton) D(ick) 1921- 37-40R
 See also SATA 4
Van Orman, Bonny 1939(?)-1987 Obituary 122
Van Orman, Richard A(lbert) 1936- CANR-34
 Earlier sketch in CA 21-24R
Van Osdol, William R(ay) 1927- 53-56
van Ostaijen, Paul 1896-1928 ....TCLC 33
Van Over, Raymond 1934- Brief entry 112
van Overbeek, Johannes 1908- CAP-1
 Earlier sketch in CA 13-14
Van Peebles, Melvin 1932- CANR-27
 Earlier sketch in CA 85-88
 See also BW
 See also CLC 2, 20
van Peursen, Cornelius Anthonie 1920- 53-56
Van Praagh, Margaret 1910-1990 ....CAP-2
 Obituary 130
 Earlier sketch in CA 17-18
Van Praagh, Peggy
 See Van Praagh, Margaret
Van Proosdy, Cornelis 1919- CANR-5
 Earlier sketch in CA 9-12R
van Ravenswaay, Charles 1911- 119
Van Rensselaer, Alexander (Taylor Mason)
 1892-1962 73-76
 See also SATA 14
Van Rensselaer, Mariana Griswold
 1851-1934 ....DLB 47
Van Rensselaer, Mrs. Schuyler
 See Van Rensselaer, Mariana Griswold
Van Rheenen, Gailyn 1946- 69-72
van Rijn, Ignatius
 See Ingram, Forrest L(eo)
Van Riper, Francis A(lbert) 1946- CANR-11
 Earlier sketch in CA 69-72
Van Riper, Frank
 See Van Riper, Francis A(lbert)
Van Riper, Guernsey Jr. 1909- CANR-6
 Earlier sketch in CA 5-8R
 See also SATA 3
Van Riper, Paul P(ritchard) 1916- CANR-31
 Earlier sketch in CA 1-4R
Van Riper, Robert 1921- 37-40R
van Rjndt, Philippe 1950- CANR-14
 Earlier sketch in CA 65-68
van Rooy, C(harles) A(ugust) 1923- 17-20R
Van Saher, Lilla 1912-1968 ....CAP-1
 Earlier sketch in CA 11-12
Vansant, Carl 1938- 37-40R
Van Schaick, Frances L.
 1912(?)-1979 Obituary 89-92
Van Scyoc, Sydney J(oyce) 1939- CANR-33
 Earlier sketches in CA 89-92, CANR-15
Van See, John
 See Vance, John Holbrook
Van Sertima, Ivan 1935- 104
Van Seters, John 1935- CANR-38
 Earlier sketch in CA 115
Van Sickle, John V(alentine) 1892- CANR-35
 Earlier sketch in CA 5-8R
Van Sickle, Neil D(avid) 1915- 41-44R
VanSickle, V. A.
 See Carhart, Arthur Hawthorne
Vansina, Jan 1929- CANR-10
 Earlier sketch in CA 65-68
Vansittart, Jane
 See Moorhouse, Hilda Vansittart
Vansittart, Peter 1920- CANR-3
 Earlier sketch in CA 1-4R
 See also CLC 42
Van Slingerland, Peter 1929- 21-24R
Van Slooten, Henry 1916- 1-4R
Van Slyck, Philip 1920- 13-16R
Van Slyke, Donald Dexter
 1883-1971 Obituary 104
Van Slyke, Helen (Lenore)
 1919-1979 ....CANR-28
 Obituary 89-92
 Earlier sketch in CA 37-40R
Van Slyke, Lyman P(age) 1929- 21-24R
Van Smith, Howard
 See Smith, Howard Van
van Someren. Liesje
 See Lichtenberg, Elisabeth Jacoba
Van Steenberghen, Fernand (Emmanuel)
 1904- 130
Van Steenwyk, Elizabeth (Ann) 1928- CANR-18
 Earlier sketch in CA 101
 See also SATA 34
Van Stockum, Hilda 1908- CANR-5
 Earlier sketch in CA 9-12R
 See also SATA 5
van Straten, Florence W(ilhelmina)
 1913- 17-20R
 Obituary 137
Van Tassel, Alfred J. 1910- 41-44R
Van Tassel, David Dirck 1928- CANR-35
 Earlier sketch in CA 103
Van Tassel, Dennie L(ee) 1939- CANR-35
 Earlier sketches in CA 57-60, CANR-8
Van Tassel, George W.
 1910-1978 Obituary 112
Van Tassel, Roger (Carleton) 1924- 45-48
van Thal, Herbert (Maurice)
 1904-1983 ....CANR-30
 Obituary 111
 Earlier sketch in CA 65-68
Van Til, Cornelius 1895- CANR-3
 Earlier sketch in CA 1-4R
Van Til, William 1911- CANR-10
 Earlier sketch in CA 25-28R
Van Tine, Warren R(ussell) 1942- 53-56
Van Trump, James D(enholm) 1908- 41-44R
Van Tuyl, Barbara 1940- 53-56
 See also SATA 11
Van Valkenburg, Samuel 1891-1976 ....5-8R
 Obituary 103
Van Valkenburgh, Paul 1941- 89-92
Van Vechten, Benjamin D(avenport) 1935- 110
Van Vechten, Carl 1880-1964 Obituary 89-92
 See also CLC 33
 See also DLB 4, 9, 51
Van Vleck, David B. 1929- 101
Van Vleck, John Hasbrouck
 1899-1980 Obituary 102
Van Vleck, L(loyd) Dale 1933- 53-56
Van Vleck, Sarita 1933- 13-16R
Van Vlissingen, Arthur 1894-1986 Obituary 120
Van Vogt, A(lfred) E(lton) 1912- CANR-28
 Earlier sketch in CA 21-24R
 See also CLC 1
 See also DLB 8
 See also SATA 14
Van Vooren, Monique 1933- 107
Van Voorhis, Linda Lyon
 1902-1989 Obituary 129
Van Voris, Jacqueline 1922- 57-60
van Vuuren, Nancy 1938- CANR-35
 Earlier sketch in CA 49-52
Van Wagenen, Gertrude
 1893-1978 Obituary 77-80
van Wageningen, J.
 See Presser, (Gerrit) Jacob
Van Wart, Alice 1948- 137
Van Waters, Miriam 1887-1974 Obituary 45-48
Van Weddingen, Marthe 1924- CANR-14
 Earlier sketch in CA 81-84
Van Wert, William F(rancis) 1945- 105
Van Winckel, Nance 1951- 131
van Witsen, Leo 1912- 106
Van Woeart, Alpheus
 See Halloway, Vance
Van Woerkom, Dorothy (O'Brien)
 1924- CANR-26
 Earlier sketches in CA 57-60, CANR-11
 See also SATA 21
Van Wormer, Joe
 See Van Wormer, Joseph Edward
Van Wormer, Joseph Edward 1913- CANR-5
 Earlier sketch in CA 9-12R
 See also SATA 35
Van Wormer, Laura (Eleanor) 1955- 127
Van Young, Eric (Julian) 1946- 122
Van Zandt, E. F.
 See Cudlipp, Edythe
Van Zandt, Roland 1918-1991 ....17-20R
 Obituary 134
Van Zante, Helen Johnson 1906- 13-16R
Van Zanten, John W(illiam) 1913- 101
van Zantwijk, Rudolf (Alexander Marinus)
 1931- 133
van Zeller, Claud 1905-1984 ....CANR-6
 Obituary 113
 Earlier sketch in CA 1-4R
van Zeller, Hubert
 See van Zeller, Claud
Vanzi, Max (Bruno) 1934- 123
Van Zwienen, Ilse Charlotte Koehn
 1929-1991 ....CANR-35
 Earlier sketch in CA 85-88
 See also SATA 28, 34
 See also SATO 67
van Zwoll, James A. 1909- CAP-1
 Earlier sketch in CA 13-14
Van Zyl Slabbert, F.
 See Slabbert, F(rederik) Van Zyl
Vaqar, Nasrollah 1920- 41-44R
Vara, Albert C. 1931- CANR-35
 Earlier sketch in CA 33-36R
Vara, Madeleine
 See Jackson, Laura (Riding)
Varah, Chad 1911- 57-60
Varandyan, Emmanuel P(aul) 1904- 65-68
Varas, Florencia
 See Olea, Maria Florencia Varas
Varda, Agnes 1928- 122
 Brief entry 116
 See also CLC 16
Vardaman, E. Jerry 1927- 17-20R
Vardaman, George T(ruett) 1920- CANR-4
 Earlier sketch in CA 1-4R
Vardaman, James M(oney) 1921- 104
Vardaman, Patricia B(lack) 1931- 37-40R
Vardamis, Alex A. 1934- 77-80
Varderi, Alejandro 1960- ....HW
Vardey, Lucinda 1949- 128
Vardre, Leslie
 See Davies, L(eslie) P(urnell)
Vardy, Steven Bela 1936- CANR-19
 Earlier sketches in CA 53-56, CANR-4
Vardys, V(ytautas) Stanley 1924- CANR-5
 Earlier sketch in CA 13-16R
Vare, Daniele 1880-1956 Brief entry 119
Vare, Ethlie Ann 1953- 127
Vare, Robert 1945- 103
Varenhorst, Barbara B(raden) 1928- 116
Varese, Louise 1890-1989 ....41-44R
 Obituary 129
Varey, Simon 1951- 135
Varg, Paul A(lbert) 1912- 118
 Brief entry 113
Varga, Andrew Charles 1917- 113
Varga, Balint Andras 1941- 132
Varga, Judy
 See Stang, Judit
Vargas, Julie S. 1938- CANR-34
 Earlier sketch in CA 57-60
Vargas Llosa, (Jorge) Mario (Pedro)
 1936- CANR-32
 Earlier sketches in CA 73-76, CANR-18
 See also CLC 3, 6, 9, 10, 15, 31, 42
 See also HW
 See also MTCW
Vargish, Thomas 1939- CANR-14
 Earlier sketch in CA 37-40R
Varia, Radu 1940- 128
Varlay, Rene G. 1927- 1-4R
Varley, Dimitry V. 1906- CAP-1
 Earlier sketch in CA 17-18
 See also SATA 10
Varley, Gloria 1932- 101
Varley, H(erbert) Paul 1931- 77-80

Varley, John (Herbert) 1947- CANR-25
Earlier sketch in CA 69-72
See also DLBY 81
Varley, John Philip
See Mitchell, Langdon (Elwyn)
Varley, Susan 1961- ....SATA 63
Varma, Baidya Nath 1921- 41-44R
Varma, Devendra P. 1923- Brief entry 113
Varma, Monika 1916- 77-80
Varnac, d'Hugues
See Prevost, Alain
Varnado, Jewel Goodgame 1915- 9-12R
Varnalis, Costas 1884-1974 Obituary 53-56
Varner, Jeannette J.
See Varner, Jeannette Johnson
Varner, Jeannette Johnson 1909- 132
Varner, John Grier 1905-1978 ....25-28R
Obituary 120
Varner, Velma V. 1916-1972 Obituary 37-40R
Varney, Carleton B(ates) 1937- CANR-16
Earlier sketch in CA 89-92
Varney, Philip 1943- 125
Varnhagen von Ense, Karl August
1785-1858 ....DLB 90
Varnhagen von Ense, Rahel 1771-1833 ....DLB 90
Vars, Gordon F(orrest) 1923- 21-24R
Vartan, Vartanig G(arabed) 1923-1988 61-64
Obituary 125
Vartanian, Aram 1922- CANR-3
Earlier sketch in CA 1-4R
Vasconcelos (Calderon), Jose
1882-1959 Brief entry 118
Vas Dias, Robert (Leonard Michael)
1931- CANR-7
Earlier sketch in CA 17-20R
Vasey, Lloyd Roland 113
Vash, Carolyn L(ee) 1934- 121
Vash, Carolyn Lee 1934- Brief entry 116
Vasil, R(aj) K(umar) 1931- CANR-14
Earlier sketch in CA 37-40R
Vasiliu, Gheorghe 1881-1957 Brief entry 123
See also Bacovia, George
Vasiliu, Mircea 1920- 21-24R
See also SATA 2
Vaske, Martin O. 1915- CANR-2
Earlier sketch in CA 5-8R
Vasquez, John A(nthony) 1945- 108
Vasquez, Richard 1928- 131
See also HW
Vass, George 1927- 37-40R
See also SATA 31, 57
Vass, Winifred Kellersberger 1917- 57-60
Vassa, Gustavus
See Equiano, Olaudah
Vassanji, M(oyez) G. 1950- 136
Vassberg, David E(rland) 1936- 131
Vassi, Marco 1937- CANR-13
Earlier sketch in CA 61-64
Vassilikos, Vassilis 1933- 81-84
See also CLC 4, 8
Vassiliou, Yannis 1949- 117
Vasta, Edward 1928- 17-20R
Vasu, Nirmala-Kumara
See Bose, N(irmal) K(umar)
Vasvary, Edmund 1888-1977 Obituary 73-76
Vatikiotis, P(anayiotis) J(erasimos)
1928- CANR-28
Earlier sketches in CA 13-16R, CANR-6
Vatter, Harold Goodhue 1910- 5-8R
Vaudrin, Bill
See Vaudrin, William
Vaudrin, William 1943-1976 ....CAP-2
Earlier sketch in CA 29-32
Vaughan, Adrian 1941- 120
Vaughan, Agnes Carr 1887- CAP-1
Earlier sketch in CA 9-10
Vaughan, Alan 1936- 81-84
Vaughan, Alden T. 1929- CANR-7
Earlier sketch in CA 17-20R
Vaughan, Beatrice
1909(?)-1972 Obituary 37-40R
Vaughan, Bill
See Vaughan, William E(dward)
Vaughan, Carter A.
See Gerson, Noel Bertram
Vaughan, Clark (Alvord) 1924- 108
Vaughan, David 1924- 77-80
Vaughan, Denis 1920- 61-64
Vaughan, Donald S(hores) 1921- CANR-10
Earlier sketch in CA 17-20R
Vaughan, Frances E. 1935- 125
Brief entry 107
Vaughan, Frederick 1935- 120
Vaughan, Harold Cecil 1923- 29-32R
See also SATA 14
Vaughan, Hilda
See Morgan, Hilda Campbell
Vaughan, James A(gnew) 1936- 49-52
Vaughan, John Edmund 1935- 61-64
Vaughan, Leo
See Lendon, Kenneth Harry
Vaughan, Marcia 1951- ....SATA 60
Vaughan, Paul 1925- 29-32R
Vaughan, Richard
See Thomas, Ernest Lewys
Vaughan, Richard Patrick 1919- 13-16R
Vaughan, Robert (Richard) 1937- 103
Vaughan, Roger 1937- 85-88
Vaughan, Sam(uel) 1928- 13-16R
See also SATA 14
Vaughan, Sheila Marie 1930- 21-24R
Vaughan, Virginia M(ason) 1947- 110
Vaughan, William E(dward) 1915-1977 ....5-8R
Obituary 69-72
Vaughan-Thomas, (Lewis John) Wynford
1908-1987 130
Vaughan Williams, Ralph
1872-1958 Brief entry 115
Vaughan Williams, Ursula Wood
1911- CANR-24
Earlier sketches in CA 9-12R, CANR-6
Vaughn, Charles L(e Claire) 1911- 41-44R
Vaughn, Donald E(arl) 1932- 21-24R
Vaughn, Jack A(lfred) 1935- 85-88
Vaughn, Jesse Wendell 1903-1968 ....1-4R
Obituary 103
Vaughn, Lewis 1950- 111
Vaughn, Michael J(effery) 1943- 37-40R
Vaughn, Richard C(lements) 1925- CANR-9
Earlier sketch in CA 21-24R
Vaughn, Robert (Francis) 1932- 61-64
Vaughn, Ruth 1935- CANR-15
Earlier sketch in CA 41-44R
See also SATA 14
Vaughn, Sally N(orthrop) 1939- 126
Vaughn, Sister Ann Carol 1922- 9-12R
Vaughn, Stephanie ....CLC 62
Vaughn, Stephen L. 1947- 101
Vaughn, Toni
See Du Breuil, (Elizabeth) L(or)inda
Vaughn, William Preston 1933- 73-76
Vaught, Jacque
See Brogan, Jacqueline Vaught
Vaupel, James W(alton) 1945- 111
Vaurie, Charles 1906-1975 ....CANR-4
Earlier sketch in CA 5-8R
Vaussard, Maurice (Rene Jean Arthur Andre)
1888- 9-12R
Vautier, Ghislaine 1932- 112
See also SATA 53
Vavra, Robert James 1935- CANR-25
Earlier sketch in CA 25-28R
See also SATA 8
Vawter, F(rancis) Bruce 1921- CANR-4
Earlier sketch in CA 1-4R
Vayda, Andrew P. 1931- 17-20R
Vayhinger, John Monroe 1916- 73-76
Vayle, Valerie
See Brooks, Janice Young
Vaz, Edmund (Winston) 1924- 108
Vazakas, Byron 1905- CAP-2
Earlier sketch in CA 25-28
Vazov, Ivan (Minchov)
1850-1921 Brief entry 121
See also TCLC 25
Vazquez Amaral, Jose 1913-1987 ....HW
Veach, William B. Templeton 1896- CAP-1
Earlier sketch in CA 9-10
Veaner, Allen B(arnet) 1929- 41-44R
Veatch, Henry Babcock 1911- CANR-6
Earlier sketch in CA 5-8R
Veatch, Robert M(arlin) 1939- CANR-11
Earlier sketch in CA 69-72
Veber, Francis 1937- 135
Veblen, Thorstein (Bunde)
1857-1929 Brief entry 115
See also TCLC 31
Vecoli, Rudolph J(ohn) 1927- CANR-26
Earlier sketches in CA 17-20R, CANR-10
Vecsey, George S. 1909(?)-1984 Obituary 114
Vecsey, George Spencer 1939- CANR-10
Earlier sketch in CA 61-64
See also SATA 9
Vedder, James S(herman) 1912- 117
Vedder, John K.
See Gruber, Frank
Vedder, Richard K(ent) 1940- 115
Vedeler, Harold C. 1903- 122
Veder, Bob 1940- 104
Vedral, Joyce L(auretta) 1943- 117
See also SATA 65
Veeck, Bill
See Veeck, William Louis Jr.
Veeck, William Louis Jr.
1914-1986 Obituary 118
Veedam, Voldemar 1912-1983 Obituary 109
Veenendaal, Cornelia 1924- 117
Vega, Janine Pommy 1942- CANR-2
Earlier sketch in CA 49-52
See also DLB 16
Veglahn, Nancy (Crary) 1937- CANR-7
Earlier sketch in CA 17-20R
See also SATA 5
Vehr, Bill 1940(?)-1988 Obituary 126
Veiga, Jose J(acinto da) 1915- CANR-33
Earlier sketches in CA 37-40R, CANR-15
Veiller, Anthony 1903-1965 ....DLB 44
Veillon, Lee 1942- 49-52
Veit, Fritz 1907- 111
Veit, Lawrence A. 1938- Brief entry 115
Veit, Stan(ley Stanford) 1929- 110
Vekemans, Roger 1921- 37-40R
Velasquez, Manuel G(onzales) 1942- 113
Veler, Richard P(aul) 1936- 49-52
Velez-Ibanez, Carlos G(uillermo) 1936- 118
See also HW
Velie, Alan R. 1937- CANR-1
Earlier sketch in CA 45-48
Velie, Lester 1908- CAP-2
Earlier sketch in CA 17-18
Velikovsky, Immanuel 1895-1979 ....CANR-15
Obituary 89-92
Earlier sketch in CA 69-72
Veliz, Claudio 1930- 25-28R
Veljanovski, (G.) Cento 1953- 128
Vella, Walter F(rancis) 1924- CANR-24
Earlier sketch in CA 45-48
Vellacott, Jo 1922- 126
Vellela, Tony 1945- 65-68
Velleman, Ruth A(nn) 1921- 110
Veloz Maggiolo, Marcio E. 1936- ....HW
Velthuijs, Max 1923- 89-92
See also SATA 53
Veltman, Vera
See Panova, Vera (Fedorovna)
Velvel, Lawrence R. 1939- 29-32R
Venable, Alan (Hudson) 1944- 45-48
See also SATA 8
Venable, Tom C(alvin) 1921- 29-32R
Venable, Vernon 1906- CAP-2
Earlier sketch in CA 21-22
Venafro, Mark
See Pizzat, Frank J(oseph)
Vencent, Gabrielle (a pseudonym) 126
Vendler, Helen (Hennessy) 1933- CANR-25
Earlier sketch in CA 41-44R
See also MTCW
Vendler, Zeno 1921- 126
Brief entry 105
Vendrovskii, David Efimovich
1879-1971 Obituary 33-36R
Vendrovsky, David
See Vendrovskii, David Efimovich
Venegas, Daniel ....DLB 82
Veness, Molly 1900(?)-1985 Obituary 118
Veness, (Winifred) Thelma 1919-1971 ....5-8R
Obituary 122
Vengroff, Richard 1945- CANR-10
Earlier sketch in CA 65-68
Venison, Alfred
See Pound, Ezra (Weston Loomis)
Veniste, Richard Ben
See Ben-Veniste, Richard
Venn, Grant 1919-1979 ....13-16R
Obituary 122
Vennard, Edwin 1902- CAP-2
Earlier sketch in CA 25-28
Vennema, Alje 1932- 101
Venner, J. G.
See Lewis, John (Noel Claude)
Venning, Corey 1924- 49-52
Venning, Hugh
See van Zeller, Claud
Venning, Michael
See Randolph, Georgiana Ann
Venter, Al(bertus) J(ohannes) 1938- 117
Venton, W. B. 1898-1976 ....CAP-2
Earlier sketch in CA 25-28
Ventura, Jeffrey
See Feinman, Jeffrey
Ventura, Piero (Luigi) 1937- CANR-39
Earlier sketch in CA 103
See also CLR 16
See also MAICYA
See also SATA 43, 61
Venturi, Denise Scott Brown
See Brown, Denise Scott
Venturi, Franco 1914- 130
Venturi, Marcello 1925- CANR-13
Earlier sketch in CA 29-32R
Venturi, Robert 1925- 61-64
Venuti, Lawrence (Michael) 1953- 120
Vequin, Capini
See Quinn, Elisabeth
Verb, M. L.
See Tammeus, William David
Verba, Sidney 1932- CANR-3
Earlier sketch in CA 1-4R
Verbeke, Gerard 1910- 131
Verbitsky, Bernardo 1907- ....HW
Vercors
See Bruller, Jean (Marcel)
Vercors, J. Bruller
See Bruller, Jean (Marcel)
Verdenius, W(illem) J(acob) 1913- 25-28R
Verdery, John D(uane) 1917- 9-12R
Verdi, Marie de
See Mencken, H(enry) L(ouis)
Verdi, Richard 1941- 128
Verdick, Mary (Peyton) 1923- CANR-4
Earlier sketch in CA 1-4R
Verdon, Dorothy
See Tralins, S(andor) Robert
Verdu, Matilde
See Cela, Camilo Jose
Verduin, John R(ichard) Jr. 1931- CANR-24
Earlier sketches in CA 21-24R, CANR-9
Verduin, Leonard 1897- 61-64
Verene, Donald Phillip 1937- CANR-15
Earlier sketch in CA 41-44R
Verey, David (Cecil Wynter)
1913-1984 ....CANR-15
Obituary 113
Earlier sketch in CA 65-68
Verey, Rosemary 1918- 130
Verga, Giovanni (Carmelo) 1840-1922 123
Brief entry 104
See also TCLC 3
Vergani, Luisa 1931- 21-24R
Vergara, Jose Manuel 1929- 97-100
Vergara, Joseph R. 1915- 29-32R
Vergara, Lisa 1948- 120
Vergara, William C(harles) 1923- 1-4R
Verghese, T. Paul
See Gregorios, Paulos Mar
Verhaeren, Emile (Adolphe Gustave)
1855-1916 Brief entry 109
See also TCLC 12
Verhalen, Philip A(ndrew) 1934- 69-72
Verhoeven, Cornelis 1928- CANR-23
Earlier sketches in CA 61-64, CANR-8
Verhoeven, Paul 1901-1975 Obituary 115
Verhonick, Phillis J.
1922(?)-1977 Obituary 73-76
Verhoogen, John 1912- 109
Verin, Velko
See Inkiow, (Janakiev) Dimiter
Verissimo, Erico (Lopes)
1905-1975 Obituary 115
Verlaine, Paul (Marie) 1844-1896 ....PC 2
Vermes, Geza 1924- 57-60
Vermes, Jean C(ampbell Pattison) 1907- 106
Vermes, Pamela 1918- 118
Vermeule, Cornelius Clarkson III 1925- 41-44R
Vermeule, E(mily) D. T. 1928- 17-20R
Vermillion, Robert 1915(?)-1987 Obituary 122
Vernadsky, George 1887-1973 Obituary 41-44R
Vernam, Glenn R. 1896-1980 ....CANR-10
Earlier sketch in CA 17-20R
Vernant, Jean-Pierre 1914- CANR-29
Earlier sketch in CA 109
Vernazza, Marcelle Wynn 1909- CANR-10
Earlier sketch in CA 17-20R
Verne, Jules (Gabriel) 1828-1905 131
Brief entry 110
See also MAICYA
See also SATA 21
See also TCLC 6
Verner, Coolie 1917-1979 ....CANR-7
Earlier sketch in CA 53-56
Verner, Gerald 1897(?)-1980 Obituary 102
See also SATA 25
Verney, Douglas Vernon 1924- 13-16R
Verney, John 1913- 65-68
See also SATA 14
Verney, Michael P(almer) 1923- CANR-6
Earlier sketch in CA 13-16R
Verney, Peter (Vivian Lloyd) 1930- CANR-19
Earlier sketch in CA 81-84
Verney, Sarah
See Holloway, Brenda W(ilmar)
Verney, Stephen Edmund 1919- 104
Vernon, Eddie
See Stone, Hoyt E(dward)
Vernon, Edward
See Coleman, Vernon
Vernon, (Georgina) Frances 1963-1991 110
Obituary 135
Vernon, Glenn M(orley) 1920- 49-52
Vernon, John 1943- 41-44R
Vernon, Judy 1945- 119
Vernon, Lee M.
See von Block, Bela W(illiam)
Vernon, Lorraine 1921- 113
Vernon, (Elda) Louise A(nderson) 1914- 53-56
See also SATA 14
Vernon, McCay 1928- 41-44R
Vernon, Philip Ewart 1905-1987 ....CANR-12
Obituary 133
Earlier sketch in CA 5-8R
Vernon, Raymond 1913- CANR-18
Earlier sketches in CA 5-8R, CANR-2
Vernon, Rosemary
See Smith, Susan Vernon
Vernon, Thomas Bowater 1939- 118
Vernon, Thomas S. 1914- 25-28R
Vernon, Tom
See Vernon, Thomas Bowater
Vernon, Walter N(ewton) Jr. 1907- CANR-12
Earlier sketch in CA 17-20R
Vernon-Jackson, Hugh (Owen Hardinge)
1925- 21-24R
Vernor, D.
See Casewit, Curtis W(erner)
Verny, Tom 1936- 73-76
Veronica, Sister Mary 1924-1977 ....17-20R
Obituary 134
Verplanck, Gulian C. 1786-1870 ....DLB 59
Verr, Harry Coe
See Kunhardt, Edith
Verral, Charles Spain 1904-1990 ....CANR-37
Obituary 131
Earlier sketches in CAP-1, CA 9-10, CANR-16
See also SATA 11
See also SATO 65
Verrette, Joyce 1939- 129
Verrill, A(lpheus) Hyatt
1871-1954 Brief entry 111
Verrone, Robert J. 1935(?)-1984 Obituary 113
See also SATA 39
Versace, Marie Teresa Rios 1917- 17-20R
See also SATA 2
Ver Steeg, Clarence L(ester) 1922- 13-16R
Versteeg, Robert John 1930- 1-4R
Verval, Alain
See Lande, Lawrence (Montague)
Verwilghen, A(lbert-) Felix 1916- 25-28R
Verwoerdt, Adriaan 1927- 17-20R
Very, Alice (N.) 1894-1977 ....21-24R
Obituary 120
Very, Jones 1813-1880 ....DLB 1
Veryan, Patricia
See Bannister, Patricia V.
Vesaas, Tarjei 1897-1970 Obituary 29-32R
See also CLC 48
Vesely, Erik 1905(?)-1970 Obituary 57-60
Vesenyi, Paul E. 1911- 53-56
Veseth, Michael 1949- 135
Vesey, A(manda) 1939- 127
See also SATA 62
Vesey, Godfrey (Norman Agmondisham)
1923- 89-92
Vesey, Paul
See Allen, Samuel W(ashington)
Vesey-FitzGerald, Brian Seymour
1900-1981 104
Obituary 105
Vesper, Karl H(ampton) 1932- 115
Vess, David M(arshall) 1925- 89-92
Vessel, Matthew F. 1912- Brief entry 108
Vesselo, I(saac) Reginald 1903- CAP-2
Earlier sketch in CA 17-18
Vestal, David 1924- 89-92
Vestal, Edith Ballard 1884-1970 ....CAP-2
Earlier sketch in CA 25-28
Vestdijk, Simon 1898-1971 Obituary 89-92
Vester, Frederic 1925- 120

Vester, Horatio 1906-1985 ... CAP-1
Obituary ... 117
Earlier sketch in CA 13-14
Vesterman, William 1942- ... 89-92
Vestly, Anne-Cath(arina) 1920- ... CANR-18
Earlier sketch in CA 85-88
See also SATA 14
Vet, T. V.
See Straiton, E(dward) C(ornock)
Vetere, Richard 1952- ... 104
Vetoe, Miklos 1936- ... 49-52
Vetter, Carole 1939- ... 25-28R
Vetter, Harold J. 1926- ... 29-32R
Vetterling-Braggin, Mary (Katherine) 1947- ... 124
Veverka, Frank B. 1923(?)-1985 Obituary ... 117
Vevers, (Henry) Gwynne 1916-1988 ... 113
Obituary ... 126
See also SATA 45, 57
Vexillum
See Banner, Hubert Stewart
Veysey, Arthur (Ernest) 1914- ... 133
Veysey, Laurence R(uss) 1932- ... 21-24R
Vezhinov, Pavel
See Gougov, Nikola Delchev
Vial, Fernand (Louis) 1905- ... CANR-21
Earlier sketch in CA 1-4R
Vialis, Gaston
See Simenon, Georges (Jacques Christian)
Vian, Boris 1920-1959 Brief entry ... 106
See also DLB 72
See also TCLC 9
Viana, Javier de 1868-1926 ... HW
Viano, Emilio C. 1942- ... 107
Viansson-Ponte, Pierre 1920-1979 ... 101
Obituary ... 85-88
Viator, Vacuus
See Hughes, Thomas
Viaud, (Louis Marie) Julien
1850-1923 Brief entry ... 107
See also Loti, Pierre
Vicar, Henry
See Felsen, Henry Gregor
Vicarion, Count Palmiro
See Logue, Christopher
Vicary, Dorothy
See Rice, Dorothy Mary
Vicchio, Stephen (John) 1950- ... 138
Vichas, Robert P. 1933- ... CANR-14
Earlier sketch in CA 29-32R
Vicker, Angus
See Felsen, Henry Gregor
Vicker, Ray 1917- ... 61-64
Vickers
See Kaufman, Wallace
Vickers, Antoinette L. 1942- ... 103
Vickers, Douglas 1924- ... CANR-11
Earlier sketch in CA 13-16R
Vickers, (Charles) Geoffrey 1894-1982 ... 41-44R
Obituary ... 106
Vickers, Hugo (Ralph) 1951- ... 128
Brief entry ... 124
Vickers, John 1916-1976 ... 9-12R
Obituary ... 134
Vickers, Roy 1888(?)-1965 ... DLB 77
Vickery, Donald M(ichael) 1944- ... 101
Vickery, Florence E. 1906- ... 37-40R
Vickery, John B. 1925- ... 57-60
Vickery, Kate
See Kennedy, T(eresa) A.
Vickery, Olga W(estland) 1925-1970 ... CANR-3
Earlier sketch in CA 1-4R
Vickery, Robert L. (Jr.) 1932- ... 49-52
Vickery, Tom Rusk 1935- ... 53-56
Vickrey, William (Spencer) 1914- ... 41-44R
Victor, Charles B.
See Puechner, Ray
Victor, David 1910(?)-1989 Obituary ... 130
Victor, Edward 1914- ... CANR-3
Earlier sketch in CA 1-4R
See also SATA 3
Victor, Joan Berg 1942- ... 105
See also SATA 30
Victor, Sam
See Hershman, Morris
Victoria 1819-1901 ... DLB 55
Vida, Nina 1933- ... 117
Vidal, Gore 1925- ... CANR-13
Earlier sketch in CA 5-8R
See also AITN 1
See also BEST 90:2
See also CLC 2, 4, 6, 8, 10, 22, 33, 72
See also DLB 6
See also MTCW
Vidal, Nicole 1928- ... 25-28R
Vidaver, Doris ... 108
Vidger, Leonard P(erry) 1920- ... CANR-5
Earlier sketch in CA 9-12R
Vidich, Arthur J. 1922- ... 115
Vidler, Alec R.
See Vidler, Alexander Roper
Vidler, Alexander Roper 1899-1991 ... CANR-5
Obituary ... 135
Earlier sketch in CA 5-8R
Vidler, Virginia (Ellen) 1928-1986 ... 69-72
Obituary ... 121
Vidor, King (Wallis) 1894(?)-1982 Obituary ... 108
Viebig, Clara 1860-1952 ... DLB 66
Vieg, John A.
See Vieg, John Albert
Vieg, John Albert 1904-1988 ... 1-4R
Obituary ... 124
Vier, Gene 1926- ... 105
Viereck, Ellen K. 1928- ... 53-56
See also SATA 14
Viereck, George Sylvester
1884-1962 Obituary ... 116
See also DLB 54
Viereck, Peter (Robert Edwin) 1916- ... CANR-1
Earlier sketch in CA 1-4R
See also CLC 4
See also DLB 5
Viereck, Phillip 1925- ... CANR-8
Earlier sketch in CA 5-8R
See also SATA 3
Viertel, Janet 1915- ... 53-56
See also SATA 10
Viertel, Joseph 1915- ... 13-16R
Viertel, Peter 1920- ... 13-16R
Viessman, Warren Jr. 1930- ... 53-56
Vieth, David M(uench) 1925- ... 5-8R
Vieth von Golssenau, Arnold Friedrich
1889-1979 ... 89-92
Vietor, John A(dolf) 1914-1982 Obituary ... 108
Viets, Roger 1738-1811 ... DLB 99
Viets, Wallace T(rowbridge) 1919- ... 17-20R
Vig, Norman Joseph 1939- ... 25-28R
Vigeland, Carl A. 1947- ... 122
Vigeveno, H(enk) S. 1925- ... 108
Vigfusson, Robin 1949- ... 106
Viggiani
See Viggiani, Guy
Viggiani, Guy 1932- ... 123
Vigil, Diego
See Vigil, James Diego
Vigil, James Diego 1938- ... 130
Vigil, Lawrence
See Finnin, (Olive) Mary
Vigliante, Mary
See Szydlowski, Mary Vigliante
Viglini, Janelle (Therese) 1933- ... 57-60
Vigna, Judith 1936- ... CANR-29
Earlier sketches in CA 77-80, CANR-13
See also SATA 15
Vigneault, Gilles 1928- ... DLB 60
Vigneras, Louis-Andre 1903- ... 65-68
Vigness, David M(artell) 1922- ... 13-16R
Vigness, Paul G. 1894- ... 41-44R
Vignone, Joseph A. 1939- ... 37-40R
Vigny, Alfred (Victor) de 1797-1863 ... DLB 119
Vigolo, Giorgio 1894-1983 ... DLB 114
Viguers, Ruth Hill 1903-1971 ... CAP-1
Obituary ... 29-32R
Earlier sketch in CA 13-16
See also SATA 6
Vikis-Freibergs, Vaira 1937- ... 53-56
Viksnins, George J(uris) 1937- ... 105
Viktoria Luise 1892-1980 Obituary ... 102
Vila, Bob
See Vila, Robert
Vila, Robert 1946- ... 106
Vilakazi, Benedict Wallet 1906-1947 ... TCLC 37
Vilar, Esther 1935- ... CANR-8
Earlier sketch in CA 49-52
Vilarino, Idea 1920- ... HW
Vildrac, Charles
See Messager, Charles
Viljoen, Helen Gill 1899-1974 ... 45-48
Obituary ... 103
Vilkitis, James R(ichard) 1941- ... 61-64
Villa, Jose Garcia 1914- ... CANR-12
Earlier sketch in CA 25-28R
Villa, Susie Hoogasian
See Hoogasian-Villa, Susie
Villada, Gene Harold Bell
See Bell-Villada, Gene Harold
Villa-Gilbert, Mariana 1937- ... 29-32R
Villanueva, Alma Luz 1944- ... 131
See also HW
Villanueva, Tino 1941- ... CANR-1
Earlier sketch in CA 45-48
See also DLB 82
See also HW
Villard, Henry Hilgard 1911-1983 Obituary ... 111
Villard, Henry S(errano) 1900- ... 17-20R
Villard, Henry 1835-1900 ... DLB 23
Villard, Oswald Garrison
1872-1949 Brief entry ... 113
See also DLB 25, 91
Villarejo, Mary (Holan) 1915- ... 9-12R
Villarejo, Oscar M(ilton) 1909- ... 17-20R
Villarreal, Jose Antonio 1924- ... 133
See also DLB 82
See also HW
Villars, Elizabeth
See Feldman, Ellen (Bette)
Villas Boas, Claudio 1916- Brief entry ... 117
Villas Boas, Orlando 1914- Brief entry ... 117
Villasenor, David V. 1913- ... 13-16R
Villasenor, Edmund
See Villasenor, Victor E(dmundo)
Villasenor, Victor
See Villasenor, Victor E(dmundo)
Villasenor, Victor E(dmundo) 1940- ... CANR-32
Earlier sketch in CA 45-48
See also HW
Villaurrutia, Xavier 1903-1950 ... HW
Villegas, Daniel Cosio
1898-1976 Obituary ... 65-68
Villemaire, Yolande 1949- ... DLB 60
Villeneuve, Jocelyne 1941- ... 132
Villere, Sidney Louis 1900- ... 69-72
Villers, Raymond 1911- ... CAP-2
Earlier sketch in CA 25-28
Villers, Robert 1921-1980 Obituary ... 93-96
Villet, Barbara 1931- ... 85-88
Villiard, Paul 1910-1974 ... CANR-10
Obituary ... 53-56
Earlier sketches in CAP-2, CA 25-28
See also SATA 20, 51
Villiers, Alan (John) 1903- ... CANR-1
Earlier sketch in CA 1-4R
See also SATA 10
Villiers, George 1628-1687 ... DLB 80
Villiers, Guy
See Goulding, Peter Geoffrey
Villiers, Marjorie 1903-1982 Obituary ... 107
Villoldo, Alberto Pedro 1949- ... 108
Vilmorin, Louise Leveque de
1902-1969 Obituary ... 104
Vilnay, Zev 1900-1988 Obituary ... 124
Vinacke, W(illiam) Edgar 1917- ... 5-8R
Vinal, Harold 1891-1965 Obituary ... 89-92
Vinas, D.
See Vinas, David
Vinas, David 1929(?)- ... HW
Vinaver, Eugene 1899- ... 13-16R
Vincent, Adrian 1917- ... 1-4R
Vincent, Charles 1945- ... 65-68
Vincent, Claire
See Allen, Charlotte Vale
Vincent, Clark E(dward) 1923- ... CANR-2
Earlier sketch in CA 1-4R
Vincent, E. Lee
See Vincent, Elizabeth Lee
Vincent, Elizabeth Lee 1897- ... CAP-2
Earlier sketch in CA 19-20
Vincent, Eric Douglas 1953- ... SATA 40
Vincent, Felix 1946- ... 118
See also SATA 41
Vincent, Gabrielle ... 126
See also CLC 13
See also CLR 13
See also MAICYA
See also SATA 61
Vincent, Howard Paton 1904- ... 65-68
Vincent, Jack E(rnest) 1932- ... CANR-19
Earlier sketch in CA 102
Vincent, Jack 1904- ... 29-32R
Vincent, Joan 1920- ... 21-24R
Vincent, John Carter
1900-1972 Obituary ... 37-40R
Vincent, John J(ames) 1929- ... CANR-26
Earlier sketches in CA 57-60, CANR-10
Vincent, John R(ussell) 1937- ... 120
Vincent, K(enneth) Steven 1947- ... 128
Vincent, Leona
See Vincent, Elizabeth Lee
Vincent, Mary Keith
See St. John, Wylly Folk
Vincent, Peter 1944- ... 37-40R
Vincent, R(aymond) J(ohn) 1943-1990 ... 77-80
Obituary ... 133
Vincent, Theodore G. 1936- ... CANR-13
Earlier sketch in CA 77-80
Vincent, William R.
See Heitzmann, William Ray
Vincent, William S(hafer) 1907- ... 41-44R
Vinciguerra, Mario 1887-1973 Obituary ... 104
Vincitorio, Gaetano L(eonard) 1921- ... 89-92
Vine, Barbara
See Rendell, Ruth (Barbara)
See also BEST 90:4
See also CLC 50
Vine, Louis L(loyd) 1922- ... CANR-3
Earlier sketch in CA 1-4R
Vine, Paul Ashley Laurence 1927- ... 21-24R
Vine, Phyllis 1945- ... 130
Vine, Sarah
See Rowland, D(onald) S(ydney)
Vineberg, Arthur (Martin) 1903-1988 ... 104
Obituary ... 125
Vineberg, Ethel (Shane) 1902- ... 85-88
Vinegar, Tom
See Gregg, Andrew K.
Viner, George 1913(?)-1983 Obituary ... 109
Viner, Jacob 1892-1970 Obituary ... 104
Vines, Alice Gilmore 1923- ... 81-84
Vines, (Henry) Ellsworth (Jr.)
1911- Brief entry ... 109
Vinest, Shaw
See Longyear, Barry Brookes
Viney, Wayne 1932- ... 103
Vineyard, Edwin Earle 1926- ... 5-8R
Vinge, Joan D(ennison) 1948- ... 93-96
See also CLC 30
See also SATA 36
Vinge, Vernor (Steffen) 1944- ... 101
Vining, Elizabeth Gray 1902- ... CANR-7
Earlier sketch in CA 5-8R
See also MAICYA
See also SATA 6
Vinogradov, Ivan M(atveyevich)
1891-1983 Obituary ... 109
Vinokur, Grigory
See Weinrauch, Herschel
Vinokurov, Yevgeny Mikhailovich
1925- Brief entry ... 116
Vinson, Elaine
See Rowland, D(onald) S(ydney)
Vinson, J(ohn) Chal(mers) 1919- ... 9-12R
Vinson, J(ohn) William
1916-1979 Obituary ... 89-92
Vinson, James (Albert) 1933- ... 120
Brief entry ... 118
Vinson, Jane 1927- ... 77-80
Vinson, Kathryn 1911- ... 5-8R
See also SATA 21
Vinson, Rex Thomas 1935- ... 101
Vinton, Bobby
See Vinton, Stanley Robert Jr.
Vinton, Eleanor W(inthrop) 1899-1977 ... 61-64
Obituary ... 73-76
Vinton, Iris 1906(?)-1988 ... 77-80
Obituary ... 124
See also SATA 24, 55
Vinton, John 1937- ... 73-76
Vinton, Stanley Robert Jr.
1935(?)- Brief entry ... 120
Vinyard, C. Dale 1932- ... 25-28R
Vinz, Mark 1942- ... 93-96
Viola, Herman J(oseph) 1938- ... CANR-23
Earlier sketches in CA 61-64, CANR-8
Viola, Lynne 1955- ... 135
Violet, Ultra
See Dufresne, Isabelle
Violett, Ellen 1925- ... 73-76
Violi, Paul 1944- ... CANR-24
Earlier sketch in CA 45-48
Violis, G.
See Simenon, Georges (Jacques Christian)
Viorst, Judith 1931- ... CANR-26
Earlier sketches in CA 49-52, CANR-2
See also BEST 90:1
See also CLR 3
See also DLB 52
See also MAICYA
See also SATA 7, 70
Viorst, Milton 1930- ... CANR-26
Earlier sketch in CA 9-12R
Vip
See Partch, Virgil Franklin II
Vipond, Don (Harry) 1932- ... 65-68
Vipont, Charles
See Foulds, Elfrida Vipont
Vipont, Elfrida
See Foulds, Elfrida Vipont
Virga, Vincent 1942- ... 107
Virgilio, Nicholas A(nthony)
1928-1989 Obituary ... 127
Virgines, George E. 1920- ... CANR-28
Earlier sketches in CA 25-28R, CANR-12
Virginius
See Connett, Eugene Virginius III
Virtanen, Reino 1910- ... CANR-4
Earlier sketch in CA 1-4R
Virtue, Noel 1947- ... 130
Vis, William Ryerson 1886-1969 Obituary ... 110
Viscardi, Henry Jr. 1912- ... CANR-5
Earlier sketch in CA 5-8R
Vischer, Helen (Cassin Lombard) Carusi
1905(?)-1986 Obituary ... 119
Vischer, Lukas 1926- ... 131
Visconti, Luchino 1906-1976 ... CANR-39
Obituary ... 65-68
Earlier sketch in CA 81-84
See also CLC 16
Viscott, David S(teven) 1938- ... CANR-26
Earlier sketch in CA 29-32R
See also AITN 1
See also SATA 65
Viscusi, W. Kip 1949- ... 138
Visher, Emily B. 1918- ... 109
Visher, Halene Hatcher 1909- ... 45-48
Visher, John Sargent 1921- ... 109
Vishniak, Mark 1883-1976 Obituary ... 69-72
Vishny, Michele 1932- ... 69-72
Visocchi, Mark 1938- ... CANR-16
Earlier sketch in CA 93-96
Visotzky, Burton L. 1951- ... 138
Visram, Rozina 1939- ... 133
Visscher, Maurice B(olks) 1901- ... 77-80
Visser, Margaret 1940- ... 123
Visser, W(illem) F(rederik) H(endrik)
1900-1968 ... CAP-2
Earlier sketch in CA 25-28
See also SATA 10
Visser 't Hooft, Willem Adolf 1900-1985 ... 9-12R
Obituary ... 116
Visson, Lynn 1945- ... 134
Visson, Vladimir 1905(?)-1976 Obituary ... 69-72
Viswanathan, S(ubrahmanyam) 1933- ... 132
Vita-Finzi, Claudio 1936- ... 89-92
Vita-Finzi, Penelope (Jean) 1939- ... 133
Vital, David 1927- ... CANR-12
Earlier sketch in CA 29-32R
Vitale, Joseph T(homas) 1951- ... 107
Vitale, Philip H. 1913- ... 17-20R
Vitek, Donna
See Vitek, Donna Kimel
Vitek, Donna Kimel 1947- ... 131
Vitek, John D(ennis) 1942- ... 124
Vitelli, James R(obert) 1920- ... 29-32R
Vitezovic, Tomislav
See Kuehnelt-Leddihn, Erik (Maria) Ritter von
Vitier, Cintio
See Vitier (y Bolanos), Cynthio
Vitier (y Bolanos), Cynthio 1921- ... HW
Vittengl, Morgan John 1928- ... 5-8R
Vittorini, Elio 1908-1966 ... 133
Obituary ... 25-28R
See also CLC 6, 9, 14
Vitz, Robert C. 1938- ... 136
Vitzthum, Richard Carleton 1936- ... 103
Vivanco, Luis Felipe 1907-1975 ... DLB 108
Vivante, Arturo 1923- ... CANR-10
Earlier sketch in CA 17-20R
See also CAAS 12
Vivante, Paolo 1921- ... 29-32R
Vivas, Eliseo 1901- ... CANR-5
Earlier sketch in CA 5-8R
Viveash, Cherry Jacqueline Lee 1929- ... CAP-1
Earlier sketch in CA 9-10
Vivelo, Jacqueline J. 1943- ... SATA 63
Vivers, Eileen Elliott 1905- ... 41-44R
Vivian, Cordy Tindell 1924- ... 49-52
Vivian, Francis
See Ashley, (Arthur) Ernest
Viviano, Benedict T(homas) 1940- ... CANR-10
Earlier sketch in CA 21-24R
Vivienne
See Entwistle, Florence Vivienne
Vizard, Stephen
See James, (David) Burnett (Stephen)
Vizedom, Monika B(asch) 1929- ... 69-72
Vizenor, Gerald Robert 1934- ... CANR-21
Earlier sketches in CA 13-16R, CANR-5

Vizinczey, Stephen 1933- 128
See also CLC 40
Vizzard, Jack
See Vizzard, John Anthony
Vizzard, John Anthony 1914- 29-32R
Vizzini, Salvatore 1926- 103
Vlach, John Michael 1948- 123
Vladeck, Bruce C. 1949- 101
Vladimirov, Leonid
See Finkelstein, Leonid Vladimirovitch
Vladimov, G.
See Vladimov, Georgii Nikolaevich
Vladimov, Georgii
See Vladimov, Georgii Nikolaevich
Vladimov, Georgii Nikolaevich 1931- 123
Vlahos, Olivia 1924- 21-24R
See also SATA 31
Vlasic, Bob
See Hirsch, Phil
Vlasic, Ivan Albert 1926- 9-12R
Vlasich, James A(nthony) 1944- 137
Vlastos, Gregory 1907-1991 130
Obituary 135
Vliet, R(ussell) G(ordon) 1929-1984 CANR-18
Obituary 112
Earlier sketch in CA 37-40R
See also CLC 22
Vlock, Laurel F(ox) 37-40R
Vloyantes, John P. 1918- 61-64
Voaden, Herman Arthur 1903- 103
See also DLB 88
Vo-Dinh, Mai 1933- CANR-29
Earlier sketches in CA 77-80, CANR-13
See also SATA 16
Vodola, Thomas M(ichael) 1925- CANR-19
Earlier sketches in CA 49-52, CANR-3
Voegeli, V(ictor) Jacque 1934- 21-24R
Voegelin, Eric (Herman Wilhelm)
1901-1985 132
Obituary 114
Voehringer, Erich F(rederick)
1905-1973 CANR-2
Obituary 41-44R
Earlier sketch in CA 1-4R
Voeks, Virginia (Wilna) 1921- 13-16R
Voelcker, Hunce 1940- 77-80
Voelkel, Robert T(ownsend) 1933- 25-28R
Voelker, John D(onaldson) 1903-1991 1-4R
Obituary 134
Voellner, Louada McCaughen
1888(?)-1986 Obituary 119
Vogan, Sara 1947-1991 134
Vogau, Boris Andreyevich
1894-1937(?) Brief entry 123
See also Pilnyak, Boris
Vogel, Alfred T(ennyson) 1906- 104
Vogel, Arthur A(nton) 1924- CANR-10
Earlier sketch in CA 25-28R
Vogel, Carole Garbuny 1951- 138
See also SATA 70
Vogel, Dan 1927- 120
Vogel, David 1947- CANR-11
Earlier sketch in CA 65-68
Vogel, Ezra F. 1930- CANR-30
Earlier sketch in CA 13-16R
Vogel, Helen Wolff 1918- 17-20R
Vogel, Hunter Bertram August
1903-1990 Obituary 131
Vogel, Ilse-Margret 1918- CANR-7
Earlier sketch in CA 13-16R
See also SATA 14
Vogel, Irving L. 1918- 122
Vogel, Jerry 1896(?)-1980 Obituary 101
Vogel, John H. Jr. 1950- 77-80
See also SATA 18
Vogel, Linda Jane 1940- 61-64
Vogel, Lucy E(laine) 49-52
Vogel, Morris J. 1945- 128
Vogel, Paula A(nne) 1951- 108
Vogel, Speed
See Vogel, Irving L.
Vogel, Stanley M(orton) 1921- 77-80
Vogel, Steve 1946- 132
Vogel, Steven 1940- 53-56
Vogel, Victor H(ugh) 1905-1978 CANR-3
Earlier sketch in CA 1-4R
Vogel, Virgil (Howard) J(oseph) 1918- CANR-10
Earlier sketch in CA 25-28R
Vogeler, Ingolf 1944- 107
Vogelgesang, Sandra Louise 1942- 57-60
Vogelgesang, Sandy
See Vogelgesang, Sandra Louise
Vogelman, Joyce 1936- 106
Vogelsang, Arthur 1942- 49-52
Vogelsinger, Hubert 1938- 25-28R
Vogenitz, David George 1930- 41-44R
Voget, Fred W. 1913- 61-64
Vogler, Roger E. 1938- 126
Vogt, Bill
See Vogt, William McKinley
Vogt, Esther Loewen 1915- CANR-7
Earlier sketch in CA 17-20R
See also SATA 14
Vogt, Evon Zartman Jr. 1918- CANR-27
Earlier sketch in CA 69-72
Vogt, Gregory SATA 45
Vogt, Gregory Max 1949- 137
Vogt, Joseph 1895- Brief entry 112
Vogt, Marie Bollinger 1921- 57-60
See also SATA 45
Vogt, William McKinley 1935- 89-92
Voight, Virginia Frances 1909- CANR-18
Earlier sketches in CA 5-8R, CANR-2
See also SATA 8
Voigt, Cynthia 1942- CANR-37
Earlier sketches in CA 106, CANR-18
See also AAYA 3
See also CLC 30
See also CLR 13
See also MAICYA
See also SATA 33, 48
Voigt, David Quentin 1926- CANR-32
Earlier sketches in CA 41-44R, CANR-14
Voigt, Ellen Bryant 1943- CANR-29
Earlier sketches in CA 69-72, CANR-11
See also CLC 54
See also DLB 120
Voigt, Erna 1925- SATA 35
Voigt, Karsten D. 1941- 113
Voigt, Lieselotte E. Kurth
See Kurth-Voigt, Lieselotte E.
Voigt, Melvin J(ohn) 1911- CANR-5
Earlier sketch in CA 13-16R
Voigt, Milton 1924- 9-12R
Voigt, Robert J(oseph) 1916- 93-96
Voigt, William Jr. 1902- 73-76
Voigt-Rother, Erna
See Voigt, Erna
Voils, Jessie Wiley CAP-2
Earlier sketch in CA 29-32
Voinovich, Vladimir (Nikolaevich)
1932- CANR-33
Earlier sketch in CA 81-84
See also CAAS 12
See also CLC 10, 49
See also MTCW
Voitle, Robert (Brown Jr.) 1919- 1-4R
Vojtech, Anna 1946- SATA 42
Volbach, Walther R(ichard) 1897- 29-32R
Volcker, Paul A(dolph) 1927- 129
Brief entry 114
Vole, Zenobia N.
See Douglas, Lauren Wright
Volgyes, Ivan 1936- CANR-20
Earlier sketch in CA 104
Volin, Michael 1911- 101
Volk, Hannah Marie
See Wormington, H(annah) M(arie)
Volkan, Vamik D(jemal) 1932- CANR-19
Earlier sketch in CA 102
Volkart, Edmund H(owell) 1919- 21-24R
Volkening, Henry T.
1902-1972 Obituary 37-40R
Volker, Roger 1934- 53-56
Volker, Roy 1924- 57-60
Volkman, Ernest 1940- 132
Volkoff, Vladimir 1932- 73-76
See also DLB 83
Volkov, Leon 1920(?)-1974 Obituary 45-48
Voll, John O(bert) 1936- 129
Vollert, Cyril (Oscar) 1901- 61-64
Vollmann, William T. 1959- 134
Vollmer, Howard M. 1928- CANR-13
Earlier sketch in CA 17-20R
Voloshinov, V. N.
See Bakhtin, Mikhail Mikhailovich
Volpe, E(rminio) Peter 1927- CANR-15
Earlier sketch in CA 37-40R
Volpe, Edmond L(oris) 1922- CANR-1
Earlier sketch in CA 1-4R
Volpe, Vernon L(ewis) 1955- 135
Voltaire 1694-1778 WLC
Voltz, Jeanne Appleton 1920- CANR-21
Earlier sketch in CA 104
Volz, Carl (Andrew) 1933- 29-32R
Volz, Marlin M(ilton) 1917- 37-40R
von Abele, Rudolph (Radama) 1922-1989 104
Obituary 127
von Albertini, Rudolf 1923- 131
von Baeyer, Hans C(hristian) 1938- 117
von Balthasar, Hans U.
See von Balthasar, Hans Urs
von Balthasar, Hans Urs 1905-1988 130
Obituary 125
Brief entry 106
von Berg, J(ohan) F(riedrich) Obituary 108
von Bertalanffy, Ludwig 1901-1972 CAP-2
Earlier sketch in CA 25-28
von Block, Bela W(illiam) 1922- 104
von Block, Sylvia 1931- CANR-7
Earlier sketch in CA 53-56
von Bothmer, Dietrich Felix 1918- 106
von Brand, Theodor C.
1900(?)-1978 Obituary 81-84
von Braun, Wernher 1912-1977 CANR-9
Obituary 69-72
Earlier sketch in CA 5-8R
von Castlehun, Friedl
See Marion, Frieda
von Cube, Irmgard
1900(?)-1977 Obituary 73-76
von Daeniken, Erich 1935- CANR-17
Earlier sketch in CA 37-40R
See also von Daniken, Erich
See also AITN 1
See also CLC 30
von Daniken, Erich
See von Daeniken, Erich
See also CLC 30
von der Gruen, Max 1926- DLB 75
von der Mehden, Fred R. 1927- 9-12R
von Doderer, Heimito
1896-1966 Obituary 25-28R
See also Doderer, Heimito von
Vondra, Josef Gert 1941- 104
von Dreele, W(illiam) H(enry) 1924- 93-96
von Eckardt, Ursula M(aria) 1925- 13-16R
Von Eckardt, Wolf 1918- 5-8R
von Elbe, Joachim 1902- 132
Von Elsner, Don Byron 1909- 1-4R
von Ende, Richard Chaffey 1907- 103
Von Erffa, Helmut (Hartmann) 1900-1979 133
von Euler, Ulf (Svante) 1905-1983 Obituary 109
von Frank, Albert J(ames) 1945- 120
von Franz, Marie-Louise 1915- 85-88
von Frisch, Karl (Ritter)
See Frisch, Karl (Ritter) von
von Frisch, Otto 1929- 101
von Fuerer-Haimendorf, Christoph 1909- 131
von Furstenberg, Egon (Edvard) 1946- 102
von Furstenberg, George Michael
1941- CANR-10
Earlier sketch in CA 65-68
von Glahn, Gerhard E(rnst) 1911- 13-16R
von Gronicka, Andre 1912- 25-28R
von Grunebaum, G(ustave) E(dmund)
1909-1972 CANR-3
Earlier sketch in CA 1-4R
Von Gunden, Heidi Cecilia 1940- 125
Vo Nguyen Giap 1912(?)- Brief entry 115
von Habsburg-Lothringen, Geza Louis Eusebius
Gebhard Ralphael Albert Maria 1940- 105
Von Hagen, Victor Wolfgang 1908- 105
See also SATA 29
von Hassell, Fey 1918- 134
von Hayek, Friedrich August
See Hayek, F(riedrich) A(ugust von)
von Heidenstam, (Carl Gustaf) Verner
See Heidenstam, (Carl Gustaf) Verner von
von Heller, Marcus
See Zachary, Hugh
von Hertzen, Heikki 1913- 37-40R
von Heyse, Paul (Johann Ludwig)
See Heyse, Paul (Johann Ludwig von)
von Hildebrand, Alice 1923- 21-24R
von Hildebrand, Dietrich 1889-1977 CANR-10
Obituary 69-72
Earlier sketch in CA 17-20R
Von Hilsheimer, George E(dwin III)
1934- 29-32R
von Hippel, Frank 1937- 93-96
von Hirsch, Andrew 1934- CANR-14
Earlier sketch in CA 81-84
von Hofe, Harold 1912- CANR-4
Earlier sketch in CA 1-4R
von Hoffman, Nicholas 1929- CANR-34
Earlier sketch in CA 81-84
von Hofmannsthal, Hugo
See Hofmannsthal, Hugo von
von Horn, Carl 1903- CAP-2
Earlier sketch in CA 21-22
von Horvath, Odon
See Horvath, Oedoen von
von Horvath, Oedoen
See Horvath, Oedoen von
von Kaschnitz-Weinberg, Marie Luise
1901-1974 127
Obituary 93-96
See also Kaschnitz, Marie Luise
Von Klemperer, Klemens 1916- 21-24R
von Klopp, Vahrah
See Malvern, Gladys
von Koenigswald, (Gustav Heinrich) Ralph
1902-1982 Obituary 110
von Koerber, Hans Nordewin 1886- 41-44R
von Lang, Jochen
See von Lang-Piechocki, Joachim
von Lang-Piechocki, Joachim 1925- 101
von Laue, Max Theodor Felix
See Laue, Max Theodor Felix von
Von Laue, Theodore Herman 1916- 9-12R
von le Fort, Gertrud (Petrea)
See le Fort, Gertrud (Petrea) von
Von Leyden, Wolfgang Marius 1911- CANR-3
Earlier sketch in CA 5-8R
von Liliencron, (Friedrich Adolf Axel) Detlev
See Liliencron, (Friedrich Adolf Axel) Detlev von
von Maltitz, Horst 1905- 77-80
Von Manstein, Erich 1887-1973 Obituary 45-48
von Meck, Galina 1891-1985 Obituary 116
von Mehren, Arthur T(aylor) 1922- 17-20R
von Mendelssohn, Felix 1918- 13-16R
Von Mering, Otto Oswald Jr. 1922- 1-4R
von Miklos, Josephine Bogdan
1900-1972 Obituary 37-40R
von Mises, Ludwig (Edler)
See Mises, Ludwig (Edler) von
von Mises, Margit
See Mises, Margit von
Von Mohrenschildt, Dimitri Sergius
1902- Brief entry 106
Von Molnar, Geza (Walter Elemer)
1932- 29-32R
von Moltke, Konrad 1941- CANR-19
Earlier sketch in CA 101
Von Moschzisker, Michael 1918- 37-40R
Vonnegut, Kurt Jr. 1922- CANR-25
Earlier sketches in CA 1-4R, CANR-1
See also AAYA 6
See also AITN 1
See also BEST 90:4
See also CDALB 1968-1988
See also CLC 1, 2, 3, 4, 5, 8, 12, 22, 40, 60
See also DLB 2, 8
See also DLBD 3
See also DLBY 80
See also MTCW
See also SSC 8
See also WLC
Vonnegut, Mark 1947- 65-68
See also AITN 2
von Neumann, John 1903-1957 Brief entry 117
von Ost, Henry Lerner 1915- 101
Von Rachen, Kurt
See Hubbard, L(afayette) Ron(ald)
von Rad, Gerhard 1901-1971 Obituary 104
von Rago, Louis J(oseph)
See Rago, Louis J(oseph von)
Von Rauch, Georg 1904- 73-76
von Rezzori (d'Arezzo), Gregor
See Rezzori (d'Arezzo), Gregor von
von Rhein, John (Richard) 1945- 120
von Riekhoff, Harald 1937- 89-92
Von Rosenstiel, Helene 1944- 105
Von Salis, Jean-R. 1901- 21-24R
von Salomon, Ernst
1902-1972 Obituary 37-40R
von Schilcher, Florian 1944- 118
von Schlabrendorff, Fabian
1907-1980 Obituary 105
von Schmidt, Eric 1931- CANR-13
Earlier sketch in CA 17-20R
See also SATA 36, 50
Von Schmidt, Harold
1896(?)-1982 Obituary 107
von Schoenhoff, Ulrike
See Frank, Rudolf
von Schuschnigg, Kurt 1897-1977 103
von Schwarzenfeld, Gertrude
See Cochrane de Alencar, Gertrude E. L.
von Staden, Heinrich 1939- 37-40R
von Staden, Wendelgard 1925- 110
von Stark, G.
See le Fort, Gertrud (Petrea) von
von Sternberg, Josef
See Sternberg, Josef von
von Storch, Anne B. 1910- CAP-2
Earlier sketch in CA 29-32
See also SATA 1
von Trapp, Maria Augusta 1905-1987 81-84
Obituary 122
See also Trapp, Maria Augusta von
von Trotta, Margarethe 1942- 126
Von Unruh, Fritz 1885-1970 Obituary 29-32R
See also Unruh, Fritz von
See also DLB 56
von Wangenheim, Chris
1942-1981 Obituary 103
von Weizsaecker, Carl Friedrich 1912- 105
von Wiegand, Charmion
1898(?)-1983 Obituary 110
Von Wiren-Garczynski, Vera 1931- 41-44R
von Wodtke, Charlotte Buel Johnson
1918-1982 112
See also Johnson, Charlotte Buel
von Wohl-Musciny, Ludwig
See de Wohl, Louis
von Wright, G(eorg) H(enrik)
See Wright, G(eorg) H(enrik) von
von Wuthenau, Alexander 1900- 65-68
von Zuehlsdorff, Volkmar J(ohannes)
1912- CANR-20
Earlier sketch in CA 5-8R
Vooren, Monique Van
See Van Vooren, Monique
Voorhees, Richard J(oseph) 1916- 5-8R
Voorhies, Barbara 1939- 104
Voorhis, Horace Jeremiah 1901-1984 CANR-6
Obituary 113
Earlier sketch in CA 1-4R
Voorhis, Jerry
See Voorhis, Horace Jeremiah
Voos, Henry 1928- 25-28R
Vorhees, Melvin B.
1904(?)-1977 Obituary 69-72
Vorobeva, Maria 1892-1984 Obituary 113
Vorpahl, Ben Merchant 1937- 41-44R
Vorspan, Albert 1924- CANR-13
Earlier sketch in CA 21-24R
Vorster, Gordon 1924- 133
See also CLC 34
Vorzimmer, Peter J. 1937- 93-96
Vos, Clarence J(ohn) 1920- 45-48
Vos, Ida 1931- 137
See also SATA 69
Vos, Nelvin (LeRoy) 1932- 17-20R
Vosburgh, Leonard (W.) 1912- SATA 15
Vosce, Trudie
See Ozick, Cynthia
Vose, Clement E(llery) 1923-1985 41-44R
Obituary 115
Vose, Ruth Hurst 1944- CANR-26
Earlier sketch in CA 109
Voskovec, George 1905-1981 Obituary 104
Voskuil, Dennis N(eal) 1944- 112
Voslensky, M(ichael) S(ergeevich) 1920- 128
Voss, Carl Hermann 1910- CANR-10
Earlier sketch in CA 21-24R
Voss, E(rnst) Theodore 1928- 37-40R
Voss, Earl H. 1922- 9-12R
Voss, George L. 1922- 57-60
Voss, James F(rederick) 1930- 41-44R
Voss, Johann Heinrich 1751-1826 DLB 90
Voss, Ralph F. 1943- 137
Voss, Thomas M(ichael) 1945- 105
Votaw, Dow 1920- 17-20R
Voureka, Amalia
See Fleming, Amalia
Vournakis, John N(icholas) 1939- 57-60
Voute, J. Peter 1906- 125
Vowles, Richard B(eckman) 1917- 25-28R
Voyageur
See Allen, Cecil J(ohn)
Voyce, Arthur 1889- CAP-1
Earlier sketch in CA 13-14
Voyle, Mary
See Manning, Rosemary (Joy)
Voynich, Ethel Lillian (Boole)
1864-1960 Obituary 104
Voysey, Margaret 1945- 108
Voysey, Michael 1920-1987 Obituary 123

Voznesensky, Andrei (Andreievich)
1933- CANR-37
Earlier sketch in CA 89-92
See also CLC 1, 15, 57
See also MTCW
Vranich, Joseph 1945-.....................138
Vrba, Rudolf 1924-.....................21-24R
Vrbovska, Anca 1905-......................81-84
Vredenburg, Harvey L. 1921-..............25-28R
Vreeland, Diana (Dalziel) 1903(?)-1989 111
Obituary 129
Vreeland, Jane D. 1915-....................21-24R
Vrettos, Theodore 1919-..................CANR-27
Earlier sketch in CA 13-16R
Vreuls, Diane 57-60
Vries, Anne de
See de Vries, Anne
Vries, Leonard de 1919-......................113
Vroman, Leo 1915-..........................49-52
Vroman, Mary Elizabeth (Gibson)
1923-1967 125
Obituary 109
See also BW
See also DLB 33
Vroom, Victor H(arold) 1932-...............9-12R
Vrooman, Jack Rochford 1929-...............45-48
Vryonis, Speros (P.) Jr. 1928-.............85-88
Vucinich, Alexander S. 1914- Brief entry 109
Vucinich, Wayne S. 1913-...................13-16R
Vugteveen, Verna Aardema 1911-..........CANR-39
Earlier sketches in CA 5-8R, CANR-3, 18
See also Aardema, Verna
Vuilleumier, Marion 1918-..................81-84
Vujica, Stanko M(irko) 1909-1976 ....41-44R
Vulliamy, Colwyn Edward
1886-1971 Obituary 89-92
Vuong, Lynette Dyer 1938-.....................117
See also SATA 60
Vuong g(ia) Thuy 1938-.....................69-72
Vyn, Kathleen 1949-........................89-92
Vyverberg, Henry (Sabin) 1921-.................109
Vyvyan, C(lara) C(oltman Rogers) 1885-..... CAP-1
Earlier sketch in CA 9-10
Vyvyan, Nigel
See Nevill, Barry St-John

W

Waage, Frederick 1943-........................104
Waagenaar, Sam 1908-.......................57-60
Waber, Bernard 1924-.....................CANR-38
Earlier sketches in CA 1-4R, CANR-2
See also MAICYA
See also SATA 40, 47
Wabun
See James, Marlise Ann
Wacher, J(ohn) S(tewart) 1927-................125
Brief entry 105
Wachhorst, Wyn 1938-..........................106
Wachs, Mark Marshall 1933-................25-28R
Wachs, Saul P(hilip) 1931- CANR-30
Earlier sketch in CA 112
Wachsberger, Ken(neth) 1949-..................138
Wachsmann, Klaus Philipp
1907- Brief entry 106
Wachtel, Albert 1939-.........................123
Wachtel, Eleanor 1947-........................134
Wachtel, Howard M(artin) 1938-.............49-52
Wachtel, Isidore H.
1909(?)-1979 Obituary 89-92
Wachtel, Paul L(awrence) 1940-................115
Wachtel, Paul Spencer 1947-...................133
Wachter, Oralee (Roberts) 1935-...............122
See also SATA 51, 61
Wachter, Susan M. 1943-.......................120
Waciuma, Wanjohi 1938-.....................77-80
Wackenroder, Wilhelm Heinrich
1773-1798 .... DLB 90
Wacker, Charles H(enry) Jr. 1925-..........73-76
Wackerbarth, Marjorie CAP-1
Earlier sketch in CA 13-14
Wadbrook, William P. 1933-.................45-48
Waddams, Herbert Montague
1911-1972 Obituary 107
Waddell, D(avid) A(lan) G(ilmour)
1927- CANR-23
Earlier sketch in CA 1-4R
Waddell, Eric (Wilson) 1939-...............45-48
Waddell, Evelyn Margaret 1918-.............53-56
See also SATA 10
Waddell, Helen (Jane) 1889-1965 102
Waddell, Jack O'(Brien) 1933-.............33-36R
Waddell, Martin 1941-....................CANR-34
Earlier sketch in CA 113
See also SATA 43
Waddington, C(onrad) H(al)
1905-1975 ....CANR-6
Obituary 61-64
Earlier sketch in CA 13-16R
Waddington, Miriam 1917- CANR-30
Earlier sketches in CA 21-24R, CANR-12
See also Merritt, E. B.
See also CLC 28
See also DLB 68
Waddington, Raymond B(ruce) 1935-.........53-56
Waddy, Charis 1909-........................69-72
Waddy, Lawrence H(eber) 1914-............CANR-7
Earlier sketch in CA 13-16R
Wade, Alan
See Vance, John Holbrook
Wade, Bob
See Wade, Robert (Allison)
Wade, Carlson 1928-.......................29-32R
Wade, David 1929-.............................103
Wade, Donald W(illiam)
1904-1988 Obituary 128
Wade, E(ileen) K(irkpatrick)
1892(?)-1985 Obituary 117
Wade, Edwin L. 1940-..........................126
Wade, Francis C(larence) 1907- CAP-1
Earlier sketch in CA 13-14
Wade, Graham 1940- CANR-25
Earlier sketch in CA 107
Wade, Harry Vincent 1894-1973 Obituary 89-92
Wade, Henry
See Aubrey-Fletcher, Henry Lancelot
See also DLB 77
Wade, Henry William Rawson 1918-..............109
Wade, Herbert
See Wales, Hugh Gregory
Wade, Hugh Mason 1913-1986 Obituary 118
Wade, Ira Owen 1896-1983 73-76
Obituary 109
Wade, Jack Warren Jr. 1948-...................131
Wade, Jennifer
See Wehen, Joy DeWeese
Wade, Jerry L(ee) 1941-....................53-56
Wade, Jewel Millsap 1937- Brief entry 107
Wade, Joanna
See Berckman, Evelyn Domenica
Wade, John Stevens 1927- CANR-6
Earlier sketch in CA 13-16R
Wade, Kit
See Carson, Xanthus
Wade, L(arry) L(ee) 1935-.................33-36R
Wade, Lawrence 1949(?)-1990 Obituary 131
Wade, Mason 1913-..........................9-12R
Wade, Nicholas (Michael Landon)
1942- CANR-16
Earlier sketch in CA 77-80
Wade, Rex A(rvin) 1936-....................61-64
Wade, Richard Clement 1922-...............17-20R
Wade, Robert
See McIlwain, David
Wade, Robert (Allison) 1920-..................108
Wade, Rosalind Herschel 1909-1989(?) CAP-1
Obituary 127
Earlier sketch in CA 9-10
Wade, Sidney 1951-............................136
Wade, Theodore E. Jr. 1936-.............SATA 37
Wade, (Sarah) Virginia 1945-..................132
Wade, (Henry) William (Rawson)
1918-.....................................CANR-4
Earlier sketch in CA 1-4R
Wade, Wyn Craig 1944-.........................103
Wadekin, Karl-Eugen
See Waedekin, Karl-Eugen
Wadepuhl, Walter 1895-.....................61-64
Wadia, Maneck S(orabji) 1931- CANR-13
Earlier sketch in CA 17-20R
Wadinasi, Sedeka
See Nall, Hiram Abiff
Wadley, Susan S(now) 1943-.................77-80
Wadlington, Walter 1931-..................33-36R
Wadlington, Warwick 1938-..................73-76
Wadsworth, Barry James 1935-..............37-40R
Wadsworth, Frank W(hittemore) 1919-........9-12R
Wadsworth, Ginger 1945-.......................134
Wadsworth, James J(eremiah)
1905-1984 .... CAP-2
Obituary 112
Earlier sketch in CA 19-20
Wadsworth, Jerry
See Wadsworth, James J(eremiah)
Wadsworth, M(arshall) D. 1936- 45-48
Wadsworth, Michael E(dwin) J(ohn)
1942- 93-96
Wadsworth, Nelson B(ingham) 1930- 65-68
Waedekin, Karl-Eugen 1921-.................73-76
Waehrer, Helen (Youngelson) 1938-..........53-56
Waelder, Robert 1900-1967 .... CAP-1
Earlier sketch in CA 13-14
Waelti-Walters, Jennifer 1942-................136
Waengler, Hans-Heinrich B. 1921- CANR-20
Earlier sketch in CA 41-44R
Waffle, Harvey W(illiam) 1904-..............5-8R
Wagar, W(alter) Warren 1932-.............CANR-3
Earlier sketch in CA 5-8R
Wagatsuma, Hiroshi 1927-..................21-24R
Wagemaker, Herbert Jr. 1929-...............93-96
Wagenaar, Theodore C(larence) 1948- 111
Wagener, Hans 1940-.......................CANR-1
Earlier sketch in CA 45-48
Wagenheim, Kal 1935- CANR-26
Earlier sketch in CA 29-32R
See also SATA 21
Wagenknecht, Edward (Charles)
1900- CANR-22
Earlier sketches in CA 1-4R, CANR-6
See also DLB 103
Wagenvoord, James 1937-..................41-44R
Wager, Walter H(erman) 1924-.............CANR-33
Earlier sketches in CA 5-8R, CANR-8
Wager, Willis Joseph 1911- 37-40R
Waggaman, William Henry
1884(?)-1978 Obituary 77-80
Waggner, George 1894-1984 Obituary 114
Waggoner, Glen 1940-..........................121
Waggoner, Hyatt H(owe) 1913-1988 ....CANR-9
Obituary 126
Earlier sketch in CA 21-24R
Waggoner, Lawrence W. 1937- 128
Wagley, Charles (Walter) 1913-1991 .....CANR-10
Obituary 136
Earlier sketch in CA 13-16R
Waglow, Irving Frederick 1915-..............1-4R
Wagman, Fredrica 1937-....................97-100
See also CLC 7
Wagman, Naomi 1937- 57-60
Wagman, Robert John 1942-..................93-96
Wagner, Anthony Richard 1908-...........CANR-20
Earlier sketches in CA 1-4R, CANR-5
Wagner, C(harles) Peter 1930- CANR-24
Earlier sketches in CA 21-24R, CANR-9
Wagner, Charles Abraham 1901- 5-8R
Wagner, David G(eorge) 1949- 114
Wagner, Denson
See Iannelli, Richard
Wagner, Doc
See Wagner, Edward J. Sr.
Wagner, Edward J. Sr.
1908(?)-1986 Obituary 118
Wagner, Edwin E(ric) 1930-.................45-48
Wagner, Elaine 1939-.......................45-48
Wagner, Eliot 1917-...........................105
Wagner, Francis S(tephen) 1911-..........CANR-8
Earlier sketch in CA 61-64
Wagner, Frederick (Reese Jr.) 1928-.........5-8R
Wagner, Geoffrey (Atheling) 1927- CANR-2
Earlier sketch in CA 1-4R
Wagner, Gordon Parsons
1915-1987 Obituary 124
Wagner, Harvey M. 1931-..................CANR-6
Earlier sketch in CA 13-16R
Wagner, Heinrich Leopold 1747-1779 ..... DLB 94
Wagner, Helmut R(udolf) 1904- CANR-19
Earlier sketches in CA 53-56, CANR-4
Wagner, Jack Russell 1916-.................49-52
Wagner, Jane 109
Wagner, Jean Pierre 1919-.................21-24R
Wagner, Jon G(regory) 1944-...................109
Wagner, Joseph Frederick
1900(?)-1974 Obituary 53-56
Wagner, Karl Edward 1945-................CANR-3
Earlier sketch in CA 49-52
Wagner, Ken(neth) 1911-...................37-40R
Wagner, Kenneth A. 1919-...................53-56
Wagner, Lilya 1940-...........................112
Wagner, Linda Welshimer 1936-............CANR-3
Earlier sketch in CA 9-12R
Wagner, Margaret D. 1949-...................5-8R
Wagner, (Griegg) Marsden 1930-.............69-72
Wagner, Michael G. 1951-......................133
Wagner, Nathaniel N(ed) 1930-..............57-60
Wagner, Peggy
See Wagner, Margaret D.
Wagner, Philip L(aurence) 1921- 41-44R
Wagner, Philip Marshall 1904-.................102
Wagner, Ray(mond) David 1924-...........CANR-19
Earlier sketches in CA 5-8R, CANR-3
Wagner, Ray Jay 1931-......................77-80
Wagner, Richard Vansant 1935- Brief entry 105
Wagner, Roy 1938-.........................41-44R
Wagner, Rudolph F(red) 1921-..............37-40R
Wagner, Ruth H(ortense) 1909-.............29-32R
Wagner, Sharon B. 1936-.................CANR-10
Earlier sketch in CA 25-28R
See also SATA 4
Wagner, Stanley P(aul) 1923-..............29-32R
Wagner, Walter F(rederick) Jr.
1926-1985 ....CANR-26
Obituary 116
Earlier sketch in CA 69-72
Wagner, Walter 1927(?)-1983(?) Obituary 109
Wagner, Wenceslas Joseph 1917- 37-40R
Wagner-Martin, Linda 1936-.............. CLC 50
Wagoner, David (Russell) 1926-...........CANR-2
Earlier sketch in CA 1-4R
See also CAAS 3
See also CLC 3, 5, 15
See also DLB 5
See also SATA 14
Wagoner, Harless D. 1918-1973 ....29-32R
Obituary 134
Wagoner, Jay J. 1923-.....................25-28R
Wagoner, John L(eonard) 1927-1984 69-72
Obituary 112
Wagoner, Walter D. 1918- 21-24R
Wagonseller, Bill R(oss) 1933-................107
Wagschal, Harry 1939-.........................108
Wagschal, Peter H(enry) 1944- CANR-19
Earlier sketch in CA 102
Wagstaff, (John) Malcolm 1940- CANR-28
Earlier sketch in CA 109
Wah, Fred(erick James) 1939- Brief entry 107
See also CLC 44
See also DLB 60
Wahking, Harold L(eroy) 1931- 29-32R
Wahl, Jan (Boyer) 1933-.................CANR-38
Earlier sketches in CA 25-28R, CANR-12
See also MAICYA
See also SAAS 3
See also SATA 2, 34
Wahl, Jean 1888-1974 Obituary 49-52
Wahl, Paul 1922-............................9-12R
Wahl, Robert (Charles) 1948-.............CANR-1
Earlier sketch in CA 49-52
Wahl, Thomas (Peter) 1931-..................9-12R
Wahlberg, Rachel Conrad 1922-..............93-96
Wahler, Robert G(ordon) 1936- Brief entry 109
Wahlke, John C(harles) 1917-............CANR-11
Earlier sketch in CA 21-24R
Wahloo, Per 1926-1975 61-64
See also CLC 7
Wahloo, Peter
See Wahloo, Per
Wahlroos, Sven 1931-.......................57-60
Wahtera, John (Edward) 1929-1985 61-64
Obituary 117
Waiblinger, Wilhelm 1804-1830 .... DLB 90
Waide, Jan 1952-..............................105
See also SATA 29
Waidson, H(erbert) Morgan 1916-.............5-8R
Waife, Marie
See Waife-Goldberg, Marie
Waife-Goldberg, Marie 1892-1985.......... CAP-2
Obituary 118
Earlier sketch in CA 25-28
Wailey, Anthony Paul 1947- 126
Wailey, Tony
See Wailey, Anthony Paul
Wain, Barry 1944-.............................122
Wain, John (Barrington) 1925- CANR-23
Earlier sketch in CA 5-8R
See also CAAS 4
See also CDBLB 1960 to Present
See also CLC 2, 11, 15, 46
See also DLB 15, 27
See also MTCW
Waine, Anthony 1946-..........................113
Wainer, Cord
See Dewey, Thomas B(lanchard)
Wainhouse, David Walter 1900-1976 ....17-20R
Obituary 65-68
Wainscott, John Milton 1910-1981 .... SATA 53
Wainscott, Ronald H(arold) 1948-..............131
Wainwright, Arthur William 1925-..............114
Wainwright, Charles Anthony 1933- 37-40R
Wainwright, David
See Stansfield, Richard Habberton
Wainwright, Geoffrey 1939- CANR-34
Earlier sketches in CA 37-40R, CANR-15
Wainwright, Gordon Ray 1937-..................113
Wainwright, Hilary 1949-......................131
Wainwright, J(oseph) Allan 1921-..........13-16R
Wainwright, Jeffrey 1944- Brief entry 122
See also DLB 40
Wainwright, John 1921-........................110
Brief entry 108
Wainwright, Loudon (Snowden)
1925(?)-1988 Obituary 127
Wainwright, Nicholas Biddle 1914-..........65-68
Wainwright, William J(udson) 1935-............120
Waisanen, F(rederick) B(rynolf) 1923- 45-48
Waite, A. E.
See Waite, Arthur Edward
Waite, Arthur Edward
1857-1942 Brief entry 121
Waite, Helen Elmira 1903-...................1-4R
Waite, P(eter) B(usby) 1922-................9-12R
See also SATA 64
Waite, Robert G(eorge) L(eeson) 1919-.......9-12R
Waite, William W(iley) 1903-.............. CAP-1
Earlier sketch in CA 13-16
Waith, Eugene M(ersereau) 1912-..........CANR-5
Earlier sketch in CA 5-8R
Waitley, Douglas 1927-...................CANR-9
Earlier sketch in CA 21-24R
See also SATA 30
Waitzmann, Dorothea 1915-.................13-16R
Wajda, Andrzej 1926-..........................102
See also CLC 16
Wakefield, Connie LaVon 1948- 65-68
Wakefield, Dan 1932-......................21-24R
See also CAAS 7
See also CLC 7
Wakefield, Donam Hahn 1927- 37-40R
Wakefield, Herbert Russell 1888-1965 ....5-8R
Wakefield, Hubert George
1915-1984 Obituary 112
Wakefield, Hugh
See Wakefield, Hubert George
Wakefield, Jean L.
See Laird, Jean E(louise)
Wakefield, R. I.
See White, Gertrude M(ason)
Wakefield, Robert A. 1916- 13-16R
Wakefield, Sherman Day
1894-1971 Obituary 29-32R
Wakefield, Tom 1935-..........................101
Wakefield, Walter Leggett 1911-............81-84
Wakeford, John 1936- Brief entry 112
Wakeham, Irene 1912-......................29-32R
Wakeley, John H(albert) 1932-.............41-44R
Wakelin, Martyn Francis 1935-..............65-68
Wakelyn, Jon L(ouis) 1938- CANR-1
Earlier sketch in CA 45-48
Wakeman, Carolyn 1943-........................126
Wakeman, Frederic (Evans) Jr. 1937-......CANR-1
Earlier sketch in CA 49-52
Wakeman, Geoffrey 1926- CANR-15
Earlier sketch in CA 37-40R
Wakeman, John 1928-...........................124
Wakeman, Robert Parker
1914(?)-1981 Obituary 104
Wakerman, Elyce 1947-.........................128
Wakil, S(heikh) P(arvez) 1935-.............85-88
Wakin, Edward 1927-.....................CANR-17
Earlier sketches in CA 5-8R, CANR-2
See also SATA 37
wa Kinyatti, Maina 1944-......................132
Wako, Mdogo
See Nazareth, Peter
Wakoski, Diane 1937-.....................CANR-9
Earlier sketch in CA 13-16R
See also CAAS 1
See also CLC 2, 4, 7, 9, 11, 40
See also DLB 5
Wakoski-Sherbell, Diane
See Wakoski, Diane
Waksman, Selman A(braham)
1888-1973 .... CAP-1
Obituary 45-48
Earlier sketch in CA 13-16
Wakstein, Allen M. 1931-..................29-32R
Walbank, F. W.
See Walbank, Frank William
Walbank, Frank William 1909- Brief entry 111
Walberg, Herbert J(ohn) 1937-..............61-64

Walch, Timothy (George) 1947- CANR-21
Earlier sketch in CA 105
Walchars, John 1912- 81-84
Walck, Henry Z. 1908(?)-1984 Obituary 114
See also SATA 40
Walcott, Derek (Alton) 1930- CANR-26
Earlier sketch in CA 89-92
See also BLC 3
See also BW
See also CLC 2, 4, 9, 14, 25, 42, 67
See also DLB 117
See also DLBY 81
See also MTCW
Walcott, Fred G. 1894- 37-40R
Walcott, John 1949- 126
Walcott, Robert 1910- CAP-1
Earlier sketch in CA 13-14
Walcutt, Charles Child 1908-1989 .... CANR-3
Obituary 128
Earlier sketch in CA 1-4R
Wald, Alan M(aynard) 1946- 129
Wald, Carol 1935- 65-68
Wald, Kenneth D. 1949- 129
Wald, Malvin (Daniel) 1917- CANR-1
Earlier sketch in CA 45-48
Wald, Richard C(harles) 108
Walde, Ralph E(ldon) 1943- 53-56
Waldeck, Peter Bruce 1940- 41-44R
Walden, Amelia Elizabeth CANR-2
Earlier sketch in CA 1-4R
See also SATA 3
Walden, Daniel 1922- 25-28R
Walden, Howard T(albot) II 1897-1981 45-48
Obituary 103
Walden, John C(layton) 1928- 53-56
Waldenfels, Hans 1931- 131
Walder, (Alan) David 1928-1978 .... CANR-17
Obituary 81-84
Earlier sketch in CA 65-68
Walder, Dennis 1943- 117
Walders, Joe 1948- 85-88
Waldheim, Kurt 1918- 89-92
Waldhorn, Arthur 1918- CANR-3
Earlier sketch in CA 1-4R
Waldinger, Ernst 1896-1970 Obituary 104
Waldman, Anne 1945- CANR-34
Earlier sketch in CA 37-40R
See also CLC 7
See also DLB 16
Waldman, Bruce 1949- .... SATA 15
Waldman, Diane 1936- CANR-26
Earlier sketch in CA 33-36R
Waldman, Eric 1914- 17-20R
Waldman, Max 1919-1981 105
Obituary 103
Waldman, Milton 1895-1976 69-72
Obituary 65-68
Waldman, Neil 1947- 128
See also SATA 51
Waldmeir, Joseph John 1923- 9-12R
Waldo, Anna Lee 1925- 85-88
Waldo, Dave
See Clarke, D(avid) Waldo
Waldo, E. Hunter
See Sturgeon, Theodore (Hamilton)
Waldo, Edward Hamilton
See Sturgeon, Theodore (Hamilton)
Waldo, Kay Cronkite 1938- 107
Waldo, Myra 93-96
Waldo, Ralph Emerson III 1944- 102
Waldo, Terry
See Waldo, Ralph Emerson III
Waldo, Willis H. 1920- 13-16R
Waldock, (Claud) Humphrey (Meredith)
1904-1981 Obituary 108
Waldorf, Paul D(ouglass) 1908- CAP-1
Earlier sketch in CA 13-16
Waldrip, Louise B. 1912- 37-40R
Waldron, Ann Wood 1924- CANR-7
Earlier sketch in CA 13-16R
See also SATA 16
Waldron, Arthur (Nelson) 1948- 135
Waldron, D'Lynn
See Waldron-Shah, Diane Lynn
Waldron, Eli 1916(?)-1980 Obituary 101
Waldron, Ingrid 1939- 53-56
Waldron, Martin O. 1925-1981 Obituary 103
Waldron-Shah, Diane Lynn 1936- 9-12R
Waldrop, Howard 1946- 118
Waldrop, Keith 1932- 117
Waldrop, Rosmarie 1935- CANR-39
Earlier sketches in CA 101, CANR-18
Waldrop, W. Earl 1910- 5-8R
Wale, Michael 81-84
Walen, Harry L(eonard) 1915- 41-44R
Wales, Hugh Gregory 1910- CANR-2
Earlier sketch in CA 5-8R
Wales, Nym
See Snow, Helen Foster
Wales, Robert 1923- 93-96
Wales, William
See Ambrose, David (Edwin)
Walesa, Lech 1943- 128
Waley, Arthur (David) 1889-1966 85-88
Obituary 25-28R
Walford, Christian
See Dilcock, Noreen
Walford, Lionel Albert
1905-1979 Obituary 85-88
Walford, Roy L(ee Jr.) 1924- 111
Walgenbach, Paul H(enry) 1923- 53-56
Walhout, Donald 1927- CANR-2
Earlier sketch in CA 5-8R
Walicki, Andrzej 1930- 101
Walinsky, Louis J(oseph) 1908- CAP-2
Earlier sketch in CA 17-18
Walinsky, Ossip J.
1887(?)-1973 Obituary 41-44R
Waliullah, Syed 1922-1971 .... 21-24R
Obituary 134
Walkden, (George) Brian 1923- CANR-10
Earlier sketch in CA 13-16R
Walkenstein, Eileen 1923- CANR-14
Earlier sketch in CA 69-72
Walker, Addison
See Walker, (Addison) Mort
Walker, Alan 1911- CANR-26
Earlier sketches in CA 13-16R, CANR-7
Walker, Alan 1949- 129
Walker, Albert L(yell) 1907- 41-44R
Walker, Alexander 1930- Brief entry 116
Walker, Alice (Malsenior) 1944- CANR-27
Earlier sketches in CA 37-40R, CANR-9
See also AAYA 3
See also BEST 89:4
See also BLC 3
See also BW
See also CDALB 1968-1988
See also CLC 5, 6, 9, 19, 27, 46, 58
See also DLB 6, 33
See also MTCW
See also SATA 31
See also SSC 5
Walker, Ardis Manly 1901- CANR-22
Earlier sketch in CA 37-40R
Walker, Augusta 1914- 21-24R
Walker, Barbara G(oodwin) 1930- 73-76
Walker, Barbara (Jeanne) K(erlin)
1921- CANR-38
Earlier sketches in CA 33-36R, CANR-16
See also SATA 4
Walker, Barbara M(uhs) 1928- .... SATA 57
Walker, Benjamin 1923- CANR-10
Earlier sketch in CA 25-28R
Walker, Bessie
See Henry, Bessie Walker
Walker, (James) Braz(elton) 1934-1983 69-72
See also SATA 45
Walker, Brooks R. 1935- 9-12R
Walker, Bruce (James) 1944- 85-88
Walker, Bryce S(tewart) 1934- 117
Walker, C(larence) Eugene 1939- CANR-28
Earlier sketches in CA 61-64, CANR-10
Walker, Charles
See Gettings, Fred
Walker, Charles R(umford) 1893-1974 .... CAP-2
Obituary 53-56
Earlier sketch in CA 17-18
Walker, Charles 1911- 17-20R
Walker, Cheryl 1947- 111
Walker, Claxton 1924- 101
Walker, Clive (Phillip) 1954- 124
Walker, D(aniel) P(ickering) 1914-1985 85-88
Obituary 116
Walker, Dale L(ee) 1935- CANR-24
Earlier sketches in CA 57-60, CANR-8
Walker, Daniel Downing 1915- CANR-2
Earlier sketch in CA 1-4R
Walker, Danton (MacIntyre)
1899-1960 Obituary 93-96
Walker, David Clifton 1942- 69-72
Walker, David G(ordon) 1926- 110
See also SATA 60
Walker, David Harry 1911- CANR-1
Obituary 137
Earlier sketch in CA 1-4R
See also CLC 14
See also SATA 8, 71
Walker, David M(axwell) 1920- CANR-22
Earlier sketches in CA 9-12R, CANR-5
Walker, David 1950- CANR-28
Earlier sketch in CA 104
Walker, Deward E(dgar) Jr. 1935- CANR-19
Earlier sketch in CA 25-28R
Walker, Diana 1925- CANR-4
Earlier sketch in CA 49-52
See also SATA 9
Walker, Donald Smith 1918- 9-12R
Walker, Doreen 1920- 135
Walker, Earl Thomas 1891- 105
Walker, Edward Joseph 1934- CANR-28
Earlier sketches in CA 21-24R, CANR-12
See also Walker, Ted
Walker, Edward L(ewis) 1914- CANR-11
Earlier sketch in CA 25-28R
Walker, Elinor 1911- 13-16R
Walker, Eric Anderson 1886-1976 .... CAP-2
Obituary 65-68
Earlier sketch in CA 13-14
Walker, Ethel Valerie 1944- 53-56
Walker, Evan 1933(?)-1982 Obituary 107
Walker, Everett 1906-1983 Obituary 109
Walker, Frank B. 1916(?)-1985 Obituary 117
Walker, Frank 1930- 69-72
See also SATA 36
Walker, Franklin (Dickerson) 1900-1979 .... 21-24R
Obituary 85-88
Walker, Geoffrey de Q(uincey) 1940- 131
Walker, Geoffrey James 1936- 93-96
Walker, George F. 1947- CANR-21
Earlier sketch in CA 103
See also CLC 44, 61
See also DLB 60
Walker, Gerald 1928- 9-12R
Walker, Gilbert James 1907-1982 Obituary 107
Walker, Glen 1937- 108
Walker, Graham S. 1956- 122
Walker, Gregory P(iers) M(ountford)
1942- 73-76
Walker, Greta 1927- 77-80
Walker, Harold Blake 1904- 17-20R
Walker, Harry
See Waugh, Hillary Baldwin
Walker, Helen M(ary) 1891-1983 Obituary 109
Walker, Hill M(ontague) 1939- 93-96
Walker, Holly Beth
See Bond, Gladys Baker
Walker, Ira
See Walker, Irma Ruth (Roden)
Walker, Irma Ruth (Roden) 1921- CANR-21
Earlier sketches in CA 5-8R, CANR-6
Walker, J.
See Crawford, John Richard
Walker, J(ohn) Ingram 1944- 112
Walker, Jack
See Thayer, Frederick C(lifton) Jr.
Walker, James Lynwood 1940- 37-40R
Walker, Janet A(nderson) 1942- 119
Walker, Jeanne Murray 1944- 111
Walker, Jeanne 1924- 61-64
Walker, Jeremy D(esmond) B(romhead)
1936- 21-24R
Walker, Joan 5-8R
Walker, John Brisben 1847-1931 .... DLB 79
Walker, John (Bruce) 1938- 120
Walker, John 1906- CANR-6
Earlier sketch in CA 5-8R
Walker, John 1933- 113
Walker, John 1947- 127
Walker, Joseph A. 1935- CANR-26
Earlier sketch in CA 89-92
See also BW
See also CLC 19
See also DLB 38
Walker, Joseph E(rdman) 1911- 37-40R
Walker, Joseph 1892-1985 Obituary 117
Walker, Kathrine Sorley
See Sorley Walker, Kathrine
Walker, Keith 1934- 121
Walker, Kenneth Francis 1924- 33-36R
Walker, Kenneth Macfarlane 1882-1966 .... 5-8R
Walker, Kenneth R(oland) 1928- 37-40R
Walker, Kenneth Richard 1931-1989 .... 17-20R
Obituary 129
Walker, Laurence C(olton) 1924- 53-56
Walker, Lawrence David 1931- 53-56
Walker, Lenore E(lizabeth) 1942- 97-100
Walker, Leo 13-16R
Walker, Lou Ann 1952- 126
See also SATA 53, 66
Walker, Louise Jean 1891-1976 Obituary 110
See also SATA 35
Walker, Lucy
See Sanders, Dorothy Lucie
Walker, Mack 1929- 9-12R
Walker, Margaret (Abigail) 1915- CANR-26
Earlier sketch in CA 73-76
See also BLC 3
See also BW
See also CLC 1, 6
See also DLB 76
See also MTCW
Walker, Margaret Pope
1901(?)-1980 Obituary 101
Walker, Mark 1953- 117
Walker, Marshall (John) 1912- 17-20R
Walker, Martin 1947- 101
Walker, Mary Alexander 1927- 104
See also SATA 61
Walker, Matthew
See Mewhinney, Bruce
Walker, Michael John
1932-1989(?) Obituary 129
Walker, Mickey 1901-1981 Obituary 108
Walker, Mildred
See Schemm, Mildred Walker
Walker, (Addison) Mort 1923- CANR-25
Earlier sketches in CA 49-52, CANR-3
See also SATA 8
Walker, Morton 1929- CANR-22
Earlier sketch in CA 85-88
Walker, Nancy A. 1942- 136
Walker, Nicolette (Daisy) Milnes 1943- 41-44R
Walker, Nigel (David) 1917- 61-64
Walker, Pamela 1948- 69-72
See also SATA 24
Walker, Peter F(ranklin) 1931- 13-16R
Walker, Peter N. 1936- CANR-14
Earlier sketch in CA 77-80
Walker, Philip (Doolittle) 1924- 133
Walker, Philip Mitchell 1943- 29-32R
Walker, Raymond Myerscough
See Myerscough-Walker, Raymond
Walker, Richard (John) 1952- 132
Walker, Richard L(ouis) 1922- CANR-7
Earlier sketch in CA 9-12R
Walker, Robert H(arris) 1924- CANR-23
Earlier sketches in CA 13-16R, CANR-7
Walker, Robert Newton 1911- 53-56
Walker, Robert W(ayne) 1948- CANR-23
Earlier sketch in CA 93-96
See also SATA 66
Walker, Roger W(illiams) 1931- 45-48
Walker, Ronald G(ary) 1945- CANR-39
Earlier sketches in CA 93-96, CANR-16
Walker, Ruth
See Walker, Irma Ruth (Roden)
Walker, Samuel 1942- 85-88
Walker, Scott 1950- 120
Walker, Sheila S(uzanne) 1944- 127
Walker, Shel
See Sheldon, Walter J.
Walker, Stanley 1898-1962 Obituary 93-96
Walker, Stella Archer 1907- 61-64
Walker, Stephen (Francis) 1941- 131
Walker, Stephen J. 1951- .... SATA 12
Walker, Stuart (Armstrong)
1880(?)-1941 Brief entry 120
Walker, Stuart H(odge) 1923- CANR-24
Earlier sketch in CA 45-48
Walker, Sydney III 1931- 21-24R
Walker, T. Michael 1937- 77-80
Walker, Ted
See Walker, Edward Joseph
See also CLC 13
See also DLB 40
Walker, Theodore J. 1922- 102
Walker, Walter (Colyear) 1912- 117
Walker, Walter (Herbert III) 1949- 117
Walker, Warren S(tanley) 1921- CANR-38
Earlier sketches in CA 9-12R, CANR-3, 16
Walker, Wendy (Alison) 1951- 131
Walker, Willard (Brewer) 1926- CANR-23
Earlier sketch in CA 45-48
Walker, William Edward 1925- 9-12R
Walker, William G(eorge) 1928- 77-80
Walker, William H. 1913- 17-20R
Walker, William Otis 1896-1981 Obituary 105
Walker, Wyatt Tee 1929- 127
Walkerley, Rodney Lewis (de Burgh)
1905- CAP-1
Earlier sketch in CA 9-10
Walkinshaw, Colin
See Reid, James Macarthur
Walkinshaw, Lawrence H(arvey) 1904- 45-48
Walkland, S(tuart) A(lan)
1925(?)-1989 Obituary 128
Walkowicz, Chris 1943- 135
Walkowitz, Daniel J(ay) 1942- 81-84
Wall, A(rthur) E(dward) P(atrick) 1925- 119
Wall, Barbara 1911- 97-100
Wall, Bennett H(arrison) 1914- 77-80
Wall, C. Edward 1942- 37-40R
Wall, Elizabeth S(pooner) 1924- 93-96
Wall, James M(cKendree) 1928- 134
Brief entry 113
Wall, John Nelson Jr. 1945- 114
Wall, Joseph Barrye 1899(?)-1985 Obituary 117
Wall, Joseph Frazier 1920- CANR-13
Earlier sketch in CA 29-32R
Wall, Maggie 1937- 65-68
Wall, Margaret
See Wall, Maggie
Wall, Martha 1910- CAP-2
Earlier sketch in CA 25-28
Wall, Mervyn 1908- 129
Wall, Michael Morris 1942- 53-56
Wall, Mike
See Wall, Michael Morris
Wall, Patrick D(avid) 1925- 17-20R
Wall, Patrick (Henry Bligh) 1916- 104
Wall, Richard 1944- 41-44R
Wall, Robert Emmet Jr. 1937- CANR-23
Earlier sketch in CA 45-48
Wall, T. D.
See Wall, Toby (Douglas)
Wall, Toby D.
See Wall, Toby (Douglas)
Wall, Toby (Douglas) 1946- 119
Wall, Wendy Somerville 1942- 49-52
Wallace, Alexander Fielding 1918-1991 .... 33-36R
Obituary 135
Wallace, Alexander Ross
1891-1982 Obituary 107
Wallace, Alfred Russel
1823-1913 Brief entry 123
Wallace, Amy 1955- CANR-27
Earlier sketch in CA 81-84
Wallace, Andrew 1930- 37-40R
Wallace, Anthony F(rancis) C(larke)
1923- CANR-13
Earlier sketch in CA 61-64
Wallace, Barbara Brooks CANR-28
Earlier sketches in CA 29-32R, CANR-11
See also SATA 4
Wallace, Ben J. 1937- 45-48
Wallace, Beverly Dobrin 1921- 101
See also SATA 19
Wallace, Bill
See Wallace, William Keith
and Wallace, William N.
See also SATA 47
Wallace, Bronwen 1945- 112
Wallace, Bruce 1920- CANR-15
Earlier sketch in CA 85-88
Wallace, Claire 1956- 138
Wallace, Daisy
See Cuyler, Margery S(tuyvesant)
Wallace, David Foster 1962- 132
See also CLC 50
Wallace, David H(arold) 1926- 25-28R
Wallace, David J. 1954- 124
Wallace, David Rains 1945- CANR-14
Earlier sketches in CA 81-84, CANR-31
Wallace, Deborah 1945- 138
Wallace, DeWitt 1889-1981 Obituary 103
Wallace, Dexter
See Masters, Edgar Lee
Wallace, Doreen
See Rash, Dora Eileen Agnew (Wallace)
Wallace, Ed(ward Tatum)
1906-1976 Obituary 69-72
Wallace, (Richard Horatio) Edgar
1875-1932 Brief entry 115
See also DLB 70
Wallace, Ernest 1906-1985 .... CANR-25
Earlier sketch in CA 13-16R
Wallace, Francis 1894(?)-1977 Obituary 73-76
Wallace, G(erald) L. 1938- 97-100
Wallace, George C(orley) 1919- Brief entry 114
Wallace, Helen Kingsbury 1897- CAP-2
Earlier sketch in CA 25-28
Wallace, Helen M(argaret) 1913- CANR-12
Earlier sketch in CA 61-64
Wallace, Henry A(gard) 1888-1965 105
Obituary 89-92

Wallace, Ian
See Pritchard, John Wallace
Wallace, Ian 1950- ... CANR-38
Earlier sketches in CA 107, CANR-25
See also MAICYA
See also SATA 53, 56
Wallace, Irving 1916-1990 ... CANR-27
Obituary ... 132
Earlier sketches in CA 1-4R, CANR-1
See also CAAS 1
See also AITN 1
See also CLC 7, 13
See also MTCW
Wallace, James Donald 1937- ... 108
Wallace, James 1947- ... 138
Wallace, Joanne (M.) 1938- ... 117
Wallace, John A(dam) 1915- ... 5-8R
See also SATA 3
Wallace, John Malcolm 1928- ... 25-28R
Wallace, K(ay) K. 1949- ... 111
Wallace, Karl R(ichards) 1906-1973 ... 101
Wallace, Lew(is) 1827(?)-1905 Brief entry ... 120
Wallace, Lewis Grant 1910- ... CAP-2
Earlier sketch in CA 23-24
Wallace, Lila Bell Acheson
1889-1984 Obituary ... 112
Brief entry ... 105
Wallace, Lillian Parker 1890-1971 ... 1-4R
Obituary ... 103
Wallace, Luther T(ompkins) 1928- ... 13-16R
Wallace, Marc J. Jr. 1944- ... 114
Wallace, Marjorie ... 101
Wallace, Michael David 1943- ... 77-80
Wallace, Michele Faith 1952- ... 108
Wallace, Mike 1918- ... 65-68
Wallace, Myron Leon
See Wallace, Mike
Wallace, Nigel
See Hamilton, Charles (Harold St. John)
Wallace, Pamela 1949- ... 105
Wallace, Pat
See Strother, Pat Wallace
Wallace, Paul A(nthony) W(ilson) 1891- ... CAP-1
Earlier sketch in CA 13-16
Wallace, Paul 1931- ... 61-64
Wallace, Philip (Adrian) Hope
See Hope-Wallace, Philip (Adrian)
Wallace, Phyllis Ann ... 105
Wallace, Richard
See Ind, Allison
Wallace, Robert Ash 1921- ... 1-4R
Wallace, Robert Kimball 1944- ... 69-72
Wallace, Robert 1932- ... CANR-10
Earlier sketch in CA 13-16R
See also SATA 37, 47
Wallace, Robin 1955- ... 128
Wallace, Roger
See Charlier, Roger H(enri)
Wallace, Ronald S(tewart) 1911- ... CANR-5
Earlier sketch in CA 9-12R
Wallace, Ronald (William) 1945- ... CANR-20
Earlier sketches in CA 57-60, CANR-6
Wallace, Ruby Ann 1923(?)- ... CANR-26
Earlier sketch in CA 112
See also BW
Wallace, Samuel E(ugene) 1935- ... 41-44R
Wallace, Sarah Leslie 1914- ... 9-12R
Wallace, Sister M. Jean
See Paxton, Mary Jean Wallace
Wallace, Sylvia ... CANR-27
Earlier sketch in CA 73-76
Wallace, Tom 1874-1961 Obituary ... 93-96
Wallace, Walter L. 1927- ... 81-84
Wallace, Willard M(osher) 1911- ... 13-16R
Wallace, William A(lan) 1935- ... 49-52
Wallace, William A(ugustine) 1918- ... 41-44R
Wallace, William Keith 1947- ... 124
See also Wallace, Bill
See also SATA 53
Wallace, William N. 1924- ... 13-16R
See also Wallace, Bill
Wallace, William Stewart
1884-1970 Obituary ... 116
Wallace-Brodeur, Ruth 1941- ... 107
See also SATA 41, 51
Wallace-Clarke, George 1916- ... 117
Wallace-Crabbe, Chris(topher Keith)
1934- ... CANR-14
Earlier sketch in CA 77-80
Wallace-Hadrill, Andrew (Frederic) 1951- ... 117
Wallace-Hadrill, D(avid) S(utherland)
1920- ... 29-32R
Wallace-Hadrill, John Michael 1916-1985 ... 5-8R
Obituary ... 118
Wallach, Erica 1922- ... 21-24R
Wallach, Ira 1913- ... 9-12R
Wallach, Janet 1942- ... CANR-38
Earlier sketch in CA 106
Wallach, Mark I(rwin) 1949- ... 69-72
Wallach, Michael A(rthur) 1933- ... CANR-26
Earlier sketches in CA 13-16R, CANR-11
Wallach, Paul I. 1927- ... CANR-8
Earlier sketch in CA 17-20R
Wallach, Robert Charles 1935- ... 107
Wallach, Sidney 1905-1979 ... 103
Obituary ... 89-92
Wallance, Gregory Joseph 1948- ... 109
Wallant, Edward Lewis 1926-1962 ... CANR-22
Earlier sketch in CA 1-4R
See also CLC 5, 10
See also DLB 2, 28
See also MTCW
Wallechinsky, David 1948- ... CANR-27
Earlier sketch in CA 61-64
Wallek, Lee
See Johnson, Curt(is Lee)
Wallen, Carl J(oseph) 1931- ... 93-96
Wallenstein, Barry J(ay) 1940- ... CANR-11
Earlier sketch in CA 45-48
Wallenstein, Meir 1903- ... CAP-1
Earlier sketch in CA 13-16
Waller, Altina L(aura) 1940- ... 112
Waller, Brown
See Fraser, W(aller) B(rown)
Waller, Charles T(homas) 1934- ... 61-64
Waller, G(ary) F(redric) 1944- ... CANR-31
Earlier sketch in CA 112
Waller, Gary
See Waller, G(ary) F(redric)
Waller, George Macgregor 1919- ... 9-12R
Waller, Gregory A(lbert) 1950- ... 127
Waller, Irene Ellen 1928- ... 109
Waller, J(ames) Irvin 1944- ... CANR-14
Earlier sketch in CA 61-64
Waller, Jane (Ashton) 1944- ... 132
Waller, John Stanier 1917- ... 45-48
Waller, Leslie 1923- ... CANR-2
Earlier sketch in CA 1-4R
See also SATA 20
Waller, Peter Louis 1935- ... 106
Waller, Robert J(ames) 1955- ... 117
Wallerstein, Immanuel 1930- ... CANR-24
Earlier sketches in CA 21-24R, CANR-9
Wallerstein, Judith (Hannah) S(aretsky)
1921- ... 124
Brief entry ... 105
See also BEST 89:3
Wallerstein, Mitchel B(ruce) 1949- ... 105
Wallerstein, Robert S(olomon) 1921- ... CANR-12
Earlier sketch in CA 33-36R
Walley, David G. 1945- ... CANR-37
Earlier sketch in CA 41-44R
Wallhauser, Henry T. 1930- ... 29-32R
Wallich, Henry C(hristopher)
1914-1988 ... CANR-6
Obituary ... 126
Earlier sketch in CA 1-4R
Wallich-Clifford, Anton 1923- ... 61-64
Wallig, Gaird (Elizabeth) 1942- ... 106
Wallin, Luke 1943- ... 130
Walling, William (Herbert) 1926- ... 103
Wallis, Charles L(angworthy) ... CANR-8
Earlier sketch in CA 5-8R
Wallis, G. McDonald
See Campbell, Hope
Wallis, George A. 1892- ... 17-20R
Wallis, Hal B.
See Wallis, Harold Brent
Wallis, Harold Brent 1898(?)-1986 Obituary ... 120
Wallis, Jim 1948- ... 102
Wallis, Keith 1930- ... 25-28R
Wallis, Kenneth F(rank) 1938- ... CANR-24
Earlier sketch in CA 45-48
Wallis, R(ichard) T(yrrell) 1941- ... 45-48
Wallis, Redmond Frankton 1933- ... 5-8R
Wallis, Robert 1900- ... CAP-2
Earlier sketch in CA 29-32
Wallis, Roy 1945- ... CANR-17
Earlier sketch in CA 97-100
Wallis, Ruth O(tis) S(awtell)
1895-1978 Obituary ... 73-76
Wallis, W(ilson) Allen 1912- ... 41-44R
Wallmann, Jeffrey M(iner) 1941- ... CANR-35
Earlier sketches in CA 77-80, CANR-14
Wallmeyer, Dick
See Wallmeyer, Richard
Wallmeyer, Richard 1931- ... 133
Wallner, Alexandra 1946- ... CANR-13
Earlier sketch in CA 73-76
See also SATA 41, 51
Wallner, John C. 1945- ... MAICYA
See also SATA 10, 51
Wallop, (John) Douglass III
1920-1985 ... CANR-13
Obituary ... 115
Earlier sketch in CA 73-76
Wallop, Lucille Fletcher 1912- ... 13-16R
Wallower, Lucille ... CANR-9
Earlier sketch in CA 21-24R
See also SATA 11
Wallraff, Charles Fredric 1909- ... 1-4R
Walls, David Stuart 1941- ... CANR-14
Earlier sketch in CA 37-40R
Walls, Dwayne E(stes) 1932- ... CANR-14
Earlier sketch in CA 41-44R
Walls, H(enry) J(ames) 1907-1988 ... 9-12R
Obituary ... 126
Walls, Ian G(ascoigne) 1922- ... 104
Walls, Ronald 1920- ... 103
Walls, William J(acob) 1885-1975 ... 81-84
Wallsten, Robert 1912- ... 101
Wallwork, Ernest (Edward) 1937- ... 41-44R
Walman, Jerome 1937- ... 125
Walmsley, Arnold Robert 1912- ... 41-44R
Walmsley, Buck
See Walmsley, Haines
Walmsley, (Ronald) Charles
1910-1983 Obituary ... 110
Walmsley, Haines 1930(?)-1983 Obituary ... 111
Walmsley, Jane ... 128
Walmsley, Leo 1892-1966 ... CAP-1
Earlier sketch in CA 11-12
Walmsley, Lewis C(alvin) 1897- ... 61-64
Walmsley, Robert 1905-1976 ... CAP-2
Earlier sketch in CA 29-32
Walmsley, Tom 1948- ... 126
Waln, Nora 1895-1964 Obituary ... 89-92
Walpole, Horace 1717-1797 ... DLB 39, 104
Walpole, Hugh (Seymour)
1884-1941 Brief entry ... 104
See also DLB 34
See also TCLC 5
Walpole, Ronald Noel 1903- ... 106
Walrath, Douglas Alan 1933- ... 120
Walrath, Jane Dwyer 1939- ... 97-100
Walrond, Eric (Derwent) 1898-1966 ... 125
See also BW
See also DLB 51
Walschap, Gerard 1898- ... 103
Walsdorf, John J(oseph) 1941- ... 115
Walser, Martin 1927- ... CANR-8
Earlier sketch in CA 57-60
See also CLC 27
See also DLB 75
Walser, Richard (Gaither) 1908- ... CANR-2
Earlier sketch in CA 5-8R
Walser, Robert 1878-1956 Brief entry ... 118
See also DLB 66
See also TCLC 18
Walsh, Ann 1942- ... SATA 62
Walsh, Annmarie Hauck 1938- ... 25-28R
Walsh, Bren(dan) 1921- ... 121
Walsh, Chad 1914-1991 ... CANR-6
Obituary ... 133
Earlier sketch in CA 1-4R
Walsh, Clune J(oseph) Jr. 1928- ... 114
Walsh, Des 1954- ... 116
Walsh, Donald Devenish 1903-1980 ... CANR-3
Obituary ... 97-100
Earlier sketch in CA 49-52
Walsh, Edward J(oseph) 1937- ... 37-40R
Walsh, Edward Warren
1930(?)-1986 Obituary ... 118
Walsh, Elizabeth M(iller) 1937- ... 120
Walsh, Ellen Stoll 1942- ... 104
See also SATA 49
Walsh, Ernest 1895-1926 Brief entry ... 109
See also DLB 4, 45
Walsh, George B. 1947(?)-1989 Obituary ... 127
Walsh, George Johnston 1889-1981 ... SATA 53
Walsh, George (Vincent) 1923- ... 109
Walsh, George (William) 1931- ... 118
Brief entry ... 114
Walsh, Gillian Paton
See Paton Walsh, Gillian
Walsh, Jack 1919(?)-1984 Obituary ... 114
Walsh, James
See Robinson, Frank M(alcolm)
Walsh, James Edward 1891-1981 Obituary ... 104
Walsh, James J(erome) 1924- ... 9-12R
Walsh, James P(atrick) 1937- ... 111
Walsh, James 1920-1986(?) Obituary ... 119
Walsh, Jill Paton
See Paton Walsh, Gillian
See also CLC 35
See also CLR 2
See also SAAS 3
Walsh, John (Dixon) 1927- ... 17-20R
Walsh, John Evangelist 1927- ... 85-88
Walsh, Justin E(arl) 1933- ... CANR-10
Earlier sketch in CA 25-28R
Walsh, Marcus 1947- ... 118
Walsh, Marnie
See Walsh, M.M.B.
Walsh, Mary Williams 1955- ... 136
Walsh, Maurice 1879-1964 ... 133
Brief entry ... 124
Walsh, Michael J. 1937- ... 106
Walsh, M.M.B. ... 101
Walsh, Myles E(ugene) 1937- ... 109
Walsh, P(atrick) G(erard) 1923- ... CANR-28
Earlier sketch in CA 25-28R
Walsh, Patricia L(ouise) 1942- ... 109
Walsh, Raoul 1887-1980 Obituary ... 102
Walsh, (Walter) Richard 1923- ... 25-28R
Walsh, Richard 1941- ... 120
Walsh, Robert 1784-1859 ... DLB 59
Walsh, Sheila 1928- ... 115
Walsh, (Michael) Stephen 1942- ... 37-40R
Walsh, (Richard) Taylor 1947- ... 73-76
Walsh, Thomas (Francis Morgan)
1908-1984 Obituary ... 114
Walsh, Timothy J(ames) 1927- ... 41-44R
Walsh, W(alter) Bruce 1936- ... 93-96
Walsh, Warren Bartlett 1909- ... CAP-2
Earlier sketch in CA 13-16
Walsh, William B(ertalan) 1920- ... CANR-4
Earlier sketch in CA 49-52
Walsh, William Henry 1913-1986 Obituary ... 119
Walsh, William 1916- ... CANR-11
Earlier sketch in CA 65-68
Walshe, M(aurice) O'C(onnell) 1911- ... 5-8R
Walshe, Peter (Aubrey) 1934- ... 130
Walshe, R(obert) D(aniel) 1923- ... CANR-21
Earlier sketch in CA 104
Walster, Elaine Hatfield
See Hatfield, Elaine (Catherine)
Walster, G. William 1941- ... 85-88
Walston, Joseph
See Walston, Marie
Walston, Marie 1925- ... 41-44R
Walt, Lewis W(illiam) 1913-1989 ... 33-36R
Obituary ... 128
Waltari, Mika (Toimi) 1908-1979 ... 9-12R
Obituary ... 89-92
Waltch, Lilla M. 1932- ... 128
Walter, Bruno
See Schlesinger, Bruno Walter
Walter, Claire 1943- ... 81-84
Walter, Dorothy Blake 1908- ... CAP-1
Earlier sketch in CA 11-12
Walter, Elizabeth ... CANR-38
Earlier sketches in CA 97-100, CANR-17
Walter, Eugene Victor 1925- ... 25-28R
Walter, Eugene 1927- ... 9-12R
Walter, Frances V. 1923- ... SATA 71
Walter, Gladys Mae 1901-1973 ... 41-44R
Walter, Hartmut 1940- ... 89-92
Walter, Ingo 1940- ... CANR-22
Earlier sketches in CA 17-20R, CANR-7
Walter, J(ulian) A(nthony) 1948- ... 120
Walter, John 1948- ... 134
Walter, Mildred Pitts 1922- ... 138
See also CLR 15
See also MAICYA
See also SAAS 12
See also SATA 45, 69
Walter, Nancy
See Holmgren, Norah
Walter, Nina Willis 1900- ... 5-8R
Walter, Otis M. 1921- ... 5-8R
Walter, Richard 1944- ... 128
Walter, Robert H(enry) K(eamer Jr.) 1922- ... 5-8R
Walter, Samuel 1916- ... 5-8R
Walter, Tony
See Walter, J(ulian) A(nthony)
Walter, William Christian
See Andersen, Hans Christian
Walter, William Grey 1910-1977 ... 103
Walters, A(lan) A(rthur) 1926- ... CANR-26
Earlier sketch in CA 29-32R
Walters, Anna L. 1946- ... 73-76
Walters, Audrey 1929- ... SATA 18
Walters, Barbara 1931- ... 65-68
See also AITN 2
Walters, Basil L(eon) 1896-1975 Obituary ... 89-92
Walters, C(harles) Glenn 1929- ... 81-84
Walters, Chad
See Smith, Richard Rein
Walters, D(avid) Gareth 1948- ... 128
Walters, Derek 1936- ... 128
Walters, Dorothy Mae Wells 1924- ... CANR-2
Earlier sketch in CA 5-8R
Walters, Dorothy 1928- ... 65-68
Walters, Dottie
See Walters, Dorothy Mae Wells
Walters, Eleanor 1955- ... 108
Walters, Helen B. ... 133
Obituary ... 121
See also SATA 50
Walters, Hugh
See Hughes, Walter (Llewellyn)
Walters, J. Donald 1926- ... 132
Walters, Jack Edward 1896-1967 ... 5-8R
Obituary ... 134
Walters, Janet Lane 1936- ... 49-52
Walters, Jennifer Waelti
See Waelti-Walters, Jennifer
Walters, John Beauchamp 1906- ... CANR-6
Earlier sketch in CA 5-8R
Walters, John Bennett Jr. 1912- ... 105
Walters, Kenneth D. 1941- ... 132
Walters, LeRoy (B. Jr.) 1940- ... 108
Walters, Nell
See Muse, Patricia (Alice)
Walters, Richard P(aul) 1935- ... 107
Walters, Rick
See Rowland, D(onald) S(ydney)
Walters, Robert Mark 1938- ... 69-72
Walters, Robert S(tephen) 1941- ... 29-32R
Walters, Ronald G(ordon) 1942- ... 85-88
Walters, Roy W(ashington) 1918- ... 93-96
Walters, Shelly
See Sheldon, Walter J.
Walters, Sister Annette 1910- ... 37-40R
Walters, Stanley D(avid) 1931- ... 53-56
Walters, Thomas N(oble) 1935- ... 65-68
Walters, Vernon A(nthony) 1917- ... 122
Waltham, Antony Clive 1942- ... CANR-26
Earlier sketches in CA 65-68, CANR-10
Walther, Fritz R(udolf) 1921- ... 132
Walther, R(ichard) E(rnest) 1921- ... 41-44R
Walther, Regis (Hills) 1917-1983 ... CANR-8
Obituary ... 111
Earlier sketch in CA 17-20R
Walther, Thomas A. 1950- ... 107
See also SATA 31
Walther, Tom
See Walther, Thomas A.
Waltman, Jerold (Lloyd) 1945- ... 117
Waltman, John L. 1946- ... 120
Waltner, Elma 1912- ... 17-20R
See also SATA 40
Waltner, Willard H. 1909- ... SATA 40
Walton, Alfred Grant 1887-1970 ... CAP-1
Earlier sketch in CA 13-14
Walton, Bobbi Smith 1949- ... 137
Walton, Bryce 1918- ... 21-24R
Walton, Clarence C. 1915- ... CANR-3
Earlier sketch in CA 1-4R
Walton, Clyde C(ameron) 1925- ... 29-32R
Walton, Craig 1934- ... 41-44R
Walton, Donald William 1917- ... 112
Walton, Douglas N(eil) 1942- ... 117
Walton, Ed(ward Hazen) 1931- ... CANR-22
Earlier sketch in CA 105
Walton, Elizabeth Cheatham ... 5-8R
Walton, Evangeline
See Ensley, Evangeline
Walton, George (H.) 1904- ... 17-20R
Walton, Hanes Jr. 1942- ... 41-44R
Walton, Henry J(ohn) 1924- ... CANR-35
Earlier sketch in CA 53-56
Walton, Izaak 1593-1683 ... CDBLB Before 1660
Walton, J(ohn) Michael 1939- ... 117
Walton, John K(immons) 1948- ... 124
Walton, John (Nicholas) 1922- ... 127
Walton, John 1910- ... CANR-5
Earlier sketch in CA 1-4R
Walton, John 1937- ... 89-92
Walton, Kendall L(ewis) 1939- ... 136
Walton, Luke
See Henderson, Bill
Walton, Ortiz Montaigne 1933- ... CANR-26
Earlier sketch in CA 45-48
Walton, Richard Eugene 1931- ... 81-84
Walton, Richard J. 1928- ... 25-28R
See also SATA 4

Walton, Robert Cutler 1932- 73-76
Walton, Ronald (Gordon) 1936- 65-68
Walton, Su 1944- 25-28R
Walton, Vicki (Elizabeth) 1949- 65-68
Walton, W. Robert 1902- 69-72
Walton, William 1909- 125
Waltrip, Lela (Kingston) 1904- 5-8R
See also SATA 9
Waltrip, Mildred 1911- .... SATA 37
Waltrip, Robert
See Short, Robert Waltrip
Waltrip, Rufus (Charles) 1898- 5-8R
See also SATA 9
Waltz, Jon R(ichard) 1929- 17-20R
Waltz, Kenneth N(eal) 1924- 37-40R
Waltzer, Herbert 1930- 41-44R
Walvin, James 1942- CANR-37
Earlier sketches in CA 49-52, CANR-1, 17
Walvoord, John F(lipse) 1910- CANR-6
Earlier sketch in CA 9-12R
Walwik, Theodore J. 1937- 25-28R
Walworth, Alice
See Graham, Alice Walworth
Walworth, Arthur 1903- 21-24R
Walworth, Nancy Zinsser 1917- CANR-3
Earlier sketch in CA 5-8R
See also SATA 14
Walz, Audrey Boyers
1907(?)-1983 Obituary 109
Walz, Edgar 1914- 29-32R
Walz, Jay (Franklin) 1907-1991 49-52
Obituary 135
Walzer, Michael 1935- CANR-15
Earlier sketch in CA 37-40R
Walzer, Norman 1943- CANR-29
Earlier sketch in CA 111
Wambaugh, Joseph (Aloysius Jr.)
1937- 33-36R
See also AITN 1
See also BEST 89:3
See also CLC 3, 18
See also DLB 6
See also DLBY 83
See also MTCW
Wamble, Gaston Hugh 1923- 5-8R
Wamble, Thelma 1916- Brief entry 106
Wamsley, Gary L(ee) 1935- CANR-3
Earlier sketch in CA 49-52
Wanamaker, A(llison) Temple 1918- 17-20R
Wand, (John) William (Charles) 1885- 103
Wandel, Joseph 1918- 93-96
Wanderer, Zev W(illiam) 1932- 105
Wandesforde-Smith, Geoffrey Albert
1943- 29-32R
Wandro, Mark 1948- 106
Wandycz, Piotr Stefan 1923- CANR-2
Earlier sketch in CA 1-4R
Wang, An 1920-1990 132
Wang, C(hing) H(sien) 1940- CANR-8
Earlier sketch in CA 61-64
Wang, (Fred) Fang Yu 1913- 37-40R
Wang, Hao 1921- 65-68
Wang, Hui-Ming 1922- 33-36R
Wang, J(en) Y(u) 1918- CANR-25
Earlier sketch in CA 45-48
Wang, John Ching-yu 1934- 41-44R
Wang, Julie C(aroline) 1947- 114
Wang, Leonard J(udah) 1926- 33-36R
Wang, Sabine E(isenberg) 1925- 37-40R
Wang, Yi Chu 1916- 61-64
Wangenheim, Chris von
See von Wangenheim, Chris
Wangensteen, Owen Harding 1898-1981 103
Wangensteen, Sarah (Anne) D(avidson)
1908- 120
Wangerin, Theodora Scharffenberg 1888- 5-8R
Wangerin, Walter Jr. 1944- CANR-34
Earlier sketch in CA 108
See also SATA 37, 45
Wangermann, Ernst 1925- 103
Wang Gungwu 1930- CANR-10
Earlier sketch in CA 65-68
Wangyal, Geshe 1901(?)-1983 Obituary 108
Wang Zhongshu 1925- 117
Waniek, Marilyn Nelson 1946- CANR-15
Earlier sketch in CA 89-92
See also DLB 120
See also SATA 60
Wankowicz, Melchoir
1892(?)-1974 Obituary 53-56
Wanlass, Stanley G(len) 1941- 61-64
Wann, Kenneth D(ouglass) 1915- 5-8R
Wannamaker, Bruce
See Moncure, Jane Belk
Wannan, Bill
See Wannan, William Fielding
Wannan, William Fielding 1915- CANR-10
Earlier sketch in CA 21-24R
Wanniski, Jude 1936- 133
Wanrooy, Willem F(rederik) 1925- 118
Wanshel, Jeff(rey Mark) 1947- CANR-13
Earlier sketch in CA 57-60
Wantland, William C(harles) 1934- 111
Wantling, William 1933-1974 105
Obituary 89-92
Waples, Douglas 1893-1978 Obituary 77-80
Wapshott, Nicholas (Henry) 1952- 135
Warbler, J. M.
See Cocagnac, Augustin Maurice(-Jean)
Warbridge, C. W.
See Woods, Clee
Warburg, Fredric (John) 1898-1981 105
Warburg, James Paul 1896-1969 ....CAP-2
Obituary 25-28R
Earlier sketch in CA 21-22
Warburg, Sandol Stoddard
See Stoddard, Sandol
See also SATA 14
Warburton, Amber Arthun
1898(?)-1976 Obituary 61-64
Warburton, Clark (Abram) 1896-1979 73-76
Obituary 89-92
Warburton, Minnie 1949- 101
Warburton, William 1698-1779 ....DLB 104
Warch, Richard 1939- 105
Warcollier, Rene 1881-1962 Obituary 112
Ward, Aileen 1919- 5-8R
See also DLB 111
Ward, Alan Joseph 1936- 73-76
Ward, Allen M(ason) 1942- 89-92
Ward, Andrew (Spencer) 1946- 81-84
Ward, Anne G. 1932- 77-80
Ward, Artemus
See Browne, Charles Farrar
Ward, Arthur Henry Sarsfield
1883-1959 Brief entry 108
See also Rohmer, Sax
Ward, Barbara
See Jackson, Barbara (Ward)
Ward, Benedicta 1933- CANR-28
Earlier sketches in CA 65-68, CANR-12
Ward, Brendan Noel 1947- 129
Ward, Charles D(uane) 1935- 33-36R
Ward, Charles Dexter
See Taylor, John (Alfred)
Ward, Charlotte
See Chesney, Marion
Ward, Chester 1907-1977 Obituary 69-72
Ward, Colin 1924- 57-60
Ward, Craig 1892-1979 Obituary 85-88
Ward, David 1938- 29-32R
Ward, Dennis 1924- 13-16R
Ward, Don(ald G.) 1911- 17-20R
Ward, Donald 1909- 109
Ward, Donald 1930- 37-40R
Ward, Douglas Turner 1930- CANR-27
Earlier sketch in CA 81-84
See also BW
See also CLC 19
See also DLB 7, 38
Ward, E. D.
See Gorey, Edward (St. John)
Ward, Ed
See Stratemeyer, Edward L.
Ward, Ed(mund O.) 1948- 114
Ward, Elizabeth Campbell 1936- 45-48
Ward, Elizabeth Honor (Shedden) 1926- 9-12R
Ward, Elizabeth 1952- 110
Ward, Eric
See Ebon, Martin
Ward, Evelyn
See Everett-Green, Evelyn
Ward, Fred 1935- 85-88
Ward, Harry Merrill 1929- CANR-2
Earlier sketch in CA 1-4R
Ward, Herman Matthew 1914- CANR-39
Earlier sketches in CA 5-8R, CANR-2, 18
Ward, Hiley Henry 1929- CANR-2
Earlier sketch in CA 1-4R
Ward, J. Alan 1937- 114
Ward, J(oseph) Neville 1915- 77-80
Ward, J(ohn) P(owell) 1937- CANR-27
Earlier sketch in CA 109
Ward, James A(rthur) 1941- 49-52
Ward, James Myron 1919-1984 Obituary 112
Ward, Jay 1920-1989 ....SATA 63
Ward, John M(anning) 1919- 21-24R
Ward, John Owen 1919- 13-16R
Ward, John (Stanton) 1917- ....SATA 42
Ward, John Stephen Keith 1938- 109
Ward, John Towers 1930-1987 ....CANR-7
Obituary 122
Earlier sketch in CA 109
Ward, John William 1922-1985 ....5-8R
Obituary 116
Ward, Jonas
See Ard, William (Thomas)
and Cox, William R(obert)
and Garfield, Brian (Wynne)
Ward, Jonathon
See Stine, Whitney Ward
Ward, Joseph A(nthony Jr.) 1931- 1-4R
Ward, Justine Bayard Cutting
1879-1975 Obituary 61-64
Ward, (John Stephen) Keith 1938- CANR-37
Earlier sketches in CA 29-32R, CANR-16
Ward, Ken 1949- 136
Ward, Lynd (Kendall) 1905-1985 ....17-20R
Obituary 116
See also DLB 22
See also MAICYA
See also SATA 2, 36, 42
Ward, Maisie 1889-1975 69-72
Obituary 53-56
Ward, Martha (Eads) 17-20R
See also SATA 5
Ward, Mary Josephine
See Ward, Maisie
Ward, Matthew 1951(?)-1990 Obituary 132
Ward, Melanie
See Curtis, Richard (Alan)
and Lynch, Marilyn
Ward, Michael 1939- 37-40R
Ward, Mrs. Humphry 1851-1920 ....DLB 18
Ward, Nathaniel 1578(?)-1652 ....DLB 24
Ward, Norman 1918- 41-44R
Ward, Olivia Tucker 1927- 57-60
Ward, Patricia A(nn) 1940- 57-60
Ward, Paul W. 1905-1976 Obituary 69-72
Ward, Pearl L(ewis) 1920- 107
Ward, Peter
See Faust, Frederick (Shiller)
Ward, (William) Peter 1943- 134
Ward, Philip C. 1932- 21-24R
Ward, Philip 1938- CANR-30
Earlier sketches in CA 25-28R, CANR-12
Ward, R(ichard) H(eron) 1910-1969 ....CAP-1
Earlier sketch in CA 11-12
Ward, R. Patrick
See Holzapfel, Rudolf Patrick
Ward, Ralph Gerard 1933- 107
Ward, Ralph T(homas) 1927- 49-52
Ward, Richard J(oseph) 1921- 41-44R
Ward, Ritchie R(unyan) 1906- 29-32R
Ward, Robert E(rnest) 1927- 49-52
Ward, Robert Elmer 1937- 49-52
Ward, Robert 1943- 104
Ward, Ronald A(rthur) 1908- 53-56
Ward, Russel (Braddock) 1914- CANR-22
Earlier sketch in CA 103
Ward, Russell A(very) 1947- 110
Ward, Stephen R(alph) 1938- 65-68
Ward, Ted (Warren) 1930- CANR-16
Earlier sketch in CA 97-100
Ward, Theodora 1890-1974 ....CAP-2
Obituary 53-56
Earlier sketch in CA 33-36
Ward, Theodore (James) 1902-1983 125
Obituary 109
See also BW
See also DLB 76
Ward, Tom
See Stratemeyer, Edward L.
Ward, Virgil S(cott) 1916- 1-4R
Ward, Waylon O. 1942- 114
Ward, William Alan Heaton
See Heaton-Ward, William Alan
Ward, William Arthur 1921- 29-32R
Ward, William B(ethea) 1912- 5-8R
Ward, William Ernest Frank 1900- CANR-19
Earlier sketches in CA 9-12R, CANR-4
Ward, William G. 1929- 21-24R
Ward, William R(eed) 1918- 61-64
Ward, Winfred O('Neil) 1933- 106
Warddel, Nora Helen
See Heron-Allen, Edward
Warde, Alan 1949- CANR-31
Earlier sketch in CA 112
Warde, William F.
See Novack, George (Edward)
Wardell, Dean
See Prince, J(ack) H(arvey)
Wardell, Phyl(lis Robinson) 1909- CAP-1
Earlier sketch in CA 11-12
Warden, G(erard) B(ryce) 1939- 29-32R
Warden, John 1936- 41-44R
Warden, Lewis (Christopher) 1913- 13-16R
Wardhaugh, Ronald 1932- 37-40R
Wardle, David 1930- 69-72
Wardle, (John) Irving 1929- 77-80
Wardle, Lynn D(ennis) 1947- 109
Wardle, Ralph Martin 1909- CANR-5
Earlier sketch in CA 1-4R
See also DLB 103
Wardman, Alan (Edgar) 1926-1986 77-80
Obituary 120
Wardman, Gordon 1948- 136
Ward-Perkins, John Bryan 1912-1981 93-96
Obituary 108
Wardroper, John (Edmund) 1923- 29-32R
Wardropper, Bruce W(ear) 1919- 13-16R
Wardropper, Ian (Bruce) 1951- 137
Ward-Thomas, Evelyn Bridget Patricia Stephens
1928- CANR-26
Earlier sketches in CA 9-12R, CANR-5
Ware, Caroline F. 1899-1990 Obituary 131
Ware, Ciji 1942- 103
Ware, Clyde 1932- 33-36R
Ware, Emma 1896(?)-1975 Obituary 57-60
Ware, George W(hitaker) 1902- 13-16R
Ware, Gilbert 1933- 65-68
Ware, Jane (O.) 1936- 133
Ware, Jean (Jones) 1914- CAP-1
Earlier sketch in CA 11-12
Ware, John
See Mabley, Edward (Howe)
Ware, Kallistos (Timothy Richard)
1934- CANR-24
Earlier sketches in CA 9-12R, CANR-7
Ware, Leon (Vernon) 1909-1976 ....CANR-2
Earlier sketch in CA 1-4R
See also SATA 4
Ware, Leonard 1900(?)-1976 Obituary 69-72
Ware, Runa Erwin CAP-2
Earlier sketch in CA 29-32
Ware, Timothy
See Ware, Kallistos (Timothy Richard)
Ware, W. Porter 1904- 105
Ware, Wallace
See Karp, David
Ware, William 1797-1852 ....DLB 1
Wareham, John 1940- 101
Warenski, Marilyn L(iston) 1931- 117
Warfel, Harry R(edcay) 1899-1971 ....CAP-1
Earlier sketch in CA 13-14
Warfield, Gerald (Alexander) 1940- 117
Warford, Jeremy J(ames) 1938- 37-40R
Wargo, Dan M. 1920- 21-24R
Warhaft, Sidney 1921- 61-64
Warhol, Andy 1928(?)-1987 ....CANR-34
Obituary 121
Earlier sketch in CA 89-92
See also BEST 89:4
See also CLC 20
Warhol, Robyn R. 1955- 135
Wark, David M(ayer) 1934- 33-36R
Wark, Ian W(illiam) 1899- CAP-2
Earlier sketch in CA 29-32
Wark, Robert R(odger) 1924- CANR-8
Earlier sketch in CA 61-64
Wark, Wesley K. 1952- 123
Warkentin, Germaine (Therese) 1933- 109
Warkentin, John 1928- 9-12R
Warland, John
See Buchanan-Brown, John
Warlimont, Walter 1894- CAP-1
Earlier sketch in CA 13-16
Warlum, Michael Frank 1940- 37-40R
Warman, (William) Eric 1904- CAP-1
Earlier sketch in CA 13-14
Warman, Henry J(ohn) 1907-1982 ....41-44R
Obituary 133
Warmbrand, Max 1896(?)-1976 Obituary 65-68
Warmbrunn, Werner 1920- 21-24R
Warmington, Brian Herbert 1924- 65-68
Warmington, E(ric) H(erbert) 1898-1987 124
Warmington, William Allan 1922- 5-8R
Warmke, Roman F. 1929- CANR-9
Earlier sketch in CA 17-20R
Warnath, Charles F. 1925- 37-40R
Warne, Clinton L. 1921- 13-16R
Warne, Colston Estey 1900-1987 Obituary 122
Warne, William E(lmo) 1905- 41-44R
Warner, Alan 1912- 104
Warner, B. F.
See Bowers, Warner Fremont
Warner, Bob
See Warner, Robert
Warner, Charles Dudley 1829-1900 ....DLB 64
Warner, Daniel S(umner) 1906-1983 ....CANR-16
Earlier sketch in CA 1-4R
Warner, Deborah Jean 1941- 108
Warner, Denis Ashton 1917- CANR-3
Earlier sketch in CA 5-8R
Warner, Edythe Records 1916-1980 ....5-8R
Obituary 134
Warner, Emily S(mith)
1902(?)-1980 Obituary 97-100
Warner, Esther S.
See Dendel, Esther (Sietmann Warner)
Warner, Francis (Robert le Plastrier)
1937- CANR-11
Earlier sketch in CA 53-56
See also CLC 14
Warner, Frank
See Richardson, Gladwell
Warner, Frank A. CANR-26
Earlier sketches in CAP-2, CA 19-20
See also SATA 1, 67
Warner, Gary 1936- 21-24R
Warner, (George) Geoffrey John 1923- 1-4R
Warner, Gertrude Chandler 1890-1979 ....CANR-3
Earlier sketch in CA 1-4R
See also SATA 9
Warner, Glen 1947- 121
Warner, H(oyt) Landon 1911- 13-16R
Warner, Harry Jr. 1922- 29-32R
Warner, Jack L(eonard)
1892-1978 Obituary 108
Warner, Jack 1896-1981 Obituary 108
Warner, James A(loysius) 1918- CANR-24
Earlier sketch in CA 45-48
Warner, John Harley 1953- 127
Warner, Ken(neth Wilson Jr.) 1928- CANR-10
Earlier sketch in CA 65-68
Warner, Kenneth (Lewis) 1915- CAP-1
Earlier sketch in CA 9-10
Warner, Langdon 1881-1955 Brief entry 112
Warner, Lucien (Hynes)
1900-1963 Obituary 112
Warner, Lucille Schulberg CANR-11
Earlier sketch in CA 69-72
See also SATA 30
Warner, Marina 1946- CANR-21
Earlier sketch in CA 65-68
See also CLC 59
Warner, Martin 1940- 137
Warner, Matt
See Fichter, George S.
Warner, Oliver (Martin Wilson)
1903-1976 ....CANR-3
Obituary 69-72
Earlier sketch in CA 1-4R
See also SATA 29
Warner, Philip 1914- CANR-18
Earlier sketch in CA 101
Warner, Rex (Ernest) 1905-1986 89-92
Obituary 119
See also CLC 45
See also DLB 15
Warner, Richard 1943- 120
Warner, Robert M(ark) 1927- CANR-7
Earlier sketch in CA 9-12R
Warner, Robert 1905- 53-56
Warner, Sam Bass Jr. 1928- CANR-39
Earlier sketches in CA 5-8R, CANR-2, 17
Warner, Seth 1927- 53-56
Warner, Sharon Oard 1952- 138
Warner, Susan (Bogert) 1819-1885 ....DLB 3, 42
Warner, Sylvia (Constance) Ashton
See Ashton-Warner, Sylvia (Constance)
Warner, Sylvia Townsend 1893-1978 ....CANR-16
Obituary 77-80
Earlier sketch in CA 61-64
See also CLC 7, 19
See also DLB 34
See also MTCW
Warner, Val 1946- CANR-23
Earlier sketch in CA 49-52
Warner, Virginia
See Brodine, Virginia Warner
Warner, W(illiam) Lloyd 1898-1970 ....CANR-2
Obituary 29-32R
Earlier sketch in CA 1-4R

Warner, Wayne E(arl) 1933- CANR-3
Earlier sketch in CA 49-52
Warner, William W(hitesides) 1920- 134
Brief entry 114
Warner-Crozetti, R(uth G.) 1913- 101
Warnick, Barbara 1946- 120
Warnock, G(eoffrey) J(ames) 1923- 21-24R
Warnock, Mary (Wilson) 1924- CANR-8
Earlier sketch in CA 5-8R
Warr, Bertram 1917-1943 .... DLB 88
Warr, Peter B(ryan) 1937- 25-28R
Warrack, Graeme Matthew
1913-1985 Obituary 115
Warrack, John 1928- CANR-5
Earlier sketch in CA 13-16R
Warre, Michael 1922-1987 Obituary 121
Warren, Andrew
See Tute, Warren (Stanley)
Warren, Austin 1899-1986 ....17-20R
Obituary 120
Warren, Betsy
See Warren, Elizabeth Avery
Warren, Bill 1943- 118
Warren, Billy
See Warren, William Stephen
Warren, Cathy ....SATA 46, 62
Warren, Charles Marquis
1913(?)-1990 Obituary 132
Warren, Dave
See Wiersbe, Warren W(endell)
Warren, David 1943- 77-80
Warren, Donald Irwin 1935- CANR-1
Earlier sketch in CA 45-48
Warren, Donald R. 1933- 111
Warren, Doug(las) 1935- CANR-34
Earlier sketch in CA 61-64
Warren, E(ugene) H(oward) Jr. 1943- 111
Warren, Earl 1891-1974 123
Obituary 49-52
Warren, Elizabeth
See Supraner, Robyn
Warren, Elizabeth Avery 1916- CANR-8
Earlier sketch in CA 5-8R
See also SATA 38, 46
Warren, (Francis) Eugene 1941- CANR-1
Earlier sketch in CA 49-52
Warren, Frank A. III 1933- Brief entry 115
Warren, Gordon Harris 1944- 114
Warren, Harold Ostrander Jr.
1910-1985 Obituary 116
Warren, Harris G(aylord) 1906- CANR-5
Earlier sketch in CA 1-4R
Warren, Harry
See Guaragna, Salvatore
Warren, James E(dward) Jr. 1908- CANR-24
Earlier sketch in CA 21-24R
Warren, James Hugo Jr.
1928(?)-1983 Obituary 110
Warren, James Vaughn
1915-1990 Obituary 130
Warren, Jefferson T(rowbridge) 1912- 41-44R
Warren, John Byrne Leicester
See De Tabley, Lord
Warren, (William) John 1937- 138
Warren, Joyce W(illiams) 1935- 77-80
See also SATA 18
Warren, Kenneth 1931- 109
Warren, Lansing 1894-1987 Obituary 124
Warren, Lella 1899-1982 Obituary 113
See also DLBY 83
Warren, Louis Austin 1885-1983 ....CANR-21
Obituary 110
Earlier sketch in CA 5-8R
Warren, Louise 1909(?)-1981 Obituary 104
Warren, Lucian (Crissey) 1913-1988 101
Obituary 126
Warren, Mary Bondurant 1930- CANR-27
Earlier sketches in CA 73-76, CANR-12
Warren, Mary Douglas
See Greig, Maysie
Warren, Mary Phraner 1929- CANR-5
Earlier sketch in CA 53-56
See also SATA 10
Warren, Matthew Madison
1907-1986 Obituary 119
Warren, Mercy Otis 1728-1814 .... DLB 31
Warren, Michael 1935- 112
Warren, Patricia Nell 1936- CANR-1
Earlier sketch in CA 45-48
Warren, Peter Whitson 1941- CANR-5
Earlier sketch in CA 53-56
Warren, Richard M. 1925- 112
Warren, Robert Penn 1905-1989 ....CANR-10
Obituary 129
Earlier sketch in CA 13-16R
See also AITN 1
See also CDALB 1968-1988
See also CLC 1, 4, 6, 8, 10, 13, 18, 39, 53, 59
See also DLB 2, 48
See also DLBY 80, 89
See also MTCW
See also SATA 46, 63
See also SSC 4
See also WLC
Warren, Roland L(eslie) 1915- CANR-26
Earlier sketches in CA 57-60, CANR-10
Warren, Sandra K. 1944- 138
Warren, Sidney 1916- 25-28R
Warren, Thomas (Bratton) 1920- 103
Warren, Thomas L(eo) 1937- 111
Warren, Vernon
See Chapman, G(eorge) W(arren) Vernon
Warren, Virginia Burgess 1913- 13-16R
Warren, W(ilfred) Lewis 1929- CANR-21
Earlier sketch in CA 1-4R
Warren, W(illiam) Preston 1901- 37-40R

Warren, William Stephen 1882-1968 .... CAP-2
Earlier sketch in CA 21-22
See also SATA 9
Warrender, James Howard
1922-1985 Obituary 116
Warrick, Patricia Scott 1925- CANR-25
Earlier sketches in CA 61-64, CANR-8
See also SATA 35
Warriner, Charles K(ing) 1920- 41-44R
Warriner, John 1907(?)-1987 Obituary 123
See also SATA 53
Warrner, Thomas W(endell) 1955- 118
Warry, J(ohn) G(ibson) 1916- 5-8R
Warsaw, Irene CAP-1
Earlier sketch in CA 13-16
Warsh
See Warshaw, Jerry
Warsh, David (Lewis) 1944- 118
Warsh, Lewis 1944- CANR-24
Earlier sketches in CA 61-64, CANR-9
Warshaw, Jerry 1929- CANR-14
Earlier sketch in CA 37-40R
See also SATA 30
Warshaw, Leon J(oseph) 1917- 107
Warshofsky, Fred 1931- 9-12R
See also SATA 24
Warshofsky, Isaac
See Singer, Isaac Bashevis
Wartels, Nat(han) 1902-1990 Obituary 130
Warth, Robert D(ouglas) 1921- 9-12R
Wartofsky, Marx W(illiam) 1928- 41-44R
Wartofsky, (William) Victor 1931- 29-32R
Warton, Joseph 1722-1800 ....DLB 104, 109
Warton, Thomas 1728-1790 ....DLB 104, 109
Wartski, Maureen (Ann Crane) 1940- 89-92
See also SATA 37, 50
Waruk, Kona
See Harris, (Theodore) Wilson
Warung, Price 1855-1911 .... TCLC 45
Warwick, Alan R(oss) 1900-1973 112
See also SATA 42
Warwick, Christopher 1949- 110
Warwick, Dennis 1930- 73-76
Warwick, Dolores
See Frese, Dolores Warwick
Warwick, Donald P(hillip) 1934- 118
Warwick, Jack 1930- 29-32R
Warwick, James 1894(?)-1983 Obituary 110
Warwick, Jarvis
See Garner, Hugh
Warwick, Ray 1911(?)-1983 Obituary 109
Warwick, Roger 1912-1991 109
Obituary 135
Warzeski, Walter C. 1929- 37-40R
Wa-Sha-Quon-Asin
See Belaney, Archibald Stansfeld
Wa-sha-quon-asin
See Belaney, Archibald Stansfeld
Washburn, (Henry) Bradford (Jr.)
1910- CANR-3
Earlier sketch in CA 49-52
See also SATA 38
Washburn, Charles 1890(?)-1972 Obituary 104
Washburn, Dorothy K(oster) 1945- CANR-24
Earlier sketch in CA 106
Washburn, Jan(ice) 1926- 93-96
See also SATA 63
Washburn, Mark 1948- 77-80
Washburn, O(swell) A(aron) 1914- 57-60
Washburn, Sherwood L(arned)
1911- Brief entry 105
Washburn, Wilcomb Edward 1925- 41-44R
Washburne, Carleton W(olsey) 1889- CAP-1
Earlier sketch in CA 13-16
Washburne, Heluiz Chandler 1892-1970 .... CAP-1
Obituary 104
Earlier sketch in CA 11-12
See also SATA 10, 26
Washington, Alex
See Harris, Mark
Washington, Booker T(aliaferro) 1856-1915 125
Brief entry 114
See also BLC 3
See also BW
See also SATA 28
See also TCLC 10
Washington, Chester Lloyd
1902-1983 Obituary 110
Washington, George 1732-1799 .... DLB 31
Washington, Gladys J(oseph) 1931- 29-32R
Washington, Harold R(obert) 1935- 112
Washington, Ida Harrison 1924- CANR-35
Earlier sketch in CA 107
Washington, Joseph R(eed) Jr. 1930- 9-12R
Washington, (Catherine) Marguerite Beauchamp
1892-1972 .... CAP-1
Earlier sketch in CA 9-10
Washington, Mary Helen 1941- CANR-26
Earlier sketch in CA 65-68
See also BW
Washington, Pat Beauchamp
See
Washington, (Catherine) Marguerite Beauchamp
Washton, Nathan S(eymour) 1916- 53-56
Wasiolek, Edward 1924- CANR-6
Earlier sketch in CA 1-4R
Waskin, Yvonne 1923- 21-24R
Waskow, Arthur I(rwin) 1933- CANR-4
Earlier sketch in CA 5-8R
Wasley, Robert S(echrist) 1918- 17-20R
Wasmuth, William J. 1925- CANR-24
Earlier sketch in CA 45-48
Wason, Betty
See Wason, Elizabeth
Wason, Elizabeth 1912- CANR-2
Earlier sketch in CA 1-4R
Wason, P(eter) C(athcart) 1924- 45-48

Wasow, Mona 1933- 110
Wass, Sir Douglas (William Gretton) 1923- 138
Wassenbergh, Henri Abraham 1924- 21-24R
Wasser, Henry H. 1919- CANR-8
Earlier sketch in CA 21-24R
Wasserfall, Adel 1918- CANR-6
Earlier sketch in CA 1-4R
Wasserman, Aaron O(sias) 1927- 53-56
Wasserman, Burton 1929- 53-56
Wasserman, Dale 1917- 49-52
Wasserman, Earl R(eeves) 1913-1973 ...... CAP-2
Earlier sketch in CA 17-18
Wasserman, Gary 1944- 69-72
Wasserman, Harvey 1945- CANR-27
Earlier sketch in CA 45-48
Wasserman, Jack 1921- 61-64
Wasserman, John L. 1938- 77-80
Wasserman, Mark 1946- 125
Wasserman, Max Judd 1895-1977 ....CANR-4
Earlier sketch in CA 5-8R
Wasserman, Paul 1924- CANR-25
Earlier sketches in CA 1-4R, CANR-1
Wasserman, Pauline 1943- CANR-24
Earlier sketch in CA 110
Wasserman, Selma (Ginsberg) 1929- 5-8R
Wasserman, Sheldon 1940- CANR-24
Obituary 137
Earlier sketches in CA 65-68, CANR-9
Wassermann, (Karl) Jakob
1873-1934 Brief entry 104
See also DLB 66
See also TCLC 6
Wasserstein, Abraham 1921- 109
Wasserstein, Bruce 1947- 37-40R
Wasserstein, Susan 1952- 107
Wasserstein, Wendy 1950- 129
Brief entry 121
See also CABS 3
See also CLC 32, 59
Wasserstrom, Richard Alan 1936- CANR-6
Earlier sketch in CA 1-4R
Wasserstrom, (Jacob) William
1922-1985 ....9-12R
Obituary 115
Wassersug, Joseph D. 1912- 17-20R
Wassil, Aly 1930- 17-20R
Wassmer, Arthur C(harles) 1947- 103
Wassner, Selig O. 1923- 25-28R
Wasson, Ben 1899(?)-1982 Obituary 114
Wasson, Chester R(eynolds) 1906- CANR-10
Earlier sketch in CA 13-16R
Wasson, David Atwood 1823-1887 .... DLB 1
Wasson, Donald 1914(?)-1976 Obituary 69-72
Wasson, John M. 1928- 45-48
Wasson, R(obert) Gordon 1898- Brief entry 116
Wasti, Syed R(azi) 1929- CANR-7
Earlier sketch in CA 13-16R
Waswo, Richard 1939- 53-56
Watanabe, Hitoshi 1919- 73-76
Watanabe, Ruth T(aiko) 1916- 37-40R
Watanabe, Shigeo 1928- 112
See also CLR 8
See also MAICYA
See also SATA 32, 39
Waten, Judah Leon 1911- 101
Water, Silas
See Loomis, Noel M(iller)
Waterfield, Gordon 1903-1987 61-64
Obituary 124
Waterfield, Robin (Everard) 1914- 49-52
Waterford, Van
See Wanrooy, Willem F(rederik)
Waterhouse, Charles 1924- 29-32R
Waterhouse, Ellis K(irkham) 1905-1985 65-68
Obituary 117
Waterhouse, Keith (Spencer) 1929- CANR-38
Earlier sketch in CA 5-8R
See also CLC 47
See also DLB 13, 15
See also MTCW
Waterhouse, Larry G(ene) 1944- 37-40R
Waterhouse, Roger 1940- 129
Waterlow, Charlotte 1915- 25-28R
Waterman, Andrew (John) 1940- CANR-31
Earlier sketch in CA 109
See also DLB 40
Waterman, Arthur E. 1926- 17-20R
Waterman, Bic
See Joseph, Stephen M.
Waterman, Cary (Martha) 1942- 103
Waterman, Charles F(rederick) 1913- 49-52
Waterman, Guy 1932- 97-100
Waterman, John Thomas 1918- CANR-8
Earlier sketch in CA 5-8R
Waterman, Laura 1939- 97-100
Waterman, Leroy 1875-1972 .... CAP-1
Obituary 33-36R
Earlier sketch in CA 19-20
Waterman, Margaret 1909- 37-40R
Waterman, Richard Alan
1914-1971 Obituary 111
Watermeier, Daniel J(ude) 1940- 73-76
Water Rat
See Jones, Stephen (Phillip)
Waters, Bob 1921(?)-1987 Obituary 122
Waters, Brian Power
See Power-Waters, Brian
Waters, Chocolate 1949- 77-80
Waters, Chris
See Waters, Harold A(rthur)
Waters, D(avid) W(atkin) 1911- 25-28R
Waters, Enoch P. 1910(?)-1987 134
Obituary 122
Waters, Ethel 1896-1977 81-84
Obituary 73-76

Waters, Frank (Joseph) 1902- CANR-18
Earlier sketches in CA 5-8R, CANR-3
See also CAAS 13
See also DLBY 86
Waters, Harold A(rthur) 1926- 53-56
Waters, John F(rederick) 1930- CANR-23
Earlier sketch in CA 37-40R
See also SATA 4
Waters, John 1946- 130
Brief entry 126
Waters, K(enneth) H(ugh) 1912- 120
Waters, Marianne
See Waters, Chocolate
Waters, Mary-Alice 1942- CANR-9
Earlier sketch in CA 61-64
Waters, Michael 1949- CANR-27
Earlier sketches in CA 65-68, CANR-10
See also DLB 120
Waters, Roger 1944-
See Pink Floyd
See also CLC 35
Waters, Thomas F(rank) 1926- 81-84
Waters, William R(oland) 1920- 49-52
Waterston, Albert 1907- CAP-1
Earlier sketch in CA 13-14
Waterston, Barbara Johns 1940- 25-28R
Waterston, (Margaret) Elizabeth (Hillman)
1922- 69-72
Waterton, Betty (Marie) 1923- CANR-28
Earlier sketch in CA 111
See also SATA 34, 37
Wathen, Richard B. 1917- 37-40R
Wathern, Peter 1947- 105
Watjen, Carolyn L. T. 85-88
Watkin, David (John) 1941- CANR-26
Earlier sketch in CA 29-32R
Watkin, Edward Ingram
1888-1981 Obituary 103
Watkin, Lawrence Edward 1901- 81-84
Watkins, A(rthur) M(artin) 1924- CANR-7
Earlier sketch in CA 9-12R
Watkins, Alan (Rhun) 1933- 104
Watkins, Arthur Rich 1916- 41-44R
Watkins, Arthur Thomas Levi 1907-1965 ......5-8R
Watkins, Arthur V(ivian)
1886-1973 Obituary 111
Watkins, Evan Paul 1946- 104
Watkins, Floyd C. 1920- CANR-18
Earlier sketches in CA 1-4R, CANR-2
Watkins, Frances Ellen
See Harper, Frances Ellen Watkins
Watkins, Gerrold
See Malzberg, Barry N(athaniel)
Watkins, Glenn (Elson) 1927- Brief entry 117
Watkins, Gordon R(onald) 1930- 37-40R
Watkins, Grace F. 1927- 21-24R
Watkins, Gwen(doline Mary) 1923- 116
Watkins, J(ohn) W(illiam) N(evill) 1924- 21-24R
Watkins, Jane 1929- 77-80
Watkins, Joan C.
See Casale, Joan T(herese)
Watkins, John C(umming) Jr. 1935- 113
Watkins, John G(oodrich) 1913- CANR-38
Earlier sketches in CA 1-4R, CANR-1, 17
Watkins, Keith 1931- 106
Watkins, Mark Hanna
1903-1976 Obituary 65-68
Watkins, Mary M. 1950- CANR-20
Earlier sketch in CA 104
Watkins, Mel 1940- 89-92
Watkins, Paul 1964- 132
See also CLC 55
Watkins, Peter 1934- 109
See also SATA 66
Watkins, Ralph J(ames) 1896-1984 45-48
Obituary 113
Watkins, (Arthur) Ronald (Dare) 1904- 53-56
Watkins, Ronald J(oseph) 1945- 133
Watkins, T(homas) H(enry) 1936- CANR-31
Earlier sketches in CA 37-40R, CANR-14
Watkins, Tobias 1780-1855 .... DLB 73
Watkins, Vernon Phillips 1906-1967 .... CAP-1
Obituary 25-28R
Earlier sketch in CA 9-10
See also CLC 43
See also DLB 20
Watkins, William Jon 1942- 41-44R
Watkinson, Valerie
See Elliston, Valerie Mae (Watkinson)
Watkins-Pitchford, Denys James
1905-1990 ....CANR-38
Obituary 132
Earlier sketches in CA 9-12R, CANR-4
See also SAAS 4
See also SATA 6
See also SATO 66
Watkyn, Arthur
See Watkins, Arthur Thomas Levi
Watland, Charles D(unton) 1913-1972 ...... CAP-2
Earlier sketch in CA 25-28
Watling, James 1933- .... SATA 67
Watlington, Patricia (Sue) 1933- 37-40R
Watmough, David 1926- CANR-33
Earlier sketches in CA 85-88, CANR-15
See also DLB 53
Watney, John B(asil) 1915- CANR-5
Earlier sketch in CA 9-12R
Watney, Sanders Obituary 109
Watson, (John Hugh) Adam 1914- CANR-17
Earlier sketch in CA 25-28R
Watson, Alan
See Watson, William Alexander Jardine
Watson, Alan D(ouglas) 1942- CANR-6
Earlier sketch in CA 57-60
Watson, Aldren A(uld) 1917- CANR-39
Earlier sketches in CA 81-84, CANR-4
See also SATA 36, 42

Watson, Andrew Samuel 1920- 45-48
Watson, Anthony I. 1926-1990 Obituary 132
Watson, B. S.
See Teitelbaum, Michael
Watson, Barbara Bellow 77-80
Watson, Bernard B(ennett)
1911-1977 Obituary 69-72
Watson, Billy 1938- 77-80
Watson, Burton (DeWitt) 1925- CANR-18
Earlier sketches in CA 5-8R, CANR-3
Watson, Charles N(elles Jr.) 1939- 113
Watson, Charles S(t. Denis) Jr. 1934- 61-64
Watson, Clarissa 69-72
Watson, Clyde 1947- CANR-39
Earlier sketches in CA 49-52, CANR-4
See also CLR 3
See also MAICYA
See also SATA 5, 68
Watson, Colin 1920-1983 ....CANR-2
Obituary 108
Earlier sketch in CA 1-4R
Watson, Cynthia 1957- 137
Watson, David Christopher Knight
1934(?)-1984 Obituary 112
Watson, David Robin 1935- 109
Watson, David 1934- CANR-24
Earlier sketch in CA 45-48
Watson, Derek 1948- 129
Watson, Donald Stevenson 1909- CAP-1
Earlier sketch in CA 13-14
Watson, E(lliot) L(ovegood) Grant
1885-1970 .... CAP-1
Earlier sketch in CA 11-12
Watson, Elaine 1921- 115
Watson, Ernest W(illiam) 1884-1969 ....5-8R
Obituary 134
Watson, Eunice L. 1932- 65-68
Watson, F. J. B.
See Watson, Francis John Bagott
Watson, Fletcher Guard (Jr.) 1912- 5-8R
Watson, Francis John Bagott
1907- Brief entry 116
Watson, Francis (Leslie)
1907-1988 Obituary 127
Watson, Francis M(arion) 1921- 105
Watson, Frank
See Ames, Francis H.
Watson, Gayle Hudgens
See Hudgens, A(lice) Gayle
Watson, George (Grimes) 1927- CANR-20
Earlier sketches in CA 13-16R, CANR-5
Watson, George (Henry) 1936- 77-80
Watson, Goodwin 1899(?)-1976 Obituary 69-72
Watson, Graham (Angus) 1913- 104
Watson, Harold M. 1924- 37-40R
Watson, Harry Legare 1949- 111
Watson, Helen Orr 1892-1978 ....5-8R
Obituary 77-80
See also SATA 24
Watson, (George) Hugh (Nicholas) Seton
See Seton-Watson, (George) Hugh (Nicholas)
Watson, Ian 1943- CANR-24
Earlier sketch in CA 61-64
Watson, Irving S.
See Mencken, H(enry) L(ouis)
Watson, J. R. 1934- CANR-39
Earlier sketches in CA 97-100, CANR-18
Watson, J(ohn) Steven 1916- 5-8R
Watson, J(ames) Wreford 1915-1990 .....CANR-19
Obituary 132
Earlier sketch in CA 25-28R
Watson, Jack Brierley 1927- 104
Watson, James B(ennett) 1918- 41-44R
Watson, James D(ewey) 1928- 25-28R
Watson, James Gray 1939- 29-32R
Watson, James 1936- CANR-4
Earlier sketch in CA 53-56
See also SATA 10
Watson, Jane Werner 1915- CANR-8
Earlier sketch in CA 5-8R
See also SATA 3, 54
Watson, Janet Lynch
See Lynch-Watson, Janet
Watson, Jean 1936- CANR-16
Earlier sketch in CA 89-92
Watson, John A(rthur) F(ergus) 1903- 65-68
Watson, John H.
See Farmer, Philip Jose
Watson, Julia 1943- CANR-15
Earlier sketch in CA 41-44R
Watson, Ken 1925(?)-1984 Obituary 114
Watson, Leland Hale 1926-1989 Obituary 130
Watson, Lyall 1939- CANR-24
Earlier sketches in CA 57-60, CANR-8
Watson, Margaret Goodrich 1913- 13-16R
Watson, Mark Skinner
1887-1966 Obituary 89-92
Watson, Mary Gordon
See Gordon-Watson, Mary
Watson, Nan Marriott
See Marriott-Watson, Nan
Watson, Nancy Dingman CANR-4
Earlier sketch in CA 49-52
See also SATA 32
Watson, O(scar) Michael 1936- 33-36R
Watson, Patricia Seets 1930- 121
Watson, Patrick 1929- 97-100
Watson, Patty Jo (Andersen) 1932- CANR-13
Earlier sketch in CA 77-80
Watson, Pauline 1925- CANR-29
Earlier sketches in CA 69-72, CANR-11
See also SATA 14
Watson, Peter L(eslie) 1944- 53-56
Watson, Philip S(aville) 1909- 104
Watson, Richard A(bernethy) 1923- CANR-25
Earlier sketch in CA 45-48
Watson, Richard A(llan) 1931- 77-80
Watson, Richard F.
See Silverberg, Robert
Watson, Richard Jesse 1951- ....SATA 62
Watson, Richard L(yness) Jr. 1914- 17-20R
Watson, Robert I(rving)
1909-1980 Obituary 111
Watson, Robert N(athaniel) 1953- 118
Watson, Robert (Winthrop) 1925- CANR-4
Earlier sketch in CA 1-4R
Watson, Roderick (Bruce) 1943- 102
Watson, Russell 1939- 77-80
Watson, Sally (Lou) 1924- CANR-3
Earlier sketch in CA 5-8R
See also SATA 3
Watson, Sara Ruth 1907- 37-40R
Watson, Sheila 1909- ....AITN 2
See also DLB 60
Watson, Steven 1947- 135
Watson, Thomas Jr. ....BEST 90:4
Watson, Thomas J(oel) 1948- 109
Watson, Thomas J(ohn) Jr. 1914- 138
Watson, Tom Jr. 1918- 21-24R
Watson, Wendy (McLeod) 1942- CANR-39
Earlier sketches in CA 49-52, CANR-4
See also MAICYA
See also SATA 5
Watson, Wilfred 1911- ....DLB 60
Watson, Will
See Floren, Lee
Watson, William Alexander Jardine
1933- CANR-12
Earlier sketch in CA 13-16R
Watson, William 1917- 9-12R
Watson Taylor, Elizabeth 1915- ....SATA 41
Watson-Watt, Robert A(lexander)
1892-1973 ....CAP-1
Obituary 45-48
Earlier sketch in CA 13-14
Watstein, Esther 1928- 57-60
Watt, (John) David (Henry) 1932-1987 133
Obituary 122
Watt, Donald Beates 1893-1977 Obituary 73-76
Watt, Donald Cameron
See Cameron Watt, Donald
Watt, Donald 1938- 41-44R
Watt, Douglas (Benjamin) 1914- 69-72
Watt, Frank Hedden 1889-1981 Obituary 105
Watt, Frederick B. 1901- 129
Watt, George Steven Harvie
See Harvie-Watt, George Steven
Watt, (Raymond Egerton) Harry
1906-1987 Obituary 122
Watt, Ian 1917- 13-16R
Watt, John Robertson 1934- 37-40R
Watt, Kenneth E(dmund) F(erguson)
1929- 61-64
Watt, Richard M(artin) 1930- 5-8R
Watt, Ruth M. 1919- CANR-10
Earlier sketch in CA 57-60
Watt, Thomas 1935- 37-40R
See also SATA 4
Watt, W(illiam) Montgomery 1909- CANR-21
Earlier sketches in CA 1-4R, CANR-6
Wattel, Harold Louis 1921- 126
Wattenbarger, James L(orenzo) 1922- 106
Wattenberg, Ben J. 1933- CANR-33
Earlier sketch in CA 57-60
Wattenberg, William W(olff) 1911- 21-24R
Wattenmaker, Richard J. 1941- 104
Watters, Barbara H(unt) 1907-1984 ....CANR-3
Obituary 111
Earlier sketch in CA 5-8R
Watters, (Walter) Pat(terson) 1927- CANR-8
Earlier sketch in CA 21-24R
Watters, R(eginald) E(yre) 1912- 25-28R
Watterson, Bill 1958- 134
See also AAYA 9
See also SATA 66
Watterson, Henry 1840-1921 ....DLB 25
Watterson, Joseph 1900-1972 ....CAP-2
Obituary 33-36R
Earlier sketch in CA 25-28
Watt-Evans, Lawrence
See Evans, Lawrence Watt
Wattie, Margaret
See 'Espinasse, Margaret
Wattles, Santha Rama Rau 1923- CANR-1
Earlier sketch in CA 1-4R
Watts, A. J.
See Watts, Anthony J(ohn)
Watts, Al(bert) L. 1934- 85-88
Watts, Alan (James) 1925- 108
Watts, Alan (Wilson) 1915-1973 ....CANR-32
Obituary 45-48
Earlier sketch in CA 41-44R
See also DLB 16
Watts, Ann Chalmers 1938- 53-56
Watts, Anthony J(ohn) 1942- CANR-11
Earlier sketch in CA 25-28R
Watts, (Anna) Bernadette 1942- CANR-31
Earlier sketch in CA 29-32R
See also SATA 4
Watts, Charles Edwin 1929- CANR-2
Earlier sketch in CA 5-8R
Watts, David 1935- 53-56
Watts, Elizabeth (Bailey) Smithgall
1941- CANR-12
Earlier sketch in CA 73-76
Watts, Emily Stipes 1936- 81-84
Watts, Ephraim
See Horne, Richard Henry
Watts, Franklin (Mowry) 1904-1978 ....CANR-9
Obituary 89-92
Earlier sketches in CAP-2, CA 25-28
See also SATA 21, 46
Watts, Harold H(olliday) 1906- CAP-2
Earlier sketch in CA 13-14
Watts, Harriet M(ayor) 1933- 45-48
Watts, Helen L. Hoke 1903-1990 73-76
Obituary 131
See also Hoke, Helen
See also SATA 15
Watts, Irene N(aemi) 1931- ....SATA 56
Watts, Isaac 1674-1748 ....DLB 95
See also SATA 52
Watts, J(ames) Wash(ington)
1896-197 (?) CANR-20
Earlier sketch in CA 1-4R
Watts, James K(ennedy) M(offitt)
1955- ....SATA 59
Watts, John D. W. 1921- 21-24R
Watts, John (Francis) 1926- CANR-21
Earlier sketch in CA 25-28R
Watts, Lew 1922- 41-44R
Watts, Mabel Pizzey 1906- CANR-3
Earlier sketch in CA 1-4R
See also SATA 11
Watts, May Theilgaard 1893-1975 ....41-44R
Watts, Meredith W(ayne Jr.) 1941- CANR-24
Earlier sketch in CA 45-48
Watts, Michael J(ohn) 1951- 122
Watts, Nigel 1957- 130
Watts, Peter Christopher 1919- CANR-12
Earlier sketch in CA 69-72
Watts, Reginald John 1931- CANR-30
Earlier sketch in CA 29-32R
Watts, Richard (Jr.) 1898-1981 Obituary 102
Watts, Ronald L(ampman) 1929- 21-24R
Watts, Sarah Miles 1934- 65-68
Watts, Stephen 1910- 5-8R
Watts, Thomas D(ale) 1941- 117
Watts, William 1930- CANR-1
Earlier sketch in CA 45-48
Watzlawick, Paul 1921- CANR-4
Earlier sketch in CA 9-12R
Waud, Elizabeth
See Tattersall, M(uriel Joyce)
Waugh, Albert E(dmund) 1902-1985 ....37-40R
Obituary 115
Waugh, Alec
See Waugh, Alexander Raban
Waugh, Alexander Raban 1898-1981 .....CANR-22
Obituary 104
Earlier sketch in CA 17-20R
Waugh, Auberon (Alexander) 1939- CANR-22
Earlier sketches in CA 45-48, CANR-6
See also CLC 7
See also DLB 14
Waugh, C. C. Roessel
See Waugh, Carol-Lynn Roessel
and Waugh, Charles G(ordon)
Waugh, Carol-Lynn Roessel 1947- 107
See also SATA 41
Waugh, Charles
See Waugh, Charles G(ordon)
Waugh, Charles G(ordon) 1943- 123
Brief entry 118
Waugh, Coulton 1896(?)-1973 Obituary 41-44R
Waugh, Dorothy CANR-1
Earlier sketch in CA 1-4R
See also SATA 11
Waugh, Evelyn (Arthur St. John)
1903-1966 ....CANR-22
Obituary 25-28R
Earlier sketch in CA 85-88
See also CDBLB 1914-1945
See also CLC 1, 3, 8, 13, 19, 27, 44
See also DLB 15
See also MTCW
See also WLC
Waugh, Harriet 1944- CANR-22
Earlier sketch in CA 85-88
See also CLC 6
Waugh, Harry 1904- 21-24R
Waugh, Hillary Baldwin 1920- CANR-2
Earlier sketch in CA 1-4R
Waugh, Linda R(uth) 1942- CANR-16
Earlier sketch in CA 89-92
Waugh, Nancy Collier 1930- 45-48
Waugh, Virginia
See Sorensen, Virginia
Waughburton, Richard
See Sykes, Christopher (Hugh)
Wauthier, Claude Rene 1923- 73-76
Wavell, Stewart Brooke 1921- 13-16R
Wax, Emmanuel 1911-1983 Obituary 109
Wax, Jimmy
See Wax, Emmanuel
Wax, Judith 1932(?)-1979 101
Obituary 85-88
Wax, Murray L(ionel) 1922- 37-40R
Wax, Rosalie (Amelia) H. 1911- 45-48
Wax, Sheldon 1928(?)-1979 Obituary 85-88
Wax, William Edward 1956- 133
Waxberg, Joseph David 1922- 108
Waxman, Chaim I(saac) 1941- CANR-19
Earlier sketch in CA 103
Waxman, Ruth B(ilgray) 1916- 93-96
Way, Irene 1924- 93-96
Way, Peter (Howard) 1936- Brief entry 115
Way, Robert E(dward) 1912- 57-60
Way, Walter L. 1931- 57-60
Way, Wayne
See Humphries, Adelaide M.
Wayburn, Peggy 1921- CANR-24
Earlier sketch in CA 45-48
Waylan, Mildred
See Harrell, Irene B(urk)
Wayland, Patrick
See O'Connor, Richard
Waymack, W(illiam) W(esley)
1888-1960 Obituary 93-96
Wayman, Alex 1921- 104
Wayman, Dorothy G. 1893-1975 65-68
Obituary 61-64
Wayman, Norbury Lansing 1912- 41-44R
Wayman, Thomas Ethan 1945- 101
See also Wayman, Tom
Wayman, Tom
See Wayman, Thomas Ethan
See also DLB 53
Wayman, Tony Russell 1929- 25-28R
Wayne, Alice
See Ressler, Alice
Wayne, Anderson
See Dresser, Davis
Wayne, David
See Balsiger, David (Wayne)
Wayne, Donald
See Dodd, Wayne (Donald)
Wayne, Doreen 29-32R
Wayne, Frances
See Wedge, Florence
Wayne, Jane Ellen 1936- CANR-20
Earlier sketches in CA 49-52, CANR-4
Wayne, (Anne) Jenifer 1917-1982 105
Obituary 108
See also SATA 32
Wayne, Jerry 1919- 29-32R
Wayne, John 1907-1979 85-88
Wayne, Joseph
See Overholser, Wayne D.
Wayne, Kyra Petrovskaya 1918- CANR-4
Earlier sketch in CA 1-4R
See also SATA 8
Wayne, Mary Collier 1913- 57-60
Wayne, Michael 1947- 112
Wayne, Philip
See Powell, Philip Wayne
Wayne, Richard
See Decker, Duane
Wayne, Stephen J(ay) 1939- CANR-20
Earlier sketches in CA 53-56, CANR-5
Wayne, Valerie 1945- 137
Wayre, Philip 1921- 89-92
Ways, C. R.
See Blount, Roy (Alton) Jr.
Ways, Max 1905-1985 Obituary 116
Waystaff, Simon
See Swift, Jonathan
Wazyk, Adam 1905-1982 Obituary 114
Wead, R(oy) Douglas 1946- CANR-20
Earlier sketch in CA 69-72
Weaks, Mary Louise 1961- 136
Weal, Michele 1936- 61-64
Weales, Gerald (Clifford) 1925- CANR-3
Earlier sketch in CA 5-8R
See also SATA 11
Wear, Ted Graham
See Wear, Theodore G(raham)
Wear, Theodore G(raham) 1902- CAP-1
Earlier sketch in CA 9-10
Weare, Ralston B.
See La Barre, Weston
Weare, Walter B(urdette) 1938- 73-76
Wearin, Otha D(onner) 1903-1990 ....CANR-5
Obituary 131
Earlier sketch in CA 13-16R
Wearing, J. P. CANR-19
Earlier sketch in CA 102
Wearne, Alan (Richard) 1948- 126
Weart, Edith L. 1898(?)-1977 Obituary 69-72
Weart, Spencer R(ichard) 1942- CANR-29
Earlier sketch in CA 25-28R
Weary, Ogdred
See Gorey, Edward (St. John)
Weatherall, Norman Leigh 1902- CAP-1
Earlier sketch in CA 11-12
Weatherby, Harold L(erow) Jr. 1934- 45-48
Weatherby, W(illiam) J(ohn) CANR-12
Earlier sketch in CA 17-20R
Weathercock, The
See Romaine, Lawrence B.
Weatherford, J. McIver
See Weatherford, Jack McIver
Weatherford, Jack
See Weatherford, Jack McIver
Weatherford, Jack McIver 1946- CANR-30
Earlier sketch in CA 111
Weatherford, Richard M(orris) 1939- 53-56
Weatherford, Willis Duke Jr. 1916- 5-8R
Weatherhead, A(ndrew) Kingsley
1923- CANR-3
Earlier sketch in CA 5-8R
Weatherhead, Leslie D(ixon)
1893-1976 ....CANR-4
Obituary 61-64
Earlier sketch in CA 5-8R
Weatherly, Edward H(owell) 1905- 5-8R
Weatherly, (John) Max 1921- 13-16R
Weatherly, Owen M. 1915- 5-8R
Weatherly, Tom 1942- CANR-25
Earlier sketch in CA 45-48
See also BW
See also DLB 41
Weathers, Wesley Wayne 1942- 111
Weathers, Winston 1926- CANR-8
Earlier sketch in CA 21-24R
Weatherwax, Rudd (B.)
1908(?)-1985 Obituary 115
Weatherwise, Abe
See Sagendorph, Robb Hansell
Weaver, Anthony Frederick 1913- 13-16R
Weaver, Bertrand 1908-1973 ....CAP-1
Obituary 45-48
Earlier sketch in CA 13-16
Weaver, Carl H(arold) 1910- 73-76
Weaver, Charley
See Arquette, Cliff(ord)
Weaver, David H(ugh) 1946- 111

Weaver, Denis 1906-1984 Obituary 114
Weaver, Earl S(idney) 1930- 116
Weaver, Earle
See Willets, Walter E.
Weaver, Frank Parks 1904- 104
Weaver, Gordon (Allison) 1937- CANR-26
Earlier sketches in CA 25-28R, CANR-10
Weaver, Harriett E. 1908- CANR-20
Earlier sketches in CA 5-8R, CANR-5
See also SATA 65
Weaver, Herbert 1905- 61-64
Weaver, Horace R. 1915- 13-16R
Weaver, James H. 1933- 17-20R
Weaver, Jerry L(ee) 1939- 69-72
Weaver, John D(owning) 1912- CANR-4
Earlier sketch in CA 9-12R
Weaver, John L. 1949- 112
See also SATA 42
Weaver, Katherine Grey Dunlap 1910- 37-40R
Weaver, Kitty
See Weaver, Katherine Grey Dunlap
Weaver, Leon Hiram 1913- 5-8R
Weaver, Mateman
See Greene, A(lvin) C(arl)
Weaver, Michael D. 1961- 126
Weaver, Peter Malcolm 1927- 13-16R
Weaver, Peter 1925- CANR-15
Earlier sketch in CA 85-88
Weaver, R(obert) Kent 1953- 138
Weaver, Richard L. II 1941- CANR-23
Earlier sketch in CA 106
Weaver, Robert C(lifton) 1907- 9-12R
Weaver, Robert 1921- ....DLB 88
Weaver, Thomas 1929- CANR-13
Earlier sketch in CA 61-64
Weaver, Ward
See Mason, F(rancis) van Wyck
Weaver, Warren Jr. 1923- 41-44R
Weaver, Warren 1894-1978 89-92
Obituary 81-84
Weaver, William Woys 1947- 123
Weaver, William 1923- 116
Brief entry 112
Webb, Anthony
See Wilson, N(orman) Scarlyn
Webb, Barbara (Helen) 1929- 103
Webb, (Stephen) Barry 1947- 135
Webb, (Martha) Beatrice (Potter)
1858-1943 Brief entry 117
See also Potter, Beatrice
See also TCLC 22
Webb, Bernice Larson CANR-15
Earlier sketch in CA 37-40R
Webb, Bob
See Forrest-Webb, Robert
Webb, C(harles) R(ichard) Jr. 1919- 5-8R
Webb, Charles (Richard) 1939- 25-28R
See also CLC 7
Webb, Christopher
See Wibberley, Leonard (Patrick O'Connor)
Webb, Clifford (Cyril) 1895-1972 105
Webb, Eugene 1938- 29-32R
Webb, Forrest
See Forrest-Webb, Robert
Webb, Francis Charles 1925-1973 101
Webb, Frank J. ....DLB 50
Webb, George Ernest 1952- 113
Webb, Harri 1920- 104
Webb, Harry 1887-1984 Obituary 113
Webb, Henry J(ameson) 1915- 17-20R
Webb, Herschel (F.) 1924-1983 ....5-8R
Obituary 109
Webb, Holmes 1904- CAP-2
Earlier sketch in CA 25-28
Webb, Igor 1941- 109
Webb, Jack (Randolph)
1920-1982 Obituary 108
Brief entry 106
Webb, James (C. N.) 1946-1980 103
Webb, James H(enry) Jr. 1946- 81-84
See also CLC 22
Webb, James Watson 1802-1884 ....DLB 43
Webb, Jean Francis 1910- CANR-21
Earlier sketches in CA 5-8R, CANR-6
See also SATA 35
Webb, Jon (Edgar) 1905(?)-1971 Obituary 104
Webb, Karl (Eugene) 1938- 105
Webb, Kaye 1914- ....SATA 60
Webb, Kempton E. 1931- 13-16R
Webb, Kenneth B(eals) 1902- 97-100
Webb, Lance 1909- CANR-10
Earlier sketch in CA 13-16R
Webb, Lionel
See Hershman, Morris
Webb, Lucas
See Burgess, M(ichael) R(oy)
Webb, Margot S. 1914- 77-80
Webb, Margot 1934- 134
See also SATA 67
Webb, Martha G.
See Wingate, (Martha) Anne (Guice)
Webb, Mary (Gladys Meredith)
1881-1927 Obituary 123
See also DLB 34
See also TCLC 24
Webb, Mary H(aydn) 1938- CANR-28
Earlier sketch in CA 61-64
Webb, Melody Rae 1946- 126
Webb, Mena 1915- 127
Webb, Michael (Dennis Puzey) 1937- 124
Webb, Michael Gordon 1940- 109
Webb, Michael (Jack) 1953- 137
Webb, Mrs. Sidney
See Webb, (Martha) Beatrice (Potter)
Webb, Muriel S(chlosberg)
1913-1977 ....CANR-36
Obituary 134
Earlier sketch in CA 17-20R
Webb, Nancy (Bukeley) 1915- CANR-21
Earlier sketch in CA 1-4R
Webb, Neil
See Rowland, D(onald) S(ydney)
Webb, Pauline M(ary) 1927- CANR-24
Earlier sketches in CA 61-64, CANR-8
Webb, Peggy (Elaine Hussey) 1942- 123
Webb, Peter B(randram) 1941- CANR-24
Earlier sketch in CA 106
Webb, Phyllis 1927- CANR-23
Earlier sketch in CA 104
See also CLC 18
See also DLB 53
Webb, R(obert) K(iefer) 1922- 25-28R
Webb, Richard 37-40R
Webb, Robert Forrest-
See Forrest-Webb, Robert
Webb, Robert 1947- 118
Webb, Rodman B. 1941- CANR-28
Earlier sketch in CA 110
Webb, Ross A. 1923- 37-40R
Webb, Rozana 1908- 29-32R
Webb, Ruth Enid Borlase Morris 1926- 9-12R
Webb, Samuel C(lement) 1934- 69-72
Webb, Sharon 1936- CANR-32
Earlier sketch in CA 113
See also SATA 41
Webb, Sidney (James)
1859-1947 Brief entry 117
See also TCLC 22
Webb, Spider
See Gohman, Fred Joseph
Webb, Stephen S(aunders) 1937- 104
Webb, Walter Prescott 1888-1963 Obituary 113
See also DLB 17
Webb, Willard 1903-1978 Obituary 77-80
Webb, Wilfred (Griffin) 1919- 25-28R
Webb, Wilse B(ernard) 1920- CANR-3
Earlier sketch in CA 1-4R
Webbe, Gale D(udley) 1909- 5-8R
Webber, Andrew Lloyd
See Lloyd Webber, Andrew
See also CLC 21
Webber, Bert
See Webber, Ebbert T(rue)
Webber, Ebbert T(rue) 1921- CANR-39
Earlier sketches in CA 45-48, CANR-2, 17
Webber, George J(ulius)
1899-1982(?) Obituary 108
Webber, Gordon 1912-1986 89-92
Obituary 120
Webber, Irma E(leanor Schmidt) 1904- 69-72
See also SATA 14
Webber, Joan Malory 1930-1978 ....CANR-7
Earlier sketch in CA 5-8R
Webber, Robert (Eugene) 1933- CANR-37
Earlier sketches in CA 89-92, CANR-16
Webber, (Edwin) Ronald 1915- CANR-4
Earlier sketch in CA 53-56
Webber, Ross A. 1934- 29-32R
Webber, Thomas L(ane) 1947- 85-88
Weber, Alfons 1921- 29-32R
See also SATA 8
Weber, Brom 1917- 13-16R
Weber, Bruce 1942- CANR-21
Earlier sketch in CA 97-100
Weber, Burton Jasper 1934- 103
Weber, C(larence) A(dam) 1903- CANR-37
Earlier sketches in CA 37-40R, CANR-13
Weber, Carl J(efferson) 1894-1966 ....CANR-3
Earlier sketch in CA 5-8R
Weber, David J. 1940- CANR-14
Earlier sketch in CA 37-40R
Weber, David R(yder) 1943- 89-92
Weber, Debora 1955- ....SATA 58
Weber, Doron 1955- 138
Weber, Eric 1942- CANR-15
Earlier sketch in CA 101
Weber, Eugen 1925- CANR-2
Earlier sketch in CA 5-8R
Weber, Eugene 1939- 41-44R
Weber, Francis J. 1933- CANR-4
Earlier sketch in CA 9-12R
Weber, Frank George 1932- 45-48
Weber, Gerard Peter 1918- 9-12R
Weber, Hans H. 1935- 61-64
Weber, Hans-Ruedi 1923- CANR-2
Earlier sketch in CA 5-8R
Weber, J(ohn) Sherwood 1918-1978 ....37-40R
Obituary 77-80
Weber, James A(mbrose) 1932- 102
Weber, Janice 121
Weber, Jean-Paul 1917- 45-48
Weber, Jerome C(harles) 1938- 73-76
Weber, Judith E(ichler) 1938- ....SATA 64
Weber, Ken(neth J.) 1940- CANR-39
Earlier sketch in CA 116
Weber, Lenora Mattingly 1895-1971 ....CAP-1
Obituary 29-32R
Earlier sketch in CA 19-20
See also CLC 12
See also SATA 2, 26
Weber, Marc 1950- CANR-1
Earlier sketch in CA 49-52
Weber, Max 1864-1920 Brief entry 109
Weber, Michael P. 127
Weber, Nancy 1942- 101
Weber, Nathan 1942- 111
Weber, Nicholas F(ox) 1947- 120
Weber, Paul J. 1937- 137
Weber, R. David 1941- 127
Weber, Ralph Edward 1926- CANR-2
Earlier sketch in CA 5-8R
Weber, Robert L(emmerman) 1913- 53-56
Weber, Ronald 1934- 115
Weber, Rubin
See Rubinstein, S(amuel) Leonard
Weber, Sarah Appleton
See Appleton, Sarah
Weber, Simon 1910(?)-1987 Obituary 124
Weber, William A(lfred) 1918- 77-80
Weber, William J(ohn) 1927- CANR-25
Earlier sketch in CA 69-72
See also SATA 14
Weberman, Ben(jamin) 1923- 77-80
Webster, Alice Jane Chandler
1876-1916 Brief entry 116
See also SATA 17
Webster, Anthony 1923(?)-1987 Obituary 123
Webster, Augusta 1837-1894 ....DLB 35
Webster, Brenda S. 1936- 53-56
Webster, C(onstance) Muriel 1906- 49-52
Webster, Cyril Charles 1909- CAP-2
Earlier sketch in CA 25-28
Webster, David Endicott 1929- 25-28R
Webster, David 1930- 29-32R
See also SATA 11
Webster, Donald Blake Jr. 1933- 37-40R
Webster, Donald 1926- 118
Webster, Douglas 1920-1986 ....13-16R
Obituary 118
Webster, Edna Robb 1896- 69-72
Webster, Elizabeth 1918- 117
Webster, Ernest 1923- 132
Webster, Frank V. CANR-27
Earlier sketches in CAP-2, CA 19-20
See also SATA 1, 67
Webster, Frederick E. Jr. 1937- CANR-14
Earlier sketch in CA 37-40R
Webster, Gary
See Garrison, Webb B(lack)
Webster, Graham 1915- 49-52
Webster, Grant T. 1933- 104
Webster, Harvey (Curtis) 1906- 41-44R
Webster, J(ames) Carson 1905- 45-48
Webster, James 1925-1981 ....CANR-29
Obituary 104
Earlier sketch in CA 73-76
See also SATA 17, 27
Webster, Jan 1924- CANR-14
Earlier sketch in CA 77-80
Webster, Jean
See Webster, Alice Jane Chandler
Webster, John
1579(?)-1634(?) ....CDBLB Before 1660
See also DC 2
See also DLB 58
See also WLC
Webster, Josh (Lew) 1949- 113
Webster, Margaret 1905-1972 Obituary 37-40R
Webster, Noah
See Knox, William
Webster, Noah
1758-1843 ....DLB 1, 37, 42, 43, 73
Webster, Norman William 1920- 104
Webster, Paul Francis 1907-1984 Obituary 112
Webster, Paul 1916- 41-44R
Webster, Randolph Wyatt 1900- CAP-1
Earlier sketch in CA 19-20
Webster, Richard A. 1928- 21-24R
Webster, S(tanley) Eric 1919-1971 ....CAP-1
Earlier sketch in CA 17-18
Webster, Staten Wentford 1928- 21-24R
Webster, Thomas Bertram Lonsdale
1905-1974 105
Obituary 107
Webster, Tony
See Webster, Anthony
Wechman, Robert Joseph 1939- CANR-24
Earlier sketch in CA 45-48
Wechsberg, Joseph 1907-1983 ....CANR-34
Obituary 109
Earlier sketch in CA 105
Wechsler, David 1896-1981 Obituary 103
Wechsler, Harold S(tuart) 1946- 110
Wechsler, Henry 1932- CANR-7
Earlier sketch in CA 17-20R
Wechsler, Herbert 1909- CANR-24
Earlier sketch in CA 1-4R
Wechsler, Herman J. 1904-1976 65-68
Obituary 61-64
See also SATA 20
Wechsler, James A(rthur) 1915-1983 101
Obituary 110
Wechsler, Judith Glatzer 1940- CANR-8
Earlier sketch in CA 57-60
Wechsler, Louis K. 1905- 65-68
Wechter, Nell Wise 1913- 57-60
See also SATA 60
Weck, Thomas L. 1942- 128
See also SATA 62
Weckstein, Richard (Selig) 1924- 49-52
Wedberg, Anders 1913-1978 Obituary 77-80
Wedd, Kate
See Gregory, Philippa
Wedda, John A. 1911- 17-20R
Wedde, Ian 1946- 104
Wedderburn, Dorothy (Enid Cole)
1925- Brief entry 113
Wedderburn, K(enneth) W(illiam) 1927- 77-80
Wedding, Dan 1949- 93-96
Wedding, Donald Keith 1934- 41-44R
Weddle, Ethel Harshbarger 1897- CANR-4
Earlier sketch in CA 9-12R
See also SATA 11
Weddle, Ferris 1922- 17-20R
Weddle, Robert S(amuel) 1921- 9-12R
Wedeck, Harry E(zekiel) 1894- CANR-4
Earlier sketch in CA 1-4R
Wedeen, Shirley Ullman 1926- 17-20R
Obituary 137
Wedekind, (Benjamin) Frank(lin)
1864-1918 Brief entry 104
See also DLB 118
See also TCLC 7
Wedel, Alfred R(aphael) 1934- 117
Wedel, Alton F. 21-24R
Wedel, Cynthia Clark 1908-1986 Obituary 120
Wedel, Janine (R.) 1957- 132
Wedel, Leonard E. 1909- 21-24R
Wedel, Theodore Otto 1892-1970 ....CANR-4
Earlier sketch in CA 5-8R
Wedel, Waldo R(udolph) 1908- 126
Brief entry 105
Wedell, Eberhard (Arthur Otto) George
1927- 104
Wedemeyer, Albert C(oady)
1897-1989 Obituary 130
Wedge, Bryant (Miner) 1921- CANR-10
Earlier sketch in CA 13-16R
Wedge, Florence 1919- 5-8R
Wedgwood, C(icely) V(eronica) 1910- CANR-21
Earlier sketch in CA 105
See also MTCW
Wedgwood, Pamela
See Tudor-Craig, Pamela
Wedlock, Eldon D(yment) Jr. 1942- 128
Weed, Florence C(ollins)
1897(?)-1983 Obituary 109
Weed, Joseph J(ohn) 1901- 25-28R
Weeden, Robert B(arton) 1933- 85-88
Weedon, Chris 1952- 121
Weekes, Mark Kinkead
See Kinkead-Weekes, Mark
Weekes, Richard V. 1924- 13-16R
Weekley, Ian George 1933- 113
Weekly, William G(eorge)
1890(?)-1983 Obituary 111
Weeks, Albert L. 1923- 13-16R
Weeks, Brigitte 1943- 132
Weeks, Christopher 1930- 21-24R
Weeks, Constance Tomkinson 1915- 17-20R
Weeks, (Norman) Donald CANR-25
Earlier sketch in CA 45-48
Weeks, Edward (Augustus)
1898-1989 ....CANR-36
Obituary 128
Earlier sketch in CA 85-88
Weeks, Edward J(oseph) 1902- CAP-1
Earlier sketch in CA 13-14
Weeks, Francis W(illiam) 1916- Brief entry 111
Weeks, Grace E(zell) 1923- 49-52
Weeks, H(erbert) Ashley 1903- 45-48
Weeks, Jeffrey 1945- 108
Weeks, John (Stafford) 1928- 77-80
Weeks, Kent M(cCuskey) 1937- Brief entry 112
Weeks, Lewis G(eorge)
1893-1977 Obituary 69-72
Weeks, Philip 1949- 110
Weeks, Robert Lewis 1924- 13-16R
Weeks, Robert P(ercy) 1915- 13-16R
Weeks, Sheldon G. 1931- CANR-30
Earlier sketches in CA 21-24R, CANR-13
Weeks, Thelma E(vans) 1921- 57-60
Weems, J. Eddie Jr.
See Weems, John Edward
Weems, John Edward 1924- CANR-19
Earlier sketches in CA 1-4R, CANR-4
Weems, Mason Locke
1759-1825 ....DLB 30, 37, 42
Weenolsen, Hebe CANR-34
Earlier sketch in CA 111
Weer, William
See Kaufman, I(sadore)
Weerts, Richard Kenneth 1928- 49-52
Wees, Frances Shelley 1902-1982 ....CANR-3
Earlier sketch in CA 5-8R
See also SATA 58
Wees, W(ilfred) R(usk) 1899- 61-64
Weesner, Theodore 105
Weevers, Peter 1944- ....SATA 59
Wegelin, Christof 1911- 45-48
Wegen, Ron(ald) ....SATA 44
Weglyn, Michi(ko Nishiura) 1926- 85-88
Wegner, Fritz 1924- ....SATA 20
Wegner, Robert E. 1929- 17-20R
Wehen, Joy DeWeese CANR-3
Earlier sketch in CA 5-8R
Wehlitz, (Annie) Lou(ise) Rogers 1906- 5-8R
Wehmeyer, Lillian (Mabel) Biermann
1933- CANR-8
Earlier sketch in CA 61-64
Wehringer, Cameron K(ingsley) 1924- 25-28R
Wehrle, Edmund S(heridan) 1930- 65-68
Wehrli, Eugene S(tanley) 1923- 45-48
Wehrwein, Austin C(arl) 1916- 77-80
Wei, Yung 1937- 49-52
Weichel, Kim 1951- 107
Weida, Bill
See Weida, William J.
Weida, William J. 1942- 135
Weidegar, Paula 1939- 65-68
Weideman, Ryan 1941- 137
Weidenbaum, Murray L(ew) 1927- CANR-14
Earlier sketch in CA 37-40R
Weidenfeld, Sheila Rabb 1943- 89-92
Weider, Ben 1923- 108
Weidhorn, Manfred 1931- 53-56
See also SATA 60
Weidlein, Edward R(ay)
1887-1983 Obituary 110
Weidman, Jerome 1913- CANR-1
Earlier sketch in CA 1-4R
See also AITN 2
See also CLC 7
See also DLB 28

Weidman, John 1946- 109
Weidman, Judith L(ynne) 1941- CANR-25
Earlier sketch in CA 107
Weidner, Edward William 1921- 13-16R
Weiers, Ronald M. 1941- CANR-19
Earlier sketch in CA 25-28R
Weigand, George R(obert) J(oseph)
1917- 13-16R
Weigand, Hermann J(ohn) 1892-1985 ....CAP-1
Obituary 117
Earlier sketch in CA 13-14
Weigel, George 1951- 125
Weigel, Gustave 1906-1964 Obituary 107
Weigel, John A(rthur) 1912- 57-60
Weiger, John George 1933- CANR-20
Earlier sketch in CA 104
Weigert, Andrew J(oseph) 1934- 109
Weigert, Edith 1894- CAP-2
Earlier sketch in CA 29-32
Weigert, Hans Werner
1902(?)-1983 Obituary 111
Weightman, Gavin 1945- 120
Weightman, J(ohn) G(eorge) 1915- CANR-5
Earlier sketch in CA 9-12R
Weigl, Bruce 1949- CANR-30
Earlier sketch in CA 110
See also DLB 120
Weigle, Luther Allan 1880-1976 77-80
Obituary 69-72
Weigle, Marta 1944- CANR-26
Earlier sketches in CA 69-72, CANR-11
Weigley, Russell F(rank) 1930- CANR-19
Earlier sketches in CA 5-8R, CANR-2
Weihofen, Henry 1904- 37-40R
Weihs, Erika 1917- 93-96
See also SATA 15
Weik, Mary Hays 1898(?)-1979 ....21-24R
Obituary 93-96
See also SATA 3, 23
Weil, Andrew (Thomas) 1942- CANR-20
Earlier sketch in CA 73-76
Weil, Ann Yezner 1908-1969 ....5-8R
Obituary 103
See also SATA 9
Weil, Dorothy 1929- 93-96
Weil, Gordon L(ee) 1937- CANR-12
Earlier sketch in CA 73-76
Weil, Herbert S. Jr. 1933- 21-24R
Weil, Irwin 1928- 21-24R
Weil, James L(ehman) 1929- CANR-36
Earlier sketches in CA 93-96, CANR-16
Weil, Jerry 1928- 1-4R
Weil, Joseph 1875-1976 Obituary 65-68
Weil, Lisl 1910- CANR-2
Earlier sketch in CA 49-52
See also SATA 7
Weil, Mildred 45-48
Weil, Robert 1955- 125
Weil, Roman L(ee) 1940- CANR-14
Earlier sketch in CA 37-40R
Weil, Simone (Adolphine)
1909-1943 Brief entry 117
See also TCLC 23
Weil, Ulric Henry 113
Weilbacher, William Manning 1928- 108
Weilerstein, Sadie Rose 1894- 5-8R
See also SATA 3
Weill, Gus 1933- CANR-7
Earlier sketch in CA 53-56
Weiman, Eiveen 1925- 108
Weimann, Jeanne Madeline 1943- 108
Weimar, Karl S(iegfried) 1916- 5-8R
Weimer, Arthur M(artin) 1909-1987 ....1-4R
Obituary 122
Weimer, Ferne 1950- 137
Weimer, Maryellen 1947- 135
Wein, Jacqueline 1938- 93-96
Weinbaum, Raquel
See Vinas, David
Weinbaum, Stanley Grauman
1902(?)-1935 Brief entry 110
See also DLB 8
Weinberg, Arthur 1915-1989 ....CANR-15
Obituary 127
Earlier sketch in CA 25-28R
Weinberg, Bernard 1909-1973 Obituary 106
Weinberg, Daniel H. 1949- 120
Weinberg, Daniela 1936- 104
Weinberg, David Henry 1945- 89-92
Weinberg, Edgar 1917-1985 Obituary 117
Weinberg, Florence M(ay) 1933- 37-40R
Weinberg, Gerald M(arvin) 1933- CANR-18
Earlier sketch in CA 89-92
Weinberg, Gerhard L(udwig) 1928- CANR-3
Earlier sketch in CA 9-12R
Weinberg, H. Barbara 134
Weinberg, Helen A(rnstein) 1927- 73-76
Weinberg, Herman G(ershon)
1908-1983 ....CANR-29
Obituary 111
Earlier sketch in CA 45-48
Weinberg, Ian 1938-1969 ....CAP-2
Earlier sketch in CA 21-22
Weinberg, Janet Hopson
See Hopson, Janet L(ouise)
Weinberg, Julius R(udolph) 1908-1971 ....CAP-1
Earlier sketch in CA 17-18
Weinberg, Julius 1922- 37-40R
Weinberg, Kenneth G. 1920- 41-44R
Weinberg, Kerry 29-32R
Weinberg, Kurt 1912- 41-44R
Weinberg, Larry
See Weinberg, Lawrence (E.)
Weinberg, Lawrence (E.) ....SATA 48
Weinberg, Lila (Shaffer) 25-28R
Weinberg, Martin S(tephen) 1939- CANR-15
Earlier sketch in CA 41-44R
Weinberg, Meyer 1920- CANR-4
Earlier sketch in CA 1-4R
Weinberg, Nathan Gerald 1945- 104
Weinberg, Robert Charles
1901-1974 Obituary 45-48
Weinberg, Robert E(dward) 1946- 97-100
Weinberg, Samuel Kirson 1912- CANR-1
Earlier sketch in CA 1-4R
Weinberg, Sanford Bruce 1950- 109
Weinberg, Steven 1933- CANR-36
Earlier sketches in CA 53-56, CANR-5
Weinberg, Werner 1915- CANR-16
Earlier sketch in CA 41-44R
Weinberger, Betty Kiralfy 1932- 65-68
Weinberger, Caspar W(illard) 1917- 133
Weinberger, Eliot 1949- 117
Weinberger, Leon J. 1926- 77-80
Weinberger, Marvin I(rvin) 1954- 113
Weinberger, Miro (Leonard) 1970- 135
Weinberger, Paul E. 1931-1983(?) 29-32R
Obituary 134
Weinbrot, Howard D. 1936- Brief entry 107
Weiner, Andrew D(avid) 1943- Brief entry 111
Weiner, Annette B. 1933- 93-96
Weiner, Bernard 1935- 57-60
Weiner, Charles 1931- 134
Brief entry 109
Weiner, Dora B(ierer) 1924- 25-28R
Weiner, Edith M. 1948- 127
Weiner, Egon 1906-1987 97-100
Obituary 123
Weiner, Elliot 1943- 122
Weiner, Florence 1931- 25-28R
Weiner, Henri
See Longstreet, Stephen
Weiner, Herbert 5-8R
Weiner, Howard L. 1944- 127
Weiner, Hyman J(oseph) 1926- 49-52
Weiner, Irving B(ernard) 1933- CANR-27
Earlier sketch in CA 29-32R
Weiner, J(oseph) S(idney) 1915-1982 114
Weiner, Jonathan (David) 1953- 123
Weiner, Kay Bain 1932- 136
Weiner, Leonard 1927- 21-24R
Weiner, Linda 1943- 114
Weiner, Marcella Bakur 1925- Brief entry 105
Weiner, Myron 1931- CANR-4
Earlier sketch in CA 1-4R
Weiner, Neal (Orlove) 1942- 118
Weiner, Neil S(herman) 1936- 119
Weiner, Richard 1927- 89-92
Weiner, Sandra 1922- 49-52
See also SATA 14
Weiner, Skip
See Weiner, Stewart
Weiner, Stewart 1945- CANR-16
Earlier sketch in CA 89-92
Weiner, Tim 1956- 135
Weinfield, Henry 1949- 37-40R
Weingand, Darlene E. 1937- 115
Weingarden, Lauren S. 1948- 128
Weingart, L(aurence) O. 1931- 17-20R
Weingarten, Henry 57-60
Weingarten, Roger 1945- CANR-10
Earlier sketch in CA 61-64
Weingarten, Violet (Brown) 1915-1976 ....CANR-7
Obituary 65-68
Earlier sketch in CA 9-12R
See also SATA 3, 27
Weingartner, Charles 1922- 49-52
See also SATA 5
Weingartner, James J(oseph) 1940- 93-96
Weingartner, Rudolph H(erbert) 1927- 13-16R
Weingast, David E(lliott) 1912- 5-8R
Weinhaus, Carol L. 1947- 137
Weinhouse, Beth 1957- 128
Weinig, Jean Maria 1920- CANR-12
Earlier sketch in CA 29-32R
Weinig, Sister Mary Anthony
See Weinig, Jean Maria
Weininger, Benjamin Isaac
1905-1988 Obituary 126
Weininger, Richard
1887(?)-1979 Obituary 89-92
Weinland, James D(avid) 1894- 57-60
Weinman, Benzion 1897-1987 Obituary 121
Weinman, Irving 1937- 122
Weinman, Paul 1940- CANR-29
Earlier sketches in CA 77-80, CANR-13
Weinrauch, Herschel 1905- CAP-1
Earlier sketch in CA 13-16
Weinreb, Lloyd L(obell) 1936- 69-72
Weinreich, Beatrice Silverman 1928- 129
Weinrich, A(nna) K(atharina) H(ildegard)
1933- CANR-37
Earlier sketches in CA 37-40R, CANR-16
Weinryb, Bernard D(ov) 1905- CANR-25
Earlier sketch in CA 45-48
Weinstein, Allen 1937- CANR-26
Earlier sketch in CA 41-44R
Weinstein, Arnold 1927- 9-12R
Weinstein, Bernard L(ee) 1942- 111
Weinstein, Bob 1941- 120
Weinstein, Brian 1937- 21-24R
Weinstein, Donald 1926- 13-16R
Weinstein, Fred 1931- 65-68
Weinstein, Gerald 1930- 25-28R
Weinstein, Grace W(ohlner) 1935- CANR-26
Earlier sketches in CA 61-64, CANR-10
Weinstein, Howard 1954- CANR-23
Earlier sketch in CA 107
Weinstein, Jacob Joseph 1902-1974 110
Obituary 108
Weinstein, James 1926- 21-24R
Weinstein, Leo 1921- Brief entry 110
Weinstein, Mark A. 1937- 25-28R
Weinstein, Marlene 1946- 45-48
Weinstein, Martin E. 1934- 85-88
Weinstein, Michael A(lan) 1942- 129
Weinstein, Michael 1898- CAP-1
Earlier sketch in CA 13-14
Weinstein, Nathan
See West, Nathanael
Weinstein, Nathan von Wallenstein
See West, Nathanael
Weinstein, Norman Charles 1948- CANR-31
Earlier sketch in CA 37-40R
Weinstein, Robert A. 1914- 29-32R
Weinstein, Sol 1928- 13-16R
Weinstein, Warren 1941- 93-96
Weinstock, Herbert 1905-1971 ....CANR-2
Obituary 33-36R
Earlier sketch in CA 1-4R
Weinstock, John M(artin) 1936- 81-84
Weinstock, M(oshe) D(avid) 1922- 131
Weinstone, William W.
1898(?)-1985 Obituary 117
Weinswig, Melvin H. 1935- Brief entry 107
Weintal, Edward 1901-1973 Obituary 41-44R
Weintraub, Dov 1926-1985 ....CANR-36
Earlier sketch in CA 109
Weintraub, Karl Joachim 1924- 25-28R
Weintraub, Linda 1942- 135
Weintraub, Robert E. 1925-1983 Obituary 110
Weintraub, Rodelle (Selma) 1933- 97-100
Weintraub, Sidney 1914-1983 ....CANR-6
Obituary 110
Earlier sketch in CA 1-4R
Weintraub, Sidney 1922- CANR-26
Earlier sketch in CA 108
Weintraub, Stanley 1929- CANR-22
Earlier sketches in CA 1-4R, CANR-2
See also DLB 111
Weintraub, Wiktor 1908-1988 ....CANR-3
Obituary 126
Earlier sketch in CA 5-8R
Weintraub, William 1926- 1-4R
Weinwurm, George F(elix) 1935- 33-36R
Weinzweig, Helen 1915- 106
Weir, Alice M.
See McLaughlin, Emma Maude
Weir, Carol S. 1924- 125
Weir, J(ohn) E(dward) 1935- 118
Weir, Joan 1928- CANR-31
Earlier sketch in CA 112
Weir, John
See Cross, Colin (John)
Weir, LaVada CANR-9
Earlier sketch in CA 21-24R
See also SATA 2
Weir, Molly 1920- CANR-12
Earlier sketch in CA 29-32R
Weir, Nancie MacCullough 1933- 65-68
Weir, Peter (Lindsay) 1944- 123
Brief entry 113
See also CLC 20
Weir, Robert M(cColloch) 1933- 93-96
Weir, Rosemary (Green) 1905- CANR-10
Earlier sketch in CA 13-16R
See also SATA 21
Weir, Thomas R(obert) 1912- 41-44R
Weir, Walter 1909- 5-8R
Weis, Elisabeth 1944- 112
Weis, Jack 1932- 105
Weis, Margaret (Edith) 1948- CANR-34
Earlier sketch in CA 111
See also SATA 38
Weis, Norman D(wight) 1923- 61-64
Weis, Rene (Jean Alphonse) 1953- 127
Weisberg, Barry 33-36R
Weisberg, Gabriel P(aul) 1942- 73-76
Weisberg, Harold 1913- 41-44R
Weisberg, Joseph Gotland
1911-1984 Obituary 112
Weisberg, Joseph S(impson) 1937- 107
Weisberg, Richard H(arvey) 1944- 128
Weisberger, Bernard A(llen) 1922- CANR-7
Earlier sketch in CA 5-8R
See also SATA 21
Weisberger, Eleanor (Burt) 1920- 97-100
Weisbord, Albert 1900(?)-1977 Obituary 69-72
Weisbord, Marvin R(oss) 1931- CANR-9
Earlier sketch in CA 65-68
Weisbord, Robert G. 1933- Brief entry 109
Weisbord, Vera Buch 1895-1987 73-76
Obituary 123
Weisbrod, Burton Allen 1931- CANR-21
Earlier sketches in CA 45-48, CANR-1
Weisbrot, Robert (S.) 1951- 131
Weisbuch, Robert 1946- 104
Weisburd, Martin Harold
1940(?)-1978 Obituary 77-80
Weise, R. Eric 1933- 41-44R
Weisenborn, Guenther 1902-1969 Obituary 114
See also Weisenborn, Gunther
See also DLB 69
Weisenborn, Gunther
See Weisenborn, Guenther
See also DLB 69
Weisenburger, Francis Phelps 1900- CAP-1
Earlier sketch in CA 17-18
Weisenfeld, Murray 1923- 104
Weiser, David K. 1944- 127
Weiser, Eric 1907- 17-20R
Weiser, Marjorie P(hillis) K(atz) 1934- 103
See also SATA 33
Weisgal, Meyer W(olf)
1894-1977 Obituary 89-92
Weisgard, Leonard Joseph 1916- 9-12R
See also MAICYA
See also SATA 2, 30
Weisgerber, Charles A(ugust)
1912-1977 ....41-44R
Weisgerber, Jean 1924- 65-68
Weisgerber, Robert A(rthur) 1929- 49-52
Weisheipl, James A(thanasius) 1923- CANR-15
Earlier sketch in CA 41-44R
Weisheit, Eldon 1933- CANR-14
Earlier sketch in CA 29-32R
Weisinger, Mort 1915- 9-12R
Weiskopf, Bob
See Weiskopf, Robert J.
Weiskopf, Robert J. 1914- 123
Obituary 118
Weisman, Alan H. 1947- 127
Weisman, Herman M. 1916- 9-12R
Weisman, John 1942- CANR-1
Earlier sketch in CA 45-48
Weisman, Marilee 1939- 65-68
Weisman, Mary-Lou 1937- 109
Weismann, Donald L(eroy) 1914- 33-36R
Weismiller, Edward Ronald 1915- CANR-1
Earlier sketch in CA 1-4R
Weiss, Abraham 1895-1971 Obituary 104
Weiss, Adelle 1920- 81-84
See also SATA 18
Weiss, Allen 1918- 109
Weiss, Ann E(dwards) 1943- CANR-28
Earlier sketches in CA 45-48, CANR-1, 11
See also MAICYA
See also SAAS 13
See also SATA 30, 69
Weiss, Arthur 1912- 25-28R
Weiss, Bennet A. Jr.
1926(?)-1983 Obituary 109
Weiss, Beno 1933- 123
Weiss, Bernard J(acob) 1936- 109
Weiss, Dale Eugene 1947- 114
Weiss, David 1909- CANR-12
Earlier sketch in CA 13-16R
Weiss, David 1928- 121
Weiss, Edna
See Barth, Edna
Weiss, Edna Smith 1916- 5-8R
Weiss, Elizabeth S(chwartz) 1944- CANR-11
Earlier sketch in CA 61-64
Weiss, Ellen 1953- 113
See also SATA 44
Weiss, Ernst 1882-1940 ....DLB 81
Weiss, Francis Joseph
1899(?)-1975 Obituary 53-56
Weiss, G(ustav) A(dolf) M(ichael) 1922- 41-44R
Weiss, Gaea (Laughingbird) 1941- 119
Weiss, Harry B(ischoff) 1883-1972 45-48
Weiss, Harvey 1922- CANR-38
Earlier sketches in CA 5-8R, CANR-6
See also CLR 4
See also MAICYA
See also SATA 1, 27
Weiss, Herbert F. 1930- 21-24R
Weiss, Irving J. 1921- CANR-10
Earlier sketch in CA 17-20R
Weiss, Jaqueline Shachter 1926- 119
See also SATA 65
Weiss, Jess E(dward) 1926- CANR-38
Earlier sketch in CA 49-52
Weiss, Joan Talmage 1928- CANR-2
Earlier sketch in CA 5-8R
Weiss, John 1818-1879 ....DLB 1
Weiss, John 1927- 17-20R
Weiss, Jonathan A(rthur) 1939- 93-96
Weiss, Kenneth M(onrad) 1941- 101
Weiss, Leatie 1928- 65-68
See also SATA 50
Weiss, Leonard W(inchell) 1925- CANR-6
Earlier sketch in CA 5-8R
Weiss, Lillian Obituary 104
Weiss, Louise 1893-1983 Obituary 109
Weiss, M(orton) Jerome 1926- CANR-9
Earlier sketch in CA 17-20R
Weiss, M. Jerry
See Weiss, M(orton) Jerome
Weiss, Malcolm E. 1928- CANR-11
Earlier sketch in CA 25-28R
See also SATA 3
Weiss, Margaret R. 1923(?)-1992 57-60
Obituary 137
Weiss, Melford Stephen 1937- 53-56
Weiss, Miriam
See Schlein, Miriam
Weiss, Miriam (Strauss) 1905- CAP-2
Earlier sketch in CA 29-32
Weiss, Morris S(amuel) 1915- 89-92
Weiss, Nancy J(oan) 1944- CANR-13
Earlier sketch in CA 77-80
Weiss, Nicki 1954- CANR-26
Earlier sketch in CA 108
See also SATA 33
Weiss, Paul
See Weiss, Paul A(lfred)
Weiss, Paul A(lfred) 1898-1989 Obituary 129
Weiss, Paul 1901- CANR-3
Earlier sketch in CA 5-8R
See also CAAS 12
Weiss, Peg 125
Weiss, Peter (Ulrich) 1916-1982 ....CANR-3
Obituary 106
Earlier sketch in CA 45-48
See also CLC 3, 15, 51
See also DLB 69
Weiss, Renee Karol 1923- 41-44R
See also SATA 5
Weiss, Robert M. 1929- 37-40R
Weiss, Robert S(tuart) 1925- 25-28R
Weiss, Roger W(illiam) 1930- 45-48
weiss, ruth 1928- 122
Weiss, Samuel A(bba) 1922- 41-44R
Weiss, Sanford 1927- 25-28R
Weiss, (Paul) Shandor 1954- 120

Weiss, Theodore (Russell) 1916- 9-12R
See also CAAS 2
See also CLC 3, 8, 14
See also DLB 5
Weiss, Thomas J(oseph) 1942- 105
Weiss, Winfried (Ferdinand) 1937- 117
Weissberg, Michael P. 1942- 126
Weissberger, L. Arnold 1907-1981 Obituary 103
Weissbort, Daniel 1935- CANR-2
Earlier sketch in CA 45-48
Weisse, Christian Felix 1726-1804 .... DLB 97
Weissenborn, Hellmuth
1898-1982 Obituary 107
See also SATA 31
Weisskopf, Kurt 1907- 25-28R
Weisskopf, Thomas E. 1940- 130
Weisskopf, Victor Frederick 1908- 107
Weisskopf, Walter A(lbert) 1904- 37-40R
Weissman, Benjamin M(urry) 1917- 73-76
Weissman, Dick
See Weissman, Richard
Weissman, Jack 1921- 13-16R
Weissman, Paul 1932- 45-48
Weissman, Philip
1911(?)-1972 Obituary 33-36R
Weissman, Richard 1935- 81-84
Weissman, Rozanne 1942- 101
Weissman, Stephen R(ichard) 1941- CANR-11
Earlier sketch in CA 57-60
Weissman, Steve
See Weissman, Stephen R(ichard)
Weissmann, Gerald 1930- 126
Weissmuller, Johnny
See Weissmuller, Peter John
Weissmuller, Peter John
1904-1984 Obituary 111
Weisstein, Ulrich W(erner) 1925- 21-24R
Weisstub, D(avid) N(orman) 1944- 29-32R
Weist, Dwight 1910- 132
Weith, Warren 1926- 114
Weithorn, Stanley S(tephen) 1924- 13-16R
Weitz, Henry 1911- 41-44R
Weitz, John 1923- 29-32R
Weitz, Martin Mishli 1909- CANR-13
Earlier sketches in CAP-2, CA 17-18
Weitz, Morris 1916-1981 ....CANR-7
Obituary 102
Earlier sketch in CA 5-8R
Weitz, Raanan 1913- CANR-1
Earlier sketch in CA 45-48
Weitzel, Edwin A(nthony)
1905-1988 Obituary 127
Weitzel, Eugene Joseph 1927- 5-8R
Weitzel, Tony
See Weitzel, Edwin A(nthony)
Weitzenhoffer, Andre M(uller) 1921- 5-8R
Weitzman, Alan 1933- 29-32R
Weitzman, Arthur J(oshua) 1933- 53-56
Weitzman, Elliot D. 1929-1983 Obituary 110
Weitzman, Martin L(awrence) 1942- 117
Weitzmann, Kurt 1904- CANR-35
Earlier sketch in CA 41-44R
Weixlmann, Joe
See Weixlmann, Joseph Norman
Weixlmann, Joseph Norman 1946- 109
Weizenbaum, Joseph 1923- Brief entry 113
Weizman, Ezer 1924- 111
Weizman, Savine Gross 1929- 131
Weizsaecker, Carl Friedrich von
See von Weizsaecker, Carl Friedrich
Welber, Robert 104
See also SATA 26
Welbourn, F(rederick) B(urkewood)
1912- 21-24R
Welburn, Ron(ald Garfield) 1944- CANR-17
Earlier sketches in CA 45-48, CANR-1
See also BW
Welch, Ann Courtenay (Edmonds)
1917- CANR-18
Earlier sketches in CA 9-12R, CANR-3
Welch, Bob
See Welch, Robert Lynn
Welch, Charles Scott
See Smith, LeRoi Tex
Welch, Claude E(merson) Jr. 1939- CANR-32
Earlier sketches in CA 41-44R, CANR-14
Welch, Cyril 1939- 118
Welch, D'Alte Aldridge 1907-1970 Obituary 104
See also SATA 27
Welch, David 1950- 130
Welch, (Maurice) Denton
1915-1948 Brief entry 121
See also TCLC 22
Welch, Don(ovan LeRoy) 1932- CANR-20
Earlier sketch in CA 104
Welch, Finis R. 1938- 118
Welch, George Patrick 1901-1976 .... CAP-1
Obituary 65-68
Earlier sketch in CA 13-14
Welch, Gita (Bernardo) Honwana 1948- 138
Welch, Herbert 1862-1969 .... CAP-1
Earlier sketch in CA 13-16
Welch, Holmes (Hinkley) 1921- 21-24R
Welch, J(oseph) Edmund 1922- 57-60
Welch, James 1940- 85-88
See also CLC 6, 14, 52
Welch, Jean-Louise
See Kempton, Jean Welch
Welch, Jerome A. 1933- 65-68
Welch, June Rayfield 1927- 41-44R
Welch, Kathleen E(thel) 1951- 136
Welch, Kenneth Frederick 1917- 105
Welch, Lew(is Barrett Jr.)
1926-1971(?) Obituary 113
See also DLB 16
Welch, Liliane 1937- CANR-27
Earlier sketch in CA 110
Welch, Martha McKeen 1914- Brief entry 114
See also SATA 45
Welch, Mary Ross 1918- 53-56
Welch, Mary-Scott (Stewart) 1914- 104
Welch, Michael Irene 1940- 97-100
Welch, Patrick
See Welch, George Patrick
Welch, Pauline
See Bodenham, Hilda Morris
Welch, Richard Edwin Jr. 1924- 85-88
Welch, Robert H(enry) W(inborne) Jr.
1899-1985 Obituary 114
Welch, Robert Lynn 1956- 112
Welch, Ronald
See Felton, Ronald Oliver
Welch, Rowland
See Davies, L(eslie) P(urnell)
Welch, Stuart Cary 1928- 103
Welch, Timothy L. 1935- 85-88
Welch, William A. 1915(?)-1976 Obituary 65-68
Welch, William 1917- Brief entry 115
Welcher, Jeanne K. 1922- Brief entry 116
Welcher, Rosalind 1922- CANR-25
Earlier sketch in CA 45-48
Welchman, Gordon 1906(?)-1985 Obituary 117
Welcome, John
See Brennan, John N(eedham) H(uggard)
Weld, Philip S(altonstall Sr.)
1914-1984 Obituary 114
Welding, Patsy Ruth 1924- 61-64
Weldon, Fay 1933(?)- CANR-16
Earlier sketch in CA 21-24R
See also CDBLB 1960 to Present
See also CLC 6, 9, 11, 19, 36, 59
See also DLB 14
See also MTCW
Weldon, John F(rederick Stover) 1948- 113
Weldon, John 1890(?)-1963 Obituary 115
See also MacNamara, Brinsley
Weldon, Lynn Leroy 1930- 97-100
Weldon, Michael J(ames) 1952- 117
Weldon, Rex
See Rimel, Duane (Weldon)
Weldon, (Nathaniel) Warren (Jr.) 1919- 29-32R
Welfare, Humphrey 1950- 124
Welfare, Simon 1946- 133
Welfle, Richard A. 1901- CAP-1
Earlier sketch in CA 13-14
Welfling, Weldon 1912-1978 Obituary 111
Welford, A(lan) T(raviss) 1914- CANR-5
Earlier sketch in CA 13-16R
Welk, Lawrence 1903- 134
Brief entry 105
Welke, Elton 1941- 65-68
Welker, David 1917- 57-60
Welker, Robert Henry 1917- 89-92
Welker, Robert L(ouis) 1924- 9-12R
Welkowitz, Joan 1929- 53-56
Well, Alan Stewart
See Sewart, Alan
Welland, Colin
See Williams, Colin
Welland, Dennis (Sydney Reginald)
1919- CANR-2
Earlier sketch in CA 5-8R
Wellard, James (Howard) 1909-1987 ......CANR-3
Obituary 122
Earlier sketch in CA 5-8R
Wellborn, Charles 1923- 29-32R
Wellborn, Fred W(ilmot) 1894- 9-12R
Wellborn, Grace Pleasant 1906- CAP-2
Earlier sketch in CA 17-18
Wellek, Rene 1903- CANR-8
Earlier sketch in CA 5-8R
See also CAAS 7
See also CLC 28
See also DLB 63
Wellen, Edward (Paul) 1919- 85-88
Weller, Allen Stuart 1907- CANR-24
Earlier sketch in CA 1-4R
Weller, Charles 1911- 21-24R
Weller, George (Anthony) 1907- 65-68
See also SATA 31
Weller, Michael 1942- 85-88
See also CLC 10, 53
Weller, Paul 1958- .... CLC 26
Weller, Robert P(aul) 1953- 118
Weller, Sheila 1945- 77-80
Wellershoff, Dieter 1925- CANR-37
Earlier sketches in CA 89-92, CANR-16
See also CLC 46
Welles, Margery Miller 1923-1985 Obituary 115
Welles, (George) Orson 1915-1985 93-96
Obituary 117
See also CLC 20
Welles, Samuel Gardner
1913(?)-1981 Obituary 105
Welles, Winifred 1893-1939 Brief entry 112
See also SATA 27
Wellesbourne, Peter
See Williams, P(eter) F(airney)
Wellesley, Gerald 1885-1972 Obituary 104
Wellesley, Kenneth 1911- 106
Wellesz, Egon Joseph
1885-1974 Obituary 53-56
Wellford, Harrison 1940- Brief entry 111
Welling, Kathryn M. 1952- 127
Welling, William 1924- 81-84
Wellington, C(harles) Burleigh 1920- 1-4R
Wellington, Harry H(illel) 1926- 25-28R
Wellington, Jean Willett 1922- 1-4R
Wellington, John H. 1892- CAP-2
Earlier sketch in CA 25-28
Wellington, Kate
See Schulze, Hertha
Wellington, Monica 1957- 136
See also SATA 67
Wellington, R(ichard) A(nthony) 1919- 61-64
Wellisch, Hans H(anan) 1920- 102
Wellisz, Leopold T. 1882-1972 Obituary 37-40R
Wellman, Alice 1900-1984 89-92
See also SATA 36, 51
Wellman, Carl (Pierce) 1926- 37-40R
Wellman, Frederick L(ovejoy) 1897- 77-80
Wellman, Henry Q. 1945- 37-40R
Wellman, Mac 1945- .... CLC 65
Wellman, Manly Wade 1903-1986 ....CANR-16
Obituary 118
Earlier sketches in CA 1-4R, CANR-6
See also CLC 49
See also SATA 6, 47
Wellman, Paul I(selin) 1898-1966 ....CANR-16
Obituary 25-28R
Earlier sketch in CA 1-4R
See also SATA 3
Wellman, William A(ugustus)
1896-1975 Obituary 61-64
Wells, Allen 1951- 125
Wells, Anna Mary 1906- CANR-2
Earlier sketch in CA 5-8R
Wells, Arvin Robert 1927- 1-4R
Wells, Bella Fromm 1901(?)-1972 Obituary 104
Wells, C(olin) M(ichael) 1933- 41-44R
Wells, Carolyn 1869(?)-1942 Brief entry 113
See also DLB 11
See also TCLC 35
Wells, Charles Jeremiah 1800-1879 .... DLB 32
Wells, David Franklin 1928- Brief entry 108
Wells, Dee (Alberta) 1925- 85-88
See also AITN 1
Wells, (William) Dicky 1910- 61-64
Wells, Donald A(rthur) 1917- 21-24R
Wells, Edward
See Wellsted, W. Raife
Wells, Ellen B(aker) 1934- 103
Wells, Evelyn 53-56
Wells, George A(lbert) 1926- CANR-32
Earlier sketches in CA 81-84, CANR-15
Wells, George Philip 1901-1985 Obituary 117
Wells, H(erbert) G(eorge) 1866-1946 121
Brief entry 110
See also CDBLB 1914-1945
See also DLB 34, 70
See also MTCW
See also SATA 20
See also SSC 6
See also TCLC 6, 12, 19
See also WLC
Wells, Harold P(hilmore) 1925- CANR-10
Earlier sketch in CA 65-68
Wells, Harry Kohlsaat 1911-1976 ....5-8R
Obituary 65-68
Wells, Helen
See Campbell, Hope
Wells, Helen 1910-1986 ....CANR-37
Earlier sketch in CA 29-32R
See also MAICYA
See also SATA 2, 49
Wells, Henry W(illis) 1895-1978 ....CANR-28
Obituary 77-80
Earlier sketch in CA 81-84
Wells, Hondo
See Whittington, Harry (Benjamin)
Wells, J. Wellington
See de Camp, L(yon) Sprague
Wells, James B(uchanan) 1909- 45-48
Wells, James M. 1917- 17-20R
Wells, Jerome C(ovell) 1936- 41-44R
Wells, Jessica
See Buckland, Raymond
Wells, Joel F(reeman) 1930- CANR-23
Earlier sketch in CA 13-16R
Wells, John Campbell 1936- 104
Wells, John Jay
See Coulson, Juanita (Ruth)
Wells, John Warren 1938- CANR-4
Earlier sketch in CA 49-52
Wells, June
See Swinford, Betty (June Wells)
Wells, Kenneth McNeill 1905- CAP-1
Earlier sketch in CA 13-14
Wells, Lawrence 1941- 120
Wells, Leon W. 1925- 17-20R
Wells, Linton 1893-1976 97-100
Obituary 61-64
Wells, Lisa
See Raucina, Thomas Frank
Wells, Louis T(ruitt) Jr. 1937- 65-68
Wells, M. Gawain 1942- 101
Wells, Marian (Louise Bradfield) 1931- 113
Wells, Merle William 1918- CANR-37
Earlier sketches in CA 85-88, CANR-16
Wells, Nigel 1944- 118
Wells, Patricia 1946- 132
Wells, Peter D. 1936- 25-28R
Wells, Robert
See Welsch, Roger L(ee)
Wells, (Frank Charles) Robert 1929- 97-100
Wells, Robert Vale 1943- CANR-12
Earlier sketch in CA 73-76
Wells, Robert W(ayne) 1918- CANR-2
Earlier sketch in CA 49-52
Wells, Robert 1947- .... DLB 40
Wells, Roger 1947- 136
Wells, Ronald Vale 1913- CANR-14
Earlier sketch in CA 37-40R
Wells, Rosemary 1943- 85-88
See also CLC 12
See also CLR 16
See also MAICYA
See also SAAS 1
See also SATA 18, 69
Wells, Samuel F(ogle Jr.) 1935- 104
Wells, Samuel J(ames III) 1936- 123
Wells, Stanley W(illiam) 1930- CANR-29
Earlier sketches in CA 21-24R, CANR-10
Wells, Theodora (Westmont) 1926- 134
Brief entry 113
Wells, Tim 1954- 129
Wells, Tobias
See Forbes, DeLoris (Florine) Stanton
Wells, Tom H. 1917- 21-24R
Wells, Walter 1937- 25-28R
Wells, William D(eWitt) 1926- CANR-13
Earlier sketch in CA 61-64
Wells, William Thomas
1908-1990(?) Obituary 130
Wells-Barnett, Ida B. 1862-1931 .... DLB 23
Wellsted, W. Raife 1929- 125
Wellstone, Paul David 1944- 107
Wellwarth, George E(manuel) 1932- CANR-3
Earlier sketch in CA 9-12R
Welmers, William Evert 1916- 104
Wels, Alena 1938(?)-1985 Obituary 115
Wels, Byron G(erald) 1924- CANR-8
Earlier sketch in CA 61-64
See also SATA 9
Welsby, Paul A(ntony) 1920- 129
Welsch, Erwin Kurt 1935- 17-20R
Welsch, Glenn Albert 1915- CANR-10
Earlier sketch in CA 13-16R
Welsch, Roger L(ee) 1936- CANR-9
Earlier sketch in CA 21-24R
Welsey, Richard (Errol) 1945- CANR-27
Welsh, Alexander 1933- CANR-6
Earlier sketch in CA 5-8R
Welsh, Andrew 1937- 110
Welsh, Anne 1922- 101
Welsh, David
See Hills, C(harles) A(lbert) R(eis)
Welsh, David J(ohn) 1920- 17-20R
Welsh, Frank (Reeson) 1931- 135
Welsh, George Schlager 1918- 17-20R
Welsh, James Michael 1938- CANR-20
Earlier sketches in CA 53-56, CANR-4
Welsh, John R(ushing) 1916-1974 ....37-40R
Welsh, Ken 1941- CANR-13
Earlier sketch in CA 77-80
Welsh, Marion E. 1910- 118
Welsh, Mary
See Hemingway, Mary Welsh
Welsh, Mary Flynn 1910(?)-1984 Obituary 112
See also SATA 38
Welsh, Paul 1911- 104
Welsh, Peter C(orbett) 1926- 25-28R
Welsh, Stanley L. 1928- 103
Welsh, Susan
See Collins, Margaret (Brandon James)
Welsh, William A(llen) 1940- CANR-25
Earlier sketch in CA 45-48
Welsman, Ernest 1912- 5-8R
Welt, Elly 127
Welt, Louis G(ordon) 1913-1974 Obituary 45-48
Welter, Erich 1900-1982 Obituary 107
Welter, Paul (R.) 1928- 121
Welter, Rush (Eastman) 1923- CANR-2
Earlier sketch in CA 5-8R
Weltge, Ralph (William) 1930- 21-24R
Welthy, Soni Halstead 1933- 13-16R
Weltmann, Lutz 1901- CAP-1
Earlier sketch in CA 11-12
Weltner, Linda R(iverly) 1938- 105
See also SATA 38
Weltsch, Robert 1891-1982 Obituary 108
Welty, Eudora 1909- CANR-32
Earlier sketch in CA 9-12R
See also CABS 1
See also CDALB 1941-1968
See also CLC 1, 2, 5, 14, 22, 33
See also DLB 2, 102
See also DLBY 87
See also MTCW
See also SSC 1
See also WLC
Welty, Joel Carl 1901- CANR-2
Earlier sketch in CA 5-8R
Welty, S. F.
See Welty, Susan F.
Welty, Susan F. 1905- CAP-2
Earlier sketch in CA 17-18
See also SATA 9
Welwood, John 1943- 120
Welzenbach, Lanora F.
See Miller, Lanora
Wemple, Suzanne Fonay 1927- 106
Wenar, Charles 1922- 93-96
Wende, Philip 1939- 29-32R
Wendel, Francois Jean 1905- CAP-1
Earlier sketch in CA 13-14
Wendel, Natalja Rose 1900- 61-64
Wendel, Thomas H(arold) 1924- 53-56
Wendel, Tim 1956- 105
Wendelin, Rudolph 1910- ....SATA 23
Wendell, Barrett 1855-1921 .... DLB 71
Wender, Dorothea 1934- CANR-24
Earlier sketch in CA 45-48
Wender, Paul H. 1934- CANR-26
Earlier sketch in CA 109
Wenders, Wim 1945- 93-96
Wendland, Michael F(letcher) 1946- CANR-9
Earlier sketch in CA 65-68
Wendland, Mike
See Wendland, Michael F(letcher)
Wendorf, Patricia 1928- 113
Wendorf, Richard (Harold) 1948- CANR-36
Earlier sketch in CA 114
Wendroff, Zalman
See Vendrovskii, David Efimovich
Wendrowsky, Zalman
See Vendrovskii, David Efimovich
Wendt, Albert 1939- 57-60

Wendt, Gerald L(ouis)
  1891-1973 Obituary 45-48
Wendt, Ingrid 1944- 117
Wendt, Jo Ann 1935- 109
Wendt, Lloyd 1908- CANR-25
  Earlier sketch in CA 102
Wendt, Viola (Sophia) 1907- 104
Wendzel, Robert L. 1938- 112
Weng, Byron S. J. 1934- CANR-16
  Earlier sketch in CA 41-44R
Weng, Hsing Ching
  See Weng, Wan-go
Weng, Wan-go 1918- 97-100
Wengenroth, Edith Flack Ackley
  1887-1970 Obituary 104
Wengenroth, Stow 1906-1978 Obituary 104
Wenger, (Anna) Grace 1919- 13-16R
Wenger, J(ohn) C(hristian) 1910- CANR-21
  Earlier sketches in CA 1-4R, CANR-6
Wengert, Norman Irving 1916- 85-88
Wengrov, Charles 1925- CANR-7
  Earlier sketch in CA 5-8R
Wenham, John W(illiam) 1913- 57-60
Wenhe, Mary B. 1910- 65-68
Wen I-to 1899-1946 ....TCLC 28
Wenk, Edward Jr. 1920- 53-56
Wenkam, Robert 1920- CANR-4
  Earlier sketch in CA 53-56
Wenkart, Heni
  See Wenkart, Henny
Wenkart, Henny 1928- 9-12R
Wennblom, Ralph D.
  1922(?)-1986 Obituary 121
Wenner, Jann S(imon) 1946- 101
Wenner, Kate 1947- 77-80
Wenner, Lettie McSpadden 1937- 65-68
Wenner, Manfred W. 1936- 29-32R
Wenner, Sim 1922- 1-4R
Wennerstrom, Mary H(annah) 1939- 134
  Brief entry 110
Wensing, Michael G. 1950- 118
Wensinger, Arthur S(tevens) 1926- CANR-33
  Earlier sketches in CA 37-40R, CANR-15
Wentink, Andrew Mark 1948- 105
Wentworth, Barbara
  See Pitcher, Gladys
Wentworth, Elise H(ughes) 1931- 77-80
Wentworth, Harold 1904- CAP-1
  Earlier sketch in CA 13-14
Wentworth, Michael J(ustin) 1938- 118
Wentworth, Patricia 1878-1961 ....DLB 77
Wentworth, Robert
  See Hamilton, Edmond
Wentz, Frederick K(uhlman) 1921- 9-12R
Wentz, Walter B. 1929- CANR-10
  Earlier sketch in CA 25-28R
Wenzel, Siegfried 1928- 21-24R
Weores, Sandor 1913-1989 Obituary 127
Wepman, Dennis 1933- 120
Wepman, Joseph M. 1907- 45-48
Weppner, Robert S. 1936- 121
Werblow, Dorothy N.
  1908-1972 Obituary 37-40R
Were, Gideon S(aulo) 1934- CANR-11
  Earlier sketch in CA 65-68
Werenskiold, Marit 1942- 130
Werfel, Franz (V.) 1890-1945 Brief entry 104
  See also DLB 81
  See also TCLC 8
Werich, Jan 1905(?)-1980 Obituary 102
Werking, Richard Hume 1943- Brief entry 113
Werkley, Caroline E(Isea) 29-32R
Werkman, Sidney L(ee) 1927- 49-52
Werkmeister, Lucyle (Thomas) 1908- 5-8R
Werkmeister, W(illiam) H(enry) 1901- 21-24R
Werlich, David P(atrick) 1941- 81-84
Werlich, Robert 1924- 9-12R
Werlin, Herbert Holland 1932- 61-64
Werlock, Abby Holmes P(otter) 1942- 137
Wermuth, Paul C(harles Joseph) 1925- 13-16R
Werne, Benjamin 1904-1978 Obituary 77-80
Wernecke, Herbert Henry 1895- 5-8R
Werner, Alfred 1911-1979 Obituary 89-92
Werner, D. Michael 1950- 120
Werner, Elsa Jane
  See Watson, Jane Werner
Werner, Emmy Elizabeth 1929- 57-60
Werner, Eric 1901-1988 ....13-16R
  Obituary 126
Werner, Hans 1946- 131
Werner, Hazen G. 1895- 17-20R
Werner, Herma 1926- CANR-34
  Earlier sketches in CA 85-88, CANR-15
  See also SATA 41, 47
Werner, Jane
  See Watson, Jane Werner
Werner, Jayne S(usan) 1944- 112
Werner, John R(oland) 1930- 41-44R
Werner, K.
  See Casewit, Curtis W(erner)
Werner, Karl Ferdinand 1924- 131
Werner, M(orris) R(obert) 1897-1981 107
  Obituary 104
Werner, Peter Howard 1944- CANR-4
  Earlier sketch in CA 53-56
Werner, Victor (Emile) 1894-1980 ....29-32R
  Obituary 93-96
Werner, Vivian 1921- 105
Werner, Zacharias 1768-1823 ....DLB 94
Wernette, J(ohn) Philip 1903- 5-8R
Wernick, Robert 1918- 97-100
Wernick, Saul 1921- 81-84
Werning, Waldo J. 1921- CANR-10
  Earlier sketch in CA 13-16R
Wernstedt, Frederick L(age) 1921- 21-24R
Werr, Donald F. 1920- 21-24R
Werry, Richard R. 1916- 9-12R
Wersba, Barbara 1932- CANR-38
  Earlier sketches in CA 29-32R, CANR-16
  See also AAYA 2
  See also CLC 30
  See also CLR 3
  See also DLB 52
  See also MAICYA
  See also SAAS 2
  See also SATA 1, 58
Wershoven, Carol Jean 1947- 112
Werstein, Irving 1914(?)-1971 73-76
  Obituary 29-32R
  See also SATA 14
Wert, Lynette L(emon) 1938- 106
Wertenbaker, Lael (Tucker) 1909- CANR-18
  Earlier sketches in CA 5-8R, CANR-3
Wertenbaker, Thomas Jefferson
  1879-1966 ....5-8R
Wertenbaker, William 1938- 97-100
Werth, Alexander 1901-1969 ....CAP-1
  Obituary 25-28R
  Earlier sketch in CA 13-16
Werth, Kurt 1896- 81-84
  See also SATA 20
Wertham, Fredric 1895-1981 ....5-8R
  Obituary 105
Wertheim, Arthur Frank 1935- 97-100
Wertheim, Bill 1944- 37-40R
Wertheim, Stanley 1930- 41-44R
Wertheimer, Barbara M(ayer) 1926(?)-1983 129
  Obituary 110
Wertheimer, Leonard 1914- 116
Wertheimer, Linda Brief entry 123
Wertheimer, Marilyn L(ou) 1928- 102
Wertheimer, Max 1880-1943 Brief entry 123
Wertheimer, Michael (Matthew) 1927- CANR-2
  Earlier sketch in CA 1-4R
Wertheimer, Richard F(rederick) II
  1943- 29-32R
Wertheimer, Roger 1942- 37-40R
Werther, William B(lanchfield) Jr.
  1947- CANR-21
  Earlier sketch in CA 105
Werthman, Michael S(cott) 1939- 89-92
Wertime, Theodore A(llen) 1919-1982 109
  Obituary 106
Wertmueller, Lina 1928- CANR-39
  Earlier sketch in CA 97-100
  See also CLC 16
Werts, Margaret F. 1915- 102
Wertsman, Vladimir (F.) 1929- CANR-20
  Earlier sketches in CA 61-64, CANR-31, 8
Wertz, Richard W(ayne) 1933- 45-48
Wertz, S. K.
  See Wertz, Spencer K.
Wertz, Spencer K. 1941- 125
Wesander, Bioern Kenneth
  See Cox, P(atrick) Brian
Wesberry, James Pickett 1906- 85-88
Weschcke, Carl L(ouis) 1930- 61-64
Wesche, L(ilburn) E(dgar) 1929- 93-96
Wesche, Percival A. 1912- 49-52
Weschler, Lawrence 1952- 135
Weschler, Louis F(redrick) 1933- 41-44R
Wescott, Glenway 1901-1987 ....CANR-23
  Obituary 121
  Earlier sketch in CA 13-16R
  See also CLC 13
  See also DLB 4, 9, 102
Wescott, Roger W. 1925- 25-28R
Wesencraft, Charles Frederick 1928- 61-64
Wesker, Arnold 1932- CANR-33
  Earlier sketches in CA 1-4R, CANR-1
  See also CAAS 7
  See also CDBLB 1960 to Present
  See also CLC 3, 5, 42
  See also DLB 13
  See also MTCW
Weslager, C(linton) A(lfred) 1909- CANR-24
  Earlier sketches in CA 21-24R, CANR-9
Wesley, Alison
  See Barnes, Michael
Wesley, Charles H(arris) 1891-1987 101
  Obituary 123
Wesley, Charles 1707-1788 ....DLB 95
Wesley, Elizabeth
  See McElfresh, (Elizabeth) Adeline
Wesley, George R(andolph) 1931- 41-44R
Wesley, James
  See Rigoni, Orlando (Joseph)
Wesley, John 1703-1791 ....DLB 104
Wesley, Mary 1912- 49-52
  See also MTCW
  See also SATA 66
Wesley, Richard (Errol) 1945- 57-60
  See also BW
  See also CLC 7
  See also DLB 38
Wesling, Donald 1939- 101
Wesner, Maralene 1935- 112
Wesner, Miles 1933- 112
Wess, Martin 1906(?)-1975 Obituary 104
Wessel, Andrew E(rnest) 1925- 73-76
Wessel, Carl John 1911-1984 Obituary 113
Wessel, Helen (Strain) 1924- CANR-11
  Earlier sketch in CA 13-16R
Wessel, Milton R(alph) 1923- 89-92
Wessel, Robert H. 1921- 1-4R
Wesselmann, Tom 1931- 108
Wessels, William L. 1889- 5-8R
Wesser, Robert F. 1933- 21-24R
Wessler, Ruth Ann 1938- 29-32R
Wessman, Alden E(benhart) 1930- 21-24R
Wesson, Joan
  See Pittock, Joan (Hornby)
Wesson, Robert G(ale) 1920-1991 ....CANR-18
  Obituary 134
  Earlier sketches in CA 9-12R, CANR-3
West, Allan M(orrell) 1910- 109
West, Anna 1938- 106
  See also SATA 40
West, Anthony C(athcart Muir) 1910- CANR-31
  Earlier sketch in CA 69-72
West, Anthony (Panther) 1914-1987 ....CANR-19
  Obituary 124
  Earlier sketches in CA 45-48, CANR-3
  See also CLC 50
  See also DLB 15
West, Barbara
  See Price, Olive
West, Betty 1921- CANR-7
  Earlier sketch in CA 5-8R
  See also SATA 11
West, Beverly Henderson 1939- 119
West, Bill
  See West, William G.
West, Bonnie 1946- 114
West, Bruce 1951- ....SATA 63
West, C. P.
  See Wodehouse, P(elham) G(renville)
West, Charles Converse 1921- 81-84
West, Colin 1951- 136
West, D(onald) J(ames) 1924- CANR-20
  Earlier sketches in CA 13-16R, CANR-5
West, David (Alexander) 1926- 21-24R
West, Delno C(loyde) Jr. 1936- 57-60
West, Dick Sheppard 1920-1989 Obituary 130
West, Don 1928- 57-60
West, Dorothy
  See Benson, Mildred (Augustine Wirt)
West, Dorothy 1907- ....DLB 76
West, E(dwin) G(eorge) 1922- CANR-29
  Earlier sketch in CA 25-28R
West, Earle H(uddleston) 1925- 53-56
West, Edward Nason 1909- CAP-2
  Earlier sketch in CA 19-20
West, Edwin G.
  See West, E(dwin) G(eorge)
West, Elliot 1924- 17-20R
West, Elmer D(alton) 1907-1991 ....CAP-1
  Obituary 135
  Earlier sketch in CA 13-14
West, Emily Govan 1919- 109
  See also SATA 38
West, Emmy
  See West, Emily Govan
West, Eugenia Lovett 85-88
West, Francis Horner 1909- 118
West, Francis (James) 1927- CANR-3
  Earlier sketch in CA 5-8R
West, Frank H.
  See West, Francis Horner
West, Fred 1918- 5-8R
West, G(eorge) Allen Jr. 1915- 17-20R
West, George Algernon
  1893-1980 Obituary 97-100
West, Gertrude 110
West, Gordon 1896- CAP-1
  Earlier sketch in CA 13-14
West, Henry Woolliscroft 1925- 41-44R
West, Herbert B(uell) 1916- 53-56
West, Herbert Faulkner 1898-1974 ....CAP-2
  Obituary 53-56
  Earlier sketch in CA 19-20
West, J. B.
  See West, J. Bernard
West, J. Bernard 1913(?)-1983 120
  Obituary 110
West, James
  See Withers, Carl A.
West, James King 1930- 45-48
West, James L(emuel) W(ills III) 1946- 131
West, (Mary) Jane 1939(?)-1981 Obituary 104
West, Jerry
  See Svenson, Andrew E(dward)
West, (Mary) Jessamyn 1902-1984 ....CANR-27
  Obituary 112
  Earlier sketch in CA 9-12R
  See also CLC 7, 17
  See also DLB 6
  See also DLBY 84
  See also MTCW
  See also SATA 37
West, John Anthony 1932- 81-84
West, John Foster 1918- 13-16R
West, John Frederick 1929- 103
West, Joyce (Tarlton) 1908- 106
West, Kirkpatrick
  See Harris, F(rank) Brayton
West, Leonard J(ordan) 1921- 41-44R
West, Lindsay
  See Weber, Nancy
West, Mae 1893-1980 89-92
  Obituary 102
  See also DLB 44
West, Marion B(ond) 1936- 101
West, Mark
  See Runyon, Charles W.
West, Morris L(anglo) 1916- CANR-24
  Earlier sketch in CA 5-8R
  See also CLC 6, 33
  See also MTCW
West, Muriel (Leitzell) 1903- CAP-1
  Earlier sketch in CA 13-16
West, Nancy Richard
  See Westphal, Wilma Ross
West, Nathanael 1903-1940 125
  Brief entry 104
  See also CDALB 1929-1941
  See also DLB 4, 9, 28
  See also MTCW
  See also TCLC 1, 14, 44
West, Owen
  See Koontz, Dean R(ay)
West, Pat
  See Strother, Pat Wallace
West, Paul 1930- CANR-22
  Earlier sketch in CA 13-16R
  See also CAAS 7
  See also CLC 7, 14
  See also DLB 14
West, Ray B(enedict) Jr. 1908- CANR-3
  Earlier sketch in CA 1-4R
West, Rebecca 1892-1983 ....CANR-19
  Obituary 109
  Earlier sketch in CA 5-8R
  See also CLC 7, 9, 31, 50
  See also DLB 36
  See also DLBY 83
  See also MTCW
West, Richard S(edgewick) Jr.
  1902-1968 ....CAP-1
  Earlier sketch in CA 13-16
West, Richard Samuel 1955- 130
West, Robert C(raig) 1947- 89-92
West, Robert Frederick 1916- 5-8R
West, Robert H(unter) 1907- 37-40R
West, Thomas R(eed) 1936- 124
  Brief entry 118
West, Token
  See Humphries, Adelaide M.
West, Trudy
  See West, Gertrude
West, Uta 1928- 85-88
West, V(ictoria Mary) Sackville
  See Sackville-West, V(ictoria Mary)
West, Ward
  See Borland, Harold Glen
West, William G. 1930- CANR-14
  Earlier sketch in CA 37-40R
Westall, Robert (Atkinson) 1929- CANR-18
  Earlier sketch in CA 69-72
  See also CLC 17
  See also CLR 13
  See also MAICYA
  See also SAAS 2
  See also SATA 23, 69
Westberg, Granger E(llsworth) 1913- CANR-6
  Earlier sketch in CA 1-4R
Westbie, Constance 1910- 85-88
Westbrook, Adele 41-44R
Westbrook, Max (Roger) 1927- 37-40R
Westbrook, Perry D(ickie) 1916- CANR-21
  Earlier sketches in CA 1-4R, CANR-6
Westbrook, Robert 1945- 25-28R
Westbrook, Wayne W(illiam) 1939- 97-100
Westbury, Ian Douglas 1939- Brief entry 106
Westby, David L. 1929- 45-48
Westby-Gibson, Dorothy Pauline 1920- 17-20R
Westcott, Cynthia 1898-1983 ....5-8R
  Obituary 109
Westcott, Jan Vlachos 1912- CANR-2
  Earlier sketch in CA 1-4R
Westcott, Kathleen
  See Abrahamsen, Christine Elizabeth
Westcott, W(illiam) F(ranklin) 1949- 113
Westcott-Jones, K(enneth) 1921- CANR-4
  Earlier sketch in CA 53-56
Westebbe, Richard (Manning) 1925- 45-48
Westell, Anthony 1926- 101
Westerberg, Christine 1950- 61-64
  See also SATA 29
Westergaard, John (Harald) 1927- CANR-11
  Earlier sketch in CA 69-72
Westerhoff, John H(enry) III 1933- CANR-17
  Earlier sketches in CA 45-48, CANR-1
Westerink, Leendert Gerrit 1913- 93-96
Westerman, Percy F(rancis)
  1876-1959 Brief entry 110
Westermann, Claus 1909- CANR-15
  Earlier sketch in CA 81-84
Westermeier, Clifford P(eter) 1910- 45-48
Westermeyer, Joseph John 1937- 109
Western, J(ohn) R(andle) 1928-1971 ....CAP-2
  Earlier sketch in CA 21-22
Western, John (Charles) 1947- 105
Western, Mark
  See Crisp, Anthony Thomas
(The) Western Spy
  See Dillon, John M(yles)
Westervelt, Virginia Veeder 1914- CANR-10
  Earlier sketch in CA 61-64
  See also SATA 10
Westfall, David 1927- 117
Westfall, Don C. 1928-1973 ....CAP-2
  Earlier sketch in CA 17-18
Westfall, Ralph (Libby) 1917- 5-8R
Westfall, Richard S(amuel) 1924- 21-24R
Westfeldt, Lulie 1896- CAP-1
  Earlier sketch in CA 13-14
Westheimer, David 1917- CANR-2
  Earlier sketch in CA 1-4R
  See also SATA 14
Westhues, Kenneth 1944- CANR-11
  Earlier sketch in CA 25-28R
Westin, Alan F(urman) 1929- CANR-10
  Earlier sketch in CA 13-16R
Westin, Av(ram) 1929- 77-80
Westin, Jeane Eddy 1931- 85-88
Westin, Richard A(xel) 1945- CANR-37
  Earlier sketch in CA 115
Westing, Arthur H(erbert) 1928- CANR-38
  Earlier sketches in CA 41-44R, CANR-17
Westing, John Howard 1911- 9-12R
Westlake, Aubrey Thomas
  1893-1985 Obituary 119

Westlake, Donald E(dwin) 1933- CANR-16
Earlier sketch in CA 17-20R
See also CAAS 13
See also CLC 7, 33
Westlake, Helen Gum 1927- 41-44R
Westlake, Michael 1942- 127
Westland, Lynn
See Joscelyn, Archie L.
Westley, Bruce H(utchinson) 1915- CANR-2
Earlier sketch in CA 1-4R
Westley, Dick
See Westley, Richard John
Westley, Richard John 1928- 112
Westley, William A. 1920- 37-40R
Westling, Louise (Hutchings) 1942- 133
Westlund, Joseph 1936- 118
Westmacott, Mary
See Christie, Agatha (Mary Clarissa)
Westman, Barbara 105
See also SATA 70
Westman, Jack C(onrad) 1927- 93-96
Westman, Paul (Wendell) 1956- 106
See also SATA 39
Westman, Wesley C(harles) 1936- 29-32R
Westminster, Aynn
See Mundis, Hester
Westmore, Ann 1953- 109
Westmore, Frank 1923(?)-1985 Obituary 116
Westmoreland, Reg(inald Conway)
1926- 29-32R
Westmoreland, William C(hilds) 1914- 101
See also SATA 63
Westoff, Charles Francis 1927- 81-84
Westoff, Leslie Aldridge 1928- 77-80
Weston, Alan J(ay) 1940- 73-76
Weston, Allen
See Hogarth, Grace (Weston Allen)
and Norton, Andre
Weston, Ann
See Pitcher, Gladys
Weston, Burns H. 1933- 29-32R
Weston, Carolyn 1921- 107
Weston, Christine (Goutiere)
1904-1989 Obituary 128
Weston, Corinne Comstock 1919- CANR-21
Earlier sketch in CA 1-4R
Weston, Glen E(arl) 1922- 49-52
Weston, Helen Gray
See Daniels, Dorothy
Weston, J(ohn) Fred(erick) 1916- CANR-1
Earlier sketch in CA 1-4R
Weston, John
See Davies, John Evan Weston
Weston, John (Harrison) 1932- 17-20R
See also SATA 21
Weston, Joseph H(arry)
1911(?)-1983 Obituary 111
Weston, Martha 1947- 129
See also SATA 53
Weston, Paul B(rendan) 1910- 13-16R
Weston, Rubin Francis 1921- 104
Weston, Susan B(rown) 1943- 81-84
Weston-Smith, M. 1956- 93-96
Westphal, Arnold Carl 1897- ......SATA 57
Westphal, Barbara Osborne 1907- CAP-1
Earlier sketch in CA 11-12
Westphal, Clarence 1904- CAP-2
Earlier sketch in CA 17-18
Westphal, Siegfried 1902-1982 Obituary 107
Westphal, Wilma Ross 1907- 21-24R
Westphall, Victor 1913- 119
Westrup, J(ack) A(llan) 1904-1975 Obituary 115
Westsmith, Kim 1945- 57-60
Westwater, Sister Agnes Martha 1929- 21-24R
Westwood, Gordon
See Schofield, Michael
Westwood, Gwen 1915- CANR-19
Earlier sketch in CA 25-28R
Westwood, J(ohn) N(orton) 1931- CANR-20
Earlier sketches in CA 13-16R, CANR-5
Westwood, Jennifer 1940- CANR-29
Earlier sketches in CA 65-68, CANR-9
See also SATA 10
Westwood, Richard E. 1921- 137
Wetcheek, J. L.
See Feuchtwanger, Lion
Wetenhall, John 1957- 136
Wetering, Janwillem van de
See van de Wetering, Janwillem
Wetherald, Agnes Ethelwyn 1857-1940 ......DLB 99
Wetherbee, Winthrop (III) 1938- CANR-28
Earlier sketches in CA 73-76, CANR-12
Wetherby, Terry (Lynne) 1943- 102
Wetherell, Elizabeth
See Warner, Susan (Bogert)
Wetherell, W(alter) D(avid) 1948- 138
Wetherell-Pepper, Joan Alexander 1920- 9-12R
Wetherill, Peter Michael 1932- CANR-12
Earlier sketch in CA 61-64
Wethey, Harold E(dwin) 1902-1984 ......CANR-2
Obituary 113
Earlier sketch in CA 1-4R
Wetmore, Alexander 1886-1978 85-88
Obituary 81-84
Wetmore, Ruth Y. 1934- 57-60
Wetmore, Thomas Hall 1915- 25-28R
Wetmore, William T. 1930- 9-12R
Wettenhall, Roger (Llewellyn) 1931- CANR-26
Earlier sketch in CA 109
Wetter, Gustav A(ndreas) 1911- 9-12R
Wettlaufer, George 1935- 57-60
Wettlaufer, Nancy 1939- 57-60
Wettstein, Howard K(enneth) 1943- 105
Wetzel, (Earl) Donald 1921- 25-28R
Wetzel, Elizabeth 1930- 114
Wetzel, Friedrich Gottlob 1779-1819 ......DLB 90
Wetzel, Richard D(ean) 1935- 85-88
Weverka, Robert 1926- CANR-2
Earlier sketch in CA 49-52
Wevers, Richard Franklin 1933- Brief entry 106
Wevill, David 1937- 13-16R
Wexler, Jean Stewart 1921- 65-68
Wexler, Jerome (LeRoy) 1923- 73-76
See also SATA 14
Wexler, Joyce Piell 1947- 97-100
Wexler, Norman 1926- Brief entry 116
Wexler, Richard 1953- 135
Wexley, John 1907-1985 Obituary 115
Wexley, Kenneth N. 93-96
Weyand, Alexander Mathias 1892- 5-8R
Weybright, Victor 1903-1978 Obituary 89-92
Weygant, Noemi CANR-2
Earlier sketch in CA 45-48
Weyl, Joachim 1915-1977 Obituary 73-76
Weyl, Nathaniel 1910- CANR-5
Earlier sketch in CA 9-12R
Weyl, Woldemar A.
1901(?)-1975 Obituary 61-64
Weyler, Rex 1947- 110
Weyn, Suzanne 1955- ......SATA 63
Weyrauch, Walter O(tto) 1919- CANR-10
Earlier sketch in CA 13-16R
Weyrich, Paul M(ichael) 1942- 118
Wezel, Johann Karl 1747-1819 ......DLB 94
Wezeman, Frederick Hartog
1915-1981 ......CANR-6
Obituary 106
Earlier sketch in CA 9-12R
Whale, John (Hilary) 1931- 101
Whalen, Barbara G. 1928- 120
Whalen, Charles William Jr. 1920- 105
Whalen, George J. 1939- CANR-16
Earlier sketch in CA 89-92
Whalen, Philip 1923- CANR-39
Earlier sketches in CA 9-12R, CANR-5
See also CLC 6, 29
See also DLB 16
Whalen, Richard J(ames) 1935- CANR-32
Earlier sketch in CA 13-16R
Whalen, Terry (Anthony) 1944- 127
Whalen, William Joseph 1926- CANR-4
Earlier sketch in CA 1-4R
Whaley, Barton Stewart 1928- 41-44R
Whaley, Donald L. 1934- 33-36R
Whaley, Joyce Irene 1923- ......SATA 61
Whaley, Russell Francis 1934- 57-60
Whaling, Frank 1934- CANR-32
Earlier sketch in CA 113
Whalley, Dorothy 1911- CAP-1
Earlier sketch in CA 9-10
Whalley, George 1915-1983 101
See also DLB 88
Whalley, Janet 1945- 117
Whalley, Joyce Irene 103
Whalon, Marion K(elley) 1913- 119
Wharf, Michael
See Weller, George (Anthony)
Wharmby, Margot CANR-24
Earlier sketches in CA 17-20R, CANR-8
See also SATA 63
Wharton, Annabel Jane 123
Wharton, Anthony
See McAllister, Alister
Wharton, Anthony P.
See McAllister, Alister
Wharton, Clifton R(eginald) Jr. 1926- 41-44R
Wharton, David B(ailey) 1914- 73-76
Wharton, Edith (Newbold Jones)
1862-1937 132
Brief entry 104
See also CDALB 1865-1917
See also DLB 4, 9, 12, 78
See also MTCW
See also SSC 6
See also TCLC 3, 9, 27
See also WLC
Wharton, Elizabeth Austin
1920-1985 Obituary 116
Wharton, Gary C(harles) 1940- 45-48
Wharton, George Frederick III 1952- 109
Wharton, James
See Mencken, H(enry) L(ouis)
Wharton, Joanna
See Hamel Peifer, Kathleen
Wharton, John Franklin 1894-1977 81-84
Obituary 73-76
Wharton, William (a pseudonym) 93-96
See also CLC 18, 37
See also DLBY 80
Whateley, Leslie Violet Lucy Evelyn Mary
1899-1987 Obituary 123
Whatmore, Leonard Elliott 1912- 13-16R
Whatmough, Joshua 1897- 5-8R
Whealey, Robert 1930- 127
Wheat, Cathleen Hayhurst 1904- CAP-1
Earlier sketch in CA 17-18
Wheat, (Marcus) Ed(ward Jr.) 1926- 118
Wheat, Gilbert Collins Jr. 1927- 1-4R
Wheat, Joe Ben 1916- 41-44R
Wheat, Leonard F. 1931- 29-32R
Wheat, Patte 1935- CANR-19
Earlier sketch in CA 101
Wheatcroft, Andrew (Jonathan Maclean)
1944- 110
Wheatcroft, Geoffrey 1945- 124
Wheatcroft, John 1925- CANR-14
Earlier sketch in CA 37-40R
Wheatcroft, Stephen F(rederick) 1921- 5-8R
Wheatley, Arabelle 1921- ......SATA 16
Wheatley, Dennis (Yeats) 1897-1977 ......CANR-9
Obituary 73-76
Earlier sketch in CA 5-8R
See also DLB 77
See also MTCW
Wheatley, Jon 1931- 29-32R
Wheatley (Peters), Phillis 1754(?)-1784 ......BLC 3
See also CDALB 1640-1865
See also DLB 31, 50
See also PC 3
See also WLC
Wheatley, Richard C(harles) 1904- CAP-1
Earlier sketch in CA 11-12
Wheatley, Ronald 1923(?)-1985 Obituary 115
Wheatley, Vera (Semple) CAP-1
Earlier sketch in CA 13-16
Wheat-Lieber, Patte
See Wheat, Patte
Wheaton, Anne (Williams)
1892-1977 Obituary 69-72
Wheaton, Bruce R. 1944- CANR-22
Earlier sketch in CA 104
Wheaton, Philip D(amon) 1916- 104
Wheaton, William L. C. 1913-1978 ......CANR-3
Earlier sketch in CA 1-4R
Whedon, Julia
See Schickel, Julia Whedon
Whedon, Margaret B(runssen) 1926- 105
Whedon, Peggy
See Whedon, Margaret B(runssen)
Wheeler, Allen 1903-1984 Obituary 111
Wheeler, Bayard O. 1905- 41-44R
Wheeler, Bonnie G(rant) 1943- 109
Wheeler, Burton K(endall)
1882-1975 Obituary 53-56
Wheeler, Charles Stearns 1816-1843 ......DLB 1
Wheeler, Charles (Thomas) 1892-1974 ......CAP-2
Obituary 53-56
Earlier sketch in CA 29-32
Wheeler, Cindy 1955- CANR-31
Earlier sketch in CA 110
See also SATA 40, 49
Wheeler, David L. 1934- 37-40R
Wheeler, David Raymond 1942- 73-76
Wheeler, Douglas L. 1937- 29-32R
Wheeler, (Charles) Gidley 1938- CANR-24
Earlier sketch in CA 107
Wheeler, (John) Harvey 1918- CANR-17
Earlier sketches in CA 45-48, CANR-1
Wheeler, Helen Rippier CANR-14
Earlier sketches in CA 17-20R, CANR-31
Wheeler, Hugh (Callingham) 1912-1987 89-92
Obituary 123
Wheeler, J(oseph) Clyde 1910- 1-4R
Wheeler, Janet D. CANR-26
Earlier sketches in CAP-2, CA 19-20
See also SATA 1
Wheeler, Jesse H(arrison) Jr. 1918- 45-48
Wheeler, John Archibald 1911- 57-60
Wheeler, Keith 1911- CANR-7
Earlier sketch in CA 5-8R
Wheeler, Leslie A. 1945- CANR-11
Earlier sketch in CA 65-68
Wheeler, Lora Jeanne 1923- 33-36R
Wheeler, Margaret 1916- CAP-2
Earlier sketch in CA 25-28
Wheeler, Mary Jane 29-32R
Wheeler, Michael 1943- CANR-9
Earlier sketch in CA 65-68
Wheeler, Molly 1920- 29-32R
Wheeler, Monroe 1900-1988 Obituary 126
See also DLB 4
Wheeler, (Robert Eric) Mortimer
1890-1976 ......CANR-32
Obituary 65-68
Earlier sketch in CA 77-80
Wheeler, Opal 1898- ......SATA 23
Wheeler, Paul 1934- 25-28R
Wheeler, Penny Estes 1943- 33-36R
Wheeler, Raymond Milner
1919-1982 Obituary 106
Wheeler, Richard Paul 1943- 108
Wheeler, Richard S(eabrook) 1928- 45-48
Wheeler, Richard 1922- CANR-25
Earlier sketches in CA 17-20R, CANR-8
Wheeler, Robert C(ordell) 1913- 61-64
Wheeler, Ron 1954- 136
Wheeler, Ruth Carr 1899- 5-8R
Wheeler, Sessions S(amuel) 1911- CANR-25
Earlier sketch in CA 17-20R
Wheeler, Thomas C. 1927- 104
Wheeler, Thomas H(utchin) 1947- 93-96
Wheeler, Tom
See Wheeler, Thomas H(utchin)
Wheeler, W(illiam) Lawrence 1925- 13-16R
Wheeler-Bennett, John 1902-1975 65-68
Obituary 61-64
Wheelis, Allen B. 1915- 17-20R
Wheelock, Arthur Kingsland Jr. 1943- 107
Wheelock, (Kinch) Carter 1924- 61-64
Wheelock, Frederic M(elvin) 1902-1987 97-100
Obituary 124
Wheelock, John Hall 1886-1978 ......CANR-14
Obituary 77-80
Earlier sketch in CA 13-16R
See also CLC 14
See also DLB 45
Wheelock, Martha E. 1941- 25-28R
Wheelwright, Edward Lawrence
1921- CANR-21
Earlier sketch in CA 103
Wheelwright, John 1592(?)-1679 ......DLB 24
Wheelwright, John 1897-1940 ......DLB 45
Wheelwright, Julie (Diana) 1960- 130
Wheelwright, Philip (Ellis) 1901-1970 ......CAP-2
Earlier sketch in CA 23-24
Wheelwright, Richard 1936- 33-36R
Wheelwright, Steven C. 1943- 119
Whelan, Elizabeth M(urphy) 1943- CANR-24
Earlier sketches in CA 57-60, CANR-8
See also SATA 14
Whelan, Gloria (Ann) 1923- 101
Whelan, James Robert 1933- 102
Whelan, Joseph P(aul) 1932- 41-44R
Wheldon, Huw (Pyrs) 1916-1986 107
Obituary 118
Whelpton, (George) Eric 1894-1981 ......CANR-5
Obituary 103
Earlier sketch in CA 9-12R
Whelpton, Pascal K(idder) 1893-1964 ......CANR-16
Earlier sketch in CA 1-4R
Whelton, Clark 1937- 69-72
Whenham, (Ernest) John 1946- 127
Whetstone, Colonel Pete
See Noland, C. F. M.
Whetten, Lawrence L. 1932- CANR-27
Earlier sketches in CA 61-64, CANR-11
Whetten, Nathan Laselle 1900- 1-4R
Whicher, John F. 1919- 17-20R
Whicher, Stephen E. 1915-1961 ......DLB 111
Whicker, Alan (Donald) 1925- 130
Whidden, Mary Bess 1936- 126
Whiffen, Marcus 1916- CANR-12
Earlier sketch in CA 61-64
Whigham, Peter 1925-1987 ......CANR-28
Obituary 123
Earlier sketch in CA 25-28R
Whinney, Margaret Dickens
1897-1975 Obituary 61-64
Whinnom, Keith 1927-1986 Obituary 118
Whipkey, Kenneth Lee 1932- CANR-4
Earlier sketch in CA 53-56
Whipple, A(ddison) B(eecher) C(olvin)
1918- 125
See also SATA 64
Whipple, Beverly 1941- CANR-30
Earlier sketch in CA 109
Whipple, Cal
See Whipple, A(ddison) B(eecher) C(olvin)
Whipple, Chandler (Henry) 1905- 25-28R
Whipple, Dorothy 1893- CAP-1
Earlier sketch in CA 13-14
Whipple, Edwin Percy 1819-1886 ......DLB 1, 64
Whipple, Fred Lawrence 1906- CAP-1
Earlier sketch in CA 11-12
Whipple, George 1927- 119
Whipple, James B. 1913- 29-32R
Whipple, Maurine 1910- 5-8R
Whisenand, Paul M. 1935- CANR-22
Earlier sketch in CA 69-72
Whisenhunt, Donald W(ayne) 1938- CANR-9
Earlier sketch in CA 57-60
Whisler, John A(lbert) 1951- 109
Whisler, Thomas Lee 1920- Brief entry 115
Whisnant, Charleen
See Swansea, Charleen
Whisnant, David E(ugene) 1938- 41-44R
Whistler, Laurence 1912- CANR-19
Earlier sketches in CA 9-12R, CANR-3
Whistler, Reginald John 1905-1944 ......SATA 30
Whistler, Rex
See Whistler, Reginald John
Whiston, Lionel (Abney) 1895- 69-72
Whitacre, Donald (DuMont) 1920- 69-72
Whitaker, Alexander 1585-1617 ......DLB 24
Whitaker, Arthur Preston
1895-1979 Obituary 112
Whitaker, Ben(jamin Charles George)
1934- 53-56
Whitaker, C(leophaus) S(ylvester) Jr.
1935- CANR-28
Earlier sketch in CA 29-32R
Whitaker, Carl A. 1912- Brief entry 114
Whitaker, Daniel K. 1801-1881 ......DLB 73
Whitaker, David 1930-1980 ......21-24R
Obituary 134
Whitaker, Dorothy Stock 1925- 13-16R
Whitaker, Frederic 1891-1980 ......CANR-4
Obituary 97-100
Earlier sketch in CA 5-8R
Whitaker, Gilbert R(iley) Jr. 1931- 9-12R
Whitaker, Haddon 1908(?)-1982 Obituary 105
Whitaker, James W. 1936- 102
Whitaker, John O(gden) Jr. 1935- 105
Whitaker, Malachi Taylor
1895-1976 Obituary 104
Whitaker, Mary 1896(?)-1976 Obituary 65-68
Whitaker, Peter 1952- 124
Whitaker, Rod 1931- 29-32R
Whitaker, Rogers E(rnest) M(alcolm)
1899-1981 Obituary 103
Whitaker, Shelagh (Dunwoody) 1930- 125
Whitaker, T(ommy) J(ames) 1949- 53-56
Whitaker, Thomas R(ussell) 1925- 25-28R
Whitaker, Urban George Jr. 1924- 9-12R
Whitaker, W(illiam) Denis 1915- 128
Whitbeck, George W(alter) 1932- 73-76
Whitbread, Jane
See Levin, Jane Whitbread
Whitbread, Leslie George 1917- 37-40R
Whitbread, Thomas (Bacon) 1931- 13-16R
Whitburn, Joel (Carver) 1939- CANR-32
Earlier sketches in CA 33-36R, CANR-15
Whitby, Henry Augustus Morton
1898-1969 ......CAP-1
Earlier sketch in CA 11-12
Whitby, Sharon
See Peters, Maureen
Whitby, Thomas J. 1919- 126
Whitcher, Frances Miriam 1814-1852 ......DLB 11
Whitcomb, Edgar D(oud) 1918- 21-24R
Whitcomb, Hale C(hristy) 1907- CAP-2
Earlier sketch in CA 29-32
Whitcomb, Helen Hafemann CANR-6
Earlier sketch in CA 13-16R
Whitcomb, Ian 1941- CANR-8
Earlier sketch in CA 57-60
Whitcomb, John C(lement) 1924- CANR-4
Earlier sketch in CA 1-4R

Whitcomb, Jon 1906-1988 .... CAP-1
Obituary 125
Earlier sketch in CA 13-16
See also SATA 10, 56
Whitcomb, Meg W. 1930- 123
Whitcomb, Noel 1918- 134
Whitcomb, Philip W(right) 1891- 73-76
White, A(drian) N(icholas) Sherwin
See Sherwin-White, A(drian) N(icholas)
White, Alan CANR-3
Earlier sketch in CA 45-48
White, Alan R(ichard) 1922- 25-28R
Obituary 137
White, Alex Sandri
1916(?)-1983(?) Obituary 108
White, Alice Violet 1922- CANR-13
Earlier sketch in CA 61-64
White, Alicen 77-80
White, Allon (H.) 1951-1988 128
White, Amber Blanco
See Blanco White, Amber
White, Andrew Dickson 1832-1918 .... DLB 47
White, Andrew 1579-1656 .... DLB 24
White, Anne Hitchcock 1902-1970 Obituary 108
See also SATA 33
White, Anne S(hanklin) 93-96
White, Anne Terry 1896-1980 .... 9-12R
Obituary 135
See also SATA 2
White, Anthony Gene 1946- CANR-12
Earlier sketch in CA 73-76
White, Antonia 1899-1980 104
Obituary 97-100
White, Babington
See Braddon, Mary Elizabeth
White, Barbara A(nne) 1942- CANR-29
Earlier sketch in CA 109
White, Barbara Ehrlich 1936- 136
White, Beatrice (Mary Irene)
1902-1986 Obituary 119
White, Benjamin V(room) 1908- 101
White, Benton R. 1949- 124
White, Bessie (Felstiner)
1892(?)-1986 Obituary 121
See also SATA 50
White, Betty 1917- 5-8R
White, Brian Terence 1927- 105
White, Burton L(eonard) 1929- CANR-4
Earlier sketch in CA 45-48
White, Carl M(ilton) 1903-1983 .... 13-16R
Obituary 111
White, Carol Hellings 1939- 81-84
White, Carol 1946- 111
White, (Edwin) Chappell 1920- 25-28R
White, Claire Nicolas 1925- CANR-25
Earlier sketch in CA 108
White, Curtis 1951- CANR-27
Earlier sketch in CA 110
White, Cynthia L(eslie) 1940- 37-40R
White, Dale
See Place, Marian T(empleton)
White, Dan S(eligsberger) 1939- 97-100
White, David Manning 1917- CANR-4
Earlier sketch in CA 1-4R
White, David Omar 1927- 17-20R
White, Dori 1919- 37-40R
See also SATA 10
White, Dorothy Shipley CAP-1
Earlier sketch in CA 13-14
White, Douglas M(alcolm) 1909- CANR-4
Earlier sketch in CA 1-4R
White, E(lwyn) B(rooks) 1899-1985 .... CANR-37
Obituary 116
Earlier sketches in CA 13-16R, CANR-16
See also AITN 2
See also CLC 10, 34, 39
See also CLR 1, 21
See also DLB 11, 22
See also MAICYA
See also MTCW
See also SATA 2, 29, 44
White, Edgar (B.) 1947- CANR-27
Earlier sketch in CA 61-64
See also BW
See also DLB 38
White, Edmund (Valentine III) 1940- CANR-36
Earlier sketches in CA 45-48, CANR-3, 19
See also AAYA 7
See also CLC 27
See also MTCW
White, Edward M. 1933- 37-40R
White, Elijah (Brockenborough III) 1938- 69-72
White, Eliza Orne 1856-1947 .... YABC 2
White, Elizabeth H(erzog)
1901(?)-1972 Obituary 37-40R
White, Elizabeth Wade 1906- 97-100
White, Elliott 1936- 127
White, Elmer G. 1926-1979 .... 21-24R
Obituary 134
White, Emmons E(aton) 1891-1982 73-76
Obituary 133
White, Eric Walter 1905-1985 .... CAP-1
Obituary 117
Earlier sketch in CA 11-12
White, Ethel Lina 1887-1944 Brief entry 108
See also DLB 77
White, Eugene E. 1919- 13-16R
White, F(rederick) Clifton 1918- 113
White, Florence M(eiman) 1910- 41-44R
See also SATA 14
White, Frank 1944- 126
White, G(eorge) Edward 1941- CANR-12
Earlier sketch in CA 69-72
White, Gerald Taylor 1913- CANR-2
Earlier sketch in CA 5-8R
White, Gertrude M(ason) 1915- 81-84
White, Gillian Mary 1936- 17-20R
White, Glenn M. 1918(?)-1978 93-96
Obituary 81-84
White, Gordon Eliot 1933- 101
White, H. T.
See Engh, Rohn
White, Harrison C(olyar) 1930- 45-48
White, Harry
See Whittington, Harry (Benjamin)
White, Hayden V. 1928- 128
White, Helen Constance 1896- 5-8R
White, Henry Kirke 1785-1806 .... DLB 96
White, Hilda Crystal 1917- 5-8R
White, Horace 1834-1916 Brief entry 119
See also DLB 23
White, Howard Ashley 1913-1991 .... 29-32R
Obituary 133
White, Howard B. 1912(?)-1974 Obituary 53-56
White, Hugh Clayton 1936- 45-48
White, Hugh Vernon 1889- 5-8R
White, Irvin L(inwood) 1932- CANR-8
Earlier sketch in CA 57-60
White, James Boyd 1938- CANR-30
Earlier sketch in CA 111
White, James Dillon
See White, Stanley
White, James F(loyd) 1932- CANR-24
Earlier sketch in CA 107
White, James L. Obituary 115
White, James P(atrick) 1940- CANR-11
Earlier sketch in CA 69-72
White, James 1913- 109
White, James 1928- CANR-4
Earlier sketch in CA 53-56
White, Jane
See Brady, Jane
White, Jane Neal 1918- 110
White, Jerry E(ugene) 1937- 129
White, Jerry S. 1946- 130
White, John Albert 1910- CAP-2
Earlier sketch in CA 23-24
White, John Baker
See Baker White, John
White, John H(enry) 1945- 124
Brief entry 117
White, John Hoxland Jr. 1933- 25-28R
White, John I(rwin) 57-60
White, John K(enneth) 1952- CANR-39
Earlier sketch in CA 116
White, John W. 1939- CANR-13
Earlier sketch in CA 37-40R
White, John Wesley 1928- CANR-31
Earlier sketch in CA 29-32R
White, John 1924- CANR-20
White, Jon (Ewbank) Manchip 1924- CANR-32
Earlier sketches in CA 13-16R, CANR-15
See also CAAS 4
White, Joyce C(arol) 1952- 112
White, Jude Gilliam 1947- CANR-23
Earlier sketch in CA 106
See also Deveraux, Jude
White, K(enneth) D(ouglas) 1908- CANR-12
Earlier sketch in CA 69-72
White, K(enneth) Owen 1902- CAP-2
Earlier sketch in CA 17-18
White, Karol Koenigsberg 1938- 5-8R
White, Katharine Sergeant
1892-1977 Obituary 104
White, Kenneth Steele 1922- 93-96
White, Kenneth 1936- 25-28R
White, Laurence B(arton) Jr. 1935- CANR-24
Earlier sketches in CA 65-68, CANR-9
See also SATA 10
White, Lawrence H(enry) 1954- 118
White, Lawrence J. 1943- CANR-31
Earlier sketches in CA 37-40R, CANR-14
White, Lawrence 1942- 115
White, Lee A. 1886-1971 Obituary 115
White, Leslie A(lvin) 1900-1975 .... CANR-3
Obituary 57-60
Earlier sketch in CA 1-4R
White, Leslie Turner 1903- CAP-1
Earlier sketch in CA 13-14
White, Lionel 1905- 103
White, Lonnie J(oe) 1931- 13-16R
White, Lucia 123
White, Lynn (Townsend) Jr. 1907-1987 .... CANR-2
Obituary 122
Earlier sketch in CA 5-8R
White, M(ary) E(llen) 1938- 21-24R
White, Margaret B(lackburn) 1936- 115
White, Martin 1943- .... SATA 51
White, Mary Alice 1920- 9-12R
White, Matthew (Hagy) 1956- 129
White, Maurine
See Miller (Riis), Maurine
White, Maury 1919- 77-80
White, Melvin R(obert) 1911- CANR-18
Earlier sketch in CA 21-24R
White, Minor (Martin) 1908-1976 .... CANR-10
Obituary 65-68
Earlier sketch in CA 17-20R
White, Morton Gabriel 1917- CANR-35
Earlier sketches in CA 5-8R, CANR-7
White, Nancy Bean 1922- 13-16R
White, Ned 1946- 129
White, Nicholas P. 1942- 73-76
White, Nola (Joan) 1942- 128
White, Norval (Crawford) 1926- 77-80
White, Orion F(orrest) 1938- 53-56
White, Osmar (Egmont Dorkin) 1909- 130
Brief entry 105
White, Owen R(oberts) 1945- 41-44R
White, Patricia (Ann) 1937- 117
White, Patrick C. T. 1924- 85-88
White, Patrick (Victor Martindale)
1912-1990 81-84
Obituary 132
See also CLC 3, 4, 5, 7, 9, 18, 65, 69
See also MTCW
White, Paul Dudley 1886-1973 Obituary 45-48
White, Paul Hamilton Hume 1910- CANR-23
Earlier sketches in CA 5-8R, CANR-7
White, Paulette Childress 1948- 111
White, Percival 1887-1970 .... CANR-2
Earlier sketch in CA 1-4R
White, Philip L(loyd) 1923- 81-84
White, Phyllis Dorothy James 1920- CANR-17
Earlier sketch in CA 21-24R
See also James, P. D.
See also MTCW
White, Poppy Cannon 1906(?)-1975 65-68
Obituary 57-60
White, R. S. 1948- 127
White, Ramy Allison CANR-26
Earlier sketches in CAP-2, CA 19-20
See also SATA 1, 67
White, Randall 1945- 121
White, Ray Lewis 1941- CANR-9
Earlier sketch in CA 21-24R
White, Reginald E(rnest) O(scar)
1914- CANR-21
Earlier sketches in CA 5-8R, CANR-5
White, Reginald James 1905-1971 108
Obituary 104
White, Rhea A(melia) 1931- 77-80
White, Richard Alan 1944- 97-100
White, Richard C(lark) 1926- 45-48
White, Richard Grant 1821-1885 .... DLB 64
White, Richard 1931- 110
White, Robb 1909- CANR-1
Earlier sketch in CA 1-4R
See also CLR 3
See also SAAS 1
See also SATA 1
White, Robert B(enjamin) Jr.
1930- Brief entry 118
White, Robert I. 1908- 1-4R
White, Robert Lee 1928- 17-20R
White, Robert Mitchell II 1915- 73-76
White, Robert R(ankin) 1942- 123
White, (William) Robin(son) 1928- CANR-20
Earlier sketches in CA 9-12R, CANR-4
White, Ronald C(edric) Jr. 1939- 93-96
White, Ruth C. 1942- 111
See also SATA 39
White, Ruth M(argaret) 1914- 17-20R
White, Ruth Morris
1902(?)-1978 Obituary 81-84
White, Sarah Harriman 1929- 9-12R
White, Sheldon Harold 1928- 105
White, Stanhope 1913- 21-24R
White, Stanley 1913- CANR-6
Earlier sketch in CA 9-12R
White, Stephanie F(rances) T(hirkell)
1942- 17-20R
White, Stephen D(aniel) 1945- 93-96
White, Stephen (Leonard) 1945- 134
White, Steve
See McGarvey, Robert
White, Steven F(orsythe) 1955- CANR-30
Earlier sketch in CA 112
White, Susan J. 1949- 126
White, Suzanne 1938- 77-80
White, T(erence) H(anbury)
1906-1964 .... CANR-37
Earlier sketch in CA 73-76
See also CLC 30
See also MAICYA
See also SATA 12
White, Ted
See White, Theodore Edwin
White, Terence de Vere 1912- CANR-3
Earlier sketch in CA 49-52
See also CLC 49
White, Teri 1946- 132
Brief entry 127
White, Theo Ballou 1903-1978 Obituary 111
White, Theodore Edwin 1938- CANR-12
Earlier sketch in CA 21-24R
White, Theodore H(arold) 1915-1986 ..... CANR-33
Obituary 118
Earlier sketches in CA 1-4R, CANR-3
See also MTCW
White, Thomas Justin Jr.
1919-1987 Obituary 122
White, Timothy (Thomas Anthony)
1952- .... SATA 60
White, W. D. 1926- 37-40R
White, W(illiam) J(ohn) 1920-1980 .... 13-16R
Obituary 97-100
White, Walter
See White, Walter F(rancis)
See also BLC 3
White, Walter F(rancis) 1893-1955 124
Brief entry 115
See also White, Walter
See also DLB 51
See also TCLC 15
White, William Jr. 1934- CANR-31
Earlier sketches in CA 37-40R, CANR-14
See also SATA 16
White, William A(nthony) P(arker)
1911-1968 .... CAP-1
Obituary 25-28R
Earlier sketch in CA 11-12
See also Boucher, Anthony
White, William Allen 1868-1944 Brief entry 108
See also DLB 9, 25
White, William F(rancis) 1928- CANR-1
Earlier sketch in CA 45-48
White, William Hale 1831-1913 Brief entry 121
See also Rutherford, Mark
White, William J(oseph) 1926- 97-100
White, William L(indsay) 1900-1973 101
Obituary 41-44R
White, William L. 1937-1985 Obituary 114
White, William Luther 1931- 29-32R
White, William S(mith) 1907- 5-8R
White, William 1910- CANR-29
Earlier sketch in CA 21-24R
White, Zita
See Denholm, Therese Mary Zita White
Whitebird, J(oanie) 1951- CANR-25
Earlier sketch in CA 69-72
White-Bowden, Susan 1939- 120
Whitechurch, Victor L(orenzo)
1868-1933 Brief entry 116
See also DLB 70
White Elk, Michael
See Walker, T. Michael
Whitefield, Ann
See Stone, Susan Berch
Whiteford, Andrew H(unter) 1913- CANR-26
Earlier sketch in CA 45-48
Whitefriar
See Hiscock, Eric
Whitehall, Harold 1905-1986 .... CAP-2
Obituary 118
Earlier sketch in CA 21-22
Whitehead, Alfred North
1861-1947 Brief entry 117
See also DLB 100
Whitehead, Barbara (Maude) 1930- 97-100
Whitehead, Catherine Sarah 1960- 131
Whitehead, Don(ald) F. 1908-1981 .... 9-12R
Obituary 102
See also SATA 4
Whitehead, E(dward) A(nthony) 1933- 65-68
See also CLC 5
Whitehead, (Walter) Edward 1908-1978 81-84
Obituary 77-80
Whitehead, Evelyn Annette Eaton 1938- 104
Whitehead, Frank S. 1916- 37-40R
Whitehead, G(eorge) Kenneth 1913- CANR-8
Earlier sketch in CA 61-64
Whitehead, James D(ouglas) 1939- 105
Whitehead, James 1936- 77-80
See also DLBY 81
Whitehead, John (Randolph) 1924- 120
Whitehead, John W. 1946- 117
Whitehead, Kate
See Whitehead, Catherine Sarah
Whitehead, Raymond Leslie 1933- 77-80
Whitehead, Robert J(ohn) 1928- CANR-13
Earlier sketch in CA 37-40R
Whitehead, William Grant
1943-1987 Obituary 124
Whitehead, William 1715-1785 .... DLB 84, 109
Whitehill, Arthur M(urray Jr.) 1919- CANR-13
Earlier sketch in CA 77-80
Whitehill, Walter Muir 1905-1978 .... CANR-6
Obituary 77-80
Earlier sketch in CA 13-16R
Whitehorn, Alan (James) 1946- 138
Whitehorn, Katharine
See Lyall, Katharine Elizabeth
Whitehouse, Arch
See Whitehouse, Arthur George Joseph
Whitehouse, Arthur George Joseph
1895-1979 .... CANR-4
Obituary 89-92
Earlier sketch in CA 5-8R
See also SATA 14, 23
Whitehouse, David (Bryn) 1941- 131
Whitehouse, Elizabeth S(cott)
1893-1968 .... CAP-1
Earlier sketch in CA 13-14
See also SATA 35
Whitehouse, Franklin S. Jr.
1934-1985 Obituary 117
Whitehouse, Jack E(dward) 1933- 111
Whitehouse, Jeanne 1939- 103
See also SATA 29
Whitehouse, Roger 1939- 57-60
Whitehouse, Ruth D(elamain) 1942- 118
Whitehouse, W(alter) A(lexander)
1915- CANR-3
Earlier sketch in CA 1-4R
Whitelaw, William Menzies
1890(?)-1974 Obituary 45-48
Whiteley, Denys Edward Hugh
1914-1987 Obituary 123
Whiteley, George 1909(?)-1990 Obituary 132
Whitelock, Dorothy 1901-1982 129
Obituary 107
Whiteman, (David) Bruce 1952- 132
Whiteman, Maxwell 1914- CANR-10
Earlier sketch in CA 21-24R
Whiteman, Paul 1890(?)-1967 Obituary 113
Whitemore, Hugh (John) 1936- 132
See also CLC 37
Whitesell, (James) Edwin 1909- 41-44R
Whitesell, Faris Daniel 1895- 5-8R
Whiteside, Lynn W. 1908- 25-28R
Whiteside, Robert L(eo) 1907- 53-56
Whiteside, Thomas 1918(?)- Brief entry 109
Whitesitt, Linda (Marie) 1951- 129
Whiteson, Leon 1930- CANR-16
Earlier sketch in CA 21-24R
Whitfield, George J(oshua) N(ewbold)
1909- CAP-1
Earlier sketch in CA 11-12
Whitfield, James Monroe 1822-1871 ...... DLB 50
Whitfield, John Humphreys 1906- 9-12R
Whitfield, Phil(ip John) 1944- 97-100
Whitfield, Raoul 1897(?)-1945 Brief entry 109
Whitfield, Shelby 1935- 49-52

Whitfield, Stephen J(ack) 1942- 61-64
Whitford, Bessie 1885(?)-1977 Obituary 69-72
Whitford, Frank 1941- 97-100
Whitin, Thomson McLintock 1923- CANR-3
Earlier sketch in CA 1-4R
Whiting, Allen S(uess) 1926- 125
Brief entry 105
Whiting, Beatrice Blyth 1914- 5-8R
Whiting, Charles E.
1914(?)-1980 Obituary 97-100
Whiting, Frank M. 1907- 101
Whiting, John (Robert) 1917-1963 102
Obituary 89-92
See also DLB 13
Whiting, Kenneth R. 1913- CANR-5
Earlier sketch in CA 5-8R
Whiting, Nathan 1946- 41-44R
Whiting, Percy H(ollister) 1880- CAP-1
Earlier sketch in CA 13-16
Whiting, Robert L(ouis) 1918- 17-20R
Whiting, Robert 1942- 102
Whiting, Samuel 1597-1679 ....DLB 24
Whiting, Thomas A. 1917- CANR-3
Earlier sketch in CA 1-4R
Whitinger, R. D.
See Place, Marian T(empleton)
Whitington, R(ichard) S. 1912- 77-80
Whitlam, (Edward) Gough 1916- 109
Whitley, George
See Chandler, A(rthur) Bertram
Whitley, Mary Ann
See Sebrey, Mary Ann
Whitley, Oliver R. 1918- 77-80
Whitlock, Baird W(oodruff) 1924- 112
Whitlock, Brand 1869-1934 Brief entry 110
See also DLB 12
Whitlock, Glenn E(verett) 1917- 21-24R
Whitlock, Pamela 1921(?)-1982 Obituary 107
See also SATA 31
Whitlock, Quentin A(rthur) 1937- 109
Whitlock, Ralph 1914- CANR-20
Earlier sketch in CA 101
See also SATA 35
Whitlock, Virginia Bennett Obituary 37-40R
Whitlow, Roger 1940- 41-44R
Whitman, Albery Allson 1851-1901 ....DLB 50
Whitman, Alden (Rogers) 1913-1990 ....CANR-29
Obituary 132
Earlier sketch in CA 17-20R
See also DLBY 91
Whitman, (Evelyn) Ardis 1905(?)-1990 ....9-12R
Obituary 131
Whitman, Bertha Yerex
1892-1984 Obituary 114
Whitman, Cedric H(ubbell)
1916-1979 ....CANR-27
Obituary 120
Earlier sketch in CA 17-20R
Whitman, David (deFreudiger) 1955- 113
Whitman, Edmund Spurr 1900- 17-20R
Whitman, Howard 1915(?)-1975 Obituary 53-56
Whitman, John 1944- CANR-11
Earlier sketch in CA 61-64
Whitman, Marina von Neumann 1935- 17-20R
Whitman, Martin J. 1924- 104
Whitman, Robert Freeman 1925- 81-84
Whitman, Ruth (Bashein) 1922- CANR-31
Earlier sketches in CA 21-24R, CANR-12
Whitman, Sarah Helen (Power)
1803-1878 ....DLB 1
Whitman, Virginia Bruner 1901- CANR-4
Earlier sketch in CA 5-8R
Whitman, W(illiam) Tate 1909- CAP-1
Earlier sketch in CA 11-12
Whitman, Walt(er)
1819-1892 ....CDALB 1640-1865
See also DLB 3, 64
See also PC 3
See also SATA 20
See also WLC
Whitman, Wanda Obituary 65-68
Whitmarsh, Anne (Mary Gordon) 1933- 106
Whitmont, Edward C. 1912- 115
Whitmore, Charles (Stanleigh) 1949- 117
Whitmore, Cilla
See Gladstone, Arthur M.
Whitmore, Eugene 1895- 5-8R
Whitmore, George 1945-1989 ....CANR-30
Obituary 128
Earlier sketch in CA 102
Whitnah, Donald R(obert) 1925- 9-12R
Whitnah, Dorothy L. 1926- CANR-16
Earlier sketch in CA 93-96
Whitnell, Barbara
See Hutton, Ann
Whitney, Alec
See White, Alan
Whitney, Alex(andra) 1922- 53-56
See also SATA 14
Whitney, Byrl A(lbert) 1901- CAP-1
Earlier sketch in CA 13-14
Whitney, Charles Allen 1929- 81-84
Whitney, Cornelius Vanderbilt 1899- 85-88
Whitney, Craig Richard 1943- 131
Whitney, Dallas (Cole) 1952- 117
Whitney, David
See Malick, Terrence
Whitney, David C(harles) 1921- CANR-5
Earlier sketch in CA 9-12R
See also SATA 29, 48
Whitney, Eleanor Noss 1938- CANR-6
Earlier sketch in CA 13-16R
Whitney, Elizabeth Dalton 1906- 21-24R
Whitney, George D(ana) 1918- 93-96
Whitney, Hallam
See Whittington, Harry (Benjamin)
Whitney, J(ohn) D(enison) 1940- CANR-3
Earlier sketch in CA 49-52
Whitney, J. L. H.
See Trimble, Jacquelyn W(hitney)
Whitney, John Hay 1904-1982 Obituary 106
Whitney, John Raymond 1920- 105
Whitney, Leon F(radley) 1894-1973 ....CANR-5
Earlier sketch in CA 5-8R
Whitney, Malika Lee 1946- 133
Whitney, Marie Louise (Schroeder) Hosford
1925(?)- Brief entry 113
Whitney, Marylou
See Whitney, Marie Louise (Schroeder) Hosford
Whitney, Peter Dwight 1915- 9-12R
Whitney, Phyllis A(yame) 1903- CANR-38
Earlier sketches in CA 1-4R, CANR-3, 25
See also AITN 2
See also BEST 90:3
See also CLC 42
See also MAICYA
See also SATA 1, 30
Whitney, Robert Frost
1906(?)-1986 Obituary 119
Whitney, Ruth Reinke 1928- 133
Whitney, Sharon 1937- ....SATA 63
Whitney, Steve(n) 1946- 81-84
Whitney, Thomas P(orter) 1917- 104
See also SATA 25
Whiton, James Nelson 1932- 13-16R
Whitridge, Arnold 1891-1989 ....9-12R
Obituary 127
Whitrow, Gerald James 1912- CANR-3
Earlier sketch in CA 5-8R
Whitson
See Warren, Peter Whitson
Whitson, Skip 1944- 118
Whitt, Anne Hall
See Thompson, Anne Hall Whitt
Whitt, Richard 1944- 81-84
Whittaker, C(harles) R(ichard) 1929- 131
Whittaker, Kathryn Putnam 1931- 13-16R
Whittaker, Otto (Jr.) 1916- 25-28R
Whittaker, Robert Harding 1920- 105
Whittemore, Charles P(ark) 1921- 9-12R
Whittemore, Don 69-72
Whittemore, L(ouis) H(enry) 1941- 45-48
Whittemore, Mildred 1946- 9-12R
Whittemore, (Edward) Reed (Jr.) 1919- CANR-4
Earlier sketch in CA 9-12R
See also CAAS 8
See also CLC 4
See also DLB 5
Whittemore, Robert Clifton 1921- 9-12R
Whitten, Jamie L(loyd) 1910- CAP-2
Earlier sketch in CA 23-24
Whitten, Leslie H(unter) 1928- CANR-29
Earlier sketch in CA 17-20R
Whitten, Mary Evelyn 1922- 17-20R
Whitten, Norman E(arl) Jr. 1937- 17-20R
Whittet, G(eorge) S(orley) 1918- 21-24R
Whittet, T. D.
See Whittet, Thomas Douglas
Whittet, Thomas Douglas
1915-1987 Obituary 122
Whittick, Arnold 1898- CAP-1
Earlier sketch in CA 11-12
Whittier, John Greenleaf
1807-1892 ....CDALB 1640-1865
See also DLB 1
Whitting, Philip (David) 1903- 97-100
Whittingham, Harry E(dward) Jr. 1918- 5-8R
Whittingham, Jack 1910-1972 Obituary 37-40R
Whittingham, Richard 1939- CANR-36
Earlier sketch in CA 37-40R
Whittington, Geoffrey 1938- CANR-20
Earlier sketch in CA 104
Whittington, H(orace) G(reeley) 1929- 21-24R
Whittington, Harry (Benjamin) 1915- CANR-5
Earlier sketch in CA 21-24R
Whittington, Peter
See Mackay, James (Alexander)
Whittington-Egan, Richard 1924- CANR-20
Earlier sketches in CA 9-12R, CANR-5
Whittle, Amberys R(ayvon) 1935- 45-48
Whittle, Tyler
See Tyler-Whittle, Michael Sidney
Whittlebot, Hernia
See Coward, Noel (Peirce)
Whittlesey, E(unice) S. 1907- 93-96
Whittlesey, Susan 1938- 29-32R
Whitton, Charlotte (Elizabeth)
1896-1975 Obituary 89-92
Whitton, John Boardman 1892- CAP-2
Earlier sketch in CA 23-24
Whitton, Kenneth S(tuart) 1925- 131
Whittow, J. B.
See Whittow, John B(yron)
Whittow, John B(yron) 1929- 120
Whitworth, John McKelvie 1942- 77-80
Whitworth, John 1945- 131
Whitworth, Reginald Henry 1910- 109
Whitworth, William 1937- 37-40R
Whiz, Walter
See Johnson, Curt(is Lee)
Wholey, Dennis 1938- 127
Whone, Herbert 1925- CANR-24
Earlier sketch in CA 108
Whorton, James C(lifton) 1942- 77-80
Whorton, M. Donald 1946- 117
Whritner, John Alden 1935- 45-48
Whyard, Florence 1917- 129
Whyatt, Frances
See Boyd, Shylah
Whybray, Roger Norman 1923- 89-92
Whynott, Douglas (Vernon) 1950- 115
Whyte, Fredrica (Harriman) 1905- CAP-1
Earlier sketch in CA 11-12
Whyte, Henry Malcolm 1920- CANR-3
Earlier sketch in CA 5-8R
Whyte, Iain Boyd 1947- 132
Whyte, James Huntington 1909- 5-8R
Whyte, John D. 1940- 129
Whyte, Lancelot Law 1896-1972 ....CAP-1
Earlier sketch in CA 13-16
Whyte, Lewis (Gilmour)
1906-1986 Obituary 121
Whyte, Mal(colm Kenneth Jr.) 1933- 106
See also SATA 62
Whyte, Martin King 1942- 81-84
Whyte, (Harry Archibald) Maxwell 1908- 105
Whyte, Robert Orr 1903- Brief entry 106
Whyte, Ron 1942(?)-1989 132
Obituary 129
See also SATA 63
Whyte, Sibly
See Stine, Henry Eugene
Whyte, William Foote 1914- CANR-18
Earlier sketches in CA 1-4R, CANR-3
Whyte, William H(ollingsworth) 1917- 9-12R
Wiarda, Howard J(ohn) 1939- CANR-21
Earlier sketches in CA 53-56, CANR-4
Wiat, Philippa
See Ferridge, Philippa
Wibbelsman, Charles J(oseph) 1945- 128
See also SATA 59
Wibberley, Leonard (Patrick O'Connor)
1915-1983 ....CANR-3
Obituary 111
Earlier sketch in CA 5-8R
See also CLR 3
See also SATA 2, 36, 45
Wiberg, Harald (Albin) 1908- ....SATA 40
Wice, Aubrey (Agnew)
1913(?)-1985 Obituary 119
Wice, Paul B(ernard) 1942- 57-60
Wick, Carter
See Wilcox, Collin
Wick, John W(illiam) 1935- CANR-15
Earlier sketch in CA 41-44R
Wick, Stuart Mary
See Freeman, Kathleen
Wick, Wendy
See Reaves, Wendy Wick
Wicke, Charles R(obinson) 1928- 37-40R
Wicke, Edith Schreiber
See Schreiber-Wicke, Edith
Wickenden, Elizabeth 1909- 1-4R
Wickenden, Leonard Daniel
1913(?)-1989 Obituary 130
Wickens, Delos D(onald) 1909- CAP-1
Earlier sketch in CA 13-16
Wickens, James F. 1933- 57-60
Wicker, Brian 1929- 17-20R
Wicker, Ireene 1905(?)-1987 69-72
Obituary 124
See also SATA 55
Wicker, Randolfe Hayden 1938- 45-48
Wicker, Thomas Grey 1926- CANR-21
Earlier sketch in CA 65-68
See also Wicker, Tom
Wicker, Tom
See Wicker, Thomas Grey
See also CLC 7
Wickers, David 1944- 77-80
Wickersham, Edward Dean 1927-1966 ....5-8R
Wickersham, Joan Barrett 1957- 105
Wickert, Erwin 1915- 132
Wickert, Frederic R(obinson) 1912- 21-24R
Wickes, George 1923- 9-12R
Wickes, Kim 1947- 109
Wickett, Ann 1942- 122
Wickett, William Harold Jr. 1919- 108
Wickey, Gould 1891- 25-28R
Wickham, Edward Ralph 1911- 5-8R
Wickham, Glynne (William Gladstone)
1922- CANR-7
Earlier sketch in CA 5-8R
Wickham, Jean 1903- 69-72
Wickham, Mary Fanning
See Bond, Mary Fanning Wickham
Wickham, Thomas Frederick 1926- 13-16R
Wicklein, John (Frederick) 1924- 106
Wickremasinghe, Esmond
1920(?)-1985 Obituary 117
Wickremasinghe, S(ugiswara) A(beywardena)
1901-1981 Obituary 108
Wicks, Ben 1926- 73-76
Wicks, Harold Vernon Jr. 1931- 102
Wicks, Harry
See Wicks, Harold Vernon Jr.
Wicks, Jared 1929- CANR-21
Earlier sketch in CA 25-28R
Wicks, John H. 1936- 17-20R
Wicks, Robert J(ohn) 1946- 113
Wicks, Robert Stewart 1923- 17-20R
Wickstrom, Lois 1948- 106
Wickwar, (William) Hardy 1903- 57-60
Wickwire, Franklin B(acon) 1931- 21-24R
Wickwire, Mary Botts 1935- 104
Wicomb, Zoe 1948- 127
Widdemer, Mabel Cleland 1902-1964 ....5-8R
See also SATA 5
Widdemer, Margaret CANR-4
Obituary 77-80
Earlier sketch in CA 5-8R
Widder, (John) Arthur (Jr.) 1928- 5-8R
Widder, Milton 1907(?)-1985 Obituary 118
Widell, Helene 1912- 37-40R
Wideman, John Edgar 1941- CANR-14
Earlier sketch in CA 85-88
See also BLC 3
See also BW
See also CLC 5, 34, 36, 67
See also DLB 33
Widener, Alice 1905(?)-1985 Obituary 114
Widener, Don(ald) 1930- 37-40R
Widenor, William C(ramer) 1937- 102
Widerberg, Siv 1931- 53-56
See also SATA 10
Widgery, Alban G(regory) 1887- 5-8R
Widgery, David 1947- 69-72
Widgery, Jan 1920- 17-20R
Widick, B. J. 1910- 9-12R
Widicus, Wilbur W(ilson) Jr. 1932- 53-56
Widman, F. Lisle 1919(?)-1983 Obituary 111
Widmer, Eleanor (Rackow) 1925- 17-20R
Widmer, Emmy Louise 1925- 29-32R
Widmer, Kingsley 1925- CANR-3
Earlier sketch in CA 1-4R
Widutis, Florence 1912(?)-1989 128
Wiebe, Katie Funk 1924- 132
Wiebe, M(elvin) G(eorge) 1939- 114
Wiebe, Robert H(uddleston) 1930- 5-8R
Wiebe, Rudy (H.) 1934- 37-40R
See also CLC 6, 11, 14
See also DLB 60
Wiebenson, Dora (Louise) 1926- 37-40R
Wiecek, William Michael 1938- 37-40R
Wiechert, Ernst 1887-1950 ....DLB 56
Wieck, Fred D(ernburg)
1910-1973 Obituary 104
Wieckert, Jeanne E. (Lentz) 1939- 89-92
Wiecking, Anna M. 1887-1973 ....CAP-1
Earlier sketch in CA 13-14
Wieczynski, Joseph L. 1934- 37-40R
Wied, Martina 1882-1957 ....DLB 85
Wiedemann, Thomas (E. J.) 1950- 138
Wieder, Laurance 1946- CANR-8
Earlier sketch in CA 57-60
Wieder, Robert S(hannon) 1944- 85-88
Wiederumb, Trotzhard
See Steiner, Gerolf
Wiedner, Donald L(awrence) 1930- 13-16R
Wiegand, Charmion von
See von Wiegand, Charmion
Wiegand, G(uenther) Carl 1906- 21-24R
Wiegand, William G(eorge) 1928- 9-12R
Wieghart, James G. 1933- 77-80
Wiegner, Kathleen K(napp) 1938- 93-96
Wiehl, Andrew (M.) 1904- 89-92
Wieland, Christoph Martin 1733-1813 ....DLB 97
Wieland, George F(red) 1936- 89-92
Wiells, Helen
See Cameron, (Barbara) Anne
Wieman, Harold F(rancis) 1917- 61-64
Wieman, Henry N(elson) 1884-1975 61-64
Obituary 57-60
Wiemer, Rudolf Otto 1905- CANR-25
Earlier sketches in CA 21-24R, CANR-9
Wienandt, Elwyn A(rthur) 1917- 41-44R
Wiener, Allen J. 1943- 125
Wiener, Daniel N(orman) 1921- 37-40R
Wiener, Harvey Shelby 1940- 102
Wiener, Joan
See Bordow, Joan (Wiener)
Wiener, Joel H. 1937- CANR-14
Earlier sketches in CA 37-40R, CANR-31
Wiener, Jon
See Wiener, Jonathan M.
Wiener, Jonathan M. 1944- 115
Wiener, Joshua M(ark) 1949- 133
Wiener, Leigh Auston 1929- 108
Wiener, M. Jean 1896-1982 Obituary 107
Wiener, Martin J. 1941- 85-88
Wiener, Norbert 1894-1964 Obituary 107
Wiener, Philip P(aul) 1905- CAP-1
Obituary 137
Earlier sketch in CA 9-10
Wiener, Sally Dixon 1926- 101
Wiener, Sam
See Dolgoff, Sam
Wiener, Solomon 1915- CANR-7
Earlier sketch in CA 17-20R
Wieners, John 1934- 13-16R
See also CLC 7
See also DLB 16
Wieniewska, Celina
See Janson-Smith, Celina
Wienpahl, Paul D(e Velin) 1916- 9-12R
Wier, Allen 1946- 77-80
Wier, Dara 1949- CANR-27
Earlier sketch in CA 77-80
Wier, Ester (Alberti) 1910- 9-12R
See also DLB 52
See also SATA 3
Wiersbe, Warren W(endell) 1929- CANR-23
Earlier sketches in CA 5-8R, CANR-7
Wiersma, Stanley M(arvin) 1930- CANR-11
Earlier sketch in CA 29-32R
Wiersma, William Jr. 1931- CANR-1
Earlier sketch in CA 45-48
Wierwille, Victor Paul 1916-1985 ....CANR-2
Obituary 116
Earlier sketch in CA 5-8R
Wierzynski, Gregory H(ieronim) 1939- 73-76
Wierzynski, Kazimierz 1894-1969 Obituary 115
Wiese, Arthur E(dward) 1946- 73-76
Wiese, Kurt 1887-1974 ....9-12R
Obituary 49-52
See also MAICYA
See also SATA 3, 24, 36
Wiesel, Elie(zer) 1928- CANR-8
Earlier sketch in CA 5-8R
See also CAAS 4
See also AAYA 7
See also AITN 1
See also CLC 3, 5, 11, 37
See also DLB 83
See also DLBY 87
See also MTCW
See also SATA 56

Wiesen, Allen E. 1939- 29-32R
Wiesenfarth, Joseph (John) 1933- CANR-8
Earlier sketch in CA 5-8R
Wiesenfeld, Joe 1947- 131
Wiesenthal, Simon 1908- CANR-13
Earlier sketch in CA 21-24R
Wiesner, Jerome B(ert) 1915- 13-16R
Wiesner, Portia
See Takakjian, Portia
Wiesner, William 1899- 41-44R
See also SATA 5
Wiest, Claire (Johnson) 1930- CANR-34
Earlier sketch in CA 113
Wigal, Donald 1933- CANR-14
Earlier sketch in CA 81-84
Wigan, Anthony Obituary 110
Wigan, Bernard (John) 1918- 13-16R
Wigan, Christopher
See Bingley, David Ernest
Wigan, Tony
See Wigan, Anthony
Wigforss, Ernst 1882(?)-1977 Obituary 69-72
Wigg, George (Edward Cecil)
1900-1983 Obituary 115
Wiggin, Kate Douglas (Smith) 1856-1923 137
See also MAICYA
Wiggin, Kate Douglas
1856-1923 Brief entry 111
See also DLB 42
See also YABC 1
Wiggin, Maurice (Samuel) 1912- CANR-5
Earlier sketch in CA 9-12R
Wiggin, Paul 1934- 25-28R
Wiggins, Arthur W. 1938- 53-56
Wiggins, Charles W(illiam) 1937- 41-44R
Wiggins, David 1933- 118
Wiggins, Jack G(illmore) 1926- 41-44R
Wiggins, James B(ryan) 1935- 37-40R
Wiggins, James Russell 1903- 133
See also AITN 2
Wiggins, James Wilhelm 1914- 17-20R
Wiggins, Marianne 1947- 130
See also BEST 89:3
See also CLC 57
Wiggins, Robert A. 1921- 13-16R
Wiggins, Sam P. 1919- 21-24R
Wigginton, Eliot 1942- 101
See also AITN 1
Wigglesworth, Michael 1631-1705 .... DLB 24
Wigham, Eric Leonard 1904- 109
Wight, Frederick S.
See Wight, Frederick Stallknecht (Van Buren)
Wight, Frederick Stallknecht (Van Buren)
1902-1986 Obituary 120
Wight, James Alfred 1916- 77-80
See also Herriot, James
See also SATA 44, 55
Wight, (Robert James) Martin
1913-1972 .... CAP-2
Earlier sketch in CA 21-22
Wightman, Edith Mary
1939(?)-1983(?) Obituary 111
Wightman, George Brian Hamilton 1933- 107
Wighton, Charles Ernest 1913- 5-8R
Wighton, Rosemary Neville 1925- 9-12R
Wigmore
See Fabricius, Johan (Johannes)
Wignall, Anne 1912- 97-100
Wignell, Edel 1936- 137
See also SATA 69
Wigner, Eugene Paul 1902- CAP-2
Earlier sketch in CA 25-28
Wigoder, Geoffrey Bernard 1922- 105
Wihl, Gary 120
Wiig, Howard (Calvert) 1940- 61-64
Wijasuriya, D(onald) E(arlian) K(ingsley)
1934- 81-84
Wik, Reynold M. 1910- CANR-14
Earlier sketch in CA 81-84
Wikander, Matthew H. 1950- 125
Wike, Edward L. 1922- 37-40R
Wikland, Ilon 1930- Brief entry 111
See also SATA 32
Wikler, Madeline 1943- 117
Wikramanayake, Marina 1938- 45-48
Wiksell, Milton J. 1910- 5-8R
Wiksell, Wesley 1906- CAP-1
Earlier sketch in CA 17-18
Wilber, Charles G(rady) 1916- CANR-21
Earlier sketch in CA 41-44R
Wilber, Charles K. 1935- 134
Brief entry 113
Wilber, Donald N(ewton) 1907- CANR-2
Earlier sketch in CA 5-8R
See also SATA 35
Wilbers, Stephen 1949- 106
Wilbert, Johannes 1927- 124
Brief entry 118
Wilbourn, Carole C(ecile) 1940- CANR-14
Earlier sketch in CA 81-84
Wilbur, C. Keith 1923- CANR-28
Earlier sketches in CA 25-28R, CANR-11
See also SATA 27
Wilbur, C(larence) Martin 1908- 85-88
Wilbur, Crane 1887(?)-1973 Obituary 45-48
Wilbur, James B(enjamin) III 1924- CANR-14
Earlier sketch in CA 37-40R
Wilbur, Marguerite Eyer 1889- CAP-1
Earlier sketch in CA 11-12
Wilbur, Richard (Purdy) 1921- CANR-29
Earlier sketches in CA 1-4R, CANR-2
See also CABS 2
See also CLC 3, 6, 9, 14, 53
See also DLB 5
See also MTCW
See also SATA 9
Wilbur, William H(ale) 1888- CAP-1
Earlier sketch in CA 13-14
Wilburn, Jean Alexander 1915- 21-24R
Wilburn, Kathy 1948- .... SATA 68
Wilburn, Ralph G(lenn) 1909- CAP-1
Earlier sketch in CA 17-18
Wilby, Basil Leslie 1930- CANR-19
Earlier sketch in CA 103
Wilcher, Robert 1942- 121
Wilckens, Ulrich 1928- Brief entry 114
Wilcock, John 1927- CANR-2
Earlier sketch in CA 1-4R
Wilcocks, Julie 1943- 110
Wilcox, Clair 1898-1970 ....CANR-4
Earlier sketch in CA 5-8R
Wilcox, Collin 1924- CANR-14
Earlier sketches in CA 21-24R, CANR-31
Wilcox, Daniel 1941- 53-56
Wilcox, Dennis L. 1941- CANR-14
Earlier sketch in CA 37-40R
Wilcox, Desmond (John) 1931- CANR-21
Earlier sketch in CA 69-72
Wilcox, Donald J(ames) 1938-1991 109
Obituary 134
Wilcox, Earl J(unior) 1933- 111
Wilcox, Francis (Orlando) 1908-1985 ....37-40R
Obituary 115
Wilcox, Fred A(llen) 1940- 129
Wilcox, Helen (Elizabeth) 1955- 136
Wilcox, Herbert 1891-1977 57-60
Obituary 118
Wilcox, Howard 1913(?)-1987 Obituary 122
Wilcox, James (P.) 1949- 129
Brief entry 125
Wilcox, Jess
See Hershman, Morris
Wilcox, John T(homas) 1933- 45-48
Wilcox, Michael (Denys) 1943- 77-80
Wilcox, Paul L(orentus) 1899- 69-72
Wilcox, R(uth) Turner 1888-1970 ....5-8R
Obituary 29-32R
See also SATA 36
Wilcox, Richard L. 1918-1978 Obituary 77-80
Wilcox, Robert K(alleen) 1943- CANR-24
Earlier sketch in CA 77-80
Wilcox, Roger P. 1916- 21-24R
Wilcox, Tamara 1940- CANR-19
Earlier sketch in CA 97-100
Wilcox, Virginia Lee 1911- 37-40R
Wilcox, Walter 1920-1983 Obituary 110
Wilcox, Wayne Ayres 1932-1974 ....CANR-4
Obituary 49-52
Earlier sketch in CA 5-8R
Wilcoxon, George Dent Jr. 1913- 93-96
Wild, Jocelyn 1941- 116
See also SATA 46
Wild, John D(aniel) 1902-1972 Obituary 37-40R
Wild, Peter 1940- 37-40R
See also CLC 14
See also DLB 5
Wild, Robert A(nthony) 1940- 111
Wild, Robin (Evans) 1936- 116
See also SATA 46
Wild, Rolf H(einrich) 1927- 81-84
Wildavsky, Aaron (B.) 1930- CANR-30
Earlier sketches in CA 1-4R, CANR-2
Wilde, Alan 1929- CANR-31
Earlier sketch in CA 110
Wilde, D. Gunther
See Hurwood, Bernhardt J.
Wilde, Daniel U(nderwood) 1937- 57-60
Wilde, Jean T(oeplitz)
1898-1973 Obituary 45-48
Wilde, Jennifer
See Huff, T(om) E.
Wilde, Jocelyn
See Toombs, John
Wilde, Kathey
See King, Patricia
Wilde, Larry 1928- CANR-26
Earlier sketches in CA 25-28R, CANR-10
Wilde, Meta Carpenter (Doherty) 1907- 81-84
Wilde, Oscar (Fingal O'Flahertie Wills)
1854(?)-1900 119
Brief entry 104
See also CDBLB 1890-1914
See also DLB 10, 19, 34, 57
See also SATA 24
See also TCLC 1, 8, 23, 41
See also WLC
Wilde, Richard Henry 1789-1847 .... DLB 3, 59
Wilde, W(illiam) H(enry) 1923- CANR-11
Earlier sketch in CA 69-72
Wildeblood, Peter 1923- 65-68
Wilden, Anthony 1935- CANR-28
Earlier sketch in CA 37-40R
Wildenhain, Marguerite 1896- 77-80
Wilder, Alec
See Wilder, Alexander Lafayette Chew
Wilder, Alexander Lafayette Chew
1907-1980 104
Obituary 102
Wilder, Amos Niven 1895- 81-84
Wilder, Billy
See Wilder, Samuel
See also CLC 20
See also DLB 26
Wilder, Charlotte Elizabeth
1898(?)-1980 Obituary 97-100
Wilder, Cherry
See Grimm, Cherry Barbara
Wilder, Gene
See Silberman, Jerome
Wilder, John Bunyan 1914- 5-8R
Wilder, Joseph 1895-1976 Obituary 116
Wilder, Laura (Elizabeth) Ingalls 1867-1957 137
Brief entry 111
See also CLR 2
See also DLB 22
See also MAICYA
See also SATA 15, 29
Wilder, Robert D. 1916- 41-44R
Wilder, Robert (Ingersoll) 1901-1974 .... CAP-2
Obituary 53-56
Earlier sketch in CA 13-14
Wilder, Roy (E.) Jr. 1914- 121
Wilder, Samuel 1906- 89-92
See also Wilder, Billy
Wilder, Stephen
See Marlowe, Stephen
Wilder, Thornton (Niven) 1897-1975 ....13-16R
Obituary 61-64
See also AITN 2
See also CLC 1, 5, 6, 10, 15, 35
See also DC 1
See also DLB 4, 7, 9
See also MTCW
See also WLC
Wilders, John (Simpson) 1927- 21-24R
Wilder-Smith, A(rthur) E(rnest) 1915- CANR-27
Earlier sketches in CA 57-60, CANR-11
Wildes, Harry Emerson 1890- 57-60
Wildgans, Anton 1881-1942 .... DLB 118
Wild Horse Annie
See Johnston, Velma B.
Wilding, Ann
See Budd, Mavis
Wilding, Michael 1942- CANR-24
Earlier sketch in CA 104
Wildman, Allan K. 1927- 105
Wildman, Eugene 1938- 25-28R
Wildman, John Hazard 1911- 37-40R
Wildman, Louis Robert 1941- CANR-5
Earlier sketch in CA 13-16R
Wildmon, Donald E(llis) 1938- CANR-13
Earlier sketch in CA 61-64
Wildrick, Stanley B. 1894-1984 Obituary 112
Wilds, Nancy Alexander 1926- 13-16R
Wildsmith, Alan 1937- 97-100
Wildsmith, Brian 1930- CANR-35
Earlier sketch in CA 85-88
See also CLR 2
See also MAICYA
See also SAAS 5
See also SATA 16, 69
Wilenski, Peter Stephen 1939- 109
Wilenski, R(eginald) H(oward) 1887-1975 61-64
Obituary 57-60
Wilensky, Harold L. 1923- CANR-34
Earlier sketches in CA 41-44R, CANR-15
Wilentz, Gay (A.) 1950- 138
Wilentz, Joan Steen 1930- 25-28R
Wilentz, Ted
See Wilentz, Theodore
Wilentz, Theodore 1915- 29-32R
Wiles, David K(imball) 1942- CANR-7
Earlier sketch in CA 53-56
Wiles, Domini 1942- 102
Wiles, Gordon Pitts 1909- 108
Wiles, John 1924- 9-12R
Wiles, Kimball 1913-1969 ....CANR-4
Earlier sketch in CA 5-8R
Wiles, Maurice Frank 1923- 108
Wiles, Peter John de la Fosse 1919- 5-8R
Wiles, Roy McKeen 1903- CAP-1
Earlier sketch in CA 19-20
Wiley, Bell
See Strauss, Frances Goetzmann
Wiley, Bell I(rvin) 1906-1980 ....CANR-4
Obituary 97-100
Earlier sketch in CA 5-8R
See also DLB 17
Wiley, David Sherman 1935- CANR-29
Earlier sketches in CA 61-64, CANR-12
Wiley, Farida A(nna) 1887(?)-1986 Obituary 121
Wiley, Jack 1936- CANR-8
Earlier sketch in CA 61-64
Wiley, Jay Wilson 1913- 5-8R
Wiley, John P. Jr. 1936- 89-92
Wiley, Karla H(ummel) 1918- 61-64
Wiley, Margaret L.
See Marshall, Margaret Wiley
Wiley, Paul L(uzon) 1914-1979 ....CANR-10
Earlier sketch in CA 5-8R
Wiley, Peter (Booth) 1942- 131
Wiley, Ralph 1952- 136
Wiley, Raymond A(loysius) 1923- 37-40R
Wiley, Richard 1944- 129
Brief entry 121
See also CLC 44
Wiley, Stan
See Hill, John S(tanley)
Wiley, Tom 1906- 25-28R
Wiley, William Leon 1903- 111
Wilf, Alexander 1905(?)-1981 Obituary 103
Wilford, Allen 1948- 128
Wilford, John Noble 1933- CANR-15
Earlier sketch in CA 29-32R
Wilford, Walton T. 1937- 49-52
Wilgus, A(lva) Curtis 1897- CANR-3
Earlier sketch in CA 5-8R
Wilgus, D(onald) K(night) 1918-1989 ....37-40R
Obituary 130
Wilhelm, Hans 1945- 119
See also SATA 58
Wilhelm, Hellmut 1905- 5-8R
Wilhelm, James Jerome 1932- CANR-32
Earlier sketch in CA 17-20R
Wilhelm, John R(emsen) 1916- 5-8R
Wilhelm, Kate
See Wilhelm, Katie Gertrude
See also CAAS 5
See also CLC 7
See also DLB 8
Wilhelm, Kathryn Stephenson 1915- 13-16R
Wilhelm, Katie Gertrude 1928- CANR-36
Earlier sketches in CA 37-40R, CANR-17
See also Wilhelm, Kate
See also MTCW
Wilhelm, Paul A. 1916- 61-64
Wilhelm, Walt 1893- 29-32R
Wilhelm II
See Hohenzollern, Friedrich Wilhelm (Victor Albert)
Wilhelmina
See Cooper, Wilhelmina (Behmenburg)
Wilhelmsen, Frederick D(aniel) 1923- CANR-3
Earlier sketch in CA 1-4R
Wilhoit, Francis M(arion) 1920- 126
Brief entry 109
Wilk, David 1951- CANR-4
Earlier sketch in CA 53-56
Wilk, Gerard H(ermann) 1902- 69-72
Wilk, Max 1920- CANR-37
Earlier sketches in CA 1-4R, CANR-1, 16
Wilk, Richard R(alph) 1953- 120
Wilke, Ekkehard-Teja 1941- 65-68
Wilke, Harold H(enry) 1914- 132
Wilke, Ulfert (Stephan) 1907- CAP-1
Earlier sketch in CA 13-16
Wilken, Robert L(ouis) 1936- CANR-16
Earlier sketch in CA 29-32R
Wilkening, Howard (Everett) 1909- 89-92
Wilkens, Emily 1917- 103
Wilkerson, Cynthia
See Levinson, Leonard
Wilkerson, David R(ay) 1931- 41-44R
Wilkerson, Hugh 1939- 104
Wilkerson, Loree A. R(andleman) 1923- 17-20R
Wilkerson, Rich(ard Preston) 1952- 123
Wilkes, Edward T. 1889-1983 Obituary 111
Wilkes, George 1817-1885 .... DLB 79
Wilkes, Glenn Newton 1928- CANR-17
Earlier sketch in CA 1-4R
Wilkes, Ian (Henry) 1932- 41-44R
Wilkes, John W(illiam) 1924- 25-28R
Wilkes, Paul 1938- CANR-15
Earlier sketch in CA 81-84
Wilkes, Peter 1937- 125
Wilkes, William Alfred 1910- 45-48
Wilkes-Hunter, R(ichard) 13-16R
Wilkie, Angus 1958- 128
Wilkie, Brian 1929- 13-16R
Wilkie, James W. 1936- 21-24R
Wilkie, Jane 1917- 102
Wilkie, Katharine E(lliott) 1904-1980 ....21-24R
Obituary 125
See also SATA 31
Wilkie, Kenneth 1942- 85-88
Wilkin, Eloise (Burns) 1904-1987 124
See also MAICYA
See also SATA 49, 54
Wilkins, Alfred T. Jr. 1949- 129
Wilkins, Beatrice (Brunson) 1928- 61-64
Wilkins, Burleigh Taylor 1932- 105
Wilkins, Ernest J. 1918- 53-56
Wilkins, Frances 1923- 73-76
See also SATA 14
Wilkins, H. Ford 1901(?)-1983 Obituary 111
Wilkins, Kathleen Sonia 1941- 104
Wilkins, Kay S.
See Wilkins, Kathleen Sonia
Wilkins, Kirby L. 1936- 127
Wilkins, Leslie T. 1915- CANR-22
Earlier sketches in CA 17-20R, CANR-7
Wilkins, Marilyn (Ruth) 1926- 105
See also SATA 30
Wilkins, Marne
See Wilkins, Marilyn (Ruth)
Wilkins, Mary
See Freeman, Mary Eleanor Wilkins
Wilkins, Mary Huiskamp 1926- CANR-18
Earlier sketches in CA 5-8R, CANR-2
See also Calhoun, Mary
Wilkins, Mesannie 1891- CAP-2
Earlier sketch in CA 25-28
Wilkins, Mira 1931- Brief entry 112
Wilkins, Roger (Wood) 1932- 117
Brief entry 109
See also BW
Wilkins, Ronald J(ohn) 1916- CANR-16
Earlier sketch in CA 93-96
Wilkins, Roy 1901-1981 104
See also BW
Wilkins, Skip
See Wilkins, Alfred T. Jr.
Wilkins, Thurman 1915- 5-8R
Wilkins, William R(ichard) 1933- 61-64
Wilkinson, Alec 1952- 109
Wilkinson, Anne 1910-1961 .... DLB 88
Wilkinson, (Thomas) Barry 1923- .... SATA 32, 50
Wilkinson, Bertie 1898- 9-12R
Wilkinson, Bonaro
See Overstreet, Bonaro (Wilkinson)
Wilkinson, Brenda 1946- CANR-26
Earlier sketch in CA 69-72
See also BW
See also CLR 20
See also SATA 14
Wilkinson, Bud
See Wilkinson, Charles B(urnham)
Wilkinson, (John) Burke 1913- 9-12R
See also SATA 4
Wilkinson, C. E. 1948- 109
Wilkinson, Charles B(urnham) 1916- 105
Wilkinson, Charlotte Jefferson 69-72
Wilkinson, Clyde Winfield 1910- 1-4R

Wilkinson, David 93-96
Wilkinson, Doris Yvonne 1936- 29-32R
Wilkinson, Elizabeth C. 1926- 123
Wilkinson, Ernest Leroy 1899-1978 .... CANR-3
Earlier sketch in CA 49-52
Wilkinson, G(eoffrey) K(edington) 1907- 1-4R
Wilkinson, J(oseph) F. 1925- 105
Wilkinson, James Hardy
1919-1986 Obituary 120
Wilkinson, James Harvie III 1944- 101
Wilkinson, John (Donald) 1929- 9-12R
Wilkinson, John Thomas 1893-1980 107
Obituary 104
Wilkinson, L(ancelot) P(atrick)
1907-1985 .... CANR-20
Obituary 116
Earlier sketches in CA 5-8R, CANR-3
Wilkinson, Lorna Hilda Kathleen 1909- CAP-1
Earlier sketch in CA 13-14
Wilkinson, Louis (Umfreville)
1881-1966 Obituary 116
Wilkinson, Maxwell Penrose
1905(?)-1985 Obituary 116
Wilkinson, Norman Beaumont
1910-1983 .... 37-40R
Obituary 126
Wilkinson, Patrick
See Wilkinson, L(ancelot) P(atrick)
Wilkinson, Paul 1937- CANR-14
Earlier sketch in CA 77-80
Wilkinson, Richard Gerald 1943- 45-48
Wilkinson, (William) Roderick 1917- 13-16R
Wilkinson, Ronald 1920- 5-8R
Wilkinson, Rosemary C(halloner)
1924- CANR-17
Earlier sketches in CA 49-52, CANR-1
Wilkinson, Rupert Hugh 1936- 9-12R
Wilkinson, Sylvia 1940- 17-20R
See also AITN 1
See also DLBY 86
See also SATA 39, 56
Wilkinson, Walter 1888-1970 Obituary 104
Wilkinson, (Arthur) Warren (Jr.) 1945- 132
Wilkinson, William Cleaver 1833-1920 .... DLB 71
Wilkinson, Winifred
See Hausmann, Winifred
Wilkon, Jozef 1930- 107
See also MAICYA
See also SATA 31, 71
Wilks, Brian 1933- 69-72
Wilks, Ed 1928(?)-1984 Obituary 114
Wilks, John 1922- 73-76
Wilks, Michael Thomas 1947- 110
See also SATA 44
Wilks, Mike
See Wilks, Michael Thomas
Wilks, Yorick 1939- 73-76
Will
See Lipkind, William
Will, Clifford M(artin) 1946- 136
Will, Frederic 1928- CANR-16
Earlier sketches in CA 49-52, CANR-1
Will, Frederick L(udwig) 1909- 13-16R
Will, George F(rederick) 1941- CANR-32
Earlier sketch in CA 77-80
See also BEST 90:3
See also MTCW
Will, Lawrence Elmer 1893- CAP-2
Earlier sketch in CA 17-18
Will, Lester J. 1908(?)-1984 Obituary 111
Will, Robert E(rwin) 1928- 17-20R
Will, W(ilbur) Marvin 1937- 118
Willan, Anne 1938- CANR-6
Earlier sketch in CA 57-60
Willan, Thomas Stuart 1910- 9-12R
Willans, Jean Stone 1924- 65-68
Willard, Barbara (Mary) 1909- CANR-15
Earlier sketch in CA 81-84
See also CLR 2
See also MAICYA
See also SAAS 5
See also SATA 17
Willard, Beatrice E(lizabeth) 1925- 41-44R
Willard, Charles
See Armstrong, John Byron
Willard, Charlotte 1914-1977 81-84
Obituary 73-76
Willard, Dallas (Albert) 1935- 116
Willard, Mildred Wilds 1911-1978 .... 21-24R
Obituary 135
See also SATA 14
Willard, Nancy 1936- CANR-39
Earlier sketches in CA 89-92, CANR-10
See also CLC 7, 37
See also CLR 5
See also DLB 5, 52
See also MAICYA
See also MTCW
See also SATA 30, 37, 71
Willard, Portman
See Norwood, Victor G(eorge) C(harles)
Willard, Samuel 1640-1707 .... DLB 24
Willcock, M(alcolm) M(aurice) 1925- 65-68
Willcox, A(lexander) R(obert) 1911- 118
Willcox, Donald J. 1933- 49-52
Willcox, Isobel 1907- 111
See also SATA 42
Willcox, Sheila 1936- 73-76
Willcox, William Bradford 1907-1985 .... CANR-3
Obituary 117
Earlier sketch in CA 5-8R
Wille, Janet Neipris 1936- CANR-30
Earlier sketch in CA 109
Willee, Albert William 1916-1982 109
Willeford, Betsy Ann 1939- 132
Willeford, Charles (Ray III)
1919-1988 .... CANR-15
Obituary 125
Earlier sketch in CA 33-36R
Willeford, William 1929- 25-28R
Willem, John M. 1909-1979 .... CAP-1
Obituary 93-96
Earlier sketch in CA 17-18
Willems, Emilio 1905- 105
Willems, J. Rutherford 1944- CANR-23
Earlier sketch in CA 45-48
Willen, Diane 1943- 117
Willens, Doris 1924- 127
Willens, Harold 1914- 132
Willensky, Elliot 1933-1990 .... 29-32R
Obituary 131
Willenson, Kim Jeremy 1937- 103
Willenz, June A. 1924- 121
Willerding, Margaret F(rances) 1919- 57-60
Willes, Mary (Janette) 1927- 120
Willets, F(rederick) W(illiam) 1930- 21-24R
Willets, Walter E. 1924- 25-28R
Willett, Brother Franciscus 1922- 13-16R
Willett, Edward R(ice) 1923- CANR-21
Earlier sketches in CA 5-8R, CANR-2
Willett, Frank 1925- 25-28R
Willett, Jincy 1946- 127
Willett, John (William Mills) 1917- CANR-4
Earlier sketch in CA 9-12R
Willett, T(erence) C(harles) 1918- 37-40R
Willett, Thomas D(unaway) 1942- 108
Willetts, R(onald) F(rederick) 1915- CANR-2
Earlier sketch in CA 5-8R
Willey, Basil 1897-1978 .... 9-12R
Obituary 135
Willey, Darrell S. 1925- 41-44R
Willey, F. T.
See Willey, Frederick Thomas
Willey, Fred
See Willey, Frederick Thomas
Willey, Frederick Thomas
1910-1987 Obituary 124
Willey, Gordon R(andolph) 1913- CANR-2
Earlier sketch in CA 5-8R
Willey, John C(offin) 1914-1990 Obituary 131
Willey, Keith (Greville) 1930- CANR-9
Earlier sketch in CA 21-24R
Willey, Margaret 1950- 117
Willey, Peter (Robert Everard) 1922- 13-16R
Willey, R(oy) DeVerl 1910-197 (?) CAP-2
Earlier sketch in CA 19-20
Willey, Richard J(ames) 1934- 41-44R
Willey, Robert
See Ley, Willy
Willgoose, Carl E(dward) 1916- CANR-6
Earlier sketch in CA 13-16R
Wilhelm, Sidney M(clarty) 1934- 9-12R
Willhoite, Michael A. 1946- .... SATA 71
William, Maurice 1882(?)-1973 Obituary 45-48
William II
See Hohenzollern, Friedrich Wilhelm (Victor Albert)
William of Auvergne 1190(?)-1249 .... DLB 115
William of Conches 1090(?)-1154(?) .... DLB 115
William of Sherwood 1200(?)-1266(?) .... DLB 115
Williams, Alan F. 1933- 49-52
Williams, (Timothy) Alden 1932- 41-44R
Williams, Alice Cary 1892-1983 65-68
Obituary 111
Williams, Alice Davis 1901- 113
Williams, Amanda Kyle 1957- 138
Williams, Ann Jr. 1951-1985 Obituary 117
Williams, Anne
See Steinke, Ann E(lizabeth)
Williams, Aston R. 1912- 21-24R
Williams, Aubrey L(ake) 1922- CANR-6
Earlier sketch in CA 1-4R
Williams, Barbara 1925- CANR-17
Earlier sketches in CA 49-52, CANR-1
See also SATA 11
Williams, Barbara 1937- .... SATA 62
Williams, Barry 1932- 29-32R
Williams, Ben A(mes) Jr. 1915- 116
Williams, Ben Ames 1889-1953 .... DLB 102
Williams, Benjamin Buford 1923- 113
Williams, Benjamin H(arrison)
1889-1974 .... CANR-29
Earlier sketch in CA 37-40R
Williams, Bernard (Arthur Owen) 1929- 130
Brief entry 112
Williams, Bert Nolan 1930- 103
Williams, Beryl
See Epstein, Beryl (M. Williams)
Williams, Bill
See Crawford, William (Elbert)
Williams, Brad 1918- CANR-1
Earlier sketch in CA 1-4R
Williams, Brian (Peter) 1943- .... SATA 54
Williams, Bruce R(odda) 1919- 13-16R
Williams, Burton John 1927- 41-44R
Williams, Byron (Leigh) 1934- 29-32R
Williams, C(hester) Arthur Jr. 1924- CANR-2
Earlier sketch in CA 1-4R
Williams, C(lifford) Glyn 1928- 29-32R
Williams, C(hristopher) J(ohn) F(ardo)
1930- 103
Williams, C(harles) K(enneth) 1936- 37-40R
See also CLC 33, 56
See also DLB 5
Williams, Carl C(arnelius) 1903- 45-48
Williams, Carol M. 1917- 65-68
Williams, Carol T(raynor) 1935- 112
Williams, Catharine M(elissa) 1903- 37-40R
Williams, Cecil B(rown) 1901-1966 .... CAP-1
Earlier sketch in CA 11-12
Williams, Chancellor 1905- .... DLB 76
Williams, Charles
See Collier, James L(incoln)
Williams, Charles (Walter Stansby)
1886-1945 Brief entry 104
See also DLB 100
See also TCLC 1, 11
Williams, Chester
See Schechter, William
Williams, Christian 1943- 130
Williams, Cicely 1907-1985 57-60
Obituary 117
Williams, Claerwen 1938- 102
Williams, Clayton (Wheat) 1895-1983 125
Williams, Clyde C. 1881-1974 .... CAP-2
Earlier sketch in CA 23-24
See also SATA 8, 27
Williams, Coe
See Harrison, C. William
Williams, Colin W(ilbur) 1921- CANR-19
Earlier sketch in CA 25-28R
Williams, Colin 1934- 109
Williams, Cris
See De Cristoforo, R(omeo) J(ohn)
Williams, Cyril Glyndwr 1921- CANR-15
Earlier sketch in CA 37-40R
Williams, D.
See Ronald, David William
Williams, (Walter) Dakin 1919- Brief entry 116
Williams, Daniel Day 1910-1973 .... CANR-1
Obituary 45-48
Earlier sketch in CA 1-4R
Williams, David A. 1922- 29-32R
Williams, David (Eliot) 1939- 123
Williams, David (Frank)
1909-1983 Obituary 109
Williams, David Glenwood 1918- 5-8R
Williams, David L. 1940- CANR-10
Earlier sketch in CA 25-28R
Williams, David Rhys 1890- 5-8R
Williams, David Ricardo 1923- CANR-26
Earlier sketch in CA 101
Williams, David 1926- 122
Williams, David 1939- 73-76
Williams, David 1945- 97-100
Williams, Denis (Joseph Ivan) 1923- CANR-17
Earlier sketch in CA 93-96
See also DLB 117
Williams, Dorian 1914- CANR-3
Earlier sketch in CA 9-12R
Williams, (Marcia) Dorothy 1945- .... SATA 71
Williams, Duncan 1927- 41-44R
Williams, E(ric) C(yril) 1918- 97-100
Williams, E(rnest) N(eville) 1917- 9-12R
Williams, Edward Ainsworth
1907-1976 Obituary 65-68
Williams, Edward Bennett 1920-1988 .... 1-4R
Obituary 126
Williams, Edward Francis
1903-1970 Obituary 29-32R
Williams, Edward G. 1929- 29-32R
Williams, Edward J(erome) 1935- CANR-10
Earlier sketch in CA 21-24R
Williams, Edward K. 1923-1966 .... CAP-1
Earlier sketch in CA 13-16
Williams, Edward V(inson) 1935- 121
Williams, Edwin B(ucher) 1891-1975 .... 5-8R
Obituary 57-60
Williams, Edwin E(veritt) 1913- 45-48
Williams, Edwina Dakin
1885(?)-1980 Obituary 97-100
Williams, Eirlys O(lwen) 1929- CAP-1
Earlier sketch in CA 9-10
Williams, Elizabeth
See Dohen, Dorothy M.
Williams, (George) Emlyn 1905-1987 .... CANR-36
Obituary 123
Earlier sketch in CA 104
See also CLC 15
See also DLB 10, 77
See also MTCW
Williams, Emmett 1925- CANR-2
Earlier sketch in CA 45-48
Williams, Eric (Ernest) 1911-1983 .... CANR-28
Obituary 111
Earlier sketch in CA 9-12R
See also SATA 14, 38
Williams, Eric (Eustace) 1911-1981 125
Obituary 103
See also BW
Williams, Ernest Wells
1896(?)-1980 Obituary 97-100
Williams, Estelle S. 1908- 123
Williams, Ethel L. 37-40R
Williams, F(rederick) Winston 1935- 103
Williams, Ferelith Eccles
See Eccles Williams, Ferelith
See also SATA 22
Williams, Frances B.
See Browin, Frances Williams
Williams, Frances Leigh 1909- 13-16R
Williams, Frances Marion 1919- 57-60
Williams, Frances 1935- 25-28R
Williams, Francis Stewart 1921-1974 .... 37-40R
Williams, Francis 1903-1970 Obituary 104
Williams, Frank B(royles) Jr. 1913- 118
Williams, Frederick D(eForrest) 1918- 65-68
Williams, Frederick (Dowell) 1933- 136
Williams, G(erhard) Mennen
1911-1988 Obituary 124
Williams, G. Robert 1948- 108
Williams, Garth (Montgomery) 1912- 134
See also DLB 22
See also MAICYA
See also SAAS 7
See also SATA 18, 66
Williams, Geoffrey J(ames) 1936- 118
Williams, Geoffrey (John) 1943- 29-32R
Williams, George C(hristopher) 1926- 73-76
Williams, George (Guion) 1902- 13-16R
Williams, George Huntston 1914- CANR-16
Earlier sketches in CA 1-4R, CANR-1
Williams, George (Joseph) III 1949- 125
Williams, George M(ason Jr.) 1940- 61-64
Williams, George W(alton) 1922- 9-12R
Williams, George Washington
1849-1891 .... DLB 47
Williams, Geraint 1942- 124
Williams, Gertrude 1897-1983 Obituary 109
Williams, Gilbert M. 1917- 61-64
Williams, Glanmor 1920- 5-8R
Williams, Glanville Llewelyn 1911- 106
Williams, Gluyas 1888-1982 Obituary 108
See also AITN 2
Williams, Gordon
See Williams, Gordon M(aclean)
Williams, Gordon Leslie 1933- 110
Williams, Gordon M(aclean) 1934(?)- 130
Brief entry 116
Williams, Greer 1909- CANR-10
Earlier sketch in CA 13-16R
Williams, Gregory 1952- 109
Williams, Griffith Wynne 1897-1972 .... CAP-2
Earlier sketch in CA 25-28
Williams, Gurney III 1941- CANR-30
Earlier sketch in CA 69-72
Williams, Guy Neal 1953- 77-80
Williams, Guy R(ichard) 1920- CANR-31
Earlier sketch in CA 13-16R
See also SATA 11
Williams, (David) Gwyn 1904- 103
Williams, Hank Jr. 1949- Brief entry 117
Williams, Harold A(nthony) 1916- 37-40R
Williams, Harold (Claude Noel)
1914-1990 Obituary 131
Williams, Harold R(oger) 1935- 53-56
Williams, Harold S(tannett) 1898- CANR-20
Earlier sketches in CA 9-12R, CANR-5
Williams, Harold Workman
See Wilson, Halsey William
Williams, Hawley
See Heyliger, William
Williams, Hazel Pearson 1914- 57-60
Williams, Heathcote 1941- 21-24R
See also DLB 13
Williams, Henry
See Manville, W(illiam) H(enry)
Williams, Henry Lionel
1895-1974 Obituary 45-48
Williams, Herbert Lee 1918- CANR-29
Earlier sketch in CA 1-4R
Williams, Herbert (Lloyd) 1932- CANR-12
Earlier sketch in CA 29-32R
Williams, Hermann Warner Jr. 1908-1974 .... 5-8R
Obituary 53-56
Williams, Hiram D. 1917- 13-16R
Williams, Hosea L(orenzo) 1926- 49-52
Williams, Howard L(loyd) 1950- 117
Williams, Howard Russell 1915- 13-16R
Williams, Hugh (Anthony Glanmor)
1904-1969 .... CAP-2
Earlier sketch in CA 25-28
Williams, Hugh Steadman 1935- 132
Williams, Hugo 1942- 17-20R
See also CLC 42
See also DLB 40
Williams, Ioan Miles 1941- CANR-11
Earlier sketch in CA 25-28R
Williams, Ira E. Jr. 1926- 53-56
Williams, Irving G(regory) 1915- 41-44R
Williams, Isaac 1802-1865 .... DLB 32
Williams, J(ames) David Lewis
See Lewis-Williams, J(ames) David
Williams, J(ames) Earl 1922- 41-44R
Williams, J(ohn) H(argreaves) Harley 9-12R
Williams, J. R.
See Williams, Jeanne
Williams, J(ohn) Rodman 1918- 81-84
Williams, J. Walker
See Wodehouse, P(elham) G(renville)
Williams, J. X.
See Ludwig, Myles Eric
and Offutt, Andrew J(efferson V)
Williams, Jay G(omer) 1932- 41-44R
Williams, Jay 1914-1978 .... CANR-39
Obituary 81-84
Earlier sketches in CA 1-4R, CANR-2
See also CLR 8
See also MAICYA
See also SATA 3, 24, 41
Williams, Jeanne 1930- 25-28R
See also SATA 5
Williams, (Edward) Jeffery 1920- 132
Williams, Jenny 1939- 112
See also SATA 60
Williams, Jeremy (Napier) Howard
See Howard-Williams, Jeremy (Napier)
Williams, Jerome 1926- CANR-1
Earlier sketch in CA 49-52
Williams, Joan 1928- 1-4R
See also DLB 6
Williams, Joel
See Jennings, John (Edward Jr.)
Williams, John A(lfred) 1925- CANR-26
Earlier sketches in CA 53-56, CANR-6
See also CAAS 3
See also BLC 3
See also BW
See also CLC 5, 13
See also DLB 2, 33
Williams, John Alden 1928- CANR-2
Earlier sketch in CA 1-4R
Williams, John B. 1919- 93-96
Williams, John Burr 1900-1989 Obituary 129
Williams, John D(elane) 1938- 57-60

Williams, John (Edward) 1922- ... CANR-2
Earlier sketch in CA 1-4R
See also DLB 6
Williams, John Edwin 1928- ... 93-96
Williams, John G(ordon) 1906- ... CAP-2
Earlier sketch in CA 23-24
Williams, John G. 1915- ... 120
Williams, John Hartley 1942- ... 130
Williams, John Henry 1887-1980 Obituary ... 105
Williams, John (Herbert) 1908-1976 ... CANR-10
Earlier sketch in CA 13-16R
Williams, John Hoyt 1940- ... 128
Williams, John R(yan) 1919- ... 37-40R
Williams, John Stanley 1925- ... CAP-1
Earlier sketch in CA 9-10
Williams, John Stuart 1920- ... 65-68
Williams, John 1954- ... 129
Williams, Jonathan (Chamberlain) 1929- ... CANR-8
Earlier sketch in CA 9-12R
See also CAAS 12
See also CLC 13
See also DLB 5
Williams, Joy 1944- ... CANR-22
Earlier sketch in CA 41-44R
See also CLC 31
Williams, Joyce E(layne) 1937- ... 104
Williams, Juan 1954- ... 125
Williams, Juanita da Lomba Jones 1925- ... 37-40R
Williams, June Vanleer ... 131
Williams, Justin Sr. 1906- ... 101
Williams, Karen Lynn 1952- ... 133
See also SATA 66
Williams, Kate
See Flynn, Donald R(obert)
Williams, Kenneth 1926-1988 Obituary ... 125
Williams, Kim 1924(?)-1986 Obituary ... 120
Williams, Kit 1946(?)- ... 107
See also CLR 4
See also SATA 44
Williams, L(aurence) F(rederic) Rushbrook
See Rushbrook Williams, L(aurence) F(rederic)
Williams, L(eslie) Pearce 1927- ... 65-68
Williams, Lady
See Williams, Gertrude
Williams, Lawrence K(enneth) 1930- ... 29-32R
Williams, Lawrence 1916(?)-1983 Obituary ... 108
Williams, Lee E(rskine) II 1946- ... 41-44R
Williams, LeRoy T. 1944- ... 120
Williams, Leslie 1941- ... 107
See also SATA 42
Williams, Linda 1946- ... 110
Williams, Linda 1948- ... SATA 59
Williams, Liza 1928- ... 102
Williams, Loring G. 1924-1974 ... CAP-2
Earlier sketch in CA 29-32
Williams, Louise Bonino 1904(?)-1984 Obituary ... 114
See also SATA 39
Williams, Lovett E(dward) Jr. 1935- ... 109
Williams, Lynn
See Hale, Arlene
Williams, Marcia 1932- ... 123
Williams, Margaret (Anne) 1902- ... 21-24R
Williams, Margaret (Vyner) 1914- ... 25-28R
Williams, Mark 1951- ... 138
Williams, Martha E(thelyn) 1934- ... 125
Williams, Martin 1924- ... 49-52
Obituary ... 137
Williams, Mary Alice 1949- Brief entry ... 123
Williams, Mary C(ameron) 1923- ... 57-60
Williams, Mary Elizabeth 1909-1976 Obituary ... 65-68
Williams, Mary McGee 1925- ... 25-28R
Williams, Mary Pat 1946- ... 112
Williams, Mason 1938- ... 25-28R
Williams, Maureen 1951- ... 85-88
See also SATA 12
Williams, Melvin D(onald) 1933- ... 73-76
Williams, Merryn 1944- ... CANR-15
Earlier sketch in CA 41-44R
Williams, Michael
See St. John, Wylly Folk
Williams, Michael 1935- ... 133
Williams, Miller 1930- ... 13-16R
See also DLB 105
Williams, Mona (Goodwyn) 1916- ... 81-84
Williams, Nancy M(argaret) 1929- ... 122
Williams, Ned 1909- ... 13-16R
Williams, Neville (John) 1924-1977 Obituary ... 111
Williams, Noel Trevor St. John 1918- ... 41-44R
Williams, Norman 1952- ... 118
See also CLC 39
Williams, Oliver F(ranklin) 1939- ... CANR-35
Earlier sketch in CA 114
Williams, Oliver P(erry) 1925- ... 37-40R
Williams, Ora (Ruby) 1926- ... 73-76
Williams, Oscar 1900-1964 ... CANR-6
Earlier sketch in CA 1-4R
Williams, Otis (C.) 1941- ... 130
Williams, P(eter) F(airney) 1931- ... 121
Williams, Patrick J.
See Butterworth, W(illiam) E(dmund III)
Williams, Patrick 1950- ... 129
Williams, Patti 1936- ... 73-76
Williams, Paul (Hamilton) 1940- ... 121
Williams, Paul O(sborne) 1935- ... CANR-24
Earlier sketch in CA 106
Williams, Paul (Revere) 1894-1980 Obituary ... 93-96
Williams, Paul (Steven) 1948- ... 81-84
Williams, Penry (Herbert) 1925- ... 128
Williams, Pete
See Faulknor, Cliff(ord Vernon)
Williams, Peter W(illiam) 1944- ... CANR-30
Earlier sketch in CA 112
Williams, Peter 1937- ... 138
Williams, Philip Lee 1950- ... 129
Williams, Philip Maynard 1920-1984 Obituary ... 114
Williams, Philip W(alter) 1941- ... CANR-11
Earlier sketch in CA 69-72
Williams, Phyllis S(awyer) 1931- ... 65-68
Williams, Ralph Mehlin 1911- ... 5-8R
Williams, Ralph Vaughan
See Vaughan Williams, Ralph
Williams, Randall Herbert Monier
See Monier-Williams, Randall Herbert
Williams, Raymond (Brady) 1935- ... 132
Williams, Raymond (Henry) 1921-1988 ... CANR-33
Obituary ... 124
Earlier sketch in CA 21-24R
See also DLB 14
See also MTCW
Williams, Rebecca (Yancy) 1899-1976 Obituary ... 65-68
Williams, Richard Hays 1912- ... CANR-2
Earlier sketch in CA 1-4R
Williams, Richard Lippincott 1910- ... 101
Williams, Robert C. 1938- ... CANR-14
Earlier sketch in CA 37-40R
Williams, Robert Coleman 1940- ... 21-24R
Williams, Robert Deryck 1917-1986 ... 103
Obituary ... 120
Williams, Robert G. 1948- ... 125
Williams, Robert Hugh 1907(?)-1983 Obituary ... 109
Williams, Robert L(ewis) 1903- ... CANR-10
Earlier sketch in CA 13-16R
Williams, Robert Moore 1907-1977 Obituary ... 102
Williams, Robert P. 1906(?)-1977 Obituary ... 69-72
Williams, Robin M(urphy) Jr. 1914- ... 13-16R
Williams, Roger J(ohn) 1893-1988 ... CANR-7
Obituary ... 124
Earlier sketch in CA 17-20R
Williams, Roger L(awrence) 1923- Brief entry ... 112
Williams, Roger M(iller) 1934- ... 37-40R
Williams, Roger Neville 1943- ... 37-40R
Williams, Roger 1603(?)-1683 ... DLB 24
Williams, Ronald Ralph 1906-1979 ... CANR-7
Earlier sketch in CA 13-16R
Williams, Rosalind
See Fergusson, Rosalind (Joyce)
Williams, Rosalind H. 1944- ... 109
Williams, Rose
See Ross, W(illiam) E(dward) D(aniel)
Williams, Rowan (Douglas) 1950- ... 128
Williams, Russell J(ohn) 1944- ... 104
Williams, Samm-Art
See Williams, Samuel Arthur
See also DLB 38
Williams, Samuel Arthur 1946- ... 123
Brief entry ... 117
See also Williams, Samm-Art
See also BW
Williams, Selma R(uth) 1925- ... CANR-1
Earlier sketch in CA 49-52
See also SATA 14
Williams, Sherley Anne 1944- ... CANR-25
Earlier sketch in CA 73-76
See also BLC 3
See also BW
See also DLB 41
Williams, Shirley
See Williams, Sherley Anne
Williams, Simon 1943- ... 133
Williams, Slim
See Williams, Clyde C.
Williams, Stanley W. 1917- ... 17-20R
Williams, Stephen 1926- Brief entry ... 114
Williams, Stirling B(acot) Jr. 1943- ... 29-32R
Williams, Strephon Kaplan 1934- ... CANR-20
Earlier sketch in CA 102
Williams, Suzanne (Bullock) 1953- ... SATA 71
Williams, T(erence) C(harles) 1925- ... 29-32R
Williams, T(homas) David 1929- ... 123
Williams, T(homas) Harry 1909-1979 ... CANR-3
Earlier sketch in CA 1-4R
See also DLB 17
Williams, Tennessee 1911-1983 ... CANR-31
Obituary ... 108
Earlier sketch in CA 5-8R
See also CABS 3
See also AITN 1, 2
See also CDALB 1941-1968
See also CLC 1, 2, 5, 7, 8, 11, 15, 19, 30, 39, 45, 71
See also DLB 7
See also DLBD 4
See also DLBY 83
See also MTCW
See also WLC
Williams, Theodore C(urtis) 1930- ... 69-72
Williams, Thomas (Alonzo) 1926-1990 ... CANR-2
Obituary ... 132
Earlier sketch in CA 1-4R
See also CLC 14
Williams, Thomas (Andrew) 1931- ... 49-52
Williams, Thomas Howard 1935- ... 13-16R
Williams, Tina
See Wiles, Domini
Williams, Trevor Illtyd 1921- ... 109
Williams, Ursula Moray
See Moray Williams, Ursula
See also SATA 3
Williams, (George) Valentine 1883-1946 Brief entry ... 111
See also DLB 77
Williams, Vera B. 1927- ... CANR-38
Earlier sketch in CA 123
See also CLR 9
See also MAICYA
See also SATA 33, 53
Williams, Vergil L(ewis) 1935- ... CANR-9
Earlier sketch in CA 57-60
Williams, Wallace Edward 1926- Brief entry ... 105
Williams, Walter
See Williams, Walter E(dward)
Williams, Walter E(dward) 1936- Brief entry ... 123
Williams, Walter G(eorge) 1903- ... CAP-1
Earlier sketch in CA 13-16
Williams, Walter L(ee) 1948- ... 127
Williams, (Margaret) Wetherby ... CANR-3
Earlier sketch in CA 45-48
Williams, Willard F(orest) 1921- ... 13-16R
Williams, William Appleman 1921-1990 ... CANR-3
Obituary ... 131
Earlier sketch in CA 1-4R
See also DLB 17
Williams, William C.
See Williams, William Carlos
Williams, William Carlos 1883-1963 ... CANR-34
Earlier sketch in CA 89-92
See also CDALB 1917-1929
See also CLC 1, 2, 5, 9, 13, 22, 42, 67
See also DLB 4, 16, 54, 86
See also MTCW
Williams, William David 1917- ... 5-8R
Williams, William H(enry) 1936- ... CANR-36
Earlier sketch in CA 69-72
Williams, William P(roctor) 1939- ... CANR-23
Earlier sketch in CA 45-48
Williams, Wirt (Alfred Jr.) 1921-1986 ... 9-12R
Obituary ... 119
See also DLB 6
Williams-Ellis, (Mary) Amabel (Nassau Strachey) 1894-1984 ... 105
Obituary ... 114
See also SATA 29, 41
Williams-Ellis, Clough 1883- ... 13-16R
Williamson, Alan (Bacher) 1944- ... 57-60
Williamson, Anthony George 1932- ... 101
Williamson, Audrey (May) 1913-1986(?) ... CANR-3
Obituary ... 118
Earlier sketch in CA 49-52
Williamson, Bruce 1893-1984 Obituary ... 111
Williamson, Bruce 1930- ... 101
Williamson, Chilton Jr. 1947- ... 102
Williamson, Chilton 1916- ... 13-16R
Williamson, Claude C(harles) H. 1891- ... CAP-1
Earlier sketch in CA 17-18
Williamson, Craig (Burke) 1943- ... CANR-16
Earlier sketch in CA 29-32R
Williamson, David (Geoffrey) 1927- ... 134
Williamson, David Keith 1942- ... 103
See also CLC 56
Williamson, David L(ouis) 1937- ... 111
Williamson, Doug 1944- ... 136
Williamson, Duncan 1928- ... 123
Williamson, Edward 1908-1984 Obituary ... 113
Williamson, Ellen Douglas 1905-1984 ... CANR-39
Obituary ... 114
Earlier sketch in CA 17-20R
Williamson, Eugene L. (Jr.) 1930- ... 9-12R
Williamson, Geoffrey 1897- ... 9-12R
Williamson, Gerald Neal 1932- ... CANR-34
Earlier sketch in CA 112
Williamson, Glen 1909- ... CANR-9
Earlier sketch in CA 57-60
Williamson, H(enry) D(arvall) 1907- ... 65-68
Williamson, Harold Francis 1901- ... 5-8R
Williamson, Henry 1895-1977 ... CANR-36
Obituary ... 73-76
Earlier sketch in CA 81-84
See also MTCW
See also SATA 30, 37
Williamson, J. N.
See Williamson, Gerald Neal
Williamson, J. Peter 1929- ... CANR-6
Earlier sketch in CA 1-4R
Williamson, Jack
See Williamson, John Stewart
See also CAAS 8
See also CLC 29
See also DLB 8
Williamson, Jeffrey G(ale) 1935- ... CANR-39
Earlier sketches in CA 85-88, CANR-18
Williamson, Joanne Small 1926- ... 13-16R
See also SATA 3
Williamson, John Butler 1943- ... 89-92
Williamson, John G(rant) 1933- ... 45-48
Williamson, John (Gordon) 1949- ... 138
Williamson, John Stewart 1908- ... CANR-23
Earlier sketch in CA 17-20R
See also Williamson, Jack
Williamson, Joseph 1895-1988 ... CAP-1
Obituary ... 125
Earlier sketch in CA 11-12
Williamson, Juanita V. 1917- ... 37-40R
Williamson, Karina 1928- ... 127
Williamson, Lamar Jr. 1926- ... 89-92
Williamson, Moncrieff 1915- ... 102
Williamson, Norma (Goff) 1934- ... 65-68
Williamson, Oliver E(aton) 1932- ... 81-84
Williamson, Porter B(eyers) 1916- ... CANR-28
Earlier sketch in CA 110
Williamson, Rene de Visme 1908- ... CANR-13
Earlier sketches in CAP-1, CA 17-18
Williamson, Richard 1930- ... 37-40R
Williamson, Richard 1935- ... 109
Williamson, Robert C(lifford) 1916- ... 21-24R
Williamson, Robin (Duncan Harry) 1943- ... 102
Williamson, Robin (Martin Eyre) 1938- ... 29-32R
Williamson, Stanford Winfield 1916- ... 5-8R
Williamson, Tony
See Williamson, Anthony George
Williamson, William Bedford 1918- ... CANR-6
Earlier sketch in CA 1-4R
Williamson, William Landram 1920- ... 9-12R
Willie, Charles V(ert) 1927- ... CANR-31
Earlier sketches in CA 41-44R, CANR-14
Willie, Frederick
See Lovecraft, H(oward) P(hillips)
Willig, George 1949- ... 102
Willig, John M. 1913-1982 Obituary ... 107
Willig, Rosette F. 1950- ... 114
Willimon, William H(enry) 1946- ... 106
Willing, Jules Z. 1914-1981 ... 108
Willing, Martha Kent 1920- ... 37-40R
Willingham, Calder (Baynard Jr.) 1922- ... CANR-3
Earlier sketch in CA 5-8R
See also CLC 5, 51
See also DLB 2, 44
See also MTCW
Willingham, John J. 1935- ... 37-40R
Willingham, John R(obert) 1919- ... 17-20R
Willings, David 1932- ... 111
Willis, (George) Anthony Armstrong 1897-1976 ... 69-72
Willis, Arthur J(ames) 1895-1983 ... CANR-5
Obituary ... 111
Earlier sketch in CA 5-8R
Willis, Charles
See Clarke, Arthur C(harles)
Willis, Cleve E(dward) 1942- ... 123
Brief entry ... 118
Willis, Connie 1945- ... CANR-35
Earlier sketch in CA 114
Willis, Corinne Denneny ... 21-24R
Willis, Donald C(halmers) 1947- ... CANR-15
Earlier sketch in CA 41-44R
Willis, Donald J. 1919- ... 127
Willis, E(dward) David 1932- ... 37-40R
Willis, Edgar E(rnest) 1913- ... 5-8R
Willis, Edward Henry
See Willis, Ted
Willis, Ellen Jane 1941- ... 106
Willis, F(rank) Roy 1930- ... 13-16R
Willis, Irene 1929- ... CANR-10
Earlier sketch in CA 65-68
Willis, James 1928- ... 109
Willis, Jeanne (Mary) 1959- ... 128
See also SATA 61
Willis, Jerry W. 1943- ... 85-88
Willis, John A(lvin) 1916- ... 17-20R
Willis, John H(oward) Jr. 1929- ... 37-40R
Willis, John Ralph 1938- ... 121
Willis, Margaret 1899- ... CANR-19
Earlier sketches in CA 5-8R, CANR-3
Willis, Maud
See Lottman, Eileen
Willis, Meredith Sue 1946- ... CANR-16
Earlier sketch in CA 85-88
Willis, Nathaniel Parker 1806-1867 ... DLB 3, 59, 73, 74
Willis, Resa 1949- ... 138
Willis, Roy (Geoffrey) 1927- ... CANR-17
Earlier sketch in CA 77-80
Willis, Samuel
See Parker, Hershel
Willis, Sharon O(zell) 1938- ... 37-40R
Willis, Stanley E. II 1923- ... 21-24R
Willis, Ted 1918- ... CANR-23
Earlier sketches in CA 9-12R, CANR-7
Willis, Val 1946- ... 130
Willis, Wayne 1942- ... 29-32R
Willison, George F(indlay) 1896-1972 ... CAP-1
Obituary ... 37-40R
Earlier sketch in CA 13-14
Willison, Marilyn Murray 1948- ... 105
Willke, John Charles 1925- ... CANR-24
Earlier sketches in CA 65-68, CANR-9
Willkens, William H(enry) R(obert) 1919- ... 21-24R
Willmington, Harold L. 1932- ... 49-52
Willmott, Peter 1923- ... 21-24R
Willmott, Phyllis 1924- ... 117
Willner, Ann Ruth 1924- ... 21-24R
Willner, Dorothy 1927- ... 53-56
Willnow, Ronald D. 1933- ... 77-80
Willock, Colin 1919- ... CANR-10
Earlier sketch in CA 13-16R
Willock, Ruth ... 13-16R
Willoughby, Cass
See Olsen, T(heodore) V(ictor)
Willoughby, Charles Andrew 1892-1972 Obituary ... 104
Willoughby, David P(atrick) 1901- ... 37-40R
Willoughby, Elaine Macmann 1926- ... 101
Willoughby, Glynn
See Allentuck, Andrew
Willoughby, Hugh
See Harvey, Nigel
Willoughby, Lee Davis
See Avallone, Michael (Angelo, Jr)
and Brandner, Gary
and DeAndrea, William L(ouis)
and Toombs, John
and Webb, Jean Francis
Willoughby, William Reid 1910- ... 1-4R
Willrich, Mason 1933- ... 77-80
Willrich, Ted L. 1924- ... 29-32R
Wills, A(lfred) J(ohn) 1927- ... 21-24R
Wills, Christopher 1938- ... 132
Wills, David Hilary 1904-1985 Obituary ... 117
Wills, Garry 1934- ... CANR-1
Earlier sketch in CA 1-4R

Wills, Geoffrey
See Staal, Cyril
Wills, Jean 1929- CANR-22
Earlier sketch in CA 105
Wills, John E(lliot) Jr. 1936- 45-48
Wills, Jonathan 1947- 69-72
Wills, Maurice Morning 1932- Brief entry 105
Wills, Maury
See Wills, Maurice Morning
Wills, Millicent A(gatha)
1901(?)-1988 Obituary 125
Wills, Philip Aubrey 1907-1978 81-84
Wills, Thomas
See Ard, William (Thomas)
Willson, A(mos) Leslie Jr. 1923- 9-12R
Willson, Mary F(rances) 1938- 129
Willson, Meredith 1902-1984 49-52
Obituary 113
Willson, Robina Beckles
See Beckles Willson, Robina (Elizabeth)
See also SATA 27
Willumsen, Dorrit (Kirsten) 1940- 131
Willwerth, James 1943- 57-60
Willy
See Colette, (Sidonie-Gabrielle)
Willy, Colette
See Colette, (Sidonie-Gabrielle)
Willy, Margaret (Elizabeth) 1919- 9-12R
Wilma, Dana
See Faralla, Dana
Wilmer, Clive 1945- 130
Brief entry 122
See also DLB 40
Wilmer, Dale
See Miller, (H.) Bill(y)
and Wade, Robert (Allison)
Wilmer, Valerie (Sybil) 1941- 85-88
Wilmerding, John 1938- 111
Wilmeth, Don B(urton) 1939- CANR-19
Earlier sketch in CA 102
Wilmore, Gayraud S(tephen Jr.) 1921- 134
Brief entry 114
Wilmore, Jack H(arrison) 1938- 129
Wilmore, Sylvia (Joan) Bruce 1914- 89-92
Wilmot, Anthony 1933- 77-80
Wilmot, William (Wallace) 1943- CANR-7
Earlier sketch in CA 57-60
Wilms, Barbara 1941- 57-60
Wilmshurst, Rea 1941- 127
Wilmut, Roger (Francis) 1942- CANR-19
Earlier sketch in CA 102
Wilner, Eleanor 1937- CANR-37
Earlier sketches in CA 93-96, CANR-16
Wilner, Herbert 1925-1977 ....CANR-3
Earlier sketch in CA 45-48
Wilroy, Mary Edith (Farr)
1910-1987 Obituary 122
Wilsher, Ann
See Henisch, Bridget Ann
Wilshire, Bruce W(ithington) 1932- 77-80
Wilson, A(lfred) Jeyaratnam 1928- CANR-12
Earlier sketch in CA 61-64
Wilson, A(ndrew) N(orman) 1950- 122
Brief entry 112
See also CLC 33
See also DLB 14
Wilson, Abraham 1899(?)-1983 Obituary 110
Wilson, Adrian 1923-1988 132
Obituary 125
Wilson, Alison M. 1932- 120
Wilson, Alton H(orace) 1925- 61-64
Wilson, Andrew 1923- 29-32R
Wilson, Angus (Frank Johnstone)
1913-1991 ....CANR-21
Obituary 134
Earlier sketch in CA 5-8R
See also CLC 2, 3, 5, 25, 34
See also DLB 15
See also MTCW
Wilson, Arthur M(cCandless) 1902-1979 61-64
Obituary 89-92
Wilson, Arthur 1595-1652 ....DLB 58
Wilson, August 1945- 122
Brief entry 115
See also BLC 3
See also BW
See also CLC 39, 50, 63
See also DC 2
See also MTCW
Wilson, Augusta Jane Evans
1835-1909 ....DLB 42
Wilson, Barbara
See Janifer, Laurence M(ark)
Wilson, Barbara Ker
See Ker Wilson, Barbara
Wilson, Beth P(ierre) CANR-1
Earlier sketch in CA 49-52
See also SATA 8
Wilson, Betty 1923- 97-100
Wilson, Brian 1942- ....CLC 12
Wilson, Bryan R(onald) 1926- CANR-19
Earlier sketches in CA 5-8R, CANR-3
Wilson, Budge 1927- 121
See also Wilson, Marjorie
See also SATA 55
Wilson, Callie C(oe) 1917- 124
Wilson, Camilla Jeanne 1945- 61-64
Wilson, Cammy
See Wilson, Camilla Jeanne
Wilson, Carlos 1941- 61-64
Wilson, Carole
See Wallmann, Jeffrey M(iner)
Wilson, Carolyn 1938- 21-24R
Wilson, Carroll L(ouis) 1910-1983 89-92
Obituary 109
Wilson, Carter 1941- 17-20R
See also SATA 6
Wilson, Catherine 1951- 132
Wilson, (Lindsay) Charles 1932- 65-68
Wilson, Charles McMoran 1882-1977 ....CAP-2
Obituary 69-72
Earlier sketch in CA 21-22
Wilson, Charles Morrow 1905-1977 ....CANR-4
Earlier sketch in CA 5-8R
See also SATA 30
Wilson, Charles (P.) 1939- 135
Wilson, Charles Reagan 1948- 105
Wilson, Chris(topher Paul) 1949- 125
Wilson, Christine
See Geach, Christine
Wilson, Christopher B.
1910(?)-1985 Obituary 117
See also SATA 46
Wilson, Clifford (Allan) 1923- 93-96
Wilson, Clifton E. 1919- 21-24R
Wilson, Clyde N(orman Jr.) 1941- 116
Wilson, Colin 1931- CANR-33
Earlier sketches in CA 1-4R, CANR-1, 22
See also CAAS 5
See also CLC 3, 14
See also DLB 14
See also MTCW
Wilson, Craig R. 1947- 57-60
Wilson, Crane
See O'Brien, Cyril C(ornelius)
Wilson, D. A.
See Wilson, Derek (Alan)
Wilson, D(udley) B(utler) 1923- 21-24R
Wilson, Dagmar 1916- ....SATA 31
Wilson, Dale 1894-1987 ....CAP-1
Obituary 121
Earlier sketch in CA 13-14
Wilson, Daniel J(oseph) 1949- 117
Wilson, Dave
See Floren, Lee
Wilson, David
See MacArthur, D(avid) Wilson
Wilson, David Allen 1926- CANR-7
Earlier sketch in CA 5-8R
Wilson, (Anthony) David 1927- 97-100
Wilson, David Henry 1937- CANR-32
Earlier sketch in CA 113
Wilson, David L(ee) 1943- 112
Wilson, David Scofield 1931- 106
Wilson, David 1942- CANR-38
Earlier sketches in CA 93-96, CANR-16
Wilson, Deirdre (Susan Moir) 1941- 97-100
Wilson, Derek A.
See Wilson, Derek (Alan)
Wilson, Derek (Alan) 1935- 123
Brief entry 115
Wilson, Dick
See Wilson, Richard Garratt
Wilson, Dirk
See Pohl, Frederik
Wilson, Don(ald) 1932- 81-84
Wilson, Don W(hitman) 1942- 61-64
Wilson, (Alan) Doric 1939- 129
Wilson, Dorothy Clarke 1904- CANR-6
Earlier sketch in CA 1-4R
See also SATA 16
Wilson, Douglas L. 1935- 37-40R
Wilson, (Archibald) Duncan 1911- 103
Wilson, E(dward) Raymond 1896-1987 61-64
Obituary 122
Wilson, Earl (Dean) 1939- 118
Wilson, (Harvey) Earl 1907-1987 69-72
Obituary 121
Wilson, Edmund 1895-1972 ....CANR-1
Obituary 37-40R
Earlier sketch in CA 1-4R
See also CLC 1, 2, 3, 8, 24
See also DLB 63
See also MTCW
Wilson, Edward A(rthur)
1886-1970 Obituary 116
See also SATA 38
Wilson, Edward M(eryon)
1906-1977 Obituary 114
Wilson, Edward O(sborne) 1929- CANR-16
Earlier sketch in CA 61-64
See also CAAS 16
See also MTCW
Wilson, Edward T(homas) 1941- 129
Wilson, Elena 1907(?)-1979 Obituary 89-92
Wilson, Elizabeth Z. 1951- 123
Wilson, Ellen (Janet Cameron) 49-52
Obituary 103
See also SATA 9, 26
Wilson, Eric (H.) 1940- CANR-20
Earlier sketch in CA 101
See also SATA 32, 34
Wilson, Erica CANR-23
Earlier sketches in CA 53-56, CANR-7
See also SATA 51
Wilson, Erle (Alexander Mann) 1898- 5-8R
Wilson, Ernest Charles 1896- 29-32R
Wilson, Ethel Davis (Bryant) 1888(?)-1980 102
See also CLC 13
See also DLB 68
See also MTCW
Wilson, Eugene E. 1887(?)-1974 Obituary 49-52
Wilson, Eugene Smith 1905-1981 Obituary 103
Wilson, Evan M(orris) 1910-1984 129
Obituary 112
Wilson, Everett K(eith) 1913- 93-96
Wilson, F(rank) P(ercy) 1889-1963 ....CANR-1
Earlier sketch in CA 1-4R
Wilson, F(rancis) Paul 1946- 138
Wilson, Forbes (Kingsbury) 1910- 126
Brief entry 112
Wilson, Forrest 1918- CANR-7
Earlier sketch in CA 53-56
See also SATA 27
Wilson, Fran
See Wilson, Frances Engle
Wilson, Frances Engle 1922- 130
Wilson, Francesca Mary
1888-1981 Obituary 103
Wilson, Francis Graham
1901-1976 Obituary 65-68
Wilson, Frank (Avray) 1914- CAP-1
Earlier sketch in CA 11-12
Wilson, Frank J. 1887-1970 ....CAP-1
Earlier sketch in CA 13-16
Wilson, Frank L(eondus) 1941- 57-60
Wilson, Fred 1937- 37-40R
Wilson, G(eorge) B(ulkeley) L(aird)
1908-1984 111
Obituary 114
Wilson, Gahan 1930- CANR-19
Earlier sketch in CA 25-28R
See also SATA 27, 35
Wilson, Garff B(ell) 1909- 45-48
Wilson, George C. 1927- 124
Wilson, George M(acklin) 1937- 25-28R
Wilson, George W(ilton) 1928- CANR-7
Earlier sketch in CA 17-20R
Wilson, Gina 1943- 106
See also SATA 34, 36
Wilson, Glenn Daniel 1942- CANR-21
Earlier sketch in CA 104
Wilson, (Leslie) Granville 1912- CANR-11
Earlier sketch in CA 69-72
See also SATA 14
Wilson, Gregory
See DeLamotte, Roy Carroll
Wilson, H. W.
See Wilson, Halsey William
Wilson, Halsey William
1868-1954 Brief entry 118
Wilson, (James) Harold 1916- CANR-16
Earlier sketch in CA 53-56
Wilson, Harold Stacy 1935- 41-44R
Wilson, Harriet E. Adams
1828(?)-1863(?) ....BLC 3
See also DLB 50
Wilson, Harriett (Charlotte) 1916- CANR-16
Earlier sketch in CA 1-4R
Wilson, Harris W(ard) 1919- 21-24R
Wilson, Harry Leon 1867-1939 Brief entry 108
See also DLB 9
Wilson, Hazel (Hutchins) 1898- CANR-6
Earlier sketch in CA 1-4R
See also SATA 3
Wilson, Helen Helga (Mayne) CANR-4
Earlier sketch in CA 9-12R
Wilson, Helen Van Pelt 1901- 105
Wilson, Howard Allan 1927- Brief entry 106
Wilson, Howard Hazen
1908-1978 Obituary 77-80
Wilson, Ian (William) 1941- 85-88
Wilson, Iris Higbie
See Engstrand, Iris (H.) Wilson
Wilson, Isaiah Herbert 1909-1990 Obituary 131
Wilson, Ivor (Arthur) 1924- CAP-1
Earlier sketch in CA 11-12
Wilson, J(anice) J. 1936- 97-100
Wilson, J(ohn) Tuzo 1908- 45-48
Wilson, Jack 1937- 21-24R
Wilson, Jacqueline 1945- CANR-38
Earlier sketches in CA 45-48, CANR-1, 17
See also SATA 52, 61
Wilson, Jacques M(arcel) P(atrick) 1920- 49-52
Wilson, James C(lyde) 1948- 111
Wilson, James Orville 1895- CAP-1
Earlier sketch in CA 11-12
Wilson, James Q(uinn) 1931- 128
Brief entry 116
Wilson, James Robert 1917- 1-4R
Wilson, James Vernon 1881- CAP-1
Earlier sketch in CA 9-10
Wilson, Jaye 1938- 104
Wilson, Jeanne (Patricia Pauline)
1920- CANR-12
Earlier sketch in CA 69-72
Wilson, Jerry V(ernon) 1928- CANR-7
Earlier sketch in CA 57-60
Wilson, Jim
See Wilson, James Vernon
Wilson, Joan Hoff 1937- 134
Brief entry 105
Wilson, Joe
See Wilson, Joseph T(homas)
Wilson, John A(braham) R(oss) 1911- 41-44R
Wilson, John A. 1900(?)-1976 Obituary 69-72
Wilson, John Boyd 1928- CANR-5
Earlier sketch in CA 9-12R
Wilson, John (Anthony) Burgess 1917- CANR-2
Earlier sketch in CA 1-4R
See also Burgess, Anthony
See also CLC 8, 10, 13
See also MTCW
Wilson, John C.
See Morrow, Felix
Wilson, John Dover 1881-1969 102
Obituary 93-96
Wilson, John F(rederick) 1933- Brief entry 117
Wilson, John Foster 1919- 109
Wilson, John Harold 1900-1982 Obituary 107
Wilson, John Oliver 1938- 129
Wilson, John R. M. 1944- 69-72
Wilson, (Richard) John (McMoran) 1924- 117
Wilson, John Stuart Gladstone 1916- CANR-11
Earlier sketch in CA 13-16R
Wilson, John T(odd) 1914-1990 Obituary 132
Wilson, John 1588-1667 ....DLB 24
Wilson, John 1785-1854 ....DLB 110
Wilson, John 1922- ....SATA 22
Wilson, Joseph T(homas) 1936- 117
Wilson, Joyce M(uriel Judson) CANR-12
Earlier sketch in CA 17-20R
See also SATA 21
Wilson, Julia 1927- 21-24R
Wilson, Jussem
See Wilson, Nelly
Wilson, Justin 116
Wilson, Katharine M(argaret) 1895- 89-92
Wilson, Keith 1927- CANR-9
Earlier sketch in CA 21-24R
See also CAAS 5
Wilson, Keith 1929- 121
Wilson, Kenneth G(eorge) 1923- 5-8R
Wilson, Kenneth L(ee) 1916- 29-32R
Wilson, Kenneth L.
1897(?)-1979 Obituary 85-88
Wilson, L(eland) Craig 1925- 37-40R
Wilson, Lanford 1937- 17-20R
See also CABS 3
See also CLC 7, 14, 36
See also DLB 7
Wilson, Larman C. 1930- CANR-14
Earlier sketch in CA 37-40R
Wilson, Leigh Allison 1957- 117
Wilson, Leonard G(ilchrist) 1928- CANR-7
Earlier sketch in CA 57-60
Wilson, Libby
See Wilson, Elizabeth Z.
Wilson, Lionel 1924- 105
See also SATA 31, 33
Wilson, Logan 1907- 45-48
Wilson, Lois (M.) 1927- 134
Wilson, Louis D(oull) 1917- 93-96
Wilson, Louis Round 1876-1980 Obituary 93-96
Wilson, M(orris) Emett 1894- 5-8R
Wilson, Major L(oyce) 1926- 57-60
Wilson, Margaret Gibbons 1943- 101
Wilson, Margaret (Wilhemina)
1882-1973 Obituary 113
See also DLB 9
Wilson, Margery
See Strayer, Sara Barker
Wilson, Margo 1942- CANR-31
Earlier sketch in CA 110
Wilson, Marie B(eatrice) 1922- 53-56
Wilson, Marjorie
See Wilson, Budge
See also SATA 51
Wilson, Mary
See Roby, Mary Linn
Wilson, Mary C(hristina) 1950- 128
Wilson, Maurice (Charles John) 1914- ......SATA 46
Wilson, (Daphne) Merna 1930- 109
Wilson, Michael 1914-1978 85-88
Obituary 77-80
See also DLB 44
Wilson, Mitchell 1913-1973 ....CANR-3
Obituary 41-44R
Earlier sketch in CA 1-4R
Wilson, Monica Hunter 1908-1982 ....CANR-6
Obituary 108
Earlier sketch in CA 1-4R
Wilson, N(igel) G(uy) 1935- 127
Wilson, N(orman) Scarlyn 1901- CANR-5
Earlier sketch in CA 5-8R
Wilson, Neil 1944- 133
Wilson, Neill C(ompton) 1889- 5-8R
Wilson, Nelly 1930- 106
Wilson, Nick
See Ellis, Edward S(ylvester)
Wilson, Noel Avon 1914- 73-76
Wilson, Pat 1910- CANR-12
Earlier sketch in CA 29-32R
Wilson, Paul C(arroll) 1944- 77-80
Wilson, Paul R(ichard) 1942- Brief entry 109
Wilson, Penelope Coker
See Hall, Penelope C(oker)
Wilson, Peter (Cecil) 1913-1984 Obituary 113
Wilson, Peter N. 1928- 25-28R
Wilson, Phillip (John) 1922- 57-60
Wilson, Phoebe Rous
1924(?)-1980 Obituary 101
Wilson, Phyllis Starr 1928- 69-72
Wilson, R(oger) H(arris) L(ebus) 1920- 13-16R
Wilson, Raymond 1925- CANR-17
Earlier sketch in CA 97-100
Wilson, Richard Garratt 1928- 106
Wilson, Richard Guy 1940- CANR-21
Earlier sketch in CA 93-96
Wilson, Richard Lawson
1905-1981 Obituary 102
Wilson, Richard Trevor 1938- 118
Wilson, Richard W(hittingham) 1933- 73-76
Wilson, Robert Anton 1932- CANR-18
Earlier sketch in CA 65-68
Wilson, Robert (Edward) 1951- 124
Wilson, Robert L. 1925-1991 ....CANR-9
Obituary 134
Earlier sketch in CA 57-60
Wilson, Robert M(ills) 1929- CANR-25
Earlier sketches in CA 21-24R, CANR-9
Wilson, Robert M. 1944- CANR-2
Earlier sketch in CA 49-52
See also CLC 7, 9
See also MTCW
Wilson, Robert McLachlan 1916- 109
Wilson, Robert McLiam 1964- 132
See also CLC 59
Wilson, Robert N(eal) 1924- 17-20R
Wilson, Robert Renbert 1898-1975 ....CANR-23
Earlier sketch in CA 45-48
Wilson, Robin Scott 1928- 101
Wilson, Robley (Conant) Jr. 1930- CANR-14
Earlier sketch in CA 77-80
Wilson, Rodney N. Usher
See Usher-Wilson, Rodney N.
Wilson, Roger Burdett 1919- 45-48

Wilson, Ron(ald William) 1941- 112
  See also SATA 38
Wilson, Ronald E(merson) 1932- 105
Wilson, Rosalind Baker 1923- 132
Wilson, (Edward) Ross (Armitage) 1914- 5-8R
Wilson, Rudy 1950- 136
Wilson, Samuel Jr. 1911- CANR-6
  Earlier sketch in CA 53-56
Wilson, Sandra 1944- 102
Wilson, Sarah 1934- 127
  See also SATA 50
Wilson, Sloan 1920- CANR-1
  Earlier sketch in CA 1-4R
  See also CLC 32
Wilson, Snoo 1948- 69-72
  See also CLC 33
Wilson, Steve 1943- 73-76
Wilson, Theodore A(llen) 1940- 37-40R
Wilson, Thomas C(ave)
  1907-1984 Obituary 112
Wilson, Thomas Williams Jr. 1912- CANR-3
  Earlier sketch in CA 5-8R
Wilson, Tom 1931- 106
  See also SATA 30, 33
Wilson, Trevor (Gordon) 1928- 53-56
Wilson, W(illiam) Harmon 1905- 37-40R
Wilson, Walt(er N.) 1939- 69-72
  See also SATA 14
Wilson, Wayne 1946- 136
Wilson, Wesley M. 1927- 9-12R
Wilson, Wilfrid George 1910- CAP-2
  Earlier sketch in CA 21-22
Wilson, William A(lbert) 1933- 105
Wilson, William E(dward) 1906-1988 .... CANR-2
  Obituary 125
  Earlier sketch in CA 5-8R
Wilson, William H(enry) 1935- 13-16R
Wilson, William J. 1935- CANR-1
  Earlier sketch in CA 45-48
Wilson, William P. 1922- 124
Wilson, William Ritchie 1911- 41-44R
Wilson, William S(mith) 1932- 81-84
  See also CLC 49
Wilson, Woodrow 1856-1924 .... DLB 47
Wilson, Z. Vance 1950- 120
Wilson-Kastner, Patricia 1944- 126
Wilt, David (Edward) 1955- 137
Wilt, Fred(erick Loren) 1920- CANR-9
  Earlier sketch in CA 57-60
Wilt, Judith 1941- CANR-12
  Earlier sketch in CA 57-60
Wiltgen, Ralph M(ichael) 1921- CANR-11
  Earlier sketch in CA 25-28R
Wilton, (James) Andrew (Rutley) 1942- 97-100
Wilton, Elizabeth 1937- CANR-28
  Earlier sketch in CA 69-72
  See also SATA 14
Wilton, Hal
  See Pepper, Frank S.
Wilton-Ely, John 1937- 128
Wiltse, Charles M(aurice) 1907-1990 .... CANR-3
  Obituary 131
  Earlier sketch in CA 1-4R
Wiltse, David 1940- CANR-22
  Earlier sketch in CA 105
Wiltsee, Joseph L. 1920- 110
Wiltz, Chris(tine) 1948- CANR-24
  Earlier sketch in CA 106
Wiltz, John Edward 1930- 9-12R
Wilwerding, Walter Joseph 1891-1966 .... CAP-1
  Earlier sketch in CA 13-16
  See also SATA 9
Wimmer, Larry T(urley) 1935- 101
Wimmer, Mike 1961- .... SATA 70
Wimsatt, James I(rving) 1927- CANR-13
  Earlier sketch in CA 61-64
Wimsatt, W(illiam) K(urtz) Jr.
  1907-1975 .... CANR-3
  Obituary 61-64
  Earlier sketch in CA 1-4R
  See also DLB 63
Winans, A(llan) D(avis Jr.) 1936- CANR-12
  Earlier sketch in CA 57-60
Winans, Christopher 1950- 133
Winans, Edgar Vincent 1930- 5-8R
Winant, Fran 1943- 53-56
Winawer, Bonnie P. (Josephs) 1938- 17-20R
Wincelberg, Shimon 1924- 45-48
Winch, D(avid) M(onk) 1933- 45-48
Winch, Donald N. 1935- 123
Winch, John
  See Campbell, (Gabrielle) Margaret (Vere)
Winch, Michael Bluett 1907- CAP-1
  Earlier sketch in CA 11-12
Winch, Peter G(uy) 1926- 29-32R
Winch, Robert F(rancis) 1911-1977 .... CANR-24
  Earlier sketch in CA 25-28R
Winch, Terence 1945- 93-96
Winchell, Carol Ann 1936- CANR-7
  Earlier sketch in CA 61-64
Winchell, Constance M(abel) 1896-1983 .... CAP-1
  Obituary 109
  Earlier sketch in CA 9-10
Winchell, Wallace 1914- 53-56
Winchell, Walter 1897-1972 101
  Obituary 33-36R
  See also DLB 29
Winchester, A(lbert) M(cCombs) 1908- 41-44R
Winchester, Clarence 1895-1981 Obituary 104
Winchester, James H(ugh) 1917-1985 .... 17-20R
  Obituary 117
  See also SATA 30, 45
Winchester, Otis 1933- 21-24R
Winchester, Simon 1944- 107
Winckelmann, Johann Joachim
  1717-1768 .... DLB 97
Winckler, Paul A(lbert) 1926- 102
Wind, Edgar 1900-1971 Obituary 104
Wind, Herbert Warren 1916- CANR-6
  Earlier sketch in CA 1-4R
Windal, Floyd W(esle 1930- 9-12R
Windchy, Eugene G. 1930- 41-44R
Windeler, Robert 1944- 102
Winder, Alvin E. 1923- 93-96
Winder, George Herbert 1895- CAP-1
  Earlier sketch in CA 11-12
Winder, Mavis Areta 1907- 21-24R
Winder, R(ichard) Bayly 1920-1988 .... 17-20R
  Obituary 126
Winders, Gertrude Hecker CANR-6
  Earlier sketch in CA 1-4R
  See also SATA 3
Windham, Basil
  See Wodehouse, P(elham) G(renville)
Windham, Donald 1920- CANR-6
  Earlier sketch in CA 1-4R
  See also DLB 6
Windham, Douglas M(acArthur) 1943- 29-32R
Windham, Joan 1904- 21-24R
Windham, Kathryn T(ucker) 1918- CANR-11
  Earlier sketch in CA 69-72
  See also SATA 14
Windle, William Frederick 1898-1985 108
  Obituary 115
Windley, Charles Ellis 1942- 65-68
Windmiller, Marshall 1924- 21-24R
Windmuller, John P. 1923- CANR-10
  Earlier sketch in CA 25-28R
Windolph, F(rancis) Lyman 1889-1978 .... 41-44R
Windrich, Elaine 1921- 131
Windrow, Martin
  See Windrow, Martin Clive
Windrow, Martin C.
  See Windrow, Martin Clive
Windrow, Martin Clive 1944- 134
  Brief entry 110
  See also SATA 68
Windsor, Alan 1931- 127
Windsor, Annie
  See Shull, Margaret Anne Wyse
Windsor, Claire
  See Hamerstrom, Frances
Windsor, Duane 1947- 111
Windsor, Duke of
  See Edward VIII
Windsor, Gerard (Charles) 1944- 124
Windsor, Merrill C(ranston Jr.) 1924-1990 113
  Obituary 133
Windsor, Patricia (Frances) 1938- CANR-19
  Earlier sketches in CA 49-52, CANR-4
  See also SATA 30
Windsor, Philip 1935- CANR-8
  Earlier sketch in CA 5-8R
Windsor, Rex
  See Armstrong, Douglas Albert
Windsor, Rudolph R. 1935- Brief entry 107
Windsor, (Bessie) Wallis Warfield (Spencer) Simpson
  1896-1986 Obituary 119
Windsor-Liscombe, Rhodri 1946- 129
Windsor-Richards, Arthur (Bedlington)
  1904- CAP-1
  Earlier sketch in CA 11-12
Wine, Dick
  See Posner, Richard
Wine, Sherwin T. 1928- 93-96
Wineapple, Brenda 1949- 133
Winearls, Jane 1908- 103
Wineberg, Henry J. 1905(?)-1983 Obituary 109
Winebrenner, D(aniel) Kenneth 1908- CAP-1
  Earlier sketch in CA 9-10
Winebrenner, Hubert W. Jr. 1937- 127
Winebrenner, Hugh
  See Winebrenner, Hubert W. Jr.
Winegardner, Mark 1961- 127
Winegarten, Renee 1922- 65-68
Winehouse, Irwin 1922- 9-12R
Winek, Charles L(eone) 1936- 65-68
Winer, Bart 1919(?)-1989 Obituary 127
Winer, Deborah Grace 1961- 136
Winer, Elihu 1914- Brief entry 111
Winer, Richard 1929- CANR-12
  Earlier sketch in CA 73-76
Wines, Roger (Andrew) 1933- 21-24R
Winetrout, Kenneth 1912- 21-24R
Winfield, Arthur M.
  See Stratemeyer, Edward L.
Winfield, Edna
  See Stratemeyer, Edward L.
Winfield, Fairlee E(lizabeth) 1929- 118
Winfield, Gerald Freeman
  1908-1984 Obituary 113
Winfield, Leigh
  See Youngberg, Norma Ione (Rhoads)
Winford, Donald C. 1945- 137
Winfrey, Dorman H(ayward) 1924- 17-20R
Winfrey, John Crawford 1935- 57-60
Winfrey, Lee 1932- 69-72
Wing, Cliff W(aldron) Jr. 1922- 49-52
Wing, Donald G(oddard)
  1904-1972 Obituary 37-40R
Wing, Frances (Scott) 1907- CAP-1
  Earlier sketch in CA 17-18
Wing, George Douglas 1921- 17-20R
Wing, J(ohn) K(enneth) 1923- CANR-28
  Earlier sketch in CA 29-32R
Wing, Jennifer Patai 1942- 57-60
Wing, R. L.
  See Aero, Rita
Wing, Willis Kingsley 1899-1985 Obituary 116
Wingate, (Martha) Anne (Guice) 1943- 116
Wingate, Gifford W(endel) 1925- 65-68
Wingate, Isabel B(arnum) 1901-1987 .... 21-24R
  Obituary 122
Wingate, John (Allan) 1920- CANR-24
  Earlier sketch in CA 77-80
Wingate, John Williams 1899- 9-12R
Wingenbach, Charles E.
  See Wingenbach, Gregory C(harles)
Wingenbach, Gregory C(harles) 1938- 13-16R
Winger, Fred E. 1912- 13-16R
Winger, Howard W(oodrow) 1914- CANR-7
  Earlier sketch in CA 17-20R
Wingert, Paul S. 1900(?)-1974 Obituary 53-56
Wingfield, Sheila (Claude) 1906-1992 130
  Obituary 136
  Brief entry 108
Wingfield Digby, George (Frederick)
  1911-1989 .... CAP-1
  Obituary 127
  Earlier sketch in CA 11-12
Wingler, Hans M(aria) 1920- CANR-14
  Earlier sketch in CA 29-32R
Wingo, E(lvis) Otha 1934- 37-40R
Wingo, Glenn Max 1913- 5-8R
Wingo, T(ullius) Lowdon Jr. 1923- 21-24R
Wingo, Walter (Scott) 1931- 81-84
Wingren, Gustaf F(redrik) 1910- 13-16R
Wingrove, David (John) 1954- 133
  See also CLC 68
Winick, Charles 1922- 134
  Brief entry 109
Winick, Myron 1929- 107
Winick, Steven 1944- 61-64
Wink, Richard L(ee) 1930- 93-96
Wink, Walter Philip 1935- CANR-36
  Earlier sketches in CA 37-40R, CANR-15
Winkelman, Donald M. 1934- 41-44R
Winkler, Allan M(ichael) 1945- 81-84
Winkler, Anthony C. 1942- 123
Winkler, Bee (Finkelberg) 1919- 13-16R
Winkler, Erhard M(ario) 1921- 89-92
Winkler, Franz E. 1907- 5-8R
Winkler, Henry R(alph) 1916- CANR-10
  Earlier sketch in CA 17-20R
Winkler, John J(oseph)
  1943-1990 Obituary 131
Winkler, Paul 1898-1982 Obituary 107
Winkler, Win Ann 1935- 73-76
Winkless, Nels(on Brock) III 1934- 57-60
Winks, Donald 1928- 25-28R
Winks, Robin William 1930- CANR-30
  Earlier sketches in CA 5-8R, CANR-3
  See also SATA 61
Winkworth, Stephen 1939- 127
Winn, Albert Curry 1921- 106
Winn, Alison
  See Wharmby, Margot
Winn, Charles S. 1932- CANR-23
  Earlier sketch in CA 69-72
Winn, Chris 1952- 117
  See also SATA 42
Winn, Ira Jay 1929- 57-60
Winn, James Anderson 1947- 120
Winn, Janet Bruce 1928- 105
  See also SATA 43
Winn, Laura Rocke 1902- CAP-1
  Earlier sketch in CA 13-14
Winn, Marie 1936(?)- 111
  See also SATA 38
Winn, Ralph Bubrich 1895- 5-8R
Winn, Rowland (Denys Guy)
  1916-1984 Obituary 114
Winn, Wilkins B(owdre) 1928- 49-52
Winnegrad, Mark Harris 1948- 77-80
Winner, Anna K(ennedy) 1900- 29-32R
Winner, Irene P(ortis) 1923- CANR-14
  Earlier sketch in CA 41-44R
Winner, Michael Robert 1935- 137
Winner, Percy 1899-1974 Obituary 45-48
Winner, Thomas G(ustav) 1917- CANR-15
  Earlier sketch in CA 37-40R
Winner, Viola Hopkins 1928- CANR-4
  Earlier sketch in CA 53-56
Winnett, Fred Victor 1903- 37-40R
Winnett, Thomas 1921- CANR-22
  Earlier sketches in CA 61-64, CANR-7
Winnick, Karen B(eth) B(inkoff) 1946- 73-76
  See also SATA 51
Winnicott, Donald (Woods) 1896-1971 .... CAP-1
  Earlier sketch in CA 13-14
Winnifrith, Thomas John 1938- CANR-25
  Earlier sketch in CA 108
Winnikoff, Albert 1930- 29-32R
Winnington, Alan 1910(?)-1983 Obituary 111
Winnington-Ingram, R(eginald) P(epys)
  1904- 129
Winograd, Terry (Allen) 1946- 128
Winokur, Joan Gelman 1935- 41-44R
Winokur, Jon 1947- 132
Winokur, Stephen 1941- 89-92
Winold, Allen 1929- 17-20R
Winsberg, Morton D. 1930- 13-16R
Winsborough, Hal (Liman) H. 1932- 9-12R
Winsett, Marvin Davis 1902- 1-4R
Winship, Elizabeth 1921- 41-44R
Winship, Laurence Leathe
  1890-1975 Obituary 104
Winslade, William J(oseph) 1941- 118
Winslow, Dean Hendricks Jr.
  1934-1972 .... 37-40R
  Obituary 41-44R
Winslow, Donald
  See Zoll, Donald Atwell
Winslow, Gerald A. 109
Winslow, John Hathaway 1932- 37-40R
Winslow, Martha
  See Rickett, Frances
Winslow, Ola Elizabeth 1885(?)-1977 .... CANR-3
  Obituary 73-76
  Earlier sketch in CA 1-4R
Winslow, Pauline Glen CANR-18
  Earlier sketch in CA 101
Winslow, Pete
  See Winslow, Dean Hendricks Jr.
Winslow, Richard E(lliott) III 1934- 129
Winslow, Robert W(allace)
  1940- Brief entry 108
Winslow, Ron(ald A.) 1949- 103
Winslow, Thyra Samter
  1893-1961 Obituary 89-92
Winslowe, John
  See Richardson, Gladwell
Winslowe, John R.
  See Richardson, Gladwell
Winsor, Justin 1831-1897 .... DLB 47
Winsor, Kathleen 1919- 97-100
Winsor, Mary P(ickard) 1943- 69-72
Winsor, Roy (William) 1912-1987 65-68
  Obituary 122
Winspear, Alban Dewes 1899- 45-48
Winspear, Violet 1928- 122
Winstanley, Michael J. 1949- 129
Winstanley, (Jane) Rita 1955- 128
Winston, Alexander 1909- CAP-2
  Earlier sketch in CA 25-28
Winston, Carl H. 1-4R
Winston, Clara 1921-1983 .... 25-28R
  Obituary 113
  See also SATA 39, 54
Winston, Daoma 1922- CANR-1
  Earlier sketch in CA 45-48
Winston, Douglas Garrett 41-44R
Winston, Eric V(on) A(rthur) 1942- 29-32R
Winston, Henry 1911-1986 Obituary 121
Winston, Kenneth I(rwin) 1940- 117
Winston, Krishna 1944- 104
Winston, Martin Bradley 1948- 118
Winston, Michael R(ussell) 1941- 113
Winston, Mike
  See King, Florence
Winston, R(obert) A(lexander)
  1907-1974 .... CAP-2
  Obituary 49-52
  Earlier sketch in CA 25-28
Winston, Richard 1917-1979 .... 25-28R
  Obituary 93-96
  See also SATA 54
Winston, Sarah 1912- 29-32R
Winstone, H(arry) V(ictor) F(rederick)
  1926- CANR-21
  Earlier sketch in CA 104
Wint, Guy 1910-1969 .... CANR-3
  Earlier sketch in CA 1-4R
Winter, Abigail
  See Schere, Monroe
Winter, Alice 1919- 13-16R
Winter, Bevis (Peter) 1918- CANR-8
  Earlier sketch in CA 5-8R
Winter, Caryl 1944- 117
Winter, Colin O'Brien 1928-1981 Obituary 105
Winter, David Brian 1929- CANR-20
  Earlier sketch in CA 103
Winter, David G(arrett) 1939- 57-60
Winter, Denis 1940- 118
Winter, Douglas E. 1950- 118
Winter, Edward H(enry) 1923- 1-4R
Winter, Elmer L(ouis) 1912- 13-16R
Winter, Gibson 1916- 49-52
Winter, Ginny Linville 1925- CANR-1
  Earlier sketch in CA 1-4R
Winter, Gordon 1912- CANR-14
  Earlier sketch in CA 77-80
Winter, Herbert R(einhold) 1928- 45-48
Winter, J(erry) Alan 1937- 41-44R
Winter, J. M. 1945- 73-76
Winter, John F. 1913- 104
Winter, Kari J. 1960- 137
Winter, Keith 1906-1983 Obituary 109
Winter, Klaus 1928- 29-32R
Winter, Leslie 1940- CANR-6
  Earlier sketch in CA 1-4R
Winter, Michael Morgan 1930- CAP-1
  Earlier sketch in CA 11-12
Winter, Milo (Kendall) 1888-1956 .... SATA 21
Winter, Nathan H. 1926- 21-24R
Winter, Paula Cecelia 1929- 107
  See also SATA 48
Winter, R. R.
  See Winterbotham, R(ussell) R(obert)
Winter, Ralph K(arl Jr.) 1935- 122
  Brief entry 118
Winter, Roger 1931- 37-40R
Winter, Ruth (Nancy G.) 1930- 37-40R
Winter, William D(avid) 1927- 25-28R
Winter, William O(rville) 1918- 49-52
Winterbotham, F(rederick) W(illiam)
  1897-1990 57-60
  Obituary 130
Winterbotham, R(ussell) R(obert)
  1904-1971 .... 1-4R
  Obituary 103
  See also SATA 10
Winterbotham, Russ
  See Winterbotham, R(ussell) R(obert)
Winterfeld, Henry 1901- 77-80
  See also SATA 55
Wintergreen, John P.
  See Ryskind, Morrie
Wintergreen, Warren
  See Adamson, Joseph III
Winterich, John 1891-1970 Obituary 29-32R
Winternitz, Emanuel 1898-1983 .... CANR-20
  Obituary 110
  Earlier sketch in CA 25-28R
Winterowd, W. Ross 1930- 17-20R
Winters, Anne 1939- 122
Winters, Bayla 1921- 21-24R

Winters, Bernice
See Winters, Bayla
Winters, Catherine (Mary) 1951- 118
Winters, Donald L(ee) 1935- 29-32R
Winters, Francis Xavier 1933- 61-64
Winters, J. C.
See Cross, Gilbert B.
Winters, Janet Lewis
See Lewis, Janet
See also CLC 41
See also DLBY 87
Winters, John D(avid) 1917- 9-12R
Winters, Jon
See Cross, Gilbert B.
Winters, Marian 1924-1978 101
Obituary 81-84
Winters, Marjorie
See Henri, Florette
Winters, Mike 1930- 119
Winters, Nina 1944- .... SATA 62
Winters, Rosemary
See Breckler, Rosemary
Winters, Shelley
See Schrift, Shirley
Winters, (Arthur) Yvor 1900-1968 .... CAP-1
Obituary 25-28R
Earlier sketch in CA 11-12
See also CLC 4, 8, 32
See also DLB 48
See also MTCW
Winterson, Jeanette 1959- 136
See also CLC 64
Winterton, Gayle
See Adams, William Taylor
Winterton, Paul 1908- CANR-6
Earlier sketch in CA 5-8R
See also Garve, Andrew
Winther, Barbara 1926- CANR-17
Earlier sketch in CA 97-100
Winther, Oscar Osburn 1903-1970 .... CANR-2
Earlier sketch in CA 1-4R
Winther, Sophus Keith 1893- 5-8R
Winthrop, Elizabeth
See Mahony, Elizabeth Winthrop
Winthrop, Henry 1910- 73-76
Winthrop, John Jr. 1606-1676 .... DLB 24
Winthrop, John 1588-1649 .... DLB 24, 30
Wintle, Anne 29-32R
Wintle, Justin (Beecham) 1949- CANR-13
Earlier sketch in CA 77-80
Winton, Calhoun 1927- 9-12R
Winton, Chester Allen 1941- 89-92
Winton, Harry N(athaniel) M(cQuillian)
1907-1977(?) CANR-29
Earlier sketch in CA 41-44R
Winton, John
See Pratt, John
Winton, Kate Barber
1882(?)-1974 Obituary 53-56
Wintrobe, Maxwell M(yer) 1901-1986 133
Obituary 121
Wintterle, John F(rancis) 1927- 29-32R
Wintz, Cary D. 1943- 137
Wintz, Jack 1936- 109
Winwar, Frances 1900- 89-92
Winward, Stephen Frederick 1911- 9-12R
Winward, (Richard) Walter 1938- 105
Wippel, John Francis 1933- 114
Wippler, Migene Gonzalez
See Gonzalez-Wippler, Migene
Wirkus, Tom E(dward) 1933- 37-40R
Wirsing, Marie E(milia) 1931- 45-48
Wirt, Ann
See Benson, Mildred (Augustine Wirt)
Wirt, Frederick Marshall 1924- CANR-31
Earlier sketch in CA 112
Wirt, Mildred A.
See Benson, Mildred (Augustine Wirt)
Wirt, Sherwood Eliot 1911- CANR-33
Earlier sketches in CA 41-44R, CANR-15
Wirt, William 1772-1834 .... DLB 37
Wirt, Winola Wells 1905(?)-1986 93-96
Obituary 120
Wirtenberg, Patricia Z(arrella) 1932- 61-64
See also SATA 10
Wirth, Arthur G. 1919- CANR-10
Earlier sketch in CA 21-24R
Wirth, Beverly 1938- 118
See also SATA 63
Wirth, John D(avis) 1936- CANR-26
Earlier sketch in CA 29-32R
Wirth, Niklaus 1934- CANR-21
Earlier sketch in CA 105
Wirth, Thomas 1941- 117
Wirths, Claudine (Turner) G(ibson) 1926- 126
See also SATA 64
Wirtz, (William) Willard 1912- 101
Wisberg, Aubrey 1909(?)-1990 97-100
Obituary 131
Wisberg, Marian Aline 1923- 109
Wisbeski, Dorothy (Gross) 1929- 9-12R
Wisbey, Herbert Andrew Jr. 1919- 13-16R
Wischnitzer, Rachel 1885(?)-1989 Obituary 130
Wisdom, (Arthur) John (Terence Dibben)
1904- 25-28R
Wisdom, Kenny
See Grogan, Emmett
Wisdome, Thomas
See Dunbar, Charles Stuart
Wise, Arthur 1923- 9-12R
Wise, Charles C(onrad) Jr. 1913- CANR-9
Earlier sketch in CA 21-24R
Wise, David 1930- CANR-2
Earlier sketch in CA 1-4R
Wise, Ernie
See Wiseman, Ernest
Wise, Gene 1936- 93-96
Wise, Helen Dickerson 1928- Brief entry 106
Wise, Herbert H(erschel) 1928- 108
Wise, James Waterman
1901-1983 Obituary 111
Wise, John E(dward) 1905-1974 .... CAP-1
Obituary 49-52
Earlier sketch in CA 13-16
Wise, John 1652-1725 .... DLB 24
Wise, Leonard 77-80
Wise, Raymond L. 1895- 21-24R
Wise, S(ydney) F(rancis) 1924- CANR-16
Earlier sketch in CA 21-24R
Wise, Stephen S(amuel)
1874-1949 Brief entry 117
Wise, Terence 1935- 89-92
Wise, William 1923- CANR-6
Earlier sketch in CA 13-16R
See also SATA 4
Wise, Winifred E. 25-28R
See also SATA 2
Wisely, Rae 1938- 106
Wiseman, Adele 1928- 77-80
See also DLB 88
Wiseman, Ann (Sayre) 1926- CANR-9
Earlier sketch in CA 65-68
See also SATA 31
Wiseman, Anne Marie (Murray) 1932- 5-8R
Wiseman, B(ernard) 1922- CANR-24
Earlier sketches in CA 5-8R, CANR-8
See also SATA 4
Wiseman, Christopher S(tephen) 1936- 113
Wiseman, David 1916- CANR-30
Earlier sketch in CA 109
See also SATA 40, 43
Wiseman, Donald John 1918- 89-92
Wiseman, Ernest 1925- 129
Wiseman, Francis Jowett 1905- CAP-1
Earlier sketch in CA 13-14
Wiseman, Frederick 1930- .... CLC 20
Wiseman, James R(ichard) 1934- CANR-1
Earlier sketch in CA 45-48
Wiseman, Robert F(rederick) 1935- 77-80
Wiseman, T(imothy) P(eter) 1940- CANR-18
Earlier sketches in CA 45-48, CANR-1
Wiseman, Thomas 1931- 25-28R
Wisenthal, J. L. 1940- 126
Wiser, William 37-40R
Wish, Harvey 1909-1968 .... CANR-3
Earlier sketch in CA 1-4R
Wishard, Armin 1941- 37-40R
Wishart, David J(ohn) 1946- 124
Brief entry 118
Wishart, E(rnest) E(dward)
1902-1987 Obituary 123
Wishart, Henry
See Shepherd, Robert Henry Wishart
Wishinsky, Frieda 1948- 138
See also SATA 70
Wiskemann, Elizabeth Obituary 111
Wisler, G(ary) Clifton 1950- 129
See also SATA 46, 58
Wisler, Gene C(harles) 1920- 9-12R
Wisloff, Carl Johan Fredrik 1908- CAP-1
Earlier sketch in CA 13-14
Wismer, Donald (Richard) 1946- CANR-28
Earlier sketch in CA 109
See also SATA 59
Wisner, Bill
See Wisner, William L.
Wisner, George 1812-1849 .... DLB 43
Wisner, William L. 1914(?)-1983 111
Obituary 110
See also SATA 42
Wisneski, Henry 1940- 57-60
Wisniewski, David 1953- 132
Wisse, Ruth R(oskies) 1936- 37-40R
Wissmann, Ruth Leslie CANR-2
Earlier sketch in CA 5-8R
Wister, John C(aspar) 1887-1982 Obituary 109
Wister, Owen 1860-1938 Brief entry 108
See also DLB 9, 78
See also SATA 62
See also TCLC 21
Wistrich, Robert Solomon 1945- 107
Wiswall, F(rank) L(awrence) Jr. 1939- 29-32R
Wiswell, Ella Lury 1909- 111
Wiswell, Thomas George 1910- CANR-2
Earlier sketch in CA 5-8R
Wiswell, Tom
See Wiswell, Thomas George
Witchel, Dinah B(rown) 1936- 105
Witcombe, R(ick) T(rader) 1943- 132
Witcover, Jules 1927- 25-28R
Witcutt, William Purcell 1907- CAP-1
Earlier sketch in CA 11-12
Witemeyer, Hugh 1939- 25-28R
Witham, (Phillip) Ross 1917- 105
See also SATA 37
Witham, W(illiam) Tasker 1914- 13-16R
Witheford, Hubert 1921- 102
Wither, George 1588-1667 .... DLB 121
Witheridge, Elizabeth P(lumb) 1907- 97-100
Withers, Carl A. 1900-1970 .... CANR-30
Earlier sketch in CA 73-76
See also SATA 14
Withers, Charles W. J. 1954- 128
Withers, E. L.
See Potter, G(eorge) W(illiam Jr.)
Withers, Josephine 1938- 101
Withers, Sara Cook 1924- 17-20R
Withers, William 1905-1987 .... 13-16R
Obituary 121
Witherspoon, Frances
1887(?)-1973 Obituary 45-48
Witherspoon, Irene Murray 1913- CANR-1
Earlier sketch in CA 1-4R
Witherspoon, John 1723-1794 .... DLB 31
Witherspoon, Mary Elizabeth 1919- 77-80
Witherspoon, Naomi Long
See Madgett, Naomi Long
Witherspoon, Thomas E. 1934- 81-84
Witherup, William 1935- 133
Withey, J(oseph) A(nthony) 1918- 25-28R
Withim, Gloria 1929- 112
Withington, William Adriance 1924- CANR-14
Earlier sketch in CA 41-44R
Withorn, Ann 1947- 125
Withrow, Dorothy E. 1910- 21-24R
Withrow, William Henry 1839-1908 .... DLB 99
Witkacy
See Witkiewicz, Stanislaw Ignacy
Witke, Roxane 1938- 69-72
Witker, Kristi 77-80
Witkiewicz, Stanislaw Ignacy
1885-1939 Brief entry 105
See also TCLC 8
Witkin, Erwin 1926- 37-40R
Witkin, Herman A. 1916-1979 .... CANR-1
Earlier sketch in CA 1-4R
Witkin, Lee D(aniel) 1935-1984 Obituary 114
Witkin-Lanoil, Georgia Hope 1943- 120
Witmer, Helen L(eland) 1898-1979 .... CAP-2
Obituary 89-92
Earlier sketch in CA 25-28
Witt, Harold (Vernon) 1923- CANR-39
Earlier sketches in CA 1-4R, CANR-1, 17
Witt, Howell Arthur John 1920- 109
Witt, Hubert 1935- CANR-28
Earlier sketches in CA 65-68, CANR-12
Witt, James F. 1937- 89-92
Witt, John (Clermont) 1907-1982 Obituary 106
Witt, Reginald Eldred 1907-1980 .... 37-40R
Obituary 97-100
Witt, Ronald Gene 1932- 126
Witt, Shirley Hill 1934- CANR-5
Earlier sketch in CA 53-56
See also SATA 17
Wittanen, Etolin 1907- .... SATA 55
Witte, Ann Dryden 1942- CANR-26
Earlier sketch in CA 107
Witte, Glenna Finley 1925- CANR-26
Earlier sketches in CA 13-16R, CANR-10
See also AITN 1
Witte, John 1948- 93-96
Wittels, Harriet Joan 1938- 107
See also SATA 31
Witten, Herbert F. 1920- 5-8R
Witten, Ian H(ugh) 1947- CANR-28
Earlier sketch in CA 111
Wittenberg, Judith Bryant 1938- 102
Wittenberg, Philip 1895-1987 .... CAP-2
Obituary 122
Earlier sketch in CA 23-24
Wittenberg, Rudolph M. 1906-1986 .... CANR-22
Earlier sketch in CA 69-72
Wittermans, Elizabeth (Pino) 17-20R
Witters, Weldon L. 1929- 93-96
Wittfogel, Karl A(ugust)
1896-1988 Obituary 125
Wittgenstein, Ludwig (Josef Johann)
1889-1951 Brief entry 113
Wittich, Claus 1932- 113
Wittich, Walter A(rno) 1910- 49-52
Wittig, Alice J(osephine) 1929- 101
Wittig, Monique 1935(?)- 135
Brief entry 116
See also CLC 22
See also DLB 83
Witting, Clifford 1907- 1-4R
Wittke, Carl (Frederick)
1892-1971 Obituary 29-32R
Wittkofski, Joseph Nicholas 1912- 9-12R
Wittkower, Rudolf 1901-1971 Obituary 33-36R
Wittkowski, Wolfgang 1925- CANR-24
Earlier sketches in CA 61-64, CANR-8
Wittliff, William D. 1940- 123
Wittlin, Alma S(tephanie) 45-48
Wittlin, Jozef 1896-1976 .... CANR-3
Obituary 65-68
Earlier sketch in CA 49-52
See also CLC 25
Wittlin, Thaddeus (Andrew) 1909- CANR-2
Earlier sketch in CA 45-48
Wittman, Sally (Anne Christensen) 1941- 107
See also SATA 30
Wittmer, Joe 1937- 45-48
Wittner, Lawrence S(tephen) 1941- CANR-33
Earlier sketch in CA 25-28R
Witton, Dorothy 73-76
Witton-Davies, Carl(yle) 1913- 9-12R
Wittreich, Joseph Anthony Jr. 1939- CANR-28
Earlier sketches in CA 29-32R, CANR-12
Wittrock, M(erlin) C(arl) 1931- CANR-2
Earlier sketch in CA 49-52
Wittwer, Sylvan Harold 1917- CANR-35
Earlier sketch in CA 114
Witty, Helen E. S(troop) 1921- 105
Witty, Paul 1898-1976 73-76
Obituary 65-68
See also SATA 30, 50
Witty, Robert G(ee) 1906- CAP-2
Earlier sketch in CA 23-24
Witucke, Virginia 1937- 37-40R
Witwer, Andrew S. 1920(?)-1990 Obituary 132
Witze, Claude 1909(?)-1977 Obituary 73-76
Wixman, Ronald 1947- 122
Wixom, Hartt 1933- 120
Wizard, Mariann G(arner) 1946- 37-40R
Wobbe, R(oland) A(rthur) 1938- 102
Woddis, Hillel Chayim Keith
1914- Brief entry 114
Woddis, Jack
See Woddis, Hillel Chayim Keith
Wodehouse, Lawrence 1934- CANR-19
Earlier sketches in CA 53-56, CANR-4
Wodehouse, P(elham) G(renville)
1881-1975 .... CANR-33
Obituary 57-60
Earlier sketches in CA 45-48, CANR-3
See also AITN 2
See also CDBLB 1914-1945
See also CLC 1, 2, 5, 10, 22
See also DLB 34
See also MTCW
See also SATA 22
See also SSC 2
Woden, George
See Slaney, George Wilson
Wodge, Dreary
See Gorey, Edward (St. John)
Wodhams, (Herbert) Jack 1931- 115
Woebcke, Mary-Jane 1933- 25-28R
Woehr, Richard (Arthur) 1942- 57-60
Woehrlin, William F(rederick) 1928- 45-48
Woelfel, James W(arren) 1937- 41-44R
Woelfl, Paul A(loysius) 1913- 17-20R
Woerner, Karl Heinrich 1910-1969 Obituary 110
Woessner, Nina C. 1933- 29-32R
Woessner, Warren (Dexter) 1944- CANR-14
Earlier sketch in CA 37-40R
Woestemeyer, Ina Faye
See Van Noppen, Ina (Faye) W(oestemeyer)
Woestendiek, (William) John (Jr.) 1953- 133
Brief entry 127
Woetzel, Robert K(urt) 1930-1991 .... CANR-6
Obituary 135
Earlier sketch in CA 5-8R
Woffinden, Bob 1948- 135
Wofford, Azile (May) 1896- 5-8R
Wofford, Harris (Llewellyn) 1926- 129
Wofsey, Marvin M(ilton) 1913- 105
Wogaman, J(ohn) Philip 1932- CANR-20
Earlier sketch in CA 25-28R
Wogaman, Philip
See Wogaman, J(ohn) Philip
Wohl, Gerald 1934- 17-20R
Wohl, James P(aul) 1937- 77-80
Wohl, Paul 1901(?)-1985 Obituary 115
Wohl, Robert 1936- 104
Wohlberg, Meg 1905-1990 Obituary 133
See also SATA 41
See also SATO 66
Wohlgelernter, Maurice 1921- CANR-6
Earlier sketch in CA 13-16R
Wohl-Musciny, Ludwig von
See de Wohl, Louis
Wohlmuth, Ed 1935- 124
Wohlrabe, Raymond A. 1900-1977 .... CANR-3
Earlier sketch in CA 1-4R
See also SATA 4
Wohlstetter, Albert J. 1913- 129
Wohmann, Gabriele 1932- .... DLB 75
Woititz, Janet G. CANR-19
Earlier sketch in CA 101
Woito, Robert (Severin) 1937- 120
Woiwode, L.
See Woiwode, Larry (Alfred)
Woiwode, Larry (Alfred) 1941- CANR-16
Earlier sketch in CA 73-76
See also CLC 6, 10
See also DLB 6
Wojahn, David (Charles) 1953- 136
Wojciechowska, Maia (Teresa) 1927- CANR-4
Earlier sketch in CA 9-12R
See also AAYA 8
See also CLC 26
See also CLR 1
See also MAICYA
See also SAAS 1
See also SATA 1, 28
Wojtyla, Karol
See John Paul II, Pope
Wolberg, Arlene Robbins
1907-1989 Obituary 130
Wolberg, Lewis Robert 1905-1988 .... CANR-19
Obituary 124
Earlier sketches in CA 45-48, CANR-2
Wolcot, John 1738-1819 .... DLB 109
Wolcott, Harry F(letcher) 1929- 65-68
Wolcott, Leonard Thompson CANR-28
Earlier sketches in CA 13-16R, CANR-11
Wolcott, Patty 1929- 57-60
See also SATA 14
Wolcott, Roger 1679-1767 .... DLB 24
Wold, Allen L. 1943- CANR-22
Earlier sketch in CA 105
See also SATA 64
Wold, Jo Anne 1938- 61-64
See also SATA 30
Wold, Marguerite Hurrey 1914- 53-56
Wold, Ruth 1923- 37-40R
Woldendorp, R(ichard) 1927- CANR-12
Earlier sketch in CA 29-32R
Woldin, Beth Weiner 1955- 102
See also SATA 34
Woldin, Judd 1925- Brief entry 122
Wolf, Adolf Hungry
See Hungry Wolf, Adolf
Wolf, Arnold Jacob 1924- 29-32R
Wolf, Arnold Veryl 1916-1975 Obituary 104
Wolf, Barbara Herrman 1932- 57-60
Wolf, Bernard 1930- Brief entry 115
See also SATA 37
Wolf, Charlotte (Elizabeth) 1926- 29-32R
Wolf, Christa 1929- 85-88
See also CLC 14, 29, 58
See also DLB 75
See also MTCW
Wolf, Daniel 1955- 136
Wolf, Deborah Goleman 1938- 97-100

Wolf, Donald J(oseph) 1929- 13-16R
Wolf, Edwin II 1911-1991 ....CANR-4
Obituary 133
Earlier sketch in CA 1-4R
Wolf, Eric R(obert) 1923- 17-20R
Wolf, Frank L(ouis) 1924- 57-60
Wolf, Frank 1940- 57-60
Wolf, Fred Alan 1934- 115
Wolf, Frederick
See Dempewolff, Richard F(rederic)
Wolf, George D(ugan) 1923- 29-32R
Wolf, George 1890(?)-1980 Obituary 97-100
Wolf, Harold A. 1923- 13-16R
Wolf, Harvey 1935- 57-60
Wolf, Hazel Catharine 1907- 5-8R
Wolf, Herbert C(hristian) 1923- 13-16R
Wolf, Jack C(lifford) 1922- 57-60
Wolf, Jacqueline 1928- 109
Wolf, John B(aptist) 1907- 9-12R
Wolf, Karl E(verett) 1921- 17-20R
Wolf, Kirsten 1959- 137
Wolf, Leonard 1923- CANR-3
Earlier sketch in CA 49-52
Wolf, Margery 1933- 138
Wolf, Marguerite Hurrey 1914- 53-56
Wolf, Marvin J(ules) 1941- 117
Wolf, Michael D(avid) 1953- 121
Wolf, Miriam Bredow 1895- CAP-1
Earlier sketch in CA 9-10
Wolf, Peter (Michael) 1935- 53-56
Wolf, Ray 1948- 107
Wolf, Robert Charles 1955- 109
Wolf, S. K.
See Wolf, Sarah (Elizabeth)
Wolf, Sarah (Elizabeth) 1936- 132
Wolf, Thomas H(oward) 1916- 69-72
Wolf, William 103
Wolf, William B. 1920- CANR-26
Earlier sketches in CA 17-20R, CANR-10
Wolf, William C(harles) Jr. 1933- 41-44R
Wolf, William J(ohn) 1918- CANR-29
Earlier sketch in CA 111
Wolfbein, Seymour L(ouis) 1915- CANR-6
Earlier sketch in CA 13-16R
Wolfe, Alan 1942- 108
Wolfe, Alvin William 1928- CANR-28
Earlier sketch in CA 1-4R
Wolfe, Bernard 1915-1985 ....CANR-3
Obituary 117
Earlier sketch in CA 1-4R
Wolfe, Bertram D(avid) 1896-1977 ....5-8R
Obituary 69-72
Wolfe, Burton H. 1932- 25-28R
See also SATA 5
Wolfe, Charles Keith 1943- CANR-34
Earlier sketches in CA 77-80, CANR-15
Wolfe, Christopher (F.) 1949- 123
Wolfe, Don Marion 1902-1976 Obituary 65-68
Wolfe, (George) Edgar 1906- CAP-2
Earlier sketch in CA 25-28
Wolfe, Elizabeth
See Lederer, Paul Joseph
Wolfe, Gary K(ent) 1946- 129
Wolfe, Gene (Rodman) 1931- CANR-32
Earlier sketches in CA 57-60, CANR-6
See also CAAS 9
See also CLC 25
See also DLB 8
Wolfe, George C. 1954- ....CLC 49
Wolfe, George Willoughby (Hooper)
1894(?)-1983 Obituary 111
Wolfe, Gerard R(aymond) 1926- CANR-11
Earlier sketch in CA 69-72
Wolfe, Harry Deane 1901-1975 ....41-44R
Wolfe, Harvey 1938- 45-48
Wolfe, Henry C. 1898(?)-1976 Obituary 69-72
Wolfe, Herbert S(now) 1898- CAP-1
Earlier sketch in CA 13-16
Wolfe, J(ames) N(athan)
1927-1988 Obituary 124
Wolfe, James H(astings) 1934- 93-96
Wolfe, Jane 1957- 133
Wolfe, John N. 1910(?)-1974 Obituary 53-56
Wolfe, Josephine Brace 1917- 5-8R
Wolfe, Linda 138
Brief entry 129
See also BEST 90:1
Wolfe, Louis 1905- CANR-3
Earlier sketch in CA 5-8R
See also SATA 8
Wolfe, Margaret Ripley 1947- 128
Wolfe, Martin 1920- 37-40R
Wolfe, Michael
See Williams, Gilbert M.
Wolfe, Michael 1945- 123
Wolfe, Peter (Bernard) 1929-1986 Obituary 121
Wolfe, Peter 1933- CANR-8
Earlier sketch in CA 21-24R
Wolfe, Randolph 1946- CANR-20
Earlier sketch in CA 104
Wolfe, Richard J(ames) 1928- CANR-30
Earlier sketch in CA 110
Wolfe, Rinna (Evelyn) 1925- 105
See also SATA 38
Wolfe, Ron 1945- 109
Wolfe, Roy I. 1917- 13-16R
Wolfe, Sidney M(anuel) 1937- 127
Wolfe, Thomas (Clayton) 1900-1938 132
Brief entry 104
See also CDALB 1929-1941
See also DLB 9, 102
See also DLBD 2
See also DLBY 85
See also MTCW
See also TCLC 4, 13, 29
See also WLC
Wolfe, Thomas Kennerly Jr. 1930- CANR-33
Earlier sketches in CA 13-16R, CANR-9
See also Wolfe, Tom
See also MTCW
Wolfe, Thomas W. 1914- 93-96
Wolfe, Tom
See Wolfe, Thomas Kennerly Jr.
See also AAYA 8
See also AITN 2
See also BEST 89:1
See also CLC 1, 2, 9, 15, 35, 51
Wolfe, (William) Willard 1936- 93-96
Wolfe, Winifred 1929-1981 ....CANR-10
Obituary 105
Earlier sketch in CA 17-20R
Wolfenden, George
See Beardmore, George
Wolfenden, John Frederick 1906-1985 106
Obituary 114
Wolfenstein, E. Victor 1940- 21-24R
Wolfenstein, Martha
1911(?)-1976 Obituary 69-72
Wolfers, Michael 1938- 136
Wolfert, Helen 1904- CAP-2
Earlier sketch in CA 17-18
Wolff, Alexander 1957- ....SATA 63
Wolff, Anthony 1938- 49-52
Wolff, (Jenifer) Ashley 1956- 118
See also SATA 50
Wolff, Charlotte 1904-1986 ....CANR-15
Obituary 120
Earlier sketch in CA 37-40R
Wolff, Cynthia Griffin 1936- 49-52
Wolff, David
See Maddow, Ben
Wolff, Diane 1945- 77-80
See also SATA 27
Wolff, Edward N(athan) 1946- 132
Wolff, Egon 1926- ....HW
Wolff, Ernst 1910- 73-76
Wolff, Geoffrey (Ansell) 1937- CANR-29
Earlier sketch in CA 29-32R
See also CLC 41
Wolff, Hans Walter 1911- 130
Wolff, Helen 1906- 117
Brief entry 113
Wolff, Janet L(oeb) 1924- 5-8R
Wolff, Janet 1943- 77-80
Wolff, John U(lrich) 1932- CANR-18
Earlier sketch in CA 102
Wolff, Jurgen M(ichael) 1948- 57-60
Wolff, Konrad (Martin) 1907-1989 ....37-40R
Obituary 130
Wolff, Kurt H(einrich) 1912- CANR-39
Earlier sketches in CA 49-52, CANR-1, 17
Wolff, Maritta 1918- 17-20R
Wolff, Mary Evaline 1887-1964 Obituary 116
Wolff, Michael 1930- CANR-19
Earlier sketch in CA 25-28R
Wolff, Miles 1945- CANR-14
Earlier sketch in CA 73-76
Wolff, Richard D(avid) 1942- 73-76
Wolff, Robert Jay 1905-1977 ....25-28R
Obituary 73-76
See also SATA 10
Wolff, Robert Lee 1915-1980 Obituary 102
Wolff, Robert Paul 1933- 103
Wolff, Ruth 1909(?)-1972 Obituary 37-40R
Wolff, Sonia
See Levitin, Sonia (Wolff)
Wolff, Tobias (Jonathan Ansell) 1945- 117
Brief entry 114
See also BEST 90:2
See also CLC 39, 64
Wolff, Victoria 1910- 111
Wolff, Virginia Euwer 1937- 107
Wolffe, B. P.
See Wolffe, Bertram (Percy)
Wolffe, Bertram (Percy)
1923(?)-1988 Obituary 124
Wolff-Salin, Mary 1932- 122
Wolfgang, Marvin E(ugene) 1924- 5-8R
Wolfinger, Raymond E(dwin)
1931- Brief entry 112
Wolfle, Dael (Lee) 1906- 49-52
Wolfman, Augustus
1908(?)-1974 Obituary 53-56
Wolfman, Bernard 1924- 41-44R
Wolf-Phillips, Leslie 1929- 21-24R
Wolfram, Walter A. 1941- 29-32R
Wolfskill, George 1921- CANR-1
Earlier sketch in CA 1-4R
Wolfson, Evelyn 1937- ....SATA 62
Wolfson, Harry Austryn 1887-1974 ....CAP-2
Obituary 53-56
Earlier sketch in CA 19-20
Wolfson, Murray 1927- 17-20R
Wolfson, P(incus) J. 1903- 5-8R
Wolfson, Randy M(eyers) 1952- 120
Wolfson, Robert J(oseph) 1925- 93-96
Wolfson, Susan 1947- 120
Wolfson, Victor 1910-1990 ....33-36R
Obituary 131
Wolfthal, Diane (Bette) 1949- 135
Wolgast, Elizabeth H(ankins) 1929- 113
Wolgensinger, Bernard 1935- 37-40R
Wolins, Leroy 1927- 107
Woliston, Jack 1916(?)-1990 Obituary 131
USAitzer, Hilma 1930- CANR-18
Earlier sketch in CA 65-68
See also CLC 17
See also SATA 31
Wolitzer, Meg 1959- CANR-18
Earlier sketch in CA 107
See also AAYA 6
Wolk, Allan 1936- 77-80
Wolkers, Jan (Hendrik) 1925- Brief entry 116
Wolkoff, Judie (Edwards) Brief entry 115
See also SATA 37
Wolkstein, Diane 1942- CANR-32
Earlier sketches in CA 37-40R, CANR-14
See also SATA 7
Woll, Peter 1933- 13-16R
Wollaston, Nicholas 1926- 25-28R
Wolle, Muriel Sibell 1898- CAP-1
Earlier sketch in CA 13-14
Wollheim, Donald A(llen) 1914-1990 ....CANR-19
Obituary 135
Earlier sketches in CA 1-4R, CANR-1
See also SATO 69
Wollheim, Richard Arthur 1923- 101
Wollman, Nathaniel 1915- Brief entry 106
Wollstonecraft, Mary
1759-1797 ....CDBLB 1789-1832
See also DLB 39, 104
Wolman, Benjamin B. 1908- CANR-11
Earlier sketch in CA 13-16R
Wolman, Harold L. 1942- 37-40R
Wolman, William 1927- 1-4R
Wolny, P.
See Janeczko, Paul B(ryan)
Woloch, Isser 1937- CANR-12
Earlier sketch in CA 29-32R
Woloszynowski, Julian
1898-1978 Obituary 85-88
Wolozin, Harold 1920- 37-40R
Wolpe, Berthold (Ludwig)
1905-1989 Obituary 129
Wolpe, Joseph 1915- 17-20R
Wolpert, Stanley A(lbert) 1927- CANR-15
Earlier sketch in CA 21-24R
Wolrige Gordon, Anne 1936- 103
Wolsch, Robert Allen 1925- 57-60
Wolseley, Roland E. 1904- CANR-39
Earlier sketches in CA 1-4R, CANR-1, 17
Wolsk, David 1930- 21-24R
Wolstein, Benjamin 1922- 9-12R
Wolter, Allan B(ernard) 1913- 106
Wolters, O(liver) W(illiam) 1915- 21-24R
Wolters, Raymond 1938- 29-32R
Wolters, Richard A. 1920- CANR-18
Earlier sketches in CA 5-8R, CANR-3
See also SATA 35
Wolterstorff, Nicholas Paul 1932- 69-72
Woltman, Frederick (Enos)
1905-1970 Obituary 89-92
Wolverton, Robert E(arl) 1925- 37-40R
Wolz, Henry G(eorge) 1905- 106
Womack, Brantly 1947- 114
Womack, David A(lfred) 1933- CANR-7
Earlier sketch in CA 53-56
Womack, Don (L.) 1922- 25-28R
Womack, John Jr. 1937- 45-48
Womack, Peter 1952- 128
Womack, Steven (James) 1952- 133
Womack, Thomas Hale 1952- 133
Womble, Vernon G.
1942(?)-1979 Obituary 89-92
Womer, Frank B(urton) 1921- 45-48
Womersley, Peter (John Walter) 1941- 118
Won, Ko
See Ko, Won
Wonder, Alvin
See Lourie, Dick
Wonder, Stevie
See Morris, Steveland Judkins
See also CLC 12
Wonders, Anne
See Passel, Anne W(onders)
Wonders, William C(lare) 1924- 41-44R
Wondratschek, Wolf 1943- ....DLB 75
Wondriska, William 1931- CANR-4
Earlier sketch in CA 1-4R
See also SATA 6
Wong, Bing W. 1922- 73-76
Wong, J(ohn) Y(ue-Wo) 1946- 126
Wong, Jade Snow 1922- 109
See also CLC 17
Wong, Lin Ken 1931- 13-16R
Wong, May 1944- 25-28R
Wong, Molly 1920- 93-96
Wong, Roderick 1932- 65-68
Wonnacott, Paul 1933- 21-24R
Wonnacott, Ronald J(ohnston) 1930- CANR-14
Earlier sketch in CA 29-32R
Wonnacott, Thomas H(erbert) 1935- CANR-14
Earlier sketch in CA 45-48
Wood, A(rthur) Skevington 1916- CANR-18
Earlier sketches in CA 9-12R, CANR-3
Wood, Abigail
See Marks, Jane (A. Steinberg)
Wood, Allen Tate 1947- 97-100
Wood, Allen W(illiam) 1942- CANR-37
Earlier sketches in CA 29-32R, CANR-17
Wood, Anne (Savage) 1937- ....SATA 64
Wood, Audrey 137
See also MAICYA
Wood, Audrey 1905-1985 Obituary 118
See also CLR 26
See also SATA 44, 50
Wood, Barbara 1947- CANR-15
Earlier sketch in CA 85-88
Wood, Bari 1936- CANR-13
Earlier sketch in CA 81-84
Wood, Barry 1940- CANR-36
Earlier sketch in CA 29-32R
Wood, Benjamin 1820-1900 Brief entry 120
See also DLB 23
Wood, Bruce 1943- 57-60
Wood, Bryce 1909-1985(?) CANR-19
Earlier sketch in CA 1-4R
Wood, Catherine
See Etchison, Birdie L(ee)
Wood, Charles Gerald 1932- 106
See also DLB 13
Wood, Charles Monroe 1944- 125
Wood, Charles Osgood III 1933- 109
Wood, Charles T(uttle) 1933- CANR-30
Earlier sketch in CA 17-20R
Wood, Chauncey 1935- 37-40R
Wood, Christopher (Hovelle) 1935- 29-32R
Wood, Christopher 1941- CANR-36
Earlier sketch in CA 103
Wood, Clement Biddle 1925- 21-24R
Wood, David (Bowne) 1945- 93-96
Wood, David G. 1919- 126
Wood, David M(ichael) 1934- Brief entry 109
Wood, David 1944- 97-100
Wood, Derek Harold 1930- CANR-16
Earlier sketch in CA 93-96
Wood, Don 1945- 136
See also CLR 26
See also MAICYA
See also SATA 44, 50
Wood, Donald 1926- 45-48
Wood, Donna (Marie) 1949- CANR-18
Earlier sketch in CA 97-100
Wood, Dorothy Adkins 1912-1975 ....CANR-6
Earlier sketch in CA 13-16R
Wood, E(dward) Rudolf 1907- CANR-3
Earlier sketch in CA 9-12R
Wood, Edgar A(llardyce) 1907- 77-80
See also SATA 14
Wood, Elizabeth A(rmstrong) 1912- CANR-30
Earlier sketch in CA 25-28R
Wood, Esther
See Brady, Esther Wood
Wood, Forrest G(len) 1931- 25-28R
Wood, Frances Elizabeth 107
See also SATA 34
Wood, Fred M. 1921- CANR-26
Earlier sketches in CA 13-16R, CANR-10
Wood, Frederic C(onger) Jr. 1932-1970 ....CAP-2
Earlier sketch in CA 25-28
Wood, Frederick Thomas 1905- CANR-5
Earlier sketch in CA 5-8R
Wood, G(eorge) R(obert) Harding
1878-1968 ....CAP-1
Earlier sketch in CA 9-10
Wood, Gordon R(eid) 1913- 77-80
Wood, Gordon S(tewart) 1933- 25-28R
Wood, Harley Weston 1911- 109
Wood, Harold A(rthur) 1921- 17-20R
Wood, (Elizabeth) Harriet Harvey
See Harvey Wood, (Elizabeth) Harriet
Wood, Herbert Fairlie 1914-1967 110
Obituary 108
Wood, J(ohn) Howard 1901-1988 Obituary 127
Wood, James (Alexander Fraser)
1918-1984 ....CANR-16
Earlier sketches in CA 1-4R, CANR-1
Wood, James E(dward) Jr. 1922- CANR-28
Earlier sketches in CA 29-32R, CANR-12
Wood, James L(eslie) 1941- CANR-8
Earlier sketch in CA 57-60
Wood, James Playsted 1905- CANR-3
Earlier sketch in CA 9-12R
See also SATA 1
Wood, James 1889(?)-1975 Obituary 57-60
Wood, Janet L(ouise) Sims
See Sims-Wood, Janet L(ouise)
Wood, Joanna E. 1867-1927 ....DLB 92
Wood, John A(rmstead Jr.) 1932- 125
Brief entry 108
Wood, John C(unningham) 1952- 133
Wood, John Thomas 1939- 77-80
Wood, John 1947- 136
Wood, Jonathan 1945- 128
Wood, Joyce 1928- 25-28R
Wood, June S(mallwood) 1931- 61-64
Wood, Kenneth 1922- CANR-26
Earlier sketches in CA 69-72, CANR-11
Wood, Kerry
See Wood, Edgar A(llardyce)
Wood, Kirk
See Stahl, Le Roy
Wood, Larry
See Wood, Marylaird
Wood, Laura N.
See Roper, Laura Wood
Wood, Lee Blair 1893-1982 Obituary 106
Wood, Leland Foster 1885- 1-4R
Wood, Leon J(ames) 1918-1976 ....CANR-26
Earlier sketch in CA 29-32R
Wood, Leonard C(lair) 1923- 37-40R
Wood, Leslie A(lfred) 1930- 29-32R
Wood, (James) Lew(is) 1928- 65-68
Wood, Linda C(arol) 1945- 110
See also SATA 59
Wood, Lorna 1913- 69-72
Wood, Margaret I(sabel) 1926- 97-100
Wood, Margaret (L. E.) 1910- 13-16R
Wood, Marion N(ewman) 1909- 61-64
Wood, Mary 1915- 21-24R
Wood, Marylaird CANR-21
Earlier sketch in CA 81-84
Wood, Maurice Arthur Ponsonby 1916- 109
Wood, Michael 1936- 37-40R
Wood, Mrs. Henry 1814-1887 ....DLB 18
Wood, Nancy 1936- CANR-9
Earlier sketch in CA 21-24R
See also SATA 6
Wood, Neal (Norman) 1922- 1-4R
Wood, Owen 1929- ....SATA 64
Wood, Pat
See Baxter, Patricia E. W.
Wood, Paul W(inthrop) 1922- 61-64
Wood, Peggy 1892-1978 Obituary 77-80
Wood, Peter Weston 1953- 125
Wood, Peter 1930- 93-96

Wood, Phyllis Anderson 1923- CANR-14
Earlier sketch in CA 37-40R
See also SATA 30, 33
Wood, R(ichard) Coke 1905-1979 ....CANR-7
Earlier sketch in CA 53-56
Wood, Ramsay 1943- 103
Wood, Raymund F(rancis) 1911- 61-64
Wood, Robert Coldwell 1923- 1-4R
Wood, Robert L. 1925- 21-24R
Wood, Robert Paul 1931- CANR-5
Earlier sketch in CA 53-56
Wood, Robert S(tephen) 1938- CANR-7
Earlier sketch in CA 57-60
Wood, Robin
See Wood, Robert Paul
Wood, Ruth C. 37-40R
Wood, Ruzena (Alenka Valda) 1937- 135
Wood, Sara
See Bowen-Judd, Sara (Hutton)
Wood, Serry
See Freeman, G(raydon) L(a Verne)
Wood, Susan Macduff 1941- 132
Wood, Susan 1946- 108
Wood, Sydney (Herbert) 1935- CANR-31
Earlier sketch in CA 112
Wood, Thomas W(esley) Jr. 1920- 81-84
Wood, Ursula
See Vaughan Williams, Ursula Wood
Wood, W(illiam) J. 1917- 135
Wood, Wallace 1927-1981 Obituary 108
See also SATA 33
Wood, Walter Hunt Sr.
1916(?)-1987 Obituary 124
Wood, William .... DLB 24
Wood, William P(reston) 1951- 118
Woodall, Corbet 1929(?)-1982 Obituary 106
Woodall, Mary 1901-1988 Obituary 125
Woodall, Ronald 1935- 73-76
Woodard, Bronte 1941(?)-1980 Obituary 101
Woodard, Carol 1929- 73-76
See also SATA 14
Woodard, Christopher R. 1913- 13-16R
Woodard, Gloria (Jean) H(iner) 1937- 45-48
Woodberry, George Edward
1855-1930 ....DLB 71, 103
Woodberry, Joan (Merle) 1921- CANR-6
Earlier sketch in CA 9-12R
Woodbridge, Benjamin 1622-1684 .... DLB 24
Woodbridge, Hensley Charles 1923- CANR-3
Earlier sketch in CA 9-12R
Woodbridge, Kenneth 1910- 127
Woodbridge, Linda 1945- 118
Woodbridge, Sally
See Woodbridge, Sally B(yrne)
Woodbridge, Sally B(yrne) 1930- 129
Woodburn, Arthur 1890-1978 Obituary 108
Woodburn, John Henry 1914- CANR-4
Earlier sketch in CA 1-4R
See also SATA 11
Woodbury, David Oakes 1896-1981 ...... SATA 62
Woodbury, Frank
See Chapman, Frank M(onroe)
Woodbury, Lael J(ay) 1927- 81-84
Woodbury, Marda 1925- CANR-17
Earlier sketch in CA 97-100
Woodbury, Mildred Fairchild
1894-1975 Obituary 57-60
Woodbury, Richard B(enjamin)
1917- Brief entry 109
Woodcock, Bruce 1948- 119
Woodcock, George 1912- CANR-1
Earlier sketch in CA 1-4R
See also CAAS 6
See also DLB 88
Woodcott, Keith
See Brunner, John (Kilian Houston)
Wooden, Kenneth 1935- 81-84
Wooden, Warren W(alter) 1941-1983 132
Wooden, Wayne S(tanley) 1943- 109
Woodfield, William Read 1928- 9-12R
Woodford, Arthur M(acKinnon) 1940- CANR-7
Earlier sketch in CA 53-56
Woodford, Bruce P(owers) 1919- 57-60
Woodford, Frank B(ury) 1903-1967 .... CAP-1
Earlier sketch in CA 13-16
Woodford, Jack
See Woolfolk, Josiah Pitts
Woodford, Peggy 1937- 104
See also SATA 25
Woodford, Susan 1938- 128
Woodforde, John 1925- CANR-10
Earlier sketch in CA 25-28R
Woodgate, Mildred Violet 9-12R
Woodham-Smith, Cecil (Blanche Fitzgerald)
1896-1977 77-80
Obituary 69-72
Woodhead, Leslie 1937- 128
Woodhead, Peter 1944- 124
Woodhouse, Barbara (Blackburn)
1910-1988 ....CANR-30
Obituary 126
Earlier sketches in CA 5-8R, CANR-13
See also SATA 63
Woodhouse, C(hristopher) M(ontague)
1917- Brief entry 108
Woodhouse, Charles Platten 1915- 105
Woodhouse, Edward J(ames) 1946- 117
Woodhouse, Martin (Charlton) 1932- CANR-16
Earlier sketch in CA 21-24R
Woodhull, Victoria C. 1838-1927 .... DLB 79
Woodin, Ann Snow 1926- 13-16R
Woodin, Noel 1929- 1-4R
Wooding, Dan 1940- 102
Wooding, Sharon
See Wooding, Sharon L(ouise)
Wooding, Sharon L(ouise) 1943- 136
See also SATA 66
Woodiwiss, Kathleen E(rin) 1939- CANR-23
Earlier sketch in CA 89-92
See also BEST 90:1
See also MTCW
Wood-Legh, Kathleen Louise
1901-1981 Obituary 105
Woodley, Winifred
See Hedden, Worth Tuttle
Woodman, Anthony John 1945- CANR-23
Earlier sketches in CA 61-64, CANR-8
Woodman, Bill
See Woodman, William
Woodman, Harold D. 1928- CANR-9
Earlier sketch in CA 21-24R
Woodman, James Monroe 1931- 17-20R
Woodman, Jim
See Woodman, James Monroe
Woodman, John E. 1932(?)-1983 Obituary 109
Woodman, Loring 1942- 45-48
Woodman, Richard 1944- 132
Woodman, William 1936- 125
Woodmason, Charles 1720(?)- .... DLB 31
Woodrell, Daniel 1953- 121
Woodress, James (Leslie Jr.) 1916- CANR-3
Earlier sketch in CA 5-8R
See also DLB 111
Woodrew, Greta 1930- 106
Woodrich, Mary Neville 1915- 25-28R
See also SATA 2
Woodring, Carl (Ray) 1919- 5-8R
Woodring, Paul (Dean) 1907- 17-20R
Woodrock, R. A.
See Cowlishaw, Ranson
Woodroffe, John
See Woodroffe, John George
Woodroffe, John George
1865-1936 Brief entry 121
Woodroof, Horace M(alcolm) 1906- CAP-2
Earlier sketch in CA 29-32
Woodruff, Archibald Mulford Jr. 1912-1984 105
Obituary 113
Woodruff, Asahel D(avis) 1904- 1-4R
Woodruff, Elvira 1951- 138
See also SATA 70
Woodruff, J(ohn) Douglas 1897-1978 107
Woodruff, John Douglas
1897-1978 Obituary 104
Woodruff, Judy (Carline) 1946- CANR-13
Earlier sketch in CA 73-76
Woodruff, Marian
See Goudge, Eileen
Woodruff, Philip
See Mason, Philip
Woodruff, Robert W.
See Mencken, H(enry) L(ouis)
Woodruff, Sue (Carolyn) 1943- 117
Woodruff, William 1916- 101
Woodrum, Lon 1901- 104
Woods, B(obby) W(illiam) 1930- CANR-19
Earlier sketch in CA 25-28R
Woods, Clee 1893- 108
Woods, Constance
See McComb, K(atherine Woods)
Woods, Donald H. 1933- 25-28R
Woods, Donald 1933- 121
Brief entry 114
Woods, Elizabeth 1940- 101
Woods, Frederick 1932- CANR-7
Earlier sketch in CA 17-20R
Woods, George A(llan) 1926-1988 ....29-32R
Obituary 126
See also SATA 30, 57
Woods, Geraldine 1948- 97-100
See also SATA 42, 56
Woods, Gerard
See Bosch, Henry G(erard)
Woods, Gregory 1953- 129
Woods, Harold 1945- 97-100
See also SATA 42, 56
Woods, James M. 1952- 125
Woods, Joan (LeSueur) 1932- 9-12R
Woods, John A(ubin) 1927- 13-16R
Woods, John B(arrie) 1933- Brief entry 107
Woods, John David 1939- 37-40R
Woods, John E(dmund) 1938- 104
Woods, John (Hayden) 1937- CANR-11
Earlier sketch in CA 57-60
Woods, John 1926- CANR-23
Earlier sketch in CA 13-16R
Woods, Kenneth F. 1930- 13-16R
Woods, L. B. 1938- 112
Woods, L(awrence) Milton 1932- 127
Woods, Lawrence
See Lowndes, Robert A(ugustine) W(ard)
Woods, Margaret S(taeger) 1911- 81-84
Woods, Margaret 1921- 21-24R
See also SATA 2
Woods, Michael 1952- 137
Woods, Nat
See Stratemeyer, Edward L.
Woods, Oliver (Frederick John Bradley)
1911-1972 Obituary 114
Woods, P. F.
See Bayley, Barrington J(ohn)
Woods, Pamela 1938- 106
Woods, Ralph L(ouis) 1904- CANR-2
Earlier sketch in CA 5-8R
Woods, Randall Bennett 1944- Brief entry 106
Woods, Richard G(lenn) 1933- 109
Woods, Richard (John) 1941- CANR-4
Earlier sketch in CA 53-56
Woods, Samuel H(ubert) Jr. 1926- 25-28R
Woods, Sara
See Bowen-Judd, Sara (Hutton)
Woods, Shadrach 1923-1973 Obituary 45-48
Woods, Sharon 1949- 125
Woods, Sherryl 1944- 120
Woods, Shirley E(dwards) Jr. 1934- 119
Woods, Sister Frances Jerome 1913- 21-24R
Woods, Stockton
See Forrest, Richard (Stockton)
Woods, Stockton
See Forrest, Richard (Stockton)
Woods, Stuart 1938- 93-96
Woods, William 77-80
Woods, William Crawford 1944- 29-32R
Woodside, Alexander Barton 1938- 123
Woodson, Carter G. 1875-1950 .... DLB 17
Woodson, Jack
See Woodson, John Waddie Jr.
Woodson, Jeff
See Oglesby, Joseph
Woodson, John Waddie Jr. 1913- .... SATA 10
Woodson, Leslie H(arold) 1929- 41-44R
Woodson, Meg
See Baker, Elsie
Woodson, Robert L. 1937- 127
Woodson, Thomas (Miller) 1931- 104
Woodson, Wesley E(dward) 1918- 37-40R
Woodstone, Arthur 69-72
Woodward, Bob
See Woodward, Robert Upshur
Woodward, C(omer) Vann 1908- CANR-17
Earlier sketches in CA 5-8R, CANR-2
See also DLB 17
Woodward, Carl Raymond 1890-1974 ......41-44R
Woodward, (Landon) Cleveland
1900-1986 ....SATA 10, 48
Woodward, Daniel Holt 1931- 37-40R
Woodward, David B(rainerd) 1918- 65-68
Woodward, David Reid 1939- 114
Woodward, David 1909-1986 Obituary 120
Woodward, Douglas P. 1954- 135
Woodward, E. L.
See Woodward, Ernest Llewellyn
Woodward, Ernest Llewellyn
1890-1971 Obituary 111
Woodward, G(eorge) W(illiam) O(tway)
1924- CANR-3
Earlier sketch in CA 5-8R
Woodward, Grace Steele 1899- CAP-1
Earlier sketch in CA 9-10
Woodward, Helen Beal
1914(?)-1982 Obituary 108
Woodward, Helen Rosen 1882- 5-8R
Woodward, Herbert N(orton) 1911- 65-68
Woodward, Hildegard 1898- 5-8R
Woodward, James B(rian) 1935- CANR-2
Earlier sketch in CA 49-52
Woodward, John (O.)
1922(?)-1988 Obituary 125
Woodward, John (William) 1920- 21-24R
Woodward, John 1945- 113
Woodward, Lilian
See Marsh, John
Woodward, Llewellyn
See Woodward, Ernest Llewellyn
Woodward, Ralph Lee Jr. 1934- 21-24R
Woodward, Robert H(anson) 1925- 17-20R
Woodward, Robert Upshur 1943- CANR-31
Earlier sketch in CA 69-72
See also MTCW
Woodward, Stanley (Wingate) 1890- 5-8R
Woodward, Thomas B. 1937- 114
Woodward, W. Mary 1921- 45-48
Woodworth, Constance
1911-1983 Obituary 109
Woodworth, David (Perrin) 1932- 37-40R
Woodworth, G(eorge) Wallace
1902-1969 .... CAP-1
Earlier sketch in CA 13-16
Woodworth, G(eorge) Walter 1903- CAP-1
Earlier sketch in CA 19-20
Woodworth, Hugh (MacCallum)
1906-1978 Obituary 107
Woodworth, Steven E(dward) 1961- 135
Woody, Regina Jones 1894- CANR-3
Earlier sketch in CA 5-8R
See also SATA 3
Woody, Robert H(enley) 1936- 93-96
Woody, Russell O(wen) Jr. 1934- 17-20R
Woodyard, David O. 1932- 21-24R
Woodyard, George 1934- 81-84
Woolard, Edgar 1899(?)-1978 Obituary 77-80
Wooldridge, Rhoda 1906- 77-80
See also SATA 22
Wooldridge, William C(harles) 1943- CANR-25
Earlier sketch in CA 45-48
Woolery, George W(illiam) 1931- 122
Wooley, John (Steven) 1949- 109
Woolf, Daniel J(ames) 1916- 5-8R
Woolf, Douglas 1922- CANR-2
Earlier sketch in CA 1-4R
Woolf, Harry 1923- CANR-1
Earlier sketch in CA 1-4R
Woolf, James Dudley 1914- 37-40R
Woolf, Leonard S(idney) 1880-1969 ......CANR-39
Obituary 25-28R
Earlier sketch in CA 5-8R
See also DLB 100
Woolf, Robert G(ary) 1928- 73-76
Woolf, S. J.
See Woolf, Stuart (Joseph)
Woolf, Stuart (Joseph) 1936- Brief entry 118
Woolf, (Adeline) Virginia 1882-1941 130
Brief entry 104
See also CDBLB 1914-1945
See also DLB 36, 100
See also MTCW
See also SSC 7
See also TCLC 1, 5, 20, 43
See also WLC
Woolfe, H(arold) Geoffrey 1902- CAP-1
Earlier sketch in CA 11-12
Woolfenden, John R(ichards) 1904- 113
Woolfolk, Joanna Martine 1940- 110
Woolfolk, Josiah Pitts
1894-1971 Obituary 29-32R
Woolfolk, Robert L(ee IV) 1947- Brief entry 112
Woolfolk, William 1917- 113
Woolgar, (George) Jack 1894- 17-20R
Woollam, William Gifford 1921- 9-12R
Woollcott, Alexander (Humphreys)
1887-1943 Brief entry 105
See also DLB 29
See also TCLC 5
Woolley, A(lban) E(dward Jr.) 1926- CANR-14
Earlier sketch in CA 41-44R
Woolley, (Lowell) Bryan 1937- CANR-4
Earlier sketch in CA 49-52
Woolley, Catherine 1904- CANR-6
Earlier sketch in CA 1-4R
See also SATA 3
Woolley, Davis Collier 1908-1971 Obituary 116
Woolley, Geoffrey Harold 1892-1968 .... CAP-1
Earlier sketch in CA 11-12
Woolley, Herbert B(allantyne)
1917-1978 Obituary 81-84
Woolley, Richard van der Riet
1906-1986 Obituary 121
Woolley, (Alfred) Russell 1899- 5-8R
Woolls, (Esther) Blanche 1935- CANR-39
Earlier sketch in CA 126
Woolman, David S. 1916- 29-32R
Woolman, John 1720-1772 ....DLB 31
Woolner, Frank 1916- 53-56
Woolner, Thomas 1825-1892 ....DLB 35
Woolrich, Cornell
See Hopley-Woolrich, Cornell George
Woolrych, Austin (Herbert) 1918- 1-4R
Woolsey, Arthur (Wallace) 1906- 45-48
Woolsey, Janette 1904- CANR-2
Earlier sketch in CA 1-4R
See also SATA 3
Woolsey, Sarah Chauncy
1835(?)-1905 Brief entry 115
See also DLB 42
Woolson, Constance Fenimore
1840-1894 ....DLB 12, 74
Woolson, Roland S. Jr.
1930(?)-1977 Obituary 104
Woon, Basil 1894(?)-1974 Obituary 49-52
Wooster, Claire 1942- 101
Wooster, Ralph A(ncil) 1928- CANR-2
Earlier sketch in CA 5-8R
Wooster, Robert 1956- 124
Wooten, James (Terrell) 1937- Brief entry 112
Wootten, Morgan 1931- 101
Wootters, John (Henry Jr.) 1928- 113
Wootton, Anthony 1935- 129
Wootton, Barbara (Frances Adam)
1897-1988 Obituary 126
Wootton, (Devere) Gareth 1937- 117
Wootton, (John) Graham (George)
1917- CANR-10
Earlier sketch in CA 5-8R
Worblefister, Petunia
See Gribbin, Lenore S.
Worboys, Anne(tte Isobel) Eyre CANR-9
Earlier sketch in CA 65-68
Worcester, Dean A(mory) Jr. 1918- 21-24R
Worcester, Donald E(mmet) 1915- CANR-19
Earlier sketches in CA 1-4R, CANR-4
See also SATA 18
Worcester, Gurdon Saltonstall 1897- CAP-1
Earlier sketch in CA 11-12
Worcester, Joseph Emerson 1784-1865 .... DLB 1
Worcester, Robert (Milton) 1933- 134
Worchel, Stephen 1946- CANR-37
Earlier sketches in CA 89-92, CANR-16
Worden, Alfred M(errill) 1932- 101
Worden, William L. 1910- CAP-1
Earlier sketch in CA 13-16
Wordsworth, Dorothy 1771-1855 .... DLB 107
Wordsworth, Elizabeth 1840-1932 .... DLB 98
Wordsworth, Jonathan 1932- CANR-20
Earlier sketch in CA 29-32R
Wordsworth, William
1770-1850 .... CDBLB 1789-1832
See also DLB 93, 107
See also PC 4
See also WLC
Worell, Judith 1928- CANR-7
Earlier sketch in CA 57-60
Work, Alison R. 1956- 128
Work, Robert E. 1928(?)-1986 Obituary 121
Work, Virginia 1946- 113
See also SATA 45, 57
Working, Russell (Craig) 1959- 124
Workman, Samuel K(linger) 1907- CAP-2
Earlier sketch in CA 23-24
Workman, William D(ouglas) Jr. 1914- 5-8R
Works, John 1949- 123
Worland, Stephen T. 1923- 21-24R
Worley, Robert Cromwell 1929- Brief entry 108
Worline, Bonnie Bess 1914- 69-72
See also SATA 14
Worlock, Derek John Harford 1920- 103
Worm, Piet 1909- 81-84
Wormall, Francis 1904(?)-1972 Obituary 104
Wormald, Jenny 1942- CANR-32
Earlier sketch in CA 112
Wormald, (Charles) Patrick 1947- 132
Worman, Charles G(ordon) 1933- 119
Worman, Eli
See Weil, Roman L(ee)
Wormell, Deborah 1946-1979 Obituary 114
Wormington, H(annah) M(arie) 1914- CANR-3
Earlier sketch in CA 45-48
Wormley, Cinda
See Kornblum, Cinda

Wormley, Stanton Lawrence 1909- CANR-12
Earlier sketch in CA 73-76
Wormser, Baron Chesley 1948- 110
Wormser, Rene A(lbert) 1896-1981 ......CANR-11
Obituary 104
Earlier sketch in CA 13-16R
Wormser, Sophie 1897- 65-68
See also SATA 22
Worner, Karl Heinrich
See Woerner, Karl Heinrich
Woroniak, Alexander 1920- 41-44R
Woronoff, Jon 1938- CANR-29
Earlier sketches in CA 29-32R, CANR-11
Woronov, Naomi 1938- 132
Worrall, Ambrose A(lexander)
1899-1972 .... CAP-2
Earlier sketch in CA 29-32
Worrall, Olga (Nathalie) 1906- 29-32R
Worrell, Albert C(adwallader) 1913- 37-40R
Worrell, Eric 1924-1987 Obituary 123
Worrick, Roberta 1941-1989 Obituary 129
Worsley, Dale 1948- 104
Worsley, Gump
See Worsley, Lorne (John)
Worsley, Lorne (John) 1929- Brief entry 111
Worster, Donald E(ugene) 1941- CANR-12
Earlier sketch in CA 57-60
Worsthorne, Peregrine 1923- 45-48
Worswick, Clark 1940- 104
Worth, C. Brooke 1908- 101
Worth, Dean S(toddard) 1927- Brief entry 112
Worth, Douglas 1940- CANR-9
Earlier sketch in CA 65-68
Worth, Fred L. 1943- 97-100
Worth, Helen 1913- 13-16R
Worth, Margaret
See Strickland, Margot
Worth, Richard 1945- ....SATA 46, 59
Worth, Sol 1922(?)-1977 81-84
Obituary 73-76
Worth, Valerie
See Bahlke, Valerie Worth
See also CLR 21
See also MAICYA
See also SATA 8, 70
Wortham, John David 1941- 37-40R
Worthen, Blaine Richard 1936- CANR-15
Earlier sketch in CA 85-88
Worthington, Edgar Barton 1905- 109
Worthington, Janet Evans 1942- 115
Worthington, Marjorie (Muir)
1898(?)-1976 ....CANR-2
Obituary 65-68
Earlier sketch in CA 1-4R
Worthington, Phoebe 1910- ....SATA 52
Worthington, Robin (Ann) 1932- 114
Worthley, Jean Reese 1925- 77-80
Worthy, James C(arson) 1910- 117
Worthy, Morgan 1936- 65-68
Worthylake, Mary Moore 1904- CANR-4
Earlier sketch in CA 1-4R
Wortis, Avi 1937- CANR-12
Earlier sketch in CA 69-72
See also Avi
See also MAICYA
See also SATA 14
Wortley, Ben Atkinson 1907-1989 57-60
Obituary 129
Wortman, Marlene Stein 1937- 112
Wortman, Max S(idones) Jr. 1932- CANR-16
Earlier sketch in CA 21-24R
Wortman, Richard 1938- CANR-9
Earlier sketch in CA 21-24R
Wortman, (Leo) Sterling
1923-1981 Obituary 108
Worton, Stanley N(elson) 1923- 57-60
Wortsman, Peter 1952- 137
Woshinsky, Oliver H(anson) 1939- 127
Brief entry 109
Wosmek, Frances 1917- CANR-26
Earlier sketches in CA 29-32R, CANR-11
See also SATA 29
Wotton, SirHenry 1568-1639 .... DLB 121
Woudenberg, Paul Richard 1927- 69-72
Woudhuysen, Jan Frank 1942- 107
Woudstra, Marten H. 1922- CANR-19
Earlier sketch in CA 25-28R
Wouil, George
See Slaney, George Wilson
Wouk, Herman 1915- CANR-33
Earlier sketches in CA 5-8R, CANR-6
See also CLC 1, 9, 38
See also DLBY 82
See also MTCW
Woutat, Donald 1944- 136
Woy, James Bayly 1927- 13-16R
Woychuk, Denis 1953- ....SATA 71
Woychuk, N(icholas) A(rthur) 1915- 13-16R
Woytinsky, Emma S(hadkhan)
1893-1969 .... CAP-1
Earlier sketch in CA 17-18
Woznicki, Andrew N(icholas) 1931- CANR-24
Earlier sketch in CA 45-48
Wrage, Ernest J. 1911-1965 ....1-4R
Wragg, David William 1946- CANR-4
Earlier sketch in CA 53-56
Wragg, E(dward) C(onrad) 1938- CANR-23
Earlier sketches in CA 57-60, CANR-8
Wragg, Joanna DiCarlo 1941- 133
Wraight, A(aron) Joseph 1913- 21-24R
Wrede, Patricia C(ollins) 1953- 134
See also AAYA 8
See also SATA 67
Wreen, Michael 1950- 117
Wreford, James
See Watson, J(ames) Wreford
Wreggitt, Andrew 1955- 138
Wren, Chris Obituary 108
Wren, Christopher S. 1936- 21-24R
Wren, Daniel Alan 1932- 41-44R
Wren, Ellaruth
See Elkins, Ella Ruth
Wren, M. K.
See Renfroe, Martha Kay
Wren, Melvin C(larence) 1910- 37-40R
Wren, Percival Christopher
1885-1941 Brief entry 123
Wren, Robert Meriwether 1928- 106
Wren, Thomas Edward 1938- 77-80
Wren, Wilfrid John 1930- 109
Wrench, David F(razer) 1932- 41-44R
Wrench, (John) Evelyn (Leslie) 1882-1966 ....5-8R
Wrenn, John H(aughton) 1920- 1-4R
Wrenn, Robert L. 1933- 29-32R
Wrenn, Tony P(entecost) 1938- 89-92
Wrenn, Winnie Holden
1886(?)-1979 Obituary 89-92
Wriggins, Sally Hovey 1922- 97-100
See also SATA 17
Wriggins, W(illiam) Howard 1918- 61-64
Wright, A(nthony) Colin 1938- 120
Wright, A. D. 1947- 129
Wright, A(mos) J(asper) 1952- 93-96
Wright, Alice E(dwards) 1905-1980 104
Wright, Andrew (Howell) 1923- 17-20R
Wright, Anna (Maria Louisa Perrott) Rose
1890-1968 Obituary 109
See also SATA 35
Wright, Arthur Frederick 1913-1976 ......CANR-33
Obituary 69-72
Earlier sketch in CA 77-80
Wright, Austin McGiffert 1922- CANR-4
Earlier sketch in CA 1-4R
Wright, Austin 1904- 61-64
Wright, Barton A(llen) 1920- CANR-8
Earlier sketch in CA 61-64
Wright, Basil Charles 1907-1987 105
Obituary 123
Wright, Beatrice A(nn) 1917- CANR-12
Earlier sketch in CA 21-24R
Wright, Benjamin Fletcher 1900-1976 77-80
Obituary 69-72
Wright, Betty Ren ....SATA 48, 63
Wright, Brooks 1922- 25-28R
Wright, Bruce S(tanley) 1912-1975 .... CAP-2
Earlier sketch in CA 19-20
Wright, Burton 1917- 81-84
Wright, C. D. 1949- ....DLB 120
Wright, Carolyne L(ee) 1949- 111
Wright, (Julia) Celeste Turner 1906- CAP-1
Earlier sketch in CA 9-10
Wright, Charles Alan 1927- CANR-37
Earlier sketches in CA 45-48, CANR-1, 16
Wright, Charles David 1932-1978 104
Wright, Charles H(oward) 1918- 61-64
Wright, Charles (Penzel Jr.) 1935- CANR-36
Earlier sketches in CA 29-32R, CANR-23
See also CAAS 7
See also CLC 6, 13, 28
See also DLBY 82
See also MTCW
Wright, Charles R(obert) 1927- CANR-1
Earlier sketch in CA 45-48
Wright, Charles Stevenson 1932- CANR-26
Earlier sketch in CA 9-12R
See also BLC 3
See also BW
See also CLC 49
See also DLB 33
Wright, Christopher 1926- 9-12R
Wright, Cobina Obituary 115
Wright, (Charles) Conrad 1917- 21-24R
Wright, Constance Choate 1897-1987 ....13-16R
Obituary 121
Wright, Cynthia Challed 1953- 77-80
Wright, D(avid) G(ordon) 1937- 65-68
Wright, D(onald) I(an) 1934- CANR-3
Earlier sketch in CA 49-52
Wright, Dare 1926(?)- 93-96
See also SATA 21
Wright, David (John Murray) 1920- CANR-3
Earlier sketch in CA 9-12R
See also CAAS 5
Wright, David McCord 1909-1968 .... CAP-2
Earlier sketch in CA 17-18
Wright, Deil S(pencer) 1930- 13-16R
Wright, Denis (Arthur Hepworth) 1911- 81-84
Wright, Don(ald Conway) 1934- CANR-20
Earlier sketch in CA 104
Wright, Dorothy 1910- 13-16R
Wright, Edward A(rlington) 1906- 29-32R
Wright, Elizabeth Atwell
1919-1976 Obituary 65-68
Wright, Enid Meadowcroft (LaMonte)
1898-1966 .... CAP-2
Earlier sketch in CA 17-18
See also SATA 3
Wright, Eric 1929- 132
Brief entry 127
Wright, Esmond 1915- CANR-6
Earlier sketch in CA 1-4R
See also SATA 10
Wright, F(rank) J(oseph) 1905- 9-12R
Wright, Frances Fitzpatrick 1897- CAP-1
Earlier sketch in CA 13-14
See also SATA 10
Wright, Frances J.
See Crothers, J(essie) Frances
Wright, Frances 1795-1852 ....DLB 73
Wright, Francesca
See Robins, Denise (Naomi)
Wright, Frank Cookman Jr.
1904-1982 Obituary 107
Wright, Frank Gardner 1931- 136
Wright, G(eorge) Ernest 1909-1974 ....CANR-2
Obituary 53-56
Earlier sketch in CA 1-4R
Wright, G(eorg) H(enrik) von
1916- Brief entry 112
Wright, Gavin Peter 1943- CANR-15
Earlier sketch in CA 89-92
Wright, George B(urton) 1912- 21-24R
Wright, George Nelson 1921- CANR-1
Earlier sketch in CA 45-48
Wright, George T(haddeus Jr.) 1925- 5-8R
Wright, Gordon 1912- 9-12R
Wright, Grahame 1947-1977 103
Wright, H(arold) Bunker 1907- 5-8R
Wright, H(ugh) Elliott 1937- CANR-14
Earlier sketch in CA 37-40R
Wright, H(arry) Norman 1937- CANR-32
Earlier sketches in CA 57-60, CANR-8
Wright, Harold Bell 1872-1944 Brief entry 110
See also DLB 9
Wright, Harrison M(orris) 1928- 41-44R
Wright, Helen L(ouise) 1932- 116
Wright, Helen 1914- 9-12R
Wright, Helena (Rosa Lowenfeld)
1887-1982 Obituary 110
Wright, Herbert Curtis 1928- 105
Wright, Howard W(ilson) 1915-1992 ....CANR-3
Obituary 136
Earlier sketch in CA 5-8R
Wright, Ione Stuessy 1905- CAP-1
Earlier sketch in CA 13-14
Wright, Irene Aloha 1879-1972 Obituary 33-36R
Wright, J(ames) Leitch Jr. 1929- 21-24R
Wright, J(oseph) Patrick (Jr.) 1941- 103
Wright, J(ohn) Robert 1936- 111
Wright, J(ohn) Stafford 1905- CANR-11
Earlier sketch in CA 57-60
Wright, Jack R.
See Harris, Mark
Wright, James (Arlington) 1927-1980 .....CANR-34
Obituary 97-100
Earlier sketches in CA 49-52, CANR-4
See also AITN 2
See also CLC 3, 5, 10, 28
See also DLB 5
See also MTCW
Wright, James Bowers 1950- 127
Wright, James C(laud) Jr. 1922- 49-52
Wright, Jay 1935- 73-76
See also DLB 41
Wright, Jim
See Wright, James Bowers
Wright, Jim
See Wright, James C(laud) Jr.
Wright, John D(ean) Jr. 1920- 117
Wright, John Eugene Jr. 1931- 112
Wright, John J(oseph) 1909-1979 ....CANR-2
Earlier sketch in CA 1-4R
Wright, John L. 1937- 131
Wright, John S(herman) 1920- CANR-6
Earlier sketch in CA 5-8R
Wright, John S(hup) 1910- 37-40R
Wright, Judith (Arandell) 1915- CANR-31
Earlier sketch in CA 13-16R
See also CLC 11, 53
See also MTCW
See also SATA 14
Wright, Katrina
See Gater, Dilys
Wright, Keith 1963- 136
Wright, Kenneth
See del Rey, Lester
Wright, L(afayette) Hart 1917-1983 ....CANR-32
Obituary 109
Earlier sketch in CA 41-44
Wright, L(aurali) R. 138
See also CLC 44
Wright, Larry 1940- Brief entry 122
Wright, Lawrence 1947- 93-96
Wright, Leigh Richard 1925- 93-96
Wright, Leonard M(arshall) Jr. 1923- CANR-13
Earlier sketch in CA 61-64
Wright, Linda Raney 1945- CANR-11
Earlier sketch in CA 69-72
Wright, Louis Booker 1899-1984 ....CANR-1
Obituary 112
Earlier sketch in CA 1-4R
See also DLB 17
Wright, M(aureen) R(osemary) 131
Wright, Mary Clabaugh 1917-1970 Obituary 109
Wright, Mary Pamela Godwin 1917- CAP-1
Earlier sketch in CA 9-10
Wright, Michael R(obert) 1901- CAP-1
Earlier sketch in CA 13-16
Wright, Monte Duane 1930- 41-44R
Wright, Muriel H(azel)
1889-1975 Obituary 57-60
Wright, Nancy Means 104
See also SATA 38
Wright, Nathalia 1913- 120
Wright, Nathan Jr. 1923- 37-40R
Wright, Nathaniel Jr.
See Wright, Nathan Jr.
Wright, Norman Edgar 1927- 101
Wright, Olgivanna Lloyd
1900(?)-1985 Obituary 115
Wright, (Mary) Patricia 1932- CANR-26
Earlier sketches in CA 65-68, CANR-10
Wright, Peter (Maurice) 1916- 128
Wright, Philip Arthur 1908- CAP-1
Earlier sketch in CA 11-12
Wright, (Philip) Quincy 1890-1970 ....CANR-5
Obituary 29-32R
Earlier sketch in CA 5-8R
Wright, R(obert) Glenn 1932- 111
Wright, R(obert) H(amilton) 1906- CANR-7
Earlier sketch in CA 17-20R
See also SATA 6
Wright, R(ichard) I(rwin) Vane
See Vane-Wright, R(ichard) I(rwin)
Wright, Rayburn B. 1922-1990 Obituary 131
Wright, Rebecca 1942- 105
Wright, Richard B(ruce) 1937- 85-88
See also CLC 6
See also DLB 53
Wright, Richard J. 1935- 89-92
Wright, Richard (Nathaniel) 1908-1960 108
See also AAYA 5
See also BLC 3
See also BW
See also CDALB 1929-1941
See also CLC 1, 3, 4, 9, 14, 21, 48
See also DLB 76, 102
See also DLBD 2
See also MTCW
See also SSC 2
See also WLC
Wright, Rick 1945-
See Pink Floyd
See also CLC 35
Wright, Robert (Alan) 1957- 129
Wright, Robert Lee 1920- CANR-13
Earlier sketch in CA 17-20R
Wright, Robert Roy 1917- 9-12R
Wright, Robin (B.) 1948- 131
Brief entry 119
Wright, Ronald (William Vernon) Selby
1908- CANR-6
Earlier sketch in CA 1-4R
Wright, Rosalie Muller 1942- 77-80
Wright, Rosalind 1952- 61-64
Wright, Rowland
See Wells, Carolyn
Wright, Russel 1904-1976 Obituary 69-72
Wright, Sarah E. 1928- 37-40R
See also BW
See also DLB 33
Wright, Sewall 1889-1988 Obituary 125
Wright, Stephen 1922- CANR-1
Earlier sketch in CA 49-52
Wright, Stephen 1946- .... CLC 33
Wright, Sylvia 1917-1981 ....29-32R
Obituary 104
Wright, T. M. 1947- 120
Wright, T(erence) R(oy) 1951- 125
Wright, Theodore P(aul) Jr. 1926- CANR-9
Earlier sketch in CA 13-16R
Wright, Theon 1904- Brief entry 109
Wright, Walter Francis 1912- 5-8R
Wright, Willard Hull 1894-1982 Obituary 107
Wright, Willard Huntington
1888-1939 Brief entry 115
See also Van Dine, S. S.
Wright, William C(ook) 1939- 41-44R
Wright, William E(dward) 1926- 21-24R
Wright, William 1930- CANR-23
Earlier sketches in CA 53-56, CANR-7
See also CLC 44
Wrightfrierson
See Wright-Frierson, Virginia
Wright-Frierson, Virginia 1949- .... SATA 58
Wrightsman, Lawrence S(amuel) Jr.
1931- CANR-11
Earlier sketch in CA 21-24R
Wrightson, (Alice) Patricia 1921- CANR-36
Earlier sketches in CA 45-48, CANR-3, 19
See also AAYA 5
See also CLR 4, 14
See also MAICYA
See also SAAS 4
See also SATA 8, 66
Wrigley, Chris (John) 1947- 129
Wrigley, E(dward) A(nthony) 1931- 129
Wrigley, Elizabeth S(pringer) 1915- 41-44R
Wriston, Henry M(erritt) 1889-1978 .... CAP-1
Obituary 77-80
Earlier sketch in CA 11-12
Wrobel, Sylvia (Burroughs) 1941- 65-68
Wroblewski, Sergius C(harles) 1918- CANR-8
Earlier sketch in CA 5-8R
Wrone, David R(ogers) 1933- CANR-6
Earlier sketch in CA 57-60
Wrong, Dennis H(ume) 1923- 81-84
Wronker, Lili
See Wronker, Lili Cassel
Wronker, Lili Cassel 1924- .... SATA 10
Wronski, Stanley P(aul) 1919- 13-16R
Wroth, Lawrence Counselman
1884-1970 Obituary 29-32R
Wroth, LadyMary 1587-1653(?) .... DLB 121
Wrottesley, A(rthur) J(ohn) F(rancis)
1908- 45-48
Wryde, Dogear
See Gorey, Edward (St. John)
Wrzos, Joseph Henry 1929- 49-52
Wu, Hsiu-Kwang 1935- 17-20R
Wu, John C(hing) H(siung) 1899-1986 104
Obituary 118
Wu, Joseph S. 1934- 97-100
Wu, K(uo) C(heng) 1903-1984 ....1-4R
Obituary 113
Wu, Nelson I(kon) 1919- 9-12R
Wu, Silas H. L. 1929- 37-40R
Wu, William F(ranking) 1951- 109
Wu, Yuan-li CANR-12
Earlier sketch in CA 17-20R
Wuamett, Victor 1941- 134
Wubben, Hubert H(ollensteiner) 1928- 102
Wubben, John 1938- 65-68
Wucherer, Ruth Marie 1948- CANR-8
Earlier sketch in CA 61-64

Wu Ching-hsiung
See Wu, John C(hing) H(siung)
WuDunn, Sheryl 1959- 132
Wuellner, Flora Slosson 1928- 53-56
Wuerpel, Charles E(dward) 1906- 105
Wul, Stefan
See Pairault, Pierre
Wulf, Helen Harlan 1913- 53-56
Wulfekoetter, Gertrude 1895- 1-4R
Wulff, Lee 1905-1991 61-64
Obituary 134
Wulff, Robert M. 1926- 49-52
Wulffson, Don L. 1943- CANR-19
Earlier sketch in CA 102
See also SATA 32
Wulforst, Harry David 1923- 125
Wuliger, Betty 1921- 65-68
Wullstein, L(eroy) H(ughes) 1931- 29-32R
Wulstan, David 1937- 127
Wunder, John Remley 1945- CANR-37
Earlier sketch in CA 107
Wunderlich, Ray C. Jr. 1929- 37-40R
Wundt, Wilhelm
See de Mille, Richard
Wundt, Wilhelm (Max)
1832-1920 Brief entry 121
Wunnakyawhtin U Ohn Ghine
See Maurice, David (John Kerr)
Wunsch, James S(tevenson) 1946- 136
Wunsch, Josephine (McLean) 1914- CANR-34
Earlier sketches in CA 1-4R, CANR-15
See also SATA 64
Wuorinen, John H(enry)
1897-1969 Obituary 111
Wuorio, Eva-Lis 1918- 77-80
See also SATA 28, 34
Wurdemann, Audrey
See Auslander, Audrey (May) Wurdemann
Wurfel, Seymour W(alter) 1907- 73-76
Wurlitzer, Rudolph 1938(?)- 85-88
See also CLC 2, 4, 15
Wurmbrand, Heinrich Richard 1909- CANR-27
Earlier sketch in CA 61-64
Wurmser, Leon 1931- 106
Wurtman, Judith J(oy) 1937- 113
Wuthnow, Robert 1946- CANR-15
Earlier sketch in CA 65-68
Wu Tien-wei 1922- 118
Wyandotte, Steve
See Thomas, Stanley
Wyant, William K(eblinger) 1913- 108
Wyatt, Arthur R(amer) 1927- 1-4R
Wyatt, B. D.
See Robinson, Spider
Wyatt, David K(ent) 1937- 29-32R
Wyatt, David M. 1948- 132
Wyatt, Dorothea E(dith) 1909- CAP-2
Earlier sketch in CA 23-24
Wyatt, James
See Robinson, Louie Jr.
Wyatt, Jane
See Bradbury, Bianca (Ryley)
Wyatt, Joan 1934- 97-100
Wyatt, John 1925- CANR-22
Earlier sketch in CA 105
Wyatt, Rachel 1929- 101
Wyatt, Richard Jed 1939- 115
Wyatt, Robert John 1931- 73-76
Wyatt, Stanley P(orter Jr.) 1921-1980 ....9-12R
Obituary 120
Wyatt, Stephen (John) 1948- CANR-34
Earlier sketches in CA 81-84, CANR-15
Wyatt, Wesley Butler
See Torme, Mel(vin Howard)
Wyatt, (Alan) Will 1942- 101
Wyatt, William F. Jr. 1932- 37-40R
Wyatt, Woodrow Lyle 1918- 103
Wyatt-Brown, Bertram 1932- CANR-21
Earlier sketch in CA 25-28R
Wycherley, R(ichard) E(rnest) 1909- 77-80
Wycherley, William
1641-1715 ....CDBLB 1660-1789
See also DLB 80
Wyckoff, Charlotte Chandler 1893-1966 ....CAP-2
Earlier sketch in CA 17-18
Wyckoff, D(onald) Daryl 1936-1985 ....CANR-7
Obituary 114
Earlier sketch in CA 57-60
Wyckoff, Edith Hay 1916- 107
Wyckoff, James M. 1918- CANR-39
Earlier sketch in CA 17-20R
Wyckoff, (Gregory) Jerome 1911- 9-12R
Wyckoff, Peter (Gerritsen) 1914- 41-44R
Wyckoff, Ralph W(alter) G(raystone)
1897- 73-76
Wyckoff, Russell L. 1916(?)-1984 Obituary 112
Wycoff, Mary Elizabeth Jordon 1932- 13-16R
Wyden, Peter H. 1923- 105
Wyeth, Betsy James 1921- 89-92
See also SATA 41
Wyeth, N(ewell) C(onvers) 1882-1945 ....MAICYA
See also SATA 17
Wyeth, Paul James Logan
1920-1982 Obituary 107
Wykes, Alan 1914- CANR-2
Earlier sketch in CA 1-4R
Wykstra, Ronald A. 1935- Brief entry 106
Wyld, Lionel D(arcy) 1925- CANR-4
Earlier sketch in CA 1-4R
Wylder, Delbert E(ugene) 1923- CANR-12
Earlier sketch in CA 29-32R
Wylder, Edith (Perry) 1925- 29-32R
Wylder, Edward C. 1921- 9-12R
Wyler, Brenda (Florence) 1951- CANR-19
Earlier sketch in CA 89-92
Wyler, Rose 1909- 93-96
See also SATA 18
Wyler, William 1902-1981 Obituary 108
Wylie, Betty Jane CANR-21
Earlier sketch in CA 105
See also SATA 48
Wylie, C(larence) Ray(mond) Jr.
1911- CANR-36
Earlier sketch in CA 45-48
Wylie, Craig 1908-1976 Obituary 69-72
Wylie, Elinor (Morton Hoyt)
1885-1928 Brief entry 105
See also DLB 9, 45
See also TCLC 8
Wylie, Francis E(rnest) 1905- CANR-37
Earlier sketch in CA 73-76
Wylie, Jeff
See Wylie, Francis E(rnest)
Wylie, Joanne 1928- 118
Wylie, John Anthony Hamilton
1919-1987 Obituary 123
Wylie, Jonathan 1945- 120
Wylie, Laura
See Matthews, Patricia (Anne)
Wylie, Laurence William 1909- 21-24R
Wylie, Laurie
See Matthews, Patricia (Anne)
Wylie, Max (Melville) 1904-1975 97-100
Obituary 61-64
Wylie, Philip (Gordon) 1902-1971 ....CAP-2
Obituary 33-36R
Earlier sketch in CA 21-22
See also CLC 43
See also DLB 9
Wylie, Ruth C(arol) 1920- 89-92
Wylie, Turrell V(erl) 1927- 41-44R
Wylie, William P(ercy) 1898- 5-8R
Wyllie, Eugene D(onald) 1929- 123
Brief entry 118
Wyllie, John (Vectis Carew) 1914- CANR-5
Earlier sketch in CA 9-12R
Wyllie, Peter J(ohn) 1930- CANR-5
Earlier sketch in CA 53-56
Wyly, Rachel Lumpkin 1892- CAP-2
Earlier sketch in CA 25-28
Wyman, David S. 1929- 25-28R
Wyman, Donald 1903- CANR-2
Earlier sketch in CA 5-8R
Wyman, Leland C(lifton)
1897-1988 Obituary 124
Wyman, Marc
See Howith, Harry
Wyman, Mark 1938- CANR-36
Earlier sketch in CA 101
Wyman, Mary Alice
1889(?)-1976 Obituary 61-64
Wyman, Oliver
See Holmes, Olive
Wyman, Walker D(e Marquis) 1907- CANR-36
Earlier sketch in CA 17-20R
Wymark, Olwen Margaret 1932- 104
Wymer, Norman (George) 1911- 104
See also SATA 25
Wymer, Thomas L(ee) 1938- 105
Wynand, Derk 1944- CANR-17
Earlier sketch in CA 77-80
Wynants, Miche 1934- ....SATA 31
Wynar, Bohdan S(tephen) 1926- CANR-27
Earlier sketches in CA 17-20R, CANR-10
Wynar, Christine L(oraine) 1933- 73-76
Wynar, Lubomyr R(oman) 1932- CANR-31
Earlier sketches in CA 73-76, CANR-14
Wynard, Talbot
See Hamilton, Charles (Harold St. John)
Wynd, Oswald Morris 1913- CANR-39
Earlier sketches in CA 1-4R, CANR-1
Wynder, Mavis Areta
See Winder, Mavis Areta
Wyndham, Esther
See Lutyens, Mary
Wyndham, Everard Humphrey 1888- CAP-1
Earlier sketch in CA 13-14
Wyndham, Francis (Guy Percy) 1924- 131
Brief entry 126
Wyndham, John
See Harris, John (Wyndham Parkes Lucas) Beynon
Wyndham, Lee
See Hyndman, Jane Andrews Lee
Wyndham, Robert
See Hyndman, Robert Utley
Wynes, Charles E. 1929- 9-12R
Wyness, (James) Fenton 1903- CAP-1
Earlier sketch in CA 11-12
Wynette, Tammy
See Pugh, Wynette
Wynia, Gary W. 1942- 133
Wynkoop, Mildred Bangs 1905- 57-60
Wynkoop, Sally 1944- 41-44R
Wynkoop, William M. 1916- 21-24R
Wynn, Alfred
See Brewer, Fredric (Aldwyn)
Wynn, Allan 1920-1987 Obituary 123
Wynn, D(ale) Richard 1918- CANR-4
Earlier sketch in CA 1-4R
Wynn, Daniel Webster 1919-1983 ....25-28R
Obituary 133
Wynn, Graeme 1946- 127
Wynn, John Charles 1920- CANR-2
Earlier sketch in CA 1-4R
Wynn, (Francis Xavier Aloysius James Jeremiah) Keenan
1916-1986 Obituary 120
Wynn, Neil A(lan) 1947- 113
Wynne, Brian
See Garfield, Brian (Wynne)
Wynne, Edward A. 1928- 130
Wynne, Frank
See Garfield, Brian (Wynne)
Wynne, Greville (Maynard)
1919-1990 Obituary 131
Wynne, Lewis Nicholas 1943- 128
Wynne, May
See Knowles, Mabel Winifred
Wynne, Nancy Blue 1931- 85-88
Wynne, Paul 1943(?)-1990 Obituary 132
Wynne, Ronald D(avid) 1934- 102
Wynne, Thorne D. 1908- 5-8R
Wynne-Davies, Marion 1958- 133
Wynne-Jones, Tim(othy) 1948- CANR-39
Earlier sketch in CA 105
See also CLR 21
See also SATA 67
Wynne-Thomas, Peter 1934- 118
Wynne-Tyson, Esme 1898- 21-24R
Wynne-Tyson, (Timothy) Jon (Lyden)
1924- 17-20R
Wynn-Jones, Michael 1941- CANR-14
Earlier sketch in CA 69-72
Wynot, Edward D(avis) Jr. 1943- 105
Wynter, Edward (John) 1914- 69-72
See also SATA 14
Wynyard, Talbot
See Hamilton, Charles (Harold St. John)
Wyon, Olive 1890- CAP-1
Earlier sketch in CA 11-12
Wyrick, V(ictor) Neil Jr. 1928- 13-16R
Wyschogrod, Edith 1930- Brief entry 111
Wyschogrod, Michael 1928- 89-92
Wyse, Lois (Helene) 1926- 108
See also BEST 89:3
Wyse, Marion 1952- 123
Wysor, Bettie 1928- CANR-13
Earlier sketch in CA 77-80
Wyss, Johann David Von 1743-1818 ....MAICYA
See also SATA 27, 29
Wyss, Max Albert 1908-1977 106
Wyss, Thelma Hatch 1934- 29-32R
See also SATA 10
Wyss, Wallace A(lfred) 1944- 124
Brief entry 107
Wyszynski, Stefan 1901-1981 Obituary 108
Wyvis, Ben
See Munro, (Macfarlane) Hugh
Wyzanski, Charles E(dward) Jr.
1906-1986 ....CAP-1
Obituary 120
Earlier sketch in CA 17-18

X

Xaveria, M. Barton
See Barton, M. Xaveria
Xaveria, Sister
See Barton, M. Xaveria
Xavier I
See Horne, Frank (Smith)
Xeno
See Lake, Kenneth R(obert)
Ximenes, Ben Cuellar Jr. 1911- 5-8R
Xixx, Jezebel Q.
See Borgmann, Dmitri A(lfred)

Y

Yaari, Ehud 1945- 37-40R
Yabes, Leopoldo Y(abes) 1912- 101
Yablokoff, Herman 1903-1981 Obituary 108
Yablonsky, Lewis 1924- 21-24R
Yabsley, Suzanne 1949- 124
Yacine, Kateb 1929- 9-12R
Yacorzynski, George Kassimer 1907- 1-4R
Yacowar, Maurice 1942- 41-44R
Yadin, (Rav-Aloof) Yigael 1917-1984 ....CANR-6
Obituary 113
Earlier sketch in CA 9-12R
See also SATA 55
Yaeger, Bart
See Strung, Norman
Yafa, Stephen H. 1941- 21-24R
Yaffe, Alan
See Yorinks, Arthur
Yaffe, Barbara 1953- 85-88
Yaffe, James 1927- CANR-12
Earlier sketch in CA 5-8R
Yaffe, Richard 1903- 69-72
Yager, Jan 1948- CANR-30
Yager, Rosemary 1909- 1-4R
Yaggy, Duncan 1938- 116
Yaggy, Elinor 1907- 89-92
Yahil, Leni 29-32R
Yahraes, Herbert 1905- 81-84
Yahuda, Joseph 1900- CAP-1
Earlier sketch in CA 11-12
Yaker, Henri (Marc) 1922- Brief entry 109
Yakobson, Helen B(ates) 1913- 17-20R
Yakobson, Sergius O.
1901-1979 Obituary 89-92
Yakovenko, L.
See Kopelev, Lev (Zinovievich)
Yakovetic, Joe
See Yakovetic (Joseph Sandy)
Yakumo Koizumi
See Hearn, (Patricio) Lafcadio (Tessima Carlos)
Yalden, Derek William 1940- 69-72
Yale, Wesley W(oodworth) 1900- CAP-2
Earlier sketch in CA 29-32
Yale, William 1888(?)-1975 Obituary 57-60
Yalem, Ronald J(oseph) 1926- 17-20R
Yalman, Ahmet Emin
1888-1972 Obituary 37-40R
Yalom, Irvin D. 1931- ....BEST 90:1
Yalom, Marilyn K. 1932- 117
Yamada, Mitsuye (May) 1923- 77-80
Yamaguchi, J(ohn) Tohr 1932- 17-20R
Yamaguchi, Marianne (Illenberger)
1936- 29-32R
See also SATA 7
Yamamoto, J(erry) Isamu 1947- 77-80
Yamamoto, Kaoru 1932- CANR-12
Earlier sketch in CA 25-28R
Yamamoto, Michiko 1936- 132
Yamanouchi, Hisaaki 1934- 93-96
Yamasaki, Minoru 1912-1986 Obituary 118
Yamauchi, Edwin M(asao) 1937- CANR-19
Earlier sketches in CA 45-48, CANR-3
Yan, Chiou-Shuang Jou 1934- Brief entry 105
Yanaga, Chitoshi 1903- CAP-2
Earlier sketch in CA 25-28
Yanagimura, Shimpu
See Verwilghen, A(lbert-) Felix
Yancey, Philip D(avid) 1949- CANR-18
Earlier sketch in CA 101
Yancey, William L(ayton) 1938- 21-24R
Yancy, Robert J(ames) 1944- 57-60
Yandell, Keith E. 1938- 37-40R
Yanev, Peter (Ivanov) 1946- 77-80
Yaney, George L(evings) 1930- 104
Yaney, Joseph P(aul) 1939- CANR-9
Earlier sketch in CA 65-68
Yanez, Agustin 1904-1980 131
See also HW
Yanez, Jose Donoso
See Donoso (Yanez), Jose
Yang, C(hing) K(un) 1911- 5-8R
Yang, Jay 1941- ....SATA 12
Yang, Linda (Gureasko) 1937- 57-60
Yang, Richard F. S. 1918- CANR-10
Earlier sketch in CA 25-28R
Yang, Sung Chul 1939- 117
Yang-Jen
See Shu, Austin Chi-wei
Yang Zhong Mei 1945- 132
Yanikian, Gourgen Migirdic
1895-1984 Obituary 112
Yaniv, Avner 1942- 126
Yankelovich, Daniel 1924- 105
Yanker, Gary 1947- 37-40R
Yankowitz, Susan 1941- CANR-39
Earlier sketches in CA 45-48, CANR-1, 17
Yannarella, Philip A(nthony) 1942- 73-76
Yannatos, James 1929- 102
Yannella, Donald 1934- CANR-25
Earlier sketches in CA 57-60, CANR-8
Yanoff, Morris 1907- 108
Yanouzas, John N(icholas) 1928- 41-44R
Yanovsky, Basile S.
See Yanovsky, V(assily) S(emenovich)
Yanovsky, V(assily) S(emenovich)
1906-1989 97-100
Obituary 129
See also CLC 2, 18
Yans-McLaughlin, Virginia 1943- 89-92
Yant, Martin 1949- 134
Yao, Esther Lee 1944- CANR-29
Earlier sketch in CA 111
Yarber, Robert Earl 1929- 49-52
Yarborough, Betty Hathaway 1927- 45-48
Yarbro, Chelsea Quinn 1942- CANR-25
Earlier sketches in CA 65-68, CANR-9
Yarbrough, Camille 1938- 125
Brief entry 105
See also BW
Yarbrough, Ira 1910(?)-1983 Obituary 110
See also SATA 35
Yarbrough, Stephen R. 1950- 138
Yarbrough, Tinsley E(ugene) 1941- 109
Yarde, Jeanne Betty Frances 1925- CANR-23
Earlier sketch in CA 105
Yardley, Alice 1913- Brief entry 106
Yardley, Herbert O(sborn)
1889-1958 Brief entry 121
Yardley, Jonathan 1939- 73-76
Yardley, Richard Q(uincy)
1903-1979 Obituary 89-92
Yaremko, Michael 1914-1970 ....CAP-2
Earlier sketch in CA 25-28
Yarmey, A(lexander) Daniel 1938- CANR-17
Earlier sketch in CA 101
Yarmolinsky, Adam 1922- 37-40R
Yarmolinsky, Avrahm (Abraham)
1890-1975 ....CANR-7
Obituary 61-64
Earlier sketch in CA 5-8R
Yarmon, Morton 1916- 9-12R
Yarn, David H(omer) Jr. 1920- 17-20R
Yarnall, Sophia
See Jacobs, Sophia Yarnall
Yarnell, Allen 1942- 101
Yaroslava
See Mills, Yaroslava Surmach
Yarrow, Arnold 1920- 106
Yarrow, Marian J(eanette Radke)
1918- Brief entry 105
Yarrow, P(hilip) J(ohn) 1917- 13-16R
Yarry, Mark Robert 1940- 110
Yar-Shater, Ehsan O(llah) 1920- 37-40R
Yartz, Frank Joseph 65-68
Yarwood, Doreen 1918- CANR-18
Earlier sketch in CA 101
Yaseen, Leonard C(layton)
1912-1989 Obituary 129

Yashima, Taro
See Iwamatsu, Jun Atsushi
See also CLR 4
Yastrzemski, Carl (Michael Jr.) 1939- 104
Yates, A(lan) G(eoffrey) 1923-1985 ....CANR-3
Obituary 116
Earlier sketch in CA 1-4R
Yates, Alan
See Yates, A(lan) G(eoffrey)
Yates, Alayne 1929- 81-84
Yates, Alfred 1917- 21-24R
Yates, Aubrey J(ames) 1925- 9-12R
Yates, Brock W(endel) 1933- 9-12R
Yates, David O.
See Womack, David A(lfred)
Yates, Donald A(lfred) 1930- 41-44R
Yates, Dornford
See Mercer, Cecil William
See also DLB 77
Yates, Elizabeth 1905- CANR-21
Earlier sketches in CA 1-4R, CANR-6
See also MAICYA
See also SAAS 6
See also SATA 4, 68
Yates, Frances A(melia) 1899-1981 ....CANR-30
Obituary 105
Earlier sketch in CA 57-60
Yates, Gerard Francis
1907-1979 Obituary 89-92
Yates, J. Michael 1938- 21-24R
See also DLB 60
Yates, Madeleine 1937- 109
Yates, Norris W(ilson) 1923- 9-12R
Yates, Paul 1954- Brief entry 117
Yates, Peter Bertram
1909-1976 Obituary 65-68
Yates, Raymond F(rancis)
1895-1966 Obituary 110
See also SATA 31
Yates, Richard 1926- CANR-10
Earlier sketch in CA 5-8R
See also CLC 7, 8, 23
See also DLB 2
See also DLBY 81
Yates, W(illiam) E(dgar) 1938- 49-52
Yatron, Michael 1921- 37-40R
Yauch, Wilbur Alden 1904-1982 Obituary 106
Yaukey, David (William) 1927- 61-64
Yaukey, Grace S(ydenstricker) 1899- CANR-1
Earlier sketch in CA 1-4R
See also SATA 5
Yavetz, Zvi 1925- CANR-16
Earlier sketch in CA 29-32R
Yavitz, Boris 1923- 114
Yaw, Yvonne 1936- 65-68
Yawetz, Zwy
See Yavetz, Zvi
Yazijian, Harvey Z. 1948- 107
Yeadon, David 1942- 104
Yeager, Allan Edward 1943- 101
Yeager, Leland B(ennett) 1924- 125
Yeager, Peter C(leary) 1949- 131
Yeager, Randolph O. 1912- 130
Yeager, Robert Cushing 1942- 102
Yeager, W(illard) Hayes 1897- CAP-2
Earlier sketch in CA 19-20
Yeakley, Marjory Hall 1908- CANR-2
Earlier sketch in CA 1-4R
See also SATA 21
Yearley, Clifton K(rebs) Jr. 1925- 13-16R
Yearns, W(ilfred) Buck 1918- 134
Yearsley, Ann 1753-1806 ....DLB 109
Yearwood, Richard M(eek) 1934- 37-40R
Yeates, Mabel
See Pereira, Harold Bertram
Yeates, Maurice 1938- CANR-14
Earlier sketch in CA 41-44R
Yeatman, Linda 1938- 117
See also SATA 42
Yeats, W. B.
See Yeats, William Butler
Yeats, William Butler 1865-1939 127
Brief entry 104
See also CDBLB 1890-1914
See also DLB 10, 19, 98
See also MTCW
See also TCLC 1, 11, 18, 31
See also WLC
Yeats-Brown, F(rancis Charles Claypon)
1886-1944 Brief entry 119
Yeazell, Ruth Bernard 1947- CANR-28
Earlier sketch in CA 102
Yeck, John D(avid) 1912- 13-16R
Yee, Albert H(oy) 1929- CANR-1
Earlier sketch in CA 49-52
Yee, Chiang
See Chiang Yee
Yee, Min S. 1938- 101
Yee, Paul (R.) 1956- 135
See also SATA 67
Yeganeh, Mohammed 1923- 5-8R
Yeh, George K(ung)-C(hao)
1904-1981 Obituary 108
Yeh, Wei-lien
See Yip, Wai-lim
Yehiya, Eliezer Don
See Don-Yehiya, Eliezer
Yehoshua, Abraham B. 1936- 33-36R
See also CLC 13, 31
Yelin, Shulamis S. 121
Yellen, Samuel 1906- 1-4R
Yellen, Sherman 1932- 29-32R
Yellin, Carol Lynn (Gilmer) 1920- 17-20R
Yellin, David G(ilmer) 1916- Brief entry 115
Yellin, Jean Fagan 1930- 41-44R
Yellowitz, Irwin 1933- CANR-4
Earlier sketch in CA 45-48
Yelton, Donald Charles 1915- 106
Yelverton, Eric Esskildsen 1888-1964 ....CAP-1
Earlier sketch in CA 9-10
Yen Ching-hwang 1937- 136
Yen-Ping, Shen 1896(?)-1981 Obituary 103
Yenser, Stephen 1941- CANR-36
Earlier sketch in CA 114
Yensid, Retlaw
See Disney, Walt(er Elias)
Yeo, Cedric Arnold 1905- CAP-1
Earlier sketch in CA 17-18
Yeo, Wilma (Lethem) 1918- 25-28R
See also SATA 24
Yeoman, John 1934- 106
See also SATA 28
Yeomans, Patricia Henry 1917- 97-100
Yep, Laurence Michael 1948- CANR-1
Earlier sketch in CA 49-52
See also AAYA 5
See also CLC 35
See also CLR 3, 17
See also DLB 52
See also MAICYA
See also SATA 7, 69
Yepsen, Roger B(ennet) Jr. 1947- CANR-35
Earlier sketch in CA 114
See also SATA 59
Yerbury, Grace D. 1899- 37-40R
Yerby, Frank G(arvin) 1916-1991 ....CANR-16
Obituary 136
Earlier sketch in CA 9-12R
See also BLC 3
See also BW
See also CLC 1, 7, 22
See also DLB 76
See also MTCW
Yergin, Daniel H. 103
Yerian, Cameron John 73-76
See also SATA 21
Yerian, Margaret A. 73-76
See also SATA 21
Yermakov, Nicholas 1951- 118
Yerushalmi, Yosef Hayim 1932- Brief entry 112
Yeselson, Abraham 1921-1978 Obituary 77-80
Yesenin, Sergei Alexandrovich
See Esenin, Sergei (Alexandrovich)
Yeshayahu, Yisrael 1910-1979 Obituary 89-92
Yeshurun, Avot 1904-1992 132
Obituary 136
Yessian, Mark R(obert) 1942- CANR-10
Earlier sketch in CA 25-28R
Yetman, Norman R(oger) 1938- 29-32R
Yetska
See Ironside, Jetske
Yette, Samuel F(rederick) 1929- 102
Yeung Yue-man 1938- 110
Yevtushenko, Yevgeny (Alexandrovich)
1933- CANR-33
Earlier sketch in CA 81-84
See also CLC 1, 3, 13, 26, 51
See also MTCW
Yezierska, Anzia 1885(?)-1970 126
Obituary 89-92
See also CLC 46
See also DLB 28
See also MTCW
Yezzo, Dominick 1947- 53-56
Yglesias, Helen 1915- CANR-15
Earlier sketch in CA 37-40R
See also CLC 7, 22
See also MTCW
Yglesias, Jose 1919- CANR-32
Earlier sketch in CA 41-44R
See also HW
Yglesias, Rafael 1954- 37-40R
Yiannopoulos, A(thanassios) N(ikolaos)
1928- CANR-27
Earlier sketch in CA 1-4R
Yim, Kwan Ha 1929- 101
Yin, Robert K(uo-zuir) 1941- CANR-1
Earlier sketch in CA 49-52
Yinger, J(ohn) Milton 1916- 89-92
Yip, Wai-lim 1937- 33-36R
Yllo, Kersti 1953- 119
Ylvisaker, Paul 1921- CANR-16
Obituary 137
Earlier sketches in CA 1-4R, CANR-1
Yngve, Victor H(use) 1920- 57-60
Yntema, Theodore O(tte)
1900-1985 Obituary 117
Yoakum, Robert 1922- 77-80
Yochelson, Samuel
1906(?)-1976 Obituary 69-72
Yochim, Louise Dunn 1909- 37-40R
Yocom, Charles Frederick 1914- CANR-7
Earlier sketch in CA 17-20R
Yoder, Dale 1901- CANR-2
Earlier sketch in CA 1-4R
Yoder, Don 1921- 85-88
Yoder, Glee 1916- CANR-9
Earlier sketch in CA 21-24R
Yoder, J(ames) Willard 1902- 37-40R
Yoder, Janice D(ana) 1952- 114
Yoder, Jess 1922- 45-48
Yoder, John H(oward) 1927- 13-16R
Yoder, Marie Angeline 1914- 5-8R
Yoder, Norman M. 1915- 21-24R
Yoder, Paton 1912- 93-96
Yoder, Sanford Calvin 1879- CAP-1
Earlier sketch in CA 13-16
Yoffe, Elkhonon (Hona) 1928- 126
Yogiji, Harbhajan Singh Khalsa 1929- 93-96
Yogman, Michael W. 1947- 126
Yohe, W(illiam) Frederick 1943- 49-52
Yohn, David Waite 1933- 41-44R
Yohn, Rick 1937- CANR-8
Earlier sketch in CA 61-64
Yoingco, Angel Q. 1921- CANR-11
Earlier sketch in CA 25-28R
Yoken, Melvin B(arton) 1939- 65-68
Yokoyama, Toshio 1947- 136
Yola, Yerima
See Kirk-Greene, Anthony (Hamilton Millard)
Yolen, Jane (Hyatt) 1939- CANR-29
Earlier sketches in CA 13-16R, CANR-11
See also AAYA 4
See also CLR 4
See also DLB 52
See also MAICYA
See also SAAS 1
See also SATA 4, 40
Yolen, Steven H. 1942- 73-76
Yolen, Will(iam Hyatt) 1908-1985 ....CANR-29
Obituary 118
Earlier sketches in CA 5-8R, CANR-5
Yolton, John W(illiam) 1921- CANR-14
Earlier sketch in CA 37-40R
Yone, Edward Michael Law
See Law Yone, Edward Michael
Yonemura, Margaret V. S. 1928- 29-32R
Yonge, Charlotte (Mary)
1823-1901 Brief entry 109
See also DLB 18
See also SATA 17
Yonge, (Charles) Maurice
1899-1986 Obituary 118
Yonker, Nicholas J(unior) 1927- 117
Yoo, Grace S.
See Yoo, Young H(yun)
Yoo, Young H(yun) 1927- 41-44R
Yoo, Yushin 1940- CANR-2
Earlier sketch in CA 45-48
Yooll, Andrew M(ichael) Graham
See Graham-Yooll, Andrew M(ichael)
Yoors, Jan 1922(?)-1977 81-84
Obituary 73-76
Yora, Shandrin M(arion) 1937- 120
Yorburg, Betty 1926- CANR-16
Earlier sketch in CA 29-32R
Yorck, Ruth (Landshoff)
1909-1966 Obituary 25-28R
Yordan, Philip 1913(?)- 129
Brief entry 116
Yorick, A. P.
See Tindall, William York
Yorinks, Arthur 1953- CANR-38
Earlier sketch in CA 106
See also CLR 20
See also MAICYA
See also SATA 33, 49
York, Amanda
See Dial, Joan
York, Andrew
See Nicole, Christopher Robin
York, Carol Beach 1928- CANR-6
Earlier sketch in CA 1-4R
See also SATA 6
York, Elizabeth
See York, Margaret Elizabeth
York, Georgia
See Hoffman, Lee
York, Helen 1918- CANR-4
Earlier sketch in CA 53-56
York, Herbert (Frank) 1921- 29-32R
York, Jeremy
See Creasey, John
York, Lorraine (M.) 1958- 129
York, Margaret Elizabeth 1927- 103
York, Pauline
See Howl, Marcia (Yvonne Hurt)
York, Phyllis 1937- 132
York, Rebecca
See Buckholtz, Eileen (Garber)
and Glick, Ruth (Burtnick)
York, Reginald O(scar) 1942- 117
York, Simon
See Heinlein, Robert A(nson)
York, Susannah 1941- 130
York, Thomas (Lee) 1940- 73-76
York, William 1950- 107
Yorke, Henry Vincent 1905-1974 85-88
Obituary 49-52
See also Green, Henry
See also CLC 13
Yorke, Katherine
See Ellerbeck, Rosemary (Anne L'Estrange)
Yorke, Malcolm 1938- 131
Yorke, Margaret
See Larminie, Margaret Beda
Yorke, Ritchie 1944- 77-80
Yorke, Roger
See Bingley, David Ernest
Yorke, Susan 1915- CANR-1
Earlier sketch in CA 1-4R
Yorkist
See Morrah, Dermot (Michael Macgregor)
Yoseloff, Martin 1919- 45-48
Yoseloff, Thomas 1913- 77-80
Yoshida, (Katsumi) Jim 1921- 41-44R
Yoshida, Shigeru 1878-1967 Obituary 113
Yoshimasu Gozo 1939- 126
Yoskowitz, Irving
See Younger, Irving
Yost, Charles W(oodruff) 1907-1981 ....CANR-3
Obituary 104
Earlier sketch in CA 9-12R
Yost, Edna 1889-1971 ....1-4R
Obituary 103
See also SATA 26
Yost, Elwy McMurran 1925- 126
Yost, F(rank) Donald 1927- 29-32R
Yost, Graham 1959- 129
Yost, Nellie Snyder 1905- CANR-16
Earlier sketch in CA 29-32R
Yost, Stanley K. 1924- 9-12R
Youcha, Geraldine 1925- 93-96
Youd, C. S.
See Youd, (Christopher) Samuel
See also SAAS 6
Youd, (Christopher) Samuel 1922- CANR-37
Earlier sketch in CA 77-80
See also Christopher, John
and Youd, C. S.
See also MAICYA
See also SATA 30, 47
Youdale, Peter J. 1928- 45-48
Youman, Roger J(acob) 1932- 65-68
Youmans, E(lmer) Grant 1907- CAP-2
Earlier sketch in CA 23-24
Youmans, Marlene 1953- 77-80
Young, Agatha
See Young, Agnes Brooks
Young, Agnes Brooks 1898-1974 Obituary 109
Young, Ahdele Carrine 1923- 107
Young, Al(bert James) 1939- CANR-26
Earlier sketch in CA 29-32R
See also BLC 3
See also BW
See also CLC 19
See also DLB 33
Young, Alan R(oger) 1941- 89-92
Young, Alan 1930- CANR-6
Earlier sketch in CA 57-60
Young, Alison 1922- CANR-29
Earlier sketch in CA 53-56
Young, Allan Edward 1939- 125
Young, Allen 1941- CANR-39
Earlier sketches in CA 101, CANR-18
Young, Andrew (John) 1885-1971 ....CANR-29
Earlier sketches in CA 5-8R, CANR-7
See also CLC 5
Young, Angela
See Yardley, Alice
Young, Anne P(atricia) 1921- 65-68
Young, Anne Steele 1923- 129
Young, Arthur C(lements) 1923- 25-28R
Young, Arthur N(ichols) 1890-1984 ....9-12R
Obituary 113
Young, Axel
See McDowell, Michael
Young, Bernice Elizabeth 1931- 37-40R
Young, Bertram Alfred 1912- 105
Young, Billie 1936- 53-56
Young, Bob
See Young, James Robert
and Young, Robert W(illiam)
Young, Brittany
See Young, Sandra
Young, Carrie
See Young, Ahdele Carrine
Young, Carter Travis
See Charbonneau, Louis (Henry)
Young, Catherine
See Olds, Helen Diehl
Young, Catherine Alicia 1963- 136
Young, Cathy
See Young, Catherine Alicia
Young, Charles M(atthew) 1951- 93-96
Young, Charles R(obert) 1927- 13-16R
Young, Chesley Virginia 1919- 33-36R
Young, Chic
See Young, Murat Bernard (Chic)
Young, Clarence CANR-27
Earlier sketches in CAP-2, CA 19-20
See also SATA 1, 67
Young, Collier
See Bloch, Robert (Albert)
Young, Collier 1908(?)-1980 Obituary 103
Young, Dallas M. 1914- 17-20R
Young, David C(harles) 1937- 41-44R
Young, David P(ollock) 1936- CANR-24
Earlier sketches in CA 21-24R, CANR-9
Young, David S(amuel D'arcy) 1946- 113
Young, Dean (Wayne) 1938- 130
Young, Delbert Alton 1907-1975 105
Young, Dennis R(alph) 1943- Brief entry 107
Young, Dick 1918(?)-1987 Obituary 123
Young, Donald Ramsey
1898-1977 Obituary 69-72
Young, Donald (Richard) 1933- CANR-12
Earlier sketch in CA 13-16R
Young, Dorothea Bennett 1924- CANR-13
Earlier sketch in CA 13-16R
See also SATA 31
Young, Douglas (Cuthbert Colquhoun)
1913-1973 ....CAP-1
Obituary 45-48
Earlier sketch in CA 17-18
Young, Ed (Tse-chun) 1931- 130
Brief entry 116
See also CLR 27
See also MAICYA
See also SATA 10
Young, Edgar Berryhill 1908- 104
Young, Edith 49-52
Young, Edward
See Reinfeld, Fred
Young, Edward J(oseph) 1907-1968 ....CAP-1
Earlier sketch in CA 11-12
Young, Edward 1683-1765 ....DLB 95
Young, (Cecil) Edwyn 1913-1988 Obituary 124
Young, Elaine L.
See Schulte, Elaine L(ouise)
Young, Eleanor R. 1918- 37-40R
Young, Elisabeth Larsh 1910- 81-84
Young, Elizabeth 108
Young, Ellin Dodge 1932- 106
Young, Everett
See Cosby, Yvonne Shepard
Young, Ezra P(orter) 1902- 113
Young, Francis A(lfred) 1907- 130

Young, Francis Brett 1884-1954 Brief entry 122
Young, Frank Carl 1907- CAP-1
Earlier sketch in CA 13-14
Young, Frank Wilbur 1928- Brief entry 108
Young, Fred(erick) L(ee) 1922- 25-28R
Young, G(eorge) M(alcolm) 1882-1959 Brief entry 120
Young, Gary 1951- 117
Young, George Berkeley 1913-1988 Obituary 124
Young, George F(rederick) W(illiam) 1937- 57-60
Young, George Kennedy 1911-1990 Obituary 131
Young, Gregory G. 1929- Brief entry 110
Young, Harold Chester 1932- 129
Brief entry 109
Young, Harold H(erbert) 1903- CAP-2
Earlier sketch in CA 19-20
Young, Howard Thomas 1926- 9-12R
Young, Hugo (John Smelter) 1938- CANR-28
Earlier sketch in CA 25-28R
Young, I(sador) S. 1902- 102
Young, Ian (George) 1945- CANR-27
Earlier sketches in CA 29-32R, CANR-11
Young, J(ames) Harvey 1915- CANR-6
Earlier sketch in CA 1-4R
Young, J(ohn) Z(achary) 1907- CANR-19
Earlier sketch in CA 101
Young, James Allan 1934- 116
Young, James D(ean) 1925- Brief entry 111
Young, James Douglas 1921- 25-28R
Young, James J(oseph) 1940- CANR-16
Earlier sketch in CA 93-96
Young, James O(wen) 1943- 49-52
Young, James Robert 1921- 93-96
Young, James V(an) 1936- 69-72
Young, Jan
See Young, Janet Randall
Young, Janet Randall 1919- CANR-5
Earlier sketch in CA 5-8R
See also SATA 3
Young, Jessica (Hankinson) Brett
See Brett-Young, Jessica (Hankinson)
Young, Jim 1930- 109
Young, Jock 1942- 104
Young, John K(arl) 1951- 135
Young, John Orr 1886-1976 Obituary 65-68
Young, John Parke 1895- 5-8R
Young, John V. 1909- 121
Young, John Wesley 1951- 138
Young, John Wray 1907- 45-48
Young, John 1920- CANR-1
Earlier sketch in CA 45-48
Young, John 1934- 134
Young, Jordan Marten 1920- 21-24R
Young, Karen M. 1942- 138
Young, Kenneth T(odd) 1916-1972 Obituary 37-40R
Young, Kenneth 1916-1985 .....CANR-3
Obituary 118
Earlier sketch in CA 9-12R
Young, Leontine R(uth) 1910-1988 ..... CAP-1
Obituary 126
Earlier sketch in CA 11-12
Young, Lesley 1949- 110
Young, Lois Horton 1911-1981 .....9-12R
See also SATA 26
Young, Louise B. 1919- CANR-10
Earlier sketch in CA 25-28R
See also SATA 64
Young, Louise Merwin 1903- CAP-1
Earlier sketch in CA 11-12
Young, M(erwin) Crawford 1931- 13-16R
Young, Mahonri 1911- 81-84
Young, Margaret B(uckner) 1922- 21-24R
See also SATA 2
Young, Margaret Labash 1926- 134
Brief entry 110
Young, Marguerite CAP-1
Earlier sketch in CA 13-16
Young, Marjorie W(illis) 85-88
Young, Martin 1947- 127
Young, Mary Elizabeth Reardon 1901(?)-1981 Obituary 105
Young, Mary Elizabeth 1929- 37-40R
Young, Mary Lou Daves 1918-1991 126
Obituary 135
Young, Michael (Dunlop) 1915- 101
Young, Miriam 1913-1974 .....37-40R
Obituary 53-56
See also SATA 7
Young, Morris N. 1909- 33-36R
Young, Murat Bernard (Chic) 1901-1973 Obituary 41-44R
Young, Nacella
See Tate, Velma
Young, Neil 1945- 110
See also CLC 17
Young, Noel 1922- 57-60
Young, Norman J(ames) 1930- 77-80
Young, Oran R(eed) 1941- 112
Brief entry 109
Young, Otis E. Jr. 1925- 53-56
Young, Pam 1943- 109
Young, (Rodney Lee) Patrick (Jr.) 1937- 69-72
See also SATA 22
Young, Paul Thomas 1892-1978 .....CANR-3
Earlier sketch in CA 1-4R
Young, Pauline Vislick 1896- 5-8R
Young, Percy M(arshall) 1912- CANR-31
Earlier sketch in CA 13-16R
See also SATA 31
Young, Perry Deane 1941- 57-60
Young, Peter Alan 1934- 107
Young, Peter 1915- 13-16R
Young, Philip
See Steward, Samuel M(orris)
Young, Philip 1918-1991 .....CANR-6
Obituary 135
Earlier sketch in CA 9-12R
Young, R(obert) V(aughan) 1947- 127
Young, Ralph Aubrey 1902(?)-1980 Obituary 97-100
Young, Richard E(merson) 1932- 29-32R
Young, Richard Knox 1913- 13-16R
Young, Richard Phillip 1940- 29-32R
Young, Robert
See Payne, (Pierre Stephen) Robert
Young, Robert Doran 1928- CANR-17
Earlier sketch in CA 29-32R
Young, Robert J(ohn) 1942- 101
Young, Robert W(illiam) 1916-1969 .....CANR-5
Earlier sketch in CA 5-8R
See also SATA 3
Young, Robert 1944- 123
Young, Rose
See Harris, Marion Rose (Young)
Young, Ruth 1884-1983 Obituary 111
Young, Ruth 1946- 136
See also SATA 67
Young, Sandra 1952- 124
Young, Scott A(lexander) 1918- CANR-20
Earlier sketches in CA 9-12R, CANR-5
See also SATA 5
Young, Seymour Dilworth 1897- CAP-2
Earlier sketch in CA 29-32
Young, Stanley (Preston) 1906-1975 Obituary 57-60
Young, Stark 1881-1963 105
Obituary 89-92
See also DLB 9, 102
Young, Stephen M(arvin) 1889(?)-1984 Obituary 114
Young, Thomas
See Yoseloff, Thomas
Young, Thomas Daniel 1919- CANR-14
Earlier sketch in CA 37-40R
Young, Vernon 1912-1986 45-48
Obituary 120
Young, Virginia Brady 1921- 61-64
Young, Virginia G(arton) 1919- 13-16R
Young, Vivien
See Gater, Dilys
Young, Waldemar 1880-1938 ..... DLB 26
Young, Warren C(ameron) 1913- 13-16R
Young, Warren R(ichard) 1926- 21-24R
Young, Wayland 1923- 13-16R
Young, Whitney M(oore) Jr. 1921-1971 .....CANR-25
Earlier sketches in CAP-1, CA 13-14
See also BW
Young, William C(urtis) 1928- 45-48
Young, William H(enry) 1912- 21-24R
Young, William J. 1938- 109
Young, William 1918- 45-48
Youngberg, Norma Ione (Rhoads) 1896- 9-12R
Youngberg, Ruth Tanis 1915- 107
Youngblood, Ila Dell 1926- 125
Youngblood, Ronald F. 1931- CANR-30
Earlier sketches in CA 37-40R, CANR-14
Young-Bruehl, Elisabeth 1946- 131
Youngdahl, Benjamin E(manuel) 1897-1970 ..... CAP-2
Earlier sketch in CA 21-22
Youngdahl, Reuben K(enneth Nathaniel) 1911-1968 .....5-8R
Obituary 103
Younge, Sheila 1945(?)-1977 Obituary 73-76
Younger, Edward Eugene 1909-1979 Obituary 89-92
Younger, George Colman the 1762-1836 ..... DLB 89
Younger, Irving 1932-1988 Obituary 125
Younger, Paul 1935- 101
Younger, R(onald) M(ichel) 1917- CANR-10
Earlier sketch in CA 17-20R
Younger, Richard D(avis) 1921- 9-12R
Younghusband, Eileen (Louise) 1902-1981 Obituary 108
Younghusband, Francis (Edward) 1863-1942 Brief entry 113
Youngman, Henny 1906(?)- 134
Brief entry 107
Youngquist, Walter 1921- 61-64
Youngren, J(ohn) Alan 1937- 108
Youngs, Betty F(errell) 1928- 33-36R
Youngs, Betty 1934-1985 117
See also SATA 42, 53
Youngs, Frederic A. Jr. 1936- Brief entry 112
Youngs, J. William T. Jr. 1941- CANR-10
Earlier sketch in CA 65-68
Youngs, Robert W(ells) 1913- 13-16R
Younie, William John 1932- 21-24R
Younin, Wolf 1908(?)-1984 Obituary 112
Younker, Lucas 1942- 65-68
Yount, John A(lonzo) 1935- CANR-5
Earlier sketch in CA 45-48
Yourcenar, Marguerite 1903-1987 .....CANR-23
Earlier sketch in CA 69-72
See also CLC 19, 38, 50
See also DLB 72
See also DLBY 88
See also MTCW
Youree, Gary 1931- CANR-2
Earlier sketch in CA 49-52
Youssef, Edwar Kolta Faltas
See al-Kharrat, Edwar
Yousuf, Ahmed
See Essop, Ahmed
Youtie, Herbert Chayyim 1904-1980 Obituary 97-100
Yowa
See McMurray, Nancy A(rmistead)
Yoxall, Harry W(aldo) 1896-1984 .....13-16R
Obituary 113
Yoxen, Edward (John) 1950- 123
Yu, Anthony C. 1938- Brief entry 110
Yu, Beongcheon 1925- Brief entry 108
Yu, Charles
See Targ, William
Yu, David C. 1918- 37-40R
Yu, Elena S. H. 1947- 125
Brief entry 109
Yu, Frederick T. C. 1921- 9-12R
Yu, George T(zuchiao) 1931- 17-20R
Yu, Pauline (Ruth) 1949- 122
Brief entry 118
Yu, Sui
See Chou, Eric
Yu, Ying-shih 1930- 25-28R
Yuan, Lei Chen
See De Jaegher, Raymond-Joseph
Yuan, T'ung-li 1895-1965 ..... CAP-1
Earlier sketch in CA 9-10
Yudell, Lynn D. 1943- 29-32R
Yudewitz, Hyman 1906- 93-96
Yudkin, John 1910- 13-16R
Yudkin, Leon Israel 1939- CANR-12
Earlier sketch in CA 29-32R
Yudkin, Michael D(avid) 1938- 29-32R
Yudof, Mark G(eorge) 1944- 109
Yu-ho, Tseng
See Ecke, Betty Tseng Yu-ho
Yuill, P. B.
See Williams, Gordon M(aclean)
Yuill, Phyllis Jean (Marquart) 1941- 65-68
Yuill, William Edward 1921- CANR-2
Earlier sketch in CA 1-4R
Yukawa, Hideki 1907-1981 Obituary 108
Yuki
See Inoue, Yukitoshi
Yule, Andrew 1936- 129
Yuma, Dan
See Dunham, Robert
Yun, Tan
See Lin, Adet J(usu)
Yunck, John A(dam) III 1917- 9-12R
Yungblut, John R(ichard) 1913- 41-44R
Yunkel, Ramar
See Martin, Jose L(uis)
Yunkel, Ramar
See Martin, Jose L(uis)
Yurchenco, Henrietta 1916- 37-40R
Yurick, Sol 1925- CANR-25
Earlier sketch in CA 13-16R
See also CLC 6
Yurieff, Zoya I(osifovna) 1922- Brief entry 109
Yurka, Blanche 1887-1974 .....9-12R
Obituary 120
Yusko, A(aron) A(llen) 1935- 65-68
Yu Zhuoyun 1918- 132
Yuzyk, Paul 1913- CANR-18
Earlier sketch in CA 101
Yzermans, Vincent Arthur 1925- 13-16R

Z

Zabaneh, Natalia (Shefka) 1946- 105
Zabeeh, Farhana 1919- 41-44R
Zabih, Sepehr 1925- CANR-9
Earlier sketch in CA 21-24R
Zabilka, Gladys M. 1917- 5-8R
Zablocki, Benjamin 1941- 37-40R
Zablocki, Clement J(ohn) 1912-1983 Obituary 111
Zabolotskii, Nikolai Alekseevich 1903-1958 Brief entry 116
Zabriskie, George 1919(?)-1989 Obituary 128
Zacek, Jane Shapiro 1938- 109
Zacek, Joseph Frederick 1930- 37-40R
Zach, Cheryl (Byrd) 1947- 124
See also SATA 51, 58
Zach, Nathan 1930- Brief entry 105
Zachariae, Friedrich Wilhelm 1726-1777 ..... DLB 97
Zacharias, Lee
See Zacharias, Lela Ann
Zacharias, Lela Ann 1944- CANR-27
Earlier sketch in CA 85-88
Zacharis, John C. 1936- 73-76
Zachary, Elizabeth 1928- 109
Zachary, Hugh 1928- CANR-13
Earlier sketch in CA 21-24R
Zachary, Saul 1934- 129
Zacher, Christian Keeler 1941- 105
Zacher, Mark W. 1938- 85-88
Zacher, Robert Vincent 1917- 1-4R
Zack, Arnold M(arshall) 1931- CANR-19
Earlier sketches in CA 9-12R, CANR-3
Zade, Mirzo Tursun
See Tursun-Zade, Mirzo
Zadeh, Norman 1950- 61-64
Zadravec, Katharine E. 1933(?)-1989 Obituary 128
Zaehner, Robert Charles 1913-1974 Obituary 109
Zaffo, George J. ..... SATA 42
Zaffuto, Anthony A(ngelo) 1926- 101
Zafren, Herbert C(ecil) 1925- CANR-25
Earlier sketch in CA 45-48
Zagar, J. Janko 1921- 121
Zagarell, Sandra A(belson) 1943- 118
Zagat, Arthur Leo 1895(?)-1949 Brief entry 110
Zagona, Salvatore Vincent 1920- Brief entry 108
Zagoren, Marc Alan 1940- 132
Zagoren, Ruby 1922-1974 ..... CAP-1
Earlier sketch in CA 17-18
Zagoria, Donald S. 1928- CANR-16
Earlier sketch in CA 21-24R
Zagorin, Perez 1920- CANR-36
Earlier sketch in CA 53-56
Zagst, Michael (Sidney) 1950- 121
Zaharias, Babe Didrikson
See Zaharias, Mildred Ella Didrikson
Zaharias, Mildred Ella Didrikson 1914(?)-1956 Brief entry 117
Zaharopoulos, George K. 1933- 41-44R
Zahava, Irene 1951- 57-60
Zahl, Paul Arthur 1910-1985 Obituary 117
Zahler, Helene S. 1911-1981 Obituary 104
Zahn, Curtis 1912- CANR-5
Earlier sketch in CA 5-8R
Zahn, Frank 1936- 97-100
Zahn, Gordon C(harles) 1918- 9-12R
Zahn, Muriel 1894- 5-8R
Zahn, Timothy 1951- 123
Zahniser, Marvin R(alph) 1934- 21-24R
Zahorchak, Michael G(eorge) 1929- CANR-15
Earlier sketch in CA 41-44R
Zahorski, Kenneth J. 1939- 123
Zaid, Barry 1938- ..... SATA 51
Zaidenberg, Arthur 1908(?)-1990 108
Obituary 131
See also SATA 34
See also SATO 66
Zaidi, S(yed) M(ohammad) Hafeez 1929- CANR-25
Earlier sketch in CA 45-48
Zainu'ddin, Ailsa
See Zainu'ddin, Ailsa G(wennyth) Thomson
Zainu'ddin, Ailsa G(wennyth) Thomson 1927- CANR-12
Earlier sketch in CA 29-32R
Zajonc, Robert Boleslaw 1923- Brief entry 106
Zakaria, Haji Ahmad 1947- 138
Zakarian, John J. 1937- 132
Zakarian, Richard H(achadoor) 1925- 41-44R
Zakia, Richard D(onald) 1925- CANR-9
Earlier sketch in CA 65-68
Zaknic, Ivan 1938- 138
Zakon, Alan J. 1935- 17-20R
Zakuta, Leo 1925- 17-20R
Zalamea, Luis 1921- 17-20R
Zalan, Magda 1936- 112
Zalben, Jane Breskin 1950- CANR-4
Earlier sketch in CA 49-52
See also SATA 7
Zald, Mayer N(athan) 1931- CANR-28
Earlier sketches in CA 17-20R, CANR-8
Zaldivar, Fulgencio Batista y
See Batista y Zaldivar, Fulgencio
Zaleski, Eugene 1918- 77-80
Zaleznik, Abraham 1924- CANR-37
Earlier sketch in CA 73-76
Zali, Paul M. 1922- Brief entry 108
Zalis, Paul 1952- 138
Zalkind, Sheldon S(tanley) 1922- 65-68
Zall, Paul M. 1922- CANR-20
Earlier sketches in CA 1-4R, CANR-6
Zaller, Angelika Bita CANR-36
Earlier sketches in CA 77-80, CANR-13
Zaller, Robert 1940- CANR-32
Earlier sketches in CA 77-80, CANR-13
Zallinger, Jean (Day) 1918- ..... SATA 14
Zallinger, Peter Franz 1943- 108
See also SATA 49
Zalon, Jean E(ugenia) 1919- 102
Zaltkovich, Charles T(heodore) 1917- 5-8R
Zaltman, Gerald 1938- CANR-7
Earlier sketch in CA 17-20R
Zalzanick, Sheldon 1928- 77-80
Zamble, Edward 1942- Brief entry 108
Zamiatin, Yevgenii
See Zamyatin, Evgeny Ivanovich
Zamonski, Stanley W. 1919- 9-12R
Zamora, Bernice (B. Ortiz) 1938- ..... DLB 82
See also HW
Zamoyski, Adam (Stefan Jan Maria Sariusz) 1949- 103
Zamoyta, Vincent C. 1921- 21-24R
Zampaglione, Gerardo 1917- CANR-14
Earlier sketch in CA 77-80
Zamyatin, Evgeny Ivanovich 1884-1937 Brief entry 105
See also TCLC 8, 37
Zand, Dale Ezra 1926- 111
Zand, Herbert 1923-1970 ..... DLB 85
Zand, Roxanne 1952- 138
Zander, Alvin Frederick 1913- CANR-19
Earlier sketch in CA 1-4R
Zanderbergen, George
See May, Julian
Zaner, Richard M(orris) 1933- CANR-16
Earlier sketch in CA 29-32R
Zanetti, J(oaquin) Enrique 1885-1974 Obituary 45-48
Zangger, Eberhard 1958- 138
Zangrando, Robert L. 1932- 25-28R
Zangwill, Israel 1864-1926 Brief entry 109
See also DLB 10
See also TCLC 16
Zangwill, Oliver Louis 1913- 109
Zanjani, Sally Springmeyer 120
Zants, Emily 1937- 37-40R
Zanuck, Daryl F(rancis) 1902-1979 Obituary 93-96
Zapata Olivella, Manuel 1920- ..... DLB 113
See also HW

Zappa, Francis Vincent Jr. 1940- 108
See also Zappa, Frank
Zappa, Frank
See Zappa, Francis Vincent Jr.
See also CLC 17
Zappler, Lisbeth 1930- CANR-4
Earlier sketch in CA 49-52
See also SATA 10
Zar, Rose 1923- 117
Zara, Louis 1910- CAP-2
Earlier sketch in CA 13-14
Zarchy, Harry 1912- CANR-2
Earlier sketch in CA 1-4R
See also SATA 34
Zarcone, Vincent P(eter) Jr. 1937- 61-64
Zarefsky, David (Harris) 1946- Brief entry 109
Zaremba, Eve 1930- 133
Zaremba, Joseph 1923- Brief entry 112
Zaretsky, Eli 1940- CANR-37
Earlier sketch in CA 85-88
Zaring, Jane (Thomas) 1936- 108
See also SATA 40, 51
Zarins, Joyce Audy
See dos Santos, Joyce Audy
See also SATA 57
Zariski, Raphael 1925- 49-52
Zarnecki, George 1915- CANR-10
Earlier sketch in CA 57-60
Zarnecki, Jerzy
See Zarnecki, George
Zarnow, Teryl 1951- 135
Zarnowitz, Victor 1919- 21-24R
Zarro, Richard A(llen) 1946- 33-36R
Zartman, I(ra) William 1932- CANR-5
Earlier sketch in CA 9-12R
Zarucchi, Jeanne Morgan 1955- 138
Zaslavskaya, Tatyana (Ivanovna) 1924- 138
Zaslavsky, Claudia 1917- CANR-1
Earlier sketch in CA 49-52
See also SATA 36
Zasloff, J. J.
See Zasloff, Joseph J(ermiah)
Zasloff, Joseph J(ermiah) 1925- 129
Brief entry 116
Zaslow, Morris 1918- CANR-24
Earlier sketch in CA 45-48
Zassenhaus, Hiltgunt 1916- 49-52
See also AITN 1
Zastrow, Charles 1942- 127
Zastrow, Erika
See Massey, Erika
Zatlin, Phyllis 1938- CANR-36
Earlier sketches in CA 41-44R, CANR-15
Zatlin-Boring, Phyllis
See Zatlin, Phyllis
Zatlin Boring, Phyllis
See Zatlin, Phyllis
Zatuchni, Gerald I. 1935- 37-40R
Zaturenska, Marya 1902-1982 ....CANR-22
Obituary 105
Earlier sketch in CA 13-16R
See also CLC 6, 11
Zauberman, Alfred 1903-1984 Obituary 112
Zavala, Albert 1930- Brief entry 117
Zavala, Iris M(ilagros) 1936- CANR-32
Earlier sketches in CA 45-48, CANR-1
See also HW
Zavarzadeh, Mas'ud 1938- 106
Zavatsky, Bill
See Zavatsky, William Alexander
Zavatsky, William Alexander 1943- CANR-1
Earlier sketch in CA 49-52
Zavattini, Cesare 1902-1989 130
Zavin, Benjamin B. 1920(?)-1981 Obituary 103
Zavin, Theodora 1922- 53-56
Zavrian, Suzanne (Ostro) 1928- 113
Zawadsky, Patience 1927- CANR-24
Earlier sketches in CA 21-24R, CANR-9
Zawadzki, Edward S. 1914-1967 .... CAP-2
Earlier sketch in CA 17-18
Zawodny, J(anusz) K(azimierz) 1921- CANR-11
Earlier sketch in CA 13-16R
Zax, Melvin 1928- CANR-36
Earlier sketch in CA 37-40R
Zayas-Bazan, Eduardo 1935- CANR-37
Earlier sketch in CA 53-56
Zdenek, Marilee 1934- 102
Zea, Leopoldo 1912- CANR-16
Earlier sketch in CA 29-32R
Zeavin, Edna A. 1930- 138
Zebel, Sydney H. 1914- 1-4R
Zebot, Cyril A. 1914-1989 Obituary 128
Zebouni, Selma A(ssir) 1930- 17-20R
Zebrowski, George (T.) 1945- CANR-30
Earlier sketch in CA 41-44R
See also DLB 8
See also SATA 67
Zec, Philip 1910(?)-1983 Obituary 110
Zech, Paul 1881-1946 .... DLB 56
Zeck, Gerald Anthony 1939- 114
See also SATA 40
Zeck, Gerry
See Zeck, Gerald Anthony
Zeckendorf, William 1905- 73-76
Zeckhauser, Richard Jay 1940- 126
Zed, Dr.
See Penrose, Gordon
Zedler, Beatrice H(ope) 1916- CANR-36
Earlier sketch in CA 41-44R
Zedler, Empress Young 1908- 41-44R
Zee, A. 138
Zeeveld, W(illiam) Gordon 1902-1975 ......41-44R
Zeff, Stephen A(ddam) 1933- CANR-19
Earlier sketches in CA 9-12R, CANR-3
Zegart, Arthur 1917(?)-1989 Obituary 127
Zegger, Robert Elie 1932- 41-44R
Zehna, Peter W(illiam) 1925- CANR-1
Earlier sketch in CA 1-4R
Zehnle, Richard F(rederick) 1933- 29-32R
Zehnpfennig, Gladys Burandt 1910- CANR-5
Earlier sketch in CA 5-8R
Zehring, John William 1947- 117
Zei, Alki 77-80
See also CLR 6
See also SATA 24
Zeidenstein, Harvey 1932- 57-60
Zeidman, Irving 1908- CAP-2
Earlier sketch in CA 21-22
Zeidner, Lisa 1955- 110
See also DLB 120
Zeiger, Henry A(nthony) 1930- 9-12R
Zeiger, Larry
See King, Larry
Zeigerman, Gerald 1939- 21-24R
Zeigfreid, Karl
See Fanthorpe, R(obert) Lionel
Zeigler, L(uther) Harmon 1936- CANR-10
Earlier sketch in CA 13-16R
Zeilik, Michael 1946- CANR-36
Earlier sketch in CA 65-68
Zeisel, Hans 1905- CANR-6
Obituary 137
Earlier sketch in CA 1-4R
Zeit, Calvin
See Barasch, Marc Ian
Zeitlin, Irving M. 1928- CANR-37
Earlier sketch in CA 21-24R
Zeitlin, Jonathan (Hart) 1955- 121
Zeitlin, Joseph 1906- 49-52
Zeitlin, Maurice 1935- CANR-26
Earlier sketches in CA 13-16R, CANR-10
Zeitlin, Patty 1936- CANR-12
Earlier sketch in CA 25-28R
Zeitlin, Solomon 1888(?)-1976 77-80
Obituary 69-72
Zeitz, James (Victor) 1940- 110
Zeka, Valentin
See Sokolov, Valentin
Zekman, Pamela (Lois) 1944- 106
Zekowski, Arlene 1922- CANR-1
Earlier sketch in CA 45-48
Zelazny, Roger (Joseph) 1937- CANR-26
Earlier sketch in CA 21-24R
See also AAYA 7
See also CLC 21
See also DLB 8
See also MTCW
See also SATA 39, 57
Zeldin, Jesse 1923- 49-52
Zeldis, Chayym 1927- CANR-6
Earlier sketch in CA 1-4R
Zelditch, Morris Jr. 1928- 53-56
Zeldner, Max 1907- CAP-1
Earlier sketch in CA 13-14
Zeldovich, Ia(kov) B(orisovich)
1914-1987 Obituary 124
Zeleny, Jindrich 1922- 132
Zeleny, Lawrence 1904- 61-64
Zeleny, Leslie D(ay) 1898- 45-48
Zelermyer, William 1914- CANR-28
Earlier sketch in CA 1-4R
Zeligs, Meyer A(aron) 1909-1978 .... CAP-2
Obituary 77-80
Earlier sketch in CA 23-24
Zeligs, Rose 57-60
Zelinka, Sydney 1906(?)-1981 Obituary 102
Zelinsky, Paul O. 1953- CANR-38
Earlier sketch in CA 121
See also MAICYA
See also SATA 33, 49
Zelinsky, Wilbur 1921- 13-16R
Zelizer, Viviana A. 1946- 125
Zelk, Zoltan 1906-1981 Obituary 103
Zelko, Harold Philip 1908- CANR-1
Earlier sketch in CA 1-4R
Zell, Hans M(artin) 1940- CANR-32
Earlier sketch in CA 113
Zellan, Audrey Penn
See Penn, Audrey
See also SATA 22
Zeller, Belle 1903- 57-60
Zeller, Frederic 1924- 132
Zeller, Frederick A. 1931- 21-24R
Zellerbach, Merla 1930- 1-4R
Zellers, Parker 1927- 37-40R
Zellmann-Finkbeiner, Peter 1942- 49-52
Zellner, Arnold 1927- 41-44R
Zelman, Aaron S(hepard) 1946- 101
Zelman, Anita 1924- 101
Zelmer, A(dam) C(harles) Lynn 1943- CANR-16
Earlier sketch in CA 89-92
Zelomek, A. Wilbert
1900-1980 Obituary 97-100
Zelver, Patricia (Farrell) 1923- 29-32R
Zemach, Harve
See Fischtrom, Harvey
See also SATA 3
Zemach, Kaethe 1958- CANR-8
Earlier sketch in CA 57-60
See also SATA 39, 49
Zemach, Margot 1931-1989 ....CANR-38
Obituary 128
Earlier sketch in CA 97-100
See also MAICYA
See also SATA 21, 59, 70
Zeman, Jarold Knox 1926- 101
Zeman, Zbynek Anthony Bohuslav 1928- 69-72
Zemansky, Mark W(aldo)
1900-1981 Obituary 105
Zend, Robert 1929- 115
Zender, Karl F(rancis) 1937- 110
Zenger, John Peter 1697-1746 ....DLB 24, 43
Zenkovsky, Serge A. 1907- CANR-2
Earlier sketch in CA 1-4R
Zenowich, Christopher 1954- 134
Zens, Patricia Martin 1926-1972 ....5-8R
Obituary 120
See also SATA 50
Zentner, Carola 1927- 65-68
Zentner, Peter 1932- 29-32R
Zepeda, Ofelia 1954- 114
Zephir, Jacques J(oseph) 1925- 45-48
Zepke, Brent Eric 1943- CANR-13
Earlier sketch in CA 69-72
Zepp, Ira G(ilbert) Jr. 1929- 135
Brief entry 114
Zerafa, Judy 1941- 113
Zerbe, Jerome (B.) 1904-1988 ....CANR-37
Obituary 126
Earlier sketch in CA 17-20R
Zerby, Lewis Kenneth 1916- 49-52
Zerden, Sheldon 1924- CANR-10
Earlier sketch in CA 25-28R
Zerin, Edward 1920- 5-8R
Zerman, Melvyn Bernard 1930- CANR-14
Earlier sketch in CA 77-80
See also SATA 46
Zernov, Nicolas (Michael) 1898-1980 ......CANR-6
Earlier sketch in CA 9-12R
Zerof, Herbert G. 1934- 85-88
Zesmer, David M(ordecai) 1924- 65-68
Zeta
See Cope, (Vincent) Zachary
Zetford, Tully
See Bulmer, (Henry) Kenneth
Zetler, Robert L. 1908- 1-4R
Zetterling, Mai (Elisabeth) 1925- 126
Brief entry 111
Zettl, Herbert (Lorenz) 1929- 41-44R
Zettler, Howard G. 1926- Brief entry 113
Zettner, Pat 1940- 138
See also SATA 70
Zeuner, Frederick E(verard) 1905-1963 ....5-8R
Zevi, Bruno 1918- CANR-18
Earlier sketch in CA 101
Zevin, Ben David 1896(?)-1984 Obituary 114
Zevin, Jack 1940- 93-96
Zevin, Robert B(rooke) 1936- 117
Zeydel, Edwin H(ermann) 1893-1973 ....5-8R
Obituary 103
Zeyher, Lewis R. 1906- 25-28R
Zgusta, Ladislav 1924- 41-44R
Zhang Jie 1937- 133
Zhang Xinxin 1953- 134
Zhdanov, Andrei A(lexandrovich)
1896-1948 Brief entry 117
See also TCLC 18
Zheludkov, Sergei 1909(?)-1984 Obituary 111
Zhivkova, Lyudmila (Todorova)
1942-1981 Obituary 108
Zholkovsky, Alexander K(onstantinovich)
1937- 133
Zhukov, Georgi K(onstantinovich)
1896(?)-1974 Obituary 110
Ziadeh, Farhat Jacob 1917- CANR-14
Earlier sketch in CA 25-28R
Ziadeh, Nicola A(bdo) 1907- 29-32R
Ziavras, Charles E.
See Jarvis, Charles E(fthemios)
Zibart, Carl F. 1907- 73-76
Zidek, Anthony 1936- 17-20R
Zidek, Tony
See Zidek, Anthony
Ziedonis, Arvids Jr. 1931- 57-60
Ziefle, Helmut W(ilhelm) 1939- 130
Zieg, Joan (Gallina) 116
Ziegel, Vic 1938(?)- Brief entry 122
Ziegelmueller, George (William) 1930- 45-48
Ziegenhagen, Eduard A(rthur) 1935- CANR-25
Earlier sketch in CA 45-48
Ziegenhagen, Eric ....CLC 55
Zieger, Robert H. 1938- 29-32R
Ziegfeld, Edwin Henry 1905-1987 Obituary 123
Ziegfeld, Richard E(van) 1948- 109
Ziegler, Alan 1947- CANR-3
Earlier sketch in CA 49-52
Ziegler, Arthur P(aul) Jr. 1937- 57-60
Ziegler, Bette 1940- 81-84
Ziegler, Charles E. 1953- 126
Ziegler, Donald J(enks) 1924- 25-28R
Ziegler, Edward K(rusen) 1903- 57-60
Ziegler, Elsie Reif 1910- 1-4R
Ziegler, Isabelle 1904- 25-28R
Ziegler, Jack (Denmore) 1942- 109
See also SATA 60
Ziegler, Jean 1934- 97-100
Ziegler, Jesse H(unsberger) 1913- CANR-19
Earlier sketch in CA 25-28R
Ziegler, Philip (Sandeman) 1929- 49-52
Ziegler, Raymond J. 1922- 13-16R
Ziegler, Richard S. 1931- 101
Ziegler, Ronald M(elvin) 1935- 102
Ziegler, (Karl Reinhart Ludwig) Theobald
1846-1918 Brief entry 119
Ziel, Ron 1939- 21-24R
Zielinski, David 1953- 132
Ziemer, Gregor (Athalwin) -
1899-198 (?) CANR-26
Earlier sketches in CAP-1, CA 13-14
Ziemer, Paul 1921(?)-1985 Obituary 117
Ziemian, Joseph 1922-1971 65-68
Ziemienski, Dennis (Theodore) 1947- ..... SATA 10
Ziemke, Donald C(harles) 1929- 5-8R
Ziemke, Earl F(rederick) 1922- 37-40R
Zierold, Norman (John) 1927- 17-20R
Zieroth, Dale 1946- 117
See also DLB 60
Ziesler, J(ohn) A(nthony) 1930- CANR-1
Earlier sketch in CA 45-48
Zietlow, E(dward) R. 1932- CANR-7
Earlier sketch in CA 17-20R
Zietlow, Paul Nathan 1935- 93-96
Ziewacz, Lawrence E. 1942- 125
Zif, Jay Jehiel 1936- 37-40R
Ziff, Gil 1938- 106
Ziff, Larzer 1927- CANR-25
Earlier sketches in CA 13-16R, CANR-7
Zigler, Edward F(rank) 1930- CANR-33
Earlier sketches in CA 41-44R, CANR-15
Zigrosser, Carl 1891-1975 Obituary 111
Zijderveld, Anton C(ornelis) 1937- CANR-12
Earlier sketch in CA 29-32R
Zikmund, Barbara Brown 1939- 117
Zikmund, Joseph II 1937- CANR-15
Earlier sketch in CA 65-68
Zilahy, Lajos 1891(?)-1974 Obituary 53-56
Zilbergeld, Bernie 1939- 112
Zilbert, Edward R(udolph) 1925- 118
Zilboorg, Caroline (Crawford) 1948- 137
Zilg, Gerard Colby 1945- 57-60
Ziliox, Marc
See Fichter, George S.
Zillah
See Macdonald, Zillah K(atherine)
Zilmer, Bertram G.
1899(?)-1976 Obituary 65-68
Zilversmit, Arthur 1932- 25-28R
Zim, Herbert S(pencer) 1909- CANR-17
Earlier sketch in CA 13-16R
See also CLR 2
See also MAICYA
See also SAAS 2
See also SATA 1, 30
Zim, Sonia Bleeker 1909-1971 ....CANR-3
Obituary 33-36R
Earlier sketch in CA 1-4R
See also Bleeker, Sonia
Ziman, H(erbert) D(avid)
1902-1983 Obituary 110
Ziman, John M(ichael) 1925- CANR-29
Earlier sketch in CA 25-28R
Zimbardo, Philip G(eorge) 1933- 85-88
Zimbardo, Rose (Abdelnour) 1932- 17-20R
Zimelman, Nathan 1921- 133
See also SATA 37, 65
Zimet, Melvin 1913- 73-76
Zimet, Sara (Florence) Goodman 1929- 25-28R
Zimiles, Martha Rogers 1946- 41-44R
Zimiles, Murray 1941- 41-44R
Zimin, Alexander 1920-1980 Obituary 97-100
Zimmer, A(rno) B. 1945- 105
Zimmer, Anne Y(oung) 1920- 85-88
Zimmer, Basil G(eorge) 1920- 13-16R
Zimmer, Dirk 1943- ....SATA 65
Zimmer, Eric 1932- 61-64
Zimmer, Herbert 1924- 1-4R
Zimmer, Jill Schary
See Robinson, Jill
Zimmer, Maude Files 1905- 25-28R
Zimmer, Paul J. 1934- CANR-27
Earlier sketch in CA 21-24R
See also DLB 5
Zimmer, Timothy W. L. 1947- 29-32R
Zimmerli, Walther Theodor
1907-1983 Obituary 111
Zimmerman, Bill
See Zimmerman, William
Zimmerman, Bill 1940- 69-72
Zimmerman, Bruce 1952- 131
Zimmerman, Carle C(lark) 1897-1983 .....CANR-21
Earlier sketch in CA 25-28R
Zimmerman, Dale A. 1928- 124
Zimmerman, David R(adoff) 1934- 57-60
Zimmerman, Deirdre A. 1959- 120
Zimmerman, Ed 1933(?)-1972 Obituary 37-40R
Zimmerman, Eleanor (Goedeke) 1916- 61-64
Zimmerman, Everett (Lee) 1936- 110
Zimmerman, Franklin B(ershir) 1923- CANR-12
Earlier sketch in CA 13-16R
Zimmerman, Fred W(esley) 1921- CANR-2
Earlier sketch in CA 1-4R
Zimmerman, Gary 1951- 107
Zimmerman, Gordon G(lenn) 1922- 13-16R
Zimmerman, Irene 1907- 37-40R
Zimmerman, Irla Lee 1923- 57-60
Zimmerman, Isidore 1917(?)-1983 Obituary 111
Zimmerman, Joseph Francis 1928- CANR-37
Earlier sketches in CA 5-8R, CANR-2, 17
Zimmerman, Mary K. 1945- 81-84
Zimmerman, Michael E(dward) 1946- 108
Zimmerman, Naoma 1914- 1-4R
See also SATA 10
Zimmerman, Paul A(lbert) 1918- Brief entry 109
Zimmerman, Paul D. 115
Zimmerman, Paul Lionel 1932- CANR-10
Earlier sketch in CA 25-28R
Zimmerman, Robert
See Dylan, Bob
Zimmerman, Toni
See Ortner-Zimmerman, Toni
Zimmerman, Velma E. 1902- 29-32R
Zimmerman, William 1936- 53-56
Zimmerman, William 1940- 69-72
Zimmermann, Arnold E. 1909- 101
See also SATA 58
Zimmermann, Caroline A(nna) 1944- 102
Zimmermann, Ethel Agnes 1909-1984 129
Obituary 112
Zimmermann, Jon E(mil) 1933- 101
Zimmeth, Mary
See Schomaker, Mary Zimmeth
Zimmy
See Stratemeyer, Edward L.
Zimnik, Reiner 1930- 77-80
See also CLR 3
See also SATA 36

Zimpel, Lloyd 1929- 37-40R
Zimring, Franklin E(ster) 1942- 93-96
Zimroth, Evan 1943- 93-96
Zimroth, Peter L. 1943- 93-96
Zimunya, (Bonas) Musaemura 1949- 133
Zinbarg, Edward D(onald) 1934- 21-24R
Zinberg, Norman E(arl) 1921-1989 CANR-16
Obituary 128
Earlier sketch in CA 85-88
Zindel, Bonnie 1943- CANR-31
Earlier sketch in CA 105
See also SATA 34
Zindel, Paul 1936- CANR-31
Earlier sketch in CA 73-76
See also AAYA 2
See also CLC 6, 26
See also CLR 3
See also DLB 7, 52
See also MAICYA
See also MTCW
See also SATA 16, 58
Ziner, Feenie
See Ziner, Florence
Ziner, Florence 1921- CANR-1
Earlier sketch in CA 1-4R
See also SATA 5
Zines, Leslie 1930- 137
Zingara, Professor
See Leeming, Joseph
Zink, David D(aniel) 1927- CANR-3
Earlier sketch in CA 45-48
Zink, Lubor Jan 1920- CANR-9
Earlier sketch in CA 65-68
Zinke, George William 1904- 5-8R
Zinkin, Taya (Nathalie) Ettinger 1918- CANR-2
Earlier sketch in CA 1-4R
Zinn, Howard 1922- CANR-33
Earlier sketches in CA 1-4R, CANR-2
Zinner, Paul E(rnest) 1922- 1-4R
Zinner, Stephen H. 1939- 119
Zinnes, Harriet CANR-21
Earlier sketches in CA 45-48, CANR-1
Zinov'Ev, A. A.
See Zinoviev, Alexander (Aleksandrovich)
Zinoviev, Alexander (Aleksandrovich)
1922- 133
Brief entry 116
See also CAAS 10
See also CLC 19
Zinsser, William (Knowlton) 1922- CANR-31
Earlier sketches in CA 17-20R, CANR-12
Zintz, Miles V(ernon) 1918- 29-32R
Ziolkowski, Theodore (Joseph) 1932- CANR-12
Earlier sketch in CA 13-16R
Ziomek, Henryk 1922- CANR-30
Earlier sketches in CA 45-48, CANR-1
Zion, Eugene 1913-1975 81-84
Obituary 61-64
See also SATA 18
Zion, Gene
See Zion, Eugene
Zionts, Stanley 1937- 49-52
Zipes, Jack (David) 1937- CANR-9
Earlier sketch in CA 65-68
Zipser, Arthur 1909- 113
Ziring, Lawrence 1928- CANR-29
Earlier sketches in CA 73-76, CANR-13
Zisfein, Melvin Bernard 1926- 108
Zisk, Betty H(ershberger) 1930- CANR-25
Earlier sketch in CA 45-48
Ziskind, Sylvia 1906- 29-32R
Zistel, Era CANR-19
Earlier sketch in CA 25-28R
Zito, George V(incent) 1923- 113
Zitta, Victor 1926- 21-24R
Zivkovic, Peter D(ragi) 1929- 53-56
Zjawin, Dorothy 1945- 111
Zmijewsky, Boris 1946- CANR-20
Earlier sketch in CA 69-72
Zneimer, John (Nicolas) 1925- 29-32R
Zobel, Hiller B(ellin) 1932- 21-24R
Zobel, Louise Purwin 1922- 110
Zober, Martin 1918- 37-40R
Zochert, Donald (Paul Jr.) 1938- 81-84
Zodhiates, Spiros 1922- CANR-10
Earlier sketch in CA 21-24R
Zodikoff, David H(yman) 1933- 37-40R
Zodrow, John 1944- 77-80
Zoellner, Robert 1926- 57-60
Zoffer, Gerald R. 1926(?)-1982 Obituary 107
Zohar, Danah 1944- 124
Brief entry 118
Zohn, Arnold 1924-1985 Obituary 116
Zohn, Harry 1923- CANR-25
Earlier sketches in CA 25-28R, CANR-10
Zoilus
See Lovecraft, H(oward) P(hillips)
Zola, Emile (Edouard Charles Antoine)
1840-1902 138
Zola, Emile 1840-1902 Brief entry 104
See also TCLC 1, 6, 21, 41
See also WLC
Zola, Irving Kenneth 1935- 107
Zola, Marion (Joy) 1945- 108
Zolar
See King, Bruce
Zolberg, Aristide R(odolphe) 1931- 21-24R
Zolbrod, Leon M(ax) 1930- 57-60
Zolbrod, Paul G(eyer) 1932- CANR-10
Earlier sketch in CA 21-24R
Zolf, Larry 1934- 101
Zoline, Pamela 1941- CLC 62
Zoll, Donald Atwell 1927- 5-8R
Zolla, Elemire 1926- CANR-6
Earlier sketch in CA 9-12R
Zollinger, Gulielma 1856-1917 Brief entry 109
See also SATA 27
Zollinger, Norman 1921- 81-84
Zollitsch, Herbert G(eorge) 1916- 13-16R
Zollschan, George K(arl) 1930- 13-16R
Zolotas, Xenophon
See Zolotas, Xenophon E(uthymiou)
Zolotas, Xenophon E(uthymiou) 1904- 133
Zolotow, Charlotte S(hapiro) 1915- CANR-38
Earlier sketches in CA 5-8R, CANR-3, 18
See also CLR 2
See also DLB 52
See also MAICYA
See also SATA 1, 35
Zolotow, Maurice 1913-1991 CANR-1
Obituary 133
Earlier sketch in CA 1-4R
Zolynas, Al(girdas Richard) 1945- 105
Zonia, Dhimitri 1921- SATA 20
Zonik, Eleanor Dorothy 1918- 13-16R
Zonis, Marvin 1936- 37-40R
Zonker, Patricia 85-88
Zook, David H(artzler) Jr. 1930- 1-4R
Obituary 103
Zook, Deborah
See Green, Deborah
Zook, Paul D(avid) 1912- 5-8R
Zopf, Paul E(dward) Jr. 1931- 37-40R
Zophy, Jonathan Walter 1945- 104
Zorach, William 1887-1966 CAP-1
Earlier sketch in CA 13-16
Zorn, Eric 1958- 134
Zorn, Robert L. 1938- 115
Zornes, Jeanne Doering 1947- 113
Zornow, William Frank 1920- 41-44R
Zoshchenko, Mikhail (Mikhailovich)
1895-1958 Brief entry 115
See also TCLC 15
Zosky, Brenda 1942- 89-92
Zotos, Stephanos 21-24R
Zschokke, Heinrich 1771-1848 DLB 94
Zsoldos, Laszlo 1925- 37-40R
Zubek, John P(eter) 1925- 37-40R
Zubin, Joseph 1900-1990 CANR-30
Obituary 133
Earlier sketch in CA 17-20R
Zubly, John Joachim 1724-1781 DLB 31
Zu-Bolton, Ahmos II 1935- DLB 41
Zubrow, Ezra B. W. 1945- CANR-10
Earlier sketch in CA 65-68
Zubrowski, Bernard 1939- 104
See also SATA 35
Zubrzycki, Jerzy (George) 1920- CANR-10
Earlier sketch in CA 21-24R
Zucchi, John E. 1955- 138
Zuck, Lowell H(ubert) 1926- 65-68
Zucker, Adolf Eduard 1890-1971 Obituary 116
Zucker, David Hard 1938- 37-40R
Zucker, David 1947- 138
Zucker, Dolores Mae Bolton CANR-7
Earlier sketch in CA 17-20R
Zucker, Jack 1935- 29-32R
Zucker, Jerry 1950- 138
Zucker, Martin 1937- CANR-30
Earlier sketch in CA 112
Zucker, Miriam S. 1962- 128
Zucker, Moses 1902-1987 Obituary 123
Zucker, Norman L(ivingston) 1933- 17-20R
Zucker, Paul 1888-1971 CAP-2
Obituary 29-32R
Earlier sketch in CA 23-24
Zuckerman, Alan S(aul) 1945- CANR-22
Earlier sketch in CA 105
Zuckerman, Arthur J(acob) 1907- 41-44R
Zuckerman, Edward (Ben) 1948- 123
Zuckerman, Harriet 1937- 136
Zuckerman, Mary Ellen 1954- 137
Zuckerman, Michael 1939- 37-40R
Zuckerman, Seth (Abram) 1961- 124
Zuckerman, Solly 1904- CANR-28
Earlier sketch in CA 65-68
Zuckerman, Yitzhak 1917-1981 Obituary 108
Zuckermann, George 1916- 53-56
Zuckmayer, Carl 1896-1977 69-72
See also CLC 18
See also DLB 56
Zudeck, Darryl 1961- SATA 61
Zuelke, Ruth E. 1924- 13-16R
Zuelzer, Wolf(gang) W(illiam) 1909-1987 110
Obituary 122
Zuesse, Evan M. 1940- 105
Zug, Margaret Philbrook 1945(?)-1976 69-72
Zugsmith, Leane 1903-1969 Obituary 115
Zuk, Georges
See Skelton, Robin
Zukerman, Eugenia 1944- 110
Zukin, Sharon 131
Zukofsky, Louis 1904-1978 CANR-39
Obituary 77-80
Earlier sketch in CA 9-12R
See also CLC 1, 2, 4, 7, 11, 18
See also DLB 5
See also MTCW
Zulaika, Joseba 1948- 137
Zulauf, Sander W(illiam) 1946- 101
Zulawski, Marek 1908-1985 Obituary 116
Zulli, Floyd (Jr.) 1922-1980 37-40R
Obituary 108
Zumbo, Jim 1940- 109
Zumwalt, Elmo Russell Jr. 1920- 85-88
Zumwalt, Elmo Russell III
1946(?)-1988 Obituary 126
Zumwalt, Eva 1936- CANR-9
Earlier sketch in CA 65-68
Zundel, Veronica (Elsa) 1953- 120
Zunder, William (Limbery) 1938- 117
Zunkel, Charles Edward 1905- 57-60
Zunkel, Cleda 1903- 57-60
Zunser, Jesse 1898-1985 Obituary 118
Zunz, Olivier J. 1946- 110
Zupa, G. Anthony
See Zeck, Gerald Anthony
Zupko, Ronald Edward 1938- CANR-13
Earlier sketch in CA 37-40R
Zupnick, I(rving) L(awrence) 1920- 45-48
Zurcher, Arnold John
1903(?)-1974 Obituary 49-52
Zurcher, Louis A(nthony) Jr. 1936- CANR-15
Earlier sketch in CA 41-44R
Zurhorst, Charles (Stewart Jr.) 1913- CANR-1
Earlier sketch in CA 45-48
See also SATA 12
Zuriff, G(erald) E(ugene) 1943- 123
Zurita (Canessa), Raul 1951- 131
See also HW
zur Muehlen, Hermynia 1883-1951
See zur Muhlen, Hermynia
See also DLB 56
zur Muhlen, Hermynia
See zur Muehlen, Hermynia
See also DLB 56
Zuromskis, Diane
See Stanley, Diane
Zuromskis, Diane Stanley
See Stanley, Diane
Zusne, Leonard 1924- 81-84
Zuwaylif, Fadil H. 1932- CANR-25
Earlier sketch in CA 45-48
Zuwiyya, Jalal (Zakariya) 1932- 77-80
Zwaanstra, Henry 1936- Brief entry 105
Zwar, Desmond L(aurence) G(audin) 1931- 107
Zwarensteyn, Hendrik 1913-1976 5-8R
Obituary 103
Zwart, Pieter (Hendrik) 1938- 53-56
Zweifel, Frances W. 1931- CANR-12
Earlier sketch in CA 73-76
See also SATA 14
Zweig, Arnold 1887-1968 Obituary 115
See also DLB 66
Zweig, Ferdynand 1896-1988 Obituary 125
Zweig, Friderike M(aria Burger Winternitz)
1882-1971 Obituary 114
Zweig, Paul 1935-1984 85-88
Obituary 113
See also CLC 34, 42
Zweig, Ronald W. 1949- 124
Zweig, Stefan 1881-1942 Brief entry 112
See also DLB 81, 118
See also TCLC 17
Zwerdling, Alex 1932- 57-60
Zwerenz, Gerhard 1925- 33-36R
Zwerger, Lisbeth 1954- MAICYA
See also SAAS 13
See also SATA 66
Zwerling, L. Steven 1938- 61-64
Zwibak, Jacques 1902- 77-80
Zwick, Peter Ronald 1942- 116
Zwicky, Fritz 1898-1974 Obituary 49-52
Zwiebach, Burton 1933- 57-60
Zwinger, Ann (H.) 1925- CANR-30
Earlier sketches in CA 33-36R, CANR-13
See also SATA 46
Zwirn, Jerrold 1943- 109
Zworykin, Vladimir Kosma
1889-1982 Obituary 107
Zyla, Wolodymyr T(aras) 1919- CANR-2
Earlier sketch in CA 45-48
Zylberberg, Michael 1907-1971 CAP-2
Earlier sketch in CA 29-32
Zylbercweig, Zalman
1894-1972 Obituary 37-40R
Zyskind, Harold 1917-1990 57-60
Obituary 130
Zytaruk, George John 1927- 110
Zytowski, Donald G(lenn) 1929- 29-32R